D0461646

The Statesman's Yearbook 2020

The Statesman's Yearbook 2020

The Politics, Cultures and Economies of the World

palgrave
macmillan

Springer Nature Limited
Published annually since 1864

The Statesman's Yearbook 2020
ISBN 978-1-349-95939-6   ISBN 978-1-349-95940-2 (eBook)
ISBN 978-1-349-95941-9 (Bundle)
https://doi.org/10.1057/978-1-349-95940-2

This Palgrave Macmillan imprint is published by the registered company Springer Nature Limited.
The registered company address is: The Campus, 4 Crinan Street, London, N1 9XW, United Kingdom.

Preface

It was in the middle of the 19th century that the then British Prime Minister, Robert Peel, suggested to Alexander Macmillan that he should publish 'a handbook presenting in a compact shape a picture of the actual conditions, political and social, of the various states in the civilised world'. The first edition of *The Statesman's Yearbook* was eventually published in January 1864.

Our redesigned 156th edition keeps tabs on our uncertain world with its numerous elections and government changes. In Brazil and Mexico, the two largest countries in Latin America, 'populist' leaders—one right-wing and one left-wing—were elected as divisive politics seemed to be increasingly the order of the day. Elsewhere, the USA and China, the world's dominant economies, ramped up their trade war, while the UK struggled to navigate its way through Brexit. Meanwhile, the devastating fallout of Syria's civil war continued to have an impact across the world. Never have we needed more a compact picture of the current global political and economic situation.

With more than 150 years of history, *The Statesman's Yearbook* has an illustrious past, and all our previous editions are available as individual eBooks. They are also part of Palgrave's and Springer's eBook collections. For details see https://link.springer.com/bookseries/15683. In early 2019 we also published a new title—*The Statesman's Yearbook Companion*. This provides detailed biographies of past leaders and figureheads not found in *The Statesman's Yearbook* itself, and includes comprehensive chronologies of natural disasters and key political events, as well as overviews of major global cities. It also contains infographics commemorating the anniversaries of key historical events as well as a number of synopses of relevant and related publications.

We always welcome feedback, so please email us with any comments at sybcomments@palgrave.com

Nicholas Heath-Brown
Publisher, *The Statesman's Yearbook*

2018 in 1,000 words

Two questions vexed political commentators throughout 2018: would the UK's intended withdrawal from the European Union (Brexit) in March 2019 be confirmed or derailed and what would US President Donald Trump do next? UK Prime Minister Theresa May's efforts to establish a government consensus on acceptable terms for Brexit were consistently undermined by Eurosceptics within her own Conservative Party, prompting damaging cabinet resignations, and by Northern Ireland's Democratic Unionists, on whom the government was reliant to maintain its parliamentary majority. The stark divisions were laid bare in December as she controversially deferred a crucial House of Commons vote on her proposed deal (reached with other EU leaders the previous month), acknowledging that the agreement would likely be rejected. She also survived a motion of no confidence in her party leadership triggered by disgruntled Conservative MPs, but with a less than overwhelming endorsement.

US President Trump's second year in office proved as unpredictable as the first. In May he announced that he was withdrawing the USA from the 2015 six-nation agreement with Iran limiting the Islamic Republic's nuclear development programme and reimposing sanctions. He then reversed his bellicose stance towards communist North Korea, staging an historic meeting with his counterpart, Kim Jong-un, in June at which they agreed to work towards denuclearization of the Korean peninsula (although there was little apparent progress by the year's end). In July Trump and Russian President Vladimir Putin conducted their first-ever, and seemingly convivial, summit meeting, during which Trump again rejected US intelligence claims of Russian interference in the US elections in 2016. However, in October he announced that the USA would withdraw from a 31-year-old arms limitation agreement with Russia on intermediate-range nuclear weapons in Europe, accusing the Russians of breaking its terms. He was similarly not averse to upsetting long-standing allies, clashing with other Western leaders at a G7 summit over climate change and trade issues and demanding other NATO members increase their defence spending.

Further discord within the Trump administration saw the dismissal of Rex Tillerson as secretary of state (and his replacement by Mike Pompeo) and Jeff Sessions as attorney-general, as well as the resignation of James Mattis as defence secretary over the President's decision in December to withdraw US troops from Syria after claiming that Islamic State extremists had been defeated. The Republicans also lost control of the US House of Representatives at the mid-term elections in November, which heralded a partial government shutdown at the end of the year as the resurgent Democrats refused to approve Trump's funding demands for a border wall with Mexico to block immigrants from across Central America.

The global threat from a damaging trade war between the USA and China escalated during the year as Trump progressively imposed tariffs on Chinese products to stop what he claimed had been the systematic theft of US intellectual property. China similarly retaliated before both sides agreed a temporary suspension in December of further punitive action to allow for more negotiation. More positively, the USA, Canada and Mexico reached an accord to supersede the 24-year-old trilateral North American Free Trade Agreement.

Meanwhile, voters in Egypt, Russia and Turkey re-elected authoritarian presidents, as Brazil, Italy and Mexico returned new populist administrations and Colombia opted for a conservative presidential candidate. Former international cricketer Imran Khan became prime minister of Pakistan, while the ruling National Front coalition was ousted in Malaysia as the opposition's Mahathir Mohamad, at 92, became the world's oldest premier. Emmerson Mnangagwa and his ZANU-PF party claimed a controversial electoral victory in Zimbabwe, and long-delayed polling in the Democratic Republic of the Congo finally went ahead in December to elect a successor to Joseph Kabila.

New prime ministers took office in Australia and Spain, while Cyril Ramaphosa replaced Jacob Zuma as president in South Africa and Raúl Castro gave way to fellow communist Miguel Díaz-Canel in Cuba. And as China's parliament voted to abolish presidential term limits, paving the way for incumbent Xi Jinping to retain the office indefinitely, Germany's Angela Merkel relinquished the leadership of her Christian Democrat party ahead of the pending completion of her final term as chancellor. Other significant developments included a peace deal between Ethiopia and Eritrea, ending the state of war existing between them since 1998, as well as The Gambia's readmission as a member of the Commonwealth and Macedonia's historic agreement with Greece to change its official name to North Macedonia and resolve a festering bilateral dispute. Greece meanwhile completed its financial bailout obligations, ending eight years of austerity and economic oversight by the EU and International Monetary Fund, in sharp contrast to Venezuela where huge numbers of citizens were fleeing violence, hyperinflation and food and medicine shortages under Nicolás Maduro's leftist government. And a damning report by the United Nations highlighted the continuing inaction on the part of Myanmar's government over atrocities perpetrated against the country's Muslim Rohingya minority.

The civil war in Syria seemingly drew to a close, with President Bashar al-Assad's regime and its Russian and Iranian backers having gained ascendancy over most rebel groups. At the same time, the Turkish government stepped up military intervention in northern Syria in its campaign against Kurdish separatism. Tentative peace talks were initiated between the Saudi Arabian-backed government and Shia Muslim Houthi rebels in Yemen, where famine and disease exacerbated a humanitarian crisis. The Saudi regime, and particularly the crown prince, meanwhile incurred international opprobrium for alleged complicity in the murder of Jamal Khashoggi, a journalist and prominent government critic, in the Saudi consulate in Istanbul, Turkey. There was also outrage over the poisoning with a nerve agent of a Russian dissident and his daughter in the UK, allegedly by Russian intelligence officers, prompting the expulsion of Russian diplomats by many Western countries.

Natural disasters were never far from the headlines, notably earthquakes and tsunamis in Indonesia, wildfires in the USA and flooding in Japan, while the commemoration of the centenary of the end of the First World War added a poignant reminder of the consequences of breakdowns in international dialogue.

World Population Developments

1950

1.	China	544,419,000
2.	India	376,325,000
3.	USSR	181,037,000
4.	USA	158,804,000
5.	Japan	82,802,000
6.	Indonesia	69,543,000
7.	Brazil	53,975,000
8.	West Germany	50,958,000
9.	UK	50,616,000
10.	Italy	46,599,000

2017

1.	China	1,409,517,000
2.	India	1,339,180,000
3.	USA	324,459,000
4.	Indonesia	263,991,000
5.	Brazil	209,288,000
6.	Pakistan	197,016,000
7.	Nigeria	190,886,000
8.	Bangladesh	164,670,000
9.	Russia	143,990,000
10.	Mexico	129,163,000

2050

1.	India	1,658,978,000
2.	China	1,364,457,000
3.	Nigeria	410,638,000
4.	USA	389,592,000
5.	Indonesia	321,551,000
6.	Pakistan	306,940,000
7.	Brazil	232,688,000
8.	Bangladesh	201,927,000
9.	Congo, Democratic Republic of the	197,404,000
10.	Ethiopia	190,870,000

Source: United Nations World Population Prospects (2017 Revision)

Largest Urban Agglomerations

1950

1.	New York-Newark, USA	12,338,000
2.	Tokyo, Japan	11,275,000
3.	London, United Kingdom	8,361,000
4.	Osaka, Japan[1]	7,005,000
5.	Paris, France	6,283,000
6.	Moscow, USSR	5,356,000
7.	Buenos Aires, Argentina	5,166,000
8.	Chicago, USA	4,999,000
9.	Calcutta, India	4,604,000
10.	Shanghai, China	4,288,000

[1] Plus major neighbouring cities, including Kobe and Kyoto.

2015

1.	Tokyo, Japan	37,256,000
2.	Delhi, India	25,866,000
3.	Shanghai, China	23,482,000
4.	Mexico City, Mexico	21,340,000
5.	São Paulo, Brazil	20,883,000
6.	Mumbai (Bombay), India	19,316,000
7.	Osaka, Japan[1]	19,305,000
8.	Cairo, Egypt	18,820,000
9.	New York-Newark, USA	18,648,000
10.	Beijing, China	18,421,000

[1] Plus major neighbouring cities, including Kobe and Kyoto.

2025

1.	Tokyo, Japan	37,036,000
2.	Delhi, India	34,666,000
3.	Shanghai, China	30,482,000
4.	Dhaka, Bangladesh	24,653,000
5.	Cairo, Egypt	23,074,000
6.	São Paulo, Brazil	22,990,000
7.	Mexico City, Mexico	22,752,000
8.	Beijing, China	22,596,000
9.	Mumbai (Bombay), India	22,089,000
10.	New York-Newark, USA	19,154,000

Source: United Nations Department of Economic and Social Affairs/Population Division, World Urbanization Prospects (2018 Revision)

The Political

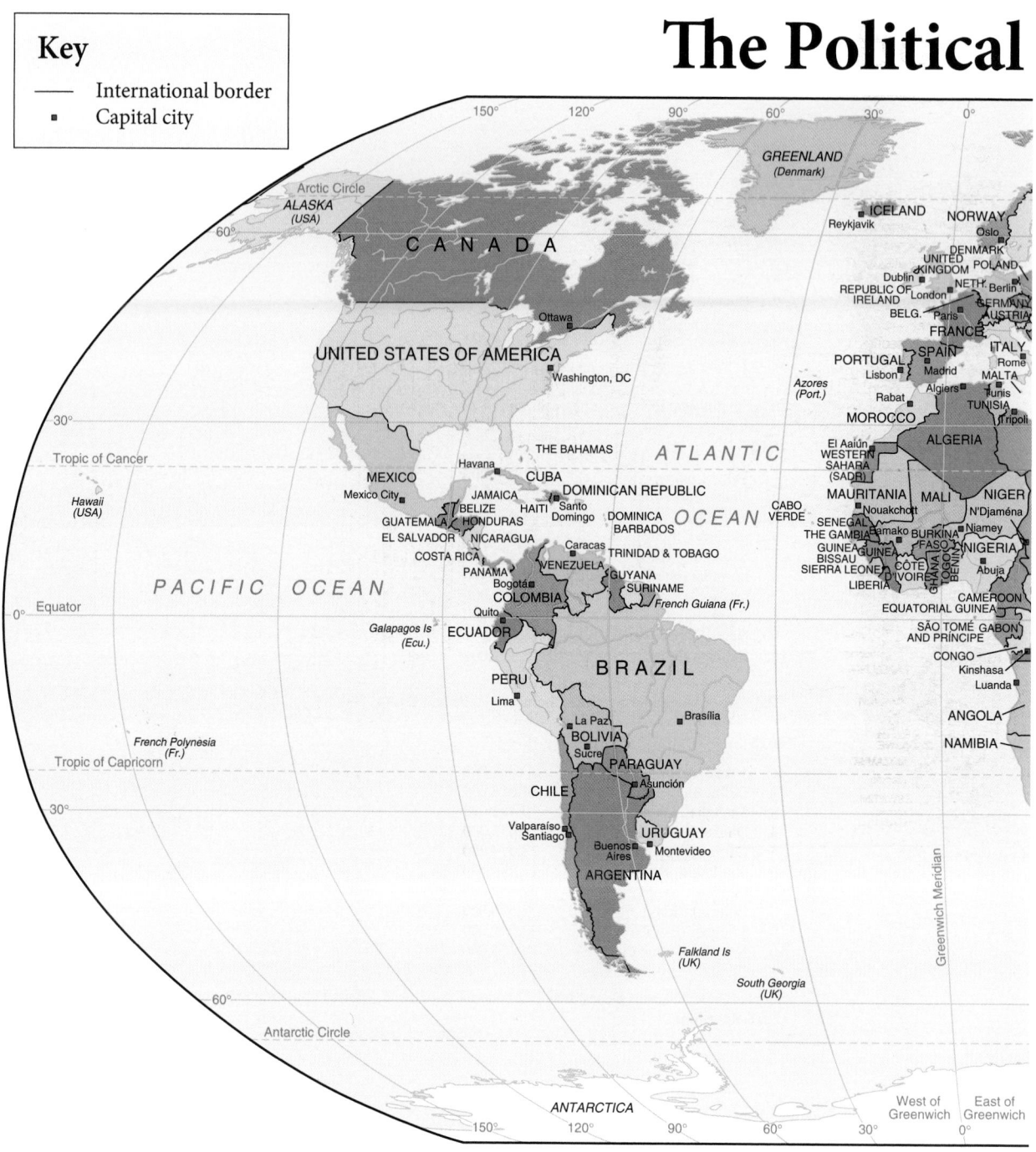

Key

— International border
▪ Capital city

World

N
W · E
S

30° 60° 90° 120° 150° 180°

Svalbard (Nor.)

Arctic Circle

SWEDEN FINLAND
Helsinki ESTONIA
Stockholm LATVIA
LITHUANIA Moscow
BELARUS
UKRAINE
HUNGARY MOLDOVA
ROMANIA
BULGARIA GEORGIA
GREECE ARMENIA AZERBAIJAN
TURKEY TURKMENISTAN
CYPRUS SYRIA
LEBANON
ISRAEL IRAQ
JORDAN IRAN
Cairo KUWAIT
LIBYA EGYPT BAHRAIN UNITED ARAB
QATAR EMIRATES
Riyadh Muscat
SAUDI
ARABIA OMAN
CHAD SUDAN ERITREA YEMEN
Khartoum Sana'a
Addis DJIBOUTI
Ababa SOMALIA
CENTRAL SOUTH ETHIOPIA
AFRICAN SUDAN Juba
REPUBLIC Juba
UGANDA KENYA
RWANDA Nairobi
CONGO BURUNDI Dodoma
(DEM. REP.) TANZANIA
ZAMBIA MALAWI COMOROS
Lusaka
ZIMBABWE MADAGASCAR
BOTSWANA Harare
Gaborone MOZAMBIQUE
Windhoek Maputo MAURITIUS
SOUTH ESWATINI
AFRICA Pretoria
LESOTHO
Cape Bloemfontein
Town

RUSSIA

60°

KAZAKHSTAN
Astana
MONGOLIA
Ulaanbaatar
UZBEKISTAN
Tashkent KYRGYZSTAN
TAJIKISTAN Beijing NORTH KOREA
Kabul Pyongyang
AFGHANISTAN Islamabad Seoul
PAKISTAN CHINA SOUTH Tokyo
NEPAL BHUTAN KOREA JAPAN
New BANGLADESH
Delhi Taipei
INDIA MYANMAR 30°
Naypyidaw LAOS Hanoi Taiwan (China) Tropic of Cancer
Yangon THAILAND VIETNAM Manila
Bangkok CAMBODIA Manila PACIFIC OCEAN
Phnom Penh
Sri Jayewardenepura SRI LANKA PHILIPPINES MARSHALL
Kotte PALAU ISLANDS
MALDIVES Kuala Lumpur BRUNEI MICRONESIA KIRIBATI
SINGAPORE MALAYSIA
Equator 0°
SEYCHELLES NAURU
INDIAN INDONESIA PAPUA
Jakarta NEW GUINEA SOLOMON ISLANDS
OCEAN TIMOR-LESTE Port TUVALU
Moresby
SAMOA
VANUATU
FIJI TONGA
Tropic of Capricorn
AUSTRALIA
30°
Canberra
NEW
ZEALAND
Wellington

60°

Antarctic Circle

ANTARCTICA

30° 60° 90° 120° 150° 180°

0   2000 miles
0   4000 km

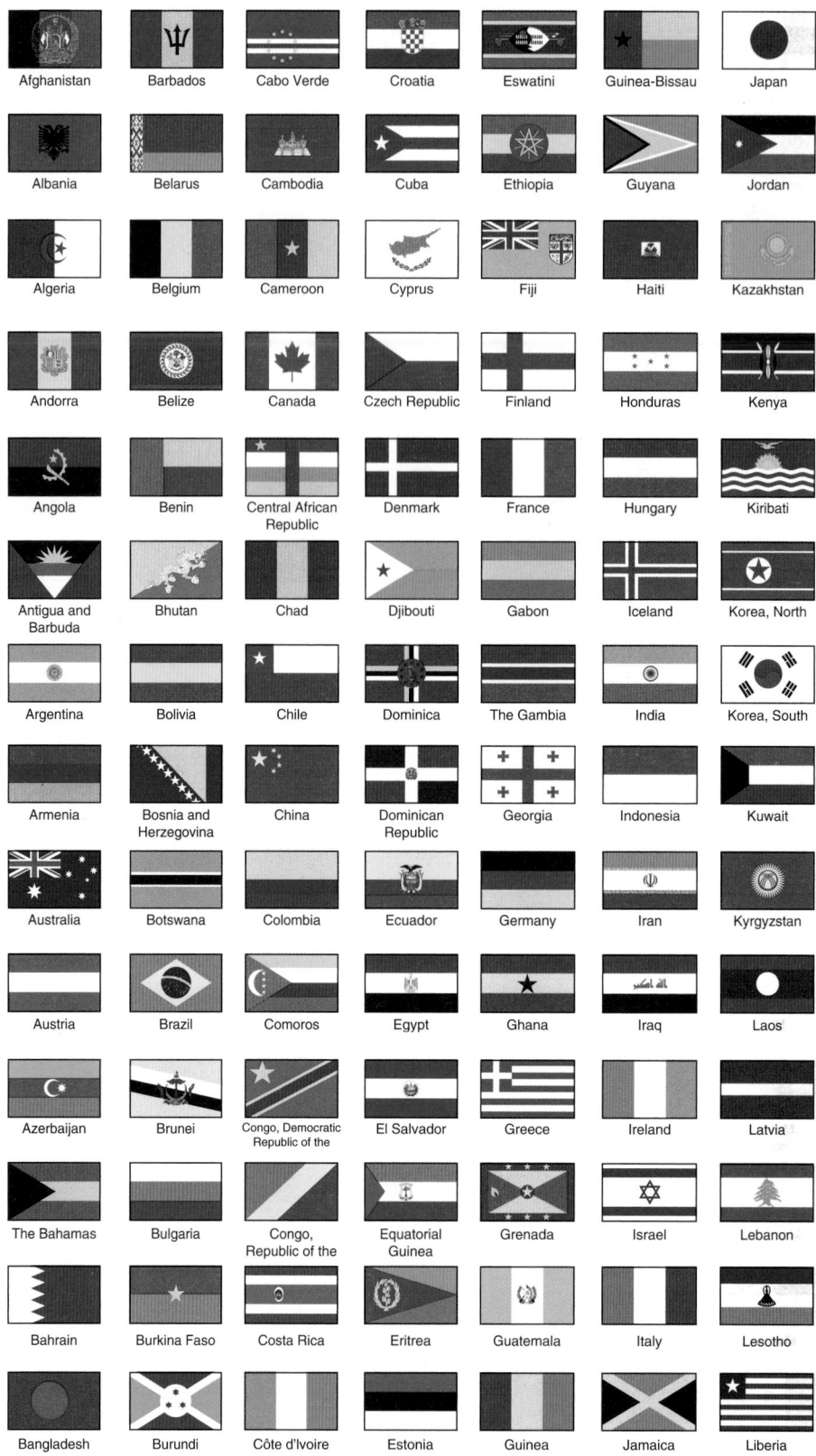

Afghanistan	Barbados	Cabo Verde	Croatia	Eswatini	Guinea-Bissau	Japan
Albania	Belarus	Cambodia	Cuba	Ethiopia	Guyana	Jordan
Algeria	Belgium	Cameroon	Cyprus	Fiji	Haiti	Kazakhstan
Andorra	Belize	Canada	Czech Republic	Finland	Honduras	Kenya
Angola	Benin	Central African Republic	Denmark	France	Hungary	Kiribati
Antigua and Barbuda	Bhutan	Chad	Djibouti	Gabon	Iceland	Korea, North
Argentina	Bolivia	Chile	Dominica	The Gambia	India	Korea, South
Armenia	Bosnia and Herzegovina	China	Dominican Republic	Georgia	Indonesia	Kuwait
Australia	Botswana	Colombia	Ecuador	Germany	Iran	Kyrgyzstan
Austria	Brazil	Comoros	Egypt	Ghana	Iraq	Laos
Azerbaijan	Brunei	Congo, Democratic Republic of the	El Salvador	Greece	Ireland	Latvia
The Bahamas	Bulgaria	Congo, Republic of the	Equatorial Guinea	Grenada	Israel	Lebanon
Bahrain	Burkina Faso	Costa Rica	Eritrea	Guatemala	Italy	Lesotho
Bangladesh	Burundi	Côte d'Ivoire	Estonia	Guinea	Jamaica	Liberia

Libya	Micronesia	Niger	Qatar	Sierra Leone	Syria	United Arab Emirates
Liechtenstein	Moldova	Nigeria	Romania	Singapore	Tajikistan	United Kingdom
Lithuania	Monaco	North Macedonia	Russia	Slovakia	Tanzania	United States of America
Luxembourg	Mongolia	Norway	Rwanda	Slovenia	Thailand	Uruguay
Madagascar	Montenegro	Oman	St Kitts and Nevis	Solomon Islands	Timor-Leste	Uzbekistan
Malawi	Morocco	Pakistan	St Lucia	Somalia	Togo	Vanuatu
Malaysia	Mozambique	Palau	St Vincent and the Grenadines	South Africa	Tonga	Vatican City State
Maldives	Myanmar	Panama	Samoa	South Sudan	Trinidad and Tobago	Venezuela
Mali	Namibia	Papua New Guinea	San Marino	Spain	Tunisia	Vietnam
Malta	Nauru	Paraguay	São Tomé and Príncipe	Sri Lanka	Turkey	Yemen
Marshall Islands	Nepal	Peru	Saudi Arabia	Sudan	Turkmenistan	Zambia
Mauritania	Netherlands	Philippines	Senegal	Suriname	Tuvalu	Zimbabwe
Mauritius	New Zealand	Poland	Serbia	Sweden	Uganda	
Mexico	Nicaragua	Portugal	Seychelles	Switzerland	Ukraine	

Key World Facts

World population in 2019	7,715 million (3,892 million males and 3,823 million females)
World population under 30 in 2019	3,775 million
World population over 60 in 2019	1,020 million
World population over 100 in 2019	543,000
World median age (both sexes)	30·6
Number of births worldwide every day	386,000
Number of deaths worldwide every day	160,000
Number of women married before the age of 18	720 million
Number of women married before the age of 15	250 million
World economic growth rate in 2018	3·6% (3·8% in 2017)
Number of illiterate adults	750 million
Number of unemployed people	173 million
Average world life expectancy	74·2 years for females; 69·8 years for males
Annual world population increase	81·8 million people
Number of people living outside country of birth	258 million, or more than 3% of the world's population
Fertility rate	2·5 births per woman
Urban population	55·3% of total population
World trade in 2017	US$35,754 billion
Annual world defence expenditure	US$1,739 billion
Number of cigarettes smoked	5,700 billion a year
Number of internet users	4·3 billion
Number of emails sent per day	281·1 billion
Number of Facebook users	2·3 billion
Number of mobile phone subscriptions	7·7 billion
Percentage of women in national parliaments	24.3%
Percentage of senior management positions held by women	24%
Number of people living in extreme poverty	736 million
Number of people living in slums	881 million
Number of undernourished people	821 million
Number of overweight adults	1·9 billion
Number of obese adults	672 million
Number of people lacking clean drinking water	844 million
Number of people lacking basic sanitation	2·3 billion
Number of people living with HIV/AIDS	36·9 million
Number of people suffering from depression worldwide	322 million
Annual carbon dioxide emissions	37·1 billion tonnes

Acknowledgements

Editors and Credits

Editors

Frederick Martin	1864–1883
Sir John Scott-Keltie	1883–1926
Mortimer Epstein	1927–1946
S. H. Steinberg	1946–1969
John Paxton	1969–1990
Brian Hunter	1990–1997
Barry Turner	1997–2014

Credits

Publisher	Nicholas Heath-Brown
Research Editor	Allan Cohen
Editorial Assistant	Eleanor Gaffney
Researchers	Daniel Smith
	Richard German
	Robert McGowan
	Jill Fenner
	Thanh Tuan Chu
	Noah Nzeribe
	Victoria Nolte
	Alexander Stilwell
	Sara Hussain
	Justine Foong
	Sharita Oomeer
	Jessica Soltys

email: sybcomments@palgrave.com

Chronology

March 2018–February 2019

Week beginning 4 March 2018

In El Salvador's parliamentary elections, the Nationalist Republican Alliance won 37 of a possible 84 seats in the Legislative Assembly (42·3% of the vote), ahead of the Farabundo Martí National Liberation Front (FMLN) with 23 (24·4%), the Grand Alliance for National Unity (GANA) 11 (11·5%), the National Coalition (PCN) 8 (10·8%), the Christian Democratic Party (PDC) 3 (3·2%) and Democratic Change 1 (0·9%). An independent candidate also won a seat.

In parliamentary elections in Italy, Matteo Salvini's centre-right coalition won 265 of 630 seats in the Chamber of Deputies (including the League with 125 seats), the Five Star Movement 227, Matteo Renzi's centre-left coalition 122 (including the Democratic Party, 112), and Free and Equal 14. In the Senate, Salvini's coalition won 137 of 315 seats (including the League, 58), the Five Star Movement 112, Renzi's coalition 60, and Free and Equal 4.

Stef Blok was appointed minister of foreign affairs in the Netherlands.

In Sierra Leone's parliamentary elections, the All People's Congress (APC) won 68 of 132 seats returned by popular vote; the Sierra Leone People's Party (SLPP), 48; Coalition for Change, 8; National Grand Coalition, 4; independents, 3. One seat remained vacant and an additional 12 were allocated for elected chiefs. In the first round of presidential elections, Julius Maada Bio of the SLPP received 43·3% of the vote and Samura Kamara of the APC 42·7%. There were 14 other candidates. The run-off held at the end of the month was won by Bio with 51·8% of the vote, against 48·2% for Kamara.

Week beginning 11 March 2018

Sebastián Piñera was sworn in as Chile's president.

In Colombia's parliamentary polling, the Liberal Party won 35 of 166 elected seats in the House of Representatives with 16·6% of the vote, the Democratic Center 32 (16·0%), the Radical Change Party 30 (14·4%), the Social National Unity Party 25 (12·4%), the Conservative Party 21 (12·2%) and the Green Alliance 9 (5·9%). Five seats were reserved for the Revolutionary Alternative Force of the Common People (formerly the rebel group FARC) and one for the vice-presidential runner-up in elections due in May 2018. The Democratic Center won 19 of the 102 Senate seats (16·4% of the vote), the Radical Change Party 16 (14·1%), the Conservative Party 15 (12·6%), the Liberal Party 14 (12·4%), the Social National Unity Party 14 (12·1%) and the Green Alliance 10 (8·6%). Again, five seats were reserved for the Revolutionary Alternative Force of the Common People and also one for the presidential runner-up in the May 2018 elections.

In elections to Cuba's National Assembly, all 605 nominally independent candidates received the requisite 50% of votes for election.

Khadga Prasad Oli, Nepal's prime minister, won a parliamentary confidence vote by 208 votes to 60. Five days later Pradeep Gyawali was sworn in as foreign minister

Robert Kaliňák resigned as Slovakia's minister of the interior. Three days later Robert Fico resigned as prime minister and was succeeded by Peter Pellegrini, whose cabinet included Tomás Drucker as interior minister.

In South Sudan, Stephen Dhieu Dau was dismissed as minister of finance and was succeeded by Salvatore Garang Mabiordit.

In Grenada's elections to the House of Representatives, the ruling New National Party won all 15 seats for the second consecutive time, with 58·9% of the votes cast against 40·5% for the National Democratic Congress.

An electoral college comprising members of Nepal's parliament and provincial assemblies re-elected Bidhya Devi Bhandari as president in preference to her opponent, Kumari Laxmi Rai.

US President Donald Trump dismissed Rex Tillerson as secretary of state and nominated Mike Pompeo, director of the Central Intelligence Agency, to succeed him.

The German *Bundestag* re-elected Angela Merkel as chancellor by 364 votes to 315. Her cabinet included Olaf Scholz as finance minister, Heiko Maas as foreign minister and Horst Seehofer as interior minister.

Miro Cerar resigned as Slovenia's prime minister, although he stayed on in a caretaker capacity.

Bakir Izetbegović assumed the chairmanship of Bosnia and Herzegovina's presidency.

China's parliament re-elected Xi Jinping as president and Li Keqiang as premier, while also electing Wang Qishan as vice-president. Gen. Wei Fenghe was named minister of defence and Liu Kun minister of finance.

Ameenah Gurib-Fakim resigned as president of Mauritius, with vice president Barlen Vyapoory taking over the post in an acting capacity.

Week beginning 18 March 2018

Vladimir Putin was re-elected president in Russia with 76·7% of the votes cast. Pavel Grudinin (Communist Party of the Russian Federation) took 11·8% of the vote; Vladimir Zhirinovsky (Liberal Democratic Party) 5·6%. Five other candidates received less than 2% of the vote each.

Paula-Mae Weekes was sworn in as Trinidad and Tobago's president.

In parliamentary elections in Antigua and Barbuda, the ruling Labour Party won 15 of 17 seats with 59·2% of the vote, with the United Progressive Party taking one seat (37·1%) and the Barbuda People's Movement one seat (1·4%). The Democratic National Alliance claimed 1·9% of the vote but won no seats. Paul 'Chet' Greene was appointed foreign minister in the new cabinet.

President Htin Kyaw resigned in Myanmar, with first vice president Myint Swe replacing him in an acting capacity. A week later Myint Swe lost to Win Myint in a parliamentary vote for the presidency by 403 votes to 211.

Peru's president Pedro Pablo Kuczynski resigned. First vice-president Martín Vizcarra replaced him and nominated César Villanueva as prime minister.

Week beginning 25 March 2018

In a cabinet reshuffle in Jamaica, Nigel Clarke became finance minister and Horace Chang security minister.

Abdel Fattah al-Sisi was re-elected in Egypt's presidential elections with 97·1% of the vote.

Week beginning 1 April 2018

In Botswana, Mokgweetsi Masisi, who had been serving as vice-president, was sworn in as president. He succeeded Ian Khama, who left office the previous day having completed the maximum term allowed by the constitution. Slumber Tsogwane became vice-president, Vincent T. Seretse minister of international affairs and co-operation, Shaw Kgathi minister of defence, justice and security, and Ontefetse K. Matambo finance minister.

After an inconclusive first round of presidential elections in Costa Rica in February, there was a run-off between Fabricio Alvarado Muñoz of the National Restoration Party (25·0% of the first-round vote) and Carlos Alvarado Quesada of the Citizens' Action Party (21·6%). Alvarado Quesada won with 60·7% of the vote against 39·3% for Alvarado Muñoz. Turnout was 66·5%.

Stefano Palmieri (Repubblica Futura) and Matteo Ciacci (Civic 10) were sworn in as San Marino's Captains Regent.

Abiy Ahmed was sworn in as Ethiopia's prime minister. His cabinet included Motuma Mekassa as defence minister, Abraham Tekeste as finance minister and Workneh Gebeyehu as foreign minister.

In Peru, César Villanueva took office as prime minister, with Gen. José Modesto Huerta as defence minister, David Tuesta as finance minister, Néstor Popolizio as foreign minister and Gen. Mauro Medina as interior minister.

Julius Maada Bio became Sierra Leone's president. He subsequently appointed David Francis as chief minister, Jacob Saffa as minister of finance, Alie Kabba as minister of foreign affairs and Edward Soluku as minister of internal affairs.

Sri Lanka's prime minister Ranil Wickremesinghe survived a no-confidence vote in parliament by 122 votes to 76.

Henrique Meirelles resigned as Brazil's minister of finance and was replaced by Eduardo Guardia.

Following a cabinet reshuffle in Rwanda, Uzziel Ndagijimana was appointed finance minister.

Week beginning 8 April 2018

In Hungary's parliamentary elections, the alliance of Fidesz-Hungarian Civic Alliance and the Christian Democratic People's Party (Fidesz-MPSz and KDNP) won 133 of 199 seats, Movement for a Better Hungary (Jobbik) 26, and the alliance of the Hungarian Socialist Party and Dialogue for Hungary (MSzP-Párbeszéd) 20. Five other groupings or independents gained ten seats or less. Turnout was 69·7%.

Armen Sarkissian was sworn in as Armenia's president and the government of Karen Karapetyan resigned. Karapetyan was succeeded eight days later by Serzh Sargsyan, who was elected by 77 to 17 parliamentary votes. His government included Vigen Sargsyan as defence minister, Vardan Aramyan as finance minister and Edward Nalbandian as foreign minister. However, protests led Serzh Sargsyan to resign within a week and Karapetyan returned as acting prime minister.

In Azerbaijan's presidential elections, Ilham Aliyev of the New Azerbaijan Party was re-elected with 86·0% of votes cast, beating seven other candidates.

Zoran Zaev, prime minister of Macedonia (renamed North Macedonia in February 2019), survived a parliamentary no-confidence motion by 62 votes to 40.

Ibrahim Yacouba resigned as Niger's foreign minister and was replaced by Kalla Ankourao.

In Tonga, 'Akosita Lavulavu was dismissed as minister of internal affairs. Deputy prime minister Semisi Lafu Kioa Sika assumed the portfolio on an interim basis.

Week beginning 15 April 2018

President José Mário Vaz of Guinea-Bissau appointed Aristides Gomes as prime minister, as well as minister of economy and finance. Eduardo Costa Sanha remained defence minister, with João Ribeiro Có becoming foreign minister and Mutaro Djaló interior minister.

In Montenegro's presidential elections, Milo Đukanović of the Democratic Party of Socialists of Montenegro was elected with 53·9% of votes cast, defeating independent candidate Mladen Bojanić (33·4%). Five other candidates took less than 10% each. Turnout was 63·9%.

Tomáš Drucker resigned as Slovakia's minister of the interior. Prime minister Peter Pellegrini assumed the portfolio in an acting capacity before Denisa Saková took on the role permanently a week later.

In a cabinet reshuffle in Burundi, Ezéchiel Nibigira was named foreign minister.

In Cuba, Miguel Díaz-Canel secured the approval of the National Assembly to become president of the Council of State and of the Council of Ministers.

Kyrgyzstan's prime minister, Sapar Isakov, resigned after losing a no-confidence vote in parliament by 101 votes to five. He was succeeded by the ruling coalition's candidate, Muhamedkaliy Abulgaziyev. Changes in the new government included Kashkar Dzhunushaliev as minister of internal affairs.

Ibrahim Ghandour was dismissed as Sudan's foreign minister, with Mohamed Abdalla Idris taking over on an interim basis.

Azerbaijan's parliament approved Novruz Mammadov as prime minister.

Week beginning 22 April 2018

In Paraguay's presidential elections, Mario Abdo Benítez of the National Republican Association–Colorado Party (ANR–PC) was elected with 46·4% of the vote, against 42·7% for Efraín Alegre of the Authentic Radical Liberal Party (PLRA). There were eight other candidates. Turnout was 61·4%. In parliamentary elections held the same day, the

ANR–PC won 42 seats in the Chamber of Deputies, the PLRA 29, the Beloved Fatherland Party 3 and the National Encounter Party 2. Four other parties won one seat each. In the Senate the ANR–PC won 18 seats, the PLRA 13, the Guasú Front 6, the Beloved Fatherland Party 3 and the Hagamos Party 2. Three other parties won one seat each.

Jean-Marie Reynaldo Brunet became Haiti's interior minister following a cabinet reshuffle.

In South Sudan, Martin Elia Lomuro took over as foreign minister in an acting capacity after Deng Alor Kuol was removed from office.

Mohamed Mursal Sheikh Abdirahman resigned as Somalia's defence minister.

In Pakistan, Khawaja Asif vacated the foreign affairs portfolio after he was disqualified from parliament, with Tehmina Janjua temporarily assuming his responsibilities. The following day Miftah Ismail was appointed minister of finance.

Mike Pompeo was sworn in as US secretary of state.

In Ecuador, Patricio Zambrano resigned as defence minister and César Navas as interior minister. They were replaced by Oswaldo Jarrín and Mauro Toscanini respectively.

Week beginning 29 April 2018

In the UK, Amber Rudd resigned as home secretary. She was replaced by Sajid Javid.

Gabon's Constitutional Court ordered the resignation of the prime minister, Emmanuel Issoze-Ngondet, after his government failed to hold timely elections. However, he was reappointed three days later by president Ali Bongo Ondimba. Régis Immongault Tatangani was named foreign minister in the new administration.

In Peru, the government of prime minister César Villanueva won a parliamentary vote of confidence by 94 votes to 19.

The government of Chad, led by prime minister Albert Pahimi Padacké, resigned the day before a new constitution came into force that abolished the post of prime minister.

Week beginning 6 May 2018

Long-delayed parliamentary elections were held in Lebanon. The Hizbollah-Amal alliance won 40 of 128 seats, the Free Patriotic Movement and its allies 29, the Future Movement and its allies 20, the Lebanese Forces and its allies 15 and the Progressive Socialist Party 9. Other parties won four seats or fewer. Turnout was 49·2%. On 24 May parliament charged incumbent prime minister Saad al-Hariri with forming a new government.

Issa Mahamat Abdelmahmout was appointed Chad's finance minister.

Vladimir Putin was sworn in for a new term as Russia's president. The government of Dmitry Medvedev resigned but Medvedev was immediately nominated by Putin for an additional term as premier and won parliamentary approval the following day by 374 votes to 56.

Serbia's minister of finance, Dušan Vujović, resigned. Prime minister Ana Brnabić took over the portfolio in an acting capacity before appointing Siniša Mali to the post permanently.

Losaline Ma'asi was named Tonga's minister of internal affairs.

Carlos Alvarado was sworn in as Costa Rica's president. His cabinet included Rocío Aguilar as finance minister and Epsy Campbell Barr as foreign minister.

Nikol Pashinyan was elected Armenia's prime minister by parliament with 59 of 101 votes in a second round of voting (the first round the previous week having proved inconclusive). Davit Tonoyan was subsequently appointed defence minister, Atom Janjughazyan finance minister and Zohrab Mnatsakanyan foreign minister.

In Malaysia's parliamentary elections, the Alliance of Hope gained 113 of 222 seats and 50·9% of the votes cast (with the predominant partner, the People's Justice Party, winning 49 seats). The ruling National Front coalition won 79 seats, the Ideas of Prosperity coalition 18, the Sabah Heritage Party 8, independent candidates 3 and the United Sabah Alliance 1. Mahathir Mohamad became prime minister for a second time at the age of 92. Mohamad Sabu was named minister of defence, Lim Guan Eng finance minister and Muhyiddin Yassin home affairs minister.

Hungary's parliament re-elected Viktor Orbán as prime minister by 134 votes to 28. Eight days later he named a government with Tibor Benkő as defence minister and Mihály Varga finance minister. Péter Szijjártó remained as foreign minister and Sándor Pintér as interior minister.

Pakistan's minister of defence, Khurram Dastgir Khan, took on the foreign affairs portfolio as well. However, at the start of the following month Nasir-ul-Mulk was appointed caretaker premier—ahead of parliamentary elections in July—and named Abdullah Hussain Haroon as minister of defence and foreign affairs, along with Shamshad Akhtar as minister of finance and Azam Khan as minister of the interior.

In elections to Iraq's National Assembly, the Forward (Saairun) alliance won 54 of 329 seats, ahead of the Conquest (al-Fatah) alliance with 47, the Victory (Nasr) alliance with 42, the Kurdistan Democratic Party and the State of Law Coalition with 25 each, the National (al-Wataniya) coalition with 21, the National Wisdom Movement with 19, the Patriotic Union of Kurdistan with 18 and the Arab Decision Alliance with 14. The remaining 64 seats went to smaller parties and coalitions.

In Timor-Leste's parliamentary elections, the Alliance for Change and Progress won 49·6% of votes cast and 34 of 65 seats, ahead of the Revolutionary Front for an Independent East Timor (FRETILIN) with 34·2% and 23 seats, the Democratic Party 8·1% and 5 seats and the Democratic Development Forum 5·5% and 3 seats. Turnout was 81·0%.

Week beginning 13 May 2018

Richard Martínez became Ecuador's finance minister.

In a cabinet reshuffle in Sudan, Ibrahim Hamid was appointed interior minister and al-Dirdiri Mohamed Ahmed foreign minister.

Guinea's government, led by Mamady Youla, resigned. Youla was succeeded as prime minister by Ibrahima Kassory Fofana. Nine days later Mamadi Camara was sworn in as finance minister.

Week beginning 20 May 2018

Milo Đjukanović became Montenegro's president.

In Venezuela's presidential elections, incumbent Nicolás Maduro (Great Patriotic Pole, led by the United Socialist Party of Venezuela) was re-elected president with 67·8% of the votes cast, ahead of Henri Falcón (Progressive Advance) with 20·9%, Javier Bertucci (ind.) with 10·8% and Reinaldo Quijada (Popular Political Unit 89) with 0·4%. Turnout was 46·1%.

In Italy, the League and the Five Star Movement nominated Giuseppe Conte as premier. Over the next ten days, president Sergio Mattarella first invited Conte to form a government before the mandate passed to Carlo Cottarelli and then back to Conte. Conte was sworn in as prime minister at the beginning of June. His cabinet included Elisabetta Trenta as defence minister, Five Star Movement leader Luigi di Maio as economic development minister, Giovanni Tria as finance minister, Enzo Moavero Milanese as foreign affairs minister and League leader Matteo Salvini as interior minister.

Hassan Ali Mohamed was appointed Somalia's minister of defence in a cabinet reshuffle.

In parliamentary elections in Barbados, all 30 seats were won by the Barbados Labour Party with 74·6% of the votes cast. The ruling Democratic Labour Party as well as three other parties and independents failed to win any seats.

Madagascar's Constitutional Court ruled that president Hery Rajaonarimampianina must dissolve the government and form a new national union administration.

Kyaw Win resigned as Myanmar's minister of finance and was replaced by Soe Win.

Week beginning 27 May 2018

Hugo Martínez resigned as El Salvador's foreign minister in order to contest the presidential elections scheduled for February 2019. Carlos Castaneda took over the portfolio in an acting capacity.

Prime minister Mariano Rajoy of Spain lost a no-confidence vote in parliament by 180 votes to 169. He was succeeded the following day by Pedro Sánchez of the Spanish Socialist Workers' Party. Sánchez subsequently appointed a government including Margarita Robles as minister of defence, María Jesús Montero minister of finance, Josep Borrell minister of foreign affairs and Fernando Grande-Marlaska minister of interior affairs.

Autonomous government was restored in Catalonia after it had been suspended from October 2017 following the region's disputed independence referendum.

Week beginning 3 June 2018

In Slovenia's parliamentary elections, the Slovenian Democratic Party won 25 seats with 24·9% of votes cast; the Marjan Šarec List 13 with 12·6%; and the Social Democrats and the Modern Centre Party 10 seats each with 9·9% and 9·7% respectively. Five other parties won fewer than ten seats, and two seats were allocated to the Italian and Hungarian national minorities. Turnout was 52·6%.

Hani Al-Mulki resigned as prime minister of Jordan. Omar Razzaz was sworn in as his successor ten days later, taking responsibility for the defence portfolio as well. Izzidine Kanakrieh was named finance minister, while Ayman Safadi and Samir Mubaidin stayed on as minister of foreign affairs and of the interior respectively.

Madagascar's prime minister Olivier Mahafaly Solonandrasana resigned, with Christian Ntsay replacing him two days later. His government included Eloi Alphonse Maxime Dovo as foreign minister and Tianarivelo Razafimahefa as interior minister. Gen. Béni Xavier Rasolofonirina and Vonintsalama Sehenosoa Andriambololona continued as minister of defence and finance respectively.

David Tuesta resigned as Peru's finance minister and was replaced by Carlos Oliva three days later.

After Abdel Fattah al-Sisi was sworn in for a second term as Egypt's president, Sherif Ismail resigned as prime minister. Two days later al-Sisi invited Mostafa Madbouly to form a new government, which was sworn in the following week with Mohamed Ahmed Zaki as minister of defence, Mohamed Maait minister of finance, Sameh Hassan Shoukry Selim minister of foreign affairs and Mahmoud Tawfiq minister of the interior.

The president of the Czech Republic, Miloš Zeman, invited prime minister Andrej Babiš to appoint a new cabinet, which was sworn in three weeks later. It included Lubomír Metnar as defence minister and Jan Hamáček as minister of the interior and acting foreign minister. Alena Schillerová stayed on as finance minister.

Lotfi Brahem was dismissed as interior minister in Tunisia, with minister of justice Ghazi Jéribi taking over the portfolio in an acting capacity.

In Ukraine, Olexandr Danyliuk was dismissed by parliament as finance minister. Oksana Markarova replaced him in an acting capacity the following day.

José Valencia Amores was named Ecuador's foreign minister.

Week beginning 10 June 2018

In a cabinet reshuffle in Mauritania, Ismail Ould Cheikh Ahmed was appointed foreign minister.

Giorgi Kvirikashvili resigned as Georgia's prime minister. He was succeeded by Mamuka Bakhtadze, who appointed a cabinet including Nikoloz Gagua as finance minister and David Zalkaliani as foreign minister. Levan Izoria was retained as minister of defence, as was Giorgi Gakharia as minister of internal affairs.

Begench Gundogdyev was appointed Turkmenistan's defence minister and Yaylym Berdyev national security minister.

Nicolás Dujovne, Argentina's economy minister, was additionally made finance minister.

In Venezuela, Delcy Rodríguez was named executive vice president.

In Greece, prime minister Alexis Tsipras's government survived a parliamentary no-confidence vote by 153 votes to 127.

Week beginning 17 June 2018

After an inconclusive first round of voting in Colombia's presidential elections the previous month, Iván Duque Márquez (Grand Alliance for Colombia) won the run-off with 54·0% against 41·8% for Gustavo Petro (List of Decency). Turnout was 53·0%.

Prime minister Charlot Salwai survived a parliamentary no-confidence vote in Vanuatu by 38 votes to 11.

Taur Matan Ruak was sworn in as Timor-Leste's prime minister. His government included Filomeno Paixão as minister of defence and Dionísio Babo as foreign minister.

Week beginning 24 June 2018

In Turkey's presidential elections, incumbent Recep Tayyip Erdoğan (Justice and Development Party) won after the first round of voting with 52·6% of votes, beating Muharrem İnce of the Republican People's Party (30·6%) and four other candidates who each received less than 10%. In parliamentary elections on the same day the People's Alliance won 344 of the 600 seats with 53·7% of votes cast (295 seats for the ruling Justice and Development Party and 49 for the Nationalist Movement Party), against 189 seats and 33·9% for the Nation Alliance (with the Republican People's Party taking 146 seats and the İyi Party 43) and 67 seats and 11·7% for the Peoples' Democratic Party. Turnout was 86·2%.

Losaline Ma'asi was sworn in as minister of internal affairs in Tonga.

The government of Viorica Dăncilă survived a no-confidence vote in Romania's parliament.

In a cabinet reshuffle in The Gambia, Ousainou Darboe was appointed vice president, Mambury Njie finance minister and Mamadou Tangara foreign minister.

Week beginning 1 July 2018

In Mexico's presidential elections, Andrés Manuel López Obrador of the Movimiento Regeneración Nacional (National Regeneration Movement/MORENA) won 53·2% of the vote, Ricardo Anaya of the Partido Acción Nacional (National Action Party/PAN) 22·3%, José Antonio Meade of the ruling Partido Revolucionario Institucional (Institutional Revolutionary Party/PRI) 16·4%, Jaime Rodríguez Calderón (ind.) 5·2% and Margarita Zavala (ind.) 0·1%. Turnout was 63·4%. Elections for the General Congress were held on the same day. In elections to the Chamber of Deputies, the National Regeneration Movement won 191 of the 500 seats, the National Action Party 81, the Labour Party 61, the Social Encounter Party 56, the Institutional Revolutionary Party 45, the Citizens' Movement 27, the Party of the Democratic Revolution 21, the Ecologist Green Party of Mexico 16 and the New Alliance Party 2. In elections to the Senate, the National Regeneration Movement won 55 seats, the National Action Party 23, the Institutional Revolutionary Party 13, and six other parties each won 8 seats or fewer.

Kangi Lugola was named as Tanzania's minister of home affairs.

In Malaysia, Saifuddin Abdullah was appointed foreign minister.

Week beginning 8 July 2018

Recep Tayyip Erdoğan was sworn in for a new term as Turkey's president. Fuat Oktay was named vice-president, Hulusi Akar defence minister and Berat Albayrak finance minister. Mevlüt Çavuşoğlu retained the foreign affairs portfolio and Süleyman Soylu continued as interior minister.

Reflecting political divisions within the UK government over prime minister Theresa May's negotiating policy on Britain's pending withdrawal from the European Union ('Brexit'), David Davis and Boris Johnson resigned from their respective posts as secretary of state for exiting the EU and as foreign secretary. They were replaced by Dominic Raab and Jeremy Hunt, respectively, in a consequent cabinet reshuffle.

The government of prime minister Andrej Babiš won a parliamentary vote of confidence in the Czech Republic by 105 votes to 91.

Salva Kiir Mayardit was sworn in for a further three years as president in South Sudan. The following week Nhial Deng Nhial was named as foreign minister.

Following a reshuffle in Taiwan, Su Jain-rong became finance minister and Hsu Kuo-yung interior minister.

Colombia's president-elect, Iván Duque, nominated Alberto Carrasquilla as minister of finance, Carlos Holmes Trujillo as foreign minister and Nancy Patricia Gutiérrez as interior minister. Four days later Guillermo Botero was named defence minister.

Jack Guy Lafontant resigned as Haiti's premier.

Week beginning 15 July 2018

The government of prime minister Narendra Modi in India survived a parliamentary no-confidence motion with 325 votes to 126.

In Cuba, the new president, Miguel Díaz-Canel, retained Gen. Leopoldo Cintra Frías as defence minister, Lina Pedraza Rodríguez as finance minister, Bruno Rodríguez Parrilla as foreign minister and Vice Adm. Julio César Gandarilla as interior minister.

Week beginning 22 July 2018

In Slovenia, president Borut Pahor declined to nominate a prime minister since the leaders of the two main parties could not command sufficient parliamentary support.

Hichem Fourati was appointed interior minister in Tunisia.

In Pakistan's parliamentary elections, the Pakistan Movement for Justice/Pakistan Tehreek-e-Insaf (led by Imran Khan) gained 149 of the National Assembly's 342 elected seats and received 31·8% of votes cast; the Pakistan Muslim League (N) won 82 seats (24·3%), the Pakistan People's Party 54 (13·0%); Muttahida Majlis-e-Amal 15 (4·8%); and the Muttahida Qaumi Movement 7 (1·4%). The remaining seats went to smaller parties and non-partisans. Turnout was 51·6%.

Week beginning 29 July 2018

In parliamentary elections in Cambodia, the ruling Cambodian People's Party claimed all 125 seats with 83·0% of votes cast.

In Zimbabwe, there were presidential and parliamentary elections. Incumbent Emmerson Mnangagwa of the Zimbabwe African National Union-Patriotic Front (ZANU-PF) won the presidential poll with 50·8% of the vote. Nelson Chamisa of the Movement for Democratic Change Alliance (MDC Alliance) was second with 44·3%. There were 21 other candidates who received less than 1% of the vote each. Of the 270 House of Assembly seats contested on the same day, ZANU-PF won 179 seats against 88 for the MDC Alliance. Two other parties and an independent won one seat each; 12 seats remained vacant. Of the 80 available seats in the Senate, ZANU-PF won 34, the MDC Alliance 25 and the Movement for Democratic Change-Tsvangirai (MDC-T) 1.

Carlos Castaneda was sworn in as El Salvador's foreign minister, having previously held the post in an acting capacity.

Emmanuel Macron's government in France survived two no-confidence votes in parliament.

Morocco's finance minister Mohamed Boussaid was dismissed, with Mohamed Benchaaboun replacing him on a permanent basis nearly three weeks later.

Week beginning 5 August 2018

President Jovenel Moïse nominated Jean-Henry Céant for premier in Haiti.

In a cabinet reshuffle in Trinidad and Tobago, Stuart Young was appointed minister of national security.

Iván Duque became Colombia's president.

Nurlan Yermekbayev was appointed minister of defence in Kazakhstan.

Dasho Tshering Wangchuk became chief adviser of a pre-election interim government in Bhutan. The following day Wangchuk assumed responsibility for the home and foreign affairs portfolios, with Dasho Karma Ura appointed finance adviser.

Week beginning 12 August 2018

After a first round of voting for Mali's presidency two weeks earlier, incumbent Ibrahim Boubacar Keïta defeated Soumaïla Cissé in a run-off with 67·2% of votes cast against 32·8%. Turnout was 42·7% in the first round and 34·5% in the second.

Mario Abdo Benítez became Paraguay's president. Gen. Bernardino Soto was named defence minister, Benigno López finance minister, Luis Castiglioni foreign minister and Juan Ernesto Villamayor interior minister.

Atal Bihari Vajpayee, twice prime minister of India (1996, 1998–2004), died.

Imran Khan was elected prime minister in Pakistan by 176 National Assembly votes against 96 for his opponent, Shahbaz Sharif. His cabinet included Pervez Khattak as minister of defence, Asad Umar finance minister and Shah Mehmood Qureshi foreign minister. Khan took the interior portfolio himself.

Marjan Šarec's appointment as prime minister of a centre-left coalition government in Slovenia was approved by the parliament.

Belarus's president Alyaksandr Lukashenka dismissed Andrei Kobyakov as premier and replaced him with Syarhey Rumas.

Kofi Annan, the general-secretary of the United Nations from 1997 to 2006, died.

Week beginning 19 August 2018

Scott Morrison replaced Malcolm Turnbull as Australia's prime minister and leader of the Liberal Party. Morrison defeated Peter Dutton in a leadership contest called after Turnbull's resignation. Three days earlier, Dutton had resigned as minister of home affairs after unsuccessfully challenging Turnbull for the leadership. Morrison announced a cabinet retaining Dutton as minister of home affairs, and with Christopher Pyne as defence minister and Marise Payne as foreign minister.

Week beginning 26 August 2018

Iran's parliament voted by 137 to 121 to remove Massoud Karbasian from his post as minister of finance.

A new cabinet was announced in the Comoros, in which Said Ali Chayhane retained the finance portfolio while Mohamed El-Amine Souef remained foreign minister and Mohamed Daoudou interior minister.

Alexis Charitsis was appointed Greece's interior minister in a cabinet reshuffle.

Following a cabinet reshuffle in South Korea, Jeong Kyeong-doo became minister of defence.

Maksim Yermalovich was named Belarus's finance minister.

In Fiji, Jioji Konrote was re-elected president by parliament. There were no other candidates.

Week beginning 2 September 2018

In Rwanda's parliamentary elections, president Paul Kagame's Rwandan Patriotic Front won 40 of the 53 directly elected seats, the Social Democratic Party 5, the Liberal Party 4, the Democratic Green Party 2 and the Social Party Imberakuri also 2.

Diego Pary became Bolivia's foreign minister.

In Mali, Ibrahim Boubacar Keïta was sworn in for a second term as president. He reappointed Soumeylou Boubèye Maïga as prime minister, whose cabinet included Tiémoko Sangaré as defence minister, Boubou Cissé as finance minister, Kamissa Camara as foreign minister and Brig.-Gen. Salif Traoré as security minister.

In indirect elections in Pakistan, Arif Alvi of the Pakistan Movement for Justice/Pakistan Tehreek-e-Insaf was elected president by federal and provincial lawmakers, winning 353 votes against 185 for Fazlur Rehman (Muttahida Majlis-e-Amal) and 124 for Aitzaz Ahsan (Pakistan People's Party).

Vincent Mhlanga was named acting prime minister in Eswatini (formerly known as Swaziland). Bheki Bhembe became finance minister, Joel Musa Nhleko foreign minister and Anthony Masilela home affairs minister, each in an acting capacity.

Haiti's prime minister-designate, Jean-Henry Céant, nominated Enol Joseph as defence minister, Ronald Décembre finance minister and Bocchit Edmond foreign minister, with Jean-Marie Reynaldo Brunet remaining as interior minister.

Hun Sen was re-elected prime minister by Cambodia's parliament.

Madagascar's president Hery Rajaonarimampianina resigned in accordance with the constitution, 60 days ahead of presidential elections. Senate president Rivo Rakotovao took over in an acting capacity.

In Zimbabwe, president Emmerson Mnangagwa named a new cabinet including Oppah Muchinguri-Kashiri as defence minister, Mthuli Ncube as finance minister and Cain Mathema as home affairs minister, while Lieut.-Gen. (retd) Sibusiso Moyo kept the foreign affairs portfolio.

Week beginning 9 September 2018

Sudan's president Omar Hassan Ahmed al-Bashir dissolved the government of prime minister Bakri Hassan Saleh. Motazz Moussa was sworn in as Saleh's successor the next day. Moussa took on the finance portfolio himself and named Gen. Awad Mohamed Ahmed bin Auf as defence minister and Ahmed Bilal Othman as interior minister. Al-Dirdiri Mohamed Ahmed stayed on as foreign minister.

In Sweden's parliamentary elections, the ruling Swedish Social Democratic Party won 100 seats with 28·3% of votes cast, the Moderate Party 70 with 19·8%, the Sweden Democrats 62 with 17·5%, the Centre Party 31 with 8·6%, the Left Party 28 with 8·0%, the Christian Democratic Party 22 with 6·3%, the Liberal Party 20 with 5·5% and the Green Party 16 with 4·4%. Turnout was 87·2%.

Slovenia's parliament approved Marjan Šarec's cabinet, with Karl Erjavec as defence minister, Andrej Bertoncelj finance minister, former prime minister Miro Cerar foreign minister and Boštjan Poklukar interior minister.

Sentje Lebona resigned as defence minister in Lesotho, with 'Mampho Mokhele appointed his interim successor.

Nigeria's finance minister, Kemi Adeosun, resigned, with Zainab Ahmed replacing him in an acting capacity.

In two rounds of parliamentary elections in Mauritania, the ruling Union for the Republic won 89 of 157 seats and Tewassoul 14.

Week beginning 16 September 2018

Alikhan Smailov became Kazakhstan's finance minister.

In Peru, the government of César Villanueva won a parliamentary vote of confidence by 82 votes to 22.

Mladen Marinov was named as Bulgaria's interior minister.

In Eswatini's parliamentary elections, 55 independent candidates were elected with ten more chosen and appointed by King Mswati III. Of the 30 candidates subsequently assigned to senatorial posts in the Swazi legislature, ten were elected by parliament and 20 were appointed by the King.

Dang Thi Ngoc Thinh became acting president in Vietnam following the death of the incumbent, Tran Dai Quang.

Week beginning 23 September 2018

In the Maldives' presidential elections, Ibrahim Mohamed Solih (Maldivian Democratic Party) won 58·4% of the vote against incumbent Abdulla Yameen (Progressive Party of Maldives) with 41·6%. Turnout was 89·2%.

Moldova's Constitutional Court reconfirmed the temporary suspension of Igor Dodon as president in response to his refusal to appoint ministers.

Week beginning 30 September 2018

Dominica's parliament re-elected Charles Savarin as president.

Gérard Collomb resigned as France's interior minister, with Christophe Castaner replacing him on a permanent basis two weeks later.

Barham Salih was elected president in Iraq by parliament in a second round of voting after the first round proved inconclusive. He was elected by 219 votes to 122 after his nearest rival, Fuad Hussein, announced his withdrawal. Salih then nominated Adil Abdul-Mahdi as prime minister.

In San Marino, Mirco Tomassoni (Democratic Socialist Left) and Luca Santolini (Civic10) were sworn in as Captains Regent.

Takeshi Iwaya was appointed Japan's defence minister.

Denis Mukwege and Nadia Murad were jointly awarded the Nobel Peace Prize for their efforts to end the use of sexual violence as a weapon of war and armed conflict.

In parliamentary elections in Latvia, Harmony won 23 of the 100 available seats (19·8% of the vote), Who Owns the State? 16 (14·4%), the New Conservative Party 16 (13·6%), Development/For! 13 (12·0%), the National Alliance 13 (11·0%), the Union of Greens and Farmers 11 (9·9%) and New Unity 8 (6·7%). Turnout was 54·6%.

Week beginning 7 October 2018

In elections for Bosnia and Herzegovina's tripartite presidency, Milorad Dodik won the Serb seat (with 53·9% of the vote against 43·0% for Mladen Ivanić), Šefik Džaferović the Bosniak seat (with 36·5% against 33·6% for Denis Bećirović) and Željko Komšić the Croat seat (with 54·1% against 34·6% for Dragan Čović). In parliamentary elections, the Party of Democratic Action won 9 of 42 seats, the Alliance of Independent Social Democrats 6, the Social Democratic Party 5, the Croat Democratic Union 5, the Serb Democratic Party 3 and the Democratic Front 3. A number of smaller parties each took one or two seats.

In the first round of Brazil's presidential elections, Jair Bolsonaro of the Social Liberal Party won 46·0% of votes cast, Fernando Haddad of the Workers' Party (PT) 29·3%, Ciro Gomes of the Democratic Labour Party (PDT) 12·5%, Geraldo Alckmin of the Brazilian Social Democracy Party (PSDB) 4·8% and João Amoêdo of the New Party (NOVO) 2·5%. Eight other candidates each received less than 2%. In the second round run-off held three weeks later, Bolsonaro won with 55·1% of the vote against 44·9% for Haddad. Turnout in the first round was 79·7% and in the run-off 78·7%. In the parliamentary elections held alongside the first round of the presidential vote, the Workers' Party won 56 of 513 seats in the Chamber of Deputies, the Social Liberal Party 52, the Progressive Party 37, the Brazilian Democratic Movement 34, the Social Democratic Party 34, the Republic Party 33, the Brazilian Socialist Party 32 and the Brazilian Republican Party 30. More than 20 other parties won seats.

In Cameroon's presidential elections, incumbent Paul Biya of the Cameroon People's Democratic Movement won with 71·3% of the vote against 14·2% for Maurice Kamto (Cameroon Renaissance Movement). Turnout was 53·9%.

In parliamentary elections in São Tomé and Príncipe, the Independent Democratic Action won 25 of the 55 available seats with 41·8% of the vote, the Movement for the Liberation of São Tomé and Príncipe/Social Democratic Party 23 (40·3%), the coalition of Democratic Convergence Party, Union for Democracy and Development, and Democratic Movement Force of Change 5 (9·5%) and Movement of Independent Citizens of São Tomé and Príncipe (MCISTP) 2 (2·1%). Turnout was 80·7%.

Nhlanhla Nene resigned as minister of finance in South Africa and was replaced by Tito Mboweni.

Erlan Abdyldayev resigned as Kyrgyzstan's foreign minister and was succeeded by Chingiz Aidarbekov.

Teodoro Locsin, Jr was appointed foreign secretary in the Philippines.

In Portugal, José Alberto Azeredo Lopes resigned as national defence minister and was replaced by João Gomes Cravinho.

Week beginning 14 October 2018

In parliamentary elections in Luxembourg, the Christian Social People's Party won 21 seats (28·3% of the vote), the Democratic Party 12 (16·9%), the Socialist Workers' Party 10 (17·6%), the Greens (Déi Gréng) 9 (15·1%), the Alternative Democratic Reform Party 4 (8·3%), the Pirate Party 2 (6·4%) and the Left 2 (5·5%). Turnout was 89·7%. Two days later Grand Duke Henri asked incumbent Xavier Bettel to form a new government

Nikol Pashinyan resigned as Armenia's prime minister, paving the way for fresh elections in December.

Tomáš Petříček was named foreign minister in the Czech Republic.

Following a cabinet reshuffle in Ethiopia, Aisha Mohammed became defence minister and Ahmed Shide finance minister.

Greece's foreign minister, Nikos Kotzias, resigned. Prime minister Alexis Tsipras took over the foreign affairs portfolio.

Bhutan held the second round of parliamentary elections, a month after the first round. The 47 seats were contested by four parties in the first round, with the two parties that won the highest number of votes progressing to the second round. In the second round the Druk Nyamrup Tshogpa won 30 of the 47 seats (55·0% of the vote) and the Druk Phuensum Tshogpa 17 seats (45·0%). Turnout was 66·4% in the first round and 71·5% in the second. Lotay Tshering of the Druk Nyamrup Tshogpa was appointed prime minister. Early the next month, he named Namgay Tshering as finance minister, Tandi Dorji as foreign minister and Sherub Gyeltshen as home affairs minister.

In a cabinet reshuffle in Rwanda, Maj.-Gen. Albert Murasira was named minister of defence and Richard Sezibera foreign minister.

Wim Kok, the Dutch prime minister from 1994 until 2002, died.

Week beginning 21 October 2018

Following a cabinet reshuffle in Iran, Farhad Dejpasand became minister of economy and finance.

In Vietnam, Nguyen Phu Trong was approved as president by parliament by 476 votes to 1.

The government of Boyko Borisov in Bulgaria survived a parliamentary no-confidence motion by 133 votes to 99.

Mulatu Teshome Wirtu resigned as Ethiopia's president. Sahle-Work Zewde was elected by parliament to succeed him, becoming the country's first female president.

Adil Abdul-Mahdi was sworn in as Iraq's prime minister. Fuad Hussein was appointed minister of finance and Mohammed Ali al-Hakeem minister of foreign affairs.

In Ireland's presidential elections, Michael D. Higgins (independent) was re-elected with 55·8% of the vote, ahead of Peter Casey (independent) with 23·3%, Seán Gallagher (independent) 6·4%, Liadh Ní Riada (Sinn Féin) 6·4%, Joan Freeman (independent) 6·0% and Gavin Duffy (independent) 2·2%. Turnout was 43·9%.

In Sri Lanka, Ranil Wickremesinghe was dismissed as prime minister by the president, Maithripala Sirisena. Mahinda Rajapaksa, a former president and prime minister, was sworn in as his successor, although Wickremesinghe rejected his dismissal. Rajapaksa also assumed the finance portfolio, while Sarath Amunugama was appointed foreign minister.

Fatmir Xhafaj resigned as Albania's minister of the interior.

Eswatini's King Mswati III appointed Ambrose Mandvulo Dlamini as prime minister. In the cabinet announced the following week, Neal Reijkenberg was named finance minister, Thuli Dladla foreign minister and Princess Lindiwe home affairs minister.

The second round of elections to Gabon's National Assembly were held, three weeks on from the first round. The Gabonese Democratic Party won 98 of 143 seats, the Democrats took 11, the Restoration of Republican Values 6, the Social Democrats of Gabon 5 and the Heritage and Modernity Rally 4. A further eight parties took ten seats in total, with eight going to independents. One seat remained vacant.

Week beginning 28 October 2018

In Mauritania, Yahya Ould Hademine resigned as prime minister and was succeeded by Mohamed Salem Ould Béchir. Mohamed Ould Ghazouani was named minister of defence.

Week beginning 4 November 2018

Following the USA's mid-term elections, the Democrats won control of the House of Representatives, winning 235 seats against 199 for the Republicans. The Republicans retained control of the Senate, with 53 seats against 45 for the Democrats and two independents.

In a cabinet reshuffle, Nicholas Dausi was appointed Malawi's minister of homeland security.

Jeff Sessions resigned as attorney general in the USA at president Donald Trump's behest, with Matthew G. Whitaker replacing him in an acting capacity.

Susil Premajayantha became Sri Lanka's home affairs minister. However, the following day president Maithripala Sirisena dissolved parliament and called new elections for two months later. The Supreme Court then issued a stay order on the dissolution until a final ruling in December at which it dismissed Sirisena's action as unconstitutional.

In a cabinet reshuffle in Chad, Daoud Yaya Brahim was named minister of defence and Mahamat Abali Salah minister of territorial administration and public security.

Guinea-Bissau's minister of the interior, Mutaro Djaló, was dismissed.

Hong Nam-ki became South Korea's finance minister.

Week beginning 11 November 2018

Sander Loones was appointed Belgium's minister of defence.

In the Marshall Islands, president Hilda Heine survived a parliamentary no-confidence vote, which was tied at 16 votes each.

Malusi Gigaba resigned as South Africa's minister of home affairs. Siyabonga Cwele was appointed his successor on a permanent basis nine days later.

In parliamentary elections in Fiji, the FijiFirst Party won 27 of the available 51 seats (50·0% of votes cast), ahead of the Social Democratic Liberal Party 21 (39·9%) and the National Federation Party 3 (7·4%). Turnout was 71·3%.

Avigdor Lieberman resigned as minister of defence in Israel, with prime minister Binyamin Netanyahu assuming the portfolio.

The British government agreed a draft plan negotiated with the European Union on the UK's pending withdrawal, which was subsequently endorsed by other EU government heads later in the month. Several UK cabinet and junior ministers resigned in protest at its terms.

Ibrahim Mohamed Solih was sworn in as president of the Maldives. His cabinet included Mariya Ahmed Didi as minister of defence, Ibrahim Ameer as finance minister, Abdulla Shahid as foreign minister and Sheikh Imran Abdulla as home affairs minister.

Week beginning 18 November 2018

Mihai-Viorel Fifor resigned as Romania's defence minister and was replaced by Gabriel-Beniamin Leş the following day.

Milorad Dodik assumed the chairmanship of the presidency of Bosnia and Herzegovina.

Andres Anvelt stepped down as Estonia's minister of the interior. Katri Raik was appointed his successor six days later.

Oksana Markarova became Ukraine's finance minister.

Evaristo Carvalho, president of São Tomé and Príncipe, dissolved the government of prime minister Patrice Trovoada and appointed Jorge Bom Jesus to the premiership a week later.

The government of prime minister Andrej Babiš in the Czech Republic survived a parliamentary no-confidence vote by nine votes.

In Sweden, interim prime minister Stefan Löfven was charged with forming a government after parliament rejected the nominations of Ulf Kristersson and Annie Lööf earlier in the month.

Taiwan's president, Tsai Ing-wen, rejected the resignation of prime minister Lai Ching-te.

Week beginning 25 November 2018

In a cabinet reshuffle, Mohammad Khalid Rahmon was named Syria's interior minister.

Latvia's president, Raimonds Vējonis, charged Aldis Gobzems with forming a new government after Jānis Bordāns had announced his failure to do so earlier in the month.

In a presidential run-off in Georgia, the independent candidate, Salome Zourabichvili, won with 59·5% of the vote against 40·5% for Grigol Vashadze of the United National Movement. There had been 23 other candidates in the first round of voting in October.

Miroslav Lajčák resigned as Slovakia's foreign minister.

Mongolia's prime minister, Ukhnaagiin Khurelsukh, survived a parliamentary no-confidence motion by 40 votes to 33.

George H. W. Bush, who served as president of the USA from 1989–93, died.

Following a first round of voting for Bahrain's 40-seat parliament the previous week, a second round was held. The following day the government resigned in line with the constitution. Two days later the king reappointed prime minister Sheikh Khalifa bin Salman Al-Khalifa, who then formed a cabinet including Sheikh Salman bin Khalifa Al-Khalifa as the new minister of finance. A record six women were returned in the elections.

Andrés Manuel López Obrador was sworn in as Mexico's president. His cabinet included Luis Crescencio Sandoval as minister of defence, Carlos Urzúa Macías as finance minister, Marcelo Ebrard Casaubón as foreign affairs and Olga Sánchez Cordero as interior minister.

Week beginning 2 December 2018

The Maldives' minister of home affairs, Imran Abdulla, resigned but was reappointed on the same day.

In São Tomé and Príncipe, prime minister Jorge Bom Jesus appointed Óscar Sousa as minister of defence and the interior, Osvaldo Vaz as finance minister and Elsa Teixeira Pinto as foreign minister.

Iraq's prime minister Adil Abdul-Mahdi nominated Faisal al-Jarba as defence minister and Falih al-Fayadh as interior minister.

The Court of Appeal in Sri Lanka issued an order prohibiting Mahinda Rajapaksa from acting as prime minister following president Sirisena's earlier dissolution of parliament and dismissal of the incumbent premier, Ranil Wickremesinghe. Rajapaksa resigned 12 days after the ruling, with Wickremesinghe returning as prime minister four days later and retaining his previous cabinet in their posts.

María Alejandra Vicuña resigned as Ecuador's vice-president, with Otto Sonnenholzner taking over the role a week later.

Vanuatu's prime minister Charlot Salwai survived a parliamentary no-confidence motion by 31 votes to 19, and another 17 days later by 36 votes to 13.

In a cabinet reshuffle in Laos, Maj.-Gen. Vilay Lakhamfong was named minister of public security.

The new government of Xavier Bettel took office in Luxembourg. It included François Bausch as defence minister and Taina Bofferding as interior minister, with Jean Asselborn retaining the foreign affairs portfolio and Pierre Gramegna staying as finance minister.

In Switzerland, Ueli Maurer was elected president for 2019 with 201 of 209 votes. Viola Amherd was appointed minister of defence.

Adylbek Kasymaliev resigned as Kyrgyzstan's finance minister. He was replaced a week later by Baktygul Jeenbaeva.

Miroslav Lajčák withdrew his resignation as Slovakia's foreign minister.

The president of the USA, Donald Trump, nominated William P. Barr as attorney general.

Week beginning 9 December 2018

In parliamentary elections in Armenia, the My Step Alliance—led by prime minister Nikol Pashinyan—won 88 seats with 70·4% of votes cast, Prosperous Armenia 26 seats (8·3%) and Bright Armenia 18 (6·4%). Turnout was 48·6%.

Following a cabinet reshuffle in Belgium, Didier Reynders became defence minister, Alexander De Croo finance minister and Pieter De Crem interior minister.

Latvia's president, Raimonds Vējonis, withdrew his nomination of Aldis Gobzems for prime minister.

Epsy Campbell Barr resigned as Costa Rica's foreign minister, with Lorena Aguilar Revelo taking over in an acting capacity.

Carwyn Jones resigned as the first minister of Wales. He was replaced the following day by Mark Drakeford.

Poland's government, led by Mateusz Morawiecki, won a confidence vote in parliament by 231 votes to 181.

Édouard Philippe's government in France survived a parliamentary no-confidence vote, with the motion receiving only 70 of the 289 votes required to pass.

The Central African Republic's foreign minister, Charles Armel-Doubane, was dismissed and replaced by Sylvie Baïpo-Temon.

Sweden's parliament rejected Stefan Löfven as prime minister by 200 votes to 116.

Week beginning 16 December 2018

Salome Zourabichvili was sworn in as president of Georgia.

After a cabinet reshuffle in Lesotho, Tefo Mapesela was sworn in as minister of defence.

Charles Michel resigned as Belgium's prime minister, although his government was expected to continue in a caretaker capacity until elections scheduled for 26 May 2019.

In Madagascar's presidential run-off election, Andry Rajoelina won with 55·7% of the vote against Marc Ravalomanana with 44·3%. There were 34 further candidates in the first round. Turnout was 54·2% in the first round and 48·1% in the run-off.

In Romania, Viorica Dăncilă's government survived a parliamentary no-confidence vote, with the motion receiving only 161 votes of the 233 needed to pass.

In Togo's parliamentary elections, the ruling Union for the Republic won 59 of 91 seats, the Union of Forces for Change 7, the New Togolese Commitment 3, the Patriotic Movement for Democracy and Development 2, the Movement of Centrist Republicans 1 and the Pan-African Democratic Party 1. Independents took 18 seats. Turnout was 59·3%.

James Mattis resigned as US defence secretary, with Patrick Shanahan appointed his successor in an acting capacity.

In Guyana, the government of Moses Nagamootoo lost a confidence vote in parliament by 33 votes to 32.

Week beginning 23 December 2018

Asadullah Khalid was named Afghanistan's acting minister of defence and Amrullah Saleh acting minister of the interior.

In St Kitts and Nevis, the government of prime minister Timothy Harris survived a no-confidence vote in parliament.

Beibut Atamkulov became Kazakhstan's foreign minister.

In Gabon, the Constitutional Court confirmed the results of the October parliamentary elections, so ending the government of Emmanuel Issoze-Ngondet.

Following a cabinet reshuffle in Saudi Arabia, Ibrahim Al-Assaf became foreign minister.

After a cabinet reshuffle in Albania, Anila Denaj became finance minister and Gent Cakaj foreign minister.

In Italy, the government of Giuseppe Conte won a parliamentary confidence vote with 327 votes to 228.

Week beginning 30 December 2018

In parliamentary elections in Bangladesh, the Awami League gained 257 seats against the National Party/Jatiya Party (Ershad) with 22 seats, the Bangladesh Nationalist Party with six seats and the Workers Party of Bangladesh with three seats. Five parties won two seats or less, while three seats went to independents.

In much-delayed presidential elections in the Democratic Republic of the Congo, Félix Tshisekedi (Union for Democracy and Social Progress) won with 38·6% of the vote, followed by Martin Fayulu (Lamuka coalition) with 34·8% and Emmanuel Ramazani Shadary (People's Party for Reconstruction and Democracy) with 23·8%. Turnout was 47·6%. In the parliamentary elections held on the same day the People's Party for Reconstruction and Democracy won 52 of 500 seats; the Alliance of the Democratic Forces of Congo 41 and the Union for Democracy and Social Progress 32. The remaining seats were won by 17 other parties or coalitions with 15 seats vacant.

Jair Bolsonaro was sworn in as Brazil's president. His government included Fernando Azevedo e Silva as minister of defence, Paulo Guedes as minister of finance and Ernesto Araújo as minister of foreign affairs.

David Bernhardt became the USA's acting interior secretary following Ryan Zinke's departure from the post.

In Bangladesh, president Abdul Hamid invited the prime minister, Sheikh Hasina Wajed, to form a new government, which included Mustafa Kamal as finance minister and Abulkalam Abdul Momen as foreign minister. Asaduzzaman Khan remained minister of home affairs.

Joseph Dion Ngute became prime minister in Cameroon.

Komi Sélom Klassou resigned as Togo's prime minister.

Week beginning 6 January 2019

Malaysia's Muhammad V resigned as king. He was succeeded by Sultan Abdullah at the end of the month.

President Raimonds Vējonis asked Krišjānis Kariņš to form a government in Latvia. His administration was approved by the *Saeima* two weeks later. Artis Pabriks was named minister of defence, Jānis Reirs finance minister and Sandis Ģirģens interior minister. Edgars Rinkēvičs retained the foreign affairs portfolio.

Jim Yong Kim announced his resignation as World Bank president.

Manuel Ventura became Costa Rica's foreign minister.

In a cabinet reshuffle in Cuba, Meisi Bolaños was appointed finance minister.

Taiwan's premier, Lai Ching-te, resigned along with his government. Su Tseng-chang succeeded him the following day, naming a largely unchanged cabinet.

Julien Nkoghe Bekale became Gabon's prime minister and Abdu Razzaq Guy Kambogo was appointed foreign minister.

Week beginning 13 January 2019

Panos Kammenos resigned as Greece's minister of defence, with Adm. Evangelos Apostolakis replacing him a day later.

In Armenia, Nikol Pashinyan was reappointed premier. He named a largely unchanged cabinet, which was sworn in at the end of the month.

Albania's parliament approved a cabinet reshuffle in which the prime minister, Edi Rama, took charge of the foreign affairs portfolio but immediately delegated responsibility for it to Gent Cakaj, whose nomination president Ilir Meta had previously rejected.

Greece's prime minister, Alexis Tsipras, won a parliamentary vote of confidence by 151 votes to 148.

In Sweden, Stefan Löfven was nominated by the parliamentary speaker as prime minister. Löfven secured sufficient parliamentary approval two days later, winning 115 votes to 153 against (175 being needed to veto the appointment). He named Mikael Damberg as his interior minister.

In the UK, prime minister Theresa May survived a parliamentary no-confidence vote by 325 votes to 306.

Paul Kaba Thiéba resigned as prime minister in Burkina Faso, with Christophe Dabiré succeeding him six days later. Moumina Chérif Sy was named minister of defence, Lassané Kaboré finance minister and Ousséni Compaoré security minister. Alpha Barry was retained as foreign minister.

Amrullah Saleh, Afghanistan's acting interior minister, resigned, with Hamdullah Mohib, the national security adviser, assuming his responsibilities.

Andry Rajoelina was sworn in as Madagascar's president. Prime minister Christian Ntsay and his government resigned on the same day but Rajoelina reappointed Ntsay two days later. Gen. Léon Richard Rakotonirina was named defence minister, Richard Randriamandrato finance minister and Naina Andriantsitohaina foreign minister. Tianarivelo Razafimahefa was reappointed interior minister.

Week beginning 20 January 2019

Following a cabinet reshuffle in Tonga, the deputy prime minister, Semisi Sika, became acting foreign minister while the health minister, Saia Piukala, became acting internal affairs minister.

In a cabinet reshuffle in Norway, Ingvil Smines Tybring-Gjedde was appointed public security minister.

Félix Tshisekedi was sworn in as president of the Democratic Republic of the Congo.

Week beginning 27 January 2019

Fiji's defence minister, Inia Seruiratu, additionally assumed the foreign affairs portfolio.

Rami Hamdallah, the Palestinian National Authority prime minister, tendered his resignation, with the rest of his government stepping down the following day.

Prime minister Allen Chastanet survived a no-confidence vote in St Lucia's parliament by 11 votes to 6.

In Lebanon, prime minister Saad al-Hariri appointed Elias Bou Saab as defence minister and Raya El Hasan as interior minister. Ali Hassan Khalil and Gebran Bassil were retained as finance minister and foreign minister, respectively.

Kristalina Georgieva assumed office as acting president of the World Bank.

Week beginning 3 February 2019

In El Salvador's presidential elections, Nayib Bukele (Grand Alliance for National Unity) won with 53·1% of votes cast, ahead of Carlos Calleja (Nationalist Republican Alliance) with 31·7%, Hugo Martínez (Farabundo Martí National Liberation Front) 14·4% and Josué Alvarado (Vamos) 0·8%.

US president Donald Trump nominated David Bernhardt as interior secretary.

In a cabinet reshuffle in Lesotho, Mokoto Hloaele was appointed minister of home affairs.

Week beginning 10 February 2019

Egypt's president, Abdel Fattah al-Sisi, assumed the chairmanship of the African Union.

Massoud Andarabi became Afghanistan's acting interior minister.

Bakhodir Kurbanov was appointed Uzbekistan's minister of defence.

In Gabon, Rose Christiane Ossouka Raponda was sworn in as defence minister.

Yerlan Turgumbayev became Kazakhstan's internal affairs minister.

Azali Assoumani temporarily stood down as president in the Comoros in accordance with constitutional requirements given his candidacy for the presidential elections to be held the following month.

After his budget was rejected by parliament, Spain's prime minister Pedro Sánchez called early elections scheduled for April.

Georgios Katrougalos became Greece's foreign minister.

Saad al-Hariri's government won a confidence vote in Lebanon's parliament by 111 votes to 6.

Week beginning 17 February 2019

Israel's premier, Binyamin Netanyahu, named Yisrael Katz as acting foreign minister.

Burkina Faso's prime minister, Christophe Dabiré, won a parliamentary confidence vote by 84 votes to 19, with 23 abstentions.

Edmundo Mendes became Guinea-Bissau's interior minister.

In Portugal, António Costa's government survived a parliamentary no-confidence motion by 115 votes to 103.

In Kazakhstan, the government of Bakhytzhan Sagintayev resigned. Askar Mamin succeeded to the premiership, naming a largely unchanged cabinet.

Simplice Sarandji resigned as prime minister in the Central African Republic, with Firmin Ngrébada replacing him the following week.

Omar al-Bashir, president of Sudan, dissolved Motazz Moussa's government. Moussa was replaced as prime minister two days later by Mohamed Tahir Ayala. Mustafa Youssef was named new finance minister.

In Nigeria's presidential elections, incumbent Muhammadu Buhari (All Progressives Congress) won a further term with 55·6% of votes cast, defeating Atiku Abubakar (People's Democratic Party), who took 41·2%. There were a further 71 candidates. Turnout was 34·7%.

Week beginning 24 February 2019

Parliamentary elections were held in Moldova, with the Party of Socialists of the Republic of Moldova winning 34 seats (31·2% of the vote), NOW Platform DA and PAS (an alliance of the Dignity and Truth Platform Party and the Party of Action and Solidarity) 27 (26·8%), the Democratic Party of Moldova 30 (23·6%) and the Republican Socio-Political Movement Equality 7 (8·3%). Turnout was 49·2%.

In Senegal's presidential elections, incumbent Macky Sall won 53·8% of the vote, ahead of former prime minister Idrissa Seck with 20·5%, Ousmane Sonko with 15·7%, Issa Sall with 4·1% and Madické Niang with 1·6%. Turnout was 66·2%.

France-Albert René, president of the Seychelles from 1977 until 2004, died.

Contents

Key Global Organizations

United Nations (UN)

Origin and Aims The United Nations is an association of states, or inter-governmental organizations, pledged to maintain international peace and security and to co-operate in solving international political, economic, social, cultural and humanitarian problems. The name 'United Nations' was devised by US President Franklin D. Roosevelt and was first used in the Declaration by United Nations of 1 Jan. 1942, during the Second World War, when 26 nations pledged to continue fighting the Axis Powers.

The United Nations Charter was drawn up by the representatives of 50 countries at the United Nations Conference on International Organization, which met in San Francisco from 25 April to 26 June 1945. Delegates started with proposals worked out by the representatives of China, the Soviet Union, the United Kingdom and the United States at Dumbarton Oaks (Washington, D.C.) from 21 Aug. to 28 Sept. 1944. The Charter was signed on 26 June 1945 by the representatives of the 50 countries. Poland, which was not represented at the Conference, signed later and became one of the original 51 member states. The United Nations came into existence officially on 24 Oct. 1945, with the deposit of the requisite number of ratifications of the Charter with the US Department of State. United Nations Day is celebrated on 24 Oct.

In recent years, most of the UN's work has been devoted to helping developing countries. Major goals include the protection of human rights; saving children from starvation and disease; providing relief assistance to refugees and disaster victims; countering global crime, drugs and disease; and assisting countries devastated by war and the long-term threat of landmines.

Members New member states are admitted by the General Assembly on the recommendation of the Security Council. The Charter provides for the suspension or expulsion of a member for violation of its principles, but no such action has ever been taken. The UN has 193 member states, comprising every internationally recognized sovereign state, with the exception of the Holy See. (For a list of these, *see* below.)

Finance Contributions from member states constitute the main source of funds. These are in accordance with a scale specified by the Assembly, and determined primarily by the country's share of the world economy and ability to pay, in the range 0·001%–22·000%. The Organization is prohibited by law from borrowing from commercial institutions.

A Working Group on the Financial Situation of the United Nations was established in 1994 to address the long-standing financial crisis caused by non-payment of assessed dues by many member states. Unpaid assessed contributions stood at US$1·6bn. as of 30 April 2018.

Official languages: Arabic, Chinese, English, French, Russian and Spanish.

Structure The UN has five principal organs established by the founding Charter (formerly six). All have their headquarters in New York except the International Court of Justice, which has its seat in The Hague. These core bodies work through dozens of related agencies, operational programmes and funds, and through special agreements with separate, autonomous, intergovernmental agencies, known as Specialized Agencies, to provide a programme of action in the fields of peace and security, justice and human rights, humanitarian assistance, and social and economic development. The five principal UN organs are:

1. The General Assembly

The General Assembly, composed of all members, with each member having one vote. Meeting once a year, proceedings begin on the Tuesday of the third week of Sept. The 73rd Session opened on 18 Sept. 2018.

At least three months before the start of each session, the Assembly elects a new President, 21 Vice-Presidents and the chairs of its six main committees, listed below. To ensure equitable geographical representation, the presidency of the Assembly rotates each year among the five geographical groups of states: Africa, Asia, Eastern Europe, Latin America and the Caribbean, and Western Europe and other States. Special sessions may be convoked by the Secretary-General if requested by the Security Council, by a majority of members, or by one member if the majority of the members concur. Emergency sessions may be called within 24 hours at the request of the Security Council on the vote of any nine Council members, or a majority of United Nations members, or one member if the majority of members concur. Decisions on important questions, such as peace and security, new membership and budgetary matters, require a two-thirds majority; other questions require a simple majority of members present and voting.

The work of the General Assembly is divided between six Main Committees, on which every member state is represented: the Disarmament and International Security Committee (First Committee); the Economic and Financial Committee (Second Committee); the Social, Humanitarian and Cultural Committee (Third Committee); the Special Political and Decolonization Committee (Fourth Committee); the Administrative and Budgetary Committee (Fifth Committee); and the Legal Committee (Sixth Committee).

There is also a General Committee charged with the task of co-ordinating the proceedings of the Assembly and its Committees, and a Credentials Committee, which examines the credentials of representatives of Member States. The General Committee consists of 28 members: the President and 21 Vice-Presidents of the General Assembly and the chairs of the six main committees. The Credentials Committee consists of nine members appointed by the Assembly on the proposal of the President at each session. In addition, the Assembly has a number of subsidiary organs, divided into Boards (of which there were 7 in Jan. 2019), Commissions (7), Committees (31), Assemblies and Councils (4) and Working Groups, etc. (16).

The General Assembly has the right to discuss any matters within the scope of the Charter and, with the exception of any situation or dispute on the agenda of the Security Council, may make recommendations accordingly. Occupying a central position in the UN, the Assembly receives reports from other organs, admits new members, directs activities for development, sets policies and determines programmes for the Secretariat and approves the UN budget. The Assembly appoints the Secretary-General, who reports annually to it on the work of the Organization.

Under the 'Uniting For Peace' resolution (377) adopted by the General Assembly in Nov. 1950, the Assembly is also empowered to take action if the Security Council, because of a lack of unanimity of its permanent members, fails to exercise its primary responsibility for the maintenance of international peace and security in any case where there appears to be a threat to the peace, breach of the peace or act of aggression. In this event, the General Assembly may consider the matter immediately with a view to making appropriate recommendations to members for collective measures, including, in the case of a breach of the peace or act of aggression, the use of armed force to maintain or restore international peace and security.

The first Emergency Special Session of the Assembly was called in 1956 during the Suez Crisis by Yugoslavia, which cited Resolution 377; demands were made for the withdrawal of British, French and Israeli troops from Egypt. On the Assembly's recommendations, the United Nations Emergency Force (UNEF I) was formed as the UN's first armed peacekeeping force.

Over the years a number of programmes and funds have been established to address particular humanitarian and development concerns. These bodies usually report to the General Assembly. They include: the United Nations Children's Fund (UNICEF); Office of the United Nations High Commissioner for Refugees (UNHCR); United Nations Conference on Trade and Development (UNCTAD); United Nations Development Programme (UNDP) and Population Fund (UNFPA); United Nations Environment Programme (UNEP); United Nations World Food Programme (WFP); United Nations Office on Drugs and Crime (UNODC).

© Springer Nature Limited 2020
Palgrave Macmillan (ed.), *The Statesman's Yearbook 2020*,
https://doi.org/10.1057/978-1-349-95940-2_1

Website: http://www.un.org/ga
President: María Fernanda Espinosa Garcés (Ecuador) was elected President for the 73rd Session in 2018.

2. The Security Council

The Security Council has primary responsibility for the maintenance of international peace and security. Under the Charter, the Security Council alone has the power to take decisions that member states are obligated to carry out. A representative of each of its members must be present at all times at UN Headquarters, but it may meet elsewhere as best facilitates its work.

The Presidency of the Council rotates monthly, according to the English alphabetical order of members' names. The Council consists of 15 members: five permanent and ten non-permanent elected for a two-year term by a two-thirds majority of the General Assembly. Each member has one vote. Retiring members are not eligible for immediate re-election. Any other member of the United Nations may participate without a vote in the discussion of questions specially affecting its interests.

Decisions on procedural questions are made by an affirmative vote of at least nine members. On all other matters, the affirmative vote of nine members must include the concurring votes of all permanent members (subject to the provision that when the Council is considering methods for the peaceful settlement of a dispute, parties to the dispute abstain from voting). Consequently, a negative vote from a permanent member has the power of veto. If a permanent member does not support a decision but does not wish to veto it, it may abstain. From 1945–91 the USSR employed its veto 119 times, the USA 69 times, the UK 32 times, France 18 times and China three times (including once before the People's Republic of China took over Taiwan's seat at the UN in 1971). From 1992–Jan. 2019 the Russian Federation vetoed 22 resolutions, the USA 16 and China ten; France and the UK did not veto any resolutions.

According to Article 29 of the United Nations Charter, the Security Council can establish subsidiary bodies as needed for the performance of its functions. All existing committees and working groups consist of the 15 members of the Council. The mandate of subsidiary organs, whether they are committees or working groups, can cover procedural matters or substantive issues.

Committees include a Counter-Terrorism Committee established in the wake of the Sept. 2001 attacks in the USA, a Non-Proliferation Committee and a Military Staff Committee. There are also sanctions committees, standing committees and *ad hoc* bodies. In addition the Security Council has responsibility for peacekeeping operations and political missions, as well as international courts and tribunals. The Peacebuilding Commission, acting as an advisory body, supports peace efforts in countries emerging from conflict.

The Council also makes recommendations to the Assembly on the appointment of the Secretary-General and, with the Assembly, elects the judges of the International Court of Justice.

Peacekeeping The Charter contains no explicit provisions for peacekeeping operations (PKOs), yet they have the highest profile of all the UN's operations. PKOs are associated with humanitarian intervention though their emergence was primarily a result of the failure of the Charter's collective security system during the Cold War and the absence of a UN Force. The end of the Cold War and the rise of intra-state conflict led to a proliferation of PKOs from the late 1980s and a greater proportion of armed missions. However, notable failures in the early and mid-1990s, such as the missions to Somalia in 1993 and to Rwanda in 1994, account for a drop in PKOs and shorter mandates. In 1992 then Secretary-General Boutros Boutros-Ghali presented the 'Agenda for Peace', which laid out four phases to prevent or end conflict: preventative diplomacy; peacemaking with civilian and military means; peacekeeping, in its traditional sense of operations in the field; and post-conflict peace-building, an area seen as comparatively neglected in previous missions. The then Secretary-General Kofi Annan presented a report aimed at conflict prevention in July 2001 emphasizing inter-agency co-operation and long-term strategies to prevent regional instability. There have been 72 peacekeeping operations in total since 1948. The first mission—consisting of unarmed observers—was to monitor the ceasefire during the First Arab–Israeli War.

Recent History In Nov. 2002 the Security Council held Iraq in 'material breach' of disarmament obligations. Weapons inspectors, led by Hans Blix (Sweden), returned to Iraq four years after their last inspections. Amid suspicion that Iraq was failing to comply, the USA, the UK and Spain reserved the right to disarm Iraq without a further Security Council resolution. Other Council members, notably China, France, Germany and Russia, opposed such action. In April 2003 US forces, supported by the UK, brought an end to Saddam Hussein's rule. In June 2004 the UN recognized the transfer of sovereignty to the interim government of Iraq. In 2005 the Council referred cases to the International Criminal Court (ICC) for the first time, asking the court to investigate the situation in Darfur, Sudan. Instability in Sudan saw the establishment of peacekeeping missions in Darfur (2007), the disputed Abyei region and newly independent South Sudan (both 2011). Other peacekeeping missions established in recent years have included Liberia (2003), Côte d'Ivoire (2004), Haiti (2004), Timor-Leste (2006), Democratic Republic of the Congo (2010), Libya (2011), Mali (2013), the Central African Republic (2014) and, again, Haiti (2017). In April 2012 the Security Council established a mission in Syria to monitor the cessation of armed violence and to oversee a UN–League of Arab States six-point peace plan. However, with continuing violence obstructing implementation of the mandate, the mission was ended in Aug. 2012. While UN sanctions have been tightened against North Korea in response to weapons tests carried out by Pyongyang, those against Iran were lifted in Jan. 2016 following implementation of the Joint Comprehensive Plan of Action limiting Iran's nuclear development activities. In 2015 the UN launched the Sustainable Development Goals agenda, comprising 17 specific targets to be achieved over 15 years, designed as a successor programme to the Millennium Development Goals. In Jan. 2017 António Guterres took office as the UN's Secretary-General. In Nov. that year the UN imposed its strongest sanctions to date on North Korea in response to Pyongyang's continued nuclear testing programme. A month later the UN General Assembly supported a non-binding resolution effectively rejecting the USA's recognition of Jerusalem as the capital of Israel. In Aug. 2018 the UN issued a report on military atrocities against Myanmar's Muslim Rohingya minority in 2017 that called for the investigation and prosecution of the country's senior generals for genocide.

Reform The composition of the Security Council, with its five permanent members having qualified as the principal Second World War victors, has been subject to intense debate in recent years. The lack of permanent representation from Latin America and the Caribbean or from Africa and the Islamic World is frequently cited to demonstrate that the Council is unrepresentative. However, reform is in the hands of the permanent members and a unanimous agreement has proved elusive. In Sept. 2004 Brazil, Germany, India and Japan (the G4) launched a joint bid for permanent membership, along with a seat for an African state. In March 2005 then Secretary-General Annan proposed either six new permanent members and three new non-permanent members or the election of a new type of member, eight of which would be elected for a four-year period. The World Summit in Sept. 2005 failed to agree on Security Council reform but pledged to continue negotiations.

Permanent Members China, France, Russian Federation, UK, USA (Russian Federation took over the seat of the former USSR in Dec. 1991).

Non-Permanent Members Côte d'Ivoire, Equatorial Guinea, Kuwait, Peru and Poland (until 31 Dec. 2019); Belgium, Dominican Republic, Germany, Indonesia and South Africa (until 31 Dec. 2020).

Finance The budget for UN peacekeeping operations in 2018–19 is US$6·7bn.

3. The Economic and Social Council (ECOSOC)

The Economic and Social Council (ECOSOC) is responsible under the General Assembly for co-ordinating international economic, social, cultural, educational, health and related matters.

The Council consists of 54 member states elected by a two-thirds majority of the General Assembly for a three-year term. Members are elected according to the following geographic distribution: Africa, 14 members; Asia, 11; Eastern Europe, 6; Latin America and Caribbean, 10; Western Europe and other States, 13. A third of the members retire each year. Retiring members are eligible for immediate re-election. Each member has one vote. Decisions are made by a majority of the members present and voting.

The Council holds one five-week substantive session a year, alternating between New York and Geneva, and one organizational session in New York. The substantive session includes a high-level meeting attended by Ministers, to discuss economic and social issues. Special sessions may be held if required. The President is elected for one year and is eligible for immediate re-election.

The subsidiary machinery of ECOSOC includes:

Eight Functional Commissions Statistical Commission; Commission on Population and Development; Commission for Social Development; Commission on the Status of Women; Commission on Narcotic Drugs (and Subcommission on Illicit Drug Traffic and Related Matters in the Near and Middle East); Commission on Crime Prevention and Criminal Justice; Commission on Science and Technology for Development; United Nations Forum on Forests.

Five Regional Economic Commissions ECA (Economic Commission for Africa, Addis Ababa, Ethiopia); ESCAP (Economic and Social Commission for Asia and the Pacific, Bangkok, Thailand); ECE (Economic Commission for Europe, Geneva, Switzerland); ECLAC (Economic Commission for Latin America and the Caribbean, Santiago, Chile); ESCWA (Economic Commission for Western Asia, Beirut, Lebanon).

Three Standing Committees Committee for Programme and Co-ordination; Commission on Non-Governmental Organizations; Committee on Negotiations with Intergovernmental Agencies.

In addition, the Council may consult international non-governmental organizations (NGOs) and, after consultation with the member concerned, with national organizations. Over 3,000 organizations have consultative status. NGOs may send observers to ECOSOC's public meetings and those of its subsidiary bodies, and may submit written statements relevant to its work. They may also consult with the UN Secretariat on matters of mutual concern. The term of office of the members listed below expires on 31 Dec. of each year.

Members Andorra (2019), Angola (2021), Armenia (2021), Azerbaijan (2019), Belarus (2020), Benin (2019), Brazil (2021), Cambodia (2019), Cameroon (2019), Canada (2021), Chad (2019), China (2019), Colombia (2019), Denmark (2019), Ecuador (2020), Egypt (2021), El Salvador (2020), Eswatini (2019), Ethiopia (2021), France (2020), Germany (2020), Ghana (2020), India (2020), Iran (2021), Ireland (2020), Jamaica (2021), Japan (2020), Kenya (2021), South Korea (2019), Luxembourg (2021), Malawi (2020), Mali (2021), Malta (2020), Mexico (2020), Morocco (2020), Netherlands (2021), Norway (2019), Pakistan (2021), Paraguay (2021), Philippines (2020), Romania (2019), Russian Federation (2019), St Vincent and the Grenadines (2019), Saudi Arabia (2021), Sudan (2020), Togo (2020), Turkey (2020), Turkmenistan (2021), Ukraine (2021), UK (2019), USA (2021), Uruguay (2020), Venezuela (Bolivarian Republic of) (2019), Yemen (2019).

Finance In 2013, US$25,840m. in socio-economic development assistance grants was provided through the organizations of the UN system.

4. The International Court of Justice (ICJ)

The International Court of Justice (ICJ) is the principal judicial organ of the UN. It has a dual role: to settle in accordance with international law the legal disputes submitted to it by States; and to give opinions on legal questions referred to it by authorized international organs and agencies.

The Court operates under a Statute of the United Nations Charter. Only States may apply to and appear before the court. The Court is composed of 15 judges, each of a different nationality, elected by an absolute majority by the General Assembly and the Security Council to nine-year terms of office. The composition of the Court must reflect the main forms of civilization and principal legal systems of the world. For a number of years the composition of the Court has maintained the following geographical balance: five seats on the bench are occupied by judges from Western Europe and other western states, three seats are occupied by African judges, three by Asian judges, two by judges from Eastern Europe and two by judges from Latin America. Elections are held every three years for one-third of the seats; retiring judges may be re-elected. Judges do not represent their respective governments but sit as independent magistrates. They must have the qualifications required in their respective countries for appointment to the highest judicial offices, or be jurists of recognized competence in international law. Candidates are nominated by the national panels of jurists in the Permanent Court of Arbitration (PCA) established by The Hague Conventions of 1899 and 1907. The Court elects its own President and Vice-President for a three-year term, and is permanently in session.

Decisions are taken by a majority of judges present, subject to a quorum of nine members, with the President having a casting vote. Judgment is final and without appeal, but a revision may be applied for within ten years from the date of the judgment on the ground of new decisive evidence. When the Court does not include a judge of the nationality of a State party to a case, that State has the right to appoint a judge *ad hoc* for that case. While the Court normally sits in plenary session, it can form chambers of three or more judges to deal with specific matters. Judgments by chambers are considered as rendered by the full Court.

Judges The nine-year terms of office of the judges currently serving end on 5 Feb. of each year indicated: Abdulqawi A. Yusuf, President (Somalia, 2027); Xue Hanqin, Vice-President (China, 2021); Ronny Abraham (France, 2027); Mohamed Bennouna (Morocco, 2024); Dalveer Bhandari (India, 2027); Antônio Augusto Cançado Trindade (Brazil, 2027); James Crawford (Australia, 2024); Joan E. Donoghue (USA, 2024); Giorgio Gaja (Italy, 2021); Kirill Gevorgian (Russia, 2024); Yuji Iwasawa (Japan, 2021); Patrick L. Robinson (Jamaica, 2024); Nawaf Salam (Lebanon, 2027); Julia Sebutinde (Uganda, 2021); Peter Tomka (Slovakia, 2021).

Competence and Jurisdiction In contentious cases, only States may apply to or appear before the Court. The conditions under which the Court will be open to non-member states are laid down by the Security Council. The jurisdiction of the Court covers all matters that parties refer to it and all matters provided for in the Charter or in treaties and conventions in force. Disputes concerning the jurisdiction of the Court are settled by the Court's own decision. The Court may apply in its decision:

(a) international conventions;
(b) international custom;
(c) the general principles of law recognized by civilized nations;
(d) as subsidiary means for the determination of the rules of law, judicial decisions and the teachings of highly qualified publicists. If the parties agree, the Court may decide a case *ex aequo et bono*.

Since 1946 the Court has delivered 145 judgments on disputes concerning *inter alia* land frontiers and maritime boundaries, territorial sovereignty, the use of force, interference in the internal affairs of States, diplomatic relations, hostage-taking, the right of asylum, nationality, guardianship, rights of passage and economic rights.

The Court may also give advisory opinions on legal questions referred to it by the General Assembly, the Security Council, other duly authorized UN organs and agencies of the UN system.

Since 1946 the Court has given 28 advisory opinions, concerning *inter alia* admission to United Nations membership, reparation for injuries suffered in the service of the United Nations, the territorial status of South-West Africa (Namibia) and Western Sahara, expenses of certain United Nations operations, the status of human rights informers, the threat or use of nuclear weapons and legal consequences of the construction of a wall in the Occupied Palestinian Territory.

Finance Parties before the Court are not required to pay fees or administrative or linguistic costs, since these are borne by the UN. The only expenses incurred by States parties to cases before the ICJ are the fees of their counsel and advocates. States that would, however, experience financial difficulties may apply to the Trust Fund set up in 1989 by the Secretary-General of the UN. The Court's budget for the biennium 2016–17 was US$45·8m.

Official languages: French and English.
Headquarters: Peace Palace, Carnegieplein 2, 2517 KJ The Hague, Netherlands.
Website: http://www.icj-cij.org
Registrar: Philippe Couvreur (Belgium).

5. The Secretariat

The Secretariat services the other four organs of the UN, carrying out their programmes, providing administrative support and information. It has a staff of 6,400 at the UN Headquarters in New York and a further 33,700 at other duty stations around the world. At its head is the Secretary-General, appointed by the General Assembly on the recommendation of the Security Council for a five-year, renewable term. The Secretary-General acts as chief administrative officer in all meetings of the General Assembly, Security Council and Economic and Social Council. An Office of Internal Oversight, established in 1994 under the tenure of former Secretary-General Boutros

Boutros-Ghali (Egypt), pursues a cost-saving mandate to investigate and eliminate waste, fraud and mismanagement within the system. The Secretary-General is assisted by Under-Secretaries-General and Assistant Secretaries-General. A new position of Deputy Secretary-General was agreed by the General Assembly in Dec. 1997 to assist in the running of the Secretariat and to raise the economic, social and development profile of the UN. Peacekeeping operations (PKOs) are chiefly run by Secretariat officials, who present a report to, and are authorized by, the Security Council.

Finance   The financial year coincides with the calendar year. The budget for the two-year period 2018–19 is US\$5·40bn.

Headquarters: United Nations Plaza, New York, NY 10017, USA.
Website: http://www.un.org
Secretary-General: António Guterres (in office since 1 Jan. 2017, Portugal).
Deputy Secretary-General: Amina J. Mohammed (in office since 1 Jan. 2017, Nigeria).

Secretaries-General since 1945

1945–46	UK	Gladwyn Jebb (acting)
1946–52	Norway	Trygve Halvdan Lie
1953–61	Sweden	Dag Hammarskjöld
1961–71	Burma	Sithu U Thant
1972–81	Austria	Kurt Waldheim
1982–91	Peru	Javier Pérez de Cuéllar
1992–96	Egypt	Boutros Boutros-Ghali
1997–2006	Ghana	Kofi Atta Annan
2007–16	South Korea	Ban Ki-moon
2017–	Portugal	António Guterres

The Trusteeship Council was one of the principal organs, but has been inactive since 1994. It was established to ensure that governments responsible for administering Trust Territories take adequate steps to prepare them for self-government or independence. It consisted of the five permanent members of the Security Council. The task of decolonization was completed in 1994, when the Security Council terminated the Trusteeship Agreement for the last of the original UN Trusteeships (Palau), administered by the USA. All Trust Territories attained self-government or independence either as separate States or by joining neighbouring independent countries. The Council formally suspended operations on 1 Nov. 1994 following Palau's independence. By a resolution adopted on 25 May 1994 the Council amended its rules of procedure to drop the obligation to meet annually and agreed to meet as occasion required.

The proposal from then Secretary-General Kofi Annan, in the second part of his reform programme, in July 1997, was that it should be used as a forum to exercise their 'trusteeship' for the global commons, environment and resource systems. However, in his 2005 report, *In Larger Freedom*, Annan called for the deletion of the Council from the UN Charter.

Current Leaders
António Guterres

Position
Secretary-General

Introduction
António Manuel de Oliveira Guterres took office as Secretary-General of the United Nations on 1 Jan. 2017. Having served as Portugal's prime minister from 1995–2002, his UN appointment marked the first time that the position had been taken by a former head of government.

Early Life
Guterres was born on 30 April 1949 in Lisbon. Between 1966 and 1972 he studied electronic engineering at the capital's Instituto Superior Técnico. A Catholic activist in the Juventude Universitária Católica (1968–72), he joined the Socialist Party (Partido Socialista; PS) during the 1974 revolution. He was a participant in post-revolution provisional governments and elected to the National Assembly in 1976, serving in the ministry of economics and finance until 1979. A member of the committee on European integration, which negotiated Portugal's entry into the European Union in 1986, he

returned to domestic politics the following year. Aiming to strengthen the PS in opposition, he promoted centrist policies and in 1992 he succeeded President Jorge Sampaio as party leader.

In the 1995 elections Guterres was elected prime minister with 43·9% of votes, ending ten years of rule by the centre-right Social Democrats (Partido Social Democrata; PSD). Winning with a centrist manifesto, he pledged to concentrate on social welfare, education and crime. He also planned a strict budgetary policy to prepare Portugal for adoption of the European single currency. In his first term, investment increased, public services and transport were improved and unemployment fell to 5%. Portugal adopted the single currency in 1999.

In Oct. 1999 Guterres was re-elected prime minister with 44·1% of votes while the PS's parliamentary representation increased from 112 to 115 seats, although still short of an absolute majority. The following month he was also elected chairman of the Socialist International, having previously served a seven-year term as the organization's vice president.

In 2000 a 10% increase in international oil prices and concerns over rising crime levels led to public discontent and the opposition mounted an unsuccessful no-confidence vote in parliament. Portugal had meanwhile taken over the EU presidency in the first half of the year. Guterres promoted a policy of encouraging greater labour mobility within the Union and in 2001 he called for more power for the European Commission and the European Parliament. Domestically, increased public spending caused economic problems and opposition politicians criticized the €400m. to be spent on hosting the Euro 2004 football tournament. In Dec. 2001 Guterres resigned as prime minister and called early elections.

In 2002 the PSD leader, José Manuel Durão Barroso, replaced him as prime minister. Guterres continued in his role as president of the Socialist International until 2006, while in June 2005 he became High Commissioner for Refugees at the United Nations. His ten years as head of that agency coincided with a series of refugee crises, including in Syria, Iraq and Afghanistan, and he was outspoken in his calls for Western countries to offer greater assistance to migrants. In Feb. 2016 he submitted his nomination as Portugal's candidate for the role of UN Secretary-General. After a strong performance in public hearings at the General Assembly, he was elected to the position in Oct. 2016 and took office on 1 Jan. 2017.

Career in Office
Guterres was elected despite expectations that the UN would appoint its first female Secretary-General. Against that backdrop, he nominated Amina J. Mohammed of Nigeria as deputy Secretary-General and she assumed office on the same day. On taking office Guterres appealed for 2017 to be a year for peace. However, in a depressing appraisal at the end of the year he warned that 'unfortunately, in fundamental ways, the world has gone in reverse... conflicts have deepened and new dangers have emerged'. Alluding to the crisis over North Korea's nuclear and missile tests, he said that global anxieties about nuclear weapons were the highest since the Cold War, while adding that climate change was accelerating, inequalities were growing and that there had been horrific violations of human rights. He concluded: 'As we begin 2018, I call for unity... We can settle conflicts, overcome hatred and defend shared values. But we can only do that together.'

One year on in Dec., while acknowledging some reasons for optimism such as a rapprochement between Ethiopia and Eritrea and tentative peace talks in the conflicts in Yemen and South Sudan, Guterres again issued a gloomy global assessment: 'Last New Year, I issued a red alert, and the dangers I mentioned still persist... Climate change is running faster than we are. Geopolitical divisions are deepening... and record numbers of people are moving in search of safety and protection. Inequality is growing. And people are questioning a world in which a handful of people hold the same wealth as half of humanity.' He nevertheless maintained that the United Nations would 'resolve to confront threats, defend human dignity and build a better future—together'.

Member States of the UN

The 193 member states, with percentage scale of contributions to the Regular Budget in 2018 and year of admission:

	% contribution	*Year of admission*
Afghanistan	0·006	1946
Albania	0·008	1955
Algeria	0·161	1962

(continued)

	% contribution	Year of admission		% contribution	Year of admission
Andorra	0·006	1993	The Gambia	0·001	1965
Angola	0·010	1976	Georgia	0·008	1992
Antigua and Barbuda	0·002	1981	Germany[8]	6·389	1973
Argentina[1]	0·892	1945	Ghana	0·016	1957
Armenia	0·006	1992	Greece[1]	0·471	1945
Australia[1]	2·337	1945	Grenada	0·001	1974
Austria	0·720	1955	Guatemala[1]	0·028	1945
Azerbaijan	0·060	1992	Guinea	0·002	1958
The Bahamas	0·014	1973	Guinea-Bissau	0·001	1974
Bahrain	0·044	1971	Guyana	0·002	1966
Bangladesh	0·010	1974	Haiti[1]	0·003	1945
Barbados	0·007	1966	Honduras[1]	0·008	1945
Belarus[1,2]	0·056	1945	Hungary	0·161	1955
Belgium[1]	0·885	1945	Iceland	0·023	1946
Belize	0·001	1981	India[1]	0·737	1945
Benin	0·003	1960	Indonesia[9]	0·504	1950
Bhutan	0·001	1971	Iran[1]	0·471	1945
Bolivia[1]	0·012	1945	Iraq[1]	0·129	1945
Bosnia and Herzegovina[3]	0·013	1992	Ireland, Rep. of	0·335	1955
Botswana	0·014	1966	Israel	0·430	1949
Brazil[1]	3·823	1945	Italy	3·748	1955
Brunei	0·029	1984	Jamaica	0·009	1962
Bulgaria	0·045	1955	Japan	9·680	1956
Burkina Faso	0·004	1960	Jordan	0·020	1955
Burundi	0·001	1962	Kazakhstan	0·191	1992
Cabo Verde	0·001	1975	Kenya	0·018	1963
Cambodia	0·004	1955	Kiribati	0·001	1999
Cameroon	0·010	1960	Korea, North	0·005	1991
Canada[1]	2·921	1945	Korea, South	2·039	1991
Central African Rep.	0·001	1960	Kuwait	0·285	1963
Chad	0·005	1960	Kyrgyzstan	0·002	1992
Chile[1]	0·399	1945	Laos	0·003	1955
China[1]	7·921	1945	Latvia	0·050	1991
Colombia[1]	0·322	1945	Lebanon[1]	0·046	1945
Comoros	0·001	1975	Lesotho	0·001	1966
Congo, Dem. Rep. of the[4]	0·008	1960	Liberia[1]	0·001	1945
Congo, Rep. of the	0·006	1960	Libya	0·125	1955
Costa Rica[1]	0·047	1945	Liechtenstein	0·007	1990
Côte d'Ivoire	0·009	1960	Lithuania	0·072	1991
Croatia[5]	0·099	1992	Luxembourg[1]	0·064	1945
Cuba[1]	0·065	1945	Madagascar	0·003	1960
Cyprus	0·043	1960	Malaŵi	0·002	1964
Czech Republic[6]	0·344	1993	Malaysia[10]	0·322	1957
Denmark[1]	0·584	1945	Maldives	0·002	1965
Djibouti	0·001	1977	Mali	0·003	1960
Dominica	0·001	1978	Malta	0·016	1964
Dominican Republic[1]	0·046	1945	Marshall Islands	0·001	1991
Ecuador[1]	0·067	1945	Mauritania	0·002	1961
Egypt[1,7]	0·152	1945	Mauritius	0·012	1968
El Salvador[1]	0·014	1945	Mexico[1]	1·435	1945
Equatorial Guinea	0·010	1968	Micronesia	0·001	1991
Eritrea	0·001	1993	Moldova	0·004	1992
Estonia	0·038	1991	Monaco	0·010	1993
Eswatini	0·002	1968	Mongolia	0·005	1961
Ethiopia[1]	0·010	1945	Montenegro[11]	0·004	2006
Fiji	0·003	1970	Morocco	0·054	1956
Finland	0·456	1955	Mozambique	0·004	1975
France[1]	4·859	1945	Myanmar[12]	0·010	1948
Gabon	0·017	1960	Namibia	0·010	1990

(continued) *(continued)*

	% contribution	Year of admission
Nauru	0·001	1999
Nepal	0·006	1955
Netherlands[1]	1·482	1945
New Zealand[1]	0·268	1945
Nicaragua[1]	0·004	1945
Niger	0·002	1960
Nigeria	0·209	1960
North Macedonia[5]	0·007	1993
Norway[1]	0·849	1945
Oman	0·113	1971
Pakistan	0·093	1947
Palau	0·001	1994
Panama[1]	0·034	1945
Papua New Guinea	0·004	1975
Paraguay[1]	0·014	1945
Peru[1]	0·136	1945
Philippines[1]	0·165	1945
Poland[1]	0·841	1945
Portugal	0·392	1955
Qatar	0·269	1971
Romania	0·184	1955
Russia[1,13]	3·088	1945
Rwanda	0·002	1962
St Kitts and Nevis	0·001	1983
St Lucia	0·001	1979
St Vincent and the Grenadines	0·001	1980
Samoa	0·001	1976
San Marino	0·003	1992
São Tomé and Príncipe	0·001	1975
Saudi Arabia[1]	1·146	1945
Senegal	0·005	1960
Serbia[1,14,15]	0·032	1945
Seychelles	0·001	1976
Sierra Leone	0·001	1961
Singapore[16]	0·447	1965
Slovakia[6]	0·160	1993
Slovenia[5]	0·084	1992
Solomon Islands	0·001	1978
Somalia	0·001	1960
South Africa[1]	0·364	1945
South Sudan	0·003	2011
Spain	2·443	1955
Sri Lanka	0·031	1955
Sudan	0·010	1956
Suriname	0·006	1975
Sweden	0·956	1946
Switzerland	1·140	2002
Syria[1,17]	0·024	1945
Tajikistan	0·004	1992
Tanzania[18]	0·010	1961
Thailand	0·291	1946
Timor-Leste	0·003	2002
Togo	0·001	1960
Tonga	0·001	1999
Trinidad and Tobago	0·034	1962
Tunisia	0·028	1956
Turkey[1]	1·018	1945
Turkmenistan	0·026	1992
Tuvalu	0·001	2000

	% contribution	Year of admission
Uganda	0·009	1962
Ukraine[1]	0·103	1945
United Arab		
Emirates	0·604	1971
UK[1]	4·463	1945
USA[1]	22·000	1945
Uruguay[1]	0·079	1945
Uzbekistan	0·023	1992
Vanuatu	0·001	1981
Venezuela[1]	0·571	1945
Vietnam	0·058	1977
Yemen[19]	0·010	1947
Zambia	0·007	1964
Zimbabwe	0·004	1980

[1]Original member.
[2]As Byelorussia, 1945–91.
[3]Pre-independence (1992) as part of Yugoslavia, which was an original member.
[4]As Zaïre, 1960–97.
[5]Pre-independence (1991) as part of Yugoslavia, which was an original member.
[6]Pre-partition Czechoslovakia (1945–92) was an original member.
[7]As United Arab Republic, 1958–71, following union with Syria (1958–61).
[8]Pre-unification (1990) as two states: the Federal Republic of Germany and the German Democratic Republic.
[9]Withdrew temporarily, 1965–66.
[10]As the Federation of Malaya till 1963, when the new federation of Malaysia (including Singapore, Sarawak and Sabah) was formed.
[11]Pre-independence (2006) as part of Yugoslavia, which was an original member, from 1945–2003 and Serbia and Montenegro from 2003–06.
[12]As Burma, 1948–89.
[13]As USSR, 1945–91.
[14]As Yugoslavia, 1945–2003, and Serbia and Montenegro, 2003–06.
[15]Excluded from the General Assembly in 1992; readmitted in Nov. 2000.
[16]As part of Malaysia, 1963–65.
[17]As United Arab Republic, by union with Egypt, 1958–61.
[18]As two states: Tanganyika, 1961–64, and Zanzibar, 1963–64, prior to union as one republic under new name.
[19]As Yemen, 1947–90, and Democratic Yemen, 1967–90, prior to merger of the two.

The USA is the leading contributor to the Peacekeeping Operations Budget, with 28·4344% of the total in 2018, followed by China (10·2377%), Japan (9·6800%), Germany (6·3890%), France (6·2801%), UK (5·7683%), Russia (3·9912%) and Italy (3·7480%). All other countries contribute less than 3%.

Publications *Yearbook of the United Nations.* New York, 1947 ff.—*UN Chronicle* (quarterly).—*Monthly Bulletin of Statistics.*—*Resolutions and Decisions Adopted by the General Assembly* (annual; in three volumes).—*Report of the Secretary-General of the United Nations on the Work of the Organization.* 1946 ff.—*Charter of the United Nations and Statute of the International Court of Justice.*—*Security Council: Index to Proceedings; Resolutions and Decisions; Report.*—*Economic and Social Council: Index to Proceedings; Resolutions and Decisions; Report.*—*Demographic Yearbook.* New York, 1948 ff.—*The United Nations Today.* New York, 2008.—*Statistical Yearbook.* New York, 1947 ff. (regional versions for: Africa; Asia and the Pacific; Latin America and the Caribbean).—*World Economic and Social Survey.* New York, 1947 ff.—*Economic and Social Survey of Asia and the Pacific.* New York, 1946 ff.—*Economic Survey of Latin America and the Caribbean.* New York, 1948 ff.—*Economic Survey of Europe.* New York, 1948 ff.—*Economic Development in Africa Report.* Geneva, 2000 ff.—*International Trade Statistics Yearbook* (annual; in two volumes). 1992 ff.—*World Economic Situation and Prospects.* 1999 ff.—*Energy Statistics Yearbook.* 1956 ff.—*The United Nations Disarmament Yearbook.* 1976 ff.—*Review of Maritime Transport.* 1968 ff.—*World Statistics Pocketbook.* 1976 ff.—*World Youth Report* (biennial), 2003 ff.—*United Nations Reference Guide in the Field of Human Rights.* UN Centre for Human Rights, 1993.

(*continued*)

Universal Declaration of Human Rights

On 10 Dec. 1948 the General Assembly of the United Nations adopted and proclaimed the Universal Declaration of Human Rights.

Preamble

Whereas recognition of the inherent dignity and of the equal and inalienable rights of all members of the human family is the foundation of freedom, justice and peace in the world,

Whereas disregard and contempt for human rights have resulted in barbarous acts which have outraged the conscience of mankind, and the advent of a world in which human beings shall enjoy freedom of speech and belief and freedom from fear and want has been proclaimed as the highest aspiration of the common people,

Whereas it is essential, if man is not to be compelled to have recourse, as a last resort, to rebellion against tyranny and oppression, that human rights should be protected by the rule of law,

Whereas it is essential to promote the development of friendly relations between nations,

Whereas the peoples of the United Nations have in the Charter reaffirmed their faith in fundamental human rights, in the dignity and worth of the human person and in the equal rights of men and women and have determined to promote social progress and better standards of life in larger freedom,

Whereas Member States have pledged themselves to achieve, in co-operation with the United Nations, the promotion of universal respect for and observance of human rights and fundamental freedoms,

Whereas a common understanding of these rights and freedoms is of the greatest importance for the full realization of this pledge,

Now, Therefore THE GENERAL ASSEMBLY proclaims THIS UNIVERSAL DECLARATION OF HUMAN RIGHTS as a common standard of achievement for all peoples and all nations, to the end that every individual and every organ of society, keeping this Declaration constantly in mind, shall strive by teaching and education to promote respect for these rights and freedoms and by progressive measures, national and international, to secure their universal and effective recognition and observance, both among the peoples of Member States themselves and among the peoples of territories under their jurisdiction.

Article 1

All human beings are born free and equal in dignity and rights. They are endowed with reason and conscience and should act towards one another in a spirit of brotherhood.

Article 2

Everyone is entitled to all the rights and freedoms set forth in this Declaration, without distinction of any kind, such as race, colour, sex, language, religion, political or other opinion, national or social origin, property, birth or other status. Furthermore, no distinction shall be made on the basis of the political, jurisdictional or international status of the country or territory to which a person belongs, whether it be independent, trust, non-self-governing or under any other limitation of sovereignty.

Article 3

Everyone has the right to life, liberty and security of person.

Article 4

No one shall be held in slavery or servitude; slavery and the slave trade shall be prohibited in all their forms.

Article 5

No one shall be subjected to torture or to cruel, inhuman or degrading treatment or punishment.

Article 6

Everyone has the right to recognition everywhere as a person before the law.

Article 7

All are equal before the law and are entitled without any discrimination to equal protection of the law. All are entitled to equal protection against any discrimination in violation of this Declaration and against any incitement to such discrimination.

Article 8

Everyone has the right to an effective remedy by the competent national tribunals for acts violating the fundamental rights granted him by the constitution or by law.

Article 9

No one shall be subjected to arbitrary arrest, detention or exile.

Article 10

Everyone is entitled in full equality to a fair and public hearing by an independent and impartial tribunal, in the determination of his rights and obligations and of any criminal charge against him.

Article 11

(1) Everyone charged with a penal offence has the right to be presumed innocent until proved guilty according to law in a public trial at which he has had all the guarantees necessary for his defence.

(2) No one shall be held guilty of any penal offence on account of any act or omission which did not constitute a penal offence, under national or international law, at the time when it was committed. Nor shall a heavier penalty be imposed than the one that was applicable at the time the penal offence was committed.

Article 12

No one shall be subjected to arbitrary interference with his privacy, family, home or correspondence, nor to attacks upon his honour and reputation. Everyone has the right to the protection of the law against such interference or attacks.

Article 13

(1) Everyone has the right to freedom of movement and residence within the borders of each state.

(2) Everyone has the right to leave any country, including his own, and to return to his country.

Article 14

(1) Everyone has the right to seek and enjoy in other countries asylum from persecution.

(2) This right may not be invoked in the case of prosecutions genuinely arising from non-political crimes or from acts contrary to the purposes and principles of the United Nations.

Article 15

(1) Everyone has the right to a nationality.

(2) No one shall be arbitrarily deprived of his nationality nor denied the right to change his nationality.

Article 16

(1) Men and women of full age, without any limitation due to race, nationality or religion, have the right to marry and to found a family. They are entitled to equal rights as to marriage, during marriage and at its dissolution.

(2) Marriage shall be entered into only with the free and full consent of the intending spouses.

(3) The family is the natural and fundamental group unit of society and is entitled to protection by society and the State.

Article 17

(1) Everyone has the right to own property alone as well as in association with others.

(2) No one shall be arbitrarily deprived of his property.

Article 18

Everyone has the right to freedom of thought, conscience and religion; this right includes freedom to change his religion or belief, and freedom, either alone or in community with others and in public or private, to manifest his religion or belief in teaching, practice, worship and observance.

Article 19

Everyone has the right to freedom of opinion and expression; this right includes freedom to hold opinions without interference and to seek, receive and impart information and ideas through any media and regardless of frontiers.

Article 20

(1) Everyone has the right to freedom of peaceful assembly and association.
(2) No one may be compelled to belong to an association.

Article 21

(1) Everyone has the right to take part in the government of his country, directly or through freely chosen representatives.
(2) Everyone has the right of equal access to public service in his country.
(3) The will of the people shall be the basis of the authority of government; this will shall be expressed in periodic and genuine elections which shall be by universal and equal suffrage and shall be held by secret vote or by equivalent free voting procedures.

Article 22

Everyone, as a member of society, has the right to social security and is entitled to realization, through national effort and international co-operation and in accordance with the organization and resources of the State, of the economic, social and cultural rights indispensable for his dignity and the free development of his personality.

Article 23

(1) Everyone has the right to work, to free choice of employment, to just and favourable conditions of work and to protection against unemployment.
(2) Everyone, without any discrimination, has the right to equal pay for equal work.
(3) Everyone who works has the right to just and favourable remuneration ensuring for himself and his family an existence worthy of human dignity, and supplemented, if necessary, by other means of social protection.
(4) Everyone has the right to form and to join trade unions for the protection of his interests.

Article 24

Everyone has the right to rest and leisure, including reasonable limitation of working hours and periodic holidays with pay.

Article 25

(1) Everyone has the right to a standard of living adequate for the health and well-being of himself and his family, including food, clothing, housing and medical care and necessary social services, and the right to security in the event of unemployment, sickness, disability, widowhood, old age or other lack of livelihood in circumstances beyond his control.
(2) Motherhood and childhood are entitled to special care and assistance. All children, whether born in or out of wedlock, shall enjoy the same social protection.

Article 26

(1) Everyone has the right to education. Education shall be free, at least in the elementary and fundamental stages. Elementary education shall be compulsory. Technical and professional education shall be made generally available and higher education shall be equally accessible to all on the basis of merit.
(2) Education shall be directed to the full development of the human personality and to the strengthening of respect for human rights and fundamental freedoms. It shall promote understanding, tolerance and friendship among all nations, racial or religious groups, and shall further the activities of the United Nations for the maintenance of peace.
(3) Parents have a prior right to choose the kind of education that shall be given to their children.

Article 27

(1) Everyone has the right freely to participate in the cultural life of the community, to enjoy the arts and to share in scientific advancement and its benefits.
(2) Everyone has the right to the protection of the moral and material interests resulting from any scientific, literary or artistic production of which he is the author.

Article 28

Everyone is entitled to a social and international order in which the rights and freedoms set forth in this Declaration can be fully realized.

Article 29

(1) Everyone has duties to the community in which alone the free and full development of his personality is possible.
(2) In the exercise of his rights and freedoms, everyone shall be subject only to such limitations as are determined by law solely for the purpose of securing due recognition and respect for the rights and freedoms of others and of meeting the just requirements of morality, public order and the general welfare in a democratic society.
(3) These rights and freedoms may in no case be exercised contrary to the purposes and principles of the United Nations.

Article 30

Nothing in this Declaration may be interpreted as implying for any State, group or person any right to engage in any activity or to perform any act aimed at the destruction of any of the rights and freedoms set forth herein.

United Nations System

Programmes and Funds

Social and economic development, aimed at achieving a better life for people everywhere, is a major part of the UN system of organizations. At the forefront of efforts to bring about such progress is the United Nations Development Programme (UNDP), the UN's global development network. UNDP works with people at all levels of society to help build nations that can withstand crisis, and drive and sustain the kind of growth that improves the quality of life for everyone. In 2014 UNDP programmes helped: empower people and build more resilient communities in 161 countries; create nearly 1m. jobs, 41% of them for women; strengthen livelihoods in low-income communities, benefitting 11·2m. people; combat climate change and mitigate its impacts in 140 countries; register 18m. new voters, including nearly 4m. in Afghanistan; train 2m. health workers to fight HIV/AIDS, tuberculosis and malaria; improve energy access for 1·3m. people.

UNDP assistance is provided only at the request of governments and in response to their priority needs, integrated into overall national and regional plans. Its activities are funded entirely through voluntary contributions outside the regular UN budget. 80% of UNDP's core programme resources go to low-income countries and Least Developed Countries (LDCs), with more than 50% of UNDP's core programme resources going to Africa. Headquartered in New York, the UNDP is governed by a 36-member Executive Board, representing both developing and developed countries.

In addition to its regular programmes, UNDP administers various special-purpose funds, such as the *UN Capital Development Fund (UNCDF)*, which offers a unique combination of investment capital, capacity building and technical advisory services to promote microfinance and local development in the LDCs and the *United Nations Volunteers (UNV)*, which is the UN focal point for promoting and harnessing volunteerism for effective development. Together with the World Bank and the United Nations Environment Programme (UNEP), UNDP is one of the three implementing agencies of the Global Environment Facility (GEF), the world's largest fund for protecting the environment.

UNDP works with governments and local communities on their own solutions to global and national development challenges. In each country office, the UNDP Resident Representative normally also serves as the Resident Coordinator of development activities for the UN system as a whole.

Administrator: Achim Steiner (Brazil/Germany).

United Nations development and humanitarian agencies include the *United Nations Children's Fund (UNICEF)*. It was established in 1946 by the United Nations General Assembly as the United Nations International Children's Emergency Fund, to meet the emergency needs of children of post-war Europe. In 1953 the organization became a permanent part of the UN and its mandate was expanded to carry out long-term programmes to benefit children worldwide. Guided by the Convention on the Rights of the Child and its Optional Protocols and the Convention on the Elimination of All Forms of Discrimination Against Women, UNICEF supports programmes to improve the wellbeing of children and women in more than 150 countries and territories. UNICEF also provides relief and rehabilitation assistance in emergencies.

UNICEF's strategic plan for 2018–21 is rooted in the aim of realizing the rights of every child, especially the most disadvantaged. UNICEF's strategy to achieve this incorporates several strands, including:

(a) Every child survives and thrives
(b) Every child learns
(c) Every child is protected from violence and exploitation
(d) Every child lives in a safe and clean environment
(e) Every child has an equitable chance in life

UNICEF's work in recent years has contributed to progress towards several Millennium Development Goals, including the steady decline of under-five mortality; a reduction in the number of primary-age out-of-school children; a decrease in the number of underweight children aged under five; an increase in birth registration; sustainable access to safe drinking water; and prevention of mother-to-child transmission and new infections among young people of HIV.

Executive Director: Henrietta H. Fore (USA).

The *United Nations Population Fund (UNFPA)* became operational in 1969 and is the leading provider of United Nations assistance in the field of population. Its mandate is to build the knowledge and the capacity to respond to needs in population and family planning; to promote awareness in both developed and developing countries of population problems and possible strategies to deal with these problems; to assist their population problems in the forms and means best suited to the individual countries' needs; to assume a leading role in the United Nations system in promoting population pro-grammes, and to co-ordinate projects supported by the Fund.

UNFPA's mission is to ensure that every pregnancy is wanted, every childbirth is safe and every young person's potential is fulfilled. Since UNFPA started working in 1969 the number of women dying from compli-cations of pregnancy or childbirth has been halved. It works in more than 150 countries and territories that are home to the vast majority of the world's people. In 2015 UNFPA total gross contribution revenue was US$979·5m. Main programme expenses by focus area are: maternal and new-born health, 26·2%; family planning, 24·6%; programme co-ordination and assistance, 10·4%. UNFPA's *The State of World Population* report is published annually.

Executive Director: Dr Natalia Kanem (Panama).

The *United Nations Environment Programme (UNEP)*, established in 1972, works to encourage sustainable development through sound environ-mental practices everywhere. UNEP has its headquarters in Nairobi, Kenya and regional offices in Bangkok, Geneva, Manama, Panama City and Washington, D.C. Its activities cover a wide range of issues, from atmosphere and terrestrial ecosystems, to the promotion of environmental science and information, to an early warning and emergency response capacity to deal with environmental disasters and emergencies. UNEP's present priorities include: environmental information, assessment and research; enhanced co-ordination of environmental conventions and development of policy instruments; fresh water; technology transfer and industry; and support to Africa. Information networks and monitoring systems established by the UNEP include: the Global Environment Information Exchange Network (INFOTERRA); Global Resource Information Database (GRID); the Inter-national Register of Potentially Toxic Chemicals (IRPTC); and the recent UNEP.net, a web-based interactive catalogue and multifaceted portal that offers access to environmentally relevant geographic, textual and pictorial information. In June 2000 the World Conservation and Monitoring Centre (WCMC) based in Cambridge, UK became UNEP's key biodiversity assess-ment centre. UNEP's latest state-of-the-environment report is *Frontiers 2017: Emerging Issues of Environmental Concern*.

Executive Director: Erik Solheim (Norway).

Other UN programmes working for development include: the *UN Con-ference on Trade and Development (UNCTAD)*, which promotes interna-tional trade, particularly by developing countries, in an attempt to increase their participation in the global economy; and the *World Food Programme (WFP)*, the world's largest international food aid organization, which is dedicated to both emergency relief and development programmes.

The *United Nations Human Settlements Programme (UN-Habitat)*, which assists over 600m. people living in health-threatening housing condi-tions, was established in 1978. The 58-member Governing Council, Habitat's governing body, meets every two years. The Centre serves as the focal point for human settlements action and the co-ordination of activities within the UN system.

The *United Nations Office on Drugs and Crime* (UNODC) educates the world about the dangers of drug abuse; strengthens international action against drug production, trafficking and drug related crime; promotes efforts to reduce drug abuse, particularly among the young and vulnerable; builds local, national and international partnerships to address drug issues; provides information, analysis and expertise on the drug issue; promotes international co-operation in crime prevention and control; supports the development of criminal justice systems; and assists member states in addressing the chal-lenges and threats posed by the changing nature of transnational organized crime.

Executive Director: Yury Fedotov (Russia).

The UN work in crime prevention and criminal justice aims to lessen the human and material costs of crime and its impact on socio-economic devel-opment. The UN Congress on the Prevention of Crime and Treatment of Offenders has convened every five years since 1955 and provides a forum for the presentation of policies and progress. The Thirteenth Crime Congress (Doha, 2015) had as its theme 'Integrating crime prevention and criminal justice into the wider United Nations agenda to address social and economic challenges and to promote the rule of law at the national and international levels, and public participation'. The *Commission on Crime Prevention and Criminal Justice*, a functional body of ECOSOC, established in 1992, seeks to strengthen UN activities in the field, and meets annually in Vienna. The interregional research and training arm of the UN crime and criminal justice programme is the *United Nations Interregional Crime and Justice Research Institute (UNICRI)* in Rome.

Humanitarian assistance to refugees and victims of natural and man-made disasters is also an important function of the UN system. The main refugee organizations within the system are the *Office of the United Nations High Commissioner for Refugees (UNHCR)* and the *United Nations Relief and Works Agency for Palestine Refugees in the Near East (UNRWA)*.

UNHCR was created in 1951 to resettle 1·2m. European refugees left homeless in the aftermath of the Second World War. It was initially envisioned as a temporary office with a projected lifespan of three years. However, in 2003, in a move to strengthen UNHCR's capacity to carry out its work more effectively, the General Assembly removed the time limitation on the organization's mandate and extended it indefinitely, until 'the refugee problem is solved'. Today, with some 58·0m. persons of concern across the globe, UNHCR has become one of the world's principal humanitarian agencies. Its Executive Committee currently comprises 98 member states. With its Headquarters in Geneva, UNHCR has a national and international staff of 11,000 working in 130 countries. The organization has twice been awarded the Nobel Peace Prize. UNHCR is a subsidiary organ of the United Nations General Assembly.

The work of UNHCR is humanitarian and non-political. International protection is its primary function. Its main objective is to promote and safeguard the rights and interests of refugees. In so doing UNHCR devotes special attention to promoting access to asylum and seeks to improve the legal, material and physical safety of refugees in their country of residence. Crucial to this status is the principle of *non-refoulement*, which prohibits the expulsion from or forcible return of refugees to a country where they may have reason to fear persecution. UNHCR pursues its objectives in the field of protection by encouraging the conclusion of intergovernmental legal instru-ments in favour of refugees, by supervising the implementation of their provisions and by encouraging governments to adopt legislation and admin-istrative procedures for the benefit of refugees. UNHCR is often called upon to provide material assistance (e.g. the provision of food, shelter, medical care and essential supplies) while durable solutions are being sought. Durable solutions generally take one of three forms: voluntary repatriation, local integration or resettlement in another country.

UNHCR co-operates both multilaterally and bilaterally with a wide range of partners in order to fulfil its mandate for refugees and other people of concern to the Office. Partners include UN co-ordination bodies, other UN agencies and departments, intergovernmental organizations, non-governmental organiza-tions (NGOs), universities and research institutes, regional organizations, foun-dations and corporate entities from the private sector, as well as governments, host communities and refugee and other displaced population representatives. In response to calls by the international community to improve the global humanitarian response capacity, today UNHCR is playing an active role in the inter-agency 'cluster leadership approach' with respect to protecting and assisting internally displaced persons. UNHCR's involvement is focused on conflict-generated situations of internal displacement, where it leads the protection 'cluster', the camp co-ordination and camp management 'cluster' and the emergency shelter 'cluster'. At present, UNHCR is funded almost entirely by voluntary contributions. In 2016 UNHCR's expenditure amounted to US$3·96bn.

High Commissioner: Filippo Grandi (Italy).

UNRWA was created by the General Assembly in 1949 as a temporary, non-political agency to provide relief to the nearly 750,000 people who became refugees as a result of the disturbances during and after the creation of the State of Israel in the former British Mandate territory of Palestine. 'Palestine refugees', as defined by UNRWA's mandate, are persons or descendants of persons whose normal residence was Palestine for at least two years prior to the 1948 conflict and who, as a result of the conflict, lost their homes and means of livelihood. UNRWA has also been called upon to help persons displaced by renewed hostilities in the Middle East in 1967. The situation of Palestine refugees in south Lebanon, affected in the aftermath of the 1982 Israeli invasion of Lebanon, was of special concern to the Agency in 1984. UNRWA provides education, health, relief and social services to eligible refugees among the 4·8m. registered Palestine refugees in its five fields of operation: Jordan, Lebanon, Syria, the West Bank and the Gaza Strip. Its mandate is renewed at intervals by the UN General Assembly, and in Dec. 2016 was extended until 30 June 2020. The regular budget for 2015 amounted to US$743·8m.

Commissioner-General: Pierre Krähenbühl (Switzerland).

The *Office of the High Commissioner for Human Rights (OHCHR)* represents the world's commitment to universal ideals of human dignity. The UN's activities in the field of human rights are the primary responsibility of the High Commissioner for Human Rights, a post established in 1993 under the direction and authority of the Secretary-General. The High Commissioner is nominated by the Secretary-General for a four-year term, renewable once. The principal co-ordinating human rights organ of the UN was until mid-2006 the 53-member Commission on Human Rights, set up by ECOSOC in 1946. On 15 March 2006 the UN General Assembly voted overwhelmingly to abolish the Commission after it was criticized for having member countries with poor human rights records. A 47-member *Human Rights Council* was established as its successor and held its first session in June 2006. In June 2018 the USA withdrew from the Council, accusing the organization of political bias.

High Commissioner: Michelle Bachelet (Chile).

Research and Training Institutes
There are six research and training institutes within the UN, all of them autonomous.

United Nations Institute for Disarmament Research (UNIDIR) Established in 1980 to undertake research on disarmament and security with the aim of assisting the international community in their disarmament thinking, decisions and efforts. Through its research projects, publications, small meetings and expert networks, UNIDIR promotes creative thinking and dialogue on both current and future security issues, through examination of topics as varied as tactical nuclear weapons, refugee security, computer warfare, regional confidence-building measures and small arms.

Address: Palais des Nations, 1211 Geneva 10, Switzerland.
Website: http://www.unidir.org

United Nations Institute for Training and Research (UNITAR) Founded in 1965, UNITAR is the leading UN institute offering training on global and strategic challenges. As an autonomous body within the UN system, UNITAR is led by an Executive Director, governed by a Board of Trustees and is supported by voluntary contributions from governments, intergovernmental organizations, foundations and the private sector. With nearly 40,000 beneficiaries in 2015 the Institute provides short executive training to national and local government officials of UN member states and civil society representatives around the world. UNITAR aims to meet the growing demand, especially from the least developed countries, for capacity development in the fields of environment, peace, security and diplomacy, and governance.

Address: Palais des Nations, 1211 Geneva 10, Switzerland.
Website: http://www.unitar.org

United Nations Interregional Crime and Justice Research Institute (UNICRI) Established in 1967 to support countries worldwide in crime prevention and criminal justice, UNICRI offers technical co-operation, research and training at various levels for governments and the international community as a whole. The institute particularly focuses on security and counter-terrorism, counter-trafficking and preventing money laundering.

Address: 10 Viale Maestri del Lavoro, 10127 Turin, Italy.
Website: http://www.unicri.it

United Nations Research Institute for Social Development (UNRISD) Established in 1963 to conduct multidisciplinary research into the social dimensions of contemporary problems affecting development, it aims to provide governments, development agencies, grassroots organizations and scholars with a better understanding of how development policies and processes of economic, social and environmental change affect different social groups.

Address: Palais des Nations, CH-1211 Geneva 10, Switzerland.
Website: http://www.unrisd.org

United Nations System Staff College (UNSSC) Established in 2002 as the pre-eminent learning arm of the UN, the College develops, co-ordinates and provides cross-organization training programmes with a view to strengthening collaboration within the UN system and increasing operational effectiveness. The UNSCC reaches an average of 7,000 beneficiaries worldwide every year.

Address: Viale Maestri del Lavoro 10, 10127 Turin, Italy.
Website: http://www.unssc.org/home

United Nations University (UNU) Sponsored jointly by the UN and UNESCO, UNU is guaranteed academic freedom by a charter approved by the General Assembly in 1973. It is governed by the UNU Council, composed of 13 appointed members who serve six-year terms (in an individual capacity, not as representatives of their countries), three *ex officio* members (the UN Secretary-General, the UNESCO Director-General and the UNITAR Executive Director) and the UNU Rector. Unlike a traditional university with a campus, students and faculty, it works through networks of collaborating institutions and individuals to undertake multidisciplinary research on problems of human survival, development and welfare; and to strengthen research and training capabilities in developing countries. It also provides postgraduate fellowships and PhD internships to scholars and scientists from developing countries. The University focuses its work within two programme areas: peace and governance, and environment and development.

Address: 5–53–70 Jingumae, Shibuya-ku, Tokyo 150-8925, Japan.
Website: http://www.unu.edu

Other UN Entities
In addition to the operational programmes and funds and the research and training institutes there are several other entities that fall within the UN system.

International Computing Centre (ICC) The Centre was established in 1971 as a common service, providing a wide range of Information and Communication Technology Services, on a cost recovery basis, to its users worldwide. More than 25 organizations, funds and programmes of the UN system currently use its services and participate in its governance.

Address: Palais des Nations, CH-1211 Geneva 10, Switzerland.
Website: http://www.unicc.org

Joint UN Programme on HIV/AIDS (UNAIDS) In 1996 the Assembly reviewed implementation of the global strategy for the prevention and control of AIDS, and progress of the Joint UN Programme on HIV/AIDS (UNAIDS), which became operational in 1996. The impact of the HIV/AIDS epidemic was seen to be expanding and intensifying, particularly in developing countries, and new resource mobilization mechanisms were called for to support countries in combating HIV/AIDS. UNAIDS brings together the HIV/AIDS responses of 11 co-sponsor UN agencies, providing an overall framework for action and ensuring better co-ordination between its members. The co-sponsor agencies are: International Labour Organization (ILO), Office of the United Nations High Commissioner for Refugees (UNHCR), United Nations Children's Fund (UNICEF), United Nations Development Programme (UNDP), United Nations Educational, Scientific and Cultural Organization (UNESCO), United Nations Entity for Gender Equality and the Empowerment of Women (UN Women), United Nations Office on Drugs and Crime (UNODC), United Nations Population Fund (UNFPA), World Bank, World Food Programme (WFP) and World Health Organization (WHO). The proposed budget for 2016–17 amounted to US$484·8m.

Address: 20 avenue Appia, 1211 CH-Geneva 27, Switzerland.
Website: http://www.unaids.org

UN Office for Project Services (UNOPS) Established in 1995, the self-funding unit provides a range of services for other organizations in the UN system, the private sector, NGOs and academic institutions. Services offered include procurement, recruitment and human resources, and loan supervision.

Address: Marmorvej 51, PO Box 2695, 2100 Copenhagen, Denmark.
Website: http://www.unops.org

United Nations Entity for Gender Equality and the Empowerment of Women (UN Women) Established in July 2010, UN Women supports international political negotiations to formulate globally agreed standards for gender equality and helps UN member states to implement those standards by providing expertise and financial support. It merges and builds on the work of four previously distinct parts of the UN system: the Division for the Advancement of Women (DAW), the International Research and Training Institute for the Advancement of Women (INSTRAW), the Office of the Special Adviser on Gender Issues and Advancement of Women (OSAGI) and the United Nations Development Fund for Women (UNIFEM).

Address: 220 East 42nd St., New York, NY 10017, USA.
Website: http://www.unwomen.org

United Nations Office for Disaster Risk Reduction (UNISDR) Established in 1999 after the UN General Assembly adopted an international strategy for disaster reduction, UNISDR is the focal point in the UN system for the co-ordination of disaster risk reduction (DRR) and the implementation of the international blueprint for DRR. Its core areas of work include ensuring DRR is applied to climate change adaptation, increasing investments for DRR, building disaster-resilient cities, schools and hospitals, and strengthening the international system for DRR.

Address: 9–11 rue de Varembé, CH-1202 Geneva, Switzerland.
Website: http://www.unisdr.org

Information

The *UN Statistics Division* in New York provides a wide range of statistical outputs and services for producers and users of statistics worldwide, facilitating national and international policy formulation, implementation and monitoring. It produces printed publications of statistics and statistical methods in the fields of international merchandise trade, national accounts, demography and population, gender, industry, energy, environment, human settlements and disability, as well as general statistics compendiums including the *Statistical Yearbook* and *World Statistics Pocketbook*. Many of its databases are available on CD-ROM and the internet.

Website: http://unstats.un.org
UN Visitor Centre. Department of Public Information, United Nations Headquarters, Room GA-1B-31, New York, NY 10017.
Website: http://visit.un.org
UN Information Centres. UN information centres are located in 63 countries around the world.
Website: https://unic.un.org

Specialized Agencies of the UN

The intergovernmental agencies related to the UN by special agreements are separate autonomous organizations which work with the UN and each other through the co-ordinating machinery of the Economic and Social Council. Of these, 19 are 'Specialized Agencies' within the terms of the UN Charter, and report annually to ECOSOC.

Food and Agriculture Organization of the United Nations (FAO)

Origin In 1943 the International Conference on Food and Agriculture, at Hot Springs, Virginia, set up an Interim Commission, based in Washington, with a remit to establish an organization. Its Constitution was signed on 16 Oct. 1945 in Quebec City. Today, membership totals 194 countries plus one member organization and two associate members. The European Union was made a member as a 'regional economic integration organization' in 1991.

Aims and Activities The aims of FAO are to raise levels of nutrition and standards of living; to improve the production and distribution of all food and agricultural products from farms, forests and fisheries; to improve the living conditions of rural populations; and, by these means, to eliminate hunger. Its priority objectives are to encourage sustainable agriculture and rural development as part of a long-term strategy for the conservation and management of natural resources; and to ensure the availability of adequate food supplies, by maximizing stability in the flow of supplies and securing access to food by the poor.

In carrying out these aims, FAO promotes investment in agriculture, better soil and water management, improved yields of crops and livestock, agricultural research and the transfer of technology to developing countries; and encourages the conservation of natural resources and rational use of fertilizers and pesticides; the development and sustainable utilization of marine and inland fisheries; the sustainable management of forest resources and the combating of animal disease. Technical assistance is provided in all of these fields, and in nutrition, agricultural engineering, agrarian reform, development communications, remote sensing for climate and vegetation, and the prevention of post-harvest food losses. In addition, FAO works to maintain global biodiversity with the emphasis on the genetic diversity of crop plants and domesticated animals; and plays a major role in the collection, analysis and dissemination of information on agricultural production and commodities. Finally, FAO acts as a neutral forum for the discussion of issues, and advises governments on policy, through international conferences like the *World Food Summit* in 1996, the *World Food Summit: five years later* in 2002 and the *World Summit on Food Security* in 2009, all held in Rome.

Special FAO programmes help countries prepare for, and provide relief in the event of, emergency food situations, in particular through the rehabilitation of agriculture after disasters. The *Special Programme for Food Security*, launched in 1994, is designed to assist target countries to increase food production and productivity as rapidly as possible, primarily through the widespread adoption by farmers of available improved production technologies, with the emphasis on high-potential areas. FAO provides support for the global co-ordination of the programme and helps attract funds. The *Emergency Prevention System for Transboundary Animal and Plant Pests and Diseases (EMPRES)*, established in 1994, strengthens FAO's existing contribution to the prevention, control and eradication of diseases and pests before they compromise food security, with locusts and rinderpest among its priorities. *The Global Information and Early Warning System (GIEWS)* provides current information on the world food situation and identifies countries threatened by shortages to guide potential donors. The interagency Food Insecurity and Vulnerability Information and Mapping System initiative (FIVIMS) was established in 1997, with FAO as its Secretariat. Together with the UN, FAO sponsors the *World Food Programme (WFP)*.

Finance The FAO regular budget for the 2018–19 biennium was US$1,005·6m. FAO's overall programme of work is funded by assessed and voluntary contributions. Member countries' assessed contributions comprise the regular budget, set at the biennial FAO Conference.

The total FAO Budget planned for 2018–19 was US$2·6bn. Of this amount 39% was to come from assessed contributions paid by member countries, with 61% mobilized through voluntary contributions from members and other partners.

The voluntary contributions provided by members and other partners support technical and emergency (including rehabilitation) assistance to governments for clearly defined purposes linked to the results framework, as well as direct support to FAO's core work. The voluntary contributions were expected to reach approximately US$1·6bn. in 2018–19.

In 2014–15, 304 projects totalling US$98·7m. were approved for development support.

Organization The FAO Conference, composed of all members, meets every other year to determine policy and approve the FAO's budget and programme. The 49-member Council, elected by the Conference, serves as FAO's governing body between conference sessions. Much of its work is carried out by dozens of regional or specialist commissions, such as the Asia-Pacific Fishery Commission, the European Commission on Agriculture and the Commission on Plant Genetic Resources. The Director-General is elected for a renewable six-year term.

Headquarters: Viale delle Terme di Caracalla, 00153 Rome, Italy.
Website: http://www.fao.org
Director-General: José Graziano da Silva (Brazil).

Publications *Unasylva,* 1947 ff.—*The State of Food and Agriculture,* 1947 ff.—*FAO Statistical Yearbook: World Food and Agriculture,* 2004 ff. (regional versions for: Africa; Asia and the Pacific; Europe and Central Asia; Latin America and the Caribbean; Near East and North Africa).—*Commodity Market Review* (biennial), 1961 ff.—*FAO Yearbook of Forest Products,* 1947 ff.—*FAO Yearbook. Fishery and Aquaculture Statistics.—The State of World Fisheries and Aquaculture* (biennial).—*The State of Food Insecurity in the World,* 1999 ff.—*The State of the World's Forests,* 1995 ff.—*World Watch List: for Domestic Animal Diversity.* 3rd ed. 2000.—*Food and Nutrition in Numbers* (online only). 2014.

International Bank for Reconstruction and Development (IBRD) — The World Bank

Origin Conceived at the UN Monetary and Financial Conference at Bretton Woods (New Hampshire, USA) in July 1944, the IBRD, frequently called the World Bank, began operations in June 1946, its purpose being to provide funds, policy guidance and technical assistance to facilitate economic development in its poorer member countries. The Group comprises four other organizations: the International Development Association (IDA), which provides interest-free loans and grants to governments of the poorest countries; the International Finance Corporation (IFC), which provides loans, equity and technical assistance to stimulate private sector investment in developing countries; the Multilateral Investment Guarantee Agency (MIGA), which provides guarantees against losses caused by non-commercial risks to investors in developing countries; and the International Centre for Settlement of Investment Disputes (ICSID), which provides international facilities for conciliation and arbitration of investment disputes.

Members Afghanistan, Albania, Algeria, Angola, Antigua and Barbuda, Argentina, Armenia, Australia, Austria, Azerbaijan, The Bahamas, Bahrain, Bangladesh, Barbados, Belarus, Belgium, Belize, Benin, Bhutan, Bolivia, Bosnia and Herzegovina, Botswana, Brazil, Brunei, Bulgaria, Burkina Faso, Burundi, Cabo Verde, Cambodia, Cameroon, Canada, Central African Republic, Chad, Chile, China, Colombia, Comoros, Democratic Republic of the Congo, Republic of the Congo, Costa Rica, Côte d'Ivoire, Croatia, Cyprus, Czech Republic, Denmark, Djibouti, Dominica, Dominican Republic, Ecuador, Egypt, El Salvador, Equatorial Guinea, Eritrea, Estonia, Eswatini, Ethiopia, Fiji, Finland, France, Gabon, The Gambia, Georgia, Germany, Ghana, Greece, Grenada, Guatemala, Guinea, Guinea-Bissau, Guyana, Haiti, Honduras, Hungary, Iceland, India, Indonesia, Iran, Iraq, Ireland, Israel, Italy, Jamaica, Japan, Jordan, Kazakhstan, Kenya, Kiribati, South Korea, Kosovo, Kuwait, Kyrgyzstan, Laos, Latvia, Lebanon, Lesotho, Liberia, Libya, Lithuania, Luxembourg, Madagascar, Malawi, Malaysia, Maldives, Mali, Malta, Marshall Islands, Mauritania, Mauritius, Mexico, Micronesia, Moldova, Mongolia, Montenegro, Morocco, Mozambique, Myanmar, Namibia, Nauru, Nepal, Netherlands, New Zealand, Nicaragua, Niger, Nigeria, North Macedonia, Norway, Oman, Pakistan, Palau, Panama, Papua New Guinea, Paraguay, Peru, Philippines, Poland, Portugal, Qatar, Romania, Russia, Rwanda, St Kitts and Nevis, St Lucia, St Vincent and the Grenadines, Samoa, San Marino, São Tomé and Príncipe, Saudi Arabia, Senegal, Serbia, Seychelles, Sierra Leone, Singapore, Slovakia, Slovenia, Solomon Islands, Somalia, South Africa, South Sudan, Spain, Sri Lanka, Sudan, Suriname, Sweden, Switzerland, Syria, Tajikistan, Tanzania, Thailand, Timor-Leste, Togo, Tonga, Trinidad and Tobago, Tunisia, Turkey, Turkmenistan, Tuvalu, Uganda, Ukraine, United Arab Emirates, UK, USA, Uruguay, Uzbekistan, Vanuatu, Venezuela, Vietnam, Yemen, Zambia, Zimbabwe.

Activities The Bank obtains its funds from the following sources: capital paid in by member countries; sales of its own securities; sales of parts of its

loans; repayments; and net earnings. A resolution of the Board of Governors of 27 April 1988 provides that the paid-in portion of the shares authorized to be subscribed under it will be 3%.

The Bank is self-supporting, raising most of its money on the world's financial markets. In the fiscal year ending 30 June 2015 allocable income totalled US$686m., compared to US$769m. for the year ending 30 June 2014.

In the fiscal year 2015 the Bank lent US$23·5bn. for 112 new operations. Cumulative lending had totalled US$629bn. by June 2015.

The Consultative Group to Assist the Poor (CGAP) works toward a world in which everyone has access to the financial services they need to improve their lives. Established in 1995 and housed at the World Bank, CGAP combines a pragmatic approach to market development with an evidence-based advocacy platform to advance poor people's access to finance. Its global network of members includes over 30 development agencies, private foundations and national governments that share a common vision of improving the lives of poor people with better access to finance.

For the purposes of its analytical and operational work, in 2017 the IBRD characterized economies as follows: low income (average annual *per capita* gross national income of $1,005 or less); lower middle income (between $1,006 and $3,955); upper middle income (between $3,956 and $12,235); and high income ($12,236 or more).

A wide variety of technical assistance is at the core of IBRD's activities. It acts as executing agency for a number of pre-investment surveys financed by the UN Development Programme. There are more than 100 offices in countries throughout the world. The Bank maintains a staff college, the *World Bank Institute* in Washington, D.C., for senior officials of member countries.

Access to Information Effective 1 July 2010, the World Bank Policy on Access to Information marked a pivotal shift in the World Bank's approach to making information available to the public. Now the public can obtain more information about projects under preparation, projects under implementation, analytic and advisory activities, and Board proceedings. The policy also includes a clear process for making information publicly available and a right to appeal if information seekers believe they were improperly or unreasonably denied access to information or there is a public interest case to override an exception that restricts certain information.

Organization As of Feb. 2019 the Bank had 189 members, each with voting power in the institution, based on shareholding which in turn is based on a country's economic growth. The president is selected by the Bank's Board of Executive Directors. The initial term is five years, with a second of five years or less.

Current Leaders
Kristalina Georgieva

Position
Interim President

Introduction
Kristalina Georgieva became interim president of the World Bank Group in Feb. 2019, following the unexpected resignation of Jim Yong Kim. The Bulgarian-born economist and academic had begun work at the World Bank in the 1990s, specializing in sustainable development, and also previously served as a vice-president of the European Commission.

Early Life
Georgieva was born on 13 Aug. 1953 in Sofia, Bulgaria, and studied political economy and sociology at the Karl Marx Higher Institute of Economics in Sofia (now the University of National and World Economy). Awarded a doctorate in economic science in 1977, she went on to become an associate professor at the university and remained there until 1991. Two years later, she joined the World Bank in Washington, D.C., in the USA as an environmental economist. She later became its director in charge of environmental strategy, policies and lending.

In 2004 Georgieva moved to Moscow and served for three years as the World Bank's director for the Russian Federation. She then returned to Washington D.C, and led policy and lending operations in infrastructure, urban development, agriculture, environment and social development. As vice-president and corporate secretary of the World Bank from 2008–10, she liaised between senior management and the Bank's shareholder countries, playing a key role in reforming the organization's governance in the wake of the 2008 international financial crisis.

In 2010 she was approved as the European Union's commissioner for international co-operation, humanitarian aid and crisis response. She oversaw humanitarian relief for the survivors of earthquakes in Haiti and Chile and flooding in Pakistan. Her tenure saw an increase in spending on aid and improvements in efficiency through schemes such as the Disaster Risk Management Knowledge Centre. In 2014 she was appointed the European Commission's vice-president for budget and human resources.

Georgieva returned to the World Bank in Oct. 2016, when she was appointed Chief Executive Officer. When Jim Yong Kim unexpectedly resigned as World Bank president in Jan. 2019, more than three years before the end of his term, the Bank announced that Georgieva would take over in an interim capacity.

Career in Office
As interim president, Georgieva will lead the organization's work to end extreme poverty by 2030, reduce inequality and boost shared prosperity around the world.

European office: 66 avenue d'Iéna, 75116 Paris, France. *London office:* Milbank Tower, 12th Floor, 21–24 Milbank, London, SW1P 4QP, England. *Tokyo office:* 10th Floor, Fukoku Seimei Building, 2-2-2 Uchisaiwai-cho, Chiyoda-ku, Tokyo 100-0011 Japan.

Headquarters: 1818 H St., NW, Washington, D.C., 20433, USA.
Website: http://www.worldbank.org
Interim President: Kristalina Georgieva (Bulgaria).

Publications World Bank Annual Report.—Publications and e-Products e-Catalog (biannual).*—World Development Report* (annual).*—Environment Matters at the World Bank* (annual).*—World Bank Research Digest* (quarterly).*—World Development Indicators* (annual).*—World Bank Research E-Newsletter* (monthly).*—Handbook on Impact Evaluation: Quantitative Methods and Practices* (online only). 2010.*—The New Microfinance Handbook: A Financial Market System Perspective* (online only). 2013.

International Development Association (IDA)
A lending agency established in 1960 and administered by the IBRD to provide assistance on concessional terms to the poorest developing countries. Its resources consist of subscriptions and general replenishments from its more industrialized and developed members, special contributions and transfers from the net earnings of IBRD. Officers and staff of the IBRD serve concurrently as officers and staff of the IDA at the World Bank headquarters (*see* above). In fiscal year 2015 IDA commitments totalled US$19bn.; new commitments totalled 191 new operations. Since 1960 IDA has lent US$312bn. to 112 countries.

Headquarters: 1818 H St., NW, Washington, D.C., 20433, USA.
Website: http://ida.worldbank.org
President: Kristalina Georgieva (Bulgaria).

International Finance Corporation (IFC)
Established in 1956 to help strengthen the private sector in developing countries, through the provision of long-term loans, equity investments, quasi-equity instruments, standby financing, and structured finance and risk management products. It helps to finance new ventures and assist established enterprises as they expand, upgrade or diversify. In partnership with other donors, it provides a variety of technical assistance and advisory services to public and private sector clients. To be eligible for financing, projects must be profitable for investors, must benefit the economy of the country concerned, and must comply with IFC's environmental and social guidelines.

The majority of its funds are borrowed from the international financial markets through public bond issues or private placements. Total capital at 30 June 2018 was US$26·1bn. In fiscal year 2018 IFC's long-term investment commitments totalled US$23·3bn., including US$11·7bn. mobilized from investment partners. It has 184 members.

Headquarters: 2121 Pennsylvania Ave., NW, Washington, D.C., 20433, USA.
Website: http://www.ifc.org
President: Kristalina Georgieva (Bulgaria).
Chief Executive Officer: Philippe Le Houérou (France).

Publications Annual Report (online only), 1995 ff.*—Sustain* (online only).*—Doing Business* (online only), 2004 ff.

Multilateral Investment Guarantee Agency (MIGA)
Established in 1988 to encourage the flow of foreign direct investment to, and among, developing member countries, MIGA is the insurance arm of the World Bank. It provides investors with investment guarantees against non-commercial risk, such as expropriation and war, and gives advice to governments on improving climate for foreign investment. It may insure up to 90% of an investment, with a current limit of US$50m. per project. In March 1999 the Council of Governors adopted a resolution for a capital increase for the Agency of approximately US$850m. In addition US$150m. was transferred to MIGA by the World Bank as operating capital. In Jan. 2019 it had 181 member countries. Like IDA and ICSID, it is located at the World Bank headquarters in Washington (*see* above).

Headquarters: 1818 H St., NW, Washington, D.C., 20433, USA.
Website: http://www.miga.org
President: Kristalina Georgieva (Bulgaria).

International Centre for Settlement of Investment Disputes (ICSID)
Founded in 1966 to promote increased flows of international investment by providing facilities for the conciliation and arbitration of disputes between governments and foreign investors. The Centre does not engage in such conciliation or arbitration. This is the task of conciliators and arbitrators appointed by the contracting parties, or as otherwise provided for in the Convention. Recourse to conciliation and arbitration by members is entirely voluntary.

In Jan. 2019 its Convention had 162 signatory countries. 423 cases had been concluded by it and 240 were pending. Disputes involved a variety of investment sectors: agriculture, banking, construction, energy, health, industrial, mining and tourism.

ICSID also undertakes research, publishing and advisory activities in the field of foreign investment law. Like IDA and MIGA, it is located at the World Bank headquarters in Washington (*see* above).

Headquarters: 1818 H St., NW, MSN J2-200, Washington, D.C., 20433, USA.
Website: https://icsid.worldbank.org
Secretary-General: Meg Kinnear (Canada).

Publications ICSID Annual Report.—ICSID Review: Foreign Investment Law Journal (three times a year).*—Investment Laws of the World.—Investment Treaties.—ICSID Convention, Regulations and Rules.—The ICSID Caseload – Statistics* (biannual).

International Civil Aviation Organization (ICAO)
Origin The Convention providing for the establishment of the ICAO was drawn up by the International Civil Aviation Conference held in Chicago in 1944. A Provisional International Civil Aviation Organization (PICAO) operated for 20 months until the formal establishment of ICAO on 4 April 1947. The Convention on International Civil Aviation superseded the provisions of the Paris Convention of 1919 and the Pan American Convention on Air Navigation of 1928.

Functions It assists international civil aviation by establishing technical standards for safety and efficiency of air navigation and promoting simpler procedures at borders; develops regional plans for ground facilities and services needed for international flying; disseminates air-transport statistics and prepares studies on aviation economics; fosters the development of air law conventions and provides technical assistance to states in developing civil aviation programmes.

Organization The principal organs of ICAO are an Assembly, consisting of all members of the Organization, and a Council, which is composed of 36 states elected by the Assembly for three years, which meets in virtually continuous session. In electing these states, the Assembly must give adequate representation to: (1) states of major importance in air transport; (2) states which make the largest contribution to the provision of facilities for the international civil air navigation; and (3) those states not otherwise included whose election would ensure that all major geographical areas of the world were represented. The budget approved for 2016 was $99·0m. CDN.

Headquarters: 999 Robert-Bourassa Blvd, Montreal, Quebec, Canada H3C 5H7.
Website: http://www.icao.int

President of the Council: Dr Olumuyiwa Benard Aliu (Nigeria).
Secretary-General: Fang Lui (China).

Publications   Annual Report of the Council.—ICAO Journal (quarterly).—
ICAO Training Report (biannual).—*ICAO Regional Report.*

International Fund for Agricultural Development (IFAD)

The idea for an International Fund for Agricultural Development arose at the 1974 World Food Conference. An agreement to establish IFAD entered into force on 30 Nov. 1977, and the agency began its operations the following month. IFAD is an international financial institution and a United Nations specialized agency dedicated to eradicating rural poverty in developing countries. It mobilizes resources from its 176 member countries to provide low-interest loans and grants to help middle and low-income member countries fight poverty in their poor rural communities. IFAD works with national partners to design and implement innovative initiatives that fit within national policies and systems. These enable poor rural people to access the assets, services, knowledge, skills and opportunities they need to overcome poverty. Since starting operations in 1978, IFAD has invested more than US$17bn. in around 1,000 projects and programmes that have reached some 500m. people.

Organization   The highest body is the Governing Council, on which all 176 member countries are represented. Operations are overseen by an 18-member Executive Board (with 18 alternate members), which is responsible to the Governing Council. The Fund works with many partner institutions, including the World Bank, regional development banks and financial agencies, and other UN agencies; many of these co-finance IFAD programmes and projects.

Headquarters: Via Paolo di Dono 44, 00142 Rome, Italy.
Website: http://www.ifad.org
President: Gilbert F. Houngbo (Togo).

Publications   Annual Report, 1997 ff.—*Polishing the Stone.* 2007.—*What Meets the Eye: Images of Rural Poverty.* 2003.

International Labour Organization (ILO)

Origin   The ILO was established in 1919 under the Treaty of Versailles as an autonomous institution associated with the League of Nations. An agreement establishing its relationship with the UN was approved in 1946, making the ILO the first Specialized Agency to be associated with the UN. An intergovernmental agency with a tripartite structure, in which representatives of governments, employers and workers participate, it seeks through international action to improve labour and living conditions, to promote productive employment and social justice for working people everywhere. On its fiftieth anniversary in 1969 it was awarded the Nobel Peace Prize. In Jan. 2019 it numbered 187 members.

Functions   The ILO's programme and budget set out four strategic objectives for the Organization at the turn of the century: i) to promote and realize fundamental principles and rights at work; ii) to create greater opportunities for women and men to secure decent employment and income; iii) to enhance the coverage and effectiveness of social protection for all; iv) to strengthen tripartism and social dialogue. The International Labour Conference 2017 adopted a budget of US$784·1m. for the 2018–19 biennium.

One of the ILO's principal functions is the formulation of international standards in the form of International Labour Conventions and Recommendations. Member countries are required to submit Conventions to their competent national authorities with a view to ratification. If a country ratifies a Convention it agrees to bring its laws into line with its terms and to report periodically how these regulations are being applied. More than 8,000 ratifications of 189 Conventions had been deposited by 31 Jan. 2016. Procedures are in place to ascertain whether Conventions thus ratified are effectively applied. Recommendations do not require ratification, but member states are obliged to consider them with a view to giving effect to their provisions by legislation or other action. By 31 Jan. 2016 the International Labour Conference had adopted 204 Recommendations.

In June 1998 delegates to the 86th International Labour Conference adopted an ILO Declaration on Fundamental Principles and Rights at Work, committing the Organization's member states to respect the principles inherent in a number of core labour standards: the right of workers and employers to freedom of association and the effective right to collective bargaining, and

to work toward the elimination of all forms of forced or compulsory labour, the effective abolition of child labour and the elimination of discrimination in respect of employment and occupation.

Activities   In addition to its research and advisory activities, the ILO now conducts more than 1,000 technical co-operation programmes in over 80 countries with the help of some 60 donor institutions worldwide. The ILO has decentralized most such activities to its regional, area and branch offices in over 40 countries. Decent Work Country Programmes have been established as the main vehicle for delivery of ILO support to countries.

The ILO's standard-setting and technical co-operation are reinforced by an extensive research, training, education and publications programme. It has established two specialized educational institutions: the *International Institute for Labour Studies* in Geneva, and the *International Centre for Advanced Technical and Vocational Training* in Turin.

The *International Institute for Labour Studies* promotes the study and discussion of policy issues. The core theme of its activities is the interaction between labour institutions, development and civil society in a global economy. It identifies emerging social and labour issues by opening up new areas for research and action; and encourages systematic dialogue on social policy between the tripartite constituency of the ILO and the international academic community, and other public opinion-makers.

The *International Training Centre* was set up in 1965 to lead the training programmes implemented by the ILO as part of its technical co-operation activities. Member states and the UN system also call on its resources and experience, and a UN Staff College was established on the Turin Campus in 1996.

In June 2009 the International Labour Conference unanimously adopted a 'Global Jobs Pact' to address the social and employment impact of the recent international financial and economic crisis. The Pact promotes a productive recovery centred on investments, employment and social protection. It provides an internationally agreed basis for policy-making designed to reduce the time lag between economic recovery and a recovery with decent work opportunities.

Organization   The International Labour Conference is the supreme deliberative organ of the ILO; it meets annually in Geneva. National delegations are composed of two government delegates, one employers' delegate and one workers' delegate. The Governing Body, elected by the Conference, is the Executive Council. It is composed of 28 government members, 14 workers' members and 14 employers' members. Ten governments of countries of industrial importance hold permanent seats on the Governing Body. These are: Brazil, China, France, Germany, India, Italy, Japan, Russia, UK and USA. The remaining 18 government members are elected every three years. Workers' and employers' representatives are elected as individuals, not as national candidates.

Headquarters: International Labour Office, 4 route des Morillons, CH-1211 Geneva 22, Switzerland.
Website: http://www.ilo.org
Email: ilo@ilo.org
Director-General: Guy Ryder (United Kingdom).
Governing Body Chairperson: Claudio Julio de la Puente Ribeyro (Peru).

Publications include: *International Labour Review* (annual; in three volumes).—*Bulletin of Labour Statistics* (quarterly).—*Official Bulletin* and *International Journal of Labour Research* (biannual).—*Yearbook of Labour Statistics* (online only).—*World Employment and Social Outlook* (biannual).—*Encyclopaedia of Occupational Health and Safety.—Key Indicators of the Labour Market (KILM).—International Social Security Review* (quarterly).—*Global Wage Report* (biennial).

International Maritime Organization (IMO)

Origin   The International Maritime Organization (formerly the InterGovernmental Maritime Consultative Organization) was established as a specialized agency of the UN by a convention drafted in 1948 at a UN maritime conference in Geneva. The Convention became effective on 17 March 1958 when it had been ratified by 21 countries, including seven with at least 1m. gross tons of shipping each. The IMCO started operations in 1959 and changed its name to the IMO in 1982.

Functions   To facilitate co-operation among governments on technical matters affecting merchant shipping, especially concerning safety and security at sea; to prevent and control marine pollution caused by ships; to facilitate international maritime traffic. The IMO is responsible for convening international maritime conferences and for drafting international maritime conventions. It also provides technical assistance to countries wishing to develop their maritime activities, and acts as a depositary authority for international conventions regulating maritime affairs. *The World Maritime University (WMU)*, at Malmö, Sweden, was established in 1983; the *IMO International Maritime Law Institute (IMLI)*, at Valletta, Malta and the *IMO International Maritime Academy*, at Trieste, Italy, both in 1989.

Organization The IMO has 174 members and three associate members. The Assembly, composed of all member states, normally meets every two years. The 40-member Council acts as governing body between sessions. There are four principal committees (on maritime safety, legal matters, marine environment protection and technical co-operation), which submit reports or recommendations to the Assembly through the Council, and a Secretariat. Total expenditure in 2017 amounted to £51,215,000.

Headquarters: 4 Albert Embankment, London, SE1 7SR, UK.
Website: http://www.imo.org
Email: info@imo.org
Secretary-General: Kitack Lim (South Korea).

Publication IMO News (quarterly).

International Monetary Fund (IMF)

Established in 1945 as an independent organization, the International Monetary Fund began financial operations on 1 March 1947. An agreement of mutual co-operation with the UN came into force on 15 Nov. 1947. The first amendment to the Articles of Agreement, creating the special drawing right (SDR), the IMF's reserve asset, took effect on 28 July 1969. The second amendment took effect on 1 April 1978, and established a new code of conduct for exchange arrangements in the wake of the collapse of the par value system. The third amendment came into force on 11 Nov. 1992; it allowed for the suspension of voting and related rights of any member that failed to settle its outstanding obligations to the IMF. The fourth Amendment, in force from 10 Aug. 2009, provided for a special one-time allocation of SDRs. A fifth amendment, effective 18 Feb. 2011, expanded the Fund's investment authority. The sixth amendment, which took effect on 3 March 2011, strengthened the representation of emerging economies through *ad hoc* quota increases. On 26 Jan. 2016 the seventh amendment, concerning quota and governance reform, was enacted.

Members Afghanistan, Albania, Algeria, Angola, Antigua and Barbuda, Argentina, Armenia, Australia, Austria, Azerbaijan, The Bahamas, Bahrain, Bangladesh, Barbados, Belarus, Belgium, Belize, Benin, Bhutan, Bolivia, Bosnia and Herzegovina, Botswana, Brazil, Brunei, Bulgaria, Burkina Faso, Burundi, Cabo Verde, Cambodia, Cameroon, Canada, Central African Republic, Chad, Chile, China, Colombia, Comoros, Democratic Republic of the Congo, Republic of the Congo, Costa Rica, Côte d'Ivoire, Croatia, Cyprus, Czech Republic, Denmark, Djibouti, Dominica, Dominican Republic, Ecuador, Egypt, El Salvador, Equatorial Guinea, Eritrea, Estonia, Eswatini, Ethiopia, Fiji, Finland, France, Gabon, The Gambia, Georgia, Germany, Ghana, Greece, Grenada, Guatemala, Guinea, Guinea-Bissau, Guyana, Haiti, Honduras, Hungary, Iceland, India, Indonesia, Iran, Iraq, Ireland, Israel, Italy, Jamaica, Japan, Jordan, Kazakhstan, Kenya, Kiribati, South Korea, Kosovo, Kuwait, Kyrgyzstan, Laos, Latvia, Lebanon, Lesotho, Liberia, Libya, Lithuania, Luxembourg, Madagascar, Malawi, Malaysia, Maldives, Mali, Malta, Marshall Islands, Mauritania, Mauritius, Mexico, Micronesia, Moldova, Mongolia, Montenegro, Morocco, Mozambique, Myanmar, Namibia, Nauru, Nepal, Netherlands, New Zealand, Nicaragua, Niger, Nigeria, North Macedonia, Norway, Oman, Pakistan, Palau, Panama, Papua New Guinea, Paraguay, Peru, Philippines, Poland, Portugal, Qatar, Romania, Russia, Rwanda, St Kitts and Nevis, St Lucia, St Vincent and the Grenadines, Samoa, San Marino, São Tomé and Príncipe, Saudi Arabia, Senegal, Serbia, Seychelles, Sierra Leone, Singapore, Slovakia, Slovenia, Solomon Islands, Somalia, South Africa, South Sudan, Spain, Sri Lanka, Sudan, Suriname, Sweden, Switzerland, Syria, Tajikistan, Tanzania, Thailand, Timor-Leste, Togo, Tonga, Trinidad and Tobago, Tunisia, Turkey, Turkmenistan, Tuvalu, Uganda, Ukraine, United Arab Emirates, UK, USA, Uruguay, Uzbekistan, Vanuatu, Venezuela, Vietnam, Yemen, Zambia, Zimbabwe.

Aims To promote international monetary co-operation, the expansion of international trade and exchange rate stability; to assist in the removal of exchange restrictions and the establishment of a multilateral system of payments; and to alleviate any serious disequilibrium in members' international balance of payments by making the financial resources of the IMF available to them, usually subject to economic policy conditions.

Activities The IMF is mandated to oversee the international monetary system and monitor the economic and financial policies of its member countries. The IMF highlights possible risks to domestic and external stability and advises on policy adjustments.

Lending A core responsibility of the IMF is to provide loans to member countries experiencing balance of payments problems. This financial assistance enables countries to rebuild their international reserves, stabilize their currencies, continue paying for imports and restore conditions for strong economic growth, while undertaking policies to correct underlying problems. Unlike development banks, the IMF does not lend for specific projects.

The IMF has various loan instruments, or 'facilities', that are tailored to address the specific circumstances of its diverse membership. Non-concessional loans are provided mainly through Stand-By Arrangements (SBAs) and the Extended Fund Facility (which is useful primarily for longer-term needs). The Flexible Credit Line (FCL) was introduced in 2009, for countries with very strong fundamentals, policies and track records of policy implementation.

The IMF also offers special financing facilities for low-income countries. A new Poverty Reduction and Growth Trust, effective from Jan. 2010, incorporates: the Extended Credit Facility, which provides flexible medium-term support; the Standby Credit Facility, which addresses short-term and precautionary needs; and the Rapid Credit Facility, which offers emergency support with limited conditionality. The IMF also provides emergency assistance to support recovery from natural disasters and conflicts, in some cases at concessional interest rates.

A major reform of the IMF's lending facilities took place in March 2009. Conditions linked to IMF loan disbursements are to be better focused and more adequately tailored to the varying strengths of countries' policies and fundamentals. The flexibility of the SBA has been enhanced. In addition, access limits have been doubled, the cost and maturity structure of the Fund's lending has been simplified and its lending facilities have been streamlined.

Technical assistance The IMF provides technical assistance in its areas of core expertise: macroeconomic policy, tax policy and revenue administration, expenditure management, monetary policy, the exchange rate system, financial sector sustainability, and macroeconomic and financial statistics. About 90% of IMF technical assistance goes to low and lower-middle income countries. The IMF operates nine regional technical assistance centres: in the Pacific (Fiji), the Caribbean (Barbados), five in Africa (Gabon, Ghana, Mali, Mauritius and Tanzania), the Middle East (Lebanon) and Central America (Guatemala).

Finances Quota subscriptions from member countries are the IMF's main source of financing. A member's quota is largely determined by its economic position relative to other members; it is also linked to their drawing rights on the IMF, their voting power and their share of SDR allocations. Quotas are generally reviewed at least every five years, although the 15th General Quota Review, which under normal circumstances would have been completed in Dec. 2015, has been delayed until at least 2019. The IMF can supplement its resources through borrowing if it believes that resources might fall short of members' needs.

The General Arrangements to Borrow (GAB) and New Arrangements to Borrow (NAB) are credit arrangements between the IMF and a group of member countries and institutions to provide supplementary resources to the IMF to deal with an exceptional situation that poses a threat to the stability of that system. The GAB, established in 1962, enables the IMF to borrow specified amounts of currencies from 11 industrial countries (or their central banks) under certain circumstances, at market-related rates of interest. The potential credit available to the IMF under the GAB totals SDR 17bn., with an additional SDR 1·5bn. available under an associated arrangement with Saudi Arabia. The NAB, which came into effect in 1998, is a set of credit arrangements between the IMF and 38 member countries and institutions. Importantly, the NAB is the facility of first and principal recourse vis-à-vis the GAB. The maximum amount of resources available to the IMF under the NAB and GAB is SDR 370bn.

In April 2009 the G20 agreed to increase the lending resources available to the IMF by up to US$500bn., thereby tripling total pre-crisis lending resources. The increase was to be made through immediate bilateral financing from IMF member countries and by subsequently incorporating this financing into an expanded and more flexible NAB increased by up to US$500bn. This objective was achieved by Sept. 2009.

Bilateral loans   Under such an agreement, the member normally commits to allow the Fund to make drawings up to a specified ceiling during the period for which drawings can be made. In 2009 the IMF signed a number of bilateral loan agreements.

IMF notes   Some official creditors may prefer to invest in paper or notes issued by the IMF. In 2009 the IMF's Executive Board approved a new framework for issuing notes to the official sector. China was the first country to have signed such a note purchase agreement.

SDR allocations   The IMF may allocate SDRs to members in proportion to their IMF quotas. Such an allocation provides each member with a costless asset. There have been three general SDR allocations, made in response to a long-term global need for reserve assets: (i) SDR 9·3bn., distributed in 1970–72; (ii) SDR 12·3bn., distributed in 1979–81; and (iii) SDR 162·1bn., distributed in Aug. 2009. A special one-off allocation of SDRs amounting to SDR 21·5bn. was implemented on 9 Sept. 2009. This allocation was for those countries that joined the Fund after 1981—more than one fifth of the IMF membership—and had never received an SDR allocation. As a result of reforms implemented in Jan. 2016, the combined quotas of the IMF's then 188 members totalled US$659bn.

Governance reform   Implemented on 28 April 2008 this reform made quotas more responsive to economic realities by increasing the representation of fast-growing economies while at the same time giving low-income countries more say in the IMF's decision making. The reform built on an initial step agreed by the IMF's membership in Sept. 2006 to have *ad hoc* quota increases for four countries—China, South Korea, Mexico and Turkey. In Dec. 2010 the IMF Board of Governors approved a shift in quota share to dynamic emerging markets and developing countries of more than 6% using the quota formulas at the time as the basis. The reforms came into effect in Jan. 2016 as part of the IMF's 14th General Quota Review.

Organization   The highest authority is the Board of Governors; each member government is represented. The Board of Governors has delegated many of its powers to the 24 executive directors in Washington, D.C., who are appointed or elected by individual member countries or groups of countries. The managing director is selected by the executive directors and serves as chairman of the Executive Board, but may not vote except in case of a tie. The term of office is for five years, but may be extended or terminated at the discretion of the executive directors. The managing director is responsible for the ordinary business of the IMF, under the direction of the executive directors, and supervises a staff of about 2,400. There are three deputy managing directors. As of Jan. 2019 the IMF had 189 members.

The IMF Institute is a specialized department providing training in macroeconomic analysis and policy, and related subjects, for officials of member countries. In addition to training offered in Washington, D.C., the IMF also offers training for country officials through a network of seven regional training institutes and programmes. These are: the IMF-Singapore Regional Training Institute; the Africa Training Institute (in Mauritius); the Joint Partnership for Africa (in Côte d'Ivoire); the Joint China-IMF Training Program (in Dalian, China); the IMF-Middle East Center for Economics and Finance (in Kuwait); the Joint Regional Training Center for Latin America (in Brazil); and the Joint Vienna Institute (in Austria).

Current Leaders
Christine Lagarde

Position
Managing Director

Introduction
Christine Lagarde became managing director of the IMF in July 2011 against a backdrop of global financial instability and uncertainty. The 11th consecutive European to head the Fund, she promised to give more voting power to developing nations. Her key challenges have included formulating the IMF response to sovereign debt crises and revitalizing global economic growth. Her appointment for a second term in the post was approved in Feb. 2016.

Early Life
Born on 1 Jan. 1956 in Paris, Christine Lagarde attended school in Le Havre, France and Holton-Arms School in Bethesda, Maryland, USA before studying law at the Université de Paris X-Nanterre. After obtaining a master's degree from the Institut d'études politiques d'Aix-en-Provence, in 1981 she joined the Paris office of international law firm Baker & McKenzie, specializing in anti-trust law, employment law, and acquisitions and mergers.

Made a partner in 1987, she served on the executive committee from 1995–2004, moving to Chicago in 1999 when she became chairman of the global executive committee. As a member of a Washington-based think tank, the Centre for Strategic and International Studies, Lagarde headed the US–Poland defence industries working group from 1995–2002, promoting the interests of US and Polish companies.

She returned to France in 2005 to serve as minister for foreign trade in Dominique de Villepin's government, overseeing the growth of exports. She was minister of agriculture and fisheries from May–June 2007, before being appointed finance minister by President Sarkozy. With the onset of the global economic crisis in 2008 she gained a reputation as an astute negotiator, winning praise domestically for her representation of French interests on the international stage. In 2010 she was closely involved in the negotiations over IMF bailout loans for eurozone countries.

IMF managing director Dominique Strauss-Kahn resigned in May 2011, accused of sexual assault, and Lagarde emerged as the favourite to replace him, ahead of Agustín Carstens of Mexico. She was backed by the USA and, despite widely expressed concern over continued European dominance of the Fund, she also won support from the BRIC nations of Brazil, Russia, India and China.

Career in Office
Lagarde took office on 5 July 2011, promising to implement reforms to IMF governance, including more voting power for emerging nations. Her main preoccupation, however, has been the containment of sovereign debt crises in economically advanced countries around the world, and particularly in the eurozone where the IMF has contributed financial support to several countries in an international effort to sustain the viability of the European single currency.

In Oct. 2013 she acknowledged that the worldwide financial turmoil had shaken faith in prosperity through globalization, but stressed the need for continued international policy collaboration in the face of 'transitions on an epic scale'. A year later she called for resolute policies to prevent economic growth from settling into a 'new mediocre', with unacceptably low job creation and inclusion. She was similarly downbeat in Dec. 2015, commenting that the world faced another year of 'disappointing and uneven' growth. She approved the first rise that month in borrowing costs in the USA since 2006 as necessary, but warned that higher interest rates, economic slowdown in China and depressed commodity markets could undermine the already tepid and vulnerable global recovery. Earlier, in Nov. that year, she heralded the inclusion of China's *yuan* in the basket of currencies that comprise the IMF's lending reserves.

In Oct. 2017 Lagarde delivered a more optimistic global economic assessment. She said that, measured by GDP, nearly 75% of the world was experiencing an upswing, reflecting a cyclical pick-up in the advanced economies, especially in Europe and Japan, strong markets in China and India, and a brighter outlook in other emerging and developing economies. Nevertheless, she said that persistent low growth since the global financial crisis had exposed long-standing inabilities to adapt to technological change and global integration. Also, there remained threats from high levels of debt in many countries, excessive risk-taking in financial markets and corruption. In Dec. Lagarde maintained that the UK referendum decision in June 2016 to leave the European Union was already having a negative impact and that the UK's weaker growth in 2017 was in contrast to accelerating activity in the rest of the world.

In Oct. 2018 she cautioned that global growth had not only plateaued but was also spread more unevenly among countries. Moreover, risks had begun to materialize from rising trade protection, while global public and private debt—at an all-time high—could provoke capital outflows and economic instability in emerging markets. She added that the IMF needed to press ahead with the financial regulatory agenda to address the issue of sustainability, including the existential threat of climate change

In Dec. 2015 a French judicial commission had ruled that Lagarde should stand trial for alleged negligence over a controversial decision she had made regarding the use of public money in 2008 while minister of finance in France. Although she was convicted in Dec. 2016, the court did not hand down any punishment and the IMF board said that it retained full confidence in her continued leadership.

Headquarters: 700 19th St., NW, Washington, D.C., 20431, USA; 1900 Pennsylvania Ave., NW, Washington, D.C., 20431, USA. European offices in Paris and Brussels and regional offices in Tokyo and Warsaw.
Website: http://www.imf.org
Email: publicaffairs@imf.org
Managing Director: Christine Lagarde (France).

Publications Annual Report of the Executive Board.—Annual Report on Exchange Arrangements and Exchange Restrictions.—International Financial Statistics (monthly).—*IMF Survey* (online).—*IMF Economic Review* (quarterly).—*World Economic Outlook* (biannual).—*Global Financial Stability Report* (biannual).—*Finance and Development* (quarterly).—*Fiscal Monitor* (biannual).—More publications information may be found online at: http://www.imf.org/en/publications.

International Telecommunication Union (ITU)
Origin Founded in Paris in 1865 as the International Telegraph Union, the International Telecommunication Union took its present name in 1934 and became a specialized agency of the United Nations in 1947. Therefore, the ITU is the world's oldest intergovernmental body.

Functions To maintain and extend international co-operation for the improvement and rational use of telecommunications of all kinds, and promote and offer technical assistance to developing countries in the field of telecommunications; to promote the development of technical facilities and their most efficient operation to improve the efficiency of telecommunication services, increasing their usefulness and making them, so far as possible, generally available to the public; to harmonize the actions of nations in the attainment of these ends.

Organization The supreme organ of the ITU is the Plenipotentiary Conference, which normally meets every four years. A 48-member Council, elected by the Conference, meets annually in Geneva and acts as the ITU's governing body in the interval between Plenipotentiary Conferences. A General Secretariat manages the administrative and financial aspects of the ITU's activities. The Secretary-General is also elected by the Conference. The ITU is made up of three sectors: Radiocommunication Sector; Telecommunication Standardization Sector; and Telecommunication Development Sector. The ITU has 193 member countries; a further 700 scientific and technical companies, public and private operators, broadcasters and other organizations are also members.

Headquarters: Place des Nations, CH-1211 Geneva 20, Switzerland.
Website: http://www.itu.int
Email: itumail@itu.int
Secretary-General: Houlin Zhao (China).

United Nations Educational, Scientific and Cultural Organization (UNESCO)
Origin UNESCO's Constitution was signed in London on 16 Nov. 1945 by 37 countries and the Organization came into being in Nov. 1946 on the premise that: 'Since wars begin in the minds of men, it is in the minds of men that the defences of peace must be constructed'. In Jan. 2019 UNESCO had 195 members including the UK, which rejoined in 1997 having left in 1985, and the USA, which rejoined in 2003 having left in 1984. There are also 11 associate members that are not members of the UN (Anguilla, Aruba, British Virgin Islands, Cayman Islands, Curaçao, Faroe Islands, Macao, Montserrat, New Caledonia, Sint Maarten and Tokelau).

Aims and Activities UNESCO's primary objective is to contribute to peace and security in the world by promoting collaboration among the nations through education, science, communication, culture and the social and human sciences in order to further universal respect for justice, democracy, the rule of the law, human rights and fundamental freedoms, affirmed for all peoples by the UN Charter. Africa and gender equality are the Organization's two chief global priorities.

Education Various activities support and foster national projects to renovate education systems and develop alternative educational strategies towards a goal of lifelong education for all. The World Development Forum in Dakar in

2000 set an agenda for progress towards this aim expressed as six goals. Two of these, attaining universal primary education by 2015 and gender parity in schooling by 2005, were also UN Millennium Development Goals. Three elements define the context for pursuing this purpose: promoting education as a fundamental right, improving the quality of education and stimulating experimentation, innovation and policy dialogue.

Science UNESCO seeks to promote international scientific co-operation and encourages scientific research designed to improve living conditions and to protect ecosystems. Several international programmes to better understand the Earth's resources towards the advancement of sustainable development have been initiated, including the Man and the Biosphere (MAB) programme, the International Hydrological Programme (IHP), the Intergovernmental Oceanographic Commission (IOC) and the International Geoscience Programme (IGCP).

Culture Promoting the preservation of heritage, both tangible and intangible, cultural diversity and intercultural dialogue is the principal priority of UNESCO's cultural programmes. UNESCO's World Heritage List, now covering 1,092 sites around the world, promotes the preservation of monuments, cultural landscapes and natural sites.

Communication Activities are geared to promoting the free flow of information, freedom of expression, press freedom, media independence and pluralism. Another priority is to promote multilingualism on the internet, bridge the digital divide and help disadvantaged groups participate in the knowledge societies created through the information and communication technologies. To this end, UNESCO promotes access to public domain information, as well as encouraging the creation of local content.

Social and Human Sciences UNESCO works to advance knowledge and intellectual co-operation in order to facilitate social transformations conducive to justice, freedom, peace and human dignity. It seeks to identify evolving social trends and develops and promotes principles and standards based on universal values and ethics, such as the *Universal Declaration on the Human Genome and Human Rights* (1997) and the *International Declaration on Human Genetic Data* (2003).

Organization The General Conference, composed of representatives from each member state, meets biennially to decide policy, programme and budget. A 58-member Executive Board elected by the Conference meets twice a year and there is a Secretariat. The approved budget for the biennium 2016–17 was US$667m., with significant extra-budgetary contributions for specific programmes provided by both public and private bodies.

There are also ten separate UNESCO institutes and centres: the International Bureau of Education (IBE), in Geneva; the UNESCO Institute for Lifelong Learning (UIL), in Hamburg; the International Institute for Educational Planning (IIEP), in Paris and Buenos Aires; the International Institute for Capacity Building in Africa (IICBA), in Addis Ababa; the International Institute for Higher Education in Latin America and the Caribbean (IESALC), in Caracas; the Institute for Information Technologies in Education (IITE), in Moscow; the UNESCO Institute for Statistics (UIS), in Montreal; the UNESCO International Centre for Technical and Vocational Education and Training (UNEVOC), in Bonn; the UNESCO-IHE Institute for Water Education (UNESCO-IHE), in Delft; and the International Centre for Theoretical Physics (ICTP), in Trieste.

Headquarters: UNESCO House, 7 place Fontenoy, 75007 Paris, France; 1 rue Miollis, 75015 Paris, France.
Website: http://www.unesco.org
Director-General: Audrey Azoulay (France).

Periodicals (published quarterly) *Museum International; International Social Science Journal; The UNESCO Courier; Prospects; World Heritage Review.*

United Nations Industrial Development Organization (UNIDO)
Origin UNIDO was established by the UN General Assembly in 1966 and became a UN specialized agency in 1985.

Aims and Activities UNIDO helps developing countries in the formulation of policies and programmes in the field of industrial development; analyses trends, disseminates information and co-ordinates activities in their industrial development; acts as a forum for consultations and negotiations directed towards the industrialization of developing countries; and provides technical co-operation to developing countries for the implementation of their development plans for sustainable industrialization in their public and private sectors.

UNIDO focuses its efforts on three thematic priority areas: poverty reduction through productive activities; trade capacity-building; and energy and the environment. Activities under the thematic priorities are reflected in UNIDO's medium-term programme frameworks and biennial programme documents.

Organization As part of the United Nations common system, UNIDO has the responsibility for promoting industrialization throughout the developing world, in co-operation with its 168 member states. Its headquarters are in Vienna, Austria. UNIDO maintains a field network of 47 regional and country offices around the world. UNIDO maintains offices in Brussels, Geneva and New York.

The General Conference meets every two years to determine policy and approve the budget. The 53-member Industrial Development Board (membership according to constitutional lists) is elected by the General Conference. The General Conference also elects a 27-member Programme and Budget Committee for two years and appoints a Director-General for four years.

Finance UNIDO's financial resources come from the regular and operational budgets, as well as voluntary contributions. The regular and operational budget for 2017 amounted to €86·2m. More than half of UNIDO's funding comes from voluntary contributions. The regular budget derives mainly from assessed contributions from member states with a marginal proportion provided from such other sources as interest income, sales publications and government contributions to the UNIDO field offices.

The Constitution of UNIDO provides for 6% of the net regular budget to be used for the Regular Programme of Technical Cooperation. These resources are primarily used for supporting the Organization's operational and normative activities. The operational budget derives mainly from support cost income (of 5–13%) earned from the implementation of technical co-operation activities. Technical co-operation is funded mainly from voluntary contributions from donor countries and institutions as well as UNDP, the Multilateral Fund for the Implementation of the Montreal Protocol, the Global Environment Facility and the Common Fund for Communities.

Headquarters: Vienna International Centre, Wagramerstr. 5, POB 300, A-1400 Vienna, Austria.
Website: http://www.unido.org
Director-General: Li Yong (China).

Publications UNIDO Annual Report.—Making It (quarterly).—*UNIDO Times* (newsletter).—*The International Yearbook of Industrial Statistics 2015.—Industrial Development Report 2016.—Introduction to Inclusive and Sustainable Industrial Development.* 2015.

Universal Postal Union (UPU)

Origin The UPU was established in 1875, when the Universal Postal Convention adopted by the Postal Congress of Berne on 9 Oct. 1874 came into force. It has 192 member countries.

Functions The UPU provides co-operation between postal services and helps to ensure a universal network of up-to-date products and services. To this end, UPU members are united in a single postal territory for the reciprocal exchange of correspondence. A Specialized Agency of the UN since 1948, the UPU is governed by its Constitution, adopted in 1964 (Vienna), and subsequent protocol amendments (1969, Tokyo; 1974, Lausanne; 1984, Hamburg; 1989, Washington; 1994, Seoul; 1999, Beijing; 2004, Bucharest; 2008, Geneva).

Organization It is composed of a Universal Postal Congress which meets every four years; a 41-member Council of Administration, which meets annually and is responsible for supervising the affairs of the UPU between Congresses; a 40-member Postal Operations Council; and an International Bureau which functions as the permanent Secretariat, responsible for strategic planning and programme budgeting. A new UPU body, the Consultative Committee, was created at the Bucharest Congress. This committee represents the external shareholders of the postal sector as well as UPU member countries. The budget for annual expenditure in 2019 was 65·5m. Swiss francs.

Headquarters: Weltpoststrasse 4, 3015 Berne, Switzerland.
Website: http://www.upu.int
Director-General: Bishar Abdirahman Hussein (Kenya).

Publications Annual Report; ICTs, new services and transformation of the Post. 2010.—*Postal Economics in Developing Countries: Posts, Infrastructure of the 21st Century?* 2008.—*Postal Statistics* (annual).—*Union Postale* (quarterly); Universal POST*CODE® DataBase (online only); *Bucharest World Postal Strategy.* 2004.

World Health Organization (WHO)

Origin An International Conference convened by the UN Economic and Social Council to consider a single health organization resulted in the adoption on 22 July 1946 of the Constitution of the World Health Organization, which came into force on 7 April 1948.

Functions WHO's objective, as stated in the first article of the Constitution, is 'the attainment by all peoples of the highest possible level of health'. As the directing and co-ordinating authority on international health, it establishes and maintains collaboration with the UN, specialized agencies, governments, health administrations, professional and other groups concerned with health. The Constitution also directs WHO to assist governments to strengthen their health services; to stimulate and advance work to eradicate diseases; to promote maternal and child health, mental health, medical research and the prevention of accidents; to improve standards of teaching and training in the health professions, and of nutrition, housing, sanitation, working conditions and other aspects of environmental health. The Organization is also empowered to propose conventions, agreements and regulations, and make recommendations about international health matters; to develop, establish and promote international standards concerning foods, biological, pharmaceutical and similar substances; to revise the international nomenclature of diseases, causes of death and public health practices.

Methods of work Co-operation in country projects is undertaken only on the request of the government concerned, through the six regional offices of the Organization. Worldwide technical services are made available by headquarters. Expert committees, chosen from the 47 advisory panels of experts, meet to advise the Director-General on a given subject. Scientific groups and consultative meetings are called for similar purposes. To further the education of health personnel of all categories, seminars, technical conferences and training courses are organized, and advisors, consultants and lecturers are provided. WHO awards fellowships for study to nationals of member countries.

Activities The main thrust of WHO's activities in recent years has been towards promoting national, regional and global strategies for the attainment of the main social target of the member states: 'Health for All in the 21st Century', or the attainment by all citizens of the world of a level of health that will permit them to lead a socially and economically productive life. Almost all countries indicated a high level of political commitment to this goal; and guiding principles for formulating corresponding strategies and plans of action were subsequently prepared.

WHO has organized its responsibilities into four priorities: enhancing global health security, which includes preventing, detecting and containing disease outbreaks, preparing the world for controlling pandemic influenza, combating new diseases such as SARS, preparing for emergencies and responding quickly to minimize death and suffering; accelerating progress on the Millennium Development Goals (MDGs) by reducing maternal and child mortality, tackling the global epidemics of HIV/AIDS, tuberculosis and malaria, promoting safe drinking water and sanitation, promoting gender equality and increasing access to essential medicines; responding to non-communicable disease such as cardiovascular diseases, diabetes and cancers by reducing smoking, promoting a healthy diet and physical activity and reducing violence and road traffic crashes; promoting equity in health through strengthening health systems to reach everyone, particularly the most vulnerable people.

World Health Day is observed on 7 April every year. The 2019 theme for World Health Day was 'Universal health coverage: everyone, everywhere'. World No Tobacco Day is held on 31 May each year; International Day Against Drug Abuse on 26 June; World AIDS Day on 1 Dec.

The number of cancer cases is expected to increase by 37% between 2007 and 2030. The incidence of lung cancers in women and prostate cancers in men in the Western world is becoming far more prevalent. The incidence of other cancers is also rising rapidly, especially in developing countries. Heart disease and stroke, the leading causes of death in richer nations, will become more common in poorer countries. The number of people affected by diabetes has risen from 171m. in 2000 to 387m. in 2014, and has been forecast by the International Diabetes Federation to increase to 592m. by 2030. There is likely to be a huge rise in some mental and neurological disorders, especially dementias and particularly Alzheimer's disease, which is projected to affect 34m. people by 2025. In 2013 an estimated 650m. people suffered from mental and neurological disorders. Dementia affected an estimated 36m. people in 2012 and some 50m. world-wide suffered from epilepsy.

These projected increases are reported to be owing to a combination of factors, not least population ageing and the rising prevalence of unhealthy lifestyles. Average life expectancy at birth globally was 71 years in 2014. It is around 50 years in a few low-income countries, well over 70 years in many countries and exceeds 80 years in some. In 2014 there were an estimated 589m. people over 65. By 2030 that number is expected to rise to 995m., representing nearly 12% of the world's population.

According to WHO, the top ten causes of death in the world in 2016 were: coronary (ischaemic) heart disease, 9·4m. deaths; stroke, 5·8m.; chronic obstructive pulmonary disease, 3·0m.; lower respiratory infections, 3·0m.; Alzheimer disease and other dementias, 2·0m.; trachea, bronchus and lung cancers, 1·7m.; diabetes mellitus, 1·6m.; road injury, 1·4m.; diarrhoeal diseases, 1·4m.; tuberculosis, 1·3m. Tobacco kills nearly 6m. people each year. In total, its use is responsible for the death of almost one in ten adults worldwide.

In response, WHO has called for an intensified and sustained global campaign to encourage healthy lifestyles and attack the main risk factors responsible for many of these diseases: unhealthy diet, inadequate physical activity, smoking and obesity.

The WHO Framework Convention on Tobacco Control (WHO FCTC) was developed in response to the globalization of the tobacco epidemic, and is the first global health treaty negotiated under the auspices of the World Health Organization. The provisions in the Treaty require countries to ban tobacco advertising, sponsorship and promotion; establish new packaging and labelling of tobacco products with prominent health warnings; establish smoking bans in public places, increase price and tax on tobacco products; and strengthen legislation to clamp down on tobacco smuggling, among other measures.

Good progress has been made towards several MDGs. The number of children globally who died before their fifth birthday fell from 12·7m. in 1990 to 6·3m. in 2013. Women dying as a result of pregnancy or childbirth declined from 532,000 in 1990 to 303,000 in 2015. Instances of underweight children aged five or under in the developing world fell from 28% in 1990 to 17% in 2013. Around the world, new HIV infections declined by 38% between 2001 and 2013 while those dying from the disease fell by 43% between 2003 and 2015. Malaria deaths fell by 48% between 2000 and 2015.

World Health Statistics 2016: Monitoring health for the Sustainable Development Goals compiles data from worldwide sources on health-related issues including access to health, life expectancy and death from main diseases. The report puts these results in perspective and promotes healthier lifestyles in accordance with the WHO Sustainable Development Goals agenda. Primarily it strives for universal health coverage and for health equality among and within countries by 2030.

Organization The principal organs of WHO are the World Health Assembly, the Executive Board and the Secretariat. Each of the 194 member states has the right to be represented at the Assembly, which meets annually in Geneva. The 34-member Executive Board is composed of technically qualified health experts designated by as many member states as elected by the Assembly. The Secretariat consists of technical and administrative staff headed by a Director-General, who is appointed for not more than two five-year terms. Health activities in member countries are carried out through regional organizations which have been established in Africa (Brazzaville), South-East Asia (New Delhi), Europe (Copenhagen), Eastern Mediterranean (Cairo) and Western Pacific (Manila). The Pan American Sanitary Bureau in Washington serves as the regional office of WHO for the Americas. It is the oldest international health agency in the world and is the Secretariat of the Pan American Health Organization (PAHO).

Finance The proposed programme budget for 2018–19 amounted to US$4·4bn.

Current Leaders
Tedros Adhanom Ghebreyesus

Position
Director-General

Introduction
Dr Tedros Adhanom Ghebreyesus was elected director-general of the WHO for a five-year term in May 2017. The first African to lead the United Nations agency, he is a specialist in malaria control and Ethiopia's former minister of health.

Early Life
Tedros Adhanom Ghebreyesus was born in the city of Asmara, Ethiopia, on 23 Nov. 1965. Graduating in biology from the University of Asmara in 1986, he went on to work for the local health authority. He undertook further study in the UK, initially at University of London's School of Tropical Medicine and then at the University of Nottingham, where in 2000 he was awarded a doctorate on malaria transmission and control in Ethiopia.

The following year he was appointed head of Tigre's regional health bureau and oversaw a modernization programme. He became a state minister for health in 2003 and in 2005 he was promoted to national health minister by then prime minister, Meles Zenawi. He led ambitious reforms to the country's health system—notably by creating more than 3,500 medical centres. Links were forged with international health organizations and foundations and he served on the boards of several initiatives including, from 2009–11, the Global Fund to fight AIDS, tuberculosis and malaria.

In 2012 Tedros was appointed Ethiopia's minister for foreign affairs amid a reshuffle organized by the new prime minister, Hailemariam Desalegn. He went on to lead the negotiations of the Addis Ababa Action Agenda, in which 193 countries committed financing to achieve the UN's Sustainable Development Goals. He also served as chair of the executive council of the African Union (AU) in 2014. In May 2016 Tedros announced he would be standing for the post of director-general of the WHO, with backing from the AU. He was elected with more than two-thirds of the vote on 23 May 2017.

Career in Office
After taking office on 1 July 2017 Tedros said that universal healthcare would be central to his leadership. He added that other WHO priorities included the health impacts of climate and environmental change. He courted controversy early in his tenure as he was forced to rescind his choice in Oct. that year of former President Robert Mugabe of Zimbabwe as a WHO goodwill ambassador in response to widespread condemnation.

In Oct. 2019 Tedros convened a meeting of the WHO Emergency Committee in response to a new outbreak of the Ebola virus in the Democratic Republic of the Congo. It was decided not to declare a public health crisis at that time, although the Committee remained deeply concerned and emphasized that response activities needed to be intensified and that ongoing vigilance was critical.

Headquarters: 20 avenue Appia, CH-1211 Geneva 27, Switzerland.
Website: http://www.who.int
Director-General: Dr Tedros Adhanom Ghebreyesus (Ethiopia).

Publications World Health Report (annual).—*World Health Statistics* (annual).—*Bulletin of the World Health Organization* (monthly).—*WHO Technical Report Series* (annual).—*Consolidated guidelines on HIV prevention, diagnosis, treatment and care for key populations.* 2014.—*Global update on the health sector response to HIV, 2014.* 2014.—*Consolidated strategic information guidelines for HIV in the health sector.* 2015.—*International Health Regulations.* 2005.—*WHO Drug Information* (quarterly).—*Weekly Epidemiological Record.*—*International travel and health.*—*The International Pharmacopoeia (Ph. Int.).*

World Intellectual Property Organization (WIPO)
Origin The World Intellectual Property Organization (WIPO) was established in 1967 following the conclusion of the Convention Establishing the World Intellectual Property Organization in Stockholm. It was given a mandate by its member states to promote the protection of intellectual property (IP) through co-operation among states and in collaboration with other international organizations. The WIPO Convention entered into force on 26 April 1970 and WIPO became a specialized agency of the United Nations in 1974.

Aims and Activities WIPO administers 26 treaties that deal with different legal and administrative aspects of intellectual property, notably the Paris Convention for the Protection of Industrial Property, the Patent Cooperation Treaty and the Bern Convention for the Protection of Literary and Artistic Works. WIPO is dedicated to developing a balanced and accessible international intellectual property (IP) system that rewards creativity, stimulates innovation and contributes to economic development while safeguarding the public interest.

In Dec. 2008 WIPO member states adopted a new strategic framework for the Organization comprising nine strategic goals that are designed to enable WIPO to more effectively respond to an evolving technological, cultural and geo-economic environment. In addition to goals relating to the balanced evolution of the international normative framework of IP, to facilitating the use of IP for development and to the provision of premier global IP services, WIPO's new goals include a focus on building respect for IP; on developing global IP infrastructure; on responsive communication; on becoming a world reference source for IP information; and on addressing IP in relation to global policy challenges such as climate change, public health and food security.

WIPO's activities fall broadly into three clusters of activities, namely: the progressive development of international IP law; IP capacity-building programmes to support the efficient use of IP, particularly in developing countries; and services to industry that facilitate the process of obtaining IP rights in multiple countries. Also, alternative dispute resolution options for private parties are available through the WIPO Arbitration and Mediation Center.

Organization As at Jan. 2019 WIPO had 191 member states. WIPO is unique among the family of UN organizations in that it is largely self-financing. The budget for the 2016–17 biennium was 707·0m. Swiss francs. Over 90% of the Organization's budget comes from earnings derived from the services that WIPO provides to industry and the private sector. The remainder of the budget is made up mainly of revenue generated by WIPO's Arbitration and Mediation Center, the sale of publications and contributions from member states.

Official languages: Arabic, Chinese, English, French, Russian and Spanish.
Headquarters: 34 chemin des Colombettes, CH-1211 Geneva 20, Switzerland.
Website: http://www.wipo.int
Director-General: Francis Gurry (Australia).

Periodicals PCT Gazette (weekly).—*PCT Newsletter* (monthly).—*International Designs Bulletin* (weekly).—*WIPO Gazette of International Marks* (weekly).—*WIPO Magazine* (6 a year).

World Meteorological Organization (WMO)

Origin A 1947 (Washington) Conference of Directors of the International Meteorological Organization (est. 1873) adopted a Convention creating the World Meteorological Organization. The WMO Convention became effective on 23 March 1950 and WMO was formally established. It was recognized as a Specialized Agency of the UN in 1951.

Functions (1) To facilitate worldwide co-operation in the establishment of networks of stations for the making of meteorological observations as well as hydrological and other geophysical observations related to meteorology, and to promote the establishment and maintenance of centres charged with the provision of meteorological and related services; (2) to promote the establishment and maintenance of systems for the rapid exchange of meteorological and related information; (3) to promote standardization of meteorological and related observations and ensure the uniform publication of observations and statistics; (4) to further the application of meteorology to aviation, shipping, water problems, agriculture and other human activities; (5) to promote activities in operational hydrology and to further close co-operation between meteorological and hydrological services; and (6) to encourage research and training in meteorology and, as appropriate, to assist in co-ordinating the international aspects of such research and training.

Organization WMO has 185 member states and six member territories responsible for the operation of their own meteorological services. Congress, which is its supreme body, meets every four years to approve policy, programme and budget, and adopt regulations. The Executive Council meets at least once a year to prepare studies and recommendations for Congress, and supervises the implementation of Congress resolutions and regulations. It has

37 members, comprising the President and three Vice-Presidents, as well as the Presidents of the six Regional Associations (Africa, Asia, South America, North America, Central America and the Caribbean, South-West Pacific, Europe), whose task is to co-ordinate meteorological activity within their regions, and 27 members elected in their personal capacity. There are eight Technical Commissions composed of experts nominated by members of WMO, whose remit includes the following areas: basic systems, climatology, instruments and methods of observation, atmospheric sciences, aeronautical meteorology, agricultural meteorology, hydrology, oceanography and marine meteorology. A permanent Secretariat is maintained in Geneva. There are four regional offices for Africa, Asia and the South-West Pacific, the Americas and Europe. The expected regular budget for 2017 was 65·2m.

Headquarters: 7 bis, avenue de la Paix, Case Postale 2300, CH-1211 Geneva 2, Switzerland.
Website: https://public.wmo.int/en
Email: wmo@wmo.int
Secretary-General: Petteri Taalas (Finland).

Publications WMO Bulletin (biannual).—*MeteoWorld* (quarterly).

World Tourism Organization (UNWTO)

Origin Established in 1925 in The Hague as the International Congress of Official Tourist Traffic Associations. Renamed the International Union for Official Tourism Organizations after the Second World War when it moved to Geneva, it was renamed the World Tourism Organization in 1975 and moved its headquarters to Madrid the following year.

The World Tourism Organization became an executing agency of the United Nations Development Programme in 1976 and in 1977 a formal co-operation agreement was signed with the UN itself. With a UN resolution on 23 Dec. 2003 the World Tourism Organization became a specialized agency of the United Nations.

Aims The World Tourism Organization exists to help nations throughout the world maximize the positive impacts of tourism, such as job creation, new infrastructure and foreign exchange earnings, while at the same time minimizing negative environmental or social impacts.

Membership The World Tourism Organization has three categories of membership: full membership which is open to all sovereign states; associate membership which is open to all territories not responsible for their external relations; and affiliate membership which comprises a wide range of organizations and companies working either directly in travel and tourism or in related sectors. In Jan. 2019 the World Tourism Organization had 158 full members, six associate members and more than 500 affiliate members.

Organization The General Assembly meets every two years to approve the budget and programme of work and to debate topics of vital importance to the tourism sector. The Executive Council is the governing board, responsible for ensuring that the organization carries out its work and keeps within its budget. The World Tourism Organization has six regional commissions—Africa, the Americas, East Asia and the Pacific, Europe, the Middle East and South Asia—which meet at least once a year. Specialized committees of World Tourism Organization members advise on management and programme content.

Headquarters: Poeta Joan Maragall 42, 28020 Madrid, Spain.
Website: http://www.unwto.org
Email: comm@unwto.org
Secretary-General: Zurab Pololikashvili (Georgia).

Publications UNWTO Annual Report.—*Yearbook of Tourism Statistics* (annual).—*UNWTO Tourism Highlights* (annual).—*Compendium of Tourism Statistics* (annual).—*Travel and Tourism Barometer* (6 a year).—*UNWTO News* (monthly).

Other Organs Related to the UN

International Atomic Energy Agency (IAEA)

Origin An intergovernmental agency, the IAEA was established in 1957 under the aegis of the UN and reports annually to the General Assembly. Its Statute was approved on 26 Oct. 1956 at a conference at UN Headquarters.

Functions To enhance the contribution of atomic energy to peace, health and prosperity throughout the world; and to ensure that Agency assistance and activities are not used for any military purpose. In addition, under the terms of the Nuclear Non-Proliferation Treaty (NPT), non-nuclear-weapon states are required to allow the IAEA to verify that their nuclear activities are peaceful. Similar responsibilities are given to the IAEA as part of the nuclear-weapon-free zone treaties in Latin America, the South Pacific, Africa and Southeast Asia.

Activities The IAEA gives advice and technical assistance to developing countries on a wide range of aspects of nuclear power development. In addition, it promotes the use of radiation and isotopes in agriculture, industry, medicine and hydrology through expert services, training courses and fellowships, grants of equipment and supplies, research contracts, scientific meetings and publications. In 2015 support for operational projects for technical co-operation involved 3,477 expert and lecturer assignments, 5,126 meeting participants, 2,722 participants in training courses and 1,852 fellows and scientific visitors.

The IAEA uses technical measures ('safeguards') to verify that nuclear equipment or materials are used exclusively for peaceful purposes. IAEA safeguards were applied in 2015 in 181 States, with 2,114 inspections conducted. The five nuclear-weapon states recognized by the NPT (China, France, Russia, UK and USA) are not required to accept safeguards but have concluded Voluntary Offer Agreements that permit the IAEA access to some of their civil nuclear activities.

Organization The Statute provides for an annual General Conference, a 35-member Board of Governors and a Secretariat headed by a Director-General and currently staffed by nearly 2,500 people from over 100 countries. The IAEA had 170 member states in Jan. 2019.

There are also research laboratories in Austria and Monaco. In addition, the *International Centre for Theoretical Physics* was established in Trieste, Italy, in 1964, and is operated jointly by UNESCO and the IAEA.

Headquarters: Vienna International Centre, PO Box 100, A-1400 Vienna, Austria.
Website: http://www.iaea.org
Director General: Yukiya Amano (Japan).

Publications *AEA Annual Report.—IAEA Bulletin* (quarterly).—*INIS Reference Series.—Nuclear Fusion* (monthly).—*Nuclear Safety Review* (annual).—*IAEA International Law Series.*—International *Nuclear Information System (INIS).—Technical Reports Series.* For a full list of IAEA publications, visit the website: http://www.iaea.org/Publications/index.html

World Trade Organization (WTO)
Origin The WTO came into being on 1 Jan. 1995. The bulk of the WTO's current work comes from the 1986–94 negotiations called the Uruguay Round and earlier negotiations under the General Agreement on Tariffs and Trade (GATT), which was created in 1948.

Aims and Activities The WTO agreements have been negotiated and signed by the bulk of the world's trading nations and provide the legal ground rules for international commerce. They act as contracts, binding governments to keep their trade policies within agreed limits. The goal is to help producers of goods and services, exporters and importers conduct their business, while allowing governments to meet social and environmental objectives. The system's overriding purpose is to help trade flow as freely as possible.

The WTO agreements cover goods, services and intellectual property. They spell out the principles of liberalization and the permitted exceptions. They include individual countries' commitments to lower customs tariffs and other trade barriers, and to open and keep open services markets. They set procedures for settling disputes. The agreements are not static; they are renegotiated from time to time and new agreements can be added to the package. The WTO began new negotiations under the 'Doha Development Agenda' launched in Nov. 2001. In Dec. 2013 all 159 member countries agreed to the 'Bali package', an agreement to facilitate cross-border trade. It was the first comprehensive agreement between all members in the organization's history and analysts estimated that it could add up to US$1trn. to the global economy.

Governments are required to make their trade policies transparent by notifying the WTO about laws in force and measures adopted. Various WTO councils and committees seek to ensure that these requirements are being followed and that WTO agreements are being properly implemented. All WTO members must undergo periodic scrutiny of their trade policies and practices, each review containing reports by the country concerned and the WTO Secretariat.

The Dispute Settlement Understanding written into the WTO agreements provides a neutral procedure based on an agreed legal foundation when conflicts of interest arise between trading nations. Countries bring disputes to the WTO if they think their rights under the agreements are being infringed. Judgments by specially appointed independent experts are based on interpretations of the agreements and individual countries' commitments.

Special provision is provided for developing countries, including longer time periods to implement agreements and commitments, measures to increase their trading opportunities and support to help them build their trade capacity, to handle disputes and to implement technical standards. The WTO organizes hundreds of technical co-operation missions to developing countries annually. It also holds numerous courses each year in Geneva for government officials. Aid for Trade aims to help developing countries improve the skills and infrastructure needed to expand their trade.

The WTO maintains regular dialogue with non-governmental organizations, parliamentarians, other international organizations, the media and the general public on various aspects of the WTO and the ongoing Doha negotiations, with the aim of enhancing co-operation and increasing awareness of WTO activities.

Organization As of Jan. 2019 the WTO had 164 members, accounting for around 95% of world trade. The WTO is run by its member governments and derives its income from annual contributions from its members. All major decisions are made by the membership as a whole, either by ministers (who usually meet at least once every two years) or by their ambassadors or delegates (who meet regularly in Geneva). Day-to-day work in between the ministerial conferences is handled by three bodies: the General Council, the Dispute Settlement Body and the Trade Policy Review Body. All three consist of all the WTO members. The previous GATT Secretariat now serves the WTO, which has no resources of its own other than its operating budget. The budget for 2018 was 197,203,900 Swiss francs.

Headquarters: Centre William Rappard, 154 rue de Lausanne, CH-1211 Geneva 2, Switzerland.
Website: http://www.wto.org
Email: enquiries@wto.org
Director-General: Roberto Azevêdo (Brazil).

Publications include *Annual Report.—World Trade Report* (annual).—*International Trade Statistics* (annual).—*Trade Policy Reviews.*

Preparatory Commission for the Comprehensive Nuclear-Test-Ban Treaty Organization (CTBTO)
The Preparatory Commission for the Comprehensive Nuclear-Test-Ban Treaty Organization (CTBTO Preparatory Commission) is an international organization established by the States Signatories to the Treaty on 19 Nov. 1996. It carries out the necessary preparations for the effective implementation of the Treaty, and prepares for the first session of the Conference of the States Parties to the Treaty.

The Preparatory Commission consists of a plenary body composed of all the States Signatories, and the Provisional Technical Secretariat (PTS). Upon signing the Treaty a state becomes a member of the Commission. Member states oversee the work of the Preparatory Commission and fund its activities. The Commission's main task is the establishment of the 337 facility International Monitoring System and the International Data Centre, its provisional operation and the development of operational manuals. The Comprehensive Nuclear-Test-Ban Treaty prohibits any nuclear weapon test explosion or any other nuclear explosion anywhere in the world. As of Jan. 2019 the Treaty had 184 States Signatories and 167 ratifications.

See also Nuclear Non-Proliferation Treaty (NPT) on page 77.

Headquarters: Vienna International Centre, PO Box 1200, A-1400 Vienna, Austria.
Website: http://www.ctbto.org
Email: info@ctbto.org
Executive Secretary: Lassina Zerbo (Burkina Faso).

Organization for the Prohibition of Chemical Weapons (OPCW)
The OPCW is responsible for the implementation of the Chemical Weapons Convention (CWC), which became effective on 29 April 1997. The principal

organ of the OPCW is the Conference of the States Parties, composed of all the members of the Organization.

Given the relative simplicity of producing chemical warfare agents, the verification provisions of the CWC are far-reaching. The routine monitoring regime involves submission by States Parties of initial and annual declarations to the OPCW and initial visits and systematic inspections of declared weapons storage, production and destruction facilities. Verification is also applied to chemical industry facilities which produce, process or consume dual-use chemicals listed in the convention.

The OPCW also co-ordinates assistance to any State Party that falls victim of chemical warfare as it fosters international co-operation in the peaceful application of chemistry.

By Jan. 2019 a total of 193 countries and territories were States Parties to the Chemical Weapons Convention.

Headquarters: Johan de Wittlaan 32, 2517 JR The Hague, Netherlands.
Website: http://www.opcw.org
Director General: Ahmet *Üzümcü* (Turkey).

UN Conventions

Convention on the Rights of Persons with Disabilities

The UN Convention on the Rights of Persons with Disabilities was adopted on 13 Dec. 2006 and came into force on 3 May 2008. With 82 signatories to the Convention and 44 signatories to the Optional Protocol, it holds the record for the highest number of signatories to a UN convention on its opening day. As of Jan. 2019 it had 161 signatories.

The Convention recognizes the human rights of disabled people who have physical, mental and/or sensory long-term impairments that may affect their full participation in society. Article 1 lays out the convention's aim 'to promote, protect and ensure the full and equal enjoyment of all human rights and fundamental freedoms by all persons with disabilities, and to promote respect for their inherent dignity'. Member states are obliged to ensure the equality and non-discrimination, health, education and employment of disabled people. Every four years, each member state must submit a report on relevant measures taken. A committee of 18 independent experts monitors the implementation of the convention and normally meets in Geneva, Switzerland twice a year.

Headquarters: Secretariat for the Convention on the Rights of Persons with Disabilities (SCRPD), Division for Inclusive Social Development (DISD), Department of Economic and Social Affairs (DESA), United Nations Secretariat (29th Floor), 405 E 42nd Street, New York, NY 10017, USA.
Website: https://www.un.org/development/desa/disabilities/convention-on-the-rights-of-persons-with-disabilities.html
Email: enable@un.org

United Nations Convention to Combat Desertification

The United Nations Convention to Combat Desertification (UNCCD) was adopted in Paris in 1994 and came into force in Dec. 1996. Its 197 signatory parties (196 states and the EU) meet every other year and work to combat the effects of desertification, drought and land degradation. Specific attention is paid to Africa, where desertification is most prevalent. The ten-year strategy covering 2008–18 focuses on improving living conditions of affected parties, improving the condition of affected ecosystems and mobilizing resources to build relationships between national and international participants.

The UNCCD encourages co-operation between nations and with international non-governmental organizations. The body also works closely with the Convention on Biological Diversity (CBD) and the United Nations Framework Convention on Climate Change (UNFCCC). In March 2014 Canada became the first member state to withdraw from the convention, having announced its intention to do so a year earlier with then Prime Minister Stephen Harper claiming that it had become too bureaucratic. He maintained that less than a fifth of the money that Canada gave to the organization went on programming.

Headquarters: United Nations Convention to Combat Desertification, UN Campus, Platz der Vereinten Nationen 1, 53113 Bonn, Germany.
Website: http://www.unccd.int
Email: secretariat@unccd.int
Executive Secretary: Monique Barbut (France).

United Nations Framework Convention on Climate Change

The Convention was produced at the 1992 UN Conference on Environment and Development with the stated aim of reducing global greenhouse gas emissions to 'a level that would prevent dangerous anthropogenic (human induced) interference with the climate system'. Signatories agreed to take account of climate change in their domestic policy and to develop national programmes that would slow its progress. However, no mandatory targets were established for the reduction of emissions so the treaty remained legally non-binding. Instead it operates as a 'framework' document, with provisions for regular updates and amendments. By Jan. 2019, 196 states and territories plus the European Union had signed and ratified the Convention.

The first of these additions was the Kyoto Protocol in 1997. Under the protocol, 37 developed countries were committed to reducing their collective emissions of six greenhouse gases to at least 5% below 1990 levels. These targets were scheduled to be met in the period 2008–12. By 2012 results were mixed. The EU had reduced emissions by 21·0% and Russia by 50·3%, while the USA's had risen by 2·7%, Canada's by 42·2%, New Zealand's by 111·4% and Turkey's by 163·3%. In Dec. 2011 Canada announced it would be the first signatory to formally withdraw from the agreement. A second commitment period of the Kyoto Protocol began on 1 Jan. 2013. The USA has not ratified the protocol. China and India, also amongst the world's top five producers of emissions, are exempt from the protocol's constraints by virtue of their status as developing countries.

The members of the UNFCCC meet on an annual basis. The conference in Indonesia in 2007 led to the creation of the 'Bali Roadmap', which timetables negotiations for a protocol to succeed Kyoto, a process continued at the 2008 conference in Poland. The subsequent Copenhagen Accord of 2009 was not legally binding and failed to set out concrete measures for tackling climate change. The 2011 conference, held in Durban, South Africa, advanced negotiations on the implementation of the Kyoto Protocol, the Bali Action Plan and the Cancún Agreements. At the 18th conference in Doha, Qatar in 2012 plans were laid for the development of a successor protocol by 2015 to be implemented by 2020. The 2014 conference, in Lima, Peru, saw a framework agreement approved by 194 nations for setting national pledges for submission at the conference in Paris, France in 2015. The Paris conference duly concluded a global agreement on countering climate change, although no country-specific goals were set. Follow-up conferences were hosted in Marrakesh, Morocco, in Nov. 2016, Bonn, Germany, in Nov. 2017 and Katowice, Poland, in Dec. 2018. A further conference was scheduled to take place in Chile in Nov. 2019. However, in June 2017 President Donald Trump announced his intention to withdraw the USA from the agreement.

Headquarters: United Nations Framework Convention on Climate Change, UN Campus, Platz der Vereinten Nationen 1, 53113 Bonn, Germany.
Website: http://unfccc.int
Executive Secretary: Patricia Espinosa (Mexico).

Further Reading

United Nations (UN)

Baehr, Peter R. and Gordenker, Leon, *The United Nations: Reality and Ideal.* 2005

Binder, Martin, *The United Nations and the Politics of Selective Humanitarian Intervention.* 2017

Carnegie Commission on Preventing Deadly Conflict, Preventing Deadly Conflict: Final Report with Executive Summary. 1997

Cavalcante, Fernando, *Peacebuilding in the United Nations.* 2019

Cortright, D. and Lopez, G. A., *The Sanctions Decade: Assessing UN Strategies in the 1990s.* 2000

Fraser, Trudy, *Maintaining Peace and Security?: The United Nations in a Changing World.* 2014

Gareis, S. B., *The United Nations: An Introduction.* 2nd ed. 2012

Hoopes, T. and Brinkley, D., *FDR and the Creation of the UN.* 1998

Karlsrud, John, *The UN at War: Peace Operations in a New Era.* 2017

Kennedy, Paul, *The Parliament of Man: The Past, Present, and Future of the United Nations.* 2006

Knight, W. Andy, *Adapting the United Nations to a Postmodern Era.* 2nd ed. 2005

Meisler, S., *United Nations: The First Fifty Years.* 1998

New Zealand Ministry of Foreign Affairs and Trade, *United Nations Handbook 2018–19.* 2018

Price, Richard and Zacher, Mark W., *United Nations and Global Security.* 2004

Tannam, Etain, *International Intervention in Ethnic Conflict: A Comparison of the European Union and the United Nations.* 2014

Specialized Agencies of the UN

Phillips, David A., *Reforming the World Bank: Twenty Years of Trial – and Error.* 2011

Steil, Benn, *The Battle of Bretton Woods: John Maynard Keynes, Harry Dexter White, and the Making of a New World Order.* 2013

Stone, D. L. and Wright, C., *The World Bank and Governance.* 2006

The World Bank, *A Guide to the World Bank.* 3rd ed. 2011

Woods, N., *The Globalizers: The IMF, the World Bank and Their Borrowers.* 2007

Xu, Yi-Chong and Weller, Patrick, *Inside the World Bank: Exploding the Myth of the Monolithic Bank.* 2009

International Monetary Fund (IMF)

Ahamed, Liaquat, *Money and Tough Love: On Tour with the IMF.* 2014

Copelovitch, Mark S., *The International Monetary Fund in the Global Economy: Banks, Bonds, and Bailouts.* 2010

Dhingra, Vasudha, *The International Monetary Fund and the World Bank: Aspects of Convergence and Divergence.* 2010

Samans, Richard, Uzan, Marc and Lopez-Claros, Augusto, *The International Monetary System, the IMF, and the G-20: A Great Transformation in the Making?* 2007

Steil, Benn, *The Battle of Bretton Woods: John Maynard Keynes, Harry Dexter White, and the Making of a New World Order.* 2013

Woods, N., *The Globalizers: The IMF, the World Bank and Their Borrowers.* 2007

Other Organs Related to the UN

Bohne, Eberhard, *The World Trade Organization: Institutional Development and Reform.* 2010

Fulton, Richard and Buterbaugh, Kevin, *The WTO Primer: Tracing Trade's Visible Hand through Case Studies.* 2008

Narlikar, Amrita, Daunton, Martin and Stern, Robert M. (eds.) *The Oxford Handbook on the World Trade Organization.* 2012

Europe

European Union (EU)

Origin The Union is founded on the existing European communities set up by the Treaties of Paris (1951) and Rome (1957), supplemented by revisions, the Single European Act in 1986, the Maastricht Treaty on European Union in 1992, the Treaty of Amsterdam in 1997, the Treaty of Nice in 2000 and the Treaty of Lisbon in 2009.

Members (28). Austria, Belgium, Bulgaria, Croatia, Cyprus (Greek-Cypriot sector only), the Czech Republic, Denmark, Estonia, Finland, France, Germany, Greece, Hungary, Ireland, Italy, Latvia, Lithuania, Luxembourg, Malta, the Netherlands, Poland, Portugal, Romania, Slovakia, Slovenia, Spain, Sweden and the UK (although British membership was due to lapse following due legal process in the wake of a national referendum in June 2016 that favoured withdrawal by a narrow majority).

History European disillusionment with nationalism after the Second World War fostered a desire to bind key European states—France and (West) Germany—to each other and prevent future conflict. In 1946 Winston Churchill called for a moral union in the form of a 'united states of Europe'. Unsupported by the British Government, Churchill chaired the 1948 European Congress of The Hague, a meeting of 800 Europeanists that resulted in the creation of the *Council of Europe*, a European assembly of nations whose aim (Art. 1 of the Statute) was: 'to achieve a greater unity between its members for the purpose of safeguarding and realizing the ideals and principles which are their common heritage'.

The formation of the *Benelux Economic Union* in 1948 provided a model for a regional customs union; the free movement of goods, people, capital and services was achieved by 1960. Further European integration and the eradication of tariff trade barriers were encouraged by the US-financed European Recovery Program (Marshall Plan) and the *Organisation for European Economic Co-operation* (later the *OECD*). Western European co-operation was also spurred on by distrust of Soviet power in the East, leading to the Brussels Treaty of 1948; the collective defence pact that established the *Western European Union (WEU)*. The North Atlantic Treaty of 1949 cemented Western European (and American) security co-operation.

Jean Monnet, a French economic advisor, suggested joint development to solve Franco-German tensions over the industrial power of the Ruhr and Saarland. Monnet's plan was championed by the French foreign minister, Robert Schuman, whose Declaration of 9 May 1950 (now celebrated as Europe Day) proposed the pooling of coal and steel production. Belgium, France, the Federal Republic of Germany, Italy, Luxembourg and the Netherlands signed the Treaty of Paris establishing the *European Coal and Steel Community (ECSC)*, regarded as a first step towards a united Europe. However, the *European Defence Community (EDC)* of 1952 was rejected by the French Parliament, ending hopes for a *European Political Community*. Encouraged by the success of the ECSC, European integrationists pressed for further economic co-operation. The *European Economic Community (EEC)* and the *European Atomic Energy Community (EAEC* or *Euratom)* were subsequently created under separate treaties signed in Rome on 25 March 1957. The treaties provided for the establishment by stages of a common market with a customs union at its core, the development of common transport and agricultural policies, and the promotion of growth and research in the nuclear industries for peaceful purposes. Euratom was awarded monopoly powers of acquisition of fissile materials for civil purposes (it is not concerned with the military uses of nuclear power).

The executives of the three communities (ECSC, Euratom, EEC) were amalgamated by a treaty signed in Brussels in 1965, forming a single Council and single Commission of the European Communities, which today constitutes the core of the EU. The Commission is advised on matters relating to Euratom by a Scientific and Technical Committee.

Enlargement On 30 June 1970 membership negotiations began between the European Community and the UK, Denmark, Ireland and Norway. On 22 Jan. 1972 all four countries signed a Treaty of Accession but Norway rejected membership in a referendum in Nov. The UK, Denmark and Ireland became full members on 1 Jan. 1973 (though Greenland exercised its autonomy under the Danish Crown to secede in 1985). Greece joined on 1 Jan. 1981; Spain and Portugal on 1 Jan. 1986. The former German Democratic Republic entered into full membership on reunification with Federal Germany in Oct. 1990 and, following referenda in favour, Austria, Finland and Sweden became members on 1 Jan. 1995. In a referendum in Nov. 1994 Norway again rejected membership. On 1 May 2004 a further ten countries became members—Cyprus, the Czech Republic, Estonia, Hungary, Latvia, Lithuania, Malta, Poland, Slovakia and Slovenia. On 1 Jan. 2007 Bulgaria and Romania also became members. Most recently Croatia became a member on 1 July 2013.

Single European Act The enlarging of the Community resulted in renewed efforts to promote European integration, culminating in the signing in 1986 of the Single European Act. The SEA represented the first major revision of the Treaty of Rome. It provided for greater involvement of the European Parliament in the decision-making process and it extended Qualified Majority Voting (QMV). The SEA also removed barriers within the EEC to movement and transnational business.

Maastricht Treaty on European Union Following German reunification, closer European integration was pursued in the political as well as economic spheres. The Maastricht Summit of Dec. 1991 produced a new framework— a European Union based on three 'pillars': a central pillar of the existing European Communities and two supporting pillars based on formal intergovernmental co-operation. One pillar comprised a Common Foreign and Security Policy (CFSP) and the other focused on justice and home affairs, including policing, immigration and law enforcement. Signed in Feb. 1992, the Treaty on European Union laid down a timetable for the creation of a common currency (subject to specific conditions, including an opt-out clause for the UK). The Community Charter of Fundamental Social Rights for Workers, signed in 1989 by all members except the UK, was strengthened by a protocol, allowing member states to use EC institutions to co-ordinate social policy. The UK agreed to abide to the protocol in 1998. Ratification by member states of the Maastricht Treaty proved controversial. In June 1992 it was rejected in a Danish referendum but approved in a second referendum in May 1993. Ratification was finally completed during 1993, with the UK ratifying on 2 Aug. The European Union (EU) came into being officially on 1 Nov. that year.

Treaty of Amsterdam The Turin Inter-Governmental Conference (IGC) of 1996 failed to advance the reform programme, in part because of the British Conservative Government's opposition to extending EU powers. The election in 1997 of a more Europeanist Labour Government led to the adoption of most of the IGC's proposals at the Amsterdam summit in 1997. Designed to further political integration, the Treaty did little more than adjust the institutions to prepare for EU enlargement. Strengthened policies included police co-operation, freedom of movement and the promotion of employment. Elements of the justice and home affairs 'pillar' were transferred to the Communities. The Treaty also allows for member states to progress with selected areas of policy at different rates.

Treaty of Nice Many of the problems unanswered at Amsterdam were left until the Dec. 2000 IGC at Nice. However, the tense summit failed to find consensus on key institutional reforms. The Treaty included a reweighting of votes in the Council of Ministers, adjustments to the composition of the Commission and several extensions to QMV. Ireland rejected the Treaty in a referendum in June 2001; this was reversed in the referendum in Oct. 2002. The Treaty came into effect on 1 Feb. 2003.

Charter of Fundamental Rights The Charter, based on the Universal Declaration of Human Rights (UDHR), contains several provisions such as workers' rights and the right to good administration that are not included in the political and civil rights of the European Convention on Human Rights (ECHR).

© Springer Nature Limited 2020
Palgrave Macmillan (ed.), *The Statesman's Yearbook 2020*,
https://doi.org/10.1057/978-1-349-95940-2_2

The Treaty was proclaimed by the European Parliament, the Commission and the Council—at the Nice IGC in 2000—but was not incorporated in the Treaty of Nice.

European Convention In Dec. 2001 the Laeken European Conference adopted the Declaration on the Future of the European Union, committing the EU to becoming more democratic, transparent and effective, while opening the way to a constitution for the people of Europe. The European Council set up a convention, comprising 105 members—chaired by Valéry Giscard d'Estaing, a former French president—to draft the Treaty establishing a Constitution for Europe (the EU constitution), to be ratified by all member states. The Treaty was to confer legal personality on the European Union, giving it the right to represent itself as a single body under international law. The constitution included provision for a President of the European Council, to replace the current six-month rotating presidency, to be elected by member states for 2½-year terms. The European Parliament was to be granted co-legislative powers in all policy areas with the Council. A new position of Union Minister of Foreign Affairs would have merged the responsibilities of the external relations Commissioner and the High Representative for the CFSP. The constitution incorporated the Charter of Fundamental Rights. Member states would have had reduced powers of veto, although the veto was to have remained in key areas including taxation, defence and foreign policy. Plans for the new constitution to be ready for EU governments to sign after the ten new members joined on 1 May 2004 were dropped when the Brussels summit of Dec. 2003 ended in stalemate over the weighting of voting rights in the Council of Ministers. On 29 Oct. 2004 the Treaty was approved for ratification by the 25 member countries, either by referendum or parliamentary vote. On 29 May 2005, after nine countries had ratified the Treaty, France became the first to reject it; the Netherlands followed suit three days later. Subsequently a further seven countries ratified the Treaty. In addition, Bulgaria and Romania ratified the constitution as part of their preparations for joining the EU. With ratification in the Czech Republic, Denmark, Ireland, Poland, Portugal, Sweden and the UK delayed indefinitely, the treaty's progress stalled.

In June 2007 the European Council initiated talks on a replacement Reform Treaty (the Treaty of Lisbon). Drafting was completed in Oct. 2007, with the intention that the treaty should be signed and ratified by all member governments in time for the European parliamentary elections of June 2009. The treaty removes much of the constitutional terminology in the draft constitution text, reduces the reach of the European charter of human rights and allows for individual states to opt out of certain legislative areas. It does, nonetheless, retain many of the draft constitution's provisions, including a reformed EU presidency, a representative for EU foreign affairs and security and the recognition of the EU as a full legal personality. The treaty was subject to ratification in the parliaments of member countries. There were calls in several countries for the reform to be put to a public vote, but only Ireland was required by its constitution to hold a referendum. The treaty was rejected in the Irish referendum held on 13 June 2008 but accepted in a second referendum on 2 Oct. 2009. On 3 Nov. 2009 the Czech Republic was the final nation to ratify the treaty, which came into effect on 1 Dec. 2009. On 1 Jan. 2010 Herman Van Rompuy, formerly Belgium's prime minister, was sworn in as the first president of the European Council.

Recent and Future Enlargement On 15 July 1997 the European Commission adopted *Agenda 2000*, which included a detailed strategy for consolidating the Union through enlargement as far eastwards as Ukraine, Belarus and Moldova. It recommended the early start of accession negotiations with the Czech Republic, Estonia, Hungary, Poland and Slovenia under the provision of Article O of the Maastricht Treaty, whereby 'any European State may apply to become a member of the Union' (subject to the Copenhagen Criteria set by the European Council at its summit in 1993).

In 2002 it was announced that ten countries would be ready to join in 2004: Cyprus, the Czech Republic, Estonia, Hungary, Latvia, Lithuania, Malta, Poland, Slovakia and Slovenia. Following a series of referenda held in 2003 they all became members on 1 May 2004. Bulgaria and Romania signed an accession treaty in April 2005 and became members on 1 Jan. 2007. Entry talks with Croatia began in Oct. 2005—it was recognized as an official candidate country in June 2004—in response to greater co-operation with the International Criminal Tribunal for the former Yugoslavia. It signed the accession treaty in Dec. 2011 and became the 28th country to join the EU on 1 July 2013. Turkey became an official candidate country in Dec. 1999 and talks on membership began in Oct. 2005. However, they then stalled for a number of years over several key areas. They were briefly revived in Dec. 2015 before

stalling once more in 2016 when the European Parliament passed a resolution in Nov. to suspend talks until the government in Ankara relaxed its hard-line response to an attempted coup in July. Switzerland applied for membership in May 1992 but this was rejected by a Swiss referendum later that year. The first Switzerland-EU summit, in 2004, brought Switzerland closer to the EU with a series of bilateral agreements. A referendum in June 2005 approved joining the Schengen Accord (*see* below). North Macedonia (at the time, the former Yugoslav Republic of Macedonia) applied for membership in March 2004. Montenegro applied for membership in Dec. 2008, as did Albania in April 2009, Iceland in July 2009, Serbia in Dec. 2009, and Bosnia and Herzegovina in Feb. 2016. North Macedonia became an official candidate country in Dec. 2005, as did Iceland in June 2010, Montenegro in Dec. 2010, Serbia in March 2012 and Albania in June 2014. However, in June 2013 Iceland formally suspended negotiations until after a national referendum and in March 2015 the government requested that 'Iceland should not be regarded as a candidate country for EU membership'. A new coalition formed in Nov. 2017 showed little sign of reversing the policy.

Recent History In Nov. 2009 Herman Van Rompuy was elected as the European Council's first permanent president—and in effect the first president of the EU. In Dec. 2009 the Lisbon Treaty entered into force.

The impact of the global financial crisis was felt acutely within the EU. In 2010 Greece became the first eurozone economy to seek an EU bailout, with Ireland, Portugal, Spain and Cyprus all following suit by March 2013. In Dec. 2013 Ireland became the first nation to exit its bailout programme. These sovereign debt crises raised fundamental questions about the strength of the euro and the future direction of the EU.

Three new financial supervisory bodies were inaugurated in Jan. 2011: the European Banking Authority, the European Insurance and Occupational Pensions Authority, and the European Securities and Markets Authority. In Jan. 2012 a 'fiscal pact' aimed at limiting government spending and borrowing (with penalties for those countries breaching limits) was signed by all of the then 27 EU members except the Czech Republic and the UK. In Oct. 2012 the European Stability Mechanism was inaugurated with a maximum lending capacity of €500bn., creating a permanent bailout fund.

The EU was awarded the Nobel Peace Prize in 2012 for its six decades of work promoting peace, democracy and human rights. In July 2013 Croatia became the EU's 28th member state. In 2014 the EU condemned Russia's 'clear violation of Ukrainian sovereignty' following its annexation of Crimea and imposed a number of punitive measures including diplomatic sanctions, asset freezes and visa bans. Also in 2014 Jean-Claude Juncker, former prime minister of Luxembourg, succeeded José Manuel Barroso as European Commission president and Donald Tusk, the former Polish premier, took over from Herman Van Rompuy as European Council president.

The EU has contended with unusually high levels of migration since 2015 as its members have received well over 1m. asylum applications (particularly from people fleeing the civil war in Syria). Germany has received more applications than any other EU state.

EU cohesion was undermined further in June 2016 as the UK electorate, citing dissatisfaction with lack of sovereignty, immigration control and democratic legitimacy, voted in a national referendum to opt for withdrawal from the Union. In March 2017 the UK government triggered the mechanism that began a two-year period of negotiations to agree precise terms for the withdrawal. As of Feb. 2019 the UK was scheduled to leave on 29 March 2019 but in Jan. 2019 the British parliament rejected a draft withdrawal agreement reached in Nov. 2018 between the EU and the UK prime minister, Theresa May, who subsequently sought to renegotiate its terms relating to Irish border arrangements.

Also in 2017, the EU declined a direct mediation role following Catalonia's unilateral declaration of independence from Spain that was rejected by the central government in Madrid.

Objectives The Maastricht Treaty claimed the ultimate goal of the EU is 'an ever closer union among the peoples of Europe, in which decisions are taken as closely as possible to the citizen'. However, there are competing views over what that 'union' should be: political confederation or federation or primarily economic union. Priorities include: economic and monetary union; further expansion of the scope of the Communities; implementation of a common foreign and security policy; and development in the fields of justice and home affairs. The Lisbon Strategy, presented in 2000, strives to turn the EU into 'the most competitive and dynamic knowledge-based economy in the world'. Yet tensions remain over how to balance economic growth measures and social welfare provisions.

Structure The EU's main institutions are: the European Commission, an independent policy-making executive with powers of proposal; the Council of the European Union (known informally as the Council of Ministers), a decision-making body drawn from the national governments (headed by a permanent president since ratification of the Treaty of Lisbon); the European Council, which defines the general political direction and priorities of the EU; the European Parliament, which has joint legislative powers in most policy areas and final say over the EU budget; the Court of Justice of the European Union, including the EU's supreme court; the European Court of Auditors, which checks the financing of the EU's activities; and the European Central Bank, which is responsible for maintaining price stability in the euro area.

Defence At the 1999 Helsinki European Conference, plans were drawn up for the formation of a rapid response capability that could be deployed at short notice. The success of Operation Artemis in 2003 (when an EU peacekeeping force, spearheaded by France, intervened in the humanitarian crisis in the Democratic Republic of the Congo) led to the statement at the Franco-British summit in Nov. 2003 that the EU should be able and willing to deploy forces within 15 days in response to a UN request. The 'EU Battlegroup Concept' was approved in 2004, reached its initial operational capability in Jan. 2005 and its full operational capability in Jan. 2007. The battlegroups are considered to be the smallest self-sufficient military unit capable of stand-alone operations or deployment in the initial phase of larger operations. The battlegroups are particularly suited for tasks such as conflict prevention, evacuation and humanitarian operations; however, they have yet to be deployed. There are currently 18 battlegroups, typically consisting of around 1,500 personnel. Two battlegroups remain on standby at any one time, rotating every six months. The European Union's first ever peacekeeping force (EUFOR) officially started work in North Macedonia (then Macedonia) on 31 March 2003.

The European Union Institute for Security Studies (EUISS) was created by a Council Joint Action in July 2001 with the status of an autonomous agency. It contributes to the development of the Common Foreign and Security Policy (CFSP) through research and debate on major security and defence issues. The European Defence Agency, headed by Federica Mogherini, the EU's High Representative, was founded by the Council in July 2004 to improve defence co-ordination, especially crisis management.

Major Policy Areas
The major policy areas of the EU were laid down in the 1957 Treaty of Rome, which guaranteed certain rights to the citizens of all member states. Economic discrimination by nationality was outlawed, and member states were bound to apply 'the principle that men and women should receive equal pay for equal work'.

The Single Internal Market The core of the process of economic integration is characterized by the removal of obstacles to the four fundamental freedoms of movement for persons, goods, capital and services. Under the Treaty, individuals or companies from one member state may establish themselves in another country (for the purposes of economic activity) or sell goods or services there on the same basis as nationals of that country. With a few exceptions, restrictions on the movement of capital have also been ended. Under the Single European Act the member states bound themselves to achieve the suppression of all barriers to free movement of persons, goods and services by 31 Dec. 1992. Since then the economies of the member states have expanded to such an extent that in 2007 the EU replaced the USA as the world's largest economy.

The *Schengen Accord* abolished border controls on persons and goods between certain EU states plus Norway and Iceland. It came into effect on 26 March 1995 and was signed by Austria, Belgium, Denmark, Finland, France, Germany, Greece, Iceland, Italy, Luxembourg, the Netherlands, Norway, Portugal, Spain and Sweden. Ireland and the United Kingdom were the only EU member states at the time that decided not to participate in the accord. The ten countries that joined the EU in 2004 signed the treaty, which came into force in nine of them (the Czech Republic, Estonia, Hungary, Latvia, Lithuania, Malta, Poland, Slovakia and Slovenia) on 21 Dec. 2007. Only Cyprus has yet to implement it. Switzerland became the 25th country to join the Schengen area on 12 Dec. 2008 and Liechtenstein the 26th on 19 Dec. 2011. Other signatory countries still to implement it are Bulgaria, Croatia and Romania, which signed as part of their accession terms. Six countries—Austria, Denmark, France, Germany, Norway, and Sweden—imposed controls on some or all of their borders with neighbouring Schengen countries in the wake of the migration crisis that escalated in the course of 2015 and the Paris Islamist attacks in Nov. of that year.

Economic and Monetary Union The establishment of the single market provided for the next phase of integration: economic and monetary union. The *European Monetary System (EMS)* was founded in March 1979 to control inflation, protect European trade from international disturbances and ultimately promote convergence between the European economies. At its heart was the *Exchange Rate Mechanism (ERM)*. The ERM is run by the finance ministries and central banks of the EU countries on a day-to-day basis; monthly reviews are carried out by the EU Monetary Committee (finance ministries) and the EU Committee of Central Bankers. Sweden is not in the ERM; the UK suspended its membership on 17 Sept. 1992. In Jan. 1995 Austria joined the ERM. Finland followed in 1996, and in Nov. that year the Italian *lira*, which had been temporarily suspended, was readmitted.

With the introduction of the euro, exchange rates have been fixed for all member countries. The member countries are Austria, Belgium, Cyprus, Estonia, Finland, France, Germany, Greece, Ireland, Italy, Latvia, Lithuania, Luxembourg, Malta, the Netherlands, Portugal, Slovakia, Slovenia and Spain.

European Monetary Union (EMU) The single European currency with 11 member states came into operation in Jan. 1999, although it was not until 2002 that the currency came into general circulation. Greece subsequently joined in Jan. 2001, Slovenia in Jan. 2007, Cyprus and Malta in Jan. 2008, Slovakia in Jan. 2009, Estonia in Jan. 2011, Latvia in Jan. 2014 and Lithuania in Jan. 2015. The euro became legal tender from 1 Jan. 2002 across the region (apart from in Cyprus, Estonia, Latvia, Lithuania, Malta, Slovakia and Slovenia). National currencies were phased out by the end of Feb. 2002 in the 12 countries that were using the euro from 1 Jan. 2002. The eurozone is the world's second largest economy after the USA in terms of output and the largest in terms of trade. EMU currency consists of the euro of 100 cents. EU member countries not in the EMU select a central rate for their currency in consultation with members of the euro bloc and the European Central Bank. The rate is set according to an assessment of each country's chances of joining the eurozone.

An agreement on the legal status of the euro and currency discipline, the Stability and Growth Pact, was reached by all member states at the Dublin summit on 13 Dec. 1996. Financial penalties are meant to be applied to member states running a GDP deficit (negative growth) of up to 0·75%. If GDP falls between 0·75% and 2%, EU finance ministers have discretion as to whether to apply penalties. France and Germany exceeded their deficit limits repeatedly despite the efforts of the Commission to penalize them, resulting in the Council of Ministers' decision to relax the regulations in 2005 in an effort to make the law more enforceable. Members running an excessive deficit are automatically exempt from penalties in the event of a natural disaster or if the fall in GDP is at least 2% over one year.

In Jan. 2012 the Treaty on Stability, Coordination and Governance in the Economic and Monetary Union (also known as a 'fiscal compact') was signed by 25 of the then 27 EU member states. It was designed to co-ordinate budget policy across the eurozone in a bid to prevent further unmanageable sovereign debt. The move followed a widespread debt crisis resulting from the global economic downturn, with Ireland, Greece and Portugal all requiring bailouts. The Czech Republic and the UK, both outside the eurozone, declined to sign the treaty.

Environment The Single European Act made the protection of the environment an integral part of economic and social policies. Public support for EU environmental activism is strong, as is made clear by the success of Green parties in the parliamentary elections. Community policy aims to prevent pollution (the Prevention Principle), rectify pollution at source, impose the costs of prevention or rectification on the polluters themselves (the Polluter Pays Principle), and promote sustainable development. The European Environment Agency (*see* page 36) was established to ensure that policy was based on reliable scientific data.

In March 2002 the then 15 EU member states agreed to the 1997 Kyoto Protocol to the United Nations Framework Convention on Climate Change, which committed the EU to reduce its emissions of greenhouse gases by 8% of 1990 levels between 2008–12. By 2012 EU emissions had fallen by 21·0%, although three of the 15 nations failed to achieve their national targets.

The Common Agricultural Policy (CAP) The objectives set out in the Treaty of Rome are to increase agricultural productivity, to ensure a fair standard of living for the agricultural community, to stabilize markets, to assure supplies, and to ensure reasonable consumer prices. In Dec. 1960 the Council laid down the fundamental principles on which the CAP is based: a single market, which calls for common prices, stable currency parities and the harmonizing of health and veterinary legislation; Community preference, which protects the single Community market from imports; common financing which seeks to improve agriculture and to stabilize markets against world price fluctuations through market intervention, with levies and refunds on exports. The CAP has made the EU virtually self-sufficient in food.

Following the disappearance of stable currency parities, artificial currency levels have been applied in the CAP. This factor, together with overproduction owing to high producer prices, meant that the CAP consumed about two-thirds of the Community budget. In May 1992 it was agreed to reform the CAP and to control over-production by reducing the price supports to farmers by 29% for cereals, 15% for beef and 5% for dairy products. In June 1995 the guaranteed intervention price for beef was decreased by 5%. In July 1996 agriculture ministers agreed a reduction in the set-aside rate for cereals from 10% to 5%. Fruit and vegetable production subsidies were fixed at no more than 4% of total marketed production, rising to 4·5% in 1999. Compensatory grants are made available to farmers who remove land from production or take early retirement. The CAP reform aims to make the agricultural sector more responsive to supply and demand.

Customs Union and External Trade Relations Goods or services originating in one member state have free circulation within the EU, which implies common arrangements for trade with the rest of the world. Member states can no longer make bilateral trade agreements with third countries; this power has been ceded to the EU. The Customs Union was achieved in July 1968.

In Oct. 1991 a treaty forming the *European Economic Area (EEA)* was approved by the member states of the then EC and European Free Trade Association (EFTA). The EEA consists of the 28 EU members plus Iceland, Liechtenstein and Norway. Although a Swiss referendum rejected ratification of the EEA in Dec. 1992, Switzerland has a bilateral agreement with the EU.

As part of the accession process, the EU has Stabilisation and Association Agreements in force with Albania, Bosnia and Herzegovina, Kosovo, North Macedonia, Montenegro and Serbia. Customs unions came into force with Andorra in 1991, Turkey in 1995 and San Marino in 2002. Association agreements, which could lead to customs union, have been made with several states in the former USSR, the Middle East, North Africa and Central America.

Free trade agreements are in force with more than 30 countries and territories (often as a component of other agreements). There are partnership and co-operation agreements with a number of Eastern European and Central Asian states (as well as Iraq).

In June 2013 the European Commission and the USA launched negotiations on a Transatlantic Trade and Investment Partnership. However, the future of the proposed deal has been uncertain since the UK's decision in June 2016 to leave the EU and Donald Trump's election as president in the USA later the same year. Talks with Canada on a Comprehensive Economic and Trade Agreement began in May 2009. As part of the agreement, over 99% of import tariffs will be removed in an attempt to create new market access opportunities in services and investment. The agreement was signed in Oct. 2016 and came into force provisionally in Sept. 2017 but will not be fully implemented until it has been ratified by all EU member states.

In the Development Aid sector, the EU has an agreement (the Cotonou Agreement, signed in 2000, the successor of the Lomé Convention, originally signed in 1975 but renewed and enlarged in 1979, 1984 and 1989) with 77 African, Caribbean and Pacific (ACP) countries that removes customs duties without reciprocal arrangements for most of their imports to the Community. Since 2002, under the terms of the Cotonou Agreement, the EU and all participating ACP nations have been in talks to establish Economic Partnership Agreements (EPAs) designed to end non-reciprocal trade agreements that conflict with WTO rules. As of Sept. 2018 EPAs had been concluded with 50 ACP countries covering over 900m. people on four continents.

The application of common duties has been conducted mainly within the framework of the *General Agreement on Tariffs and Trade (GATT)*, which was succeeded in 1995 by the establishment of the World Trade Organization.

Fisheries The Common Fisheries Policy (CFP) came into effect in Jan. 1983. All EU fishermen have equal access to the waters of member countries (a zone extending up to 200 nautical miles from the shore), with the total allowable catch for each species being set and shared out between member countries according to pre-established quotas. In some cases 'historic rights' apply, as well as special rules to preserve marine biodiversity and ensure sustainable fishing.

A number of agreements are operating with third countries and territories (with Cabo Verde, the Cook Islands, Côte d'Ivoire, Greenland, Liberia, Madagascar, Mauritania, Mauritius, Senegal and the Seychelles) allowing reciprocal fishing rights. When Greenland withdrew from the Community in 1985, EU boats retained their fishing rights subject to quotas and limits, which were revised in 1995 owing to concern about the overfishing of Greenland halibut.

Transport Failure to create a common transport policy, as expected by the Treaty of Rome, led in 1982 to parliamentary proceedings against the Council at the Court of Justice. Under the Maastricht Treaty, the Community must contribute to the establishment and development of Trans-European Networks (TENs) in the areas of transport, telecommunications and energy infrastructures. Funding is via the Connecting Europe Facility (CEF), which has a budget of €29·3bn. for 2014–20. Of this, €23·2bn. is allocated to transport projects (up from €8·0bn. for 2007–13). Common transport policy includes safety agreements, such as lorry weight and driver hours limits, the easing of border crossings for commercial vehicles and progress towards a common transport market. Rail plans include a 35,000 km high-speed train (HST) network, incorporating France's TGV and Germany's ICE networks.

Competition The Competition (anti-trust) law of the EU is based on two principles: that businesses should not seek to nullify the creation of the common market by the erection of artificial national (or other) barriers to the free movement of goods; and that there should not be any abuse of dominant positions in any market. These two principles have led to the outlawing of prohibitions on exports to other member states, of price-fixing agreements and of refusal to supply; and to the refusal by the Commission to allow mergers or takeovers by dominant undertakings in specific cases.

Funds There are two Structural Funds: the *European Regional Development Fund* (promoting economic and social cohesion through the reduction of imbalances between regions or social groups) and the *European Social Fund* (combating unemployment, developing human resources and promoting integration into the labour market). These Structural Funds along with the Cohesion Fund are the financial instruments of EU regional policy, which is intended to narrow the development disparities among regions and member states.

Finances The budget (or Multiannual Financial Framework) for 2014–20 totals €960bn., representing a real terms cut of 3·3% on the 2007–13 budget (the first cut in EU history). The reduction, opposed by many members, was championed by major net-contributors including Finland, Germany, the Netherlands, Sweden and the UK.

Spending is divided under five broad headings: smart and inclusive growth (47%); sustainable growth: natural resources (39%); global Europe (6%); administration (6%); and security and citizenship (2%).

EU revenue in €1m.:

	2017
Customs duties	25,406·7
GNI-based own resource	78,620·0
VAT-based own resource	16,947·3
Miscellaneous	19,049·2
Total	139,023·2

Expenditure for 2017 was €137,379·1m., of which common agricultural policy spending accounted for €56,454·7m. (41·4% of the total).

The resources of the Community (the levies and duties mentioned above, and up to a 1·4% VAT charge) have been agreed by Treaty. The Budget is made by the Council and the Parliament acting jointly as the Budgetary Authority. The Parliament has control, within a certain margin, of non-obligatory expenditure (where the amount to be spent is not set out in the legislation concerned), and can also reject the Budget. Otherwise, the Council decides.

Official languages: Bulgarian, Croatian, Czech, Danish, Dutch, English, Estonian, Finnish, French, German, Greek, Hungarian, Irish, Italian, Latvian, Lithuanian, Maltese, Polish, Portuguese, Romanian, Slovak, Slovenian, Spanish and Swedish.

Website: http://europa.eu

EU Institutions

European Commission

The European Commission consists of 28 members. The Commission President is selected by a consensus of member state heads of government and serves a five-year term. The Commission acts as the EU executive body and as guardian of the Treaties. In this it has the right of initiative (putting proposals to the Council of Ministers for action) and of execution (once the Council has decided). It can take the other institutions or individual countries before the European Court of Justice should any of these fail to comply with European Law. Decisions on legislative proposals made by the Commission are taken in the Council of the European Union. Members of the Commission swear an oath of independence, distancing themselves from partisan influence from any source. The Commission operates through 47 Directorates-General and services. As of Feb. 2019 there were also six executive agencies set up for fixed periods to manage EU programmes. They were: the Consumers, Health and Food Executive Agency (CHAFEA); the Education, Audiovisual and Culture Executive Agency (EACEA); the European Research Council Executive Agency (ERC Executive Agency); the Executive Agency for Small and Medium-sized Enterprises (EASME); the Innovation and Networks Executive Agency (INEA); and the Research Executive Agency (REA).

At the European Summit held in Nice in Dec. 2000 it was decided that from 2005 each EU member state would have one commissioner until the number of members reached 27 (which happened on 1 Jan. 2007). Under the terms of the Treaty of Lisbon, in 2014 the Commission was to comprise representatives from two-thirds of the member states on a rotating basis. However, in Dec. 2008 it was agreed that even if the Treaty of Lisbon entered force (which it did on 1 Dec. 2009), the principle of one commissioner per member state would be maintained. It was a position upheld by the European Council in May 2013 for the Commission that was to take office on 1 Nov. 2014.

The current Commission took office in Nov. 2014. Members, their nationality and political affiliation in their respective countries (C-Christian Democrat/Conservative; S-Socialist/Social Democrat; L-Liberal; Ind-Independent) in Jan. 2019 were as follows:

President: Jean-Claude Juncker (Luxembourg, C).

The commissioners are:

First vice-president: Frans Timmermans (Netherlands, S); responsible for better regulation, interinstitutional relations, the rule of law and the charter of fundamental rights.

Vice-president: Federica Mogherini (Italy, S); high representative of the Union for foreign affairs and security policy.

Vice-president: Andrus Ansip (Estonia, L); responsible for the digital single market.

Vice-president: Maroš Šefčovič (Slovakia, S); responsible for energy union.

Vice-president: Valdis Dombrovskis (Latvia, C); responsible for the euro and social dialogue (also in charge of financial stability, financial services and capital markets union).

Vice-president: Jyrki Katainen (Finland, C); responsible for jobs, growth, investment and competitiveness.

Agriculture and Rural Development: Phil Hogan (Ireland, C).

Budget and Human Resources: Günther Oettinger (Germany, C).

Climate Action and Energy: Miguel Arias Cañete (Spain, C).

Competition: Margrethe Vestager (Denmark, L).

Digital Economy and Society: Mariya Gabriel (Bulgaria, C).

Economic and Financial Affairs, Taxation and Customs: Pierre Moscovici (France, S).

Education, Culture, Youth and Sport: Tibor Navracsics (Hungary, C).

Employment, Social Affairs, Skills and Labour Mobility: Marianne Thyssen (Belgium, C).

Environment, Maritime Affairs and Fisheries: Karmenu Vella (Malta, S).

European Neighbourhood Policy and Enlargement Negotiations: Johannes Hahn (Austria, C).

Health and Food Safety: Vytenis Andriukaitis (Lithuania, S).

Humanitarian Aid and Crisis Management: Christos Stylianides (Cyprus, C).

Internal Market, Industry, Entrepreneurship and SMEs: Elżbieta Bieńkowska (Poland, C).

International Co-operation and Development: Neven Mimica (Croatia, S).

Justice, Consumers and Gender Equality: Věra Jourová (Czech Republic, L).

Migration, Home Affairs and Citizenship: Dimitris Avramopoulos (Greece, C).

Regional Policy: Corina Crețu (Romania, S).

Research, Science and Innovation: Carlos Moedas (Portugal, C).

Security Union: Julian King (UK, Ind).

Trade: Cecilia Malmström (Sweden, L).

Transport: Violeta Bulc (Slovenia, L).

Current Leaders

Jean-Claude Juncker

Position
President

Introduction
On 15 July 2014 former Luxembourg premier Jean-Claude Juncker became the first elected president of the European Commission under provisions in the 2009 Treaty of Lisbon. He succeeded José Manuel Barroso when he took office on 1 Nov. 2014 and is scheduled to serve a five-year term.

Early Life
Juncker was born in Redange-sur-Attert in Luxembourg on 9 Dec. 1954. He studied law at the University of Strasbourg and was admitted to the Bar of Luxembourg in Feb. 1980. An active member of the Christian Social Party (CSV), he chaired its youth organization from 1979–84. Appointed state secretary for employment and social affairs in 1982, he was elected to parliament for the first time in 1984 and became minister of labour, social security and budget. When Luxembourg held the presidency of the European Community in 1985, Juncker chaired the council of ministers for social affairs and the budget.

In 1990 he was elected leader of the CSV. As president of the Council of the European Union's economic and financial affairs council in 1991, he was among the co-authors of the Treaty of Maastricht. He was a governor of the World Bank from 1989–95, and from 1995–2013 was the country's representative governor of the European Investment Bank and the International Monetary Fund.

In Jan. 1995 he was appointed prime minister. In Oct. 2000 his government oversaw the abdication of Grand Duke Jean in favour of his son, Prince Henri. Following his re-election in 2004, Juncker formed a coalition government with the Socialist Workers' Party (LSAP). From Jan.–June 2005 he headed Luxembourg's six-month presidency of the European Union. From 2005–13 he served as the permanent president of the Eurogroup of eurozone finance ministers. At the height of the 2008–09 financial crisis, he played a key role in drafting several national bailout packages.

In the June 2009 elections the CSV increased its representation in the Chamber of Deputies and Juncker began his fourth term as prime minister at the head of a CSV–LSAP coalition. On 11 July 2013 he resigned as prime minister and called for snap elections following claims of misconduct by the country's security agency, which the prime minister oversees. He remained head of a caretaker government until Dec. 2013 when he was succeeded by Xavier Bettel.

On 7 March 2014 Juncker was elected as the lead candidate of the European People's Party (EPP) for the presidency of the European Commission. The European Council approved his candidacy on 27 June, and on 15 July the European Parliament elected him with 422 votes from 729 cast.

Career in Office
To boost growth and employment across Europe, in Nov. 2014 Juncker launched a €315bn. strategic investment scheme in partnership with the European Investment Bank. He has also supported negotiations for an EU–US free trade treaty and advocated the creation of a digital single market. Although a champion of tax reform in the EU, Juncker has been plagued by claims that under his premiership Luxembourg turned into a major European centre of corporate tax avoidance.

In 2015 Juncker's Commission sought to develop a co-ordinated approach to managing the burgeoning refugee crisis generated by mass migration into the EU, particularly from Syria, Iraq, Kosovo, Albania and Afghanistan.

A firm believer in European integration, Juncker has often been accused of being a 'federalist' by his Eurosceptic critics. He has expressed willingness to discuss repatriating some powers back to member states, but has stood firm on key treaty mainstays such as the free movement of people—a position at odds with British demands for reforms, which led to the UK's controversial decision in a national referendum in June 2016 to withdraw from membership of the EU.

Against the backdrop of an increasing terrorist threat, Russian military assertiveness and the reverberations of conflict in the Middle East, Juncker stressed the need for an integrated European defence policy in his 'state of the union' address in Sept. 2016.

In his next review in Sept. 2017, Juncker gave a positive vision for the economic future of Europe, although he lamented the UK's 'tragic' decision to leave the Union. He proposed more help for all the remaining 27 EU countries to join the single currency as well as a range of institutional reforms, including combining the presidencies of the European Commission and European Council as a single directly-elected position. He also repeated his support for the establishment of a fully-fledged European defence union by 2025 and of a European cybersecurity agency. As the EU and Japan approached the successful conclusion of negotiations on a free trade agreement (reached in Dec.), Juncker said that he also intended to start trade talks with Australia and New Zealand. However, he ruled out Turkey's accession to the EU in the foreseeable future. Juncker again pressed for greater European integration in his next state of the union address in Sept. 2018, calling on governments to pool their sovereignty in order to boost the EU's collective economic, political and military power.

In Dec. 2017, following first-phase talks on the UK's withdrawal from the EU (Brexit), both parties reached agreement in principle on the mutual protection of the rights of each other's resident citizens, on the UK's financial divorce settlement and on the need to address Northern Ireland's unique border circumstances with the Irish Republic. Juncker welcomed the advance as 'the breakthrough we needed' to progress to the second, more complex, phase of negotiations in 2018.

However, such optimism proved premature as UK Prime Minister Theresa May's Brexit strategy was consistently undermined through the year by domestic political opposition and dissension within her ruling Conservative Party. In Dec. 2018 Juncker stated that the UK's pending withdrawal (scheduled for 29 March 2019) without a conclusive agreement would be a catastrophe and also that it was 'unreasonable for parts of the British public to believe that it is for the EU alone to propose a solution for all future British problems'. He appealed to the UK government: 'Get your act together and then tell us what you want.' The UK parliament subsequently voted on 29 Jan. 2019 for a renegotiation of a central element (on the Irish border) of withdrawal terms already agreed between Prime Minister May and the EU the previous Nov., which Juncker rejected and claimed had further increased the chances of a disorderly Brexit.

Headquarters: 170 rue de la Loi/Wetstraat, B-1049 Brussels, Belgium.
Website: https://europa.eu/european-union/about-eu/institutions-bodies/euro pean-commission_en
Secretary-General: Martin Selmayr (Germany).

Statistical Office of the European Communities (Eurostat)

Eurostat is a directorate-general of the European Commission. Its mission is to provide the EU with a high-quality statistical service. It receives data collected according to uniform rules from the national statistical institutes of member states, then consolidates and harmonizes the data, before making them available to the public. The data are available from the Eurostat website.

Address: Joseph Bech Building, 5 Rue Alphonse Weicker, L-2721 Luxembourg.
Website: http://ec.europa.eu/eurostat

Council of the European Union (Council of Ministers)

The Council of Ministers consists of ministers from the 28 national governments and is the only institution which directly represents the member states' national interests. It is the Union's principal decision-making body. Here, members legislate for the Union, set its political objectives, co-ordinate their national policies and resolve differences between themselves and other institutions. The presidency rotates every six months. Romania had the presidency during the first half of 2019 and Finland has the presidency during the second half of 2019; Croatia will have it during the first half of 2020 and Germany during the second half of 2020. Romania, Finland and Croatia are co-operating in a triple presidency over an 18-month period. There is only one Council, but it meets in different configurations depending on the items on the agenda. The meetings are held in Brussels, except in April, June and Oct. when all meetings are in Luxembourg. Around 100 formal ministerial sessions are held each year.

Decisions are taken either by qualified majority vote or by unanimity. Since the entry into force of the Single European Act in 1987 an increasing number of decisions are by majority vote, although some areas such as taxation and social security, immigration and border controls are reserved to unanimity. At the Nice Summit in Dec. 2000 agreement was reached that a further 39 articles of the EU's treaties would move to qualified majority voting. 26 votes were then needed to veto a decision (blocking minority), and member states were allocated the following number of votes: France, Germany, Italy and the UK, 10; Spain, 8; Belgium, Greece, the Netherlands and Portugal, 5; Austria and Sweden, 4; Denmark, Finland and the Republic of Ireland, 3; Luxembourg, 2. During a six-month transitional period that followed the accession of the ten new member states on 1 May 2004 these vote weightings remained unchanged, while the new members were allocated the following number of votes: Poland, 8; Czech Republic and Hungary, 5; Estonia, Latvia, Lithuania, Slovakia and Slovenia, 3; Cyprus and Malta, 2. When Bulgaria and Romania joined the EU on 1 Jan. 2007 the allocation of vote weightings became: France, Germany, Italy and the UK, 29; Poland and Spain, 27; Romania, 14; the Netherlands, 13; Belgium, the Czech Republic, Greece, Hungary and Portugal, 12; Austria, Bulgaria and Sweden, 10; Denmark, Finland, the Republic of Ireland, Lithuania and Slovakia, 7; Cyprus, Estonia, Latvia, Luxembourg and Slovenia, 4; Malta 3. After Croatia joined the EU on 1 July 2013, it received a vote weighting of seven while those for other members remained the same. Qualified majority voting was extended following the introduction of the Treaty of Lisbon. On 1 Nov. 2014 an amended procedure, the 'double majority' rule, was introduced. When the Council votes on a proposal by the Commission or the EU's High Representative for Foreign Affairs and Security Policy, a qualified majority is reached if 55% of EU countries vote in favour (16 out of 28) and the proposal is supported by countries representing at least 65% of the total EU population. When the Council votes on a proposal not made by the Commission or the High Representative, a decision is adopted if there are 72% of EU country votes in favour and they represent at least 65% of the EU population. Each member state has a national delegation in Brussels known as the Permanent Representation, headed by Permanent Representatives, senior diplomats whose committee (Coreper) prepares ministerial sessions. Coreper meets weekly and its main task is to ensure that only the most difficult and sensitive issues are dealt with at ministerial level.

The General Secretariat of the Council provides the practical infrastructure of the Council at all levels and prepares the meetings of the Council and the European Council by advising the Presidency and assisting the Coreper and the various committees and working groups of the Council.

Legislation The Community's legislative process starts with a proposal from the Commission (either at the suggestion of its services or in pursuit of its declared political aims) to the Council, or in the case of co-decision, to both the Council and the European Parliament. The Council generally seeks the views of the European Parliament on the proposal, and the Parliament adopts a formal Opinion after consideration of the matter by its specialist Committees. The Council may also (and in some cases is obliged to) consult the Economic and Social Committee and the Committee of the Regions which similarly deliver an opinion. When these opinions have been received, the Council will decide. Most decisions are taken on a majority basis, but will take account of reservations expressed by individual member states.

Provisions of the Treaties and secondary legislation may be either directly applicable in member states or only applicable after member states have enacted their own implementing legislation. Community law, adopted by the Council (or by Parliament and the Council in the framework of the co-decision procedure) may take the following forms: (1) *Regulations*, which are of general application and binding in their entirety and directly applicable in all member states; (2) *Directives*, which are binding upon each member state as to the result to be achieved within a given time, but leave to the national authorities the choice of form and method of achieving this result; and (3) *Decisions*, which are binding in their entirety on their addressees. In addition the Council and Commission can issue recommendations, opinions, resolutions and conclusions which are essentially political acts and not legally binding.

Transparency In order to make its decision-making process more transparent to the European citizens, the Council has, together with the European Parliament and the Commission, introduced a set of rules concerning public access to the documents of the three institutions. A considerable number of Council documents can be accessed electronically via the Council's public register of documents, whereas other documents which may not be directly accessible can be released to the public upon request. With a view to ensure the widest possible access to its decision-making process, some Council debates and deliberations are open to the public.

Headquarters: 175 rue de la Loi/Wetstraat, B-1048 Brussels, Belgium.
Website: http://www.consilium.europa.eu/en/council-eu
Secretary-General: Jeppe Tranholm-Mikkelsen (Denmark).

The European Council

Since 1974 Heads of State or Government have met at least twice a year (until the end of 2002 in the capital of the member state currently exercising the presidency of the Council of the European Union, since 2003 primarily in Brussels) in the form of the European Council or European Summit as it is commonly known. Its membership includes the President of the European Commission, and the President of the European Parliament is invited to make a presentation at the opening session. The European Council has become an increasingly important element of the Union, setting priorities, giving political direction, providing the impetus for its development and resolving contentious issues that prove too difficult for the Council of the European Union. It has a direct role to play in the context of the Common Foreign and Security Policy (CFSP) when deciding upon common strategies, and at a more general level, when deciding upon the establishing of closer co-operation between member states within certain policy areas covered by the EU-treaties. Moreover, during recent years, the European Council has played a preponderant role in defining the general political guidelines within key policy areas with a bearing on growth and employment and in the context of the strengthening of the EU as an area of freedom, security and justice. With the entry into force of the Treaty of Lisbon on 1 Dec. 2009, it has become a full EU institution.

Current Leaders
Donald Tusk

Position
President

Introduction
Donald Tusk, the centre-right prime minister of Poland from 2007–14, became the European Union's first president of the European Council from an eastern EU member state on 1 Dec. 2014 and was re-elected to the post on 9 March 2017 despite the opposition of a hostile government in his native Poland.

Early Life
Donald Franciszek Tusk was born on 22 April 1957 in Gdańsk. He read history at the University of Gdańsk and, as a long-time critic of the communist administration, helped to establish the student committee of the Solidarity movement, which grew out of nationwide industrial unrest in 1980. He subsequently co-founded the Independent Polish Students' Association (NZS). Following the authorities' crackdown on Solidarity in 1981, Tusk and other activists were forced underground. He earned a living as a builder, an experience subsequently presented as evidence of his empathy with 'ordinary people'.

In the late 1980s Tusk left Solidarity for the nascent liberal movement and in 1991 joined the Liberal Democratic Congress (KLD), which contested the first multi-party elections in Oct. that year on a free-market platform of privatization, freedom of movement and accession to the EU. Tusk took one of the KLD's 37 seats in the *Sejm* (the Polish parliament). Although he was re-elected as a deputy in the 1993 elections, the KLD fared poorly and in March 1994 merged with the Democratic Union to form a new centre-right party, Freedom Union (UW). The UW secured 13·4% of the vote in the 1997 elections and became a junior partner in Jerzy Buzek's coalition government. Tusk was elected to the Senate and from 1998–2001 served as vice-speaker.

Having failed to win the chairmanship of the UW in 2000, Tusk resigned from the party and helped launch Civic Platform (PO) in early 2001, with Maciej Płażyński at the helm. The PO performed strongly in the 2001 elections, taking 65 seats in the *Sejm* and becoming the largest opposition party. In June 2003 Tusk became the PO's chairman. He was a vocal critic of the left-leaning SLD government, particularly its economic policies. Although Tusk's standing improved as the SLD became mired in corruption scandals, he failed in his 2005 bid for the presidency, losing to Lech Kaczyński of the Law and Justice Party. Later in 2005 the PO suffered further electoral defeat to Law and Justice, led by Jarosław Kaczyński (Lech's twin brother), who became prime minister.

Tusk remained leader of the PO and took a more aggressive approach in the run-up to the early election called for Oct. 2007, which followed the collapse of the Law and Justice-led coalition amid corruption allegations. He accused Kaczyński of incompetence on international relations and of failing to prevent the mass movement of Poles to Britain and Ireland in search of work. He campaigned to speed up privatization, lower taxes and reduce business bureaucracy to encourage investors. In parliamentary elections on 21 Oct. 2007 the PO emerged victorious and Tusk took office as prime minister in Nov.

Tusk pledged to create jobs and promote economic development by cutting bureaucracy and regulation. However, the global financial meltdown of 2008 undermined Poland's growth prospects and prompted the government to launch an economic stimulus programme and to negotiate a one-year US$20·6bn. credit line with the IMF, which was approved in May 2009.

On the international stage, Tusk oversaw the withdrawal in Oct. 2008 of Poland's last troops stationed in Iraq. Plans agreed in 2008 for Poland to host a controversial missile defence shield for the USA were abandoned in Sept. 2009 when the US president announced the scrapping of key elements of the system. Tusk nevertheless insisted that the USA and Poland would remain close allies. In July 2011 Poland assumed the EU's six-month rotating presidency for the first time since its accession in 2004.

In Oct. 2011 Tusk's PO was returned to power. However, having introduced unpopular fiscal measures in May 2012—including pension reform and increasing the retirement age—his administration lost ground in opinion polls to the opposition Law and Justice Party. In Oct. that year the government narrowly won a parliamentary vote of confidence after pledging US$95bn. in infrastructure and other investments to boost growth. In 2013 Tusk's administration survived further parliamentary confidence votes but anti-government sentiment continued over the unpopular fiscal measures.

Tusk was selected as the next president of the European Council in Aug. 2014, winning support from a number of EU leaders including the UK's David Cameron, and took office on 1 Dec. 2014, succeeding Herman Van Rompuy. He resigned as Polish prime minister on 9 Sept. 2014.

Career in Office
Working alongside European Commission president Jean-Claude Juncker and charged with priority-setting, mediation and chairing meetings of EU leaders, Tusk has continued to try to navigate a course through a number of critical challenges since taking office. These have included the revitalization of the eurozone economy, the EU's fractious relations with Russia over its interference in Ukraine and Syria and its threat to the security of its Baltic neighbours, Greece's financial crisis, the UK's controversial vote to leave the EU (Brexit) in a national referendum in June 2016 and subsequent complex withdrawal negotiations, the rise of nationalist populism in some EU states, and credible management of a migration crisis caused by the mass influx of refugees from beyond the EU's borders. Other issues on his agenda have included forging a single EU market in digital services, a centralized 'energy union' and a free trade deal with the USA.

In Nov. 2018, regarding the Brexit process, the European Council endorsed a withdrawal agreement and political declaration reached between EU negotiators and UK Prime Minister Theresa May. However, a divided and hostile UK parliament failed to sanction the provisions and, at end of Jan. 2019, voted for a renegotiation of a central element of the terms (on the status of the Irish border), which Tusk said the EU would not countenance. He subsequently stressed in early Feb. that his priority was to avoid a 'no-deal' scenario but added: 'I've been wondering what that special place in hell looks like for those who promoted Brexit without even a sketch of a plan of how to carry it [out] safely'—which provoked a hostile response from Brexit supporters in the UK.

Headquarters: 175 rue de la Loi/Wetstraat, B-1048 Brussels, Belgium.
Website: http://www.consilium.europa.eu/en/european-council
President: Donald Tusk (Poland).

European Parliament
The European Parliament consists of 751 members (up from 736 elected in 2009 before Croatia joined the European Union, but down from 766 prior to the May 2014 elections). All EU citizens may stand or vote in their adoptive country of residence. Germany returned 96 members in 2014 (and returned 99 in 2009), France 74 (72 in 2009), Italy and the UK 73 each (72 each in 2009), Spain 54 (50 in 2009), Poland 51 (50 in 2009), Romania 32 (33 in 2009), the Netherlands 26 (25 in 2009), Belgium, Czech Republic, Greece, Hungary and Portugal 21 each (22 each in 2009), Sweden 20 (18 in 2009),

Austria 18 (17 in 2009), Bulgaria 17 (17 in 2009), Denmark, Finland and Slovakia 13 each (13 each in 2009), Croatia, Ireland and Lithuania 11 each (12 each for Ireland and Lithuania in 2009—Croatia only became a member of the European Union in 2013), Latvia and Slovenia 8 each (Latvia with 8 in 2009 and Slovenia with 7), Cyprus, Estonia, Luxembourg and Malta 6 each (6 each in 2009, apart from Malta with 5). Turnout declined from 62·0% at the first direct elections in 1979 to 42·6% in 2014.

Political groupings In Jan. 2019 the European People's Party (EPP) had 217 seats, Progressive Alliance of Socialists and Democrats (S&D) 187, European Conservatives and Reformists (ECR) 75, Alliance of Liberals and Democrats for Europe (ALDE) 68, European United Left/Nordic Green Left (GUE/NGL) 52, Greens/European Free Alliance (Greens/EFA) 52, Europe of Freedom and Direct Democracy (EFDD) 41, Europe of Nations and Freedom (ENF) 37, Non-attached members (NI) 22.

The Parliament has a right to be consulted on a wide range of legislative proposals and forms one arm of the Community's Budgetary Authority. Under the Single European Act, it gained greater authority in legislation through the 'concertation' procedure under which it can reject certain Council drafts in a second reading procedure. Under the Maastricht Treaty, it gained the right of 'co-decision' on legislation with the Council of Ministers on a restricted range of domestic matters. The President of the European Council must report to the Parliament on progress in the development of foreign and security policy. It also plays an important role in appointing the President and members of the Commission. It can hold individual commissioners to account and can pass a motion of censure on the entire Commission, a prospect that was realized in March 1999 when the Commission, including the President, Jacques Santer, was forced to resign following an investigation into mismanagement and corruption. Parliament's seat is in Strasbourg where the one-week plenary sessions are held each month. In the Chamber, members sit in political groups, not as national delegations. The other two main bodies are the Bureau—consisting of the President, 14 Vice-Presidents and five Quaestors (in a consultative capacity) elected for a two-and-a-half year period—which is responsible for budgetary and administration issues, and the Conference of Presidents, which is a governing body composed of the presidents of each of the parliament's political groups.

Location: Bât. Altiero Spinelli, Wiertzstraat 60, B-1047 Brussels, Belgium; WIC, Allée du Printemps, BP 1024, F-67070 Strasbourg Cedex, France; Plateau du Kirchberg, BP 1601, L-2929 Luxembourg, Luxembourg.
Website: http://www.europarl.europa.eu
President: Antonio Tajani (Italy, EPP).

Court of Justice of the European Union
The Court of Justice of the European Union consists of two courts: the Court of Justice (the highest court in the European Union in matters of EU law, created in 1952 and composed of 28 Judges and eight Advocates General) and the General Court (created in 1988 as the Court of First Instance). A Civil Service Tribunal, created in 2004, was dissolved in 2016. Since their establishment the courts have delivered more than 15,000 judgments.

Address: Rue du Fort Niedergrünewald, L-2925 Luxembourg.
Website: http://curia.europa.eu
President of the Court of Justice: Koen Lenaerts (Belgium).
President of the General Court: Marc Jaeger (Luxembourg).

European Court of Auditors
The European Court of Auditors was established by a treaty of 22 July 1975 which took effect on 1 June 1977. It consists of 28 members (one from each member state) and was raised to the status of a full EU institution by the 1993 Maastricht Treaty. It audits the accounts and verifies the implementation of the budget of the EU.

Address: 12, rue Alcide De Gasperi, L-1615 Luxembourg.
Website: http://eca.europa.eu
President: Klaus-Heiner Lehne (Germany).

European Central Bank
The European System of Central Banks (ESCB) is composed of the European Central Bank (ECB) and 28 National Central Banks (NCBs). The NCBs of the member states not participating in the euro area are members with special status; while they are allowed to conduct their respective national monetary policies, they do not take part in decision-making

regarding the single monetary policy for the euro area and the implementation of these policies. The Governing Council of the ECB makes a distinction between the ESCB and the 'Eurosystem' which is composed of the ECB and the 19 fully participating NCBs.

Members The 19 fully participating National Central Banks are from: Austria, Belgium, Cyprus, Estonia, Finland, France, Germany, Greece, Ireland, Italy, Latvia, Lithuania, Luxembourg, Malta, Netherlands, Portugal, Slovakia, Slovenia and Spain. The other nine EU members (those which do not use the euro as their currency) have special status.

Functions The primary objective of the ESCB is to maintain price stability. Without prejudice to this, the ESCB supports general economic policies in the Community with a view to contributing to the achievement of the objectives of the Community. Tasks to be carried out include: i) defining and implementing the monetary policy of the Community; ii) conducting foreign exchange operations; iii) holding and managing the official foreign reserves of the participating member states; iv) promoting the smooth operation of payment systems; v) supporting the policies of the competent authorities relating to the prudential supervision of credit institutions and the stability of the financial system.

The ECB has the exclusive right to issue banknotes within the Community.

Organization The ESCB is governed by the decision-making bodies of the ECB: the 25-member Governing Council and the Executive Board. The Governing Council is the supreme decision-making body and comprises all members of the Executive Board plus the governors of the NCBs forming the Eurosystem. The Executive Board comprises the president, vice-president and four other members, appointed by common accord of the heads of state and government of the participating member states. There is also a General Council which will exist while there remain members with special status.

Address: Sonnemannstrasse 20, 60314 Frankfurt am Main, Germany.
Website: https://www.ecb.europa.eu/ecb
Email: info@ecb.europa.eu
President: Mario Draghi (Italy).

European Systemic Risk Board
Founded in 2010 to oversee the financial system of the European Union and prevent and mitigate systemic risk. An independent body within the European System of Financial Supervision, its secretariat is provided by the European Central Bank.

Address: c/o European Central Bank, Sonnemannstrasse 22, 60314 Frankfurt am Main, Germany.
Website: http://www.esrb.europa.eu

Other EU Structures

European Investment Bank (EIB)
The EIB is the financing institution of the European Union, created by the Treaty of Rome in 1958 as an autonomous body set up to finance capital investment furthering European integration. To this end, the Bank raises its resources on the world's capital markets where it mobilizes significant volumes of funds on favourable terms. It directs these funds towards capital projects promoting EU economic policies. Outside the Union the EIB implements the financial components of agreements concluded under European Union development aid and co-operation policies. The members of the EIB are the member states of the European Union, who have all subscribed to the Bank's capital. Its governing body is its Board of Governors consisting of the ministers designated by each of the member states, usually the finance ministers.

Address: 98–100 Blvd Konrad Adenauer, L-2950 Luxembourg.
Website: http://www.eib.org
President and Chairman of the Board: Werner Hoyer (Germany).

European Investment Fund
Founded in 1994 as a subsidiary of the European Investment Bank and the European Union's specialized financial institution. It has a dual mission that combines the pursuit of objectives such as innovation, the creation of employment and regional development with maintaining a commercial

approach to investments. It particularly provides venture capital and guarantee instruments for the growth of small and medium-sized enterprises (SMEs). In 2002 it began advising entities in the setting up of financial enterprise and venture capital and SME guarantee schemes.

Address: 37B avenue J. F. Kennedy, L-2968 Luxembourg.
Website: http://www.eif.org

European Data Protection Supervisor

The European Data Protection Supervisor protects those individuals whose data are processed by the EU institutions and bodies by advising on new legislation and implications, processing and investigating complaints, and promoting a 'data protection culture' and awareness. The present incumbent is Giovanni Buttarelli (Italy).

Address: Rue Montoyer 30, B-1000 Brussels, Belgium.
Website: http://www.edps.europa.eu/EDPSWEB
Email: edps@edps.europa.eu

European Ombudsman

The Ombudsman was inaugurated in 1995 and deals with complaints from citizens, companies and organizations concerning maladministration in the activities of the institutions and bodies of the European Union. The present incumbent is *Emily* O'Reilly (Ireland).

Address: Bâtiment Václav Havel, Allée Spach, F-67070 Strasbourg, France; Montoyer-Science, 30 rue Montoyer, B-1000 Bruxelles, Belgium.
Website: http://www.ombudsman.europa.eu

Advisory Bodies

There are two main consultative committees whose members are appointed in a personal capacity and are not bound by any mandatory instruction.

1. European Economic and Social Committee The 350-member committee is consulted by the Council of Ministers or by the European Commission, particularly with regard to agriculture, free movement of workers, harmonization of laws and transport. It is served by a permanent and independent General Secretariat, headed by a Secretary-General.

Address: Rue Belliard 99, B-1040 Brussels, Belgium.
Website: http://www.eesc.europa.eu
Secretary-General: Gianluca Brunetti (Italy).

2. Committee of the Regions A political assembly which provides representatives of local, regional and city authorities with a voice at the heart of the European Union. Established by the Maastricht Treaty, the Committee consists of 350 full members and an equal number of alternates appointed for a four-year term. It must be consulted by the European Commission and Council of Ministers whenever legislative proposals are made in areas which have repercussions at the regional or local level. The Committee can also draw up opinions on its own initiative, which enables it to put issues on the EU agenda.

Address: Bâtiment Jacques Delors, Rue Belliard 99–101, B-1040 Brussels, Belgium.
Website: http://cor.europa.eu
President: Karl-Heinz Lambertz (Belgium).

Main EU Agencies

Agency for the Cooperation of Energy Regulators

Launched in 2011 to assist and coordinate the work of national regulatory authorities, ensuring the proper functioning of the single European market in gas and electricity.

Address: Trg republike 3, 1000 Ljubljana, Slovenia.
Website: http://www.acer.europa.eu

Body of European Regulators for Electronic Communications

Established in 2009 to help the European Commission and national regulatory authorities implement EU regulations on electronic communications.

Address: Zigfrīda Annas Meierovica Bulvaris 14, 2nd Floor, Riga, LV-1050, Latvia.
Website: http://berec.europa.eu

Community Plant Variety Office

Launched in 1995 to administer a system of plant variety rights. The system allows Community Plant Variety Rights (CPVRs), valid throughout the European Union, to be granted for new plant varieties as sole and exclusive form of Community intellectual property rights.

Address: 3 Blvd Maréchal Foch, F-49000 Angers, France.
Website: http://www.cpvo.europa.eu

Euratom Supply Agency

The 1957 Euratom Treaty created the European Atomic Energy Community to coordinate member states' research programmes into the peaceful use of nuclear energy. The Euratom Supply Agency came into operation in 1960 with the task of ensuring a regular and equitable supply of ores, source materials and special fissile materials into EU member countries. In 2008 the Agency was also entrusted with the creation of a 'nuclear market observatory'. Today Euratom pools knowledge, infrastructure and funding for nuclear energy within the EU, as well as supervising safety standards.

Address: Complexe Euroforum, 1 rue Henri Schnadt, L-2530 Luxembourg.
Website: http://ec.europa.eu/euratom/index.html

European Agency for Safety and Health at Work

Founded in 1996 in order to serve the information needs of people with an interest in occupational safety and health.

Address: 12 Santiago de Compostela (Edificio Miribilla), 5th Floor, E-48003 Bilbao, Spain.
Website: http://osha.europa.eu

European Agency for the operational management of large-scale IT systems in the area of freedom, security and justice

Established in 2012 to provide a viable, long-term solution for the management of large-scale information systems in the areas of freedom, security and justice.

Address: EU House, 6th Floor, Rävala pst 4, 10143 Tallinn, Estonia.
Website: http://www.eulisa.europa.eu

European Asylum Support Office

Founded in 2011 to enhance co-operation within the EU on asylum matters and to assist member states in meeting their obligations to protect people in need. It also provides support to member states whose asylum systems are under particular pressure.

Address: MTC Block A, Winemakers Wharf, Grand Harbour Valletta, MRS 1917, Malta.
Website: http://easo.europa.eu

European Aviation Safety Agency

Established in 2002 to establish and maintain a high uniform level of civil aviation safety in Europe. It offers technical expertise to the European Commission, such as assisting in the drafting of aviation safety regulations, and carries out executive tasks including the certification of aeronautical products and organizations involved in their design, production and maintenance.

Address: Konrad-Adenauer-Ufer 3, 50668 Cologne, Germany.
Website: http://www.easa.europa.eu

European Banking Authority

Established in 2011 as part of the European System of Financial Supervisors to ensure financial stability by effective and consistent regulation and supervision across the European banking sector. Its chief task is to advise on the creation of a European Single Rulebook setting out harmonized prudential rules for all EU financial institutions. It also promotes convergence of supervisory practices and assesses risks and vulnerabilities within the region's banking sector.

Address: One Canada Square (Floor 46), Canary Wharf, London, E14 5AA, UK.
Website: http://eba.europa.eu

European Border and Coast Guard Agency

Generally known as 'Frontex' and officially called the European Agency for the Management of Operational Cooperation at the External Borders until 2016, the agency was established in 2004 to facilitate co-operation between member states in managing external borders. It assists in the training of national border guards, provides risk analyses and where necessary offers technical and operational assistance at external borders. It works in conjunction with other relevant EU partners, such as Europol.

Address: Plac Europejski 6, 00-844 Warsaw, Poland.
Website: http://www.frontex.europa.eu

European Centre for Disease Prevention and Control

Established in 2004 to help strengthen Europe's defences against infectious diseases, such as influenza, SARS and HIV/AIDS. It co-operates with a network of partners across the EU and the EEA/EFTA member states to strengthen and develop continent-wide disease surveillance and early warning systems. By pooling Europe's health knowledge, it provides analyses of risks posed by new and emerging infectious diseases.

Address: Gustav III:S Boulevard 40, 169 73 Solna, Sweden.
Website: http://ecdc.europa.eu

European Centre for the Development of Vocational Training

Generally known as 'Cedefop', it was set up to help policy-makers and practitioners of the European Commission, the member states and social partner organizations across Europe make informed choices about vocational training policy.

Address: Europe 123, 570 01 Thessaloniki, Greece.
Website: http://www.cedefop.europa.eu

European Chemicals Agency

Established in 2007 to manage the Registration, Evaluation, Authorisation and Restriction of Chemicals (REACH) system of the EU. There is a staff of approximately 200.

Address: Annankatu 18, 00121 Helsinki, Finland.
Website: http://echa.europa.eu

European Defence Agency

Established in 2004 to improve the EU's defence capabilities in the field of crisis management and to sustain the European Security and Defence Policy.

Address: Rue des Drapiers/Lakenweversstraat 17–23, B-1050 Brussels, Belgium.
Website: http://www.eda.europa.eu

European Environment Agency

Launched in 1993 to orchestrate and put to strategic use information of relevance to the protection and improvement of Europe's environment. It has a mandate to ensure objective, reliable and comprehensive information on the environment at European level. The Agency carries out its tasks through the European Information and Observation Network (EIONET). Membership is open to countries outside the EU and currently includes all EU countries, Iceland, Liechtenstein, Norway, Switzerland and Turkey. There are a further six co-operating countries.

Address: Kongens Nytorv 6, 1050 Copenhagen K, Denmark.
Website: http://eea.europa.eu

European External Action Service

Launched in 2011 as the European Union's diplomatic service, the Service is charged with assisting the High Representative for Foreign Affairs and Security Policy to carry out the EU's common foreign and security policy.

Address: EEAS Building, 9A Rond Point Schuman, B-1046 Brussels, Belgium.
Website: http://eeas.europa.eu

European Fisheries Control Agency

Established in 2005 as the Community Fisheries Control Agency to oversee compliance with the 2002 reforms of the common fisheries policy. It was renamed the European Fisheries Control Agency from 1 Jan. 2012.

Address: Edificio Odriozola, Avenida García Barbón 4, E-36201 Vigo, Spain.
Website: http://efca.europa.eu

European Food Safety Authority

Founded in 2002 to provide independent scientific advice on all matters with a direct or indirect impact on food safety.

Address: Via Carlo Magno 1A, 43126 Parma, Italy.
Website: http://efsa.europa.eu

European Foundation for the Improvement of Living and Working Conditions

Launched in 1975 to contribute to the planning and establishment of better living and working conditions. The Foundation's role is to provide findings, knowledge and advice from comparative research managed in a European perspective, which respond to the needs of the key parties at the EU level.

Address: Wyattville Rd, Loughlinstown, Dublin, D18 KP65, Ireland.
Website: http://www.eurofound.europa.eu

European GNSS Agency

Established in 2004 as the European GNSS Supervisory Authority to manage the public interests related to and to be the regulatory authority for the European global navigation satellite system, taking over tasks previously assigned to the Galileo Joint Undertaking. It was renamed the European GNSS Agency in 2010.

Address: Janovského 438/2, Holešovice, 170 00 Prague 7, Czech Republic.
Website: http://gsa.europa.eu

European Institute for Gender Equality

Established in 2007 to support the EU and its member states in their efforts to promote gender equality, to fight discrimination based on sex and to raise awareness about gender equality issues.

Address: Gedimino pr. 16, LT-01103 Vilnius, Lithuania.
Website: http://eige.europa.eu

European Institute of Innovation and Technology

Established in 2008 and operational since 2010, the European Institute of Innovation and Technology seeks to foster Europe's ability to innovate in order to address emerging social problems and develop new consumer products.

Address: Infopark 1/E, Neumann János utca, 1117 Budapest, Hungary.
Website: http://eit.europa.eu

European Insurance and Occupational Pensions Authority

Founded in 2011 as part of the European System of Financial Supervisors. Its chief task is to rebuild trust in the financial system by supporting stability and the transparency of markets and financial products across the EU. It aims to protect policyholders, pension scheme members and beneficiaries.

Address: Westhafenplatz 1, 60327 Frankfurt am Main, Germany.
Website: http://eiopa.europa.eu

European Joint Undertaking for ITER and the Development of Fusion Energy

Also known as Fusion for Energy (F4E), the agency was established in 2007 for a 35-year period. It is responsible for providing Europe's contribution to ITER, the international nuclear fusion research project. It also supports fusion research and development initiatives through the Broader Approach Agreement signed with Japan.

Address: c/ Josep Pla, n° 2, Torres Diagonal Litoral, Edificio B3, 08019 Barcelona, Spain.
Website: http://fusionforenergy.europa.eu

European Maritime Safety Agency

Established in 2003 to enhance the EU's pre-existing range of legal tools to deal with incidents resulting in serious casualties or pollution in European waters and coastlines. The agency gives advice to member states and offers support to the directorate-general of energy and transport. As well as the 28 member states, it also covers Norway and Iceland. The Agency is active across issues including maritime safety controls, classification societies and port reception facilities for hazardous substances. It plays a major role in harmonizing member states' methodologies in post-accident investigations.

Address: Praça Europa 4, Cais do Sodré, 1249-206 Lisbon, Portugal.
Website: http://emsa.europa.eu

European Medicines Agency

Founded in 1995 (as European Agency for the Evaluation of Medicinal Products) to evaluate the quality and effectiveness of health products for human and veterinary use.

Address: 30 Churchill Place, Canary Wharf, London, E14 5EU, UK.
Website: http://www.ema.europa.eu

European Monitoring Centre for Drugs and Drug Addiction

Established in 1993 to provide the European Union and its member states with objective, reliable and comparable information on a European level concerning drugs and drug addiction and their consequences.

Address: Praça Europa 1, Cais do Sodré, 1249-289 Lisbon, Portugal.
Website: http://emcdda.europa.eu

European Network and Information Security Agency

Established in 2004 to serve as a centre of expertise on the digital economy, providing advice to member states and EU institutions in matters of network and information security.

Address: Science and Technology Park of Crete (ITE), Vassilika Vouton, 700 13 Heraklion, Greece.
Website: http://enisa.europa.eu

European Securities and Markets Authority

Founded in 2011 as part of the European System of Financial Supervisors to oversee the integrity, transparency and efficient functioning of the European securities markets. It is also charged with enhancing investor protection.

Address: 103 rue de Grenelle, 75007 Paris, France.
Website: http://www.esma.europa.eu

European Training Foundation

Launched in 1995 to contribute to the process of vocational education and training reform that is currently taking place within the EU's partner countries and territories.

Address: Villa Gualino, viale Settimio Severo 65, I-10133 Turin, Italy.
Website: http://etf.europa.eu

European Union Agency for Fundamental Rights

In 2007 the FRA succeeded the European Monitoring Centre on Racism and Xenophobia, which was established in 1997. It seeks to provide assistance and expertise to relevant institutions and authorities in relation to fundamental rights when implementing Community law.

Address: Schwarzenbergplatz 11, A-1040 Vienna, Austria.
Website: http://fra.europa.eu

European Union Agency for Law Enforcement Cooperation (Europol)

Founded in 1994 to exchange criminal intelligence between EU countries. Its precursor was the Europol Drugs Unit; the European Police Office (Europol) took up its activities in 1999, and was renamed as the European Union Agency for Law Enforcement Cooperation in 2017. Europol's current mandate includes the prevention and combat of illicit drug trafficking, illegal immigration networks, vehicle trafficking, trafficking in human beings including child pornography, forgery of money, terrorism and associated money laundering activities. There are about 700 staff members from all member states. Of these, 130 are Europol Liaison Officers working for their national police, gendarmerie, customs or immigration services. The 2015 budget was €95·4m.

Address: Eisenhowerlaan 73, 2517 KK The Hague, Netherlands.
Website: http://www.europol.europa.eu

European Union Agency for Law Enforcement Training (CEPOL)

Known as the European Police College (CEPOL) until 2016, the agency was established in 2005 to encourage cross-border cooperation in the fight against crime, maintenance of public security and law and order by bringing together senior police officers across Europe.

Address: 1066 Budapest, Ó utca 27, Hungary.
Website: http://www.cepol.europa.eu

European Union Agency for Railways

Established in 2004 to reinforce safety and interoperability of railways throughout Europe. It has a staff of 100, most of whom come from the European railway sector.

Address: 120 rue Marc Lefrancq, 59300 Valenciennes, France.
Website: http://www.era.europa.eu

European Union Institute for Security Studies

Established in 2001 to help support and develop the EU's common foreign and security policy (CFSP) by offering analyses and forecasting to the High Representative for Foreign Affairs and Security Policy.

Address: 100 avenue de Suffren, 75015 Paris Cedex 16, France.
Website: http://www.iss.europa.eu

European Union Intellectual Property Office

Renamed from the Office for Harmonization in the Internal Market in 2016, the Office was established in 1994, and is responsible for registering Community trade marks and designs. Both Community trade marks and Community designs confer their proprietors a uniform right, which covers all member states of the EU by means of one single application and one single registration procedure.

Address: Avenida de Europa 4, E-03008 Alicante, Spain.
Website: https://euipo.europa.eu

European Union Satellite Centre

Set up in 2002 to support the EU's common foreign and security policy (CFSP) by providing analyses of satellite imagery and collateral data.

Address: Apdo. de Correos 511, Torrejón de Ardoz 28850, Madrid, Spain.
Website: https://www.satcen.europa.eu

Single Resolution Board

Established as an independent EU agency in 2015, the SRB is charged with overseeing the orderly resolution of failing banking institutions established in member states. It works in partnership with national resolution authorities, as well as the European Central Bank, the European Commission and assorted other international institutions.

Address: Treurenberg 22, B-1049 Brussels, Belgium.
Website: http://srb.europa.eu

The European Union's Judicial Cooperation Unit

Generally known as 'Eurojust', it was established in 2002 to stimulate and improve the coordination of investigations and prosecutions among the judicial authorities of the EU member states when dealing with serious cross-border and organized crime.

Address: Johan de Wittlaan 9, 2517 JR The Hague, Netherlands.
Website: http://eurojust.europa.eu

Translation Centre for the Bodies of the European Union

Established in 1994, the Translation Centre's mission is to meet the translation needs of the other decentralized Community agencies. It also participates in the Interinstitutional Committee for Translation and Interpretation.

Address: Bâtiment Drosbach, 12E rue Guillaume Kroll, L-1882 Luxembourg.
Website: http://cdt.europa.eu

In Jan. 2019 there were also seven joint undertakings in areas of strategic importance for the European Union as part of 'Horizon 2020'.

EU general information The Office for Official Publications of the European Communities is the publishing house of the institutions and other bodies of the European Union. It is responsible for producing and distributing EU publications on all media and by all means.

Address: 2 rue Mercier, L-2985 Luxembourg.
Website: http://publications.europa.eu

Publications *Official Journal of the European Union* (every working day).—*General Report on the Activities of the European Union* (annual).—*Report on Competition Policy* (annual).—*The European Union Explained.* For a full list of European Union publications, visit the website: http://europa.eu/publications/index_en.htm

Black Sea Economic Cooperation (BSEC)

Founded in 1992 to promote economic co-operation in the Black Sea region. Priority areas of interest include: trade and economic development; banking and finance; communications; energy; transport; agriculture and agro-industry; healthcare and pharmaceutics; environmental protection; tourism; science and technology; exchange of statistical data and economic information; combating organized crime, illicit trafficking of drugs, weapons and radioactive materials, all acts of terrorism and illegal immigration.

Members Albania, Armenia, Azerbaijan, Bulgaria, Georgia, Greece, Moldova, Romania, Russia, Serbia, Turkey, Ukraine.

Observers Austria, Belarus, Black Sea Commission, Croatia, Czech Republic, Egypt, Energy Charter Secretariat, European Commission, France, Germany, International Black Sea Club, Hungary, Israel, Italy, Poland, Slovakia, Tunisia, USA.
    The *Parliamentary Assembly of the Black Sea Economic Cooperation* is the BSEC parliamentary dimension. The *BSEC Business Council* is composed of representatives from the business circles of the member states. The *Black Sea Trade and Development Bank* is considered as the financial pillar of the BSEC. There is also an *International Center for Black Sea Studies* and a *Coordination Center for the Exchange of Statistical Data and Economic Information.*

Headquarters: Darüşşafaka Cad. Seba Center İş Merkezi, No: 45 Kat 3, İstinye, 34460 Sarıyer, İstanbul, Turkey.
Website: http://www.bsec-organization.org
Email: info@bsec-organization.org
Secretary-General: Michael B. Christides (Greece).

Central European Initiative (CEI)

In Nov. 1989 Austria, Hungary, Italy and the then Yugoslavia met on Italy's initiative to form an economic and political co-operation group in the region.

Members Albania, Belarus, Bosnia and Herzegovina, Bulgaria, Croatia, Czech Republic, Hungary, Italy, Moldova, Montenegro, North Macedonia, Poland, Romania, Serbia, Slovakia, Slovenia, Ukraine.

Address: Executive Secretariat, Via Genova 9, 34121 Trieste, Italy.
Website: http://www.cei.int
Email: cei@cei.int
Secretary General: Giovanni Caracciolo di Vietri (Italy).

CERN – The European Organization for Nuclear Research

Founded in 1954, CERN is the world's leading particle physics research centre. By studying the behaviour of nature's fundamental particles, CERN aims to find out what our Universe is made of and how it works. CERN's biggest accelerator, the Large Hadron Collider (LHC), became operational in Sept. 2008. One of the beneficial byproducts of CERN activity is the Worldwide Web, developed at CERN to give particle physicists easy access to shared data. One of Europe's first joint ventures, CERN now has a membership of 22 member states: Austria, Belgium, Bulgaria, Czech Republic, Denmark, Finland, France, Germany, Greece, Hungary, Israel, Italy, the Netherlands, Norway, Poland, Portugal, Romania, Slovak Republic, Spain, Sweden, Switzerland, United Kingdom. Some 12,000 scientists, half of the world's particle physicists, use CERN's facilities. They represent 600 institutions and universities and 120 nationalities.

Address: CH-1211 Geneva 23, Switzerland.
Website: http://home.cern
Email: cern.reception@cern.ch
Director-General: Fabiola Gianotti (Italy).

Council of Europe

Origin and Membership In 1948 the Congress of Europe, bringing together at The Hague nearly 1,000 influential Europeans from 26 countries, called for the creation of a united Europe, including a European Assembly. This proposal, examined first by the Ministerial Council of the Brussels Treaty Organization, then by a conference of ambassadors, was at the origin of the Council of Europe, which is, with its 47 member States, the widest organization bringing together all European democracies. The Statute of the Council was signed at London on 5 May 1949 and came into force two months later.
    The founder members were Belgium, Denmark, France, Ireland, Italy, Luxembourg, the Netherlands, Norway, Sweden and the UK. Turkey and Greece joined in 1949, Iceland in 1950, the Federal Republic of Germany in 1951 (having been an associate since 1950), Austria in 1956, Cyprus in 1961, Switzerland in 1963, Malta in 1965, Portugal in 1976, Spain in 1977, Liechtenstein in 1978, San Marino in 1988, Finland in 1989, Hungary in 1990, Czechoslovakia (after partitioning, the Czech Republic and Slovakia rejoined in 1993) and Poland in 1991, Bulgaria in 1992, Estonia, Lithuania, Romania and Slovenia in 1993, Andorra in 1994, Albania, Latvia, Moldova, North Macedonia (then Macedonia) and Ukraine in 1995, Croatia and Russia in 1996, Georgia in 1999, Armenia and Azerbaijan in 2001, Bosnia and Herzegovina in 2002, Serbia in 2003 (as Serbia and Montenegro until 2006), Monaco in 2004 and Montenegro in 2007.
    Membership is limited to European states which 'accept the principles of the rule of law and of the enjoyment by all persons within [their] jurisdiction of human rights and fundamental freedoms'. The Statute provides for both withdrawal (Article 7) and suspension (Articles 8 and 9). Greece withdrew during 1969–74.

Aims and Achievements Article 1 of the Statute states that the Council's aim is 'to achieve a greater unity between its members for the purpose of safeguarding and realizing the ideals and principles which are their common heritage and facilitating their economic and social progress'; 'this aim shall be pursued … by discussion of questions of common concern and by agreements and common action'. The only limitation is provided by Article 1 (d), which excludes 'matters relating to national defence'.
    The main areas of the Council's activity are: human rights, the media, social and socio-economic questions, education, culture and sport, youth, public health, heritage and environment, local and regional government, and legal co-operation. As of Jan. 2019, 194 Conventions, Agreements and Protocols had entered into force covering such matters as social security, cultural affairs, conservation of European wildlife and natural habitats, protection of archaeological heritage, extradition, medical treatment, equivalence of degrees and diplomas, the protection of television broadcasts, adoption of children, transportation of animals, cybercrime and the manipulation of sports competitions.

European Social Charter The Charter defines the rights and principles which are the basis of the Council's social policy, and guarantees a number of social and economic rights to the citizen, including the right to work, the right to form workers' organizations, the right to social security and assistance, the right of the family to protection and the right of migrant workers to protection and assistance. Two committees, comprising independent and government experts, supervise the parties' compliance with their obligations under the Charter. A revised charter, incorporating new rights such as protection for those without jobs and opportunities for workers with family responsibilities, was opened for signature on 3 May 1996 and entered into force on 1 July 1999.

Human rights The promotion and development of human rights is one of the major tasks of the Council of Europe. The European Convention on Human Rights, signed in 1950, set up special machinery to guarantee internationally fundamental rights and freedoms. The European Commission of Human Rights which was set up has now been abolished and has been replaced by the new European Court of Human Rights, which came into operation on 1 Nov. 1998. The European Court of Human Rights in Strasbourg, set up under the European Convention on Human Rights as amended, is composed of a number of judges equal to that of the Contracting States (currently 47). There is no restriction on the number of judges of the same nationality. Judges are elected by the Parliamentary Assembly of the Council of Europe for a term of six years. The terms of office of one half of the judges elected at the first election expired after three years, so as to ensure that the terms of office of one half of the judges are renewed every three years. Any Contracting State (State application) or individual claiming to be a victim of a violation of the Convention (individual application) may lodge directly with the Court in Strasbourg an application alleging a breach by a Contracting State of one of the Convention rights.

President of the European Court of Human Rights: Guido Raimondi (Italy).

The Development Bank formerly the Social Development Fund, was created in 1956. The main purpose of the Bank is to give financial aid in the spheres of housing, vocational training, regional planning and development.

The *European Youth Foundation* provides money to subsidize activities by European youth organizations in their own countries.

Structure Under the Statute, two organs were set up: an intergovernmental *Committee of [Foreign] Ministers* with powers of decision and recommendation to governments, and an interparliamentary deliberative body, the *Parliamentary Assembly* (referred to in the Statute as the Consultative Assembly)—both served by the Secretariat. A Joint Committee acts as an organ of co-ordination and liaison between the two and gives members an opportunity to exchange views on matters of important European interest. In addition, a number of committees of experts have been established. On municipal matters the Committee of Ministers receives recommendations from the Congress of Local and Regional Authorities of Europe. The Committee meets at ministerial level once a year; the ministers' deputies meet once a week. The chairmanship of the Committee is rotated on a six-monthly basis.

The *Parliamentary Assembly* consists of 318 parliamentarians elected or appointed by their national parliaments (Albania 4, Andorra 2, Armenia 4, Austria 6, Azerbaijan 6, Belgium 7, Bosnia and Herzegovina 5, Bulgaria 6, Croatia 5, Cyprus 3, the Czech Republic 7, Denmark 5, Estonia 3, Finland 5, France 18, Georgia 5, Germany 18, Greece 7, Hungary 7, Iceland 3, Ireland 4, Italy 18, Latvia 3, Liechtenstein 2, Lithuania 4, Luxembourg 3, Malta 3, Moldova 5, Monaco 2, Montenegro 3, Netherlands 7, North Macedonia 3, Norway 5, Poland 12, Portugal 7, Romania 10, Russia 18, San Marino 2, Serbia 7, Slovakia 5, Slovenia 3, Spain 12, Sweden 6, Switzerland 6, Turkey 12, Ukraine 12, UK 18). It meets three times a year for approximately a week.

Although without legislative powers, the Assembly acts as the powerhouse of the Council, initiating European action in key areas by making recommendations to the Committee of Ministers. As the widest parliamentary forum in Western Europe, the Assembly also acts as the conscience of the area by voicing its opinions on important current issues. These are embodied in Resolutions. The Ministers' role is to translate the Assembly's recommendations into action, particularly as regards lowering the barriers between the European countries, harmonizing their legislation or introducing, where possible, common European laws, abolishing discrimination on grounds of nationality, and undertaking certain tasks on a joint European basis.

Official languages: English and French.
Headquarters: Council of Europe, Avenue de l'Europe, F-67075 Strasbourg Cedex, France.
Website: http://www.coe.int
Secretary-General: Thorbjørn Jagland (Norway).

Publications European Yearbook.—Yearbook on the Convention on Human Rights.—Catalogue of Publications (annual).—*Council of Europe –*
Highlights (annual). Information on other bulletins and documents is available on the Council of Europe's website: https://book.coe.int/eur/en

Council of the Baltic Sea States

Established in 1992 in Copenhagen following a conference of ministers of foreign affairs.

Members Denmark, Estonia, Finland, Germany, Iceland, Latvia, Lithuania, Norway, Poland, Russia, Sweden and the European Commission.

Aims To promote co-operation in the Baltic Sea region in the field of trade, investment and economic exchanges, combating organized crime, civil security, culture and education, transport and communication, energy and environment, human rights and assistance to democratic institutions.

The Council meets at ministerial level once a year, chaired by rotating foreign ministers; it is the supreme decision-making body. Between annual sessions the Committee of Senior Officials and three working groups meet at regular intervals. In 1999 ministers of energy of the CBSS member states agreed to achieve the goal of creating effective, economically and environmentally sound and more integrated energy systems in the Baltic Sea region. Nine summits at the level of heads of government of CBSS member states and the President of the European Commission have taken place; in 1996 and then every other year since up to and including 2012. The 2014 CBSS summit was due to be held in Turku, Finland, but was cancelled owing to the Ukraine crisis and the annexation of Crimea by Russia. The Baltic Sea Region Energy Cooperation (BASREC) is made up of energy ministers from the region and is chaired by the energy minister from the chair country of the CBSS.

Official language: English.
CBSS Secretariat: Strömsborg, PO Box 2010, 103 11 Stockholm, Slussplan 9, Sweden.
Website: http://www.cbss.org
Email: cbss@cbss.org
Director General of the Secretariat: Maira Mora (Latvia).

Danube Commission

History and Membership The Danube Commission was constituted in 1949 according to the Convention regarding the regime of navigation on the Danube signed in Belgrade on 18 Aug. 1948. The Belgrade Convention, amended by the Additional Protocol of 26 March 1998, declares that navigation on the Danube from Kelheim to the Black Sea (with access to the sea through the Sulina arm and the Sulina Canal) is equally free and open to the nationals, merchant shipping and merchandise of all states as to harbour and navigation fees as well as conditions of merchant navigation. The Commission holds annual sessions and is composed of one representative from each of its 11 member countries: Austria, Bulgaria, Croatia, Germany, Hungary, Moldova, Romania, Russia, Serbia, Slovakia and Ukraine.

Functions To ensure that the provisions of the Belgrade Convention are carried out; to establish a uniform buoying system on all navigable waterways; to establish the basic regulations for navigation on the river and ensure facilities for shipping; to co-ordinate the regulations for river, customs and sanitation control as well as the hydrometeorological service; to collect relevant statistical data concerning navigation on the Danube; to propose measures for the prevention of pollution of the Danube caused by navigation; and to update its recommendations regularly with a view to bringing them in line with European Union regulations on inland waterway navigation.

Official languages: German, French and Russian.
Headquarters: Benczúr utca 25, 1068 Budapest, Hungary.
Website: http://www.danubecommission.org
Email: secretariat@danubecom-intern.org
President: Gordan Grlić Radman (Croatia).
Director-General: Petar Margić (Croatia).

European Bank for Reconstruction and Development (EBRD)

History The European Bank for Reconstruction and Development was established in 1991 when communism was collapsing in central and eastern

Europe and ex-Soviet countries needed support to nurture a new private sector in a democratic environment.

Activities The EBRD is the largest single investor in the region and mobilizes significant foreign direct investment beyond its own financing. It is owned by 67 countries and two intergovernmental institutions. But despite its public sector shareholders, it invests mainly in private enterprises, usually together with commercial partners. Today the EBRD uses the tools of investment to help build market economies and democracies in 30 countries from Central Europe to Central Asia.

It provides project financing for banks, industries and businesses, for both new ventures and investments in existing companies. It also works with publicly-owned companies, to support privatization, restructuring of state-owned firms and improvement of municipal services. The EBRD uses its close relationship with governments in the region to promote policies that will bolster the business environment. Respect for the environment is part of the strong corporate governance attached to all EBRD investments.

Organization All the powers of the EBRD are vested in a Board of Governors, to which each member appoints a governor, generally the minister of finance or an equivalent. The Board of Governors delegates powers to the Board of Directors, which is responsible for the direction of the EBRD's general operations and policies. The President is elected by the Board of Governors and is the legal representative of the EBRD. The President conducts the current business of the Bank under the guidance of the Board of Directors.

Headquarters: One Exchange Square, London, EC2A 2JN, UK.
Website: http://www.ebrd.com
President: Sir Suma Chakrabarti (India).
Secretary-General: Enzo Quattrociocche (Italy).

European Broadcasting Union (EBU)

Founded in 1950 by western European radio and television broadcasters, the EBU is the world's largest professional association of national broadcasters, with 71 active members in 56 countries of Europe, North Africa and the Middle East, and 34 associate members worldwide. The EBU merged with the OIRT, its counterpart in eastern Europe, in 1993.

The EBU's members operate nearly 2,000 television and radio channels between them, along with numerous online platforms. Together, they reach audiences of more than 1bn. people around the world, broadcasting in more than 120 languages.

The EBU operates the News Exchange, which distributes many thousands of news items a year. Euroradio relays concerts, operas, sports fixtures and major news events via its satellite and IP network. The EBU's Eurovision Operations Department has a permanent network comprising more than 100 satellite channels on eight different satellites, and a fibre network with almost 200 nodes spanning the globe.

Headquarters: L'Ancienne Route 17A, Postal Box 45, CH-1218 Grand-Saconnex, Geneva, Switzerland.
Website: http://www.ebu.ch
Email: ebu@ebu.ch
Director-General: Noel Curran *(Ireland)*.

European Free Trade Association (EFTA)

History and Membership The Stockholm Convention establishing the Association was signed on 4 Jan. 1960 and entered into force on 3 May 1960. Founder members were Austria, Denmark, Norway, Portugal, Sweden, Switzerland and the UK. With the accession of Austria, Denmark, Finland, Portugal, Sweden and the UK to the EU, EFTA was reduced to four member countries: Iceland, Liechtenstein, Norway and Switzerland. In June 2001 the Vaduz Convention was signed. It liberalizes trade further among the four EFTA States in order to reflect the Swiss–EU bilateral agreements.

Activities Free trade in industrial goods among EFTA members was achieved by 1966. Co-operation with the EU began in 1972 with the signing of free trade agreements and culminated in the establishment of a *European Economic Area (EEA)*, encompassing the free movement of goods, services, capital and labour throughout EFTA and the EU member countries. The Agreement was signed by all members of the EU and EFTA on 2 May

1992, but was rejected by Switzerland in a referendum on 6 Dec. 1992. The agreement came into force on 1 Jan. 1994.

The main provisions of the EEA Agreement are: free movement of products within the EEA from 1993 (with special arrangements to cover food, energy, coal and steel); EFTA to assume EU rules on company law, consumer protection, education, the environment, research and development, and social policy; EFTA to adopt EU competition rules on anti-trust matters, abuse of a dominant position, public procurement, mergers and state aid; EFTA to create an EFTA Surveillance Authority and an EFTA Court; individuals to be free to live, work and offer services throughout the EEA, with mutual recognition of professional qualifications; capital movements to be free with some restrictions on investments; EFTA countries not to be bound by the Common Agricultural Policy (CAP) or Common Fisheries Policy (CFP).

The EEA-EFTA states have established a Surveillance Authority and a Court to ensure implementation of the Agreement among the EFTA-EEA states. Political direction is given by the EEA Council which meets twice a year at ministerial level, while ongoing operation of the Agreement is overseen by the EEA Joint Committee. Legislative power remains with national governments and parliaments.

EFTA has formal relations with several other states. Free trade agreements have been signed with Turkey (1991), Israel and Czechoslovakia (1992, with protocols on succession with the Czech Republic and Slovakia in 1993), Poland and Romania (1992), Bulgaria and Hungary (1993), Estonia, Latvia, Lithuania and Slovenia (1995), Morocco (1997), the Palestine Liberation Organization on behalf of the Palestinian Authority (1998), Mexico and North Macedonia (then the former Yugoslav Republic of Macedonia) (2000), Jordan and Croatia (2001), Singapore (2002), Chile (2003), Lebanon and Tunisia (2004), South Korea (2005), the Southern African Customs Union (2006), Egypt (2007), Canada and Colombia (2008), Albania, the Gulf Co-operation Council and Serbia (2009), Peru and Ukraine (2010), Hong Kong and Montenegro (2011), Bosnia and Herzegovina and Central American States (Costa Rica and Panama) (2013), Central American States (Guatemala) (2015), Georgia and the Philippines (2016) and Ecuador and Indonesia (2018). Agreements with the countries that have joined the European Union in the meantime have been replaced by the relevant arrangements between the EFTA states and the EU. Negotiations on free trade agreements are ongoing with Algeria (although negotiations were on hold as at Jan. 2019), Central American States (Honduras) (also on hold as at Jan. 2019), India, Malaysia, Mercosur, Russia, Belarus and Kazakhstan (although as at Jan. 2019 negotiations with these latter three countries were on hold), Thailand (also on hold as at Jan. 2019) and Vietnam. There are currently Joint Declarations on Co-operation with Mongolia (2007), Mauritius (2009), Pakistan (2012), Myanmar (2013), Moldova and Nigeria (2017) and Kosovo (2018).

Organization The operation of the free trade area among the EFTA states is the responsibility of the EFTA Council which meets regularly at ambassadorial level in Geneva. The Council is assisted by a Secretariat and standing committees. Each EFTA country holds the chairmanship of the Council for six months. For EEA matters there is a separate committee structure.

Brussels Office (EEA matters, press and information): 12–16 Rue Joseph II, B-1000 Brussels, Belgium.
Headquarters: 9–11 rue de Varembé, CH-1211 Geneva 20, Switzerland.
Website: http://www.efta.int
Email: mail.gva@efta.int
Secretary-General: Henri Gétaz (Switzerland).

Publications *Convention Establishing the European Free Trade Association.—EFTA Annual Report* (online only)*.—EFTA Factsheets.—EFTA Bulletin.—This is EFTA* (annual)*.—EFTA Commemorative Publications.—EEA Supplements.—EFTA Study on Certification and Marks in Europe.* 2008.—*EFTA/EU Statistical Cooperation Handbook.* 2011.

European Space Agency (ESA)

History Established in 1975, replacing the European Space Research Organization (ESRO) and the European Launcher Development Organization (ELDO).

Members Austria, Belgium, Czech Republic, Denmark, Estonia, Finland, France, Germany, Greece, Hungary, Ireland, Italy, Luxembourg, the

Netherlands, Norway, Poland, Portugal, Romania, Spain, Sweden, Switzerland, United Kingdom. Slovenia is an associate member. Canada takes part in some projects under a co-operation agreement.

Activities ESA is the intergovernmental agency in Europe responsible for the exploitation of space science, research and technology for exclusively peaceful purposes. Its aim is to define and put into effect a long-term European space policy that allows Europe to remain competitive in the field of space technology. It has a policy of co-operation with various partners on the basis that pooling resources and sharing work will boost the effectiveness of its programmes. Its space plan covers the fields of science, Earth observation, telecommunications, navigation, space segment technologies, ground infrastructures, space transport systems and microgravity research.

Headquarters: 24 rue du Général Bertrand, 75345 Paris Cedex 7, France
Website: http://www.esa.int
Director-General: Johann-Dietrich Woerner (Germany).

European Trade Union Confederation (ETUC)

Established in 1973, the ETUC is recognized by the EU, the Council of Europe and EFTA as the only representative cross-sectoral trade union organization at a European level. It has grown steadily with a membership of 90 National Trade Union Confederations from 38 countries and ten European Industry Federations with a total of 45m. members. The Congress meets every four years; the 13th Statutory Congress took place in Paris in Sept.–Oct. 2015.

Address: 5 Blvd Roi Albert II, B-1210 Brussels, Belgium.
Website: http://www.etuc.org
Email: etuc@etuc.org
General Secretary: Luca Visentini (Italy).

Nordic Council

Founded in 1952 as a co-operative link between the parliaments and governments of the Nordic states. The co-operation focuses on Intra-Nordic co-operation, co-operation with Europe/EU/EEA and co-operation with the adjacent areas. The Council consists of 87 elected MPs and the committees meet several times a year, as required. Every year the Nordic Council grants prizes for literature, music, nature and environment.

Members Denmark (including the Faroe Islands and Greenland), Finland (including Åland), Iceland, Norway, Sweden.

Address: Ved Stranden 18, DK-1061 Copenhagen K, Denmark.
Website: http://www.norden.org
Email: nordisk-rad@norden.org
President: Jessica Polfjärd (Sweden).

Nordic Development Fund (NDF)

NDF is a multilateral development finance institution established by the five Nordic countries, Denmark, Finland, Iceland, Norway and Sweden. In 1989 NDF began its operations providing soft loans for social and economic development. It entered a new phase in 2009 and changed its focus to grant aid for climate change-related projects. By 2015 NDF had approved 85 projects with a total value of €235·7m. for climate change projects in 17 countries.

Address: Fabianinkatu 34, PO Box 185, FI-00171 Helsinki, Finland.
Website: http://www.ndf.fi
Email: info.ndf@ndf.fi
Managing Director (acting): Leena Klossner (Finland).

Nordic Investment Bank (NIB)

The Nordic Investment Bank, which commenced operations in 1976, is a multilateral financial institution owned by Denmark, Estonia, Finland, Iceland, Latvia, Lithuania, Norway and Sweden. It finances public and private projects both within and outside the Nordic area. Priority is given to projects furthering economic co-operation between the member countries or improving the environment. Focal points include the neighbouring areas of the member countries.

Address: Fabianinkatu 34, PO Box 249, FI-00171 Helsinki, Finland.
Website: http://www.nib.int
Email: info@nib.int
President: Henrik Normann (Denmark).

Organization for Security and Co-operation in Europe (OSCE)

The OSCE is a pan-European security organization of 57 participating states. It has been recognized under the UN Charter as a primary instrument in its region for early warning, conflict prevention, crisis management and post-conflict rehabilitation.

Origin Initiatives from both NATO and the Warsaw Pact culminated in the first summit Conference on Security and Co-operation in Europe (CSCE) attended by heads of state and government in Helsinki on 30 July–1 Aug. 1975. It adopted the *Helsinki Final Act* laying down ten principles governing the behaviour of States towards their citizens and each other, concerning human rights, self-determination and the interrelations of the participant states. The CSCE was to serve as a multilateral forum for dialogue and negotiations between East and West.

The Helsinki Final Act comprised three main sections: 1) politico-military aspects of security: principles guiding relations between and among participating States and military confidence-building measures; 2) co-operation in the fields of economics, science and technology and the environment; 3) co-operation in humanitarian and other fields.

From CSCE to OSCE The Paris Summit of Nov. 1990 set the CSCE on a new course. In the Charter of Paris for a New Europe, the CSCE was called upon to contribute to managing the historic change in Europe and respond to the new challenges of the post-Cold War period. At the meeting, members of NATO and the Warsaw Pact signed an important Treaty on Conventional Armed Forces in Europe (CFE) and a declaration that they were 'no longer adversaries' and did not intend to 'use force against the territorial integrity or political independence of any state'. All 34 participants adopted the Vienna Document comprising Confidence and Security-Building Measures (CSBMs), which pertain to the exchange of military information, verification of military installations, objection to unusual military activities etc., and signed the Charter of Paris. The Charter sets out principles of human rights, democracy and the rule of law to which all the signatories undertake to adhere, and lays down the basis for East-West co-operation and other future action. The 1994 Budapest Summit recognized that the CSCE was no longer a conference and on 1 Jan. 1995 the CSCE changed its name to the Organization for Security and Co-operation in Europe (OSCE).

Members Albania, Andorra, Armenia, Austria, Azerbaijan, Belarus, Belgium, Bosnia and Herzegovina, Bulgaria, Canada, Croatia, Cyprus, Czech Republic, Denmark, Estonia, Finland, France, Georgia, Germany, Greece, Holy See, Hungary, Iceland, Ireland, Italy, Kazakhstan, Kyrgyzstan, Latvia, Liechtenstein, Lithuania, Luxembourg, Malta, Moldova, Monaco, Mongolia, Montenegro, Netherlands, North Macedonia, Norway, Poland, Portugal, Romania, Russian Federation, San Marino, Serbia, Slovak Republic, Slovenia, Spain, Sweden, Switzerland, Tajikistan, Turkey, Turkmenistan, Ukraine, UK, USA and Uzbekistan. *Partners for co-operation:* Afghanistan, Algeria, Australia, Egypt, Israel, Japan, Jordan, South Korea, Morocco, Thailand and Tunisia.

Organization The OSCE's regular body for political consultation and decision-making is the Permanent Council. Its members, the Permanent Representatives of the OSCE participating States, meet weekly in the Hofburg Congress Center in Vienna to discuss and take decisions on all issues pertinent to the OSCE. The Forum for Security Co-operation (FSC), which deals with arms control and confidence- and security-building measures, also meets weekly in Vienna. Summits—periodic meetings of Heads of State or Government of OSCE participating States—set priorities and provide orientation at the highest political level. In the years between these summits, decision-making and governing power lies with the *Ministerial Council*, which is made up of the Foreign Ministers of the OSCE participating States. In addition, a Senior Council also meets once a year in special session as the Economic Forum. The Chairman-in-Office has overall responsibility for executive action and agenda-setting. The Chair rotates annually.

The Secretary-General acts as representative of the Chairman-in-Office and manages OSCE structures and operations.

The Secretariat is based in Vienna and includes a *Conflict Prevention Centre* which provides operational support for OSCE field missions. The OSCE employs about 3,500 staff, including some 2,900 in its field operations.

The *Office for Democratic Institutions and Human Rights* is located in Warsaw. It is active in monitoring elections and developing national electoral and human rights institutions, providing technical assistance to national legal institutions, and promoting the development of the rule of law and civil society.

The *Office of the Representative on Freedom of the Media* is located in Vienna. Its main function is to observe relevant media developments in OSCE participating States with a view to providing an early warning on violations of freedom of expression.

The *Office of the High Commissioner on National Minorities* is located in The Hague. Its function is to identify and seek early resolution of ethnic tensions that might endanger peace, stability or friendly relations between the participating States of the OSCE.

The budget for 2016 was €141·1m.

Headquarters: Wallnerstrasse 6, A-1010 Vienna, Austria.
Website: http://www.osce.org
Email: pm@osce.org
Chairperson-in-Office: Miroslav Lajčák (Slovakia).
Secretary-General: Thomas Greminger (Switzerland).

Further Reading

Main EU Agencies

Bale, Tim, *European Politics*. 4th ed. 2017

Bond, Martyn, *The Council of Europe: Structure, History and Issues in European Politics*. 2011

Bootle, Roger, *The Trouble with Europe*. 2014

Brown, Stuart A., *The European Commission and Europe's Democratic Process*. 2016

Brunnermeier, Markus K., James, Harold and Landau, Jean-Pierre, *The Euro and the Battle of Ideas*. 2016

Bulmer, Simon and Paterson, William E., *Germany and the European Union: Europe's Reluctant Hegemon*. 2018

Buonanno, Laurie and Nugent, Neill, *Policies and Policy Processes of the European Union*. 2013

Chang, Michele, *Economic and Monetary Union*. 2016

Charter, David, *Europe: In or Out?: Everything You Need to Know*. 2014

Christiansen, Thomas, Kirchner, Emil and Wissenbach, Uwe, *The European Union and China*. 2018

Christiansen, Thomas and Reh, Christine, *Constitutionalizing the European Union*. 2009

Church, Clive H. and Phinnemore, David, *The Penguin Guide to the European Treaties: From Rome to Maastricht, Amsterdam, Nice and Beyond*. 2002.—*Understanding the European Constitution: An Introduction to the EU Constitutional Treaty*. 2005

Cook, C. and Paxton, J., *European Political Facts of the Twentieth Century*. 2000

Copsey, Nathaniel, *Rethinking the European Union*. 2015

Davies, N., *Europe: A History*. 1997

Déloye, Yves and Bruter, Michael, (eds.) *Encyclopaedia of European Elections*. 2007

Dinan, Desmond, *Ever Closer Union? An Introduction to the European Union*. 4th ed. 2010.—Europe Recast: A History of European Union. 2nd ed. 2014

Dinan, Desmond, Nugent, Neill and Paterson, William E. (eds) *The European Union in Crisis*. 2017

Dod's European Companion. Occasional

Duke, Simon, *Europe as a Stronger Global Actor: Challenges and Strategic Responses*. 2016

Farnell, John and Irwin Crookes, Paul, *The Politics of EU-China Economic Relations*. 2016

Forsberg, Tuomas and Haukkala, Hiski, *The European Union and Russia*. 2016

Gänzle, Stefan and Sens, Allen G. (eds.) *The Changing Politics of European Security: Europe Alone?* 2007

Hantrais, Linda, *Social Policy in the European Union*. 2007

Hefftler, Claudia, Neuhold, Christine, Rozenberg, Olivier and Smith, Julie, (eds.) *The Palgrave Handbook of National Parliaments and the European Union*. 2015

Holland, Martin and Doidge, Mathew, *Development Policy of the European Union*. 2013

Howorth, Jolyon, *Security and Defence Policy in the European Union*. 2nd ed. 2014

Jacobs, Francis B., *The EU after Brexit: Institutional and Policy Implications*. 2018

Keukeleire, Stephan and Delreux, Tom, *The Foreign Policy of the European Union*. 2nd ed. 2014

Lovec, Marko, *The European Union's Common Agricultural Policy Reforms*. 2016

McCormick, John, *The European Superpower*. 2006.—*Understanding the European Union*. 7th ed. 2017.—*European Union Politics*. 2nd ed. 2015

McGuire, Steven and Smith, Michael, *The European Union and the United States: Competition and Convergence in the Global Arena*. 2008

Mazower, M., *Dark Continent: Europe's 20th Century*. 1998

Menon, Anand, *Europe: the State of the Union*. 2008

Mindus, Patricia, *European Citizenship after Brexit*. 2017

Nugent, Neill, *European Union Enlargement*. 2004.—*The Government and Politics of the European Union*. 8th ed. 2017

Nugent, Neill and Rhinard, Mark, *The European Commission*. 2nd ed. 2015

Phinnemore, David and McGowan, Lee, *A Dictionary of the European Union*. 6th ed. 2013

Phinnemore, David and Warleigh-Lack, Alex, (eds.) *Reflections on European Integration: 50 Years of the Treaty of Rome*. 2009

Pisani-Ferry, Jean, *The Euro Crisis and its Aftermath*. 2014

Ripoll Servent, Ariadna, *The European Parliament*. 2017

Saurugger, Sabine and Terpan, Fabien, *The Court of Justice of the European Union and the Politics of Law*. 2016

Stiglitz, Joseph, *The Euro And Its Threat to the Future Of Europe*. 2016

Tannam, Etain, *International Intervention in Ethnic Conflict: A Comparison of the European Union and the United Nations*. 2014

Tocci, Nathalie, *Framing the EU Global Strategy*. 2017

Tömmel, Ingeborg, *The European Union: What it is and how it works*. 2014

Van Middelaar, Luuk, *The Passage to Europe: How a Continent Became a Union*. 2013

Vollaard, Hans, *European Disintegration: A Search for Explanations*. 2018

Wallace, Helen, Pollack, Mark and Young, Alasdair, (eds.) *Policy-Making in the European Union*. 6th ed. 2010

Wallace, Paul, *The Euro Experiment*. 2015

Webber, Douglas, *European Disintegration? The Politics of Crisis in the European Union*. 2018

Wessels, Wolfgang, *The European Council*. 2015

Organization for Security and Co-operation in Europe (OSCE)

Freeman, J., *Security and the CSCE Process: the Stockholm Conference and Beyond*. 1991

Galbreath, David J., *The Organization for Security and Co-operation in Europe*. 2007

Other Organizations

Alliance of Small Island States (AOSIS)

The Alliance of Small Island States was established in 1990 by a coalition of small island and low-lying coastal nations. It seeks to co-ordinate members' lobbying efforts within the United Nations system in relation to the environmental and developmental challenges facing them—especially the adverse effects of climate change.

Organization The AOSIS has no formal charter or permanent Secretariat. However, there is a Bureau, made up of the chairperson and two vice-chairs, appointed from the UN Permanent Representatives of countries from each of the organization's three regional groupings (the Caribbean; the Pacific; and Africa, Indian Ocean, Mediterranean and South China Sea).

Members As of Jan. 2019 AOSIS comprised 37 nation states (plus the New Zealand dependencies of the Cook Islands and Niue): Antigua and Barbuda, The Bahamas, Barbados, Belize, Cabo Verde, Comoros, Cuba, Dominica, Dominican Republic, Fiji, Federated States of Micronesia, Grenada, Guinea-Bissau, Guyana, Haiti, Jamaica, Kiribati, Maldives, Marshall Islands, Mauritius, Nauru, Palau, Papua New Guinea, St Kitts and Nevis, St Lucia, St Vincent and the Grenadines, Samoa, Singapore, Seychelles, São Tomé and Príncipe, Solomon Islands, Suriname, Timor-Leste, Tonga, Trinidad and Tobago, Tuvalu and Vanuatu. A further five non-sovereign territories have observer status.

Website: http://aosis.org
Chairperson: Thoriq Ibrahim (Maldives).

Amnesty International (AI)

Origin Founded in 1961 by British lawyer Peter Benenson as a one-year campaign for the release of prisoners of conscience, Amnesty International has grown to become a worldwide organization, winning the Nobel Peace Prize in 1977.

Activities AI is a worldwide movement of people campaigning for human rights. It acts independently and impartially to promote respect for internationally recognized human rights standards.

Historically, the focus of AI's campaigning has been: to free all prisoners of conscience (a term coined by Peter Benenson); to ensure a prompt and fair trial for all political prisoners; to abolish the death penalty, torture and other cruel, inhuman or degrading punishments; to end extrajudicial executions and 'disappearances'; to fight impunity by working to ensure perpetrators of such abuses are brought to justice. AI is independent of any government or political ideology, and neither supports nor opposes the views of the victim it seeks to protect.

AI has over 3m. members, subscribers and regular donors in more than 150 countries. Major policy decisions are taken by an International Council comprising representatives from all national sections. AI's national sections, members and supporters are primarily responsible for funding the movement. In 2015 Amnesty International raised €278m. for human rights work.

Every year AI produces a global report detailing human rights violations in all regions of the world.

International Secretariat: 1 Easton St., London, WC1X 0DW, UK.
Website: http://www.amnesty.org
Email: contactus@amnesty.org
Secretary-General: Kumi Naidoo (South Africa).

Bank for International Settlements (BIS)

Origin Founded on 17 May 1930, the Bank for International Settlements is the world's oldest international financial organization.

Activities The BIS fosters international monetary and financial co-operation and serves as a bank for central banks. It acts as a forum to promote discussion and policy analysis among central banks and within the international financial community, a centre for economic and monetary research and an agent or trustee in connection with international financial operations.

As its customers are central banks and international organizations, the BIS does not accept deposits from, or provide financial services to, private individuals or corporate entities.

The head office is in Basle, Switzerland, and there are representative offices in Hong Kong and Mexico City.

Representative Office for Asia and the Pacific: 78th Floor, Two International Finance Centre, 8 Finance St., Central, Hong Kong SAR, People's Republic of China.
Representative Office for the Americas: Torre Chapultepec, Rubén Dario 281, Col. Bosque de Chapultepec, 11580 México, D. F., Mexico.
Headquarters: Centralbahnplatz 2, CH-4051 Basle, Switzerland.
Website: http://www.bis.org
Email: email@bis.org
Chairman of the Board of Directors: Jens Weidmann (Germany).

Commonwealth

The Commonwealth is a free association of sovereign independent states. It numbered 53 members in Jan. 2019. With a membership of over 2bn. people, it represents around 30% of the world's population. There is no charter, treaty or constitution; the association is expressed in co-operation, consultation and mutual assistance for which the Commonwealth Secretariat is the central co-ordinating body.

Origin The Commonwealth was first defined by the Imperial Conference of 1926 as a group of 'autonomous Communities within the British Empire, equal in status, in no way subordinate one to another in any aspect of their domestic or external affairs, though united by a common allegiance to the Crown, and freely associated as members of the British Commonwealth of Nations'. The basis of the association changed from one owing allegiance to a common Crown, and the modern Commonwealth was born in 1949 when the member countries accepted India's intention of becoming a republic at the same time as continuing 'her full membership of the Commonwealth of Nations and her acceptance of the King as the symbol of the free association of its independent member nations and as such the Head of the Commonwealth'. In Jan. 2019 the Commonwealth consisted of 32 republics and 21 monarchies, of which 16 are the Queen's realms. All acknowledge the Queen symbolically as Head of the Commonwealth. The Queen's legal title rests on the statute of 12 and 13 Will. III, c. 3, by which the succession to the Crown of Great Britain and Ireland was settled on the Princess Sophia of Hanover and the 'heirs of her body being Protestants'.

A number of territories, formerly under British jurisdiction or mandate, did not join the Commonwealth: Egypt, Iraq, Transjordan, Myanmar (then Burma), Palestine, Sudan, British Somaliland and Aden. Seven countries (Ireland in 1948, South Africa in 1961, Pakistan in 1972, Fiji in 1987, Zimbabwe in 2003, The Gambia in 2013 and the Maldives in 2016) have left the Commonwealth. Pakistan was readmitted to the Commonwealth in 1989, South Africa in 1994, Fiji in 1997 and The Gambia in 2018. Nigeria was fully suspended in 1995 for violation of human rights but was fully reinstated on 29 May 1999. Pakistan was suspended from the Commonwealth's councils following a coup in Oct. 1999 but was readmitted in May 2004. It was again suspended in Nov. 2007 after then President Musharraf declared emergency rule but was readmitted in May 2008. Fiji was suspended from the Commonwealth's councils in June 2000 following a coup there but was readmitted in Dec. 2001 following the restoration of democracy. They were again suspended from the councils following the coup of Dec. 2006 and fully suspended from membership in Sept. 2009, before being readmitted in Sept. 2014 following the first parliamentary elections in more than eight years. Zimbabwe was suspended from the Commonwealth's

© Springer Nature Limited 2020
Palgrave Macmillan (ed.), *The Statesman's Yearbook 2020*,
https://doi.org/10.1057/978-1-349-95940-2_3

councils for a year on 19 March 2002 for a 'high level of politically motivated violence' during the vote that saw then President Robert Mugabe re-elected. In March 2003 it was suspended for a further nine months. The suspension was extended at the Abuja meeting in Dec. 2003. Mugabe responded by withdrawing Zimbabwe from the Commonwealth. Mozambique, admitted in Nov. 1995, was the first member state not to have been a member of the former British Commonwealth or Empire.

Member States of the Commonwealth

The 53 member states, with year of admission:

	Year of admission
Antigua and Barbuda	1981
Australia[1]	1931
The Bahamas	1973
Bangladesh	1972
Barbados	1966
Belize	1981
Botswana	1966
Brunei[2]	1984
Cameroon	1995
Canada[1]	1931
Cyprus	1961
Dominica	1978
Eswatini	1968
Fiji[3]	1997
The Gambia[4]	2018
Ghana	1957
Grenada	1974
Guyana	1966
India	1947
Jamaica	1962
Kenya	1963
Kiribati	1979
Lesotho	1966
Malaŵi	1964
Malaysia	1957
Malta	1964
Mauritius	1968
Mozambique	1995
Namibia	1990
Nauru[5]	1968
New Zealand[1]	1931
Nigeria[6]	1960
Pakistan[7]	1989
Papua New Guinea	1975
Rwanda	2009
St Kitts and Nevis	1983
St Lucia	1979
St Vincent and the Grenadines	1979
Samoa	1970
Seychelles	1976
Sierra Leone	1961
Singapore	1965
Solomon Islands	1978
South Africa[8]	1994
Sri Lanka	1948
Tanzania	1961
Tonga[2]	1970
Trinidad and Tobago	1962
Tuvalu	1978

(continued)

	Year of admission
Uganda	1982
United Kingdom	1931
Vanuatu	1980
Zambia	1964

[1]Independence given legal effect by the Statute of Westminster 1931.
[2]Brunei and Tonga had been sovereign states in treaty relationship with Britain.
[3]Fiji left in 1987 but rejoined in 1997. Fiji was suspended in 2009 but readmitted as a full member in 2014.
[4]Left 2013, rejoined 2018.
[5]Nauru joined as a special member on independence in 1968. It became a full member in 1999 but its status was changed back to that of a special member in 2006.
[6]Nigeria was suspended in 1995 but readmitted as a full member in 1999.
[7]Left 1972, rejoined 1989.
[8]Left 1961, rejoined 1994.

Aims and Conditions of Membership Membership involves acceptance of certain core principles, as set out in the Harare Declaration of 1991, and is subject to the approval of other member states. The Harare Declaration charted a course to take the Commonwealth into the 21st century affirming members' continued commitment to the Singapore Declaration of 1971, by which members committed themselves to the pursuit of world peace and support of the UN.

The core principles defined by the Harare Declaration are: political democracy, human rights, good governance and the rule of law, and the protection of the environment through sustainable development. Commitment to these principles was made binding as a condition of membership at the 1993 Heads of Government meeting in Cyprus.

The Millbrook Action Programme of 1995 aims to support countries in implementing the Harare Declaration, providing assistance in constitutional and judicial matters, running elections, training and technical advice. Violations of the Harare Declaration will provoke a series of measures by the Commonwealth Secretariat, including: expression of disapproval, encouragement of bilateral actions by member states, appointment of fact-finders and mediators, stipulation of a period for the restoration of democracy, exclusion from ministerial meetings, suspension of all participation and aid and finally punitive measures including trade sanctions. A nine-member *Commonwealth Ministerial Action Group on the Harare Declaration* (*CMAG*) may be convened by the Secretary-General as and when necessary to deal with violations. The Group held its first meeting in Dec. 1995. Its terms of reference are as set out in the Millbrook Action Programme.

The *Commonwealth Parliamentary Association* was founded in 1911. As defined by its constitution, its objectives are to 'promote knowledge of the constitutional, legislative, economic, social and cultural aspects of parliamentary democracy'. Its principal governing body is the General Assembly, which meets annually during the Commonwealth Parliamentary Conference and is composed of members attending that Conference as delegates. The Association elects a 35-member Executive Committee, which controls and manages the activities and business of the Association.

Commonwealth Secretariat The Commonwealth Secretariat is an international body at the service of all 53 member countries. It provides the central organization for joint consultation and co-operation in many fields. It was established in 1965 by Commonwealth Heads of Government as a 'visible symbol of the spirit of co-operation which animates the Commonwealth', and has observer status at the UN General Assembly.

The Secretariat disseminates information on matters of common concern, organizes and services meetings and conferences, co-ordinates many Commonwealth activities, and provides expert technical assistance for economic and social development through the multilateral Commonwealth Fund for Technical Co-operation. The Secretariat is organized in divisions and sections which correspond to its main areas of operation: political affairs, economic affairs, human rights, gender affairs, youth affairs, education, information, law, health and a range of technical assistance and advisory services.

Commonwealth Heads of Government Meetings (CHOGMs) Outside the UN, the CHOGM remains the largest intergovernmental conference in the world. Meetings are held every two years. The 2002 CHOGM in Coolum,

Australia, scheduled for Oct. 2001 but postponed following the attacks on the United States of 11 Sept. 2001, was dominated by the Zimbabwe issue, as was the meeting held in Abuja, Nigeria in Dec. 2003. The last meeting was held in April 2018 in London. A host of Commonwealth organizations and agencies are dedicated to enhancing inter-Commonwealth relations and the development of the potential of Commonwealth citizens. They are listed in the *Commonwealth Yearbook*, which is published by the Secretariat.

Commonwealth Day is celebrated on the second Monday in March each year. The theme for 2019 was 'A connected Commonwealth'.

Overseas Territories and Associated States There are 14 United Kingdom overseas territories (*see* pages 1289–93), seven Australian external territories (*see* pages 153–4), two New Zealand dependent territories and two New Zealand associated states (*see* pages 903–4). A dependent territory is a territory belonging by settlement, conquest or annexation to the British, Australian or New Zealand Crown.

United Kingdom Overseas Territories administered through the Foreign and Commonwealth Office comprise, in the Indian Ocean: British Indian Ocean Territory; in the Mediterranean: Gibraltar, the Sovereign Base Areas of Akrotiri and Dhekelia in Cyprus; in the Atlantic Ocean: Bermuda, Falkland Islands, South Georgia and South Sandwich Islands, British Antarctic Territory, St Helena and Dependencies (Ascension and Tristan da Cunha); in the Caribbean: Montserrat, British Virgin Islands, Cayman Islands, Turks and Caicos Islands, Anguilla; in the Western Pacific: Pitcairn Group of Islands.

The Australian external territories are: Ashmore and Cartier Islands, Australian Antarctic Territory, Christmas Island, Cocos (Keeling) Islands, Coral Sea Islands, Heard and McDonald Islands, and Norfolk Island. The New Zealand external territories are: Tokelau Islands and the Ross Dependency. The New Zealand associated states are: Cook Islands and Niue.

Headquarters: Marlborough House, Pall Mall, London, SW1Y 5HX, UK.
Website: http://www.thecommonwealth.org
Email: info@commonwealth.int
Secretary-General: Baroness Scotland of Asthal (UK/Dominica).

Selected publications Commonwealth Yearbook.—The Commonwealth at the Summit: Communiqués of Commonwealth Heads of Government Meetings. 1997. For a full list of Commonwealth publications, visit the website: http://www.commonwealthofnations.org/publications

Commonwealth of Independent States (CIS)

The Commonwealth of Independent States, founded on 8 Dec. 1991 in Belarus, is a community of independent states that proclaimed itself the successor to the Union of Soviet Socialist Republics (USSR) in some aspects of international law and affairs. When negotiations on its founding began in 1990, it sought to embrace all the 15 constituent republics of the USSR at that date. The founding members—Russia, Belarus and Ukraine—were subsequently joined by Armenia, Azerbaijan, Georgia, Kazakhstan, Kyrgyzstan, Moldova, Tajikistan, Turkmenistan and Uzbekistan. However, Turkmenistan withdrew as a permanent member in 2005 to become an associate member and Georgia withdrew altogether in 2009.

Member states are committed to recognizing the independence and sovereignty of other members, to respecting human rights including those of national minorities and to observing existing boundaries. Members agreed that Russia should take up the seat at the United Nations formerly occupied by the USSR. In March 1994 the CIS was accorded observer status at the UN. Ukraine's continued involvement with the CIS (as a participating state rather than as a full member) was thrown into doubt after Russia's annexation of Crimea in March 2014, with some politicians calling for a complete withdrawal. In Aug. 2016 Ukraine protested to the CIS over its plans to send monitors to Russian State Duma elections in Crimea.

The principal organs of the CIS, according to the agreement concluded in Alma-Ata on 21 Dec. 1991, are the Council of Heads of States and the Council of Heads of Government. There is also a Council of Defence Ministers, established in Feb. 1992, and a Council of Foreign Ministers (Dec. 1993). The Secretariat is the standing working organ.

Headquarters: 220030 Minsk, Kirova 17, Belarus.
Website (Russian only): http://www.cis.minsk.by
Email: info@e-cis.info
Executive Secretary: Sergei Lebedev (Russia).

Eurasian Economic Union (EEU)

The EEU came into being on 1 Jan. 2015 as the successor organization to the Eurasian Economic Community (EurAsEC, founded in 2000). It was established by treaty in May 2014 and provides for the free movement of goods, services, capital and labour across member states.

Membership As of Jan. 2019 there were five member states: Armenia, Belarus, Kazakhstan, Kyrgyzstan and Russia.

Organization The Supreme Council is the highest authority, consisting of the heads of state of the members. There is also an Intergovernmental Council, made up of the heads of government. The Eurasian Economic Commission serves as the permanent regulatory body, charged with supporting the operation and development of the Union and drafting proposals for economic integration. The Court of the EEU seeks to ensure the uniform application of all relevant treaties.

Eurasian Economic Commission Headquarters: 2 Letnikovskaya St., Bldg 1/2, Moscow 115114, Russia.
Website: http://www.eaeunion.org
Email: info@eecommission.org
Chairman of the Board of the Eurasian Economic Commission: Tigran Sargsyan (Armenia).

International Air Transport Association (IATA)

Founded in 1945 for inter-airline co-operation in promoting safe, reliable, secure and economical air services, IATA has approximately 290 members from 120 nations worldwide. IATA is the successor to the International Air Traffic Association, founded in The Hague in 1919, the year of the world's first international scheduled services.

Main offices: IATA Centre, Route de l'Aéroport 33, PO Box 416, CH-1215 Geneva, Switzerland. 800 Place Victoria, PO Box 113, Montreal, Quebec, Canada H4Z 1M1.
Website: http://www.iata.org
Director-General: Alexandre de Juniac (France).

International Committee of the Red Cross (ICRC)

The International Committee of the Red Cross (ICRC) is a Swiss-based impartial, neutral and independent organization ensuring humanitarian protection and assistance for victims of war and other situations of violence.

Established in 1863, the ICRC is a founding member of the International Red Cross and Red Crescent Movement and of international humanitarian law, notably the Geneva Conventions.

The ICRC is mandated by the international community to be the guardian and promoter of international humanitarian law. It has a permanent mandate under international law to take impartial action for prisoners, the wounded and sick, and civilians affected by conflict.

The ICRC aims to ensure that civilians not taking part in hostilities are spared and protected; to visit prisoners of war and security detainees and ensure that they are treated humanely and according to recognized international standards that forbid torture and other forms of abuse; to transmit messages to and reunite family members separated by armed conflict; to help find missing persons; to offer or facilitate access to basic health care facilities; to provide food, safe drinking water, sanitation and shelter in emergencies; to promote respect for, monitor compliance with and contribute to the development of international humanitarian law; to help reduce the impact of mines and explosive remnants of war on people; and to support national Red Cross and Red Crescent Societies to prepare for and respond to armed conflict and situations of violence.

The ICRC is a global presence with offices in over 80 countries and some 14,500 staff worldwide. Its HQ is in Geneva, Switzerland.

Headquarters: 19 avenue de la Paix, CH-1202 Geneva, Switzerland.
Website: http://www.icrc.org
President: Peter Maurer (Switzerland).

International Criminal Court (ICC)

Origin As far back as 1946 an international congress called for the adoption of an international criminal code prohibiting crimes against humanity and the prompt establishment of an international criminal court, but for more than 40 years little progress was made. In 1989 the end of the Cold War brought a dramatic increase in the number of UN peacekeeping operations and a world where the idea of establishing an International Criminal Court became more viable. The United Nations Conference of Plenipotentiaries on the Establishment of an International Criminal Court took place from 15 June–17 July 1998 in Rome, Italy.

Aims and Activities The International Criminal Court is a permanent court for trying individuals who have been accused of committing genocide, war crimes and crimes against humanity, and is thus a successor to the *ad hoc* tribunals set up by the UN Security Council to try those responsible for atrocities in the former Yugoslavia and Rwanda. Ratification by 60 countries was required to bring the statute into effect. The court began operations on 1 July 2002 with 139 signatories and after ratification by 76 countries. As of Jan. 2019 there had been 124 ratifications, although in Oct. 2017 Burundi became the first country to leave the ICC, citing bias against African countries. Earlier in the year, the governments of The Gambia and South Africa had reversed earlier declarations that they too would withdraw. The Court's first trial, with Thomas Lubanga facing war crimes charges for his role in the Democratic Republic of the Congo's civil war, opened on 26 Jan. 2009 and was not concluded until 14 March 2012. Lubanga was found guilty of conscripting and enlisting children under the age of 15 and using them to participate in hostilities.

Judges The International Criminal Court's first 18 judges were elected in Feb. 2003, with six serving for three years, six for six years and six for nine years. Every three years six new judges are elected. At present the 18 judges, with the year in which their term of office is scheduled to end, are: *Rosario Salvatore Aitala (Italy, 2027);* Tomoko Akane (Japan, 2027); *Reine Alapini-Gansou (Benin, 2027); Solomy Balungi Bossa* (Uganda, 2027); Chung Chang-ho (South Korea, 2024); Chile Eboe-Osuji (Nigeria, 2021); Robert Fremr (Czech Republic, 2021); Geoffrey A. Henderson (Trinidad and Tobago, 2021); Olga Venecia Herrera Carbuccia (Dominican Republic, 2021); Piotr Hofmański (Poland, 2024); *Luz del Carmen Ibáñez Carranza (Peru, 2027);* Péter Kovács (Hungary, 2024); Antoine Kesia-Mbe Mindua (Democratic Republic of the Congo, 2024); Howard Morrison (United Kingdom, 2021); Raul Pangalangan (Philippines, 2021); Marc Pierre Perrin de Brichambaut (France, 2024); Kimberly Prost (Canada, 2027); Bertram Schmitt (Germany, 2024).

Prosecutor Fatou Bensouda (The Gambia) was unanimously elected the second prosecutor of the Court on 12 Dec. 2011 and succeeded Luis Moreno-Ocampo (Argentina) on 16 June 2012.

Headquarters: Oude Waalsdorperweg 10, 2597 AK The Hague, Netherlands.
Website: http://www.icc-cpi.int
President: Chile Eboe-Osuji (Nigeria).

International Institute for Democracy and Electoral Assistance (IDEA)

Created in 1995, International IDEA is an intergovernmental organization that supports sustainable democratic change through providing comparative knowledge, assisting in democratic reform, and influencing policies and politics. International IDEA focuses on the ability of democratic institutions to deliver a political system marked by public participation and inclusion, representative and accountable government, responsiveness to citizens' needs and aspirations, and the rule of law and equal rights for all citizens.

Aims and Activities International IDEA undertakes work through three activity areas: providing comparative knowledge derived from practical experience on democracy-building processes—elections and referendums, constitutions, political parties, women's political empowerment and democracy self-assessments—from diverse contexts around the world; assisting political actors in reforming democratic institutions and processes, and engaging in political processes when invited to do so; influencing democracy-building policies and assistance to political actors.

Membership International IDEA had 30 full member states and one observer state in Jan. 2019.

Organization International IDEA has regional operations in Latin America, Africa, the Middle East, Asia and the Pacific, and has a staff of over 70 worldwide.

Headquarters: Strömsborg, 103 34 Stockholm, Sweden.
Website: http://www.idea.int
Secretary-General: Yves Leterme (Belgium).

International Mobile Satellite Organization (IMSO)

Founded in 1979 as the International Maritime Satellite Organization (Inmarsat) to establish a satellite system to improve maritime communications for distress and safety and commercial applications. Its competence was subsequently expanded to include aeronautical and land mobile communications. Privatization, which was completed in April 1999, transferred the business to a newly created company and the Organization remains as a regulator to ensure that the company fulfils its public services obligations. The company has taken the Inmarsat name and the Organization uses the acronym IMSO. In Jan. 2019 the Organization had 104 member parties.

Organization The Assembly of all Parties to the Convention meets every two years.

Headquarters: 4 Albert Embankment, London, SE1 7SR, UK.
IMSO Website: http://www.imso.org
Email: info@imso.org
Inmarsat Website: http://www.inmarsat.com
Director General, IMSO: Capt. Moin Ahmed (Bangladesh).
Chief Executive, Inmarsat Ltd: Rupert Pearce (United Kingdom).

International Olympic Committee (IOC)

Founded in 1894 by French educator Baron Pierre de Coubertin, the International Olympic Committee is an international non-governmental, non--profit organization whose members act as the IOC's representatives in their respective countries, not as delegates of their countries within the IOC. The Committee's main responsibility is to supervise the organization of the summer and winter Olympic Games. It owns all rights to the Olympic symbols, flag, motto, anthem and Olympic Games.

Aims 'To contribute to building a peaceful and better world by educating youth through sport, practised without discrimination of any kind and in the Olympic Spirit, which requires mutual understanding with a spirit of friendship, solidarity and fair play.'

Finances The IOC receives no public funding. Its only source of funding is from private sectors, with the substantial part of these revenues coming from television broadcasters and sponsors.

Address: Villa du Centenaire, Quai d'Ouchy 1, CH-1006 Lausanne, Switzerland.
Website: http://www.olympic.org
Email: studies.centre@olympic.org
President: Thomas Bach (Germany).

International Organisation of La Francophonie

The International Organisation of La Francophonie represents 88 countries and provinces/regions (including 27 with observer status) using French as an official language. It estimates that there are 220m. French speakers worldwide. Objectives include the promotion of peace, democracy, and economic and social development, through political and technical co-operation. The Secretary-General is based in Paris.

Members Member states and governments: Albania, Andorra, Armenia, Belgium, French Community of Belgium, Benin, Bulgaria, Burkina Faso, Burundi, Cambodia, Cameroon, Canada, Canada–New Brunswick, Canada–Quebec, Cape Verde, Central African Republic, Chad, Comoros, Democratic Republic of the Congo, Republic of the Congo, Côte d'Ivoire, Cyprus, Djibouti, Dominica, Egypt, Equatorial Guinea, France, Gabon,

Ghana, Greece, Guinea, Guinea-Bissau, Haiti, Kosovo, Laos, Lebanon, Luxembourg, Madagascar, Mali, Morocco, Mauritius, Mauritania, Moldova, Monaco, New-Caledonia, Niger, North Macedonia, Qatar, Romania, Rwanda, Saint Lucia, São Tomé and Príncipe, Senegal, Serbia, Seychelles, Switzerland, Togo, Tunisia, United Arab Emirates, Vanuatu, Vietnam. *Observers:* Argentina, Austria, Bosnia and Herzegovina, Canada-Ontario, Costa Rica, Croatia, Czech Republic, Dominican Republic, Estonia, Gambia, Georgia, Hungary, Ireland, South Korea, Latvia, Lithuania, Louisiana, Malta, Mexico, Montenegro, Mozambique, Poland, Slovakia, Slovenia, Thailand, Ukraine, Uruguay.

Headquarters: 19–21 avenue Bosquet, 75007 Paris, France.
Website (limited English): http://www.francophonie.org
Secretary-General: Louise Mushikiwabo (Rwanda).

International Organization for Migration (IOM)

Established in 1951, the International Organization for Migration (IOM) is the principal intergovernmental organization in the field of migration.

Members (172 as of Jan. 2019) Afghanistan, Albania, Algeria, Angola, Antigua and Barbuda, Argentina, Armenia, Australia, Austria, Azerbaijan, Bahamas, Bangladesh, Belarus, Belgium, Belize, Benin, Bolivia, Bosnia and Herzegovina, Botswana, Brazil, Bulgaria, Burkina Faso, Burundi, Cabo Verde, Cambodia, Cameroon, Canada, Central African Republic, Chad, Chile, China, Colombia, Comoros, Democratic Republic of the Congo, Republic of the Congo, Cook Islands, Costa Rica, Côte d'Ivoire, Croatia, Cuba, Cyprus, Czech Republic, Denmark, Djibouti, Dominica, Dominican Republic, Ecuador, Egypt, El Salvador, Eritrea, Estonia, Eswatini, Ethiopia, Fiji, Finland, France, Gabon, Gambia, Georgia, Germany, Ghana, Greece, Grenada, Guatemala, Guinea, Guinea-Bissau, Guyana, Haiti, Holy See, Honduras, Hungary, Iceland, India, Iran, Ireland, Israel, Italy, Jamaica, Japan, Jordan, Kazakhstan, Kenya, Kiribati, South Korea, Kyrgyzstan, Latvia, Laos, Lesotho, Liberia, Libya, Lithuania, Luxembourg, Madagascar, Malawi, Maldives, Mali, Malta, Marshall Islands, Mauritania, Mauritius, Mexico, Micronesia, Moldova, Mongolia, Montenegro, Morocco, Mozambique, Myanmar, Namibia, Nauru, Nepal, Netherlands, New Zealand, Nicaragua, Niger, Nigeria, North Macedonia, Norway, Pakistan, Palau, Panama, Papua New Guinea, Paraguay, Peru, Philippines, Poland, Portugal, Romania, Rwanda, St Kitts and Nevis, St Lucia, St Vincent and the Grenadines, Samoa, São Tomé and Príncipe, Senegal, Serbia, Seychelles, Sierra Leone, Slovakia, Slovenia, Solomon Islands, Somalia, South Africa, South Sudan, Spain, Sri Lanka, Sudan, Suriname, Sweden, Switzerland, Tajikistan, Tanzania, Thailand, Timor-Leste, Togo, Tonga, Trinidad and Tobago, Tunisia, Turkey, Turkmenistan, Tuvalu, Uganda, Ukraine, UK, Uruguay, USA, Vanuatu, Venezuela, Vietnam, Yemen, Zambia, Zimbabwe.

Activities IOM works to help ensure the orderly and humane management of migration, to promote international co-operation on migration issues, to assist in the search for practical solutions to migration problems and to provide humanitarian assistance to migrants in need, be they refugees, displaced persons or other uprooted people. The IOM Constitution gives explicit recognition to the link between migration and economic, social and cultural development, as well as to the right of freedom of movement of persons. IOM's operational budget for 2018 was US$956·5m.

Official languages: English, French and Spanish.
Headquarters: Route des Morillons 17, POB 17, CH-1211 Geneva 19, Switzerland.
Website: http://www.iom.int
Email: hq@iom.int
Director-General: António Vitorino (Portugal).

International Organization for Standardization (ISO)

Established in 1947, the International Organization for Standardization is a non-governmental federation of national standards bodies from 162 countries worldwide, one from each country. ISO's work results in international agreements which are published as International Standards. The first ISO standard was published in 1951 with the title 'Standard reference temperature for industrial length measurement'.

Some 19,500 ISO International Standards are available on subjects in such diverse fields as information technology, textiles, packaging, distribution of goods, energy production and utilization, building, banking and financial services. ISO standardization activities include the widely recognized ISO 9000 family of quality management system and standards and the ISO 14000 series of environmental management system standards. Standardization programmes are now being developed in completely new fields, such as food safety, security, social responsibility and the service sector.

Mission To promote the development of standardization and related activities in the world with a view to facilitating the international exchange of goods and services, and to developing co-operation in the spheres of intellectual, scientific, technological and economic activity.

Headquarters: BIBC II, 8 Chemin de Blandonnet, CP 401, CH-1214 Vernier, Geneva, Switzerland.
Website: http://www.iso.org
Email: central@iso.org
President: John Walter (Canada).

International Road Federation (IRF)

The IRF is a non-profit, non-political service organization whose purpose is to encourage better road and transportation systems worldwide and to help apply technology and management practices to give maximum economic and social returns from national road investments.

Founded following the Second World War, over the years the IRF has led major global road infrastructure developments, including achieving 1,000 km of new roads in Mexico in the 1950s, and promoting the Pan-American Highway linking North and South America. The IRF works together with members and associates in 118 countries, promoting social and economic benefits that flow from well planned and environmentally sound road transport networks. It publishes *World Road Statistics*, covering over 200 countries and territories.

Headquarters: Madison Place, 500 Montgomery St., Fifth Floor, Alexandria, Virginia 22314, USA.
Website: https://www.irf.global
Email: info@IRF.global
Chairman: Abdullah A. Al-Mogbel (Saudi Arabia).

International Seabed Authority (ISA)

The ISA is an autonomous international organization established under the UN Convention on the Law of the Sea (UNCLOS) of 1982 and the 1994 Agreement relating to the implementation of Part XI of the UNCLOS. It came into existence on 16 Nov. 1994 and became fully operational in June 1996.

The administrative expenses are met from assessed contributions from its members. Membership numbered 168 in Jan. 2019; the budget for the biennium 2015–16 was US$15,743,143.

The UNCLOS covers almost all ocean space and its uses: navigation and overflight, resource exploration and exploitation, conservation and pollution, fishing and shipping. It entitles coastal states and inhabitable islands to proclaim a 12-mile territorial sea, a contiguous zone, a 200-mile exclusive economic zone and an extended continental shelf (in some cases). Its 320 Articles and nine Annexes constitute a guide for behaviour by states in the world's oceans, defining maritime zones, laying down rules for drawing sea boundaries, assigning legal rights, duties and responsibilities to States, and providing machinery for the settlement of disputes.

Organization The Assembly, consisting of representatives from all member states, is the supreme organ. The 36-member Council, elected by the Assembly, includes the four largest importers or consumers of seabed minerals, four largest investors in seabed minerals, four major exporters of the same, six developing countries representing special interests and 18 members from all the geographical regions. The Council is the executive organ of the Authority. There are also two subsidiary bodies: the Legal and Technical Commission (currently 24 experts) and the Finance Committee (currently 15 experts). The Secretariat serves all the bodies of the Authority and under the 1994 Agreement is performing functions of the Enterprise (until such time as it starts to operate independently of the Secretariat). The Enterprise is the organ through which the ISA carries out deep seabed activities directly or through joint ventures.

Activities   In July 2000 the ISA adopted the Regulations for Prospecting and Exploration for Polymetallic Nodules in the Area. Pursuant thereto, it signed exploration contracts with eight contractors who have submitted plans of work for deep seabed exploration. These are: Institut Français de Recherche pour l'Exploitation de la Mer (IFREMER) and Association Française pour l'Etude de la Recherche des Nodules (AFERNOD), France; Deep Ocean Resources Development Co. Ltd (DORD), Japan; State Enterprise Yuzhmorgeologiya, Russian Federation; China Ocean Minerals Research and Development Association (COMRA); Interoceanmetal Joint Organiza-tion (IOM), a consortium sponsored by Bulgaria, Cuba, Czech Republic, Poland, Russia and Slovakia; the government of the Republic of Korea; the Republic of India; and the Federal Institute for Geosciences and Natural Resources, Germany.

Workshops are held on a range of topics, normally once a year. In the past these have included: environmental management needs for exploration and exploitation of deep seabed minerals; a standardized system of data interpre-tation; and prospects for international collaboration in marine environmental research.

Headquarters: 14–20 Port Royal St., Kingston, Jamaica.
Website: http://www.isa.org.jm
Secretary-General: Michael W. Lodge (United Kingdom).

Publications   Handbook 2013.—Selected Decisions and Documents from the Authority's Sessions.—various others.

International Telecommunications Satellite Organization (ITSO)

Founded in 1964 as Intelsat, the organization was the world's first commer-cial communications satellite operator. Today, with capacity on a fleet of geostationary satellites and expanding terrestrial network assets, Intelsat continues to provide connectivity for telephony, corporate network, broad-cast and internet services.

Organization   In 2001 the member states of the organization implemented restructuring by transferring certain assets to Intelsat Ltd, a new commercial company under the supervision of the International Telecommunications Satellite Organization, now known as ITSO. In 2009 Intelsat Ltd moved its corporate headquarters to Luxembourg and became Intelsat S.A. ITSO's mission is to ensure that Intelsat provides public telecommunications ser-vices, including voice, data and video, on a global and non-discriminatory basis. The governing body of ITSO is the Assembly of Parties, which normally meets every other year. The Executive Organ is headed by the Director-General and is responsible to the Assembly of Parties. The Director-General supervises and monitors Intelsat's provision of public telecommuni-cations services. There were 149 member countries in Jan. 2019.

Headquarters: 4400 Jenifer St., NW, Suite 332, Washington, D.C., 20015, USA.
Website: http://www.itso.int
Director-General: Patrick Masambu (Uganda).

International Trade Union Confederation (ITUC)

Origin   Founded in Nov. 2006, the ITUC was formed through a unification process that included the merger of the International Confederation of Free Trade Unions (ICFTU) and the World Confederation of Labour (WCL) with the addition of several national centres that had not been affiliated with either organization. The WCL was established in 1920 as the International Feder-ation of Christian Trade Unions, but went briefly out of existence in 1940 owing to the suppression of affiliated unions by the Nazi and Fascist regimes. It reconstituted in 1945 and became the WCL in 1968. The founding congress of the ICFTU took place in London in Dec. 1949 following the withdrawal of some Western trade unions from the World Federation of Trade Unions (WFTU), which was founded in 1945 but had come under Communist control.

In Jan. 2019 the ITUC represented 207m. members of 331 affiliates in 163 countries and territories.

Aims   The ITUC aims to defend and promote the rights of workers, partic-ularly the right to trade union organization and collective bargaining; to combat discrimination at work and in society; to ensure that social concerns are put at the centre of global economic, trade and finance policies; to support young people's rights at work; and to promote the involvement of women in trade unions. Its main priorities are: Count Us In!; Countries at Risk; Domes-tic Workers; Global Coherence; Global Governance of Migration; and Organising.

Organization   The Congress meets every four years to set policies and to elect the General Secretary and the General Council, composed of 70 mem-bers, which is the main decision-making body between congresses. The President and Deputy Presidents are appointed by the General Council. The Founding Congress was held in Vienna in Nov. 2006. Its second Congress was held in 2010 in Vancouver, its third in Berlin in 2014 and its fourth in Copenhagen in 2018.

The ITUC has regional organizations for Africa, the Americas, the Arab countries, Asia-Pacific and Europe. It has offices that deal with the Interna-tional Labour Organization (Geneva), the United Nations, the World Bank and the International Monetary Fund (Washington, D.C.) and the Interna-tional Maritime Organization (London). There are also offices in Moscow and Sarajevo.

The ITUC is a member of the Council of Global Unions, which was created in 2006 as a tool for structured co-operation and co-ordination.

Headquarters: Bd du Roi Albert II, N°5, bte 1, B-1210 Brussels, Belgium.
Website: http://www.ituc-csi.org
Email: info@ituc-cso.org
President: Ayuba Wabba (Nigeria).
General Secretary: Sharan Burrow (Australia).

International Tribunal for the Law of the Sea (ITLOS)

The International Tribunal for the Law of the Sea (ITLOS), founded in Oct. 1996 and based in Hamburg, adjudicates on disputes relating to the interpre-tation and application of the United Nations Convention on the Law of the Sea. The Convention gives the Tribunal jurisdiction to resolve a variety of international law of the sea disputes such as the delimitation of maritime zones, fisheries, navigation and the protection of the marine environment. Its Seabed Disputes Chamber has compulsory jurisdiction to resolve disputes amongst States, the International Seabed Authority, companies and private individuals, arising out of the exploitation of the deep seabed. The Tribunal also has compulsory jurisdiction in certain instances to protect the rights of parties to a dispute or to prevent serious harm to the marine environment, and over the prompt release of arrested vessels and their crews upon the deposit of a security. The Tribunal is composed of 21 judges, elected by signatories from five world regional blocs: five each from Africa and Asia; four from Western Europe and other States; four from Latin America and the Carib-bean; and three from Eastern Europe. The judges serve a term of nine years, with one third of the judges' terms expiring every three years.

Headquarters: Am Internationalen Seegerichtshof 1, 22609 Hamburg, Germany.
Website: http://www.itlos.org
Email: itlos@itlos.org
Registrar: Philippe Gautier (Belgium).

Inter-Parliamentary Union (IPU)

Founded in 1889 by William Randal Cremer (UK) and Frédéric Passy (France), the Inter-Parliamentary Union was the first permanent forum for political multilateral negotiations. The Union is a centre for dialogue and parliamentary diplomacy among legislators representing every political sys-tem and all the main political leanings in the world. It was instrumental in setting up what is now the Permanent Court of Arbitration in The Hague.

Activities   The IPU fosters contacts, co-ordination and the exchange of experience among parliaments and parliamentarians of all countries; con-siders questions of international interest and concern, and expresses its views on such issues in order to bring about action by parliaments and parliamen-tarians; contributes to the defence and promotion of human rights—an essential factor of parliamentary democracy and development; contributes to better knowledge of the working and development of representative institutions and to the strengthening of representative democracy.

Membership The IPU had 178 members and 12 associate members in Jan. 2019.

Headquarters: Chemin du Pommier 5, C.P. 330, CH-1218 Le Grand Saconnex, Geneva 19, Switzerland.
Website: http://www.ipu.org
Email: postbox@ipu.org
President: Gabriela Cuevas Barron (Mexico).
Secretary-General: Martin Chungong (Cameroon).

INTERPOL (International Criminal Police Organization)

Organization INTERPOL was founded in 1923, disbanded in 1938 and reconstituted in 1946. The International Criminal Police Organization—INTERPOL was created to ensure and promote the widest possible mutual assistance between all criminal police authorities within the limits of the law existing in the different countries worldwide and the spirit of the Universal Declaration of Human Rights, and to establish and develop all institutions likely to contribute effectively to the prevention and suppression of ordinary law crimes.

Aims INTERPOL provides a co-ordination centre (General Secretariat) for its 194 member countries. Its priority areas of activity concern criminal organizations, public safety and terrorism, drug-related crimes, financial crime and high-tech crime, trafficking in human beings and tracking fugitives from justice. INTERPOL centralizes records and information on international offenders; it operates a worldwide communication network.

INTERPOL's General Assembly is held annually. The General Assembly is the body of supreme authority in the organization. It is composed of delegates appointed by the members of the organization.

The Executive Committee, which meets four times a year, supervises the execution of the decisions of the General Assembly. The Executive Committee is composed of the president of the organization, the three vice-presidents and nine delegates.

The General Secretariat is the centre for co-ordinating the fight against international crime. Its activities, undertaken in response to requests from the police services and judicial authorities in its member countries, focus on crime prevention and law enforcement.

As of Jan. 2019 INTERPOL's regional offices were located in Abidjan, Bangkok, Buenos Aires, Harare, Nairobi, San Salvador and Yaoundé.

Headquarters: 200 Quai Charles de Gaulle, 69006 Lyon, France.
Website: http://www.interpol.int
President: Kim Jong Yang (South Korea).

Islamic Development Bank

The Agreement establishing the IDB (Banque islamique de développement) was adopted at the Second Islamic Finance Ministers' Conference held in Jeddah, Saudi Arabia in Aug. 1974. The Bank, which is open to all member countries of the Organisation of Islamic Cooperation, commenced operations in 1975. Its main objective is to foster economic development and social progress of member countries and Muslim communities individually as well as jointly in accordance with the principles of the Sharia. It is active in the promotion of trade and the flow of investments among member countries, and maintains a Special Assistance Fund for member countries suffering natural calamities. The Fund is also used to finance health and educational projects aimed at improving the socio-economic conditions of Muslim communities in non-member countries. A US$1·5bn. IDB Infrastructure Fund was launched in 1998 to invest in projects such as power, telecommunications, transportation, energy, natural resources, petro-chemical and other infrastructure-related sectors in member countries.

Members (57 as of Jan. 2019) Afghanistan, Albania, Algeria, Azerbaijan, Bahrain, Bangladesh, Benin, Brunei, Burkina Faso, Cameroon, Chad, Comoros, Côte d'Ivoire, Djibouti, Egypt, Gabon, The Gambia, Guinea, Guinea-Bissau, Guyana, Indonesia, Iran, Iraq, Jordan, Kazakhstan, Kuwait, Kyrgyzstan, Lebanon, Libya, Malaysia, Maldives, Mali, Mauritania, Morocco, Mozambique, Niger, Nigeria, Oman, Pakistan, Palestine, Qatar, Saudi Arabia, Senegal, Sierra Leone, Somalia, Sudan, Suriname, Syria, Tajikistan, Togo, Tunisia, Turkey, Turkmenistan, Uganda, United Arab Emirates, Uzbekistan, Yemen.

Official language: Arabic. Working languages: English and French.
Headquarters: 8111 King Khalid St, Al Nuzlah Al Yamania Dist. Unit No. 1, Jeddah 22332–2444, Saudi Arabia.
Website: http://www.isdb.org
Email: info@isdb.org
President: Bandar Hajjar (Saudi Arabia).

Médecins Sans Frontières/Doctors Without Borders (MSF)

Origin Médecins Sans Frontières/Doctors Without Borders was founded in 1971 by a small group of doctors and journalists who believed that all people have a right to emergency relief.

Functions MSF was one of the first non-governmental organizations to provide both urgently needed medical assistance and to publicly bear witness to the plight of the people it helps. Today MSF is an international medical humanitarian organization with 19 sections and several additional offices around the world. Every year MSF sends around 3,000 volunteer doctors, nurses, other medical professionals, logistical experts, water and sanitation engineers, and administrators to join approximately 25,000 locally hired staff to provide medical aid in over 60 countries. MSF was awarded the 1999 Nobel Peace Prize.

Headquarters: MSF International Office, 78 Rue de Lausanne, CP 1016, CH-1211 Geneva 1, Switzerland.
Website: http://www.msf.org
International President: Dr Joanne Liu (Canada).
Secretary-General: Christopher Lockyear (UK).

Nobel Prizes

When the scientist, industrialist and inventor Alfred Nobel died in 1896, he made provision in his will for his fortune to be used for prizes in Physics, Chemistry, Physiology or Medicine, Literature and Peace. The Norwegian Nobel Committee awards the Nobel Peace Prize, and the Nobel Foundation in Stockholm (founded 1900; Mailing address: Box 5232, SE-10245, Stockholm, Sweden) awards the other four prizes plus the Sveriges Riksbank Prize in Economic Sciences in Memory of Alfred Nobel (often referred to as the Nobel Memorial Prize in Economic Sciences). The Prize Awarding Ceremony takes place on 10 Dec., the anniversary of Nobel's death. The last ten recipients of the Nobel Peace Prize, worth 9m. Sw. kr. in 2017 (up from 8m. Sw. kr. for the previous five years), are:

2009 – Barack Obama (USA) for his extraordinary efforts to strengthen international diplomacy and co-operation between peoples.
2010 – Liu Xiaobo (China) for his long and non-violent struggle for fundamental human rights in China.
2011 – Ellen Johnson-Sirleaf (Liberia), Leymah Gbowee (Liberia) and Tawakkul Karman (Yemen) for their non-violent struggle for the safety of women and for women's rights to full participation in peace-building work.
2012 – the European Union (EU) for its contribution for over six decades to the advancement of peace and reconciliation, democracy and human rights.
2013 – the Organization for the Prohibition of Chemical Weapons (OPCW) for its extensive work to eliminate chemical weapons.
2014 – Kailash Satyarthi (India) and Malala Yousafzai (Pakistan) for their struggle against the suppression of children and young people and for the right of all children to education.
2015 – National Dialogue Quartet (Tunisia) for its decisive contribution to the building of a pluralistic democracy in Tunisia in the wake of the Jasmine Revolution of 2011.
2016 – Juan Manuel Santos (Colombia) for his resolute efforts to bring the country's more than 50-year-long civil war to an end.
2017 – the International Campaign to Abolish Nuclear Weapons (ICAN) for its work to draw attention to the catastrophic humanitarian consequences of any use of nuclear weapons and for its ground-breaking efforts to achieve a treaty-based prohibition of such weapons.
2018 – Denis Mukwege (Democratic Republic of Congo) and Nadia Murad (Iraq) for their efforts to end the use of sexual violence as a weapon of war and armed conflict.

Sveriges Riksbank Prize in Economic Sciences in Memory of Alfred Nobel

The Sveriges Riksbank Prize in Economic Sciences in Memory of Alfred Nobel was set up by the Swedish central bank in 1968. The last ten recipients of the prize, worth 9m. Sw. kr. in 2017 (up from 8m. Sw. kr. for the previous five years), are:

2009 – Elinor Ostrom (USA) for her analysis of economic governance, especially the commons, and Oliver E. Williamson (USA) for his analysis of economic governance, especially the boundaries of the firm.
2010 – Peter A. Diamond (USA), Dale T. Mortensen (USA) and Christopher A. Pissarides (Cyprus) for their analysis of markets with search frictions.
2011 – Thomas J. Sargent (USA) and Christopher A. Sims (USA) for their empirical research on cause and effect in macroeconomy.
2012 – Alvin E. Roth (USA) and Lloyd S. Shapley (USA) for the theory of stable allocations and the practice of market design.
2013 – Eugene Fama (USA), Lars Peter Hansen (USA) and Robert J. Shiller (USA) for their empirical analysis of asset prices.
2014 – Jean Tirole (France) for his analysis of market power and regulation.
2015 – Sir Angus Deaton (UK/USA) for his analysis of consumption, poverty and welfare.
2016 – Oliver Hart (UK/USA) and Bengt Holmström (Finland) for their contributions to contract theory.
2017 – Richard H. Thaler (USA) for his contributions to behavioural economics.
2018 – William D. Nordhaus (USA) for integrating climate change into long-run macroeconomic analysis, and Paul M. Romer (USA) for integrating technological innovations into long-run macroeconomic analysis.

North Atlantic Treaty Organization (NATO)

Origin On 4 April 1949 the foreign ministers of Belgium, Canada, Denmark, France, Iceland, Italy, Luxembourg, the Netherlands, Norway, Portugal, the UK and the USA signed the North Atlantic Treaty, establishing the *North Atlantic Alliance*. In 1952 Greece and Turkey acceded to the Treaty; in 1955 the Federal Republic of Germany; in 1982 Spain; in 1999 the Czech Republic, Hungary and Poland; in 2004 Bulgaria, Estonia, Latvia, Lithuania, Romania, Slovakia and Slovenia; in 2009 Albania and Croatia; and in 2017 Montenegro, bringing the total to 29 member countries.

Functions The Alliance was established as a defensive political and military alliance of independent countries in accordance with the terms of the UN Charter. Its fundamental role is to safeguard the freedom and security of its members by political and military means. It also encourages consultation and co-operation with non-NATO countries in a wide range of security-related areas to help prevent conflicts within and beyond the frontiers of its member countries. NATO promotes democratic values and is committed to the peaceful resolution of disputes. If diplomatic efforts fail, it has the military capacity needed to undertake crisis-management operations alone or in co-operation with other countries and international organizations.

Reform and Transformation of the Alliance Following the demise of the Warsaw Pact in 1991, and the improved relations with Russia, NATO established security dialogue and co-operation with the states of Central and Eastern Europe and those of the former USSR. These changes were reflected in the publication in 1991 of a new Strategic Concept for the Alliance outlining NATO's enduring purpose and nature, and its fundamental security tasks. Further changes in the security environment during the 1990s led to the development of the current Strategic Concept, published in 1999 to address new risks such as terrorism, ethnic conflict, human rights abuses, political instability, economic fragility, and the spread of nuclear, biological and chemical weapons and their means of delivery. A new Strategic Concept, which reflects new and emerging security threats, was published at a NATO summit meeting in Nov. 2010.

The Euro-Atlantic Partnership In 1991 the North Atlantic Co-operation Council (NACC) was established as a forum for dialogue with former Warsaw Pact countries. The NACC was replaced in 1997 by the Euro-Atlantic Partnership Council (EAPC), which brings together all 50 NATO and partner countries in the Euro-Atlantic area for dialogue and consultation on political and security-related issues. It provides the overall political framework for NATO's co-operation with partner countries and the bilateral relationships developed between NATO and individual partner countries under the Partnership for Peace (PfP) programme, which was launched in 1994.

Since its launch, the PfP programme has been adapted to expand and intensify political and military co-operation throughout Europe. Core objectives are: the facilitation of transparency in national defence planning and budgeting processes; democratic control of defence forces; members' maintenance of capability and readiness to contribute to operations under the authority of the UN; development of co-operative military relations with NATO (joint planning, training and exercises) in order to strengthen participants' ability to undertake missions in the fields of peacekeeping, search and rescue, and humanitarian operations; development, over the longer term, of forces better able to operate with those of NATO member forces. NATO will consult with any active partner which perceives a direct threat to its territorial integrity, political independence or security.

One of the most tangible aspects of co-operation between partner countries and NATO has been their individual participation in NATO-led peace-support operations. In Jan. 2019 NATO had 21 PfP partners: Armenia, Austria, Azerbaijan, Belarus, Bosnia and Herzegovina, Finland, Georgia, Ireland, Kazakhstan, Kyrgyzstan, Malta, Moldova, North Macedonia (then the former Yugoslav Republic of Macedonia), Russia, Serbia, Sweden, Switzerland, Tajikistan, Turkmenistan, Ukraine and Uzbekistan.

Country Relations On 27 May 1997 in Paris, NATO and Russia signed the Founding Act on Mutual Relations, Co-operation and Security, committing themselves to build together a lasting peace in the Euro-Atlantic area, and establishing a new forum for consultation and co-operation called the NATO-Russia Permanent Joint Council. In May 2002 the Permanent Joint Council was replaced by a new NATO-Russia Council which brought together all NATO member countries and Russia in a forum in which they would work as equal partners, identifying and pursuing opportunities for joint action in areas of common concern. However, NATO's ties with Russia deteriorated during 2014 when Moscow sanctioned the annexation of Crimea following the ousting of Ukraine's pro-Russian president, Viktor Yanukovych, in Feb. of that year.

At the meeting in Sintra, Portugal in May 1997 a NATO-Ukraine Charter on a Distinctive Partnership was drawn up and signed in Madrid in July, establishing the NATO-Ukraine Commission (NUC). Dialogue and co-operation has become well-established with NATO and individual allies supporting Ukraine's ongoing reform efforts, particularly in the defence and security sectors.

NATO launched the Mediterranean Dialogue with six countries of the Mediterranean (Egypt, Israel, Jordan, Mauritania, Morocco and Tunisia) in 1995. In 1997 allied foreign ministers agreed to enhance the Dialogue. A new committee, the Mediterranean Co-operation Group, was established to take the Mediterranean Dialogue forward and Algeria joined in March 2000. Later, in 2004, NATO also launched the İstanbul Co-operation Initiative that aims to develop bilateral co-operation with countries in the broader Middle East. Bahrain, Kuwait, Qatar and the United Arab Emirates have since joined the Initiative.

Relations with other international organizations NATO is gradually developing a strategic partnership with the European Union. Efforts to strengthen the security and defence role of NATO's European allies were initially organized through the Western European Union (WEU) during the 1990s, when there was a growing realization of the need for European countries to further develop defence capabilities and to assume greater responsibility for their common security. In 2000 the crisis management responsibilities of the WEU were increasingly assumed by the EU. Institutionalized relations between NATO and the EU were launched in 2001. The political principles underlying the NATO-EU relationship were set out in the Dec. 2002 NATO-EU Declaration on ESDP (European Security and Defence Policy). These decisions paved the way for the two organizations to work out the modalities for the transfer of responsibilities to the EU for the NATO-led military operations in North Macedonia (then the former Yugoslav Republic of Macedonia) in 2003 and, from Dec. 2004, in Bosnia and Herzegovina.

NATO and the UN share a commitment to maintaining international peace and security and have been co-operating in this area since the early 1990s with consultations established between NATO and UN specialized bodies on a range of issues including crisis management, combating human trafficking, mine action and the fight against terrorism.

NATO and the OSCE work together to build security and promote stability in the Euro-Atlantic area, co-operating at both the political and the operational level in areas such as conflict prevention, crisis management and addressing new security threats.

Operations   One of the most significant aspects of NATO's transformation has been the decision to undertake peace-support and crisis-management operations in the Euro-Atlantic area and further afield.

In the wake of the disintegration of the former Yugoslavia, the Alliance has focused much of its attention on the Balkans. NATO first committed itself to peacekeeping in Bosnia and Herzegovina in Dec. 1995, through the NATO-led Implementation Force (IFOR), which was replaced by the Stabilization Force (SFOR) in 1996. Improvements in the security situation allowed NATO to hand over its operation to the EU in Dec. 2004.

Since 1999, following a 78-day air campaign against the Yugoslav regime to bring an end to the violent repression of ethnic Albanians, NATO has led a peacekeeping mission in Kosovo (the Kosovo Force, or KFOR). NATO also intervened in North Macedonia (then the former Yugoslav Republic of Macedonia) at the request of the government to help avoid a civil war in 2001, and maintained a small peacekeeping presence there until March 2003, when the operation was handed over to the EU.

Following the attacks on New York and Washington, D.C. on 11 Sept. 2001, NATO invoked article five of the Washington Treaty (the collective defence clause) for the first time in its history, declaring it considered the attack on the USA as an attack against all members of the Alliance. It subsequently launched a series of initiatives aimed at curtailing terrorist activity. Operation *Active Endeavour* was a maritime operation led by NATO's naval forces to detect and deter terrorist activity in the Mediterranean. It was succeeded by Operation *Sea Guardian* in Oct. 2016. Operation *Eagle Assist* was one of the measures requested by the USA in the aftermath of the attacks in Sept. 2001. Aircraft from NATO's Airborne Warning and Control System (AWACS) patrolled American airspace from mid-Oct. 2001 to mid-May 2002.

In Aug. 2003 NATO took over responsibility for the International Security Assistance Force (ISAF) in Afghanistan. Initially centred on the capital, Kabul, by Oct. 2006 it covered the entire country. Troop numbers peaked at 140,000 in 2011, but ISAF ceased combat operations at the end of 2014. On 1 Jan. 2015 the NATO-led Operation *Resolute Support* began to train, advise and assist the Afghan National Security Forces. As of Dec. 2018 its personnel numbered 16,919.

From 2004 until 2011 NATO helped train Iraqi military personnel and supported the development of security institutions in Iraq. From 2005 to 2007 it provided logistical support to the African Union's mission in Darfur, Sudan.

In late 2008 NATO conducted counter-piracy operations in the Gulf of Aden, where piracy threatened to undermine international humanitarian efforts in Africa, as well as the safety of commercial maritime routes and international navigation. From 2009 until the end of 2016 NATO conducted a similar operation off the Horn of Africa.

From March until Oct. 2011 a coalition of NATO allies and partners conducted Operation *Unified Protector* in Libya. Using only air and sea resources, its aim was to protect civilians, enforce an air embargo and maintain a no-fly zone. It was widely regarded as instrumental in the downfall of the Libyan leader, Col. Gaddafi.

Since the establishment in 1998 of the Euro-Atlantic Disaster Response Co-ordination Centre to serve as a focal point for co-ordinating the disaster-relief efforts of NATO member states and partner countries, NATO plays an increasingly important role in humanitarian relief. Most notably, in 2005 some NATO capabilities and forces were deployed to support relief efforts following Hurricane Katrina in the USA and the devastating earthquake in Pakistan and in 2010 after the Haitian earthquake and flooding in Pakistan.

In Sept. 2014 the outgoing NATO Secretary General, Anders Fogh Rasmussen, identified Russian aggression in Ukraine and the militant Islamic State group's advance in the Middle East as the chief threats to Western security. In the same month NATO announced the creation of a rapid-deployment 'spearhead' force, which numbered 40,000 personnel by 2016. In July that year the Alliance also agreed to station multinational battalions from early 2017 in Estonia, Latvia, Lithuania and Poland—each considered a front-line target in any potential Russian expansionism.

Defence capabilities   This widened scope of NATO military operations is radically transforming the military requirements of the Alliance. The large defence forces of the past are being replaced by more flexible, mobile forces which are able to deploy at significant distances from their normal operating bases and to engage in the full range of missions, ranging from high-intensity combat to humanitarian support. A modernization process was launched at the Prague Summit in 2002 to ensure that NATO could effectively deal with the security challenges of the 21st century and measures to enhance the Alliance's military operational capabilities were agreed. A new capabilities initiative (the Prague Capabilities Commitment) and a NATO Response Force were created and the Alliance's military command structure streamlined. In addition, steps were taken to increase efforts in the areas of intelligence sharing and crisis response arrangements, as well as greater co-operation with partner countries. Five nuclear, biological and chemical (NBC) weapons defence initiatives were also endorsed, as well as the creation of a multinational chemical, biological, radiological and nuclear battalion. At subsequent NATO summit meetings in İstanbul in 2004 and Riga in 2006, further initiatives were taken to promote the Alliance's ongoing transformation.

Organization   The North Atlantic Council (NAC) is the highest decision-making body and forum for consultation within the Atlantic Alliance. Composed of Permanent Representatives of all the member countries, it meets at least once a week and also meets at higher levels involving foreign ministers, defence ministers or heads of state or government. The authority and powers of decision-making and status and validity of its decisions remain the same at whatever level it meets. All decisions are taken on the basis of consensus, reflecting the collective will of all member governments. The NAC is the only body within the Atlantic Alliance which derives its authority explicitly from the North Atlantic Treaty.

The Military Committee is responsible for making recommendations to the NAC and the Defence Planning Committee on military matters and for supplying guidance to the Allied Commanders. Composed of the Chiefs-of-Staff of member countries (Iceland, which has no military forces, may be represented by a civilian), the Committee is assisted by an International Military Staff. It meets at Chiefs-of-Staff level at least twice a year but remains in permanent session at the level of national military representatives. The military command structure of the Alliance is divided into two strategic commands, one based in Europe and the other based in the USA.

Finance   The greater part of each member country's contribution to NATO, in terms of resources, comes indirectly through its expenditure on its own national armed forces and on its efforts to make them interoperable with those of other members so that they can participate in multinational operations. Member countries usually incur the deployment costs involved whenever they volunteer forces to participate in NATO-led operations, although in 2006 agreement was reached on using common funding for some aspects of deployments on a trial basis.

Member countries make direct contributions to three budgets managed directly by NATO: namely the Civil Budget, the Military Budget and the Security Investment Programme. Member countries pay contributions to each of these budgets in accordance with agreed cost-sharing formulae broadly calculated in relation to their ability to pay.

Under the terms of the Partnership for Peace strategy, partner countries undertake to make available the necessary personnel, assets, facilities and capabilities to participate in the programme, and share the financial cost of any military exercises in which they participate.

Current Leaders

Jens Stoltenberg
Position
Secretary General

Introduction
Jens Stoltenberg became Secretary General of NATO on 1 Oct. 2014. Previously a three-term prime minister of Norway, he is a social democrat with a reputation for consensus-building. He succeeded Denmark's Anders Fogh Rasmussen at NATO. His term of office was extended in Dec. 2017 for a further two years.

Early Life
Jens Stoltenberg was born in Oslo on 16 March 1959, the son of politicians (his father, Thorvald, served as Norway's defence minister). He studied economics at Oslo University, where he joined the Norwegian Labour

Party (Det Norske Arbeiderpartiet, DNA). In 1985 he was appointed leader of the Labour Youth League and from 1985–89 was vice president of the International Union of Socialist Youth. He also worked briefly at the National Statistics Office and was an economics lecturer at Oslo University before serving for two years as leader of the Oslo Labour Party (1990–92).

Elected a member of the *Storting* (parliament) for Oslo in the Sept. 1993 general election, Stoltenberg served as minister of trade and energy from 1993–96 and oversaw Norway's accession to the European Economic Area in 1994. In Oct. 1996 he was named minister of finance, a post he held for a year until the DNA lost power to the conservative Christian People's Party, led by Kjell Magne Bondevik. When Bondevik resigned in March 2000, Stoltenberg (by then deputy leader of the DNA) was asked to form a government as the youngest prime minister in Norway's history.

Having ushered in controversial reforms to the welfare state, Stoltenberg suffered a heavy defeat in the parliamentary elections of Sept. 2001 to a centre-right coalition led by Bondevik. A DNA party leadership battle between Stoltenberg and Thorbjørn Jagland (leader since 1992) ensued with Stoltenberg emerging victorious. He became prime minister for a second time on 17 Oct. 2005, following the victory of a coalition comprising the DNA, Socialist Left Party and the Centre Party. Stoltenberg vowed to further reform the welfare system and develop Norway's knowledge-based economy.

In 2006 his administration approved the expansion of exploration in the oil- and gas-rich Barents Sea and also the merger of Norway's two largest energy companies, Statoil and Norsk Hydro (with the government having a controlling stake in the combined group). Stoltenberg withdrew the small Norwegian military contingent from Iraq, but contributed nearly 600 troops to the NATO-led peacekeeping force in Afghanistan. In Sept. 2009 his centre-left coalition was returned to power in parliamentary elections. In 2010 he finalized an agreement with Russia to resolve a long-running border dispute over the Barents Sea. The rapprochement continued with the creation, in 2012, of a visa-free zone along the boundary between the two countries.

In July 2011 a right-wing extremist set off a bomb in central Oslo, killing eight people, before going on a shooting rampage at a Labour Party youth camp near the capital and murdering another 69 victims. Stoltenberg responded to the attacks by calling for 'more democracy, more openness'. He sought re-election at the 2013 elections, but his coalition failed to secure a majority, despite the Labour Party winning most seats and the highest share of the vote. He was succeeded as prime minister on 16 Oct. 2013 by Erna Solberg.

Career in Office
In March 2014 Stoltenberg was named Secretary General of NATO, an appointment championed by German Chancellor Angela Merkel. Upon assuming office, he was faced with an escalating security crisis in Ukraine. Stoltenberg, who as Norway's prime minister had sought closer ties with Russia, nonetheless fiercely criticized its annexation of Crimea, stating that the action offered a 'brutal reminder of the necessity of NATO'. He responded by deploying warships in the Black Sea and fighter planes in neighbouring NATO members.

Citing Russian aggression and the rise of the militant Islamic State movement, Stoltenberg said in Nov. 2014 that 'threats are coming closer' and called on European member states to arrest the cuts in defence spending that had left the USA shouldering an increasingly large burden of the NATO budget. Despite Russian opposition, in 2015 NATO members formally invited Montenegro to join the Alliance in a reaffirmation, according to Stoltenberg, of its open door policy towards potential member states, including Georgia. Montenegro subsequently became the 29th full member of the Alliance in June 2017.

In response to increasing nervousness about Russian military ambitions in Eastern Europe, NATO agreed in June 2016 to further multinational troop deployments in the three Baltic states and Poland. Concerns then arose about the USA's continued commitment to the Alliance as aspiring presidential candidate Donald Trump was ambivalent about defending those member states that did not fulfil their defence spending obligations. However, in Nov. 2016 Trump, as president-elect, jointly affirmed with Stoltenberg NATO's 'enduring importance' to Western security.

In Dec. 2017 the Alliance partners agreed to extend Stoltenberg's appointment until the end of Sept. 2019, having 'full confidence in his ability to continue his dedicated work to advance NATO's adaptation to the security challenges of the 21st century'.

Ongoing Russian military assertiveness and further aggression against Ukraine heralded NATO's staging, in Oct.–Nov. 2018, of its largest military exercise since the end of the Cold War, stretching from Iceland to Finland. In Dec. Stoltenberg criticized Russia's 'pattern of disrespect for the borders of its neighbours' and restated NATO's solidarity with Georgia and Ukraine and support for their membership aspirations.

Headquarters: NATO, Blvd Leopold III, B-1110 Brussels, Belgium.
Website: http://www.nato.int
Secretary General: Jens Stoltenberg (Norway).

Publications For a full list of NATO publications, visit the website: http://www.nato.int/cps/en/natolive/publications.htm

Organisation for Economic Co-operation and Development (OECD)

Origin Founded in 1961 to replace the Organisation for European Economic Co-operation (OEEC), which was established in 1948 and linked to the Marshall Plan. The change of title marks the Organisation's altered status and functions: it ceased to be a European body with the accession of Canada and USA as full members and became a forum of global influence adding development to its list of core priorities. The Organisation aims to promote policies designed to achieve the highest sustainable economic growth and employment, as well as raising standards of living in member countries, while maintaining financial stability, thereby contributing to the development of the world economy; to contribute to sound economic expansion in member as well as non-member economies in the process of economic development; and to contribute to the expansion of world trade on a multilateral, non-discriminatory basis in accordance with international obligations.

Members Australia, Austria, Belgium, Canada, Chile, Czech Republic, Denmark, Estonia, Finland, France, Germany, Greece, Hungary, Iceland, Ireland, Israel, Italy, Japan, South Korea, Latvia, Lithuania, Luxembourg, Mexico, Netherlands, New Zealand, Norway, Poland, Portugal, Slovakia, Slovenia, Spain, Sweden, Switzerland, Turkey, UK and USA. Discussions that began in May 2007 on the possible future accession of Russia were suspended in March 2014 following its annexation of Crimea. Colombia and Costa Rica are currently in accession talks.

Activities The OECD's main fields of work are: economic policy; statistics; energy; development co-operation; sustainable development; public governance and territorial development; international trade; financial and enterprise affairs; tax policy and administration; food, agriculture and fisheries; environment; science, technology and industry; biotechnology and biodiversity; education; employment, labour and social affairs; entrepreneurship, small and middle-sized enterprises; and local development.

Relations with non-members In order to ensure its continuing relevance as a hub for dialogue and action on globally significant policy issues, the OECD has developed an active global relations strategy and maintains co-operative relations with many economies outside the OECD. Officials from non-member economies increasingly discuss policy with their counterparts from member countries and conduct peer assessments while sharing each other's policy experiences. In 2007 the OECD launched a process of enhanced engagement with five countries whose engagement in the work of the OECD is particularly important for the fulfilment of the Organisation's mandate to promote policy convergence and global economic development: Brazil, China, India, Indonesia and South Africa. It aims to bring these countries closer to the OECD by engaging them actively in the OECD's analytical and policy development work, while supporting their own reform processes.

Other activities with non-OECD members are grouped around Global Forums in 12 policy areas. Created by Committees as stable, active networks of policy makers in OECD member and non-member economies, as well as other stakeholders, the Global Forums focus on: agriculture, biotechnology, competition, development, education, environment, finance, international investment, the knowledge economy, public governance, taxation and trade. A regional approach provides for targeted co-operation with non-OECD economies in Europe, Asia, Latin America, the Middle East and Northern Africa (MENA), and in Africa more generally, where the OECD supports the objectives of the New Partnership for Africa's Development (NEPAD) and the initiatives of the African Partnership Forum.

Relations with developing countries Developing countries participate in many of the OECD's above-mentioned activities with non-members. The principal body dealing with issues related to development co-operation is the Development Assistance Committee (DAC). Its 30 members (the 36 OECD members excluding Chile, Estonia, Israel, Latvia, Lithuania, Mexico and Turkey plus the European Union) are major aid donors, collectively providing US$145·0bn. in 2016. The DAC largely focuses on how to spend and invest this aid so as to help its partners achieve the Millennium Development Goals and produces analysis and guidance on a range of topics, including aid for trade, aid effectiveness, capacity development, poverty reduction, environment, conflict and fragility, gender equality, good governance, evaluation and aid architecture.

The OECD Development Centre links OECD member countries and developing countries in Africa, Asia and Latin America by helping policy-makers in OECD and developing countries find solutions to the challenges of development, poverty alleviation and the curbing of inequality through recommendations designed to promote constructive policy change. Annual publications include the *Latin American Economic Outlook* and, jointly with the African Development Bank, the *African Economic Outlook*.

Relations with other international organizations Under a protocol signed at the same time as the OECD Convention, the European Commission takes part in the work of the OECD. EFTA may also send representatives to attend OECD meetings. Formal relations also exist with the Asian Development Bank, Inter-American Development Bank, World Bank, IMF, UNCTAD, WHO and the Parliamentary Assemblies of the Council of Europe and NATO.

Relations with civil society Consultations with civil society organizations (CSOs) take place across the whole range of the OECD's work. The Business and Industry Advisory Committee to the OECD (BIAC) and the Trade Union Advisory Committee to the OECD (TUAC) have consultative status enabling them to discuss subjects of common interest and be consulted in a particular field by the relevant OECD Committee or its officers. Since 2000 the OECD has organized the annual OECD Forum, an international public conference offering business, labour and civil society the opportunity to discuss key issues of the 21st century with government ministers and leaders of international organizations.

Organization The governing body of the OECD is the Council, comprising representatives of each member country and in which the European Commission participates. It usually meets once a year at the level of government ministers, with a rotating chairmanship at ministerial level among member governments. The Council also meets regularly, under the chairmanship of the Secretary-General at the level of Permanent Representatives to OECD (ambassadors who head resident diplomatic missions). It is responsible for all questions of general policy and may establish subsidiary bodies as required to achieve the aims of the Organisation. Decisions and recommendations of the Council are adopted by consensus of all its members.

An Executive Committee, a Budget Committee and an External Relations Committee assist the Council although they have limited decision-making power within their fields of competence. In addition, the Executive Committee in Special Session meets, usually twice a year, and is attended by senior government officials. Most of the work of the OECD is prepared and carried out by about 250 specialized bodies (Committees, Working Parties, etc.). All members are normally represented on these bodies, except a few which have a more restricted membership. Funding is by member state contributions based on a formula related to their size and economy.

The International Energy Agency (IEA) and the Nuclear Energy Agency (NEA) are also part of the OECD system.

Headquarters: 2 rue André Pascal, 75775 Paris Cedex 16, France.
Website: http://www.oecd.org
Secretary-General: Angel Gurría (Mexico).
Deputy Secretaries-General: Ludger Schuknecht (Germany), Masamichi Kono (Japan).

Publications include: *OECD Factbook* (annual).—*Economic, Environmental and Social Statistics (annual).—OECD Policy Briefs* (20 a year).—*OECD Economic Surveys* (by country).—*Environmental Performance Reviews* (by country).—*OECD Economic Outlook* (twice a year).—*Economic Policy Reform: Going for Growth* (annual).—*OECD-FAO Agricultural Outlook* (annual).—*Education at a Glance (annual).—OECD Employment Outlook* (annual).—*OECD Science, Technology and Industry Outlook* (biennial).—*International Migration Outlook* (annual).—*Health at a Glance* (biennial).—*Society at a Glance* (biennial).—*OECD Health Statistics (online only).—Financial Market Trends* (twice a year).—*International Trade by Commodity Statistics* (annual).—*Main Economic Indicators* (monthly).—*Energy Balances* (annual).—*World Energy Outlook* (annual).—*National Accounts* (quarterly and annual).—*African Economic Outlook* (annual).—*OECD Observer* (quarterly).—*Development Co-operation Report* (annual). For a full list of OECD publications, visit the website: http://www.oecdbookshop.org

Organisation of Islamic Cooperation (OIC)

Founded in 1969, the objectives of the OIC are to promote Islamic solidarity among member states; to consolidate co-operation among member states in the economic, social, cultural, scientific and other vital fields of activities, and to carry out consultations among member states in international organizations; to endeavour to eliminate racial segregation, discrimination and to eradicate colonialism in all its forms; to take the necessary measures to support international peace and security founded on justice; to strengthen the struggle of all Muslim peoples with a view to safeguarding their dignity, independence and national rights; to create a suitable atmosphere for the promotion of co-operation and understanding among member states and other countries. Originally known as the Organization of the Islamic Conference, it changed its name in June 2011.

Members (57 as of Jan. 2019) Afghanistan, Albania, Algeria, Azerbaijan, Bahrain, Bangladesh, Benin, Brunei, Burkina Faso, Cameroon, Chad, Comoros, Côte d'Ivoire, Djibouti, Egypt, Gabon, The Gambia, Guinea, Guinea-Bissau, Guyana, Indonesia, Iran, Iraq, Jordan, Kazakhstan, Kuwait, Kyrgyzstan, Lebanon, Libya, Malaysia, Maldives, Mali, Mauritania, Morocco, Mozambique, Niger, Nigeria, Oman, Pakistan, Palestine, Qatar, Saudi Arabia, Senegal, Sierra Leone, Somalia, Sudan, Suriname, Syria*, Tajikistan, Togo, Tunisia, Turkey, Turkmenistan, Uganda, United Arab Emirates, Uzbekistan, Yemen. *Observers.* Bosnia and Herzegovina, Central African Republic, Russia, Thailand, Turkish Republic of Northern Cyprus. *Suspended since Aug. 2012.

Headquarters: PO Box 178, Jeddah 21411, Saudi Arabia.
Website: http://www.oic-oci.org
Secretary-General: Dr Yousef bin Ahmad Al-Othaimeen (Saudi Arabia).

Union for International Cancer Control (UICC)

Founded in 1933, the UICC (formerly the International Union Against Cancer) is an international non-governmental association of over 1,000 member organizations in 163 countries.

Objectives The UICC is the only non-governmental organization dedicated exclusively to the global control of cancer. Its objectives are to advance scientific and medical knowledge in research, diagnosis, treatment and prevention of cancer, and to promote all other aspects of the campaign against cancer throughout the world. Particular emphasis is placed on professional and public education.

Membership The UICC is made up of voluntary cancer leagues, patient organizations, associations and societies as well as cancer research and treatment centres and, in some countries, ministries of health.

Activities The UICC creates and carries out programmes around the world in collaboration with several hundred volunteer experts, most of whom are professionally active in UICC member organizations. It promotes co-operation between cancer organizations, researchers, scientists, health professionals and cancer experts, with a focus in four key areas: building and enhancing cancer control capacity, tobacco control, population-based cancer prevention and control, and transfer of cancer knowledge and dissemination. The next UICC World Cancer Congress is scheduled to take place in Kuala Lumpur, Malaysia in Oct. 2018.

Address: 31–33 avenue Giuseppe Motta, CH-1202 Geneva, Switzerland.
Website: http://www.uicc.org
Email: info@uicc.org
President: Sanchia Aranda (Australia).
Chief Executive Officer: Cary Adams (UK).

Unrepresented Nations and Peoples Organization (UNPO)

UNPO is an international organization created by nations and peoples around the world who are not represented in the world's principal international organizations, such as the UN. Founded in 1991, UNPO had 43 members as at Jan. 2019 representing more than 250m. people worldwide.

Membership Open to all nations and peoples unrepresented, subject to adherence to the five principles that form the basis of UNPO's charter: equal right to self-determination of all nations and peoples; adherence to internationally accepted human rights standards; to the principles of democracy; promotion of non-violence; and protection of the environment. Applicants must show that they constitute a 'nation or people' as defined in the Covenant.

Functions and Activities UNPO offers an international forum for occupied nations, indigenous peoples, minorities and oppressed majorities, who struggle to regain their lost countries, preserve their cultural identities, protect their basic human and economic rights, and safeguard their environment.

It does not represent those peoples; rather it assists and empowers them to represent themselves more effectively. To this end, it provides professional services and facilities as well as education and training in the fields of diplomacy, human rights law, democratic processes, conflict resolution and environmental protection. Members, private foundations and voluntary contributions fund the Organization.

In total six former members of UNPO (Armenia, Belau, Estonia, Georgia, Latvia and Timor-Leste) subsequently achieved full independence and gained representation in the UN. Belau is now called Palau. Current members Bougainville and Kosovo have achieved a degree of political autonomy. Kosovo declared itself an independent state in 2008, although both Serbia and Russia oppose its sovereignty.

Headquarters: Rue du Pépin 54, B-1000, Brussels, Belgium.
Website: http://www.unpo.org
Email: unpo.brussels@unpo.org
General Secretary: Ralph Bunche (USA).

Publication *UNPO News* (quarterly).

World Council of Churches

The World Council of Churches was formally constituted on 23 Aug. 1948 in Amsterdam. In Jan. 2019 member churches numbered 363 from more than 110 countries.

Origin The World Council was founded by the coming together of Christian movements, including the overseas mission groups gathered from 1921 in the International Missionary Council, the Faith and Order Movement, and the Life and Work Movement. On 13 May 1938, at Utrecht, a provisional committee was appointed to prepare for the formation of a World Council of Churches.

Membership The basis of membership (1975) states: 'The World Council of Churches is a fellowship of Churches which confess the Lord Jesus Christ as God and Saviour according to the Scriptures and therefore seek to fulfil together their common calling to the glory of the one God, Father, Son and Holy Spirit.' Membership is open to Churches which express their agreement with this basis and satisfy such criteria as the Assembly or Central Committee may prescribe. Today, Churches of Protestant, Anglican, Orthodox, Old Catholic and Pentecostal confessions from all over the world belong to this fellowship. The Roman Catholic Church is not a member of the WCC but works closely with it.

Activities The WCC's Central Committee comprises the Programme Committee and the Finance Committee. Within the Programme Committee there are advisory groups on issues relating to communication, women, justice, peace and creation, youth, ecumenical relations and inter-religious relations. Following the WCC's 8th General Assembly in Harare, Zimbabwe in 1998 the work of the WCC was restructured. Activities were grouped into four 'clusters'—Relationships; Issues and Themes; Communication; and Finance, Services and Administration. The Relationships cluster comprises four teams (Church and Ecumenical Relations, Regional Relations and Ecumenical Sharing, Inter-Religious Relations and International Relations), as well as two programmes (Action by Churches Together and the Ecumenical Church Loan Fund). The Issues and Themes cluster comprises four teams (Faith and Order; Mission and Evangelism; Justice, Peace and Creation; and Education and Ecumenical Formation).

Organization The governing body of the World Council, consisting of delegates specially appointed by the member Churches, is the Assembly, which meets every seven or eight years to frame policy. It has no legislative powers and depends for the implementation of its decisions upon the action of member Churches. The 10th General Assembly, held in Busan, South Korea from 30 Oct.–8 Nov. 2013, had as its theme 'God of life, lead us to justice and peace'. The 11th General Assembly is scheduled to take place in Karlsruhe, Germany, in 2021. A 150-member Central Committee meets annually to carry out the Assembly mandate, with a smaller 26-member Executive Committee meeting twice a year.

Headquarters: 150 route de Ferney, CP 2100, CH-1211 Geneva 2, Switzerland.
Website: http://www.oikoumene.org
General Secretary: Rev. Dr Olav Fykse Tveit (Norway).

Publications *WCC Annual Review.—Directory of Christian Councils.* 1985.—*Dictionary of the Ecumenical Movement.* 1991.—*A History of the Ecumenical Movement.* 1993.—*Ecumenical Review* (quarterly).—*International Review of Mission* (biannual).

World Customs Organization

Established in 1952 as the Customs Co-operation Council, the World Customs Organization is an intergovernmental body with worldwide membership, whose mission it is to enhance the effectiveness and efficiency of customs administrations throughout the world. It has 183 member countries or territories.

Headquarters: Rue du Marché, 30, B-1210 Brussels, Belgium.
Website: http://www.wcoomd.org
Secretary-General: Kunio Mikuriya (Japan).

World Federation of Trade Unions (WFTU)

Origin and History The WFTU was founded on a worldwide basis in 1945 at the international trade union conferences held in London and Paris, with the participation of all the trade union centres in the countries of the anti-Hitler coalition. The aim was to reunite the world trade union movement at the end of the Second World War. The acute political differences among affiliates, especially the east–west confrontation in Europe on ideological lines, led to a split. A number of affiliated organizations withdrew in 1949 and established the ICFTU. The WFTU now draws its membership from the industrially developing countries like India, Vietnam and other Asian countries, Brazil, Peru, Cuba and other Latin American countries, Syria, Lebanon, Kuwait and other Arab countries, and it has affiliates and associates in more than 20 European countries. It has close relations with the International Confederation of Arab Trade Unions, the Organization of African Trade Union Unity as well as the All-China Federation of Trade Unions. The 18th Congress was held in Mexico City in March 2018. There are ten Trade Unions Internationals (TUIs) constituted within the WFTU.

The WFTU has 92m. members in 126 countries. It has regional offices in Damascus, Havana, Johannesburg, Libreville, New Delhi and Nicosia and Permanent Representatives accredited to the UN in New York, the FAO in Rome, the ILO in Geneva and UNESCO in Paris.

Headquarters: 40 Zan Moreas St., 117 45 Athens, Greece.
Website: http://www.wftucentral.org
Email: info@wftucentral.org
President: Mzwandile Michael Makwayiba (South Africa).
General Secretary: George Mavrikos (Greece).

Further Reading

Amnesty International (AI)

Power, Jonathan, *Like Water on Stone: The Story of Amnesty International.* 2001

Commonwealth

The Cambridge History of the British Empire. 8 vols. 1929 ff.
Judd, D. and Slinn, P., *The Evolution of the Modern Commonwealth.* 1982
Madden, F. and Fieldhouse, D. (eds.) *Selected Documents on the Constitutional History of the British Empire and Commonwealth.* 1994
Mayall, James, (ed.) *The Contemporary Commonwealth.* 2009
McIntyre, W. D., *The Significance of the Commonwealth, 1965–90.* 1991

Eurasian Economic Union (EEU)

Vinokurov, Evgeny, *Introduction to the Eurasian Economic Union.* 2018

International Committee of the Red Cross (ICRC)

Forsythe, David P., *The Humanitarians: The International Committee of the Red Cross.* 2005
Forsythe, David P. and Rieffer-Flanagan, Barbara Ann J., *The International Committee of the Red Cross: A Neutral Humanitarian Actor.* 2007
Moorehead, Caroline, *Dunant's Dream: War, Switzerland and the History of the Red Cross.* 1998

International Criminal Court (ICC)

Baker, Michael N. (ed.) *International Criminal Court: Developments and U.S. Policy.* 2012
Mendes, Errol, *Peace and Justice at the International Criminal Court: A Court of Last Resort.* 2010
Reydams, Luc, *Universal Jurisdiction: International and Municipal Perspectives.* 2003
Schabas, William A., *An Introduction to the International Criminal Court.* 4th ed. 2011

Struett, Michael J., *The Politics of Constructing the International Criminal Court: NGOs, Discourse, and Agency.* 2008

INTERPOL (International Criminal Police Organization)

Martha, Rutsel Silvestre J., *The Legal Foundations of INTERPOL.* 2010

North Atlantic Treaty Organization (NATO)

Cook, D., *The Forging of an Alliance.* 1989
Cottey, Andrew, *Security in 21st Century Europe.* 2nd ed. 2012
Edström, Håkan and Gyllensporre, Dennis, (eds.) *Pursuing Strategy: NATO Operations from the Gulf War to Gaddafi.* 2012
Hallams, Ellen, Ratti, Luca and Zyla, Ben, (eds.) *NATO Beyond 9/11: The Transformation of the Atlantic Alliance.* 2013
Matláry, Janne Haaland and Petersson, Magnus, (eds.) NATO's European Allies: Military Capability and Political Will. 2013
Sloan, Stanley R., *Permanent Alliance?: NATO and the Transatlantic Bargain from Truman to Obama.* 2010
Song, Yanan, *The US Commitment to NATO in the Post-Cold War Period.* 2016
Webber, Mark, Sperling, James and Smith, Martin A., *NATO's Post-Cold War Trajectory: Decline or Regeneration?* 2012

World Council of Churches

Castro, E., *A Passion for Unity.* 1992
Van Elderen, M. and Conway, M., *Introducing the World Council of Churches.* 1991

Africa

African Development Bank

Established in 1964 to promote economic and social development in Africa.

Regional members (54) Algeria, Angola, Benin, Botswana, Burkina Faso, Burundi, Cabo Verde, Cameroon, Central African Republic, Chad, Comoros, Democratic Republic of the Congo, Republic of the Congo, Côte d'Ivoire, Djibouti, Egypt, Equatorial Guinea, Eritrea, Eswatini, Ethiopia, Gabon, The Gambia, Ghana, Guinea, Guinea-Bissau, Kenya, Lesotho, Liberia, Libya, Madagascar, Malaŵi, Mali, Mauritania, Mauritius, Morocco, Mozambique, Namibia, Niger, Nigeria, Rwanda, São Tomé and Príncipe, Senegal, Seychelles, Sierra Leone, Somalia, South Africa, South Sudan, Sudan, Tanzania, Togo, Tunisia, Uganda, Zambia, Zimbabwe.

Non-regional members (27) Argentina, Austria, Belgium, Brazil, Canada, China, Denmark, Finland, France, Germany, India, Italy, Japan, South Korea, Kuwait, Luxembourg, Netherlands, Norway, Portugal, Saudi Arabia, Spain, Sweden, Switzerland, Turkey, UAE, UK, USA.

Within the ADB Group are the African Development Fund (ADF) and the Nigeria Trust Fund (NTF). The ADF, established in 1972, provides development finance on concessional terms to low-income Regional Member Countries which are unable to borrow on the non-concessional terms of the African Development Bank. Membership of the Fund is made up of 27 non-African State Participants and the African Development Bank. The NTF is a special ADB fund created in 1976 by agreement between the Bank Group and the Government of the Federal Republic of Nigeria. Its objective is to assist the development efforts of low-income Regional Member Countries whose economic and social conditions and prospects require concessional financing.

Official languages: English and French.
Headquarters: Avenue Joseph Anoma, 01 BP 1387, Abidjan 01, Côte d'Ivoire.
Website: http://www.afdb.org
President: Akinwumi Adesina (Nigeria).

African Export–Import Bank (Afreximbank)

Established in 1987 under the auspices of the African Development Bank to facilitate, promote and expand intra-African and extra-African trade. Membership is made up of three categories of shareholders: Class 'A' Shareholders consisting of African governments, African central banks and sub-regional and regional financial institutions and economic organizations; Class 'B' Shareholders consisting of African public and private financial institutions; and Class 'C' Shareholders consisting of international financial institutions, economic organizations and non-African states, banks, financial institutions and public and private investors.

Official languages: English, French, Arabic and Portuguese.
Headquarters: 72B El Maahad El Eshteraky St., Heliopolis, Cairo 11341, Egypt.
Website: http://www.afreximbank.com
President and Chairman of the Board: Benedict Okey Oramah (Nigeria).

African Union (AU)

History The Fourth Extraordinary Session of the Assembly of the Heads of State and Government of the Organization of African Unity (OAU) held in Sirté, Libya on 9 Sept. 1999 decided to establish an African Union. At Lomé, Togo on 11 July 2000 the OAU Assembly of the Heads of State and Government adopted the Constitutive Act of the African Union, which was later ratified by the required two-thirds of the member states of the Organization of African Unity (OAU); it came into force on 26 May 2001. The Lusaka Summit, in July 2001, gave a mandate to translate the transformation of the Organization of African Unity into the African Union, and on 9 July 2002 the Durban Summit, in South Africa, formally launched the African Union.

Members Algeria, Angola, Benin, Botswana, Burkina Faso, Burundi, Cabo Verde, Cameroon, Central African Republic, Chad, Comoros, Democratic Republic of the Congo, Republic of the Congo, Côte d'Ivoire, Djibouti, Egypt, Equatorial Guinea, Eritrea, Eswatini, Ethiopia, Gabon, The Gambia, Ghana, Guinea, Guinea-Bissau, Kenya, Lesotho, Liberia, Libya, Madagascar, Malaŵi, Mali, Mauritania, Mauritius, Morocco, Mozambique, Namibia, Niger, Nigeria, Rwanda, Sahrawi Arab Democratic Republic (Western Sahara), São Tomé and Príncipe, Senegal, Seychelles, Sierra Leone, Somalia, South Africa, South Sudan, Sudan, Tanzania, Togo, Tunisia, Uganda, Zambia, Zimbabwe.

Aims The African Union aims to promote unity, solidarity, cohesion and co-operation among the peoples of Africa and African states, and at the same time to co-ordinate efforts by African people to realize their goals of achieving economic, political and social integration.

Activities The African Union became fully operational in July 2002, and is working towards establishing the organs stipulated in the constitutive act. These include a Pan-African parliament, an Economic, Social and Cultural Council (ECOSOCC) and a Peace and Security Council (which have now been inaugurated), plus a Central Bank (which has not yet been launched).

The African Court on Human and Peoples' Rights was established in 2004. A protocol to set up an African Court of Justice entered into force in 2009, but has been superseded by a plan to create an African Court of Justice and Human Rights—also incorporating the African Court on Human and Peoples' Rights—which as of Jan. 2019 had yet to be established. Supporters of the proposal hope that this court will eventually supplant the International Criminal Court in prosecuting human rights abuses in Africa.

The African Union has established several peacekeeping forces, including in Burundi (2003–04), the Darfur region of Sudan (initially from 2004, and as part of a hybrid AU–UN mission since 2007), Somalia (since 2007) and the Central African Republic (since 2013).

Official languages: Arabic, English, French, Portuguese, Spanish and Swahili.
Headquarters: POB 3243, Roosevelt St. (Old Airport Area), W21K19 Addis Ababa, Ethiopia.
Website: http://www.au.int
Chairman: Abdel Fattah al-Sisi (Egypt).
Chair of the African Union Commission: Moussa Faki Mahamat (Chad).

Bank of Central African States (BEAC)

The Bank of Central African States (Banque des Etats de l'Afrique Centrale) was established in 1973 when a new Convention of Monetary Co-operation with France was signed. The five original members, Cameroon, Central African Republic, Chad, Republic of the Congo and Gabon, were joined by Equatorial Guinea in 1985. Under its Convention and statutes, the BEAC is declared a 'Multinational African institution in the management and control of which France participates in return for the guarantee she provides for its currency'.

Official language: French.
Headquarters: 736 avenue Monseigneur Vogt, 1917 Yaoundé, Cameroon.
Website (French only): http://www.beac.int
Governor: Abbas Mahamat Tolli (Chad).

Central Bank of West African States (BCEAO)

Established in 1962, the Central Bank of West African States (Banque Centrale des Etats de l'Afrique de l'Ouest) is the common central bank of the eight member states that form the West African Monetary Union

© Springer Nature Limited 2020
Palgrave Macmillan (ed.), *The Statesman's Yearbook 2020*,
https://doi.org/10.1057/978-1-349-95940-2_4

(WAMU). It has the sole right of currency issue throughout the Union territory and is responsible for the pooling of the Union's foreign exchange reserve; the management of the monetary policy of the member states; the keeping of the accounts of the member states treasury; and the definition of the banking law applicable to banks and financial establishments.

Members Benin, Burkina Faso, Côte d'Ivoire, Guinea-Bissau, Mali, Niger, Senegal, Togo.

Official language: French.
Headquarters: Avenue Abdoulaye Fadiga, 3108 Dakar, Senegal.
Website: http://www.bceao.int
Governor: Tiémoko Meyliet Koné (Côte d'Ivoire).

Common Market for Eastern and Southern Africa (COMESA)

COMESA is an African economic grouping of 19 member states who are committed to the creation of a Common Market for Eastern and Southern Africa. It was established in 1994 as a building block for the African Economic Community and replaced the Preferential Trade Area for Eastern and Southern Africa, which had been in existence since 1981.

Members Burundi, Comoros, Democratic Republic of the Congo, Djibouti, Egypt, Eritrea, Eswatini, Ethiopia, Kenya, Libya, Madagascar, Malaŵi, Mauritius, Rwanda, Seychelles, Sudan, Uganda, Zambia, Zimbabwe.

Objectives To facilitate the removal of the structural and institutional weaknesses of member states so that they are able to attain collective and sustainable development.

Activities COMESA's Free Trade Area (FTA) was launched on 31 Oct. 2000 at a Summit of Heads of States and Government in Lusaka, Zambia. The FTA participating states have zero tariff on goods and services produced in these countries.

In addition to creating the policy environment for freeing trade, COMESA has also created specialized institutions like the Eastern and Southern African Trade and Development Bank (PTA Bank), the PTA Reinsurance Company (ZEP-RE), the Clearing House and the COMESA Court of Justice, to provide the required financial infrastructure and service support. COMESA has also promoted a political risk guarantee scheme, the Africa Trade Insurance Agency (ATI), a Leather and Leather Products Institute (LLPI), as well as a cross-border insurance scheme, the COMESA Yellow Card.

Official languages: English, French and Portuguese.
Headquarters: COMESA Secretariat, COMESA Centre, Ben Bella Rd, PO Box 30051, 10101 Lusaka, Zambia.
Website: http://www.comesa.int
Email: info@comesa.int
Secretary General: Chileshe Kapwepwe (Zambia).

East African Community (EAC)

The East African Community (EAC) was formally established on 30 Nov. 1999 with the signing in Arusha, Tanzania of the Treaty for the Establishment of the East African Community. The Treaty envisaged the establishment of a Customs Union, as the entry point of the Community, a Common Market, subsequently a Monetary Union and ultimately a Political Federation of the East African States. In Nov. 2003 the EAC partner states signed a Protocol on the Establishment of the East African Customs Union, which came into force on 1 Jan. 2005. The Common Market came into force on 1 July 2010. There are plans to introduce a single currency in EAC member countries by 2024.

Members Burundi, Kenya, Rwanda, South Sudan, Tanzania, Uganda.

Headquarters: EAC Close, Afrika Mashariki Rd, PO Box 1096, Arusha, Tanzania.
Website: http://www.eac.int
Email: eac@eachq.org
Secretary General: Liberat Mfumukeko (Burundi).

East African Development Bank (EADB)

Established originally under the Treaty for East African Co-operation in 1967 with Kenya, Tanzania and Uganda as signatories, a new Charter for the Bank (with the same signatories) came into force in 1980. Rwanda was admitted as a member in 2008. Under the original Treaty the Bank was confined to the provision of financial and technical assistance for the promotion of industrial development in member states but with the new Charter its remit was broadened to include involvement in agriculture, forestry, tourism, transport and the development of infrastructure, with preference for projects which promote regional co-operation.

Official language: English.
Headquarters: 4 Nile Ave., PO Box 7128, Kampala, Uganda.
Website: http://www.eadb.org
Director General: Vivienne Yeda (Kenya).

Economic Community of Central African States (CEEAC)

The Economic Community of Central African States (Communauté Economique des Etats de l'Afrique Centrale) was established in 1983 to promote regional economic co-operation and to establish a Central African Common Market. There are plans for both a common market and a single currency.

Members Angola, Burundi, Cameroon, Central African Republic, Chad, Democratic Republic of the Congo, Republic of the Congo, Equatorial Guinea, Gabon, Rwanda, São Tomé and Príncipe.

Headquarters: BP 2112, Libreville, Gabon.
Website (French only): http://www.ceeac-eccas.org
Email: contact@ceeac-eccas.org
Secretary General: Ahmad Allam-Mi (Chad).

Economic Community of West African States (ECOWAS)

Founded in 1975 as a regional common market, ECOWAS later also became a political forum involved in the promotion of a democratic environment and the pursuit of fundamental human rights. In July 1993 it revised its treaty to assume responsibility for the regulation of regional armed conflicts, acknowledging the inextricable link between development and peace and security. Thus it now has a new role in conflict management and prevention through its Mediation and Security Council, which monitors the moratorium on the export, import and manufacture of light weapons and ammunition. However, it still retains a military arm, the Economic Community of West African States Monitoring Group (generally known as ECOMOG). It is also involved in the war against drug abuse and illicit drug trafficking. There are plans to introduce a single currency, the *eco*, in ECOWAS member countries in 2020.

Members Benin, Burkina Faso, Cabo Verde, Côte d'Ivoire, The Gambia, Ghana, Guinea, Guinea-Bissau, Liberia, Mali, Niger, Nigeria, Senegal, Sierra Leone, Togo.

Organization The institutions of ECOWAS are: the Commission, the Community Parliament, the Community Court of Justice and the ECOWAS Bank for Investment and Development.

Official languages: English, French and Portuguese.
Headquarters: 101 Yakubu Gowon Crescent, Asokoro, Abuja, Nigeria.
Website: http://www.ecowas.int
ECOWAS Commission President: Jean-Claude Kassi Brou (Côte d'Ivoire).

Intergovernmental Authority on Development

The Intergovernmental Authority on Development was created on 21 March 1996 and has its origins in the Intergovernmental Authority on Drought and Development, which had been established in 1986. It has three priority areas of co-operation: conflict prevention, management and humanitarian affairs; infrastructure development; food security and environment protection.

Members Djibouti, Eritrea, Ethiopia, Kenya, Somalia, South Sudan, Sudan, Uganda.

Headquarters: Ave. Georges Clemenceau, PO Box 2653, Djibouti, Republic of Djibouti.
Website: http://igad.int
Executive Secretary: Mahboub Maalim (Kenya).

Lake Chad Basin Commission

Established by a Convention and Statute signed on 22 May 1964 by Cameroon, Chad, Niger and Nigeria, and later by the Central African Republic (Sudan has also been admitted as an observer), to regulate and control utilization of the water and other natural resources in the Basin; to initiate, promote and co-ordinate natural resources development projects and research within the Basin area; and to examine complaints and promote settlement of disputes, with a view to promoting regional co-operation.

In Dec. 1977, at Enugu in Nigeria, the 3rd summit of heads of state of the commission signed the protocol for the Harmonization of the Regulations Relating to Fauna and Flora in member countries, and adopted plans for the multi-donor approach towards major integrated development for the conventional basin. An international campaign to save Lake Chad following a report on the environmental degradation of the conventional basin was launched by heads of state at the 8th summit of the Commission in Abuja in March 1994. Lake Chad has declined in size from 25,000 sq. km in the 1960s to its current size of 2,500 sq. km. The 10th summit, held in N'Djaména in 2000, saw agreement on a US$1m. inter-basin water transfer project.

Official languages: English and French.
Headquarters: Place de la Grande Armée, P. O. Box 727, N'Djaména, Chad.
Website: http://www.cblt.org/en/lake-chad-basin-commission
Executive Secretary: Mamman Nuhu (Nigeria).

Niger Basin Authority

As a result of a special meeting of the Niger River Commission (established in 1964), to discuss the revitalizing and restructuring of the organization to improve its efficiency, the Niger Basin Authority was established in 1980. Its responsibilities cover the harmonization and co-ordination of national development policies; the formulation of the general development policy of the Basin; the elaboration and implementation of an integrated development plan of the Basin; the initiation and monitoring of an orderly and rational regional policy for the utilization of the waters of the Niger River; the design and conduct of studies, researches and surveys; the formulation of plans, the construction, exploitation and maintenance of structure, and the elaboration of projects.

Members Benin, Burkina Faso, Cameroon, Chad, Côte d'Ivoire, Guinea, Mali, Niger, Nigeria.

Official languages: English and French.
Headquarters: 288 avenue du Fleuve Niger, Plateau, Niamey, Niger.
Website: http://www.abn.ne
Email: sec-executif@abn.ne
Executive Secretary: Abderahim Bireme Hamid (Chad).

Southern African Customs Union (SACU)

Established by the Customs Union Convention between the British Colony of Cape of Good Hope and the Orange Free State Boer Republic in 1889, the Southern African Customs Union was extended in 1910 to include the then Union of South Africa and British High Commission Territories in Africa and remained unchanged after these countries gained independence. South Africa was the dominant member with sole-decision making power over customs and excise policies until the 2002 SACU Agreement which created a permanent Secretariat, a Council of Ministers headed by a minister from one of the member states on a rotational basis, a Customs Union Commission, Technical Liaison Committees, a SACU tribunal and a SACU tariff board.

Members Botswana, Eswatini, Lesotho, Namibia, South Africa.

Aims To promote economic development through regional co-ordination of trade.

Headquarters: Private Bag 13285, Windhoek 9000, Namibia.
Website: http://www.sacu.int

Email: info@sacu.int
Executive Secretary: Paulina Mbala Elago (Namibia).

Southern African Development Community (SADC)

The Southern African Development Co-ordination Conference (SADCC), the precursor of the Southern African Development Community (SADC), was formed in Lusaka, Zambia on 1 April 1980, following the adoption of the Lusaka Declaration—*Southern Africa: Towards Economic Liberation*—by the nine founding member states.

Members The nine founder member countries were Angola, Botswana, Eswatini, Lesotho, Malawî, Mozambique, Tanzania, Zambia and Zimbabwe. Comoros, The Democratic Republic of the Congo, Madagascar, Mauritius, Namibia, the Seychelles and South Africa have since joined. The Seychelles left in July 2004 but rejoined in Aug. 2007. As a result there are now 16 members.

Aims and Activities SADC's Common Agenda includes the following: the promotion of sustainable and equitable economic growth and socio-economic development that will ensure poverty alleviation with the ultimate objective of its eradication; the promotion of common political values, systems and other shared values that are transmitted through institutions that are democratic, legitimate and effective; and the consolidation and maintenance of democracy, peace and security.

In contrast to the country-based co-ordination of sectoral activities and programmes, SADC has now adopted a more centralized approach through which the 21 sectoral programmes are grouped into four clusters; namely: Trade, Industry, Finance and Investment; Infrastructure and Services; Food, Agriculture and Natural Resources; Social and Human Development and Special Programmes.

SADC has made significant progress in implementing its integration agenda since the 1992 Treaty came into force. Since then, more than 20 Protocols to spearhead the sectoral programmes and activities have been signed. Those Protocols that have entered into force include: Immunities and Privileges; Combating Illicit Drugs; Energy; Transport, Communications and Meteorology; Shared Watercourse Systems; Mining; Trade; Education and Training; Tourism; and Health.

Official languages: English, French and Portuguese.
Headquarters: SADC House, Plot No. 54385, Central Business District, Private Bag 0095, Gaborone, Botswana.
Website: http://www.sadc.int
Email: registry@sadc.int
Executive Secretary: Dr Stergomena Lawrence Tax (Tanzania).

Tripartite Free Trade Area (TFTA)

The Tripartite Free Trade Area is a free trade agreement negotiated by the Common Market for Eastern and Southern Africa (COMESA), the Southern African Development Community (SADC) and the East African Community (EAC). It was launched in June 2015 by 26 African nations. The accord envisages a trading block of over 600m. people with a combined GDP of some US$1trn. As of Jan. 2019, 24 nations had signed the agreement.

Members (subject to ratification) Angola, Botswana, Burundi, Comoros, Democratic Republic of the Congo, Djibouti, Egypt, Eritrea, Eswatini, Ethiopia, Kenya, Lesotho, Libya, Madagascar, Malawî, Mauritius, Mozambique, Namibia, Rwanda, Seychelles, South Africa, Sudan, Tanzania, Uganda, Zambia, Zimbabwe.

Address: c/o TradeMark Southern Africa, 1st Floor Building 41, CSIR Campus, Meiring Naude Rd, Brummeria, Pretoria 0001, South Africa.
Email: info@comesa-eac-sadc-tripartite.org

West African Development Bank (BOAD)

The West African Development Bank (Banque Ouest Africaine de Développement) was established in Nov. 1973 by an Agreement signed by the member states of the West African Monetary Union (UMOA), now the West African Economic and Monetary Union (UEMOA).

Aims To promote balanced development of the States of the Union and to achieve West African economic integration.

Members Benin, Burkina Faso, Côte d'Ivoire, Guinea-Bissau, Mali, Niger, Senegal, Togo.

Official language: French.
Headquarters: 68 avenue de la Libération, BP 1172 Lomé, Togo.
Website: http://www.boad.org
Email: boadsiege@boad.org
President: Christian Adovèlandé (Benin).

West African Economic and Monetary Union (UEMOA)

Founded in 1994, the UEMOA (Union Economique et Monétaire Ouest Africaine) aims to reinforce the competitiveness of the economic and financial activities of member states in the context of an open and rival market and a rationalized and harmonized juridical environment; to ensure the convergence of the macroeconomic performances and policies of member states; to create a common market among member states; to co-ordinate the national sector-based policies; and to harmonize the legislation, especially the fiscal system, of the member states.

Members Benin, Burkina Faso, Central Bank of West African States, Côte d'Ivoire, Guinea-Bissau, Mali, Niger, Senegal, Togo.

Headquarters: 380 avenue Professeur Joseph Ki-Zerbo, 01 BP 543, Ouagadougou 01, Burkina Faso.
Website (French only): http://www.uemoa.int
Email: commission@uemoa.int
President: Abdallah Boureima (Nigeria).

Further Reading

African Union (AU)

Makinda, Samuel M., and Okumu, F. Wafula, *The African Union: Challenges of Globalization, Security, and Governance.* 2007
Miller-Jones, Edward R., *The African Union: Aiming to Unify the Continent.* 2010
Muthri, Tim, Akopari, John and Ndinga-Mavumba, Angela, (eds.) *The African Union and its Institutions.* 2008
New Zealand Ministry of Foreign Affairs and Trade, *African Union Handbook 2018.* 2018
Welz, Martin, *Integrating Africa: Decolonization's Legacies, Sovereignty and the African Union.* 2012

Economic Community of West African States (ECOWAS)

Jaye, Thomas, Garuba, Dauda and Amadi, Stella, (eds.) *ECOWAS and the Dynamics of Conflict and Peace-building.* 2011

Agency for the Prohibition of Nuclear Weapons in Latin America and the Caribbean (OPANAL)

The Agency (Organismo para la Proscripción de las Armas Nucleares en la América Latina y el Caribe) was established following the Cuban missile crisis to guarantee implementation of the world's first Nuclear-Weapon-Free-Zone (NWFZ) in the region. Created by the Treaty of Tlatelolco (1967), OPANAL is an inter-governmental agency responsible for ensuring that the requirements of the Treaty are enforced. OPANAL has played a major role in establishing other NWFZs throughout the world.

Organization The Agency consists of three main bodies: the General Conference which meets for biennial sessions and special sessions when deemed necessary; the Council of OPANAL consisting of five member states which meet every two months plus special meetings when necessary; and the Secretariat General.

Members of the Treaty Antigua and Barbuda, Argentina, The Bahamas, Barbados, Belize, Bolivia, Brazil, Chile, Colombia, Costa Rica, Cuba, Dominica, Dominican Republic, Ecuador, El Salvador, Grenada, Guatemala, Guyana, Haiti, Honduras, Jamaica, Mexico, Nicaragua, Panama, Paraguay, Peru, St Kitts and Nevis, St Lucia, St Vincent and the Grenadines, Suriname, Trinidad and Tobago, Uruguay, Venezuela.

Headquarters: Calle Milton 61, Colonia Anzures, Delegación Miguel Hidalgo, C. P. 11590, México, D. F., Mexico.
Website: http://www.opanal.org
Email: info@opanal.org
Secretary-General: Luiz Filipe de Macedo Soares (Brazil).

Andean Community

On 26 May 1969 an agreement was signed by Bolivia, Chile, Colombia, Ecuador and Peru establishing the Cartagena Agreement (also referred to as the Andean Pact or the Andean Group). Chile withdrew from the Group in 1976. Venezuela, which was actively involved, did not sign the agreement until 1973. In 1997 Peru announced its withdrawal for five years. In 2006 Venezuela left as a result of Colombia and Peru signing bilateral trade agreements with the USA.

The Andean Free Trade Area came into effect on 1 Feb. 1993 as the first step towards the creation of a common market. Bolivia, Colombia, Ecuador and Peru have fully liberalized their trade. A Common External Tariff for imports from third countries has been in effect since 1 Feb. 1995.

In March 1996 at the Group's 8th summit in Trujillo in Peru, the then member countries (Bolivia, Colombia, Ecuador, Peru, Venezuela) set up the Andean Community, to promote greater economic, commercial and political integration between member countries under a new Andean Integration System (SAI).

The member countries and bodies of the Andean Integration System are working to establish an Andean Common Market and to implement a Common Foreign Policy, a social agenda, a Community policy on border integration, and policies for achieving joint macroeconomic targets.

Organization The Andean Presidential Council, composed of the presidents of the member states, is the highest-level body of the Andean Integration System (SAI). The Commission and the Andean Council of Foreign Ministers are legislative bodies. The General Secretariat is the executive body and the Andean Parliament is the deliberative body of the SAI. The Court of Justice, which began operating in 1984, resolves disputes between members and interprets legislation. The SAI has other institutions: Andean Development Corporation (CAF), Latin American Reserve Fund (FLAR), Simón Bolívar Andean University, Andean Business Advisory Council, Andean Labour Advisory Council and various Social Agreements.

Further to the treaty signed by 12 South American countries in May 2008, it is anticipated that the Andean Community will gradually be integrated into the Union of South American Nations.

Official language: Spanish.
Headquarters: Avda Paseo de la República 3895, San Isidro, Lima 27, Peru.
Website: http://www.comunidadandina.org
Email: correspondencia@comunidadandina.org
Secretary-General: Jorge Hernando Pedraza (Colombia).

Association of Caribbean States (ACS)

The Convention establishing the ACS was signed on 24 July 1994 in Cartagena de Indias, Colombia, with the aim of promoting consultation, co-operation and concerted action among all the countries of the Caribbean, comprising 25 full member states and three (now eight) associate members.

Members Antigua and Barbuda, The Bahamas, Barbados, Belize, Colombia, Costa Rica, Cuba, Dominica, Dominican Republic, El Salvador, Grenada, Guatemala, Guyana, Haiti, Honduras, Jamaica, Mexico, Nicaragua, Panama, St Kitts and Nevis, St Lucia, St Vincent and the Grenadines, Suriname, Trinidad and Tobago, Venezuela.

Associate members Aruba, British Virgin Islands, Curacao, France on behalf of (French Guiana, St Barthélemy and St Martin), Guadeloupe, Martinique, Sint Maarten and The Netherlands Antilles (on behalf of Saba and Sint Eustatius).

The CARICOM Secretariat, the Latin American Economic System (SELA), the Central American Integration System (SICA) and the Permanent Secretariat of the General Treaty on Central American Economic Integration (SIECA) were declared Founding Observers of the ACS in 1996. The United Nations Economic Commission for Latin America and the Caribbean (ECLAC) and the Caribbean Tourism Organization (CTO) were admitted as Founding Observers in 2000 and 2001 respectively.

Functions The objectives of the ACS are enshrined in the Convention and are based on the following: the strengthening of the regional co-operation and integration process, with a view to creating an enhanced economic space in the region; preserving the environmental integrity of the Caribbean Sea which is regarded as the common patrimony of the peoples of the region; and promoting the sustainable development of the Greater Caribbean. Its current focal areas are trade, transport, sustainable tourism and natural disasters.

Organization The main organs of the Association are the Ministerial Council and the Secretariat. There are Special Committees on: Trade Development and External Economic Relations; Sustainable Tourism; Transport; Natural Disasters; Budget and Administration. There is also a Council of National Representatives of the Special Fund responsible for overseeing resource mobilization efforts and project development.

Headquarters: ACS Secretariat, 5–7 Sweet Briar Rd, St Clair, PO Box 660, Port of Spain, Trinidad and Tobago.
Website: http://www.acs-aec.org
Secretary-General: Dr June Soomer (St Lucia).

Caribbean Community (CARICOM)

Origin The Treaty of Chaguaramas establishing the Caribbean Community and Common Market was signed by the prime ministers of Barbados, Guyana, Jamaica and Trinidad and Tobago at Chaguaramas, Trinidad, on 4 July 1973.

Six additional countries and territories (Belize, Dominica, Grenada, St Lucia, St Vincent and the Grenadines, Montserrat) signed the Treaty on 17 April 1974, and the Treaty came into effect for those countries on

© Springer Nature Limited 2020
Palgrave Macmillan (ed.), *The Statesman's Yearbook 2020*,
https://doi.org/10.1057/978-1-349-95940-2_5

1 May 1974. Antigua acceded to membership on 4 July that year; St Kitts and Nevis on 26 July; The Bahamas on 4 July 1983 (not Common Market); Suriname on 4 July 1995.

Members Antigua and Barbuda, The Bahamas, Barbados, Belize, Dominica, Grenada, Guyana, Haiti, Jamaica, Montserrat, St Kitts and Nevis, St Lucia, St Vincent and the Grenadines, Suriname, and Trinidad and Tobago. Anguilla, Bermuda, the British Virgin Islands, the Cayman Islands and the Turks and Caicos Islands are associate members.

Objectives The Caribbean Community has the following objectives: improved standards of living and work; full employment of labour and other factors of production; accelerated, co-ordinated and sustained economic development and convergence; expansion of trade and economic relations with third States; enhanced levels of international competitiveness; organization for increased production and productivity; the achievement of a greater measure of economic leverage and effectiveness of member states in dealing with third States, groups of States and entities of any description; enhanced co-ordination of member states' foreign and foreign economic policies; enhanced functional co-operation.

At its 20th Meeting in July 1999 the Conference of Heads of Government of the Caribbean Community approved for signature the agreement establishing the Caribbean Court of Justice. They mandated the establishment of a Preparatory Committee comprising the Attorneys General of Barbados, Guyana, Jamaica, St Kitts and Nevis, St Lucia and Trinidad and Tobago assisted by other officials, to develop and implement a programme of public education within the Caribbean Community and to make appropriate arrangements for the inauguration of the Caribbean Court of Justice prior to the establishment of the CARICOM Single Market and Economy. To this end at its 23rd Meeting in July 2002 the Heads of Government agreed on immediate measures to inaugurate the Court by the second half of 2003, although delays meant it was not inaugurated until April 2005. Among the measures adopted was the establishment of a Trust Fund with a one-time settlement of US$100m. to finance the Court.

Structure The Conference of Heads of Government is the principal organ of the Community, and its primary responsibility is to determine and provide the policy direction for the Community. It is the final authority on behalf of the Community for the conclusion of treaties and for entering into relationships between the Community and international organizations and States. It is responsible for financial arrangements to meet the expenses of the Community.

The Community Council of Ministers is the second highest organ of the Community and consists of Ministers of Government responsible for Community Affairs. The Community Council has primary responsibility for the development of Community strategic planning and co-ordination in the areas of economic integration, functional co-operation and external relations.

The Secretariat is the principal administrative organ of the Community. The Secretary-General is appointed by the Conference (on the recommendation of the Community Council) for a term not exceeding five years, and may be reappointed. The Secretary-General is the Chief Executive Officer of the Community and acts in that capacity at all meetings of the Community Organs.

Associate Institutions Caribbean Development Bank (CDB); University of Guyana (UG); University of the West Indies (UWI); Caribbean Law Institute (CLI)/Caribbean Law Institute Centre (CLIC); Organisation of Eastern Caribbean States.

Official language: English.
Headquarters: Caribbean Community (CARICOM) Secretariat, Turkeyen, Greater Georgetown, Guyana.
Website: http://www.caricom.org
Email: registry@caricom.org
Secretary-General: Irwin LaRocque (Dominica).

Caribbean Development Bank (CDB)

Established in 1969 by 16 regional and two non-regional members. Membership is open to all states and territories of the region and to non-regional states that are members of the UN or its Specialized Agencies or of the International Atomic Energy Agency.

Members—regional countries and territories: Anguilla, Antigua and Barbuda, The Bahamas, Barbados, Belize, British Virgin Islands, Cayman Islands, Dominica, Grenada, Guyana, Haiti, Jamaica, Montserrat, St Kitts and Nevis, St Lucia, St Vincent and the Grenadines, Suriname, Trinidad and Tobago, Turks and Caicos Islands. *Other regional countries:* Brazil, Colombia, Mexico, Venezuela. *Non-regional countries:* Canada, China, Germany, Italy, United Kingdom.

Function To contribute to the economic growth and development of the member countries of the Caribbean and promote economic co-operation and integration among them, with particular regard to the needs of the less developed countries.

Headquarters: PO Box 408, Wildey, St Michael, Barbados, WI BB11000.
Website: http://www.caribank.org
President: William Warren Smith (Jamaica).

Central American Bank for Economic Integration (CABEI)

Established in 1960, the Bank is the financial institution created by the Central American Economic Integration Treaty and aims to implement the economic integration and balanced economic growth of the member states.

Regional members Belize, Costa Rica, Dominican Republic, El Salvador, Guatemala, Honduras, Nicaragua, Panama..

Non-regional members Argentina, Colombia, Mexico, Taiwan, Spain, Cuba.

Official languages: Spanish and English.
Headquarters: Apartado Postal 772, Tegucigalpa, DC, Honduras.
Website: http://www.bcie.org
President: Dante Mossi (Honduras).

Central American Integration System (SICA)

The Central American Integration System (SICA) was established in Dec. 1991 and became operational in Feb. 1993. SICA is the successor body to the Organization of Central American States, which was suspended in 1973 after a war between El Salvador and Honduras (which were both member countries). It aims to achieve political, economic, social, cultural and ecological integration in Central America and transform the area into a region of peace, liberty, democracy and development.

Members Belize, Costa Rica, Dominican Republic, El Salvador, Guatemala, Honduras, Nicaragua and Panama.

Activities The Framework Treaty on Democratic Security in Central America, signed in 1995, seeks to achieve a proper 'balance of forces' in the region, intensify the fight against trafficking of drugs and arms, and reintegrate refugees and displaced persons.

Headquarters: Final Bulevar Cancillería, Distrito El Espino, Ciudad Merliot, Antiguo Cuscatlán, La Libertad, El Salvador.
Website: http://www.sica.int
Email: info.sgsica@sica.int
Secretary-General: Vinicio Cerezo Arévalo (Guatemala).

Eastern Caribbean Central Bank (ECCB)

The Eastern Caribbean Central Bank was established in 1983, replacing the East Caribbean Currency Authority (ECCA). Its purpose is to regulate the availability of money and credit; to promote and maintain monetary stability; to promote credit and exchange conditions and a sound financial structure conducive to the balanced growth and development of the economies of the territories of the participating governments; and to actively promote, through means consistent with its other objectives, the economic development of the territories of the participating governments.

Members Anguilla, Antigua and Barbuda, Dominica, Grenada, Montserrat, St Kitts and Nevis, St Lucia, St Vincent and the Grenadines.

Official language: English.
Headquarters: PO Box 89, Bird Rock, Basseterre, St Kitts and Nevis.

Website: http://www.eccb-centralbank.org
Email: info@eccb-centralbank.org
Governor: Timothy Antoine (Grenada).

Inter-American Development Bank (IDB)

The IDB, the oldest and largest regional multilateral development institution, was established in 1959 to help accelerate economic and social development in Latin America and the Caribbean. The Bank's original membership included 19 Latin American and Caribbean countries and the USA. Today, membership totals 48 nations, including non-regional members.

Members Argentina, Austria, The Bahamas, Barbados, Belgium, Belize, Bolivia, Brazil, Canada, Chile, China, Colombia, Costa Rica, Croatia, Denmark, Dominican Republic, Ecuador, El Salvador, Finland, France, Germany, Guatemala, Guyana, Haiti, Honduras, Israel, Italy, Jamaica, Japan, South Korea, Mexico, the Netherlands, Nicaragua, Norway, Panama, Paraguay, Peru, Portugal, Slovenia, Spain, Suriname, Sweden, Switzerland, Trinidad and Tobago, UK, USA, Uruguay, Venezuela.

Activities The Bank's total lending up to 2017 was US$272bn. for projects with a total cost of over US$552bn. Its lending in 2017 amounted US$11·4bn.

Current lending priorities include poverty reduction and social equity, modernization and integration, and the environment. The Bank has a Fund for Special Operations for lending on concessional terms for projects in countries classified as economically less developed. An additional facility, the Multilateral Investment Fund (MIF), was created in 1992 to help promote and accelerate investment reforms and private-sector development throughout the region.

The Board of Governors is the Bank's highest authority. Governors are usually Ministers of Finance, Presidents of Central Banks or officers of comparable rank. The IDB has country offices in each of its borrowing countries, and in Paris and Tokyo.

Official languages: English, French, Portuguese and Spanish.
Headquarters: 1300 New York Ave., NW, Washington, D.C., 20577, USA.
Website: http://www.iadb.org
President: Luis Alberto Moreno (Colombia).

Latin American Economic System (SELA)

Established in 1975 by the Panama Convention, SELA (Sistema Económico Latinoamericano) promotes co-ordination on economic issues and social development among the countries of Latin America and the Caribbean.

Members Argentine, The Bahamas, Barbados, Belize, Bolivia, Brazil, Chile, Colombia, Cuba, Dominican Republic, Ecuador, El Salvador, Guatemala, Guyana, Haiti, Honduras, Jamaica, Mexico, Nicaragua, Panama, Paraguay, Peru, Suriname, Trinidad and Tobago, Uruguay, Venezuela.

Official languages: English, French, Portuguese and Spanish.
Headquarters: Torre Europa, Pisos 4 y 5, Avenida Francisco de Miranda, Urb. Campo Alegre, Caracas 1060, Venezuela.
Website: http://www.sela.org
Permanent Secretary: Javier Paulinich Velarde (Peru).

Latin American Integration Association (ALADI/LAIA)

The ALADI was established to promote freer trade among member countries in the region.

Members (13) Argentina, Bolivia, Brazil, Chile, Colombia, Cuba, Ecuador, Mexico, Panama, Paraguay, Peru, Uruguay and Venezuela.

Observers (28) Andean Development Corporation (CAF), China, Costa Rica, Dominican Republic, El Salvador, European Commission, Guatemala, Honduras, Ibero-American General Secretariat (SEGIB), Inter-American Development Bank, Inter-American Institute for Cooperation on Agriculture (IICA), Italy, Japan, South Korea, Latin American Economic System (SELA), Nicaragua, Organization of American States (OAS), Pan American Health Organization/World Health Organization (PAHO/WHO), Pakistan, Portugal, Romania, Russia, San Marino, Spain, Switzerland, Ukraine, UN Development Programme, UN Economic Commission for Latin America and the Caribbean (ECLAC).

Official languages: Portuguese and Spanish.
Headquarters: Calle Cebollatí 1461, Barrio Palermo, Casilla de Correos 20005, 11200 Montevideo, Uruguay.
Website: http://www.aladi.org
Email: sgaladi@aladi.org
Secretary-General: Alejandro de la Peña (Mexico).

Latin American Reserve Fund

Established in 1991 as successor to the Andean Reserve Fund, the Latin American Reserve Fund assists in correcting payment imbalances through loans with terms of up to four years and guarantees extended to members, to co-ordinate their monetary, exchange and financial policies and to promote the liberalization of trade and payments in the Andean sub-region.

Members Bolivia, Colombia, Costa Rica, Ecuador, Paraguay, Peru, Uruguay, Venezuela.

Official language: Spanish.
Headquarters: Avenida 82, N° 12-18, piso 7, Box 241523, Bogotá, DC, Colombia.
Website: http://www.flar.net
Email: flar@flar.net
Executive President: José Darío Uribe (Colombia).

Organisation of Eastern Caribbean States (OECS)

Founded in 1981 when seven eastern Caribbean states signed the Treaty of Basseterre agreeing to co-operate with each other to promote unity and solidarity among the members.

Members Antigua and Barbuda, Dominica, Grenada, Montserrat, St Kitts and Nevis, St Lucia, St Vincent and the Grenadines. Anguilla, the British Virgin Islands and Martinique have associate membership.

Functions As set out in the Treaty of Basseterre: to promote co-operation among the member states and to defend their sovereignty and independence; to assist member states in the realization of their obligations and responsibilities to the international community with due regard to the role of international law as a standard of conduct in their relationships; to assist member states in the realization of their obligations and responsibilities to the international community with due regard to the role of international issues; to establish and maintain, where possible, arrangements for joint overseas representation and common services; to pursue these through its respective institutions by discussion of questions of common concern and by agreement on common action.

The Authority is the highest decision-making body of the OECS, comprising the heads of government of the member countries. The OECS is administered by a Central Secretariat (based in Castries, St Lucia), headed by a director general who is responsible to the Authority. The Secretariat is divided into four principal divisions: the division of the office of the director general; social and sustainable development division; corporate services division; and economic affairs division.

In June 2010 a Revised Treaty of Basseterre was signed. It came into effect in Jan. 2011, establishing the OECS Economic Union. Under its terms, member states agreed to the removal of trade barriers, the free movement of labour and capital, the establishment of a regional assembly of parliamentarians and the implementation of a common external tariff. Membership of the Economic Union initially comprised Antigua and Barbuda, Dominica, Grenada, St Kitts and Nevis, St Lucia, and St Vincent and the Grenadines.

Official language: English.
Headquarters: Morne Fortune, PO Box 179, Castries, St Lucia.
Website: http://www.oecs.org
Director-General: Dr Didacus Jules (St Lucia).

Organization of American States (OAS)

Origin On 14 April 1890 representatives of the American republics, meeting in Washington at the First International Conference of American States, established an International Union of American Republics and, as its central office, a Commercial Bureau of American Republics, which later became the Pan-American Union. This international organization's object was to foster mutual understanding and co-operation among the nations of the western hemisphere. This led to the adoption on 30 April 1948 by the Ninth International Conference of American States, at Bogotá, Colombia, of the Charter of the Organization of American States. This co-ordinated the work of all the former independent official entities in the inter-American system and defined their mutual relationships. The Charter of 1948 was subsequently amended by the Protocol of Buenos Aires (1967) and the Protocol of Cartagena de Indias (1985).

Members Antigua and Barbuda, Argentina, The Bahamas, Barbados, Belize, Bolivia, Brazil, Canada, Chile, Colombia, Costa Rica, Cuba (suspended 1962*), Dominica, Dominican Republic, Ecuador, El Salvador, Grenada, Guatemala, Guyana, Haiti, Honduras, Jamaica, Mexico, Nicaragua, Panama, Paraguay, Peru, St Kitts and Nevis, St Lucia, St Vincent and the Grenadines, Suriname, Trinidad and Tobago, USA, Uruguay, Venezuela. *In June 2009 the OAS voted to lift Cuba's suspension, although *Cuba* had stated that it did *not wish to rejoin* the organization.

Permanent Observers Albania, Algeria, Angola, Armenia, Austria, Azerbaijan, Belgium, Benin, Bosnia and Herzegovina, Bulgaria, China, Croatia, Cyprus, Czech Republic, Denmark, Egypt, Equatorial Guinea, Estonia, EU, Finland, France, Georgia, Germany, Ghana, Greece, Holy See, Hungary, Iceland, India, Ireland, Israel, Italy, Japan, Kazakhstan, South Korea, Latvia, Lebanon, Liechtenstein, Lithuania, Luxembourg, Malta, Monaco, Montenegro, Morocco, the Netherlands, Nigeria, North Macedonia, Norway, Pakistan, Philippines, Poland, Portugal, Qatar, Romania, Russia, Saudi Arabia, Serbia, Slovakia, Slovenia, Spain, Sri Lanka, Sweden, Switzerland, Thailand, Tunisia, Turkey, Ukraine, UK, Vanuatu, Yemen.

Aims and Activities To strengthen the peace and security of the continent; promote and consolidate representative democracy; promote by co-operative action economic, social and cultural development; and achieve an effective limitation of conventional weapons.

In Sept. 2001 an Inter-American Democratic Charter was adopted, declaring: 'The peoples of the Americas have a right to democracy and their governments have an obligation to promote and defend it.' The Charter compels the OAS to take action against any member state that disrupts its own democratic institutions.

Organization Under its Charter the OAS accomplishes its purposes by means of:

(a) The General Assembly, which meets annually. The Secretary-General is elected by the General Assembly for five-year terms. The General Assembly approves the annual budget which is financed by quotas contributed by the member governments. The proposed budget for 2018 amounted to US$81·6m.

(b) The Meeting of Consultation of Ministers of Foreign Affairs, held to consider problems of an urgent nature and of common interest.

(c) The Councils: The Permanent Council, which meets on a permanent basis at OAS headquarters and carries out decisions of the General Assembly, assists the member states in the peaceful settlement of disputes, acts as the Preparatory Committee of that Assembly, submits recommendations with regard to the functioning of the Organization, and considers the reports to the Assembly of the other organs. The Inter-American Council for Integral Development (CIDI) directs and monitors OAS technical co-operation programmes.

(d) The Inter-American Juridical Committee which acts as an advisory body to the OAS on juridical matters and promotes the development and codification of international law. 11 jurists, elected for four-year terms by the General Assembly, represent all the American States.

(e) The Inter-American Commission on Human Rights which oversees the observance and protection of human rights. Seven members elected for four-year terms by the General Assembly represent all the OAS member states.

(f) The General Secretariat, which is the central and permanent organ of the OAS.

(g) The Specialized Conferences, meeting to deal with special technical matters or to develop specific aspects of inter-American co-operation.

(h) The Specialized Organizations, intergovernmental organizations established by multilateral agreements to discharge specific functions in their respective fields of action, such as women's affairs, agriculture, child welfare, Indian affairs, geography and history, and health.

Headquarters: 17th St. and Constitution Ave., NW, Washington, D.C., 20006-4499, USA.
Website: http://www.oas.org
Secretary-General: Luis Almagro (Uruguay).

Pacific Alliance

Origin and Aims The Pacific Alliance was founded in June 2012 through the Pacific Alliance Framework Agreement. The group had informally come together with the signing of the Lima Declaration a year earlier.

Its principal aims are to encourage free trade and economic integration between member states, facilitate freedom of movement and pursue multilateral ties with other regions. A number of jointly-run embassies and consulates have been opened.

Organization The Alliance holds regular summits attended by heads of member states. This is the leading decision-making body. There is also a Council of Ministers, comprising ministers of foreign affairs and foreign trade, as well as a High-Level Group made up of their deputy ministers.

Membership In Jan. 2019 there were four members: Chile, Colombia, Mexico and Peru. Costa Rica and Panama were in the process of joining as of Jan. 2019. Countries with observer status in Jan. 2019 were: Argentina, Australia, Austria, Belarus, Belgium, Canada, China, Croatia, Czech Republic, Denmark, Dominican Republic, Ecuador, Egypt, El Salvador, Finland, France, Georgia, Germany, Greece, Guatemala, Haiti, Honduras, Hungary, India, Indonesia, Israel, Italy, Japan, South Korea, Lithuania, Morocco, Netherlands, New Zealand, Norway, Paraguay, Poland, Portugal, Romania, Serbia, Singapore, Slovakia, Slovenia, Spain, Sweden, Switzerland, Thailand, Trinidad and Tobago, Turkey, UAE, Ukraine, UK, USA, Uruguay.

Website: http://alianzapacifico.net
Email: comunicaciones@alianzapacifico.net
President pro tempore: Ollanta Humala Tasso (Peru).

Secretariat for Central American Economic Integration (SIECA)

SIECA (Secretaría de Integración Económica Centroamericana) was created by the General Treaty on Central American Economic Integration in Dec. 1960. The General Treaty incorporates the Agreement on the Regime for Central American Integration Industries. In Oct. 1993 the Protocol to the General Treaty on Central Economic Integration, known as the Guatemala Protocol, was signed.

Members Costa Rica, El Salvador, Guatemala, Honduras, Nicaragua, Panama.

Official language: Spanish.
Headquarters: 4a Avenida 10–25, Zona 14, Ciudad de Guatemala, Guatemala.
Website: http://www.sieca.int
Email: info@sieca.int
Secretary-General: Melvin Enrique Redondo (Honduras).

Southern Common Market (MERCOSUR)

Founded in March 1991 by the Treaty of Asunción between Argentina, Brazil, Paraguay and Uruguay, MERCOSUR committed the signatories to the progressive reduction of tariffs culminating in the formation of a common market on 1 Jan. 1995. This duly came into effect as a free trade zone affecting 90% of commodities. A common external tariff averaging 14% applies to 80% of trade with countries outside MERCOSUR. Details were agreed at foreign minister level by the Protocol of Ouro Preto signed on 17 Dec. 1994.

In 1996 Chile negotiated a free trade agreement with MERCOSUR which came into effect on 1 Oct. Subsequently Bolivia, Chile, Colombia, Ecuador, Guyana, Peru and Suriname have all been granted associate member status. Bolivia began the accession process to full membership in 2012. Mexico and New Zealand have observer status. Venezuela, which had associate membership between 2004 and 2006, became the fifth member of MERCOSUR in

July 2006, although it was not going to have full voting rights until all the other full members had ratified its entry into the organization. Paraguay was the only country still to approve Venezuela's full membership, but it was suspended from MERCOSUR in June 2012 following the impeachment of its president, Fernando Lugo. With Paraguay suspended, Venezuela was then formally admitted in July 2012. Paraguay was readmitted in Aug. 2013 after the swearing-in ceremony of its new democratically-elected president, Horacio Cartes. Venezuela was temporarily suspended in Dec. 2016 for failing to meet membership requirements and indefinitely suspended in Aug. 2017.

Organization   The member states' foreign ministers form a Council responsible for leading the integration process, the chairmanship of which rotates every six months. The permanent executive body is the Common Market Group of member states, which takes decisions by consensus. There is a Trade Commission and Joint Parliamentary Commission, an arbitration tribunal whose decisions are binding on member countries, and a Secretariat in Montevideo.

Further to the treaty signed by 12 South American countries in May 2008, it is anticipated that MERCOSUR will gradually be integrated into the Union of South American Nations.

Headquarters: Dr Luis Piera 1992, Piso 1, 11200 Montevideo, Uruguay.
Website (Spanish and Portuguese only): http://www.mercosur.int
President pro tempore: Mauricio Macri (Argentina).

Union of South American Nations (UNASUR)

History   Established in May 2008 in Brazil, it is anticipated that the Union of South American Nations will eventually supersede MERCOSUR and the Andean Community, creating an enlarged customs union with a single market, parliament, Secretariat and central bank, based on the European Union structure. UNASUR is the successor body to the now defunct South American Community of Nations (CSN/SACN), founded in 2004. Despite initial problems, progress was made at UNASUR's fourth Summit in Nov. 2010 culminating in the 'Georgetown Declaration', with the attending heads of state and government and foreign ministers highlighting their commitment to working together to achieve a better South America. The Treaty establishing UNASUR became effective on 11 March 2011.

Organization   There is a permanent Secretariat based in Quito, Ecuador. A proposed South American parliament is planned for Cochabamba, Bolivia. The heads of state of member nations meet annually.

Members   Argentina, Bolivia, Brazil, Chile, Colombia, Ecuador, Guyana, Paraguay (suspended following the impeachment of President Fernando Lugo in June 2012 but then readmitted in Aug. 2013 following the swearing-in of Horacio Cartes as its new democratically-elected president), Peru, Suriname, Uruguay, Venezuela.

Official languages: Portuguese, Spanish, Dutch and English.
Headquarters: Av. Manuel Córdova Galarza, Mitad del Mundo, 170311 Quito, Ecuador.
Website: http://www.unasursg.org
Email: secretaria.general@unasursg.org
Secretary-General: Vacant.

Further Reading

Caribbean Community (CARICOM)

Payne, Anthony, *The Political History of CARICOM.* 2007

Asian Development Bank

A multilateral development finance institution established in 1966 to promote economic and social progress in the Asian and Pacific region, the Bank's strategic objectives are to foster economic growth, reduce poverty, improve the status of women, support human development (including population planning) and protect the environment.

The bank's capital stock is owned by 67 member countries, 48 regional and 19 non-regional. The bank makes loans and equity investments, and provides technical assistance grants for the preparation and execution of development projects and programmes; promotes investment of public and private capital for development purposes; and assists in co-ordinating development policies and plans in its developing member countries (DMCs).

The bank gives special attention to the needs of smaller or less developed countries, giving priority to projects that contribute to the economic growth of the region and promote regional co-operation. Loans from ordinary capital resources on non-concessional terms account for about 80% of cumulative lending. Loans from the bank's principal special fund, the Asian Development Fund, are made on highly concessional terms almost exclusively to the poorest borrowing countries.

Regional members Afghanistan, Armenia, Australia, Azerbaijan, Bangladesh, Bhutan, Brunei, Cambodia, China, Cook Islands, Fiji, Georgia, Hong Kong, India, Indonesia, Japan, Kazakhstan, Kiribati, South Korea, Kyrgyzstan, Laos, Malaysia, Maldives, Marshall Islands, Micronesia, Mongolia, Myanmar, Nauru, Nepal, New Zealand, Pakistan, Palau, Papua New Guinea, Philippines, Samoa, Singapore, Solomon Islands, Sri Lanka, Taiwan, Tajikistan, Thailand, Timor-Leste, Tonga, Turkmenistan, Tuvalu, Uzbekistan, Vanuatu and Vietnam.

Non-regional members Austria, Belgium, Canada, Denmark, Finland, France, Germany, Ireland, Italy, Luxembourg, Netherlands, Norway, Portugal, Spain, Sweden, Switzerland, Turkey, UK, USA.

Organization The bank's highest policy-making body is its Board of Governors, which meets annually. Its executive body is the 12-member Board of Directors (each with an alternate), eight from the regional members and four non-regional. The ADB has resident missions in a number of countries. There are also three representative offices: in Tokyo, Frankfurt and Washington, D.C.

Official language: English.
Headquarters: 6 ADB Avenue, Mandaluyong City 1550, Metro Manila, Philippines.
Website: https://www.adb.org
President: Takehiko Nakao (Japan).

Asian Infrastructure Investment Bank (AIIB)

The Chinese government announced proposals for the establishment of the Asian Infrastructure Investment Bank in Oct. 2013. Articles of agreement, which form the bank's legal basis, were adopted in May 2015 and the institution was formally launched in Dec. that year, with an initial capitalization of US$100bn.

Aims and Activities The bank aims to provide financial backing for infrastructure development projects in Asia and to promote regional co-operation to address development challenges. It approved its first four projects within six months of launching, of which three were joint ventures with existing institutions (the single solo project being a scheme to electrify 2·5m. rural homes in Bangladesh). At its inaugural annual meeting in June 2016 the bank signed off projects worth in excess of US$500m.

Organization The senior decision-making body is the Board of Governors, comprising one governor from each member state. A Board of Directors, made up of 12 Governors, oversees the day-to-day running of the organization. There is also a Secretariat, headed by the Secretary-General.

Members On 25 Dec. 2015 the AIIB came into force when ratification passed the statutory requirement of at least ten countries holding over 50% of initial capital stock subscriptions. As of Jan. 2019 there were 44 regional members and 26 non-regional members.

Official languages: Chinese, English and French.
Headquarters: B-9 Financial St., Xicheng District, Beijing 100-33, China.
Website: http://www.aiib.org
Email: information@aiib.org
President: Liqun Jin (China).

Asia-Pacific Economic Co-operation (APEC)

Origin and Aims APEC was established in 1989 to take advantage of the interdependence among Asia-Pacific economies, by facilitating economic growth for all participants and enhancing a sense of community in the region. Begun as an informal dialogue group, APEC is the premier forum for facilitating economic growth, co-operation, trade and investment in the Asia-Pacific region. APEC has a membership of 21 economic jurisdictions that together account for 40% of the world population, 43% of world trade and 55% of world GDP. APEC is working to achieve what are referred to as the 'Bogor Goals' of free and open trade and investment in the Asia-Pacific area.

Members Australia, Brunei, Canada, Chile, China, Hong Kong, Indonesia, Japan, South Korea, Malaysia, Mexico, New Zealand, Papua New Guinea, Peru, Philippines, Russia, Singapore, Taiwan, Thailand, USA and Vietnam.

Activities APEC works in three broad areas to meet the Bogor Goals. These three broad work areas, known as APEC's 'Three Pillars', are: Trade and Investment Liberalisation—reducing and eliminating tariff and non-tariff barriers to trade and investment, and opening markets; Business Facilitation—reducing the costs of business transactions, improving access to trade information and co-ordinating policy and business strategies to facilitate growth, and free and open trade; Economic and Technical Co-operation—assisting member economies build the necessary capacities to take advantage of global trade and the new economy. In 2018 Papua New Guinea hosted APEC meetings under the theme *'Harnessing Inclusive Opportunities, Embracing the Digital Future'*. The host for 2019 is Chile, using the theme *'Connecting People, Building the Future'*.

Official language: English.
Headquarters: 35 Heng Mui Keng Terrace, Singapore 119616.
Website: http://www.apec.org
Email: info@apec.org
Executive Director: Dr Rebecca Fatima Sta Maria (Singapore).

Association of South East Asian Nations (ASEAN)

History and Membership ASEAN is a regional intergovernmental organization formed by the governments of Indonesia, Malaysia, the Philippines, Singapore and Thailand through the Bangkok Declaration which was signed by their foreign ministers on 8 Aug. 1967. Brunei joined in 1984, Vietnam in 1995, Laos and Myanmar in 1997 and Cambodia in 1999. Papua New Guinea and Timor-Leste also have observer status. The ASEAN Charter, signed in Nov. 2007, established the group as a legal entity and created permanent representation for members at its Secretariat in Jakarta.

Objectives The main objectives are to accelerate economic growth, social progress and cultural development, to promote active collaboration and mutual assistance in matters of common interest, to ensure the political and economic stability of the South East Asian region, and to maintain close co-operation with existing international and regional organizations with similar aims.

© Springer Nature Limited 2020
Palgrave Macmillan (ed.), *The Statesman's Yearbook 2020*,
https://doi.org/10.1057/978-1-349-95940-2_6

Activities Principal projects concern economic co-operation and development, with the intensification of intra-ASEAN and global trade; joint research and technological programmes; co-operation in transportation and communications; promotion of tourism, South East Asian studies, cultural, scientific, educational and administrative exchanges. An *ASEAN Free Trade Area (AFTA)* agreement was signed in 1992. ASEAN member countries have in the meantime made significant progress in the lowering of intra-regional tariffs through the Common Effective Preferential Tariff (CEPT) Scheme for AFTA. The *ASEAN Charter* of 2007 established a schedule for the elimination of non-tariff barriers and other restrictions on trade. On 1 Jan. 2010 ASEAN signed a free trade agreement with China, creating the world's largest free trade area by population (encompassing 1·9bn. people) and the third largest by economic value.

Heads of government who met in Bangkok in Dec. 1995 established a South-East Asia Nuclear-Free Zone, which was extended to cover offshore economic exclusion zones. Individual signatories were to decide whether to allow port visits or transportation of nuclear weapons by foreign powers through territorial waters. The first formal meeting of the *ASEAN Regional Forum (ARF)* to discuss security issues in the region took place in July 1994 and was attended by the then six members (Brunei, Indonesia, Malaysia, Philippines, Singapore and Thailand). Also in attendance were ASEAN's dialogue partners (Australia, Canada, the EU, Japan, South Korea, New Zealand and the USA), consultative partners (China and Russia) and observers (Laos, Papua New Guinea and Vietnam). The *ARF* ministerial meeting now takes place on an annual basis.

ASEAN is committed to resolving the dispute over sovereignty of the Spratly Islands, a group of more than 100 small islands and reefs in the South China Sea. Some or all of the largely uninhabited islands have been claimed by Brunei, China, Malaysia, the Philippines, Taiwan and Vietnam. The disputed areas have oil and gas resources. The subject dominated the April 2013 ASEAN summit after tensions rose in 2012 as China pressed its claims, and did so once more at the 2014 summit (following clashes between Chinese and Vietnamese coastguard vessels in disputed waters) and again at the 2015 and 2016 summits. In 2017 ASEAN leaders expressed 'grave concern' at growing tensions prompted by North Korea's ongoing programme of nuclear weapons testing. The following year's summit was dominated by concerns regarding the growing tensions between China and the USA.

The *ASEAN Economic Community (AEC)* was established in Dec. 2015. Originally outlined in 1997, the AEC aims to produce a single market across all ASEAN member states.

Organization The highest authority is the meeting of Heads of Government, which takes place twice annually. The highest policy-making body is the annual Meeting of Foreign Ministers, commonly known as AMM, the ASEAN Ministerial Meeting, which convenes in each of the member countries on a rotational basis in alphabetical order. The AEM (ASEAN Economic Meeting) meets each year to direct ASEAN economic co-operation. The AEM and AMM report jointly to the heads of government at summit meetings. The central Secretariat in Jakarta is headed by the Secretary-General, a post that revolves among the member states in alphabetical order every five years.

Official language: English.
Headquarters: 70A Jl. Sisingamangaraja, Jakarta 12110, Indonesia.
Website: http://www.asean.org
Email: public@asean.org
Secretary-General: Dato Paduka Lim Jock Hoi (Brunei).

ASEAN-Mekong Basin Development Co-operation (Mekong Group)
The ministers and representatives of Brunei, Cambodia, China, Indonesia, Laos, Malaysia, Myanmar, Philippines, Singapore, Thailand and Vietnam met in Kuala Lumpur on 17 June 1996 and agreed the following objectives for the Group: to co-operate in the economic and social development of the Mekong Basin area and strengthen the link between it and ASEAN member countries, through a process of dialogue and common project identification.

Priorities include: development of infrastructure capacities in the fields of transport, telecommunications, irrigation and energy; development of trade and investment-generating activities; development of the agricultural sector to enhance production; sustainable development of forestry resources and development of mineral resources; development of the industrial sector, especially small to medium enterprises; development of tourism; human resource development and support for training; co-operation in the fields of science and technology.

Colombo Plan

History Founded in 1950 to promote the development of newly independent Asian member countries, the Colombo Plan has grown from a group of seven Commonwealth nations into an organization of 25 countries. Originally the Plan was conceived for a period of six years but the Consultative Committee gave the Plan an indefinite life span in 1980.

Members Afghanistan, Australia, Bangladesh, Bhutan, Brunei, Fiji, India, Indonesia, Iran, Japan, South Korea, Laos, Malaysia, Maldives, Mongolia, Myanmar, Nepal, New Zealand, Pakistan, Papua New Guinea, Philippines, Saudi Arabia, Singapore, Sri Lanka, Thailand, USA and Vietnam.

Aims The aims of the Colombo Plan are: (1) to provide a forum for discussion, at local level, of development needs; (2) to facilitate development assistance by encouraging members to participate as donors and recipients of technical co-operation; and (3) to execute programmes to advance development within member countries. The Plan currently has the following programmes: Programme for Public Administration (PPA); South-South Technical Co-operation Data Bank Programme (SSTC/DB); Drug Advisory Programme (DAP); Programme for Private Sector Development (PPSD); Colombo Plan Staff College for Technician Education (CPSC).

Structure The Consultative Committee is the principal policy-making body of the Colombo Plan. Consisting of all member countries, it meets every two years to review the economic and social progress of members, exchange views on technical co-operation programmes and review the Plan's activities. The Colombo Plan Council represents each member government and meets several times a year to identify development issues, recommend measures to be taken and ensure implementation.

Headquarters: 556 Bauddhaloka Mawatha, Colombo 8, Sri Lanka.
Website: http://www.colombo-plan.org
Secretary-General: Phan Kieu Thu (Vietnam).

Economic Co-operation Organization (ECO)

The Economic Co-operation Organization (ECO) is an intergovernmental regional organization established in 1985 by Iran, Pakistan and Turkey and the successor of the Regional Co-operation for Development (RCD). ECO was expanded in 1992 to include seven new members: Afghanistan, Azerbaijan, Kazakhstan, Kyrgyzstan, Tajikistan, Turkmenistan and Uzbekistan. The organization's objectives, stipulated in its Charter, the Treaty of İzmir, include the promotion of conditions for sustained economic growth in the region. Transport and communications, trade and investment, and energy are the high priority areas in ECO's scheme of work although industry, agriculture, health, science and education, drug control and human development are also on the agenda.

The Council of Ministers (COM) remains the highest policy and decision-making body of the organization, meeting at least once a year and chaired by rotation among the member states.

ECO Summits were instituted with the First Summit held in Tehran in 1992. A further 12 Summits have been held since then, most recently in Islamabad in March 2017.

The long-term perspectives and priorities of ECO are defined in the form of two Action Plans: the Quetta Plan of Action and the İstanbul Declaration and Economic Co-operation Strategy.

ECO enjoys observer status with the United Nations, World Trade Organization and the Organisation of Islamic Cooperation.

Headquarters: 1 Golbou Alley, Kamranieh St., 19519-33114, Tehran, Islamic Republic of Iran.
Website: http://www.eco.int
Email: registry@eco.int
Secretary-General: Hadi Soleimanpour (Iran).

Pacific Islands Forum (PIF)

In Oct. 2000 the South Pacific Forum changed its name to the Pacific Islands Forum. As the South Pacific Forum it held its first meeting of Heads of Government in New Zealand in 1971. The Agreement Establishing the Forum Secretariat defines the membership of the Forum and the Secretariat. Decisions are reached by consensus. The administrative arm of the Forum, known officially as the Pacific Islands Forum Secretariat, is based in Suva, Fiji. In Oct. 1994 the Forum was granted observer status to the UN.

Members Australia, Cook Islands, Fiji, French Polynesia, Kiribati, Marshall Islands, Micronesia, Nauru, New Caledonia, New Zealand, Niue, Palau, Papua New Guinea, Samoa, Solomon Islands, Tonga, Tuvalu and Vanuatu. *Associate Members.* Tokelau. *Observers.* The ACP Group, American Samoa, Asian Development Bank, the Commonwealth, Guam, the Commonwealth of the Northern Marianas, the United Nations, Wallis and Futuna, Western and Central Pacific Fisheries Commission, and the World Bank. *Special Observers.* International Organization for Migration, Timor-Leste.

Functions The Secretariat's mission is to provide policy options to the Pacific Islands Forum, and to promote Forum decisions and regional and international co-operation. The organization seeks to promote political stability and regional security; enhance the management of economies and the development process; improve trade and investment; and efficiently manage the resources of the Secretariat.

Activities The Secretariat has four core divisions: Trade and Investment; Political and International Affairs; Development and Economic Policy; Corporate Services. It provides policy advice to members on social, economic and political issues. Since 1989 the Forum has held Post Forum Dialogues with key dialogue partners at ministerial level. There are currently 18 partners: Canada, China, Cuba, EU, France, Germany, India, Indonesia, Italy, Japan, South Korea, Malaysia, Philippines, Spain, Thailand, Turkey, UK and USA.

Organization Established in 1972, the South Pacific Bureau for Economic Co-operation (SPEC) began as a trade bureau before being reorganized as the South Pacific Forum Secretariat in 1988. The Secretariat is headed by a Secretary-General and Deputy Secretary-General who form the Executive. The governing body is the Forum Officials Committee, which acts as an intermediary between the Secretariat and the Forum. The Secretariat operates four Trade Offices in Auckland, Beijing, Sydney and Tokyo.

The Secretary-General is the permanent Chair of the Council of Regional Organisations in the Pacific (CROP), which brings together nine main regional organizations in the Pacific region: Forum Fisheries Agency (FFA); Pacific Aviation Safety Office (PASO); Pacific Islands Development Programme (PIDP); Pacific Islands Forum Secretariat (PIFS); Pacific Power Association (PPA); Secretariat for the Pacific Community (SPC); Secretariat of the Pacific Regional Environment Programme (SPREP); South Pacific Tourism Organisation (SPTO); and University of the South Pacific (USP).

Official language: English.
Headquarters: Ratu Sukuna Rd, Suva, Fiji.
Website: http://www.forumsec.org
Email: info@forumsec.org
Secretary-General: Dame Meg Taylor (Papua New Guinea).

Secretariat of the Pacific Community (SPC)

Until Feb. 1998 known as the South Pacific Commission, this is a regional intergovernmental organization founded in 1947 under an agreement commonly referred to as the Canberra Agreement. It is funded by assessed contributions from its 26 members and by voluntary contributions from member and non-member countries, international organizations and other sources.

Members American Samoa, Australia, Cook Islands, Fiji, France, French Polynesia, Guam, Kiribati, Marshall Islands, Federated States of Micronesia, Nauru, New Caledonia, New Zealand, Niue, Northern Mariana Islands, Palau, Papua New Guinea, Pitcairn Islands, Samoa, Solomon Islands, Tokelau, Tonga, Tuvalu, USA, Vanuatu, and Wallis and Futuna.

Functions The SPC has three main areas of work: land resources, marine resources and social resources. It conducts research and provides technical assistance and training in these areas to member Pacific Island countries and territories of the Pacific.

Organization The Conference of the Pacific Community is the governing body of the Community. Its key focus is to appoint the Director-General, to consider major national or regional policy issues and to note changes to the Financial and Staff Regulations approved by the CRGA, the Committee of Representatives of Governments and Administrations. It meets every two years. The CRGA meets once a year and is the principal decision-making organ of the Community. There are also regional offices in Fiji and Micronesia.

Headquarters: 95 Promenade Roger Laroque, BP D5, 98848 Nouméa Cedex, New Caledonia.
Website: http://www.spc.int
Email: spc@spc.int
Director-General: Dr Colin Tukuitonga (New Zealand).

Shanghai Cooperation Organisation (SCO)

Origin and Aims The Shanghai Cooperation Organisation was founded in June 2001, having evolved out of the Shanghai Five grouping formed in 1996. All member states come from the Eurasia region.

Its principal aims are to promote closer defence, economic and cultural co-operation between member states and to 'strengthen mutual confidence and good neighbourly relations'.

Organization The SCO's highest decision-making organ is the Heads of State Council, which meets once a year, as does a Heads of Government Council. There are also regular meetings of member states' foreign ministers and other government officials. In addition, there are two permanent bodies—a Secretariat based in Beijing, China and a Regional Counter-Terrorism Structure in Tashkent, Uzbekistan. The SCO has observer status at the UN General Assembly.

Membership As of Jan. 2019 there were eight permanent members: China, India, Kazakhstan, Kyrgyzstan, Pakistan, Russia, Tajikistan and Uzbekistan. There are also four observer states (Afghanistan, Belarus, Iran and Mongolia) and six dialogue partners (Armenia, Azerbaijan, Cambodia, Nepal, Sri Lanka and Turkey). The SCO now comprises member states accounting for over 40% of the world's population.

Headquarters: 7 Ritan Rd, Chaoyang District, Beijing 100600, China.
Website: http://eng.sectsco.org
Email: sco@sectsco.org
Secretary-General: Vladimir Norov (Uzbekistan).

South Asian Association for Regional Co-operation (SAARC)

SAARC was established to accelerate the process of economic and social development in member states. The foreign ministers of the seven member countries met for the first time in New Delhi in Aug. 1983 and adopted the Declaration on South Asian Regional Co-operation whereby an Integrated Programme of Action (IPA) was launched. The charter establishing SAARC was adopted at the first summit meeting in Dhaka in Dec. 1985.

Members Afghanistan, Bangladesh, Bhutan, India, Maldives, Nepal, Pakistan, Sri Lanka. *Observers.* Australia, China, EU, Iran, Japan, South Korea, Mauritius, Myanmar, USA.

Objectives To promote the welfare of the peoples of South Asia; to accelerate economic growth, social progress and cultural development; to promote and strengthen collective self-reliance among members; to promote active collaboration and mutual assistance in the economic, social, cultural, technical and scientific fields; to strengthen co-operation with other developing countries and among themselves. Agreed areas of co-operation under the *Integrated Programme of Action (IPA)* include agriculture and rural development; human resource development; environment, meteorology and forestry; science and technology; transport and communications; energy; and social development.

A SAARC Preferential Trading Arrangement (SAPTA) designed to reduce trade tariffs between SAARC member states was signed in April 1993, entering into force in Dec. 1995. In 1998 at the Tenth Summit in Colombo, the importance of achieving a South Asian Free Trade Area (SAFTA) as mandated by the Malé Summit in 1997 was reiterated and it was decided to set up a Committee of Experts to work on drafting a comprehensive treaty regime for creating a free trade area. The Colombo Summit agreed that the text of this regulatory framework would be finalized by 2001.

Organization The highest authority of the Association rests with the heads of state or government, who meet annually at Summit level. The Council of Foreign Ministers, which meets twice a year, formulates policy, reviews progress and decides on new areas of co-operation. The Council is supported by a Standing Committee of Foreign Secretaries, by the Programming Committee and by 11 Technical Committees which are responsible for individual areas of SAARC's activities. There is a Secretariat in Kathmandu, headed by a Secretary-General, who is assisted in his work by seven Directors, appointed by the Secretary-General upon nomination by member states for a period of three years which may in special circumstances be extended.

Official language: English.
Headquarters: PO Box 4222, Tridevi Sadak, Kathmandu, Nepal.
Website: http://www.saarc-sec.org
Email: saarc@saarc-sec.org
Secretary-General: Amjad Hussain B. *Sial* (Pakistan).

Further Reading

Association of South East Asian Nations (ASEAN)

Ba, Alice D. and Beeson, Mark, *Contemporary Southeast Asia.* 3rd ed. 2017.

Beeson, Mark, *Regionalism & Globalization in East Asia: Politics, Security & Economic Development.* 2nd ed. 2014.—*Institutions of the Asia-Pacific: ASEAN, APEC and Beyond.* 2008

Hayton, Bill, *The South China Sea: The Struggle for Power in Asia.* 2014

Huang, Jing and Billo, Andrew, (eds.) *Territorial Disputes in the South China Sea.* 2014

Huang, Xiaoming and Young, Jason, *Politics in Pacific Asia: An Introduction.* 2016

Jarvis, Darryl S. L. and Welch, Anthony, (eds.) *ASEAN Industries and the Challenge from China.* 2011

Jones, Lee, *ASEAN, Sovereignty and Intervention in Southeast Asia.* 2011

Kaplan, Robert D., *Asia's Cauldron: The South China Sea and the End of a Stable Pacific.* 2014

Lee, Yoong Yoong, *ASEAN Matters! Reflecting on the Association of Southeast Asian Nations.* 2011

Pennisi di Floristella, Angela, *The ASEAN Regional Security Partnership.* 2015

Arab Fund for Economic and Social Development (AFESD)

Established in 1968, the Fund commenced operations in 1974.

Functions AFESD is an Arab regional financial institution that assists the economic and social development of Arab countries through: financing development projects, with preference given to overall Arab development and to joint Arab projects; encouraging the investment of private and public funds in Arab projects; and providing technical assistance services for Arab economic and social development.

Members Algeria, Bahrain, Djibouti, Egypt, Iraq, Jordan, Kuwait, Lebanon, Libya, Mauritania, Morocco, Oman, Palestine, Qatar, Saudi Arabia, Somalia, Sudan, Syria, Tunisia, United Arab Emirates, Yemen.

Headquarters: PO Box 21923, Safat 13080, Kuwait.
Website: http://www.arabfund.org
Email: HQ@arabfund.org
Director General and Chairman of the Board of Directors: Abdulatif Y. al-Hamad (Kuwait).

Arab Monetary Fund (AMF)

Origin The Agreement establishing the Arab Monetary Fund was approved by the Economic Council of the League of Arab States in April 1976 and the first meeting of the Board of Governors was held on 19 April 1977.

Aims To assist member countries in eliminating payments and trade restrictions, in achieving exchange rate stability, in developing capital markets and in correcting payments imbalances through the extension of short- and medium-term loans; the co-ordination of monetary policies of member countries; and the liberalization and promotion of trade and payments, as well as the encouragement of capital flows among member countries.

Members Algeria, Bahrain, Comoros, Djibouti, Egypt, Iraq, Jordan, Kuwait, Lebanon, Libya, Mauritania, Morocco, Oman, Palestine, Qatar, Saudi Arabia, Somalia, Sudan, Syria, Tunisia, United Arab Emirates, Republic of Yemen.

Headquarters: PO Box 2818, Abu Dhabi, United Arab Emirates.
Website: http://www.amf.org.ae
Director General and Chairman of the Board of Directors: Dr Abdulrahman Bin Abdullah Al-Humaidi (Saudi Arabia).

Arab Organization for Agricultural Development (AOAD)

The AOAD was established in 1970 and commenced operations in 1972. Its aims are to develop natural and human resources in the agricultural sector and improve the means and methods of exploiting these resources on scientific bases; to increase agricultural productive efficiency and achieve agricultural integration between the Arab States and countries; to increase agricultural production with a view to achieving a higher degree of self-sufficiency; to facilitate the exchange of agricultural products between the Arab States and countries; to enhance the establishment of agricultural ventures and industries; and to increase the standards of living of the labour force engaged in the agricultural sector.

Organization The structure comprises a General Assembly consisting of ministers of agriculture of the member states, an Executive Council, a Secretariat General, seven technical departments—Food Security, Human Resources Development, Water Resources, Studies and Research, Projects Execution, Technical Scientific Co-operation, and Financial Administrative Department—and two centres—the Arab Center for Agricultural Information and Documentation, and the Arab Bureau for Consultation and Implementation of Agricultural Projects.

Members Algeria, Bahrain, Comoros, Djibouti, Egypt, Iraq, Jordan, Kuwait, Lebanon, Libya, Mauritania, Morocco, Oman, Palestine, Qatar, Saudi Arabia, Somalia, Sudan, Syria*, Tunisia, United Arab Emirates, Republic of Yemen. *Membership suspended since Nov. 2011.

Official languages: Arabic (English and French used in translated documents and correspondence).
Headquarters: 7 Amarat Street, Box 474, Al-Amarat, Khartoum, Sudan.
Website: http://www.aoad.org
Email: info@aoad.org
Director General: Ibrahim Adam Ahmed Al-Dikhiri (Sudan).

Gulf Co-operation Council (GCC)

Origin Also referred to as the Co-operation Council for the Arab States of the Gulf (CCASG), the Council was established on 25 May 1981 on signature of the Charter by Bahrain, Kuwait, Oman, Qatar, Saudi Arabia and the United Arab Emirates.

Aims To assure security and stability of the region through economic and political co-operation; promote, expand and enhance economic ties on solid foundations, in the best interests of the people; co-ordinate and unify economic, financial and monetary policies, as well as commercial and industrial legislation and customs regulations; achieve self-sufficiency in basic foodstuffs.

Organization The Supreme Council formed by the heads of member states is the highest authority. Its presidency rotates, based on the alphabetical order of the names of the member states. It holds one regular annual session in addition to a mid-year consultation session. Attached to the Supreme Council are the Commission for the Settlement of Disputes and the Consultative Commission. The Ministerial Council is formed of the Foreign Ministers of the member states or other delegated ministers and meets quarterly. The Secretariat consists of the following sectors: Political Affairs, Military Affairs, Legal Affairs, Human and Environment Affairs, Information Centre, Media Department, Gulf Standardization Organization (GSO), GCC Patent Office, Secretary-General's Office, GCC Delegation in Brussels, Technical Telecommunications Bureau in Bahrain. In Jan. 2003 it launched a customs union, introducing a 5% duty on foreign imports across the trade bloc.

Finance The annual budget of the GCC Secretariat is shared equally by the six member states.

Headquarters: PO Box 7153, Riyadh-11462, Saudi Arabia.
Website (Arabic only): http://www.gcc-sg.org
Secretary-General: Abdul Latif bin Rashid al-Zayani (Bahrain).

League of Arab States

Origin The League of Arab States (often referred to as the Arab League) is a voluntary association of sovereign Arab states, established by a Pact signed in Cairo on 22 March 1945 by the representatives of Egypt, Iraq, Saudi Arabia, Syria, Lebanon, Jordan and Yemen. It seeks to promote closer ties among member states and to co-ordinate their economic, cultural and security policies with a view to developing collective co-operation, protecting national security and maintaining the independence and sovereignty of member states, in order to enhance the potential for joint Arab action across all fields.

Members Algeria, Bahrain, Comoros, Djibouti, Egypt, Iraq, Jordan, Kuwait, Lebanon, Libya, Mauritania, Morocco, Oman, Palestine, Qatar, Saudi Arabia, Somalia, Sudan, Syria*, Tunisia, United Arab Emirates and Republic of Yemen. *Observers.* Brazil, Eritrea, India and Venezuela. *Membership suspended since Nov. 2011 after calls for the government to end violence against civilian protesters by a set date were ignored.

Palgrave Macmillan (ed.), *The Statesman's Yearbook 2020*,
https://doi.org/10.1057/978-1-349-95940-2_7

Aims and Activities In the political field, the League is entrusted with defending the supreme interests and national causes of the Arab world through the implementation of joint action plans at regional and international levels. It examines any disputes that may arise between member states with a view to finding a peaceful resolution. The Joint Defence and Economic Co-operation Treaty signed in 1950 provided for the establishment of a Joint Defence Council as well as an Economic Council (renamed the Economic and Social Council in 1977). Economic, social and cultural activities constitute principal and vital elements of the joint action initiative.

Against the backdrop of the 2011 Arab Spring, the League backed a UN resolution authorizing action in Libya against Col. Gaddafi's air defences and suspended Syria for its government's oppression of the opposition movement. At the 2012 Arab League summit, Syria's seat was granted in principle to the opposition, although it remained vacant as of Dec. 2016. In March 2014 Secretary-General Nabil al-Araby had stated that it would not be filled until the opposition had completed the formation of its institutions. In 2011 the League supported a Palestinian bid for UN recognition and in 2014 championed an unsuccessful move to push through a UN resolution calling for an Israeli–Palestinian peace deal within 12 months and the withdrawal of Israeli troops from the disputed territory by 2017. In Feb. 2017 the League accused Israel of 'stealing the land' of Palestinians following the passage of an Israeli law legalizing Jewish outposts in the occupied West Bank.

Arab Common Market An Arab Common Market came into operation on 1 Jan. 1965. Initial plans to abolish customs duties on agricultural products, natural resources and industrial products by incremental reductions never came to fruition although the concept remains an ambition shared by many people in the Arab world.

Organization The machinery of the League consists of a Council, 11 specialized ministerial committees entrusted with drawing up common policies for the regulation and advancement of co-operation in their fields (information, internal affairs, justice, housing, transport, social affairs, youth and sports, health, environment, telecommunications and electricity), and a permanent Secretariat.

The League is considered to be a regional organization within the framework of the United Nations at which its Secretary-General is an observer. It has permanent delegations in New York and Geneva for the UN and in Addis Ababa for the African Union, as well as offices in a number of cities throughout the world.

Headquarters: Tahrir Square, 11642 Cairo, Egypt.
Website (Arabic only): http://www.lasportal.org
Secretary-General: Ahmed Aboul Gheit (Egypt).

Organization of Arab Petroleum Exporting Countries (OAPEC)

Established in 1968 to promote co-operation and close ties between member states in economic activities related to the oil industry; to determine ways of safeguarding their legitimate interests, both individual and collective, in the oil industry; to unite their efforts so as to ensure the flow of oil to consumer markets on equitable and reasonable terms; and to create a favourable climate for the investment of capital and expertise in their petroleum industries.

Members Algeria, Bahrain, Egypt, Iraq, Kuwait, Libya, Qatar, Saudi Arabia, Syria, Tunisia*, United Arab Emirates. *Tunisia's membership was made inactive in 1986.

Headquarters: PO Box 20501, Safat 13066, Kuwait.
Website: http://www.oapecorg.org
Email: oapec@oapecorg.org
Secretary-General: Abbas Ali Naqi (Kuwait).

Organization of the Petroleum Exporting Countries (OPEC)

Origin and Aims Founded in Baghdad in 1960 by Iran, Iraq, Kuwait, Saudi Arabia and Venezuela. The principal aims are: to unify the petroleum policies of member countries and determine the best means for safeguarding their interests, individually and collectively; to devise ways and means of ensuring

the stabilization of prices in international oil markets with a view to eliminating harmful and unnecessary fluctuations; and to secure a steady income for the producing countries, an efficient, economic and regular supply of petroleum to consuming nations, and a fair return on their capital to those investing in the petroleum industry. It is estimated that OPEC members possess 75% of the world's known reserves of crude petroleum, of which about two-thirds are in the Middle East. OPEC countries account for about 43% of world oil production (55% in the mid-1970s).

Members (Jan. 2019) Algeria, Angola, Republic of the Congo, Ecuador, Equatorial Guinea, Gabon, Iran, Iraq, Kuwait, Libya, Nigeria, Saudi Arabia, United Arab Emirates and Venezuela. Membership applications may be made by any other country having substantial net exports of crude petroleum, which has fundamentally similar interests to those of member countries. Gabon became an associated member in 1973 and a full member in 1975, but in 1996 withdrew owing to difficulty in meeting its percentage contribution. However, it rejoined in July 2016. Ecuador joined the Organization in 1973 but left in 1992; it then rejoined in Oct. 2007. Indonesia joined in 1962 but left in 2008 as it had ceased to be an oil exporter; it then rejoined in Jan. 2016 despite being a net oil importer, only to leave again in Dec. of the same year. The Republic of the Congo joined in June 2018. Qatar left in Jan. 2019, with the country expected to focus instead on its natural gas potential.

Organization The main organs are the Conference, the Board of Governors and the Secretariat. The Conference, which is the supreme authority meeting at least twice a year, consists of delegations from each member country, normally headed by the respective minister of oil, mines or energy. All decisions, other than those concerning procedural matters, must be adopted unanimously.

Headquarters: Helferstorferstrasse 17, A-1010 Vienna, Austria.
Website: http://www.opec.org
Secretary-General: Mohammad Sanusi Barkindo (Nigeria).

Publications *Annual Statistical Bulletin.—Annual Report.—OPEC Bulletin* (monthly).—*Monthly Oil Market Report.—World Oil Outlook* (annual).—*OPEC General Information.* 2012.—*OPEC Statute.* 2012.

OPEC Fund for International Development

The OPEC Fund for International Development (OFID) was established in 1976 as the OPEC Special Fund, with the aim of providing financial aid on concessional terms to developing countries (other than OPEC member states) and international development agencies whose beneficiaries are developing countries. In 1980 the Fund was transformed into a permanent autonomous international agency and renamed the OPEC Fund for International Development. It is administered by a Ministerial Council and a Governing Board. Each member country is normally represented on the Council by its finance minister, or if not then by another designated person.

The initial endowment of the fund amounted to US$800m. By the end of Sept. 2015 OFID's total approved commitments (including public sector operations, private sector operations, trade finance operations, grants and contributions to other institutions) stood at US$18,871m. OFID had approved 3,504 operations by 30 Sept. 2015, including US$11,020m. for project financing, US$724m. for balance-of-payments support, US$333m. for programme funding and US$281m. for debt relief under the *Highly Indebted Poor Countries Initiative*. In addition, and through its private sector window, OFID had approved financing worth a total of US$2,482m. in 229 operations in support of private sector entities in Africa, Asia, Latin America, the Caribbean and Europe. Through its grants programme OFID had also committed a total of US$613m. in support of a wide range of initiatives, ranging from technical assistance, research and emergency aid to dedicated operations to combat HIV/AIDS and hardship in Palestine.

Headquarters: Parkring 8, POB 995, A-1011 Vienna, Austria.
Website: http://www.ofid.org
Director-General: Abdulhamid Alkhalifa (Saudi Arabia).

Further Reading

Gulf Co-operation Council (GCC)
Twinam, J. W., *The Gulf, Co-operation and the Council: an American Perspective.* 1992

League of Arab States

Bouhamidi, Soumia, *The Role of the League of Arab States: Mediating and Resolving Arab-Arab Conflicts*. 2011

Gomaa, A. M., *The Foundation of the League of Arab States*. 1977

Organization of the Petroleum Exporting Countries (OPEC)

Parra, Francisco, *Oil Politics: A Modern History of Petroleum*. 2010

Yergin, Daniel, *The Quest: Energy, Security and the Remaking of the Modern World*. 2011

Environmental Organizations

Friends of the Earth International

Origin Friends of the Earth was founded in 1971 by a network of environmental activists from France, Sweden, the UK and the USA.

Mission The organization aims to 'collectively ensure environmental and social justice, human dignity, and respect for human rights and peoples' rights so as to ensure sustainable societies'.

Organization Friends of the Earth International comprises 75 national member groups, with a combined membership of individuals exceeding 2m. around the world in some 5,000 local activist groups. A small, central Secretariat operates out of Amsterdam in the Netherlands and co-ordinates major campaigns, but grassroots activities are tailored by the relevant national or regional group.

Headquarters: PO Box 19199, 1000 GD Amsterdam, Netherlands.
Website: http://www.foei.org
Chair: Karen Nansen (Uruguay).

Global Environment Facility (GEF)

Origin The Global Environment Facility is an independent financial organization that brings together 183 countries in partnership with international institutions, civil society bodies and the private sector to address global environmental issues and support national development initiatives. It was established in 1991 under the aegis of the World Bank, becoming a permanent, separate institution in 1994.

Activities As of Jan. 2019 the GEF had provided US$17·9bn. in grants and co-financed more than 4,500 projects in 170 countries totalling US$93·2bn. since 1991. It also serves as the financial mechanism for the Convention on Biological Diversity, the UN Framework Convention on Climate Change, the Stockholm Convention on Persistent Organic Pollutants, the UN Convention to Combat Desertification and the Minamata Convention on Mercury (an agreement to protect human health and the environment from the effects of mercury emissions).

Organization There is a GEF Assembly comprising representatives of each member country that meets every three to four years. The GEF Council is the main governing body, developing, adopting and evaluating specific programmes. The Secretariat is based in Washington, D.C., and there are also a scientific and technical advisory panel, an evaluation office and a number of agencies managing particular projects.

Headquarters: 1899 Pennsylvania Ave., NW, Washington, D.C., 20006, USA.
Website: http://www.thegef.org
Chief Executive Officer and Chair: Dr Naoko Ishii (Japan).

Greenpeace International

Origin Greenpeace evolved out of a series of environmental and anti-nuclear protests in Canada in the late 1960s and early 1970s. In 1985 it became the focus of international attention when agents of the French security services blew up the organization's flagship, *Rainbow Warrior*, while it was in Auckland Harbour, New Zealand.

Mission Greenpeace is an independent global environmental organization that aims to secure a planet 'that is ecologically healthy and able to nurture life in all its diversity'. It campaigns to: prevent pollution and abuse of the Earth's land, oceans, air and fresh water; end all nuclear threats; and promote peace, global disarmament and non-violence.

Organization Greenpeace International has its headquarters in Amsterdam in the Netherlands, from where it co-ordinates worldwide campaigns and monitors and advises national and regional offices in 41 countries.

Financial contributions from governments, political parties and commercial organizations are not accepted. Funding is provided by individual supporters and foundation grants. In 2013 Greenpeace had 3m. individual supporters.

Headquarters: Ottho Heldringstraat 5, 1066 AZ Amsterdam, Netherlands.
Website: http://www.greenpeace.org
Executive Directors: Bunny McDiarmid (New Zealand) and Jennifer Morgan (USA).

World Wide Fund for Nature (WWF)

Origin WWF was officially formed and registered as a charity on 11 Sept. 1961. The first National Appeal was launched in the United Kingdom on 23 Nov. 1961, shortly followed by the United States and Switzerland.

Mission WWF has as its mission preserving genetic, species and ecosystem diversity; ensuring that the use of renewable natural resources is sustainable now and in the longer term, for the benefit of all life on Earth; promoting actions to reduce to a minimum pollution and the wasteful exploitation and consumption of resources and energy. WWF's ultimate goal is to stop, and eventually reverse, the accelerating degradation of our planet's natural environment, and to help build a future in which humans live in harmony with nature.

Organization WWF is the world's largest and most experienced independent conservation organization with over 5m. supporters (including 1·1m. in the USA). As at Jan. 2019 there were national offices in 72 countries and territories.

The National Organizations carry out conservation activities in their own countries and contribute technical expertise and funding to WWF's international conservation programme. The Programme Offices implement WWF's fieldwork, advise national and local governments, and raise public understanding of conservation issues.

Address: Rue Mauverney 28, CH-1196 Gland, Switzerland.
Website: http://wwf.panda.org
Director General: Marco Lambertini (Italy).
President Emeritus: HRH The Prince Philip, Duke of Edinburgh.
President: Pavan Sukhdev (India).

© Springer Nature Limited 2020
Palgrave Macmillan (ed.), *The Statesman's Yearbook 2020*,
https://doi.org/10.1057/978-1-349-95940-2_8

Treaties

Antarctic Treaty

Antarctica is an island continent some 15·5m. sq. km in area which lies almost entirely within the Antarctic Circle. Its surface is composed of an ice sheet over rock, and it is uninhabited except for research and other workers in the course of duty. It is in general ownerless: for countries with territorial claims, *see* ARGENTINA; AUSTRALIA: Australian Antarctic Territory; CHILE; FRANCE: Southern and Antarctic Territories; NEW ZEALAND: Ross Dependency; NORWAY: Queen Maud Land; UNITED KINGDOM: British Antarctic Territory.

12 countries which had maintained research stations in Antarctica during International Geophysical Year, 1957–58 (Argentina, Australia, Belgium, Chile, France, Japan, New Zealand, Norway, South Africa, the USSR, the UK and the USA) signed the Antarctic Treaty (Washington Treaty) on 1 Dec. 1959. Austria, Belarus, Brazil, Bulgaria, Canada, China, Colombia, Cuba, Czech Republic, Denmark, Ecuador, Estonia, Finland, Germany, Greece, Guatemala, Hungary, Iceland, India, Italy, Kazakhstan, North Korea, South Korea, Malaysia, Monaco, Mongolia, the Netherlands, Pakistan, Papua New Guinea, Peru, Poland, Portugal, Romania, Slovakia, Spain, Sweden, Switzerland, Turkey, Ukraine, Uruguay and Venezuela subsequently acceded to the Treaty. The Treaty reserves the Antarctic area south of 60° S. lat. for peaceful purposes, provides for international co-operation in scientific investigation and research, and preserves, for the duration of the Treaty, the *status quo* with regard to territorial sovereignty, rights and claims. The Treaty entered into force on 23 June 1961. The 53 nations party to the Treaty (29 consultative or voting members and 24 non-consultative parties) meet biennially.

An agreement reached in Madrid in April 1991 and signed by all 39 parties in Oct. imposes a ban on mineral exploitation in Antarctica for 50 years, at the end of which any one of the 29 voting parties may request a review conference. After this the ban may be lifted by agreement of three quarters of the nations then voting, which must include the present 29.

Headquarters: Maipú 757 Piso 4, C1006ACI, Buenos Aires, Argentina.
Website: http://www.ats.aq

Email: ats@ats.aq
Executive Secretary: Albert Lluberas (Uruguay).

Nuclear Non-Proliferation Treaty (NPT)

The Treaty on the Non-Proliferation of Nuclear Weapons opened for signatories on 1 July 1968. It came into force on 5 March 1970. A review meeting takes place every five years. The initial treaty was limited to a 25-year term but it was extended indefinitely in 1995.

The treaty aims to prevent the spread of nuclear weapons and weapons technology, to promote co-operation in the peaceful uses of nuclear energy and to further the goal of achieving nuclear disarmament and general and complete disarmament. The International Atomic Energy Agency (*see* page 22–3) is responsible for setting safeguards to ensure compliance.

Of the treaty's 191 members only five have nuclear weapon capabilities: China, France, Russia, UK and USA. Three states known or believed to have developed nuclear weapons have not ratified the treaty: India, Israel and Pakistan. North Korea withdrew from the treaty in 2003, the only state to have done so.

See also Preparatory Commission for the Comprehensive Nuclear-Test-Ban Treaty Organization (CTBTO) on page 23.

Website: http://www.un.org/disarmament/WMD/Nuclear/NPT.shtml

Further Reading

Antarctic Treaty

Elliott, L. M., *International Environmental Politics: Protecting the Antarctic.* 1994

Triggs, Gillian D. (ed.) *The Antarctic Treaty Regime: Law, Environment and Resources.* 2009

Leading Think Tanks

African Centre for the Constructive Resolution of Disputes (ACCORD)

Founded 1992. Non-governmental conflict management institution established to influence the process of negotiation and conflict resolution in South Africa. The Institution's focus has since broadened to include the entire African continent. ACCORD specializes in conflict management, conflict analysis and conflict prevention.

Address: 2 Golf Course Drive, Mt Edgecombe 4320, South Africa.
Website: http://www.accord.org.za
Executive Director: Vasu Gounden.

American Enterprise Institute (for Public Policy Research)

Founded 1943. Private, non-partisan think tank based around principles of private liberty, individual opportunity and free enterprise. Six principal research areas: economics; foreign and defence policy; health; legal and constitutional studies; political and public opinion studies; social and cultural studies.

Address: 1789 Massachusetts Ave., NW, Washington, D.C., 20036, USA.
Website: http://www.aei.org
President: Arthur C. Brooks.

Asian Development Bank Institute

Founded 1997. Leading institute engaged in building capacity, skills and knowledge related to poverty reduction and other areas that support long-term growth and competitiveness in developing economies in the Asia-Pacific region. Research covers inclusive and sustainable growth, regional co-operation and integration, and governance for policies and institutions.

Address: Kasumigaseki Bldg 8F, 3-2-5 Kasumigaseki, Chiyoda-ku, Tokyo 100-6008, Japan.
Website: http://www.adbi.org
Dean: Naoyuki Yoshino.

Atlantic Council

Founded 1961. Non-partisan, non-profit think tank seeking to promote constructive leadership and engagement in international affairs. As a member of the Atlantic Treaty Association, research programmes are based on the principle that a healthy transatlantic relationship is fundamental to maintaining a strong international system. Programmes relate to international security, sustainable energy, regional development and global economic growth.

Address: 1030 15th St., NW, 12th Floor, Washington, D.C., 20005, USA.
Website: http://www.atlanticcouncil.org
President and Chief Executive Officer: Frederick Kempe.

Barcelona Centre for International Affairs (CIDOB)

Founded 1973. Independent, non-partisan research centre that aims to become a point of reference in the field of international and development studies, generate ideas, undertake activities that increase awareness of belonging to a global community, and foster greater understanding of and between societies. Main thematic areas: security and development; globalization and regionalism; human rights and citizenship.

Address: C/ Elisabets 12, 08001 Barcelona, Spain.
Website: http://www.cidob.org
President: Antoni Segura.

Brookings Institution

Founded 1916. Independent, frequently cited as the world's best think tank. Goals are to strengthen American democracy; foster the economic and social welfare, security and opportunity of all Americans; and secure a more open, safe, prosperous and co-operative international system. Priority research areas include energy and climate, growth through innovation, managing global change, and opportunity and wellbeing.

Address: 1775 Massachusetts Ave., NW, Washington, D.C., 20036, USA.
Website: http://www.brookings.edu
President: John Rutherford Allen.

Bruegel

Founded 2004. Independent European think tank working in the field of international economics. Research areas: emerging powers and global governance structures; Europe's macroeconomic and structural challenges; competitiveness, innovation and financial regulation; climate change and energy.

Address: Rue de la Charité 33, B-1210 Saint-Josse-ten-Noode, Brussels, Belgium.
Website: http://www.bruegel.org
Director: Guntram B. Wolff.

Carnegie Endowment for International Peace

Founded 1910. Independent think tank specializing in international affairs with particular focus on Russia and Eurasia, China, the Indian subcontinent/South Asia, globalization, non-proliferation and security affairs. Aims to advance co-operation between nations and promote active international engagement by the USA and become 'the first truly multinational—ultimately global—think tank'. Offices in Washington, D.C., Moscow, Beijing, Beirut and Brussels.

Address: 1779 Massachusetts Ave., NW, Washington, D.C., 20036-2103, USA.
Website: http://www.carnegieendowment.org
President: William J. Burns.

Carnegie Middle East Center

Founded in 2006 as part of the Carnegie Endowment for International Peace's Middle East programme. Public policy think tank and research centre that aims to better inform the process of political change in the Arab Middle East and deepen understanding of the complex security and economic issues that affect it. Programmes: Middle East economies; Arab politics; regional relations; security.

Address: Lazarieh Tower, Building No 2026 1210, Fifth Floor, Emir Bechir St., Beirut, 11-1061 Riad El Solh, Lebanon.
Website: http://www.carnegie-mec.org
Director: Mahi Yahia.

Carnegie Moscow Center

Founded in 1994 as a subdivision of the Carnegie Endowment for International Peace. Analyses the most important issues in international affairs and Russian domestic and foreign policy, as well as the regions they affect. Programmes: economic policy; foreign and security policy; non-proliferation; religion, society and security; Russian domestic politics and political institutions; society and regions.

Address: 16/1 Tverskaya, Moscow 125009, Russia.
Website: http://www.carnegie.ru
Director: Dmitry Trenin.

© Springer Nature Limited 2020
Palgrave Macmillan (ed.), *The Statesman's Yearbook 2020*,
https://doi.org/10.1057/978-1-349-95940-2_10

Cato Institute

Founded 1977. Non-profit public policy research foundation based on the principles of the American Revolution—limited government, free markets, individual liberty and peace. Comprises Centers for Constitutional Studies, Educational Freedom, Global Liberty and Prosperity, Representative Government and Trade Policy Studies.

Address: 1000 Massachusetts Ave., NW, Washington, D.C., 20001-5403, USA.
Website: http://www.cato.org
President: Peter N. Goettler.

Center for American Progress

Founded 2003. Organization dedicated to improving the lives of Americans through progressive ideas and action. Research issues: domestic; economy; national security; energy and environment; media and progressive values.

Address: 1333 H St., NW, 10th Floor, Washington, D.C., 20005, USA.
Website: http://www.americanprogress.org
President: Neera Tanden.

Center for Strategic and International Studies

Founded in 1962 during the Cold War to find ways for the USA to sustain its prominence and prosperity as a force for good in the world. Bipartisan, non-profit organization that conducts research and analysis and develops policy initiatives that look into the future and anticipate change. Research focuses on defence and security, energy and climate change, global health, global trends and forecasting, governance, human rights, technology, and trade and economics.

Address: 1616 Rhode Island Ave., NW, Washington, D.C., 20036, USA.
Website: http://www.csis.org
President: John J. Hamre.

Centre for Economic Policy Research

Founded 1983. Non-profit, educational research network that promotes independent, objective analysis and public discussion of open economies and the relations among them. Programmes: development economics; financial economics; industrial organization; international macroeconomics; international trade and regional economics; labour economics; public policy.

Address: 33 Great Sutton St., London, EC1V 0DX, UK.
Website: http://www.cepr.org
President: Beatrice Weder di Mauro.

Centre for European Policy Studies

Founded 1983. Independent institute specializing in European affairs. Research programmes: economic and social welfare policies; energy, climate change and sustainable development; EU neighbourhood, foreign and security policy; financial markets and institutions; justice and home affairs; politics and European institutions; regulatory policy; trade developments and agricultural policy.

Address: 1 Place du Congrès, B-1000 Brussels, Belgium.
Website: http://www.ceps.eu
Director: Daniel Gros.

Centre for International Governance Innovation (CIGI)

Founded 2001. Autonomous body focused on international governance. The organization aims to support research, form networks, advance policy debate and generate ideas for multilateral governance improvements. CIGI's research programmes focus on: global economy, global security and politics, and international law. Its interdisciplinary work includes collaboration with policy, business and academic communities around the world.

Address: 67 Erb St. West, Waterloo, ON, Canada N2L 6C2.
Website: https://www.cigionline.org
President: Rohinton P. Medhora.

Chatham House (Royal Institute of International Affairs)

Founded 1920. Leading independent think tank whose research centres on three areas: energy, environment and resource governance; international economics; regional and security studies. Established the 'Chatham House Rule' that aids free and open debate by allowing for anonymity of speakers at meetings. Sister organization of Council on Foreign Relations in New York.

Address: 10 St James's Square, London, SW1Y 4LE, UK.
Website: http://www.chathamhouse.org
Director: Dr Robin Niblett.

China Institute of International Studies (CIIS)

Founded 1956. The think tank of China's ministry of foreign affairs focuses on global politics and economics and the decision-making process of the central government. Research at the Institute centres on medium and long-term policy issues of strategic importance, specifically those concerning international politics and the world economy.

Address: 3 Toutiao, Taijichang, Beijing 100005, China.
Website: http://www.ciis.org.cn
President: Qi Zhenhong.

China Institutes of Contemporary International Relations

Founded 1965. Influential research institution of international studies devoted to a wide range of political, economic, diplomatic, military and social issues spanning all continents as well as issues related to Hong Kong, Macao and Taiwan. A key research area is the United States and the Sino–US relationship.

Address: A-2 Wanshousi, Haidian District, Beijing 100081, China.
Website (Chinese only): http://www.cicir.ac.cn
President: Yuan Peng.

Chinese Academy of Social Sciences

Founded 1977. China's highest academic research organization in the fields of philosophy and social sciences. Comprises 32 research institutes, three research centres and a graduate school. Research covers 120 key areas.

Address: 5 Jianguomennei Dajie, Beijing 100732, China.
Website: http://cass.cssn.cn
President: Xie Fuzhan.

Council on Foreign Relations

Founded 1921. Independent think tank that seeks to foster better understanding of the world and the foreign policy choices facing the USA and other countries. Research by the David Rockefeller Studies Program centres on major geopolitical areas but also covers global health, international institutions and global governance, national security, science and technology and US foreign policy. Sister organization of Chatham House in London.

Address: The Harold Pratt House, 58 East 68th St., New York, NY 10065, USA.
Website: http://www.cfr.org
Chairman: David M. Rubenstein.
President: Richard N. Haass.

Danish Institute for International Studies

Founded 2002 by the Danish parliament. Independent institution engaged in research in international affairs in order to assess the security and foreign policy situation of Denmark. Research units: defence and security; foreign policy and EU studies; global economy, regulation and development; holocaust and genocide; migration; natural resources and poverty; politics and governance; the Middle East.

Address: Østbanegade 117, 2100 Copenhagen, Denmark.
Website: http://www.diis.dk
Chairman of the Board: Henrik Halkier.

European Council on Foreign Relations

Founded 2007. Pan-European think tank that conducts European foreign policy research and promotes a more integrated European foreign policy in support of shared European interests and values. Main programmes: Russia and wider Europe; China; democracy, human rights and the rule of law.

Address: 4th Floor, Tennyson House, 159–165 Great Portland St., London, W1W 5PA, UK.
Website: http://www.ecfr.eu
Director: Mark Leonard.

Fraser Institute

Founded 1974. Independent non-partisan research and educational organization that aims to measure, study and communicate the impact of competitive markets and government interventions on the welfare of individuals. Research covers taxation, government spending, health care, school performance and trade.

Address: 4th Floor, 1770 Burrard St., Vancouver, BC, Canada V6J 3G7.
Website: http://www.fraserinstitute.org
President: Niels Veldhuis.

French Institute of International Relations (IFRI)

Founded 1979. The Institut Français des Relations Internationales is an independent research and debate institution dedicated to international affairs. Research centres on geographic regions as well as economy; energy; Franco–German relations; health/environment; migration; identities and citizenship; security and defence; space; and sport.

Address: 27 rue de la Procession, 75740 Paris Cedex 15, France.
Website: http://www.ifri.org
President: Thierry de Montbrial.

Friedrich Ebert Foundation (Friedrich-Ebert-Stiftung; FES)

Founded in 1925 as a political legacy of Germany's first democratically elected president, Friedrich Ebert. Non-profit foundation committed to the advancement of public policy issues in the spirit of the basic values of social democracy. Focuses on democracy promotion and international dialogue on the central topics of international politics, globalization, and economic, social and political development in the world.

Address: Berliner Haus, Hiroshimastrasse 17, 10785 Berlin, Germany; Bonner Haus, Godesberger Allee 149, 53175 Bonn, Germany.
Website (German only): http://www.fes.de
Chairman: Kurt Beck.

Fundação Getulio Vargas

Founded 1944. Higher education establishment dedicated to social sciences research to develop the socio-economic position of Brazil. Research covers business, citizenship, education, finance, justice, health, history, law, macro and microeconomics, politics, pollution, poverty and unemployment, sustainable development and welfare.

Address: Praia de Botafogo 190, Rio de Janeiro, 22250-900 Brazil.
Website: http://www.fgv.br
President: Carlos Ivan Simonsen Leal.

German Council on Foreign Relations

Founded 1945. Independent, non-partisan and non-profit membership organization and think tank that promotes public debate on foreign policy. Research programmes focus on: China; energy policy; European integration; global economics; international security policy; Middle East; Russia/Eurasia; transatlantic relations.

Address: Rauchstrasse 17–18, 10787 Berlin, Germany.
Website: https://dgap.org
President: Dr Arend Oetker.

German Development Institute (DIE)

Founded 1964. One of the leading think tanks for global development and international co-operation worldwide. It develops policy-relevant concepts, advises ministries, governments and international organizations, and refers to current policy issues. Research areas: bi- and multilateral development co-operation; sustainable economic and social development; governance, statehood and security; environmental policy and natural resources management; world economy and development financing.

Address: Tulpenfeld 6, 53113 Bonn, Germany.
Website: http://www.die-gdi.de
Acting Director: Imme Scholz.

German Institute for International and Security Affairs (Stiftung Wissenschaft und Politik; SWP)

Founded 1962. Independent scientific establishment that conducts practically oriented research on the basis of which it then advises the Bundestag and the German federal government on foreign and security policy issues. Research divisions: EU integration; EU external relations; international security; the Americas; Russian Federation/CIS; Middle East and Africa; Asia; global issues.

Address: Ludwigkirchplatz 3–4, 10719 Berlin, Germany.
Website: http://www.swp-berlin.org
Director: Prof. Dr Volker Perthes.

Heritage Foundation

Founded 1973. Conservative think tank aiming to formulate and promote public policies based on the principles of free enterprise, limited government, individual freedom, traditional American values and a strong national defence. Target audience includes members of Congress, key congressional staff members, policymakers in the executive branch, the news media, and the academic and public policy communities.

Address: 214 Massachusetts Ave., NE, Washington, D.C., 20002-4999, USA.
Website: http://www.heritage.org
President: Kay Coles James.

Human Rights Watch

Founded 1978. Non-profit, non-governmental organization dedicated to protecting the human rights of people around the world. Research topics include: arms; children's rights; counterterrorism; disability rights; health; international justice; migrants; press freedom; refugees; terrorism; torture; women's rights.

Address: 350 Fifth Avenue, 34th floor, New York, NY 10118-3299, USA.
Website: http://www.hrw.org
Executive Director: Kenneth Roth.

Institute for Defence Studies and Analyses (IDSA)

Founded 1965. Non-partisan, autonomous body funded by the Indian ministry of defence that has played a key role in shaping India's foreign and security policies. It aims to promote national and international security by generating and disseminating knowledge on defence and security-related issues.

Address: 1 Development Enclave, Rao Tula Ram Marg, New Delhi 110010, India.
Website: http://www.idsa.in
Director General: Sujan R. Chinoy.

Institute of World Economy and International Relations

Founded 1956. Non-profit organization that carries out applied socio-economic, political and strategic research. Research areas include: current global problems; economic theory; economic, social and political problems of the transition period in Russia; forecasting and analysis of world economy dynamics and socio-political developments; international politics; military and strategic problems; theory of international relations; theory of social and political processes.

Address: 23 Profsoyuznaya St., Moscow 117997, Russia.
Website: http://www.imemo.ru
Director: Alexander A. Dynkin.

International Crisis Group

Founded 1995. Independent, non-profit organization committed to preventing and resolving deadly conflict. Combines field-based analysis, policy advice and high-level advocacy to highlight potential future conflicts, resolve peace negotiations and advise governments and intergovernmental bodies.

Address: 149 avenue Louise, Level 24, B-1050 Brussels, Belgium.
Website: http://www.crisisgroup.org
President: Robert Malley.

International Institute for Strategic Studies (IISS)

Founded 1958. Independent organization, considered the world's leading authority on political-military conflict. Research programme themes: conflict; defence and military analysis; economics and conflict resolution; non-proliferation and disarmament; transnational threats and international political risk; transatlantic dialogue on climate change and security.

Address: Arundel House, 13–15 Arundel St., Temple Place, London, WC2R 3DX, UK.
Website: http://www.iiss.org
Director-General: Dr John Chipman.

Japan Institute of International Affairs (JIIA)

Founded 1959. Private, non-partisan institute committed to research on foreign affairs and security issues. Examines Japanese foreign policy, provides policy recommendations to the government and disseminates information on international relations to the public. JIIA aims to serve as an indispensable resource on international affairs.

Address: 3rd Floor Toranomon Mitsui Building, 3-8-1 Kasumigaseki, Chiyodaku, Tokyo 100-0013, Japan.
Website: http://www2.jiia.or.jp
President and Director General: Kenichiro Sasae.

Kiel Institute for the World Economy (Institut für Weltwirtschaft an der Universität Kiel; IfW)

Founded 1914. Independent, international centre for research in global economic affairs, economic policy consulting, economic education and documentation. Research areas: the global division of labour; knowledge creation and growth; the environment and natural resources; poverty reduction, equity and development; monetary policy under market imperfections; financial markets and macroeconomic activity; reforming the welfare society.

Address: Kiellinie 66, 24105 Kiel, Germany.
Website: http://www.ifw-kiel.de
President: Prof. Dennis Snower.

Konrad Adenauer Foundation (Konrad-Adenauer-Stiftung)

Founded in 1955 as the Society for Christian Democratic Civic Education and renamed in 1964. Political foundation that focuses on consolidating democracy, the unification of Europe and the strengthening of transatlantic relations, as well as on development co-operation.

Address: Klingelhöferstrasse 23, 10785 Berlin, Germany; Rathausallee 12, 53757 Sankt Augustin, Germany.
Website: http://www.kas.de
Chairman: Dr Norbert Lammert.

Korea Development Institute (KDI)

Founded 1971. Think tank set up by the government aiming to make substantial contributions to the economic and social development of Korea. Research focuses on providing policy recommendations and guidance based on in-depth analyses of international and domestic economic conditions and projections.

Address: 263 (Bangok-dong, Korea Development Institute) Namsejong-ro, Sejong-si 30149, South Korea.
Website: http://www.kdi.re.kr
President: Choi Jeong-pyo.

Korea Institute for International Economic Policy (KIEP)

Founded 1990. Think tank under the affiliation of the South Korean government. The main function of the organization is to advise the government on all kinds of international economic policy topics. Research programmes focus on: international macroeconomics and finance; international trade; northeast Asian economies; Asia-Pacific; Europe, Americas and Eurasia.

Address: Building C, Sejong National Research Complex, 370, Sicheong-daero, Sejong-si, South Korea.
Website: http://www.kiep.go.kr
President: Jae-Young Lee.

National Bureau of Economic Research (NBER)

Founded 1920. Private, non-profit, non-partisan research organization dedicated to promoting a greater understanding of how the economy works. Concentrates on four types of empirical research: developing new statistical measurements, estimating quantitative models of economic behaviour, assessing the economic effects of public policies and projecting the effects of alternative policy proposals.

Address: 1050 Massachusetts Ave., Cambridge, Massachusetts 02138-5398, USA.
Website: http://www.nber.org
President: Dr James Poterba.

Netherlands Institute of International Relations 'Clingendael'

Founded 1983. Non-profit, independent think tank for international relations. Identifies and analyses emerging political and social developments for the benefit of government and the general public. Programmes include: diplomatic studies; European studies; security and conflict; international energy.

Address: Clingendael 7, 2597 VH The Hague, Netherlands.
Website: http://www.clingendael.nl
General Director: Monika Sie Dhian Ho.

Peterson Institute for International Economics

Founded 1981. Private, non-profit, non-partisan research institution devoted to the study of international economic policy. Research encompasses country and regional studies, debt and development, globalization, international finance and macroeconomics, international trade and investment, and US economic policy.

Address: 1750 Massachusetts Ave., NW, Washington, D.C., 20036-1903, USA.
Website: http://www.iie.com
Chairman: Michael A. Peterson.

RAND Corporation

Founded in 1948 out of US military research and development during World War II by Douglas Aircraft. Independent, non-profit organization dedicated to promoting scientific, educational and charitable purposes for the public welfare. Research areas include health, education, national security, international affairs, law and business, and the environment. Houses three federally funded research and development centres sponsored by the US defence department: the RAND Arroyo Center, providing research and analysis for the army; the RAND National Defense Research Institute; and RAND Project Air Force.

Address: 1776 Main St., Santa Monica, CA 90401-3208, USA.
Website: http://www.rand.org
President: Michael D. Rich.

Royal United Services Institute

Founded 1831. Leading independent think tank engaged in cutting-edge defence and security research. The institution brings to the fore vital policy issues and offers expertise to policy makers. Principal research areas: defence, industries and society; UK defence; terrorism; nuclear weapons and nuclear arms control; cyber-security; conflict, war and culture.

Address: 61 Whitehall, London, SW1A 2ET, UK.
Website: http://www.rusi.org
Chairman: William Hague.

Stockholm International Peace Research Institute (SIPRI)

Founded in 1966 by the Swedish parliament. Independent international institute dedicated to research into conflict, armaments, arms control and disarmament. Compiles detailed studies on multilateral peace operations, military expenditure, arms transfers and arms embargoes.

Address: Signalistgatan 9, SE-169 72 Solna, Sweden.
Website: http://www.sipri.org
Director: Dan Smith.

Transparency International

Founded 1993. Non-partisan global civil society organization seeking to create change towards a world free of corruption. Global priorities: combating corruption in politics, public contracting and the private sector; international anti-corruption conventions; poverty and development.

Address: Alt-Moabit 96, 10559 Berlin, Germany.
Website: http://www.transparency.org
Chair of the Board of Directors: Delia Ferreira Rubio.

Urban Institute

Founded 1968. Independent think tank founded by the Lyndon B. Johnson administration committed to developing evidence-based insights into the efficiency of government programmes. It helped design and monitor the implementation of the Affordable Care Act (ACA) under the Obama administration. The organization conducts impartial data research on issues including taxes, health and health policy, housing and housing finance, economic growth and productivity, immigration, education and poverty.

Address: 2100 M St., NW, Washington, D.C., 20037, USA.
Website: https://www.urban.org
President: Sarah Rosen Wartell.

Woodrow Wilson International Center for Scholars

Founded in 1968 by an act of Congress as a memorial to former US president Woodrow Wilson. Non-partisan, it promotes and develops relations between policy-makers and academic scholars. Research covers most public policy areas, specializing in the field of international affairs.

Address: Ronald Reagan Building and International Trade Center, One Woodrow Wilson Plaza, 1300 Pennsylvania Ave., NW, Washington, D.C., 20004-3027, USA.
Website: http://www.wilsoncenter.org
Director, President and Chief Executive Officer: Jane Harman.

Afghanistan

Da Afganistan Islami Jomhoriyat—Jamhuri-ye Islami-ye Afganistan (Islamic Republic of Afghanistan)

Capital: Kabul
Population projection, 2020: 38·05m.
GNI per capita, 2017: (PPP$) 1,824
HDI/world rank, 2017: 0·498/168=
Internet domain extension: .af

Key Historical Events

Excavations near Kandahar in southern Afghanistan have revealed Neolithic settlements dating to 5000 BC. Later settlements indicate trade links with cities in the Indus Valley and Mesopotamia. Aryan tribes that settled in Afghanistan's northern plains near Balkh (Bactria) from around 1500 BC gave way to successive Persian dynasties, including the Acaemanid Empire (550 BC–330 BC) ruled by Darius the Great from Persepolis after 515 BC.

Alexander the Great conquered Bactria in 328 BC but his rule was short-lived and the region fell first to the Seleucid, then to the Parthian empires. Buddhism was spread by the Yuechi, who invaded from the northeast and established the Kushan dynasty at Peshawar in around 200 BC. The famous Buddha statues at Bamiyan, destroyed in 2001 by the Taliban, dated from the 3rd and 5th centuries AD. Scythians, White Huns and Turkish Tu-Kuie invaded in the first half of the first millennium. The Muslim conquest of Afghanistan began with the arrival of Arab settlers in AD 642, though it was during the reign of Mahmud of Ghazni (998–1030) that the region became a thriving cultural centre. Mahmud was succeeded by smaller dynasties, all of which fell to Genghis Khan's Mongol invasion in 1219.

Following Genghis Khan's death in 1227, chiefs and princes vied for supremacy until, late in the 14th century, one of his descendants, Timur-i Lang, incorporated Afghanistan into his central Asian empire. Babur, a descendant of Timur and founder of India's Moghul dynasty at the beginning of the 16th century, made Kabul his capital, although power later transferred to Delhi and Agra. The early sixteenth century also saw the rise of the Safavid dynasty in Iran which ruled over western Afghanistan, while the Shaibanid Uzbeks controlled northern Afghanistan and territory stretching northward across central Asia.

The early 18th century was marked by Afghan tribes revolting against foreign occupation. Ahmad Shah Durrani, a Pashtun, became the founder of modern Afghanistan following the death of the Persian ruler, Nadir Shah, in 1747. The subsequent rule by Dost Muhammad, who became Amir in 1826, was overshadowed by the power struggle between Britain, dominant in India, and the expanding Russian empire. The British attempt to oust Dost Muhammad sparked the first Afghan War (1838–42), during which the British were forced to retreat by an armed rebellion in Kabul in 1841.

Dost Muhammad returned from exile and governed for the next 20 years. British attempts to delineate India's northwest frontier and prevent Russian advances led to another invasion of Afghanistan in 1878, when British-Indian troops seized the Khyber Pass. Abd Ar-Rahman Khan, who became the Amir of Afghanistan in 1880, abolished the traditional regional centres of power and consolidated his government in Kabul. Border treaties were signed with Russia and British India. Following the Anglo-Russian agreement of 1907 Afghanistan's independence was guaranteed, although foreign affairs remained under British control until the 1919 Treaty of Rawalpindi. King Amanullah introduced Western-style reforms in the 1920s but development was restricted by tribal wars and banditry.

Záhir Shah took power in 1933 and ruled for 40 years, bringing stability and the expansion of education. In 1964 he established parliamentary democracy. In 1973 his cousin and brother-in-law, and a former prime minister, Mohammed Daoud, led a military coup and abolished the constitution to declare a republic. In April 1978 President Daoud was killed in a further coup which installed a pro-Soviet government. The new president, Noor Mohammad Taraki, was overthrown in Sept. 1979, whereupon the USSR invaded in Dec. to install Babrak Karmal in power.

In Dec. 1986 Sayid Mohammed Najibullah became president with civil war continuing between government and rebel Muslim forces. The USSR gave military support to the authorities while the USA backed the rebels. In the mid-1980s the UN began negotiating the withdrawal of Soviet troops and the establishment of a national unity government. The first Soviet troops withdrew in early 1988. After talks in Nov. 1991 with Afghan opposition movements ('mujahideen'), the USSR transferred its support from the Najibullah regime to an 'Islamic Interim Government'. As mujahideen insurgents closed in on Kabul on 16 April 1992 President Najibullah stepped down but fighting continued.

In 1994 a newly formed militant Islamic movement, the 'Taliban' (which translates as 'students'), took Kabul, apparently with Pakistani support. The Taliban, most of whose leaders were Pashtuns, were in turn defeated by the troops of President Rabbani. However, in Sept. 1996 Taliban forces recaptured Kabul and set up an interim government under Mohamed Rabbani. Afghanistan was declared an Islamic state under Sharia law. Government forces counter-attacked but a new Taliban offensive, launched in Dec. 1996, took most of the country. The opposition Northern Alliance controlled the northeast of the country. Under the Taliban, irregular forces were disarmed, roads cleared of bandits, and towns and villages rebuilt. Only three countries—Pakistan, Saudi Arabia and the United Arab Emirates—recognized the Taliban as the legal government.

In March 2001 Afghanistan was widely condemned for destroying the ancient Buddha statues at Bamiyan. In May 2001 the Taliban refused to extradite Osama bin Laden, a Saudi militant who led the al-Qaeda jihadist network, to the USA to face charges connected to the bombing of American embassies in Kenya and Tanzania in 1998. Bin Laden had fought in the 1980s against the Soviet occupiers and had subsequently used the country as a base for his organization's operations. In Sept. 2001 Ahmed Shah Masood, leader of the Northern Alliance, was killed by two suicide bombers.

Following the al-Qaeda attacks on the USA on 11 Sept. 2001, Saudi Arabia and the United Arab Emirates broke off relations with Afghanistan and the USA unsuccessfully put pressure on the Taliban to hand over bin Laden. Consequently the USA launched air strikes on 7 Oct. On 13 Nov. the Northern Alliance took the capital Kabul, effectively bringing an end to Taliban rule. With the surrender of Kandahar the Taliban lost control of their last stronghold. On 27 Nov. representatives of rival factions, but excluding the Taliban, joined UN-sponsored talks on Afghanistan's future. Hamid Karzai, a Pashtun tribal leader, was chosen to head an interim power-sharing council which took office in Dec. He was appointed president of the transitional government in June 2002. He survived an assassination attempt in Sept. 2002 and won re-election in 2004 and 2009 (the latter in a disputed contest). Following a meeting of international donors in London in 2006, Afghanistan was pledged US$10bn. in reconstruction aid over a five-year period.

Since Aug. 2003 the government has attempted to assert its authority with the help of the NATO-controlled International Security Assistance Force (ISAF), operating under a UN mandate. By 2007 the international force was battling a resurgent Taliban supported by around a quarter of the population in the south of the country. At the London Conference in Jan. 2010 it was agreed to increase ISAF personnel numbers from 96,000 to 135,000 in the course of 2010.

In May 2012 NATO endorsed plans to withdraw foreign combat troops by 2014. In Sept. 2012 the USA suspended the training of police recruits after a spate of attacks apparently carried out by members of the military and police forces with links to the Taliban. In Dec. 2014 NATO's US-led International Security Assistance Force (ISAF)—which numbered 140,000 troops at its peak in 2011—ended its mission. However, as at May 2017 more than 13,500 personnel were retained in the country to train, advise and assist the Afghan National Security Forces as part of Operation *Resolute Support*.

Territory and Population

Afghanistan is bounded in the north by Turkmenistan, Uzbekistan and Tajikistan, east by China, east and south by Pakistan and west by Iran.

The area is 652,230 sq. km (251,830 sq. miles). The last census was in 1979. In 2011, 22·9% of the population lived in urban areas.

© Springer Nature Limited 2020
Palgrave Macmillan (ed.), *The Statesman's Yearbook 2020*,
https://doi.org/10.1057/978-1-349-95940-2_11

The UN gives a projected population for 2020 of 38·05m. Afghanistan's population has doubled since the early 1990s.

Successive wars in Afghanistan resulted in one of the world's largest refugee crises. Prior to the withdrawal of Soviet troops in 1989 there were more than 6m. Afghan refugees, mainly in Pakistan, Iran and to a lesser extent Western Europe, Australia and North America. In the first half of the 1990s large numbers began to return, but after the Taliban came to power in 1996 repatriation slowed. As a consequence of the US-led war in Afghanistan beginning in Oct. 2001, numbers of refugees to Pakistan and Iran increased dramatically. In the meantime more than 5m. Afghans have returned to their country since a UN-sponsored programme began in early 2002, but as at the end of 2016 there were still 2·5m. Afghan refugees living abroad—the second highest by nationality and 18% of the global total. According to humanitarian agencies in Jan. 2002 there were almost 1·2m. internally displaced persons in Afghanistan. Approximately half of the internally displaced persons in Afghanistan moved prior to the events of Sept. 2001, for reasons such as drought and food scarcity. There were still 1,798,000 internally displaced persons at the end of 2016. In 2016 thousands of Afghan refugees returned to the country from Pakistan following a security crackdown against undocumented foreigners there and the tightening of border controls.

The country is divided into 34 regions *(velayat)*. Area and estimated population in 2009:

Region	Area (sq. km)	Population (1,000)
Badakhshan	44,059	860
Badghis	20,591	449
Baghlan	21,118	819
Balkh	17,249	1,169
Bamyan	14,175	405
Daikondi	18,200	417
Farah	48,471	459
Faryab	20,293	900
Ghazni	22,915	1,111
Ghowr	36,479	625
Helmand	58,584	836
Herat	54,778	1,676
Jawzjan	11,798	485
Kabul	4,462	3,569
Kandahar	54,022	1,080
Kapisa	1,842	400
Khost	4,152	520
Konar	4,942	408
Kondoz	8,040	900
Laghman	3,843	404
Logar	3,880	355
Nangarhar	7,727	1,358
Nimroz	41,005	149
Nurestan	9,225	134
Paktika	19,482	499
Paktiya	6,432	394
Panjshir	3,610	139
Parwan	5,974	600
Samangan	11,262	350
Saripul	15,999	505
Takhar	12,333	886
Uruzgan	12,600	317
Vardak	8,938	540
Zabul	17,343	275

The capital, Kabul, had an estimated population of 2·94m. in 2009. Other towns (with population estimates, 2009): Herat (395,000), Kandahar (363,000), Mazar i Sharif (334,000), Jalalabad (188,000).

Main ethnic groups: Pashtuns, 38%; Tajiks, 25%; Hazaras, 19%; Uzbeks, 6%; others, 12%. The official languages are Pashto and Dari.

Social Statistics

Based on 2008 estimates: birth rate, 46·5 per 1,000 population; death rate, 19·6 per 1,000. Infant mortality (2010), 103 per 1,000 live births. Life expectancy at birth, 2013, was 62·2 years for women and 59·7 years for men. Fertility rate, 2008, 6·6 births per woman. In spite of the ongoing conflict in the country, Afghanistan has made significant progress in recent years in reducing maternal mortality. The number of deaths per 100,000 live births among mothers was reduced from 1,100 in 2000 to 400 in 2013.

Climate

The climate is arid, with a big annual range of temperature and very little rain, apart from the period Jan. to April. Winters are very cold, with considerable snowfall, which may last the year round on mountain summits. Kabul, Jan. 27°F (–2·8°C), July 76°F (24·4°C). Annual rainfall 13" (338 mm).

Constitution and Government

UN sanctions were imposed in 1999 but were withdrawn following the collapse of the Taliban regime. Following UN-sponsored talks in Bonn, Germany in Nov. 2001, on 22 Dec. 2001 power was handed over to an Afghan Interim Authority, designed to oversee the restructuring of the country until a second stage of government, the Transitional Authority, could be put into power. This second stage resulted from a *Loya Jirga* (Grand Council), an assembly of elders that convened between 10–16 June 2002. The Loya Jirga established the Transitional Islamic State of Afghanistan. A constitutional commission was established, with UN assistance, to help the Constitutional Loya Jirga prepare a new constitution. A draft constitution was produced for public scrutiny in Nov. 2003 and was approved by Afghanistan's Loya Jirga on 4 Jan. 2004. The new constitution creates a strong presidential system, providing for a *President* and two *Vice Presidents*, and a bicameral parliament. The constitution imposes a limit of two five-year terms for a president. The lower house is the 249-member House of the People (*Wolesi Jirga*), directly elected for a five-year term, and the upper house the 102-member House of Elders (*Meshrano Jirga*). The upper house is elected in three divisions. The provincial councils elect one third of its members for a four-year term. The district councils elect the second third of the members for a three-year term. The president appoints the remaining third for a five-year term. At least one woman is elected to the *Wolesi Jirga* from each of the country's 32 regions, and half of the president's appointments to the *Meshrano Jirga* must be women. The constitution reserves 25% of the seats in the *Wolesi Jirga* for women. The president appoints ministers, the attorney general and central bank governor with the approval of the *Wolesi Jirga*. Cabinet ministers must be university graduates. Presidential and parliamentary elections, the first in 25 years, were scheduled for June 2004 but were put back to Oct. 2004. The parliamentary elections were subsequently delayed again and were set to be held in April 2005, but were postponed a further time until Sept. 2005. In Dec. 2005 an elected parliament sat for the first time since 1973.

National Anthem

'Daa watan Afghanistan di' ('This land is Afghanistan'); words by Abdul Bari Jahani, tune by Babrak Wassa.

Recent Elections

Elections for the 249-member House of the People took place on 18 Sept. 2010; all elected representatives were non-partisan. There were widespread voting irregularities and at least 14 people died in election-related violence. Nearly a quarter of the ballot was declared void owing to fraud. Turnout was approximately 40%.

Presidential elections, representing the first democratic transfer of power in Afghanistan's history, were held on 5 April 2014. The Taliban had pledged to disrupt the elections, and a massive security operation was launched by the government to prevent attacks on polling stations. Sporadic violence and a shortage of ballot papers was reported across the country after 6·6m. people turned out to vote. Abdullah Abdullah of the National Coalition took 44·9% of the vote, Mohammad Ashraf Ghani Ahmadzai (ind.) 31·5%, Zalmai Rassoul (ind.) 11·5%, Abdul Rasul Sayyaf (Islamic Dawa) 7·1%, Qutbuddin

Hilal (ind.) 2·7% and Gul Agha Sherzai (ind.) 1·6%. Two other candidates both obtained less than 1% of the vote. As no candidate secured the necessary 50% or more of the vote to win outright, a run-off between Abdullah and Ghani took place on 7 June 2014. Ghani won with 56·4% of the vote against Abdullah with 43·6%, but Abdullah claimed that there was widespread fraud and refused to concede defeat. 8·1m. people voted in the second round.

Current Government

President: Ashraf Ghani Ahmadzai; b. 1949 (Pashtun; sworn in 29 Sept. 2014).

Vice Presidents: Abdul Rashid Dostum (Uzbek); Sarwar Danish (Hazara).

Chief Executive (Prime Minister): Abdullah Abdullah; b. 1960 (Tajik–Pashtun; sworn in 29 Sept. 2014).

In Feb. 2019 the government was composed as follows:

Minister of Agriculture and Livestock: Nasir Ahmad Durani. *Borders and Tribal Affairs:* Gul Aqa Shirzai. *Commerce and Industries:* Homayoun Rasa. *Communication and Information Technology:* Shahzadgul Aryubi. *Counter-Narcotics:* Salamat Azimi. *Defence (acting):* Asadullah Khalid. *Economy:* Mohammad Mustafa Mastoor. *Education (acting):* Mohammad Ibrahim Shinwari. *Energy and Water:* Ali Ahmad Osmani. *Finance:* Eklil Hakimi. *Foreign Affairs:* Salahuddin Rabbani. *Hajj and Religious Endowments:* Faiz Muhammad Usmani. *Higher Education:* Najibullah Khawaja Omari. *Information and Culture (acting):* Hasina Safi. *Interior (acting):* Massoud Andarabi. *Justice:* Abdul Basir Anwar. *Labour, Social Affairs, Martyrs and the Disabled:* Faizullah Zaki. *Mines and Petroleum (acting):* Nargis Nehan. *Public Health:* Firuzuddin Firuz. *Public Works:* Yama Yari. *Refugees:* Sayed Hussain Alemi Balkhi. *Rural Development:* Mujib Rahman Karimi. *Transport and Civil Aviation:* Hamidullah Tahmasi. *Urban Development:* Sayed Saadat Mansoor Naderi. *Women's Affairs:* Dilbar Nazari. *Attorney General:* Mohammad Farid Hamidi. *Head of National Directorate of Security:* Mohammed Masoom Stanekzai. *National Security Adviser:* Mohammad Hanif Atmar.

Afghan Parliament: http://www.parliament.af

Current Leaders

Ashraf Ghani Ahmadzai

Position
President

Introduction
Ashraf Ghani became president in Sept. 2014, heading a national unity government. A modernizer and former finance minister with experience at the World Bank, Ghani pledged to rebuild the economy, tackle corruption and work with parties from across the political spectrum.

Early Life
Born on 12 Feb. 1949 in Logar province, Ghani was educated in Kabul and graduated from the American University of Beirut in 1973. From 1973–77 he taught anthropology at Kabul University before studying for a PhD at Columbia University, New York, USA. He taught briefly at the University of California, Berkeley, then at John Hopkins University, Baltimore, from 1983–91. From 1991–2001 he worked for the World Bank, where he was involved in reviewing country strategies. During this time he helped pioneer a new approach that emphasized building coalitions for reform and working with local people.

In 2002, after the ousting of the Taliban government, he became special adviser to President Hamid Karzai and helped organize the *Loya Jirga* (Grand Council). The same year he was appointed adviser to Lakhdar Brahimi, the UN Secretary-General's special envoy to Afghanistan. In this role he was involved in drawing up the Bonn Agreement, which laid out a programme for transition to democratic government. From 2002–04 he served as finance minister in the Transitional Administration, implementing the launch of a new currency and introducing the concept of a 'double-compact' between aid donors and the Afghan government, and the government and the Afghan people.

Following the 2004 general election, Ghani left government to become chancellor of Kabul University. In 2006 he co-founded the Institute for State Effectiveness, which advises on methods for building accountable governments and civil societies. From 2010–13 he served as chairman of the Transition Coordination Commission, overseeing the transfer of security from foreign troops to Afghan forces. In 2014 he stood for the presidency, promising to build a strong economy and promote unity and security. He won in the second round of voting in June 2014 but the result was disputed amid allegations of electoral fraud. Months of negotiations were finally resolved by a power-sharing deal that saw Ghani's runner-up, Abdullah Abdullah, appointed chief executive officer, with ministerial posts divided between their followers.

Career in Office
Ashraf Ghani was sworn in on 29 Sept. 2014 at the head of a national unity government. His early months saw him struggle to appoint a full contingent of ministers, and holding his diverse government together posed a key challenge, along with tackling corruption, combating continuing armed attacks by the Taliban and managing relations with Pakistan.

In Dec. 2014 the US-led military coalition formally ended its combat mission against the Taliban after 13 years, although some personnel were to be retained in the country to train and support the Afghan security forces. However, in response to a resurgence of Taliban attacks and a marked deterioration in the security outlook from 2015, the then US president Barack Obama twice extended the deployment of about 8,400 retained US combat troops to help with counter-terrorism operations, and in Aug. 2017 his successor, Donald Trump, announced that he was sending additional forces to the country.

Taliban insurgent attacks and bombings nevertheless persisted, notably an assault in Aug. 2018 on Ghazni, a strategic provincial capital, in which several hundred people were killed in days of fighting before government forces regained control of the city. Despite the violence, the first parliamentary elections in eight years took place across the country in Oct., although the voter turnout was low amid Taliban warnings of retribution.

Defence

In 2013 military expenditure totalled US$2,898m. (US$93 per capita), representing 13·8% of GDP.

Since the fall of the Taliban, Afghanistan has had an all-volunteer professional-army. The UN-mandated international force, ISAF, assisted the government in the maintenance of security throughout the country until its mandate expired at the end of 2014. It had been led by NATO since 2003. About 13,500 personnel have been retained to train, advise and assist the Afghan National Security Forces in the context of Operation *Resolute Support*.

Army

The decimation of the Taliban's armed forces left Afghanistan without an army. A multi-ethnic Afghan National Army was created in Dec. 2002. Personnel numbered approximately 179,000 in Aug. 2014 (up from 12,000 in 2004).

Air Force

Afghanistan's air forces were severely damaged with all planes destroyed by US military operations in 2001, but the Afghan Air Force (the Afghan National Army Air Corps until June 2010) is being rebuilt. In Sept. 2014 it had approximately 6,800 personnel.

International Relations

Afghanistan was the world's largest recipient of foreign aid every year from 2010 until 2014 (peaking at US$6·9bn. in 2011). Foreign aid has fallen since then and Syria has replaced Afghanistan as the largest recipient.

Economy

In 2012 agriculture accounted for 25% of GDP, industry 21% and services 54%.

Afghanistan featured among the ten most corrupt countries in the world in a 2018 survey of 180 countries carried out by the anti-corruption organization Transparency International.

Overview

Afghanistan is one of the world's poorest countries with formidable development, humanitarian and governance challenges. After the removal of the Taliban regime in 2001, work began on reconstructing an economy impoverished by more than 20 years of conflict, periodic earthquakes and drought.

In 2014 the country was still among the bottom 10% of nations on the UN Human Development Index. Unemployment and poverty remain widespread. The presence of large and active militant groups (including the Taliban), poor governance and endemic corruption also restrict short- and long-term prospects.

The authorities have taken some steps towards establishing economic stability. Real GDP growth averaged over 10% annually in the five years to 2010–11 and revenue collection increased. However, the withdrawal of most remaining international troops in 2014, together with uncertainty surrounding the transfer of political power and the exposure of weaknesses in the banking sector, impaired investor confidence, prompting a decline in GDP growth that year to 1·3% from 3·9% the previous year. In late 2014 international donors reaffirmed their support after the government pledged to restore confidence in the banking sector and lift revenue collection. The government also stated its commitment to combatting corruption and countering the financing of terrorism. Nonetheless, opium production remains an integral part of the economy, with the trade accounting for 4% of GDP in 2014.

Growth averaged 1·8% per year in the period 2014–17, reflecting ongoing political and social instability that has undermined consumer demand and private investment. Unfavourable weather conditions have also stunted growth, given the agricultural sector's importance as its primary driver.

The poverty rate was measured at 55% in 2016–17, up from 38% five years earlier, while about 40% of children aged under five suffer from chronic malnutrition. Comprehensive reforms to spur investor confidence—allied to an upswing in domestic and regional security—are vital for long-term growth.

Currency

The *afghani* (AFN) was introduced in Oct. 2002 with one of the new notes worth 1,000 old *afghani* (AFA). The old *afghani* had been trading at around 46,000 to the US$. There was inflation of 4·4% in 2016 and 5·0% in 2017.

Budget

The fiscal year begins on 21 March. Revenues in 2012–13 were 260,600m. afghani and expenditures 188,200m. afghani. Grants accounted for 59·8% of revenues in 2012–13; current expenditure accounted for 97·1% of expenditures.

Performance

Real GDP growth was 1·0% in 2015, 2·2% in 2016 and 2·7% in 2017. Total GDP in 2017 was US$20·8bn.

Banking and Finance

Da Afghanistan Bank undertakes the functions of a central bank, holding the exclusive right of note issue. Founded in 1939, its current *Governor* is Khalilullah Sediq. The banking sector has undergone major reconstruction since the removal of the Taliban government in 2001, with a number of new private banks having opened in the meantime.

In 2010 the banking system came under scrutiny after Kabul Bank, a leading commercial bank used by the government to pay civil servants and members of the security forces, was unable to account for US$910m. amid allegations of fraud and mismanagement. It was subsequently bailed out by the central bank to avert a collapse.

Total external debt in 2010 was US$2,297m., which was equivalent to 21% of GNI.

Energy and Natural Resources

Environment

Carbon dioxide emissions from the consumption of energy were the equivalent of 0·3 tonnes per capita in 2011.

Electricity

Installed capacity was 0·43m. kW in 2011–12. Production was 1,005m. kWh in 2011–12 with consumption per capita 128 kWh. In 2016, 84% of the population had access to electricity compared to only 43% in 2010.

Oil and Gas

Proven natural gas reserves were 50bn. cu. metres in 2013. Production in 2012 was 168m. cu. metres.

Minerals

There are deposits of barite, coal, copper, emerald, lapis lazuli, salt and talc. Mining, particularly of copper, is considered to be the country's best prospect for economic growth. In spite of the instability, Afghanistan is still one of the world's leading producers of lapis lazuli.

Agriculture

The greater part of Afghanistan is mountainous but there are many fertile plains and valleys. In 2007 there were an estimated 8·53m. ha. of arable land and 0·13m. ha. of permanent cropland; 2·25m. ha. were irrigated in 2007. The agricultural population was approximately 16·0m. in 2007, of whom around 5·08m. were economically active.

Output, 2013, in 1,000 tonnes: wheat, 5,169; grapes, 611; rice, 512; barley, 514; maize, 312; potatoes, 303. Opium production in 2001 was just 185 tonnes (down from 4,565 tonnes in 1999), but in 2002 it went up to 3,400 tonnes. Estimated potential production reached a record 9,000 tonnes in 2017, up from 4,800 tonnes in 2016. The area under cultivation in 2017 was a record 328,000 ha. (up from 201,000 ha. in 2016). It had been just 7,606 ha. in 2001. Afghanistan accounts for around 90% of the world's opium. In Feb. 2001 the United Nations Drug Control Programme reported that opium production had been almost totally eradicated after the Taliban outlawed the cultivation of poppies. As a result in 2001 Myanmar became the largest producer of opium, but since then Afghanistan has again been the leading producer.

Livestock (2013): sheep, 13·1m.; goats, 7·0m.; cattle, 5·2m.; asses, 1·5m.; horses, 171,000; camels, 170,000; chickens, 12m.

Forestry

In 2015 forests covered 1·35m. ha., or 2% of the total land area. Timber production in 2011 was 3·42m. cu. metres.

Fisheries

In 2015 the total catch was estimated to be 1,000 tonnes, exclusively from inland waters.

Industry

Major industries include natural gas, fertilizers, cement, coal mining, small vehicle assembly plants, building, carpet weaving, cotton textiles, clothing and footwear, leather tanning and fruit canning.

Labour

The labour force in 2013 was 7,983,000 (5,569,000 in 2003). 49·0% of the population aged 15–64 was economically active in 2013. In the same year 9·2% of the population was unemployed.

Afghanistan had 86,000 people living in slavery according to the Walk Free Foundation's 2013 *Global Slavery Index*.

International Trade

Imports and Exports

Total imports (2010), US$2,218m.; exports US$388·5m. Main imports: mineral fuels, lubricants and related materials; food and live animals; manufactured goods; machinery and transport equipment. Main exports: opium (illegal trade); food and live animals; manufactured goods; inedible crude materials (excluding fuels). The illegal trade in opium is the largest source of export earnings and accounts for half of Afghanistan's GDP. Main import sources in 2010 were Uzbekistan (21·1%), China (13·7%), Pakistan (11·6%) and Germany (8·2%) The leading export destination in 2010 was Pakistan (38·9%), followed by India (16·8%), Turkey (9·0%) and Iran (8·2%).

Imports and exports were largely unaffected by the sanctions imposed during the Taliban regime.

Communications

Roads

There were 42,150 km of roads in 2006, of which 29·3% were paved. A large part of the road network is in a poor state of repair as a result of military action, but rebuilding is under way. In Jan. 2003 women regained the right to drive after a ten-year ban. 431,600 passenger cars (15 per 1,000 inhabitants in 2007) and 153,600 lorries and vans were in use in 2008.

Rail

Historically, Afghanistan has lacked its own railway system although two short stretches of railway extend inside the country from the Uzbek and Turkmen networks. In Feb. 2012 the first major Afghan-run railway opened to commercial traffic at a cost of US$170m., covering 75 km from Hairatan, a town on the border with Uzbekistan, to Mazar i Sharif. It is hoped it will be integrated into a wider network being developed as part of a Central Asia Regional Economic Co-operation programme.

Civil Aviation

There is an international airport at Kabul (Khwaja Rawash Airport). The national carrier is Ariana Afghan Airlines, which in 2010 operated direct flights from Kabul to Amritsar, Baku, Delhi, Dubai, Dushanbe, Frankfurt, Islamabad, İstanbul, Jeddah, Kuwait, Mashad, Moscow, Riyadh, Tehran and Urumqi, as well as domestic services. In 2014 it carried 253,040 passengers, up from 226,266 in 2013. The UN sanctions imposed on 14 Nov. 1999 included the cutting off of Afghanistan's air links to the outside world. In Jan. 2002 Ariana Afghan Airlines resumed services and Kabul airport was reopened. The airport was heavily bombed during the US campaign and although it is now functioning with some civilian flights it is still being used extensively by the military authorities. Afghanistan's first private airline, Kam Air, was launched in Nov. 2003.

Shipping

There are practically no navigable rivers. A port has been built at Qizil Qala on the Oxus and there are three river ports on the Amu Darya, linked by road to Kabul. The container port at Kheyrabad on the Amu Darya river has rail connections to Uzbekistan.

Telecommunications

There were 23,424,000 mobile phone subscriptions in 2014 (748·8 per 1,000 inhabitants) and 102,000 landline telephone subscriptions (3·3 per 1,000 inhabitants). In 2014, 6·4% of the population were internet users. In March 2012 there were 257,000 Facebook users.

Social Institutions

According to the 2017 *Fragile States Index*—a list published jointly by the Fund for Peace and *Foreign Policy* magazine—Afghanistan was ranked as the country ninth most vulnerable to conflict or collapse. The index is based on 12 indicators of state vulnerability across social, political and economic categories.

Justice

A Supreme Court was established in June 1978. It retained its authority under the Taliban regime.

Under the Taliban, a strict form of Sharia law was followed. This law, which was enforced by armed police, included prohibitions on alcohol, television broadcasts, internet use and photography, yet received its widest condemnation for its treatment of women. Public executions and amputations were widely used as punishment under the regime.

The Judicial Reform Commission is in the process of establishing a civil justice system in accordance with Islamic principles, international standards, the rule of law and Afghan legal traditions. The death penalty is still in force. There were five confirmed judicial executions in 2017 and three in 2018. In 2015 the World Justice Project *Rule of Law Index*, which provides data on how the rule of law is experienced by the general public across eight categories, ranked Afghanistan 100th of 102 countries for criminal justice and 101st for civil justice.

The population in penal institutions in 2012 was 25,289 (76 per 100,000 of national population).

Education

Adult literacy was an estimated 38·2% in 2015 (51·5% among males but only 23·9% among females).

In 2007 there were 4,718,077 pupils at primary schools (37% female) with 110,312 teaching staff and 1,035,782 at secondary schools (26% female) with 32,817 teaching staff. There were around 9,000 schools in 2008. Schools are often burned down and insurgents have attacked both teachers and pupils.

In 2009 there were 19 public universities and higher education institutions. There are also a number of private universities including the American University of Afghanistan. In 2008–09 there were 95,000 students

(18% female) in tertiary education and 3,000 academic staff. Kabul University had some 8,000 students in 2006. Formerly one of Asia's finest educational institutes, Kabul University lost many of its staff during the Taliban regime, and following the US bombing attacks it was closed down, although it has since reopened.

In areas controlled by the Taliban education was forbidden for girls. Boys' schools taught only religious education and military training. Female teachers and pupils returned to education after five years of exclusion in 2002, and now nearly 40% of pupils and 30% of teachers are female.

Health

Afghanistan is one of the least successful countries in the battle against undernourishment. In 2015, 26·8% of the population were undernourished.

In *Water: At What Cost? The State of the World's Water 2016*, WaterAid reported that 44·7% of the population does not have access to safe water—the eighth highest percentage of any nation.

The bombing of Afghanistan beginning in Oct. 2001 severely disrupted the supply of aid to the country and left much of the population exposed to starvation, but progress since has resulted in more than 60% of the population now having access to basic health services compared to under 10% in 2001.

In 2005 there were 5,970 physicians, 900 dentistry personnel and 14,930 nursing and midwifery personnel in Afghanistan.

Religion

The predominant religion is Islam. According to a study by the Pew Research Center entitled *Mapping the Global Muslim Population*, around 84–89% of the population in 2009 were Sunni Muslims and 10–15% Shias.

The Taliban provoked international censure in 2001 by forcing the minority population of Afghan Hindus and Sikhs to wear yellow identification badges.

Culture

World Heritage Sites

There are two UNESCO sites in Afghanistan: the Minaret and Archaeological Remains of Jam (inscribed in 2002), a 12th century minaret; the Cultural Landscape and Archaeological Remains of the Bamiyan Valley (2003), including the monumental Buddha statues destroyed by the Taliban in 2001.

Press

Afghanistan had approximately 540 newspapers in 2008 including 16 paid-for dailies. The main dailies were *Hewad*, *Anis* and the English language publications *Daily Outlook Afghanistan* and *Kabul Times*.

Tourism

Owing to the political situation the tourism industry has been negligible since 2001. It is estimated that around 3,000–4,000 tourists visit the country annually.

Calendar

In 2002 the Afghan Interim Authority replaced the lunar calendar with the traditional Afghan solar calendar. The solar calendar had previously been used in Afghanistan until 1999 when it was changed by the Taliban authorities who wanted the country to adopt the system used in Saudi Arabia. The change back to the solar calendar means the current year is 1397.

Diplomatic Representatives

Of Afghanistan in the United Kingdom (31 Prince's Gate, London, SW7 1QQ)
    Ambassador: Said Tayeb Jawad.

Of the United Kingdom in Afghanistan (15th St., Roundabout Wazir Akbar Khan, PO Box 334, Kabul)
    Ambassador: Vacant.
    Chargé d'Affaires a.i.: Giles Lever.

Of Afghanistan in the USA (2341 Wyoming Ave., NW, Washington, D.C., 20008)
    Ambassador: Vacant.
    Chargé d'Affaires a.i.: Madina Qasimi.

Of the USA in Afghanistan (Great Masood Rd, Wazir Akbar Khan, Kabul)
  Ambassador: John R. Bass.

Of Afghanistan to the United Nations
  Ambassador: Mahmoud Saikal.

Of Afghanistan to the European Union
  Ambassador: Wali J. Monawar.

Further Reading

Cowper-Coles, Sherard, *Cables from Kabul: The Inside Story of the West's Afghanistan Campaign.* 2011

Dalrymple, William, *Return of a King: The Battle for Afghanistan, 1839–42.* 2013

Ewans, Martin, *Afghanistan, A New History.* 2001

Gall, Carlotta, *The Wrong Enemy: America in Afghanistan, 2001–14.* 2014

Goodson, Larry, *Afghanistan's Endless War: State Failure, Regional Politics and the Rise of the Taliban.* 2001

Griffiths, John, *Afghanistan: A History of Conflict.* 2001

Hopkins, B. D., *The Making of Modern Afghanistan.* 2008

Hyman, A., *Afghanistan under Soviet Domination, 1964–1991.* 3rd ed. 1992

Magnus, Ralph H. and Naby, Eden, *Afghanistan: Mullah, Marx and Mujahid.* Revised ed. 2002

Maley, William, *The Afghanistan Wars.* 2nd ed. 2009

Margolis, Eric, *War at the Top of the World: The Struggle for Afghanistan, Kashmir and Tibet.* 2001

Nojumi, Neamatollah, *The Rise of the Taliban in Afghanistan.* 2001

Snetkov, Aglaya and Aris, Stephen, *The Regional Dimensions to Security.* 2013

Steele, Jonathan, *Ghosts of Afghanistan: The Haunted Battleground.* 2011

Vogelsang, Willem, *The Afghans.* 2002

National Statistical Office: Central Statistics Office, Ansar-i-Watt, Kabul.

Website: http://cso.gov.af/en

Albania

Republika e Shqipërisë (Republic of Albania)

Capital: Tirana
Population projection, 2020: 2·94m.
GNI per capita, 2017: (PPP$) 11,886
HDI/world rank, 2017: 0·785/68
Internet domain extension: .al

Key Historical Events

Albania was originally part of Illyria which stretched along the eastern coastal region of the Adriatic. By 168 BC the Romans, having conquered Illyria, administered it as a province (Illyricum). From AD 395 Illyria, as part of the eastern Byzantine empire, submitted to waves of Slavic invasions. During the middle ages the name Albania gained currency, possibly deriving from Albanoi, the name of an Illyrian tribe. Ottoman intrusion began in the 14th century and, despite years of resistance under the leadership of national hero Gjergj Kastrioti, Turkish suzerainty was imposed from 1478. During the 15th and 16th centuries, many Albanians fled to southern Italy to escape Ottoman rule and conversion to Islam. After the Russo-Turkish war of 1877–78 there were demands for independence from Turkey. With the defeat of Turkey in the Balkan war of 1912, Albanian nationalists proclaimed independence and set up a provisional government.

In the First World War Albania was a battlefield for opposing occupation forces. Albania was admitted to the League of Nations on 20 Dec. 1920. In Nov. 1921 its 1913 frontiers were confirmed with minor alterations. Although declared a republic in 1925, Albania became a monarchy from Sept. 1928 until April 1939 when Italy's dictator, Mussolini, invaded and set up a puppet state. During the Second World War Albania suffered first Italian and then German occupation. Resistance was led by royalist, nationalist republican and Communist movements, often at odds with each other. The Communists had the support of Josip Broz Tito's Yugoslav partisans, who were instrumental in forming the Albanian Communist Party on 8 Nov. 1941. Communists dominated the Anti-Fascist National Liberation Committee which became the Provisional Democratic Government on 22 Oct. 1944 after the German withdrawal, with Enver Hoxha at its head.

Relations with Tito's Yugoslavia became increasingly strained as Hoxha strove to keep Albania from becoming a satellite of its neighbour, as it pursued its own brand of socialism independently of Moscow. In Albania, large estates were broken up and the land distributed, with collectivization imposed from 1955–59. However, the close ties forged with the USSR of Joseph Stalin were severed during the late 1950s and early 1960s when Stalin's successor as Soviet leader, Nikita Khrushchev, embarked on a campaign of de-Stalinization and achieved rapprochement with Yugoslavia. China replaced the Soviet Union as Albania's patron until the end of the Maoist phase in 1977. The regime then adopted a policy of 'revolutionary self-sufficiency'.

Following the collapse of the USSR, the People's Assembly legalized opposition parties. The Communists won the first multi-party elections in April 1991, but soon resigned from office following a general strike. They were replaced by a coalition government, which collapsed in Dec. 1991, and then by an interim technocratic administration. A new, non-Communist government was elected in March 1992.

In 1997 Albania was disrupted by financial crises caused by the collapse of fraudulent pyramid finance schemes. A period of violent anarchy led to the fall of the administration and to fresh elections which returned a Socialist led government. A UN peacekeeping force withdrew in Aug. 1997, but sporadic violence continued.

In April 1999 the Kosovo crisis, which led to NATO air attacks on Yugoslav military targets, prompted a flood of refugees into Albania.

Having won a decisive victory in the 2001 elections, the ruling Socialist Party lost power to the opposition Democratic Party in July 2005. The Democrats won a further term in government in July 2009 but lost to the Socialist Party at the general election of June 2013, after which Socialist leader Edi Rama became prime minister. Albania joined NATO in April 2009 and was recommended for EU candidate membership status by the European Commission in June 2014.

Territory and Population

Albania is bounded in the north by Montenegro and Serbia, east by North Macedonia, south by Greece and west by the Adriatic. The area is 28,703 sq. km (11,082 sq. miles). The population at the census of Oct. 2011 was 2,821,977 giving a density of 98·3 per sq. km. Population estimate, Jan. 2018: 2,870,324.

The UN gives a projected population for 2020 of 2·94m.

In 2011, 52·9% of the population lived in urban areas. The capital is Tirana (population in 2011, 418,495); other large towns (population in 2011) are Durrës (113,249), Vlorë (79,513), Elbasan (78,703), Shkodër (76,000; estimate), Fier (55,845) and Korçë (51,152).

The country is administratively divided into 12 counties, subdivided into 61 municipalities.

Counties	Area (sq. km)	2018 population (estimate)
Berat	1,798	127,431
Dibër	2,586	120,978
Durrës	766	289,628
Elbasan	3,199	278,547
Fier	1,890	298,144
Gjirokastër	2,884	62,952
Korçë	3,711	210,178
Kukës	2,374	77,394
Lezhë	1,620	126,800
Shkodër	3,562	204,994
Tirana	1,652	883,996
Vlorë	2,706	189,282

In most cases prefectures are named after their capitals. The one exception is Dibër, where the capital is Peshkopi.

The vast majority of the population are Albanians, with small Greek, Roma, Aromanian and Macedonian minorities.

The official language is Albanian.

Social Statistics

2007: births, 33,163; deaths, 14,528. Rates in 2007 (per 1,000): births, 10·5; deaths, 4·6. Infant mortality, 2010, was 16 per 1,000 live births. Fertility rate (number of births per woman), 1·9 in 2008. Annual population growth rate, 2008–10, 0·4%. Life expectancy at birth, 2007, was 73·4 years for men and 79·8 years for women. Abortion was legalized in 1991.

Climate

Mediterranean-type, with rainfall mainly in winter, but thunderstorms are frequent and severe in the great heat of the plains in summer. Winters in the highlands can be severe, with much snow. Tirana, Jan. 44°F (6·8°C), July 75°F (23·9°C). Annual rainfall 54" (1,353 mm). Shkodër, Jan. 39°F (3·9°C), July 77°F (25°C). Annual rainfall 57" (1,425 mm).

Constitution and Government

A new constitution was adopted on 28 Nov. 1998. The supreme legislative body is the single-chamber *Parliament* of 140 deputies. As from April 2009 all members are elected through proportional representation, for four-year terms. Where no candidate wins an absolute majority, a run-off election is held. The *President* is elected by parliament for a five-year term.

© Springer Nature Limited 2020
Palgrave Macmillan (ed.), *The Statesman's Yearbook 2020*,
https://doi.org/10.1057/978-1-349-95940-2_12

National Anthem

'Rreth Flamurit të përbashkuar' ('The flag that united us in the struggle'); words by A. S. Drenova, tune by C. Porumbescu.

Recent Elections

Parliamentary elections took place on 25 June 2017. The Socialist Party won 74 of the 140 seats with 48·3% of votes cast; the Democratic Party, 43 with 28·8% of the votes; the Socialist Movement for Integration, 19 (14·3%); the Party for Justice, Integration and Unity, 3 (4·8%); the Social Democratic Party, 1 (1·0%). Turnout was 46·8%.

Parliament elected Ilir Meta (Socialist Movement for Integration; LSI) president on 28 April 2017 in a fourth round after votes on 19, 20 and 27 April had failed to result in the required three-fifths majority.

Current Government

President: Ilir Meta; b. 1969 (LSI; sworn in 24 July 2017).

In Feb. 2019 the government comprised:

Prime Minister: Edi Rama; b. 1964 (PS; sworn in 15 Sept. 2013).

Deputy Prime Minister: Erion Braçe.

Minister of Agriculture and Rural Development: Blendi Çuçi. *Culture:* Elva Margariti. *Defence:* Olta Xhaçka. *Education, Sports and Youth:* Besa Shahini. *Europe and Foreign Affairs (acting):* Gent Cakaj. *Finance and Economy:* Anila Denaj. *Health and Social Care:* Ogerta Manastirliu. *Infrastructure and Energy:* Belinda Balluku. *Interior:* Sandër Lleshaj. *Justice:* Etilda Gjonaj. *Tourism and Environment:* Blendi Klosi.

Minister of State for Diaspora Affairs: Pandeli Majko. *Minister of State for Entrepreneurship:* Eduard Shalsi. *Minister of State for Relations with the Parliament:* Elisa Spiropali.

Albanian Parliament (Albanian only): http://www.parlament.al

Current Leaders

Ilir Meta

Position

President

Introduction

Ilir Meta, a former prime minister, was elected president by parliament on 28 April 2017.

Early Life

Ilir Meta was born in Çorovodë in the municipality of Skrapar. He studied economics and politics at the University of Tirana, also becoming fluent in English and Italian. He was elected as a member of parliament for the Socialist Party of Albania (PS) in 1992, serving variously as first deputy chairman of the foreign affairs commission, deputy prime minister and minister of co-ordination. In Oct. 1999 he was elected prime minister.

In 2004 Meta left the PS to form the Socialist Movement for Integration and also became a member of the International Commission on the Balkans. He had adopted a pragmatic approach to the issue of the historic diaspora of Albanians, dealing with problems of illegal migrants and extremists in co-operation with international aid organizations while rejecting the idea of uniting all ethnic Albanians under a single flag. As one of the founders of the Albanian Euro-Socialist Youth Movement, Meta has been an advocate of integration with the European Union.

As premier, Meta made it a priority to improve relations with key trading partners including Germany, Italy and Greece. He also sought to stabilize the economy through privatization of strategic sectors, upgrading the transport infrastructure and improving law and order.

After resigning as prime minister in Jan. 2002 amid PS infighting, he was foreign minister in the government of Pandeli Majko until 2003 (a role he resumed from 2009–10). He then served as chairman of parliament from 2013–17.

Career in Office

Meta was elected as Albania's president with 87 of a possible 140 parliamentary votes in April 2017 and was sworn in on 24 July.

Edi Rama

Position

Prime Minister

Introduction

A former mayor of Tirana, Edi Rama became prime minister in June 2013 at the head of a socialist coalition. A modernizer known internationally for his work in urban regeneration, he has promised to achieve EU membership.

Early Life

Edi Rama was born on 4 July 1964 in Tirana. He became politically active while a student and was a founding member of the Movement for Democracy, which campaigned for reforms. For much of the 1990s he followed a career as a painter in Paris, exhibiting internationally.

In 1998 he returned to Albania to become minister of culture, youth and sport in Fatos Nano's government. He was elected mayor of Tirana in 2000, serving for three consecutive terms until 2011. In this role he tackled the decline of the city centre, restoring parks and widening roads, but critics accused him of concentrating on cosmetic solutions rather than improving basic services. He also faced allegations of corruption and mismanagement of public funds.

In 2005 he became leader of the Socialist Party (PS) and in 2009 contested the general election at the head of a five-party coalition. After a turbulent campaign, featuring competing promises of EU integration, incumbent Prime Minister Sali Berisha's coalition was declared victorious. Rama challenged the result, leading his party in a series of parliamentary boycotts and demonstrations. In 2013 the PS formed a new coalition, the Alliance for a European Albania, with other left-wing parties, including the Socialist Movement for Integration that had defected from Berisha's government. Campaigning on pledges to introduce democratic reforms and speed up EU integration, Rama's coalition won 83 of 140 seats.

Career in Office

Rama took office on 15 Sept. 2013. His appointment of six women to the cabinet was widely viewed as a signal of his modernizing credentials.

With the aim of achieving EU membership for Albania, he sought to tackle corruption and organized crime, implement democratic reforms, reduce unemployment and stabilize the economy, and in April 2018 the European Commission recommended that Albania be allowed to start talks on joining.

Although allegations in June 2015 of voting irregularities in local government elections fuelled parliamentary tensions between his ruling coalition and the opposition Democratic Party, Rama's Socialist Party won the majority of seats in parliamentary elections in June 2017 and subsequent government changes in Aug. included new defence, interior and finance ministers. In Oct. 2018 Rama announced that Fatmir Xhafaj, a controversial political figure under pressure from the opposition for his alleged links to organized crime and for human rights violations in the 1980s, had resigned as interior minister.

In Nov. 2014, against the backdrop of continuing bilateral tensions over the status of Kosovo, Rama had made the first visit by an Albanian prime minister to Serbia in nearly 70 years. The Serbian prime minister then made a similarly landmark visit to Albania in May 2015.

Defence

Since 1 Jan. 2010 Albania has had an all-volunteer professional army. Strength of the Joint Forces Command was 8,150 in 2011. In 2013 defence expenditure totalled US$182m. (US$61 per capita), representing 1·4% of GDP.

Army

The Albanian Land Force—part of the Albanian Armed Forces—comprises a rapid reaction brigade, a commando regiment, an area support brigade, a logistics battalion and a communications battalion. Equipment in 2011 included three main battle tanks.

Navy

The Albanian Naval Force—part of the Albanian Armed Forces—had three patrol boats in 2011. The Albanian Coast Guard had 13 riverine patrol boats in 2011 plus 12 coastal patrol boats and nine other patrol boats. There are naval bases at Durrës and Vlorë.

Air Force

The Albanian Air Force—part of the Albanian Armed Forces—operated 16 helicopters in 2011 (including seven Agusta Bell 206s).

International Relations

Albania applied to join the EU in April 2009 and was granted candidate status in June 2014.

Economy

In 2013 agriculture accounted for 22·5% of GDP, industry 26·4% and services 51·1%.

Overview

Formerly a closed state with a centrally-planned economy, Albania's transition to a middle-income country has not been without problems. Notably, while poverty fell by about half to 12·4% between 2002 and 2008, it had risen again to 14·3% as of 2012. Economic growth averaged 6% per year from 2004 to 2008 but only 3% per year from 2009 to 2011, and just over 1% between 2012 and 2014. Remittances contributed 12–15% of GDP before the global financial crisis took hold in 2008, but a subsequent decline (which saw them account for only 5·7% of GDP in 2015) reflected the high number of Albanians competing for work in the troubled economies of Italy and Greece.

The agricultural sector accounts for 43·3% of employment but contributes only around 20% of GDP annually. The ongoing shift towards industry and services has been supported by strong foreign direct investment, equivalent to some 8–9% of GDP by the mid-2010s, which in turn has been propelled by large-scale energy projects. The economy has historically suffered from poor infrastructure and energy shortages.

Albania imports far more than it exports, reflected in a 13% current account deficit predicted for 2016. However, public debt was on a downward trajectory as of 2015 and fiscal consolidation is slowly countering a large informal economy. In Feb. 2014 the IMF approved a three-year US$457m. loan to support the government's reform programme. Albania became a member of NATO in 2009 and has applied for European Union membership.

Currency

The monetary unit is the *lek* (ALL), notionally of 100 *qindars*. In Sept. 1991 the lek (plural, *lekë* or leks) was pegged to the ecu at a rate of 30 leks = one ecu. In June 1992 it was devalued from 50 to 110 to US$1. There was inflation of 1·3% in 2016 and 2·0% in 2017.

Foreign exchange reserves were US$1,180m. in July 2005, total money supply was 184,249m. leks and gold reserves totalled 69,000 troy oz.

Budget

The fiscal year is the calendar year. In 2011 general government revenue was 330,450m. leks (324,721m. leks in 2010) and expenditure 305,621m. leks (300,878m. leks in 2010).

Principal sources of revenue in 2011 were: taxes on goods and services, 188,259m. leks; social security contributions, 56,627m. leks; taxes on income, profits and capital gains, 50,249m. leks. Main items of expenditure by economic type in 2011 were: social benefits, 132,639m. leks; compensation of employees, 67,446m. leks; interest, 41,121m. leks.

VAT is 20%.

Performance

Total GDP in 2017 was US$13·0bn. Since the economy contracted by 10·2% in 1997 following the collapse of pyramid finance schemes, Albania has enjoyed consistently strong growth and managed to avoid recession in 2009. Every year between 1998 and 2001 and again from 2003 to 2008 real GDP growth was in excess of 5%. More recently there was a growth of 2·2% in 2015, 3·4% in 2016 and 3·8% in 2017.

Banking and Finance

The central bank and bank of issue is the Bank of Albania, founded in 1925 with Italian aid as the Albanian State Bank and renamed in 1993. Its *Governor* is Gent Sejko. In 2015 there were 16 banks, of which 13 were majority foreign-owned. The largest banks are Banka Kombëtare Tregtare (National Commercial Bank) and Raiffeisen Bank Shqipëri (Raiffeisen Albania).

Albania's external debt amounted to US$4,736m. in 2010, up from US$2,054m. in 2005 and US$1,070m. in 2000—this was equivalent to 40·5% of GNI (up from 24·1% in 2005).

A stock exchange opened in Tirana in 1996.

Energy and Natural Resources

Environment

Albania's carbon dioxide emissions from the consumption of energy in 2011 were the equivalent of 1·4 tonnes per capita (compared to the European average of 7·1 tonnes per capita).

Electricity

Although virtually all of the electricity is generated by hydro-electric power plants only 35% of potential hydro-electric sources are currently being used. Electricity capacity was an estimated 1·59m. kW in 2011. Production was 3·99bn. kWh in 2011 and consumption per capita 2,272 kWh. Albania imported 3,475m. kWh of electricity in 2011.

Oil and Gas

Oil reserves in 2014 were 168m. bbls. Crude oil production in 2011, 5·9m. bbls. Natural gas reserves in 2014 totalled 0·8bn. cu. metres; output in 2011 was 16m. cu. metres.

Minerals

Mineral wealth is considerable and includes lignite, chromium, copper and nickel. Output (in 1,000 tonnes): copper ore (2005), 73; chromite (2005), 66.

Agriculture

In 2007 the agricultural population was an estimated 1·37m., of whom around 620,000 were economically active. Only 24% of the land area is suitable for cultivation; 15% of Albania is used for pasture. In 2007 there were 578,000 ha. of arable land and 120,000 ha. of permanent cropland. 106,530 ha. were irrigated in 2007.

In 2007 there were 369,598 agricultural holdings. Since 1995 owners have been permitted to buy and sell agricultural land. In 2007 there were 10,833 tractors in use and 1,643 harvester-threshers.

Production (in 1,000 tonnes), 2007: total grains, 494 (including wheat 250 and maize 216); watermelons, 190; tomatoes, 160; potatoes, 155; grapes, 147; onions, 73; cucumbers and gherkins, 50. Livestock, 2007: sheep, 1,853,000; goats, 876,000; cattle, 577,000; pigs, 147,000; horses, 46,000; chickens, 4,712,000.

Forestry

Forests covered 772,000 ha. in 2015 (28% of the total land area), mainly oak, elm, pine and birch. Timber production in 2011 was 1·18m. cu. metres.

Fisheries

The total catch in 2015 amounted to 6,278 tonnes (4,796 tonnes from sea fishing and 1,482 tonnes from inland fishing).

Industry

Output is small, and the principal industries are agricultural product processing, textiles, oil products and cement. Closures of loss-making plants in the chemical and engineering industries built up in the Communist era led to a 60% decline in the two years after the collapse of the USSR and the subsequent political changes in Albania. Output in 2007 unless otherwise indicated (in 1,000 tonnes): cement (2008), 737; rolled steel (2008), 194; wheat and blended flour, 191; distillate fuel oil, 82; residual fuel oil, 32; sawnwood (estimate), 97,000 cu. metres; beer, 36·6m. litres.

Labour

The labour force in 2013 was 1,287,000 (1,322,000 in 2003). 62·9% of the population aged 15–64 was economically active in 2013. In the same year 16·0% of the population was unemployed.

The official minimum wage in 2010 was 16,120 leks. Minimum wages may not fall below one-third of maximum.

Albania had 11,000 people living in slavery according to the Walk Free Foundation's 2013 *Global Slavery Index*.

International Trade

Imports and Exports

In 2009 imports (c.i.f.) amounted to US$4,548·3m. and exports (f.o.b.) to US$1,087·9m.

Principal imports in 2009: manufactured goods, 25·3%; machinery and transport equipment, 22·6%; food and livestock, 12·1%; mineral fuels, lubricants and related materials (including petroleum and petroleum products), 11·8%. Leading exports in 2009: clothing and apparel, 26·8%; footwear, 19·4%; petroleum and petroleum products, 8·3%; manufactures of metal, 4·8%.

Main import sources in 2009 were: Italy, 26·1%; Greece, 15·5%; China, 7·2%; Germany, 6·5%. Main export markets in 2009 were: Italy, 62·8%; Greece, 7·4%; Slovakia, 5·5%; China, 4·8%.

Communications

Roads

In 2009 there were around 15,000 km of roads including 3,412 km of national or primary roads. There were 237,932 passenger cars in 2007, as well as 29,506 buses and coaches and 59,645 lorries and vans. There were 384 fatalities in road accidents in 2007.

Rail

Total length in operation in 2012 was 399 km. Passenger-km travelled in 2012 came to 16m. and freight tonne-km to 25m.

Civil Aviation

After Albanian Airlines ceased operations in Nov. 2011 Belle Air, a low-cost carrier founded in 2005, became the *de facto* national carrier. However, it in turn ceased operations in Nov. 2013. In 2006 scheduled airline traffic of Albania-based carriers flew 2m. km, carrying 213,000 passengers (all on international flights). The main airport is Mother Teresa International Airport at Rinas, 25 km from Tirana, which handled 1,394,688 passengers in 2009.

Shipping

In Jan. 2014 there were 28 ships of 300 GT or over registered, totalling 40,000 GT. The main port is Durrës, with secondary ports being Vlorë, Sarandë and Shëngjin.

Telecommunications

In 2010 there were 333,000 landline telephone subscriptions (equivalent to 103·9 per 1,000 inhabitants) and 2,692,000 mobile phone subscriptions (or 840·2 per 1,000 inhabitants). In 2009, 41·2% of the population were internet users. Fixed internet subscriptions totalled 105,000 in 2009 (32·9 per 1,000 inhabitants). In March 2012 Albania had 1·06m. Facebook users.

Social Institutions

Out of 178 countries analysed in the 2017 *Fragile States Index*—a list published jointly by the Fund for Peace and *Foreign Policy* magazine—Albania was ranked the 55th least vulnerable to conflict or collapse. The index is based on 12 indicators of state vulnerability across social, political and economic categories.

Justice

A new criminal code was introduced in June 1995. The administration of justice (made up of First Instance Courts, The Courts of Appeal and the Supreme Court) is presided over by the *Council of Justice*, chaired by the President of the Republic, which appoints judges to courts. A Ministry of Justice was re-established in 1990 and a Bar Council set up. In Nov. 1993 the number of capital offences was reduced from 13 to six and the death penalty was abolished for women. In 2000 the death penalty was abolished for peacetime offences; it was abolished for all crimes in 2007.

The prison population in Sept. 2015 was 5,455 (189 per 100,000 of national population). In 2015 the World Justice Project *Rule of Law Index*, which provides data on how the rule of law is experienced by the general public across eight categories, ranked Albania 54th of 102 countries for criminal justice and 59th for civil justice.

Education

Primary education is free and compulsory from six to 14 years. Secondary education is also free and lasts four years. Pupils who fail exams at 14 are required to remain in school until the age of 16.

Secondary education is divided into three categories: general; technical and professional; vocational. There were, in 2008–09, 75,000 children enrolled in nursery schools and 4,000 teachers; 12,000 primary school teachers with 236,000 pupils; and 355,000 pupils and 24,000 teachers at secondary schools. In 2008–09 there were nine public universities, two academies (Academy of Arts and Academy of Sports), the Inter-University Center of Albanological Studies, the Academy of Public Order and the Military University. In Sept. 2008 there were 21 private universities. Adult literacy in 2008 was 95·9% (97·3% among males and 94·7% among females).

In 2007 public expenditure on education came to 3·3% of GDP and represented 11·1% of total government expenditure.

Health

Medical services are free, though medicines are charged for. In 2008 there were 41 public hospitals providing 29·1 beds per 10,000 population. There were 2,039 GPs, 1,587 specialized physicians and 12,746 nurses in 2008.

The budget for expenditure on health in 2007 was 24,104m. leks (8·4% of the total budget).

In *Water: At What Cost? The State of the World's Water 2016*, WaterAid reported that 4·9% of the population does not have access to safe water.

Welfare

The retirement age is 65 (men) and 60 (women). To be eligible for a full state pension contributions over 35 years are required. There is a partial pension with between 15 and 35 years of contributions. Old-age benefits consist of a basic pension and an earnings-related increment. The basic pension is adjusted annually according to average paid contributions.

Unemployment benefit was 6,850 leks per month as of 2012.

Religion

At the 2011 census the declared religious adherence of the population included: Muslims (mainly Sunnis, but with a significant Bektashi Shia minority), 56·7%; Catholics, 10·0%; Orthodox, 6·7%. The remainder follow other religions or are atheists. The Roman Catholic Church has five dioceses in the country, including two archdioceses. The Autocephalous Orthodox Church of Albania is headed by Anastasios, Archbishop of Tirana, Durrës and All Albania (b. 1929). In Feb. 2019 there was one cardinal.

Culture

World Heritage Sites

In 1992 Butrint was added to the UNESCO World Heritage List (reinscribed in 1999 and 2007). Butrint is a settlement in the southwest of the country, near the port of Sarandë, which was inhabited from 800 BC and is now a major site of archaeological investigation. The site was extended for protection after looting in 1997. The historic town of Gjirokastër was added in 2005 (reinscribed in 2008) and is a rare example of a well-preserved Ottoman town built around the 13th century. Ancient and Primeval Beech Forests of the Carpathians and Other Regions of Europe (2007 and 2017) are shared with Austria, Belgium, Bulgaria, Croatia, Germany, Italy, Romania, Slovakia, Slovenia, Spain and Ukraine.

Press

In 2008 there were 28 paid-for dailies (combined circulation of 77,000) and 82 paid-for non-dailies. The leading newspaper in terms of circulation is *Shekulli*.

Tourism

In 2012 there were a record 3,156,000 international tourist arrivals, excluding same-day visitors (up from 2,469,000 in 2011); tourism expenditure in 2012 totalled US$1,623m.

Festivals

The main festivals are Tirana International Contemporary Art Biennial (Sept.–Oct.), Tirana Autumn (Nov.), a music and arts festival, and the Tirana International Film Festival (Nov.–Dec.).

Diplomatic Representatives

Of Albania in the United Kingdom (33 St George's Drive, London, SW1V 4DG)
Ambassador: Qirjako Qirko.

Of the United Kingdom in Albania (Rruga Skënderbeg 12, Tirana)
Ambassador: Duncan Norman, MBE.

Of Albania in the USA (2100 S St., NW, Washington, D.C., 20036)
Ambassador: Floreta Faber.

Of the USA in Albania (Rruga Elbasanit 103, Tirana)
Ambassador: Vacant.
Chargé d'Affaires a.i.: Leyla Moses-Ones.

Of Albania to the United Nations
Ambassador: Besiana Kadare.

Of Albania to the European Union
Ambassador: Suela Janina.

Further Reading

Bezemer, Dirk J. (ed.) *On Eagle's Wings: The Albanian Economy in Transition.* 2009
Vickers, M. and Pettifer, J., *The Albanian Question: Reshaping the Balkans.* 2009
National Statistical Office: Albanian Institute of Statistics, Blv. Zhan d'Ark, Nr. 3, Tirana.
Website: http://www.instat.gov.al

Algeria

© Springer Nature Limited 2020
Palgrave Macmillan (ed.), *The Statesman's Yearbook 2020*,
https://doi.org/10.1057/978-1-349-95940-2_13

Jumhuriya al-Jazairiya ad-Dimuqratiya ash-Shabiya (People's Democratic Republic of Algeria)

Capital: Algiers
Population projection, 2020: 43·33m.
GNI per capita, 2017: (PPP$) 13,802
HDI/world rank, 2017: 0·754/85
Internet domain extension: .dz

Key Historical Events

Algeria came under French control in the 1850s. French settlers assumed political and economic power at the expense of the indigenous Muslim population. In Nov. 1954 the *Front de Libération Nationale* (FLN), representing the Muslim majority, declared open warfare against the French administration. Fierce fighting continued unabated until March 1962 when a ceasefire was agreed between the French government and the nationalists. Against the wishes of the French in Algeria, Gen. de Gaulle conceded Algerian independence on 3 July 1962.

The Political Bureau of the FLN took over the functions of government, a National Constituent Assembly was elected and the Republic was declared on 25 Sept. 1962. One of the founders of the FLN, Ahmed Ben Bella, became prime minister, and president the following year. On 15 June 1965 the government was overthrown by a junta of army officers, who established a Revolutionary Council under Col. Houari Boumedienne. After ten years of rule, Boumedienne proposed elections for a president and a National Assembly. A new constitution was accepted in a referendum in Nov. 1976 and Boumedienne was elected president unopposed. With all parties except the FLN banned from participating, a National Assembly was elected in Feb. 1977.

Following the death of the president in Dec. 1978 the Revolutionary Council again took over the government. The Islamic Salvation Front (FIS) was banned in March 1992. The head of state, Mohamed Boudiaf, was assassinated on 29 July 1992 and a campaign of terrorism by fundamentalists followed. Unrest among Berbers, Algeria's main ethnic community, erupted into violence in May 2001, resulting in 60 deaths in the Berber region of Kabylie. In March 2002 President Bouteflika agreed to grant the Berber language 'national' status alongside Arabic. The state of emergency declared in Feb. 1992 was not lifted until Feb. 2011, following a series of strikes and protests.

In Jan. 2013 Islamist militants seized a gas complex in the Sahara Desert populated by both Algerian and international workers. Algerian special forces stormed the complex after a four-day siege but the operation ended in heavy loss of life. France had used Algerian airspace earlier in the month to launch counter-insurgency operations against Islamist militants active in neighbouring northern Mali.

Territory and Population

Algeria is bounded in the west by Morocco and Western Sahara, southwest by Mauritania and Mali, southeast by Niger, east by Libya and Tunisia, and north by the Mediterranean Sea. It has an area of 2,381,741 sq. km (919,595 sq. miles) and is the largest country in Africa. Population (census 2008) 34,080,030 (16,847,283 female); density, 14·3 per sq. km. In 2011, 67·1% of the population lived in urban areas.

The UN gives a projected population for 2020 of 43·33m.

2·5m. Algerians live in France.

86% of the population speak Arabic, 14% Berber; French is widely spoken. A law of Dec. 1996 made Arabic the sole official language, but in March 2002 Tamazight, the Berber language, was made a national language.

The 2008 census populations of the 48 *wilayat* (provincial councils) were as follows:

Adrar	399,714
Aïn Defla	766,013
Aïn Témouchent	371,239
Algiers (El Djazaïr)	2,988,145
Annaba	609,499
Batna	1,119,791
Béchar	270,061
Béjaia	912,577
Biskra	721,356
Blida	1,002,937
Bordj Bou Arreridj	628,475
Bouira	695,583
Boumerdès	802,083
Chlef	1,002,088
Constantine (Qacentina)	938,475
Djelfa	1,092,184
El Bayadh	228,624
El Oued	647,548
El Tarf	408,414
Ghardaia	363,598
Guelma	482,430
Illizi	52,333
Jijel	636,948
Khenchela	386,683
Laghouat	455,602
Mascara	784,073
Médéa	819,932
Mila	766,886
Mostaganem	737,118
M'Sila	990,591
Naâma	192,891
Oran (Ouahran)	1,454,078
Ouargla	558,558
Oum El Bouaghi	621,612
Relizane	726,180
Saida	330,641
Sétif	1,489,979
Sidi-bel-Abbès	604,744
Skikda	898,680
Souk Ahras	438,127
Tamanrasset	176,637
Tébessa	648,703
Tiaret	846,823
Tindouf	49,149[1]
Tipaza	591,010
Tissemsilt	294,476
Tizi-Ouzou	1,127,607
Tlemcen	949,135

[1]Excluding Saharawi refugees in camps.

The capital is Algiers (2008 census population, 2,364,230). Other major towns (with 2008 census populations over 200,000): Oran, 803,329;

Constantine, 448,028; Annaba, 342,703; Blida, 331,779; Batna, 289,504; Djelfa, 265,833; Sétif, 252,127; Sidi-bel-Abbès, 210,146; Biskra, 204,661.

Social Statistics

2007 estimates: births, 783,000; deaths, 149,000; marriages, 325,000. Rates (2007 estimates): births, 23·0 per 1,000; deaths, 4·4 per 1,000. Infant mortality in 2010 was 31 per 1,000 live births. Expectation of life (2007), 73·6 years for females and 70·8 years for males. Annual population growth rate, 1998–2008, 1·5%. Fertility rate, 2008, 2·4 births per woman.

Climate

Coastal areas have a warm temperate climate, with most rain in winter, which is mild, while summers are hot and dry. Inland, conditions become more arid beyond the Atlas Mountains. Algiers, Jan. 54°F (12·2°C), July 76°F (24·4°C). Annual rainfall 30" (762 mm). Biskra, Jan. 52°F (11·1°C), July 93°F (33·9°C). Annual rainfall 6" (158 mm). Oran, Jan. 54°F (12·2°C), July 76°F (24·4°C). Annual rainfall 15" (376 mm).

Constitution and Government

A referendum was held on 28 Nov. 1996. The electorate was 16,434,527; turnout was 79·6%. The electorate approved by 85·8% of votes cast a new constitution which defines the fundamental components of the Algerian people as Islam, Arab identity and Berber identity. It was signed into law on 7 Dec. 1996. Political parties are permitted, but not if based on a separatist feature such as race, religion, sex, language or region. The President appoints the prime minister and cabinet ministers.

In Feb. 2016 parliament adopted a series of constitutional reforms including the reintroduction of a two-term limit on the presidency (a measure that had been lifted in 2008 so enabling the incumbent president, Abdelaziz Bouteflika, to run for a third term). Nonetheless, Bouteflika was permitted to complete his fourth term, due to finish in 2019. The role of premier, meanwhile, is to be filled by a member of the largest party in parliament. Other measures included preventing citizens with dual nationality from running for high office, creating an independent electoral commission and recognizing the Amazigh language of the indigenous Berber population as an official language.

Parliament is bicameral: a 462-member *National People's Assembly* elected by direct universal suffrage using proportional representation (389 prior to the elections of May 2012), and a 144-member *Council of the Nation*, one-third nominated by the President and two-thirds indirectly elected by the 48 local authorities. The Council of the Nation debates bills passed by the National Assembly which become law if a three-quarters majority is in favour.

National Anthem

'Qassaman bin nazilat Il-mahiqat' ('We swear by the lightning that destroys'); words by Moufdi Zakaria, tune by Mohamed Fawzi.

Government Chronology

(FLN = National Liberation Front; PRS = Revolutionary Socialist Party; RND = National Rally for Democracy; n/p = non-partisan)
    Heads of State since 1962.

President of the Provisional Executive		
1962	FLN	Abderrahmane Farès
Chairman of the National Constituent Assembly		
1962	FLN	Ferhat Abbas
President of the Republic		
1962–65	FLN	Ahmed Ben Bella
Chairman of the Revolutionary Council		
1965–76	military/FLN	Houari Boumedienne
Presidents of the Republic		
1976–78	FLN	Houari Boumedienne
1979–92	FLN	Chadli Bendjedid
Chairman of the Constitutional Council		
1992	FLN	Abdelmélik Benhabilès

(*continued*)

High Council of State (HCE) (collective presidency)		
1992	military	Gen. Khaled Nezzar
	FLN	Ali Hussain Kafi
	FLN	Ali Haroun
	n/p	El-Tidjani Haddam
Chairman of the HCE		
1992	PRS	Mohamed Boudiaf
High Council of State (HCE) (collective presidency)		
1992	n/p	Redha Malek
	military	Gen. Khaled Nezzar
	FLN	Ali Hussain Kafi
	FLN	Ali Haroun
	n/p	El-Tidjani Haddam
Chairman of the HCE		
1992–94	FLN	Ali Hussain Kafi
Presidents of the Republic		
1994–99	n/p, RND	Liamine Zéroual
1999–	n/p	Abdelaziz Bouteflika
Prime Ministers since 1962		
1962–63	FLN	Ahmed Ben Bella
1979–84	FLN	Mohammed Abdelghani
1984–88	FLN	Abdelhamid Brahimi
1988–89	FLN	Kasdi Merbah
1989–91	FLN	Mouloud Hamrouche
1991–92	FLN	Sid Ahmed Ghozali
1992–93	FLN	Belaid Abdessalam
1993–94	n/p	Redha Malek
1994–95	n/p	Mokdad Sifi
1995–98	n/p, RND	Ahmed Ouyahia
1998–99	n/p	Smail Hamdani
1999–2000	n/p	Ahmed Benbitour
2000–03	FLN	Ali Benflis
2003–06	RND	Ahmed Ouyahia
2006–08	FLN	Abdelaziz Belkhadem
2008–12	RND	Ahmed Ouyahia
2012–14	n/p	Abdelmalek Sellal
2014	n/p	Youcef Yousfi (acting)
2014–17	n/p	Abdelmalek Sellal
2017	FLN	Abdelmadjid Tebboune
2017–19	RND	Ahmed Ouyahia
2019–	n/p	Noureddine Bedoui

Recent Elections

In presidential elections on 17 April 2014 Abdelaziz Bouteflika won a fourth term of office, gaining 81·5% of the votes cast; former prime minister Ali Benflis (ind.) received 12·2% of votes cast; Abdelaziz Belaid (Front for the Future), 3·4%; Louisa Hanoune, 1·4%; Ali Fawzi Rebaine, 1·0%; Moussa Touati, 0·6%. Turnout was 51·7%.

Parliamentary elections were held on 4 May 2017. The Front de Libération Nationale/National Liberation Front won 164 of 462 seats; Rassemblement National Démocratique/National Rally for Democracy, 97; Mouvement de la Société pour la Paix/Movement of Society for Peace, 33; Rassemblement de l'Espoir de l'Algérie/Rally for Hope for Algeria, 19. Independents took 28 seats and the remainder went to minor parties. Turnout was 38·3%.

Current Government

President and Minister of National Defence: Abdelaziz Bouteflika; b. 1937 (ind.; sworn in 27 April 1999 and re-elected 8 April 2004, 9 April 2009 and 17 April 2014). In March 2019 the government comprised:
    Prime Minister, and Minister of Interior, Local Government and Regional Planning: Noureddine Bedoui; b. 1959 (ind.; sworn in 12 March 2019).

Deputy Prime Minister, and Minister of Foreign Affairs: Ramtane Lamamra.

Minister of Agriculture, Rural Development and Fisheries: Abdelkader Bouazghi.*Commerce:* Said Djellab. *Communication:* Djamel Kaouane. *Culture:* Azzedine Mihoubi. *Energy:* Mustapha Guitouni. *Environment and Renewable Energies:* Fatma Zohra Zerouati. *Finance:* Abderrahmane Raouia. *Health, Population and Hospital Reform:* Mokhtar Hazbellaoui. *Higher Education and Scientific Research:* Tahar Hadjar. *Housing, Urban Planning and Cities:* Abdelwahid Temmar. *Industry and Mines:* Youcef Yousfi. *Justice and Keeper of the Seals:* Tayeb Louh. *Labour, Employment and Social Security:* Mourad Zemali. *Moudjahidine (War Veterans):* Tayeb Zitouni. *National Education:* Nouria Benghebrit. *National Solidarity, Families and Women's Affairs:* Ghania Eddalia. *Post, and Information and Communication Technologies:* Houda-Imane Feraoun. *Public Works and Transport:* Abdelghani Zaalane. *Relations with Parliament:* Mahdjoub Bedda. *Religious Affairs and Waqfs:* Mohamed Aïssa. *Tourism and Handicrafts:* Abdelkader Benmessaoud. *Vocational Education and Training:* Mohamed Mebarki. *Water Resources:* Hocine Necib. *Youth and Sports:* Mohamed Hattab. *Secretary General of the Government:* Ahmed Noui.

Office of the President (Arabic and French only): http://www.elmouradia.dz

---

Current Leaders

Abdelaziz Bouteflika

Position
President

Introduction
Abdelaziz Bouteflika became president in April 1999 following disputed elections, vowing to improve Algeria's weak economy and end civil discord. Improvements in the economy and state reform have since been slow. However, the significant reduction in Islamist rebel violence following an amnesty in 1999 was a key factor in Bouteflika's re-election in 2004, making him the first Algerian leader to be returned to power in a democratic vote since the country's independence. His charter for peace and national reconciliation was approved in a national referendum in Sept. 2005. He won a further term in the election of April 2009, having secured earlier parliamentary approval in Nov. 2008 of constitutional changes allowing him to run for a third consecutive term of office. In the wake of social unrest and anti-government protests in early 2011, Bouteflika lifted the long-standing state of emergency and set up a committee to consider further constitutional and democratic reform. In April 2014 he was re-elected for a fourth term but, facing declining health and nationwide opposition, he dropped his bid for further re-election in March 2019.

Early Life
Bouteflika was born on 2 March 1937 in Morocco. In 1956 he joined the Armée de Libération Nationale—a wing of the Front de Libération Nationale (FLN; National Liberation Front), and was involved in secret talks with the French authorities that led to Algerian independence in 1962.

Bouteflika joined the government of Ahmed Ben Bella as minister of youth, sport and tourism and was appointed foreign minister in 1963. He retained the position in the government of Houari Boumedienne. Having failed to secure military support to succeed Boumedienne, he was pushed out of the political mainstream. In 1981 he was charged with corruption and forced into exile. However, with the charges dropped, he re-entered Algeria in Jan. 1987. He rejoined the FLN congress in 1989 and was elected to the central committee. In Dec. 1998 he announced his intention to contest the presidency. At the elections, he won almost three-quarters of the vote after his six opponents all stood down from the race the day before polling, accusing him of vote rigging.

Career in Office
Having become president and commanding army support, Bouteflika declared that his primary aim was to end Algeria's many years of civil unrest. In July 1999 parliament passed the National Harmony Law, which offered an amnesty to all rebels who had not been directly responsible for loss of life. A national referendum in Sept. 1999 approved the amnesty scheme, with nearly 99% in favour. Violence by some Islamist groups has since continued but at a greatly reduced rate. In foreign policy, he has

striven to improve relations with neighbouring Morocco, while on the economic front he has encouraged the further development of the country's large oil and gas reserves.

Bouteflika's relations with his prime ministers have been turbulent. Ahmed Benbitour, prime minister from Dec. 1999 to Aug. 2000, resigned over divergent attitudes on economic recovery. His successor, Ali Benflis, was a personal friend and the leader of the largest party, the FLN. However, Benflis's reformist agenda was too radical for Bouteflika, who feared violent insurrection. Bouteflika appointed Ahmed Ouyahia to succeed Benflis.

Benflis refused to support the president's bid for re-election in 2004, instead announcing his own candidacy, supported by the FLN, in Oct. 2003. However, Bouteflika's bid was supported by a coalition of the Rassemblement National Démocratique (RND; National Rally for Democracy), the Islamic Mouvement de la Société pour la Paix (MSP; Movement of the Society for Peace) and also renegade members of the FLN. The elections on 8 April 2004 gave Bouteflika a resounding victory with 85% of the vote in a 58% turnout—against just 6% for Benflis. International observers declared the elections free and fair, despite opposition claims of electoral fraud. His dramatic win was ascribed to the much improved security situation and a steadily growing economy, despite high unemployment.

Bouteflika pledged to investigate the disappearance of around 7,000 Algerians, allegedly killed or imprisoned by the security forces during the 1990s. Improving relations with the Berber community was also a priority, and he promised reform of Algeria's family law, which he described as unfair to women. In Sept. 2005 his charter for peace and national reconciliation to end the civil war, envisaging a limited amnesty and compensation for some victims of violence, was approved in a national referendum. A six-month amnesty from March–Aug. 2006 resulted in the release of some 2,200 Islamist militants (except those accused of the most serious crimes) from prison. However, incidents of terrorism increased again, particularly in Aug. 2008 when almost 60 people were killed in a series of bombings in towns to the east of Algiers.

In May 2006 Bouteflika appointed Abdelaziz Belkhadem as prime minister in place of Ahmed Ouyahia, but reinstated the latter in June 2008. In Nov. Algeria's parliament overwhelmingly approved constitutional amendments that abolished presidential term limits, paving the way for Bouteflika to retain the presidency in the election held on 9 April 2009. However, discontent over housing shortages, unemployment and low wages was reflected in unrest in 2009–10. Further disorder in early 2011, echoing widespread anti-government protests across much of the Arab world, led Bouteflika to promise democratic constitutional amendments. In the May 2012 parliamentary elections the ruling coalition headed by the FLN won a majority of seats in the National Assembly, and in Sept. Bouteflika named Abdelmalek Sellal as the new prime minister.

In Jan. 2013, in the wake of conflict in neighbouring Mali, militant Islamists attacked an isolated gas installation in southeast Algeria and took the foreign workers hostage. The government ordered special forces to storm the plant, which they retook after four days, but at least 37 foreign workers died.

In Nov. 2013 Bouteflika was nominated to run for re-election and was subsequently returned for a fourth consecutive term in April 2014, beating his nearest rival Ali Benflis with 81·5% of the vote. In May 2014 the government proposed constitutional changes, envisaging greater parliamentary powers, the reinstatement of a two-term limit for the presidency and official status for the Berber language. These amendments were passed by parliament in Feb. 2016. The previous month the security service directorate known as DRS was dissolved to be replaced by a new agency under presidential direction. In May 2017 the FLN-led coalition again won a majority of seats in the National Assembly elections and Bouteflika subsequently appointed Abdelmadjid Tebboune as the new premier in place of Abdelmalek Sellal. However, he dismissed Tebboune after less than three months in office and appointed in his place Ahmed Ouyahia, a former prime minister.

Having effectively withdrawn from public view following two strokes since 2013, speculation about Bouteflika's health fuelled persistent rumours that he had relinquished real power to a clique within the economic, political and military elite. Then in early 2019 he registered to run for a fifth term in office, prompting nationwide protests that led him to withdraw his candidacy in March and to postpone the presidential elections scheduled for April. At the same time Ahmed Ouyahia resigned as prime minister and was replaced by Noureddine Bedoui.

In April 2018 Bouteflika had decreed three days of national mourning after 257 people were killed in the country's worst-ever plane crash.

Noureddine Bedoui

Position
Prime Minister

Introduction
Noureddine Bedoui became prime minister in March 2019. He was appointed by the then president, Abdelaziz Bouteflika, following the resignation of Ahmed Ouyahia. Bedoui previously served as minister of vocational training and of the interior.

Early Life
Bedoui was born on 22 Dec. 1959 in Aïn Taya, in the province of Algiers. He graduated from the National School of Administration in city of Algiers and subsequently held several administrative and ministerial posts at local, provincial and national levels. He served in executive positions in the cities of Tizi-Ouzou, Annaba, Bologhine and Aïn Touila. He was also secretary general of the province of Oran and served as governor in the provinces of Sidi Bel-Abbès, Bordj Bou Arreridj, Sétif and Constantine.

On 11 Sept. 2013 Bedoui was appointed minister of vocational education and training. He held the position until 14 May 2015, when he was appointed minister of the interior. He remained in that role until March 2019.

In Feb. 2019 Bouteflika announced his intention to seek a fifth presidential term. Opposition protests broke out soon after amid accusations of corruption and calls for broad changes to the system of government. On 11 March Ahmed Ouyahia resigned as prime minister. Bouteflika withdrew his candidacy for re-election the same day and appointed Bedoui to replace Ouyahia.

Career in Office
Bedoui took office on 12 March 2019, faced with leading a government in the midst of ongoing popular protests and internal turmoil. On 26 March Gaïd Salah, the deputy minister of national defence, called on a Constitutional Council to declare Bouteflika unfit for office.

Defence

Conscription is for 12 months.

Military expenditure totalled US$9,957m. in 2013, equivalent to US$261 per capita and representing 4·7% of GDP.

Army

There are six military regions. The Army had a strength of 110,000 (approximately 75,000 conscripts) in 2011. The Directorate of National Security maintains National Security Forces of 16,000. The Republican Guard numbers 1,200 personnel and the Gendarmerie 20,000. There were in addition legitimate defence groups (self-defence militia and communal guards) numbering around 150,000.

Navy

Naval personnel in 2011 totalled about 6,000. The Navy's 45 vessels included four submarines and three frigates. The main naval bases are at Algiers, Annaba and Mers el Kebir.

Air Force

The Air Force in 2011 had some 14,000 personnel; equipment included 125 combat-capable aircraft and 33 attack helicopters.

International Relations

The land border between Algeria and Morocco has been closed since 1994 following a hotel bombing in Marrakesh in which the Moroccan authorities suspected Algerian involvement.

Economy

In 2016 agriculture contributed 13·3% of GDP, industry 37·8% and services 48·9%.

Overview

The economy, which is heavily dependent on public spending and the sale of hydrocarbons (oil and gas), has expanded every year since 1995. Rising oil prices prompted particularly robust growth from 2003. Algeria was largely shielded from the global financial crisis thanks to its limited exposure to international financial markets and a very low external debt. However, with oil and gas accounting for two-thirds of total government revenues each year, there is a need for economic diversification. The services and construction sectors are gradually expanding and non-hydrocarbon growth amounted to 5·5% in 2015.

In 1994 an IMF-sponsored programme for economic reconstruction educed inflation and set in place a free-market economy. However, it was a further decade before privatization made significant strides. The creation of new private sector jobs is essential, as unemployment remains high despite growth and government initiatives bringing it down to 9·8% in 2013 from 15·3% in 2005 (although it has gone up slightly in the meantime). Unemployment is especially acute among women and the young. While Algeria faced relatively little disruption during the 'Arab Spring' uprisings of 2011, regional fragility threatens longer-term growth prospects.

Currency

The unit of currency is the *Algerian dinar* (DZD) of 100 *centimes*. Foreign exchange reserves were US$146,130m. in Sept. 2009, with gold reserves 5·58m. troy oz. Total money supply was 4,071·5bn. dinars in June 2009. Inflation rates (based on IMF statistics):

2008	2009	2010	2011	2012	2013	2014	2015	2016	2017
4·9%	5·7%	3·9%	4·5%	8·9%	3·3%	2·9%	4·8%	6·4%	5·6%

The dinar was devalued by 40% in April 1994.

Budget

The fiscal year starts on 1 Jan. In 2011 budgetary central government revenue totalled 5,897bn. dinars and expenditure 4,308bn. dinars. Principal sources of revenue in 2011 were: taxes on income, profits and capital gains, 3,550bn. dinars; taxes on goods and services, 1,548bn. dinars. Main items of expenditure by economic type in 2011: compensation of employees, 1,733bn. dinars; social benefits, 870bn. dinars.

The standard rate of VAT was increased from 17% to 19% with effect from 1 Jan. 2017.

Performance

Real GDP growth rates (based on IMF statistics):

2008	2009	2010	2011	2012	2013	2014	2015	2016	2017
2·4%	1·6%	3·6%	2·8%	3·4%	2·8%	3·8%	3·7%	3·2%	1·4%

Total GDP was US$170·4bn. in 2017.

Banking and Finance

The central bank and bank of issue is the Banque d'Algérie. The *Governor* is Mohammed Loukal. In Jan. 2016 there were 20 commercial banks, of which six were public and 14 private.

Foreign debt fell from US$25,388m. in 2000 to US$16,871m. in 2005 and further to US$5,276m. in 2010 (representing just 3·4% of GNI).

There is a stock exchange in Algiers.

Energy and Natural Resources

Environment

Algeria's carbon dioxide emissions from the consumption of energy in 2011 were the equivalent of 3·3 tonnes per capita.

Electricity

Installed capacity was 11·5m. kW in 2011. Production in 2011 was 51·22bn. kWh, with consumption per capita 1,353 kWh.

Oil and Gas

A law of Nov. 1991 permits foreign companies to acquire up to 49% of known oil and gas reserves. Oil production in 2013 was 68·9m. tonnes; oil reserves (2013) totalled 12·2bn. bbls. Production of natural gas in 2017 was 91·2bn. cu. metres; proven reserves in 2017 were 4·3trn. cu. metres.

Minerals

Output in 2013 (in 1,000 tonnes): limestone (estimate), 22,000; gypsum, 2,078; phosphate rock, 1,151; iron ore, 1,067; pozzolan, 388; calcite, 267;

feldspar, 259; aggregates, crushed stone and gravel, 54·9m. cu. metres; construction sand, 2·6m. cu. metres. There are also deposits of mercury, silver, gold, copper, antimony, kaolin, marble, onyx, salt and coal.

Agriculture

Much of the land is unsuitable for agriculture. The northern mountains provide grazing. There were 7·47m. ha. of arable land in 2014 and 0·97m. ha. of permanent crops. An estimated 1·36m. ha. were equipped for irrigation in 2014.

The chief crops in 2013 were (in 1,000 tonnes): potatoes, 4,887; wheat, 3,299; watermelons, 1,501; barley, 1,499; onions, 1,359; tomatoes, 975; oranges, 891; dates, 848; olives, 579; grapes, 571; chillies and green peppers, 482; apples, 456; carrots and turnips, 396.

Livestock, 2013: sheep, 26·6m.; goats, 4·9m.; cattle, 1·9m.; camels, 344,000; asses, 134,000; chickens (estimate), 130m. Livestock products, 2013 (in 1,000 tonnes): poultry meat (estimate), 288; lamb and mutton, 280; beef and veal, 140; eggs, 347; cow's milk, 3,368; sheep's milk (estimate), 351; goat's milk (estimate), 304.

Forestry

Forests covered 1·96m. ha. in 2015, or 1% of the total land area. Timber production in 2011 was 8·39m. cu. metres.

Fisheries

The total catch in 2015 amounted to 96,405 tonnes, exclusively from marine waters.

Industry

Output (2014 unless otherwise specified, in 1,000 tonnes): cement. 11,555; gas oil and diesel oil, 9,027; fuel oil, 6,594; petrol, 3,007; jet fuels, 2,001; flour, 507; crude steel, 415; pig iron (2012), 350; woven cotton fabrics, 7·6m. metres; beer (2012), 0·4m. litres. Production in units (2014): TV sets, 48,900; refrigerators, 47,900; tractors, 4,075; lorries, 530.

Labour

The labour force in 2013 was 12,088,000 (9,648,000 in 2003). 46·5% of the population aged 15–64 was economically active in 2013. In 2016, 10·5% of the population was unemployed.

Algeria had 71,000 people living in slavery according to the Walk Free Foundation's 2013 *Global Slavery Index*.

International Trade

Imports and Exports

Goods imports were US$56,618·1m. in 2014 (US$54,910·0m. in 2013) and goods exports US$63,227·8m. (US$65,998·1m. in 2013).

Principal imports in 2014 were machinery and transport equipment (38·0%), manufactured goods, and food, animals and beverages; main exports in 2014 were mineral fuels and lubricants (97·4%), chemicals, and food, animals and beverages.

The leading import supplier in 2010 was France (14·9%), followed by China and Italy; the leading export destination in 2010 was the USA (24·2%), followed by Italy and Spain.

Communications

Roads

There were, in 2008, 111,261 km of roads including 29,146 km of highways and main roads. There were 2,042,800 passenger cars (58 cars per 1,000 inhabitants in 2005) and 1,166,200 lorries and vans in use in 2006.

Rail

In 2011 there were 3,720 km of 1,432 mm route (254 km electrified) and 1,090 km of 1,055 mm gauge. The railways carried 6·9m. tonnes of freight and 24·7m. passengers in 2008.

A metro system opened in Algiers in Nov. 2011, 28 years after work on the project first began.

Civil Aviation

The main airport is Algiers International Airport (also known as Houari Boumedienne Airport). Some international services also use airports at Annaba, Constantine and Oran. The national carrier is the state-owned Air Algérie, which in 2013 carried 4,703,000 passengers (3,182,000 on international flights). In 2010 it flew to more than 30 international destinations and also operated on domestic routes. There were direct international flights in 2010 with other airlines to around 20 destinations. In 2012 Houari Boumedienne Airport handled 5,404,971 passengers (3,824,009 on international flights) and 25,359 tonnes of freight.

Shipping

In Jan. 2014 there were 41 ships of 300 GT or over registered, totalling 733,000 GT. Skikda, the leading port, handled 25,323,000 tonnes of cargo in 2013.

Telecommunications

In 2014 mobile phone subscribers numbered 37,113,130 (929·5 per 1,000 persons). In the same year there were 3,098,787 main (fixed) telephone lines. 18·1% of the population were internet users in 2014. In June 2012 there were 3·6m. Facebook users.

Government plans to privatize Algérie Télécom, the major state-owned telecommunications company, were rejected in Feb. 2009. Mobilis, a subsidiary of Algérie Télécom, is one of three mobile phone networks operating in the country. It has the second largest market share, behind Djezzy and ahead of Nedjma.

Social Institutions

Out of 178 countries analysed in the 2017 *Fragile States Index*—a list published jointly by the Fund for Peace and *Foreign Policy* magazine—Algeria was ranked the joint 77th most vulnerable (along with Bolivia) to conflict or collapse. The index is based on 12 indicators of state vulnerability across social, political and economic categories.

Justice

The judiciary is constitutionally independent. Judges are appointed by the Supreme Council of Magistrature chaired by the President of the Republic. Criminal justice is organized as in France. The Supreme Court is at the same time Council of State and High Court of Appeal. The death penalty is in force for terrorism.

The population in penal institutions in May 2013 was 60,000 (162 per 100,000 of national population).

Education

Adult literacy in 2006 was 72·6% (81·3% among males and 63·9% among females). In 2007 there were 171,000 children in pre-primary education. There were 4,079,000 pupils in primary schools in 2007, and 4,585,000 pupils in secondary schools in 2009.

The leading institute of higher education is the University of Algiers, founded in 1909 although Algerians were not admitted until 1946. In 2007 there were 901,562 students in tertiary education and 31,683 academic staff.

In 2008 expenditure on education came to 4·3% of GDP and represented 20·3% of total government expenditure.

Health

In 2007 there were 40,857 physicians, 11,010 dentistry personnel and 8,232 pharmaceutical personnel. There were 61,800 hospital beds in 2007. Health spending accounted for 4·4% of GDP in 2007.

In *Water: At What Cost? The State of the World's Water 2016*, WaterAid reported that 16·4% of the population does not have access to safe water.

Welfare

Welfare payments to 7·4m. beneficiaries on low incomes were introduced in 1992.

Religion

The 1996 constitution made Islam the state religion, established a consultative *High Islamic Council*, and forbids practices 'contrary to Islamic morality'. In 2010 the population was 97·9% Muslim according to estimates by the Pew Research Center's Forum on Religion & Public Life, with 1·8% religiously unaffiliated and 0·2% Christian. The vast majority of citizens are Sunni Muslims. Hundreds of foreign nationals, including priests and nuns, were killed over ten years of civil conflict that began in 1991.

Culture

World Heritage Sites

There are seven UNESCO sites in Algeria: Al Qal'a of Beni Hammad (inscribed in 1980), the 11th century ruined capital of the Hammadid emirs; Tassili n'Ajjer (1982), a group of over 15,000 prehistoric cave drawings; the M'zab Valley (1982), a tenth century community settlement of the Ibadites; Djémila (1982), or Cuicul, a mountainous Roman town; Tipasa (1982), an ancient Carthaginian port; Timgad (1982), a military colony founded by the Roman emperor Trajan in AD 100; the Kasbah of Algiers (1992), the medina of Algiers.

Press

Algeria had 65 paid-for daily newspapers in 2008 (including five sports dailies), with a combined average daily circulation of 2·16m. There were also 226 non-dailies in 2008.

Tourism

In 2014 there were 2,301,000 non-resident visitors (down from 2,733,000 in 2013).

Diplomatic Representatives

Of Algeria in the United Kingdom (1–3 Riding House St., London, W1W 7DR)
    Ambassador: Amar Abba.

Of the United Kingdom in Algeria (3 Chemin Capitaine Hocine Slimane [ex Chemin des Glycines], Algiers)
    Ambassador: Barry Lowen.

Of Algeria in the USA (2118 Kalorama Rd, NW, Washington, D.C., 20008)
    Ambassador: Madjid Bouguerra.

Of the USA in Algeria (5 Chemin Cheikh Bachir Ibrahimi, Algiers)
    Ambassador: John P. Desrocher.

Of Algeria to the United Nations
    Ambassador: Sabri Boukadoum.

Of Algeria to the European Union
    Ambassador: Amar Belani.

Further Reading

Ageron, C.-R., *Modern Algeria: a History from 1830 to the Present.* 1991

Eveno, P., *L'Algérie.* 1994

Heggoy, A. A. and Crout, R. R., *Historical Dictionary of Algeria.* 1995

Roberts, Hugh, *The Battlefield: Algeria 1998–2002, Studies in a Broken Polity.* 2003

Ruedy, J., *Modern Algeria: the Origins and Development of a Nation.* 1992

Stora, B., *Histoire de l'Algérie depuis l'Indépendance.* 1994

Volpi, Frédéric, *Islam and Democracy: The Failure of Dialogue in Algeria, 1998–2001.* 2003

Willis, M., *The Islamist Challenge in Algeria: A Political History.* 1997

National Statistical Office: Office National des Statistiques, 8–10 rue des Moussebilines, Algiers.

Website (French only): http://www.ons.dz

Andorra

Principat d'Andorra (Principality of Andorra)

Capital: Andorra la Vella
Population projection, 2020: 77,000
GNI per capita, 2017: (PPP$) 47,574
HDI/world rank, 2017: 0·858/35
Internet domain extension: .ad

Key Historical Events

Excavations near St Julia de Loria near Andorra's southern border have revealed Neolithic artifacts dating to around 4,500 BC. The Andosini, a Basque-speaking tribe subdued by Hannibal in 218 BC, were the first recorded inhabitants of the Pyrenean state. By the early fifth century AD Roman garrisons in the area came under attack from Germanic tribes including the Vandals, Visigoths and Alans. They crossed the Pyrenees and controlled swathes of Iberia over the next three centuries, before succumbing to Moorish advances from North Africa. An Arab–Berber army led by Tariq Ibn Ziyad reached the Pyrenees in around 720 and pushed into France. The Moors' defeat at Poitiers by Charles Martell in 732 forced them back towards Iberia; in Andorra, locals fought alongside Charlemagne's forces led by his son, Louis I (the Pious). As a reward, a new feudal state, tasked with protecting France from Iberian raids, was established under the Count of Urgel.

The Acte de Paréage of 1278 placed Andorra under the joint suzerainty of the Catalan bishop of La Seu de Urgel and the Comte de Foix. In 1419 they allowed notable families from across Andorra's six parishes to establish the 24-member Council of the Land—among the first parliaments in Europe. The rights vested in the house of Foix passed by marriage to that of Bearn and, on the accession of Henri IV in 1589, to the French crown. Suzerainty was relinquished by the French revolutionary government after 1793 but was restored by Napoleon in an imperial decree 13 years later. When Catalonia was annexed to the French Empire in 1812, Andorra was briefly absorbed into the district of Puigcerda before French title passed to the president of France.

The construction of a road to the Spanish town of La Seu de Urgel in 1911 paved the way to deeper integration with western Europe, with postal communications launched in 1928 and a large French-built power station a year later. Calls for electoral rights and control of natural resources grew in the 1930s, briefly led in 1934 by a White Russian émigré, Boris Skosyrev, who, with widespread local support proclaimed himself King Boris I and promised to modernize the country.

During the Second World War Andorra was neutral and was used as a smuggling route from Vichy France to Spain. Development gathered pace in the 1950s and 1960s, with improvements in infrastructure (including ski resorts). In 1970 women were given the right to vote and the electoral age was lowered to 18 in 1985. Andorra became a parliamentary democracy in May 1993 after the approval of a new constitution in a referendum. Civil rights were increased, including the provision for a sovereign judiciary and legislation for trade unions and political parties.

Territory And Population

The co-principality of Andorra is situated in the eastern Pyrenees on the French–Spanish border. The country is mountainous and has an average altitude of 1,996 metres. Area, 464 sq. km. In lieu of a census, a register of population is kept. The estimated population at 31 Dec. 2017 was 74,794; density, 161 per sq. km.

The UN gives a projected population for 2020 of 77,000.

In 2010, 88% of the population lived in urban areas.

The chief towns are Andorra la Vella, the capital (population, 19,230 in 2016) and Escaldes-Engordany (14,521); other towns are Sant Julià de Lòria, Encamp and La Massana. In 2010, 38·8% of the residential population were Andorran, 31·4% Spanish, 15·4% Portuguese and 6·0% French.

Catalan is the official language, but Spanish and French are widely spoken.

Social Statistics

Births in 2006 numbered 843 (10·4 per 1,000 inhabitants) and deaths 260 (3·2). Life expectancy (2006): males, 78 years; females, 85 years. Annual population growth rate, 2000–05, 3·5%. Fertility rate, 2008, 1·3 births per woman (one of the lowest rates in the world). Infant mortality in 2010 was three per 1,000 live births.

Climate

Escaldes-Engordany, Jan. 35·8°F (2·1°C), July 65·8°F (18·8°C). Annual rainfall 34·9" (886 mm).

Constitution and Government

The joint heads of state are the co-princes—the President of the French Republic and the Bishop of Urgel.

A new democratic constitution was approved by 74·2% of votes cast at a referendum on 14 March 1993. The electorate was 9,123; turnout was 75·7%. The new constitution, which came into force on 4 May 1993, makes the co-princes a single constitutional monarch and provides for a parliament, the unicameral *General Council of the Valleys*, with 28 members, two from each of the seven parishes and 14 elected by proportional representation from the single national constituency, for four years. In 1982 an *Executive Council* was appointed and legislative and executive powers were separated. The General Council elects the President of the Executive Council, who is the head of the government.

There is a *Constitutional Court* of four members who hold office for eight-year terms, renewable once.

National Anthem

'El Gran Carlemany, mon pare' ('Great Charlemagne, my father'); words by Juan Bautista Benlloch y Vivò, tune by Enric Marfany Bons.

Recent Elections

Elections to the General Council were held on 1 March 2015. The Democrats for Andorra (DA) won 15 seats (37·0% of the vote); the Liberals of Andorra 8 (27·7%); the Alliance of the Social Democratic Party of Andorra, the Greens and Citizens' Initiative 3 (23·5%); and Social Democracy and Progress 2 (11·7%). Turnout was 65·6%.

Current Government

In Feb. 2019 the government comprised:

President, Executive Council: Antoni Martí; b. 1963 (Democrats for Andorra; sworn in 12 May 2011).

Minister for Culture, Youth and Sports: Olga Gelabert Fàbrega. *Economy, Competitiveness and Innovation:* Gilbert Saboya. *Education and Higher Education:* Eric Jover. *Environment, Agriculture and Sustainability:* Sílvia Calvó. *Finance:* Jordi Cinca. *Foreign Affairs:* Maria Ubach. *Health:* Carles Alvarez. *Land Management:* Jordi Torres. *Public Service and Administrative Reform:* Eva Descarrega. *Social Affairs, Justice and Interior:* Xavier Espot. *Tourism and Commerce:* Francesc Camp.

Government Website (Catalan only): http://www.govern.ad

© Springer Nature Limited 2020
Palgrave Macmillan (ed.), *The Statesman's Yearbook 2020*,
https://doi.org/10.1057/978-1-349-95940-2_14

Current Leaders

Antoni Martí Petit

Position
President of the Executive Council

Introduction
Antoni Martí Petit became the president of the executive council (*de facto* prime minister) after his party, the Democrats for Andorra, gained an absolute majority in parliamentary elections held in April 2011. He and his party won a further term at the general election of March 2015. An architect and the former mayor of Escaldes-Engordany, Andorra's second city, Martí pledged to open up the state to foreign investment.

Early Life
Born in Escaldes-Engordany in 1963, Martí studied architecture at the University of Toulouse. He was elected to parliament in 1994. In 2003 he became mayor of Escaldes-Engordany, winning re-election to the post four years later. Towards the end of his second term he was elected to lead the centre-right Democrats for Andorra, which had been formed in Feb. 2011.

Early parliamentary elections were called for April 2011 after the dissolution of Andorra's General Council following deadlock over budget legislation. Martí's party defeated the incumbent Social Democrats.

Career in Office
Martí was elected head of government by parliament on 11 May and sworn in the following day. Although he had campaigned against the introduction of personal income tax, in June 2013 he bowed to pressure from the European Union and announced that Andorra would bring in the tax. He had also promised to end the protectionism that has previously discouraged inward investment. His party won another outright majority at the polls in March 2015 despite losing five seats, securing Martí a second term in office.

International Relations

The 1993 constitution empowers Andorra to conduct its own foreign affairs, with consultation on matters affecting France or Spain.

Economy

Overview

The mainstay of the economy is tourism, which accounts for 80% of GDP annually. In 2015 there were 7·9m. visitors, attracted by Andorra's duty-free status and its thriving resorts. The country is also a leading offshore financial centre—in 2014 the finance and insurance industry represented 20·9% of GDP and was the fastest-growing sector of the economy, expanding at 10% compared to overall GDP growth of 2·3% that year.

With only 5% of territory classified as arable land, most food is imported. While not a member of the European Union, Andorra is a member of the EU Customs Union and uses the euro single currency. It is treated as an EU member for trade in manufactured goods but not for agricultural products.

The country has long come under pressure from its European neighbours to tackle tax evasion. Efforts to address this issue saw the Organisation for Economic Co-operation and Development remove Andorra from its List of Uncooperative Tax Havens in May 2009. In June 2014 Andorra committed to automatic exchange of information in tax matters. In 2012 a 10% business tax was introduced, followed by a 2% sales tax in 2013 and, under EU pressure, a flat-rate income tax of 10% in 2015.

Currency

Since 1 Jan. 2002 Andorra has been using the *euro* (EUR). Inflation was 1·6% in 2010 (0·0% in 2009 and 2·0% in 2008).

Budget

In 2014 revenue was €568,600,000 and expenditure also €568,600,000.
VAT at 4·5% was introduced on 1 Jan. 2013.

Performance

The economy grew by 2·3% in 2014 and 0·8% in 2015. Total GDP was US$3·0bn. in 2017.

Banking and Finance

The banking sector, with its tax haven status, contributes substantially to the economy. Leading banks include: Andbank; MoraBanc; Banca Privada d'Andorra, SA; Crèdit Andorrà Group; and BancSabadell d'Andorra, SA.

Energy and Natural Resources

Electricity

Installed capacity was an estimated 32,000 kW in 2011. Production in 2011 was 91m. kWh. Over 80% of electricity consumed has to be imported.

Agriculture

In 2011 there were some 2,400 ha. of arable land (5% of total). Tobacco and potatoes are principal crops. The principal livestock activity is sheep raising.

Forestry

Forests covered 16,000 ha. in 2015, or 34% of the total land area.

Industry

Labour

Only 1% of the workforce is employed in agriculture, the rest in tourism, commerce, services and light industry. Manufacturing consists mainly of cigarettes, cigars and furniture.

International Trade

Andorra is a member of the EU Customs Union for industrial goods, but is a third country for agricultural produce. There is a free economic zone.

Imports and Exports

In 2010 imports were valued at €1,143m. and exports at €41m.
The main imports in 2010 were: clothing and footwear (€169m.); food (€167m.); fuel (€117m.). Main exports are motor vehicles, electronic products, and clothing and footwear. Leading import suppliers in 2010 were: Spain, 63·8%; France, 18·7%; Germany, 4·7%. Spain is by far the biggest export market, followed by France and Germany.

Communications

Roads

There were 76,616 motor vehicles in 2012 including 52,038 private cars and 13,154 motorcycles and mopeds. A total of 4,111,528 vehicles entered the country in 2012 (4,178,116 in 2011).

Civil Aviation

The nearest airport is Seo de Urgel, over the border in Spain 12 km to the south of Andorra.

Telecommunications

In 2010 there were 38,171 landline telephone subscriptions, equivalent to 449·8 per 1,000 inhabitants. There were 65,500 mobile phone subscriptions in 2010 (771·8 per 1,000 inhabitants). Andorra had 785·3 internet users per 1,000 inhabitants in 2009. Fixed internet subscriptions totalled 32,000 in 2009 (382·6 per 1,000 inhabitants).

Social Institutions

Justice

Justice is administered by the High Council of Justice, comprising five members appointed for single six-year terms. The independence of judges is constitutionally guaranteed. Judicial power is exercised in civil matters in the first instance by Magistrates' Courts and a Judge's Court. Criminal justice is administered by the *Corts*, consisting of the judge of appeal, a general attorney and an attorney nominated for five years alternately by each of the co-princes. There is also a *raonador* (ombudsman) elected by the General Council of the Valleys.

The International Centre for Prison Studies estimated in 2014 that 59·6% of prisoners had yet to receive a trial.

Education

Free education in French- or Spanish-language schools is compulsory: six years primary starting at six years, followed by four years secondary. A Roman Catholic school provides education in Catalan. In 2007 there were 4,427 pupils in primary schools and 3,819 in secondary schools.

Health

In 2010 there was one public hospital; in 2009 there were 41 general practitioners, 220 medical specialists, 51 dentists and stomatologists, 309 nurses and 78 pharmacists.

Religion

The Roman Catholic is the established church, but the 1993 constitution guarantees religious liberty. In 2011 around 90% of the population were Catholics.

Culture

World Heritage Sites

There is one UNESCO site in Andorra: Madriu-Perafita-Claror Valley (entered on the list in 2004 and 2006).

Press

In 2008 there were three daily newspapers with a combined circulation of about 32,000. *Diari d'Andorra* and *El Periodic d'Andorra* are paid-for, while *Bondia* is free. *L'Esportiu*, a daily Catalan-language sports paper, is included in *Diari d'Andorra*. In the 2013 *World Press Freedom Index* compiled by Reporters Without Borders, Andorra was ranked fifth out of 179 countries.

Tourism

Tourism is one of the mainstays of the economy. In 2014 there were 2,363,000 non-resident tourist arrivals (excluding same-day visitors).

Festivals

In March the Big Snow festival in the ski resort of Arinsal combines music and winter sports. A jazz festival, the International Colours of Music Festival, is held in Escaldes-Engordany every July.

Diplomatic Representatives

Of Andorra in the United Kingdom
  Ambassador: Vacant.
  Chargé d'Affaires a.i.: Cristina Mota Gouveia (resides in Andorra).

Of the United Kingdom in Andorra
  Ambassador: Simon Manley, CMG (resides in Madrid).

Of Andorra in the USA (2 United Nations Plaza, 25th Floor, N.Y. 10017)
  Ambassador: Elisenda Vives Balmaña.

Of the USA in Andorra
  Ambassador: Richard Duke Buchan III (resides in Madrid).

Of Andorra to the United Nations
  Ambassador: Elisenda Vives Balmaña.

Of Andorra to the European Union
  Ambassador: Esther Rabasa Grau.

Further Reading

A Strategic Assessment of Andorra. 2000
National Statistical Office: Edifici Administratiu de Govern, Carrer de les Boïgues. Edif. les Boigues, 3a, AD700 Escaldes-Engordany.
Website: http://www.estadistica.ad

Angola

República de Angola (Republic of Angola)

Capital: Luanda
Population projection, 2020: 32·83m.
GNI per capita, 2017: (PPP$) 5,790
HDI/world rank, 2017: 0·581/147
Internet domain extension: .ao

Key Historical Events

Khoisan hunter-gatherers were in southern Angola at least 23,000 years ago. From AD 1000 Bantu-speaking groups moved south from the borders of present-day Cameroon and Nigeria. Substantial numbers of settlers arrived in present-day Angola during the 13th century, displacing Khoisan groups. Several powerful Bantu kingdoms developed, including the Bakongo, across northern Angola, parts of present-day Democratic Republic of the Congo, Republic of the Congo and Gabon, and the Ndongo kingdom further south. The name Angola is derived from Ngola a Kiluanje, the traditional title of the ruler of the Ndongo.

Portuguese vessels commanded by Diogo Cão reached Angola in 1482. Relations between Portugal and the Bakongo were initially cordial and a few Portuguese missionaries, craftsmen and merchants settled on Angola's coast. However, tensions rose in the 16th century as Portugal's colonial ambitions grew. Slaves were transported to São Tomé and Príncipe and later, Brazil, the Caribbean and North America.

Centred on Luanda, and, from 1617, Benguela, the slave trade used local clans as intermediaries. In 1665 Portuguese forces and their African allies defeated the Bakongo king, Antonio I, at the Battle of Mbwila, after which it splintered into small chieftaincies. The Ndongo kingdom went the same way in 1671. Nonetheless, several central and eastern Angolan kingdoms remained into the 18th century but were eventually undermined by the slave trade and Portuguese exploration of the interior. Portuguese control of Angola and its other African colonies was weakened after 1807, when Napoleon's armies forced the Portuguese court into exile in Brazil.

Political instability in Portugal between 1820 and 1834 spread to Angola, with uprisings and an army mutiny that toppled the colony's governor. But slave traders prospered from new markets in Brazil, Cuba and southern America, even after the progressive Portuguese prime minister, the Marquês de Sá da Bandeira, outlawed the trade in 1836. It is estimated that by 1850 four million Angolans had been enslaved and shipped overseas.

From the 1830s the Portuguese expanded to the south and east from Luanda. British forces held back Portuguese control of Cabinda and the mouth of the River Congo but both Cabinda and Massabi were annexed in 1883. Portugal's claims to Angola were outlined at the 1884 Berlin Conference and treaties with rival colonial powers were agreed by 1900.

By this time, a massive forced labour system had replaced slavery as the basis for the plantation economy and, later, the mining sector. Forced labour and British financing helped construct major rail routes, including one linking the port of Lobito with the copper zones of the Belgian Congo and what is now Zambia.

Economic growth did not translate into social development for native Angolans. The Portuguese encouraged white immigration, especially after 1950, which intensified racial antagonisms. As decolonization progressed elsewhere in Africa, Portugal rejected calls for independence. Nonetheless, three main militant movements had emerged by 1961: the Popular Movement for the Liberation of Angola (MPLA) led by Agostinho Neto; the National Front for the Liberation of Angola (FNLA), led by Holden Roberto; and the National Union for the Total Independence of Angola (UNITA), led by Jonas Savimbi.

A 1974 coup d'état in Portugal established a leftist military government in Lisbon that agreed, in the Alvor Accords of 1975, to hand power in Angola over to a coalition of the three movements. The ideological differences between the three led to armed conflict, with FNLA and UNITA forces attempting to wrest control of Luanda from the MPLA. South African involvement and civil war continued until the New York Agreement of 1988 saw South Africa withdraw from Angola and Namibia. Cuba also agreed to the phased withdrawal of its troops.

A peace agreement was signed by all sides on 31 May 1991, allowing for a national army to be formed and multi-party elections to be held. In Sept. 1992 the MPLA won elections and José Eduardo dos Santos was re-elected president. UNITA's Jonas Savimbi rejected the result and resumed the war, seizing 70% of the country.

On 20 Nov. 1994 a peace agreement was signed in Lusaka, allowing for UNITA to share in government. In Jan. 1998 Savimbi met with President dos Santos but talks foundered and fighting resumed. Meanwhile, Angolan troops fought in the Democratic Republic of the Congo alongside the forces of President Kabila in his efforts to quash a Rwandan-backed rebellion in the east of his country. They remained after the assassination of Kabila in Jan. 2001 but renewed hopes of peace resulted in withdrawal in Jan. 2002. In Feb. 2002 Savimbi was killed in fighting with Angolan government troops. On 4 April 2002 the Angolan army and UNITA agreed a ceasefire. More than half a million Angolans had died in the unrest.

Following the ceasefire oil production increased and investment flowed, notably from China, despite some remaining pockets of unrest. In Sept. 2008 the MPLA, still under dos Santos, won a landslide in the first multi-party elections for 16 years. The expected presidential election was repeatedly delayed until direct presidential elections were abolished by a new constitution in Jan. 2010.

Territory and Population

Angola is bounded in the north by the Republic of the Congo, north and northeast by the Democratic Republic of the Congo, east by Zambia, south by Namibia and west by the Atlantic Ocean. The area is 1,246,700 sq. km (481,354 sq. miles) including the province of Cabinda, an exclave of territory separated by 30 sq. km of the Democratic Republic of the Congo's territory. Angola's first census in more than 40 years was held in May 2014; when the population was 25,789,024, giving a density of 20·7 per sq. km. In 2010, 58·5% of the population were living in urban areas. More than 300,000 Angolan refugees have returned to the country since the civil war ended in 2002. The number of Portuguese in Angola rose from 45,000 in 2007–08 to 92,000 a year later. By 2015 the figure was over 100,000.

The UN gives a projected population for 2020 of 32·83m.

Area, population and chief towns of the provinces:

Province	Area (in sq. km)	Population 2014 census (in 1,000)	Chief town
Bengo	31,371	356·6	Caxito
Benguela	31,788	2,231·4	Benguela
Bié	70,314	1,455·3	Kuito
Cabinda	7,270	716·1	Cabinda
Cunene	89,342	990·1	Ondjiva
Huambo	34,274	2,019·6	Huambo
Huíla	75,002	2,497·4	Lubango
Kuando-Kubango	199,049	534·0	Menongue
Kwanza Norte	24,190	443·4	Ndalatando
Kwanza Sul	55,660	1,881·9	Sumbe
Luanda	2,418	6,945·4	Luanda
Lunda Norte	102,783	862·6	Dundo
Lunda Sul	45,649	537·6	Saurimo
Malanje	97,602	986·4	Malanje
Moxico	223,023	758·6	Luena
Namibe	58,137	495·3	Namibe
Uíge	58,698	1,483·1	Uíge
Zaire	40,130	594·4	Mbanza Congo

© Springer Nature Limited 2020
Palgrave Macmillan (ed.), *The Statesman's Yearbook 2020*,
https://doi.org/10.1057/978-1-349-95940-2_15

The most important towns are Luanda, the capital (2014 census population, 6·76m.), Huambo, Lobito, Benguela, Kuito, Lubango, Malanje and Namibe.

The main ethnic groups are Umbundo (Ovimbundo), Kimbundo, Bakongo, Chokwe, Ganguela, Luvale and Kwanyama.

Portuguese is the official language. Bantu and other African languages are also spoken.

Social Statistics

Life expectancy at birth, 2013, 50·4 years for males and 53·4 years for females. 2008 births (estimates), 775,000; deaths, 306,000. Estimated birth rate in 2008 was 43 per 1,000 population; estimated death rate, 17. Annual population growth rate, 2000–08, 2·9%. Fertility rate, 2008, 5·8 births per woman; infant mortality, 2010, 98 per 1,000 live births.

Climate

The climate is tropical, with low rainfall in the west but increasing inland. Temperatures are constant over the year and most rain falls in March and April. Luanda, Jan. 78°F (25·6°C), July 69°F (20·6°C). Annual rainfall 13" (323 mm). Lobito, Jan. 77°F (25°C), July 68°F (20°C). Annual rainfall 14" (353 mm).

Constitution and Government

Under the Constitution adopted at independence, the sole legal party was the MPLA. In Dec. 1990, however, the MPLA announced that the Constitution would be revised to permit opposition parties. The supreme organ of state is the 220-member *National Assembly*. For the 2008 elections 30% of seats were guaranteed for women. There is an executive *President*, elected for renewable terms of five years, who appoints a *Council of Ministers*.

In Dec. 2002 Angola's ruling party and the UNITA party of former rebels agreed on a new constitution. The president would keep key powers, including the power to name and to remove the prime minister. The president will also appoint provincial governors, rather than letting voters elect them, but the governor must be from the party that received a majority of votes in that province. A draft constitution was submitted to the constitutional commission of the Angolan parliament for consideration in Jan. 2004.

A new constitution was adopted on 21 Jan. 2010 and came into effect on 5 Feb. although the opposition party UNITA boycotted the vote. Direct presidential elections were abolished. Instead the party with the majority in parliament chooses the president. A two five-year term limit was introduced although it did not take effect until after the parliamentary elections in Aug. 2012. The president was also made responsible for judicial appointments while the office of prime minister was replaced by that of a vice-president to be appointed by the president.

National Anthem

'O Pátria, nunca mais esqueceremos' ('Oh Fatherland, never shall we forget'); words by M. R. Alves Monteiro, tune by R. A. Dias Mingas.

Government Chronology

Presidents since 1975. (MPLA = Popular Movement for the Liberation of Angola)

1975–79	MPLA	António Agostinho Neto
1979–2017	MPLA	José Eduardo dos Santos
2017–	MPLA	João Manuel Gonçalves Lourenço

Recent Elections

In parliamentary elections held on 23 Aug. 2017 (and on 26 Aug. in 15 constituencies) the electorate was 9,317,294. Turnout was 76·1%. The Popular Movement for the Liberation of Angola/MPLA gained 150 seats in the National Assembly with 61·1% of votes cast, the National Union for the Total Independence of Angola/UNITA 51 with 26·7%, Broad Convergence for the Salvation of Angola–Electoral Coalition/CASA–CE 16 with 9·4%,

Social Renewal Party 2 with 1·4% and the National Front for the Liberation of Angola 1 with 0·9%.

Current Government

President: João Lourenço; b. 1954 (MPLA; sworn in 26 Sept. 2017).
   Vice-President: Bornito de Sousa.
   In Feb. 2019 the government comprised:
   Minister of State for Economic and Social Development: Manuel José Nunes Júnior. *Minister of State and Head of the Security Office of the President:* Pedro Sebastião. *Minister of State and Head of the Civil Office of the President:* Frederico Manuel dos Santos e Silva Cardoso.
   Minister of Agriculture and Forestry: Marcos Alexandre Nhunga. *Attorney General:* Hélder Fernando Pitta Gróz. *Construction and Public Works:* Manuel Tavares de Almeida. *Culture:* Carolina Cerqueira. *Economy and Planning:* Pedro Luís da Fonseca. *Education:* Maria Cândida Teixeira. *Energy and Water:* João Baptista Borges. *Environment:* Paula Cristina Francisco Coelho. *Finance:* Augusto Archer de Sousa Mangueira. *Fisheries and the Sea:* Victória Francisco Lopes Cristóvão de Barros Neto. *Foreign Affairs:* Manuel Domingos Augusto. *Former Combatants and Veterans of the Homeland:* João Ernesto dos Santos 'Liberdade'. *Health:* Sílvia Paula Valentim Lutucuta. *Higher Education, Science, Technology and Innovation:* Maria do Rosário Bragança Sambo. *Hotels and Tourism:* Maria Ângela Teixeira de Alva Sequeira Bragança. *Industry:* Bernarda Gonçalves Martins Henriques da Silva. *Interior:* Ângelo de Barros da Veiga Tavares. *Justice and Human Rights:* Francisco Manuel Monteiro de Queiroz. *Lands and State Reform:* Adão Francisco Correia de Almeida. *Mineral Resources and Petroleum:* Diamantino Pedro Azevedo. *National Defence:* Salviano de Jesus Sequeira. *Parliamentary Affairs:* Rosa Luís de Sousa Micolo. *Public Administration, Labour and Social Security:* Jesus Faria Maiato. *Social Action, Family and Women's Issues:* Victória Francisco Correia da Conceição. *Social Communication:* Aníbal João da Silva Melo. *Spatial Planning and Housing:* Ana Paula Chantre Luna de Carvalho. *Telecommunications and Information Technologies:* José Carvalho da Rocha. *Trade:* Jofre Van-Dúnem Júnior. *Transport:* Ricardo Viegas de Abreu. *Youth and Sport:* Ana Paula Sacramento Neto.
   Government Website: http://www.governo.gov.ao

Current Leaders

João Lourenço
Position
President

Introduction
João Lourenço was sworn in as president on 26 Sept. 2017, succeeding José Eduardo dos Santos who had been in office for 38 years. Lourenço had previously been the vice-president of the ruling Popular Movement for the Liberation of Angola (MPLA) and had served as minister of defence.

Early Life
João Manuel Gonçalves Lourenço was born in Lobito, Benguela Province, in what was then Portuguese Angola, on 5 March 1954. After Angola secured its independence in 1975, he fought on the side of the MPLA government against its previous partner in the anti-colonial struggle, the National Union for the Total Independence of Angola (UNITA), in a civil war that lasted until 2002.

In 1978 he travelled to the then Soviet Union (which supported the MPLA in the civil war) to study at a military academy, where he completed his military training and was awarded a degree in historical sciences. On his return he quickly rose through the ranks of the MPLA.

In 1984 Lourenço was appointed governor of the eastern province of Moxico. Between 1992 and 1997 he served as secretary for information in the MPLA, and in 1998 was appointed secretary-general of the party. However, his rise was halted at the 2003 party congress when he was demoted amid speculation that dos Santos perceived him as a presidential rival.

Lourenço's appointment as defence minister in 2014 heralded the end of his period in the political wilderness, and in Aug. 2016 he was confirmed as vice-president of the MPLA. The decision of dos Santos to step down from the presidency after parliamentary elections in Aug. 2017, at which the MPLA won a comfortable majority in the National Assembly, was a surprise and cleared the way for his party deputy to succeed him.

Career in Office

On coming to power, Lourenço was tasked with reshaping an economy suffering the effects of a steep decline in oil prices, while rampant inflation and widespread government corruption provided further obstacles to reform. Nevertheless, in Nov. 2017 he removed Isabel dos Santos, daughter of the previous president, from her position as head of the country's state oil company, Sonangol, and in early 2018 sacked her brother, José Filomeno dos Santos, from his position as head of the country's sovereign wealth fund. Furthermore, in Sept. José Filomeno was arrested for suspected embezzlement and money laundering and his father stepped down from leadership of the ruling MPLA.

Defence

Conscription is for two years. Defence expenditure totalled US$6,049m. in 2013 (US$326 per capita), representing 4·8% of GDP.

Army

In 2011 the Army had 42 regiments. Total strength was 100,000. In addition the paramilitary Rapid Reaction Police numbered 10,000.

Navy

Naval personnel in 2011 totalled about 1,000 with 14 operational vessels. There is a naval base at Luanda.

Air Force

The National Air Force (FAN), initially formed in 1976 as the Angolan People's Air Force (FAPA) and renamed in 2007, had 6,000 personnel in 2011. There were 92 combat-capable aircraft in 2011 and 44 attack helicopters.

Economy

In 2011 agriculture accounted for 9% of GDP, industry 62% and services 29%.

Overview

Despite four decades of civil war, Angola has emerged as Africa's second largest oil exporter. Oil income accounts for more than 75% of budgetary revenue each year. The economy grew by 15% per year on average between 2004 and 2007 as oil production increased and the country's infrastructure was rebuilt. Although Angola has a wealth of other natural resources, including diamonds, coffee, fish and timber, the economy remains vulnerable to oil price shocks. Poverty is widespread.

As a result of declining oil prices in 2008–09 Angola experienced a sharp contraction in its revenues and international reserves, prompting macroeconomic instability. Further plunging oil prices in 2014—coupled with a fall in oil production—highlighted the over-reliance on the sector, with GDP growth falling to 4·8% from 6·8% the previous year. Growth then averaged -1·4% per year between 2015 and 2017, with the budget deficit reaching 5·3% of GDP in 2017.

Structural reforms and diversification are key to the economy's long-term prospects.

Currency

The unit of currency is the *kwanza* (AOA), introduced in Dec. 1999, replacing the *readjusted kwanza* at a rate of 1 kwanza = 1m. readjusted kwanzas. Foreign exchange reserves were US$2,017m. in July 2005 and money supply was 103,304m. kwanzas. Inflation, which had reached 4,146% in 1996, was 30·7% in 2016 and 29·8% in 2017.

Budget

Revenues in 2012 were 4,892bn. kwanzas and expenditures 4,223bn. kwanzas. Petroleum tax revenue accounted for 76·7% of revenues in 2012; current expenditure accounted for 76·8% of expenditures.

Performance

Total GDP was US$124·2bn. in 2017. The civil war meant GDP growth in 1993 was negative, at −24·0%, but a recovery followed and in 2007 and 2008 it was 22·6% and 13·8% respectively, mainly thanks to booming diamond exports and post-war rebuilding. Angola's growth in both 2007 and 2008 was among the highest in the world. More recently there was real GDP growth of 0·9% in 2015. However, falling oil prices then led to a recession with the economy shrinking by 2·6% in 2016 and 2·5% in 2017.

Banking and Finance

The Banco Nacional de Angola is the central bank and bank of issue (*Governor*, José de Lima Massano). All banks were state-owned until the sector was reopened to commercial competition in 1991. The largest banks in Dec. 2010 were: Banco Africano de Investimentos (BAI), with assets of US$8,373m.; Banco Espirito Santo Angola (BESA), with assets of US$7,892m.; Banco de Fomento Angola, with assets of US$6,435m.

Total external debt in 2010 was US$18,562m., equivalent to 24·6% of GNI.

Energy and Natural Resources

Environment

In 2011 Angola's carbon dioxide emissions from the consumption of energy were the equivalent of 1·7 tonnes per capita.

Electricity

Installed capacity was an estimated 1·2m. kW in 2011. Production in 2011 was 5·65bn. kWh, with consumption per capita 280 kWh.

Oil and Gas

Oil is produced mainly offshore and in the Cabinda exclave. Oil production and supporting activities contribute more than half of Angolan GDP and provide the government with 80% of revenues. Angola's oil production ranks among the fastest-growing in the world. A new US$8bn. oil refinery has been under construction near Lobito for many years but work on it was suspended in Aug. 2016. Only Nigeria among sub-Saharan African countries produces more oil. It is believed that there are huge oil resources yet to be discovered. Proven oil reserves in 2013 were 12·7bn. bbls. Total production (2013) 87·4m. tonnes. Proven natural gas reserves (2013) 366bn. cu. metres; production, 2011, 730m. cu. metres.

Minerals

Mineral production in Angola is dominated by diamonds and 90% of all workers in the mining sector work in the diamond industry. Production in 2009 was an estimated 13·8m. carats. Angola has billions of dollars worth of unexploited diamond fields. In 2000 the government regained control of the nation's richest diamond provinces from UNITA rebels. Other minerals produced (2009 estimates) include granite, 50,000 cu. metres; salt, 35,000 tonnes. Iron ore, phosphate, manganese and copper deposits exist.

Agriculture

In 2013 there were an estimated 4·9m. ha. of arable land and 0·3m. ha. of permanent crops. An estimated 86,000 ha. were equipped for irrigation in 2013. Principal crops (with 2014 production unless otherwise indicated, in 1,000 tonnes): cassava, 7,639; bananas (2013), 3,095; sweet potatoes, 1,929; maize, 1,687; cabbages, kale, etc. (2013), 1,135; potatoes, 671; sugarcane, 510 (estimate); pineapples (2013), 479; dry beans, 402; palm fruit oil, 281 (estimate).

Livestock (2013): 4·8m. cattle, 4·2m. goats, 2·6m. pigs, 1·1m. sheep and 27m. chickens.

Forestry

In 2015, 57·86m. ha., or 46% of the total land area, was covered by forests. Timber production in 2011 was 5·20m. cu. metres.

Fisheries

Total catch in 2011 came to an estimated 273,000 tonnes, mainly from sea fishing.

Industry

The principal industries are petroleum, diamonds, uranium, food processing, fisheries and textiles. Output, 2010 unless otherwise indicated (in 1,000 tonnes): cement (2010 estimate), 1,500; residual fuel oil, 620; distillate fuel oil, 530; jet fuel, 303; petrol, 65; sugar (2008), 10.

Labour

In 2010 the estimated economically active population numbered 8,533,000 (53% males), up from 6,238,000 in 2000.

Angola had 17,000 people living in slavery according to the Walk Free Foundation's 2013 *Global Slavery Index.*

International Trade

Imports and Exports

In 2007 imports (c.i.f.) totalled US$15,048m. (US$9,586m. in 2006); exports (f.o.b.), US$38,997m. (US$31,862m. in 2006).

Main exports, 2007 (in US$1m.): crude oil, 36,417; diamonds, 1,552; manufactures, 359. Oil accounts for 97% of exports. Chief import suppliers are Portugal, China, the USA and Brazil. Principal export markets are China, the USA, India and Taiwan.

Communications

Roads

The road network was destroyed during the 27-year long civil war that ended in 2002. Since then efforts to clear around 7m. landmines and rebuild roads and bridges have reopened most of the main routes and by 2010 there were over 62,000 km of roads. In 2007 there were 671,060 vehicles registered.

Rail

Prior to the civil war there was in excess of 2,900 km of railway (predominantly 1,067 mm gauge track), but much of the network was damaged during the war. However, restoration and redevelopment of the network is now under way, notably the Benguela Railway, linking the port city of Lobito with Huambo in Angola's rich farmlands and neighbouring Democratic Republic of the Congo and Zambia.

Civil Aviation

There is an international airport at Luanda (Fourth of February). The national carrier is Linhas Aéreas de Angola (TAAG), which in 2013 carried 1,322,000 passengers (669,000 on domestic flights and 653,000 on international flights). It operated direct flights in 2010 to Bangui, Brazzaville, Cape Town, Douala, Harare, Johannesburg, Lisbon, Lusaka, Praia, Rio de Janeiro, São Paulo, São Tomé and Windhoek, as well as domestic services. There were direct flights in 2010 with other airlines to Abidjan, Addis Ababa, Bamako, Beijing, Brussels, Douala, Dubai, Frankfurt, Johannesburg, Lisbon, London, Maputo, Moscow, Paris, Pointe-Noire, Port Harcourt, Port-Gentil and Windhoek.

Shipping

There are ports at Luanda, Lobito and Namibe, and oil terminals at Malongo, Lobito and Soyo. In Jan. 2014 there were 29 ships of 300 GT or over registered, totalling 25,000 GT.

Telecommunications

In 2010 there were 303,200 main (fixed) telephone lines but mobile phone subscribers numbered 8·91m. There were 32·8 internet users per 1,000 inhabitants in 2009. Fixed internet subscriptions totalled 320,000 in 2009 (17·2 per 1,000 inhabitants). In June 2012 there were 433,000 Facebook users.

Social Institutions

Out of 178 countries analysed in the 2017 *Fragile States Index*—a list published jointly by the Fund for Peace and *Foreign Policy* magazine—Angola was ranked the 32nd most vulnerable to conflict or collapse. The index is based on 12 indicators of state vulnerability across social, political and economic categories.

Justice

The Supreme Court and Court of Appeal are in Luanda. The death penalty was abolished in 1992. In 2002–03 the US government's Agency for International Development assisted in the modernization of the judicial system. Measures including the introduction of a court case numbering system were intended to reduce legal costs and attract foreign investment.

The population in penal institutions in June 2013 was 21,634 (105 per 100,000 of national population).

Education

The education system provides three levels of general education totalling eight years, followed by schools for technical training, teacher training or pre-university studies. In 2011 there were 5,026,803 pupils and 118,158 teachers at primary schools, 884,982 pupils and 32,279 teachers at secondary schools, and 142,798 students with 7,863 academic staff in tertiary education. Angola has a number of public and private universities. The oldest and largest university is the Agostinho Neto University (formerly the University of Luanda and later the University of Angola). The oldest private university is the Catholic University of Angola, which was founded in 1997. The adult literacy rate was an estimated 70·0% in 2009 (82·9% among males and 57·6% among females).

In 2010 government expenditure on education came to 3·5% of GDP.

Health

In 2009 there were 2,956 physicians and 29,592 nursing and midwifery personnel. In 2005 there were eight hospital beds per 10,000 population.

In *Water: At What Cost? The State of the World's Water 2016*, WaterAid reported that 51·0% of the population does not have access to safe water—the third highest percentage of any nation. 41% of the population were undernourished in the period 2005–07, down from 61% in 1995–97.

Religion

A study by the Pew Research Center's Forum on Religion & Public Life estimated that there were 17·3m. Christians in 2010 and 790,000 followers of folk religions. A further 980,000 people had no religious affiliation. Catholics account for around 65% of Christians and Protestants 35%. In Feb. 2019 there was one cardinal.

Culture

Press

The government-owned *Jornal de Angola* (circulation of 42,000) was the only daily newspaper in 2008. The *Diario da República* is the official gazette. There are 12 private weekly publications and four smaller regional weeklies.

Tourism

In 2012 there were a record 528,000 non-resident tourists (up from 91,000 in 2002 and 195,000 in 2007), bringing revenue of US$711m.

Festivals

The Luanda International Jazz Festival was first held in 2009.

Diplomatic Representatives

Of Angola in the United Kingdom (22 Dorset St., London, W1U 6QY)
Ambassador: Dr Rui Jorge Carneiro Mangueira.

Of the United Kingdom in Angola (Rua 17 de Setembro No. 4, Caixa, Luanda 1244)
Ambassador: Jessica Hand.

Of Angola in the USA (2108 16th St., NW, Washington, D.C., 20009)
Ambassador: Agostinho Tavares da Silva Neto.

Of the USA in Angola (32 rua Houari Boumedienne, Luanda)
Ambassador: Nina Fite.

Of Angola to the United Nations
Ambassador: Maria de Jesus dos Reis Ferreira.

Of Angola to the European Union
Ambassador: Georges Rebelo Chikoti.

Further Reading

Anstee, M. J., *Orphan of the Cold War: the Inside Story of the Collapse of the Angolan Peace Process, 1992–93.* 1996
Brittain, Victoria, *Death of Dignity: Angola's Civil War.* 1999
Guimarães, Fernando Andersen, *The Origins of the Angolan Civil War: Foreign Intervention and Domestic Political Conflict.* 2001
Hodges, Tony, *Angola: Anatomy of an Oil State.* 2004
National Statistical Office: Instituto Nacional de Estatística, Rua Ho-Chi-Minh, C.P. 1215, Luanda.

Antigua and Barbuda

Capital: St John's
Population projection, 2020: 105,000
GNI per capita, 2017: (PPP$) 20,764
HDI/world rank, 2017: 0·780/70=
Internet domain extension: .ag

Key Historical Events

The islands of Antigua and Barbuda were populated by Arawak-speaking people from at least 1000 BC. By 1493, when Columbus passed Antigua, it was occupied by Carib Indians. English settlers arrived in 1632. Sugar plantations, using slave labour, were established in the 1650s. As British colonies, Antigua and Barbuda formed part of the Leeward Islands Federation from 1871 until 1956 when they became a separate Crown Colony. This was merged into the West Indies Federation from Jan. 1958 until May 1962 and became an Associated State of the UK on 27 Feb. 1967. Antigua and Barbuda gained independence on 1 Nov. 1981.

Territory and Population

Antigua and Barbuda comprises three islands of the Lesser Antilles situated in the eastern Caribbean with a total land area of 442 sq. km (171 sq. miles); it consists of Antigua (280 sq. km), Barbuda, 40 km to the north (161 sq. km) and uninhabited Redonda, 40 km to the southwest (one sq. km). The population at the census of May 2011 was 85,567 (1,634 on Barbuda); density, 194 per sq. km. In 2011, 30·4% of the population lived in urban areas.

The UN gives a projected population for 2020 of 105,000.

The chief town is St John's, the capital, on Antigua (22,219 inhabitants in 2011). The only settlement on Barbuda is Codrington.

English is the official language; local dialects are also spoken.

Social Statistics

Expectation of life, 2009: males, 73 years; females, 76. Annual population growth rate, 2010–15, 1·1%. 2007: births, 1,240; deaths, 504. Infant mortality in 2010 was 7 per 1,000 live births; fertility rate, 2008, 2·1 births per woman.

Climate

A tropical climate, but drier than most West Indies islands. The hot season is from May to Nov., when rainfall is greater. Mean annual rainfall is 40" (1,000 mm).

Constitution and Government

H.M. Queen Elizabeth, as Head of State, is represented by a Governor-General appointed by her on the advice of the Prime Minister. There is a bicameral legislature, comprising a 17-member *Senate* appointed by the Governor-General and an 18-member *House of Representatives* (with 17 members elected by universal suffrage for a five-year term plus the Speaker). The Governor-General appoints a Prime Minister and, on the latter's advice, other members of the Cabinet.

Barbuda is administered by a nine-member directly-elected council.

National Anthem

'Fair Antigua and Barbuda'; words by N. H. Richards, tune by W. G. Chambers.

Recent Elections

At the elections to the House of Representatives of 21 March 2018 the ruling Antigua and Barbuda Labour Party (ABLP) won 15 seats with 59·2% of votes cast, the United Progressive Party (UPP) 1 with 37·2% and the Barbuda People's Movement (BPM) 1 with 1·4%. Turnout was 76·5%.

Current Government

Governor-General: Rodney Williams (in office since 14 Aug. 2014).

In Feb. 2019 the ABLP government comprised:

Prime Minister, and Minister of Finance and Corporate Governance: Gaston Browne; b. 1967 (ABLP; in office since 13 June 2014).

Senior Minister, and Minister of Public Utilities, Civil Aviation and Energy: Robin Yearwood.

Minister of Agriculture, Fisheries and Barbuda Affairs: Dean Jonas. *Attorney General:* Steadroy 'Cutie' Benjamin. *Education, Science and Technology:* Michael Browne. *Health, Wellness and the Environment:* Molwyn Joseph. *Housing, Lands and Urban Renewal:* Maria Browne. *Information, Broadcasting, Telecommunications and Information Technology:* Melford Nicholas. *Investment and Trade:* Asot Michael. *Social Transformation, Human Resource Development, Youth and Gender Affairs:* Samantha Marshall. *Tourism and Economic Development:* Charles Max Fernandez. *Foreign Affairs, International Trade and Immigration:* Paul 'Chet' Greene. *Sports, Culture, National Festivals and the Arts:* Daryl Matthew. *Works:* Lennox Weston.

Government Website: http://www.ab.gov.ag

Current Leaders

Gaston Browne

Position
Prime Minister

Introduction
Gaston Browne took office as prime minister on 13 June 2014 after leading the Antigua and Barbuda Labour Party (ABLP) to a landslide victory at the general election. He prioritized reviving the economy, reducing crime and lowering unemployment. He remained in office after the March 2018 general election when the ABLP won 15 of the 17 parliamentary seats.

Early Life
Gaston Browne was born in the township of Potter Village on 9 Feb. 1967 and moved to the UK to attend City Banking College, London before completing a post-graduate degree at the University of Manchester.

Back in Antigua, Browne worked for various public and private organizations. He served as a senior manager with the Swiss American Banking Group (which later became the Global Bank of Commerce), managing assets in excess of US$400m. In 1999 he was elected to parliament representing the constituency of St. John's City West for the ABLP. He went on to defend his seat at the elections of 2004, 2009 and 2014. He was appointed minister of planning in the administration of Lester Bird (1994–2004), subsequently adding trade to his portfolio. In 2003 he was caught up in a scandal involving improper payments from a US financier while negotiating a land swap, but was never charged with any offence.

On 26 Nov. 2012, Browne won the party leadership from the incumbent, Lester Bird. It was the first time that the leadership had been held by someone not from the Bird family, although on the same day Browne announced the date of his wedding to Maria Bird, Lester's niece. On 12 June 2014 the ABLP defeated the ruling United Progressive Party, winning 14 of 17 parliamentary seats, and Browne became premier.

Career in Office
Browne's main task on taking office was to plan the revival of the economy. He has aimed to attract more foreign direct investment, including from emerging economies and from China, and to expand the trade and tourism sectors. He has also spoken out against the terms of an IMF loan arranged by the previous government, and announced that his government was in talks with Venezuela for alternative finance. In Sept. 2017 Barbuda was devastated by Hurricane Irma, prompting Browne to describe the evacuated island as 'barely habitable'.

In a constitutional referendum in Nov. 2018 (the first in the country's history), the proposed amendment to replace the London-based Judicial Committee of the Privy Council by the Caribbean Court of Justice as the country's final court of appeal failed to reach the required quorum of valid votes in favour.

Defence

The Antigua and Barbuda Defence Force (ABDF) numbers 170 and has four units: the Antigua and Barbuda Regiment, the Service and Support Unit, the Coast Guard and the Antigua and Barbuda Cadet Corps. There are 75 reserves.

In 2013 defence expenditure totalled US$26m. (US$286 per capita), representing 2·1% of GDP.

Army
The strength of the Army section of the Defence Force was 125 in 2011.

Navy
There was a naval force of 45 operating two patrol craft in 2011.

Economy

In 2014 agriculture accounted for 1·9% of GDP, industry 19·2% and services 78·9%.

Overview
Antigua and Barbuda, a member of the Organisation of Eastern Caribbean States, relies heavily on tourism, construction and light manufacturing, but its limited economic base experiences significant volatility. The credit crisis from 2008 prompted the collapse of the country's largest financial institution, while a sharp fall in tourism and foreign direct investment inflows resulted in the economy contracting by over 20% by 2012.

In 2014, however, tourism enjoyed a steady recovery, supported by the strengthening US economy. Average annual GDP growth was recorded at 3·1% between 2012 and 2014. The average public debt (general government gross debt as a percentage of GDP) was 92·4% between 2010 and 2014.

Currency
The unit of currency is the *East Caribbean dollar* (XCD), issued by the Eastern Caribbean Central Bank. Foreign exchange reserves in June 2010 were US$121m. and total money supply was EC$653m. There was deflation of 0·5% in 2016 but then inflation of 2·5% in 2017.

Budget
In 2013 revenues totalled EC$599·1m. and expenditures EC$743·6m. Tax revenue accounted for 92·7% of revenues in 2013; current expenditure accounted for 94·2% of expenditures.

Performance
The economy grew by 4·1% in 2015, 5·3% in 2016 and 2·8% in 2017. Total GDP was US$1·5bn. in 2017.

Banking and Finance
The Eastern Caribbean Central Bank based in St Kitts functions as a central bank. The *Governor* is Timothy Antoine. Investment banking and financial services play an important role in the economy. Leading banks include Antigua Commercial Bank, Caribbean Union Bank Ltd, Eastern Caribbean Amalgamated Bank Ltd and Global Bank of Commerce Ltd. In 1981 Antigua established an offshore banking sector. The offshore sector is regulated by the Financial Services Regulatory Commission, a statutory body.

Energy and Natural Resources

Environment
In 2011 Antigua and Barbuda's carbon dioxide emissions from the consumption of energy were the equivalent of 6·7 tonnes per capita.

Electricity
Capacity in 2011 was 84,000 kW. Production was estimated at 325m. kWh in 2011 and consumption per capita was about 3,687 kWh.

Agriculture
In 2014 there were around 4,000 ha. of arable land and 1,000 ha. of permanent crops. Production (2013 estimate) of fruits and vegetables, 12,500 tonnes (notably melons and mangoes).

Livestock (2013 estimates): goats, 27,000; sheep, 14,000; cattle, 5,000; pigs, 5,000; chickens, 150,000.

Forestry
Forests covered 10,000 ha., or 22% of the total land area, in 2015.

Fisheries
Total catch in 2014 came to 3,114 tonnes, exclusively from sea fishing.

Industry

Manufactures include beer, cement, stoves, refrigerators, fans, garments and rum (molasses imported from Guyana).

Labour
In 2008, 38,500 people were in employment. The main areas of activity were: hotels and restaurants, 5,800; wholesale and retail trade, repair of motor vehicles, motorcycles and personal and household goods, 5,500; public administration and defence, and compulsory social security, 5,000. The hourly minimum wage was raised to EC$7·50 (US$2·78) in Jan. 2008.

International Trade

Imports and Exports
Imports in 2010 (c.i.f.) totalled US$361·3m. and exports (f.o.b.) US$34·8m. The main trading partners were the USA, China and the UK for imports; and the USA, the UK and Panama for exports.

Communications

Roads
In 2012 there were about 1,170 km of roads. 20,100 vehicles were in use in 2009, including 13,400 passenger cars and 5,300 commercial vehicles.

Civil Aviation
V. C. Bird International Airport is near St John's. There were flights in 2010 to nearly 30 international destinations. A domestic flight links the airports on Antigua and Barbuda.

Shipping
The main port is St John's Harbour. In Jan. 2014 there were 1,178 ships of 300 GT or over registered, totalling 10,277,000 GT. Antigua and Barbuda is a 'flag of convenience' country.

Telecommunications
There were 41,700 fixed telephone lines in 2010, or 470·5 per 1,000 inhabitants. Mobile phone subscribers numbered 163,900 in 2010. There were 742·0 internet users per 1,000 inhabitants in 2009. Fixed internet subscriptions totalled 15,600 in 2009 (177·7 per 1,000 inhabitants).

Social Institutions

Out of 178 countries analysed in the 2017 *Fragile States Index*—a list published jointly by the Fund for Peace and *Foreign Policy* magazine— Antigua and Barbuda was ranked the 48th least vulnerable to conflict or collapse. The index is based on 12 indicators of state vulnerability across social, political and economic categories.

Justice
Law is based on UK common law as exercised by the Eastern Caribbean Supreme Court (ECSC) on St Lucia. There are Magistrates' Courts and a Court of Summary Jurisdiction. Appeals lie to the Court of Appeal of ECSC, or ultimately to the UK Privy Council. Antigua and Barbuda was one of ten countries to sign an agreement in Feb. 2001 establishing a Caribbean Court of Justice to replace the British Privy Council as the highest civil and criminal court. In the meantime the number of signatories has risen to 12. The court was inaugurated at Port of Spain, Trinidad on 16 April 2005 although Antigua and Barbuda has yet to accept it as its court of last resort.

The population in penal institutions in July 2013 was 371 (equivalent to 403 per 100,000 of national population).

Education

Adult literacy was an estimated 98·9% in 2009. In 2007 there were 11,569 pupils at primary schools and 7,838 pupils at secondary schools. The University of Health Sciences Antigua is a private medical school, the University of the West Indies School of Continuing Studies offers adult training and the Antigua State College offers technical and teacher training. Antigua is a partner in the regional University of the West Indies.

In 2009 public expenditure on education came to 2·8% of GDP.

Health

There is one general hospital, a private clinic, seven health centres and 17 associated clinics. A new medical centre at Mount St John's opened in Feb. 2009. In the period 2000–06 there were two physicians per 10,000 inhabitants. In 2005 there were 16 dentists, 175 nurses, and 15 pharmacists and pharmacy assistants.

In *Water: At What Cost? The State of the World's Water 2016*, WaterAid reported that 2·1% of the population does not have access to safe water.

Welfare

The state operates a Medical Benefits Scheme providing free medical attention, and a Social Security Scheme, providing age and disability pensions and sickness benefits.

Religion

In 2010 an estimated 93·0% of the population were Christians (mainly Protestants) and 3·6% folk religionists according to the Pew Research Center's Forum on Religion & Public Life.

Culture

Press

The main newspapers are *The Antigua Sun* and *The Daily Observer*, with a combined circulation of 9,000 in 2008.

Tourism

Tourism is the main industry, contributing about 70% of GDP and 80% of foreign exchange earnings and related activities. In 2014 there were 249,316 tourist arrivals by air, 522,342 cruise passengers arrivals and 17,922 yacht arrivals.

Festivals

Of particular interest are the International Sailing Week (April–May), the Annual Tennis Championship (May) and the Mid-Summer Carnival (July–Aug.).

World Heritage Sites

The Antigua Naval Dockyard and Related Archaeological Sites was inscribed on the UNESCO World Heritage List in 2016.

Diplomatic Representatives

Of Antigua and Barbuda in the United Kingdom (2nd Floor, 45 Crawford Pl., London, W1H 4LP)
High Commissioner: Karen-Mae Hill.

Of the United Kingdom in Antigua and Barbuda
High Commissioner: Janet Douglas, CMG (resides in Bridgetown, Barbados).

Of Antigua and Barbuda in the USA (3216 New Mexico Ave., NW, Washington, D.C., 20016)
Ambassador: Sir Ronald Sanders.

Of the USA in Antigua and Barbuda
Ambassador: Linda S. Taglialatela (resides in Bridgetown, Barbados).

Of Antigua and Barbuda to the United Nations
Ambassador: Walton Alfonso Webson.

Of Antigua and Barbuda to the European Union
Ambassador: Vacant.

Further Reading

Dyde, Brian, *The Unsuspected Isle: A History of Antigua.* 2000
Nicholson, Desmond, *Antigua, Barbuda and Redonda: A Historical Sketch.* 1991

Argentina

República Argentina (Argentine Republic)

Capital: Buenos Aires
Population projection, 2020: 45·51m.
GNI per capita, 2017: (PPP$) 18,461
HDI/world rank, 2017: 0·825/47
Internet domain extension: .ar

Key Historical Events

Before European colonization two main indigenous American groups and numerous nomadic tribes inhabited the region that is now Argentina, constituting a population of some 300,000. Both groups—the Diaguita people in the northwest, and the Guarani people in the south and east—created the basis for a permanent agricultural civilization. The Diaguita also prevented the powerful Inca from expanding their empire from Bolivia into Argentina.

Europeans first came to Argentina in the early 16th century. The explorer Sebastian Cabot established the first Spanish settlement in 1526. He reported Argentina's natural silver resources, possibly inspiring the name *Argentina* ('of silver'). Ten years later Pedro de Mendoza founded Buenos Aires; however, it was not until 1580 that the region's indigenous peoples, weakened by European diseases as much as European military campaigns, were finally defeated and Spanish rule established.

Largely neglected as Spain looked instead to the riches of Peru, most settlers in Argentina came from the neighbouring colonies of Chile, Peru and Paraguay. Missions established by the Roman Catholic Church played an important part in the colonizing process.

In 1776 Buenos Aires, known throughout the 18th century as a smuggler's haunt, was made a free port at the centre of a viceroyalty comprising Argentina, Uruguay, Paraguay and Bolivia. As trade with Europe increased, Buenos Aires adopted European enlightenment and was seen as more cosmopolitan than its rivals.

When Spain came under Napoleonic control the British attacked Buenos Aires, first in 1806 and then again in 1807. On both occasions the city was able to repel the invasions without help from Spanish forces. This was a spur to the independence movement.

Independence

Having separated from Paraguay in 1814, Argentina gained its independence from Spain in 1816. Unable to control its outlying regions, it lost Bolivia in 1825 and Uruguay in 1828. In the early years of independence, the country was embroiled in internal struggles between the Unitarists and the Federalists. Unitarists wanted a strong central government, particularly as Britain agreed to recognize Argentinian independence only if it could devise a government representing the whole country. Federalists, on the other hand, advocated regional control, as each province had formed its own political regime, based on local interests and reinforced by military leaders dominant since the war.

In 1827 Argentinians joined forces with Uruguay to repel a Brazilian invasion, thereby securing independence for Uruguay and encouraging Argentinian unification. From 1835–52, the Federalists held power under Gen. Juan Manuel de Rosas, an important landowner and commander of a rural militia. Governor of Buenos Aires from 1829, Rosas proved a formidable leader who used a secret police force, the Mazorca, to defeat his opponents. He also consolidated church support, compelling priests to display his portrait at the altar.

Britain seized the Falkland Islands (Islas Malvinas) in 1833, while Bolivia, Paraguay and Uruguay continued to isolate the federation. In 1838, following a trade dispute with Uruguay, Argentinian political exiles gained French support in an attempt to overthrow Rosas. But he remained in power until 1853 when he was ousted by Gen. Justo José de Urquiza. The Unitarists inaugurated a new constitution to achieve a more stable government, although Urquiza's overthrow by Santiago Derquai led to another civil war. An agreement between Urquiza and Gen. Bartolomé Mitre, governor of Buenos Aires, saw a return to stability and established the city as the seat of government.

In a period of strong economic growth, schools were built, public works started and liberal reforms instituted. From 1865–70 Argentina was involved in the War of the Triple Alliance, joining with Uruguay and Brazil in a campaign against Paraguay. This ultimately strengthened the newly centralized Argentina. From 1880–86 Argentina thrived under the leadership of Gen. Julio Roca. A Federalist, Roca nevertheless retained Buenos Aires as the capital. During his second term of office, Roca made peace with Chile after years of dispute over territory.

As a magnet for European immigration, the political system came under pressure to broaden its representation. Italian and Spanish immigrants established the new Socialist, Anarchist and Unión Cívica Radical parties. This latter became the main political force and under the leadership of Hipólito Irigoyen won their first presidential election in 1916, following Roque Sáenz Peña's electoral reforms of 1910–14. The conservatives regained power in 1930, supported by the military, and the activities of radicals were restricted until Gen. Augustín Pedro Justin, heading a coalition of conservatives, radicals and independent socialists, was elected in 1931. Political and economic reforms resulted in trade agreements with Britain which strengthened the economy.

Perón

Although Argentina remained neutral at the outbreak of the Second World War, another coup in 1943 brought Gen. Juan Domingo Perón to power. He chose to side with the allies and declared war on the axis powers.

Perón led a regime that was autocratic but populist and nationalistic, winning presidential elections in 1946 and 1951 with the support of the urban working class. His success was reinforced by his second wife Eva Duarte de Perón, 'Evita'. Acting as *de facto* minister of health and labour, she awarded wage increases that led to inflation. Her death in 1952 combined with Perón's increasing authoritarianism and his excommunication from the church, led to a fall in his popularity. In 1955 a coup by the armed forces sent him into exile.

In 1957 Argentina reverted to the constitution of 1853, and a year later Arturo Frondizi was elected president. With US financial aid, Frondizi attempted to stabilize the economy but faced heavy criticism from left-wing parties and from the Peronists. Frondizi also fell out of favour with the military, whose intervention continued to overshadow Argentinian politics. When the Peronists achieved the highest number of votes in elections in 1962 the military took control, banning the Peronists, along with the Communist party, before elections in 1963. Arturo Illia, a moderate liberal, was elected and many political prisoners were released. An attempted return by Perón in 1964 drove the military to install Gen. Carlos Onganía as president. Responding to popular resistance, the military eventually allowed the re-election of Perón in 1973.

After Perón's death in 1974 his third wife, María Estela Martínez de Perón, 'Isabelita', succeeded, becoming the Americas' first woman chief of state. She was deposed by military coup two years later and the army's commander-in-chief, Gen. Jorge Videla, became president. Once in power, Videla dissolved Congress, banned trade unions and imposed military control. Censorship and military curfews were imposed and the secret police was active. The savagely repressive regime implemented what became known as the 'Dirty War' when up to 15,000 of Videla's opponents disappeared, almost certainly tortured and executed.

Falklands War

Videla was succeeded by Gen. Leopoldo Galtieri, the army commander-in-chief. In April 1982, in an effort to distract attention from internal tension, Galtieri invaded the Falkland Islands. The subsequent defeat helped to precipitate Galtieri's fall in July 1982. Decades of state intervention, regulation, inward looking policies and special interest subsidies had caused economic chaos. Presidential elections held in Oct. 1983 restored civilian rule under Raúl Alfonsín, leader of the middle-class Unión Cívica Radical. Despite attempting to redress the finances of the bloated public sector,

© Springer Nature Limited 2020
Palgrave Macmillan (ed.), *The Statesman's Yearbook 2020*,
https://doi.org/10.1057/978-1-349-95940-2_17

growing unemployment and four-figure inflation led to a Peronist victory in the 1989 elections and Carlos Menem became Argentina's new president.

After an attempted military coup in Dec. 1990, Menem met allegations of corruption in the country's privatization programme by reshuffling his government. Economy Minister Domingo Cavallo's plan to stabilize the economy allowed Menem to alter the constitution in 1994 to permit his re-election for a second term.

By 1999, with economic recession and high unemployment, Menem's popularity had plummeted. In the election that year, Fernando de la Rúa of the centrist Alliance became the first president in a decade from outside of the Peronist party. Menem was later accused of illegal arms deals but was released by a federal court and announced his intention to return to politics.

A state of emergency was introduced in Dec. 2001 as Argentina verged on bankruptcy. De la Rúa resigned on 20 Dec. 2001 after days of rioting and looting. Three interim presidents held power over a period of just 11 days before another Peronist, Eduardo Duhalde, was elected president by Congress. With the economy still in crisis, Duhalde held office until the election of Néstor Kirchner in May 2003. He was succeeded by his wife, Cristina Fernández de Kirchner, four years later. She enjoyed a relatively powerful presidency benefiting from a strong legislative majority, during which Argentina became the first Latin American country to legalize same-sex marriage. Mauricio Macri was elected president in Oct. 2015, taking over from Fernández, who had completed her constitutionally limited mandate of two successive terms.

Territory and Population

The second largest country in South America, the Argentine Republic is bounded in the north by Bolivia, in the northeast by Paraguay, in the east by Brazil, Uruguay and the Atlantic Ocean, and the west by Chile. The republic consists of 23 provinces and one federal district. Area (in sq. km) and census population (in 1,000) in 2010:

Provinces	Area	Population	Capital	Population
Buenos Aires	307,571	15,625	La Plata	643
Catamarca	102,602	368	Catamarca	159
Chaco	99,633	1,055	Resistencia	291
Chubut	224,686	509	Rawson	25
Córdoba	165,321	3,309	Córdoba	1,317
Corrientes	88,199	993	Corrientes	346
Entre Ríos	78,781	1,236	Paraná	247
Formosa	72,066	530	Formosa	222
Jujuy	53,219	673	San Salvador de Jujuy	258
La Pampa	143,440	319	Santa Rosa	103
La Rioja	89,680	334	La Rioja	179
Mendoza	148,827	1,739	Mendoza	115
Misiones	29,801	1,102	Posadas	275
Neuquén	94,078	551	Neuquén	232
Río Negro	203,013	639	Viedma	53
Salta	155,488	1,214	Salta	521
San Juan	89,651	681	San Juan	109
San Luis	76,748	432	San Luis	170
Santa Cruz	243,943	274	Río Gallegos	96
Santa Fé	133,007	3,195	Santa Fé	391
Santiago del Estero	136,351	874	Santiago del Estero	252
Tierra del Fuego	21,571	127	Ushuaia	57
Tucumán	22,524	1,448	San Miguel de Tucumán	549
Federal Capital	200	2,890	Buenos Aires	2,890

Argentina also claims territory in Antarctica.

The area is 2,780,400 sq. km (excluding the claimed Antarctic territory) and the population at the 2010 census 40,117,096, giving a density of 14 per sq. km.

The UN gives a projected population for 2020 of 45·51m.

In 2011, 92·6% of the population were urban.

In April 1990 the National Congress declared that the Falklands and other British-held islands in the South Atlantic were part of the new province of Tierra del Fuego formed from the former National Territory of the same name. The 1994 constitution reaffirms Argentine sovereignty over the Falkland Islands.

The population of the main metropolitan areas at the 2010 census was: Buenos Aires, 13,588,171; Córdoba, 1,453,865; Rosario, 1,236,089; Mendoza, 937,154; Tucumán, 794,327; La Plata, 787,294.

97% speak the national language, Spanish, while 2% speak Italian and 1% other languages. The 2010 census population included 1,805,957 persons born outside Argentina (550,713 born in Paraguay, 345,272 in Bolivia, 191,147 in Chile, 157,514 in Peru and 147,499 in Italy).

Social Statistics

2010 births, 756,176; deaths, 318,602. Rates, 2010 (per 1,000 population): birth, 18·7; death, 7·9. Infant mortality, 2010, 12 per 1,000 live births. Life expectancy at birth, 2013, 72·6 years for males and 79·9 years for females. Annual population growth rate, 2005–10, 0·9%; fertility rate, 2013, 2·2 births per woman. Argentina legalized same-sex marriage in July 2010.

Climate

The climate is warm temperate over the pampas, where rainfall occurs in all seasons, but diminishes towards the west. In the north and west, the climate is more arid, with high summer temperatures, while in the extreme south conditions are also dry, but much cooler. Buenos Aires, Jan. 74°F (23·3°C), July 50°F (10°C). Annual rainfall 37" (950 mm). Bahía Blanca, Jan. 74°F (23·3°C), July 48°F (8·9°C). Annual rainfall 21" (523 mm). Mendoza, Jan. 75°F (23·9°C), July 47°F (8·3°C). Annual rainfall 8" (190 mm). Rosario, Jan. 76°F (24·4°C), July 51°F (10·6°C). Annual rainfall 35" (869 mm). San Juan, Jan. 78°F (25·6°C), July 50°F (10°C). Annual rainfall 4" (89 mm). San Miguel de Tucumán, Jan. 79°F (26·1°C), July 56°F (13·3°C). Annual rainfall 38" (970 mm). Ushuaia, Jan. 50°F (10°C), July 34°F (1·1°C). Annual rainfall 19" (475 mm).

Constitution and Government

On 10 April 1994 elections were held for a 230-member constituent assembly to reform the 1853 constitution. The Justicialist National Movement (Peronist) gained 39% of votes cast and the Radical Union 20%. On 22 Aug. 1994 this assembly unanimously adopted a new constitution. This reduces the presidential term of office from six to four years, but permits the President to stand for two terms. The President is no longer elected by an electoral college, but directly by universal suffrage. A presidential candidate is elected with more than 45% of votes cast, or 40% if at least 10% ahead of an opponent; otherwise there is a second round. The Constitution reduces the President's powers by instituting a *Chief of Cabinet*. The bicameral *National Congress* consists of a *Senate* and a *Chamber of Deputies*. The Senate comprises 72 members (one-third of the members elected every two years to six-year terms). The Chamber of Deputies comprises 257 members (one-half of the members elected every two years to four-year terms) directly elected by universal suffrage. Voting is compulsory for citizens aged 18 to 70 and—with effect from the mid-term elections of Oct. 2013—optional for those aged 16 and 17.

National Anthem

'Oíd, mortales, el grito sagrado: Libertad' ('Hear, mortals, the sacred cry of Liberty'); words by V. López y Planes, 1813; tune by J. Blas Parera.

Government Chronology

Presidents since 1944. (FREJULI = Justicialista Liberation Front; FV = Front for Victory; PJ = Justicialist Party; PL = Labour Party; PP = Peronist Party; PRO = Republican Proposal; UCR = Radical Civic

Union; UCRI = Radical Intransigent Civic Union; UCRP = People's Radical Civic Union)

1944–46	military	Edelmiro Julián Farrell Plaul
1946–55	military/PL/PP	Juan Domingo Perón Sosa
1955	military	Eduardo A. Lonardi Doucet
1955–58	military	Pedro Eugenio Aramburu Cilveti
1958–62	UCRI	Arturo Frondizi Ercoli
1962–63	UCRI	José María Guido
1963–66	UCRP	Arturo Umberto Illia Francesconi
1966–70	military	Juan Carlos Onganía Carballo
1970–71	military	Roberto Marcelo Levingston Laborda
1971–73	military	Alejandro Agustín Lanusse Gelly
1973	FREJULI	Héctor José Cámpora Demaestre
1973	FREJULI	Raúl Alberto Lastiri
1973–74	PJ	Juan Domingo Perón Sosa
1974–76	PJ	María Estela Martínez de Perón
1976–81	military	Jorge Rafael Videla
1981	military	Roberto Eduardo Viola
1981–82	military	Leopoldo Fortunato Galtieri
1982–83	military	Reynaldo Benito Bignone
1983–89	UCR	Raúl Ricardo Alfonsín
1989–99	PJ	Carlos Saúl Menem
1999–2001	UCR	Fernando de la Rúa
2002–03	PJ	Eduardo Duhalde
2003–07	PJ	Néstor Carlos Kirchner
2007–15	FV	Cristina Fernández de Kirchner
2015–	PRO	Mauricio Macri

Recent Elections

In the first round of presidential elections held on 25 Oct. 2015 Daniel Scioli (Front for Victory) won 37·1% of the vote, followed by Mauricio Macri (Let's Change coalition) with 34·2%, Sergio Massa (United for a New Alternative coalition) with 21·4%, Nicolás del Caño (Workers' Left Front) 3·2%, Margarita Stolbizer (the Progressives coalition) 2·5% and Adolfo Rodriguez Saá (Federal Commitment) 1·6%. Turnout was 81·2%. In the second round run-off on 22 Nov., Macri won with 51·4% of the vote against Scioli with 48·6%. Turnout was 80·9%.

In elections to the Chamber of Deputies held on 22 Oct. 2017, 127 of the 257 seats that were not contested at the previous elections in Oct. 2015 were at stake. Following the elections, Let's Change and its allies held 107 seats, the Citizen's Unity Front 67, the Justicialist Party 40, United for a New Alternative 21, the Socialist Left 4 and others 19.

Current Government

President: Mauricio Macri; b. 1959 (Republican Proposal; sworn in 10 Dec. 2015).

Vice-President: Gabriela Michetti.

In Feb. 2019 the cabinet comprised:

Chief of the Cabinet: Marcos Peña. *Minister of Defence:* Oscar Raúl Aguad Beily. *Treasury:* Nicolás Dujovne. *Education, Culture, Science and Technology:* Alejandro Finocchiaro. *Foreign Affairs and Worship:* Jorge Marcelo Faurie. *Health and Social Development:* Dr Carolina Stanley. *Interior, Public Works and Housing:* Rogelio Frigerio. *Justice and Human Rights:* Germán Carlos Garavano. *Production and Labour:* Dante Enrique Sica. *Security:* Patricia Bullrich. *Transport:* Guillermo Javier Dietrich. *Secretary General of the Presidency:* Fernando de Andreis.

Office of the President (Spanish only): http://www.presidencia.gov.ar

Current Leaders

Mauricio Macri

Position

President

Introduction

Mauricio Macri became president in Dec. 2015, at the head of a centre-right coalition. He promised to boost growth by implementing liberal economic policies.

Early Life

Born in Tandil in Buenos Aires province on 8 Feb. 1959, Macri studied civil engineering at the Pontifical Catholic University of Argentina. He then undertook graduate studies in finance and economics at the Universidad del CEMA, at Columbia Business School and at the Wharton School of the University of Pennsylvania in the USA. From the mid-1980s he worked in various companies within his family's Socma Group, rising to become president of car manufacturer Sevel Argentina in 1994.

In 1991 he was kidnapped by a group of Argentinian police officers and released after 12 days, reportedly after payment of a multi-million dollar ransom—an incident that influenced him to enter politics. From 1995–2003 he served as president of the popular Boca Juniors football club. His tenure saw the club achieve success and gained him an increased public profile. In 2003 he founded the centre-right Commitment to Change party, and unsuccessfully contested the Buenos Aires mayoral elections. In 2005 the party was relaunched as Republican Proposal and Macri was elected to parliament. He was elected mayor of Buenos Aires at the second attempt in 2007, and re-elected in 2011. In office he won praise for investing in public transport and city infrastructure, although his attempt to set up a metropolitan police force was more controversial.

In 2015 he formed the Let's Change coalition comprising his own Republican Proposal, the Radical Civic Union and several smaller parties. He then headed its presidential election campaign, pledging to re-invigorate the economy with free-market policies, strengthen institutions and build better relationships with the USA and Europe. Having performed well enough in the first round to force a run-off, Macri won a surprise second round victory in Nov. with 51·4% of the vote.

Career in Office

Macri took office on 10 Dec. 2015 and moved swiftly to implement key economic policies, cutting export taxes on agricultural products and removing currency controls. In Feb. 2016 he also reached an agreement with overseas bondholders to settle multi-billion dollar debts that had restricted Argentina's access to international credit markets. He meanwhile sought to address widespread inequality and corruption and signalled a conservative stance on social issues, such as abortion. Despite some labour unrest over job cuts and Macri's reformist economic policies, his Let's Change coalition made significant gains in mid-term congressional elections in Oct. 2017.

His major challenge nevertheless remained the revival of the sluggish economy and containment of high inflation. In May 2018, amid a rapid slide in the value of the currency, his government raised interest rates dramatically. He also turned to the International Monetary Fund for a $50bn. standby loan, public hostility to which prompted a 24-hour strike in June bringing much of the country to a standstill.

Defence

Conscription was abolished in 1994. In 2013 defence expenditure totalled US$5,104m. (US$120 per capita), representing 1·0% of GDP (compared to over 8% in 1981).

Army

In 2013 the Army was 38,500 strong. There are no reserves formally established or trained.

There is a paramilitary gendarmerie of 18,000 run by the ministry of interior.

Navy

In 2013 the Argentinian Navy included three diesel submarines, five destroyers and six frigates. Total personnel was 20,000 including 2,000 in Naval Aviation and 2,500 marines. Main bases are at Puerto Belgrano, Mar del Plata and Ushuaia.

The Naval Aviation Service had 23 combat-capable aircraft in 2013, including Super-Etendard strike aircraft, and 14 helicopters, including Agusta/Sikorsky ASH-3H Sea Kings.

Air Force

The Air Force is organized into Air Operations, Air Regions, Logistics and Personnel Commands. There were (2013) 14,600 personnel and 100 combat-capable aircraft including A-4 Skyhawk and Mirage III jet fighters.

Economy

Agriculture contributed 7·2% of GDP in 2013, industry 28·5% and services 64·3%.

In Jan. 2006 the government repaid the country's entire US$9·57bn. debt to the IMF ahead of schedule.

Overview

With the third largest economy in Latin America, Argentina is rich in natural resources, boasts a vibrant agricultural sector and has a well-educated workforce. However, it has long been locked into a debilitating cycle of boom and bust. After GDP growth of 2·4% in 2013, the economy contracted by 2·5% in 2014. The economy remains vulnerable to weak external demand, low global prices for agricultural products, slow internal consumption growth and, as of 2016, the deep recession in Brazil (its largest trading partner).

In the 1980s the economy contracted at an average annual rate of 0·7% following a period of macroeconomic mismanagement. Structural reforms, market liberalization and a convertibility plan (establishing a currency peg to the US dollar) in 1991 helped stabilize the economy for most of the 1990s. The fixed exchange rate regime survived the Mexican and Asian financial crises but the balance of payments was unable to withstand the pressure caused by subsequent shocks. By the fourth quarter of 1998 the economy was in recession.

In Dec. 2001 Argentina recorded the largest sovereign debt default in history and in Jan. 2002 abandoned convertibility. From 1999–2002 the economy contracted by 18·4%, leaving over half the population in poverty. Strong recovery between 2003 and 2007 was underpinned by a firm fiscal policy, debt restructuring and favourable international market conditions. Unemployment fell and the urban poverty rate dropped from 48% in 2003 to 10% in 2010.

Argentina weathered the 2008–09 global financial crisis, with strong growth in 2010 supported by high agricultural yields and exports, notably of soybean and beef products. In June 2010 Argentina concluded an US$18·3bn. debt swap process, in which bad debts stemming from the 2001 default were exchanged for new bonds. This, combined with the earlier restructuring, enabled the government to settle 92% of the US$100bn. default debt. However, those bondholders who rejected the swap offers subsequently won a series of judgments in US courts ordering Argentina to pay.

The economy slowed in 2012, with investor confidence undermined in April that year by the nationalization of oil firm YPF, restrictions on imports and currency tightening in an attempt to bolster reserves. In early 2014 the government devalued the peso by 20% and tightened fiscal policy, but in July 2014 the country defaulted for the eighth time in its history after a legal stand-off with its 'hold-out' bondholders. In an effort to preserve international reserves, which fell to an eight-year low in Aug. 2014, the government further increased limits on imports, making it costly for local manufacturers to obtain raw materials.

A new president, Mauricio Macri, took office in Dec. 2015. He promptly cut export taxes on agricultural products, removed currency controls and, in Feb. 2016, reached an agreement with outstanding overseas bondholders to settle those debts that had restricted Argentina's access to international credit markets.

Inflation has remained high, with the official figure of 10·6% in 2013 being much lower than some independent estimates putting it in the region of 40%. In 2016 the Central Bank aimed to target inflation with reforms to boost business confidence.

Currency

The monetary unit is the *peso* (ARS). In Dec. 2015 foreign exchange controls were lifted and the peso was allowed to float freely. However, in July 2017 the central bank intervened to halt further declines after the peso reached historic lows against the US dollar. There was inflation of 25·7% in 2017.

Gold reserves were 1·76m. troy oz in Sept. 2009; foreign exchange reserves were US$43,111m. Total money supply was 107,615m. pesos in Aug. 2009.

Budget

Revenues in 2015 totalled 1,102,452m. pesos and expenditures 1,096,200m. pesos. Tax revenue accounted for 57·5% of revenues in 2015; current expenditure accounted for 86·7% of expenditures.

VAT is 21% (reduced rates, 10·5% and 2·5%).

Performance

There was real GDP growth of 2·7% in 2015. Argentina suffered a recession in 2016 when the economy shrank by 1·8%, before a recovery saw growth of 2·9% in 2017.

Total GDP was US$637·6bn. in 2017.

Banking and Finance

The total assets of the Argentine Central Bank (BCRA) in Dec. 2007 were 228·92bn. pesos. The *President* of the Central Bank is Guido Sandleris. In early 2002 banks and financial markets were temporarily closed as an emergency measure in response to the economic crisis that made the country virtually bankrupt. In Dec. 2014 there were 65 banks (of which 53 were private and 12 public), 15 finance companies and one credit co-operative.

In 2010 total external debt was US$127,849m., representing 36·1% of GNI.

There is a main stock exchange at Buenos Aires, which was the best performing exchange in the world in 2014 with an annual gain of 58·9%. There are also exchanges in Córdoba, Rosario, Mendoza and La Plata.

Energy and Natural Resources

Environment

Argentina's carbon dioxide emissions from the consumption of energy in 2011 were the equivalent of 4·7 tonnes per capita. An *Environmental Performance Index* compiled in 2016 ranked Argentina 43rd of 180 countries, with 79·8%. The index examined various factors in nine areas—agriculture, air quality, biodiversity and habitat, climate and energy, fisheries, forests, health impacts, water and sanitation, and water resources.

Electricity

Installed capacity in 2011 was 33·8m. kW. Electric power production (2011) was 129,892m. kWh (including 31,901m. kWh hydro-electric and 6,371m. kWh nuclear); consumption per capita in 2011 was 3,427 kWh. In 2015 there were three nuclear reactors operational.

Oil and Gas

Oil production (2013) was 30·5m. tonnes. Reserves were 2·4bn. bbls in 2013. The oil industry was privatized in 1993 but the country's largest oil firm, YPF, was renationalized in 2012. Natural gas extraction in 2013 was 35·5bn. cu. metres. Reserves were 300bn. cu. metres in 2013. The main area in production is the Neuquen basin in western Argentina, with over 40% of the total oil reserves and nearly half the gas reserves. Argentina has vast mostly untapped shale gas reserves that could help revive the economy in the future. Natural gas accounts for approximately 45% of all the energy consumed in Argentina.

Minerals

Minerals (with production in 2005) include clays (6·4m. tonnes), salt (1·8m. tonnes), borates (632,792 tonnes), aluminium (270,714 tonnes), bentonite (247,101 tonnes), copper (187,317 tonnes), coal (110,000 tonnes in 2007), zinc (30,227 tonnes of metal), lead (10,683 tonnes of metal), silver (264 tonnes), gold (27,904 kg), granite, marble and tungsten. Production from the US$1·1bn. Alumbrera copper and gold mine, the country's biggest mining project, in Catamarca province in the northwest, started in 1997. In 1993 the mining laws were reformed and state regulation was swept away, creating a more stable tax regime for investors. In 1997 Argentina and Chile signed a treaty laying the legal and tax framework for mining operations straddling the 5,000 km border, allowing mining products to be transported out through both countries.

Agriculture

In 2007 there were around 32·5m. ha. of arable land and 1·0m. ha. of permanent crops. 1·56m. ha. were irrigated in 2006. The agricultural population was an estimated 3·18m. in 2008, of whom 1·42m. were economically active. In 2009 there were 4·40m. ha. of organic agricultural land (the second largest area after Australia), representing 3·3% of the total area under agriculture.

Livestock (2009 estimates): cattle, 50,750,000; sheep, 12,450,000; goats, 4,250,000; horses, 3,680,000; pigs, 2,270,000. In 2008–09 greasy wool production was 54,000 tonnes; milk (in 2007), 9,527m. litres; eggs (in 2007), 696m. dozen.

Crop production (in 1,000 tonnes) in 2006–07: soybeans, 47,500; sugar-cane (2008 estimate), 29,950; maize, 21,800; wheat, 14,500; sunflower seeds, 3,500; potatoes (2008 estimate), 1,950. Cotton, vine, citrus fruit, olives and *yerba maté* (Paraguayan tea) are also cultivated. Argentina is the world's leading producer of sunflower seeds, and is now the fifth largest wine producer (15,046,000 hectolitres in 2007) after Italy, France, Spain and the USA; it ranked seventh in the world in 2007 for wine exports and eighth for wine consumption.

Forestry

The forest area was 27·11m. ha., or 10% of the total land area, in 2015. Timber production in 2011 was 14·62m. cu. metres.

Fisheries

Fish landings in 2015 amounted to 814,300 tonnes, almost exclusively from sea fishing.

Industry

Production, 2007 unless otherwise indicated (in 1,000 tonnes): distillate fuel oil, 10,970; cement, 9,602; crude steel, 5,388; petrol, 4,846; pig iron, 4,389; residual fuel oil, 4,267; sugar (2006), 2,312; paper (2006), 1,721; jet fuel, 1,283; polyethylene, 575; synthetic rubber, 54. Motor vehicles produced in 2007 totalled 350,735; car tyres, 12,079,000; motorcycles, 225,397.

Labour

In 2012 the labour force in urban areas totalled 16·90m., of which 15·66m. were employed and 1·24m. were unemployed. The urban unemployment rate was 7·3% in 2012.

Argentina had 35,000 people living in slavery according to the Walk Free Foundation's 2013 *Global Slavery Index*.

International Trade

Imports and Exports

Goods imports were US$65,323·4m. in 2014 (US$73,655·5m. in 2013) and goods exports US$68,335·1m. (US$76,633·9m. in 2013).

Principal imports in 2014 were machinery and transport equipment (41·7%), chemicals, and mineral fuels and lubricants; main exports in 2014 were food, animals and beverages (42·2%), machinery and transport equipment, and crude materials and animal and vegetable oils.

The leading import supplier in 2010 was Brazil (31·3%), followed by China and the USA; the leading export destination in 2010 was Brazil (21·2%), followed by China and Chile.

Communications

Roads

In 2012 there were 228,512 km of roads, of which 34·6% were paved. The four main roads constituting Argentina's portion of the Pan-American Highway were opened in 1942. Vehicles in use in 2007 totalled 12,399,900. In 2005, 3,443 people were killed in road accidents.

Rail

Much of the 34,000 km state-owned network (on 1,000 mm, 1,435 mm and 1,676 mm gauges) was privatized in 1993–94. 30-year concessions were awarded to five freight operators; long-distance passenger services are run by contractors to the requirements of local authorities. Metro, light rail and suburban railway services are also operated by concessionaires.

The rail company carrying the most passengers is Trenes de Buenos Aires (190m. in 2008); Ferrosur Roca carries the most freight (5·1m. tonnes in 2005–06).

The metro and light rail network in Buenos Aires extended to 75 km in 2005. A light railway opened in Mendoza in 2012, with a total length of 12·5 km.

Civil Aviation

The main airport is Ministro Pistarini International Airport—also known as Ezeiza International Airport—which serves Buenos Aires and handled 7,910,048 passengers in 2009 (7,461,727 passengers on international flights). The second busiest airport is Aeroparque Jorge Newbery, also serving Buenos Aires, which handled 6,449,344 passengers in 2009. It is much more important as a domestic airport, with only 524,934 passengers on international flights in 2009. The national carrier, Aerolíneas Argentinas, was privatized in 1990 but renationalized in Sept. 2008. In 2010 it operated direct flights to Asunción, Auckland, Barcelona, Bogotá, Caracas, Florianópolis, Lima, Madrid, Miami, Montevideo, Porto Alegre, Punta del Este, Rio de Janeiro, Rome, Salvador, Santa Cruz, Santiago, São Paulo and Sydney, as well as domestic services. There were direct international flights with other airlines in 2010 to Asunción, Atlanta, Barcelona, Belo Horizonte, Bogotá, Cape Town, Cayo Coco, Cochabamba, Curitiba, Dallas, Florianópolis, Frankfurt, Guayaquil, Havana, Houston, Johannesburg, Kuala Lumpur, La Paz, Lima, London, Los Angeles, Madrid, Mexico City, Miami, Montevideo, New York, Panama City, Paris, Porto Alegre, Punta Cana, Punta del Este, Quito, Recife, Rio de Janeiro, Salvador, San José (Costa Rica), Santa Cruz, Santiago, São Paulo, Sydney, Toronto and Washington, D.C.

In 2006 scheduled airline traffic of Argentinian-based carriers flew 101m. km, carrying 6,636,000 passengers (1,818,000 on international flights).

Shipping

In Jan. 2014 there were 34 ships of 300 GT or over registered, totalling 229,000 GT. The leading ports are Bahía Blanca, Buenos Aires and San Lorenzo–San Martín.

Telecommunications

The telephone service Entel was privatized in 1990. The sell-off split Argentina into two monopolies, operated by Telefónica Internacional de España, and a holding controlled by France Télécom and Telecom Italia. In 2000 the industry was opened to unrestricted competition. In 2014 mobile phone subscriptions numbered 66·4m. (1,588·0 per 1,000 persons). In the same year there were 9·6m. main (fixed) telephone lines. In 2014, 64·7% of the population were internet users. In June 2012 there were 19·0m. Facebook users.

Social Institutions

Out of 178 countries analysed in the 2017 *Fragile States Index*—a list published jointly by the Fund for Peace and *Foreign Policy* magazine—Argentina was ranked the 39th least vulnerable to conflict or collapse. The index is based on 12 indicators of state vulnerability across social, political and economic categories.

Justice

Justice is administered by federal and provincial courts. The former deal only with cases of a national character, or those in which different provinces or inhabitants of different provinces are parties. The chief federal court is the Supreme Court, with five judges whose appointment is approved by the Senate. Other federal courts are the appeal courts, at Buenos Aires, Bahía Blanca, La Plata, Córdoba, Mendoza, Tucumán and Resistencia. Each province has its own judicial system, with a Supreme Court (generally so designated) and several minor chambers. The death penalty was reintroduced in 1976—for the killing of government, military police and judicial officials, and for participation in terrorist activities—but was abolished in 2008. In 2012 there were 2,888 homicides (rate of 7·0 per 100,000 population). The population in penal institutions in Dec. 2011 was 60,789 (147 per 100,000 of national population). Argentina was ranked 59th of 102 countries for criminal justice and 42nd for civil justice in the 2015 World Justice Project *Rule of Law Index*, which provides data on how the rule of law is experienced by the general public across eight categories.

The police force is centralized under the Federal Security Council.

Education

Adult literacy was 98% in 2008.

In 2005, 1,324,529 children attended pre-school institutions, 6,510,382 pupils were in basic general education, 1,545,992 in 'multimodal' secondary schooling and 509,134 in higher non-universities.

In 2006, in the public sector, there were 39 universities (including one technical university and one art institute) and university institutes of aeronautics, military studies, naval and maritime studies, and police studies. In the private sector, there were 40 universities (including seven Roman Catholic universities) and ten university institutes. In 2006 there were 1,304,003 students attending public universities and 279,373 at private universities.

In 2006 public expenditure on education came to 4·6% of GDP and 14·0% of total government spending.

Health

Free medical attention is obtainable from public hospitals. In the period 2006–12 Argentina had 47 hospital beds per 10,000 population. There were 38·6 physicians for every 10,000 inhabitants in the period 2007–13. Spending on health amounted to 7·3% of GDP in 2013.

In *Water: At What Cost? The State of the World's Water 2016*, WaterAid reported that 0·9% of the population does not have access to safe water.

Welfare

Until the end of 1996 trade unions had a monopoly in the handling of the compulsory social security contributions of employees, but private insurance agencies are now permitted to function alongside them.

Social security system expenditure (in 1m. pesos):

	2012	*2013*[1]
Social security benefits including pensions	204,357	270,076
Family allowances	24,386	32,644
Pension transfers	954	1,771
Unemployment insurance	575	569
Other	6,238	7,870
Total	*236,509*	*312,929*

[1]Budgeted figures.

Religion

The Roman Catholic religion is supported by the State; according to estimates by the Pew Research Center's Forum on Religion & Public Life there were 31·02m. Catholics in 2010. There were four cardinals in Feb. 2019. Jorge Mario Bergoglio was a cardinal from 2001 until March 2013, when he was selected to succeed Benedict XVI as Pope. The Pew Research Center estimates that in 2010 there were also 2·96m. Protestants, 440,000 other Christians (including Latter-day Saints/Mormons), 400,000 Muslims, 330,000 folk religionists and 200,000 Jews.

Culture

World Heritage Sites

Argentina's heritage sites as classified by UNESCO (with year entered on list) are: Los Glaciares National Park (1981), the Iguazu National Park (1984), the Ischigualasto and Talampaya Natural Parks (2000) and Los Alerces National Park (2017). The Cueva de las Manos (Cave of Hands, 1999), in Patagonia, contains cave art that is between 1,000 and 10,000 years old. The Península Valdés (1999) in Patagonia protects several endangered species of marine mammal. The Jesuit Block and Estancias of Córdoba (2000) are the principal buildings of the Jesuit community from the 17th and 18th century. The Quebrada de Humahuaca (2003) is a valley on the Camino Inca trade route. Shared with Brazil, the Jesuit Missions of the Guaranis (1984) encompasses the ruins of five Jesuit missions. Shared with Bolivia, Chile, Colombia, Ecuador and Peru, Qhapaq Ñan, Andean Road System (2014) is an extensive Inca communication, trade and defence network of roads covering 30,000 km. Shared with Belgium, France, Germany, India, Japan and Switzerland, the Architectural Work of Le Corbusier, an Outstanding Contribution to the Modern Movement (2016), consists of 17 sites that were built over a period of a half-century.

Press

In 2014 there were 47 daily newspapers with a combined average daily circulation of 1·4m. The main newspapers are *Clarín*, *La Nación* and *Diario Popular*.

Tourism

In 2011 a record 5,705,000 tourists visited Argentina (excluding same-day visitors), of which 4,760,000 were from elsewhere in the Americas and 739,000 were from Europe.

Festivals

Carnival is celebrated in Feb.–March. The Grape Harvest Festival (Fiesta Nacional de la Vendimia) takes place in Mendoza at the end of Feb. Mar del Plata holds an annual National Sea Festival (Dec.–Jan.) and International Film Festival (Nov.). Cosquín Rock (Feb.) and, in Buenos Aires, Pepsi music festival (Sept.–Oct.), Personal Fest (Oct.–Dec.) and Bue Festival (Nov.), are the leading pop and rock festivals. Buenos Aires Tango Festival takes place in Feb.–March.

Diplomatic Representatives

Of Argentina in the United Kingdom (65 Brook St., London, W1K 4AH)
Ambassador: Carlos Sersale di Cerisano.

Of the United Kingdom in Argentina (Dr Luis Agote 2412, 1425 Buenos Aires)
Ambassador: Mark Kent.

Of Argentina in the USA (1600 New Hampshire Ave., NW, Washington, D.C., 20009-2512)
Ambassador: Fernando Oris de Roa.

Of the USA in Argentina (Av. Colombia 4300, 1425 Buenos Aires)
Ambassador: Edward Prado.

Of Argentina to the United Nations
Ambassador: Martín García Moritán.

Of Argentina to the European Union
Ambassador: Héctor Marcelo Cima.

Further Reading

Bethell, L. (ed.) *Argentina since Independence.* 1994

Levey, Cara, Ozarow, Daniel and Wylde, Christopher, (eds) *Argentina Since the 2001 Crisis: Recovering the Past, Reclaiming the Future.* 2014

Levitsky, Steven, *Argentine Democracy: The Politics of Institutional Weakness.* 2006

Pion-Berlin, David, *Broken Promises? The Argentine Crisis and Argentine Democracy.* 2006

Powers, Nancy R., *Grassroots Expectations of Democracy and Economy: Argentina in Comparative Perspective.* 2001

Romero, Luis Alberto, *A History of Argentina in the Twentieth Century;* translated from Spanish. 2002

National library: Biblioteca Nacional, Calle Agüero 2502, C1425EID Buenos Aires.

Website (Spanish only): http://www.bn.gov.ar

National Statistical Office: Instituto Nacional de Estadística y Censos (INDEC), Av. Presidente Julio A. Roca 609, P.B. C1067ABB Buenos Aires.

Website: http://www.indec.gov.ar

Armenia

Hayastani Hanrapetoutiun (Republic of Armenia)

Capital: Yerevan
Population projection, 2020: 2·94m.
GNI per capita, 2017: (PPP$) 9,144
HDI/world rank, 2017: 0·755/83=
Internet domain extension: .am

Key Historical Events

Some of the world's earliest settlements, dating from around 6200 BC, were built on the Armenian plateau, part of the 'fertile crescent' encompassing Anatolia, Mesopotamia and the Levant. Independent culture and language developed and trade flourished with neighbouring civilizations. By 900 BC the kingdom of Urartu had taken root, centred on Lake Van (now in Turkey), until falling to the Assyrian and Scythian empires in the sixth century BC.

In 190 BC a Hellenistic Armenian state emerged from the remnants of Alexander the Great's short-lived empire. Led by King Artaxias, Greater Armenia reached its peak around 70 BC, stretching from central Anatolia to the Levant, Syria and northwestern Persia. The imperialistic ambitions of King Tigranes ended in defeat against Rome, with Armenia becoming a tributary kingdom. Christianity was adopted as the state religion in AD 301. The Sassanid Persians overran Armenia in AD 328, although the persecution of Christians kindled nationalism, particularly after the partition of the kingdom in AD 387 between Persia and Rome.

Despite successive domination by Persian, Byzantine and Arab forces between the fifth and ninth centuries, Armenian identity was maintained by nobles ('nakharars') with highly militarized fiefdoms. In 884 sovereignty was restored under the Bagrunti dynasty, which oversaw prosperity and urban development for over 150 years.

Byzantine forces recaptured Armenia in 1040 but were overwhelmed by Seljuk Turks at the battle of Manzikert in 1071. The expansion of the Mongol empire forced Armenians, led by Prince Reuben, westward to the former Byzantine province of Cilicia. A new state was founded, centred on Sis, and prospered on trade between the Mediterranean, the Middle East and Central Asia, until conquered by Mamlik Turks in 1337.

There were further Mongol attacks until, following the death of the great Turkic warrior Tamerlane in 1405, the western part of the Armenian plateau came under Ottoman Turkish control, while its eastern reaches were dominated by Persia. Led by the merchants, many Armenians migrated, establishing communities in Constantinople and Tiflis.

Russian expansion into the Caucasus in the early 19th century resulted in eastern Armenia becoming a Russian province in 1828. Following Russia's victory in the Russo–Turkish War in 1878, the province incorporated Kars, Ardahan and Batumi. Western Armenia remained under the waning Ottoman Empire. The brutal reign of Sultan Abdul-Hamid II led to an uprising in 1894, with between 100,000 and 300,000 dying in reprisal massacres over the following two years.

The ultranationalist Committee of Union and Progress, which led the Ottoman government from 1913, has been blamed for the systematic killing in 1915 of between 600,000 and 1·5m. Armenians. Turkey and Azerbaijan deny this amounted to genocide, arguing that the number of deaths was inflated and resulted from inter-ethnic violence during the First World War.

On 28 May 1918 the Democratic Republic of Armenia became an independent state. Violent clashes with the newly established republics of Georgia and Azerbaijan followed. Hopes that its former provinces in eastern Anatolia would be returned to Armenia as outlined in the 1920 Treaty of Sèvres were dashed when opposing Turkish and Red Army forces invaded the country. The Treaty of Kars, which ended Bolshevik–Turkish hostilities in Oct. 1921, ceded Mount Ararat and the ancient city of Ani to Turkey. The Armenian Soviet Socialist Republic became one of the 15 constituent republics of the USSR in Dec. 1922.

The collapse of the Soviet Union prompted a declaration of independence in Sept. 1991. The new president, Levon Ter-Petrosyan, led the country into the Commonwealth of Independent States. Hostilities with Azerbaijan over sovereignty of Nagorno-Karabakh erupted in 1988, intensifying into full-scale war in 1992. A ceasefire was agreed in 1994, with 30,000 having lost their lives and up to 1m. Armenians and Azeris displaced. A new constitution in July 1995 led to elections. Ter-Petrosyan was re-elected in 1996, though OSCE observers noted 'serious irregularities' in electoral procedures.

Ter-Petrosyan was succeeded by Robert Kocharyan in 1998. On 27 Oct. 1999 gunmen invaded parliament and killed the premier, Vazgen Sargsyan, and seven other officials. Aram Sargsyan was named his brother's successor. Kocharyan won a second presidential term in 2003, amid renewed complaints of voting irregularities. Thousands marched against the president in Yerevan in April 2004. Serzh Sargsyan, whose right-wing Republican Party took a third of seats in the 2007 parliamentary election, became president in Feb. 2008. When tens of thousands of opposition supporters took to the streets, a state of emergency was declared.

The historic visit of the then Turkish president, Abdullah Gül, in Sept. 2008 seemed to herald a rapprochement between the two nations, although Sargsyan's calls to establish diplomatic relations and open borders have gone unheeded.

Territory and Population

Armenia covers an area of 29,743 sq. km (11,484 sq. miles). It is bounded in the north by Georgia, in the east by Azerbaijan and in the south and west by Iran and Turkey.

The 2011 census population was 3,018,854; population density, 101 per sq. km. Jan. 2018 estimate: 2,972,700. Armenians account for 97·9%, Kurds 1·3% and Russians 0·5%—in 1989, prior to the Nagorno-Karabakh conflict, 2·6% of the population were Azeris. Approximately 64% lived in urban areas in 2009.

The UN gives a projected population for 2020 of 2·94m.

There are an estimated 8m. Armenians worldwide, mainly living in Russia, the USA and Georgia as well as in Armenia itself.

The capital is Yerevan (estimated population of 1,077,600 in 2018). Other large towns are Gyumri (formerly Leninakan) (114,500, 2018 estimate) and Vanadzor (formerly Kirovakan) (79,300, 2018 estimate).

The official language is Armenian.

Social Statistics

2010 births, 44,825; deaths, 27,921; marriages, 17,984; divorces, 2,097. Rates, 2010 (per 1,000 population): birth, 13·8; death, 8·6; marriage, 5·5; divorce, 0·9. Infant mortality, 2010, 18 per 1,000 live births. Annual population growth rate, 2008–10, 0·2%. Life expectancy at birth, 2013, 71·3 years for men and 78·0 years for women; fertility rate, 2013, 1·7 births per woman.

Climate

Summers are very dry and hot although nights can be cold. Winters are very cold, often with heavy snowfall. Yerevan, Jan. –9°C, July 28°C. Annual rainfall 318 mm.

Constitution and Government

The constitution was adopted by a nationwide referendum on 5 July 1995. It has been amended twice since, in 2005 and 2015. The head of state is the President, elected for a single seven-year term. Starting with the March 2018 election, the President is elected by the National Assembly (having previously been directly elected). The 2015 amendments also reduced the President's executive powers in favour of Parliament. Parliament is the 132-member *Azgayin Zhoghov* (National Assembly). Four seats are reserved for national minorities.

National Anthem

'Mer Hayrenik, azat ankakh' ('Land of our fathers, free and independent'); words by M. Nalbandyan, tune by B. Kanachyan.

Recent Elections

The 2018 presidential election marked the first time since a constitutional amendment of Dec. 2015 that the president was chosen by the National Assembly instead of being elected by direct suffrage. Armen Sarkissian, an independent and the only candidate, was elected on 2 March 2018 with 90 of 101 votes.

Parliamentary elections were held on 9 Dec. 2018. The My Step Alliance—led by Prime Minister Nikol Pashinyan—won 88 seats with 70·4% of votes cast, Prosperous Armenia 26 seats (8·3%) and Bright Armenia 18 (6·4%). Turnout was 48·6%.

Current Government

President: Armen Sarkissian; b. 1953 (ind.; took office on 9 April 2018).

In Feb. 2019 the coalition government comprised:

Prime Minister: Nikol Pashinyan; b. 1975 (Civil Contract; since 8 May 2018).

Deputy Prime Ministers: Tigran Avinyan; Mher Grigoryan.

Minister of Agriculture (acting): Gegham Gevorgyan. *Culture:* Vacant. *Defence:* Davit Tonoyan. *Diaspora Affairs:* Vacant. *Economic Development and Investments:* Tigran Khachatryan. *Education and Science:* Arayik Harutyunyan. *Emergency Situations:* Feliks Tsolakyan. *Energy Infrastructure and Natural Resources (acting):* Garegin Baghramyan. *Finance:* Atom Janjughazyan. *Foreign Affairs:* Zohrab Mnatsakanyan. *Health:* Arsen Torosyan. *Justice:* Artak Zeynalyan. *Labour and Social Affairs:* Zaruhi Batoyan. *Nature Protection:* Erik Grigoryan. *Sport and Youth Affairs (acting):* Gabriel Ghazaryan. *Territorial Administration and Development:* Suren Papikyan. *Transport, Communication and Information Technologies:* Hakob Arshakyan.

Government Website: http://www.gov.am

Current Leaders

Armen Sarkissian

Position
President

Introduction
An academic and diplomat, Armen Sarkissian succeeded Serzh Sargsyan as president of Armenia in April 2018. Following a constitutional amendment in 2015, he was elected in March 2018 by parliament rather than by direct suffrage.

Early Life
Armen Sarkissian was born in Yerevan in the Armenian Soviet Socialist Republic on 23 June 1953 and graduated in theoretical physics and mathematics from the Yerevan State University. He was a professor of physics at the same university from 1976–84 before becoming head of the department of computer modelling. In 1982 he additionally became a visiting research fellow (and later a professor) at the University of Cambridge in the UK. He is also a member of the National Academy of Sciences of Armenia.

In 1991 he was appointed ambassador to the UK (the Republic of Armenia's first ambassadorial appointment to the West) and held a series of concurrent roles over that decade, including senior ambassador to Europe, ambassador to the European Union, and to Belgium, Luxembourg, the Netherlands and the Vatican. He also briefly served as prime minister, a position he held for a year from 1996 before returning to his diplomatic role. His programme of reform as premier included liberalization of the media, anti-corruption measures and strengthening of democratic institutions. He then worked for a number of academic institutions and international organizations from 2000 and in 2013 began a third stint as ambassador to the UK before becoming president on 9 April 2018.

Career in Office
Sarkissian's main challenges included consolidating his nation's democratic institutions while confronting corruption, promoting the free-market economy and protecting the freedom of the press. More immediately, however, he faced turmoil over the election and then resignation in April of former president Serzh Sargsyan as prime minister amid anti-government protests that prompted the appointment in his place of opposition leader Nikol Pashinyan on 8 May. Pashinyan promised an early parliamentary election and subsequently resigned in Oct., paving the way for the dissolution of the legislature and polling in early Dec. in which his My Step Alliance, formed in Aug. 2018, won a landslide victory.

Nikol Pashinyan

Position
Prime Minister

Introduction
Nikol Pashinyan is a journalist-turned-politician who led a peaceful political upheaval in 2018 and was twice elected prime minister that year.

Early Life
Born on 1 June 1975 in northeast Armenia, Pashinyan was active in the Karabakh Movement that was formed in the late 1980s to call for Armenian-dominated Nagorno-Karabakh to secede from Azerbaijan and become part of Armenia.

Pashinyan studied journalism at Yerevan State University from 1991 but was expelled in 1995 before completing his degree after he spoke out against university corruption. Between 1999 and 2012 he edited *Haykakan Zhamanak* (*The Armenian Times*). Calling for the impeachment of the then president, Robert Kocharyan, Pashinyan helped to found the Impeachment Union electoral bloc in advance of the 2007 parliamentary elections.

Pashinyan's focus then shifted to the presidential election of 2008. He joined the election office of Levon Ter-Petrosyan, who had been the first president of Armenia, and was detained several times during the campaign period. Pashinyan denounced the increasing use of force against opposition activists, which came to a head on 1 March 2008 when an estimated 100 civilians were arrested and at least ten were killed. Pashinyan was wanted on charges of mass disorder but evaded arrest until June 2009 when he turned himself in. He was among those released in a general amnesty for political prisoners in May 2011. In 2012 he became a member of the National Assembly, leading the Civil Contract party.

A referendum in 2015 saw Armenia become a parliamentary republic. From March 2018, as it became apparent that the incumbent president, Serzh Sargsyan (who had promised after the referendum to step down from presidential office in 2018), was not going to be ruled out as a prime ministerial candidate, Pashinyan spearheaded a wave of popular protests that forced Sargsyan to resign as premier in April only one week after taking office.

Sargsyan's Republican Party then blocked Pashinyan's election as prime minister on 1 May, despite him being the only candidate. This led to renewed protests and a general strike on 2 May. Pashinyan's eventual election by parliament on 8 May was welcomed by Russian President Vladimir Putin.

Career in Office
On 16 Oct. Pashinyan resigned and announced new elections. His My Step Alliance won over 70% of the vote and thereby unseated the opposition's previous majority. One of Pashinyan's biggest challenges is implementing the economic changes that he has championed. He needs to focus on attracting investment to the country, addressing the problem of a dwindling population through repatriation, and invigorating key sectors such as technology.

Defence

There is conscription for 24 months. Total active forces numbered 48,834 in 2011, including 25,880 conscripts.

Defence expenditure in 2013 totalled US$447m. (US$150 per capita), representing 4·3% of GDP.

There is a Russian military base in Armenia with 3,303 personnel in 2011.

Army

Troop levels were 45,846 in 2011, plus air and defence aviation forces of 1,927, air/air defence joint command forces of 1,061 and paramilitary forces of 6,694. There are approximately 210,000 Armenians who have received some kind of military service experience within the last 15 years.

International Relations

There is a dispute over the mainly Armenian-populated enclave of Nagorno-Karabakh, which lies within Azerbaijan's borders—Armenia and Azerbaijan are technically still at war with sporadic fighting continuing, most recently in Feb. 2017.

Economy

In 2014 agriculture contributed 20·4% of GDP, industry 28·5% and services 51·1%.

Overview

After independence in 1991 most agricultural land was privatized. By the end of 2000, with support from the IMF and the World Bank, over 80% of medium and large enterprises and 90% of small enterprises had also been privatized. Following reforms in 2001 to strengthen the business environment and promote exports and investment, there were several years of double-digit economic growth.

Since the global financial crisis that began in 2008, growth has been driven by construction, mining and services, while the contribution of agriculture has declined. Remittances have also been important. The poverty rate peaked at 35% in 2010, largely as a result of high long-term unemployment. In 2015 GDP grew by 3·3%, which was down from 7·1% in 2012 and below the average of 13·1% from 2002 to 2007 but an improvement on 2009 when the economy shrank by 14·2%. The fiscal deficit fell by nearly 75% between 2010 and 2012, but has since increased to reach 4·8% of GDP in 2015.

Currency

In Nov. 1993 a new currency unit, the *dram* (AMD) of 100 *lumma*, was introduced to replace the rouble. Inflation had been 5,273% in 1994. More recently there was deflation of 1·4% in 2016 and then inflation of 0·9% in 2017. Foreign exchange reserves were US$2049m. in Aug. 2009 and total money supply was 365,877bn. drams.

Budget

Budgetary central government revenue totalled 880,851m. drams in 2011 and expenditure 812,315m. drams. Tax revenues in 2011 were 653,960m. drams. Main items of expenditure by economic type in 2011 were social benefits (256,414m. drams) and use of goods and services (171,452m. drams).

VAT is 20%.

Performance

There was real GDP growth of 3·3% in 2015, 0·3% in 2016 and 7·5% in 2017 (the highest rate since 2007). Total GDP in 2017 was US$11·5bn.

Banking and Finance

The *Chairman* of the Central Bank (founded in 1993) is Arthur Javadyan. In 2008 there were 22 commercial banks. There are commodity and stock exchanges in Yerevan and Gyumri.

In 2010 total foreign debt was US$6,103m., representing 64·8% of GNI.

Energy and Natural Resources

Environment

Armenia's carbon dioxide emissions from the consumption of energy in 2011 were the equivalent of 3·9 tonnes per capita.

Electricity

Output of electricity in 2011 was 7·4bn. kWh. Capacity was 3·5m. kW in 2011. Consumption per capita was 2,059 kWh in 2011. A nuclear plant closed in 1989 was reopened in 1995 because of the blockade of the electricity supply by Azerbaijan.

Minerals

There are deposits of copper, zinc, aluminium, molybdenum, marble, gold and granite.

Agriculture

The chief agricultural area is the valley of the Arax and the area round Yerevan. Here there are cotton plantations, orchards and vineyards.

Almonds, olives and figs are also grown. In the mountainous areas the chief pursuit is livestock raising. In 2013 there were 448,000 ha. of arable land and 57,000 ha. of permanent crops. Major agricultural production (in tonnes in 2013): potatoes, 661,000; wheat, 312,000; tomatoes, 276,000; grapes, 241,000; watermelons, 208,000; barley, 189,000. Livestock (2013): cattle, 661,000; sheep, 646,000; pigs, 145,000; chickens (estimate), 3·8m.

Forestry

In 2015 forests covered 0·33m. ha., or 12% of the total land area. Timber production in 2011 was 2·08m. cu. metres.

Fisheries

The total catch in 2012 came to 861 tonnes, exclusively from inland waters.

Industry

Among the chief industries are chemicals, producing mainly synthetic rubber and fertilizers, the extraction and processing of building materials, ginning- and textile mills, carpet weaving and food processing (including winemaking).

Labour

The labour force in 2013 was 1,536,000 (1,452,000 in 2003). 67·3% of the population aged 15–64 was economically active in 2013. In 2015, 17·7% of the population was unemployed.

Armenia had 11,000 people living in slavery according to the Walk Free Foundation's 2013 *Global Slavery Index*.

International Trade

Imports and Exports

Imports and exports for calendar years in US$1m.:

	2005	2006	2007	2008	2009
Imports c.i.f.	1,691·5	2,194·4	3,052·6	4,101·2	3,174·6
Exports f.o.b.	937·0	1,004·0	1,121·2	1,055·0	684·0

The main import suppliers in 2009 were Russia (24·8%), China (9·0%) and Ukraine (6·4%). Principal export markets were Germany (16·8%), Russia (15·6%) and USA (9·7%). Machinery and transport equipment account for 24% of Armenia's imports, manufactured goods 21%, and mineral fuels and lubricants 15%. Manufactured goods (in particular non-ferrous metals and iron and steel) account for 45% of Armenia's exports, crude materials (excluding fuels) 20%, and beverages and tobacco 13%.

Communications

Roads

There were 7,515 km of road network in 2007, of which 89·8% were paved. In 2007 there were 289,800 passenger cars and 25,679 buses and coaches. There were 371 fatalities as a result of road accidents in 2007.

Rail

Total length in 2010 was 826 km of 1,520 mm gauge. Passenger-km travelled in 2010 came to 50m. and freight tonne-km to 346m.

There are a metro and a tramway in Yerevan.

Civil Aviation

There is an international airport at Yerevan (Zvartnots), which handled 1,443,557 passengers and 8,323 tonnes of freight in 2009. In April 2013 the Armenian flag carrier, Armavia, ceased operations. In 2010 there were direct flights from Yerevan to over 40 international destinations.

Telecommunications

There were 589,900 fixed telephone lines in 2010 (190·8 per 1,000 inhabitants). Mobile phone subscribers numbered 3·87m. in 2010. There were 153·0 internet users per 1,000 inhabitants in 2009. Fixed internet subscriptions totalled 96,000 in 2010 (31·1 per 1,000 inhabitants). In March 2012 there were 283,000 Facebook users.

Social Institutions

Out of 178 countries analysed in the 2017 *Fragile States Index*—a list published jointly by the Fund for Peace and *Foreign Policy* magazine—Armenia was ranked the 77th least vulnerable to conflict or collapse. The index is based on 12 indicators of state vulnerability across social, political and economic categories.

Justice

The court system is regulated by the Judicial Code, which was adopted in 2007 and substantially amended in 2009. The Code provides for a three-tiered courts system, with courts of first instance, courts of appeal and a Court of Cassation (the highest court except for matters of constitutional justice). The population in penal institutions in Jan. 2013 was 4,756 (164 per 100,000 of national population). The death penalty was abolished in 2003.

Education

Armenia's literacy rate was over 99% in 2008. In 2007, 48,015 children attended pre-school institutions. There were 127,546 pupils in primary schools with 6,606 teaching staff; and 336,877 pupils in secondary schools with 43,372 teaching staff. At the tertiary level there were 107,398 students in 2007 and 12,521 academic staff.

Public expenditure on education in 2006 came to 2·6% of GNI.

Health

In 2006 there were 12,388 physicians, 18,574 paramedics and 140 hospitals with 14,276 beds.

Welfare

In 2008 there were 523,839 pensioners. The average monthly pension was 21,370 drams in 2008.

Religion

Armenia adopted Christianity in AD 301, thus becoming the first Christian nation in the world. The Armenian Apostolic Church is headed by its Catholicos (Karekin II, b. 1951) whose seat is at Echmiatsin, and who is head of all the Armenian (Gregorian) communities throughout the world. In 2013 it numbered 9m. adherents, two-thirds of whom lived outside of Armenia. There is a second see located at Antelias in Lebanon—the Catholicos of Cilicia is Aram I (b. 1947). An estimated 87% of the population belonged to the Armenian Apostolic Church in 2010 according to the Pew Research Center's Forum on Religion & Public Life. The largest religious minority is Armenian Catholicism.

Culture

World Heritage Sites

There are three UNESCO sites in Armenia: the Monasteries of Haghpat and Sanahin (inscribed in 1996 and 2000); the Monastery of Geghard and the Upper Azat Valley (2000); the Cathedral and Churches of Echmiatsin and the Archaeological Site of Zvartnots (2000).

Press

In 2008 there were 11 paid-for daily newspapers and 49 paid-for non-dailies with a combined circulation of 116,000.

Tourism

In 2014 there were 1,204,000 international tourist arrivals (excluding same-day visitors), up from 575,000 in 2009.

Diplomatic Representatives

Of Armenia in the United Kingdom (25A Cheniston Gdns, London, W8 6TG)
> *Ambassador:* Vacant.
> *Chargé d'Affaires a.i.:* Armen Liloyan.

Of the United Kingdom in Armenia (34 Baghramyan Ave., Yerevan 0019)
> *Ambassador:* Judith Margaret Farnworth.

Of Armenia in the USA (2225 R St., NW, Washington, D.C., 20008)
> *Ambassador:* Grigor Hovhannissian.

Of the USA in Armenia (1 American Ave., Yerevan 0082)
> *Ambassador:* Vacant.
> *Chargé d'Affaires a.i.:* Rafik Mansour.

Of Armenia to the United Nations
> *Ambassador:* Mher Margaryan.

Of Armenia to the European Union
> *Ambassador:* Tatoul Markarian.

Further Reading

De Waal, Thomas, *Black Garden: Armenia and Azerbaijan Through Peace and War.* 2003.—*Great Catastrophe: Armenians and Turks in the Shadow of Genocide.* 2015

Hovannisian, R. G., *The Republic of Armenia.* 4 vols. 1996

National Statistical Office: National Statistical Service of the Republic of Armenia, Republic Ave, 3 Government House, Yerevan 0010.

Website: http://www.armstat.am

Australia

Commonwealth of Australia

Capital: Canberra
Population projection, 2020: 25·40m.
GNI per capita, 2017: (PPP$) 43,560
HDI/world rank, 2017: 0·939/3
Internet domain extension: .au

Key Historical Events

The Australian landmass, reaching northwards to Papua New Guinea and including Tasmania in the south, was inhabited in prehistoric times until adverse climatic conditions led to an exodus between 15,000 and 25,000 years ago. Stone tools date to 2000–1000 BC. The Aboriginal society was based on extended family groups. At maximum there were 1m. Aborigines, using 200 different languages. By the early 18th century contact was made with traders from the area of modern Indonesia and Papua New Guinea.

Australia was sighted in 1522 by compatriot explorers of the Portuguese Ferdinand Magellan and in 1642 the Dutch explorer Abel Tasman mapped what is now Tasmania and part of New Zealand's east coast. By the middle of the century the Dutch had charted the western part of Australia, calling it New Holland.

But while the Dutch, Portuguese and Spanish made the early running in charting the continent, it was the discovery of the east coast by Capt. James Cook in 1770 that prompted colonization. Over several voyages he charted the Torres Strait and 8,000 kilometres of coastline. Having lost their penal settlements in the American War of Independence, the British decided to send convicts to Australia. Botany Bay was selected as the first settlement.

By 1800 convicts had established legal rights as crown subjects. Many freed men were able to make a successful living. However, there were several uprisings against penal rule culminating in the Rum Rebellion of 1808, in which John Macarthur led a troop of New South Wales officers against Gov. William Bligh. The response of the British government was to appoint Lachlan Macquarie, who promoted reform.

His tenure began a period of development in which Australia ceased to be primarily a penal settlement. The crossing of the Blue Mountains in 1813 was the first of many expeditions which led to discovery of vast areas of grazing land, although sealing and whaling were more important than agriculture until the 1830s. Macquarie's benevolent despotism rewarded freed men and several of the more talented were appointed to official posts. He did much to develop Sydney, instigating public works and establishing a bank and currency. His policies caused concern in London and in 1822 he was forced to resign.

The Aboriginal question remained unresolved. The early assumption that the Aboriginal people were nomadic meant that Britain had claimed much of the Australian land without an agreement of purchase from the natives. There was some peaceful interaction with the Aborigines but resentment grew as British encroachment damaged Aboriginal culture. Diseases brought in by the colonists decimated the Aboriginal population. By the late 18th century there was widespread and persistent conflict. The most notable Aboriginal resistance leader was Pemulwuy (killed in 1802) who fought battles at Hawkesbury and Parramatta. Between 1820–50 the indigenous population fell from 600,000 to 300,000.

Trade and Prosperity

The wool trade took off in the middle of the 19th century. With the introduction of the Merino sheep between 1830–50, Australia's share of the British wool market rose from 10% to 50%, accounting for 90% of all Australia's exports. The pastoral economy boomed and from the 1830s the population was swollen by 'free immigrants' from Britain. A settler population of 30,000 in 1820 grew to over 1·1m. in 1860. The economy was further boosted by the discovery of copper and gold in several locations and by 1850 Victoria accounted for one third of the world's gold supply. The gold rushes attracted prospectors from Britain, the USA, Western and Central Europe and China.

Sydney, Melbourne, Adelaide and Perth all grew during these boom decades, developing their own institutions and gradually attaining a degree of self-rule. New South Wales, Tasmania and Victoria were granted full parliamentary control of their own affairs in 1855, with South Australia and the newly formed Queensland following in the next five years. However, the UK government retained control of foreign policy and kept a power of veto.

By the 1860s there was a culture of bushranging as epitomized by Ned Kelly. Bad relations between settlers, immigrant workers and the Aboriginal population persisted. The population passed 3m. in 1888. In the 1890s recession the economy shrank by 30%. Unemployment among skilled workers stood at 30% in 1893 and was higher among unskilled workers, for whom records were not kept. Problems were exacerbated by a severe drought in the east of the country.

Social and Constitutional Reform

Trade unionism grew from the 1870s, gaining strength in the 1890s. Between 1899, when a first Labor government took power in Queensland, and the outbreak of the First World War, Labor was in government in every state. Union membership included a third of all workers. The 1890s witnessed the emergence of the federalist movement, with Sydney hosting conventions in 1891 and 1897–98. On 1 Jan. 1901 the six separately constituted colonies of New South Wales, Victoria, Queensland, South Australia, Western Australia and Tasmania were federated under the Commonwealth of Australia, the designation of 'colonies' being at the same time changed into that of 'states'—except in the case of Northern Territory, which was transferred from South Australia to the Commonwealth as a 'territory' on 1 Jan. 1911. A bicameral parliament was established while the states retained certain powers. Foreign policy continued to be guided by London and in 1907 Australia gained dominion status. By the following year there was female suffrage for the national and all state legislatures.

The Labor Party formed its first national government in 1904 and their old allies in the protectionist parties forged an alliance with free trade parties, forming the Liberal Party to challenge Labor's growth. A period in which the government switched between Labor and the Liberals saw pension and welfare reforms. The growing fear of an Asian (and especially Japanese) threat—Britain was reluctant to keep a strong military presence in the Pacific—led to the development of the army and navy.

In 1911 a site in New South Wales was designated the Australian capital, to be known as Canberra. Construction began in 1923 and the Federal Parliament was opened in Canberra in 1927. With the outbreak of the First World War Australia rallied to the British cause but at significant cost. Around 330,000 Australian troops served in the war—60,000 died and over 150,000 were wounded. Such losses caused unrest and conscription was rejected by referendum in 1916. In addition Australia lost its markets in France, Belgium and Germany, which together accounted for 30% of its exports. The economy contracted by 10% in 1914 and unemployment soared.

The Labor Party, in power at the start of the war, gave way to a national government. The effect of the war years kept Labor out of power until 1929. The early 1920s was a period of recovery, assisted by an influx of 200,000 immigrants from Britain. Sydney and Melbourne expanded to a point where they accounted for a third of the Australian population. However, the economy (with the notable exception of the wool industry) relied on government subsidy, leaving it exposed in the depression which followed the 1929 Wall Street Crash. Under Labor public spending was cut, a 10% reduction in wages imposed and the currency devalued by 25%. Unemployment approached 30%. The government collapsed but the depression had the long-term effect of radicalizing the trade unions.

Jo Lyons and the recently formed United Australia Party took over the government. Lyons was succeeded by Robert Menzies in 1939. The late 1930s saw deteriorating relations with Japan but broad support for the policy of appeasement of Nazi Germany. However, when war became inevitable, Australia again rallied to the imperial cause. 100,000 Australian troops were killed or wounded. Fear of Japan escalated after Pearl Harbor and Darwin was attacked in 1942. These events marked a watershed in foreign relations with the Labor prime minister, John Curtin, commenting that 'Australia looks to America, free from any pangs about our traditional links of friendship to Britain.'

Post-War Recovery

The war encouraged the rapid expansion of Australian industry and the 1950s and 1960s were something of a golden age. Robert Menzies led successive Liberal governments from 1949–66. The population nearly doubled as immigration from Britain and continental Europe was encouraged. Unemployment was consistently low and the economy tripled in size during the two decades. Aware of its 'junior partner' status in the relationship with America, Australia undertook nuclear development with Britain. In 1951 it entered the ANZUS group with New Zealand and the USA and three years later joined the South-East Asian Treaty Organization. Australia's new found confidence was reflected in the success of the 1956 Melbourne Olympics.

The growing number of non-English speaking immigrants accentuated racial problems, with a succession of governments holding to a monocultural policy. The future of the Aboriginal population was one of assimilation. The movement for Aboriginal rights grew after the war, with a strike by Aboriginal workers at Pilbara in 1946 marking a new phase in the conflict. It climaxed in 1966 when an Aboriginal demand for equal pay in Northern Australia turned into demands for land. There was a swathe of moderate reforms favouring the Aboriginal population between 1959–67 but at the same time the assimilation policy allowed for the forced removal of large numbers of children from their families. The last of the Aboriginal reserves was taken over in the 1960s. The policy of forced removal of children did not prompt a formal apology from the Australian government until 2008.

When Menzies retired in 1966 he was followed by a succession of leaders who weakened the standing of the Liberals. Australia's participation in the Vietnam War also drew criticism. Gough Whitlam led the Labor Party to power in 1972 and oversaw a radical administration. He withdrew Australian forces from Vietnam, set about modernizing the education and health programmes and funded extensive urban renewal. Government expenditure doubled over his three years in office and Australia was ill-prepared when the global oil crisis struck in 1974.

Whitlam's Liberal opponents, many of whom regarded him as a dangerous maverick, led a parliamentary revolt. A failure to win approval for the national budget led to a constitutional crisis in which the Governor-General John Kerr (himself recommended for the post by Whitlam) dismissed the prime minister and invited Malcolm Fraser to form an administration. Fraser believed that Australian society had become overly dependent on the state. He authorized cuts in public spending but was unable to counter rising unemployment and inflation and was voted out of government in 1983.

Free Market Politics

Bob Hawke took power at the head of a Labor government, assisted by his finance minister (and successor as prime minister), Paul Keating. Their terms of office, spanning 1983–96, saw a shift in Labor's stance on state control and economic planning to allow for an ambitious programme of privatization and financial deregulation. Trade with Asia took on increasing importance and Hawke stood fully behind US foreign policy. In March 1986 the Australia Act abolished the remaining legislative, executive and judicial controls of the British Parliament. By the end of the decade unemployment stood at a respectable 6% but the Australian dollar had suffered a 40% loss of value in 1986 and foreign debt stood at around 30% of GNP. Keating described the recession of the late 1980s as 'necessary'.

Keating took over the premiership in 1991 and mounted a programme of economic reform. He was replaced in 1996 by the Liberal, John Howard, who pressed on with economic reforms and won re-election two years later. The Aboriginal question continued to test every government. There were some symbolic gestures such as the return of Ayers Rock (with its Aboriginal name Uluru restored) in 1988. The High Court's Mabo ruling of 1992, which overturned a previous ruling that the Aboriginal title to land had not survived British settlement, raised expectations. Keating officially acknowledged injustices to the Aboriginal population when the 'Native Title' legislation was passed in Dec. 1993. Howard's tenure, however, saw disputes over indigenous land rights following a 1996 court ruling against Aboriginal access to cultural sites owned by non-Aboriginals.

A referendum to decide if Australia should become a republic was held on 6 Nov. 1999. 54·9% were in favour of the monarchy with Queen Elizabeth II as head of state, against 45·1% for a republic with a president chosen by parliament. In foreign policy Howard agreed to military involvement in UN peacekeeping in Timor-Leste and NATO action against Serbia.

His government's approach to immigration came under the spotlight in July 2001, when a refugee-laden Norwegian cargo ship was caught in a diplomatic gridlock between Australia, the UN and Norway. Its passengers were eventually diverted to Papua New Guinea, with Howard assuming a firm and populist stance against asylum seekers. He won a further term of office at the elections of Nov. 2001. The Liberals also won the elections of Oct. 2004. Howard pursued an interventionist foreign policy in the Pacific region—with notable success in the peacekeeping mission to the Solomon Islands—and committed Australia to the US-led war in Iraq in 2003. Labor returned to power with victory in the elections of Nov. 2007, led by Kevin Rudd. After a steep decline in popularity in early 2010, he was succeeded by Australia's first female prime minister, Julia Gillard, in June that year.

Following the election in Aug. 2010 she remained prime minister in Australia's first hung parliament since 1940. The Liberal–National Coalition under Tony Abbott then won the elections of Sept. 2013 but Abbott was replaced as premier in Sept. 2015 by Malcolm Turnbull, who also displaced him as Liberal Party leader. After the Senate twice voted down a government bill, Turnbull called early elections for July 2016 and secured a slim majority.

Territory and Population

Australia, excluding external territories, covers a land area of 7,692,024 sq. km, extending from Cape York (10° 41' S) in the north some 3,680 km to South East Cape, Tasmania (43° 39' S), and from Cape Byron, New South Wales (153° 39' E) in the east some 4,000 km west to Steep Point, Western Australia (113° 9' E). External territories under the administration of Australia comprise the Ashmore and Cartier Islands, Australian Antarctic Territory, Christmas Island, the Cocos (Keeling) Islands, the Coral Sea Islands, the Heard and McDonald Islands and Norfolk Island. For these *see* pages 153–4.

Growth in census population has been:

1901	3,774,310
1911	4,455,005
1921	5,435,734
1947	7,579,358
1961	10,508,186
1966	11,599,498
1971	12,755,638
1976	13,915,500
1981	15,053,600
1986	15,763,000
1991	16,852,258
1996	17,752,829
2001	18,769,249
2006	19,855,288
2011	21,507,717
2016	23,401,892

Of the 2016 census population, 50·7% were female.

The UN gives a projected population for 2020 of 25·40m.

At the census of 9 Aug. 2016 density was 3·0 per sq. km. In 2015, 85·7% of the population lived in urban areas.

Areas and populations of the States and Territories at the 2016 census:

States and Territories	Area (sq. km)	Population	Per sq. km
Australian Capital Territory (ACT) including Jervis Bay Territory	2,431	397,397	163·5
Northern Territory (NT)	1,349,129	228,833	0·2
New South Wales (NSW)	800,642	7,480,228	9·3
Queensland (Qld)	1,730,648	4,703,192	2·7
South Australia (SA)	983,482	1,676,653	1·7
Victoria (Vic.)	227,416	5,926,624	26·1
Tasmania (Tas.)	68,401	509,965	7·5
Western Australia (WA)	2,529,875	2,474,410	1·0

Resident population in the state/territory capitals (2016 census figures):

Capital	State	Population
Canberra	ACT	396,857
Darwin	NT	136,826
Sydney	NSW	4,823,991
Brisbane	Qld	2,270,800
Adelaide	SA	1,295,714
Hobart	Tas.	222,356
Melbourne	Vic.	4,485,211
Perth	WA	1,943,858

The median age of the 2016 census population was 38 years.

Australians born overseas (census 2016), 6,163,667 (26·3%—up from 24·6% in 2011 and the highest proportion anywhere in the industrialized world), of whom 907,570 were born in England, 518,466 in New Zealand and 509,555 in China.

Aboriginals have been included in population statistics only since 1967. At the 2016 census 649,171 people identified themselves as being of indigenous origin (2·8% of the total population). A 1992 High Court ruling that the Meriam people of the Murray Islands had land rights before the European settlement reversed the previous assumption that Australia was *terra nullius* before that settlement. The Native Title Act setting up a system for deciding claims by Aborigines came into effect on 1 Jan. 1994.

Overseas arrivals and departures:

	Permanent arrival numbers	Permanent departure numbers	Net permanent gain
2010	83,540	20,000	63,530
2011	83,980	19,280	64,690
2012	85,960	19,100	66,860
2013	95,280	19,570	75,710

In 2013–14, 163,017 people who were born overseas became Australian citizens.

The national language is English.

Social Statistics

Life expectancy at birth, 2010–12, 79·9 years for males and 84·3 years for females.

Statistics for years ended 30 June:

	Births	Deaths	Marriages	Divorces
2009	301,253	140,760	120,118	49,448
2010	303,318	143,473	121,176	50,240
2011	301,617	146,932	121,752	48,935
2012	309,582	147,098	123,244	49,917
2013	308,065	147,678	118,962	47,638

In 2012 the median age for marrying was 31·4 years for males and 29·4 for females. In Dec. 2017 both houses of parliament passed a bill to legalize same-sex marriage. Infant mortality, 2012, was 3·3 per 1,000 live births. Population growth rate in 2014, 1·4%; fertility rate, 2013, 1·9 births per woman.

Suicide rates (per 100,000 population, 2013): 10·9 (men, 16·4; women, 5·5).

UNICEF reported that 17·5% of children in Australia in 2014 lived in relative poverty (living in a household in which disposable income—when adjusted for family size and composition—is less than 60% of the national median income), compared to 9·2% in Denmark (the world's lowest rate).

In the Human Development Index, or HDI (measuring progress in countries in longevity, knowledge and standard of living), Australia was ranked second (behind Norway) in the 2015 rankings published in the annual Human Development Report.

Climate

Over most of the continent, four seasons may be recognized. Spring is from Sept. to Nov., summer from Dec. to Feb., autumn from March to May and winter from June to Aug., but because of its great size there are climates that range from tropical monsoon to cool temperate, with large areas of desert as well. In northern Australia there are only two seasons, the wet one lasting from Nov. to March, but rainfall amounts diminish markedly from the coast to the interior. Central and southern Queensland are subtropical, north and central New South Wales are warm temperate, as are parts of Victoria, Western Australia and Tasmania, where most rain falls in winter. Canberra, Jan. 68°F (20°C), July 42°F (5·6°C). Annual rainfall 25" (635 mm). Adelaide, Jan. 73°F (22·8°C), July 52°F (11·1°C). Annual rainfall 21" (528 mm). Brisbane, Jan. 77°F (25°C), July 58°F (14·4°C). Annual rainfall 45" (1,153 mm). Darwin, Jan. 83°F (28·3°C), July 77°F (25°C). Annual rainfall 59" (1,536 mm). Hobart, Jan. 62°F (16·7°C), July 46°F (7·8°C). Annual rainfall 23" (584 mm). Melbourne, Jan. 67°F (19·4°C), July 49°F (9·4°C). Annual rainfall 26" (659 mm). Perth, Jan. 74°F (23·3°C), July 55°F (12·8°C). Annual rainfall 35" (873 mm). Sydney, Jan. 71°F (21·7°C), July 53°F (11·7°C). Annual rainfall 47" (1,215 mm).

Constitution and Government

Federal Government. Under the Constitution legislative power is vested in a Federal Parliament, consisting of the Queen, represented by a Governor-General, a Senate and a House of Representatives. Under the terms of the constitution there must be a session of parliament at least once a year.

The *Senate* (Upper House) comprises 76 Senators (12 for each State voting as one electorate and, as from Aug. 1974, two Senators respectively for the Australian Capital Territory and the Northern Territory). Senators representing the States are chosen for six years. The terms of Senators representing the Territories expire at the close of the day next preceding the polling day for the general elections of the House of Representatives. In general, the Senate is renewed to the extent of one-half every three years, but in case of disagreement with the House of Representatives, it, together with the House of Representatives, may be dissolved, and an entirely new Senate elected. Elections to the Senate are on the single transferable vote system; voters list candidates in order of preference. A candidate must reach a quota to be elected, otherwise the lowest-placed candidate drops out and his or her votes are transferred to other candidates.

The *House of Representatives* (Lower House) consists, as nearly as practicable, of twice as many Members as there are Senators, the numbers chosen in the several States being in proportion to population as shown by the latest statistics, but not less than five for any original State. The 150 membership is made up as follows: New South Wales, 48; Victoria, 37; Queensland, 30; South Australia, 11; Western Australia, 15; Tasmania, 5; ACT, 2; Northern Territory, 2. Elections to the House of Representatives are on the alternative vote system; voters list candidates in order of preference, and if no one candidate wins an overall majority, the lowest-placed drops out and his or her votes are transferred. The first Member for the Australian Capital Territory was given full voting rights as from the Parliament elected in Nov. 1966. The first Member for the Northern Territory was given full voting rights in 1968. The House of Representatives continues for three years from the date of its first meeting, unless sooner dissolved.

Every Senator or Member of the House of Representatives must be a subject of the Queen, be of full age, possess electoral qualifications and have resided for three years within Australia. The franchise for both Houses is the same and is based on universal (males and females aged 18 years) suffrage. Compulsory voting was introduced in 1925. If a Member of a State Parliament wishes to be a candidate in a federal election, he must first resign his State seat.

Executive power is vested in the *Governor-General*, advised by an Executive Council. The Governor-General presides over the Council, and its members hold office at his pleasure. All Ministers of State, who are members of the party or parties commanding a majority in the lower House, are members of the Executive Council under summons. A record of proceedings of meetings is kept by the Secretary to the Council. At Executive Council meetings the decisions of the Cabinet are (where necessary) given legal form, appointments made, resignations accepted, proclamations, regulations and the like made.

The policy of a ministry is, in practice, determined by the Ministers of State meeting without the Governor-General under the chairmanship of the Prime Minister. This group is known as the *Cabinet*. In Labor governments all Ministers have been members of Cabinet; in Liberal and National Country Party governments, only the senior ministers. Cabinet meetings are private and deliberative, and records of meetings are not made public. The Cabinet does not form part of the legal mechanisms of government; the decisions it takes have, in themselves, no legal effect. The Cabinet substantially controls, in ordinary circumstances, not only the general legislative programme of Parliament but the whole course of Parliamentary proceedings. In effect, though not in form, the Cabinet, by reason of the fact that all Ministers are members of the Executive Council, is also the dominant element in the executive government of the country.

The legislative powers of the Federal Parliament embrace: trade and commerce, shipping, etc.; taxation, finance, banking, currency, bills of exchange, bankruptcy, insurance, defence, external affairs, naturalization and aliens, quarantine, immigration and emigration; the people of any race for whom it is deemed necessary to make special laws; postal, telegraph and like services; census and statistics; weights and measures; astronomical and meteorological observations; copyrights; railways; conciliation and arbitration in disputes extending beyond the limits of any one State; social services; marriage, divorce, etc.; service and execution of the civil and criminal process; recognition of the laws, Acts and records, and judicial proceedings of the States. The Senate may not originate or amend money bills. Disagreement with the House of Representatives may result in dissolution and, in the last resort, a joint sitting of the two Houses. The Federal Parliament has limited and enumerated powers, the several State parliaments retaining the residuary power of government over their respective territories. If a State law is inconsistent with a Commonwealth law, the latter prevails.

The Constitution also provides for the admission or creation of new States. Proposed laws for the alteration of the Constitution must be submitted to the electors, and they can be enacted only if approved by a majority of the States and by a majority of all the electors voting.

The Australia Acts 1986 removed residual powers of the British government to intervene in the government of Australia or the individual States.

In Feb. 1998 an Australian Constitutional Convention voted for Australia to become a republic. In a national referendum, held on 6 Nov. 1999, 54·9% voted against Australia becoming a republic.

State Government
In each of the six States (New South Wales, Victoria, Queensland, South Australia, Western Australia, Tasmania) there is a State government whose constitution, powers and laws continue, subject to changes embodied in the Australian Constitution and subsequent alterations and agreements, as they were before federation. The system of government is basically the same as that described above for the Commonwealth—i.e. the Sovereign, her representative (in this case a Governor), an upper and lower house of Parliament (except in Queensland, where the upper house was abolished in 1922), a cabinet led by the Premier and an Executive Council. Among the more important functions of the State governments are those relating to education, health, hospitals and charities, law, order and public safety, business undertakings such as railways and tramways, and public utilities such as water supply and sewerage. In the domains of education, hospitals, justice, the police, penal establishments, and railway and tramway operation, State government activity predominates. Care of the public health and recreative activities are shared with local government authorities and the Federal government; social services other than those referred to above are now primarily the concern of the Federal government; the operation of public utilities is shared with local and semi-government authorities.

Administration of Territories
Since 1911 responsibility for administration and development of the Australian Capital Territory (ACT) has been vested in Federal Ministers and Departments. The ACT became self-governing on 11 May 1989. The ACT House of Assembly has been accorded the forms of a legislature, but continues to perform an advisory function for the Minister for the Capital Territory.

On 1 July 1978 the Northern Territory of Australia became a self-governing Territory with expenditure responsibilities and revenue-raising powers broadly approximating those of a State.

National Anthem
'Advance Australia Fair' (adopted 19 April 1984; words and tune by P. D. McCormick). The 'Royal Anthem' (i.e. 'God Save the Queen') is used in the presence of the Royal Family.

Government Chronology
Prime Ministers since 1945. (ALP = Australian Labor Party; CP = Australian Country Party; LP = Liberal Party)

1945	ALP	Francis Michael (Frank) Forde
1945–49	ALP	Joseph Benedict (Ben) Chifley
1949–66	LP	Robert Gordon Menzies
1966–67	LP	Harold Edward Holt
1967–68	CP	John (Jack) McEwen (acting)
1968–71	LP	John Grey Gorton
1971–72	LP	William (Bill) McMahon
1972–75	ALP	(Edward) Gough Whitlam
1975–83	LP	(John) Malcolm Fraser
1983–91	ALP	Robert James Lee (Bob) Hawke
1991–96	ALP	Paul John Keating
1996–2007	LP	John Winston Howard
2007–10	ALP	Kevin Michael Rudd
2010–13	ALP	Julia Eileen Gillard
2013	ALP	Kevin Michael Rudd
2013–15	LP	Anthony John (Tony) Abbott
2015–18	LP	Malcolm Bligh Turnbull
2018–	LP	Scott John Morrison

Recent Elections
The 45th Parliament was elected on 2 July 2016.

House of Representatives
The ruling Liberal–National Coalition won 76 seats and 42·1% of the primary vote (of which Liberal Party, 45 and 28·6%; Liberal National Party of Queensland (LNP), 21 and 8·6%; and National Party of Australia (NP), 10 and 4·6%). The opposition Labor Party (ALP) won 69 seats with 34·7% of the primary vote; Australian Greens 1 (10·2%); Nick Xenophon Team 1 (1·8%); Katter's Australian Party 1 (0·5%). Independents took two seats.

Senate
As at Feb. 2018 the make-up of the Senate was Coalition (Liberal Party/Liberal National Party/National Party/Country Liberal Party), 29; Australian Labor Party, 26; Greens, 9; Pauline Hanson's One Nation, 3; Nick Xenophon Team, 3; ind., 2; Liberal Democrats, 1; Derryn Hinch's Justice Party, 1; Australian Conservatives, 1. One seat was vacant.

Current Government
Governor-General: Sir Peter Cosgrove, AK, MC; b. 1947 (took office on 28 March 2014).

In March 2019 the cabinet comprised:

Prime Minister: Scott Morrison; b. 1968 (Liberal Party; in office since 24 Aug. 2018).

Deputy Prime Minister, and Minister for Infrastructure, Transport and Regional Development: Michael McCormack.

Attorney-General: Christian Porter. *Minister for Agriculture and Water Resources:* David Littleproud. *Communications, and the Arts:* Mitch Fifield. *Defence:* Christopher Pyne. *Defence Industry:* Linda Reynolds. *Education:* Dan Tehan. *Energy:* Angus Taylor. *Environment:* Melissa Price. *Families and Social Services:* Paul Fletcher. *Finance and the Public Service:* Mathias Cormann. *Foreign Affairs:* Marise Payne *Health:* Greg Hunt. *Home Affairs:* Peter Dutton. *Indigenous Affairs:* Nigel Scullion. *Industry, Science and Technology:* Karen Andrews. *Jobs, Industrial Relations and Women:* Kelly O'Dwyer. *Regional Services, Sport, Local Government and Decentralization:* Bridget McKenzie. *Resources and Northern Australia:* Matthew Canavan. *Small and Family Business, and Skills and Vocational Education:* Michaelia Cash. *Trade, Tourism and Investment:* Simon Birmingham. *Treasurer:* Josh Frydenberg.

The *Speaker* is Tony Smith (LP).
The *President*of the Senate is Scott Ryan (LP).
Leader of the Opposition: Bill Shorten (ALP).
Government: http://www.gov.au

Current Leaders

Scott Morrison
Position
Prime Minister

Introduction
Scott Morrison was sworn in as premier in Aug. 2018 following the resignation of Malcolm Turnbull. A former civil servant, Morrison is socially conservative and well known for his tough stance on immigration. He was the fifth prime minister to take office in five years.

Early Life
Scott Morrison was born on 13 May 1968 in Sydney, Australia. The son of a policeman, he attended Sydney Boys High School and graduated in economic geography from the University of New South Wales. Morrison worked as a civil servant in the Property Council of Australia until 1995, before taking a position at the Tourism Council of Australia. In 1998 he moved to New Zealand to work as director of the newly established Office of Tourism and Sport.

Returning to Australia in 2000, he entered the political scene and led the New South Wales division of the centre-right Liberal Party. Following two further years in the tourism sector, Morrison decided to stand as the Liberal Party candidate for the Division of Cook, a parliamentary seat in the south of Sydney. After a controversial pre-selection ballot, he won the seat in the federal election on 24 Nov. 2002, which delivered a sweeping win for the Labor Party. Morrison was appointed shadow minister for housing and local government under Malcolm Turnbull.

When Tony Abbott became leader of the opposition Liberal Party in Dec. 2009, Morrison served on the shadow cabinet committee on border protection where his hard-line stance on immigration drew criticism. Following the victory of the Liberal-National coalition in the federal election of Sept. 2013, Morrison became minister for immigration and border protection and led Operation Sovereign Borders, a strategy to stop unauthorized boats from entering Australian waters.

When Turnbull ousted Abbott as prime minister in Sept. 2015, he appointed Morrison as his Treasurer. His priorities were to reduce government spending and reform the tax system, which included an anti-avoidance measure known as the Google tax. Following a royal commission into the banking and financial services industry in early 2018, Morrison announced new civil and criminal penalties for financial misconduct. Further infighting in the Liberal Party led to a leadership challenge in Aug. 2018 by the right-wing home affairs minister Peter Dutton. It was unsuccessful, but Turnbull stepped down shortly afterwards, triggering a second ballot. Morrison emerged as the compromise candidate, defeating Dutton and Julie Bishop to become party leader and prime minister. He was sworn in on 24 Aug. 2018.

Career in Office
Morrison attempted to play down concerns about political instability in Australia ahead of federal elections due in 2019. He said his administration was committed to free trade, maintaining a strong economy and boosting security. He also announced the conclusion of a free-trade arrangement with Indonesia and pledged that Canberra would increase its involvement in the Pacific Islands.

Defence

The Minister for Defence has responsibility under legislation for the control and administration of the Australian Defence Force (ADF). The Chief of the Defence Force is vested with command of the ADF. He is the principal military adviser to the Minister. The Chief of Navy, the Chief of Army and the Chief of Air Force command the Royal Australian Navy, Australian Army and Royal Australian Air Force respectively. They have delegated authority from the Chief of Defence Force Staff and the Secretary to administer matters relating to their particular Service. Conscription was abolished in 1972.

2013 defence expenditure was US$25,967m., amounting to US$1,166 per capita and representing 1·6% of GDP. In the period 2011–15 Australia's spending on major weapons was the fifth highest in the world, accounting for 3·6% of the global total.

Having contributed to the 2003 US-led invasion of Iraq, the last Australian troops left the country in July 2009. Australian troops served with the International Security Assistance Force (ISAF) in Afghanistan in Feb. 2014, although the mission's mandate expired at the end of the year. As at May 2017 Australia contributed 270 troops to the more than 13,500 personnel charged with training, advising and assisting the Afghan National Security Forces under the aegis of Operation *Resolute Support*.

Army
The strength of the Army was 28,246 in 2011. The effective strength of the Army Reserve was 15,840.

Women have been eligible for combat duties since 1993.

Navy
The all-volunteer Navy had 14,250 personnel in 2011, with a reserve of 2,000. Equipment in 2011 included six diesel-powered submarines and 12 frigates. It was announced in April 2016 that the French shipbuilder DCNS had won a $A50bn. deal to build a fleet of 12 new submarines in South Australia.

The main naval bases are at Sydney and Perth with further bases at Cairns and Darwin.

Air Force
The Royal Australian Air Force (RAAF) operated 142 combat-capable aircraft including F/A-18F Super Hornets in 2011. Personnel in 2011 numbered 14,056. There is also an Australian Air Force Reserve, 2,600-strong.

Economy

In 2013 agriculture contributed 2% of GDP, industry 27% and services 71%.

According to the anti-corruption organization Transparency International, Australia ranked 13th in the world in a 2018 survey of the countries with the least corruption in business and government. It received 77 out of 100 in the annual index.

Australia gave US$3·0bn. in international aid in 2017, equivalent to 0·23% of GNI (compared to the UN target of 0·7%).

Overview
Australia has abundant natural resources, including coal, iron, copper, gold, natural gas and uranium. The export sector is driven by mining, as well as by agriculture. There are, however, concerns about the long-term dependency on commodity resources owing to external fluctuations in prices. The country boasts maximum international credit rating status and has promoted itself to global and regional businesses (especially in the financial sector) as an ideal location for administrative and support operations. According to the World Bank, the country ranked 14th out of 189 economies for the ease of doing business in 2017.

Prior to the global financial crisis of 2008–09 the economy had experienced 17 years of robust expansion. Reforms in the 1980s and early 1990s had liberalized the previously heavily protected and regulated economy, while increased competition and technological advances helped drive productivity growth (which averaged 1·7% annually over the period 1991–2000—six times greater than that for the previous decade). Reform and good fiscal management facilitated growth even in the face of the Asian financial crisis of 1997–98 and the US downturn of 2001–02.

The buoyant domestic economy withstood the impact of a severe drought in 2003 and a global slowdown, while a commodities boom helped cushion a fall in the housing market from its 2004 peak. The terms of trade then improved by 30% from 2005–08 to register their highest level for over 50 years. Near full employment in 2007 saw joblessness at its lowest since the mid-1970s, while the National Reform Agenda agreed in 2006 aimed to lift long-term productivity and workforce participation. Per capita GDP has now become one of the highest in the world, with services accounting for a high proportion of output.

In the global financial crisis Australia did not suffer as much as other advanced nations. The government initially implemented a US$50bn. stimulus package and cut interest rates. Also, continued robust export demand from China and India helped the economy escape recession in 2009, with the second-best performance among OECD countries (after Poland) that year. With a low risk of serious contraction, the Reserve Bank of Australia (RBA) then adopted a tighter monetary policy and temporarily raised interest rates. In 2010 the fiscal stimulus was reduced and the mining sector experienced another boom, with strong demand from emerging economies in Asia. Between 2007 and 2014 real disposable income increased cumulatively by an average of 3·6%. However, in Jan. 2016 the RBA acknowledged that the exchange rate had been overvalued since 2014, exacerbating falling prices in key commodities such as iron ore and oil.

In Jan. 2011 severe flooding in Queensland, which contributes about 19% of national output and produces 80% of the country's coking coal, was followed by a cyclone that together led to reduced production and an increase in the budget deficit. The cost of clean-up and rebuilding was estimated at $A30bn., prompting the government to announce a levy on middle- and high-income earners, budget cuts and delays to infrastructure projects. In March 2017 another cyclone hit Queensland, affecting crops, tourism and infrastructure, and temporarily disrupting coal exports.

Between 2014 and 2016 unemployment reached its highest levels since 2002, peaking in Oct. 2014 at 6·4%. However, by Oct. 2017 it had declined to 5·4%, its lowest rate since 2013. Annual GDP growth averaged 2·7% in the five years to 2016.

The economy remains susceptible to the effects of the European debt crisis and the economic slowdown in its largest trading partner, China. However, in 2016 there were increases in key commodity prices (including oil, iron ore and coal), reflecting higher Chinese demand (along with lower Chinese domestic iron ore production that year), and Australia recorded its first increase in its terms of trade since 2013. Nevertheless, weak investment and productivity growth is expected to exert a drag on potential medium- to long-term economic performance. In March 2018 Australia and ten other countries bordering the Pacific (although not the USA) signed the Comprehensive and Progressive Agreement for Trans-Pacific Partnership.

In 2016 labour market improvements, expansion in major trading markets and low interest rates supported increased household consumption. However, high household debt and slow growth in real wages pose risks for the Australian economy in the medium-to-long term. Over the long term, a rise in the number of older people and increasing health care costs are expected to make greater demands on public expenditure.

Currency

On 14 Feb. 1966 Australia adopted a system of decimal currency. The currency unit, the Australian dollar (AUD), is divided into 100 *cents*.

Foreign exchange reserves were US$34,857m. in Sept. 2009 and gold reserves 2·57m. troy oz. Total money supply was $A376·5bn. in July 2009.

Inflation rates (based on OECD statistics):

2008	2009	2010	2011	2012	2013	2014	2015	2016	2017
4·3%	1·8%	2·9%	3·3%	1·7%	2·5%	2·5%	1·5%	1·3%	2·0%

Budget

The fiscal year is 1 July–30 June. In Aug. 1998 the Commonwealth government introduced a tax reform package including, from 2000, the introduction of a Goods and Services Tax (GST) at a 10% rate, with all the revenues going to the states in return for the abolition of a range of other indirect taxes; the abolition of Financial Assistance Grants to states; the abolition of wholesale sales tax (which is levied by the Commonwealth government); cuts in personal income tax; and increases in social security benefits, especially for families. In the 2013–14 Mid-Year Economic and Fiscal Outlook an underlying cash deficit of $A47·0bn. (3·0% of GDP) was anticipated in 2013–14, a deficit increase of $A29·0bn. since the 2013–14 budget.

The Australian Government levies income taxes. State expenditure is backed by federal grants. Australian Government expenses and revenue outcomes (in $A1m.):

	2012–13	2013–14
Total expense (by function)	393,896	419,402
General public services	26,339	35,667
Defence	22,057	23,064
Public order and safety	4,031	4,477

(continued)

	2012–13	2013–14
Education	28,468	29,669
Health	67,264	70,252
Social security and welfare	131,803	140,561
Housing and community amenities	5,281	6,045
Recreation and culture	3,553	3,749
Fuel and energy	5,955	6,749
Agriculture, fisheries and forestry	2,407	2,384
Mining, manufacturing and construction	3,016	3,548
Transport and communication	12,788	17,935
Other economic affairs	10,263	10,444
Other purposes	70,671	64,858
Total revenue (by source)	*370,447*	*386,149*
Income tax		
Individuals and other withholding taxes	159,779	167,915
Company tax	67,811	68,625
Superannuation funds	7,473	6,147
Fringe benefits tax	3,970	4,285
Resource rent taxes	1,914	1,785
Indirect tax		
Sales taxes	51,349	56,819
Excise duty	25,709	25,647
Customs duty	8,172	9,282
Carbon pricing mechanism	5,047	4,744
Other indirect taxes	3,206	3,820
Non-tax revenue	36,017	37,080

Performance

Real GDP growth rates (based on OECD statistics):

2008	2009	2010	2011	2012	2013	2014	2015	2016	2017
2·5%	1·9%	2·5%	2·7%	3·9%	2·2%	2·5%	2·5%	2·6%	2·2%

In fiscal year 2018 (July 2017–June 2018) the GDP growth rate was 2·8%. Australia has experienced economic growth every year since 1992—the longest period of uninterrupted economic growth in any developed country. During much of the 1990s the real GDP growth rate, along with lower inflation, made the Australian economic performance one of the best in the OECD area. In 2017 total GDP was US$1,323·4bn.

Banking and Finance

From 1 July 1998 a new financial regulatory framework based on three agencies was introduced by the Australian government, following recommendations by the Financial System Inquiry. The framework included changes in the role of the Reserve Bank of Australia and creation of the Australian Prudential Regulation Authority (APRA) with responsibility for the supervision of deposit-taking institutions (comprising banks, building societies and credit unions), friendly societies, life and general insurance companies and superannuation funds. It further involved replacement of the Australian Securities Commission with the Australian Securities and Investments Commission (ASIC) with responsibility for the regulation of financial services and Australia's 1·2m. companies.

The banking system comprises:

(a) The Reserve Bank of Australia is the central bank. It has two broad responsibilities—monetary policy and the maintenance of financial stability, including stability of the payments system. It also issues Australia's currency notes and provides selected banking and registry services to Commonwealth Government customers and some overseas official institutions. Within the Reserve Bank there are two Boards: the Reserve Bank Board and the Payments System Board; the *Governor* (present incumbent, Philip Lowe) is the Chairman of each.

At 30 June 2016 total assets of the Reserve Bank of Australia were $A167,489m., including gold and foreign currency investments, $A77,446m.; and Australian dollar securities, $A88,500m. At 30 June 2016 capital and reserves were $A23,912m. and main liabilities were Australian notes on issue, $A70,209m.; and deposits, $A61,210m.

A wholly owned subsidiary of the Reserve Bank (Note Printing Australia Limited) manufactures currency notes and other security documents for Australia and for export.

(b) Four major banks: (i) The Commonwealth Bank of Australia; (ii) the Australia and New Zealand Banking Group Ltd; (iii) Westpac Banking Corporation; (iv) National Australia Bank.

(c) The Commonwealth Bank of Australia has a subsidiary—Commonwealth Development Bank. There are nine other Australian-owned banks—Adelaide Bank Ltd, AMP Bank Ltd, Bank of Queensland Ltd, Bendigo Bank Ltd, Elders Rural Bank (50% owned by Bendigo Bank Ltd), Macquarie Bank Ltd, Members Equity Pty Ltd, St George Bank Ltd and Suncorp-Metway Ltd.

(d) There are ten banks incorporated in Australia which are owned by foreign banks and 30 branches of foreign banks (these figures include five foreign banks which have both a subsidiary and a branch presence in Australia).

(e) According to the Australian Prudential Regulation Authority (APRA), as at 30 June 2016 there were 80 authorized banks with Australian banking assets of $A4,116·2bn., with 5,357 branches, 32,156 reported ATMs and 934,001 reported EFTPOS (electronic funds transfer at point of sale) terminals. As at 30 June 2016 there were four building societies with assets of $A11·9bn. and 66 credit unions with assets of $A39·8bn.

Total foreign direct investment in 2017 was US$46·4bn., up from a record US$20·5bn. in 2015. At the end of 2017 foreign direct investment stocks totalled US$662·3bn.

Australia's gross external debt amounted to US$1,331,026m. in June 2012.

There is an Australian Stock Exchange (ASX) in Sydney.

Energy and Natural Resources

Environment

Australia's carbon dioxide emissions from the consumption of energy were the equivalent of 19·6 tonnes per capita in 2011. An *Environmental Performance Index* compiled in 2016 ranked Australia 13th of 180 countries, with 87·2%. The index examined various factors in nine areas—agriculture, air quality, biodiversity and habitat, climate and energy, fisheries, forests, health impacts, water and sanitation, and water resources.

Electricity

Electricity supply is the responsibility of the State governments. In 2014–15 total production (and consumption) was 252,360m. kWh. Coal was the main fuel source for electricity generation in 2013–14, accounting for 61% of the total, with gas accounting for 22% and hydro 7%. Residential customers accounted for 27·3% of consumption in 2013–14.

Oil and Gas

In the year ending 30 June 2014 the Carnarvon Basin (off the coast of Western Australia) produced 42·9bn. cu. metres of natural gas, representing 65·2% of the total Australian output of 65·8bn. cu. metres. Natural gas consumption was 41·7bn. cu. metres in 2016. The Carnarvon and Perth Basins are the largest producers of crude oil and condensate with output of 82·0m. bbls in the financial year 2013–14. Total crude oil and condensate production was 126·7m. bbls in 2013–14, a reduction of 5·1% over the previous year. Oil reserves at the end of 2013 totalled 4·0bn. bbls and natural gas reserves 3·7trn. cu. metres..5

Minerals

Australia is the world's largest producer of bauxite and alumina. It is the world's fourth largest producer of diamonds, ranking second for industrial-grade diamonds after Russia. It is also the third largest gold and uranium producer. Black coal is Australia's major source of energy. Reserves are large (Dec. 2014: 63bn. economically recoverable tonnes) and easily worked. The main fields are in New South Wales and Queensland. Brown coal (lignite) reserves are mined principally in Victoria and South Australia. In 2013–14 raw coal production was 563m. tonnes; lignite production (2011–12), 69m. tonnes; and iron ore and concentrates, 678m. tonnes.

Production of other major minerals in 2013–14 (in tonnes): bauxite, 80·0m.; alumina, 21·5m.; salt (estimate), 11·9m.; manganese ore and concentrates (estimate), 7·4m.; zinc (estimate), 1·5m.; nickel, 214,000; uranium, 5,710; silver (estimate), 1,898; gold (estimate), 274. Diamond production, 2013–14: 11·3m. carats.

Agriculture

In 2013–14 there were an estimated 128,489 establishments mainly engaged in agriculture; the estimated total area of land under agricultural use in the year ending 30 June 2014 was 406·3m. ha. (about 53% of total land area). Gross value of agricultural production in the same year, $A50·9bn., including (in $A1bn.) cattle and calves slaughtering, 8·5; sheep and lamb slaughtering, 2·6; wheat, 8·0; milk, 4·7; wool, 2·5. In the year ending 30 June 2014 there were 25·7m. ha. of crops. An estimated 2·36m. ha. of crops and pastures were irrigated in 2013–14. Important crops in the year ending 30 June 2014 (estimates): sugarcane (30·5m. tonnes from 160;0·4m. ha.); wheat (25·3m. tonnes from 12·6m. ha.); barley (9·2m. tonnes from 3·8m. ha.); canola (3·8m. tonnes from 2·7m. ha.); grain sorghum (1·3m. tonnes from 0·5m. ha.); oats (1·3m. tonnes from 0·7m. ha.). In 2013–14 an estimated 1·56m. tonnes of grapes were harvested from 146,405 ha. of vines.

Beef cattle farming represents the largest sector, accounting for around 55% of farming establishments. Livestock totals at June 2014 (estimates): beef cattle and calves, 26·3m.; dairy cattle, 2·8m.; pigs, 2·3m.; sheep and lambs, 72·6m. Livestock products (in 1,000 tonnes) in 2014 unless otherwise indicated: beef and veal, 2,595; lamb and mutton, 721; pigmeat, 362; chicken meat, 1,141; wool (2013–14), 419. Milk in 2013–14, 9,372m. litres.

Estimated fruit and vegetable production in year ending 30 June 2014 (in 1,000 tonnes): potatoes, 1,171; oranges, 350; tomatoes, 326; apples, 267; onions, 256; bananas, 254; carrots, 243.

Wine production (2014): 11,863,000 hectolitres. Exports of wine in 2014 rose by 1·9% compared to 2013 and were worth $A1·82bn. Australia was both the fifth largest wine producer in the world and the fifth largest exporter in 2015.

In 2013 organic crops were grown in an area covering 17·2m. ha. (the largest area of any country in the world), representing 4·2% of all farmland.

Australia is the world's leading wool producer; only China has more sheep.

Forestry

The Federal government is responsible for forestry at the national level. Each State is responsible for the management of publicly owned forests. Total forest cover was 124·7m. ha. in 2013–14 (16% of Australia's land area). The major part of wood supplies derives from coniferous (softwood) plantations, of which there were 1,024,200 ha. in 2013–14. Australia also had 963,200 ha. of broadleaved (hardwood) plantation in 2013–14. Timber production in 2014 was 30·01m. cu. metres.

Fisheries

The Australian Fishing Zone covers an area 16% larger than the Australian land mass and is the third largest fishing zone in the world, but fish production is insignificant by world standards owing to low productivity of the oceans. The major commercially exploited species are prawns, rock lobster, abalone, tuna, other fin fish, scallops, oysters and pearls. Total fisheries production in 2013–14 came to 227,123 tonnes with a gross value of $A2·5bn. In the same year aquaculture production was 74,913 tonnes with a gross value of $A1·0bn. which represented 40% of the total value of fisheries production.

Industry

The leading companies by market capitalization as at March 2019 were: BHP Billiton Ltd (Australian/British), a resources company (US$133·2bn.); the Commonwealth Bank of Australia (US$93·5bn.); and Westpac Banking (US$76·2bn.).

In 2013–14 manufacturing contributed 6·5% to Australia's GDP. As at 30 June 2016, an estimated 837,609 people worked in manufacturing, 7·0% of Australia's total employed.

Manufacturing by sector in 2013–14:

	Wages and salaries in $A1m.	Sales and service income in $A1m.
Food, beverages and tobacco	12,566	99,976
Textiles, clothing, footwear and leather products	1,467	7,587
Wood, pulp and paper products	3,474	20,054

(continued)

	Wages and salaries in $A1m.	Sales and service income in $A1m.
Printing (including the reproduction of recorded media)	2,051	8,265
Petroleum, coal, basic chemical and associated products	4,608	65,256
Polymer and rubber products	2,608	14,022
Non-metallic mineral products	2,898	18,063
Primary and fabricated metal products	11,615	80,972
Transport equipment	5,658	30,756
Machinery and equipment	7,064	33,069
Furniture and other manufacturing	1,373	7,651

Manufactured products in 2012–13 (unless otherwise indicated) included: clay bricks, 1,312m.; portland cement, 9·5m. tonnes; ready-mixed concrete, 25m. cu. metres; newsprint (2014), 365,000 tonnes; crude steel (2014), 4·6m. tonnes; pig iron (2014), 3·3m. tonnes; automotive gasoline (2013–14), 14,478m. litres; diesel oil (2013–14), 12,456m. litres; aviation turbine fuel (2013–14), 5,009m. litres; beer (2014), 1,691m. litres.

Labour

In Feb. 2016 the total labour force (persons aged 15 and over) numbered 12,740,200 (5,916,700 females). There were 11,952,500 employed persons in Feb. 2016 (46% females) with 3,674,600 in part-time employment (69% females). The majority of wage and salary earners have had their minimum wages and conditions of work prescribed in awards by the Industrial Relations Commission. In Oct. 1991 the Commission decided to allow direct employer-employee wage bargaining, provided agreements reached are endorsed by the Commission. In some States, some conditions of work (e.g. weekly hours of work, leave) are set down in State legislation. Average weekly wage, May 2016, $A1,516·00 (men, $A1,613·50; women, $A1,352·10). The minimum wage was raised to $A18·93 an hour from 1 July 2018. Average weekly hours worked by full-time employed males, 2010–11: 41·2 hours; females, 37·2. Four weeks annual leave is standard. In Feb. 2016 part-time work accounted for 31% of all employment in Australia. Foreign-born workers made up 28·8% of the labour force as at Aug. 2014, the highest share of any major industrialized nation.

Employees in all States are covered by workers' compensation legislation and by certain industrial award provisions relating to work injuries.

In 2015 there were 228 industrial disputes recorded, which accounted for 83,400 working days lost (71,400 in 2014). In these disputes 73,300 workers were involved.

As at Feb. 2016 health care and social assistance (12·7% of employed persons) and retail trade (10·9%) were the largest employers, ahead of the construction industry (8·9%) and professional, scientific and technical services (8·6%).

The following table shows the annual average percentage distribution of employed persons as at Nov. 2013:

	Employed persons (%)
Professionals	22·1
Clerical and administrative workers	14·6
Technicians and trades workers	14·6
Managers	12·8
Community and personal service workers	9·9
Labourers	9·8
Sales workers	9·4
Machinery operators and drivers	6·8

In Dec. 2017, 730,600 persons were unemployed, of whom, according to the OECD in 2017, 23·5% had been unemployed for more than one year. The unemployment rate in Dec. 2018 was 5·0% (down slightly from 5·6% in 2017 as a whole).

Australia had 3,000 people living in slavery according to the Walk Free Foundation's 2013 *Global Slavery Index*.

International Trade

In 1990 Australia and New Zealand completed a Closer Economic Relations agreement (initiated in 1983) which establishes free trade in goods. Net foreign debt was $A865·5bn. as at 30 June 2014 (an increase of 8·6% on the previous year). In 1998 the effect of the Asian meltdown on exports resulted increasingly in shipments of commodities and exports of manufactures and some services being redirected to other destinations, notably the USA and Europe. Merchandise imports increased by 12·0% in 2011–12 against the previous year while exports rose by 7·4%.

Imports and Exports

The Australian customs tariff provides for preferences to goods produced in and shipped from certain countries as a result of reciprocal trade agreements. These include the UK, New Zealand, Canada and Ireland.

In 2014 merchandise imports totalled $A252,338m. ($A240,540m. in 2013); merchandise exports in 2014 totalled $A265,994m. ($A261,959m. in 2013).

Leading commodity imports, 2014 (in $A1m.): crude petroleum oils, 20,050; refined petroleum, 18,579; passenger motor vehicles, 17,566; telecommunications equipment and parts, 9,845; medicaments (including veterinary), 7,497; computers, 7,316. Most valuable commodity exports, 2014 (in $A1m.): iron ore and concentrates, 66,008; coal, 37,999; natural gas, 17,743; gold, 13,460; crude petroleum, 10,564; beef, 7,751. Although the resources sector accounts for the majority of Australia's exports, education (international students studying in Australia) is actually the third largest export.

Australia is the world's largest exporter of iron ore and metallurgical coal and the world's third largest exporter of liquefied natural gas.

Trade in goods and services by bloc or country in 2013–14 (in $A1m.):

	Imports	Exports
APEC	220,498	266,325
ASEAN	61,424	37,063
EU	63,486	21,812
China	52,399	99,426
Japan	21,084	51,019
Korea, South	12,671	22,476
Malaysia	12,704	7,231
New Zealand	11,180	11,467
Singapore	18,114	10,949
UK	12,850	7,837
USA	41,327	17,138

China accounts for 23% of Australia's foreign trade in goods and services combined.

Communications

Roads

At 30 June 2012 there were an estimated 900,083 km of roads (around 42·7% of which were sealed), including 51,847 km of highways.

As at 31 Jan. 2016 registration totals were: 13,876,007 passenger vehicles, 2,985,592 light commercial vehicles, 576,423 trucks, 96,582 buses and 828,965 motorcycles.

In 2014, 1,056 persons were killed in road accidents (less than half the 1989 total of 2,407).

Rail

Privatization of government railways began in Victoria in 1994 with West Coast Railway and Hoys Transport being granted seven-year franchises. Specialised Container Transport (SCT) won the first private rail freight franchise in 1995 followed by TNT (now Toll Holdings). Australian National Railway Commission was sold by the Commonwealth Government in Nov. 1997 and in Feb. 1999 V/Line Freight Corporation, owned by the Victorian Government, was sold to Freight Australia. Rail passenger services in Victoria were franchised in mid-1999. The Australian Railroad Group acquired Western Australia's government rail freight operation, Westrail, in Nov. 2000. In Jan. 2002 Toll Holdings and Lang acquired the rolling stock of the National Rail Corporation (NRC) and New South Wales freight carrier,

FreightCorp. These two sales left Queensland Rail (QR) as the only government-owned rail freight operator in Australia. In July 2010 it was split into two separate companies with Queensland Rail as the State government-owned corporation responsible for passenger services and QR National, which was privatized in Nov. 2010, for freight.

In 2012 Australia had 33,299 route-km of open track of which 17,034 km were standard gauge (1,435 mm), 12,595 km were narrow gauge (1,067 mm), 3,281 km were narrow gauge (610 mm) and 389 km dual gauge; a total of 3,300 route-km were electrified. In 2014–15 a total of 1·24bn. tonnes of freight were carried; passengers carried totalled approximately 849m. urban; 50m. non-urban.

Under various Commonwealth–State standardization agreements, all the State capitals are now linked by standard gauge track. The 'AustralAsia Rail Project', which involved the construction of 1,420 km standard gauge railway between Alice Springs and Darwin, has been completed and passenger services from Adelaide through Alice Springs and on to Darwin commenced in Feb. 2004.

There are also private industrial and tourist railways, and tramways in Adelaide, Melbourne and Sydney. In the latter two cities there are also metro systems.

Civil Aviation

Qantas Airways is Australia's principal international airline. In 1992 Qantas merged with Australian Airlines, and in 1993, 25% of the company was purchased by British Airways. After it was floated on the stock exchange in the mid-1990s it was 55% Australian-owned and 45% foreign-owned. Under current law 51% must be Australian-owned. The second largest airline is Virgin Australia, which was established in 2000 as a low-cost carrier and initially called Virgin Blue. The largest low-cost carrier is now Jetstar Airways, a subsidiary of Qantas. A total of 54 international airlines operated scheduled air services to and from Australia in 2014. There are 11 international airports, the main ones being Adelaide, Brisbane, Cairns, Darwin, Melbourne, Perth and Sydney. In 2014–15 passenger movements totalled a record 147,353,391 (an increase of 0·6% on the previous financial year); domestic and regional passenger numbers totalled 113,486,916 and international 33,866,475; international freight increased by 6·3% to a record 936,733 tonnes; international mail decreased by 0·3% to 40,395 tonnes.

Sydney (Kingsford Smith) handled the most traffic (26·5%) in Australia in 2014–15 (39,021,357 passengers, of which 25,513,156 on domestic and regional flights), followed by Melbourne International (21·7%) and Brisbane (14·9%).

In 2015 a total of 60·1m. passengers were carried on domestic flights (including charter flights). Domestic airlines were deregulated in Oct. 1990.

In 2014–15 there were 192 certified and 135 registered aerodromes in Australia and its external territories. At 30 June 2015 there were 15,287 registered aircraft on the Australian Civil Aircraft Register including 2,125 helicopters and 386 balloons.

Shipping

The chief ports are Brisbane, Dampier, Fremantle, Gladstone, Hay Point, Melbourne, Newcastle, Port Hedland, Port Kembla, Sydney and Weipa. Port Hedland overtook Dampier as Australia's busiest port in 2008–09, and in 2013–14 handled 372,301,000 tonnes of cargo (369,927,000 tonnes loaded and 2,374,000 tonnes discharged) compared to 177,528,000 tonnes for Dampier (176,900,000 tonnes loaded and 628,000 tonnes discharged). Iron ore exports to China are the principal factor behind the rapid growth of Dampier and Port Hedland (both of which are in Western Australia) during the 2000s. Melbourne, the busiest container port, handled 2·5m. TEUs (twenty-foot equivalent units) in 2013–14.

In Jan. 2014 there were 108 ships of 300 GT or over registered, totalling 851,000 GT. The Australian-controlled fleet comprised 74 vessels of 1,000 GT or over in July 2014, of which 28 were under the Australian flag and 46 under foreign flags.

Telecommunications

In 1989 the domestic market became a regulated monopoly with Telstra as the government-owned company providing all services and, in 1991, a duopoly (with Optus) in fixed network services. In 1993 Vodafone joined Telstra and Optus in the provision of mobile phone services. A new regulatory regime was created by the introduction of the Telecommunications Act 1997 and both markets were opened to wholesale and retail competition. There is no limit to the number of carriers that can hold licences under the

new arrangements and at 30 June 2015 there were 229 licensed carriers. The Australian Communications and Media Authority (ACMA) and the Australian Competition and Consumer Commission (ACCC) are the primary regulators with responsibility for the industry's development. The privatization of Telstra was completed in Nov. 2006.

In 2013 there were 10,350,000 main (fixed) telephone lines, down from 10,709,000 in 2009. Mobile phone subscriptions numbered 24,940,000 in 2013 (1,068·4 per 1,000 persons). In 2013, 83·5% of the population aged 15 or over were internet users. The fixed broadband penetration rate in Dec. 2016 was 30·1 subscribers per 100 inhabitants. In Dec. 2017 there were 15·0m. Facebook users (61% of the population).

Social Institutions

Out of 178 countries analysed in the 2017 *Fragile States Index*—a list published jointly by the Fund for Peace and *Foreign Policy* magazine—Australia was ranked the joint sixth least vulnerable (along with Ireland) to conflict or collapse. The index is based on 12 indicators of state vulnerability across social, political and economic categories.

Justice

The judicial power of the Commonwealth of Australia is vested in the High Court of Australia (the Federal Supreme Court), in the Federal courts created by the Federal Parliament (the Federal Court of Australia and the Family Court of Australia) and in the State courts invested by Parliament with Federal jurisdiction.

High Court

The High Court consists of a Chief Justice and six other Justices, appointed by the Governor-General in Council. The Constitution confers on the High Court original jurisdiction, *inter alia*, in all matters arising under treaties or affecting consuls or other foreign representatives, matters between the States of the Commonwealth, matters to which the Commonwealth is a party and matters between residents of different States. Federal Parliament may make laws conferring original jurisdiction on the High Court, *inter alia*, in matters arising under the Constitution or under any laws made by the Parliament. It has in fact conferred jurisdiction on the High Court in matters arising under the Constitution and in matters arising under certain laws made by Parliament.

The High Court may hear and determine appeals from its own Justices exercising original jurisdiction, from any other Federal Court, from a Court exercising Federal jurisdiction and from the Supreme Courts of the States. It also has jurisdiction to hear and determine appeals from the Supreme Courts of the Territories. The right of appeal from the High Court to the Privy Council in London was abolished in 1986.

Other Federal Courts

Since 1924, four other Federal courts have been created to exercise special Federal jurisdiction, i.e. the Federal Court of Australia, the Family Court of Australia, the Australian Industrial Court and the Federal Court of Bankruptcy. The Federal Court of Australia was created by the Federal Court of Australia Act 1976 and began to exercise jurisdiction on 1 Feb. 1977. It exercises such original jurisdiction as is invested in it by laws made by the Federal Parliament including jurisdiction formerly exercised by the Australian Industrial Court and the Federal Court of Bankruptcy, and in some matters previously invested in either the High Court or State and Territory Supreme Courts. The Federal Court also acts as a court of appeal from State and Territory courts in relation to Federal matters. Appeal from the Federal Court to the High Court will be by way of special leave only. The State Supreme Courts have also been invested with Federal jurisdiction in bankruptcy.

State Courts

The general Federal jurisdiction of the State courts extends, subject to certain restrictions and exceptions, to all matters in which the High Court has jurisdiction or in which jurisdiction may be conferred upon it.

Industrial Tribunals

The chief federal industrial tribunal is the Australian Conciliation and Arbitration Commission, constituted by presidential members (with the status of judges) and commissioners. The Commission's functions include settling industrial disputes, making awards, determining the standard hours of work and wage fixation. Questions of law, the judicial interpretation of awards and imposition of penalties in relation to industrial matters are dealt with by the Industrial Division of the Federal Court.

At 30 June 2014 the prison population was 33,791 (185·6 per 100,000 of national population). In 2015 the World Justice Project *Rule of Law Index*, which provides data on how the rule of law is experienced by the general public across eight categories, ranked Australia 10th of 102 countries for criminal justice and 15th for civil justice.

Each State has its own individual police service which operates almost exclusively within its State boundaries. State police investigations include murder, robbery, street-level drug dealing, kidnapping, domestic violence and motor vehicle offences.

The role of the Australian Federal Police (AFP) is to enforce Commonwealth criminal law and protect Commonwealth and national interests from crime in Australia and overseas. Responsibilities include combating organized crime, trans-national crime, money laundering, illicit drug trafficking, e-crime, the investigation of fraud against the Australian Government and handling special references from Government. The AFP also provides a protection service to dignitaries and crucial witnesses as well as community policing services to the people of the Australian Capital Territory, Jervis Bay and Australia's External Territories.

Total Australian Federal Police personnel as at 30 June 2014 was 6,853, including 3,620 sworn police, 639 sworn protective service officers and 2,582 unsworn staff. In 2013–14 there were approximately 55,000 sworn police officers in total in Australia.

Education

The governments of the Australian States and Territories have the major responsibility for education, including the administration and substantial funding of primary, secondary, and technical and further education. In most States, a single education department is responsible for these three levels but in Queensland, Western Australia and the Northern Territory, separate departments deal with school-based and technical and further education issues.

School attendance is compulsory between the ages of six (five in Tasmania) and 17 years (with the exception of the Northern Territory where the leaving age is 15 years), at either a government school or a recognized non-government educational institution. Between the ages of 16 and 17 in some states students have the option of undertaking vocational training, apprenticeships or other government approved learning programmes. Many children attend pre-schools for a year before entering school (usually in sessions of two–three hours, for two–five days per week). Government schools are usually co-educational and comprehensive. Non-government schools have been traditionally single-sex, particularly in secondary schools, but there is a trend towards co-education. Tuition is free at government schools, but fees are normally charged at non-government schools.

In 2016 there were 6,634 government (and 2,780 non-government) primary and secondary schools with 2,465,628 (1,313,028) full-time equivalent pupils and 176,819 (99,511) full-time equivalent teachers.

Vocational education and training (VET) is essentially a partnership between the Commonwealth, the States and Territories and industry. The Commonwealth is involved in VET through an agreed set of national arrangements for sharing responsibility with the States and Territories. In 2016 publicly-funded VET programmes were offered by some 53 Technical and Further Education (TAFE) institutes and other government institutions. A further 381 community education providers and 1,558 other providers (mainly private providers) delivering VET were at least partly publicly funded. In 2016 there were 1·3m. people enrolled in publicly funded VET courses.

As at June 2016 there was a total of 137 higher education providers approved to receive Commonwealth Government funding through the Higher Education Support Act 2003, of which 38 were publicly-funded universities and 99 were other education institutions with students on accredited higher education courses. Most of these institutions operate under State and Territory legislation although several operate under Commonwealth legislation. There are also three completely privately-funded universities (Bond University in Queensland, the University of Notre Dame Australia in Western Australia and Torrens University Australia in South Australia) and numerous private higher education providers in a range of specialist fields. Institutions established by appropriate legislation are autonomous and have the authority to accredit their own programmes and are primarily responsible for their own quality assurance. There were 1·37m. students in higher education in 2014; fields of study with the largest number of students in 2014 were management and commerce (26·1%); society and culture (21·8%); health (15·3%); and education (9·7%).

The higher education sector contributes a significant proportion of the research and research training undertaken in Australia. The Australian Research Council provides advice on research issues and administers the allocation of some research grants to higher education sector researchers and institutions.

The Commonwealth Government offers a number of programmes which provide financial assistance to students. The Youth Allowance is available for eligible full-time students aged 16 to 24, depending on the circumstances of study. Austudy is available to eligible full-time students aged over 25. Abstudy provides financial assistance for eligible Aboriginal and Torres Strait Islanders who undertake full-time or part-time study. AIC—the Assistance for Isolated Children scheme—provides special support to families whose children are isolated from schooling or who have physical disabilities.

Most students contribute to the cost of their higher education through the Higher Education Contribution Scheme (HECS). They can choose to make an upfront contribution (with a 25% discount) or to defer all or part of their payment until their income reaches a certain level when they must begin repaying their contribution through the taxation system. Overseas students generally pay full tuition fees. Universities are also able to offer full-fee places in postgraduate courses and to a limited number of domestic undergraduate students.

International education is increasingly important, with 347,560 enrolments by overseas students at Australian educational institutions in 2014, an increase of 5·8% on the previous year; 25·3% of higher education students were foreign.

Total operating expenses of Australian Government on education in 2013–14 were \$A81,375m. Private expenditure on education in 2013–14 amounted to \$A42,388m. The figures include government grants to the private sector which are also included in the operating expenses of Australian governments.

The adult literacy rate is at least 99%.

Health

In 2011–12 there were 753 public hospitals (including 17 psychiatric hospitals) and 592 private hospitals; there were 87,549 hospital beds (3·9 per 1,000 population). Australia had 334,100 registered nurses and midwives in 2012 and 34,632 general practitioners in 2015–16; there were 23,382 physiotherapists as at 31 Dec. 2012. The Royal Flying Doctor Service serves remote areas. Total government expenditure on health goods and services (public and private sectors) in 2011–12 was \$A140·2bn. (\$A130·3bn. in the previous year), representing 9·5% of GDP. In 2011–12, 57·1% of Australians aged 18 years and over had private health insurance.

In 2015 there were an estimated 25,313 HIV cases, with 1,025 new diagnoses during the year.

In 2011–12, 63% of the adult population (men, 70%; women, 56%) aged 18 years and over were considered overweight or obese, compared to 61% in 2007–08.

Welfare

All Commonwealth government social security pensions, benefits and allowances are financed from the Commonwealth government's general revenue. In addition, assistance is provided for welfare services.

Age Pensions—age pensions are payable to both men and women aged 65 years and 6 months or more who have lived in Australia for a specified period and, unless permanently blind, also satisfy an income and assets test. On 1 July 2017 the minimum age for both men and women's eligibility was raised from 65 to 65 years and 6 months. It is increasing by six month every two years, until it reaches 67 by 1 July 2023. In the year ending 30 June 2017, 2,498,765 age pensioners received a total of \$A4·2bn.

Disability Support Pension (DSP)—payable to persons aged 16 years or over with a physical, intellectual or psychiatric impairment of at least 20%, assessed as being unable to work for at least 15 hours a week. DSP for those of 21 years or over is paid at the same rate as Age Pensions and is subject to the same means test except for those who are permanently blind. In the year ending 30 June 2017, 758,911 disability support pensioners received a total of \$A16·3bn.

Carer Payment—payable to a person unable to support themselves owing to providing constant care and attention at home for a severely disabled person aged 16 or over, or a person who is frail aged, either permanently or for an extended period. Since 1 July 1998 Carer Payment has been extended to carers of children under 16 years of age with profound disabilities. Subject to income and assets tests, the rate of Carer Payment is the same as for other pensions. In the year ending 30 June 2017, 263,874 carers received a total of \$A5·1bn.

Carer Allowance—supplementary payment to a person providing constant care and attention at home for an adult or child with a disability or severe medical condition. The allowance is not income or assets tested. In the year ending 30 June 2017, 610,068 carers received a total of $A2·2bn.

Sickness Allowance—paid to those over school-leaving age but below Age Pension age who are unable to work or continue full-time study temporarily owing to illness or injury. Eligibility rests on the person having a job or study course to which they can return. In the year ending 30 June 2017 a total of $A95·8m. was paid to 6,336 beneficiaries.

Family Tax Benefit (FTB)—Family Tax Benefit Part A is paid to assist families with children under 21 years of age or dependent full-time students aged 21–24 years; Family Tax Benefit Part B provides additional assistance to families with only one income earner and children under 16 years of age or dependent full-time students aged 16–18 years. Both benefits are subject to an income and assets test. In the year ending 30 June 2017 FTB Part A and Part B payments were made to a total of 2·7m. families.

Parenting Payment (Single) and (Partnered)—is paid to assist those who care for children under 16, with income and assets under certain amounts, and have been an Australian resident for at least two years or a refugee or have become a lone parent while an Australian resident. Parenting Payment (Single) is paid to lone parents under pension rates and conditions; Parenting Payment (Partnered) is paid to one of the parents in the couple. In the year ending 30 June 2017, 255,801 Parenting Payment (Single) beneficiaries and 94,198 Parenting Payment (Partnered) beneficiaries received a total of $A5·6bn.

Newstart Allowance (NSA)—payable to those who are unemployed and are over 21 years of age but less than Age Pension age. Eligibility is subject to income and assets tests and recipients must satisfy the 'activity test' whereby they are actively seeking and willing to undertake suitable paid work, including casual and part-time work. To be eligible for benefit a person must have resided in Australia for at least 12 months preceding his or her claim or intend to remain in Australia permanently; unemployment must not be as a result of industrial action by that person or by members of a union to which that person is a member. In the year ended 30 June 2017 a total of $A10·0bn. was paid to 733,088 NSA beneficiaries.

Youth Allowance—replaced five former schemes for young people, including the Youth Training Allowance. In the year ending 30 June 2017 a total of $A3·1bn. was paid to 305,368 YA beneficiaries.

Austudy—means tested payment for students or apprentices aged 25 years and over. In the year ending 30 June 2017 a total of $A583·7m. was paid to 42,642 beneficiaries.

Service Pensions—are paid by the Department of Veterans' Affairs. Male veterans who have reached the age of 60 years or are permanently unemployable, and who served in a theatre of war, are eligible subject to an income and assets test. The minimum age for female veterans' eligibility was lifted in six-monthly increments every two years until 1 Jan. 2014 when it also became 60 years. Partners of service pensioners are also eligible, provided that they do not receive a pension from the Department of Social Security. Disability pension is a compensatory payment in respect of incapacity attributable to war service. It is paid at a rate commensurate with the degree of incapacity and is free of any income test. In the year ended 30 June 2017, $A2,485·4m. for service pensions and $A3,163·5m. for disability and war widows' dependants' pensions were paid out; at 30 June 2017 there were 106,970 service pensioners and 153,474 disability and war widow(er)s' pensioners.

In addition to cash benefits, welfare services are provided, either directly or through State and local government authorities and voluntary agencies, for people with special needs.

Medicare—covers: automatic entitlement under a single public health fund to medical and optometrical benefits of 75% of the Medical Benefits Schedule fee, with a maximum patient payment for any service where the Schedule fee is charged; access without direct charge to public hospital accommodation and to inpatient and outpatient treatment by doctors appointed by the hospital; the restoration of funds for community health to approximately the same real level as 1975; a reduction in charges for private treatment in shared wards of public hospitals, and increases in the daily bed subsidy payable to private hospitals.

The Medicare programme is financed in part by a 2·0% levy on taxable incomes, with low income cut-off points, which were $A21,655 p.a. for a single person in 2016–17 and $A36,541 for a family; there is an extra income threshold for each child (lower threshold in 2016–17 of $A3,356). From 1 July 2012 a banded levy surcharge was introduced: single individuals with taxable incomes of $A90,001–105,000p.a., 1%; $A105,001–140,000p.a., 1·25%; $A140,001 and over p.a., 1·5%; couples and families with combined taxable incomes who do not have private hospital cover through private health insurance, $A180,001–210,000, 1%; $A210,001–280,000, 1·25%; $A280,001 and over p.a., 1·5%.

Medicare benefits are available to all persons ordinarily resident in Australia. Visitors from the UK, New Zealand, Italy, Sweden, the Netherlands and Malta have immediate access to necessary medical treatment, as do all visitors staying more than six months.

Religion

Under the Constitution the Commonwealth cannot make any law to establish any religion, to impose any religious observance or to prohibit the free exercise of any religion. The following percentages refer to those religions with the largest number of adherents at the census of 2016. Answering the census question on religious adherence was not obligatory, however.

Christian, 52·1% of population (including: Catholic, 22·6%; Anglican, 13·3%; Uniting Church, 3·7%; Presbyterian and Reformed, 2·3%; Eastern Orthodox, 2·1%; Baptist, 1·5%; Pentecostal, 1·0%; Lutheran, 0·7%). Religions other than Christian, 8·2% (including: Islam, 2·6%; Buddhism, 2·4%; Hinduism, 1·9%; Sikhism, 0·5%; Judaism, 0·4%). Other religions, 0·4%; no religion, 30·1%; not stated 9·1%.

The Anglican Church of Australia first ordained women as priests in 1992. Women have been ordained as bishops since May 2008. In Feb. 2019 the Roman Catholic Church had two cardinals.

Jupp, James, (ed.) *The Encyclopedia of Religion in Australia.* 2009
Thompson, R. C., *Religion in Australia, a History.* 1995

Culture

World Heritage Sites

There are 19 sites under Australian jurisdiction that appear on the UNESCO World Heritage List. They are (with year entered on list): Great Barrier Reef (1981), Kakadu National Park (1981, 1987 and 1992), Willandra Lakes Region (1981), Tasmanian Wilderness (1982 and 1989), Lord Howe Island Group (1982), Gondwana Rainforests of Australia (1986 and 1994), Uluru-Kata Tjuta National Park (1987 and 1994), Wet Tropics of Queensland (1988), Shark Bay (1991), Fraser Island (1992), Australian Fossil Mammal Sites (Riversleigh/Naracoorte) (1994), Heard and McDonald Islands (1997), Macquarie Island (1997), the Greater Blue Mountains Area (2000), Purnululu National Park (2003), Royal Exhibition Building and Carlton Gardens in Melbourne (2004), Sydney Opera House (2007), Australian Convict Sites in New South Wales, Tasmania, Western Australia and Norfolk Island (2010), and Ningaloo Coast (2011).

Press

There were 49 English daily metropolitan newspapers in 2013 (two national, ten metropolitan and 37 regional). There are also ten metropolitan Sunday newspapers. The papers with the largest circulations in June 2013 were the *Sunday Telegraph* (New South Wales), with an average of 541,749 per issue; the *Sunday Herald Sun* (Victoria), with an average of 485,943 per issue; and the Saturday edition of the *Herald Sun* (Victoria), with an average of 416,662 per issue. In 2013 there were two free dailies, *mX* (with three editions, published in Brisbane, Melbourne and Sydney) and *Manly Daily*.

Source: Audited Media Association of Australia; ABC Paid Media Audit

Tourism

In 2017 the total number of overseas visitors for the year stood at 8·8m. (a 6·5% increase on the previous year). The top source countries for visitors in 2017 were New Zealand (1,356,400); China (1,355,500); USA (781,000); UK (731,900); Japan (434,600); and Singapore (434,400). In 2016–17 tourism accounted for a 3·2% share of total GDP.

Festivals

Among the largest events are the Sydney Festival (running for three weeks each Jan., with over 500 performers from across the arts), the National Multicultural Festival in Canberra (Feb.), the Perth International Arts Festival (Feb.), the Brisbane Festival (July) and the Melbourne International Arts Festival (Oct.). Adelaide and Darwin have their own large events too. Each June the Dreaming Festival in Woodford celebrates Indigenous culture. Among the biggest rock and pop festivals are the Big Day Out (Jan.–Feb.) and Future Music Festival (Feb.–March) concerts held across different locations in Sydney, Melbourne, Brisbane, Adelaide and Perth. However, the Big Day Out's future is in jeopardy owing to falling ticket sales. Other music festivals include Tamworth Country

Music Festival (Jan.), Canberra's National Folk Festival (Easter) and Bluesfest at Byron Bay (also Easter). The Melbourne International Film Festival (July–Aug.) is the largest film festival in the southern hemisphere with over 190,000 annual admissions.

Diplomatic Representatives

Of Australia in the United Kingdom (Australia House, Strand, London, WC2B 4LA)
High Commissioner: George Brandis, QC.

Of the United Kingdom in Australia (Commonwealth Ave., Yarralumla, Canberra, A.C.T. 2600)
High Commissioner: Menna Rawlings, CMG.

Of Australia in the USA (1601 Massachusetts Ave., NW, Washington, D.C., 20036)
Ambassador: Joseph Benedict Hockey.

Of the USA in Australia (21 Moonah Pl., Yarralumla, Canberra, A.C.T. 2600)
Ambassador: Vacant.
Chargé d'Affaires a.i.: James Carouso.

Of Australia to the United Nations
Ambassador: Gillian Bird.

Of Australia to the European Union
Ambassador: Mark Higgie.

Australian Capital Territory

Key Historical Events
The area that is now the Australian Capital Territory (ACT) was explored in 1820 by Charles Throsby who named it Limestone Plains. Settlement commenced in 1824. In 1901 the Commonwealth constitution stipulated that a land tract of at least 260 sq. km in area and not less than 160 km from Sydney be reserved as a capital district. The Canberra site was adopted by the Seat of Government Act 1908. The present site was surrendered by New South Wales and accepted by the Commonwealth in 1909. By subsequential proclamation the Territory became vested in the Commonwealth from 1 Jan. 1911. The Jervis Bay Territory was acquired by the Commonwealth of Australia from New South Wales in 1915 in order that the national seat of government at Canberra would have access to the sea. In 1911 an international competition for the city plan had been won by W. Burley Griffin of Chicago but construction was delayed by the First World War. It was not until 1927 that Canberra became the seat of government. Located on the Molonglo River surrounding an artificial lake, it was built as a compromise capital to stop squabbling between Melbourne and Sydney following the 1901 Federation of Australian States.

In Dec. 1988 self-government was proclaimed and in May 1989 the first ACT assembly was elected.

Territory and Population
The total area is 2,431 sq. km (including Jervis Bay Territory). Around 60% is hilly or mountainous. Timbered mountains are located in the south and west, and plains and hill country in the north. The ACT lies within the upper Murrumbidgee River catchment, in the Murray-Darling Basin. The Murrumbidgee flows throughout the Territory from the south, and its tributary, the Molonglo, from the east. The Molonglo was dammed in 1964 to form Lake Burley Griffin. Population at the 2011 census excluding Jervis Bay Territory was 357,222 (2006: 324,034).

The Jervis Bay Territory (73 sq. km) is independent and administered by central government although the laws of the ACT apply. Population at the 2011 census was 378 (2006: 368).

Social Statistics
2014: births, 5,552; deaths, 1,813; marriages, 1,523; divorces, 1,278. Infant mortality rate (per 1,000 live births), 2·3. Expectation of life, 2014: males, 81·4 years; females, 85·2 years.

Climate
ACT has a continental climate, characterized by a marked variation in temperature between seasons, with warm to hot summers and cold winters.

Constitution and Government
The ACT became self-governing on 11 May 1989. It is represented by two members in the Commonwealth House of Representatives and two senators.

The parliament of the ACT, the *Legislative Assembly*, consists of 17 members elected for a three-year term. Its responsibilities are at State and Local government level. The Legislative Assembly elects a Chief Minister and a four-member cabinet.

Recent Elections
At the elections of 15 Oct. 2016 ACT Labor won 12 seats with 38·4% of the vote, Canberra Liberals 11 with 36·7% and the Greens 2 with 10·3%.

Current Government
In March 2019 the Labor–Green government comprised the following:
Chief Minister, Treasurer, Minister for Social Inclusion and Equality, Tourism and Special Events, and Trade, Industry and Investment: Andrew Barr.
Deputy Chief Minister, Minister for Education, Early Childhood Development, Housing and Suburban Development, Prevention of Domestic and Family Violence, Sport and Recreation, and Women: Yvette Berry. *Environment and Heritage, Planning and Land Management, and Police and Emergency Services:* Mick Gentleman. *Health and Wellbeing, Higher Education, Medical and Health Research, Transport, and Vocational Education and Skills:* Meegan Fitzharris. *Climate Change and Sustainability, Corrections and Justice Health, Justice, Consumer Affairs and Road Safety, and Mental Health:* Shane Rattenbury. *City Services, Community Services and Facilities, Multicultural Affairs, and Roads:* Chris Steel. *Aboriginal and Torres Strait Islander Affairs, Disability, Children, Youth and Families, Employment and Workplace Safety, Government Services and Procurement, and Urban Renewal:* Rachel Stephen-Smith. *Attorney General, Minister for the Arts and Cultural Events, Building Quality Improvement, Business Regulatory Services, and Seniors and Veterans:* Gordon Ramsay.

ACT Government Website: http://www.act.gov.au

Economy

Budget
The ACT fully participates in the federal-state model underpinning the Australian Federal System. As a city-State, the ACT Government reflects State and local (municipal) government responsibilities, which is unique within the federal system. However, the ACT is treated equitably with the other Australian jurisdictions regarding the distribution of federal funding.

In 2006 the Territory recorded total income of $A3,436m. (including the Territory's share of operating surplus from Joint Ventures accounted for using the Equity Method) and incurred expenditure of $A3,065m. achieving a surplus of $A372m. on accrual basis.

Banking and Finance
According to the Australian Prudential Regulation Authority, as at 30 June 2006 there were ten authorized banks with 66 branches; one building society with four branches and seven credit unions with 31 branches.

Energy and Natural Resources

Electricity
See New South Wales.

Agriculture
Sheep and/or beef cattle farming is the main agricultural activity. In 2005–06 there were 99 farming establishments with an estimated total area of 44,910 ha. Gross value of agricultural production in 2009–10: $A10·7m.

Forestry
There are about 10,000 ha. of plantation forest in the ACT (approximately 3·96% of the land area). Most of the area is managed for the production of softwood timber. The established pine forests, such as Kowen, Stromlo, Uriarra and Pierces Creek, are in the northern part of the Territory. After harvesting, 500–1,000 ha. of land are planted with new pine forest each year. No native forests or woodlands have been cleared for plantation since the mid-1970s.

Industry
Manufacturing industries in the year ended 30 June 2007 employed 4,967 persons and generated sales and service income of $A1,162m.

Labour

In June 2007 there were 187,900 employed persons and 6,000 unemployed persons, giving an unemployment rate of 3·1%.

In the year ending Feb. 2006, 25·7% of the ACT labour force was employed in public administration and defence; 14·9% in property and business services; 11·6% in retail trade. The average weekly wage in Nov. 2010 was $A1,468·20 (males $A1,550·80, females $A1,370·50).

International Trade

Imports and Exports

In 2009–10 foreign merchandise imports were valued at $A5m.; exports at $A4m. Major sources of imports for 2009–10 (figures in $A1,000): Austria, 1,737; USA, 810; France, 660. Major export destinations (figures in $A1,000): Germany, 2,380; Saudi Arabia, 729; Hong Kong, 600. Principal commodity imports in 2009–10 were (with values in $A1,000): artwork and antiques, 1,558; telecommunications equipment and parts, 771; electrical machinery and parts, 518. Principal commodity exports (with values in $A1,000): gold coins and legal tender coins, 1,129; heating and cooling equipment, 729; optical instruments, 71.

Communications

Roads

In 2007 there were an estimated 3,023 km of roads. At 31 March 2006 there were 224,076 vehicles registered in the ACT. In 2007 there were 14 road accident fatalities.

Civil Aviation

In 2009–10 Canberra International Airport handled 3,258,396 passengers.

Social Institutions

Justice

In the year ending 30 June 2011 there were 26,087 criminal incidents recorded by police. During the same year there were 740 full-time sworn police officers in the ACT and 206 unsworn police staff.

Education

In Feb. 2006 there were 221 schools comprising 82 pre-schools, 139 primary and secondary schools (including colleges) and five special schools. Of these 177 were government schools. There were a total of 60,142 full-time students. There were four higher education institutions in 2006: the Signadou Campus of the Australian Catholic University (ACU) had 596 students enrolled; the Australian National University, 14,476 students; the University of Canberra, 11,632; and the Australian Defence Force Academy, 2,136.

Health

The ACT is serviced by three public and 12 private hospitals (nine of the private hospitals are free-standing day hospital facilities only). At 30 June 2006 there were 2,056 medical practitioners, 4,469 registered nurses and 264 dentists.

Welfare

In 2005–06 there were 18,468 age pensioners (5·7% of ACT population); 7,281 persons received disability support pension (2·2%).

Religion

At the 2006 census 60·2% of the population were Christian. Of these, 46·5% were Roman Catholic and 27·8% Anglican. Non-Christian religions accounted for 6·2%, the largest groups being Buddhists, Muslims and Hindus.

Culture

Tourism

In the year ending March 2009, 156,885 international visitors came to the ACT. Of these, the largest proportion (19%) was from the UK. At Dec. 2008 there were 56 hotels, guest houses and serviced apartments employing 2,467 persons.

Northern Territory

Key Historical Events

The Northern Territory, after forming part of New South Wales, was annexed on 6 July 1863 to South Australia. After the agreement of 7 Dec. 1907 for the transfer of the Northern Territory to the Commonwealth, it passed to the control of the Commonwealth government on 1 Jan. 1911. On 1 Feb. 1927 the Northern Territory was divided into two territories but in 1931 it was again administered as a single territory. The Legislative Council for the Northern Territory, constituted in 1947, was reconstituted in 1959. In that year, citizenship rights were granted to Aboriginal people of 'full descent'. On 1 July 1978 self-government was granted.

Territory and Population

The Northern Territory's total area is 1,349,129 sq. km and includes adjacent islands. It has 5,100 km of mainland coastline and 2,100 km of coast around the islands. The greater part of the interior consists of a tableland with excellent pasturage. The southern part is generally sandy and has a small rainfall.

The 2011 census population was 211,945 (2006, 192,898). The capital, seat of government and principal port is Darwin, on the north coast; 2011 census population, 120,586. Other main areas of population (2011 census, Local Government Areas) are Palmerston (27,703); Alice Springs (25,186); and Katherine (9,187). There are also a number of large self-contained Aboriginal communities. People identifying themselves as indigenous numbered 56,776 at the 2011 census.

Social Statistics

2014 totals: births, 4,026; deaths, 1,168; marriages, 820; divorces, 366. Infant mortality rate per 1,000 live births, 5·2. Life expectancy, 2014: 75·4 years for males and 78·9 for females. The annual rates per 1,000 population in 2014 were: births, 16·5; deaths, 4·8; marriages, 3·3; divorces, 1·5.

Climate

See AUSTRALIA: Climate.

The highest temperature ever recorded in the NT was 118·9°F (48·3°C) at Finke in 1960, while the lowest recorded temperature was 18·5°F (–7·5°C) at Alice Springs in 1976.

Constitution and Government

The Northern Territory (Self-Government) Act 1978 established the Northern Territory as a body politic as from 1 July 1978, with Ministers having control over and responsibility for Territory finances and the administration of the functions of government as specified by the Federal government. Regulations have been made conferring executive authority for the bulk of administrative functions.

The Northern Territory has federal representation, electing one member to the House of Representatives and two members to the Senate.

The *Legislative Assembly* has 25 members, directly elected for a period of four years. The *Administrator* (Vicki O'Halloran) appoints Ministers on the advice of the Leader of the majority party.

Recent Elections

In parliamentary elections held on 27 Aug. 2016 the Australian Labor Party won 18 seats against two for the Country Liberal Party. Five independents were elected. Turnout was 73·7%.

Current Government

Administrator: Vicki O'Halloran.

The Labor ministry was as follows in March 2019:

Chief Minister, Minister for Northern Australia, and Trade and Major Projects, Business and Innovation, Defence Jobs and Veterans' Affairs, Treaty, and Children: Michael Gunner.

Deputy Chief Minister, Treasurer, and Minister for Police, Fire and Emergency Services, and Multicultural Affairs: Nicole Manison. *Attorney-General, and Minister for Justice, Health, Disabilities, and the Arafura Games:* Natasha Fyles. *Local Government, Housing and Community Development, and Public Employment:* Gerald McCarthy. *Tourism, Sport and Culture, and Corporate and Information Services:* Lauren Moss. *Environment and Natural Resources, Infrastructure, Planning and Logistics, and Climate Change:* Eva Lawler. *Territory Families, and Renewables, Energy and Essential Services:* Dale Wakefield. *Education, Aboriginal Affairs, and Workforce Training:* Selena Uibo. *Primary Industry and Resources:* Paul Kirby.

NT Government Website: http://www.nt.gov.au

Economy

Budget

In 2013–14 general government revenue totalled $A4,925m. of which $A3,626m. current grants and $A242m. sales of goods and services.

Expenditure in 2013–14 totalled \$A5,126m. including \$A1,937m. employee benefits expense and \$A804m. current grants.

Banking and Finance

According to the Australian Prudential Regulation Authority, as at 30 June 2006 there were seven authorized banks with 39 branches; and six credit unions with 24 branches.

Energy and Natural Resources

Electricity

The Power and Water Corporation supplies power to 72 indigenous and remote communities as well as the major centres. In the year ended 30 June 2009 total electricity generated was 1,525 GWh; total consumption was 1,748m. kWh. Total installed capacity at 30 June 2009 was 473 MW.

Oil and Gas

The Timor Sea is a petroleum producing province with five fields and more than 22m. cu. ft of known gas reserves. Gas is currently supplied from the Palm Valley and Mereenie fields in the onshore Amadeus Basin to the Channel Island Power Station in Darwin via one of Australia's longest onshore gas pipelines. The estimated total value of oil and gas production in 2009–10 was \$A2,401·4m., a decrease of \$A64·4m. on 2008–09. The Northern Territory produced 1,789 megalitres of crude oil and 509m. cu. metres of natural gas in 2006–07.

Minerals

Mining is the major contributor to the Territory's economy. Compared to 2005–06 the overall value of production in the mining industry rose by 51·2% in 2006–07. Value of major mineral commodities production in 2006–07 (in \$A1m.): manganese, 982; zinc/lead concentrate, 566; alumina, 483; gold, 421; uranium oxide, 273; bauxite, 167; crushed rock, 13.

Agriculture

In the year ending June 2007 there were 640 agricultural establishments with a total area under holding of 61·2m. ha. Gross value of agricultural production in the year ending June 2007 rose by 21·8% to \$A373m. Beef cattle production constitutes the largest farming industry. Total value of livestock slaughter and products in the year ending June 2007 was \$A243m., an increase of 8·4% on the previous year. In the same year fruit production totalled (in tonnes): mangoes, 13,937; bananas, 1,701; table grapes, 1,327. Estimated value of the Northern Territory crocodile industry in 2010–11 was \$A10·1m. with 64,835 kg of meat produced.

Forestry

In 2006 there were 27m. ha. of native forest, accounting for 20·2% of the Territory's total land area. As at June 2006 the total native forest cover consisted of 406,000 ha. closed forest, 7,139,000 ha. open forest and 25,290,000 ha. woodland. Total area of plantation forest was 26,000 ha., consisting mainly of softwoods. Hardwood plantations of fast-growing Acacia Mangium have been established on the Tiwi Islands for the production of woodchip for paper pulp. In addition, a number of operations for the production of sandalwood oil and neem products have been established near Batchelor.

Fisheries

Estimated total fisheries production in 2005–06 came to 8,257 tonnes with a gross value of \$A98·0m. In the same year, aquaculture had a gross value of \$A26·0m.

Industry

In the year ended 30 June 2007 the sales and service income generated by manufacturing industry was \$A2,765m.; 4,634 persons were employed and salaries totalled \$A283m. In Nov. 2006, 15,300 persons were employed in the wholesale and retail trade.

Labour

The labour force totalled 104,700 in Jan. 2007, of whom 102,100 were employed. The unemployment rate was 2·5%, down from 6·4% in Jan. 2006. The average weekly wage in Nov. 2006 was \$A847·90 (males \$A975·50, females \$A724·80).

International Trade

Imports and Exports

In 2009–10 foreign merchandise imports were valued at \$A3,051m.; exports at \$A4,980m. Major sources of imports for 2009–10 (figures in \$A1m.): Singapore, 550; Kuwait, 331; Japan, 169; USA, 131; Thailand, 93. Major export destinations (figures in \$A1m.): Japan, 1,952; China, 1,225; USA, 446; Indonesia, 339; Oman, 187. Principal commodity imports in 2009–10 were (with values in \$A1m.): natural gas, 1,219; refined petroleum, 529; non-electric engines and motors, 138. Principal exports (with values in \$A1m.): natural gas, 1,771; manganese ores and concentrates, 902; zinc ores and concentrates, 235.

Communications

Roads

In 2007 there were an estimated 22,187 km of roads. The number of registered motor vehicles (excluding tractors and trailers) at 31 March 2006 was 114,015, including 73,302 passenger vehicles, 28,872 light commercial vehicles, 4,725 trucks, 2,989 buses and 3,950 motorcycles. There were 75 road accident fatalities in 2008. The death rate on the Northern Territory's roads in 2008 was, at 34·1 per 100,000 people, nearly five times higher than the rate for Australia as a whole.

Rail

In 1980 Alice Springs was linked to the Trans-continental network by a standard (1,435 mm) gauge railway to Tarcoola in South Australia (830 km). A 1,410 km standard gauge line operates between Darwin and Alice Springs. This \$A1·3bn. AustralAsia Railway project links Darwin and Adelaide. The first train to complete the journey of 1,860 miles arrived in Darwin on 3 Feb. 2004.

Civil Aviation

Darwin and most regional centres in the Territory are serviced by daily flights to all State capitals and major cities. In 2010 there were direct international services connecting Darwin to Indonesia (Bali), Singapore, Timor-Leste and Vietnam. In 2009–10 Darwin airport handled 1,569,007 passengers (1,191,208 on domestic airlines); and Alice Springs 681,295 passengers (681,255 domestic).

Shipping

In 2008–09, 1,578 commercial vessels called at Northern Territory ports. General cargo imported in 2008–09 was 333,249 mass tonnes and general cargo exported was 247,324 mass tonnes.

Social Institutions

Justice

Voluntary euthanasia for the terminally ill was legalized in 1995 but the law was overturned by the Federal Senate on 24 March 1997. The first person to have recourse to legalized euthanasia died on 22 Sept. 1996.

Police personnel (sworn and unsworn) at 30 June 2007, 1,703 including 78 Aboriginal community police officers. In 2006–07 the Territory had two prisons with a daily average of 833 prisoners held.

Education

Education is compulsory from the age of six to 15 years. There were (Aug. 2006) 28,506 full-time students enrolled in 151 government schools and 9,074 enrolled in 35 non-government schools. Teaching staff in government and non-government schools totalled 3,205. The proportion of Indigenous students in the Territory is high, comprising 38·9% of all primary and secondary students at Aug. 2006. Bilingual programmes operate in some Aboriginal communities where traditional Aboriginal culture prevails.

The Northern Territory University (NTU), founded in 1989 by amalgamating the existing University College of the Northern Territory and the Darwin Institute of Technology, joined with Alice Springs's Centralian College in 2004 to form the Charles Darwin University. In 2011, 8,744 students were enrolled in higher education courses of whom 4·7% were identified as Indigenous. The Batchelor Institute of Indigenous Tertiary Education, which provides higher and vocational education and training for Aboriginal and Torres Straits Islanders, had 355 students enrolled in higher education courses in 2011 and 2,550 in Vocational Education and Training

(VET) courses. In 2010–11 there were 24,054 enrolments in the Northern Territory's Vocational Education and Training activities.

Health
In 2006–07 there were five public hospitals with a total of 600 beds and one private hospital. Community health services are provided from urban and rural Health Centres including mobile units. Remote communities are served by resident nursing staff, aboriginal health workers and in larger communities, resident GPs. Emergency services are supported by the Aerial Medical Services throughout the Territory.

Welfare
Total social security and welfare expenditure for 2006–07 was $A175,331m. In the same year payments for welfare services for the aged totalled $A17,276m. and disability welfare services expenditure was $A50,811m.

Religion
Religious affiliation at the 2006 census: Roman Catholic, 21·1%; Anglican, 12·3%; Uniting Church, 7·0%; Lutheran, 3·9%; Baptist, 2·4%; other Christian, 8·0%; non-Christians, 5·1%; no religion, 23·1%; not stated, 17·1%.

Culture

Tourism
In 2009 a total of 1·4m. people visited the Northern Territory, a decrease of 1·9% from the previous year. In the same year tourist expenditure was $A1·8bn. Tourism is the second largest revenue earner after the mining industry.

New South Wales

Key Historical Events
The name New South Wales was applied to the entire east coast of Australia when Capt. James Cook claimed the land for the British Crown on 23 Aug. 1770. The separate colonies of Tasmania, South Australia, Victoria and Queensland were proclaimed in the 19th century. In 1911 and 1915 the Australian Capital Territory around Canberra and Jervis Bay was ceded to the Commonwealth. New South Wales was thus gradually reduced to its present area. The first settlement was made at Port Jackson in 1788 as a penal settlement. A partially elective council was established in 1843 and responsible government in 1856.

Gold discoveries from 1851 brought an influx of immigrants, and responsible government was at first unstable, with seven ministries holding office in the five years after 1856. Bitter conflict arose from land laws enacted in 1861. Lack of transport hampered agricultural expansion.

New South Wales federated with the other Australian states to form the Commonwealth of Australia in 1901.

Territory and Population
New South Wales (NSW) is situated between the 29th and 38th parallels of S. lat. and 141st and 154th meridians of E. long., and comprises 800,642 sq. km, inclusive of Lord Howe Island, 17 sq. km, but exclusive of the Australian Capital Territory (2,352 sq. km) and 67 sq. km at Jervis Bay.

The population at the 2011 census was 6,917,658 (6,549,177 at 2006 census), of which 3,508,780 were female. In 2011 there were nine people per sq. km. Although NSW comprises only 10·4% of the total area of Australia, 33·0% of the Australian population live there. During the year ended June 2010, 42,300 permanent settlers arrived in New South Wales (47,000 in the year to June 2009).

The population of Sydney at the 2011 census was 4,391,674. Outside of Sydney the resident populations of the large sub-state regions at the 2011 census were: Newcastle and Lake Macquarie, 342,605; Illawarra, 275,983; Hunter Valley excluding Newcastle, 243,246; Richmond-Tweed, 227,619; Capital Region, 207,822; Mid North Coast, 201,110; Central West, 196,742; New England and North West, 176,194; Riverina, 150,120; Southern Highlands and Shoalhaven, 137,007; Coffs Harbour-Grafton, 130,604; Far West and Orana, 113,591; Murray, 110,317.

Lord Howe Island, 31° 33' 4" S., 159° 4' 26" E., which is part of New South Wales, is situated about 702 km northeast of Sydney; area, 1,654 ha., of which only about 120 ha. are arable; resident population (2011 census), 360 (185 females). The Island, which was discovered in 1788, is of volcanic origin. Mount Gower, the highest point, reaches a height of 866 metres.

The Lord Howe Island Board manages the affairs of the Island and supervises the Kentia palm-seed industry.

Social Statistics
Statistics for calendar years:

	Live births	Deaths	Marriages	Divorces
2011	99,054	50,661	41,720	13,917
2012	98,508	49,314	40,981	14,607
2013	100,462	50,396	40,373	13,820
2014	91,074	52,320	41,277	13,706

The annual rates per 1,000 of mean estimated resident population in 2014 were: births, 12·1; deaths, 7·0; marriages, 5·5; divorces, 1·8; infant mortality, 3·5 per 1,000 live births. Expectation of life in 2014: males, 80·2 years; females, 84·4.

Climate
See AUSTRALIA: Climate.

Constitution and Government
Within the State there are three levels of government: the Commonwealth government, with authority derived from a written constitution; the State government with residual powers; the local government authorities with powers based upon a State Act of Parliament, operating within incorporated areas extending over almost 90% of the State.

The Constitution of New South Wales is drawn from several diverse sources; certain Imperial statutes such as the Commonwealth of Australia Constitution Act (1900); the Australian States Constitution Act (1907); an element of inherited English law; amendments to the Commonwealth of Australia Constitution Act; the (State) Constitution Act; the Australia Acts of 1986; the Constitution (Amendment) Act 1987 and certain other State Statutes; numerous legal decisions; and a large amount of English and local convention.

The Parliament of New South Wales may legislate for the peace, welfare and good governance of the State in all matters not specifically reserved to the Commonwealth government. The State Legislature consists of the Sovereign, represented by the Governor, and two Houses of Parliament, the *Legislative Council* (upper house) and the *Legislative Assembly* (lower house). Australian citizens aged 18 and over, and other British subjects who were enrolled prior to 26 Jan. 1984, men and women aged 18 years and over, are entitled to the franchise. Enrolment and voting is compulsory. The optional preferential method of voting is used for both houses. The Legislative Council has 42 members elected for a term of office equivalent to two terms of the Legislative Assembly, with 21 members retiring at the same time as the Legislative Assembly elections. The whole State constitutes a single electoral district. The Legislative Assembly has 93 members elected in single-seat electoral districts for a maximum period of four years.

Recent Elections
In elections held on 28 March 2015 the ruling Liberal–National Coalition won 54 of 93 seats (the Liberals 37 and the Nationals 17), the Australian Labor Party 34, the Greens 3 and ind. 2.

Current Government
Governor: David Hurley, AC, DSC.

The New South Wales Liberal–National ministry was as follows in March 2019:

Premier: Gladys Berekljan (b. 1970).

Deputy Premier, and Minister for Regional New South Wales, Skills, and Small Business: John Barilaro. *Treasurer, and Minister for Industrial Relations:* Dominic Perrottet. *Primary Industries, Regional Water, and Trade and Industry:* Niall Blair. *Resources, Energy and Utilities, and the Arts:* Don Harwin. *Planning, and Housing:* Anthony Roberts. *Transport and Infrastructure:* Andrew Constance. *Health, and Medical Research:* Brad Hazzard. *Education:* Rob Stokes. *Attorney General:* Mark Speakman. *Police, and Emergency Services:* Troy Grant. *Finance, Services and Property:* Victor Dominello. *Family and Community Services, Social Housing, and Prevention of Domestic Violence and Sexual Assault:* Pru Goward. *Lands and Forestry, and Racing:* Paul Toole. *Counter Terrorism, Corrections, and*

Veterans' Affairs: David Elliott. *Environment, Local Government, and Heritage:* Gabrielle Upton. *Western Sydney, WestConnex, and Sport:* Stuart Ayres. *Roads, Maritime and Freight:* Melinda Pavey. *Innovation and Better Regulation:* Matt Kean. *Tourism and Major Events:* Adam Marshall. *Mental Health, Women, and Ageing:* Tanya Davies. *Early Childhood Education, and Aboriginal Affairs:* Sarah Mitchell. *Multiculturalism, and Disability Services:* Ray Williams.

NSW Government Website: http://www.nsw.gov.au

Economy

Budget
In 2006–07 general government expenses by the State totalled $A42,892m.; revenue was $A42,196m. In the same year State government revenue from taxes amounted to $A16,719m.; grants and subsidies totalled $A17,625m.

Performance
In 2012–13 the gross state product of New South Wales represented 31·3% of Australia's total GDP.

Banking and Finance
According to the Australian Prudential Regulation Authority, as at 30 June 2006 there were 27 authorized banks with 1,525 branches; seven building societies with 153 branches; and 87 credit unions with 397 branches.

Energy and Natural Resources

Electricity
In 2008–09, 79,750 GWh were produced, of which 7·2% was from renewable sources. Black coal is the main fuel source for electricity generation in the state, producing 88·8% of the total output in 2008–09. Total installed capacity in 2010 was around 18,000 MW.

Oil and Gas
No natural gas is produced in NSW. Almost all gas is imported from the Moomba field in South Australia plus, since 2001, a small amount from Bass Strait.

Minerals
New South Wales contains extensive mineral deposits. In 2008–09 there were 60 coal mines directly employing 16,914 people. The value of metallic minerals produced in 2008–09 was $A2·59bn.; construction materials, $A346m. Output of principal products, 2008–09 (in tonnes): coal, 182·0m.; copper, 158,000; zinc, 122,000; lead, 73,000; zircon, 56,000; silver, 71; gold, 28.

Agriculture
NSW accounts for around 21% of the value of Australia's total agricultural production with a gross value of $A8,359·2m. in 2009–10. In the year ending 30 June 2010 there were 43,115 farming establishments with a total area under holding of 59m. ha. of which 6·9m. ha. were under crops.

Principal crops in 2009–10 with production in 1,000 tonnes: wheat for grain, 5,350; barley, 1,236; sorghum, 581; canola, 281. Value of crops, 2009–10, came to $A4·2bn. with wheat totalling $A1·2bn. and cotton $A453m.

The total area under vines in 2010 was 42,621 ha; wine grape production totalled 442,608 tonnes.

Orange production in 2009–10 was 192,500 tonnes (49% of the Australian total); apple production in 2007–08 was 44,900 tonnes.

2009–10 gross value of livestock products was $A1·3bn., including wool produced, $A641m.; and milk, $A522m. In the year ended 31 Aug. 2010 production (in tonnes) of beef and veal, 471,947; lamb and mutton, 133,637; pork, 63,691.

Forestry
The area of native and planted forests managed by State Forests of NSW in 2008–09 totalled 2·41m. ha.; there were 204,828 ha. of softwood and 46,483 ha. of hardwood plantation. In 2008–09, 2·66m. cu. metres of sawlogs and veneer logs were harvested.

Fisheries
Estimated total fisheries production in 2005–06 came to 27,916 tonnes with a gross value of $A143·3m. In the same year aquaculture production was an estimated 5,212 tonnes with a gross value of $A45·03m.

Industry

A wide range of manufacturing is undertaken in the Sydney area, and there are large iron and steel works near the coalfields at Newcastle and Port Kembla. Around one-third of Australian manufacturing takes place in NSW.

Manufacturing establishments' operations in the year ended 30 June 2007:

Industry	No. of persons employed (1,000)	Wages and salaries ($A1m.)	Sales and service income ($A1m.)
Food, beverages and tobacco	69·6	3,238	25,074
Primary and fabricated metal products	50·2	2,701	20,720
Chemicals, and chemical and rubber product manufacturing	28·2	1,655	12,463
Machinery and equipment	41·5	2,326	12,111
Wood and paper products	19·0	898	6,468
Transport equipment	17·4	946	4,745
Non-metallic mineral products	13·4	780	4,139
Printing, publishing and recorded media	21·9	944	4,068
Textiles, clothing, footwear and leather products	17·2	561	3,276
Petroleum and coal product manufacturing	1·9	—	—
Furniture and other manufacturing	11·0	—	—
Total manufacturing	291·3	14,712[1]	111,442[1]

[1]Although the totals include figures for both petroleum and coal product manufacturing and furniture and other manufacturing the individual figures are not available for those categories.

Labour
In 2007 the labour force totalled 3,493,200 persons, of whom 3,319,300 were employed: 476,100 in retail trade; 429,800 in property and business services; 347,300 in health and community services; 325,300 in manufacturing; 287,200 in construction; and 222,100 in education. There were 173,900 unemployed (a rate of 5·0%) in June 2007. The average weekly wage in Nov. 2005 was $A1,089·00 (males $A1,157·40, females $A973·90).

Industrial tribunals are authorized to fix minimum rates of wages and other conditions of employment. Their awards may be enforced by law, as may be industrial agreements between employers and organizations of employees, when registered.

International Trade

Imports and Exports
In 2009–10 foreign merchandise imports were valued at $A76,004m.; exports at $A31,173m. Major sources of imports for 2009–10 (figures in $A1m.): China, 18,370; USA, 8,948; Japan, 5,856; Germany, 4,134; Malaysia, 2,953. Major export destinations (figures in $A1m.): Japan, 8,306; China, 3,225; South Korea, 3,112; USA, 2,275; New Zealand, 2,191. Principal commodity imports in 2009–10 were (with values in $A1m.): medicaments (including veterinary), 6,322; telecommunications equipment and parts, 5,421; passenger motor vehicles, 4,882; computers, 4,806; crude petroleum, 3,954. Principal commodity exports (with values in $A1m.): coal, 8,460; copper ores and concentrates, 1,797; aluminium, 1,624; medicaments (including veterinary), 1,325; refined petroleum, 1,114.

Communications

Roads

At 30 June 2006 there were 183,120 km of public roads in total. The Roads and Traffic Authority of New South Wales is responsible for the administration and upkeep of major roads. In 2006 there were 20,699 km of roads under its control, comprising 4,250 km of national highways, 13,503 km of state roads and 2,946 km of regional and local roads.

The number of registered motor vehicles (excluding tractors and trailers) at 31 March 2006 was 4,268,631, including 3,395,905 passenger vehicles, 587,713 light commercial vehicles, 133,662 trucks, 20,733 buses and 122,211 motorcycles. There were 510 road accident fatalities in 2006.

Rail

Rail Corporation New South Wales (RailCorp) was formed in 2004 following a merger of the State Rail Authority and Rail Infrastructure Corporation. RailCorp owns, operates and maintains the rail tracks and related infrastructure, and provides metropolitan and long distance passenger services and access to rail freight operators. In the year ended 30 June 2009, 304·8m. passengers were carried on CityRail and 1·7m. on CountryLink. Also open for traffic are 325 km of Victorian government railways which extend over the border, 68 km of private railways (mainly in mining districts) and 53 km of Commonwealth government-owned track.

A tramway opened in Sydney in 1996. There is also a small overhead railway in the city centre.

Civil Aviation

Sydney Airport (Kingsford Smith) is the major airport in New South Wales and Australia's principal international air terminal. In 2002 it was sold to Macquarie Airports. As well as domestic flights, in 2010 there were direct international services connecting Sydney with nearly 50 destinations. In 2009–10 it handled a total of 34,462,117 passengers (21,394,601 on domestic airlines). It is also the leading airport for freight, handling 377,896 tonnes of international freight in 2009–10.

Shipping

The main ports are at Sydney, Newcastle and Port Kembla. In 2008–09, 4,664 commercial vessels called at New South Wales ports. General cargo imported in 2008–09 was 8,418,728 mass tonnes and general cargo exported was 7,177,701 mass tonnes.

Social Institutions

Justice

Legal processes may be conducted in Local Courts presided over by magistrates or in higher courts (District Court or Supreme Court) presided over by judges. There is also an appellate jurisdiction. Persons charged with more serious crimes must be tried before a higher court.

The Children's Court deals with certain matters, including care and protection cases and criminal cases, involving children under 18. There are also a number of tribunals exercising special jurisdiction, e.g. the Industrial Commission and the Compensation Court.

As at 30 June 2006 there was a daily average of 9,911 persons held in prison. Police personnel (sworn) at 30 June 2006, 14,634.

Education

The State government maintains a system of free primary and secondary education, and attendance at school is compulsory from the age of six years of age. Since Jan. 2010 it has been compulsory for young people aged 15–17 to remain in school or, by arrangement, take part in an approved education and training pathway such as an apprenticeship or traineeship. Non-government schools are subject to government inspection.

In Aug. 2006 there were 2,187 government schools with 740,415 pupils (434,366 primary, 306,049 secondary) and 51,385 teachers, and 912 non-government schools with 369,902 pupils (185,963 primary, 183,939 secondary) and 26,775 teachers. There were 297,200 students in higher education in 2005, with the largest numbers enrolled in management and commerce (29·1% of total enrolments) and society and culture (23·7%). Student enrolments in 2006: University of Sydney (founded 1850), 45,039; University of New England at Armidale (incorporated 1954), 17,854; University of New South Wales (founded 1949), 37,836; University of Newcastle (granted autonomy 1965), 22,997; University of Wollongong (founded 1951), 22,754; Macquarie University in Sydney (founded 1964), 31,660; University of Technology, Sydney, 32,708; University of Western Sydney, 35,061; Charles Sturt University, 34,261; Southern Cross University (founded 1994), 14,092. Colleges of advanced education were merged with universities in 1990. Post-school technical and further education is provided at State TAFE colleges. Enrolments in 2010 totalled 583,200.

Health

In 2006–07 there were 228 public and 173 private hospitals. In 2005–06 there were 27,918 medical practitioners, 4,358 dentists and 82,740 registered nurses.

Welfare

The number of age and disability pensions at 30 June 2007 was: age, 633,312; disability support, 226,955. There were 146,720 newstart allowance, 110,014 youth allowance and 130,038 single parent payments current at 30 June 2007.

Direct State government social welfare services are limited, for the most part, to the assistance of persons not eligible for Commonwealth government pensions or benefits, and the provision of certain forms of assistance not available from the Commonwealth government. The State also subsidizes many approved services for needy persons.

Religion

At the 2006 census 28·2% of the population were Roman Catholic and 21·8% Anglican. These two religions combined had nearly 3·3m. followers.

Culture

Tourism

In 2009, 2·7m. overseas visitors arrived for short-term visits, a 2·1% decrease on the previous year. The UK represented the major source of international visitors with 13·9%; followed by New Zealand, 13·2%; USA, 11·2%.

Queensland

Key Historical Events

Queensland was discovered by Capt. Cook in 1770. From 1778 it was part of New South Wales and was made a separate colony, with the name of Queensland, by letters patent of 8 June 1859, when responsible government was conferred. Although by 1868 gold had been discovered, wool was the colony's principal product. The first railway line was opened in 1865. Queensland federated with the other Australian states to form the Commonwealth of Australia in 1901. In 1982 Brisbane hosted the Commonwealth Games. Severe flooding in Dec. 2010 and Jan. 2011 killed at least 30 people and affected over 200,000, with damage estimated to have cost $A30bn.

Territory and Population

Queensland comprises the whole northeastern portion of the Australian continent, including the adjacent islands in the Pacific Ocean and in the Gulf of Carpentaria. Area, 1,730,648 sq. km.

At the 2011 census the population was 4,332,739 (3,904,532 at 2006 census). At the 2011 census there were 155,825 Aboriginals and Torres Strait Islanders. Statistics on birthplaces from the 2011 census are as follows: Australia, 73·7%; New Zealand, 4·4%; England, 4·1%; South Africa, 0·8%; India, 0·7%; Philippines, 0·7%.

Brisbane, the capital, had at the time of the 2011 census a resident population of 2,065,996. Outside of Brisbane the resident populations of the major large sub-state regions at the 2011 census were: Gold Coast, 507,642; Sunshine Coast, 306,909; Logan-Beaudesert, 290,430; Ipswich, 281,790; Wide Bay, 273,267; Cairns, 224,436; Townsville, 217,897.

Social Statistics

Statistics (including Aboriginals) for calendar years:

	Births	Deaths	Marriages	Divorces
2011	63,253	27,414	25,560	11,393
2012	63,837	28,300	26,276	11,317
2013	63,354	27,901	25,015	10,861
2014	63,066	28,704	24,918	10,699

The annual rates per 1,000 population in 2014 were: births, 13·4; deaths, 6·1; marriages, 5·3; divorces, 2·3. The infant mortality rate in 2014 was 4·4 per 1,000 live births. Life expectancy, 2014: 79·9 years for males, 84·2 for females.

Climate

A typical subtropical to tropical climate. High daytime temperatures during Oct. to March give a short spring and long summer. Centigrade temperatures in the hottest inland areas often exceed the high 30s before the official commencement of summer on 1 Dec. Daytime temperatures in winter are quite mild, in the low- to mid-20s. Average rainfall varies from about 150 mm in the desert in the extreme southwestern corner of the State to about 4,000 mm in parts of the sugar lands of the wet northeastern coast, the latter being the wettest part of Australia.

Constitution and Government

Queensland, formerly a portion of New South Wales, was formed into a separate colony in 1859, and responsible government was conferred. The power of making laws and imposing taxes is vested in a parliament of one house—the *Legislative Assembly*—which comprises 93 members, returned for four-year terms by a system of full-preferential voting.

Queensland elects 26 members to the Commonwealth House of Representatives.

The Elections Act 1983 provides franchise for all males and females, 18 years of age and over, qualified by six months' residence in Australia and three months in the electoral district.

Recent Elections

In Legislative Assembly elections on 25 Nov. 2017 the ruling Labor Party (ALP) won 48 seats, the Liberal National Party (LNP) 39 and Katter's Australian Party 3. The Greens, One Nation and an independent candidate won a single seat each.

Current Government

Governor of Queensland: Paul de Jersey, AC (took office on 29 July 2014).

In March 2019 the ALP administration was as follows:

Premier and Minister for Trade: Annastacia Palaszczuk.

Deputy Premier, Treasurer, and Minister for Aboriginal Affairs and Torres Strait Islander Partnerships: Jackie Trad. *Agricultural Industry Development and Fisheries:* Mark Furner. *Attorney General, and Minister for Justice:* Yvette D'Ath. *Child Safety, Youth and Women, and Prevention of Domestic and Family Violence:* Dianne Farmer. *Communities, and Disability Services and Seniors:* Coralee O'Rourke. *Education, and Industrial Relations:* Grace Grace. *Employment and Small Business, and Training and Skills Development:* Shannon Fentiman. *Environment and the Great Barrier Reef, Science, and the Arts:* Leeanne Enoch. *Fire and Emergency Services:* Craig Crawford. *Health, and Ambulance Services:* Steven Miles. *Housing and Public Works, Digital Technology, and Sport:* Mick de Brenni. *Innovation and Tourism Industry Development, and the Commonwealth Games:* Kate Jones. *Local Government, Racing, and Multicultural Affairs:* Stirling Hinchliffe. *Natural Resources, Mines and Energy:* Anthony Lynham. *Police, and Corrective Services:* Mark Ryan. *State Development, Manufacturing, Infrastructure and Planning:* Cameron Dick. *Transport and Main Roads:* Mark Bailey.

Government Website: http://www.qld.gov.au

Economy

Budget

In 2006–07 general government expenses by the state were expected to total \$A28,825m.; revenue and grants received were expected to be \$A29,070m.

Performance

Queensland's 2012–13 gross state product represented 19·1% of Australia's total GDP.

Banking and Finance

According to the Australian Prudential Regulation Authority, as at 30 June 2006 there were 16 authorized banks with 1,151 branches; six building societies with 151 branches; and 24 credit unions with 148 branches.

Energy and Natural Resources

Electricity

In 2008, 81% of electricity came from coal-fired power stations, 15% from gas and 4% from renewable energy. As at 31 Dec. 2008 total installed capacity was 12,487 MW.

Minerals

There are large reserves of coal, bauxite, gold, copper, silver, lead, zinc, nickel, phosphate rock and limestone. The state is the largest producer of black coal in Australia. Most of the coal produced comes from the Bowen Basin coalfields in central Queensland. Copper, lead, silver and zinc are mined in the northwest and the State's largest goldmines are in the north. The total value of metallic minerals in 2008–09 was \$A6·24bn. In 2008–09 there were 55 coal mines in operation producing 190·55m. tonnes of saleable coal (an increase of 5·6% on the previous year); and at 30 June 2009, 37,000 persons were employed in mining.

Agriculture

Queensland is Australia's leading beef-producing state and its chief producer of fruit and vegetables. In 2015–16 there were 18,153 agricultural businesses farming 127·6m. ha. The gross value of agricultural production in 2015–16 was \$A13·2bn. which comprised crops, \$A5·8bn.; livestock disposals, \$A6·9bn.; and livestock products, \$A0·5bn. Livestock numbered (at 30 June 2005) 11,380,000 beef cattle; 4,949,000 sheep and lambs; and 666,000 pigs. Total value of wool production, 2007–08: \$A103m.

Forestry

Of a total of 56m. ha. of forests and woodlands in 2007, 9% was in national parks, World Heritage areas and other conservation reserves, while 5% was native forests in multiple use such as timber production. Queensland plantation forests comprise around 0·4% (225,000 ha.) of the state's total forest cover and supply around 10% of Australia's wood and paper products. The forestry industry is an important part of the state's economy, employing more than 19,000 people with an annual turnover of \$A2·7bn.

Source: *Australia's Forests at a Glance 2007.* Australian Government Dept. of Agriculture, Fisheries and Forestry, Bureau of Rural Sciences publication, 2007.

Fisheries

Estimated total fisheries production in 2005–06 came to 34,417 tonnes with a gross value of \$A322·6m. In the same year aquaculture production was an estimated 5,290 tonnes with a gross value of \$A66·12m.

Industry

In the year ended 30 June 2016 wholesale trade sales and service income was \$A81,251m., retail trade \$A78,244m., construction \$A76,491m. and manufacturing \$A74,678m. Retail trade employs the most people, with 249,000 at end June 2016.

Labour

At Nov. 2006 the labour force numbered 2,163,900, of whom 2,082,900 (947,100 females) were employed. In June 2007 unemployment stood at 3·4%, down from 4·5% in June 2006. The average weekly wage in Nov. 2005 was \$A959·60 (males \$A1,014·00, females \$A866·70).

International Trade

Imports and Exports

In 2009–10 foreign merchandise imports were valued at \$A31,046m.; exports at \$A43,277m. Major sources of imports for 2009–10 (figures in \$A1m.): China, 3,629; Japan, 3,625; USA, 3,356; Papua New Guinea, 2,081; Malaysia, 1,899. Major export destinations (figures in \$A1m.): Japan, 9,763; China, 6,922; India, 5,254; South Korea, 4,724; Taiwan, 2,461. Principal commodity imports in 2009–10 were (with values in \$A1m.): crude petroleum, 4,247; passenger motor vehicles, 3,204; refined petroleum, 2,425; goods vehicles, 1,757; gold, 1,459. Principal commodity exports (with values in \$A1m.): coal, 20,527; beef, 2,492; copper, 1,444; aluminium, 1,001; lead ores and concentrates, 878.

Communications

Roads

In 2007 there were an estimated 180,818 km of roads open to the public. The number of registered motor vehicles (excluding tractors and trailers) at 31 March 2006 was 2,897,867, including 2,138,364 passenger vehicles, 520,070 light commercial vehicles, 103,967 trucks, 16,516 buses and 110,501 motorcycles. There were 360 road accident fatalities in 2007.

Rail

In July 2010 Queensland Rail was divided into two separate companies with Queensland Rail as the State government-owned corporation responsible for passenger services and QR National, which was privatized in Nov. 2010, for freight. Total length of line as at 30 June 2009 was 8,038 km. In 2008–09, 66·0m. passengers and 247·7m. tonnes of freight were carried.

Civil Aviation

Queensland is well served with a network of air services, with overseas and interstate connections. Subsidiary companies provide planes for taxi and charter work, and the Flying Doctor Service operates throughout western Queensland. In 2009–10 Brisbane handled 18,897,115 passengers (13,670,871 on domestic airlines); Cairns, 3,549,828 passengers (2,795,344 on domestic airlines). As well as domestic flights, there were direct international services in 2010 from Brisbane to Brunei, Fiji, Hong Kong, India, Indonesia, Japan, Malaysia, Nauru, New Caledonia, New Zealand, Papua New Guinea, Philippines, Samoa, Singapore, Solomon Islands, South Korea, Taiwan, Thailand, UAE, USA and Vanuatu, and from Cairns to Hong Kong, Guam, Japan, New Zealand, Papua New Guinea and Singapore. The number of aircraft registered at 31 Dec. 2005 was 2,715.

Shipping

Queensland has 14 modern trading ports, two community ports and a number of non-trading ports. In 2008–09 general cargo imported through Queensland ports was 5,152,027 mass tonnes and general cargo exported was 5,296,748 mass tonnes. There were 6,553 commercial ship calls during 2008–09.

Social Institutions

Justice

Justice is administered by Higher Courts (Supreme and District), Magistrates' Courts and Children's Courts. The Supreme Court comprises the Chief Justice and 21 judges; the District Courts, 34 district court judges. Stipendiary magistrates preside over the Magistrates' and Children's Courts, except in the smaller centres, where justices of the peace officiate. A parole board may recommend prisoners for release.

Total police personnel (sworn and unsworn) at 30 June 2007 was 13,548. As at 30 June 2005 the average daily number of prisoners stood at 5,354.

Education

Education is compulsory between the ages of six and 16 years and is provided free in government schools. From 2008 students aged 15–17 must remain in school or, by arrangement, take part in an approved education and training pathway such as an apprenticeship or traineeship.

Primary and secondary education comprises 12 years of full-time formal schooling, and is provided by both the government and non-government sectors. In Aug. 2008 the State administered 1,250 schools with 308,771 primary students and 171,079 secondary students. In 2008 there were 40,189 teachers in government schools. There were 463 private schools in Aug. 2008 with 123,795 primary students and 102,817 secondary students. Educational programmes at private schools were provided by 17,320 teachers in 2008. In 2010 there were 303,000 subject enrolments in Vocational Education and Training activities. The one private and eight publicly-funded universities had approximately 190,000 full-time students in 2007.

Health

In 2006–07 there were 173 public acute hospitals and four public psychiatric hospitals. There were 51 private free-standing day hospital facilities and 57 private acute and psychiatric hospitals in 2006–07. In 2009 the percentage of Queensland adults considered overweight or obese rose to 55·3% of the State's population.

Welfare

Welfare institutions providing shelter and social care for the aged, people with a disability and children are maintained or assisted by the State. A child health service is provided throughout the State. Age, invalid, widows', disability and war service pensions, family allowances, and unemployment and sickness benefits are paid by the Federal government. The number of age and disability pensions at 30 June 2007 was: age, 344,648; disability support, 135,863. There were 75,144 newstart allowance, 58,024 youth allowance and 85,710 single parent payments current at 30 June 2007.

Religion

Religious affiliation at the 2006 census: Roman Catholic, 24·0%; Anglican, 20·4%; Uniting Church, 7·2%; Presbyterian and Reformed, 3·7%; Lutheran, 2·0%; Baptist, 1·9%; other Christian, 7·2%; non-Christian, 3·3%; no religion, 18·6%; not stated, 11·7%.

Culture

Tourism

Overseas visitors to Queensland in the year ending March 2011 totalled 2·0m., the main source being from New Zealand (accounting for 20·0% of tourists), the UK (11·0%), Japan (10·4%) and China (9·8%).

South Australia

Key Historical Events

South Australia was surveyed by Tasman in 1644 and charted by Flinders in 1802. It was made into a British province by letters of patent of Feb. 1836, and a partially elective legislative council was established in 1851. From 6 July 1863 the Northern Territory was placed under the jurisdiction of South Australia until the establishment of the Commonwealth of Australia in 1911.

Territory and Population

The total area of South Australia is 983,482 sq. km. The settled part is divided into counties and hundreds. There are 49 counties proclaimed, and 535 hundreds, covering 23m. ha., of which 19m. ha. are occupied. Outside this area there are extensive pastoral districts, covering 76m. ha., 49m. of which are under pastoral leases.

The 2011 census population was 1,596,572 (2006 census: 1,514,337). There were a total of 30,431 Aboriginal and Torres Strait Islanders at the 2011 census.

At the 2011 census Adelaide had a population of 1,225,235 persons (76·7% of South Australia's total population). Urban centres outside this area at the 2011 census include: Mount Gambier, 27,755; Whyalla, 21,991; Murray Bridge, 16,708; Port Lincoln, 15,221; Port Pirie, 14,043; Port Augusta, 13,658.

Social Statistics

Statistics for calendar years:

	Live Births	Deaths	Marriages	Divorces
2011	19,892	12,665	8,115	3,506
2012	20,433	13,178	7,697	3,511
2013	20,090	12,804	8,353	3,343
2014	20,384	13,262	7,973	3,211

The rates per 1,000 population in 2014 were: births, 12·1; deaths, 7·9; marriages, 4·7; divorces, 1·9. The infant mortality rate in 2014 was 2·6 per 1,000 live births. Life expectancy for 2014 was 80·1 years for men and 84·3 years for women.

Climate

Most of the state has an arid or semi-arid climate, with as little as 150 mm of rainfall per annum in desert areas. Oodnadatta, a town north of Adelaide on the outskirts of the Simpson Desert, recorded Australia's highest reliably-measured temperature at 50·7°C (123·3°F) on 2 Jan. 1960.

Constitution and Government

The present Constitution dates from 24 Oct. 1856. It vests the legislative power in an elected Parliament, consisting of a *Legislative Council* and a *House of Assembly*. The former is composed of 22 members. Eleven members are elected at alternate elections for a term of at least six years and are elected on the basis of preferential proportional representation with the State as one multi-member electorate. The House of Assembly consists of 47 members elected by a preferential system of voting for the term of a Parliament (four years). Election of members of both Houses takes place by secret ballot. Voting is compulsory for those on the Electoral Roll. The qualifications of an elector are to be an Australian citizen, or a British subject who was, at some time within the period of three months commencing on 26 Oct. 1983, enrolled under the Repealed Act as an Assembly elector or enrolled on an electoral roll maintained under the Commonwealth or a Commonwealth

Territory, must be at least 18 years of age and have lived in the subdivision for which the person is enrolled for at least one month. By the Constitution Act Amendment Act 1894 the franchise was extended to women, who voted for the first time at the general election of 25 April 1896. Certain persons are ineligible for election to either House.

The executive power is vested in a Governor appointed by the Crown and an Executive Council, consisting of the Governor and the Ministers of the Crown. The Governor has the power to dissolve the House of Assembly but not the Legislative Council, unless that Chamber has twice consecutively with an election intervening defeated the same or substantially the same bill passed in the House of Assembly by an absolute majority.

Recent Elections

The House of Assembly, elected on 17 March 2018, consisted of the following members: Liberal Party (LP), 25; Australian Labor Party (ALP), 19; Independent (ind.), 3.

Current Government

Governor: Hieu Van Le.

In March 2019 the Liberal administration comprised:

Premier: Steven Marshall.

Deputy Premier, and Attorney General: Vickie Chapman. *Minister for Child Protection:* Rachel Sanderson. *Education:* John Gardner. *Energy and Mining:* Dan van Holst Pellekaan. *Environment and Water:* David Speirs. *Health and Wellbeing:* Stephen Wade. *Human Services:* Michelle Lensink. *Industry and Skills:* David Pisoni. *Police, Emergency Services and Correctional Services, and Recreation, Sport and Racing:* Corey Wingard. *Primary Industries and Regional Development:* Tim Whetstone. *Trade, Tourism and Investment:* David Ridgway. *Transport, Infrastructure and Local Government, and Planning:* Stephan Knoll. *Treasurer:* Robert Lucas.

SA Government Website: http://www.sa.gov.au

Economy

Budget

Estimated government sector revenue and expenses ($A1m.):

	2004–05	*2005–06*	*2006–07*
Revenue	10,592	11,088	11,264
Expenditure	10,368	10,942	11,173

In 2006–07 State government revenue from taxes amounted to $A3,086m.; grants and subsidies totalled $A5,792m.

Performance

South Australia's 2012–13 gross state product represented 6·3% of Australia's total GDP.

Banking and Finance

According to the Australian Prudential Regulation Authority, as at 30 June 2006 there were 14 authorized banks with 439 branches; one building society with one branch; and 14 credit unions with 75 branches.

Energy and Natural Resources

Electricity

In 2010 installed capacity was 4,508 MW. In 2008–09 electricity generated from renewable sources constituted 14·8% of electricity production and 16·4% of consumption.

Minerals

The principal metallic minerals produced are copper, iron ore, uranium oxide, gold and silver. The total value of metallic minerals produced in 2005–06 was $A2,077m. including copper, $A1,444m.; uranium oxide, $A288m.; iron ore, $A191m. Total value of opal production (2005–06), $A25·1m. In 2005–06 there were 4,141 persons employed in mining.

Agriculture

In 2006–07 there were 15,835 establishments mainly engaged in agriculture with a total area under holding of 50·1m. ha. of which 4·4m. ha. were under crops. The gross value of agricultural production in 2006–07 was $A3·7bn.

Total value of wool production, $315·2m. Value of chief crops in 2006–07: wheat, $A341m.; barley, $A226m.; potatoes, $A179m. Production of grapes was 586,000 tonnes with virtually all being used for winemaking (vineyards' total area, 73,407 ha., including 3,548 ha. not yet bearing). Fruit culture is extensive with citrus and orchard fruits. The most valuable vegetable crops are potatoes, onions and carrots.

Livestock, 2006–07: sheep and lambs, 11,641,000; cattle, 1,242,000; pigs, 360,000. Gross value of livestock slaughtered, 2006–07, $A895·0m.

Forestry

Total area of plantations at 31 Dec. 2006 totalled 172,000 ha. Production of sawn timber in 2005–06 was 493,900 cu. metres.

Fisheries

Estimated total fisheries production in 2005–06 came to 69,400 tonnes with a gross value of $A466·8m. In the same year aquaculture production was an estimated 16,935 tonnes with a gross value of $A214·5m.

Industry

Total sales and service income in manufacturing industry in 2015–16 was $A22,531m., including $A4,133m. from food product manufacturing, $A3,241m. from transport equipment manufacturing and $A2,783m. from beverage and tobacco product manufacturing. In the same year there were 67,000 persons employed in the manufacturing sector (including 17,100 in food product manufacturing, 7,700 in transport equipment manufacturing and 7,300 in beverage and tobacco product manufacturing) with wages and salaries totalling $A4,187m.

Labour

In Aug. 2007 the labour force stood at 799,700. There were 38,100 unemployed in June 2007, a rate of 4·8%. The average weekly wage in Nov. 2005 was $A950·60 (males $A982·40, females $A891·00).

International Trade

Imports and Exports

In 2009–10 foreign merchandise imports were valued at $A6,446m.; exports at $A8,135m. Major sources of imports for 2009–10 were (figures in $A1m.): Singapore, 977; China, 964; Japan, 756; Thailand, 512; USA, 504. Major export destinations (figures in $A1m.): China, 1,251; USA, 956; Japan, 680; India, 599; UK, 531. Principal commodity imports in 2009–10 were (with values in $A1m.): refined petroleum, 972; passenger motor vehicles, 609; goods vehicles, 303; vehicle parts and accessories, 228. Principal commodity exports (with values in $A1m.): alcoholic beverages, 1,344; iron ore and concentrates, 624; copper ores and concentrates, 619; copper, 560.

Communications

Roads

In 2007 there were an estimated 92,027 km of roads. The number of registered motor vehicles (excluding tractors and trailers) at 31 March 2006 was 1,137,957, including 915,059 passenger vehicles, 145,643 light commercial vehicles, 34,994 trucks, 4,413 buses and 33,772 motorcycles. In 2007 there were 124 road accident fatalities.

Rail

In Aug. 1997 the passenger operations of Australian National Railways were sold to Great Southern Railway and the freight operations to Australian Southern Railroad. In 2012 there were 3,899 route-km of open railway. TransAdelaide operates 120 km of railway in the metropolitan area of Adelaide. In 2009–10, 20m. tonnes of freight were carried.

There is a tramway in Adelaide that runs from the city centre to the coast. A joint South Australia and Northern Territory project, The AustralAsia Rail Project between Alice Springs and Darwin, carried its first passenger train in Feb. 2004.

Civil Aviation

The main airport is Adelaide International Airport, which handled 7,015,509 passengers (5,993,091 on domestic airlines) in 2009–10. In 2010 there were direct international services to China (Hong Kong), Fiji, Indonesia (Bali), Malaysia, New Zealand and Singapore.

Shipping

There are ten state and five private deep-sea ports. In 2008–09, 1,501 commercial vessels arrived in South Australia. General cargo imported in

2008–09 was 1,090,330 mass tonnes and general cargo exported was 2,233,279 mass tonnes.

Social Institutions

Justice

There is a Supreme Court, which incorporates admiralty, civil, criminal, land and valuation, and testamentary jurisdiction; district criminal courts, which have jurisdiction in many indictable offences; and magistrates courts, which include the Youth Court. Circuit courts are held at several places. At 30 June 2009 the police force numbered 5,762. The prison population at 30 June 2013 was 2,266.

Education

Education is compulsory for children between the ages of six and 16 years although most children are enrolled at age five or soon after. Since Jan. 2009 it has been compulsory for young people to remain in full-time education or training until they reach the age of 17. Primary and secondary education at government schools is secular and free. In March 2006 there were 805 schools operating, of which 602 were government and 203 non-government schools. In that year there were 107,611 children in government and 49,767 in non-government primary schools, and 63,576 children in government and 35,424 in non-government secondary schools. In 2010 there were 123,900 enrolments in Vocational Education and Training activities. There were 32,266 students enrolled at the University of South Australia in 2005; University of Adelaide, 19,224; and Flinders University of South Australia, 15,110.

Health

In 2006–07 there were 79 public hospitals and 54 private hospitals. Beds available in public and private hospitals totalled 7,188.

Welfare

The number of age and disability pensions at 30 June 2007 was: age, 178,184; disability support, 68,159. There were 37,133 newstart allowance, 28,176 youth allowance and 31,923 single parent payments current at 30 June 2007.

Religion

Religious affiliation at the 2006 census: Catholic, 305,205; Anglican, 207,715; Uniting Church, 151,553; Lutheran, 71,251; Orthodox, 44,912; Baptist, 26,146; Presbyterian and Reformed, 21,030; other Christians, 78,252; non-Christians, 59,557; no religion, 367,161; not stated, 181,555.

Culture

Tourism

In the year ended 30 June 2007 international visitors totalled 375,500 (around 48% from Europe), an increase of 8·5% on the previous year. At 30 June 2007 there were 253 hotels, motels, guest houses and serviced apartments with 11,547 rooms.

Tasmania

Key Historical Events

Abel Janszoon Tasman discovered Van Diemen's Land (Tasmania) on 24 Nov. 1642. The island became a British settlement in 1803 as a dependency of New South Wales. In 1825 its connection with New South Wales was terminated and in 1851 a partially elected Legislative Council was established. In 1856 a fully responsible government was inaugurated. On 1 Jan. 1901 Tasmania was federated with the other Australian states into the Commonwealth of Australia.

Territory and Population

Tasmania is a group of islands separated from the mainland by Bass Strait with an area (including islands) of 68,401 sq. km, of which 63,447 sq. km form the area of the main island. The population at the 2011 census was 495,354 (476,481 at the 2006 census), including 414,261 born in Australia, 19,470 in England and 4,927 in New Zealand.

The largest cities and towns (with populations at the 2011 census) are: Hobart (211,656), Launceston (79,046), Devonport (43,224) and Burnie (17,334).

Social Statistics

Statistics for calendar years:

	Births	Deaths	Marriages	Divorces
2011	6,608	4,245	2,329	1,096
2012	6,168	4,459	2,913	1,161
2013	6,049	4,444	2,400	972
2014	5,935	4,476	2,526	1,009

The annual rates per 1,000 of the mean resident population in 2014 were: births, 11·5; deaths, 8·7; marriages, 4·9; divorces, 2·0. Infant mortality rate, 2014, 5·2 per 1,000 live births. Expectation of life, 2014: males, 78·8 years; females, 82·5 years.

Climate

Mostly a temperate maritime climate. The prevailing westerly airstream leads to a west coast and highlands that are cool, wet and cloudy, and an east coast and lowlands that are milder, drier and sunnier.

Constitution and Government

Parliament consists of the Governor, the *Legislative Council* and the *House of Assembly*. The Council has 15 members, elected by adults with six months' residence. Members sit for six years, with either two or three retiring annually. There is no power to dissolve the Council. The House of Assembly has 25 members; the maximum term for the House of Assembly is four years. Women received the right to vote in 1903. Proportional representation was adopted in 1907, the method now being the single transferable vote in five member constituencies.

A Minister must have a seat in one of the two Houses.

Recent Elections

At the elections of 3 March 2018 the ruling Liberal Party won 13 seats in the House of Assembly, the Australian Labor Party 10 and the Tasmanian Greens 2.

Current Government

Governor: Kate Warner.

In March 2019 the Liberal government comprised:

Premier, and Minister for Tourism, Hospitality and Events, Heritage, Trade, and Parks: Will Hodgman (took office on 31 March 2014).

Deputy Premier, and Minister for Education and Training, Infrastructure, and Advanced Manufacturing and Defence Industries: Jeremy Rockliff.

Treasurer, and Minister for State Growth, and Local Government: Peter Gutwein. *Minister for Health, Police, Fire and Emergency Management, and Science and Technology:* Michael Ferguson. *Attorney General, and Minister for Racing, Justice, Corrections, the Arts, and the Environment:* Elise Archer. *Sport and Recreation, Aboriginal Affairs, Women, and Disability Services and Community Development:* Jacquie Petrusma. *Primary Industries and Water, Energy, and Veterans' Affairs:* Guy Barnett. *Resources, and Building and Construction:* Sarah Courtney. *Human Services, Housing, and Planning:* Roger Jaensch.

TAS Government Website: http://www.tas.gov.au

Economy

Budget

Consolidated Revenue Fund receipts and expenditure, in $A1m., for financial years ending 30 June:

	2005–06	2006–07
Revenue	3,572	3,695
Expenditure	3,453	3,680

In 2007–08 estimated State government revenue from taxes amounted to $A752m.; grants and subsidies, $A2,391m.

Banking and Finance

According to the Australian Prudential Regulation Authority, as at 30 June 2006 there were seven authorized banks with 126 branches; one building society with nine branches; and three credit unions with 22 branches.

Energy and Natural Resources

Electricity

As at 30 June 2008 installed capacity was 2,510 MW; total electricity generated in 2007–08 was 8,269 GWh.

Minerals

Output of principal metallic minerals in 2010–11 was (in 1,000 tonnes): iron ore pellets, 1,840; zinc, 93; lead, 29; copper, 25; tin, 5.

Agriculture

In 2015–16 there were 2,330 agricultural businesses farming 1·5m. ha. The gross value of agricultural production in 2015–16 was $A1,485m. Principal crops in 2015–16 with production in 1,000 tonnes: potatoes, 251; onions, 59; carrots, 57; wheat, 53; apples, 31; barley, 16. Livestock, 2005–06: meat cattle, 501,000; sheep and lambs, 2,963,000; pigs, 17,000. Wool produced during 2007–08 was 9,900 tonnes and had a value of $A71·2m.

Forestry

Indigenous forests, which cover a considerable part of the State, support sawmilling and woodchipping industries. Production of sawn timber in 2005–06 was 364,300 cu. metres. Newsprint and paper are produced from native hardwoods.

Fisheries

Estimated total fisheries production in 2005–06 came to 39,298 tonnes with a gross value of $A435·0m. In the same year aquaculture production was an estimated 22,756 tonnes with a gross value of $A247·2m.

Industry

The most important manufactures for export are refined metals, woodchips, newsprint and other paper manufactures, pigments, woollen goods, fruit pulp, confectionery, butter, cheese, preserved and dried vegetables, sawn timber and processed fish products. The electrolytic-zinc works at Risdon produce zinc, sulphuric acid, superphosphate, sulphate of ammonia, cadmium and other by-products. At George Town, large-scale plants produce refined aluminium and manganese alloys. In the year ending 30 June 2006 employment in manufacturing establishments was 21,400; wages and salaries totalled $A941m.

Labour

In 2006–07 the labour force stood at 238,000. In the same year there were 13,500 unemployed, a rate of 5·7%. The average weekly wage in Nov. 2005 was $A911·40 (males $A955·90, females $A827·60).

International Trade

Imports and Exports

In 2009–10 foreign merchandise imports were valued at $A715m.; exports at $A3,005m. Major sources of imports for 2009–10 were (figures in $A1m.): Singapore, 131; USA, 72; Peru, 71; China, 67; Indonesia, 39. Major export destinations (figures in $A1m.): China, 457; Japan, 421; South Korea, 299; Taiwan, 294; Hong Kong, 284. Principal commodity imports in 2009–10 were (with values in $A1m.): refined petroleum, 114; cocoa, 65; zinc ores and concentrates, 39; animal feed, 28. Principal commodity exports (with values in $A1m.): zinc, 578; aluminium, 383; wood in chips or particles, 263; copper ores and concentrates, 201.

Communications

Roads

In 2007 there were an estimated 19,618 km of roads open to general traffic. The number of registered motor vehicles (excluding tractors and trailers) at 31 March 2006 was 374,846, including 271,365 passenger vehicles, 74,586 light commercial vehicles, 12,639 trucks, 2,219 buses and 10,488 motorcycles. In 2007 there were 45 road accident fatalities.

Rail

Tasmania's rail network, incorporating 867 km of railways, is primarily a freight system with no regular passenger services. There are some small tourist railways, notably the newly rebuilt 34 km Abt Wilderness Railway on the west coast.

Civil Aviation

Regular passenger and freight services connect the south, north and northwest of the State with the mainland. The main airports (Hobart and Launceston) handled 1,855,849 and 1,131,326 passengers respectively in 2009–10.

Shipping

There are four major commercial ports: Burnie, Devonport, Launceston and Hobart. In 2008–09, 1,905 commercial vessels called at Tasmanian ports.

General cargo imported in 2008–09 was 2,412,126 mass tonnes and general cargo exported was 2,775,214 mass tonnes. Passenger ferry services connect Tasmania with the mainland and offshore islands.

Social Institutions

Justice

The Supreme Court of Tasmania is a superior court of record, with both original and appellate jurisdiction, and consists of a Chief Justice and five puisne judges. There are also inferior civil courts with limited jurisdiction.

In 2008–09 there were 31,615 recorded offences, including 25,635 against property; 4,884 against the person; and 547 fraud and similar offences. Total police personnel (sworn and unsworn) at 30 June 2009 was 1,723. The prison population at 30 June 2013 was 483.

Education

Education is controlled by the State and is free, secular and compulsory between the ages of five and 16. Since Jan. 2008 it has been compulsory for students aged 16–17 to remain in school or, by arrangement, take part in an approved education and training pathway such as an apprenticeship or traineeship. In 2007, 212 government schools had a total enrolment of 58,926 pupils; 67 private schools had a total enrolment of 22,933 pupils.

In 2010 there were 49,600 students in Vocational Education and Training activities.

Tertiary education is offered at the University of Tasmania and the Australian Maritime College. In 2007 the University (established 1890) had 20,019 students and the Australian Maritime College 1,726 students.

Health

In 2006–07 there were 27 public hospitals with 1,353 beds and eight private hospitals with 948 beds, a total of 4·7 beds per 1,000 population.

Welfare

The number of age and disability pensions at 30 June 2007 was: age, 54,481; disability support, 24,948. There were 15,087 newstart allowance, 10,830 youth allowance and 11,631 single parent payments current at 30 June 2007.

Religion

At the census of 2006 the following numbers of adherents of the principal religions were recorded (476,481 in total): Anglican Church, 139,379; Roman Catholic, 87,784; Uniting Church, 27,507; Presbyterian and Reformed, 12,125; Baptist, 8,664; other Christian, 30,614; not stated, 58,135; no religion, 102,577; non-Christian, 9,696.

Culture

Tourism

In 2007, 815,200 adult visitors arrived in Tasmania (748,500 in 2004).

Victoria

Key Historical Events

The first permanent settlement was formed at Portland Bay in 1834. A government was established in 1839. Victoria, formerly a portion of New South Wales, was proclaimed a separate colony in 1851 at much the same time as gold was discovered. A new constitution giving responsible government to the colony was proclaimed on 23 Nov. 1855. This event had far-reaching effects, as the population increased from 76,162 in 1850 to 589,160 in 1864. By this time the impetus for the search for gold had waned and new arrivals made a living from pastoral and agricultural holdings and from the development of manufacturing industries. Victoria federated with the other Australian states to form the Commonwealth of Australia in 1901.

Territory and Population

The State has an area of 227,416 sq. km. The 2011 census population was 5,354,042 (4,932,422 at 2006 census). Victoria has the greatest proportion of people from non-English-speaking countries of any State or Territory, with (2011 census) 2·1% from India, 1·8% from China and 1·4% from Italy.

The 2011 census population of Melbourne was 3,999,982. Resident populations in 2011 of the major large sub-state regions: Latrobe-Gippsland, 255,858; Geelong, 250,651; Hume, 159,294; North West, 147,428; Ballarat,

146,235; Bendigo, 140,696; Shepparton, 124,894; Warrnambool and South West, 120,659.

Social Statistics

Statistics for calendar years:

	Births	Deaths	Marriages	Divorces
2011	71,444	36,552	28,944	12,271
2012	77,405	35,760	29,901	12,483
2013	73,969	35,916	27,584	11,663
2014	74,224	38,042	28,872	11,711

The annual rates per 1,000 of the mean resident population in 2014 were: births, 12·7; deaths, 6·5; marriages, 4·9; divorces, 2·0. Infant mortality rate, 2014, 2·8 per 1,000 live births. Expectation of life, 2014: males, 81·1 years; females, 84·7 years.

Climate

See AUSTRALIA: Climate.

Constitution and Government

Victoria, formerly a portion of New South Wales, was, in 1851, proclaimed a separate colony, with a partially elective Legislative Council. In 1856 responsible government was conferred, the legislative power being vested in a parliament consisting of a *Legislative Council* (Upper House) and a *Legislative Assembly* (Lower House). At present the Council consists of 44 members who are elected for two terms of the Assembly, with half of the seats up for renewal at each election. The Assembly consists of 88 members, elected for four years from the date of its first meeting unless sooner dissolved by the Governor. Members and electors of both Houses must be aged 18 years and Australian citizens or those British subjects previously enrolled as electors, according to the Constitution Act 1975. Single voting (one elector one vote) and compulsory preferential voting apply to Council and Assembly elections. Enrolment for Council and Assembly electors is compulsory. The Council may not initiate or amend money bills, but may suggest amendments in such bills other than amendments which would increase any charge. A bill shall not become law unless passed by both Houses.

In the exercise of the executive power the Governor is advised by a Cabinet of responsible Ministers. Section 50 of the Constitution Act 1975 provides that the number of Ministers shall not at any one time exceed 22, of whom not more than six may sit in the Legislative Council and not more than 17 may sit in the Legislative Assembly.

Recent Elections

In elections to the Legislative Assembly on 24 Nov. 2018 the Australian Labor Party (ALP) won 55 seats with 42·9% of votes cast; the Liberal Party (LP) 21 (30·4%); the National Party (NP) 6 (4·8%); the Greens 3 (10·7%); ind. 3 (6·1%). Turnout was 90·2%.

In the simultaneous elections to the Legislative Council the ALP won 18 seats, the LP 10, Derry Hinch's Justice Party 3 and the Liberal Democratic Party 2. The Animal Justice Party, Fiona Patten's Reason Party, the Greens, the NP, the Shooters, Fishers and Farmers, Sustainable Australia and Transport Matters won a single seat each.

Current Government

Governor: Linda Dessau, AM.

The Labor ministry was as follows in March 2019:

Premier: Daniel Andrews.

Deputy Premier, and Minister for Education: James Merlino.

Leader of the Government in the Legislative Council, Special Minister of State, and Minister for Aboriginal Affairs, and Priority Precincts: Gavin Jennings. *Minister for Regional Development, Agriculture, and Resources:* Jaclyn Symes. *Treasurer, and Minister for Economic Development, and Industrial Relations:* Tim Pallas. *Transport Infrastructure:* Jacinta Allan. *Crime Prevention, Corrections, Youth Justice, and Victim Support:* Ben Carroll. *Energy, Environment and Climate Change, and Solar Homes:* Lily D'Ambrosio. *Child Protection, and Disability, Ageing and Carers:* Luke Donnellan. *Mental Health, Equality, and Creative Industries:* Martin Foley. *Attorney General, and Minister for Workplace Safety:* Jill Hennessy. *Public Transport, and Ports and Freight:* Melissa Horne. *Consumer Affairs, Gaming and Liquor Regulation, and Suburban Development:* Marlene Kairouz. *Health, and Ambulance Services:* Jenny Mikakos. *Police and Emergency Services, and Water:* Lisa Neville. *Jobs, Innovation and Trade, Tourism, Sport and Major Events, and Racing:* Martin Pakula. *Roads, Road Safety and the Transport Accident Commission, and Fishing and Boating:* Jaala Pulford. *Veterans:* Robin Scott. *Local Government, and Small Business:* Adem Somyurek. *Training and Skills, and Higher Education:* Gayle Tierney. *Prevention of Family Violence, Women, and Youth:* Gabrielle Williams. *Planning, Housing and Multicultural Affairs:* Richard Wynne. *Cabinet Secretary:* Mary-Anne Thomas.

VIC Government Website: http://www.vic.gov.au

Economy

Budget

In 2007–08 general government expenses by the state were estimated to total $A33,315·4m.; revenue and grants received were expected to increase by 2·9% to $A33,701·2m. ($A32,749·1m. in 2006–07).

Performance

In 2012–13 Victoria's gross state product represented 22·2% of Australia's total GDP.

Banking and Finance

The major trading banks in Victoria are the Commonwealth Bank of Australia, the Australia and New Zealand Banking Group, the Westpac Banking Corporation, the National Australia Bank, the St George Bank, the Bank of Queensland, Suncorp-Metway Bank, HSBC Bank Australia, Elders Rural Bank and the Bendigo Bank. According to the Australian Prudential Regulation Authority, as at 30 June 2006 there were 21 authorized banks with 1,282 branches; two building societies with five branches; and 45 credit unions with 139 branches.

Energy and Natural Resources

Electricity

In 1993 the State government began a major restructure of the government-owned electricity industry along competitive lines. The distribution sector was privatized in 1995, and four generator companies in 1997.

Total installed capacity in 2009 was 9,577 MW, of which brown coal 6,555 MW (69%), natural gas 1,943 MW (20%) and renewable sources 1,079 MW (11%). Over 90% of electricity generated is supplied by brown coal-fired generating stations in the Latrobe Valley.

Oil and Gas

Crude oil in commercially recoverable quantities was first discovered in 1967 in two large fields offshore, in East Gippsland in Bass Strait, between 65 and 80 km from land. These fields, with 20 other fields since discovered, have been assessed as containing initial recoverable oil reserves of 4,063m. bbls. Production of crude oil peaked at 450,000 bbls per day in 1985 but declined to 83,000 bbls per day in the fiscal year 2005–06, representing 19·5% of Australia's total production. Estimated remaining oil reserves as at May 2009 was 400·0m. bbls.

Natural gas was discovered offshore in East Gippsland in 1965. The initial recoverable gas reserves were 272·0m. cu. metres. Estimated remaining gas reserves (30 June 2005), 88·68m. cu. metres. Production of natural gas (2008–09), 9,374m. cu. metres.

Liquefied petroleum gas is produced after extraction of the propane and butane fractions from the untreated oil and gas.

Brown Coal

Major deposits of brown coal are located in the Latrobe Valley in the Central Gippsland region and comprise approximately 89% of the total resources in Victoria. In 2005 the resource was estimated to be 41,500 megatonnes, of which about 37,400 megatonnes were economically recoverable.

The primary use of these reserves is to fuel electricity generating stations. Production of brown coal in 2005–06 was 71·2m. tonnes.

Minerals

Production: limestone (2006–07), 1,565,433 tonnes; kaolin (2007–08), 151,669 tonnes. In 2007–08, 5,632 kg of gold were produced.

Agriculture

In the year ending 30 June 2007 there were 37,410 agricultural establishments (excluding those with an estimated value of agricultural operations less than $A5,000) with a total area of 13·3m. ha. of which around 3·4m. ha. were under crops. Gross value of agricultural production, 2006–07, $A8·7bn. Principal crops in 2006–07 with estimated production in 1,000 tonnes: wheat, 879; barley, 605; oats, 134; canola, 42.

Gross value of livestock production in 2006–07 totalled $A2·6bn., including wool production $A498m.

Grape growing, particularly for winemaking, is an important activity. In 2006–07, 308,501 tonnes of wine grapes were produced from 38,650 ha. of vineyards (including 1,904 ha. not yet bearing).

Forestry
Commercial timber production is an increasingly important source of income. As at Dec. 2006 there were 396,000 ha. of plantation. Of Victoria's 7·9m. ha. of native forest (Dec. 2005), 6·6m. ha. (83·4%) were publicly owned (3·1m. ha. in conservation reserves).

Fisheries
Estimated total fisheries production in 2005–06 came to 18,903 tonnes with a gross value of $A127·2m. In the same year aquaculture production was an estimated 3,034 tonnes with a gross value of $A21·6m.

Industry
Total sales and service income in manufacturing industry in 2014–15 was $A104,039m., including $A28,609m. from food product manufacturing, $A12,587m. from transport equipment manufacturing and $A7,947m. from basic chemical and chemical product manufacturing. In the same year there were 246,800 persons employed in the manufacturing sector (including 63,100 in food product manufacturing, 26,500 in transport equipment manufacturing and 24,900 in fabricated metal product manufacturing) with wages and salaries totalling $A16,212m.

Labour
At Aug. 2007 there were 2,706,600 persons in the labour force of whom 2,583,700 were employed: wholesale and retail trade, 503,600; finance, insurance, property and business services, 431,400; manufacturing, 330,600; health and community services, 264,000; construction, 211,900; education, 193,900; culture, recreation, personal and other services, 180,300; accommodation, cafes and restaurants, 118,100; transport and storage, 105,900; government administration and defence, 82,400; agriculture, forestry and fishing, 78,400; communication services, 50,100; electricity, gas and water supply, 20,400; mining, 12,600. There were 122,900 unemployed persons in Aug. 2007, a rate of 4·5%. The average weekly wage in Nov. 2005 was $A1,010·10 (males $A1,055·70, females $A915·00).

International Trade

Imports and Exports
In 2009–10 foreign merchandise imports were valued at $A53,121m.; exports at $A18,427m. Major sources of imports for 2009–10 were (figures in $A1m.): China, 10,477; USA, 6,024; Japan, 5,108; Germany, 3,655; Thailand, 2,727. Major export destinations (figures in $A1m.): China, 2,380; New Zealand, 1,989; Japan, 1,561; USA, 1,514; Saudi Arabia, 1,069. Principal commodity imports in 2009–10 were (with values in $A1m.): passenger motor vehicles, 4,582; crude petroleum, 3,291; refined petroleum, 1,916; goods vehicles, 1,502; vehicle parts and accessories, 1,362. Principal commodity exports (with values in $A1m.): passenger motor vehicles, 1,560; aluminium, 1,106; medicaments (including veterinary), 1,072; wool and other animal hair, 884; milk and cream, 876.

Communications

Roads
In 2007 there were an estimated 151,000 km of roads open to general traffic. The number of registered motor vehicles (excluding tractors and trailers) at 31 March 2006 was 3,740,726, including 2,997,856 passenger vehicles, 483,097 light commercial vehicles, 119,533 trucks, 16,508 buses and 114,438 motorcycles. There were 333 road accident fatalities in 2006.

Rail
The Victorian rail network is owned by the Victorian RailTrack Corporation (VicTrack), a Victorian Government corporation. Three interlinked rail networks operate in Victoria, comprising: 1,213 km of standard gauge interstate and intrastate non-urban track leased to the Australian Rail Track Corporation; 400 km of urban broad gauge track franchised to Metro Trains Melbourne, the metropolitan network access manager and passenger service operator; and 3,278 km of intrastate, non-urban rail network franchised to V/Line Passenger, the network access provider and regional passenger operator.

The regional intrastate rail network is leased to and managed by V/Line Passenger. Approximately 3m. tonnes of freight is transported on the intrastate rail network annually. There were more than 12m. passenger trips taken on regional train services in 2008–09.

Two new operators commenced operation from 30 Nov. 2009 following a competitive worldwide tender. The new train franchise agreement was awarded to Metro Trains Melbourne (Metro) and the new tram franchise to Keolis Downer EDI (KDR). The contracts operate for eight years with a possible extension of seven years based on good performance.

Melbourne's 249 km tramway and light rail network is operated by KDR (branded as Yarra Trams) across 28 main routes and had approximately 178·1m. passenger boardings in 2008–09. Melbourne's metropolitan passenger rail network, operated by Metro, comprises 15 lines and approximately 2,000 daily metropolitan rail services and had approximately 213·9m. passenger boardings in 2008–09.

Civil Aviation
Melbourne (Tullamarine) Airport, Australia's second busiest airport after Sydney, handled 25,917,963 passengers in 2009–10 (19,828,176 on domestic airlines). Total international freight handled in 2009–10 was 199,033 tonnes (also the second highest total after Sydney). In 2010 there were direct international services to Abu Dhabi, Auckland, Bali, Bangkok, Beijing, Chicago, Christchurch, Doha, Dubai, Guangzhou, Hanoi, Ho Chi Minh City, Hong Kong, Honolulu, Jakarta, Johannesburg, Kuala Lumpur, London, Los Angeles, Macau, Manila, Mauritius, Nadi, Phuket, Queenstown, Seoul, Shanghai, Singapore and Wellington.

Shipping
The four major commercial ports are at Melbourne, Geelong, Portland and Hastings. In 2008–09, 4,189 commercial vessels called at Victorian ports. General cargo imported in 2008–09 was 12,452,210 mass tonnes and general cargo exported was 12,885,409 mass tonnes.

Social Institutions

Justice
There is a Supreme Court with a Chief Justice and 21 puisne judges. There are a county court, magistrates' courts, a court of licensing and a bankruptcy court.

In 1996–97 the State's prisons were upgraded with three new facilities developed, owned and operated by the private sector. In 2006–07 approximately 36% of Victoria's prison population was accommodated in the two private prisons still operating (one of the prisons having been returned to public ownership and operation in Nov. 2000). There are 12 public prisons remaining. At 30 June 2007 the number of prisoners held stood at 4,183. Police personnel at 30 June 2007, 14,078.

Education
In Feb. 2006 there were 1,606 government schools with 307,577 pupils in primary schools and 222,827 in secondary schools. In the same year there were 694 non-government schools with 140,683 pupils at primary schools; and 153,039 pupils at secondary schools.

All higher education institutions, excluding continuing education and technical and further education (TAFE), now fall under the Unified National System, and can no longer be split into universities and colleges of advanced education. In addition, a number of institutional amalgamations and name changes occurred in the 12 months prior to the commencement of the 1992 academic year. In 2010 there were 520,000 enrolments in Vocational Education and Training activities.

There are ten publicly funded higher education institutions including eight State universities, Marcus Oldham College and the Australian Catholic University (partly privately funded), and the Melbourne University Private, established in 1998. In 2005 there were 292,761 students in higher education.

Health

In 2006–07 there were 144 public hospitals with 12,434 beds, and 144 private hospitals with 6,675 beds. Total government outlay on health in 2006–07 was $A6,716m.

Welfare

Victoria was the first State of Australia to make a statutory provision for the payment of Age Pensions. The Act came into operation on 18 Jan. 1901, and continued until 1 July 1909, when the Australian Invalid and Old Age Pension Act came into force. The Social Services Consolidation Act, which came into operation on 1 July 1947, repealed the various legislative enactments relating to age and invalid pensions, maternity allowances, child endowment, unemployment and sickness benefits and, while following in general the Acts repealed, considerably liberalized many of their provisions.

The number of age and disability pensions at 30 June 2007 was: age, 493,728; disability support, 169,694. There were 105,264 newstart allowance, 93,007 youth allowance and 90,551 single parent payments current at 30 June 2007.

Religion

There is no State Church, and no State assistance has been given to religion since 1875. At the 2006 census the following were the enumerated numbers of the principal religions: Catholic, 1,355,904; Anglican, 671,774; Uniting Church, 274,056; Orthodox, 224,038; Presbyterian and Reformed, 143,146; other Christian, 316,887; Buddhist, 132,633; Muslim, 109,369; Hindu, 42,310; Jewish, 41,108; no religion, 1,007,415; not stated, 550,309.

Culture

Tourism

For the year ending June 2007 the number of short-term overseas visitors to Australia who specified Victoria as their main destination was 1·4m. (28·4% of total overseas visitors to Australia), with 1·02m. nominating 'holiday' or 'visiting friends/relatives' as purpose of their trip. The UK represented the major source of international visitors with 16·1%; followed by New Zealand (16·0%), China (9·9%), USA (8·6%), Singapore (4·5%) and Japan (4·2%).

Source: International Visitor Survey, year ending June 2007

Western Australia

Key Historical Events

In 1791 the British navigator George Vancouver took possession of the country around King George Sound. In 1826 the government of New South Wales sent 20 convicts and a detachment of soldiers to form a settlement then called Frederickstown. The following year, Capt. James Stirling surveyed the coast from King George Sound to the Swan River, and in May 1829 Capt. Charles Fremantle took possession of the territory. In June 1829 Capt. Stirling founded the Swan River Settlement (now the Commonwealth State of Western Australia) and the towns of Perth and Fremantle. He was appointed Lieut.-Governor.

Grants of land were made to the early settlers until, in 1850, with the colony languishing, they petitioned for the colony to be made a penal settlement. Between 1850 and 1868 (in which year transportation ceased), 9,668 convicts were sent out. In 1870 partially representative government was instituted. Western Australia federated with the other Australian states to form the Commonwealth of Australia in 1901.

In the 1914–18 war Western Australia provided more volunteers for overseas military service in proportion to population than any other State. The worldwide depression of 1929 brought unemployment (30% of trade union membership), and in 1933 over two-thirds voted to leave the Federation. While there were modest improvements in the standard of living through the 1930s, it was the 1939–45 war which brought full employment. Japanese aircraft attacked the Western Australia coast in 1942. Talk of a 'Brisbane line', which would abandon the West to invasion, only served to reinforce Western Australia's sense of isolation from the rest of the nation. The post-war years saw increasing demand for wheat and wool but the 1954–55 decline in farm incomes led to diversification. Work began in the early 1950s on steel production and oil processing. Oil was discovered in 1953 but it was not until 1966 that it was commercially exploited. The discovery of deposits of iron ore in the Pilbara, bauxite in the Darling scarp, nickel in Kambalda and ilmenite from sand led to the State becoming a major mineral producer by 1965.

Territory and Population

Western Australia has an area of 2,529,875 sq. km and 12,500 km of coastline.

The population at the 2011 census was 2,239,170 (1,959,088 at 2006 census). In 2011, 62·9% were born in Australia. Perth, the capital, had a 2011 census population of 1,728,867.

Principal local government areas outside the metropolitan area at the 2011 census: Mandurah, 69,903; Albany, 33,650; Bunbury, 31,348; Kalgoorlie-Boulder, 30,841; Busselton, 30,330; Port Hedland, 15,044.

Social Statistics

Statistics for calendar years:

	Births	Deaths	Marriages	Divorces
2011	32,259	12,724	12,665	5,020
2012	33,627	13,339	12,968	5,073
2013	34,516	13,414	12,886	5,268
2014	35,403	13,787	13,287	4,518

The annual rates per 1,000 of the mean resident population in 2014 were: births, 13·8; deaths, 5·4; marriages, 5·2; divorces, 1·8. Infant mortality rate, 2014, 2·5 per 1,000 live births. Expectation of life, 2014: males, 80·5 years; females, 84·9 years.

Climate

Western Australia is a region of several climate zones, ranging from the tropical north to the semi-arid interior and Mediterranean-style climate of the southwest. Most of the State is a plateau between 300 and 600 metres above sea level. Except in the far southwest coast, maximum temperatures in excess of 40°C have been recorded throughout the State. The normal average number of sunshine hours per day is 8·0.

Constitution and Government

The *Legislative Council* consists of 36 members elected for a term of four years. There are six electoral regions for Legislative Council elections. Each electoral region returns six members. Each member represents the entire region.

There are 59 members of the *Legislative Assembly*, each member representing one of the 59 electoral districts of the State. Members are elected for a period of up to four years. A system of proportional representation is used to elect members.

Recent Elections

In elections to the Legislative Assembly on 11 March 2017 the opposition Labor Party (ALP) won 41 seats with 42·2% of votes cast; the Liberal Party (LP) won 13 with 31·2%; and the National Party (NP), 5 with 5·4%. Turnout was 86·9%.

Current Government

Governor: Kim Beazley, AC.

Lieut.-Governor: Wayne Martin, AC.

In March 2019 the Cabinet comprised:

Premier, and Minister for Public Sector Management, State Development, Jobs and Trades, and Federal–State Relations: Mark McGowan (ALP).

Deputy Premier, and Minister for Health, and Mental Health: Roger Cook. *Education and Training:* Sue Ellery. *Environment, Disability Services, and Electoral Affairs:* Stephen Dawson. *Police, and Road Safety:* Michelle Roberts. *Regional Development, Agriculture and Food, and Ports:* Alannah MacTiernan. *Emergency Services, and Corrective Services:* Francis Logan. *Local Government, Heritage, and Culture and the Arts:* David Templeman. *Attorney General, and Commerce:* John Quigley. *Seniors and Ageing, Volunteering, and Sport and Recreation:* Mick Murray. *Treasurer, and Minister for Finance, Aboriginal Affairs, and Lands:* Ben Wyatt. *Tourism, Racing and Gaming, Small Business, Defence Issues, and Citizenship and Multicultural Interests:* Paul Papalia. *Mines and Petroleum, Energy, and Industrial Relations:* Bill Johnston. *Transport, and Planning:* Rita Saffioti. *Housing, Veterans Issues, Youth, and Asian Engagement:* Peter Tinley. *Child Protection, Women's Interests, Prevention of Family and Domestic Violence, and Community Services:* Simone McGurk. *Water, Fisheries, Forestry, Innovation and ICT, and Science:* Dave Kelly.

WA Government Website: http://wa.gov.au

Economy

Budget
Revenue and expenditure (in $A1m.) in years ending 30 June:

	2005–06	2006–07	2007–08[1]
Revenue	16,123	16,510	17,593
Expenditure	14,141	15,234	16,141

[1]Projected.

A general government net operating surplus of $A1,853m. was projected for 2006–07, a decrease of $A812m. on the 2005–06 outcome.

Performance
Western Australia's 2012–13 gross state product represented 16·0% of Australia's total GDP, up from 10·8% in 2002–03 and 9·8% in 1992–93.

Banking and Finance
According to the Australian Prudential Regulation Authority, as at 30 June 2006 there were 15 authorized banks with 519 branches; one building society with 19 branches; and 16 credit unions with 41 branches.

Energy and Natural Resources

Electricity
In 2008–09 electricity consumption was 31,343 GWh of which 979 GWh (3·1%) was from renewable sources.

Oil and Gas
Petroleum continued to be the State's largest resource sector with sales increasing by 33% to $A22·3bn. in 2008. Owing to low oil prices in 2008–09 the value of crude oil sales decreased by 12% to $A7·7bn.; output was 81·4m. bbls. The State accounts for 66% of Australia's oil and condensate production.

Western Australia has significant natural gas resources and, with a $A2·4bn. expansion of the North West Shelf liquefied natural gas (LNG) project, exports are forecast to rise by around $A1bn. Total natural gas production, 2005–06: 25,887 gigalitres.

Source: Western Australian Department of Mineral and Petroleum Resources.

Minerals
Mining is a significant contributor to the Western Australia economy. The State is the world's largest producer of iron ore, accounting for 37% of global iron ore production.

Principal minerals produced in 2016–17 were: iron ore, 793·1m. tonnes; gold, 203 tonnes; diamonds, 12·6m. carats; coal, 6·8m. tonnes.

Agriculture
In the year ending 30 June 2017 there were 83·8m. ha. of agricultural land. Gross value of agricultural production in 2016–17 totalled $A9·0bn., representing 15% of Australia's agricultural production.

Principal crops in 2017 with estimated production in 1,000 tonnes: wheat, 7,600; barley, 3,800; canola, 1,900; oats, 480; lupins, 450.

Value of livestock products in 2009 totalled $A691m. Total value of wool produced in 2016–17 was $A826m.

Forestry
The area of State forests and timber reserves at 30 June 2010 was 1,427,954 ha. In 2009–10 sawlog production totalled 769,780 cu. metres, of which plantation softwood sawlogs and veneer logs 570,556 cu. metres and Jarrah and Karri hardwoods 183,816 cu. metres.

Fisheries
Estimated total fisheries production in 2007–08 came to 29,301 tonnes with a gross value of $A448·4m., of which $A216·9m. from rock lobster. In the same year aquaculture production was an estimated 1,013 tonnes with a gross value of $A122·8m. Pearling is the most valuable form of aquaculture in the State with the Pearl Oyster Fishery producing an estimated $A113m. worth of pearls from wild captured and hatchery produced oysters in 2007–08.

Industry
Total sales and service income in manufacturing industry in 2015–16 was $A53,413m., including $A22,916m. from primary metal and metal product manufacturing, $A4,764m. from basic chemical and chemical product manufacturing and $A4,284m. from food product manufacturing. In the same year there were 87,500 persons employed in the manufacturing sector (including 15,800 in food product manufacturing, 13,500 in fabricated metal product manufacturing and 9,800 in machinery and equipment manufacturing) with wages and salaries totalling $A6,222m.

Labour
The labour force comprised 1,054,800 employed and 44,500 unemployed persons in 2005 (an unemployment rate of 4·1%). The average weekly wage in Nov. 2005 was $A1,054·80 (males $A1,148·60, females $A863·40).

International Trade

Imports and Exports
In 2009–10 foreign merchandise imports were valued at $A27,939m.; exports at $A83,357m. Major sources of imports for 2009–10 were (figures in $A1m.): Thailand, 4,528; USA, 2,822; China, 2,820; Singapore, 2,543; Japan, 2,244. Major export destinations (figures in $A1m.): China, 30,801; Japan, 14,245; India, 8,584; South Korea, 6,694; UK, 4,494. Principal commodity imports in 2009–10 were (with values in $A1m.): gold, 6,200; crude petroleum, 3,229; refined petroleum, 1,966; pumps (excluding liquid pumps) and parts, 1,747; passenger motor vehicles, 1,528. Principal commodity exports (with values in $A1m.): iron ore and concentrates, 34,125; gold, 13,659; crude petroleum, 8,810; natural gas, 6,016; wheat, 1,677.

Communications

Roads
In 2007 there were an estimated 152,262 km of roads open to general traffic. The number of registered motor vehicles (excluding tractors and trailers) at 31 March 2006 was 1,600,566, including 1,205,266 passenger vehicles, 254,164 light commercial vehicles, 63,316 trucks, 11,051 buses and 59,675 motorcycles. In 2008 there were 209 road accident fatalities.

Rail
Transperth is responsible for metropolitan rail services and Transwa for rail passenger services to regional areas. In 2005–06, 34·1m. passenger journeys were made on urban services. In 2009–10, 442m. tonnes of freight were carried.

Civil Aviation
An extensive system of regular air services operates for passengers, freight and mail. In 2009–10 Perth International Airport handled 9,992,583 passengers (6,606,335 on domestic airlines). In 2010 there were direct international services to Brunei, China (Hong Kong), Indonesia, Japan, Malaysia, Mauritius, New Zealand, Singapore, South Africa, Thailand and the UAE.

Shipping
In 2008–09, 5,869 commercial vessels called at Western Australian ports (1,789 at Dampier and 1,774 at Fremantle). General cargo imported in 2008–09 was 10,334,358 mass tonnes and general cargo exported was 10,968,803 mass tonnes.

Social Institutions

Justice
Justice is administered by a Supreme Court, consisting of a Chief Justice, 16 other judges and two masters; a District Court comprising a chief judge and 20 other judges; a Magistrates Court, a Chief Stipendiary Magistrate, 37 Stipendiary Magistrates and Justices of the Peace. All courts exercise both civil and criminal jurisdiction except Justices of the Peace who deal with summary criminal matters only. Juvenile offenders are dealt with by the Children's Court. The Family Court also forms part of the justice system.

At 30 June 2005 there was a daily average of 3,482 prisoners held. At 30 June 2006 police personnel stood at 6,875.

Education
School attendance is compulsory from the age of six until the end of the year in which the child attains 16 years. Since Jan. 2008 young people aged 15–17 have been obliged to remain in school or, by arrangement, take part in an

approved education and training pathway such as an apprenticeship or traineeship.

In Aug. 2006 there were 777 government primary and secondary schools (with 16,737 full-time equivalent teaching staff) providing free education to 131,294 primary and 83,064 secondary students; in the same year there were 303 non-government schools for 51,577 primary and 53,828 secondary students.

Higher education is available through four state universities and one private (Notre Dame). In 2010 there were 166,000 enrolments in Vocational Education and Training activities. In 2006 there were approximately 98,745 students in tertiary education at the University of Western Australia, Murdoch University, the University of Notre Dame Australia, Curtin University of Technology and the Edith Cowan University.

Health

In 2006–07 there were 94 acute public hospitals and one public psychiatric hospital; and 23 acute and psychiatric private hospitals and 20 private free-standing day hospitals.

Welfare

The Department for Community Development is responsible for the provision of welfare and community services throughout the State. The number of age and disability pensions at 30 June 2007 was: age, 166,239; disability support, 58,467. There were 27,650 newstart allowance, 26,001 youth allowance and 37,900 single parent payments current at 30 June 2007.

Religion

At the census of 2006 the principal denominations were: Catholic, 464,005; Anglican, 400,480; Uniting Church, 74,333; Presbyterian and Reformed, 43,807; Baptist, 32,730; other Christian, 147,171. There were 97,916 persons practising non-Christian religions and 448,435 persons had no religion.

Culture

Tourism

In the year ending March 2007 there were 634,000 overseas visitors. Of these, 26·9% were from the UK, 9·1% from Singapore, 7·5% from New Zealand and 7·1% from Japan.

Ashmore and Cartier Islands

Ashmore Islands (known as Middle, East and West Islands) and Cartier Island are situated in the Indian Ocean, some 320 km off the northwest coast of Australia (area, 5 sq. km). They were placed under Commonwealth authority in 1931 and accepted as the Territory of Ashmore and Cartier Islands in 1933. It was the intention that the Territory should be administered by the state of Western Australia but, owing to administrative difficulties, it was deemed in 1913 to form part of the Northern Territory. The islands are uninhabited, but Indonesian fishing boats operate within them. The islands and their waters may hold considerable oil reserves.

Australian Antarctic Territory

All the islands and territories (other than Adélie Land) situated south of 60° S. lat. and lying between 160° E. long. and 45° E. long. (area, 6,119,818 sq. km) were placed under the authority of the Commonwealth of Australia in 1933. The boundaries of Adélie Land were fixed by a French decree in 1938 as the islands and territories south of 60° S. lat. lying between 136° E. long. and 142° E. long. Legislation in 1954 provided that the laws in force in the Australian Capital Territory are generally applicable in the Australian Antarctic Territory.

There are research stations at Mac.Robertson Land (Mawson), Princess Elizabeth Land (Davis) and Wilkes Land (Casey). The Australian Antarctic Division also operates a station on Macquarie Island.

Christmas Island

Christmas Island is an isolated peak in the Indian Ocean, lat. 10° 25' 22" S., long. 105° 39' 59" E. (area, 136·7 sq. km). The climate is tropical. The island was annexed by the UK in 1888, placed under the administration of the Governor of the Straits Settlements in 1889 and incorporated with the Settlement of Singapore in 1900. Sovereignty was transferred to the Australian government in 1958. Under federal legislation passed in 1992, Commonwealth and state laws applying in Western Australia are generally applicable in the Territory. Population at the 2016 census was 1,843.

The Shire of Christmas Island has nine members elected for terms of four years. Every two years half of the positions are elected.

Administrator: Natasha Griggs (since 5 Oct. 2017).

The Australian dollar is legal tender. Extraction and export of rock phosphate dust is the main industry. There are scheduled flights to and from Perth. A high school provides education under the Western Australian curriculum for kindergarten through to Year 12. About 50% of the population are Buddhists or Taoists, 30% Christians and 16% Muslims.

Cocos (Keeling) Islands

Situated in the Indian Ocean at 12° 05' S. lat. and 96° 53' E. long (2,950 km northwest of Perth), the islands comprise two separate coral atolls with a total area of about 14·2 sq. km. They are low-lying, flat and thickly covered by coconut palms. Temperatures range over the year from 68°F (20°C) to 88°F (31°C) and annual rainfall averages 80" (2,000 mm).

The main islands are: West Island (the largest, about 14 km long), home to most of the European community; Home Island, occupied by the Cocos Malay community; Direction, South and Horsburgh Islands, and North Keeling Island. Population at the 2016 census was 544, distributed between Home Island (74%) and West Island (26%).

The islands were discovered in 1609 by Capt. William Keeling but remained uninhabited until 1826. In 1857 they were annexed to the British Empire; the governments of Ceylon and Singapore held jurisdiction at different periods until they were placed under the authority of the Australian government in 1955. An Administrator, appointed by the Governor-General, is the government's representative. The Shire of Cocos (Keeling) Islands has seven members elected for terms of four years. Every two years half of the elected members' terms expire.

Administrator: Natasha Griggs (since 5 Oct. 2017).

The Australian dollar is legal tender. There are scheduled flights to and from Perth.

About 85% of the population are Muslim and 15% Christian.

Coral Sea Islands

The Coral Sea Islands, which became a Territory of the Commonwealth of Australia in 1969, comprise scattered reefs and islands over an area of about 1m. sq. km. The Territory is uninhabited apart from a meteorological station on Willis Island.

Heard and Mcdonald Islands

These islands, about 2,500 miles southwest of Fremantle, were transferred from British to Australian control from 1947. Heard Island is about 43 km long and 21 km wide; Shag Island is about 8 km north of Heard. The total area is 412 sq. km. The McDonald Islands are 42 km to the west of Heard. Heard is an active stratovolcano that erupted most recently in 2016. A volcano on McDonald Island had been dormant for 75,000 years until 1992 and erupted most recently in 2005. Research programmes have been conducted on the islands by the Australian National Antarctic Research Expedition.

Norfolk Island

The island is situated 29° 02' S. lat. 167° 57' E. long. (area, 3,455 ha). The climate is sub-tropical. Permanent population at 2016 census was 1,748 (685 born in Australia, 381 in Norfolk Island and 303 in New Zealand). The island was formerly part of the colony of New South Wales and then of Van Diemen's Land (now Tasmania). A penal colony between 1788–1814 and 1825–55, it was separated from Tasmania in 1856 and placed under the jurisdiction of the state of New South Wales. Following legislation in 1913 the island was accepted as an Australian external territory. It had partial self-government from 1979 until legislation in 2015 instituted the transition to an elected Regional Council (from July 2016) and an extension of federal government responsibilities.

Descendants of the *Bounty* mutineer families constitute the 'original' settlers and are known locally as 'Islanders', while later settlers, mostly from Australia and New Zealand, are identified as 'mainlanders'. Descendants of the Pitcairn Islanders make up around a quarter of the permanent population.

An *Administrator*, appointed by the Governor-General, is the senior government representative. The capital is Kingston. A new elected representative body, the five-member Norfolk Island Regional Council, was inaugurated in July 2016. Elections to the Regional Council were held on 28 May 2016. The Australian government has assumed responsibility for funding and delivering essential services including welfare and health benefits, while Norfolk Islanders now pay Australian taxes.

Administrator: Eric Hutchinson (since April 2017).

The Australian dollar is legal tender.

There are scheduled flights to Australia and New Zealand.

A school is run by the New South Wales Department of Education for children aged 5 to 12. 40% of the population are Anglicans.

Further Reading

Australia

Australian Bureau of Statistics (ABS). *Year Book Australia*, 1901–2012.—*Australia at a Glance*, since 1994.—*Australian Economic Indicators* (absorbed *Monthly Summary of Statistics*) since 1994.—*Australian Social Trends*, 1994–2014. ABS also provide numerous online specialized statistical summaries.

Arthur, Bill and Morphy, Frances, *The Macquarie Atlas of Indigenous Australia*. 2006

Australian Encyclopædia. 12 vols. 1983

Blainey, G., *A Short History of Australia*. 1996

The Cambridge Encyclopedia of Australia. 1994

Concise Oxford Dictionary of Australian History. 2nd ed. 1995

Davison, Graeme, *et al*., (eds) *The Oxford Companion to Australian History*. 2nd ed. 2002

Docherty, J. D., *Historical Dictionary of Australia*. 1993

Foster, S. G., Marsden, S. and Russell, R. (compilers) *Federation. A guide to records*. 2000

Gilbert, A. D. and Inglis, K. S. (eds)*Australians: a Historical Library*. 5 vols. 1988

Hirst, John, *The Sentimental Nation: The Making of the Australian Commonwealth*. 2000.—*Australia's Democracy: A Short History*. 2002

Irving, H. (ed.) *The Centenary Companion to Australian Federation*. Revised ed. 2010

Knightley, Phillip, *Australia: A biography of a Nation*. 2000

Macintyre, S., *A Concise History of Australia*. 2000

Oxford History of Australia. vol 2: 1770–1860. 1992. vol 5: 1942–88. 1990

Peel, Mark and Twomey, Christina, *A History of Australia*. 2011

Ward, Stuart, *Australia and the British Embrace: The Demise of the Imperial Ideal*. 2002

More specialized titles are listed under RELIGION, *above.*

National library: The National Library, Parkes Place, Parkes, Canberra, ACT 2600.

Website: http://www.nla.gov.au

National Statistical Office: Australian Bureau of Statistics (ABS), ABS House, 45 Benjamin Way, Belconnen, ACT 2617. The statistical services of the states are integrated with the Bureau. *Australian Statistician:* David Kalisch.

ABS Website: http://www.abs.gov.au

Australian Capital Territory

Statistical Information: The State office of the Australian Bureau of Statistics (ABS) is at Level 5, QBE Insurance Building, 33–35 Ainslie Ave., Canberra City. Publications include: *Australian Capital Territory in Focus*. Annual (from 1994); *Australian Capital Territory at a Glance*, Annual (from 1995).

Sources: ACT in Focus 1307.8, Labour Force, Australia 6203.0 and *Labour Force, New South Wales and Australian Capital Territory 6201.1.*

Northern Territory

Statistical Information: The State office of the Australian Bureau of Statistics (ABS) is at 7th Floor, AANT House, 81?Smith St., Darwin. Publications include: *Northern Territory at a Glance*. Annual (from 1994); *Regional Statistics, Northern Territory*. Annual (with exception of 1996) from 1995; and National Regional Profile: Northern Territory (from 2002).

The Northern Territory: Annual Report. Dept. of Territories, Canberra, from 1911. Dept. of the Interior, Canberra, from 1966–67. Dept. of Northern Territory, from 1972

Australian Territories, Dept. of Territories, Canberra, 1960 to 1973. Dept. of Special Minister of State, Canberra, 1973–75. Department of Administrative Services, 1976

Donovan, P.F., *A Land Full of Possibilities: A History of South ?Australia's Northern Territory 1863–1911*. 1981.—*At the Other End of ?Australia: The Commonwealth and the Northern Territory 1911–1978*. 1984

Heatley, A., *Almost Australians: the Politics of Northern Territory Self-Government*. 1990

Powell, A., *Far Country: A Short History of the Northern Territory*. 1996 (Powell 1996)

State library: Northern Territory Library, Parliament House, State Sq., Darwin.

Website: https://ntl.nt.gov.au

New South Wales

Statistical Information: The NSW Government Statistician's Office was established in 1886, and in 1957 was integrated with the Commonwealth Bureau of Census and Statistics (now called the Australian Bureau of Statistics). The state office of the Australian Bureau of Statistics is at 5th Floor, St Andrews House. Sydney Sq., Sydney. Publications include: *New South Wales in Focus*. Replaces *New South Wales Yearbook*. Annual, since 2005.—*Regional Statistics, New South Wales.*

State library: The State Library of NSW, Macquarie St., Sydney.

Website: http://www.sl.nsw.gov.au

Queensland

Statistical Information: The State office of the Australian Bureau of Statistics is at Level 3, 639 Wickham St., Brisbane. *A Queensland Official Year Book* was issued in 1901, the annual *ABC of Queensland Statistics* from 1905 to 1936 with exception of 1918 and 1922, *Queensland at a Glance* from 2000 to 2011 and *Qld Stats* from 2005 to 2011. *National Regional Profile: Queensland* (online only). Selected statistics available at *website:* http://www.abs.gov.au

Johnston, W. R., *A Bibliography of Queensland History*. 1981.—*The Call of the Land: A History of Queensland to the Present Day*. 1982

Johnston, W. R. and Zerner, M., *Guide to the History of Queensland*. 1985

State library: The State Library of Queensland, Queensland Cultural Centre, PO Box 3488, South Bank, South Brisbane.

Website: http://www.slq.qld.gov.au

Local Statistical Office: Office of Economic and Statistical Research, PO Box 15037, City East, Qld 4002.

Website: http://www.qgso.qld.gov.au

South Australia

Statistical Information: The State office of the Australian Bureau of Statistics (ABS) is at 7th Floor East, Commonwealth Centre, 55 Currie St., Adelaide. Although the first printed statistical publication was the *Statistics of South Australia, 1854*, with the title altered to *Statistical Register* in 1859, there is a manuscript volume for each year back to 1838. These contain simple records of trade, demography, production, etc. and were prepared only for the information of the Colonial Office; one copy was retained in the State.

ABS publications include the *South Australian Year* Book (now discontinued), *South Australia at a Glance* from 1979 to 2009 and *SA Stats* from 2005 to 2011. *National Regional Profile: South Australia* (online only). Selected statistics available at *website:* http://www.abs. gov.au

Gibbs, R. M., *A History of South Australia: from Colonial Days to the Present*. 3rd ed. revised. 1995

Prest, Wilfred, Round, Kerrie and Fort, Carol, (eds) *The Wakefield Companion to South Australian History*. 2002

State library: The State Library of South Australia, Corner North Terrace and Kintore Avenue, Adelaide SA 5000.

Website: http://www.slsa.sa.gov.au

Tasmania

Statistical Information: The State Government Statistical Office (200 Collins St., Hobart), established in 1877, became in 1924 the Tasmanian Office of the Australian Bureau of Statistics, but continues to serve State statistical needs as required.

Main publications: *Tasmanian Year Book.* Annual (from 1967; biennial from 1986), now discontinued.—*Tasmania at a Glance.* Annual (from 1994).—*Statistics–Tasmania.* Annual (from 2002 to 2008).—*Tasmanian State and Regional Indicators.* Quarterly (from 2007 to 2010).—*Tasmanian Key Indicators* (from 2006 to 2011).—*National Regional Profile: Tasmania* (online only).

Email address: Sales and Inquiries: client.services@abs.gov.au

Website: http://www.abs.gov.au

Robson, L., *A History of Tasmania. Vol. 1: Van Diemen's Land from the Earliest Times to 1855.* 1983.—*A History of Tasmania. Vol. 2: Colony and State from 1856 to the 1980s.* 1990

State library: The State Library of Tasmania, 91 Murray St., Hobart, TAS 7000.

Website: http://www.statelibrary.tas.gov.au

Victoria

Statistical Information: The State office of the Australian Bureau of Statistics is at 5th Floor, Commercial Union Tower, 485 LaTrobe Street, Melbourne. Publications: *Victorian Year Book.* Annual, 1873–2002.—*State and Regional Indicators.* Quarterly, Sept. 2001–Dec. 2010.

State library: The State Library of Victoria, 328 Swanston St., Melbourne 3000.

Website: http://www.slv.vic.gov.au

Western Australia

Statistical Information: The State Government Statistician's Office was established in 1897 and now functions as the Western Australian Office of the Australian Bureau of Statistics (Level 15, Exchange Plaza, Sherwood Court, Perth). Publications include: *Western Australia at a Glance,* Annual (1997–2014). *Western Australian Statistical Indicators,* Quarterly (Sept. 2000–2010).

Crowley, F. K., *Australia's Western Third: A History of Western Australia from the First Settlements to Modern Times.* (Rev. ed.) 1970

Stannage, C. T. (ed.) *A New History of Western Australia.* 1981

State library: State Library of Western Australia, 25 Francis Street, Perth Cultural Centre, Perth WA 6000.

Website: http://www.slwa.wa.gov.au

Austria

Republik Österreich (Austrian Republic)

Capital: Vienna
Population projection, 2020: 8·78m.
GNI per capita, 2017: (PPP$) 45,415
HDI/world rank, 2017: 0·908/20
Internet domain extension: .at

Key Historical Events

The oldest historical site in Austria is at the Gudenus caves in the Kremstal valley, where hunters' stone implements and bones dating from the Paleolithic Age have been found. The Early Iron Age Hallstatt culture prevailed from around 750–400 BC, covering the area north of the Alps, large parts of Slovakia, the north Balkans and Hungary. This area became renowned for its ceramics, ornamental Hallstatt burial grounds and the development of salt mining.

In the fifth century BC Celtic tribes stormed the eastern Alps, their culture named after the site in Switzerland (La-Tène) where tools, weapons and other artefacts were found. La-Tène culture showed Greek and Etruscan influences. Around the middle of the second century BC some of these tribes united to found Noricum, the first recognizable state on Austrian territory. In 113 BC a treaty of friendship was signed between Rome and Noricum. Around 15 BC Noricum was incorporated into the Roman Empire. Present day Austria (with parts of Germany, Switzerland, Slovenia and Hungary) was eventually divided into the three Roman provinces of Raetia, Noricum and Pannonia.

Germanic tribes, in particular the Marcomanni and Quadi, later known as Bavarians, invaded in AD 166–80. Emperor Marcus Aurelius campaigned against them from Vindobona (Vienna), where he died in battle in AD 180. His successors fought unsuccessfully against the Alemanni and other invading tribes. Brigantium (Bregenz) became a border town of the Roman Empire after a peace agreement was signed with the Alemanni.

Charlemagne conquered the Bavarian duke Tassilo III and the Avars at the end of the 8th century and established a territory in the Danube Valley known as the Ostmark in 803. The church of Salzburg (Roman Juvavum) was founded at the end of the 8th century and consequently became the Bavarian-Frankish spiritual centre and archbishopric. Christianity spread throughout the region, led by the Slav apostles Cyril and Methodius.

The Magyar invasions culminated in the battle for Vienna in 881 and the loss of Lower Austrian territories. The Babenbergs took over the margravate of Bavaria in 976 under Leopold I. The name 'Ostarichi', originating from Old High German, first appeared in a document of Emperor Otto III in 996. In 1156 the margravate of Austria became a separate duchy.

From 1160–1200 Vienna, the most important trading town on the Danube, became the residence of the art-loving Babenberger dukes, receiving its town charter in 1198. In 1246 the last Babenberger, Friedrich II, fell in the battle of Leitha against King Bela IV of Hungary. Count Rudolf IV of Habsburg was elected German King Rudolf I in 1273 and set about conquering the former Babenberg lands, naming his son Duke Albert I the sole ruler in 1283. From the rule of Albert's son and successor Frederick I onwards, the territory of the Habsburgs was known as the *dominium Austriae*.

Holy Roman Empire

In 1452 Frederick III became Holy Roman Emperor. In one of the first of a series of dynastic marriages to expand the Habsburg realm, his son Maximilian I was married to Mary, the heiress of Burgundy. The marriage of their son, Philip the Handsome, to Juana, the heiress of the Spanish crowns, forged a massive and disparate Habsburg inheritance, encompassing Spain and its empire, Hungary, Bohemia, the Burgundian Netherlands and territory in Italy. Austria was harried by the Ottoman Turks, whose armies had advanced across southeast Europe as far as Hungary under Sultan Süleyman the Magnificent. A truce was agreed after the Ottoman defeat at Vienna in 1529.

The Reformation brought Protestantism to Austria but was resisted by Rudolf II. Brought up a strict Catholic, he embraced the Counter-Reformation in 1576. Tensions between Protestants and Catholics came to a head with the Defenestration of Prague in 1618, which led to the Thirty Years War. Peace was restored by the Treaty of Westphalia in 1648.

Philip, a grandson of Louis XIV of France, was designated heir to the last of the Spanish Habsburgs, Charles II. During the subsequent War of the Spanish Succession, Holland and England joined the coalition forces. Peace negotiations at Rastatt awarded Austria Spanish territory in Italy and the Netherlands. Austrian boundaries reached their furthest limit in 1720.

In 1740 Emperor Charles VI died without a male heir. By pragmatic sanction, his daughter Maria Theresa was allowed to succeed him as the first female Habsburg ruler, though she was denied the Imperial crown. Challenged by Prussia, the War of the Austrian Succession divided the two alliances of Bavaria, France, Spain and Prussia against Austria, Holland and Great Britain. Maria Theresa introduced a number of reforms aimed at strengthening the Habsburg monarchy. The army was doubled in size, a public education system was introduced and administrative and financial structures were overhauled, centralizing government and laying the foundations of a modern state. During the Seven Years' War (1756–63) Maria Theresa aimed to reconquer Silesia, lost in the War of the Austrian Succession. However, the Austrians, bereft of allies, were defeated at Burkersdorf in July 1762. Silesia was settled on Prussia by the Peace of Hubertusburg.

Enlightened Despotism

In 1772 Austria, Prussia and Russia carried out the first partition of Poland, with Austria gaining Galicia. Maria Theresa's youngest daughter of 16 children, Marie-Antoinette, married Louis XVI, thus achieving a closer political alliance with France. Maria Theresa was succeeded by Joseph, her eldest son. Also a reformist, and heavily influenced by the Enlightenment, Joseph II proclaimed the Edict of Toleration in 1781, giving more rights to faiths other than Catholicism. He also abolished serfdom and homogenized land tax laws. Not all of these changes were popular, such as the introduction of German as the official language in the Hungarian government. His heavy-handed reforms provoked resistance, leading to a revolt in the Austrian Netherlands opposing absolutist rule. In the face of widespread opposition to his reforms, Joseph revoked a number of them in 1790.

From 1792–1815 the Habsburgs were involved in almost continuous warfare. Austria and Prussia voiced their disapproval of the ideals of the French Revolution in the Declaration of Pillnitz. Ill-received by the French government, this led to a declaration of war followed by 23 years of hostilities and five separate wars. During the first, second and third coalition wars Vienna was occupied twice by French troops. Napoleon defeated Austria in the Battle of Austerlitz in 1805, forcing Francis to surrender his title of Holy Roman Emperor and to hand over one of his daughters, Archduchess Marie Louise, in marriage. After Napoleon was defeated and exiled to Elba in 1814, the Congress of Vienna met to re-establish Europe's internal borders. Leading Austria's foreign policy, Prince von Metternich created the German confederation of 35 states and four free cities to succeed the Holy Roman Empire.

With the growth of the cities in the first half of the 19th century came an expansion of the markets for agricultural goods. The first Austrian railway, the Kaiser-Ferdinand Nordbahn, was built between Linz and Budweis and steam navigation started on the Danube. An uprising in Vienna in 1848 forced the Habsburgs to flee the city and Metternich to resign. Ferdinand I abdicated in Dec. and was succeeded by his 18-year-old nephew, Francis Joseph I. The pan-European wave of revolution spread to Hungary, where the fight for emancipation was led by Lajos Kossuth. The Habsburgs refused to accept Hungary's independence and enlisted Russian aid to quell the uprising. Italian and Slavic revolts followed. In 1859, during the Austro-Italian war, the Habsburgs were defeated and Italy was unified.

The German unification campaign was headed by Otto von Bismarck, who expanded Prussian influence by isolating Austria from her allies. This led to the Austro-Prussian war of 1866. Austria's defeat at the battle of Königgrätz stripped it of all presiding powers over Germany. The loss of Venetia in 1867 added a further blow to the shrinking Habsburg empire.

© Springer Nature Limited 2020
Palgrave Macmillan (ed.), *The Statesman's Yearbook 2020*,
https://doi.org/10.1057/978-1-349-95940-2_20

Forced to compromise with Hungary, Emperor Francis Joseph I negotiated the 'Ausgleich' in 1867, giving Hungary its own constitution and quasi-independent status. Francis Joseph was henceforth recognized as the Apostolic king of Hungary and emperor of Austria within the Austro-Hungarian monarchy, also referred to as the Dual Monarchy. Foreign policy, the army and finances were administered jointly.

German Alliance
In 1879 Austria entered the Dual Alliance with the German Reich and the two states pledged mutual support in the eventuality of Russian aggression. Italy joined in 1882, making a Triple Alliance. Tensions between Austria and Russia heightened over territory in the Balkans, with an uprising in Macedonia in 1903. King Alexander of Serbia was assassinated while the Serbs were fighting for the unification of the Southern Slavs. The Habsburg empire responded with a livestock embargo, known as the Pig War. Austria-Hungary then annexed the two provinces of Bosnia and Herzegovina in 1908, prompting a Serb revolt and protests by the pan-Slav movement. Austria tried to gain control over Serbia during the Balkan wars of 1912–13. In June 1914 the heir to the Habsburg throne, Archduke Franz Ferdinand, and his wife were assassinated in Sarajevo by a Bosnian nationalist. The refusal of Serbia to accept the blame led to an Austrian declaration of war on Serbia in July. German backing for Austria encompassed a settling of its own scores with France and Russia. Austria was obliged to support Germany against France and Russia. Germany declared war on Russia and France in early Aug., beginning the First World War. The Austro-Hungarian army suffered major setbacks and the monarchy began to crumble after Francis Joseph I's death in 1916. His great-nephew, Charles I of Austria, succeeded him, trying but failing to achieve a secret truce with the Allies. A series of strikes, mutiny in the army and navy, and food shortages were among the factors that defeated Austro-Hungarian forces in the spring and summer of 1918. About 1·2m. soldiers from Austria-Hungary died during the war.

Emperor Charles I issued a manifesto on 17 Oct. 1918 guaranteeing the independence of the non-German speaking states. Each province established a national council which then developed into a government. The Poles declared themselves an independent unified state in Warsaw on 7 Oct. 1918; the Czechs founded an independent republic in Prague and the Southern Slavs merged with Serbia. An armistice was agreed on 3 Nov. and the Hungarian government announced its complete separation from Austria. Within days Austria and Hungary declared republics. The Habsburg monarchy was formally dissolved on 11 Nov. with the abdication of Charles I. The Treaty of Saint Germain in 1919 stipulated that the German–Austrian lands were not permitted to unite (*Anschluss*) with Germany without the consent of the League of Nations. Austria was declared a federal state on 1 Oct. 1920.

Nazism
The economic crises of the 1920s led to the rise of a nationalist movement much influenced by Germany's adoption of National Socialism. When Engelbert Dollfuss of the conservative Christian Socialists became chancellor in 1932 he faced Nazi and Marxist opposition. He dissolved parliament and governed by emergency decree, founding the conservative Fatherland Front in 1933. The anti-Marxist Heimwehr (home defence forces) supported him. When the Social Democrats fought back they were defeated by Dollfuss with the backing of the Heimwehr. All political parties except the Fatherland Front were subsequently banned. On 25 July 1934 a Nazi gang murdered Dollfuss but was forced to surrender and the coup leaders were executed. Dollfuss's successor, Kurt Schuschnigg, signed the Austrian–German agreement whereby Germany recognized Austria's sovereignty in return for Austria calling itself a German state. German Nazis pressurized Schuschnigg to allow them more influence, Hitler demanding that leading Nazis take on top positions in the Austrian cabinet. Schuschnigg planned a plebiscite to decide upon Anschluss but on 12 March 1938 German forces marched into Austria, establishing a Nazi government led by Arthur Seyss-Inquart. Renamed 'Ostmark', Austria was put under the central authority of the German Third Reich. After anti-Nazis were rounded up a plebiscite held on 10 April 1938 showed over 99% support for Hitler.

The Allied Moscow conference of 1943 agreed Austrian independence along the demarcation lines of 1937. The borders were finally set at the Yalta conference of Feb. 1945. On 13 April 1945 Vienna was liberated by Soviet troops. Two weeks later, Dr Karl Renner proclaimed a provisional government and Austria a republic, recognized officially by Western powers at the Potsdam conference. The first elections were held in Nov., with former Nazis excluded from voting. Leopold Figl of the Austrian People's Party (Christian Socialists) became the first chancellor of the Second Republic, with Karl Renner as its first president. The Paris treaty of Sept. 1946 granted autonomy for South Tyrol within Italy, the Allies refusing to return it to Austria. Financial support from the United Nations and the Marshall Plan enabled Austria to begin rebuilding its economy.

Post-War Period
The Soviet Union, Britain, France and the USA occupied Austria until 1955, when the country reaffirmed its neutrality. Full sovereignty was restored by the State Treaty in Vienna. Anschluss between Austria and Germany or restoration of the Habsburgs were expressly prohibited. The rights of ethnic minorities were guaranteed and former German assets confiscated by the Western allies were returned. The Soviet Union, however, demanded reparations including US$150m. for former German businesses. Austria became a member of the United Nations in 1955 and subsequently joined EFTA in 1959 and the OECD in 1960.

The first all-socialist cabinet was formed in 1970 under Chancellor Bruno Kreisky, who established economic stability and prosperity throughout the 1970s. The late 1970s saw the emergence of the Green party, with the planned construction of a nuclear power station becoming a central political issue. Kreisky's achievements were followed by political scandals which led to his resignation in 1983. Kurt Waldheim (elected as secretary general of the UN in 1971) became Austrian president in 1986 despite allegations of a Nazi past. Although this was never proved, the affair caused him to be placed on the USA's list of undesirable aliens.

Austria became a member of the European Union in 1995. In 1999 the far-right Freedom Party (FPÖ)—whose then leader, Jörg Haider, was regarded as a 'dangerous extremist' by leaders of other EU states—secured its best-ever result in a national election and subsequently joined a coalition government with the centre-right People's Party (ÖVP). The Social Democratic Party (SPÖ) emerged from further legislative elections in 2006 and 2008 as the largest party and entered into fragile coalition governments with the ÖVP. The partnership was renewed following the Sept. 2013 polls, but increasing voter concern over a surge of migrants and refugees into the country from 2015 led to a resurgence of far-right electoral support. In presidential elections in May 2016 the FPÖ candidate, Norbert Hofer, was narrowly beaten by Alexander Van der Bellen, a former Green party leader standing as an independent, although the Constitutional Court annulled the result in July because of apparent polling irregularities. Nevertheless, Van der Bellen again defeated Hofer in rerun elections in Dec. 2016.

Territory and Population
Austria is bounded in the north by Germany and the Czech Republic, east by Slovakia and Hungary, south by Slovenia and Italy, and west by Switzerland and Liechtenstein. It has an area of 83,879 sq. km (32,386 sq. miles), including 1,444 sq. km (558 sq. miles) of inland waters. Population (2011) 8,401,940; density, 101·9 per sq. km. Austria has now adopted a register-based method of calculating the population rather than a traditional census, and had a full register-based census in 2011 for the first time. Previous population censuses: (1923) 6·53m., (1934) 6·76m., (1951) 6·93m., (1971) 7·49m., (1981) 7·56m., (1991) 7·96m., (2001) 8·03m. In 2011, 67·8% of the population lived in urban areas. In Jan. 2018 the population was estimated at 8,822,267.

The UN gives a projected population for 2020 of 8·78m.

In 2011, 88·8% of residents were of Austrian nationality. The countries of origin of the principal minorities in Jan. 2012 were: Germany (153,000); Serbia and Montenegro combined, including Kosovo (136,000); Turkey (114,000); Croatia (57,000); Romania (48,000).

The areas, populations and capitals of the nine federal states:

Federal States	Area (sq. km)	Population at censuses (2001)	(2011)	State capitals
Vienna (Wien)	415	1,550,261	1,714,227	Vienna
Lower Austria (Niederösterreich)	19,186	1,545,794	1,614,693	St Pölten
Burgenland	3,962	277,558	285,685	Eisenstadt
Upper Austria (Oberösterreich)	11,980	1,376,607	1,413,762	Linz
Salzburg	7,156	515,454	529,066	Salzburg

(continued)

Federal States	Area (sq. km)	Population at censuses (2001)	Population at censuses (2011)	State capitals
Styria (Steiermark)	16,401	1,183,246	1,208,575	Graz
Carinthia (Kärnten)	9,538	559,346	556,173	Klagenfurt
Tyrol	12,640	673,543	709,319	Innsbruck
Vorarlberg	2,601	351,048	370,440	Bregenz

Populations of the main towns at the census of 2011 (and 2001): Vienna, 1,714,227 (1,550,261); Graz, 261,726 (226,241); Linz, 189,889 (183,614); Salzburg, 145,270 (142,808); Innsbruck, 119,617 (113,457); Klagenfurt, 94,483 (90,145); Villach, 59,324 (57,492); Wels, 58,591 (56,481); St Pölten, 51,955 (49,117).

The official language is German. For orthographical changes agreed in 1996 see GERMANY: Territory and Population.

Social Statistics

Statistics, 2014: live births, 81,722 (rate of 9·6 per 1,000 population); deaths, 78,252 (rate of 9·2 per 1,000 population); infant deaths, 249; marriages, 37,458; divorces, 16,647. In 2011 there were 1,286 suicides (rate of 15·3 per 100,000 population), of which 973 males and 313 females. Average annual population growth rate, 2007–11, 0·4%. Life expectancy at birth, 2011, 83·4 years for women and 78·1 years for men. In 2013 the most popular age range for marrying was 30–34 for males and 25–29 for females. Infant mortality, 2010, was four per 1,000 live births; fertility rate, 2013, 1·4 children per woman. In 2011, 130,208 people immigrated into Austria and 94,604 emigrants left Austria. Net immigration in 2011, at 35,604, was the highest since 2005. Asylum applications totalled 17,503 in 2013, up from 12,841 in 2008. Austria was ranked 37th in a gender gap index of 145 countries compiled by the World Economic Forum for its *Global Gender Gap Report 2015*. The annual index considers economic, political, education and health criteria.

Climate

The climate is temperate and from west to east in transition from marine to more continental. Depending on the elevation, the climate is also predominated by alpine influence. Winters are cold with snowfall. In the eastern parts summers are warm and dry.

Vienna, Jan. 0·0°C, July 20·2°C. Annual rainfall 624 mm. Graz, Jan. –1·0°C, July 19·4°C. Annual rainfall 825 mm. Innsbruck, Jan. –1·7°C, July 18·1°C. Annual rainfall 885 mm. Salzburg, Jan. –0·9°C, July 18·6°C. Annual rainfall 1,174 mm.

Constitution and Government

The constitution of 1 Oct. 1920 was revised in 1929 and restored on 1 May 1945. Austria is a democratic federal republic comprising nine states *(Länder)*, with a federal *President (Bundespräsident)* directly elected for not more than two successive six-year terms, and a bicameral National Assembly which comprises a National Council and a Federal Council.

The National Council *(Nationalrat)* comprises 183 members directly elected for a five-year term by proportional representation in a three-tier system by which seats are allocated at the level of 43 regional and nine state constituencies, and one federal constituency. Any party gaining 4% of votes cast nationally is represented in the National Council. In 2007 Austria's voting age was reduced to 16—the lowest for national elections in the EU.

The Federal Council *(Bundesrat)* has 61 members appointed by the nine states for the duration of the individual State Assemblies' terms; the number of deputies for each state is proportional to that state's population. In Feb. 2019 the ÖVP held 22 of the 61 seats, the SPÖ 21, the FPÖ 16 and the Greens 2.

The head of government is the *Federal Chancellor*, who is appointed by the President (usually the head of the party winning the most seats in National Council elections). The *Vice Chancellor*, the *Federal Ministers* and the *State Secretaries* are appointed by the President at the Chancellor's recommendation.

National Anthem

'Land der Berge, Land am Strome' ('Land of mountains, land on the river'); words by Paula Preradovic; tune attributed to Mozart.

Government Chronology

Presidents since 1945. (FPÖ = Freedom Party, ÖVP = Austrian People's Party; SPÖ = Social Democratic Party; n/p = non-partisan)

1945–50	SPÖ	Karl Renner
1951–57	SPÖ	Theodor Körner
1957–65	SPÖ	Adolf Schärf
1965–74	SPÖ	Franz Joseph Jonas
1974–86	SPÖ	Rudolf Kirchschläger
1986–92	ÖVP	Kurt Josef Waldheim
1992–2004	ÖVP	Thomas Klestil
2004–16	SPÖ	Heinz Fischer
2016–17	SPÖ/ÖVP/FPÖ	Doris Bures; Karlheinz Kopf; Norbert Hofer (joint acting presidents)
2017–	n/p	Alexander Van der Bellen

Federal Chancellors since 1945.

1945	SPÖ	Karl Renner
1945–53	ÖVP	Leopold Figl
1953–61	ÖVP	Julius Raab
1961–64	ÖVP	Alfons Gorbach
1964–70	ÖVP	Josef Klaus
1970–83	SPÖ	Bruno Kreisky
1983–86	SPÖ	Alfred (Fred) Sinowatz
1986–97	SPÖ	Franz Vranitzky
1997–2000	SPÖ	Viktor Klima
2000–07	ÖVP	Wolfgang Schüssel
2007–08	SPÖ	Dr Alfred Gusenbauer
2008–16	SPÖ	Werner Faymann
2016	ÖVP	Reinhold Mitterlehner (acting)
2016–17	SPÖ	Christian Kern
2017–	ÖVP	Sebastian Kurz

Recent Elections

Elections to the National Council were held on 15 Oct. 2017. The Austrian People's Party (ÖVP) won 62 seats with 31·5% of votes cast; the Social Democratic Party (SPÖ), 52 with 26·9%; the Freedom Party (FPÖ), 51 with 26·0%; the New Austria (NEOS), 10 with 5·3%; Peter Pilz List (PILZ), 8 with 4·4%. Turnout was 80·0%.

In the first round of presidential elections held on 24 April 2016 Norbert Hofer (FPÖ) won 35·1% of the vote against 21·3% for Alexander Van der Bellen (ind. but affiliated to the Greens), 18·9% for Irmgard Griss (ind.), 11·3% for Rudolf Hundstorfer (SPÖ), 11·1% for Andreas Khol (ÖVP) and 2·3% for Richard Lugner (ind.). Turnout was 68·5%. A second round run-off between Hofer and Van der Bellen took place on 22 May 2016. Van der Bellen won with 50·3% of the vote against Hofer with 49·7%. Turnout was 72·7%. However, the Constitutional Court later annulled the result after the Freedom Party had challenged the outcome and the court announced that the election would be rerun. The repeat presidential run-off was held on 4 Dec. 2016. Van der Bellen won with 53·8% of the vote against Hofer with 46·2%. Turnout was 74·2%.

European Parliament

Austria has 18 representatives. At the May 2014 elections turnout was 45·4% (46·0% in 2009). The ÖVP won 5 with 27·0% of votes cast (political affiliation in European Parliament: European People's Party); the SPÖ 5 with 24·1% (Progressive Alliance of Socialists and Democrats); the FPÖ, 4 with 19·7% (non-attached); the Greens, 3 with 14·5% (Greens/European Free Alliance); the NEOS, 1 with 8·1% (Alliance of Liberals and Democrats for Europe).

Current Government

President: Alexander Van der Bellen; b. 1944 (ind.; took office on 26 Jan. 2017).

Following the elections of Oct. 2017 the ÖVP and the FPÖ agreed in Dec. 2017 to form a coalition. In Feb. 2019 the government comprised the following:

Chancellor: Sebastian Kurz; b. 1986 (ÖVP; took office on 18 Dec. 2017).

Vice Chancellor, and Minister of Civil Service and Sport: Heinz-Christian Strache (FPÖ).

Minister of Agriculture, Forestry, Environment and Water Management: Elisabeth Köstinger (ÖVP). *Defence:* Mario Kunasek (FPÖ). *Education:* Heinz Fassmann (ind.). *Europe, Integration and Foreign Affairs:* Karin Kneissl (ind.). *Families and Youth:* Juliane Bogner-Strauss (ÖVP). *Finance:* Hartwig Löger (ind.). *Health and Women's Affairs, and Labour, Social Affairs and Consumer Protection:* Beate Hartinger-Klein (FPÖ). *Interior:* Herbert Kickl (FPÖ). *Justice:* Josef Moser (ind.). *Science, Research and Economy:* Margarete Schramböck (ind.). *Transport, Innovation and Technology:* Norbert Hofer (FPÖ). *Minister without Portfolio:* Gernot Blümel (ÖVP).

Government Website: http://www.austria.gv.at

Current Leaders

Alexander Van der Bellen

Position
President

Introduction
Alexander Van der Bellen was elected president in Dec. 2016 with the backing of the Green Party and took office on 26 Jan. 2017.

Early Life
Alexander Van der Bellen was born in Vienna on 18 Jan. 1944 into an aristocratic family of Dutch and Russian origin. His parents had fled to Austria during the Stalinist era. He graduated in economics from the University of Innsbruck in 1970 and began working at the same institution in 1976, becoming a professor four years later. Between 1990 and 1994 he was dean of economics and social sciences at the University of Vienna.

Van der Bellen had been a member of the Social Democratic Party but in 1994 became a member of the National Council (*Nationalrat*) representing the Green Party. Five years later, he was named chair of the Green faction in parliament. However, he resigned that position following the general election of Sept. 2008 when the party lost votes for the first time in a decade. Van der Bellen left parliament altogether in 2012 to join the Vienna city council.

He ran as an independent candidate for the state presidency in May 2016, although he had the *de facto* backing of the Greens. After he was declared the winner by a narrow margin, the result was annulled by the Constitutional Court in July, citing irregularities in the counts. However, he won again in the Dec. rerun, gaining 53·8% of the vote.

Career in Office
An outspoken advocate of the European Union, which he has characterized as a 'United States of Europe', he had warned in the presidential election campaign that victory for his rival Norbert Hofer of the far-right Freedom Party could herald Austria's exit from the EU. Van der Bellen has also spoken out against nationalism and anti-immigrant sentiment (having called himself the 'child of immigrants') and supports gay marriage. In Oct. 2017 federal parliamentary elections saw a strong voter swing to the right, positioning Sebastian Kurz, the leader of the conservative Austrian People's Party, to become chancellor.

Sebastian Kurz

Position
Chancellor

Introduction
Sebastian Kurz, chairman of the Austrian People's Party (ÖVP), became Chancellor on 18 Dec. 2017.

Early Life
Born on 27 Aug. 1986 in Vienna, Kurz had an early interest in politics. He joined the youth wing of the ÖVP in 2003, was elected its provincial chairman in 2007 and became federal chairman of the ÖVP in 2008. He suspended his law studies at the University of Vienna to focus on his political career.

From 2010–11, Kurz served as a member of Vienna's *Landtag* and the municipal council, and in April 2011 he was appointed state secretary for integration within the federal ministry of the interior. Elected to parliament in the 2013 legislative elections, he was named minister for Europe, integration and foreign affairs in Dec. that year. During his tenure he chaired the Committee of Ministers of the Council of Europe in 2014, hosted the Vienna Conference on the Humanitarian Impact of Nuclear Weapons in the same year and pushed through controversial legal reforms related to the funding of Islamic institutions in 2015. During Europe's migrant crisis in 2016, he closed the Western Balkans route to refugees, calling for more effective control of the European Union's external borders. In Sept. 2015 he was elected chairman of the political academy of the ÖVP.

In May 2017, following the unexpected resignation of Reinhold Mitterlehner, Kurz was elected party chairman with 98% of votes. Ahead of the Oct. legislative elections, he rebranded the ÖVP, appealing to left and far-right voters and securing the party 31·5% of the vote. It subsequently entered into a coalition with the far-right Freedom Party (FPÖ) and Kurz was sworn in as Chancellor in Dec.

Career in Office
At 31, Kurz became the world's youngest national leader, promising to lower taxes and restrict immigration whilst balancing Austria's commitment to the EU. In June 2016 he controversially proposed an 'axis of the willing' between Germany, Italy and Austria to curb illegal migration ahead of Austria's assumption of the rotating presidency of the EU Council the following month.

Defence

The Federal President is C.-in-C. of the armed forces. Conscription is for a six-month period, with liability for at least another 30 days' reservist refresher training spread over eight to ten years. Conscientious objectors can instead choose to undertake nine months' civilian service. In Jan. 2013 a referendum was held on whether to continue with conscription; 59·8% of votes cast were in favour of maintaining compulsory military service. Since 2005 the total 'on mobilization strength' of the forces has been reduced from 110,000 to 55,000 troops. In 2010 approximately 1,200 personnel were deployed in peace support operations in places such as Afghanistan, Bosnia and Herzegovina, Cyprus, the Democratic Republic of the Congo, the Golan Heights and Kosovo.

Defence expenditure in 2013 totalled US$3,232m. (US$393 per capita), representing 0·8% of GDP.

Army

The Army is structured in four brigades and nine provincial military commands. Two brigades are mechanized and two are infantry brigades. The mechanized brigades are equipped with Leopard 2/A4 main battle tanks. One of the infantry brigades is earmarked for airborne operations and the other is specialized in mountain operations. M-109 armoured self-propelled guns equip the artillery battalions. In addition to these standing units, some ten infantry battalions under the direction of the provincial military commands are available on mobilization. Active personnel, 2010, 50,000 including 25,000 conscripts. Women started to serve in the armed forces in 1998.

Air Force

The Air Force Command comprises two brigades (one air support and one air defence), approximately 150 aircraft and a number of fixed and mobile radar stations. Some 15 Eurofighter interceptors equip a surveillance wing responsible for the defence of the Austrian air space and a fighter-bomber wing operates SAAB 105s. Helicopters including the S-70 Black Hawk equip six squadrons for transport/support, communication, observation, and search and rescue duties. Fixed-wing aircraft including PC-6s, PC-7s, and C-130 Hercules are operated as trainers and for transport.

Economy

In 2012 agriculture accounted for 2% of GDP, industry 28% and services 70%.

According to the anti-corruption organization Transparency International, Austria ranked equal 14th in the world in a 2018 survey of the countries with the least corruption in business and government. It received 76 out of 100 in the annual index.

Austria gave US$1·3bn. in international aid in 2017, equivalent to 0·30% of GNI (compared to the UN target of 0·7%).

Overview

Austria has a well-developed market economy with a skilled labour force. Banking and insurance dominate economic activity, although the industrial sector is also important.

Austria has had one of the strongest productivity growth rates in the Organisation for Economic Co-operation and Development (OECD) since the late 1990s, while maintaining an employment rate above the OECD average. The economy has benefited from increasing integration with central and Eastern European countries, expanding its market share as foreign direct investment into the region has grown. Economic and monetary union within the European Union has also added momentum and encouraged market liberalization, with many companies coming under foreign (particularly German) ownership. Social partnership in the labour market has ensured wage moderation and low unemployment. Tourism is also important, reflecting Austria's Alpine appeal.

GDP growth averaged 2·8% annually over the four years before the global financial crisis in 2008 led to recession and a 3·6% contraction in 2009. Despite quickly recovering, the economy has nevertheless continued to feel the effects of the regional slowdown, with growth falling to 0·8% in 2014 from 3·0% in 2011, reflecting weak external and domestic demand. However, growth rose to 2·0% in 2016—its highest level in five years—thanks to accelerating rates of consumer spending and fixed investment.

Government debt, which had stood at 84·2% of GDP in 2014, fell slightly to 83·5% in 2016. However, despite hopes of a sharp decrease on the back of strong growth, declining government interest payments and the winding-down of bad bank liabilities, the IMF has forecast that the rate will exceed 70% for at least the medium term.

House price dynamics have raised some concerns in recent years, but pressures eased in 2017 with a pick-up in residential construction. In 2012 the government agreed an austerity package of US$36·6bn. to balance the budget by 2016. By 2014 the deficit stood at 2·7% of GDP—down from a peak of 5·3% in 2009. It continued to decline, measuring 0·8% in 2017. Nonetheless, Austria's ageing population could upset the fiscal sustainability of pension spending.

Currency

On 1 Jan. 1999 the *euro* (EUR) became the legal currency in Austria at the irrevocable conversion rate of 13·7603 schillings to one euro. The euro, which consists of 100 cents, has been in circulation since 1 Jan. 2002. On the introduction of the euro there was a 'dual circulation' period before the schilling ceased to be legal tender on 28 Feb. 2002.

Inflation rates (based on OECD statistics):

2008	2009	2010	2011	2012	2013	2014	2015	2016	2017
3·2%	0·4%	1·7%	3·6%	2·6%	2·1%	1·5%	0·8%	1·0%	2·2%

Foreign exchange reserves were US$5,269m. in Sept. 2009 and gold reserves 9·00m. troy oz. Total money supply was €96,422m. in Aug. 2009.

Budget

Central government revenue and expenditure in €1m.:

	2009	2010	2011
Revenue	101,033	104,711	109,137
Expenditure	109,759	114,090	115,914

Austria's budget deficit in 2017 was 0·8% of GDP (2016, 1·6%; 2015, 1·0%). The required target set by the EU is a deficit of no more than 3%.

The standard rate of VAT is 20%, with a special rate of 19% in two border regions (reduced rates, 13% and 10%).

Performance

Real GDP growth rates (based on OECD statistics):

2008	2009	2010	2011	2012	2013	2014	2015	2016	2017
1·2%	−3·6%	1·9%	3·0%	0·6%	0·0%	0·8%	1·1%	2·0%	2·7%

Total GDP was US$416·6bn. in 2017.

Banking and Finance

The Oesterreichische Nationalbank, central bank of Austria, opened on 1 Jan. 1923 but was taken over by the German Reichsbank on 17 March 1938. It was re-established on 3 July 1945. Its *Governor* is Ewald Nowotny. At 31 Dec. 2011 it had assets of €99,348m.

In 2011 banking and insurance accounted for 4·6% of gross domestic product at current prices. In 2010 an average of 124,789 individuals were engaged in banking and insurance (78,309 in banking and credit institutions, 28,101 in insurance companies and pension funds and 18,379 in other financial and insurance services).

In 2011 there were 824 bank and credit institution head offices and 4,441 branch offices. The leading banks with total assets in Dec. 2010 (in €1m.) were: Erste Group, 205,938; Bank Austria, 193,049; Raiffeisen Zentralbank Österreich, 136,497.

Gross external debt amounted to US$779,544m. in June 2012.

There is a stock exchange in Vienna (VEX). It is one of the oldest in Europe.

Energy and Natural Resources

In 2011, 30·9% of energy consumption came from renewables (wind power, solar power, hydro-electric power, tidal power, geothermal energy and biomass), compared to the European Union average of 13·0%. A target of 34% has been set by the EU for 2020.

Environment

Austria's carbon dioxide emissions from the consumption of energy were the equivalent of 8·4 tonnes per capita in 2011. An *Environmental Performance Index* compiled in 2016 ranked Austria 18th of 180 countries, with 86·6%. The index examined various factors in nine areas—agriculture, air quality, biodiversity and habitat, climate and energy, fisheries, forests, health impacts, water and sanitation, and water resources.

Austria is one of the world leaders in recycling. In 2012 an estimated 62% of municipal waste was composted or recycled.

Electricity

The Austrian electricity market was fully liberalized on 1 Oct. 2001. Installed capacity was 22·8m. kW in 2011. Production in 2011 was 65·70bn. kWh. Consumption per capita, 2011: 8,763 kWh. Renewable sources accounted for 68·0% of electricity consumption in 2013—the highest share in the EU.

Oil and Gas

The commercial production of petroleum began in the early 1930s. Production of crude oil, 2011: 5·0m. bbls. Crude oil reserves, 2011, were 50m. bbls.

The Austrian gas market was fully liberalized on 1 Oct. 2002. Production of natural gas, 2011: 1,873m. cu. metres. Natural gas reserves in 2013 amounted to 11bn. cu. metres.

Minerals

The most important minerals are sand and gravel (2011 production, 25,063,350 tonnes), limestone (2011 production, 21,570,972 tonnes), dolomite (2011 production, 3,710,729 tonnes) and granite and granulite (2011 production, 3,034,265 tonnes).

Agriculture

In 2010 the agricultural workforce numbered 413,755 (520,984 in 2005). There were 173,317 farms in 2010. There were 1·35m. ha. of arable land in 2013 and 65,000 ha. of permanent crops. In 2011 Austria set aside 542,600 ha. (19·7% of its agricultural land—the highest percentage in the European Union) for the growth of organic crops. Food and live animals accounted for 5·8% of exports and 6·7% of imports in 2014.

The chief products in 2010 (area in 1,000 ha.; yield in tonnes) were as follows: barley (168·9, 777,961); grain maize (179·8, 1,692,450); potatoes (22·0, 671,722); silo maize (81·2, 3,557,330); sugar beets (44·8, 3,131,666); wheat (302·9, 1,517,805). Other important agricultural products include apples (197,413 tonnes in 2010) and pears (8,185 tonnes in 2010). Wine production in 2015 totalled 2,268,403 hectolitres.

Livestock in 2011: cattle, 1,976,527; pigs, 3,004,907; sheep, 361,183; poultry, 14,644,413.

Forestry

Forested area in 2015, 3·87m. ha. (47% of the land area). Of the total area under forests 3% was primary forest in 2015, 53% other naturally regenerated forest and 44% planted forest. Growing stock was 1,155m. cu. metres in 2015 (927m. cu. metres coniferous and 228m. cu. metres broadleaved). Felled timber, in 1,000 cu. metres: 2008, 21,795·4; 2009, 16,727·4; 2010, 17,831·0.

Fisheries

Total catch in 2015 came to 350 tonnes, exclusively from inland waters.

Industry

The leading companies by market capitalization in Austria in March 2019 were: OMV Group, an oil and gas company (US$21·5bn.); Erste Group, a banking group (US$19·0bn.); and Raiffeisen Bank International, a regional banking group (US$11·2bn.).

Production (in 1,000 tonnes): pig iron (2007), 5,808; paper and paperboard (2007), 5,199; cement (2008), 5,309; distillate fuel oil (2007), 3,461; petrol (2007), 1,702; residual fuel oil (2007), 880; sawnwood (2007), 11·26m. cu. metres; beer (2010), 883·4m. litres.

Labour

Of 3,421,755 employees in 2011 (annual average), 573,571 worked in the manufacturing and production of goods; 529,976 in public administration and defence, and compulsory social security; 518,188 in wholesale and retail trade, and the repair of motor vehicles; 233,994 in human health and social work; 184,548 in accommodation and food service activities. In 2011 there were an average of 73,800 job vacancies.

The unemployment rate in Dec. 2018 was 4·6% (down from 5·5% in 2017 as a whole), compared to the European Union average of 7·3%.

There were no recorded strikes between 2005 and 2009.

Austria has one of the lowest average retirement ages but reforms passed in 1997 now make it less attractive to retire before 60. Only 15% of men and 6% of women in the 60–65 age range work, although the legal retirement ages are 60 for women and 65 for men.

International Trade

Imports and Exports

In 2014 imports were valued at €129,847m. (€130,707m. in 2013) and exports €128,106m. (€125,812m. in 2013).

Leading import suppliers in 2011 (% of total imports) were: Germany, 38·2%; Italy, 6·5%; Switzerland, 5·4%; China, 4·9%; Czech Republic, 3·7%; USA, 2·9%. Principal export markets in 2011 (% of total exports) were: Germany, 31·2%; Italy, 7·7%; USA, 5·2%; Switzerland, 4·9%; France, 4·1%; Czech Republic 3·9%.

In 2011 chemicals, manufactured goods classified chiefly by material and miscellaneous manufactured articles accounted for 42·5% of Austria's imports and 47·7% of exports; machinery and transport equipment 31·8% of imports and 37·8% of exports; food, live animals, beverages and tobacco 6·3% of imports and 6·7% of exports; mineral fuels, lubricants and related materials 12·0% of imports and 3·4% of exports; inedible crude materials (except fuels), and animal and vegetable oil and fats 5·5% of imports and 3·5% of exports.

Trade Fairs

Vienna ranked as the second most popular convention city in 2016 according to the International Congress and Convention Association. Vienna hosted 186 international association meetings that year.

Communications

Roads

In 2007 the road network totalled 107,262 km (Autobahn, 1,677 km; highways, 10,408 km; secondary roads, 23,657 km). In 2007 passenger cars in use numbered 4,245,600, lorries and vans 372,600, buses and coaches 9,300, and motorcycles and mopeds 642,800. There were 691 fatalities in road accidents in 2007.

Rail

The Austrian Federal Railways (ÖBB) has been restructured and was split up into ten new companies, which became operational on 1 Jan. 2005. Length of route in 2011, 5,500 km, of which 3,763 km were electrified. There are also a number of private railways. In 2011, 244·0m. passengers and 107·6m. tonnes

of freight were carried by Federal Railways. There is a metro and tramway in Vienna, and tramways in Gmunden, Graz, Innsbruck and Linz.

Civil Aviation

There are international airports at Vienna (Schwechat), Graz, Innsbruck, Klagenfurt, Linz and Salzburg. The national airline is Austrian Airlines, which was privatized after a takeover by Lufthansa in Sept. 2009. In April 2015 Tyrolean Airways merged into Austrian Airlines. In 2010, 65 other airlines had scheduled flights to and from Vienna. In 2011, 312,502 commercial aircraft and 25,704,655 passengers arrived and departed; 227,938 tonnes of freight and 13,551 tonnes of mail were handled. In 2011 Vienna handled 21,069,398 passengers and 218,835 tonnes of freight. Austrian Airlines carried 11,261,000 passengers in 2011. In 2010 there were direct international services to more than 140 destinations from Vienna, 30 from Salzburg, 24 from Graz, 17 from Linz and 16 from Innsbruck.

Shipping

The Danube is an important waterway. Goods traffic (in 1,000 tonnes): 10,714 in 2012; 10,710 in 2013; 10,122 in 2014; 8,599 in 2015 (including the Rhine-Main-Danube Canal).

Telecommunications

Österreichische Industrie Holding AG, the Austrian investment and privatization agency, holds a 28·4% stake in Telekom Austria. In 2014 mobile phone subscriptions numbered 12,952,600 (1,519·1 per 1,000 persons). In the same year there were 3,254,700 main (fixed) telephone lines. In 2014, 81·0% of the population were internet users. In March 2012 there were 2·8m. Facebook users.

Social Institutions

Out of 178 countries analysed in the 2017 *Fragile States Index*—a list published jointly by the Fund for Peace and *Foreign Policy* magazine— Austria was ranked the 13th least vulnerable to conflict or collapse. The index is based on 12 indicators of state vulnerability across social, political and economic categories.

Justice

The Supreme Court of Justice *(Oberster Gerichtshof)* in Vienna is the highest court in civil and criminal cases. In addition, in 2012 there were four Courts of Appeal *(Oberlandesgerichte)*, 20 High Courts *(Landesgerichte)* and 141 District Courts *(Bezirksgerichte)*. There are also a Supreme Constitutional Court *(Verfassungsgerichtshof)* and a Supreme Administrative Court *(Verwaltungsgerichtshof)*, both seated in Vienna. In 2011 a total of 540,007 criminal offences were reported to the police and 36,461 people were convicted of offences. The population in penal institutions in Jan. 2013 was 8,273 (98 per 100,000 of national population). In 2015 the World Justice Project *Rule of Law Index*, which provides data on how the rule of law is experienced by the general public across eight categories, ranked Austria fifth of 102 countries for criminal justice and eighth for civil justice.

Education

In 2015–16 there were 4,522 general compulsory schools (including special education) with 72,696 teachers and 567,544 pupils. Secondary schools totalled 347 in 2015–16, with 22,417 teachers and 207,070 pupils. Secondary technical and vocational colleges numbered 309 in 2015–16, with 133,447 pupils.

The dominant institutions of higher education are the 16 public universities and six colleges of arts. Student fees were introduced in 2001, but in 2008 the government decided to eliminate fees for Austrian nationals who complete their studies within the minimum time.

In the winter term 2015–16 there were 280,445 students (73,795 foreign) enrolled at the public universities and 10,990 (5,160 foreign) at the colleges of arts. In 1994 Higher Technical Study Centres *(Fachhochschul-Studiengänge,* FHS) were established, which are private, but government-dependent, institutions. A federal law was passed in 1999 to allow the accreditation of private universities. In 2016 there were 12 accredited private universities.

In 2013 public expenditure on education came to 5·6% of GDP and 11·0% of total government spending. The adult literacy rate is at least 99%.

Health

In 2015 there were 44,002 doctors, 4,906 dentists and 60,171 nurses and midwives. In the same year there were 278 hospitals and 65,138 hospital beds. In 2014 Austria spent 11·0% of its GDP on health.

Welfare

Maternity/paternity leave is until the child's second birthday. A new parenting allowance was introduced on 1 Jan. 2002, replacing the maternity/paternity allowance. The latest formula is based on family benefit financed from the Family Fund. The basic allowance is €436 per month for a maximum of three years. In June 2003 a reform of the pensions system was approved involving the reduction of pension benefits by 10%, an increase in the workers' contribution period from 40 to 45 years and a gradual increase in the retirement age. As at Feb. 2018 the minimum retirement age was 65 years for males and 60 years for females, with the latter set to increase incrementally to 65 years between 2024 and 2033. There were 2,705,480 pensioners in Dec. 2011.

Religion

In 2012 there were 5·36m. Roman Catholics (5·92m. in 2001). There were an estimated 574,000 Muslims in 2012 (339,000 in 2001). Orthodox Christians number around 500,000 and Evangelical Lutherans 300,000. The Roman Catholic Church has two ecclesiastical provinces and seven suffragan dioceses. In Feb. 2019 there was one cardinal.

Culture

World Heritage Sites

There are ten UNESCO sites in Austria. They are: the historic centre of the city of Salzburg (inscribed in 1996); the Palace and gardens of Schönbrunn (1996); Hallstatt-Dachstein Salzkammergut cultural landscape (1997); Semmering Railway (1998); the historic centre of the city of Graz (1999); the Wachau cultural landscape (2000); and the historic centre of the city of Vienna (2001).

Austria shares the Cultural Landscape of Fertö/Neusiedlersee site (2001) with Hungary. Ancient and Primeval Beech Forests of the Carpathians and Other Regions of Europe (2007 and 2017) are shared with Albania, Belgium, Bulgaria, Croatia, Germany, Italy, Romania, Slovakia, Slovenia, Spain and Ukraine. The Prehistoric Pile dwellings around the Alps (2011) are shared with France, Germany, Italy, Slovenia and Switzerland.

Press

There were 18 daily newspapers and 273 non-daily newspapers in 2014. The most popular newspaper is the mass-market tabloid *Kronen Zeitung*, with an average daily circulation of 815,000 in 2014. In the 2011–12 *World Press Freedom Index* compiled by Reporters Without Borders, Austria ranked fifth out of 179 countries.

Tourism

In 2011, 13,359 hotels and boarding houses had a total of 594,357 beds available; in the same year 23,012,000 non-resident tourists stayed in holiday accommodation and international tourist spending came to €14·3bn. Of 126,002,551 overnight stays in tourist accommodation in 2011, 35,296,997 were by Austrians and 47,389,531 by Germans.

Festivals

The main festivals are the Salzburg Festival, held every July–Aug. (263,501 visitors in 2015), the Bregenz Festival, also held in July–Aug. (259,425 visitors in 2013) and the Mörbisch Festival on the Lake (131,560 visitors in 2015), again held in July–Aug. Popular music festivals include Snowbombing music and snow sports festival in Mayrhofen (April), Vienna Jazz Fest (May–July), Donauinselfest in Vienna (June) and Nova Rock Festival at Nickelsdorf (June).

Diplomatic Representatives

Of Austria in the United Kingdom (18 Belgrave Mews West, London, SW1X 8HU)
Ambassador: Dr Michael Zimmermann.

Of the United Kingdom in Austria (Jaurèsgasse 12, 1030 Vienna)
Ambassador: Leigh Turner, CMG.

Of Austria in the USA (3524 International Court, NW, Washington, D.C., 20008)
Ambassador: Wolfgang A. Waldner.

Of the USA in Austria (Boltzmanngasse 16, 1090 Vienna)
Ambassador: Trevor D. Traina.

Of Austria to the United Nations
Ambassador: Jan Kickert.

Of Austria to the European Union
Permanent Representative: Nikolaus Marschik.

Further Reading

Austrian Central Statistical Office. *Main publications: Statistisches Jahrbuch für die Republik Österreich.* New Series from 1950. Annual.—*Statistische Nachrichten.* Monthly.—*Beiträge zur österreichischen Statistik.—Statistik in Österreich 1918–1938.* [Bibliography] 1985.—*Veröffentlichungen des Österreichischen Statistischen Zentralamtes 1945–1985.* [Bibliography] 1990.—*Republik Österreich, 1945–1995.*

Bischof, Günter, Pelinka, Anton and Gehler, Michael, (eds) *Austria in the European Union.* 2002.—*Austrian Foreign Policy in Historical Context.* 2005

Brook-Shepherd, G., *The Austrians: a Thousand-Year Odyssey.* 1997

Bruckmüller, Ernst, *Austrian Nation: Cultural Consciousness and Socio-Political Processes.* 2003

Pick, Hella, *Guilty Victim: Austria from the Holocaust to Haider.* 2000

Steininger, Rolf, *Austria in the Twentieth Century.* 2002

Wolfram, H. (ed.) *Österreichische Geschichte.* 10 vols. 1994

National library: Österreichische Nationalbibliothek, Josefsplatz, 1015 Vienna.

Website: http://www.onb.ac.at

National Statistical Office: Austrian Central Statistical Office, Guglgasse 13, A-1110 Vienna.

Website: http://www.statistik.at

Azerbaijan

Azarbaijchan Respublikasy (Republic of Azerbaijan)

Capital: Baku
Population projection, 2020: 10·10m.
GNI per capita, 2017: (PPP$) 15,600
HDI/world rank, 2017: 0·757/80=
Internet domain extension: .az

Key Historical Events

Rock art at Gobustan, close to Azerbaijan's Caspian Sea coast, dates from 20,000 BC. Part of southern Azerbaijan came under the influence of the Assyrian Empire around 800 BC and was later subsumed into the ancient kingdoms of Manue, Urartu and Medea. During the 6th century BC the Persian Akhemenid dynasty held sway in what was known as Caucasian Albania, fortified by the Zoroastrian religion. Persian influence continued in the form of the Parthian Empire from around 200 BC, followed by periods of Roman rule. The Arshakid dynasty, installed by the Romans to control much of the Caucasus, survived until the Persian Sassanid Empire in the 4th century AD.

Sassanid power reached its zenith under Khosrau II around AD 620, with a sphere of influence stretching from Egypt to the Caucasus, central Asia and northwest India. Arab tribes, newly united around Islam, made incursions into Azerbaijan from the mid-7th century. From 750 the territory came under the rule of Caliph Abu Abbas, whose Abbasid dynasty was centred on Baghdad.

Arab control of Azerbaijan was waning by the late 10th century and the region dissolved into numerous fiefdoms, including Shirvan (centred on Shemakha) and Arran (based at Terter). The 11th century saw an influx of nomadic Oghuz Turks under the Seljuk dynasty from Central Asia. This began a process of Turkification that continued for the next three centuries, punctuated by Mongol incursions including the Golden Horde in 1319 and Timur in 1380.

At the end of the 15th century Azerbaijan became the power base of the Safavid dynasty, centred on Ardabil (now in northern Iran). Shah Ismail I forged a kingdom that controlled all Persia by 1520 and which promoted the Shia branch of Islam as the state religion. There was conflict with Ottoman Turkey, which followed Sunni Muslim traditions, and the Safavids shifted their focus eastwards from Azerbaijan, eventually establishing their capital in Esfahan.

The overthrow of Safavid control in Azerbaijan in 1722 preceded increasing Russian influence in the region, which led to the annexation of Georgia by Tsar Alexander I and the control of the khanates in Azerbaijan. By 1807 Nakhichevan remained the only independent khanate, although Russian forces had to fight off Persian challenges for control. The territory of the present Azerbaijan was acquired by Russia from Persia through the treaties of Gulistan (1813) and Turkmenchai (1828). This period of Russian rule was marked by an influx of Armenians into western Azerbaijan, fleeing persecution from Ottoman Turkey and Persia.

Azerbaijan's oil industry, centred on Baku, began to develop in the 1870s. By the early 20th century half the world's production was supplied from Baku. Tensions between Azeris and Armenians rose against the backdrop of revolutions in Russia (1905–07) and Iran (1906–11), prompting the rise of Azeri nationalism. Following the Bolshevik revolution in 1917, Azerbaijan joined with Armenia and Georgia to form the short-lived Transcaucasian Federation. On 28 May 1918 the Azerbaijani Democratic Republic was declared, with Gandja as its capital. The fledgling nation was soon occupied, first by Ottoman troops and then by British forces until they withdrew in Aug. 1919. After the Red Army achieved victory in Russia's civil war in early 1920, it moved swiftly to secure control of oil-rich Azerbaijan, reaching Baku on 28 April 1920.

In 1922 Azerbaijan joined the Transcaucasian Soviet Federal Socialist Republic, led by Nariman Narimanov. Stalin's administrative reorganization of 1936 made Azerbaijan a separate Soviet Republic, forcing it to break links with other Turkic and Islamic states. Mass killings, deportations and imprisonments followed, reaching their height in the Stalinist purges of 1937. Baku's oilfields were an objective for Nazi forces in the Second World War but their defeat at Stalingrad meant that Azerbaijan remained under Soviet control.

Conflict with Armenia over the enclave of Nagorno-Karabakh (now Artsakh) escalated in 1988, leading to violent expulsions of Armenians in Azerbaijan and Azeris in Armenia. In 'Black January' 1990 Soviet tanks moved into Baku following rioting and over 100 civilians were killed. War broke out between the two countries in 1992 after the Armenian population of Nagorno-Karabakh declared independence from Azerbaijan. A ceasefire was agreed in 1994 but the dispute over territory remains unsettled, despite the efforts of the Organization for Security and Co-operation in Europe's Minsk Group (co-chaired by France, Russia and the USA) to broker a peace.

On 18 Aug. 1991 the Supreme Soviet of Azerbaijan declared independence from the crumbling Soviet Union. Following an attempted coup in June 1993, Heidar Aliyev was appointed president by the National Assembly and then confirmed in a general election in Oct. Parliament ratified association with the Commonwealth of Independent States on 20 Sept. 1993. A treaty of friendship and co-operation was signed with Russia on 3 July 1997 and Aliyev was re-elected in Oct. 1998, although the administration of the election was criticized by international observers. Following serious illness, Aliyev stood down from the presidency in Oct. 2003. He controversially appointed his son, Ilham, as the party's sole presidential candidate. Ilham Aliyev duly won the presidential election of 15 Oct. 2003 but international observers again criticized the contest as falling below accepted standards. He was re-elected in both 2008 and 2013.

Territory and Population

Azerbaijan is bounded in the west by Armenia, in the north by Georgia and the Russian Federation (Dagestan), in the east by the Caspian sea and in the south by Turkey and Iran. Its area is 86,600 sq. km (33,430 sq. miles), and it includes the Nakhichevan Autonomous Republic and the largely Armenian-inhabited Artsakh (formerly Nagorno-Karabakh).

The population at the 2009 census was 8,922,447 (50·5% females); density, 103 per sq. km. In 2011, 52·1% of the population lived in urban areas. The population breaks down into 91·6% Azerbaijanis, 2·0% Lezgis, 1·3% Armenians and 1·3% Russians (2009 census). Population estimate, Jan. 2013: 9,356,500.

The UN gives a projected population for 2020 of 10·10m.

Chief cities (estimates of Jan. 2013): Baku, 1,200,300; Gandja 322,600; Sumgait 290,500. There are 66 districts and 13 cities.

The official language is Azeri. On 1 Aug. 2001 Azerbaijan abolished the use of the Cyrillic alphabet and switched to using Latin script.

Social Statistics

In 2009: births, 152,139; deaths, 52,514; marriages, 78,072; divorces, 7,784. Rates, 2009 (per 1,000 population): births, 17·2; deaths, 5·9; infant mortality (2010, per 1,000 live births), 39. Life expectancy in 2013: 73·9 years for females and 67·6 years for males. Annual population growth rate, 2005–12, 1·3%; fertility rate, 2013, 1·9 children per woman.

Climate

The climate is almost tropical in summer and the winters slightly warmer than in regions north of the Caucasus. Cold spells do occur, however, both on the high mountains and in the enclosed valleys. There are nine climatic zones. Baku, Jan. –6°C, July 25°C. Annual rainfall 318 mm.

Constitution and Government

Parliament is the 125-member *Melli-Majlis*, with all seats elected from single-member districts. A constitutional referendum and parliamentary elections were held on 12 Nov. 1995. Turnout for the referendum was 86%. The

© Springer Nature Limited 2020
Palgrave Macmillan (ed.), *The Statesman's Yearbook 2020*,
https://doi.org/10.1057/978-1-349-95940-2_21

new constitution was approved by 91·9% of votes cast. As a result of a referendum held on 24 Aug. 2002 a number of changes were made to the constitution, including the distribution of the *Melli-Majlis* seats—previously, 25 seats were distributed proportionally among political parties. The validity of the outcome of the referendum was questioned by international observers. In a referendum on 18 March 2009 a measure to abolish presidential term limits was approved, with 91·8% of votes cast in favour. In a referendum on 18 March 2009 a measure to abolish the two-term presidential limit was approved, with 91·8% of votes cast in favour. A further amendment, approved by referendum in Sept. 2016, extended the length of the presidential term from five to seven years.

National Anthem

'Azerbaijan! Azerbaijan!'; words by A. Javad, tune by U. Hajibeyov.

Recent Elections

At elections on 11 April 2018 Ilham Aliyev of the New Azerbaijan Party (YAP) was re-elected president with 86·0% of votes cast. The independent candidate Zahid Oruj won 3·1%, Sardar Mammadov of the Azerbaijan Democratic Party (ADP) won 3·0% and Gudrat Hasanguliyev of the Whole Azerbaijan Popular Front Party (PFPWA) also 3·0%. There were four other candidates who received less than 2% of the vote each.

At the parliamentary elections held on 1 Nov. 2015 the YAP gained 70 seats, Civic Solidarity 2, and ind. and others 52. One seat was vacant. Turnout was 55·5%.

Current Government

President: Ilham Aliyev; b. 1961 (YAP; sworn in 31 Oct. 2003 and re-elected in Oct. 2008, Oct. 2013 and April 2018).

Vice-President: Mehriban Aliyeva.

In Feb. 2019 the government comprised:

Prime Minister: Novruz Mammadov; b. 1947 (YAP; in office since 21 April 2018).

First Deputy Prime Minister: Yaqub Eyyubov. *Deputy Prime Ministers:* Hajibala Abutalybov; Ali Ahmadov; Ali Hasanov.

Minister of Agriculture: Inam Karimov. *Culture:* Abulfaz Garayev. *Defence:* Zakir Hasanov. *Defence Industry:* Vacant. *Ecology and Natural Resources:* Mukhtar Babayev. *Economy:* Shahin Mustafayev. *Education:* Jeyhun Bayramov. *Emergency Situations:* Kamaladdin Heydarov. *Energy:* Parviz Shahbazov. *Finance:* Samir Sharifov. *Foreign Affairs:* Elmar Mamedyarov. *Health:* Ogtay Shiraliyev. *Interior:* Ramil Usubov. *Justice:* Fikret Mamedov. *Labour and Social Protection:* Sahil Babayev. *Taxes:* Mikayil Jabbarov. *Transport, Communications and Information Technologies:* Ramin Guluzade. *Youth and Sport:* Azad Rahimov.

Office of the President: http://www.president.az

Current Leaders

Ilham Aliyev

Position

President

Introduction

Ilham Aliyev succeeded his father, Heidar Aliyev, as president in Oct. 2003. The Moscow-educated politician has presided not only over a rapidly-growing economy until the collapse in oil prices from 2014, but also increasing repression of political opposition. He was re-elected president in Oct. 2008, Oct. 2013 and April 2018, although opposition groups dismissed the polls as neither free nor fair.

Early Life

Ilham Heidar oglu Aliyev was born in Baku, capital of the Soviet Socialist Republic of Azerbaijan, on 24 Dec. 1961. His father was Heidar Aliyev, who became deputy prime minister of the Soviet Union under Mikhail Gorbachev and, in Oct. 1993, president of Azerbaijan. Ilham Aliyev graduated in history from the Moscow State Institute for International Relations in 1982. He subsequently gained a PhD in history and began teaching at the Institute. Plans to enter the diplomatic service were curtailed by the collapse of the Soviet Union in 1991 and he established 'business interests' in Moscow and İstanbul. Between 1991 and 1994 his flamboyant lifestyle attracted media attention and he was accused of accumulating large gambling debts.

In May 1994 Ilham Aliyev was appointed vice president of Azerbaijan's state oil company. Four months later President Aliyev signed a 30-year deal valued at more than US$7bn. with eight foreign companies to develop the country's substantial oil reserves. In 1995 Ilham Aliyev was elected to parliament and was subsequently appointed president of the national Olympic committee and head of the Azerbaijan delegation to the Council of Europe. In Dec. 1999 he became a deputy of the ruling New Azerbaijan Party (YAP) and, in 2001, was appointed party vice president.

Following the surprise resignation of Prime Minister Artur Rasizade in Aug. 2003, Heidar Aliyev appointed his son as prime minister. The move was approved by a 101–1 vote in the National Assembly but opposition parties boycotted the election. Critics took the move as proof that the increasingly frail president planned to hand over power to his son (an amendment to the constitution in Aug. 2002 providing for the prime minister to become interim president in the event that the president dies in office or is incapacitated). A few weeks before the presidential elections of Oct. 2003 Heidar Aliyev pulled out of the running, leaving Ilham as the YAP's candidate.

Official results gave Aliyev victory with 76·8% of the vote but opposition parties staged mass protests over alleged intimidation and fraud, charges backed by international observers. Aliyev was sworn in as the president on 31 Oct. 2003. His father died on 12 Dec. 2003.

Career in Office

For most of his tenure Aliyev has overseen a rapidly expanding economy, a consequence of the discovery of offshore gas fields, high international oil prices (until 2014) and the completion of pipelines crossing from the Caucasus to Turkey. However, unemployment and poverty levels nonetheless have remained high, especially in rural areas.

Aliyev released a number of opposition figures from prison in March 2005 following international pressure, particularly from the Council of Europe. However, his administration was criticized for intimidating opposition activists in the run-up to parliamentary elections in Nov. 2005. The YAP, led by Aliyev since March 2005, won 56 of 125 parliamentary seats but the Organization for Security and Co-operation in Europe's international election observer mission reported harassment and vote buying. The opposition Azadlig party refused to accept the election results and organized mass protests in Nov. and Dec. 2005. In Nov. 2006 an independent broadcaster was closed down and a newspaper evicted from offices in Baku. These measures were denounced by the opposition as a clampdown by the regime on freedom of speech. In Oct. 2008 Western observers judged that Aliyev's overwhelming re-election as president was an improvement on the conduct of previous polls but still fell short of fully-democratic standards. A constitutional amendment to abolish presidential term limits was approved in a referendum in March 2009 with nearly 92% of the vote, allowing Aliyev to stand for election a third time. In Nov. 2010 the YAP won a majority of seats in parliamentary elections, although international monitors again cited widespread voting irregularities. There were repeated demonstrations against Aliyev's regime in 2011 but protesters' demands for democratic reforms were rejected and a continuing security crackdown on civil society imposed. Aliyev was nonetheless returned to office again in Oct. 2013 with a landslide victory, while the YAP maintained its dominance in further parliamentary polling in Nov. 2015 that the opposition boycotted and international observers declined to monitor. Furthermore, in Sept. 2016 voters in a referendum approved a series of constitutional amendments including an extension of the presidential term from five to seven years and the creation of the post of first vice-president (a position subsequently awarded to his wife, Mehriban, in Feb. 2017).

In Feb. 2006 Aliyev met Armenia's then president, Robert Kocharian, in Paris, France, but the two failed to agree on a 'declaration of principles' on the disputed territory of Nagorno-Karabakh (now Artsakh). Azerbaijan has continued to reject any move towards independence for the Armenian enclave, despite several Russian-brokered meetings between Aliyev and the then Armenian president Serzh Sargsyan to find a political settlement over the territory. Sporadic border fighting has meanwhile continued, notably in 2008, 2012, 2014, 2016 and 2017.

Novruz Mammadov

Position

Prime Minister

Introduction

Novruz Mammadov, an academic-turned-politician, was appointed prime minister by President Ilham Aliyev in April 2018, succeeding Artur Rasizade who had served in the post almost continuously since July 1996.

Early Life

Novruz Mammadov was born on 15 March 1947 in Nakhichevan, an autonomous territory within the then Azerbaijan Soviet Socialist Republic prior to the break-up of the Soviet Union and Azerbaijan's declaration of independence in Aug. 1991. Having studied French at the Azerbaijani Pedagogical Foreign Languages Institute (APFLI), he initially worked as an interpreter in Algeria (for two periods from 1967–68 and from 1978–81) and in Guinea (from 1971–73). He was later awarded a postgraduate PhD in philology from the APFLI where he became an instructor and then dean of the French language faculty. From 1995–97 he served as French language interpreter/translator to the President of Azerbaijan (the late Heidar Aliyev, father of the present incumbent) and subsequently held the political position of assistant to the President for foreign policy issues and head of the state foreign policy department before his appointment as premier in April 2018.

Mammadov was meanwhile concurrently chair of French Language Lexicology and Methodology at the Azerbaijani Foreign Languages University from 2003–18. He has authored numerous academic articles and books, translated notable works and also been awarded several state honours.

Career in Office

Following the return of Ilham Aliyev for a fourth consecutive presidential term in early elections boycotted by opposition parties on 11 April 2018, Mammadov was nominated as the new prime minister on 21 April. On the same day his candidature was approved by parliament and his cabinet was announced with no changes to key ministerial personnel. A staunch Aliyev loyalist, Mammadov defended the early presidential poll, stating that it was 'crucial for resolving important issues facing the state and mobilizing political and economic resources more effectively for the new era . . . with a view to increase the effectiveness of reforms on the agenda'.

Defence

Conscription is for 18 months, or 12 in the case of university graduates. In 2013 defence spending reached US$3·3bn., up from US$0·4bn. a decade earlier. Defence expenditure in 2013 was equivalent to US$209 per capita and represented 2·6% of GDP.

Army

Personnel, 2011, 56,840. In addition there is a reserve force of 300,000 Azerbaijanis who have received some kind of military service experience within the last 15 years. There is also a paramilitary Ministry of the Interior militia of more than 15,000 and a border guard of approximately 5,000.

Navy

The flotilla is based at Baku on the Caspian Sea. Personnel numbered about 2,200 in 2011. Equipment in 2011 included eight patrol and coastal combatants.

Air Force

How many ex-Soviet aircraft are usable is not known but in 2011 there were 44 combat-capable aircraft and 26 attack helicopters. Personnel, 7,900 in 2011.

International Relations

There is a dispute with Armenia over the status of the chiefly Armenian-populated Azerbaijani enclave of Artsakh (formerly Nagorno-Karabakh). A ceasefire was negotiated from 1994 with 20% of Azerbaijan's land in Armenian hands and with 1m. Azeri refugees and displaced persons. Nonetheless, sporadic fighting has since continued.

Economy

In 2015 agriculture accounted for 6·8% of GDP, industry 49·3% and services 43·9%.

Overview

The economy is heavily reliant on oil. In 1994 the government signed a production-sharing agreement with a consortium of foreign companies to develop oil deposits in the Caspian Sea and transport oil from Azerbaijan to Turkey via Georgia through the Baku-Tbilisi-Ceyhan and Shah Deniz pipelines. In 1999 the State Oil Fund was created to manage the oil boom. Its assets were valued at US$37·6bn. at the end of the first quarter of 2018.

GDP growth averaged 2·4% per year between 2011 and 2015. However, a decline in the oil price, as well as a fall-off in exports, induced a contraction of 3·1% in 2016, prompting the central bank to tighten monetary policy. Growth then recovered to 0·1% in 2017.

Following independence in 1991, Azerbaijan suffered from corruption, distortion and weak social infrastructure. Nonetheless, in the first decade of this century the economy consistently had one of the world's fastest growth rates (measuring 34·5% in 2006) and was well equipped to weather the global financial crisis that hit in 2008. Fiscal stimulus and a stable exchange rate prevented non-oil growth falling below 3%, while the central bank provided support to state enterprises, including provision for losses on overseas investments.

Strong oil-based growth combined with increased wages and well-targeted social programmes helped reduce the poverty rate from 50% in 2001 to 5% in 2013. However, inequalities in income, health and education have remained high, and a small increase in the poverty rate was observed in 2016, tied to the overall economic challenges of the country.

In the longer term the authorities must seek to reduce dependence on oil and gas revenues. According to the IMF, diversification is dependent on stimulating private sector development by improving governance and the business environment. While there have been encouraging signs since 2013, corruption, limited access to finance and a weak financial sector remain major obstacles.

Currency

The *manat* (AZM) of 100 *gyapiks* replaced the *rouble* in Jan. 1994. It was in turn replaced in Jan. 2006 by the *new manat* (AZN), also of 100 *gyapiks*, at 1 new manat = 5,000 manats. It was devalued by 33·5% against the US dollar in Feb. 2015 and again by 47·6% in Dec. of the same year, following which Azerbaijan adopted a floating exchange rate regime. Inflation was 12·6% in 2016 and 13·0% in 2017. Foreign exchange reserves were US$1,028m. in July 2005 and total money supply was 3,846·1bn. manats.

Budget

Budgetary central government revenue in 2011 totalled 15,831·7m. manats and expenditure 7,827·7m. manats.

Principal sources of revenue in 2011 were: grants, 9,006·7m. manats; taxes on goods and services, 2,865·1m. manats; taxes on income, profits and capital gains, 2,861·6m. manats. Main items of expenditure by economic type in 2011: compensation of employees, 1,750·3m. manats; grants, 1,150·7m. manats; use of goods and services, 916·2m. manats.

Performance

Total GDP was US$40·7bn. in 2017. Until 2010 Azerbaijan had one of the fastest-growing economies in the world. Real GDP growth was 28·0% in 2005, 34·5% in 2006 and 25·5% in 2007—the highest rates of any country in each of these years. This was largely thanks to the oil boom at the time. More recently the economy grew by 0·6% in 2015. A recession followed in 2016 as a consequence of the global fall in oil prices, with the economy contracting by 3·1%. There was only a very slight recovery in 2017 when GDP grew by 0·1%.

Banking and Finance

The central bank and bank of issue is the National Bank (*Chairman*, Dr Elman Rustamov). The largest of the 44 commercial banks in Dec. 2011 was the International Bank of Azerbaijan (the only state-owned bank), with assets of US$6·2bn. The largest private bank is Bank Standard.

In 2010 total external debt was US$6,974m., representing 14·9% of GNI.

Energy and Natural Resources

Environment

Azerbaijan's carbon dioxide emissions from the consumption of energy were the equivalent of 3·4 tonnes per capita in 2011.

Electricity

Output was 20·3bn. kWh in 2011; consumption per capita in 2011 was 2,132 kWh. Capacity in 2011 was 6·4m. kW.

Oil and Gas

The most important industry is crude oil extraction. Baku is at the centre of oil exploration in the Caspian. Partnerships with Turkish, Western European and US companies have been forged.

In 2013 oil reserves totalled 7·0bn. bbls. A century ago Azerbaijan produced half of the world's oil, but output today is just 1% of the total (although production started to increase in the late 1990s, rising every year between 1997 and 2010). Oil production in 2013 was 43·4m. tonnes. In July 1999 BP Amoco announced a major natural gas discovery in the Shah Deniz offshore field, with reserves of at least 700bn. cu. metres and perhaps as much as 1,000bn. cu. metres. There were proven reserves of 900bn. cu. metres in 2013. Natural gas production in 2013 amounted to 16·2bn. cu. metres—up from just 6·1bn. cu. metres in 2006.

Accords for the construction of an oil pipeline from Baku, the Azerbaijani capital, on the Caspian Sea through Georgia to Ceyhan in southern Turkey (the BTC pipeline) were signed in Nov. 1999. Work on the pipeline began in Sept. 2002 and it was officially opened in May 2005.

A gas pipeline from Baku through Georgia to Erzurum in Turkey (the South Caucasus pipeline) was commissioned in 2006, allowing Azerbaijan to become a net exporter of natural gas.

Minerals

The republic is rich in natural resources: iron, bauxite, manganese, aluminium, copper ores, lead, zinc, precious metals, sulphur pyrites, nepheline syenites, limestone and salt. Cobalt ore reserves have been discovered in Dashkasan, and Azerbaijan has the largest iodine-bromine ore reserves of the former Soviet Union (the Neftchala region has an iodine-bromine mill).

Agriculture

In 2008 the total area devoted to agriculture was 4·8m. ha. In 2007 there were 1·85m. ha. of arable land and 0·22m. ha. of permanent crops. 1·43m. ha. were irrigated in 2007. In 2009, 38% of the economically active population was engaged in agriculture, hunting and forestry. Principal crops include grain, cotton, rice, grapes, citrus fruit, vegetables, tobacco and silk.

Output of main agricultural products (in 1,000 tonnes) in 2008: wheat, 1,646; potatoes, 1,077; barley, 606; tomatoes, 438; watermelons, 408; apples, 205.

Livestock (2009): cattle, 2·28m.; goats, 591,000; sheep, 7·69m.; poultry, 22m. Livestock products (2008, in 1,000 tonnes): beef and veal, 77; poultry, 52; mutton and goat meat, 46; cow's milk, 1,382; eggs, 1·0bn. units.

Forestry

In 2015 forests covered 1·14m. ha., or 14% of the total land area. Timber production in 2011 was 7,000 cu. metres.

Fisheries

Total fish catch in 2015 came to 568 tonnes, exclusively from inland waters.

Industry

There are oil extraction and refining, oil-related machinery, iron and steel, aluminium, copper, chemical, cement, building materials, timber, synthetic rubber, salt, textiles, food and fishing industries. Production (2014) in 1,000 tonnes: gas oil and diesel oil, 2,946; cement (2013), 2,296; petrol, 1,238; bread and bakery products, 746; jet fuels, 709. Output of other products: footwear (2014), 180,400 pairs.

Labour

In 2009 the economically active workforce numbered 4,331,800. The main areas of activity were: agriculture, hunting and forestry, 1,562,400; wholesale and retail trade/repair of motor vehicles, motorcycles and personal and household goods, 661,500; education, 346,900; public administration and defence/social security, 277,200. The unemployment rate in 2009 was 6·0%. The average monthly salary in 2009 was 298 manats.

Azerbaijan had 33,000 people living in slavery according to the Walk Free Foundation's 2013 *Global Slavery Index*.

International Trade

Imports and Exports

Goods imports were US$9,178·6m. in 2014 (US$10,763·4m. in 2013) and goods exports US$21,751·7m. (US$23,904·1m. in 2013).

Principal imports in 2014 were machinery and transport equipment (37·7%), manufactured goods, and food, animals and beverages; main exports in 2014 were mineral fuels and lubricants (92·8%), food, animals and beverages, and manufactured goods.

The leading import supplier in 2010 was Russia (17·4%), followed by Turkey and Germany; the leading export destination in 2010 was Italy (33·1%), followed by France and Israel.

Communications

Roads

There were 59,141 km of roads (6,928 km highways and main roads) in 2006. Passenger cars in use in 2006 totalled 548,979 (57 per 1,000 inhabitants in 2005). In addition, there were 9,916 lorries and vans, and 27,474 buses and coaches. There were 1,107 fatalities as a result of road accidents in 2007.

Rail

Total length in 2011 was 2,079 km of 1,524 mm gauge (1,244 km electrified). Passenger-km travelled in 2011 came to 1,660m. and freight tonne-km to 7·8bn.

There is a metro and tramway in Baku and a tramway in Sumgait.

Civil Aviation

There is an international airport at Baku. Azerbaijan Airlines, the national airline, had international flights in 2010 to Aktau, Ankara, Astrakhan, Dubai, İstanbul, London, Milan, Moscow, Paris, Rostov, St Petersburg, Tel Aviv and Urumqi. There were direct flights in 2010 with other airlines to Almaty, Ashgabat, Atyrau, Dnepropetrovsk, Donetsk, Dushanbe, Ekaterinburg, Frankfurt, İstanbul, Kabul, Khanty-Mansiysk, Kyiv, London, Mineralnye Vody, Minsk, Moscow, Nizhnevartovsk, Nizhny Novgorod, Novosibirsk, Odesa, Riga, St Petersburg, Samara, Surgut, Tashkent, Tbilisi, Tehran, Tyumen, Urumqi and Vienna. In 2005 scheduled airline traffic of Azerbaijan-based carriers flew 14·8m. km, carrying 494,800 passengers.

Shipping

In Jan. 2014 there were 99 ships of 300 GT or over registered, totalling 485,000 GT. Baku is the main port.

Telecommunications

In 2011 there were 1,684,000 landline telephone subscriptions (180·9 per 1,000 inhabitants) and 10,120,000 mobile phone subscriptions (1,087·5 per 1,000 inhabitants). There were 274·0 internet users per 1,000 inhabitants in 2009. Fixed internet subscriptions totalled 871,000 in 2010 (94·8 per 1,000 inhabitants). In March 2012 there were 782,000 Facebook users.

Social Institutions

Out of 178 countries analysed in the 2017 *Fragile States Index*—a list published jointly by the Fund for Peace and *Foreign Policy* magazine—Azerbaijan was ranked the 81st most vulnerable to conflict or collapse. The index is based on 12 indicators of state vulnerability across social, political and economic categories.

Justice

The number of recorded crimes in 2009 was 22,830, including 236 murders or attempted murders (604 in 1995); there were 259 crimes per 1,000 inhabitants.

The population in penal institutions in Sept. 2009 was 20,470 (228 per 100,000 of national population).

The death penalty was abolished in 1998.

Education

In 2009–10 there were 7,048 pupils at 368 primary schools, 79,069 pupils at 853 secondary schools and 1,272,361 pupils at 3,299 joint primary and secondary schools. There were a total of 173,299 teachers in primary and secondary schools. 107,954 children were enrolled at pre-school institutions. In 2009–10 there were 117,934 students and 12,813 teaching staff at 37 state higher educational institutions and 21,260 students and 2,120 teaching staff at 16 non-state higher educational institutions. There were 43 institutes of higher education in Baku, with 110,131 students in 2009–10. The Azerbaijan Academy of Sciences, founded in 1945, has 31 research institutes. Adult literacy is 98·8%.

In 2010 public expenditure on education came to 2·8% of GDP and represented 8·8% of total government expenditure.

Health

In 2009 there were 752 state and private hospitals with 67,800 beds. There were 32,503 physicians in 2009 (377 per 100,000 population). In 2006 there were 71,265 nursing and midwifery personnel, 2,431 dentistry personnel and 1,074 pharmaceutical personnel.

In *Water: At What Cost? The State of the World's Water 2016*, WaterAid reported that 13·0% of the population does not have access to safe water.

Welfare

In Jan. 2016 there were 781,000 age pensioners and 519,000 other pensioners.

Religion

Azerbaijan is a secular state. In 2010 Muslims (mostly Shia) accounted for an estimated 97% of the population according to the Pew Research Center's Forum on Religion & Public Life, the balance being mainly Russian Orthodox, Armenian Apostolic and Jewish.

Culture

World Heritage Sites

There are two UNESCO World Heritage sites in Azerbaijan: the Walled City of Baku with the Shirvanshah's Palace and Maiden Tower (2000), which was damaged by an earthquake in 2000, and the Gobustan rock art cultural landscape (2007).

Press

In 2008 Azerbaijan published 32 paid-for daily newspapers with a combined circulation of 120,000. The leading paid-for daily is *Yeni Müsavat*, with an average daily circulation of 25,000 in 2008.

Tourism

In 2012 there were 2,484,000 non-resident visitors; spending by tourists totalled US$2,634m. in 2012.

Diplomatic Representatives

Of Azerbaijan in the United Kingdom (4 Kensington Court, London, W8 5DL)
  Ambassador: Tahir Taghizadeh.

Of the United Kingdom in Azerbaijan (45 Khagani St., AZ-1010 Baku)
  Ambassador: Carole Crofts.

Of Azerbaijan in the USA (2741 34th St., NW, Washington, D.C., 20008)
  Ambassador: Elin Emin Oglu Suleymanov.

Of the USA in Azerbaijan (111 Azadliq Prospect, AZ-1007 Baku)
  Ambassador: Vacant.
  Chargé d'Affaires a.i.: William R. Gill.

Of Azerbaijan to the United Nations
  Ambassador: Yashar Teymur oglu Aliyev.

Of Azerbaijan to the European Union
  Ambassador: Fuad Eldar oglu Isgandarov.

Artsakh

Established in 1923 as an Autonomous Region within Azerbaijan, in 1989 the area was placed under a 'special form of administration' subordinate to the USSR government. In Sept. 1991 the regional Soviet and the Shaumyan district Soviet jointly declared a Nagorno-Karabakh republic, which proclaimed itself independent in Dec. 1991. The autonomous status of the region was meanwhile abolished by the Azerbaijan Supreme Soviet in Nov. 1991, and a presidential decree of Jan. 1992 placed the region under direct rule. The desire of the largely Armenian population to be separated from Muslim Azerbaijan led to ethnic conflict, culminating in Armenian occupation of the region in 1993. Since May 1994 there has been a nominal ceasefire. In a referendum in Dec. 2006, 99% of votes favoured declaring the territory a sovereign state, but Azerbaijan, the USA, the EU and the OSCE all refused to recognize the results. Negotiations to end the deadlock, which have been conducted within the OSCE Minsk Group, have since proved fruitless and 2014 saw the worst clashes in two decades. Further fighting, resulting in dozens of deaths, erupted in April 2016 before Moscow instigated another ceasefire. It was renamed the Republic of Artsakh (or just Artsakh) in March 2017.

Area, 4,400 sq. km; population (Dec. 2008 est.), 139,900 (mainly Armenians, with some Russians and others). Capital, Khankendi.

President: Bako Sahakyan.

Nakhichevan

This territory, on the borders of Turkey and Iran, forms part of Azerbaijan although separated from it by the territory of Armenia. It was annexed by Russia in 1828. In June 1923 it was constituted as an Autonomous Region within Azerbaijan and in 1924 it was elevated to the status of Autonomous Republic. The 1996 Azerbaijani Constitution defines it as an Autonomous State within Azerbaijan.

Area, 5,500 sq. km; population (2009 census), 398,400. Capital, Nakhichevan.

Chairman of the Supreme Council: Vasif Talybov.
Prime Minister: Alovsat Bakhshiyev.

Approximately 70% of the economically active population are engaged in agriculture, particularly cotton and tobacco growing.

Further Reading

Azerbaijan

Azerbaijan. A Country Study. 2004
Chorbajian, Levon, *The Making of Nagorno-Karabagh: From Secession to Republic.* 2001
De Waal, Thomas, *Black Garden: Armenia and Azerbaijan Through Peace and War.* 2003
Swietochowski, T., *Russia and a Divided Azerbaijan.* 1995
Van Der Leeuw, C., *Azerbaijan.* 1999
National Statistical Office: The State Statistical Committee of the Republic of Azerbaijan, Inshaatchilar Av., Baku AZ1136.
Website: https://www.stat.gov.az

The Bahamas

Commonwealth of The Bahamas

Capital: Nassau
Population projection, 2020: 407,000
GNI per capita, 2017: (PPP$) 26,681
HDI/world rank, 2017: 0·807/54
Internet domain extension: .bs

Key Historical Events

The islands that make up The Bahamas were first inhabited by Lucayan clans, an Arawak-speaking people who migrated from Cuba from the 7th century and whose ancestors originated in the Amazon Basin. By the 15th century their population may have reached 40,000, with sizeable settlements across several islands. Christopher Columbus made landfall on one of the easterly islands (known to the Lucayans as Guanahani) on 12 Oct. 1492 and named it San Salvador.

Relations between the indigenous population and the Spanish explorers were initially cordial but diseases carried by the Europeans took a heavy toll. Meanwhile, large numbers of Lucayans were transported to Hispaniola and other Spanish colonies across the Caribbean to develop mines and settlements and dive for pearls. By the 1530s The Bahamas were all but uninhabited.

English puritans and freed West African slaves fleeing conflict in Bermuda during the 1640s settled on an island they named Eleuthera. A further wave of settlers from England and Bermuda founded Charles Town on New Providence Island in 1656. It was renamed Nassau in 1695 in honour of King William III of Orange-Nassau, and cotton, tobacco and sugarcane plantations were established. The myriad islands and shoals became notorious as hideouts for hundreds of buccaneers, notably Blackbeard (Edward Teach), who plundered ships plying the increasingly busy route between America, the Caribbean and Europe.

The British Crown took control of The Bahamas in 1717, although Britain and Spain both claimed ownership of the islands until the matter was decided in Britain's favour by the 1793 Peace of Paris. As the first Governor of The Bahamas, Woodes Rogers led a sweeping crackdown on piracy and set up a representative assembly. Following American independence, several thousand Loyalists and their slaves moved out of Florida and Carolina to settle in The Bahamas.

Nassau enjoyed a brief period of prosperity during the American Civil War, becoming a key base for the Confederacy. Fast steamships evaded the Union's blockade of Southern ports in the early 1860s, trading cotton from Carolina for British military equipment and luxury goods. However, victory for the Union in 1865 precipitated economic decline until fortunes revived in the 1920s and early 1930s when the islands became a hub for rum smuggling to the Prohibition-era USA.

During the Second World War The Bahamas became an important naval base overseen by the Duke of Westminster (formerly King Edward VIII). Installed as Governor in Aug. 1940, he helped quell civil unrest over low wages, but is remembered for describing The Bahamas as a 'third-rate British colony'. Tourism and offshore banking developed in the 1950s, bolstered by a free-trade zone. Internal self-government was granted in 1964, with the first legislative elections held three years later. The centrist Progressive Liberal Party (PLP) emerged victorious and Lynden Pindling became premier.

Pindling led The Bahamas to independence on 10 July 1973 and oversaw a rapid expansion of tourism and financial services. However, his administration was dogged by allegations of corruption and links to Colombian drug-smuggling syndicates. Hubert Ingraham became prime minister in Aug. 1992 after his centre-left Free National Movement (FNM) won an absolute majority in the general election, ending 25 years of rule under Pindling. Ingraham was succeeded in 2002 by Perry Christie but served a second term as prime minister from 2007 until 2012, when the PLP was returned to power.

Territory and Population

The Commonwealth of The Bahamas consists of over 700 islands and inhabited cays off the southeast coast of Florida extending for about 260,000 sq. miles. Only 22 islands are inhabited. Land area, 5,382 sq. miles (13,939 sq. km).

The areas and populations of the 19 divisions used for the most recent census in 2010 were as follows:

	Area (in sq. km)	Population
New Providence	207	246,329
Grand Bahama	1,373	51,368
Abaco	1,681	17,224
Eleuthera	484	8,202
Andros	5,957	7,490
Exuma and Cays	290	6,928
Long Island	596	3,094
Biminis	23	1,988
Harbour Island	8	1,762
Spanish Wells	26	1,551
Cat Island	388	1,522
San Salvador	163	940
Inagua	1,551	913
Berry Islands	31	807
Acklins	497	565
Crooked Island	241	330
Mayaguana	285	277
Rum Cay	78	99
Ragged Island	36	72

Total census population for 2010 was 351,461.

The UN gives a projected population for 2020 of 407,000.

In 2011, 84·3% of the population were urban. The capital is Nassau on New Providence Island (246,329 in 2010). Other large towns are Freeport (on Grand Bahama), West End (also on Grand Bahama) and Coopers Town (on Abaco).

English is the official language. Creole is spoken among Haitian immigrants.

Social Statistics

2008 estimated births, 5,600; deaths, 2,000. Rates, 2008 estimates (per 1,000 population): birth, 16·7; death, 6·0; infant mortality (per 1,000 live births), 2010, 14. Expectation of life was 72·1 years for males and 78·2 years for females in 2013. Annual population growth rate, 2005–10, 1·8%; fertility rate, 2008, 2·0 children per woman.

Climate

Winters are mild and summers pleasantly warm. Most rain falls in May, June, Sept. and Oct., and thunderstorms are frequent in summer. Rainfall amounts vary over the islands from 30" (750 mm) to 60" (1,500 mm). Nassau, Jan. 71°F (21·7°C), July 81°F (27·2°C). Annual rainfall 47" (1,179 mm).

Constitution and Government

The Commonwealth of The Bahamas is a free and democratic sovereign state. Executive power rests with Her Majesty the Queen, who appoints a Governor-General to represent her, advised by a Cabinet whom he appoints. There is a bicameral legislature. The *Senate* comprises 16 members all

© Springer Nature Limited 2020
Palgrave Macmillan (ed.), *The Statesman's Yearbook 2020*,
https://doi.org/10.1057/978-1-349-95940-2_24

appointed by the Governor-General for five-year terms, nine on the advice of the Prime Minister, four on the advice of the Leader of the Opposition, and three after consultation with both of them. The *House of Assembly* consists of 39 members elected from single-member constituencies for a maximum term of five years.

National Anthem

'Lift up your head to the rising sun, Bahamaland'; words and tune by T. Gibson.

Recent Elections

In parliamentary elections held on 10 May 2017 the Free National Movement (FNM) won 57·0% of votes cast and 35 out of 39 seats (9 in 2012) against the ruling Progressive Liberal Party (PLP) with 37·0% and 4 seats (29 in 2012).

Current Government

Governor-General: Dame Marguerite Pindling; b. 1932 (sworn in 8 July 2014).

In Feb. 2019 the cabinet was composed as follows:

Prime Minister: Hubert Minnis; b. 1954 (FNM; took office on 11 May 2017).

Deputy Prime Minister and Minister of Finance: K. Peter Turnquest.

Minister of Agriculture and Marine Resources: Michael Pintard. *Education:* Jeffrey Lloyd. *Environment and Housing:* Romauld Ferreira. *Financial Services, Trade and Industry, and Immigration:* Brent Symonette. *Foreign Affairs:* Darren Henfield. *Health:* Dr Duane Sands. *Labour:* Dion Foulkes. *Legal Affairs and Attorney General:* Carl Bethel. *National Security:* Marvin Dames. *Social Services and Urban Development:* Frankie Campbell. *Tourism and Aviation:* Dionisio D'Aguilar. *Transport and Local Government:* Renward Wells. *Works:* Desmond Bannister. *Youth, Sports and Culture:* Lanisha Rolle.

Government Website: http://www.bahamas.gov.bs

Current Leaders

Hubert Minnis

Position
Prime Minister

Introduction
Hubert Minnis of the Free National Movement (FNM) became prime minister in May 2017.

Early Life
Minnis was born in Bain Town and graduated in biology from the University of Minnesota in the USA before undertaking medical studies at the University of the West Indies (UWI) and in London in the UK. He then practised as a doctor in the UK prior to his return to the Bahamas, where he became president of the national medical association, served on the medical council and also lectured at the UWI.

After entering parliament in May 2007, he was appointed minister of health. Following the FNM's election defeat in 2012, Minnis was unanimously elected party leader after Hubert Ingraham resigned. However, in Dec. 2016 Minnis faced a leadership challenge after seven of his party's ten members of parliament resigned. Loretta Butler-Turner briefly succeeded him as leader but he returned to the post in April 2017, a month before scheduled elections.

Career in Office
Following the FNM's victory over the Progressive Liberal Party of incumbent Prime Minister Perry Christie, Minnis was sworn in as premier on 11 May 2017. He promised tougher parliamentary regulation and more transparent dealings, as well as pledging to reform the education system and to champion incentives to stimulate homegrown industries.

Defence

The Royal Bahamas Defence Force is a primarily maritime force tasked with naval patrols and protection duties in the extensive waters of the archipelago. Personnel in 2011 numbered 860. The base is at Coral Harbour on New Providence Island.

In 2013 defence expenditure totalled US$64m. (US$201 per capita), representing 0·8% of GDP.

Navy

In 2011 the Navy operated 18 patrol craft and three aircraft.

Economy

Services contributed 78·9% to GDP in 2013, with industry accounting for 19·2% and agriculture 1·9%.

Overview

The economy is heavily dependent on tourism and offshore banking. In 2016 tourism and related activities, notably construction, accounted for approximately 36% of GDP and 53% of total employment, while financial services, including offshore banking, accounted for 20% of GDP and around 25% of employment.

Prior to the global financial crisis annual growth had been robust (averaging 2·1% between 2000 and 2007), boosted by the construction of new resorts and second homes. However, the crisis saw a collapse in tourism with GDP contracting in 2009 by 4·2% while unemployment rose. Output began to recover in 2010, but annual growth in the five years to 2016 averaged just 0·2% and central government debt reached 63·9% of GDP in 2015. Short-term growth remains over-reliant on tourism (especially from the USA, which accounts for 80% of visitors).

Currency

The unit of currency is the *Bahamian dollar* (BSD) of 100 *cents.* American currency is generally accepted. There was deflation of 0·3% in 2016 but then inflation of 1·4% in 2017. Foreign exchange reserves were US$1522m. in Dec. 2017 and total money supply was B$2,585m.

Budget

The fiscal year is 1 July–30 June.

Budgetary central government revenues in 2014–15 (provisional) were B$1,698m. (including tax revenue, 88·3%) and expenditures B$1,714m. (including compensation of employees, 37·3%; subsidies, 19·3%; use of goods and services, 19·3%).

VAT of 12% was introduced on 1 July 2018.

Performance

There was real GDP growth of 1·0% in 2015. The Bahamas suffered a recession in 2016 when the economy shrank by 1·7%, before a slight recovery saw growth of 1·4% in 2017. Total GDP was US$12·2bn. in 2017.

Banking and Finance

The Central Bank of The Bahamas was established in 1974. Its *Governor* is John A. Rolle. The Bahamas is an important centre for offshore banking. Financial business produces about 15% of GDP. In 2007, 245 banks and trust companies were licensed. Leading Bahamian-based banks include The Bank of Bahamas Ltd, The Commonwealth Bank Ltd and Private Investment Bank Ltd. There is also a Development Bank.

Gross external debt amounted to US$1,287m. in June 2012.

A stock exchange, the Bahamas International Securities Exchange (BISX) based in Nassau, was inaugurated in May 2000.

Energy and Natural Resources

Environment

Carbon dioxide emissions from the consumption of energy were the equivalent of 11·6 tonnes per capita in 2011.

Electricity

In 2011 installed capacity was 0·6m. kW, all thermal. Output in 2011 was approximately 1·77bn. kWh; consumption per capita in 2011 was 4,821 kWh.

Oil and Gas

The Bahamas does not have reserves of either oil or gas, but oil is refined in The Bahamas. The Bahamas Oil Refining Company (BORCO), in Grand Bahama, operates as a terminal which trans-ships, stores and blends oil.

Minerals

Aragonite is extracted from the seabed.

Agriculture

In 2013 there were some 8,000 ha. of arable land and 4,000 ha. of permanent crops. Production (in 1,000 tonnes), 2013 estimates: sugarcane, 58; grapefruit, 21; bananas, 10; tomatoes, 6.

Livestock (2013 estimates): goats, 15,000; sheep, 7,000; pigs, 5,000; chickens, 3m.

Forestry

In 2015 forests covered 0·52m. ha. or 51% of the total land area. Timber production in 2011 was 50,000 cu. metres.

Fisheries

Total catch in 2012 amounted to 19,462 tonnes, exclusively from sea fishing.

Industry

Tourism and offshore banking are the main industries. Two industrial sites, one in New Providence and the other in Grand Bahama, have been developed as part of an industrialization programme. The main products are pharmaceutical chemicals, salt and rum.

Labour

The labour force in 2013 was 220,000 (165,000 in 2003). 80·2% of the population aged 15–64 was economically active in 2013. In the same year 16·2% of the population was unemployed.

International Trade

There is a free trade zone on Grand Bahama. Although a member of CARICOM, The Bahamas is not a signatory to its trade protocol.

Imports and Exports

Imports and exports for calendar years in US$1m.:

	2006	2007	2008	2009	2010
Imports c.i.f.	2,984	3,103	3,230	2,699	2,862
Exports f.o.b.	509	670	702	585	620

In 2010 the principal imports were (in US$1m.): mineral fuels, lubricants and related materials, 687; machinery and transport equipment, 494; food and live animals, 427. The principal exports were (in US$1m.): mineral fuels, lubricants and related materials, 160; food and live animals, 75; machinery and transport equipment, 74. In 2010 the USA was the source of 91% of imports; the main export markets were the USA (76%) and the UK (5%).

Communications

Roads

There are approximately 2,700 km of roads, of which about 60% are paved. In 2007 there were around 27,100 vehicles in use.

Civil Aviation

There are international airports at Nassau and Freeport (Grand Bahama Island). The national carrier is the state-owned Bahamasair, which in 2010 flew to Fort Lauderdale, Havana, Miami, Orlando and the Turks and Caicos Islands, as well as providing services between different parts of The Bahamas. There were direct international flights in 2010 with other airlines to Atlanta, Atlantic City, Baltimore, Birmingham (USA), Boston, Buffalo, Calgary, Cayman Islands, Charlotte, Cleveland, Dallas/Fort Worth, Detroit, Fort Lauderdale, Frankfurt, Havana, Holguín, Houston, Kingston, Little Rock, London, Louisville, Miami, Montego Bay, Montreal, Myrtle Beach, New Orleans, New York, Orlando, Philadelphia, Pittsburgh, Toronto, the Turks and Caicos Islands and Washington, D.C. In 2006 scheduled airline traffic of Bahamas-based carriers flew 8m. km, carrying 1,033,000 passengers (456,000 on international flights).

Shipping

In Jan. 2014 there were 1,144 ships of 300 GT or over registered, totalling 48·21m. GT (giving The Bahamas the world's sixth largest fleet by gross tonnage). Of the 1,144 vessels registered, 310 were general cargo ships, 306 oil tankers, 262 bulk carriers, 128 passenger ships, 81 liquid gas tankers and 57 container ships. The Bahamas is a 'flag of convenience' country.

Telecommunications

There were 129,300 fixed telephone lines in 2010 (377·1 per 1,000 inhabitants) and mobile phone subscribers numbered 428,400. There were 338·8 internet users per 1,000 inhabitants in 2009. Fixed internet subscriptions totalled 38,600 in 2009 (114·0 per 1,000 inhabitants). In June 2012 there were 164,000 Facebook users.

Social Institutions

Out of 178 countries analysed in the 2017 *Fragile States Index*—a list published jointly by the Fund for Peace and *Foreign Policy* magazine—The Bahamas was ranked the 45th least vulnerable to conflict or collapse. The index is based on 12 indicators of state vulnerability across social, political and economic categories.

Justice

English Common Law is the basis of the Bahamian judicial system, although there is a large volume of Bahamian Statute Law. The highest Tribunal in the country is the Court of Appeal. New Providence has 14 Magistrates' Courts, Grand Bahama has three and Abaco one.

The strength of the police force (2017) was 2,600 officers.

There were 122 murders in 2014 (a rate of 33·0 per 100,000 population). The death penalty is in force, although no executions have been carried out since 2000. The population in penal institutions in Aug. 2012 was 1,600 (444 per 100,000 of national population).

Education

Education is compulsory between five and 16 years of age. In 2012 there were 210 schools (52 independent). In 2010 there were 33,977 pupils with 2,402 teachers in primary schools and 34,406 pupils with 2,837 teachers in secondary education. Courses lead to The Bahamas General Certificate of Secondary Education (BGCSE). Independent schools provide education at primary, secondary and high school levels.

The four institutions offering higher education are: the government-sponsored College of The Bahamas, established in 1974; the University of the West Indies (regional), affiliated with The Bahamas since 1960; The Bahamas Hotel Training College, sponsored by the ministry of education and the hotel industry; and The Bahamas Technical and Vocational Institute, established to provide basic skills. Several schools of continuing education offer secretarial and academic courses.

Health

In the period 2005–12 there were 28 physicians per 10,000 inhabitants, two dentists per 10,000 persons and 41 nursing and midwifery personnel per 10,000. Over the same period there were 31 hospital beds per 10,000 inhabitants. In 2014 total expenditure on health accounted for 7·7% of GDP. Private expenditure on health in 2014 represented 54·1% of total expenditure on health and government expenditure 45·9%.

In *Water: At What Cost? The State of the World's Water 2016*, WaterAid reported that 1·6% of the population does not have access to safe water.

Welfare

Social Services are provided by the Department of Social Services, a government agency which grants assistance to restore, reinforce and enhance the capacity of the individual to perform life tasks, and to provide for the protection of children in The Bahamas.

The Department's divisions include: community support services, child welfare, family services, senior citizens, disability affairs, Family Island and research planning, training and community relations.

Religion

In 2010 the population was an estimated 96% Christian (mainly Protestant) according to the Pew Research Center's Forum on Religion & Public Life. Most of the remainder of the population is religiously unaffiliated.

Culture

Press

There were four paid-for dailies in 2008.

Tourism

Tourism is the most important industry, accounting for about 60% of GDP. In 2015 there were 1,390,911 overnight tourist arrivals by air and 4,721,182 sea arrivals (1,343,093 overnight tourist arrivals by air and 4,977,075 sea arrivals in 2014).

Festivals

Junkanoo is the quintessential Bahamian celebration, a parade or 'rush-out' characterized by colourful costumes, goatskin drums, cowbells, horns and a brass section. It is staged in the early hours of 26 Dec. and the early hours of 1 Jan.

Diplomatic Representatives

Of The Bahamas in the United Kingdom (10 Chesterfield St., London, W1J 5JL)
  High Commissioner: Ellison Edroy Greenslade.

Of the United Kingdom in The Bahamas
  High Commissioner: Asif Ahmad, CMG (resides in Kingston, Jamaica).

Of The Bahamas in the USA (2220 Massachusetts Ave., NW, Washington, D.C., 20008)
  Ambassador: Sidney Stanley Collie.

Of the USA in The Bahamas (42 Queen St., Nassau)
  Ambassador: Vacant.
  Chargé d'Affaires a.i.: Stephanie Bowers.

Of The Bahamas to the United Nations
  Ambassador: Sheila Carey.

Of The Bahamas to the European Union
  Ambassador: Vacant.
  Chargé d'Affaires a.i.: Frank Davis.

Further Reading

Cash, P., *et al., Making of Bahamian History.* 1991
Craton, M. and Saunders, G., *Islanders in the Stream: a History of the Bahamian People.* 2 vols. 1998
Storr, Virgil Henry, *Enterprising Slaves and Master Pirates: Understanding Economic Life in The Bahamas.* 2004
National Statistical Office: Department of Statistics, Clarence A. Bain Building, Thompson Blvd, PO Box N-3904, Nassau.
Website: http://www.bahamas.gov.bs/statistics

Bahrain

Al-Mamlaka Al-Bahrayn (Kingdom of Bahrain)

Capital: Manama
Population projection, 2020: 1·70m.
GNI per capita, 2017: (PPP$) 41,580
HDI/world rank, 2017: 0·846/43
Internet domain extension: .bh

Key Historical Events

The natural springs and safe anchorages of the northern reaches of Bahrain island were home to the Dilmun civilization 5,000 years ago, which traded goods such as Omani copper with Mesopotamia and the Indus Valley civilization. From the 6th century BC the archipelago came under the influence of various Persian dynasties—initially the Achaemenids, and then, from the 3rd century BC, the Parthians followed by the Sassanids.

The Christian faith gained some influence during the 4th century, and from around AD 630 Bahrain became one of the first places to embrace Islam. It developed as a centre of Shia Islamic scholarship, benefited from trade with Baghdad (capital of the Abbasid Caliphate from AD 750) and became internationally famed for its pearls. Portuguese forces, which had captured Hormuz in 1505, invaded Bahrain in 1521 and controlled the archipelago for the next 80 years. A succession of Sunni governors from Hormuz proved unpopular with the Shia population, and the Persian army, led by Imam Quli-Khan, ousted the Portuguese in 1602.

In 1783 Bahrain passed into the hands of the Al-Khalifa Sunni dynasty from Qatar, and Manama developed as a cosmopolitan port, linked to British India, Ottoman Basra and Qajar Persia. In the late 18th century Persia and Oman attempted to take control of Bahrain but both were repelled. Wishing to protect British Indian trade against frequent pirate attacks in the Persian Gulf, Britain proposed a peace treaty that was signed by local sheikhs in 1820, including Bahrain's Al-Khalifas. A further maritime truce, established in 1835, was frequently violated, most notably when Bahrain attacked Qatar in 1867. A counter-attack the next year led to over 1,000 deaths, and was followed by the Anglo–Bahraini agreement, by which Bahrain renounced its territorial claims in Qatar. Bahrain was a British protectorate in all but name and by 1880 it had become the region's pre-eminent trading centre.

Bahrain was the site of the first attempts to drill for crude oil in the Gulf, with offshore extraction beginning in the early 1930s (although reserves have proved smaller than elsewhere in the region). Following Britain's ending of its treaty agreements with the Persian Gulf sheikhdoms in 1968, there was an attempt to form a regional union. However, when terms could not be agreed, Bahrain declared its independence, which was granted on 16 Dec. 1971. Sheikh Isa bin Salman Al-Khalifa became the nation's Amir. A constitution ratified in June 1973 provided for a National Assembly of 30 members (popularly elected for a four-year term), plus a 14-member cabinet (appointed by the Amir). However, in 1975 the assembly was dissolved and the Amir began ruling by decree.

In 1986 the opening of the King Fahd Causeway connected Bahrain to the Saudi Arabian mainland. Sheikh Isa died in March 1999 and was replaced as Amir by his son, Sheikh Hamad bin Isa Al-Khalifa. In Feb. 2002 the country became a constitutional monarchy and Sheikh Hamad proclaimed himself king. The first parliamentary elections for almost three decades (and the first to include women voters and candidates) were held in Oct. of the same year. Manama's reputation as a prosperous and stable city suffered in Feb. 2011 when security forces attacked protesters (at times numbering more than 100,000) who were demanding greater political freedom and equality for the majority Shia population.

Territory and Population

The Kingdom of Bahrain forms an archipelago of 36 low-lying islands in the Persian Gulf, between the Qatar peninsula and the mainland of Saudi Arabia. The total area is 771 sq. km.

The island of Bahrain (578 sq. km) is connected by a 2·4 km causeway to the second largest island, Muharraq to the northeast, and by a causeway with the island of Sitra to the east. A causeway links Bahrain with Saudi Arabia. From Sitra, oil pipelines and a causeway carrying a road extend out to sea for 4·8 km to a deep-water anchorage.

In March 2001 the International Court of Justice ruled on a long-standing dispute between Bahrain and Qatar over the boundary between the two countries and ownership of certain islands. Both countries accepted the decision.

Total census population in 2010 was 1,234,571 (males, 768,414; females, 466,157) of which 568,399 were Bahraini and 666,172 non-Bahraini. Among Bahrainis 50·5% of the population in 2010 were males but among non-Bahrainis 72·2% were males. Population estimate, July 2016: 1,423,726. The population density was 1,715 per sq. km in 2010. In 2011, 88·7% of the population were urban.

The UN gives a projected population for 2020 of 1·70m.

There are four governorates: Capital, Muharraq, Northern, Southern. Manama, the capital and commercial centre, had an estimated population of 398,000 in 2014. Other towns are Muharraq, Rifa'a, Hamad Town, Al-Ali and Isa Town.

Arabic is the official language. English is widely used in business.

Social Statistics

Statistics, 2009: births, 17,841; deaths, 2,387. Rates (per 1,000 population) in 2009: birth, 15·1; death, 2·0. Infant mortality (per 1,000 live births), 9 (2010). Life expectancy at birth, 2007, was 74·2 years for men and 77·4 years for women. Annual population growth rate, 2005–12, 4·7%; fertility rate, 2008, 2·3 children per woman. In 2006 there were 4,714 marriages and 1,130 divorces.

Climate

The climate is pleasantly warm between Dec. and March but from June to Sept. the conditions are very hot and humid. The period June to Nov. is virtually rainless. Bahrain, Jan. 66°F (19°C), July 97°F (36°C). Annual rainfall 5·2" (130 mm).

Constitution and Government

The ruling family is the Al-Khalifa who have been in power since 1783.

The constitution changing Bahrain from an Emirate to a Kingdom dates from 14 Feb. 2002. The new constitutional hereditary monarchy has a bicameral legislature, inaugurated on 14 Dec. 2002. National elections for a legislative body took place on 24 and 31 Oct. 2002 (the first since the National Assembly was adjourned 27 years earlier). One chamber *(Council of Representatives)* is a directly elected assembly while the second (upper) chamber, a *Shura* consultative council of experts, is appointed by the King. Both chambers have 40 members. All Bahraini citizens over the age of 21—men and women—are able to vote for the elected assembly. In the Oct. 2002 national elections women stood for office for the first time.

National Anthem

'Bahrain ona, baladolaman' ('Our Bahrain, secure as a country'); words by M. S. Ayyash, tune anonymous.

Government Chronology

Heads of State since 1942.

Hakims	
1942–61	Sheikh Salman bin Hamad Al-Khalifa
1961–71	Sheikh Isa bin Salman Al-Khalifa

(continued)

© Springer Nature Limited 2020
Palgrave Macmillan (ed.), *The Statesman's Yearbook 2020*,
https://doi.org/10.1057/978-1-349-95940-2_25

Amirs	
1971–99	Sheikh Isa bin Salman Al-Khalifa
1999–2002	Sheikh Hamad bin Isa Al-Khalifa
King	
2002–	Sheikh Hamad bin Isa Al-Khalifa

Recent Elections

Elections to the 40-member Council of Representatives were held on 24 Nov. 2018 with a run-off on 1 Dec. 2018. The main opposition group had been dissolved in 2016 and its members banned from participating. A record six women were elected. Turnout in the first round was officially put at 67% but opposition groups claimed that it was no more than 30%.

Current Government

The present king (formerly Amir), HH Sheikh Hamad bin Isa Al-Khalifa, KCMG (b. 1950), succeeded on 6 March 1999 and became king on 14 Feb. 2002.

In Feb. 2019 the cabinet was composed as follows:

Prime Minister: Sheikh Khalifa bin Salman Al-Khalifa; b. 1936. He is currently the longest-serving prime minister of any sovereign country, having been Bahrain's prime minister since it became independent in Aug. 1971.

First Deputy Prime Minister: Salman bin Hamad Al-Khalifa.

Deputy Prime Ministers: Sheikh Mohammed bin Mubarak Al-Khalifa; Sheikh Ali bin Khalifa Al-Khalifa; Jawad bin Salem Al-Arrayed; Sheikh Khalid bin Abdulla Al-Khalifa.

Minister of Cabinet Affairs: Mohammad bin Ibrahim Al-Mutawa. *Interior:* Sheikh Rashid bin Abdulla Al-Khalifa. *Foreign Affairs:* Sheikh Khalid bin Ahmed bin Mohammad Al-Khalifa. *Finance:* Sheikh Salman bin Khalifa Al-Khalifa. *Education:* Majid Ali Al-Nuaymi. *Electricity and Water Affairs:* Abdulhussain Mirza. *Justice, Islamic Affairs and Endowments:* Sheikh Khalid bin Ali Al-Khalifa. *Works, Municipalities and Urban Planning:* Issam bin Abdulla Khalaf. *Labour and Social Development:* Jameel Humaidan. *Transport and Telecommunications:* Kamal bin Ahmed Mohammed. *Housing:* Basim bin Yacub Al-Hamar. *Shura Council and House of Representatives Affairs:* Ghanim bin Fadhel Al-Buainain. *Health:* Faeqa bint Saeed Al-Saleh. *Youth and Sports Affairs:* Aymen Tawfiq Almoayyed. *Defence Affairs:* Maj.-Gen. Abdulla Al Nuaimi. *Industry, Commerce and Tourism:* Zayed bin Rashid Al-Zayani. *Information Affairs:* Ali bin Mohammed Al-Rumaihi. *Oil:* Shaikh Mohammed bin Khalifa Al Khalifa.

Government Website: http://www.bahrain.bh

Current Leaders

HH Sheikh Hamad bin Isa Al-Khalifa

Position

King

Introduction

HH Sheikh Hamad bin Isa Al-Khalifa became Amir in March 1999. In Feb. 2001 his national action charter, encompassing a range of reforms, was approved by popular referendum. The state became a kingdom and Sheikh Hamad's title was changed to King. The king is the supreme authority, with members of his ruling Sunni Muslim family holding most senior political and military positions. Bahrain has not been immune to popular disaffection with the political status quo that spread across much of the Arab world from 2011 but Sheikh Hamad has maintained a repressive response to pro-democracy demands, particularly among the Shia majority population.

Early Life

Sheikh Hamad bin Isa Al-Khalifa was born on 28 Jan. 1950 in Rifa'a, Bahrain. He was educated in Bahrain and the UK before pursuing a military career. He attended Mons Officer Cadet School in Aldershot, UK, and continued his military training at the US Army Command and Staff College in Fort Leavenworth, Kansas. In 1968 he founded the Bahrain Defence Force (BDF) and served as the minister of defence from 1971–88.

Bahrain has been headed by the Al-Khalifa family since 1783 and Sheikh Hamad was crown prince from 1964 until he succeeded his father as head of state in early 1999. He also became supreme commander of the BDF. His interest in Arabian horses led him to establish the Amiri Stables in 1977.

Career in Office

On becoming Amir, Sheikh Hamad implemented changes to the running of the country. In June 1999 he released all political prisoners and in 2002 reintroduced parliamentary elections, with women granted the right to vote for the first time. He created the supreme judicial council and scrapped old state security laws. These reforms were based on his national action charter, which won 98% approval in a referendum in Feb. 2001.

The parliamentary elections of Oct. 2002 were the first to be held since Sheikh Isa bin Salman Al-Khalifa dissolved the first elected parliament in 1975. Sheikh Isa's subsequent suspension of the constitution and ensuing rule by decree led to widespread civil unrest amongst the Shia majority but the 2002 elections ensured the House of Deputies included a dozen Shia MPs. It is estimated that over 50% of the public voted, despite calls from Islamist parties for a boycott.

Sheikh Hamad encouraged the expansion of the role of women within Bahraini society and politics. In 2000 he appointed four women to the consultative council and in April 2004 Nada Haffadh became the first woman to head a government ministry when she became health minister. In April 2005 Alees Samaan became the first woman, and the first non-Muslim, to chair a parliamentary session.

In a bid to ease inter-religious tensions, Sheikh Hamad pardoned Shia opposition leader Sheikh Abdel Amir Al-Jamin in July 1999, the day after he was sentenced to ten years imprisonment for inciting hostility. Despite support for his reforms, mainly among the Sunni minority population, thousands attended marches in 2005 to demand a fully elected government. Parliamentary elections in Nov. and Dec. 2006 resulted in a stronger showing by the opposition Shia Al-Wefaq group, campaigning against broad social grievances such as unemployment, poor services and corruption.

Discontent among the Shia majority continued, provoking frequent public protests in poorer areas outside the predominantly Sunni capital of Manama in the early months of 2008. In the run-up to the Oct. 2010 parliamentary elections Shia opposition leaders were arrested, accused of instigating violent protests to overthrow the government. However, the Shia Al-Wefaq party won 18 seats in the elections to become the single largest group in the House of Deputies. The incumbent prime minister was meanwhile reappointed and asked to form a new cabinet. In the early months of 2011 political discontent across the Arab world spread to Bahrain. Pro-democracy demonstrations prompted Sheikh Hamad to initially make conciliatory gestures to the Shia opposition before declaring martial law and calling in Saudi military support in March that year to forcefully suppress the protests. Sporadic unrest nevertheless continued, prompting the government to announce a ban in Oct. 2012 on all demonstrations and gatherings.

In Feb. 2013 opposition groups agreed to a dialogue with the government and in March Crown Prince Salman bin Hamad Al-Khalifa, considered less hard-line than other members of the ruling family, was appointed first deputy prime minister. However, any hopes of a political reconciliation faded in the wake of renewed demonstrations and the withdrawal from talks in Sept. that year of the main Shia opposition representatives. The government suspended further contacts in Jan. 2014 and Al-Wefaq was subsequently formally dissolved by court order in July 2016. The political scene has remained unstable against a background of continuing sporadic Shia protests and increasing repression by the Sunni authorities. Furthermore, in Oct. 2017 the appeal court confirmed an earlier ruling ordering the dissolution of the main secular opposition group, the National Democratic Action Society (Wa'ad), for alleged incitement to violence and in early Nov. 2018 sentenced the banned Al-Wefaq leader Sheikh Ali Salman to life imprisonment on charges of spying. A predominantly pro-government parliament was then returned in subsequent two-stage legislative elections on 24 Nov. and 1 Dec., including a record six women candidates, although opposition groups disputed official voter turnout figures.

In June 2017 Bahrain, along with Saudi Arabia, the United Arab Emirates and Egypt, severed diplomatic relations and cut transport links with Qatar, accusing the Gulf state of supporting terrorism and aligning with Iran.

Defence

The Crown Prince is C.-in-C. of the armed forces. An agreement with the USA in Oct. 1991 gave port facilities to the US Navy and provided for mutual manoeuvres.

In 2013 defence expenditure totalled US$1,394m. (up from US$943m. in 2011), with spending per capita US$1,088. The 2013 expenditure represented 5·0% of GDP.

Army

The Army consists of one armoured brigade, one infantry brigade, one artillery brigade, one special forces battalion and one air defence battalion. Personnel, 2011, 6,000. In addition there is a National Guard of approximately 2,000 and a paramilitary police force of 11,260.

Navy

The Naval force based at Mina Sulman numbered 700 in 2011.

Air Force

Personnel (2011), 1,500. Equipment includes 39 combat-capable aircraft and 28 attack helicopters.

Economy

Crude petroleum and natural gas contributed 26·1% of GDP in 2013, finance and real estate 20·1%, manufacturing 14·7%, and public administration and defence 12·2%.

Overview

Despite having one of the more diversified economies in the Gulf region, Bahrain relies on oil for 60% of all exports, 70% of government revenue and almost a quarter of GDP. The country also competes with Malaysia to be the world's leading Islamic banking centre.

The tourism sector suffered as a result of civil unrest that erupted in 2011. The economy as a whole, however, weathered the global downturn well, and in the five years to 2016 annual GDP growth averaged 3·7%. Nonetheless, public debt—which reached 75·2% of GDP in 2016—is in breach of the 60% threshold required by the prospective Gulf Co-operation Council currency union and poses a threat to long-term prosperity. In addition, vulnerability to further civil unrest, as well as regional tensions and low monetary reserves (the result of declining oil prices since 2015), have held back growth in the tourism and financial services sectors.

Currency

The unit of currency is the *Bahraini dinar* (BHD), divided into 1,000 *fils*. In Feb. 2005 foreign exchange reserves were US$1,742m. Total money supply was BD3,458m. in March 2016 and gold reserves were 150,000 troy oz. There was inflation of 2·8% in 2016 and 1·4% in 2017.

Budget

Budgetary central government revenue in 2013 totalled BD2,942m. and expenditure BD2,857m. Oil accounts for 70% of government revenues.

VAT of 5% was introduced on 1 Jan. 2019.

Performance

Total GDP in 2017 was US$35·3bn. Real GDP growth was 2·9% in 2015, 3·5% in 2016 and 3·8% in 2017.

Banking and Finance

The Central Bank of Bahrain (*Governor*, Rasheed Mohammed Al-Maraj) has central banking powers. The banking and financial sector generates around a quarter of GDP. In Sept. 2010 there were 15 locally incorporated commercial banks, 15 foreign commercial banks, 76 wholesale banks and 27 representative offices; assets totalled US$216·4bn.

There is a stock exchange in Manama linked with those of Kuwait and Oman.

Energy and Natural Resources

Environment

Bahrain's carbon dioxide emissions from the consumption of energy in 2011 accounted for 24·9 tonnes per capita. An *Environmental Performance Index* compiled in 2016 ranked Bahrain 86th of 180 countries, with 70·1%. The index examined various factors in nine areas—agriculture, air quality, biodiversity and habitat, climate and energy, fisheries, forests, health impacts, water and sanitation, and water resources.

Electricity

In 2011 installed capacity was an estimated 3·2m. kW; 13·83bn. kWh were produced in 2011. Electricity consumption per capita was 10,788 kWh in 2011.

Oil and Gas

In 1931 oil was discovered. Operations were at first conducted by the Bahrain Petroleum Co. (BAPCO) under concession. In 1975 the government assumed a 60% interest in the oilfield and related crude oil facilities of BAPCO. Oil reserves in 2011 were 125m. bbls and production 69m. bbls. Refinery distillation output amounted to 12·7m. tonnes in 2011.

There were known natural gas reserves of 200bn. cu. metres in 2013. Production in 2013 was 15·8bn. cu. metres. Gas reserves are government-owned.

Water

Water is obtained from artesian wells and desalination plants and there is a piped supply to Manama, Muharraq, Isa Town, Rifa'a and most villages.

Minerals

Aluminium is Bahrain's oldest major industry after oil and gas; production in 2009 was 847,738 tonnes.

Agriculture

In 2014 there were some 2,000 ha. of arable land and 3,000 ha. of permanent crops. Production, 2013 estimates (in tonnes): dates, 11,500; tomatoes, 4,100; aubergines, 1,300; lemons and limes, 1,100.

Livestock (2014 estimates): sheep, 40,000; goats, 18,500; cattle, 10,500; chickens, 550,000.

In 2013 an estimated 16,900 tonnes of lamb and mutton, 6,500 tonnes of poultry meat, 2,800 tonnes of eggs and 8,900 tonnes of fresh milk were produced.

Fisheries

The total catch in 2014 was 15,854 tonnes, exclusively from sea fishing.

Industry

The largest company by market capitalization in Bahrain in April 2015 was Ahli United Bank (US$4·8bn.).

Industry is being developed with foreign participation: aluminium smelting (and ancillary industries), shipbuilding and repair, petrochemicals, electronics assembly and light industry.

Traditional crafts include boatbuilding, weaving and pottery.

Labour

The labour force in 2013 was 750,000 (more than double the 358,000 in 2003). 71·8% of the population aged 15–64 was economically active in 2013. In the same year 3·7% of the population was unemployed. Bahrain is highly dependent on foreign workers, with the private sector employing around six times more foreigners than Bahraini nationals.

International Trade

Bahrain, along with Kuwait, Oman, Qatar, Saudi Arabia and the United Arab Emirates entered into a customs union in Jan. 2003.

Imports and Exports

Goods imports were US$14,249·1m. in 2012 (US$17,643·3m. in 2011) and goods exports US$16,621·2m. (US$22,561·9m. in 2011).

Principal imports in 2012 were machinery and transport equipment (29·0%), mineral fuels and lubricants, and manufactured goods; main exports in 2012 were mineral fuels and lubricants (59·7%), manufactured goods, and crude materials and animal and vegetable oils.

The leading import supplier in 2010 was Brazil (18·0%), followed by China and Japan; the leading export destination in 2010 was Saudi Arabia (25·5%), followed by Qatar and India.

Communications

Roads

A 25 km causeway links Bahrain with Saudi Arabia. In 2008 there were 3,942 km of roads, including 475 km of main roads and 563 km of secondary roads. Bahrain has one of the densest road networks in the world. In 2008 there were 310,200 passenger cars in use (404 per 1,000 inhabitants in 2007). In 2007 there were 91 fatalities in road accidents.

Civil Aviation

The national carrier is Gulf Air, now fully owned by the government of Bahrain after the other three former partners, Qatar, Abu Dhabi and Oman, withdrew in 2002, 2006 and 2007 respectively. In 2010 Gulf Air flew to about 40 international destinations. In 2014 Bahrain International Airport handled 8·10m. passengers (all on international flights) and 219,332 tonnes of freight. In 2012 scheduled airline traffic of Bahrain-based carriers flew 83·5m. km; passenger-km totalled 14·4bn. in the same year.

Shipping

In Jan. 2014 there were 12 ships of 300 GT or over registered, totalling 301,000 GT. The port of Mina Sulman is a free transit and industrial area.

Telecommunications

Bahrain's telecommunications industry was fully liberalized on 1 July 2004. In 2014 there were 2,328,994 mobile phone subscriptions (1,732·7 per 1,000 inhabitants) and 284,684 landline telephone subscriptions (equivalent to 211·8 per 1,000 inhabitants). 91·0% of the population were internet users in 2014. Fixed internet subscriptions totalled 287,572 in 2014 (213·9 per 1,000 inhabitants). In March 2012 there were 346,000 Facebook users.

Social Institutions

Out of 178 countries analysed in the 2017 *Fragile States Index*—a list published jointly by the Fund for Peace and *Foreign Policy* magazine—Bahrain was ranked the 61st least vulnerable to conflict or collapse. The index is based on 12 indicators of state vulnerability across social, political and economic categories.

Justice

The new constitution which came into force in Feb. 2002 included the creation of an independent judiciary. The State Security Law and the State Security Court were both abolished in the lead-up to the change to a constitutional monarchy.

The population in penal institutions in 2012 was 2,307 (275 per 100,000 of national population). The death penalty is still in force and was last used in Jan. 2017.

Education

Adult literacy was 91% in 2008. Government schools provide free education from primary to technical college level. Schooling is in three stages: primary (six years), intermediate (three years) and secondary (three years). Secondary education may be general or specialized. In 2005–06 there were 67,528 primary school pupils, 32,359 intermediate school pupils and 29,223 secondary school pupils; there were a total of 203 schools and 10,836 teachers in 2005–06 including two religious institutes with 1,197 male students and 114 teachers.

In the private sector there were 56 schools with 34,378 pupils and 2,629 teachers in 2005–06.

There were 16 universities and similar institutions in 2005–06 with 29,678 students; and 2,392 persons attending adult education centres.

In 2006 expenditure on education came to 10·8% of total government spending.

Health

There is a free medical service for all residents. In the period 2006–12 Bahrain had 21 hospital beds per 10,000 population. Over the period 2007–13 there were 9·2 physicians for every 10,000 inhabitants, 23·7 nursing and midwifery personnel for every 10,000 and 2·4 dentistry personnel per 10,000.

Welfare

In 1976 a pensions, sickness benefits and unemployment, maternity and family allowances scheme was established. Employers contribute 7% of salaries and Bahraini employees 11%. In 2009, 27,503 persons received state welfare payments totalling BD13,904,790. A total of BD6,548,490 was paid out to pensioners, and BD2,183,460 to families.

Religion

Islam is the state religion. According to the Pew Research Center's Forum on Religion & Public Life, in 2010 the population was an estimated 70·3% Muslim (of whom around two-thirds Shia and a third Sunni), with 14·5% Christian and 9·8% Hindu.

Culture

World Heritage Sites

In 2005 Qal'at Al-Bahrain archaeological site was added to the UNESCO World Heritage List (reinscribed in 2008). The site was an area of human occupation from about 2300 BC to the 16th century. It is now a site of major excavation. Pearling was added to the list in 2012. The site, consisting of urban properties in Muharraq City, a fort, the seashore and oyster beds, is an exceptional illustration of the cultural tradition of pearling, which brought prosperity to the Persian Gulf between the 2nd and early 20th centuries.

Press

There were eight daily newspapers in 2008 with a combined average daily circulation of 155,000. The only independent newspaper was shut down by the government in June 2017.

Tourism

In 2012 there were 8,062,000 foreign visitors (up from 6,732,000 in 2011, but down from the record high of 11,952,000 in 2010 before the Arab Spring of early 2011 and the subsequent turmoil experienced by Bahrain).

Diplomatic Representatives

Of Bahrain in the United Kingdom (30 Belgrave Sq., London, SW1X 8QB)
    Ambassador: Sheikh Fawaz bin Mohammed Al-Khalifa.

Of the United Kingdom in Bahrain (21 Government Ave., Manama 306, PO Box 114, Bahrain)
    Ambassador: Simon Martin, CMG.

Of Bahrain in the USA (3502 International Drive, NW, Washington, D.C., 20008)
    Ambassador: Sheikh Abdulla Rashed Abdulla Al-Khalifa.

Of the USA in Bahrain (Building No. 979, Rd No. 3119, Block 331, Zinj District, Manama)
    Ambassador: Justin H. Siberell.

Of Bahrain to the United Nations
    Ambassador: Jamal Fares Al-Ruwae.

Of Bahrain to the European Union
    Ambassador: Bahiya Jawad Al-Jishi.

Further Reading

Bahrain Monetary Authority. *Quarterly Statistical Bulletin.*
Central Statistics Organization. *Statistical Abstract.* Annual
Al-Khalifa, A. and Rice, M. (eds) *Bahrain through the Ages.* 1993
Al-Khalifa, H. bin I., *First Light: Modern Bahrain and its Heritage.* 1995
Joyce, Miriam, *Bahrain from the Twentieth Century to the Arab Spring.* 2012
Moore, Philip, *Bahrain: A New Era.* 2001
National Statistical Office: Central Statistics Organization, Council of Ministers, Manama.
Open Data Portal: http://www.data.gov.bh

Bangladesh

Gana Prajatantri Bangladesh (People's Republic of Bangladesh)

Capital: Dhaka
Population projection, 2020: 169·78m.
GNI per capita, 2017: (PPP$) 3,677
HDI/world rank, 2017: 0·608/136
Internet domain extension: .bd

Key Historical Events

India's Maurya Empire established Buddhism in Bengal (*Bangla*) in the 3rd century BC. The Buddhist Pala Dynasty ruled Bengal and Bihar independently from AD 750, exporting Buddhism to Tibet. Hinduism regained dominance under the Sena Dynasty in the 11th century until the Muslim invasions in 1203–04. Rule from Delhi was broken in the 14th century by local Bengali kings. The Afghan adventurer Sher Shah conquered Bengal in 1539 and defeated the Mughal Emperor Humayun, creating an extensive administrative empire in North India. However, Mughal power was re-established by Akbar in 1576.

The Portuguese arrived in the 15th century, drawn to the rich Bengali cotton trade. They were followed by the Dutch and the British, whose East India Company was centred at Calcutta. The Nawab of Bengal was defeated by Robert Clive's army at the Battle of Plassey in 1757. British rule was maintained through the mainly Hindu *zamindar* land-owners and the Company was replaced by the Crown in 1858.

The partition of Bengal in 1905 was an attempt to undermine the nationalist influence of the *bhadralok*, the Hindu middle-classes, by forming a Muslim-dominated eastern province. Religious violence increased and political interests were represented by newly formed parties, including the All-India Muslim League. The partition was reversed in 1912. Tensions between the Muslim and Hindu communities escalated in the 1930s. The League suffered electoral defeat in 1936 but calls for a Muslim state were strengthened by the Pakistan Resolution of 1940. An agreement between Hindu and Muslim leaders to create an independent, secular Bengal was resisted by Mahatma Gandhi. Further violence, such as the Great Calcutta Killing in 1946, put pressure on the administration and India was hastily partitioned—East Bengal was united with the northwestern Muslim provinces as Pakistan. East Pakistan (as East Bengal became under the 1956 constitution) received 0·7m. Muslims, while over 2·5m. Hindus left for India.

Relations with West Pakistan were strained from the outset. Bengali demands for recognition of their language and resentment of preferential investment in their western partner led to the formation of the Awami League in 1949 to represent Bengali interests. Led by Sheikh Mujibur Rahman (Mujib), the Awami League triumphed as part of the 'United Front' in elections in 1954 but its government was dismissed by Governor-General Ghulam Mohammad after two months. A military government was installed from 1958–62 and in 1966 Mujib was arrested. Civilian government was again suspended in 1969 and in elections in 1970–71 the Awami League won all East Pakistani seats. While talks to form a government foundered, President Yahya Khan sent troops to the East and suspended the assembly, provoking a civil disobedience campaign. On 25 March 1971 the army began a crackdown. Members of the Awami League were arrested or fled to Calcutta, where they declared a provisional Bengali government. 10m. Bengalis fled to India to escape the bloody repression. India, with Soviet support, invaded on 3 Dec. 1971, forcing the surrender of the Pakistani army on 16 Dec. Mujib was released to become prime minister of independent Bangladesh.

Bangladesh suffered famine in 1974 and disorder led to Mujib assuming the presidency with dictatorial powers. Assassinated in Aug. 1975, a coup brought to power Maj.-Gen. Ziaur Rahman, who turned against the former ally, India. Rahman was assassinated in 1981. Hussain Mohammad Ershad became martial law administrator in 1982 and president in 1983. Ershad's National Party triumphed in parliamentary elections in May 1986 but presidential elections in Oct. were boycotted by opposition parties. A campaign of demonstrations and national strikes forced Ershad's resignation in 1990. Rahman's widow, Khaleda, became prime minister after her Bangladesh Nationalist Party won nearly half the seats. The victory in 1996 of the Bangladesh Awami League (as the post-independence Awami League became) brought Mujib's daughter, Sheikh Hasina Wajed, to the premiership but Khaleda Zia returned to power in 2001.

A state of emergency was declared in Jan. 2007 and elections were postponed following several weeks of violence that claimed more than 40 lives. Sheikh Hasina Wajed became prime minister for a second time when the Bangladesh Awami League won elections held in Dec. 2008, at which time the state of emergency was lifted. She was re-elected in 2014 in polls boycotted by the opposition. In May 2013 a garment factory in Dhaka collapsed, killing over 1,100 people and highlighting the plight of the country's low paid factory workers. From late 2016 and through 2017, Bangladesh received a surge of Muslim Rohingya migrants fleeing persecution in Myanmar.

Territory and Population

Bangladesh is bounded in the west and north by India, east by India and Myanmar and south by the Bay of Bengal. The area is 147,570 sq. km (56,977 sq. miles). In 1992 India granted a 999-year lease of the Tin Bigha corridor linking Bangladesh with its enclaves of Angarpota and Dahagram. The most recent census took place in March 2011; population, 144,043,697 (72,109,796 males), giving a density of 976 persons per sq. km.

The UN gives a projected population for 2020 of 169·78m.

In 2011, 28·6% of the population lived in urban areas. The country is administratively divided into eight divisions (since Sept. 2015), subdivided into 64 districts (*zila*). Area (in sq. km) and population (in 1,000) at the March 2011 census of the then seven divisions:

	Area	*Population*
Barisal division	13,297	8,326
Chittagong division	33,771	28,423
Dhaka division[1]	31,120	47,424
Khulna division	22,272	15,688
Rajshahi division	18,197	18,485
Rangpur division	16,317	15,788
Sylhet division	12,596	9,910

[1]In 2015 Mymensingh division was formed by taking four districts from Dhaka.

The populations of the chief cities (2011 census) were as follows:

Dhaka[1]	7,033,075
Chittagong	2,592,439
Khulna	663,342
Narayanganj	543,090
Sylhet	479,837
Tongi	476,350
Rajshahi	449,756
Bogra	350,397
Barisal	328,278
Comilla	326,386

[1]Metropolitan area, 11,086,309.

The official language is Bengali. English is also in use for official, legal and commercial purposes.

© Springer Nature Limited 2020
Palgrave Macmillan (ed.), *The Statesman's Yearbook 2020*,
https://doi.org/10.1057/978-1-349-95940-2_26

Social Statistics

2008 estimated births, 3,429,000; deaths, 1,054,000. In 2008 the birth rate was an estimated 21·4 per 1,000 population; death rate, 6·6; infant mortality, 2010, 38 per 1,000 live births (down from 99 per 1,000 in 1990). Life expectancy at birth, 2013, 71·5 years for females and 69·9 years for males. Annual population growth rate, 2000–08, 1·6%; fertility rate, 2008, 2·3 births per woman (down from 4·4 in 1990). Bangladesh has made some of the best progress in recent years in reducing child mortality. The number of deaths per 1,000 live births among children under five was reduced from 143 in 1990 to 48 in 2010. A UNICEF report published in 2014 revealed that 39% of women aged 20–49 had been married or in union before the age of 15, the highest percentage of any country.

Climate

A tropical monsoon climate with heat, extreme humidity and heavy rainfall in the monsoon season, from June to Oct. The short winter season (Nov.–Feb.) is mild and dry. Rainfall varies between 50" (1,250 mm) in the west to 100" (2,500 mm) in the southeast and up to 200" (5,000 mm) in the northeast. Dhaka, Jan. 66°F (19°C), July 84°F (28·9°C). Annual rainfall 81" (2,025 mm). Chittagong, Jan. 66°F (19°C), July 81°F (27·2°C). Annual rainfall 108" (2,831 mm).

Constitution and Government

Bangladesh is a unitary republic. The Constitution came into force on 16 Dec. 1972 and provides for a parliamentary democracy. The head of state is the *President*, elected by parliament every five years, who appoints a *Vice-President*. A referendum of Sept. 1991 was in favour of abandoning the executive presidential system and opted for a parliamentary system. There is a *Council of Ministers* to assist the President. The President appoints ministers. A 2011 constitutional amendment provided for a single-chamber parliament of 350 members, 300 directly elected every five years and 50 reserved for women, elected by the 300 MPs based on proportional representation in parliament. There have been 16 amendments to the Constitution altogether.

National Anthem

'Amar Sonar Bangla, ami tomay bhalobashi' ('My Bengal of gold, I love you'); words and tune by Rabindranath Tagore.

Government Chronology

Presidents since 1971. (BAL = Bangladesh Awami League; BJD = Bangladesh Jatiyatabadi Dal/Bangladesh Nationalist Party; JD = National Party; n/p = non-partisan)

1971–72	BAL	Sayeed Nazrul Islam (acting)
1971–72	BAL	Sheikh Mujibur Rahman
1972–73	n/p	Abu Sayeed Chowdhury
1973–75	BAL	Mohammad Mohammadullah
1975	BAL	Sheikh Mujibur Rahman
1975	BAL	Khandakar Mushtaq Ahmed
1975–77	n/p	Abu Sadat Mohammad Sayem
1977–81	military/BJD	Ziaur Rahman
1981–82	BJD	Abdus Sattar
1982–83	n/p	Abul Fazal Ahsanuddin Chowdhury
1983–90	military/JD	Hossain Mohammad Ershad
1991–96	BJD	Abdur Rahman Biswas
1996–2001	n/p	Shahabuddin Ahmed
2001–02	BJD	A. Q. M. Badruddoza Chowdhury
2002–09	n/p	Iajuddin Ahmed
2009–13	BAL	Zillur Rahman
2013–	BAL	Abdul Hamid

Heads of government since 1971.

Prime Ministers		
1971–72	BAL	Tajuddin Ahmed
1972–75	BAL	Sheikh Mujibur Rahman
1975	BAL	Mohammad Mansoor Ali
Chief Martial Law Administrators		
1975	military	Ziaur Rahman
1975–76	n/p	Abu Sadat Mohammad Sayem
1976–79	military/BJD	Ziaur Rahman
Prime Ministers		
1979–82	BJD	Shah Azizur Rahman
1984–86	JD	Ataur Rahman Khan
1986–88	JD	Mizanur Rahman Chowdhury
1988–89	JD	Moudud Ahmed
1989–90	JD	Kazi Zafar Ahmed
1991–96	BJD	Khaleda Zia
1996	n/p	Mohammad Habibur Rahman
1996–2001	BAL	Sheikh Hasina Wajed
2001	n/p	Latifur Rahman
2001–06	BJD	Khaleda Zia
2006–07	n/p	Iajuddin Ahmed
2007–09	n/p	Fakhruddin Ahmed
2009–	BAL	Sheikh Hasina Wajed

Recent Elections

Abdul Hamid was elected president unopposed on 22 April 2013 after incumbent Zillur Rahman died on 20 March 2013.

In parliamentary elections of 30 Dec. 2018 the Bangladesh Awami League (BAL) gained 257 seats against the National Party/Jatiya Party (Ershad) with 22 seats, the Bangladesh Nationalist Party (BNP) with six seats and the Workers Party of Bangladesh (WPB) with three seats. The Jatiya Samajtantrik Dal (JASAD), the Bikalpa Dhara Bangladesh (BDB) and Gano Forum (GF) gained two seats each. The National Party/Jatiya Party (Manju) and the Bangladesh Tarikat Federation won one seat each. Three seats went to independents and one seat remained vacant. There were incidents of violence, threats and harassment and allegations of electoral irregularities.

Current Government

President: Abdul Hamid; b. 1944 (Bangladesh Awami League; since 14 March 2013—acting until 24 April 2013).

In Feb. 2019 the government comprised:

Prime Minister, and Minister of Public Administration, Defence, Power, Energy and Mineral Resources, and Women and Children Affairs, in Charge of Cabinet Division and Armed Forces Division: Sheikh Hasina Wajed; b. 1947 (BAL; since 6 Jan. 2009, having previously held office from June 1996–July 2001).

Minister for Agriculture: Abdur Razzak. *Chittagong Hill Tracts Affairs:* Bir Bahadur Ushwe Sing. *Commerce:* Tipu Munshi. *Education:* Dipu Moni. *Environment, Forest and Climate Change:* Mohammad Shahab Uddin. *Finance:* Mustafa Kamal. *Food:* Sadhan Chandra Majumber. *Foreign Affairs:* Abulkalam Abdul Momen. *Health and Family Welfare:* Zahid Maleque. *Home Affairs:* Asaduzzaman Khan. *Housing and Public Works:* Rezaul Karim Hira. *Industries:* Nurul Majid Mahmud Humayun. *Information:* Muhammad Hasan Mahmud. *Land:* Saifuzzaman Chowdhury. *Law, Justice and Parliamentary Affairs:* Anisul Huq. *Liberation War Affairs:* Mozammel Haque. *Local Government, Rural Development and Co-operatives:* Tajul Islam. *Planning:* Muhammad Abdul Mannan. *Posts, Telecommunications and Information Technology:* Mustafa Jabbar. *Railways:* Nurul Islam Sujon. *Road Transport and Bridges:* Obaidul Quader. *Science and Technology:* Yeafesh Osman. *Social Welfare:* Nuruzzaman Ahmed. *Textiles and Jute:* Golam Dastagir Gazi.

There were 19 Ministers of State as at Feb. 2019.

Government Website: http://www.bangladesh.gov.bd

Current Leaders

Sheikh Hasina Wajed

Position

Prime Minister

Introduction

Sheikh Hasina, leader of the Bangladesh Awami League (BAL), was elected prime minister in Dec. 2008 after two years of military government. It was her second term as premier, having previously served from 1996–2001. She was returned to office following parliamentary elections in Jan. 2014 and again in Dec. 2018.

Early Life

Born on 28 Sept. 1947 in Tungipara, Bangladesh, Sheikh Hasina is the oldest child of Bangabandhu Sheikh Mujibar Rahman, former leader of the AL (which later became the BAL) and the nation's first head of state following the 1971 liberation war with Pakistan.

Hasina was a member of the AL's student Chhatra League while at Dhaka University, from where she graduated in 1973. In 1981 she was elected head of the BAL despite being in self-imposed exile, six years after the assassinations of her father, mother and three siblings.

Her chief political rival has been BJD leader Khaleda Zia, widow of the assassinated military president Ziaur Rahman, who had taken power following the death of Hasina's father. Throughout the 1980s and early 1990s Hasina worked to remove the military government, including a BAL boycott of Zia's government in 1994. In 1996 a civilian caretaker government was established ahead of elections, which Hasina won with a landslide to become prime minister. However, Bangladesh descended into chaos and in 2001 Transparency International ranked it the most corrupt country in the world.

The BJD regained power in elections in 2001, after which political violence involving BJD and BAL supporters escalated. In 2007 a military-backed caretaker government seized control and implemented emergency rule. Hasina was arrested on charges of corruption, extortion and murder and was briefly jailed before her release to seek medical care in the USA. Despite attempts to prevent her return, she arrived in Bangladesh in time to lead the BAL to election victory in Dec. 2008.

Career in Office

Hasina's primary challenge was to re-establish national stability. Internationally, relations with India were consolidated by trade and co-operation pacts and by agreements on border enclaves and the establishment of transit routes across Bangladesh to India's remote northeastern states. However, in domestic affairs the Nov. 2010 eviction, backed by a High Court order, of Khaleda Zia from her home in Dhaka sparked protests by BJD supporters and opposition boycotts of parliament.

In Jan. 2012 the army claimed to have uncovered a coup plot by officers hostile to the government, and stability was further undermined by anti-Hasina unrest through the rest of that year and 2013. Hasina meanwhile sought to amend the constitution and repeal the requirement (since 1996) that governments cede power to an independent caretaker administration ahead of an election. This provoked further political violence in the run-up to polling in Jan. 2014 and an electoral boycott by the BJD. The BAL won an overwhelming parliamentary majority in a low voter turnout but Hasina's victory was widely seen as lacking legitimacy. In April 2014 Khaleda Zia and other leading BJD figures were sent for trial on charges of corruption and embezzlement, and in Feb. 2015 she was further charged with instigating an opposition arson attack. She was eventually sentenced to five years imprisonment for corruption in Feb. 2018. Subsequent student protests from April to Aug. 2018 prompted an increasingly repressive crackdown by the government on dissent and opposition, including draconian legislation regulating online publishing and social media, ahead of parliamentary elections in Dec. that were won by the BAL.

From Nov. 2015 three senior members of the opposition Islamist Jaamat-e-Islami party were executed for war crimes during the country's war of independence in 1971 and in July 2016 Islamist militants attacked a restaurant popular with foreign nationals in Dhaka, killing 20 hostages before security forces ended the siege.

In 2017 the country suffered a series of floods and landslides that killed several hundred people and displaced thousands more, while the government was confronted by an escalating refugee crisis resulting from the mass influx of minority Muslim Rohingya people from neighbouring Myanmar fleeing persecution and violence by the country's military.

Defence

The supreme command of defence services is vested in the president. Defence expenditure in 2013 totalled US$1,652m. (US$10 per capita), representing 1·2% of GDP.

Army

Strength (2011) 126,153. There are also a 5,000-strong specialized police unit (the Armed Police), 20,000 security guards (Ansars) and the Bangladesh Rifles (border guard) numbering 38,000.

Navy

Naval bases are at Chittagong, Dhaka, Kaptai and Khulna. In 2011 the fleet included five frigates, 42 patrol and coastal combatants, and five mine sweepers. Personnel in 2011 numbered 16,900.

Air Force

Personnel strength (2011) 14,000. There were 74 combat-capable aircraft and 23 helicopters in 2011.

Economy

In 2011 agriculture accounted for 18% of GDP, industry 28% and services 54%.

Overview

The economy has achieved impressive and steady growth, doubling in size between 2006 and 2013 and remaining resilient throughout the global financial crisis. Growth declined only moderately to 5·9% in 2009 from 6·0% the previous year. The textiles and garments sector has fared particularly well. GDP growth between 2013 and 2016 averaged 6·5% per year.

Although the service sector is the dominant contributor to GDP, around half of the population is employed in agriculture and fishing. Despite political upheaval, international reserves have strengthened (tripling between 2011–12 and 2016–17) as a result of strong remittances and exports. The current account surplus reached a record 3·5% of GDP in 2009, before falling to 1·4% in 2015.

Good progress has been made on structural and tax reforms, although power and gas shortages continue to hold back growth and the application of public–private partnerships has been slow. In addition, low skill levels, poor governance and a weak infrastructure remain obstacles to sustained development and poverty reduction. The economy is also prone to downturns in export demand, while ongoing social unrest and political instability are additional long-term hurdles to progress.

Currency

The unit of currency is the *taka* (BDT) of 100 *poisha*, which was floated in 1976. Foreign exchange reserves in July 2009 were US$7,636m., gold reserves were 113,000 troy oz and total money supply was Tk.646,660m. Inflation was 5·7% in 2016 and 5·6% in 2017.

Budget

The fiscal year ends on 30 June. Budget, 2014–15: revenue, Tk.1,829·5bn.; expenditure, Tk.2,371·2bn.

VAT is 15%.

Performance

Real GDP growth was 6·8% in 2015, 7·2% in 2016 and 7·4% in 2017. Total GDP was US$249·7bn. in 2017.

Banking and Finance

Bangladesh Bank is the central bank (*Governor*, Fazle Kabir). There were 56 banks in Dec. 2015 of which six were state-owned commercial banks. Eight of the 39 private commercial banks in Dec. 2015 were full-fledged Islamic banks. In 2008 the Bangladesh Bank had deposits of Tk.211,805m. Sonali Bank Limited is the largest of the nationalized commercial banks, with deposits of Tk.406,152m. at 31 Dec. 2009.

In 2010 total foreign debt was US$24,963m., representing 22·8% of GNI. There are stock exchanges in Dhaka and Chittagong.

Energy and Natural Resources

Environment

Bangladesh's carbon dioxide emissions from the consumption of energy in 2011 were the equivalent of 0·4 tonnes per capita.

The *Climate Change and Environmental Risk Atlas 2014* produced by Maplecroft, a risk analytics company, ranked Bangladesh as the country facing the highest economic and social risk from climate change by 2025.

Electricity

Installed capacity was an estimated 6·6m. kW in 2010–11. Electricity generated, 2010–11, 44·06bn. kWh; consumption per capita in 2010–11 was 288 kWh. Bangladesh's first nuclear power plant is under construction at Rooppur, with work on the first reactor having started in 2017 and on a second reactor in 2018.

Oil and Gas

In 2013 Bangladesh had proven natural gas reserves of 300bn. cu. metres. Total natural gas production in 2013 amounted to 21·9bn. cu. metres.

Minerals

The principal minerals are lignite, limestone, china clay and glass sand. There are coal reserves of an estimated 2bn. tonnes. Production (2012–13, in 1,000 tonnes): marine salt, 1,439; coal, 855; granite, 281.

Agriculture

There were an estimated 7·7m. ha. of arable land in 2013 and 0·8m. ha. of permanent crops. Around 5·5m. ha. were equipped for irrigation in 2013. Bangladesh is a major producer of jute: production, 2013, 1,391,000 tonnes. Rice is the most important food crop; production in 2013 (in 1m. metric tonnes), 51·53. Other major crops in 2013 (1m. tonnes): potatoes, 8·60; sugarcane, 4·43; maize, 1·55; wheat, 1·26; onions, 1·17. Livestock in 2013: goats (estimate), 55·60m.; cattle, 23·34m.; sheep (estimate), 1·90m.; buffalo (estimates), 1·47m.; chickens, 249m. Livestock products in 2013 (estimates in tonnes): goat meat, 204,000; beef and veal, 192,000; poultry meat, 174,000; goat's milk, 2·62m.; cow's milk, 838,000; hen's eggs, 287,000. Bangladesh is the second largest producer of goat's milk, after India.

Forestry

In 2015 the area under forests was 1·43m. ha., or 11% of the total land area. Timber production in 2011 was 27·41m. cu. metres.

Fisheries

Bangladesh is a major producer of fish and fish products. The total catch in 2015 amounted to 1,623,837 tonnes, of which 1,023,991 tonnes came from inland waters. Only China and India have larger annual catches of freshwater fish. Aquaculture production totalled 1,308,515 tonnes in 2010 (the fifth highest in the world).

Industry

Manufacturing contributed 17·3% of GDP in 2013. The principal industries are jute and cotton textiles, tea, paper, newsprint, cement, chemical fertilizers and light engineering. In 2013 industrial output grew by 9·6%. There were 42,792 manufacturing establishments with ten or more workers in 2012.

Labour

In 2010 the economically active workforce totalled 56,651,000 over the age of 15 years (39,477,000 males). The main areas of activity (in 1,000) were: agriculture, forestry and fishing, 25,727; wholesale and retail trade, and repair of motor vehicles, motorcycles and personal and household goods, 7,557; manufacturing, 6,737. In 2010, 4·5% of the workforce aged 15 or over were unemployed. For the five-year period 2007–12 the National Minimum Wage Board established the minimum monthly wage at Tk.1,500 (equivalent to US$19) for all economic sectors not covered by industry-specific wages. The minimum wage in the garment industry was raised from Tk.3,000 (US$37) per month to Tk.5,300 (US$68) per month in 2013, but this still ranks among the lowest of any country.

Bangladesh had 0·34m. people living in slavery according to the Walk Free Foundation's 2013 *Global Slavery Index*, the tenth highest total of any country.

International Trade

Imports and Exports

Goods imports were US$41,221·7m. in 2011 (US$30,503·8m. in 2010) and goods exports US$24,313·7m. (US$19,231·0m. in 2010).

Principal imports in 2011 were manufactured goods (25·5%), machinery and transport equipment, and crude materials and animal and vegetable oils; main exports in 2011 were miscellaneous manufactured articles including garments (81·1%), manufactured goods, and food, animals and beverages.

The leading import sources are China, India and Kuwait. Leading export markets are the USA, Germany and the UK.

Communications

Roads

In 2015 there were 3,813 km of national highways, 4,247 km of regional highways and 13,242 km of district roads plus secondary and rural roads. In 2007 there were 158,100 passenger cars and 168,600 vans and lorries. There were 3,160 fatalities as a result of road accidents in 2006.

Rail

In 2005 there were 2,855 km of railways, comprising 660 km of 1,676 mm gauge, 1,830 km of metre gauge and 365 km of dual gauge. Passenger-km travelled in 2008 came to 402·4m. and freight tonne-km to 952m.

Civil Aviation

There are international airports at Dhaka (Hazrat Shahjalal) and Chittagong, and eight domestic airports. Biman Bangladesh Airlines was state-owned until July 2007 when it became a public limited company. In addition to domestic routes, in 2010 it operated international services to 16 destinations. There were direct international flights in 2010 with other airlines to 27 destinations. In 2009 Dhaka's Hazrat Shahjalal International Airport handled 4,254,427 passengers and 147,239 tonnes of freight. In 2012 scheduled airline traffic of Bangladesh-based carriers flew 67·9m. km; passenger-km totalled 8·1bn. in the same year.

Shipping

In Jan. 2014 there were 171 ships of 300 GT or over registered, totalling 959,000 GT. The main port is Chittagong, which handled 44,237,000 tonnes of cargo in 2013. There is also a seaport at Mongla. There are 8,000 km of navigable inland waterways.

Telecommunications

Mobile phone subscribers numbered 126,866,091 in 2014 (800·4 per 1,000 inhabitants). There were 974,181 main telephone lines in the same year. Fixed internet subscriptions totalled 3,093,171 in 2014 (19·5 per 1,000 inhabitants). In 2014, 9·6% of the population were internet users. In March 2012 there were 2·5m. Facebook users.

Social Institutions

Out of 178 countries analysed in the 2017 *Fragile States Index*—a list published jointly by the Fund for Peace and *Foreign Policy* magazine— Bangladesh was ranked the 39th most vulnerable to conflict or collapse. The index is based on 12 indicators of state vulnerability across social, political and economic categories.

Justice

The Supreme Court comprises an Appellate and a High Court Division, the latter having control over all subordinate courts. Judges are appointed by the President and retire at 65. There are benches at Comilla, Rangpur, Jessore, Barisal, Chittagong and Sylhet, and courts at District level.

The population in penal institutions in April 2013 was 72,104 (42 per 100,000 of national population). The International Centre for Prison Studies estimated in 2014 that 73·8% of prisoners had yet to receive a trial. The death penalty is still in force. There were six executions in 2017 but none in 2018. In 2015 the World Justice Project *Rule of Law Index*, which provides data on how the rule of law is experienced by the general public across eight categories, ranked Bangladesh 88th of 102 countries for criminal justice and 93rd for civil justice.

Education

In 2007 there were 16·3m. pupils and 364,494 teaching staff at primary schools; 10·4m. pupils and 413,746 teaching staff at secondary schools; 1·1m. students and 60,915 academic staff in tertiary education. In 2006 there were 78 universities, 42 medical colleges, 171 polytechnic institutes and 3,197 general colleges.

Adult literacy was an estimated 55·9% in 2009 (60·7% among males and 51·0% among females).

In 2007 public expenditure on education came to 2·4% of GNI and 15·8% of total government spending.

Health

In 2008 there were 2,860 hospitals and health complexes with 74,400 beds. There were 49,994 registered physicians in 2008, and 2,344 dentistry personnel and 39,471 nursing and midwifery personnel in 2005.

In *Water: At What Cost? The State of the World's Water 2016*, WaterAid reported that 13·1% of the population does not have access to safe water. Bangladesh ranked as the country with the eighth largest number of people living without access to safe water (21·1m. in 2015).

Religion

Islam is the state religion, although the constitution states that other religions may be practised in peace and harmony. According to the Pew Research Center's Forum on Religion & Public Life the population was 89·8% Muslim in 2010, with Hindus accounting for 9·1%. In Feb. 2019 there was one Roman Catholic cardinal.

Culture

World Heritage Sites

There are three UNESCO sites in Bangladesh: the Historic Mosque City of Bagerhat (inscribed in 1985); the Ruins of the Buddhist Vihara at Paharpur (1985); the Sundarbans (1997), 140,000 ha. of mangrove forest.

Press

In 2008 there were 430 paid-for daily newspapers with a combined circulation of 1·5m.

Tourism

In 2014 there were 125,000 non-resident tourists (267,000 in 2009).

Diplomatic Representatives

Of Bangladesh in the United Kingdom (28 Queen's Gate, London, SW7 5JA)
High Commissioner: Saida Muna Tasneem.

Of the United Kingdom in Bangladesh (United Nations Rd, Baridhara, PO Box 6079, Dhaka 1212)
High Commissioner: Alison Blake.

Of Bangladesh in the USA (3510 International Drive, NW, Washington, D.C., 20007)
Ambassador: Mohammad Ziauddin.

Of the USA in Bangladesh (Madani Ave., Baridhara, Dhaka 1212)
Ambassador: Earl R. Miller.

Of Bangladesh to the United Nations
Ambassador: Masud Bin Momen.

Of Bangladesh to the European Union
Ambassador: Mohammed Shahdat Hossain.

Further Reading

Bangladesh Bureau of Statistics. *Statistical Yearbook of Bangladesh.—Statistical Pocket Book of Bangladesh.*

Baxter, Craig, *Historical Dictionary of Bangladesh.* 2003

Lewis, David, *Bangladesh: Politics, Economy and Civil Society.* 2011

Riaz, Ali, *God Willing: The Politics of Islamism in Bangladesh.* 2004.—*Unfolding State: The Transformation of Bangladesh.* 2005

Sawada, Yasuyuki, Mahmud, Minhaj and Kitano, Naohiro, (eds) *Economic and Social Development of Bangladesh: Miracle and Challenges.* 2017

Van Schendel, Willem, *A History of Bangladesh.* 2009

National Statistical Office: Bangladesh Bureau of Statistics, Ministry of Planning, E-27/A, Agargaon, Sher-e-banglanagar, Dhaka 1207.

Website: http://www.bbs.gov.bd

Barbados

Capital: Bridgetown
Population projection, 2020: 288,000
GNI per capita, 2017: (PPP$) 15,843
HDI/world rank, 2017: 0·800/58=
Internet domain extension: .bb

Key Historical Events

Archaeological evidence suggests Barbados was inhabited by Barrancoid Indians from at least 1,000 BC, and by Arawak and Carib people for about 400 years from around AD 1,000. However, Portuguese mariners who landed in 1536 reported that the island was uninhabited. The Portuguese named it Los Barbados—meaning 'bearded', seemingly a reference to the appearance of local fig trees.

Lacking obvious mineral resources, the island remained unsettled until an Englishman, William Courteen, established Jamestown in 1627. English colonists began cultivating cotton, tobacco and indigo, before developing plantations using sugarcane shipped from Dutch Brazil in the 1650s. Plantation owners initially imported English and Irish servants and prisoners, but then turned to West Africa, principally the Gold Coast, for slave labour. Hundreds of thousands of slaves were shipped to Barbados over the next two centuries. While many worked on the sugar plantations, others were re-exported to other slave-owning colonies in the Caribbean and North America.

Barbados became the dominant sugar producer in the Caribbean—by the end of the 18th century there were 745 plantations and a population of more than 80,000. Bridgetown, the capital, became the third largest settlement in English America, behind Boston and Port Royal, Jamaica. Revolts against harsh working conditions erupted in the early 19th century, the most notable of which was an 1816 slave uprising led by Bussa, a ranger on one of the largest plantations. Bussa's Rebellion took place nine years after the British had abolished the slave trade, but not slavery itself. Slaves in Barbados were not fully emancipated until 1838, at the end of an 'apprenticeship period' that followed the official abolition of slavery in the British Empire in 1834.

In 1876 a British proposal for a confederation of Barbados and the Windward Islands triggered riots in Bridgetown. Politics remained dominated by wealthy merchants of English and Scottish descent until the 1930s, when the nascent trade union movement challenged the established order against a backdrop of worsening conditions linked to the Great Depression. Grantley Adams founded the Barbados Progressive League, later renamed the Barbados Labour Party (BLP), in 1938. It campaigned for improved conditions for workers, economic development and the extension of political rights. Universal suffrage was introduced in 1951, followed by cabinet government three years later. Adams was elected premier of Barbados in 1958, the year in which the island joined the short-lived ten-member West Indies Federation.

Full internal self-government was attained in Oct. 1961. Errol Barrow, founder of the Democratic Labour Party (DLP), was elected prime minister that year and led the island to independence on 30 Nov. 1966. He served as the nation's first president until ousted in Sept. 1976. Power has been held alternately by the BLP and DLP for the duration of the country's post-independence history.

Territory and Population

Barbados lies to the east of the Windward Islands. Area 430 sq. km (166 sq. miles). In 2010 the census population was 277,821; density, 646·1 per sq. km.

The UN gives a projected population for 2020 of 288,000.

In 2011, 45·1% of the population were urban. Bridgetown is the principal city: population (including suburbs), 122,000 in 2011. The country is divided into 11 parishes.

The official language is English.

Social Statistics

In 2007: births registered, 3,537; deaths registered, 2,213; birth rate, 12·9 per 1,000 population; death rate, 8·1 per 1,000 population; infant mortality (2010), 17 per 1,000 live births. Expectation of life, 2007, males 74·0 years and females 79·7. Population growth rate, 2005, 0·3%; fertility rate, 2008, 1·5 children per woman.

Climate

An equable climate in winter, but the wet season, from June to Nov., is more humid. Rainfall varies from 50" (1,250 mm) on the coast to 75" (1,875 mm) in the higher interior. Bridgetown, Jan. 76°F (24·4°C), July 80°F (26·7°C). Annual rainfall 51" (1,275 mm).

Constitution and Government

The head of state is the British sovereign, represented by an appointed Governor-General. The bicameral Parliament consists of a Senate and a House of Assembly. The *Senate* comprises 21 members appointed by the Governor-General, 12 being appointed on the advice of the Prime Minister, two on the advice of the Leader of the Opposition and seven at the Governor-General's discretion. The *House of Assembly* comprises 30 members elected every five years. In 1963 the voting age was reduced to 18.

The *Privy Council* is appointed by the Governor-General after consultation with the Prime Minister. It consists of 12 members and the Governor-General as chairman. It advises the Governor-General in the exercise of the royal prerogative of mercy and in the exercise of his disciplinary powers over members of the public and police services.

National Anthem

'In plenty and in time of need'; words by Irvine Burgie, tune by C. Van Roland Edwards.

Recent Elections

In the general election of 24 May 2018 the Barbados Labour Party (BLP) won all 30 seats (74·6% of the total vote) against the ruling Democratic Labour Party (DLP), who failed to win any seats. Three other parties and independents also failed to win any seats.

Current Government

Governor-General: Dame Sandra Mason; b. 1949.

In Feb. 2019 the government comprised:

Prime Minister, and Minister of Finance, Economic Affairs and Investment: Mia Mottley; b. 1965 (BLP; sworn in 25 May 2018).

Minister of Agriculture and Food Security: Indar Weir. *Attorney General and Minister of Legal Affairs:* Dale Marshall. *Creative Economy, Culture and Sports:* John King. *Education, Technological and Vocational Training and Leader of Government Business:* Santia Bradshaw. *Energy and Water Resources:* Wilfried Abrahams. *Environment and National Beautification:* Trevor Prescod. *Foreign Affairs and Foreign Trade:* Jerome Walcott. *Health and Wellness:* Jeffrey Bostic. *Home Affairs:* Edmund Hinkson. *Housing, Lands and Rural Development:* George Payne. *Information, Broadcasting and Public Affairs:* Lucille Moe. *Innovation, Science and Smart Technology:* Kay McConney. *International Business and Industry:* Ronald Toppin. *Labour and Social Partnership Relations:* Colin Jordan. *Maritime Affairs and the Blue Economy:* Kirk Humphrey. *People's Empowerment and the Elderly:* Cynthia Forde. *Small Business, Entrepreneurship and Commerce:* Dwight Sutherland. *Tourism and International Transport:* Kerrie Symmonds. *Transport, Works and Maintenance:* William Duguid. *Youth and Community Empowerment:* Adrian Forde.

Government of Barbados Information Network: http://www.gov.bb

Current Leaders

Mia Mottley

Position
Prime Minister

Introduction
Mia Mottley became the country's first female prime minister in May 2018 at the head of a Barbados Labour Party (BLP) government. The BLP won all 30 parliamentary seats in that month's election—the first time that had happened since the country gained independence.

Early Life
Mottley was born on 1 Oct. 1965. She was educated in Barbados and the USA, before graduating in law from the London School of Economics in the UK in 1986.

She entered politics in 1991, serving as an opposition senator until 1994. The BLP then formed a government and Mottley became minister of education, youth affairs and culture. In 1996 she was appointed party general-secretary and five years later became minister of home affairs and attorney-general. In 2003 she was named deputy prime minister, and a cabinet reshuffle in 2006 saw her additionally take on the economic affairs and development portfolio.

The BLP lost the 2008 election, precipitating the resignation of Owen Arthur as party leader. Mottley replaced him, becoming the nation's country's first female leader of the opposition. However, tensions within the BLP led to Mottley relinquishing the role, with Arthur returning to the post.

Mottley became leader again in 2013 but could not secure victory for the party at that year's general election. In the run-up to the 2018 election, she ran on a platform of eradicating government corruption and battling growing debt.

Career in Office
The BLP won all the seats in the House of Assembly in the election of 24 May 2018. Mottley was sworn in as prime minister the following day. Among her primary tasks was to address the high level of national debt (measured at 175% of GDP in June 2018). She announced that domestic creditors would be prioritized, prompting defaults on several international obligations that resulted in a downgrading of the national credit rating.

Defence

The Barbados Defence Force has a strength of about 610. In 2013 defence expenditure totalled US$33m. (US$115 per capita), representing 0·7% of GDP.

Army

Army strength was 500 with reserves numbering 430 in 2011.

Navy

A small maritime unit numbering 110 (2011) operates six patrol vessels. The unit is based in the St Ann's Fort area at the Garrison, Bridgetown.

Economy

In 2012 finance and real estate contributed 26·4% to GDP; followed by trade, tourism and restaurants, 20·2%; public administration and defence, 11·3%; and transport and communications, 10·0%.

Overview

Barbados is the wealthiest and most developed economy in the Eastern Caribbean. Once agriculture-based, it has diversified over the decades, with services accounting for 87% of GDP in 2016 and tourism in particular contributing 40%. The global financial crisis took a heavy toll as GDP shrank by an average of 0·5% per year between 2008 and 2013, although growth reached 2·2% in 2015 and 2·3% in 2016. Public debt had reached 111% of GDP at the end of 2016, up from 60% in 2009. Meanwhile, government bonds lost 8% of their value in early 2014, reflecting a pattern seen around the Caribbean that saw regional neighbours, including Belize and Jamaica, default on their debt.

The government has embarked on a range of measures to reduce the deficit, including cutting 13% of civil service jobs (about 3,000 positions) and freezing wage growth for other public workers. It has also sought to stem the decline in foreign reserves resulting from an initial fall in tourist numbers following the financial crash in Europe and North America. In 2016 Barbados Port Inc. completed a BDS$115m. project that included new cruise ship mooring facilities and the acquisition of specialized cargo equipment, with the aim of expanding the tourist and freight sectors.

While the IMF has praised measures to raise VAT rates and public transportation tariffs, it recommends broadening the tax base, streamlining government operations and reducing public spending in the interests of cutting public debt to a manageable level. Unemployment, despite declining from 11·6% in 2013 to 9·7% in 2016, remains a major challenge.

Currency

The unit of currency is the *Barbados dollar* (BBD), usually written as BDS$, of 100 *cents*, which is pegged to the US dollar at BDS$2=US$1. Inflation was 1·5% in 2016 and 4·4% in 2017. Total money supply was BDS$2,686m. and foreign exchange reserves were US$725m. in May 2009.

Budget

The financial year runs from 1 April. Budgetary central government revenue and expenditure (in BDS$1m.):

	2008–09	2009–10	2010–11
Revenue	2,662·5	2,531·7	2,410·4
Expenditure	2,957·0	3,035·6	3,112·3

Tax revenue accounted for 92·9% of revenues in 2010–11. Main sources of expenditure in 2010–11 were compensation of employees, 28·4%; subsidies, 28·0%; interest, 15·7%.

VAT is 17·5% (reduced rate, 6%).

Performance

The economy grew by 2·2% in 2015 and 2·3% in 2016. However, there was then negative growth of 0·2% in 2017. Total GDP in 2017 was US$4·8bn.

Banking and Finance

The central bank and bank of issue is the Central Bank of Barbados (*Governor*, Cleviston Haynes), which was established in 1972. In 2014 there were seven commercial banks and bank holding companies licensed to operate in Barbados plus 12 trusts, finance and merchant banks. Commercial banks hold 60% of the financial sector's assets. In 2012 banks had total assets amounting to BDS$11,878m. There were 4,016 international business companies registered in Barbados in 2014.

There is a stock exchange which participates in the regional Caribbean exchange.

Energy and Natural Resources

Environment

Carbon dioxide emissions from the consumption of energy in 2011 were the equivalent of 5·0 tonnes per capita.

Electricity

Production in 2011, 1,049m. kWh. Capacity in 2011 was 0·2m. kW. Consumption per capita was 3,722 kWh in 2011.

Oil and Gas

Crude oil production in 2011 was 300,000 bbls and reserves 1·8m. bbls. Output of natural gas (2011) 17m. cu. metres.

Agriculture

The agricultural sector accounted for 1·8% of GDP in 2013 (3·7% in 1993). Of the total labour force in 2013, 2·7% were employed in agriculture. Of the total area of Barbados (42,995 ha.), about 11,000 ha. are arable land, which is intensively cultivated. In 2013, 4,240 ha. were under sugarcane cultivation. Production, 2013 (in tonnes): sugarcane, 173,085; coconuts (estimate), 2,200; sweet potatoes, 1,220; tomatoes, 989; bananas (2012 estimate), 950; cucumbers and gherkins, 824; yams, 749; avocados (2012 estimate), 700.

Meat and dairy products, 2013 (in tonnes): poultry, 13,702; pork, 2,498; beef, 140; cow's milk, 5,082; eggs, 2,966.

Livestock (2013 estimates): pigs, 23,000; sheep, 13,000; cattle, 11,000; chickens, 3·6m.

Forestry

Timber production in 2011 was 11,000 cu. metres. In 2015 forests covered 6,000 ha. or 15% of the total land area.

Fisheries

The total catch in 2012 was 1,363 tonnes, exclusively from sea fishing.

Industry

Industry has traditionally been centred on sugar, but there is also light manufacturing and component assembly for export. In 2013, 17,400 tonnes of raw sugar were produced.

Labour

The labour force in 2013 was 161,900 (up from 149,500 in 2003). 80·8% of the population aged 15–64 was economically active in 2013. In the same year 11·6% of the population was unemployed.

International Trade

Imports and Exports

Trade in US$1m.:

	Imports (c.i.f.)	Exports (f.o.b.)
2006	1,628·6	441·2
2007	1,298·7	314·2
2008	1,744·3	454·2
2009	1,340·7	322·7
2010	1,196·2	313·7

In 2010 imports (in US$1m.) were mainly from the USA (525·7), Trinidad and Tobago (85·9), the UK (64·2) and China (57·8). Principal export markets in 2010 were (in US$1m.) the USA (78·2), the UK (52·6), Trinidad and Tobago (26·5) and St Lucia (18·2).

The main imports are machinery and transport equipment; food and live animals; manufactured goods. The main exports are chemicals and petroleum products; manufactured articles; beverages.

Communications

Roads

Barbados has some 1,600 km of roads. In 2007 there were 103,500 passenger cars, 15,200 lorries and vans, and 630 buses and coaches. There were 38 deaths as a result of road accidents in 2007.

Civil Aviation

Grantley Adams International Airport is 16 km from Bridgetown. In 2009 it handled 1,939,059 passengers (down from 2,165,125 in 2008) and 21,098 tonnes of freight (up from 19,479 in 2008). There were flights in 2010 to Antigua, Atlanta, Beef Island, Boston, Canouan Island, Charlotte, Curaçao, Dominica, Fort de France, Frankfurt, Georgetown, Grenada, Kingston, London, Manchester, Miami, Montreal, New York, Philadelphia, Port of Spain, St Kitts, St Lucia, St Maarten, St Vincent, San Juan, Tobago and Toronto.

Shipping

There is a deep-water harbour at Bridgetown. In Jan. 2014 there were 92 ships of 300 GT or over registered, totalling 614,000 GT. Barbados is a 'flag of convenience' country.

Telecommunications

In 2011 there were 141,000 landline telephone subscriptions (equivalent to 513·5 per 1,000 inhabitants) and 348,000 mobile phone subscriptions (1,270·1 per 1,000 inhabitants). Fixed broadband subscriptions totalled 68,000 in 2013 (240·0 per 1,000 inhabitants). In Dec. 2011 Barbados had 118,000 Facebook users.

Social Institutions

Out of 178 countries analysed in the 2017 *Fragile States Index*—a list published jointly by the Fund for Peace and *Foreign Policy* magazine—Barbados was ranked the 40th least vulnerable to conflict or collapse. The index is based on 12 indicators of state vulnerability across social, political and economic categories.

Justice

Justice is administered by the Supreme Court and Justices' Appeal Court, and by magistrates' courts. All have both civil and criminal jurisdiction. There are a Chief Justice, three judges of appeal, five puisne judges of the Supreme Court and nine magistrates. The death penalty is authorized. Barbados was one of ten countries to sign an agreement in Feb. 2001 establishing a Caribbean Court of Justice (CCJ) to replace the British Privy Council as the highest civil and criminal court. In the meantime the number of signatories has risen to 12. The court was inaugurated at Port of Spain, Trinidad on 16 April 2005. Barbados is one of only four countries, along with Belize, Dominica and Guyana, to have accepted it as its court of final appeal.

The population in penal institutions in June 2013 was 1,507 (521 per 100,000 of national population).

Education

The adult literacy rate is at least 98%. There were 23 public and seven private secondary schools in 2016. Education is free in all government-owned and government-maintained institutions from primary to university level. There were 22,584 pupils at primary schools in 2007 with 1,553 teaching staff and 20,855 pupils at secondary schools in 2006 with 1,430 teaching staff.

In 2005 public expenditure on education came to 6·9% of GDP and 16·4% of total government spending.

In 2007 there were 11,405 students in higher education and 786 academic staff. One of the three main campuses of the University of the West Indies is in Barbados, at Cave Hill.

Health

Expenditure on health represented 7·4% of GDP in 2012. In the period 2005–12 there were 18 physicians per 10,000 inhabitants and 49 nursing and midwifery personnel per 10,000.

In *Water: At What Cost? The State of the World's Water 2016*, WaterAid reported that 0·3% of the population does not have access to safe water.

Welfare

The National Insurance and Social Security Scheme provides contributory sickness, age, maternity, disability and survivors benefits. Sugar workers have their own scheme.

Religion

In 2010 there were an estimated 240,000 Protestants and 10,000 Roman Catholics according to the Pew Research Center's Forum on Religion & Public Life, with the remainder of the population being unaffiliated or following other religions.

Culture

World Heritage Sites

Historic Bridgetown and its Garrsion, an outstanding example of British colonial architecture, was inscribed on the UNESCO World Heritage List in 2011.

Press

In 2008 there were two daily newspapers, the *Barbados Advocate* (est. 1895) and the *Daily Nation* (est. 1973). The *Daily Nation* has an average daily circulation of 33,000; the *Barbados Advocate*, 15,000.

Tourism

In 2014 there were 519,635 overnight tourist arrivals by air (of which 186,858 were from the United Kingdom) and 684,608 cruise ship visitors, up from 508,520 and 570,263 respectively in 2013.

Festivals

The National Cultural Foundation organizes three annual national festivals: the nine-day Congaline Carnival which begins in the last week of April; Crop Over, a three-week festival held from mid-July until Aug.; the National Independence Festival of Creative Arts (NIFCA) which runs throughout Nov. The biggest music festivals are the Barbados Jazz Festival (Jan.) and Gospelfest (May). Other festivals include the Holetown Festival (Feb.), which commemorates the anniversary of the first settlement of Barbados, Holders Season (March), an arts festival at St James, and the Oistins Fish Festival (March–April).

Diplomatic Representatives

Of Barbados in the United Kingdom (1 Great Russell St., London, WC1B 3ND)
High Commissioner: Guy Arlington Hewitt.

Of the United Kingdom in Barbados (Lower Collymore Rock, PO Box 676, Bridgetown)
High Commissioner: Janet Douglas, CMG.

Of Barbados in the USA (2144 Wyoming Ave., NW, Washington, D.C., 20008)
Ambassador: Vacant.
Chargé d'Affaires a.i.: Jane Elizabeth Brathwaite.

Of the USA in Barbados (Wildey Business Park, Wildey, St Michael, BB 14006, Bridgetown)
Ambassador: Linda S. Taglialatela.

Of Barbados to the United Nations
Ambassador: Henrietta Elizabeth Thompson.

Of Barbados to the European Union
Ambassador: Vacant.
Chargé d'Affaires a.i.: Nicholas Cox.

Further Reading

Beckles, H., *A History of Barbados: from Amerindian Settlement to Nation-State.* 1990
Carmichael, Trevor A. (ed.) *Barbados: Thirty Years of Independence.* 1998
Carter, R. and Downes, A. S., *Analysis of Economic and Social Development in Barbados: A Model for Small Island Developing States.* 2000
Hoyos, F. A., *Tom Adams: a Biography.* 1988.—*Barbados: A History from the Amerindians to Independence.* 2nd ed. 1992
National Statistical Office: Barbados Statistical Service, Fairchild Street, Bridgetown.
Website: http://www.barstats.gov.bb

Belarus

Respublika Belarus (Republic of Belarus)

Capital: Minsk
Population projection, 2020: 9·42m.
GNI per capita, 2017: (PPP$) 16,323
HDI/world rank, 2017: 0·808/53
Internet domain extension: .by

Key Historical Events

There is evidence of Neolithic settlement dating to 4000 BC at Asaviec in northern Belarus. During the third and second millennia BC, parts of present-day Belarus were settled by Finno-Ugric tribes, as well as groups migrating along the Dniepr river and from the southern Baltic. Slavic tribes, notably the Kryvichans, gained dominance between the 5th and 8th centuries AD, seeing off Huns and Avars from the eastern steppes. The territory came under the sway of Kyivan Rus during the 9th century, although the Duchy of Polotsk challenged Kyiv and Novgorod for control of the northern reaches until its decline in the late 12th century. The Duchy of Turau and Pinsk to the south also became powerful during this period.

Kyiv's influence waned in the 13th century and raids by Mongol horsemen in the 1220s and 1230s left the area weak and open to conquest by the Dukes of Lithuania, initially under Mindaugas. Grand Duke Ladislaus Jagiełło's marriage to a Polish princess, Jadwiga, in 1385 made him king of Poland and a powerful rival to Muscovy, and several wars ensued between the two over access to the Baltic Sea, with Belarus one of the battlegrounds.

Jewish settlers arrived in Belarus in the late 14th century, initially in the cities of Brest and Hrodna. Belarusian culture flourished until the Polish–Lithuanian union in 1569, which put Polish rulers in the ascendency. The Commonwealth reached its zenith in the early 17th century then gradually declined until partitions in 1772, 1793 and 1795 saw control of all Belarusian territory pass to the Russian empire. By the 1830s Russification had taken hold, with the Polish language outlawed in schools and the Russian Orthodox church dominant.

Poverty and hardship under Tsarist rule led to significant emigration, notably by Jews to the USA, and fuelled rebellion. In 1863 anti-Russian uprisings erupted across the eastern Baltic region, led in Belarus by Kastus Kalinouski. By the 1880s several organizations championed Belarusian independence, although the movement gained little ground until the Russian Revolution of 1905, when bans on a free press and non-Russian languages were lifted. The outbreak of the First World War brought a million Russian troops into Belarus, with as many of the local population fleeing or being evacuated.

In March 1918 the first all-Belarusian Congress in Minsk declared an independent republic, but nine months later the Bolshevik government in Smolensk proclaimed the Byelorussian Soviet Socialist Republic (BSSR). A battlefield in the Russo–Polish war, it was divided by the Treaty of Riga in 1921, with 40% of the territory coming under Polish rule.

In Sept. 1939 the Red Army annexed western Belarus and western Ukraine, setting the stage for the region's devastation. Up to 300,000 people were deported under Stalin prior to the German offensive in June 1941. During the three years of Nazi occupation 2·2m. people died, including almost all the Jewish population, and over 1m. buildings were destroyed. The Red Army liberated Minsk in July 1944 and Belarus was fully integrated into the Soviet Union at the end of the war, becoming the most militarized Soviet Republic and a centre for light industry.

Gorbachev's reforms of the mid-1980s encouraged demands for greater freedom. On 25 Aug. 1991 Belarus declared independence, with the reformist Stanislau Shushkevich becoming head of state. Alyaksandr Lukashenka who, in 1991, had opposed the dissolution of the USSR, was elected president in July 1994. By 1996 only 11% of state enterprises had been privatized and the pro-Russian government worked to establish a Russia–Belarus Union. A referendum held in Nov. 1996 extended the president's term of office from three to five years and increased his powers.

The government maintained its political stranglehold at the 2008 parliamentary election, winning all seats. Lukashenka remained defiant in the face of domestic and international pressure for reform. In Dec. 2010 he secured a further presidential term, although the opposition and international observers alleged vote rigging. He was re-elected again in Oct. 2015 in an election that passed off more peacefully than its 2010 counterpart but that nonetheless prompted more accusations of irregularities.

Territory and Population

Belarus is situated along the western Dvina and Dnieper. It is bounded in the west by Poland, north by Latvia and Lithuania, east by Russia and south by Ukraine. The area is 207,600 sq. km (80,155 sq. miles). The capital is Minsk. Other important towns are Homel, Vitebsk, Mahilyou, Bobruisk, Hrodno and Brest. On 2 Nov. 1939 western Belorussia was incorporated with an area of over 108,000 sq. km and a population of 4·8m. Census population, 2009, 9,503,807; density, 45·8 per sq. km. Estimate, Jan. 2018: 9,491,823.

The UN gives a projected population for 2020 of 9·42m.

In 2011, 75·2% of the population lived in urban areas. Major ethnic groups: 81·2% Belarusians, 11·4% Russians, 3·9% Poles, 2·4% Ukrainians.

Belarus comprises six regions and one municipality. Areas and populations:

Province	Area sq. km	Population (2018 estimate)	Capital	Population (2018 estimate)
Brest	32,800	1,384,476	Brest	347,576
Homel	40,400	1,415,749	Homel	535,693
Hrodno	25,100	1,043,681	Hrodno	370,919
Mahilyou	29,100	1,058,746	Mahilyou	381,353
Minsk	39,800	1,426,525	Minsk	—
Minsk City	350	1,982,444	—	—
Vitebsk	40,100	1,180,202	Vitebsk	370,298

Belarusian and Russian are both official languages.

Social Statistics

2013 births, 118,463 (rate of 12·5 per 1,000 population); deaths, 125,872 (rate of 13·3 per 1,000 population); marriages, 87,127; divorces, 36,105. Annual population growth rate, 2005–12, –0·5%. Life expectancy at birth, 2013, was 64·2 years for men and 75·8 years for women. Infant mortality, 2010, four per 1,000 live births; fertility rate, 2013, 1·5 children per woman.

Climate

Moderately continental and humid with temperatures averaging 20°F (–6°C) in Jan. and 64°F (18°C) in July. Annual precipitation is 22–28" (550–700 mm).

Constitution and Government

A new constitution was adopted on 15 March 1994. It provides for a *President* who must be a citizen of at least 35 years of age, have resided for ten years in Belarus and whose candidacy must be supported by the signatures of 70 deputies or 100,000 electors. At a referendum held on 17 Oct. 2004, 86·2% of votes cast were in favour of the abolition of the two-term limit on the presidency. The vote was widely regarded as fraudulent.

There is a 12-member *Constitutional Court*. The chief justice and five other judges are appointed by the president.

© Springer Nature Limited 2020
Palgrave Macmillan (ed.), *The Statesman's Yearbook 2020*,
https://doi.org/10.1057/978-1-349-95940-2_28

Four referenda held on 14 May 1995 gave the president powers to dissolve parliament; work for closer economic integration with Russia; establish Russian as an official language of equal status with Belarusian; and introduce a new flag.

At a further referendum of 24 Nov. 1996 turnout was 84%. 79% of votes cast were in favour of the creation of an upper house of parliament nominated by provincial governors and 70% in favour of extending the presidential term of office by two years to five years. The Supreme Soviet was dissolved and a 110-member lower *House of Representatives* established, whose members are directly elected by universal adult suffrage every four years. The upper chamber is the *Council of the Republic* (64 seats, 56 members elected by regional councils and eight members appointed by the president, all for four-year terms). In practice, since 1996 the Belarusian parliament has only had a ceremonial function.

National Anthem

'My Bielarusy' ('We, the Belarusians'); words by M. Klimkovich and U. Karyzna, tune by Nester Sakalowski.

Government Chronology

Heads of State since 1991.

Chairmen of the Supreme Council	
1991–94	Stanislau Stanislavavich Shushkevich
1994	Myechyslau Ivanavich Hryb
President	
1994	Alyaksandr Rygorovich Lukashenka

Recent Elections

Parliamentary elections were held on 11 Sept. 2016. 110 deputies were elected. Independent candidates won 94 seats, the Communist Party 8, the Belarusian Patriotic Party 3, the Republican Party of Labour and Justice 3 and the United Civic Party 1. Turnout was 74·7%. According to international observers the elections suffered significant shortcomings relating to restrictive political rights. For the first time since 2000 an opposition party member was elected. Including one of the independents, two opposition candidates in total won seats.

Presidential elections were held on 11 Oct. 2015. Alyaksandr Lukashenka was re-elected with 83·5% of votes cast against 4·4% for Tatsiana Karatkevich, 3·3% for Sergei Gaidukevich and 1·7% for Nikolai Ulakhovich. Turnout was 87·2%. Independent observers noted several violations during the poll while accepting that there was a slight improvement on the previous two elections.

Current Government

President: Alyaksandr Lukashenka; b. 1954 (sworn in 20 July 1994 and re-elected in Sept. 2001, March 2006, Dec. 2010 and Oct. 2015).

 Prime Minister: Syarhey Rumas; b. 1969 (took office on 18 Aug. 2018).
 In Feb. 2019 the government comprised:

 First Deputy Prime Minister: Alexander Turchin. *Deputy Prime Ministers:* Vladimir Kukarev; Igor V. Lyashenko; Igor Petrishenko; Mikhail I. Rusyi.

 Minister for Agriculture and Food: Leonid Zayats. *Anti-Monopoly Regulation and Trade:* Vladimir Koltovich. *Architecture and Construction:* Dmitry Mikulenok. *Communications and Information Technology:* Kanstantsin Shulhan. *Culture:* Yuri Bondar. *Defence:* Maj.-Gen. Andrei Ravkov. *Economy:* Dmitry Krutoi. *Education:* Igor Karpenko. *Emergencies:* Vladimir Vashchenko. *Energy:* Viktar Karankevich. *Finance:* Maksim Yermalovich. *Foreign Affairs:* Vladimir Makei. *Forestry:* Vitaly Drozhzha. *Health:* Valery Malashko. *Housing and Communal Services:* Alexandr Terekhov. *Industry:* Pavel Utyupin. *Information:* Alexandr Karlyukevich. *Internal Affairs:* Igor Shunevich. *Justice:* Oleg Slizhevsky. *Labour and Social Protection:* Irina Kostevich. *Natural Resources and Environmental Protection:* Andrei Khudyk. *Sports and Tourism:* Sergei Kovalchuk. *Taxes and Duties:* Sergei Nalivaiko. *Trade:* Vladimir Koltovich. *Transport and Communications:* Anatoly Sivak.

Government Website: http://www.government.by

Current Leaders

Alyaksandr Rygorovich Lukashenka

Position
President

Introduction
Alyaksandr Lukashenka has been president since 1994. A communist from an early age, he has strengthened his powers within the constitution but has drawn international condemnation for his autocratic leadership and human rights abuses against political opponents and journalists.

Early Life
Lukashenka was born on 30 Aug. 1954 in Kepys. After studying history and agricultural economics, he taught at the Mahilyou Teaching Institute and the Belarusian SSR Agro-economics Academy. He was a member of Komsomol, a young communists' group, before working on collective farms. After working in local politics, he became a deputy on the Belarusian Supreme Council in 1990. When Belarus gained independence the following year, he opposed the formation of the CIS, set up by Russia, Belarus and the Ukraine, as well as the nationalist and free market tendencies of Stanislau Shushkevich (the first post-independence leader). By the time of the 1994 presidential elections, Shushkevich had been forced to stand down. Campaigning on a pro-Russian manifesto, Lukashenka won in a second round run-off with former prime minister (1990–94) Vyachaslau Kebich, receiving 80·1% of votes.

Career in Office
Following his election, Lukashenka set about increasing presidential powers and strengthening state control. Countering Shushkevich's efforts to promote Belarusian culture, he reinstated Russian as the official language and sought closer ties, not always successfully, with the Russian Federation. Trade agreements were made with Russia and several other former Soviet states. In 1996 he pressed through constitutional changes to give himself more power and to extend his term of office by two years to 2001. He reversed reforms made by his predecessor after the collapse of the Soviet Union and secured control over the state-owned media and security services. He also rejected Shushkevich's previous moves towards privatization.

Lukashenka used his presidential decree to impose restrictions on opponents and journalists, with the international community accusing him of disregarding democracy.

In the 2000 parliamentary elections, his supporters won 81 of 110 seats. The following year he won a second presidential term, taking 75·6% of the vote against 15·4% for Uladzimir Hancharyk. Both elections were criticized by international observers as undemocratic, with many opposition politicians either boycotting them or remaining in exile. International organizations continued to criticize Lukashenka's repressive regime during 2002 (when the authorities expelled an OSCE delegation) and 2003. The USA meanwhile passed legislation allowing the provision of financial support to the opposition in Belarus.

Further parliamentary elections and a referendum were held on 17 Oct. 2004. No opposition candidates won a parliamentary seat in the poll, while Lukashenka claimed overwhelming support in the referendum for his intention to change the constitution and run for another presidential term. The results were dismissed as fraudulent by most international observers, human rights activists and opposition politicians.

Lukashenka was re-elected for a further term in March 2006, again amid accusations of vote rigging. From April 2006 the EU and the USA imposed travel bans and asset freezes on various Belarusian officials, including Lukashenka, deemed responsible for electoral fraud and civil repression.

In 2007 Belarus was in dispute with Russia over oil supplies, price rises and unpaid debts, and in May that year Belarus's bid for a seat on the United Nations Human Rights Council was rejected.

In the spring of 2008 relations with the USA deteriorated further, as Lukashenka's government expelled US diplomats for criticizing Belarus's human rights record. In Sept. 2008 candidates loyal to the president were again returned to every seat in parliamentary elections considered by European monitors to be only marginally less flawed than previous polls.

Following the lifting of the EU's travel ban in Oct. 2008, Lukashenka visited the Vatican in April 2009 for talks with then Pope Benedict XVI in his first official visit to Western Europe since the mid-1990s.

Tensions with Russia over energy trading continued. In Jan. 2010 the Belarus government threatened to cut electricity deliveries to the Russian Baltic enclave of Kaliningrad and there was a further dispute in June that year over Belarus's unpaid debts and transit fees. Russia began reducing gas supplies and Lukashenka threatened to disrupt Russian gas and oil deliveries to Europe before the situation was resolved.

The EU reinstated the travel ban on Lukashenka in response to accusations of human rights violations ahead of the presidential election in Dec. 2010, in which he claimed another overwhelming victory. Subsequent protests in Minsk were broken up by force and there were mass arrests of opposition activists. In April 2011 a terrorist attack on a metro station in the capital was cited by Lukashenka as a plot to destabilize the country. Against a background of increasing social unrest, the economy continued to suffer in 2011, with rising inflation, a sharp devaluation of the currency, declining financial support from Russia and debt-servicing difficulties. In Jan. 2012 new legislation imposed restrictions on access to foreign websites, while in parliamentary elections in Sept., which were boycotted by opposition groups, loyal Lukashenka supporters again secured every assembly seat. In April 2013 concerns over the management of the country's energy sector prompted Lukashenka to replace both the minister for energy and the director-general of Belenergo, the state-owned energy corporation. In Dec. 2014 he dismissed the prime minister, Mikhail Myasnikovich, along with several other cabinet members and the chief of the central bank amid deteriorating economic conditions. He chose close ally Andrei Kobyakov as the new premier.

Lukashenka was re-elected for a fifth consecutive term following his convincing victory at the Oct. 2015 presidential elections. Despite foreign observers stating that there appeared to be less repression than had been seen during previous elections, prominent opposition leaders were barred from taking part. However, in parliamentary polling in Sept. 2016 two opposition candidates secured seats in the House of Representatives.

In Sept. 2017 Belarus and Russia staged joint military exercises close to their borders with NATO's Eastern European member countries, heightening concerns in the West about a return to Cold War geopolitics.

Following a corruption scandal involving the embezzlement of health service funds, Lukashenka in Aug. 2018 dismissed Andrei Kobyakov as prime minister and replaced him with Syarhey Rumas, formerly head of the state-owned Development Bank.

Defence

Conscription is for 18 months, or 12 in the case of university and college graduates. A treaty with Russia of April 1993 co-ordinates their military activities. All nuclear weapons had been transferred to Russia by Dec. 1996. Total active armed forces in 2011 numbered 72,940. In addition there are Ministry of Interior paramilitary troops numbering 110,000.

Defence expenditure in 2012 totalled US$552m. (US$57 per capita), representing 1·0% of GDP.

Army

In 2011 Army personnel numbered 29,600. In addition there were 289,500 reserves. Equipment in 2011 included 515 main battle tanks (T-72s and T-80s).

Air Force

In 2011 the Air Force and Air Defence Forces operated 128 combat-capable aircraft, including MiG-29s, Su-24s, Su-25s and Su-27s, and 50 attack helicopters. Personnel, 2011, 18,170.

International Relations

A treaty of friendship with Russia was signed on 21 Feb. 1995. A further treaty signed by the respective presidents on 2 April 1997 provided for even closer integration.

Economy

Manufacturing contributed 26·1% to GDP in 2012; followed by trade and hotels, 14·7%; finance and real estate, 9·7%; and services, 8·7%.

Overview

Following the collapse of the Soviet Union, the economy underperformed relative to other transition economies. From 1991 to 1995 it contracted at an average annual rate of 8·1% compared to the 0·6% experienced by other Eastern European economies. In 1995 President Lukashenka reinstated price controls, state intervention in private enterprise and the obstruction of foreign investment. In spite of this, the economy grew at an annual average rate of 6·9% in the decade 1996–2005.

The economy is largely sustained by Russian oil subsidies and the processing and re-export of Russian oil at Belarus's two refining centres, Mozyr and Naftan. The global financial crisis that began in 2008 led to a loss of external financing and a sharp decline in exports, exacerbated by an already high current account deficit and low reserves. A balance of payments crisis in 2011 as a result of unsustainably loose macroeconomic policies then prompted soaring inflation and a rise in the poverty rate rose from 5·2% in 2010 to 7·3% in 2011 before a subsequent decline to 5·5% in 2013.

Stabilization measures implemented from mid-2011 included a more flexible exchange rate regime, fiscal consolidation and constrained credit growth. In addition, oil and gas agreements with Russia saw lower-priced imports. Annual GDP growth averaged 1·7% between 2010 and 2017 but a higher poverty rate of 5·7% was recorded in 2017.

Currency

The *rouble* was retained under an agreement of Sept. 1993 and a treaty with Russia on monetary union of April 1994. Foreign currencies ceased to be legal tender in Oct. 1994. Only banknotes are issued—there are no coins in circulation. In Jan. 2000 the Belarusian rouble was revalued at 1 new rouble (BYR) = 1,000 old roubles (BYB). In Nov. 2000 President Lukashenka and President Putin of Russia agreed the introduction of a single currency, but plans to introduce the Russian rouble to Belarus have since been postponed indefinitely. The inflation rate in 1994 was 2,221% but has since fallen. Inflation was 11·8% in 2016 and 6·0% in 2017, the lowest rate since Belarus became independent in 1991. Foreign exchange reserves in Sept. 2009 were US$3,142m., total money supply was 8,914·8bn. roubles and gold reserves were 740,000 troy oz.

Budget

Budgetary central government revenue in 2015 totalled 175,682bn. roubles and expenditure 144,552bn. roubles.

Principal sources of revenue in 2015 were: taxes on goods and services, 78,650bn. roubles; taxes on international trade and transactions, 39,586bn. roubles; grants, 8,369bn. roubles. Main items of expenditure by economic type in 2015: grants, 37,467bn. roubles; compensation of employees, 30,929bn. roubles; use of goods and services, 27,267bn. roubles.

VAT is 20%.

Performance

Belarus experienced a two-year recession in 2015 (when the economy contracted by 3·8%) and 2016 (when it shrank by 2·5%). There was then real GDP growth of 2·4% in 2017. Total GDP in 2017 was US$54·4bn.

Banking and Finance

The central bank is the National Bank (*Chairman*, Pavel Kallaur). In 2013 there were 32 commercial banks. The largest banks are Belarusbank, Belagroprombank, BPS-Sberbank and Belinvestbank.

In 2010 total external debt was US$25,726m., equivalent to 47% of GNI. There is a stock exchange in Minsk.

Energy and Natural Resources

Environment

Carbon dioxide emissions from the consumption of energy were the equivalent of 7·0 tonnes per capita in 2011.

Electricity

Installed capacity was an estimated 8·4m. kW in 2011. Production was 32·19bn. kWh in 2011. Consumption per capita in 2011 was 3,997 kWh. Construction of the country's first nuclear power plant at Ostrovets—a joint Belarusian-Russian project—began in Nov. 2013, with a first reactor scheduled to become operational during 2019 and a second in 2020.

Oil and Gas

In 2011 output of crude petroleum totalled 12m. bbls; reserves in 2011 were 198m. bbls. Natural gas production in 2011 was 220m. cu. metres; reserves were 2·8bn. cu. metres in 2013.

Minerals

Particular attention has been paid to the development of the peat industry with a view to making Belarus as far as possible self-supporting in fuel. There are over 6,500 peat deposits. There are rich deposits of rock salt and of iron ore.

Agriculture

Output of main agricultural products (in 1m. tonnes) in 2012: potatoes, 6·91; milk, 6·77; sugar beets, 4·77; wheat, 2·55; barley, 1·92; rye, 1·08; meat, 0·91; oats, 0·42; cheese, 0·15; eggs, 3,846m. units. As of 1 Jan. 2013 there were 4·37m. cattle; 4·24m. pigs; 92,000 horses; and 42·4m. poultry.

Agricultural land makes up 42·5% of the country's land area. At the beginning of 2013 there were 5·52m. ha. of arable land and 119,900 ha. of permanent crops. There were 1,530 agricultural organizations and 2,436 private (peasant) farms in 2012. Agricultural organizations accounted for 75% of agricultural output in 2012, and private (peasant) farms and households 25%. Agricultural output grew by 6·6% in 2012 compared to 2011.

Forestry

Forests occupied 8·63m. ha., or 42% of the land area, in 2015. There are valuable reserves of oak, elm, maple and white beech. Timber production in 2011 was 10·36m. cu. metres.

Fisheries

The total catch in 2015 came to 869 tonnes, exclusively from inland waters. Aquaculture production totalled 16,265 tonnes in 2010 (95% of total fish production).

Industry

Belarus has a well-developed industry sector. Output in 2012: (in 1,000 tonnes) distillate fuel oil, 11,667; cement, 4,906; potassium fertilizers, 4,831; petrol, 3,729; steel, 2,869; paper and paperboard, 381; sausages, 299; chemical fibres, 239; (in units) tractors, 71,030; lorries, 24,668; buses, 2,271; dump trucks, 1,671; (in 1,000 units) pneumatic rubber tyres, 5,732; refrigerators and freezers, 1,263; TV sets, 594; washing machines, 324; (in 1m. sq. metres) textiles, 184; carpets, 13; (in 1m. litres) beer, 432; distilled alcoholic beverages, 194; (in 1m. pairs) hosiery, 133·7; footwear, 16·5.

Around 75% of GDP is produced by state-owned companies.

Labour

The labour force in 2013 was 4,482,700 (4,665,400 in 2003). 66·1% of the population aged 15–64 was economically active in 2013. In the same year 6·0% of the population was unemployed.

Belarus had 11,000 people living in slavery according to the Walk Free Foundation's 2013 *Global Slavery Index*.

International Trade

In Jan. 2010 Belarus joined a customs union with Kazakhstan and Russia, which was superseded by the Eurasian Economic Union in Jan. 2015.

Imports and Exports

In 2013 imports were valued at US$37,203m. and exports at US$43,023m. The main import suppliers in 2013 were Russia (53·2%), Germany (7·1%), China (6·6%), Ukraine (4·8%) and Poland (3·7%). Principal export markets were Russia (45·3%), Ukraine (11·3%), the Netherlands (9·0%), Germany (4·7%) and Lithuania (2·9%). Main import commodities are crude petroleum including gas condensates, natural gas, motor cars, pharmaceutical products and communications equipment. Export commodities include petroleum products, milk and dairy products, potash fertilizers, crude petroleum including gas condensates, trucks and tractors.

Communications

Roads

In 2013 there were 101,030 km of roads (87·0% paved), including 15,735 km of national roads. There were 2,670,567 passenger cars in use as of 1 Jan. 2014 (282 per 1,000 inhabitants). In 2013 public transport totalled 10,546m. passenger-km and freight 25,603m. tonne-km. There were 894 fatalities as a result of road accidents in 2013.

Rail

In 2013 there were 5,490 km of railways in use (1,520 mm gauge), of which 1,013 km were electrified. Passenger-km travelled in 2013 came to 9bn. and freight tonne-km to 44bn.

Civil Aviation

The main airport is Minsk National Airport, which handled 2,593,559 passengers in 2014 and 19,900 tonnes of freight. The national carrier is Belavia, which in 2017 operated on domestic routes and also flew to more than 50 international destinations. In 2014 Belavia carried 1,973,000 passengers.

Telecommunications

In 2011 there were 4,208,000 landline telephone subscriptions (equivalent to 440·2 per 1,000 inhabitants) and 10,694,900 mobile phone subscriptions (or 1,118·8 per 1,000 inhabitants). In 2011, 39·6% of the population were internet users. In March 2012 there were 409,000 Facebook users.

Social Institutions

Out of 178 countries analysed in the 2017 *Fragile States Index*—a list published jointly by the Fund for Peace and *Foreign Policy* magazine—Belarus was ranked the 84th least vulnerable to conflict or collapse. The index is based on 12 indicators of state vulnerability across social, political and economic categories.

Justice

The death penalty is retained following the constitutional referendum of Nov. 1996; there were at least two executions in 2017 and at least four in 2018. Belarus is the only European country that still uses the death penalty.

180,427 crimes were reported in 2007. There were 39,552 prisoners in 2007, at a rate of 408 prisoners per 100,000 population. Belarus was ranked 43rd of 102 countries for criminal justice and 30th for civil justice in the 2015 World Justice Project *Rule of Law Index*, which provides data on how the rule of law is experienced by the general public across eight categories.

Education

Adult literacy rate in 2008 was over 99%. In 2007 there were 365,298 children and 50,568 teachers at pre-school institutions, 362,282 pupils and 22,990 teachers at primary schools, 772,584 pupils and 99,011 teachers in secondary schools, and 576,679 students and 42,603 academic staff at institutions of tertiary education.

In 2007 there were 56 higher educational establishments (46 public and ten private) of which eight were general universities and 24 specialized universities (including four medical, three agricultural, three economics and three technical). There were also seven academies and 14 institutes. In 2007 there were 354,988 people enrolled at state higher education establishments.

Public expenditure on education in 2007 came to 5·3% of GNI.

Health

In 2007 there were 46,965 doctors (48·5 per 10,000 population), 1,964 dentists, 79,941 nurses, 4,921 midwives and 4,179 pharmacists. There were 112·4 hospital beds per 10,000 population in 2007. Belarus has the highest alcohol consumption rate of any country, at an average of 17·5 litres of alcohol per adult per year in the period 2008–10 compared to the global average of 6·2 litres per person.

In *Water: At What Cost? The State of the World's Water 2016*, WaterAid reported that 0·3% of the population does not have access to safe water.

Welfare

To qualify for an old-age pension men must be age 60 with 25 years of insurance coverage and women must be 55 with 20 years of insurance coverage. Minimum old-age pension is 25% of the average per capita subsistence budget. The maximum pension is 75% of wage base. Benefits are adjusted periodically according to changes in the minimum wage, which in 2009 was 229,000 roubles a month.

Religion

The Orthodox Church claims the most adherents. There is a Roman Catholic archdiocese of Minsk and Mahilyou, and three dioceses. According to a report published by the ministry of foreign affairs in 2011 an estimated 58·9% of the population were believers. Of these, 82% were Orthodox, 12% Catholic and the remainder followers of other religions.

Culture

World Heritage Sites

There are four UNESCO sites in Belarus: the Mir Castle Complex, begun in the 15th century (inscribed on the list in 2000); the Radziwill Family complex at Nesvizh (2005); the Belovezhskaya Pushcha/Białowieża Forest site (1979, 1992 and 2014), shared with Poland, and the Struve Geodetic Arc (2005). The Arc is a chain of survey triangulations spanning from Norway to the Black Sea that helped establish the exact shape and size of the earth and is shared with nine other countries.

Press

In Jan. 2013 there were about 1,500 registered print media in Belarus, of which more than 1,100 were non-state media. The most widely read paper is *Sovetskaya Belarussiya,* with a daily circulation of about 400,000. There are also Belarusian editions of the Russian daily *Komsomolskaya Pravda* and weekly *Argumenty i Fakty.*

Tourism

In 2011 there were 115,700 foreign tourists on organized trips. Spending by tourists totalled US$747m. in 2011.

Diplomatic Representatives

Of Belarus in the United Kingdom (6 Kensington Court, London, W8 5DL)
  Ambassador: Sergei Aleinik.

Of the United Kingdom in Belarus (37 Karl Marx St., Minsk 220030)
  Ambassador: Fionna Gibb.

Of Belarus in the USA (1619 New Hampshire Ave., NW, Washington, D.C., 20009)
  Ambassador: Vacant.
  Chargé d'Affaires a.i.: Pavel Shidlovsky.

Of the USA in Belarus (46 Starovilenskaya, Minsk 220002)
  Ambassador: Vacant.
  Chargé d'Affaires a.i.: Jenifer H. Moore.

Of Belarus to the United Nations
  Ambassador: Valentin Rybakov.

Of Belarus to the European Union
  Ambassador: Aleksandr Mikhnevich.

Further Reading

Balmaceda, Margarita M., *Independent Belarus: Domestic Determinants, Regional Dynamics and Implications for the West.* 2003

Korosteleva, Elena, *Contemporary Belarus: Between Democracy and Dictatorship.* 2002

Marples, D. R., *Belarus: from Soviet Rule to Nuclear Catastrophe.* 1996

White, Stephen, *Postcommunist Belarus.* 2004

Zaprudnik, J., *Belarus at the Crossroads in History.* 1993

National Statistical Office: Ministry of Statistics and Analysis of the Republic of Belarus, 12 Partizansky Avenue, Minsk 220070.

Website: http://www.belstat.gov.by

Belgium

Royaume de Belgique Koninkrijk België (Kingdom of Belgium)

Capital: Brussels
Population projection, 2020: 11·62m.
GNI per capita, 2017: (PPP$) 42,156
HDI/world rank, 2017: 0·916/17=
Internet domain extension: .be

Key Historical Events

The Neanderthal Mousterian culture of the Ardennes region produced flint tools between 80–35,000 years ago. Omalien tribes of the early Neolithic period (5–4000 BC) developed settled agricultural practices, sophisticated tools and decorated black pottery. The Bronze Age Hilversum culture left evidence of contact overseas in Wessex, southern England. During the pre-Roman period Celtic and Germanic tribes moved across the region. Much of northern Gaul and southern Britain was settled by a Celtic group known as the Belgae, forming numerous tribes including the seafaring Morini and Menapii in what is now Flanders and the bellicose Nervii in Artois. In alliance with Germanic and other Belgic tribes, the Nervii led resistance to the invasion of Julius Caesar in 59 BC, succumbing five years later. Roman control was extended as far north as the Rhine and the area divided into the provinces of Gallia Belgica and Germania Inferior. Several tribes survived as Roman administrative *civitates*.

The network of Roman power, based around wealthy *villae* (country estates), declined from the mid-3rd century AD, despite the campaigns of Julian, who became emperor in AD 361. The massive influx of Germanic tribes (known commonly as the Barbarian invasions) over the Rhine in 406/7 effectively brought Roman rule in Belgium to an end. Chief among the German tribes were the Franks, who settled in Toxandria (modern Brabant). The Frankish Merovingian Empire, established by Childeric I, was based at Tournai and extended by Childeric's son, Clovis. The successors to the Merovingians, the Pippins (or Carolingians), ruled all but in name from Austrasia in the Ardennes. A partnership between the nobility and the church allowed the expansion of Frankish power north and east across the Rhine, bringing Christianity to the Low Countries by the 7th century, under the sees of Arras, Tournai, Cambrai and, from 720, Liège.

The death of Louis the Pious in 840 precipitated the fragmentation of Charlemagne's huge empire. Viking attacks on the Low Countries came at the end of the 8th century, intensifying in the period 841–75. Resistance began under Charlemagne; provincial princes capitalized on the fortification process and land reclamation to increase their own power. Baldwin 'Iron Arm', count of Flanders, fortified Ghent around 867, cementing his authority over the Flemish towns. His successors extended control into Artois (and to Hainault by personal union) in defiance of the French kings. Philippe IV of France was defeated in 1302 at the Battle of the Golden Spurs at Kortrijk, Flanders and formally recognized Flemish independence. Flanders' alliance with England during the Hundred Years War created an advantageous trading relationship, especially the importation of English wool for the textile industry. Bruges (Brugge), Ypres and Ghent flourished and in the 14th century had to be forcibly restrained from becoming city-states by Philip of Burgundy.

Other principalities emerged in the wake of the Carolingian empire, most notably the duchies of Brabant and Limburg and the prince-bishopric of Liège. Their union was forged under the dukes of Burgundy. The marriage of Philip the Bold, duke of Burgundy, to Margaret of Flanders in 1369 was the first step towards what became the Burgundian *Kreis* (lands) under Emperor Charles V. The addition of Hainault-Holland, Namur and Luxembourg encouraged Burgundian ambitions of centralization and even a unitary empire, vainly attempted by Duke Charles the Bold in the 1470s. The provinces and towns jealously guarded their imperial and local privileges and resisted the high taxation imposed by their Burgundian lord. Burgundian authority was reinforced by the 1477 marriage of Charles's daughter (and heir), Mary, to the Habsburg Maximilian of Austria, later Holy Roman Emperor, beginning over three centuries of Habsburg rule in the Low Countries.

Trade Centres

Bruges became the principal market of northwest Europe in the 14th century but after the silting of its waterways ceded its role in the 1490s to Antwerp. The volume of Portuguese and English traders and Italian financiers testified to the importance of Antwerp as a mercantile and financial centre; the *Antwerpen beurs* (stock exchange) was established in 1531. Antwerp's population reached 100,000 in the mid-16th century. The artistic achievements of the 15th century were supported by court patronage. Artists such as Rogier van der Weyden in Brussels and Jan van Eyck in Ghent formed part of a Flemish school that greatly influenced northern European art. The University of Louvain (Leuven), founded in 1425, was a centre of Dutch Humanism made famous by scholars such as Erasmus.

Dynastic pressures increased with the marriage of Archduke Philip the Handsome to the heiress of the Spanish crowns, Joanna the Mad, leaving the Netherlands (the Burgundian Low Countries, including Belgium) under the supervision of governors-general in Brussels. Centralization continued under Philip's son, Charles of Ghent (Holy Roman Emperor Charles V), who regulated the succession to his Burgundian territories by pragmatic sanction. However, it was the imposition of a new ecclesiastical hierarchy by Charles's son, Philip II of Spain, that unified opposition in the Netherlands.

The Netherlands was highly receptive to non-conformist ideas, most notably those of Jean Calvin, whose influence had extended to Antwerp by 1545. Appealing to the urban middle classes and the lower nobility, Calvinism suffered repression, especially after the radical iconoclasm of 1566. The following year Philip sent the duke of Alba to stamp out the religious and political uprisings, sparking revolution in Holland and other northern provinces. The execution of the counts of Hoorne and Egmond in Brussels in 1568 reinforced opposition to Spanish rule.

The secession of the northern Netherlands was partly the result of the inability of the Spanish armies to penetrate the marshes and dendritic waterways of Holland and Zeeland. Although Alba managed to reassert Philip's authority in the south, his armies never retook the provinces north of the Rhine after 1574. Separation was also caused by the extreme demands of the northern Calvinists, who alienated the more Catholic southern provinces. However, a measure of unity was achieved at the Pacification of Ghent after the atrocities of the 'Spanish Fury'—Spanish troops massacred 7,000 people in Antwerp in 1576.

In 1578 Philip appointed as governor-general Alessandro Farnese, duke of Parma, who ejected Protestants from the governments of the southern provinces and waged successful campaigns against the revolutionaries. The Union of Arras (1579), led by Flanders and Hainault, accepted the sovereignty of the Spanish king, supported Catholicism and ended the revolt of the southern provinces. In reaction the northern provinces drew up the Union of Utrecht, thus marking the birth of the 'Dutch Republic', though Philip was not rejected as sovereign in the north until 1581. Farnese took Antwerp in 1585, effectively creating the boundaries of the renegade Dutch state. Although fighting resumed after the Twelve Year Truce (1609–21), the Habsburg government accepted the independence of the Dutch Netherlands at the Peace of Westphalia in 1648.

The Spanish Netherlands was governed autonomously for much of the 17th century—Liège remained neutral in the revolt and separate until 1795. Antwerp was at first eclipsed as the principal trading centre of the region by Dutch Amsterdam, which attracted many of the south's skilled artisans and merchants. Economic recovery was helped by new industries such as linen production and diamond processing in Antwerp. Art was dominated by the Baroque style, patronized by the Catholic Church and adopted by Rubens, Van Dyck and Jordaens.

© Springer Nature Limited 2020
Palgrave Macmillan (ed.), *The Statesman's Yearbook 2020*,
https://doi.org/10.1057/978-1-349-95940-2_29

War of Succession

The death of Charles II of Spain without an heir in 1700 caused a constitutional crisis and the War of the Spanish Succession. Philip of Anjou, the heir-designate and a grandson of Louis XIV of France, was urged to hand over the Spanish Netherlands to France. The intervention of England and the Dutch was motivated by the fear of either Franco-Spanish union or the reuniting of the Austrian and Spanish Habsburgs. The Spanish Netherlands were finally settled on Emperor Charles VI after the Treaty of Utrecht in 1713, thus bringing the Netherlands under the sway of the Austrian Habsburgs.

Dynastic succession was again the cause of war after the death of Charles VI in 1740. By pragmatic sanction, his daughter, Archduchess Maria Theresa, succeeded to the Habsburg territories but was barred from the Imperial crown (it was secured for her husband, Francis Stephen of Lorraine). Supported by Great Britain, the Dutch and the Hungarian diet, Maria Theresa's armies repelled the French from the Austrian Netherlands, establishing her authority by the Treaty of Aix-la-Chapelle in 1748 (though she lost Silesia to Prussia). Her reign saw great economic gains in the Netherlands and the beginning of industrial capitalism thanks to good trading relations with Great Britain.

The Austrian regime lost popular support under Maria Theresa's successor, Emperor Joseph II, whose abolition of local privileges and his attempts to exchange the Austrian Netherlands for Bavaria made him highly unpopular. Coupled with his attacks on the power of the Catholic Church, his 'Belgian' subjects—conservatives and progressives alike—revolted in 1789. The bulk of Joseph's forces being engaged on the Ottoman frontier, the Austrian army was easily routed at Turnhout. Conservative elements were victorious in the 'Brabant Revolution' and proclaimed the United States of Belgium in 1790.

Although Joseph's brother, Leopold II, reasserted Austrian authority, the seeds of revolution had been sown, encouraged by events in France. Republican France invaded Belgium in 1795, ending the independence and religious rule of Liège. Discontent with French rule was immediate, partly in reaction to military conscription, persecution of the Church and the denial of autonomy. After peasant uprisings in 1798 the Napoleonic consulate agreed a compromise with the papacy and the Belgian church, ending persecution.

Towards Independence

Napoleon's defeat in 1814 left Belgium in the hands of the Great Powers. Belgium was reunified with the Dutch Netherlands as the Kingdom of the Netherlands at the Congress of Vienna. Despite cultural and linguistic affinities, the relationship between the two Netherlands was uneasy. Belgium, ruled by the Dutch William of Orange, was under-represented in the States General and its French-speaking elite alienated by the declaration of Dutch as the sole legal language. The two economies were in contrast, the Dutch being primarily mercantile while the Belgian was geared towards mechanized industry. Belgium was one of the first areas of continental Europe to adopt the innovations of the Industrial Revolution, most notably in the Ghent textile industry and coal mining in Hainaut. The loss of the French market in 1814 and William's refusal to increase tariffs to protect Belgian industry impacted heavily on the Belgian economy.

Dissent paved the way for the Belgian Revolution of 1830. The secession of Belgium was secured by the intervention of France and Britain, which recognized Belgian independence in 1831. Repelled by the French, William accepted the loss of Belgium in 1838. Limburg and Luxembourg were partitioned and a liberal constitution implemented. The great powers insisted on a Belgian monarch and Prince Leopold of Saxe-Coburg was duly installed.

A Liberal government came to power in 1847 after three devastating harvests. The Liberal prime minister, Walthère Frère-Orban, championed the removal of church control of the schools. The Schools War dominated the political agenda and saw a conservative counter-offensive with the establishment of a network of independent Catholic schools. A conservative Catholic victory in 1884 brought Auguste Beernaert to the premiership. Closely associated with the Flemish revivalists, Beernaert managed the Flemish Equality Law, giving the Flemish language the same rights as French. Changes in the electoral system brought in full male suffrage (over 25 years of age) in 1893.

The Congo

Belgian foreign policy was bound by recognition (and imposition) of neutrality. King Leopold II, set on expanding his kingdom, looked to Africa. The Belgian Congo, acquired as his personal possession in 1885, was soon infamous for colonial abuse and exploitation. After widespread international condemnation, the 'Congo Free State' was formally annexed by Belgium in 1908, thus curbing Leopold's inhuman regime. In Europe, threats were perceived to the west and east. Attempts by Albert I (reigned 1909–34) to arm Belgium against French and German aggression were frustrated by the domestic pacifist movement led by Beernaert. Belgian neutrality was violated by Germany in 1914 after Albert's refusal to allow German free passage. Albert remained with his army on the Yser River throughout the First World War, supported by Allied troops. Neutrality, seen by many Belgians as a hindrance, was abolished under the Treaty of Versailles in 1919; Belgium was awarded the provinces of Eupen and Malmédy and jurisdiction over Ruanda-Urundi from the defeated Germany.

Economic reconstruction after the First World War included an economic union with Luxembourg in 1921. The Belgian Congo was exploited for its minerals. Constitutional changes allowed for equal suffrage of all men over 21 (women were denied the vote until 1948) and the formal linguistic separation of Flanders and Wallonia (excluding Brussels).

The 1930s was a time of rising unemployment and concern over German ambitions. Germany invaded Belgium on 10 May 1940. Capitulation after just 18 days made King Leopold III unpopular, despite his refusal to flee to France (and later to London) with the government. Resistance was active for much of the Second World War. Insurgents managed to protect the port of Antwerp, crucial for Allied support, during the liberation of Belgium in Sept. 1944.

The post-war economy made a speedy recovery but political unity foundered on the royal question. A referendum on the return of the king from imprisonment in Austria caused violent protest in Wallonia and in 1951 Leopold abdicated in favour of his son, Baudouin.

European Union

Belgium embarked on international co-operation under the leadership of Prime Minister Paul-Henri Spaak. Economic union with Luxembourg was re-established and extended to include the Netherlands, forming the Benelux Economic Union. In 1949 Belgium joined the North Atlantic Treaty Organization (NATO) and in 1951 the European Coal and Steel Community (ECSC). Encouraged by the success of the ECSC, plans were laid for the establishment of two more communities. The European Economic Community (EEC) and the European Atomic Energy Community (Euratom) were subsequently created under separate treaties signed in Rome on 25 March 1957.

The administration of the Belgian Congo resisted political reform and demands for greater participation until the 1950s. After violent protest and agitation, local government reform was passed in 1957 but was too late to quell the independence movement, led by Patrice Lumumba. In 1959 the Belgian government rushed through a decolonization programme, leaving the Congo abruptly in 1960. Rwanda and Burundi became independent in 1962.

A milestone in domestic politics was reached in 1958 with the School Pact, ending a century of conflict between secularists and conservative Catholics. Prime Minister Gaston Eyskens negotiated a guarantee of funding for state secondary schools and private religious schools. Relations between Walloon and Flemish society became difficult as a result of the decline of Walloon industry. Strikes and discontent with government subsidies set Belgium on the course of federalization. After the division of Brabant along linguistic lines Belgium officially became a federal state in 1993. King Baudouin, who died in 1993, was respected for his even-handed approach to Belgium's divided society and seen as an important symbol of unity. He was succeeded by his brother, Albert II.

Following elections in June 2007 in which the Christian Democratic and Flemish/New Flemish Alliance won most seats but fell short of an overall majority, no new government was formed for 282 days. After a period of interim administration a coalition took office in March 2008. However, Prime Minister Yves Leterme resigned in Dec. 2008 after criticism of the government's role in the bailing-out of Fortis Bank. He was succeeded by Herman Van Rompuy but returned for another term in Nov. 2009 when Van Rompuy left to become the first president of the European Council. Leterme's coalition collapsed six months later after a dispute over francophone voting rights.

With the parliamentary election of June 2010 resulting in no party having an absolute majority, attempts to form a coalition followed. Fundamental differences between the Flemish separatist New Flemish Alliance and the

Francophone Socialist Party led to breakdowns in negotiations. After a series of failed talks, it was only in Dec. 2011 that Elio Di Rupo, leader of the Socialist Party, formed a government comprising six parties. Without an administration for 541 days, Belgium has the record for failing to form a new government following an election.

In Nov. 2015 Brussels-based militants linked to the Islamic State jihadist movement launched assaults in Paris, France, that killed 130 people. In March 2016 Islamic State bombers then attacked transport targets in Brussels, killing 35.

Territory and Population

Belgium is bounded in the north by the Netherlands, northwest by the North Sea, west and south by France, and east by Germany and Luxembourg. Its area is 30,528 sq. km. Population (at 1 Jan. 2015), 11,209,044 (5,703,950 females); density, 367·2 per sq. km. The Belgian exclave of Baarle-Hertog in the Netherlands has an area of seven sq. km and a population (2010) of 2,504. There were 1,195,122 resident foreign nationals as at 1 Jan. 2013. In 2011, 97·4% of the population lived in urban areas.

The UN gives a projected population for 2020 of 11·62m.

Dutch (Flemish) is spoken by the Flemish section of the population in the north, French by the Walloon south. The linguistic frontier passes south of the capital, Brussels, which is bilingual. Some German is spoken in the east. Each language has official status in its own community. (Bracketed names below signify French/Dutch alternatives.)

Area, population and chief towns of the ten provinces on 1 Jan. 2012:

Province	Area (sq. km)	Population	Chief Town
Flemish Region			
Antwerp	2,867	1,781,904	Antwerp (Antwerpen/Anvers)
East Flanders	2,982	1,454,716	Ghent (Gent/Gand)
West Flanders	3,144	1,169,990	Bruges (Brugge)
Flemish Brabant	2,106	1,094,751	Leuven (Louvain)
Limburg	2,422	849,404	Hasselt
Walloon Region			
Hainaut (Henegouwen)	3,786	1,328,196	Mons (Bergen)
Liège (Luik)	3,862	1,083,400	Liège (Luik)
Namur (Namen)	3,666	480,105	Namur (Namen)
Walloon Brabant	1,091	385,990	Wavre (Waver)
Luxembourg	4,440	273,638	Arlon (Aarlen)

Population of the regions on 1 Jan. 2012: Brussels-Capital Region, 1,138,854; Flemish Region, 6,350,765; Walloon Region, 3,546,329.

The most populous towns, with population on 1 Jan. 2012:

Brussels (Brussel/Bruxelles)[1]	1,138,854
Antwerp (Antwerpen/Anvers)	502,604
Ghent (Gent/Gand)	248,242
Charleroi	203,871
Liège (Luik)	195,576
Bruges (Brugge)	117,170
Namur (Namen)	110,096
Leuven (Louvain)	97,656
Mons (Bergen)	93,072
Mechelen (Malines)	82,325
Aalst (Alost)	81,853
La Louvière	78,774
Kortrijk (Courtrai)	75,219
Hasselt	74,588
St Niklaas (St Nicolas)	72,883
Ostend (Oostende/Ostende)	70,284
Tournai (Doornik)	69,593

(continued)

Genk	65,264
Seraing	63,575
Roeselare (Roulers)	58,823
Mouscron (Moeskroen)	56,011
Verviers	55,936

[1] 19 communes.

Social Statistics

Statistics for calendar years:

	Births	Deaths	Marriages	Divorces
2005	118,002	103,278	43,141	30,840
2006	121,382	101,587	44,813	29,189
2007	120,663	100,658	45,561	30,081
2008	128,049	104,587	45,613	35,366
2009	127,297	104,509	43,303	32,606

In 2010 Belgium received 19,941 asylum applications, equivalent to 1·9 per 1,000 inhabitants. Annual population growth rate, 2005–10, 0·7%. Life expectancy at birth, 2009, was 77·2 years for men and 82·4 years for women. 2009 birth rate (per 1,000 population): 11·8; death rate: 9·7. Infant mortality, 2008, 3·8 per 1,000 live births; fertility rate, 2013, 1·9 children per woman. In 2003 Belgium became the second country to legalize same-sex marriage.

Climate

Cool temperate climate influenced by the sea, giving mild winters and cool summers. Brussels, Jan. 36°F (2·2°C), July 64°F (17·8°C). Annual rainfall 33" (825 mm). Ostend, Jan. 38°F (3·3°C), July 62°F (16·7°C). Annual rainfall 31" (775 mm).

Constitution and Government

According to the constitution of 1831, Belgium is a constitutional, representative and hereditary monarchy. The legislative power is vested in the King, the federal parliament and the community and regional councils. The King convokes parliament after an election or the resignation of a government, and has the power to dissolve it in accordance with Article 46 of the Constitution.

The reigning King is **Philippe**, born 15 April 1960, who succeeded his father, Albert II, on 21 July 2013. Married on 4 Dec. 1999 to Mathilde d'Udekem d'Acoz, daughter of Count d'Udekem d'Acoz and Countess Anna Maria Komorowska. *Offspring:* Princess Elisabeth, b. 25 Oct. 2001 (heiress apparent); Prince Gabriel, b. 20 Aug. 2003; Prince Emmanuel, b. 4 Oct. 2005; Princess Eléonore, b. 16 April 2008.

Other principal members of the royal family (indicated in bold): **Albert II**, b. 6 June 1934, reigned 9 Aug. 1993–21 July 2013. Married on 2 July 1959 to **Paola** Ruffo di Calabria, daughter of Don Fuleo and Donna Gazelli de Rossena. **Princess Astrid**, b. 5 June 1962, daughter of Albert II, married Archduke **Lorenz** of Austria, 22 Sept. 1984. *Offspring:* Prince Amedeo, b. 21 Feb. 1986, married Elisabetta Maria Rosboch von Wolkenstein, 5 July 2014; Princess Maria Laura, b. 26 Aug. 1988; Prince Joachim, b. 9 Dec. 1991; Princess Luisa Maria, b. 11 Oct. 1995; Princess Laetitia Maria, b. 23 April 2003. **Prince Laurent**, son of Albert II, b. 19 Oct. 1963, married **Claire** Coombs, 12 April 2003. *Offspring:* Princess Louise, b. 6 Feb. 2004; Prince Nicolas, b. 13 Dec. 2005; Prince Aymeric, b. 13 Dec. 2005.

A constitutional amendment of June 1991 permits women to accede to the throne.

The King received an annual allowance of €11,554,000 for 2016. Albert II's allowance had dropped to €906,000 by 2016 following his abdication in 2013. Princess Astrid received an annual allowance of €315,000 for 2016 and Prince Laurent €302,000.

Constitutional reforms begun in Dec. 1970 culminated in May 1993 in the transformation of Belgium from a unitary into a 'federal state, composed of communities and regions'. The communities are three in number and based on language: Flemish, French and German. The regions also number three, and are based territorially: Flemish, Walloon and the Brussels-Capital Region.

Since 1995 the federal parliament has consisted of a 150-member Chamber of Representatives, directly elected by obligatory universal suffrage from 20 constituencies on a proportional representation system for four-year terms, and a Senate. Following the inconclusive 2010 elections that left Belgium without a working government for over 500 days, a package of constitutional reforms was agreed, including an extension of government terms of office from four to five years and the end of direct elections to the Senate. Furthermore, the electoral constituency of Brussels-Halle-Vilvoorde was abolished, with each province and the federal capital becoming its own constituency. Brussels-Halle-Vilvoorde had been a touchstone for Franco-Flemish tensions for several years, which was regarded as a significant factor in the impasse in forming a government after the 2010 election.

Since the elections held on 25 May 2014 the Senate comprises 60 members (previously 71), of whom 50 are appointed by and from Community and Regional parliaments (29 by the Flemish parliament; 10 by the parliament of the French Community; 8 by the Walloon parliament; 2 by the French-speaking group in the Brussels-Capital Region parliament; and 1 by the parliament of the German-speaking Community). These senators co-opt a further ten senators (six Dutch-speaking and four French-speaking). The state reform that introduced these changes also devolved an array of powers from federal government to the regions and language communities.

The federal parliament's powers relate to constitutional reform, federal finance, foreign affairs, defence, justice, internal security, social security and some areas of public health. The Senate is essentially a revising chamber, though it may initiate certain legislation, and is equally competent with the Chamber of Representatives in matters concerning constitutional reform and the assent to international treaties.

The number of ministers in the federal government is limited to 15. The Council of Ministers, apart from the Prime Minister, must comprise an equal number of Dutch- and French-speakers. Members of parliament, if appointed ministers, are replaced in parliament by the runner-up on the electoral list for the minister's period of office. Community and regional councillors may not be members of the Chamber of Representatives or Senate.

National Anthem

'La Brabançonne'; words by L. A. Dechet, tune by F. Van Campenhout. The Flemish version is 'O dierbaar België, O heilig land der vaad'ren' ('Noble Belgium, for ever a dear land').

Government Chronology

Prime Ministers since 1939. (BSP/PSB = Belgian Socialist Party; CD&V = Christian Democratic and Flemish; CVP = Christian People's Party; CVP/PSC = Christian People's/Social Christian Party; MR = Reformist Movement; PS = Socialist Party; VLD = Flemish Liberals and Democrats)

1939–45	CVP/PSC	Hubert Pierlot
1945–46	BSP/PSB	Achille Van Acker
1946	BSP/PSB	Paul-Henri Spaak
1946	BSP/PSB	Achille Van Acker
1946–47	BSP/PSB	Camille Huysmans
1947–49	BSP/PSB	Paul-Henri Spaak
1949–50	CVP/PSC	Gaston Eyskens
1950	CVP/PSC	Jean Pierre Duvieusart
1950–52	CVP/PSC	Louis Marie Joseph Pholien
1952–54	CVP/PSC	Jean Marie Van Houtte
1954–58	BSP/PSB	Achille Van Acker
1958–61	CVP/PSC	Gaston Eyskens
1961–65	CVP/PSC	Théodore Lefèvre
1965–66	CVP/PSC	Pierre Charles Harmel
1966–68	CVP/PSC	Paul Vanden Boeynants
1968–73	CVP	Gaston Eyskens
1973–74	BSP/PSB	Edmond Jules Leburton
1974–78	CVP	Leo Tindemans
1978–79	CVP	Paul Vanden Boeynants

(continued)

1979–81	CVP	Wilfried Martens
1981	CVP	Mark Eyskens
1981–92	CVP	Wilfried Martens
1992–99	CVP	Jean-Luc Dehaene
1999–2008	VLD	Guy Verhofstadt
2008	CD&V	Yves Leterme
2008–09	CD&V	Herman Van Rompuy
2009–11	CD&V	Yves Leterme
2011–14	PS	Elio Di Rupo
2014–	MR	Charles Michel

Recent Elections

Elections to the 150-member Chamber of Representatives were held on 25 May 2014. The New Flemish Alliance (N-VA) won 33 seats with 20·3% of votes cast; the Socialist Party (PS) 23 seats (11·7%); the Reformist Movement (MR) 20 (9·6%); Christian Democratic and Flemish (CD&V) 18 (11·6%); Open Flemish Liberals and Democrats (Open Vld) 14 (9·8%); Socialist Party Alternative (sp.a) 13 (8·8%); the Humanist Democratic Centre (CDH) 9 (5·0%); Green (Groen) 6 (5·3%); Ecolo 6 (3·3%); Flemish Interest (VB) 3 (3·7%); the Workers' Party Coalition (PVDA-PTB) 2 (3·7%); Francophone Democratic Federalists (FDF) 2 (1·8%); and the People's Party (PP) 1 (1·5%). Turnout was 89·4%.

Voting for the 40 electable seats in the Senate last took place on 13 June 2010. N-VA won 9 seats; PS, 7; CD&V, sp.a, MR and Open Vld, 4 each; VB, 3; Ecolo and Humanist Democratic Centre, 2 each; and Groen!, 1. There were also 31 indirectly elected senators. However, starting with the May 2014 elections the Senate is no longer directly elected, and appointments are instead made by community and regional parliaments.

European Parliament

Belgium has 21 representatives. At the May 2014 elections turnout was 89·6% (90·4% in 2009). The N-VA won 4 seats with 16·8% of the vote (political affiliation in European Parliament: European Conservatives and Reformists); the Open Vld, 3 with 12·8% (Alliance of Liberals and Democrats for Europe); the PS, 3 with 10·7% (Progressive Alliance of Socialists and Democrats); the MR, 3 with 9·9% (Alliance of Liberals and Democrats for Europe); the CD&V, 2 with 12·6% (European People's Party); sp.a, 1 with 8·3% (Progressive Alliance of Socialists and Democrats); Groen, 1 with 6·7% (Greens/European Free Alliance); Ecolo, 1 with 4·3% (Greens/European Free Alliance); the VB, 1 with 4·3% (non-attached); the CDH, 1 with 4·1% (European People's Party); the Christian-Social Party, 1 with 0·2% (European People's Party).

Current Government

In Feb. 2019 the caretaker government comprised:

Prime Minister: Charles Michel; b. 1975 (MR; sworn in 11 Oct. 2014).

Deputy Prime Ministers: Kris Peeters (CD&V; also *Minister of Employment, Economy and Consumers, in Charge of Foreign Trade, Poverty Alleviation, Equal Opportunities and People with Disabilities*); Alexander De Croo (Open Vld; also *Minister of Finance, and Co-operation and Development, in Charge of the Fight Against Fiscal Fraud*); Didier Reynders (MR; also *Minister of Foreign and European Affairs, and Defence, in Charge of Beliris and Federal Cultural Institutions*).

Minister for Security and Interior: Pieter De Crem (CD&V). *Justice, in Charge of the Buildings Agency:* Koen Geens (CD&V). *Social Affairs and Public Health, and Asylum and Migration:* Maggie De Block (Open Vld). *Pensions:* Daniel Bacquelaine (MR). *Energy, Environment and Sustainable Development:* Marie-Christine Marghem (MR). *Budget and Civil Service, in Charge of the National Lottery and Science Policy:* Sophie Wilmès (MR). *Mobility, in Charge of Air Traffic Safety (Belgocontrol) and the National Society of Belgian Railways:* François Bellot (MR). *Middle Classes, the Self-Employed, Small and Medium-Sized Enterprises, Agriculture and Social Integration, in Charge of Cities:* Denis Ducarme (MR). *Digital Agenda, Telecommunications and Post, in Charge of Administrative Simplification, the Fight against Social Fraud, the Protection of Privacy and the North Sea:* Philippe De Backer.

Government Website: http://www.belgium.be

Current Leaders

Charles Michel

Position

Prime Minister

Introduction

Charles Michel became prime minister in Oct. 2014, heading a centre-right coalition in which his Reformist Movement (MR) is the only French-speaking party.

Early Life

Born on 21 Dec. 1975 in Namur, in the Wallonia region of Belgium, Michel studied law at the Université Libre de Bruxelles (ULB) and the University of Amsterdam. After graduating in 1998 he was admitted to the Brussels Bar. His political career began when he joined the Jodoigne youth wing of the Liberal Reformist Party in 1991, serving as its chairman from 1992–99. He became a councillor for Walloon Brabant in 1994 and was vice-chairman of the provincial council from 1995–99.

Elected as a member of the federal parliament in June 1999, he resigned in 2000 to become minister for interior affairs and civil service in the Walloon parliament, a post he held until July 2004. He was then a city councillor for Wavre, the capital of Walloon Brabant, until Nov. 2006 and became mayor of Wavre in Dec. that year.

From 2004 he was a spokesman for the MR, an alliance principally of Francophone parties. After winning re-election to the federal parliament in June 2007, he was appointed minister for development co-operation in Dec. that year, holding the post in three successive governments until in 2010 he successfully contested his party's leadership. He resigned as minister to head the MR in Feb. 2011

In the May 2014 general elections the MR emerged as the third largest party behind the Flemish separatist New Flemish Alliance (N-VA) and the Socialist Party. After initial attempts to form a government foundered, Michel oversaw negotiations and formed a coalition with three Flemish-speaking parties. The inclusion of the N-VA, as well as the MR's position as the administration's sole French-speaking party, brought criticism from other Francophone parties who refused to enter government with separatists. The coalition agreement committed the government to economic austerity measures aimed at cutting €11bn. from the budget over five years.

Career in Office

Michel took office on 11 Oct. 2014. The main cabinet posts were divided equally between representatives of Flemish- and French-speaking parties, in accordance with Belgian law. His early months in office saw strikes and protests against austerity measures. His main challenges were implementing economic reforms in the face of opposition from centre-left parties and trade unions, while at the same time managing tensions within the coalition.

In Nov. 2015 Michel's government raised the security alert in Brussels to the maximum level and staged armed police raids in response to the risk of an Islamist terror onslaught similar to a series of devastating attacks that month inflicted on Paris in neighbouring France by suspects who had apparently been based in the Belgian capital. In March 2016, days after the capture in Brussels of one of the suspected ringleaders of the Paris attacks, Islamic State-linked bombers struck Brussels' Zaventem Airport and the city's metro system; 35 people died and hundreds were injured. Then in June 2017 security forces killed a suspected Islamist suicide bomber following a small explosion in the central railway station in the capital.

In early Dec. 2018 the N-VA quit the ruling coalition government in protest at Michel's support for a controversial United Nations agreement on regulating migration, leaving the prime minister heading a minority administration. Michel resigned later that month but stayed on in a caretaker capacity at the King's request pending the next federal elections scheduled for May 2019.

Defence

Conscription was abolished in 1994 and the Armed Forces were restructured, with the aim of progressively reducing the size and making more use of civilian personnel. Since 1 Jan. 2002 they have been organized into one unified structure consisting of four main components: the Land Component (Army), Naval Component (Navy), Air Component (Air Force) and Medical Component.

In Dec. 2015 the Belgian government approved the Strategic Defence Plan for 2030 based on a multilateral partnership with NATO, the EU and the UN. It includes plans for €9·2bn. worth of spending on equipment, personnel and research across the forces and in cyber intelligence in the period to 2030.

In 2013 defence expenditure totalled US$5,294m. (US$507 per capita), representing 1·0% of GDP (compared to the NATO target of 2%).

Army

The Land Component (formerly Army) has five 'capacities': the command capacity, the combat capacity, the support capacity, the services capacity and the training capacity. Total strength (2011) 12,544. In addition there are 1,400 reserves. All tracked vehicles are in the process of being phased out in favour of wheeled vehicles. The transition was ongoing as of Feb. 2018.

Navy

The Naval Component (formerly Navy), based at Ostend and Zeebrugge, includes two frigates and five minehunters. Under the Strategic Defence Plan for 2030, plans were announced to add two new frigates and six mine countermeasure vessels. Personnel (2011) totalled 1,590.

The naval air arm comprised three Aérosptiale Alouette III helicopters in 2011.

Air Force

The Air Component (formerly Belgian Air Force) has a strength of (2011) 5,739 personnel. There are two tactical wings, based at Florennes and Kleine Brogel. Equipment in 2011 included 88 combat-capable aircraft (mostly Lockheed Martin F-16s). Under the Strategic Defence Plan for 2030, it is envisaged that a further 34 fighter jets will be added.

Economy

Services contributed 76% of GDP in 2012, with industry accounting for 23% and agriculture 1%.

According to the anti-corruption organization Transparency International, Belgium ranked 17th in the world in a 2018 survey of the countries with the least corruption in business and government. It received 75 out of 100 in the annual index.

Belgium gave US$2·2bn. in international aid in 2017, equivalent to 0·45% of GNI (compared to the UN target of 0·7%).

Overview

With a strategic geographical location within the European Union and sophisticated transport links, Belgium's open and highly developed economy is closely linked with those of its main partners—Germany, France and the Netherlands. Its main industries include chemicals, pharmaceuticals and auto-manufacture. However, with little in the way of natural resources, the country is a net importer of raw materials.

Economic activity slowed at the end of 2007 and into 2008 as a result of low private consumption and investment as well as negative export growth stemming from the global financial crisis. Bankruptcies increased by 12·5% year-on-year in Dec. 2008. The end of that year also saw a downturn in manufacturing, although consumer confidence and activity in the trade and construction sectors experienced a slow recovery. In Oct. 2008 the French bank BNP Paribas bailed out the Belgian wing of Fortis, the Belgian–Dutch bank conglomerate, the Dutch part having been nationalized the same month.

A slow recovery in GDP growth began in the third quarter of 2009 and continued through 2010, when GDP expanded by 2·7% owing to modest increases in private consumption and exports. However, growth declined to 1·8% in 2011 as confidence weakened in tandem with a significant slowdown across the rest of the eurozone. From the third quarter of 2012 until mid-2013 Belgium experienced recession as quarterly growth rates averaged –0·3% before a modest recovery came in 2014 of 1·3%. There followed growth of 1·7% in 2015 and 1·5% in 2016.

Historically, Belgium has suffered from low labour mobility and wage inflexibility, which has contributed to long-term unemployment. In 2016 unemployment stood at 11·1% among people aged between 55 and 64 and 39·9% among those aged 15 to 24. Employment rates for the prime-age working population were comparable to international levels. The jobless rate among ethnic minorities is twice that of native Belgians, largely because of poor education and language barriers.

After more than 500 days under a caretaker government, the establishment of a working coalition that assumed office in Dec. 2011 contributed to a measurable improvement in financial market conditions. In 2009 the government deficit had reached its highest level in decades, at 5·4% of GDP. However, consolidation efforts reduced it to 4% in 2011 and 3% in 2014. Pension and unemployment insurance reforms were introduced, while the decision to ensure further devolution of power to regions and communities increased stability. The banking system has become less complex and less leveraged, with around two-thirds of bank assets under foreign ownership. Also, the financial authorities have committed to strengthening banking supervision through implementation of the Basel III and Solvency II regulatory frameworks.

Long-term demographic patterns pose a major challenge. In addition to an increasing public debt (105·7% of GDP in 2016), the OECD expects the old-age ratio to double by 2050, constricting economic growth and putting pressure on public finances and services. Continued eurozone uncertainty, slow recovery across the continent and political instability (exacerbated by the European migrant crisis) also point to an uncertain outlook for the economy.

Currency

On 1 Jan. 1999 the *euro* (EUR) became the legal currency in Belgium at the irrevocable conversion rate of BEF40·3399 to EUR1. The euro, which consists of 100 cents, has been in circulation since 1 Jan. 2002. On the introduction of the euro there was a 'dual circulation' period before the Belgian franc ceased to be legal tender on 28 Feb. 2002.

Inflation rates (based on OECD statistics):

2008	2009	2010	2011	2012	2013	2014	2015	2016	2017
4·5%	0·0%	2·3%	3·4%	2·6%	1·2%	0·5%	0·6%	1·8%	2·2%

In Sept. 2009 gold reserves were 7·32m. troy oz and foreign exchange reserves US$8,060m. Total money supply was €97,656m. in Aug. 2009.

Budget

Central government revenue and expenditure in €1m. for calendar years:

	2009	2010	2011[1]
Revenue	136,828	144,721	152,046
Expenditure	153,631	156,228	165,478

[1]Provisional.

Principal sources of revenue in 2010: taxes on income, profits and capital gains, €50,491m.; social security contributions, €47,848m.; taxes on goods and services, €35,699m. Main items of expenditure by economic type in 2010: social benefits, €77,900m.; grants, €41,922m.; interest, €11,296m.

Belgium's budget deficit in 2017 was 0·9% of GDP (2016, 2·4%; 2015, 2·5%). The required target set by the EU is a budget deficit of no more than 3%.

VAT is 21% (reduced rates, 12% and 6%).

Performance

Real GDP growth rates (based on OECD statistics):

2008	2009	2010	2011	2012	2013	2014	2015	2016	2017
0·8%	−2·3%	2·7%	1·8%	0·2%	0·2%	1·3%	1·7%	1·5%	1·7%

Total GDP in 2017 was US$492·7bn.

Banking and Finance

The National Bank of Belgium was established in 1850. The *Governor* is Jan Smets. Its shares are listed on Euronext (Brussels).

The law of 22 Feb. 1998 adapted the status of the National Bank of Belgium in view of the realization of the Economic and Monetary Union.

The National Bank of Belgium is within the European System of Central Banks framework in charge of the issue of banknotes, the execution of exchange rate policy and monetary policy. Furthermore, it is the Bank of banks and the cashier of the federal state.

The law of 2 Aug. 2002 relating to the supervision of the financial sector and financial services integrated the supervision of banks and insurance corporations into one institution, the Banking, Finance and Insurance Commission.

The Royal Decree of 3 March 2011 concerning the evolution of the supervisory architecture for the financial sector transferred the responsibilities for the prudential supervision of the financial sector from the Banking, Finance and Insurance Commission to the National Bank of Belgium. The Banking, Finance and Insurance Commission was transformed into the Financial Services and Markets Authority, responsible for the integrity of the financial markets and consumer protection.

On 30 June 2013, 100 credit institutions with a balance sheet totalling €1,088bn. were established in Belgium: 40 governed by Belgian law and 60 by foreign law, all supervised by the National Bank of Belgium. 512 collective investment institutions (130 Belgian and 382 foreign) were marketed in Belgium and supervised by the Financial Services and Markets Authority; and 64 investment firms were operating in Belgium with the approval of the National Bank of Belgium (stockbroking firms) and the Financial Services and Markets Authority (other investment firms).

Gross external debt totalled US$1,379,070m. in June 2012.

There is a stock exchange (a component of Euronext) in Brussels. Euronext was created in Sept. 2000 through the merger of the Amsterdam, Brussels and Paris stock exchanges.

Energy and Natural Resources

In 2011 an estimated 4% of energy consumption came from renewables (wind power, solar power, hydro-electric power, tidal power, geothermal energy and biomass), compared to the European Union average of 13%. A target of 13% has been set by the EU for 2020.

Environment

Belgium's carbon dioxide emissions from the consumption of energy were the equivalent of 13·4 tonnes per capita in 2011.

Electricity

The production of electricity amounted to 90·2bn. kWh in 2011; consumption per capita (2011) was 8,429 kWh. Installed capacity (2011) was 20·1m. kW. 54% of production in 2011 was nuclear-produced. Belgium had seven operational nuclear reactors in 2010.

Minerals

Belgium's mineral resources are very limited; the most abundantly occurring mineral is calcite.

Agriculture

There were, in 2006, 1,382,390 ha. under cultivation, of which 841,666 ha. were arable land. There were 49,850 farms in 2006.

	Area (ha.)		Production (tonnes)	
Chief crops	2005	2006	2005	2006
Barley	39,965	49,008	301,647	367,348
Beet (fodder)	3,750	3,423	371,694	330,290
Beet (sugar)	85,527	82,912	5,983,173	5,666,621
Chicory	15,649	8,210	704,821	371,238
Maize (fodder)	163,825	161,178	7,745,553	6,600,738
Maize grain	54,256	56,500	634,088	575,898
Potatoes	64,952	67,267	2,780,865	2,592,820
Wheat	204,209	201,330	1,737,552	1,661,958

At the May 2006 agricultural census there were 6,294,904 pigs, 2,663,076 cattle, 153,976 sheep, 34,799 horses, 27,985 goats and 32,866,650 poultry.

Forestry

In 2015 forest covered 0·68m. ha. (23% of the total land area). Timber production in 2011 was 5·13m. cu. metres.

Fisheries

In 2011 the Belgian fishing fleet numbered 89 vessels of 15,800 gross tonnes. Total catch in 2012 was 24,659 tonnes, almost entirely from marine waters.

Industry

The leading companies by market capitalization in March 2019 were: Anheuser-Busch InBev, a beverages company (US$184·3bn.); KBC, a banking group (US$36·0bn.); and Solvay, an advanced materials and speciality chemicals company (US$14·3bn.).

Output, 2007 unless otherwise indicated, in 1,000 tonnes: distillate fuel oil, 12,737; crude steel (2006), 11,238; cement (2006), 8,192; residual fuel oil, 7,391; petrol, 5,041; sugar (2005), 3,394; beer (2006), 1,784·1m. litres; mineral water (2006), 1,066·8m. litres.

Labour

In 2010 (Labour Force Survey), 60,686 persons worked in the primary sector (agriculture, fishing and mining), 1,049,239 in the secondary sector (industry and construction) and 3,298,598 in the tertiary sector (services). The unemployment rate was 5·5% in Dec. 2018. In French-speaking Wallonia the rate is more than double that in Dutch-speaking Flanders.

International Trade

In 1922 the customs frontier between Belgium and Luxembourg was abolished; their foreign trade figures are amalgamated.

Imports and Exports

Trade in €1m.:

	Imports	Exports
2007	300,298·2	314,449·4
2008	317,044·0	320,806·0
2009	253,344·5	265,609·8

Leading imports and exports (in €1m.):

| | Imports | | Exports | |
	2008	2009	2008	2009
Chemicals and pharmaceutical products	62,438·6	59,436·0	71,991·1	71,047·5
Machinery and appliances	43,127·1	34,190·4	38,929·6	30,623·7
Vehicles and transport equipment	36,280·9	28,441·7	35,631·2	26,805·3
Mineral products	52,198·0	31,730·0	32,099·4	20,356·2
Base metals	27,684·2	17,318·5	32,022·4	20,364·1
Plastics and rubber	15,943·8	12,968·4	25,575·6	20,913·3
Food industry	10,416·9	10,065·6	12,715·3	12,490·4
Textile and textile articles	12,202·7	9,122·2	12,107·5	10,558·9
Precious stones and precious metals	12,053·8	8,368·5	12,992·5	9,866·5
Vegetable products	9,094·6	8,104·3	7,680·4	6,927·8

Trade by selected countries (in €1m.):

| | Imports from | | Exports to | |
	2008	2009	2008	2009
China	5,805·9	5,014·4	2,788·4	3,382·2
France	28,294·5	24,183·4	38,931·9	31,601·4
Germany	37,860·9	30,747·0	38,302·6	29,933·4
India	2,668·8	1,992·9	4,756·0	4,250·5
Italy	7,436·3	6,359·2	9,818·4	7,573·1
Japan	5,660·9	5,102·2	1,187·5	1,058·5
Luxembourg	2,714·8	1,681·9	5,479·6	4,126·5
Netherlands	57,334·6	41,667·0	30,339·9	24,573·4

(continued)

| | Imports from | | Exports to | |
	2008	2009	2008	2009
Poland	2,445·4	2,143·3	3,958·6	3,103·4
Russia	4,759·0	3,552·6	2,976·1	1,668·3
Spain	5,277·4	4,469·3	7,064·9	5,488·0
Sweden	5,195·6	3,169·3	3,332·1	2,420·8
Switzerland	2,382·8	2,163·1	3,307·8	2,305·8
UK	14,594·9	10,444·9	15,676·1	12,805·6
USA	9,955·0	8,017·7	8,567·8	7,588·8

In 2009 fellow EU-member countries accounted for 54·0% of imports and 50·5% of exports.

Communications

Roads

Length of roads, 2006: motorways, 1,763 km; national roads, 12,585 km; secondary roads, 1,349 km; local roads, 136,559 km. Belgium has one of the densest road networks in the world. In 2007 there were 5,006,300 passenger cars in use, 29,000 buses and coaches, 696,700 lorries and vans, and 371,500 motorcycles and mopeds. Road accidents caused 994 fatalities in both 2008 and 2009 (1,470 in 2000).

Rail

The main Belgian lines were a State enterprise from their inception in 1834. In 1926 the Société Nationale des Chemins de Fer Belges (SNCB) was formed to take over the railways. In 2005 SNCB was divided into separate operating and infrastructure companies. The length of railway operated in 2005 was 3,696 km (electrified, 3,110 km). In 2008, 217m. passengers and 55·5m. tonnes of freight were carried.

The regional transport undertakings Société Régionale Wallonne de Transport and Vlaamse Vervoermaatschappij operate tramways around Charleroi (20 km) and from De Panne to Knokke (55 km). There is also a metro and tramway in Brussels (175 km), and tramways in Antwerp (57 km) and Ghent (30 km). An urban commuter rail network around Brussels is partially open but may not be completed until 2025 or later.

Civil Aviation

The former national airline SABENA (*Société anonyme belge d'exploitation de la navigation aérienne*) was set up in 1923. However, in Nov. 2001 it filed for bankruptcy. Its successor, Delta Air Transport (DAT), a former SABENA subsidiary, was given a new identity in Feb. 2002 as SN Brussels Airlines. In Nov. 2006 SN Brussels Airlines merged with Virgin Express and since March 2007 has been trading under the name Brussels Airlines.

The busiest airport is Brussels National Airport (Zaventem), which handled 19,232,284 passengers in 2013 and 400,282 tonnes of freight. Charleroi is the second busiest airport in terms of passenger numbers and Liège the third busiest.

Shipping

In Jan. 2014 there were 75 ships of 300 GT or over registered, totalling 4·14m. GT. Of the 75 vessels registered, 22 were bulk carriers, 19 liquid gas tankers, 18 general cargo ships, 14 oil tankers and two passenger ships. Antwerp is Europe's second busiest port in terms of total cargo handled after Rotterdam and the third busiest in terms of container traffic after Rotterdam and Hamburg. In 2013, 190,849,000 tonnes of cargo were handled at the port of Antwerp (92,974,000 tonnes loaded and 97,875,000 tonnes discharged), with total container throughput 8,578,000 TEUs (twenty-foot equivalent units).

The length of navigable inland waterways was 1,516 km in 2008; 190·3m. tonnes of freight were carried on inland waterways in 2014.

Telecommunications

In 2014 mobile phone subscriptions numbered 12,734,724 (1,142·7 per 1,000 persons). In the same year there were 4,532,475 main (fixed) telephone lines. 85·0% of the population were internet users in 2014. The fixed broadband penetration rate in 2014 was 359·9 subscribers per 1,000 inhabitants. In March 2012 there were 4·6m. Facebook users.

Social Institutions

Out of 178 countries analysed in the 2017 *Fragile States Index*—a list published jointly by the Fund for Peace and *Foreign Policy* magazine—Belgium was ranked the 16th least vulnerable to conflict or collapse. The index is based on 12 indicators of state vulnerability across social, political and economic categories.

Justice

Judges are appointed for life. There are a court of cassation, five courts of appeal and assize courts for political and criminal cases. There are 27 judicial districts, each with a court of first instance. In each of the 222 cantons is a justice and judge of the peace. There are also various special tribunals. There is trial by jury in assize courts. The death penalty, which had been in abeyance for 45 years, was formally abolished in 1991.

The Gendarmerie ceased to be part of the Army in Jan. 1992.

The population in penal institutions in Jan. 2013 was 12,126 (108 per 100,000 of national population). Owing to overcrowding in Belgian prisons some inmates have since Feb. 2010 been accommodated at Tilburg prison in the Netherlands. In 2015 the World Justice Project *Rule of Law Index*, which provides data on how the rule of law is experienced by the general public across eight categories, ranked Belgium 20th of 102 countries for criminal justice and 16th for civil justice.

In Aug. 2003 a new act reformed war crimes legislation introduced in 1993 which allowed for charges to be brought against foreign nationals accused of abuses committed outside Belgian jurisdiction. The amendment requires that either accuser or defendant be a citizen of or resident in Belgium.

Education

Following the constitutional reform of 1988, education is the responsibility of the three Communities (the French Community, the Flemish Community and the German-speaking Community). Education is free and compulsory from the age of six to 18, although from 16 to 18 it may be part-time.

In 2007 there were 411,951 children and 29,550 teaching staff in pre-primary schools; 732,411 pupils and 65,378 teaching staff in primary schools; 825,293 pupils and (2006) 81,873 teaching staff in secondary schools; and 393,687 students and 26,298 academic staff in tertiary education. There were 16 universities and 73 non-university colleges and institutes in 2006–07. There are five royal academies of fine arts and six royal conservatoires at Brussels (one Flemish and one French), Liège, Ghent, Antwerp and Mons.

Public expenditure on education in 2005 amounted to 6·0% of GNI and represented 12·1% of total government expenditure.

The adult literacy rate is at least 99%.

Health

On 31 Dec. 2006 there were 42,326 physicians, 8,423 dentists and 12,109 pharmacists. There were 210 hospitals with 55,000 beds in 2007. Total health spending accounted for 9·4% of GDP in 2007. In Jan. 2000 the Belgian government agreed to decriminalize the use of cannabis. Euthanasia became legal on 24 Sept. 2002. The Belgian Chamber of Representatives had given its approval on 16 May 2002 to a measure adopted by the Senate on 26 Oct. 2001. Belgium was the second country to legalize euthanasia, after the Netherlands.

Welfare

Expenditure on social security, 2006: wage earners, €50,774·6m.; self-employed, €3,858·9m. Expenditure on pensions, 2006: wage earners, €15,324·6m.; self-employed, €2,192·3m.

The retirement age for men and women is 65. In Oct. 2014 the four parties negotiating the formation of the new government announced that the state pension age will rise to 66 in 2025 and further to 67 in 2030. A full pension is 60% of average lifetime earnings (75% for married couples). Based on size and sustainability of payments, a report by Aon Consulting in Nov. 2005 rated Belgium as the country with the worst pensions system of the 15 pre-expansion EU countries.

Religion

The Constitution provides for freedom of religion. Traditionally, Roman Catholicism has been the majority religion but it has been in rapid decline—according to the Pew Research Center's Forum on Religion &

Public Life, an estimated 62% of the population in 2010 were Catholics, 29% religiously unaffiliated and 6% Muslim. There are nine Roman Catholic dioceses including the Archdiocese of Mechelen-Brussel. In Feb. 2019 there were two cardinals.

Culture

World Heritage Sites

Belgium has 13 sites which have been included on the UNESCO world heritage list. They are: the Flemish Béguinages (1998); the four lifts on the Canal du Centre and their environs (1998); La Grand Place in Brussels (1998); the historic centre of Bruges (2000); the major town houses of the architect Victor Horta in Brussels (2000); the Neolithic flint mines at Spiennes (2000); Notre Dame cathedral in Tournai (2000); the Plantin-Moretus Museum, a Renaissance printing and publishing house (2005); Stoclet House in Brussels, a house designed by artists of the Vienna Secession movement (2009); and Major Mining Sites of Wallonia, the four best-preserved mining sites of the country dating back to the late 17th century (2012).

Belgium shares the belfries of Belgium and France (1999 and 2005) with France; Ancient and Primeval Beech Forests of the Carpathians and Other Regions of Europe (2007 and 2017) are shared with Albania, Austria, Bulgaria, Croatia, Germany, Italy, Romania, Slovakia, Slovenia, Spain and Ukraine; and the Architectural Work of Le Corbusier, an Outstanding Contribution to the Modern Movement (2016), with Argentina, France, Germany, India, Japan and Switzerland.

Press

In 2013 there were 25 daily newspapers (23 paid-for and two free) with a combined circulation of 1,520,000. There were 14 newspaper online editions in 2012 with 3,818,000 unique daily visitors.

Tourism

In 2014 there were 17,068,872 overnight stays by non-resident visitors, including 4,144,256 by visitors from the Netherlands and 2,449,842 by visitors from France. A total of 11,293,395 overnight stays were for leisure, holiday and recreation purposes, 3,554,876 for conferences, congresses and seminars and 2,220,601 for other business purposes.

Festivals

The country's largest festival is Gentse Feesten (July), which has been held annually in Ghent since 1843 and combines music and theatre. The main rock and pop festivals are Graspop Metal Meeting (June) at Dessel, Rock Werchter (July) at Werchter near Leuven, Klinkers (July–Aug.) in Bruges, Pukkelpop (Aug.) in Hasselt and Marktrock (Aug.) in Leuven.

Diplomatic Representatives

Of Belgium in the United Kingdom (17 Grosvenor Cres., London, SW1X 7EE)
    Ambassador: Rudolph Huygelen.

Of the United Kingdom in Belgium (Ave. d'Auderghem 10, 1040 Brussels)
    Ambassador: Alison Rose.

Of Belgium in the USA (3330 Garfield St., NW, Washington, D.C., 20008)
    Ambassador: Dirk Jozef M. Wouters.

Of the USA in Belgium (Blvd du Régent 27, 1000 Brussels)
    Ambassador: Ronald J. Gidwitz.

Of Belgium to the United Nations
    Ambassador: Marc Pecsteen de Buytswerve.

Of Belgium to the European Union
    Permanent Representative: François Roux.

Further Reading

The Institut National de Statistique. *Statistiques du commerce extérieur* (monthly). *Bulletin de Statistique.* Bi-monthly. *Annuaire Statistique de la Belgique* (from 1870).—*Annuaire statistique de poche* (from 1965).
Service Fédéral d'Information. *Guide de l'Administration Fédérale.* Occasional
Arblaster, Paul, *A History of the Low Countries.* 2005

Blom, J. C. H. and Lamberts, E. (eds) *History of the Low Countries.* Revised ed. 2006

Deprez, K., and Vos, L., *Nationalism in Belgium—Shifting Identities, 1780–1995.* 1998

Deschouwer, Kris, *The Politics of Belgium: Governing a Divided Society.* 2nd ed. 2012

Fitzmaurice, J., *The Politics of Belgium: a Unique Federalism.* 1996

Hermans, T. J., *et al.,* (eds) *The Flemish Movement: a Documentary History.* 1992

Witte, Els, *Political History of Belgium from 1830 Onwards.* 2000

National library: Bibliothèque royale de Belgique, 4 Boulevard de l'Empereur, B-1000 Brussels.

Website (Dutch and French only): http://www.kbr.be

National Statistical Office: Institut national de statistique, Rue de Louvain 44, 1000 Brussels.

Website: http://statbel.fgov.be

Belize

Capital: Belmopan
Population projection, 2020: 398,000
GNI per capita, 2017: (PPP$) 7,166
HDI/world rank, 2017: 0·708/106=
Internet domain extension: .bz

Key Historical Events

Evidence of farming settlements at Cuello in northern Belize dates to around 2000 BC. Over the following centuries Mayan towns and villages encompassed Belize, Mexico's Yucatán peninsula and much of Guatemala. The city of Caracol, near Belize's border with Guatemala, is estimated to have spread over 140 sq. km, with some 180,000 residents at its height in the 7th century AD. However, the Mayan civilization declined rapidly after 900 AD for reasons that are still unclear. Construction of the great pyramid temples ceased, literacy was abandoned and subsistence farming returned.

By 1525 the Spanish adventurer, Hernán Cortés, established a base in Honduras. From 1543 Melchor and Alonso Pacheco took control of land around Tipu in southern Belize, which became part of the Spanish Empire. However, Spanish control was limited and Tipu became a centre of Mayan resistance in the late 1630s. By the 1640s British buccaneers were attacking Spanish ships from havens along Belize's coast. Some established settlements and traded logwood, then used in dyes. After the capture of Jamaica from Spain in 1655 they were joined by demobilized British soldiers and sailors.

Spanish attempts to expel the British settlers ended with the defeat of the commander of Yucatán, Arturo O'Neill, at the Battle of St George's Caye in 1798. Belize was part of Britain's 'informal empire' during the 18th century. Logwood and mahogany were harvested by slaves with British Honduras, as it was known, a focal point for Central American trade until the Panama railway was completed in 1855. In 1862 British Honduras was declared a British colony with a Legislative Assembly and a lieutenant-governor under the governor of Jamaica. The administrative connection with Jamaica was severed in 1884.

Belize's small economy was hit by the depression in the 1930s and the capital, Belize City, was laid waste by a hurricane in Sept. 1931. Widespread protests over unemployment and poor living conditions in the mid-1930s were led by Antonio Soberanis Gómez. The establishment of the General Workers' Union became one of the foundations of Belize's nationalist movement after the Second World War. The People's United Party (PUP), formed in 1950, became the dominant political force under George Price. Universal suffrage was introduced in 1964 and thereafter the majority of the legislature were elected rather than appointed.

The road to independence from Britain was complicated by turbulent relations with Guatemala, which had long claimed Belize as its territory. Price rejected calls for an 'associated state' of Guatemala and full independence was achieved on 21 Sept. 1981, prompting Guatemala to threaten war. Price served as Belize's first prime minister until his party was defeated by the United Democratic Party (UDP) under Manuel Esquivel in Dec. 1984. Guatemala officially recognized Belize as an independent sovereign nation in Sept. 1991. But a border dispute rumbled on, remaining unresolved at the time of Dean Barrow's election as prime minister in Feb. 2008, following a landslide victory for the UDP.

Territory and Population

Belize is bounded in the north by Mexico, west and south by Guatemala and east by the Caribbean. Fringing the coast there are three atolls and some 400 islets (cays) in the world's second longest barrier reef (140 miles), which was declared a world heritage site in 1996. Area, 22,965 sq. km.

There are six districts as follows, with area, 2010 census population and chief city:

District	Area (in sq. km)	Population	Chief City	Population
Belize	4,307	95,292	Belize City	57,169
Cayo	5,196	75,046	San Ignacio/ Santa Elena	17,878
Corozal	1,860	41,061	Corozal	10,287
Orange Walk	4,636	45,946	Orange Walk	13,709
Stann Creek	2,554	34,323	Dangriga	9,591
Toledo	4,413	30,785	Punta Gorda	5,351

Population at the 2010 census, 324,528; density, 14·1 per sq. km. Estimate, July 2018: 398,050.

The UN gives a projected population for 2020 of 398,000.

The capital is Belmopan (2010 census population, 13,931). In 2010, 45·0% of the population were urban.

English is the official language. Spanish is widely spoken. In 2010 the main ethnic groups were Mestizo (Spanish-Maya), 49·7%; Creole (African descent), 20·8%; Mayans, 9·9%; and Garifuna (Caribs), 4·6%.

Social Statistics

2009 births (est.), 8,000; deaths (est.), 1,000. In 2009 the estimated birth rate per 1,000 was 25 and the death rate 4; infant mortality in 2010 was 14 per 1,000 live births. Life expectancy in 2013 was 70·9 years for males and 77·1 for females. Annual population growth rate, 2005–10, 2·5%; fertility rate, 2013, 2·7 children per woman.

Climate

A tropical climate with high rainfall and small annual range of temperature. The driest months are Feb. and March. Belize City, Jan. 74°F (23·3°C), July 81°F (27·2°C). Annual rainfall 76" (1,890 mm).

Constitution and Government

The head of state is the British sovereign, represented by an appointed Governor-General. The Constitution, which came into force on 21 Sept. 1981, provided for a National Assembly, with a five-year term, comprising a 32-member *House of Representatives* (31 elected by universal suffrage plus the Speaker), and a *Senate* consisting of 13 members, six appointed by the Governor-General on the advice of the Prime Minister, three on the advice of the Leader of the Opposition, one on the advice of the Belize Council of Churches and the Evangelical Association of Churches, one on the advice of the Belize Chamber of Commerce and Industry and the Belize Business Bureau and one on the advice of the National Trade Union Congress of Belize and the Civil Society Steering Committee plus the Senate President.

National Anthem

'O, Land of the Free'; words by S. A. Haynes, tune by S. W. Young.

Recent Elections

In elections to the House of Representatives held on 4 Nov. 2015 the ruling United Democratic Party won 19 of 31 seats with 50·5% of votes cast and the People's United Party 12 with 47·8%. Turnout was 72·7%.

© Springer Nature Limited 2020
Palgrave Macmillan (ed.), *The Statesman's Yearbook 2020*,
https://doi.org/10.1057/978-1-349-95940-2_30

Current Government

Governor-General: Sir Colville Young, GCMG; b. 1932 (sworn in 17 Nov. 1993).

In Feb. 2019 the cabinet comprised the following:

Prime Minister, and Minister of Finance, and Labour, Local Government, Rural Development, Energy, Public Utilities, Public Service, and Elections and Boundaries: Dean Barrow; b. 1951 (United Democratic Party/UDP; sworn in 8 Feb. 2008).

Deputy Prime Minister: Patrick Faber (also *Minister of Education, Science and Technology, Culture, Youth and Sports*).

Minister of Agriculture, Fisheries, Forestry, the Environment, Sustainable Development, and Immigration: Godwin Hulse. *Defence:* John Saldivar. *Economic Development, Petroleum, Investment, Trade and Commerce:* Erwin Contreras. *Health:* Pablo Marin. *Home Affairs and Foreign Affairs:* Wilfred Elrington. *Housing and Urban Development:* Michael Finnegan. *Human Development, Social Transformation and Poverty Alleviation:* Anthony Martinez. *Natural Resources:* Hugo Patt. *Tourism and Civil Aviation:* Jose Manuel Heredia, Jr. *Transport and National Emergency Management:* Edmond Castro. *Works:* Rene Montero. *Attorney General:* Michael Peyrefitte.

Government Website: http://www.belize.gov.bz

Current Leaders

Dean Barrow

Position

Prime Minister

Introduction

Dean Barrow, leader of the United Democratic Party (UDP), won a landslide victory in the Feb. 2008 general election to become Belize's first black prime minister. He took office promising to root out corruption, reduce crime and reform the faltering economy. He was returned for a second term in March 2012 and for an unprecedented third in Nov. 2015.

Early Life

Dean Barrow was born on 2 March 1951 in Belize City and was educated at St Michael's College. He studied law at the University of the West Indies, Barbados, and the Norman Manley Law School in Kingston, Jamaica. He entered the legal profession in 1975, joining his uncle Dean Lindo's Church Street Chambers in Belize City and becoming a partner in 1977. In the early 1980s he completed a master's degree in international relations at the University of Miami.

In 1983 Barrow was elected to Belize City council. He successfully contested the Dec. 1984 general election for the UDP, winning the Queen's Square division. He was appointed attorney general and minister of foreign affairs, serving until 1989 when the UDP lost office. In 1989 Barrow set up with Rodwell Williams the law firm Barrow & Williams which has acted for influential clients including the Belize Bank and Belize Telecommunications Ltd (BTL). In 1990 Barrow became deputy leader of the UDP.

With the UDP victory at the 1993 general election, Barrow returned to his previous posts of attorney general and minister of foreign affairs but also took on responsibility for the national security, immigration and nationality, and media portfolios. This concentration of power attracted some criticism. In 1998, after the UDP lost all but three seats in the general election, Barrow became party head and oversaw the securing of seven seats in the 2003 election.

In opposition, Barrow argued for greater transparency in public finances and advocated building public infrastructure. In the Feb. 2008 general election the UDP upset predictions of a close result to win 25 out of 31 seats. Barrow took office as prime minister on 8 Feb. 2008 and on 11 Feb. announced his new cabinet with himself as minister of finance.

Career in Office

Barrow's early months in office were dominated by investigations into a financial scandal inherited from the previous administration, involving the alleged misuse of US$20m. of overseas grants. With politicians, the Belize Bank and a health care company all implicated, Barrow requested US assistance to set up an audit. Among his other major challenges were the revitalization of the economy, and implementing a programme to build houses, roads and health centres. The ongoing problem of crime was

highlighted in Sept. 2011 as the US government added Belize to a blacklist of countries considered to be producers of or transit routes for illegal drugs. The UDP won the parliamentary election of March 2012 albeit with a reduced majority, giving Barrow a second term in office. The UDP nonetheless won further parliamentary elections in March 2012 and Nov. 2015, extending Barrow's premiership to a third consecutive term.

In Aug. 2016 Belize's High Court decriminalized homosexuality, controversially ruling the existing law unconstitutional.

In April 2018 voters in a referendum in Guatemala (in a very low turnout) approved the filing of a claim with the International Court of Justice demanding sovereignty over half of Belize's territory. Belize is expected to hold a similar referendum in due course on the historical dispute.

Defence

The Belize Defence Force numbers around 1,050 (2011) with 700 reservists. There are three infantry battalions, three reserve companies, a support group and an air wing.

In 2013 defence expenditure totalled US$18m. (US$53 per capita), representing 1·1% of GDP.

International Relations

In 2018 Guatemala's electorate voted in favour of filing a claim with the International Court of Justice demanding sovereignty over 53% of Belize.

Economy

In 2011 agriculture accounted for 13% of GDP, industry 23% and services 64%.

Overview

Belize is classified as an upper-middle income country by the World Bank. The largest industries are services, garment production, food processing, tourism, construction and crude oil production. In 2016 agricultural produce (including sugar, citrus fruits, bananas and papayas) comprised over 50% of total exports, whilst the service sector accounted for over 60% of GDP. Marine products are also exported. A Commercial Free Zone was established in 1994 and foreign direct investment increased substantially from 2000.

Annual GDP growth rates had averaged 7% in the 1980s but declined to less than 4% over the period 2000–10. Belize weathered the global financial crisis relatively well compared to other Caribbean Community countries and managed to avoid recession. GDP growth then averaged 2·9% per year between 2010 and 2014 (spurred by increased agricultural exports and tourist arrivals), before falling back to an average of 1·7% annually between 2015 and 2017.

In Feb. 2007 the government restructured 98% of its external debt, worth US$900m., although national debt remains a concern. The government renationalized Belize Telemedia and Belize Electricity Limited in 2011, prompting Standard & Poor's international agency to downgrade the country's sovereign credit rating from 'B' to 'B–'. In Feb. 2012 it was further downgraded to a lowly 'CCC+'. However, further investment in sugar and non-traditional agricultural products subsequently boosted the economic outlook, resulting in a further rating reclassification to 'B–/B' in Nov. 2014. Public debt was put at 95·5% of GDP in 2017.

It was estimated in 2017 that over 40% of the Belizean population lived in poverty, while unemployment stood at 12·0% in the same year. The International Monetary Fund has highlighted improving the business environment and addressing the widening current account deficit as key to stronger growth.

Currency

The unit of currency is the *Belize dollar* (BZD) of 100 *cents.* Since 1976 $B2 has been fixed at US$1. Total money supply was $B651m. in Aug. 2009 and foreign exchange reserves were US$207m. There was inflation of 0·7% in 2016 and 1·1% in 2017.

Budget

Revenues in 2011–12 were $B843·6m. and expenditures $B889·8m. Tax revenues accounted for 81·5% of total revenues; current expenditure accounted for 82·0% of total expenditures.

A Goods and Services Tax (GST) was introduced in July 2006, initially of 10% and since April 2010 of 12·5%.

Performance

There was real GDP growth of 3·8% in 2015. Belize suffered a recession in 2016 when the economy shrank by 0·5%, before a slight recovery saw growth of 0·8% in 2017. Total GDP in 2017 was US$1·8bn.

Banking and Finance

A Central Bank was established in 1981 (*Governor*, Joy Grant). In 2014 there were five commercial banks, not including offshore banks. Three were based in Belize (Atlantic Bank, Belize Bank and Heritage Bank) and two were multinational banks with branches in Belize (FirstCaribbean International Bank and Scotiabank). The oldest and largest bank is Belize Bank.

Energy and Natural Resources

Environment

Carbon dioxide emissions from the consumption of energy were the equivalent of 1·5 tonnes per capita in 2011.

Electricity

Installed capacity in 2011 was 144,000 kW. Production was 322m. kWh in 2011 and consumption per capita 1,558 kWh.

Oil and Gas

After several years of exploration, oil was discovered in 2005 by Belize Natural Energy. It is the only company producing oil in Belize. Production of crude oil was 4,300 bbls per day in 2010.

Agriculture

In 2013 there were an estimated 78,000 ha. of arable land and 32,000 ha. of permanent crops. Output, 2013 (in 1,000 tonnes): sugarcane, 1,078; oranges (estimate), 230; bananas (estimate), 102; maize, 72. Livestock (2013 estimates): cattle, 114,000; pigs, 22,000; sheep, 13,000; horses, 6,000; mules, 5,000; chickens, 1·6m.

Forestry

In 2015, 1·37m. ha. (60% of the total land area) were under forests. Timber production in 2011 was 167,000 cu. metres.

Fisheries

The total catch in 2012 amounted to 149,806 tonnes, exclusively from sea fishing.

Industry

Manufacturing is mainly confined to processing agricultural products and timber. There is also a clothing industry. Sugar production in 2006 was 113,000 tonnes; molasses, 42,000 tonnes.

Labour

The labour force in 2013 was 149,600 (100,800 in 2003). 68·3% of the population aged 15–64 was economically active in 2013. In the same year 11·7% of the population was unemployed.

International Trade

Imports and Exports

Merchandise imports in 2014 totalled US$1,004·3m. (US$931·2m. in 2013) and merchandise exports US$359·1m. (US$411·4m. in 2013).

Principal imports in 2014 were food, animals and beverages (21·7%) followed by machinery and transport equipment (21·4%); main exports in 2014 were food, animals and beverages (55·5%) followed by mineral fuels and lubricants (16·3%).

The leading import supplier in 2010 was the USA (47·9%), followed by Mexico and China; the leading export destination in 2010 was the USA (49·1%), followed by the UK and Costa Rica.

Communications

Roads

In 2006 there were 575 km of main roads and 2,432 km of other roads. There were 40,000 passenger cars in use in 2006 and 14,800 trucks and vans. In 2006 there were 68 deaths as a result of road accidents.

Civil Aviation

There is an international airport (Philip S. W. Goldson) in Belize City. The national carrier is Maya Island Air, which operates scheduled domestic services and charter flights to Guatemala and Honduras. There were direct flights in 2010 with other airlines to Atlanta, Charlotte, Dallas, Houston, Los Angeles, Miami, Minneapolis/St Paul, New York, San Pedro Sula and San Salvador. In 2013 Philip S. W. Goldson International handled 542,833 passengers (449,291 in 2008).

Shipping

The main port is Belize City, with a modern deep-water port able to handle containerized shipping. There are also ports at Commerce Bight and Big Creek. In Jan. 2014 there were 409 ships of 300 GT or over registered, totalling 1,570,000 GT. Of the 409 vessels registered, 288 were general cargo ships, 52 bulk carriers, 47 oil tankers, 11 passenger ships, six container ships and five liquid gas tankers. Belize is a 'flag of convenience' country.

Telecommunications

In 2011 there were 28,800 landline telephone subscriptions (equivalent to 90·7 per 1,000 inhabitants) and 203,100 mobile phone subscriptions (or 638·7 per 1,000 inhabitants). Fixed broadband subscriptions totalled 10,000 in 2012 (29·6 per 1,000 inhabitants).

Social Institutions

Out of 178 countries analysed in the 2017 *Fragile States Index*—a list published jointly by the Fund for Peace and *Foreign Policy* magazine— Belize was ranked the 64th least vulnerable to conflict or collapse. The index is based on 12 indicators of state vulnerability across social, political and economic categories.

Justice

Each of the six judicial districts has summary jurisdiction courts (criminal) and district courts (civil), both of which are presided over by magistrates. There are a Supreme Court, a Court of Appeal and a Family Court. There are a Director of Public Prosecutions, a Chief Justice and two Puisne Judges. Belize was one of ten countries to sign an agreement in Feb. 2001 establishing a Caribbean Court of Justice (CCJ) to replace the British Privy Council as the highest civil and criminal court. In the meantime the number of signatories has risen to 12. The court was inaugurated at Port of Spain, Trinidad on 16 April 2005. Belize became the third country to abolish appeals to the Privy Council and accept the CCJ as its court of last resort in June 2010.

The population in penal institutions in Dec. 2012 was 1,562 (476 per 100,000 of national population). Belize's prison population rate ranks in the top ten in the world. Belize was ranked 97th of 102 countries for criminal justice and 64th for civil justice in the 2015 World Justice Project *Rule of Law Index*, which provides data on how the rule of law is experienced by the general public across eight categories.

Education

Education is in English. State education is managed jointly by the government and the Roman Catholic and Anglican Churches. It is compulsory for children between five and 14 years and primary education is free. In 2008–09 there were 53,000 pupils at primary schools and 32,000 at secondary schools. There are two government-maintained schools for children with special needs. There is a teacher training college. The University College of Belize opened in 1986. The University of the West Indies maintains an extramural department in Belize City.

In 2009 public expenditure on education came to 6·1% of GDP. Expenditure on education was 18·7% of total government spending in 2008.

Health

In 2006 there were 11 hospitals with 12 beds per 10,000 persons. There were 263 physicians, 12 dentists, 441 nurses and 46 pharmacists. Medical services in rural areas are provided by health care centres and mobile clinics.

In *Water: At What Cost? The State of the World's Water 2016*, WaterAid reported that 0·5% of the population does not have access to safe water.

Religion

In 2010 there were an estimated 160,000 Roman Catholics and 110,000 Protestants according to the Pew Research Center's Forum on Religion & Public Life, with the remainder of the population being unaffiliated or following other religions.

Culture

World Heritage Sites

The Belize Barrier Reef Reserve System was inscribed on the UNESCO World Heritage List in 1996.

Press

There are no daily newspapers although there were eight non-dailies in 2008, the largest of which were *Belize Times*, *The Amandala Press* and *The Reporter*.

Tourism

There were 716 hotels and 7,111 hotel rooms in 2011. In 2012 there were 917,869 visitors of which 277,135 stayed overnight and 640,734 arrived on cruise ships.

Festivals

The Belize Carnival is celebrated in the week before Lent begins, with particularly extravagant celebrations in San Pedro. There is also a series of Lobsterfests (at which lobsters prepared in many different ways are consumed) held at different venues throughout June and July. 10 Sept. is St George's Caye Day, held in memory of the defeat of Spanish forces in 1798 and including a battle re-enactment. National Independence Day follows on 21 Sept.

Diplomatic Representatives

Of Belize in the United Kingdom (3rd Floor, 45 Crawford Pl., London, W1H 4LP)
High Commissioner: Perla Maria Perdomo.

Of the United Kingdom in Belize (North Ring Rd/Melhado Parade, PO Box 91, Belmopan, Belize)
High Commissioner: Claire Evans, OBE.

Of Belize in the USA (2535 Massachusetts Ave., NW, Washington, D.C., 20008)
Ambassador: Francisco Daniel Gutierez.

Of the USA in Belize (Floral Park Rd, Belmopan, Cayo)
Ambassador: Vacant.
Chargé d'Affaires a.i.: Keith R. Gilges.

Of Belize to the United Nations
Ambassador: Lois Michele Young.

Of Belize to the European Union
Ambassador: Dylan Vernon.

Further Reading

Leslie, Robert, (ed.) *A History of Belize: Nation in the Making.* 3rd ed. 1997
Shoman, Assad, *Thirteen Chapters of a History of Belize.* 1994
Sutherland, Anne, *The Making of Belize: Globalization in the Margins.* 1998
Twigg, Alan, *Understanding Belize: A Historical Guide.* 2006
National Statistical Office: Statistical Institute of Belize, 1902 Constitution Drive, Belmopan.
Website: http://www.sib.org.bz

Benin

République du Bénin (Republic of Benin)

Capital: Porto-Novo
Population projection, 2020: 12·12m.
GNI per capita, 2017: (PPP$) 2,061
HDI/world rank, 2017: 0·515/163
Internet domain extension: .bj

Key Historical Events

The ancient rainforest stretching along the West African coast was home to hunter-gatherers for millennia, although there is scant evidence of early settlement. Present-day Benin lay beyond the influence of the powerful Edo/Benin civilization that emerged in the Niger delta during the 12th century. Oral history recounts that the Aja people migrated south in the 13th century and founded Allada, which expanded to encompass Abomey and the coastal settlement of Ajashe (later named Porto-Novo by Portuguese explorers). Abomey prospered as the 16th century progressed, drawing in other ethnic groups such as the Fon and eventually forging the Kingdom of Dahomey. The dynasty expanded to the south and west, led by Te-Agdanlin, who came from a powerful family in the region and who made contact with European mariners.

By the late 17th century Dahomey had joined the slave trade—acquiring young men from neighbouring areas and selling them to Portuguese, French, Dutch and British traders through coastal middlemen in return for weapons and other manufactured goods. By the 1730s about 20,000 slaves were being transported annually—mostly through the port of Oiudah—and the area became known as the Slave Coast. As it strengthened, Dahomey came into frequent conflict with the Yoruba kingdom of Oyo, which captured Abomey in 1738 and forced the payment of an annual tribute for decades.

Under King Ghezo, who ruled from 1818–58, Dahomey developed as a military and cultural centre, famed for its Amazon female fighting force. A military victory over the declining Oyo empire in 1823 finally brought an end to Dahomey's tributary status. In the 1840s Ghezo came under pressure from the British to end the slave trade and traditions including human sacrifice. A wealth of natural resources and the prospect of trade in commodities such as palm oil made the kingdom a target in the European scramble for Africa from the 1870s. In 1878 King Glele agreed to French demands for a protectorate at Cotonou and similar concessions were later granted over Porto-Novo. Opposition to French control, led by Glele's son Béhanzin, sparked the Franco-Dahomean war in 1892.

Following the defeat of Dahomey and the abolition of the monarchy in 1894, the French occupied territory inland up to the River Niger and absorbed Dahomey into French West Africa. Protests against French rule mounted after the Second World War and in 1946 Dahomey was designated a French overseas territory. After becoming independent on 1 Aug. 1960 civilian government led by Hubert Maga was beset by periods of instability, economic difficulties, ethnic rivalries and unrest.

In Oct. 1972 Gen. Mathieu Kérékou seized power and installed a left-wing regime. In 1975 Kérékou renamed the country the People's Republic of Benin. A constitution was adopted in 1977 based on a single Marxist-Leninist party, the People's Revolutionary Party of Benin, which held exclusive power until 1989. Political newcomer Yayi Boni, running as an independent, was elected president in 2006 and oversaw a gradual improvement in the economy. His close ally, cotton businessman Patrice Talon, succeeded him in March 2016.

Territory and Population

Benin is bounded in the east by Nigeria, north by Niger and Burkina Faso, west by Togo and south by the Gulf of Guinea. The area is 114,763 sq. km, and the population (2013 census) 10,008,749; density, 87·2 per sq. km.

The UN gives a projected population for 2020 of 12·12m.

In 2011, 42·5% of the population were urban.

The areas and populations of the 12 departments are as follows:

Department	Sq. km	Census (2013)
Alibori	26,242	867,463
Atacora	20,499	772,262
Atlantique	3,233	1,398,229
Borgou	25,856	1,214,249
Collines	13,931	717,477
Couffo	2,404	745,328
Donga	11,126	543,130
Littoral	79	679,012
Mono	1,605	497,243
Ouémé	1,281	1,100,404
Plateau	3,264	622,372
Zou	5,243	851,580

Cotonou, the largest city, had a population of 679,012 in 2013 and Porto-Novo, the capital, 264,320; other major towns are Abomey-Calavi, Godomey and Parakou.

There are about 40 different ethnic groups, the largest being the Fon, Adja, Yoruba and Bariba.

The official language is French. Over 50 indigenous languages are spoken.

Social Statistics

2006 (estimates) births, 303,000; deaths, 79,000. Rates, 2006 estimates (per 1,000 population): births, 38·7; deaths, 10·1. Infant mortality, 2010 (per 1,000 live births), 73. Expectation of life in 2007 was 59·8 years for males and 62·1 for females. Annual population growth rate, 2010–15, 2·8%. Fertility rate, 2008, 5·4 children per woman.

Climate

In coastal parts there is an equatorial climate, with a long rainy season from March to July and a short rainy season in Oct. and Nov. The dry season increases in length from the coast, with inland areas having rain only between May and Sept. Porto-Novo, Jan. 82°F (27·8°C), July 78°F (25·6°C). Annual rainfall 52" (1,300 mm). Cotonou, Jan. 81°F (27·2°C), July 77°F (25°C). Annual rainfall 53" (1,325 mm).

Constitution and Government

The Benin Party of Popular Revolution (PRPB) held a monopoly of power from 1977 to 1989.

In Feb. 1990 a 'National Conference of the Active Forces of the Nation' proclaimed its sovereignty and appointed Nicéphore Soglo prime minister of a provisional government. At a referendum in Dec. 1990, 93·2% of votes cast were in favour of the new constitution, which introduced a presidential regime. The *President* is directly elected for renewable five-year terms. Parliament is the unicameral *National Assembly* of 83 members elected by proportional representation for four-year terms.

A 30-member advisory *Social and Economic Council* was set up in 1994. There is a *Constitutional Court.*

National Anthem

'L'Aube Nouvelle' ('The Dawn of a New Day'); words and tune by Gilbert Jean Dagnon.

Recent Elections

In the first round of presidential elections held on 6 March 2016 Lionel Zinsou (Cowry Forces for an Emerging Benin) won 28·4% of the vote against Patrice Talon (ind.) with 23·8%, Sébastien Ajavon (ind.) with 23·0%, Abdoulaye Bio-Tchané (Alliance for a Triumphant Benin) with 8·8% and Pascal Koupaki (New Consciousness Rally) with 5·9%. 28 other candidates won less than 2% of the vote each. Talon won the second round run-off on 20 March 2016 with 65·4% against Zinsou with 34·6%. Turnout was 64·0% in the first round and 66·1% in the second round.

Parliamentary elections were held on 26 April 2015. The Cowry Forces for an Emerging Benin–Amana Alliance, a coalition supporting then President Yayi Boni, won 33 of 83 seats; Union Makes the Nation, 13; Democratic Renewal Party, 10; Benin Rebirth Party–Patriotic Revival Party, 7; National Alliance for Development and Democracy, 5; Sun Alliance, 4; United Democratic Forces, 4; the Scout Alliance, 2; Alliance for a Triumphant Benin, 2; Union for Benin, 2; the Atao Network, 1.

Current Government

President: Patrice Talon; b. 1958 (ind.; sworn in 6 April 2016).

In Feb. 2019 the government comprised:

Ministers of State: Pascal Irénée Koupaki (also *Secretary General of the Presidency*); Abdoulaye Bio Tchané (*in Charge of Planning and Development*).

Minister of Agriculture, Livestock and Fisheries: Gaston Dossouhoui. *Decentralization and Local Government:* Barnabé Dassigli. *Digital Economy and Communication:* Aurélie Adam Soulé. *Economy and Finance:* Romuald Wadagni. *Energy:* Dona Jean-Claude Houssou. *Foreign Affairs and Co-operation:* Aurélien Agbénonci. *Health:* Benjamin Hounkpatin. *Higher Education and Scientific Research:* Marie-Odile Attanasso. *Industry and Commerce:* Serges Ahissou. *Infrastructure and Transport:* Alassane Séidou. *Interior and Public Security:* Sacca Lafia. *Justice and Legislation and Keeper of the Seals:* Sévérin Quenum. *Labour and Civil Service:* Adidjatou Mathys. *Pre-Primary and Primary Education:* Karimou Salimane. *Quality of Life and Sustainable Development:* José Didier Tonato. *Secondary and Technical Education and Vocational Training:* Mahougnon Kakpo. *Small and Medium-Sized Enterprise, and Employment Promotion:* Modeste Kérékou. *Social Affairs and Microfinance:* Bintou Chabi Adam. *Tourism, Culture and Sports:* Oswald Homeky. *Water and Mines:* Samou Séidou Adambi. *Minister Delegate in the Presidency in Charge of National Defence:* Fortunet Alain Nouatin.

Government Website (French only): http://www.gouv.bj

Current Leaders

Patrice Talon

Position
President

Introduction
Patrice Talon became president of Benin on 20 March 2016. Having amassed a fortune from the cotton industry, he was a close ally of former president Yayi Boni (who was in power from 2006–16) before being accused in 2012 of plotting a coup. He was pardoned in 2014.

Early Life
Patrice Guillaume Athanase Talon was born in Ouidah on 1 May 1958. He earned a baccalaureate in Dakar, Senegal, before joining the science faculty of the University of Dakar. He subsequently went into agribusiness in Paris, France.

In 1985 he returned to Benin and established the Société de Distribution Intercontinentale (SDI), which supplied agricultural products to the cotton industry. In the 1990s Benin began to privatize the industry and Talon used his close ties with government to establish a near monopoly, earning him the nickname 'king of cotton'.

Talon was one of the chief financial backers of Yayi Boni's election campaign in 2006 and again in 2011. In 2009 and 2011 respectively his company, Benin Control, acquired two nationally important enterprises, Sodeco and PVI. However, in 2012 Yayi Boni accused Talon of mismanagement and financial misappropriation before taking Sodeco and PVI into state control. The president also accused his former ally of plotting to poison him and to orchestrate a coup.

Talon fled to Paris but was officially pardoned in 2014, although a number of charges against him remain unresolved. In 2015 US business magazine *Forbes* listed him as the 15th richest individual in sub-Saharan Africa with personal wealth of some US$400m.

Career in Office
During his 2016 presidential campaign Talon promised to reform the state and harness the country's 'collective drive'. In particular, he pledged to reform the courts and to dilute executive powers, although his proposal to restrict the presidency to a single six-year term was narrowly rejected by parliament in April 2017. After taking office, he named lawyer Joseph Djogbénou (who previously defended him against the coup charges) as minister of justice and included three women in his first government.

Defence

There is selective conscription for 18 months. Defence expenditure totalled US$86m. in 2013 (US$9 per capita), representing 1·0% of GDP.

Army

The Army strength (2011) was 4,300, with an additional 2,500-strong paramilitary gendarmerie.

Navy

Personnel in 2011 numbered about 200; the force is based at Cotonou.

Air Force

The Air Force has suffered a shortage of funds and operates no combat aircraft. Personnel, 2011, 250.

Economy

Agriculture, forestry and fishing contributed 33·0% to GDP in 2013; followed by trade and restaurants, 15·9%; finance and real estate, 10·6%; and transport and communications, 10·1%.

Overview

In the first decade of this century the economy grew on average by 3·9% per year. GDP growth slipped to 2·6% in 2010, lower than predicted as a result of flooding and weak exports, but then averaged 5% per year between 2012 and 2017. Foreign direct investment (predominantly focused on oil exploration) decreased by 14% between 2015 and 2016, while average inflation stood at 1·2% between 2012 and 2016.

The services and agricultural sectors dominate, accounting for more than 75% of GDP in 2016, with cotton production particularly important. The Agricultural Productivity and Diversification Program launched in 2011 seeks to implement improved technologies to develop food security and diversify production.

Benin's geographical location makes it an important transit point for exports from neighbouring countries including Burkina Faso and Nigeria. Benin aims to become an emerging economy by 2025 by achieving the United Nations Millennium Development Goals. However, regional disparities, high levels of poverty, corruption and inefficiency are impediments to long-term growth.

Currency

The unit of currency is the *franc CFA* (XOF) with a parity of 655·957 francs CFA to one euro. Total money supply was 394,434m. francs CFA in June 2005 and foreign exchange reserves were US$692m. There was deflation of 0·8% in 2016 but inflation of 0·1% in 2017.

Budget

The fiscal year is the calendar year. In 2014 revenues were 902·4bn. francs CFA and expenditures 960·2bn. francs CFA.

VAT is 18%.

Performance

Real GDP growth was 2·1% in 2015, 4·0% in 2016 and 5·6% in 2017. Total GDP was US$9·3bn. in 2017.

Banking and Finance

The bank of issue and the central bank is the regional Central Bank of West African States (BCEAO). The *Governor* is Tiémoko Meyliet Koné. In 2009 there were 13 banks and one financial institute. The Caisse Autonome d'Amortissement du Bénin manages state funds.

Total foreign debt was US$1,221m. in 2010, representing 18% of GNI.

Energy and Natural Resources

Environment

Benin's carbon dioxide emissions from the consumption of energy in 2011 were the equivalent of 0·6 tonnes per capita.

Electricity

Installed capacity in 2011 was an estimated 171,000 kW. In 2011 production was 154m. kWh; Benin also imported 925m. kWh. Consumption per capita in 2011 was 110 kWh.

Oil and Gas

The Semé oilfield, located 15 km offshore, was discovered in 1968. Production commenced in 1982 but ceased in 2004. Crude petroleum reserves in 2011 were 8m. bbls.

Agriculture

Benin's economy is underdeveloped, and is dependent on subsistence agriculture. In 2013 an estimated 2·7m. ha. were arable and 0·5m. ha. permanent crops; about 23,000 ha. were suitable for irrigation in 2013. Production in 1,000 tonnes in 2014 (unless otherwise indicated): cassava, 4,067; yams, 3,221; maize, 1,354; palm fruit oil, 583 (estimate); seed cotton, 382; tomatoes (2013), 332; rice, 234; cottonseed, 180 (estimate); groundnuts, 145.

Livestock, 2014: cattle, 2,222,000; goats, 1,755,000; sheep, 878,000; pigs, 431,000; chickens, 19m.

Livestock products, 2013 (in 1,000 tonnes): beef and veal, 31; goat meat, 5; pork and pork products, 5; poultry meat, 24; eggs, 13; milk, 42.

Forestry

In 2015 there were 4·31m. ha. of forest (39% of the total land area), mainly in the north. Timber production in 2011 was 6·79m. cu. metres.

Fisheries

Total catch in 2015 was 36,477 tonnes, mainly freshwater fish.

Industry

Only about 2% of the workforce is employed in industry. The main activities include palm-oil processing, brewing and the manufacture of cement, sugar and textiles. Also important are cigarettes, food, construction materials and petroleum. Production (2007 unless otherwise specified, in 1,000 tonnes): cement (2010 estimate), 40; cottonseed oil, 22; groundnut oil (estimate), 10; raw sugar, 10; sawnwood, 84,000 cu. metres.

Labour

The estimated labour force numbered 3,825,000 in 2010 (54% males), up from 3,212,000 in 2005. Approximately half of the economically active population is engaged in agriculture, fishing and forestry.

Benin had 80,000 people living in slavery according to the Walk Free Foundation's 2013 *Global Slavery Index*.

International Trade

Commercial and transport activities, which make up 36% of GDP, are extremely vulnerable to developments in neighbouring Nigeria, with which there is a significant amount of illegal trade.

Imports and Exports

Merchandise imports in 2014 totalled US$3,596·1m. (US$2,940·7m. in 2013) and merchandise exports US$951·0m. (US$602·0m. in 2013).

Principal imports in 2014 were food, animals and beverages (45·1%) followed by machinery and transport equipment, and mineral fuels and lubricants; main exports in 2014 were crude materials and animal and vegetable oils (35·0%) followed by machinery and transport equipment, and food, animals and beverages.

The main import partners are France, China and Côte d'Ivoire. Principal export partners are China, Nigeria and India.

Communications

Roads

Benin had some 15,700 km of roads in 2010, of which about 6,100 km were main roads. Passenger cars in use in 2007 totalled 149,300, buses and coaches 1,100, and lorries and vans 35,700.

Rail

In 2005 there were 438 km of metre gauge railway. In 2007 railways carried 0·1m. tonnes of freight. Passenger services were suspended in 2007 but have since resumed on a limited basis.

Civil Aviation

The international airport is at Cotonou (Cadjehoun), which in 2012 handled 466,778 passengers (all on international flights) and 5,237 tonnes of freight. Westair Benin, the only operational airline based in the country, was founded in 2002. In 2010 there were direct flights to 17 destinations in Africa as well as Paris.

Shipping

There is a port at Cotonou, which handled 7,841,000 tonnes of cargo in 2013 (864,000 tonnes loaded and 6,977,000 tonnes discharged).

Telecommunications

Mobile phone subscribers numbered 10,562,647 in 2014 (996·5 per 1,000 persons). In the same year there were 195,662 main (fixed) telephone lines. 5·3% of the population were internet subscribers in 2014.

Social Institutions

Out of 178 countries analysed in the 2017 *Fragile States Index*—a list published jointly by the Fund for Peace and *Foreign Policy* magazine—Benin was ranked the 73rd most vulnerable to conflict or collapse. The index is based on 12 indicators of state vulnerability across social, political and economic categories.

Justice

The Supreme Court is at Cotonou. There are Magistrates Courts and a *tribunal de conciliation* in each district. The legal system is based on French civil law and customary law.

The population in penal institutions in 2010 was 6,908 (75 per 100,000 of national population). 74·9% of prisoners had yet to receive a trial according to 2014 estimates by the International Centre for Prison Studies. The death penalty was abolished in Aug. 2011.

Education

Adult literacy rate was 41% in 2008. In 2015 there were 2,238,185 pupils in primary schools with 49,688 teaching staff and 963,787 pupils in secondary schools with 93,366 teaching staff. There were 42,603 students in higher education in 2006. The leading institution in the tertiary sector is the National University of Benin (Université Nationale du Bénin), located in Cotonou.

In 2006 public expenditure on education came to 3·9% of GNI and 18·0% of total government spending.

Health

In 2006 there were 1,088 physicians, 3,563 nurses and 999 midwives. There were three hospital beds per 10,000 inhabitants in 2006.

In *Water: At What Cost? The State of the World's Water 2016*, WaterAid reported that 22·1% of the population does not have access to safe water.

Religion

In 2010 there were an estimated 4·7m. Christians, 2·1m. Muslims and 1·6m. folk religionists according to the Pew Research Center's Forum on Religion & Public Life. A further 450,000 people had no religious affiliation. Catholics account for around 56% of Christians and Protestants 43%. Voodoo became an official religion in 1996.

Culture

World Heritage Sites

The Royal Palaces of Abomey joined the World Heritage List in 1985 (reinscribed in 2007). They preserve the remains of the palaces of 12 kings who ruled the former kingdom of Abomey between 1625 and 1900. The W-Arly-Pendjari Complex (1996 and 2017) is shared with Burkina Faso and Niger. It includes the largest and most important continuum of terrestrial, semi-aquatic and aquatic ecosystems in the West African savannah belt.

Press

In 2008 there were 38 daily newspapers with an average circulation of 50,000. The main newspapers are *Le Matinal*, *Les Echos du Jour* and the government-controlled *La Nation*.

Tourism

In 2011 there were 209,000 non-resident tourists. Tourist spending totalled US$188m. in 2011.

Diplomatic Representatives

Of Benin in the United Kingdom
   Ambassador: Vacant (resides in Paris).
   Honorary Consul: Vacant (Millennium House, Humber Rd, London, NW2 6DW).

Of the United Kingdom in Benin
   Ambassador: Iain Walker (resides in Accra, Ghana).

Of Benin in the USA (2124 Kalorama Rd, NW, Washington, D.C., 20008)
   Ambassador: Hector Sedozan Ruffin Festus Posset.

Of the USA in Benin (Marina Ave., Cotonou)
   Ambassador: Vacant.
   Chargé d'Affaires a.i.: Laura Hruby.

Of Benin to the United Nations
   Ambassador: Jean-Claude do Rego.

Of Benin to the European Union
   Ambassador: Richard Zacharie Akplogan.

Further Reading

Bay, E., *Wives of the Leopard: Gender, Politics, and Culture in the Kingdom of Dahomey.* 1998
National Statistical Office: Institut National de la Statistique et de l'Analyse Économique, 01 BP 323, Cotonou.
Website (French only): http://www.insae-bj.org

Bhutan

Druk-yul (Kingdom of Bhutan)

Capital: Thimphu
Population projection, 2020: 835,000
GNI per capita, 2017: (PPP$) 8,065
HDI/world rank, 2017: 0·612/134=
Internet domain extension: .bt

Key Historical Events

Indigenous Monpa clans established settlements in the eastern Himalayas by around 2000 BC. Buddhism was brought to Bhutan in the 7th century AD when Tibetan lamas (monks) founded monasteries at Bumthang and Kyichi, although animist beliefs persisted among the scattered villages. It was the arrival in 1616 of a monk, Zhabdrung Nawang Namgyal, fleeing persecution in Tibet, which led to the foundation of the kingdom of Bhutan. Over a period of 35 years Zhabdrung and his followers built fortresses and monasteries and established the Drukpa sect of Buddhism as well as a dual system of governance known as the Chhoesid. Power was split between the Deb Raja, the head of secular affairs (responsible for four regional governors) and the Dharma Raja, the spiritual head who was charged with enacting laws. In 1720 the Ch'ing dynasty took control of Tibet, claiming suzerainty of it and neighbouring Bhutan.

Tensions between Bhutan and Bengal to the south culminated in a Bhutanese invasion of Cooch Behar in 1772. This prompted the governor of the province to seek military assistance from the British who had defeated the Nawab of Bengal in 1757. Skirmishes continued for two years until peace was brokered by Tashi Lama, then Regent of Tibet. British attempts to develop trade with Bhutan in the 1780s were unsuccessful and new tensions emerged when British India took control of neighbouring Assam in 1826. In 1864 British India claimed ownership of a strip of southern Bhutan known as the Duars. It was formally ceded to India the following year, although the Treaty of Sinchula provided for an annual subsidy to Bhutan as compensation.

In 1907 the office of Dharma Raja came to an end. The governor of Tongsa, Ugyen Wangchuck, was then chosen as Maharajah of Bhutan, the first of a hereditary line (the title is now King of Bhutan). He concluded a treaty with British India in 1910 which allowed for internal autonomy with British control of foreign policy in return for doubling Britain's annual subsidy. After Indian independence, a treaty of 1949 returned the Duars to Bhutan. The kingdom continued to manage its internal affairs while India inherited control of Bhutan's defence and foreign affairs.

When Communist Chinese forces invaded Tibet in 1950, Bhutan was claimed as part of 'Greater Tibet'. In response, India closed the Bhutan–Tibet border and upgraded roads linking Bengal with Bhutan. Amid mounting Indo-Sino tensions in the early 1960s, Bhutan established a small army, trained and equipped by India. The reign of the third king, Jigme Dorji Wangchuk (1952–72), was marked by gradual economic development and an opening up to the outside world. The 151-seat National Assembly was established in 1952 and Bhutan became a member of the United Nations in 1971, since when relations with China have slowly thawed.

In the early 1990s, tens of thousands of 'illegal immigrants', mostly Nepali-speaking Hindus, were forcibly expelled from southern and western Bhutan. Twenty years on, there are still more than 85,000 people claiming to be Bhutanese refugees in camps set up by the UNHCR in eastern Nepal, although around 23,000 have been resettled in the USA and Europe since March 2008. Bhutan was ruled from 1972–2006 by King Jigme Singye Wangchuck. He abdicated in Dec. 2006 in favour of his son, Jigme Kesar Namgyel Wangchuck. In Dec. 2007 and March 2008 Bhutan held its first democratic parliamentary elections. The leader of the Druk Phuensum Tshogpa (Bhutan Peace and Prosperity Party), Jigme Thinley, took office as the first elected prime minister of Bhutan on 9 April 2008.

Territory and Population

Bhutan is situated in the eastern Himalayas, bounded in the north by Tibet and on all other sides by India. In 1949 India retroceded 83 sq. km of Dewangiri, annexed in 1865. Area 38,394 sq. km (14,824 sq. miles); 2017 census population, 727,145 (380,453 males), giving a density of 19 per sq. km.

The UN gives a projected population for 2020 of 835,000.

In 2017, 37·8% of the population lived in urban areas. A Nepalese minority makes up 30–35% of the population, mainly in the south. The capital is Thimphu (2017 population, 138,736). The country is divided into 20 districts (*dzongkhag*).

The official language is Dzongkha.

Social Statistics

2008 (estimates) births, 14,800 (rate of 21·5 per 1,000 population); deaths, 4,900 (rate of 7·1 per 1,000 population). Life expectancy at birth, 2013, was 68·0 years for men and 68·7 years for women. Infant mortality, 2010, 44 per 1,000 live births. Annual population growth rate, 2000–08, 2·5%; fertility rate, 2008, 2·6 children per woman.

Climate

The climate is largely controlled by altitude. The mountainous north is cold, with perpetual snow on the summits, but the centre has a more moderate climate, though winters are cold, with rainfall under 40" (1,000 mm). In the south, the climate is humid sub-tropical and rainfall approaches 200" (5,000 mm).

Constitution and Government

Bhutan's first formal constitution came into force on 18 July 2008, after a period of almost seven years of planning. There is a bicameral parliament. The lower house is the *National Assembly* (with a maximum of 55 members but currently with 47, all elected) and the upper house the 25-member *National Council* (with 20 members elected and five appointed by the king). Executive power is vested in the *Council of Ministers*.

The reigning King is Jigme Kesar Namgyel Wangchuck (born 1980), who succeeded his father King Jigme Singye Wangchuck (abdicated 14 Dec. 2006). He was crowned on 6 Nov. 2008. Married on 13 Oct. 2011 to Jetsun Pema (b. 4 June 1990). *Offspring:* Prince Jigme Namgyel Wangchuck, b. 5 Feb. 2016. With the introduction of democratic elections in 2007–08, the King's role became more ceremonial. Nonetheless, all leading political parties have affirmed their loyalty to the monarchy, which remains central to political life.

In 1907 the Tongsa Penlop (the governor of the province of Tongsa in central Bhutan), Sir Ugyen Wangchuck, GCIE, KCSI, was elected as the first hereditary Maharaja of Bhutan. The Bhutanese title is Druk Gyalpo, and his successors are addressed as King of Bhutan. The stated goal is to increase Gross National Happiness.

National Anthem

'Druk tsendhen koipi gyelknap na' ('In the Thunder Dragon Kingdom'); words by Gyaldun Dasho Thinley Dorji, tune by A. Tongmi.

Recent Elections

Bhutan's first ever elections were held on 31 Dec. 2007 when 15 members (all independents) were elected to the National Council (the non-partisan upper house of Bhutan's bicameral parliament). A further five members were elected on 29 Jan. 2008. In the third National Council elections, 20 members (again, all independents) were elected in single-member constituencies on 20 April 2018. A further five members were appointed by the king.

© Springer Nature Limited 2020
Palgrave Macmillan (ed.), *The Statesman's Yearbook 2020*,
https://doi.org/10.1057/978-1-349-95940-2_32

Two rounds of elections for Bhutan's National Assembly were held on 15 Sept. and 18 Oct. 2018. The 47 seats were contested by four parties in the first round, with the two parties that won the highest number of votes progressing to the second round. In the second round the Druk Nyamrup Tshogpa (DNT), led by Lotay Tshering, won 30 of the 47 seats with 55·0% of the vote against the Druk Phuensum Tshogpa (DPT; Bhutan Peace and Prosperity Party), led by Pema Gyamtsho, which gained 17 seats and 45·0% of the vote. Turnout was 66·4% in the first round and 71·5% in the second.

Current Government

In Feb. 2019 the government comprised:

Prime Minister: Lotay Tshering; b. 1968 (Druk Nyamrup Tshogpa; took office on 7 Nov. 2018).

Minister for Agriculture and Forests: Yeshey Penjor. *Economic Affairs:* Loknath Sharma. *Education:* Jai Bir Rai. *Finance:* Namgay Tshering. *Foreign Affairs:* Tandi Dorji. *Health:* Dechen Wangmo. *Home and Cultural Affairs:* Sherub Gyeltshen. *Information and Communications:* Karma Donnen Wangdi. *Labour and Human Resources:* Ugyen Dorji. *Works and Human Settlement:* Dorji Tshering.

Government Website: http://www.bhutan.gov.bt

Current Leaders

Lotay Tshering

Position
Prime Minister

Introduction
Lotay Tshering became prime minister of Bhutan in Nov. 2018.

Early Life
Lotay Tshering was born on 14 March 1968 in Dalukha village, Mewang Gewog, in Bhutan's capital district of Thimphu. He graduated in medicine and surgery from Dhaka University in Bangladesh in 2001. In 2007 he received a World Health Organization fellowship to study urology at the Medical College of Wisconsin in the United States, later becoming the only practising trained urologist in Bhutan. In 2010 he completed medical fellowships at the Singapore General Hospital and Okayama University in Japan. He also served as a consulting surgeon and urologist at the National Referral Hospital in Thimphu, treated patients on behalf of the king's mobile medical unit, and hosted a television programme on health and medicine. In 2005 he had received the Unsung Hero of Compassion Award from the Dalai Lama.

In 2013 he resigned as a civil servant in the ministry of health to pursue a career in front-line politics but lost a bid for parliament as a candidate of the Druk Nyamrup Tshogpa (Bhutan United Party). The following year he was awarded a master's degree in business administration from Australia's University of Canberra. He was elected president of the Druk Nyamrup Tshogpa in May 2018, ahead of parliamentary elections later in the year. Under his leadership, the party adopted the slogan 'Narrowing the Gap' and promised to deliver programmes addressing youth unemployment, crop insurance schemes, and shortfalls in health and social services. His party emerged from the elections as the largest in parliament and Tshering was sworn in as premier on 7 Nov. 2018.

Career in Office
Tshering made his first international trip as prime minister in Dec. 2018 when he visited India, Bhutan's primary trade partner and source of financial aid. Tshering aims to transform the country's relationship with India from dependency to partnership, and to this end has championed new ventures in tourism and hydro-electric power.

Defence

Army

In 2008 the Royal Bhutan Army had a strength of 8,000. It is lightly armed, mainly with weapons supplied by India. There is also a small Air Arm.

Economy

Agriculture accounted for 17·7% of GDP in 2014, with industry accounting for 42·9% and services 39·4%.

Overview

Although its economy has historically been based on subsistence agriculture and cottage industry, Bhutan is considered a development success story following a remarkable period of economic expansion and improvement in human development indicators. GDP growth averaged 8·1% in the decade 2003–13, while the poverty rate reduced from 31·7% in 2003 to 12·0% in 2012, and GDP per capita nearly doubled from 2004–14. There was further robust growth averaging 4·8% per year between 2013 and 2017. Developments in hydro-power and related construction, as well as growth in domestic services, have been the driving forces behind economic prosperity.

The country has benefited from its proximity to India, which typically is the destination for over 80% of Bhutan's exports and the source of 75% of its imports. The currency, the *ngultrum*, is pegged to the Indian rupee and the Indian government finances a large part of Bhutan's budget expenditures.

Agriculture employs over 40% of the labour force, although its share of GDP has steadily declined. Sales of cement, production of which is one of the country's few large-scale industries, have grown since about 2005, reflecting strong performance in the construction and manufacturing sectors. Public expenditure, guided by the government ideology of Gross National Happiness, is focused on health and education.

Public debt stood at 111·5% of GDP in 2017, much of which was incurred through hydro-power projects, and such a high level remains a key challenge. In terms of ease of doing business, Bhutan rose in the World Bank's annual *Doing Business* rankings from 125th of 189 countries in 2015 to 76th in 2017.

Currency

The unit of currency is the *ngultrum* (BTN) of 100 *chetrum*, at parity with the Indian rupee. Indian currency is also legal tender. Foreign exchange reserves were US$632m. in Jan. 2008 and total money supply was Nu12,575bn. Inflation was 7·6% in 2016 and 5·8% in 2017.

Budget

Budgetary central government revenue and expenditure (in Nu1m.):

	2011–12	2012–13	2013–14
Revenue	32,796	30,613	37,425
Expenditure	19,915	21,226	21,715

Taxes accounted for 42·6% of revenues in 2013–14 and grants 38·0%; compensation of employees accounted for 38·1% of expenditures and use of goods and services 31·8%.

Performance

Real GDP growth was 6·2% in 2015, 7·3% in 2016 and 7·4% in 2017. Total GDP in 2017 was US$2·5bn.

Banking and Finance

The Royal Monetary Authority (founded 1982; *Governor,* Dasho Penjore) acts as the central bank. Assets (June 2010) Nu38·25bn. Financial sector total assets were Nu55·29bn. in June 2010 with the country's four commercial banks accounting for 90·6% of assets. The oldest and largest commercial bank is the Bank of Bhutan, which was established in 1968 and operated as the central bank until 1982. The headquarters are at Phuentsholing with 26 branches throughout the country. It is 80%-owned by the government of Bhutan and 20%-owned by the Indian government. There is also a development bank (the Bhutan Development Finance Corporation) and a stock exchange in Thimphu.

In 2010 Bhutan's total external debt amounted to US$898m., equivalent to 63·3% of GNI.

Energy and Natural Resources

Environment

Bhutan's carbon dioxide emissions from the consumption of energy in 2011 were the equivalent of 0·5 tonnes per capita.

Electricity

Installed capacity in 2010–11 was 1·5m. kW (nearly all hydro-electric). Production (2010–11) was 7·1bn. kWh. Consumption per capita in 2010–11 was 2,495 kWh. Bhutan exports around 75% of the electricity that it produces, mainly to India. There are four major hydro-electric plants in operation, three of which were financed by neighbouring India. Four further installations are under construction.

Minerals
Large deposits of limestone, marble, dolomite, slate, graphite, lead, copper, coal, talc, gypsum, beryl, mica, pyrites and tufa have been found. Most mining activity (principally limestone, coal, slate and dolomite) is on a small-scale. Output, 2010: dolomite, 1,192,000 tonnes; limestone, 716,000 tonnes; gypsum, 344,000 tonnes; coal, 88,000 tonnes.

Agriculture
The agricultural area in 2007 was an estimated 562,000 ha. In 2007 there were an estimated 128,000 ha. of arable land and 27,000 ha. of permanent crops. The chief products (2007 estimated production in 1,000 tonnes) are rice (74), maize (62), potatoes (61), oranges (37), dried chillies and peppers (11) and ginger (10).

Livestock (2005): cattle, 381,000; goats (estimate), 30,000; pigs, 28,000; horses, 25,000; sheep, 18,000.

Forestry
In 2015, 2·76m. ha. (72% of the land area) were forested. Timber production in 2011 was 5·03m. cu. metres.

Industry
Industries in Bhutan include cement, wood products, processed fruits, alcoholic beverages and calcium carbide. In 2014 manufacturing accounted for 8·6% of GDP. 2012 production (estimates): cement, 521,000 tonnes; wood-based panels, 29,000 cu. metres; particle board, 27,000 cu. metres; sawnwood, 27,000 cu. metres.

Labour
The labour force in 2013 was 393,400 (273,300 in 2003). 74·8% of the population aged 15–64 was economically active in 2013. In the same year 2·9% of the population was unemployed.

International Trade
Financial support is received from India, the UN and other international aid organizations.

Imports and Exports
The following table shows the value of Bhutan's foreign trade (in US$1m.):

	Imports (f.o.b.)	Exports (c.i.f.)
2006	418·9	413·9
2007	498·1	674·5
2008	543·3	521·4
2009	529·4	495·8
2010	853·8	413·5

India is by far the biggest trading partner. In 2010 the leading import suppliers (in US$1m.) were: India (640·8); South Korea (43·8); Thailand (21·6). The main export markets in 2010 (in US$1m.) were: India (340·8); Hong Kong (47·8); Bangladesh (19·8). Major imports are machinery and transport equipment, manufactured goods, and mineral fuels and lubricants. Hydro-power, ferrosilicon and cement are the main exports.

Communications

Roads
In 2006 there were about 4,153 km of roads, of which 1,577 km were highways. In 2007 there were 19,600 passenger cars, 180 buses and coaches, 5,400 lorries and vans, and 7,500 motorcycles and mopeds. A number of sets of traffic lights were installed during the late 1990s but all have subsequently been removed as they were considered to be eyesores. There had previously been just one set. There were 111 fatalities in road accidents in 2007.

Rail
Bhutan does not currently have a railway network but there are plans for a line funded by India that would potentially provide links between a number of towns in Bhutan and India.

Civil Aviation
In 2010 Drukair flew from Paro to Bagdogra (in India), Bangkok, Delhi, Dhaka, Kathmandu and Kolkata. In 2012 scheduled airline traffic of Bhutan-based carriers flew 3·0m. km; passenger-km totalled 307m. in the same year.

Telecommunications
There were 26,300 fixed telephone lines in 2010 (36·2 per 1,000 inhabitants). Mobile phone subscribers numbered 394,300 in 2010. There were 136·0 internet users per 1,000 inhabitants in 2010. Fixed internet subscriptions totalled 6,700 in 2009 (9·3 per 1,000 inhabitants).

Social Institutions
Out of 178 countries analysed in the 2017 *Fragile States Index*—a list published jointly by the Fund for Peace and *Foreign Policy* magazine—Bhutan was ranked the 83rd most vulnerable to conflict or collapse. The index is based on 12 indicators of state vulnerability across social, political and economic categories.

Justice
The High Court consists of eight judges appointed by the King. There is a Magistrate's Court in each district, under a *Thrimpon*, from which appeal is to the High Court at Thimphu. The death penalty, which had not been used for 40 years, was abolished in 2004.

The population in penal institutions in July 2011 was 1,001 (135 per 100,000 of national population).

Education
In 2008–09 there were 109,000 pupils and 4,000 teachers in primary schools and 57,000 pupils with 3,000 teachers in secondary schools. In 2006 there were 4,141 students in tertiary education and 375 academic staff. Adult literacy was 52·8% in 2005.

In 2005 public expenditure on education came to 7·1% of GNI and 17·2% of total government spending.

Health
In 2006 there were 29 hospitals with 1,133 beds, 176 basic health units and 514 outreach clinics. There were two doctors per 10,000 population in 2005. Free health facilities are available to 90% of the population.

Religion
The state religion of Bhutan is the Drukpa Kagyupa, a branch of Mahayana Buddhism. Around 23% of the population is Hindu according to the Pew Research Center's Forum on Religion & Public Life.

Culture

Press
Until 2006 there was only one newspaper, the government-controlled *Kuensel*, which is published in English, Dzongkha and Nepali. Two private non-dailies were launched in 2006. The country's first daily paper, the English-language *Bhutan Today*, was launched in 2008 and had an average daily circulation of 18,000 that year. Although still published, it no longer appears daily.

Tourism
Bhutan was not formally opened to foreign tourists until 1974, but tourism is now the largest source of foreign exchange. In 2013, 116,000 tourists visited Bhutan (up from 28,000 in 2008).

Festivals
Bhutan's most famous festival is Tshechu, a religious celebration of Guru Padsambhava held throughout the country at the end of the harvest. The Thimphu Tshechu takes place around mid-Sept. and includes spectacular masked dances performed by monks. Other important festivals include Dromche (to honour the protective deities of the Bhutanese people) and Jambay Lhakhan Drup (including a fire dance to promote fertility).

Diplomatic Representatives

Of Bhutan in the United Kingdom
Honorary Consul: Michael R. Rutland (2 Windacres, Warren Rd, Guildford, Surrey, GU1 2HG).

Of Bhutan to the United Nations
Ambassador: Doma Tshering.

Of Bhutan to the European Union
Ambassador: Pema Choden.

Further Reading

Crossette, B., *So Close to Heaven: The Vanishing Buddhist Kingdoms of the Himalayas.* 1995
Parmanand, Parashar, *The Politics of Bhutan: Retrospect and Prospect.* 2002
Rahul, Ram, *Royal Bhutan: A Political History.* 1997
Savada, A. M. (ed.) *Nepal and Bhutan: Country Studies.* 1993
Sinha, A. C., *Bhutan: Ethnic Identity and National Dilemma.* 1998.—*Himalayan Kingdom Bhutan: Tradition, Transition and Transformation.* 2002
National Statistical Office: National Statistics Bureau, Thimphu.
Website: http://www.nsb.gov.bt

Bolivia

Estado Plurinacional de Bolivia (Plurinational State of Bolivia)

Capital: Sucre
Seat of government: La Paz
Population projection, 2020: 11·54m.
GNI per capita, 2017: (PPP$) 6,714
HDI/world rank, 2017: 0·693/118
Internet domain extension: .bo

Key Historical Events

Archaeological evidence from the Bolivian Amazon's Llanos de Moxos region points to hunter-gatherer settlements dating from 8000 BC. Small farming settlements were established by 1500 BC on the Altiplano high plains to the southeast of Lake Titicaca and one of them, Tiwanaku, developed sophisticated irrigation techniques that by AD 800 may have supported hundreds of thousands of people. However, the Tiwanaku civilization appears to have waned after AD 950 when there was a shift to drier climatic conditions. In the mid-15th century the area around Lake Titicaca came under the control of the Quechua-speaking Inca people, originally from the Cusco valley. Under Huayna Capac (1464–1527) the empire stretched along the Andes from Ecuador to Chile.

By the late 1520s the Inca civilization was waning, beset by internal rivalries and a feud between Huayna Capac's two sons, Huasca and Atahualpa. The Spanish, led by Francisco Pizarro and Diego de Almagro, landed on the Ecuadorian coast in 1531, building alliances with local groups who resented Inca rule. After victory at the 1532 Battle of Cajamara, the Spanish conquistadors took Cusco. The Alto Peru high plains briefly came under the control of Almagro, and then Pizarro following the former's assassination in 1538. In that year La Plata (later Sucre) was established as the capital of Alto Peru. It was controlled after 1542 by the Viceroyalty of Peru, which for a time had jurisdiction over all the Spanish colonies in South America.

Having liberated Colombia and Venezuela in the 1820s, Simón Bolívar sent Antonio José de Sucre to counter Spanish royalists further south. Peru's independence came after a prolonged guerrilla war and victory for Bolívar and Sucre's forces in the battles of Junin and Ayacucho in 1824. Alto Peru was declared the Republic of Bolivia on 6 Aug. 1825, with Bolívar its president. A presidential successor, Andrés de Santa Cruz, forged a short-lived union with Peru until 1839. Bolivia's political and military weaknesses—exposed during the 1879–83 War of the Pacific—led to its loss of access to lucrative coastal and nitrate resources to Chile.

Economically weak and politically unstable, Bolivia lost further territory to Brazil (1903) and Paraguay (following the Chaco War, 1932–35). Poverty and poor working conditions fuelled the rise of the National Revolutionary Movement (MNR) in the 1940s. The MNR took power in 1952 after an armed revolt, led by Víctor Paz Estenssoro. His reforms included the granting of universal suffrage, land redistribution and nationalization of mines, as well as an overhaul of the education system and greater rights for indigenous peoples. A military coup staged by Vice-President René Barrientos Ortuño in 1964 brought the first of a succession of military governments. Col. Hugo Banzer Suárez's dictatorship (1971–78) became notorious for human rights abuses and political suppression.

Civilian rule was restored in 1982 when Dr Siles Zuazo became president. He introduced reforms embracing free markets and open trade, which restored stability but widened the gap between rich and poor. After several attempts to return to high office, Banzer was elected president again in 1997. His four-year term was dominated by attempts to strengthen law and order and fight drug trafficking. Amid growing discontent over rising fuel prices and mounting poverty, Evo Morales Ayma was elected as Bolivia's first indigenous president in Dec. 2005. He was re-elected in Dec. 2009 with 64% of the vote and again in Oct. 2014 with 61%.

Territory and Population

Bolivia is a landlocked state bounded in the north and east by Brazil, south by Paraguay and Argentina, and west by Chile and Peru, with an area of some 1,098,581 sq. km (424,165 sq. miles). A coastal strip of land on the Pacific passed to Chile after a war in 1884. In 1953 Chile declared Arica a free port and Bolivia has certain privileges there.

Population (2012 census): 10,059,856 (5,040,409 females); density, 9·2 per sq. km. In 2011, 67·0% of the population lived in urban areas.

The UN gives a projected population for 2020 of 11·54m.

Area and population of the departments (capitals in brackets) at the 2001 and 2012 censuses:

Departments	Area (sq. km)	Census (2001)	Census (2012)
Beni (Trinidad)	213,564	362,521	422,008
Chuquiaca (Sucre)	51,524	531,522	581,347
Cochabamba (Cochabamba)	55,631	1,455,711	1,762,761
La Paz (La Paz)	133,985	2,350,466	2,719,344
Oruro (Oruro)	53,588	391,870	494,587
Pando (Cobija)	63,827	52,525	110,436
Potosí (Potosí)	118,218	709,013	828,093
Santa Cruz (Santa Cruz de la Sierra)	370,621	2,029,471	2,657,762
Tarija (Tarija)	37,623	391,226	483,518
Total	*1,098,581*	*8,274,325*	*10,059,856*

Population (2012 census, in 1,000) of the principal towns: Santa Cruz de la Sierra, 1,442; El Alto, 847; La Paz, 759; Cochabamba, 632; Oruro, 265; Sucre, 239; Tarija, 180; Potosí, 176; Sacaba, 150.

Spanish along with the Amerindian languages Quechua and Aymará are all official languages; Tupi Guaraní is also spoken. 41% of the population identified themselves as indigenous at the 2012 census.

Social Statistics

In 2008 births totalled an estimated 263,000 (birth rate of 27·1 per 1,000 population); deaths totalled an estimated 73,000 (rate, 7·5 per 1,000); infant mortality (2010), 42 per 1,000 live births, the highest in South America. Expectation of life (2013) was 65·1 years for men and 69·5 years for women. Annual population growth rate, 2000–08, 1·9%. Fertility rate, 2008, 3·5 children per woman (the highest in South America).

Climate

The varied geography produces different climates. The low-lying areas in the Amazon Basin are warm and damp throughout the year, with heavy rainfall from Nov. to March; the Altiplano is generally dry between May and Nov. with sunshine but cold nights in June and July, while the months from Dec. to March are the wettest. La Paz, Jan. 55·9°F (13·3°C), July 50·5°F (10·3°C). Annual rainfall 20·8" (529 mm). Sucre, Jan. 58·5°F (14·7°C), July 52·7°F (11·5°C). Annual rainfall 20·1" (510 mm).

Constitution and Government

Bolivia's first constitution was adopted on 19 Nov. 1826. The present constitution, the fifteenth, came into effect following its acceptance in a referendum on 25 Jan. 2009 and defined Bolivia as 'a United Social State of Plurinational Communitarian Law'. Under its terms, running to 411 articles, the majority indigenous population has been granted increased rights (including recognition of indigenous systems of justice), state control is

© Springer Nature Limited 2020
Palgrave Macmillan (ed.), *The Statesman's Yearbook 2020*,
https://doi.org/10.1057/978-1-349-95940-2_33

extended over the exploitation of natural resources and regional autonomy is enhanced. The separation of church and state is recognized and land reforms in favour of indigenous populations enshrined. A new 'plurinational Legislative Assembly', consisting of a 130-member *Chamber of Deputies* and a 36-member *Senate*, took office following elections in Dec. 2009. The constitution also allows for the president to serve a maximum of two consecutive terms. In a referendum in Feb. 2016 an amendment that would have allowed Morales to seek a further term in 2019 was narrowly rejected. However, in Nov. 2017 the Constitutional Court overturned the referendum result and scrapped term limits, opening the way for Evo Morales to stand for a fourth term at elections scheduled for Oct. 2019.

National Anthem

'Bolivianos, el hado propicio' ('Bolivians, a favourable destiny'); words by José Ignacio Sanjinés, tune by Leopoldo Benedetto Vincenti.

Government Chronology

Heads of State since 1943. (ADN = Nationalist Democratic Action; FRB = Front of the Bolivian Revolution; MAS = Movement Towards Socialism; MIR = Movement of Revolutionary Left; MNR = Nationalist Revolutionary Movement; MNRI = Nationalist Revolutionary Movement of the Left; PSD = Social Democratic Party; PURS = Party of the Republican Socialist Union; n/p = non-partisan)

President of the Republic		
1943–46	military	Gualberto Villarroel López
Presidents of the Provisional Junta of Government		
1946	n/p	Néstor Guillén Olmos
1946–47	n/p	Tomás Monje Gutiérrez
Presidents of the Republic		
1947–49	PURS	José Enrique Hertzog Garaizábal
1949–51	PURS	Mamerto Urriolagoitia Harriague

President of the Military Junta of Government		
1951–52	military	Hugo Ballivián Rojas
Presidents of the Republic		
1952	MNR	Hernán Siles Zuazo
1952–56	MNR	Ángel Víctor Paz Estenssoro
1956–60	MNR	Hernán Siles Zuazo
1960–64	MNR	Ángel Víctor Paz Estenssoro

Presidents of the Military Junta of Government		
1964	military	Alfredo Ovando Candía
1964–65	military	René Barrientos Ortuño
1965–66	military	René Barrientos Ortuño; Alfredo Ovando Candía
1966	military	Alfredo Ovando Candía

Presidents of the Republic		
1966–69	FRB	René Barrientos Ortuño
1969	PSD-FRB	Luis Adolfo Siles Salinas
1969–70	military	Alfredo Ovando Candía
1970–71	military	Juan José Torres González

(continued)

1971–78	military	Hugo Banzer Suárez
1978	military	Juan Pereda Asbún

President of the Military Junta of Government		
1978–79	military	David Padilla Arancibia

Presidents of the Republic		
1979	military	Alberto Natusch Busch
1980–81	military	Luis García Meza Tejada
1981–82	military	Celso Torrelio Villa
1982	military	Guido Vildoso Calderón
1982–85	MNRI	Hernán Siles Zuazo
1985–89	MNR	Ángel Víctor Paz Estenssoro
1989–93	MIR	Jaime Paz Zamora
1993–97	MNR	Gonzalo Sánchez de Lozada
1997–2001	ADN	Hugo Banzer Suárez
2001–02	ADN	Jorge Fernando Quiroga Ramírez
2002–03	MNR	Gonzalo Sánchez de Lozada
2003–05	MNR	Carlos Diego Mesa Gisbert
2005–06	n/p	Eduardo Rodríguez Veltzé
2006–	MAS	Evo Morales Ayma

Recent Elections

Presidential elections were held on 12 Oct. 2014. Evo Morales Ayma (Movement Towards Socialism) won 61·0% of votes cast against 24·5% for Samuel Doria Medina (Democratic Unity), 9·1% for Jorge Quiroga (Christian Democratic Party), 2·7% for Juan del Granado (Movement without Fear) and 2·7% for Fernando Vargas (Green Party of Bolivia).

In elections to the Chamber of Deputies, also held on 12 Oct. 2014, the Movement Towards Socialism won 84 seats, Democratic Unity 33, the Christian Democratic Party 11, Movement without Fear 1 and Green Party of Bolivia 1. Of the 130 seats, 69 (53·1%) are held by women. Only Rwanda and Cuba have a higher percentage of female MPs. In Senate elections of the same day Movement Towards Socialism won 25 seats, Democratic Unity 9 and the Christian Democratic Party 2.

Current Government

President: Evo Morales Ayma; b. 1959 (Movement Towards Socialism; sworn in 22 Jan. 2006 and re-elected 6 Dec. 2009 and 12 Oct. 2014).

Vice-President: Álvaro García Linera.

In Feb. 2019 the cabinet was composed as follows:

Minister of Communication: Gisela López. *Culture and Tourism:* Wilma Alanoca Mamani. *Defence:* Javier Zavaleta. *Economy and Public Finance:* Mario Alberto Guillén. *Education:* Roberto Iván Aguilar Gómez. *Energy:* Rafael Alarcón. *Environment and Water:* Carlos Ortuño. *Foreign Relations:* Diego Pary. *Health:* Rodolfo Rocabado. *Hydrocarbons:* Luis Alberto Sánchez. *Interior:* Gabriela Montaño. *Justice and Institutional Transparency:* Héctor Arce. *Labour, Employment and Social Security:* Héctor Hinojosa. *Mining and Metals:* César Navarro. *Planning:* Mariana Prado. *Presidency:* Alfredo Rada. *Productive Development and Pluralist Economics:* Eugenio Rojas. *Public Works, Services and Housing:* Milton Claros Hinojosa. *Rural Development and Lands:* César Hugo Cocarico Yana. *Sport:* Tito Rolando Montaño Rivera.

Office of the President (Spanish only): http://www.presidencia.gob.bo

Current Leaders

Juan Evo Morales Ayma

Position

President

Introduction

Evo Morales Ayma became Bolivia's first indigenous president in Jan. 2006, promising to transform the fortunes of South America's poorest country. The former coca farmer and left-wing activist has sought to embed a state-led socialist economy and strengthen presidential powers, and has been a leading critic of US foreign policies. He was re-elected in Dec. 2009 and again in Oct. 2014.

Early Life

Evo Morales Ayma was born in the mining town of Orinoca, Oruro on 26 Oct. 1959. When the mines began to close in the early 1980s, his family moved to become coca farmers in Chapare. Morales became a leader of the *cocaleros* and during the 1990s clashed with successive governments, particularly that of the former right-wing military dictator, Hugo Banzer Suárez. Banzer joined the US 'war on drugs' and introduced a five-year plan to eradicate coca cultivation and pressurize the *cocaleros* into growing alternative crops. In 1997 Morales, by then a member of the Movement Towards Socialism (MAS), was elected to Congress where he continued to fight the government's policy, arguing that coca consumption was an accepted part of daily life for workers and that the West had a responsibility to suppress cocaine demand.

In Jan. 2002 he was removed from Congress on a terrorism charge related to riots in Sacaba over coca eradication, though many claimed his dismissal followed pressure from the US embassy. Morales nevertheless declared his candidacy for the congressional and presidential elections, held in June 2002, on a platform of nationalizing strategic industries, providing basic services for all, land reform and tackling corruption. The MAS came second with 20·9% of the vote, with Morales crediting much of his success to inflammatory comments made against him by the then US ambassador. Refusing to join a coalition with the Nationalist Revolutionary Movement (MNR), led by President Gonzalo Sánchez de Lozada, the MAS became the leading opposition party.

Following a general strike, Morales was involved in an uprising that led to the ousting of de Lozada in Oct. 2003. He was also a key figure in mass protests in La Paz in April 2005 calling for an end to poverty and a greater share of profits from the country's gas reserves. A blockade led to food and fuel shortages in La Paz and when clashes erupted between the police and protesters, Carlos Mesa, the new president, fled the city. In fresh elections in Dec. 2005, Morales defeated the conservative former president, Jorge Quiroga, with 53·7% of the vote, and was sworn in as president on 22 Jan. 2006.

Career in Office

Morales promised 'equality and justice' for the poor and marginalized, and a new constitution providing greater legal representation and more rights for indigenous people. His choice of inexperienced left-wing activists to fill most of the cabinet led to comparisons with Venezuela's late president, Hugo Chávez, with whom Morales swiftly signed an energy co-operation accord. Close links were also forged with communist Cuba, but relations with the USA remained strained (leading to the expulsion of the US ambassador and the suspension of operations of the US drug enforcement agency in Bolivia in Oct.–Nov. 2008).

On 1 May 2006 Morales announced the nationalization of Bolivia's oil and gas industry. The decree required foreign energy companies already operating in the market, including Brazil's Petrobras, to accept harsh new contracts within six months. However, a temporary suspension was announced in Aug. owing to shortage of finance, and the terms accepted by foreign companies by the end of Oct. were less draconian than in the May decree.

In July 2006 Morales and the MAS won elections for a new Constituent Assembly to revise the constitution, but fell well short of the two-thirds majority needed to rewrite it at will. This led MAS delegates to introduce a controversial measure in Sept. allowing the Assembly to approve individual clauses by simple majority vote. Opponents feared the loss of regional autonomy and the greater centralization of political power in the president's hands. There was also resistance from large landowners to Morales's land redistribution reform in favour of the indigenous majority, which passed into law in Nov. 2006. Although Morales retained popular support, he remained locked in a power struggle over the proposed constitution with the wealthier eastern departments. In response, he staged a recall referendum on his leadership in Aug. 2008, which he won convincingly. In Oct. Congress approved the text of the new constitution, which was accepted in a referendum in Jan. 2009.

Presidential and parliamentary elections in Dec. 2009 returned Morales to office in a landslide victory, while his MAS won majorities in the Chamber of Deputies and Senate. Morales resumed the nationalization programme, taking over four electricity companies in May 2010, but he also faced strikes and

protests—the first such opposition since he took office in 2006—against his government's restrictive wage policy. In Oct. 2010 Morales and the Peruvian leader signed an accord allowing landlocked Bolivia to build its own Pacific port on a small stretch of Peru's coastline.

There were further mass demonstrations in early 2011 against a government proposal to raise fuel prices sharply, and again in Aug.–Sept. that year against a controversial plan to build a highway through a rainforest reserve. Both initiatives were subsequently dropped. In mid-2012 Morales announced another electricity nationalization, this time of the Bolivian subsidiary of the Spanish power company REE. He also faced strikes by government workers, particularly police officers, over pay.

In April 2013 the Constitutional Court ruled that Morales was entitled to seek re-election in 2014 on the grounds that his first term in office had predated the 2009 constitution and did not therefore count towards the two-term limit. In the same month he expelled the US Agency for International Development from the country, accusing the humanitarian organization of trying to undermine his government.

Morales was re-elected to a third term as president following the elections of 12 Oct. 2014, in which the MAS also retained a substantial parliamentary majority. Then in Sept. 2015 Congress voted to amend the constitution allowing Morales to stand for a fourth presidential term subject to approval in a referendum. The proposed change was narrowly rejected in the vote held in Feb. 2016, but in Nov. 2017 the Constitutional Court controversially overturned the referendum outcome, paving the way for Morales to again contest elections due in 2019.

In Oct. 2018, despite Morales's optimistic expectations, the International Court of Justice rejected Bolivia's longstanding claim that Chile was obligated to negotiate the landlocked country's 'sovereign access to the sea'.

Defence

In 2013 defence expenditure totalled US$373m., with spending per capita US$36. The 2013 expenditure represented 1·3% of GDP.

Army

There are six military regions. Strength (2009): 34,800 (25,000 conscripts), including a Presidential Guard infantry regiment under direct headquarters command.

Navy

A small force exists for river and lake patrol duties. Despite being landlocked, Bolivia's naval personnel totalled 4,800 in 2009, including 1,700 marines. There were six Naval Districts in 2009. The Navy had 73 vessels in 2009, including 54 patrol craft.

Air Force

The Air Force, established in 1923, had 33 combat-capable aircraft and 15 armed helicopters in 2009. Personnel strength (2009): 6,500 (including conscripts).

Economy

In 2012 agriculture accounted for 13·0% of GDP, industry 38·7% and services 48·3%.

Bolivia's 'shadow' (black market) economy is estimated to constitute approximately 63% of the country's official GDP, one of the highest percentages of any country in the world.

Overview

Bolivia is a lower-middle income country with an economy based on international trading of minerals, natural gas and agricultural goods. Hydrocarbon income accounts for about 30% of total revenue, making Bolivia vulnerable to fluctuations in global commodity prices. It is also among the world's largest producers of coca (the raw material for cocaine).

Growth has been volatile over the decades. The 1960s and 1970s were boom years owing to a flourishing mining sector and capital inflows, while the 1980s were marked by hyperinflation, high debt and political crises. In the 1990s consumption-driven expansion led to an average annual investment growth rate of 4–5%. The state also privatized some utilities, but by the end of the decade growth was slowing owing to the knock-on effect of economic upheaval in Brazil and Argentina—both major trading partners—and averaged 3·3% per year over the period 1996–2005.

As a result of development in the domestic services, construction and commodities sectors, growth then revived, averaging 5·1% per year between 2006 and 2014. The country also maintained current account and fiscal surpluses (until 2013) that enabled it to build reserves while also expanding public investment. External debt fell from 52·5% of GNI in 2006 to below 30% in 2014. In 2015 international reserves equated to 46% of GDP, while public sector deposits in the Central Bank reached 27% of GDP. However, the economy slowed again that year, largely in response to the declining international oil price. International reserves fell from US$15·1bn. in late 2014 to US$10bn. in 2016.

The poverty rate declined from over 60% in 2005 to 39% in 2015, while the Gini coefficient (a measure of income inequality) dropped from 0·59 to 0·49 between 2005 and 2013. However, Bolivia remains among the poorest countries in Latin America.

Currency
The unit of currency is the *boliviano* (BOB) of 100 *centavos*, which replaced the *peso* on 1 Jan. 1987 at a rate of one boliviano = 1m. pesos. Inflation was 3·6% in 2016 and 2·8% in 2017. In June 2009 foreign exchange reserves were US$7,099m., total money supply was 26,680bn. bolivianos and gold reserves totalled 911,000 troy oz.

Budget
Central government revenue was 54,450m. bolivianos in 2011 and expenditure 56,358m. bolivianos. Income taxes accounted for 58·6% of revenues in 2011 and taxes on hydrocarbons 29·7%; current expenditure accounted for 64·3% of expenditures and capital expenditure 35·7%.

The nominal rate of VAT is 13%, corresponding to an actual rate of 14·94%.

Performance
Real GDP growth was 4·9% in 2015, 4·3% in 2016 and 4·2% in 2017. Total GDP was US$37·5bn. in 2017.

Banking and Finance
The Central Bank (*President*, Pablo Ramos Sánchez) is the bank of issue. In 2013 there were 13 licensed banks in Bolivia. The largest banks are Banco Mercantil Santa Cruz, Banco Nacional de Bolivia and Banco BISA.

In 2010 total external debt was US$5,267m., representing 27·8% of GNI. There is a stock exchange in La Paz.

Energy and Natural Resources

Environment
In 2011 Bolivia's carbon dioxide emissions from the consumption of energy were the equivalent of 1·4 tonnes per capita.

Electricity
Installed capacity was 1·7m. kW in 2011. Production from all sources in 2011 was 7·22bn. kWh, of which 4·87bn. kWh thermal and 2·35bn. kWh hydroelectric; consumption per capita was 700 kWh in 2011.

Oil and Gas
There are petroleum and natural gas deposits in the Tarija, Santa Cruz and Cochabamba areas. Production of oil in 2010 was 12,607,000 bbls. Reserves in 2011 were 465m. bbls. The US$2·2bn. Bolivia–Brazil pipeline was completed in 2000 and is the longest natural gas pipeline in South America. The 3,150 km pipeline connects Bolivia's gas sources with the southeast regions of Brazil. Natural gas output in 2013 was 20·8bn. cu. metres, with proven reserves of 300bn. cu. metres. In May 2006 Bolivia nationalized the oil and natural gas industries and six months later, in Nov., Bolivia signed up 40 new contracts with oil and natural gas enterprises.

Minerals
Mining accounted for 4% of GDP in 2005. Tin-mining had been the mainstay of the economy until the collapse of the international tin market in 1985. Estimated production in 2005 (preliminary, in tonnes): zinc, 157,019; tin, 18,694; lead, 11,093; antimony, 5,225; wolfram, 658; silver, 420; gold, 8,906 fine kg.

Agriculture
In 2014, 31% of employed persons were engaged in agriculture. In the same year there were approximately 4·47m. ha. of arable land. Output in 1,000

tonnes in 2014 was: sugarcane, 7,599; soybeans, 2,814; potatoes, 1,064; maize, 1,007; sorghum, 656; rice, 484; plantains, 427; bananas, 283; cassava, 246. In 2012, 41,000 tonnes of coca (the source of cocaine) were grown. Since 1987 Bolivia has received international (mainly US) aid to reduce the amount of coca grown, with compensation for farmers who co-operate. Bolivia (not Brazil) is the largest producer of brazil nuts (45,000 tonnes in 2012).

Livestock, 2013: sheep, 9,288,000; cattle, 8,847,000; pigs, 2,864,000; goats, 2,371,000; llamas (2005), 2,130,000; asses, 635,000 (estimate); horses, 488,000 (estimate); alpacas (2005), 255,000; chickens, 191m.

Forestry
Forests covered 54·76m. ha. (51% of the land area) in 2015. Tropical forests with woods ranging from the 'iron tree' to the light balsa are exploited. Timber production in 2011 was 3·28m. cu. metres.

Fisheries
In 2014 the total catch was 6,990 tonnes, exclusively from inland waters.

Industry
In 2012 industry accounted for 38·7% of GDP, with manufacturing contributing 13·5%. The principal manufactures are mining, petroleum, smelting, foodstuffs, tobacco and textiles.

Labour
The labour force in 2013 was 5,025,100 (3,913,600 in 2003). 74·2% of the population aged 15–64 was economically active in 2013. In the same year 2·6% of the population was unemployed. In April 2013 the minimum wage was raised from 1,000 bolivianos to 1,200 bolivianos a month.

Bolivia had 30,000 people living in slavery according to the Walk Free Foundation's 2013 *Global Slavery Index*.

International Trade
An agreement of Jan. 1992 with Peru gives Bolivia duty-free transit for imports and exports through a corridor leading to the Peruvian Pacific port of Ilo from the Bolivian frontier town of Desaguadero, in return for Peruvian access to the Atlantic via Bolivia's roads and railways.

Imports and Exports
In 2005 imports (f.o.b.) amounted to US$2,191·8m.; exports (f.o.b.) US$2,810·4m. Main import commodities are road vehicles and parts, machinery for specific industries, cereals and cereal preparations, general industrial machinery, chemicals, petroleum, food, and iron and steel. Main export commodities are natural gas, soybeans and products, fuels, zinc, metallic tin, silver ore, metallic gold and nuts.

Main import suppliers in 2005 (provisional, in US$1m.): Brazil, 486·0; Argentina, 370·2; USA, 294·2; Chile, 154·3; Peru, 145·6; Japan, 135·9. Main export markets in 2005 (provisional, in US$1m.): Brazil, 1,011·6; USA, 385·3; Argentina, 260·5; Colombia, 180·5; Venezuela, 154·3; Japan, 134·3.

Communications

Roads
The total length of the road system was 82,288 km in 2011, of which 15,983 km were highways, national or main roads. Total passenger cars in use in 2007 numbered 174,900, lorries and vans 468,800, and buses and coaches 7,000. There were 1,073 road accident fatalities in 2007.

Rail
In 2007 the railway network totalled 2,866 km of metre gauge track. Passenger-km travelled in 2007 came to 313m. and freight tonne-km in 2005 to 1,027m.

Civil Aviation
The three international airports are La Paz (El Alto), Santa Cruz de la Sierra (Viru Viru) and Cochabamba (Jorge Wisterman). The main airline is Aerosur, which in 2007 ran scheduled services to Asunción, Buenos Aires, Lima, Salta and São Paulo, as well as internal services. The operations of Lloyd Aéreo Boliviano, for many years the national airline, were suspended in April 2007 owing to financial problems but charter flights were resumed in Dec. In Oct. 2007 the government announced the creation of a new airline, Boliviana de Aviación, as a successor flag carrier. It began commercial flights in March

2009 and in Feb. 2018 ran scheduled services to Barcelona, Buenos Aires, Madrid and Salta (in Argentina) as well as internal services. In 2005 scheduled airline traffic of Bolivian-based carriers flew 17·1m. km, carrying 1,396,400 passengers.

Shipping
Lake Titicaca and about 19,000 km of rivers are open to navigation. In Jan. 2014 there were 46 ships of 300 GT or over registered, totalling 80,000 GT. Bolivia is a 'flag of convenience' country.

Telecommunications
In 2008 President Evo Morales nationalized Entel, Bolivia's leading telecommunications company. It had been privatized in 1995 and was a subsidiary of Telecom Italia. There were 879,800 landline telephone subscriptions in 2011 (equivalent to 87·2 per 1,000 inhabitants) and 8,353,300 mobile phone subscriptions (or 828·0 per 1,000 inhabitants). Fixed broadband subscriptions totalled 154,100 in 2013 (14·8 per 1,000 inhabitants). In June 2012 there were 1·6m. Facebook users.

Social Institutions
Out of 178 countries analysed in the 2017 *Fragile States Index*—a list published jointly by the Fund for Peace and *Foreign Policy* magazine—Bolivia was ranked the joint 77th most vulnerable (along with Algeria) to conflict or collapse. The index is based on 12 indicators of state vulnerability across social, political and economic categories.

Justice
Justice is administered by the Supreme Court, superior department courts (of five or seven judges) and courts of local justice. The Supreme Court, with headquarters at Sucre, is divided into two sections, civil and criminal, of five justices each, with the Chief Justice presiding over both. Members of the Supreme Court are chosen on a two-thirds vote of Congress. The death penalty was abolished for ordinary crimes in 1997.

The population in penal institutions in 2013 was 14,770 (140 per 100,000 of national population). 83·2% of prisoners had yet to receive a trial according to 2014 estimates by the International Centre for Prison Studies. Bolivia was ranked 99th of 102 countries for criminal justice and 95th for civil justice in the 2015 World Justice Project *Rule of Law Index*, which provides data on how the rule of law is experienced by the general public across eight categories.

Education
Adult literacy was 90·7% in 2008 (male, 95·9%; female, 86·8%). Primary instruction is free and obligatory between the ages of six and 14 years. In 2007–08 there were 1,508,000 pupils and (2006–07) 62,000 teachers in primary schools, 1,060,000 pupils and (2006–07) 58,000 teachers in secondary schools; there were an estimated 353,000 students and 16,000 academic staff in tertiary education in 2006–07.

In 2005 there were ten universities, two technical universities, one Roman Catholic university, one musical conservatory, and colleges in the following fields: business, six; teacher training, four; industry, one; nursing, one; technical teacher training, one; fine arts, one; rural education, one; physical education, one. Bolivia's largest university is the Universidad Mayor de San Andrés, in La Paz, founded in 1830. There were 37 private universities in 2006–07.

In 2006 public expenditure on education came to 6·3% of GDP.

Health
In the period 2000–10 there were 12·2 physicians for every 10,000 population and 21·3 nursing and midwifery personnel per 10,000 population. There were 241 hospitals with 9,886 hospital beds (one per 954 persons) in 2005.

In *Water: At What Cost? The State of the World's Water 2016*, WaterAid reported that 10·0% of the population does not have access to safe water.

Welfare
The pensions and social security systems in Bolivia were reformed in 2010. Instead of a defined-contribution system based on privately managed individual capitalization accounts (introduced in 1996), a defined-benefit publicly managed pension system was reintroduced. In 2008 the solidarity bonus (Bonosol) was replaced by a new universal pension (Renta Dignidad). The new universal pension—worth approximately US$340 a year—is paid to all Bolivians over the age of 60.

Religion
The State is independent from religion. The Roman Catholic Church was disestablished in 2009. It has four archdioceses, six dioceses, five apostolic vicariates and two territorial prelatures. In 2010 there were an estimated 7·9m. Roman Catholics and 1·4m. Protestants according to the Pew Research Center's Forum on Religion & Public Life, with most of the remainder of the population being unaffiliated. In Feb. 2019 the Roman Catholic Church had one cardinal.

Culture

World Heritage Sites
There are seven UNESCO sites in Bolivia: the City of Potosí (inscribed in 1987), the largest industrial mining complex of the 16th century; the Jesuit Missions of the Chiquitos (1990), six settlements for converted Indians built between 1696 and 1760; the Historic City of Sucre (1991), containing 16th century colonial architecture; El Fuerte de Samaipata (1998), a pre-Hispanic sculptured rock and political and religious centre; Noel Kempff Mercado National Park (2000), a 1,523,000 ha. park in the Amazon Basin; and Tiwanaku: Spiritual and Political Centre of the Tiwanaku Culture (2000), monumental remains from AD 500 to 900. Shared with Argentina, Chile, Colombia, Ecuador and Peru, Qhapaq Ñan, Andean Road System (2014) is an extensive Inca communication, trade and defence network of roads covering 30,000 km.

Press
There were 25 paid-for daily newspapers in 2008 with a combined circulation of 145,000. The top-selling daily is the tabloid *El Deber*, with an average daily circulation of 15,000 (30,000 on Sundays).

Tourism
In 2014 there were 871,000 international tourists (excluding same-day visitors), up from 599,000 in 2009.

Diplomatic Representatives
Of Bolivia in the United Kingdom (106 Eaton Sq., London, SW1W 9AD)
> *Ambassador:* Vacant.
> *Chargé d'Affaires a.i.*: Giovanna Lenny Vidal Sejas.

Of the United Kingdom in Bolivia (Avenida Arce 2732, La Paz)
> *Ambassador:* Jeff Glekin.

Of Bolivia in the USA (3014 Massachusetts Ave., NW, Washington, D.C., 20008)
> *Ambassador:* Vacant.
> *Chargé d'Affaires a.i.:* Rafael Pablo Antonio Canedo Daroca.

Of the USA in Bolivia (Avenida Arce 2780, La Paz)
> *Ambassador:* Vacant.
> *Chargé d'Affaires a.i.:* Bruce Williamson.

Of Bolivia to the United Nations
> *Ambassador:* Sacha Sergio Llorenti Solíz.

Of Bolivia to the European Union
> *Ambassador:* Nestor Gabriele Bellavite.

Further Reading

Jemio, Luis Carlos, *Debt, Crisis and Reform in Bolivia: Biting the Bullet.* 2001

Klein, Herbert S., *A Concise History of Bolivia.* 2003

Morales, Waltraud Q., *Bolivia.* 2004

Muñoz-Pogossian, Betilde, *Electoral Rules and the Transformation of Bolivian Politics: The Rise of Evo Morales.* 2008

National Statistical Office: Instituto Nacional de Estadística, Av. José Carrasco 1391, CP 6129, La Paz.

Website (Spanish only): http://www.ine.gob.bo

Bosnia and Herzegovina

Republika Bosna i Hercegovina (Republic of Bosnia and Herzegovina)

Capital: Sarajevo
Population projection, 2020: 3·50m.
GNI per capita, 2017: (PPP$) 11,716
HDI/world rank, 2017: 0·768/77
Internet domain extension: .ba

Key Historical Events

Settled by Slavs in the 7th century, Bosnia was conquered by the Turks in 1463 when much of the population was gradually converted to Islam. At the Congress of Berlin (1878) the territory was assigned to Austria-Hungary under nominal Turkish suzerainty. Austria-Hungary's outright annexation in 1908 contributed to the outbreak of the First World War. After 1918 Bosnia and Herzegovina became part of a new Kingdom of Serbs, Croats and Slovenes. Its name was changed to Yugoslavia in 1929. (*See* SERBIA and MONTENEGRO for developments up to and beyond the Second World War.)

In Oct. 1991 the National Assembly adopted a 'Memorandum on Sovereignty' supporting Bosnian autonomy within a Yugoslav federation. Though boycotted by Serbs, a referendum in March 1992 supported independence and an agreement was reached by Muslims, Serbs and Croats to set up three autonomous ethnic communities under a central Bosnian authority.

Bosnia and Herzegovina declared independence on 5 April 1992. Fighting broke out between the Serb, Croat and Muslim communities, with heavy casualties in Sarajevo, Muslim territorial losses and a refugee exodus.

In Aug. 1992 the UN Security Council authorized force to ensure the delivery of humanitarian aid. Internationally sponsored peace talks were held in Geneva in 1993, but fighting continued. In April 1993 the UN established havens for Muslim civilians in Sarajevo, Srebrenica and Goražde.

In Dec. 1994 Bosnian Serbs and Muslims signed a countrywide interim ceasefire. Bosnian Croats also signed in Jan. 1995. However, Croatian Serbs and the Muslim secessionist forces under Fikret Abdić continued fighting. On 16 June 1995 Bosnian government forces launched an attack to break the Bosnian Serb siege of Sarajevo. On 11 July Bosnian Serb forces began to occupy UN security zones despite retaliatory NATO air strikes, and on 28 Aug. shelled Sarajevo. In July Srebrenica was the scene of the worst massacre of the war, when Bosnian Serb troops killed over 7,000 Muslim men and boys. Dutch peacekeeping forces protecting the area failed to prevent the massacre.

To stop the shelling of UN safe areas, NATO aircraft attacked Bosnian Serb military installations on 30–31 Aug. On 26 Sept. in Washington the foreign ministers of Bosnia, Croatia and Yugoslavia (the latter negotiating for the Bosnian Serbs) agreed a draft Bosnian constitution under which a central government would handle foreign affairs and commerce and a Serb Zone, while a Muslim-Croat Federation administered internal affairs. A ceasefire came into force on 12 Oct. 1995.

In Dayton (Ohio) on 21 Nov. 1995 the prime ministers of Bosnia, Croatia and Yugoslavia initialled a US-brokered peace agreement. The Bosnian state was divided into a Muslim-Croat Federation containing 51% of Bosnian territory and a Serb Republic containing 49%. A central government authority representing all ethnic groups with responsibility for foreign and monetary policy and citizenship issues was established and free elections held. On 20 Dec. 1995 a NATO contingent (IFOR) took over from UN peacekeeping forces and set up a 4 km separation zone between the Serb and Muslim-Croat territories. After a year IFOR was replaced by SFOR, a 'Stabilization Force'. On 2 Dec. 2004 a 7,000-strong European Union force 'EUFOR' took over from SFOR.

Territory and Population

The republic is bounded in the north and west by Croatia, in the east by Serbia and in the southeast by Montenegro. It has a coastline of only 20 km with no harbours. Its area is 51,210 sq. km, including 210 sq. km of inland waters. The capital is Sarajevo.

The population at the 1991 census—when present-day Bosnia and Herzegovina was still part of Yugoslavia—was 4,377,033, of which the predominating ethnic groups were Muslims (1,905,829), Serbs (1,369,258) and Croats (755,892). Bosnia and Herzegovina is made up of three 'constituent' peoples: Bosniaks (Bosnian Muslims), Croats and Serbs. Census population, 2013, 3,473,078; density, 68·1 per sq. km. Census population of the principal cities in 2013: Sarajevo, 348,363; Banja Luka, 135,059; Tuzla, 74,457; Zenica, 70,553. According to a 2008 report by the ministry of human rights and refugees of Bosnia and Herzegovina around 1·35m. Bosnians live abroad, mainly in the USA, Germany, Serbia, Austria and Slovenia.

The UN gives a projected population for 2020 of 3·50m.

In 2011, 49·2% of the population lived in urban areas.

In accordance with the Dayton Agreement the country is divided into two entities: the Federation of Bosnia and Herzegovina (51% of the territory) and Republika Srpska, sometimes referred to as the Serb Republic (49% of the territory). In addition there is a self-governing unit, Brčko District, which is a *de facto* third entity in the northeast of the country. *See also* CONSTITUTION AND GOVERNMENT *below.*

The official languages are Bosnian, Croatian and Serbian.

Social Statistics

2010 births, 33,779; deaths, 34,633. Rates per 1,000, 2010: birth, 8·8; death, 9·0. Annual population growth rate, 2000–08, 0·3%. Life expectancy at birth, 2013, was 73·8 years for men and 78·9 years for women. Infant mortality, 2010, eight per 1,000 live births; fertility rate, 2013, 1·3 children per woman (the joint lowest in the world).

Climate

The climate is generally continental with steady rainfall throughout the year, although in areas nearer the coast it is more Mediterranean.

Constitution and Government

On 18 March 1994 in Washington, D.C., USA, Bosnian Muslims ('Bosniaks') and Croats reached an agreement for the creation of a federation of cantons with a central government responsible for foreign affairs, defence and commerce. It was envisaged that there would be a president elected by a two-house legislature alternating annually between the nationalities.

On 31 May 1994 the National Assembly approved the creation of the Bosniak-Croat federation (the Federation of Bosnia and Herzegovina). Alija Izetbegović remained the unitary states's president. An interim government with Hasan Muratović as prime minister was formed on 30 Jan. 1996.

The Dayton Agreement including the new constitution was signed and came into force on 14 Dec. 1995. The government structure was established in 1996 as follows:

Heading the state is a three-member *Presidency* (one Bosniak, one Croat, one Serb) with a rotating president. The Presidency is elected by direct universal suffrage, and is responsible for foreign affairs and the nomination of the prime minister. There is a two-chamber parliament: the *House of Representatives* (which meets in Sarajevo) comprises 42 directly elected deputies, two-thirds Bosniak and Croat and one-third Serb; and the *House of Peoples* (which meets in Lukavica) comprises five Bosniak, five Croat and five Serb delegates.

Below the national level the country is divided into two self-governing entities along ethnic lines.

© Springer Nature Limited 2020
Palgrave Macmillan (ed.), *The Statesman's Yearbook 2020*,
https://doi.org/10.1057/978-1-349-95940-2_34

The Bosniak-Croat Federation of Bosnia and Herzegovina (Federacija Bosna i Hercegovina) is headed by a President and Vice-President, a 98-member Chamber of Representatives and a 58-member Chamber of Peoples. The Serb Republic (Republika Srpska) is also headed by an elected President and Vice-President, and there is a National Assembly of 83 members, elected by proportional representation.

Central government is conducted by a *Council of Ministers*, which comprises Bosniak and Serb Co-Prime Ministers and a Croat Deputy Prime Minister. The Co-Prime Ministers alternate in office every week.

National Anthem

'Intermezzo'; tune by Dušan Šestić; no words.

Recent Elections

Elections were held on 7 Oct. 2018 for the Presidium and the federal parliament. Elected to the Presidency were: Šefik Džaferović (Bosniak; Party of Democratic Action—SDA); Željko Komšić (Croat; Democratic Front—DF); and Milorad Dodik (Serb; Alliance of Independent Social Democrats—SNSD). In the parliamentary elections the SDA won 9 seats with 17·0% of the vote, the SNSD 6 (16·0%), the Social Democrat Party (SDP) 5 (9·1%), the Croat Democratic Union (HDZ BiH) 5 (9·0%), the Serb Democratic Party (SDS) 3 (9·8%) and the Democratic Front (DF) 3 (5·8%). A number of smaller parties each took one or two seats.

Current Government

Presidency Chairman: Milorad Dodik (Serb; Alliance of Independent Social Democrats—SNSD); took rotating presidency on 20 Nov. 2018. *Presidency Members:* Šefik Džaferović (Bosniak; Party of Democratic Action—SDA); Željko Komšić (Croat; Democratic Front—DF).

In Feb. 2019 the cabinet comprised:

Chairman of the Council of Ministers (Prime Minister): Denis Zvizdić (Bosniak, SDA); b. 1964 (in office since 11 Feb. 2015).

Minister of Civil Affairs: Adil Osmanović. *Communications and Transport:* Ismir Jusko. *Defence:* Marina Pendeš. *Finance and Treasury:* Vjekoslav Bevanda. *Foreign Affairs:* Igor Crnadak. *Foreign Trade and Economic Relations:* Mirko Šarović. *Human Rights and Refugees:* Semiha Borovac. *Justice:* Josip Grubeša. *Security:* Dragan Mektić.

High Representative for Bosnia and Herzegovina: Valentin Inzko (Austria); b. 1949 (in office since 26 March 2009).

Office of the High Representative: http://www.ohr.int

Current Leaders

Milorad Dodik

Position
President

Introduction
Milorad Dodik became presidency chairman on 20 Nov. 2018. He is the Serb member of the country's tripartite presidency that rotates every eight months between representatives of the country's three main ethnic groups.

Early Life
Born in Banja Luka on 12 March 1959, Dodik graduated in political sciences from the University of Belgrade in 1983. From 1986–90 he was chairman of the executive board of the Municipal Assembly of Laktasi. When the first multi-party elections were held in 1990 he was elected to parliament as a candidate of the Union of Reform Forces. He formed the Independent Members of the Parliament Caucus (in opposition to the ruling Serb Democratic Party), which was a precursor to the Party of Independent Social Democrats that eventually became the Alliance of Independent Social Democrats, of which he became president.

Dodik was prime minister of Republika Srpska from 1998–2001, during which time he offered to co-operate with war crimes tribunals. Following the 2006 general election he became prime minister for a second time before leaving the position in 2010 to become president.

On 7 Oct. 2018 Dodik was elected to Bosnia's three-person presidency, representing the Serbs, and became presidency chairman on 20 Nov. 2018.

Career in Office
In his inauguration speech, Dodik stated that the interests of Republika Srpska would be his priority, later announcing his intention to replace 16 ambassadors appointed by his predecessor and accusing them of not working to that end. Although supportive of the nation's bid to join the European Union, he is opposed to NATO membership, pushing instead for Serbia's alignment with Russia. His critics argue that his hard-line Serb nationalist position threatens the fragile Dayton peace agreement that ended the Bosnian war in 1995.

Defence

Defence expenditure in 2012 totalled US$231m. (US$60 per capita), representing 1·4% of GDP.

An EU-led peacekeeping contingent 'EUFOR' took over military operations from the NATO-led 'SFOR' on 2 Dec. 2004. Its mission is to focus on the apprehension of indicted war criminals and counter-terrorism, and provide advice on defence reform. Initially numbering 7,000 personnel, the strength has since been reduced and in 2015 stood at 600.

Army

Reform of the defence forces began in 2003 and resulted, in 2006, in the establishment of a single state army (in place of the previously separate armed forces of the Federation of Bosnia and Herzegovina and the Serb Republic). Its personnel—including that of the Air Force and Anti-Air Defence Brigade—totalled 9,205 in 2011. The Army had 334 main battle tanks in 2011 plus 127 armoured personnel carriers and 137 armoured infantry fighting vehicles.

Air Force

The Air Force and Anti-Aircraft Defence was established in 2006. It had 19 combat-capable aircraft and 45 helicopters in 2011.

Economy

In 2016 agriculture accounted for 7·7% of GDP, industry 28·1% and services 64·2%.

Overview

Infrastructure and output were damaged by war in the early 1990s but growth has been largely continuous since the Dayton Accords ended fighting in 1995. In the post-war decade GDP growth increased by over two-thirds and the poverty level dropped from 20% to 14%. The economy then fell into recession in 2009 following the onset of the global financial crisis. The government agreed a stand-by arrangement with the International Monetary Fund to cushion the impact of the deteriorating external environment and adopted policies to redress fiscal and structural imbalances, with additional financing from the World Bank and European Union.

The economy rebounded in 2011 with growth of 1%, although it briefly returned to recession in 2012. It was dealt a new blow in May 2014 when heavy flooding—affecting one-third of the country—damaged infrastructure and disrupted trade flows. GDP growth then averaged 3·1% per year from 2015–17. Public debt in 2017 was measured at 43·5% of GDP. The financial sector plays an important role in the economy, although banking is dominated by foreign institutions.

Membership of the Central European Free Trade Agreement was achieved in Sept. 2007. The country was recognized as a potential candidate for EU membership in 2003, although it is yet to join.

Currency

A new currency, the *konvertibilna marka* (BAM) consisting of 100 *pfennig*, was introduced in June 1998. Initially trading at a strict 1-to-1 against the Deutsche Mark, it is now pegged to the euro at a rate of 1·95583 convertible marks to the euro. There was deflation of 1·1% in 2016 but inflation of 1·2% in 2017. Total money supply was 7,011bn. convertible marks in Aug. 2011.

Budget

Budgetary central government revenue in 2014 was 6,469m. convertible marks; expenditure was 6,082m. convertible marks. VAT of 17% was introduced on 1 Jan. 2006.

Performance

Real GDP growth was 3·1% in 2015, 3·2% in 2016 and 3·0% in 2017. Total GDP was US$18·2bn. in 2017.

Banking and Finance

There is a Central Bank (*Governor*, Senad Softić). In 2005 there were 28 commercial banks (19 in the Federation and 9 in the Serb Republic).

In 2010 total external debt was US$8,457m., representing 48·8% of GNI. There are stock exchanges in Banja Luka and Sarajevo.

Energy and Natural Resources

Environment

Bosnia and Herzegovina's carbon dioxide emissions from the consumption of energy in 2011 were the equivalent of 7·1 tonnes per capita.

Electricity

Bosnia and Herzegovina is rich in hydro-electric potential and is a net exporter of electricity. Installed capacity was estimated at 4·3m. kW in 2011. Production in 2011 was 15·28bn. kWh. In 2011 consumption per capita was 3,592 kWh.

Minerals

Output in 2008: lignite, 11·2m. tonnes; crushed stone, 4·4m. tonnes; iron ore, 2·7m. tonnes; gravel, 1·5m. tonnes; bauxite, 1·0m. tonnes; aluminium, 156,000 tonnes.

Agriculture

In 2007 there were 1·02m. ha. of arable land and 95,000 ha. of permanent crops. 2009 production (in 1,000 tonnes): maize, 963; potatoes, 414; wheat, 256; plums, 156; cabbage and kale, 82; barley, 77; apples, 72; tomatoes, 46. Livestock in 2009: cattle, 458,000; pigs, 529,000; sheep, 1,055,000; poultry, 18·7m.

Source: Agency for Statistics of Bosnia and Herzegovina

Forestry

In 2015 forests covered 2·19m. ha., or 43% of the total land area. Timber production in 2011 was 3·85m. cu. metres.

Fisheries

Estimated total fish catch in 2015: 305 tonnes (almost exclusively freshwater).

Industry

Industry accounted for 28·0% of GDP in 2010, with manufacturing contributing 13·7%. Output in 2008 (in 1,000 tonnes): cement, 1,406; crude steel, 608; lime, 216.

Labour

The active labour force totalled 1,157,940 in April 2010 (62% males). Unemployment in April 2010 was 27·2% (25·6% for men and 29·9% for women). Among 15–24 year olds it was 57·5%[1]. Bosnia and Herzegovina had 14,000 people living in slavery according to the Walk Free Foundation's 2013 *Global Slavery Index*.

[1]Source: Agency for Statistics of Bosnia and Herzegovina

International Trade

Imports and Exports

Goods imports were US$10,990·4m. in 2014 (US$10,295·2m. in 2013) and goods exports US$5,892·1m. (US$5,687·5m. in 2013).

Principal imports in 2014 were manufactured goods (21·5%) followed by machinery and transport equipment, and mineral fuels and lubricants; main exports in 2014 were miscellaneous manufactured articles (25·5%), manufactured goods, and machinery and transport equipment.

The leading import supplier in 2010 was Croatia (15·1%), followed by Serbia and Germany; the leading export destination in 2010 was Germany (15·3%), followed by Croatia and Serbia.

Communications

Roads

In 2005 there were an estimated 22,419 km of roads (4,104 km main roads). Passenger cars numbered 473,076 in 2007 (123 per 1,000 inhabitants). There were 428 road accident fatalities in 2007.

Source: Agency for Statistics of Bosnia and Herzegovina

Rail

There were 1,017 km of railways in 2008 (771 km electrified). It is estimated that up to 80% of the rail network was destroyed in the civil war, and it was not until July 2001 that the first international services were resumed. There are two state-owned rail companies—the Railway of the Federation of Bosnia and Herzegovina (ŽFBH) and the Railway of the Serb Republic (ŽRS). In 2008 ŽFBH carried 528,000 passengers and 8·1m. tonnes of freight while ŽRS carried 727,000 passengers and 5·0m. tonnes of freight.

Civil Aviation

There are airports at Sarajevo (Butmir), Tuzla, Banja Luka and Mostar. In 2010 there were direct flights to 14 European destinations. In 2012 Sarajevo handled 580,058 passengers (all international) and 1,858 tonnes of freight.

Telecommunications

In 2011 there were 955,900 landline telephone subscriptions (equivalent to 254·8 per 1,000 inhabitants) and 3,171,300 mobile phone subscriptions (or 845·2 per 1,000 inhabitants). In the same year there were 365,000 fixed broadband subscriptions and 346,000 mobile broadband subscriptions.

Social Institutions

Out of 178 countries analysed in the 2017 *Fragile States Index*—a list published jointly by the Fund for Peace and *Foreign Policy* magazine—Bosnia and Herzegovina was ranked the 86th least vulnerable to conflict or collapse. The index is based on 12 indicators of state vulnerability across social, political and economic categories.

Justice

The population in penal institutions in the Federation of Bosnia and Herzegovina in April 2008 was 1,750; in the Serb Republic the prison population was 928 in Sept. 2007. Bosnia and Herzegovina was ranked 37th of 102 countries for criminal justice and 51st for civil justice in the 2015 World Justice Project *Rule of Law Index*, which provides data on how the rule of law is experienced by the general public across eight categories.

Education

The adult literacy rate was 98% in 2008. In 2008–09 there were 174,000 pupils in primary schools, 334,000 in secondary schools and 105,000 students in tertiary education. The largest university is the University of Sarajevo, established in 1949 but with its origins dating back to 1531.

Health

In 2005 there were 5,540 physicians, 18,332 nursing and midwifery personnel, 629 dentistry personnel and 308 pharmaceutical personnel. In 2005 there were 30 hospital beds per 10,000 inhabitants.

In *Water: At What Cost? The State of the World's Water 2016*, WaterAid reported that 0·1% of the population does not have access to safe water.

Welfare

There were 509,000 pensioners in 2006. Only around 30% of the population over 65 receives an old-age pension. The average monthly pension was 246·6 convertible marks in 2006.

Religion

According to estimates by the Pew Research Center's Forum on Religion & Public Life, in 2010 the vast majority of the population was Christian (1·98m., of which 1·44m. Orthodox Christians and 0·54m. Catholics) or Muslim (1·70m., most of whom were Sunnis). In Feb. 2019 the Roman Catholic Church had one cardinal.

Culture

World Heritage Sites

There are three UNESCO World Heritage sites in Bosnia and Herzegovina: the Old Bridge area of the Old City of Mostar (inscribed on the list in 2005), an important Ottoman frontier town, and the Mehmed Paša Sokolović Bridge in Višegrad (2007), constructed in the 16th century.

Bosnia and Herzegovina shares the Stećci Medieval Tombstones Graveyards (2016) with Croatia, Montenegro and Serbia.

Press

There were seven paid-for daily newspapers in 2008 with a combined circulation of 75,000 and 46 paid-for non-dailies.

Tourism

In 2014, 536,000 non-resident tourists stayed in holiday accommodation (up from 311,000 in 2009 and 171,000 in 2000).

Diplomatic Representatives

Of Bosnia and Herzegovina in the United Kingdom (5–7 Lexham Gdns, London, W8 5JJ)
Ambassador: Valentina Marinčić.

Of the United Kingdom in Bosnia and Herzegovina (39a Hamdije Cemerlica St., 71000 Sarajevo)
Ambassador: Matthew Field.

Of Bosnia and Herzegovina in the USA (2109 E St., NW, Washington, D.C., 20037)
Ambassador: Vacant.
Chargé d'Affaires a.i.: Milenko Mišić.

Of the USA in Bosnia and Herzegovina (1 Robert C. Frasure St., 71000 Sarajevo)
Ambassador: Maureen Cormack.

Of Bosnia and Herzegovina to the United Nations
Ambassador: Ivica Dronjić.

Of Bosnia and Herzegovina to the European Union
Ambassador: Emina Merdan.

Further Reading

Bieber, Florian, *Post-War Bosnia: Ethnicity, Inequality and Public Sector Governance.* 2005
Burg, Steven L. and Shoup, Paul S., *The War in Bosnia-Herzegovina.* 1999
Hoare, Marko Attila, *The History of Bosnia: From the Middle Ages to the Present Day.* 2006
Malcolm, N., *Bosnia: a Short History.* 3rd ed. 2002
National Statistical Office: Agency for Statistics of Bosnia and Herzegovina, Zelenih beretki 26, 71000 Sarajevo.
Website: http://www.bhas.ba

Botswana

Lefatshe la Botswana (Republic of Botswana)

Capital: Gaborone
Population projection, 2020: 2·42m.
GNI per capita, 2017: (PPP$) 15,534
HDI/world rank, 2017: 0·717/101=
Internet domain extension: .bw

Key Historical Events

The Tswana or Batswana people are the principal inhabitants of the country formerly known as Bechuanaland. The territory was declared a British protectorate in 1895 administered by the High Commissioner in South Africa until the post was abolished in 1964. Proposals for the merging of Bechuanaland and the other two High Commission Territories into South Africa were strongly opposed. Economically, however, the country was closely tied to that of South Africa and has remained so. In Dec. 1960 Bechuanaland received its first constitution. Further constitutional change brought self-government in 1965 and independence on 30 Sept. 1966. Botswana had difficulties with the neighbouring settler regime in Rhodesia, until that country became Zimbabwe in 1980. Relations with South Africa were also strained until the ending of apartheid. Today Botswana is one of the few African countries to enjoy stability and (2009 apart) a fast-growing economy.

Territory and Population

Botswana is bounded in the west and north by Namibia, northeast by Zambia and Zimbabwe, and east and south by South Africa. The area is 581,730 sq. km. 2011 census population, 2,024,904; density, 3·5 per sq. km.

The UN gives a projected population for 2020 of 2·42m.

In 2011, 61·8% of the population were urban.

The country is divided into ten districts (Central, Chobe, Ghanzi, Kgalagadi, Kgatleng, Kweneng, North East, North West, South East and Southern).

The main towns (2011 census population) are Gaborone (231,592), Francistown (98,961), Molepolole (66,466), Maun (60,263), Mogoditshane (58,079), Serowe (50,820), Selebi-Phikwe (49,411), Kanye (47,007), Mochudi (44,815) and Mahalapye (43,289).

The official languages are Setswana and English. Setswana is spoken by over 90% of the population and English by approximately 40%. More than ten other languages, including Herero, Hottentot, Kalanga, Mbukushu, San and Sekgalagadi are spoken in various tribal areas. The main ethnic groups are the Tswana (79%) and the Kalanga (11%). Botswana is one of Africa's most homogenous countries.

Social Statistics

2008 (estimates) births, 47,000; deaths, 23,000. Rates, 2008 estimates (per 1,000 population): births, 24·5; deaths, 12·1. Infant mortality, 2010 (per 1,000 live births), 36. Expectation of life in 2013 was 62·1 years for males and 66·8 for females. In 2013, 21·9% of all adults between 15 and 49 were infected with HIV. Annual population growth rate, 2000–08, 1·4%. Fertility rate, 2008, 2·9 children per woman.

Climate

In winter, days are warm and nights cold, with occasional frosts. Summer heat is tempered by prevailing northeast winds. Rainfall comes mainly in summer, from Oct. to April, while the rest of the year is almost completely dry with very high sunshine amounts. Gaborone, Jan. 79°F (26·1°C), July 55°F (12·8°C). Annual rainfall varies from 650 mm in the north to 250 mm in the southeast. The country is prone to droughts.

Constitution and Government

The Constitution was adopted in March 1965 and became effective on 30 Sept. 1966. It provides for a republican form of government headed by the President with three main organs: the Legislature, the Executive and the Judiciary. The executive rests with the President who is responsible to the National Assembly. The President is elected for five-year terms by the National Assembly.

The *National Assembly* consists of 63 members, of which 57 are elected by universal suffrage, four are specially elected members and two, the President and the Speaker, are *ex officio*.

Elections are held every five years. Voting is on the first-past-the-post system.

There is also a *House of Chiefs* to advise the government. It consists of the Chiefs of the eight tribes who were autonomous during the days of the British protectorate, plus four members elected by and from among the sub-chiefs in four districts; these 12 members elect a further three politically independent members.

National Anthem

'Fatshe leno la rona' ('Blessed be this noble land'); words and tune by K. T. Motsete.

Government Chronology

Presidents since 1966. (BDP = Botswana Democratic Party)

1966–80	BDP	Seretse Khama
1980–98	BDP	Quett Ketumile Joni Masire
1998–2008	BDP	Festus Gontebanye Mogae
2008–18	BDP	Lieut.-Gen. Seretse Khama Ian Khama
2018–	BDP	Mokgweetsi Masisi

Recent Elections

In National Assembly elections held on 24 Oct. 2014 the Botswana Democratic Party (BDP) gained 37 seats with 46·5% of the vote, the Umbrella for Democratic Change 17 with 30·0% and the Botswana Congress Party 3 with 20·4%. Turnout was 84·8%.

Current Government

President: Mokgweetsi Masisi; b. 1961 (BDP; sworn in 1 April 2018).

Vice-President: Slumber Tsogwane.

In Feb. 2019 the cabinet was as follows:

Minister of Presidential Affairs, Governance and Public Administration: Nonofo Molefhi. *Defence, Justice and Security:* Shaw Kgathi. *Agricultural Development and Food Security:* Patrick Ralotsia. *Infrastructure and Housing Development:* Vincent T. Seretse. *Basic Education:* Bagalatia Arone. *Environment, Natural Resources Conservation and Tourism:* Tshekedi Khama. *Finance and Economic Development Planning:* Ontefetse K. Matambo. *International Affairs and Co-operation:* Unity Dow. *Health and Wellness:* Dr Alfred Madigele. *Employment, Labour Productivity and Skills Development:* Tshenolo Mabeo. *Land Management, Water and Sanitation Services:* Kefentse Mzwinila. *Local Government and Rural Development:* Pelonomi Venson-Moitoi. *Mineral Resources, Green Technology and Energy Security:* Eric M. Molale. *Investment, Trade and Industry:* Bogolo Kenewendo. *Transport and Communications:* Onkokame K. Mokaila. *Youth Empowerment, Sport and Culture Development:* Thapelo Olopeng. *Tertiary Education, Research, Science and Technology:* Ngaka Ngaka. *Nationality, Immigration and Gender Affairs:* Dorcas Makgato.

Government Website: http://www.gov.bw

© Springer Nature Limited 2020
Palgrave Macmillan (ed.), *The Statesman's Yearbook 2020*,
https://doi.org/10.1057/978-1-349-95940-2_35

Current Leaders

Mokgweetsi Masisi

Position
President

Introduction
Mokgweetsi Masisi, leader of the Botswana Democratic Party (BDP), became president on 1 April 2018. His inauguration marked the fifth peaceful transition of power in one of Africa's strongest democracies.

Early Life
Mokgweetsi Eric Keabetswe Masisi was born on 21 July 1963. His father, Edison Masisi, was a cabinet minister and National Assembly speaker. In 1984 the younger Masisi graduated in English and History from the University of Botswana. He then worked as a social studies teacher before focusing on university curriculum development at his *alma mater* in 1987. He obtained a master's degree in education from Florida State University in the USA in 1989 and returned home to work on curriculum development again in 1990. From 1995–2003 he worked with UNICEF as an education project officer, during which time he was posted to conflict-ridden Afghanistan.

In the 2009 general elections, Masisi won the parliamentary seat of Moshupa, which he continues to represent. He was appointed assistant minister for presidential affairs and public administration in Oct. 2009, becoming minister in Jan. 2011. In April 2014 he was named acting minister of education and undertook the role on a permanent basis following the Oct. 2014 general elections. On 12 Nov. 2014 President Ian Khama appointed him vice-president. In July 2015 Masisi was elected as chair of the BDP and, following the end of Khama's second term in office, was sworn in as president on 1 April 2018.

Career in Office
As interim president until elections scheduled for Oct. 2019, Masisi needed to address high levels of corruption, unemployment, economic inequality and poverty while attempting to reduce the nation's over-reliance on the mineral sector. He was expected to face strong opposition from a coalition of parties intent on toppling the BDP, which has been in power since 1966.

Defence

In 2013 defence expenditure totalled US$438m. (US$206 per capita), representing 2·4% of GDP.

Army

The Army personnel (2011) numbered 8,500. There is also a 1,500-strong paramilitary force.

Air Force

The Air Wing operated 30 combat-capable aircraft in 2011 and numbered 500.

Economy

Services accounted for 58·9% of GDP in 2014, industry 38·7% and agriculture 2·4%.

Overview

Botswana has enjoyed consistently high economic growth since gaining independence in 1966. This has reflected its long-term political stability relative to regional neighbours and has been fuelled by the diamond industry. However, with the World Bank suggesting that diamond reserves could be depleted by 2028, economic diversification is a key priority.

In 2015 the economy contracted by 1·7% owing to weak demand for diamond exports, severe drought and persistent electricity and water supply shortages. However, real GDP growth soon resumed, measuring 4·3% in 2016 and 2·4% in 2017, driven by expansion in non-mining sectors allied to an upturn in diamond demand. Meanwhile, in 2016 inflation was estimated at 2·8%—outside the medium-term objective range of 3%–6%—as a result of low domestic demand and modestly increasing prices of imports, and, after three years of surpluses, the budget went into deficit before recovering to a

modest surplus in 2017. Also in 2017, public debt fell to 22·3% of GDP, well below the statutory ceiling of 40%.

Despite entering the ranks of upper-middle income nations, Botswana suffers from high unemployment, a lack of skilled labour (aggravated by the prevalence of HIV/AIDS) and one of the highest levels of inequality in the world. Almost 20% of the population lived below the poverty line in 2014, with rural areas particularly affected. This problem is exacerbated by discriminatory policies against tribal peoples.

Currency

The unit of currency is the *pula* (BWP) of 100 *thebe*. The pula was devalued by 7·5% in Feb. 2004 and 12·5% in May 2005. Inflation was 2·8% in 2016 and 3·3% in 2017. Foreign exchange reserves were US$8,423m. in July 2009 and total money supply was P6,789bn.

Budget

The fiscal year begins in April. Budgetary central government revenue in 2010–11 totalled P31,838·6m. and expenditure P28,774·1m. Principal sources of revenue in 2010–11 were: taxes on income, profits and capital gains, P9,362·1m.; taxes on international trade and transactions, P6,208·3m.; taxes on goods and services, P4,899·3m. Main items of expenditure by economic type in 2010–11: wages and salaries, P10,308·0m.; use of goods and services, P7,940·7m.; social contributions, P1,590·9m.

VAT is 12%.

Performance

Botswana suffered a recession in 2015 when the economy shrank by 1·7% as a consequence of declining diamond production. However, a recovery followed with real GDP growth of 4·3% in 2016 and 2·4% in 2017. Total GDP in 2017 was US$17·4bn.

Banking and Finance

There were ten commercial banks and three statutory banks in 2016. Total assets of the banking sector were P80,640m. in Dec. 2016. The Bank of Botswana (*Governor*, Moses Dinekere Pelaelo), established in 1976, is the central bank. The National Development Bank, founded in 1964, has six regional offices, and agricultural, industrial and commercial development divisions. The Botswana Co-operative Bank is banker to co-operatives and to thrift and loan societies. The government-owned Post Office Savings Bank (Botswana Post) operates throughout the country.

In 2010 external debt totalled US$1,709m., representing 11·6% of GNI. There is a stock exchange in Gaborone.

Energy and Natural Resources

Environment

Botswana's carbon dioxide emissions from the consumption of energy in 2011 were the equivalent of 2·3 tonnes per capita.

Electricity

Installed capacity was 152,000 kW in 2011. Production in 2010 was 430m. kWh. The coal-fired power station at Morupule supplies cities and major towns.

Minerals

Botswana is the world's second biggest diamond producer in terms of value with production estimated to be worth US$3·65bn. in 2014. Diamonds were first discovered in Botswana in 1967. Debswana, a partnership between the government and De Beers, runs four mines. Most of the diamonds produced come from two mines located at Jwaneng and Orapa. Coal reserves are estimated at 17bn. tonnes. There is also copper, salt and soda ash. Diamond production in 2013, 23·2m. carats (the second largest quantity after Russia). Other mineral production, 2013: coal, 1,496,000 tonnes; salt, 521,000 tonnes; soda ash, 228,000 tonnes; copper (mine output, copper content), 51,000 tonnes; gold, 1,205 kg.

Agriculture

70% of the total land area is desert. 80% of the population is rural, 71% of all land is 'tribal', protected and allocated to maintain small farmers, foster commercial ranching and prevent over-grazing. Agriculture provides a livelihood for over 70% of the population, but accounts for only 2·4% of GDP (2014). In 2013, 277,000 ha. were arable and an estimated 2,000 ha. permanent crops. There were 3,371 tractors in 2008. Cattle-rearing is the chief industry after diamond-mining, and the country is more a pastoral than an agricultural one, crops depending entirely upon the rainfall. In 2007 an estimated 295,000 persons were economically active in agriculture. In 2014 there were: goats, 1·6m.; cattle, 1·6m.; sheep, 227,000; asses, 227,000; chickens, 1·0m.

Production in 2014 (in 1,000 tonnes) included: maize, 28; sorghum, 14; millet, 4; onions (estimate), 3.

17% of the land is set aside for wildlife conservation and 20% for wildlife management areas, with four national parks and game reserves.

Forestry

Forests covered 10·84m. ha., or 19% of the total land area, in 2015. There are forest nurseries and plantations. Concessions have been granted to harvest 7,500 cu. metres in Kasane and Chobe Forestry Reserves, and up to 2,500 cu. metres in the Masame area. In 2011, 791,000 cu. metres of roundwood were cut.

Fisheries

In 2015 the total catch was 81 tonnes, exclusively from inland waters.

Industry

In 2014 industry accounted for 38·7% of GDP, with manufacturing contributing 6·0%. The most important sector is the diamond industry. A diamond-processing plant opened in Gaborone in March 2008. Meat is processed, and beer, soft drinks, textiles and foodstuffs manufactured. Rural technology is being developed and traditional crafts encouraged.

Labour

The labour force in 2013 was 1,128,700 (867,600 in 2003). 78·9% of the population aged 15–64 was economically active in 2013. In the same year 17·6% of the population was unemployed.

Botswana had 14,000 people living in slavery according to the Walk Free Foundation's 2013 *Global Slavery Index*.

International Trade

Botswana is a member of the Southern African Customs Union (SACU) with Eswatini, Lesotho, Namibia and South Africa. There are no foreign exchange restrictions.

Imports and Exports

Merchandise imports in 2013 totalled US$7,433·5m. (US$8,025·3m. in 2012) and merchandise exports US$7,573·3m. (US$5,971·2m. in 2012).

Principal imports in 2013 were manufactured goods (37·0%) followed by machinery and transport equipment, and mineral fuels and lubricants; main exports in 2013 were manufactured goods (82·7%), crude materials and animal and vegetable oils, and machinery and transport equipment. Diamonds accounted for 82·9% of Botswana's exports in 2013.

The leading import supplier in 2010 was South Africa (72·8%), followed by the UK and China; the leading export destination in 2010 was the UK (55·5%), followed by South Africa and Norway.

Communications

Roads

In 2005 the total road network was estimated to be 25,798 km (32·6% paved). In Dec. 2008 there were 256,498 motor vehicles registered. There were 497 deaths in road accidents in 2007.

Rail

The main line from Mafeking in South Africa to Bulawayo in Zimbabwe traverses Botswana. The total length of the rail system was 888 km in 2005, including two branch lines. In 2006, 426,894 passengers and 1,712,607 tonnes of freight were carried.

Civil Aviation

There are international airports at Gaborone (Sir Seretse Khama) and at Maun and six domestic airports. The national carrier is the state-owned Air Botswana, which in 2013 carried 265,000 passengers (173,000 on international flights). In 2010 direct international flights were operated to Harare, Johannesburg and Nairobi as well as domestic services. In Oct. 1999 an Air Botswana pilot who had been suspended two months earlier crashed an empty passenger plane into the airline's two serviceable aeroplanes at Gaborone Airport, killing himself and destroying the airline's complete fleet in the process. In 2012 Gaborone handled 403,372 passengers.

Telecommunications

In 2011 there were 149,600 landline telephone subscriptions (equivalent to 73·7 per 1,000 inhabitants) and 2,900,300 mobile phone subscriptions (or 1,428·2 per 1,000 inhabitants). In 2011, 7·0% of the population were internet users. In June 2012 there were 224,000 Facebook users.

Social Institutions

Out of 178 countries analysed in the 2017 *Fragile States Index*—a list published jointly by the Fund for Peace and *Foreign Policy* magazine—Botswana was ranked the 59th least vulnerable to conflict or collapse. The index is based on 12 indicators of state vulnerability across social, political and economic categories.

Justice

Law is based on the Roman-Dutch law of the former Cape Colony, but judges and magistrates are also qualified in English common law. The Court of Appeal has jurisdiction in respect of criminal and civil appeals emanating from the High Court, and in all criminal and civil cases and proceedings. Magistrates' courts and traditional courts are in each administrative district. As well as a national police force there are local customary law enforcement officers. The death penalty is still in force; there were no executions in 2017 but two in 2018. The population in penal institutions in Dec. 2012 was 4,241 (205 per 100,000 of national population). Botswana was ranked 27th of 102 countries for criminal justice and 33rd for civil justice in the 2015 World Justice Project *Rule of Law Index*, which provides data on how the rule of law is experienced by the general public across eight categories. Both rankings were the highest of any African country.

Education

Adult literacy rate in 2008 was 83%. Basic free education, introduced in 1986, consists of seven years of primary and three years of junior secondary schooling. In 2005 enrolment in primary schools was 326,500 with 13,472 teaching staff, and 168,720 pupils at secondary level with 12,371 teaching staff. There were 10,950 students is higher education in 2005 with 529 academic staff. 'Brigades' (community-managed private bodies) provide lower-level vocational training. The Department of Non-Formal Education offers secondary-level correspondence courses and is the executing agency for the National Literacy Programme.

In 2009 total expenditure on education came to 8·2% of GNI and 16·2% of total government spending.

Health

In 2007 there were 17 primary hospitals, one mental hospital, three referral hospitals, 14 district hospitals, 277 clinics and 338 health posts. There were also six private hospitals and 167 private medical clinics. In 2006 there were 591 doctors and 5,006 nurses.

In *Water: At What Cost? The State of the World's Water 2016*, WaterAid reported that 3·8% of the population does not have access to safe water.

Religion

Freedom of worship is guaranteed under the Constitution. In 2010 there were an estimated 1·32m. Protestants and 120,000 Roman Catholics according to the Pew Research Center's Forum on Religion & Public Life, with most of the remainder of the population being unaffiliated or folk religionists.

Culture

World Heritage Sites

Tsodilo was created a UNESCO World Heritage Site in 2001. It is the site of over 4,500 prehistoric rock paintings in the Kalahari Desert. The Okavango Delta, comprising permanent marshlands and seasonally flooded plains, was inscribed on the list in 2014.

Press

The government-owned *Daily News* is distributed free (circulation, 2008: 65,000). There is one other daily, the independent *Mmegi* ('The Reporter'), and 14 non-dailies.

Tourism

There were 1,544,000 international tourists (excluding same-day visitors) in 2013. Of these, 1,182,000 were from elsewhere in Africa, 151,000 from Europe and 150,000 from the Americas.

Diplomatic Representatives

Of Botswana in the United Kingdom (6 Stratford Pl., London, W1C 1AY)
High Commissioner: Dr John Ndebele G. Seakgosing.

Of the United Kingdom in Botswana (Plot 1079–1084, Main Mall, off Queens Rd, Gaborone).
High Commissioner: Katharine Ransome.

Of Botswana in the USA (1531 New Hampshire Ave., NW, Washington, D.C., 20036)
Ambassador: David John Newman.

Of the USA in Botswana (PO Box 90, Gaborone)
Ambassador: Vacant.
Chargé d'Affaires a.i.: Kali Jones.

Of Botswana to the United Nations
Ambassador: Collen Vixen Kelapile.

Of Botswana to the European Union
Ambassador: Samuel Otsile Outlule.

Further Reading

Central Statistics Office. *Statistical Bulletin* (Quarterly).

Ministry of Information and Broadcasting. *Botswana Handbook.—Kutlwano* (Monthly).

Hillbom, Ellen and Bolt, Jutta, *Botswana—A Modern Economic History: An African Diamond in the Rough.* 2018

Molomo, M. G. and Mokopakgosi, B. (eds) *Multi-Party Democracy in Botswana.* 1991

Perrings, C., *Sustainable Development and Poverty Alleviation in Sub-Saharan Africa: the Case of Botswana.* 1995

National Statistical Office: Central Statistics Office, Private Bag 0024, Gaborone.

Brazil

República Federativa do Brasil (Federative Republic of Brazil)

Capital: Brasília (Federal District)
Population projection, 2020: 213·86m.
GNI per capita, 2017: (PPP$) 13,755
HDI/world rank, 2017: 0·759/79
Internet domain extension: .br

Key Historical Events

Evidence of human habitation in Brazil dates to 9000 BC. Before the Portuguese discovery and occupation of Brazil there was a large indigenous population fragmented into smaller tribes. The largest was the Tupi-Guarani, which survived the sub-tropical environment by clearing land for crops.

The first Europeans to encounter the indigenous peoples were exiled criminals, or *degredados*, and Jesuit missionaries. The first Portuguese contact with Brazil was Pedro Alvares Cabral who left Lisbon in 1500 with orders to travel along the Cape of Good Hope route discovered by the Portuguese navigator Vasco da Gama in 1497–98. In an attempt to avoid storms he set a course more westerly than da Gama's and was carried still farther westward, landing in a place he named *Terra da Vera Cruz* (Land of the True Cross) and later renamed *Terra do Brasil* (Land of Brazil).

Although the official motive for Portuguese exploration was religious—the conversion of the natives to the Catholic faith—the greater incentive was to find a direct all-water trade route with Asia and thereby break Italy's commercial domination. Early Portuguese economic activity in Brazil revolved around the exploitation of the huge timber (Brazilwood) resources. This was soon superseded by sugarcane and, to a lesser extent, tobacco, harvested on plantations that sprang up in the interior in the 16th and 17th centuries. As these industries came to dominate the economy the need for large-scale labour became more pressing. Where the indigenous people proved unsuitable or unavailable, largely owing to ill health from newly introduced European diseases, millions of Africans were enslaved and shipped to the region.

The first attempt to establish a working government came in 1533 when the Portuguese divided the land into 15 captaincies, subdivided into leagues and ruled by selected governors (*donatários*). In 1549 John III sought to establish a more centralized power structure and appointed Tomé de Sousa as governor general, ruling from the newly founded capital, Salvador (Bahia). In 1567 Governor-General Mem da Sá founded Rio de Janeiro to protect its harbour from French incursions. During the Union of Portugal and Spain (1580–1640), Brazil became subject to attacks from Spanish enemies, notably the Netherlands, whose forces were not expelled until 1654.

The Portuguese settlers had set about conquering the vast Brazilian interior by the late 17th century. Early excursions were made by *bandeirantes*, men pursuing private enterprise and dreams of personal wealth. They discovered the first gold in the region at Minas Gerais in 1695. This opened up a new resource for exploitation by the Portuguese crown. Rio de Janeiro benefited greatly and in 1763 became the colonial capital in place of Salvador. Recife and Ouro Preto were the other major colonial urban centres.

The third quarter of the 18th century saw Spain accept many of Portugal's claims in the region. Portuguese Prime Minister Sebastião José de Carvalho e Mello ended the rule of the *donatários,* expelled the Jesuits, gave new freedoms to the native population and established two companies to regulate Brazilian trade. As Brazilian government became increasingly centralized a burgeoning nationalism emerged, most famously in the failed rebellion against the Portuguese led by Joaquim José da Silva Xavier (Tiradentes) in 1789.

In 1807 an invasion of Portugal by Napoleon Bonaparte forced the royal family to flee Portugal and take refuge in Rio, declaring it the temporary capital of the Portuguese Empire. In 1816 King João VI ascended the Portuguese throne but for five years refused to return to Lisbon. While in Brazil he initiated reforms which ended Portugal's commercial monopoly and in 1815 granted Brazil equal status with Portugal when he established the United Kingdom of Portugal, Brazil and the Algarves. On his return to Portugal João's son, Pedro, became Brazil's regent.

Independence

Pedro's regency ran into trouble when the Cortes (the Portuguese parliamentary body) demanded his return to Portugal. The Cortes repealed many of João's reforms and sought to reduce it to its earlier colonial status. When, in Sept. 1822, the Cortes decided to reduce Pedro's powers he called for Brazilian independence. On 1 Dec. 1822 he was crowned Constitutional Emperor and Perpetual Defender of Brazil. The United States recognized Brazil's independence in May 1824 followed by Portugal itself in 1825.

Pedro was forced to abdicate in 1831 following a disastrous war with Argentina and a financial crisis deepened by his promise to free the slaves. He left his five-year old son Pedro II as the ruler in waiting. In 1840 Pedro II succeeded after nine years of weak rule and civil strife. By 1847, Pedro was established as a leader free of political influences. He ruled for nearly 50 years and despite uprisings Brazil remained relatively stable and its economy strong.

Pedro was instrumental in the overthrow of Juan Manuel de Rosas in Argentina in the 1850s and became involved in Uruguay's civil war in the 1860s. In the 1870s the three nations united to repel the advances of the Paraguayan forces of Francisco Solano López. Pedro outlawed the slave trade in 1854. Emancipation was achieved in 1888 when three-quarters of a million slaves were freed without compensation to their owners. In 1889 Gen. Manuel Deodoro da Fonseca led a military revolt which forced Pedro's abdication. In Feb. 1891 Brazil became a Federal Republic with Fonseca elected as its first president. Forced to resign when he attempted to bypass congress, he was succeeded by Floriano Peixoto who used the military to restore order. In 1894 he was replaced by Brazil's first civilian head of state, Prudente de Morais. He and his immediate successors enjoyed relative peace as Brazil grew rich on coffee exports.

Brazil underwent significant territorial expansion in the early years of the 20th century during the Baron of Rio Branco's tenure as foreign minister. As well as winning 900,000 sq. km of land from other South American nations, he pursued close relations with the USA and UK, which led to a declaration of war against Germany in 1917. However, by the 1920s there was growing internal resentment at the wealth of the coffee barons and in 1922 a failed military coup initiated eight years of civil strife. Amid economic crisis in 1930 Getúlio Vargas lost the presidential election but was swept to power by a military junta which dismissed the legitimately elected government.

The constitution of 1934 provided for universal suffrage and three years later a new constitution, drafted in the aftermath of a failed coup, gave Vargas greatly extended power. During his period of rule some areas, including São Paulo, saw considerable industrial development, helping Brazil to create a modern economy. In the 1940s the first steel plant was built in the state of Rio de Janeiro at Volta Redonda with US financing. In 1942 Brazil followed the lead of the USA and declared war against the Axis powers. In Oct. 1945 the military staged a coup and Vargas was forced to step down.

Economic Problems

The subsequent election was won by Eurico Gaspar Dutra, a favourite of Vargas, whose government set presidential terms at five years and reduced the power of central government. Vargas was returned to power in 1950 but failed to dominate as he had previously. Brazil's economic problems spiralled and in 1954 Vargas was implicated in the attempted murder of a journalist. When the High Command demanded his resignation Vargas shot himself.

Juscelino Kubitschek, popularly known as JK, was elected president in 1956. He launched road and hydro-electric schemes and built a new capital, Brasília. It was hoped these programmes would be the catalyst for the development of Brazil's huge interior but instead brought uncontrollable inflation. The presidency of Jânio Quadros in 1961 was marked by his decoration of Che Guevara in a public ceremony. Antagonizing the right-

© Springer Nature Limited 2020
Palgrave Macmillan (ed.), *The Statesman's Yearbook 2020*,
https://doi.org/10.1057/978-1-349-95940-2_36

wing military, he resigned after six months in office. Vice-President João Goulart took over but his leftist policies led to his overthrow by the military in 1964.

There followed 20 years of single party rule and censored press. Humberto Castelo Branco was installed as president in April 1964. Chosen by the military to enforce fundamental political and economic reforms, Branco instead sought to introduce change through democratic channels. He narrowly survived a coup in 1965 but was forced by the military powerbrokers to take a radical line. Laws passed in Oct. 1965 suspended political parties and gave the president emergency powers. An ostensibly two-party state was created, consisting of the government-backed National Renewal Alliance (ARENA) and the Brazilian Democratic Movement (MDB). The MDB declined to field a candidate at the presidential elections of 1966 and ARENA's Costa e Silva took the presidency.

Brazil's military regime was not as brutal as those of Chile or Argentina, but at its height, around 1968 and 1969 when Costa e Silva awarded himself emergency powers, the use of torture was widespread. Costa e Silva had a stroke in Aug. 1970 and was replaced by Gen. Emílio Garrastazú Médici in Oct. He was succeeded in early 1974 by Gen. Ernesto Geisel. Geisel promoted measures to reduce censorship and increase political freedom but reverted to political oppression when electoral victory was in doubt. In April 1977 he dismissed congress when it failed to pass judicial reforms and governed using emergency powers. He resigned in 1979 to be replaced by his favoured successor, Gen. João Baptista de Oliveira Figueiredo. The generals benefited from the Brazilian economic miracle in the late 1960s and '70s, when the economy was growing by more than an annual 10%. However, uncoordinated growth led to rampant bureaucracy, corruption and inflation.

Return to Democracy

Unable to contain hyperinflation, the government authorized the restitution of political rights. In 1980 a militant working-class movement sprang up under the charismatic leadership of a worker, Lula da Silva (better known as Lula). Popular opposition, together with economic problems, forced Figueiredo to adopt the *abertura* (opening)—a slow process of returning to democratic government.

Tancredo Neves, leader of the Partido do Movimento Democratico Brasiliero (PMDB), the main opposition party, surprised his military opponents by winning the 1985 elections, but died shortly before taking power. José Sarney, his vice-president, guided the country through the transition from military to civilian rule as well as overseeing the drafting and implementation of a new democratic constitution. But the country drifted into the economic chaos afflicting the whole continent, with finance ministers changing frequently and foreign debt reaching CR$115,000m. Price and wage freezes set out in Sarney's Cruzado Plan succeeded only briefly in bringing down inflation. In the presidential run-off of Dec. 1989 voters backed two of Sarney's most vociferous critics, with Fernando Collor de Mello narrowly defeating Labour Party candidate, Lula.

Collor, of the National Reconstruction party, promised reductions in inflation and corruption. In March 1990 he confiscated 80% of every bank account worth more than US$1,200, promising to release them 18 months later with interest. He also announced the privatization of state-owned companies and the opening of Brazilian markets to foreign competition and capital. By 1992 Collor's government had failed to reach many of its targets and was embroiled in scandals and corruption, some of which were linked directly to his family. Inflation was again spiralling. Parliament, under public pressure, forced an impeachment and Itamar Franco, Collor's vice-president, took office until elections were held in Oct. 1994. Under Franco inflation leapt towards 3,000% but his fourth finance minister, Fernando Henrique Cardoso, introduced successful economic reforms.

In 1994 Cardoso was elected president for the Partido da Social Democracia Brasiliera, formed in 1990 by PMDB dissidents. He oversaw an economic revolution that included a radical privatization programme, the lowering of trade barriers and the introduction of a new currency, the *real*. A constitutional amendment in 1997 provided for consecutive presidential terms and the following year Cardoso won re-election at a time when Brazil was feeling the effects of the economic turbulence in the Far East. In Jan. 1999 the *real* was devalued, losing 35% of its value against the dollar in two months. In Cardoso's second term the public debt reached US$260bn. and the government was forced to reduce spending on health and welfare while increasing taxes. His government failed to address the problems of inequality

and corruption and at the 2002 presidential elections Cardoso's successor, José Serra, was defeated by the left-wing leader, Luiz Inácio Lula da Silva.

Lula, the country's first elected socialist president, pledged to combat Brazil's widespread poverty while co-operating with the business sector and international community. In May 2003 he invited the Democratic Movement into government to ensure the passage of key economic reforms. In 2011 Dilma Rousseff, also of the Workers' Party, succeeded him to become Brazil's first female president. Despite growing social protest over the struggling economy, she was re-elected in 2014. However, she became increasingly embroiled in a major corruption scandal involving Petrobras, the state-owned oil conglomerate, while she had been company chair between 2003 and 2010. Rising indignation over the scandal and Rousseff's alleged misuse of public funds led Congress to pursue impeachment proceedings against her in 2016. In Aug. she was removed from office and replaced by former vice-president Michel Temer for the remainder of her term. Temer's tenure also became increasingly unpopular and he did not stand in the Dec. 2018 presidential elections, which were won by Jair Bolsonaro, a radical right-wing populist.

Territory and Population

Brazil is bounded in the east by the Atlantic and on its northern, western and southern borders by all the South American countries except Chile and Ecuador. The total area (including inland waters) is 8,514,877 sq. km. It is the world's fifth largest country and occupies 47·8% of South America. Area and population as at the census of 2010:

Federal Unit and Capital	Area (sq. km)	Census population 2010
North	3,853,327	
Rondônia (Porto Velho)	237,576	1,562,409
Acre (Rio Branco)	164,165	733,559
Amazonas (Manaus)	1,559,161	3,483,985
Roraima (Boa Vista)	224,299	450,479
Pará (Belém)	1,247,690	7,581,051
Amapá (Macapá)	142,815	669,526
Tocantins (Palmas)	277,621	1,383,445
North-East	1,554,257[1]	
Maranhão (São Luís)	331,983	6,574,789
Piauí (Teresina)	251,529	3,118,360
Ceará (Fortaleza)	148,826	8,452,381
Rio Grande do Norte (Natal)	52,797	3,168,027
Paraíba (João Pessoa)	56,440	3,766,528
Pernambuco (Recife)	98,312	8,796,448
Alagoas (Maceió)	27,768	3,120,494
Sergipe (Aracaju)	21,910	2,068,017
Bahia (Salvador)	564,693	14,016,906
South-East	924,511	
Minas Gerais (Belo Horizonte)	586,528	19,597,330
Espírito Santo (Vitória)	46,078	3,514,952
Rio de Janeiro (Rio de Janeiro)	43,696	15,989,929
São Paulo (São Paulo)	248,209	41,262,199
South	576,410	
Paraná (Curitiba)	199,315	10,444,526
Santa Catarina (Florianópolis)	95,346	6,248,436
Rio Grande do Sul (Porto Alegre)	281,749	10,693,929
Central West		1,606,372
Mato Grosso (Cuiabá)	903,358	3,035,122
Mato Grosso do Sul (Campo Grande)	357,125	2,449,024
Goiás (Goiânia)	340,087	6,003,788
Distrito Federal (Brasília)	5,802	2,570,160
Total	8,514,877	190,755,799

[1]Including disputed areas between states of Piauí and Ceará.

Population density, 2010, 22·4 per sq. km. The 2010 census showed 93,406,990 males and 97,348,809 females. The urban population comprised 84·3% of the population in 2010. July 2018 population estimate, 208,494,900.

The UN gives a projected population for 2020 of 213·86m.

The official language is Portuguese.

Population of principal cities (2010 census):

São Paulo	11,152,344
Rio de Janeiro	6,320,446
Salvador	2,674,923
Brasília	2,482,210
Fortaleza	2,452,185
Belo Horizonte	2,375,151
Manaus	1,792,881
Curitiba	1,751,907
Recife	1,537,704
Porto Alegre	1,409,351
Belém	1,381,475
Goiânia	1,297,076
Guarulhos	1,221,979
Campinas	1,061,540
São Gonçalo	998,999
São Luís	958,522
Maceió	932,129
Duque de Caxias	852,138
Natal	803,739
Nova Iguaçu	787,563
Campo Grande	776,242
Teresina	767,557
São Bernardo do Campo	752,658
João Pessoa	720,785
Santo André	676,407
Osasco	666,740
Jaboatão dos Guararapes	630,595
São José dos Campos	617,106
Ribeirão Preto	602,966
Contagem	601,400
Uberlândia	587,266
Sorocaba	580,655
Aracaju	571,149
Cuiabá	540,814
Feira de Santana	510,635
Juiz de Fora	510,378

The principal metropolitan areas (census, 2010) were São Paulo (19,683,975), Rio de Janeiro (11,835,708), Belo Horizonte (5,414,701), Porto Alegre (3,958,985), Brasília (3,717,728), Recife (3,690,547), Fortaleza (3,615,767), Salvador (3,573,973), Curitiba (3,174,201) and Campinas (2,797,137).

Approximately 54% of the population of Brazil is White, 40% mixed White and Black, and 5% Black. There are some 260,000 native Indians. Less than 0·5% of the population are immigrants.

Social Statistics

The total number of registered live births in 2006 was 2,799,128 (rate of 15·4 per 1,000 population); deaths, 1,020,211 (5·6); marriages, 889,828 (4·9); divorces 162,244 (0·9). The average age at first marriage in 2006 was 28·3 years for men and 25·4 for women. Brazil legalized same-sex marriage in May 2013. Life expectancy in 2006 was 68·5 years for males and 76·1 for females. Annual population growth rate, 2000–05, 1·5%; infant mortality, 2010, 17 per 1,000 live births (down from 50 per 1,000 in 1990); fertility rate, 2006, 2·0 children per woman. The number of deaths per 1,000 live births among children under five was reduced from 59 in 1990 to 19 in

2010. Brazil's recent economic advances have enabled 36m. people to move out of extreme poverty since the Workers' Party came to power in 2003. Brazil was ranked 85th in a gender gap index of 145 countries compiled by the World Economic Forum for its *Global Gender Gap Report 2015*. The annual index considers economic, political, education and health criteria.

Climate

Because of its latitude, the climate is predominantly tropical, but factors such as altitude, prevailing winds and distance from the sea cause certain variations, though temperatures are not notably extreme. In tropical parts, winters are dry and summers wet, while in Amazonia conditions are constantly warm and humid. The northeast *sertão* is hot and arid, with frequent droughts. In the south and east, spring and autumn are sunny and warm, summers are hot, but winters can be cold when polar air-masses impinge. Brasília, Jan. 72°F (22·3°C), July 68°F (19·8°C). Annual rainfall 60" (1,512 mm). Belém, Jan. 78°F (25·8°C), July 80°F (26·4°C). Annual rainfall 105" (2,664 mm). Manaus, Jan. 79°F (26·1°C), July 80°F (26·7°C). Annual rainfall 92" (2,329 mm). Recife, Jan. 80°F (26·6°C), July 77°F (24·8°C). Annual rainfall 75" (1,907 mm). Rio de Janeiro, Jan. 83°F (28·5°C), July 67°F (19·6°C). Annual rainfall 67" (1,758 mm). São Paulo, Jan. 75°F (24°C), July 57°F (13·7°C). Annual rainfall 62" (1,584 mm). Salvador, Jan. 80°F (26·5°C), July 74°F (23·5°C). Annual rainfall 105" (2,669 mm). Porto Alegre, Jan. 75°F (23·9°C), July 62°F (16·7°C). Annual rainfall 59" (1,502 mm).

Constitution and Government

The present Constitution came into force on 5 Oct. 1988, the eighth since independence. The *President* and *Vice-President* are elected for a four-year term. To be elected candidates must secure 50% plus one vote of all the valid votes, otherwise a second round of voting is held to elect the President between the two most voted candidates. Voting is compulsory for men and women between the ages of 18 and 70 apart from illiterates (for whom it is optional); it is also optional for persons from 16 to 18 years old and persons over 70. A referendum on constitutional change was held on 21 April 1993. Turnout was 80%. 66·1% of votes cast were in favour of retaining a republican form of government, and 10·2% for re-establishing a monarchy. 56·4% favoured an executive presidency, 24·7% parliamentary supremacy.

A constitutional amendment of June 1997 authorizes the re-election of the President for one extra term of four years.

Congress consists of an 81-member *Senate* (three Senators per federal unit plus three from the Federal District of Brasília) and a 513-member *Chamber of Deputies*. The Senate is directly elected (two-thirds of it and one-third of it elected for eight years in rotation every four years). The Chamber of Deputies is elected by universal franchise for four years. There is a *Council of the Republic* which is convened only in national emergencies.

Baaklini, A. I., *The Brazilian Legislature and Political System*. 1992

Kingstone, Peter and Power, Timothy, (eds.) *Democratic Brazil Revisited*. 2008

Martinez-Lara, J., *Building Democracy in Brazil: the Politics of Constitutional Change*. 1996

Montero, Alfred, *Brazilian Politics: Reforming a Democratic State in a Changing World*. 2006

Skidmore, Thomas E., *Brazil: Five Centuries of Change*. 2009

National Anthem

'Ouviram do Ipiranga às margens plácidas de um povo heróico o brado retumbante' ('The peaceful banks of the Ipiranga heard the resounding cry of an heroic people'); words by J. O. Duque Estrada, tune by F. M. da Silva.

Government Chronology

Presidents since 1930. (ARENA = National Renewal Alliance; PMDB = Brazilian Democratic Movement Party; PRN = Party for National Reconstruction; PSD = Social Democratic Party; PSDB = Brazilian Social Democracy Party; PSL = Social Liberal Party; PT = Workers' Party; PTB = Brazilian Labour Party; n/p = non-partisan)

1930–45	n/p	Getúlio Dornelles Vargas
1945–46	n/p	José Linhares
1946–51	military/PSD	Eurico Gaspar Dutra
1951–54	PTB	Getúlio Dornelles Vargas
1954–56	PTB	João Fernandes de Campos Café (Filho)
1956–61	PSD	Juscelino Kubitschek de Oliveira
1961	n/p	Jânio da Silva Quadros
1961–64	PTB	João Belchior Marques Goulart
1964–67	military	Humberto de Alencar Castelo Branco
1967–69	military	Artur da Costa e Silva
1969	Triumvirate (military)	Augusto Hamann Rademaker Grünewald, Aurélio de Lyra Tavares, Márcio de Souza e Mello
1969–74	military/ARENA	Emílio Garrastazú Médici
1974–79	military/ARENA	Ernesto (Beckmann) Geisel
1979–85	military/ARENA/PDS	João Baptista de Oliveira Figueiredo
1985–90	PMDB	José Sarney Costa
1990–92	PRN	Fernando Affonso Collor de Mello
1992–95	n/p	Itamar Augusto Cautiero Franco
1995–2003	PSDB	Fernando Henrique Silva Cardoso
2003–11	PT	Luiz Inácio Lula da Silva
2011–16	PT	Dilma Rousseff
2016–19	PMDB	Michel Temer
2019–	PSL	Jair Bolsonaro

Recent Elections

In presidential elections held on 7 Oct. 2018, Jair Bolsonaro of the Social Liberal Party (PSL) won 46·0% of votes cast, Fernando Haddad of the Workers' Party (PT) 29·3%, Ciro Gomes of the Democratic Labour Party (PDT) 12·5%, Geraldo Alckmin of the Brazilian Social Democracy Party (PSDB) 4·8% and João Amoêdo of the New Party (NOVO) 2·5%. Eight other candidates received less than 2·0% of the vote each. In the second round run-off on 28 Oct., Bolsonaro won with 55·1% of the vote against 44·9% for Haddad. Turnout in the first round was 79·7% and in the run-off 78·7%.

Parliamentary elections were also held on 7 Oct. 2018 for the Chamber of Deputies.

In the elections to the 513-seat Chamber of Deputies, the Workers' Party (PT) won 56 seats; Social Liberal Party (PSL), 52; Progressive Party (PP), 37; Brazilian Democratic Movement (MDB), 34; Social Democratic Party (PSD), 34; Republic Party (PR), 33; Brazilian Socialist Party (PSB), 32; Brazilian Republican Party (PRB), 30; Brazilian Social Democracy Party (PSDB), 29; Democrats (DEM), 29; Democratic Labour Party (PDT), 28; Solidarity (SD), 13; Podemos (PODE), 11; Socialism and Liberty Party (PSOL), 10; Brazilian Labour Party (PTB), 10; Communist Party of Brazil (PCdoB), 9; New Party (NOVO), 8; Popular Socialist Party (PPS), 8; Republican Party of the Social Order (PROS), 8; Social Christian Party (PSC), 8. A further ten parties took 34 seats in total.

Following the Senate elections of 7 Oct. 2018 the MDB had 12 seats; PSDB, 8; DEM, 7; PDT, 6; PP, 6; PSD, 6; PT, 6; PSB, 5; Sustainability Network (REDE), 5; PSL, 4; PTB, 4; Humanist Party of Solidarity (PHS), 2; PPS, 2; PR, 2; PODE, 1; PRB, 1; Progressive Republican Party (RRP), 1; PROS, 1; PSC, 1; SD, 1.

Current Government

President: Jair Bolsonaro; b. 1955 (Social Liberal Party; since 1 Jan. 2019).
  Vice-President: Hamilton Mourão.
  In Feb. 2019 the coalition government comprised:
  Minister of Agriculture, Livestock and Supply: Tereza Cristina. *Attorney General:* André Luiz Mendonça. *Citizenship:* Osmar Terra. *Defence:* Fernando

Azevedo e Silva. *Economy:* Paulo Guedes. *Education:* Ricardo Vélez Rodriguez. *Environment:* Ricardo de Aquino Salles. *Foreign Relations:* Ernesto Araújo. *Health:* Luiz Henrique Mandetta. *Infrastructure:* Tarcísio Gomes de Freitas. *Justice and Public Security:* Sérgio Moro. *Mines and Energy:* Bento Costa Lima. *Regional Development:* Gustavo Canuto. *Science, Technology, Innovation and Communication:* Marcos Pontes. *Tourism:* Marcelo Álvaro Anonio. *Transparency, Supervision and Control:* Wagner Rosário. *Women, Family and Human Rights:* Damares Alves. *Chief of Staff of the Presidency:* Onyx Lorenzoni. *Secretary of the Government:* Carlos Alberto dos Santos Cruz. *Secretary General of the Presidency:* Gustavo Bebianno.
  President of the Chamber of Deputies: Rodrigo Maia.
Government Website: http://www.brasil.gov.br

Current Leaders

Jair Bolsonaro

Position
President

Introduction
Jair Bolsonaro became president in Jan. 2019 on a platform of tackling the endemic corruption that has characterized Brazilian politics over recent years. However, his radical populist views on race, gender and sexuality, allied to pledges to further militarize the police and loosen public gun laws, make him a divisive figure in national politics.

Early Life
Bolsonaro was born on 21 March 1955 in Glicério, in the southwest state of São Paulo. He graduated from the Agulhas Negras military academy in 1977 and began a career in the army. In 1986 he was reprimanded for his comments in a magazine about low pay in the armed forces. Two years later, he joined the reserve army with the rank of captain while also running for the Rio de Janeiro City Council as a member of the Christian Democratic Party. In 1990 he was elected to the lower chamber of Congress, retaining his seat for 27 years.

In July 2018 he was nominated as a presidential candidate by the conservative Social Liberal Party, with Gen. Hamilton Mourão as his running mate. In Sept. 2018 Bolsonaro was stabbed while on the election campaign trail, but on 7 Oct. he emerged as the leading candidate after the first round of voting with 40% support. Three weeks later he defeated the Workers' Party candidate, Fernando Haddad, in a run-off poll. In the wake of political scandals and rising crime, Bolsonaro's promises to tackle corruption and empower citizens with liberal gun laws won support from a disenchanted youth vote that was too young to remember military rule and from an older voting public seeking a return of law and order.

Career in Office
Addressing the annual World Economic Forum at Davos in Jan. 2019, Bolsonaro promised investment in safety and security in a bid to attract visitors to the country. He also stressed the need to balance the preservation of the environment and biodiversity alongside economic progress, and argued for a lowering of the tax burden and making the economy more accessible to foreign trade.

Defence

Conscription is for nine to 12 months.
  In 2013 defence expenditure totalled US$34,730m. (US$173 per capita), representing 1·4% of GDP. Brazil was responsible for 49% of South America's military spending in 2013.
  As at 31 Jan. 2013, 2,202 personnel (including 2,170 troops) were deployed in UN peacekeeping operations.

Army
There are seven military commands and 12 military regions. Strength, 2011, 190,000 (including 70,000 conscripts). Equipment in 2011 included 267 main battle tanks.

Navy
The principal ship of the Navy until it was decommissioned in Feb. 2017 was Brazil's only aircraft carrier, the 32,700-tonne *São Paulo* (formerly the French *Foch*). It had been commissioned in 1963 and purchased in 2000.

The main ships now are six multipurpose frigates, two anti-submarine warfare frigates, one training frigate and five diesel submarines.

Naval bases are at Rio de Janeiro, Salvador, Natal, Belém, Rio Grande and São Paulo, with river bases at Brasília, Ladário and Manaus.

Active personnel in 2011 totalled 59,000, including 15,000 Marines and 2,500 in Naval Aviation.

Air Force

The Air Force has four commands: COMGAR (operations), COMDABRA (aerospace defence), COMGAP (logistics) and COMGEP (personnel). There are seven air regions. Personnel strength, 2011, 69,480. There were 235 combat aircraft in 2011, including Mirage F-2000s and F-5Es.

Economy

Agriculture accounted for 5·2% of GDP in 2014, industry 24·0% and services 70·8%.

In Dec. 2005 the government repaid the country's entire US$15·5bn. debt to the IMF two years ahead of schedule.

Overview

Brazil's economy has experienced rapid expansion over the last few decades to become the eighth largest in the world and the largest in Latin America. The country has an abundance of natural resources and is the ninth largest energy producer in the world. Oil reserves were estimated at 12·4bn. bbls in 2018, with further offshore natural gas and oil deposits yet to be fully exploited. It is also the fourth largest food exporter in the world and is a major research centre for biotechnology and genetic sciences.

However, while there is a diverse industrial sector—principally textiles, cement, iron ore, tin, steel, automobiles and aircraft-part manufacturing—the economy remains over-reliant on commodity exports. Sluggish growth, coupled with fiscal slippage and a weakening external account, led to Standard & Poor's international credit rating agency downgrading the country's sovereign debt rating in 2013, and it was further reduced to junk status in 2015 as Brazil experienced a prolonged recession. Moreover, the energy sector has been threatened by weak market conditions and the impact of corruption scandals involving the government and Petrobras, the state-controlled petroleum giant.

The country's growth rate decelerated steadily from an annual average of 4·5% between 2006 and 2010 to 2·4% between 2011 and 2014. GDP then contracted by 3·5% in both 2015 and 2016 respectively. Economic instability, as a result of the fall in commodity prices, coupled with ongoing political crises have undermined the confidence of consumers and investors. After falling for eight consecutive quarters, growth resumed in 2017 (initially driven by the agriculture sector) and recorded a rise of 1% for the year as a whole. Although investment is still weak, falling inflation (partly reflecting lower food prices and reduced demand) has buoyed consumer purchasing power. Fiscal policy must address the high level of public debt, which reached 78·4% of GDP in 2017. Meanwhile, unemployment fell from its 2017 peak of 14% to 11·7% by late 2018.

Brazil's economic and social progress lifted 29m. people out of poverty between 2003 and 2014 and saw inequality drop significantly—the Gini coefficient (a statistical measure of inequality) fell by 6·6 percentage points in the same period, down to 51·5%. The income level of the poorest 40% of the population rose, on average, 7·1% in real terms between 2003 and 2014, compared to a 4·4% income growth for the population as a whole. Extreme poverty (those living on less than US$1·25 a day) fell from 7·2% to 3·8% between 2005 and 2012, according to the United Nations Children's Fund, but had risen again to 6·1% in 2013.

Brazil's medium-term outlook depends on the success of growth-enhancing reforms. Raising productivity and competitiveness is the main challenge, along with refocusing social spending and reducing ineffective industrial subsidies. President Bolsonaro, who took office in Jan. 2019 and also assumed the economics portfolio, has promised reforms to hasten recovery, including an overhaul of the state pension system.

Currency

The unit of currency is the *real* (BRL) of 100 *centavos*, which was introduced on 1 July 1994 to replace the former *cruzeiro real* at a rate of 1 real (R$1) = 2,750 cruzeiros reais (CR$2,750). The *real* was devalued in Sept. 1994, March 1995, June 1995 and Jan. 1999, when it was allowed to float. Inflation rates (based on IMF statistics):

2008	2009	2010	2011	2012	2013	2014	2015	2016	2017
5·7%	4·9%	5·0%	6·6%	5·4%	6·2%	6·3%	9·0%	8·7%	3·4%

In 1990 inflation had been 2,948%.

In Sept. 2009 foreign exchange reserves were US$215,978m. (US$32,434m. in 2000); gold reserves totalled 1·08m. troy oz. Total money supply in Aug. 2009 was R$201,761m.

Budget

Central government revenue and expenditure (in R$1m.):

	2009	2010	2011
Revenue	772,793	987,943	1,035,457
Expenditure	851,259	1,006,188	1,089,901

Principal sources of revenue in 2011 were: taxes on income, profits and capital gains, R$294,313m.; taxes on goods and services, R$277,984m.; social security contributions, R$258,278m. Main items of expenditure by economic type in 2011: social benefits, R$340,516m.; interest, R$249,419m.; grants, R$188,339m.

Performance

Real GDP growth rates (based on IMF statistics):

2008	2009	2010	2011	2012	2013	2014	2015	2016	2017
5·1%	−0·1%	7·5%	4·0%	1·9%	3·0%	0·5%	−3·5%	−3·5%	1·0%

Total GDP in 2017 was US$2,055·5bn.

Banking and Finance

On 31 Dec. 1964 the Banco Central do Brasil (*President*, Roberto Campos Neto) was founded as the national bank of issue and at May 2010 had total assets of R$1,192·4bn.

The Banco do Brasil/Bank of Brazil (founded in 1853 and reorganized in 1906) is a state-owned commercial bank; it had 4,048 branches in 2007 throughout the country. In Nov. 2008 Banco Itaú and Unibanco agreed to merge in a move that created South America's biggest bank, Itaú Unibanco, with assets in 2010 of R$651bn. (US$366bn.). In March 2007 total deposits in banks were R$386·8bn.

In Nov. 1998 the IMF announced a US$41·5bn. financing package to help shore up the Brazilian economy. In Aug. 2001 it gave approval for a new US$15bn. stand-by credit, and in Aug. 2002 granted an additional US$30bn. loan to try to prevent a financial meltdown that was threatening to devastate the region. In Dec. 2005 Brazil repaid all its IMF debts.

Brazil received US$62·7bn. worth of foreign direct investment in 2017, down from US$73·1bn. in 2014. At the end of 2017 foreign direct investment stocks totalled US$778·3bn.

In 2010 total external debt amounted to US$346,978m. (equivalent to 16·9% of GNI), up from US$187,526m. in 2005.

There is a stock exchange in São Paulo.

Energy and Natural Resources

Environment

Brazil's carbon dioxide emissions from the consumption of energy in 2011 were the equivalent of 2·4 tonnes per capita. An *Environmental Performance Index* compiled in 2016 ranked Brazil 46th of 180 countries, with 78·9%. The index examined various factors in nine areas—agriculture, air quality, biodiversity and habitat, climate and energy, fisheries, forests, health impacts, water and sanitation, and water resources.

Brazil has the world's biggest river system and about a quarter of the world's primary rainforest. Current environmental issues are deforestation in the Amazon Basin, air and water pollution in Rio de Janeiro and São Paulo (the world's fourth largest city), and land degradation and water pollution caused by improper mining activities. Contaminated drinking water causes 70% of child deaths.

Electricity

Hydro-electric power accounts for about 78% of Brazil's total electricity output, although its share has been gradually falling—from around 93% in 1990—as the proportion of electricity generated from fossil fuels has been rising. Brazil was only the ninth largest electricity producer overall in the world in 2011, but the second largest producer of hydro-electric power (behind only China). Installed electric capacity (2011) was 117·1m. kW, of which 82·5m. kW hydro-electric. Production cannot meet demand, making Brazil a net importer of electricity. There were two nuclear power plants in 2014, supplying some 2·9% of total output. A third nuclear plant is currently under construction and is expected to become operational around 2023. There are plans for a further four plants to be built by 2030. Production (2011) 531,759 GWh. Consumption per capita in 2011 was 2,882 kWh.

Oil and Gas

There are 13 oil refineries, of which 11 are state-owned. Oil production in 2017 was a record 142·7m. tonnes, up from 95·4m. tonnes in 2007. Proven oil reserves rose to 15·6bn. bbls in 2013. Brazil began to open its markets in 1999 by inviting foreign companies to drill for oil, and in 2000 the monopoly of the state-owned Petrobras on importing oil products was removed. In Nov. 2007 the discovery of a huge offshore oilfield was announced off Brazil's southeastern Atlantic coast that could increase the country's oil reserves by as much as 40%. The Tupi field, which contains reserves estimated at between 5bn. and 8bn. bbls of oil, is the largest new oilfield discovered since Kazakhstan's Kashagan field in 2000. Oil now contributes 12% of total GDP. It has been suggested that by 2020 Brazil could be the world's fifth largest oil producer.

Natural gas production in 2013 was a record 21·3bn. cu. metres with reserves of 500bn. cu. metres. One of the most significant developments has been the construction of the 3,150-km Bolivia–Brazil gas pipeline, one of Latin America's biggest infrastructure projects, costing around US$2bn. (£1·2bn.). The pipeline runs from the Bolivian interior across the Brazilian border at Puerto Suárez-Corumbá to the far southern port city of Porto Alegre. Gas from Bolivia began to be pumped to São Paulo in 1999.

Ethanol

Brazil is the second largest producer of ethanol (after the USA) and the second largest exporter. Production, almost exclusively from sugarcane, totalled 21·1bn. litres in 2012 (also 21·1bn. litres in 2011 but 26·2bn. litres in 2010). Ethanol accounts for half of all the transport fuel used in Brazil.

Minerals

The chief minerals are bauxite, gold, iron ore, manganese, nickel, phosphates, platinum, tin and uranium. Output figures, 2012 unless otherwise indicated (in 1,000 tonnes): phosphate rock, 44,560 (2011); bauxite, 33,260; hard coal, 12,704; salt, 7,482; asbestos (crude ore), 4,365 (2011 estimate); manganese (gross weight), 2,796; magnesite, 2,232; aluminium, 1,436; chromium (crude ore), 473; copper, 223; barytes, 186; zinc, 164; nickel ore, 139; graphite (concentrate), 88; zirconium, 20; lead (lead content in concentrate), 17; tin (tin content), 14. Deposits of coal exist in Rio Grande do Sul, Santa Catarina and Paraná. Total reserves are estimated at 9,920m. tonnes in 2005.

Iron is found chiefly in Minas Gerais, notably the Cauê Peak at Itabira. Proven reserves of iron ore amounted to around 15,800m. tonnes in 2005. Total output of iron ore, 2013 was 386·3m. tonnes. Brazil is the second largest producer of iron ore after China.

Gold is chiefly from Pará, Mato Grosso and Minas Gerais; total production (2013), 79·6 kg. Silver output (2013), 72·5 kg. Diamond output in 2013 was an estimated 49,000 carats, mainly from Minas Gerais and Mato Grosso.

Agriculture

In 2007 the agricultural population was an estimated 23·06m. There were 5·2m. farms in 2006. There were some 59·5m. ha. of arable land in 2007 and 7·0m. ha. of permanent crops.

Production (in tonnes):

	2004	2005
Apples	980,203	850,535
Bananas	6,583,564	6,703,400
Beans	2,967,007	3,021,641
Cassava	23,926,553	25,872,015

(continued)

	2004	2005
Coconut (1,000 fruits)	2,078,226	2,079,291
Coffee	2,465,710	2,140,169
Cotton	3,801,382	3,668,283
Grapes	1,291,382	1,232,564
Maize	41,787,558	35,113,312
Onions	1,157,562	1,137,684
Oranges	18,313,717	17,853,443
Pineapples (1,000 fruits)	1,477,299	1,528,313
Potatoes	3,047,083	3,130,174
Rice	13,277,008	13,192,863
Soya	49,549,941	51,182,074
Sugarcane	415,205,835	422,956,646
Tomatoes	3,515,567	3,452,973
Wheat	5,818,846	4,658,790

Brazil is the world's leading producer of sugarcane, oranges and coffee—production of all three is more than double that of any other country. Harvested coffee area, 2005, 2,325,920 ha., principally in the states of Minas Gerais, Espírito Santo, São Paulo and Paraná. Harvested cocoa area, 2005, 625,384 ha. Bahia furnished 65% of the output in 2005. Two crops a year are grown. Brazil accounts for more than a quarter of annual coffee production worldwide. Harvested castor-bean area, 2005, 230,911 ha. Tobacco is grown chiefly in Rio Grande do Sul and Santa Catarina.

Rubber is produced chiefly in the states of São Paulo, Mato Grosso, Bahia, Espírito Santo and Minas Gerais. Output, 2005, 172,847 tonnes.

Livestock, 2005: cattle, 207·2m.; pigs, 34·1m.; sheep, 15·6m.; goats, 10·3m.; horses, 5·8m.; mules, 1·4m.; asses, 1·2m.; chickens and other poultry, 999·0m.

Livestock products, 2005 (in 1,000 tonnes): beef and veal, 6,346; pork and pork products, 2,157; poultry meat, 7,866; milk, 24·6bn. litres; hen's eggs, 2·8bn. dozen; wool, 11; honey, 34.

Forestry

With forest lands covering 493,538,000 ha. in 2015, only Russia had a larger area of forests. Other wooded land covered a further 39,535,000 ha. in 2015. Brazil's forests account for 12% of global forest cover. In 2015, 59·0% of the total land area of Brazil was under forests. The annual loss of 984,000 ha. of forests between 2010 and 2015 was the biggest in any country in the world over the same period. Of the total area under forests 41% was primary forest in 2015, 57% other naturally regenerated forest and 2% planted forest.

Timber production in 2011 totalled 284·02m. cu. metres, a figure exceeded only in the USA, India and China. In 1996 the government ruled that Amazonian landowners could log only 20% of their holdings instead of 50%, as had previously been permitted. In 2008 the government pledged to end net deforestation and reduce deforestation in the Amazon by 80% by 2020. Amazon deforestation in 2011–12, at 4,571 sq. km, was around a sixth of the 2003–04 total and at its lowest level since records began. There was, however, an increase again in 2012–13, to 5,891 sq. km.

Fisheries

In 2012 the fishing industry had a catch of 842,987 tonnes, of which 576,945 tonnes came from sea fishing and 266,042 tonnes from inland fishing. Aquaculture production totalled 479,399 tonnes in 2010.

Industry

The leading companies by market capitalization in Brazil in March 2019 were: Petrobras, a petroleum company (US$92·6bn.); Itaú Unibanco (US$87·0bn.); and Vale (US$77·4bn.).

The main industries are textiles, shoes, chemicals, cement, lumber, iron ore, tin, steel, aircraft, motor vehicles and parts, and other machinery and equipment. The National Iron and Steel Co. at Volta Redonda, State of Rio de Janeiro, furnishes a substantial part of Brazil's steel. Production (in 1,000 tonnes): cement (2008), 51,970; pig iron (2008), 34,871; distillate fuel oil (2007), 34,035; crude steel (2008), 33,716; sugar (2007), 28,226; rolled steel (2008), 24,693; petrol (2007), 15,733; residual fuel oil (2007), 15,707; cellulose (2008), 12,697; paper (2008), 9,409. Output of other products in 2007: 68·43m. mobile phones; 37·54m. rubber tyres for cars; 12·84m. TV sets; 2·55m. motor vehicles (2008); soft drinks, 12,642·2m. litres; beer, 10,020·2m. litres.

Labour

The labour force in 2013 was 108,384,600 (90,365,500 in 2003). 75·0% of the population aged 15–64 was economically active in 2013. A constitutional amendment of 1996 prohibits the employment of children under 14 years. There is a minimum monthly wage, which was increased from R$622 to R$678 with effect from 1 Jan. 2013. In Sept. 2013, 4·9% of the workforce was unemployed based on figures from six of Brazil's largest metropolitan areas (down from 10·9% in Sept. 2004 and 7·7% in Sept. 2009).

Brazil had 0·21m. people living in slavery according to the Walk Free Foundation's 2013 *Global Slavery Index*.

International Trade

In 1990 Brazil repealed most of its protectionist legislation. Import tariffs on some 13,000 items were reduced in 1995. In 1991 the government permitted an annual US$100m. of foreign debt to be converted into funds for environmental protection.

Imports and Exports

Merchandise imports and exports for calendar years (in US$1m.):

	2012	2013	2014
Imports	223,149·1	239,620·9	229,060·1
Exports	242,579·8	242,178·1	225,098·4

Principal imports in 2014 were machinery and transport equipment (36·4%) followed by chemicals, and mineral fuels and lubricants; main exports in 2014 were crude materials and animal and vegetable oils (29·3%), food, animals and beverages, and machinery and transport equipment.

The leading import supplier in 2010 was the USA (15·1%), followed by China and Argentina; the leading export destination in 2010 was also the USA (9·7%), again followed by China and Argentina.

Communications

Roads

In 2006 there were 1,600,000 km of roads, of which 73,009 km were federal roads. In 2007 there were 37,978,000 vehicles in use, including 30,283,000 passenger cars. In 2006, 407,685 persons were injured in road accidents and 35,155 were killed.

Rail

The Brazilian railways have largely been privatized: all six branches of the large RFFSA network are now under private management. The largest areas of the network are now run by América Latina Logística (12,883 km of metre gauge in 2007) and Ferrovia Centro-Atlântica (7,080 km of metre gauge). The Rio de Janeiro suburban network is run by SuperVia (128m. passengers in 2008) and the São Paulo network by Cia Paulista de Trens Metropolitanos (390m. passengers in 2005). In 2010 the government announced plans to develop South America's first high-speed rail service linking Rio de Janeiro and São Paulo, which was originally intended to be operational in time for the 2016 Olympic Games. However, following repeated delays as at March 2018 there was no confirmed start date for the project.

Several other freight routes operate independently and are mainly used by the mining industry. There are metros in Belo Horizonte (30 km), Brasília (40 km), Fortaleza (24 km), Porto Alegre (31 km), Recife (39 km), Rio de Janeiro (46 km), Salvador (7 km), São Paulo (57 km) and Teresina (15 km).

Civil Aviation

There are major international airports at Rio de Janeiro-Galeão (Antonio Carlos Jobim International) and São Paulo (Guarulhos) and some international flights from Brasília, Porto Alegre, Recife and Salvador. The main airlines are LATAM (created in June 2012 when the Brazilian carrier TAM merged with LAN Airlines, Chile's largest airline), Gol (a low-cost airline launched in 2001) and Azul Brazilian Airlines (usually just known as Azul), founded in 2008. In 2005 TAM carried 17,109,193 passengers and Varig 13,268,869 passengers. Varig was previously Brazil's biggest airline but was surpassed by TAM and was bought by Gol in April 2007. In 2014 LATAM

carried 67,833,000 passengers, making it the world's seventh largest airline on the basis of passengers carried.

Brazil's busiest airport is Guarulhos (São Paulo), which handled 18,795,596 passengers in 2007, followed by Congonhas (São Paulo) with 15,244,401 passengers (all on domestic flights) and Brasília International (Presidente Juscelino Kubitschek International Airport) with 11,119,872 passengers. In Feb. 2012 Guarulhos was one of three Brazilian airports to be privatized.

Shipping

There are some 60,000 km of inland waterways although only about 13,000 km are used. Itaqui (which handled 135,421,000 tonnes of cargo in 2013), Tubarão and Santos are the leading ports. In 2013 Santos, the leading container port, handled 3·45m. TEUs (twenty-foot equivalent units). In Jan. 2014 there were 105 ships of 300 GT or over registered, totalling 1·65m. GT. Of the 105 vessels registered, 37 were oil tankers, 20 general cargo ships, 13 container ships, 12 bulk carriers, 12 liquid gas tankers and 11 passenger ships.

Telecommunications

Mobile phone services were opened to the private sector in 1996. In 2014 there were 280,728,799 mobile phone subscriptions (1,389·5 per 1,000 persons). The largest mobile operators are Vivo (owned by Spain's Telefónica), Claro (owned by Mexico's América Móvil) and TIM Brasil (owned by Telecom Italia). There were 44,128,188 main (fixed) telephone lines in 2014. In the same year 57·6% of the population were internet users. In June 2012 Brazil had 51·2m. Facebook users, the second highest total after the USA (26% of the population).

Social Institutions

Out of 178 countries analysed in the 2017 *Fragile States Index*—a list published jointly by the Fund for Peace and *Foreign Policy* magazine—Brazil was ranked the 69th least vulnerable to conflict or collapse. The index is based on 12 indicators of state vulnerability across social, political and economic categories.

Justice

There is a Supreme Federal Court of Justice at Brasília composed of 11 judges, and a Supreme Court of Justice; all judges are appointed by the President with the approval of the Senate. There are also Regional Federal Courts, Labour Courts, Electoral Courts and Military Courts. Each state organizes its own courts and judicial system in accordance with the federal Constitution.

In Dec. 1999 then President Cardoso created the country's first intelligence agency (the Brazilian Intelligence Agency) under civilian rule. It replaced informal networks which were a legacy of the military dictatorship, and helps authorities crack down on organized drug gangs.

The prison population was 607,731 in June 2014 (301 per 100,000 of national population). Around half of all inmates in Brazil's prisons are still awaiting trial. The annual murder rate is among the highest of any country at 30 per 100,000 population in 2016 (when there were a record 62,517 murders), around six times that of the USA. In 2015 the World Justice Project *Rule of Law Index*, which provides data on how the rule of law is experienced by the general public across eight categories, ranked Brazil 68th of 102 countries for criminal justice and 48th for civil justice.

Education

Elementary education is compulsory from seven to 14. Adult literacy in 2008 was 90·0% (male, 89·8%; female, 90·2%). In 2006 there were 107,375 pre-primary schools, with 5,588,153 pupils and 310,241 teachers; 159,016 elementary schools, with 33,282,663 pupils and 1,665,341 teachers; 24,131 secondary schools, with 8,906,820 pupils and 519,935 teachers. In 2006, 97·6% of children between the ages of seven and 14 were enrolled at schools.

In 2014 there were 8,072,146 students in tertiary education (more than double the number in 2003) with 425,842 academic staff. Brazil had 2,391 higher education institutions in 2013, of which 301 were public and 2,090 were private. Of the 301 public institutions, 106 were federal and 195 state or municipal.

In 2008 total expenditure on education came to 5·4% of GDP. Expenditure on education was 16·1% of total government spending in 2007.

Health

In 2005 there were 62,483 hospitals, clinics and health centres (18,496 private). There were a total of 443,210 beds at hospitals, clinics and health centres in 2005 (294,244 private). In 2007, 329,041 doctors, 219,827 dentists, 178,546 nurses and 104,098 pharmacists were registered with Brazil's national health system. In 2006 there were 115 physicians per 100,000 population.

Brazil has been one of the most successful countries in the developing world in the campaign against AIDS. The death rate from HIV/AIDS fell from 9·6 deaths per 100,000 people in 1996 to 6·0 in 2006.

In *Water: At What Cost? The State of the World's Water 2016*, WaterAid reported that 1·9% of the population does not have access to safe water.

Welfare

Old-age pensions begin at 65 years (men) or 60 years (women) for employees and the urban self-employed, and ages 60 (men) or 55 (women) for the rural self-employed. To qualify there must be at least 35 years contributions for men or 30 years contributions for women. The maximum monthly age pension was R$5,189·82 in 2016 and the minimum monthly age pension was R$880·00.

Unemployment benefits vary depending on insurance but, as a general rule, cover 50% of average earnings in the last three months of employment, up to three times the minimum wage. The minimum benefit is 100% of the minimum monthly wage (R$678 in Jan. 2013).

Family allowances are granted to low-income families with one or more children under the age of 14 or with disabled children attending school. In 2016, R$37·18 was paid a month for each child if the insured's earnings did not exceed R$725·02. If the insured's earnings were between R$725·03 and R$1,089·72 the monthly payment fell to R$26·20.

Religion

According to the Pew Research Center's Forum on Religion & Public Life the population was an estimated 88·9% Christian in 2010, with folk religionists accounting for 2·8% and a further 7·9% unaffiliated. Only the USA has more Christians, although Brazil has the most Catholics of any country (an estimated 133·7m. in 2010). The Roman Catholic Church has 44 ecclesiastical provinces, each headed by an archbishop. These ecclesiastical provinces are in turn subdivided into 215 dioceses. The Archbishop of São Salvador da Bahia (Murilo Sebastião Ramos Krieger) is also the Primate of Brazil. In Feb. 2019 there were ten Roman Catholic cardinals.

Culture

World Heritage Sites

The sites under Brazilian jurisdiction entered on the UNESCO World Heritage List (with year entered) are: the Historic Town of Ouro Preto (1980), the centre of the gold rush founded at the end of the 17th century; the Historic Centre of Olinda (1982), founded by the Portuguese in the 16th century and largely rebuilt in the 18th century; the centre of Salvador de Bahia, Brazil's first capital (1549–1763), with its early mix of European, African and Amerindian cultures and many colonial buildings; and the Sanctuary of Bom Jesus do Congonhas, an ornate church dating to the late 18th century (both 1985); the Iguaçu National Park (1986), with its 2,700 metre waterfall and an impressive range of flora and fauna, shared with the Iguazu National Park in Argentina; Brasília (1987), Brazil's purpose built capital city; Serra da Capivara National Park (1991) including cave paintings over 25,000 years old; the Historic Centre of São Luís (1997), which has examples of late 17th-century architecture; the Historic Centre of Diamantina, a colonial village inhabited by diamond prospectors in the 18th century; the Discovery Coast Atlantic Forest Reserves, incorporating eight separate areas protecting 100,000 ha. of Atlantic forest; and Atlantic Forest Southeast Reserves, covering 470,000 ha. over 25 protected areas (all 1999); the Pantanal Conservation Area (2000), incorporating four protected areas covering 188,000 ha. and offering access to a major freshwater wetland ecosystem; the Central Amazon Conservation Complex, covering over 6m. ha. of Amazon basin (2000 and 2003); the Cerrado Protected Areas, comprising Chapada dos Veadeiros and Emas National Parks, home to a diverse tropical ecosystem; Brazilian Atlantic Islands, comprising Fernando de Noronha and Atol das Rocas Reserves, protecting important marine flora and fauna such as dolphins and turtles and a large concentration of tropical seabirds; the Historic Centre of Goiás, established by colonizing powers in the 18th and 19th centuries (all 2001); São Francisco Square in the town of São Cristóvão, a Franciscan complex dating from the late 17th century (2010); Rio de Janeiro: Carioca Landscapes between the Mountain and the Sea, key natural elements that have shaped the city including the peaks of the Tijuca mountains, the Botanical Gardens, Corcovado Mountain and its statue of Christ, the hills around Guanabara Bay and the extensive designed landscapes along Copacabana Bay (2012); Pampulha Modern Ensemble (2016), a cultural and leisure centre that included a ballroom, a casino, the Golf Yacht Club and the São Francisco de Assis church; and Valongo Wharf Archaeological Site (2017), originally built for the landing of African slaves and located in the former harbour area of Rio de Janeiro.

Brazil shares the Jesuit Missions of the Guaranis (1983 and 1984), the ruins of five Jesuit missions in the tropical rainforest dating from the 17th and 18th centuries, with Argentina.

Press

There were 784 daily newspapers in 2014 with a combined circulation of 8,478,000. In the same year there were 123 newspapers with online editions. The daily newspapers with the highest circulation are *Folha de S. Paulo* and the tabloid *Super Notícia*. In the 2013 *World Press Freedom Index* compiled by Reporters Without Borders, Brazil was ranked 108th out of 179 countries.

Tourism

In 2012, 5,677,000 tourists visited Brazil (up from 5,433,000 in 2011 and 3,785,000 in 2002). In 2011 the largest number of tourists came from elsewhere in the Americas (3,402,000); 1,663,000 European tourists visited the country, down from 1,938,000 in 2007. Receipts in 2012 totalled US$6·89bn. (US$6·83bn. in 2011).

Festivals

New Year's Eve in Rio de Janeiro is always marked with special celebrations, with a major fireworks display at Copacabana Beach. Immediately afterwards, preparations start for Carnival, which in 2020 will be held from 21–26 Feb. Other notable cultural festivals include the Parintins Folk Festival, held at the end of June and attracting over 40,000 people, and the Bahia Carnival, held in Salvador in Feb. to celebrate African influences in the region.

Diplomatic Representatives

Of Brazil in the United Kingdom (14–16 Cockspur St., London, SW1Y 5BL)
    Ambassador: Claudio Frederico de Matos 'Fred' Arruda.

Of the United Kingdom in Brazil (Quadra 801, Conjunto K, Lote 08, Av. das Nações-Asa Sul, CEP 70408-900, Brasília)
    Ambassador: Vijay Rangarajan, CMG.

Of Brazil in the USA (3006 Massachusetts Ave., NW, Washington, D.C., 20008)
    Ambassador: Sérgio Silva do Amaral.

Of the USA in Brazil (Av. das Nações, Quadra 801, Lote 03, CEP 70403-900, Brasília, D.F.)
    Ambassador: Vacant.
    Chargé d'Affaires a.i.: William Popp.

Of Brazil to the United Nations
    Ambassador: Mauro Vieira.

Of Brazil to the European Union
    Ambassador: Marcos Galvão.

Further Reading

Banco Central do Brasil: *Boletim do Banco Central do Brasil* (monthly).
Instituto Brasileiro de Geografia e Estatística: *Anuário Estatístico do Brasil.—Indicadores IBGE* (monthly).
Baer, Werner, *The Brazilian Economy: Growth and Development.* 7th ed. 2013
Brainard, Lael and Martinez-Diaz, Leonardo, (eds) *Brazil as an Economic Superpower?: Understanding Brazil's Changing Role in the Global Economy.* 2009
Burns, Bradford E., *A History of Brazil.* 1993
Casanova, Lourdes and Kassum, Julian, *The Political Economy of an Emerging Global Power: In Search of the Brazil Dream.* 2014
Eakin, Marshall C., *Brazil: The Once and Future Country.* 1997

Falk, P. S. and Fleischer, D. V., *Brazil's Economic and Political Future.* 1988

Fausto, Boris, *A Concise History of Brazil.* 1999

Klein, Herbert, *Brazil Since 1980.* 2006

Levine, Robert M., *History of Brazil.* 2003

Love, Jospeh L. and Baer, Werner, (eds) *Brazil Under Lula: Economy, Politics, and Society Under the Worker-President.* 2009

Reid, Michael, *Brazil: The Troubled Rise of a Global Power.* 2014

Riordan, Roett, *The New Brazil.* 2011

Rohter, Larry, *Brazil on the Rise: The Story of a Country Transformed.* 2010

For other more specialized titles see under CONSTITUTION AND GOVERNMENT *above.*

National library: Biblioteca Nacional, Avenida Rio Branco 219, 22040-008 Rio de Janeiro, RJ.

National Statistical Office: Instituto Brasileiro de Geografia e Estatística (IBGE), Avenida Franklin Roosevelt 166, 20021-120 Rio de Janeiro, RJ. *President:* Roberto Olinto.

Website: http://www.ibge.gov.br

Brunei

Negara Brunei Darussalam (State of Brunei Darussalam)
Capital: Bandar Seri Begawan
Population projection, 2020: 445,000
GNI per capita, 2017: (PPP$) 76,427
HDI/world rank, 2017: 0·853/39=
Internet domain extension: .bn

Key Historical Events

Records from Chinese and Arab seafarers dating back 1,400 years mention settlements on the northwest coast of Borneo that may have been forerunners to those in modern Brunei. From the early ninth century Vijayapura, which ancient Chinese texts refer to as a highly developed port, came under the control of the Srivjaya Empire (centred on Palumbang on the island of Sumatra). Trade with China blossomed from the late 10th century, with Song dynasty merchants seeking camphor from the hinterland they knew as Po-ni. By the 14th century Po-ni was under the influence of both the Javanese Majapahit Empire and Ming Dynasty Chinese traders.

In the mid-15th century Melaka emerged as the key port in the region, boasting a prosperous society of Malays, Sumatrans, Javans, Gujaratis, Arabs, Persians, Filipinos and Chinese. Following its capture by Portuguese merchants in 1511, Muslim traders were forced to seek alternative ports. Among them was Brunei, where an independent sultanate was established. The reign of Bolkiah (1485–1521) is considered a 'golden age' during which Brunei developed into a prosperous realm that extended across northern Borneo (modern Sabah and Sarawak), the Sulu archipelago and parts of the Philippines (Manila Bay). The Portuguese explorer Ferdinand Magellan reached Brunei in 1521 and his Venetian navigator, Antonio Pigafetta, described the riches of Rajah Siripadah's court, including gold, pearls the size of hen's eggs, porcelain and tame elephants.

Skirmishes with Spanish naval forces in the 1560s left the Brunei sultanate weakened and it lost control of Manila in 1571 followed shortly by Sulu (both in the Philippines). The Spanish mounted an invasion of Brunei in 1578 until a cholera outbreak forced them to retreat after two months. The sultanate's influence waned further in the 17th century, with much of the region coming under the influence of Bugis warriors from the island of Sulawesi, renowned for their navigational and commercial abilities. Dutch and British influence in the East Indies increased in the 18th and 19th centuries and by the 1880s Brunei had lost much of its territory to the British adventurer James Brooke, who was granted the title of Rajah of Sarawak in 1841. Brunei became a British protectorate in 1888 and from 1906 Britain effectively established indirect rule.

The discovery of oil near the River Seria in 1929 brought great prosperity, with production reaching 6m. bbls per year by 1940. Brunei was occupied by Japanese forces in Dec. 1941, eight days after the attack on Pearl Harbor. After the Japanese surrendered in Sept. 1945 Brunei was governed by the British Military Administration, which was staffed mainly by Australians. In 1959 Sultan Omar Saifuddian III signed a new constitution that saw the Sultan become Supreme Head of State, although Britain retained responsibility for foreign affairs.

In 1962, fearful of the rise of the leftist Brunei People's Party, Sultan Omar declared a state of emergency and began ruling by decree. The following year Brunei decided against joining the Federation of Malaysia and remained a British dependency. Hassanal Bolkiah became Sultan in Oct. 1967 following his father's abdication. Full independence was achieved in Jan. 1984 and over the following decade Bolkiah strengthened his grip on power. He outlawed political parties and in 1991 introduced the conservative Malay Muslim Monarchy ideology upon which the nation's political and social institutions are based. Parliament was reopened in Sept. 2004 with 21 appointed members and the constitution was amended to allow for the appointment of elected representatives, although no date for elections has been set.

Territory and Population

Brunei, on the coast of Borneo, is bounded in the northwest by the South China Sea and on all other sides by Sarawak (Malaysia), which splits it into two parts, the smaller portion forming the Temburong district. Area, 5,765 sq. km (2,226 sq. miles). Population (2016 census) 417,256 (214,104 males), giving a density of 72·4 per sq. km.

The UN gives a projected population for 2020 of 445,000.

In 2011, 76·1% of the population lived in urban areas. The four districts are Brunei/Muara (2016 census: 289,630), Belait (69,062), Tutong (48,313) and Temburong (10,251). The capital is Bandar Seri Begawan (2016 census, provisional: 202,715); other large towns are Kuala Belait and Seria. Ethnic groups include Malays (66%) and Chinese (10%).

The official language is Malay but English is in use.

Social Statistics

2005 births, 6,933; deaths, 1,072. Rates, 2005: birth per 1,000 population, 18·7; death, 2·9. There were 2,018 marriages in 2005. Life expectancy in 2007: males, 74·9 years; females, 79·6. Annual population growth rate, 1995–2005, 2·5%. Infant mortality, 2010, six per 1,000 live births; fertility rate, 2005, 2·1 children per woman. Brunei was ranked 88th in a gender gap index of 145 countries compiled by the World Economic Forum for its *Global Gender Gap Report 2015*. The annual index considers economic, political, education and health criteria.

Climate

The climate is tropical marine, hot and moist, but nights are cool. Humidity is high and rainfall heavy, varying from 100" (2,500 mm) on the coast to 200" (5,000 mm) inland. There is no dry season. Bandar Seri Begawan, Jan. 80°F (26·7°C), July 82°F (27·8°C). Annual rainfall 131" (3,275 mm).

Constitution and Government

The Sultan and Yang Di Pertuan of Brunei Darussalam is HM Sultan Haji Hassanal Bolkiah Mu'izzadin Waddaulah. He succeeded on 5 Oct. 1967 at his father's abdication and was crowned on 1 Aug. 1968. On 10 Aug. 1998 his son, Oxford-graduate Prince Al-Muhtadee Billah, was inaugurated as Crown Prince and heir apparent.

On 29 Sept. 1959 the Sultan promulgated a constitution, but parts of it have been in abeyance since Dec. 1962 under emergency powers assumed by the Sultan. The Legislative Council (*Majlis Masyuarat Megeri*) was suspended in 1984 but reconvened in Sept. 2004 following a constitutional amendment that allowed for the first elections since 1962, with a third of 45 members to be directly elected. However, no direct elections had taken place by Jan. 2017 when the Sultan appointed a new 33-member Legislative Council comprised of *ex officio* cabinet members, titled persons, persons of distinction and district representatives. As both the head of state and head of government, the Sultan also presides over an appointed Council of Cabinet Ministers that assists with executive matters, and is additionally advised by the Council of Succession, the Privy Council, the Religious Council and the Adat Istiadat Council, which deal with state customs and cultural affairs.

National Anthem

'Ya Allah, lanjutkan lah usia' ('God bless His Majesty'); words by P. Rahim, tune by H. Sagap.

Current Government

In Feb. 2019 the Council of Ministers was composed as follows:
Prime Minister, Minister of Defence, Finance, and Foreign Affairs and Trade: HM Sultan Haji Hassanal Bolkiah Mu'izzadin Waddaulah (the Sultan).

Minister of Communications: Abdul Mutalib bin Pehin Orang Kaya Seri Setia Dato Paduka Haji Mohammad Yusof. *Culture, Youth and Sports:* Maj.-Gen. Dato Paduka Seri Haji Aminuddin Ihsan bin Pehin Orang Kaya Saiful Mulok Dato Seri Paduka Haji Abidin. *Defence (No. 2):* Pehin Datu Lailaraja Maj.-Gen. (retd) Dato Paduka Seri Haji Awang Halbi bin Haji Mohammad Yussof. *Development:* Dato Seri Paduka Haji Suhaimi bin Haji Gafar. *Education:* Dato Paduka Haji Hamzah bin Haji Sulaiman. *Energy and Industry:* Dato Paduka Haji Mat Suny bin Haji Mohammad Hussein. *Finance (No. 2):* Dato Seri Paduka Haji Mohammadd Amin Liew bin Abdullah. *Foreign Affairs and Trade (No. 2):* Dato Seri Paduka Haji Erywan bin Pehin Datu Pekerma Jaya Haji Mohammad Yusof. *Health:* Dato Paduka Dr Haji Mohammad Isham bin Jaafar. *Home Affairs:* Pehin Orang Kaya Seri Kerna Dato Seri Setia Awang Haji Abu Bakar bin Haji Apong. *Primary Resources and Tourism:* Dato Seri Setia Haji Ali bin Haji Apong. *Religious Affairs:* Pehin Udana Khatib Dato Paduka Seri Setia Ustaz Awang Haji Badaruddin bin Pengarah Dato Paduka Haji Othman.

Senior Minister at the Prime Minister's Office: HRH Prince Haji Al-Muhtadee Billah. *Ministers in the Prime Minister's Office:* Pehin Orang Kaya Laila Setia Bakti Diraja Dato Laila Utama Haji Awang Isa bin Pehin Datu Perdana Manteri Dato Laila Utama Haji Awang Ibrahim; Dato Seri Paduka Haji Abdul Mokti bin Haji Mohammad Daud.

Office of the Prime Minister: http://www.pmo.gov.bn

Current Leaders

Sultan Sir Hassanal Bolkiah (Sultan of Brunei)

Position
Head of State

Introduction
The Sultan was crowned Brunei's 29th head of state on 1 Aug. 1968 following the abdication of his father the previous year and on 5 Oct. 2017 he celebrated the 50th anniversary of his succession. He is among the world's richest men.

Early Life
The Sultan was born on the 15 July 1946 in Bandar Seri Begawan. He was educated in Darussalam, Brunei and Malaysia. He became the Crown Prince of Brunei in 1961 and in 1966–67 he enlisted as an officer cadet at the Royal Military Academy in Sandhurst in the UK.

In 1978 he led the mission to London which paved the way for Brunei to become a sovereign state. On 1 Jan. 1984 a treaty of friendship ended British control over Brunei's foreign affairs and defence.

Career in Office
The Sultan is head of government as well as head of state. He is prime minister, minister of defence and minister of finance. Under the 1959 constitution and the Malay Muslim Monarchy tradition, he is assisted by a council of cabinet ministers, a privy council, council of succession and a religious council. A legislative council (a third of whose 45 members will, following a constitutional amendment in Sept. 2004, be directly elected) is to be revived, although elections have yet to be scheduled.

In May 2010 the Sultan reshuffled non-royal members of the cabinet, appointing the first female minister and raising the position of attorney general to cabinet rank. In May 2014 a Sharia-based Islamic legal code was introduced for the sultanate's majority Muslim population. In further cabinet changes in Oct. 2015 the Sultan took over the foreign affairs and trade portfolio previously held by Prince Haji Mohammad Bolkiah, and former education minister Dato Seri Setia Haji Awang Abu Bakar bin Haji Apong was appointed home affairs minister.

Brunei's wealth originates from the country's large oil and gas reserves, although earnings from overseas investments have exceeded those from exports. The people of Brunei enjoy high subsidies and pay no taxes.

Defence

In 2013 military expenditure totalled US$416m. (US$1,002 per capita), representing 2·5% of GDP.

Army

The armed forces are known as the Task Force and contain the naval and air elements. Only Malays are eligible for service. Strength (2011): 4,900.

There is a Gurkha reserve unit of 400–500.

Navy

The Royal Brunei Armed Forces Flotilla includes three fast missile-armed attack craft. Personnel in 2011 numbered 1,000.

Air Force

The Royal Brunei Air Force (formerly known as the Air Wing) was formed in 1965. Personnel (2011), 1,100. There are no combat aircraft.

Economy

In 2012 industry contributed 71·1% to GDP, services 28·2% and agriculture 0·7%. The fall in oil prices in 1997–98 led to the setting up of an Economic Council to advise the Sultan on reforms. In 1998 an investigation was mounted into the Amedeo Corporation, Brunei's largest private company, run by Prince Jefri, the Sultan's brother. Amedeo collapsed with large debts.

Overview

Oil and gas production annually accounts for around 98% of exports, 93% of government revenues and 68% of GDP. Brunei is the fourth largest producer of oil in southeast Asia and has one of the highest standards of living in the world. GDP per capita was US$38,563 in 2013, behind only Singapore and Hong Kong in Asia. In March 2018 Brunei and ten other countries bordering the Pacific (although not the USA) signed the Comprehensive and Progressive Agreement for Trans-Pacific Partnership.

Growth averaged 1·2% per year between 2003 and 2012. However, low global energy prices were responsible for a GDP contraction of 3·8% between mid-2013 and early 2015. Also, the budget deficit was expected to reach 16% of GDP in the fiscal year 2015–16, down from a 28% surplus in 2011–12.

With declining oil and gas supplies, the government embarked on a process of economic diversification, and in 2014 the non-energy sector grew by 1·9% on the back of high public spending. Rainforests cover 70% of the country and eco-tourism is ripe for development. The country also aims to become a major financial centre. The central bank has implemented regulatory reform and improved the financial infrastructure, although future prospects may be limited because banks are unable to set their own loan rates.

Currency

The unit of currency is the *Brunei dollar* (BND) of 100 cents, which is at parity with the Singapore dollar (also legal tender). There was deflation of 0·7% in 2016 and of 0·2% in 2017.

Budget

The financial year runs from 1 April–31 March. Revenues in 2009–10 totalled B$6,393m.; expenditures were B$6,639m. Tax revenues accounted for 58·5% of revenues in 2009–10; current expenditure accounted for 70·6% of total expenditures.

Performance

The economy contracted by 0·4% in 2015 and 2·5% in 2016. Brunei then came out of its four-year recession in 2017 when there was real GDP growth of 1·3%. Total GDP in 2017 was US$12·1bn.

Banking and Finance

The Monetary Authority of Brunei Darussalam (*Chairman:* Haji Al-Muhtadee Billah) is the note-issuing monetary authority. At Aug. 2016 there were seven conventional banks and one Islamic bank. Total bank assets in June 2017 were B$17,305m.

The International Brunei Exchange Ltd (IBX) established an international securities exchange in May 2002.

Energy and Natural Resources

Environment

Brunei's carbon dioxide emissions from the consumption of energy were the equivalent of 21·7 tonnes per capita in 2011.

Electricity

Installed capacity was an estimated 0·8m. kW in 2011. Production in 2011 was 3·73bn. kWh and consumption per capita 9,163 kWh.

Oil and Gas

The Seria oilfield, discovered in 1929, has passed its peak production. The high level of crude oil production is maintained through the increase of offshore oilfields production. Output was 6·6m. tonnes in 2013. The crude oil is exported directly, and only a small amount is refined at Seria for domestic uses. There were proven oil reserves of 1·1bn. bbls in 2013.

Natural gas is produced (12·2bn. cu. metres in 2013) at one of the largest liquefied natural gas plants in the world and is exported to Japan. There were proven reserves of 300bn. cu. metres in 2013.

Agriculture

In 2014 there were about 5,000 ha. of arable land and 6,000 ha. of permanent crops. The main crops produced in 2013 were (estimates, in 1,000 tonnes): cassava, 3; cucumbers and gherkins, 2; bananas, 1; pineapples, 1; pumpkins, squash and gourds, 1; rice, 1; spinach, 1.

Livestock in 2012: buffaloes, 2,439; goats, 6,850; pigs (estimate), 1,100; sheep (estimate), 4,000; chickens, 17m.

Livestock products (2013 estimates, in 1,000 tonnes): beef and veal, 1; poultry meat, 27; eggs, 7.

Forestry

Forests covered 0·38m. ha., or 72% of the total land area, in 2015. Most of the interior is under forest, containing large potential supplies of serviceable timber. In 2015, 69% of forest area was primary forest. Timber production in 2011 was 119,000 cu. metres.

Fisheries

The 2012 catch totalled 3,938 tonnes, exclusively from sea fishing.

Industry

Although Brunei has long been dependent on its oil and gas industry, the government has begun a programme of diversification, recognizing oil and gas as non-renewable resources. Greater emphasis is now placed on other sectors such as manufacturing, services, tourism and high technology industries, but oil still accounted for over 60% of total GDP in 2011.

Labour

The labour force in 2013 was 200,400 (167,200 in 2003). 67·4% of the population aged 15–64 was economically active in 2013. In the same year 3·8% of the population was unemployed.

International Trade

Imports and Exports

Merchandise imports in 2014 totalled US$3,598·7m. (US$3,612·4m. in 2013) and merchandise exports US$10,508·8m. (US$11,447·2m. in 2013).

Principal imports in 2014 were machinery and transport equipment (38·6%) followed by manufactured goods, and food, animals and beverages; main exports in 2014 were mineral fuels and lubricants (92·5%), chemicals, and machinery and transport equipment.

The leading import supplier in 2010 was Malaysia (21·6%), followed by Singapore and Japan; the leading export destination in 2010 was Japan (30·6%), followed by Indonesia and South Korea.

Communications

Roads

There were an estimated 3,560 km of roads in 2005; 77·2% of all roads were paved in 2005. The main road connects Bandar Seri Begawan with Kuala Belait and Seria. In 2007 there were 252,700 passenger cars in use (649 per 1,000 inhabitants—one of the highest rates in the world), 16,700 vans and lorries, 1,500 buses and coaches, and 12,200 motorcycles and mopeds. There were 38 fatalities in road accidents in 2005.

Civil Aviation

Brunei International Airport (Bandar Seri Begawan) handled 1,262,343 passengers (all international) in 2005. The national carrier is the state-owned Royal Brunei Airlines (RBA). In 2006 RBA operated services to Auckland, Bangkok, Brisbane, Darwin, Denpasar Bali, Dubai, Frankfurt, Ho Chi Minh City, Hong Kong, Jakarta, Jeddah, Kota Kinabalu, Kuala Lumpur, London, Manila, Perth, Shanghai, Sharjah, Singapore, Surabaya and Sydney. RBA carried 1·10m. passengers in 2013, up slightly from 1·03m. in 2012 although down from a peak of 1·35m. in 2010.

Shipping

Regular shipping services operate from Singapore, Hong Kong, Sarawak and Sabah to Bandar Seri Begawan, and there is a daily passenger ferry between Bandar Seri Begawan and Labuan. In Jan. 2014 there were 14 ships of 300 GT or over registered, totalling 519,000 GT.

Telecommunications

There is a telephone network linking the main centres. Brunei had an estimated 412,900 mobile phone subscriptions in 2009 (or 1,033·0 per 1,000 inhabitants) and 80,500 fixed telephone lines. There were 787·8 internet users per 1,000 inhabitants in 2009. Fixed internet subscriptions totalled 100,000 in 2009 (255·6 per 1,000 inhabitants). In March 2012 there were 234,000 Facebook users.

Social Institutions

Out of 178 countries analysed in the 2017 *Fragile States Index*—a list published jointly by the Fund for Peace and *Foreign Policy* magazine—Brunei was ranked the 57th least vulnerable to conflict or collapse. The index is based on 12 indicators of state vulnerability across social, political and economic categories.

Justice

The Supreme Court comprises a High Court and a Court of Appeal and the Magistrates' Courts. The High Court receives appeals from subordinate courts in the districts and is itself a court of first instance for criminal and civil cases. The Judicial Committee of the Privy Council in London is the final court of appeal. Sharia Courts—applicable only to the nation's Muslims, who constitute some two-thirds of the population—have traditionally focused on resolving personal and family disputes. However, in Oct. 2013 the Sultan announced that a stricter Sharia code would be introduced; this entered force in May 2014.

The population in penal institutions in Sept. 2012 was 507 (122 per 100,000 of national population).

Education

The government provides free education to all citizens from pre-school up to the highest level at local and overseas universities and institutions. In 2005 there were 12,999 children and 701 teachers in pre-primary education; 46,012 pupils and 4,548 teachers in primary education; 41,107 pupils and 3,907 teachers in secondary education; 4,154 students and 658 academic staff in tertiary education. The University of Brunei Darussalam was founded in 1985; in 2006 there were also eight technical and vocational colleges, one teacher training college and an institute of advanced education.

Estimated adult literacy rate, 2009, 95·3% (male, 96·8%; female, 93·7%). Public expenditure on education in 2010 came to 2·0% of GDP.

Health

Medical and health services are free to citizens and those in government service and their dependants. Citizens are sent overseas, at government expense, for medical care not available in Brunei. Flying medical services are provided to remote areas. In 2005 there were four government hospitals and the Jerudong Park private hospital with a total of 1,154 beds; there were 390 physicians, 73 dentists, 1,789 nurses, 748 midwives and 41 pharmacists.

Religion

The official religion is Islam. In 2010, 75·1% of the population were Muslims (mostly Sunnis of Malay origin) according to estimates by the Pew Research Center's Forum on Religion & Public Life. There are also some Christians, Buddhists and folk religionists.

Culture

Press

In 2008 there were three daily newspapers with an average circulation of 41,000. The *Borneo Bulletin* and the *Brunei Times* are English-language papers, while *Media Permata* is a Malay paper.

Tourism

In 2015, 218,213 non-resident tourists (excluding same-day visitors) arrived by air—up from 200,989 in 2014 but down from 224,904 in 2013.

Festivals

The national day is celebrated on 23 Feb.

Diplomatic Representatives

Of Brunei in the United Kingdom (19/20 Belgrave Sq., London, SW1X 8PG)
High Commissioner: Vacant.
Acting high Commissioner: Pengiran Rooslina Weti Pengiran Haji Kamaludin.

Of the United Kingdom in Brunei (2.01, 2nd Floor, Block D, Kompleks Bangunan Yayasan Sultan Haji Hassanal Bolkiah, Jalan Pretty, Bandar Seri Begawan, PO Box 2197)
High Commissioner: Richard Lindsay.

Of Brunei in the USA (3520 International Court, NW, Suite 300, Washington, D.C., 20008)
Ambassador: Serbini Ali.

Of the USA in Brunei (Simpang 336-52-16-9 Jalan Duta, Bandar Seri Begawan, BC4115)
Ambassador: Vacant.
Chargé d'Affaires a.i.: Scott E. Woodward.

Of Brunei to the United Nations
Ambassador: Hajah Noor Qamar binti Haji Sulaiman.

Of Brunei to the European Union
Ambassador: Abu Sufian bin Haji Ali.

Further Reading

Department of Economic Planning and Development, Prime Minister's Office. *Brunei Darussalam Statistical Yearbook.*

Cleary, M. and Wong, S. Y., *Oil, Economic Development and Diversification in Brunei.* 1994

Saunders, G., *History of Brunei.* 1996

Sidhu, Jatswan S, *Historical Dictionary of Brunei Darussalam.* 2010

National Statistical Office: Department of Statistics, Department of Economic Planning and Development, Prime Minister's Office, Block 2A, Jalan Ong Sum Ping, Bandar Seri Begawan, BA 1311.

Website: http://www.depd.gov.bn/SitePages/National%20Statistics.aspx

Bulgaria

Republika Bulgaria (Republic of Bulgaria)

Capital: Sofia
Population projection, 2020: 6·94m.
GNI per capita, 2017: (PPP$) 18,740
HDI/world rank, 2017: 0·813/51
Internet domain extension: .bg

Key Historical Events

Neolithic settlements in central Bulgaria dating from 6000 BC are among the oldest man-made structures yet discovered. Thracian tribes entered the Balkans from the east around 1500 BC, establishing fortified villages. By 500 BC Thracian rulers were under Hellenic influence and Greek colonists founded settlements on the Black Sea coast. Thrace was conquered by Philip of Macedonia in 324 BC and later absorbed into the eastern (Byzantine) Roman Empire, along with Moesia to the north.

Semi-nomadic Turkic clans entered the region-among them Bulgars who united under Khan Kublat in 632. They formed alliances with Slavic tribes during the sixth and seventh centuries and defeated the Byzantines in 681. The first Bulgarian state, centred on Pliska, was characterized by intermarriage between various ethnic groups and the rise of the Slavic language and Orthodox Christianity (adopted by Boris I in 864). Tsar Simeon moved the capital to Preslav in 893. Subsequent tsars battled with Byzantium and the expanding Kievan Rus. Preslav fell in 971, followed by a westward shift and defeat to the Byzantines in 1014.

Ivan Asen I's defeat of the Byzantines in 1187 heralded the Second Bulgarian Empire, centred on Tarnovo. It held sway until the late 13th century, when invading Mongols divided the territory into rival principalities. Following battles at Kosovo (1389) and Nikopol (1396), Bulgaria was absorbed into the Ottoman Empire.

Uprisings against feudal rule occurred at Tarnovo in 1598 and 1668. The failed siege of Vienna in 1683, plus growing Austrian and Russian influence, contributed to a gradual decline in Ottoman dominance in the Balkans.

Bulgaria's 'national awakening' began in 1762 with the publication of Paisi Khilandarski's *History of the Bulgarian Slavs*. Calls for a separate Bulgarian church in the mid-19th century developed into broader revolutionary movements in the 1860s. The Russo-Turkish war of 1877–78 and the subsequent Treaties of San Stefano and Berlin paved the way for an autonomous principality of Bulgaria.

After Austria annexed Bosnia in 1908, Prince Ferdinand Saxe-Coburg-Gotha became Tsar of independent Bulgaria. To block Austrian expansion into the Balkans, Russia encouraged Greece, Serbia, Montenegro and Bulgaria to attack Turkey (First Balkan War, 1912). The dispute that followed Bulgaria's claims to Macedonia led to the Second Balkan War and the entry of Bulgaria into the First World War in 1915 on the side of Germany and Austria-Hungary.

In 1918 Ferdinand abdicated in favour of his son, Boris III. Parliamentary government was ended by a military coup in 1934. A year later, Boris established a royal dictatorship.

Bulgaria entered the Second World War in March 1941 allied to Germany. In Sept. 1944 the USSR declared war. An alliance of Communists, agrarians and pro-Soviet army officers led by Kimon Georgiev seized power and a referendum in 1946 abolished the monarchy and established Bulgaria as a republic and one-party state. The government was aligned with Moscow under the authoritarian Todor Zhivkov from 1954. In Nov. 1989 reformers within the Communist Party forced Zhivkov's resignation. Multi-party elections in Oct. 1991 were won by the centre-right Union of Democratic Forces, which formed a coalition with the predominantly ethnic-Turkish Movement for Rights and Freedom. Zhelyu Zhelev became the first directly-elected president in Jan. 1992.

Petar Stoyanov, elected as an anti-Communist pro-reform president in 1996, failed to contain political and economic unrest. In June 2001 the former King, Simeon Saxe-Coburg-Gotha, became premier. Bulgaria joined NATO in 2004 and in 2005 the Socialist leader, Sergey Stanishev, replaced Simeon as prime minister and led Bulgaria into the European Union on 1 Jan. 2007.

The general election of July 2009 was won by the Citizens for the European Development of Bulgaria (GERB), led by Boyko Borisov. However, he resigned amid anti-government protests in Feb. 2013 and his government was replaced by a technocratic administration. Borisov was nevertheless returned as premier at the head of a GERB-Reformist Bloc coalition following the general election of Oct. 2014 before standing down again in Nov. 2016 in the face of continuing popular disaffection with mainstream politics. In the ensuing polls in March 2017, GERB remained the largest parliamentary party and Borisov formed another coalition administration in May with the nationalist United Patriots.

Territory and Population

The area of Bulgaria is 111,370 sq. km (42,614 sq. miles). It is bounded in the north by Romania, east by the Black Sea, south by Turkey and Greece, and west by Serbia and North Macedonia. The country is divided into 28 districts.

Area and population in 2011 (census):

District	Area (sq. km)	Population
Blagoevgrad	6,290	323,552
Bourgas	7,644	415,817
Dobrich	4,720	189,677
Gabrovo	1,896	122,702
Haskovo	5,560	246,238
Kardzhali	3,228	152,808
Kyustendil	3,086	136,686
Lovech	4,141	141,422
Montana	3,634	148,098
Pazardzhik	4,332	275,548
Pernik	2,366	133,530
Pleven	4,645	269,752
Plovdiv	5,978	683,027
Razgrad	2,401	125,190
Rousse	2,859	235,252
Shumen	3,393	180,528
Silistra	2,845	119,474
Sliven	3,536	197,473
Smolyan	3,209	121,752
Sofia (city)	1,329	1,291,591
Sofia (district)	6,969	247,489
Stara Zagora	5,129	333,265
Targovishte	2,710	120,818
Varna	3,822	475,074
Veliko Tarnovo	4,666	258,494
Vidin	3,025	101,018
Vratsa	3,602	186,848
Yambol	3,355	131,447
Total	*111,370*	*7,364,570*

The capital, Sofia, has district status.

The population of Bulgaria at the census of 2011 was 7,364,570 (females, 3,777,999); population density 66·3 per sq. km. Bulgaria's population has been declining since the mid-1980s. It has been falling at such a rate that in 2017 it was even less than it had been in 1950. The United Nations predicts that it will lose nearly a quarter of its population by 2050. In 2011, 71·7% of the population were urban. In Dec. 2017 the population was estimated at 7,050,034.

© Springer Nature Limited 2020
Palgrave Macmillan (ed.), *The Statesman's Yearbook 2020*,
https://doi.org/10.1057/978-1-349-95940-2_38

The UN gives a projected population for 2020 of 6·94m.

Population of principal towns (2011 census): Sofia, 1,202,761; Plovdiv, 338,153; Varna, 334,870; Bourgas, 200,271; Rousse, 149,642; Stara Zagora, 138,272; Pleven, 106,954; Sliven, 91,620; Dobrich, 91,030.

Ethnic groups at the 2011 census: Bulgarians, 5,664,624; Turks, 588,318; Roma, 325,343. The actual number of Roma is estimated to be closer to 750,000.

Bulgarian is the official language.

Social Statistics

2008: live births, 77,712; deaths, 110,523; marriages, 27,722; divorces, 14,104. Rates per 1,000 population, 2008: birth, 10·2; death, 14·5; marriage, 3·6; divorce, 1·9; infant mortality, 11 per 1,000 live births (2010). There were 37,272 reported abortions in 2006. In 2005 the most popular age range for marrying was 25–29 for males and 20–24 for females. Expectation of life in 2007 was 69·6 years among males and 76·7 years among females. The annual population growth rate for the period 2010–15 was –0·6%, giving Bulgaria one of the fastest declining populations of any country. Fertility rate, 2008, 1·4 children per woman.

Climate

The southern parts have a Mediterranean climate, with winters mild and moist and summers hot and dry, but further north the conditions become more Continental, with a larger range of temperature and greater amounts of rainfall in summer and early autumn. Sofia, Jan. 28°F (–2·2°C), July 69°F (20·6°C). Annual rainfall 25·4" (635 mm).

Constitution and Government

A new constitution was adopted at Tarnovo on 12 July 1991. The *President* is directly elected for not more than two five-year terms. Candidates for the presidency must be at least 40 years old and have lived for the last five years in Bulgaria. American-style primary elections were introduced in 1996; voting is open to all the electorate.

The 240-member *National Assembly* is directly elected by proportional representation. The *President* nominates a candidate from the largest parliamentary party as *Prime Minister*.

National Anthem

'Gorda stara planina' ('Proud and ancient mountains'); words and tune by T. Radoslavov.

Government Chronology

(BKP = Bulgarian Communist Party; BSP = Bulgarian Socialist Party; GERB = Citizens for the European Development of Bulgaria; NMS = National Movement Simeon II; NMSP = National Movement for Stability and Progress; SDS = Union of Democratic Forces; Zveno = People's League Zveno; n/p = non-partisan)

Heads of State since 1943.

King		
1943–46	Simeon II (Simeon Sakskoburggotski)	
Chairman of Provisional Presidency		
1946–47	BKP	Vasil Petrov Kolarov
Chairmen of the Presidium of the National Assembly		
1947–50	BKP	Mincho Kolev Neychev
1950–58	BKP	Georgi Parvanov Damyanov
1958–64	BKP	Dimitar Ganev Varbanov
1964–71	BKP	Georgi Traykov Girovski
Chairmen of the Council of State		
1971–89	BKP	Todor Khristov Zhivkov
1989–90	BKP	Petar Toshev Mladenov
Presidents of the Republic		
1990	n/p	Petar Toshev Mladenov

(continued)

1990–97	SDS	Zhelyu Mitev Zhelev
1997–2002	SDS	Petar Stefanov Stoyanov
2002–12	BSP	Georgi Sedefchov Parvanov
2012–17	GERB	Rosen Asenov Plevneliev
2017–	n/p	Rumen Georgiev Radev

Prime Ministers since 1944.

1944–46	Zveno	Kimon Gheorgiev Stoyanov
1946–49	BKP	Georgi Mihaylov Dimitrov
1949–50	BKP	Vasil Petrov Kolarov
1950–56	BKP	Vulko Velov Chervenkov
1956–62	BKP	Anton Tanev Yugov
1962–71	BKP	Todor Khristov Zhivkov
1971–81	BKP	Stanko Todorov Georgiev
1981–86	BKP	Grisha Stanchev Filipov
1986–90	BKP	Georgi Ivanov Atanasov
1990	BSP	Andrey Karlov Lukanov
1990–91	n/p	Dimitar Popov
1991–92	SDS	Filip Dimitrov Dimitrov
1992–94	n/p	Lyuben Borisov Berov
1995–97	BSP	Zhan Vasilev Videnov
1997–2001	SDS	Ivan Yordanov Kostov
2001–05	NMS	Simeon Borisov Sakskoburggotski
2005–09	BSP	Sergey Dimitrievich Stanishev
2009–13	GERB	Boyko Metodiev Borisov
2013	n/p	Marin Raikov Nikolov (interim)
2013–14	n/p	Plamen Vasilev Oresharski
2014	n/p	Georgi Bliznashki (interim)
2014–17	GERB	Boyko Metodiev Borisov
2017	NMSP	Ognyan Stefanov Gerdzhikov (interim)
2017–	GERB	Boyko Metodiev Borisov

Recent Elections

Presidential elections were held in two rounds on 6 and 13 Nov. 2016. Rumen Radev won the first round with 25·4% of votes cast, ahead of Tsetska Tsacheva with 22·0%, Krasimir Karakachanov with 15·0%, Veselin Mareshki with 11·2%, Plamen Oresharski with 6·6% and Traycho Traykov with 5·9%. There were 15 other candidates. In the second round Radev won with 59·4% of the vote against Tsacheva with 36·2%. Turnout was 56·3% in the first round and 50·4% in the second.

Parliamentary elections were held on 26 March 2017. Citizens for the European Development of Bulgaria (GERB) won 95 of 240 seats with 33·5% of the vote; the Bulgarian Socialist Party-led BSP–Left Bulgaria won 80 seats with 27·9% of the vote; the United Patriots—an electoral alliance of nationalist parties—won 27 seats with 9·3%; the Movement for Rights and Freedom— a predominantly ethnic Turkish minority party—won 26 seats with 9·2%; Volya won 12 seats with 4·2%. Turnout was 54·1%.

European Parliament

Bulgaria has 17 representatives. At the May 2014 elections turnout was 36·1% (39·0% in 2009). GERB won 6 seats with 30·4% of the vote (political affiliation in European Parliament: European People's Party); the Coalition for Bulgaria, 4 with 18·9% (Progressive Alliance of Socialists and Democrats); the Movement for Rights and Freedoms, 4 with 17·3% (Alliance of Liberals and Democrats for Europe); Bulgaria without Censorship, 2 with 10·7% (European Conservatives and Reformists); the Reformist Bloc, 1 with 6·5% (European People's Party).

Current Government

President: Rumen Radev; b. 1963 (ind.; in office since 22 Jan. 2017).

Vice President: Iliana Iotova.

In Feb. 2019 the government comprised:

Prime Minister: Boyko Borisov; b. 1959 (Citizens for the European Development of Bulgaria/GERB; sworn in 4 May 2017, having previously been prime minister from July 2009–March 2013 and Nov. 2014–Jan. 2017).

Deputy Prime Minister: Tomislav Donchev. *Deputy Prime Minister for Economic and Demographic Policy:* Valeri Simeonov. *Deputy Minister for Public Order and Security, and Minister of Defence:* Krasimir Karakachanov. *Deputy Prime Minister for Judiciary Reform, and Minister of Foreign Affairs:* Ekaterina Zaharieva.

Minister of Agriculture, Food and Forestry: Rumen Porodzanov. *Culture:* Boil Banov. *Economy:* Emil Karanikolov. *Education and Science:* Krasimir Valchev. *Energy:* Temenuzhka Petkova. *Environment and Water:* Neno Dimov. *Finance:* Vladislav Goranov. *Health:* Kiril Ananiev. *Interior:* Mladen Marinov. *Justice:* Tsetska Tsacheva. *Labour and Social Policy:* Biser Petkov. *Regional Development and Public Works:* Petya Avramova. *Tourism:* Nikolina Angelkova. *Transport, Information Technologies and Communications:* Rossen Jeliazkov. *Youth and Sports:* Krasen Kralev. *Minister for the EU Presidency:* Lilyana Pavlova.

Government Website: http://www.government.bg

Current Leaders

Rumen Radev

Position

President

Introduction

Rumen Radev took office as president on 22 Jan. 2017, after winning the Nov. 2016 election. A pro-Russian former air force commander, he is considered a political novice.

Early Life

Rumen Georgiev Radev was born on 18 June 1963 in Dimitrovgrad and graduated from the Georgi Benkovski Bulgarian Air Force University in 1987. He joined the air force as a junior pilot and in 2003 received a master's degree in strategic studies from the Air War College at Maxwell Air Force Base in Alabama, USA. Rising through the ranks of the air force, he became a commander in 2014 but resigned his post in July 2016 over a disagreement about NATO policing of air space.

In Aug. 2016 Radev launched his presidential candidacy as an independent. He gained the backing of the Bulgarian Socialist Party (BSP), which subsequently selected him as its candidate. On 13 Nov. he defeated the candidate of the ruling GERB coalition, Tsetska Tsacheva, with 59·4% of votes. The result prompted Prime Minister Boyko Borisov to resign the following day. On 22 Jan. 2017 Radev replaced Rosen Plevneliev as president.

Career in Office

Radev's success was fuelled by public discontent at perceived failures by previous governments to address corruption and poverty in a country ranked as the European Union's poorest. There was also widespread concern over thousands of foreign migrants stranded in the country, many of whom were attempting to flee the civil war in Syria and reach Western Europe.

Seen as a critic of the conservative political status quo, Radev has stressed the importance of national security, the prevention of the migrant influx and a desire for closer ties with Moscow (including the lifting of EU sanctions imposed after Russia's annexation of Crimea in Ukraine). He has nonetheless pledged to maintain Bulgaria's membership of the EU and NATO.

Boyko Borisov

Position

Prime Minister

Introduction

Boyko Metodiev Borisov, the leader of the Citizens for the European Development of Bulgaria (GERB) party, was sworn in for a third term as premier on 4 May 2017. He had resigned from his first term in Feb. 2013 amid mass protests and his second term was similarly undermined. His resignation in Nov. 2016 prompted fresh elections in March 2017, at which GERB again remained the largest party, and Borisov subsequently formed a new coalition government.

Early Life

Borisov was born in Bankya in June 1959. He graduated in engineering in 1982 and taught at the interior ministry's police academy from 1985–90. He resigned in 1990 to found one of Bulgaria's largest security firms, IPON. Having been named chief secretary of the interior ministry in 2001, he gave up the post in 2005 to run for mayor of Sofia, serving until 2009.

Borisov founded the centre-right GERB in Dec. 2006. The party won the largest share of votes in Bulgaria's first European parliamentary elections in June 2007 and joined the European People's Party group in early 2008.

Career in Office

GERB emerged from national elections in July 2009 as the largest party. Borisov was sworn in as prime minister on 27 July, pledging to balance the economy, restore EU trust in Bulgaria and reduce the nation's energy dependence on Russia. However, his tenure was marred by allegations of official corruption. He announced the resignation of his government in Feb. 2013 amid violent nationwide protests. Elections, scheduled for July 2013, were brought forward to May. GERB again emerged as the largest party but Borisov refused President Plevneliev's invitation to form a government, leading to the formation of a technocratic administration supported by the Bulgarian Socialist Party. This government, plagued by the same protests that had derailed its predecessor, was dissolved in Aug. 2014.

In elections in Oct. 2014 GERB won more than twice as many seats as its nearest rival. Borisov took office again in Nov. at the head of a new coalition government. However, he faced a catalogue of problems on resuming his premiership, including the perceived weakness of his coalition, high energy prices and rampant corruption. Following the heavy defeat of his party's candidate in presidential elections in Nov. 2016 he again stood down from office. He was nevertheless reinstated as premier in May 2017 after GERB emerged as the largest party in parliamentary elections in March that year. In Sept. 2018 parliament approved a cabinet reshuffle and subsequently rejected a no-confidence motion against Borisov's government the following month.

Defence

Since 1 Jan. 2008 Bulgaria has had an all-volunteer professional army. Following restructuring the total strength of the armed forces has been reduced from more than 68,000 in 2002 to less than 32,000 in 2011.

Defence expenditure in 2013 totalled US$751m. (US$108 per capita), representing 1·4% of GDP.

Army

In 2011 the Army had a strength of 16,304. In addition there are reserves of 250,500, 12,000 border guards and 18,000 railway and construction troops.

Navy

The Navy, mostly ex-Soviet or Soviet-built, includes one old diesel submarine and two small frigates. The Naval Aviation Wing operates three armed helicopters. Major naval bases are at Atiya and Varna. Personnel in 2011 totalled 3,471, with 7,500 reservists.

Air Force

The Air Force had (2011) 6,706 personnel, with 45,000 reservists. There were 62 combat-capable aircraft in 2011, including MiG-21s, MiG-29s and Su-25s, and 18 attack helicopters.

International Relations

At the European Union's Helsinki Summit in Dec. 1999 Bulgaria, along with five other countries, was invited to begin full membership negotiations in Feb. 2000. Bulgaria joined the EU on 1 Jan. 2007. It became a member of NATO on 29 March 2004.

Economy

Transport, communications, trade and restaurants contributed 21·8% to GDP in 2011; followed by mining, public utilities and manufacturing, 21·2%; finance and real estate, 15·0%; public administration and defence, 10·8%; and services, 6·8%.

Overview

Bulgaria is classified as an upper-middle income economy by the World Bank, with a per capita income of US$8,032 in 2017.

Its post-communist transition to a market economy in the 1990s was slow, and in 1997 the collapse of the banking system led to a currency crisis and a sharp decline in GDP. However, having applied for membership of the European Union, the government implemented a programme of comprehensive reforms to promote macroeconomic stability and stimulate growth between 2000 and 2007 (when EU accession was attained). The government ran fiscal surpluses between 2004 and 2008, while public debt fell from over 70% of GDP in 2000 to 13·3% in 2008—the second lowest debt level in the EU. Between 2000 and 2008 GDP per capita rose by 6·6% per year, Bulgaria's highest growth rate to date.

Following the global financial crisis that began in 2008, the economy maintained stability through prudent macroeconomic supervision and by restricting public debt (measured at 24·4% of GDP in 2017). However, the country remains one of the poorest in the EU. Average annual GDP per capita growth slowed to 2·6% between 2008 and 2017, while income per capita measured only 24% of the EU average in 2017.

Currency

The unit of currency is the *lev* (BGN) of 100 *stotinki*. In May 1996 the lev was devalued by 68%. A new *lev* was introduced on 5 July 1999, at 1 new *lev* = 1,000 old *leva*. Runaway inflation (123·0% in 1996 rising to 1,061% in 1997) forced the closure of 14 banks in 1996. However, by 1999 the rate had slowed to 2·6%. There was deflation of 1·3% in 2016 but inflation of 1·2% in 2017. The lev is pegged to the euro at one euro = 1·95583 new leva. Foreign exchange reserves were US$16,100m. in Aug. 2009, gold reserves were 1·28m. troy oz and total money supply was 17,869bn. leva.

Budget

The fiscal year is the calendar year.

Central government revenue and expenditure (in 1m. new leva):

	2009	2010	2011
Revenue	23,292	21,924	23,651
Expenditure	21,631	21,754	23,728

Bulgaria reported a budget surplus of 1·1% of GDP in 2017 and 0·2% of GDP in 2016 following a deficit of 1·7% of GDP in 2015. The required target set by the EU is a budget deficit of no more than 3%.

VAT is 20% (reduced rate, 9%). There is a flat income tax rate of 10%.

Performance

Total GDP in 2017 was US$56·8bn. The economy grew by 3·6% in 2015, 3·9% in 2016 and 3·6% again in 2017.

Banking and Finance

The National Bank (*Governor*, Dimitar Radev) is the central bank and bank of issue. There is also a Currency Board, established in 1997. The largest Bulgarian bank in terms of assets is UniCredit Bulbank (assets of 11·52bn. leva in Dec. 2009). Other major banks are DSK Bank (the last state bank to be privatized, in 2003), United Bulgarian Bank and Raiffeisenbank Bulgaria. In June 2014 there were runs on the country's third and fourth biggest lenders, First Investment Bank and Corporate Commercial Bank, despite the IMF declaring the banking system 'stable and liquid' earlier in the month.

In 2010 total external debt was US$48,077m., representing 104·8% of GNI.

There is a stock exchange in Sofia.

Energy and Natural Resources

In 2011, 13·8% of energy consumption came from renewables (wind power, solar power, hydro-electric power, tidal power, geothermal energy and biomass), compared to the European Union average of 13·0%. A target of 16% has been set by the EU for 2020.

Environment

Bulgaria's carbon dioxide emissions from the consumption of energy were the equivalent of 7·4 tonnes per capita in 2011.

Electricity

In 2012 there were two nuclear reactors in use, at the country's sole nuclear power plant in Kozloduy (dating from the 1970s). The two oldest of the plant's six reactors closed in Dec. 2002. A further two closed in Dec. 2006, as a condition of Bulgaria's accession to the EU. To compensate, the government had approved plans to complete a nuclear plant in Belene, started in the 1980s but suspended in 1990. However, the project was abandoned by the Borisov government in March 2012. Installed electrical capacity was 10·2m. kW in 2011. Output, 2011, 50·8bn. kWh (59% thermal, 32% nuclear and 7% hydro-electric). Consumption per capita: 5,473 kWh (2011).

Oil and Gas

Oil is extracted in the Balchik district on the Black Sea coast, in an area 100 km north of Varna, and at Dolni Dubnik near Pleven. There are refineries at Bourgas (annual capacity 5m. tonnes) and Dolni Dubnik (7m. tonnes). Crude oil production (2011) was 0·2m. bbls. Bulgaria is heavily dependent on Russia for oil and gas.

Minerals

Output in 2010 (in tonnes): lignite, 29·38m.; hard coal, 26,000. There are also deposits of gold, silver and copper.

Agriculture

In 2013 the total area of land in agricultural use was 4,995,000 ha. (45·0% of the overall territory of the country); there were around 3·48m. ha. of arable land and 135,000 ha. of permanent crop land.

Production in 2014 (in 1,000 tonnes): wheat, 5,347; maize, 3,137; sunflower seeds, 2,011; barley, 852; rapeseed, 528; grapes (2013), 326; potatoes, 133. Bulgaria produced 130,500 tonnes of wine in 2013.

Livestock (2014), in 1,000: sheep, 1,370; pigs, 586; cattle, 576; goats, 289; chickens, 11,665.

Forestry

In 2015 forests covered 3·82m. ha., or 35% of the total land area. Timber production in 2011 totalled 6·21m. cu. metres.

Fisheries

In 2015 total catch was 8,829 tonnes, almost exclusively from sea fishing.

Industry

In 2005 the total output of industrial enterprises was 35,260m. new leva, of which 31,459m. new leva (89·2%) came from the private and 3,801m. new leva (10·8·%) from the public sector.

Output in 1,000 tonnes (2007 unless otherwise indicated): cement (2005), 3,618; distillate fuel oil, 2,376; crude steel, 1,909; rolled steel (2005), 1,817; residual fuel oil, 1,550; petrol, 1,466; pig iron, 1,069; paper and paperboard (2010), 248; nitrogenous fertilizers, 185. Production of other products: cotton fabrics (2005), 67·7m. sq. metres; silk fabrics (2005), 18·3m. sq. metres; woollen fabrics (2005), 9·9m. sq. metres; 17·4bn. cigarettes (2006).

Labour

A total of 2,949,600 persons were in employment in 2011, with the leading areas of activity as follows: manufacturing, 601,600; wholesale and retail trade, and repair of motor vehicles and motorcycles, 538,400; construction, 225,300; public administration and defence, and compulsory social security, 225,300; agriculture, forestry and fishing, 200,500. The unemployment rate was 12·3% in June 2012, up from 11·3% in 2011 as a whole and 5·6% in 2008. The monthly minimum wage was raised from 270 leva to 290 leva in May 2012.

Bulgaria had 28,000 people living in slavery according to the Walk Free Foundation's 2013 *Global Slavery Index*.

International Trade

Imports and Exports

Goods imports were US$34,740·0m. in 2014 (US$34,306·8m. in 2013) and goods exports US$29,386·5m. (US$29,512·3m. in 2013).

Principal imports in 2014 were machinery and transport equipment (23·4%) followed by mineral fuels and lubricants, and manufactured goods; main exports in 2014 were manufactured goods (22·1%), machinery and transport equipment, and miscellaneous manufactured articles.

The leading import supplier in 2010 was Russia (16·1%), followed by Germany and Italy; the leading export destination in 2010 was Germany (10·6%), followed by Italy and Romania.

Communications

Roads

In 2005 Bulgaria had 40,231 km of roads, including 331 km of motorways and 2,961 km of main roads. In 2007 there were 1,971,500 passenger cars (257 per 1,000 inhabitants), 262,900 lorries and vans, 26,300 buses and coaches, and 78,900 motorcycles and mopeds. In 2005 public transport totalled 13·7bn. passenger-km. In 2007, 9,827 persons were injured in road accidents and 1,006 were killed.

Rail

In 2011 there were 3,947 km of 1,435 mm gauge railway (2,862 km electrified) and 125 km of 760 mm gauge. Passenger-km travelled in 2011 came to 2·07bn. and freight tonne-km to 3·17bn.

There is a tramway and a 31 km long metro in Sofia.

Civil Aviation

There is an international airport at Sofia (Vrazhdebna), which handled 3,467,455 passengers (3,266,427 on international flights) and 16,246 tonnes of freight in 2012. The flag carrier is Bulgaria Air, which in 2010 operated direct services to Amsterdam, Athens, Barcelona, Beirut, Berlin, Brussels, Bucharest, Budapest, Frankfurt, Larnaca, London, Madrid, Malaga, Moscow, Palma, Paphos, Paris, Rome, Tel Aviv, Tripoli (Libya), Vienna, Warsaw and Zürich, as well as internal services. In 2015 it carried 1,271,610 passengers, of which 920,156 were on scheduled international flights.

Shipping

In Jan. 2014 there were 37 ships of 300 GT or over registered, totalling 204,000 GT. Bourgas is a fishing and oil port. Varna is the other main port.

Telecommunications

The Bulgarian Telecommunications Company was privatized in Jan. 2004. In 2011 there were 2,310,800 landline telephone subscriptions (equivalent to 310·3 per 1,000 inhabitants) and 10,475,100 mobile phone subscriptions (or 1,406·8 per 1,000 inhabitants). In 2011, 51·0% of the population were internet users. In March 2012 there were 2·4m. Facebook users.

Social Institutions

Out of 178 countries analysed in the 2017 *Fragile States Index*—a list published jointly by the Fund for Peace and *Foreign Policy* magazine—Bulgaria was ranked the 47th least vulnerable to conflict or collapse. The index is based on 12 indicators of state vulnerability across social, political and economic categories.

Justice

A law of Nov. 1982 provides for the election (and recall) of all judges by the National Assembly. There are a Supreme Court, 28 provincial courts (including Sofia) and regional courts. Jurors are elected at the local government elections. The Prosecutor General and judges are elected by the Supreme Judicial Council established in 1992.

The population in penal institutions in Oct. 2012 was 10,996 (151 per 100,000 of national population). The maximum term of imprisonment is 20 years. The death penalty was abolished for all crimes in 1998. 21·1% of prisoners had yet to receive a trial according to 2014 estimates by the International Centre for Prison Studies. In 2015 the World Justice Project *Rule of Law Index*, which provides data on how the rule of law is experienced by the general public across eight categories, ranked Bulgaria 50th of 102 countries for criminal justice and 44th for civil justice.

Education

Adult literacy rate was 98·4% in 2011. Education is free, and compulsory for children between the ages of 7 and 16.

In 2012–13 there were 5,067 educational establishments: 2,070 kindergartens, 2,112 general and special schools, 494 vocational schools, 338 vocational training centres (offering programmes for adults to obtain professional qualifications) and 53 tertiary education institutions (including 36 state universities or equivalent institutions and nine private universities). There were 102,488 teaching staff (23,456 in higher education) and 1,294,682 pupils and students (283,959 in higher education); 128 schools (with 9,367 pupils), 323 vocational training centres (with 21,627 students) and 16 higher institutions (with 49,849 students) were private. The Academy of Sciences was founded in 1869.

In 2010 public expenditure on education came to 4·1% of GDP and 10·8% of total government spending.

Health

All medical services are free. Private medical services were authorized in 1991. In 2012 there were 312 hospitals. Bulgaria had 66 hospital beds per 10,000 inhabitants in 2012. There were 28,643 physicians, 6,706 dentists and 35,350 nurses and midwives in 2012. In 2009 total health spending represented 7·2% of GDP.

In *Water: At What Cost? The State of the World's Water 2016*, WaterAid reported that 0·6% of the population does not have access to safe water.

Welfare

In 2000 Bulgaria's official retirement age remained unchanged since the Soviet era at 60 years (men) and 55 years (women). However, as part of EU accession reform, the age level increased gradually until 2009 when retirement ages were 63 (men) and 60 (women). They have continued to rise since then, and in 2016 were 63 years and 10 months for men (with a period of social insurance cover of 38 years and 2 months) and 60 years and 10 months for women (with a period of social insurance cover of 35 years and 2 months). The minimum old-age pension at the normal retirement age is 161·38 leva a month with the required number of contributions.

The family allowance is 37 leva a month for the first child, 85 leva for the second, 130 leva for the third, 140 leva for the fourth and an additional 20 leva for each subsequent child. Benefits are doubled for disabled children

In order for a person to be eligible for unemployment benefits they must have been working and making social insurance contributions for at least nine of the previous 15 months.

Religion

'The traditional church of the Bulgarian people' (as it is officially described) is that of the Eastern Orthodox Church. It was disestablished under the 1947 constitution. In 1953 the Bulgarian Patriarchate was revived. The Patriarch is Neofit (enthroned Feb. 2013). The seat of the Patriarch is at Sofia. The Bulgarian Orthodox Church has 15 dioceses, of which 13 are in Bulgaria and two abroad—one covering the United States, Canada and Australia, and the other Central and Western Europe. According to the Pew Research Center's Forum on Religion & Public Life the Orthodox population numbered an estimated 6·22m. in 2010. There were also 1·02m. indigenous Muslims (Pomaks) in 2010 and 310,000 people who were religiously unaffiliated.

Culture

Plovdiv is one of two European Capitals of Culture for 2019. The title attracts large European Union grants.

World Heritage Sites

There are ten Bulgarian sites that appear on the UNESCO World Heritage List. They are (with year entered on list): Boyana Church (1979); Madara Rider (1979), an 8th century sculpture carved into a rock face; Rock-hewn Churches of Ivanovo (1979); Thracian Tomb of Kazanlak (1979); Ancient City of Nessebar (1983); Srebarna Nature Reserve (1983); Pirin National Park (1983); Rila Monastery (1983 and 2008); Thracian tomb of Sveshtari (1985). Ancient and Primeval Beech Forests of the Carpathians and Other Regions of Europe (2007 and 2017) are shared with Albania, Austria, Belgium, Croatia, Germany, Italy, Romania, Slovakia, Slovenia, Spain and Ukraine.

Press

In 2012 there were 57 daily newspapers with a combined daily circulation of 639,000. The two biggest circulation paid-for dailies are *Telegraph* (which was only launched in 2005) and *Trud*, the only title from the socialist era that survived after 1989. A total of 8,263 book titles were published in 2012, including 2,171 fiction titles for adults.

Tourism

There were 6,541,000 non-resident tourists in 2012 (5,151,000 in 2007). Earnings from tourism were US$4,202m. in 2012.

Festivals

The Surva International Festival of Masquerade Games in Pernik takes place every two years in Jan. and is one of the most important celebrations of traditional folkloric culture in the country. Classical music is showcased at the March Music Days festival in Rousse while the Spirit of Bourgas pop and dance music festival takes place in Aug.

Diplomatic Representatives

Of Bulgaria in the United Kingdom (186–188 Queen's Gate, London, SW7 5HL)
   Ambassador: Konstantin Stefanov Dimitrov.

Of the United Kingdom in Bulgaria (9 Moskovska St., Sofia 1000)
   Ambassador: Emma Hopkins.

Of Bulgaria in the USA (1621 22nd St., NW, Washington, D.C., 20008)
   Ambassador: Tihomir Anguelov Stoytchev.

Of the USA in Bulgaria (16 Kozyak St., 1408 Sofia)
   Ambassador: Eric Rubin.

Of Bulgaria to the United Nations
   Ambassador: Georgi Panayotov.

Of Bulgaria to the European Union
   Permanent Representative: Dimiter Tzantchev.

Further Reading

Central Statistical Office. *Statisticheski Godishnik.—Statisticheski Spravochnik* (annual).—*Statistical Reference Book of Republic of Bulgaria* (annual).

Crampton, Richard J., *A Concise History of Bulgaria*. 2nd ed. 2005

National Statistical Office: Natsionalen Statisticheski Institut, 2 P. Volov St., 1038 Sofia.

Website: http://www.nsi.bg

Burkina Faso

République Démocratique du Burkina Faso (Democratic Republic of Burkina Faso)

Capital: Ouagadougou
Population projection, 2020: 20·90m.
GNI per capita, 2017: (PPP$) 1,650
HDI/world rank, 2017: 0·423/183
Internet domain extension: .bf

Key Historical Events

Iron-age artefacts found at Boura in southern Burkina Faso suggest settlement dating from around the 3rd century AD. The West African state, much of which is a plateau forming the headwaters of the Volta River, was the scene of several competing kingdoms from the 9th century. The Songhai Empire, centred on Gao (in present-day Mali) controlled the northeast of Burkina Faso, as well as much of Niger and parts of Mali. It developed as a powerful Islamic state, reaching its peak under Sonni Ali Ber (1465–92) and Askia Mohammed (1492–1529), before sliding into civil war. Further undermined by prolonged drought and disease, it fell to Morocco in 1591.

Mossi clans, famed for their horsemanship, entered the high plains from the south during the 12th century and eventually established five independent kingdoms—Tenkodogo, Yatenga, Gourma, Zandoma and Ouagadougou. Ouagadougou emerged as the most powerful. The Mossi resisted Islamic crusades and attacks by the Songhai and Malian empires for centuries, and frequently fought to retain control of trans-Saharan trade routes.

French forces, who had established Saint-Louis in present-day Senegal as a trading post as early as 1659, did not engage in the transatlantic slave trade to the same extent as their British, Portuguese and Spanish counterparts. However, a major French military expansion inland got under way in the late 1850s, led by Gen. Louis Faidherbe. The French encountered considerable resistance but their superior weaponry led to the signing of several treaties with African leaders.

French troops led by Paul Voulet and Julien Chanoine conquered Ouagadougou in Sept. 1896 and within two years the territory of Burkina Faso was loosely under French control. In June 1898 France and Britain agreed on the demarcation of their colonial borders. Upper Volta, as Burkina Faso was then called, was one of six colonies comprising French West Africa, administered by a single governor-general based in Dakar, Senegal.

France made Upper Volta a separate colony in 1919, only to abolish it in 1932 and divide the territory between the Ivory Coast (now Côte d'Ivoire), French Sudan (now Mali) and Niger. In 1947 the territory of Upper Volta was reconstituted as a territory within French West Africa. In 1958 it was granted the status of autonomous republic within the French Community before winning full independence on 5 Aug. 1960.

Upper Volta remained a desperately poor country often hit by drought, particularly from 1972–74 and again from 1982–84. The military has held power for most of the period since independence. In Aug. 1983 Capt. Thomas Sankara, a leading radical, led a coup before heading a left-wing regime allied to the Soviet Union and Cuba. The country was renamed Burkina Faso (meaning 'the land of honest men') in 1984. Sankara was overthrown and killed in another coup on 15 Oct. 1987, the fifth since 1960, mounted by his former friend, Capt. Blaise Compaoré. Establishing himself as a key power-broker in the region, he won a fourth consecutive presidential election in 2010. However, popular protests in 2014 against planned constitutional changes allowing the president to extend his rule resulted in Compaoré being forced from office by the military. He was succeeded by Michel Kafando, who held power in an interim capacity until Roch Marc Christian Kaboré won the presidential election of Nov. 2015. In Jan. 2016 Islamist militants killed 29 people in an attack on a hotel and café in the capital, Ouagadougou.

Territory and Population

Burkina Faso is bounded in the north and west by Mali, east by Niger and south by Benin, Togo, Ghana and Côte d'Ivoire. Area: 270,764 sq. km; 2006 census population, 14,017,262, giving a density of 51·8 per sq. km. In 2011 the population was 26·5% urban.

The UN gives a projected population for 2020 of 20·90m.

The largest cities in 2006 were Ouagadougou, the capital (1,475,223), Bobo-Dioulasso (489,967), Koudougou (88,184), Banfora (75,917), Ouahigouya (73,153) and Pouytenga (60,618).

The country is administratively divided into 13 regions (with capitals): Boucle du Mouhoun (Dédougou), Cascades (Banfora), Centre (Ouagadougou), Centre-Est (Tenkodogo), Centre-Nord (Kaya), Centre-Ouest (Koudougou), Centre-Sud (Manga), Est (Fada N'Gourma), Hauts-Bassins (Bobo-Dioulasso), Nord (Ouahigouya), Plateau-Central (Ziniaré), Sahel (Dori), Sud-Ouest (Gaoua).

The principal ethnic groups are the Mossi (48%), Fulani (10%), Bobo (7%), Lobi (7%), Mandé (7%), Grosi (5%), Gurma (5%), Sénoufo (5%) and Tuareg (3%).

French is the official language.

Social Statistics

2008 births (estimates), 719,000; deaths, 198,000. Estimated birth rate in 2008 was 47·2 per 1,000 population; estimated death rate, 13·0. Burkina Faso has one of the youngest populations of any country, with 73% of the population under the age of 30 and 45% under 15. Annual population growth rate, 2000–08, 3·3%. Expectation of life at birth, 2013, 56·9 years for females and 55·7 for males. Infant mortality, 2010 (per 1,000 live births), 93. Fertility rate, 2008, 5·9 children per woman.

Climate

A tropical climate with a wet season from May to Nov. and a dry season from Dec. to April. Rainfall decreases from south to north. Ouagadougou, Jan. 76°F (24·4°C), July 83°F (28·3°C). Annual rainfall 36" (894 mm).

Constitution and Government

At a referendum in June 1991 a new constitution was approved; there is an executive presidency and a multi-party system. Parliament consists of the 127-member *National Assembly,* elected by universal suffrage. The *Chamber of Representatives,* a consultative body representing social, religious, professional and political organizations, was abolished in 2002.

National Anthem

'Contre la férule humiliante' ('Against the shameful fetters'); words by T. Sankara, tune anonymous.

Recent Elections

At the presidential elections of 29 Nov. 2015 Roch Marc Christian Kaboré was elected with 53·5% of votes cast, defeating Zéphirin Diabré with 29·7% and 12 other candidates. Turnout was 60·0%.

Parliamentary elections were also held on 29 Nov. 2015. The People's Movement for Progress (MPP) won 55 out of 127 seats; Union for Progress and Reform (UPC), 33; Congress for Democracy and Progress (CDP), 18; Union for Rebirth/Sankarist Movement (UNIR/PS), 5; Alliance for Democracy and Federation–African Democratic Rally (ADF–RDA), 3; New Era for Democracy (NTD), 3; National Rebirth Party (PAREN), 2; New Alliance of Faso (NAFA), 2. Six other parties won one seat each. Turnout was 60·1%.

Current Government

In Feb. 2019 the government comprised:

President: Roch Marc Christian Kaboré; b. 1957 (People's Movement for Progress; since 29 Dec. 2015).

Prime Minister: Christophe Dabiré; b. 1948 (since 24 Jan. 2019).

Ministers of State: Moumina Chérif Sy (also *Minister of National Defence and Veterans' Affairs*); Siméon Sawadogo (also *Minister of Territorial Administration, Decentralization and Social Cohesion*).

Minister of African Integration and Expatriate Affairs: Paul Robert Tiendrébéogo. *Agriculture and Hydro-Agricultural Development:* Salif Ouédraogo. *Animal Resources and Fisheries:* Sommanogo Koutou. *Commerce, Industry and Handicrafts:* Harouna Kaboré. *Communication and Relations with Parliament:* Rémis Fulgance Dandjinou. *Culture, Arts and Tourism:* Abdoul Karim Sango. *Development of the Digital Economy and Postal Services:* Hadja Fatimata Ouattara. *Economy, Finance and Development:* Lassané Kaboré. *Energy:* Bachir Ismaël Ouédraogo. *Environment, the Green Economy and Climate Change:* Batio Bassière. *Foreign Affairs and Co-operation:* Alpha Barry. *Health:* Léonie Claudine Lougué. *Higher Education, Scientific Research and Innovation:* Alkassoum Maïga. *Human Rights and Civic Promotion:* Maminata Ouattara. *Infrastructure:* Eric Wendmanegda Bougouma. *Justice and Keeper of the Seals:* René Bagoro. *Mines and Quarries:* Oumarou Idani. *National Education, Literacy, and Promotion of National Languages:* Stanislas Ouaro. *Public Service, Labour and Social Security:* Séni Ouédraogo. *Security:* Ousséni Compaoré. *Sport and Recreation:* Daouda Azoupiou. *Transport, Urban Mobility and Road Safety:* Vincent Dabilgou. *Urban Affairs and Habitat:* Maurice Dieudonné Bonanet. *Water and Sanitation:* Niouga Ambroise Ouédraogo. *Women, National Solidarity, Family, and Humanitarian Action:* Hélène Marie Laurence Ilboudo. *Youth and Promotion of Youth Entrepreneurship:* Salifo Tiemtoré.

Government Website (French only): http://www.gouvernement.gov.bf

Current Leaders

Roch Marc Christian Kaboré

Position
President

Introduction
Roch Kaboré took office as president on 29 Dec. 2015 after a comfortable election victory. A former banker, prime minister and president of the National Assembly, Kaboré was a long-standing ally of President Blaise Compaoré during most of his 27 years in office.

Early Life
Roch Marc Christian Kaboré was born in Ouagadougou on 25 April 1957. He read economics at the University of Dijon in France, before obtaining a master's degree in business administration in 1980. He then returned home and joined the International Bank of Burkina Faso (BIB).

He was key to the surge of revolutionary feeling that culminated in the 1983 coup orchestrated by Compaoré and which saw Thomas Sankara become president. In 1984 Kaboré was named director-general of the BIB. Five years later he supported Compaoré's overthrow of Sankara.

Kaboré became Compaoré's minister for transport and communications in 1989 and, after heading several other ministries, served as prime minister from 1994–96. Until 2014 he remained a key Compaoré loyalist and a central figure in the National Assembly, acting as its president from 2002–12. In 1999 he served as national secretary of Compaoré's Congress for Democracy and Progress (CDP), and four years later took the post of party chairman.

In Jan. 2014 Kaboré defected from the CDP to form and lead the People's Movement for Progress (MPP). The MPP opposed a constitutional amendment that would allow Compaoré to serve another presidential term. Mass uprisings forced Compaoré to flee in Oct. 2014 after 27 years in power. An interim government took over and Kaboré was elected president in Nov. 2015. The elections were the first in the country's history to be widely considered free and fair.

Career in Office
Kaboré made ambitious pledges to 'build a new Burkina Faso' and break with the previous regime. Specifically, he promised to curb executive power and strengthen governance, invest in health and education, provide better access to clean water and support small-to-medium agricultural enterprises.

The plans were estimated by the MPP to require US$11bn. over five years, which Kaboré aimed to finance primarily through private sector investment and by clamping down on fraud. A new government, announced in Jan. 2016 and headed by Paul Kaba Thiéba (in which Kaboré initially held the defence portfolio), held office until Jan. 2019 when Thiéba resigned and was replaced as prime minister by Christophe Dabiré.

In Jan. 2016 suspected Islamist extremists launched an assault on a hotel in Ouagadougou, killing almost 30 people before security forces ended the attack, and a similar number died in further raids in the capital on a restaurant in Aug. 2017 and on the French embassy and an army base in March 2018.

Defence

There are three military regions. Defence expenditure totalled US$153m. in 2013 (US$9 per capita), representing 1·3% of GDP.

Army

Strength (2011), 6,400 with a paramilitary Gendarmerie of 4,200. In addition there is a People's Militia of 45,000.

Air Force

Personnel total (2011), 600 with two combat-capable aircraft.

Economy

Agriculture, forestry and fisheries contributed 30·2% of GDP in 2011; followed by public administration, defence and services, 17·1%; mining and quarrying, 11·6%; trade and hotels, 11·2%; and manufacturing, 6·8%.

Overview

Landlocked Burkina Faso is one of the poorest countries in the world. 80% of the population exists by subsistence farming and less than 10% of the land is cultivable without irrigation. It is Africa's largest cotton grower, and cultivated some 80% of its crop from genetically modified (GM) seeds in 2010. However, plans were announced in 2016 to end GM cultivation, as producers have claimed that the seeds result in crops of a lower quality and value. Producers estimated their resultant losses between 2011 and 2016 at around US$80m.

Gold is the main export, although a reduction in commodity prices contributed to a slowdown in growth in 2014, which was further exacerbated by the impact of the Ebola virus outbreak in West Africa.

Greater political stability and a resolution of the civil conflict in neighbouring Côte d'Ivoire have allowed for the restoration of important transport links, improving mid- to long-term economic prospects. Nonetheless, the economy faces significant challenges from a fast-growing population and must seek to tackle the national debt while improving infrastructure. In 2015 the IMF agreed provision of US$100m. in budgetary support via the World Bank.

Currency

The unit of currency is the *franc CFA* (XOF) with a parity of 655·957 francs CFA to one euro. Foreign exchange reserves were US$520m. in June 2005 and total money supply was 375,711m. francs CFA. There was deflation of 0·2% in 2017 but inflation of 0·4% in 2017.

Budget

Budgetary central government revenues in 2014 totalled 1,321bn. francs CFA (1,442bn. francs CFA in 2013) and expenses were 887bn. francs CFA (819bn. francs CFA in 2013). Taxes accounted for 71·2% of revenues in 2014 and compensation of employees 49·3% of expenses.

VAT is 18%.

Performance

Real GDP growth was 3·9% in 2015, 5·9% in 2016 and 6·4% in 2017. Total GDP was US$12·9bn. in 2017.

Banking and Finance

The bank of issue which functions as the central bank is the regional Central Bank of West African States (BCEAO; *Governor*, Tiémoko Meyliet Koné). There are seven other banks and three credit institutions.

In 2010 external debt totalled US$2,053m., representing 23·3% of GNI. There is a stock exchange in Ouagadougou.

Energy and Natural Resources

Environment

Burkina Faso's carbon dioxide emissions from the consumption of energy in 2011 were the equivalent of 0·1 tonnes per capita.

Electricity

Production of electricity (2011) was 530m. kWh. Thermal capacity in 2011 was 238,000 kW; hydro-electric capacity in 2011 was 32,000 kW. Total installed capacity was 270,000 kW in 2011. Consumption per capita was 64 kWh in 2011.

Minerals

There are deposits of manganese, zinc, limestone, phosphate and diamonds. Gold production was 5,482 kg in 2008.

Agriculture

In 2007 there were about 5·2m. ha. of arable land and 60,000 ha. of permanent crops. An estimated 55,000 ha. were equipped for irrigation in 2013. There were four tractors per 10,000 ha. of arable land in 2006. The agricultural population in 2007 totalled approximately 13·56m., of whom 6·12m. were economically active. Production (2013, in 1,000 tonnes): sorghum, 1,880; maize, 1,585; millet, 1,079; seed cotton, 766; cowpeas (estimate), 569; sugarcane (estimate), 480; cottonseed (estimate), 430; groundnuts, 350; rice, 305; cotton lint (estimate), 280.

Livestock (2013): goats, 13·5m.; sheep, 9·0m.; cattle, 8·9m.; pigs, 2·3m.; asses, 1·1m.; chickens, 33m. Livestock products, 2013 (in 1,000 tonnes): beef and veal, 131; goat meat, 35; pork and pork products (estimate), 33; poultry meat (estimate), 38; cow's milk, 139; goat's milk, 113; eggs (estimate), 60.

Forestry

In 2015 forests covered 5·35m. ha., or 20% of the total land area. Timber production in 2011 was 14·13m. cu. metres.

Fisheries

In 2015 total catch was 20,750 tonnes, exclusively from inland waters.

Industry

In 2014 manufacturing contributed 6·0% of GDP. Industry in Burkina Faso is underdeveloped and employs only 10% of the workforce. Industry is mainly centred around food processing, brewing and textiles.

Labour

The labour force in 2013 was 7,695,400 (5,625,600 in 2003). 85·1% of the population aged 15–64 was economically active in 2013. In the same year 3·3% of the population was unemployed.

Burkina Faso had 0·11m. people living in slavery according to the Walk Free Foundation's 2013 *Global Slavery Index*.

International Trade

Imports and Exports

In 2010 imports totalled US$2,048·2m. and exports US$1,288·1m. Principal import suppliers, 2010: Côte d'Ivoire, 16·0%; France, 10·3%; China, 9·7%; Togo, 4·5%. Principal export markets, 2010: Switzerland, 63·5%; South Africa, 11·2%; Singapore, 4·9%; United Kingdom, 3·0%. Machinery and transport equipment accounted for 22·9% of the country's imports in 2010; gold (including gold plated with platinum) accounted for 68·6% of exports in 2010.

Communications

Roads

The road system comprised approximately 61,000 km in 2011 (including approximately 15,300 km of classified roads). There were 97,100 passenger cars (seven per 1,000 inhabitants), 55,700 lorries and vans, and 356,400 motorcycles and mopeds in use in 2007.

Rail

The railway from Abidjan in Côte d'Ivoire to Kaya (600 km of metre gauge within Burkina Faso) is operated by the mixed public-private company Sitarail, a concessionaire to both governments.

Civil Aviation

The international airports are Ouagadougou (which handled 485,815 passengers in 2012) and Bobo-Dioulasso. The national carrier is Air Burkina, which in 2010 flew to Abidjan, Accra, Bamako, Cotonou, Dakar, Douala, Libreville, Lomé, Marseille, N'Djaména, Niamey and Paris in addition to operating on domestic routes. In 2013 Air Burkina carried 129,000 passengers (122,000 on international flights).

Telecommunications

In 2011 there were 141,500 landline telephone subscriptions (equivalent to 8·3 per 1,000 inhabitants) and 7,628,100 mobile phone subscriptions (or 452·7 per 1,000 inhabitants). Fixed broadband subscriptions totalled 14,300 in 2012 (0·9 per 1,000 inhabitants). In June 2012 there were 116,000 Facebook users.

Social Institutions

Out of 178 countries analysed in the 2017 *Fragile States Index*—a list published jointly by the Fund for Peace and *Foreign Policy* magazine—Burkina Faso was ranked the joint 44th most vulnerable (along with Malaŵi) to conflict or collapse. The index is based on 12 indicators of state vulnerability across social, political and economic categories.

Justice

Civilian courts replaced revolutionary tribunals in 1993. A law passed in April 2000 split the supreme court into four separate entities—a constitutional court, an appeal court, a council of state and a government audit office. The death penalty, which had not been used since 1988, was abolished in 2018.

The population in penal institutions in Dec. 2012 was 4,899 (28 per 100,000 of national population). In 2015 the World Justice Project *Rule of Law Index*, which provides data on how the rule of law is experienced by the general public across eight categories, ranked Burkina Faso 70th of 102 countries for both criminal justice and civil justice.

Education

In 2007 adult literacy was 28·7%, among the lowest in the world. The 1994–96 development programme established an adult literacy campaign, and centres for the education of 10–15-year-old non-school attenders. In 2007 there were 1,561,258 pupils at primary schools with 32,760 teaching staff. During the period 1990–95 only 24% of females of primary school age were enrolled in school but by 2006 this had increased to 42%. In 2007 there were 352,376 pupils and 12,498 teaching staff in secondary schools, and 33,459 students in higher education with 1,886 academic staff.

In 2006 public expenditure on education came to 4·5% of GNI and 15·4% of total government expenditure.

Health

In 2007 there were three national hospitals, nine regional hospitals and 75 medical centres. There were 441 physicians, 38 dentists, 4,262 nurses, 604 midwives and 58 pharmacists in the public sector in 2007.

In *Water: At What Cost? The State of the World's Water 2016*, WaterAid reported that 17·7% of the population does not have access to safe water.

Religion

According to estimates by the Pew Research Center's Forum on Religion & Public Life, in 2010 the population was 61·6% Muslim (nearly all Sunnis) with 22·5% Christian (mainly Catholic) and 15·4% folk religionists. In Feb. 2019 the Roman Catholic Church had one cardinal.

Culture

World Heritage Sites

The Ruins of Loropéni were inscribed on the UNESCO World Heritage List in 2009. At least 1,000 years old, Loropéni is the best preserved of ten similar fortresses in the Lobi area and is part of a larger group of around 100 stone-built enclosures with ties to the trans-Saharan gold trade. The W-Arly-Pendjari Complex (1996 and 2017) is shared with Benin and Niger. It includes the largest and most important continuum of terrestrial, semi-aquatic and aquatic ecosystems in the West African savannah belt.

Press

There were five dailies (two government-owned) with a combined circulation of 36,000 in 2008. The leading newspaper in terms of circulation is *Le Pays*.

Tourism

In 2011, 238,000 foreign tourists stayed in hotels or similar accommodation.

Diplomatic Representatives

Of Burkina Faso in the United Kingdom
 Ambassador: Jacqueline Zaba Nikiema (resides in Brussels).
 Honorary Consul: Vacant.

Of the United Kingdom in Burkina Faso
 Ambassador: Iain Walker (resides in Accra, Ghana).

Of Burkina Faso in the USA (2340 Massachusetts Ave., NW, Washington, D.C., 20008)
 Ambassador: Seydou Kaboré.

Of the USA in Burkina Faso (Secteur 15, Ouaga 2000, Ave. Sembène Ousmane, rue 15.873, Ouagadougou)
 Ambassador: Andrew Young.

Of Burkina Faso to the United Nations
 Ambassador: Yemdaogo Eric Tiaré.

Of Burkina Faso to the European Union
 Ambassador: Jacqueline Marie Zaba Nikiéma.

Further Reading

Nnaji, B. O., *Blaise Compaoré: Architect of the Burkina Faso Revolution.* 1991

National Statistical Office: Institut National de la Statistique et de la Démographie (INSD), Ave. Pascal Zagre, Ouaga 2000, 01 BP 374, Ouagadougou.

Website (French only): http://www.insd.bf

Burundi

Republika y'Uburundi (Republic of Burundi)

Capital: Bujumbura
Population projection, 2020: 11·94m.
GNI per capita, 2017: (PPP$) 702
HDI/world rank, 2017: 0·417/185
Internet domain extension: .bi

Key Historical Events

From 1890 Burundi was part of German East Africa and from 1919 part of Ruanda-Urundi, administered by Belgium as a League of Nations mandate. The country gained independence on 1 July 1962. In April 1972 fighting between rebels from Burundi and neighbouring countries and the ruling Tutsi, apparently aiming to destroy Tutsi hegemony, killed up to 120,000. Following the deposition of Presidents Micombero and Bagaza by the army on 1 Nov. 1976 and 3 Sept. 1987 respectively, Maj. Pierre Buyoya, a Tutsi, assumed the presidency on 1 Oct. 1987.

On 1 June 1993 Buyoya was defeated in elections by Melchior Ndadaye, who became the country's first elected president and the first Hutu president. However, on 21 Oct. 1993 he and six ministers were killed in an attempted military coup. Another wave of Tutsi-Hutu violence cost thousands of lives. On 6 April 1994 the new president, Cyprien Ntaryamira, was also killed, possibly assassinated, together with the president of Rwanda.

On 25 July 1996 the army seized power, installing Buyoya as president for the second time. In June 1998 Buyoya drew up a transitional power-sharing arrangement, with two vice-presidents—one Hutu and one Tutsi—replacing the prime minister. However, extremists on both sides denounced it. In July 2001 it was agreed that a three-year transitional government should be installed with Buyoya as president and Domitien Ndayizeye, a Hutu, as vice-president for the first 18 months, after which the roles would be reversed. Fighting nevertheless continued until a ceasefire was eventually signed in Dec. 2002 by the government and the Forces for the Defense of Democracy (FDD), the country's principal rebel movement. In Oct. 2003 the FDD and the government sealed a peace deal to implement the 2002 ceasefire.

In March 2005 a new power-sharing constitution won popular approval and Pierre Nkurunziza became president in Aug. that year. In April 2009 the Forces for National Liberation, the last remaining rebel group, gave up its campaign of violence and became a legitimate political party. In June 2010 and July 2015 Nkurunziza won further terms as president.

Territory and Population

Burundi is bounded in the north by Rwanda, east and south by Tanzania and west by the Democratic Republic of the Congo, and has an area of 27,830 sq. km (10,745 sq. miles) including 2,150 sq. km of inland water (830 sq. miles). The population at the 2008 census was 8,053,574 (4,088,668 females); density, 314 per sq. km. In 2011, 11·3% of the population lived in urban areas (the smallest proportion of any country in the world).

The UN gives a projected population for 2020 of 11·94m.

There are 18 provinces (since March 2015), named after their chief towns apart from Bujumbura Rural. These are subdivided into 129 communes. The 17 provinces at the time of the 2008 census (with 2008 populations) were: Bubanza (338,023), Bujumbura Mairie (497,166), Bujumbura Rural (555,933), Bururi (574,013), Cankuzo (228,873), Cibitoke (460,435), Gitega (725,223), Karusi (436,443), Kayanza (585,412), Kirundo (628,256), Makamba (430,899), Muramvya (292,589), Muyinga (632,409), Mwaro (273,143), Ngozi (660,717), Rutana (333,510), Ruyigi (400,530). A new province, Rumonge, came into existence in March 2015 and was created from five communes previously belonging to Bujumbura Rural and Bururi.

The capital, Bujumbura, had a population of 497,166 in 2008. Other large towns are Gitega, Ngozi and Rumonge.

There are four ethnic groups—Hutu (Bantu, forming 81% of the total); Tutsi (Nilotic, 16%); Lingala (2%); Twa (pygmoids, 1%). The local language, Kirundi, and French are both official languages. Swahili is spoken in the commercial centres.

Social Statistics

2008 estimates: births, 278,000; deaths, 112,000. Rates, 2008 estimates (per 1,000 population): birth, 34·5; death, 13·9. Life expectancy at birth, 2013, was 52·2 years for men and 56·1 years for women. Infant mortality, 2010, 88 per 1,000 live births. Annual population growth rate, 2000–08, 2·8%; fertility rate, 2008, 4·6 children per woman.

Climate

An equatorial climate, modified by altitude. The eastern plateau is generally cool, the easternmost savannah several degrees hotter. The wet seasons are from March to May and Sept. to Dec. Bujumbura, Jan. 73°F (22·8°C), July 73°F (22·8°C). Annual rainfall 33" (825 mm).

Constitution and Government

The constitution of 1981 provided for a one-party state. In Jan. 1991 the government of President Maj. Pierre Buyoya, leader of the sole party, the Union for National Progress (UPRONA), proposed a new constitution which was approved by a referendum in March 1992 (with 89% of votes cast in favour), legalizing parties not based on ethnic group, region or religion and providing for presidential elections by direct universal suffrage. In 2001, following years of civil war, a multi-ethnic broad-based transition government was established. On 28 Feb. 2005 citizens voted overwhelmingly to adopt a new constitution laying the foundations for the end of a 12-year civil war, with 92% of votes cast in favour of the constitution. The constitution gives Tutsis (who have traditionally held power in Burundi but only make up 15% of the population) 40% of seats in the National Assembly, while the Hutus, who constitute 83% of the population, are given 60% of the seats. Initially, the president was only permitted to serve a maximum of two five-year terms. However, in May 2015 the constitutional court ruled controversially that Nkurunziza could seek a third term, since it would be only the second time he was pursuing popular election (having originally been appointed to the post by parliamentary vote). He was duly re-elected in July 2015, sparking widespread unrest.

In May 2018 a range of constitutional amendments were approved with 73% support in a disputed referendum. The presidential term was increased from five to seven years from 2020. Other provisions included ending the requirement to have two vice-presidents (one from the governing party and one from the opposition) in favour of a single vice-president (appointed from the opposition) to serve alongside the newly-created position of prime minister (whom the president will select from the ruling party).

Burundi has a bicameral legislature, consisting of the *National Assembly* of 121 members, with 100 members elected to serve five-year terms and 21 co-opted members, and the *Senate* of 43 members (36 elected and seven appointed, including four former presidents).

National Anthem

'Burundi Bwacu' ('Dear Burundi'); words by a committee, tune by M. Barengayabo.

Recent Elections

Pierre Nkurunziza was re-elected president on 21 July 2015 with 69·4% of votes cast. Agathon Rwasa came second with 19·0% of the vote followed by Gerard Nduwayo with 2·1% and five other candidates who took less than 2% each. Several opposition parties boycotted the election amid controversy over Nkurunziza's eligibility for a third term. Turnout was 73·4%.

At the parliamentary elections of 29 June 2015 the ruling National Council for the Defense of Democracy–Forces for the Defense of Democracy (CNDD–FDD) won 77 of 100 available seats with 60·3% of the vote, the

© Springer Nature Limited 2020
Palgrave Macmillan (ed.), *The Statesman's Yearbook 2020*,
https://doi.org/10.1057/978-1-349-95940-2_40

Hope for Burundians coalition 21 with 11·2% and Union for National Progress 2 with 2·5%. Turnout was 74·3%. In indirect Senate elections held on 24 July 2015 the National Council for the Defense of Democracy–Forces for the Defense of Democracy won 33 of 36 available seats, the Union for National Progress 2 and the National Forces of Liberation 1. Three ethnic Twa members were appointed to the Senate as were four former presidents. The opposition boycotted the elections.

Current Government

President: Pierre Nkurunziza; b. 1963 (CNDD–FDD; sworn in 26 Aug. 2005 and re-elected 28 June 2010 and 21 July 2015).

In Feb. 2019 the government comprised:

First Vice-President: Gaston Sindimwo. *Second Vice-President:* Joseph Butore.

Minister of Civil Service, Labour and Employment: Félix Mpozeriniga. *Commerce, Industry and Tourism:* Jean-Marie Niyokindi. *Communication and the Media:* Serges Ndayiragije. *Culture and Sports:* Pélate Niyonkuru. *Decentralization and Institutional Reform:* Jean Bosco Hitimana. *Education, and Vocational and Professional Training:* Janvière Ndirahisha. *Environment, Agriculture and Livestock:* Déo Guide Rurema. *Finance, Budget and Economic Co-operation and Development:* Domitien Ndihokubwayo. *Foreign Affairs:* Ezéchiel Nibigira. *Higher Education and Scientific Research:* Gaspard Banyankimbona. *Human Rights, Social Affairs and Gender:* Martin Nivyabandi. *Interior, Patriotic Education and Local Development:* Pascal Barandagiye. *Justice, Civil Protection and Keeper of the Seals:* Aimée-Laurentine Kanyana. *National Defence and War Veterans:* Emmanuel Ntahomvukiye. *Public Health and the Fight Against Aids:* Dr Thaddée Ndikumana. *Public Security and Emergency Situations:* Alain-Guillaume Bunyoni. *Transport, Public Works, Infrastructure and Regional Development:* Jean-Bosco Ntunzwenimana. *Water, Energy and Mining:* Côme Manirakiza. *Youth, Posts and Information Technology:* Evelyne Butoyi. *Minister in the Presidency in Charge of East African Community Affairs:* Isabelle Ndahayo. *Minister in the Presidency in Charge of Good Governance and Planning:* Jeanne d'Arc Kagayo.

Government Website: http://www.burundi.gov.bi

Current Leaders

Pierre Nkurunziza

Position
President

Introduction
Pierre Nkurunziza, an ethnic Hutu, became president in Aug. 2005 in the country's first democratic elections since the start of the civil war in 1993. He was re-elected in 2010 and again, more controversially, in July 2015. His administration has attracted criticism for economic mismanagement, corruption and intolerance of opposition.

Early Life
Born in Bujumbura on 18 Dec. 1963, Nkurunziza attended primary school in Ngozi, where in 1972 his father was killed in ethnic violence, and secondary school in Gitega. He studied physical education at the University of Burundi in Bujumbura and graduated in 1990.

Civil war followed the assassination in Oct. 1993 of Burundi's first ethnic Hutu president, Melchior Ndadaye, and Nkurunziza joined the National Council for the Defense of Democracy–Forces for the Defense of Democracy (CNDD–FDD) as a soldier. The group was one of several rebel Hutu groups that fought the Tutsi-dominated army, in a conflict that had killed thousands by the late 1990s. By 1998 Nkurunziza was co-ordinating the activities of the armed and political wings of the CNDD–FDD. That year he was sentenced to death by a Burundian court for alleged involvement in ambushes, but was granted immunity during peace talks that culminated in the Arusha Peace Accord of Aug. 2000.

Elected chairman of the CNDD–FDD in 2001, Nkurunziza began negotiations with Burundi's transitional government. In Nov. 2003 he signed a ceasefire accord, winning official recognition of the CNDD–FDD as a political party. He became state minister of good governance in the transitional government, helping to forge a power-sharing agreement and timetable for democratic elections.

Following CNDD–FDD victories in elections in June and July 2005, Nkurunziza was nominated as the party's presidential candidate. He won an overwhelming victory in a vote by parliament (acting as an electoral college) on 19 Aug. and was sworn in a week later.

Career in Office
President Nkurunziza appointed a cabinet of 20 ministers comprising 11 Hutus and nine Tutsis in accordance with the quotas stipulated in the constitution. He promised free primary education for all children with immediate effect as well as aid for the return of Burundian refugees from Tanzania and Rwanda. In Aug. 2006 an alleged coup attempt prompted a government crackdown on opposition and the arrest of several prominent political and military figures. The following month the government signed a ceasefire agreement with the Palipehutu–FNL rebel group which finally entered the peace process. In 2007 the United Nations completed its peacekeeping mandate in Burundi. In April 2008 there was a renewal of fighting between government forces and the FNL before another ceasefire was negotiated the following month. Then, in April 2009, the FNL officially disarmed and transformed into a legal political party.

Nkurunziza was re-elected overwhelmingly at presidential elections on 28 June 2010, but opposition members dismissed the legitimacy of the poll. In parliamentary elections in July that year, boycotted by the opposition, the CNDD–FDD was returned with a large majority, prompting a sporadic resurgence of violence across the country in 2011 and 2012. In June 2013 the president approved controversial legislation restricting media freedom.

Concerns over his authoritarianism were further heightened in March 2014 when several opposition party activists were jailed for life for insurrection for having attempted to attend a political rally in the capital. At the same time, Nkurunziza unsuccessfully sought parliamentary approval for constitutional amendments that would allow him to run for a third term in office and could politically marginalize the Tutsi minority. However, in May 2015 the Constitutional Court ruled in favour of his re-election bid amid allegations of intimidation of the judiciary, prompting months of widespread protests. In June the CNDD–FDD claimed victory in legislative elections and the following month Nkurunziza won his third term in polling marred by violence and an opposition boycott. In March 2016, in response to the continuing political unrest, the European Union suspended direct aid to Nkurunziza's government.

Following a campaign marred by violence, nearly 80% of voters in a referendum approved constitutional changes increasing the presidential term of office from five to seven years and allowing Nkurunziza to run for a further two terms after his current one ends in 2020.

Defence

A new National Defence Force combining government forces and rebels from the FDD was created following the Oct. 2003 peace settlement.

Defence expenditure totalled US$64m. in 2013 (US$6 per capita), representing 2·5% of GDP.

Army
The Army had a strength (2011) of 20,000 including an air wing.

Air Force
There were 200 air wing personnel in 2011 with one combat-capable aircraft and two attack helicopters.

Economy

In 2014 agriculture accounted for 39·3% of GDP, industry 18·3% and services 42·4%.

Overview
Being landlocked and among the world's poorest countries, Burundi is dependent on foreign aid, which constitutes around 50% of the annual government budget. 90% of the population relies on subsistence agriculture. Private sector development is impeded by poor infrastructure, with less than 5% of households having access to electricity, and government suffers from high levels of corruption. The economy is driven by coffee and tea exports and, to a lesser extent, gold, sugar, cotton and hides. Ethnic tensions exacerbated by the civil war that ended in 2005 persist, particularly in light of the Tutsi minority effectively controlling the coffee trade.

Nonetheless, the World Bank named Burundi among the world's top economic reformers in 2013 and the country was granted preferential access to the European Union market. However, while it was hoped that a rebound in coffee production and investment in large-scale construction projects would accelerate GDP growth, the economy slowed in 2014 and political instability in 2015 led to a recession, which continued in 2016. Climate change poses a further threat to the economy, particularly the vital agricultural sector. Vulnerability to international food and fuel price rises, a high debt burden, continuing political tension and lack of infrastructure remain long-term challenges to growth.

Currency

The unit of currency is the *Burundi franc* (BIF) of 100 *centimes*. There was inflation of 5·5% in 2016, rising to 16·6% in 2017. In July 2005 gold reserves were 1,000 troy oz and foreign exchange reserves US$88m. Total money supply was estimated at 310bn. Burundi francs in March 2009.

Budget

Total revenues in 2011 were 667·5bn. Burundi francs and expenditures 789·0bn. Burundi francs. Tax revenue accounted for 65·1% of revenues in 2011; current expenditure accounted for 72·8% of expenditures.

VAT of 18% was introduced in July 2009, replacing the 17% transaction tax.

Performance

Owing to the unstable political and social environment the economy contracted by 4·0% in 2015 and 1·0% in 2016. There was then zero growth in 2017. Total GDP in 2017 was US$3·5bn.

Banking and Finance

The Bank of the Republic of Burundi is the central bank and bank of issue. Its *Governor* is Jean Ciza. The largest commercial banks in 2007 were Interbank Burundi (assets of US$126m.), Banque de Crédit de Bujumbura (US$110m.) and Banque Commerciale du Burundi (US$67m.). Consolidated assets of financial institutions totalled 42·5bn. Burundi francs in 2009. In 2010 foreign debt totalled US$537m., representing 33·8% of GNI.

Energy and Natural Resources

Environment

Burundi's carbon dioxide emissions from the consumption of energy in 2011 were the equivalent of less than 0·1 tonnes per capita.

Electricity

Installed capacity was estimated at 33,000 kW in 2011. Production was 143m. kWh in 2011. Consumption per capita in 2011 was 25 kWh. In 2016 only 8% of the population had access to electricity.

Minerals

Gold is mined on a small scale. Deposits of nickel (280m. tonnes) and vanadium remain to be exploited. There are proven reserves of phosphates of 17·6m. tonnes.

Agriculture

The main economic activity is agriculture, which contributed 39% of GDP in 2014. In 2013 an estimated 1·2m. ha. were arable and 350,000 ha. were permanent crops. 23,000 ha. were equipped for irrigation in 2013. Beans, cassava, maize, sweet potatoes, groundnuts, peas, sorghum and bananas are grown according to the climate and the region.

The main cash crop is coffee, of which about 95% is arabica. It accounts for 90% of exports, and taxes and levies on coffee constitute a major source of revenue. Production (2013) 36,000 tonnes. The main agricultural crops (2013 production, in 1,000 tonnes) are bananas (2,236), cassava (2,234), sweet potatoes (840), dry beans (225), sugarcane (223) and maize (162).

Livestock (2013): 2,489,000 goats, 778,000 cattle, 388,000 pigs, 353,000 sheep and 3m. chickens.

Forestry

Forests covered 0·28m. ha., or 11% of the total land area, in 2015. Timber production in 2011 was 10·28m. cu. metres, the majority of it for fuel.

Fisheries

In 2012 the total catch was 12,309 tonnes, exclusively from inland waters.

Industry

In 2013 production of sugar totalled 28,000 tonnes. Other major products are (2009 output): beer (136·6m. litres), soft drinks (28·7m. litres) and cigarettes (514m. units).

Labour

The labour force in 2013 was 4,799,400 (3,287,700 in 2003). 83·6% of the population aged 15–64 was economically active in 2013. In the same year 7·0% of the population was unemployed.

Burundi had 71,000 people living in slavery according to the Walk Free Foundation's 2013 *Global Slavery Index*.

International Trade

Imports and Exports

Imports and exports for calendar years in US$1m.:

	2006	2007	2008	2009	2010
Imports c.i.f.	433·6	423·0	315·2	344·8	832·5
Exports f.o.b.	228·5	156·2	141·8	112·9	275·5

Main exports are coffee, gold and tea. Leading imports are road vehicles, medicinal and pharmaceutical products, and cement. In 2010 main import sources (in US$1m.) were: Belgium (101·0); China (101·0); Japan (78·0). Leading export markets in 2010 (in US$1m.) were: Switzerland (74·2); UK (36·8); Belgium (35·8).

Communications

Roads

Burundi has some 12,300 km of roads. There were 15,500 passenger cars (two per 1,000 inhabitants) and 32,700 lorries and vans in use in 2007.

Civil Aviation

There were direct flights to Dar es Salaam, Kigali, Mwanza and Nairobi in 2010. Air Burundi is the state-owned national airline, but it has not been operational since Sept. 2009. Bujumbura International airport handled 291,838 passengers and 3,054 tonnes of freight in 2012.

Shipping

There are lake services from Bujumbura to Kigoma (Tanzania) and Kalémie (Democratic Republic of the Congo). The main route for exports and imports is via Kigoma, and thence by rail to Dar es Salaam.

Telecommunications

There were 32,600 fixed telephone lines in 2010 (3·9 per 1,000 inhabitants) and mobile phone subscribers numbered 1·15m. There were 21·0 internet users per 1,000 inhabitants in 2010. Fixed internet subscriptions totalled 5,000 in 2009 (0·6 per 1,000 inhabitants).

Social Institutions

Out of 178 countries analysed in the 2017 *Fragile States Index*—a list published jointly by the Fund for Peace and *Foreign Policy* magazine—Burundi was ranked the joint 17th most vulnerable (along with Pakistan) to conflict or collapse. The index is based on 12 indicators of state vulnerability across social, political and economic categories.

Justice

There are a Supreme Court, an appeal court and a court of first instance at Bujumbura, and provincial courts in each provincial capital.

The death penalty was abolished in April 2009. The population in penal institutions in Feb. 2013 was 6,477 (72 per 100,000 of national population). The International Centre for Prison Studies estimated in 2014 that 51·8% of prisoners had yet to receive a trial.

Education

Adult literacy rate was 66% in 2008. In 2007 there were 1,490,844 pupils in primary schools with 28,671 teachers and 209,945 pupils in secondary schools with 7,501 teachers. There were 15,623 students in higher education in 2007 and 1,007 academic staff. The leading institution in the tertiary sector is the Université du Burundi, located in Bujumbura.

In 2005 public expenditure on education came to 5·2% of GNI.

Health

In 2016 there were 542 physicians and 6,914 nursing and midwifery personnel. In 2006 there were seven hospital beds per 10,000 inhabitants (up from less than one per 10,000 in 1996).

In *Water: At What Cost? The State of the World's Water 2016*, WaterAid reported that 24·1% of the population does not have access to safe water.

Religion

According to estimates by the Pew Research Center's Forum on Religion & Public Life, in 2010 the population was 91·5% Christian with the remainder being folk religionists and Muslims. Around four-fifth of Christians are Catholics and the rest Protestants.

Culture

Press

There was one state-controlled daily newspaper (*Le Renouveau*) in 2008 with a circulation of 20,000.

Tourism

There were 142,000 foreign tourists in 2010 (212,000 in 2009).

Diplomatic Representatives

Of Burundi in the United Kingdom (Uganda House, Second Floor, 58–59 Trafalgar Sq., London, WC2N 5DX)
  Ambassador: Ernest Ndabashinze.

Of the United Kingdom in Burundi
  Ambassador: Jo Lomas (resides in Kigali, Rwanda).

Of Burundi in the USA (2233 Wisconsin Ave., NW, Suite 212, Washington, D.C., 20007)
  Ambassador: Vacant.
  Chargé d'Affaires a.i.: Benjamin Manirakiza.

Of the USA in Burundi (No. 50 Ave. des Etats-Unis, 110-01-02, Bujumbura)
  Ambassador: Anne S. Casper.

Of Burundi to the United Nations
  Ambassador: Albert Shingiro.

Of Burundi to the European Union
  Ambassador: Vacant.
  Chargé d'Affaires a.i.: Venant Ntabona.

Further Reading

Lemarchand, R., *Burundi: Ethnic Conflict and Genocide.* 1996

Melson, Robert, *Genocide and Crisis in Central Africa: Conflict Roots, Mass Violence and Regional War.* 2001

National Statistical Office: Service des Études et Statistiques, Ministère du Plan, B. P. 1156, Bujumbura.

Website (French only): http://www.isteebu.bi

Cabo Verde

República de Cabo Verde (Republic of Cabo Verde)

Capital: Praia
Population projection, 2020: 567,000
GNI per capita, 2017: (PPP$) 5,983
HDI/world rank, 2017: 0·654/125=
Internet domain extension: .cv

Key Historical Events

During centuries of Portuguese rule the islands were gradually peopled with Portuguese, slaves from Africa and people of mixed African-European descent who formed the majority. While retaining some African culture, the Cabo Verdians spoke Portuguese or the Portuguese-derived Crioulo (Creole) language and became Catholics. In 1956 nationalists from Cape Verde (now officially known as Cabo Verde) and Portuguese Guinea founded the *Partido Africano da Independência da Guiné e Cabo Verde* (PAIGC). In the 1960s the PAIGC waged a successful guerrilla war. On 5 July 1975 Cape Verde became independent, ruled by the PAIGC, which was already the ruling party in the former Portuguese colony of Guinea-Bissau. But resentment at Cape Verdians' privileged position in Guinea-Bissau led to the end of the ties between the two countries' ruling parties. Although the PAIGC retained its name in Guinea-Bissau, in Jan. 1981 it was renamed the *Partido Africano da Independência do Cabo Verde* (PAICV) in Cape Verde. The constitution of 1981 made the PAICV the sole legal party, but in Sept. 1990 the National Assembly abolished its monopoly and free elections were permitted. In Oct. 2013 the government informed the United Nations that the country would henceforth be designated Cabo Verde rather than Cape Verde.

Territory and Population

Cabo Verde is situated in the Atlantic Ocean 620 km off west Africa and consists of ten islands (Boa Vista, Brava, Fogo, Maio, Sal, Santa Luzia, Santo Antão, São Nicolau, São Tiago and São Vicente) and five islets. The islands are divided into two groups, named Barlavento (windward) and Sotavento (leeward). The total area is 4,033 sq. km (1,557 sq. miles). The 2010 census population was 491,875 (248,282 female), giving a density of 122 per sq. km. In 2010, 62% of the population lived in urban areas.

The UN gives a projected population for 2020 of 567,000.

Over 600,000 Cabo Verdeans live abroad (more than the population in the country), mainly in the USA.

Areas and populations of the islands:

Island	Area (sq. km)	Population census 2000	Population census 2010
Santo Antão	779	47,170	43,915
São Vicente[1]	227	67,163	76,140
São Nicolau	388	13,647	12,817
Sal	216	14,816	25,779
Boa Vista	620	4,209	9,162
Barlavento	*2,230*	*147,005*	*167,813*
Maio	269	6,754	6,952
São Tiago	991	236,631	274,044
Fogo	476	37,431	37,071
Brava	64	6,804	5,995
Sotavento	*1,803*	*287,620*	*324,062*

[1]Including Santa Luzia island, which is uninhabited.

The main towns are Praia, the capital, on São Tiago (127,832, 2010 census population) and Mindelo on São Vicente (70,468, 2010 census population). It is estimated that around 71% of the population are of mixed African and European descent, with 28% African (mainly Fulani, Balanta and Mandyako) and 1% European. The official language is Portuguese; a creole (Crioulo) is in ordinary use.

Social Statistics

2008 estimates: births, 12,000; deaths, 2,000. Rates, 2008 estimates (per 1,000 population): birth, 24·1; death, 5·0. Annual population growth rate, 2000–08, 1·6%. Annual emigration varies between 2,000 and 10,000. Life expectancy at birth, 2013, was 71·1 years for men and 78·8 years for women. Infant mortality, 2010, 29 per 1,000 live births; fertility rate, 2008, 2·7 children per woman. Cabo Verde has had one of the largest reductions in its fertility rate of any country in the world over the past quarter of a century, having had a rate of 5·3 births per woman in 1990.

Climate

The climate is arid, with a cool dry season from Dec. to June and warm dry conditions for the rest of the year. Rainfall is sparse, rarely exceeding 5" (127 mm) in the northern islands or 12" (304 mm) in the southern ones. There are periodic severe droughts. Praia, Jan. 72°F (22·2°C), July 77°F (25°C). Annual rainfall 10" (250 mm).

Constitution and Government

The Constitution was adopted in Sept. 1992 and was revised in 1995 and 1999. The President is elected for five-year terms by universal suffrage. There is a 72-member National Assembly (Assembleia Nacional), elected for five-year terms.

National Anthem

'Cântico da Liberdade' ('Song of Freedom'); words by A. S. Lopes, tune by A. H. T. Silva.

Recent Elections

Elections for the National Assembly of 72 members were held on 20 March 2016. Turnout was 66·0%. The Movement for Democracy (MPD) won 40 seats with 54·5% of votes cast, the African Party for the Independence of Cabo Verde (PAICV) won 29 seats with 38·2% and the Democratic and Independent Cabo Verdean Union won 3 with 6·9%. Three smaller parties failed to win any seats.

In presidential elections held on 2 Oct. 2016 Jorge Carlos Fonseca was re-elected with 74·1% of the vote against Albertino Graça with 22·5% and Joaquim Monteiro with 3·4%. Turnout was 35·5%.

Current Government

President: Jorge Carlos Fonseca; b. 1950 (MPD; sworn in 9 Sept. 2011 and re-elected 2 Oct. 2016).

In Feb. 2019 the government comprised:

Prime Minister: Ulisses Correia e Silva; b. 1962 (MPD; sworn in 22 April 2016).

Deputy Prime Minister and Minister of Finance: Olavo Correia.

Minister of Agriculture and Environment: Gilberto Silva. *Culture and Creative Industries:* Abraão Vicente. *Education, Family and Social Inclusion:* Maritza Rosabal Peña. *Foreign Affairs, Communities and Defence:* Luís Felipe Tavares. *Health and Social Security:* Arlindo do Rosário. *Industry, Commerce and Energy:* Alexandre Monteiro. *Infrastructure, Spatial Planning and Housing:* Eunice Silva. *Internal Administration:* Paulo Costa Rocha. *Justice and Labour:* Janine Lélis. *Parliamentary Affairs and Sport:* Fernando Elísio Freire. *Tourism and Transport, and Maritime Economy:* José Gonçalves.

Government Website (Portuguese only): http://www.governo.cv

© Springer Nature Limited 2020
Palgrave Macmillan (ed.), *The Statesman's Yearbook 2020*,
https://doi.org/10.1057/978-1-349-95940-2_41

Current Leaders

Jorge Carlos Fonseca

Position
President

Introduction
Jorge Carlos Fonseca was elected president in Aug. 2011, having previously served as foreign minister. As leader of the main opposition party, the Movement for Democracy (MPD), he pledged co-operation with the ruling African Party for the Independence of Cabo Verde (PAICV) to boost economic growth and to strengthen representative democracy. He was re-elected in Oct. 2016 with an increased share of the popular vote.

Early Life
Born on 20 Oct. 1950 in São Velenti, Jorge Carlos de Almeida Fonseca was educated in Praia and Mindelo, before studying law at the University of Lisbon. He returned to Cape Verde in 1975 when the island gained independence from Portugal. From 1975–77 he served under the ruling African Party for the Independence of Guinea and Cape Verde (PAIGC) as director general of emigration. From 1977–79 he was secretary general at the ministry of foreign affairs.

Returning to academic life, he worked at the University of Lisbon from 1982 before becoming a professor of criminal law at Lisbon's National Institute of Legal Medicine in 1987. From 1989–90 he was a resident director and associate professor of law and public administration at the University of East Asia, Macau. As a founder member of the centrist MPD in 1990, he helped negotiate Cape Verde's first multi-party elections in Jan. 1991, in which he was elected to parliament. He served as minister of foreign affairs in the MPD government from 1991–93, before leaving the party to co-found the Democratic Convergence Party (PCD) in 1994.

Representing a coalition of minor parties, he stood unsuccessfully for the presidency in 2001. For the next decade he pursued a career as an academic and political activist. He co-founded the Law and Justice Foundation in 2004 and was appointed president of the Higher Institute of Legal and Social Sciences in Praia. He fought the Aug. 2011 presidential election as the MPD candidate, promising to sustain economic growth and build the island's infrastructure. He won in the second round with close to 55% of the vote.

Career in Office
Fonseca took office on 9 Sept. 2011, pledging to work with the governing PAICV to maintain political stability and attract inward investment. In March 2016 his MPD secured control of the National Assembly in parliamentary elections and in Oct. he was returned to the presidency for a second term. His main challenge remains boosting the economy to reduce high unemployment in an uncertain global economic climate.

Defence

National service is by selective conscription. The President of the Republic is C.-in-C. of the armed forces. Defence expenditure totalled US$9m. in 2013 (US$18 per capita), representing 0·5% of GDP.

Army

The Army is composed of two battalions and had a strength of 1,000 in 2011.

Navy

There is a coast guard of about 100 (2011) with three patrol and coastal combatants.

Air Force

The Air Force had under 100 personnel and no combat aircraft in 2011.

Economy

Agriculture contributed 10·0% of GDP in 2016, industry 19·4% and services 70·6%.

Overview

Tourism is the main engine of the economy, providing around 75% of annual GDP. The economy is also heavily dependent on remittances, which account for some 20% of GDP and provide vital stocks of foreign currency. The country has few natural resources, although frozen marine products are an important source of exports.

Real GDP growth averaged over 7% between 2003 and 2008 but dropped to under 1% in 2013, with declining consumer and business confidence leading to a fall in foreign direct investment. Economic growth then recovered to 4·7% in 2016—up from 1·0% in 2015—as tourism receipts increased, domestic demand improved and energy prices remained low. Nonetheless, deflation and high unemployment remain serious barriers to long-term prospects. Partly owing to the phasing out of a public investment programme, central government debt fell from 7·4% of GDP in 2014 to 4·5% in 2015. However, public debt was estimated at 118% of GDP in 2015, up from 94·7% in 2013.

Cabo Verde's insularity is a challenge to long-term growth but it is hoped that a programme of urban renewal will support an expansion of entrepreneurship. Many of the country's socio-economic indicators are encouraging—life expectancy is among the highest in sub-Saharan Africa and, by 2011, 86% of the total population lived less than half an hour from a health centre. Similarly, the adult literacy rate, estimated at 87%, is strong by regional standards, although disparities persist between men and women.

Cabo Verde has traditionally been vulnerable to the vagaries of global economic developments. Given the fixed exchange rate with the euro, it is vital for the country to rebuild fiscal buffers to absorb future shocks. Diversification within and beyond the tourism sector, along with a more flexible labour market, will help to this end. Safeguards are also needed against the threats posed by climate change, especially rising sea levels, and natural disasters—an active volcano on the island of Fogo last erupted in Nov. 2014.

Currency

The unit of currency is the *Cabo Verde escudo* (CVE) of 100 *centavos*, which is pegged at 110·265 to the euro. Foreign exchange reserves were US$164m. in June 2005 and total money supply was 25,156m. escudos. There was deflation of 1·4% in 2016 but inflation of 0·8% in 2017.

Budget

Budgetary central government revenues in 2011 were 37,300m. escudos (including taxes, 29,187m. escudos) and expenditures 33,929m. escudos (including compensation of employees, 5,993m. escudos).

VAT is 15%.

Performance

Real GDP growth was 1·0% in 2015, 4·7% in 2016 and 4·0% in 2017. Total GDP in 2017 was US$1·8bn.

Banking and Finance

The Banco de Cabo Verde is the central bank (*Governor*, João Serra) and bank of issue, and was also previously a commercial bank. Its latter functions have been taken over by the Banco Comercial do Atlântico, mainly financed by public funds. The Caixa Econômica de Cabo Verde (CECV) has been upgraded into a commercial and development bank. Two foreign banks have also been established there. In addition, the Fundo de Solidariedade Nacional acts as the country's leading savings institution while the Fundo de Desenvolvimento Nacional administers public investment resources and the Instituto Caboverdiano channels international aid.

External debt totalled US$857m. in 2010 and represented 54·3% of GNI.

There is a stock exchange in Mindelo.

Energy and Natural Resources

Environment

Cabo Verde's carbon dioxide emissions from the consumption of energy in 2011 were the equivalent of 0·8 tonnes per capita.

Electricity

Installed capacity was 109,000 kW in 2011. Production was 362m. kWh in 2011. Consumption per capita in 2011 was 738 kWh.

Minerals

Salt is obtained on the islands of Sal, Boa Vista and Maio. Volcanic rock (pozzolana) is mined for export. There are also deposits of kaolin, clay, gypsum and basalt.

Agriculture

Some 10–15% of the land area is suitable for farming. In 2013 an estimated 55,000 ha. were arable and 4,000 ha. permanent crops, mainly confined to inland valleys. About 4,000 ha. were equipped for irrigation in 2013. The chief crops (production, 2013, in 1,000 tonnes) are: sugarcane, 28; tomatoes (estimate), 14; bananas, 10; sweet potatoes, 9; potatoes, 8; onions, 7.

Livestock (2013): 190,000 goats; 85,000 pigs; 23,000 cattle; 15,000 asses.

Forestry

In 2015 the forest area was 90,000 ha., or 22% of the total land area.

Fisheries

In 2012 the total catch was 20,189 tonnes, exclusively from marine waters.

Industry

The main industries are the manufacture of paint, beer, soft drinks, rum, flour, cigarettes, canned tuna and shoes.

Labour

In 2010 the estimated economically active population was 221,000 (57% males).

International Trade

Imports and Exports

Merchandise imports in 2013 totalled US$726·4m. (US$754·8m. in 2012) and merchandise exports US$69·2m. (US$55·8m. in 2012).

Principal imports in 2013 were food, animals and beverages (30·1%), mineral fuels and lubricants, and machinery and transport equipment; main exports in 2013 were food, animals and beverages (86·1%), manufactured goods, and crude materials and animal and vegetable oils.

The leading import supplier in 2010 was Portugal (45·5%), followed by the Netherlands; the leading export destination in 2010 was Spain (68·2%), followed by Portugal.

Communications

Roads

There are approximately 1,400 km of roads. In 2007 there were 49,800 vehicles in use.

Civil Aviation

Amilcar Cabral International Airport, at Espargos on Sal, is a major refuelling point on flights to Africa and Latin America. A new international airport, Praia International Airport, has been built at Praia on São Tiago, and was opened in 2005. Transportes Aéreos de Cabo Verde (TACV), the national carrier, provided services to most of the other islands in 2010, and internationally to Bissau, Boston, Dakar, Fortaleza, Las Palmas, Lisbon and Paris. In 2006 Amilcar Cabral International Airport handled 562,972 passengers and 1,415 tonnes of freight. In 2012 scheduled airline traffic of Cabo Verde-based carriers flew 6·6m. km; passenger-km totalled 965m. in the same year.

Shipping

The main ports are Mindelo and Praia. In Jan. 2014 there were 21 vessels of 300 GT or over registered, totalling 30,000 GT. There are regular ferry service between the islands.

Telecommunications

In 2011 there were 74,500 landline telephone subscriptions (equivalent to 148·8 per 1,000 inhabitants) and 396,400 mobile phone subscriptions (or 791·9 per 1,000 inhabitants). There were 296·7 internet users per 1,000 inhabitants in 2009. Fixed internet subscriptions totalled 12,900 in 2009 (26·3 per 1,000 inhabitants).

Social Institutions

Out of 178 countries analysed in the 2017 *Fragile States Index*—a list published jointly by the Fund for Peace and *Foreign Policy* magazine—Cabo Verde was ranked the 73rd least vulnerable to conflict or collapse.

The index is based on 12 indicators of state vulnerability across social, political and economic categories.

Justice

There is a network of People's Tribunals, with a Supreme Court in Praia. The Supreme Court is composed of a minimum of five Judges, of whom one is appointed by the President, one elected by the National Assembly and the other by the Supreme Council of Magistrates.

The population in penal institutions in 2012 was 1,348 (267 per 100,000 of national population). The death penalty was abolished in 1981.

Education

Adult literacy in 2009 was estimated at 84·8% (90·1% among males and 80·2% among females). Primary schooling is followed by lower (13–15 years) and upper (16–18 years) secondary education options. In 2005–06 there were 3,196 primary school teachers for 81,162 pupils; and 2,363 teachers for 52,969 pupils at secondary schools. There are two universities: the Jean Piaget University of Cabo Verde and the University of Cabo Verde.

In 2007 public expenditure on education came to 5·9% of GNI.

Health

Cabo Verde's main hospitals are located in Praia and Mindelo. There is a network of health centres and clinics. In 2005 there were 21 hospital beds per 10,000 inhabitants. There were 217 physicians and 471 nurses in 2006.

In *Water: At What Cost? The State of the World's Water 2016*, WaterAid reported that 8·3% of the population does not have access to safe water.

Religion

According to the Pew Research Center's Forum on Religion & Public Life, in 2010 the population was an estimated 89·1% Christian with a further 9·1% being religiously unaffiliated and the remainder followers of other religions. Around 90% of Christians are Catholics. In Feb. 2019 there was one cardinal.

Culture

World Heritage Sites

Cidade Velha, the historic centre of Ribeira Grande, was inscribed on the UNESCO World Heritage List in 2009. It was the first European colonial town to be built in the tropics.

Press

In 2008 there were 12 non-daily newspapers although no dailies. The most popular newspaper is the weekly *A Semana*.

Tourism

In 2014 there were 494,000 non-resident tourists staying at hotels and similar establishments, down from 503,000 in 2013. Travel and tourism contributes more than 40% to Cabo Verde's GDP and is the driving force behind the economy.

Festivals

Festivals include the São Vicente Creole Carnival (Feb.) and the music festivals, Gamboa Festival in São Tiago (May) and São Vicente Baia das Gatas Festival (Aug.).

Diplomatic Representatives

Of Cabo Verde in the United Kingdom
    Ambassador: Vacant (resides in Brussels).
    Chargé d'Affaires a.i.: Octavio Bento Gomes.
    Honorary Consul: Anne-Marie Dias Borges (33 Buckthorne Rd, London, SE4 2DG).

Of the United Kingdom in Cabo Verde
    Ambassador: George Hodgson (resides in Dakar, Senegal).

Of Cabo Verde in the USA (3415 Massachusetts Ave., NW, Washington, D.C., 20007)
    Ambassador: Carlos Alberto Wahnon de Carvalho Veiga.

Of the USA in Cabo Verde (Rua Abilio Macedo 6, Praia)
  Ambassador: Vacant.
  Chargé d'Affaires a.i.: Marissa Scott.

Of Cabo Verde to the United Nations
  Ambassador: José Luis Fialho Rocha.

Of Cabo Verde to the European Union
  Ambassador: José Filomeno de Carvalho Dias Monteiro.

Further Reading

Foy, C., *Cape Verde: Politics, Economics and Society.* 1988
Lobban, Richard, *Historical Dictionary of the Republic of Cape Verde.* 1995.—*Cape Verde: Crioulo Colony to Independent Nation.* 1998
Meintel, D., *Race, Culture, and Portuguese Colonialism in Cabo Verde.* 1984
National Statistical Office: Instituto Nacional de Estatística, Praia.
Website (limited English): http://ine.cv/en

Cambodia

Preah Reach Ana Pak Kampuchea (Kingdom of Cambodia)

Capital: Phnom Penh
Population projection, 2020: 16·72m.
GNI per capita, 2017: (PPP$) 3,413
HDI/world rank, 2017: 0·582/146
Internet domain extension: .kh

Key Historical Events

Neolithic communities, probably linked to migration from southeast China, were established by 1000 BC in the Kompong Cham province of eastern Cambodia. From around 300 BC the Indianized Funan kingdom held sway across much of present-day Cambodia with trading links to China, India, the Middle East and Rome. The state of Chenla broke away from Funan control during the 6th century and over the next 300 years its influence spread to western Cambodia, central Laos and northern Thailand. Cambodia's southern coast came under Javanese control in the eighth century, forcing Khmer-speaking groups inland. The crowning of Jayavarman II as a deva-raja (or god king) in 802 heralded a long period of regional Khmer domination centred around Angkor.

The Indian-influenced civilization prospered with the development of agriculture and trade, notably under King Yasovarman I around 900 AD and during the reign of Suryavarman II (1113–50), when the temple complex at Angkor Wat was constructed. The empire was attacked by the Islamic Kingdom of Champa (now in central Vietnam) in the 12th and 13th centuries and was subsequently vulnerable to Thai incursions from Ayudhya. Thai forces sacked Angkor in 1432, ushering in a period of dominance by the kings of Siam on Cambodia's western frontier and pressure from Annam to the east. Cambodian nobility established a capital at Phnom Penh in the 16th century, although its influence was limited and the city was sacked by Rama I of Siam in 1772. In 1811–12 Siamese and Vietnamese forces fought for control of Cambodia, with the kingdom coming under Vietnam's control in 1835–40. King Ang Doung wrested back control in 1848 and appealed for military assistance from France, a major naval force in the region with bases in southern Vietnam. Under King Norodom I, a French protectorate was established in 1863, although resentment grew as French control extended beyond foreign affairs and defence. Rebellions were suppressed in the 1870s and 1880s and Cambodia became part of the Union of Indochina in 1887.

Anti-French feeling strengthened in 1940–41 when the Vichy French submitted to Japanese demands for bases in Cambodia. Son Ngoc Thanh was one of the leaders of a nascent nationalist movement after French control was reasserted in 1945. Having returned to Cambodia in 1951, he joined the Khmer Issarak guerrillas to fight the French. Independence was achieved on 9 Nov. 1953, the result of deft diplomacy by King Norodom Sihanouk and France's increasingly weak position in a war against Vietnam's communist revolutionaries. Sihanouk abdicated in 1955 to form the popular Socialist Party which dominated the general election of that year. He served as the country's leader until 1970 when he was deposed by the US-backed Lon Nol amid growing communist incursions from North Vietnam, a rapidly deteriorating economy and political corruption.

The country's name was changed to the Khmer Republic in Oct. 1970. US forces attacked Cambodia's communist strongholds, which led to the rise of the Khmer Rouge. In 1973 direct US involvement came to an end, precipitating a civil war between the Khmer Republic and the United National Cambodian Front (including the Khmer Rouge), supported by North Vietnam and China. After unsuccessful attempts to capture Phnom Penh in 1973 and 1974, the Khmer Rouge, led by Pol Pot, overthrew Lon Nol's government in April 1975.

Renaming the country Democratic Kampuchea, Pol Pot instituted a harsh and highly centralized regime. All cities and towns were forcibly evacuated and citizens set to work in the fields. Intellectuals, members of the professional classes and people identified as enemies of the Khmer Rouge were murdered in their hundreds of thousands and many more died as a result of disease, malnutrition and overwork, resulting in the loss of an estimated 2m. Cambodian lives from 1975–79. In response to repeated border attacks, Vietnam invaded Cambodia in 1978. On 7 Jan. 1979 Phnom Penh was captured by the Vietnamese and Pol Pot fled. During the 1980s the country was destabilized by warring factions fighting both the Vietnamese and the Khmer Rouge. On 23 Oct. 1991 an agreement was signed in Paris by the warring factions and 19 countries, instituting a UN-monitored ceasefire.

A new constitution was promulgated in 1993 restoring parliamentary monarchy. The Khmer Rouge continued hostilities, refusing to take part in the 1993 elections, and by 1996 had split into two factions. The leader of one faction, Ieng Sary, had been sentenced to death *in absentia* for genocide but was pardoned in Sept. 1996. In Nov. 1996 Ieng Sary and 4,000 of his troops joined with government forces. Prince Norodom Ranariddh, styled as First Prime Minister of the Royal Government, was exiled in July 1997 and coup-leader Hun Sen appointed himself prime minister. In March 1998 Ranariddh returned with a Japanese-brokered plan to ensure 'fair and free' elections, which took place in July 1998. Against a background of violence Hun Sen's Cambodian People's Party (KPK) declared victory.

King Norodom Sihanouk abdicated in Oct. 2004 for health reasons and was succeeded by his son, Norodom Sihamoni. In July 2007 UN-backed tribunals investigated allegations of genocide by the Khmer Rouge. The KPK claimed victory in the parliamentary elections of July 2008 and announced that it would remain in coalition with the depleted Royalist FUNCINPEC (National United Front for an Independent, Neutral, Peaceful and Co-operative Cambodia).

Territory and Population

Cambodia is bounded in the north by Laos and Thailand, west by Thailand, east by Vietnam and south by the Gulf of Thailand. It has an area of about 181,035 sq. km (69,898 sq. miles).

Population, 13,395,682 (2008 census), of whom 6,879,628 were females; density, 74·0 per sq. km. In 2011, 20·4% of the population lived in urban areas.

The UN gives a projected population for 2020 of 16·72m.

The capital, Phnom Penh, had a population of 1,242,992 in 2008. Other cities are Battambang and Siem Reap. Khmers make up around 90% of the population. There are also Vietnamese, Chinese and ethnic hill tribes.

Khmer is the official language.

Social Statistics

2008 estimated births, 360,000; deaths, 121,000. Rates, 2008 estimates (per 1,000 population): births, 24·7; deaths, 8·3. Infant mortality, 2010 (per 1,000 live births), 43. Expectation of life in 2013 was 69·1 years for males and 74·5 for females. Annual population growth rate, 2000–08, 1·7%. Fertility rate, 2008, 2·9 children per woman, down from 5·8 births per woman in 1990.

Climate

A tropical climate, with high temperatures all the year. Phnom Penh, Jan. 78°F (25·6°C), July 84°F (28·9°C). Annual rainfall 52" (1,308 mm).

Constitution and Government

A parliamentary monarchy was re-established by the 1993 constitution. King Norodom Sihamoni (b. 14 May 1953; appointed 14 Oct. 2004 and sworn in on 29 Oct. 2004) was chosen in the first ever meeting of the nine-member Throne Council following the abdication of his father King Norodom Sihanouk (1922–2012) on health grounds. As the Cambodian constitution allowed for a succession only in the event of the monarch's death, a new law had to be approved after King Norodom Sihanouk announced his abdication.

Cambodia has a bicameral legislature. There is a 125-member *National Assembly*, which on 14 June 1993 elected Prince Sihanouk head of state. On

21 Sept. 1993 it adopted a constitution (promulgated on 24 Sept.) by 113 votes to five with two abstentions making him monarch of a parliamentary democracy. Its members are elected by popular vote to serve five-year terms. There is also a 62-member *Senate*, established in 1999.

National Anthem

'Nokoreach' ('Royal kingdom'); words by Chuon Nat, tune adapted from a Cambodian folk song.

Recent Elections

Parliamentary elections were held on 29 July 2018. The ruling Cambodian People's Party (CPP) won all 125 seats with 76·8% of the vote (up from 68 and 48·8% in 2013). Turnout was 83·0%. The election was described as flawed and a sham after the Supreme Court dissolved the country's main opposition party, with various international governments dismissing the results.

Current Government

In Feb. 2019 the government comprised:

Prime Minister: Hun Sen; b. 1951 (CPP; sworn in 30 Nov. 1998 and reappointed 14 July 2004, 25 Sept. 2008, 24 Sept. 2013 and 6 Sept. 2018, having first become prime minister in 1985).

Deputy Prime Ministers: Bin Chhin (also *Minister in Charge of the Office of the Council of Ministers*); Aun Porn Moniroth (also *Minister of Economy and Finance*); Prak Sokhon (also *Minister of Foreign Affairs and International Co-operation*); Sar Kheng (also *Minister of Internal Affairs*); Chea Sophara (also *Minister of Land Management, Urban Affairs and Construction*); Men Sam An (also *Minister of National Assembly–Senate Relations and Inspection*); Gen. Tea Banh (also *Minister of Defence*); Hor Nam Hong; Yim Chhai Ly; Ke Kim Yan.

Minister of Agriculture, Forestry and Fisheries: Veng Sakhon. *Civil Service:* Pich Bunthin. *Commerce:* Pan Sorasak. *Cults and Religions:* Him Chhem. *Culture and Fine Arts:* Phoeung Sakona. *Education, Youth and Sports:* Hang Chuon Naron. *Environment:* Say Samal. *Health:* Mam Bun Heng. *Industry and Handicrafts:* Cham Prasidh. *Information:* Khieu Kanharith. *Justice:* Ang Vong Vathana. *Labour and Vocational Training:* Ith Sam Heng. *Mines and Energy:* Suy Sem. *Planning:* Chhay Than. *Posts and Telecommunications:* Tram Iv Tek. *Public Works and Transport:* Sun Chanthol. *Rural Development:* Ouk Rabun. *Social Affairs, Veterans and Youth Rehabilitation:* Vorng Saut. *Tourism:* Thong Khon. *Water Resources and Meteorology:* Lim Kean Hor. *Women's Affairs:* Ing Kantha Phavi.

Government Website: http://www.pressocm.gov.kh

Current Leaders

Hun Sen

Position

Prime Minister

Introduction

Hun Sen has been the dominant figure in Cambodian politics since becoming prime minister in 1985. His tenure has coincided with national recovery from the rule of the Khmer Rouge in the 1970s and the subsequent occupation by Vietnamese forces, although he has been criticized for the repressive tactics he has used to retain power. Despite the economy having suffered from endemic corruption and a failure to attract foreign investment, Hun Sen has moved it away from state socialism towards one based on free market principles. A UN-backed tribunal to investigate charges of genocide against prominent Khmer Rouge figures has sought to conclude that turbulent period in the nation's history.

Early Life

Hun Sen was born into a peasant family in Kompang in 1951 and was educated in Phnom Penh by Buddhist monks. In 1970 he joined the Khmer Rouge, losing an eye in battle in 1975, but in 1977 he joined anti-Khmer Rouge forces operating out of Vietnam. After Vietnamese troops invaded Kampuchea in 1979, Hun Sen was appointed foreign minister in the newly established People's Republic of Kampuchea. He became prime minister in 1985.

Career in Office

On assuming office, Hun Sen was confronted with a country in turmoil as pro- and anti-Vietnamese forces waged guerrilla war. In 1989 Vietnamese forces withdrew from the country, which was renamed the State of Cambodia. Buddhism was re-established as the state religion and Hun Sen announced the end of state socialism. In 1991 the UN brokered a peace treaty and a transitional government was installed, with Prince Sihanouk as head of state.

FUNCINPEC, the royalist party of Prince Norodom Ranariddh, was victorious at the 1993 elections but Hun Sen refused to relinquish power. A compromise government was formed with Ranariddh as first prime minister and Hun Sen as his deputy. However, in 1997 Hun Sen received international condemnation and saw Cambodia expelled from ASEAN for deposing Ranariddh while he was absent from the country. The Cambodian People's Party (CPP) won the 1998 elections but did not gain enough seats to form a government. Hun Sen agreed to head a coalition that included FUNCINPEC. Ranariddh, who had been found guilty *in absentia* of arms smuggling, received a royal pardon and was named president of the National Assembly. Also in 1998, Pol Pot died, having been sentenced to life imprisonment for his crimes the previous year.

At the general elections of 2003 the CPP emerged as the single biggest party but fell short of the two-thirds majority required to form the government. The opposition FUNCINPEC and Sam Rainsy parties agreed to join a ruling coalition but not under Hun Sen. However, the King finally confirmed Hun Sen as head of government in July 2004, after almost a year without a properly functioning administration.

After winning Senate approval, Cambodia began talks with the UN on a tribunal to try former Khmer Rouge leaders for genocide. Negotiations were protracted and in 2003 the UN concluded that the tribunal was unlikely to function alongside Cambodia's existing judicial system, which claimed precedence over international law. The issue was further complicated by Khmer Rouge leaders transferring allegiance to the government in the years following Pol Pot's fall from power. Hun Sen himself was a soldier in the Khmer Rouge, though he denied claims that he ever held a senior position. Nevertheless, the UN-backed tribunal, run by Cambodian and international judges, finally held its first public hearing in Nov. 2007 and achieved its first conviction (of a prison commandant) in July 2010. Preliminary hearings against three senior Khmer Rouge figures began in June 2011 and their trial started in Nov. that year. Of the three, Ieng Sary died in March 2013 while Nuon Chea and Khieu Samphan received life sentences for crimes against humanity in Aug. 2014. In Nov. 2018 they were additionally convicted of genocide.

Meanwhile, in 2003 a Thai celebrity had suggested that the religious complex of Angkor Wat had been stolen by Cambodia from Thailand. The comments caused outrage in Cambodia and led to a siege of the Thai embassy in Phnom Penh. Then in 2004 Hun Sen threatened to boycott a joint Asian-European summit if, as the European Union was requesting, Myanmar was banned from attending. Cambodia's entry into the World Trade Organization was ratified in Aug. 2004 after long delays.

Other significant domestic problems confronting Hun Sen's government at that time included deforestation and the spread of AIDS. In Aug.-Sept. 2006 he also pushed two controversial measures through the National Assembly curtailing the right of parliamentarians to speak openly without fear of prosecution and imposing a ban on adultery.

Following public criticism by Hun Sen, Prince Ranariddh resigned as president of the National Assembly and in March 2007 was sentenced *in absentia* to 18 months imprisonment for breach of trust over the sale of the FUNCINPEC headquarters.

On 26 Sept. 2008 Hun Sen was reappointed prime minister after the CPP had secured over two-thirds of the seats in National Assembly elections in July that were criticized by EU monitors as falling short of international standards.

In Oct. 2008 tensions between Cambodia and Thailand worsened as border skirmishes resulted in the deaths of two Cambodian soldiers in a disputed area around Preah Vihear, an ancient temple and (since July 2008) a UNESCO World Heritage site. Exchanges of gunfire on the border were reported in the spring of 2009 and again in Feb. and April 2011 before the International Court of Justice (ICJ) ruled in July that year that both sides should withdraw their forces from the area. In Nov. 2013 the ICJ ruled in favour of Cambodian sovereignty in the dispute, which was welcomed by Hun Sen.

In Sept. 2010 exiled opposition leader Sam Rainsy was sentenced *in absentia* to ten years imprisonment by a Cambodian court for disinformation and manipulating public documents. However, he was subsequently pardoned and returned from exile in July 2013. National Assembly elections that month were again won by the CPP amid opposition allegations of voting irregularities. Sam Rainsy's Cambodia National Rescue Party (CNRP) made significant gains in the poll but refused to take up its parliamentary seats and maintained a year-long protest campaign against the results until July 2014 when Hun Sen agreed to electoral reforms. Political tensions remained despite the apparent truce and were exacerbated by the removal of the deputy opposition leader, Kem Sokha, as vice president of the National Assembly in Oct. 2015 in a vote that was boycotted by the CNRP. In Nov. 2015 an arrest warrant was issued against Sam Rainsy over a conviction for defamation in 2011 and in Sept. 2016 Kem Sokha was sentenced to five months' imprisonment in what opposition supporters deemed a campaign of political intimidation by Hun Sen through the courts. The following month the CNRP resumed its parliamentary boycott over alleged threats from the CPP.

In Feb. 2017 Sam Rainsy resigned as head of the CNRP. In the same month the parliament approved a legislative change barring anyone convicted of an offence from running for public office. In apparent response by the government to a strong showing by the CNRP in local elections the following June, Kem Sokha, who had been elected party leader in March in place of Sam Rainsy, was again arrested in Sept. on treason charges. Then, in Nov., at the government's behest and ahead of parliamentary elections due in July 2018, the Supreme Court dissolved the CNRP and outlawed more than 100 politicians on the grounds that they were plotting a foreign-backed revolution.

Following the CPP's overwhelming victory in the July 2018 polling, claiming all 125 National Assembly seats, the parliament subsequently re-elected Hun Sen as prime minister for a further term in Sept.

Defence

The King is C.-in-C. of the Royal Cambodian Armed Forces (RCAF). Conscription has not been implemented since 1993 although it is authorized. Defence expenditure in 2013 totalled US$394m. (US$26 per capita), representing 2·5% of GDP.

Army

Strength in 2011 was an estimated 75,000. There are also provincial forces numbering some 45,000 and paramilitary local forces organized at village level.

Navy

Naval personnel in 2011 totalled about 2,800 including a naval infantry of 1,500. In 2011 the Navy had 11 patrol boats.

Air Force

Aviation operations were resumed in 1988, initially under the aegis of the Army and since 1993 as part of the RCAF. Personnel (2011), 1,500. There were 24 combat-capable aircraft in 2011.

Economy

Agriculture accounted for 30·5% of GDP in 2014, industry 27·1% and services 42·4%.

Overview

The economy was devastated by the Khmer Rouge regime of 1975–79, when trade collapsed to an agrarian barter system, the industrial base was destroyed, and the banking system and domestic currency abolished. Economic recovery remained slow until the Paris Peace Accord of 1991 brought about a ceasefire in the civil war. At the time of signing, Cambodia faced rapid inflation, exchange rate depreciation, monetary instability, negative real interest rates and high fiscal deficits. Since the Accord, and with the aid of the World Bank and the IMF, the government has tried to restore monetary stability and improve fiscal performance. Privatization of state-owned enterprises was completed by 1996 and the trade regime was liberalized as Cambodia joined the Association of South East Asian Nations in 1999 and later acceded to the World Trade Organization in 2004.

After more than two decades of strong economic growth, Cambodia had achieved lower-middle income status in 2015, with gross national income per capita reaching US$1,070 (PPP). This was driven by solid performances in the clothing, tourism, paddy and milled rice, and construction sectors. The country sustained an average annual growth rate of 7·6% from 1994–2015,

ranking it sixth in the world for economic expansion over the period. Although solid growth of 7·0% was maintained in 2016, the economy nonetheless remains vulnerable to international shocks and natural disasters.

Improving fiscal management is a long-term objective, with the public deficit standing at 2·7% of GDP in 2016 and gross public debt at 33%. Public expenditure is set to rise as a result of the growing public sector wage bill, although revenues have also increased as a result of more efficient tax collection.

Although Cambodia remains among the poorest countries outside of Africa, the poverty rate declined from 47·8% in 2007 to 13·5% in 2014. About 90% of the poor reside in the countryside. Improving health and education provision are priorities—33% of children under five have stunted growth and 79% of the population did not have access to a piped water supply in 2015.

To secure long-term prosperity the government must also address high levels of corruption and income inequality, as well as maintain macroeconomic stability, enhance economic diversification and export competitiveness, develop the private sector and better manage the country's natural resources.

Currency

The unit of currency is the *riel* (KHR) of 100 *sen*. In July 2005 total money supply was 1,222·4bn. riels, foreign exchange reserves were US$937m. and gold reserves 400,000 troy oz. There was inflation of 3·0% in 2016 and 2·9% in 2017.

Budget

In 2014 revenues were 10,517bn. riels and expenditures 14,168bn. riels. Tax revenue accounted for 84·2% of revenues in 2014; current expenditure accounted for 61·6% of expenditures.

VAT is 10%.

Performance

The economy grew by 7·0% in both 2015 and 2016 and 6·9% in 2017. With the exception of the negligible 0·1% growth in 2009, Cambodia's economy has grown at more than 5·0% every year since 1998. Total GDP in 2017 was US$22·2bn.

Banking and Finance

Banking and money were banned during the rule of the Khmer Rouge from 1975–79. The National Bank of Cambodia (*Governor*, Chea Chanto), which was founded in 1954 and re-established in Oct. 1979 after the fall of the Khmer Rouge, is the bank of issue. In 2011 there were 31 commercial banks, seven specialized banks and 32 licensed microfinance institutions. The largest banks in Dec. 2011 were Acleda Bank (with assets of US$1·49bn.), Canadia Bank and Cambodian Public Bank.

In 2010 external debt totalled US$4,676m., equivalent to 43·4% of GNI.

A stock exchange opened in Phnom Penh in July 2011 and started trading in April 2012.

Energy and Natural Resources

Environment

Carbon dioxide emissions from the consumption of energy in 2011 were the equivalent of 0·3 tonnes per capita in 2011.

The *Climate Change and Environmental Risk Atlas 2014* produced by Maplecroft, a risk analytics company, ranked Cambodia as the country facing the eighth highest economic and social risk from climate change by 2025.

Electricity

Installed capacity was 570,000 kW in 2011. Production (2011) was 1,053m. kWh; consumption per capita was 185 kWh.

Oil and Gas

Oil was discovered in 2005 off the coast of Cambodia. The reserves are estimated to total at least 400m. bbls. Oil production is expected to commence during 2019 and construction of the first phase of the country's first oil refinery is also expected to be completed in the course of 2019.

Minerals

There are phosphates and high-grade iron ore deposits. Some small-scale gold panning and gem (mainly zircon) mining is carried out.

Agriculture

The majority of the population is engaged in agriculture, fishing or forestry. Before the spread of war in the 1970s the high productivity provided for a low but well-fed standard of living for the peasant farmers, the majority of whom owned the land they worked before agriculture was collectivized. The war and unwise pricing policies led to a disastrous reduction in production, so much so that the country became a net importer of rice. Private ownership of land was restored by the 1989 constitution. In 2013 there were around 3·80m. ha. of arable land and 155,000 ha. of permanent crops.

A crop of 9·32m. tonnes of rice was produced in 2014. Production of other crops, 2014 estimates (in 1,000 tonnes): cassava, 8,835; sugarcane, 624; maize, 550; soybeans, 162; bananas (2013), 155.

Livestock (2011): cattle, 3·41m.; pigs, 2·10m.; buffaloes, 690,000; poultry, 24m.

Livestock products, 2013 estimates (in 1,000 tonnes): meat, 198; eggs, 23; milk, 23.

Forestry

Some 9·46m. ha., or 54% of the land area, were covered by forests in 2015. Timber exports have been banned since Dec. 1996. Rubber plantations are a valuable asset with production at around 40,000 tonnes per year. Timber production in 2011 was 8·47m. cu. metres.

Fisheries

2015 catch was 608,193 tonnes (mainly from inland waters).

Industry

Some development of industry had taken place before the spread of open warfare in 1970, but little was in operation by the 1990s except for rubber processing, sea-food processing, jute sack making and cigarette manufacture. Garment manufacture, rice milling, wood and wood products, rubber, cement and textiles production are the main industries. In the private sector small family concerns produce a wide range of goods. Light industry is generally better developed than heavy industry.

Labour

The labour force in 2013 was 8,446,300 (6,311,500 in 2003). 84·9% of the population aged 15–64 was economically active in 2013. In the same year 0·3% of the population was unemployed.

Cambodia had 0·11m. people living in slavery according to the Walk Free Foundation's 2013 *Global Slavery Index*.

International Trade

Imports and Exports

In 2010 imports (c.i.f.) totalled US$4,902·5m. (US$3,905·7m. in 2009); exports (f.o.b.), US$5,590·1m. (US$4,992·0m. in 2009).

Main imports are: textile yarn, fabrics and finished articles; road vehicles; specialized machinery; gold. Main exports are: textile yarn, fabrics and finished articles; printed matter; specialized machinery; road vehicles.

Major import sources, 2010: China (24·2%), Thailand (14·1%) and Hong Kong (11·3%). Principal export destinations, 2010: USA (34·1%), Hong Kong (24·8%) and Singapore (7·7%).

Communications

Roads

There were 39,704 km of roads in 2009, of which 8·2% were paved. In 2005 there were 195,300 passenger cars in use plus 3,200 buses and coaches, 32,100 lorries and vans and 566,300 motorcycles and mopeds. There were 1,545 fatalities in road accidents in 2007.

Rail

All official rail services had been suspended by 2009 owing to the dilapidated state of the 600 km metre gauge network. However, a rehabilitation project began in 2006 and freight services were resumed in Oct. 2010 between Phnom Penh and Touk Meas. In April 2016 passenger services were restored between Phnom Penh and the coastal town of Sihanoukville. A route between Phnom Penh and Poipet—on the border with Thailand and a departure point for trains to Bangkok—opened in 2018.

Civil Aviation

Phnom Penh International Airport handled 1,587,986 passengers in 2009 and Siem Reap International Airport 1,255,166. The flag carrier is Cambodia Angkor Air (51% state-owned), which began services in 2009. The former national airline, Royal Air Cambodge, had gone bankrupt in 2001.

Shipping

The main deep-sea port is Sihanoukville. There are also international ports at Phnom Penh and Koh Kong. In Jan. 2014 there were 563 ships of 300 GT or over registered, totalling 1,343,000 GT. Cambodia is a 'flag of convenience' country.

Telecommunications

Cambodia had 20,451,982 mobile phone subscriptions in 2014 (1,327·3 for every 1,000 persons) but only 361,056 main (fixed) telephone lines (23·4 per 1,000 population). 9% of the population were internet users in 2014.

Social Institutions

Out of 178 countries analysed in the 2017 *Fragile States Index*—a list published jointly by the Fund for Peace and *Foreign Policy* magazine—Cambodia was ranked the 50th most vulnerable to conflict or collapse. The index is based on 12 indicators of state vulnerability across social, political and economic categories.

Justice

The population in penal institutions in Nov. 2012 was 15,397 (106 per 100,000 of national population). The International Centre for Prison Studies estimated in 2014 that 63·6% of prisoners had yet to receive a trial. The death penalty was abolished in 1989. In 2015 the World Justice Project *Rule of Law Index*, which provides data on how the rule of law is experienced by the general public across eight categories, ranked Cambodia last of 102 countries for civil justice and 98th for criminal justice.

Education

In 2016–17 there were 12,889 schools of which 7,144 were primary, 1,699 lower secondary and 486 upper secondary. There were 190,148 pupils in pre-primary schools and 4,888 teaching staff in 2016–17; 2,022,061 pupils and 46,149 teaching staff in primary schools; 585,971 pupils at lower secondary level and 28,782 teaching staff; and at upper secondary level 12,625 teaching staff for 279,480 pupils. There were 217,364 students in tertiary education in 2015 and 12,246 academic staff. Adult literacy in 2008 was 78%.

In 2007 public expenditure on education came to 1·7% of GNI and 12·4% of total government spending.

Health

In 2011 there were 2,391 doctors (including 91 specialists), 8,433 nurses and 3,748 midwives.

In *Water: At What Cost? The State of the World's Water 2016*, WaterAid reported that 24·5% of the population does not have access to safe water.

Religion

The constitution of 1989 reinstated Buddhism as the state religion; it had an estimated 13·69m. adherents in 2010 according to the Pew Research Center's Forum on Religion & Public Life. There are small Muslim, folk religionist and Protestant minorities.

Culture

World Heritage Sites

There are three UNESCO world heritage sites in Cambodia: Angkor (inscribed in 1992), an archaeological park that was the site of various capitals of the Khmer Empire from the 9th to the 15th centuries containing the Temple of Angkor Wat and the Bayon Temple at Angkor Thom; the Temple of Preah Vihear (2008), an outstanding example of Khmer architecture that dates back to the first half of the 11th century and is composed of a series of sanctuaries linked by a system of pavements and staircases; and the Temple Zone of Sambor Prei Kuk, Archaeological Site of Ancient Ishanapura (2017), the capital of the Chenla Empire that flourished in the late sixth and early seventh centuries AD.

Press

There were 22 paid-for daily newspapers in 2008 with a combined circulation of 60,000, including the English-language *Cambodia Daily*.

Tourism

In 2014 there were 4,503,000 international tourist arrivals (excluding same-day visitors), up from just 2,162,000 in 2009.

Diplomatic Representatives

Of Cambodia in the United Kingdom (64 Brondesbury Park, London, NW6 7AT)
Ambassador: Dr Soeung Ratchavy.

Of the United Kingdom in Cambodia (27–29 St. 75, Sangkat Srah Chak, Khan Daun Penh, Phnom Penh, 12201)
Ambassador: Tina Redshaw.

Of Cambodia in the USA (4530 16th St., NW, Washington, D.C., 20011)
Ambassador: Chum Sounry.

Of the USA in Cambodia (1 St. 96, Sangkat Wat Phnom, Khan Daun Phen, Phnom Penh)
Ambassador: Vacant.
Chargé d'Affaires a.i.: Michael Newbill.

Of Cambodia to the United Nations
Ambassador: Sovann Ke.

Of Cambodia to the European Union
Ambassador: Piseth Nom.

Further Reading

Chandler, D. P., *A History of Cambodia*. 4th ed. 2007
Etcheson, Craig, *After the Killing Fields: Lessons from the Cambodian Genocide*. 2005
Gottesman, Evan R., *Cambodia After the Khmer Rouge: Inside the Politics of Nation Building*. 2004
Strangio, Sebastian, *Hun Sen's Cambodia*. 2014
National Statistical Office: National Institute of Statistics, Ministry of Planning, 386 Preah Monivong Blvd, Boeung Keng Kong 1, Phnom Penh.
Website: http://www.nis.gov.kh

Cameroon

République du Cameroun (Republic of Cameroon)

Capital: Yaoundé
Population projection, 2020: 25·96m.
GNI per capita, 2017: (PPP$) 3,315
HDI/world rank, 2017: 0·556/151
Internet domain extension: .cm

Key Historical Events

Neolithic settlements at Shum Laka and Abeke date from between 5000 and 4000 BC. From around 500 BC Bantu-speaking farmers originating in central Cameroon began migrating to the east and south and, over the next 2,000 years, dispersed across most of the African continent. The Sao civilization developed in the far north, close to Lake Chad, from around 600 AD. It developed ties with the Kanem kingdom, which for a time controlled trans-Saharan trade.

By the 14th century Sao was reduced to small, scattered settlements under the control of the Kotoko state, itself comprised of several kingdoms across northern Cameroon including the Makari, Mara and Kousseri. The Duala, mainly located in the coastal lowlands, made contact with Portuguese, Dutch and British mariners during the 15th and 16th centuries, with Fernando Gomes reaching the Wouri river in 1472 and naming it Rio dos Camarões (or 'shrimp river').

The Duala acted as middlemen between European explorers and tribes in the interior, trading ivory, palm oil and slaves. The port of Bimbia and its surrounding area became the focal point for the slave trade, with hundreds of thousands shipped to plantations in São Tomé and Príncipe, Equatorial Guinea, the Caribbean and the Americas.

By the early 1800s much of Cameroon's coastal trade was under British control, although its influence inland remained limited. The north was increasingly Islamic following the arrival of Fulani settlers from the north-west, led by Uthman Dan Fodio. In 1858 an English naval engineer and missionary, Alfred Saker, founded the colony of Victoria (Limbe), which relied on exports of gold, ivory and palm oil after the demise of the slave trade.

British colonial operations centred on Lagos were supplanted by German influence in 1884 when a treaty between the Duala and Gustav Nachtigal (on behalf of Kaiser Wilhelm) created the protectorate of Kamerun. The port of Kamerunstadt (Douala) was developed and roads, bridges and settlements (including the future capital, Yaoundé) were established inland using forced labour.

In 1915 a combined force of British, French and Belgian troops defeated the German administrators. After the First World War the territory was governed briefly by Britain and France, before partition. The British sector encompassed two small provinces along the border with Nigeria (the North and South Cameroons), administered from Lagos, while the French sector (Cameroun) aligned with most of the former German colony. Both areas became mandated territories under the League of Nations in 1922 and, after the Second World War, Trust Territories of the newly established UN.

In French Cameroun the Union des Populations du Cameroun (UPC) was founded in 1948 to call for independence and 'reunification' with British Cameroons. In 1955 uprisings organized by the UPC broke out in several towns. From 1958 more moderate parties, such as l'Union Camerounaise of Ahmadou Ahidjo, were permitted to work towards independence within the French administration. This was achieved on 1 Jan. 1960 when Ahidjo was inaugurated as president. In a referendum on 11 Feb. 1961 British Southern Cameroons voted to join the new federal republic of Cameroon, while British Northern Cameroons chose to join Nigeria.

Re-elected in 1965 and 1970, Ahidjo became increasingly authoritarian and by 1976 opposition parties were outlawed. He stepped down, apparently for health reasons, in 1982, to be succeeded by Paul Biya, a Christian from the south. Cameroon faced economic hardship in the late 1980s linked to the depletion of oil reserves, sparking demands for democracy.

Biya narrowly won the first multi-party elections in Oct. 1992. Tensions with Nigeria over the potentially oil-rich Bakassi peninsula erupted in 1994, with flare-ups continuing until Nigeria retracted its claims in Aug. 2008. Biya won presidential elections in 1997, 2004 and 2011, although opposition parties rejected the results on each occasion amid claims of widespread fraud.

Territory and Population

Cameroon is bounded in the west by the Gulf of Guinea, northwest by Nigeria, east by Chad and the Central African Republic, and south by the Republic of the Congo, Gabon and Equatorial Guinea. The total area is 475,650 sq. km (land area, 466,050 sq. km). On 29 March 1994 Cameroon asked the International Court of Justice to confirm its sovereignty over the oil-rich Bakassi peninsula, occupied by Nigerian troops. The dispute continued for eight years, with Equatorial Guinea also subsequently becoming involved. In Oct. 2002 the International Court of Justice rejected Nigeria's claims and awarded the peninsula to Cameroon. All parties agreed to accept the Court's judgment. At the 2005 census the population was 17,463,836 (50·6% female); Jan. 2010 estimate, 19,406,100, giving a density of 41·6 per sq. km.

The UN gives a projected population for 2020 of 25·96m.

In 2011, 59·2% of the population were urban.

The areas, populations and chief towns of the ten provinces are:

Province	Sq. km	Census 2005	Chief town	Census 2005
Adamaoua	63,701	884,289	Ngaoundéré	152,698
Centre	68,953	3,098,044	Yaoundé	1,817,524
Est	109,002	771,755	Bertoua	88,462
Extrême-Nord	34,263	3,111,792	Maroua	201,371
Littoral	20,248	2,510,263	Douala	1,906,962
Nord (Bénoué)	66,090	1,687,959	Garoua	235,996
Nord-Ouest	17,300	1,728,953	Bamenda	269,530
Ouest	13,892	1,720,047	Bafoussam	239,287
Sud	47,191	634,655	Ebolowa	64,980
Sud-Ouest	25,410	1,316,079	Buéa	90,090

The population is composed of Sudanic-speaking people in the north (Fulani, Sao and others) and Bantu-speaking groups, mainly Bamileke, Beti, Bulu, Tikar, Bassa and Duala, in the rest of the country. The official languages are French and English (although about 80% of the country is French-speaking and only around 20% English-speaking).

Social Statistics

2008 estimates: births, 704,000; deaths, 271,000. Rates, 2008 estimates (per 1,000 population): birth, 36·9; death, 14·2. Annual population growth rate, 2000–08, 2·3%. Infant mortality, 2010, 84 per 1,000 live births. Life expectancy in 2013: males, 53·9 years; females, 56·2. Fertility rate, 2008, 4·6 children per woman.

Climate

An equatorial climate, with high temperatures and plentiful rain, especially from March to June and Sept. to Nov. Further inland, rain occurs at all seasons. Yaoundé, Jan. 76°F (24·4°C), July 73°F (22·8°C). Annual rainfall 62" (1,555 mm). Douala, Jan. 79°F (26·1°C), July 75°F (23·9°C). Annual rainfall 160" (4,026 mm).

Constitution and Government

The constitution was approved by referendum on 20 May 1972 and became effective on 2 June; it was amended in Jan. 1996. It provides for a *President* as head of state and government. The President is directly elected for a seven-year term, and there is a *Council of Ministers* whose members must not be members of parliament. A constitutional bill removing a two-term presidential limit was adopted in April 2008.

The *National Assembly*, elected by universal adult suffrage for five years, consists of 180 representatives. After 1966 the sole legal party was the Cameroon People's Democratic Movement (RDPC), but in Dec. 1990 the National Assembly legalized opposition parties. The 1996 amendment to the constitution established a 100-seat *Senate*, although elections to it were not held until April 2013.

National Anthem

'O Cameroon, Thou Cradle of our Fathers'/'O Cameroun, Berceau de nos Ancêtres'; words by R. Afame, tune by R. Afame, S. Bamba and M. Nko'o.

Government Chronology

Presidents since 1960. (RDPC = Cameroon People's Democratic Movement; UC = Cameroonian Union; UNC = Cameroonian National Union)

| 1960–82 | UC, UNC | Ahmadou Babatoura Ahidjo |
| 1982– | UNC, RDPC | Paul Biya |

Recent Elections

Presidential elections were held on 7 Oct. 2018. Incumbent Paul Biya was re-elected with 71·3% of the votes ahead of Maurice Kamto with 14·2% and Cabral Libii with 6·3%. There were six other candidates. Turnout was 53·9%.

National Assembly elections were held on 30 Sept. 2013. The ruling Cameroon People's Democratic Movement (Rassemblement Démocratique du Peuple Camerounais; RDPC) won 148 seats, Social-Democratic Front (Front Social-Démocratique; SDF) 18, National Union for Democracy and Progress (Union Nationale pour la Démocratie et le Progrès; UNDP) 5, Democratic Union of Cameroon (Union Démocratique du Cameroun; UDC) 4, Union of the Peoples of Cameroon (Union des Populations du Cameroun; UPC) 3, Cameroon Renaissance Movement (Mouvement Pour la Renaissance du Cameroun; MRC) 1 and Movement for the Defence of the Republic (Mouvement pour la Défense de la République; MDR) 1.

First elections to the Senate took place on 14 April 2013. The Cameroon People's Democratic Movement won 56 seats of the 70 contested with 73% of the vote; the opposition Social-Democratic Front obtained 14 seats with 17%. The remaining 30 seats are appointed.

Current Government

President: Paul Biya; b. 1933 (RDPC; assumed office 6 Nov. 1982, elected 14 Jan. 1984, re-elected 24 April 1988, also 10 Oct. 1992, 12 Oct. 1997, 11 Oct. 2004 and once again re-elected 9 Oct. 2011).

In Feb. 2019 the cabinet comprised:

Prime Minister: Joseph Dion Ngute; b. 1954 (RDPC; sworn in 4 Jan. 2019).

Ministers of State: Ferdinand Ngoh Ngoh (also *Secretary General of the Presidency*); Jacques Fame Ndongo (also *Minister of Higher Education*).

Minister for Agriculture and Rural Development: Gabriel Mbairobe. *Arts and Culture:* Pierre Ismaël Bidoung Kpwatt. *Basic Education:* Laurent Serge Etoundi Ngoa. *Commerce:* Luc Magloire Mbarga Atangana. *Communication:* René Sadi. *Decentralization and Local Government:* Elanga Obam George. *Economy, Planning and Regional Development:* Alamine Ousmane Mey. *Employment and Vocational Training:* Bakary Issa Tchiroma. *Energy and Water Resources:* Gaston Eloundou Essomba. *Environment and Nature Protection:* Pierre Hélé. *External Relations:* Mbella Mbella Lejeune. *Finance:* Louis-Paul Motaze. *Forests and Wildlife:* Jules Doret Ndongo. *Housing and Urban Development:* Célestine Ketcha Courtès. *Labour:* Grégoire Owona. *Livestock, Fisheries and Animal Industries:* Dr Taiga. *Mines, Industry and Technological Development:* Gabriel Dodo Ndoke. *Posts and Telecommunications:* Minette Libom Li Likeng. *Promotion of Women and Family Affairs:* Marie Thérèse Abena Ondoa. *Public Health:* Malachie Manaouda. *Public Service and Administrative Reforms:* Joseph Lé.

Public Works: Emmanuel Nganou Djoumessi. *Scientific Research and Innovation:* Madeleine Tchuenté. *Secondary Education:* Pauline Egbe Nalova Lyonga. *Small and Medium-Sized Enterprises, Social Economy and Handicrafts:* Achille Bassilekin III. *Social Affairs:* Pauline Irène Nguene. *Sports and Physical Education:* Narcisse Mouelle Kombi. *State Property, Surveys and Land:* Henri Eyebe Ayissi. *Territorial Administration:* Paul Atanga Nji. *Transport:* Jean Ernest Masséna Ngalle Bibehe. *Youth Affairs:* Mounouna Foutsou.

Minister Delegate at the Ministry of Justice and Keeper of the Seals: Jean de Dieu Momo. *Minister Delegate at the Ministry of Transport:* Zakariaou Njoya. *Minister Delegate at the Presidency in Charge of Public Contracts:* Ibrahim Talba Malla. *Minister Delegate at the Presidency in Charge of Relations with Parliament:* Bolvine Wakata.

Office of the President: http://www.prc.cm

Current Leaders

Paul Biya

Position
President

Introduction
President since 1982, Biya has kept tight political control over Cameroon. Despite some concessions to democracy, his regime has been dogged by allegations of widespread corruption. His international profile has been low, although he has maintained close relations with France, the former colonial ruler.

Early Life
Born on 13 Feb. 1933 in Mvomeka'a, Sud Province, Biya attended a Catholic mission school and, in the early 1950s, a seminary. He specialized in philosophy at the Lycée Général Leclerc in Yaoundé before studying law at the Université de la Sorbonne, Paris. His postgraduate studies included a diploma in public law from the Institut des Hautes Etudes d'Outre-Mer.

Biya's political career began in 1962 as chargé de mission at the Presidency of the Republic. He became secretary-general of the ministry of national education in 1965. In 1970 he was made a minister of state, serving as secretary-general to the Presidency. On 30 June 1975 Biya was appointed prime minister by President Ahmadou Ahidjo. An amendment to the constitution in 1979, designating the prime minister as successor to the president in case of vacancy, allowed Biya to assume the presidency on 6 Nov. 1982 following Ahidjo's resignation.

Career in Office
The succession, although constitutional, was not peaceful. In Aug. 1983 Biya forced Ahidjo into exile, and then consolidated his position by replacing Ahidjo's northern supporters with fellow southerners. Direct presidential elections by universal suffrage were instituted in Jan. 1984, which Biya won. Despite his initial democratic and modernizing aspirations, freedom of speech and the press were soon curtailed, largely as a result of problems with the old regime. The Republican Guard revolt of April 1984 provoked Biya to reform the sole political party, the Cameroon National Union (UNC), which was seen as Ahidjo's personal support base. Transformed into the Cameroon People's Democratic Movement (RDPC; Rassemblement Démocratique du Peuple Camerounais), it elected Biya as party president in March 1985.

In the early 1980s Cameroon's economy suffered from a downturn in the commodity export trade. Biya only admitted the severity of the economic crisis in 1987, submitting the national economy to scrutiny and assistance from the World Bank. Despite popular dissatisfaction, he was re-elected in April 1988.

Opposition political parties were legalized in Dec. 1990, although the delay in organizing multi-party elections and a ban on opposition party meetings caused rioting and a general strike in 1991. Biya relented in Oct. promising elections, which took place in March 1992. The RDPC was forced into coalition with the Movement for the Defence of the Republic (MDR; Mouvement pour la Défense de la République) to attain a majority in the National Assembly. Biya himself was re-elected in Oct. by a narrow majority.

Conflict over the Bakassi Peninsula, on the Nigerian border, and its oil and fishing rights began when the Nigerian leader Gen. Abacha sent troops to claim the area. Biya responded with military force and appealed to the International Court of Justice, which ruled in Cameroon's favour in 2002 (with Cameroon eventually taking control of the territory in Aug. 2008).

The presidential elections of Oct. 1997 were boycotted by the three main opposition parties after a year of popular unrest. The removal of elected mayors after the 1996 municipal elections and the Supreme Court's controversial rulings concerning the May 1997 National Assembly elections were two of the more prominent causes of the boycott. Biya was re-elected with a large majority of the vote.

By that time, Biya's presidency was marked by anglophone separatist unrest and allegations of corruption and human rights abuses. The secessionist Southern Cameroon National Council (SCNC), claiming to represent the country's 5m. English speakers, was targeted by the government and its leaders charged with treason. In 1998 Transparency International, the Berlin-based anti-corruption organization, classed Cameroon as the most corrupt country of the 85 covered by their survey. Amnesty International meanwhile claimed that extrajudicial executions and politically-motivated detentions were continuing despite international pressure.

In parliamentary elections in 2002 the RDPC won 149 of the 180 seats in National Assembly. On 11 Oct. 2004 Biya was re-elected for a further presidential term with over 70% of the vote, although opposition parties alleged widespread fraud and international observers said the poll lacked credibility in key areas. By 2006 new measures against corruption were in place, including a law requiring the declaration of assets by public officials and the establishment of an anti-corruption commission. In the 2007 legislative elections the RDPC retained its overwhelming majority and in April 2008 parliament approved a controversial constitutional amendment enabling Biya to run for a third term of office. He again secured re-election in Oct. 2011 by a landslide margin, claiming 78% of the vote. In Nov. 2012 Biya celebrated 30 years in executive power and in Sept. 2013 the RDPC maintained its dominance in National Assembly elections. He was returned again for a seventh presidential term in Oct. 2018 in an election marked by a low voter turnout.

Terrorist attacks in the north of the country by Boko Haram, an Islamist extremist group operating mainly in Nigeria, have escalated since 2015, threatening Cameroon's security and political stability and undermining its trade and tourism industry. There were also increasing tensions in 2017 between the country's Anglophone and majority Francophone populations. In Nov. 2018 up to 80 children and a teacher were abducted from a school in Bamenda in the northwest of the country by suspected English-speaking separatists, although many were subsequently released.

Defence

The President of the Republic is C.-in-C. of the armed forces. Defence expenditure totalled US$393m. in 2013 (US$19 per capita), representing 1·4% of GDP.

Army

Total strength (2011) is 12,500 and includes a Presidential Guard; there is a Gendarmerie 9,000 strong.

Navy

Personnel in 2011 numbered about 1,300. There are bases at Douala (HQ), Limbe and Kribi.

Air Force

Aircraft availability is low because of funding problems. Personnel (2011), 300–400. There were nine combat-capable aircraft in 2011.

Economy

In 2013 agriculture, fishing and forestry contributed 20·8% of GDP; followed by trade and hotels, 18·4%; manufacturing, 13·4%; finance and real estate, 10·6%; and public administration and defence, 7·8%.

Overview

Cameroon became an oil exporter in 1977, with production peaking in 1985. The country came to be regarded as an African success story in the early 1980s. However, an economic reversal was triggered in 1985 by a sharp fall in prices for primary products including cocoa and oil. Underlying the external trade shock were weak economic and political structures, a fiscal crisis and an overvalued exchange rate. In 1994 the currency was devalued.

A programme of privatization began in 1995, taking in the export, infrastructure, banking and insurance sectors. In 1996, supported by the IMF and World Bank, the government adopted structural reforms and macroeconomic policies encompassing forestry, banking, transportation and privatization of public utilities. Despite these reforms, corruption and poor resource management remained.

The Heavily Indebted Poor Countries Initiative and the Multilateral Debt Relief Initiative helped reduce the country's debt burden from 51·8% of GDP in 2005 to 9·5% in 2008. However, the debt level subsequently increased to stand at 33·9% of GDP in 2017.

Average annual real GDP growth was 3% over the period 2007–11. In 2011 and 2012 it expanded at a rate above 4% each year, and averaged 5·7% per year between 2012 and 2017. The inflation rate had fluctuated during the 1990s and early 2000s, but was contained at 2·2% between 2013 and 2017. High economic growth, however, has not been reflected in improved social indicators. Although declining since 1950s, the poverty rate remained close to 37·5% in 2017. Moreover, Cameroon's Human Development Index ranking is among the lowest in the world.

The economy remains overly dependent on its trading partners' economic health. Exports fell in the aftermath of the global financial and eurozone debt crises that began in 2008, and any further downturn in eurozone fortunes—the eurozone representing Cameroon's main trading partner—represents a significant threat to the short- to medium-term outlook.

Currency

The unit of currency is the *franc CFA* (XAF) with a parity of 655·957 francs CFA to one euro. In June 2005 foreign exchange reserves were US$759m. (negligible in 1997), total money supply was 757,006m. francs CFA and gold reserves were 30,000 troy oz. Inflation was 0·9% in 2016 and 0·6% in 2017.

Budget

The financial year used to end on 30 June but since 2003 has been the calendar year. In 2013 revenues totalled 2,727bn. francs CFA and expenditures 3,223bn. francs CFA.

VAT is 19·25%.

Performance

Real GDP growth was 5·7% in 2015, 4·6% in 2016 and 3·5% in 2017. Total GDP in 2017 was US$34·8bn.

Banking and Finance

The Banque des Etats de l'Afrique Centrale (*Governor*, Abbas Mahamat Tolli) is the sole bank of issue. The largest commercial banks are Afriland First Bank, Banque internationale du Cameroun pour l'épargne et le crédit (BICEC) and Société générale des banques au Cameroun (SGBC).

External debt totalled US$2,964m. in 2010 and represented 13·5% of GNI.

The Douala Stock Exchange was opened in 2003.

Energy and Natural Resources

Environment

Cameroon's carbon dioxide emissions from the consumption of energy in 2011 were the equivalent of 0·4 tonnes per capita.

Electricity

Installed capacity in 2011 was 1·0m. kW. Total production in 2011 was 6·00bn. kWh (73% hydro-electric), with consumption per capita 283 kWh. Cameroon is rich in hydro-electric potential, of which only a very small proportion is currently exploited.

Oil and Gas

Oil production (2011), mainly from Kole oilfield, was 22m. bbls. In 2014 there were proven reserves of 200m. bbls. In June 2000 the World Bank approved funding for a 1,000-km US$4bn. pipeline to run from 300 new oil wells in Chad through Cameroon to the Atlantic Ocean. Oil started pumping in July 2003. Natural gas reserves in 2014 totalled 135bn. cu. metres; output in 2011 was 284m. cu. metres.

Minerals

Tin ore and limestone are extracted. There are deposits of aluminium, bauxite, uranium, nickel, gold, cassiterite and kyanite. Aluminium production in 2008 was 89,700 tonnes.

Agriculture

In 2013 there were an estimated 6·20m. ha. of arable land and 1·55m. ha. of permanent crops. Around 29,000 ha. were equipped for irrigation in 2013. Main agricultural crops (with 2013 production in 1,000 tonnes): cassava, 4,596; plantains, 3,692; palm fruit oil (estimate), 2,450; maize, 1,647; taro, 1,551; bananas, 1,538; sugarcane (estimate), 1,200; sorghum (estimate), 1,150; tomatoes, 954; groundnuts, 636.

Livestock (2014 estimates): 6·0m. cattle; 4·7m. goats; 4·0m. sheep; 1·8m. pigs; 50m. chickens.

Livestock products (in 1,000 tonnes), 2013 estimates: meat, 335; milk, 253; eggs, 16.

Forestry

Forests covered 18·82m. ha. in 2015 (40% of the total land area), ranging from tropical rain forests in the south (producing hardwoods such as mahogany, ebony and sapele) to semi-deciduous forests in the centre and wooded savannah in the north. Timber production in 2011 was 12·17m. cu. metres.

Fisheries

In 2012 the total catch was an estimated 140,000 tonnes (mainly from inland waters).

Industry

Manufacturing is largely small-scale. Output in 1,000 tonnes (2007 unless otherwise indicated): cement (2005), 1,026; distillate fuel oil, 694; kerosene, 404; petrol, 390; residual fuel oil, 387. In 2005, 444m. litres of beer and 1·8bn. cigarettes were produced. There are also factories producing shoes, soap, oil and food products.

Labour

The total labour force numbered 8,906,000 in 2013. 70% of employed persons work in agriculture.

Cameroon had 0·15m. people living in slavery according to the Walk Free Foundation's 2013 *Global Slavery Index*.

International Trade

Imports and Exports

Merchandise imports in 2013 totalled US$6,657·2m. (US$6,515·1m. in 2012) and merchandise exports US$4,520·9m. (US$4,275·0m. in 2012).

Principal imports in 2013 were mineral fuels and lubricants (23·5%) followed by machinery and transport equipment, and food, animals and beverages; main exports in 2013 were mineral fuels and lubricants (55·9%), food, animals and beverages, and crude materials and animal and vegetable oils.

The leading import supplier in 2010 was Nigeria (18·2%), followed by France and China; the leading export destination in 2010 was Spain (18·5%), followed by the Netherlands and Italy.

Communications

Roads

There were about 122,222 km of roads in 2017, of which 5·8% were national roads. In 2005 there were 174,900 passenger cars, 56,200 lorries and vans, 15,600 buses and coaches, and 65,600 motorcycles and mopeds. In 2007 there were 990 deaths in road accidents.

Rail

Cameroon Railways (Camrail), 977 km in 2011, link Douala with Nkongsamba and Ngaoundéré, with branches from M'Banga to Kumba and Makak to M'Balmayo. In 2011 railways carried 1·5m. passengers and 1·6m. tonnes of freight.

Civil Aviation

There are international airports at Douala, Garoua and Yaoundé (Nsimalen). In 2011 Douala handled 746,092 passengers. The flag carrier, Camair-Co, was founded in 2011 and operates mainly on domestic routes with international services to Cotonou and N'Djaména. In 2012 scheduled airline traffic of Cameroon-based carriers flew 2·7m. km; passenger-km totalled 638m. in the same year.

Shipping

The main port is Douala; other ports are Bota, Campo, Garoua (only navigable in the rainy season), Kribi and Limbo-Tiko.

Telecommunications

There were 496,500 fixed telephone lines in 2010 (25·3 per 1,000 inhabitants) and mobile phone subscribers numbered 8·16m. In 2010 there were 40·0 internet users per 1,000 inhabitants. In the same year 1·9% of households had internet access at home. In June 2012 there were 494,000 Facebook users.

Social Institutions

Out of 178 countries analysed in the 2017 *Fragile States Index*—a list published jointly by the Fund for Peace and *Foreign Policy* magazine—Cameroon was ranked the 26th most vulnerable to conflict or collapse. The index is based on 12 indicators of state vulnerability across social, political and economic categories.

Justice

The Supreme Court sits at Yaoundé, as does the High Court of Justice (consisting of nine titular judges and six surrogates all appointed by the National Assembly). There are magistrates' courts situated in the provinces.

The population in penal institutions in Dec. 2011 was 24,000 (119 per 100,000 of national population). The International Centre for Prison Studies estimated in 2014 that 62·2% of prisoners had yet to receive a trial. Cameroon was ranked 91st of 102 countries for criminal justice and 96th for civil justice in the 2015 World Justice Project *Rule of Law Index*, which provides data on how the rule of law is experienced by the general public across eight categories.

Education

In 2007 there were 217,284 children and 12,349 teaching staff at pre-primary schools. There were 3,120,357 pupils in primary schools in 2007 with 70,230 teaching staff and 750,777 secondary level pupils with (2006) 43,193 teaching staff.

In 2007, 132,134 students were in tertiary education with 3,040 academic staff. There were six public universities and five private universities in 2007. The adult literacy rate in 2008 was 76%.

Public expenditure on education came to 3·9% of GNI in 2007 and 17·0% of total government spending.

Health

In 2010 there were 1,712 physicians, 10,714 nursing and midwifery personnel, 58 dentistry personnel and 42 pharmaceutical personnel. There were 15 hospital beds per 10,000 population in 2006.

In *Water: At What Cost? The State of the World's Water 2016*, WaterAid reported that 24·4% of the population does not have access to safe water.

Religion

In 2010 there were an estimated 7·6m. Roman Catholics, 6·2m. Protestants, 3·6m. Muslims and 0·7m. folk religionists according to the Pew Research Center's Forum on Religion & Public Life. A further 1·1m. people had no religious affiliation. In Feb. 2019 there was one cardinal.

Culture

World Heritage Sites

The Dja Faunal Reserve was inscribed on the UNESCO World Heritage List in 1987. Surrounded by the Dja River, it is one of Africa's largest rainforests. Sangha Trinational, a transboundary conservation complex situated in Cameroon, Central African Republic and the Republic of the Congo, was added to the UNESCO World Heritage List in 2012. The site consists of three contiguous national parks totalling around 750,000 ha. Much of it is unaffected by human activity and features a wide range of humid tropical forest ecosystems with rich flora and fauna.

Press

In 2008 there was one national government-owned daily newspaper with a circulation of 25,000, four privately-owned dailies and about 200 other privately owned-newspapers that appeared at irregular intervals.

Tourism

In 2013 there were 912,000 international tourist arrivals (excluding same-day visitors), up from 812,000 in 2012 and 480,000 in 2008.

Festivals

The Cameroon National Festival takes place on 20 May. The Ngonda festival in Douala takes place over ten days ending on the first Sunday of Dec. and involves water ceremonies of the jengu cult.

Diplomatic Representatives

Of Cameroon in the United Kingdom (84 Holland Park, London, W11 3SB)
High Commissioner: Albert Fotabong Njoteh.

Of the United Kingdom in Cameroon (Ave. Winston Churchill, Centre Region 547, Yaoundé)
High Commissioner: Rowan James Laxton.

Of Cameroon in the USA (3400 International Drive, NW, Washington, D.C., 20008)
Ambassador: Etoundi Essomba.

Of the USA in Cameroon (Ave. Rosa Parks, BP 817, Yaoundé)
Ambassador: Peter Henry Barlerin.

Of Cameroon to the United Nations
Ambassador: Michel Tommo Monthe.

Of Cameroon to the European Union
Ambassador: Daniel Evina Abe'e.

Further Reading

Ardener, E., *Kingdom on Mount Cameroon: Studies in the History of the Cameroon Coast 1500–1970.* 1996

Gros, Jean-Germain, *Cameroon: Politics and Society in Critical Perspective.* 2003

National Statistical Office: Institut National de la Statistique du Cameroun, Ministère de l'Economie, de la Planification et de l'Aménagement du Territoire, Yaoundé.

Website: http://www.statistics-cameroon.org

Canada

Capital: Ottawa
Population projection, 2020: 37·60m.
GNI per capita, 2017: (PPP$) 43,433
HDI/world rank, 2017: 0·926/12
Internet domain extension: .ca

Key Historical Events

The first habitation in Canada dates from the last stages of the Pleistocene Ice Age up to 30,000 years ago. Tribes from Central and Northern Asia crossed the Bering Strait by a land bridge in search of mammoth, bison and elk. These hunter-gatherers were the forefathers of some of Canada's native people referred to today as the First Nations. There are currently two other Aboriginal groups; the Inuit (Arctic people, formerly known as Eskimos) and the Métis. The Inuit were one of the last groups to arrive, around 1000 BC, whereas the Métis evolved from the union of natives and Europeans (mostly French).

The numerous tribes that made up the First Nations consisted of 12 major language groups with a number of sub groups with diverse spiritual beliefs, laws and customs. Around 6000 BC, during the Boreal Archaic age, the glaciers of the Canadian Shield melted and lakes were formed. The Iroquois speaking tribes, including the Mohawks and the Huron, settled along the St Lawrence River and the Great Lakes. Excellent farmers, they lived in large communities. Trade flourished but tribal wars were common. By 1000 BC the Early Woodland Culture had developed in the east. Among the eight tribes were the Algonquin, one of the largest language groups, who spread west to the Plains to hunt buffalo along with the Blackfoot, Sioux and Cree. The tribes of the Pacific Coast, such as the Tlingit and Salish, made a living from whaling and salmon fishing and enjoyed a more elaborate social structure. The peoples in the north around Yukon and Mackenzie River basins and the Inuit around the Arctic were nomadic hunters foraging for limited food in small family groups. However, one factor common to all was that they were self-governing and politically independent.

In 1963 remains of a Viking settlement were found at L'Anse aux Meadows in Newfoundland and Labrador dating from AD 1000. Trade had been established between the Norse men and the Inuit but settlements were abandoned when the Norse withdrew from Greenland. John Cabot, an Italian navigator, commissioned by King Henry VII of England in 1497, charted the coasts around Labrador and Newfoundland and found large resources of fish. The Frenchman, Jacques Cartier, discovered the Gulf of St Lawrence in 1534 and claimed it for the French crown. In the following years fisheries were set up by the English and French with Indians bringing valuable furs, mostly beaver, to trade for iron and other goods. Realising the potential, the French sent Samuel de Champlain in 1604 to establish a fur trade and organize a settlement. This he achieved in 1605 in an area called Acadia (now New Brunswick, Nova Scotia and Prince Edward Island). The French traded with the Algonquin and Huron and supported them during fierce raids by the Iroquois. In retaliation the Iroquois later became the fur trading allies of the Dutch and then the English. Champlain, having founded Quebec City, went on to explore Huron territory, now central Ontario, and is considered by many to be the father of New France.

English–French Rivalry

In opposition to French expansion, England sent explorers such as Martin Frobisher, William Baffin and Henry Hudson to claim new territory. Colonies sprang up along the English coast and the Hudson Bay Company was formed in 1670 to gain a fur-trading monopoly over the area. Rivalry between the English and French for trade at Hudson Bay persisted throughout the 17th century. In 1713 the Treaty of Utrecht, signed by Queen Anne of England and Louis XIV, gave England complete control of the Hudson Bay territory, Acadia and Newfoundland. France, however, retained Cape Breton Island, the St Lawrence Islands and fishing rights in Newfoundland. Led by Gen. Wolfe, Britain's victory over France at the Battle of the Plains of Abraham in 1759 gained Quebec, and in 1760 Montreal too was taken. This brought an end to the Seven Years' War (1756–63) confirmed in 1763 by the Treaty of Paris by which all French Canadian territory was ceded to the British.

Relations with Indian tribes formerly allied to the French were strained and there was much resentment at the invasion of their lands by white settlers. The Royal Proclamation of 1763, administered by the Indian Department, ruled that aboriginal peoples could only sell land to crown representatives. Numerous treaties were signed over the following decades, redistributing thousands of acres of land. To soothe the British rule of a French speaking colony, the British government passed the Quebec Act in 1774 allowing French Canadians religious and linguistic freedom, the right to collect tithes and recognition of French civil law.

The attack on Montreal in 1775, during the American War of Independence, failed and Americans, loyal to Britain, sought refuge in Canada. Around 50,000 emigrated to Nova Scotia, from which New Brunswick was created in 1784. In an attempt to keep the peace the Constitutional Act of 1791 divided Quebec into Lower Canada (mostly French) and Upper Canada (mostly British from America).

Exploration continued on the Pacific Coast and into the Plains and the Northwest. Capt. James Cook charted the Pacific Coast from Vancouver to Alaska in 1778. From trading posts set up by the Hudson Bay Company (HBC) expeditions were made by traders including Samuel Hearne who, in 1771, was the first man to reach the Arctic Ocean by land. A rival company, the North West Company (NWC), was set up in Montreal in 1783. In 1793 Alexander Mackenzie, from the NWC, crossed the Rocky Mountains and reached the coast making him the first man to cross the continent. Competition between the two companies erupted into violence between new settlers and established traders including the Métis who were hired, mainly by NWC, to transport furs and supply food. To resolve the conflict the British government pressed for the merger of the two companies. This was achieved in 1821.

After the American war against Britain in Canada in 1812 (which ended in stalemate), large numbers of English, Scottish and Irish settlers swelled the English-speaking population. By 1837 radical reformers were seeking accountable government with a broader electorate. Rebellions led by William Lyon Mackenzie in Upper Canada and by Louis-Joseph Papineau in Lower Canada were quashed by government troops. Following a report by Lord Durham, who was sent from England as governor-general to conduct an enquiry, the two colonies were united under one central government in 1841 with both enjoying equal representation. Vancouver Island was acknowledged to be British by the Oregon Boundary Treaty of 1846. The 1850s saw a significant period of growth. Railways were built and industry and commerce thrived, enhanced by the Reciprocity Treaty of 1854 with the USA.

Dominion Status

However, by the 1860s ethnic clashes had made Canada almost ungovernable. The American Civil War also posed a threat. Three political leaders, George Étienne Cartier (Conservative–Canada East), George Brown (Reform Movement–Canada West) and John A. Macdonald (Conservative–Canada West) formed a coalition government in 1864. Nova Scotia, New Brunswick and the Canadas (now Ontario and Quebec) were united in 1867 as the Dominion of Canada. What became known as the Constitution Act, confirmed the language and legal rights of the French and provided for the division of power between the federal government and the provinces. John Macdonald was elected prime minister.

One of the first actions of the new federal government was to purchase the Northwest Territories from the HBC, a move that led to rebellion by white settlers and the Métis, under Louis Riel. The result was the creation of Manitoba in 1870 with political power divided between the French and English. British Columbia joined the federation in 1871 and Prince Edward Island in 1873. The former agreed to join on the promise of a federally financed railway. To make way for new settlers from 1868–77, treaties were negotiated with Indians from Ontario to the Rocky Mountains. In return for moving to reserves the Indians were to receive financial support and other concessions. They were also to be assimilated into Christian society. In the years following the government failed in its obligations and many Plains

Palgrave Macmillan (ed.), *The Statesman's Yearbook 2020*,
https://doi.org/10.1057/978-1-349-95940-2_44

Indians suffered poverty, starvation and disease. Later legislation even outlawed traditional practices such as the Sun Dance and the potlatch (exchange of gifts). Many Métis had moved out of Manitoba and settled further west but were not awarded the same rights as those of the Aboriginal Indians. Resistance grew, and Riel, who had emigrated to Montana, was urged to lead a revolt. In response, troops were rushed in by rail and the rebellion was crushed. The importance of the railway became evident and money was found for its completion across the Rockies. The new railway was opened in 1885, the same year in which Riel was executed.

Prosperity and Reform

Following the death of Macdonald in 1891, the Liberal leader Wilfrid Laurier came to power in 1896 and there followed a period of growth and stability. Mineral resources were found in British Columbia and Ontario as well as gold which precipitated the Klondike gold rush of 1897. The Yukon Territory was established in 1898 to ensure Canadian jurisdiction over the exploitation of gold. The provinces of Saskatchewan and Alberta were created in 1905, each with its own premier and elected assembly. By 1911 the population in the provinces had doubled and there was a powerful business sector. When reformers called for action to alleviate conditions in overcrowded cities, health and welfare programmes were introduced. A new women's movement campaigned for equal rights and women's suffrage. Anti-monopoly legislation was passed in 1910. However, much industrial investment was backed by American money and many French Canadians began to agitate for autonomy. In 1910 Laurier founded the Canadian Navy with the provision that in time of war it would be placed under British command. This further angered the French Canadians. Laurier's decision to negotiate a new trade agreement with the USA, coupled with the navy issue, lost him the 1911 election to the Conservatives. Robert Laird Borden became prime minister.

When the First World War broke out in 1914 thousands of British-born Canadians volunteered to fight. At first troops were under British command, but by the time conscription had been introduced in 1917 they were under Canadian leadership. Around 60,000 men lost their lives in the battles of Ypres, Vimy Ridge and Passchendaele, and another 173,000 were wounded. Having won recognition for its contribution to the war effort, Canada participated as an independent state at the Paris Peace Conference and joined the League of Nations. French Canadians had been bitterly opposed to conscription and to counteract this Borden formed a joint government of Liberals and Conservatives. This was split into the English speaking Unionists and the French speaking Liberals. At the election in 1917 the Unionists won every province but Quebec.

Women's suffrage was granted in 1918. 1921 saw the Liberals back in power under William Lyon Mackenzie King who strove to unify the nation and gain autonomy. This was achieved in 1931 by the Statute of Westminster in which Canada was granted complete independence. In the same year Norway formally recognized the Canadian title to the Sverdrup group of Arctic islands. Canada thus holds sovereignty in the whole Arctic sector north of the Canadian mainland.

Following the Wall Street Crash of 1929, the country chose the Conservatives under the leadership of Richard Bedford Bennett in the election of 1930. Despite measures to alleviate the effects of the depression and the severe drought in the prairies, Bennett was unsuccessful and in 1935 King was re-elected. King introduced a new Reciprocity Treaty (1936) with the USA, nationalized the Bank of Canada, created the Canadian Broadcasting Corporation and made available federal money to provide social services.

Post-War Politics

Canada's contribution in the Second World War was even more extensive than that in the First World War although casualties were lower. A post-war plan introduced unemployment insurance, family allowances, veterans' benefits, subsidized housing, health plans and improved pensions. Industrial controls were lifted and trade was encouraged. Canada became a founder member of the United Nations in 1945 and has been active in a peacekeeping role ever since. King retired in 1948 to be succeeded by Louis St Laurent, a Quebec lawyer, who won an overwhelming victory in 1949. In the same year, Newfoundland—including Labrador—became a Canadian province thus completing the Confederation. Also in that year, Canada joined NATO.

An amendment to the Indian Act in 1959 increased opportunities for Indians to influence decisions affecting them, and in 1960 the federal government granted the franchise to all Indians, with several provinces following suit.

For 20 years after 1950 Canada enjoyed growth, prosperity and a 'baby boom'. The face of industrial Canada changed with the discovery of radium,

petroleum and natural gas. Canada took a more active part in foreign affairs, especially in the 1956 Suez war when Lester B. Pearson, external affairs minister, won the Nobel Peace Prize. The North American Air Defense Command (NORAD) was formed with the USA in 1957. In the same year, after 22 years of Liberal rule, the Conservatives won the election with John Diefenbaker as leader. However, internal struggles and an economic recession saw the return of the Liberals in 1963 under Pearson. During his five years as prime minister Canada gained a national flag, a social security system and medical care for all its citizens.

Having chosen Pierre Trudeau to succeed Pearson, the Liberals won the 1968 election. At the same time there was a revival of French nationalism, especially in Quebec, with the formation of the Parti Québécois (PQ) led by René Lévesque. Keen to preserve national unity, Trudeau passed the Official Languages Act in 1969 which affirmed the equality of French and English in all governmental activities. However, in 1970 he had to send troops into Quebec following the murder of the Labour minister, Pierre Laporte, by the separatist Front de Libération du Québec. In 1976 a pledge on separatism won the PQ the provincial election and French became the official language of Quebec. Despite these milestones, a referendum to make the province an independent country was rejected by Quebec voters in 1980.

Indian Rights

In the sixties and seventies Indians sought special rights and settlement of their outstanding treaty claims. The National Indian Brotherhood was formed in 1968 to represent the interest of Indians at federal level. By 1973 the Department of Indian Affairs and Northern Development was instructed to resolve these claims. In 1982, with the exception of Quebec, the country agreed to a new constitution giving Canada, as opposed to the British Parliament, prerogative over all future constitutional changes. At the same time a charter of Rights and Freedoms was introduced recognizing the nation's multi-cultural heritage, affirming the existing rights of native peoples and the principle of equality of benefits to the provinces.

Retiring in 1984, Trudeau was succeeded by John Turner who was ousted the same year by the Conservative leader Brian Mulroney. In 1987 at a meeting in Meech Lake, a series of constitutional amendments were drawn up to win Quebec's acceptance of the new constitution. English Canadians objected to the Meech Lake Accord and it was rejected by Newfoundland and Manitoba. This failure sparked another separatist revival in Quebec leading to the drafting of the Charlottetown Accord incorporating extensive amendments, including recognition of Quebec as a 'distinct society', offering better representation in parliament, and self-government for indigenous peoples. This was defeated in a national referendum in 1992.

Mulroney negotiated a free trade agreement with the United States which went into effect in 1989. This was followed in 1994 by North American Free Trade Agreement (NAFTA) with the USA and Mexico. Voter opposition coupled with a recession in the early nineties forced Mulroney to resign in 1993. He was replaced by Kim Campbell, Canada's first female prime minister. In the Oct. election of that year, Campbell and the Conservatives suffered a major defeat retaining only two of their 154 seats. Led by Jean Chrétien, the Liberals won 177 seats and the Reform Party 52 seats. The PQ became the major opposition party with 54 seats.

Another referendum on Quebec's independence from Canada failed narrowly in 1995. Again in 1997 leaders of all provinces and territories (apart from Quebec) met in Calgary and signed a declaration recognizing the 'unique character' of Quebec's society. The following year the Supreme Court ruled that Quebec was prohibited from declaring itself independent without first negotiating an agreement with the federal government and other provinces.

In the 1990s further protests were made by native peoples anxious to claim their territory. In 1997 the Supreme Court ruled that two aboriginal groups had title to 22,000 square miles of ancestral lands in British Columbia. The following year a formal apology was issued by the government for the treatment Indian and Inuit peoples had received since the arrival of the Europeans. After decades of complex negotiations, the Inuit were granted their own territory of Nunavut in 1999, an area once part of the Northwest Territories. In the same year the government agreed that Indians and the Inuit should have the right of self-government.

Following a period of economic growth Chrétien's government made major tax cuts in 2000. In an attempt to form a more effective opposition, the Reform Party accepted the 'united alternative' proposed by party leader Preston Manning which resulted in the Canadian Alliance (Canadian Reform Conservative Alliance), a broad-based conservative party with Stockwell Day as its first leader. However, with the Progressive Conservative Party declining to join forces, Chrétien was returned for a third term in Nov. 2000 with an increased majority.

Chrétien stood down from the premiership in late 2003 and was replaced by his Liberal colleague, Paul Martin. Martin and his party soon became embroiled in a financial scandal over misuse of government money for advertising. In the Jan. 2006 general election the Conservative Party, led by Stephen Harper, defeated the Liberals, taking power for the first time in 12 years. In Dec. 2011 Canada became the first country to formally withdraw from the Kyoto Protocol. From Oct. 2014 the air force took part in US-led air strikes against Islamic State militants in Iraq and Syria. A year later Harper was replaced as premier by Liberal leader, Justin Trudeau.

Territory and Population

Canada is bounded in the northwest by the Beaufort Sea, north by the Arctic Ocean, northeast by Baffin Bay, east by the Davis Strait, Labrador Sea and Atlantic Ocean, south by the USA and west by the Pacific Ocean and USA (Alaska). The area is 9,984,670 sq. km, of which 891,163 sq. km are fresh water. 2016 census population, 35,151,728 (50·8% female), giving a density of 3·9 per sq. km. In 2011, 81·1% of the population were urban.

The UN gives a projected population for 2020 of 37·60m.

Population at previous censuses:

1861	3,229,633
1871	3,689,257
1881	4,324,810
1891	4,833,239
1901	5,371,315
1911	7,206,643
1921	8,787,949
1931	10,376,786
1941	11,506,655
1951	14,009,429
1961	18,238,247
1971	21,568,311
1976[1]	22,992,604
1981	24,343,181
1986[1]	25,309,331
1991	27,296,859[2]
1996[1]	28,848,761[2]
2001	30,007,094
2006[1]	31,612,897
2011	33,476,688
2016	35,151,728

[1]It became a statutory requirement to conduct a census every five years in 1971. [2]Excludes data from incompletely enumerated Indian reserves and Indian settlements.

Figures from the 2016 National Household Survey on the population according to ethnic origin (leading categories) were[1]:

Canadian	11,135,965
English	6,320,085
Scottish	4,799,005
French origins	4,680,820
Irish	4,627,000
German	3,322,405
Chinese	1,769,195
Italian	1,587,965
First Nations (North American Indian)	1,525,570
East Indian	1,374,710
Ukrainian	1,359,655
Dutch	1,111,655
Polish	1,106,585

(continued)

Filipino	837,130
Russian	622,445

[1]Census respondents who reported multiple ethnic origins are counted for each origin they reported.

The aboriginal population (those persons identifying with at least one aboriginal group, and including North American Indian, Métis or Inuit) numbered 1,673,785 in 2016. In 2011, 55·4% of the population gave their mother tongue as English and 20·4% as French (English and French are both official languages); 4·7% of the population reported speaking at least two languages at home, compared to 17·5% in 2011. In 2016 foreign-born residents numbered 7,540,830 and accounted for 21·5% of the total population; 1,212,075 people immigrated into Canada between 2011 and 2016, 61·8% of whom were from Asia (including the Middle East), 11·6% from Europe, 13·4% from Africa, 9·9% from the Caribbean, Central and South America and 2·7% from the USA.

In 2011 the vast majority of the foreign-born population (94·8%) lived in four provinces: Ontario (with 53·3%), British Columbia (17·6%), Quebec (14·4%) and Alberta (9·5%).

Nunavut had the biggest population increase between 2011 and 2016 with 12·7%, while the New Brunswick had the smallest population growth at –0·5%.

Populations of Census Metropolitan Areas (CMA) and Cities (proper), 2011 census:

	CMA	City proper
Toronto	5,583,064	2,615,060
Montreal	3,824,221	1,649,519
Vancouver	2,313,328	603,502
Ottawa-Gatineau	1,236,324	—
Ottawa	—	883,391
Gatineau	—	265,349
Calgary	1,214,839	1,096,833
Edmonton	1,159,869	812,201
Quebec	765,706	516,622
Winnipeg	730,018	663,617
Hamilton	721,053	519,949
Kitchener	477,160	366,151
London	474,786	219,153
St Catharines-Niagara	392,184	—
St Catharines	—	131,400
Niagara Falls	—	82,997
Halifax	390,328	390,096
Oshawa	356,177	149,607
Victoria	344,615	80,017
Windsor	319,246	210,891
Saskatoon	260,600	222,189
Regina	210,556	193,100
Sherbrooke	201,890	154,601
St John's	196,966	106,172
Barrie	187,013	135,711
Kelowna	179,839	117,312
Abbotsford	170,191	133,497
Greater Sudbury	160,770	160,274
Kingston	159,561	123,363
Saguenay	157,790	144,746
Trois-Rivières	151,773	131,338
Guelph	141,097	121,688

Social Statistics

Statistics for period from July–June:

	Live births	Deaths
2006–07	360,916	233,825
2007–08	373,695	236,525

(continued)

	Live births	Deaths
2008–09	380,767	239,930
2009–10	383,585	244,677

Average annual population growth rate, 2000–10, 1·1%. Birth rate, 2009–10 (per 1,000 population), 11·2; death rate, 7·2. Suicides, 2011, 3,728 (10·8 per 100,000 population). Life expectancy at birth, 2013, was 79·3 years for men and 83·6 years for women. Infant mortality, 2010, five per 1,000 live births; fertility rate, 2013, 1·7 children per woman. Canada legalized same-sex marriage in 2005.

Climate

The climate ranges from polar conditions in the north to cool temperate in the south, but with considerable differences between east coast, west coast and the interior, affecting temperatures, rainfall amounts and seasonal distribution. Winters are very severe over much of the country, but summers can be very hot inland. *See* individual provinces for climatic details.

Constitution and Government

In Nov. 1981 the Canadian government agreed on the provisions of an amended constitution, to the end that it should replace the British North America Act and that its future amendment should be the prerogative of Canada. These proposals were adopted by the Parliament of Canada and were enacted by the UK Parliament as the Canada Act of 1982. This was the final act of the UK Parliament in Canadian constitutional development. The Act gave to Canada the power to amend the Constitution according to procedures determined by the Constitutional Act 1982. The latter added to the Canadian Constitution a charter of Rights and Freedoms, and provisions which recognize the nation's multi-cultural heritage, affirm the existing rights of native peoples, confirm the principle of equalization of benefits among the provinces, and strengthen provincial ownership of natural resources.

Under the Constitution legislative power is vested in Parliament, consisting of the Queen, represented by a Governor-General, a Senate and a House of Commons. The members of the *Senate* are appointed until age 75 by summons of the Governor-General under the Great Seal of Canada. Members appointed before 2 June 1965 may remain in office for life. The Senate consists of 105 senators: 24 from Ontario, 24 from Quebec, 10 from Nova Scotia, 10 from New Brunswick, 6 from Manitoba, 6 from British Columbia, 6 from Alberta, 6 from Saskatchewan, 6 from Newfoundland and Labrador, 4 from Prince Edward Island, 1 from Yukon, 1 from the Northwest Territories, and 1 from Nunavut. Each senator must be at least 30 years of age and reside in the province for which he or she is appointed. The *House of Commons*, which consists of 338 members, is elected by universal secret suffrage, by a first-past-the-post system. Legislation that came into force in May 2007 stipulates that elections will be held on the third Monday of Oct. in the fourth calendar year following the previous general election, except when a government loses a vote of confidence. Representation is based on the population of all the provinces taken as a whole with readjustments made after each census. State of the parties in the Senate (March 2019): Independent Senators Group, 58; Conservatives, 31; Liberals, 9; non-affiliated, 7.

The First Nations have representation in the *Assembly of First Nations* (*National Chief:* Perry Bellegarde, elected Dec. 2014).

The office and appointment of the Governor-General are regulated by letters patent of 1947. In 1977 the Queen approved the transfer to the Governor-General of functions discharged by the Sovereign. The Governor-General is assisted by a *Privy Council* composed of Cabinet Ministers.

Canada: The State of the Federation. Queen's Univ., annual
Canadian Parliamentary Guide. Annual.
Bejermi, J., *Canadian Parliamentary Handbook.* 2008
Cairns, A. C., *Charter versus Federalism: the Dilemmas of Constitutional Reform.* 1992
Courtney, John and Smith, David, *The Oxford Handbook of Canadian Politics.* 2010
Fox, P. W. and White, G., *Politics Canada.* 8th ed. 1995
Hogg, P. W., *Constitutional Law of Canada.* 2001
Kernaghan, K., *Public Administration in Canada: a Text.* 1991
Mahler, G., *Contemporary Canadian Politics, 1970–1994: an Annotated Bibliography.* 2 vols. 1995
Reesor, B., *The Canadian Constitution in Historical Perspective.* 1992
Tardi, G., *The Legal Framework of Government: a Canadian Guide.* 1992

National Anthem

'O Canada, our home and native land'/'O Canada, terre de nos aïeux'; words by R. S. Weir/A. Routhier, tune by C. Lavallée.

Government Chronology

Prime Ministers since 1935. (CPC = Conservative Party of Canada; LP = Liberal Party; PC = Progressive Conservative Party)

1935–48	LP	William Lyon Mackenzie King
1948–57	LP	Louis Stephen Saint Laurent
1957–63	PC	John George Diefenbaker
1963–68	LP	Lester Bowles Pearson
1968–79	LP	Pierre Elliott Trudeau
1979–80	PC	Charles Joseph (Joe) Clark
1980–84	LP	Pierre Elliott Trudeau
1984	LP	John Napier Turner
1984–93	PC	Martin Brian Mulroney
1993	PC	Avril Phaedra (Kim) Campbell
1993–2003	LP	Joseph Jacques Jean Chrétien
2003–06	LP	Paul Joseph Martin, Jr
2006–15	CPC	Stephen Joseph Harper
2015–	LP	Justin Pierre James Trudeau

Recent Elections

At the elections of 19 Oct. 2015 the opposition Liberal Party won 184 of 338 seats (up from 34 of 308 seats in 2011) with 39·5% of votes cast, securing a huge victory over the ruling Conservative Party with 99 seats and 31·9% of the vote (down from 167 in 2011 with 39·6%). The New Democratic Party won 44 seats with 19·7% (102 in 2011 with 30·6%); the Bloc Québécois 10 with 4·7% (4 in 2011 with 6·0%); and the Green Party 1 with 3·5% (1 in 2011 with 3·9%). Turnout was 68·5% (61·4% in 2011).

Current Government

Governor-General: Julie Payette (b. 1963; sworn in 2 Oct. 2017).

In March 2019 the Liberal Party cabinet comprised:

Prime Minister, and Minister of Governmental Affairs and Youth: Justin Trudeau; b. 1971 (Liberal Party; took office on 4 Nov. 2015).

Minister of Agriculture and Agri-Food: Marie-Claude Bibeau. *Border Security and Organized Crime Reduction:* Bill Blair. *Canadian Heritage and Multiculturalism:* Pablo Rodriguez. *Crown-Indigenous Relations:* Carolyn Bennett. *Democratic Institutions:* Karina Gould. *Employment, Workforce Development and Labour:* Patricia A. Hajdu. *Environment and Climate Change:* Catherine McKenna. *Families, Children and Social Development:* Jean-Yves Duclos. *Finance:* Bill Morneau. *Fisheries, Oceans and the Canadian Coast Guard:* Jonathan Wilkinson. *Foreign Affairs:* Chrystia Freeland. *Health:* Ginette Petitpas Taylor. *Immigration, Refugees and Citizenship:* Ahmed D. Hussen. *Indigenous Services:* Seamus O'Regan. *Infrastructure and Communities:* François-Philippe Champagne. *Innovation, Science and Economic Development:* Navdeep Singh Bains. *Intergovernmental and Northern Affairs and Internal Trade:* Dominic LeBlanc. *International Trade Diversification:* Jim Carr. *Justice and Attorney General:* David Lametti. *National Defence:* Harjit Sajjan. *National Revenue:* Diane Lebouthillier. *Natural Resources:* Amarjeet Sohi. *Public Safety and Emergency Preparedness:* Ralph Goodale. *Public Services and Procurement:* Carla Qualtrough. *Rural Economic Development:* Bernadette Jordan. *Science and Sport:* Kirsty Duncan. *Seniors:* Filomena Tassi. *Small Business and Export Promotion:* Mary Ng. *Status of Women, and International Development:* Maryam Monsef. *Tourism, Official Languages and La Francophonie:* Mélanie Joly. *Transport:* Marc Garneau. *Veterans' Affairs:* Lawrence MacAulay. *Leader of the Government in the House of Commons:* Bardish Chagger. *President of the Treasury Board and Minister of Digital Government:* Jane Philpott.

Of the 35 ministers, 17 are currently women.
The *Leader of the Opposition* is Andrew Scheer.
Speaker of the House of Commons: Geoff Regan.
Office of the Prime Minister: http://www.pm.gc.ca

Current Leaders

Justin Trudeau

Position
Prime Minister

Introduction
Justin Trudeau was sworn in as prime minister in Oct. 2015. He has led the Liberal Party of Canada since 2013 and is the son of Pierre Trudeau, one of the country's longest serving Liberal prime ministers (from 1968–79 and 1980–84).

Early Life
Justin Pierre James Trudeau was born in Ottawa on 25 Oct. 1971. The oldest of three boys, he grew up at the premier's official residence until the Liberal government was defeated in 1979. His parents, meanwhile, separated in 1977.

Trudeau attended Collège Jean-de-Brébeuf in Montreal. In 1994 he graduated in English literature from McGill University, where he was an active member of the debating union. Four years later he received a degree in education from the University of British Columbia, before working as a teacher in Vancouver.

He came to public attention in Oct. 2000 when he delivered a eulogy at his father's state funeral. Thereafter, he built his public profile as he promoted various causes and appeared regularly on television and radio. He subsequently abandoned his master's degree in environmental geography at McGill to dedicate himself to a political career. In 2008 he ran in the parliamentary election as the Liberal candidate for the Montreal riding of Papineau and narrowly defeated Bloc Québécois incumbent Vivian Barbot. He co-chaired the Liberal Party's 2009 national convention in Vancouver and until 2011 held several party positions responsible for youth, citizenship, immigration and sport.

In March 2012 Trudeau fought a boxing match against Conservative senator Patrick Brazeau to raise money for cancer research. In the same year, he announced his intentions to contest the Liberal leadership, which he won in 2013. His election prompted a surge in popular support that lifted the party from third to first in the polls. Trudeau went on to lead his party to victory in the 2015 federal election.

Career in Office
Trudeau pledged to prioritize transparency in the execution of his office and to re-engage with the press following the sometimes uneasy relationship between his Conservative predecessor, Stephen Harper, and the media. Trudeau appointed a young cabinet, with half of the positions taken by women, while he himself took charge of the intergovernmental affairs and youth portfolios.

One of his first acts in office was to agree to sign the landmark accord reached at a United Nations conference in Paris, France, in Dec. 2015 on countering climate change. Despite opposition from the country's energy-producing provinces, in Oct. 2016 the House of Commons approved his plan to impose a national carbon tax (of $10 CDN per metric ton, rising to $50 CDN in 2022) starting in 2018 in a bid to meet Canada's emission reduction targets under the Paris accord.

Meanwhile, his government's promise to end Canada's involvement in air strikes against Islamic State jihadists in the Middle East was implemented in Feb. 2016. Domestically, he pledged to pursue a pro-choice abortion policy, the legalization of marijuana use (which was achieved in 2018), gender parity, senate reform, improved relations with First Nations indigenous peoples and a reform of the first-past-the-post voting system in time for the 2019 election.

Trudeau's voter approval rating continued to rise throughout his first year in office, but in Feb. 2017 his government abandoned the campaign promise to change the voting system claiming that momentum for reform had waned, which prompted condemnation from political opponents. Nevertheless, in April that year his party held on to power in five by-elections across the country, leaving the Liberals with an undiminished majority in parliament. Trudeau has also faced criticism over his approach to Canada's indigenous peoples, few of whom joined the celebrations for Canada's 150th birthday in

July 2017, although in Aug. he overhauled the indigenous affairs portfolio as part of a ministerial reshuffle and reiterated his commitment to a relationship based on recognition of rights, respect and partnership.

In Oct. 2016 Canada signed a major, and long-delayed, trade deal with the European Union. However, there was uncertainty over the future of the North American Free Trade Agreement (NAFTA) between the USA, Canada and Mexico. The new US president, Donald Trump, had initially threatened to abandon NAFTA, but in July 2017 his trade representative outlined the administration's goals for a renegotiation. While the US imposition of tariffs on imports of Canadian steel and aluminium in June 2018 contributed to an apparent souring of Trudeau's personal relations with Trump, the Canadian government nevertheless agreed in Sept. to join a new trade accord previously reached in July between the USA and Mexico that largely preserved the NAFTA provisions. The new arrangement is referred to as USMCA (the US–Mexico–Canada Agreement).

Defence

The armed forces have been unified since 1968 as the Canadian Armed Forces (usually referred to as the Canadian Forces). The three commands are the Canadian Army (known until Aug. 2011 as Land Force Command), the Royal Canadian Navy (Maritime Command until Aug. 2011) and the Royal Canadian Air Force (Air Command until Aug. 2011). In 2011 the active armed forces numbered 65,700; reserves, 33,950.

In 2010 defence expenditure totalled US$20,240m. (US$600 per capita), representing 1·3% of GDP.

Army

The Canadian Army numbered 34,800 in 2011; reserves numbered 23,150. It had 121 main battle tanks in 2011 and 1,220 armoured personnel carriers.

Navy

The naval combatant force is headquartered at Halifax (Nova Scotia), and includes four diesel submarines, three destroyers and 12 helicopter-carrying frigates. Naval personnel in 2011 numbered about 11,000, with 4,150 reserves. The main bases are Halifax, where about two-thirds of the fleet is based, and Esquimalt (British Columbia).

Air Force

The Royal Canadian Air Force numbered 19,900 in 2011 with 95 combat-capable aircraft (mainly CF-18s). There were also 2,350 primary reservists in 2011.

Economy

Services accounted for 68·9% of GDP in 2011, industry 29·4% and agriculture 1·7%.

According to the anti-corruption organization Transparency International, Canada ranked equal ninth in the world in a 2018 survey of the countries with the least corruption in business and government. It received 81 out of 100 in the annual index.

Canada gave US$4·3bn. in international aid in 2017, equivalent to 0·26% of GNI (compared to the UN target of 0·7%).

Overview

Canada has the tenth largest economy in the world and, with vast natural resources, is a major exporter of energy, food and minerals. It has the third largest oil reserves in the world after Venezuela and Saudi Arabia and is the world's fourth largest natural gas exporter. However, a collapse in world oil prices since mid-2014 has put pressure on the country's primary industry. As a party to the Canada–USA–Mexico Agreement (which superseded the North American Free Trade Agreement in late 2018), it is closely integrated economically with the USA, its largest trading partner.

Canada suffered during the 2008–09 global financial crisis and the economy dropped into recession as GDP fell by 2·9% in 2009. A recovery followed, with growth averaging 2·3% per year between 2010 and 2017, reflecting sound macroeconomic and financial sector management. The central bank maintained low interest rates throughout the recovery, encouraging an increase in consumer spending. However, this also contributed to large increases in house prices, especially in Vancouver and Toronto, which together represent one third of the national market. Household debt is also high in relation to disposable income.

Job creation has seen employment in real terms increase steadily, and the unemployment rate fell to a 40-year low of 5·8% in 2018. Consumer price inflation stood at 2·0% in 2018 (above the mid-point of the Bank of Canada's 1–3% target range despite exchange rate depreciation). However, high housing prices—accompanied by high household debt levels—remain a challenge.

The Liberal government elected in Oct. 2015 that brought an end to a decade of Conservative rule has maintained its predecessor's aim to rebalance the export base by pursuing free trade agreements with emerging economies in Asia and Latin America (where Canada has historically had little presence). In March 2018 Canada and ten other countries bordering the Pacific (although not the USA) signed the Comprehensive and Progressive Agreement for Trans-Pacific Partnership, which came into force for the initial six ratifying countries on 30 Dec. 2018. The administration has also advocated fiscal stimulus and public investment to boost long-term growth potential, and has pledged to introduce reforms to the government-backed system of mortgage insurance in a bid to discourage risky lending.

Currency

The unit of currency is the *Canadian dollar* (CAD) of 100 *cents*. In Sept. 2009 gold reserves were 0·11m. troy oz and foreign exchange reserves totalled US$46,327m. Total money supply was $434,519m. CDN in Dec. 2008.

Inflation rates (based on OECD statistics):

2008	2009	2010	2011	2012	2013	2014	2015	2016	2017
2·4%	0·3%	1·8%	2·9%	1·5%	0·9%	1·9%	1·1%	1·4%	1·6%

Budget

In 2012–13 budgetary revenues totalled $256·6bn. CDN and total expenses $275·6bn. CDN, giving a federal deficit of $18·9bn. CDN. The deficit had been $26·3bn. CDN in 2011–12 and $55·6bn. CDN in 2009–10.

In 2012–13 revenue included (in $1bn. CDN): personal income tax, 125·7; corporate income tax, 35·0; goods and services tax, 28·8; employment insurance premium revenues, 20·4. Expenses in 2012–13 included (in $1bn. CDN): direct programme operating expenses, 78·0; elderly benefits, 40·3; direct programme transfer payments, 34·9; public debt charges, 29·2.

On 1 Jan. 1991 a 7% Goods and Services Tax (GST) was introduced, superseding a 13·5% Manufacturers' Sales Tax. This was reduced to 6% from 1 July 2006 and 5% from 1 Jan. 2008. A Harmonized Sales Tax (HST) that combines the GST and the regional Provincial Sales Tax (PST) into a single value added sales tax applies in five provinces: New Brunswick (15%), Newfoundland and Labrador (15%), Nova Scotia (15%), Ontario (13%) and Prince Edward Island (15%). Following a referendum held in Aug. 2011, British Columbia—which had been using HST—reinstated the GST/PST system on 1 April 2013.

Performance

Real GDP growth rates (based on OECD statistics):

2008	2009	2010	2011	2012	2013	2014	2015	2016	2017
1·0%	−2·9%	3·1%	3·1%	1·7%	2·5%	2·9%	1·0%	1·4%	3·0%

Real GDP grew by 1·8% in 2018 according to Statistics Canada. Total GDP was US$1,653·0bn. in 2017.

Banking and Finance

The Bank of Canada (established 1935) is the central bank and bank of issue. The *Governor* (Stephen Poloz) is appointed by the Bank's directors for seven-year terms. The Minister of Finance owns the capital stock of the Bank on behalf of Canada. Banks in Canada are chartered under the terms of the Bank Act, which imposes strict conditions on capital reserves, returns to the federal government, types of lending operations, ownership and other matters. As of June 2008 there were 20 domestic banks, 24 foreign bank subsidiaries, 22 full service foreign bank branches and seven foreign bank lending branches operating in Canada; these manage over $2·7trn. CDN in assets between them. Chartered banks accounted collectively for over 70% of the total assets of the Canadian financial services sector, with the six largest domestic banks (Canadian Imperial Bank of Commerce, Bank of Nova Scotia, Bank of Montreal, National Bank of Canada, TD Canada Trust and Royal Bank of Canada) accounting for over 90% of the total assets held by the banking industry. In 2011 there were 2,090 automated bank machines per

1m. of the adult population. The First Nations Bank was founded in Dec. 1996 to provide finance to Inuit and Indian entrepreneurs.

The activities of banks are monitored by the federal Office of the Superintendent of Financial Institutions (OSFI), which reports to the Minister of Finance. Canada's federal financial institutions legislation is reviewed at least every five years. Significant legislative changes were made in 1992, updating the regulatory framework and removing barriers separating the activities of various types of financial institutions. In 1999 legislation was passed allowing foreign banks to establish operations in Canada without having to set up Canadian-incorporated subsidiaries. In 2001 Bill C-8, establishing the Financial Consumer Agency of Canada (the FCAC), was implemented. It aimed to foster competition in the financial sector and provide a holding company option allowing additional organizational flexibility to banks and insurance companies. The FCAC is responsible for enforcing consumer-related provisions of laws governing federal financial institutions.

Foreign direct investment was US$24·2bn. in 2017, down from US$45·6bn. in 2015. At the end of 2017 foreign direct investment stocks totalled US$1,084·4bn.

In June 2012 Canada's gross external debt amounted to US$1,202,858m.

There are stock exchanges at Calgary (Alberta Stock Exchange), Montreal, Toronto, Vancouver and Winnipeg.

Energy and Natural Resources

Environment

Canada's carbon dioxide emissions from the consumption of energy in 2011 were the equivalent of 16·2 tonnes per capita.

An *Environmental Performance Index* compiled in 2016 ranked Canada 25th of 180 countries, with 85·1%. The index examined various factors in nine areas—agriculture, air quality, biodiversity and habitat, climate and energy, fisheries, forests, health impacts, water and sanitation, and water resources.

Electricity

Generating capacity, 2011, 138·7m. kW. Production, 2010, 602·00bn. kWh (351·46bn. kWh hydro-electric, 151·02bn. kWh thermal, 90·66bn. kWh nuclear and 8·87bn. kWh other); consumption per capita was 16,887 kWh in 2010. There were 18 nuclear reactors in use in 2010. Canada is one of the world's leading exporters of electricity, with 44·4bn. kWh in 2010.

Oil and Gas

Oil reserves in 2017 were 168·9bn. bbls (97% oil sands reserves in Alberta and 3% conventional crude oil and condensate reserves), ranking Canada third after Venezuela and Saudi Arabia. Natural gas reserves in 2017 were 1·9trn. cu. metres. Production of oil in 2017 was a record 236·3m. tonnes; natural gas production was 176·3bn. cu. metres. The oil sands of Alberta accounted for 64% of Canada's oil production in 2017.

Canada's first off-shore field, 250 km off Nova Scotia, began producing in June 1992.

Minerals

Mineral production in 1,000 tonnes (in 2014): sand and gravel, 223,407; coal, 69,035; iron ore, 43,173; salt, 14,473; potash, 10,818 (the highest of any country in the world); lignite (2012 estimate), 10,000; aluminium (2012), 2,800; lime, 1,995; gypsum, 1,793; peat, 1,178; copper, 654; zinc, 323; nickel, 218; uranium, 9·8; cobalt, 3·9; lead, 3·6. Silver production in 2014 was 472 tonnes; gold, 151 tonnes; diamonds (2012), 10·5m. carats.

Agriculture

Grain growing, dairy farming, fruit farming, ranching and fur farming are all practised. In 2011 there were 293,295 farm operators (a decline of 10·1% from 2006) and 297,683 paid employees.

The total farm area in 2011 was 648,127 sq. km (7·1% of the total land area). There were 205,730 farms in 2011 (down from 229,373 in 2006); average size, 315 ha. There were 685,914 tractors in 2011 and 90,903 combine harvesters.

Total farm cash receipts (2015), $59,430,885,000 CDN. The following table shows the value of receipts for selected agricultural commodities in 2015 (in $1m. CDN):

Total crops	*31,639*
Canola (rapeseed)	7,995
Corn	1,854

(continued)

Lentils	2,250
Soybeans	2,389
Wheat	5,081
Livestock and products	*25,666*
Beef	10,509
Dairy	6,028
Hogs	4,225
Poultry	2,796

Output (in 1,000 tonnes) and harvested area (in 1,000 ha.) of selected crops:

	Output		Harvested area	
	2012	*2013*	*2012*	*2013*
Wheat	27,205	37,530	9,630	10,626
Canola (rapeseeds)	13,869	18,551	8,912	8,197
Maize	13,060	14,194	1,418	1,480
Barley	8,012	10,237	2,997	2,866
Soybeans	5,086	5,359	1,680	1,869
Potatoes	4,590	4,620	148	142
Peas	3,400	4,014	1,485	1,356[1]
Oats	2,830	3,906	1,168	1,284
Lentils	1,538	2,262	1,018	1,101
Linseeds	489	731	397	433
Sugar beets	599	599	10	9
Tomatoes	490	396	6	6
Carrots and turnips	401	349	8	8
Beans	335	259[1]	130	93[1]
Cucumbers and gherkins	231[1]	228[1]	2	2
Rye	337	223	140	109
Cabbages, Brussels sprouts, etc.	207	205	10	10

[1]Estimate.

Canada is the world's largest producer of rapeseeds and the second largest producer of oats.

Fruit production in 2015, in 1,000 tonnes: apples, 373; blueberries, 183; cranberries, 161; grapes, 88; strawberries, 23; peaches, 21; raspberries, 11; pears, 9.

Livestock

In parts of Saskatchewan and Alberta, stockraising is still carried on as a primary industry, but the livestock industry of the country at large is mainly a subsidiary of mixed farming. The following table shows the numbers of livestock (in 1,000) by provinces in the third quarter of 2016:

Provinces	*Total cattle and calves (including dairy cows)*	*Dairy cows*	*Sheep and lambs*	*Pigs[1]*
Newfoundland and Labrador	12·2	5·8	2·2	—
Prince Edward Island	62·7	13·6	6·8	44·3
Nova Scotia	82·5	22·2	27·8	—
New Brunswick	68·5	18·4	7·7	49·2
Quebec	1,185·0	351·1	240·0	4,315·0
Ontario	1,739·1	303·0	321·0	3,197·7
Manitoba	1,250·0	42·4	77·0	3,035·0
Saskatchewan	2,745·0	26·4	124·0	1,190·0
Alberta	5,370·0	82·5	185·0	1,515·0
British Columbia	690·0	74·0	50·0	86·0
Total	13,205·0	939·4	1,041·5	13,450·0

[1]First quarter of 2016.

Other livestock totals (2015 estimates): chickens, 683m.; turkeys, 21·5m.

Livestock Products

Slaughterings in 2015: pigs, 21·35m.; cattle, 2·92m.; sheep, 0·73m. Products, 2014 (in 1,000 tonnes): pork and pork products, 1,977; poultry meat (estimate), 1,254; beef and veal, 1,056; horse meat (estimate), 29; lamb and mutton, 17; cow's milk (estimate), 8,394; hens' eggs, 443; cheese, 407; honey, 35; hides, 77.

Forestry

Forests and other wooded land make up nearly half of Canada's landmass. Forestry is of great economic importance, and forestry products (pulp, newsprint, building timber) constitute Canada's most valuable exports. In 2015 Canada had 347·07m. ha. of forest land (9% of the world's forest cover) and 40·87m. ha. of other wooded land. 2·4m. ha. were burned by forest fires in 2011. 148·18m. cu. metres of roundwood was produced in 2011.

Fur Trade

In 2009, 730,915 wildlife pelts (valued at $14,847,952 CDN) and 2,279,810 ranch-raised pelts (valued at $146,991,034 CDN) were produced.

Fisheries

In 2012 landings of commercial fisheries totalled 832,768 tonnes with a value of $2,188m. CDN. More than 96% of the total catch in 2012 was from sea fishing; in 2012 Atlantic landings totalled 673,923 tonnes and Pacific landings 129,519 tonnes, with freshwater fish totalling 29,326 tonnes. Value of sea fish landed in 2012 was $2,121m. CDN and of freshwater fish $67m. CDN. Imports of fishery commodities were valued at US$2,688m. in 2012 and exports at US$4,213m.

Industry

The leading companies by market capitalization in Canada in March 2019 were: Royal Bank of Canada (US$113·4bn.); Toronto-Dominion Bank (US$107·8bn.); and Bank of Nova Scotia (US$75·0bn.).

Value of manufacturing sales for all industries in 2015 was $609,499·5m. CDN. Principal sales by subsector: transportation equipment, $122,964·9m. CDN; food, $95,697·8m. CDN; petroleum and coal products, $59,335·7m. CDN; chemicals, $48,566·8m. CDN; primary metals, $44,738·6m. CDN; machinery, $34,742·5m. CDN; fabricated metal products, $34,448·6m. CDN; plastics and rubber products, $27,953·0m. CDN; paper, $26,867·9m. CDN; wood products, $26,011·8m. CDN; computer and electronic products, $13,688·0m. CDN; non-metallic mineral products, $12,941·3m. CDN; beverage and tobacco products, $12,456·3m. CDN; furniture and related products, $11,620·5m. CDN.

According to the World Bank's *Doing Business 2016* Canada is the third easiest country in which to start a business, after New Zealand and Macedonia (now North Macedonia).

Labour

In 2015 the labour force was 19,278,000 (10,182,400 males; 9,095,600 females), of whom 17,946,600 (9,422,700 males, 8,523,900 females) were employed. The unemployment rate in Dec. 2018 was 5·6% (down from 6·3% in 2017 as a whole).

In 2011 an average of about one hour per employee was lost to labour disputes, amounting to an estimated 1,967,000 workdays lost in the year; at provincial level, New Brunswick lost the most time to labour disputes (4·5 hours per employee).

Canada had 6,000 people living in slavery according to the Walk Free Foundation's 2013 *Global Slavery Index*.

International Trade

A North American Free Trade Agreement (NAFTA) between Canada, Mexico and the USA was signed on 7 Oct. 1992 and came into force on 1 Jan. 1994.

Imports and Exports

Total value of imports and exports of goods in US$1m.:

	2012	*2013*	*2014*
Imports	462,366·2	461,764·1	462,000·0
Exports	454,099·0	456,605·4	472,866·1

Canada is heavily dependent on foreign trade. In 2011 imports of goods and services were equivalent to 31·7% of GDP and exports equivalent to 30·4%. The trade deficit that Canada experienced in 2009 at the height of the global economic downturn was the country's first in 15 years.

Principal imports in 2014 were machinery and transport equipment (41·3%), manufactured goods, and miscellaneous manufactured articles; main exports in 2014 were mineral fuels and lubricants (27·2%), machinery and transport equipment, and manufactured goods.

Leading import suppliers in 2010: USA, 50·4%; China, 11·0%; Mexico, 5·5%; Japan, 3·3%; Germany, 2·8%; UK, 2·7%. Leading export markets in 2010: USA, 74·8%; UK, 4·1%; China, 3·3%; Japan, 2·3%; Mexico, 1·3%; Germany, 1·0%.

Communications

Roads
In 2015 there were more than 1,300,000 two-lane equivalent lane-km of public roads; about 34% of the road network is paved. Ontario, Quebec, Saskatchewan and Alberta accounted for 77% of the total road length. The National Highway System, spanning over 38,000 lane-km in 2014 (but representing only 3·7% of the public road network), includes the Trans-Canada Highway and other major east–west and north–south highways.

Registered road motor vehicles totalled 23,923,806 in 2015; they comprised 22,067,778 light vehicles, 591,897 medium duty trucks (weighing 4,500–14,999 kg), 464,322 heavy duty trucks (15,000 kg or more), 90,551 buses and 709,258 motorcycles and mopeds.

There were 1,951 fatalities (a rate of 5·5 deaths per 100,000 population) in road accidents in 2013.

Rail
In 2015 the Canadian Rail System had 45,200 km of track. Canada has two great trans-continental systems: the Canadian National Railway system (CN), a body privatized in 1995 that operates the largest network with 22,205 km of routes in 2015, and the Canadian Pacific Railway (CP), with 11,600 km. Other railways own 11,395 km of track. A government-funded organization, VIA Rail, operates passenger services in all regions of Canada; 4·2m. passengers were carried in 2010.

There are metros in Montreal and Toronto, and tram/light rail systems in Calgary, Edmonton, Ottawa, Toronto and Vancouver.

Civil Aviation
Civil aviation is under the jurisdiction of the federal government. The technical and administrative aspects are supervised by Transport Canada, while the economic functions are assigned to the Canadian Transportation Agency.

The busiest Canadian airport is Toronto Pearson International, which in 2012 handled 34,912,029 passengers (21,265,866 on international flights), ahead of Vancouver International, with 17,742,065 passengers (9,170,801 on domestic flights) and Montreal (Pierre Elliot Trudeau International), with 13,798,672 passengers (8,466,108 on international flights). Toronto is also the busiest airport for freight, handling 417,022 tonnes in 2012.

Air Canada (privatized in 1989) is the largest full-service airline and largest provider of scheduled passenger services in the Canadian market, carrying 34·9m. revenue passengers in 2012; it took over its main competitor, Canadian Airlines, in 2000. Other major Canadian airlines are Air Transat and WestJet.

Shipping
In Jan. 2014 there were 181 ships of 300 GT or over registered, totalling 1·46m. GT. Of the 181 vessels registered, 109 were passenger ships, 29 oil tankers, 30 general cargo ships, 12 bulk carriers and one container ship.

In 2011 the total tonnage handled by Canadian ports was 466·1m. tonnes (289·7m. loaded and 176·5m. unloaded). Canada's leading port in terms of cargo handled is Vancouver. Other major ports are Saint John, Montreal, Sept-Iles and Quebec City.

The major canals are those of the St Lawrence Seaway. Main commodities moved along the seaway are grain, iron ore, coal, other bulk and steel. The St Lawrence Seaway Management Corporation was established in 1998 as a non-profit making corporation to operate the Canadian assets of the seaway for the federal government under a long-term agreement with Transport Canada.

In 2010 total traffic on the Montreal-Lake Ontario (MLO) section of the seaway was 26,920,000 tonnes; on the Welland Canal section it was 29,180,000 tonnes. There were 3,925 vessel transits in 2010, generating $60·7m. CDN in toll revenue.

Telecommunications
Telecommunications in Canada is dominated by three companies—Bell, Rogers and Telus. In 2013 there were 28,360,000 mobile phone subscriptions (806·1 per 1,000 persons). In the same year retail access lines numbered 16,921,000. A 2010 survey found that 78% of households had a mobile phone and 13% only had a mobile phone; 17% only had a landline. In 2012, 81·5% of households had internet access. The fixed broadband penetration rate in Dec. 2010 was 30·7 subscribers per 100 inhabitants. In Dec. 2011 there were 17·1m. Facebook users (49% of the population).

Social Institutions

Out of 178 countries analysed in the 2017 *Fragile States Index*—a list published jointly by the Fund for Peace and *Foreign Policy* magazine—Canada was ranked the joint ninth least vulnerable (along with New Zealand) to conflict or collapse. The index is based on 12 indicators of state vulnerability across social, political and economic categories.

Justice
The courts in Canada are organized in a four-tier structure. The Supreme Court of Canada, based in Ottawa, is the highest court, having general appellate jurisdiction in civil and criminal cases throughout the country. It is comprised of a Chief Justice and eight puisne judges appointed by the Governor-in-Council, with a minimum of three judges coming from Quebec. The second tier consists of the Federal Court of Appeal and the various provincial courts of appeal. The third tier consists of the Federal Court (which replaced the Exchequer Court in 1971), the Tax Court of Canada and the provincial and territorial superior courts (which include both a court of general trial jurisdiction and a provincial court of appeal). The majority of cases are heard by the provincial courts, the fourth tier in the hierarchy. They are generally divided within each province into various divisions defined by the subject matter of their respective jurisdictions (for example a Traffic Division, a Small Claims Division, a Family Division and a Criminal Division).

There were 1,863,675 Criminal Code Offences (excluding traffic) reported in 2015 (down from 2,440,650 in 1998). Crimes of violence in 2015 totalled 380,795 (up from 300,058 in 1998), including 219,068 assaults, 22,080 robberies, 774 attempted murders and 604 homicides. In 2011–12 the average daily population in penal institutions (including youth offenders) was 40,544 (118 per 100,000 of national population). The death penalty was abolished for all crimes in 1998. In 2018 Canada became the second country (after Uruguay) to legalize the recreational use of marijuana.

Canada was ranked 17th of 102 countries for criminal justice and 18th for civil justice in the 2015 World Justice Project *Rule of Law Index*, which provides data on how the rule of law is experienced by the general public across eight categories.

Police
Total police officers in Canada in 2015 numbered 68,777 (192 officers per 100,000 population), including 14,332 female officers; the proportion of women in higher ranks has increased from 5·5% in 2005 to 12·4% in 2015. Policing costs in 2014–15 totalled $13·88bn. CDN.

Royal Canadian Mounted Police (RCMP)
The RCMP is Canada's national police force maintained by the federal government. Established in 1873 as the North-West Mounted Police, it became the Royal Northwest Mounted Police in 1904. Its sphere of operations was expanded in 1918 to include all of Canada west of Thunder Bay, Ontario. In 1920 the force absorbed the Dominion Police and its headquarters was transferred from Regina, Saskatchewan to Ottawa, Ontario. Its title also changed to Royal Canadian Mounted Police. The RCMP is responsible to the Minister of Public Safety and Emergency Preparedness Canada and is controlled by a Commissioner who is empowered to appoint peace officers in all the provinces and territories of Canada.

The responsibilities of the RCMP are national in scope. The administration of justice within the provinces, including the enforcement of the Criminal Code of Canada, is the responsibility of provincial governments, but all the provinces except Ontario and Quebec have entered into contracts with the RCMP to enforce criminal and provincial laws under the direction of the respective Attorneys-General. In these eight provinces the RCMP is under agreement to provide police services to municipalities as well. The RCMP is also responsible for all police work in the three territories—Yukon, Northwest Territories and Nunavut—enforcing federal law and territorial ordinances.

The RCMP has 15 divisions plus its Headquarters in Ottawa. Each division, managed by a Commanding Officer, roughly approximates to provincial boundaries. Air and marine services supply support to the divisions. In Sept. 2015 the Force had a total strength of 28,461 including regular members, special constables, civilian members and public service employees. There are also 112 dog teams across Canada.

Supporting Canada's law enforcement agencies, the RCMP's National Police Services comprises the Canadian Police College, Canadian Police Information Centre, Criminal Intelligence Service Canada, Forensic Science and Identification Services, Canadian Firearms Program, Violent Crime Linkage Analysis System and National Sex Offender Registry.

Education
Under the Constitution the provincial legislatures have powers over education. These are subject to certain qualifications respecting the rights of denominational and minority language schools. School board revenues derive from local taxation on real property, and government grants from general provincial revenue.

In 2009–10 there were 5,077,021 pupils enrolled in elementary and secondary public schools and 337,600 educators (including teaching support staff and administrators).

The federal government shares responsibility with First Nations for the provision of education to children ordinarily resident on reserve and attending provincial, federal or band-operated schools. In 2011–12 the government provided $1·55bn. CDN in support for 116,400 First Nations students in elementary and secondary education and $322m. CDN for 22,000 at postsecondary level. About 60% of First Nations children attend schools on reserves, while 40% go off reserve to schools under provincial authority. Funding is also provided for postsecondary tuition, books and living allowances for students residing on or off reserve.

The Association of Universities and Colleges of Canada represents 97 public and private not-for-profit universities and degree-level colleges. In 2010–11 there were 912,000 full-time and 325,581 part-time students enrolled in universities and 520,584 full-time and 197,172 part-time students enrolled in colleges. Full-time faculty staff in universities numbered 44,934 (16,448 women) in 2010–11. According to data from the 2011 National Household Survey and Statistics Canada, 11,782,700 adults aged between 25 and 64 had a postsecondary qualification; 4,755,420 had a university degree and 3,913,710 had a college diploma. The proportion of adults with a high school diploma or equivalent as their highest level of educational attainment was 23·2%.

The adult literacy rate is at least 99%.

In 2010 public education expenditure represented 5·5% of GDP.

Health
Constitutional responsibility for health care services rests with the provinces and territories. Accordingly, Canada's national health insurance system consists of an interlocking set of provincial and territorial hospital and medical insurance plans conforming to certain national standards rather than a single national programme. The Canada Health Act (which took effect from April 1984 and consolidated the original federal health insurance legislation) sets out the national standards that provinces and territories are required to meet in order to qualify for full federal health contributions, including: provision of a comprehensive range of hospital and medical benefits; universal population coverage; access to necessary services on uniform terms and conditions; portability of benefits; and public administration of provincial and territorial insurance plans. From 1996–97 the federal government's contribution to provincial health and social programmes was consolidated into a single block transfer—the Canada Health and Social Transfer (CHST). However, following reforms introduced by the 2003 Accord on Health Care Renewal to improve health spending accountability it was split into the Canada Health Transfer (CHT) for health and the Canada Social Transfer (CST) for post-secondary education, social service and social assistance in April 2004. The CHT is the federal government's largest transfer—in 2017–18 the provinces and territories were scheduled to receive $37·2bn. CDN, up from $36·1bn. CDN in 2016–17.

Over and above this health transfer, the federal government also provides financial support for such provincial and territorial extended health care service programmes as nursing-home care, certain home care services, ambulatory health care services and adult residential care services.

The approach taken by Canada is one of state-sponsored health insurance. The advent of insurance programmes produced little change in the ownership of hospitals, almost all of which are owned by non-government non-profit corporations, or in the rights and privileges of private medical practice. Patients are free to choose their own general practitioner. Except for a small percentage of the population whose care is provided for under other legislation (such as serving members of the Canadian Armed Forces and inmates of federal penitentiaries), all residents are eligible, regardless of whether they are in the workforce. Benefits are available without upper limit so long as they are medically necessary, provided any registration obligations are met.

In addition to the benefits qualifying for federal contributions, provinces and territories provide additional benefits at their own discretion. Most fund their portion of health costs out of general provincial and territorial revenues. Most have charges for long-term chronic hospital care geared, approximately, to the room and board portion of the OAS–GIS payment mentioned under Welfare *below*. Health spending accounted for 10·9% of GDP in 2011.

In 2010 there were 69,648 physicians, giving a rate of 2·1 per 1,000 population; in 2011 there were 319,026 nursing and midwifery personnel (9·3 per 1,000 population); and in 2012 there were 35,555 pharmacists (1·0 per 1,000 population).

In *Water: At What Cost? The State of the World's Water 2016*, WaterAid reported that 0·2% of the population does not have access to safe water.

Welfare
The social security system provides financial benefits and social services to individuals and their families through programmes administered by federal, provincial and municipal governments and voluntary organizations. Federally, Human Resources and Skills Development is responsible for research into the areas of social issues, provision of grants and contributions for various social services and the administration of income security programmes, including the Old Age Security (OAS) programme, the Guaranteed Income Supplement, the Allowance and the Canada Pension Plan (CPP).

The Old Age Security pension is payable to persons 65 years of age and over who satisfy the residence requirements stipulated in the Old Age Security Act. The amount payable, whether full or partial, is also governed by stipulated conditions, as is the payment of an OAS pension to a recipient who absents himself from Canada. OAS pensioners with little or no income apart from OAS may, upon application, receive a full or partial supplement known as the Guaranteed Income Supplement (GIS). Entitlement is normally based on the pensioner's income in the preceding year, calculated in accordance with the Income Tax Act (which excepts OAS income). The spouse or common-law partner (same sex or opposite sex since the Modernization of Benefits and Obligations Act of 2000) of an OAS pensioner, meeting specific citizenship/residency requirements and aged 60 to 64, may be eligible for a full or partial benefit called the Allowance (introduced in 1975 and formerly known as the Spouse's Allowance). The Allowance is payable, on application, to spouses/partners of individuals receiving OAS and GIS, where the couple's joint income is classified as low. An Allowance for the Survivor (introduced in 1985) is available to persons aged 60–64 whose spouse or common-law partner has died and where the survivor has not entered into a subsequent marriage or common law relationship. The Allowance and Allowance for the Survivor stop when the recipient becomes eligible for the OAS at age 65.

As of 1 July 2011 the maximum OAS pension was $533·70 CDN monthly; the maximum Guaranteed Income Supplement was $723·65 CDN monthly for a single pensioner or a married pensioner whose spouse or common law partner was not receiving an OAS pension, and $479·84 CDN monthly for each spouse of a married couple/common law partner where both were pensioners.

The Canada Pension Plan is designed to provide workers with a basic level of income protection in the event of retirement, disability or death. Benefits may be payable to a contributor, a surviving spouse or an eligible child. Actuarially adjusted retirement benefits may begin as early as age 60 or as late as age 70. Benefits are determined by the contributor's earnings and contributions made to the Plan. Contribution is compulsory for most employed and self-employed Canadians aged 18 to 65. The CPP does not operate in Quebec, which has exercised its constitutional prerogative to establish a similar plan. In 2011 the maximum monthly retirement pension payable under CPP was $960·00 CDN; the maximum disability pension was $1,153·37 CDN; and the maximum surviving spouse's pension was $576·00 CDN (for survivors 65 years of age and over). The survivor pension payable to a surviving spouse under 65 (maximum of $529·09 CDN in 2011) is composed of two parts: a flat-rate component and an earnings-related portion.

The CPP is financed through mandatory contributions from employers, employees and the self-employed, and through revenue generated from investments. The combined contribution rate is 9·9% of earnings between the year's basic exemption ($3,500 CDN in 2010) and the year's maximum pensionable earnings ($47,200 CDN in 2010). The contribution rate (maximum rate of $4,326·30 CDN in 2010) is split equally between employers and employees, while the self-employed pay both shares. Changes to the CPP were introduced incrementally between 2011 and 2016 whereby the monthly pension amount has been increased by a larger percentage if taken after age 65 and decreases by a larger percentage if taken before 65.

The Canada Pension Plan Investment Board, an independent investment organization separate from the CPP, was established to invest excess CPP funds in a diversified portfolio of securities, beginning operations in April 1998. A total of 5·3m. Canadians received Canada Pension Plan benefits amounting to $38·7bn. CDN in fiscal year 2014–15. Social security agreements co-ordinate the operation of the Old Age Security and the CPP with the comparable social security programmes of certain other countries.

Canada Child Tax Benefit (CCTB) is a tax-free monthly payment made to eligible families to help them with the cost of raising children under 18. Included with the CCTB is the National Child Benefit Supplement (NCBS), a monthly benefit for low-income families with children.

Religion

Membership of main religious denominations (2011 National Household Survey data):

Roman Catholic	12,728,885
United Church	2,007,610
Anglican	1,631,845
Muslim	1,053,945
Baptist	635,840
Christian Orthodox	550,690
Hindu	497,960
Pentecostal	478,705
Lutheran	478,185
Presbyterian	472,385
Sikh	454,965
Buddhist	366,830
Jewish	329,500
Mennonite	175,880

A total 7,850,605 people described themselves as not having any religious affiliation. In Feb. 2019 the Roman Catholic Church had three cardinals.

Culture

World Heritage Sites

Sites under Canadian jurisdiction which appear on UNESCO's world heritage list are (with year entered on list): L'Anse aux Meadows National Historic Site (1978), the remains of an 11th-century Viking settlement in Newfoundland and Labrador; Nahanni National Park (1978), containing canyons, waterfalls and a limestone cave system—fauna includes wolves, grizzly bears, caribou, Dall's sheep and mountain goats; Dinosaur Provincial Park (1979), in Alberta, a major area for fossil discoveries, including 35 species of dinosaur; SGaang Gwaii (Anthony Island) (1981), illustrating the Haida people's art and way of life; Head-Smashed-In Buffalo Jump (1981), in southwest Alberta, incorporating an aboriginal camp—the name relates to the aboriginal custom of killing buffalo by chasing them over a precipice; Wood Buffalo National Park (1983), in north-central Canada, home to America's largest population of wild bison as well as important fauna; Canadian Rocky Mountain Parks (1984 and 1990), incorporating the neighbouring parks of Banff, Jasper, Kootenay and Yoho, as well as the Mount Robson, Mount Assiniboine and Hamber provincial parks, and the Burgess Shale fossil site; Historic District of Québec (1985), retaining aspects of its French colonial past; Gros Morne National Park (1987), in Newfoundland and Labrador; Old Town Lunenburg (1995), a well-

preserved British colonial settlement established in 1753; Miguasha Park (1999), among the world's most important fossil sites for fish species of the Devonian age, forerunners of the first four-legged, air-breathing terrestrial vertebrates (tetrapods); Rideau Canal (2007), a 19th century monumental canal running from Ottawa to Kingston Harbour; Joggins Fossil Cliffs (2008), a 689 ha. palaeontological site along the coast of Nova Scotia; Landscape of Grand Pré in Nova Scotia (2012), a symbolic reference landscape for the Acadian way of life and deportation; Red Bay Basque Whaling Station (2013), one of the best-preserved examples of the European whaling tradition, located in Newfoundland and Labrador; Mistaken Point (2016), a fossil site located at the southeastern tip of Newfoundland, consisting of a narrow 17 km-long strip of rugged coastal cliffs; and Pimachiowin Aki (2018), a landscape of rivers, lakes, wetlands and boreal forest.

Two UNESCO World Heritage Sites fall under joint Canadian and US jurisdiction: Kluane/Wrangell-St Elias/Glacier Bay/Tatshenshini-Alsek (1979, 1992 and 1994), parks in Yukon, British Columbia and Alaska, include the world's largest non-polar icefield, glaciers and high peaks, and important fauna; Waterton Glacier International Peace Park (1995), in Alberta and Montana, with collections of plant and mammal species as well as prairie, forest, and alpine and glacial features.

Press

In 2014 there were 95 daily papers with a total average circulation of 5·31m.; *The Globe and Mail* had the largest circulation at 358,000 in 2014, followed by *Toronto Star* with 343,000. *Le Journal de Montréal* is the largest francophone daily with an average daily circulation in 2014 of 233,000.

Tourism

In 2012 foreign visitors made 16,344,000 overnight trips to Canada (up from 16,014,000 in 2011 but down from 20,057,000 in 2002). Of these, 12,395,000 came from elsewhere in the Americas, 2,299,000 from Europe and 1,286,000 from East Asia and the Pacific. The USA was by far the biggest tourist market in 2012, followed by the UK, France, Germany and China. In 2012, 609,500 were employed in tourism.

Festivals

Canada Day, held on 1 July, is marked nationwide with firework displays, parades and parties. The Quebec Winter Festival is held each Feb. The Calgary Stampede (the world's largest rodeo, incorporating a series of concerts and a carnival) is in July. Also in July are the Québec Festival d'Été/Summer Festival (featuring music and art performances) and the Montréal Juste Pour Rire/Just for Laughs comedy festival. The Toronto international film festival takes place in Sept. and the Vancouver international film festival is the following month. Popular music festivals include the Montreal International Jazz Festival and North by Northeast in Toronto in June, the Ottawa International Jazz Festival in June–July, Ottawa Bluesfest and Halifax Rocks in July and Osheaga in Montreal in July–Aug. Les FrancoFolies de Montréal, a festival dedicated to francophone music, is held every summer.

Diplomatic Representatives

Of Canada in the United Kingdom (Canada House, Trafalgar Sq., London, SW1Y 5BJ)
   High Commissioner: Janice Charette.

Of the United Kingdom in Canada (80 Elgin St., Ottawa, K1P 5K7)
   High Commissioner: Susan le Jeune d'Allegeershecque, CMG.

Of Canada in the USA (501 Pennsylvania Ave., NW, Washington, D.C., 20001)
   Ambassador: David Brookes MacNaughton.

Of the USA in Canada (490 Sussex Drive, Ottawa, K1N 1G8)
   Ambassador: Kelly Craft.

Of Canada to the United Nations
   Ambassador: Marc André Blanchard.

Of Canada to the European Union
   Ambassador: Daniel Costello.

Canadian Provinces

General Details

The ten provinces each have a separate parliament and administration, with a Lieut.-Governor, appointed by the Governor-General in Council at the head of the executive. They have full powers to regulate their own local affairs and dispose of their revenues, provided that they do not interfere with the action and policy of the central administration. Among the subjects assigned exclusively to the provincial legislatures are: the amendment of the provincial constitution, except as regards the office of the Lieut.-Governor; property and civil rights; direct taxation for revenue purposes; borrowing; management and sale of Crown lands; provincial hospitals, reformatories, etc.; shop, saloon, tavern, auctioneer and other licences for local or provincial purposes; local works and undertakings, except lines of ships, railways, canals, telegraphs, etc., extending beyond the province or connecting with other provinces, and excepting also such works as the Canadian Parliament declares are for the general good; marriages, administration of justice within the province; education. On 18 July 1994 the federal and provincial governments signed an agreement easing inter-provincial barriers on government procurement, labour mobility, transport licences and product standards. Federal legislation of Dec. 1995 grants provinces a right of constitutional veto.

For the administration of the three territories *see* Northwest Territories, Nunavut and Yukon *below*.

Areas of the ten provinces and three territories (Northwest Territories, Nunavut and Yukon) (in sq. km) and population at recent censuses:

Province	Land area	Total land and fresh water area	Population, 2001	Population, 2006	Population, 2011
Newfoundland and Labrador (NL)	373,872	405,212	512,930	505,469	514,536
Prince Edward Island (PEI)	5,660	5,660	135,294	135,851	140,204
Nova Scotia (NS)	53,338	55,284	908,007	913,462	921,727
New Brunswick (NB)	71,450	72,908	729,498	729,997	751,171
Quebec (Que.)[1]	1,365,128	1,542,056	7,237,479	7,546,131	7,903,001
Ontario (Ont.)[1]	917,741	1,076,395	11,410,046	12,160,282	12,851,821
Manitoba (Man.)[1]	553,556	647,797	1,119,583	1,148,401	1,208,268
Saskatchewan (Sask.)[1]	591,670	651,036	978,933	968,157	1,033,381
Alberta (Alta.)[1]	642,317	661,848	2,974,807	3,290,350	3,645,257
British Columbia (BC)[1]	925,186	944,735	3,907,738	4,113,487	4,400,057
Nunavut (Nvt.)	1,936,113	2,093,190	26,745	29,474	31,906
Northwest Territories (NWT)	1,183,085	1,346,106	37,360	41,464	41,462
Yukon (YT)	474,391	482,443	28,674	30,372	33,897

[1]Excludes population data from incompletely enumerated Indian reserves and Indian settlements.

Local Government

Under the terms of the British North America Act the provinces are given full powers over local government. All local government institutions are, therefore, supervised by the provinces, and are incorporated and function under provincial acts.

The acts under which municipalities operate vary from province to province. A municipal corporation is usually administered by an elected council headed by a mayor or reeve, whose powers to administer affairs and to raise funds by taxation and other methods are set forth in provincial laws, as is the scope of its obligations to, and on behalf of, the citizens. Similarly, the types of municipal corporations, their official designations and the requirements for their incorporation vary between provinces. The following table sets out the classifications as at the 2011 census:

	Economic regions	Census divisions
NL	4	11
PEI	1	3[1]
NS	5	18[1]

(*continued*)

	Economic regions	Census divisions
NB	5	15[1]
Que.	17	98[2]
Ont.	11	49[3]
Man.	8	23
Sask.	6	18
Alta.	8	19
BC	8	29[4]
Nvt.	1	3[5]
NWT	1	6[5]
YT	1	1[6]

[1]Counties.
[2]81 municipalités régionales de comté, 12 territoires équivalents, 5 divisions de recensement.
[3]20 counties, 10 districts, 9 census divisions, 6 regional municipalities, 3 united counties, 1 district municipality.
[4]28 regional districts, 1 region.
[5]Regions.
[6]Territory.

Alberta

Key Historical Events

The southern half of Alberta was administered from 1670 as part of Rupert's land by the Hudson's Bay Company. Trading posts were set up after 1783 when the North West Company took a share in the fur trade. In 1869 Rupert's Land was transferred from the Hudson's Bay Company (which had absorbed its rival in 1821) to the new Dominion and in the following year this land was combined with the former Crown land of the North Western Territories to form the Northwest Territories. In 1882 'Alberta' first appeared as a provisional 'district', consisting of the southern half of the present province. In 1905 the Athabasca district to the north was added when provincial status was granted to Alberta.

Territory and Population

The area of the province is 661,848 sq. km, 642,317 sq. km being land area and 16,531 sq. km water area. The population at the 2016 census was 4,067,175. The urban population (2011), centres of 1,000 or over, was 83% and the rural 17%. Population (2011 census) of the 18 cities, as well as the two largest specialized municipalities: Calgary, 1,096,833; Edmonton, 812,201; Red Deer, 90,564; Lethbridge, 83,517; St Albert, 61,466; Medicine Hat, 60,005; Grande Prairie, 55,032; Airdrie, 42,564; Spruce Grove, 26,171; Leduc, 24,279; Fort Saskatchewan, 19,051; Lloydminster (Alberta portion), 18,032; Camrose, 17,286; Chestermere, 14,824; Cold Lake, 13,839; Brooks, 13,676; Wetaskiwin, 12,525; Lacombe, 11,707; Specialized Municipality of Strathcona County (Sherwood Park), 92,490; Specialized Municipality of Wood Buffalo (Fort McMurray), 65,565.

Social Statistics

Births in 2013–14 numbered 56,078 and deaths 23,233. In 2012 the infant mortality rate was 4·3 per 1,000 live births. Life expectancy in the period 2009–11 was 83·5 years for females and 79·1 years for males.

Climate

Alberta has a continental climate of warm summers and cold winters—extremes of temperature. For the capital city, Edmonton, the hottest month is usually July (mean 17·5°C), while the coldest are Dec. and Jan. (−12°C). Rainfall amounts are greatest between May and Sept. In a year, the average precipitation is 461 mm (19·6") with about 129·6 cm of snowfall.

Constitution and Government

The constitution of Alberta is contained in the British North America Act of 1867, and amending Acts; also in the Alberta Act of 1905, passed by the Parliament of the Dominion of Canada, which created the province out of the then Northwest Territories. The province is represented by six members in the Senate and 34 in the House of Commons of Canada.

The executive is vested nominally in the *Lieut.-Governor*, who is appointed by the federal government, but actually in the *Executive Council* or the Cabinet of the legislature. Legislative power is vested in the Assembly in the name of the Queen.

Members of the 87-member *Legislative Assembly* are elected by the universal vote of adults, 18 years of age and older.

Recent Elections

In elections on 5 May 2015 the opposition New Democratic Party won 40·6% of the vote (taking 54 of 87 seats), the Wildrose Party 24·2% (21), the ruling Progressive Conservative Party 27·8% (10), the Liberal Party 4·2% (1) and the Alberta Party 2·3% (1). Turnout was 53·7%. The Progressive Conservative Party had been in power continuously since 1971.

Current Government

Lieut.-Governor: Lois Mitchell (sworn in 12 June 2015).

As of March 2019 the members of the Executive Council were as follows:
Premier and President of Executive Council: Rachel Notley; b. 1964 (New Democratic; sworn in 24 May 2016).

Deputy Premier and Minister of Health: Sarah Hoffman. *Transportation:* Brian Mason. *Education:* David Eggen. *Economic Development and Trade:* Deron Bilous. *President of the Treasury Board and Minister of Finance:* Joseph Ceci. *Justice and Solicitor General:* Kathleen Ganley. *Environment and Parks:* Shannon Phillips. *Agriculture and Forestry:* Oneil Carlier. *Municipal Affairs:* Shaye Anderson. *Energy:* Margaret McCuaig-Boyd. *Community and Social Services:* Irfan Sabir. *Children's Services and Status of Women:* Danielle Larivee. *Seniors and Housing:* Lori Sigurdson. *Indigenous Relations:* Richard Feehan. *Labour:* Christina Gray. *Service Alberta:* Brian Malkinson. *Culture and Tourism:* Ricardo Miranda. *Advanced Education:* Marlin Schmidt. *Infrastructure:* Sandra Jansen.

Office of the Premier: http://premier.alberta.ca

Economy

GDP per person in 2014 was $91,183 CDN.

Budget

Total revenue in 2008–09 was $51,388m. CDN (own source revenue, $47,005m. CDN; specific purpose transfers, $3,159m. CDN; general purpose transfers, $1,224m. CDN). Total expenditures in 2008–09 amounted to $49,201m. CDN (including: health, $13,119m. CDN; education, $11,509m. CDN; transportation and communication, $5,469m. CDN).

Performance

Real GDP grew by 5·7% in 2011 (the second highest rate of any of the Canadian provinces and territories that year) and then 4·5% in 2012 (the highest rate of any of the provinces or territories).

Energy and Natural Resources

Electricity

Electricity generation totalled 63·6bn. kWh in 2013 (44·9bn. kWh conventional steam), representing 10·4% of Canada's production.

Oil and Gas

Oil sands underlie some 140,200 sq. km of Alberta, the three major deposits being: the Athabasca, Cold Lake, and Peace River deposits. Some 20% (28,040 sq. km) of the Athabasca deposit can be recovered by open-pit mining techniques. The rest of the Athabasca, and all the deposits in the other areas, are deeper reserves which must be developed through *in situ* techniques. These reserves reach depths of 75 metres. In 2012 Alberta produced 556,000 bbls per day of conventional crude oil and 1·8m. bbls per day of synthetic crude oil and non-upgraded bitumen. The 2012 value of Albertan producers' sales of conventional crude oil plus upgraded and non-upgraded bitumen was $67·5bn. CDN. Alberta accounted for 81% of Canada's total crude oil production in 2017.

Natural gas is found in abundance in numerous localities. In 2012, 3,450bn. cu. ft valued at $8·4bn. CDN were produced in Alberta.

Minerals

Coal production in 2012 was 28·0m. tonnes with 6·4m. tonnes of coal being exported.

The value of mineral production in 2011 (excluding oil and gas) was $2,696m. CDN.

Agriculture

There were 40,638 farms in Alberta in 2016 with a total area of 20,335,534 ha.; 10,223,079 ha. were land in crop in 2016. The majority of farms are made up of cattle, followed by grains and oilseed, and wheat. For particulars of livestock *see* CANADA: Agriculture.

Farm cash receipts in 2016 totalled $13,498·2m. CDN of which crops contributed $6,676·0m. CDN, livestock and products $6,125·8m. CDN and direct payments $696·4m. CDN.

Forestry

Alberta is covered by 38m. ha. of provincially owned Crown forest. In 2014 roundwood harvested totalled 23·3m. cu. metres. Revenue from logging activities in 2012 amounted to $850,368 CDN. According to the Labour Force Survey 19,617 people were employed in the forest industry in 2015.

Industry

The leading manufacturing industries are food and beverages, petroleum refining, metal fabricating, wood industries, primary metal, chemicals and chemical products and non-metallic mineral products.

Manufacturing shipments had a total value of $73·5bn. CDN in 2012. Greatest among these shipments were (in $1bn. CDN): refined petroleum, 19·7; food and beverages, 12·7; chemicals and chemical products, 11·6; machinery, 8·2.

Total retail sales in 2017 were $80·3bn. CDN.

Labour

In 2015 the labour force was 2,449,200 (1,099,800 females), of whom 2,301,100 (1,038,700) were employed. The unemployment rate in 2015 was 6·0%.

International Trade

Imports and Exports

Alberta's exports were valued at a record $80·6bn. CDN in 2007, an increase of 3·7% on 2006. The largest export markets were the USA, China, Japan, Mexico and the Netherlands, which together accounted for 93% of Alberta's international exports. Energy accounted for 68% of exports in 2007.

Communications

Roads

In 2005 there were 30,800 km of provincial highways and 153,500 km of local roads.

On 31 March 2005 there were 2,459,926 motor vehicles registered.

Rail

Alberta's railway network comprises approximately 7,000 route-km of track and represents about 16% of the overall Canadian network. There are light rail networks in Edmonton (23·7 km) and Calgary (58·4 km).

Civil Aviation

Calgary International is Canada's fourth busiest airport (handling 11,775,000 passengers in 2010) and Edmonton the fifth busiest (5,981,000 passengers in 2010).

Telecommunications

In 2013, 90·1% of households had at least one mobile phone (the highest rate of any of the Canadian provinces) and 21·2% of households only had a mobile phone. 83% of households had home internet access in 2010.

Social Institutions

Justice

The Supreme Judicial authority of the province is the Court of Appeal. Judges of the Court of Appeal and Court of Queen's Bench are appointed by the Federal government and hold office until retirement at the age of 75. There are courts of lesser jurisdiction in both civil and criminal matters. The Court of Queen's Bench has full jurisdiction over civil proceedings. A Provincial Court which has jurisdiction in civil matters up to $2,000 CDN is presided over by provincially appointed judges. Youth Courts have power to try boys and girls 12–17 years old inclusive for offences against the Young Offenders Act.

The jurisdiction of all criminal courts in Alberta is enacted in the provisions of the Criminal Code. The system of procedure in civil and criminal cases conforms as nearly as possible to the English system. In 2009–10, 53,375 Criminal Code cases were disposed of in an adult criminal court. In 2010 there were 77 homicides (a rate of 2·1 per 100,000 population).

Education

Schools of all grades are included under the term of public school (including those in the separate school system, which are publicly supported). The same board of trustees controls the schools from kindergarten to university entrance. In 2014–15 there were 608,109 pupils enrolled in grades 1–12, including private schools and special education programmes. There are eight universities in the province, the largest of which are Athabasca University (with 42,300 part-time students in 2018), the University of Alberta (with 38,820 students in 2018) and the University of Calgary (with 32,710 students in 2018).

Culture

Tourism

Alberta attracted 4,896,000 visitors from outside the province in 2014 of which 3,228,000 were from elsewhere in Canada and 1,668,000 from other countries (including 772,000 from the USA). It is known for its mountains, museums, parks and festivals. Total tourism expenditures in 2014 were $8·3bn. CDN.

British Columbia

Key Historical Events

British Columbia, formerly known as New Caledonia, was first administered by the Hudson's Bay Company. In 1849 Vancouver Island was given crown colony status and in 1853 the Queen Charlotte Islands became a dependency. The discovery of gold on the Fraser river and the subsequent influx of population resulted in the creation in 1858 of the mainland crown colony of British Columbia, to which the Strikine Territory (established 1862) was later added. In 1866 the two colonies were united.

Territory and Population

British Columbia has an area of 944,735 sq. km of which land area is 925,186 sq. km. The capital is Victoria. The province is bordered westerly by the Pacific Ocean and Alaska Panhandle, northerly by the Yukon and Northwest Territories, easterly by the Province of Alberta and southerly by the USA along the 49th parallel. A chain of islands, the largest of which are Vancouver Island and the Queen Charlotte Islands, affords protection to the mainland coast.

The population at the 2016 census was 4,648,055. The principal metropolitan areas and cities and their population census for 2011 are as follows: Metropolitan Vancouver (including Burnaby and Surrey), 2,313,328; Metropolitan Victoria, 344,615; Abbotsford (amalgamated with Matsqui), 133,497; Kelowna, 117,312; Kamloops, 85,678; Nanaimo, 83,810; Chilliwack, 77,936; Prince George, 71,974; Vernon, 38,150; Penticton, 32,877; Campbell River, 31,186; Courtenay, 24,099; Cranbrook, 19,319; Fort St John, 18,609; Port Alberni, 17,743; Salmon Arm, 17,464.

Social Statistics

Births in 2013–14 numbered 43,781 and deaths 32,985. In 2012 the infant mortality rate was 3·8 per 1,000 live births. Life expectancy in the period 2009–11 was 84·4 years for females and 80·3 years for males.

Climate

The climate is cool temperate, but mountain influences affect temperatures and rainfall considerably. Driest months occur in summer. Vancouver, Jan. 36°F (2·2°C), July 64°F (17·8°C). Annual rainfall 58" (1,458 mm).

Constitution and Government

The British North America Act of 1867 provided for eventual admission into Canadian Confederation, and on 20 July 1871 British Columbia became the sixth province of the Dominion.

British Columbia has a unicameral legislature of 85 elected members. Government policy is determined by the *Executive Council* responsible to the Legislature. The *Lieut.-Governor* is appointed by the Governor-General of Canada, usually for a term of five years, and is the head of the executive government of the province.

The *Legislative Assembly* is elected for a maximum term of five years. Every Canadian citizen 18 years and over, having resided a minimum of six months in the province, duly registered, is entitled to vote. The province is represented in the Federal Parliament by 42 members in the House of Commons and six Senators.

Recent Elections

At the Legislative Assembly elections of 9 May 2017 the ruling Liberal Party won 40·4% of the vote and 43 of the 87 seats, the New Democratic Party 40·3% and 41 seats and the Green Party 16·8% and three seats.

Current Government

Lieut.-Governor: Janet Austin (sworn in 24 April 2018).
　The Liberal Executive Council comprised in March 2019:
　　Premier and President of the Executive Council: John Horgan.
　　Deputy Premier and Minister of Finance: Carole James.
　　Minister of Advanced Education, Skills and Training: Melanie Mark. *Agriculture:* Lana Popham. *Attorney General:* David Eby. *Children and Family Development:* Katrine Conroy. *Citizens' Services:* Jinny Sims. *Education:* Rob Fleming. *Energy, Mines and Petroleum Resources:* Michelle Mungall. *Environment and Climate Change Strategy:* George Heyman. *Forests, Lands, Natural Resource Operations and Rural Development:* Doug Donaldson. *Health:* Adrian Dix. *Indigenous Relations and Reconciliation:* Scott Fraser. *Jobs, Trade and Technology:* Bruce Ralston. *Labour:* Harry Bains. *Mental Health and Addictions:* Judy Darcy. *Municipal Affairs and Housing:* Selina Robinson. *Public Safety and Solicitor General:* Mike Farnworth. *Social Development and Poverty Reduction:* Shane Simpson. *Tourism, Arts and Culture:* Lisa Beare. *Transportation and Infrastructure:* Claire Trevena.
　Office of the Premier: http://www.gov.bc.ca/prem

Economy

GDP per person in 2014 was $51,136 CDN.

Budget

Total revenue in 2008–09 was $48,949m. CDN (own source revenue, $42,334m. CDN; specific purpose transfers, $4,951m. CDN; general purpose transfers, $1,663m. CDN). Total expenditures in 2008–09 amounted to $51,533m. CDN (including: health, $14,960m. CDN; education, $11,853m. CDN; social services, $7,242m. CDN).

Performance

Real GDP grew by 2·8% in 2011 and 2·4% in 2012.

Energy and Natural Resources

Electricity

Electricity generation totalled 64·1bn. kWh in 2013 (58·2bn. kWh hydro), representing 10·5% of Canada's production.

Oil and Gas

In 2013 natural gas production, from the northeastern part of the province, was 105m. cu. metres per day.

Minerals

Coal, copper, gold, zinc, silver and molybdenum are the most important minerals produced but natural gas amounts to approximately half of the value of mineral and fuel extraction. The total value of mineral production in 2014 was $6·8bn. CDN. In 2014 the most valuable commodities (production in $1m. CDN) were: copper, 2,366; gold, 532; molybdenum, 260; sand and gravel, 231; stone, 81.

Agriculture

Only 3% of the total land area is arable or potentially arable. Farm holdings (19,844 in 2006) cover 2·8m. ha. with an average size of 143 ha. Farm cash receipts in 2007 were $2·4bn. CDN, led by dairy products valued at $424m. CDN, floriculture and nursery products valued at $404m. CDN and poultry and eggs valued at $382m. CDN. For particulars of livestock see CANADA: Agriculture.

Forestry

Around 49·9m. ha. are considered productive forest land of which 48·0m. ha. are provincial crown lands managed by the ministry of forests.

Approximately 96% of the forested land is coniferous. The total timber harvest in 2007 was 72·9m. cu. metres. Output of forest-based products, 2007: lumber, 3·7m. cu. metres; plywood (2006), 1·6m. cu. metres; pulp, 4·7m. tonnes; newsprint, paper and paperboard, 2·5m. tonnes.

Fisheries

In 2006 the total landed value of the catch was $786m. CDN; wholesale value $1·3bn. CDN. Salmon (wild and farmed) generated 53% of the wholesale value of seafood products, followed by groundfish and shellfish. In 2006, 7,800 people worked in the commercial fishery, aquaculture and fish processing industries.

Industry

The value of shipments from all manufacturing industries reached $43·4bn. CDN in 2012, including wood ($7·9bn. CDN), food ($7·2bn. CDN), paper ($4·5bn. CDN) and primary metals ($2·6bn. CDN).

Labour

In 2015 the labour force was 2,457,600 (1,159,700 females), of whom 2,306,200 (1,095,800) were employed. The unemployment rate in 2015 was 6·2%.

International Trade

Imports and Exports

Imports in 2007 totalled $38,687m. CDN in value, while exports amounted to $31,459m. CDN. The USA is the largest market for products exported through British Columbia customs ports ($19,009m. CDN in 2007), followed by Japan ($4,102m. CDN) and People's Republic of China, excluding Hong Kong ($1,744m. CDN).

Wood products accounted for 22·7% of exports in 2007, energy products 19·6%, pulp and paper products 16·2%, machinery and equipment 11·0% and metallic mineral products 10·9%.

Communications

Roads

The National Highway System included 7,026 km of roads in British Columbia in Dec. 2009. In 2015 there were 3,092,030 road motor vehicles registered.

Rail

The province is served by two transcontinental railways, the Canadian Pacific Railway and the Canadian National Railway. Passenger service is provided by VIA Rail, a Crown Corporation, and the publicly owned British Columbia Railway. In 1995 the American company Amtrak began operating a service between Seattle and Vancouver after a 14-year hiatus. British Columbia is also served by the freight trains of the B.C. Hydro and Power Authority, the Northern Alberta Railways Company and the Burlington Northern and Southern Railways Inc. The combined route-mileage of mainline track operated by the CPR, CNR and BCR totals 6,800 km. The system also includes CPR and CNR wagon ferry connections to Vancouver Island, between Prince Rupert and Alaska, and interchanges with American railways at southern border points. There is a light rail system in Vancouver, opened in 1985 (50 km). A commuter rail service linking Vancouver and the Fraser Valley was established in 1995 (69 km).

Civil Aviation

Vancouver International Airport is Canada's second busiest airport. It handled 16,254,000 passengers in 2010, up from 15,660,000 in 2009. The second busiest in British Columbia is Victoria International Airport. It handled 1,464,000 passengers in 2010, down from 1,491,000 in 2009.

Shipping

The major ports are Vancouver (the largest dry cargo port on the North American Pacific coast), Prince Rupert and ports on the Fraser River. Other deep-sea ports include Nanaimo, Port Alberni, Campbell River, Powell River, Kitimat, Stewart and Squamish. Total cargo shipped through the port of Vancouver in 2007 was 82·7m. tonnes. 961,000 cruise passengers visited Vancouver in 2007.

British Columbia Ferries—one of the largest ferry systems in the world—connect Vancouver Island with the mainland and also provide service to other coastal points; in 2006–07, over 21m. passengers and more than 8·5m. vehicles were carried. Service by other ferry systems is also provided between Vancouver Island and the USA. The Alaska State Ferries connect Prince Rupert with centres in Alaska.

Telecommunications

In 2013, 87·1% of households had at least one mobile phone and 23·1% of households only had a mobile phone (the highest rate of any of the Canadian provinces). 84% of households had home internet access in 2010.

Social Institutions

Justice

The judicial system is composed of the Court of Appeal, the Supreme Court, County Courts and various Provincial Courts, including Magistrates' Courts and Small Claims Courts. The federal courts include the Supreme Court of Canada and the Federal Court of Canada.

In 2009–10, 40,467 Criminal Code cases were disposed of in an adult criminal court. In 2010 there were 83 homicides (a rate of 1·8 per 100,000 population).

Education

Education, free up to Grade 12 level, is financed jointly from municipal and provincial government revenues. Attendance is compulsory from the age of five to 16. There were 582,691 pupils enrolled in 1,634 public schools from kindergarten to Grade 12 in Sept. 2007.

The universities had a full-time enrolment of 114,536 for 2006–07. Enrolment at the six universities (2006–07): the University of British Columbia, 48,293; Simon Fraser University, 24,842; University of Victoria, 19,372; Thompson Rivers University, 14,711; University of Northern British Columbia, 3,672; Royal Roads University, 3,646. There were three university-colleges in 2006: Kwantlen University College, Surrey; Malaspina University-College, Nanaimo; University College of the Fraser Valley, Abbotsford. British Columbia also had 12 colleges and five institutes in 2006: Camosun College, Victoria; Capilano College, North Vancouver; College of New Caledonia, Prince George; College of the Rockies, Cranbrook; Douglas College, New Westminster; Langara College, Vancouver; North Island College, Courtenay; Northern Lights College, Dawson Creek; Northwest Community College, Terrace; Okanagan College, Kelowna; Selkirk College, Castlegar; Vancouver Community College, Vancouver; British Columbia Institute of Technology, Burnaby; Emily Carr Institute of Art and Design, Vancouver; Institute of Indigenous Government, Burnaby; Justice Institute of British Columbia, New Westminster; Nicola Valley Institute of Technology, Merritt.

Televised distance education and special programmes through KNOW, the Knowledge Network of the West, are also provided.

Health

The government operates a hospital insurance scheme giving universal coverage after a qualifying period of three months' residence in the province. In 2015 there were 199 hospital establishments. In the same year there were 23·2 physicians per 10,000 population. The provincial government spent an estimated $12·1bn. CDN on health programmes in 2006–07. 38% of the government's total expenditure was for health care in 2005–06.

Culture

Tourism

British Columbia's greatest attractions are the city of Vancouver, and the provincial parks and ecological reserves that make up the Protected Areas System. In 2015 there were 4,925,916 international overnight arrivals in the province (3,263,395 from the USA).

Manitoba

Key Historical Events

Manitoba was known as the Red River Settlement before it entered the dominion in 1870. During the 18th century its only inhabitants were fur-trappers, but a more settled colonization began in the 19th century. The area was administered by the Hudson's Bay Company until 1869 when it was purchased by the new dominion. In 1870 it was given provincial status. It was enlarged in 1881 and again in 1912 by the addition of part of the Northwest Territories.

Territory and Population

The area of the province is 647,797 sq. km (250,114 sq. miles), of which 553,556 sq. km are land and 94,241 sq. km water. From north to south it is 1,225 km, and at the widest point it is 793 km.

The population at the 2016 census was 1,278,365. The 2011 census showed the following figures for areas of population of over 10,000 people: Winnipeg, the province's capital and largest city, 730,018; Brandon, 46,061; Steinbach, 13,524; Portage la Prairie, 12,996; Thompson, 12,829; Winkler, 10,670.

Social Statistics

Births in 2013–14 numbered 16,248 and deaths 10,588. In 2012 the infant mortality rate was 5·9 per 1,000 live births. Life expectancy in the period 2009–11 was 82·2 years for females and 77·7 years for males.

Climate

The climate is cold continental, with very severe winters but pleasantly warm summers. Rainfall amounts are greatest in the months May to Sept. Winnipeg, Jan. –3°F (–19·3°C), July 67°F (19·6°C). Annual rainfall 21" (539 mm).

Constitution and Government

The provincial government is administered by a *Lieut.-Governor* assisted by an *Executive Council* (Cabinet), which is appointed from and responsible to a *Legislative Assembly* of 57 members elected for five years. Women were enfranchised in 1916. The province is represented by six members in the Senate and 14 in the House of Commons of Canada.

Recent Elections

In elections to the Legislative Assembly held on 19 April 2016 the Progressive Conservative Party of Manitoba won 40 of 57 seats (53·4% of the vote), the New Democratic Party of Manitoba 14 seats (25·6%) and the Liberal Party 3 seats (14·2%). Turnout was 57·6%.

Current Government

Lieut.-Governor: Janice Filmon (took office on 19 June 2015).

The members of the Progressive Conservative Party of Manitoba government in March 2019 were:

Premier, President of the Executive Council, and Minister of Intergovernmental Affairs and International Relations: Brian Pallister; b. 1954.

Deputy Premier and Minister of Families: Heather Stefanson.

Minister of Agriculture: Ralph Eichler. *Crown Services:* Colleen Mayer. *Education and Training:* Kelvin Goertzen. *Finance:* Scott Fielding. *Growth, Enterprise and Trade:* Blaine Pedersen. *Health, Seniors and Active Living:* Cameron Friesen. *Indigenous and Northern Relations:* Eileen Clarke. *Infrastructure:* Ron Schuler. *Justice and Attorney General:* Cliff Cullen. *Municipal Relations:* Jeff Wharton. *Sport, Culture and Heritage:* Cathy Cox. *Sustainable Development:* Rochelle Squires.

Manitoba Government Website: http://www.gov.mb.ca

Economy

GDP per capita was $50,051 CDN in 2014.

Budget

Total revenue in 2008–09 was $14,715m. CDN (own source revenue, $10,788m. CDN; general purpose transfers, $2,458m. CDN; specific purpose transfers, $1,469m. CDN). Total expenditures in 2008–09 amounted to $15,025m. CDN (including: health, $4,470m. CDN; education, $3,237m. CDN; social services, $1,901m. CDN).

Performance

Real GDP grew by 2·1% in 2011, rising to 3·3% in 2012.

Energy and Natural Resources

Electricity

Electricity generation totalled 35·9bn. kWh in 2013 (35·4bn. kWh hydro), representing 5·9% of Canada's production.

Oil and Gas

Oil production in 2010 was a record 11·7m. bbls. The estimated value of oil sold in 2010 was $907m. CDN, up 45·3% from 2009.

Minerals

Principal minerals mined are nickel, zinc, copper, gold and small quantities of silver. The value of mineral production increased 24·0% in 2010 to $1,663·5m. CDN. At $674m. CDN, nickel is Manitoba's most important mineral product, accounting for 26·2% of the province's total value of mineral production. Copper accounted for 24·6% of the value of mineral production in 2010, with a large increase in price and an 8·0% gain in the province's output. Zinc, which accounts for 10·3% of mineral production value, also saw a jump in price, while its volume of production was steady in 2010. Gold was 10·8% of mineral production value, with strong growth in both price and production in Manitoba.

Agriculture

Rich farmland is the main primary resource, although the area in farms is only about 18% of the total land area. In 2010 total farm cash receipts increased by 0·1% to $4·85bn. CDN. Crop receipts fell 2·2% to $2·74bn. CDN but livestock receipts increased 6·2% to $1·76bn. CDN. Crop receipts accounted for 61% of total market receipts while livestock accounted for 39%. Within crops, the oilseeds share increased compared to wheat during the 2000s, illustrating its growing importance to Manitoba agriculture. For particulars of livestock *see* CANADA: Agriculture.

Fisheries

From about 57,000 sq. km of rivers and lakes, the value of fisheries production to fishers was about $27·0m. CDN in 2008–09 representing about 12,130 tonnes of fish. Pickerel, pike, sauger and whitefish are the principal varieties of fish caught.

Industry

Manitoba's diverse manufacturing sector is the province's largest industry, accounting for approximately 10·7% of total GDP. The value of manufacturing shipments declined by 1·6% in 2010 to $14·4bn. CDN.

Labour

In 2015 the labour force was 674,100 (317,400 females), of whom 636,200 (299,400) were employed. The unemployment rate in 2015 was 5·6%.

International Trade

Imports and Exports

In 2015 Manitoba's merchandise imports totalled $13·7bn. CDN (of which imports from the USA $9·5bn. CDN) and exports $20·9bn. CDN (of which exports to the USA $16·3bn. CDN). China was the second biggest import supplier in 2015 ahead of Japan and Mexico, and the second biggest export market ahead of Mexico and Germany. In 2013 the main imports were agricultural machinery, tractors and gas turbines; main exports were wheat, crude oil and nickel.

Communications

Roads

The National Highway System included 2,095 km of roads in Manitoba in Dec. 2015. In 2016 there were 1,137,179 vehicle registrations in the province of which 857,033 were road motor vehicles, 199,564 trailers and 80,582 off-road, construction and farm vehicles.

Rail

The province has about 5,650 km of commercial track, not including industrial track, yards and sidings. Most of the track belongs to the country's two national railways. Canadian Pacific owns about 1,950 km and Canadian National about 2,400 km. The Hudson Bay Railway, operated by Denver-based Omnitrax, has about 1,300 km of track. Fort Worth-based Burlington Northern's railcars are moved in Manitoba on CN and CP tracks and trains.

Civil Aviation

Winnipeg (James Armstrong Richardson International Airport) was Canada's eighth busiest airport in 2010, handling 3,385,000 passengers (3,372,000 in 2009).

Telecommunications

In 2013, 82·9% of households had at least one mobile phone and 18·5% of households only had a mobile phone. 73% of households had home internet access in 2010.

Social Institutions

Justice

In 2009–10, 16,849 Criminal Code cases were disposed of in an adult criminal court. In 2010 there were 45 homicides (a rate of 3·6 per 100,000 population)

Education

Education is controlled through locally elected school divisions. There were 181,446 students enrolled in the province's public schools in the 2007–08 school year. Student teacher ratios (including all instructors but excluding school-based administrators) averaged one teacher for every 17·6 students in 2006–07.

Manitoba has seven public post-secondary institutions. They are the University of Manitoba, founded in 1877; the University of Winnipeg; Brandon University; the Collège universitaire de Saint Boniface; Red River College (in Winnipeg); Assiniboine Community College (at Brandon); and University College of the North (at The Pas). The University of Manitoba (the largest university) had 29,929 students in fall 2015. Provincial core government expenditure on education and training for the 2015–16 fiscal year was budgeted at $2·69bn. CDN.

Culture

Tourism
Between 2009 and 2010 Manitoba recorded a 14·1% increase in total visitor numbers. In 2009 visitors spent $1·2bn. CDN (representing 2·8% of GDP). The province received a total of 6,910,000 visits in 2009 of which 371,000 were from the USA and 82,000 from other foreign countries. 24,800 people were employed in tourism-related jobs in 2009.

New Brunswick

Key Historical Events

Visited by Jacques Cartier in 1534, New Brunswick was first explored by Samuel de Champlain in 1604. With Nova Scotia, it originally formed one French colony called Acadia. It was ceded by the French in the Treaty of Utrecht in 1713 and became a permanent British possession in 1759. It was first settled by British colonists in 1764 but was separated from Nova Scotia, and became a province in June 1784 as a result of the influx of United Empire Loyalists. Responsible government from 1848 consisted of an executive council, a legislative council (later abolished) and a House of Assembly. In 1867 New Brunswick entered the Confederation.

Territory and Population

The area of the province is 72,908 sq. km (28,150 sq. miles), of which 71,450 sq. km (27,587 sq. miles) is land area. The 2016 census counted 747,101 people in New Brunswick. At the time of the 2011 census, 64·9% of the population reported English only as their mother tongue, 31·6% reported French only and 2·5% reported only a non-official language.

The seven urban centres of the province and their respective populations based on 2011 census figures are: Moncton, 138,644; Saint John, 127,761; Fredericton (capital), 94,268; Bathurst, 33,484; Miramichi, 28,115; Edmundston, 21,903; Campbellton (part only), 14,520. The official languages are English and French.

Social Statistics

Births in 2013–14 numbered 6,827 and deaths 6,832. In 2012 the infant mortality rate was 5·7 per 1,000 live births. Life expectancy in the period 2009–11 was 83·1 years for females and 78·4 years for males.

Climate

A cool temperate climate, with rain in all seasons but temperatures modified by the influence of the Gulf Stream. Annual average total precipitation in Fredericton: 1,131 mm. Warmest month, July (average high) 25·6°C.

Constitution and Government

The government is vested in a *Lieut.-Governor*, appointed by the Queen's representative in New Brunswick, and a *Legislative Assembly* of 55 members, each of whom is individually elected to represent the voters in one constituency or riding. The political party with the largest number of elected representatives, after a Provincial election, forms the government.

The province has ten appointed members in the Canadian Senate and elects ten members in the House of Commons.

Recent Elections

Elections to the provincial assembly were held on 24 Sept. 2018. The opposition Progressive Conservative Party won 22 seats (with 31·9% of the vote), the ruling Liberal Party 21 seats (with 37·8%), and the People's Alliance and the Green Party 3 seats each with 12·6% and 11·9% respectively.

Current Government

Lieut.-Governor: Jocelyne Roy-Vienneau (took office on 23 Oct. 2014).

The members of the Progressive Conservative government were as follows in March 2019:

Premier and President of Executive Council Office: Blaine Higgs; b. 1954.
Deputy Premier, and Minister of Tourism, Heritage and Culture: Robert Gauvin.

Minister of Aboriginal Affairs: Jake Stewart. *Agriculture, Aquaculture and Fisheries:* Ross Wetmore. *Economic Development and Small Business:* Mary Wilson. *Education and Early Childhood Development:* Dominic Cardy. *Energy and Resource Development:* Mike Holland. *Environment and Local Government:* Jeff Carr. *Finance, and President of the Treasury Board:* Ernie Steeves. *Health:* Hugh 'Ted' Flemming. *Intergovernmental Affairs:* Gregory Thompson. *Justice, and Attorney General:* Andrea Anderson-Mason. *Post-Secondary Education, Training and Labour:* Trevor Holder. *Public Safety:* Carl Urquhart. *Social Development:* Dorothy Shephard. *Service New Brunswick:* Sherry Wilson. *Transportation and Infrastructure:* Bill Oliver.
Government of New Brunswick Website: http://www.gnb.ca

Economy

GDP per capita in 2014 was $42,482 CDN.

Budget
Total revenue in 2008–09 was $8,978m. CDN (own source revenue, $6,313m. CDN; general purpose transfers, $1,824m. CDN; specific purpose transfers, $840m. CDN). Total expenditures in 2008–09 amounted to $9,373m. CDN (including: health, $3,245m. CDN; education, $1,886m. CDN; debt charges, $945m. CDN).

Performance
Real GDP grew by 0·6% in 2011 but then contracted by 0·4% in 2012.

Energy and Natural Resources

Electricity
Hydro-electric, thermal and nuclear generating stations of NB Power had an installed capacity of 3,142 MW at 31 March 2010, consisting of 14 generating stations. Electricity generation totalled 13·9bn. kWh in 2013 (4·4bn. kWh conventional steam), representing 2·3% of Canada's production.

Minerals
The total value of mineral production in 2014 was $439m. CDN. The major minerals mined are zinc, silver and lead. Among non-metallic minerals, peat, stone and sulphur are of importance.

Agriculture
The total area under crops was 151,996 ha. in 2006. Farms numbered 2,776 and averaged 142 ha. (census 2006). Potatoes account for 33% of total farm cash receipts and dairy products 11%. New Brunswick is self-sufficient in fluid milk and supplies a processing industry. For particulars of livestock *see* CANADA: Agriculture. Net farm income in 2005 was $25·4m. CDN.

Forestry
New Brunswick contains some 6m. ha. of productive forest lands. The value of shipments of forest products in 2008 was $1·25bn. CDN; the value of manufacturing shipments for the wood-related industries was $871m. CDN. In 2008 nearly 13,000 people were employed in all aspects of the forest industry.

Fisheries
Commercial fishing is one of the most important primary industries of the province, employing 6,366 in 2007. Landings in 2005 (117,295 tonnes) amounted to $197m. CDN. In 2005 molluscs and crustaceans ranked first with a value of $178m. CDN, 90% of the total landed value. Exports in 2005, totalling $653·4m. CDN, went mainly to the USA and Japan.

Industry

Important industries include food and beverages, paper and allied industries, and timber products.

Labour
In 2015 the labour force was 390,200 (188,000 females), of whom 351,800 (174,300) were employed. The unemployment rate in 2015 was 9·8%.

International Trade

Imports and Exports

New Brunswick's location, with deepwater harbours open throughout the year and container facilities at Saint John, makes it ideal for exporting. The main exports include lumber, wood pulp, newsprint, refined petroleum products and electricity. In 2009 the major trading partners of the province were the USA with 86% of total exports, followed by the Netherlands with 3%. Imports totalled $9,396m. CDN while exports reached $9,902m. CDN in 2009.

Communications

Roads

There are 21,423 km of roads in the Provincial Highway system, of which 8,333 km consists of arterial, collector and local roads that provide access to most areas. The main highway system, including approximately 964 km of the Trans-Canada Highway, links the province with the principal roads in Quebec, Nova Scotia and Prince Edward Island, as well as the Interstate Highway System in the eastern seaboard states of the USA. At 31 March 2009 total road motor vehicle registrations numbered 524,300 of which 489,507 were vehicles weighing less than 4,500 kilograms, 7,662 were vehicles weighing 4,500 kilograms to 14,999 kilograms, 4,643 were vehicles weighing 15,000 kilograms or more, 3,086 were buses and 19,399 were motorcycles and mopeds.

Rail

New Brunswick is served by the Canadian National Railways, Springfield Terminal Railway, New Brunswick Southern Railway, New Brunswick East Coast Railway, Le Chemin de fer de la Matapédia et du Golfe and VIA Rail. The Salem-Hillsborough rail is popular with tourists.

Civil Aviation

There are three major airports at Fredericton, Moncton and Saint John. There are also a number of small regional airports.

Shipping

New Brunswick has five major ports. The Port of Saint John handles approximately 20m. tonnes of cargo each year including forest products, steel, potash and petroleum. The Port of Belledune is a deep-water port and open all year round. Other ports are Dalhousie, Bayside/St Andrews and Miramichi.

Telecommunications

In 2013, 80·5% of households had at least one mobile phone and 13·0% of households only had a mobile phone. 70% of households had home internet access in 2010.

Social Institutions

Justice

In 2015, 41,597 Criminal Code offences were reported, including 11 homicides.

Education

Public education is free and non-sectarian.

There were, in Sept. 2009, 106,394 students (including kindergarten) and 7,896 full-time equivalent/professional educational staff in the province's 322 schools.

There are four universities. The University of New Brunswick at Fredericton (founded 13 Dec. 1785 by the Loyalists, elevated to university status in 1823 and reorganized as the University of New Brunswick in 1859) had 9,706 students (2015–16); the Université de Moncton at Moncton, 4,981 students; Mount Allison University at Sackville, 2,423 students; St Thomas University at Fredericton had 2,096 students.

Culture

Tourism

New Brunswick has a number of historic buildings as well as libraries, museums and other cultural sites. Tourism is one of the leading contributors to the economy. In 2007 tourism revenues reached $1·4bn. CDN.

Newfoundland and Labrador

Key Historical Events

Archaeological finds at L'Anse aux Meadows in northern Newfoundland show that the Vikings established a colony here in about AD 1000. This site is the only known Viking colony in North America. Newfoundland was discovered by John Cabot on 24 June 1497, and was soon frequented in the summer months by the Portuguese, Spanish and French for its fisheries. It was formally occupied in Aug. 1583 by Sir Humphrey Gilbert on behalf of the English Crown but various attempts to colonize the island remained unsuccessful. Although British sovereignty was recognized in 1713 by the Treaty of Utrecht, disputes over fishing rights with the French were not finally settled until 1904. By the Anglo-French Convention of 1904, France renounced her exclusive fishing rights along part of the coast, granted under the Treaty of Utrecht, but retained sovereignty of the offshore islands of St Pierre and Miquelon. Self-governing from 1855, the colony remained outside of the Canadian confederation in 1867 and continued to govern itself until 1934, when a commission of government appointed by the British Crown assumed responsibility for governing the colony and Labrador. This body controlled the country until union with Canada in 1949.

Territory and Population

Area, 405,212 sq. km (156,452 sq. miles), of which freshwater, 31,340 sq. km (12,100 sq. miles). In March 1927 the Privy Council decided the boundary between Canada and Newfoundland in Labrador. This area, now part of the Province of Newfoundland and Labrador, is 294,330 sq. km (113,641 sq. miles) of land area.

Newfoundland island's coastline is punctuated with numerous bays, fjords and inlets, providing many good deep water harbours. Approximately one-third of the area is covered by water. Grand Lake, the largest body of water, has an area of about 530 sq. km. Good agricultural land is generally found in the valleys of the Terra Nova River, the Gander River, the Exploits River and the Humber River, which are also heavily timbered. The Strait of Belle Isle separates the island from Labrador to the north. Bordering on the Canadian province of Quebec, Labrador is a vast, pristine wilderness and extremely sparsely populated (approximately 10 sq. km per person). Labrador's Lake Melville is 2,934 sq. km and its highest peak, Mount Caubvick, is 1,700 metres.

The population at the 2016 census was 519,716. The capital of the province is the City of St John's (2011 census population, 106,172). The other cities are Mt Pearl (24,284 in 2011) and Corner Brook (19,886); important towns are Conception Bay South (24,848), Paradise (17,695), Grand Falls-Windsor (13,725), Gander (11,054), Happy Valley-Goose Bay (7,552), Torbay (7,397), Labrador City (7,367), Portugal Cove-St Philip's (7,366), Stephenville (6,719), Clarenville (6,036), Bay Roberts (5,818) and Marystown (5,506).

Social Statistics

Births in 2013–14 numbered 4,484 and deaths 4,849. In 2012 the infant mortality rate was 5·5 per 1,000 live births. Life expectancy in the period 2009–11 was 82·0 years for females and 77·1 years for males.

Climate

The cool temperate climate is marked by heavy precipitation, distributed evenly over the year, a cool summer and frequent fogs in spring. St. John's, Jan. –4°C, July 15·8°C. Annual rainfall 1,240 mm.

Constitution and Government

Until 1832 Newfoundland was ruled by a British Governor. In that year a Legislature was brought into existence, but the Governor and his Executive Council were not responsible to it. Under the constitution of 1855, the government was administered by the *Governor* appointed by the Crown with an *Executive Council* responsible to the House of Assembly.

Parliamentary government was suspended in 1933 on financial grounds and Government by Commission was inaugurated on 16 Feb. 1934. Confederation with Canada was approved by a referendum in July 1948. In the Canadian Senate on 18 Feb. 1949 Royal Assent was given to the terms of union of Newfoundland and Labrador with Canada, and on 23 March 1949, in the House of Lords, London, Royal Assent was given to an amendment to the British North America Act, made necessary by the inclusion of Newfoundland and Labrador as the tenth Province of Canada. Since April 1949 Newfoundland and Labrador has had a *Lieut.-Governor* rather than a Governor, and its House of Assembly (comprised of 48 members) was reconstituted.

The province is represented by six members in the Senate and by seven members in the House of Commons of Canada.

Recent Elections

Elections were held on 30 Nov. 2015. The Liberal Party won 31 of the 40 seats in the House of Assembly with 57·2% of the vote; the Progressive Conservative Party, 7 (30·1%); and the New Democratic Party, 2 (12·1%).

Current Government

Lieut.-Governor: Judy Foote (assumed office 3 May 2018).

In March 2019 the Liberal cabinet was composed as follows:

Premier, President of the Executive Council, and Minister of Intergovernmental and Indigenous Affairs, and Labrador Affairs: Dwight Ball (sworn in 14 Dec. 2015).

Minister of Fisheries and Land Resources: Gerry Byrne. *Natural Resources:* Siobhan Coady. *Transportation and Works:* Steve Crocker. *Children, Seniors and Social Development:* Lisa Dempster. *Service NL:* Sherry Gambin-Walsh. *Health and Community Services:* Dr John Haggie. *Education and Early Childhood Development:* Al Hawkins. *Tourism, Culture, Industry and Innovation:* Christopher Mitchelmore. *Finance and President of the Treasury Board:* Tom Osborne. *Justice and Public Safety, and Attorney General:* Andrew Parsons. *Advanced Education, Skills and Labour:* Bernard Davis. *Municipal Affairs and Environment:* Graham Letto.

Office of the Premier: http://www.premier.gov.nl.ca/premier

Economy

GDP per capita was $63,345 CDN in 2014.

Budget

Total revenue in 2008–09 was $8,374m. CDN (own source revenue, $4,396m. CDN; general purpose transfers, $3,280m. CDN; specific purpose transfers, $697m. CDN). Total expenditures in 2008–09 amounted to $7,121m. CDN (including: health, $2,228m. CDN; education, $1,535m. CDN; transportation and communication, $588m. CDN).

Performance

Real GDP grew by 3·1% in 2011, but then contracted by 4·5% in 2012.

Energy and Natural Resources

Electricity

Newfoundland and Labrador is served by two large physically independent electrical systems with a total of 7,412 MW of operational electrical generating capacity and 23 small isolated systems primarily supplied by diesel-fuelled internal combustion generators. In 2011 total provincial electricity generation equalled 41·2bn. kWh, of which about 97% was from hydro-electric sources. Approximately 73% of total electricity generation was exported outside the province. Electricity service for a total of 274,000 retail customers is provided by two utilities and regulated by the Board of Commissioners of Public Utilities.

Oil and Gas

Newfoundland and Labrador is home to three active offshore oil projects: Hibernia, Terra Nova and White Rose. In 2011 oil production from Hibernia reached 56·3m. bbls. The Terra Nova development started producing oil in Jan. 2002 and in 2003 produced more than 40m. bbls, although production declined in 2011 to 15·7m. bbls. Production at the White Rose development started in Nov. 2005 and reached 25·2m. bbls in 2011. A fourth development, Hebron, began oil production in late 2017.

Minerals

The mineral resources are vast but only partially documented. Large deposits of iron ore, with an ore reserve of over 5,000m. tonnes at Labrador City, Wabush City and in the Knob Lake area, are supplying approximately half of Canada's production. Other large deposits of iron ore are known to exist in the Julienne Lake area. The Central Mineral Belt, which extends from the Smallwood Reservoir to the Atlantic coast near Makkovik, holds uranium, copper, beryllium and molybdenite potential.

The percentage share of mineral shipment value in 2015 stood at 52% for iron ore and 32% for nickel. Other major mineral products were copper and gold. The value of mineral shipments in 2015 totalled $2·9bn. CDN.

Agriculture

Farm receipts in 2011 were $124·8m. CDN, an increase of 5·8% on 2010. In 2011 dairy products contributed $43·3m. CDN, crops $18·2m. CDN, eggs $17·1m. CDN and furs $15·8m. CDN. For particulars of livestock *see* CANADA: Agriculture.

Forestry

The province's forestry industry has an estimated value of $286m. CDN annually. The main areas are pulp and paper, sawmilling, harvesting and value-added enterprises. Newsprint shipments totalled 254,626 tonnes in 2015 with an estimated value of $174·5m. CDN. Lumber mills and saw-log operations produced 81·2m. bd ft in 2011.

Fisheries

Fish landings in 2015 totalled approximately 240,800 tonnes, with the associated landed value reaching an all-time high of $738m. CDN. Shellfish accounted for 58·9% of total landings and 82·5% of landed value. Approximately 17,500 people were employed in the fishing industry in 2015.

Industry

The total value of manufacturing shipments in 2012 was $7·3bn. CDN, a 32·0% increase on 2011, mainly owing to higher production of refined petroleum products. Other significant contributors were fish products and newsprint.

Labour

In 2015 the labour force was 270,800 (129,700 females), of whom 236,200 (116,900) were employed. The unemployment rate in 2015 was 12·8%.

Communications

Roads

In 2012 there were 20,210 km of roads, of which 11,703 km were paved. In 2010 there were 334,912 motor vehicles registered.

Rail

The Quebec North Shore and Labrador Railway operated both freight and passenger services on its 588 km main line from Sept-Iles, Quebec, to Shefferville, Quebec and its 58 km spur line from Ross Bay Junction to Labrador City, Newfoundland. In 2013 iron ore freight totalled 19·6m. tonnes.

Civil Aviation

The province is linked to the rest of Canada by regular air services provided by Air Canada and a number of smaller air carriers.

Shipping

Marine Atlantic, a federal crown corporation, provides a freight and passenger service all year round from Channel-Port aux Basques to North Sydney, Nova Scotia; and seasonal ferries connect Argentia with North Sydney, and Lewisporte with Goose Bay, Labrador.

Telecommunications

In 2013, 85·9% of households had at least one mobile phone and 15·8% of households had three or more mobile phones. 74% of households had home internet access in 2010.

Social Institutions

Justice

In 2009–10, 4,846 Criminal Code cases were disposed of in an adult criminal court. In 2010 there were four homicides (a rate of 0·8 per 100,000 population).

Education

In 2014–15 total enrolment for elementary and secondary education was 67,293 and full-time equivalent teachers numbered 5,379; total number of schools was 264 in 2013–14. Memorial University, offering courses in arts, humanities and social sciences, professional programmes and sciences, had 18,420 students in 2014–15 (14,225 full-time).

Culture

Tourism

In 2014, 507,900 non-resident tourists (497,900 in 2013) spent approximately $491·1m. CDN in the province.

Nova Scotia

Key Historical Events

Nova Scotia was visited by John and Sebastian Cabot in 1497–98. In 1605 a number of French colonists settled at Port Royal. The old name of the colony, Acadia, was changed in 1621 to Nova Scotia. The French were granted possession of the colony by the Treaty of St-Germain-en-Laye (1632). In 1654 Oliver Cromwell sent a force to occupy the settlement. Charles II, by the Treaty of Breda (1667), restored Nova Scotia to the French. It was finally ceded to the British by the Treaty of Utrecht in 1713. In the Treaty of Paris (1763) France resigned all claims and in 1820 Cape Breton Island united with Nova Scotia. Representative government was granted as early as 1758 and a fully responsible Legislative Assembly was established in 1848. In 1867 the province entered the dominion of Canada.

Territory and Population

The area of the province is 55,284 sq. km (21,345 sq. miles), of which 53,338 sq. km are land area and 1,946 sq. km water area. The population at the 2016 census was 923,598.

Population of the major urban areas (2011 census): Halifax Regional Municipality, 390,096; Cape Breton Regional Municipality, 97,398. Principal towns (2011 census): Truro, 12,059; Amherst, 9,717; New Glasgow, 9,562; Bridgewater, 8,241; Yarmouth, 6,761; Kentville, 6,094.

Social Statistics

Births in 2013–14 numbered 8,613 and deaths 8,966. In 2012 the infant mortality rate was 4·6 per 1,000 live births. Life expectancy in the period 2009–11 was 82·6 years for females and 78·1 years for males.

Climate

A cool temperate climate, with rainfall occurring evenly over the year. The Gulf Stream moderates the temperatures in winter so that ports remain ice-free. Halifax, Jan. 23·7°F (−4·6°C), July 63·5°F (17·5°C). Annual rainfall 54" (1,371 mm).

Constitution and Government

Under the British North America Act of 1867 the legislature of Nova Scotia may exclusively make laws in relation to local matters, including direct taxation within the province, education and the administration of justice. The legislature of Nova Scotia consists of a *Lieut.-Governor*, appointed and paid by the federal government, and holding office for five years, and a *House of Assembly* of 52 members, chosen by popular vote at least every five years. The province is represented in the Canadian Senate by ten members, and in the House of Commons by 11.

Recent Elections

At the provincial elections of 30 May 2017 the ruling Liberal Party won 27 seats (39·5% of the vote), the Progressive Conservatives 17 (35·7%) and the New Democratic Party 7 (21·5%). Turnout was 53·9%.

Current Government

Lieut.-Governor: Arthur Joseph LeBlanc (assumed office 28 June 2017).

The members of Nova Scotia's Liberal cabinet in March 2019 were:
Premier, President of the Executive Council, and Minister of Intergovernmental Affairs, Aboriginal Affairs, and Regulatory Affairs and Service Effectiveness: Stephen McNeil.

Deputy Premier, Deputy President of the Executive Council, and Minister of Finance and Treasury Board: Karen Casey. *Agriculture, and Fisheries and Aquaculture:* Keith Colwell. *Attorney General and Minister of Justice, and Labour Relations:* Mark Furey. *Business, Service Nova Scotia, and Trade:* Geoff MacLellan. *Communities, Culture and Heritage, Seniors, and the Voluntary Sector:* Leo Glavine. *Community Services:* Kelly Regan. *Education and Early Childhood Development:* Zach Churchill. *Energy and Mines:* Derek Mombourquette. *Environment:* Margaret Miller. *Health and Wellness, and Gaelic Affairs:* Randy Delorey. *Immigration, and Acadian Affairs and Francophonie:* Lena Metlege Diab. *Internal Services, and Communications Nova Scotia:* Patricia Arab. *Lands and Forestry:* Iain Rankin. *Labour and Advanced Education:* Labi Kousoulis. *Municipal Affairs:* Chuck Porter. *Public Service Commission, and African Nova Scotia Affairs:* Tony Ince. *Transportation and Infrastructure Renewal:* Lloyd Hines.
Government of Nova Scotia Website: http://www.gov.ns.ca

Economy

GDP per capita was $41,466 CDN in 2014.

Budget

Total revenue in 2008–09 was $11,074m. CDN (own source revenue, $7,507m. CDN; general purpose transfers, $2,387m. CDN; specific purpose transfers, $1,181m. CDN). Total expenditures in 2008–09 amounted to $11,259m. CDN (including: health, $3,314m. CDN; education, $2,777m. CDN; social services, $1,189m. CDN).

Performance

Real GDP grew by 0·7% in 2011 but then fell by 0·3% in 2012.

Energy and Natural Resources

Electricity

Electricity generation totalled 10·5bn. kWh in 2013 (8·5bn. kWh conventional steam), representing 1·9% of Canada's production.

Oil and Gas

Significant finds of offshore natural gas are currently under development. Gas is flowing to markets in Canada and the USA (the pipeline was completed in 1999). Total marketable gas receipts for 2005 was 3·9bn. cu. metres.

Minerals

The total value of mineral production in 2014 was $198m. CDN. The mineral industry is dominated by the production of industrial minerals and structural materials.

Agriculture

In 2006 there were 3,795 farms in the province with 116,609 ha. of land under crops. Dairying, poultry and egg production, livestock and fruit growing are the most important branches. Farm cash receipts for 2005 were $453·4m. CDN. Cash receipts from sale of dairy products were $107·0m. CDN, with total milk and cream sales of 166·7m. litres. The production of poultry meat in 2005 was 37,030 tonnes, of which 33,508 tonnes were chicken and 3,522 tonnes were turkey. Egg production in 2005 was 17·9m. dozen. For particulars of livestock see CANADA: Agriculture.

The main fruit crops in 2005 were apples, 39,372 tonnes; blueberries, 16,239 tonnes; strawberries, 1,769 tonnes.

Forestry

The estimated forest area of Nova Scotia is 15,830 sq. miles (40,990 sq. km), of which about 28% is owned by the province. Softwood species represented 89·4% of the 6,254,716 cu. metres of the forest round products produced in 2005. Employment in the forest sector was 4,100 persons in 2005.

Fisheries

The fisheries of the province in 2005 had a landed value of $647m. CDN of sea fish; including lobster fishery, $339m. CDN; and crab fishery, $73m. CDN. Aquaculture production in 2005 was 8,917 tonnes with a value of $40·4m. CDN; finfish accounted for 64% of total value while shellfish made up the remainder.

Industry

The number of employees in manufacturing establishments was 29,900 in 2014; wages and salaries totalled $1,567m. CDN as at Dec. 2014. The value of shipments in 2005 was $10,596m. CDN, and the leading industries were food, paper production, and plastic and rubber products.

Labour

In 2015 the labour force was 490,200 (240,100 females), of whom 448,100 (223,300) were employed. The unemployment rate in 2015 was 8·6%.

International Trade

Imports and Exports

Total of imports and exports to and from Nova Scotia (in $1m. CDN):

	2002	2003	2004	2005
Imports	5,140	5,816	6,590	6,989
Exports	5,345	5,477	5,859	5,815

The main exports in 2005 included fish and fish products, natural gas and paper. Major trading partners were the USA with 80·1% of total exports, followed by Japan and the United Kingdom.

Communications

Roads
In 2005 there were 26,000 km of highways, of which 13,600 km were paved. The Trans Canada and 100 series highways are limited access, all-weather, rapid transit routes. The province's first toll road opened in Dec. 1997. In 2005 total road vehicle registrations numbered 561,325 and over 600,000 persons had road motor vehicle operators licences.

Rail
The province has an 805 km network of mainline track operated predominantly by Canadian National Railways. The Cape Breton and Central Nova Scotia Railway operates between Truro and Cape Breton Island. The Windsor and Hantsport Railway operates in the Annapolis Valley region. VIA Rail operates the Ocean for six days a week, a transcontinental service between Halifax and Montreal.

Civil Aviation
Halifax (Robert L. Stanfield International Airport) was Canada's seventh busiest airport in 2010, handling 3,509,000 passengers. There are other major airports at Sydney and Yarmouth.

Shipping
Ferry services connect Nova Scotia to the provinces of Newfoundland and Labrador, Prince Edward Island and New Brunswick as well as to the USA. The deep-water, ice-free Port of Halifax handles about 14m. tonnes of cargo annually.

Telecommunications
In 2013, 82·9% of households had at least one mobile phone and 17·2% of households only had a mobile phone. 77% of households had home internet access in 2010.

Social Institutions

Justice
The Supreme Court (Trial Division and Appeal Division) is the superior court of Nova Scotia and has original and appellate jurisdiction in all civil and criminal matters unless they have been specifically assigned to another court by Statute. An appeal from the Supreme Court, Appeal Division, is to the Supreme Court of Canada.

In 2009–10, 11,760 Criminal Code cases were disposed of in an adult criminal court. In 2010 there were 21 homicides (a rate of 2·2 per 100,000 population).

Education
Public education in Nova Scotia is free, compulsory and undenominational through elementary and high school. Attendance is compulsory to the age of 16. In 2015–16 there were 118,152 students in public elementary and secondary schools. Public and private elementary and secondary education expenditure in 2015–16 totalled $1·67bn. CDN. The province has 11 degree-granting institutions. The Nova Scotia Agricultural College is located at Truro. The Technical University of Nova Scotia, which grants degrees in engineering and architecture, amalgamated with Dalhousie University and is now known as DalTech.

The Nova Scotia government offers financial support and organizational assistance to local school boards for provision of weekend and evening courses in academic and vocational subjects, and citizenship for new Canadians.

Health
A provincial retail sales tax of 8% provides funds for free hospital in-patient care up to ward level and free medically required services of physicians. The Queen Elizabeth II Hospital in Halifax is the overall referral hospital for the province and, in many instances, for the Atlantic region. The Izaak Walton Killam Hospital provides similar regional specialization for children.

Welfare
General and specialized welfare services in the province are under the jurisdiction of the Department of Community Services. The provincial government funds all of the costs.

Culture

Tourism
Tourism revenues were $1·3bn. CDN in 2005. Total number of visitors in 2005 was 2,114,000.

Ontario

Key Historical Events
The French explorer Samuel de Champlain explored the Ottawa River from 1613. The area was governed by the French, first under a joint stock company and then as a royal province, from 1627 and was ceded to Great Britain in 1763. A constitutional act of 1791 created the province of Upper Canada, largely to accommodate loyalists of English descent who had immigrated after the United States war of independence. Upper Canada entered the Confederation as Ontario in 1867.

Territory and Population
The area is 1,076,395 sq. km (415,596 sq. miles), of which some 917,741 sq. km (354,340 sq. miles) are land area and some 158,654 sq. km (61,256 sq. miles) are lakes and fresh water rivers. The province extends 1,690 km (1,050 miles) from east to west and 1,730 km (1,075 miles) from north to south. It is bounded in the north by the Hudson and James Bays, in the east by Quebec, in the west by Manitoba, and in the south by the USA, the Great Lakes and the St Lawrence Seaway.

The census population in 2016 was 13,448,494. Population of the principal cities (2011 census):

Toronto[1]	2,615,060
Ottawa	883,391
Mississauga	713,443
Brampton	523,911
Hamilton	519,949
London	366,151
Markham	301,709
Vaughan	288,301
Kitchener	219,153
Windsor	210,891
Richmond Hill	185,541
Oakville	182,520
Burlington	175,779
Greater Sudbury	160,274
Oshawa	149,607
Barrie	135,711
St Catharines	131,400
Cambridge	126,748
Kingston	123,363
Whitby	122,022
Guelph	121,688
Thunder Bay	108,359

[1]The new City of Toronto was created on 1 Jan. 1998 through the amalgamation of seven municipalities: Metropolitan Toronto and six local area municipalities of Toronto, North York, Scarborough, Etobicoke, East York and York.

There are over 1m. French-speaking people and 0·25m. native Indians. An agreement with the Ontario government of Aug. 1991 recognized Indians' right to self-government.

Social Statistics
Births in 2013–14 numbered 142,970 and deaths 96,883. In 2012 the infant mortality rate was 4·9 per 1,000 live births. Life expectancy in the period 2009–11 was 83·9 years for females and 79·8 years for males.

Climate
A temperate continental climate, but conditions can be quite severe in winter, though proximity to the Great Lakes has a moderating influence on temperatures. Ottawa, average temperature, Jan. −10·8°C, July 20·8°C. Annual

rainfall (including snow) 911 mm. Toronto, average temperature, Jan. −4·5°C, July 22·1°C. Annual rainfall (including snow) 818 mm.

Constitution and Government

The provincial government is administered by a *Lieut.-Governor*, a cabinet and a single-chamber 107-member *Legislative Assembly* elected by a general franchise for a period of no longer than five years. The minimum voting age is 18 years. The province is represented by 24 members in the Senate and 121 in the House of Commons of Canada.

Recent Elections

At the elections on 7 June 2018 to the Legislative Assembly the opposition Progressive Conservative Party won 76 of a possible 124 seats (with 40·5% of the vote), the New Democratic Party 40 seats (33·6%), the governing Liberal Party 7 seats (19·6%) and the Green Party 1 seat (4·6%). Turnout was 58·0%.

Current Government

Lieut.-Governor: Elizabeth Dowdeswell (in office since 23 Sept. 2014).

In March 2019 the Executive Council comprised:

Premier, and Minister of Intergovernmental Affairs: Douglas Robert 'Doug' Ford; b. 1964 (sworn in 29 June 2018).

Deputy Premier, and Minister of Health and Long-Term Care: Christine Elliott.

Minister of Agriculture, Food and Rural Affairs: Ernie Hardeman. *Attorney General, and Minister of Francophone Affairs:* Caroline Mulroney. *Children, Community and Social Services, and Minister Responsible for Women's Affairs:* Lisa MacLeod. *Community Safety and Correctional Services:* Sylvia Jones. *Economic Development, Job Creation and Trade, and Government House Leader:* Todd Smith. *Education:* Lisa Thompson. *Energy, Northern Development and Mines, and Indigenous Affairs:* Greg Rickford. *Environment, Conservation and Parks:* Rod Phillips. *Finance, and Chair of the Cabinet:* Victor Fedeli. *Government and Consumer Services:* Bill Walker. *Infrastructure:* Monte McNaughton. *Labour:* Laurie Scott. *Municipal Affairs and Housing:* Steve Clark. *Natural Resources and Forestry:* John Yakabuski. *Seniors and Accessibility:* Raymond Cho. *Tourism, Culture and Sport:* Michael Tibollo. *Training, Colleges and Universities:* Merrilee Fullerton. *Transportation:* Jeff Yurek. *President of the Treasury Board:* Peter Bethlenfalvy.

Office of the Premier: http://www.premier.gov.on.ca

Economy

GDP per person in 2014 was $52,785 CDN.

Budget

Total revenue in 2008–09 was $141,577m. CDN (own source revenue, $123,412m. CDN; specific purpose transfers, $13,958m. CDN; general purpose transfers, $4,207m. CDN). Total expenditures in 2008–09 amounted to $147,581m. CDN (including: health, $45,239m. CDN; education, $35,155m. CDN; social services, $20,374m. CDN).

Performance

Real GDP grew by 2·6% in 2011 and then 1·7% in 2012.

Energy and Natural Resources

Electricity

Electricity generation totalled 149·8bn. kWh in 2013 (93·1bn. kWh nuclear), representing 24·5% of Canada's production. Ontario ranks second after Quebec for electricity production.

Oil and Gas

Ontario is Canada's leading petroleum refining region. The province's five refineries have an annual capacity of 170m. bbls (27m. cu. metres).

Minerals

The total value of mineral production in 2014 was $11·0bn. CDN. In 2014 the most valuable commodities (production in $1m. CDN) were: gold, 3,376; nickel, 1,867; copper, 1,453; stone, 649; cement, 603. Total direct employment in the mining industry was 27,000 in 2013.

Agriculture

In 2006, 57,211 census farms operated on 5,386,453 ha.; total gross farm receipts in 2005 (excluding forest products sold) were $10·3bn. CDN. Net farm income in 2005 totalled $341·8m. CDN. For particulars of livestock *see* CANADA: Agriculture.

Forestry

The forested area totals 69·1m. ha., approximately 65% of Ontario's total area. Composition of Ontario forests: conifer, 56%; mixed, 26%; deciduous, 18%. The total growing stock (62% conifer, 38% hardwood) equals 5·3bn. cu. metres with an annual harvest level of 23m. cu. metres.

Industry

Ontario is Canada's most industrialized province, with GDP in 2007 of $532,842m. CDN, or 40·5% of the Canadian total. In 2006 manufacturing accounted for 19·1% of Ontario's GDP.

Leading manufacturing industries include: motor vehicles and parts; office and industrial electrical equipment; food processing; chemicals; and steel.

In 2006 Ontario was responsible for about 43% ($177·4bn. CDN) of Canada's merchandise exports, and for 96% ($69·2bn. CDN) of exports of motor vehicles and motor vehicle parts.

Labour

In 2015 the labour force was 7,426,100 (3,546,100 females), of whom 6,923,200 (3,316,100) were employed. The unemployment rate in 2015 was 6·8%.

International Trade

Imports and Exports

Ontario's imports were $241·7bn. CDN in 2008, up from $240·3bn. CDN in 2007. Exports were $188·8bn. CDN in 2008, down from $202·5bn. CDN.

Communications

Roads

Almost 40% of the population of North America is within one day's drive of Ontario. The National Highway System included 6,836 km of roads in Ontario in Dec. 2015. In 2016 there were 11,948,296 vehicle registrations in the province of which 8,538,070 were road motor vehicles, 2,680,796 trailers and 729,430 off-road, construction and farm vehicles.

Rail

In 2007 there were 17 short lines (eight provincially-licensed freight railways, four provincially-licensed tourist railways and five federally-licensed railways), plus the provincially-owned Ontario Northland Railway. The Canadian National and Canadian Pacific Railways operate in Ontario. Total track length, approximately 11,800 km. There is a metro and tramway network in Toronto.

Civil Aviation

Toronto's Lester B. Pearson International Airport is Canada's busiest, handling 30,911,000 passengers in 2010 (29,326,000 in 2009).

Shipping

The Great Lakes/St Lawrence Seaway, a 3,747 km system of locks, canal and natural water connecting Ontario to the Atlantic Ocean, has 95,000 sq. miles of navigable waters and serves the water-borne cargo needs of four Canadian provinces and 17 American States.

Telecommunications

In 2013, 87·4% of households had at least one mobile phone and 22·0% of households only had a mobile phone. 81% of households had home internet access in 2010.

Social Institutions

Justice

In 2015 there were 3,991 criminal code violations per 100,000 population, compared to a national average of 5,888 per 100,000 population.

Education

There is a provincial system of publicly financed elementary and secondary schools as well as private schools. Publicly financed elementary and secondary schools had a total enrolment of 1,368,283 pupils in 2014–15 (932,976 elementary and 435,307 secondary) and 89,295 teaching staff.

There are 22 publicly funded universities (Algoma, Brock, Carleton, Guelph, Hearst, Lakehead, Laurentian, McMaster, Nipissing, OCAD, Ontario Institute of Technology, Ottawa, Queen's, Royal Military College, Ryerson, Toronto, Trent, Waterloo, Western, Wilfred Laurier, Windsor and York). The University of Toronto is the largest university in both Ontario and Canada, with 87,363 students in 2015–16. York University is Ontario's second largest university, with 52,418 students in 2015–16, and Ryerson University the third largest (43,757 students in 2015–16). All publicly funded universities receive operating grants from the Ontario government. There are also 24 publicly financed Colleges of Applied Arts and Technology.

Government funding for education in Ontario in 2005–06 was $17·2bn. CDN.

Health
Ontario Health Insurance Plan health care services are available to eligible Ontario residents at no cost. The Ontario Health Insurance Plan (OHIP) is funded, in part, by an Employer Health Tax.

Prince Edward Island

Key Historical Events
The first recorded European visit was by Jacques Cartier in 1534, who named it Isle St-Jean. In 1719 it was settled by the French, but was taken from them by the English in 1758, annexed to Nova Scotia in 1763, and constituted a separate colony in 1769. Named Prince Edward Island in honour of Prince Edward, Duke of Kent, in 1799, it joined the Canadian Confederation on 1 July 1873.

Territory and Population
The province lies in the Gulf of St Lawrence, and is separated from the mainland of New Brunswick and Nova Scotia by Northumberland Strait. The area of the island is 5,660 sq. km (2,185 sq. miles). The population at the 2016 census was 142,907. Population of the principal cities (2011): Charlottetown (capital), 34,562; Summerside, 14,751.

Social Statistics
Births in 2013–14 numbered 1,429 and deaths 1,311. In 2012 the infant mortality rate was 3·5 per 1,000 live births. Life expectancy in the period 2009–11 was 82·9 years for females and 78·2 years for males.

Climate
The cool temperate climate is affected in winter by the freezing of the St Lawrence, which reduces winter temperatures. Charlottetown, Jan. –3°C to –11°C, July 14°C to 23°C. Annual rainfall 853·5 mm.

Constitution and Government
The provincial government is administered by a *Lieut.-Governor-in-Council* (Cabinet) and a *Legislative Assembly* of 27 members who are elected for up to five years. The province is represented by four members in the Senate and four in the House of Commons of Canada.

Recent Elections
At provincial elections on 4 May 2015 the governing Liberal Party won 18 of the available 27 seats (with 40·8% of the vote), the Progressive Conservatives took eight seats (37·4%) and the Greens took one seat (10·8%). The New Democratic Party won no seats (11·0%). Turnout was 85·9%.

Current Government
Lieut.-Governor: Antoinette Perry, O.PEI (sworn in 20 Oct. 2017).

The Liberal Party Executive Council was composed as follows in March 2019:

Premier: Wade MacLauchlan; b. 1954.

Minister of Transportation, Infrastructure and Energy: Paula Biggar. *Education, Early Learning and Culture, and Justice and Public Safety, and Attorney General:* Jordan Brown. *Communities, Land and Environment:* Richard Brown. *Workforce and Advanced Learning:* Sonny Gallant. *Agriculture and Fisheries:* Robert Henderson. *Health and Wellness:* Robert Mitchell. *Family and Human Services:* Tina Mundy. *Rural and Regional Development:* Pat Murphy. *Finance:* Heath MacDonald. *Economic Development and Tourism:* Chris Palmer.

Office of the Premier: http://www.gov.pe.ca/premier

Economy
GDP per person was $41,071 CDN in 2014.

Budget
Total revenue in 2008–09 was $1,576m. CDN (own source revenue, $1,006m. CDN; general purpose transfers, $367m. CDN; specific purpose transfers, $204m. CDN). Total expenditures in 2008–09 amounted to $1,673m. CDN (including: health, $491m. CDN; education, $409m. CDN; transportation and communication, $137m. CDN).

Performance
There was real GDP growth of 1·6% in 2011 and 1·0% in 2012.

Energy and Natural Resources

Electricity
Electricity generation totalled 0·9bn. kWh in 2013 (mainly wind energy).

Oil and Gas
In 2006 Prince Edward Island had more than 400,000 ha. under permit for oil and natural gas exploration.

Agriculture
Total area of farmland occupies approximately half of the total land area of 566,177 ha. Farm cash receipts in 2015 were $477m. CDN, with cash receipts from potatoes accounting for nearly 50% of the total. Cash receipts from dairy products, cattle and soybeans followed in importance. For particulars of livestock, *see* CANADA: Agriculture.

Forestry
Forests cover about 45% of Prince Edward Island's land surface. In 2013 roundwood harvested totalled 360,000 cu. metres. Domestic exports of pulp and paper products in 2015 were valued at $21,148,231 CDN.

Fisheries
The total catch of 114·8m. lb in 2008 had a landed value of $155·2m. CDN. Lobsters accounted for $100·7m. CDN; other shellfish, $44·0m. CDN; pelagic and estuarial, $9·7m. CDN; groundfish, $0·4m. CDN; seaplants, $0·4m. CDN.

Industry
The primary industries are agriculture, fisheries and tourism. Aerospace, bioscience, information technology and renewable energy are also important. Value of manufacturing sales in 2015 was $1,600·5m. CDN. The total value of retail trade in 2015 was $2,073·4m. CDN.

Labour
In 2015 the labour force was 81,700 (39,800 females), of whom 73,200 (36,200) were employed. The unemployment rate in 2015 was 10·4%.

Communications

Roads
In 2006 there were 3,700 km of paved highway and 1,900 km of unpaved road as well as 1,200 bridge structures. The Confederation Bridge, a 12·9 km two-lane bridge that joins Borden-Carleton with Cape Jourimain in New Brunswick, was opened in June 1997. A bus service operates twice daily to the mainland.

Civil Aviation
Prince Edward Island's busiest airport is Charlottetown, which handled 285,000 passengers in 2010 (271,000 in 2009). There were direct flights in 2010 to Edmonton, Halifax, Montreal, Ottawa and Toronto.

Shipping
Car ferries link the Island to New Brunswick year-round, with ice-breaking ferries during the winter months. Ferry services are operated to Nova Scotia from late April to mid-Dec. A service to the Magdalen Islands (Quebec) operates from 1 April to 31 Jan. The main ports are Summerside and Charlottetown, with additional capacity provided at Souris and Georgetown.

Telecommunications
In 2013, 78·5% of households had at least one mobile phone and 13·5% of households only had a mobile phone. 73% of households had home internet access in 2010.

Social Institutions

Justice

In 2009–10, 1,215 Criminal Code cases were disposed of in an adult criminal court. There were no homicides in 2010.

Education

~~In 2014 there were 10,717 elementary students and 9,447 secondary students~~ in both private and public schools. The University of Prince Edward Island had 4,015 undergraduate students and 389 graduate students in 2014. There are two community colleges—Holland College and the French-language Collège de l'Île.

Estimated government expenditure on education, 2013–14, $230·9m. CDN.

Culture

Tourism

In 2015 there were 1,410,316 visitors to Prince Edward Island, of which 1,191,255 were from elsewhere in Canada and 99,527 from the USA.

Quebec—Québec

Key Historical Events

Quebec was known as New France from 1534 to 1763; as the province of Quebec from 1763 to 1790; as Lower Canada from 1791 to 1846; as Canada East from 1846 to 1867, and when, by the union of the four original provinces, the Confederation of the Dominion of Canada was formed, it again became known as the province of Quebec (Québec).

The Quebec Act, passed by the British Parliament in 1774, guaranteed to the people of the newly conquered French territory in North America security in their religion and language, their customs and tenures, under their own civil laws. In a referendum on 20 May 1980, 59·5% voted against 'separatism'. At a further referendum on 30 Oct. 1995, 50·6% of votes cast were against Quebec becoming 'sovereign in a new economic and political partnership' with Canada. The electorate was 5m.; turnout was 93%. On 20 Aug. 1998 Canada's supreme court ruled that Quebec was prohibited by both the constitution and international law from seceding unilaterally from the rest of the country but that a clear majority in a referendum would impose a duty on the Canadian government to negotiate. Both sides claimed victory. On 27 Nov. 2006 Canada's parliament passed a motion recognizing that 'the Québécois form a nation within a united Canada'.

Territory and Population

The area of Quebec (as amended by the Labrador Boundary Award) is 1,542,056 sq. km (595,388 sq. miles), of which 1,365,128 sq. km is land area (including the Territory of Ungava, annexed in 1912 under the Quebec Boundaries Extension Act). The population at the 2016 census was 8,164,361. At the time of the 2011 census, 78·1% of the population reported French only as their mother tongue, 7·7% reported English only and 12·3% reported only a non-official language.

Principal cities (2011 census populations): Montreal, 1,649,519; Quebec (capital), 516,622; Laval, 401,553; Gatineau, 265,349; Longueuil, 231,409; Sherbrooke, 154,601; Saguenay, 144,746; Lévis, 138,769; Trois-Rivières, 131,338; Terrebonne, 106,322; Saint-Jean-sur-Richelieu, 92,394; Repentigny, 82,000; Brossard, 79,273; Drummondville, 71,852; Saint-Jérôme, 68,456; Granby, 63,433; Blainville, 53,510; Sainte-Hyacinthe, 53,236; Shawnigan, 50,060.

Social Statistics

Births in 2013–14 numbered 88,250 and deaths 61,050. In 2012 the infant mortality rate was 5·0 per 1,000 live births. Life expectancy in the period 2009–11 was 83·6 years for females and 79·4 years for males.

Climate

Cool temperate in the south, but conditions are more extreme towards the north. Winters are severe and snowfall considerable, but summer temperatures are quite warm. Quebec, Jan. −12·5°C, July 19·1°C. Annual rainfall 1,123 mm. Montreal, Jan. −10·7°C, July 20·2°C. Annual rainfall 936 mm.

Constitution and Government

There is a *Legislative Assembly* consisting of 125 members, elected in 125 electoral districts for four years. The province is represented by 24 members in the Senate and 78 in the House of Commons of Canada.

Recent Elections

At the elections of 1 Oct. 2018 the Coalition Avenir Québec won 74 seats with 37·4% of votes cast, the federalist Quebec Liberal party 32 seats with 24·8%, Québec Solidaire 10 seats with 16·1% and the separatist Parti Québécois 9 seats with 17·1%. Turnout was 66·4%.

Current Government

Lieut.-Governor: J. Michel Doyon (took office on 24 Sept. 2015).
Members of the Coalition Avenir Québec cabinet in March 2019:
Premier: François Legault; b. 1957.
Deputy Premier, and Minister of Public Security: Geneviève Guilbault. Education and Higher Education: Jean-François Roberge. Economy and Innovation: Pierre Fitzgibbon. Chair of the Conseil du trésor: Christian Dubé. Transport: François Bonnardel. Family: Mathieu Lacombe. Agriculture, Fisheries and Food: André Lamontagne. Forests, Wildlife and Parks: Pierre Dufour. Culture and Communications: Nathalie Roy. Health and Social Services: Danielle McCann. Finance: Eric Girard. Environment and the Fight Against Climate Change: Benoit Charette. Government House Leader, and Minister of Immigration, Diversity and Inclusiveness: Simon Jolin-Barrette. Justice: Sonia LeBel. International Relations and La Francophonie: Nadine Girault. Municipal Affairs and Housing: Andrée Laforest. Energy and Natural Resources: Jonatan Julien. Labour, Employment and Social Solidarity: Jean Boulet. Tourism: Caroline Proulx.
Government of Quebec Website: http://www.gouv.qc.ca

Economy

GDP per person in 2014 was $45,048 CDN.

Budget

Total revenue in 2008–09 was $101,392m. CDN (own source revenue, $85,211m. CDN; general purpose transfers, $9,332m. CDN; specific purpose transfers, $6,849m. CDN). Total expenditures in 2008–09 amounted to $107,491m. CDN (including: health, $24,620m. CDN; social services, $24,516m. CDN; education, $19,940m. CDN).

Performance

There was real GDP growth in 2011 of 2·0% and in 2012 of 1·5%.

Energy and Natural Resources

Electricity

Electricity generation totalled 206·8bn. kWh in 2013 (205·0bn. kWh hydro), representing 33·7% of Canada's production (the highest of any province or territory). Quebec is among the largest producers of hydro-electric power in the world.

Water

There are 4,500 rivers and 500,000 lakes in Quebec, which possesses 3% of the world's freshwater resources.

Minerals

For 2013 the value of mineral production was $8,095m. CDN. Chief minerals: iron ore, $2,821m. CDN; gold, $1,659m. CDN; nickel, $497m. CDN; zinc, $256m. CDN; copper, $240m. CDN. Non-metallic minerals produced include: titanium-dioxide, sulphur, salt, peat and quartz (silica). Among the building materials produced in 2013 were: stone, $494m. CDN; cement, $359m. CDN; sand and gravel, $121m. CDN.

Agriculture

In 2011 the agricultural area was 3,341,333 ha. The production of the principal crops was (2011 in 1,000 tonnes):

Crops	Production
Tame hay	3,900
Corn for grain	3,125
Fodder corn	2,000
Soya	800
Oats	223
Barley	196
Wheat	116
Mixed grains	42
Canola	36

There were 29,437 farms operating in 2011. Cash receipts, 2011, $7,968m. CDN (livestock and livestock products, 61·6%; crops, 30·2%; direct payments, 8·2%). Quebec was a net importer of food and agricultural produce in 2011. For particulars of livestock *see* CANADA: Agriculture.

Forestry

Forests cover an area of 761,100 sq. km. 343,214 sq. km are classified as accessible productive forest, of which 276,968 sq. km are public and 66,246 sq. km are privately owned.

Quebec leads the Canadian provinces in newsprint production, having nearly half of the Canadian estimated total. In 2012 the pulp and paper industry in Quebec had 44 factories, the annual production capacity of which totals 6·7m. tonnes.

Fisheries

The principal fish and seafood are Greenland halibut, Atlantic halibut, herring, snow crab, lobster and shrimp. The landed value in 2011 of fish, seafood and shellfish was $149m. CDN.

Industry

In 2010 there were 21,127 industrial establishments in the province; employees, 413,425; salaries and wages, $19,289m. CDN; value of shipments, $129,794m. CDN. Among the leading industries are primary metal manufacturing, food, transportation equipment, chemicals, and pulp and paper mills.

Labour

In 2015 the labour force was 4,434,200 (2,099,400 females), of whom 4,097,000 (1,960,200) were employed. The unemployment rate in 2015 was 7·6%.

International Trade

Imports and Exports

In 2014 Quebec's imports were valued at $90·2bn. CDN; value of exports, $75·8bn. CDN.

Communications

Roads

In 2013 there were approximately 185,000 km of roads. There were 6,082,303 motor vehicles registered in 2012.

Rail

There were (2013) 6,631 km of railway. There is a metro system in Montreal, which has four lines (71 km altogether) and 68 stations.

Civil Aviation

Quebec's busiest airports are Montreal (Pierre Elliott Trudeau International), which is the third busiest in Canada and handled 12,700,000 passengers in 2010, and Quebec City (Jean Lesage International Airport).

Telecommunications

In 2013, 78·4% of households had at least one mobile phone and 17·7% of households only had a mobile phone. 73% of households had home internet access in 2010.

Social Institutions

Justice

In 2015, 345,122 Criminal Code offences were reported; there were 77 homicides.

Education

Education is compulsory for children aged 6–16. Pre-school education and elementary and secondary training are free in some 2,362 public schools. There are 72 school boards. They are organized along linguistic lines, 60 French, nine English and three special school boards that serve native students in the Côte-Nord and Nord-du-Québec regions. 12·7% of the student population attends private schools: in 2010–11, 359 establishments were authorized to provide pre-school, elementary and secondary education. After six years of elementary and five years of secondary school education, students attend Cegep, a post-secondary educational institution. In 2010–11 college, pre-university and technical training for young and adult students

was provided by 48 Cegeps, 11 government schools and 47 private establishments.

In 2010–11 there were: in pre-kindergartens and kindergartens, 93,884 pupils; in primary schools, 461,632; in secondary schools, 351,540; in general education for adults, 309,376; in colleges (post-secondary, non-university), 218,000; and in universities, 281,948.

The operating expenditures of education institutions totalled $14,321·3m. CDN in 2012–13. This included $5,179·9m. CDN for universities and colleges, and $9,141·3m. CDN for public and private primary and secondary schools.

In 2010–11 the province had 18 universities and affiliated schools of which seven were major universities: four French-language universities—Université Laval (Quebec, founded 1852), Université de Montréal (opened 1876 as a branch of Laval, independent 1920), Université de Sherbrooke (founded 1954), Université du Québec (founded 1968, comprising ten regional branches); and three English-language universities—McGill University (Montreal, founded 1821), Bishop's University (Lennoxville, founded 1843) and Concordia University (Montreal, granted a charter 1975). Université de Montréal has two affiliated schools: HEC Montréal (École des Hautes Études Commerciales), a business school founded in 1907; and École Polytechnique de Montréal, an engineering school founded in 1873. In 2010–11 there were 188,843 full-time university students and 89,169 part-time.

Health

Quebec's socio-health network consisted of 294 public and private establishments in 2009, of which 191 were public.

Saskatchewan

Key Historical Events

Saskatchewan derives its name from its major river system, which the Cree Indians called 'Kis-is-ska-tche-wan', meaning 'swift flowing'. It officially became a province when it joined the Confederation on 1 Sept. 1905.

In 1670 Charles II granted to Prince Rupert and his friends a charter covering exclusive trading rights in 'all the land drained by streams finding their outlet in the Hudson Bay'. This included what is now Saskatchewan. The trading company was first known as The Governor and Company of Adventurers of England; later as the Hudson's Bay Company. In 1869 the Northwest Territories was formed, and this included Saskatchewan. The North-West Mounted Police Force was inaugurated four years later. In 1882 the District of Saskatchewan was formed and in 1885 the Canadian Pacific Railway's transcontinental line was completed, bringing a stream of immigrants to southern Saskatchewan. The Hudson's Bay Company surrendered its claim to territory in return for cash and land around the existing trading posts.

Territory and Population

Saskatchewan is bounded in the west by Alberta, in the east by Manitoba, in the north by the Northwest Territories and in the south by the USA. The area of the province is 651,036 sq. km (251,365 sq. miles), of which 591,670 sq. km is land area and 59,366 sq. km is water. The population at the 2016 census was 1,098,352. Population of cities, 2011 census: Saskatoon, 222,189; Regina (capital), 193,100; Prince Albert, 35,129; Moose Jaw, 33,274; Yorkton, 15,669; Swift Current, 15,503; North Battleford, 13,888; Estevan, 11,054; Weyburn, 10,484; Lloydminster, 9,772; Martensville, 7,716; Humboldt, 5,678; Melfort, 5,576.

Social Statistics

Births in 2013–14 numbered 15,345 and deaths 9,684. In 2012 the infant mortality rate was 5·5 per 1,000 live births. Life expectancy in the period 2009–11 was 82·2 years for females and 77·2 years for males.

Climate

A cold continental climate, with severe winters and warm summers. Rainfall amounts are greatest from May to Aug. Regina, Jan. 0°F (–17·8°C), July 65°F (18·3°C). Annual rainfall 15" (373 mm).

Constitution and Government

The provincial government is vested in a *Lieut.-Governor*, an *Executive Council* and a *Legislative Assembly* of 58 seats, elected for five years. Women were given the franchise in 1916. The province is represented by six members in the Senate and 14 in the House of Commons of Canada.

Recent Elections

In elections on 4 April 2016 the Saskatchewan Party (SP) won 51 of 61 seats (62·4% of the vote) and the New Democrats (NDP) 10 (30·2%).

Current Government

Lieut.-Governor: W. Thomas Molloy (took office 21 March 2018).

The Saskatchewan Party ministry comprised the following in March 2019:

Premier, President of the Executive Council and Minister of Intergovernmental Affairs: Scott Moe.

Deputy Premier and Minister of Education: Gordon Wyant. *Advanced Education:* Tina Beaudry-Mellor. *Agriculture:* David Marit. *Central Services:* Ken Cheveldayoff. *Corrections and Policing:* Christine Tell. *Crown Investments:* Joe Hargrave. *Energy and Resources:* Bronwyn Eyre. *Environment:* Dustin Duncan. *Finance:* Donna Harpauer. *Government Relations:* Warren Kaeding. *Health:* Jim Reiter. *Highways and Infrastructure:* Lori Carr. *Justice and Attorney General, and Labour Relations and Work Safety:* Don Morgan. *Parks, Culture and Sport:* Gene Makowsky. *Social Services:* Paul Merriman. *Trade and Export Development, and Immigration and Careers Training:* Jeremy Harrison.

Office of the Premier: http://www.gov.sk.ca/premier

Economy

GDP per capita in 2014 was $73,760 CDN.

Budget

Total revenue in 2008–09 was $17,032m. CDN (own source revenue, $14,955m. CDN; specific purpose transfers, $1,734m. CDN; general purpose transfers, $343m. CDN). Total expenditures in 2008–09 amounted to $14,325m. CDN (including: health, $4,189m. CDN; education, $3,365m. CDN; transportation and communication, $1,363m. CDN).

Performance

There was real GDP growth in 2011 of 5·8% (the highest rate of any of the Canadian provinces or territories that year) and in 2012 of 3·1%.

Energy and Natural Resources

Electricity

SaskPower (the Saskatchewan Power Corporation) generated 20,969m. kWh in 2011, 55% of which came from coal-fired power plants.

Minerals

In 2011 mineral sales were valued at $21,290m. CDN, of which (in $1m. CDN): petroleum, 12,369; potash, 6,853; others (including uranium, salt, natural gas, sand and gravel), 2,068.

Agriculture

Agriculture accounted for 11·4% of the provincial GDP in 2011, second to the mining sector which accounted for 13·4%. Saskatchewan normally produces about two-thirds of Canada's wheat. Wheat production in 2012 (in 1,000 tonnes) was 12,727·3 from 13·1m. acres; canola, 6,137·1 from 11·2m. acres; barley, 2,351·4 from 2·6m. acres; oats, 1,236·9 from 1·3m. acres; flax, 381·0 from 775,000 acres; rye, 148·6 from 310,000 acres. Livestock (1 July 2012): cattle and calves, 2·9m.; swine, 1·1m.; sheep and lambs, 127,000. Poultry in 2012: chickens, 26·6m.; turkeys, 883,000. Cash income from the sale of farm products in 2012 was $11,828m. CDN. At the 2011 census there were 36,952 farms in the province covering an area of 26,019,885 ha. (with 14,032,487 ha. of land under crops).

The South Saskatchewan River irrigation project, the main feature of which is the Gardiner Dam, was completed in 1967. It will ultimately provide for an area of 0·2m. to 0·5m. acres of irrigated cultivation in Central Saskatchewan. As of 2012, 247,158 acres were intensively irrigated. Total irrigated land in the province, 339,583 acres.

Forestry

Over half of Saskatchewan's area is forested, but only 117,000 sq. km are of commercial value at present. Forest products sales totalled $949m. CDN in 2016.

Fisheries

In 2010 commercial freshwater fisheries landings had a total weight of 2,731 tonnes (of which whitefish 1,137 tonnes) and a value of $3,192,000 CDN.

Industry

In 2011 there were 1,682 manufacturing establishments, employing 27,785 persons. In 2011 manufacturing value added totalled $4,424·6m. CDN; sale of manufactured goods totalled $12,577·5m. CDN. In 2012 total value of building permits was $3,114m. CDN. Total public and private investment in construction was $14,382m. CDN.

Labour

In 2015 the labour force was 604,100 (275,800 females), of whom 573,700 (263,100) were employed. The unemployment rate in 2015 was 5·0%.

Communications

Roads

In 2005 there were 26,168 km of provincial highways and 198,375 km of municipal roads (including prairie trails). Motor vehicles registered totalled 750,640 (2005). Bus services are provided by two major lines.

Rail

In 2005 there were approximately 9,513 km of railway track.

Civil Aviation

Saskatchewan's busiest airports are Saskatoon and Regina, which handled 1,196,000 and 1,102,000 passengers in 2010 respectively.

Telecommunications

In 2013, 86·1% of households had at least one mobile phone and 20·9% of households only had a mobile phone. 76% of households had home internet access in 2010.

Social Institutions

Justice

In 2009–10, 21,665 Criminal Code cases were disposed of in an adult criminal court. In 2010 there were 34 homicides (a rate of 3·3 per 100,000 population).

Education

In 2005–06 there were 28 school divisions serving 107,331 elementary pupils, 59,801 high-school students and 1,577 students enrolled in special classes. The Saskatchewan Institute of Applied Science and Technology (SIAST) had approximately 13,200 full-time and 29,000 part-time and extension course registration students in 2005–06.

The University of Saskatchewan was established at Saskatoon in 1907. In 2005–06 it had 15,300 full-time students, 4,000 part-time students and 961 full-time academic staff. The University of Regina, established in 1974, had 9,678 full-time and 2,977 part-time students and 425 full-time academic staff in 2005–06.

Culture

Tourism

In 2016 approximately 12·5m. visits were made to and within the province. In the same year tourists spent $2·2bn. CDN.

The Northwest Territories

Key Historical Events

The Territory was developed by the Hudson's Bay Company and the North West Company (of Montreal) from the 17th century. The Canadian government bought out the Hudson's Bay Company in 1869 and the Territory was annexed to Canada in 1870. The Arctic Islands lying north of the Canadian mainland were annexed to Canada in 1880.

A plebiscite held in March 1992 approved the division of the Northwest Territories into two separate territories. (For Nunavut *see* CONSTITUTION AND GOVERNMENT *below,* and NUNAVUT *on page* 301).

Territory and Population

The Northwest Territories comprises all that portion of Canada lying north of the 60th parallel of N. lat. except those portions within Nunavut, Yukon and the provinces of Quebec and Newfoundland and Labrador. The total area of the Territories was 3,426,320 sq. km, but since the formation of Nunavut is now 1,346,106 km. Of its five former administrative regions—Fort Smith,

Inuvik, Kitikmeot, Keewatin and Baffin—only Fort Smith and Inuvik remain in the Northwest Territories.

The population at the 2016 census was 41,786. The capital is Yellowknife, population (2011); 19,234. Other main centres (with population in 2011): Hay River (3,606), Inuvik (3,463), Fort Smith (2,093), Behchokò (1,926). Iqaluit and Rankin Inlet, formerly in the Northwest Territories, are now in Nunavut. In Aug. 2003 an agreement was reached for the Tlicho First Nation to assume control over 39,000 sq. km of land in the Northwest Territories (including Canada's two diamond mines), creating the largest single block of First Nations-owned land in Canada.

Social Statistics
Births in 2013–14 numbered 695 and deaths 198. In 2012 the infant mortality rate was 4·4 per 1,000 live births. Life expectancy in the period 2009–11 was 80·1 years for females and 76·3 years for males.

Climate
Conditions range from cold continental to polar, with long hard winters and short cool summers. Precipitation is low. Yellowknife, Jan. mean high −24·7°C, low −33°C; July mean high 20·7°C, low 11·8°C. Annual rainfall 26·7 cm.

Constitution and Government
The Northwest Territories is governed by a *Premier*, with a cabinet (the *Executive Council*) of eight members including the *Speaker*, and a *Legislative Assembly*, who choose the premier and ministers by consensus. There are no political parties. The Assembly is composed of 19 members elected for a four-year term of office. A *Commissioner* of the Northwest Territories is the federal government's senior representative in the Territorial government. The seat of government was transferred from Ottawa to Yellowknife when it was named Territorial Capital on 18 Jan. 1967. On 10 Nov. 1997 the governments of Canada and the Northwest Territories signed an agreement so that the territorial government could assume full responsibility to manage its elections.

Legislative powers are exercised by the Executive Council on such matters as taxation within the Territories in order to raise revenue, maintenance of justice, licences, solemnization of marriages, education, public health, property, civil rights and generally all matters of a local nature. The territory is represented by one member in the Senate and one in the House of Commons of Canada.

The Territorial government has assumed most of the responsibility for the administration of the Northwest Territories but political control of Crown lands. In a Territory-wide plebiscite in April 1982, a majority of residents voted in favour of dividing the Northwest Territories into two jurisdictions, east and west. Constitutions for an eastern and western government have been under discussion since 1992. A referendum was held in Nov. 1992 among the Inuit on the formation of a third territory, **Nunavut** ('Our Land'), in the eastern Arctic. Nunavut became Canada's third territory on 1 April 1999.

Recent Elections
On 23 Nov. 2015, 19 members (MLAs) were returned to the 18th Legislative Assembly. There were 59 candidates, 16 of whom were incumbents. All members are independent.

Current Government
Commissioner: Margaret M. Thom (since Sept. 2017).
      Members of the Executive Council of Ministers in March 2019:
      Premier, and Minister of the Executive, and Indigenous Affairs: Bob McLeod.
      Deputy Premier, and Minister of Environment and Natural Resources, and Finance: Robert C. McLeod. *Health and Social Services:* Glen Abernethy. *Municipal and Community Affairs:* Alfred Moses. *Education, Culture and Employment:* Caroline Cochrane. *Industry, Tourism and Investment, and Infrastructure:* Wally Schumann. *Lands, and Justice:* Louis Sebert.
Government of the Northwest Territories Website: http://www.gov.nt.ca

Economy
GDP per person in 2014 was $107,572 CDN, the highest of any Canadian province or territory.

Budget
Total revenue in 2008–09 was $1,624m. CDN (own source revenue, $593m. CDN; general purpose transfers, $820m. CDN; specific purpose transfers, $211m. CDN). Total expenditures in 2008–09 amounted to $1,730m. CDN (including: health, $377m. CDN; education, $316m. CDN; social services, $153m. CDN).

Performance
The Northwest Territories experienced a recession in 2011 with real GDP growth of −8·1%, but there was a slight recovery in 2012 when real GDP grew by 2·2%.

Energy and Natural Resources
Oil and Gas
Crude petroleum production was 578,000 cu. metres in 2015; natural gas production was 86m. cu. metres in 2015.

Minerals
The total value of mineral production in 2014 was $1,882m. CDN. Diamonds are by far the most important commodity ($1,791m. CDN in 2014). Tungsten ($84m. CDN in 2014) is the other major mineral mined.

Forestry
Forest land area in the Northwest Territories consists of 61·4m. ha., about 18% of the total land area. The principal trees are white and black spruce, jack-pine, tamarack, balsam poplar, aspen and birch. In 2015, 18,000 cu. metres of timber were produced.

Trapping and Game
Wildlife harvesting is the largest economic activity undertaken by aboriginal residents in the Northwest Territories. The value of the subsistence food harvest is estimated at $28m. CDN annually in terms of imports replaced. Fur-trapping (the most valuable pelts being white fox, wolverine, beaver, mink, lynx and red fox) was once a major industry, but has been hit by anti-fur campaigns. In 2009–10, 27,489 pelts worth $830,921 CDN were sold.

Fisheries
Fish marketed through the Freshwater Fish Marketing Corporation in 2005–06 totalled 734,000 kg at a value of $705,000 CDN, principally whitefish, northern pike and trout.

Industry
Mining is the largest private sector industry, with major mines for ore including gold, uranium and diamonds. Oil and gas exploration and development onshore and offshore are also becoming important.

Communications
Roads
The Mackenzie Route connects Grimshaw, Alberta, with Hay River, Pine Point, Fort Smith, Fort Providence, Rae-Edzo and Yellowknife. The Mackenzie Highway extension to Fort Simpson and a road between Pine Point and Fort Resolution have both been opened.

Highway service to Inuvik in the Mackenzie Delta was opened in spring 1980, extending north from Dawson, Yukon as the Dempster Highway. The Liard Highway connecting the communities of the Liard River valley to British Columbia opened in 1984.

In 2014 there were a total of 38,185 vehicle registrations, including 27,087 passenger motor vehicles and 5,806 trailers.

Rail
There is one small railway system in the north which runs from Hay River, on the south shore of Great Slave Lake, 435 miles south to Grimshaw, Alberta, where it connects with the Canadian National Railways, but it is not in use.

Civil Aviation
The busiest airport is Yellowknife, which handled 319,000 passengers in both 2009 and 2010.

Shipping
A direct inland-water transportation route for about 1,700 miles is provided by the Mackenzie River and its tributaries, the Athabasca and Slave rivers. Subsidiary routes on Lake Athabasca, Great Slave Lake and Great Bear Lake

total more than 800 miles. Communities in the eastern Arctic are resupplied by ship each summer via the Atlantic and Arctic Oceans or Hudson Bay.

Social Institutions

Justice
In 2009–10, 1,706 Criminal Code cases were disposed of in an adult criminal court. In 2010 there was one homicide (a rate of 2·3 per 100,000 population).

Education
The Education System in the Northwest Territories is comprised of eight regional bodies (boards) that have responsibilities for the K-12 education programme.

For the 2010–11 school year there were 46 public plus three (Catholic) private schools operating in the NWT. Within this system there were 758 teachers, excluding those at Aurora College and community learning centres, for 8,576 students. 98% of students have access to high school programmes in their home communities. There is a full range of courses available in the school system, including academic, French immersion, Aboriginal language, cultural programmes, and technical and occupational programmes.

A range of post-secondary programmes are available through the Northwest Territories' Aurora College. The majority of these programmes are offered at the three main campus locations: Inuvik, Yellowknife and Fort Smith.

Health
In 2011 there were eight health authorities. Expenditure on health and social services totalled $349·7m. CDN in 2009–10.

Welfare
Welfare services are provided by professional social workers. Facilities included (2006): family violence services in seven communities, eight helplines, seven group homes or shelters and one residential treatment centre.

Nunavut

Key Historical Events
Inuit communities were to be found in what is now the Canadian Arctic between 4500 BC and AD 1000. By the 19th century these communities were under the jurisdiction of the Northwest Territories. In 1963 the Canadian government first introduced legislation to divide the territory, a proposal that failed at the order paper stage. In 1973 the Comprehensive Land Claims Policy was established which sought to define the rights and benefits of the Aboriginal population in a land claim settlement agreement. The Northwest Territories Legislative Assembly voted in favour of dividing the territory in 1980, and in a public referendum of 1982, 56% of votes cast were also for the division. In 1992 the proposed boundary was ratified in a public vote and the Inuit population approved their land claim settlement. A year later, the Nunavut Act (creating the territory) and the Nunavut Land Claim Agreement Act were passed by parliament. Iqaluit was selected as the capital in 1995.

On 15 Feb. 1999 Nunavut held elections for its Legislative Assembly. The territory was officially designated and the government inaugurated on 1 April 1999.

Territory and Population
The total area of the region is 2,093,190 sq. km or about 21% of Canada's total mass, making Nunavut Canada's largest territory. It contains seven of Canada's 12 largest islands and two-thirds of the country's coastline. The territory is divided into three regions: Qikiqtaaluk (Baffin), Kivalliq (Keewatin) and Kitikmeot. The total population at the 2016 census was 35,944. The population is divided up into 25 communities of which the largest is in the capital Iqaluit, numbering 7,740 (2016).

The native Inuit language is Inuktitut.

Social Statistics
Births in 2013–14 numbered 885 and deaths 182. In 2012 the infant mortality rate was 21·4 per 1,000 live births. Life expectancy in the period 2009–11 was 73·9 years for females and 68·8 years for males.

Climate
Conditions range from cold continental to polar, with long hard winters and short cool summers. In Iqaluit there can be as little as four hours sunshine per day in winter and up to 21 hours per day at the summer solstice. Iqaluit, Jan. mean high –22°C; July mean high, 15°C.

Constitution and Government
Government is by a *Legislative Assembly* of 22 elected members, who then choose a leader and ministers by consensus. There are no political parties. Government is highly decentralized, consisting of ten departments spread over 11 different communities. By 2020 Inuktitut is intended to be the working language of government but government agencies will also offer services in English and French. Although the Inuits are the dominant force in public government, non-Inuit citizens have the same voting rights. The territory is represented by one member in the Senate and one in the House of Commons of Canada.

Recent Elections
Legislative Assembly elections were held on 30 Oct. 2017. There were 72 non-partisan candidates; 22 were elected.

Current Government
Commissioner: Nellie Taptaqut Kusugak (since May 2015—acting until June 2015).

In March 2019 the cabinet was as follows:

Premier, and Minister of Executive and Intergovernmental Affairs, Aboriginal Affairs, Environment, and Energy: Joe Savikataaq (took office on 14 June 2018).

Deputy Premier, and Minister of Economic Development and Transportation: David Akeeagok.

Minister of Community and Government Services, and Human Resources: Lorne Kusugak. *Education, Culture and Heritage, and Languages:* David Joanasie. *Finance and Chairman of the Financial Management Board, and Health:* George Hickes. *Family Services:* Elisapee Sheutiapik. *Justice:* Jeannie Ehaloak.

Government of Nunavut Website: http://www.gov.nu.ca

Economy
GDP per person was $68,924 CDN in 2014.

Currency
The Canadian dollar is the standard currency.

Budget
Total revenue in 2008–09 was $1,385m. CDN (general purpose transfers, $979m. CDN; specific purpose transfers, $224m. CDN; own source revenue, $182m. CDN). Total expenditures in 2008–09 amounted to $1,402m. CDN (including: health, $287m. CDN; education, $243m. CDN; housing, $194m. CDN).

Performance
Real GDP grew by 4·8% in 2011 and 1·2% in 2012.

Energy and Natural Resources

Minerals
There are two lead and zinc mines operating in the High Arctic region. There are also known deposits of copper, gold, silver and diamonds.

Hunting and Trapping
Most communities still rely on traditional foodstuffs such as caribou and seal. The Canadian government now provides meat inspections so that caribou and musk ox meat can be sold across the country.

Fisheries
Fishing is still very important in Inuit life. The principal catches are shrimp, scallops and arctic char.

Industry
The main industries are mining, tourism, fishing, hunting and trapping and arts and crafts production.

Labour
In 2013 the labour force numbered 14,500, of whom 12,500 were in employment. The employment rate in 2013 was 48·5% for Inuit and 89·3% for non-Inuit.

Communications

Roads

There is one 21 km government-maintained road between Arctic Bay and Nanisivik. There are a few paved roads in Iqaluit and Rankin Inlet, but most are unpaved. Some communities have local roads and tracks but Kivalliq has no direct land connections with southern Canada.

Civil Aviation

The busiest airport is Iqaluit, which handled 129,000 passengers in 2010.

Shipping

There is an annual summer sea-lift by ship and barge for transport of construction materials, dry goods, non-perishable food, trucks and cars.

Telecommunications

In 2010, 85% of households had telephones. Because of the wide distances between communities, there is a very high rate of internet use in Nunavut. However, line speeds are slow and there is a problem with satellite bounce.

Social Institutions

Justice

In 2009–10, 1,494 Criminal Code cases were disposed of in an adult criminal court. In 2010 there were six homicides (a rate of 18·1 per 100,000 population—by some way the highest of any Canadian province or territory).

Education

Approximately one quarter of Nunavut's population aged over 15 have less than Grade 9 schooling. Training and development is seen as central to securing a firm economic foundation for the province.

Courses in computer science, business management and public administration may be undertaken at Arctic College. In 2010–11 there were 42 schools with 8,855 students.

Health

There is one hospital in Iqaluit. 26 health centres provide nursing care for communities. For more specialized treatment, patients of Qikiqtaaluk may be flown to Montreal, patients in Kivalliq to Churchill or Winnipeg and patients in Kitikmeot to Yellowknife's Stanton Regional Hospital.

Culture

Tourism

Nunavut has four national parks—Auyuittuq, Quttinirpaaq, Sirmilik and Ukkusiksalik—offering the opportunity of seeing Inuit life first-hand. Tourism generates $30m. CDN per year for the Territory, with 20% of visitors arriving on cruise ships. During the 2008 high season (June–Oct.) there were 33,000 visitors.

Yukon

Key Historical Events

The territory owes its fame to the discovery of gold in the Klondike at the end of the 19th century. Formerly part of the Northwest Territories, the Yukon joined the Dominion as a separate territory on 13 June 1898.

Yukon First Nations People lived a semi-nomadic subsistence long before the region was established as a territory. The earliest evidence of human activity was found in caves containing stone tools and animal bones estimated to be 20,000 years old. The Athapaskan cultural linguistic tradition to which most Yukon First Nations belong is more than 1,000 years old. The territory's name comes from the native 'Yu-kun-ah' for the great river that drains most of this area.

The Yukon was created as a district of the Northwest Territories in 1895. The Klondike Gold Rush in the late 1890s saw thousands pouring into the gold fields of the Canadian northwest. Population at the peak of the rush reached 40,000. This event spurred the federal government to set up basic administrative structures in the Yukon. The territory was given the status of a separate geographical and political entity with an appointed legislative council in 1898. In 1953 the capital was moved south from Dawson City to Whitehorse, where most of the economic activity was centred. The federal government granted the Yukon responsible government in 1979.

The *Yukon Act* of 1 April 2003 gave the territory more control over its own governance and changed its name from the Yukon Territory to Yukon.

Territory and Population

The territory consists of one city, three towns, four villages, two hamlets, 13 unincorporated communities and eight rural communities. It is situated in the northwestern region of Canada and comprises 482,443 sq. km of which 8,052 sq. km is fresh water.

The population at the 2016 census was 35,874. Yukon had the fastest-growing population of any Canadian province or territory between 2006 and 2011, with an 11·6% increase over the five-year period.

Principal centres in 2011 were Whitehorse, the capital, 23,276; Dawson City, 1,319; Watson Lake, 802; Haines Junction, 593; Carmacks, 503.

Yukon represents 4·8% of Canada's total land area.

Social Statistics

Births in 2013–14 numbered 439 and deaths 221. In 2012 the infant mortality rate was 2·2 per 1,000 live births. Life expectancy in the period 2009–11 was 79·6 years for females and 75·2 years for males.

Climate

Temperatures in Yukon are usually more extreme than those experienced in the southern provinces of Canada. A cold climate in winter with moderate temperatures in summer provide a considerable annual range of temperature and moderate rainfall.

Whitehorse, Jan. –18·7°C (–2·0°F), July 14°C (57·2°F). Annual precipitation 268·8 mm. Dawson City, Jan. –30·7°C (–23·3°F), July 15·6°C (60·1°F). Annual precipitation 182·7 mm.

Constitution and Government

Yukon was constituted a separate territory on 13 June 1898. The *Yukon Legislative Assembly* consists of 19 elected members and functions in much the same way as a provincial legislature. The seat of government is at Whitehorse. It consists of an *Executive Council* with parliamentary powers similar to those of a provincial cabinet. The Yukon government consists of 14 departments, as well as a Workers' Compensation Health and Safety Board and four Crown corporations. The territory is represented by one member in the Senate and one in the House of Commons of Canada.

Recent Elections

At elections held on 7 Nov. 2016 the Liberal Party took 11 of the available 19 seats; the Yukon Party 6; and the New Democratic Party 2.

Current Government

Commissioner: Angélique Bernard (took office on 12 March 2018).

In March 2019 the Liberal Party Ministry comprised:

Premier, Minister of the Executive Council Office, and Finance: Sandy Silver.

Deputy Premier, and Minister of Energy, Mines, and Resources, and Economic Development: Ranj Pillai. *Justice, and Education:* Tracy-Anne McPhee. *Community Services:* John Streicker. *Health and Social Services, and Environment:* Pauline Frost. *Highways and Public Works, and Public Service Commission:* Richard Mostyn. *Tourism and Culture:* Jeanie Dendys.

Government of Yukon Website: http://www.gov.yk.ca

Economy

GDP per person was $70,370 CDN in 2014.

Budget

Total revenue in 2008–09 was $990m. CDN (general purpose transfers, $575m. CDN; own source revenue, $254m. CDN; specific purpose transfers, $160m. CDN). Total expenditures in 2008–09 amounted to $1,019m. CDN (including: transportation and communication, $165m. CDN; education, $157m. CDN; health, $138m. CDN).

Performance

Real GDP grew by 4·3% in 2011 and then 2·6% in 2012.

Energy and Natural Resources

Electricity

Electricity generation totalled 0·4bn. kWh in 2013 (mainly hydro).

Minerals

Gold and silver are the chief minerals. There are also deposits of lead, zinc, copper, tungsten and iron ore. Gold deposits, both hard rock and placer, are being mined.

The total value of mineral production in 2014 was $408m. CDN. In 2014 the most valuable commodities (production in $1m. CDN) were: copper, 159; gold, 123; silver, 57.

Agriculture

Many areas have suitable soils and climate for the production of forages, vegetables, domestic livestock and game farming. The greenhouse industry is Yukon's largest horticulture sector.

In 2016 there were 142 farms operating full- and part-time. The total area of farms was 10,330 ha. of which 6,801 ha. were under production.

Gross farm receipts in 2016 were estimated at $4·3m. CDN. Total farm capital at market value in 2006 was $66·1m. CDN.

Forestry

The forests, covering 281,000 sq. km of the territory, are part of the great Boreal forest region of Canada, which covers 58% of Yukon.

Fur Trade

The fur-trapping industry is considered vital to rural and remote residents and especially First Nations people wishing to maintain a traditional lifestyle. In 2009, 2,324 wildlife pelts (valued at $199,546 CDN) were produced.

Fisheries

Commercial fishing concentrates on chinook salmon, chum salmon, lake trout and whitefish.

Industry

The key sectors of the economy are tourism and government.

Labour

The 2006 labour force average was 16,200, of whom 15,500 were employed.

International Trade

Imports and Exports

In 2012 merchandise imports were valued at $86·1m. CDN and merchandise exports at $215·6m. CDN. Resource-based goods accounted for 95·6% of the value of Yukon's exports in 2012; manufactured goods accounted for 62·2% of imports.

Communications

Roads

The Alaska Highway and branch highway systems connect Yukon's main communities with Alaska, the Northwest Territories, southern Canada and the United States. The 733 km Dempster Highway north of Dawson City connects with Inuvik, in the Northwest Territories. In 2006 there were 4,902·5 km of roads maintained by the government of Yukon: 3,780·8 km is primary (including the 998·1 km Alaska Highway); 1,121·7 km is secondary. Vehicles registered in 2006 totalled 29,003 (excluding buses, motorcycles and trailers), including 26,621 passenger vehicles.

Rail

The 176 km White Pass and Yukon Railway connected Whitehorse with year-round ocean shipping at Skagway, Alaska, but was closed in 1982. A modified passenger service was restarted in 1988 to take cruise ship tourists from Skagway to Carcross, Yukon, over the White Pass summit.

Civil Aviation

The busiest airport is Whitehorse (Erik Nielsen Whitehorse International Airport), which handled 230,000 passengers in 2010.

Shipping

The majority of goods are shipped into the territory by truck over the Alaska and Stewart-Cassiar Highways. Some goods are shipped through the ports of Skagway and Haines, Alaska, and then trucked to Whitehorse for distribution throughout the territory.

Social Institutions

Justice

In 2009–10, 1,050 Criminal Code cases were disposed of in an adult criminal court. In 2010 there was one homicide (a rate of 2·9 per 100,000 population).

Education

The Yukon Department of Education operates (with the assistance of elected school boards) the territory's 29 schools, both public and private, from kindergarten to grade 12. In May 2006 there were 5,148 pupils. There is also one French First Language school and three Roman Catholic schools. The total enrolment figure for Yukon College in 2005–06 was 5,057. The Whitehorse campus is the administrative and programme centre for 13 other campuses located throughout the territory. In 2005–06 a total of 600 full-time and 4,457 part-time students enrolled in programmes and courses.

Health

In 2006 there were two hospitals with 71 staffed beds, 14 health centres, 74 resident doctors and 16 resident dentists.

Culture

Tourism

In 2006, 396,377 visitors came to Yukon. Tourism is the largest private sector employer. In 2005 approximately 80% of employees in Yukon worked for businesses that reported some level of tourism revenue. In 2005, 15% of businesses generated more than a third of gross revenues from tourism.

Further Reading

Canada

Canadian Annual Review of Politics and Public Affairs. From 1960
Canadian Encyclopedia. 2000
Brown, R. C., *An Illustrated History of Canada.* 1991
Dawson, R. M. and Dawson, W. F., *Democratic Government in Canada.* 5th ed. 1989
Fierlbeck, Katherine, *The Development of Political Thought in Canada: An Anthology.* 2005
Jackson, R. J. and Jackson, D., *Politics in Canada: Culture, Institutions, Behaviour and Public Policy.* 7th ed. 2009
O'Reilly, Marc, *Handbook of Canadian Foreign Policy.* 2006
Silver, A. I. (ed.) *Introduction to Canadian History.* 1994
Other more specialized titles are listed under CONSTITUTION AND GOVERNMENT *above.*
Library and Archives Canada: 395 Wellington Street, Ottawa, K1A 0N4. *Librarian and Archivist of Canada:* Guy Berthiaume.
National Statistical Office: Statistics Canada, 150 Tunney's Pasture Driveway, Ottawa, Ontario, K1A 0T6. *Chief Statistician:* Anil Arora.
Website: http://www.statcan.gc.ca

Alberta

Savage, H., Kroetsch, R., Wiebe, R., *Alberta.* 1993
Statistical office: Alberta Finance, Statistics, Room 259, Terrace Bldg, 9515–107 St., Edmonton, AB T5K 2C3.
Websites: http://www.albertacanada.com; http://www.finance.alberta.ca/aboutalberta/index.html

British Columbia

Barman, J., *The West beyond the West: a History of British Columbia.* 1991
Statistical office: BC STATS, Ministry of Finance and Corporate Relations, P.O. Box 9410, Stn. Prov. Govt., Victoria V8W 9V1.
Website: http://www.bcstats.gov.bc.ca

Manitoba

Statistical office: Manitoba Bureau of Statistics, 910–386 Broadway, Winnipeg, MB, Canada, R3C 3R6.
Website: https://www.gov.mb.ca/mbs

New Brunswick

Industrial Information: Dept. of Business New Brunswick, Fredericton. *Economic Information:* Dept. of Finance, New Brunswick Statistics Agency, Fredericton. *General Information:* Communications New Brunswick, Fredericton.

Newfoundland and Labrador

Statistical office: Newfoundland & Labrador Statistics Agency, POB 8700, St John's, NL A1B 4J6.
Website: http://www.stats.gov.nl.ca

Nova Scotia

Statistical office: Statistics Division, Department of Finance, POB 187, Halifax, Nova Scotia B3J 2N3.
Website: http://www.novascotia.ca/finance/en/home/default.aspx

Ontario

Statistical Information: Annual publications of the Ontario Ministry of Finance include: *Ontario Statistics; Ontario Budget; Public Accounts; Financial Report.*

Prince Edward Island

Baldwin, D. O., *Abegweit: Land of the Red Soil.* 1985

Quebec—Québec

Dickinson, J. A. and Young, B., *A Short History of Quebec.* 4th ed. 2008
Statistical office: Institut de la statistique du Québec, 200 chemin Sainte-Foy, Québec, G1R 5T4.
Website: http://www.stat.gouv.qc.ca

Saskatchewan

Archer, J. H., *Saskatchewan: A History.* 1980
Statistical office: Bureau of Statistics, 9th Floor, 2350 Albert St., Regina, SK, S4P 4A6.

Website: http://www.saskatchewan.ca/government/government-data/bureau-of-statistics

The Northwest Territories

Northwest Territories—2017: By the Numbers. Online only
Zaslow, M., *The Opening of the Canadian North 1870–1914.* 1971
Statistical office: Bureau of Statistics, Government of the Northwest Territories, PO Box 1320, Yellowknife, NWT X1A 2L9.
Website: http://www.statsnwt.ca

Nunavut

The Nunavut Handbook. 2004

Yukon

Annual Report of the Government of Yukon.
Yukon Executive Council, *Annual Statistical Review.*
Berton, P., *Klondike.* (Rev. ed.) 1987
Coates, K. and Morrison, W., *Land of the Midnight Sun: A History of the Yukon.* 1988
Statistical office: Bureau of Statistics, Executive Council Office, Box 2703, Whitehorse, Yukon Y1A 2C6. There is also a Yukon Archive at Yukon College, Whitehorse.
Website: http://www.eco.gov.yk.ca/stats

Central African Republic

République Centrafricaine

Capital: Bangui
Population projection, 2020: 4·92m
GNI per capita, 2017: (PPP$) 663
HDI/world rank, 2017: 0·367/188
Internet domain extension: .cf

Key Historical Events

One of the four territories of French Equatorial Africa, the Central African Republic became independent on 13 Aug. 1960. A constitution of 1976 provided for a parliamentary democracy to be known as the Central African Empire. President Bokassa became Emperor Bokassa I. He was overthrown in 1979. In 1981 Gen. André Kolingba took power, initiating a gradual return to constitutional rule.

On 5 June 1996, following an army mutiny, President Patassé accepted an agreement brokered by France which led to the formation of a government of national unity. But mutineers demanded the replacement of President Patassé. France chaired a mediation committee of various neighbouring French-speaking states. An agreement to end the mutiny was signed in 1997 and a peacekeeping force from neighbouring states, MISAB, was set up. Conflicts between the mutineers and MISAB continued until a ceasefire was concluded on 2 July 1997. There was an attempted coup on 28 May 2001, allegedly led by Gen. Kolingba, who had been the country's military ruler from 1981 to 1993. However, it failed following several days of fighting in and around the capital, Bangui. Fighting erupted once more in Oct. 2002 after another coup attempt. In March 2003 a further coup saw Gen. François Bozizé, a former army chief, seize power.

Bozizé claimed victory in the presidential election of May 2005. Despite reaching peace agreements in 2008 with two of the three main rebel groups in the country, his tenure was marked by violent civil unrest. In Sept. 2007 the UN established a peacekeeping force to protect civilians affected by the fighting in Darfur in neighbouring Sudan, withdrawing the mission three years later. In Jan. 2011 Bozizé won a further term in office. However, in March 2013 he fled the country following a coup by Séléka coalition rebel forces led by Michel Djotodia, who suspended the constitution and dissolved parliament. Djotodia was sworn in as president in Aug. 2013, with the UN secretary-general Ban Ki-moon condemning the 'total breakdown of law and order' in the country. Amid increasing sectarian violence, Djotodia resigned in Jan. 2014 and was replaced as president by Catherine Samba-Panza, the mayor of Bangui, on an interim basis. At its peak in 2014, 930,000 people were internally displaced by the conflict, with 190,000 refugees fleeing to neighbouring countries between Dec. 2013 and Aug. 2014. In April 2014 the UN agreed to send a 12,000-strong peacekeeping force to the country but violence continued to plague the country into 2015. In March 2016 the swearing in of Faustin-Archange Touadéra following his victory in presidential elections the previous month heralded an end to the period of transitional government.

Territory and Population

The republic is bounded in the north by Chad, northeast by Sudan, east by South Sudan, south by the Democratic Republic of the Congo and the Republic of the Congo, and west by Cameroon. Area, 622,984 sq. km (240,534 sq. miles). At the last census, in 2003, the population was 3,895,139. The United Nations gave an estimated population for 2013 of 4·50m.; density, 7 per sq. km. In 2011, 39·2% of the population were urban.

The UN gives a projected population for 2020 of 4·92m.

The country is administratively divided into 14 prefectures, the two economic prefectures of Nana Grebizi and Sangha M'baéré and the autonomous commune of Bangui (with capitals): Bamingui-Bangoran (Ndele), Bangui (Bangui), Basse-Kotto (Mobaye), Haute-Kotto (Bria), Haut-M'bomou (Obo), Kemo (Sibut), Lobaye (M'baiki), Mambere Kadéi (Berbérati), M'bomou (Bangassou), Nana Grebizi (Kaga-Bandoro), Nana-Mambere (Bouar), Ombella-M'poko (Bimbo), Ouaka (Bambari), Ouham (Bossangoa), Ouham-Pendé (Bozoum), Sangha M'baéré (Nola), Vakaga (Birao).

The capital, Bangui, had an estimated population in 2014 of 781,000. Other main towns are Bimbo, Berbérati, Carnot, Bambari and Bouar.

There are a number of ethnic groups, the largest being Gbaya (34%), Banda (27%) and Mandja (21%).

Sango and French are the official languages.

Social Statistics

2008 births (estimates), 154,000; deaths, 74,000. Estimated birth rate in 2008 was 35·4 per 1,000 population; estimated death rate, 17·0. Infant mortality, 2010 (per 1,000 live births), 106. Expectation of life in 2013 was 48·3 years for males and 52·1 for females. Annual population growth rate, 2000–08, 1·8%. Fertility rate, 2008, 4·8 children per woman.

Climate

A tropical climate with little variation in temperature. The wet months are May, June, Oct. and Nov. Bangui, Jan. 31·9°C, July 20·7°C. Annual rainfall 1,289·3 mm. Ndele, Jan. 36·3°C, July 30·5°C. Annual rainfall 203·6 mm.

Constitution and Government

Under the Constitution adopted by a referendum on 21 Nov. 1986, the sole legal political party was the *Rassemblement Démocratique Centrafricain*. In Aug. 1992 the Constitution was revised to permit multi-party democracy. Further constitutional reforms followed a referendum in Dec. 1994, including the establishment of a *Constitutional Court*. Following the coup of March 2003 Gen. François Bozizé suspended the constitution and dissolved parliament. However, at a referendum on 5 Dec. 2004, 90·4% of voters approved the adoption of a new constitution; voter participation was 77·4%. The new constitution resembled the previous one but permitted the President to serve not more than two terms of five years. However, the constitution was suspended by Michel Djotodia after he seized power in March 2013.

A new constitution was promulgated on 30 March 2016, after receiving 93% backing in a referendum held the previous Dec. It established a Senate to operate in addition to the pre-existing 140-member National Assembly, and retained the limit of two five-year presidential terms. A special criminal court to try particularly serious crimes and a national election authority were also set up.

National Anthem

'La Renaissance' ('Rebirth'); words by B. Boganda, tune by H. Pepper.

Recent Elections

In the first round of presidential elections held on 30 Dec. 2015, former prime minister Anicet-Georges Dologuélé won 23·8% of the vote against Faustin-Archange Touadéra (another former prime minister) with 19·4%, Désiré Nzanga Kolingba with 12·6% and Martin Ziguélé (a third former prime minister) with 10·8%. A further 26 candidates took part in the poll. The incumbent acting president Catherine Samba-Panza was barred from participating under rules set by the transitional government. Touadéra won the second round run-off on 14 Feb. 2016 with 62·7% of the vote against Dologuélé with 37·3%.

Parliamentary elections were held on 30 Dec. 2015. The result of the first round was annulled owing to irregularities, and a rerun held on 14 Feb. and 31 March 2016. Independents won 60 of 140 seats, the National Union for Democracy and Progress 16, the Central African Union for Renewal 11, the Movement for the Liberation of the Central African People 10 and the Central African Democratic Rally 8. A number of smaller parties won the remaining seats.

© Springer Nature Limited 2020
Palgrave Macmillan (ed.), *The Statesman's Yearbook 2020*,
https://doi.org/10.1057/978-1-349-95940-2_45

Current Government

In March 2019 the government comprised the following:

President: Faustin-Archange Touadéra; b. 1957 (ind.; sworn in 30 March 2016).

Prime Minister: Firmin Ngrébada; b. 1968 (ind.; sworn in 27 Feb. 2019).

Minister of Agriculture and Rural Development: Honoré Feizoure. *Arts, Culture and Tourism:* Dieudonné Ndomaté. *Civil Service:* Bertin Béa. *Commerce and Industry:* Hugues Tchemeuni. *Communication and the Media:* Ange-Maxime Kazagui. *Economy, Planning and Co-operation:* Félix Moloua. *Energy Development and Water Resources:* Guismala Amza. *Environment and Sustainable Development:* Thierry Kamach. *Finance and Budget:* Henri-Marie Dondra. *Foreign Affairs and Central Africans Abroad:* Sylvie Baïpo-Temon. *Health and Population:* Pierre Somsé. *Higher Education:* Jean-Jacques Sanzé. *Humanitarian Action and National Reconciliation:* Virginie Mbaïkoua. *Interior, in Charge of Public Security:* Brig.-Gen. Henri Wanzet-Linguissara. *Justice, Human Rights and Keeper of the Seals:* Flavien Mbata. *Labour, Employment, Social Protection and Vocational Training:* Jean-Christophe Nguinza. *Livestock and Animal Health:* Souleymane Daouda. *Mines and Geology:* Léopold Mboli-Fatrane. *Modernization of the Administration and Innovation of the Public Service Sector:* Adama Chaïbou. *National Defence and Reconstruction of the Army:* Marie-Noëlle Koyara. *Posts and Telecommunication:* Justin Gourna-Zacko. *Primary, Secondary and Technical Education, and Literacy:* Aboubakar Moukadas-Nouré. *Promotion of Women, Family and Children:* Aline-Gisèle Pana. *Public Works and Road Maintenance:* Moustapha Moctar. *Scientific Research and Technological Innovation:* Ginette Amara. *Small and Medium Businesses, Handicrafts and Informal Sector:* Mireille Sanghami. *Territorial Administration, Decentralization and Local Development:* Augustin Yangana-Yahoté. *Transport and Civil Aviation:* Arnaud Djoubaye-Abazène. *Urban Affairs, Town Planning and Housing:* Gina Lawson Roosalem. *Water, Forests, Hunting and Fishing:* Amit Idriss. *Youth and Sports:* Régis Lionel Dounda. *Minister in Charge of Disarmament, Demobilization, Reintegration and Repatriation:* Maxime Mokom. *Minister in Charge of La Francophonie and State Protocol:* Chancel Sekode Ndeugbayi. *Minister in Charge of Relations with Institutions:* Eugénie Lucienne Ngbondo. *General Secretariat of the Government:* Maxime Balalou.

Office of the Prime Minister (French only): http://primature.govcf.org

Current Leaders

Faustin-Archange Touadéra

Position
President

Introduction
A former prime minister, Faustin-Archange Touadéra was elected president on 14 Feb. 2016. Widely considered to have been an outsider in the presidential race, he faced a formidable task in reconciling a country riven by civil war since 2013.

Early Life
Touadéra was born 21 April 1957 in Bangui, one of ten children. He studied at the Universities of Bangui and Abidjan before earning a doctorate in mathematics from Lille University of Science and Technology in France.

After returning from Lille in 1987 he became an assistant mathematics lecturer at the University of Bangui and, from 1989, vice-dean of its faculty of science. In 1992 he was appointed director of the Teachers' Training College in Bangui. He joined the Inter-State Committee for the Standardisation of Mathematics Programs in French-speaking Countries and the Indian Ocean in 1999, serving as committee president from 2001–03. In 2004 he earned a second doctorate in mathematics from the University of Yaoundé in Cameroon and became vice-chancellor of the University of Bangui. A year later he was appointed rector of the University of Bangui.

In 2008, with the country increasingly volatile under President François Bozizé, Prime Minister Élie Doté resigned and Bozizé invited the largely unknown Touadéra to succeed him. To appease rebel forces, Touadéra was instructed by Bozizé to form a national unity government in 2009. Unrest nonetheless continued and in 2013 Séléka rebels staged a coup, prompting Touadéra and his family to spend six months on a United Nations base before leaving for Lille.

At the 2015 presidential election Touadéra ran as an independent against 29 other candidates. He defeated Anicet-Georges Dologuélé, who had run with Bozizé's endorsement, after two rounds of voting.

Career in Office
Touadéra was sworn in on 30 March 2016. Although the election process was fraught with accusations of fraud, his appointment was widely welcomed by the international community and accepted by Dologuélé. Touadéra's challenge has been to oversee the disarmament, demobilization and reintegration of rebel forces, while trying to foster reconciliation in a country that has seen more than 1m. people displaced internally and across borders since 2013. However, continuing violence between Christian and Muslim militias escalated in 2017, as did attacks on United Nations peacekeepers, raising fears of genocide. In early 2018 the International Committee of the Red Cross warned that about half of the population was in need of humanitarian aid.

Defence

Selective national service for a two-year period is in force.

Defence expenditure totalled an estimated US$54m. in 2011 (approximately US$11 per capita), representing around 2·5% of GDP.

In Dec. 2013, 1,600 French troops were deployed to the Central African Republic to try to restore order after months of violence. An African Union-led peacekeeping mission, initially numbering 6,000 personnel, was also deployed in Dec. 2013 as the conflict worsened. In Sept. 2014 a UN operation, the United Nations Multidimensional Integrated Stabilization Mission in the Central African Republic (MINUSCA), took over peacekeeping responsibilities. In March 2019 it had 15,045 deployed personnel.

Army

The Army consisted (2011) of about 2,000 personnel. There is an infantry regiment and a territorial defence regiment. In addition there are some 1,000 personnel in the paramilitary Gendarmerie.

Navy

The Army includes a small naval wing operating a handful of patrol craft.

Air Force

Personnel strength (2011) was 150. There are no combat aircraft.

Economy

Agriculture, fishing and forestry contributed 50·2% to GDP in 2011; followed by trade, hotels and restaurants, 12·4%; finance and real estate, 6·4%; manufacturing, 6·2%; transport and communications, 5·4%.

Overview

Despite being rich in natural resources—including diamonds, gold, timber and uranium—and having favourable agricultural conditions, the Central African Republic is one of the world's poorest countries. Political turmoil and armed conflict, along with droughts, a landlocked geography, poor transport infrastructure and government mismanagement have hampered growth for decades.

A *coup d'état* in 2003 preceded two years of transition culminating in legislative and presidential elections in May 2005. The return to representative government prompted the strongest economic expansion for a decade. GDP growth was around 4% in 2006 owing to increased private consumption following the resumption of regular salary payments to civil servants, a pick-up in investment, recovery in diamond and timber exports, and an upturn in agriculture (the economy's largest sector).

A series of external shocks, including the breakdown of a major hydropower plant, a price surge in imported commodities and the global economic downturn, led to slower growth and accelerated inflation from 2008. However, the current account deficit narrowed to 7·7% of GDP in 2009 from 10·3% the previous year, reflecting improvements in terms of trade as a result of lower oil costs and rising diamond prices.

In June 2009 the country completed its IMF-led Heavily Indebted Poor Countries Initiative, so qualifying for additional aid. In June 2012 the government signed an extended credit facility with the IMF. As of 2015 total debt stood at 48·5% of GDP. A coup in 2013 led to a surge in sectarian violence that resulted in thousands of deaths and the displacement of around 1m. people by the end of the year, which led to GDP contracting by almost

37%. In Jan. 2014 the World Bank announced US$100m. in assistance to restore key government services and secure food supplies and health care. It was hoped that presidential and parliamentary elections held in early 2016 would promote more stable socio-political conditions and an improved economic outlook.

Currency
The unit of currency is the *franc CFA* (XAF) with a parity of 655·957 francs CFA to one euro. Total money supply in June 2005 was 98,664m. francs CFA, with foreign exchange reserves US$132m. and gold reserves 11,000 troy oz. Inflation was 4·6% in 2016 and 4·1% in 2017.

Budget
Budgetary central government revenues in 2012 (provisional) were 201,430m. francs CFA and expenditures 104,889m. francs CFA.
VAT is 19%.

Performance
Total GDP in 2017 was US$1·9bn. There was real GDP growth of 4·8% in 2015, 4·5% in 2016 and 4·3% in 2017.

Banking and Finance
The Banque des Etats de l'Afrique Centrale (BEAC) acts as the central bank and bank of issue. The *Governor* is Abbas Mahamat Tolli. There are three commercial banks, a development bank and an investment bank.
In 2010 external debt totalled US$385m., representing 19% of GNI.

Energy and Natural Resources

Environment
The Central African Republic's carbon dioxide emissions from the consumption of energy in 2011 were the equivalent of 0·1 tonnes per capita.

Electricity
Installed capacity was an estimated 44,000 kW in 2011. Production in 2011 was estimated at 174m. kWh (around 84% hydro-electric). Consumption per capita in 2011 was about 39 kWh.

Minerals
In 2011 an estimated 243,000 carats of gem diamonds and 81,000 carats of industrial diamonds were mined; and 53 kg of gold. There are also oil, uranium and other mineral deposits that are for the most part unexploited.

Agriculture
In 2013 there were around 1·8m. ha. of arable land and 80,000 ha. of permanent crop land. The main crops (production 2012, in 1,000 tonnes) are cassava, 684; yams (estimate), 460; maize, 162; groundnuts, 149; bananas (estimate), 128; taro (estimate), 125; sugarcane (estimate), 100; plantains (estimate), 85; sorghum, 46.
Livestock, 2011: goats, 5·74m.; cattle, 4·18m.; pigs, 1·0m.; sheep, 386,000; chickens, 6·6m.

Forestry
There were 22·17m. ha. of forest in 2015, or 36% of the total land area. The extensive hardwood forests, particularly in the southwest, provide mahogany, obeche and limba. Timber production in 2011 was 2·73m. cu. metres.

Fisheries
The catch in 2015 was estimated at 28,000 tonnes, exclusively from inland waters.

Industry
In 2011 manufacturing accounted for 6·2% of GDP. The country's small industrial sector includes factories producing wood products, cotton fabrics, footwear and beer.

Labour
The labour force in 2013 was 2,236,000 (1,777,000 in 2003). 79·2% of the population aged 15–64 was economically active in 2013. In the same year 7·4% of the population was unemployed. The Central African Republic had 32,000 people living in slavery according to the Walk Free Foundation's 2013 *Global Slavery Index*.

International Trade

Imports and Exports
Imports and exports for calendar years in US$1m.:

	2005	2006	2007	2008	2009
Imports c.i.f.	185·3	140·4	197·8	185·0	211·7
Exports f.o.b.	110·7	109·8	131·1	114·2	80·5

Principal imports in 2009 (in US$1m.) were: cereal and cereal preparations (27·2); fruit and vegetables (23·7); medicinal and pharmaceutical products (23·3). Leading exports in 2009 (in US$1m.) were: industrial diamonds (49·6); wood (24·9); coffee (1·8).
In 2009 major import sources (in US$1m.) were: France (48·0); USA (33·0); Cameroon (18·6); China (16·8). Major export markets in 2009 (in US$1m.) were: Belgium (47·1); China (7·5); France (7·5); Germany (6·8).

Communications

Roads
There were 20,278 km of roads in 2010, including 5,044 km of highways or main roads. In 2007 there were 1,200 passenger cars, 58 lorries and vans, and 4,500 motorcycles and mopeds. There were 583 road accident deaths in 2007.

Civil Aviation
There is an international airport at M'Poko, near Bangui, which handled 124,940 passengers (91,854 on international flights) in 2012. In 2010 there were direct services operating to Brazzaville, Casablanca, Cotonou, Douala, Luanda, Nairobi, Paris and Tripoli. The only airline based in the Central African Republic is Karinou Airlines, which was founded in 2012 as African Airlines and renamed in 2013.

Shipping
Timber and barges are taken to Brazzaville (Republic of the Congo).

Telecommunications
There were 12,000 fixed telephone lines in 2010 (2·7 per 1,000 inhabitants). Mobile phone subscribers numbered 1·02m. in 2010. There were 1,410 wireless broadband subscriptions in 2012 and 120 fixed internet subscriptions in 2010. In June 2012 there were 144,000 Facebook users.

Social Institutions
According to the 2017 *Fragile States Index*—a list published jointly by the Fund for Peace and *Foreign Policy* magazine—the Central African Republic was ranked as the country third most vulnerable to conflict or collapse. The index is based on 12 indicators of state vulnerability across social, political and economic categories.

Justice
The Criminal Court and Supreme Court are situated in Bangui. There are 16 high courts throughout the country. The population in penal institutions in Nov. 2011 was 845 (19 per 100,000 of national population). 70·2% of prisoners had yet to receive a trial according to 2014 estimates by the International Centre for Prison Studies.

Education
Adult literacy rate was an estimated 55·2% in 2009 (69·1% among males and 42·1% among females).
In 2011 there were 648,370 pupils in primary schools with 7,974 teaching staff and 126,017 pupils in secondary schools with 1,886 teaching staff. The University of Bangui, founded in 1969, is the leading institution in the tertiary sector. There were 13,289 students in 2011 with 384 academic staff at institutes of tertiary education.
Public expenditure on education was 1·2% of GDP in 2011.

Health
In 2006 there were 12 hospital beds per 10,000 population. In 2009 there were 205 physicians, 1,097 nursing and midwifery personnel, 12 dentistry personnel and 12 pharmaceutical personnel. Expenditure on health in 2005

came to 4·0% of GDP and represented 10·9% of total government expenditure.

In *Water: At What Cost? The State of the World's Water 2016*, WaterAid reported that 31·5% of the population does not have access to safe water.

Religion

In 2010 there were an estimated 2·67m. Protestants, 1·26m. Roman Catholics and 0·37m. Muslims according to the Pew Research Center's Forum on Religion & Public Life. In Feb. 2019 there was one cardinal.

Culture

World Heritage Sites

The Manovo-Gounda St Floris National Park was inscribed on the UNESCO World Heritage List in 1988. Poaching and violence led to the park's closure to tourism in 1997. Sangha Trinational, a transboundary conservation complex situated in Cameroon, the Central African Republic and the Republic of the Congo, was added to the UNESCO World Heritage List in 2012. The site consists of three contiguous national parks totalling around 750,000 ha. Much of it is unaffected by human activity and features a wide range of humid tropical forest ecosystems with rich flora and fauna.

Press

In 2008 there were 30 newspapers, of which six were dailies with a circulation of 5,000.

Tourism

In 2010, 54,000 non-resident tourists—excluding same-day visitors—arrived by air (27,000 from other African countries).

Diplomatic Representatives

Of the Central African Republic in the United Kingdom
    Ambassador: Vacant (resides in Paris).

Of the United Kingdom in the Central African Republic
    Ambassador: Rowan James Laxton (resides in Yaoundé, Cameroon).

Of the Central African Republic in the USA (2704 Ontario Rd, NW, Washington, D.C., 20009)
    Ambassador: Martial Ndoubou.

Of the USA in the Central African Republic (Ave. David Dacko, Bangui)
    Ambassador: Lucy Tamlyn.

Of the Central African Republic to the United Nations
    Ambassador: Ambroisine Kpongo.

Of the Central African Republic to the European Union
    Ambassador: Daniel Emery Dede.

Further Reading

Kalck, Pierre, *Historical Dictionary of the Central African Republic.* 3rd ed. 2004

Titley, B., *Dark Age: The Political Odyssey of Emperor Bokassa.* 1997

National Statistical Office: Division des Statistiques, des Études Économiques et Sociales, BP 696, Bangui.

Website (French only): http://www.stat-centrafrique.com

Chad

République du Tchad (Republic of Chad)

Capital: N'Djaména
Population projection, 2020: 16·29m.
GNI per capita, 2017: (PPP$) 1,750
HDI/world rank, 2017: 0·404/186
Internet domain extension: .td

Key Historical Events

France proclaimed a protectorate over Chad in 1900 and in July 1908 the territory was incorporated into French Equatorial Africa. It became a separate colony in 1920, and in 1946 one of the four constituent territories of French Equatorial Africa. It achieved full independence on 11 Aug. 1960. Conflicts between the government and secessionist groups, particularly in the Muslim north and centre, from 1965 led to civil war. In 1982 Hissène Habré gained control of the country. In June 1983 Libyan-backed forces reoccupied some territory but a ceasefire took effect in Sept. 1987. Rebel forces of the Popular Salvation Movement led by Idriss Déby entered Chad from Sudan in Nov. 1990. On 4 Dec. 1990 Déby declared himself President.

In Feb. 2000 Hissène Habré was charged with torture and barbarity and put under house arrest in Senegal, where he remained as of 2013 despite having been sentenced to death by a Chadian court *in absentia*. In 2016 he was sentenced to life imprisonment on charges including crimes against humanity, torture and slavery by a special criminal court convened by the African Union operating within the Senegalese judicial system. He was also ordered to pay compensation to victims totalling several million US dollars.

Déby won disputed presidential elections in 2001, 2006 and 2011 and militant rebels have remained active throughout his tenure. Cross-border clashes between Chadian and Sudanese forces severely strained relations between the two countries and resulted in the deployment of a UN peace-keeping force in the area between 2007 and 2010.

Territory and Population

Chad is bounded in the west by Cameroon, Nigeria and Niger, north by Libya, east by Sudan and south by the Central African Republic. In Feb. 1994 the International Court of Justice ruled that the Aozou Strip along the Libyan border, occupied by Libya since 1973, was part of Chad. Area, 1,284,000 sq. km. The population at the 2009 census was 11,039,873.

The UN gives a projected population for 2020 of 16·29m.

In 2011, 28·2% of the population were urban. The capital is N'Djaména with 951,458 inhabitants (2009 census), other large towns being (2009 census figures) Moundou (137,251), Abéché (97,963) and Sarh (97,224). About half the population lives in the southern belt (the southernmost 20% of the country's territory), where most of the major cities are located including N'Djaména. Whereas in the south of the country most people are settled, in the north, east and centre people are generally nomadic or semi-nomadic.

Following administrative reforms of 2002 and 2008, Chad's 14 prefectures were divided into 22 regions, including the City of N'Djaména (which is a commune governed by a special statute). In 2012 Ennedi Region was divided into Ennedi-Est and Ennedi-Ouest. The 23 regions are (with 2009 census population and capital): Barh el Ghazel, population 257,267 (Moussoro); Batha, 488,458 (Ati); Bourkou, 93,584 (Faya); Chari-Baguirmi, 578,425 (Massénya); Ennedi-Est, 113,862 (Am-Djarass); Ennedi-Ouest, 59,744 (Fada); Guéra, 538,359 (Mongo); Hadjer-Lamis, 566,858 (Massakory); Kanem, 333,387 (Mao); Lac, 433,790 (Bol); Logone Occidental, 689,044 (Moundou); Logone Oriental, 779,339 (Doba); Mandoul, 628,065 (Koumra); Mayo-Kebbi Est, 774,782 (Bongor); Mayo-Kebbi Ouest, 564,470 (Pala); Moyen-Chari, 588,008 (Sarh); N'Djaména, 951,418 (N'Djaména); Ouaddaï, 721,166 (Abéché); Salamat, 302,301 (Am-Timan);

Sila, 387,461 (Goz Beïda); Tandjilé, 661,906 (Laï); Tibesti, 25,483 (Bardaï); Wadi Fira, 508,383 (Biltine).

The official languages are French and Arabic, but more than 100 different languages and dialects are spoken. The largest of the more than 200 ethnic groups is the Sara of southern Chad (27·7% of the total population), followed by the Sudanic Arabs (11·5%).

Social Statistics

2008 estimates: births, 499,000; deaths, 182,000. Rates, 2008 estimates (per 1,000 population): births, 45·7; deaths, 16·7. Chad has one of the youngest populations of any country, with 73% of the population under the age of 30 and 45% under 15. Annual rate of growth, 2000–08, 3·3%. Expectation of life in 2013 was 50·3 years among males and 52·1 among females. Infant mortality, 2010 (per 1,000 live births), 99. Fertility rate, 2008, 6·2 children per woman.

Climate

A tropical climate, with adequate rainfall in the south, though Nov. to April are virtually rainless months. Further north, desert conditions prevail. N'Djaména, Jan. 75°F (23·9°C), July 82°F (27·8°C). Annual rainfall 30" (744 mm).

Constitution and Government

After overthrowing the regime of Hissène Habré, Idriss Déby proclaimed himself *President* and was sworn in on 4 March 1991.

A law of Oct. 1991 permits the formation of political parties provided they are not based on regionalism, tribalism or intolerance. There are more than 70 political parties.

The constitution, approved in 1996, defines Chad as a unitary state. The head of state is the *President*, elected by universal suffrage. On 26 May 2004 the *National Assembly* passed an amendment scrapping the two-term limit on the presidency, replacing it with an age limit of 70. The amendment was approved by referendum in June 2005. In May 2018 parliament adopted a series of constitutional reforms abolishing the role of prime minister and reintroducing the two-term limit on the presidency. Nonetheless, this measure will only be implemented after the 2021 presidential election, allowing Idriss Déby to seek two further terms. A further amendment extended the length of the presidential term from five to six years.

The National Assembly has 188 members, elected for a four-year term. A *Senate* was stipulated in the 1996 constitution, but has yet to be created.

National Anthem

'Peuple tchadien, debout et à l'ouvrage' ('People of Chad, arise and take up the task'); words by L. Gidrol, tune by P. Villard.

Recent Elections

Presidential elections were held on 10 April 2016. Turnout was 76·1%. Incumbent Idriss Déby won re-election, with 61·6% of the vote, against 12·8% for Saleh Kebzabo and 10·7% for Laoukein Kourayo Médard. There were 11 other candidates.

In parliamentary elections held on 13 Feb. 2011 (the first since April 2002) the Patriotic Salvation Movement (MPS) of President Idriss Déby and allied parties won 131 seats, the National Union for Democracy and Renewal (UNDR) 10, the Union for Renewal and Democracy (URD) 8, the National Rally for Democracy in Chad (RNDT) 6 and the Federation Action for the Republic (FAR) 4. A number of smaller parties each took one or two seats. Turnout was 56·6%.

Current Government

President: Lieut.-Gen. Idriss Déby; b. 1952 (MPS; in office since Dec. 1990 and re-elected 3 July 1996, 20 May 2001, 3 May 2006, 25 April 2011 and 10 April 2016).

In Feb. 2019 the government comprised:

Ministers of State: Delwa Kassiré Koumakoye (also *Minister in the Presidency*); Kalzeubé Pahimi Deubet (also *Minister Secretary General of the Presidency*).

Minister of Civil Aviation, Transport and Meteorology: Mahamat Tahir Orozi. *Communications, and Government Spokesperson:* Oumar Yaya Hissein. *Economy, Planning and Development:* Issa Doubragne. *Environment, Water and Fisheries:* Sidick Abdelkerim Haggar. *Finance and Budget:* Allali Mahamat Abakar. *Foreign Affairs, African Integration, International Co-operation and Chadians Abroad:* Mahamat Zene Chérif. *Higher Education, Research and Innovation:* David Houdeingar Ngarimaden. *Infrastructure, Transport and Rural Development:* Abdramane Mouctar Mahamat. *Justice and Keeper of the Seals, in Charge of Human Rights:* Djimet Arabi. *Livestock and Animal Production:* Gayang Souaré. *Mines, Industrial Development, Trade Development and Private Sector Development:* Ahmat Mahamat Bâchir. *National Education and Civic Promotion:* Aboubakar Assidick Tchoroma. *Oil and Energy:* Boukar Michel. *Posts, and New Information Technologies:* Ndolenodji Alixe Naïmbaye. *Production, Irrigation and Agricultural Infrastructure:* Lydie Beassemda. *Promotion of Youth, Sports and Employment:* Mahamat Nassour Abdoulaye. *Public Health:* Aziz Mahamat Saleh. *Public Service, Employment and Social Dialogue:* Ali Mbodou Mbodoumi. *Spatial Planning, Housing Development and Urban Development:* Achta Ahmat Bremé. *Territorial Administration, Public Security and Local Governance:* Mahamat Abali Salah. *Tourism Development, Culture and Handicrafts:* Madeleine Alingué. *Vocational Training and Small Businesses:* Ruth Madjidian Padja. *Women, Child Protection and National Solidarity:* Djalal Ardjoun Khalil. *Deputy Minister at the Presidency in Charge of National Defence, Veterans' Affairs and Victims of War:* Daoud Yaya Brahim. *Minister Secretary General of the Government in Charge of Relations with the National Assembly:* Mariam Mahamat Nour.

Office of the President (Arabic and French only): https://www.presidence.td

Current Leaders

Idriss Déby

Position

President

Introduction

Lieut.-Gen. Idriss Déby became president in Feb. 1991 after participating in a coup to overthrow Hissène Habré. He oversaw multi-party elections, but opponents have cited electoral irregularities or largely boycotted Déby's victories in subsequent presidential contests up to April 2016. His political survival has been attributed in large part to the presence of French forces in the country, while his tenure has been marked by civil war and an overspill of fighting from conflicts in neighbouring countries, hindering attempts at reducing Chad's extreme poverty.

Early Life

Déby was born in 1952 into the Bidyate clan of the Zaghawa peoples. While serving in the army he helped Hissène Habré take power in 1982, overthrowing Goukouni Oueddei in a coup. His relationship with Habré declined and in 1989 Déby was accused of involvement in an alleged coup and went into exile in Sudan. In Dec. 1990, as head of the Patriotic Salvation Movement (MPS) and with the support of Libya, he removed Habré from power. Déby was proclaimed president in Feb. 1991 and in 1993 was appointed interim head of a transitional government charged with preparing democratic elections to be held within a year.

Career in Office

Déby went on to establish a multi-party constitution and triumphed at presidential elections held in 1996. The MPS won elections to the Legislative Assembly the following year.

Déby has had to cope with tensions between the largely Arab-Muslim north and the mainly Christian and animist south. In 1998 there was a surge in rebel activity in the north, spearheaded by the Movement for Democracy and Justice in Chad (MDJT), led by Déby's former defence minister Youssouf Togoimi. In early 2002 Libyan leader Col. Gaddafi, formerly a supporter of Chadian rebel movements, brokered a peace agreement which included provision for an amnesty for MDJT members. It soon failed but in Jan. 2003 the government reached a peace agreement with the rebel National Resistance Army in the east and in Dec. that year a new accord was signed with the MDJT.

Déby was re-elected in 2001 although the electoral commission discounted results from 25% of polling stations for electoral irregularities. Six of Déby's defeated rivals were subsequently arrested for 'inciting violence and civil disobedience' but were later released as human rights organizations and trade unions pressed for a general strike. A constitutional amendment in June 2005 permitted him to stand for a third term of office, which he did successfully in May 2006. He was returned again in April 2011, claiming 89% of the vote, although the main opposition parties continued to boycott the polls.

From 2003 fighting spilled over the border from Darfur in neighbouring Sudan, prompting a large influx of refugees to Chad. Chad accused Sudan of supporting Chadian rebels, who made unsuccessful assaults on the capital, N'Djaména, in April 2006 and Feb. 2008. The government meanwhile declared a state of emergency in eastern provinces in Nov. 2006 and again in Oct. 2007. In March 2008 Déby and Sudan's president signed an accord aimed at stopping hostilities. However, alleged Chadian involvement in a rebel attack on Omdurman in Sudan in May prompted Sudan to sever diplomatic relations and Déby to cut economic links in retaliation. In Jan. 2009 several rebel groups united to form the Union of Resistance Forces (UFR), which in May launched a major offensive in eastern Chad from bases in Sudan. The offensive was repelled but the action exacerbated tensions between the Chadian and Sudanese governments until Jan. 2010 when both sides stated their readiness to normalize relations. In April that year the Chad–Sudan border reopened seven years after the Darfur conflict had forced its closure.

In 2013 Chadian troops supported French military action against Islamist insurgents in Mali. They were also involved in efforts to stabilize the security situation in neighbouring Central African Republic following a coup in March that year. However, relations were soured after the Central African Republic accused Chadian troops of colluding with rebel forces and in May 2014 Déby's government announced that it would close the border between the two countries. Since early 2015 the Chadian army has participated in regional military operations against the militant Islamist Boko Haram movement based in northeast Nigeria, whose raids and suicide bombings have spread to Chad, Niger and Cameroon.

Déby made numerous cabinet changes during 2013, including the appointment in Nov. of Kalzeubé Pahimi Deubet as prime minister following Djimrangar Dadnadji's resignation after less than a year in office. In a further reshuffle in Aug. 2015 he appointed new finance, public security and territorial administration ministers. In Feb. 2016 Deubet resigned and was replaced by Albert Pahimi Padacké. Déby was subsequently re-elected president for a fifth term in April that year, although with only 62% of the vote, and in April 2018 parliament approved a new constitution expanding his presidential powers and abolishing the post of prime minister.

In 2016 Déby held the year-long chairmanship of the African Union.

Defence

There are seven military regions. Total armed forces personnel numbered 25,350 in 2011, including republican guards. Defence expenditure totalled an estimated US$202m. in 2012 (approximately US$18 per capita), representing around 2% of GDP.

Army

In 2011 the strength was about 17,000–20,000 although it is being reorganized. In addition there was a paramilitary Gendarmerie of 4,500 and a Republican Guard of 5,000.

Air Force

Personnel (2011), 350 including 11 combat-capable aircraft and three attack helicopters.

Economy

In 2011 mining contributed 29·7% to GDP; followed by trade and hotels, 17·9%; agriculture, 15·8%; finance and real estate, 12·3%; public administration and defence, 8·1%.

Overview

Chad is ranked among the poorest countries in the world. The agrarian sector supports 80% of the population and accounts for over half of GDP.

The country's post-independence history has been characterized by instability and conflict arising from ethnic and religious tensions. Development has been further hindered by droughts and primitive infrastructure. Although oil-related investments and the completion of the Chad–Cameroon oil pipeline in July 2003 saw real GDP growth peak at over 30% in 2004, the economy entered recession in 2016 with a contraction of 6·4%, resulting from a decline in oil prices, lower government spending and challenges in domestic security. GDP per capita, which had stood at US$973 in 2012, declined to US$664 in 2016.

The majority of oil revenues have been earmarked for priority sectors including education, health care, infrastructure and rural development. Overdependence on hydrocarbons is nonetheless a significant long-term challenge, especially given price volatility.

Chad became a member of the Economic Community of Central African States in 2004. The currency is pegged to the euro and managed by the Banque des Etats de l'Afrique Centrale.

Currency

The unit of currency is the *franc CFA* (XAF) with a parity of 655·957 francs CFA to one euro. There was deflation of 1·1% in 2016 and of 0·9% in 2017. Foreign exchange reserves were US$214m. in June 2005, total money supply was 213,920m. francs CFA and gold reserves were 11,000 troy oz.

Budget

Revenues in 2013 (provisional) were 1,181bn. francs CFA (petroleum revenue, 63·4%) and expenditures 1,464bn. francs CFA (current expenditure, 56·2%).

VAT is 18%.

Performance

Chad's growth in 2010 was among the highest in the world at 13·5%. In 2004 there had been growth of 33·6%, thanks mainly to the construction of an oil pipeline from landlocked Chad to neighbouring Cameroon's Atlantic coast. Chad became the world's newest oil producer at the time in 2003, and as a result in 2004 recorded the highest economic growth of any country. More recently there was real GDP growth of 1·8% in 2015. However, declining oil prices then led to a recession with the economy contracting by 6·4% in 2016 and 3·1% in 2017. Total GDP in 2017 was US$10·0bn.

Banking and Finance

The Banque des Etats de l'Afrique Centrale (*Governor*, Abbas Mahamat Tolli) is the bank of issue. Other leading banks include: Banque Agricole du Soudan au Tchad; Banque Commerciale du Chari; Banque Internationale de l'Afrique au Tchad; Commercial Bank Tchad; Financial Bank Tchad; and Société Générale Tchadienne de Banque.

In 2010 foreign debt totalled US$1,733m., representing 25·7% of GNI.

Energy and Natural Resources

Environment

Carbon dioxide emissions from the consumption of energy were the equivalent of less than 0·1 tonnes per capita in 2011.

Electricity

Installed capacity was estimated at 41,000 kW in 2011. Production in 2011 amounted to about 218m. kWh. Consumption per capita was an estimated 18 kWh in 2011. Only 9% of the population had access to electricity in 2016 (31% in urban areas but just 2% in rural areas).

Oil and Gas

There is an oilfield in the Doba basin. In June 2000 the World Bank approved funding for a 1,070-km US$4bn. pipeline to run from 300 new oil wells in Chad through Cameroon to the Atlantic Ocean. Oil started pumping in July 2003. Oil production in 2013 was 5·0m. tonnes. Proven reserves totalled 1·5bn. bbls in 2013. Revenue in 2008 was US$1·9bn.

Minerals

Salt (about 4,000 tonnes per annum) is mined around Lake Chad, and there are deposits of uranium, gold, iron ore and bauxite. There are small-scale workings for gold and iron.

Agriculture

Some 80% of the workforce is involved in subsistence agriculture and fisheries. In 2014 an estimated 4·5m. ha. were arable and 35,000 ha. permanent crops. Cotton growing (in the south) and animal husbandry (in the central zone) are the most important branches. Production, 2011 estimates (in 1,000 tonnes): sorghum, 648; groundnuts, 414; yams, 400; sugarcane, 390; millet, 319; cassava, 230; maize, 195; rice, 173.

Livestock, 2011 estimates: cattle, 7,650,000; goats, 6,750,000; sheep, 3,100,000; camels, 1,435,000; chickens, 5·6m.

Forestry

In 2015 the area under forests was 4·88m. ha., or 4% of the total land area. Timber production in 2011 was 7·95m. cu. metres.

Fisheries

Total catches, from Lake Chad and the Chari and Logone rivers, were 120,020 tonnes in 2014.

Industry

Output in 1,000 tonnes (2010): sugar, 38; groundnut oil (estimate), 31; cottonseed oil (estimate), 3.

Labour

The labour force in 2013 was 4,874,000 (3,415,000 in 2003). 71·9% of the population aged 15–64 was economically active in 2013. In the same year 7·1% of the population was unemployed.

Chad had 86,000 people living in slavery according to the Walk Free Foundation's 2013 *Global Slavery Index*.

International Trade

Imports and Exports

Imports (c.i.f.) in 2009 totalled US$1,950m.; exports (f.o.b.) in 2009 totalled US$2,800m.

Main import suppliers are France, USA and Germany. Main export markets are Portugal, Germany and USA. The principal imports are machinery and transportation equipment, industrial goods and tobacco. Mineral fuels and oils account for the majority of exports.

Communications

Roads

In 2006 there were around 40,000 km of roads. 18,900 passenger cars were in use in 2006, plus 3,300 buses and coaches, 35,400 lorries and vans, and 63,000 motorcycles and mopeds. In 2007 there were 840 deaths in road accidents.

Civil Aviation

There is an international airport at N'Djaména, from which there were direct flights in 2010 to Abidjan, Addis Ababa, Cotonou, Douala, Johannesburg, Ouagadougou, Paris and Tripoli (Libya). There were 5,286 aircraft movements in 2011.

Telecommunications

There were 51,200 fixed telephone lines in 2010 (4·6 per 1,000 inhabitants). Mobile phone subscribers numbered 2·61m. in 2010. There were 17·0 internet users per 1,000 inhabitants in 2010. Fixed internet subscriptions totalled 4,600 in 2009 (0·4 per 1,000 inhabitants).

Social Institutions

According to the 2017 *Fragile States Index*—a list published jointly by the Fund for Peace and *Foreign Policy* magazine—Chad was ranked as the country eighth most vulnerable to conflict or collapse. The index is based on 12 indicators of state vulnerability across social, political and economic categories.

Justice

There are criminal courts and magistrates courts in N'Djaména, Moundou, Sarh and Abéché, with a Court of Appeal situated in N'Djaména.

The population in penal institutions in 2010 was 4,775 (43 per 100,000 of national population). 63·4% of prisoners had yet to receive a trial according to 2014 estimates by the International Centre for Prison Studies. The death penalty is still in force, and was used in 2015 when ten members of the Boko Haram Islamist group were executed. It had previously not been used since 2003.

Education

In 2007 there were 1,324,298 pupils in primary schools with 21,933 teaching staff and 314,470 pupils in secondary schools with 9,555 teaching staff. In 2005 there were 10,468 students with 1,100 academic staff at institutes of tertiary education. Adult literacy rate was 33% in 2008.

In 2005 public expenditure on education came to 2·3% of GNI.

Health

In 2005 there were four hospital beds per 10,000 population; there were four physicians per 100,000 population and 19 nurses and midwives per 100,000 in the period 2006–13.

In *Water: At What Cost? The State of the World's Water 2016*, WaterAid reported that 49·2% of the population does not have access to safe water—the fourth highest percentage of any nation. Chad has made significant progress in the reduction of undernourishment in the past 20 years. Between 1993 and 2013 the proportion of undernourished people declined from 56% of the population to 35%.

Religion

The northern and central parts of the country are predominantly Muslim. There were an estimated 6·21m. Muslims (both Sunnis and Shias) and 4·56m. Christians (more Catholics than Protestants) in 2010 according to the Pew Research Center's Forum on Religion & Public Life. Most of the remainder of the population is religiously unaffiliated, with some followers of folk religions.

Culture

Press

There are no daily newspapers; there were five non-dailies in 2008, including the government-owned *Info-Tchad*. Combined circulation was 4,000.

Tourism

In 2014 there were 122,000 non-resident tourists (excluding same-day visitors).

World Heritage Sites

The Lakes of Ounianga were added to the UNESCO World Heritage List in 2012. The site includes 18 permanent interconnected lakes in a desert setting, a remarkable natural phenomenon that is still to be fully understood. In 2016 Ennedi Massif: Natural and Cultural Landscape was also added to the list. The sandstone features have been sculpted over time by water and wind erosion into a plateau featuring valleys and canyons.

Diplomatic Representatives

Of Chad in the United Kingdom
    Ambassador: Sem Amine Abba Sidick (resides in Brussels).

Of the United Kingdom in Chad
    Ambassador: Rowan James Laxton (resides in Yaoundé, Cameroon).

Of Chad in the USA (2401 Massachusetts Ave., NW, Washington, D.C., 20008)
    Ambassador: Ngote Gali Koutou.

Of the USA in Chad (Chagoua Round Point, BP 413, N'Djaména)
    Ambassador: Vacant.
    Chargé d'Affaires a.i.: Richard K. Bell.

Of Chad to the United Nations
    Ambassador: Ali Alefei Moustapha.

Of Chad to the European Union
    Ambassador: Ammo Aziza Baroud.

Further Reading

National Statistical Office: Institut National de la Statistique, des Etudes Economiques et Démographiques, BP 453 N'Djaména.

Chile

República de Chile (Republic of Chile)

Capitals: Santiago (Administrative), Valparaíso (Legislative)
Population projection, 2020: 18·47m.
GNI per capita, 2017: (PPP$) 21,910
HDI/world rank, 2017: 0·843/44
Internet domain extension: .cl

Key Historical Events

Archaeological evidence suggests the earliest settlements of hunter-gatherers in Chile date from around 10,500 BC. They were probably the descendants of Paleo-Indians who crossed from Siberia by way of the Bering Strait (at various times a land bridge). Prior to the arrival of Europeans, the indigenous peoples included the Atacameno, living in small settlements in the northern deserts, the Araucanians, farmers in the more temperate valleys of central Chile, and the Chono, Alacaluf and Yahgan tribes from the mountainous southern areas.

Ferdinand Magellan was the first European to catch sight of what is now Chile when, in 1520, he sailed through the bleak archipelago at the tip of South America en route for the Pacific Ocean. Fifteen years later a Spanish expeditionary force, led by Diego de Almagro, set off from the newly captured Inca city of Cusco to explore land to the south. Almagro travelled as far as the Itata river but came under repeated attacks from hostile Araucanians and was unable to establish a foothold. He returned to Peru in 1536, with news only of 'a cursed land without gold, inhabited by savages of the worst kind.' Five years passed before the next Spanish expedition to Chile left Cusco, headed by Pedro de Valdivia. After months of hardship, battles with Araucanians and internal divisions, Valdivia's forces established the settlement of Santiago in early 1541. In the next ten years the Spanish built fortified towns at Concepción, La Serena, Valdivia and Villarrica. North of Concepción, they began to convert the Araucanians to Christianity and established mines run on forced labour. Subjugating the indigenous people south of Concepción, however, proved difficult. In that region, Araucanians known as Mapuche fought hard and quickly adapted their weapons and tactics to become effective guerrilla fighters. Fifty years after Valdivia's forces arrived in Chile, the colony remained a frontier, dependent on the Viceroyalty of Peru and governed by military officers based in dispersed fort towns. Gold was discovered but the wealth it generated was minimal compared with the riches that poured out of Mexico and Peru.

Opposition to Spain

Following further military defeats at the hands of the Mapuche and the destruction of Concepción in an earthquake in 1570, King Felipe II of Spain named a veteran conquistador, Rodrigo de Quiroga, as governor of Chile. After 1575 Quiroga attempted to quell rebellion with a brutal campaign against the Araucanians, capturing them for forced labour and mutilating their feet to prevent escape. A subsequent governor, Garcia Onez de Loyola, attempted to moderate these abuses, but was killed at the battle of Curalaba in 1598. Subsequently, all major Spanish settlements south of the Bíobío river were destroyed or abandoned. In 1600 the king of Spain granted a permanent military subsidy to fund the war in Chile and in 1608 he signed a royal decree legalizing the enslavement of 'rebellious' Indians. At around this time, coastal settlements such as Valparaíso came under attack from English and Dutch adventurers and pirates in search of wealth and as part of a prolonged effort to force Spain to allow other nations to trade with its colonies. The relative lack of mineral wealth in Chile led the 5,000 or so Spanish settlers to develop a pastoral and agricultural society; they grew a wide range of cereals and raised livestock. North of the Bíobío river, there was considerable intermarriage and the rapid growth of a mestizo (mixed Amerindian and European) group. The social status of mestizos was determined by the extent to which they were Hispanicized and by their kinship ties with the landed class.

In 1664 the governorship of Chile passed to Francisco de Meneses, an opportunist who took advantage of the warfare economy, taxing ships unless they carried his merchandise. He demanded bribes and accumulated vast wealth from the slave trade. An earthquake that shook Lima in 1687 disrupted the supply of food to the Peruvian city for some years. Chilean merchants cashed in by shipping wheat from the country's central belt and there was a rapid expansion in wheat production. The wheat 'boom' continued until 1700 with trade controlled by a clique of merchants who colluded with corrupt officials. Attempts by successive governors to make peace with the Mapuche (the Pact of Quillin) ended in failure, and sporadic fighting continued throughout the 17th and 18th centuries. Many thousands of Mapuche migrated eastwards across the Andes to Argentina.

Bourbon Rule

The Habsburg dynasty's rule over Spain ended in 1700. They were succeeded by the Bourbons who gave the *audiencia* of Chile (based in Santiago) greater independence from the Viceroyalty of Peru. One of the most charismatic governors of the Bourbon era was the Irish-born Ambrosio O'Higgins, who presided over increased economic production and strengthened the military. In 1791 he also outlawed forced labour. Economic links with Argentina increased after it became the Viceroyalty of the Río de la Plata in 1776 and by the end of the 18th century Chile was engaging in direct trade with Europe. Freer trade brought with it knowledge of politics abroad, particularly the spread of liberalism in Europe and American independence. The Royal University of San Felipe was established at Santiago in 1758 but most educated Chileans followed the traditional ideology of the Spanish crown and the Roman Catholic Church, while the majority of mestizos and Araucanians remained illiterate and subordinate.

The French Revolution and Napoleon Bonaparte's subsequent invasion of Spain in 1807 eventually led to greater autonomy and independence. On 18 Sept. 1810 the Santiago elite, employing the town council as a junta, announced their intention to govern the colony until Fernando VII was reinstated. They remained loyal to the ousted Spanish king but insisted they had the right to rule and immediately relaxed trade restrictions. Chile's first government was led by José Miguel Carrera Verdugo. Carrera and his brothers, as well as Bernardo O'Higgins (son of former governor Ambrosio O'Higgins) soon saw the opportunity to replace temporary self-rule with permanent independence, although others remained loyal to Spain. 1814 saw the start of the Reconquest (*La Reconquista*), and the Spanish authorities managed to reassert control of Chile by winning the Battle of Rancagua. O'Higgins and many of the Chilean rebels escaped to Argentina, from where they plotted to liberate their country. O'Higgins won the support of the revolutionary government in Buenos Aires under José de San Martín. Their joint forces freed Chile in 1817, defeating the Spaniards and their supporters at the Battle of Chacabuco.

Independence

Bernardo O'Higgins ruled Chile from 1817–23, formally proclaiming independence on 12 Feb. 1818 at Talca. He founded schools and expelled the remaining Spaniards but his authoritarian style and attempted reforms of the land tenure system caused unrest among the powerful landowners. A succession of poor harvests forced him to abdicate in 1823. Civil conflict continued throughout the 1820s, owing largely to a split between the Chilean oligarchs and the army. The harmful effects on the economy prompted conservatives to seize control in 1830. Diego Portales reached a compromise between the oligarchs and promulgated a constitution in 1833, beginning a prolonged period of political stability and economic revival. A free port was created at Valparaíso to encourage trade with foreign, especially British, merchants. Chilean landowners and merchants profited from new markets in California and Australia in the 1850s. Economic improvement was underpinned by discoveries of silver and copper in northern Chile and significant coal deposits around Concepción. The period after 1860, known as the 'Liberal Republic', saw the emergence of rival political groups influenced by economic, scientific and literary ideas from Europe. Great Britain became the main trading partner and British entrepreneurs invested in the railways and the modernization of the ports.

Palgrave Macmillan (ed.), *The Statesman's Yearbook 2020*,
https://doi.org/10.1057/978-1-349-95940-2_48

Access to valuable saltpetre (potassium nitrate) deposits in the far north, bordering Peru and Bolivia, led to the War of the Pacific (1879–83), in which the Chilean army and navy prevailed. During the presidency of José Manuel de Balmaceda (1886–91) the government attempted to use revenue from mineral extraction to strengthen its administration, a policy opposed by the oligarchs who forced Balmaceda's abdication. Thereafter Chile's presidential republic was transformed into a parliamentary republic. The next 20 years saw the emergence of new political parties representing the emerging working and middle classes. The Democratic Party was formed in 1887 to represent artisans and urban workers, while the Radical Party was backed by the middle class. Marxist ideology spread among workers in the late 1890s and the Socialist Party was established in 1901. By the start of the 20th century Chile was becoming increasingly urbanized as workers poured into the cities from rural areas. Society was polarized, with parts of Santiago and Valparaíso mirroring prosperous and elegant European cities, while the masses remained largely poverty stricken and illiterate.

The outbreak of the First World War, with Britain and Germany on opposite sides, brought disaster to the Chilean economy. Demand for saltpetre fell away and thousands of workers lost their jobs. The reformist president Arturo Alessandri Palma was elected in 1920 but his initiatives were blocked by the legislature and he resigned. The army intervened and returned Alessandri to power in 1925, after which the constitution was amended to strengthen the executive at the expense of the legislature. It established a presidential republic, separated church and state, and enshrined new labour and welfare legislation. Attempts to reduce the power of the oligarchs failed. Alessandri resigned for a second time and was replaced by Carlos Ibáñez del Campo in 1927. His military dictatorship led to improvements in education and public services but also failed to address the economic power of the oligarchs. The world depression of the 1930s was hard on Chile as demand for mineral exports plummeted. A democratic-leftist coalition, the Popular Front, took power following the elections of 1938. Chile remained neutral in the Second World War until 1942 when President Juan Antonio Ríos declared war on Germany, Italy and Japan.

Conflict with the USA

The Radical Party joined with the Communists to field a left-wing Radical, Gabriel González Videla, for president in the 1946 election. Once in office, González Videla (president, 1946–52) turned against his Communist allies, expelling them from his cabinet and banning the party in 1948. He also severed relations with the Soviet Union, prompting accusations of a Cold War agreement with the United States. The early 1950s were characterized by slow economic growth, spiralling inflation and increasing social demands. By 1952 Chileans were alienated by multi-party politics and reacted by turning to two symbols of the past: first, the 1920s dictator Ibáñez and, following the 1958 elections, the son of former president Alessandri. The Christian Democrat party, under the leadership of Eduardo Frei Montalva, undertook a 'Chileanization programme', wresting back control from the US-owned copper mines and making progress in land reform by establishing peasant co-operatives. There were also advances in education and housing. The agrarian reforms increased support for the various Socialist and Communist parties. In 1969 they formed the Popular Unity coalition, headed by Salvador Allende Gossens, who was elected president in 1970. Allende nationalized many private companies, attempted to improve conditions for the working classes and established ties with other socialist states. The first year was heralded a success, but in 1971–72 Chile was afflicted by rapid inflation and shortages of foods and consumer goods. The United States, which had become by far the largest foreign investor in the decades that followed the Second World War, withdrew much of its backing.

In Sept. 1973, with covert American support, the armed forces staged a coup and Allende died during an assault on the presidential palace in Santiago. Gen. Augusto Pinochet was installed as president. The military closed Congress, censored the media, purged the universities and banned Marxist parties and union activities. It is estimated that over 3,000 of Allende's supporters lost their lives, over 30,000 were forced into exile and more than 130,000 were arrested over a three-year period. The return to market capitalism led to steady economic improvement from 1976 but falling copper prices and mounting foreign debt led to spiralling inflation and growing unemployment in the early 1980s. In 1981 a new constitution was approved, guaranteeing an eight-year extension to Pinochet's rule but also allowing a transition to civilian government by the end of the decade. The first free elections since the 1973 coup took place in Dec. 1989 and Patricio Aylwin Azócar emerged victorious, heading a coalition of left and centrist

parties. The 1990s saw a rapid strengthening of the economy, underpinned by large inflows of foreign investment.

Pinochet remained head of the military until 1998, after which he claimed his constitutional right to become a senator for life (and hence immune from prosecution). While visiting Britain for medical treatment in 1998, Pinochet was arrested and held on human rights charges instigated by Spain. In early 2000 he returned to Chile after the British government ruled he was too ill to be extradited to Spain to face charges. Stripped of his immunity from prosecution, he died in Dec. 2006 without facing trial. On his election in Jan. 2000, Ricardo Lagos Escobar, leader of the Coalition of Parties for Democracy (CPD) pledged to reform the labour code, increase the minimum wage, introduce unemployment insurance and provide better health care, education and housing. In 2003 allegations of corruption damaged investor confidence.

In Jan. 2006 Michelle Bachelet, of the centre-left Concertación coalition, became Chile's first female president. In March 2010 she was succeeded by Sebastián Piñera, leader of the rightist Coalition for Change. In May 2013 his government reached a landmark free trade agreement with regional partners Colombia, Mexico and Peru. In Dec. 2013 Bachelet was returned to the presidency with a convincing majority to become the first two-term president of the post-Pinochet era. Piñera was then elected for a second term in the presidential polling in Nov.–Dec. 2017, reflecting a wave of conservatism sweeping South America.

Territory and Population

Chile is bounded in the north by Peru, east by Bolivia and Argentina, and south and west by the Pacific Ocean. The area is 756,096 sq. km (291,928 sq. miles) excluding the claimed Antarctic territory. Many islands to the west and south belong to Chile: the Islas Juan Fernández (147 sq. km with a population of 792 in 2012) lie about 600 km west of Valparaíso, and the volcanic Isla de Pascua (Easter Island or Rapa Nui, 164 sq. km with a population of 5,761 in 2012), lies about 3,000 km west-northwest of Valparaíso. Small uninhabited dependencies include Sala y Goméz (400 km east of Easter Is.), San Félix and San Ambrosio (1,000 km northwest of Valparaíso, and 20 km apart) and Islas Diego Ramírez (100 km southwest of Cape Horn).

In 1940 Chile declared, and in each subsequent year has reaffirmed, its ownership of the sector of the Antarctic lying between 53° and 90° W. long., and asserted that the British claim to the sector between the meridians 20° and 80° W. long. overlapped the Chilean by 27°. There are ten Chilean bases in Antarctica. A law of 1955 put the governor of Magallanes in charge of the 'Chilean Antarctic Territory' which has an area of 1,250,258 sq. km and a population of 127 in 2012.

In Jan. 2014 the International Court of Justice ruled on a case brought by Peru claiming a large area of Pacific waters extending from its territorial border with Chile and incorporating valuable fishing grounds. Peru was awarded an extension to its maritime area of some 50,000 sq. km, although many of the most lucrative fishing areas remain under Chilean jurisdiction.

The census population in April 2017 was 17,574,003. This equated to a density of 23·2 per sq. km. 89·2% of the population lived in urban areas in 2011.

The UN gives a projected population for 2020 of 18·47m.

Area, population and capitals of the 15 regions at the time of the 2017 census:

Region	Area (sq. km)	Population	Capital
Antofagasta	126,049	607,534	Antofagasta
Araucanía	31,842	957,224	Temuco
Arica-Parinacota	16,873	226,068	Arica
Atacama	75,176	286,168	Copiapó
Aysén	108,494	103,158	Coihaique
Biobío[1]	37,063	2,037,414	Concepción
Coquimbo	40,580	757,586	La Serena
Libertador General B. O'Higgins	16,387	914,555	Rancagua
Los Lagos	48,584	828,708	Puerto Montt
Los Ríos	18,430	384,837	Valdivia

(continued)

Region	Area (sq. km)	Population	Capital
Magallanes y de la Antártica Chilena	132,297	166,533	Punta Arenas
Maule	30,296	1,044,950	Talca
Metropolitana de Santiago	15,403	7,112,808	Santiago
Tarapacá	42,226	330,558	Iquique
Valparaíso	16,396	1,815,902	Valparaíso

[1] A 16th region, Ñuble, was created in Sept. 2018 with three provinces taken from Biobío region.

The capital is Santiago; population (urban agglomeration, 2017) 6,160,040. Other major cities are Puente Alto, Viña del Mar, Antofagasta, Valparaíso and San Bernardo. In a 2011 survey 59% of the population described themselves as being white, 30% mestizo and 6% indigenous. Language and culture remain of European origin, with Mapudungun-speaking (mainly Mapuche) Indians the only sizeable minority.

The official language is Spanish.

Social Statistics

2007 births, 240,569; deaths, 93,000; marriages, 57,792. Rates, 2007 (per 1,000 population): birth, 14·6; death, 5·6; marriage, 3·5. Divorce was only made legal in 2004. In Aug. 2017 legislation was passed that partially lifted the ban on abortion in cases where the mother's life is at risk, the pregnancy results from rape or the foetus has a fatal defect. Annual population growth rate, 2008–10, 0·9%. Infant mortality, 2010 (per 1,000 live births), 8. In 2009 the most popular age range for marrying was 25–29 for both males and females. Expectation of life at birth (2013): males, 77·1 years; females, 82·7 years. Chile has the highest life expectancy in South America. Fertility rate, 2008, 1·9 children per woman. In 2012, 69·6% of all births were outside of marriage.

Climate

With its enormous range of latitude and the influence of the Andean Cordillera, the climate of Chile is very complex, ranging from extreme aridity in the north, through a Mediterranean climate in Central Chile, where winters are wet and summers dry, to a cool temperate zone in the south, with rain at all seasons. In the extreme south, conditions are very wet and stormy. Santiago, Jan. 67°F (19·5°C), July 46°F (8°C). Annual rainfall 15" (375 mm). Antofagasta, Jan. 69°F (20·6°C), July 57°F (14°C). Annual rainfall 0·5" (12·7 mm). Valparaíso, Jan. 64°F (17·8°C), July 53°F (11·7°C). Annual rainfall 20" (505 mm).

Constitution and Government

A new constitution was approved by 67·5% of the voters on 11 Sept. 1980 and came into force on 11 March 1981. It provided for a return to democracy after a minimum period of eight years. Gen. Pinochet would remain in office during this period after which the government would nominate a single candidate for President. At a plebiscite on 5 Oct. 1988 then President Pinochet was rejected as a presidential candidate by 54·6% of votes cast. The Constitution has been amended on a number of occasions since then. Until 2012 voting was compulsory for people who had registered (although Chileans could choose if they wanted to register). Now all eligible Chileans are automatically registered but voting is no longer mandatory.

The *President* is directly elected for a non-renewable four-year term. Parliament consists of a 155-member *Chamber of Deputies* and a *Senate* of 43 members. In March 2006 the Senate became fully elected, by abolishing non-elected senators and eliminating life seats for former presidents. Senators are elected for an eight-year term.

Santiago is the administrative capital of Chile but since 11 March 1990 Valparaíso has been the legislative capital.

National Anthem

'Dulce patria, recibe los votos' ('Sweet Fatherland, receive the vows'); words by E. Lillo, tune by R. Carnicer.

Government Chronology

Heads of State since 1942. (APL = Popular Liberating Alliance; FP = Popular Front; PC = Conservative Party; PDC = Christian Democratic Party; PS = Socialist Party; RN = National Renewal)

Presidents of the Republic		
1942–46	FP	Juan Antonio Ríos Morales
1946–52	FP	Gabriel González Videla
1952–58	APL	Carlos Ibáñez del Campo
1958–64	PC	Jorge Alessandri Rodríguez
1964–70	PDC	Eduardo Nicanor Frei Montalva
1970–73	PS	Salvador Allende Gossens

Military Junta		
1973–74		Gen. Augusto J. R. Pinochet (chair); Gen. César Raúl Benavides Escobar; Admr. José Toribio Merino Castro; Gen. Gustavo Leigh Guzmán; Gen. Fernando Matthei Aubel; Gen. César Mendoza Durán; Gen. Rodolfo Stange Oelckers

Presidents of the Republic		
1974–90	military	Augusto J. R. Pinochet
1990–94	PDC	Patricio Aylwin
1994–2000	PDC	Eduardo Frei Ruiz-Tagle
2000–06	PS	Ricardo Froilán Lagos
2006–10	PS	Michelle Bachelet
2010–14	RN	Sebastián Piñera Echenique
2014–18	PS	Michelle Bachelet
2018–	RN	Sebastián Piñera Echenique

Recent Elections

In the presidential run-off held on 17 Dec. 2017, centre-right former president Sebastián Piñera (ind.) was elected after leaving the presidency in 2014, polling 54·6% against the leftist candidate Alejandro Guillier (ind.), with 45·4%. Six other candidates had participated in the first round of voting on 19 Nov. 2017. Turnout was 46·7% in the first round and 49·0% in the second round.

In elections to the Chamber of Deputies on 19 Nov. 2017 Chile Vamos won 72 seats with 38·7% of the vote (National Renewal, 36 and 17·8%; Independent Democratic Union, 30 and 16·0%; Political Evolution, 6 and 4·3%) against 43 seats (24·0%) for the Force of the Majority (Socialist Party, 19 and 9·8%; Party for Democracy, 8 and 6·1%; Communist Party, 8 and 4·6%; Social Democrat Radical Party, 8 and 3·6%); 20 (16·4%) for Broad Front (Democratic Revolution, 10 and 5·7%; Humanist Party, 5 and 4·2%; Liberal Party, 2 and 0·8%; Equality Party, 1 and 2·2%; Green Ecologist Party, 1 and 2·1%; Power, 1 and 1·5%); 14 (10·7%) for Democratic Convergence (Christian Democratic Party, 14 and 10·3%); 4 (1·9%) for the Green Regionalist Coalition (Social Green Regionalist Federation, 4 and 1·6%). For All Chile and an independent candidate won the two remaining seats. Elections for 23 of the 43 seats in the Senate were held on the same day. Chile Vamos won 12 seats; Force of the Majority, 7; Democratic Convergence, 3; and Broad Front, 1.

Current Government

President: Sebastián Piñera; b. 1949 (RN; sworn in 11 March 2018, having previously been president from March 2010–March 2014).

In Feb. 2019 the government comprised:

Minister of Agriculture: Antonio Walker. *Culture, Arts and Heritage:* Consuelo Valdés. *Economy, Development and Tourism:* José Ramón Valente. *Education:* Marcela Cubillos. *Energy:* Susana Jiménez. *Environment:* Carolina Schmidt. *Foreign Affairs:* Roberto Ampuero. *Health:* Emilio Santelices. *Housing and Urban Planning:* Cristián Monckeberg. *Interior and Public Security:* Andrés Chadwick. *Justice and Human Rights:* Hernán Larraín. *Labour and Social Welfare:* Nicolás Monckeberg. *Mining:* Baldo Prokurica. *National Defence:* Alberto Espina. *Public Lands:* Felipe Ward. *Public Works:* Juan Andrés Fontaine. *Social Development:* Alfredo Moreno. *Sport:* Pauline Kantor. *Transport and Telecommunications:* Gloria Hutt.

Treasury: Felipe Larraín. *Women and Gender Equality:* Isabel Plá. *General Secretary of the Government:* Cecilia Pérez. *General Secretary of the Presidency:* Gonzalo Blumel.
Government Website: http://www.gob.cl

Current Leaders

Sebastián Piñera

Position
President

Introduction
Sebastián Piñera, a businessman and right-of-centre politician, became president on 11 March 2018 for a second time, having previously served from 2010–14.

Early Life
Miguel Juan Sebastián Piñera Echenique was born on 1 Dec. 1949 in Santiago, the son of a diplomat. He grew up in Belgium, New York (USA) and Chile, graduating in economics from the Pontifical Catholic University of Chile in 1971 and working as a university tutor for two years. He then gained a doctorate from Harvard University in the USA in 1976. Returning to Chile, he taught economics while amassing personal wealth by establishing a credit card business and, from 1977–80, serving as general manager of the Bank of Talca. By 2017 he was ranked 745th on *Forbes* magazine's annual global rich list.

In 1989 Piñera entered politics to lead the presidential campaign of Hernán Büchi, a former finance minister. From 1990–98 he was senator for East Santiago, representing the centre-right National Renewal (RN) party. During this period he served on the Senate financial committee and in 1992 made an unsuccessful attempt to win the party's presidential candidacy. In 1993 he created the Future Foundation, later renamed the Foundation for Culture and Society, to develop policies on social justice, human rights and the environment.

From 2001–04 Piñera was RN president and in 2005 he contested the state presidential election, coming second to Michelle Bachelet. He made another bid for the presidency in Dec. 2009 and won with 52% of the vote in the run-off election in Jan. 2010, ending 22 years of centre-left rule. He took office in March 2010 as Chile struggled to cope with the impact of the previous month's earthquake in which hundreds died and about half a million homes were destroyed. He sought to restore the social fabric by unveiling a US$8·4bn. reconstruction plan, while also seeking to rebuild the economy and achieve a balanced budget. He gained international recognition for his close involvement in the successful rescue of 33 trapped miners in Oct. 2010. However, he faced a sharp decline in popularity in 2011 and 2012 in the face of mass student protests demanding more investment in state education. He did not contest the presidential election of 2013 and left office in March 2014 to be succeeded by Michelle Bachelet. In the Dec. 2017 run-off election Piñera faced Alejandro Guillier of Bachelet's New Majority (Nueva Mayoría) coalition and secured a comfortable win with 54·6% of votes. He began his second presidential term on 11 March 2018.

Career in Office
Piñera's electoral victory underscored a wave of conservatism sweeping through South America. While his first tenure had been marked by a vibrant economy underpinned by booming prices for copper (Chile's leading export) at that time, his second term began in more sluggish economic circumstances.

He has pledged to unite the country's political factions, jump-start economic growth (based around recovering copper prices), ease industry regulations, narrow the budget deficit and promote business-friendly policies. He also promised to make Chile the first country in Latin America to achieve 'developed nation' status in the Organisation for Economic Co-operation and Development. However, his centre-right coalition lacks a majority in Congress where it faces resistance.

Defence

Conscription is compulsory when there are not enough voluntary recruits. Military service lasts for a maximum of 12 months in the Army and 22 months in the Air Force and the Navy.

In 2013 defence expenditure totalled US$4,594m. (US$267 per capita), representing 1·6% of GDP. In 1985 defence spending had accounted for 10% of GDP.

Army

Strength (2011): 35,000 (including 11,000 conscripts) with 40,000 reserves. There is a 44,700-strong force of *Carabineros* (paramilitary police).

Navy

The principal ships of the Navy are an ex-British destroyer, four diesel submarines and seven frigates. There is a Naval Air Service numbering 600 personnel with 22 combat-capable aircraft.

Naval personnel in 2011 totalled 16,299 (807 conscripts) including 3,616 marines. There are HQs at Iquique, Puerto Montt, Punta Arenas, Talcahuano and Valparaíso.

Air Force

Strength (2011) was 7,760 personnel (460 conscripts). There are 59 combat-capable aircraft made up largely of F-16s.

Economy

Agriculture accounted for 4·3% of GDP in 2016, industry 31·3% and services 64·4%.

Overview

Chile had one of Latin America's fastest-growing economies in the decade to 2013, averaging around 4·6% per year. However, GDP growth fell to 1·8% in 2014 and 2·3% in 2015, as a result of a slowdown in the mining sector (reflecting declining copper prices) and reduced private consumption. The fiscal balance moved from a surplus of 0·5% of GDP in 2013 to a deficit of 2·1% in 2015. Tax reforms implemented in 2015 aim to increase fiscal revenue in order to finance additional expenditures in education while reducing the fiscal gap. The current account deficit as of 2015 was almost entirely covered by net foreign direct investment (FDI) flows. In March 2018 Chile and ten other countries bordering the Pacific (although not the USA) signed the Comprehensive and Progressive Agreement for Trans-Pacific Partnership.

Chile's economy was liberalized under the Pinochet regime (1973–90) and reform continued under the democratic governments of the 1990s, when it had the highest FDI-to-GDP ratio in the region. The percentage of the population considered poor (those living on US$2·50 per day) declined from 7·7% in 2003 to 2·0% in 2014; moderate poverty (under US$4 per day) also fell, from 20·6% to 6·8% in the same period. Moreover, between 2003 and 2014 the average income of the poorest 40% of the population increased by 4·9%, a figure considerably above the average income growth of the population as a whole (3·3%).

Chile enjoys both political stability and a strong business environment, with a well-developed institutional framework. The country still faces important challenges, however, and macroeconomic management must improve if inclusive medium- and long-term growth is to be achieved.

Currency

The unit of currency is the *Chilean peso* (CLP) of 100 *centavos*. The peso was revalued 3·5% against the US dollar in Nov. 1994. In Sept. 1999 the managed exchange-rate system was abandoned and the peso allowed to float. Inflation rates (based on OECD statistics):

2008	2009	2010	2011	2012	2013	2014	2015	2016	2017
8·7%	0·4%	1·4%	3·3%	3·0%	1·9%	4·4%	4·3%	3·8%	2·2%

In Aug. 2009 gold reserves were 8,000 troy oz and foreign exchange reserves US$23,711m. Total money supply was 9,687·2bn. pesos in May 2009.

Budget

The fiscal year is the calendar year.
Budgetary central government revenue and expenditure (in 1bn. pesos):

	2009	2010	2011
Revenue	17,709·9	23,352·4	26,941·6
Expenditure	20,176·2	22,141·1	23,465·0

Principal sources of revenue in 2011 were: taxes on goods and services, 11,531·1bn. pesos; taxes on income, profits and capital gains, 7,483·9bn.

pesos; social security contributions, 1,623·8bn. pesos. Main items of expenditure by economic type in 2011: social benefits, 5,752·7bn. pesos; compensation of employees, 4,946·9bn. pesos; subsidies, 3,289·1bn. pesos.

VAT is 19%.

Performance

Real GDP growth rates (based on OECD statistics):

2008	2009	2010	2011	2012	2013	2014	2015	2016	2017
3·5%	−1·5%	5·9%	6·0%	5·4%	4·1%	1·8%	2·3%	1·2%	1·6%

Total GDP in 2017 was US$277·1bn.

Banking and Finance

The Superintendencia de Bancos e Instituciones Financieras, affiliated to the finance ministry, is the banking supervisory authority. There are a Central Bank and a State Bank. The Central Bank was made independent of government control in March 1990. The *Governor* is Mario Marcel. There were 21 domestic and six foreign banks in 2005. In Jan. 2005 deposits in domestic banks totalled 25,779,053m. pesos; in foreign banks, 2,163,183m. pesos, and in other finance companies, 4,829,090m. pesos.

External debt totalled US$86,349m. in 2010 and represented 45·9% of GNI.

There are stock exchanges in Santiago and Valparaíso.

Energy and Natural Resources

Environment

Chile's carbon dioxide emissions from the consumption of energy in 2011 were the equivalent of 4·6 tonnes per capita.

Electricity

Installed capacity was 17·6m. kW in 2011. Production of electricity was 65·71bn. kWh in 2011, of which 32% was hydro-electric. Consumption per capita in 2011 was 3,839 kWh.

Oil and Gas

Production of crude oil, 2011, was 2·0m. bbls. Natural gas production, 2011, was 1·6bn. cu. metres. Chile imports nearly all of its oil and around 75% of the natural gas that it consumes.

Minerals

The wealth of the country consists chiefly in its minerals. Chile is the world's largest copper producer; copper is the most important source of foreign exchange and government revenues. Production, 2013, 5,851,000 tonnes. Chile is also the largest producer of lithium. Coal is low-grade and mining is difficult. Production, 2013, 2,902,000 tonnes.

Output of other minerals, 2013 unless otherwise indicated (in tonnes): iron ore (2012), 9,088,000; salt, 6,577,000; limestone, 6,246,000; lithium carbonate, 52,358; molybdenum, 38,715; zinc, 29,759; silver, 1,174. Gold (51,309 kg in 2013), nitrate, iodine and sodium sulphate are also produced.

Agriculture

In 2007, 1·29m. ha. were arable land and 0·46m. ha. permanent crops. 0·96m. ha. were irrigated in 2007. There were 400 tractors and 66 harvester-threshers per 10,000 ha. of arable land in 2006.

Principal crops were as follows:

Crop	Area harvested, 1,000 ha. 2013	Production, 1,000 tonnes 2013
Maize	143	1,519
Wheat	254	1,475
Sugar beets	18	1,186
Potatoes	50	1,159
Tomatoes	13	836
Oats	127	680
Onions	7	338[1]
Rapeseed	41	156

[1]Estimate.

Fruit production, 2013 estimates (in 1,000 tonnes): grapes, 2,376; apples, 1,729; peaches and nectarines, 371; plums, 314; kiwi fruit, 272; pears, 230; lemons and limes, 158. Wine production in 2013 totalled 1,282,000 tonnes.

Livestock, 2013: sheep (estimate), 3·4m.; cattle, 3·0m.; pigs, 2·8m.; goats, 462,000; horses (2011 estimate), 310,000; poultry (estimate), 80m. Livestock products, 2013 (in 1,000 tonnes): pork and pork products, 550; beef and veal, 206; poultry meat, 676; cow's milk, 2,149; eggs, 209.

Forestry

In 2015, 17·74m. ha., or 24% of the total land area, was under forests. Of the total area under forests 30% was primary forest in 2015, 53% other naturally regenerated forest and 17% planted forest. Timber production in 2011 was 55·15m. cu. metres.

Fisheries

The catch in 2015 was 1,786,633 tonnes. Exports of fishery commodities in 2010 were valued at US$3·40bn., against imports of US$255m. Chile is one of the leading aquaculture producers, with 701,062 tonnes in 2010. Only Norway produces more farmed salmon. Chile is also a major producer of fishmeal, with 2009 production second only to that of Peru at 641,000 tonnes.

Industry

The leading companies by market capitalization in Chile in March 2019 were: Falabella, a retail company (US$23·6bn.); SQM, a strategic industry company (US$15·1bn.); and Empresas CMPC, a pulp and paper company (US$10·0bn.).

Output of major products in 1,000 tonnes: sulphuric acid, 5,132 (2010); cement (2012), 4,722; distillate fuel oil (2007), 3,623; residual fuel oil (2007), 2,445; petrol (2007), 2,349. Output of other products: soft drinks (2013), 1,387m. litres; beer (2007), 550m. litres; 5·04m. motor tyres (2008).

Labour

The labour force in 2013 was 8,603,000 (6,372,000 in 2003). 67·4% of the population aged 15–64 was economically active in 2013. In Dec. 2018, 7·1% of the active population was unemployed (up from 6·7% in 2017 as a whole).

Chile had 38,000 people living in slavery according to the Walk Free Foundation's 2013 *Global Slavery Index*.

International Trade

Imports and Exports

Goods imports were US$72,344·3m. in 2014 (US$79,172·8m. in 2013) and goods exports US$76,639·2m. (US$76,684·1m. in 2013).

Main imports in 2014 were machinery and transport equipment (34·2%), mineral fuels and lubricants, and manufactured goods; main exports in 2014 were crude materials and animal and vegetable oils (34·0%), manufactured goods, and food, animals and beverages.

The leading import source in 2010 was China (17·6%), followed by the USA and Argentina; the leading export market in 2010 was China (24·6%), followed by Japan and the USA.

Communications

Roads

In 2013 there were approximately 78,000 km of national roads, but only 23·1% were paved. There were approximately 3,000 km of concession roads and approximately 14,000 km of local roads. In 2007 there were 1,701,036 passenger cars, 849,282 trucks and vans, 170,217 buses and coaches and 63,257 motorcycles and mopeds. In 2006 there were 2,280 road accident fatalities.

Rail

The total length of railway lines was (2014) 5,529 km, about a fifth of which was electrified, of broad- and metre-gauge. The state railway (EFE) transported 11·3m. passengers in 2005. Freight operations are in the hands of the semi-private companies Ferronor, Pacifico and the Antofagasta (Chili) and Bolivia Railway (973 km, metre-gauge) which links the port of Antofagasta with Bolivia and Argentina. Passenger-km travelled in 2008 came to 759m. and freight tonne-km in 2006 to 3,660m.

There are metro systems in Santiago (46·2 km) and Valparaíso (42·5 km).

Civil Aviation

There are international airports at Antofagasta, Arica, Easter Island (Isla de Pascua), Iquique, Puerto Montt, Punta Arenas and Santiago (Comodoro Arturo Merino Benítez). The largest airline is LATAM, created in June 2012 when the Chilean carrier LAN Airlines (formerly LAN-Chile) merged with TAM, Brazil's largest airline. In 2014 LATAM carried 67,833,000 passengers, making it the world's seventh largest airline on the basis of passengers carried. In 2012 Santiago handled 14,168,282 passengers (6,753,584 on international flights).

Shipping

In Jan. 2014 there were 82 ships of 300 GT or over registered, totalling 515,000 GT. The leading ports are Antofagasta, Arica, Iquique, Puerto Ventanas, San Antonio, Talcahuano/San Vicente and Valparaíso.

Telecommunications

In 2012 there were 3,281,000 main (fixed) telephone lines. In the same year mobile phone subscriptions numbered 23,941,000. There were 4,933,000 mobile broadband subscriptions in 2012 and 2,154,000 fixed broadband subscriptions. In June 2012 there were 9·4m. Facebook users.

Social Institutions

Out of 178 countries analysed in the 2017 *Fragile States Index*—a list published jointly by the Fund for Peace and *Foreign Policy* magazine—Chile was ranked the 29th least vulnerable to conflict or collapse. The index is based on 12 indicators of state vulnerability across social, political and economic categories.

Justice

There are a High Court of Justice in the capital, 16 courts of appeal distributed over the republic, courts of first instance in the departmental capitals and second-class judges in the sub-delegations.

The population in penal institutions in July 2013 was 46,718 (266 per 100,000 of national population). In 2015 the World Justice Project *Rule of Law Index*, which provides data on how the rule of law is experienced by the general public across eight categories, ranked Chile 32nd of 102 countries for both criminal justice and civil justice.

The death penalty for ordinary crimes was abolished in 2001.

Education

In 2007–08 there were 402,000 children at pre-primary schools, 1·66m. primary school pupils and 1·59m. pupils at secondary level. Adult literacy rate in 2008 was 99%.

In 2012 there were 1,118,773 students in higher education. There were 60 universities with 619,681 students, 45 professional institutes with 282,436 students and 69 technical training centres with 131,769 students.

In 2007 public expenditure on education came to 3·8% of GNI and represented 18·2% of total government expenditure.

Health

There were 418 hospitals in 2008. Over the period 2007–13 there were 10·2 physicians for every 10,000 inhabitants and 1·4 nursing and midwifery personnel for every 10,000.

In *Water: At What Cost? The State of the World's Water 2016*, WaterAid reported that 1·0% of the population does not have access to safe water.

Welfare

In 1981 Chile abolished its state-sponsored pension plan and became the first country to establish private mandatory retirement savings. The system is managed by competitive private companies called AFPs (Pension Fund Administrators). Employees are required to save 13% of their pay. In April 2005 it had 7,132,983 members and assets of 35,051,470m. pesos. In 2005 about 65% of the population over the age of 14 had private health insurance.

Religion

In 2010 there were an estimated 12·29m. Roman Catholics, 2·66m. Protestants and 0·35m. other Christians according to the Pew Research Center's Forum on Religion & Public Life. A further 1·47m. people had no religious affiliation and there were 0·26m. folk religionists. The Roman Catholic Church has five ecclesiastical provinces, each headed by an archbishop. In Feb. 2019 there were three cardinals.

Culture

World Heritage Sites

Chile's six UNESCO protected sites are the Rapa Nui National Park, the Churches of Chiloé, the Historic Quarter of the Seaport of Valparaíso, the Humberstone and Santa Laura Saltpeter Works, and the Sewell Mining Town. Entered on the list in 1995, the Rapa Nui National Park encompasses much of the coastline of Easter Island and protects the shrines and statues (*Moai*) carved between the 10th–16th centuries. On the island of Chiloé off the Región de Los Lagos coastline, wooden churches were built by Jesuit missionaries at the turn of the 17th century. The churches were entered on the list in 2000. The Valparaíso site was inscribed on the list in 2003 as a model of urban and architectural development in 19th-century Latin America. The Humberstone and Santa Laura Saltpeter Works were inscribed in 2005 and are where workers from Peru, Chile and Bolivia formed a distinctive communal pampinos culture. The Sewell Mining Town, inscribed in 2006, is an example of the company towns that existed in the early 20th century in many remote parts of the world. Shared with Argentina, Bolivia, Colombia, Ecuador and Peru, Qhapaq Ñan, Andean Road System (2014) is an extensive Inca communication, trade and defence network of roads covering 30,000 km.

Press

In 2012 there were 65 daily newspapers (60 paid-for and five free) and 42 non-dailies (39 paid-for and three free). The dailies had a combined average daily circulation of 689,000 in 2012.

Tourism

There were 3,069,792 non-resident overnight tourists in 2011 (2,766,007 in 2010). Tourist receipts were US$3,134m. in 2014.

Diplomatic Representatives

Of Chile in the United Kingdom (37–41 Old Queen St., London, SW1H 9JA)
  Ambassador: David Gallagher.

Of the United Kingdom in Chile (Av. El Bosque Norte 0125, Las Condes, Santiago)
  Ambassador: Jamie Bowden.

Of Chile in the USA (1732 Massachusetts Ave., NW, Washington, D.C., 20036)
  Ambassador: Oscar Alfonso Sebastian Silva Navarro.

Of the USA in Chile (Av. Andrés Bello 2800, Las Condes, Santiago)
  Ambassador: Vacant.
  Chargé d'Affaires a.i.: Baxter Hunt.

Of Chile to the United Nations
  Ambassador: Milenko Skoknic Tapia.

Of Chile to the European Union
  Ambassador: Raúl Fernandez Daza.

Further Reading

Bizzarro, Salvatore, *Historical Dictionary of Chile.* 2005
Collier, S. and Sater, W. F., *A History of Chile, 1808–1994.* 1996
Hojman, D. E., *Chile: the Political Economy of Development and Democracy in the 1990s.* 1993.—(ed.) *Change in the Chilean Countryside: from Pinochet to Aylwin and Beyond.* 1993
Oppenheim, L. H., *Politics in Chile: Democracy, Authoritarianism and the Search for Development.* 1993
Rector, John L., *The History of Chile.* 2006
National Statistical Office: Instituto Nacional de Estadísticas (INE), Paseo Bulnes 418, Santiago.
Website (Spanish only): http://www.ine.cl

China

Zhonghua Renmin Gonghe Guo (People's Republic of China)

Capital: Beijing (Peking)
Population projection, 2020: 1,424·55m.
GNI per capita, 2017: (PPP$) 15,270
HDI/world rank, 2017: 0·752/86=
Internet domain extension: .cn

Key Historical Events

An embryonic Chinese state emerged in the fertile Huang He (Yellow River) basin before 4000 BC. Chinese culture reached the Chang Jiang (Yangtze) basin by 2500 BC and within 500 years the far south was also within the Chinese orbit. Four thousand years ago the Xia dynasty ruled in the Huang He basin. About 1500 BC it was supplanted by the Shang dynasty, the cultural ancestor of modern China.

As Shang civilization spread, in the west the Shang came into conflict with the Zhou, whose rulers replaced the Shang dynasty around 1000 BC. Under the Zhou, a centralized administration developed. In about 500 BC one court official, Kongfuzi (Confucius), outlined his vision of society. Confucianism, which introduced a system of civil service recruitment through examination, remained dominant until the mid-20th century.

The Zhou expanded the Chinese state south beyond the Chang Jiang. In 221 BC the ruler of Qin became the first emperor of China. He built an empire extending from the South China Sea to the edge of Central Asia where work was begun on the Great Wall of China. The Qin dynasty standardized laws, money and administration throughout the empire but it was short-lived. By 206 BC the state had divided into three.

Reunification came gradually under the Han dynasty (202 BC–AD 200) with its efficient, centralized bureaucracy. A nation with boundaries similar to those of modern China was created. But peripheral territories proved too distant to hold and the Han empire fell to rebellion and invasion. It was followed by the Jin (265–316) and Sui (589–612) dynasties, interspersed by internecine war and anarchy. Reunification was achieved by the Tang dynasty which brought prosperity to China from 618–917, before falling to separatism.

Under the Song (960–1127), the balance of power shifted south. The Song state lost control of the area north of the Chang Jiang in 1126 when nomads from Manchuria invaded. A declining Song empire survived in the south until 1279.

Genghis Khan

The northern invaders were overthrown by the Mongols, led by Genghis Khan (c. 1162–1227), who went on to claim the rest of China. In 1280 Kublai Khan (1251–94), who had founded the Yuan dynasty in 1271, swept into southern China. The Mongol Yuan dynasty adopted Chinese ways but was overthrown by a nationalist uprising in 1368, led by Hongwu (1328–98), a former beggar who established the Ming dynasty.

The Ming empire collapsed in a peasants' revolt in 1644. The capital, Beijing (Peking), was only 64 km from the Great Wall and vulnerable to attack from the north. Within months the peasants' leader was swept aside by the Manchus, whose Qing dynasty ruled China until 1911. Preoccupied with threats from the north, China neglected its southern coastal frontier. The Portuguese, who landed on the Chinese coast in 1516, were followed by the Dutch in 1622 and the English in 1637.

The Qing empire expanded into Mongolia, Tibet, Vietnam and Kazakhstan. But by the 19th century, under pressure from rural revolts ignited by crippling taxation and poverty, the Qing dynasty was crumbling. Two Opium Wars (1838–42; 1856–58) forced China to allow the import of opium from India into China, while Britain, France, Germany and other European states gained concessions in 'treaty ports' that virtually came under foreign rule.

The Taiping Rebellion (1851–64) set up a revolutionary egalitarian state in southern China. The European powers intervened to crush the rebellion and in 1860 British and French forces invaded Beijing and burnt the imperial palace. Further trading concessions were demanded. A weakened China was defeated by Japan in 1895 and lost both Taiwan and Korea.

The xenophobic Boxer Rebellion, led by a secret society called the Fists of Righteous Harmony, broke out in 1900. The Guangxu emperor (1875–1908) attempted modernization in the Hundred Days Reform, but was taken captive by the conservative dowager empress Cixi who harnessed the Boxer Rebellion to her own ends. The rebellion was put down by European troops in 1901. China was then divided into zones of influence between the major European states and Japan.

With imperial authority weakened, much of the country was ripe for rebellion. In 1911 the Kuomintang (Guomintang or Nationalist movement) of Sun Yet-sen (Sun Zhong Shan; 1866–1925) overthrew the imperial system. The authoritarian Yuan Shih-kai ruled as president from 1913 to 1916. Following the overthrow of Yuan, China disintegrated into warlord anarchy.

In 1916 Sun founded a republic in southern China but the north remained beyond his control. Reorganizing the Nationalist party on Soviet lines, Sun co-operated with the Communists to re-establish national unity. But rivalry between the two parties increased, particularly after the death of Sun in 1925.

Nationalism and Communism

After Sun's death the nationalist movement was taken over by his ally Chiang Kai-shek (Jiang Jie Shi; 1887–1976). As commander in chief of the Nationalist army from 1925, Chiang's power grew. In April 1927 his campaign to suppress the Chinese Communist Party saw thousands of Communists slaughtered. The survivors fled to the far western province of Jiangxi. In 1928 Chiang's army entered Beijing. With the greater part of the country under Chiang's rule, he made Nanjing the capital. In 1934 the Communists were forced to retreat from Jiangxi province. Led by Mao Zedong (Mao Tse-tung; 1893–1976) they trekked for more than a year on the 5,600-mile Long March, eventually taking refuge in Shaanxi province.

In 1931 the Japanese invaded Manchuria. By 1937 they had seized Beijing and most of coastal China. The Nationalists and Communists finally co-operated against the invader but struggled against the superior Japanese forces.

During the Second World War (1939-45), a Nationalist government ruled unoccupied China ineffectually from a temporary capital in Chongqing. At the end of the war, Nationalist–Communist co-operation was short-lived. The Soviet Union sponsored the Communist Party, which marched into Manchuria in 1946, beginning a civil war that lasted until 1949. Although the Nationalist forces of Chiang Kai-shek received support from some western countries, particularly the United States, the Communists were victorious. On 1 Oct. 1949 Mao declared the People's Republic of China in Beijing.

Chiang fled with the remains of his Nationalist forces to Taiwan, where he established a government that claimed to be a continuation of the Republic of China. At first recognized as the government of China by most Western countries, Taiwan kept China's Security Council seat at the United Nations until 1971. Chiang's authoritarian regime was periodically challenged by Red China, which bombed Taiwan's small offshore islands near the mainland. In the 1960s and 1970s, Taiwan gradually lost recognition as the legitimate government and in 1978 the USA recognized the People's Republic of China.

Expansionism

In 1950 China invaded Tibet, independent since 1916. Chinese rule quickly alienated the Tibetans who rebelled in 1959. The Tibetan religious leader, the Dalai Lama, was forced to flee to India. Since then, the settlement of large numbers of ethnic Chinese in the main cities of Tibet has threatened to swamp Tibetan culture.

During the 1950s and 1960s China was involved in a number of border disputes and wars in neighbouring states. The Communists posted 'volunteers' to fight alongside Communist North Korea during the Korean War (1950–53). There were clashes on the Soviet border in the 1950s and the Indian border in the 1960s, when China occupied some Indian territory.

From the establishment of the People's Republic of China, Communist China and the Soviet Union were allies. Communist China initially depended upon Soviet assistance for economic development. A Soviet-style five-year plan was put into action in 1953, but the relationship with Moscow was already showing signs of strain. By the end of the 1950s the Soviet Union and China were rivals, spurring the Chinese arms race. Chinese research into atomic weapons culminated in the testing of the first Chinese atomic bomb in 1964.

Mao introduced rapid collectivization of farms in 1955. The plan was not met with universal approval in the Communist Party but its implementation demonstrated Mao's authority over the fortunes of the nation. In 1956 he launched the doctrine of letting a 'hundred flowers bloom', encouraging intellectual debate. However, the new freedoms took a turn Mao did not expect and led to the questioning of the role of the party. Strict controls were reimposed and free-thinkers were sent to work in the countryside to be 're-educated'.

In May 1958 Mao launched another ill-fated policy, the Great Leap Forward. To promote rapid industrialization and socialism, the collectives were reorganized into larger units. Neither the resources nor trained personnel were available for this huge task. Backyard blast furnaces were set up to increase production of iron and steel. The Great Leap Forward was a disaster. It is believed that 30m. died from famine. Soviet advice against the project was ignored and a breakdown in relations with Moscow came in 1963, when Soviet assistance was withdrawn. A rapprochement with the United States was achieved in the early 1970s.

Cultural Revolution

Having published his 'Thoughts' in the 'Little Red Book' (as it is known in the West) in 1964, Mao set the Cultural Revolution in motion. Militant students were organized into groups of Red Guards to attack the party hierarchy. Anyone perceived to lack enthusiasm for Mao Zedong Thought was denounced. Thousands died as the students lost control and the army was eventually called in to restore order.

After Mao's death in 1976 the Gang of Four, led by Mao's widow Jiang Qing, attempted to seize power. These hard-liners were denounced and arrested. China effectively came under the control of Deng Xiaoping. Deng pursued economic reform. The country was opened to Western investment. Special Economic Zones and 'open cities' were designated and private enterprise gradually returned.

Improved standards of living and a thriving economy increased expectations for civil liberties. The demand for political change climaxed in demonstrations by workers and students in April 1989, following the funeral of Communist Party leader Hu Yaobang. In Beijing where demonstrators peacefully occupied Tiananmen Square, they were evicted by the military who opened fire, killing more than 1,500. Hard-liners took control of the government, and martial law was imposed from May 1989 to Jan. 1990.

Since 1989 the leadership has concentrated on economic development. Hong Kong was returned to China from British rule in 1997 (for the background, *see* page 330) and Macao from Portuguese rule in 1999. The late 1990s saw a cautious extension of civil liberties but Chinese citizens are still denied most basic political rights.

Beijing was chosen for the 2008 Olympic Games. China's treatment of Tibet came under the international spotlight in the build-up to the games, following violent protests in Tibet's capital city, Lhasa.

The arrest by Japan of a Chinese trawler in disputed waters in 2010 marked the beginning of heightened tensions between the two nations in the East and South China Seas. In 2011 China became the world's second largest national economy. In Nov. 2012 the Communist Party congress selected Xi Jinping to succeed Hu Jintao as president from March 2013. In Sept. that year, former leadership hopeful Bo Xilai received a life sentence for corruption in one of China's highest-profile trials in decades.

In Oct. 2015 the government announced the end of the country's one-child policy. A month later, the presidents of China and Taiwan met for talks—the first time that leaders from the respective territories had met since 1949. On the economic front, GDP growth in 2015 was at its lowest level for a quarter of a century.

Territory and Population

China is bounded in the north by Russia and Mongolia; east by North Korea, the Yellow Sea and the East China Sea, with Hong Kong and Macao as enclaves on the southeast coast; south by Vietnam, Laos, Myanmar, India, Bhutan and Nepal; west by India, Pakistan, Afghanistan, Tajikistan, Kyrgyzstan and Kazakhstan. The total area (including Taiwan, Hong Kong and Macao) is estimated at 9,572,900 sq. km (3,696,100 sq. miles). A law of Feb. 1992 claimed the Spratly, Paracel and Diaoyutasi Islands. An agreement

of 7 Sept. 1993 at prime ministerial level settled Sino-Indian border disputes which had first emerged in the war of 1962.

China's sixth national census was held on 1 Nov. 2010. The total population of the 31 provinces, autonomous regions and municipalities and of servicemen on the mainland was 1,339,724,852 (652,872,280 females, representing 48·73%); density, 140 per sq. km. China's population in 2010 represented 19% of the world's total population. The population rose by 73,899,804 (or 5·84%) since the census in 2000. There were 665,575,306 urban residents, accounting for 49·68% of the population; compared to the 2000 census, the proportion of urban residents rose by 13·46% (reflecting the increasing migration from the countryside to towns and cities since the economy was opened up in the late 1970s). Population estimate, Dec. 2016: 1,382,710,000.

China has a fast-growing ageing population. Whereas in 1980 only 5·2% of the population was aged 65 or over and by 2010 this had increased to 8·2%, by 2030 it is expected to rise to 17·2%. Long-term projections suggest that in 2050 as much as 27·6% of the population will be 65 or older. The population is expected to peak at 1·42m. around 2028 and then begin to decline to such an extent that by around 2050 it will be back to the 2011 level. China is set to lose its status as the world's most populous country to India in about 2022.

The UN gives a projected population for 2020 of 1,424·55m.

1979 regulations restricting married couples to a single child, a policy enforced by compulsory abortions and economic sanctions, were widely ignored, and it was admitted in 1988 that the population target of 1,200m. by 2000 would have to be revised to 1,270m. From 1988 peasant couples were permitted a second child after four years if the first born was a girl, a measure to combat infanticide. In 1999 China started to implement a more widespread gradual relaxation of the one-child policy. In Dec. 2013 the Standing Committee of the National People's Congress (NPC) approved a resolution allowing couples to have two children if either parent was an only child. The one-child policy was formally abandoned altogether from 1 Jan. 2016.

An estimated 50m. persons of Chinese origin lived abroad in 2012.

A number of widely divergent varieties of Chinese are spoken. The official 'Modern Standard Chinese' is based on the dialect of North China. Mandarin in one form or another is spoken by 885m. people in China, or around 70% of the population of mainland China. The Wu language and its dialects has some 77m. native speakers and Cantonese 66m. Around 400m. people in China cannot speak Mandarin. The ideographic writing system of 'characters' is uniform throughout the country, and has undergone systematic simplification. In 1958 a phonetic alphabet (*Pinyin*) was devised to transcribe the characters, and in 1979 this was officially adopted for use in all texts in the Roman alphabet. The previous transcription scheme (*Wade*) is still used in Taiwan and Hong Kong.

Mainland China is administratively divided into 22 provinces, five autonomous regions (originally entirely or largely inhabited by ethnic minorities, though in some regions now outnumbered by Han immigrants) and four government-controlled municipalities. These are in turn divided into 332 prefectures, 658 cities (of which 265 are at prefecture level and 393 at county level), 2,053 counties and 808 urban districts.

Government-controlled municipalities	Area (1,000 sq. km)	2010 census population (1,000)	Density per sq. km (2010)	Capital
Beijing	16·8	19,612	1,167	—
Chongqing	82·0	28,846	352	—
Shanghai	6·2	23,019	3,713	—
Tianjin	11·3	12,939	1,145	—
Provinces				
Anhui	139·9	59,500	425	Hefei
Fujian	123·1	36,894	300	Fuzhou
Gansu[1]	366·5	25,575	70	Lanzhou
Guangdong[1]	197·1	104,320	529	Guangzhou
Guizhou[1]	174·0	34,749	200	Guiyang
Hainan[1]	34·3	8,671	253	Haikou
Hebei[1]	202·7	71,854	354	Shijiazhuang
Heilongjiang[1]	463·6	38,314	83	Haerbin
Henan	167·0	94,030	563	Zhengzhou

(*continued*)

Government-controlled municipalities	Area (1,000 sq. km)	2010 census population (1,000)	Density per sq. km (2010)	Capital
Hubei[1]	187·5	57,238	305	Wuhan
Hunan[1]	210·5	65,701	312	Changsha
Jiangsu	102·6	78,661	767	Nanjing
Jiangxi	164·8	44,568	270	Nanchang
Jilin[1]	187·0	27,453	147	Changchun
Liaoning[1]	151·0	43,746	290	Shenyang
Qinghai[1]	721·0	5,627	8	Xining
Shaanxi	195·8	37,327	191	Xian
Shandong	153·3	95,793	625	Jinan
Shanxi	157·1	35,712	227	Taiyuan
Sichuan[1]	487·0	80,418	165	Chengdu
Yunnan[1]	436·2	45,967	105	Kunming
Zhejiang[1]	101·8	54,427	535	Hangzhou
Autonomous regions				
Guangxi Zhuang	220·4	46,024	209	Nanning
Inner Mongolia	1,177·5	24,706	21	Hohhot
Ningxia Hui	66·4	6,301	95	Yinchuan
Tibet[2]	1,221·6	3,002	2	Lhasa
Xinjiang Uighur	1,646·9	21,816	13	Urumqi

[1]Also designated minority nationality autonomous area. [2]See also Tibet below.

Population of largest cities in 2010: Shanghai, 20·22m.; Beijing (Peking), 16·45m.; Shenzhen, 10·36m.; Guangzhou (Canton), 9·70m.; Tianjin, 9·29m.; Dongguan, 7·27m.; Wuhan, 6·84m.; Foshan, 6·77m.; Chengdu, 6·32m.; Chongqing, 6·26m.; Nanjing, 5·83m.; Shenyang, 5·72m.; Xian, 5·21m.; Hangzhou, 5·16m.; Haerbin, 4·60m.; Suzhou, 4·08m.; Dalian, 3·90m.; Zhengzhou, 3·68m.; Shantou, 3·64m.; Jinan, 3·53m.; Qingdao, 3·52m.; Changchun, 3·41m.; Kunming, 3·28m.; Changsha, 3·19m.; Taiyuan, 3·15m.; Xiamen, 3·12m.; Hefei, 3·10m.; Urumqi (Wulumuqi), 2·85m.; Fuzhou, 2·82m.; Shijiazhuang, 2·77m.; Wuxi, 2·76m.; Zhongshan, 2·74m.; Wenzhou, 2·69m.; Nanning, 2·66m.; Ningbo, 2·58m.; Guiyang, 2·52m.; Lanzhou, 2·44m.; Zibo, 2·26m.; Changzhou, 2·26m.; Nanchang, 2·22m.; Xuzhou, 2·21m.; Tangshan, 2·13m.

China has 56 ethnic groups. According to the 2010 census 1,225,932,641 people (91·51%) were of Han nationality and 113,792,211 (8·49%) were from national minorities (including Zhuang, Manchu, Hui, Miao, Uighur, Yi, Tujia, Mongolian and Tibetan). Compared with the 2000 census, the Han population increased by 66,537,177 (5·74%), while the ethnic minorities increased by 7,362,627 (6·92%). Non-Han populations predominate in the autonomous regions, most notably in Tibet where Tibetans account for around 95% of the population.

Chang, Chiung-Fang, Lee, Che-Fu, McKibben, Sherry L., Poston, Dudley L. and Walther, Carol S. (eds.) *Fertility, Family Planning and Population Policy in China.* 2009

Li Chengrui, *A Study of China's Population.* 1992

Zhao, Zhongwei and Guo, Fei, *Transition and Challenge: China's Population at the Beginning of the 21st Century.* 2007

Tibet

Relations between Tibet and China's central government have fluctuated over the question of Tibetan independence. The borders were opened for trade with neighbouring countries in 1980. In 1984 a Buddhist seminary opened in Lhasa, the regional capital, with 200 students, and monasteries and shrines have since been renovated and reopened. There were some 46,000 monks and nuns in 2013. In 1988 Tibetan was reinstated as a 'major official language', competence in which is required of all administrative officials. In 1998 the then Chinese president, Jiang Zemin, said he was prepared to meet the Dalai Lama provided he acknowledged Chinese sovereignty over Tibet and Taiwan. In Sept. 2002 direct contact between the exiled government and China was re-established after a nine-year gap.

However, in March 2008 anti-Chinese protests in Lhasa ended in violence, with dozens reportedly killed by the Chinese authorities, and in Oct.

that year the Dalai Lama stated he had lost hope of reaching agreement with China on Tibet's status. In April 2011 he announced his retirement from active politics in favour of Lobsang Sangay, who had been elected to lead the Tibetan government-in-exile. In July 2011, shortly after US President Obama had received the Dalai Lama in Washington, China's soon-to-be president, Xi Jinping, pledged to 'smash' attempts to destabilize Tibet. By Feb. 2013 there had been over 100 reported cases of self-immolation by Tibetans protesting against Chinese rule.

The estimated population of Tibet at the end of 2012 had risen to 3·08m. from 3·00m. at the 2010 census. The average population density was 2·26 persons per sq. km in 2008, although the majority of residents live in the southern and eastern parts of the region. Birth rate (per 1,000), 2012, 15·5; death rate, 5·2. Population of Lhasa, the capital, in 2010 was 199,159.

About 80% of the population is engaged in the dominant industries of farming and animal husbandry. In 2009 the total sown area was 240,610 ha. Output in 2011: total grain crops, 937,300 tonnes; vegetables, 600,700 tonnes. In 2011 there were 14·59m. sheep and goats and 6·45m. cattle and yaks.

Tibet has over 2,000 mineral ore fields. Mining, particularly of copper and gold, has expanded rapidly since 2006 when the railway came to Tibet. Cement production, 2011: 2·35m. tonnes. Electricity consumption totalled 2·7bn. kWh in 2012.

In 2011 there were 63,108 km of roads (21,842 km in 1990). There are airports at Lhasa, Bangda and Nyingchi providing external links. In 2011, 270,800 foreign tourists visited Tibet. In July 2006 a 1,142-km railway linking Lhasa with the town of Golmud opened. It is the highest railway in the world. Direct services have subsequently been introduced between Lhasa and a number of major Chinese cities, including Beijing and Shanghai. An extension from Lhasa to Shigatse, Tibet's second largest city, became operational in Aug. 2014. In 2011 Tibet had 860 primary schools (with 294,725 pupils) and 123 secondary schools of which 22 were senior secondary schools (with 44,676 pupils), 93 junior secondary schools (with 136,371 pupils) and eight whole secondary schools. There were also six vocational secondary schools in 2011 (19,446 pupils). Tibet has six higher education institutes (the largest of which is Tibet University), with 33,198 enrolled students in total in 2011. The illiteracy rate of people aged 15 and above was 32·3% in 2011.

In 2011 there were 10,797 medical personnel (including 4,175 doctors) and 1,378 medical institutions, with a total of 9,462 beds.

Lixiong, Wang and Shakya, Tsering, *The Struggle for Tibet.* 2009

Margolis, Eric, *War at the Top of the World: The Struggle for Afghanistan, Kashmir and Tibet.* 2001

Shakya, Tsering, *The Dragon in the Land of Snows: The History of Modern Tibet since 1947.* 1999

Smith, W. W., *A History of Tibet: Nationalism and Self-Determination.* 1996

Van Schaik, Sam, *Tibet: A History.* 2011

Social Statistics

Births, 2012, 16,350,000; deaths, 9,660,000. 2012 birth rate (per 1,000 population), 12·1; death rate, 7·2. In 2005 the birth rate rose for the first time since 1987. There were 13,235,900 marriages and 3,103,800 divorces in 2012. In 2011 the marriage rate was 9·7 per 1,000 population and the divorce rate a record high 2·1 per 1,000. The divorce rate has doubled since 2003. In April 2001 parliament passed revisions to the marriage law prohibiting bigamy and cohabitation outside marriage. The suicide rate in China in 2012 was 16·2 per 100,000 population. Life expectancy at birth, 2015, was 73·6 years for men and 79·4 years for women. Infant mortality, 2015, 9 per 1,000 live births. China has made some of the best progress in recent years in reducing child mortality. The number of deaths per 1,000 live births among children under five was reduced from 54 in 1990 to 14 in 2012. Fertility rate, 2013, 1·7 births per woman (compared to over 6 in the mid-1960s). Annual population growth rate, 2010–15, 0·5%. According to the World Bank, the number of people living in poverty (less than US$1·25 a day) at purchasing power parity declined from 835m. in 1981 to 156m. in 2010.

Climate

Most of China has a temperate climate but, with such a large country, extending far inland and embracing a wide range of latitude as well as containing large areas at high altitude, many parts experience extremes of climate, especially in winter. Most rain falls during the summer, from May to

Sept., though amounts decrease inland. Monthly average temperatures and annual rainfall (2012): Beijing (Peking), Jan. 25·5°F (−3·6°C), July 81·3°F (27·4°C). Annual rainfall 28·9" (733 mm). Chongqing, Jan. 45·0°F (7·2°C), July 83·3°F (28·5°C). Annual rainfall 43·5" (1,104 mm). Shanghai, Jan. 40·5°F (4·7°C), July 85·5°F (29·7°C). Annual rainfall 43·5" (1,104 mm). Tianjin, Jan. 25·2°F (−3·8°C), July 81·0°F (27·2°C). Annual rainfall 29·7" (755 mm).

Constitution and Government

On 21 Sept. 1949 the *Chinese People's Political Consultative Conference* met in Beijing, convened by the Chinese Communist Party. The Conference adopted a 'Common Programme' of 60 articles and the 'Organic Law of the Central People's Government' (31 articles). Both became the basis of the Constitution adopted on 20 Sept. 1954 by the 1st National People's Congress, the supreme legislative body. The Consultative Conference continued to exist after 1954 as an advisory body. Three further constitutions have been promulgated under Communist rule—in 1975, 1978 and 1982 (currently in force). The latter was partially amended in 1988, 1993, 1999, 2004 and 2014, endorsing the principles of a socialist market economy and of private ownership.

The unicameral *National People's Congress* is the highest organ of state power. Usually meeting for one session a year, it can amend the constitution and nominally elects and has power to remove from office the highest officers of state. There are a maximum of 3,000 members of the Congress, who are elected to serve five-year terms by municipal, regional and provincial people's congresses. In 2018, 2,980 deputies were elected to the Congress. It elects a *Standing Committee* (which supervises the *State Council*) every five years, as well as the *President* and *Vice-President*. Term limits for the president and vice-president were abolished in 2018. When not in session, Congress business is carried on by the Standing Committee.

The State Council is the supreme executive organ and comprises the Prime Minister, Deputy Prime Ministers and State Councillors.

The *Central Military Commission* is the highest state military organ.

National Anthem

'March of the Volunteers'; words by Tien Han, tune by Nie Er.

Government Chronology

Leaders of the Communist Party of China since 1935.

Chairmen	
1935–76	Mao Zedong
1976–81	Hua Guofeng
1981–82	Hu Yaobang
General Secretaries	
1956–57	Deng Xiaoping
1980–87	Hu Yaobang
1987–89	Zhao Ziyang
1989–2002	Jiang Zemin
2002–12	Hu Jintao
2012–	Xi Jinping
De facto ruler	
1978–97	Deng Xiaoping

Heads of State since 1949.

Chairman of the Central People's Government	
1949–54	Mao Zedong
Chairmen (Presidents)	
1954–59	Mao Zedong
1959–68	Liu Shaoqi
1968–75	Dong Biwu
Chairmen of the Standing Committee of the National People's Congress	
1975–76	Zhu De
1978–83	Ye Jianying

(*continued*)

Presidents of the Republic	
1983–88	Li Xiannian
1988–93	Yang Shangkun
1993–2003	Jiang Zemin
2003–13	Hu Jintao
2013–	Xi Jinping
Prime Ministers since 1949.	
1949–76	Zhou Enlai
1976–80	Hua Guofeng
1980–87	Zhao Ziyang
1987–98	Li Peng
1998–2003	Zhu Rongji
2003–13	Wen Jiabao
2013–	Li Keqiang

Recent Elections

Elections of delegates to the 13th National People's Congress were held between Oct. 2017 and Feb. 2018 by municipal, regional and provincial people's congresses. At its annual session in March 2018 the Congress re-elected Xi Jinping as President and elected Wang Qishan as Vice-President.

Current Government

President and Chairman of Central Military Commission: Xi Jinping; b. 1953 (Chinese Communist Party; elected 14 March 2013).

Vice-President: Wang Qishan.

In Feb. 2019 the government comprised:

Premier of the State Council (Prime Minister): Li Keqiang; b. 1955 (Chinese Communist Party; appointed 15 March 2013).

Deputy Prime Ministers: Han Zheng; Sun Chunlan; Hu Chunhua; Liu He.

Minister of Agriculture and Rural Affairs: Han Changfu. *Civil Affairs:* Huang Shuxian. *Commerce:* Zhong Shan. *Culture and Tourism:* Luo Shugang. *Ecology and Environment:* Li Ganjie. *Education:* Chen Baosheng. *Emergency Management:* Wang Yupu. *Finance:* Liu Kun. *Foreign Affairs:* Wang Yi. *Housing, and Urban and Rural Development:* Wang Menghui. *Human Resources and Social Security:* Zhang Jinan. *Industry and Information Technology:* Miao Wei. *Justice:* Fu Zhenghua. *National Defence:* Gen. Wei Fenghe. *Natural Resources:* Lu Hao. *Public Security:* Zhao Kezhi. *Science and Technology:* Wang Zhigang. *State Security:* Chen Wenqing. *Transport:* Li Xiaopeng. *Veterans' Affairs:* Sun Shaocheng. *Water Resources:* E Jingping.

Heads of State Commissions: *Ethnic Affairs*, Bagatur. *National Development and Reform*, He Lifeng. *National Health*, Ma Xiaowei.

De facto power is in the hands of the Communist Party of China, which had 88·76m. members at the end of 2015. There are eight other parties, all members of the Chinese People's Political Consultative Conference.

The members of the Standing Committee of the Politburo in March 2019 were: Xi Jinping (*General Secretary*); Li Keqiang; Li Zhanshu; Wang Yang; Wang Huning; Zhao Leji; Han Zheng.

Chairman of the National People's Congress Standing Committee: Li Zhanshu.

Government Website: http://www.gov.cn

Current Leaders

Xi Jinping

Position
President

Introduction
Xi Jinping succeeded Hu Jintao as president in March 2013 at the 12th National People's Congress. Tipped for the role since his appointment as secretary general of the Chinese Communist Party (CCP) and chairman of the Central Military Commission in Nov. 2012, Xi pursued a strong style of authoritarian rule at home and a proactive and muscular foreign policy in his

first term. In Oct. 2016 the CCP gave him the title of 'core' leader, a significant honorific bracketing him with Mao Zedong and Deng Xiaoping among previous party figures although conferring no absolute powers. Then, at its five-yearly congress in Oct. 2017, the party voted to enshrine his name and ideology in the Chinese state constitution. He was subsequently re-elected in March 2018 and parliament also voted to abolish presidential term limits in a major shift from precedent.

Early Life
Xi Jinping was born on 15 June 1953 in Beijing, the son of one of the first generation of communist leaders. He joined the CCP in 1974 and, after graduating from Tsinghua University in 1979 with a degree in chemical engineering, he became secretary to the vice-premier and secretary-general of the Central Military Commission.

Xi became the Zhengding County Committee deputy secretary in Hebei province in 1982 and the following year was promoted to secretary. In 1985 he was made deputy mayor of Xiamen City, Fujian province. Having undertaken various party roles in the province, he became deputy governor of Fujian in 1999 and governor a year later.

In 2002 he moved to Zhejiang province and made his first inroads into national politics when he was named a member of the 16th Central Committee. From 2003–07 he was party secretary of Fujian, overseeing economic growth averaging 14% a year and earning a reputation as an opponent of corruption.

In March 2007 Xi transferred to Shanghai to take the role of party secretary following the dismissal of the incumbent on corruption charges. His appointment to such an important regional post was seen as a vote of confidence from the central government and he became a member of the Politburo standing committee at the 17th Party Congress in Oct. 2007. He was also made a high-ranking member of the central secretariat. On 15 March 2008 he was elected vice-president at the 11th National People's Congress and took on a number of high profile portfolios including the presidency of the Central Party School. He was also Beijing's senior representative for Hong Kong and Macao and headed up preparations for the 2008 Olympic Games in Beijing.

On 18 Oct. 2010 Xi was appointed vice-chairman of the CCP and Central Military Commission, marking him as Hu's successor. He was elected general-secretary of the CCP and chairman of the Central Military Commission by the 18th Central Committee on 15 Nov. 2012 and was sworn in as president on 14 March 2013.

Career in Office
Ahead of his presidency, Xi said little about his policy ambitions. There was hope abroad and at home that he would champion political and social reform and attempt to deal with corruption and a widening wealth gap between rich and poor and between urban and rural communities. He also faced the conundrum of how to provide adequate health care to a rapidly ageing population.

In Jan. 2014 the prospect of greater transparency and accountability under his leadership was undermined when the authorities began criminal proceedings against anti-corruption campaigners calling for public disclosure of officials' assets. This coincided with a report by a US investigative organization claiming that relatives of some of China's top political and military figures, including Xi's brother-in-law, held secret offshore financial holdings.

In other social and political affairs the CCP announced plans in Nov. 2013 to ease China's one-child policy (which was subsequently abandoned following an announcement in Oct. 2015, with effect from 2016) and to abolish the system of 're-education through labour' camps, while a party plenum called—for the first time—for markets to play a 'decisive' role in the allocation of resources. Meanwhile, in 2014 Xi was confronted by domestic political opposition in the form of militant attacks by ethnic Uighur separatists from Xinjiang region and, from Sept. that year, by widespread pro-democracy and autonomy protests in Hong Kong.

On the economic front, China's previously frenetic annual rate of growth slowed markedly in 2015, reflecting a slump in factory production and concerns over depressed oil prices, and again in 2016 to its lowest since 1990. It also heralded severe stock market turbulence into 2016 despite emergency government measures, which had negative reverberations throughout the world economy. Nevertheless, recognizing China's rise as a global economic power, the IMF in Nov. 2015 voted to add the yuan as the fifth member of its special drawing rights (SDR) currency basket alongside the US dollar, Japanese yen, British pound and the euro.

In foreign affairs, regional concerns over China's territorial and military intentions were raised in Nov. 2013 by the government's declaration of a new 'air defence identification zone' over a swathe of the East China Sea including disputed islands claimed by Japan and South Korea. There has also been friction, regionally and with the USA, over China's sovereignty claims and land reclamation operations on islands in the South China Sea, although in July 2016 an international legal tribunal ruled in favour of a challenge by the Philippines to China's sovereignty assertions—a verdict Beijing vowed to ignore. Further afield, Xi has meanwhile undertaken numerous official visits abroad, as well as attending multilateral forums, for diplomatic, trading and investment purposes. And, while in Singapore in Nov. 2015, Xi and President Ma Ying-jeou of Taiwan held the first direct talks between leaders of the two estranged governments since their split in 1949.

More recently, in 2018 Xi aimed to extend China's economic and military co-operation with Russia and also sought to defuse tensions with India over a simmering border dispute at an informal summit with Prime Minister Narendra Modi. Meanwhile, friction with the USA escalated markedly over disputed trading and commercial practices, with both countries imposing punitive trade tariffs.

Li Keqiang
Position
Premier of the State Council

Introduction
Li Keqiang took office as premier of the State Council, a role equivalent to prime minister, in March 2013, succeeding Wen Jiabao. He was re-elected in March 2018.

Early Life
Li Keqiang was born on 1 July 1955 in Dingyuan County, Anhui province. Following graduation from high school in 1974, he joined the CCP and in 1982 he graduated in law from Peking University, serving as head of the Students' Federation from 1978–82. He went on to earn a master's degree and doctorate in economics and headed the University's Communist Youth League of China (CYLC) committee. Over the following two decades he rose through the CYLC ranks, joining the secretariat of its central committee in the 1980s and serving as its first secretary in the 1990s. At this time he built up his power base and forged close ties with Hu Jintao, a fellow CYLC committee member and future Chinese president.

In 1998 Li became deputy party secretary for Henan province and a year later was appointed Henan's governor. In Dec. 2004 he was named party secretary for Liaoning province where he spearheaded a major coastal infrastructure project, the '5 Points and One Line' highway development. In 2009 this template was adopted at the national level to rejuvenate industrial northeast China. He also oversaw the rehousing of 1·5m. shanty-town residents into new apartment blocks over a three-year period.

Li advanced to national level politics when he was elected to the Politburo standing committee in Oct. 2007. He was appointed vice-premier of the State Council in March 2008, leading a medical reform programme aimed at creating an accessible public health care service. He also chaired an affordable housing programme and introduced tax reform plans. In Nov. 2012 Li was re-elected as a member of the Politburo standing committee and on 15 March 2013 became premier of the State Council at the 12th National People's Congress.

Career in Office
Regarded as the steward of the Chinese economy, Li has aimed to focus on securing China's long-term expansion and on the further provision of basic national health care, affordable housing, employment growth, regional development and cleaner energy. However, global confidence in China's economy has been shaken since 2015 as the country's growth momentum has slowed amid apparent policy differences and blunders, prompting rumours that Li was being increasingly sidelined in the governing hierarchy. He was nevertheless re-elected to the Politburo standing committee in Oct. 2017 and to the premiership in March 2018.

Having sought assurances that a recently revised US–Mexico–Canada trade agreement would not stop Canada from signing deals with other countries, Li met with Canadian Prime Minister Justin Trudeau in Nov. 2018 at an international summit in Singapore with the aim of pursuing negotiations on a bilateral free trade pact.

Defence

The Chinese president is chairman of the State and Party's Military Commissions. China is divided into seven military regions. The military commander also commands the air, naval and civilian militia forces assigned to each region.

China's armed forces (PLA: 'People's Liberation Army'), totalling nearly 3·0m. in 2013 including the paramilitary People's Armed Police (PAP) and 2·3m. excluding the PAP, are the largest of any country. However, active armed personnel numbers have halved since 1980. Moreover, in 2015 President Xi laid out plans to reform the army structure—replacing an organization based on seven regions with one based on five 'theatre commands'—and reduce the number of military personnel by a further 300,000.

Conscription is compulsory, but for organizational reasons, is selective: only some 10% of potential recruits are called up. Service is for two years. A military academy to train senior officers in modern warfare was established in 1985.

Defence expenditure in 2013 was US$112,173m. (equivalent to US$83 per capita). China's military spending more than trebled between 2007 and 2015. Defence spending in 2013 represented 1·2% of GDP, although the share has actually declined since 1990. Only the USA spent more on defence in 2013, but China's defence expenditure totalled around a fifth of that of the USA. In March 2014 it was announced that the defence budget would rise by 12·2% to US$132bn. following increases of 10·7%, 11·2% and 12·7% in the previous three years. China is the world's third largest exporter of arms after the USA and Russia, with 6·2% of the global major weapons total over the period 2012–16. In the period 2004–08 it had only been the eighth largest exporter.

As at 31 May 2016 China had 3,044 personnel serving in UN peace-keeping operations (the largest contingent of any of the five permanent members of the UN Security Council and more than the other four combined).

Nuclear Weapons

Having carried out its first test in 1964, there have been 45 tests in all at Lop Nur, in Xinjiang (the last in 1996). The nuclear arsenal consisted of approximately 270 operational warheads in Jan. 2017 according to the Stockholm International Peace Research Institute. China has been helping Pakistan with its nuclear efforts.

Army

The Army (the PLA Groundforce) is divided into main and local forces. Main forces, administered by the seven military regions in which they are stationed, but commanded by the ministry of defence, are available for operation anywhere and are better equipped. Local forces concentrate on the defence of their own regions. Ground forces are divided into infantry, armour, artillery, air defence, aviation, engineering, chemical defence and communications service arms. There are also specialized units for electronic counter-measures, reconnaissance and mapping. In 2013 there were 18 group armies covering seven military regions. They included: 17 armoured divisions and brigades; 29 mechanized infantry divisions, brigades and regiments; 30 motorized infantry divisions and brigades; nine special operations units; 19 artillery divisions and brigades; 3 amphibious brigades and divisions; two mountain brigades; 14 aviation brigades and regiments; and two guard divisions. Total strength in 2013 was 1·60m. including some 800,000 conscripts. Reserve forces are undergoing major reorganization on a provincial basis but are estimated to number some 510,000.

There is a paramilitary People's Armed Police force estimated at 660,000 under PLA command.

Navy

In Nov. 2011 the naval arm of the PLA included 71 submarines, of which three were strategic (two Jin-class and one Xia-class) and 68 tactical. By mid-2015 two more Jin-class nuclear-powered ballistic missile submarines had entered service. Surface combatant forces in Nov. 2011 included 13 destroyers and 65 frigates. Sea trials of China's first aircraft carrier, *Liaoning* (a former Soviet warship purchased from Ukraine), began in Aug. 2011. It entered service in Sept. 2012 and was initially only used for training before being declared 'combat ready' in Nov. 2016. Work on China's first domestically-built aircraft carrier began in 2015. It was launched in April 2017 and is expected to be operational by 2020.

There is a land-based naval air force of about 311 combat-capable aircraft, primarily for defensive and anti-submarine service. The force includes H-6 strategic bombers and JH-7 fighters.

The naval arm is split into a North Sea Fleet, an East Sea Fleet and a South Sea Fleet.

In 2013 naval personnel were estimated at 235,000, including 26,000 in the naval air force and 35,000 conscripts.

Air Force

The PLA Air Force organizes its command through seven military region air forces. The Air Force has an estimated 1,700 combat-capable aircraft. Equipment includes J-7 (MiG-21) interceptors (known in the West as 'Fishbed'), H-6 Chinese-built copies of Tu-16 strategic bombers, Q-5 fighter-bombers (evolved from the MiG-19 and known in the West as 'Fantan'), Su-27 fighters supplied by Russia (known in the West as 'Flanker'), J-10 Chinese-designed and produced fighters (known in the West as 'Firebird') and J-8 locally-developed fighters (known in the West as 'Finback').

Total strength (2013) was 398,000.

Economy

In 2014 agriculture accounted for 9·1% of GDP, industry 43·1% and services 47·8%. Industry was the largest contributor until 2011, while services only overtook agriculture as the second largest sector in 1985. In the late 1960s agriculture was the largest contributor towards GDP.

Overview

China's economic performance has been marked by high rates of growth for over three decades. Annual GDP increases in the early 2000s consistently exceeded 10% until the global financial crisis. China also holds the world's largest foreign exchange reserves, at more than US$3·05trn. in April 2017, although they have been falling since 2014 as the central bank strives to boost the currency in the face of large capital outflows. It is among the top recipients of foreign direct investment (FDI) and is the world's largest producer and consumer of coal. In 2005 China made the transition from net receiver of foreign aid to net donor and has established itself as a key player in Africa's economic development, becoming the largest export partner of sub-Saharan Africa in 2013. According to the World Bank, China's cumulative FDI stock in Africa totalled nearly US$34·7bn. in 2015, up from US$14·7bn. in 2011. In 2010 China overtook Japan to become the world's second largest economy after the USA. New sectors like e-commerce and online financial services are gaining momentum in an economy long dominated by export-oriented sectors. Rising trade tensions between the USA and China, however, pose a threat to longer-term prospects.

The first steps from a centrally-planned towards a more market-oriented economy were taken by Deng Xiaoping in the late 1970s. He opened the economy to foreign trade and investment, decentralized industrial management and allowed private sector development. In 2001 China became a member of the World Trade Organization, establishing trade relations with many countries. Private entrepreneurs and foreign investors have played an important role in developing the manufacturing sector, China's principal growth engine. Even before 1978 the economy was heavily skewed towards manufacturing, but following the market-oriented transition output increased significantly. During this period there was a structural shift away from large state-owned enterprises (SOEs), although these still remain an important part of the economy. Between 1997 and 2003 the government oversaw reform of SOEs, with many poorly performing businesses privatized or liquidated. Stronger firms were restructured and often listed on the stock market. Many more recent enterprises are labour-intensive as distinct from the capital-intensive SOEs. Growth has been fuelled by low added value and labour-intensive exports. However, Chinese firms are predicted to become increasingly competitive with higher added value producers, such as South Korea.

Although the global financial crisis reduced the rate of growth and inbound FDI, China's recovery was among the earliest. GDP growth averaged 7·9% in the second quarter of 2009, up from a two-decade low of 6·1% in the first quarter of that year. FDI also recovered rapidly, averaging 4·1% of GDP annually between 2009 and 2013. Growth was rooted in a stimulus package of 4trn. yuan (US$586bn. or 13% of 2008 GDP), including fiscal spending and interest rate cuts, as well as an expansionary monetary policy. Central government committed 1·18trn. yuan, with the rest coming from local government, banks and SOEs. Although exports declined by around 17% in 2009, other countries fared worse and China's share of world exports increased to nearly 13·6% in 2016 (up from 3% in 1999), making it the world's largest merchandise provider.

GDP growth in 2010 stood at more than 10% but moderated between 2011 and 2014, reflecting the global economic slowdown and diminishing dividends from past reforms. In Aug. 2015 a devaluation of the yuan sent the Shanghai stock exchange plummeting by nearly 40%, which was swiftly followed by a surge in capital outflows. The stock market meltdown lasted until Feb. 2016, with trading halted altogether for two days in Jan. that year. Nonetheless, the Shanghai exchange subsequently began a recovery and had stabilized (at around 3,000 points) by Feb. 2017. Despite stock market turbulence, the property market, which constitutes a quarter of China's GDP and is vital to the banking sector (as it accounts for a substantial amount of its collateral), remained buoyant. GDP growth declined to 6·9% in 2015 (the slowest rate in 25 years) and fell again to 6·7% in 2016 as China attempted to reduce its reliance on exports, increase domestic consumption and develop its service sector. However, China remains one of the fastest growing major economies in the world, recording expansions of 6·9% and 6·6% in 2017 and 2018, respectively, driven by exports and robust domestic household consumption.

In May 2017, for the first time since 1998, the credit rating agency Moody's downgraded China's sovereign rating. Inflation was 2·2% in 2018, up from 1·6% in 2017, while public debt was measured by the government at 50·1% of GDP (although there is wide-held suspicion that the real figure is significantly higher). Corporate debt reached 165% of GDP in 2018, with household debt—although still low—rising by 15% of GDP over the preceding five years. President Xi Jinping has targeted spending cuts and aims to curb loans to bloated SOEs.

Rapid economic advance has brought with it a number of challenges that threaten future growth. Notably, China's cost advantage has been undermined in recent years by rising wages and transportation costs, as well as weak global demand. Other concerns include rising property costs, high levels of local government debt, lack of enforcement of intellectual property rights, endemic corruption at government level and credit and investment dependence, while total social financing—a broad measure of total credit—increased by 77% of GDP between 2008 and early 2014. The stimulus package implemented by the government to boost growth increased total debt levels to more than double the value of GDP in 2016.

According to the IMF, an increase in consumer demand and a reduced dependence on exports and investment are keys to achieving stable long-term economic expansion. China's 13th five-year plan (covering 2016–20) aims to promote domestic consumption and to support innovation and entrepreneurship within a framework of balanced and sustainable development. Efforts to promote domestic consumption have seen exports' share of GDP falling from 38% in 2007 to 19·6% in 2016 and a lower investment contribution to GDP. Trade frictions are predicted to disproportionately affect smaller firms that are less able to squeeze profit margins to accommodate tariff hikes, as well as those geographical regions most reliant on exports.

The continued decline in commodity prices coupled with China's economic slowdown has had knock-on effects for commodity-exporting nations, such as Brazil, Indonesia and Argentina, given that China consumes about half of the world's steel, aluminium and nickel.

Inefficient production and outmoded equipment have meanwhile led to significant environmental problems, especially in the north of the country. Air pollution, soil erosion and a declining water table are of particular concern. China has become the world's largest consumer of coal and second largest consumer of oil after the USA. The government aims to diversify its energy sources, relying less on coal and more on nuclear and alternative energy sources. There has been heavy investment in hydro-power, including the Three Gorges Dam.

Since 1980, 600m. people have been lifted out of poverty, yet China still has the second largest number of poor in the world after India. The World Bank estimates that 98·9m. people lived below the national poverty line at the end of 2012 (equivalent to income less than US$1 per day), located mainly in remote and resource-poor regions and particularly in the west and the interior. Nonetheless, some progress has been made, with 7·2% of the rural population living below the poverty line in 2014 compared to 8·5% in 2013. A large gap remains between living standards of the urban and rural communities, between urban zones on the Chinese coast and the interior and western parts of the country, and between the urban middle classes and those who have not been able to profit from the growth of recent decades. China also faces the growing burden of an ageing population. Those aged 65 and over accounted for 10·1% of the total population in 2016, up from 6·9% in 2000.

Currency

The currency is called Renminbi (i.e. People's Currency). The unit of currency is the *yuan* (CNY) which is divided into ten *jiao*, the *jiao* being

divided into ten *fen*. The yuan was floated to reflect market forces on 1 Jan. 1994 while remaining state-controlled. For 11 years the People's Bank of China maintained the yuan at about 8·28 to the US dollar, allowing it to fluctuate but only by a fraction of 1% in closely supervised trading. In July 2005 it was revalued and pegged against a 'market basket' of currencies the central parities of which were determined every night. In July 2008, after three years of sharp appreciation, it was repegged at around 6·83 yuan to the dollar, leading to claims from some international observers that it was being kept unfairly low to boost exports. In June 2010 the government announced that the yuan would be allowed to move freely against the dollar as long as a rise or fall does not exceed 0·5% within a single day. In Aug. 2015 the yuan was devalued by a total of 4·65% on three consecutive days. In Aug. 2009 total money supply was 20,039·5bn. yuan, gold reserves were 33·89m. troy oz and foreign exchange reserves US$2,210·8bn. (US$75·4bn. in 1995). China's reserves are the highest of any country, having overtaken those of Japan in 2006.

Inflation rates (based on IMF statistics):

2008	2009	2010	2011	2012	2013	2014	2015	2016	2017
5·9%	−0·7%	3·3%	5·4%	2·6%	2·6%	2·0%	1·4%	2·0%	1·6%

China's economy overheated in the early 1990s, leading to inflation rates of 14·7% in 1993, 24·1% in 1994 and 17·1% in 1995. The 2008 rate was the highest since 1996.

Budget

Total revenue and expenditure (in 1bn. yuan):

	2011	2012	2013	2014	2015
Revenue	10,387·4	11,725·4	12,921·0	14,037·0	15,226·9
Expenditure	10,924·8	12,595·3	14,021·2	15,178·6	17,587·8

Of the total revenues in 2015 central government accounted for 6,926·7bn. yuan and local governments 8,300·2bn. yuan. Tax revenues came to 12,492·2bn. yuan in 2015 (including domestic VAT 3,110·9bn. yuan and corporate income tax 2,713·4bn. yuan) and non-tax revenues 2,734·7bn. yuan. Of the total expenditure in 2015 central government accounted for 2,554·2bn. yuan and local governments 15,033·6bn. yuan. The leading items of expenditure in 2015 were education (2,627·2bn. yuan) and social safety net and employment effort (1,901·9bn. yuan).

The standard rate of VAT is 16%.

Performance

GDP totalled US$12,237·7bn. in 2017, the second highest behind the USA. China's share of world GDP has risen from 4% in 2000 to 15% in 2016. It replaced Japan as the second largest economy in 2010. It is forecast that around 2020 China will overtake the USA to become the world's largest economy. As recently as 2000 the US economy was around eight times larger than China's. Real GDP growth rates (based on IMF statistics):

2008	2009	2010	2011	2012	2013	2014	2015	2016	2017
9·6%	9·2%	10·6%	9·5%	7·9%	7·8%	7·3%	6·9%	6·7%	6·9%

GDP growth in 2017 was 6·9% according to the National Bureau of Statistics. In spite of high growth in recent years, China's gross national income (GNI) per capita at purchasing power parity was $12,547 in 2014, compared to the Human Development Report's 'very high human development' average of $41,584.

Banking and Finance

The People's Bank of China is the central bank and bank of issue (*Governor*, Yi Gang). At the end of 2012 the banking sector included the China Development Bank, two state policy banks (the Export-Import Bank of China and the Agricultural Development Bank of China), five large commercial banks (Bank of China, Industrial and Commercial Bank of China, Agricultural Bank of China, China Construction Bank and Bank of Communications), 12 joint-stock commercial banks, 144 city commercial banks, 337 rural commercial banks and 147 rural co-operative banks. The Bank of China is responsible for foreign banking operations. In April 2003 the China Banking Regulatory Commission was launched, taking over the role of regulating and supervising the country's banks and other deposit-taking financial institutions from the central bank. Legislation in 1995 permitted the establishment of commercial banks; credit co-operatives may be transformed into banks, mainly to provide credit to small businesses. There were 1,927 rural credit co-operatives at the end of 2012. Insurance is handled by the People's Insurance Company. The Industrial and Commercial Bank of China is the world's largest bank by assets (US$3,743bn. as at 31 Dec. 2016).

Savings deposits in various forms in all banking institutions totalled 40,370·4bn. yuan in 2012; loans amounted to 67,287·5bn. yuan.

There are stock exchanges in the Shenzhen Special Economic Zone and in Shanghai. A securities trading system linking six cities (Securities Automated Quotations System) was inaugurated in 1990 for trading in government bonds.

China received a record US$136·3bn. worth of foreign direct investment in 2017, up from US$133·7bn. in 2016.

External debt totalled US$548,551m. in 2010 (up from US$145,339m. in 2000) and represented 9·3% of GNI.

Energy and Natural Resources

Environment
China's carbon dioxide emissions from the consumption of energy in 2011 accounted for 25·3% of the world total (making it the biggest emissions producer, having overtaken the USA in 2007) and were equivalent to 6·1 tonnes per capita (up from 4·5 tonnes per capita in 2007). Carbon dioxide emissions have more than doubled since 2000. An *Environmental Performance Index* compiled in 2016 ranked China 109th of 180 countries, with 65·1%. The index examined various factors in nine areas—agriculture, air quality, biodiversity and habitat, climate and energy, fisheries, forests, health impacts, water and sanitation, and water resources. Pollution is estimated to cost China about 10% of GDP annually.

Electricity
Installed generating capacity in 2011 was an estimated 1,006m. kW, compared with 299m. kW in 2000. In 2014 electricity output was 5,649,580 GWh, up from 1,355,600 GWh in 2000. Consumption per capita was 3,927 kWh in 2014. Rapidly increasing demand has meant that more than half of China's provinces have had to ration power. Sources of electricity in 2014 as percentage of total production: thermal, 75·6%; hydro-electric power, 18·8%; wind, 2·8% (China is one of the world's largest producers of wind power); and nuclear, 2·3%. In 2016 there were 35 nuclear reactors in use and 20 under construction. Generating electricity is not centralized; local units range between 30 and 60 MW of output. In Dec. 2002 China formally broke up its state power monopoly, creating instead five generating and two transmission firms. The Three Gorges dam project on the Yangtze river was launched in 1993 and is intended to produce abundant hydro-electricity (as well as helping flood control). The first three 700,000-kW generators in service at the project's hydro-power station began commercial operation in July 2003. The original specification was completed in Oct. 2008, although six more generators have been added in the meantime (bringing the total to 32). The final two generators become operational in July 2012, giving the dam an overall capacity of 22·5 GW. China surpassed Germany in terms of solar generating capacity in 2015, with 43·5 GW at the end of the year.

Oil and Gas
On-shore oil reserves are found mainly in the northeast (particularly the Daqing and Liaohe fields) and northwest. There are off-shore fields in the continental shelves of east China. Oil production was a record 211·4m. tonnes in 2014 and was 191·5m. tonnes in 2017. China is the second largest consumer of oil after the USA. Ever-growing demand has meant that increasing amounts of oil are having to be imported. A 964-km pipeline from Skovorodino in Russia to Daqing in the northeast of China was inaugurated in Jan. 2011, allowing China to increase significantly its imports of oil from the world's second largest producer. The 1,833-km Turkmenistan–China gas pipeline, bringing natural gas to Xinjiang in China via Kazakhstan and Uzbekistan, was inaugurated in Dec. 2009. This connects with China's Second West–East gas pipeline. Only the USA imports more oil. Domestic production now accounts for only 55% of consumption, compared to nearly 85% in 1998. Proven reserves in 2017 were 25·7bn. bbls.

The largest natural gas reserves are located in the western and north-central regions. Production was a record 149·2bn. cu. metres in 2017—up from 138·0bn. cu. metres in 2015—with proven reserves of 5·5trn. cu. metres in 2017.

Wind
China is the second largest producer of wind power after the USA, with 156·1bn. kWh in 2014. In 2015 total installed capacity amounted to 145,362 MW, the highest of any country and 33·6% of the world total.

Minerals
China is one of the world's leading mineral producing and consuming countries. Recoverable deposits of coal in 2012 totalled 229·9bn. tonnes, mainly distributed in north China (particularly Shanxi province and the Inner Mongolia Autonomous Region). Coal production was 3,660m. tonnes in 2012. Annual coal production has increased every year since 2000. Growing domestic demand nonetheless meant that China became a net importer of coal in 2009.

Iron ore reserves were 19·5bn. tonnes in 2012. Deposits are abundant in the anthracite field of Shanxi, in Hebei and in Shandong, and are found in conjunction with coal and worked in the northeast. Production in 2012 was 1,310m. tonnes, making China the world's largest iron ore producer. It is also the largest consumer, at around 55% of the global total in 2012.

Tin ore is plentiful in Yunnan, where the tin-mining industry has long existed. Tin production was 110,000 tonnes in 2012.

China is a major producer of wolfram (tungsten ore). There is mining of wolfram in Hunan, Guangdong and Yunnan.

Output of other minerals (in 1,000 tonnes) in 2012: salt, 69,100; bauxite, 47,000; aluminium, 37,700; zinc, 4,900; lead, 2,800; copper, 1,550. There are also reserves of diamond, nickel, barite, bismuth, graphite, gypsum, mercury, molybdenum, silver, salt, phosphate ore and sylvite. Gold production, 2012: 403 tonnes. China surpassed South Africa as the world's leading gold producer in 2007, since when its output has increased every year.

Agriculture
Agriculture accounted for approximately 10% of GDP in 2012, compared to over 50% in 1949 at the time of the birth of the People's Republic of China and over 30% in 1980. In 2015 sown areas for major crops were (in 1m. ha.): corn, 38·12; rice, 30·22; wheat, 24·14; soybeans, 8·87; tubers, 8·84; rapeseed, 7·53. Intensive agriculture and horticulture have been practised for millennia. Present-day policy aims to avert the traditional threats from floods and droughts by soil conservancy, afforestation, irrigation and drainage projects, and to increase the 'high stable yields' areas by introducing fertilizers, pesticides and improved crops. In Aug. 1998 more than 21m. ha., notably in the Yangtze valley, were under water as China experienced its worst flooding since the 1950s. The 1998 flood season claimed over 4,100 lives.

'Township and village enterprises' in agriculture comprise enterprises previously run by the communes of the Maoist era, co-operatives run by rural labourers and individual firms of a certain size. There were 1,786 state farms in 2012 with 3·18m. employees. Net per capita annual income of rural households, 2012: 7,917 yuan.

In 2014 there were an estimated 106·3m. ha. of arable land and 16·2m. ha. of permanent cropland; 70·4m. ha. were equipped for irrigation.

There were 4·85m. large/medium-sized tractors in 2012 and 17·97m. small tractors.

China is the world's leading producer of a number of agricultural crops. Production of major products (in 1m. tonnes), 2015 (unless otherwise indicated): corn, 224·63; rice, 208·23; wheat, 130·19; sugarcane, 116·97; potatoes (2014 estimate), 95·57; watermelons (2014 estimate), 75·05; sweet potatoes (2014 estimate), 71·54; cucumbers and gherkins (2014 estimate), 56·90; tomatoes (2014 estimate), 52·72; apples (2014 estimate), 40·92; cabbages, kale, etc. (2014 estimate), 33·95; aubergines (2014 estimate), 29·52; onions (2014 estimate), 22·61; spinach (2014 estimate), 22·11; garlic (2014 estimate), 20·06; seed cotton (2014 estimate), 18·53; pears (2014 estimate), 18·10; carrots and turnips (2014 estimate), 17·44; peanuts, 16·44; tangerines and mandarins (2014 estimate), 16·44. Tea production in 2015 was 2,249,000 tonnes. China ranked sixth for wine production in 2014, with 1·1m. litres, and overtook France in 2013 as the largest consumer of red wine in the world. The gross output value of farming in 2012 was 4,694,050m. yuan; and of animal husbandry, 2,718,940m. yuan.

Livestock, 2015 (unless otherwise indicated): pigs, 451,125,000; sheep, 162,062,000; goats, 148,934,000; cattle and buffaloes, 108,173,000; horses, 5,908,000; chickens (2014 estimate), 4·63bn.; ducks (2014 estimate), 665m. China has more pigs, goats, sheep, horses and chickens than any other country. It is also home to nearly two-thirds of the world's ducks. Meat production in 2015 was estimated at 86·25m. tonnes; milk, 38·70m. tonnes; eggs, 29·99m. tonnes; honey, 477,000 tonnes. China is the world's leading producer of meat, eggs and honey.

Gale, Fred, (ed.) *China's Food and Agriculture: Issues for the 21st Century.* 2012

Powell, S. G., *Agricultural Reform in China: from Communes to Commodity Economy, 1978–1990.* 1992

Forestry

In 2015 the area under forests was 208·32m. ha., or 22% of the total land area. The average annual increase in forest cover of 1,542,000 ha. between 2010 and 2015 was the highest of any country in the world. Total roundwood production in 2011 was 329·47m. cu. metres, making China the world's third largest timber producer (9·4% of the world total in 2011). It is the highest consumer of roundwood; timber consumption in 2011 totalled 375·71m. cu. metres. It is also the world's leading importer of roundwood, accounting for 35·9% of world timber imports in 2011.

Fisheries

Total catch, 2012: 16,167,443 tonnes, of which 13,869,604 tonnes were from marine waters. China's annual catch is the largest in the world, and currently accounts for approximately 18% of the world total. In 1989 the annual catch had been just 5·3m. tonnes. China's aquaculture production is also the largest in the world, at 45,468,960 tonnes in 2014. Imports of fishery commodities in 2012 were valued at US$7,441m. (the third highest behind Japan and the USA); exports were the most of any country, at US$18,211m. China's fishery commodities exports in 2012 represented approximately 13% of the global total.

Water

In 2013, the first phase of the South-to-North Water Diversion Project opened, with a second phase opening a year later. The scheme, which by 2018 provided Beijing with a third of its total supply, was estimated to have cost almost US$50bn., with a third phase still to be completed.

Industry

The leading companies by market capitalization in China in March 2019 were Alibaba, an e-commerce and data company (US$499·4bn.); Tencent Holdings, an investment holding company (US$491·3bn.); and ICBC, the world's largest commercial bank (US$311·0bn.). In Nov. 2007 PetroChina was briefly the world's largest company after its flotation on the Shanghai stock market, with a market capitalization in excess of US$1trn., although its rank has since fallen considerably.

Industry accounted for 43·1% of GDP in 2015. Cottage industries persist into the 21st century. Industrial output grew by 15·7% in 2010. Modern industrial development began with the manufacture of cotton textiles and the establishment of silk filatures, steel plants, flour mills and match factories. In 2012 there were 343,769 industrial enterprises with an annual revenue of more than 20m. yuan. Of these enterprises, 286,861 were domestically funded, 30,973 were foreign funded and 25,935 were dependent on funds from Hong Kong, Macao and Taiwan. There were 17,851 state-owned industrial enterprises in total.

Output of major products, 2015 unless otherwise indicated (in tonnes): cement, 2,359·2m.; rolled steel, 1,123·5m.; crude steel, 803·8m.; pig iron, 691·4m.; gas oil and diesel oil (2014), 176·4m.; gasoline, 121·0m.; paper and paperboard, 117·4m.; sulphuric acid, 89·8m.; chemical fertilizers, 74·3m.; fuel oil (2014), 35·4m.; yarn, 35·4m.; refined sugar, 14·7m. Also produced in 2015: cloth, 89,260m. metres; beer, 47,156·0m. litres; 1,812·6m. mobile phones; 174·4m. notebook PCs; 144·8m. colour TV sets; 142·0m. air conditioners; 79·9m. home refrigerators; 72·7m. washing machines; 68·8m. bicycles; 28·5m. cameras; 25·0m. motorcycles. China is the world's leading cement, steel and pig iron manufacturer; since 2000 output of cement has trebled, and production of crude steel has increased sixfold and of pig iron fivefold (although in 2014 pig iron production fell for the first time in more than 30 years, as did crude steel production in 2015). China overtook Japan as the world's largest producer of motor vehicles in 2009, and in 2013 produced 18·1m. cars and 4·0m. commercial vehicles.

Labour

The employed population at the 1990 census was 647·2m. (291·1m. female). By 2012 it had risen to 767·0m. (2·8m. more than in 2011), of whom 396·0m. worked in rural areas (9·0m. fewer than in 2011) and 371·0m. in urban areas (11·9m. more than in 2011). In 2015 China's registered urban jobless was 4·1%, with 9·66m. registered unemployed in the country's cities. With China's fast-growing ageing population, according to the United Nations the working-age population began to decline in 2015.

In 2012 China had 189,289 private industrial enterprises. It was not until the late 1970s that the private sector even came into existence in China.

The average annual wage of people working in urban units in 2012 was 46,769 yuan. China's Labour Law stipulates a five-day working week with no more than eight hours a day and no more than 44 hours a week. Minimum working age was fixed at 16 in 1991. Strikes over pay have become ever more frequent in China, particularly at foreign-owned facilities.

China had 2·95m. people living in slavery according to the Walk Free Foundation's 2013 *Global Slavery Index*, the second highest total of any country.

International Trade

There are five Special Economic Zones at Shenzhen, Xiamen, Zhuhai, Shantou and Hainan in which concessions are made to foreign businessmen. The Pudong New Area in Shanghai is also designated a special development area. Since 1979 joint ventures with foreign firms have been permitted. A law of April 1991 reduced taxation on joint ventures to 33%. There is no maximum limit on the foreign share of the holdings; the minimum limit is 25%.

In May 2000 the USA granted normal trade relations to China, a progression after a number of years when China was accorded 'most favoured nation' status. China subsequently joined the World Trade Organization on 11 Dec. 2001.

Saee, John, *China and the Global Economy in the 21st Century.* 2011

Imports and Exports

Trade in US$1m.:

	2012	2013	2014	2015
Imports	1,818,200	1,950,000	1,958,000	1,681,700
Exports	2,048,800	2,209,000	2,342,300	2,281,900

China is the second largest trading nation in the world, accounting for 10·3% of global merchandise imports by value in 2014 and 12·3% of global merchandise exports (up from 4·3% when it joined the WTO in 2001). It was the second largest importer in 2014 behind the USA and the largest exporter. As recently as 2004 the USA's total trade in goods was more than twice that of China. It overtook Germany as the largest exporter of goods in 2009. Its trade surplus in goods is the highest of any country. However, it has the world's highest trade deficit in services. In 2014 imports of services totalled US$382bn. but exports only US$232bn.

Main imports in 2015 (in US$1bn.): machinery and transport equipment, 682·4; non-edible raw materials, 209·7; mineral fuels, lubricants and related materials, 198·6; chemicals, 171·3. Major exports in 2015 (in US$1bn.): machinery and transport equipment, 1,059·1; miscellaneous manufactured goods, 587·5; light textile industrial products, rubber products, minerals and metallurgical products, 391·0; chemicals, 129·6.

The main trading partners were as follows in 2015 (in US$1m.):

Countries	Value of exports
Korea (Republic of)	174,563·8
USA	150,544·0
Japan	143,092·9
Germany	87,689·4
Australia	73,871·4
Malaysia	53,257·6
Brazil	44,339·3
Switzerland	41,205·1
Countries	*Value of exports*
USA	410,804·9
Hong Kong	334,290·8
Japan	135,896·9
Korea (Republic of)	101,474·6
Germany	69,216·8

(*continued*)

Countries	Value of exports
Vietnam	66,381·2
UK	59,668·0
Netherlands	59,630·2

Customs duties with Taiwan were abolished in 1980. Trade with the European Union is fast expanding, having increased from €259·5bn. in 2006 to €514·6bn. in 2016.

Communications

Roads

The total road length in 2012 was 4,237,500 km, including 96,200 km of expressways (of which there had not been any as recently as the mid-1980s); 31,885m. tonnes of freight and 35,570m. persons were transported by road that year. The number of civilian motor vehicles was 109·30m. in 2012, including 89·43m. passenger vehicles and 18·95m. trucks (more than double the number in 2008, when there were 51·00m. civilian vehicles overall including 38·39m. passenger vehicles and 11·26m. trucks). China is the world's fastest-growing car market. There were 204,196 traffic accidents in 2012, with 59,997 fatalities.

Rail

In 2013 there were 103,000 km of railway. The high-speed network, at 20,000 km in Sept. 2016, is the longest in the world. The high-speed line linking Beijing and Guangzhou, which opened in Dec. 2012, is the longest in the world at 2,293 km. The railways carried 2·53bn. passengers in 2015 and 3·36bn. tonnes of freight. China's railways are the busiest in the world, carrying 24% of global rail traffic. There are metro systems in Beijing, Changsha, Chengdu, Chongqing, Dalian, Dongguan, Foshan, Fuzhou, Guangzhou, Guiyang, Haerbin, Hangzhou, Hefei, Jinan (where the first line opened in Jan. 2019), Kunming, Nanchang, Nanjing, Nanning, Ningbo, Qingdao, Shanghai, Shenyang, Shenzhen, Shijiazhuang, Suzhou, Tianjin, Urumqi (where the first line opened in 2018), Wenzhou (where the first line opened in Jan. 2019), Wuhan, Wuxi, Xiamen and Xian.

Civil Aviation

There are major international airports at Beijing (Capital), Guangzhou (Baiyun), Hong Kong (Chek Lap Kok) and Shanghai (Hongqiao and Pudong). In 2012 there were 180 civil airports for regular flights. The national and major airlines are state-owned. The leading Chinese airlines operating scheduled services in 2013 were China Southern Airlines (91·8m. passengers), China Eastern Airlines (79·1m.) and Air China (77·7m.). Other Chinese airlines include Hainan Airlines, Shandong Airlines, Shanghai Airlines, Shenzhen Airlines, Sichuan Airlines and Xiamen Airlines. In Feb. 2010 Shanghai Airlines merged with China Eastern Airlines but they have both retained their brand and livery.

In 2013 the busiest airport was Beijing (Capital International), with 83·7m. passengers; followed by Hong Kong International (Chek Lap Kok), with 59·9m. passengers; Guangzhou (Baiyun), with 52·4m. passengers; and Shanghai (Pudong), with 47·1m. passengers. Beijing Capital was the second busiest airport in the world in 2013. As recently as 2003 it had not featured among the world's 20 busiest airports. A new airport serving Beijing, Daxing International, is scheduled to open in 2019. It is expected to be the world's largest, with eight runways and capacity for 100m. passengers per year. Hong Kong International was the world's busiest airport for cargo in 2014, handling 4,411,193 tonnes; Shanghai (Pudong) was the third busiest, with 3,181,365 tonnes. In 2012 China had a total of 2,457 scheduled flight routes, of which 2,076 were domestic air routes and 381 were international air routes. Total passenger traffic in 2012 reached 319·36m.; freight traffic totalled 5·45m. tonnes.

Regular direct flights between mainland China and Taiwan resumed in July 2008 for the first time since 1949.

Shipping

In Jan. 2014 there were 2,577 ships of 300 GT or over registered, totalling 44·45m. GT. Of the 2,577 vessels registered, 968 were bulk carriers, 583 general cargo ships, 545 oil tankers, 192 container ships, 189 passenger ships and 100 liquid gas tankers.

Mainland China's busiest port in 2012 was Ningbo-Zhoushan (handling 744·0m. tonnes of cargo), followed by Shanghai (637·4m. tonnes), Tianjin

(477·0 tonnes), Guangzhou (Canton) (435·2m. tonnes) and Qingdao (406·9m. tonnes). Shanghai overtook Singapore to become the world's busiest container port in 2010 and handled 33·6m. TEUs (twenty-foot equivalent units) in 2013. Shenzhen, mainland China's second busiest port for container traffic and the world's fourth busiest in 2012, handled 22·9m. TEUs. Hong Kong handled 23·1m. TEUs in 2012.

In Jan. 2001 the first legal direct shipping links between the Chinese mainland and Taiwanese islands in more than 50 years were inaugurated.

Inland waterways totalled 125,000 km in 2012; 4,587·0m. tonnes of freight and 257·5m. passengers were carried. In June 2003 the Three Gorges Reservoir on the Chang Jiang River, the largest water control project in the world, reached sufficient depth to support the resumption of passenger and cargo shipping.

Telecommunications

In 2013 mobile phone subscriptions numbered 1,229,113,000 (887·1 per 1,000 persons), making China the biggest market for mobile phones in the world. The number of subscriptions doubled between 2007 and 2013. The two main mobile operators are China Mobile and China Unicom. The main landline operators are China Telecom and China Netcom. In 2013 there were 226,985,000 main (fixed) telephone lines, down from a peak of 367,786,000 in 2006. In 2002 there were 55,763,000 fixed internet subscriptions, but this had increased to 180,881,000 by 2012. That year the number of wireless broadband subscriptions rose to 232,803,000. In 2012 an estimated 42·3% of the population were internet users. In March 2012 there were only 447,000 Facebook users in mainland China (less than 0·1% of the population).

Social Institutions

Out of 178 countries analysed in the 2017 *Fragile States Index*—a list published jointly by the Fund for Peace and *Foreign Policy* magazine—China was ranked the 85th most vulnerable to conflict or collapse. The index is based on 12 indicators of state vulnerability across social, political and economic categories.

Justice

Six new codes of law (including criminal and electoral) came into force in 1980, to regularize the legal unorthodoxy of previous years. There is no provision for *habeas corpus*. As well as treason and murder the death penalty may be used for rape, embezzlement, smuggling, fraud, theft, drug-dealing, bribery and robbery with violence. Amendments to the Criminal Law in 2011 and 2015 reduced the number of capital crimes—which include both violent and non-violent offences—from 68 to 55 and further to 46. China does not divulge figures on its use of the death penalty, but Amnesty International reports that China executes thousands of people annually and is the world's top executioner. Nevertheless, western analysts believe that the number of executions now is around a fifth of the yearly total in the 1990s. 'People's courts' are divided into some 30 higher, 200 intermediate and 2,000 basic-level courts, and headed by the Supreme People's Court. The latter, the highest state judicial organ, tries cases, hears appeals and supervises the people's courts. It is responsible to the National People's Congress and its Standing Committee. People's courts are composed of a president, vice-presidents, judges and 'people's assessors' who are the equivalent of jurors. 'People's conciliation committees' are charged with settling minor disputes. There are also special military courts. Procuratorial powers and functions are exercised by the Supreme People's Procuracy and local procuracies.

In March 2017 the National People's Congress passed legislation developing aspects of the 1986 General Principles of Civil Law, with effect from Oct. 2017. Among its provisions was the extension of legitimate rights and interests from Chinese citizens only to anyone conducting civil activities in the country. In addition, the statute of limitation was increased from two to three years.

The number of sentenced prisoners in mid-2015 was 1,649,804 (118 per 100,000 of national population). China was ranked 47th of 102 countries for criminal justice and 67th for civil justice in the 2015 World Justice Project *Rule of Law Index*, which provides data on how the rule of law is experienced by the general public across eight categories.

Education

An educational reform of 1985 brought in compulsory nine-year education consisting of six years of primary schooling and three years of secondary schooling, to replace a previous five-year system.

In mainland China the 2010 population census revealed the following levels of educational attainment: 119·63m. people had finished university education; 187·99m. had received senior secondary education; 519·66m. had received junior secondary education; and 358·76m. had had primary education. 54·66m. people over 15 years of age or 4·08% of the population were illiterate, although this compared favourably with a 15·88% rate of illiteracy in the 1990 census and a 6·72% rate in 2000. In 2010 adult literacy was estimated at 95·1%; youth literacy in 2010 was 99·6%.

In 2012 there were 181,251 kindergartens with 36·86m. children and 1·48m. full-time teachers; 228,585 regular primary schools with 96·96m. pupils and 5·59m. full-time teachers; 81,662 secondary schools (including: 14,205 senior secondary; 53,216 junior secondary; 5,245 specialized; 4,517 vocational; and 2,901 technical) with 94·21m. pupils and 5·99m. full-time teachers. There were also 378,751 pupils at 1,853 special education schools. Institutes of higher education, including universities, numbered 2,442 in 2012, with 23·91m. undergraduates and 1·72m. postgraduate level students, and 1·44m. full-time teaching staff. China has more than 600 private universities, almost all of which have been established since the mid-1990s. A national system of student loans was established in 1999. The number of Chinese students studying abroad went up from 3,000 in 1990 to 39,000 in 2000; it rose above 100,000 in 2002 and 200,000 in 20009, and by 2015 exceeded 500,000, making China the largest source of overseas students in the world. Chinese students account for a fifth of all international students in tertiary education in the OECD, but fewer than half return to China after finishing their studies. The number of Chinese undergraduate students in American universities in 2013–14 was 11 times as many as in 2006–07, rising from 10,000 to 110,000 in the space of seven years.

There is an Academy of Sciences with provincial branches. An Academy of Social Sciences was established in 1977.

In 2012 national government expenditure on education came to 2,124,210m. yuan and accounted for 16·9% of national government spending.

Health

Medical treatment is free only for certain groups of employees, but where costs are incurred they are partly borne by the patient's employing organization.

In 2012 there were 950,297 health institutions throughout China, including 23,170 hospitals, 912,620 local health centres, 3,490 centres for disease control and prevention, and 1,289 specialized prevention and treatment centres.

China's first AIDS case was reported in 1985. At the end of 2014 there were 501,000 reported cases of people living with HIV/AIDS. The number of deaths of people who had been living with HIV/AIDS in 2014 was 21,000.

In the first half of 2003 China was struck by an epidemic of a pneumonia-type virus identified as SARS (severe acute respiratory syndrome). The virus was first detected in southern China and was subsequently reported in over 30 other countries. According to the ministry of health, by the time the outbreak had been contained a total of 5,327 cases had been reported on the Chinese mainland; 4,959 patients were cured and discharged from hospital, and 349 died.

In *Water: At What Cost? The State of the World's Water 2016*, WaterAid reported that 4·5% of the population does not have access to safe water. China ranked as the country with the second largest number of people living without access to safe water (63·2m. in 2015).

In 2015 an estimated 47·6% of adult males and 1·8% of adult females smoked in China. A study from the same year estimated that Chinese males smoke one-third of all the world's cigarettes.

Welfare

In 2012 there were 48,078 social welfare enterprises with 4·49m. beds. Numbers (in 1,000) of beneficiaries of relief funds in 2012: urban residents receiving minimum living allowance, 21,435; rural residents receiving minimum living allowance, 53,445; persons receiving traditional relief, 796; persons in rural households entitled to the 'five guarantees' (food, clothing, medical care, housing and burial expenses), 5,456. The official retirement age for men is 60 and for women 50 (or 55 in the case of civil servants and professionals).

Religion

The government accords legality to five religions only: Buddhism, Islam, Protestantism, Roman Catholicism and Taoism. Confucianism, Buddhism and Taoism have long been practised. Confucianism has no ecclesiastical organization and appears rather as a philosophy of ethics and government. Taoism—of Chinese origin—copied Buddhist ceremonial soon after the arrival of Buddhism two millennia ago. Buddhism in return adopted many Taoist beliefs and practices. A more tolerant attitude towards religion had emerged by 1979, and the government's Bureau of Religious Affairs (since renamed the State Administration for Religious Affairs) was reactivated.

Ceremonies of reverence to ancestors have been observed by the whole population regardless of philosophical or religious beliefs.

A new quasi-religious movement, Falun Gong, was founded in 1992, but has since been banned by the authorities. The movement has claimed some 100m. adherents, although the Chinese government has disputed this.

Muslims are found in every province of China, being most numerous in the Ningxia-Hui Autonomous Region, Yunnan, Shaanxi, Gansu, Hebei, Henan, Shandong, Sichuan, Xinjiang and Shanxi.

Roman Catholicism has had a footing in China for more than three centuries. Two Christian organizations—the Chinese Patriotic Catholic Association, which declared its independence from Rome in 1958, and the Protestant Three-Self Patriotic Movement—are sanctioned by the Chinese government.

According to estimates (by the state-approved Xinhua news agency, the Chinese Academy of Social Sciences and the State Administration for Religious Affairs) there were 100m. Buddhists (more than in any other country), 23m. Christians and more than 21m. Muslims in the country in 2009. Other official figures indicate that there are 5·3m. Catholics, although unofficial estimates are much higher. The number of Christians in China is generally thought to be far higher than official numbers indicate, with so-called 'house churches' becoming ever more popular. Some analysts estimate that there are as many as 100m. Christians overall.

Legislation of 1994 prohibits foreign nationals from setting up religious organizations.

Johnson, Ian, *The Souls of China: The Return of Religion after Mao*. 2017

Culture

World Heritage Sites

There are 53 sites in the People's Republic of China that appear on the UNESCO World Heritage List. They are (with year entered on list): the Great Wall of China (1987), Zhoukoudian, the Peking Man site (1987), Imperial Palaces of the Ming and Qing Dynasties in Beijing and Shenyang (1987 and 2004), mausoleum of first Qing dynasty emperor, Beijing (1987), Taishan mountain (1987), Mogao Caves (1987), Mount Huangshan (1990), Huanglong Scenic Reserve (1992), Jiuzhaigou National Reserve (1992), Wulingyuan Scenic Reserve (1992), Chengde mountain resort and temples (1994), Potala palace, Lhasa (1994, 2000 and 2001), ancient building complex in the Wudang Mountains (1994), Qufu temple, cemetery and mansion of Confucius (1994), Mount Emei Scenic Reserve, including the Leshan Buddha (1996), Lushan National Park (1996), Lijiang old town (1997), Ping Yao old town (1997), Suzhou classical gardens (1997 and 2000), Summer Palace, Beijing (1998), Temple of Heaven, Beijing (1998), Mount Wuyi (1999), Dazu rock carvings (1999), Mount Qincheng and Dujiangyan irrigation system (2000), Xidi and Hongcun ancient villages, Anhui (2000), Longmen grottoes (2000), Ming and Qing dynasty tombs (2000, 2003 and 2004), the Yungang Grottoes (2001), the Three Parallel Rivers of Yunnan Protected Areas (2003), the Capital Cities and Tombs of the Ancient Koguryo Kingdom (2004), the historic centre of Macao (2005), the Sichuan Giant Panda sanctuaries (2006), Yin Xu (2006), Kaiping Diaolou and villages (2007), South China Karst (2007), Fuijan Tulou (2008), Mount Sanqingshan National Park (2008), Mount Wutai (2009), China Danxia, six sub-tropical areas of erosional landforms (2010), the Historic Monuments of Dengfeng (2010), the West Lake Cultural Landscape of Hangzhou (2011), Chengjiang Fossil Site, one of the earliest records of a complex marine ecosystem (2012), Xanadu, the remains of the summer capital of the Yuan Dynasty (2012), the cultural landscape of Honghe Hani Rice Terraces (2013), Xinjiang Tianshan (2013), a mountainous site comprising four components covering 606,833 ha. and an important habitat for endemic and relic flora species, the Grand Canal (2014), a vast waterway system running from Beijing to Zhejiang, Tusi Sites (2015), the remains of tribal domains whose leaders were appointed by the central government as 'Tusi', hereditary rulers of their regions from the 13th to the early 20th century, located in southwest China, Zuojiang Huashan Rock Art Cultural Landscape (2016), 38 sites of rock art that illustrate the life and rituals of the Luoyue people, Hubei Shennongjia (2016), a site that protects the largest primary forests in central

China and provides habitat for a number of rare animal species, Kulangsu, a Historic International Settlement (2017), a tiny island located on the estuary of the Chiu-lung River, Qinghai Hoh Xil (2017), the largest and highest plateau in the world, and Fanjingshan (2018), an island of metamorphic rock in Guizhou Province. Shared with Kazakhstan and Kyrgyzstan, Silk Roads: the Routes Network of Chang'an–Tianshan Corridor (2014) is a 5,000-km section of the extensive Silk Roads network stretching from Chang'an/Luoyang to the Zhetysu region in present-day Kazakhstan.

Press

China has two news agencies: Xinhua (New China) News Agency (the nation's official agency) and China News Service. In 2012 there were 1,918 newspapers and 9,867 magazines; 48,230m. copies of newspapers and 3,350m. copies of magazines were published. In 1980 there were fewer than 200 newspapers. The Communist Party newspaper, *Renmin Ribao* (People's Daily), had an average daily circulation of 2·6m. in 2012. The most widely read newspaper is *Cankao Xiaoxi*, with an average daily circulation of 3·1m. in 2012. China has the second highest circulation of daily newspapers after India, with an estimated average daily total of 137·8m. in 2014. As of Sept. 2014 it was also home to the world's two most visited online news sites: Xinhua News Agency (90·2m. unique desktop users per month) and People's Daily Online (89·1m.). In the 2013 *World Press Freedom Index* compiled by Reporters Without Borders, China ranked 173rd out of 179 countries.

In 2012, 7,920m. volumes of books were produced.

Tourism

In 2015 tourist numbers totalled 56·9m. China was the fourth most visited destination in 2015 after France, the USA and Spain. Income from tourists in 2015 was US$45·0bn., ranking it third behind the USA and Spain. Expenditure by Chinese travellers outside of mainland China for 2015 was US$249·8bn., the most of any country and more than double the next largest expenditure (that of US tourists). In 2011 both German and US travellers abroad had spent more than those from China.

Festivals

The lunar New Year, also known as the 'Spring Festival', is a time of great excitement for the Chinese people. The festivities get under way 22 days prior to the New Year date and continue for 15 days afterwards. Dates of the lunar New Year: Year of the Pig, 5 Feb. 2019; Year of the Rat, 25 Jan. 2020. Lantern Festival, or Yuanxiao Jie, is an important, traditional Chinese festival, which is on the 15th of the first month of the Chinese New Year. Guanyin's Birthday is on the 19th day of the second month of the Chinese lunar calendar. Guanyin is the Chinese goddess of mercy. Tomb Sweeping Day, as the name implies, is a day for visiting and cleaning the ancestral tomb and usually falls on 5 April. Dragon Boat Festival is called Duan Wu Jie in Chinese. The festival is celebrated on the 5th of the 5th month of the Chinese lunar calendar. The Moon Festival is on the 15th of the 8th lunar month. It is sometimes called Mid-Autumn Festival. The Moon Festival is an occasion for family reunion. China's largest rock festivals include the Midi Modern Music Festival in Beijing (May), Beijing Pop Festival (Sept.) and Modern Sky Festival, also in Beijing (Oct.).

Diplomatic Representatives

Of China in the United Kingdom (49–51 Portland Pl., London, W1B 1JL)
　　Ambassador: Liu Xiaoming.

Of the United Kingdom in China (11 Guang Hua Lu, Jian Guo Men Wai, Beijing 100600)
　　Ambassador: Barbara Woodward, DCMG, OBE.

Of China in the USA (3505 International Pl., NW, Washington, D.C., 20008)
　　Ambassador: Cui Tiankai.

Of the USA in China (55 An Jia Lou Rd, 100600 Beijing)
　　Ambassador: Terry Branstad.

Of China to the United Nations
　　Ambassador: Vacant.
　　Chargé d'Affaires a.i.: Wu Haitao.

Of China to the European Union
　　Ambassador: Zhang Ming.

Hong Kong

Xianggang

Population projection, 2020: 7·55m.
GNI per capita, 2017: (PPP$) 58,420
HDI/world rank, 2017: 0·933/7=

Key Historical Events

Hong Kong island and the southern tip of the Kowloon peninsula were ceded in perpetuity to the British Crown in 1841 and 1860 respectively. The area lying immediately to the north of Kowloon known as the New Territories was leased to Britain for 99 years in 1898. Talks began in Sept. 1982 between Britain and China over the future of Hong Kong after the lease expiry in 1997. On 19 Dec. 1984 the two countries signed a Joint Declaration by which Hong Kong became, with effect from 1 July 1997, a Special Administrative Region of the People's Republic of China, enjoying a high degree of autonomy and vested with executive, legislative and independent judicial power, including that of final adjudication. The existing social and economic systems were to remain unchanged for another 50 years. This 'one country, two systems' principle, embodied in the Basic Law, became the constitution for the Hong Kong Special Administrative Region of the People's Republic of China. In 2014 the island saw large-scale pro-democracy protests after Beijing announced that only approved candidates would be allowed to run for the post of Chief Executive at the March 2017 elections.

Territory and Population

Hong Kong ('Xianggang' in Mandarin *Pinyin*) island is situated off the southern coast of the Chinese mainland 32 km east of the mouth of the Pearl River. The area of the island is 81 sq. km. It is separated from the mainland by a fine natural harbour. On the opposite side is the peninsula of Kowloon (47 sq. km). The 'New Territories' include the mainland area lying to the north of Kowloon together with over 200 offshore islands (976 sq. km). Total area of the Territory is 1,106 sq. km, a large part of it being steep and unproductive hillside. Country parks and special areas cover over 40% of the land area. Since 1945 the government has reclaimed over 6,700 ha. from the sea, principally from the seafronts of Hong Kong and Kowloon, facing the harbour.

Based on the results of the 2016 population census Hong Kong's resident population in June 2016 was 7,336,585 and the population density 6,633 per sq. km. In 2011, 60·5% of the population were born in Hong Kong, 32·1% in other parts of China and 7·4% in the rest of the world.

In 2011, 100% of the population lived in urban areas.

The UN gives a projected population for 2020 of 7·55m.

The official languages are Chinese and English.

Social Statistics

Annual population growth rate, 2006–11, 0·7%. Vital statistics, 2010: known births, 88,600; known deaths, 42,200; registered marriages, 52,600. Rates (per 1,000): birth, 12·5; death, 6·0; marriage, 7·4; infant mortality, 2010, 1·7 per 1 000 live births (one of the lowest rates in the world). Expectation of life at birth, 2010: males, 80·0 years; females, 85·9. The median age for marrying in 2010 was 33·2 years for males and 29·8 for females. Total fertility rate, 2010, 1·1 children per woman.

Climate

The climate is sub-tropical, tending towards temperate for nearly half the year, the winter being cool and dry and the summer hot and humid, May to Sept. being the wettest months. Normal temperatures are Jan. 60°F (15·8°C), July 84°F (28·8°C). Annual rainfall 87" (2,214·3 mm).

The British Administration

Hong Kong used to be administered by the Hong Kong government. The Governor was the head of government and presided over the *Executive Council*, which advised the Governor on all important matters. The last British Governor was Chris Patten. In Oct. 1996 the Executive Council consisted of three *ex officio* members and ten appointed members, of whom one was an official member. The chief functions of the *Legislative Council* were to enact laws, control public expenditure and put questions to the administration on matters of public interest. The Legislative Council elected in Sept. 1995 was, for the first time, constituted solely by election. It comprised 60 members, of whom 20 were elected from geographical constituencies, 30 from functional constituencies encompassing all eligible persons in a workforce of 2·9m., and ten from an election committee formed by members of 18 district boards. A president was elected from and by the members.

At the elections on 17 Sept. 1995 turnout for the geographical seats was 35·79%, and for the functional seats (21 of which were contested), 40·42%. The Democratic Party and its allies gained 29 seats, the Liberal Party 10 and the pro-Beijing Democratic Alliance 6. The remaining seats went to independents.

Constitution and Government

In Dec. 1995 the Standing Committee of China's National People's Congress set up a Preparatory Committee of 150 members (including 94 from Hong Kong) to oversee the retrocession of Hong Kong to China on 1 July 1997. In Nov. 1996 the Preparatory Committee nominated a 400-member Selection Committee to select the *Chief Executive of Hong Kong* and a provisional legislature to replace the Legislative Council. The Selection Committee was composed of Hong Kong residents, with 60 seats reserved for delegates to the National People's Congress and appointees of the People's Political Consultative Conference. On 11 Dec. 1996 Tung Chee Hwa was elected Chief Executive by 80% of the Selection Committee's votes.

On 21 Dec. 1996 the Selection Committee selected a provisional legislature which began its activities in Jan. 1997 while the Legislative Council was still functioning. In Jan. 1997 the provisional legislature started its work by enacting legislation which would be applicable to the Hong Kong Special Administrative Region and compatible with the Basic Law.

Constitutionally Hong Kong is a Special Administrative Region of the People's Republic of China. The Basic Law enables Hong Kong to retain a high degree of autonomy. It provides that the legislative, judicial and administrative systems which were previously in operation are to remain in place. The Special Administrative Region Government is also empowered to decide on Hong Kong's monetary and economic policies independent of China.

In July 1997 the first-past-the-post system of returning members from geographical constituencies to the Legislative Council was replaced by proportional representation. There were 20 directly elected seats out of 60 for the first elections to the Legislative Council following Hong Kong's return to Chinese sovereignty, increasing in accordance with the Basic Law to 24 for the 2000 election with 36 indirectly elected. In the Sept. 2004 Legislative Council election (and that of Sept. 2008) 30 of the 60 seats were directly elected. For the election in Sept. 2012 the number of seats was increased to 70, with 35 directly elected and 30 indirectly elected by functional constituencies. There were also five new functional constituency seats nominated by elected District Council members. The Chief Executive is chosen by a Beijing-backed 1,200-member election committee (800 prior to the March 2012 election), although it has been stated that universal suffrage is the ultimate aim. In 2007 a timetable was announced for Hong Kong to directly elect its Chief Executive in 2017 and its Legislative Council in 2020. However, Beijing insisted that only approved candidates would be allowed to stand in 2017, prompting mass pro-democracy rallies in the territory in 2014 and formal rejection of the plan by the Legislative Council in June 2015. Beijing nevertheless refused to countenance amendments.

In July 2002 a new accountability or 'ministerial' system was introduced, under which the Chief Executive nominates for appointment 14 policy secretaries, who report directly to the Chief Executive. The Chief Executive is aided by the *Executive Council*, consisting of the three senior Secretaries of Department (the Chief Secretary, the Financial Secretary and the Secretary for Justice) and eleven other secretaries plus five non-officials.

The British Administration

Hong Kong used to be administered by the Hong Kong government. The Governor was the head of government and presided over the *Executive Council*, which advised the Governor on all important matters. The last British Governor was Chris Patten. In Oct. 1996 the Executive Council consisted of three *ex officio* members and ten appointed members, of whom one was an official member. The chief functions of the *Legislative Council* were to enact laws, control public expenditure and put questions to the administration on matters of public interest. The Legislative Council elected in Sept. 1995 was, for the first time, constituted solely by election. It comprised 60 members, of whom 20 were elected from geographical constituencies, 30 from functional constituencies encompassing all eligible persons in a workforce of 2·9m., and ten from an election committee formed by members of 18 district boards. A president was elected from and by the members.

At the elections on 17 Sept. 1995 turnout for the geographical seats was 35·79%, and for the functional seats (21 of which were contested), 40·42%. The Democratic Party and its allies gained 29 seats, the Liberal Party 10 and the pro-Beijing Democratic Alliance 6. The remaining seats went to independents.

Recent Elections

In the Legislative Council election held on 4 Sept. 2016 turnout was 58·3%, up from 53·0% at the 2012 vote. 35 of the 70 seats were directly elected, the other 35 being returned by committees and professional associations in 'functional constituencies'. Pro-Beijing parties won 40 of the 70 seats (43 of 70 in 2012); pro-democracy parties won 23 (27 of 70 in 2012); localists won 6; non-aligned won 1.

Carrie Lam was elected chief executive on 26 March 2017, receiving 777 of 1,194 votes in the Election Committee.

Current Government

In Feb. 2019 the government of the Hong Kong Special Administrative Region comprised:

Chief Executive: Carrie Lam; b. 1957 (since 1 July 2017).

Chief Secretary for Administration: Matthew Cheung Kin-chung. *Financial Secretary:* Paul Chan Mo-po. *Secretary for Justice:* Teresa Cheng Yeuk-wah. *Environment:* Wong Kam-sing. *Innovation and Technology:* Nicholas W. Yang. *Home Affairs:* Lau Kong-wah. *Financial Services and the Treasury:* James Henry Lau, Jr. *Labour and Welfare:* Law Chi-kwong. *Civil Service:* Joshua Law Chi-kong. *Security:* John Lee Ka-chiu. *Transport and Housing:* Frank Chan Fan. *Food and Health:* Sophia Chan Siu-chee. *Commerce and Economic Development:* Edward Yau Tang-wah. *Development:* Michael Wong Wai-lun. *Education:* Kevin Yueng Yun-hung. *Constitutional and Mainland Affairs:* Patrick Nip Tak-kuen.

Government Website: http://www.gov.hk

Economy

Services accounted for 92% of GDP in 2016 and industry 8%.

According to the anti-corruption organization Transparency International, Hong Kong ranked equal 14th in the world in a 2018 survey of the countries and regions with the least corruption in business and government. It received 76 out of 100 in the annual index.

Overview

Hong Kong has one of the world's most open economies and is an internationally important financial centre. The territory's economic rise was founded on its role as an international trade emporium, acting as a conduit for China's burgeoning exports. Mainland China, the USA and Japan are Hong Kong's major export partners, accounting for 51·2%, 7·2% and 5·0% of exports respectively in 2015. The island is dependent on imports of food and other resources. In 2015 it imported 49% of goods from mainland China, 7% from Taiwan and 6% from Japan.

In 2004 and 2005 the economy grew strongly on the back of a rise in Chinese tourism, healthy global demand for exports and improving domestic consumer confidence. However, the global financial crisis saw the economy shrink by 2·5% in 2009 before rebounding with a 6·8% increase the following year. Between 2010 and 2015 annual growth averaged 3·6%, supported by strong external demand. Student-led pro-democracy protests in the latter months of 2014 caused major disruption in several key business districts and threatened to weaken the local economy in the short term.

Foreign direct investment levels have been high, averaging 39% of GDP between 2010 and 2015 according to World Bank data, and the World Economic Forum ranked Hong Kong as the ninth most competitive economy in the world in its 2016 report. The government aims to tackle a housing shortage by providing 280,000 new housing units by the mid-2020s.

Currency

The unit of currency is the *Hong Kong dollar* (HKD) of 100 *cents*. It has been pegged since 1983 at a rate of HK$7·8 to the US dollar. Banknotes are issued by the Hongkong and Shanghai Banking Corporation and the Standard Chartered Bank, and, from May 1994, the Bank of China. Total money supply was HK$529,161m. in July 2009. In Aug. 2009 gold reserves were 67,000 troy oz and foreign exchange reserves were US$223,211m.

Inflation rates (based on IMF statistics):

2008	2009	2010	2011	2012	2013	2014	2015	2016	2017
4·3%	0·6%	2·3%	5·3%	4·1%	4·3%	4·4%	3·0%	2·4%	1·5%

Budget
In 2010–11 revenue totalled HK$376·5bn. and expenditure HK$323·8bn. Earnings and profits taxes accounted for 38·0% of revenues in 2010–11 and indirect taxes 26·1%; education accounted for 19·1% of expenditures and social welfare 12·6%.

Performance
GDP totalled US$341·5bn. in 2017. Real GDP growth rates (based on IMF statistics):

2008	2009	2010	2011	2012	2013	2014	2015	2016	2017
2·1%	−2·5%	6·8%	4·8%	1·7%	3·1%	2·8%	2·4%	2·2%	3·8%

In the 2016 *World Competitiveness Yearbook*, compiled by the International Institute for Management Development, Hong Kong came first in the world ranking. The annual publication ranks and analyses how a nation's business environment creates and sustains the competitiveness of enterprises.

Banking and Finance
The Hong Kong Monetary Authority acts as a central bank. The *Chief Executive* is Norman Chan. As at Dec. 2009 there were 145 banks licensed under the Banking Ordinance, of which 23 were locally incorporated. There were also 26 restricted licence banks, 28 deposit-taking companies and 71 representative offices of foreign banks. Licensed bank deposits were HK$5,193,003m. in July 2007; restricted licence bank deposits were HK$22,065m. There are three banks of issue: Bank of China (Hong Kong); The Hongkong and Shanghai Banking Corporation; and Standard Chartered Bank.

Gross external debt amounted to US$1,029,927m. in June 2012.

Total foreign direct investment in 2017 was US$104·3bn.

The principal regulator of Hong Kong's securities and futures markets is the Securities and Futures Commission. Hong Kong Exchanges and Clearing (HKEx), which was created in March 2000, owns and operates the only stock and futures exchange in Hong and their related clearing houses.

Energy and Natural Resources

Environment
Hong Kong's carbon dioxide emissions from the consumption of energy in 2011 were the equivalent of 13·2 tonnes per capita.

Electricity
Installed capacity was 12·6m. kW in 2011. Production in 2011 was 39·03bn. kWh. Hong Kong is a net importer of electricity. Consumption in 2011 was 47·41bn. kWh.

Agriculture
The local agricultural industry is directed towards the production of high quality fresh food through intensive land use and modern farming techniques. Out of the territory's total land area of 1,103 sq. km, only 60 sq. km is currently farmed. In 2006 local production accounted for 55% of live poultry consumed, 23% of live pigs and 4% of fresh vegetables. The gross value of local agricultural production totalled HK$1,184m. in 2006, with pig production valued at HK$585m., poultry production (including eggs) at HK$340m., and vegetable and flower production at HK$254m.

Fisheries
In 2015 the total catch was 145,193 tonnes, exclusively from marine waters.

Industry
The leading companies by market capitalization in Hong Kong in March 2019 were: China Mobile, a telecommunications company (US$192·6bn.); AIA Group, a life insurance company (US$111·4bn.); and CNOOC, an integrated oil company (US$78·8bn.).

Industry is mainly service-oriented. In June 2013 there were 343,006 establishments employing 2,505,081 persons in service industries and 11,609 establishments employing 103,350 persons in manufacturing industries. Establishment statistics by service type (and persons engaged) were mainly: import/export trade and wholesale, 116,335 (554,372); retail, 65,046 (264,805); social and personal services, 44,194 (460,973); professional and business services, 42,017 (344,544); financing and insurance, 21,683 (207,346); accommodation and food services, 17,201 (276,207); real estate, 15,071 (126,415).

Labour
In 2011 the size of the labour force (synonymous with the economically active population) was 3,703,100 (1,760,400 females). The persons engaged in June 2012 included 1,090,059 people in wholesale, retail and import/export trades, accommodation and food services, 664,652 in finance, insurance, real estate, professional and business services, 159,217 in the civil service, 107,637 in manufacturing and 71,721 in construction sites (manual workers only). A minimum wage of HK$28 per hour was introduced for the first time on 1 May 2011.

Unemployment stood at 3·1% in the period Sept.–Dec. 2011.

External Economic Relations

Imports and Exports
In 2009 the total value of imports was HK$2,692,356m. and total exports HK$2,469,089m. The main suppliers of imports in 2009 were mainland China (46·4%), Japan (8·8%), Taiwan (6·5%), Singapore (6·5%) and USA (5·3%). In 2009, 51·2% of total exports went to mainland China, 11·6% to the USA, 4·4% to Japan, 3·2% to Germany and 2·4% to the United Kingdom.

The chief import items in 2009 were: electrical machinery, apparatus and appliances, etc. (26·8%); telecommunications, sound recording and reproducing equipment (13·7%); office machines and automatic data processing machines (9·2%); articles of apparel and clothing accessories (4·5%). The main exports in 2009 were: electrical machinery, apparatus and appliances, etc. (26·4%); telecommunications, sound recording and reproducing equipment (16·8%); office machines and automatic data processing machines (10·1%); articles of apparel and clothing accessories (7·2%).

Communications

Roads
In 2011 there were 2,086 km of roads, over 50% of which were in the New Territories. There are 16 road tunnels, including three under Victoria Harbour. In 2011 there were 435,000 private cars, 111,000 goods vehicles, 20,000 buses and coaches, and 39,000 motorcycles and mopeds. There were 15,541 road accidents in 2011, of which 128 were fatal. A total of 26·7m. tonnes of cargo were transported by road in 2011.

A 55 km bridge (the world's longest sea bridge) linking Hong Kong, Zhuhai in Guangdong Province in mainland China and Macao opened in Oct. 2018 following a number of delays.

Hong Kong was ranked fourth for its road infrastructure in the World Economic Forum's *Global Competitiveness Report 2017–2018*.

Rail
Hong Kong's railways are run by the MTR Corporation Limited (MTRCL), a public listed company of which the government is the majority shareholder. The MTR system comprises nine railway lines serving Hong Kong Island, Kowloon and the New Territories. Its 175 km network has 82 stations and carries an average of 4·8m. passengers each day. MTR lines carried 1,545m. passengers in 2012. In addition, a Light Rail network (36·2 km and 68 stops) serves the local communities of Tuen Mun, Yuen Long and Tin Shui Wai in the New Territories; 464,000 passengers travel daily on the system. A high speed rail service between Hong Kong and Guangzhou on the mainland opened in Sept. 2018.

The electric tramway on the northern state of Hong Kong Island commenced operating in 1904 and has a total track length of 16 km. The Peak Tram, a funicular railway connecting the Peak district with the lower levels in Victoria, has a track length of 1·4 km and two tramcars (each with a capacity of 120 passengers per trip). It carries an average of 16,200 passengers daily. The Airport Express Line (35·2 km) opened in 1998 and is also operated by the MTRCL. It carried 12·7m. passengers in 2012.

In June 2013 it was estimated that 12·2m. passenger journeys were made daily on public transport (including local railways, buses, etc.).

In the World Economic Forum's *Global Competitiveness Report 2017–2018* Hong Kong ranked third for quality of rail infrastructure.

Civil Aviation
The new Hong Kong International Airport (generally known as Chek Lap Kok), built on reclaimed land off Lantau Island to the west of Hong Kong, was opened on 6 July 1998 to replace the old Hong Kong International Airport at Kai Tak, which was situated on the north shore of Kowloon Bay. More than 100 airlines now operate scheduled services to and from

Hong Kong. In 2012 Cathay Pacific Airways, the largest Hong Kong-based airline, operated approximately 105,000 passenger and cargo services to 172 destinations in 41 countries and territories around the world. Cathay Pacific carried 21,146,492 passengers and 1·4m. tonnes of cargo in 2012. Dragonair, a Cathay Pacific subsidiary, provided scheduled services to 41 cities in mainland China and Asia in 2012. In 2012 Air Hong Kong, an all-cargo operator, provided scheduled services to Bangkok, Beijing, Ho Chi Minh City, Manila, Nagoya, Osaka, Penang (via Bangkok), Seoul, Shanghai, Singapore, Taipei and Tokyo. Hong Kong International Airport handled more international freight in 2011 than any other airport. In 2011, 334,000 aircraft arrived and departed and 54m. passengers and 3·94m. tonnes of freight were carried on aircraft.

Hong Kong was second, behind only Singapore, in the rankings for air transport infrastructure in the World Economic Forum's *Global Competitiveness Report 2017–2018*.

Shipping

The port of Hong Kong handled 23·1m. TEUs (twenty-foot equivalent units) in 2012, making it the world's third busiest container port after Shanghai and Singapore. The Kwai Chung Container Port has 24 berths with 7,694 metres of quay backed by 275 ha. of cargo handling area. At the end of 2016 there were 2,513 ships (2,228 ocean-going) of 107,573,898 GT registered in Hong Kong. In 2016, 27,642 ocean-going vessels, 72,810 river cargo vessels and 84,559 river passenger vessels arrived at the port of Hong Kong. A total of 257m. tonnes of freight were handled in 2015.

Hong Kong was ranked third in the World Economic Forum's *Global Competitiveness Report 2017–2018* for the quality of its port facilities.

Telecommunications

In 2013 there were 4,546,000 main (fixed) telephone lines (equivalent to 631·1 per 1,000 population). The local fixed telecommunications network services (FTNS) market in Hong Kong was liberalized in 1995. There were 17,098,000 mobile phone subscriptions in 2013 (equivalent to 2,373·5 per 1,000 population), up from 11,580,000 in 2008 (1,661·9 per 1,000 population). The number of subscriptions doubled between 2006 and 2013. The internet market has also seen huge growth. In 2013 there were 6,892,000 wireless broadband subscriptions (956·7 per 1,000 population) and 2,220,000 fixed broadband subscriptions (308·2 per 1,000 population). The number of fixed broadband subscriptions has been declining since 2011 as more people have wireless subscriptions instead. In March 2012 there were 3·8m. Facebook users.

The external telecommunications services market has been fully liberalized since 1 Jan. 1999, and the external telecommunications facilities market was also liberalized starting from 1 Jan. 2000.

Social Institutions

Education

In 2010 the adult literacy rate was 94·6% (92·4% in 2000). Universal basic education is available to all children aged from six to 15 years. In around three-quarters of the ordinary secondary day schools teaching has been in Cantonese since 1998–99, with about a quarter of ordinary secondary day schools still using English. In 2010 there were 148,940 pupils in 951 kindergartens, 331,112 in 572 primary schools (including 40 international schools) and 458,131 in 565 secondary schools (including 27 international schools).

The University of Hong Kong (founded 1911) had 12,916 full-time and 736 part-time students in 2010–11; the Chinese University of Hong Kong (founded 1963), 13,260 full-time and 654 part-time students; the Hong Kong University of Science and Technology (founded 1991), 7,208 full-time and 26 part-time students; the Hong Kong Polytechnic University (founded 1972 as the Hong Kong Polytechnic), 13,925 full-time and 807 part-time students; the City University of Hong Kong (founded 1984 as the City Polytechnic of Hong Kong), 10,221 full-time and 11 part-time students; the Hong Kong Baptist University (founded 1956 as the Hong Kong Baptist College), 5,050 full-time and 506 part-time students; the Lingnan University (founded 1967 as the Lingnan College), 2,287 full-time and five part-time students; and the Hong Kong Institute of Education (founded 1994), 3,270 full-time and 3,706 part-time students.

Estimated total government expenditure on education in 2011–12 was HK$68·3bn. (18·6% of total government spending and 3·6% of GDP). In 2010–11: 20·1% of total government spending and 3·4% of GDP.

According to the OECD's 2015 PISA (Programme for International Student Assessment) study, 15-year-olds in Hong Kong rank second among OECD and other major countries and cities in mathematics and reading, and ninth in science. The three-yearly study compares educational achievement of pupils in over 70 countries.

Health

The Department of Health (DH) is the Government's health adviser and regulatory authority. The Hospital Authority (HA) is an independent body responsible for the management of all public hospitals. In 2009 there were 12,424 registered doctors, equivalent to 1·8 doctors per 1,000 population. In 2009 there were 2,126 dentists, 38,641 nurses and 4,525 midwives. The total number of hospital beds in 2009 was 35,062, including 26,872 beds in 38 public hospitals under the HA and 3,818 beds in 13 private hospitals. The bed-population ratio was 5·0 beds per thousand population.

The Chinese Medicine Ordinance was passed by the Legislative Council in July 1999 to establish a statutory framework to accord a professional status for Chinese medicine practitioners and ensure safety, quality and efficacy of Chinese medicine. In 2009 there were 6,048 registered Chinese medicine practitioners.

Total expenditure on health in 2009–10 amounted to HK$88,069m., an increase of 5·2% over that in 2008–09.

Justice

The Hong Kong Act of 1985 provided for Hong Kong ordinances to replace English laws in specified fields.

The courts of justice comprise the Court of Final Appeal (inaugurated 1 July 1997), which hears appeals on civil and criminal matters from the High Court; the High Court (consisting of the Court of Appeal and the Court of First Instance); the Lands Tribunal, which determines on statutory claims for compensation over land and certain landlord and tenant matters; the District Court (which includes the Family Court); the Magistracies (including the Juvenile Court); the Coroner's Court; the Labour Tribunal, which provides a quick and inexpensive method of settling disputes between employers and employees; the Small Claims Tribunal, which deals with monetary claims involving amounts not exceeding HK$50,000; and the Obscene Articles Tribunal.

While the High Court has unlimited jurisdiction in both civil and criminal matters, the District Court has limited jurisdiction. The maximum term of imprisonment it may impose is seven years. Magistracies exercise criminal jurisdiction over a wide range of offences, and the powers of punishment are generally restricted to a maximum of two years' imprisonment or a fine of HK$100,000.

After being in abeyance for 25 years, the death penalty was abolished in 1992.

75,936 crimes were reported in 2011, of which 13,100 were violent crimes. 38,327 people were arrested in 2011, of whom 8,962 were for violent crimes. The population in penal institutions was 9,067 at 31 Dec. 2011 (127 per 100,000 population).

Welfare

Social welfare programmes include social security, family services, child care, services for the elderly, medical social services, youth and community work, probation, and corrections and rehabilitation. 171 non-governmental organizations are subsidized by public funds.

The government gives non-contributory cash assistance to needy families, unemployed able-bodied adults, the severely disabled and the elderly. Caseload as at Aug. 2011 totalled 280,358. Victims of natural disasters, crimes of violence and traffic accidents are financially assisted. Estimated recurrent government expenditure on social welfare for 2011–12 was HK$42·2bn.

Religion

According to the Pew Research Center's Forum on Religion & Public Life, an estimated 56·1% of the population in 2010 had no religious affiliation, 14·3% were Christians (four-fifths Protestants and a fifth Catholics), 13·2% were Buddhists and 12·8% folk religionists. Joseph Zen Ze-kiun became Hong Kong's first cardinal in 2006. In Feb. 2019 the Roman Catholic Church had two cardinals.

Culture

Press

In 2008 there were 54 daily newspapers, of which 50 were paid-for and four free. The newspapers with the highest circulation figures are all Chinese-language papers—*Oriental Daily News, Apple Daily* and *The Sun*. The English-language paper with the highest circulation is the *South China Morning Post*. Circulation of dailies (including free papers) in 2008 was 3·6m. (2·0m. paid-for and 1·6m. free).

Tourism
There were a record 36,030,300 visitor arrivals in 2010. Expenditure associated to inbound tourism totalled HK$209,983·0m. in 2010.

Festivals
The Hong Kong Arts Festival takes place in Feb.–March and features music, theatre, dance and opera. The Hong Kong International Film Festival (Aug.–Sept.) has been running annually since 1977.

Macao

Região Administrativa Especial de Macau (Macao Special Administrative Region)
Population projection, 2020: 652,000
GDP per capita, 2015: US$75,574

Key Historical Events
Macao was visited by Portuguese traders from 1513 and became a Portuguese colony in 1557. Initially sovereignty remained vested in China, with the Portuguese paying an annual rent. In 1848–49 the Portuguese declared Macao a free port and established jurisdiction over the territory. On 6 Jan. 1987 Portugal agreed to return Macao to China on 20 Dec. 1999 when it would become a special administrative region of China, with considerable autonomy.

Territory and Population
The Macao Special Administrative Region, which lies at the mouth of the Pearl River, comprises a peninsula (9·3 sq. km) connected by a narrow isthmus to the People's Republic of China, on which is built the city of Santa Nome de Deus de Macao, the islands of Taipa (7·6 sq. km), linked to Macao by three bridges, Colôane (7·6 sq. km) linked to Taipa by a 2-km causeway, and Cotai, a strip of reclaimed land between Colôane and Taipa (6·0 km). The total area of Macao in 2016 was 30·5 sq. km. Additional land continues to be reclaimed from the sea. The population at the 2016 census was 650,834 (336,816 females); density, 21,339 people per sq. km. According to UN estimates, the entire population lived in urban areas in 2011. The official languages are Chinese and Portuguese, with the majority speaking the Cantonese dialect. Only about 4,000 people speak Portuguese as their first language.

The UN gives a projected population for 2020 of 652,000.

In 2015, 1,784 foreigners were legally registered for residency in Macao. There were 8,468 legal immigrants from mainland China.

Social Statistics
2014: births, 7,360 (11·8 per 1,000 population); deaths, 1,939 (3·1); marriages, 4,085 (6·6); divorces, 1,308 (2·1). Infant mortality, 2014, 2·0 per 1,000 live births. Life expectancy at birth (2011–14), 82·9 years.

Climate
Sub-tropical tending towards temperate, with an average temperature of 23·0°C. The number of rainy days is around a third of the year. Average annual rainfall varies from 47–87" (1,200–2,200 mm). It is very humid from May to Sept.

Constitution and Government
Macao's constitution is the 'Basic Law', promulgated by China's National People's Congress on 31 March 1993 and in effect since 20 Dec. 1999. It is a Special Administrative Region (SAR) of the People's Republic of China, and is directly under the Central People's Government while enjoying a high degree of autonomy. The *Legislative Assembly* has 33 seats of which 14 are directly elected, 12 indirectly elected by functional constituencies and seven appointed by the chief executive.

Recent Elections
At the elections held on 17 Sept. 2017 the Macau-Guangdong Union won two of 14 elected seats with 10·0% of votes cast and the Union for

Development two with 9·7%. Ten other parties won a single seat each. Turnout was 57·2%.

Fernando Chui Sai-on was re-elected chief executive for a second term on 31 Aug. 2014, receiving 380 out of 396 votes in the Election Committee.

Current Government
Chief Executive: Fernando Chui Sai-on; b. 1957 (sworn in 20 Dec. 2009 and re-elected in Aug. 2014).
Government Website: http://www.gov.mo

Economy
The gaming sector is of major importance to the economy of Macao. It accounted for 46·1% of total GDP in 2013 and provides billions of dollars in taxes. In 2014, 21·5% of the workforce was employed in gaming. In 2014 gross gaming revenue totalled US$43,307m. (nearly double the 2010 figure). However, 2014 revenues were down slightly on the 2013 total. Macao overtook Nevada as the world's largest gaming market in 2008.

Overview
After its transfer of sovereignty to the People's Republic of China in 1999, Macao achieved high growth based on tourism and gambling. China's relaxation of travel restrictions in 1999 resulted in an increase in mainland visitors to more than 20m. by 2015 out of a total of 30m. visitors. The cessation of business magnate Stanley Ho's monopoly of the local gaming industry in 2001 and its opening up to foreign competition led to an influx of foreign investment that made Macao the world's biggest gaming centre in 2008. Gambling revenues exceeded US$28bn. in 2015, having grown by more than 20% per year on average from 2008.

The economy grew by an average 7·7% per year from 2005–13, driven mainly by the gaming sector and the ongoing construction of a number of casino resorts. However, it went into recession from 2014 following China's crackdown on government corruption.

Macao's traditional manufacturing industries virtually disappeared following the transfer of much of the textile industry to the Chinese mainland and, in 2005, the termination of the Multifibre Arrangement, which had governed international textile trade flows for three decades.

Currency
The unit of currency is the *pataca* (MOP) of 100 *avos*, which is tied to the Hong Kong dollar at parity. Inflation was 2·4% in 2016 and 1·2% in 2017. Foreign exchange reserves were US$18,350m. in 2009. Total money supply was 30,608m. patacas in 2009.

Budget
In 2014 revenues totalled 161,861m. patacas; expenditures, 67,078m. patacas. Revenues from gaming tax accounted for 84·5% of total revenue in 2014; current expenditure accounted for 86·4% of expenditure.

Performance
Real GDP growth was just 1·7% in 2009 but then rose to 25·3% in 2010 and 21·7% in 2011. More recently the economy contracted by 0·9% in 2016 before growing by 9·1% in 2017. Total GDP in 2017 was US$50·4bn.

Banking and Finance
There are two note-issuing banks in Macao—the Macao branch of the Bank of China and the Macao branch of the Banco Nacional Ultramarino. The Monetary Authority of Macao functions as a central bank (*Chairman*, Benjamin Chan Sau San). Commercial business is handled (2015) by 28 banks, nine of which are local and 19 foreign. Total deposits, 2015 (including non-resident deposits), 728,785·9m. patacas. There are no foreign exchange controls within Macao.

Energy and Natural Resources

Environment
Macao's carbon dioxide emissions from the consumption of energy in 2011 were the equivalent of 2·8 tonnes per capita.

Electricity
Installed capacity was 0·47m. kW in 2013; production, 0·41bn. kWh. Macao imported 4,059m. kWh of electricity in 2013.

Oil and Gas
202,688,000 litres of fuel oil were imported in 2009.

Fisheries

The catch in 2015 was estimated at 1,500 tonnes.

Industry

Although the economy is based on gaming and tourism there is a light industrial base of textiles and garments. In 2014 the number of manufacturing establishments was 864 (food products and beverages, 284; textiles and wearing apparel, 160; publishing, printing and reproduction of recorded media, 153).

Labour

In 2015 a total of 396,500 people were in employment, including 83,500 (21·1%) in gaming and junket activities (up from 12,500 in 1999); 55,000 (13·9%), hotels, restaurants and similar activities; 54,800 (13·8%), construction; 45,000 (11·4%), wholesale and retail trade, repair of motor vehicles, motorcycles and personal and household goods; 29,800 (7·5%), real estate and business activities; 29,400 (7·4%), public administration and social security. Employment in 2015 was 98·2% of the labour force; unemployment rate stood at 1·8%.

International Trade

Imports and Exports

In 2009 imports (c.i.f.) were valued at US$4,750·9m., of which the main products were telecommunications, sound recording and reproducing equipment; petroleum and petroleum products; and gold, silverware, jewellery and articles of precious materials. In 2009 the chief import sources (in US$1m.) were: mainland China (1,451·6); Hong Kong (505·4); Japan (381·9).

2009 exports (f.o.b.) were valued at US$960·7m., of which the leading products were articles of apparel and clothing accessories; gold, silverware, jewellery and articles of precious materials; and petroleum oils and oils obtained from bituminous minerals. In 2009 the main export markets (in US$1m.) were: Hong Kong (377·5); USA (163·8); mainland China (139·9).

Communications

Roads

In 2013 there were 421 km of roads. In 2013 there were 97,721 passenger cars in use (179 cars per 1,000 inhabitants), 3,723 buses and coaches, 5,114 trucks and 119,453 motorcycles. There were 19 fatalities in road accidents in 2013.

A 55 km bridge (the world's longest sea bridge) linking Macao, Zhuhai in Guangdong Province in mainland China and Hong Kong opened in Oct. 2018 following a number of delays.

Civil Aviation

An international airport opened in Dec. 1995. In 2009 Macau International Airport handled 3,643,970 passengers and 52,464 tonnes of freight (including transit cargo). In 2013 Air Macau flew to Bangkok, Beijing, Changsha, Chengdu, Chongqing, Da Nang, Hangzhou, Hefei, Kaohsiung, Nanjing, Nanning, Ningbo, Osaka, Quanzhou, Seoul, Shanghai, Shenyang, Taipei, Taiyuan, Tokyo, Wenzhou, Xiamen and Zhengzhou.

Shipping

Regular services connect Macao with Hong Kong, 65 km to the northeast.

Telecommunications

In 2011 there were 165,500 landline telephone subscriptions (equivalent to 297·9 per 1,000 inhabitants) and 1,353,200 mobile phone subscriptions (or 2,435·0 per 1,000 inhabitants). In 2012, 82·5% of households had internet access. In March 2012 there were 205,000 Facebook users.

Social Institutions

Justice

There are a judicial district court, a criminal court and an administrative court with 24 magistrates in all.

In 2009 there were 12,406 crimes, of which 6,462 were against property. There were 930 persons in prison in Dec. 2009.

Education

There are both public and private schools. In 2014–15 there were 95 schools and colleges. Number of students in the 2014–15 academic year (with number of teachers): pre-primary, 14,552 (916); primary, 24,252 (1,722); secondary, 30,088 (2,629). In 2014–15 there were four special education schools with 624 pupils and 112 teachers. There were ten higher education institutions with student enrolment of 30,771. In 2014 there were 31 institutions offering vocational training courses, in which participants totalled 52,636.

Expenditure on education came to 1·8% of GDP in 2013 and 14·9% of total government spending in 2014.

Health

In 2009 there were 723 doctors, 108 dentists and 450 nurses working in primary health care, and 560 doctors, 14 dentists and 1,169 nurses working in hospitals. In 2009 there were 1,294 hospital beds; there were 2·4 doctors per 1,000 population.

Religion

In 2010 there were an estimated 320,000 folk religionists and 90,000 Buddhists according to the Pew Research Center's Forum on Religion & Public Life. A further 80,000 people were religiously unaffiliated. There are also small numbers of Catholics.

Culture

World Heritage Sites

The historic centre of Macao was inscribed on the UNESCO World Heritage List in 2005.

Press

In 2009 there were 14 daily newspapers (nine in Chinese, three in Portuguese and two in English) and 11 weekly newspapers (ten in Chinese and one in Portuguese).

Tourism

Tourism is one of the mainstays of the economy. In 2014 there were 31·5m. tourists (of which 21·3m. were from mainland China, 6·4m. from Hong Kong and 1·0m. from Taiwan), up from 29·3m. in 2013 and 28·1m. in 2012. Visitor spending in 2014 totalled 61,749m. patacas.

Festivals

The government-run Macao International Music Festival featuring a wide range of Chinese and Western music takes place in Oct.–Nov.

Taiwan[1]

Zhonghua Minguo ('Republic of China')

Capital: Taipei
Population projection, 2020: 23·82m.
GDP per capita, 2013: US$20,925

Key Historical Events

Taiwan, christened Ilha Formosa ('beautiful island') by the Portuguese, was ceded to Japan by China by the Treaty of Shimonoseki in 1895. After the Second World War the island was surrendered to Gen. Chiang Kai-shek who made it the headquarters for his crumbling Nationalist Government. Until 1970 the USA supported Taiwan's claims to represent all of China. Only in 1971 did the government of the People's Republic of China manage to replace that of Chiang Kai-shek at the UN. In Jan. 1979 the USA established formal diplomatic relations with the People's Republic of China, breaking off formal ties with Taiwan. Taiwan itself has continued to reject attempts at reunification, and although there have been frequent threats of direct action from mainland China (including military manoeuvres off the Taiwanese coast) the prospect of confrontation with the USA supports the status quo.

In July 1999 President Lee Teng-hui repudiated Taiwan's 50-year-old 'One China' policy—the pretence of a common goal of unification—arguing that Taiwan and China should maintain equal 'state to state' relations. This was a rejection of Beijing's view that Taiwan is no more than a renegade Chinese province which must be reunited with the mainland, by force if

---

[1] See note on transcription of names in CHINA: Territory and Population.

necessary. In the presidential election of 18 March 2000 Chen Shui-bian, leader of the Democratic Progressive Party, was elected, together with Annette Lu Hsiu-lien as his Vice President. Both supported independence although Chen Shui-bian made friendly gestures towards China and distanced himself from colleagues who wanted an immediate declaration of independence. Following his wife's indictment on embezzlement charges in Nov. 2006, President Chen survived three parliamentary attempts to impeach him. He was succeeded as president in 2008 by Ma Ying-jeou of the Nationalist Party.

In Sept. 2009 Chen Shui-bian received a life sentence (later reduced to a 19-year term) after being found guilty of multiple counts of corruption. China and Taiwan signed a free trade agreement in June 2010, which was considered a significant thawing of relations. Nonetheless, tensions remained, particularly in relation to disputed sovereignty over several islands in the East China Sea. In Jan. 2012 Ma Ying-jeou was re-elected to the presidency but the election in Jan. 2016 was won by Tsai Ing-wen, whose Democratic Progressive Party won the most seats in legislative polls at the same time—the first occasion that the Nationalist Party has not been the largest party in government since 2004.

Territory and Population

Taiwan lies between the East and South China Seas about 160 km from the coast of Fujian. The territories currently under the control of the Republic of China include Taiwan, Penghu (the Pescadores), Kinmen (Quemoy) and Lienchiang (the Matsu Islands), as well as the archipelagos in the South China Sea. Off the Pacific coast of Taiwan are Green Island and Orchid Island. To the northeast of Taiwan are the Tiaoyutai Islets. The total area of Taiwan Island, the Penghu Archipelago and the Kinmen area (including the fortified offshore islands of Quemoy and Matsu) is 36,193 sq. km (13,974 sq. miles). Population (2017), 23,571,227. The ethnic composition is 84% native Taiwanese (including 15% of Hakka), 14% of Mainland Chinese and 2% aborigine of Malayo-Polynesian origin. There were also 519,984 aboriginals of Malay origin in Dec. 2011. In 2009 Taiwan adopted *hanyu pinyin*, developed in the 1950s on mainland China, as the standard system for romanizing Chinese characters. However, by 2014 several cities, including Kaohsiung—the second largest—refused to use *hanyu pinyin* in what was widely seen as a political statement against perceived closer ties with Beijing. Population density: 642 per sq. km.

Taiwan's administrative units comprise (with 2013 populations): five special municipalities: Kaohsiung (2,779,877), New Taipei (3,954,929), Taichung (2,701,661), Tainan (1,883,208), Taipei, the capital (2,686,516); three provincial cities: Chiayi (270,872), Hsinchu (428,483), Keelung (374,914); 12 counties (*hsien*) in Taiwan Province: Changhwa (1,296,013), Chiayi (529,229), Hsinchu (530,486), Hualien (333,897), Ilan (458,456), Miaoli (565,554), Nantou (517,222), Penghu (100,400), Pingtung (852,286), Taitung (224,821), Taoyuan (2,044,023), Yunlin (707,792); two counties in Fujian Province: Kinmen (120,713), Lienchiang (12,165).

Social Statistics

In 2006 the birth rate was 9·0 per 1,000 population; death rate, 6·0 per 1,000. Population growth rate, 2006, 0·5%. Life expectancy, 2006: males, 74·1 years; females, 80·2 years. Infant mortality, 2006, 5·8 per 1,000 live births.

Climate

The climate is subtropical in the north and tropical in the south. The typhoon season extends from July to Sept. The average monthly temperatures of Jan. and July in Taipei are 59·5°F (15·3°C) and 83·3°F (28·5°C) respectively, and average annual rainfall is 84·99" (2,158·8 mm). Kaohsiung's average monthly temperatures of Jan. and July are 65·66°F (18·9°C) and 83·3°F (28·5°C) respectively, and average annual rainfall is 69·65" (1,769·2 mm).

Constitution and Government

The ROC Constitution is based on the Principles of Nationalism, Democracy and Social Wellbeing formulated by Dr Sun Yat-sen, the founding father of the Republic of China. The ROC government is divided into three main levels: central, provincial/municipal and county/city, each of which has well-defined powers.

The central government consists of the *Office of the President*, the *National Assembly*, which is specially elected only for constitutional amendment, and five governing branches called '*yuan*', namely the Executive Yuan, the Legislative Yuan, the Judicial Yuan, the Examination Yuan and the Control Yuan. Beginning with the elections to the seventh Legislative Yuan held on 12 Jan. 2008 the Legislative Yuan has 113 members (formerly 225). Of the

113 members 73 are elected under the first-past-the-post system in single-member constituencies, 34 are filled by proportional representation in accordance with a nationwide party vote and six are reserved for aboriginal candidates.

Since 1996 the president has been directly elected. Since 1997 a resolution on the impeachment of the president or vice president is no longer to be instituted by the Control Yuan but rather by the Legislative Yuan. The Legislative Yuan has the power to pass a no-confidence vote against the premier of the Executive Yuan, while the president of the Republic has the power to dissolve the Legislative Yuan. The premier of the Executive Yuan is directly appointed by the president of the Republic.

In Dec. 2003 a law came into effect allowing for referendums to be held.

National Anthem

'San Min Chu I' ('The Three Principles of the People'); words by Dr Sun Yat-sen, tune by Cheng Mao-yun.

Recent Elections

Presidential elections took place on 16 Jan. 2016. Tsai Ing-wen (Democratic Progressive Party) won 56·1% of the vote, Eric Chu Li-luan (Nationalist Party/Kuomintang) 31·0% and James Soong Chu-yu (People First Party) 12·8%.

Elections to the Legislative Yuan were also held on 16 Jan. 2016. The Democratic Progressive Party won 68 seats (50 constituency and 18 proportional); the Nationalist Party, 35 (24 constituency and 11 proportional); the New Power Party, 5; the People First Party, 3; the Non-Partisan Solidarity Union, 1; ind., 1.

Current Government

President: Tsai Ing-wen; b. 1956 (Nationalist Party/Kuomintang; sworn in 20 May 2016).

Vice President: Chen Chien-jen.

Prime Minister and President of the Executive Yuan: Su Tseng-chang; b. 1947 (Democratic Progressive Party; sworn in 14 Jan. 2019). *Vice Premier:* Chen Chi-mai. There are 12 ministries under the Executive Yuan: Culture; Economic Affairs; Education; Finance; Foreign Affairs; Health and Welfare; Interior; Justice; Labour; National Defence; Science and Technology; Transportation and Communications.

President, Control Yuan: Chang Po-ya. *President, Examination Yuan:* Wu Jin-lin. *President, Judicial Yuan:* Hsu Tzong-li. *President, Legislative Yuan:* Su Jia-chyuan. *Secretary General, Executive Yuan:* Li Meng-yen. *Minister of Culture:* Cheng Li-chiun. *Economic Affairs:* Shen Jong-chin. *Education:* Pan Wen-chung. *Finance:* Su Jain-rong. *Foreign Affairs:* Joseph Wu. *Health and Welfare:* Chen Shih-chung. *Interior:* Hsu Kuo-yung. *Justice:* Tsai Ching-hsiang. *Labour:* Hsu Ming-chun. *National Defence:* Yen De-fa. *Science and Technology:* Chen Liang-gee. *Transportation and Communications:* Lin Chia-lung. *Ministers without Portfolio:* Lin Wan-i; Chang Jing-sen; Wu Tsung-tsong; Chen Mei-ling (also *Minister of the National Development Council*); Deng Chen-chung; Tang Feng; Lo Ping-cheng; Wu Tse-cheng (also *Minister of the Public Construction Commission*); Kung Ming-hsin. *Spokesperson, Executive Yuan:* Kolas Yotaka.

A number of commissions and subordinate organizations have been formed with the resolution of the Executive Yuan Council and the Legislature to meet new demands and handle new affairs. Examples include the Mongolian and Tibetan Affairs Commission; the Mainland Affairs Council; the Fair Trade Commission; the Public Construction Commission; and the Financial Supervisory Commission. Some of these are headed by ministers without portfolio (*see* above). Other commissions, councils and agencies are headed by:

Council of Agriculture: Chen Chi-chung. *Atomic Energy Council:* Hsieh Shou-shing. *Directorate General of Budget, Accounting and Statistics:* Chu Tzer-ming. *Central Election Commission (acting):* Chen Chao-chien. *Environmental Protection Administration:* Chang Tzi-chin. *Fair Trade Commission:* Huang Mei-ying. *Financial Supervisory Commission:* Koo Li-hsiung. *Hakka Affairs Council:* Lee Yung-te. *Council of Indigenous Peoples:* Icyang Parod. *Mainland Affairs Council:* Chen Ming-tong. *National Communications Commission:* Chan Ting-i. *Ocean Affairs Council:* Lee Chung-wei. *Overseas Community Affairs Council:* Wu Hsin-hsing. *Directorate General of Personnel Administration:* Shih Ning-jye. *Transitional Justice Commission (acting):* Yang Tsui. *Veterans' Affairs Council:* Chiu Kuo-cheng. *Government Website:* http://www.ey.gov.tw

Defence

Conscription was reduced from 14 months to 12 months in 2009. The government has announced its intention to move towards a volunteer professional force—a process that was originally scheduled to start in 2011 and end in 2014 but has been delayed owing to low recruitment levels. Defence expenditure in 2013 totalled US$10,316m. (US$443 per capita), representing 2·1% of GDP.

Army

The Republic of China Army conducts ground combat missions as well as air support and airborne special operations. It was estimated to number about 200,000 personnel in 2011, with reserves numbering 1·5m. Its principal role is to defend against a possible amphibious assault from the Chinese mainland by the People's Liberation Army. In addition there are paramilitary forces totalling 17,000 personnel.

Navy

Navy personnel in 2011 totalled 45,000, with 67,000 reservists. The forces consist of four submarines, four cruisers and 22 frigates. There are also 61 missile craft for patrol and coastal defence, 12 mine-laying vehicles and 290 amphibious landing craft.

Air Force

In 2011 the air force numbered 55,000 personnel with 90,000 reservists. There were 477 combat-capable aircraft in the same year including F-5Es, F-16s and Mirage 2000-5s.

International Relations

By a treaty of 2 Dec. 1954 the USA pledged to defend Taiwan, but this treaty lapsed one year after the USA established diplomatic relations with the People's Republic of China on 1 Jan. 1979. In April 1979 the Taiwan Relations Act was passed by the US Congress to maintain commercial, cultural and other relations between USA and Taiwan through the American Institute in Taiwan and its Taiwan counterpart, the Co-ordination Council for North American Affairs in the USA, which were accorded quasi-diplomatic status in 1980. The People's Republic took over the China seat in the UN from Taiwan on 25 Oct. 1971. In May 1991 Taiwan ended its formal state of war with the People's Republic. Taiwan became a member of the World Trade Organization on 1 Jan. 2002.

In Sept. 2018 Taiwan had formal diplomatic ties with 17 countries. In Aug. 2007, 15 of the diplomatic allies sponsored an unsuccessful proposal for Taiwan to join the UN.

Economy

Overview

Taiwan has made a successful transition from an agricultural economy to one based on high-tech electronics. Economic growth averaged 8% per year over three decades from the 1970s, driven primarily by high value-added manufacturing and exports, especially in electronics and computers.

Government-owned enterprises, including banks, have been privatized. Though largely escaping the impact of the 1997 Asian financial crisis, the economy went into recession in 2001 with the first year of negative growth ever recorded and unemployment reaching record highs. Strong export performance stimulated a recovery, with annual GDP growth above 4% from 2002–08. Inflation has been consistently low and unemployment, which fell below 3% in 1999, has averaged between 4 and 6% since the turn of the century.

Owing to its heavy dependence on exports, Taiwan suffered a severe downturn as a result of the global financial crisis in 2008. Major export industries such as semiconductors and memory chips declined, unemployment reached its highest levels since 2003 and, in 2009, the economy again went into recession. A US$5·6bn. stimulus package boosted recovery and in 2010 the economy recorded its highest growth rate for nearly three decades, at 10·7%. However, growth subsequently cooled owing to lower demand from developed nations, averaging 1·9% per year between 2013 and 2016.

Tourism has grown in importance, with over 10·5m. visitors in 2016 constituting Taiwan's highest annual number to date. An ageing population and high savings rates threaten to constrain domestic demand in the future.

Currency

The unit of currency is the *New Taiwan dollar* (TWD) of 100 *cents*. Gold reserves were 13·62m. oz in Dec. 2010. There was inflation of 1·0% in 2016 and 1·1% in 2017. Foreign exchange reserves were US$382·0bn. in Dec. 2010.

Budget

In 2006 general government revenues totalled NT$2,172,436m. and expenditures NT$2,261,958m. Tax revenue accounted for 71·7% of revenues in 2006; education, science and culture accounted for 21·6% of expenditures, economic development 17·0% and general administration 15·3%.

VAT is 5%.

Performance

Taiwan sustained rapid economic growth at an annual rate of 9·2% from 1960 up to 1990. The rate slipped to 6·4% in the 1990s and 5·9% in 2000; Taiwan suffered from the Asian financial crisis, though less than its neighbours. In 2001 global economic sluggishness and the events of 11 Sept. in the USA severely affected Taiwan's economy, which contracted by 2·2%. Subsequent economic recovery led to growth of 5·4% in 2006 and 6·0% in 2007. There was negative growth of 1·6% in 2009 but again the economy bounced back, and grew by 1·4% in 2016 and 2·9% in 2017.

Banking and Finance

The Central Bank of The Republic of China (Taiwan), reactivated in 1961, regulates the money supply, manages foreign exchange and issues currency. The *Governor* is Yang Chin-long. The Bank of Taiwan is the largest commercial bank and the fiscal agent of the government. There are seven domestic banks, 38 commercial banks and 36 foreign banks.

There are two stock exchanges in Taipei.

Energy and Natural Resources

Environment

Taiwan's carbon dioxide emissions from the consumption of energy in 2011 were the equivalent of 13·4 tonnes per capita.

Electricity

Output of electricity in 2011 was 238·6m. MWh; total installed capacity was 41,401 MW. There were six units in three nuclear power stations in 2010.

Oil and Gas

Crude oil production in 2010 was 91,000 bbls; natural gas, 290m. cu. metres. Taiwan imports most of the oil and natural gas that it consumes.

Agriculture

In 2010 the cultivated area was 813,126 ha., of which 410,832 ha. were paddy fields. Rice production totalled 1,451,011 tonnes. Livestock production was valued at NT$144,614m., accounting for 34% of Taiwan's total agricultural production value.

Forestry

Forest area, 2010: 2,102,000 ha. Forest reserves: trees, 357,492,000 cu. metres; bamboo, 1,109m. poles. Timber production, 19,468 cu. metres.

Fisheries

The catch in 2015 was 987,873 tonnes, almost exclusively from sea fishing.

Industry

The largest companies in Taiwan by market capitalization in March 2015 were: Taiwan Semiconductor Manufacturing (US$120·6bn.); Hon Hai Precision Industry, an electronics manufacturer (US$43·0bn.); and Chunghwa Telecom (US$24·7bn.).

Output (in tonnes) in 2010: crude steel; 20·5m.; cement, 16·3m.; cotton fabrics, 270·5m. sq. metres; integrated circuit packages, 50·5trn. units; Global Positioning System (GPS) sets, 20·9bn. units.

Labour

In 2010 the average total labour force was 11·07m., of whom 10·49m. were employed. Of the employed population, 27·3% worked in manufacturing; 16·6% in wholesale and retail trade; 7·6% in construction; 6·9% in accommodation and food services; 5·9% in education; 5·2% in agriculture, forestry and fisheries. The unemployment rate was 5·2%.

Communications

Roads

In 2006 there were 39,286 km of roads. In 2007, 5·7m. passenger cars, 117,100 buses and coaches, 1·0m. lorries and vans, and 13·9m. motorcycles and mopeds were in use. 1,007m. passengers and 594m. tonnes of freight were transported in 2006. There were 3,140 fatalities in road accidents in 2006.

Rail

In 2010 freight traffic amounted to 14·5m. tonnes and passenger traffic to 864m. Total route length was 1,741 km. There are metro systems in Taipei (opened in 1996), Kaohsiung (opened in 2008) and Taoyuan (opened in 2017).

Civil Aviation

There are currently two international airports: Taiwan Taoyuan International Airport at Taoyuan near Taipei, and Kaohsiung International in the south. In addition there are 14 domestic airports: Taipei, Hualien, Taitung, Taichung, Tainan, Chiayi, Pingtung, Makung, Chimei, Orchid Island, Green Island, Wangan, Kinmen and Matsu (Peikan). In 2010 Taiwan Taoyuan International Airport handled 25,114,418 passengers, up from 18,681,462 in 2000.

The top airlines serving Taiwan (by capacity) as of Sept. 2011 were China Airlines (CAL), EVA Air, Cathay Pacific Airways, UNI Airways, TransAsia Airways (TNA) and Mandarin Airlines (MDA; CAL's subsidiary). In 2010, 37·5m. passengers and 1·2m. tonnes of freight were flown.

Regular direct flights between Taiwan and mainland China resumed in July 2008 for the first time since 1949.

Shipping

Maritime transportation is vital to the trade-oriented economy of Taiwan. In Jan. 2014 there were 140 ships of 300 GT or over registered, totalling 2·63m. GT. Of the 140 vessels registered, 40 were general cargo ships, 38 bulk carriers, 27 container ships, 26 oil tankers and nine passenger ships. There are six international ports: Kaohsiung, Keelung, Taichung, Hualien, Anping and Suao. The first three are container centres, Kaohsiung handling 9·98m. 20-ft equivalent units in 2013, making it the world's 13th busiest container port in terms of number of containers handled. Suao port is an auxiliary port to Keelung. In Jan. 2001 the first legal direct shipping links between Taiwanese islands and the Chinese mainland in more than 50 years were inaugurated.

Telecommunications

In 2011 there were 16,907,300 landline telephone subscribers (726·8 per 1,000 inhabitants). Taiwan's biggest telecommunications firm, the state-owned Chunghwa Telecom, lost its fixed-line monopoly in Aug. 2001. In 2011 there were 28,861,800 mobile phone subscriptions, equivalent to 1,240·7 per 1,000 persons. In 2013 there were 57·1 mobile broadband subscriptions per 100 inhabitants and 24·2 fixed broadband subscriptions per 100 inhabitants. In March 2012 there were 11·9m. Facebook users.

Social Institutions

Justice

The Judicial Yuan is the supreme judicial organ of state. Comprising 15 grand justices, since 2003 these have been nominated and, with the consent of the Legislative Yuan, appointed by the President of the Republic. The grand justices hold meetings to interpret the Constitution and unify the interpretation of laws and orders. There are three levels of judiciary: district courts and their branches deal with civil and criminal cases in the first instance; high courts and their branches deal with appeals against judgments of district courts; the Supreme Court reviews judgments by the lower courts. There is also the Supreme Administrative Court, high administrative courts and a Commission on the Disciplinary Sanctions of Public Functionaries. Criminal cases relating to rebellion, treason and offences against friendly relations with foreign states are handled by high courts as the courts of first instance.

The death penalty is still in force. There were no executions in 2017 but there was one in 2018. The population in penal institutions in April 2013 was 65,288 (280 per 100,000 of national population).

Education

Since 1968 there has been compulsory education for six to 15-year-olds with free tuition. The illiteracy rate dropped from 7·1% in 1989 to 2·5% by 2006. There were 2,654 primary schools, 1,061 secondary schools and 156 vocational schools in 2008; and 102 universities, 45 colleges and 15 junior colleges. In 2005–06 there were 1,831,913 pupils with 101,682 teaching staff at elementary schools; 951,236 pupils and 48,816 teaching staff at junior high schools; 420,608 pupils and 34,112 teaching staff at senior high schools; and 331,604 students and 15,590 teaching staff at senior vocational schools. There were 1,259,490 students in universities and colleges in 2005–06 with 48,047 academic staff.

Health

In 2011 there were 40,002 physicians (one for every 510 persons), 5,570 doctors of Chinese medicine, 133,336 nurses, 12,032 dentists and assistants, and 31,300 pharmacists and assistants.

In 2010 there were 20,691 medical facilities serving 1,119 persons per facility; there were 158,922 beds and 68·6 beds per 10,000 persons.

In 2010 cancers, heart diseases, cerebrovascular diseases, diabetes and accidents were the first five leading causes of death.

Welfare

A universal health insurance scheme came into force in 1995 as an extension to 13 social insurance plans that cover only 59% of Taiwan's population. Premium shares among the government, employer and insured are varied according to the insured statuses. By the end of 2010, 23·07m. people or 99% of the population were covered by the National Health Insurance programme.

Religion

According to estimates by the Pew Research Center's Forum on Religion & Public Life, 44·2% of the population in 2010 were folk religionists, 21·3% were Buddhists and 5·5% Christians. The remainder of the population was either religiously unaffiliated or followed other religions, including Taoism.

Culture

Press

There were 23 daily newspapers in 2008 with a circulation of 4·2m. and 21 non-dailies with a circulation of 3·8m. The biggest circulation dailies are *The Liberty Times* and *Apple Daily*.

Tourism

In 2011 there were 6,087,000 international visitors. Receipts totalled US$11,065m.

Festivals

The pop festival, Spring Scream, is held in April in Kenting.

Further Reading

China

State Statistical Bureau. *China Statistical Yearbook*
China Directory [in Pinyin and Chinese]. Annual
Adshead, S. A. M., *China in World History.* 1999
Baum, R., *Burying Mao: Chinese Politics in the Age of Deng Xiaoping.* 1994
Becker, Jasper, *The Chinese.* 2000
Breslin, Shaun, *China and the Global Political Economy.* 2007
Brown, Kerry, *Contemporary China.* 3rd ed. 2019.—*CEO, China: The Rise of Xi Jinping.* 2016
The Cambridge Encyclopaedia of China. 2nd ed. 1991
The Cambridge History of China. 14 vols. 1978 ff.
Chang, David Wen-Wei and Chuang, Richard Y., *The Politics of Hong Kong's Reversion to China.* 1999
Chang, Jung and Halliday, Jon, *Mao: The Unknown Story.* 2005
Christiansen, Thomas, Kirchner, Emil and Wissenbach, Uwe, *The European Union and China.* 2018
Cook, Sarah, Yao, Shujie and Zhuang, Juzhong, (eds) *The Chinese Economy Under Transition.* 1999
De Crespigny, R., *China This Century.* 2nd ed. 1993
Dikötter, Frank, *Mao's Great Famine: The History of China's Most Devastating Catastrophe, 1958–1962.* 2010.—*The Tragedy of Liberation: A History of the Chinese Revolution 1945–1957.* 2013.—*The Cultural Revolution: A People's History, 1962–1976.* 2016
Dillon, Michael, *China: A Modern History.* 2006
Dittmer, Lowell, *China's Deep Reform: Domestic Politics in Transition.* 2006
Dixin, Xu and Chengming, Wu, (eds) *Chinese Capitalism, 1522–1840.* 1999
Evans, R., *Deng Xiaoping and the Making of Modern China.* 1993
Fairbank, J. K., *The Great Chinese Revolution 1800–1985.* 1987.—*China: a New History.* 1992
Farnell, John and Irwin Crookes, Paul, *The Politics of EU-China Economic Relations.* 2016
French, Howard W., *China's Second Continent: How a Million Migrants are Building a New Empire in Africa.* 2014

Glassman, R. M., *China in Transition: Communism, Capitalism and Democracy.* 1991

Goldman, M., *Sowing the Seeds of Democracy in China: Political Reform in the Deng Xiaoping Era.* 1994

Guo, Jian, *Historical Dictionary of the Chinese Cultural Revolution.* 2006

Guo, Rongxing, *How the Chinese Economy Works.* 4th ed. revised. 2016

Hsü, Immanuel C. Y., *The Rise of Modern China.* 6th ed. 2000

Huang, R., *China: a Macro History.* 2nd ed. 1997

Jisheng, Yang, *Tombstone: The Untold Story of Mao's Great Famine.* 2012

Kissinger, Henry, *On China.* 2011

Kroeber, Arthur R., *China's Economy: What Everyone Needs to Know.* 2016

Kruger, Rayne, *All Under Heaven: A Complete History of China.* 2004

Lam, Willy Wo-Lap, *Chinese Politics in the Hu Jintao Era: New Leaders, New Challenges.* 2006

Lim, Louisa, *The People's Republic of Amnesia: Tiananmen Revisited.* 2014

Liu, Guoli, *China Rising: Chinese Foreign Policy in a Changing World.* 2016

Lynch, Michael, *Modern China.* 2006

Ma, Jun, *Chinese Economy in the 1990s.* 1999

MacFarquhar, Roderick, (ed.) *The Politics of China: Sixty Years of the People's Republic of China.* 3rd ed. 2011.—*The Origins of the Cultural Revolution.* 3 vols. 1998

McGregor, Richard, *The Party: the Secret World of China's Communist Rulers.* 2010.—*Asia's Reckoning: China, Japan and the Fate of US Power in the Pacific Century.* 2017

Mitter, Rana, *China's War with Japan, 1937–1945: The Struggle for Survival.* 2013

Mok, Ka-Ho, *Social and Political Development in Post-Reform China.* 1999

Osnos, Evan, *Age of Ambition: Chasing Fortune, Truth and Faith in the New China.* 2014

Pantsov, Alexander and Levine, Steven, *Deng Xiaoping: A Revolutionary Life.* 2015

Pursiainen, Christer, (ed.) *At the Crossroads of Post-Communist Modernisation: Russia and China in Comparative Perspective.* 2012

Roberts, J. A. G., *A History of China.* 3rd ed. 2011

Saich, Tony, *Governance and Politics of China.* 4th ed. 2015

Schell, Orville and Delury, John, *Wealth and Power: China's Long March to the Twenty-first Century.* 2013

Schram, S. (ed.) *Mao's Road to Power: Revolutionary Writings 1912–1949.* 7 vols. 2005

Shambaugh, David, *China Goes Global: The Partial Power.* 2013

Shenkar, Oded, *The Chinese Century: The Rising Chinese Economy and Its Impact on the Global Economy, the Balance of Power, and Your Job.* 2004

Short, Philip, *Mao: A Life.* 2000

Small, Andrew, *The China-Pakistan Axis: Asia's New Geopolitics.* 2015

Spence, Jonathan, D., *The Chan's Great Continent: China in Western Minds.* 1998.—*Mao Zedong.* 2000

Suyin, H., *Eldest Son, Zhou Enlai and The Making of Modern China.* 1995

Tsang, Steve and Men, Honghua (eds), *China in the Xi Jinping Era.* 2016

Tseng, Wanda and Cowen, David, *India's and China's Recent Experience with Reform and Growth.* 2007

Tubilewicz, Czeslaw, *Critical Issues in Contemporary China.* 2006

Weatherley, Robert, *Making China Strong.* 2014

Zha, Jianying, *Tide Players: The Movers and Shakers of a Rising China.* 2011

Other more specialized titles are listed under TERRITORY AND POPULATION; TIBET; AGRICULTURE; INTERNATIONAL TRADE; RELIGION.

National Statistical Office: National Bureau of Statistics, 57 Yuetan Nanjie, Sanlihe, Xicheng District, Beijing 100826. *Commissioner:* Ning Jizhe. *Website:* http://www.stats.gov.cn

Hong Kong

Statistical Information: The Census and Statistics Department is responsible for the preparation and collation of government statistics. These statistics are published mainly in the *Hong Kong Monthly Digest of Statistics.* The Department also publishes monthly trade statistics, economic indicators and an annual review of overseas trade, etc. *Website:* http://www.censtatd.gov.hk

Hong Kong [various years] Hong Kong Government Press

Brown, J. M. (ed.) *Hong Kong's Transitions, 1842–1997.* 1997

Buckley, R., *Hong Kong: the Road to 1997.* 1997

Chang, David Wen-Wei and Chuang, Richard Y., *The Politics of Hong Kong's Reversion to China.* 1999

Cottrell, R., *The End of Hong Kong: the Secret Diplomacy of Imperial Retreat.* 1993

Courtauld, C. and Holdsworth, M., *The Hong Kong Story.* 1997

Flowerdew, J., *The Final Years of British Hong Kong: the Discourse of Colonial Withdrawal.* 1997

Keay, J., *Last Post: the End of Empire in the Far East.* 1997

Lo, S.-H., *The Politics of Democratization in Hong Kong.* 1997

Lok, Sang Ho and Ash, Robert, *China, Hong Kong and the World Economy.* 2006

Roberts, E. V., *et al., Historical Dictionary of Hong Kong and Macau.* 1993

Shipp, S., *Hong Kong, China: a Political History of the British Crown Colony's Transfer to Chinese Rule.* 1995

Tok, Sow Keat, *Managing China's Sovereignty in Hong Kong and Taiwan.* 2013

Welsh, Frank, *A History of Hong Kong.* 2nd ed. revised. 2010

Macao

Direcção dos Serviços de Estatística e Censos. *Anuário Estatístico/Yearbook of Statistics Macau in Figures.* Annual

Porter, J., *Macau, the Imaginary City: Culture and Society, 1557 to the Present.* 1996

Roberts, E. V., *Historical Dictionary of Hong Kong and Macau.* 1993

Statistics and Census Service Website: http://www.dsec.gov.mo

Taiwan

Statistical Yearbook of the Republic of China. Annual. *The Republic of China Yearbook.* Annual. *Taiwan Statistical Data Book.* Annual. *Annual Review of Government Administration, Republic of China.* Annual.

Arrigo, L. G., *et al., The Other Taiwan: 1945 to the Present Day.* 1994

Cooper, J. F., *Historical Dictionary of Taiwan.* 1993

Hughes, C., *Taiwan and Chinese Nationalism: National Identity and Status in International Society.* 1997

Lary, Diana, *China's Republic.* 2006

Lee, Wei-chin, *Taiwan's Political Re-Alignment and Diplomatic Challenges.* 2018

Tok, Sow Keat, *Managing China's Sovereignty in Hong Kong and Taiwan.* 2013

Tsang, S. (ed.) *In the Shadow of China: Political Developments in Taiwan since 1949.* 1994

National library: National Central Library, Taipei (established 1986).

National Statistics Website: http://www.stat.gov.tw

Colombia

República de Colombia (Republic of Colombia)

Capital: Bogotá
Population projection, 2020: 50·22m.
GNI per capita, 2017: (PPP$) 12,938
HDI/world rank, 2017: 0·747/90=
Internet domain extension: .co

Key Historical Events

Cundinamarca in central Colombia shows evidence of human habitation from 10,500 BC. The central highlands became the stronghold of the Chibcha people from 550 BC, with settlements based on the cultivation of corn, potatoes and beans. Much of the north, including the Caribbean coast, was associated with the Tairona civilization whose stone dwellings and ceremonial sites date from AD 1000.

Columbus explored South America's Caribbean coast in 1498, heralding the European influx. The port of Cartagena, founded in 1533 by Pedro de Heredia, became a leading administrative and commercial centre, its wealth derived from gold mined in the Cauca valley, Antioquia and the Choco. The Spanish explorer, Gonzalo Jiménez de Quesada, founded Bogotá in 1538 and within a decade the Chibcha were conquered and the New Kingdom of Granada declared. In 1564 the Spanish Crown appointed a president, loosely attached to the viceroyalty of Peru and centred on Bogotá, with jurisdiction over Colombia, Ecuador, Panama and Venezuela. Cartagena and the districts near the gold mines prospered, while other parts of the colony remained undeveloped. Disputes with Lima led to the creation of the Viceroyalty of New Granada in 1719.

An independence movement followed the Napoleonic invasion of Spain in 1808. Antonio Nariño was a leading revolutionary figure, along with Francisco de Paula Santander and Simón Bolívar, who became an officer in the Patriot forces in 1811. Forced to flee to Jamaica when Gen. Pablo Morilla launched the Spanish reconquest in 1815, Bolívar settled in the Llanos (Colombia's eastern plains) and assembled a new army. Victory at Boyaca in 1819 secured Greater Colombia as an independent state. Following the Spanish surrender of Cartagena in 1821, Bolívar became president, ruling from Bogotá what is now Venezuela, Panama and (from 1822) Ecuador.

Separatist movements soon emerged and by 1826 Venezuela was autonomous. Ecuador withdrew three years later, with Colombia and Panama emerging as the Republic of New Granada, renamed the United States of Colombia following the signing of the Treaty of Rionegro in 1863. Politics was dominated by the reformist Liberal Party (PL) and the Conservatives, who sought to preserve Spanish and Roman Catholic heritage. Free trade led to the growth of exports, notably tobacco, quinine and coffee. Concerns over government weakness brought about a new Nationalist movement under Rafael Núñez. President from 1879, he introduced a constitution in 1886 that reversed the federalist trend and brought strong centralist control to the new Republic of Colombia. A Liberal revolt in 1899 sparked off the War of a Thousand Days, which had claimed over 100,000 lives by the time peace was achieved in 1902. The department of Panama became independent in 1903, backed by the USA, after plans for a canal across the isthmus were rejected by Colombia.

The rule of Gen. Rafael Reyes from 1904 was characterized by centralized power and industrial growth. Collapsing coffee prices caused economic hardship in the early 1930s but conditions improved under the Liberal governments of Enrique Olaya Herrera (1930–34) and Alfonso López Pumarejo (1934–38). After re-election in 1942, López Pumarejo faced a split in the PL, which culminated in an aborted coup and his resignation in 1945. The Conservatives took power the following year under Mariano Ospina Pérez, setting the stage for a civil war (*La Violencia*) that claimed 300,000 lives by 1957.

Conservatives and Liberals agreed to unite under the National Front in 1958, while other parties were banned. Several leftist guerrilla organizations emerged in the 1960s, including the Colombian Revolutionary Armed Forces (FARC), which aimed to install a Marxist regime. Generating wealth from the illegal drugs trade, it was especially influential in the rural south and east. Additionally, the National Liberation Army (ELN) was behind waves of kidnapping and violence in the mid-1990s.

In 1998 peace talks were started when a Conservative, Andrés Pastrana Arango, was elected president. FARC was granted a haven in the southeast. In 2000 Pastrana's 'Plan Colombia' initiative was launched, backed with US$1bn. from Washington to fight drug-trafficking. In 2001 FARC was accused of preparing attacks and conducting drug deals, and in Feb. 2002, following the kidnapping of a senator, Pastrana broke off peace talks. Three months later Álvaro Uribe Vélez, an independent, became president but within days declared a state of emergency after 20 died in bomb blasts in Bogotá. Relations with several rebel groups subsequently thawed, with talks with the rightist United Self-Defence Forces of Colombia (AUC) beginning in 2004 and with the ELN in 2005.

Parties loyal to Uribe secured victory in elections in 2006 and the president won a new term. In July 2007 hundreds of thousands of Colombians staged protests demanding the release of 3,000 people held hostage. The government made inroads into FARC territory in 2008 and secured the release of several high-profile hostages, including former presidential candidate Ingrid Betancourt. In July 2009 relations with Venezuela deteriorated over Colombia's plans to allow US military access to its bases and claims by Colombia that Caracas supplied arms to FARC. The two nations cut off diplomatic ties from July–Aug. 2010. In June 2010 Juan Manuel Santos, a former defence minister, became president. In Dec. that year a state of emergency was declared following floods and landslides that killed almost 300 people and affected over 2m. more.

In Oct. 2011 the US Congress signed off a free trade agreement with Colombia. In Nov. 2012 the Santos administration began peace talks with FARC. Santos secured a further term of office in May 2014. By then, FARC and the government had reached agreement in principle on three main areas of contention: land reform, participation of guerrilla fighters in political life and the illegal drugs trade. Despite a brief breakdown in the talks in Nov. 2014 after FARC fighters captured an army general, a peace deal was eventually signed in Sept. 2016. It was initially rejected in a referendum the following month, but the two sides then negotiated revised terms in Nov. 2016 that won congressional approval. The civil conflict had lasted over 50 years and resulted in 220,000 deaths.

Territory and Population

Colombia is bounded in the north by the Caribbean Sea, northwest by Panama, west by the Pacific Ocean, southwest by Ecuador and Peru, northeast by Venezuela and southeast by Brazil. The estimated area is 1,141,748 sq. km (440,829 sq. miles). Population at the last census in 2005 was 42,888,592; density, 37·6 per sq. km. June 2013 estimate, 47,121,089. More than 7·1m. Colombians protected and assisted by the Office of the United Nations High Commissioner for Refugees are displaced within the country as a consequence of civil conflict involving left-wing guerrillas since the 1960s and right-wing paramilitaries and drug gangs since the 1980s.

The UN gives a projected population for 2020 of 50·22m.

In 2011, 75·4% lived in urban areas. Population of Bogotá, the capital (census 2005): 6,824,510.

The following table gives census populations for departments and their capitals for 2005:

Departments	Area (sq. km)	Population	Capital	Population
Amazonas	109,665	67,726	Leticia	23,811
Antioquia	63,612	5,682,276	Medellín	2,175,681
Arauca	23,818	232,118	Arauca	62,634
Atlántico	3,388	2,166,156	Barranquilla	1,142,312
Bogotá[1]	1,587	6,840,116	—	—

(continued)

Departments	Area (sq. km)	Population	Capital	Population
Bolívar	25,978	1,878,993	Cartagena	842,228
Boyacá	23,189	1,255,311	Tunja	146,621
Caldas	7,888	968,740	Manizales	353,312
Caquetá	88,965	420,337	Florencia	121,898
Casanare	44,640	295,353	Yopal	90,218
Cauca	29,308	1,268,937	Popayán	226,978
Cesar	22,905	903,279	Valledupar	299,065
Chocó	46,530	454,030	Quibdó	101,134
Córdoba	25,020	1,467,929	Montería	286,575
Cundinamarca	22,623	2,280,037	Bogotá	—
Guainía	72,238	35,230	Puerto Inírida	10,793
Guaviare	42,327	95,551	San José del Guaviare	34,863
Huila	19,890	1,011,418	Neiva	295,961
La Guajira	20,848	681,575	Riohacha	136,183
Magdalena	23,188	1,149,917	Santa Marta	385,122
Meta	85,635	783,168	Villavicencio	356,464
Nariño	33,268	1,541,956	Pasto	312,377
Norte de Santander	21,658	1,243,975	Cúcuta	567,664
Putumayo	24,885	310,132	Mocoa	25,751
Quindío	1,845	534,552	Armenia	273,114
Risaralda	4,140	897,509	Pereira	371,239
San Andrés y Providencia	44	70,554	San Andrés	48,421
Santander	30,537	1,957,789	Bucaramanga	509,216
Sucre	10,917	772,010	Sincelejo	219,639
Tolima	23,562	1,365,342	Ibagué	468,647
Valle del Cauca	22,140	4,161,425	Cali	2,083,171
Vaupés	65,268	39,279	Mitú	13,066
Vichada	100,242	55,872	Puerto Carreño	10,032

[1]Capital District.

Ethnic divisions at the 2005 census: non-ethnic population (whites and mestizos), 85·9%; Afro–Colombian, 10·6%; Amerindian, 3·4%.

The official language is Spanish.

Social Statistics

2008 estimates: births, 918,000; deaths, 248,000. Rates, 2008 estimates (per 1,000 population): births, 20·4; deaths, 5·5. In 2009–10, 84% of all births were outside of marriage. Annual population growth rate, 2000–08, 1·5%. Life expectancy at birth, 2013, was 70·4 years for men and 77·7 years for women. Infant mortality, 2010, 17 per 1,000 live births; fertility rate, 2008, 2·4 children per woman. Colombia legalized same-sex marriage in April 2016. Abortion is illegal.

Climate

The climate includes equatorial and tropical conditions, according to situation and altitude. In tropical areas, the wettest months are March to May and Oct. to Nov. Bogotá, Jan. 58°F (14·4°C), July 57°F (13·9°C). Annual rainfall 42" (1,052 mm). Barranquilla, Jan. 80°F (26·7°C), July 82°F (27·8°C). Annual rainfall 32" (799 mm). Cali, Jan. 75°F (23·9°C), July 75°F (23·9°C). Annual rainfall 37" (915 mm). Medellín, Jan. 71°F (21·7°C), July 72°F (22·2°C). Annual rainfall 64" (1,606 mm).

Constitution and Government

Simultaneously with the presidential elections of May 1990, a referendum was held in which 7m. votes were cast for the establishment of a special assembly to draft a new constitution. Elections were held on 9 Dec. 1990 for this 74-member 'Constitutional Assembly' which operated from Feb. to July

1991. The electorate was 14·2m.; turnout was 3·7m. The Liberals gained 24 seats, M-19 (a former guerrilla organization), 19. The Assembly produced a new constitution which came into force on 5 July 1991. It stresses the state's obligation to protect human rights, and establishes constitutional rights to health care, social security and leisure. Indians are allotted two Senate seats. Congress may dismiss ministers, and representatives may be recalled by their electors.

The *President* is elected by direct vote. In Oct. 2005 the constitution was amended to allow a president to be re-elected for a second term. A vice-presidency was instituted in July 1991.

The legislative power rests with a *Congress* of two houses, the *Senate*, of 102 members (including two elected from a special list set aside for American Indian communities), and the *House of Representatives*, of 166 members, both elected for four years by proportional representation. Congress meets annually at Bogotá on 20 July.

In Oct. 2016 a peace agreement between the government and the rebel FARC movement, which offered hope of bringing an end to more than half a century of civil conflict, was rejected in a referendum by 50·2% to 49·8%. However, subsequent revisions to the deal won congressional approval the following month.

National Anthem

'O! Gloria inmarcesible' ('Oh unfading Glory!'); words by R. Núñez, tune by O. Síndici.

Government Chronology

Heads of State since 1945. (CD = Democratic Center; Partido de la U = Social National Unity Party; PLC = Colombian Liberal Party; PSC = Colombian Conservative Party/Colombian Social Conservative Party; n/p = non-partisan)

Presidents		
1945–46	PLC	Alberto Lleras Camargo
1946–50	PSC	Luis Mariano Ospina Pérez
1950–51	PSC	Laureano Eleuterio Gómez Castro
1951–53	PSC	Roberto Urdaneta Arbeláez
1953	PSC	Laureano Eleuterio Gómez Castro
1953–57	military	Gustavo Rojas Pinilla

Military Junta		
1957–58		Gabriel Paris Gordillo (chair); Rubén Piedrahíta Arango;
		Deogracias Fonseca Espinosa; Luis Ernesto Ordóñez Castillo;
		Rafael Navas Pardo

Presidents		
1958–62	PLC	Alberto Lleras Camargo
1962–66	PSC	Guillermo León Valencia Muñoz
1966–70	PLC	Carlos Lleras Restrepo
1970–74	PSC	Misael Eduardo Pastrana Borrero
1974–78	PLC	Alfonso López Michelsen
1978–82	PLC	Julio César Turbay Ayala
1982–86	PSC	Belisario Betancur Cuartas
1986–90	PLC	Virgilio Barco Vargas
1990–94	PLC	César Augusto Gaviria Trujillo
1994–98	PLC	Ernesto Samper Pizano
1998–2002	PSC	Andrés Pastrana Arango
2002–10	n/p	Uribe Vélez Álvaro
2010–18	Partido de la U	Juan Manuel Santos
2018–	CD	Iván Duque Márquez

Recent Elections

The first round of presidential elections were held on 27 May 2018, in which Iván Duque Márquez (Grand Alliance for Colombia) won with 39·1% of votes cast, against 25·1% for Gustavo Petro (List of Decency), 23·7% for

Sergio Fajardo (Colombia Coalition), 7·3% for Germán Vargas Lleras (Mejor Vargas Lleras) and 2·1% for Humberto de la Calle (Colombian Liberal Party–Indigenous Social Alliance Movement coalition). There were three other candidates. Turnout was 53·4%. In the run-off held on 17 June 2018, Duque was elected with 54·0% against Petro with 41·8%. Turnout for the second round was 53·0%.

Congressional elections were held on 11 March 2018. In elections to the House of Representatives the Colombian Liberal Party won 35 seats, the Democratic Center 32, Radical Change 30, the Social National Unity Party 25, the Colombian Conservative Party 21 and the Green Alliance 9. Smaller parties accounted for the remainder. In the elections to the Senate the Democratic Center won 19 seats, Radical Change 16, the Colombian Conservative Party 15, the Colombian Liberal Party and the Social National Unity Party 14 each, the Green Alliance 10, the Alternative Democratic Pole 5, the List of Decency Coalition 4 and the Independent Movement of Absolute Renovation 3.

Current Government

President: Iván Duque Márquez; b. 1976 (Democratic Center; sworn in 7 Aug. 2018).

Vice-President: Marta Lucía Ramírez.

In Feb. 2019 the government comprised:

Minister of Agriculture and Rural Development: Andrés Valencia Pinzón. *Culture:* Carmen Inés Vásquez. *Education:* María Victoria Angulo. *Environment and Sustainable Development:* Ricardo José Lozano. *Finance and Public Credit:* Alberto Carrasquilla Barrera. *Foreign Relations:* Carlos Holmes Trujillo. *Health and Social Welfare:* Juan Pablo Uribe. *Housing, Cities and Land:* Jonathan Malagón. *Information Technologies and Communications:* Sylvia Constaín. *Interior:* Nancy Patricia Gutiérrez. *Justice and Law:* Gloria María Borrero. *Labour:* Alicia Arango Olmos. *Mines and Energy:* María Fernanda Suárez. *National Defence:* Guillermo Botero Nieto. *Trade, Industry and Tourism:* José Manuel Restrepo. *Transport:* Ángela María Orozco.

Office of the President (Spanish only): http://www.presidencia.gov.co

Current Leaders

Iván Duque Márquez

Position
President

Introduction
Iván Duque Márquez was sworn in as president on 7 Aug. 2018. A former senator, he has worked as a political consultant and author, as well as serving as an adviser to the Inter-American Development Bank.

Early Life
Duque was born into a politically prominent family in Bogotá, Colombia, on 1 Aug. 1976. He read law at Sergio Arboleda University in Bogotá and later studied in Washington, D.C. in the USA, where he received a master's degree in international law from the American University and another in public policy from Georgetown University.

From 1999–2000 he served as a consultant to the Andean Development Corporation and as an adviser in the Colombian ministry of finance. He worked for the Inter-American Development Bank in Washington, D.C. from 2001–13, first as an adviser on Colombia, Peru and Ecuador and later as division chief of cultural, solidarity and creativity affairs.

Duque's political career was fostered by his mentor, former president Álvaro Uribe (from 2002–10). In 2011 Duque was appointed by the then president, Juan Manuel Santos, to assist in a United Nations (UN) investigation into Israeli military operations. He subsequently joined the Democratic Center (CD), the centre-right party founded by Uribe. In 2014 he was elected to the Senate but resigned in 2017 and was subsequently selected by Uribe as the CD's presidential candidate. He was elected in a run-off poll held in June 2018.

Career in Office
Duque has pledged to tackle violence and corruption. He is a critic of the 2016 peace accord that ended the decades-long civil war with the Colombian Revolutionary Armed Forces (FARC) and plans to introduce punitive amendments to the accord, ending amnesty for drug-traffickers and imposing harsher sentences and greater restrictions on former rebel commanders. He has also suspended the previous administration's peace talks with the National Liberation Army (ELN), pending the release of all hostages, and vowed to end the cultivation of coca, which reached an all-time high in 2018. In Sept. 2018 Duque called on the UN to establish a multinational fund to support Venezuelan refugees, approximately 1 million of whom have migrated to Colombia.

Defence

There is selective conscription for 12 to 24 months. In 2013 defence expenditure totalled US$7,016m. (US$153 per capita), representing 1·8% of GDP.

Army

Personnel (2011) 235,800; reserves number 54,700. The national police numbered (2011) 136,100.

Navy

The Navy has two diesel powered submarines, two midget submarines and four small frigates. Naval personnel in 2011 totalled 33,100. There are also 14,000 marines. An air arm operates light reconnaissance aircraft.

The Navy's main ocean base is at Cartagena.

Air Force

The Air Force has been independent of the Army and Navy since 1943, when its reorganization began with US assistance. It has 82 combat-capable aircraft. There are six combat air commands plus a command responsible for air operations in a specific geographical area. Personnel in 2011 numbered 13,758.

International Relations

It was announced in Aug. 2000 that Colombia would receive US$1·3bn. in anti drug-trafficking aid (mostly of a military nature) from the USA as part of 'Plan Colombia', a five-year long series of projects intended to serve as a foundation for stability and peace of which the focal point is the fight against drugs. By May 2005 the USA had given aid amounting to US$4·5bn.

In March 2008 Colombian forces killed a high-level member of the rebel FARC movement during an unsanctioned raid over the Ecuadorian border. A week-long diplomatic incident ensued, in which both Ecuador and Venezuela massed military personnel on their respective borders with Colombia.

Economy

In 2016 agriculture accounted for 7·1% of GDP, industry 32·6% and services 60·3%.

Overview

Colombia has among the largest economies in Latin America and is endowed with abundant natural resources. Prudent macroeconomic management, a commodity boom and improved internal security have yielded strong economic growth since the early 2000s. Nonetheless, the country has suffered from decades of violent conflicts, drug cartels and human rights violations.

Large oil and coal reserves, along with deposits of gold, silver, emeralds and platinum, have fuelled a resources-led boom that saw annual growth average 4·9% from 2010–13. However, the country has since been significantly affected by falling oil prices and deceleration in the extractive sector so that growth slowed to 4·4% in 2014 and 3·1% in 2015.

Fiscal discipline has been among the strongest in the region and enabled Colombia to maintain healthy growth rates throughout the global financial crisis that began in 2008. The IMF praised the authorities' tight policy framework, which has included inflation targeting, a flexible exchange rate and improved financial regulation. However, Colombia remains overly reliant on exports and is vulnerable to fluctuating commodity prices and financial volatility.

The oil price decline from mid-2014 has led to a significant deterioration of the fiscal and external accounts. The fiscal deficit doubled to 3·4% of GDP in 2015, prompting spending cuts, while recession in neighbouring countries (including Ecuador and Venezuela) along with lower growth in the USA have resulted in declining export revenues. The current account deficit widened to 6·5% of GDP in 2015—its highest level in over a decade.

Furthermore, despite the rapid economic development since the turn of the century, growth has not been inclusive, with 32·7% of the population classified as living below the poverty line in 2012. The country is the largest producer of cocaine in the world and it is estimated that trade in illegal drugs accounts for 3% of GDP, although production is declining.

Currency

The unit of currency is the *Colombian peso* (COP) of 100 *centavos*. Inflation rates (based on IMF statistics):

2008	2009	2010	2011	2012	2013	2014	2015	2016	2017
7·0%	4·2%	2·3%	3·4%	3·2%	2·0%	2·9%	5·0%	7·5%	4·3%

In Sept. 2009 gold reserves were 221,000 troy oz and foreign exchange reserves US$22,926m. Total money supply was 41,403bn. pesos in Aug. 2009.

Budget

In 2011 budgetary central government revenue totalled 106,031bn. dinars and expenditure 103,500bn. dinars. Principal sources of revenue in 2011 were: taxes on goods and services, 33,754bn. pesos; taxes on income, profits and capital gains, 23,325bn. pesos. Main items of expenditure by economic type in 2011: grants, 38,331bn. pesos; interest, 16,106bn. pesos.

The standard rate of VAT is 19%.

Performance

Real GDP growth rates (based on IMF statistics):

2008	2009	2010	2011	2012	2013	2014	2015	2016	2017
3·3%	1·2%	4·3%	7·4%	3·9%	4·6%	4·7%	3·0%	2·0%	1·8%

Total GDP in 2017 was US$309·2bn.

Banking and Finance

In 1923 the Bank of the Republic (*Governor*, Juan José Echavarría) was inaugurated as a semi-official central bank, with the exclusive privilege of issuing banknotes. Its note issues must be covered by a reserve in gold of foreign exchange of 25% of their value. Interest rates of 40% plus are imposed.

In 2016 there were 25 registered banks. The largest bank, Bancolombia, had assets of US$62·3bn. in 2015.

External debt totalled US$63,064m. in 2010 and represented 22·8% of GNI.

There are stock exchanges in Bogotá, Medellín and Cali.

Energy and Natural Resources

Environment

In 2011 Colombia's carbon dioxide emissions from the consumption of energy were the equivalent of 1·6 tonnes per capita.

Electricity

Installed capacity of electric power (2011) was 14·4m. kW. In 2011 production was 59·65bn. kWh and consumption per capita 1,234 kWh. Colombia exported 1,543m. kWh of electricity in 2011.

Oil and Gas

Oil production (2013) 52·9m. tonnes. Production has risen every year since 2005. Colombia's oil output has been growing at one of the fastest rates of any producer in recent years. Natural gas production in 2013 totalled 12·6bn. cu. metres. In 2013 there were proven oil reserves of 2·4bn. bbls and proven natural gas reserves of 200bn. cu. metres.

Minerals

Production (2005): gold, 35,785 kg; silver, 7,142 kg; platinum, 1,082 kg. Other important minerals include: copper, lead, mercury, manganese, nickel and emeralds (of which Colombia accounts for about 60% of world production).

Coal production (2007): 69·90m. tonnes; iron ore (2005): 498,623 tonnes; salt production (2005): 473,996 tonnes.

Agriculture

There were an estimated 1·68m. ha. of arable land in 2013 and 1·77m. ha. of permanent crops. In 2015, 16% of employed persons were engaged in agriculture.

Production, 2013 (in 1,000 tonnes): sugarcane, 34,876; palm fruit oil, 5,052; plantains, 3,307; cassava, 2,491; potatoes, 2,129; bananas, 2,099; rice, 1,997; maize, 1,779. Coca, the raw material for cocaine, was cultivated in Dec. 2017 on a record 171,000 ha., compared to just 48,000 ha. in Dec. 2012. Cut flowers are also important, with Colombia being the second largest exporter after the Netherlands. Along with coffee and bananas, cut flowers are the country's leading agricultural exports.

Livestock (2014): 24·21m. cattle; 5·90m. pigs; 913,000 goats; 822,000 horses; 726,000 sheep; 170m. chickens (estimate).

Livestock products, 2013: beef and veal, 848,000 tonnes; pork and pork products, 243,000 tonnes; poultry meat, 1·28m. tonnes (estimate); milk, 6·46m. tonnes (estimate); eggs, 668,000 tonnes (estimate).

Forestry

In 2015 the area under forests was 58·50m. ha., or 53% of the total land area. Timber production in 2011 was 12·14m. cu. metres.

Fisheries

The estimated total catch (2011) was 87,489 tonnes, of which 72% was from marine waters.

Industry

The largest companies by market capitalization in Colombia in March 2015 were Ecopetrol, a company involved in the development and production of crude oil and natural gas (US$45·7bn.); Bancolombia, the country's largest commercial bank (US$11·5bn.); and GrupoAval, a holding company engaged in a variety of financial activities (US$9·5bn.);

Production, 2007 unless otherwise indicated (in 1,000 tonnes): cement (2005), 9,959; distillate fuel oil, 4,395; residual fuel oil, 3,318; petrol, 3,164; raw sugar, 2,277; crude steel and semi-finished products, 1,245; jet fuel, 537; sawnwood, 382,000 cu. metres; passenger cars, 68,000 units.

Labour

The economically active workforce in 2014 was 23·65m., of which 21·50m. were employed. The main areas of activity in 2014 were: commerce, restaurants and hotels (employing 5·86m. persons); community, social and personal services (4·28m.); and agriculture, hunting, forestry and fishing (3·50m.). The unemployment rate was 8·9% in 2015 (down from 9·1% in 2014 and the lowest rate in 15 years).

Colombia had 0·13m. people living in slavery according to the Walk Free Foundation's 2013 *Global Slavery Index*.

International Trade

In Nov. 2006 Colombia and the USA signed a free trade agreement that eliminates tariffs on each other's goods. It was ratified in Oct. 2011 and came into effect in May 2012.

Imports and Exports

Goods imports were US$64,027·6m. in 2014 (US$59,381·2m. in 2013) and goods exports US$54,794·8m. (US$58,821·9m. in 2013).

Main imports in 2014 were machinery and transport equipment (37·0%), chemicals and manufactured goods; main exports in 2014 were mineral fuels and lubricants (65·6%), food, animals and beverages, and chemicals.

The leading import source in 2010 was the USA (25·9%), followed by China and Mexico; the leading export market in 2010 was the USA (43·1%), followed by China and Ecuador.

Communications

Roads

Total length of roads was 164,278 km in 2006 (including 14,143 km of main roads). In 2005 there were 2,686,000 vehicles in use, including 1,607,000 passenger cars. There were 5,486 road accident fatalities in 2006.

Rail

The National Railways (2,532 km of route, 914 mm gauge) went into liquidation in 1990. There are currently two concessions operating—Ferrocarril del Oeste and Red Férrea del Atlántico. Ferrocarril del Oeste carried 360,000 tonnes of freight in 2007 and Red Férrea del Atlántico 22m. tonnes in 2006. Passenger services are very limited. Total length in 2007 was 1,663 km. A metro system operates in Medellín.

Civil Aviation

The main international airports at Barranquilla, Bogotá (Eldorado), Cali, Cartagena and Medellín. The main Colombian airline is Avianca. In 2005 scheduled traffic of Colombian-based carriers flew 132·5m. km and carried 9,933,100 passengers. The busiest airport is Bogotá, which in 2014 handled 27,430,266 passengers (19,075,679 on domestic flights) and 636,657 tonnes of freight.

Shipping

In Jan. 2014 there were 22 ships of 300 GT or over registered, totalling 54,000 GT. The chief port is Cartagena, which handled 31·5m. tonnes of foreign cargo in 2013. The Magdalena River—Colombia's longest—is subject to drought, and navigation is always impeded during the dry season, but it is an important artery of passenger and goods traffic.

Telecommunications

In 2012 there were 6,291,000 main (fixed) telephone lines. In the same year mobile phone subscriptions numbered 49,066,000 (1,028·5 per 1,000 persons). There were 3,313,000 fixed internet subscriptions in 2011 and 3,093,000 wireless broadband subscriptions. In June 2012 there were 16·8m. Facebook users.

Social Institutions

Out of 178 countries analysed in the 2017 *Fragile States Index*—a list published jointly by the Fund for Peace and *Foreign Policy* magazine—Colombia was ranked the joint 69th most vulnerable (along with Israel) to conflict or collapse. The index is based on 12 indicators of state vulnerability across social, political and economic categories.

Justice

The July 1991 constitution introduced the offices of public prosecutor and public defence. The Supreme Court, at Bogotá, of 20 members, is divided into three chambers—civil cassation (six), criminal cassation (eight), labour cassation (six). Each of the 61 judicial districts has a superior court with various sub-dependent tribunals of lower juridical grade. In Dec. 1997 the constitution was amended to allow the extradition of Colombian nationals.

In 2016 there were 12,262 murders, continuing a downward trend since the high of 28,837 in 2002. Colombia's murder rate, at 25 per 100,000 persons in 2016, has more than halved in the space of 13 years. In 2016 the reported number of kidnappings totalled 205—down from 3,572 in 2000.

Colombia abolished the death penalty in 1997. The population in penal institutions in July 2013 was 118,201 (245 per 100,000 of national population). Colombia was ranked 83rd of 102 countries for criminal justice and 55th for civil justice in the 2015 World Justice Project *Rule of Law Index*, which provides data on how the rule of law is experienced by the general public across eight categories.

Education

Education between the ages of five and 15 became compulsory in 1991. Schools are both state and privately controlled. In 2007 there were 49,538 teaching staff for 1,081,343 children in pre-primary schools; 187,821 teaching staff for 5,298,567 pupils in primary schools; and 4,657,360 pupils with 164,484 teaching staff in secondary schools.

There were 32 public universities in 2007. The National University of Colombia (Universidad Nacional de Colombia), founded in 1867, is the leading institution in the tertiary sector. Colombia also has many private universities and colleges of art and music. In 2007 there were 1,372,674 students in total in higher education and 88,337 academic staff.

Adult literacy in 2008 was 93%.

In 2007 public expenditure on education came to 5·1% of GNI and represented 12·6% of total government expenditure.

Health

Over the period 2006–12 Colombia had 15 hospital beds per 10,000 population. In 2010 there were 15 physicians per 10,000 inhabitants, six nursing and midwifery personnel per 10,000 and nine dentists for every 10,000.

In *Water: At What Cost? The State of the World's Water 2016*, WaterAid reported that 8·6% of the population does not have access to safe water.

Welfare

The retirement age has been 62 for men and 57 for women since 1 Jan. 2014 (up from 60 for men and 55 for women previously); to be eligible for a state pension 1,000 weeks of contributions are required. The minimum social insurance pension is equal to the minimum wage. If a private pension is less than the minimum pension set by law, the government makes up the difference.

Unemployment benefit is a month's wage for every year of employment.

Religion

The main religion is Roman Catholicism (an estimated 38·1m. adherents in 2010 according to the Pew Research Center's Forum on Religion & Public Life), with the Archbishop of Bogotá as Primate of Colombia. The Roman Catholic Church has 13 ecclesiastical provinces, subdivided into 13 archdioceses and 52 dioceses. In Feb. 2019 there were three cardinals. The Pew Research Center estimated that there were also 4·64m. Protestants in 2010 and 3·05m. people who were religiously unaffiliated.

Culture

World Heritage Sites

There are nine UNESCO sites in Colombia. They are: the Port, Fortresses and Group of Monuments, Cartagena (1984)—on the Caribbean coast, Cartagena was one of the first cities to be founded in South America and has the most extensive fortifications in the continent; Los Katíos National Park (1994) covers 72,000 ha. in northwest Colombia; founded 200 km inland on the River Magdalena in the 1530s, the Historic Centre of Santa Cruz de Mompox (1995), or Mompós, was a focal point for colonization and a vital trade post between the Caribbean coast and the interior—its colonial aspect has been preserved; the National Archaeological Park of Tierradentro (1995) in the southwest contains statues and elaborately decorated underground tombs dating from the 6th–10th centuries; the San Agustín Archaeological Park (1995) protects religious monuments and sculptures from the 1st–8th centuries; the Malpelo Fauna and Flora sanctuary (2006) provides a critical habitat for internationally threatened marine species; the Coffee Cultural Landscape of Colombia (2011) reflects a tradition of coffee growing in small plots in the high forests; and Chiribiquete National Park—'The Maloca of the Jaguar' (2018) is the largest protected area in the country, containing over 75,000 paintings dating from 20,000 BC to present day. Shared with Argentina, Bolivia, Chile, Ecuador and Peru, Qhapaq Ñan, Andean Road System (2014) is an extensive Inca communication, trade and defence network of roads covering 30,000 km.

Press

There were 57 daily newspapers in 2014 (53 paid-for and four free); daily circulation totalled 1·53m. in 2009. The newspaper with the highest circulation is the broadsheet *El Tiempo*.

Tourism

In 2014 there were 2,565,000 international tourist arrivals (excluding same-day visitors), bringing revenue of US$3,825m.

Diplomatic Representatives

Of Colombia in the United Kingdom (3 Hans Cres., London, SW1X 0LN)
   Ambassador: Néstor Osorio Londoño.

Of the United Kingdom in Colombia (Carrera 9, No. 76–49, Piso 8, Edificio ING Barings, Bogotá)
   Ambassador: Peter Tibber.

Of Colombia in the USA (1724 Massachussetts Ave., NW, Washington, D.C., 20036)
   Ambassador: Francisco Santos Calderon.

Of the USA in Colombia (Carrera 45, No. 24B–27, Bogotá)
   Ambassador: Kevin Whitaker.

Of Colombia to the United Nations
   Ambassador: Guillermo Fernandez de Soto Valderrama.

Of Colombia to the European Union
   Ambassador: Felipe García Echeverri.

Further Reading

Departamento Administrativo Nacional de Estadística. *Boletín de Estadística.* Monthly.
Dudley, Steven, *Walking Ghosts: Murder and Guerrilla Politics in Colombia.* 2004
Hylton, Forrest, *Evil Hour in Colombia.* 2006
Palacios, Marco, *Between Legitimacy and Violence: A History of Colombia, 1875–2002.* 2006
National Statistical Office: Departamento Administrativo Nacional de Estadística (DANE), AA 80043, Zona Postal 611, Bogotá.
Website: http://www.dane.gov.co

Comoros

Union des Comores (Union of the Comoros)

Capital: Moroni
Population projection, 2020: 870,000
GNI per capita, 2017: (PPP$) 1,399
HDI/world rank, 2017: 0·503/165=
Internet domain extension: .km

Key Historical Events

The Comoros islands were inhabited from at least the first century BC—they were home to East African mariners and Malagasy-speaking seafarers from maritime southeast Asia, who were also early colonizers of Madagascar. Permanent villages on the islands of Mohéli and Mayotte date from the 8th century, established by Arab seafarers who plied trade routes along the East African coast.

Trade with Madagascar, Tanzania, Kenya, Oman and Yemen flourished between the 11th and 15th centuries. Sunni Muslim settlers from Shiraz in Persia had a profound influence on the Comoros islands in the 15th and 16th centuries, establishing sultanates and building mosques. Ibn Madjid, a celebrated navigator in the western Indian Ocean during the 15th century, noted that Domoni, on the island of Anjouan (Nzwani) was a major port used by African, Arabian, Persian and Indian vessels. Portuguese mariners reached Grande Comore in 1505, while British and Dutch merchants began visiting the islands from the start of the 17th century.

Grande Comore was divided into ten sultanates, while Anjouan and Mohéli were generally controlled by one ruler. Mayotte was briefly ruled by the former Madagascan king, Adriantsoly, in the 1830s before being captured by one of the sultans of Grande Comore. In 1841 Mayotte was purchased by France, which later sought control of the other islands. In 1886, Said Ali bin Said Omar, who by then ruled Grande Comore, was persuaded to grant France rights over the archipelago. The Comoros was declared a French protectorate in 1908. The four islands were proclaimed colonies in 1912 and administratively attached to Madagascar from 1914 until 1947 when they became a French Overseas Territory, achieving internal self-government in Dec. 1961. In referendums held on each island on 22 Dec. 1974, the three western islands voted overwhelmingly for independence, while Mayotte voted to remain French.

There have been dozens of coups or attempted takeovers since independence. In April 1999 an agreement was brokered on a federal structure for the three main islands—Grande Comore, Anjouan and Mohéli—to be known as the Union of the Comoros. However, the delegates from Anjouan did not sign the agreement. Violence broke out in the capital, Moroni, on Grande Comore against Anjouans living there. A military coup followed on 30 April 1999, led by Col. Azali Assoumani. He subsequently dissolved the government and the constitution, declaring a transitional government.

A new constitution in 2001 kept the union in place but with greater autonomy for each constituent island. Col. Azali Assoumani was elected president of the federation in April 2002, holding office until May 2006 when he was replaced by Ahmed Abdallah Mohamed Sambi. In May 2007 Mohamed Bascar, president of Anjouan, refused to stand down and held local elections in defiance of the federal government, prompting an African Union-led blockade. In March 2009 African Union and Comorian forces seized control of the island. Ikililou Dhoinine was elected president in 2011 and served a full term before Azali Assoumani narrowly won the 2016 presidential poll.

Territory and Population

The Comoros consists of three islands in the Indian Ocean between the African mainland and Madagascar with a total area of 1,862 sq. km (719 sq. miles). At the last census, in 2003, the population was 575,660 (285,590 males). The United Nations gave an estimated population for 2013 of 741,500; density, 398 per sq. km.

The UN gives a projected population for 2020 of 870,000.

In 2011, 28·3% of the population were urban.

The islands with their chief towns are: Njazídja (Grande Comore), Moroni; Nzwani (Anjouan), Mutsamudu; Mwali (Mohéli), Fomboni.

The capital, Moroni, had an estimated population in 2014 of 56,000. Other main towns are Mutsamudu, Fomboni and Domoni.

The indigenous population are a mixture of Malagasy, African, Malay and Arab peoples; the vast majority speak Comorian, an Arabized dialect of Swahili and one of the three official languages, but a small proportion speak one of the other official languages, French and Arabic, or Makua (a Bantu language).

Social Statistics

2008 births (estimates), 21,000; deaths, 4,000. Estimated birth rate in 2008 was 32·4 per 1,000 population; estimated death rate, 6·7. Annual population growth rate, 2000–08, 2·2%. Infant mortality, 63 per 1,000 live births (2010). Expectation of life in 2013 was 59·5 years among males and 62·3 among females. Fertility rate, 2008, 4·0 children per woman.

Climate

There is a tropical climate, affected by Indian monsoon winds from the north, which gives a wet season from Nov. to April. Moroni, Jan. 81°F (27·2°C), July 75°F (23·9°C). Annual rainfall, 113" (2,825 mm).

Constitution and Government

A referendum was held on 30 July 2018 to approve a new constitution. 92·3% of votes cast were in favour and turnout was 62·7%. The constitution permits the president to stand for two consecutive five-year terms, abolishes the position of vice-president and removes the requirement that the presidency rotate between the country's three main islands. Islam also became the state religion. At a previous referendum on 23 Dec. 2001, 77% of voters approved a constitution that kept the three islands as one country while granting each one greater autonomy.

The *President of the Union* is Head of State. There used to be a *Federal Assembly* comprised of 42 democratically elected officials and a 15-member *Senate* chosen by an electoral college, but these were dissolved after the 1999 coup. A new 33-member *Federal Parliament* was established following the elections of April 2004. In 2004 there were 15 deputies selected by the individual islands' parliaments and 18 by universal suffrage but this was changed to nine selected by the individual islands' parliaments and 24 by universal suffrage for the 2009 elections.

National Anthem

'Udzima wa ya Masiwa' ('The union of the islands'); words by S. H. Abderamane, tune by K. Abdallah and S. H. Abderamane.

Recent Elections

In the first round of presidential elections held on 21 Feb. 2016 Mohamed Ali Soilihi won 17·6% of the vote, Mouigni Baraka 15·1%, former president Azali Assoumani 15·0% and Fahmi Said Ibrahim 14·4%. There were 21 other candidates. Turnout was 74·4%. A second round took place on 10 April 2016, but owing to violence and electoral irregularities a partial rerun was held on 11 May. Assoumani won with 41·4% against Soilihi with 39·7% and Baraka with 18·9%.

Parliamentary elections were held on 25 Jan. and 22 Feb. 2015. The Union for the Development of the Comoros won 8 of 33 seats; Juwa Party 7; Democratic Rally of the Comoros 2; Convention for the Renewal of the Comoros 2; Rally for an Alternative of Harmonious and Integrated Development 1; and Party for the Comorian Agreement 1. Independent candidates won three seats. The remaining nine were allocated to regional assembly representatives.

© Springer Nature Limited 2020
Palgrave Macmillan (ed.), *The Statesman's Yearbook 2020*,
https://doi.org/10.1057/978-1-349-95940-2_51

Current Government

President of the Union: Azali Assoumani; b. 1959 (sworn in 26 May 2016 for a third time, having previously held office from April 1999–Jan. 2002 and May 2002–May 2006).

In Feb. 2019 the government comprised:

Ministry of Economy, and Investments, in Charge of Economic Integration Policies: Bianrifi Tharmidhi. *Energy, Agriculture, Fisheries and Environment:* Moustardoine Abdou. *Finance and Budget:* Said Ali Chayhane. *Foreign Affairs and International Co-operation:* Mohamed El-Amine Souef. *Health, Solidarity, Social Protection and Gender Promotion:* Rashid Mohamed Mbaraka Fatma. *Interior, Information, Decentralization, in Charge of Relations with Institutions and Government Spokesperson:* Mohamed Daoudou. *Justice, Islamic Affairs, Public Administration and Human Rights:* Mohamed Housseini Djamalilaili. *Maritime and Air Transport, in Charge of Tourism and Handicrafts:* Nourdine Ben Ahmed. *National Education, Higher Education and Scientific Research:* Salim Mahamoud. *Posts and Telecommunications, and Information and Communications Technologies:* Abdallah Said Sarouma. *Spatial Planning, and Urbanization, in Charge of Land Affairs:* Mohamed Chatur Badaoui. *Youth, Employment, Labour, Vocational Training, Occupational Integration, Sports, Arts and Culture:* Ladaenti Houmadi.

Office of the President (French only): http://www.beit-salam.km

Current Leaders

Azali Assoumani

Position

President

Introduction

Azali Assoumani was sworn in as president on 26 May 2016. He was previously head of state between 1999 and early 2002, after ousting the civilian president in a bloodless coup. Having been required by a new draft constitution to step down for an interim period, Assoumani was then elected to the presidency in April 2002. In May 2006, as part of an agreement that the presidency would rotate between the three islands that form the Comoros, he was succeeded by Ahmed Abdallah Mohamed Sambi. When the presidency returned to Assoumani's native island of Grande Comore (Njazídja) in 2016, he won a narrow victory over Mohamed Ali Soilihi (the incumbent Vice President).

Early Life

Azali Assoumani was born on 1 Jan. 1959 in Mitsoudjé in southwestern Grande Comore, the largest island of the French Overseas Territory of the Comoros. Between 1977 and 1980 he trained at the Royal Military Academy in Morocco. Returning to the Comoros, he joined the Comorian Armed Forces, then overseen by Col. Robert Denard, a French mercenary whose forces had overthrown President Ali Soilih in May 1978. Assoumani worked closely with the new president, Ahmed Abdullah, during the 1980s when the country was run as a federal Islamic republic. After the assassination of Abdullah by mercenaries in Nov. 1989, Assoumani became a senior officer in the Comorian Defence Force, which was formed with the assistance of the French army. Following another coup and French military intervention in 1995, Assoumani undertook further training at an army academy in France. A year later he was appointed the army's chief of staff.

In April 1999 unrest on the islands of Anjouan (Nzwani) and Mohéli (Mwali)—which had declared independence in 1997—spread to Grande Comore. Assoumani overthrew acting president Tadjidine Ben Said Massounde in a bloodless coup. He dissolved the state institutions and the constitution, assuming the duties of president, prime minister and defence minister on 30 April 1999.

Career in Office

Although he appointed a civilian prime minister, Bainrifi Tarmidi, in Dec. 1999, Assoumani remained head of state and army chief of staff until 21 Jan. 2002. He stood as a civilian candidate in the April 2002 presidential elections and emerged victorious, taking office on 26 May 2002, but international observers described the polls as flawed. Assoumani attempted to tackle poverty and high unemployment by upgrading education and technical training, reforming institutions and promoting tourism. However, he suffered a setback in legislative elections in April 2004, as his supporters won only six

of the 18 seats in the newly-established National Assembly. Despite an attempt in 2005 to draft a law that would allow Assoumani to run for a second term, he handed power to Ahmed Abdallah Mohamed Sambi on 26 May 2006. The handover to the island of Anjouan marked the first peaceful transfer of power in the Comoros's history.

In 2016 the presidency returned to Grande Comore. After a first round of voting on 21 Feb. 2016, Azali Assoumani, Mohamed Ali Soilihi and Mouigni Baraka advanced to a run-off on 10 April. Assoumani was declared the winner by a narrow margin, but reports of intimidation and voting irregularities led to some polls being rerun on 11 May. The results confirmed Assoumani's victory, and he was inaugurated on 26 May.

As well as maintaining political order in a notoriously unstable country, Assoumani promised to improve access to basic necessities and to strengthen the national economy through improved regional co-operation.

In July 2018 voters in a constitutional referendum approved the removal of presidential term limits and of the requirement for the presidency to rotate between the three main islands, allowing Assoumani to run for further terms in office.

Defence

Army

The Army numbered an estimated 1,060 in 2008.

Navy

There is no navy. The Army operates two small patrol boats that were supplied by Japan in 1982.

Economy

Agriculture and fishing accounted for 43·9% of GDP in 2010, followed by trade, restaurants and hotels 26·1%, public administration and defence 12·2% and construction 5·6%.

Overview

80% of the labour force is employed in agriculture, fishing, hunting and forestry. The primary sector is geared towards high-value export crops, chiefly vanilla and cloves, but dependency on food imports leaves the country vulnerable to global food price fluctuations. GDP is supplemented by remittances and aid. Under the 2010 Enhanced Heavily Indebted Poor Countries Initiative, the World Bank and the IMF agreed to provide assistance worth 1·1% of GDP over the period 2014–17.

Despite 3% average annual GDP growth between 2011 and 2015, the economy has not managed to achieve structural transformation. Poverty is widespread and there are severe shortages in electricity supply. The economy is constrained by a dominant public sector, an overbearing regulatory framework and limited access to credit, which has deterred private sector growth. Improving political stability offers longer-term hope of strengthening the economy.

Currency

The unit of currency is the *Comorian franc* (KMF) of 100 *centimes.* It is pegged to the euro at 491·96775 *Comorian francs* to the euro. Foreign exchange reserves were US$92m. in July 2005, total money supply was 24,096m. Comorian francs and gold reserves were 1,000 troy oz. Inflation was 1·8% in 2016 and 1·0% in 2017.

Budget

Revenues in 2014 were 64·7bn. Comorian francs and expenditures 78·0bn. Comorian francs.

VAT is 10%.

Performance

Real GDP growth was 1·0% in 2015, 2·2% in 2016 and 2·7% in 2017. In 2017 total GDP was US$0·6bn.

Banking and Finance

The Central Bank of the Comoros (*Governor*, Younoussa Imani) is the bank of issue. Chief commercial banks include the Banque Internationale des Comores, the Banque de Développement des Comores and the Banque pour l'Industrie et le Commerce-Comores.

External debt totalled US$485m. in 2010 and represented 90·1% of GNI.

Energy and Natural Resources

Environment

Carbon dioxide emissions from the consumption of energy were the equivalent of 0·2 tonnes per capita in 2011.

Electricity

In 2011 estimated installed capacity was 22,000 kW. Production was estimated at 43m. kWh in 2011; consumption per capita was an estimated 61 kWh in 2011.

Agriculture

The agricultural area in 2013 was an estimated 133,000 ha. There were about 65,000 ha. of arable land in 2013 and 53,000 ha. of permanent crops. The chief product was formerly sugarcane, but now vanilla, copra, maize and other food crops, cloves and essential oils (citronella, ylang-ylang, lemongrass) are the most important products. Production (2013 estimates in 1,000 tonnes): coconuts, 92; cassava, 70; bananas, 65; rice, 29; taro, 13.

Livestock estimates (2014): goats, 122,000; cattle, 50,000; sheep, 24,000; asses, 5,000.

Forestry

In 2015 the area under forest was 37,000 ha., or 20% of the total land area. The forested area has been severely reduced because of the shortage of cultivable land and ylang-ylang production. In 2011, 297,000 cu. metres of timber were cut.

Fisheries

The catch totalled 12,343 tonnes in 2012.

Industry

Branches include perfume distillation, textiles, furniture, jewellery, soft drinks and the processing of vanilla and copra.

Labour

The estimated economically active population in 2010 was 342,000 (53% males).

International Trade

Imports and Exports

In 2009 imports amounted to US$181·5m. (up from US$163·0m. in 2008) and exports to US$12·6m. (up from US$5·4m. in 2008).

Main import suppliers, 2006: United Arab Emirates, 30·7%; France, 21·3%; South Africa, 9·5%. Main export markets, 2006: France, 53·8%; India, 15·4%; Germany, 11·5%. The principal imports are machinery and transport equipment (35·0% of total imports in 2006), food and live animals (25·1% in 2006), cement (6·6% in 2006), petroleum and petroleum products, chemicals and related products, and iron and steel. Main exports are vanilla (53·8% in 2006) and cloves (30·8% in 2006).

Communications

Roads

In 2005 there were 849 km of roads.

Civil Aviation

There is an international airport at Moroni (International Prince Said Ibrahim). In 2009 it handled 149,071 passengers (98,638 international) and 627 tonnes of freight.

Shipping

In Jan. 2014 there were 139 ships of 300 GT or over registered, totalling 548,000 GT. The Comoros is a 'flag of convenience' country.

Telecommunications

In 2011 there were 23,600 landline telephone subscriptions (equivalent to 31·3 per 1,000 inhabitants) and 216,400 mobile phone subscriptions (or 287·1 per 1,000 inhabitants). There were 2,000 fixed internet subscriptions in 2012.

Social Institutions

Out of 178 countries analysed in the 2017 *Fragile States Index*—a list published jointly by the Fund for Peace and *Foreign Policy* magazine—the Comoros was ranked the joint 52nd most vulnerable (along with the Solomon Islands) to conflict or collapse. The index is based on 12 indicators of state vulnerability across social, political and economic categories.

Justice

Aspects of both French and Muslim law are incorporated into a consolidated code. The Supreme Court comprises seven members, two each appointed by the President and the Federal Assembly, and one by each island's Legislative Council. The death penalty is authorized for murder. The last execution was in 1996.

The International Centre for Prison Studies estimated in 2014 that 55·8% of prisoners had yet to receive a trial.

The estimated population in penal institutions in 2012 was approximately 120 (equivalent to 16 per 100,000 of national population).

Education

After two pre-primary years at Koran school, which 50% of children attend, there are six years of primary schooling for seven- to 13-year-olds followed by a four-year secondary stage attended by 25% of children. Some 5% of 17- to 20-year-olds conclude schooling at *lycées*. There were 106,700 pupils with 3,050 teaching staff in primary schools in 2005 and 43,349 pupils at secondary schools with 3,138 teaching staff. At the tertiary level there were approximately 3,000 students in 2009.

The adult literacy rate in 2009 was an estimated 74·2% (79·7% among males and 68·7% among females).

In 2008 public expenditure on education came to 7·6% of GDP.

Health

In 2009 there were 121 physicians, 21 dentistry personnel and 451 nursing and midwifery personnel. In 2006 there were 17 hospital beds per 10,000 inhabitants.

In *Water: At What Cost? The State of the World's Water 2016*, WaterAid reported that 9·9% of the population does not have access to safe water.

Religion

Islam is the official religion: 98% of the population are Muslims; there is a small Christian minority. Following the coup of April 1999 the federal government discouraged the practice of religions other than Islam, with Christians especially facing restrictions on worship.

Culture

Press

There has not been a daily newspaper since *Le Matin des Comores* ceased publication in 2006. *Le Canal*, which is published in Mayotte, is distributed in the Comoros. There were five non-dailies in 2008. *Al-Watwan* is published four days a week in French and one day a week in Arabic.

Tourism

In 2014 there were 23,000 international tourists, bringing revenue of US$48m.

Diplomatic Representatives

Of the Comoros in the United Kingdom
Honorary Consul: Khaled Chehabi (11 Park Pl., London, SW1A 1LP).

Of the United Kingdom in the Comoros
Ambassador: Phil Boyle (resides in Antananarivo, Madagascar).

Of the Comoros in the USA and to the United Nations (Temporary: c/o the Permanent Mission of the Union of the Comoros to the United Nations, 866 United Nations Plaza, Suite 418, N.Y. 10017)
Ambassador: Soilih Mohamed Soilih.

Of the USA in the Comoros
   Ambassador: Vacant (resides in Antananarivo, Madagascar).
   Chargé d'Affaires a.i.: Stuart R. Wilson.

Of the Comoros to the European Union
   Ambassador: Said Mdahoma Ali.

Further Reading

Ottenheimer, M. and Ottenheimer, H. J., *Historical Dictionary of the Comoro Islands.* 1994

Congo, Democratic Republic of the

République Démocratique du Congo

Capital: Kinshasa
Population projection, 2020: 89·51m.
GNI per capita, 2017: (PPP$) 796
HDI/world rank, 2017: 0·457/176
Internet domain extension: .cd

Key Historical Events

Bantu tribes migrated to the Congo basin from the northwest in the first millennium AD but Congo emerged as a kingdom on the Atlantic coast only in the 14th century. King Nzinga Mbemba forged diplomatic relations with Portugal after 1492. The Luba kingdom was centred on the marshy Upemba depression in the southeast. Expansion began in the late 18th century under Ilungu Sungu. In central Congo the Kuba kingdom was established in the 17th century as a federation of Bantu groups. Agriculture became the economic mainstay, strengthened by the introduction of American crops by Europeans. Trade made the Kuba elite, especially the Bushoong group, wealthy and the arts flourished. Kuba thrived until the incursions of the Nsapo in the late 19th century.

King Leopold II of the Belgians claimed the Congo Basin in 1885. Exploitation of the native population provoked international condemnation. The Belgian government then annexed the Congo in 1908. Political representation was denied the Congolese until 1957 when the colonial administration introduced the *statut des villes* in response to the revolutionary demands of the *Alliance des BaKongo* (Abako). Violence increased, instigated by the *Mouvement National Congolais* (MNC) of Patrice Lumumba. Local elections were held in Dec. 1959 and in Jan. 1960 Belgium announced a rapid independence programme. After general elections in May, the Republic of the Congo became independent on 1 June 1960, with Lumumba as prime minister and Joseph Kasavubu as president.

Independence and Anarchy

The country descended into anarchy, with the mineral-rich Katanga region declaring independence. Lumumba was ousted and in 1961 assassinated. Only in 2002 did Belgium admit to participating in his murder. Lieut.-Gen. Joseph-Désiré Mobutu (who later styled himself as Mobutu Sese Seko) seized power in 1965. He was initially seen as a strongman who could hold together the country's hundreds of tribes and language groups. He changed the country's name to Zaïre in 1971. Despite the brutality and repressiveness of his regime, in the 1970s he was feted by the USA, which launched operations from Zaïre into neighbouring Angola in support of rebels fighting the Cuban and Soviet-backed government.

After armed insurrection by Tutsi rebels in the province of Kivu, the government alleged pro-Tutsi intervention by the armies of Burundi and Rwanda and in Oct. 1996 declared a state of emergency. By Dec. the secessionist forces of Laurent-Désiré Kabila, the *Alliance des Forces Démocratiques pour la Libération du Congo-Zaïre* (AFDL), was driving the regular Zaïrean army out of Kivu and an attempt was made to establish a rebel administration, called 'Democratic Congo'. In the face of continuing rebel military successes and the disaffection of the army, the Government accepted a UN resolution demanding the end of hostilities. The Security Council asked the rebels to make a public declaration of their acceptance. However, they continued in their advance westwards, capturing Kisangani on 15 March 1997, then Kasai and Shaba, giving Kabila control of eastern Zaïre, and crucially the country's mineral wealth. After a futile attempt to deploy Serbian mercenaries, Mobutu succumbed to US and South African pressure to meet Kabila, an occasion widely regarded as a symbolic surrender. Mobutu fled on the night of 15–16 May 1997 and died of cancer four months later.

On coming to power Kabila changed the name of the country to the Democratic Republic of the Congo. Hopes for democratic and economic renewal were soon disappointed. The regime relied closely on its military backup, mainly Rwandans and eastern Congolese from the Tutsi minority who seemed more interested in eliminating tribal enemies than in establishing democracy. As a result, Rwanda and Uganda switched support to rebel forces. When Zimbabwe and Angola sent troops to help Kabila, full-scale civil war threatened. A ceasefire was negotiated in Nov. 1998 but the military build-up continued into the new year and violence intensified.

A ceasefire was signed by leaders from more than a dozen African countries in July 1999. Rival factions of the *Rassemblement Congolais pour la Démocratie* (RCD), the main rebel group, also signed the accord, but not until Sept.

Violence and Collapse

On 16 Jan. 2001 President Kabila was assassinated, allegedly by one of his bodyguards. He was succeeded by his son, Joseph. In Feb. 2001 the UN Security Council approved the deployment of 3,000 UN-supported peacekeepers. However, in early 2002 talks between the government and rebels ended without agreement. Then in July 2002 Kabila and the president of neighbouring Rwanda signed a peace deal that saw Rwanda complete the withdrawal of its forces in Oct. 2002. The Democratic Republic of the Congo and Uganda also signed a peace agreement.

The conflict, sometimes described as 'Africa's first world war', had drawn in Zimbabwe, Angola and Namibia (and, for a time, Sudan and Chad) on the side of the government, while Rwanda and Uganda backed other rival factions. The RCD was backed by Rwanda, while Uganda supported the *Mouvement de Libération du Congo* (MLC). Burundi also had troops in the country. In addition to the huge death toll, large numbers of people were displaced and sought asylum in Tanzania and Zambia. In Dec. 2002 the government and leading rebel forces reached an agreement on power-sharing. Its terms allowed for Joseph Kabila to remain as president until elections which, after several postponements, were held in July 2006. Kabila was elected president in a second round run-off in Oct. 2006 that signalled the end of the period of transitional government.

In April 2007 the Democratic Republic of the Congo resurrected the Economic Community of the Great Lakes alongside Rwanda and Burundi. Political instability within the country continued, particularly in eastern areas, where disparate rebel forces including Joseph Kony's Lord's Resistance Army were active. In Jan. 2008 the government signed a peace deal with militia groups, including that of the renegade Gen. Laurent Nkunda. However, fighting between the army and Rwandan Hutu militias (notably the Democratic Forces for the Liberation of Rwanda) had resumed by April. In Oct. the government accused Rwanda of secretly backing Nkunda. Fighting intensified and Goma, the provincial capital of Nord-Kivu, was paralysed as rebel forces encroached and some 200,000 people were displaced. In Jan. 2009 Rwandan forces arrested Nkunda, signalling a new diplomatic direction.

Peace remained elusive, however, with the UN warning that war crimes had been committed on all sides. In Nov. 2011 Joseph Kabila won a further term as president in disputed elections. In Oct. the following year rebel militias from the March 23 Movement (M23) seized control of Goma. Representatives from 11 African nations signed an accord in Feb. 2013 committing them to seeking an end to the conflict. By the end of the year the government and M23 had signed a peace agreement. Violence has nonetheless continued to beset the nation. In June 2014 Congolese troops were involved in border skirmishes with their Rwandan counterparts while in Jan. 2015 protests against constitutional changes that critics claimed would consolidate Kabila's grip on power ended in the deaths of dozens of demonstrators.

It is estimated that fighting in the country accounted for the loss of between 3m. and 5·4m. lives between 1998 and 2007 alone.

Territory and Population

The Democratic Republic of the Congo, sometimes referred to as Congo (Kinshasa), is bounded in the north by the Central African Republic, northeast by South Sudan, east by Uganda, Rwanda, Burundi and Lake

© Springer Nature Limited 2020
Palgrave Macmillan (ed.), *The Statesman's Yearbook 2020*,
https://doi.org/10.1057/978-1-349-95940-2_52

Tanganyika, south by Zambia, southwest by Angola and northwest by the Republic of the Congo. There is a 37-km stretch of coastline that gives access to the Atlantic Ocean, with the Angolan exclave of Cabinda to the immediate north, and Angola itself to the south. The area is 2,344,860 sq. km (905,360 sq. miles), including 77,810 sq. km (30,040 sq. miles) of inland waters. A census has not been held since 1984, when the population was 29,916,800. The United Nations gave an estimated population for 2013 of 71·32m.; density, 31 per sq. km. 35·9% of the population was urban in 2011.

The UN gives a projected population for 2020 of 89·51m.

There were 452,000 refugees in the country at the end of 2016, up from 383,000 a year earlier.

The country is administratively divided into 25 provinces plus Kinshasa city, as follows (with capitals): Bas-Uele (Buta), Équateur (Mbandaka), Haut-Katanga (Lubumbashi), Haut-Lomami (Kamina), Haut-Uele (Isiro), Ituri (Bunia), Kinshasa (Kinshasa), Kasai (Luebo), Kasaï-Central (Kananga), Kasai-Oriental (Mbuji-Mayi), Kongo Central (Matadi), Kwango (Kenge), Kwilu (Kikwit), Lomami (Kabinda), Lualaba (Kolwezi), Mai-Ndombe (Inongo), Maniema (Kindu), Mongala (Lisala), Nord-Kivu (Goma), Nord-Ubangi (Gbadolite), Sankuru (Lusambo), Sud-Kivu (Bukavu), Sud-Ubangi (Gemena), Tanganyika (Kalemia), Tshopo (Kisangani), Tshuapa (Boende).

The capital is Kinshasa (2010 population estimate, 8,415,000). Other main cities (with 2010 population estimates) are: Lubumbashi (1,486,000); Mbuji-Mayi (1,433,000); Kananga (846,000); Kisangani (783,000).

The population is Bantu, with minorities of Sudanese (in the north), Nilotes (northeast), Pygmies and Hamites (in the east). French is the official language, but of more than 200 languages spoken, four are recognized as national languages: Kiswahili, Tshiluba, Kikongo and Lingala. Lingala has become the *lingua franca* after French.

Social Statistics

2008 estimates: births, 2,883,000; deaths, 1,090,000. Rates (2008 estimates, per 1,000 population); birth, 44·9; death, 17·0. Annual population growth rate, 2000–08, 2·9%. Infant mortality in 2010 was 112 per 1,000 live births (the second highest in the world after Sierra Leone). Expectation of life in 2013 was 48·2 years for males and 51·8 for females. Fertility rate, 2008, 6·0 children per woman.

Climate

The climate is varied, the central region having an equatorial climate, with year-long high temperatures and rain at all seasons. Elsewhere, depending on position north or south of the Equator, there are well-marked wet and dry seasons. The mountains of the east and south have a temperate mountain climate, with the highest summits having considerable snowfall. Kinshasa, Jan. 79°F (26·1°C), July 73°F (22·8°C). Annual rainfall 45" (1,125 mm). Kananga, Jan. 76°F (24·4°C), July 74°F (23·3°C). Annual rainfall 62" (1,584 mm). Kisangani, Jan. 78°F (25·6°C), July 75°F (23·9°C). Annual rainfall 68" (1,704 mm). Lubumbashi, Jan. 72°F (22·2°C), July 61°F (16·1°C). Annual rainfall 50" (1,237 mm).

Constitution and Government

The 240-member *Constituent and Legislative Assembly* was appointed in Aug. 2000 by former President Laurent Désiré Kabila. In Aug. 2003 a new bicameral parliament of 500 members and 120 senators met in Kinshasa. A new constitution was adopted by the transitional parliament on 16 May 2005. It limited the powers of the president, who may serve a maximum of two five-year terms and lowered the minimum age for presidential candidates from 35 to 30. It also allowed a greater degree of federalism and recognized as citizens all ethnic groups at the time of independence in 1960. In a referendum held on 18–19 Dec. 2005 the constitution was approved by 83% of voters in the country's first free vote in 40 years and on 18 Feb. 2006 it was promulgated.

In accordance with the new constitution, at the 2006 presidential election the *President* was elected by direct popular vote to serve a five-year term. In the *National Assembly*, 60 members were elected by majority vote in single-member constituencies and 440 members by open list proportional representation in multi-member constituencies to serve five-year terms. The 108 members of the *Senate* were elected by indirect vote, by provincial deputies, to serve five-year terms. In Jan. 2011 constitutional amendments provided for presidential elections to take place in one round rather than two and for a candidate to win with a simple majority.

National Anthem

'Debout Congolais' ('Stand up, Congolese'); words and tune by J. Lutumba and S. Boka di Mpasi Londi.

Recent Elections

Much-delayed elections were held on 30 Dec. 2018. Incumbent Joseph Kabila was constitutionally barred from standing again. Félix Tshisekedi received 38·6% of votes cast, Martin Fayulu 34·8% and Emmanuel Ramazani Shadary 23·8%. There were 18 other candidates. Some international observers and the opposition suggested that irregularities were committed in favour of Tshisekedi.

In the parliamentary elections held on the same day the People's Party for Reconstruction and Democracy (PPRD), founded by Kabila and lead by Shadary, won 52 of 500 seats; the Alliance of the Democratic Forces of Congo (AFDC) 41 and Tshisekedi's Union for Democracy and Social Progress (UDPS) 32. The remaining seats were won by 17 other parties or coalitions with 15 seats vacant.

Current Government

President: Félix Tshisekedi; b. 1963 (sworn in 24 Jan. 2019).

In March 2019 the government comprised:

Prime Minister: Bruno Tshibala; b. 1955 (Union for Democracy and Social Progress; sworn in 7 April 2017).

Deputy Prime Minister: José Makila (also *Minister of Transport and Communication Channels*).

Ministers of State: Alexis Thambwe Mwamba (also *Minister of Justice and Keeper of the Seals, and Acting Minister of Foreign Affairs and Regional Integration*); Kangubia Mbayi Pierre (also *Minister of Budget*); Modeste Bahati Lukwebo (also *Minister of Planning, and Acting Minister of National Economy*); Lambert Matuku Memas (also *Minister of Employment, Labour and Social Welfare, and Acting Minister of External Trade*); Azarias Ruberwa (also *Minister of Decentralization and Institutional Reforms*); Michel Bongongo Ikoli (also *Minister of the Civil Service, and Acting Minister of National Defence, Veterans and Reintegration*); Jean-Pierre Lisanga Bonganga (also *Minister of Parliamentary Relations*).

Minister of Agriculture: Georges Kazadi Kabongo. *Culture and Arts:* Astrid Madiya. *Customary Affairs:* Guy Mikulu Pombo. *Development Co-operation:* John Kwet Mwan Kwet. *Environment and Sustainable Development:* Amy Ambatobe Nyongolo. *Finance:* Henri Yav Mulang (also *Acting Minister of Mines*). *Fisheries and Livestock:* Paluku Kisaka Yereyere. *Gender, Children and Family:* Chantal Safu. *Health:* Oly Ilunga Kalenga. *Higher Education and Universities:* Steve Mbikayi Mabuluki. *Human Rights:* Marie-Ange Mushobekwa (also *Acting Minister of Communications and Media*). *Hydrocarbons:* Aimé Ngoy Mukena. *Industry:* Marcel Ilunga Leu. *Infrastructure, Public Works and Reconstruction:* Thomas Luhaka (also *Acting Minister of Urban Planning and Housing*). *Interior and Security (acting):* Basile Olongo. *Land Affairs:* Lumeya Dhu-Maleguy (also *Acting Minister of Energy and Hydraulics Resources*). *Parastatals:* Wivine Mumba Matipa (also *Acting Minister of Regional Planning*). *Posts, Telecommunications, and New Information and Communication Technologies:* Emery Okundji (also *Acting Minister of Primary, Secondary and Technical Education*). *Rural Development:* Justin Bitakwira. *Scientific Research:* Heva Muakasa. *Small and Medium Enterprises:* Bienvenu Liyota. *Social Affairs:* Eugène Serufuli. *Solidarity and Humanitarian Action:* Bernard Byango Sango. *Sport and Recreation:* Papy Nyango Iziamay. *Tourism:* Franck Mwe di Malila. *Vocational Education and Handicrafts:* Pierrot Uweka Ukaba. *Youth and New Citizenship:* Maguy Kiala Bolenga. *Minister Delegate for the Congolese Living Abroad:* Emmanuel Ilunga Ngoie. *Minister Delegate at the Prime Minister's Office:* Tshibangu Kalala.

Office of the President (French only): http://www.presidentrdc.cd

Current Leaders

Félix Tshisekedi

Position
President

Introduction
Félix Tshisekedi became president in Jan. 2019, following an unexpected victory in the Dec. 2018 general election.

Félix Tshisekedi was born on 13 June 1963 in Leopoldville (now Kinshasa), the son of a politician, Etienne Tshisekedi. When his father founded the Union for Democracy and Social Progress (UDPS) in 1982 to oppose Mobutu Sese Seko's dictatorship, the family was forced into house arrest at their home village in central Kasai province.

Granted permission to leave Kasai in 1985, Tshisekedi emigrated to Brussels, Belgium. He studied at the city's Institut des Carrieres Commerciales, graduating with a diploma in marketing and communication in 1991. After working in the marketing department of an insurance company, he established a distribution firm and worked for the postal service in Brussels between 2003 and 2006.

Long active in the Congolese diaspora's political scene, Tshisekedi led the UDPS's Leuven branch in the mid-1990s. In 2008 he became the party's Brussels-based national secretary for external affairs. He contested the general election in the Democratic Republic of the Congo in Nov. 2011, winning the seat of Mbuji Mayi in Kasai-Oriental province. However, he did not take up the position amid international concerns about the transparency of the election.

Tshisekedi became vice-secretary general of the UDPS in 2016. In March 2018 he was elected to replace his father (who had died the previous year) as its leader and stood as the party's presidential candidate at elections in Dec. He unexpectedly defeated Martin Fayulu and Emmanuel Shadari, who was backed by the outgoing president, Joseph Kabila. Fayulu claimed that there was vote rigging, but the Constitutional Court dismissed his challenge and Tshisekedi was sworn in as president on 24 Jan. 2019.

Career in Office

In his inaugural address, Tshisekedi promised to prioritize peace and security, as well as to make the fight against poverty a 'great national cause'. He has targeted a tenfold increase in average income per head—to US$11·75 a day—over the next decade.

Defence

Following the overthrow of the Mobutu regime in May 1997, the former Zaïrean armed forces were in disarray. In June 2003 command of ground forces and naval forces were handed over to the RCD-Goma and MLC factions respectively as part of the power-sharing transitional government. Supreme command of the armed forces will remain in the hands of the former government faction.

A UN mission, MONUSCO, has been in the Democratic Republic of the Congo since 1999 (under the name of MONUC until June 2010). It had 18,316 uniformed personnel in Dec. 2017 (a number exceeded only by UNAMID in the Darfur region of Sudan). An additional United Nations Force Intervention Brigade has been in the eastern part of the country since 2013 to neutralize anti-government rebels. The first UN peacekeeping force to be given an offensive combat mandate, it is composed of troops from Malaŵi, South Africa and Tanzania. In Dec. 2013 it became the first UN mission to deploy drones to gather information for military intelligence.

Defence expenditure totalled US$416m. in 2013 (US$6 per capita), representing 2·2% of GDP.

Army

The total strength of the Army was estimated at 110,000–120,000 in 2011, with some 6,000–8,000 republican guards. There is an additional paramilitary National Police Force of unknown size. Equipment in 2011 included 149 main battle tanks.

Navy

Naval strength (2011), 6,700.

Air Force

Personnel (2011), 2,500, with five combat-capable aircraft.

Economy

Agriculture accounted for 45·5% of GDP in 2011 (one of the highest percentages of any country), industry 22·0% and services 32·5%.

Overview

After the end of the Second Congo War in 2003, a transitional government embarked on a number of macroeconomic reforms to bring hyperinflation

under control. This led to annual growth averaging 6·4% from 2003–08 before the global financial crisis reduced it to 2·8% in 2009. The mining industry spurred a rebound in subsequent years, with GDP expanding by 6·9% on average per year from 2010–15. However, mineral smuggling remains a serious threat to maximizing the sector's contribution to national prosperity.

Tighter fiscal and monetary policies helped bring inflation down from 550·0% in 2000 to 1·0% by 2015. It is hoped that investment in infrastructure, including transport and the electricity grid, will further boost growth. However, political stability and internal security remain fragile, with an estimated 2·3m. citizens displaced as of Sept. 2017.

Currency

The unit of currency is the *Congolese franc* (CDF) which replaced the former *zaïre* in July 1998. Total money supply was 120,605m. Congolese francs in July 2005. Inflation, which reached 23,760% in 1994, had declined to 4·0% by 2004 before rising to 46·1% in 2009. More recently it was 18·2% in 2016 and 41·5% in 2017. In May 2001 the franc was floated in an effort to overcome the economic chaos caused by three years of state control and inter-regional war.

Budget

In 2013 revenues totalled 4,797bn. Congolese francs and expenditures 5,275bn. Congolese francs.

Performance

Real GDP growth was 6·9% in 2015, 2·4% in 2016 and 3·4% in 2017. Total GDP in 2017 was US$37·2bn.

Banking and Finance

The central bank, the Banque Centrale du Congo (*Governor*, Deogratias Mutombo Mwana Nyembo), achieved independence in May 2002. In 2010 there were 23 commercial banks, two specialized financial institutions, one savings bank and 120 co-operative banks. The largest bank is Rawbank, which was only created in 2001 and had assets in 2011 of US$669·1m.

Foreign debt totalled US$5,774m. in 2010 and represented 47·1% of GNI.

Energy and Natural Resources

Environment

Carbon dioxide emissions from the consumption of energy were the equivalent of less than 0·1 tonnes per capita in 2011.

The *Climate Change and Environmental Risk Atlas 2014* produced by Maplecroft, a risk analytics company, ranked the Democratic Republic of the Congo as the country facing the seventh highest economic and social risk from climate change by 2025.

Electricity

Production (2011), 7·9bn. kWh. Installed capacity was an estimated 2·5m. kW in 2011. The Democratic Republic of the Congo is rich in untapped hydro-electric potential, but the unstable climate and poor infrastructure have made it difficult to attract investors. Consumption per capita was 121 kWh in 2011.

Oil and Gas

Production of oil in 2011 was 8·6m. bbls; reserves in 2014 were 180m. bbls. There is an oil refinery at Kinlao-Muanda.

Minerals

Production, 2013 estimates (in 1,000 tonnes): copper, 970; cobalt, 58; coal, 4; gold, 17,000 kg. Diamond production, 2013: 15·7m. carats. The Democratic Republic of the Congo is the world's largest producer of cobalt, and only Russia and Botswana produce more diamonds. The country holds an estimated 80% of the world's coltan (columbite-tantalite) reserves. Coal, tin and silver are also found.

Agriculture

In 2011, 11·4% of the total land area was agricultural of which 26·4% was arable land and 2·9% used for permanent crops. The main agricultural crops (2011 production in 1,000 tonnes) are: cassava, 15,024; sugarcane, 1,950 (estimate); palm fruit oil, 1,675 (estimate); plantains, 1,300 (estimate); maize,

1,156. Livestock (2011): goats, 4,058,000; pigs, 981,000; sheep, 905,000; cattle, 748,000; chickens, 20m.

Forestry
Forests covered 152·58m. ha. in 2015, or 67% of the land area. Timber production in 2011 was 82·32m. cu. metres.

Fisheries
The catch for 2012 was approximately 220,000 tonnes, almost entirely from inland waters.

Industry
Important industries include mining, mineral processing, consumer products, metal products, lumber and cement. Manufacturing accounted for 4·5% of GDP in 2011.

Labour
The estimated economically active population in 2010 was 25·77m. (59% males), up from 21·79m. in 2005. Agriculture employs around 65% of the total labour force.

The Democratic Republic of the Congo had 0·46m. people living in slavery according to the Walk Free Foundation's 2013 *Global Slavery Index*, the eighth highest total of any country.

International Trade

Imports and Exports
Imports in 2007 were US$5,257m.; exports were US$6,143m. Main commodities for import are consumer goods, foodstuffs, mining and other machinery, transport equipment and fuels; and for export: copper, cobalt, coffee, diamonds and crude oil. China is the principal import supplier, ahead of South Africa. China is also the biggest export market, with Zambia the second largest. China has become by far the biggest trading partner thanks to the massive growth since the early 2000s in its imports of raw materials from the Democratic Republic of the Congo.

Communications

Roads
In 2005 there were 171,250 km of roads (1·3% paved). In 2007 there were around 312,000 vehicles in use.

Rail
Total route length was 3,641 km on three gauges in 2011, of which 858 km was electrified. In 2008 the Office National des Transports carried 1·2m. passengers and in 2011 the Société Nationale des Chemins de Fer du Congo (SNCC) carried 46,000 passengers. The SNCC carried 573,000 tonnes of freight in 2011.

Civil Aviation
There is an international airport at Kinshasa (Ndjili). Other major airports are at Lubumbashi (Luano), Bukavu, Goma and Kisangani. For some years the national carrier was Hewa Bora Airways. Operations were suspended in 2011, after which FlyCongo was formed as a successor. However, it was only flying for six months before it merged with Compagnie Africaine d'Aviation, another airline based in the Democratic Republic of the Congo. In 2009 Kinshasa handled 672,347 passengers (385,923 international) and 67,544 tonnes of freight.

Shipping
About 15,000 km of the Congo River and its tributaries are navigable. Regular traffic has been established between Kinshasa and Kisangani as well as Ilebo, on the Lualaba (i.e. the river above Kisangani), on some tributaries and on the lakes. The Democratic Republic of the Congo has only 37 km of sea coast. Matadi, Kinshasa and Kalemie are the main seaports.

Telecommunications
In 2009 the Democratic Republic of the Congo had just 42,300 main (fixed) telephone lines (0·7 for every 1,000 persons), but there were 9,459,000 mobile phone subscribers (147·3 for every 1,000 persons). In 2010, 0·7%

of the population were internet users. In June 2012 there were 808,000 Facebook users.

Social Institutions
According to the 2017 *Fragile States Index*—a list published jointly by the Fund for Peace and *Foreign Policy* magazine—the Democratic Republic of the Congo was ranked as the country seventh most vulnerable to conflict or collapse. The index is based on 12 indicators of state vulnerability across social, political and economic categories.

Justice
There are a Supreme Court at Kinshasa, 11 courts of appeal, 36 courts of first instance and 24 'peace tribunals'. The death penalty is in force.

The population in penal institutions in 2010 was approximately 22,000 (33 per 100,000 of national population). The International Centre for Prison Studies estimated in 2014 that 82·0% of prisoners had yet to receive a trial.

Education
In 2007 there were 230,834 teaching staff in primary schools for 8·8m. pupils, and 2·8m. pupils in secondary schools with 179,635 teaching staff. In 2007 there were 237,836 students in higher education and 16,913 academic staff. The largest public universities are the University of Kinshasa, the University of Kisangani and the University of Lubumbashi.

Adult literacy rate was 67% in 2008.

Health
In 2009 there were 9·1 physicians and 96·1 nursing and midwifery personnel per 100,000 population.

In *Water: At What Cost? The State of the World's Water 2016*, WaterAid reported that 47·6% of the population does not have access to safe water (the seventh highest percentage of any nation). The Democratic Republic of the Congo ranked as the country with the fifth largest number of people living without access to safe water (33·9m. in 2015).

Religion
According to estimates by the Pew Research Center's Forum on Religion & Public Life, in 2010 the population was 95·8% Christian with 1·5% Muslim and 1·8% religiously unaffiliated. Around half the Christians are Catholics and half are Protestants. In Feb. 2019 there was one Roman Catholic cardinal.

Culture

World Heritage Sites
(With year entered on list). Virunga National Park (1979); Kahuzi-Biega National Park (1980); Garamba National Park (1980); Salonga National Park (1984); and Okapi Wildlife Reserve (1996).

Press
In 2008 there were 12 daily newspapers with a combined circulation of 50,000.

Tourism
In 2010 there were 81,000 non-resident tourist arrivals by air.

Diplomatic Representatives
Of the Democratic Republic of the Congo in the United Kingdom (45–49 Great Portland St., London, W1W 7LD)
Ambassador: Marie Ndjeka Opombo.

Of the United Kingdom in the Democratic Republic of the Congo (83 Ave. du Roi Baudouin, Gombe, Kinshasa)
Ambassador: Dr John Murton.

Of the Democratic Republic of the Congo in the USA (1100 Connecticut Ave., NW, Suite 725, Washington, D.C., 20036)
Ambassador: François Nkuna Balumuene.

Of the USA in the Democratic Republic of the Congo (310 Ave. des Aviateurs, Kinshasa)
    Ambassador: Michael A. Hammer.

Of the Democratic Republic of the Congo to the United Nations
    Ambassador: Ignace Gata Mavita wa Lufuta.

Of the Democratic Republic of the Congo to the European Union
    Ambassador: Vacant.
    Chargé d'Affaires a.i.: Paul-Crispin Kakhozi Bin Bulongo.

Further Reading

Gondola, Didier, *The History of Congo.* 2003
Hochschild, Adam, *King Leopold's Ghost: A Study of Greed, Terror and Heroism in Colonial Africa.* 1999
Stearns, Jason, *Dancing in the Glory of Monsters: the Collapse of the Congo and the Great War of Africa.* 2011

Congo, Republic of the

République du Congo

Capital: Brazzaville
Population projection, 2020: 5·69m.
GNI per capita, 2017: (PPP$) 5,694
HDI/world rank, 2017: 0·606/137
Internet domain extension: .cg

Key Historical Events

First occupied by France in 1882, the Congo became a territory of French Equatorial Africa from 1910–58, and then a member state of the French Community. Between 1940 and 1944, thanks to Equatorial Africa's allegiance to Gen. de Gaulle, he named Brazzaville the capital of the Empire and Liberated France. Independence was granted in 1960. A Marxist-Leninist state was introduced in 1970. Free elections were restored in 1992 but violence erupted when, in June 1997, President Lissouba tried to disarm opposition militia ahead of a fresh election. There followed four months of civil war with fighting concentrated on Brazzaville which became a ghost town. In Oct. Gen. Sassou-Nguesso proclaimed victory, having relied upon military support from Angola. President Lissouba went into hiding in Burkina Faso. A peace agreement signed in Nov. 1999 between President Sassou-Nguesso and the 'Cocoye' and 'Ninja' militias brought a period of relative stability.

Territory and Population

The Republic of the Congo, sometimes referred to as Congo (Brazzaville), is bounded by Cameroon and the Central African Republic in the north, the Democratic Republic of the Congo to the east and south, Angola and the Atlantic Ocean to the southwest and Gabon to the west, and covers 342,000 sq. km. At the census of 2007 the population was 3,697,490 (1,876,133 females); density, 11 per sq. km.

The UN gives a projected population for 2020 of 5·69m.

In 2011, 62·5% of the population were urban. Area, census population and county towns of the departments in 2007 were:

Department	Sq. km	Population	County town
Bouenza	12,266	309,073	Madingou
Capital District	100	1,373,382	Brazzaville
Cuvette	47,650	156,044	Owando
Cuvette Ouest	27,200	72,999	Ewo
Kouilou[1]	13,694	807,289	Pointe-Noire
Lékoumou	20,950	96,393	Sibiti
Likouala	66,044	154,115	Impfondo
Niari	25,941	231,271	Loubomo (Dolisie)
Plateaux	38,400	174,591	Djambala
Pool	33,955	236,595	Kinkala
Sangha	55,800	85,738	Ouesso

[1]A new department, Pointe-Noire (formerly part of Kouilou), has been created since the 2007 census.

Census population of major cities in 2007: Brazzaville, the capital, 1,373,382; Pointe-Noire, 715,334; Loubomo (Dolisie), 83,798; N'Kayi, 71,620; Impfondo, 33,911; Ouesso, 28,179. Main ethnic groups are: Kongo (48%), Sangha (20%), Teke (17%) and M'Bochi (12%).

French is the official language. Kongo languages are widely spoken. Monokutuba and Lingala serve as *lingua francas*.

Social Statistics

2008 estimates: births, 125,000; deaths, 46,000. Rates, 2008 estimates (per 1,000 population): births, 34·5; deaths, 12·9. Infant mortality, 2010 (per 1,000 live births), 61. Expectation of life in 2013 was 57·4 years for males and 60·2 for females. Annual population growth rate, 2000–08, 2·2%. Fertility rate, 2008, 4·4 children per woman.

Climate

An equatorial climate, with moderate rainfall and a small range of temperature. There is a long dry season from May to Oct. in the southwest plateaux, but the Congo Basin in the northeast is more humid, with rainfall approaching 100" (2,500 mm). Brazzaville, Jan. 78°F (25·6°C), July 73°F (22·8°C). Annual rainfall 59" (1,473 mm).

Constitution and Government

A new constitution was approved in a referendum held in Jan. 2002, providing for an increase in the president's term of office from five to seven years, for a maximum of two terms. Provision was also made for a new two-chamber legislature consisting of a National Assembly and a Senate. The president could also appoint and dismiss ministers. 84·3% of voters were in favour of the draft constitution and 11·3% against. Turnout was 78%. The new constitution came into force in Aug. 2002. In Oct. 2015 proposals to remove the presidential upper age limit of 70 and to increase the allowable number of terms from two to three won 92% approval in a further referendum. The amendments came into force the following month.

There is a 151-seat *National Assembly*, with members elected for a five-year term in single-seat constituencies, and a 72-seat *Senate*, with members elected for a six-year term (one half of members every three years).

National Anthem

'La Congolaise'; words by Levent Kimbangui, tune by Français Jacques Tondra.

Recent Elections

Presidential elections were held on 20 March 2016. Incumbent Denis Sassou-Nguesso was re-elected with 60·2% of votes cast, against 15·0% for Guy Brice Parfait Kolélas and 13·7% for Jean-Marie Michel Mokoko. The turnout was 68·9%. There were six other candidates. Opposition groups refused to accept the results, claiming that they were fraudulent.

Parliamentary elections were held on 16 and 30 July 2017. President Denis Sassou-Nguesso's Congolese Labour Party won 96 out of 151 seats; Pan-African Union for Social Democracy, 8; Congolese Movement for Democracy and Integrated Development, 4; Action Movement for Renewal, 3; Dynamic for the Republic and Recovery, 3; Rally for Democracy and Social Progress, 3; Union for a People's Movement, 2. 12 other parties won one seat each and 20 went to independents.

Current Government

President: Denis Sassou-Nguesso; b. 1943 (Congolese Labour Party; sworn in 25 Oct. 1997 for a second time and re-elected in March 2002, July 2009 and March 2016, having previously held office 1979–92).

In Feb. 2019 the government comprised:

Prime Minister: Clément Mouamba (ind.; since 23 April 2016).

Vice Prime Minister (also *Minister for Civil Service, State Reform, Labour and Social Security*): Firmin Ayessa.

Minister of State and Director of Cabinet of the Head of State: Florent Tsiba. *Minister of State for Agriculture, Livestock and Fisheries:* Henri

© Springer Nature Limited 2020
Palgrave Macmillan (ed.), *The Statesman's Yearbook 2020*,
https://doi.org/10.1057/978-1-349-95940-2_53

Djombo. *Economy, Industrial Development and Promotion of the Private Sector:* Gilbert Ondongo. *Trade, Supplies and Consumer Affairs:* Claude Alphonse Nsilou.

Minister of Communications, Media and Government Spokesperson: Thierry Moungalla. *Construction, Town Planning and Housing:* Josué Rodrigue Ngouonumba. *Culture and the Arts:* Dieudonné Moyongo. *Energy and Water Resources:* Serge Blaise Zoniaba. *Finance and Budget:* Calixte Ganongo. *Foreign Affairs, Co-operation and Congolese Abroad:* Jean-Claude Gakosso. *Forest Economy and Sustainable Development:* Rosalie Matondo. *Health and Population:* Jacqueline Lydia Mikolo. *Higher Education:* Bruno Jean-Richard Itoua. *Hydrocarbons:* Jean-Marc Thystère Tchicaya. *Infrastructure and Road Maintenance:* Émile Ouosso. *Interior and Decentralization:* Raymond Zéphirin Mboulou. *Justice, Human Rights and the Promotion of Indigenous Peoples:* Ange Aimé Bininga. *Land Affairs and Public Territory, in Charge of Relations with Parliament:* Pierre Mabiala. *Mines and Geology:* Pierre Oba. *National Defence:* Charles Richard Mondjo. *Planning, Statistics and Regional Integration:* Ingrid Olga Ebouka-Babakas. *Posts, Telecommunications and Digital Economy:* Léon Juste Ibombo. *Primary and Secondary Education, and Literacy:* Anatolle Collinet Makosso. *Promotion of Women and the Involvement of Women in Development:* Inès Bertille Nefer Ingani. *Scientific Research and New Technologies:* Martin Parfait Aimé Coussoud-Mavoungou. *Small and Medium-Sized Businesses, and Handicrafts:* Yvonne Adélaïde Mougany. *Social Affairs, Humanitarian Affairs and Solidarity:* Antoinette Dinga Djondo. *Special Economic Zones:* Gilbert Mokoki. *Sports and Physical Education:* Hugues Ngouélondélé. *Technical and Vocational Training, and Employment:* Nicéphore Antoine Thomas Fila Saint Eudes. *Territorial Management and Major Projects:* Jean-Jacques Bouya. *Tourism and Environment:* Arlette Soudan Nonault. *Transport, Civil Aviation and Merchant Navy:* Fidèle Dimou. *Youth and Civic Education:* Destinée Ermela Doukaga.

Office of the President (French only): http://www.presidence.cg/accueil

Current Leaders

Denis Sassou-Nguesso

Position

President

Introduction

A military leader from the 1960s, Denis Sassou-Nguesso ruled the Republic of the Congo between 1979–92, regaining power in 1997 in a coup. He maintained Congo's one-party Marxist-Leninist state—through the Congolese Labour Party (PCT; Parti Congolais du Travail)—until 1992, when he introduced free elections in which he was defeated. Much of his tenure since 1997 has been marred by civil war and economic crises.

Early Life

Sassou-Nguesso was born in 1943 in Edou. Joining the army in 1960, he trained at the General Leclerc military school in the Congo and the Saint-Maixent military school in France. In 1963 he was involved in the overthrow of Fulbert Youlou, the first president of independent Congo from 1959, and then of his successor Alphonse Massemba-Débat (1963–68). When Marien Ngouabi took power in 1969 he introduced a Marxist-Leninist state with the newly created PCT at its core. Sassou-Nguesso joined the PCT in the same year.

In 1977 Sassou-Nguesso formed part of a military junta which took power following the assassination of Ngouabi by forces supposedly loyal to Massemba-Débat, before serving as defence minister under the leadership of Col. Joachim Yhombi-Opango (1977–79). At the same time he became vice president of the military committee. Two years later Sassou-Nguesso replaced Yhombi-Opango as president.

Career in Office

On taking power, Sassou-Nguesso introduced a new constitution with the PCT continuing to lead a one-party government. Despite signing a co-operation treaty with the USSR in 1981, Sassou-Nguesso sought a rapprochement with France and international investment in Congo's oil resources. In 1990 the party then abandoned Marxism for democratic socialism and in 1992, following a referendum, free elections were introduced. The first multi-party elections saw the defeat of Sassou-Nguesso by Pascal Lissouba of the Pan-African Union for Social Democracy. Sassou-Nguesso came third with 16·9% of votes.

Thereafter, tension between the governing and opposition parties led to recurring violence between their respective militias, including the 'Cobra' militia loyal to Sassou-Nguesso. Violence increased ahead of elections scheduled for 1997, accelerating into civil war. Sassou-Nguesso, with the aid of Angolan soldiers, finally ousted Lissouba and was sworn in as president again in Oct. 1997. Fighting erupted again in Jan. 1999 as 'Cocoye' rebels loyal to Lissouba attacked Brazzaville, and in April there was an attack on Pointe-Noire by the 'Ninja' rebels loyal to former prime minister Bernard Kolélas. Then in Aug. 1999 peace talks were held by Sassou-Nguesso, Lissouba and Kolélas at which a ceasefire was agreed.

In Jan. 2001 a new constitution increased the president's term from five to seven years and strengthened presidential powers. In elections held in March 2002, Sassou-Nguesso won 89·4% of votes. The new constitution deemed Lissouba and Kolélas ineligible to stand, while another opposition candidate, Andre Milongo, refused to participate claiming 'irregularities'. The elections were marred by violence between the 'Ninja' rebels and government forces in the Pool area of the country. Legislative elections which followed in May and June 2002 resulted in a large parliamentary majority for the PCT and its allies, although the results were criticized by international observers and provoked further militia violence. A peace agreement reached in March 2003 remained fragile. Following the parliamentary elections in mid-2007 the PCT remained the largest party in the National Assembly and in July 2009 Sassou-Nguesso was re-elected for a further seven-year presidential term, although the results were again disputed.

In a cabinet reshuffle in Sept. 2009, Sassou-Nguesso abolished the post of prime minister and assumed those duties himself. The PCT maintained its dominance in legislative elections in July–Aug. 2012. A controversial constitutional amendment that came into force in Nov. 2015 overturned a two-term limit for the president and an upper age bar of 70, so allowing Sassou-Nguesso to seek re-election. He was duly returned in March 2016 in polls that the opposition again claimed were fraudulent. The following month he reinstated the post of prime minister, appointing Clément Mouamba, an independent, as premier in a largely unchanged government. In parliamentary elections in July 2017 the PCT again secured a majority with 96 of 151 seats.

Defence

In 2012 military expenditure totalled an estimated US$325m. (approximately US$74 per capita), representing around 2·5% of GDP.

Army

Total personnel (2011) 8,000. There is a Gendarmerie of 2,000.

Navy

Personnel in 2011 totalled about 800, with six patrol boats.

Air Force

The Air Force had (2011) about 1,200 personnel; aircraft included two ground attack fighters and two attack helicopters, although none are combat-capable and their serviceability is questionable.

Economy

Agriculture produced 3·4% of GDP in 2011, industry 76·6% and services 20·0%.

Overview

Oil and petroleum production account for the bulk of export earnings having superseded forestry as the mainstay. Other mineral production is increasingly important. The country has a diverse base of natural resources including zinc, copper, lead, uranium, diamonds and natural gas. It is the largest producer of potash in Africa, producing 1·2m. tonnes in 2013. Iron ore is also important with the country possessing some of West Africa's largest deposits. Many of these remain unexploited but the Congolese government has awarded licences to a number of international mining companies. However, the economy is vulnerable to drops in commodity prices and the country remains one of the poorest in the world with 46·5% of the population below the poverty line.

The World Bank cites better management of oil revenues and improved agricultural practice as key to broad-based growth. Currently the Republic of the Congo is a net food importer, although subsistence farming dominates employment. Public debt as a percentage of GDP fell from 68·1% to 22·2%

between 2008 and 2011. GDP growth averaged 7·8% between 2008 and 2010 but then only 4·2% between 2013 and 2015.

Currency

The unit of currency is the *franc CFA* (XAF) with a parity of 655·957 francs CFA to one euro. Total money supply in June 2005 was 322,269m. francs CFA and foreign exchange reserves were US$226m. Gold reserves were 11,000 troy oz in July 2005. Inflation was 3·2% in 2016 and 0·5% in 2017.

Budget

In 2013 revenues were 3,123bn. francs CFA and expenditures 2,555bn. francs CFA. Petroleum revenue accounted for 73·5% of revenues in 2013; capital expenditure accounted for 63·1% of expenditures.

Performance

Total GDP in 2017 was US$8·7bn. Real GDP growth was 2·6% in 2015, before the economy contracted by 2·8% in 2016 and 3·1% in 2017.

Banking and Finance

The Banque des Etats de l'Afrique Centrale (*Governor*, Abbas Mahamat Tolli) is the bank of issue. There are four commercial banks and a development bank, in all of which the government has majority stakes. There is also a co-operative banking organization (Mutuelle Congolaise de l'Épargne et de Crédit).

In 2010 external debt totalled US$3,781m. and represented 43·9% of GNI.

Energy and Natural Resources

Environment

Carbon dioxide emissions from the consumption of energy in 2011 were the equivalent of 1·6 tonnes per capita.

Electricity

Installed capacity was an estimated 310,000 kW in 2011. Total production in 2011 was 1,293m. kWh and consumption per capita 312 kWh.

Oil and Gas

Oil was discovered in the mid-1960s. In 2011 production reached a record high of 15·6m. tonnes before dropping to 14·5m. tonnes in 2013. Proven reserves in 2013 were 1·6bn. bbls, including major off-shore deposits. Oil provides about 80–90% of government revenue and exports. There is a refinery at Pointe-Noire, the second largest city. There were proven natural gas reserves of 91bn. cu. metres in 2013.

Minerals

A government mine produces several metals; gold and diamonds are extracted by individuals. There are reserves of potash (4·5m. tonnes), iron ore (1,000m. tonnes), and also clay, bituminous sand, phosphates, zinc and lead.

Agriculture

In 2011, 30·9% of total land area was agricultural of which 4·7% was arable and 0·6% used for permanent crops. Production (2013 estimates, in thousand tonnes): cassava, 1,250; sugarcane, 650; palm fruit oil, 144; bananas, 104; plantains, 86; mangoes and guavas, 41; groundnuts, 33; palm oil, 27; yams, 16; maize, 14.

Livestock (2013 estimate): cattle, 337,000; goats, 325,000; sheep, 122,000; pigs, 95,000; chickens, 3m.

Forestry

In 2015 forests covered 22·33m. ha. (65% of the total land area). In 2011, 3·55m. cu. metres of timber were produced. Before the development of the oil industry, forestry was the mainstay of the economy.

Fisheries

The catch for 2012 was 81,054 tonnes, of which 43,184 tonnes were from marine waters.

Industry

Manufacturing contributed 3·4% of GDP in 2011. Production (2010): residual fuel oil, 227,000 tonnes; distillate fuel oil, 223,000 tonnes; petrol, 98,000 tonnes; sugar, 65,000 tonnes; jet fuel, 47,000 tonnes; kerosene, 34,000

tonnes; sawnwood, 179,000 cu. metres; wood-based panels, 60,000 cu. metres; veneer sheets, 35,000 cu. metres.

Labour

In 2010 the estimated economically active population was 1,637,000 (56% males), up from 1,256,000 in 2000. More than 50% of the labour force in 2010 were engaged in agriculture.

The Republic of the Congo had 31,000 people living in slavery according to the Walk Free Foundation's 2013 *Global Slavery Index*.

International Trade

Imports and Exports

Merchandise imports in 2013 totalled US$8,371·6m. (US$7,348·6m. in 2012) and merchandise exports US$10,453·1m. (US$7,437·9m. in 2012).

Principal imports in 2013 were machinery and transport equipment (78·0%), manufactured goods, and food, animals and beverages; main exports in 2013 were mineral fuels and lubricants (75·7%), machinery and transport equipment, and crude materials and animal and vegetable oils.

Leading import suppliers in 2009 were Angola (15·4%), France and Singapore. Leading export markets were the USA (13·7%), France and Taiwan.

Communications

Roads

In 2006 there were 17,000 km of roads, of which 7·1% were surfaced. Passenger cars in use in 2007 numbered 56,000 (15 per 1,000 inhabitants). There were 214 deaths in road accidents in 2007.

Rail

A railway connects Brazzaville with Pointe-Noire via Loubomo and Bilinga, and a branch links Mont-Belo with Mbinda. Total length in 2005 was 797 km (1,067 mm gauge). In 2006 passenger-km totalled 167m. and freight tonne-km 264m.

Civil Aviation

The principal airports are at Brazzaville (Maya Maya) and Pointe-Noire. In 2012 Brazzaville handled 957,472 passengers (675,193 on domestic flights) and 26,418 tonnes of freight. The national carrier is Equatorial Congo Airlines—operating as ECAir—which in 2013 carried 207,000 passengers (175,000 on domestic flights). It serves a number of cities elsewhere in Africa as well as Paris and domestic destinations.

Shipping

The only seaport is Pointe-Noire. There are some 5,000 km of navigable rivers, and river transport is an important service for timber and other freight as well as passengers.

Telecommunications

There were 9,800 fixed telephone lines in 2010 (2·4 per 1,000 inhabitants). Mobile phone subscribers numbered 3·80m. in 2010. There were 56·0 internet users per 1,000 inhabitants in 2011.

Social Institutions

Out of 178 countries analysed in the 2017 *Fragile States Index*—a list published jointly by the Fund for Peace and *Foreign Policy* magazine—the Republic of the Congo was ranked the 29th most vulnerable to conflict or collapse. The index is based on 12 indicators of state vulnerability across social, political and economic categories

Justice

The Supreme Court, Court of Appeal and a criminal court are situated in Brazzaville, with a network of *tribunaux de grande instance* and *tribunaux d'instance* in the regions.

The International Centre for Prison Studies estimated in 2014 that 75·0% of prisoners had yet to receive a trial.

The population in penal institutions in Dec. 2012 was approximately 1,300 (31 per 100,000 national population).

The death penalty, which was last used in 1982, was abolished in Nov. 2015.

Education

In 2012 there were 16,527 teaching staff for 734,493 pupils at primary schools and 18,165 secondary school teaching staff for 339,250 pupils. There were 39,303 students at tertiary level in 2012 with 3,317 academic staff. Adult literacy rate in 2011 was estimated at 79·3%.

In 2005 public expenditure on education came to 1·8% of GDP and 8·1% of total government spending.

Health

In 2005 there were 16 hospital beds for every 10,000 persons. In the period 2007–13 there was one physician per 10,000 population and eight nurses and midwives per 10,000.

In *Water: At What Cost? The State of the World's Water 2016*, WaterAid reported that 23·5% of the population does not have access to safe water.

Religion

In 2010 there were an estimated 2·08m. Protestants, 1·22m. Roman Catholics, 0·18m. other Christians and 0·11m. folk religionists according to the Pew Research Center's Forum on Religion & Public Life. A further 0·36m. people had no religious affiliation.

Culture

Press

In 2008 there were five daily newspapers with a combined circulation of 8,000.

Tourism

In 2012 there were 259,000 non-resident visitor arrivals (224,000 in 2011).

World Heritage Sites

Sangha Trinational, a transboundary conservation complex situated in Cameroon, Central African Republic and the Republic of the Congo, was added to the UNESCO World Heritage List in 2012. The site consists of three contiguous national parks totalling around 750,000 ha. Much of it is unaffected by human activity and features a wide range of humid tropical forest ecosystems with rich flora and fauna.

Diplomatic Representatives

Of the Republic of the Congo in the United Kingdom
    Ambassador: Vacant (resides in Paris).
    Honorary Consul: Louis Muzzu (3rd Floor, Holborn Gate (HRG), 26 Southampton Buildings, London, WC2A 1PN).

Of the United Kingdom in the Republic of the Congo
    Ambassador: Dr John Murton (resides in Kinshasa, Democratic Republic of the Congo).

Of the Republic of the Congo in the USA (1720 16th St., NW, Washington, D.C., 20009)
    Ambassador: Serge Mombouli.

Of the USA in the Republic of the Congo (Blvd Denis Sassou Nguesso 70–83, Section D, Centre Ville, Brazzaville).
    Ambassador: Todd Philip Haskell.

Of the Republic of the Congo to the United Nations
    Ambassador: Raymond Serge Balé.

Of the Republic of the Congo to the European Union
    Ambassador: Léon Raphaël Mokoko.

Further Reading

Thompson, V. and Adloff, R., *Historical Dictionary of the People's Republic of the Congo.* 2nd ed. 1984

National Statistical Office: Centre National de la Statistique et des Études Économiques, BP 2031, Brazzaville.

Website (French only): http://www.cnsee.org

Costa Rica

República de Costa Rica (Republic of Costa Rica)

Capital: San José
Population projection, 2020: 5·04m.
GNI per capita, 2017: (PPP$) 14,636
HDI/world rank, 2017: 0·794/63
Internet domain extension: .cr

Key Historical Events

Archaeological evidence suggests hunter-gatherers from both North and South America had settled in the area by 12,000 BC. As agriculture developed, permanent settlements appeared from around 2,500 BC. By the turn of the 16th century AD, the region was divided between some 19 major chieftainships, with a combined population of up to 500,000. European contact began with the arrival of Christopher Columbus in 1502 on his last voyage. The newly-named Costa Rica (Rich Coast) formed part of the Spanish viceroyalty of New Spain from 1540 to 1821, then of the Central American Federation until 1838 when it achieved full independence. Coffee was introduced in 1808 and became a mainstay of the economy, helping to create a peasant land-owning class.

In 1948 accusations of election fraud led to a six-week civil war, at the conclusion of which José Figueres Ferrer won power at the head of a revolutionary junta. A new constitution abolished the Army. In 1986 Óscar Arias Sánchez was elected president. He promised to prevent Nicaraguan anti-Sandinista (contra) forces using Costa Rica as a base. In 1987 he received the Nobel Peace Prize as recognition of his Central American peace plan, agreed to by the other Central American states.

Costa Rica was beset with economic problems in the early 1990s when several politicians, including President Calderón, were accused of profiting from drug trafficking. Calderón was given a five-year prison sentence in 2009 after being convicted of corruption. In Feb. 2010 the country elected its first female president, Laura Chinchilla.

She served a single term before being succeeded by Luis Guillermo Solís in May 2014, who was in turn replaced by Carlos Alvarado Quesada in May 2018.

In Dec. 2015 the International Court of Justice ruled in Costa Rica's favour over a long-running territorial dispute with Nicaragua.

Territory and Population

Costa Rica is bounded in the north by Nicaragua, east by the Caribbean, southeast by Panama, and south and west by the Pacific. The area is estimated at 51,100 sq. km (19,730 sq. miles). The population at the census of May 2011 was 4,301,712 (2,195,649 females); density, 84·2 per sq. km. In 2011, 64·9% of the population were urban.

The UN gives a projected population for 2020 of 5·04m.

There are seven provinces (with 2011 census population): Alajuela (848,146); Cartago (490,903); Guanacaste (326,953); Heredia (433,677); Limón (386,862); Puntarenas (410,929); San José (1,404,242). The largest cities are San José (estimated population of 1,330,000 in 2011), Heredia, Cartago and Alajuela. Main ethnic groups (2011): White or Mestizo 84%, Mulatto 7%, Amerindian 2%, Black or Afro-Caribbean 1%.

Spanish is the official language.

Social Statistics

Statistics for calendar years:

	Marriages	Births	Deaths
2005	25,631	71,548	16,139
2006	26,575	71,291	16,766

(*continued*)

	Marriages	Births	Deaths
2007	26,010	73,144	17,071
2008	25,034	75,187	18,021

2008 rates per 1,000 population: births, 16·9; deaths, 4·0. Annual population growth rate, 2005–10, 1·6%. Life expectancy at birth, 2013, was 77·8 years for men and 82·2 years for women. Infant mortality, 2008, 9·0 per 1,000 live births; fertility rate, 2008, 2·0 children per woman.

Climate

The climate is tropical, with a small range of temperature and abundant rain. The dry season is from Dec. to April. San José, Jan. 66°F (18·9°C), July 69°F (20·6°C). Annual rainfall 72" (1,793 mm).

Constitution and Government

The Constitution was promulgated on 7 Nov. 1949. The legislative power is vested in a single-chamber *Legislative Assembly* of 57 deputies elected for four years. The *President* and two *Vice-Presidents* are elected for four years; the candidate receiving the largest vote, provided it is over 40% of the total, is declared elected, but a second ballot is required if no candidate gets 40% of the total. Since 2003 former presidents have been permitted to stand again. Elections are normally held on the first Sunday in Feb.

The President may appoint and remove members of the cabinet.

National Anthem

'Noble patria, tu hermosa bandera' ('Noble fatherland, thy beautiful banner'); words by J. M. Zeledón Brenes, tune by M. M. Gutiérrez.

Government Chronology

Presidents since 1944. (PAC = Citizens' Action Party; PLN = National Liberation Party; PRD = Party of the Democratic Renewal; PRN = National Republican Party; PUN = National Union Party; PUSC = Social Christian Unity Party)

1944–48	PRN	Teodoro Picado Michalski
1948–49	military	José María Figueres Ferrer
1949–53	PUN	Luis Otilio Ulate Blanco
1953–58	PLN	José María Figueres Ferrer
1958–62	PUN	Mario José Echandi Jiménez
1962–66	PLN	Francisco José Orlich Bolmarcich
1966–70	PUN	José Joaquín Trejos Fernández
1970–74	PLN	José María Figueres Ferrer
1974–78	PLN	Daniel Oduber Quirós
1978–82	PRD	Rodrigo José Carazo Odio
1982–86	PLN	Luis Alberto Monge Álvarez
1986–90	PLN	Óscar Rafael Arias Sánchez
1990–94	PUSC	Rafael Ángel Calderón Fournier
1994–98	PLN	José María Figueres Olsen
1998–2002	PUSC	Miguel Ángel Rodríguez Echeverría
2002–06	PUSC	Abel Pacheco de la Espriella
2006–10	PLN	Óscar Rafael Arias Sánchez
2010–14	PLN	Laura Chinchilla Miranda
2014–18	PAC	Luis Guillermo Solís
2018–	PAC	Carlos Alvarado Quesada

© Springer Nature Limited 2020
Palgrave Macmillan (ed.), *The Statesman's Yearbook 2020*,
https://doi.org/10.1057/978-1-349-95940-2_54

Recent Elections

In presidential elections held on 4 Feb. 2018 Fabricio Alvarado Muñoz of the National Restoration Party (PREN) won 25·0% of the vote, with Carlos Alvarado Quesada of the Citizens' Action Party (PAC) winning 21·6%, Antonio Álvarez of the National Liberation Party (PLN) 18·6%, Rodolfo Piza of the Social Christian Unity Party (PUSC) 16·0% and Juan Diego Castro of the National integration Party (PIN) 9·5%. There were eight other candidates. Turnout was 65·7%. Since neither Alvarado Muñoz nor Alvarado Quesada achieved the 40% required for an outright victory, a run-off between the two candidates took place on 1 April 2018. Alvarado Quesada won with 60·7% of the vote against Alvarado Muñoz with 39·3%. Turnout in the second round was 66·5%.

In parliamentary elections held on 4 Feb. 2018 the PLN won 17 of 57 seats, the PREN 14, the PAC 10, the PUSC 9, the PIN 4, the Social Christian Republican Party (PRS) 2 and the Broad Front (FA) 1.

Current Government

President: Carlos Alvarado Quesada; b. 1980 (PAC; sworn in 8 May 2018).
In Feb. 2019 the government comprised:
First Vice-President: Epsy Campbell Barr. *Second Vice-President:* Marvin Rodríguez Cordero.
Minister of Agriculture and Livestock: Renato Alvarado. *Communication:* Nancy Marín Espinoza. *Culture and Youth:* Sylvie Durán. *Economy, Industry and Trade:* Victoria Hernández. *Education:* Edgar Mora. *Environment:* Carlos Manuel Rodríguez. *Finance:* Rocío Aguilar. *Foreign and Religious Affairs:* Manuel Ventura Robles. *Foreign Trade:* Dyalá Jiménez. *Health:* Daniel Salas Peraza. *Housing and Human Settlements:* Irene Campos Gómez. *Justice and Peace:* Marcia González. *Labour and Social Security:* Steven Núñez. *National Planning and Economic Policy:* Pilar Garrido González. *Private Sector Co-ordination:* André Garnier Kruse. *Public Security:* Michael Soto. *Public Works and Transport:* Rodolfo Méndez Mata. *Science, Technology and Telecommunications:* Luis Adrián Salazar. *Sport and Recreation:* Hernán Solano. *Status of Women:* Patricia Mora Castellanos. *Tourism:* María Amalia Revelo. *Welfare and Social Investment:* Juan Luis Bermúdez. *Minister of the Presidency:* Rodolfo Piza.

Costa Rican Parliament (Spanish only): http://www.asamblea.go.cr

Current Leaders

Carlos Alvarado

Position
President

Introduction
Carlos Alvarado, a member of the Citizens' Action Party (PAC) who had previously held several ministerial posts, was elected president in April 2018.

Early Life
Born on 14 Jan. 1980 in San José, Alvarado graduated in communication and then took a master's degree in political science from the University of Costa Rica. In 2008 he was awarded a Chevening Scholarship from the British Council, which enabled him to gain a master's degree in development studies from the University of Sussex in the UK.

In 2004 Alvarado began worked as a press officer and two years later was put in charge of the office of Alberto Salom Echeverría, deputy of the PAC. In 2009 he was an adviser on the Ottón Solís Fallas presidential campaign. Then, after working for three years in Panama, he returned to Costa Rica to work as communications director on the successful 2014 presidential campaign of Luis Guillermo Solís.

In 2014 Alvarado served as executive chairman of the Joint Social Welfare Institute and as minister of human development and social inclusion, where he spearheaded the national strategy for poverty reduction. After the resignation of Victor Morales Mora, Alvarado was appointed minister of labour and social security in April 2016. In elections for the PAC's presidential nomination held on 9 July 2017, Alvarado defeated former minister of economics, Welmer Ramos, with 56% of the votes.

Campaigning for the presidency under the slogan of 'I choose the future', Alvarado announced his intention to lead a progressive government. In the first round of voting on 4 Feb. 2018, Alvarado won 22% of the vote against 25% for Fabricio Alvarado Muñoz of the conservative National Restoration Party. As no candidate reached the 40% threshold to claim victory, a run-off was held on 1 April 2018 with Alvarado taking 61% against 39% for his opponent.

Career in Office
Alvarado faces the challenge of reducing the national deficit and reversing a sharply rising murder rate. He is also a champion of same-sex marriage, having branded his presidential opponent homophobic for his rejection of a ruling made in Jan. 2018 by the Inter-American Human Rights Court that gay marriage should be recognized by all signatory nations of the American Convention on Human Rights. Costa Rica's Supreme Court subsequently ruled the ban on same-sex marriage unconstitutional in Aug. and ordered the Legislative Assembly to amend the law within 18 months.

Defence

In 2013 defence expenditure totalled US$397m. (US$84 per capita), representing 0·8% of GDP.

Army

The Army was abolished in 1948 and replaced by a Civil Guard numbering 4,500 in 2011. In addition there is a Border Security Police of 2,500 and a Rural Guard, 2,000-strong.

Navy

The paramilitary Coast Guard Unit numbered (2011) 400.

Air Wing

There is a 400-strong Air Surveillance Unit attached to the ministry of public security, equipped with ten light planes and two helicopters.

Economy

Agriculture accounted for 5·7% of GDP in 2014, industry 22·1% and services 72·2%.

Overview

Costa Rica is classified as an upper-middle income country by the World Bank. After suffering an economic crisis in the 1980s as a result of falling prices of key exports, including bananas, pineapples and coffee, it enjoyed a period of prolonged development. Growth was driven by a large-scale diversification strategy into manufacturing, increased exports, openness to foreign investment and gradual trade liberalization. Growth averaged 5% per year throughout the 1990s and early 2000s.

Tax-free trade zones were established to attract foreign companies, which were also drawn by the country's comparative political stability and its well-educated, English-speaking population. The USA remains Costa Rica's biggest trading partner—accounting for some 40% in 2016—followed by the European Union, China and Mexico.

Economic growth reached a peak of 8·8% in 2006, but that figure had declined to 1·0% in 2009 as a consequence of the global financial crisis. In response, the government increased spending on social and labour-intensive infrastructure, enabling domestic investment and higher private consumption. The economy recovered to an average growth rate of over 3·8% per year from 2010 to 2017. Nonetheless, the overall poverty rate of 20% reported in 2017 remains a challenge.

Currency

The unit of currency is the *Costa Rican colón* (CRC) of 100 *céntimos.* The official rate is used for all imports on an essential list and by the government and autonomous institutions, and a free rate is used for all other transactions. In July 2005 total money supply was 1,101·6bn. colones, foreign exchange reserves were US$2,215m. and gold reserves were 2,000 troy oz. There was zero inflation in 2016 and inflation of 1·6% in 2017.

Budget

In 2015 budgetary central government revenues were 4,181bn. colones (3,799bn. colones in 2014) and expenditures 6,176bn. colones (5,281bn. colones in 2014).

There is a sales tax of 13%.

Performance

Costa Rica is considered to be amongst the most stable countries in Central America. The economy grew by 3·6% in 2015, 4·2% in 2016 and 3·3% in 2017. Total GDP in 2017 was US$57·1bn.

Banking and Finance

The bank of issue is the Central Bank (founded 1950) which supervises the national monetary system, foreign exchange dealings and banking operations. The bank has a board of seven directors appointed by the government, including *ex officio* the Minister of Finance and the Planning Office Director. The *President* is Olivier Castro.

There are three state-owned banks (Banco de Costa Rica, Banco Nacional de Costa Rica and Banco Popular y de Desarrollo Comunal), 17 private banks and one credit co-operative.

External debt totalled US$8,849m. in 2010 and represented 26·8% of GNI.

There is a stock exchange in San José.

Energy and Natural Resources

Environment

Costa Rica's carbon dioxide emissions from the consumption of energy in 2011 were the equivalent of 1·5 tonnes per capita.

Electricity

Installed capacity was an estimated 2·9m. kW in 2011. Production was 9·83bn. kWh in 2011; consumption per capita in 2011 was 2,067 kWh.

Minerals

In 2007 production of gold was 1,036 kg; crushed rock and rough stone, 9,260,000 tonnes; diatomite, 1,712,000 tonnes.

Agriculture

There were 0·2m. ha. of arable land in 2014 and 0·3m. ha. of permanent crops. The principal agricultural products are coffee, bananas and sugar. Cattle are also of great importance. Production figures for 2013 (in 1,000 tonnes): sugarcane, 4,411; pineapples, 2,685; bananas, 2,175; palm fruit oil, 1,304; palm oil, 300; oranges, 280; rice, 225; melons and watermelons, 191; cassava, 145; plantains, 100.

Livestock (2013 estimates): cattle, 1·3m.; pigs, 448,000; horses, 126,000; chickens, 23m.

Forestry

In 2015 forests covered 2·76m. ha., or 54% of the land area. Timber production in 2011 was 4·53m. cu. metres.

Fisheries

Total catch in 2011 amounted to an estimated 20,500 tonnes, mostly from sea fishing.

Industry

The main manufactured goods are foodstuffs, palm oil, textiles, fertilizers, pharmaceuticals, furniture, cement, tyres, canning, clothing, plastic goods, plywood and electrical equipment.

Labour

In the third quarter of 2015 the economically active population numbered 2,273,300 of which 2,063,100 were employed. The main area of employment in the period July–Sept. 2015 was trade and repairs (373,600), followed by manufacturing (241,000) and agriculture, ranching and fisheries (239,800).

International Trade

A free trade agreement was signed with Mexico in March 1994. Some 2,300 products were freed from tariffs, with others to follow over ten years. In 2007 a national referendum approved the adoption of the Central America-Dominican Republic-United States Free Trade Agreement (CAFTA-DR), which establishes a free trade zone with the Dominican Republic, El Salvador, Guatemala, Honduras, Nicaragua and the USA. It was approved by the Legislative Assembly in Nov. 2008 and subsequently entered into force on 1 Jan. 2009.

Imports and Exports

Goods imports were US$18,124·5m. in 2013 (US$18,356·0m. in 2012) and goods exports US$11,472·1m. (US$11,250·8m. in 2012).

Principal imports in 2013 were machinery and transport equipment (36·0%), manufactured goods and chemicals; main exports in 2013 were food, animals and beverages (32·6%), machinery and transport equipment, and manufactured articles.

The leading import supplier in 2010 was the USA (46·8%), followed by China and Mexico; the leading export destination in 2010 was the USA (37·4%), followed by the Netherlands and Hong Kong.

Communications

Roads

In 2007 there were 36,654 km of roads, including 7,640 km of main roads. On the Costa Rica section of the Inter-American Highway it is possible to drive to Panama during the dry season. The Pan-American Highway into Nicaragua is metalled for most of the way and a new highway between San José and Caldera opened in Jan. 2010. Passenger cars in use in 2007 numbered 525,400, buses and coaches 12,300, vans and lorries 139,600 and motorcycles and mopeds 100,100. There were 339 fatalities as a result of road accidents in 2007.

Rail

The nationalized railway system (Incofer) was closed in 1995 as a result of insufficient finances to maintain it. However, freight services and some commuter services have resumed. In 2007 passenger-km totalled 872,000 and freight tonne-km 230,000.

Civil Aviation

There are international airports at San José (Juan Santamaria) and Liberia (Daniel Oduber Quirós). The national carrier is Líneas Aéreas Costarriquenses (LACSA). In 2012 scheduled airline traffic of Costa Rican-based carriers flew 23·2m. km; passenger-km totalled 4·9bn. in the same year. San José handled 3,217,400 passengers in 2012 (2,287,416 on international flights) and 80,157 tonnes of freight.

Shipping

The chief ports are Limón on the Atlantic and Caldera on the Pacific. In Jan. 2014 there were four ships of 300 GT or over registered, totalling 4,000 GT.

Telecommunications

In 2011 there were 1,490,600 landline telephone subscriptions (equivalent to 315·4 per 1,000 inhabitants) and 4,358,100 mobile phone subscriptions (or 922·0 per 1,000 inhabitants). There were 35·6 mobile broadband subscriptions per 100 inhabitants in 2013 and 13·0 fixed broadband subscriptions per 100 inhabitants. In Dec. 2011 there were 1·6m. Facebook users.

Social Institutions

Out of 178 countries analysed in the 2017 *Fragile States Index*—a list published jointly by the Fund for Peace and *Foreign Policy* magazine—Costa Rica was ranked the 34th least vulnerable to conflict or collapse. The index is based on 12 indicators of state vulnerability across social, political and economic categories.

Justice

Justice is administered by the Supreme Court and five appeal courts divided into five chambers—the Court of Cassation, the Higher and Lower Criminal Courts, and the Higher and Lower Civil Courts. There are also subordinate courts in the separate provinces and local justices throughout the republic. There is no capital punishment.

The population in penal institutions in July 2012 was 14,963 (314 per 100,000 of national population). Costa Rica was ranked 31st of 102 countries for criminal justice and 27th for civil justice in the 2015 World Justice Project *Rule of Law Index*, which provides data on how the rule of law is experienced by the general public across eight categories.

Education

The adult literacy rate in 2011 was estimated at 96·3% (96·0% among males and 96·5% among females). Primary instruction is compulsory and free from six to 14 years; secondary education (since 1949) is also free. Primary schools are provided and maintained by local school councils, while the national government pays the teachers, besides making subventions in aid of local funds. In 2006 there were 4,026 public and private primary schools with 35,413 teachers and administrative staff and 521,505 enrolled pupils, and 752 public and private secondary schools with 24,445 teachers and 338,508 pupils. In 2015 there were 217,841 students in tertiary education. The largest of the four public universities is the University of Costa Rica (Universidad de Costa Rica). There are also a number of private universities.

In 2006 public expenditure on education came to 4·9% of GNI, representing 20·6% of total government expenditure.

Health

In 2006 there were 6,987 doctors, 2,800 dentists, 6,943 nurses, 3,058 pharmacists and 29 hospitals. There were 14 beds per 10,000 inhabitants in 2006.

In *Water: At What Cost? The State of the World's Water 2016*, WaterAid reported that 2·2% of the population does not have access to safe water.

Religion

Roman Catholicism is the state religion; it had an estimated 3·11m. adherents in 2010 according to the Pew Research Center's Forum on Religion & Public Life. The Archbishop of Costa Rica has seven bishops at Alajuela, Cartago, Ciudad Quesada, Limón, Puntarenas, San Isidro de el General and Tilarán. The Pew Research Center estimated that there were also 1·06m. Protestants in 2010. The remainder of the population are religiously unaffiliated or followers of other religions.

Culture

World Heritage Sites

Costa Rica has four sites on the UNESCO World Heritage List: Cocos Island National Park (1997 and 2002); the Area de Conservación Guanacaste (1999 and 2004); and Precolumbian Chiefdom Settlements with Stone Spheres of the Diquís (2014), a property consisting of four archaeological sites that are considered unique examples of the social, political and economic systems of the period AD 500–1500.

Costa Rica shares a UNESCO site with Panama: the Talamanca Range-La Amistad Reserves (1983 and 1990), an important cross-breeding site for North and South American flora and fauna.

Press

There were six daily newspapers in 2011 with a combined circulation of 380,000, and 50 non-dailies. The most widely read daily is *La Teja* (which was only launched in 2006), followed by *La Nación* and *Diario Extra*.

Tourism

In 2012 there were 2,343,000 non-resident tourists (excluding same-day visitors), up from 2,192,000 in 2011.

Diplomatic Representatives

Of Costa Rica in the United Kingdom (23 Woodstock Street, London, W1C 2AS)
Ambassador: Rafael Ortiz Fábrega.

Of the United Kingdom in Costa Rica (Edificio Centro Colón, Paseo Colón and Streets 38 and 40, Apartado 815, San José 1007)
Ambassador: Ross Denny.

Of Costa Rica in the USA (2114 S St., NW, Washington, D.C., 20008)
Ambassador: Fernando Llorca Castro.

Of the USA in Costa Rica (Calle 98, Vía 104, Pavas, San José)
Ambassador: Sharon Day.

Of Costa Rica to the United Nations
Ambassador: Rodrigo Alberto Carazo Zeledón.

Of Costa Rica to the European Union
Ambassador: Vacant.
Chargé d'Affaires a.i.: Andrés Vargas Ramirez.

Further Reading

Creedman, T. S., *Historical Dictionary of Costa Rica.* 2nd ed. 1991
Cruz, Consuelo, *Political Culture and Institutional Development in Costa Rica and Nicaragua: World Making in the Tropics.* 2005
National Statistical Office: Instituto Nacional de Estadística y Censos, San José.
Website (Spanish only): http://www.inec.go.cr

Côte D'ivoire

République de la Côte d'Ivoire (Republic of Côte d'Ivoire)

Capital: Yamoussoukro
Seat of government: Abidjan
Population projection, 2020: 26·17m.
GNI per capita, 2017: (PPP$) 3, 481
HDI/world rank, 2017: 0·492/170
Internet domain extension: .ci

Key Historical Events

Evidence of Neolithic settlement has been found at Boundali in northern Côte d'Ivoire but the country's forested central and southern regions are believed to have been thinly populated. From the ninth century the northwest fell under the Ghana empire and prospered from Trans-Saharan trade. From the 13th to the 17th centuries the north came under the control of the Islamic Mali empire.

Malinké ethnic groups moved southwards during the 16th and 17th centuries, founding kingdoms including Kong and Kabadugu. The central and southern regions became associated with two ethnic groups, the Kru and the Akan, the latter principally emigrants fleeing the Ashanti empire (present-day Ghana) after 1720. Of the Akan groups, the Baoulé dominated the Ivorian centre. The Gyaman kingdom, centred on Bondoukou in the east, became famous for its Muslim scholars in the 18th and 19th centuries. Various Anyi kingdoms, notably the Sanwi, held sway in the southeast.

Lacking natural harbours, Côte d'Ivoire was neglected by European traders in the 15th and 16th centuries. The first French attempt to establish a missionary station in 1637 at Assinie was abandoned for almost a century but coastal settlements developed in the 18th century, although with less slave trading than elsewhere in West Africa. In 1842 the French Admiral Bouët-Willaumez signed treaties with local chiefs establishing a French protectorate, beginning with Assinie and Grand Bassam and extending along the coast over the next 25 years.

In the early 1870s the French unsuccessfully offered Côte d'Ivoire to the British in exchange for The Gambia, which bisected the French colony of Senegal. However, rumours of gold rekindled French interest in the region and expeditions were mounted to sign treaties with inland kingdoms and the trading centres of Kong and Bondoukou. In 1893 Côte d'Ivoire was declared a French colony, with the explorer Louis-Gustave Binger as governor. He negotiated boundary treaties with Liberia and with the UK's Gold Coast colony (now Ghana), as well as exiling the Malinké chief, Samory Touré, in 1898. In 1904 Côte d'Ivoire became part of the Federation of French West Africa. Governor Gabriel Angoulvant embarked on a full military conquest in 1908, brutally suppressing revolts by the Baoulé, Dan and Bété.

Sweeping reforms to the governance of French West Africa after the Second World War saw the establishment of Côte d'Ivoire's first political party, the Democratic Party of Côte d'Ivoire. Its leader, Félix Houphouët-Boigny, eventually adopted a policy of co-operation with the French and by the mid-1950s the country was the wealthiest in French West Africa. In 1958 it became an autonomous republic within the French Community and achieved full independence on 7 Aug. 1960, with Houphouët-Boigny as president. He developed ties with the West and oversaw economic development. Revenues from agriculture (principally coffee and cocoa, but also bananas, sugar, palm oil and rubber) were invested in infrastructure, education and industry.

Resentment against one-party rule grew from the late 1980s. Under Henri Konan Bédié, who became president after Houphouët-Boigny's death in 1993, Côte d'Ivoire faced economic challenges triggered by corruption and falling prices for cash crops. In Dec. 1999 Bédié was ousted in a coup led by Gen. Robert Guéï, the country's military chief from 1990 to 1995. After Guéï declared victory in the presidential election in Oct. 2000, 2,000 people died in an uprising and Guéï fled to Benin. The veteran opposition candidate, Laurent Gbagbo, was declared the rightful winner.

In Sept. 2002 a failed coup claimed over 20 lives, including those of Gen. Guéï and the interior minister. The country descended into civil war between the rebel-held north and the government-held south. In April 2005 government, rebel and opposition leaders signed a deal to end the war but promised elections were repeatedly postponed. Under a power-sharing peace deal agreed in March 2007 between the government and rebels from the New Forces movement, the latter's leader, Guillaume Soro, became prime minister. In Dec. 2010 the electoral commission declared Gbagbo had lost the presidency to Alassane Ouattara in a run-off held the previous month. Despite international pressure to leave office, Gbagbo ignored the ruling, leading to rising tensions as both candidates claimed power. Captured in April 2011, Gbagbo was handed over to the International Criminal Court (ICC). In the Dec. 2011 parliamentary elections, Ouattara and his allies secured a majority. In March 2015 Simone Gbagbo, wife of the former president, received a 20-year prison sentence from an Ivorian court for her role in the violence that followed the election of 2010. In Jan. 2016 the trial of her husband began at the ICC in The Hague. It was still in progress as of March 2018.

Territory and Population

Côte d'Ivoire is bounded in the west by Liberia and Guinea, north by Mali and Burkina Faso, east by Ghana, and south by the Gulf of Guinea. It has an area of 322,463 sq. km (including 4,460 sq. km of inland water). A census was held in 2014 for the first time in 16 years. The population was 22,671,331 (51·7% male), giving a density of 71·3 per sq. km. The population was 51·3% urban in 2011.

The UN gives a projected population for 2020 of 26·17m.

The country is administratively divided into 12 districts and the two autonomous districts of Abidjan and Yamoussoukro (with capitals): Abidjan (Abidjan), Bas-Sassandra (San-Pédro), Comoé (Abengourou), Denguélé (Odienné), Gôh-Djiboua (Gagnoa), Lacs (Dimbokro), Lagunes (Dabou), Montagnes (Man), Sassandra-Marahoué (Daloa), Savanes (Korhogo), Vallée du Bandama (Bouaké), Woroba (Séguéla), Yamoussoukro (Yamoussoukro), Zanzan (Bondoukou).

In 2014 the census population of Abidjan was 4,395,243. Other major towns are Bouaké, Daloa, Korhogo, San-Pédro and Yamoussoukro.

There are about 60 ethnic groups, the principal ones being the Baoulé (23%), the Bété (18%) and the Sénoufo (15%). A referendum held in July 2000 on the adoption of a new constitution set eligibility conditions for presidential candidates (the candidate and both his parents had to be Ivorian). This excluded a northern Muslim leader and in effect made foreigners out of millions of Ivorians. The north of the country is predominantly Muslim and the south predominantly Christian and animist.

Approximately 10% of the population are immigrants, in particular from Burkina Faso, Mali, Guinea and Senegal.

French is the official language.

Social Statistics

2008 estimates: births, 720,000; deaths, 223,000. Rates (2008 estimates, per 1,000 population); birth, 35·0; death, 10·8. Expectation of life in 2013 was 50·0 years for males and 51·6 for females. Annual population growth rate, 2000–08, 2·2%. Infant mortality, 2010, 86 per 1,000 live births; fertility rate, 2008, 4·6 births per woman. 29% of the population are migrants.

Climate

A tropical climate, affected by distance from the sea. In coastal areas, there are wet seasons from May to July and in Oct. and Nov., but in central areas the periods are March to May and July to Nov. In the north, there is one wet season from June to Oct. Abidjan, Jan. 81°F (27·2°C), July 75°F (23·9°C). Annual rainfall 84" (2,100 mm). Bouaké, Jan. 81°F (27·2°C), July 77°F (25°C). Annual rainfall 48" (1,200 mm).

Constitution and Government

A new constitution came into force on 8 Nov. 2016, replacing the previous one dating from 2000. There is a 255-member *National Assembly* elected by universal suffrage for a five-year term and provision for a *Senate*. The *President* is also directly elected for a five-year term (renewable). He appoints and leads a Council of Ministers.

The draft constitution was approved overwhelmingly by the National Assembly and in a national referendum in Oct. 2016. Changes included the removal of the condition that presidential candidates and both parents should be Ivorian and of the age limit of 75 for those seeking election. Other provisions allowed for the new post of vice-president, the creation of a partly-elected Senate as an arm of the legislature alongside the National Assembly, and the establishment of a new chamber for traditional chiefs.

National Anthem

'L'Abidjanaise' ('Song of Abidjan'); words by M. Ekra, J. Bony and P. M. Coty, tune by P. M. Pango.

Government Chronology

Presidents since 1960. (FPI = Ivorian Popular Front; PDCI-RDA = Democratic Party of Ivory Coast-African Democratic Rally; RDR = Rally of the Republicans)

1960–93	PDCI-RDA	Félix Houphouët-Boigny
1993–99	PDCI-RDA	Aimé Henri Konan Bédié
1999–2000	military	Robert Guéï
2000–11	FPI	Laurent Gbagbo
2010–	RDR	Alassane Ouattara

Recent Elections

In presidential elections on 25 Oct. 2015 Alassane Ouattara was re-elected with 83·7% of the vote against Pascal Affi N'Guessan with 9·3% and Konan Bertin Kouadio with 3·9%. Seven other candidates took less than 1% of the vote each and turnout was 54·6%. Compared to previous elections, campaigning and voting was relatively peaceful despite a boycott by the main opposition party, the Ivorian Popular Front.

In parliamentary elections held on 18 Dec. 2016 the Rally of Houphouëtists for Democracy and Peace (including the Rally of the Republicans/RDR of President Ouattara) won 167 of 255 seats. Independents took 76 seats, the Union for Democracy and Peace in Côte d'Ivoire 6, the Ivorian Popular Front 3 and the Union for Côte d'Ivoire 3. Turnout was 34·1%.

Current Government

President and Minister of Defence: Alassane Dramane Ouattara; b. 1942 (RDR; assumed office 4 Dec. 2010, although former incumbent Laurent Gbagbo refused to surrender the office before being captured by Ouattara's forces on 11 April 2011).

Vice-President: Daniel Kablan Duncan.

In Feb. 2019 the government comprised:

Prime Minister, and Minister of Budget and State Assets: Amadou Gon Coulibaly; b. 1959 (RDR; took office on 10 Jan. 2017).

Minister of State, and Minister of Defence: Hamed Bakayoko.

Minister of African Integration and Ivorians Abroad: Ally Coulibaly. *Agriculture and Rural Development:* Mamadou Sangafowa Coulibaly. *Animal Resources and Fisheries:* Kobenan Kouassi Adjoumani. *Cities:* François Albert Amichia. *Civil Service:* Issa Coulibaly. *Commerce, Industry and the Promotion of Small and Medium-Sized Enterprises:* Souleymane Diarrassouba. *Communication and the Media, and Spokesperson of the Government:* Sidi Tiémoko Touré. *Construction, Housing, and Urban Affairs:* Bruno Nabagné Koné. *Culture and Francophonie:* Maurice Bandaman. *Digital Economy and Posts:* Claude Isaac Dé. *Economy and Finance:* Adama Koné. *Employment and Social Protection:* Pascal Abinan Kouakou. *Environment and Sustainable Development:* Joseph Seka Seka. *Foreign Affairs:* Marcel Amon Tanoh. *Handicrafts:* Sidiki Konaté. *Health and Public Hygiene:* Aouélé Eugène Aka. *Higher Education and Scientific Research:* Albert Toikeusse Mabri. *Mines and Geology:* Jean-Claude Kouassi. *Infrastructure and Road Maintenance:* Amedé Koffi Kouakou.

Interior and Security: Sidiki Diakité. *Justice, Human Rights and Keeper of the Seals:* Sansan Kambilé. *Modernization of Public Administration and Public Service Sector:* Raymonde Goudou-Coffie. *National Education, Technical Education and Vocational Training:* Kandia Kamissoko Camara. *Petroleum, Energy and Renewable Energy:* Thierry Tanoh. *Planning and Development:* Nialé Kaba. *Promotion of Youth and Youth Employment:* Mamadou Touré. *Sanitation and Hygiene:* Anne Désirée Ouloto. *Solidarity, Social Cohesion and Poverty Alleviation:* Mariatou Koné. *Sport:* Paulin Danho. *Tourism and Recreation:* Siandou Fofana. *Transport:* Amadou Koné. *Water Resources:* Laurent Tchagba. *Waters and Forests:* Alain Richard Donwahi. *Women, Family and Children:* Ramata Ly-Bakayoko.

Government Website (French only): http://www.gouv.ci

Current Leaders

Alassane Ouattara

Position
President

Introduction
Alassane Ouattara was elected president in Nov. 2010 but was initially prevented from taking office when the incumbent, Laurent Gbagbo, disputed the result. An economist who formerly worked for the IMF, Ouattara draws his support largely from the Muslim north of the country. He spent the early months of his term under UN guard as conflict waged between his supporters and those of Gbagbo before the former president's capture in April 2011. He was re-elected president in Oct. 2015.

Early Life
Alassane Ouattara was born on 1 Jan. 1942 in Dimbokro to a family with links to Burkina Faso. After graduating in business administration from the Drexel Institute of Technology in the USA, he gained an MA in 1967 and a PhD in economics in 1972, both from the University of Pennsylvania. He worked as an economist at the IMF from 1968–73, before moving to the Paris office of the Central Bank of West African States (BCEAO), becoming vice governor in 1983. From 1984–88 he was director of the African department at the IMF and served as counsellor to the managing director from 1987–88. From 1988–93 he was governor of the BCEAO.

In April 1990 Côte d'Ivoire's president, Félix Houphouët-Boigny, appointed Ouattara chairman of an inter-ministerial committee responsible for the national economic recovery programme. From Nov. 1990–Dec. 1993 he served as prime minister, acting as president for the last nine months of that period when Houphouët-Boigny fell ill. Ouattara then returned to the IMF as deputy managing director until 1999. In July 1995 he was nominated by the opposition Rally of the Republics (RDR) as its presidential candidate but was banned from standing by Gbagbo on the grounds that one of his parents was a foreign national.

In 2000, after becoming leader of the RDR, he was again banned on nationality grounds from contesting the presidency, leading to increased tensions between the Muslim north and predominantly Christian south that helped to precipitate the 2002 civil war. Ouattara finally became the RDR's presidential candidate in 2008, promising to rebuild the country and unite its people. He emerged victorious in the UN-supervised presidential election of Nov. 2010. However, Gbagbo disputed the result and refused to leave office; on 4 Dec., Gbagbo and Ouattara took rival presidential oaths.

Career in Office
The international community refused to recognize Gbagbo's presidency and on 8 Dec. 2010 the UN Security Council declared Ouattara the winner. He was also endorsed by the USA, European Union, African Union and ECOWAS. Gbagbo nonetheless remained in power, with escalating violence between the RDR and Gbagbo's supporters resulting in tens of thousands of civilians fleeing to neighbouring Liberia. By March 2011 Ouattara's forces had gained supremacy in much of the country and on 11 April captured Gbagbo and his inner circle after surrounding the presidential compound in Abidjan. Ouattara was inaugurated in May, and in Sept. a truth and reconciliation commission was set up with the aim of restoring national unity in the wake of the post-election violence.

In parliamentary elections in Dec. 2011 Ouattara's RDR and its Democratic Party ally won an overwhelming majority of seats in the National Assembly. Supporters of Gbagbo boycotted the poll and were implicated in June 2012 in an alleged anti-government plot. Ouattara subsequently dissolved the government led by Jeannot Ahoussou-Kouadio in Nov. that year over a controversial proposed change to marriage legislation and appointed foreign minister Daniel Kablan Duncan as prime minister of a new administration. Ouattara was re-elected president for a second five-year term in Oct. 2015, winning by a landslide against nine other candidates, and in Jan. 2016 Duncan was reappointed at the head of a largely unchanged government.

In June 2016 Ouattara established a review panel to draw up a new constitution, and the draft was approved comprehensively by the National Assembly and in a national referendum in Oct. that year. There were significant changes regarding the eligibility criteria for presidential candidates, as well as the creation of a bicameral legislature and the new post of vice-president, to which former prime minister Duncan was appointed in Jan. 2017 following parliamentary elections the previous month. The retention of a ban on presidential third terms of office meant that Ouattara could not stand for re-election again.

The apparent restoration of stability and security across the country following its turbulent past was disturbed by an assault in March 2016 by suspected Islamist extremists on a tourist resort near Abidjan and in Jan. 2017 when soldiers mutinied over pay and conditions and briefly took control of Bouaké, the second largest city. A further mutiny four months later prompted gun battles in Bouaké and Abidjan before a settlement was agreed with the government.

Defence

In Oct. 2011 President Alassane Ouattara announced the formation of the Forces Armées Nationale de Côte d'Ivoire, which aims to merge 29,000 veterans of the former regular army with 9,000 former rebels plus 2,000 volunteers.

Defence expenditure totalled US$751m. in 2013 (US$34 per capita), representing 2·7% of GDP.

Economy

In 2011 agriculture contributed 29·1% to GDP; followed by finance and real estate, 13·2%; trade and restaurants, 13·2%; manufacturing, 11·9%; public administration and defence, 8·3%.

Côte d'Ivoire's 'shadow' (black market) economy is estimated to constitute approximately 47% of the country's official GDP.

Overview

Côte d'Ivoire experienced a burst of economic expansion, known as the Ivorian Miracle and characterized by rapid developments in agriculture, following independence from France in 1960. However, it has seen little growth since the turn of the century against a backdrop of political insecurity.

The civil war that began in 2002 restricted growth rates at around 1% per year for most of that decade. The economy began to recover in 2008, spurred by a power-sharing peace accord in 2007 that reunified the country and a boom in the oil industry. However, the political crisis following disputed elections in 2010 led to another economic slowdown (as well as the destruction of much of the country's social infrastructure) and also had a negative impact on the West African Economic and Monetary Union (UEMOA), in which Côte d'Ivoire has the leading economy.

Nonetheless, there was a strong recovery from 2011, reinforced in June 2012 when the IMF and World Bank announced more than US$4bn. in debt relief. Annual growth averaging 9·1% in the period 2012–14 and buoyant exports, accounting for almost half of GDP, outstripped the economic performance of all other UEMOA member states. The economy then grew at an average annual rate of 8·2% between 2015 and 2017.

Key exports include cocoa, of which the country is the largest producer in the world, accounting for 30% of world supply. Coffee, petroleum, cashew nuts, and palm oil are also major export commodities. In 2015 the United Nations lifted a ban on diamond trading from the country.

Côte d'Ivoire has adopted a National Development Plan for the period 2016–20 with the goals of achieving middle-income economy status and reducing the poverty rate (which had come down to 46% by 2017). Donors have pledged $15·4bn. in a mixture of grants and loans to support the plan.

The World Bank has identified price volatility in agricultural and mining products, climate conditions, and security risks as the most critical challenges to the economy in the future.

Currency

The unit of currency is the *franc CFA* (XOF) with a parity of 655·957 francs CFA to one euro. Foreign exchange reserves were US$1,379m. in June 2005 and total money supply was 1,225·0bn. francs CFA. Inflation was 0·7% in 2016 and 0·8% in 2017.

Budget

Revenues in 2011 were 1,726bn. francs CFA (tax revenue, 86·5%) and expenditures 2,209bn. francs CFA (current expenditure, 87·1%).

VAT is 18%.

Performance

Real GDP contracted by 4·2% in 2011 as a consequence of the political crisis that paralysed the country for the early part of the year. However, there has since been a strong recovery with the economy growing in 2015 by 8·8%, in 2016 by 8·3% and in 2017 by 7·8%. Total GDP in 2017 was US$40·4bn.

Banking and Finance

The regional Banque Centrale des Etats de l'Afrique de l'Ouest is the central bank and bank of issue. The *Governor* is Tiémoko Meyliet Koné. In 2013 there were 24 banks. The African Development Bank is based in Abidjan, as is the stock exchange of Francophone West African countries—the *Bourse Régionale des Valeurs Mobilières* ('BRVM').

External debt amounted to US$11,430m. in 2010 (equivalent to 52·6% of GNI), down from US$12,138m. in 2000.

Energy and Natural Resources

Environment

Carbon dioxide emissions from the consumption of energy in 2011 were the equivalent of 0·3 tonnes per capita.

Electricity

Installed capacity was an estimated 1·6m. kW in 2011. Production in 2011 amounted to 6·10bn. kWh, with consumption per capita 283 kWh.

Oil and Gas

Petroleum has been produced (offshore) since 1977. Production (2011), 12m. bbls. Oil reserves in 2011 totalled 100m. bbls. Natural gas reserves, 2013, 28bn. cu. metres; production (2011), 1,559m. cu. metres.

Minerals

Côte d'Ivoire has large deposits of iron ores, bauxite, tantalite, diamonds, gold, nickel and manganese, most of which are untapped. Gold production totalled 6·9 tonnes in 2009. Estimated diamond production, 2008: 300,000 carats.

Agriculture

The agricultural area totalled an estimated 20·6m. ha. in 2013. 14·2% of agricultural land was arable in 2011, and 21·5% of agricultural land comprised permanent crops. 0·4% of agricultural land was equipped for irrigation in 2011. Côte d'Ivoire is the world's largest producer and exporter of cocoa beans, with an output of 1·45m. tonnes in 2013 (more than 31% of the world total). The cocoa industry has for years relied on foreign workers, but tens of thousands have left the country since the 1999 coup resulting in labour shortages. Other main crops, with 2013 production figures in 1,000 tonnes, are: yams (5,731), cassava (2,436), sugarcane (1,969), rice (1,934), palm fruit oil (1,744), plantains (1,624), maize (661).

Livestock, 2013: 1·73m. sheep, 1·59m. cattle, 1·38m. goats, 363,000 pigs and 58m. chickens.

Forestry

In 2015 forests covered 10·40m. ha., or 33% of the total land area. Of the total area under forests 6% was primary forest in 2015, 90% other naturally regenerated forest and 4% planted forest. Products include teak, mahogany and ebony. In 2011, 10·46m. cu. metres of roundwood were produced.

Fisheries

The total catch in 2014 amounted to 75,203 tonnes, of which 66,964 tonnes came from sea fishing and 8,239 tonnes from inland fishing.

Industry

Industrialization has developed rapidly since independence, particularly food processing, textiles and sawmills. Output in 2007 (in 1,000 tonnes): distillate fuel oil, 1,089; kerosene, 933; petrol, 564; residual fuel oil, 500; cement (2008 estimate), 360; sawnwood (2010), 456,000 cu. metres; veneer sheets (2008), 396,000 cu. metres.

Labour

The labour force in 2013 was 8,298,000 (6,551,000 in 2003). 67·9% of the population aged 15–64 was economically active in 2013. In the same year 4·1% of the population was unemployed. Côte d'Ivoire had 0·16m. people living in slavery according to the Walk Free Foundation's 2013 *Global Slavery Index*.

International Trade

Imports and Exports

Goods imports were US$12,483·0m. in 2013 (US$9,769·7m. in 2012) and goods exports US$12,083·8m. (US$10,861·0m. in 2012).

Principal imports in 2013 were machinery and transport equipment (36·9%), mineral fuels and lubricants, and food, animals and beverages; main exports in 2013 were food, animals and beverages (34·7%), mineral fuels and lubricants, and machinery and transport equipment.

The leading import suppliers in 2010 were Nigeria (26·3%), France and China; the leading export destinations in 2010 were the Netherlands (14·2%), the USA and Ghana.

Communications

Roads

In 2007 there were 81,996 km of roads, including 142 km of motorways. There were 314,165 passenger cars, 78,575 vans and trucks, 38,105 motorcycles and mopeds and 17,512 buses and coaches in use in 2007.

Rail

From Abidjan a metre gauge railway runs to Ouangolodougou near the border with Burkina Faso (660 km), and thence through Burkina Faso to Ouagadougou and Kaya. Operation of the railway in both countries is franchised to the mixed public-private company Sitarail.

Civil Aviation

There is an international airport at Abidjan (Félix Houphouët-Boigny Airport), which in 2012 handled 961,643 passengers (842,927 on international flights) and 16,755 tonnes of freight. The national carrier is Air Côte d'Ivoire, which in 2015 operated domestic services and flew to 19 other African countries. It was founded in 2012 after its predecessor Air Ivoire went bankrupt.

Shipping

The main port is Abidjan, which handled 21·5m. tonnes of foreign cargo in 2013. In Jan. 2014 there were two ships of 300 GT or over registered, totalling 1,000 GT.

Telecommunications

There were 223,200 fixed telephone lines in 2010 (11 per 1,000 inhabitants). Mobile phone subscribers numbered 14·91m. in 2010. In 2011 an estimated 2% of the population were internet users.

Social Institutions

Out of 178 countries analysed in the 2017 *Fragile States Index*—a list published jointly by the Fund for Peace and *Foreign Policy* magazine— Côte d'Ivoire was ranked the 21st most vulnerable to conflict or collapse. The index is based on 12 indicators of state vulnerability across social, political and economic categories.

Justice

There are 28 courts of first instance and three assize courts in Abidjan, Bouaké and Daloa, two courts of appeal in Abidjan and Bouaké, and a supreme court in Abidjan. Côte d'Ivoire abolished the death penalty in 2000.

The population in penal institutions was 7,086 (34 per 100,000 of national population) in Dec. 2012. In 2015 the World Justice Project *Rule of Law Index*, which provides data on how the rule of law is experienced by the general public across eight categories, ranked Côte d'Ivoire 64th of 102 countries for criminal justice and 43rd for civil justice.

Education

The adult literacy rate in 2009 was estimated at 55·3% (64·7% among males and 45·3% among females). In 2014 there were 3,176,874 pupils with 74,703 teachers in primary schools and 1,418,361 pupils with 63,602 teachers at secondary schools. In the same year there were 176,504 students in higher education. There were five state universities in 2013, the oldest and largest of which is the Université Félix Houphouët-Boigny in Abidjan, plus a number of private universities.

In 2008 expenditure on education came to 4·6% of GDP and 24·6% of total government spending.

Health

In 2006 there were four hospital beds per 10,000 inhabitants. In 2008 there were 2,746 physicians, 9,231 nursing and midwifery personnel, 274 dentistry personnel and 413 pharmaceutical personnel.

In *Water: At What Cost? The State of the World's Water 2016*, WaterAid reported that 18·1% of the population does not have access to safe water.

Religion

According to the Pew Research Center's Forum on Religion & Public Life, in 2010 the population was an estimated 44·1% Christian and 37·5% Muslim, with 10·2% folk religionists and 8·0% religiously unaffiliated. Around 51% of the Christians are Protestants and 48% Catholics. In Feb. 2019 there was one Roman Catholic cardinal.

Culture

World Heritage Sites

UNESCO world heritage sites in Côte d'Ivoire are: Taï National Park (inscribed on the list in 1982); the Comoé National Park (1983); the Mount Nimba Strict Nature Reserve (1981 and 1982), shared with Guinea; and the Historic Town of Grand-Bassam (2012).

Press

In 2008 there were 23 paid-for daily newspapers with an estimated combined circulation of 200,000.

Tourism

There were 380,000 non-resident visitors in 2013; spending by tourists in 2013 (excluding passenger transport) totalled US$191m.

Diplomatic Representatives

Of Côte d'Ivoire in the United Kingdom (2 Upper Belgrave St., London, SW1X 8BJ)
Ambassador: Georges Aboua.

Of the United Kingdom in Côte d'Ivoire (Cocody, Quartier Ambassades, Impasse du Belier, Rue A58, 01 BP 2581, Abidjan 01)
Ambassador: Josephine Gauld.

Of Côte d'Ivoire in the USA (2424 Massachusetts Ave., NW, Washington, D.C., 20008)
Ambassador: Mamadou Haidara.

Of the USA in Côte d'Ivoire (Riviera Golf, 01 B.P. 1712, Abidjan 01)
Ambassador: Vacant.
Chargé d'Affaires a.i.: Katherine Brucker.

Of Côte d'Ivoire to the United Nations
Ambassador: Kacou Houadja Léon Adom.

Of Côte d'Ivoire to the European Union
Ambassador: Abou Dosso.

Further Reading

Direction de la Statistique. *Bulletin Mensuel de Statistique.*
Hellweg, Joseph, *Hunting the Ethical State: The Benkadi Movement of Côte d'Ivoire.* 2011

McGovern, Mike, *Making War in Côte d'Ivoire.* 2006
Mundt, Robert J., *Historical Dictionary of Côte d'Ivoire.* 1995
National Statistical Office: Institut National de la Statistique, BP V 55, Abidjan 01.
Website (limited English): http://www.ins.ci/n

Croatia

Republika Hrvatska (Republic of Croatia)

Capital: Zagreb
Population projection, 2020: 4·12m.
GNI per capita, 2017: (PPP$) 22,162
HDI/world rank, 2017: 0·831/46
Internet domain extension: .hr

Key Historical Events

Several Neolithic cultures existed in Croatia, with Vucedol, on the Danube near present-day Vukovar, one of Europe's most important settlements between 3,000 and 2,200 BC. Illyrians settled in the region from 800 BC, establishing several kingdoms that the Romans absorbed into the provinces of Pannonia and Dalmatia from 10 AD.

Croats, a Slavic tribe thought to have originated in Ukraine and the north Caucasus, reached the Adriatic coast around 600 AD. Christianity established itself during the pontificate of Pope Agaton (678–681) and by the ninth century the region was a Frankish vassal state. Kresimir IV unified the territories of Dalmatia, Bosnia and Croatia after 1058. Invasion by King Ladislav of Hungary in 1091 led to an eight-century union with Hungary from 1102. Venetian forces, meanwhile, attacked Zadar in 1116, seizing control of the Adriatic coast as far as Dubrovnik until the end of the 18th century.

Following the battle of Mohacs in 1526, most of Croatia came under Ottoman rule but the following year the Croatian parliament (Sabor) elected Ferdinand of Habsburg as ruler in return for defence commitments. Hungary imposed Magyarization in the nineteenth century, with legislation of 1848 undermining Croatian autonomy within the Habsburg empire. Ljudevit Gaj (1809–72) spurred a Croatian nationalist awakening and in 1848–49 Josip Jelačić led an uprising against the Habsburgs. Nonetheless, when the Austro-Hungarian monarchy was established in 1867, Croatia and Slavonia were included in the Kingdom of Hungary.

Following the First World War and the collapse of the Habsburg dynasty, the Kingdom of Serbs, Croats and Slovenes was formed, initially ruled by the authoritarian Serbian king, Alexander Karađorđević. In 1928 Stjepan Radić, the founder and leader of the Croatian Peoples Peasant Party (HPSS) and a fierce critic of the king, was assassinated in Belgrade. In the aftermath, Alexander abolished the constitution but was himself assassinated in 1934.

During the Second World War an independent fascist (Ustaša) state was set up in Croatia under the aegis of the German occupiers, led by Ante Pavelić. A wave of expulsions and attacks on Serbs, Jews and Roma saw hundreds of thousands killed. However, the communist and multi-ethnic Yugoslav Partisan movement, led by Josip Tito, gained momentum and, with Soviet military assistance, had control of Yugoslavia by May 1945. Croatia became one of the country's six constituent 'Socialist Republics'.

Another national awakening—the Croatian Spring—occurred in the late 1960s, with demands for economic reform escalating into mass demonstrations. Tito responded with a crackdown, dismissing progressives within the Communist Party, imprisoning intellectuals, and banning nationalist writings and cultural institutions. Nationalist sentiment rose again after Tito's death in 1981, compounded by Yugoslavia's economic woes.

On 19 May 1991 a referendum returned 94% support for an independent sovereign Croatian state. The self-proclaimed Serb Republic of Krajina (situated within Croatia) was also declared that year. Conflict broke out between Croatian troops and Serb insurgents backed by federal forces until the arrival of a UN peacekeeping mission in early 1992. Franjo Tuđman was subsequently elected president of independent Croatia.

The new state became embroiled in the war in Bosnia and Herzegovina, supporting the Bosnian Croats first against the Bosnian Serbs and then against the Bosniaks (Muslims). In May 1995 Croatian forces retook the breakaway Serb region of Western Slavonia and on 4 Aug. 1995 the Serb Republic of Krajina was occupied, provoking an exodus of 180,000 Serb refugees. The war ended that year with the signing of the Dayton peace accords.

Stjepan Mesić, elected president in Feb. 2000 after Tuđman's death, campaigned for membership of NATO and the European Union. EU accession talks began in March 2005 but, owing to concerns about corruption, organized crime and a border dispute with Slovenia, were not completed until June 2011. Croatia joined the EU on 1 July 2013.

Territory and Population

Croatia is bounded in the north by Slovenia and Hungary, in the east by Serbia and Bosnia and Herzegovina and in the southeast by Montenegro. It includes the areas of Dalmatia, Istria and Slavonia, which no longer have administrative status. Its area is 56,542 sq. km. 2011 census population, 4,284,889; population density, 75·8 per sq. km. In Dec. 2015 the population was estimated at 4,190,669.

The UN gives a projected population for 2020 of 4·12m.

In 2011, 58·0% of the population lived in urban areas.

The area, 2011 census population and capital of the 20 counties and one city:

County	Area (sq. km)	Population	Capital
Bjelovarska-Bilogorska	2,638	119,764	Bjelovar
Brodsko-Posavska	2,027	158,575	Slavonski Brod
Dubrovačko-Neretvanska	1,782	122,568	Dubrovnik
Istarska	2,813	208,055	Pazin
Karlovačka	3,622	128,899	Karlovac
Koprivničko-Križevačka	1,734	115,584	Koprivnica
Krapinsko-Zagorska	1,230	132,892	Krapina
Ličko-Senjska	5,350	50,927	Gospić
Međimurska	730	113,804	Čakovec
Osječko-Baranjska	4,149	305,032	Osijek
Požeško-Slavonska	1,821	78,034	Požega
Primorsko-Goranska	3,590	296,195	Rijeka
Šibensko-Kninska	2,994	109,375	Šibenik
Sisačko-Moslavačka	4,448	172,439	Sisak
Splitsko-Dalmatinska	4,524	454,798	Split
Varaždinska	1,260	175,951	Varaždin
Virovitičko-Podravska	2,021	84,836	Virovitica
Vukovarsko-Srijemska	2,448	179,521	Vukovar
Zadarska	3,643	170,017	Zadar
Zagrebačka	3,078	317,606	Zagreb
Zagreb (city)	640	790,017	Zagreb

Zagreb, the capital, had a 2011 population of 688,163. Other major towns (with 2011 census population): Split (167,121), Rijeka (128,384) and Osijek (84,104).

The official language is Croatian.

Social Statistics

2012: births, 41,771 (9·8 per 1,000 population); deaths, 51,710 (12·1). 2011: marriages, 20,211 (4·6); divorces, 5,662 (1·3); suicides (2012), 776 (11·9 per 100,000). Infant mortality, 2010, five per 1,000 live births. Annual population growth rate, 2005–10, –0·2%. In 2010 the most popular age range for marrying was 25–29 for both males and females. Life expectancy at birth, 2011, was 73·8 years for males and 79·9 years for females. Fertility rate, 2013, 1·5 children per woman.

© Springer Nature Limited 2020
Palgrave Macmillan (ed.), *The Statesman's Yearbook 2020*,
https://doi.org/10.1057/978-1-349-95940-2_56

Climate

Inland Croatia has a central European type of climate, with cold winters and hot summers, but the Adriatic coastal region experiences a Mediterranean climate with mild, moist winters and hot, brilliantly sunny summers with less than average rainfall. Average annual temperature and rainfall: Dubrovnik, 16·6°C and 1,051 mm. Zadar, 15·6°C and 963 mm. Rijeka, 14·3°C and 1,809 mm. Zagreb, 12·4°C and 1,000 mm. Osijek, 11·3°C and 683 mm.

Constitution and Government

A new constitution was adopted on 22 Dec. 1990 and was revised in both 2000 and 2001. The *President* is elected for renewable five-year terms. There is a unicameral Parliament (*Hrvatski Sabor*), consisting of 151 deputies; 140 members are elected from multi-seat constituencies for a four-year term, eight seats are reserved for national minorities and three members representing Croatians abroad are chosen by proportional representation.

National Anthem

'Lijepa nasva domovino' ('Beautiful our homeland'); words by A. Mihanović, tune by J. Runjanin.

Government Chronology

(HDZ = Croatian Democratic Union; SDP = Social Democratic Party of Croatia; n/p = non-partisan)

Presidents since 1990.

1990–99	HDZ	Franjo Tuđman
2000–10	n/p	Stjepan (Stipe) Mesić
2010–15	SDP	Ivo Josipović
2015–	HDZ	Kolinda Grabar-Kitarović

Prime Ministers since 1990.

1990	HDZ	Stjepan (Stipe) Mesić
1990–91	HDZ	Josip Manolić
1991–92	HDZ	Franjo Gregurić
1992–93	HDZ	Hrvoje Šarinić
1993–95	HDZ	Nikica Valentić
1995–2000	HDZ	Zlatko Mateša
2000–03	SDP	Ivica Račan
2003–09	HDZ	Ivo Sanader
2009–11	HDZ	Jadranka Kosor
2011–16	SDP	Zoran Milanović
2016	n/p	Tihomir Orešković
2016–	HDZ	Andrej Plenković

Recent Elections

Presidential elections were held on 28 Dec. 2014. Incumbent president Ivo Josipović (ind.) received 38·5% of the vote, Kolinda Grabar-Kitarović (Croatian Democratic Union/HDZ) 37·2%, Ivan Vilibor Sinčić (Human Wall/Živi zid) 16·4% and Milan Kujundžić (Alliance for Croatia) 6·3%. Turnout was 47·1%. As no candidate received more than 50% of the vote a second round took place on 11 Jan. 2015, which Kolinda Grabar-Kitarović won with 50·7% of votes against Ivo Josipović with 49·3%. Turnout was 59·1%.

Parliamentary elections were held on 11 Sept. 2016. A coalition led by the HDZ won 61 seats (36·3% of the vote in the domestic electoral districts), the People's Coalition led by the Social Democratic Party of Croatia (SDP) 54 (33·8%), independent candidates running under the 'Bridge of Independent Lists' platform 13 (9·9%) and the Only Option Coalition 8 (6·2%). Four smaller parties and coalitions won three seats or fewer. Domestic turnout was 54·4%. In the national minority electoral district the Independent Democratic Serb Party won three seats and other national minority representatives five.

European Parliament

Croatia has 11 representatives. At the May 2014 elections turnout was 25·2%. The Croatian Democratic Union (HDZ) and its allies won 6 seats with 41·4% of votes cast, of which the HDZ itself won 4 (political affiliation in European Parliament: five for the European People's Party and one for European Conservatives and Reformists); the SDP and its allies 4 with 29·9%, of which the SDP itself won 3 (three for Progressive Alliance of Socialists and Democrats and one for Alliance of Liberals and Democrats for Europe); Croatian Sustainable Development, 1 with 9·4% (Greens/European Free Alliance).

Current Government

President: Kolinda Grabar-Kitarović; b. 1968 (HDZ; sworn in 15 Feb. 2015).
    In Feb. 2019 the government comprised:
    Prime Minister: Andrej Plenković; b. 1970 (HDZ; sworn in 19 Oct. 2016).
    Deputy Prime Ministers: Marija Pejčinović Burić (also *Minister of Foreign and European Affairs*); Damir Krstičević (also *Minister of Defence*); Predrag Štromar (also *Minister of Construction and Physical Planning*); Tomislav Tolušic (also *Minister of Agriculture*).
    Minister of Demography, Family, Youth and Social Policy: Nada Murganić. *Economy, Entrepreneurship and Crafts:* Darko Horvat. *Environmental Protection and Energy:* Tomislav Ćorić. *Finance:* Zdravko Marić. *Government Affairs:* Goran Marić. *Health:* Milan Kujundžić. *Interior:* Davor Božinović. *Justice:* Dražen Bošnjaković. *Labour and the Pension System:* Marko Pavić. *Maritime Affairs, Transport and Infrastructure:* Oleg Butković. *Public Administration:* Lovro Kuščević. *Regional Development and EU Funds:* Gabrijela Žalac. *Science and Education:* Blaženka Divjak. *Tourism:* Gari Cappelli. *Veterans' Affairs:* Tomo Medved.
    Government Website: http://www.vlada.hr

Current Leaders

Kolinda Grabar-Kitarović
Position
President

Introduction
Kolinda Grabar-Kitarović became Croatia's fourth president since gaining independence in Feb. 2015. A former foreign minister, she promised to bolster the economy and increase the country's international profile.

Early Life
Kolinda Grabar-Kitarović was born on 29 April 1968 in Rijeka. Educated mainly in Croatia, she also spent some time in high school in New Mexico, USA as an exchange student. She graduated in English and Spanish from the University of Zagreb in 1992.

From 1992–93 she worked as adviser to the international co-operation department of the ministry of science and technology, and in 1993 she joined the conservative Croatian Democratic Union (HDZ). From 1993–95 she was an adviser in the foreign ministry and served as director of its North American department from 1995–97. She also undertook diplomatic training from 1995–96 and from 1997–2000 was diplomatic counsellor at the Croatian embassy in Canada, additionally serving as deputy chief of mission.

In 2001 she returned to the foreign ministry as minister-counsellor. Having obtained a postgraduate degree in international relations from the University of Zagreb in 2000, she furthered her academic studies in the USA, at George Washington, Harvard and John Hopkins universities. In Nov. 2003 she was elected to Croatia's parliament, and served from 2003–05 as minister for European integration.

Between 2005 and 2007 she was foreign minister, overseeing preparations for Croatia's entry into the European Union and NATO. Following the HDZ's failure to win an outright majority at the 2007 general election, she left government to become ambassador to the USA from 2008–11. In July 2011 she was appointed assistant secretary general for public diplomacy at NATO, serving until 2014. In 2013 she became one of Croatia's three members of the Trilateral Commission, an international body which promotes co-operation between Europe, Pacific Asia and North America.

In 2014 Grabar-Kitarović was confirmed as HDZ candidate for the presidential elections. Campaigning on a platform of addressing Croatia's economic problems, she came narrowly behind the centre-left incumbent, Ivo Josipović, in the first round of voting in Dec. 2014. However, she won the run-off in Jan. 2015 by 50·7% to 49·3%.

Career in Office
Grabar-Kitarović took office on 18 Feb. 2015. Her challenges as president included attracting investment and maintaining social cohesion, while developing Croatia's standing within the EU and NATO. Inconclusive parliamentary elections in Nov. 2015 led to the formation of a coalition under Prime Minister Tihomir Orešković, an independent technocrat, in Jan. 2016. However, his government lost a confidence vote in June leading to further elections in Sept. that year, after which Grabar-Kitarović asked HDZ leader Andrej Plenković to form a new administration.

Andrej Plenković
Position
Prime Minister

Introduction
Andrej Plenković was sworn in as prime minister of Croatia on 19 Oct. 2016. A career diplomat who entered parliament in 2011, he came to power in the wake of snap elections after a vote of no confidence in the ruling coalition.

Early Life
Andrej Plenković was born on 8 April 1970 in Zagreb. In 1993 he graduated in law from the University of Zagreb and was later awarded a master's degree in international law. He entered the ministry of foreign affairs in 1994 and three years later he was appointed chief of the department for European integration. He was named deputy head of the Croatian mission to the European Union in 2002.

In 2005 Plenković became deputy ambassador to France, a position he held for five years. He entered party politics in 2011, when he was elected to parliament as a representative of the conservative Croatian Democratic Union (HDZ). He was then elected as a member of the European Parliament upon Croatia's accession to the EU in 2013.

Tomislav Karamarko resigned as president of the HDZ after the ruling coalition—of which it was part along with the Bridge of Independent Lists (Most)—lost a vote of confidence in June 2016. Plenković was the sole candidate to replace him. A parliamentary election was subsequently called for 11 Sept., in which the incumbent prime minister, Tihomir Orešković, did not stand. The HDZ won 61 seats against 54 for its largest rival, the People's Coalition (SDP), and agreed a new coalition with Most and parliamentary representatives of the country's ethnic minorities. Plenković was confirmed as prime minister on 19 Oct. 2016.

Career in Office
Seen as a pro-European moderate, Plenković pledged to reverse his party's shift to the right during its last abortive spell in office. However, his administration was swiftly undermined as disagreements with the junior coalition party, Most, led him to dismiss its ministers from the government in April 2017. Plenković nevertheless remained in power after striking a new deal with the liberal Croatian People's Party, representatives of national minorities and a few smaller parties. In June 2017 he appointed seven new ministers in his HDZ-led coalition that was endorsed by parliament that month and later survived a no confidence vote in Nov.

Defence

Conscription was abolished on 1 Jan. 2008. Defence expenditure in 2013 totalled US$813m. (US$182 per capita), representing 1·4% of GDP.

Army
Personnel, 2011, 11,390. Paramilitary forces include an armed police of 3,000. There are 18,500 reserves. Equipment in 2011 included 261 main battle tanks.

Navy
In 2011 the fleet included three submarines and six patrol and coastal combatants. Personnel in 2011 numbered 1,850 (250 conscripts), including two companies of marines.

Air Force
Personnel, 2011, 3,500 (including Air Defence). There were ten combat-capable aircraft (MiG-21s) in 2011.

Economy

Agriculture contributed 4·3% of GDP in 2014, industry 26·3% and services 69·4%.

Overview
Since the global financial crisis of the late 2000s, Croatia has struggled with economic stagnation. Before the downturn the economy had been growing at 4–5% annually but subsequently shrank by an average of 2·5% per year between 2009 and 2013, before recovering to 1·6% in 2015. Reliance on the eurozone for 60% of trade has left the economy exposed to regional instabilities. Foreign direct investment in 2012 was only a quarter of the 2008 total. In 2013, 19·4% of the population lived in poverty.

Agriculture is responsible for only 4% of GDP but employs 8·7% of the population. Tourism is also important; 47% of land and 39% of sea territories are designated protected natural areas of beauty and attract millions of tourists each year. A key challenge for the government is to reduce its public debt (86·7% of GDP in 2015), while encouraging investment. In particular, the transport infrastructure needs to improve for the country to take full advantage of its strategic location, especially in light of its EU accession in 2013.

Currency
On 30 May 1994 the *kuna* (HRK; a name used in 1941–45) of 100 *lipa* replaced the Croatian dinar at one kuna = 1,000 dinars. Foreign exchange reserves were US$8,529m. in July 2005 and total money supply was 38,305m. kuna. There was deflation of 1·1% in 2016 and inflation of 1·1% in 2017.

Budget
Budgetary central government revenue totalled 108,585m. kuna in 2013 (109,559m. kuna in 2012) and expenditure 123,506m. kuna (118,730m. kuna in 2012).

Principal sources of revenue in 2013 were: taxes on goods and services, 53,812m. kuna; social security contributions, 37,149m. kuna. Main items of expenditure by economic type in 2013: social benefits, 58,943m. kuna; compensation of employees, 30,462m. kuna.

Croatia had a budget surplus of 0·9% in 2017. There deficits in 2016 (0·9%) and 2015 (3·4%). The required target set by the EU for 2014 was a budget deficit of no more than 4·6%. This was to fall to 3·5% of GDP in 2015 and 3·0% of GDP in 2016.

VAT is 25%.

Performance
Croatia's economy contracted every year from 2009 to 2014, shrinking by 7·4% in 2009. However, the economy recovered and more recently there was growth of 2·4% in 2015, 3·5% in 2016 and 2·8% in 2017. Total GDP was US$54·8bn. in 2017.

Banking and Finance
The National Bank of Croatia (*Governor,* Boris Vujčić) is the bank of issue. In 2017 there were 25 registered banks. The largest banks are Zagrebačka Banka, with assets in Dec. 2017 of US$16·3bn., and Privredna Banka Zagreb. There is a stock exchange in Zagreb.

Gross external debt amounted to US$46·7bn. in June 2018.

Energy and Natural Resources

Environment
Croatia's carbon dioxide emissions from the consumption of energy in 2011 were the equivalent of 4·0 tonnes per capita.

Electricity
Installed capacity was 4·0m. kW in 2011. Output in 2011 was 10·83bn. kWh and consumption per capita 4,285 kWh.

Oil and Gas
In 2011, 4·3m. bbls of crude oil were produced. Natural gas output totalled 2·4bn. cu. metres in 2011; reserves were 25bn. cu. metres in 2013.

Minerals
Production (in 1,000 tonnes): salt (2012), 46.

Agriculture

Agriculture and fishing generate approximately 3·2% of GDP. Some 4·1% of the workforce were engaged in agriculture, hunting and forestry in 2014. Agricultural land totalled 1·2m. ha. in 2014; there were 811,067 ha. of arable land and 77,598 ha. of permanent crops. Production (in 1,000 tonnes, 2014): maize, 2,047; sugar beets, 1,392; wheat, 649; potatoes, 161; grapes, 135; soybeans, 131; sunflower seeds, 99. Livestock, 2014: pigs, 1,156,000; sheep, 605,000; cattle, 441,000; chickens, 9·8m.

Forestry

Forests covered 1·92m. ha. in 2015. In 2011, 5·26m. cu. metres of round-wood were produced.

Fisheries

Total catch in 2014 was 79,318 tonnes, almost exclusively from sea fishing. The annual catch doubled between 2006 and 2014.

Industry

In 2014 industrial production grew 1·2% in comparison with 2013. Output in 2014: cement, 2,358,000 tonnes; distillate fuel oil, 1,120,000 tonnes; petrol, 806,000 tonnes; paper and paperboard, 418,000 tonnes; residual fuel oil, 311,000 tonnes; cigarettes, 8,191m. units; cotton woven fabrics, 8m. sq. metres; beer, 341m. litres.

Labour

In 2015 the labour force numbered 1,898,000 people of whom 1,589,000 were employed. In 2015 the unemployment rate was 16·3%, down from 17·3% in 2014; youth unemployment among 15 to 24-year-olds was 43·0% (45·5% in 2014). The main area of activity in 2015 was manufacturing (employing 266,000 persons), ahead of wholesale and retail trade/repair of motor vehicles and motorcycles (225,000).

Croatia had 15,000 people living in slavery according to the Walk Free Foundation's 2013 *Global Slavery Index*.

International Trade

Imports and Exports

Imports in 2012 came to US$20,834m. Exports were valued at US$12,369m. in 2012.

Principal imports in 2012 were: mineral fuels, 23·2%; machinery and transport equipment, 22·3%; manufactured goods, 16·6%; chemicals, 13·6%; miscellaneous manufactured articles, 11·2%; food and live animals, 10·0%. Main exports in 2012 were: machinery and transport equipment, 26·8%; manufactured goods, 14·3%; mineral fuels, 13·7%; miscellaneous manufactured articles, 12·5%; chemicals, 10·9%; food and live animals, 10·0%.

In 2012 the main import suppliers were (in US$1m.): Italy (3,513); Germany (2,646); Russia (1,583); China (1,488); Slovenia (1,218). Main export markets (in US$1m.): Italy (1,892); Bosnia and Herzegovina (1,578); Germany (1,261); Slovenia (1,065); Austria (808).

Communications

Roads

There were 26,821 km of roads in 2017 (including 1,310 km of motorways and 6,969 km of highways, national and main roads). In 2017 there were 1,596,087 passenger cars, 5,698 buses and coaches, 156,724 lorries and 11,334 road tractors. 50m. passengers and 72m. tonnes of freight were carried by road transport in 2017. There were 331 deaths in road accidents in 2017.

Rail

There were 2,604 km of 1,435 mm gauge rail in 2015 (970 km electrified). In 2015 railways carried 22m. passengers and 10m. tonnes of freight. In Sept. 2010 the state-owned railway companies of Croatia, Serbia and Slovenia announced the creation of a joint venture called Cargo 10 to improve the management of freight trains along the route known as Corridor 10 that passes through all three countries.

Civil Aviation

The biggest international airports are Zagreb (Franjo Tuđman), Split and Dubrovnik. The national carrier is Croatia Airlines, which carried 1,952,000 passengers in 2012. Zagreb Airport handled 2,317,170 passengers in 2012 (1,896,129 on international flights) and 6,929 tonnes of freight, Dubrovnik 1,455,470 passengers (1,215,168 on international flights) and Split 1,393,649 passengers (1,211,067 on international flights).

Shipping

The main statistical ports in 2017 (ports that had total traffic of goods greater than or equal to 1m. tonnes) are Bakar (3·0m. tonnes), Omišalj (8·0m. tonnes), Ploče (3·2m. tonnes), Rijeka (2·6m. tonnes) and Split (2·2m. tonnes). Figures for 2017 show that 32·5m. passengers and 20·8m. tonnes of cargo were transported. In 2017 merchant shipping (passenger and cargo ships) totalled 1,681,522 GT, including liquid bulk carriers 691,472 GT.

Telecommunications

There were 1·87m. fixed telephone lines in 2010 (423·7 per 1,000 inhabitants). Mobile phone subscribers numbered 6·36m. in 2010. There were 603·2 internet users per 1,000 inhabitants in 2010. Fixed internet subscriptions totalled 1·50m. in 2009 (339·7 per 1,000 inhabitants). In March 2012 there were 1·5m. Facebook users.

Social Institutions

Out of 178 countries analysed in the 2017 *Fragile States Index*—a list published jointly by the Fund for Peace and *Foreign Policy* magazine—Croatia was ranked the 41st least vulnerable to conflict or collapse. The index is based on 12 indicators of state vulnerability across social, political and economic categories.

Justice

The population in penal institutions in Jan. 2013 was 4,741 (108 per 100,000 of national population). Croatia was ranked 29th of 102 countries for criminal justice and 45th for civil justice in the 2015 World Justice Project *Rule of Law Index*, which provides data on how the rule of law is experienced by the general public across eight categories.

Education

In 2014–15 there were 1,590 pre-school institutions with 133,764 children and 18,800 childcare workers; 888 active (self-contained) basic schools (primary schools), comprising 1,242 satellite schools and departments, with 323,195 pupils and 28,288 full-time equivalent teachers; 440 active upper secondary schools comprising 743 school units, with 178,661 pupils and 18,035 full-time equivalent teachers. In 2013–14 there were 133 institutions of higher education with 166,054 students and 11,743 full-time equivalent academic staff. In 2013–14 there were seven universities (Dubrovnik, Osijek, Pula, Rijeka, Split, Zadar and Zagreb). Adult literacy rate in 2011 was 99·1% (male, 99·6%; female, 98·7%).

In 2011 public expenditure on education came to 4·2% of GDP.

Health

In 2017 there were 74 hospitals and health resorts with 23,049 beds; and 14,810 physicians, 3,716 dentists, 30,773 nurses, 2,874 pharmacists and 1,766 midwives.

In *Water: At What Cost? The State of the World's Water 2016*, WaterAid reported that 0·4% of the population does not have access to safe water.

Welfare

To qualify for a full old-age pension an individual must have reached the age of 65 years (men) and 61 years and 6 months (women), with at least 15 years of coverage. For women the retirement age is increasing by three months a year until reaching age 65 in 2030. For both men and women it will then rise gradually until reaching age 67 in 2038. The minimum pension is calculated as 0·825% of the average gross salary for each year of the qualifying period, which as of 1 July 2016 amounted to 59·71 kuna per year of service. The average unemployment benefit was 1,817 kuna in 2015.

Religion

At the census of 2011 the principal denominations were: Roman Catholic, 3,697,143; Orthodox, 190,143; Muslims, 62,977; no religion or atheist, 163,375; not stated, 93,018. In Feb. 2019 there was one cardinal.

Culture

World Heritage Sites

Croatia has ten UNESCO protected sites: the Old City of Dubrovnik (entered on the List in 1979 and 1994), known as the 'Pearl of the Adriatic'; the Historic Complex of Split with the Palace of Diocletian (1979), including Roman Emperor Diocletian's mausoleum, now the cathedral; Plitvice Lakes National Park (1979 and 2000), a series of lakes and waterfalls and a habitat for bears and wolves; the Episcopal Complex of the Euphrasian Basilica in the Historical Centre of Poreč (1997); the Historic City of Trogir (1997), a Venetian city based on a Hellenistic plan; the Cathedral of St James in Šibenik (2000), built in the Gothic and Renaissance styles between 1431–1535; and Stari Grad Plain (2008), agricultural land on the island of Hvar that was first cultivated by the Greeks in the 4th century BC.

Croatia shares Ancient and Primeval Beech Forests of the Carpathians and Other Regions of Europe (2007 and 2017) with Albania, Austria, Belgium, Bulgaria, Germany, Italy, Romania, Slovakia, Slovenia, Spain and Ukraine. The Stećci Medieval Tombstones Graveyards (2016) are shared with Bosnia and Herzegovina, Montenegro and Serbia. The Venetian Works of Defence between the 16th and 17th Centuries: *Stato da Terra*—Western *Stato da Mar* (2017) are shared with Italy and Montenegro.

Press

In 2013 there were 13 daily newspapers. The papers with the highest circulation in 2013 were *24sata* (daily average of 108,000 copies and 1,176,000 unique monthly visitors in Dec. 2013 for its online edition), *Večerni list* and *Jutarnji list*.

Tourism

In 2014, 11·62m. non-resident tourists stayed in holiday accommodation (up from 8·69m. in 2009 and 7·91m. in 2004).

Festivals

Croatia has a number of cultural and traditional festivals, including the International Folk Dance Festival in Zagreb (July); the Zagreb Summer Festival (July–Aug.); Dubrovnik Summer Festival (July–Aug.); Split Summer Festival (July–Aug.); Alka Festival (traditional medieval tilting), Sinj (Aug.). The best-known music festivals include Mars Festival in Zagreb (May), INmusic Festival near Zagreb (June) and Garden Festival near Zadar (July).

Diplomatic Representatives

Of Croatia in the United Kingdom (21 Conway St., London, W1T 6BN)
    Ambassador: Igor Pokaz.

Of the United Kingdom in Croatia (Ivana Lučića 4, 10000 Zagreb)
    Ambassador: Andrew Dalgleish.

Of Croatia in the USA (2343 Massachusetts Ave., NW, Washington, D.C., 20008)
    Ambassador: Pjer Šimunović.

Of the USA in Croatia (Thomasa Jeffersona 2, 10010 Zagreb)
    Ambassador: W. Robert Kohorst.

Of Croatia to the United Nations
    Ambassador: Vladimir Drobnjak.

Of Croatia to the European Union
    Permanent Representative: Mato Škrabalo.

Further Reading

Central Bureau of Statistics. *Statistical Yearbook, Monthly Statistical Report, Statistical Information, Statistical Reports.*

Fisher, Sharon, *Political Change in Post-Communist Slovakia and Croatia: From Nationalist to Europeanist.* 2006

Jovanovic, Nikolina, *Croatia: A History.* Translated from Croatian. 2000

Stallaerts, Robert, *Historical Dictionary of the Republic of Croatia.* 2nd ed. 2003

Uzelac, Gordana, *The Development of the Croatian Nation: An Historical and Sociological Analysis.* 2006

National Statistical Office: Central Bureau of Statistics, 3 Ilica, 10000 Zagreb.

Website: http://www.dzs.hr

Cuba

República de Cuba (Republic of Cuba)

Capital: Havana
Population projection, 2020: 11·50m.
GNI per capita, 2017: (PPP$) 7,524
HDI/world rank, 2017: 0·777/73
Internet domain extension: .cu

Key Historical Events

Archaeological evidence from Levisa in eastern Cuba suggests Neolithic cultures date back to at least 3000 BC. Hunter-gatherers known as the Guanahatabey appear to have been pushed to the west of the island—Pinar del Río—by waves of Taíno and Ciboney (Arawak) settlers, whose origins were in South America's Orinoco river valley. The Taíno, who cultivated yucca, maize and sweet potatoes, may have numbered 350,000 on the island when Christopher Columbus reached Cuba in Oct. 1492. Diego Velázquez attempted to establish the first Spanish settlement at Baracoa in Cuba's far east in 1511 but met fierce Taíno resistance, led by Hatuay, who had fled from Spanish forces in Hispaniola. Hatuay's eventual defeat paved the way to the Spanish conquest of Cuba, initially from Baracoa which was granted city status in 1518. Other settlements were established, including at Trinidad, Sancti Spíritus and Havana, which grew into a bustling, fortified port and base for further exploration of the region. Within 50 years of their first contact with Europeans, the Taíno and Ciboney populations were almost wiped out by diseases to which they had no resistance. Tobacco and sugar plantations were developed in the 17th century, cultivated by tens of thousands of slaves imported from West Africa.

During the Seven Years' War, British forces sought to strengthen their position in the Caribbean. In 1762, led by Lord Albemarle, they attacked Havana and forced out Cuba's governor, Juan de Prado and his administrators. Spanish control was restored the following year by the Treaty of Paris, when the British traded Cuba for Florida. The authorities maintained the more liberal trade regime that the British had introduced, enabling more shipments of slaves and agricultural equipment—and prompting a surge in sugar production. By 1805 annual output had reached 34,000 tons.

Resistance to Spanish rule grew after the removal of Cuban delegates from the Spanish *Cortes* in 1837. Repeated offers by the USA to buy Cuba were rejected. Slavery was suppressed from the 1850s though not abolished until 1886. A rebellion, the Ten-Year War, broke out in 1868 and was led by Gen. Máximo Gómez. An assembly was granted the following year. However, José Martí y Pérez created the Cuban Revolutionary Party from New York and launched an invasion of Cuba in 1895 with Gómez and Antonio Maceo. The USA intervened in 1898, winning control of Cuba from Spain by the Treaty of Paris. Municipal elections in 1900 rejected annexationist policies and Cuba achieved independence in 1902. The Platt Amendment allowed for US intervention to preserve independence and stability and awarded the USA control of Guantánamo Bay. At the request of President Estrada Palma, US forces were installed on the island between 1906 and 1909. In 1912 and 1917 there were further interventions by US forces.

Gerardo Machado's dictatorial presidency began in 1925 and was ended by a coup in 1933. The Revolt of the Sergeants brought Fulgencio Batista y Zaldívar to power. The Platt Amendment was revoked and in 1940 a socially progressive constitution was inaugurated. Batista was returned at disputed elections in 1940 but was voted out of office four years later. He ran for re-election in 1952 but, with little chance of victory, led a bloodless coup before elections could be held, suspending the constitution and instigating a repressive and corrupt regime.

Fidel Castro, imprisoned in 1953 after a failed revolt, arrived from Mexico with 80 supporters in 1956. Castro and Che Guevara led a guerrilla war from the Sierra Maestra mountains and, despite US financial support, Batista fled after revolutionaries seized Havana in Jan. 1959. The USA recognized the new regime but relations soon deteriorated. Castro, as prime minister, launched a nationalization programme, seizing US assets and outlawing foreign land ownership. In Oct. 1960 the USA's trade embargo began and diplomatic relations were broken in Jan. 1961. Close relations between Cuba and the USSR provoked covert US support for the doomed Bay of Pigs invasion in April 1961, in which an offensive by a group of exiled Cubans was defeated by Castro's troops. The following month Castro declared Cuba to be a socialist state. In 1962 the USA and USSR neared nuclear conflict during the Cuban Missile Crisis, with the US Navy imposing a blockade on Cuba from 22 Oct. until 22 Nov. to force the USSR to withdraw Soviet missile bases. In return, the USA guaranteed not to invade Cuba and, in a secret deal, to withdraw missiles from Turkey. Between 1965 and 1973, 250,000 Cubans left for the USA on Freedom Flights agreed between the two nations. In 1976 a new constitution consolidated Castro's power as head of state, government and the armed forces.

Cuba continued to receive financial aid and technical advice from the USSR until the early 1990s, when subsidies were suspended. This led to a 40% drop in GDP between 1989 and 1993. The USA maintained an economic embargo against the island and relations between Cuba and the USA remained embittered for many years. From Jan. 2002 suspected al-Qaeda and Taliban prisoners were brought from Afghanistan to the military prison at the US naval base at Guantánamo Bay.

In July 2006 Castro was hospitalized and temporarily handed power to his brother, Raúl. In Feb. 2008 Fidel announced his resignation and was immediately replaced by Raúl. In April 2015 full diplomatic ties with the USA were restored after a 60-year gap. However, in 2017 the new US administration under President Donald Trump imposed trade and visa regulations as the White House adopted a harder line towards its island neighbour. Raúl Castro stood down from the leadership in April 2018, having served two terms as president, and was replaced by Miguel Díaz-Canel.

Territory and Population

The island of Cuba forms the largest and most westerly of the Greater Antilles group and lies 166 km (103 miles) south of the tip of Florida, USA. The area is 109,884 sq. km, and comprises the island of Cuba (104,339 sq. km); the Isle of Youth (Isla de la Juventud, formerly the Isle of Pines; 2,419 sq. km); and some 1,600 small isles ('cays'; 3,126 sq. km). Census population (2012), 11,167,325, giving a density of 101·6 per sq. km. The estimated population for 2017 was 11,221,060. In 2011, 75·2% of the population were urban.

The UN gives a projected population for 2020 of 11·50m.

There are (with area and 2012 populations) 15 provinces and the special Municipality of the Isle of Youth (Isla de la Juventud):

	Area (sq. km)	*Population*
La Habana (Havana)	728	2,106,146
Santiago de Cuba	6,228	1,049,084
Holguín	9,216	1,035,072
Granma	8,374	834,380
Villa Clara	8,412	791,216
Camagüey	15,386	771,905
Matanzas	11,792	694,476
Pinar del Río	8,884	587,026
Las Tunas	6,593	532,645
Guantánamo	6,168	515,428
Artemisa	4,003	494,631
Sancti Spíritus	6,777	463,458
Ciego de Avila	6,972	426,054
Cienfuegos	4,189	404,228
Mayabeque	3,744	376,825
Isla de la Juventud	2,419	84,751

© Springer Nature Limited 2020
Palgrave Macmillan (ed.), *The Statesman's Yearbook 2020*,
https://doi.org/10.1057/978-1-349-95940-2_57

The capital city, Havana, had a census population in 2012 of 2,106,146. Other major cities (2012 census populations in 1,000): Santiago de Cuba (431), Camagüey (301), Holguín (288), Guantánamo (217), Santa Clara (212), Las Tunas, (163), Bayamo (157), Cienfuegos (147), Pinar del Río (140) and Matanzas (134).

The official language is Spanish.

Social Statistics

2008 births, 122,569; deaths, 86,357; marriages, 61,852; divorces, 35,882; suicides, 1,357. Rates, 2008 (per 1,000 population): birth, 10·9; death, 7·7; marriage, 5·5; divorce, 3·2; suicide, 12·1 per 100,000 population. Infant mortality rate, 2008, 4·7 per 1,000 live births. Annual population growth rate, 2005–10, 0·0%. Life expectancy, 2013: 77·3 years for males and 81·3 for females. The fertility rate in 2008 was 1·6 births per woman.

Climate

Situated in the sub-tropical zone, Cuba has a generally rainy climate, affected by the Gulf Stream and the N.E. Trades, although winters are comparatively dry after the heaviest rains in Sept. and Oct. Hurricanes are liable to occur between June and Nov. Havana, Jan. 72°F (22·2°C), July 82°F (27·8°C). Annual rainfall 48" (1,224 mm).

Constitution and Government

A Communist Constitution came into force on 24 Feb. 1976. It was amended in July 1992 to permit direct parliamentary elections and in June 2002 to make the country's socialist system 'irrevocable'.

Legislative power is vested in the *National Assembly of People's Power*, which meets twice a year and consists of 605 deputies elected for a five-year term by universal suffrage. Citizens are entitled to vote at the age of 16. Lists of candidates are drawn up by mass organizations (trade unions, etc.). The National Assembly elects a 31-member *Council of State* as its permanent organ. The Council of State's President, who is head of state and of government, nominates and leads a Council of Ministers approved by the National Assembly.

National Anthem

'Al combate corred Bayameses' ('Run, Bayamans, to the combat'); words and tune by P. Figueredo.

Recent Elections

The Communist Party is the official state party. However, it is not a requirement that candidates for the National Assembly or municipal assemblies belong to the party. Elections to the National Assembly were held on 11 March 2018. 50% of candidates must come from municipal assemblies, with the other 50% being candidates of national or provincial importance. All 605 nominally independent candidates received the requisite 50% of votes for election.

Current Government

President: Miguel Díaz-Canel Bermúdez (b. 1960) became *President* of the Council of State and of the Council of Ministers on 19 April 2018.

In Feb. 2019 the government comprised:

First Vice-President of the Council of State and First Vice-President of the Council of Ministers: Salvador Valdés Mesa.

Vice-Presidents of the Council of Ministers: Ricardo Cabrisas Ruiz, Ramiro Valdés Menendéz, Roberto Morales Ojeda, Ulises Rosales del Toro, Inés María Chapman Waugh.

Secretary of the Council of Ministers: José Amado Ricardo Guerra.

Minister of Agriculture: Gustavo Rodríguez Rollero. *Communications:* José Luis Perdomo Di-Lella. *Construction:* René Mesa Villafaña. *Culture:* Alpidio Alonso Grau. *Defence:* Gen. Leopoldo Cintra Frías. *Domestic Trade:* Betsy Díaz Velázquez. *Economy and Planning:* Alejandro Gil Fernández. *Education:* Ena Elsa Velázquez Cobiella. *Energy and Mines:* Raúl García Barreiro. *Finance and Prices:* Meisi Bolaños Weiss. *Food Industry:* Iris Quiñones Rojas. *Foreign Relations:* Bruno Rodríguez Parrilla. *Foreign Trade and Investment:* Rodrigo Malmierca Díaz. *Higher Education:* José Ramón Saborido Loidi. *Industries:* Alfredo López Valdés. *Interior:* Vice Adm. Julio César Gandarilla. *Justice:* Oscar Silveira Martínez. *Labour and*

Social Security: Margarita Marlene González Fernández. *Public Health:* José Ángel Portal Miranda. *Science, Technology and Environment:* Elba Rosa Pérez Montoya. *Tourism:* Manuel Marrero Cruz. *Transport:* Eduardo Rodríguez Dávila.

The Congress of the Cuban Communist Party (PCC) elects a Central Committee of 150 members, which in turn appoints a Political Bureau comprising 15 members.

Government Website: http://www.minrex.gob.cu/

Current Leaders

Miguel Díaz-Canel

Position

President

Introduction

Tipped for several years as Raúl Castro's likely successor, Miguel Díaz-Canel was elected president in April 2018.

Early Life

Díaz-Canel was born on 20 April 1960 in Placetas and graduated in electronic engineering from Central University in 1982. After serving in the army, he taught at Central University from 1985, joining the Young Communist League around that time. In 1994 he became first secretary of the provincial party committee for Villa Clara province, and then took up the same position for Holguín province in 2003. In this same year, he joined the Politburo of the Communist Party of Cuba.

Díaz-Canel became minister of higher education in 2009, where he sought to reverse failing standards by introducing more rigorous university entrance tests. In 2012 he was made vice-president of the Council of Ministers. The following year Raúl Castro named Díaz-Canel as his preferred successor when his second presidential term came to an end. When Castro stepped down on 19 April 2018, Díaz-Canel was approved by parliament to take over the office. Castro, meanwhile, retained his position as head of the Communist Party.

Career in Office

Díaz-Canel has spoken of his disappointment at US President Donald Trump's decision to tighten restrictions on travel and commerce with Cuba, reversing the trend established by the Obama administration. On the domestic front, he must seek to create greater economic opportunities in a bid to stem the country's long-term brain drain. Nevertheless, a new constitution, the draft of which was released in July 2018 and subsequently approved in a national referendum in Feb. 2019, preserves Cuba's long-established one-party system despite some liberalizing reforms.

Defence

The National Defence Council is headed by the president of the republic. Conscription is for two years.

In 2011 defence expenditure totalled US$96m. (US$9 per capita).

Army

The strength was estimated at 38,000 in 2011, with 39,000 reservists. Border Guard and State Security forces total 26,500. The Territorial Militia is estimated at 1m. (reservists), all armed. In addition there is a Youth Labour Army of 70,000 and a Civil Defence Force of 50,000.

Navy

Personnel in 2011 totalled about 3,000 including some 550 marines. The Navy has seven patrol and coastal combatants, five mine warfare vessels and three support vessels. Main bases are at Cabañas and Holguín. The USA still occupies the Guantánamo naval base.

Air Force

In 2011 the Air Force had a strength of some 8,000 and 45 combat-capable aircraft. They include MiG-29, MiG-23 and MiG-21 jet fighters.

Economy

Services accounted for 74·5% of GDP in 2011, industry 20·5% and agriculture 5·0%.

Overview

The centrally planned economy is dominated by the services sector. After the withdrawal of annual subsidies worth US$4–6bn. from the former Soviet Union in 1990, the economy fell into deep recession and had to cope with falling tourism receipts, low export prices and hurricane damage. The black market is estimated to be larger than the legal economy and basic economic activities take place in the informal sector. The USA has imposed a trade embargo since 1963 and has effectively blocked access to funds from the IMF and the World Bank, although UN agencies continue to operate in Cuba. Following a thawing in bilateral relations in 2014, initial talks took place between Cuban and US officials in Jan. 2015 towards normalizing relations, with Cuba citing the lifting of the embargo as crucial. However, after a change of US administration in 2017, the new president, Donald Trump, signalled a return to a more hard-line approach to US–Cuban relations.

Following the collapse of the Soviet Union, the Havana government had helped stimulate growth through legalization of the US dollar in shops and other businesses. However, commercial transactions in dollars were banned in Nov. 2004 in response to tighter US sanctions. The economy has meanwhile received substantial aid from Venezuela in the form of heavily subsidized oil supplies.

In 2008 Hurricanes Gustav and Ike resulted in damage valued at 20% of GDP. The global financial crisis at that time also had a significant impact, leading to a decline in the value of exports (particularly nickel, Cuba's second largest foreign exchange earner after tourism) and tighter conditions for external financing. More recently, Cuba again suffered serious damage and disruption from Hurricane Irma in Sept. 2017.

Raúl Castro, who was president for ten years until April 2018, implemented some reforms to reduce the state's role in the economy. These included expansion of the private sector, legalization of private property sales and the opening up of retail services to self-employment. However, change has been slow with mixed effectiveness, reflecting the government's desire to maintain political control. The critical task of merging Cuba's two currencies—thereby equalizing the rate of exchange used by foreigners and locals—is scheduled to begin during 2018.

Currency

Since 1994 there have been two currencies in use in Cuba. However, in Oct. 2013 plans were announced to unify them although no time scale was given. The official currency ('*moneda nacional*') is the *Cuban peso* (CUP) of 100 *centavos*. The *Convertible peso* (CUC), introduced in 1994 (pegged since April 2005 at 1 Convertible peso = US$1·08), is the 'tourist' currency. The US dollar ceased to be legal tender in 2004. The average inflation rate in 2014 was estimated at 2·5%.

Budget

In 2014 revenues were 47,269m. pesos (tax revenue, 64·0%) and expenditure 49,033m. pesos (current expenditure, 94·2%).

Performance

Cuba's economic growth was officially put as 4·3% in 2008, down from 7·5% in 2007 and 12·5% in 2006. Total GDP was US$87·1bn. in 2015.

Banking and Finance

The Central Bank of Cuba (*President*, Irma Margarita Martínez Castrillón) replaced the National Bank of Cuba as the central bank in 1997. On 14 Oct. 1960 all banks were nationalized. Changes to the banking structure beginning in 1996 divested the National Bank of its commercial functions, and created new commercial and investment institutions. The Grupo Nueva Banca has majority holdings in each institution of the new structure. There were nine commercial banks in 2016 and 14 non-banking financial institutions. There were also nine representative offices of foreign banks. All insurance business was nationalized in 1964. A National Savings Bank was established in 1983.

Energy and Natural Resources

Environment

Cuba's carbon dioxide emissions from the consumption of energy were the equivalent of 2·5 tonnes per capita in 2011.

Electricity

Installed capacity was 5·9m. kW in 2011. Production was 17·8bn. kWh in 2011; consumption per capita in 2011 was 1,575 kWh.

Oil and Gas

Crude oil production (2011), 19m. bbls. There were known natural gas reserves of 71bn. cu. metres in 2013. Natural gas production (2011), 1·0bn. cu. metres.

Minerals

Iron ore abounds, with deposits estimated at 3,500m. tonnes; output (2006), 7·8m. tonnes. The output of salt was 180,000 tonnes in 2006; nickel, 74,000 tonnes (2005); chromite, 34,000 tonnes (2005); lime, 34,000 tonnes (2005). Other minerals are cobalt and silica. Nickel is Cuba's second largest foreign exchange earner, after tourism. Gold is also worked.

Agriculture

In 1959 all land over 30 *caballerías* (one caballería = 13·4m. ha. or 23·2m. acres) was nationalized and eventually turned into state farms. In 2007 there were 3·0m. ha. of arable land and 1·8m. ha. of permanent crops. Under legislation of 1993, state farms were reorganized as 'units of basic co-operative production'. Unit workers select their own managers and are paid an advance on earnings. In 1963 private holdings were reduced to a maximum of five *caballerías*. In 1994 farmers were permitted to trade on free market principles after state delivery quotas had been met. In 2008 private farmers were granted access to underused government land in the form of ten-year leases in an effort to boost food production and curb dependence on imported produce.

During the 1980s average annual sugar production totalled 7·5m. tonnes making it one of the country's most important crops. However, the negative economic impact of the collapse of the Soviet Union in 1991 followed by a series of weather disasters in subsequent years resulted in production shrinking to 3·2m. tonnes in 1998, the smallest crop for 50 years. In 2002 the government closed over half of the 156 sugar mills and by 2008 production had fallen to 1·4m. tonnes with the country relying on imports to meet domestic demand. Production of other crops in 2008 was (in 1,000 tonnes): bananas, 758; tomatoes, 576; rice, 436; sweet potatoes, 375; cassava, 340; maize, 326; oranges, 200.

In 2008 livestock included 3·8m. cattle; 1·9m. pigs; 1·1m. goats; 565,000 horses; 277,500 sheep; 29m. chickens.

Forestry

Cuba had 3·20m. ha. of forests in 2015, representing 30% of the land area. These forests contain valuable cabinet woods. Cedar is used locally for cigar boxes, and mahogany is exported. In 2011, 1·73m. cu. metres of roundwood were produced.

Fisheries

The total catch was 24,754 tonnes in 2014, of which 22,916 tonnes were from marine waters. The catch in 2014 was less than half the 2001 total and less than a third of the 1997 total.

Industry

In 2008 manufacturing accounted for 14% of GDP. All industrial enterprises used to be state-controlled, but in 1995 the economy was officially stated to comprise state property, commercial property based on activity by state enterprises, joint co-operative and private property. Production in 2007 (in 1,000 tonnes): cement, 1,812; raw sugar (2008), 1,446; residual fuel oil, 940; distillate fuel oil, 464; sulphuric acid, 428; petrol, 392; wheat and blended flour, 391; crude steel and steel semi-finished products, 247; televisions, 118,300 units; clay building bricks, 24·9m. units; cigarettes, 13·8bn. units; shoes, 721,000 pairs; soft drinks, 350·6m. litres; beer, 250·4m. litres; spirits and liqueurs, 95·1m. litres; mineral water, 33·2m. litres; cotton fabrics, 6·1m. sq. metres.

Labour

The labour force in 2013 was 5,360,000 (4,727,000 in 2003). 65·9% of the population aged 15–64 was economically active in 2013. In the same year 3·2% of the population was unemployed.

Self-employment was legalized in 1993. Under legislation of 1994 employees made redundant must be assigned to other jobs or to strategic social or economic tasks; failing this, they are paid 60% of their former salary.

International Trade

Since July 1992 foreign investment has been permitted in selected state enterprises, and Cuban companies have been able to import and export without seeking government permission. Foreign ownership is recognized in joint ventures. A free trade zone opened at Havana in 1993. In 1994 the productive, real estate and service sectors were opened to foreign investment. Legislation of 1995 opened all sectors of the economy to foreign investment except defence, education and health services. 100% foreign-owned investments and investments in property are now permitted.

The Helms-Burton Law of March 1996 gives US nationals the right to sue foreign companies investing in Cuban estate expropriated by the Cuban government.

Imports and Exports
In 2006 imports (c.i.f.) totalled US$10,173·6m. and exports (f.o.b.) US$2,980·2m. The principal exports are nickel, tobacco and medical products. Sugar used to account for more than half of Cuba's export revenues, but revenues have been gradually declining and constituted less than 1% of the total in 2006. In 2005 the chief import sources (in US$1m.) were: Venezuela (2,021·5); China (926·2); Spain (702·9); USA (520·7). The chief export markets (in US$1m.) were: Netherlands (645·1); Canada (471·4); Venezuela (434·2); Spain (159·5).

Communications

Roads
In 2007 there were 68,395 km of roads, of which 29,609 km were paved. Vehicles in use in 2008 included 236,881 passenger cars and 171,081 trucks and vans. There were 1,403 fatalities as a result of road accidents in 2008.

Rail
There were 4,066 km of public railway (1,435 mm gauge) in 2005, of which 140 km was electrified. Passenger-km travelled in 2007 came to 1,285m. and freight tonne-km to 783m. In addition, the large sugar estates have 7,162 km of lines in total on 1,435 mm, 914 mm and 760 mm gauges.

Civil Aviation
There is an international airport at Havana (José Martí). The state airline Cubana operates internal services, and in 2010 had international flights from Havana to Bogotá, Buenos Aires, Cancún, Caracas, Guatemala City, London, Madrid, Mexico City, Montreal, Moscow, Panama City, Paris, Rome, San José (Costa Rica), Santiago, Santo Domingo and Toronto. In 2012 scheduled airline traffic of Cuban-based carriers flew 15·6m. km; passenger-km totalled 2·7bn. in the same year. In 2009 Havana José Martí International handled 6,632,862 passengers and 27,339 tonnes of freight.

Shipping
The largest ports are Havana, Cienfuegos and Mariel. In Jan. 2014 there were seven ships of 300 GT or over registered, totalling 10,000 GT.

Telecommunications
In 2011 there were 1,193,400 landline telephone subscriptions (equivalent to 106·0 per 1,000 inhabitants) and 1,315,100 mobile phone subscriptions (or 116·9 per 1,000 inhabitants). In 2011, 23·2% of the population were internet users.

Social Institutions

Out of 178 countries analysed in the 2017 *Fragile States Index*—a list published jointly by the Fund for Peace and *Foreign Policy* magazine— Cuba was ranked the 60th least vulnerable to conflict or collapse. The index is based on 12 indicators of state vulnerability across social, political and economic categories.

Justice
There are a Supreme Court in Havana and seven regional courts of appeal. The provinces are divided into judicial districts, with courts for civil and criminal actions, and municipal courts for minor offences. The civil code guarantees aliens the same property and personal rights as those enjoyed by nationals.

The 1959 Agrarian Reform Law and the Urban Reform Law passed on 14 Oct. 1960 have placed certain restrictions on both. Revolutionary Summary Tribunals have wide powers.

The death penalty is still in force. There were three executions in 2003, but none since then.

The population in penal institutions in May 2012 was 57,337 (510 per 100,000 of national population).

Education
Education is compulsory (between the ages of six and 14), free and universal. In 2007 there were 883,132 pupils in primary school and 91,530 teaching staff; and 898,833 secondary school pupils with 93,311 teaching staff. There were 864,846 students and 135,800 academic staff in higher education in 2007.

There are four universities, plus ten teacher training, two agricultural, four medical and ten other higher educational institutions.

The adult literacy rate was estimated at 99·8% in 2009.

In 2007 public expenditure on education came to 13·6% of GNI and 20·6% of total government spending.

Health
At 31 Dec. 2008 there were 74,552 physicians, 107,761 nurses and 2,962 pharmacists. There were 217 hospitals in 2008 with 43,434 beds. An additional 23,834 beds were provided by other health care units.

Free medical services are provided by the state polyclinics, though a few doctors still have private practices. Health spending accounted for 11·1% of GDP in 2014. In the same year general government expenditure on health represented 95·6% of total expenditure on health.

In *Water: At What Cost? The State of the World's Water 2016*, WaterAid reported that 5·1% of the population does not have access to safe water.

Welfare
The official retirement age is 65 (men) or 60 (women). However, the qualifying age falls to 60 (men) or 55 (women) if 75% of all work or the 15 years immediately before retirement was in dangerous or arduous work. The minimum pension in 2014 was 200 pesos a month. The maximum pension is 90% of average earnings.

Cuba has a sickness and maternity support programme.

Religion

Religious liberty was constitutionally guaranteed in 1992. According to the Pew Research Center's Forum on Religion & Public Life, in 2010 an estimated 51·7% of the population was Roman Catholic, 23·0% had no religious affiliation and 17·4% were folk religionists. In 2016 Juan de la Caridad García Rodríguez (b. 1948) was nominated Archbishop of Havana by Pope Francis. The Roman Catholic Church has three ecclesiastical provinces, each headed by an archbishop. In Feb. 2019 there was one cardinal.

Culture

World Heritage Sites
There are nine UNESCO sites in Cuba: Old Havana and its fortifications (inscribed in 1982), Trinidad and the Valley de los Ingenios (19th century sugar mills; 1988), San Pedro de la Roca Castle in Santiago de Cuba (1997), Desembarco del Granma National Park (marine terraces; 1999), Viñales Valley (1999), the 19th-century coffee plantations at Sierra Maestra (2000), Alejandro de Humboldt National Park (2001), the urban historic centre of Cienfuegos (2005) and the historic centre of Camagüey (2008).

Press
There were (2008) four national daily newspapers and 15 regional and local dailies with a combined circulation of 1·8m. The most widely read newspaper is the Communist Party's *Granma*.

Tourism
Tourism is Cuba's largest foreign exchange earner. There were 2,716,317 foreign visitors in 2011 (2,429,809 in 2009 and 2,531,745 in 2010), of whom 1,002,318 were from Canada, 175,822 from the United Kingdom and 110,432 from Italy.

Diplomatic Representatives

Of Cuba in the United Kingdom (167 High Holborn, London, WC1V 6PA)
Ambassador: Teresita de Jesús Vicente Sotolongo.

Of the United Kingdom in Cuba (Calle 34, No. 702, esq. 7ma, Miramar, Havana 11300)
Ambassador: Antony Stokes, LVO.

Of Cuba in the USA (2630 16th St., NW, Washington, D.C. 20009)
Ambassador: José Ramón Cabañas Rodríguez.

Of the USA in Cuba (Calzada between L and M Streets, Vedado, Havana)
Ambassador: Vacant.
Chargé d'Affaires a.i.: Mara Tekach.

Of Cuba to the United Nations
Ambassador: Anayansi Rodríguez Camejo.

Of Cuba to the European Union
Ambassador: Norma Miguelina Goicochea Estenoz.

Further Reading

Bunck, J. M., *Fidel Castro and the Quest for a Revolutionary Culture in Cuba.* 1994
Dosal, Paul J., *Cuba Libre: A Brief History of Cuba.* 2006
Gott, Richard, *Cuba: A New History.* 2004
McKelvey, Charles, *The Evolution and Significance of the Cuban Revolution.* 2017
Mesa-Lago, C. (ed.) *Cuba: After the Cold War.* 1993
Sweig, Julia, *Inside the Cuban Revolution.* 2002
National Statistical Office: Oficina Nacional de Estadísticas, Paseo No. 60e/3ra y 5ta, Vedado, Plaza de la Revolución, Havana, CP 10400.
Website (Spanish only): http://www.one.cu

Cyprus

Kypriaki Dimokratia—Kibris Çumhuriyeti (Republic of Cyprus)

Capital: Nicosia
Population projection, 2020: 1·21m.
GNI per capita, 2017: (PPP$) 31,568
HDI/world rank, 2017: 0·869/32
Internet domain extension: .cy

Key Historical Events

Cyprus has been settled since the early Neolithic period in the 9th millennium BC. During the 2nd millennium BC Greek colonies were established and Greek culture predominated. Cyprus then came under Assyrian and Egyptian rule, subsequently becoming part of the Persian Empire. In the 2nd and 1st centuries BC the island was Hellenized. It became a Roman province in 58 BC and remained within the Roman Empire for most of the next three centuries, when Christianity was adopted.

The island became part of the Byzantine Empire in AD 364. In 488 the Church of Cyprus was confirmed as independent. Successive Arab invasions in the 7th century led to joint rule by Arabs and Byzantines until 965, when Byzantium regained sole rule. From 1191 Cyprus was attacked by Crusaders and in 1193 it became a Frankish kingdom under Guy de Lusignan. The Venetians ruled it as a dependency from 1489–1571, when it was taken by the Ottoman Turks. Under the Ottomans, the population was divided between Muslim Turks and Christian Greeks. After Greece achieved independence in 1829, some Greek Cypriots called for a union between Cyprus and Greece. On 4 June 1878 Great Britain and the Ottomans signed the Cyprus Convention, which gave Cyprus to Britain as a protectorate, in return for Britain supporting Turkey against Russia. In 1914, in response to Turkey's alliance with Germany, Britain annexed Cyprus. On 1 May 1925 it became a Crown Colony.

In the 1930s Greek Cypriots began campaigning for union with Greece (*enosis*). In 1955 the EOKA (National Organization of Cypriot Fighters), an anti-British guerrilla movement, was formed, led by Archbishop Makarios, head of the Greek Orthodox Church in Cyprus. In 1959 Greek and Turkish Cypriots agreed a constitution for an independent Cyprus and Makarios was elected president. On 16 June 1960 Cyprus became an independent state.

In Dec. 1963 conflict over proposed changes to the power-sharing mechanisms led to the Turkish Cypriots withdrawing from government. Fighting broke out and a UN peacekeeping force was deployed in 1964. Further fighting occurred in 1967–68, after which the Turkish Cypriots formed a provisional administration to run their community's affairs. Some Turkish Cypriots began to call for *taksim*, division of the island. On 15 July 1974 the Greek Cypriot National Guard staged a coup, with backing from Athens, and deposed President Makarios. On 20 July 1974 Turkey invaded. Turkish forces rapidly occupied the northern third of the island and, as the coup collapsed, enforced partition between north and south. During the fighting, and later as part of a UN-supervised population transfer, 200,000 Greek Cypriots moved south, while an estimated 65,000 Turkish Cypriots migrated north.

In Dec. 1974 Makarios returned as president. In 1975 a Turkish Cypriot Federated State was proclaimed in the north, with Rauf Denktaş its president. In 1983 the Turkish state unilaterally proclaimed itself the 'Turkish Republic of Northern Cyprus' ('TRNC'). UN-sponsored peace talks continued without success throughout the 1980s. In 1991 the UN rejected Rauf Denktaş's demands for recognition of the 'TRNC', including the right to secession. In 1998 the Greek and Cypriot governments rejected Denktaş's proposal that the Greek and Turkish communities should join in a federation recognizing 'the equal and sovereign status of Cyprus' Greek and Turkish parts'.

In 2002 Cyprus was one of ten countries to be granted EU membership starting in 2004; the 'TRNC' would be included only if UN-brokered talks to reunify the country succeeded. In Nov. 2002 the UN presented a peace plan to the Greek Cypriot and Turkish Cypriot leaders for a 'common' state with two 'component' states and a rotating presidency. In March 2003 UN-brokered talks to pave the way for reunification collapsed. However, as a goodwill measure the 'TRNC' opened the 'Green Line' separating the island's two sectors in April 2003. In a referendum held in the Greek-speaking and the Turkish-speaking areas on 24 April 2004, Turkish Cypriots voted in favour of a UN plan to reunite the island but Greek Cypriots voted overwhelmingly against. This result meant that after EU accession, EU benefits and laws would apply only to Greek Cypriots. On 1 May 2004, under these conditions, Cyprus became a member of the EU.

In Dec. 2004 Turkey extended its EU customs union agreement to Cyprus but declared that this did not amount to a recognition of Cyprus. In 2006 at UN-sponsored talks, a series of confidence building measures were agreed by Greek and Turkish Cypriots. However, in Nov. 2006 EU-Turkish talks on Cyprus broke down. Hopes of finding a solution were boosted with the election in March 2008 of President Dimitris Christofias—the EU's sole communist head of state—who vowed to revive negotiations with Turkey. A month later the Ledra Street crossing that had symbolized the island's division since its closure 44 years earlier was reopened.

However, little further progress in talks was made and in 2010 the pro-unity Mehmet Ali Talat was replaced as president of the 'TRNC' by a hard-line nationalist, Derviş Eroğlu. Tensions between Cyprus and Turkey began to grow in 2011 over oil and gas exploration rights. In Feb. 2013 Nicos Anastasiades of Democratic Rally replaced Christofias as president. A month later, with the banking sector on the point of collapse, he agreed a €10bn. bailout with the EU and IMF that saw the closure of Laiki, the country's second biggest bank.

Territory and Population

The island lies in the Mediterranean, about 60 km off the south coast of Turkey and 90 km off the coast of Syria. Area, 9,251 sq. km (3,572 sq. miles). The Turkish-occupied area is 3,355 sq. km. Population of Cyprus by ethnic group:

Ethnic group	1960 census	1973 census	1992	2011
Greek Cypriot	452,291	498,511	599,200	681,000
Turkish Cypriot	104,942	116,000	94,500[1]	90,100[1]
Others	16,333	17,267	20,000	181,000[2]
Total	*573,566*	*631,778*	*713,700[1]*	*952,100[1]*

[1]Excluding Turkish settlers and troops. [2]Including foreign workers and residents.

The 2011 census population (government-controlled area only) was 856,857.

The UN gives a projected population for 2020 of 1·21m.

70·3% of the population lived in urban areas in 2010. Principal towns with populations (2011 census): Nicosia (the capital), 239,277; Limassol, 180,201; Larnaca, 84,591; Paphos, 62,122.

As a result of the Turkish occupation of the northern part of Cyprus, 0·2m. Greek Cypriots were displaced and forced to find refuge in the south. The urban centres of Famagusta, Kyrenia and Morphou were completely evacuated. *See below* for details on the 'Turkish Republic of Northern Cyprus'. (The 'TRNC' was unilaterally declared as a 'state' in 1983 in the area of the Republic of Cyprus, which has been under Turkish occupation since 1974, when Turkish forces invaded the island. The establishment of the 'TRNC' was declared illegal by UN Security Resolutions 541/83 and 550/84. The 'TRNC' is not recognized by any country in the world except Turkey). Nicosia is a divided city, with the UN-patrolled Green Line passing through it.

Greek and Turkish are official languages. English is widely spoken.

Social Statistics

2009 births, 9,608; deaths, 5,182; marriages, 12,769; divorces, 1,738. Rates, 2009 (per 1,000 population): birth, 12·0; death, 6·5; marriage (residents of Cyprus only), 7·9; divorce, 2·2. Life expectancy at birth, 2013, was 77·9 years for males and 81·8 years for females. The World Health Organization's *World Health Statistics 2014* put Cyprus in third place in a 'healthy life expectancy' list, with an expected 74 years of healthy life for babies born in 2012. Population growth rate, 2009, 0·8%; infant mortality, 2009, 3·3 per 1,000 live births; fertility rate, 2013, 1·5 children per woman. Cyprus was ranked 100th in a gender gap index of 145 countries compiled by the World Economic Forum for its *Global Gender Gap Report 2015*. The annual index considers economic, political, education and health criteria. In 2009 the average age of first marriage (residents of Cyprus only) was 29·5 years for men and 27·4 years for women.

Climate

The climate is Mediterranean, with very hot, dry summers and variable winters. Maximum temperatures may reach 112°F (44·5°C) in July and Aug., but minimum figures may fall to 22°F (−5·5°C) in the mountains in winter. Rainfall is generally between 10" and 27" (250 and 675 mm) but it may reach 48" (1,200 mm) in the Troodos mountains. Nicosia, Jan. 50°F (10·0°C), July 83°F (28·3°C). Annual rainfall 19·6" (500 mm).

Constitution and Government

Under the 1960 constitution executive power is vested in a *President* elected for a five-year term by universal suffrage, and exercised through a Council of Ministers appointed by him or her. The *House of Representatives* exercises legislative power. It is elected by universal suffrage for five-year terms, and consists of 80 members, of whom 56 are elected by the Greek Cypriot and 24 by the Turkish Cypriot community. As from Dec. 1963 the Turkish Cypriot members have ceased to attend, and the 24 seats allocated to the Turkish Cypriot community are no longer contested. Voting is compulsory.

National Anthem

'Imnos eis tin Eleftherian' ('Hymn to Freedom'); words by Dionysios Solomos, tune by N. Mantzaros.
(Same as Greece.)

Government Chronology

Presidents since 1960. AKEL = Progressive Party of the Working People; DIKO = Democratic Party; DISI = Democratic Rally; EOKA = National Organization of Cypriot Fighters; n/p = non-partisan)

1960–74	n/p	Makarios III
1974	EOKA	Nikolaos (Nikos) Sampson
1974–77	n/p	Makarios III
1977–88	DIKO	Spyros Achilleos Kyprianou
1988–93	n/p	Georgios Vasou Vasiliou
1993–2003	DISI	Glafcos Ioannou Clerides
2003–08	DIKO	Tassos Nikolaou Papadopoulos
2008–13	AKEL	Dimitris Christofias
2013–	DISI	Nicos Anastasiades

Recent Elections

Parliamentary elections were held on 22 May 2016. The ruling Democratic Rally (DISI) won 18 of 56 available seats with 30·7% of votes cast, followed by the Progressive Party of Working People (AKEL) with 16 and 25·7%, the Democratic Party (DIKO) 9 and 14·5%, the Movement for Social Democracy (EDEK) 3 and 6·2%, the Citizens' Alliance 3 and 6·0%, the Solidarity Movement 3 and 5·2%, the Ecological and Environmental Movement (KOP) 2 and 4·8%, and the National Popular Front (ELAM) 2 and 3·7%. Turnout was 66·7%.

Presidential elections were held in Jan.–Feb. 2018. In the first round on 28 Jan. none of the nine candidates obtained the necessary 50% of the vote to win an outright majority. A second round was held on 4 Feb. between the two leading candidates, Nicos Anastasiades (DISI) and Stavros Malas (AKEL). Anastasiades won with 56·0% of the vote against 44·0% for Malas. Turnout was 71·9% in the first round and 74·0% in the second.

European Parliament

Cyprus has six representatives. At the May 2014 elections turnout was 44·0% (59·4% in 2009). The DISI won 2 seats with 37·8% of votes cast (political affiliation in European Parliament: European People's Party), AKEL 2 seats with 27·0% (European United Left/Nordic Green Left), DIKO 1 seat with 10·8% (Progressive Alliance of Socialists and Democrats) and EDEK 1 seat with 7·7% (Progressive Alliance of Socialists and Democrats).

Current Government

President: Nicos Anastasiades; b. 1946 (Democratic Rally; sworn in 28 Feb. 2013 and re-elected 4 Feb. 2018).

In Feb. 2019 the Council of Ministers consisted of:
Minister of Foreign Affairs: Nikos Christodoulides. *Finance:* Harris Georgiades. *Interior:* Constantinos Petrides. *Defence:* Savvas Angelides. *Education and Culture:* Kostas Champiaouris. *Transport, Communications and Works:* Vassiliki Anastassiadou. *Energy, Commerce, Industry and Tourism:* Yiorgos Lakkotrypis. *Agriculture, Rural Development and Environment:* Costas Kadis. *Labour, Welfare and Social Insurance:* Zeta Emilianidou. *Justice and Public Order:* Ionas Nicolaou. *Health:* Constantinos Ioannou.

Government Website: http://www.cyprus.gov.cy

Current Leaders

Nicos Anastasiades

Position
President

Introduction
Nicos Anastasiades was sworn into office on 28 Feb. 2013 following his victory in the second round of a presidential poll. The immediate priority facing his new administration was dealing with an economy and financial system in crisis. He has also endeavoured to move forward intercommunal talks with the Turkish Cypriots and was re-elected in Feb. 2018.

Early Life
Nicos Anastasiades was born on 27 Sept. 1946 in Pera Pedi, Limassol District. In 1969 he graduated in law from the National and Kapodistrian University of Athens. Two years later he completed his postgraduate studies in shipping law at University College, London, and in 1972 established his own firm, Nicos Chr. Anastasiades & Partners.

Anastasiades became a founding member of Democratic Rally (DISI) in 1976. He was active in its youth wing (NEDISI) from that date until 1990, serving as both its vice-president and president. At the 1981 general election he was voted into parliament as the representative for Limassol. In 1990 he became DISI's vice-president, a year later was named deputy parliamentary spokesman for the DISI–Democratic Party coalition and from 1993–97 served as its parliamentary spokesman. He was appointed DISI deputy president in 1995 and took the party leadership two years later, a role he has kept ever since.

In March 2012 Anastasiades was named DISI's presidential nominee after receiving 86·7% backing from the party executive. The campaign trail was dominated by the country's financial crisis, with Anastasiades pledging to finalize a bailout programme and rebuild Cyprus' economic credibility on the international stage. On 17 Feb. 2013 he won 45% of the first round vote and in a run-off a week later claimed the presidency with 57·5% support.

Career in Office
Anastasiades began his tenure working to seal a financial bailout package worth €10bn. from the IMF and European Union, which was agreed in late March 2013 after difficult negotiations and amid parliamentary hostility. In return, he was expected to implement banking and structural reforms, entailing heavy losses for uninsured depositors, and severe austerity measures. In June he sought a revision of the terms as the economy lurched further into recession. Nevertheless, in Sept. 2013 parliament adopted legislation demanded by the IMF and EU in return for the continuation of bailout instalments. Anastasiades subsequently pushed through stringent reforms and, having eased out of recession as the economy grew 0·5% in the second quarter of 2015, Cyprus exited the bailout arrangement in March 2016.

Throughout 2013 Anastasiades was also under pressure to restart talks with the 'Turkish Republic of Northern Cyprus ('TRNC'), based on the guidelines laid out in the Annan Plan (recommending the unification of

Cyprus and the 'TRNC' within a federation). In Feb. 2014 he reached an accord with the then Turkish Cypriot president paving the way for new negotiations. However, in Oct. that year escalating tensions with Turkey over exploration rights to recently discovered hydrocarbons in the eastern Mediterranean prompted the Greek-Cypriot government to suspend further talks. Renewed optimism was generated in April 2015 with the election of Mustafa Akıncı, a left-wing moderate and advocate of reunification, as the new president of the 'TRNC'. Fresh talks between the two Cypriot leaders, brokered by the UN, began the following month. However, despite positive advances and an unprecedented joint new year television address in Jan. 2016 by the two leaders, subsequent intensive negotiations failed to achieve sufficient convergence on territorial adjustment or security guarantees and collapsed in acrimony in July 2017. However, in Oct. 2017 Anastasiades announced that he planned to seek a second presidential term and pledged to reignite the settlement process. At the elections in early 2018 he was returned to office with 56·0% of the vote.

Defence

Conscription is for 14 months. In 2013 defence expenditure totalled US$460m., with spending per capita US$398. The 2013 expenditure represented 2·1% of GDP. In 1998 the then president cancelled a US$450m. contract with Russia for the deployment of S-300 anti-aircraft missiles on the island and negotiated to place them on Crete instead.

National Guard

Total strength (2011) 12,000 (10,700 conscripts). There is also a paramilitary force of some 500 armed police.

There are two British bases (Army and Royal Air Force) and some 2,800 personnel. Greek (1,150) and UN peacekeeping (954 uniformed personnel in Jan. 2017; UNFICYP) forces are also stationed on the island.

There are approximately 36,000 Turkish troops stationed in the occupied area of Cyprus. The Turkish Cypriot Security Force amounts to around 5,000 troops, with 26,000 reservists and a paramilitary armed police of approximately 150.

Navy

The Maritime Wing of the National Guard operates six vessels. In the Turkish-occupied area of Cyprus the Coast Guard operates six patrol craft.

Air Force

The Air Wing of the National Guard operates a couple of aircraft and 11 attack helicopters (Mi-35s).

Economy

Overview

The traditional leading economic sectors are tourism, financial services and real estate. The southern part of Cyprus joined the European Union in 2004 and adopted the euro in Jan. 2008. Major regulatory and institutional reform implemented after 2004 included tax incentives to attract international corporations. The economy had expanded for 35 years before the global downturn prompted shrinkage of 1·9% in 2009, followed by slow growth in 2010 and 2011 and another contraction of 2·4% in 2012.

In June 2012 Cyprus became the fifth eurozone country to request a financial bailout, having been undermined by a combination of rapid credit expansion, a property market bubble, exposure to toxic Greek debt and the knock-on effects of the eurozone crisis. After an initial deal was rejected by parliament, a rescue package valued at €10bn. was agreed in March 2013 with the banking sector close to collapse and access to the international capital markets severely curtailed. The IMF reported bank assets equivalent to 835% of GDP in 2011—more than double the eurozone average.

Nonetheless, Cyprus has shown remarkable resilience since 2013, implementing tough austerity measures to restructure and diversify its economy. The country exited recession in 2015, a year earlier than first projected, and continued to grow in 2016. Driven by strong private demand, and supported by the euro's depreciation and low energy prices, the economy recorded growth of 1·7% in 2015 and 2·8% in 2016. Unemployment, although high, also fell, from 14·9% in 2015 to 13·3% in 2016. The inflation rate was recorded at −1·5% in 2015 and −1·2% in 2016, owing to depressed oil prices and the unemployment level.

Among Cyprus's key challenges are the reduction of high levels of non-performing loans, bringing down public debt, and implementing structural reforms to increase public sector efficiency and improve the country's attractiveness as an investment destination. A strong tourism sector, the rapidly developing investment fund sector and the discovery of significant quantities of natural gas in Cypriot waters raise the prospect of a transformation of the economy in the medium to long term.

Currency

On 1 Jan. 2008 the *euro* (EUR) replaced the Cyprus pound (CYP) as the legal currency of Cyprus at the irrevocable conversion rate of £C0·585274 to one euro. There was deflation 1·5% in 2015 and 1·2% in 2016.

In July 2005 gold reserves were 465,000 troy oz, foreign exchange reserves were US$3,655m. and total money supply was £C1,504m.

Budget

General government revenue totalled €7,035m. in 2014 (€6,596m. in 2013) and expenditure €8,522m. (€7,566m. in 2013).

Principal sources of revenue in 2014 were: taxes on goods and services, €2,397m.; taxes on income, profits and gains, €1,599m. Main items of expenditure by economic type in 2014: social benefits, €2,576m.; compensation of employees, €2,299m.

Cyprus had a budget surplus of 1·8% of GDP in 2017 and of 0·3% in 2016. There was a deficit in 2015 (1·3%). The required target set by the EU is a budget deficit of no more than 3%.

The standard rate of VAT was increased from 18% to 19% in Jan. 2014. There are reduced rates of 9·0% and 5·0%.

Performance

The economy grew by 2·0% in 2015, 3·4% in 2016 and 3·9% in 2017. Total GDP was US$21·7bn. in 2017 (government-controlled area only).

Banking and Finance

The Central Bank of Cyprus, established in 1963, is the bank of issue. It regulates money supply, credit and foreign exchange and supervises the banking system. The *Governor* is Chrystalla Georghadji.

In 2012 there were six domestic banks, 35 International Banking Units and one representative office of a foreign bank. The leading banks are Bank of Cyprus, Cyprus Popular Bank and Hellenic Bank. At 31 Oct. 2012 banks' total deposits and lending amounted to €70,306m. and €71,415m. respectively.

Total foreign direct investment in 2017 was US$6·3bn., down from a high of US$7·5bn. in 2015.

There is a stock exchange in Nicosia.

Energy and Natural Resources

In 2011, 5·4% of energy consumption came from renewables (wind power, solar power, hydro-electric power, tidal power, geothermal energy and biomass), compared to the European Union average of 13·0%. A target of 13% has been set by the EU for 2020.

Environment

Carbon dioxide emissions from the consumption of energy were the equivalent of 7·8 tonnes per capita in 2011. An *Environmental Performance Index* compiled in 2016 ranked Cyprus 40th of 180 countries, with 80·2%. The index examined various factors in nine areas—agriculture, air quality, biodiversity and habitat, climate and energy, fisheries, forests, health impacts, water and sanitation, and water resources.

Electricity

Installed capacity was 1·1m. kW in 2011. Production in 2011 was 4·93bn. kWh and consumption per capita 4,415 kWh.

Oil and Gas

An offshore gas field in Cypriot waters to the south of the island was discovered in 2011. The Aphrodite field is believed to contain around 127bn. cu. metres of natural gas and was declared commercially viable in 2015.

Minerals

The principal minerals extracted in 2010 were (in 1,000 tonnes): crushed aggregate, 4,589; sand, 4,571; gravel, 4,253; crushed limestone, 250; gypsum, 240; clay, 210.

Agriculture

21% of the government-controlled area is cultivated. There were 102,400 ha. of arable land in 2008 and 37,500 ha. of permanent crops. 24,400 ha. were irrigated in 2008. About 6·3% (2008) of the economically active population were engaged in agriculture.

Chief agricultural products in 2008 (1,000 tonnes): milk, 194·9; potatoes, 115·0; citrus fruit, 111·8; meat, 100·5; fresh fruit, 52·2; grapes, 32·4; olives, 15·6; eggs, 9·9; carobs, 6·5; cereals (barley, wheat and oats), 6·3; carrots, 1·9; almonds, 0·4; other vegetables, 71·9. Livestock in 2008: cattle, 55,800; goats, 318,400; pigs, 464,900; sheep, 267,300; poultry, 2·9m.

Forestry

Total forest area in 2015 was 0·17m. ha. (19% of the land area). In 2011, 8,000 cu. metres of timber were produced.

Fisheries

Catches in 2012 totalled 1,303 tonnes; aquaculture production that year amounted to 4,334 tonnes.

Industry

The most important manufacturing industries in 2008 were: food products, other non-metallic mineral products, fabricated metal products, beverages, wood products, printing, pharmaceutical products and plastic products. The manufacturing industry in 2008 contributed 7·5% of the GDP.

Labour

Out of an average of 381,300 people in employment in 2009, 71,800 were in wholesale and retail trade/repair of motor vehicles and motorcycles; 44,300 in construction; and 34,800 in manufacturing. The unemployment rate was 7·1% in Sept. 2010. There were a total of 1,211 working days lost to strike action in 2009, up from 1,034 in 2008 but down from 10,289 in 2007.

International Trade

Imports and Exports

In 2011 imports (c.i.f.) totalled €6,311m. (€6,517m. in 2010); exports (f.o.b.), €1,404m. (€1,137m. in 2010).

Chief imports, 2009 (in €1,000): machinery, electrical equipment, sound and television recorders, 1,018,788; mineral products, 1,007,937; prepared foodstuffs, beverages, spirits and vinegar, tobacco, 542,945; products of chemical or allied industries, 514,872; vehicles, aircraft, vessels and associated transport equipment, 478,516. Chief domestic exports, 2009 (in €1,000): pharmaceutical products, 108,019; photosensitive semiconductor devices, 57,421; haloumi cheese, 41,027; potatoes, 38,094; waste and scrap, 29,900.

Main import suppliers, 2010: Greece, 18·8%; Italy, 9·4%; Germany, 8·9%; UK, 8·3%. Main export markets, 2010: Greece, 21·3%; Bunkers and ship stores, 14·3%; Germany, 9·2%; UK, 7·5%.

Communications

Roads

In 2007 the total length of roads in the government-controlled area was 12,246 km, of which 64·0% were paved. In 2007 there were 410,936 passenger cars, 117,498 trucks and vans, 3,292 buses and coaches and 41,211 motorcycles and mopeds. There were 71 deaths as a result of road accidents in 2009.

The area controlled by the government of the Republic and that controlled by the 'TRNC' are now served by separate transport systems, and there are no services linking the two areas.

Civil Aviation

Nicosia airport has been closed since the Turkish invasion in 1974. It is situated in the UN controlled buffer zone. There are international airports at Larnaca (the main airport) and Paphos. In 2009, 7,068,080 passengers, 59,092 aircraft and 38,502 tonnes of commercial freight went through these airports. Both airports have been expanded considerably to increase capacity, with new terminals at Paphos and Larnaca coming into operation in Nov. 2008 and Nov. 2009 respectively. In 2009 Larnaca handled 5,360,369 passengers and 38,092 tonnes of freight, and Paphos handled 1,707,711 passengers and 410 tonnes of freight. In 2009, 2,318,107 passengers arrived at the two airports on scheduled flights and 2,306,850 passengers departed. Cyprus Airways, the former national carrier, ceased operations in Jan. 2015.

Shipping

The two main ports are Limassol and Larnaca. In 2013, 3,041 ships of 20,667,393 net registered tons entered Cyprus ports carrying 7,610,499 tonnes of cargo from, to and via Cyprus. In Jan. 2014 there were 822 ships of 300 GT or over registered, totalling 20·34m. GT. Among the 822 vessels registered were 277 bulk carriers, 203 container ships, 184 general cargo ships and 122 oil tankers. Cyprus is a 'flag of convenience' country.

Telecommunications

In 2011 there were 405,000 landline telephone subscriptions (equivalent to 362·7 per 1,000 inhabitants) and 1,090,900 mobile phone subscriptions (or 977·1 per 1,000 inhabitants). There were 529·9 internet users per 1,000 inhabitants in 2010. Fixed internet subscriptions totalled 190,900 in 2009 (175·1 per 1,000 inhabitants). In March 2012 there were 554,000 Facebook users. CYTA (short for Cyprus Telecommunications Authority) is the state-owned national telecommunications provider. It has developed an extensive submarine fibre optic cable network linking Cyprus with neighbouring countries such as Greece, Israel and Egypt and—by extension—with the rest of the world.

Social Institutions

Out of 178 countries analysed in the 2017 *Fragile States Index*—a list published jointly by the Fund for Peace and *Foreign Policy* magazine—Cyprus was ranked the 58th least vulnerable to conflict or collapse. The index is based on 12 indicators of state vulnerability across social, political and economic categories.

Justice

There are a Supreme Court, Assize Courts and District Courts. The Supreme Court is composed of 13 judges, one of whom is the President of the Court. The Assize Courts have unlimited criminal jurisdiction. The District Courts exercise civil and criminal jurisdiction, the extent of which varies with the composition of the Bench.

A Supreme Council of Judicature, consisting of the President and Judges of the Supreme Court, is entrusted with the appointment, promotion, transfers, termination of appointment and disciplinary control over all judicial officers, other than the Judges of the Supreme Court. The Attorney-General (Costas Clerides) is head of the independent Law Office and legal adviser to the President and his Ministers.

The population in penal institutions in the government-controlled area in Sept. 2011 was 905 (106 per 100,000 of national population). The International Centre for Prison Studies estimated in 2014 that 41·8% of prisoners had yet to receive a trial.

The death penalty was abolished for all crimes in 2002.

Education

Greek-Cypriot Education. Primary education is compulsory and is provided free in six grades to children between 5 years 8 months and 11 years 8 months. A one-year pre-primary education is compulsory and is provided free by the public kindergartens. There are also schools for the deaf and blind, and nine schools for disabled children. In 2008–09 the ministry of education and culture ran 250 kindergartens for children in the age group 3–5 years 8 months; there were also 60 communal and 154 private kindergartens. There were 371 primary schools in 2008–09 with 55,552 pupils and 4,686 teachers.

Secondary education is also free and attendance for the first cycle (gymnasium) is compulsory. The secondary school lasts six years—three years at the gymnasium followed by three years at the *lykeion* (lyceum) or three years at one of the technical schools that provide technical and vocational education for industry. In 2008–09 there were 165 secondary schools with 7,652 teachers and 65,445 pupils.

Tertiary education is provided at nine public and 34 private institutions. There are three public universities: the University of Cyprus, the Open University of Cyprus and the Cyprus University of Technology, which admitted their first students in Sept. 1992, Sept. 2006 and Sept. 2007 respectively and had a combined total of 7,527 students in 2008–09. The other public institutions are the Higher Technical Institute, which provides courses lasting three to four years for technicians in civil, electrical, mechanical and marine engineering; the Cyprus Forestry College (administered by the ministry of agriculture, natural resources and environment); the Higher Hotel Institute (ministry of labour and social insurance); the Mediterranean Institute of Management (ministry of labour and social insurance); the School of Nursing (ministry of health), which runs courses lasting two to three years;

the Cyprus Police Academy, which provides a three-year training programme. Among the 34 private institutions are three private universities: the European University Cyprus, the University of Nicosia and the Frederick University. All three universities opened in Sept. 2007; they had a combined total of 10,367 students in 2008–09.

There are also various public and private institutions that provide non-formal education. These include the Apprenticeship Training Scheme and Evening Technical Classes, and other vocational and technical courses organized by the Human Resources Development Authority.

In 2008 the adult literacy rate was 98%. The percentage of the population aged 20 years and over that has attended school was 93·0% in 2008.

In 2008 public expenditure on education came to 7·5% of GDP and 16·9% of total government spending.

Health

In 2010 there were 2,442 physicians, 772 dentists, 3,930 nurses and midwives and 181 pharmacists. There were 87 registered private hospitals/clinics, six government hospitals and two rural hospitals in 2009.

Welfare

Cyprus has a compulsory earnings-related Social Insurance Scheme financed by tripartite contributions, which covers all the gainfully employed population. Employees in the broader public sector are covered by supplementary mandatory pension schemes or provident funds. A large proportion of the private sector's employees have supplementary coverage under non-statutory provident funds established by collective agreements.

Religion

The Greek Cypriots are predominantly Greek Orthodox Christians, and almost all Turkish Cypriots are Muslims (mostly Sunnis of the Hanafi sect). There are also small groups of the Armenian Apostolic Church, Roman Catholics (Maronites and Latin Rite) and Protestants (mainly Anglicans). *See also* CYPRUS: Territory and Population.

Culture

World Heritage Sites

There are three sites under Cypriot jurisdiction in the World Heritage List: Paphos (entered on the list in 1980); the churches of the Troodos region (1985, 2001); and Choirokoitia (1998). Paphos, inhabited since the Neolithic age, was a site of worship of the goddess Aphrodite and prehistoric fertility deities. The site has the remains of villas, palaces, theatres, fortresses and tombs. The Troodos region has one of the largest groups of Byzantine churches and monasteries. Decorated with murals and frescoes, they include the Church of St John Lampadistis, built between the 11th and 15th centuries. The Neolithic settlement of Choirokoitia, between Larnaca and Limassol and dating from the 7th to the 4th millennium BC, is one of the most important prehistoric sites in the eastern Mediterranean.

Press

In 2008 there were 22 paid-for dailies daily newspapers with a circulation of 103,000. The most widely read daily is *Phileleftheros*.

Tourism

There were 2,173,000 international tourist arrivals in 2010 (excluding same-day visitors), up from 2,141,000 in 2009. Most tourists in 2010 were from the UK (45·8%), followed by Russia (10·3%), Germany (6·4%) and Greece (5·9%). Tourist spending in 2010 totalled US$2,371m. There were 839 tourist establishments in 2010 with 88,234 beds.

Festivals

The capital, Nicosia, is the focal point for Independence Day festivities each Oct. Limassol hosts many of the country's largest festivals, including a ten-day Carnival as part of the nationwide Apokreo festival that precedes Easter. Each May Anthestiria (a flower festival) is held, and there are annual festivals of Shakespearean and Ancient Greek theatre.

Diplomatic Representatives

Of Cyprus in the United Kingdom (13 St James's Sq., London, SW1Y 4LB)
    High Commissioner: Euripedes L. Evriviades.

Of the United Kingdom in Cyprus (Alexander Pallis St., PO Box 21978, Nicosia 1587)
    High Commissioner: Stephen Lillie, CMG.

Of Cyprus in the USA (2211 R St., NW, Washington, D.C., 20008)
    Ambassador: Marios Lysiotis.

Of the USA in Cyprus (Metochiou and Ploutarchou Streets, Engomi 2407, Nicosia)
    Ambassador: Vacant.
    Chargé d'Affaires a.i.: Nathaniel P. Dean.

Of Cyprus to the United Nations
    Ambassador: Kornelios Korneliou.

Of Cyprus to the European Union
    Permanent Representative: Nicholas Emiliou.

'Turkish Republic of Northern Cyprus (Trnc)'

Kuzey Kıbrıs Türk Cumhuriyeti
    The Turkish Republic of Northern Cyprus, proclaimed on 15 Nov. 1983, occupies 3,355 sq. km (about 33% of the island of Cyprus) and its population at the 2011 census was 286,257. Around 36,000 members of Turkey's armed forces are also stationed in the TRNC.

Presidential elections were held over two rounds in April 2015. Mustafa Akıncı, a moderate independent and proponent of Cypriot reunification (which had been rejected by the Greek Cypriot south in 2004), won the run-off with 60·5% of the vote against conservative, incumbent president Derviş Eroğlu with 39·5%.

The 50 members of the *Legislative Assembly* are elected under a proportional representation system. In parliamentary elections in Jan. 2018 the National Unity Party won 35·6% of the vote (21 seats), the Republican Turkish Party 20·9% (12), the People's Party 17·1% (19), the Communal Democracy Party 8·6% (3), the Democratic Party-National Forces 7·8% (3) and the Rebirth Party 7·0% (2). Turnout was 66·2%.
    President: Mustafa Akıncı (since April 2015).
    Prime Minister: Tufan Erhürman (since Feb. 2018).

The Turkish lira is used as the currency. 22 banks, including 14 local private banks, were operating in 2014. Control is exercised by the Central Bank of the TRNC.

There is a free port at Famagusta and an international airport at Ercan. In 2013 there were direct flights to Turkey and indirect flights to Azerbaijan, Belgium, Germany, Hungary, Italy, Kazakhstan, Moldova, Spain, Turkmenistan, Ukraine, the UK and the USA.

There are 12 universities.

Further Reading

Cyprus

Calotychos, V., *Cyprus and Its People: Nation, Identity and Experience in an Unimaginable Community 1955–1997.* 1999

Faustmann, Hubert and Ker-Lindsay, James, *The Government and Politics of Cyprus.* 2008

Hakkı, Murat Metin, *The Cyprus Issue: A Documentary History, 1878–2006.* 2007

Hitchens, Christopher, *Hostage to History: Cyprus from the Ottomans to Kissinger.* 1997

Joseph, Joseph S., *Cyprus: Ethnic Conflict and International Politics: From Independence to the Threshold of the European Union.* 1999

Ker-Lindsay, James, *The Cyprus Problem: What Everyone Needs to Know.* 2011

Ker-Lindsay, James, (ed.) *Resolving Cyprus: New Approaches to Conflict Resolution.* 2014

Mallinson, William, *Cyprus: A Modern History.* 2005

Michael, Michális Stavrou, *Resolving the Cyprus Conflict: Negotiating History.* 2009

Pace, Roderick, *The European Union's Mediterranean Enlargement: Cyprus and Malta.* 2006

Papadakis, Yiannis, *Divided Cyprus: Modernity, History and an Island in Conflict.* 2006

Richter, Heinz, *A Concise History of Modern Cyprus: 1878–2009.* 2010

Sepos, Angelos, *The Europeanization of Cyprus: Polity, Policies and Politics.* 2008

Statistical Information: Statistical Service of the Republic of Cyprus, Michalakis Karaolis Street, 1444 Nicosia.

Website: http://www.mof.gov.cy/mof/cystat/statistics.nsf

'Turkish Republic Of Northern Cyprus (Trnc)'

Dodd, C. H. (ed.) *The Political, Social and Economic Development of Northern Cyprus.* 1993

Hanworth, R., *The Heritage of Northern Cyprus.* 1993

Ioannides, C. P., *In Turkey's Image: the Transformation of Occupied Cyprus into a Turkish Province.* 1991

Czech Republic

Česká Republika

Capital: Prague
Population projection, 2020: 10·63m.
GNI per capita, 2017: (PPP$) 30,588
HDI/world rank, 2017: 0·888/27
Internet domain extension: .cz

Key Historical Events

The area that is today the Czech Republic was originally inhabited by Celts around the 4th century BC. The Celtic Boii tribe gave the country its Latin name—Boiohaemum (Bohemia)—but was driven out by Germanic tribes. Slav tribes migrated to central Europe during the period known as the Migration of Peoples and were well established by the 6th century. The first half of the 7th century saw allied Slavonic tribes defending their territory from the Avar Empire in the Hungarian lowlands and from Frank attackers to the West.

Mojmír established The Great Moravian Empire in 830, comprising Bohemia, Moravia and Slovakia. The Empire reached its height under Moravian ruler Svatopluk but was engulfed and destroyed by the Magyars around 903–07. In 1041, after the defeat of Prince Břetislav the Restorer by the German Emperor Henry III, Bohemia became a fief of the Holy Roman Empire. Dynastic squabbles, exacerbated by German interference, weakened the power of the dukes, but in 1212 Otakar I (1197–1230) was granted a hereditary kingship from the Holy Roman Emperor who also declared the indivisibility of Bohemia as a key independent state within the realm.

A period of prosperity followed, aided by the immigration of German miners and merchants. Bohemia expanded under the last Přemysl kings. Wenceslas I (1230–53) seized Austria in 1251, though it passed to the Habsburgs when Otakar II was killed at the battle of Marchfeld in 1278. His son Wenceslas II was elected king of Poland in 1300. Wenceslas III was assassinated in 1306, thus ending the Přemysl line. After four years of struggle John of Luxemburg succeeded the throne in 1310.

John's son Charles (1346–78) became Holy Roman Emperor as Charles IV (Charles I of Bohemia) in 1355. He declared Prague the capital of the German Empire, designating the Crownlands of Bohemia to include parts of modern Germany and Poland. The Golden Bull of Nürnberg in 1356 granted the king of Bohemia first place among the empire's electors.

In what became known as the Golden Age, Charles fostered the commercial and cultural development of Bohemia. In 1348 he founded Prague University, the first university in Central Europe. Work started on the building of St Vitus cathedral, Charles Bridge and the Czech castle of the Grail in Karlstejn during his reign.

Hussite Revolution

Dissatisfaction with the Catholic church in the 14th and 15th centuries climaxed with the Hussite Revolution, the clerical reform movement associated with Jan Hus. The movement had undertones of anti-German Czech nationalism and found support amongst the urban middle classes and lesser rural gentry as well as the urban poor and peasantry. Hus was condemned as a heretic and burnt at the stake in Constance in 1415. Anti-Hussite rulings by Wenceslas IV led to the first 'Defenestration of Prague' in 1419, when Catholic councillors were thrown from the Town Hall windows. In the ensuing Hussite wars Sigismund, the Hungarian Holy Roman Emperor, failed to recover the Bohemian crown. Five crusades were launched against the Hussites in the years 1420–31, all of which were defeated.

The Hussites were eventually weakened by divisions between moderates, the Utraquists, and radicals, the Taborites (originating from the town of Tabor in South Bohemia). The latter's militant leader, Jan Žižka, was defeated in the battle of Lipany in 1434 by the Prague faction supported by Sigismund. This victory allowed for a temporary agreement between Hussite Bohemia and Catholic Europe, known as the Compacts of Basle, which reunited the Utraquist faction with Rome in 1436. A degree of post-war recovery followed under the moderate Hussite king, George of Poděbrady (1457–71), who crushed the radical Taborite dissidents.

In 1471 Vladislav Jagellonský, son of King Casimir IV of Poland, was elected King of Bohemia. His son Louis inherited the throne but was killed at Mohás fighting the Turks in 1526. From 1490, Hungary and Bohemia were both ruled by the Jagiellon Dynasty. Under their rule, the provincial diet of three estates (nobility, gentry and burgesses) enhanced the power of the nobility at the expense of the burgesses. Animosity between the Hussite church and the minority Catholic Church continued.

In 1526, after the extinction of the Jagiellon line, Czech nobles elected Archduke Ferdinand. The advent of the Habsburgs saw Roman Catholicism reintroduced. When Rudolf II (1576–1611) left Vienna to make Prague the capital of the German Empire and the seat of a papal nuncio, the city became a centre of European culture. However, religious divisions with the beginnings of the Counter-Reformation led to the second Defenestration of Prague. Two Catholic governors and their secretary were thrown from a window of Prague Castle, an action which sparked off the Thirty Years' War (1618–48). This brought political disorder and economic devastation to the country with the Habsburg forces wiping out a third of the Bohemian population. The estates deposed Emperor Ferdinand II in favour of the Calvinist Frederick V but the latter's forces were defeated at the battle of White Mountain in 1620. A period of Habsburg hegemony ensued.

After the suppression of the Taborites, the only remaining Protestant Church in Bohemia was the Unity of Czech Brethren, to which Catholics, Utraquists and Lutherans were opposed. The Czech nobility was replaced by German-speaking adventurers, the burgesses lost their rights, the peasantry suffered hardships and citizens were forced to embrace the Catholic faith or emigrate. The throne of Bohemia was made hereditary in the Habsburg Dynasty and the most important offices transferred to Vienna. Opposition was savagely repressed. The next two centuries became known as the Dark Ages.

Enlightened Despotism

In the Enlightenment of the late 18th century, Empress Maria Theresa and her son Joseph II granted freedom of worship and movement to the peasantry in 1781, a precondition for the industrial revolution of the next century which made Bohemia the most developed economy within the Empire. Bohemia and Moravia each became independent parts of the Habsburg Monarchy although, conversely, the reforms led to greater Germanization and centralization of power, threatening the Slavic identities of the Empire's subjects.

The revival of the Czech nation, which began as a cultural movement, soon progressed into a struggle for political emancipation. Calls for the promotion of the Czech language encouraged Czech nationalists to campaign for the formation of a new Czechoslovakia. It was a concept fostered by Tomáš Garrigue Masaryk, a philosophy professor at the University of Prague and Professor for Slavonic Studies at King's College, London, who was to become the first president of the Czechoslovak Republic.

Male suffrage was granted in 1906 but the chamber of deputies was constantly bypassed by the emperor. The First World War brought estrangement between the Czechs and the Germans, the latter supporting the war effort, the former seeing it as a clash of monarchy versus democracy. Masaryk went into exile in London, where he committed himself to enlisting the support of Britain, France, Russia and the United States in founding a post-war independent Czechoslovak state. He worked with other exiled Czechs and Slovaks, including Dr Edvard Beneš, who later also became president of Czechoslovakia. In 1916 a Czechoslovak National Council was set up in Paris under Masaryk's chairmanship.

In 1918 Masaryk secured the support of US president Woodrow Wilson for Czech and Slovak unity and in May the Pittsburgh agreement was signed in the USA by exiles of both lands. On 18 Oct. 1918 the National Council transformed itself into a provisional government, and was recognized by the Allies.

© Springer Nature Limited 2020
Palgrave Macmillan (ed.), *The Statesman's Yearbook 2020*,
https://doi.org/10.1057/978-1-349-95940-2_59

Creation of the State

Austria accepted President Wilson's terms on 27 Oct. 1918, and the next day a republic was proclaimed with Masaryk, almost 70, as president, and Beneš as foreign minister. In drawing up the frontiers of the new state the principles of Wilsonian self-determination were defeated by the ethnic mix; other criteria employed were the partial restoration of the historic provinces and the need to establish an economically viable and defensible state. Among the minorities were 3·25m. Sudeten Germans. Borders were confirmed in the Treaty of Versailles in June 1919 (although Hungary subsequently called for these to be reformed) along with the official recognition of the state of Czechoslovakia by the international community.

The constitution of 1920 provided for a two-chamber parliament with adult suffrage. The French Constitution and the American Declaration of Rights were both used as models. The electoral system worked so that all governments were coalitions. Slovakia was granted an assembly in 1927 but the state was basically centralist and the Slovaks maintained their own parties. Between the wars Czechoslovakia became one of the ten most developed and stable countries of the world, although it suffered severe economic depression in the 1930s.

In Nov. 1935 Masaryk was succeeded by Beneš. Meanwhile in Germany, Hitler's designs on expanding the Third Reich stirred up nationalist agitation among the Sudeten Germans. The 1930 census showed 22·3% of the Czechoslovak population were ethnic Germans. In 1933 the German National Socialist Worker's Party in Czechoslovakia, directly affiliated to the Nazi party in Germany, was banned. The Sudeten German Party, led by Konrad Henlein, was formed in its place and won 67% of the German vote in the parliamentary elections of 1935. Czechoslovakia had relied on its 1925 pact with France to defend it against the threat of German aggression, but in the Munich Conference of 29 Sept. 1938 France sided with Britain and Italy in stipulating that all districts with a German population of more than 50% should be ceded to Germany. This legitimized the annexing of the Czech Sudetenland to Germany.

On 5 Oct. 1938 Beneš resigned and went into exile in Britain, and on 15 March 1939 Hitler's troops invaded Prague, contravening the Munich agreement. Slovakia, though allied to the Germans, declared independence under the fascist leadership of Jozef Tiso. The Czech territory became the German Protectorate of Bohemia-Moravia.

Czechoslovakia suffered further territorial losses to Poland and Hungary under the Vienna Arbitration of 2 Nov. 1938. In all, it lost 30% of its territory and almost 34% of its population. Over 1m. Czechs, Slovaks and Ukrainians came under German, Polish and Hungarian rule. Hitler's declared aim was to drive the Czechs out of Central Europe. The Protectorate became a centre for arms production.

Nazi Occupation

Initial attempts at resistance were brutally crushed. On 17 Nov. 1939 German occupiers closed down all Czech universities, executed nine of the leaders of the student movement and transported scores of other students to concentration camps. In 1940 the Gestapo transformed the town of Terezín (Theresienstadt) near Prague into a concentration camp, evacuating the pre-war population to accommodate 140,000 Jews from all parts of the Reich, the majority from the Protectorate of Bohemia-Moravia. 85,000 were then transported to death camps in the East, chiefly to Auschwitz, and over 30,000 prisoners were held in the fortress. Many Communists and Czech resistance fighters also met their deaths there.

Mass expulsions were a regular feature of the Protectorate. In 1942, 30,000 people were forced to leave their homes in order to make way for the military. In another case around 5,000 families were expelled from around 30 villages in Moravia in an attempt to create an ethnic German enclave. Growing resistance led to the appointment of SS General Reinhard Heydrich, head of the Reich's Security Office, who launched a savage offensive against underground organizations and executed general Alois Elias, head of the Protectorate's government, for his connections with the Beneš government in Britain. The latter, along with the Allies, were in turn behind the assassination of Heydrich, carried out on 27 May 1942 by two paratroopers. The Nazis responded with a frenzy of terror known as the 'Heydrichiade'. Revenge murders of the entire populations of Lidice (on 10 June 1942) and Lezáky (24 June 1942) were carried out.

The Beneš government in exile in London, with Jan Šrámek as prime minister, was officially recognized by Britain and the USSR on 18 June 1941. A 20-year treaty of alliance with the USSR was signed on 12 Dec. 1943 and, in March 1945, Beneš went to Moscow to prepare for post-war government in the wake of the Soviet Army advance. Liberation by the Soviet Army and US forces was completed in 1945 following an insurrection on 5 May. Territories taken by Germans, Poles and Hungarians were restored to Czechoslovakia. Subcarparthian Ruthenia (now in Ukraine) was transferred to the USSR, creating a common border with the Soviet state.

The Sudeten Germans suffered brutal expulsions, during which up to 250,000 died, 6,000 of whom were murdered. The 'resettlement' of ethnic Germans was officially approved at the Potsdam Conference on 1 Aug. 1945, when the USA and Britain insisted on humane transfer, subsequently supervised by the Allies and the Red Cross. German or Hungarian Czechs had their citizenship taken away unless they were naturalized Czechs or Slovaks. In order to stay, German or Hungarian Czechs had to prove that they had remained faithful to the Czechoslovak Republic, had fought in the resistance or had personally suffered at the hands of fascists. Further decrees expropriated property and agricultural land. A total of 2,700,000 Germans were expelled, and in the Czech census of March 1991 only 47,000 claimed German as their nationality. A Czech–German Declaration of 21 Jan. 1997 saw both sides admit to and apologize for their atrocities during the period.

Soviet Domination

Beneš once again became president of Czechoslovakia but, under pressure from the USSR, measures were taken to confiscate and redistribute property and to take key industries into public ownership. Before 1939 the Communist party of Czechoslovakia (CPCz) had never gained more than 13% of the vote, but its patriotic stance in the late 1930s as well as its clear affiliation with the country's main liberator, the USSR, led to a sharp increase in popularity. In the elections of 26 May 1946 the Communists won almost 40% of the vote in Czech areas and 30% in Slovakia. This made the party the largest group in the new Constituent National Assembly, with 114 of the 300 seats and Klement Gottwald as premier. Its leaders pledged commitment to democratic traditions while pursuing a 'specific Czechoslovak road to socialism'.

The party's independence was first put to the test when Czechoslovakia was pressured by Stalin into withdrawing from the American Marshall Plan for European economic reconstruction, seen from Moscow as a threat to its own influence. Stalin's encouragement of the CPCz grew in the autumn of 1947 when a people's militia was formed and non-communist parties in the governing coalition found their influence eroded. In protest, 12 non-communist ministers handed in their resignations. The CPCz adroitly handled this situation to its own advantage, forcing President Beneš to appoint a predominantly communist government on 25 Feb. 1948.

A new constitution, declaring Czechoslovakia a 'people's democracy', was approved on 9 May 1948 and elections were held on 30 May with a single list of candidates, resulting in an 89% majority for the government. Beneš resigned on 2 June after refusing to ratify the Communist Constitution. 12 days later Gottwald succeeded him as President. Civil rights were severely restricted; from 1950 monasteries and convents were nationalized, with 219 monasteries being taken over by the People's Militia on the night of 13 April alone; monastic orders were abolished.

The secret service became one of the most systematic and omnipresent in the Soviet bloc. Unsubstantiated charges of treason and resistance to the communist cause led to a series of show trials and executions, with many victims from the CPCz itself. It is estimated that between 200,000 and 280,000 suffered death or persecution during the Stalin era. Stalin died on 5 March 1953, and Gottwald just a week later, but the communists maintained their grip. Workers' demonstrations in Plzeň and other Czech towns against price rises and currency reform, which devalued savings, were brutally suppressed by the military in June that year. Political trials of 'Slovak nationalists' in 1954 had many Slovak Communists imprisoned, including Gustáv Husák, who later went on to become secretary-general of the CPCz and president of Czechoslovakia.

The Soviet five-year economic plans emphasized engineering, arms production and heavy industry. A third of Czechoslovak output came from the arms industry. The service and consumer goods industries were virtually abolished and all farms collectivized. The founding of COMECON on 1 Jan. 1949 and the signing of the Warsaw Pact in 1955 limited Czechoslovakia's trading partners to the Eastern bloc.

A new constitution, introduced in 1960, reinforced the power of the Communist Party and changed the country's name to the Socialist Republic of Czechoslovakia (ČSSR).

Prague Spring

The failure of the third five-year plan to meet its targets gave a push to economic reform. A mixed economy was introduced which led to a period of cultural liberalization. Support for political reform grew within party ranks. Antonín Novotný was persuaded to resign as CPCz leader on 5 Jan. 1968. He was replaced by Alexander Dubček, leader of the Communist Party of Slovakia. On 22 March, Novotný resigned as president in favour of Gen. Ludvík Svoboda, who was elected by the National Assembly. Precipitating what became known as the Prague Spring, Dubček introduced many reforms in his pursuit of 'socialism with a human face'. New political bodies were formed, breaking up the monopoly of the Communist Party. Press censorship was abolished and restraints on freedom of expression relaxed.

The reforms caused consternation in Moscow. Brezhnev unsuccessfully put pressure on Czechoslovakia between May and Aug. He then ordered the invasion of Czechoslovakia by troops of the Warsaw Pact countries (with the exception of Romania) on 20–21 Aug. The Soviet intention of replacing Dubček and his government with more hard-line Communists failed when President Svoboda turned down Soviet nominees. Dubček and other party leaders were then abducted to Moscow and forced to sign an agreement to keep Soviet troops stationed in Czechoslovakia. The Prague Spring all but withered. The only surviving measure of reform was the introduction of the federal system on 1 Jan. 1969. Separate Czech and Slovak states came into force within a Czechoslovak federation, a move that satisfied the Slovaks who had been seeking autonomy for some time. Each state was awarded its own administration and a national council, and the National Assembly divided into two chambers. All other reforms of the Dubček administration were stamped out or reversed and the Soviet policy of 'normalization' took hold.

In protest at the Soviet repression, student Jan Palach set fire to himself in Wenceslas Square on 16 Jan. 1969. On 28 March when the Czechoslovak national ice hockey team beat the Soviets, celebrations turned into anti-Soviet demonstrations and led to many arrests. On 17 April Dubček was forced from office and replaced with the hard-liner, Gustáv Husák. Repression led to mass emigrations. So-called 'enemies of the state' were put under constant surveillance, blacklisted for jobs and their children denied university places. Freedom to travel abroad was no longer granted to ordinary citizens. Protest resurfaced again in 1977, with the signing of Charter 77 and founding of the Committee for the Defence of the Rights of the Unjustly Persecuted (VONS). These two organizations, led by artists and intellectuals, alerted the public to civil rights abuses and campaigned for civil and political rights.

Velvet Revolution

The advent of Mikhail Gorbachev's *glasnost* and *perestroika* in the mid-1980s initially changed little. Husák was replaced as leader of the CPCz by Miloš Jakeš, who had been responsible for Party purges in 1970. But there were renewed demonstrations in Aug. 1988 on the 20th anniversary of the Soviet invasion, in Oct. on the 70th anniversary of the founding of Czechoslovakia and in Jan. 1989 on the 20th anniversary of Jan Palach's suicide when the crowd was brutally dispersed and leading dissidents, including Václav Havel, arrested and imprisoned. Protests, petitions and further demonstrations followed in May, Aug. and Oct. of 1989. The fall of the Berlin Wall on 9 Nov. 1989 galvanized the pro-democracy movement. Another major demonstration by students on 17 Nov. led to further protests until the entire CPCz leadership resigned on 24 Nov. Civic Forum (OF) in the Czech Republic and the Public Against Violence (VPN) in Slovakia were formed to co-ordinate all pro-democratic forces, and an interim broad coalition 'Government of National Understanding' with a minority of Communists took over. This became known as the 'Velvet Revolution' owing to the lack of violence. Václav Havel was unanimously elected president of Czechoslovakia by the Federal Assembly on 29 Dec. 1989.

The first free elections since the Second World War were held in June 1990, with a turnout of 96·4%. The Communists were roundly defeated, and Civic Forum won 52% of the votes. Second parliamentary elections were fixed for mid-1992, by which time Civic Forum (OF) and VPN had been replaced by fully-fledged parties across the political spectrum. In the Czech lands, the right wing emerged as the strongest element, with the Civic Democratic party (ODS) the largest coalition party. Its leader, Václav Klaus, who was also finance minister, became prime minister and stayed in the post until Nov. 1997.

By contrast, in Slovakia, Vladimír Mečiar's Democratic Slovakia party and other post-communists were successful in the elections. A continuing Slovak desire for independence from Prague, along with differences in opinion on economic policy and the role of the state, strained relations between the two federal partners. An agreement to a 'velvet divorce' was reached with the two devolving into separate sovereign states from 1 Jan. 1993. Economic property was divided in accordance with a federal law of

13 Nov. 1992 and real estate became the property of the republic in which it was located. Other property was divided by specially-constituted commissions in the proportion of 2 (Czech Republic) to 1 (Slovakia) on the basis of population. Military material was also divided on the 2:1 principle, and regular military personnel were invited to choose in which army they would serve.

The Czech Republic showed the greater eagerness to become westernized. Although many feared a precipitous move towards a market economy, Klaus argued that danger lay in delaying reform, and that the creation of a market economy would lead the 'return to Europe' and the opening up of new markets.

Klaus immediately embarked on a series of radical reforms, impressing Western investors with his Thatcherite rhetoric, policies and publications. A programme of mass privatization was implemented, at first successfully, and the early to mid-nineties were a time of economic boom, with the Czech Republic a leading contender for Western trade and investment. However, many of the tough policies were not fully implemented and an increasing number of financial scandals were associated with the Klaus administration. 1997 also saw a currency crisis, where the crown devalued 12% against the dollar. Klaus was forced to resign as prime minister on 18 Nov. 1997.

Josef Tošovský formed a caretaker government until 1998 when Miloš Zeman formed a minority Social Democratic government, the country's first left-wing government since the fall of socialism. The Czech Republic joined NATO in 1999 and in 2001 Vladimír Špidla succeeded Zeman as party leader and prime minister. The Czech Republic became a member of the EU on 1 May 2004.

Following an inconclusive election in June 2006 there were seven months of political deadlock when the country was without a government. A new centre-right coalition was formed under Mirek Topolánek in Jan. 2007 but collapsed two years later. An interim government took office until July 2010 when Petr Nečas formed a coalition. Austerity measures prompted mass protests. In Dec. 2011 Václav Havel died and was given a state funeral.

In Jan. 2013 Miloš Zeman won the country's first direct presidential elections, going on to claim a second term in Jan. 2018. Nečas resigned as prime minister in June 2013 amid a corruption scandal and was succeeded by Jiří Rusnok, who headed a caretaker government until the end of the year. Bohuslav Sobotka then took over at the head of a coalition, before giving way to billionaire businessman Andrej Babiš after elections in Oct. 2017. Babiš later assembled a coalition of his own anti-corruption ANO party, the Social Democrats and the Christian and Democratic Union.

Territory and Population

The Czech Republic is bounded in the west by Germany, north by Poland, east by Slovakia and south by Austria. Minor exchanges of territory to straighten their mutual border were agreed between the Czech Republic and Slovakia on 4 Jan. 1996, but the Czech parliament refused to ratify them on 24 April 1996. Its area is 78,867 sq. km (30,451 sq. miles), including 1,620 sq. km (625 sq. miles) of inland waters. The population at the 2011 census was 10,436,560; density, 135·1 per sq. km. In 2011, 73·6% of the population lived in urban areas. In Jan. 2018 the population was estimated at 10,610,055.

The UN gives a projected population for 2020 of 10·63m.

There are 14 administrative regions *(Kraj)*, one of which is the capital, Prague (Praha).

Region	Chief city	Area in sq. km	2011 census population
Jihočeský	České Budějovice	10,057	628,336
Jihomoravský	Brno	7,196	1,163,508
Karlovarský	Karlovy Vary	3,315	295,595
Královéhradecký	Hradec Králové	4,758	547,916
Liberecký	Liberec	3,163	432,439
Moravskoslezský	Ostrava	5,427	1,205,834
Olomoucký	Olomouc	5,267	628,427
Pardubický	Pardubice	4,519	511,627
Plzeňský	Pilsen (Plzeň)	7,561	570,401
Prague (Praha)	—	496	1,268,796

(continued)

Region	Chief city	Area in sq. km	2011 census population
Středočeský	Prague (Praha)	11,015	1,289,211
Ústecký	Ústí nad Labem	5,335	808,961
Vysočina	Jihlava	6,796	505,565
Zlínský	Zlín	3,964	579,944

The census population of the principal towns in 2011 (in 1,000):

Prague (Praha)	1,269
Brno	386
Ostrava	296
Pilsen (Plzeň)	170
Liberec	103
Olomouc	101
České Budějovice	94
Hradec Králové	94
Ústí nad Labem	93
Pardubice	91
Havířov	77
Zlín	75
Kladno	68
Most	65
Opava	58

The main ethnic groups in 2011 were Czechs (64%), Moravians (5%) and Slovaks (1%). However, about 26% of the population (or more than 2·7m. people) did not answer the optional question on nationality. There were also (in 1,000): Ukrainians, 54; Poles, 39; Vietnamese, 30; Germans, 19; Russians, 18. Although only 5,000 people described themselves as being Roma in the 2011 census they are in reality estimated to number up to 300,000.

In May 2016 the government announced that it would adopt 'Czechia' as the official English-language short name for the country. The name 'Czechia'—as a geographic designation—is recognized by the United Nations Group of Experts on Geographical Names (UNGEGN), the United Nations Multilingual Terminology Database (UNTERM) and the International Organization for Standardization (ISO). 'Czech Republic' remains the official long name and is used as a political designation—for example, when referring to the country's government structure or membership in the United Nations and the European Union.

The official language is Czech.

Social Statistics

2009 births, 118,667; deaths, 107,421; marriages, 47,862; divorces, 29,133. Rates (per 1,000 population), 2009: birth, 11·3; death, 10·0; marriage, 4·6; divorce, 2·8. Life expectancy at birth, 2013, 74·6 years for males and 80·7 years for females. In 2009 the most popular age range for marrying was 30–34 for males and 25–29 for females. Annual population growth rate, 2005–10, 0·5%. Infant mortality, 2010, three per 1,000 live births; fertility rate, 2013, 1·6 children per woman.

Climate

A humid continental climate, with warm summers and cold winters. Precipitation is generally greater in summer, with thunderstorms. Autumn, with dry clear weather, and spring, which is damp, are each of short duration. Prague, Jan. 29·5°F (−1·5°C), July 67°F (19·4°C). Annual rainfall 19·3" (483 mm). Brno, Jan. 31°F (−0·6°C), July 67°F (19·4°C). Annual rainfall 21" (525 mm).

Constitution and Government

The constitution of 1 Jan. 1993 provides for a parliament comprising a 200-member *Chamber of Deputies*, elected for four-year terms by proportional representation, and an 81-member *Senate* elected for six-year terms in single-member districts, 27 senators being elected every two years. The main function of the Senate is to scrutinize proposed legislation. Senators must be at least 40 years of age, and are elected on a first-past-the-post basis, with a run-off in constituencies where no candidate wins more than half the votes cast. For the House of Representatives there is a 5% threshold; votes for parties failing to surmount this are redistributed on the basis of results in each of the eight electoral districts.

There is a *Constitutional Court* at Brno, whose 15 members are nominated by the President and approved by the Senate for ten-year terms.

Following a constitutional amendment that took effect in Oct. 2012, the *President* of the Republic is directly elected for a five-year term. Candidates standing for office must be 40 years of age. In the event of no candidate winning an absolute majority, a second round is held between the two most successful candidates. A president may not serve more than two consecutive five-year terms.

National Anthem

'Kde domov můj?' ('Where is my homeland?'); words by J. K. Tyl, tune by F. J. Škroup.

Government Chronology

(ANO = ANO 2011; ČSSD = Czech Social Democratic Party; ODS = Civic Democratic Party; SPOZ = Party of Civic Rights–Zemanovci; n/p = non-partisan)

Presidents since 1993.		
1993–2003	n/p	Václav Havel
2003–13	ODS	Václav Klaus
2013–	SPOZ	Miloš Zeman

Prime Ministers since 1993.		
1993–97	ODS	Václav Klaus
1997–98	n/p	Josef Tošovský
1998–2002	ČSSD	Miloš Zeman
2002–04	ČSSD	Vladimír Špidla
2004–05	ČSSD	Stanislav Gross
2005–06	ČSSD	Jiří Paroubek
2006–09	ODS	Mirek Topolánek
2009–10	n/p	Jan Fischer
2010–13	ODS	Petr Nečas
2013–14	n/p	Jiří Rusnok
2014–17	ČSSD	Bohuslav Sobotka
2017–	ANO	Andrej Babiš

Recent Elections

The first round of direct presidential elections took place on 12–13 Jan. 2018. None of the nine candidates secured enough votes in the first round and a run-off between incumbent Miloš Zeman (Party of Civic Rights) and Jiří Drahoš (ind.) was held on 26–27 Jan. 2018. Zeman was re-elected with 51·4% of the vote to Drahoš's 48·6%. Turnout was 61·9% in the first round and 66·6% in the second.

Elections to the Chamber of Deputies were held on 20 and 21 Oct. 2017; turnout was 60·8%. ANO 2011 (ANO) gained 78 seats with 29·6% of votes cast; the Civic Democratic Party (ODS) gained 25 with 11·3%; the Czech Pirate Party (Piráti), 22 with 10·8%; Freedom and Direct Democracy (SPD), 22 with 10·6%; the Communist Party of Bohemia and Moravia (KSČM), 15 with 7·8%; the Czech Social Democratic Party (ČSSD), 15 with 7·3%; the Christian and Democratic Union–Czechoslovak People's Party (KDU–ČSL), 10 with 5·8%; Tradition Responsibility Prosperity (TOP 09), 7 with 5·3%; Mayors and Independents (STAN), 6 with 5·2%.

Elections for a third of the 81 seats in the Senate were held on 5, 6, 12 and 13 Oct. 2018. As a result ODS and STAN each had 18 seats in the Senate; KDU–ČSL 15; ČSSD 13; ANO 2011 6; Senator 21 6. Independents held four seats and one seat remained vacant.

European Parliament

The Czech Republic has 21 representatives. At the May 2014 elections turnout was 18·2% (28·2% in 2009). ANO 2011 won 4 seats with 16·1% of votes cast (political affiliation in European Parliament: Alliance of Liberals and Democrats for Europe); TOP 09–Mayors and Independents coalition, 4 with 16·0% (European People's Party); ČSSD, 4 with 14·2% (Progressive Alliance of Socialists and Democrats); KSČM, 3 with 11·0% (European United Left/Nordic Green Left); KDU–ČSL, 3 with 10·0% (European People's Party); ODS, 2 with 7·7% (European Conservatives and Reformists); the Party of Free Citizens, 1 with 5·2% (Europe of Freedom and Direct Democracy).

Current Government

President: Miloš Zeman; b. 1944 (SPOZ; sworn in 8 March 2013).

In Feb. 2019 the coalition government consisted of:

Prime Minister: Andrej Babiš; b. 1954 (ANO 2011; sworn in 13 Dec. 2017).

First Deputy Prime Minister: Jan Hamáček (also *Minister of Interior*).
Deputy Prime Minister: Richard Brabec (also *Minister of Environment*).

Minister of Agriculture: Miroslav Toman. *Culture:* Antonín Staněk. *Defence:* Lubomír Metnar. *Education, Youth and Sports:* Robert Plaga. *Finance:* Alena Schillerová. *Foreign Affairs:* Tomáš Petříček. *Health:* Adam Vojtěch. *Industry and Trade:* Marta Nováková. *Justice:* Jan Kněžínek. *Labour and Social Affairs:* Jana Maláčová. *Regional Development:* Klára Dostálová. *Transport:* Dan Ťok.

Government Website: http://www.vlada.cz

Current Leaders

Miloš Zeman

Position
President

Introduction
Miloš Zeman, leader of the Party of Civic Rights–Zemanovci (SPOZ), was sworn in as president on 8 March 2013 following elections in Jan. He had previously served as prime minister from 1998–2002, representing the centre-left Czech Social Democratic Party (ČSSD).The president's primary role is to represent the Czech Republic abroad and make appointments to the constitutional court and central bank. Zeman has championed European integration and pledged to fight corruption.

Early Life
Miloš Zeman was born on 28 Sept. 1944 in Kolin, a town 55 km east of Prague. Having completed his schooling he was refused entry to university because of his political beliefs, but graduated from the Prague University of Economics in 1969 after undertaking external studies. After his attempts to join the Social Democratic Party were frustrated when the party was banned, he joined the Czechoslovakian Communist Party. This was in 1968 at the zenith of Dubček's Prague Spring, when the country experienced rapid liberal reform. After the Soviets crushed the movement, Zeman was expelled from the party for his opposition to Soviet 'normalization'.

After working in several sports and fitness organizations, Zeman established a forecasting centre, which was closed in 1984 by the communist regime. He then worked for an agricultural organization specializing in social systems forecasting but was dismissed from his post in 1989 after writing an article critical of the authorities.

Joining the Civic Forum, an alliance of anti-communist reformist groups, Zeman became a leading voice for the centre-left. Following the success of the Velvet Revolution and the overthrow of the communist regime in 1989, he entered parliament and became chairman of the budget and planning committee in 1990. After the Civic Forum split, he joined ČSSD in 1992 and won re-election to parliament. In 1993 he was elected party chairman, a position he retained in 1995 and 1997. Following the general elections of 1996 he was elected speaker of the parliament.

In 1997 the administration of Václav Klaus collapsed. After elections the following year in which the ČSSD emerged victorious, Zeman replaced him as prime minister. Over his four-year term Zeman reduced the pace of market reforms and privatization and advocated increased public spending. Leading a minority government, he secured an alliance with Klaus's Civic Democrats, a move that led to widespread criticism. Popular discontent resulted in demonstrations in Prague in late 1999 calling for the resignations of Zeman and Klaus to make room for a new generation of politicians. Zeman's relationship with the Czech media was strained and in 2000 national television journalists went on strike in protest at what they claimed was the politically-motivated appointment of a new director general.

On the international scene, Zeman oversaw the Czech Republic's entry into NATO in 1999. After relations with Austria became strained over a nuclear power plant dispute, Zeman resigned both his party leadership and the premiership in 2001. In 2003 he ran unsuccessfully for president and went into semi-retirement. In 2007 he left the ČSSD after a number of hostile public exchanges and established SPOZ. Despite SPOZ's shaky performance at its first elections in 2010, the party endorsed Zeman as leader and in 2012 he announced his candidature for the presidency.

Career in Office
On 8 March 2013 Zeman took office as the first president to be directly elected by universal suffrage in Czech history. He ran on a social-democratic pro-Europe platform in a heated campaign against Karel Schwarzenberg, winning support from poorer and older voters. He faced a fraught post-election political atmosphere as he sought to establish a working relationship with a politically opposed right-of-centre coalition government led by Petr Nečas.

Nečas and his cabinet resigned in June 2013 amid allegations of spying and corruption and Zeman nominated Jiří Rusnok, a former finance minister, as premier. This was opposed by the main political parties, who criticized the president for bypassing parliament and seeking to appoint a caretaker government comprised of Zeman loyalists and technocrats. In Aug. the Rusnok cabinet lost a parliamentary vote of confidence, heralding fresh elections in Oct. that proved inconclusive with no dominant party. In Nov. 2013 Zeman asked Bohuslav Sobotka of the ČSSD to try to form a new coalition government. This was eventually sworn in two months later.

At a ceremony in Prague in Nov. 2014 to mark the 25th anniversary of the Velvet Revolution, Zeman was the target of abuse from demonstrators demanding his resignation. In Sept. 2015 he rejected the EU's proposal of compulsory migrant quotas to manage the refugee flow into Europe (emanating mainly from the Syrian civil war) and remained a critic of EU asylum policy through 2016.

Parliamentary elections in Oct. 2017 saw a strong voter swing to the populist Action of Dissatisfied Citizens (ANO 2011), resulting in party leader Andrej Babiš, a billionaire industrialist and former deputy prime minister and finance minister, replacing Bohuslav Sobotka as prime minister in Dec. However, in Jan. 2018 his minority government lost a confidence vote in parliament and had to resign. Nevertheless, Zeman asked Babiš to try to form a new administration despite opposition to his reappointment, and in July the Chamber of Deputies endorsed his new coalition.

Earlier, in March 2017, Zeman had announced his intention to stand again in presidential elections scheduled for Jan. 2018, and was duly returned to office in the poll with 51·4% of the vote in a run-off.

Andrej Babiš

Position
Prime Minister

Introduction
Andrej Babiš was sworn in as prime minister on 6 Dec. 2017, having founded the centrist-populist ANO party in 2011. The second richest man in the country, Babiš took office despite facing fraud charges.

Early Life
Babiš was born on 2 Sept. 1954 in Bratislava, in present-day Slovakia. His father was a senior diplomat. Having graduated in international trade from the city's University of Economics, Babiš joined the state-controlled international trade company Petrimex and in 1980 joined the Communist Party. He disputes accusations that he worked for the state security services at that time.

In Jan. 1993, having taken up residence in the Czech Republic after the dissolution of Czechoslovakia, he became chief executive office of a Petrimex subsidiary, Agrofert. With financial assistance from undisclosed foreign sources, he acquired sole ownership of Agrofert, which became one of the country's largest conglomerates. The company purchased two leading Czech newspapers in 2013 and, the following year, a popular radio station. In 2017 Babiš was forced by conflict of interest legislation to move Agrofert and other assets into trust funds.

In Oct. 2013 the ANO contested its first legislative election, winning 47 of 200 parliamentary seats and entering a coalition government with the Social Democratic Party and Christian and Democratic Union. Babiš served as finance minister from 2014–17. At the elections in Oct. 2017 the ANO won 78 seats to make it the single biggest party in parliament. However, other parties—including the next biggest, the Civic Democratic Party (ODS)—refused to join a coalition with Babiš, who was under investigation for fraud. Babiš therefore formed a minority government.

Career in Office

On 16 Jan. 2018 Babiš lost a parliamentary vote of confidence and three days later was stripped of his parliamentary immunity after the European Union's antifraud office found 'irregularities' in payments made to an Agrofert subsidiary. Nonetheless, his position was strengthened by the re-election of his ally, President Miloš Zeman, later the same month. Despite popular protests, Zeman asked Babiš to form a new government and in July his new coalition administration with the Social Democrats was approved with Communist Party support by the Chamber of Deputies.

On the international stage, in late March Babiš pledged to expel three Russian diplomats in protest at Moscow's alleged complicity in an assassination attempt on Sergei Skripal, a former Russian double agent, on British territory.

Defence

Conscription ended in Dec. 2004 when the armed forces became all-volunteer. Defence expenditure in 2013 totalled US$2,179m. (US$214 per capita), representing 1·1% of GDP.

Army

Strength (2011) 12,383. There are also paramilitary Border Guards (3,000-strong) and Internal Security Forces (100). In 2017 the Czech government reached an agreement with Germany to integrate a Czech army brigade into a division of the German army.

Air Force

The Air Force had a strength of 4,804 in 2011 including Air Defence Forces. There were 47 combat-capable aircraft in 2011 (L-159s and JAS 39s) and 24 attack helicopters.

International Relations

In 1974 the Federal Republic of Germany and Czechoslovakia annulled the Munich agreement of 1938. On 14 Feb. 1997 the Czech parliament ratified a declaration of German–Czech reconciliation, with particular reference to the Sudeten German problems.

The Czech Republic became a member of the EU on 1 May 2004. A referendum held on 13–14 June 2003 approved accession, with 77·3% of votes cast for membership and 22·7% against. In 2000 a visa requirement for Russians entering the country was introduced as one of the conditions for EU membership.

The Czech Republic's Senate approved the European Union's Treaty of Lisbon on 6 May 2009, after the Chamber of Deputies had done so on 18 Feb. 2009. However, then President Klaus stated that he would not sign it until Ireland had ratified it (which happened after a second referendum held on 2 Oct. 2009). Klaus subsequently gave his presidential assent on 3 Nov. 2009, making the Czech Republic the last country to ratify it.

Economy

Agriculture accounted for 2·7% of GDP in 2014, industry 38·0% and services 59·3%.

Overview

Until 1996 the Czech Republic was viewed as the most successful European transition economy. Although industrial production and employment declined significantly after the communist era, job losses were contained by rising service sector opportunities and soft loans given to loss-making enterprises by state banks. After four years of 3% average annual growth, the economy fell into recession during 1997–98. In May 1997 large current account deficits fuelled a speculative attack on the *koruna*, forcing the country to adopt a tight monetary policy and fiscal austerity. Foreign direct investment (FDI) then began flowing from Western countries in 1999 and the country returned to solid growth in the early 2000s. Integration with the European Union and large-scale FDI further boosted export-oriented growth prior to the global financial crisis in 2008. The economy was severely hit by the crisis and particularly by the downturn in Germany, the country's largest trading partner. Exports and investment declined, unemployment rose and the trade deficit widened while debt increased.

GDP growth averaged just 1·1% annually between 2009 and 2014 but accelerated to 3·2% per year in the period 2015–17, led by strong domestic demand. By April 2018 the unemployment rate had fallen to a record low of 2·3%, while real wage growth reached 6·5% in the first quarter of that year. The banking system is well capitalized, liquid and profitable, with private credit growth in line with nominal GDP growth.

The short-term economic outlook is positive, characterized by strong domestic growth momentum, along with high consumer and business confidence. However, challenges remain, in particular the need to increase participation and productivity among an ageing and shrinking working population.

Currency

The unit of currency is the *koruna* (CZK) or crown of 100 *haler*, introduced on 8 Feb. 1993 at parity with the former Czechoslovakian koruna. There was inflation of 0·7% in 2016 and 2·4% in 2017. Gold reserves were 415,000 troy oz in Sept. 2009 and foreign exchange reserves were US$39,101m. Total money supply was Kč. 1,736·0bn. in Aug. 2009.

Budget

Budgetary central government revenue in 2011 totalled Kč. 993·07bn. (Kč. 984·66bn. in 2010) and expenditure Kč. 1,140·28bn. (Kč. 1,149·59bn. in 2010).

Principal sources of revenue in 2011 were: social security contributions, Kč. 352·77bn.; taxes on goods and services, Kč. 327·26bn.; taxes on income, profits and capital gains, Kč. 173·13bn. Main items of expenditure by economic type in 2011: social benefits, Kč. 444·22bn.; grants, Kč. 319·31bn.; subsidies, Kč. 92·88bn.

The Czech Republic had a budget surplus of 1·5% of GDP in 2017 and 0·7% in 2016. There was a deficit of 0·6% in 2015. The required target set by the EU is a budget deficit of no more than 3%.

VAT is 21% (reduced rates, 15% and 10%).

Performance

The economy grew by 5·3% in 2015, 2·5% in 2016 and 4·3% in 2017. Total GDP was US$215·7bn. in 2017.

Banking and Finance

The central bank and bank of issue is the Czech National Bank (*Governor*, Jiří Rusnok), which also acts as banking supervisor and regulator. Decentralization of the banking system began in 1991, and private banks began to operate. The only legal forms of domestically operating banks are joint stock companies and branches of foreign banks. The Commercial Bank and Investment Bank are privatized nationwide networks with a significant government holding. Specialized banks include the Czech Savings Bank and the Czech Commercial Bank (for foreign trade payments). Private banks tend to be on a regional basis, many of them agricultural banks. In 1997 the cabinet agreed to sell off large stakes in three of the largest state-held banks to individual foreign investors through tenders, in preparation for European Union entry. In 2000 the country's fourth largest bank, Československá obchodní banka (ČSOB), acquired the operations of the third largest bank, IPB (Investiční a Poštovní banka). The newly formed institution (which retained the name ČSOB) is the largest bank in central and Eastern Europe, with assets of US$50·2bn. in Sept. 2010. Other major banks are Česká Spořitelna (assets of US$49·3bn. in Sept. 2010) and Komerční banka (assets of US$38·5bn. in Sept. 2010). Other capital market participants are subject to the supervision of the Czech Securities Commission. Savings deposits were Kč. 2,698,236m. in 2007.

In June 2012 gross external debt amounted to US$93,069m.

Foreign direct investment was US$7·4bn. in 2017, down from US$9·8bn. in 2016.

A stock exchange was founded in Prague in 1992.

Energy and Natural Resources

In 2011, 9·4% of energy consumption came from renewables (wind power, solar power, hydro-electric power, tidal power, geothermal energy and biomass), compared to the European Union average of 13·0%. A target of 13% has been set by the EU for 2020.

Environment

The Czech Republic's carbon dioxide emissions from the consumption of energy in 2011 were the equivalent of 9·3 tonnes per capita.

Electricity

Installed capacity was 20·2m. kW in 2011. Production in 2011 was 87·5bn. kWh. 62% of electricity was produced by thermal power stations (mainly using brown coal) and 32% was nuclear. In 2010 there were six nuclear reactors in operation. Consumption per capita in 2011 was 6,636 kWh.

Oil and Gas

Natural gas reserves in 2013 totalled 4·0bn. cu. metres. Production in 2011 was 215m. cu. metres. In 2014 crude petroleum reserves were 15m. bbls; production was 1·1m. bbls in 2011.

Minerals

There are hard coal and lignite reserves (chief fields: Most, Chomutov, Kladno, Ostrava and Sokolov). Lignite production in 2010 was 43·8m. tonnes; hard coal production in 2010 was 11·4m. tonnes.

Agriculture

In 2013 there were 4,219,000 ha. of agricultural land. In the same year there were 3·15m. ha. of arable land and 0·76m. ha. of permanent crops. 34,000 ha. were equipped for irrigation in 2013. Main agricultural production figures, 2014 (1,000 tonnes): wheat, 5,442; sugar beets, 4,425; barley, 1,967; rapeseed, 1,537; maize, 832; potatoes, 698; triticale, 244. Livestock, 2014: cattle, 1·37m.; pigs, 1·62m.; sheep, 225,000; poultry, 21m. In 2013 production of meat was 504,000 tonnes; cheese (estimate), 136,000 tonnes; milk, 2·9m. tonnes; 2,160m. eggs.

Forestry

In 2015 forests covered 2·67m. ha., or 35% of the total land area. Timber production in 2011 was 15·38m. cu. metres.

Fisheries

Freshwater aquaculture (particularly carp) is an integral part of the Czech agriculture sector; production in 2010 totalled 20,420 tonnes (84% of total fish production). Fish landings in 2015 amounted to 3,841 tonnes, entirely from inland waters.

Industry

The leading company in the Czech Republic in March 2019 was ČEZ (České Energetické Závody a.s.), with a market capitalization of US$14·1bn.

In 2008 there were 1,747,020 small private businesses (of which 17,448 were incorporated), 311,309 companies and partnerships (of which 22,700 were joint-stock companies), 15,338 co-operatives and 526 state enterprises. Output (2008 unless otherwise indicated) includes: crude steel, 6·4m. tonnes; cement (2007), 4·9m. tonnes; pig iron, 4·7m. tonnes; 940,300 cars; soft drinks, 2,935·4m. litres; beer, 1,904·4m. litres.

Labour

In the fourth quarter of 2010 the economically active population numbered 5,281,800; 1·28m. persons worked in manufacturing; 589,400 in trade; 445,500 in construction; 338,300 in human health and social work activities; and 327,500 in public administration and defence. In Dec. 2018 the unemployment rate was 2·2% (down from 2·9% in 2017 as a whole).

The average monthly gross wage was Kč. 23,004 in 2010. Pay increases are regulated in firms where wages grow faster than production. Fines are levied if wages rise by more than 15% over four years. On 1 Aug. 2013 the minimum wage was increased from Kč. 8,000 a month to Kč. 8,500.

The Czech Republic had 38,000 people living in slavery according to the Walk Free Foundation's 2013 *Global Slavery Index*.

International Trade

Imports and Exports

Trading with EU and EFTA countries has increased significantly while trading with all post-communist states has fallen.

Trade, 2010, in US$1m. (2009 in brackets): imports c.i.f., 125,691 (104,850); exports f.o.b., 132,141 (112,884). In 2010 main import sources (in US$1m.) were: Germany (32,057); China (15,332); Poland (8,041); Russia (6,813); Slovakia (6,505). Main export markets in 2010

(in US$1m.) were: Germany (42,213); Slovakia (11,596); Poland (8,129); France (7,101); UK (6,443).

Principal imports in 2010 (in US$1m.) were: machinery and transport equipment (53,253); manufactured goods (21,457); chemicals and related products (12,719). Principal exports in 2010 (in US$1m.) were: machinery and transport equipment (70,592); manufactured goods (22,238); miscellaneous manufactured articles (14,131).

Communications

Roads

In 2007 there were 657 km of motorways, 6,191 km of highways and main roads, 48,736 km of secondary roads and 72,927 km of other roads, forming a total network of 128,511 km. Passenger cars in use in 2007 numbered 4,280,100 (414 per 1,000 inhabitants), and there were also 555,200 lorries and vans and 20,400 buses and coaches. Motorcycles and mopeds numbered 860,100. There were 832 deaths as a result of road accidents in 2009.

Rail

In 2011 Czech State Railways had a route length of 9,470 km (9,448 km on 1,435 mm gauge), of which 3,020 km were electrified. Passenger-km travelled in 2011 came to 6·64bn. and freight tonne-km to 13·85bn. There is a metro (44 km) and tram/light rail system (496 km) in Prague, and also tram/light rail networks in Brno, Liberec, Most, Olomouc, Ostrava and Plzeň.

Civil Aviation

There are international airports at Prague (Václav Havel), Ostrava (Leoš Janáček) and Brno (Turany). The flag carrier is Czech Airlines, which in 2007 flew 82·9m. km and carried 5,492,200 passengers (5,379,500 on international flights). In 2007 Prague handled 12,436,254 passengers; there were a total of 174,662 take-offs and landings.

Shipping

In 2014, 802,000 tonnes of freight were carried by inland waterways.

Telecommunications

In 2013 there were 2,001,000 main (fixed) telephone lines. In the same year mobile phone subscriptions numbered 13,670,000 (1,277·3 per 1,000 persons). Český Telecom was sold to the Spanish telecommunications firm Telefónica in April 2005. It has since become Telefónica O2 Czech Republic. In 2013, 74·1% of the population aged 16–74 were internet users. In March 2012 there were 3·5m. Facebook users.

Social Institutions

Out of 178 countries analysed in the 2017 *Fragile States Index*—a list published jointly by the Fund for Peace and *Foreign Policy* magazine—the Czech Republic was ranked the 27th least vulnerable to conflict or collapse. The index is based on 12 indicators of state vulnerability across social, political and economic categories.

Justice

The post-Communist judicial system was established in July 1991. This provides for a unified system of civil, criminal, commercial and administrative courts. Commercial courts arbitrate in disputes arising from business activities. Administrative courts examine the legality of the decisions of state institutions when appealed by citizens. In addition, there are military courts which operate under the jurisdiction of the ministry of defence. There is a Supreme Court, and a hierarchy of courts under the ministry of justice at republic, region and district level. District courts are courts of first instance. Cases are usually decided by Senates comprising a judge and two associate judges, though occasionally by a single judge. (Associate judges are citizens in good standing over the age of 25 who are elected for four-year terms). Regional courts are courts of first instance in more serious cases and also courts of appeal for district courts. Cases are usually decided by a Senate of two judges and three associate judges, although occasionally by a single judge. There is also a Supreme Administrative Court. The Supreme Court interprets law as a guide to other courts and functions also as a court of appeal. Decisions are made by Senates of three judges. A new Civil Code entered force in Jan. 2014.

There is no death penalty. In 2008, 343,799 crimes were reported (33·0 per 1,000 inhabitants) of which 37·2% were solved. The population in penal institutions in Aug. 2013 was 16,257. The Czech Republic was ranked 19th of 102 countries for criminal justice and 20th for civil justice in the 2015 World Justice Project *Rule of Law Index*, which provides data on how the rule of law is experienced by the general public across eight categories.

Education

Elementary education up to age 15 is compulsory. 52% of children continue their education in vocational schools and 48% move on to secondary schools. In 2007 there were 462,820 children in primary schools with 24,713 teaching staff and 937,026 secondary school pupils with (2006) 91,622 teaching staff.

In 2009 there were 73 universities, of which 26 were public, 45 private and two state—the University of Defence and the Police Academy. Private universities have only existed since 1990. There were 389,231 students at the public and private universities in 2009.

In 2006 public expenditure on education came to 4·8% of GNI and 10·5% of total government spending.

The adult literacy rate is at least 99%.

Health

At 31 Dec. 2008 there were 192 hospitals with 63,263 beds. Another 54,472 beds were available in other health establishments. There were 34,437 physicians, 6,595 dentists, 77,956 nurses, 5,583 pharmacists and 3,842 midwives in 2007. In 2008 the Czech Republic spent 7·1% of its GDP on health.

Welfare

In 2010 new legislation redefined the pension age and amount, as well as the required period of insurance. As of 2016 the retirement age for men was 63 years (with at least 32 years of coverage), and 62 years and 4 months for women with the same coverage (or less, depending on number of children raised). For those with at least 20 years but less than 32 years coverage, the retirement age was 68 years for men and 67 years and 4 months for women. The retirement age for both men and women is to increase incrementally to 65 by 2030, while the required period of coverage rose to 35 years in 2018.

The old-age pension is calculated as a flat-rate basic amount of Kč. 2,440 plus an earnings-related percentage calculated on personal assessment and the number of years of insurance. As at 31 Dec. 2012 the average monthly old-age pension was Kč. 10,778. Early pensions are available up to three years before the standard date of retirement, with the claimant required to have at least 31 to 33 years of contributions.

To qualify for unemployment benefit the applicant must have been registered as a jobseeker and have been insured for at least 12 months in the previous two years. The maximum unemployment benefit in 2016 was Kč. 15,024 per month or Kč. 16,837 per month if undergoing retraining.

Religion

According to estimates by the Pew Research Center's Forum on Religion & Public Life, 76·4% of the population was religiously unaffiliated in 2010—more than in any other country. Most of the remainder of the population are Christians (90% Catholics in 2010).

Dominik Duka (b. 1943) was installed as Archbishop of Prague and Primate of Bohemia in April 2010. In Feb. 2019 the Roman Catholic Church had one cardinal. The largest Protestant church is the Evangelical Church of Czech Brethren, which unites Calvinists and Lutherans and has about 115,000 members. In 2009 there were 25 registered churches and religious societies.

Culture

World Heritage Sites

Sites under Czech jurisdiction which appear on UNESCO's World Heritage List are (with year entered on list): Historic Centre of Prague (1992); Historic Centre of Český Krumlov (1992); Historic Centre of Telč (1992); Pilgrimage

Church of St John of Nipomuk at Zelená Hora in Žďár nad Sázavou (1994); Kutná Hora—the Historical Town Centre with the Church of Saint Barbara and the Cathedral of our Lady at Sedlec (1995); Lednice-Valtice Cultural Landscape (1996); Holašovice Historical Village Reservation (1998); Gardens and Castle at Kroměříž (1998); Litomyšl Castle (1999); Holy Trinity Column in Olomouc (2000); Tugendhat Villa in Brno (2001); and the Jewish Quarter and St Procopius's Basilica in Třebíč (2003).

Press

There were 81 daily newspapers in 2014 (79 paid-for and two free) with a combined average daily circulation of 1,209,000. In 2011 there were 417 non-dailies. The newspaper with the highest circulation is *Blesk* (daily average of 265,000 copies in 2014).

Tourism

In 2015, 8,707,000 non-resident tourists stayed in holiday accommodation. Of these, 1,767,000 were from Germany, 578,000 from Slovakia, 509,000 from the USA, 485,000 from Poland and 443,000 from the UK.

Festivals

The leading classical music festivals are the Prague Spring International Music Festival (May–June) and Smetana's Litomyšl International Opera Festival (June–July). The main popular music festivals are Rock for People in Hradec Králové (July) and Trutnov Open Air Music Festival (Aug.).

Diplomatic Representatives

Of the Czech Republic in the United Kingdom (26–30 Kensington Palace Gdns, London, W8 4QY)
    Ambassador: Libor Sečka.

Of the United Kingdom in the Czech Republic (Thunovská 14, 118 00 Prague)
    Ambassador: Nick Archer, MVO.

Of the Czech Republic in the USA (3900 Spring of Freedom St., NW, Washington, D.C., 20008)
    Ambassador: Hynek Kmoníček.

Of the USA in the Czech Republic (Tržiště 15, 118 01 Prague 1)
    Ambassador: Stephen B. King.

Of the Czech Republic to the United Nations
    Ambassador: Marie Chatardová.

Of the Czech Republic to the European Union
    Permanent Representative: Jakub Dürr.

Further Reading

Czech Statistical Office. *Statistical Yearbook of the Czech Republic.*
Krejcí, Jaroslav and Machonin, Pavel, *Czechoslovakia 1918–1992: A Laboratory for Social Change.* 1996
Leff, C. S., *National Conflict in Czechoslovakia: The Making and Remaking of a State, 1918–1987.* 1988
Simmons, M., *The Reluctant President: a Political Life of Vaclav Havel.* 1992
National Statistical Office: Czech Statistical Office, Na Padesátém 81, 100 82 Prague 10.
Website: http://www.czso.cz

Denmark

Kongeriget Danmark (Kingdom of Denmark)

Capital: Copenhagen
Population projection, 2020: 5·80m.
GNI per capita, 2017: (PPP$) 47,918
HDI/world rank, 2017: 0·929/11
Internet domain extension: .dk

Key Historical Events

Evidence of habitation exists from the Bølling period (12500–12000 BC). By 7700 BC reindeer hunters were settled on the Jutland Peninsula and around 3900 BC agriculture developed. Metal tools and weapons were imported in the Dagger Period (*c.* 2000 BC) but trading stations on the coast did not appear until around AD 300. The first towns developed in the Germanic Iron Age (AD 400–750). The first trading market was held in the 8th century in Hedeby. Denmark was converted to Christianity in 860 when Ansgar built churches in Hedeby and Ribe.

In about 936 Gorm the Old became the first king of Denmark. His successor was Harald Bluetooth, whose grandson, Canute the Great, fought successfully to incorporate England into his North Sea Empire and from 1018–35, Denmark, England and Norway were one nation. However, civil war broke out and in 1146 the kingdom was divided between Magnus the Strong and Knud Lavard. In 1157 Knud's son Valdemar was recognized as the ruler of Denmark. By 1200 Skåne, Halland and Blekinge in the South of Sweden were part of the Danish kingdom. The southern border of Denmark extended to the Eider in what is today northern Germany. In 1219 Valdemar conquered Estonia. He also established a code of law and a land register (Jordebog). The first written constitution was a coronation charter signed by Erik V in 1282.

In the 13th century, agriculture was supplemented by the expansion of fishing to supply inland Europe. Other industries also benefited and this brought with it a passion for building, particularly cathedrals and churches. Economic growth strengthened German influence. The Hanseatic League of German entrepreneurs was granted trade concessions for herring, salt and grain and also played a leading role in the country's political affairs. Valdemar IV Atterdag was crowned king in 1340. He challenged the privileges of the Hanseatic League, and was brought into conflict with Sweden over the southern provinces of Skåne, Halland and Blekinge. In 1361 Valdemar Atterdag took Gotland in one of the bloodiest of Nordic battles. When the king died in 1375, his daughter Margaret (married to King Håkon of Norway) claimed the throne on behalf of her five-year-old son Olav. After Håkon's death in 1388 she also became regent of Norway. While resisting the Hanseatic League, she succeeded in defeating her opponent Albrecht of Mecklenburg, king of Sweden, thus clearing the way to a Nordic union. In 1397, after Olav's death, Margaret's nephew Erik of Pomerania became king of Denmark, Norway and Sweden. In 1412 Erik was opposed by the Swedish nobles who resented being taxed to finance Danish wars in northern Germany. When Erik abdicated, Christian I was elected king of Denmark and Norway in 1448.

By the 16th century Scandinavia was divided between Denmark–Norway (including Iceland and Greenland) and Sweden–Finland. In 1520 a power struggle in Sweden made the country vulnerable to a Danish invasion. Christian II was crowned king of Sweden in 1520 (having assumed the thrones of Norway and Denmark in 1513) but was soon challenged by Gustav Vasa, who replaced him in Sweden in 1521. In 1523 Christian was succeeded in Denmark and Norway by Frederick I, who ended the union with Sweden. Following the Lutheran Reformation, the monarchy enhanced its power by confiscating the property of the Roman Catholic Church.

Imperial Rise and Fall

Christian IV (1577–1648) is regarded as one of Denmark's greatest rulers. Around this time overseas colonies were established, including Tranquebar (India), Danish Gold Coast (Ghana) and the Danish West Indies (the US Virgin Islands). However, in 1626 Denmark was defeated in the Thirty Years' War. Denmark lost Gotland and the Norwegian territories of Jämtland and Härjedalen to Sweden. In 1660 Sweden gained Skåne, Halland and Blekinge. A new constitution proclaimed the Danish king absolute sovereign. In 1661 the Supreme Court was established and in 1683 the law was codified.

In the Great Northern War, Denmark allied itself with Russia, the Netherlands and France, a policy which lasted for the rest of the 18th century. In the Napoleonic Wars, Denmark, smarting under the British bombardment of Copenhagen, allied itself to Napoleon. The price Denmark had to pay was signing away its rights to Norway, which it did by the treaty of Kiel in 1814. Danish possessions were now reduced to Iceland, Greenland, the Faroes and Schleswig-Holstein. Holstein was lost to Germany in 1863 and Schleswig a year later. The surrender of so much rich agricultural land, with nearly 1m. inhabitants, brought Denmark to the edge of bankruptcy. But within a few years the country had pulled itself back from one of the lowest points in its history. The economy benefited from a land-reclamation programme in Jutland. Socially, Bishop Grundtvig (founder of the folk high-schools), who reconciled patriotism with a reduced status for Denmark in European affairs, had a great influence. There were demands for a liberal constitution. In 1846 Anton Frederik Tscherning founded the Society of the Friends of the Peasant (Bondevennernes Selskab), which later became the Liberal Party (Venstre).

Social Reform

In 1901 the Left Reform Party (Venstrereformpartiet) came to power to introduce free-trade, popular education and changes in the revenue system to make income rather than land the criterion for taxation. The First World War gave neutral Denmark an improved export market but there was a shortage of raw materials. In 1929 a Social Democrat government, with Thorvald Stauning as prime minister, combined rural and urban interests in one of the most ambitious programmes of social reforms ever mounted. The 1930s Great Depression led to unemployment made worse when Britain favoured Commonwealth food imports over those from Denmark. In the late 1930s trade improved and industry expanded.

In 1939 when the Second World War broke out, Denmark again declared neutrality. On 9 April 1940 German troops entered and occupied the country. The Germans permitted Danish self-government until growing resistance led to direct rule. After the liberation a Liberal government was elected with Knud Kristensen as prime minister. Kristensen's campaign for the return of southern Schleswig from Germany brought down his government in 1947. Denmark joined NATO in 1949.

With its share of the Marshall Plan, Denmark entered on a new industrial revolution. By the mid-1950s the value of manufacturing equalled that of agriculture. However, there was a high rate of inflation. In 1953 the Social Democrats came back to power where they remained until the mid-1960s. By then the rate of inflation was higher than in any comparable country. In 1968 a centre-right coalition was elected, led by Hilmar Baunsgaard. But the change of government did not signify a change in strategy. Taxes were kept high and the budget expanded to increase social welfare. After the 1971 election, the Social Democrat leader Jens Otto Krag negotiated entry into the European Union, making Copenhagen the bridge between the Nordic capitals and Brussels. In 1982 a Conservative-led minority government was formed, led by Poul Schlüter, the first Conservative prime minister since 1901. He remained in power until 1993 when a Social Democratic coalition led by Poul Nyrup Rasmussen took office. Following the 2001 election, a right-wing government came to power under Anders Fogh Rasmussen, whose campaign for entry into the EMU (European Monetary Union) was rejected in a referendum in 2000. In Nov. 2008 Greenland approved a referendum in favour of greater autonomy from Denmark. Anders Fogh Rasmussen left office in April 2009 to become Secretary General of NATO. He was replaced by Lars Løkke Rasmussen (no relation) of the Liberal Party as prime minister. Helle Thorning-Schmidt became Denmark's first female prime minister in 2011 at the head of a left-leaning coalition but was replaced by the returning Lars Løkke Rasmussen following elections in June 2015.

© Springer Nature Limited 2020
Palgrave Macmillan (ed.), *The Statesman's Yearbook 2020*,
https://doi.org/10.1057/978-1-349-95940-2_60

Territory and Population

Denmark is bounded in the west by the North Sea, northwest and north by the Skagerrak and Kattegat straits (separating it from Norway and Sweden), and south by Germany. In Dec. 2014 Denmark made a submission to the Commission on the Limits of the Continental Shelf asserting its claim to some 895,000 sq. km beyond Greenland's nautical borders, including the North Pole.

Regions	Area (sq. km)	Population 1 Jan. 2018	Population per sq. km 2018
Capital Region (Hovedstaden)	2,561	1,822,659	711·7
Central Jutland (Midtjylland)	13,124	1,313,596	100·1
North Jutland (Nordjylland)	7,933	589,148	74·3
Zealand (Sjælland)	7,273	835,024	114·8
South Denmark (Syddanmark)	12,206	1,220,763	100·0
Total	43,098[1]	5,781,190	134·1

[1]Totals do not add up because of rounding.

Denmark has not used a traditional census since 1970, but instead uses a register-based method of calculating the population. It was the first country in the world to implement such a change.

The UN gives a projected population for 2020 of 5·80m.

In 2010 an estimated 86·7% of the population lived in urban areas. In 2010, 91·4% of the inhabitants were born in Denmark, including the Faroe Islands and Greenland.

On 1 Jan. 2017 the population of the capital, Copenhagen (comprising Copenhagen, Frediksberg and Gentofte municipalities), was 1,295,686; Aarhus, 269,022; Odense, 176,683; Aalborg, 113,417; Esbjerg, 72,261; Randers, 62,563; Kolding, 60,300; Horsens, 58,480; Vejle, 55,876; Roskilde, 50,393.

The official language is Danish.

Social Statistics

Statistics for calendar years:

	Live births	Marriages	Divorces	Deaths	Emigration	Immigration
2005	64,282	36,148	15,300	54,962	45,869	52,458
2006	64,984	36,452	14,343	55,477	46,786	56,750
2007	64,082	36,576	14,066	55,604	41,566	64,656
2008	65,038	37,376	14,695	54,591	43,490	72,749
2009	62,818	32,934	14,940	54,872	44,874	67,161

2009 rates per 1,000 population: birth, 11·4; death, 9·9. Births outside marriage: 2006, 46·4%; 2007, 46·1%; 2008, 46·2%; 2009, 46·5%. Average annual population growth rate, 2005–09, 0·5%. Suicide rate, 2006 (per 100,000 population) was 11·9 (men, 17·5; women, 6·4). Life expectancy at birth, 2008–09, was 76·5 years for males and 80·8 years for females. In 2007 the most popular age range for marrying was 30–34 for males and 25–29 for females. Denmark was the first country to legalize same-sex unions, in 1989. Infant mortality, 2009, 3·0 per 1,000 live births. Fertility rate, 2009, 1·8 births per woman. In 2009 Denmark received 3,855 asylum applications, equivalent to 0·7 per 1,000 inhabitants. In July 2002 a controversial new immigration law was introduced in an attempt to deter potential asylum seekers. Denmark legalized same-sex marriage in June 2012 (although the legislation does not apply in the Faroe Islands and Greenland).

UNICEF reported that 9·2% of children in Denmark in 2014 lived in relative poverty (living in a household in which disposable income—when adjusted for family size and composition—is less than 60% of the national median income), the lowest rate in the world

Climate

The climate is much modified by marine influences and the effect of the Gulf Stream, to give winters that may be either cold or mild and often cloudy. Summers may be warm and sunny or chilly and rainy. Generally the east is drier than the west. Long periods of calm weather are exceptional and windy conditions are common. Copenhagen, Jan. 33°F (0·5°C), July 63°F (17°C). Annual rainfall 650 mm. Esbjerg, Jan. 33°F (0·5°C), July 61°F (16°C). Annual rainfall 800 mm. In general 10% of precipitation is snow.

Constitution and Government

The present constitution is founded upon the Basic Law of 5 June 1953. The legislative power lies with the Queen and the *Folketing* (parliament) jointly. The executive power is vested in the monarch, who exercises authority through the ministers.

The reigning Queen is **Margrethe II**, b. 16 April 1940; married 10 June 1967 to Prince Henrik, b. Count de Monpezat (died 13 Feb. 2018). She succeeded to the throne on the death of her father, King Frederik IX, on 14 Jan. 1972. *Offspring:* Crown Prince Frederik, b. 26 May 1968, married 14 May 2004 Mary Elizabeth Donaldson, b. 5 Feb. 1972 (*offspring:* Prince Christian Valdemar Henri John, b. 15 Oct. 2005; Princess Isabella Henrietta Ingrid Margrethe, b. 21 April 2007; Prince Vincent Frederik Minik Alexander, b. 8 Jan. 2011; Princess Josephine Sophia Ivalo Mathilda, b. 8 Jan. 2011); Prince Joachim, b. 7 June 1969, married 18 Nov. 1995 Alexandra Manley, b. 30 June 1964, divorced 8 April 2005 (*offspring:* Prince Nikolai William Alexander Frederik, b. 28 Aug. 1999; Prince Felix Henrik Valdemar Christian, b. 22 July 2002), married 24 May 2008 Marie Cavallier, b. 6 Feb. 1976 (*offspring:* Prince Henrik Carl Joachim Alain, b. 4 May 2009; Princess Athena Marguerite Françoise Marie, b. 24 Jan. 2012).

Sisters of the Queen. Princess Benedikte, b. 29 April 1944; married 3 Feb. 1968 to Prince Richard of Sayn-Wittgenstein-Berleburg; Princess Anne-Marie, b. 30 Aug. 1946; married 18 Sept. 1964 to King Constantine of Greece.

The crown was elective from at least the tenth century but became hereditary by right in 1660. The direct male line of the house of Oldenburg became extinct with King Frederik VII on 15 Nov. 1863. In view of the death of the king, without direct heirs, the Great Powers signed a treaty at London on 8 May 1852, by the terms of which the succession to the crown was made over to Prince Christian of Schleswig-Holstein-Sonderburg-Glücksburg, and to the direct male descendants of his union with the Princess Louise of Hesse-Cassel. This became law on 31 July 1853. Linked to the constitution of 5 June 1953, a new law of succession, dated 27 March 1953, has come into force, which restricts the right of succession to the descendants of King Christian X and Queen Alexandrine, and admits the sovereign's daughters to the line of succession, ranking after the sovereign's sons.

The Queen receives a tax-free annual sum from the state. This was 79m. kroner in 2015.

The judicial power is with the courts. The monarch must be a member of the Evangelical-Lutheran Church, the official Church of the State, and may not assume major international obligations without the consent of the Folketing. The Folketing consists of one chamber. All men and women of Danish nationality of more than 18 years of age and permanently resident in Denmark possess the franchise, and are eligible for election to the Folketing, which is at present composed of 179 members; 135 members are elected by the method of proportional representation in 17 constituencies. In order to attain an equal representation of the different parties, 40 additional seats are divided among such parties which have not obtained sufficient returns at the constituency elections. Two members are elected for the Faroe Islands and two for Greenland. The term of the legislature is four years, but a general election may be called at any time. The Folketing convenes every year on the first Tuesday in Oct. Besides its legislative functions, every six years it appoints judges who, together with the ordinary members of the Supreme Court, form the *Rigsret*, a tribunal which can alone try parliamentary impeachments.

National Anthem

Denmark has two national anthems. 'Kong Kristian stod ved højen mast' ('King Christian stood by the lofty mast'; words by J. Ewald, tune by D. L. Rogert) is used on royal and military occasions. 'Der er et yndigt land' ('There is a lovely country'; words by A. Oehlenschläger, tune by H. E. Krøyer) is regarded as the civil national anthem.

Government Chronology

Prime Ministers since 1945. (KF = Conservative Party; RV = Radical Liberal Party; SD = Social Democratic Party; V = Liberal Party)

1945	SD	Vilhelm Buhl
1945–47	V	Knud Kristensen
1947–50	SD	Hans Hedtoft
1950–53	V	Erik Eriksen
1953–55	SD	Hans Hedtoft
1955–60	SD	Hans Christian Hansen
1960–62	SD	Viggo Kampmann
1962–68	SD	Jens Otto Krag
1968–71	RV	Hilmar Baunsgaard
1971–72	SD	Jens Otto Krag
1972–73	SD	Anker Jørgensen
1973–75	V	Poul Hartling
1975–82	SD	Anker Jørgensen
1982–93	KF	Poul Holmskov Schlüter
1993–2001	SD	Poul Nyrup Rasmussen
2001–09	V	Anders Fogh Rasmussen
2009–11	V	Lars Løkke Rasmussen
2011–15	SD	Helle Thorning-Schmidt
2015–	V	Lars Løkke Rasmussen

Recent Elections

Parliamentary elections were held on 18 June 2015; turnout was 85·9%. The Social Democratic Party won 47 seats, with 26·3% of mainland votes cast (44 seats with 24·8% in 2011); the Danish People's Party 37 with 21·1% (22 with 12·3%); the Liberal Party (V) 34 with 19·5% (47 with 26·7%); the Unity List—the Red-Greens 14 with 7·8% (12 with 6·7%); the Liberal Alliance 13 with 7·5% (9 with 5·0%); the Alternative 9 with 4·8% (participating for the first time); the Danish Social Liberal Party 8 with 4·6% (17 with 9·5%); the Socialist People's Party 7 with 4·2% (16 with 9·2%); and the Conservative People's Party 6 with 3·4% (8 with 4·9%). Although the Social Democratic Party won the most seats, the Liberal party-led 'Blue bloc' took 90 seats compared to 85 for the Social Democratic Party-led 'Red bloc'. The four remaining seats are reserved for representative parties from the Faroe Islands and Greenland.

European Parliament

Denmark has 13 representatives. At the May 2014 elections turnout was 56·3% (59·5% in 2009). The Danish People's Party won 4 seats with 26·6% of votes cast (political affiliation in European Parliament: European Conservatives and Reformists); the Social Democratic Party, 3 with 19·1% (Progressive Alliance of Socialists and Democrats); V, 2 with 16·7% (Alliance of Liberals and Democrats for Europe); the Socialist People's Party, 1 with 11·0% (Greens/European Free Alliance); the Conservative People's Party, 1 with 9·1% (European People's Party); People's Movement Against the EU, 1 with 8·1% (European United Left/Nordic Green Left); the Danish Social Liberal Party, 1 with 6·5% (Alliance of Liberals and Democrats for Europe).

Current Government

In Feb. 2019 the government of the Liberal Party, the Liberal Alliance and the Conservative People's Party comprised the following:

Prime Minister: Lars Løkke Rasmussen; b. 1964 (V; took office for a second time on 28 June 2015, having previously been prime minister from April 2009–Oct. 2011).

Minister for Children and Social Affairs: Mai Mercado. *Culture and Church:* Mette Bock. *Defence:* Claus Hjort Frederiksen. *Development Co-operation:* Ulla Tørnæs. *Economy and Interior:* Simon Emil Ammitzbøll-Bille. *Education:* Merete Riisager. *Employment:* Troels Lund Poulsen. *Energy, Utilities and Climate:* Lars Christian Lilleholt. *Environment and Food:* Jakob Ellemann-Jensen. *Finance:* Kristian Jensen. *Fisheries and Equal Opportunities, and Nordic Co-operation:* Eva Kjer Hansen. *Foreign Affairs:* Anders Samuelsen. *Health:* Ellen Trane Nørby. *Higher Education and Science:* Tommy Ahlers. *Immigration and Integration:* Inger Støjberg. *Industry, Business and Financial Affairs:* Rasmus Jarlov. *Justice:* Søren Pape Poulsen. *Public Innovation:* Sophie Løhde. *Seniors:* Thyra Frank. *Taxation:* Karsten Lauritzen. *Transport, Building and Housing:* Ole Birk Olesen. *Office of the Prime Minister:* http://www.stm.dk/_a_2747.html

Current Leaders

Lars Løkke Rasmussen

Position
Prime Minister

Introduction
Lars Løkke Rasmussen became prime minister for the second time in June 2015, at the head of a minority government. He was previously in office between 2009 and 2011. With his Liberal Party (V) only the third largest party in parliament, Rasmussen was reliant on the support of other parties on a vote-by-vote basis.

Early Life
Lars Løkke Rasmussen was born on 15 May 1964 in Vejle in the Syddanmark region. Prior to graduating in law from Copenhagen University in 1992, he became active in the V party. He was national chairman of the Young Liberals from 1986–89, and in 1986 also became a member of Graested-Gilleleje municipal council. In 1994 he entered parliament and in the same year became first deputy mayor of Graested-Gilleleje, serving until 1997. In 1998 he became mayor of Frederiksborg County and was appointed deputy chairman of V.

From 2001–07 he served as minister for the interior and health, overseeing municipal reforms and promoting policies to cut hospital waiting lists. Appointed finance minister in 2007, he led negotiations to share tax revenues between richer and poorer municipalities. In response to the global financial crisis in 2008, he was responsible for providing funds to troubled banks and for creating a national economic stimulus package. In Feb. 2009 he cut the rate of income tax and increased taxes on pollution—reforms that fulfilled party campaign promises but which received a mixed reception from the public and opposition parties.

Career in Office
Rasmussen became prime minister and party leader in April 2009, after the incumbent Anders Fogh Rasmussen resigned to take up the post of NATO secretary general. He reappointed substantially the same cabinet, while converting the social welfare ministry into two separate portfolios and appointing two female V MPs to head the ministry of employment and the newly-created interior and social affairs ministry. This took the proportion of women in cabinet to almost 50%, one of the highest in the world. In Dec. 2009 Rasmussen chaired the United Nations Climate Change Conference in Copenhagen, but its ultimately disappointing outcome earned him criticism from some quarters. In 2010 he announced his support for a phased withdrawal of Danish combat units from Afghanistan. On the domestic front, in May 2010 his government announced a three-year package of cuts to public expenditure, including reductions in unemployment and family benefits and foreign aid.

In 2011 the government proposed the reintroduction of border controls as part of a deal to secure the support of the right-wing Danish People's Party (DF) for pension reforms. The proposals were popular with a section of the Danish public but strained relations with the European Union (and the revised measures that were eventually implemented were revoked by the next government). In the Sept. 2011 elections Rasmussen's government lost its ability to command a majority and he resigned, although he remained in office as head of a caretaker government until the following month. In 2015 he contested the general election as part of the 'Blue bloc' alliance of centre-right parties, which included the DF. Although the V party lost seats, the 'Blue bloc' emerged victorious, with the DF becoming the second largest party in parliament.

Rasmussen took office on 28 June 2015, leading a minority administration after the DF chose not to join the government, although in Nov. 2016 he reinforced his position by concluding a coalition agreement with the Liberal Alliance and the Conservative People's Party.

Asylum seekers and refugees have been a particular area of contention in Denmark amid Europe-wide concern over migration emanating mainly from the Middle East. In Jan. 2017 the *Folketing* approved measures to deter immigration, including confiscation of migrants' valuables at the border, and in May 2018 banned the wearing of face veils by women in public place.

Defence

The armed forces of Denmark consist of the Royal Danish Army, the Royal Danish Navy, the Royal Danish Air Force and the Danish Home Guard.

Under the terms of the Danish Defence Agreement 2018–23, the government proposes an increase in the defence budget of 4·8bn. kroner between 2018 and 2023, equating to a 20% increase on defence spending as of 2017. It is intended that Denmark will also achieve the NATO target of allocating 20% of defence expenditure on investments in major equipment.

Specific proposals include establishing a brigade with enhanced capabilities, as well as fitting out the Navy's frigates with new short- and long-range missiles and sonar and anti-torpedo systems. The Danish Defence and Home Guard will also be able to mobilize approximately 20,000 soldiers, as well as deploying some 4,000 soldiers from the reserves. There will also be a new 500-soldier light infantry battalion that can be deployed on short notice to support the police and engage in protection and guard missions.

The government furthermore intends to increase the number of conscripts by 500 per year but will refrain from forcibly drafting anyone provided that at least 90% of the nation's defence needs can be met by drafting volunteers. A new situation centre is also to be established to bolster cyber defence.

Denmark has a compulsory military service with mobilization based on the constitution of 1849. This states that it is the duty of every fit man to contribute to the national defence. However, the number of young men available for military service is much greater than what is deemed necessary by the Danish National Forces. In 2013 defence expenditure totalled US$4,509m. (US$812 per capita), representing 1·4% of GDP.

Army

The Danish Army is comprised of field army formations and local defence forces. The strength of the Danish Army is approximately 10,600. The Danish Army is organized in two brigades, the first made up of professional soldiers and the second functioning as a training structure for conscripts.

Navy

The strength of the Royal Danish Navy is approximately 3,500. The two main naval bases are located at Frederikshavn and Korsør.

Air Force

The strength of the Royal Danish Air Force is approximately 3,500. The Royal Danish Air Force consists of Tactical Air Command Denmark and the Danish Air Materiel Command.

Home Guard (Hjemmeværnet)

The overall Home Guard organization comprises the Home Guard Command, the Army Home Guard, the Naval Home Guard, the Air Force Home Guard and supporting institutions. The personnel are recruited on a voluntary basis. The personnel establishment of the Home Guard is approximately 50,000 soldiers.

International Relations

In a referendum in June 1992 the electorate voted against ratifying the Maastricht Treaty for closer political union within the EU. Turnout was 82%. 50·7% of votes were against ratification, 49·3% in favour. However, a second referendum on 18 May 1993 reversed this result, with 56·8% of votes cast in favour of ratification and 43·2% against. Turnout was 86·2%. In a referendum held on 28 Sept. 2000 Danish voters rejected their country's entry into the common European currency, 53·2% opposing membership of the euro against 46·8% voting in favour. Turnout was 87·6%.

Economy

In 2016 agriculture accounted for 0·9% of GDP, industry 23·5% and services 75·6%.

According to the Berlin-based organization Transparency International, Denmark ranked first in the world in a 2018 survey of countries with the least corruption in business and government. It received 88 out of 100 in the corruption perceptions index.

Denmark gave US$2·5bn. in international aid in 2017, equivalent to 0·74% of GNI (making Denmark one of only five industrialized countries to meet the UN target of 0·7%).

Overview

Denmark's modern market economy has a high-tech agricultural sector that was its cornerstone from the 1960s. The economic structure has nonetheless changed significantly since then. Services now employ over three-quarters of the workforce and account for three-quarters of GDP, while agriculture engages only 2% of the workforce. Denmark is also a world leader in the industrial, pharmaceutical, shipping and renewable energy sectors, although the economy is reliant on raw material imports, especially for manufacturing.

Productivity growth has been weak since the late 1990s and well behind the best performers in the OECD, in response to which the government established a productivity commission in 2012.

Given its dependency on foreign trade, Denmark has been a long-time supporter of EU trade liberalization and conforms to almost all EU standardization policies. Export growth was negative in 2013 but grew by 0·2% and 0·1% in 2014 and 2015, respectively. The balance of payments surplus averaged 6·1% annually between 2013 and 2015.

The Danes enjoy an extremely high standard of living, characterized by generous government welfare subsidies. Denmark has the lowest level of income inequality in the OECD and was ranked third out of 190 countries in the World Bank's 2017 *Doing Business* report. Yet the economy faces challenges. A drastic drop in property prices in 2008 and 2009, reflecting widespread uncertainty in international real estate markets, prompted an ongoing decline despite a short respite in 2010. Meanwhile, the fall in North Sea oil and gas production coupled with lower oil prices have contributed to a drag on GDP growth that in recent years has been propped up by private consumption.

Household debt is high, averaging 260% of gross disposable income in 2015. The global financial crisis also exacerbated a cyclical slowdown, leading to increased borrowing to make up the shortfall in export demand. Low consumer and investor confidence have been additional problems. Government spending prompted a tentative recovery but could not prevent a technical recession during 2010–11. Interest rates turned negative in 2012 and remained so as of the end of 2016.

Denmark has historically had relativity low levels of unemployment but the rate reached 7·6% in 2011 before falling to 6·2% at the end of 2015. The country also faces challenges from an ageing population and a shortage of workers to replace those retiring. Nonetheless, the country's fiscal position is strong compared to most of the European Union, with public debt measuring 45·8% of GDP in 2015.

Currency

The monetary unit is the *Danish krone* (DKK) of 100 *øre*. Inflation rates (based on OECD statistics):

2008	2009	2010	2011	2012	2013	2014	2015	2016	2017
3·4%	1·3%	2·3%	2·8%	2·4%	0·8%	0·6%	0·5%	0·3%	1·1%

In Aug. 2009 foreign exchange reserves were US$67,774m., gold reserves were 2·14m. troy oz and total money supply was 832·2bn. kroner.

While not participating directly in EMU, the Danish krone is pegged to the euro in ERM-2, the successor to the exchange rate mechanism.

Budget

General government revenue in 2015 (provisional) totalled 1,084bn. kroner and expenditure 1,101bn. kroner.

Principal sources of revenue in 2015 (provisional) were: taxes on income, profits and capital gains, 584bn. kroner; taxes on goods and services, 291bn. kroner; social contributions, 20bn. kroner. Main items of expenditure by economic type in 2015 (provisional): social benefits, 376bn. kroner; compensation of employees, 326bn. kroner; use of goods and services, 184bn. kroner.

In 2017 tax revenues were 46·0% of GDP (the second highest percentage of any developed country after those of France).

Denmark registered a budget surplus of 1·1% of GDP in 2017 following a deficit of 0·4% in 2016 and 1·5% in 2015.

VAT is 25%.

Performance

Real GDP growth rates (based on OECD statistics):

2008	2009	2010	2011	2012	2013	2014	2015	2016	2017
−0·5%	−4·9%	1·9%	1·3%	0·2%	0·9%	1·6%	2·3%	2·4%	2·3%

Total GDP was US$324·9bn. in 2017.

Banking and Finance

In 2009 the accounts of the National Bank (*Governor*, Lars Rohde) balanced at 550,151m. kroner. The assets included official net foreign reserves of 370,861m. kroner. The liabilities included notes and coins totalling 60,761m. kroner. On 31 Dec. 2008 there were 138 commercial banks and savings banks, with deposits of 1,438,028m. kroner.

The two largest commercial banks are Danske Bank and Nordea Bank Danmark. The supervisory boards of all banks must include public representation.

Gross external debt totalled US$584,152m. in June 2012.

There is a stock exchange in Copenhagen.

Energy and Natural Resources

In 2011, 23·1% of energy consumption came from renewables (wind power, solar power, hydro-electric power, tidal power, geothermal energy and biomass), compared to the European Union average of 13·0%. A target of 30% has been set by the EU for 2020.

Environment

Denmark's carbon dioxide emissions from the consumption of energy in 2011 were the equivalent of 8·2 tonnes per capita. An *Environmental Performance Index* compiled in 2016 ranked Denmark 4th of 180 countries, with 89·2%. The index examined various factors in nine areas—agriculture, air quality, biodiversity and habitat, climate and energy, fisheries, forests, health impacts, water and sanitation, and water resources.

Electricity

Installed capacity was 13·6m. kW in 2011. Production (2011), 35,171m. kWh. Consumption per capita in 2011 was 6,545 kWh. In 2007 some 5,212 wind turbines produced 19·7% of output.

Oil and Gas

Oil production has been steadily declining since 2004. In 2012 production was 10·1m. tonnes with 0·7bn. bbls of proven reserves. Production of natural gas was 6·4bn. cu. metres in 2012, with proven reserves of 51bn. cu. metres. In 2011 natural gas consumption totalled 4·4bn. cu. metres.

Wind

Denmark consumed 42·1% of its electricity from wind power in 2015, the highest proportion of any country. Denmark is one of the world's largest wind-power producers, with 13·1bn. kWh in 2014.

Agriculture

Agriculture accounted for 9·7% of exports and 2·5% of imports in 2009. Land ownership is widely distributed. In 2008 there were 43,413 holdings with at least 5 ha. of agricultural area (or at least a production equivalent to that from 5 ha. of barley). There were 10,214 small holdings (with less than 10 ha.), 18,465 medium-sized holdings (10–50 ha.) and 14,734 holdings with more than 50 ha. Approximately 5·1% of all agricultural land is used for organic farming. There were 24,675 agricultural workers in 2007. In 2007 Denmark had 2·30m. ha. of arable land and 8,000 ha. of permanent cultures.

In 2008 the cultivated area was (in 1,000 ha.): grain, 1,505; green fodder and grass, 705; root crops, 84; set aside, 71; other crops, 298; pulses, 5; total cultivated area, 2,668.

Chief crops	Area (1,000 ha.)				Production (in 1,000 tonnes)			
	2006	2007	2008	2009	2006	2007	2008	2009
Wheat	686	689	638	739	4,802	4,519	5,019	5,940
Barley	679	632	717	593	3,270	3,104	3,396	3,394
Potatoes	39	41	41	39	1,361	1,626	1,705	1,618
Oats	69	66	84	67	274	312	322	315
Rye	28	30	29	44	130	135	152	238
Other root crops	46	43	41	43	2,585	3,518	2,525	2,278

Livestock, 2008 (in 1,000): pigs, 12,738; cattle, 1,564; sheep, 136; horses, 60; poultry, 15,106.

Production (in 1,000 tonnes) in 2009: pork, 1,898; beef, 137; milk, 4,733; cheese, 324; eggs, 73; butter, 37.

On 1 Jan. 2010 tractors numbered 99,700.

Forestry

The area under forests in 2015 was 0·61m. ha., or 14% of the total land area. Timber production in 2011 was 2·58m. cu. metres.

Fisheries

The total value of the fish caught was (in 1m. kroner): 1970, 854; 1980, 2,888; 1985, 3,542; 1990, 3,485; 1995, 3,020; 2000, 3,141; 2005, 2,781; 2008, 2,487; 2009, 2,154.

In 2015 the total catch was 869,066 tonnes, almost exclusively from sea fishing. Denmark is one of the leading fishing nations in the EU.

Industry

The leading companies by market capitalization in Denmark in March 2019 were: Novo Nordisk A/S, a health care company (US$116·9bn.); A. P. Møller-Mærsk, a shipping company (US$35·1bn.); and Danske Bank (US$29·1bn.).

The following table is of gross value added by kind of activity (in 1m. kroner; 2000 constant prices):

	2007	2008	2009
Total	1,229,577	1,227,087	1,169,778
Agriculture, fishing and quarrying	55,028	50,296	52,120
Manufacturing	190,818	198,674	174,528
Electricity, gas and water supply	21,252	22,931	21,895
Construction	62,040	58,498	49,900
Wholesale and retail trade	174,600	169,413	147,085
Transport, post and telecommunication	111,394	99,815	91,999
Financial and business activities	310,271	319,820	321,501
Public and personal services	304,173	307,641	310,749

In the following table 'number of jobs' refers to 18,779 local business enterprises including self-employed businesses with no employees (Nov. 2006):

Branch of industry	Number of jobs
Food, beverages and tobacco	72,508
Textiles, clothing and footwear, and leather	8,963
Wood and wood products	15,537
Paper products	44,541
Refined petroleum products	1,008
Chemicals and man-made fibres	27,940
Rubber and plastic products	21,157
Non-metallic mineral products	16,585
Basic metals	52,902
Machinery and equipment	62,976
Electrical and optical equipment	47,873
Transport equipment	15,040
Furniture and other manufactures	26,510
Total manufacturing	413,540

Labour

The labour force in 2013 was 2,902,000 (2,874,000 in 2003). 78·0% of the population aged 15–64 was economically active in 2013. In 2013, 34·9% of those in employment worked in the public sector. In Dec. 2018 the unemployment rate was 4·9% (down from 5·7% in 2017 as a whole), compared to the European Union average of 7·3%. The youth unemployment rate in the fourth quarter of 2015 was 10·7% (19·9% for the European Union as a whole).

International Trade

Imports and Exports

In 2009 imports totalled 437,998m. kroner and exports 495,577m. kroner.

Imports and exports (in 1m. kroner) for calendar years:

Leading commodities	2008		2009	
	Imports	Exports	Imports	Exports
Live animals, meat and meat preparations	7,911	33,199	7,519	31,756
Dairy products and eggs	4,297	13,438	3,267	12,346
Fish, crustaceans, etc. and preparations	10,188	16,331	8,767	14,276
Cereals and cereal preparations	6,532	5,412	4,448	5,344
Fodder for animals	7,344	5,348	6,649	5,192
Wood and cork	4,616	1,060	3,666	790
Textile fibres, yarns, fabrics, etc.	8,452	7,448	6,222	5,926
Mineral fuels, lubricants, etc.	41,598	56,804	27,974	37,592
Chemicals and plastics, etc.	31,387	27,202	24,041	26,004
Medicine and pharmaceutical products	17,119	40,630	17,654	42,503
Metals, manufacture of metals	54,553	40,348	32,100	29,658
Machinery, electrical, equipment, etc.	126,803	131,770	99,186	107,296
Transport equipment	59,488	24,566	50,049	19,243
Furniture, etc.	8,989	13,916	7,243	11,432
Clothing and clothing accessories	24,131	20,884	21,171	19,022

Distribution of foreign trade (in 1m. kroner) according to countries of origin and destination for 2009:

Countries	Imports	Exports
Austria	4,242·5	3,661·4
Belgium	15,145·2	8,033·3
Canada	2,641·3	4,931·3
China	28,780·1	11,475·4
Finland	7,547·9	11,844·6
France	15,203·1	20,631·1
Germany	92,689·5	85,607·0
Greece	1,060·1	3,556·7
Greenland	2,082·6	2,764·0
Hong Kong	1,104·9	4,844·8
Ireland	4,787·2	5,839·2
Italy	15,274·4	14,991·9
Japan	2,283·0	10,038·3
Netherlands	30,796·1	22,860·9
Norway	23,228·0	31,423·4
Poland	11,345·1	12,228·4
Russia	4,754·6	8,266·8
South Korea	2,928·9	3,103·1
Spain	6,511·3	12,847·5
Sweden	57,758·3	63,666·1
Switzerland	4,721·6	4,715·2
Turkey	4,021·7	2,879·6
United Kingdom	24,296·7	41,970·1
United States of America	15,175·8	31,018·5

In 2006 fellow European Union member countries accounted for 72·6% of imports and 69·1% of exports.

Communications

A 16-km long fixed link with Sweden was opened in July 2000 when the Öresund motorway and railway bridge between Malmö and Copenhagen was completed.

Roads

Denmark proper had (1 Jan. 2009) 1,128 km of motorways, 3,790 km of other state roads and 69,500 km of other commercial roads. Motor vehicles registered at 1 Jan. 2010 comprised 2,120,322 passenger cars, 32,300 trucks, 462,359 vans, 14,509 buses and 147,373 motorcycles. There were 5,250 casualties in road accidents in 2009, resulting in 303 fatalities.

Rail

In 2012 there were 2,131 km of state railways of 1,435 mm gauge (619 km electrified). In 2011, 219m. passengers were carried. DB Schenker Rail Scandinavia A/S (formerly the Danish State Railways Freight Division) carried 7·1m. tonnes of freight in 2012. There were also 959 km of private railways. A metro system was opened in Copenhagen in 2002.

Civil Aviation

The main international airport is at Copenhagen (Kastrup), and there are also international flights from Aalborg, Aarhus, Billund and Esbjerg. The Scandinavian Airlines System (SAS) resulted from the 1950 merger of the three former Scandinavian airlines. It is now known as Scandinavian Airlines. SAS Denmark A/S is the Danish partner (SAS Norge ASA and SAS Sverige AB being the other two). the Danish government holds 14·2% of the capital of SAS, with the Swedish government holding 14·8%. The remaining shares are listed on the stock exchanges of Copenhagen, Oslo and Stockholm.

On 1 Jan. 2009 Denmark had 1,122 aircraft with a capacity of 19,077 seats. Copenhagen (Kastrup) handled 9,848,000 departing passengers in 2009, Billund 1,151,000, Aalborg 561,000 and Aarhus 255,000.

Shipping

In Jan. 2014 there were 452 ships of 300 GT or over registered (of which 326 in the Danish International Shipping Register and 126 in the Danish Shipping Register), totalling 12·21m. GT. Of the 452 vessels registered, 161 were oil tankers, 107 were general cargo ships, 104 container ships, 75 passenger ships, three bulk carriers and two liquid gas tankers. The Danish-controlled fleet comprised 932 vessels of 1,000 GT or over in July 2014, of which 335 were under the Danish flag and 597 under foreign flags. The busiest ports are Fredericia, Aarhus and Copenhagen.

Telecommunications

In 2009 there were 2,062,000 main (fixed) telephone lines. In the same year mobile phone subscriptions numbered 7,424,000 (134·1 per 100 persons). In 2010, 86% of the population had access to the internet at home and 88% had access to a computer at home. Denmark has one of the highest fixed broadband penetration rates, at 37·7 subscribers per 100 inhabitants in Dec. 2010. In March 2012 there were 2·8m. Facebook users.

Social Institutions

According to the 2017 *Fragile States Index*—a list published jointly by the Fund for Peace and *Foreign Policy* magazine—Denmark was ranked as the country fourth least vulnerable to conflict or collapse. The index is based on 12 indicators of state vulnerability across social, political and economic categories.

Justice

The lowest courts of justice are organized in 24 tribunals *(byretter)*, where minor cases are dealt with by a single judge. The tribunal at Copenhagen has one president and 42 other judges; and Aarhus one president and 13 other judges; the other tribunals have one to 11 judges. Cases of greater consequence are dealt with by the two High Courts *(Landsretterne)*; these courts are also courts of appeal for minor cases. The Eastern High Court in Copenhagen has one president and 60 other judges; and the Western in Viborg one president and 39 other judges. From these an appeal lies to the Supreme Court in Copenhagen, composed of a president and 19 other judges. Judges under 65 years of age can be removed only by judicial sentence.

In 2009, 487,851 penal code offences were reported, including 56 homicides. In Sept. 2013 the population in penal institutions was 4,091 (73 per 100,000 of national population). Denmark was ranked second of 102 countries for criminal justice and fourth for civil justice in the 2015 World Justice Project *Rule of Law Index*, which provides data on how the rule of law is experienced by the general public across eight categories. It ranked first in the overall 2015 Index.

Education

Education has been compulsory since 1814. The first stage of the Danish education system is the basic school (education at first level). This starts with a pre-school year (education preceding the first level), which has been compulsory since the beginning of the 2009–10 school year, and continues up to and including the optional 10th year in the *folkeskole* (municipal primary and lower secondary school). In 2006, 649,000 pupils attended education at first level and second level, first stage. In 2010 the number of pupils beginning their education at pre-school was 67,174.

Of all students leaving basic school in 2007–08, 79% had commenced further education within three months. Over half of the students (53%) had elected to attend general upper-secondary education (general programmes of education at secondary level, second stage), while 25% opted for vocational education and training at secondary level, second stage.

Education that qualifies students for tertiary level education is called general upper-secondary education and comprises general upper-secondary education (general programmes of education at secondary level, second stage), such as *gymnasium* (upper-secondary school), higher preparatory examination and adult upper-secondary level courses as well as general/vocational upper-secondary education at the vocational education institutions. In 2008, 119,000 students attended general upper-secondary education and 125,000 students attended upper-secondary vocational education and training.

Higher education is divided into three levels: short-cycle higher education involves two years of training, sometimes practical, after completion of upper-secondary education (19,000 students in 2008); medium-cycle higher education involves two–four years of mainly theoretical training (64,000 students in 2008); long-cycle higher education requires more than four years of education, mainly theoretical, divided between a bachelor's degree, candidate programme and PhD programme (bachelor's students in 2008: 62,000; master's: 53,000; PhD: 6,800).

Universities have been reorganized as a result of several mergers in Jan. 2007. The universities ranked by student population are: the University of Copenhagen (founded 1479), 36,600 students; the University of Aarhus (1928), 30,100; the University of Southern Denmark (1964), 14,300; the Copenhagen Business School, 13,900; the University of Aalborg (1974), 11,300; Roskilde University (1972), 8,100; the Technical University of Denmark, 6,200; the IT University of Copenhagen, 1,300.

Other types of post-secondary education have also been reorganized through mergers of institutions. Eight university colleges have been formed with student numbers ranging from 3,000 to 13,000. The university colleges encompass: schools of nursing; schools of midwifery education; colleges of physiotherapy; social education colleges; teacher training colleges; engineering colleges. There are also post-secondary educational institutions in the cultural sector in areas such as music, architecture, media and the visual arts.

In 2008 public expenditure on education was 15·0% of total government spending.

The adult literacy rate is at least 99%.

Health

In 2005 there were 17,350 doctors (321 per 100,000 persons), 4,634 dentists, 52,843 nurses, 27,072 auxiliary nurses and 1,304 midwives. There were 59 hospitals in 2005 (20,058 beds). In 2007 Denmark spent 9·8% of its GDP on health.

Welfare

The main body of Danish social welfare legislation is consolidated in seven acts concerning: (1) public health security, (2) sick-day benefits, (3) social pensions (for early retirement and old age), (4) employment injuries insurance, (5) employment services, unemployment insurance and activation measures, (6) social assistance including assistance to disabled, rehabilitation, child and juvenile guidance, daycare institutions, care of the aged and sick, and (7) family allowances.

Public health security, covering the entire population, provides free medical care, substantial subsidies for certain essential medicines together with some dental care, and a funeral allowance. Hospitals are primarily municipal and treatment is normally free. All employed workers are granted daily sickness allowances; others can have limited daily sickness allowances. Daily cash benefits are granted in the case of temporary incapacity because of illness, injury or childbirth to all persons in paid employment. The benefit is paid up to the rate of 100% of the average weekly earnings. There is, however, a maximum rate of 3,415 kroner a week.

Social pensions cover the entire population. Entitlement to the old-age pension at the full rate is subject to the condition that the beneficiary has been ordinarily resident in Denmark for 40 years. For a shorter period of residence, the benefits are reduced proportionally. The basic amount of the old-age pension in Jan. 2007 was 174,720 kroner a year to married couples and 119,244 to single persons. Various supplementary allowances, depending on age and income, may be payable with the basic amount. The retirement age is 65, or 67 for those born before 1 July 1939. Depending on health and income, persons aged 60–64 (60–66 for those born before 1 July 1939) may apply for an early retirement pension. Persons over 65 (or 67) years of age are entitled to the basic amount. The pensions to a married couple are calculated and paid to the husband and the wife separately. Early retirement pension to a disabled person is payable at ages 18–64 (or 66) years, at a rate of 177,636 kroner to a single person. Early retirement pensions may be subject to income regulation. The same applies to the old-age pension.

Employment injuries insurance provides for disability or survivors' pensions and compensations. The scheme covers practically all employees.

Employment services are provided by regional public employment agencies. Insurance against unemployment provides daily allowances and covers about 85% of the unemployed. The unemployment insurance system is based on state subsidized insurance funds linked to the trade unions. The unemployment insurance funds had a membership of 2,065,700 in Jan. 2010.

The *Social Assistance Act* comprises three acts (the act on active social policy, the act on social service and the act on integration of foreigners). From these acts individual benefits are applied, in contrast to the other fields of social legislation which apply to fixed benefits. Total social expenditure, including hospital and health services, statutory pensions etc., amounted in the financial year 2008 to 515,935·0m. kroner.

Religion

There is complete religious liberty. The Church of the State is the Evangelical Lutheran Church in Denmark to which 80·9% of the population belonged in 2010. There are ten dioceses, each with a Bishop. The Bishop together with the Chief Administrative Officer of the county make up the diocesan-governing body, responsible for all matters of ecclesiastical local finance and general administration. Bishops are appointed by the Crown after an election by the clergy and parish council members. Each diocese is divided into a number of deaneries (107 in the whole country), each with its own Dean and Deanery Committee, who have certain financial powers. 81% of church finance derives from a voluntary tax paid by members, at a rate between 0·4–1·5% of income depending upon location. A further 12% comes from state subsidiaries and 7% from other sources, such as church lands.

Culture

World Heritage Sites

Denmark has ten sites on the UNESCO World Heritage List: the burial mounds, runic stones and church at Jelling (inscribed on the list in 1994); Roskilde Cathedral (1995); Kronborg Castle (2000); Ilulissat Icefjord (2004), the sea mouth of Sermeq Kujalleq in Greenland; Stevns Klint (2014), a 15 km-long fossil-rich coastal cliff; Christiansfield (2015), a Moravian Church settlement; the par force hunting landscape in North Zealand (2015); Kujataa Greenland: Norse and Inuit Farming at the Edge of the Ice Cap (2017), a subarctic farming landscape; and Aasivissuit-Nipisat Inuit Hunting Ground between Ice and Sea (2018), a cultural landscape containing the remains of 4,200 years of human history. Shared with Germany and the Netherlands, Wadden Sea (2014) is the largest unbroken system of intertidal sand and mud flats in the world.

Press

In 2014 there were 31 daily newspapers with a combined circulation of 1·09m. The newspaper with the largest average circulation in 2014 was *MetroXpress* (a free paper; 325,000 on weekdays). In the 2016 *World Press Freedom Index* compiled by Reporters Without Borders, Denmark ranked fourth out of 180 countries.

Tourism

In 2015 there were 49,152,744 guest nights in commercial accommodation (hotels, holiday cottages, campsites, holiday resorts, youth hostels and marinas), of which 24,731,131 were by foreigners and 24,421,614 by

Danes. The leading nationalities of the foreign visitors in 2013 were Germany (13,837,381 guest nights), Norway, Sweden, the Netherlands and the United Kingdom.

Festivals

Roskilde, one of Europe's largest music festivals, is held annually in July. Other festivals include the Winter Jazz Festival in late Jan./early Feb. which takes place across the country, Carnival in Aalborg, held every May, the Copenhagen Jazz Festival in July, Skanderborg festival (music) in Aug., Tønder Festival (folk music) in Aug., Aarhus Festival (performing arts) in Aug./Sept. and the Copenhagen International Film Festival in Sept./Oct.

Diplomatic Representatives

Of Denmark in the United Kingdom (55 Sloane St., London, SW1X 9SR)
  Ambassador: Lars Thuesen.

Of the United Kingdom in Denmark (Kastelsvej 36–40, DK-2100, Copenhagen)
  Ambassador: Dominic Schroeder.

Of Denmark in the USA (3200 Whitehaven St., NW, Washington, D.C., 20008)
  Ambassador: Lars Gert Lose.

Of the USA in Denmark (Dag Hammarskjölds Allé 24, DK-2100, Copenhagen Ø)
  Ambassador: Carla Sands.

Of Denmark to the United Nations
  Ambassador: Martin Bille Hermann.

Of Denmark to the European Union
  Permanent Representative: Kim Jørgensen.

Faroe Islands

Føroyar/Færøerne

A Norwegian province until the peace treaty of 14 Jan. 1814, the islands have been represented by two members in the Danish parliament since 1851. In 1852 they were granted an elected parliament which in 1948 secured a degree of home-rule. The islands are not part of the EU.

The archipelago is situated due north of Scotland, 300 km from the Shetland Islands, 675 km from Norway and 450 km from Iceland, with a total land area of 1,399 sq. km. There are 17 inhabited islands (the main ones being Streymoy, Eysturoy, Vágoy, Suðuroy, Sandoy and Borðoy) and numerous islets, all mountainous and of volcanic origin. Population estimate in Jan. 2018 was 50,494; density, 36·1 per sq. km. The capital is Tórshavn on Streymoy.

The official languages are Faroese and Danish.

There is a 33-member parliament, the *Løgting*, which is elected by proportional representation by universal suffrage at age 18. Parliament elects a government of at least three members that administers home rule. Denmark is represented in parliament by the *High Commissioner.*

High Commissioner: Lene Moyell Johansen (since May 2017—acting until Aug. 2017).

Prime Minister: Aksel V. Johannesen (since Sept. 2015).

Since 1940 the currency has been the Faroese *króna* (kr.), which remains freely interchangeable with the Danish krone.

Only 2% of the surface is cultivated; it is chiefly used for sheep and cattle grazing. Fishery products, including farmed salmon, represent the greater proportion of merchandise exports.

The airport is on Vágoy, from which there are regular services to Aberdeen, Billund, Copenhagen and Reykjavík. The chief port is Tórshavn, with smaller ports at Klaksvik, Vestmanna, Skálafjørður, Tvøroyri, Vágur and Fuglafjørður.

About 80% are Evangelical Lutherans and 20% are Plymouth Brethren, or belong to small communities of Roman Catholics, Pentecostalists, Adventists, Jehovah's Witnesses and Bahá'ís.

Greenland

Grønland/Kalaallit Nunaat

A Danish possession since 1380, Greenland became an integral part of the Danish kingdom in June 1953 and achieved home rule in May 1979. The territory joined the then European Economic Community (now European Union) along with Denmark in Jan. 1973, but withdrew in Jan. 1985 following a referendum. Greenland's autonomy was extended in June 2009, including increased control over law administration and energy resource revenues and the adoption of Kalaallisut (Greenlandic) as the sole official language (although most inhabitants also speak Danish).

Area, 2,166,086 sq. km, made up of 1,755,437 sq. km of ice cap and 410,449 sq. km of ice-free land. The population at 1 Jan. 2013 was 56,370, of whom 88·9% were born in Greenland; density 0·03 per sq. km. The capital is Nuuk (Godthåb).

There is a 31-member elected parliament (*Inatsisartut*), which appoints the prime minister who in turn appoints the Cabinet of ministers. Greenland also elects two representatives to the Danish parliament (*Folketing*). Denmark is represented by an appointed High Commissioner.

Following parliamentary elections in Nov. 2014, a social democrat-led coalition government was formed in Dec.

High Commissioner: Mikaela Engell (appointed 2011).

Prime Minister: Kim Kielsen (since Sept. 2014—acting until Dec. 2014).

The unit of currency is the *Danish krone.*

There are indications of significant oil deposits off the west coast of Greenland. In Jan. 2014 the government issued a series of exploration licences to international companies, reversing an earlier moratorium imposed on environmental grounds. The territory is also home to around 10% of the world's known deposits of rare-earth metals. Fishing and product-processing are the principal industries. Air Greenland operates domestic services and international flights to Denmark, Iceland and Canada.

Education is compulsory from six to 15 years. A further three years of schooling are optional. The medical service is free to all citizens. There is a central hospital in Nuuk.

About 80% of the population are Evangelical Lutherans.

Greenland has three sites on the UNESCO World Heritage List: the Ilulissat Icefjord, the sea mouth of Sermeq Kujalleq on the west coast of the island (inscribed on the list in 2004), Kujataa Greenland: Norse and Inuit Farming at the Edge of the Ice Cap, a subarctic farming landscape (inscribed on the list in 2017) and Kujataa Greenland: Norse and Inuit Farming at the Edge of the Ice Cap (2017), a subarctic farming landscape; and Aasivissuit-Nipisat Inuit Hunting Ground between Ice and Sea (inscribed on the list in 2018), a cultural landscape containing the remains of 4,200 years of human history.

Further Reading

Denmark

Statistical Information: Danmarks Statistik was founded in 1849 and reorganized in 1966 as an independent institution; it is administratively placed under the Minister of Economic Affairs and the Interior. Its main publications are: *Statistisk Årbog* (Statistical Yearbook). From 1896: *Statistiske Efterretninger* (Statistical News). *Konjunkturstatistik* (Main indicators); *Statistisk Tiårsoversigt* (Statistical Ten-Year Review).

Kongelig Dansk Hof og Statskalender. Annual

Jespersen, Knud J. V., *A History of Denmark.* 2nd ed. 2011

Larsen, Henrik, *Analysing Small State Foreign Policy in the EU: The Case of Denmark.* 2005

National library: Det kongelige Bibliotek, POB 2149, DK-1016 Copenhagen K.

National Statistical Office: Statistics Denmark, Sejrøgade 11, DK-2100 Copenhagen Ø.

Website: http://www.dst.dk

Faroe Islands

Árbók fyri Føroyar. Annual.

Rutherford, G. K. (ed.) *The Physical Environment of the Fœroe Islands.* 1982

Wylie, J., *The Faroe Islands: Interpretations of History.* 1987

National Statistical Office: Hagstova Føroya, Glyvursvegur 1, PO Box 2068, FO-165 Argir.

Website: http://www.hagstova.fo

Greenland

Statistics Greenland. *Greenland in Figures 2017* in English. Online only. *Stat Bank* in English. Online only.

Gad, F., *A History of Greenland.* 2 vols. 1970–73

Greenland National Library, P. O. Box 1011, DK-3900 Nuuk

National Statistical Office: Statistics Greenland, PO Box 1025, DK-3900 Nuuk.

Website: http://www.stat.gl

Djibouti

Jumhouriyya Djibouti (Republic of Djibouti)

Capital: Djibouti
Population projection, 2020: 1·00m.
GNI per capita, 2017: (PPP$) 3,392
HDI/world rank, 2017: 0·476/172
Internet domain extension: .dj

Key Historical Events

At a referendum held on 19 March 1967, 60% of the electorate voted for continued association with France rather than independence. France affirmed that the Territory of the Afars and the Issas was destined for independence but no date was fixed. Independence as the Republic of Djibouti was achieved on 27 June 1977. Afar rebels in the north, belonging to the Front for the Restoration of Unity and Democracy (FRUD), signed a 'Peace and National Reconciliation Agreement' with the government on 26 Dec. 1994, envisaging the formation of a national coalition government, the redrafting of the electoral roll and the integration of FRUD militants into the armed forces and civil service.

Territory And Population

Djibouti is in effect a city-state surrounded by a semi-desert hinterland. It is bounded in the northwest by Eritrea, northeast by the Gulf of Aden, southeast by Somalia and southwest by Ethiopia. The area is 23,200 sq. km (8,958 sq. miles). The population at the 2009 census was 818,159. In 2011, 76·3% of the population lived in urban areas. Around half the population in 2005 were Somali (Issa, Gadaboursi and Issaq), 35% Afar, with some Europeans (mainly French) and Arabs.

The UN gives a projected population for 2020 of 1·00m.

There are five administrative regions, plus the city of Djibouti (areas in sq. km): Ali-Sabieh (2,200); Arta (1,800); Dikhil (7,200); Djibouti (200); Obock (4,700); Tadjourah (7,100). The capital is Djibouti (2009 population, 475,322).

French and Arabic are official languages; Somali and Afar are also spoken.

Social Statistics

2008 estimates: births, 24,100; deaths, 9,300. Rates (2008 estimates, per 1,000 population); birth, 28·4; death, 11·0. 2006: marriages, 3,059; divorces, 723. Annual population growth rate, 2000–08, 1·9%. Infant mortality, 2010, 73 per 1,000 live births. Expectation of life, 2007: 53·7 years for men; 56·5 for women. Fertility rate, 2008, 3·9 children per woman.

Climate

Conditions are hot throughout the year, with very little rain. Djibouti, Jan. 78°F (25·6°C), July 96°F (35·6°C). Annual rainfall 5″ (130 mm).

Constitution and Government

The constitution, approved by referendum in 1992, permits the existence of up to four political parties. Parties are required to maintain an ethnic balance in their membership. The *President* is directly elected for a renewable six-year term. Parliament is a 65-member *National Assembly* elected for five-year terms. In April 2010 the constitution was amended to allow the president to stand for a third consecutive term. It also provided for the creation of a *Senate*.

National Anthem

'Hinjinne u sara kaca' ('Arise with strength'); words by A. Elmi, tune by A. Robleh.

Recent Elections

In the presidential election on 8 April 2016 Ismail Omar Guelleh was re-elected with 87·1% of the vote, ahead of Omar Elmi Khaireh with 7·3% and four other candidates. Turnout was 69·0%.

At the parliamentary elections of 23 Feb. 2018 the Union for a Presidential Majority won 58 of the 65 seats and the coalition between the Djibouti Union for Democracy and Justice and the Djibouti Party for Development 7. The opposition boycotted the election amid controversy over the integrity of the electoral process.

Current Government

President: Ismail Omar Guelleh; b. 1947 (People's Rally for Democracy/ RPP; sworn in 8 May 1999 and re-elected in April 2005, April 2011 and April 2016).

In Feb. 2019 the Council of Ministers comprised:

Prime Minister: Abdoulkader Kamil Mohamed; b. 1951 (RPP; took office 1 April 2013).

Minister of Agriculture, Water, Livestock and Fisheries: Mohamed Ahmed Awaleh. *Budget:* Bodeh Ahmed Robleh. *Communication, in Charge of Posts and Telecommunications:* Abdi Youssouf Sougueh. *Defence, in Charge of Relations with Parliament:* Ali Hassan Bahdon. *Economy and Finance, in Charge of Industry:* Ilyas Moussa Dawaleh. *Energy, in Charge of Natural Resources:* Yonis Ali Guedi. *Foreign Affairs and International Co-operation, and Government Spokesman:* Mahamoud Ali Youssouf. *Health:* Dr Djama Elmi Okieh. *Higher Education and Research:* Nabil Mohamed Ahmed. *Housing, Town Planning and Environment:* Moussa Mohamed Ahmed. *Infrastructure and Transport:* Mohamed Abdoulkader Moussa Helem. *Interior:* Hassan Omar Mohamed. *Justice and Penitentiary Affairs, in Charge of Human Rights:* Moumin Ahmed Cheikh. *Labour, in Charge of Administrative Reform:* Hassan Idriss Samrieh. *Muslim Affairs, Culture and Awqaf:* Moumin Hassan Barreh. *National Education and Vocational Training:* Moustapha Mohamed Mahamoud. *Promotion of Women and Family Planning:* Moumina Houmed Hassan. *Minister in the Presidency in Charge of Investments:* Ali Guelleh Aboubaker.

Government Website (French only): http://www.presidence.dj

Current Leaders

Ismail Omar Guelleh

Position
President

Introduction
Ismail Omar Guelleh was elected for a fourth term as president in April 2016. He succeeded his uncle in 1999, becoming the country's second president since independence in 1977.

Early Life
Ismail Omar Guelleh was born on 27 Nov. 1947 in Dire Dawa, Ethiopia. He is the grandson of Guelleh Batal, one of the chiefs of the Issa clan who signed the 1917 agreement placing the Issa territories under French administration. From 1974 Guelleh became increasingly involved in the fight for independence as a member of the African Popular League for Independence (LPAI). Following Djibouti's declaration of independence on 27 June 1977, Guelleh was appointed principal private secretary to the president, his uncle, Hassan Gouled Aptidon.

Guelleh became head of the security services and joined the People's Rally for Democracy (RPP) when it was established in March 1979. He became head of the party's cultural commission in 1981, the year in which Gouled made the Issa-dominated RPP the country's only legal political party, causing resentment among the Afar community. Civil war followed in 1991.

© Springer Nature Limited 2020
Palgrave Macmillan (ed.), *The Statesman's Yearbook 2020*,
https://doi.org/10.1057/978-1-349-95940-2_61

When Gouled announced that he would not contest the April 1999 presidential elections, Guelleh stood as the RPP candidate. He was sworn in as president on 8 May 1999.

Career in Office

In Feb. 2000 Guelleh signed a peace agreement with the radical faction of the Afar party, the Front for the Restoration of Unity and Democracy, ending nine years of civil war. During the multi-party elections of Jan. 2003 the coalition supporting him—the Union for a Presidential Majority—won all 65 seats, prompting accusations of vote-rigging. Ahead of the April 2005 presidential election, Guelleh pledged to tackle poverty and the dependence on food imports while boosting women's rights and institutional accountability. The opposition boycotted the polls and he was sworn in for a second six-year term with 100% of the vote. In Feb. 2008 the Union for a Presidential Majority again won all 65 seats in parliamentary elections boycotted by its rivals. A constitutional amendment allowing the president to seek a third term was then approved in April 2010, and in April 2011 Guelleh was re-elected with 80% of the vote. In subsequent parliamentary elections in Feb. 2013 and Feb. 2018 the Union for a Presidential Majority retained control of the National Assembly, and in April 2016 Guelleh won a further presidential term having previously stated he would not run again.

In Sept. 2002, in support of the US-led war on terror, Guelleh had allowed 900 US troops to be based in Djibouti. Although his government denied interference in neighbouring Somalia's affairs, US air strikes in Jan. 2007 on the retreating Islamist militias that had earlier taken control of the Somali capital, Mogadishu, and much of the south of the country, were launched from the US base. In June 2008 border clashes between troops from Djibouti and Eritrea led Guelleh to declare war with the neighbouring state. However, following the imposition of sanctions against Eritrea by the UN Security Council in Dec. 2009, both sides agreed in June 2010 to resolve their border issues peacefully. In Aug. 2017 China formally opened its first overseas military base in Djibouti.

Defence

France—Djibouti's former colonial ruler—maintains a naval base and forces numbering 1,900 as of Feb. 2014. The USA's only military base in Africa is in Djibouti, in a former French barracks. China opened a military base in Djibouti in Aug. 2017 and Saudi Arabia is currently building one.

Defence expenditure totalled an estimated US$10m. in 2011 (approximately US$13 per capita), representing around 1% of GDP.

Army

There are four military districts. The strength of the Army in 2011 was approximately 8,000. There is also a paramilitary Gendarmerie of 2,000, and an Interior Ministry National Security Force of some 2,500.

Navy

A coastal patrol is maintained. Personnel (2011 estimate), 200.

Air Force

There is a small Air Force with no combat-capable aircraft. Personnel (2011), 250.

Economy

In 2014 transport and communications contributed 25·5% of GDP; followed by trade and hotels, 16·7%; construction, 13·8%; and finance and insurance, 13·2%.

Overview

The economy relies on Djibouti's status as a free trade centre, with the government encouraging foreign investment in a bid to create the Horn of Africa's principal trading hub. By providing neighbouring landlocked Ethiopia with its main access to the sea, imports and exports from that country represent 70% of port activity at Djibouti's container terminal. The population depends heavily on food imports to meet its needs.

Djibouti weathered the global financial crisis and consequent economic downturn well, although real GDP growth at that time slowed from 5·8% in 2008 to 5·0% in 2009 and foreign direct investment (FDI) declined from 23·8% of GDP to 18·0%. By 2015 FDI stood at only 7·8%, but trade with Ethiopia and greater transhipment and port activity saw GDP growth reach 6·5% that year. High unemployment is a long-term challenge, with over 48%

of the working-age population unemployed in 2016. Meanwhile, high poverty levels (around 23% of the population fell below the poverty line in 2016) and public debt exposure threaten to impede economic progress.

Currency

The currency is the *Djibouti franc* (DJF), notionally of 100 *centimes.* Foreign exchange reserves were US$90m. in July 2005 and total money supply was 49,822m. Djibouti francs. Inflation was 2·7% in 2016 and 0·7% in 2017.

Budget

Revenues in 2013 were 90·5bn. Djibouti francs and expenditures 98·5bn. Djibouti francs.

Performance

Real GDP growth was 6·5% in 2015 and 2016, increasing to 6·7% in 2017. Total GDP in 2017 was US$1·8bn.

Banking and Finance

The Banque Centrale de Djibouti (*Governor*, Ahmed Osman Ali) is the bank of issue. There are three commercial banks and a development bank. External debt totalled US$755m. in 2009 and represented 67·4% of GNI.

Energy and Natural Resources

Environment

Djibouti's carbon dioxide emissions from the consumption of energy in 2011 were the equivalent of 1·8 tonnes per capita.

Electricity

Installed capacity in 2011 was 130,000 kW. Production in 2011 was estimated at 387m. kWh with consumption per capita an estimated 457 kWh.

Agriculture

There were 1,600 ha. of arable land in 2010. An estimated 1,000 ha. in 2010 were equipped for irrigation. Vegetable production (2010 estimate), 30,000 tonnes. The most common crops are tomatoes, mangoes, papayas and melons. Livestock (2005 estimates): goats, 512,000; sheep, 466,000; cattle, 297,000; camels, 69,000.

Forestry

In 2015 the area under forests was 6,000 ha., or 0·2% of the total land area.

Fisheries

In 2012 the catch was 2,167 tonnes, entirely from sea fishing.

Industry

Labour

The labour force in 2013 was 300,000 (227,000 in 2003). 54·6% of the population aged 15–64 was economically active in 2013. Unemployment in 2012 was 48%.

International Trade

Imports and Exports

The main economic activity is the operation of the port. Exports are largely re-exports. In 2009 imports totalled US$647·6m. and exports US$363·7m. The chief imports are cotton goods, sugar, cement, flour, fuel oil and vehicles; the chief exports are hides, cattle and coffee (transit from Ethiopia).

Main import suppliers are France, UAE, Saudi Arabia and Japan. Main export markets are Ethiopia, France, Somalia and Brazil.

Communications

Roads

In 2011 there were an estimated 1,300 km of roads.

Rail

For the lines from Djibouti to Addis Ababa, part of which lie within Djibouti, *see* ETHIOPIA: Communications. Traffic carried is mainly in transit to and from Ethiopia. A new line, the 756 km Addis Ababa–Djibouti Railway, became operational on a trial basis in Oct. 2016 and was officially opened on 1 Jan. 2018.

Civil Aviation

There is an international airport at Djibouti (Ambouli), 5 km south of Djibouti. The national carrier is Air Djibouti, which was resurrected in 2015 after having gone into liquidation in 2002. In 2016 it had flights to Addis Ababa, Berbera, Dire Dawa, Hargeisa and Mogadishu.

Shipping

Djibouti is a free port and container terminal. In 2013, 7·10m. tonnes of cargo were handled. A container terminal opened at Doraleh in 2009.

Telecommunications

There were 18,500 fixed telephone lines in 2010 (20·8 per 1,000 inhabitants). Mobile phone subscribers numbered 165,600 in 2010. There were an estimated 95 internet users per 1,000 inhabitants in 2013.

Social Institutions

Out of 178 countries analysed in the 2017 *Fragile States Index*—a list published jointly by the Fund for Peace and *Foreign Policy* magazine—Djibouti was ranked the 41st most vulnerable to conflict or collapse. The index is based on 12 indicators of state vulnerability across social, political and economic categories.

Justice

There are a Court of First Instance and a Court of Appeal in the capital. The judicial system is based on Islamic law. The death penalty was abolished for all crimes in 1994.

The population in penal institutions in 2011 was approximately 750 (83 per 100,000 of national population). The International Centre for Prison Studies estimated in 2014 that 50·0% of prisoners had yet to receive a trial.

Education

In 2007 there were 56,667 pupils and 1,597 teaching staff in primary schools, and 34,667 pupils and 1,021 teachers in secondary schools. In the same year there were 2,192 students at tertiary education institutions and 121 academic staff.

In 2010 public expenditure on education came to 4·5% of GDP.

Health

In 2007 there were a total of 1,220 hospital beds. There were 85 physicians, nine dentists, 196 nurses, 90 midwives and eight pharmacists in 2007.

In *Water: At What Cost? The State of the World's Water 2016*, WaterAid reported that 10·0% of the population does not have access to safe water.

Religion

According to the Pew Research Center's Forum on Religion & Public Life, in 2010 the population was an estimated 96·9% Muslim (Sunnis) with a small Christian minority.

Culture

Press

There are no daily newspapers; in 2008 the government-owned *La Nation* was published four times a week.

Tourism

There were 63,000 foreign tourists staying at hotels and similar establishments in 2013 (60,000 in 2012).

Diplomatic Representatives

Of Djibouti in the United Kingdom
    Ambassador: Ayeid Mousseid Yahya (resides in Paris).

Of the United Kingdom in Djibouti
    Ambassador: Dr Alastair McPhail, CMG, OBE (resides in Addis Ababa, Ethiopia).

Of Djibouti in the USA and to the United Nations (1156 15th St., NW, Suite 515, Washington, D.C., 20005)
    Ambassador: Mohamed Siad Doualeh.

Of the USA in Djibouti (B. P. 185, Lot no. 350-B, Lotissement Haramous, Djibouti)
    Ambassador: Larry Edward André.

Of Djibouti to the European Union
    Ambassador: Omar Abdi Saïd.

Further Reading

Direction Nationale de la Statistique. *Annuaire Statistique de Djibouti*
Alwan, Daoud A., *Historical Dictionary of Djibouti*.2000
National Statistical Office: Direction Nationale de la Statistique, Ministère de l'Économie et des Finances, chargé de l'Industrie, BP 13, Djibouti.
Website (French only): http://www.ministere-finances.dj.

Dominica

Commonwealth of Dominica

Capital: Roseau
Population projection, 2020: 75,000
GNI per capita, 2017: (PPP$) 8,344
HDI/world rank, 2017: 0·715/103
Internet domain extension: .dm

Key Historical Events

When Christopher Columbus sighted Dominica on 3 Nov. 1493 it was occupied by Carib Indians, who are thought to have overrun the previous inhabitants, the Arawak, from around 1300. Dominica remained a 'Carib Isle' until the 1630s, when French farmers and missionaries established sugar plantations. Control was contested between the British and French until it was awarded to the British by the Treaty of Versailles in 1783. In March 1967 Dominica became a self-governing state within the West Indies Associated States, with Britain retaining control of external relations and defence. The island became an independent republic, the Commonwealth of Dominica, on 3 Nov. 1978.

Territory and Population

Dominica is an island in the Windward group of the West Indies situated between Martinique and Guadeloupe. It has an area of 750 sq. km (290 sq. miles) and a provisional population at the 2011 census of 71,293. The population density in 2011 was 95·1 per sq. km.

In 2010, 67·2% of the population were urban. The chief town, Roseau, had 14,725 inhabitants (provisional) in 2011.

The UN gives a projected population for 2020 of 75,000.

The population is mainly of African and mixed origins, with small white and Asian minorities. There is a Kalinago (Carib) Territory with a population of around 3,000—the Kalinago people inhabited Dominica prior to European colonization.

The official language is English, although 90% of the population also speak a French Creole.

Social Statistics

Births, 2006 estimates, 1,080 (rate of 14·9 per 1,000 population); deaths, 540 (rate of 7·5); marriages (2009), 250; divorces (2009), 85. Life expectancy, 2007: male, 72 years; female, 76 years. Annual population growth rate, 2000–08, –0·2%. Infant mortality rate, 2010, 11 per 1,000 live births. Fertility rate, 2008, 2·1 births per woman.

Climate

A tropical climate, with pleasant conditions between Dec. and March, but there is a rainy season from June to Oct., when hurricanes may occur. Rainfall is heavy, with coastal areas having 70" (1,750 mm) but the mountains may have up to 225" (6,250 mm). Roseau, Jan. 76°F (24·2°C), July 81°F (27·2°C). Annual rainfall 78" (1,956 mm).

Constitution and Government

The head of state is the *President*, nominated by the *Prime Minister* and the Leader of the Opposition, and elected for a five-year term (renewable once) by the House of Assembly. The *House of Assembly* has 32 members, of whom 21 members are elected and nine nominated by the President in addition to the Speaker and the Attorney General.

National Anthem

'Isle of beauty, isle of splendour'; words by W. Pond, tune by L. M. Christian.

Recent Elections

Elections were held on 8 Dec. 2014. The ruling Dominica Labour Party (DLP) won 15 of 21 elected seats (18 in 2009) and the United Workers Party (UWP) won 6 (3 in 2009).

Current Government

President: Charles Savarin; b. 1943 (sworn in 2 Oct. 2013 and re-elected 1 Oct. 2018).

Prime Minister, and Minister for Finance, Investments, Housing and Lands: Roosevelt Skerrit; b. 1972 (DLP; sworn in 8 Jan. 2004 and again on 21 Dec. 2009 and 9 Dec. 2014).

Deputy Prime Minister, and Minister for Agriculture, Food and Fisheries: Reginald Austrie.

In Feb. 2019 the cabinet comprised:

Minister for Commerce, Enterprise and Small Business Development: Roselyn Paul. *Ecclesiastical Affairs, Family and Gender Affairs:* Catherine Daniel. *Education and Human Resource Development:* Petter Saint-Jean. *Environment, Climate Resilience, Disaster Management and Urban Renewal:* Joseph Isaac. *Foreign and CARICOM Affairs:* Francine Baron. *Health and Social Services:* Kenneth Darroux. *Information, Science, Telecommunications and Technology:* Kelver Darroux. *Justice, Immigration and National Security:* Rayburn Blackmoore. *Kalinago Affairs:* Casius Darroux. *Planning and Economic Development:* Miriam Blanchard. *Public Works, Water Resource Management and Ports:* John Collin McIntyre. *Tourism and Culture:* Robert Tonge. *Trade, Energy and Employment:* Ian Douglas. *Youth, Sports and Constituency Empowerment:* Justina Charles. *Attorney General:* Levi Peter.

Government Website: http://www.dominica.gov.dm

Current Leaders

Charles Angelo Savarin

Position
President

Introduction
Savarin was elected president by the House of Assembly in Sept. 2013. He succeeded Eliud Williams, who had served in an acting capacity since 2012. He was re-elected in Oct. 2018.

Early Life
Savarin was born on 2 Oct. 1943 in Portsmouth, Dominica and attended Dominica Grammar School and Ruskin College, Oxford. He was a teacher at Dominica Grammar School between 1963 and 1970 and also served as general secretary of the Civil Service Association from 1966 until 1983.

He was appointed chairman of the Committee for National Salvation, installed after the resignation of Prime Minister Patrick John in 1979. He was then a senator in the interim government that ruled until 1980, when Dame Eugenia Charles of the Dominica Freedom Party (DFP) was elected prime minister. Savarin contested that year's presidential elections for the DFP but lost to Mike Douglas. He served as a senator under Charles from 1980–85 and from 1983–85 was minister without portfolio with special responsibility for trade, industry and tourism.

He subsequently became a diplomat, serving as minister counsellor of the Dominica High Commission to the UK from 1985 until 1986 when he became permanent representative to the European Union and ambassador to Belgium, Luxembourg and Switzerland. He also served as principal ambassadorial spokesman on the banana trade for the African, Caribbean and Pacific States until 1993. He then returned to Dominica to become general manager of the National Development Corporation.

When Charles stepped down as DFP leader in 1995, Savarin was beaten by Brian Alleyne in the contest to succeed her. However, he replaced Charles as the party's MP in the Roseau Central Constituency and when Alleyne resigned the leadership in 1996, Savarin took over. He stayed in the role until 2007, when mounting criticism of his leadership forced him to resign.

Savarin served as minister for tourism and enterprise development, foreign affairs, trade and labour from 2000–05 and sat as a senator under the Dominica Labour Party government of 2005–13. He was minister with responsibility for the public service from 2005 until 2007, adding the public utilities, energy and ports portfolios until 2009 before substituting them for the national security, immigration and labour portfolios from 2010–13.

Career in Office
Despite strong objections from the opposition United Workers Party, Savarin was elected to the presidency by the House of Assembly on 30 Sept. 2013 and again, for a second term, on 1 Oct. 2018.

Roosevelt Skerrit

Position
Prime Minister

Introduction
Roosevelt Skerrit became Dominica's youngest ever prime minister in Jan. 2004 when he took office following the death of his predecessor, Pierre Charles. Appointed by parliamentary recommendation to lead the coalition government, he was returned as prime minister in the May 2005 general election when the Dominica Labour Party (DLP) won an outright majority, and again in Dec. 2009 and Dec. 2014.

Early Life
Roosevelt Skerrit was born in 1972 and grew up in Vieille Case in northeast Dominica. From 1994–97 he studied psychology and English at the University of Mississippi and New Mexico State University. On his return to Dominica he worked as a teacher, first in a high school then at the Dominica Community College. In 1999 he entered politics and in 2000 was elected as a DLP representative to the House of Assembly.

In the coalition government of the DLP and the Dominica Freedom Party (DFP), Skerrit served as minister for sports and youth affairs and later also for education. When Pierre Charles died of a heart attack in Jan. 2004, the then President Nicholas Liverpool appointed Skerrit as his replacement.

Career in Office
Skerrit inherited a small working majority and sought to maintain unity in the coalition government. Against a background of economic troubles, the government introduced unpopular austerity measures, with a combination of spending cuts and higher taxes prompting strikes. During his first year in office he pursued a Caribbean Community (CARICOM) initiative to raise US$50m. of aid and has subsequently been involved in developing a regional stabilization fund under the auspices of the Caribbean Development Bank.

In March 2004 Skerrit reversed Dominica's traditional policy of pursuing diplomatic ties with Taiwan in preference to relations with China, obtaining a six-year aid package from China worth US$117m. In an attempt to reduce Dominica's dependence on agriculture, the government has invested in tourism and major infrastructure projects.

In the election of 5 May 2005 Skerrit led the DLP to victory with 12 of 21 elected seats. In Sept. 2005 Dominica was one of several CARICOM countries to enter into an oil-purchasing deal with Venezuela and in Oct. 2005 he secured around US$2m. of direct US aid for public and private sector investment. The International Monetary Fund commended his government in Dec. 2006 for its successful economic programme, including significant progress in debt restructuring. In Feb. 2009 Skerrit announced that his government had secured US$49m. in grants from Venezuela within the framework of the ALBA (Alianza Bolivariana para los Pueblos de Nuestra América) trade group of leftist Latin American states. In the Dec. 2009 and Dec. 2014 general elections he again led the DLP to victory, winning 18 and then 15 of the 21 elected seats respectively, and in Oct. 2016 he survived a parliamentary vote of no confidence by 14 votes to 0.

Skerrit served a six-month tenure as chairman of CARICOM in the first half of 2010.

In Sept. 2017 Dominica suffered severe damage from Hurricane Maria, along with several other Caribbean islands.

Economy

In 2014 agriculture accounted for 15·9% of GDP, industry 14·8% and services 69·3%.

Overview
Annual GDP growth has averaged 2·0% since the early 1990s—over a percentage point less than the Caribbean mean. Traditionally the economy has relied on bananas as its main export earner, but the banana market has come under increased competition since the European Union was forced by the World Trade Organization to phase out preferential treatment for former colonies. There is also a large potential for tourism, although the sector remains underdeveloped owing to poor infrastructure and the lack of a large airport. Its relatively small scale by regional standards nevertheless ensured a limited impact on the broader economy from the global financial crisis and downturn. However, foreign direct investment and remittance inflows declined, resulting in sluggish growth from 2010–13.

Dominica is susceptible to a variety of natural disasters. In 2007 Hurricane Dean caused damage estimated at 20% of the country's GDP, while in 2015 the cost of Tropical Storm Erika's devastation was calculated at US$483m.—equivalent to 90% of GDP according to government estimates. The IMF predicted output growth would remain subdued in 2016 as the economy slowly recovers. Long-term recovery is conditional on donor grants proceeding as expected.

Currency
The *East Caribbean dollar* (XCD) and the US dollar are legal tender. Foreign exchange reserves were US$50m. in July 2005 and total money supply was EC$149m. There was zero inflation in 2016 and inflation of 0·6% in 2017.

Budget
The fiscal year begins on 1 July. Revenues for the fiscal year 2013–14 (provisional) were EC$537·1m. (including general revenue, EC$401·5m.) and expenditures EC$492·6m. (including project expense, EC$163·6m.).

The standard rate of VAT is 15% (reduced rate, 10%).

Performance
Real GDP grew by 2·6% in 2016 but contracted by 4·7% in 2017. In 2015 the economy contracted by 1·8% as a result of Tropical Storm Erika, which hit the island in Aug. of that year and significantly affected agriculture and tourism. In 2017 total GDP was US$0·6bn.

Banking and Finance
The Eastern Caribbean Central Bank based in St Kitts and Nevis functions as a central bank. The *Governor* is Timothy Antoine. As at 2016 there were four commercial banks (three foreign and one domestic), a development bank and ten credit unions. Dominica is affiliated to the Eastern Caribbean Securities Exchange in Basseterre, St Kitts and Nevis. Total foreign debt was US$293m. in 2013.

Energy and Natural Resources

Environment
Carbon dioxide emissions from the consumption of energy were the equivalent of 1·9 tonnes per capita in 2011.

Electricity
Installed capacity was 27,000 kW in 2011. Production in 2011 was 100m. kWh. Consumption per capita in 2011 was about 1,406 kWh. There are three small hydro-electric power stations.

Agriculture
Agriculture employs 26% of the labour force. In 2007 there were around 5,000 ha. of arable land and 16,000 ha. of permanent crops. Estimated production, 2013, in 1,000 tonnes: bananas, 24; grapefruit, 15; yams, 14; taro, 13; coconuts, 8; oranges, 6; plantains, 6. Livestock (2013 estimates): cattle, 14,000; goats, 10,000; sheep, 8,000; pigs, 5,000.

Forestry
In 2015 forests covered 43,000 ha., or 58% of the total land area. Of the total area under forests 61% was primary forest in 2015 and 39% other naturally regenerated forest.

Fisheries
In 2012 fish landings were 561 tonnes (all from sea fishing).

Industry

Manufactures include soap, coconut oil, copra, cement blocks, furniture and footwear. Industry produced 14·8% of GDP in 2014, although only 3·6% came from manufacturing.

Labour

Around 25% of the economically active population are engaged in agriculture, fishing and forestry. In 2006 the minimum wage was US$0·75 an hour. The unemployment rate in 2008–09 was 14·0%.

International Trade

Imports and Exports

In 2010 imports (c.i.f.) totalled US$224·6m. and exports (f.o.b.) US$34·1m. Main import sources in 2010 (in US$1m.) were: USA (98·3); Trinidad and Tobago (34·3); Venezuela (16·3). Main export markets in 2010 (in US$1m.) were: St Kitts and Nevis (6·0); Jamaica (5·9); Trinidad and Tobago (4·7).

Principal imports in 2010 (in US$1m.) were: machinery and transport equipment (51·0); mineral fuels, lubricants and related materials (38·8); food (37·0). Principal exports in 2010 (in US$1m.) were: chemicals and related products (16·5); food (7·2); miscellaneous manufactured articles (5·0).

Communications

Roads

In 2010 there were an estimated 905 km of roads, of which 82% were paved. Approximately 24,600 vehicles were registered in 2014.

Civil Aviation

There are international airports at Melville Hall and Cane Field. In 2010 there were direct flights to Antigua, Barbados, Georgetown, Guadeloupe, Porlamar (Venezuela), Puerto Rico, St Lucia and St Vincent.

Shipping

There are deep-water harbours at Roseau and Woodbridge Bay. Roseau has a cruise ship berth. In Jan. 2014 there were 51 ships of 300 GT or over registered, totalling 703,000 GT.

Telecommunications

There were 15,500 fixed telephone lines in 2010 (228·5 per 1,000 inhabitants). Mobile phone subscribers numbered 98,100 in 2010. There were 474·5 internet users per 1,000 inhabitants in 2010.

Social Institutions

Justice

There are a supreme court and 14 magistrates courts. Law is based on UK common law as exercised by the Eastern Caribbean Supreme Court on St Lucia. Dominica was one of 12 countries to sign an agreement establishing a Caribbean Court of Justice to replace the British Privy Council as the highest civil and criminal court. The court was inaugurated at Port of Spain, Trinidad on 16 April 2005. Dominica is one of only four countries, along with Barbados, Belize and Guyana, to have accepted it as its court of final appeal.

The police force has a residual responsibility for defence. The population in penal institutions in March 2013 was 266 (equivalent to 391 per 100,000 of national population). 22·7% of prisoners had yet to receive a trial according to 2014 estimates by the International Centre for Prison Studies.

Education

In 2008 adult literacy was 86%. Education is free and compulsory between the ages of five and 16 years. In 2007 there were 499 teaching staff and 8,643 pupils in primary schools, and 469 teaching staff and 7,481 pupils in general secondary level education. The leading higher education institution is Ross University School of Medicine, established in 1978. In 2007 public expenditure on education came to 5·5% of GNI.

Health

In 2005 there were 39 hospital beds per 10,000 inhabitants. There were 124 physicians and 370 nurses and midwives in 2008. Large numbers of

professional nurses take up employment abroad, especially in the USA, causing a shortage of health care workers in Dominica. In 2011 health spending represented 6·0% of GDP.

Welfare

The minimum age to qualify for an old-age pension was 61 years in 2013, incrementally rising by six months each year to reach 65 years in 2021. To be eligible, at least 500 weeks of contributions are required. In 2013 the minimum old-age pension was EC$36·90 per month.

Religion

In 2010 around 94% of the population were Christians according to the Pew Research Center's Forum on Religion & Public Life, of whom two-thirds were Catholics and a third Protestants.

Culture

World Heritage Sites

Dominica has one site on the UNESCO World Heritage List: Morne Trois Pitons National Park (1997), a tropical forest centred on the Morne Trois Pitons volcano.

Press

In 2008 there were no daily newspapers but there were four weeklies—*The Chronicle*, *The Sun*, *The Times* and *The Tropical Star*.

Tourism

In 2014 there were 81,511 overnight tourist arrivals by air, up from 78,277 in 2013 although down from the peak of 84,041 in 2006. There were 286,573 cruise ship visitors in 2014 (when there were 199 cruise ship calls), down from the peak of 532,352 in 2009 although up from 230,587 in 2013.

Festivals

The pre-Lent Carnival season usually occurs in Feb. or March each year. The Dominica Festival of Arts (DOMFESTA) runs from April to June. There is also an annual World Creole Music Festival, which is held in Oct.

Diplomatic Representatives

Of Dominica in the United Kingdom (1 Collingham Gdns, London, SW5 0HW)
   Acting High Commissioner: Janet Charles.

Of the United Kingdom in Dominica
   High Commissioner: Janet Douglas, CMG (resides in Bridgetown, Barbados).

Of Dominica in the USA (3216 New Mexico Ave., NW, Washington, D.C., 20016)
   Ambassador: Vince Henderson.

Of the USA in Dominica
   Ambassador: Linda S. Taglialatela (resides in Bridgetown, Barbados).

Of Dominica to the United Nations
   Ambassador: Loreen Ruth Bannis-Roberts.

Of Dominica to the European Union
   Ambassador: Vacant.
   Chargé d'Affaires a.i.: Sharlene Shillingford-McKimon.

Further Reading

Baker, P. L., *Centring the Periphery: Chaos, Order and the Ethnohistory of Dominica.* 1994
Honychurch, L., *The Dominica Story: a History of the Island.* 2nd ed. 1995
National Statistical Office: Central Statistical Office, Kennedy Avenue, Roseau.

Dominican Republic

República Dominicana

Capital: Santo Domingo
Population projection, 2020: 11·11m.
GNI per capita, 2017: (PPP$) 13,921
HDI/world rank, 2017: 0·736/94
Internet domain extension: .do

Key Historical Events

In 1492 Columbus discovered the island of Hispaniola, which he called La Isla Española, and which for a time was also known as Santo Domingo. The city of Santo Domingo, founded by his brother, Bartholomew, in 1496, is the oldest city in the Americas. The western third of the island—now the Republic of Haiti—was later occupied and colonized by the French, to whom the Spanish colony of Santo Domingo was also ceded in 1795. In 1808 the Dominican population routed the French at the battle of Palo Hincado. Eventually, with the aid of a British naval squadron, the French were forced to return the colony to Spanish rule, from which it declared its independence in 1821. It was invaded and held by the Haitians from 1822 to 1844, when the Dominican Republic was founded and a constitution adopted.

Thereafter the rule was dictatorship interspersed with brief democratic interludes. Between 1916 and 1924 the country was under US military occupation. From 1930 until his assassination in 1961, Rafael Trujillo used puppet presidents to remain in control after his legal terms in office ended. The conservative pro-American Joaquin Balaguer was president from 1966 to 1978. In 1986 Balaguer returned to power at the head of the Socialist Christian Reform Party, leading the way to economic reforms. But there was violent opposition to spending cuts and general austerity. The 1996 elections brought in a reforming government under Leonel Fernández of the Dominican Liberation Party (PLD), which pledged to act against corruption.

Although the PLD lost power in 2000, Fernández won a second term in 2004. He oversaw the country's entry into a free trade agreement with the USA and Central American nations in 2005. Re-elected in 2008, he was succeeded in 2012 by Danilo Medina.

Territory and Population

The Dominican Republic occupies the eastern portion (about two-thirds) of the island of Hispaniola, the western division forming the Republic of Haiti. The area is 48,671 sq. km (18,792 sq. miles). The area and 2010 census populations of the provinces and National District (Santo Domingo area) were:

	Area (in sq. km)	Population
La Altagracia	3,010	273,210
Azua	2,532	214,311
Bahoruco (Baoruco)	1,282	97,313
Barahona	1,739	187,105
Dajabón	1,021	63,955
Distrito Nacional (Santo Domingo area)	1,401	3,339,410
Duarte	1,605	289,574
Elías Piña	1,426	63,029
Espaillat	839	231,938
Hato Mayor	1,329	85,017
Hermanas Mirabal	440	92,193
Independencia	2,006	52,589
María Trinidad Sánchez	1,272	140,925
Monseñor Nouel	992	165,224
Monte Cristi	1,924	109,607

(continued)

	Area (in sq. km)	Population
Monte Plata	2,632	185,956
Pedernales	2,075	31,587
Peravia	792	184,344
Puerto Plata	1,853	321,597
La Romana	654	245,433
Samaná	854	101,494
Sánchez Ramírez	1,196	151,392
San Cristóbal	1,266	596,930
San José de Ocoa	855	59,544
San Juan	3,569	232,333
San Pedro de Macorís	1,255	290,458
Santiago	2,837	963,422
Santiago Rodríguez	1,111	57,476
El Seibo	1,787	87,680
Valverde	823	163,030
La Vega	2,287	394,205

Census population in 2010 was 9,445,281. In 2011 the population was 69·8% urban.

The UN gives a projected population for 2020 of 11·11m.

Population of the main towns (2010 census, in 1,000): Santo Domingo, the capital, 2,582; Santiago de los Caballeros, 551; Los Alcarrizos, 245; La Romana, 225; San Pedro de Macorís, 185.

The population is mainly composed of a mixed race of European (Spanish) and African descent. The official language is Spanish; about 0·18m. persons speak a Haitian-French Creole.

Social Statistics

2009 estimates: births, 216,000; deaths, 59,000. Rates, 2009 estimates (per 1,000 population): birth, 22; death, 6. Annual population growth rate, 2005–10, 1·4%. Life expectancy, 2013: male, 70·4 years; female, 76·7 years. Infant mortality, 2010, 22 per 1,000 live births. Fertility rate, 2013, 2·5 children per woman.

Climate

A tropical maritime climate with most rain falling in the summer months. The rainy season extends from May to Nov. and amounts are greatest in the north and east. Hurricanes may occur from June to Nov. Santo Domingo, Jan. 75°F (23·9°C), July 81°F (27·2°C). Annual rainfall 56" (1,400 mm).

Constitution and Government

A new constitution—the country's 38th—came into force on 26 Jan. 2010, replacing one from 1966. The Dominican Republic has had more constitutions than any other country. The new constitution's provisions included the establishment of a Constitutional Court, Council of the Judiciary and Supreme Electoral Court. It also provides for recourse to instruments of direct democracy, including referenda and plebiscites, and outlaws same-sex marriages and abortions. Furthermore, it defined Dominican nationals as children born to at least one Dominican parent. A ruling by the Constitutional Court retroactively applied this definition to 1929, effectively stripping—according to UN estimates—210,000 people of their citizenship, many of them the children of undocumented Haitian immigrants. Implementation of a 2014 naturalization law to recognize those already registered as Dominican citizens was fraught with difficulties that had not been solved by June 2015, when the government set a deadline for non-citizens to leave the country.

The *President*, who has executive power, is elected for four years by direct vote and—since 2015—may serve two consecutive terms. A second round of voting in a presidential election is authorized when no candidate secures an absolute majority in the first ballot. There is a bicameral legislature, the *Congress*, comprising a 32-member *Senate* (one member for each province and one for the National District of Santo Domingo) and a 190-member *Chamber of Deputies*, both elected for four-year terms. Citizens are entitled to vote at the age of 18.

National Anthem

'Quisqueyanos valientes, alcemos' ('Valiant Quisqueyans, Let us raise our voices'); words by E. Prud'homme, tune by J. Reyes.

Government Chronology

Heads of State since 1942. (PD = Dominican Party; PLD = Dominican Liberation Party; PR = Reformist Party; PRD = Dominican Revolutionary Party; PRSC = Social Christian Reformist Party; REP = Republican Party; UCN = National Civic Union; n/p = non-partisan)

Presidents		
1942–52	PD/military	Rafael Leonidas Trujillo Molina
1952–60	PD	Héctor Bienvenido Trujillo Molina
1960–62	PD	Joaquín Antonio Balaguer Ricardo
1962–63	REP	Rafael Filiberto Bonelly Fondeur
1963	PRD	Juan Emilio Bosch Gaviño
Chairmen of the Triumvirate		
1963	n/p	Emilio de los Santos
1963–65	UCN	Donald Joseph Reid Cabral
Chairman of Military Junta of Government		
1965	military	Pedro Bartolomé Benoit Vanderhorst
President of the Government of National Reconstruction		
1965	military	Antonio Cosme Imbert Barrera
Presidents		
1965	military	Francisco Alberto Caamaño Deñó
1965–66	PR	Héctor Federico García-Godoy Cáceres
1966–78	PR	Joaquín Antonio Balaguer Ricardo
1978–82	PRD	Silvestre Antonio Guzmán Fernández
1982	PRD	Jacobo Majluta Azar
1982–86	PRD	Salvador Jorge Blanco
1986–96	PRSC	Joaquín Antonio Balaguer Ricardo
1996–2000	PLD	Leonel Antonio Fernández Reyna
2000–04	PRD	Rafael Hipólito Mejía Domínguez
2004–12	PLD	Leonel Antonio Fernández Reyna
2012–	PLD	Danilo Medina Sánchez

Recent Elections

Presidential elections were held on 15 May 2016. Incumbent president Danilo Medina Sánchez of the ruling Dominican Liberation Party (PLD) was re-elected with 61·7% of the votes against Luis Abinader of the Modern Revolutionary Party (PRM) with 35·0%. The six other candidates received less than 2·0% of the vote each. Turnout was 69·6%.

Parliamentary elections were also held on 15 May 2016. In the election to the Chamber of the Deputies the PLD won 106 seats with 41·8% of the vote, the PRM 42 (20·4%), the Social Christian Reformist Party (PRSC) 18 (9·2%) and the Dominican Revolutionary Party (PRD) 16 (7·8%). Six smaller parties won the remaining eight seats. Turnout was 70·3%. In the Senate elections of the same day, the PLD won 26 seats and the PRM 2. The Institutional Social Democratic Bloc, the Liberal Reformist Party, the PRD and the PRSC won a seat each.

Current Government

President: Danilo Medina Sánchez; b. 1951 (PLD; sworn in 16 Aug. 2012 and re-elected 15 May 2016).

Vice-President: Margarita Cedeño de Fernández.

In Feb. 2019 the government comprised:

Secretary of State for Agriculture: Ángel Francisco Estévez Bourdierd. *Culture:* Pedro Vergés. *Defence:* Lieut.-Gen. Rubén Darío Paulino Sem. *Economy, Planning and Development:* Isidoro Santana. *Education:* Andrés Navarro García. *Energy and Mines:* Antonio Isa Conde. *Environment and Natural Resources:* Francisco Domínguez Brito. *Finance:* Donald Guerrero. *Foreign Relations:* Miguel Vargas. *Higher Education, Science and Technology:* Alejandrina Germán. *Industry and Commerce:* Nelson Toca Simó. *Interior and Police:* Carlos Amarante Baret. *Labour:* José Ramón Fadul. *Presidency:* Gustavo Montalvo. *Presidential Administration:* José Ramón Peralta. *Public Administration:* Ramón Ventura Camejo. *Public Health and Social Welfare:* Altagracia Guzmán Marcelino. *Public Works and Communications:* Gonzalo Castillo. *Sport and Recreation:* Danilo Díaz. *Tourism:* Francisco Javier García Fernández. *Women:* Janet Camilo. *Youth:* Robiamny Nadesha Balcácer Vásquez. *Attorney General:* Jean Alain Rodríguez.

Office of the President (Spanish only): http://www.presidencia.gob.do

Current Leaders

Danilo Medina Sánchez

Position
President

Introduction
Danilo Medina was elected president in May 2012, heading the Dominican Liberation Party (PLD). He was re-elected for a second four-year term in May 2016.

Early Life
Medina was born on 10 Nov. 1951 in Bohechío. After leaving school in 1965, he became involved in student associations affiliated with the Dominican Revolutionary Party (PRD). A year after moving to Santo Domingo in 1972 to further his studies, he followed PRD leader Juan Bosch into the newly founded PLD. Having abandoned his initial studies, Medina enrolled at the Instituto Tecnológico de San Domingo in 1980 and graduated in economics in 1984.

Medina was elected to congress in 1986 and again in 1990. From 1994–95 he was Bosch's head campaign strategist and also served as president of the Chamber of Deputies. In 1995 he became party spokesman and was twice secretary of state to President Leonel Fernández Reyna, from 1996–99 and 2004–06.

Medina unsuccessfully contested the presidency in 2000. In 2011, when Fernández retired, he made a second, successful, bid.

Career in Office
Medina was sworn in as president in Aug. 2012. Positioning himself away from the policies of his predecessor, he campaigned on a platform of tackling structural poverty, improving public services, fighting corruption and developing tourism and the nation's natural resources. Despite strong congressional support, he has faced public finance challenges, a bloated public sector and social tensions over corruption.

In May 2014 Medina signed legislation overturning an earlier court ruling in 2013 and reinstating the citizenship of children born in the Dominican Republic to immigrant parents in a bid to ease a source of tension with neighbouring Haiti. Nonetheless, relations remained strained following problems with implementation of the law.

Medina was sworn in for a second term in Aug. 2016, having won the May 2016 presidential election convincingly.

In May 2018 his government severed the Dominican Republic's longstanding diplomatic relations with Taiwan, switching recognition to the People's Republic of China.

Defence

In 2013 defence expenditure totalled US$378m. (US$37 per capita), representing 0·6% of GDP.

Army

There are five defence zones. The Army had a strength in 2011 of 15,000 and includes a special forces battalion and a Presidential Guard. There is a paramilitary National Police 15,000-strong.

Navy

The Navy is mainly equipped with former US vessels. Personnel in 2011 totalled 4,000, based at Santo Domingo and Las Calderas.

Air Force

The Air Force, with HQ at San Isidoro, had eight combat-capable aircraft in 2011. Personnel strength (2011), 5,500.

Economy

In 2014 agriculture accounted for 5·4% of GDP, industry 28·5% and services 66·1%.

Overview

The Dominican Republic is historically noted for its plantation crop exports of sugar, cocoa, coffee and tobacco, but their combined share of total exports has declined. The pillars of the economy are now tourism, worker remittances from the USA and the free trade zones where in-bond factories (known as *maquiladoras*) produce clothing for big name brands. In March 2007 the Dominican Republic-Central America-United States Free Trade Agreement (DR-CAFTA) came into effect, providing free access to the US market.

Economic growth was interrupted in 2003 when a banking crisis, triggered by corruption, sent the sovereign debt to the brink of default while the peso depreciated dramatically and inflation soared. Tight fiscal and monetary policy measures, as well as a resurgent US economy, helped lift the country out of crisis. Economic activity was subsequently robust, with GDP growth averaging 5·7% annually over the period 2005 to 2017, supported by both wage restraint and productivity growth. Per capita income more than doubled, inflation stabilized within the central bank's target range, and reserves grew. Strong inflows of remittances have contributed to the narrowing of the current account deficit, which reached the lowest level in a decade in 2017. However, the consolidated fiscal deficit widened to 4·6% of GDP in 2017, despite efforts to curb tax evasion.

Despite strong GDP growth since the 2003 crisis, poverty and inequality in the Dominican Republic have fallen only slowly. The country requires the completion of long-planned reforms in the electricity sector, improvement in the investment environment, simplification of the tax system and strengthening social policies.

Currency

The unit of currency is the *peso* (DOP), written as RD$, of 100 *centavos*. Gold reserves were 18,000 troy oz in July 2005, foreign exchange reserves US$1,537m. and total money supply was RD$78,490m. Inflation was 1·6% in 2016 and 3·3% in 2017.

Budget

Budgetary central government revenue totalled RD$372bn. and expenditure RD$382bn. in 2013. Tax revenues in 2013 were RD$354bn. Main items of expenditure by economic type in 2013 were compensation of employees (RD$105bn.) and grants (RD$81bn.).

VAT is 18%.

Performance

Real GDP growth was 7·0% in 2015, 6·6% in 2016 and 4·6% in 2017. Total GDP in 2017 was US$75·9bn.

Banking and Finance

In 1947 the Central Bank was established (*Governor*, Héctor Valdez Albizu). Its foreign assets were US$3,337·6m. at Sept. 2010. In 2010 there were 13 commercial banks (two foreign).

In 2010 external debt totalled US$13,045m., representing 26·2% of GNI.

The Santo Domingo Securities Exchange is a member of the Association of Central American Stock Exchanges (Bolcen).

Energy and Natural Resources

Environment

Carbon dioxide emissions from the consumption of energy in 2011 were the equivalent of 2·1 tonnes per capita.

Electricity

Installed capacity was 3·4m. kW in 2011. Production was 15·89bn. kWh in 2011; consumption per capita was 1,566 kWh. Power failures are frequent.

Minerals

Output: nickel (2011 estimate), 13,528 tonnes (mine output, metal content); gold (2009 estimate), 173 kg.

Agriculture

Agriculture and processing are the chief sources of income, sugar cultivation being the principal industry. In 2013 there were an estimated 800,000 ha. of arable land and 350,000 ha. of permanent cropland. 208,000 ha. were irrigated in 2011.

Production, 2013 (in 1,000 tonnes): sugarcane, 4,771; bananas, 1,171; rice, 724; plantains, 595; papayas, 532; pineapples, 486; avocados, 388; coconuts, 287; palm fruit oil (estimate), 262; tomatoes, 259.

Livestock in 2013 (estimates): 3·0m. cattle; 528,000 pigs; 355,000 horses; 248,000 sheep; 235,000 goats; 170m. chickens. Livestock products, 2013 (in 1,000 tonnes): meat (estimate), 466; eggs, 91; milk, 602.

Forestry

Forests and woodlands covered 1·98m. ha. in 2015, representing 41% of the total land area. In 2011, 930,000 cu. metres of timber were cut.

Fisheries

The total catch in 2015 was 11,893 tonnes, mainly from sea fishing.

Industry

Production, 2007 unless otherwise indicated (in 1,000 tonnes): cement, 4,100; residual fuel oil, 753; raw sugar, 488; petrol, 404; distillate fuel oil, 359; kerosene, 158; rum (2005), 49·9m. litres; beer (2006), 213·4m. litres; cigarettes (2006), 1·4bn. units.

Labour

The labour force in 2013 was 4,636,000 (3,804,000 in 2003). 69·2% of the population aged 15–64 was economically active in 2013. The unemployment rate in 2013 was 14·9% (14·7% in 2012).

The Dominican Republic had 23,000 people living in slavery according to the Walk Free Foundation's 2013 *Global Slavery Index*.

International Trade

On 1 March 2007 the Central America-Dominican Republic-United States Free Trade Agreement (CAFTA-DR) entered into force between the Dominican Republic and El Salvador, Guatemala, Honduras, Nicaragua and the USA. Costa Rica implemented the agreement on 1 Jan. 2009.

Imports and Exports

Trade, 2009, in US$1m.: imports (f.o.b.), 12,053·9; exports (f.o.b.), 4,690·9. Principal imports in 2009 were: machinery and transport equipment, 22·2%; mineral fuels and lubricants, 20·9%; manufactured goods, 18·2%; chemicals and related products, 11·5%. Main exports in 2009 were: miscellaneous manufactured articles, 39·4%; food, live animals, beverages and tobacco, 24·6%; manufactured goods, 16·4%; machinery and transport equipment, 11·5%. Main import suppliers, 2009: USA, 42·2%; China, 10·1%; Venezuela, 5·4%. Main export markets, 2009: USA, 61·9%; Haiti, 13·8%; Netherlands, 2·2%.

Communications

Roads

In 2005 the road network covered around 20,000 km. There were 602,700 passenger cars in 2007 (62 per 1,000 inhabitants), 525,400 lorries and vans, and 64,200 buses and coaches. The Dominican Republic has one of the world's highest road death rates, at an estimated 41·7 per 100,000 population in 2010.

Rail

The railway system has been closed down with the exception of 142 km line from Guayubin to the port of Pepillo, used primarily for the banana trade.

There is a metro in Santo Domingo.

Civil Aviation

The main airports are at Puerto Plata, Punta Cana and Santo Domingo (Las Américas). In 2009 Punta Cana was the busiest airport, handling 4,077,596 passengers. The largest airline operating in the Dominican Republic is the American low-cost airline JetBlue.

Shipping
The main ports are Santo Domingo, Puerto Plata, La Romana and Haina. In Jan. 2014 there were three ships of 300 GT or over registered, totalling 90,000 GT.

Telecommunications
In 2011 there were 1,044,200 landline telephone subscriptions (equivalent to 103·8 per 1,000 inhabitants) and 8,770,800 mobile phone subscriptions (or 872·2 per 1,000 inhabitants). In 2011, 35·5% of the population were internet users. In Dec. 2011 there were 2·5m. Facebook users.

Social Institutions

Out of 178 countries analysed in the 2017 *Fragile States Index*—a list published jointly by the Fund for Peace and *Foreign Policy* magazine—the Dominican Republic was ranked the 70th least vulnerable to conflict or collapse. The index is based on 12 indicators of state vulnerability across social, political and economic categories.

Justice
The judicial power resides in the Supreme Court of Justice, the courts of appeal, the courts of first instance, the communal courts and other tribunals created by special laws, such as the land courts. The Supreme Court supervises the lower courts. Each province forms a judicial district, as does the National District, and each has its own procurator fiscal and court of first instance. The death penalty was abolished in 1924.

The population in penal institutions in May 2013 was 24,744 (240 per 100,000 of national population). 56·5% of prisoners had yet to receive a trial according to 2014 estimates by the International Centre for Prison Studies. The Dominican Republic was ranked 69th of 102 countries for criminal justice and 56th for civil justice in the 2015 World Justice Project *Rule of Law Index*, which provides data on how the rule of law is experienced by the general public across eight categories.

Education
Primary education is free and compulsory for children between five and 14 years of age; there are also secondary, normal, vocational and special schools, all of which are either wholly maintained by the State or state-aided. In 2007 there were 1,355,085 primary school pupils with 56,744 teaching staff and 920,494 pupils at secondary level with 31,710 teaching staff. The Universidad Autónoma de Santo Domingo, founded in 1914, is the leading public university; there were 158,534 students enrolled in 2005–06. The leading private university is the Universidad Tecnológica de Santiago, created in 1976. There were 480,103 students and 18,809 academic staff in tertiary education in 2015. Adult literacy was 88% in 2007.

In 2007 public expenditure on education came to 2·6% of GNI and 11·0% of total government spending.

Health
In 2007 there were 14,479 doctors. There were 136 hospitals in 2006 with a total of 9,517 beds. In 2005 there were 20 hospital beds per 10,000 inhabitants.

In *Water: At What Cost? The State of the World's Water 2016*, WaterAid reported that 15·3% of the population does not have access to safe water.

Religion
The religion of the state is Roman Catholicism; according to estimates by the Pew Research Center's Forum on Religion & Public Life there were 6·67m. adherents in 2010 (just over two-thirds of the population). The Pew Research Center estimated that Protestants numbered 2·08m. in 2010 and 1·08m. people were religiously unaffiliated. In Feb. 2019 there was one cardinal.

Culture

World Heritage Sites
The Dominican Republic has one site on the UNESCO World Heritage List: the Colonial City of Santo Domingo (1990), which was founded in 1492, is the site of the first cathedral and university in the Americas.

Press
In 2008 there were ten dailies (eight paid-for and two free) with a combined circulation of 465,000.

Tourism
In 2014 there were 5,141,377 non-resident tourist arrivals by air (of which 4,464,643 were foreigners), up from 4,689,770 in 2013. There were 435,494 cruise ship visitors in 2014, up from 423,910 in 2013. The Dominican Republic had 66,323 hotel rooms in 2012.

Diplomatic Representatives

Of the Dominican Republic in the United Kingdom (8 Gloucester Sq., London, W2 2TJ)
Ambassador: Dr Federico Alberto Cuello Camilo.

Of the United Kingdom in the Dominican Republic (Edificio Corominas Pepin, Ave. 27 de Febrero 233, Santo Domingo)
Ambassador: Christopher Campbell.

Of the Dominican Republic in the USA (1715 22nd St., NW, Washington, D.C., 20008)
Ambassador: José Tomás Pérez Vázquez.

Of the USA in the Dominican Republic (Av. República de Colombia 57, Santo Domingo)
Ambassador: Robin S. Bernstein.

Of the Dominican Republic to the United Nations
Ambassador: Francisco A. Cortorreal.

Of the Dominican Republic to the European Union
Ambassador: Anibal de Castro.

Further Reading

Gregory, Steven, *The Devil Behind the Mirror: Globalization and Politics in the Dominican Republic*. 2006
Peguero, Valentina, *The Militarization of Culture in the Dominican Republic, from the Captains General to General Trujillo*. 2004
National Statistical Office: Oficina Nacional de Estadística, Av. México esq. Leopoldo Navarro, Edificio de Oficinas Gubernamentales 'Juan Pablo Duarte' Piso 9, Santo Domingo.

Ecuador

República del Ecuador (Republic of Ecuador)

Capital: Quito
Population projection, 2020: 17·34m.
GNI per capita, 2017: (PPP$) 10,347
HDI/world rank, 2017: 0·752/86=
Internet domain extension: .ec

Key Historical Events

Ecuador's Santa Elena peninsula has evidence of occupation by hunter-gatherers dating back to 9000 BC, with signs that the Las Vegas culture grew crops from around 6000 BC—the earliest agriculture known in the Americas. The Valdivia culture, famed for its ceramics, developed in the same coastal area from around 3000 BC. The people navigated the Pacific coast using rafts with sails and traded with groups such as the Chorrera and the Mayo Chinchipe in the foothills of the Andes mountains. The Cotocallao culture arose in the valley that is now dominated by the capital, Quito.

Tribes integrated over subsequent centuries, forging new cultures such as the Capulí in the mountains and the Manteños on the coast. The Kingdom of Quito, founded in AD 980, became an important commercial centre. The Kingdom of Cusco expanded northward from present-day Peru into Ecuador in the late 15th century, led by Topa Inca Yupanqui. By 1500 Topa's son, Emperor Huayana Capac, had overcome many local tribes and Ecuador formed the northern extent of the Inca civilization (Tawantinsuyu), with Quito its second city. Huayana Capac's sudden death led to a protracted power struggle between two of his sons—a civil war that seriously weakened the empire. The eventual victor, Atahualpa, soon had a new adversary when the Spanish adventurer, Francisco Pizarro, landed on the Ecuadorian coast in 1532. Relations between the Spanish and the Incas quickly soured and Emperor Atahualpa was captured after the Battle of Cajamarca. He was executed in 1533 and a year later Pizarro headed south and conquered Cusco. Quito, which was burned by Inca warriors to prevent its capture, became the site of a new Spanish city, along with the port of Guayaquil.

From 1543 Ecuador was part of the Spanish-ruled Viceroyalty of Peru, governed from Lima. Resentment over colonial rule was given impetus after French Emperor Napoleon's invasion of Spain in 1808, with Quito experiencing waves of revolts organized by Criolos rebels. They were inspired in part by Simón Bolívar's campaign against the Spanish monarchy in what became the Federation of Gran Colombia. His deputy, Antonio José de Sucre, was a key figure in the defeat of Spain at the Battle of Pichincha in 1822 near Quito. On 13 March 1830 the union with Gran Colombia was dissolved, creating the Republic of Ecuador. Instability characterized much of the rule of the first president, Juan José Flores, fuelled by conflict between liberals from Guayaquil and Quito-based conservatives—a schism that endured for more than a century. Development of Ecuador's institutions and infrastructure accelerated in the 1890s under President Eloy Alfaro, who was a central figure in the Liberal Revolution of 1895. From the mid-1930s, President José Maria Velasco Ibarra was deposed by military coups from four of his five presidencies. A long-standing territorial dispute with Peru erupted into war in 1941 and was not finally resolved until 1998.

From 1963 to 1966 and from 1976 to 1979 military juntas ruled the country. The second of these produced a new constitution. Presidencies were more stable but civil unrest continued in the wake of economic reforms and attempts to combat political corruption. In 1997, 2m. people marched through Quito demanding the resignation of President Abdalá Bucaram Ortiz, who was declared mentally unfit to rule. In April 2005 President Lucio Gutiérrez was ousted by Ecuador's Congress after public protest at his attempts to implement IMF-backed economic policies and his substitution of 27 out of 31 Supreme Court judges with his allies. His replacement, Alfredo Palacio, was defeated in the elections of Nov. 2006, with the socialist Rafael Correa taking over and ushering in social reforms and extending state ownership of the oil industry.

Territory and Population

Ecuador is bounded in the north by Colombia, in the east and south by Peru and in the west by the Pacific Ocean. The frontier with Peru has long been a source of dispute. It was delimited in the Treaty of Rio, 29 Jan. 1942, when, after being invaded by Peru, Ecuador lost over half her Amazonian territories. Ecuador unilaterally denounced this treaty in Sept. 1961. Fighting between Peru and Ecuador began again in Jan. 1981 over this border issue but a ceasefire was agreed in early Feb. Following a confrontation of soldiers in Aug. 1991 the foreign ministers of both countries signed a pact creating a security zone, and took their cases to the UN in Oct. 1991. On 26 Jan. 1995 further armed clashes broke out with Peruvian forces in the undemarcated mutual border area (*Cordillera del Cóndor*). On 2 Feb. talks were held under the auspices of the guarantor nations of the 1942 Protocol of Rio de Janeiro (Argentina, Brazil, Chile and the USA) but fighting continued. A ceasefire was agreed on 17 Feb., which was broken, and again on 28 Feb. On 25 July 1995 an agreement between Ecuador and Peru established a demilitarized zone along their joint frontier. The frontier was reopened on 4 Sept. 1995. Since 23 Feb. 1996 Ecuador and Peru have signed three further agreements to regulate the dispute. The dispute was settled in Oct. 1998. Confirming the Peruvian claim that the border lies along the high peaks of the Cóndor, Ecuador gained navigation rights on the Amazon within Peru.

The total area of the country is 256,369 sq. km, including the Galápagos Archipelago (8,010 sq. km), situated in the Pacific Ocean about 960 km west of Ecuador, and comprising 13 islands and 19 islets. These were discovered in 1535 by Fray Tomás de Berlanga and had a population of 25,124 in 2010. They constitute a national park, and had approximately 122,000 visitors in 2005.

Census population in 2010, 14,483,449; density, 53 per sq. km. In 2011, 67·6% lived in urban areas.

The UN gives a projected population for 2020 of 17·34m.

The country is administratively divided into 24 provinces (with capitals): Azuay (Cuenca), Bolívar (Guaranda), Cañar (Azogues), Carchi (Tulcán), Chimborazo (Riobamba), Cotopaxi (Latacunga), El Oro (Machala), Esmeraldas (Esmeraldas), Guayas (Guayaquil), Imbabura (Ibarra), Loja (Loja), Los Ríos (Babahoyo), Manabí (Portoviejo), Morona-Santiago (Macas), Napo (Tena), Orellana (Francisco de Orellana), Pastaza (Puyo), Pichincha (Quito), Santa Elena (Santa Elena), Santo Domingo de los Tsáchilas (Santo Domingo de los Colorados), Sucumbíos (Nueva Loja), Tungurahua (Ambato), Zamora-Chinchipe (Zamora), Galápagos (Puerto Baquerizo Moreno). There are also three non-delimited areas.

The population is an amalgam of European, Amerindian and African origins. Some 41% of the population is Amerindian: Quechua, Shiwiar, Achuar and Zaparo. In May 1992 they were granted title to the 1m. ha. of land they occupy in Pastaza.

The official language is Spanish. Quechua and other languages are also spoken.

Social Statistics

2008 estimates: births, 280,000; deaths, 70,000. Rates, 2008 estimates (per 1,000 population): birth, 20·8; death, 5·2. Life expectancy at birth, 2013, was 73·7 years for males and 79·4 years for females. Annual population growth rate, 2000–08, 1·1%. Infant mortality, 2010, 18 per 1,000 live births; fertility rate, 2008, 2·6 children per woman. In 2009 the most popular age for marrying was 20–24 for both men and women.

Climate

The climate varies from equatorial, through warm temperate to mountain conditions, according to altitude, which affects temperatures and rainfall. In coastal areas, the dry season is from May to Dec., but only from June to Sept. in mountainous parts, where temperatures may be 20°F colder than on the coast. Quito, Jan. 59°F (15°C), July 58°F (14·4°C). Annual rainfall 44" (1,115 mm). Guayaquil, Jan. 79°F (26·1°C), July 75°F (23·9°C). Annual rainfall 39" (986 mm).

Constitution and Government

An executive *President* and a *Vice-President* are directly elected by universal suffrage. The president appoints and leads a *Council of Ministers*, and determines the number and functions of the ministries that comprise the executive branch. Legislative power is vested in a *National Assembly* of 137 members, popularly elected by province. One seat is reserved for overseas voters. Citizens must be at least 16 years of age to vote. Voting is obligatory for all literate citizens of 18–65 years. It is optional for those aged 16 and 17 and other eligible voters.

A new constitution came into force on 20 Oct. 2008. It was drafted by a Constituent Assembly set up by then President Correa in Nov. 2007 and was approved with 63·9% of the vote in a referendum on 28 Sept. 2008. It superseded the previous constitution that had been in place for ten years. The 2008 constitution, which includes 444 articles, allows a president to run for two consecutive four-year terms, dissolve parliament and call early elections, and set monetary policy. The *National Congress* was abolished and replaced by a new *National Assembly*. The constitution also allows for tighter control of key industries, the expropriation and redistribution of idle farm land, free health care for the elderly and the legalization of same-sex civil marriages. The government can also declare some foreign loans illegitimate.

In May 2011 a package of ten changes to the constitution was passed in a referendum. The proposals included giving the executive branch of government increased influence over the appointment of Supreme Court judges, creating a body to regulate media content, extending the legal period of detention without trial, outlawing 'unjustified' wealth and restricting gambling, requiring owners of banks and media organizations to declare other commercial holdings, and banning cock- and bull-fighting.

In Feb. 2018 a constitutional amendment eliminating presidential terms limits that was introduced in 2015 was overturned by referendum. Instead, candidates may seek a single re-election. The decision ruled out the chances of former president Rafael Correa seeking a further term of office.

National Anthem

'Salve, Oh Patria, mil veces, Oh Patria' ('Hail, Oh Fatherland, a thousand times, Oh Fatherland'); words by J. L. Mera, tune by A. Neumane.

Government Chronology

Heads of State since 1944. (AD = Democratic Alliance; Alianza PAIS = Proud and Sovereign Fatherland Alliance; CFP = Concentration of Popular Forces; CID = Democratic Institutional Coalition; DP–UDC = People's Democracy–Christian Democratic Union; FNV = National Velasquista Federation; FRA = Alfarista Radical Front; ID = Democratic Left; MCDN = National Democratic Civic Movement; MSC = Social Christian Party [called PSC since 1967]; PRE = Ecuadorian Roldosist Party; PSC = Social Christian Party; PSP = Patriotic Society January 21; PUR = Republican Union Party; n/p = non-partisan)

Presidents		
1944–47	AD	José María Velasco Ibarra
1947–48	n/p	Carlos Julio Arosemena Tola
1948–52	MCDN	Galo Plaza Lasso
1952–56	FNV	José María Velasco Ibarra
1956–60	MSC	Camilo Ponce Enríquez
1960–61	FNV	José María Velasco Ibarra
1961–63	FNV	Carlos Julio Arosemena Monroy
Military Junta		
1963–66		Adm. Ramón Castro Jijón (chair); Gen. Luis Cabrera Sevilla; Col. Guillermo Freile Posso; Gen. Mario Gándara Enríquez
Presidents		
1966	n/p	Clemente Yerovi Indaburu
1966–68	CID	Otto Arosemena Gómez
1968–72	FNV	José María Velasco Ibarra
1972–76	military	Gen. Guillermo Rodríguez Lara

(continued)

Military Junta		
1976–79		Admr. Alfredo Ernesto Poveda Burbano (chair); Gen. Luis Leoro Franco; Gen. Luis G. Durán Arcentales
Presidents		
1979–81	CFP	Jaime Roldós Aguilera
1981–84	DP–UDC	Osvaldo Hurtado Larrea
1984–88	PSC	León Esteban Febres Cordero
1988–92	ID	Rodrigo Borja Cevallos
1992–96	PUR	Sixto Alfonso Durán-Ballén
1996–97	PRE	Abdalá Jaime Bucaram Ortiz
1997–98	FRA	Fabián Ernesto Alarcón Rivera
1998–2000	DP–UDC	Jorge Jamil Mahuad Witt
2000–03	DP–UDC	Gustavo Noboa Bejarano
2003–05	PSP	Lucio Edwin Gutiérrez Borbúa
2005–07	n/p	Luis Alfredo Palacio González
2007–17	Alianza PAIS	Rafael Vicente Correa Delgado
2017–	Alianza PAIS	Lenín Voltaire Moreno Garcés

Recent Elections

At the presidential elections of 19 Feb. 2017 turnout was 81·6%. Lenín Moreno won 39·4% of the vote, against 28·1% for Guillermo Lasso, 16·3% for Cynthia Viteri, 6·7% for Paco Moncayo, 4·8% for Abdalá Bucaram, Jr and 3·2% for Iván Espinel Molina. There were two other candidates who each received less than 2% of the vote. As no candidate obtained the 40% required for victory a run-off was held on 2 April 2017, which Lenín Moreno won with 51·2% of the vote against 48·8% for Guillermo Lasso. Turnout in the second round was 83·0%.

In the parliamentary elections also held on 19 Feb. 2017 the Proud and Sovereign Fatherland Alliance (Alianza PAIS) won 74 of 137 seats with 39·1% of the vote; Creating Opportunities–SUMA, 34 (20·1%); Social Christian Party, 15 (15·9%); Democratic Left, 4 (3·8%); Pachakutik Plurinational Unity Movement–New Country, 4 (2·7%); Patriotic Society Party, 2 (2·9%); Fuerza Ecuador, 1 (4·7%). Independents and regionalists took three seats. Turnout was 81·7%.

Current Government

President: Lenín Moreno; b. 1953 (Alianza PAIS; sworn in 24 May 2017).
  Vice-President: Otto Sonnenholzner.
  In Feb. 2019 the cabinet comprised:
  Minister of Agriculture and Livestock: Xavier Lazo. *Culture and Heritage:* Raúl Pérez Torres. *Economic and Social Inclusion:* Berenice Cordero Molina. *Economy and Finance:* Richard Martínez. *Education:* Milton Luna Tamayo. *Energy and Non-Renewable Natural Resources:* Carlos Pérez García. *Environment and Water:* Marcelo Mata Guerrero. *Foreign Affairs and Human Mobility:* José Valencia Amores. *Interior:* María Paula Romo. *Labour (acting):* Andres Madero Poveda. *National Defence:* Oswaldo Jarrín. *Production, Foreign Trade, Investments and Fisheries:* Pablo Campana Sáenz. *Public Health:* Verónica Espinosa Serrano. *Telecommunications and Information Society:* Guillermo León Santacruz. *Tourism:* Rosi Prado de Holguín. *Transport and Public Works:* Aurelio Hidalgo. *Urban Development and Housing:* Germán Xavier Torres Correa.

Office of the President (Spanish only): http://www.presidencia.gob.ec

Current Leaders

Lenín Moreno
Position
President

Introduction
Lenín Moreno was elected president on 2 April 2017 and took office on 24 May, having previously served as vice-president in the administration of Rafael Correa from 2007–13.

Early Life

Lenín Moreno was born on 19 March 1953 in Nova Rocafuerte in the Ecuadorian Amazon. He moved with his family to Quito and graduated in public administration from the Universidad Central del Ecuador. After working in sales and marketing, he joined the government tourism department, serving as executive director of the Pichincha chamber of tourism between 1997 and 1999.

Moreno is confined to a wheelchair and has been a high-profile campaigner to improve the status and rights of the disabled in Ecuador and the wider region. When he became vice-president in 2007, he promoted a significant increase in the state budget for disabled people and founded the Manuel Espejo Solidarity Mission for the Disabled—efforts that earned him a nomination for the Nobel Peace Prize in 2012.

Supported by incumbent Rafael Correa, Moreno made a bid for the presidency in 2017. Moreno led the first round of voting on 19 Feb. and faced the centre-right candidate, Guillermo Lasso—who pledged to reverse many of Correa's policies—in a run-off on 2 April. Moreno was declared the winner, although Lasso demanded a recount amid allegations of fraud.

Career in Office

Moreno signalled a departure from the Correa era by removing his predecessor's serving vice-president, Jorge Glas Espinel, from office in Aug. 2017. In Dec. 2017 Glas was found guilty on corruption charges and sentenced to six years in prison. Among his chief challenges were contending with a large fiscal deficit, spurring economic growth, and bridging political divisions over fractious issues including limits on press freedom.

In Feb. 2018 voters in a referendum overturned a 2015 constitutional amendment allowing presidents to serve more than two terms in office.

Defence

The country is divided into four military zones, with headquarters at Quito, Guayaquil, Cuenca and Pastaza.

In 2012 defence expenditure totalled US$1,509m. (US$99 per capita), representing 2·1% of GDP.

Army

Strength (2011) 46,500.

Navy

Navy combatant forces include two diesel submarines (although their serviceability is in doubt) and two ex-UK frigates. The Naval Aviation had 13 aircraft in 2011 but no combat-capable aircraft. Naval personnel in 2011 totalled 7,283 including 2,160 marines.

Air Force

The Air Force had a 2011 strength of 4,200 personnel and 52 combat-capable aircraft, and includes Mirage F-1s, Mirage 50s and Kfirs.

International Relations

In March 2008 Ecuador responded to a Colombian incursion into its territory, during which a senior figure in the rebel FARC movement was killed, by sending troops to the border with Colombia. Venezuela made a similar gesture in sympathy before a diplomatic solution to the stand-off came into effect a week later.

Economy

Agriculture accounted for 10·4% of GDP in 2011, industry 36·8% and services 52·8%.

Overview

In the 1980s and 1990s per capita income stagnated at a level above the Latin American average but below the world mean. The country is heavily dependent on oil exports (the extractive industries accounting for around 20% of GDP annually and underpinning public investment) and the fall in oil prices in the late 1990s, combined with natural disasters, triggered a collapse in GDP and income levels. However, higher oil prices in the early 2000s helped reinvigorate growth.

In Dec. 2008 the government announced a default on its sovereign debt—representing 80% of its private external debt—labelling it as 'illegitimate'. However, it bought back the majority of its defaulted bonds in 2009. The global financial crisis, along with volatile world oil prices and a drop in remittances, led to the slowest growth for ten years in 2009 before recovery took hold in 2010. In the five years to 2014, GDP growth averaged over 5% per annum, although it fell back to 0·2% in 2015 and the economy suffered a contraction in 2016 of 1·5%. Income poverty (measured against the national poverty line) fell from 37·6% to 22·9% between 2006 and 2016.

Currency

The monetary unit is the *US dollar*. There was inflation of 1·7% in 2016 and 0·4% in 2017. In March 2000 the government passed a law to phase out the former national currency, the *sucre*, to be replaced by the US dollar, and in April bank cash machines began dispensing dollars instead of sucres. On 11 Sept. 2000 the dollar became the only legal currency. Foreign exchange reserves were US$1,398m. in July 2005 with gold reserves of 845,000 troy oz.

Budget

Revenues in 2013 (provisional) totalled US$20·4bn. and expenditures US$25·9bn.

VAT is 12% and corporate tax 25%.

Performance

Real GDP growth was 0·1% in 2015. Ecuador then experienced a recession with the economy shrinking by 1·2% in 2016, before growing by 2·4% in 2017. Total GDP in 2016 was US$103·1bn.

Banking and Finance

The Central Bank of Ecuador (*General Manager*, Verónica Artola Jarrín), the bank of issue, with reserves of US$1,994·5m. in Dec. 2008, is modelled after the Federal Reserve Banks of the USA. There were 24 banks in Dec. 2006 with deposits of US$8,755m. Ecuador's largest private bank is Banco del Pichincha. All commercial banks must be affiliated to the Central Bank. The national monetary board is based in Quito.

In 2010 foreign debt totalled US$14,815m., representing 23·1% of GNI. There are stock exchanges in Quito and Guayaquil.

Energy and Natural Resources

Environment

Ecuador's carbon dioxide emissions from the consumption of energy in 2011 were the equivalent of 2·3 tonnes per capita.

Electricity

Installed capacity was 4·79m. kW in 2011. Production was 20·27bn. kWh in 2011; consumption per capita was 1,413 kWh.

Oil and Gas

Production of oil in 2012 was 27·1m. tonnes. Proven oil reserves, 2012, 8·2bn. bbls. In 2011 natural gas production was 359m. cu. metres. Proven reserves (2014), 6·0bn. cu. metres.

Minerals

Main products are silver, gold, copper and zinc. The country also has some iron, uranium, lead, coal, cobalt, manganese and titanium.

Agriculture

There were 1·20m. ha. of arable land in 2007 and 1·22m. ha. of permanent crops. In 2007 the agricultural population was an estimated 2·86m., of which about 1·19m. were economically active.

Main crops, in 1,000 tonnes, in 2013: sugarcane, 7,158; bananas, 5,996; palm fruit oil, 2,317; rice, 1,516; maize, 1,177; plantains, 604; potatoes, 346; palm oil (estimate), 325; mangoes and guavas, 177; cocoa beans, 128.

Livestock, 2013: cattle, 5·13m.; pigs, 1·22m.; sheep, 739,000; horses, 308,000; chickens, 164m.

Forestry

Excepting the agricultural zones and a few arid spots on the Pacific coast, Ecuador is a vast forest. 12·55m. ha., or 51% of the land area, was forested in 2015, but much of the forest is not commercially accessible. In 2011, 7·04m. cu. metres of roundwood were produced.

Fisheries

Fish landings in 2011 were 506,430 tonnes (almost entirely from sea fishing). Exports of fishery commodities were valued at US$2·49bn. in 2011.

Industry

Industry produced 36·8% of GDP in 2011, including 12·6% from manufacturing. Manufacturing grew by 5·6% in 2011. Main products include (in 1,000 tonnes): cement (2012), 6,025; residual fuel oil (2011), 3,513; distillate fuel oil (2011), 1,734; petrol (2011), 1,253.

Labour

The labour force in 2013 was 7,554,000 (6,095,000 in 2003). 71·6% of the population aged 15–64 was economically active in 2013. In the same year 4·2% of the population was unemployed.

Ecuador had 44,000 people living in slavery according to the Walk Free Foundation's 2013 *Global Slavery Index.*

International Trade

Most restrictions on foreign investment were removed in 1992 and the repatriation of profits was permitted.

Imports and Exports

Goods imports were US$27,515·4m. in 2014 (US$27,064·5m. in 2013) and goods exports US$25,730·1m. (US$24,957·6m. in 2013).

Principal imports in 2014 were machinery and transport equipment (30·0%), mineral fuels and lubricants, and chemicals; main exports in 2014 were mineral fuels and lubricants (51·7%), food, animals and beverages, and crude materials and animal and vegetable oils.

The leading import supplier in 2010 was the USA (27·9%), followed by Colombia and China; the leading export destination in 2010 was the USA (34·7%), followed by Panama and Peru.

Communications

Roads

In 2007 there were 43,670 km of roads. There were 507,500 passenger cars in 2007 (38 per 1,000 inhabitants) and 323,500 lorries and vans. There were 1,848 fatalities in road accidents in 2007.

In 1998 storms and floods on the coast, caused by El Niño, resulted in 2,000 km of roads being damaged or destroyed.

Rail

The railway network, only 10% of which was operational in 2008, has since been repaired and rebuilt. In 2015 it had a total length of 517 km.

Civil Aviation

The Ecuadorian flag carrier is Tame. There are international airports at Quito (Mariscal Sucre) and Guayaquil (José Joaquín de Olmedo). In 2009 Quito handled 4,746,292 passengers and 143,767 tonnes of freight, and Guayaquil handled 3,382,554 passengers and 55,605 tonnes of freight. A new airport at Quito opened in 2013. The old airport, which was also called Mariscal Sucre International Airport, was more central in Quito and could not be expanded to meet growing demand.

Shipping

Ecuador has three major seaports, of which Guayaquil is the most important, and six minor ones. In Jan. 2014 there were 49 ships of 300 GT or over registered, totalling 231,000 GT.

Telecommunications

In 2011 there were 2,210,600 landline telephone subscriptions (equivalent to 150·7 per 1,000 inhabitants) and 15,332,700 mobile phone subscriptions (or 1,045·5 per 1,000 inhabitants). In 2011, 31·4% of the population were internet users. In June 2012 there were 4·7m. Facebook users.

Social Institutions

Out of 178 countries analysed in the 2017 *Fragile States Index*—a list published jointly by the Fund for Peace and *Foreign Policy* magazine—Ecuador was ranked the 75th most vulnerable to conflict or collapse. The index is based on 12 indicators of state vulnerability across social, political and economic categories.

Justice

The Supreme Court in Quito, consisting of a President and 30 Justices, comprises ten chambers each of three Justices. It is also a Court of Appeal. There is a Superior Court in each province, comprising chambers (as appointed by the Supreme Court) of three magistrates each. The Superior Courts are at the apex of a hierarchy of various tribunals. There is no death penalty.

The population in penal institutions in Dec. 2012 was 21,080 (149 per 100,000 of national population). Ecuador was ranked 77th of 102 countries for criminal justice and 89th for civil justice in the 2015 World Justice Project *Rule of Law Index*, which provides data on how the rule of law is experienced by the general public across eight categories.

Education

There were an estimated 287,000 pre-primary pupils in 2007–08 and an estimated 19,000 pre-primary teachers in 2008–09. Primary education is free and compulsory. Private schools, both primary and secondary, are under some state supervision. In 2007 there were 2·04m. pupils and 90,366 teaching staff in primary schools; and 1·14m. pupils with 77,904 teaching staff in secondary schools. The oldest and largest university is the Central University of Ecuador, which was established in 1826. The first private university was established in 1988. There were 443,509 students in tertiary education in 2007 with 22,714 academic staff. Adult literacy was 84·2% in 2009 (male, 87·1%; female, 81·5%).

In 2011 total expenditure on education came to 4·3% of GDP and 11·0% of total government spending.

Health

Beds available in hospitals in 2012 totalled 23,138 (1·5 per 1,000 population). There were 31,879 physicians and 12,668 nurses in 2011.

In *Water: At What Cost? The State of the World's Water 2016*, WaterAid reported that 13·1% of the population does not have access to safe water.

Welfare

Those who qualify for a pension must have at least 480 months of contributions (at any age), or be aged 60 with 360 months of contributions, 65 with 180 months of contributions or 70 with 120 months of contributions. In 2011 the minimum monthly pension was US$132, and the maximum pension was US$1,452.

Social insurance providing lump-sum benefits for unemployment is gradually being phased out in favour of a system linking payments to income and length of employment.

Religion

The state recognizes no religion and grants freedom of worship to all. In 2010, 94·1% of the population were Christians according to estimates by the Pew Research Center's Forum on Religion & Public Life. Most of the remainder of the population was religiously unaffiliated. Of the Christians, 89% were Catholics and 10% Protestants. In Feb. 2019 there was one Roman Catholic cardinal.

Culture

World Heritage Sites

Ecuador has five sites on the UNESCO World Heritage List: the Galápagos Islands (inscribed on the list in 1978 and 2001); the City of Quito (1978); Sangay National Park (1983); the Historic Centre of Santa Ana de los Ríos de Cuenca (1999); and shared with Argentina, Bolivia, Colombia, Chile and Peru, Qhapaq Ñan, Andean Road System (2014) is an extensive Inca communication, trade and defence network of roads covering 30,000 km.

Press

There were 47 daily newspapers in 2008, with a circulation of 591,000.

Tourism

Foreign visitors numbered 1,272,000 in 2012, of whom 996,000 were from elsewhere in the Americas and 212,000 from Europe.

Diplomatic Representatives

Of Ecuador in the United Kingdom (Flat 3b, 3 Hans Cres., London, SW1X 0LS)
Ambassador: Jaime Alberto Marchán Romero.

Of the United Kingdom in Ecuador (Citiplaza Building, Naciones Unidas Ave. and República de El Salvador, 14th Floor, PO Box 17-17-830, Quito)
Ambassador: Katherine Ward, LVO.

Of Ecuador in the USA (2535 15th St., NW, Washington, D.C., 20009)
Ambassador: Francisco Benjamin Esteban Carrión Mena.

Of the USA in Ecuador (Avenida Avigiras E12–170 y Avenida Eloy Alfaro, Quito)
Ambassador: Todd C. Chapman.

Of Ecuador to the United Nations
Ambassador: Luis Gallegos Chiriboga.

Of Ecuador to the European Union
Ambassador: Vacant.
Chargé d'Affaires a.i.: Isabel Albornoz.

Further Reading

Roos, W. and van Renterghem, O., *Ecuador in Focus: A Guide to the People, Politics and Culture.* 1997

Sawyer, Suzana, *Crude Chronicles: Indigenous Politics, Multinational Oil, and Neoliberalism in Ecuador.* 2004

Selverston-Scher, M., *Ethnopolitics in Ecuador: Indigenous Rights and the Strengthening of Democracy.* 2001

National Statistical Office: Instituto Nacional de Estadística y Censos (INEC), Juan Larrea N15-36 y José Riofrío, Quito.

Website (Spanish only): http://www.ecuadorencifras.gob.ec

Egypt

Jumhuriyat Misr al-Arabiya (Arab Republic of Egypt)

Capital: Cairo
Population projection, 2020: 102·94m.
GNI per capita, 2017: (PPP$) 10,355
HDI/world rank, 2017: 0·696/115
Internet domain extension: .eg

Key Historical Events

There is evidence of pastoralism and the cultivation of cereals in southwest Egypt from as early as 7000 BC. Settlements grew along the Nile valley, though Upper and Lower Egypt only united around 3100 BC under Pharoah Menes. The subsequent Early Dynastic period was marked by flourishing trade with Sinai, the Levant and as far north as the Black Sea. The astonishing artistic and intellectual developments of the Old Kingdom began during the IVth dynasty (2575–2465 BC), when sun-worship took hold and temples and pyramids, including those at Giza, were constructed. Egypt was governed from the city of Memphis, south of modern Cairo, reaching its height during the VIth dynasty before losing power to local rulers from around 2200 BC.

Centralized power was restored at Thebes from 2134 BC. The Middle Kingdom (XIIth dynasty) saw Egypt expand south into Nubia under Amenemhat I. A cultural flowering included the invention of a writing system. The XIIth dynasty ended in 1786 BC when the region was invaded by the Hyksos, a nomadic Asiatic tribe. The New Kingdom came into being with the expulsion of the Hyksos around 1550 BC and lasted until 1050 BC. It was now that Egypt achieved its greatest territorial dominance, with Syria, Palestine and northern Iraq all under Egyptian jurisdiction. The conquests brought great prosperity and bold architecture, which reached its zenith under the XVIIIth dynasty pharaohs, Tuthmosis III and Tutankhamun.

Ancient Egyptian civilization began to fragment in conflict with Hittite invaders during the XIXth dynasty (around 1250 BC). The subsequent rise of Assyria to the northeast and Nubian conquests from the south hastened the decline. The last pharaoh was ousted by Persian invading forces led by Cambyses in 525 BC. The Persians remained in power until overrun by Alexander the Great in 332 BC. He founded the port of Alexandria, including its great lighthouse, and made the city the commercial and cultural centre of the Greek world. On his death in 305 BC, Ptolemy of Macedonia seized power, establishing a dynasty which lasted until 30 BC and the suicide of Cleopatra.

Egypt then became a province of the Roman Empire until Arabian forces invaded in AD 642, absorbing the Nile valley into the Ummayad Caliphate, centred on Damascus. The Arabic language became the official language of government in 706. The Abbasid defeat of the Ummayad dynasty in 750 brought a shift of Arab power to the new city of Baghdad. Abdullah bin Tahir sent a deputy to rule Egypt. The Fatimid caliphs, whose origins were in Tunisia, entered Egypt in 960 and founded Cairo as their capital, later establishing the Muslim university. Over the next 200 years they built an empire that stretched from Tunisia to Syria and Yemen, with extensive trade routes across the Mediterranean and into the Indian Ocean.

Weakened by the Christian Crusades, the Fatimid caliphate fell to the Ayyubid dynasty in 1169, led by Tikrit-born Saladin (Salahuddin al-Ayyubi). Operating from Damascus, he fought the Crusader States and by the end of the 12th century controlled much of the Eastern Mediterranean. Egypt was largely governed by his deputy, Karaksh. In 1250 Egypt was seized by Saif ad Din Qutuz, a Turkic former slave who founded the Mamluk Sultanate. There were frequent revolts and changes of leaders (*beys*, or princes), but the Sultanate survived until 1517 when Egypt was absorbed into the Ottoman empire.

Napoleonic forces seized the country between 1798 and 1801 but were forced out by a combined Anglo-Ottoman force. Muhammad Ali, appointed Egyptian pasha by the Ottoman emperor in 1805, swiftly destroyed the remnants of Mamluk power. He introduced sweeping political and social reforms and modernized agriculture. Like many of his predecessors he took control of Syria, Nubia and part of the Arabian peninsula. The opening of the Suez Canal during the reign of Muhammad Said Pasha in 1867 heralded an era of foreign intervention and domination, with Said selling his shares in the Suez Canal to the British in 1875. British forces occupied Alexandria and then Cairo in 1882, ruling the country through the consul general, Lord Cromer. During the First World War, Britain declared Egypt a British Protectorate, ousting the khedive, Abbas I, for supporting Germany. Calls for independence grew louder after the war ended and Fuad I ruled a partially independent Egypt from 1923.

Although Egypt was officially neutral until the last days of the Second World War, Britain was the dominant power. From 1940 it was the arena for the Desert War that saw Allied forces ultimately repel Axis attempts to occupy Egypt, take control of the Suez Canal and open up access to the oil fields of the Middle East. The decisive victory came when Gen. Montgomery's Eighth Army overpowered the German and Italian forces under Gen. Rommel at the Second Battle of El Alamein in July 1942.

Following a revolution in July 1952 led by Gen. Neguib, King Farouk abdicated in favour of his son but in 1953 the monarchy was abolished. Neguib became president but encountered opposition from the military when he attempted to move towards a parliamentary republic. Col. Gamal Abdel Nasser became head of state on 14 June 1954 (president from 1956). In 1956 Egypt nationalized the Suez Canal, a move which led Britain, France and Israel to mount military attacks against Egypt until UN and US pressure forced a withdrawal.

The 1960s and 1970s were years of conflict with Israel, notably the Six-Day War in June 1967, when Egypt (together with Syria and Jordan) declared war on Israel but were defeated despite having more troops and armaments. After the war Egypt received economic and military aid from the Soviet Union. Following Nasser's death in Sept. 1970 Muhammad Anwar Sadat took over as president. Having launched a peace initiative during a visit to Jerusalem in 1977, Sadat secured a treaty with Israel in March 1979. Sadat was assassinated on 6 Oct. 1981 and was succeeded by his vice-president, Lieut.-Gen. Muhammad Hosni Mubarak of the National Democratic Party (NDP). He gained a fifth consecutive term after emerging victorious in presidential elections in Sept. 2005 (the first multi-candidate presidential poll) to become the country's longest-serving leader since Muhammad Ali. In Jan. and Feb. 2011 he faced popular protests demanding his resignation. Despite attempts to appease the protesters through various concessions, on the 18th day of unrest Mubarak resigned and handed control to the Armed Forces Supreme Council. In June 2012 Mohamed Morsi became the nation's first democratically elected president. Soon after taking office, he was criticized for giving too much power to his allies in the Muslim Brotherhood. Mass protests were staged by Egyptians who favoured a secular administration. In July 2013 Morsi was ousted in a 'democratic coup'. Interim president Adly Mansour oversaw the passage of a new constitution in Jan. 2014 before former army commander-in-chief Abdel Fattah al-Sisi won the presidency in elections in May 2014.

Territory and Population

Egypt is bounded in the east by Israel and Palestine, the Gulf of Aqaba and the Red Sea, south by Sudan, west by Libya and north by the Mediterranean. The total area is 1,009,450 sq. km (including 6,000 sq. km of inland water), but the cultivated and settled area, that is the Nile Valley, Delta and oases, covers only 35,000 sq. km. A number of new desert cities are being developed to entice people away from the overcrowded Nile valley, where 99% of the population lives. The 2017 census population was 94,798,827; density 94·5 per sq. km.

In 2011, 43·5% of the population were urban.

The UN gives a projected population for 2020 of 102·94m.

3·9m. Egyptians were living abroad in 2006.

© Springer Nature Limited 2020
Palgrave Macmillan (ed.), *The Statesman's Yearbook 2020*,
https://doi.org/10.1057/978-1-349-95940-2_65

Area, population and capitals of the governorates (2006 and 2017 censuses):

Governorate	Area (in sq. km)	Population (2006 census)	Population (2017 census)	Capital
Alexandria	2,300	4,123,869	5,163,750	Alexandria
Aswan	62,726	1,186,482	1,473,975	Aswan
Asyut	25,926	3,444,967	4,383,289	Asyut
Behera	9,826	4,747,283	6,171,613	Damanhur
Beni Suef	10,954	2,291,618	3,154,100	Beni Suef
Cairo	3,085	6,758,581	9,539,673	Cairo
Dakahlia	3,716	4,989,997	6,492,381	Mansura
Damietta	910	1,097,339	1,496,765	Damietta
Fayum	6,068	2,511,027	3,596,954	Fayum
Gharbia	1,948	4,011,320	4,999,633	Tanta
Giza	13,184	3,143,486	8,632,021	Giza
Ismailia	5,067	953,006	1,303,993	Ismailia
Kafr El Shaikh	3,748	2,620,208	3,362,185	Kafr El Shaikh
Kalyubia	1,124	4,251,672	5,627,420	Benha
Luxor	2,410	457,286	1,250,209	Luxor
Matruh	166,563	323,381	425,624	Matruh
Menia	32,279	4,166,299	5,497,095	Menia
Menufia	2,499	3,270,431	4,301,601	Shibin Al Kom
New Valley	440,098	187,263	241,247	Al Kharija
Port Said	1,351	570,603	749,371	Port Said
Qena	10,798	3,001,681	3,164,281	Qena
Red Sea	119,099	288,661	359,888	El Gurdakah
Sharkia	4,911	5,354,041	7,163,824	Zagazig
North Sinai	27,564	343,681	450,328	Al Arish
South Sinai	31,272	150,088	102,018	At Tur
Suez	9,002	512,135	728,180	Suez
Suhag	11,022	3,747,289	4,967,409	Suhag

The capital, Cairo, had a census population in 2006 of 7,740,018. Other major cities, with populations at the 2006 census (in 1,000): Alexandria, 4,028; Giza, 3,022; Shubra Al Khayma, 1,026; Port Said, 571; Suez, 485.

Smaller cities, with 2006 populations (in 1,000): Mahalla Al Kubra, 443; Mansura, 439; Tanta, 423; Asyut, 389; Fayum, 316; Zagazig, 303; Ismailia, 293; Al Khusus, 291; Aswan, 266; Damanhur, 244; Menia, 236; Damietta, 207; Luxor (Uqsur), 202; Qena, 201.

The official language is Arabic, although French and English are widely spoken.

Social Statistics

Births (est.), 2009, 2,217,000 (28·8 per 1,000 population); deaths, 477,000 (6·2). Annual population growth rate, 2005–10, 1·7%. In 2010, 73% of the population was under 40 years old. Life expectancy at birth, 2013, was 68·8 years for males and 73·6 years for females. Fertility rate, 2013, 2·8 births per woman; infant mortality, 2010, 19 per 1,000 live births. Egypt has made some of the best progress in recent years in reducing child mortality. The number of deaths per 1,000 live births among children under five was reduced from 86 in 1990 to 21 in 2012.

Climate

The climate is mainly dry, but there are winter rains along the Mediterranean coast. Elsewhere, rainfall is very low and erratic in its distribution. Winter temperatures are comfortable everywhere, but summer temperatures are very high, especially in the south. Cairo, Jan. 56°F (13·3°C), July 83°F (28·3°C). Annual rainfall 1·2" (28 mm). Alexandria, Jan. 58°F (14·4°C), July 79°F (26·1°C). Annual rainfall 7" (178 mm). Aswan, Jan. 62°F (16·7°C), July 92°F (33·3°C). Annual rainfall (trace). Giza, Jan. 55°F (12·8°C), July 78°F (25·6°C). Annual rainfall 16" (389 mm). Ismailia, Jan. 56°F (13·3°C), July 84°F (28·9°C). Annual rainfall 1·5" (37 mm). Luxor, Jan. 59°F (15°C), July 86°F (30°C). Annual rainfall (trace). Port Said, Jan. 58°F (14·4°C), July 78°F (27·2°C). Annual rainfall 3" (76 mm).

Constitution and Government

Following the popular uprising that led to President Hosni Mubarak being deposed in Feb. 2011, a Provisional Constitution came into force to supersede the previous constitution dating from 1971. It in turn was replaced by a constitution passed into law by President Mohamed Morsi in Dec. 2012. However, he was deposed by the military in July 2013 and another new constitution was drafted by a 50-member constituent assembly.

Under the terms of this revised constitution, the *President* may serve a maximum of two four-year terms and may be impeached by parliament. The president, who must be at least 40 years old and an Egyptian citizen without a non-Egyptian parent or spouse, appoints the *Prime Minister* subject to parliamentary approval. The president also appoints the ministers of foreign affairs, the interior and justice. For two presidential terms (or eight years) from the promulgation of the constitution, the military has the right to approve the appointment of the defence minister, who must be a military officer. Parliament consists of a single chamber, the *House of Representatives*, which has the right to call a referendum on early presidential elections with a two-thirds majority. The House of Representatives consists of 596 seats, of which 448 are elected via the individual candidacy system, 120 are party-based candidates elected through lists and 28 are appointed by the president.

Islam is the state religion and the principles of *Sharia* (Islamic law) are the main source of legislation. However, freedom of belief is guaranteed by the state, as is equality of the sexes. No political party may be formed on the basis of religion, race, gender or geography. Furthermore, all forms of torture are a crime with no statute of limits. A Supreme Police Council must be consulted over any legislation pertaining to the police, while civilians may be tried by the military courts in the event of an alleged crime directed against the armed forces.

In a referendum held in Jan. 2014 (turnout: 38·6%) the constitution received 98·1% support, although then President Morsi and his Muslim Brotherhood boycotted the vote.

National Anthem

'Biladi' ('My homeland'); words and tune by S. Darwish.

Government Chronology

Heads of State since 1953. (ASU = Arab Socialist Union; LR = Liberation Rally; NDP = National Democratic Party; NU = National Union; n/p = non-partisan)

President		
1953–54	military, LR	Muhammad Neguib
Chairman of the Revolutionary Command Council		
1954	military, LR	Gamal Abdel Nasser
President		
1954	military, LR	Muhammad Neguib
Chairman of the Revolutionary Command Council		
1954–56	military, LR	Gamal Abdel Nasser
Presidents		
1956–70	NU, ASU	Gamal Abdel Nasser
1970–81	ASU, NDP	Muhammad Anwar Sadat
1981–2011	NDP	Muhammad Hosni Mubarak
Head of the Armed Forces Supreme Council		
2011–12	military	Mohamed Hussein Tantawi
Presidents		
2012–13	n/p	Mohamed Morsi
2013–14	n/p	Adly Mansour (interim)
2014–	n/p	Abdel Fattah al-Sisi

Recent Elections

In the presidential elections of 26–28 March 2018 incumbent president Abdel Fattah al-Sisi (ind.) won with 97·1% of the vote against his only opponent Moussa Mostafa Moussa (El-Ghad Party) with 2·9%. Turnout was 41·1%.

Parliamentary elections were held in two phases—a first phase from 17–28 Oct. 2015 and a second phase from 21 Nov.–2 Dec. 2015. The results for 16 seats were invalidated, leading to further run-off elections from 14–16 Dec. 2015. 351 seats went to independent candidates and 245 to party representatives. Of these the Free Egyptians Party won 65 seats, the Nation's Future Party 53, the New Wafd Party 36, the Protectors of the Homeland Party 18, the Republican People's Party 13, the Conference Party 12, the al-Nour Party 11, the Conservative Party 6 and the Democratic Peace Party 5. A further ten parties won four seats or fewer.

Current Government

President: Abdel Fattah al-Sisi; b. 1954 (ind.; sworn in 8 June 2014 and re-elected 28 March 2018).

In Feb. 2019 the government comprised:

Prime Minister, and Minister of Housing, Utilities and Urban Development: Mostafa Madbouly; b. 1966 (ind.; since 7 June 2018—acting until 14 June 2018).

Minister of Agriculture and Land Reclamation: Ezz el-Din Abu-Steit. *Antiquities:* Khaled al-Enani Ezz. *Civil Aviation:* Youssef el-Massri. *Communications and Information Technology:* Amr Ahmed Tallat. *Culture:* Inas Abdel-Dayem. *Defence and Military Production:* Mohamed Ahmed Zaki. *Education and Technical Education:* Tarek Galal Shawki Ahmed Shawki. *Electricity and Renewable Energy:* Mohamed Hamed Shaker. *Endowments:* Mohamed Mokhtar Gomaa. *Environment:* Yassmin Salah al-Din. *Finance:* Mohamed Maait. *Foreign Affairs:* Sameh Hassan Shoukry Selim. *Health and Population:* Hala Mustafa Zaid. *Higher Education and Scientific Research:* Khaled Attef Abdel-Ghaffar. *Immigration and Egyptian Expatriates Affairs:* Nabila Makram. *Interior:* Mahmoud Tawfiq. *Investment and International Co-operation:* Sahar Nasr. *Justice:* Mohamed Hossam Abdel-Rahim. *Local Development:* Mahmoud Youssry Shaarawy. *Manpower:* Mohamed Mahmoud Ahmed Saafan. *Parliamentary Affairs:* Omar Marwan. *Petroleum and Mineral Resources:* Tarek al-Molla. *Planning and Administrative Reform:* Hala Helmy al-Saeed Younis. *Public Business Sector:* Hisham Tawfik. *Social Solidarity:* Ghada Wali. *Supply and Internal Trade:* Ali al-Sayed Mosselhi. *Tourism:* Rania al-Mashat. *Trade and Industry:* Amr Adel Nassar. *Transport:* Hesham Arafat Mahdi Ahmed. *Water Resources and Irrigation:* Mohamed Abdel Ati Khalil. *Youth and Sports:* Ashraf Sobhy. *Minister of State for Military Production:* Mohamed al-Assar.

Government Website: http://www.egypt.gov.eg

Current Leaders

Abdel Fattah al-Sisi

Position
President

Introduction
A former defence minister and commander-in-chief of the armed forces, Abdel Fattah al-Sisi became president in June 2014, 11 months after overseeing the removal of President Morsi and his government. He was re-elected as president in March 2018, claiming 97·1% of the vote, but critics of his rule have met with increasing intolerance and repression.

Early Life
Born on 19 Nov. 1954 in Cairo, al-Sisi was educated at an army school and attended the Egyptian Military Academy. He rose through the ranks in the mechanized infantry brigades, while also receiving advanced training in Egypt and abroad including in the UK and the USA.

From 2008 he served as chief of staff of the northern military zone. In 2011, after President Mubarak was ousted from office, he was appointed director of military intelligence and reconnaissance and elected to the Supreme Council of the Armed Forces, which governed Egypt from Feb. 2011 to June 2012. In Aug. 2012 he was appointed commander-in-chief of the armed forces and defence minister by newly-elected President Morsi.

In June 2013, with public protests mounting against Morsi's government and its Muslim Brotherhood base, al-Sisi warned that division and conflict were a danger to the Egyptian state. The following month he announced that the army had removed Morsi from office and suspended the constitution. He oversaw the installation of an interim government, headed by Adly Mansour, in which he served as deputy prime minister as well as defence minister.

Al-Sisi called for public demonstrations of support as the army and police carried out widespread arrests of members of the Muslim Brotherhood. Violent clashes resulted in the deaths of hundreds of Morsi sympathizers in Aug. 2013, prompting domestic and international criticism. However, al-Sisi retained the support of many Egyptians and in March 2014 he resigned his military posts to contest the presidency. Campaigning on pledges to create jobs and restore faith in national institutions, he won a landslide victory in May 2014, officially garnering 96·9% of the vote.

Career in Office
Al-Sisi took office on 8 June 2014, initially raising taxes, cutting fuel subsidies and signalling his intention to diversify Egypt's overseas relations. Domestic challenges included rebalancing an economy heavily reliant on foreign aid, while maintaining political stability and handling Islamist militancy fuelled by his crackdown on the Muslim Brotherhood.

In parliamentary elections held in phases in late 2015 and marked by a low voter turnout, 57% of the new MPs were independent candidates and 43% were party-affiliated. Al-Sisi's government has since suppressed most political dissent in the name of public security against a background of militant Islamist attacks on Christian targets and Egypt's worst terror atrocity at a Sinai mosque in Nov. 2017. He has additionally challenged judicial independence, following the highest administrative court's rejection in Jan. 2017 of his proposed transfer of two islands in the Red Sea to Saudi Arabia. Subsequently, in April that year, he ratified legislation giving him the power to appoint the chief judges of the higher courts.

In Aug. 2015 al-Sisi inaugurated a major US$8bn. extension of the shipping capacity of the Suez Canal, with the aim of stimulating Egypt's economy. However, in response to continuing economic gloom, the central bank secured a US$12bn. financial bailout from the International Monetary Fund in Nov. 2016 in return for the imposition of new taxes and the floating of the Egyptian pound. Also, in an effort to attract foreign investment, a new law was passed in May 2017 aimed at reducing bureaucracy and offering tax incentives.

In June 2017 Egypt, along with Bahrain, Saudi Arabia and the United Arab Emirates, severed diplomatic relations and cut transport links with Qatar, accusing the state of supporting terrorism and aligning with Iran.

Following his re-election in March 2018, al-Sisi was sworn in for his second term as president in early June, at which point Sherif Ismail resigned as prime minister after almost three years in office and was replaced by Mostafa Madboul at the head of a new government.

Defence

Conscription is selective, and for 12–36 months, depending on the level of education. Military expenditure totalled US$5,278m. in 2013 (US$62 per capita), representing 2·0% of GDP.

Army

Estimated strength (2011) 310,000 (around 205,000 conscripts). In addition there were 375,000 reservists, a Central Security Force of 325,000, a National Guard of 60,000 and 12,000 Border Guards.

Navy

Major surface combatants include eight frigates and two corvettes. A small shore-based naval aviation branch operates 19 helicopters. There are naval bases at Al Ghardaqah, Alexandria, Hurghada, Mersa Matruh, Port Said, Port Tewfik, Safaga and Suez. Naval personnel in 2011 totalled an estimated 18,500 (including 10,000 conscripts and 2,000 coast guards).

Air Force

Until 1979 the Air Force was equipped largely with aircraft of USSR design, but subsequent re-equipment involves aircraft bought in the West, as well as some supplied by China. Strength (2011) is about 30,000 personnel (10,000 conscripts), 589 combat-capable aircraft including J-7s, F-16s and *Mirage* Vs, and 35 attack helicopters.

Economy

In 2014 agriculture accounted for 11·1% of GDP, industry 39·0% and services 49·9%.

Overview

Egypt is one of the most economically diversified countries in the Middle East, but has been embroiled in turmoil since the overthrow of Hosni Mubarak's regime in 2011.

The 1980s was a decade of macroeconomic disorder in Egypt before an IMF-backed reform programme in the 1990s helped the country achieve stability. However, the late 1990s saw a further downturn, and privatization efforts stalled in the early 2000s. In 2004 an economically liberal cabinet was appointed, reviving a structural reform agenda to generate jobs and promote foreign investment.

GDP growth then averaged 6·4% per year between 2005 and 2008, underpinned by record levels of foreign direct investment and a favourable external environment. The economy held up relatively well during the global financial crisis, with the decline in remittances and external earnings partially offset by resilient domestic demand and strong performances in the construction, communications and trade sectors.

GDP fell by 9% in the first quarter of 2011 following the revolution in Jan. of that year, before stabilizing at a growth rate averaging 3·1% per year from 2011 to 2017. However, unemployment had climbed to 12·4% and gross public debt rose to over 100% of GDP by 2017. Establishing the political and fiscal conditions for long-term economic stability remains the major challenge in the coming years.

Currency

The monetary unit is the *Egyptian pound* (EGP) of 100 *piastres*. Inflation rates (based on IMF statistics) for fiscal years:

2008	2009	2010	2011	2012	2013	2014	2015	2016	2017
11·7%	16·2%	11·7%	11·1%	8·6%	6·9%	10·1%	11·0%	10·2%	23·5%

In Nov. 2016 the government announced it would allow the pound to float, effectively devaluing it. The move was part of a package of reforms designed to secure a US$12bn. loan from the IMF. In June 2009 foreign exchange reserves were US$29,278m., gold reserves totalled 2·43m. troy oz and total money supply was £E182,991m.

Budget

The financial year runs from 1 July. Budgetary central government revenues in 2013–14 were £E457bn. and expenditures £E649bn. Taxes on income, profits and capital gains accounted for 26·5% of revenue and taxes on goods and services 23·4%. Main items of expenditure were subsidies (29·0%) and interest (26·7%).

VAT was increased from 13% to 14% in July 2017.

Performance

Real GDP growth rates (based on IMF statistics):

2008	2009	2010	2011	2012	2013	2014	2015	2016	2017
7·2%	4·7%	5·1%	1·8%	2·2%	3·3%	2·9%	4·4%	4·3%	4·2%

Total GDP in 2017 was US$235·4bn.

Banking and Finance

The Central Bank of Egypt (founded 1960) is the central bank and bank of issue. The *Governor* is Tarek Amer.

In June 2013 there were 40 banks operating in Egypt. National Bank of Egypt, the largest bank, had assets of US$50·7bn. in 2011. Other leading banks are Banque Misr (assets of US$29·4bn. in 2011), Commercial International Bank (assets of US$14·2bn. in 2011) and National Société Générale Bank (assets of US$10·4bn. in 2011).

In 2010 external debt totalled US$34,844m., representing 16·2% of GNI. There are stock exchanges in Cairo and Alexandria.

Energy and Natural Resources

Environment

Egypt's carbon dioxide emissions from the consumption of energy in 2011 were the equivalent of 2·4 tonnes per capita.

Electricity

Installed capacity was 30·1m. kW in 2011. Electricity generated in 2011 was 161·16bn. kWh. Consumption per capita was an estimated 2,010 kWh in 2011. The government aims to have 20% of power being produced from renewable sources by 2020. An agreement was signed with Russia in Nov. 2015 to build Egypt's first nuclear power plant. It is expected to be completed by 2022.

Oil and Gas

Oil was discovered in 1909. Production in 2012 was 35·4m. tonnes with 4·3bn. bbls of proven reserves.

As a result of a series of new discoveries gas reserves doubled between 1998 and 2006. Egypt began exporting natural gas in 2003 and is now a major exporter. More recently, a huge new offshore gas field in Egyptian waters in the Mediterranean Sea was discovered in 2015. Production from the new field began in Dec. 2017. A further offshore field discovered in 2018 may be even larger. Egypt is expected to become a net exporter of natural gas during 2019. In 2012 total production amounted to 60·9bn. cu. metres. There were proven natural gas reserves of 2·0trn. cu. metres in 2012.

Minerals

Production (2013 estimates, in tonnes): phosphate rock, 5·9m.; iron ore, 3·0m.; salt, 2·9m.; sand and gravel, 900,000; aluminium, 520,000; feldspar, 400,000; sandstone, 400,000; limestone, 2·0m. cu. metres.

Agriculture

There were 2·87m. ha. of arable land in 2010 and 0·80m. ha. of permanent crops. About a quarter of the arable area is land reclaimed from the desert. Irrigation is vital to agriculture and reaches most cultivated areas, covering 3·65m. ha. in 2010.

Output (in 1,000 tonnes), 2007: sugarcane, 17,014; tomatoes, 8,695; wheat, 7,379; maize, 6,930; rice, 6,877; sugar beets, 5,458; potatoes, 2,760; melons and watermelons, 2,121; oranges, 2,055; onions, 1,756. Egypt is Africa's largest producer of a number of crops, including wheat, rice, tomatoes, potatoes and oranges.

Livestock, 2012: sheep, 5·43m.; cattle, 4·95m.; goats, 4·31m.; buffaloes, 4·16m.; asses (estimate), 3·36m.; camels, 142,000; chickens (estimate), 126m. Livestock products in 2011 (in 1,000 tonnes): cow's milk, 3,107; buffalo's milk, 2,568; poultry meat, 888; beef and veal, 455; buffalo meat, 396; cheese (estimate), 634; eggs, 306.

Forestry

In 2015 forests covered 73,000 ha., representing 0·1% of the total land area. In 2011, 17·82m. cu. metres of roundwood were produced.

Fisheries

The catch in 2015 was 344,112 tonnes, of which 241,179 tonnes were freshwater fish. Aquaculture production totalled 919,585 tonnes in 2010 (70% of total fish production).

Industry

The largest company by market capitalization in Egypt in March 2015 was Commercial International Bank (US$6·7bn.).

Production, in 1,000 tonnes: cement (2007), 38,469; residual fuel oil (2007), 10,989; distillate fuel oil (2007), 8,803; crude steel (2008), 6,198; petrol (2005), 2,972; refined sugar (2011), 1,806; nitrogenous fertilizers (2012), 850; paper and paperboard (2010 estimate), 660; cotton yarn (2008), 150. Motor vehicles (2012), 56,480 units; washing machines (2008), 564,000 units; cigarettes (2008), 61·7bn. units.

Labour

The labour force in 2013 was 28,974,000 (21,796,000 in 2003). 52·7% of the population aged 15–64 was economically active in 2013. In the same year 13·2% of the population was unemployed.

Egypt had 69,000 people living in slavery according to the Walk Free Foundation's 2013 *Global Slavery Index*.

International Trade

Imports and Exports

Goods imports were US$71,337·7m. in 2014 (US$66,666·4m. in 2013) and goods exports US$26,812·2m. (US$28,779·4m. in 2013).

Main imports in 2014 were machinery and transport equipment (22·3%), manufactured goods, and food, animals and beverages; main exports in 2014 were mineral fuels and lubricants (23·4%), manufactured goods and chemicals. Egypt is the world's largest importer of wheat.

The leading import source in 2010 was the USA (9·4%), followed by China and Germany; the leading export market in 2010 was Italy (8·4%), followed by Spain and Saudi Arabia.

Communications

Roads

In 2006 there were 99,672 km of roads, of which 81·0% were paved. Vehicles in use in 2006 (in 1,000): passenger cars, 2,372 (29 per 1,000 inhabitants in 2005); lorries and vans, 1,463; motorcycles and mopeds, 751; buses and coaches, 79. There were 12,295 fatalities as a result of road accidents in 2007.

Rail

Egypt's rail network is the oldest in Africa. In 2011 there were 5,195 km of state railways (1,435 mm gauge). Passenger-km travelled in 2011 came to 40·8bn. and freight tonne-km in 2010 to 1·6bn.

There are tramway networks in Cairo, Heliopolis and Alexandria, and a metro (63 km) opened in Cairo in 1987.

Civil Aviation

There are international airports at Cairo, Luxor, Borg El Arab (serving Alexandria), Hurghada and Sharm El-Sheikh. The national carrier is Egyptair, which in 2013 carried 8,513,000 passengers (7,020,000 on international flights). In 2012 Cairo handled 14,839,421 passengers (12,865,751 on international flights). Hurghada was the second busiest airport in 2012, with 7,134,032 passengers.

Shipping

In Jan. 2014 there were 84 ships of 300 GT or over registered, totalling 917,000 GT. The Egyptian-controlled fleet comprised 125 vessels of 1,000 GT or over in July 2014, of which 44 were under the Egyptian flag and 81 under foreign flags. The leading ports are Adabeya, Alexandria, Damietta, Dekheila, Port Said and Sokhna.

Suez Canal

The Suez Canal was opened for navigation on 17 Nov. 1869 and nationalized in June 1956. By the convention of Constantinople of 29 Oct. 1888, the canal is open to vessels of all nations and is free from blockade, except in time of war. It is 190 km long, connecting the Mediterranean with the Red Sea. It has a maximum depth of 22·5 metres and a maximum width of 365 metres. Vessels of up to 210,000 DWT fully laden are able to pass through the canal. In Aug. 2014 work began on the canal's first expansion in its 145-year history. The US$8·2bn. year-long project created a 35 km parallel channel and saw the main waterway deepened, and expanded capacity from 78 vessels per day to 97. The resulting New Suez Canal was officially opened on 6 Aug. 2015.

In 2014, 17,148 vessels (net tonnage, 963m.) went through the canal; 822m. tonnes of cargo were transported. Toll revenue in 2014 was US$5,465m.

Telecommunications

In 2013 mobile phone subscriptions numbered 99,705,000 (1,215·1 per 1,000 persons) and there were 6,821,000 fixed telephone lines. In 2005 the Egyptian government sold 20% of its holding in Telecom Egypt. There were 25,553,000 wireless broadband subscriptions and 2,675,000 fixed broadband subscriptions in 2013. In June 2012 there were 11·3m. Facebook users.

Social Institutions

Out of 178 countries analysed in the 2017*Fragile States Index*—a list published jointly by the Fund for Peace and *Foreign Policy* magazine— Egypt was ranked the 36th most vulnerable to conflict or collapse. The index is based on 12 indicators of state vulnerability across social, political and economic categories.

Justice

The court system comprises: a Court of Cassation with a bench of five judges which constitutes the highest court of appeal in both criminal and civil cases; five Courts of Appeal with three judges; Assize Courts with three judges which deal with all cases of serious crime; Central Tribunals with three judges which deal with ordinary civil and commercial cases; Summary Tribunals presided over by a single judge which hear minor civil disputes and criminal offences. Contempt for religion and what is judged to be a false interpretation of the Koran may result in prison sentences.

The population in penal institutions in 2011 was approximately 66,000 (80 per 100,000 of national population). The death penalty is in force; there were at least 35 executions in 2017 and at least 61 in 2018. There have also been widespread reports of extrajudicial executions since the Arab Spring in 2011. Egypt was ranked 55th of 102 countries for criminal justice and 92nd for civil justice in the 2015 World Justice Project *Rule of Law Index*, which provides data on how the rule of law is experienced by the general public across eight categories.

Education

The adult literacy rate in 2005 was 71·4%. Free compulsory education is provided in primary schools (eight years). Secondary and technical education is also free. In 2017 there were 1,306,538 pupils at pre-primary schools; 12,161,376 pupils at primary schools and 8,938,257 pupils at secondary schools.

Al Azhar institutes educate students who intend enrolling at Al Azhar University, one of the world's oldest universities and Sunni Islam's foremost seat of learning. In 2009–10 there were 8,731 institutes in the Al Azhar system with 2,015,797 pupils.

In 2010 there were 19 public universities, Al Azhar University and 20 private universities. There were 2,645,832 students enrolled in tertiary education establishments in 2010.

Public education expenditure in 2007 was 3·7% of GNI and 12·6% of total government spending.

Health

In 2012 there were five hospital beds per 10,000 population. There were 225,565 physicians and 280,561 nurses in 2009. In 2012 health expenditure represented 5·0% of GDP.

In *Water: At What Cost? The State of the World's Water 2016*, WaterAid reported that 0·6% of the population does not have access to safe water.

Welfare

An old-age pension is available at the age of 60 with at least 120 months of contributions, or at any age with at least 240 months of contributions. For a base old-age pension, up to 2·2% of the insured's reference monthly base earnings (2·5% for arduous work or 2·8% for dangerous work) is paid for each year of contributions, up to 36 years.

Religion

Islam has constitutionally been the state religion since 1980. According to estimates by the Pew Research Center's Forum on Religion & Public Life, in 2010 there were 77·0m. Muslims (94·9% of the population) and 4·1m. Christians (5·1%). The vast majority of Muslims are Sunnis. Most Christians belong to the Coptic Orthodox Church of Alexandria but there are also some Protestants and Catholics. The Coptic Church is headed by a pope (Tawadros II, enthroned Nov. 2012). It has four metropolitan archbishops and four metropolitan bishops. In Feb. 2019 there was one cardinal in the Roman Catholic Church.

Culture

World Heritage Sites

There are seven UNESCO sites in Egypt. The first five were entered on the list in 1979. They are: Memphis and its Necropolis (the Pyramid Fields from Giza to Dahshur); Ancient Thebes with its Necropolis; Nubian Monuments from Abu Simbel to Philae; Historic Cairo; and Abu Mena. Memphis was considered one of the Seven Wonders of the World. Ancient Thebes was the capital of Egypt during the period of the middle (c. 2000 BC) and new (c. 1600 BC) kingdoms. The Nubian monuments include the temples of Ramses II in Abu Simbel and the Sanctuary of Isis in Philae. Historic Cairo, founded in the 10th century, became the centre of the Islamic world. Abu Mena was an early Christian holy city. The Saint Catherine Area was added to the list in 2002. It included Saint Catherine's Monastery, an outstanding example of an Orthodox Christian monastic settlement, dating from the 6th century AD. The area is centred on Mount Sinai (Jebel Musa or Mount Horeb). In 2005 Wadi Al-Hitan (Whale Valley) was inscribed on the list. The site is an area rich in fossil remains in Egypt's western desert.

Press

In 2008 there were 18 dailies (17 paid-for and one free) with a total average circulation of 2·74m. The leading dailies are *Al-Ahram* and *Al-Gomhuriya*.

Tourism

In 2014 there were 9,628,000 non-resident tourists (excluding same-day visitors), up from 9,174,000 in 2013 although down from the peak figure of 14,051,000 in 2010. Tourism receipts in 2014 totalled US$7,208m.

Festivals

Annual film festivals are held in Alexandria (Sept.) and Cairo (Nov.). The Arab Music Festival at the Cairo Opera House takes place in Nov.

Diplomatic Representatives

Of Egypt in the United Kingdom (26 South St., London, W1K 1DW)
    Ambassador: Tarek Adel.

Of the United Kingdom in Egypt (7 Ahmed Ragheb St., Garden City, Cairo)
    Ambassador: Sir Geoffrey Adams, KCMG.

Of Egypt in the USA (3521 International Court, NW, Washington, D.C., 20008)
    Ambassador: Yasser Reda Abdalla Ali Said.

Of the USA in Egypt (8 Kamal el-Din Salah St., Garden City, Cairo)
    Ambassador: Vacant.
    Chargé d'Affaires a.i.: Thomas H. Goldberger.

Of Egypt to the United Nations
    Ambassador: Mohamed Fathi Ahmed Edrees.

Of Egypt to the European Union
    Ambassador: Khaled Aly el Bakly.

Further Reading

CAPMAS, *Statistical Year Book, Arab Republic of Egypt*

Arafat, Alaa Al-Din, *The Rise of Islamism in Egypt.* 2017—*Egypt in Crisis: The Fall of Islamism and Prospects of Democratization.* 2018

Baker, Raymond William, *Islam without Fear: Egypt and the New Islamists.* 2006

Cook, Steven, *The Struggle for Egypt: From Nasser to Tahrir Square.* 2011

Daly, M. W. (ed.) *The Cambridge History of Egypt.* 2 vols. 2000

Ibrahim, Fouad N. and Ibrahim, Barbara, *Egypt: An Economic Geography.* 2001

Khalil, Ashraf, *Liberation Square: Inside the Egyptian Revolution and the Rebirth of a Nation.* 2012

King, J. W., *Historical Dictionary of Egypt.* 2nd ed. revised by A. Goldschmidt. 1995

Kirkpatrick, David, *Into the Hands of the Soldiers: Freedom and Chaos in Egypt and the Middle East.* 2018

Malek, J. (ed.) *Egypt.* 1993

Shenker, Jack, *The Egyptians: A Radical Story.* 2016

Turner, Barry, *Suez 1956: The Inside Story of the First Oil War.* 2007

National Statistical Office: Central Agency for Public Mobilization and Statistics (CAPMAS), Salah Salam Street, Nasr City, Cairo.

Website: http://www.capmas.gov.eg

El Salvador

República de El Salvador (Republic of El Salvador)

Capital: San Salvador
Population projection, 2020: 6·48m.
GNI per capita, 2017: (PPP$) 6,868
HDI/world rank, 2017: 0·674/121
Internet domain extension: .sv

Key Historical Events

Conquered by Spain in 1526, El Salvador remained under Spanish rule until 1821. Thereafter, El Salvador was a member of the Central American Federation comprising the states of El Salvador, Guatemala, Honduras, Nicaragua and Costa Rica until this federation was dissolved in 1839. In 1841 El Salvador declared itself an independent republic.

The country's history has been marked by political violence. The repressive dictatorship of President Maximiliano Hernandez Martínez lasted from 1931 to 1944 when he was deposed as were his successors in 1948 and 1960. The military junta that followed gave way to more secure presidential succession although left-wing guerrilla groups were fighting government troops in the late 1970s. As the guerrillas grew stronger, gaining control over a part of the country, the USA sent economic aid and assisted in the training of Salvadorean troops. A new constitution was enacted in Dec. 1983 but the presidential election was boycotted by the main left-wing organization, the Favabundo Marti National Liberation Front (FMLN). Talks between the government and the FMLN in April 1991 led to constitutional reforms in May, envisaging the establishment of civilian control over the armed forces and a reduction in their size. On 16 Jan. 1992 the government and the FMLN signed a peace agreement.

In Jan. 2001 an earthquake killed 1,200 people and left 1m. homeless. Five years later El Salvador and Honduras inaugurated their newly-defined mutual border, which had previously caused conflict between the two countries.

Mauricio Funes of the FMLN became the first left-wing president in more than 20 years when he was elected in March 2009. He was succeeded by fellow FMLN member Salvador Sánchez Cerén in June 2014.

Territory and Population

El Salvador is bounded in the northwest by Guatemala, northeast and east by Honduras and south by the Pacific Ocean. The area (including 247 sq. km of inland lakes) is 21,040 sq. km. Population (2007 census), 5,744,113 (female 53%), giving a population density of 273 per sq. km. The United Nations population estimate for 2007 was 6,083,000. The estimated population in 2014 was 6,383,000.

The UN gives a projected population for 2020 of 6·48m.

In 2007, 62·7% of the population were urban. Some 2·5m. Salvadoreans live abroad, mainly in the USA.

The republic is divided into 14 departments. Areas (in sq. km) and 2007 census populations:

Department	Area	Population	Chief town	Population
Ahuachapán	1,240	319,503	Ahuachapán	63,981
Cabañas	1,104	149,326	Sensuntepeque	15,395
Chalatenango	2,017	192,788	Chalatenango	16,976
Cuscatlán	756	231,480	Cojutepeque	41,072
La Libertad	1,653	660,652	Santa Tecla	108,840
La Paz	1,224	308,087	Zacatecoluca	42,127
La Unión	2,074	238,217	La Unión	18,046
Morazán	1,447	174,406	San Francisco	15,307
San Miguel	2,077	434,003	San Miguel	158,136

(*continued*)

Department	Area	Population	Chief town	Population
San Salvador	886	1,567,156	San Salvador	316,090[1]
San Vicente	1,184	161,645	San Vicente	36,700
Santa Ana	2,023	523,655	Santa Ana	204,340
Sonsonate	1,225	438,960	Sonsonate	49,129
Usulatán	2,130	344,235	Usulután	51,496

[1]Greater San Salvador conurbation (2007), 1,566,629.

The official language is Spanish.

Social Statistics

2008 births (est.), 112,000; deaths (est.), 32,000. Rates (2008, per 1,000 population): births (est.), 18·3; deaths (est.), 5·2. Life expectancy at birth in 2013 was 67·8 years for males and 77·1 years for females. Annual population growth rate, 2005–10, 0·5%. Infant mortality, 2010, 14 per 1,000 live births; fertility rate, 2008, 2·3 births per woman. Abortion is illegal.

Climate

Despite its proximity to the equator, the climate is warm rather than hot, and nights are cool inland. Light rains occur in the dry season from Nov. to April, while the rest of the year has heavy rains, especially on the coastal plain. San Salvador, Jan. 71°F (21·7°C), July 75°F (23·9°C). Annual rainfall 71" (1,775 mm). San Miguel, Jan. 77°F (25°C), July 83°F (28·3°C). Annual rainfall 68" (1,700 mm).

Constitution and Government

A new constitution was enacted in Dec. 1983. Executive power is vested in a *President* and *Vice-President* elected for a non-renewable term of five years. There is a *Legislative Assembly* of 84 members elected by universal suffrage and proportional representation: 64 locally and 20 nationally, for a term of three years.

National Anthem

'Saludemos la patria orgullosos' ('We proudly salute the Fatherland'); words by J. J. Cañas, tune by J. Aberle.

Government Chronology

Heads of State since 1944. (ARENA = Nationalist Republican Alliance; FMLN = Farabundo Martí National Liberation Front; PCN = National Conciliation Party; PDC = Christian Democratic Party; PRUD = Revolutionary Party of Democratic Unification; n/p = non-partisan)

Presidents		
1944–45	military	Osmín Aguirre y Salinas
1945–48	military	Salvador Castaneda Castro
Military Junta		
1948–50		Manuel de Jesús Córdova; Óscar Osorio Hernández; Reinaldo Galindo Pohl; Óscar A. Bolaños; Humberto Costa
Presidents		
1950–56	military, PRUD	Óscar Osorio Hernández
1956–60	military, PRUD	José María Lemus López

(*continued*)

© Springer Nature Limited 2020
Palgrave Macmillan (ed.), *The Statesman's Yearbook 2020*,
https://doi.org/10.1057/978-1-349-95940-2_66

Junta		
1960–61		Miguel Ángel Castillo; César Yanes Urías; Rubén Alonso Rosales; Ricardo Falla Cáceres; Fabio Castillo Figueroa; Rene Fortín Magaña

Civic Military Directory		
1961–62		José Antonio Rodríguez Porth; José Francisco Valiente; Feliciano Avelar; Aníbal Portillo; Julio Adalberto Rivera Carballo; Mariano Castro Morán

Presidents		
1962	n/p	Eusebio Rodolfo Cordón Cea
1962–67	military, PCN	Julio Adalberto Rivera Carballo
1967–72	military, PCN	Fidel Sánchez Hernández
1972–77	military, PCN	Arturo Armando Molina Barraza
1977–79	military, PCN	Carlos Humberto Romero Mena

Revolutionary Junta of Government (I)		
1979–80		Adolfo Arnaldo Majano Ramos; Jaime Abdul Gutiérrez Avendaño; Román Mayorga Quirós; Guillermo Manuel Ungo Revelo; Mario Antonio Andino

Revolutionary Junta of Government (II)		
1980		Adolfo Arnaldo Majano Ramos (military); Jaime Abdul Gutiérrez Avendaño (military); José Antonio Morales Ehrlich (PDC); éctor Miguel Dada Hirezi (PDC); José Napoleón Duarte Fuentes (PDC); José Ramón Ávalos Navarrete (n/p)

Chairman of the Revolutionary Junta of Government		
1980–82	PDC	José Napoleón Duarte Fuentes

Presidents		
1982–84	n/p	Álvaro Alfredo Magaña Borja
1984–89	PDC	José Napoleón Duarte Fuentes
1989–94	ARENA	Alfredo Félix Cristiani Burkard
1994–99	ARENA	Armando Calderón Sol
1999–2004	ARENA	Francisco Guillermo Flores Pérez
2004–09	ARENA	Elías Antonio Saca González
2009–14	FMLN	Carlos Mauricio Funes Cartagena
2014–	FMLN	Salvador Sánchez Cerén

Recent Elections

Presidential elections were held on 3 Feb. 2019. Nayib Bukele (Grand Alliance for National Unity; GANA) was elected president by 53·1% of votes cast, ahead of Carlos Calleja (Nationalist Republican Alliance; ARENA) with 31·7%, Hugo Martínez (Farabundo Martí National Liberation Front; FMLN) with 14·4% and Josué Alvarado (Vamos) with 0·8%.

In parliamentary elections on 4 March 2018 the Nationalist Republican Alliance gained 37 of a possible 84 seats in the Legislative Assembly (42·3% of the vote), ahead of the Farabundo Martí National Liberation Front (FMLN) with 23 (24·4%), the Grand Alliance for National Unity (GANA) 11 (11·5%), the National Coalition (PCN) 8 (10·8%), the Christian Democratic Party (PDC) 3 (3·2%) and Democratic Change 1 (0·9%). An independent candidate also won a seat.

Current Government

President: Salvador Sánchez Cerén; b. 1944 (FMLN; sworn in 1 June 2014).
In Feb. 2019 the cabinet comprised:
Vice-President: Óscar Ortiz.
Minister of Agriculture and Livestock: Orestes Fredesman Ortez Andrade. *Defence:* David Munguía Payés. *Economy:* Tharsis Salomón López Guzmán. *Education:* Carlos Mauricio Canjura Linares. *Environment and Natural Resources:* Lina Dolores Pohl Alfaro. *Finance:* Nelson Fuentes. *Foreign Affairs:* Carlos Castaneda. *Health:* Violeta Menjívar. *Interior:* Ramón Arístides Valencia. *Justice and Public Security:* Benito Antonio Lara Fernánde. *Labour and Social Welfare:* Sandra Guevara. *Public Works, Transport, Housing and Urban Development:* Gerson Martínez. *Tourism:* Napoleón Duarte.
Office of the President (Spanish only): http://www.presidencia.gob.sv

Current Leaders

Salvador Sánchez Cerén

Position
President

Introduction
Salvador Sánchez Cerén became president in June 2014. A member of the Farabundo Martí National Liberation Front (FMLN), he was a guerrilla leader during the country's civil war. He was due to step down from office on 1 June 2019 following presidential elections in Feb. in which he was ineligible to stand.

Early Life
Sánchez was born on 18 June 1944 in Quezaltepeque. He qualified as a teacher in 1963 and taught for ten years in public and rural schools.

In 1965 he helped establish the ANDES 21 de Junio union, the first teachers' union in the country, and associated with groups linked to the Salvadoran Communist Party. In 1972 he joined the militant guerrilla group Fuerzas Populares de Liberación Farabundo Martí (FPL), which later evolved into the FMLN. He took on roles of increasing responsibility and went underground in 1978 after serving a second prison term. During the Salvadoran Civil War (1980–92) he adopted the pseudonym Commander Leonel González. In 1984 he was made a commanding general in the FMLN and in 1992 he was a signatory to the Chapultepec Peace Accords that ended the conflict.

In the post-war period he was elected as an FMLN congressman in 2000, 2003 and 2006. From 2001–04 he served as general co-ordinator of the party and in 2006 became its Assembly leader. He was running mate to Mauricio Funes at the 2009 presidential election in which the FMLN defeated its rival, ARENA, for the first time. From 2009–14 he served as vice-president.

Career in Office
Sánchez's key challenges were a sluggish economy, poverty and social insecurity, coupled with a high homicide rate resulting from gang (*maras*) warfare. Shortly after he came to office, he ended a 2012 truce between the then government and the gangs, which had reduced the killings but fuelled allegations of illegal collusion between politicians and gangsters leading to subsequent court proceedings against public officials.

Sánchez also sought to promote the FMLN's core aims of job creation, education, social inclusion and public safety, while favouring closer Latin American integration. He supported the Bolivarian Alliance for the Peoples of Our America (ALBA), advocated a Central American Union and aimed to strengthen ties with Venezuela via the Petrocaribe oil alliance.

Defence

There is selective conscription for 12 months. In 2013 defence expenditure totalled US$154m. (US$25 per capita), representing 0·6% of GDP.

Army

Strength (2011): 13,850 (4,000 conscripts). The National Civilian Police numbers about 17,000.

Navy

There is a small Navy with 700 (2011) personnel including a special forces company. Equipment in 2011 included ten patrol boats.

Air Force

Strength (2011): 771 personnel (200 air defence). There were 16 combat-capable aircraft in 2011, plus 21 other aircraft and 35 helicopters.

Economy

Agriculture accounted for 11·0% of GDP in 2016, industry 26·5% and services 62·5%.

Overview

After going into recession in 2009, with a contraction in GDP of 3·1% as a result of the global financial crisis, growth averaged 1·9% per year between 2010 and 2015. It then measured 2·4% in both 2016 and 2017, supported by lower oil prices, the continued US recovery and a surge in remittances. Higher revenues and expenditure restraint resulted in a primary government surplus of 0·9% of GDP in 2017, although high interest payments led to an overall deficit of 2·5%. Inflation remained low at 1% that year.

Economic performance in the first few years of this century had been underpinned by wide-ranging reforms, promoting more open trade and changes to fiscal policies. In 2006 the country joined the Central America–Dominican Republic–United States Free Trade Agreement (CAFTA–DR), which has supported exports and encouraged investment.

Economic links to the USA are strong and broad-based. The USA accounts for over 90% of the total migrant and remittance inflows (worth over 17% of GDP), 50% of goods exported from El Salvador and one-third of the foreign direct investment stock.

The normalization of US monetary policy, allied to more restrictive US immigration policies, pose significant challenges for El Salvador's economy. Moreover, its long-term outlook is dependent on further domestic structural reforms.

Currency

The *dollar* (USD) replaced the *colón* as the legal currency of El Salvador in 2003. Inflation was 0·6% in 2016 and 1·0% in 2017. Foreign exchange reserves were US$1,741m. and gold reserves 326,000 troy oz in May 2005.

Budget

Budgetary central government revenue totalled US$4,096m. in 2015 and expenditure US$4,162m.

VAT is 13%.

Performance

The economy grew by 2·4% in 2015, 2·6% in 2016 and 2·3% in 2017. Total GDP in 2017 was US$24·8bn.

Banking and Finance

The bank of issue is the Central Reserve Bank (*President*, Oscar Cabrera Melgar), formed in 1934 and nationalized in 1961. In 2008 there were ten commercial banks (eight foreign). Foreign debt was US$11,069m. in 2010, representing 53% of GNI.

There is a stock exchange in San Salvador, founded in 1992.

Energy and Natural Resources

Environment

El Salvador's carbon dioxide emissions from the consumption of energy in 2011 were the equivalent of 1·0 tonnes per capita.

Electricity

Installed capacity in 2011 was 1,477,000 kW, of which 472,000 kW hydro-electric. Production in 2011 was 5·84bn. kWh; consumption per capita was 954 kWh in 2011.

Minerals

El Salvador has few mineral resources. In 2008 an estimated 1·2m. tonnes of limestone were produced. Annual marine salt production averages 30,000 tonnes.

Agriculture

27% of the land surface is given over to arable farming. There were about 682,000 ha. of arable land in 2007 and 237,000 ha. of permanent crops. From the mid-19th century until the late 20th century El Salvador's economy was dominated by coffee. More recently there has been increased competition from other countries, resulting in a significant decline in the country's coffee industry. Output, in 1,000 tonnes (2013): sugarcane, 7,163; maize, 867; sorghum, 141; dry beans, 118; mangoes and guavas (estimate), 78; oranges,

69; coconuts, 55; cocoyam (estimate), 43. Livestock (2013): 893,000 cattle; 402,000 pigs (estimate); 98,000 horses (estimate); 15·5m. chickens (estimate).

Forestry

Forest area was 0·27m. ha. (13% of the land area) in 2015. Balsam trees abound: El Salvador is the world's principal source of this medicinal gum. In 2011, 4·90m. cu. metres of roundwood were cut.

Fisheries

The catch in 2011 was 54,281 tonnes (96% from marine waters).

Industry

Production in 1,000 tonnes: cement (2006), 1,311; sugar (2005), 633; residual fuel oil (2007), 477; distillate fuel oil (2007), 229; petrol (2007), 117; paper and paperboard (2006 estimate), 56. Traditional industries include food processing and textiles.

Labour

The labour force in 2013 was 2,712,000 (2,333,000 in 2003). 65·5% of the population aged 15–64 was economically active in 2013. In the same year 5·9% of the population was unemployed.

El Salvador had 10,000 people living in slavery according to the Walk Free Foundation's 2013 *Global Slavery Index*.

International Trade

Imports and Exports

Imports and exports in calendar years (in US$1m.):

	2006	2007	2008	2009	2010
Imports c.i.f.	7,763	8,821	9,818	7,306	8,485
Exports f.o.b.	3,730	4,015	4,641	3,866	4,499

In 2010 main import sources (in US$1m.) were: USA (3,130); Guatemala (803); Mexico (752); China (483). Main export markets in 2010 (in US$1m.) were: USA (2,176); Guatemala (629); Honduras (579); Nicaragua (244). Main import commodities are chemicals and chemical products, transport equipment, and food and beverages; main export commodities are coffee, paper and paper products, and clothing.

Communications

Roads

In 2011 there were 7,298 km of roads, 53·2% of which were paved. Vehicles in use in 2011: passenger cars, 331,200; trucks and vans, 275,000. There were 12,396 road accidents in 2009 resulting in 1,033 fatalities.

Rail

There are 555 km of 914 mm gauge railway. The railway was closed from 2002–06 but a limited service resumed in 2007.

Civil Aviation

The main airport is Monseñor Óscar Arnulfo Romero International Airport (commonly known as Comalapa International Airport) in San Salvador. The national carrier is Taca International Airlines. It flies to various destinations in the USA, Mexico and all Central American countries. In 2012 scheduled airline traffic of El Salvador-based carriers flew 86·1m. km; passenger-km totalled 5·6bn. in the same year. In 2012 El Salvador International handled 2,113,740 passengers (2,051,636 on international flights) and 23,363 tonnes of freight.

Shipping

The main ports are Acajutla (which handled 4·11m. tonnes of cargo in 2013) and Cutuco.

Telecommunications

In 2010 there were 1,000,900 landline telephone subscriptions (equivalent to 161·6 per 1,000 inhabitants) and 7,700,300 mobile phone subscriptions (or 1,243·4 per 1,000 inhabitants). In 2010, 15·9% of the population were internet users. In Dec. 2011 there were 1·3m. Facebook users.

Social Institutions

Out of 178 countries analysed in the 2017 *Fragile States Index*—a list published jointly by the Fund for Peace and *Foreign Policy* magazine—El Salvador was ranked the 87th least vulnerable to conflict or collapse. The index is based on 12 indicators of state vulnerability across social, political and economic categories.

Justice

Justice is administered by the Supreme Court (six members appointed for three-year terms by the Legislative Assembly and six by bar associations), courts of first and second instance, and minor tribunals. A National Civilian Police Force numbered 17,000 by 2013. The population in penal institutions in May 2013 was 26,568 (422 per 100,000 of national population). El Salvador was ranked 81st of 102 countries for criminal justice and 58th for civil justice in the 2015 World Justice Project *Rule of Law Index*, which provides data on how the rule of law is experienced by the general public across eight categories.

There were 5,257 homicides in 2016, equivalent to 83 per 100,000 people—the highest rate of any country.

Education

The adult literacy rate in 2009 was 84·1%. Education, run by the state, is free and compulsory. In 2007 there were 229,539 children in nursery schools, 1,075,041 in primary schools and 536,017 in secondary schools. The University of El Salvador (Universidad de El Salvador), founded in 1841, is the country's oldest and largest public university. There are also several private universities. In 2007 there were 132,246 students and 8,370 academic staff in tertiary education.

In 2007 public expenditure on education came to 3·1% of GNI and 13·1% of total government spending.

Health

In 2012 there were 11 hospital beds per 10,000 population. There were 16·0 physicians for every 10,000 inhabitants in the period 2007–13.

In *Water: At What Cost? The State of the World's Water 2016*, WaterAid reported that 6·2% of the population does not have access to safe water.

Welfare

There are old age, disability and survivors' pensions and sickness, maternity and work injury benefits. The official retirement age is 55 years (women) and 60 years (men). The minimum monthly old age pension is US$207·60. Maternity benefit is equal to 75% of average monthly earnings for up to 12 weeks.

Religion

In 2010 there were an estimated 3·16m. Roman Catholics (51% of the population) and 2·21m. Protestants (36% of the population) according to the Pew Research Center's Forum on Religion & Public Life, with 680,000 people religiously unaffiliated. There is an archbishop in San Salvador and bishops at Chalatenango, San Miguel, San Vicente, Santa Ana, Santiago de María, Sonsonate and Zacatecoluca. In Feb. 2019 there was one cardinal.

Culture

World Heritage Sites

El Salvador has one site on the UNESCO World Heritage List: the Joya de Cerén Archaeological Site (1993), a pre-Hispanic farming community preserved under volcanic ash.

Press

In 2005 there were five daily newspapers with a combined circulation of 250,000.

Tourism

There were 1,255,000 non-resident tourists in 2012 (excluding same-day visitors), up from 1,184,000 in 2011.

Diplomatic Representatives

Of El Salvador in the United Kingdom (8 Dorset Sq., 1st and 2nd Floors, London, NW1 6PU)
    Ambassador: Lidia Elisabeth Hayek-Weinmann.

Of the United Kingdom in El Salvador (Torre Futura, 14th Floor, Colonia Escalón, San Salvador)
    Ambassador: Bernhard Garside.

Of El Salvador in the USA (1400 16th St., NW, Suite 100, Washington, D.C., 20036)
    Ambassador: Claudia Ivette Canjura de Centeno.

Of the USA in El Salvador (Blvd Santa Elena, Antiguo Cuscatlán, San Salvador)
    Ambassador: Jean Elizabeth Manes.

Of El Salvador to the United Nations
    Ambassador: Rubén Armando Escalante Hasbún.

Of El Salvador to the European Union
    Ambassador: Julia Emma Villatoro Tario.

Further Reading

Lauria-Santiago, Aldo and Binford, Leigh, (eds) *Landscapes of Struggle: Politics, Society and Community in El Salvador.* 2004
National Statistical Office: Dirección General de Estadística y Censos, Av. Juan Bertis No. 79, Ciudad Delgado, San Salvador.

Equatorial Guinea

República de Guinea Ecuatorial (Republic of Equatorial Guinea)

Capital: Malabo
Population projection, 2020: 1·41m.
GNI per capita, 2017: (PPP$) 19,513
HDI/world rank, 2017: 0·591/141
Internet domain extension: .gq

Key Historical Events

Equatorial Guinea consists of the island of Bioko, for centuries called Fernando Pó; other smaller islands and the mainland territory of Rio Muni. Fernando Pó was named after the Portuguese navigator Fernão do Pó. The island was ruled for three centuries by Portugal until 1778 when it was ceded to Spain. For some decades after taking possession, Spain did not have a strong presence. Britain established a naval base at Clarence (later Santa Isabel), which was central to the suppression of slave trading over a wide area. Spain asserted its rule from the 1840s when cocoa was cultivated on European-owned plantations using imported African labour. This traffic led to an international scandal in 1930 when Liberians were found to be held in virtual slavery. Later many Nigerians were employed, often in poor conditions.

African nationalist movements began in the 1950s. Internal self-government was granted in 1963 and in 1968 the colony gained independence. The two parts of Equatorial Guinea were united under Macías Nguema who established single-party rule. During his bloody dictatorship up to a third of the population was either killed or left the country. Macías was declared President-for-Life in July 1972 but was overthrown by a military coup on 3 Aug. 1979, which saw Obiang Nguema assume power.

A constitution approved by a referendum on 3 Aug. 1982 restored some institutions but a Supreme Military Council remained the sole political body until constitutional rule was resumed on 12 Oct. 1982. Obiang remained as head of state. The first multi-party elections were held in 1993, although they were boycotted by the opposition amid claims of electoral fraud. In 1996 large-scale oil and gas reserves were discovered and by the early years of the 21st century Equatorial Guinea had one of the fastest-growing economies in the world. Obiang won successive presidential elections in 1989, 1996, 2002, 2009 and 2016, despite international criticism of his authoritarian rule.

Territory and Population

The mainland part of Equatorial Guinea is bounded in the north by Cameroon, east and south by Gabon, and west by the Gulf of Guinea, in which lie the islands of Bioko (called Macías Nguema from 1973 to 1979 and before that Fernando Pó) and Annobón (called Pagalu from 1973 to 1979). The total area is 28,051 sq. km (10,831 sq. miles). Although the population at the last census in 2015 was given as 1,225,377, the United Nations does not consider this to be an accurate figure.

The UN gives a projected population for 2020 of 1·41m.

In 2011, 39·9% of the population were urban.

The seven provinces are grouped into two regions—Continental (C), chief town Bata; and Insular (I), chief town Malabo—with areas and 2015 provisional census populations as follows:

	Area (sq. km)	Population	Chief town
Annobón (I)	17	5,314	San Antonio de Palea
Bioko Norte (I)	776	300,374	Malabo
Bioko Sur (I)	1,241	34,674	Luba
Centro Sur (C)	9,931	141,986	Evinayong

(continued)

	Area (sq. km)	Population	Chief town
Kié-Ntem (C)	3,943	183,664	Ebebiyin
Litoral (C)	6,665[1]	367,348	Bata
Wele-Nzas (C)	5,478	192,017	Mongomo

[1]Including the adjacent islets of Corisco, Elobey Grande and Elobey Chico (17 sq. km).

In 2014 the capital, Malabo, had an estimated population of 145,000. In 2015 the new purpose-built, rainforest city of Djibloho was inaugurated, with a view to it replacing Malabo as the national capital in years to come.

The main ethnic group on the mainland is the Fang, which comprises 85% of the total population; there are several minority groups along the coast and adjacent islets. On Bioko the indigenous inhabitants (Bubis) constitute 60% of the population there, the balance being mainly Fang and coast people. On Annobón the indigenous inhabitants are the descendants of Portuguese slaves and still speak a Portuguese patois. The official languages are French, Portuguese and Spanish.

Social Statistics

2008 estimates: births, 25,000; deaths, 10,000. Rates (2008 estimates, per 1,000 population); birth, 38·0; death, 15·0. Life expectancy (2013): male, 51·7 years; female, 54·6. Annual population growth rate, 2000–08, 2·8%. Infant mortality, 2010, 81 per 1,000 live births; fertility rate, 2008, 5·3 births per woman.

Climate

The climate is equatorial, with alternate wet and dry seasons. In Rio Muni, the wet season lasts from Dec. to Feb.

Constitution and Government

A Constitution was approved in a plebiscite in Aug. 1982 and was amended in Jan. 1995. It provided for an 11-member Council of State, and for a 41-member House of Representatives of the People. The President presides over a Council of Ministers.

On 12 Oct. 1987 a single new political party was formed as the *Partido Democrático de Guinea Ecuatorial*. A referendum on 17 Nov. 1991 approved the institution of multi-party democracy, and a law to this effect was passed in Jan. 1992. The *Cámara de los Diputados* (*Chamber of Deputies*) has 100 seats, with members elected for a five-year term by proportional representation in multi-member constituencies. In Nov. 2011 further constitutional amendments were approved by referendum. Official results indicated 97·7% support and turnout of 91·8%, although opposition parties alleged fraud. The amendments relaxed restrictions on the number of terms the *President* can serve and on the age of incumbents (previously set at between 40 and 75 years old), and provide for the creation of a *Senate*. The Senate currently has 72 members of whom 55 are elected and 15 appointed by the president, with two other *ex officio* members.

A new position of *Vice President* was established, to be appointed by the President.

National Anthem

'Caminemos pisando las sendas' ('Let us journey treading the pathways'); words by A. N. Miyongo, tune anonymous.

Recent Elections

Presidential elections were held on 24 April 2016. President Teodoro Obiang Nguema Mbasogo of the Democratic Party of Equatorial Guinea (PDGE) won with 93·7% of the vote against Avelino Mochache Benga of the Union of the Centre Right (UCD) with 1·5% and Buenaventura Monsuy Asumu of

© Springer Nature Limited 2020
Palgrave Macmillan (ed.), *The Statesman's Yearbook 2020*,
https://doi.org/10.1057/978-1-349-95940-2_67

the Convergence for Social Democracy (CPDS) also with 1·5%. Four other candidates took less than 1·0% of the vote each. Turnout was 93·0%.

Legislative elections took place on 12 Nov. 2017. The ruling PDGE won 99 of the 100 seats in the Chamber of Deputies and all 55 directly-elected seats in the Senate. All 15 appointed members of the Senate were also from the PDGE. The remaining seat in the Chamber of Deputies was obtained by Citizens for Innovation. Turnout was 84·0%.

Current Government

President of the Supreme Military Council: Brig.-Gen. Teodoro Obiang Nguema Mbasogo; b. 1942 (PDGE; in office since 1979, most recently re-elected in April 2016).

Vice President, in Charge of Defence and Security: Teodoro Nguema Obiang Mangue.

In Feb. 2019 the government comprised:

Prime Minister, in Charge of Administrative Co-ordination: Francisco Pascual Obama Asue (PDGE; sworn in 23 June 2016).

First Deputy Prime Minister, and Minister of Interior and Local Corporations, in Charge of the Political Sector and Democracy: Clemente Engonga Nguema Onguene. *Second Deputy Prime Minister, in Charge of Relations with Parliament and Judicial Affairs:* Ángel Mesie Mibuy. *Third Deputy Prime Minister, in Charge of Human Rights:* Alfonso Nsue Mokuy.

Minister of State to the Presidency in Charge of Missions: Alejandro Evuna Owono Asangono. *Minister of State to the Presidency in Charge of Presidential Security:* Gen. Antonio Mba Nguema. *Minister of State to the Presidency of the Government in Charge of Regional Integration:* Baltasar Engonga Edjo. *Minister of State in Charge of National Security:* Nicolás Obama Nchama. *Minister of State in Charge of Health and Welfare:* Salomón Nguema Owono. *Minister of the Presidency, in Charge of External Security:* Juan-Antonio Bibang Nchuchuma. *Minister-Secretary General of the Presidency of the Government:* Baltasar Esono Oworo Nfono.

Minister of Foreign Affairs and Co-operation: Simeón Oyono Esono Angüe. *Justice, Religious Affairs and Penitentiary Institutions:* Salvador Ondo Ncumu. *National Defence:* Alejandro Bacale Ncogo. *Finance, Economy and Planning:* Lucas Abaga Nchama. *Education, Higher Education and Sports:* Jesús Engonga Ndong. *Public Works, Housing and Town Planning:* Diosdado Nsue Medja. *Labour, Employment Promotion and Social Security:* Celestino-Bonifacio Bakale Obiang. *Agriculture, Livestock, Forests and the Environment:* Nicolás Houtonji Acapo. *Fisheries and Water Resources:* Adoración Salas Chonco. *Mines and Hydrocarbons:* Gabriel Mbega Obiang Lima. *Industry and Energy:* Miguel Ekua Ondo. *Information, Press and Radio:* Eugenio Nze Obiang. *Social Affairs and Gender Equality:* María Consuelo Nguema Oyana. *Transport, Postal Services and Telecommunications:* Eucario Bacale Angüe. *Public Service and Administrative Reform:* Faustino Ndong Esono Eyang. *Trade and Promotion of Small and Medium-Sized Businesses:* Pastor Micha Ondó Bile. *Civil Aviation:* Leandro Mico Angüe. *Culture, Tourism and Promotion of Handicrafts:* Rufino Ndong Esono Nchama.

Government Website: http://www.guineaecuatorialpress.com

Current Leaders

Brig.-Gen. Teodoro Obiang Nguema Mbasogo

Position
President

Introduction
Brig.-Gen. Teodoro Obiang Nguema Mbasogo has been president of Equatorial Guinea since Aug. 1979, when he led a coup d'état against the dictatorial regime of his uncle, Macías Nguema. After introducing some liberalizing reforms, Obiang himself adopted an authoritarian form of government, leading to widespread allegations of civil rights abuses and electoral fraud. The discovery of major fossil fuel reserves in the mid-1990s created an economic boom, although Obiang has been criticized for the government's lack of transparency in administering this new wealth.

Early Life
Obiang, an ethnic Fang, was born on 5 June 1942 into the Esangui clan of Acoacán. He undertook military training in Spain and, following the election of his uncle as president of the newly independent country, was made a lieutenant. He had stints as governor of Bioko, presidential aide-de-camp and head of the military, while Macías Nguema's regime became increasingly

repressive, with around a third of the population leaving the country during the 1970s.

In Aug. 1979 Obiang ousted his uncle, who was subsequently put on trial and executed.

Career in Office
On assuming the presidency on 3 Aug. 1979 it was hoped that Obiang would implement a more liberal and democratic approach. One of his first acts was to call an amnesty on refugees and to free 5,000 political prisoners. However, he retained many of his uncle's powers and soon came under criticism. Local and national political appointments have been blighted by nepotism, which has led to some interfamilial feuding within the political and military establishments.

The discovery of large oil and gas reserves off Bioko in the mid-1990s led to a massive upturn in the economy. However, it has been widely claimed that the benefits of this oil money have failed to reach the population at large. The IMF and the World Bank demanded increased transparency concerning government oil revenues, which Obiang claimed were a state secret, and warned against an over-reliance on the limited oil reserves.

The country's first multi-party elections in 1993 were won by Obiang's Democratic Party of Equatorial Guinea (PDGE), but boycotted by most of the opposition parties. Then, in the presidential election in Feb. 1996, he was returned with a reported 99% of the vote. At the presidential election of Dec. 2002 he again claimed over 97% of the vote and opposition parties accused the government of vote rigging. Obiang's treatment of opposition politicians received condemnation from, among others, the European Union and Amnesty International and he was accused of using torture on political prisoners. There were also high-profile public trials such as the one in 2002 that resulted in the one-year imprisonment of opposition leader Fabian Nseu Guema for insulting Obiang on a website. In Nov. 2009 Obiang was again re-elected overwhelmingly as president in polling that was denounced by opposition figures as fraudulent and manipulated.

In foreign policy, Obiang has been in dispute with Gabon over the latter's long-term occupation of Mbagne, an island in the Bay of Corisco thought to contain further significant oil supplies. In 2002 he signed an agreement with Nigeria for the development of the Zafiro-Ekanga oil field along their joint maritime border.

In 2004 a plane flying from Zimbabwe was intercepted after Obiang announced it was carrying mercenaries preparing a coup against him. Those accused of involvement included Mark Thatcher (son of former British prime minister Margaret Thatcher), who was arrested in South Africa and later fined and given a suspended prison term, and British mercenary Simon Mann, arrested in Zimbabwe. Obiang claimed that the arrests were evidence of a plot by the secret services of the USA, UK and Spain to overthrow him. In Feb. 2008 Mann was extradited from Zimbabwe to stand trial for his alleged role in the coup and in July was sentenced to 34 years' imprisonment. However, he was granted a presidential pardon in Nov. 2009 on humanitarian grounds.

According to official results, voters in a referendum in Nov. 2011 overwhelmingly approved a new constitution based on the US presidential system, including a new vice presidential office and Senate and a limitation on presidential terms of office. However, opposition figures dismissed the changes as a sham. In April 2016 Obiang took 94% of the vote at presidential elections, which were again deemed to be flawed, to secure a further term. The PDGE meanwhile retained its dominance in successive parliamentary elections, most recently in Nov. 2017, although foreign observers have claimed serious irregularities in polling. Furthermore, in May 2018 the Supreme Court upheld a ban on the main opposition Citizens for Innovation party for alleged involvement in electoral violence.

In 2011 Obiang served as chair of the African Union.

Defence

In 2011 defence expenditure totalled an estimated US$8m. (around US$12 per capita).

Army
The Army consists of three infantry battalions with (2011) 1,100 personnel. There is also a paramilitary Guardia Civil.

Navy
A small force, numbering an estimated 120 in 2011 and based at Malabo and Bata, operates eight patrol and coastal combatants (although their serviceability is in doubt).

Air Force
There are four combat-capable aircraft and six attack helicopters. Personnel (2011), 100.

Economy

In 2014 agriculture accounted for 1·3% of GDP, industry 72·1% and services 26·6%.

Equatorial Guinea featured among the ten most corrupt countries in the world in a 2018 survey of 180 countries carried out by the anti-corruption organization Transparency International.

Overview
Equatorial Guinea has had one of the world's fastest-expanding economies since the discovery of oil in the 1990s, with double or triple digit growth every year from 1992 to 2004. It is the third largest oil producer in sub-Saharan Africa, behind Nigeria and Angola, and substantial gas reserves have also been discovered. Hydrocarbon exports were valued at US$11bn. in 2014.

The oil boom generated inflation averaging 4·9% annually between 2000 and 2014. However, a slowdown in hydrocarbon production, coupled with lower world commodity prices, saw GDP growth fall from an annual average of 27% between 1996 and 2009 to −2·8% between 2009 and 2015. Non-hydrocarbon growth has remained positive, with public infrastructure investment and private housing construction the main drivers.

Despite having the highest level of per capita income in sub-Saharan Africa, living standards for the majority of the population remain poor. Although the economy is equipped to make socio-economic progress, stronger institutional capacity is needed to direct resources to priority areas. The government's development agenda, *Horizon 2020*, focuses on medium-term poverty reduction and economic diversification.

Currency
On 2 Jan. 1985 the country joined the Franc Zone and the *ekpwele* was replaced by the *franc CFA* (XAF) which now has a parity value of 655·957 francs CFA to one euro. Foreign exchange reserves were US$1,416m. in June 2005 and total money supply was 209,768m. francs CFA. Inflation was 1·4% in 2016 and 0·7% in 2017.

Budget
In 2013 revenue was 3,502·0bn. francs CFA and expenditure 4,178·5bn. francs CFA. Tax revenue accounted for 86·2% of revenues in 2013; capital expenditure accounted for 81·7% of total expenditures.

Performance
Equatorial Guinea was one of the world's fastest-growing economies during much of the 1990s and 2000s thanks to the rapid expansion of its oil sector. The economy grew by a record 148·0% in 1997. In both 2007 and 2008 growth was among the highest in the world, at 15·3% and 17·8% respectively. In 2010 the global downturn resulted in the economy contracting by 8·9% that year. More recently, owing to a decline in oil revenue, another recession saw the economy shrink by 9·1% in 2015, 8·6% in 2016 and 3·2% in 2017. Total GDP in 2017 was US$12·5bn.

Banking and Finance
The Banque des Etats de l'Afrique Centrale (*Governor*, Abbas Mahamat Tolli) became the bank of issue in Jan. 1985. There were five registered banks in 2014.

Energy and Natural Resources

Environment
Carbon dioxide emissions from the consumption of energy in 2011 were the equivalent of 7·7 tonnes per capita.

Electricity
Installed capacity was an estimated 41,000 kW in 2011. Production was around 97m. kWh in 2011; consumption per capita in 2011 was approximately 135 kWh.

Oil and Gas
Oil production started in 1992 and in 2012 totalled 13·2m. tonnes, up from 5·8m. tonnes in 2000. There were proven reserves of 1·7bn. bbls in 2012.

Since oil in commercial quantities was discovered in 1995 the total stock of foreign direct investment has risen from US$0·2bn. to US$13·5bn. in 2012. Natural gas reserves were 37bn. cu. metres in 2013.

Minerals
There is some small-scale alluvial gold production.

Agriculture
There were an estimated 130,000 ha. of arable land in 2007 and 90,000 ha. of permanent crops. Subsistence farming predominates. In 2007 the agricultural population was approximately 425,000 of which about 164,000 were economically active. The major crops (estimated production, 2013 estimates, in 1,000 tonnes) are: sweet potatoes, 92; cassava, 70; plantains, 37; palm fruit oil, 36; bananas, 34; coconuts, 8; palm oil, 6; coffee, 4. Plantations in the hinterland have been abandoned by their Spanish former owners and, except for cocoa and coffee, commercial agriculture is in serious difficulties. Livestock, 2013 estimates: cattle, 5,300; goats, 9,500; pigs, 6,700; sheep, 40,000.

Forestry
In 2015 forests covered 1·57m. ha., or 56% of the total land area. Timber production in 2011 totalled 972,000 cu. metres.

Fisheries
The total catch in 2012 was 10,758 tonnes (mainly from sea fishing).

Industry

The once-flourishing light industry collapsed under the Macías regime. Oil production is now the major activity. Production of veneer sheets, 2012 estimate, 11,000 cu. metres. Food processing is also being developed.

Labour
In 2010 the estimated economically active population was 270,000 (69% males). The wage-earning non-agricultural workforce is small.

International Trade

Imports and Exports
Imports for 2007 came to US$3,098m.; exports in 2007 were valued at US$10,095m.

The main import suppliers are the Netherlands, Spain and China. The leading export markets are China, South Korea and Spain. Principal import commodities are machinery and transport equipment, and petroleum and petroleum products; principal export commodities are petroleum, cocoa and timber.

Communications

Roads
In 2015 the road network covered an estimated 2,700 km, around two-thirds of which are paved.

Civil Aviation
There is an international airport at Malabo. There were international flights in 2010 to Addis Ababa, Casablanca, Douala, Frankfurt, Madrid, Nairobi and Paris. In 2009 Malabo handled 283,981 passengers.

Shipping
Bata is the main port, handling mainly timber. The other ports are Luba, formerly San Carlos, on Bioko, and Malabo, Evinayong and Mbini on the mainland. In Jan. 2014 there were 11 ships of 300 GT or over registered, totalling 11,000 GT. Equatorial Guinea is a 'flag of convenience' country.

Telecommunications
In 2010 there were 13,500 main (fixed) telephone lines. In the same year mobile phone subscribers numbered 399,000 (570·1 per 1,000 persons). There were 60·0 internet users per 1,000 inhabitants in 2010.

Social Institutions

Out of 178 countries analysed in the 2017 *Fragile States Index*—a list published jointly by the Fund for Peace and *Foreign Policy* magazine— Equatorial Guinea was ranked the 51st most vulnerable to conflict or collapse. The index is based on 12 indicators of state vulnerability across social, political and economic categories.

Justice

The Constitution guarantees an independent judiciary. The Supreme Tribunal, the highest court of appeal, is located at Malabo. There are Courts of First Instance and Courts of Appeal at Malabo and Bata. The death penalty is legal; nine executions in Jan. 2014 were the first since 2010. A temporary moratorium on the death penalty was declared in Feb. 2014.

Education

In 2012 there were 2,400 teachers for 42,000 children in pre-primary schools; 3,500 teachers for 92,000 pupils in primary schools; and (2005) 26,000 secondary pupils with 1,300 teachers. The National University of Equatorial Guinea, founded in 1995, had 6,500 students in 2010–11. Adult literacy was an estimated 93·3% in 2009 (male, 97·0%; female, 89·8%).

Health

In 2010 there were 21 hospital beds per 10,000 inhabitants. There were 3·0 physicians for every 10,000 population over the period 2000–10 and 5·3 nursing and midwifery personnel per 10,000.

In *Water: At What Cost? The State of the World's Water 2016*, WaterAid reported that 52·1% of the population does not have access to safe water—the second highest percentage of any nation.

Religion

According to the Pew Research Center's Forum on Religion & Public Life, an estimated 81% of the population in 2010 was Roman Catholic. There are also small Protestant and Muslim minorities.

Culture

Press

There are no daily newspapers, although there are a number of periodicals that are published at varying degrees of regularity.

Tourism

The tourist industry is undeveloped and the tourism infrastructure is almost non-existent.

Diplomatic Representatives

Of Equatorial Guinea in the United Kingdom (13 Park Pl., London, SW1A 1LP)
Ambassador: Vacant.
Chargé d'Affaires a.i.: Maria Jesús Diallo Besari.

Of the United Kingdom in Equatorial Guinea
Ambassador: Rowan James Laxton (resides in Yaoundé, Cameroon).

Of Equatorial Guinea in the USA (2020 16th St., NW, Washington, D.C., 20009)
Ambassador: Miguel Ntutumu Evuna Andeme.

Of the USA in Equatorial Guinea (Malabo II Highway, Malabo)
Ambassador: Julie Furuta-Toy.

Of Equatorial Guinea to the United Nations
Ambassador: Anatolio Ndong Mba.

Of Equatorial Guinea to the European Union
Ambassador: Carmelo Nvono-Ncá.

Further Reading

Liniger-Goumaz, M., *Guinea Ecuatorial: Bibliografía General.* 7 vols. 1974–91.—*Small is Not Always Beautiful: The Story of Equatorial Guinea.* 1988.—*Historical Dictionary of Equatorial Guinea.* 2000
National Statistical Office: Dirección General de Estadísticas y Cuentas Nacionales.
Website (Spanish only): http://www.dgecnstat-ge.org

Eritrea

Hagere Ertra (State of Eritrea)

Capital: Asmara
Population projection, 2020: 5·43m.
GNI per capita, 2017: (PPP$) 1,750
HDI/world rank, 2017: 0·440/179
Internet domain extension: .er

Key Historical Events

Modern-day Eritrea and northern Ethiopia was known by Egyptian Pharaohs as the Land of Punt, a region rich in precious resources including gold and ivory. Settlers from southern Arabia brought Semitic languages and stone-building techniques. Archaeological evidence suggests Asmara, the present Eritrean capital, was the site of a settled agricultural community from at least 800 BC. During the sixth century BC Arab merchants, who traded ivory and slaves, inhabited Eritrea's coastal strip. This area and the Tigray highlands subsequently formed part of the Aksumite kingdom. At its height in the sixth century AD the kingdom, which had embraced Christianity, controlled much of the Red Sea coast from the port of Adulis (modern Zula) and traded with Mediterranean powers, as well as Persia and India.

As Aksum declined in the eighth and ninth centuries, Eritrea increasingly came under Islamic influence. The kingdom of Medri Bahri (Land of the Sea) became established around 1100, centred on Debarwa—close to Asmara. The Ottoman Empire conquered parts of Medri Bahri during the 16th century, although other influences held sway in the southeast, including the Sultanates of Adal and Aussa.

The opening of the Suez Canal in 1869 intensified the regional scramble for influence among European powers. Land around the Bay of Assab was sold to the Genoa-based Rubattino Shipping Company and developed into a port and coaling station. In the disorder that followed the death of Ethiopia's Emperor Yohannes IV in 1889, the Italian general Oreste Baratieri occupied part of the Red Sea coast and declared the new colony of Eritrea, initially centred on the port of Massawa, a former Egyptian garrison. Asmara, which became the capital in 1897, attracted considerable investment and large numbers of Italian immigrants. Under Italian dictator Benito Mussolini's rule during the late 1920s and 1930s, Eritrea was chosen to be the industrial centre of Italian East Africa—an ambition that was halted by the Second World War. British Empire forces captured Eritrea in 1941 and it remained a British protectorate for the next decade.

In 1952 the United Nations sanctioned Eritrea's federation with Ethiopia. In 1962 Ethiopia became a unitary state and Eritrea was incorporated as a province. Eritreans began an armed struggle for independence under the leadership of the Eritrean People's Liberation Front (EPLF), which culminated in the capture of Asmara in May 1991. Thereafter the EPLF maintained a *de facto* independent administration recognized by the Ethiopian government. Sovereignty was proclaimed on 24 May 1993. In 1999 fighting broke out along the border with Ethiopia, following a series of skirmishes the previous year. After the failure of international mediation, a 13-month truce ended in May 2000 when Ethiopia launched a major offensive. In June both sides agreed to an Organization of African Unity peace deal.

In 2003 the UN border commission's award of the disputed town of Badame to Eritrea was rejected by Ethiopia, leading to a standoff between the two nations. UN helicopters were banned from Eritrean airspace in Nov. 2005. The following month Eritrea expelled all North American and European UN representatives, with the UN threatening sanctions against both countries unless they adhered to the 2000 peace plan. Meanwhile, the international commission in The Hague judged that Eritrea's 1998 attacks on Ethiopia breached international law.

Eritrean relations with the UN deteriorated throughout 2006, with five UN staff expelled on charges of spying in Sept. In Nov. 2007 Eritrea agreed to a new judgment by the international boundary commission, which Ethiopia rejected. In July 2008 the UN Security Council voted to end its peacekeeping mission along the border. The previous month there were skirmishes between troops from Eritrea and Djibouti over the disputed borderlands of Ras Doumeira. In Dec. 2009 Eritrea was the subject of UN sanctions amid accusations that it was backing Islamist insurgents in Somalia. In June 2010 Djibouti and Eritrea pledged to resolve their dispute diplomatically. Regional tensions persisted, however, with Ethiopia declaring in April 2011 its support for Eritrean rebel groups campaigning for the overthrow of President Afewerki.

In June 2015 the UN accused the Eritrean government of systematic human rights abuses.

In July 2018 Afewerki and Ethiopia's Prime Minister Abiy Ahmed issued a joint declaration formally ending their countries' border conflict. Full diplomatic relations were restored and the joint border was reopened to people, goods and services.

Territory and Population

Eritrea is bounded in the northeast by the Red Sea, southeast by Djibouti, south by Ethiopia and west by Sudan. Some 300 islands form the Dahlak Archipelago, most of them uninhabited. For the dispute with Yemen over the islands of Greater and Lesser Hanish *see* YEMEN: Territory and Population. Its area is 117,600 sq. km (45,410 sq. miles), including 16,600 sq. km (6,410 sq. miles) of inland waters. There has not been a census since Eritrea became independent in 1993. United Nations population estimate, 2013, 4·65m.; density, 46 per sq. km. 22·1% of the population were urban in 2011.

The UN gives a projected population for 2020 of 5·43m.

In 2009 there were around 200,000 Eritreans living abroad, more than half of them as refugees in Sudan.

There are six regions: Anseba, Debub, Debubawi Keyih Bahri, Gash Barka, Maekel and Semenawi Keyih Bahri. The capital is Asmara (2014 estimated population, 775,000). Other large towns are Keren, Teseney and Mendefera. An agreement of July 1993 gives Ethiopia rights to use the ports of Assab and Massawa.

49% of the population speak Tigrinya and 32% Tigré, and there are seven other indigenous languages. Arabic is spoken on the coast and along the Sudanese border, and English is used in secondary schools. Arabic and Tigrinya are the official languages.

Social Statistics

2008 births (estimates), 182,000; deaths, 42,000. Estimated birth rate in 2008 was 37·0 per 1,000 population; estimated death rate, 12·4. Annual population growth rate, 2000–08, 3·7%. Life expectancy at birth, 2013, was 60·5 years for males and 65·2 years for females. Infant mortality, 2010, 42 per 1,000 live births; fertility rate, 2008, 4·6 births per woman.

Climate

Massawa, Jan. 78°F (25·6°C), July 94°F (34·4°C). Annual rainfall 8" (193 mm).

Constitution and Government

A referendum to approve independence was held on 23–25 April 1993. The electorate was 1,173,506. 99·8% of votes cast were in favour.

The transitional government consists of the *President* and a 150-member *National Assembly*. It elects the President, who in turn appoints the *State Council* made up of 14 ministers and the governors of the ten provinces. The President chairs both the State Council and the National Assembly. Eritrea is a single-party state.

National Anthem

'Ertra, Ertra, Ertra' ('Eritrea, Eritrea, Eritrea'); words by S. Beraki, tune by I. Meharezghi and A. Tesfatsion.

© Springer Nature Limited 2020
Palgrave Macmillan (ed.), *The Statesman's Yearbook 2020*,
https://doi.org/10.1057/978-1-349-95940-2_68

Recent Elections

Isaias Afewerki was elected president by the National Assembly in May 1993. Direct elections have never been held. National Assembly elections, postponed in 1998, were set to take place before the end of 2003 but have been put back indefinitely. Parliament has not met since 2002. In the meantime several dissident politicians have been jailed.

Current Government

President: Issaias Afewerki; b. 1945 (People's Front for Democracy and Justice/PFDJ, formerly the Eritrean People's Liberation Front/EPLF; elected 22 May 1993 and re-elected in May 1997).

In Feb. 2019 ministers in the State Council were:

Minister of Agriculture: Arefaine Berhe. *Defence:* Sebhat Ephrem. *Education:* Semere Russom. *Energy and Mining:* Ahmed Haj Ali. *Finance:* Berhane Abrehe. *Foreign Affairs:* Osman Saleh. *Health:* Amina Nurhussein. *Information:* Ali Abdu. *Justice:* Fozia Hashim. *Labour and Human Welfare:* Salma Hassen. *Land, Water and Environment:* Tesfai Ghebreselassie. *Marine Resources:* Tewoldi Kelati. *National Development:* Giorgis Teklemikael. *Public Works:* Abraha Asfaha. *Tourism:* Askalu Menkerios. *Trade and Industry:* Estifanos Habte. *Transport and Communications:* Woldemikael Abraha.

Ministry of Information: http://www.shabait.com

Current Leaders

Issaias Afewerki

Position
President

Introduction
Issaias Afewerki has been president of Eritrea since it achieved independence from Ethiopia in 1993, having been a leading campaigner for secession since the mid-1960s. However, his tenure has been marked by human rights abuses and the imprisonment of political opponents. In foreign policy he oversaw a state of war with neighbouring Ethiopia from 1998 (and was also accused of destabilizing the wider African sub-region) until July 2018 when a peace treaty finally ended the protracted territorial dispute.

Early Life
Issaias Afewerki was born in 1945 in Asmara, Eritrea's capital, which was then under British administration. Eritrea became part of Ethiopia in 1962 and in 1966 Afewerki joined the secessionist Eritrean Liberation Front (ELF). Having received military training in China, he became a deputy divisional commander. In 1970 he helped found the Eritrean People's Liberation Front (EPLF), becoming its general secretary in 1987.

Following the collapse of the Mengistu military regime in Ethiopia in 1991, the new government agreed to a referendum on Eritrean independence. The referendum was held in 1993 and Eritrea declared independence in May of that year. Eritrea's National Assembly selected Afewerki as the country's first president.

Career in Office
The EPLF initially suggested a multi-party political system and in the early stages of his tenure Afewerki advocated close economic relations with Ethiopia. However, in Feb. 2002 the National Assembly, composed of EPLF representatives, refused to ratify a bill on the establishment of new political parties. Multi-party elections, previously scheduled for the end of 2001, were shelved.

In 2001 Afewerki authorized the arrest of critical journalists and political opponents. The move was condemned internationally and the Italian ambassador, who had voiced concerns over human rights violations, was expelled. International aid was consequently cut. In 2002 Afewerki set out his plans for the creation of a 'responsible' press, soon after an opposition party—the Eritrean People's Liberation Front Democratic Party—had emerged to challenge him. The party was believed to have been co-founded by Mesfin Hagos, Afewerki's former defence minister.

In 1998 border disputes escalated into full-scale war between Ethiopian and Eritrean forces which resulted in 70,000 deaths. A ceasefire was agreed in June 2000, with Ethiopia withdrawing its forces under UN supervision. A

formal peace treaty was signed in Dec. 2000. Tensions remained, particularly concerning the ownership of the small border settlement of Badame, and in May 2001 the countries agreed to abide by the decision of an international boundary commission. The commission awarded Badame to Eritrea, but Ethiopia refused to accept the decision. Fears of a renewed conflict mounted in late 2005 after Eritrea expelled UN observers policing the militarized border region.

Relations with the UN deteriorated further during the autumn of 2006 as Eritrea expelled several UN peacekeeping staff for allegedly spying and moved troops into the buffer zone on the Ethiopian border in violation of the ceasefire. At the same time, the Eritrean government was accused of providing arms and supplies to the Islamist militias confronting the Ethiopian-backed transitional government in Somalia. In Nov. 2007 Eritrea accepted a border demarcation proposal by an independent boundary commission but Ethiopia rejected it. In Jan. 2008 the UN Security Council extended the mandate of its peacekeeping mission on the Eritrean-Ethiopian border for a further six months (despite Eritrean opposition), but brought it to a close at the end of July. Relations deteriorated again in March–April 2011 as Ethiopia accused Eritrea of terrorist infiltration and then declared openly that it would support Eritrean rebel forces aiming to overthrow Afewerki.

Afewerki meanwhile oversaw the restoration of diplomatic ties with Sudan and Djibouti, although relations with both countries have remained unsettled. Eritrea claimed that Islamic fundamentalist groups active within the country received backing from Khartoum, and also accused Djibouti of providing military support to Ethiopia, a claim denied by Djibouti. In June 2008 there were border clashes between troops from Djibouti and Eritrea following several weeks of rising tensions. However, following the imposition of sanctions against Eritrea by the UN Security Council in Dec. 2009, both sides agreed in June 2010 to resolve their border issues peacefully. In mid-2009 the African Union (AU) rebuked Afewerki's regime for continuing to aid Islamist insurgents in Somalia, so endangering civilians and AU peacekeeping forces, and the UN Security Council similarly acted against Eritrea with further sanctions in Dec. 2011.

In early 2013 there were reports of a brief occupation of the ministry of information by army mutineers demanding the release of political prisoners before troops loyal to Afewerki regained control of the building. In a separate incident, several military officers sought asylum in Saudi Arabia.

In 2016 Reporters Without Borders, an international non-governmental organization promoting freedom of information, ranked Eritrea in last place in its *World Press Freedom Index* for the ninth year in a row.

More positively, in July 2018 the state of war between Eritrea and Ethiopia was brought to an end following a diplomatic rapprochement between Afewerki and Abiy Ahmed, the newly appointed Ethiopian prime minister. Also, in Nov., the UN Security Council lifted the sanctions on Eritrea imposed in 2009.

Defence

Conscription is compulsory for both males and females. In theory they must complete 18 months of service but in reality national service is often indefinite. The total strength of all forces was estimated at 201,750 in 2011.

Defence expenditure totalled an estimated US$78m. in 2011 (approximately US$13 per capita and around 3% of GDP).

Army

The Army had a strength of around 200,000 in 2011. There were also approximately 120,000 reservists available.

Navy

Most of the former Ethiopian Navy is now in Eritrean hands. The main base is at Massawa. Personnel numbered 1,400 in 2011.

Air Force

Personnel numbers were estimated at 350 in 2011. There were 20 combat-capable aircraft including MiG-29s and Su-27s.

International Relations

A border dispute between Eritrea and Ethiopia broke out in May 1998. Eritrean troops took over the border town of Badame after a skirmish between Ethiopian police units and armed men from Eritrea. Ethiopia maintained that Badame and Sheraro, a nearby town, had always been part of Ethiopia and called Eritrea's action an invasion. An agreement ending hostilities was signed in June 2000, followed by a peace accord in Dec. A buffer zone was created to separate the armies but tensions still arose from time to time, notably in late 2005 following a further dispute between the two countries over Badame. There were also border skirmishes in June 2016. Then, in July 2018, the leaders of the two countries signed a joint declaration formally ending the border conflict.

Economy

In 2012 public administration and defence contributed 27·2% to GDP; followed by trade and hotels, 18·8%; agriculture, forestry and fishing, 16·3%; construction, 15·0%; and transport and communications, 12·0%.

Overview

Eritrea is one of the world's poorest countries, with an estimated two-thirds of the population living below the poverty line. Subsistence agriculture is the main economic activity, but it meets only 60–70% of the population's requirements, necessitating food imports. In the five years following Eritrea's declaration of independence in 1993 and after 30 years of war with Ethiopia, the average annual growth rate was 10·9%. However, renewed conflict with Ethiopia from 1998–2000 damaged much of the economic and social infrastructure and displaced much of the population.

A series of external shocks devastated the economy in 2008, including a drought that resulted in a harvest 75% lower than the previous year and prompted emergency imports. However, a subsequent favourable harvest, combined with a boom in gold mining and a fall in inflation from 33·0% in 2009 to 12·7% in 2010, elevated Eritrea to among the fastest-growing economies in Africa in 2011. Annual growth in 2015 was 4·8% compared to 3·4% for sub-Saharan Africa as a whole.

The budget deficit declined slightly to 10·3% of GDP in 2015 from 10·7% in 2014 as a result of increasing revenue from mining projects, improved access to aid and more focused spending programmes. Inflation remained high at 9·0% in 2015, largely because of food supply and foreign exchange vulnerabilities.

Over the medium term, the government aims to increase trade with Middle Eastern and Asian countries, to expand mining activities and the food sector and to develop tourism. However, Eritrea's economic prospects remain challenging in view of the difficult macroeconomic situation, limited physical and human capital, and residual tensions with Ethiopia. The country also continues to be impacted by political isolation and sanctions imposed by the UN Security Council over the government's alleged contribution to insecurity in the Horn of Africa.

Currency

The *nakfa* (ERN) replaced the Ethiopian currency, the *birr*, in 1997. However, its introduction led to tensions with Ethiopia, adversely affecting cross-border trade. Inflation was 9·0% in both 2016 and 2017. Total money supply was 8,063m. nafka in May 2005.

Budget

Revenues in 2008 were 4·46bn. nafka and expenditures 9·84bn. nafka.

Performance

Total GDP in 2013 was US$3·4bn. The economy shrank by 12·4% in 2001 following the end of the conflict with neighbouring Ethiopia but grew by 8·8% in 2002. More recently there was real GDP growth of 2·6% in 2015, 1·9% in 2016 and 5·0% in 2017.

Banking and Finance

The central bank is the National Bank of Eritrea (*Acting Governor*, Kibreab Woldemariam). All banks and financial institutions are state-run. There is a Commercial Bank of Eritrea with 15 branches, an Eritrean Investment and Development Bank with 13 branches, a Housing and Commercial Bank of Eritrea with seven branches and an Insurance Corporation.

In 2010 external debt totalled US$1,010m., representing 48·2% of GNI.

Energy and Natural Resources

Environment

Carbon dioxide emissions from the consumption of energy were the equivalent of 0·1 tonnes per capita in 2011.

Electricity

Installed capacity was an estimated 140,000 kW in 2011. Total production was 337m. kWh in 2011.

Minerals

There are deposits of gold, silver, copper, zinc, sulphur, nickel, chrome and potash. Basalt, limestone, marble, sand and silicates are extracted. Oil exploration is taking place in the Red Sea. Salt production totals 200,000 tonnes annually.

Agriculture

Agricultural land makes up around 75% of the country's land area. There were an estimated 690,000 ha. of arable land in 2013 and 2,000 ha. of permanent crops. 21,000 ha. were equipped for irrigation in 2013.

Main agricultural products, 2013 estimates (in 1,000 tonnes): sorghum, 138; barley, 65; wheat, 30; millet, 26; maize, 20; sesame seeds, 5.

Livestock, 2013 (estimates): sheep, 2·3m.; cattle, 2·1m.; goats, 1·8m.; camels, 370,000; chickens, 1·4m.

Livestock products, 2013 estimates (in 1,000 tonnes): beef and veal, 24; lamb and mutton, 7; goat meat, 6; camel meat, 3; chicken meat, 2; milk, 148.

Forestry

In 2015 forests covered 1·51m. ha., or 15% of the total land area. Timber production in 2011 was 1·27m. cu. metres.

Fisheries

The total catch in 2012 was 4,152 tonnes, exclusively from marine waters.

Industry

Light industry was well developed in the colonial period but capability has declined. Processed food, textiles, leatherwear, building materials, glassware and oil products are produced. Industrial production accounted for 22% of GDP in 2009, with the manufacturing sector providing 6%.

Labour

In 2010 the estimated labour force was 2,230,000 (55% males). Eritrea had 44,000 people living in slavery according to the Walk Free Foundation's 2013 *Global Slavery Index.*

International Trade

Eritrea is dependent on foreign aid for most of its capital expenditure.

Imports and Exports

In 2009 imports (c.i.f.) were valued at US$540m. and exports (f.o.b.) at US$15m. The leading imports are machinery and transport equipment, basic manufactures, and food and live animals. The main exports are drinks, leather and products, textiles and oil products. China is the principal import supplier, ahead of Egypt. China is also the biggest export market, with India the second largest.

Communications

Roads

There are some 14,000 km of roads including a number of asphalted highways. In 2007 there were 6·4 passenger cars per 1,000 inhabitants. About 500 buses operate regular services.

Rail

In 2000 the reconstruction of the 117 km Massawa–Asmara line reached Embatkala, thus opening up an 80 km stretch from Massawa on the coast. In 2003 the line was rebuilt right through to Asmara.

Civil Aviation

There is an international airport at Asmara (Yohannes IV Airport). In 2010 there were scheduled flights to Cairo, Dubai, Frankfurt, Jeddah, Khartoum, Milan, Nairobi, Rome and Sana'a. In 2012 Asmara handled 211,811 passengers (200,248 on international flights) and 2,705 tonnes of freight.

Shipping

Massawa is the main port; Assab used to be the main port for imports to Ethiopia. Both were free ports for Ethiopia until the onset of hostilities. In

Jan. 2014 there were five ships of 300 GT or over registered, totalling 12,000 GT.

Telecommunications

In 2011 there were 58,000 landline telephone subscriptions (equivalent to 10·7 per 1,000 inhabitants) and 241,900 mobile phone subscriptions (or 44·7 per 1,000 inhabitants). In 2013 there were 1,100 fixed internet subscriptions.

Social Institutions

Out of 178 countries analysed in the 2017 *Fragile States Index*—a list published jointly by the Fund for Peace and *Foreign Policy* magazine— Eritrea was ranked the 19th most vulnerable to conflict or collapse. The index is based on 12 indicators of state vulnerability across social, political and economic categories.

Justice

The legal system derives from a decree of May 1993.

Education

Adult literacy was 65% in 2008. In 2007 there were 331,855 pupils and 6,933 teaching staff in primary schools, and 218,369 pupils at secondary schools with 4,425 teaching staff. There were 10,000 students and 1,000 academic staff in tertiary education in 2009–10. In 2006 public expenditure on education came to 2·4% of GNI.

Health

In 2006 there were 12 hospital beds per 10,000 inhabitants. There were five physicians per 100,000 population and 58 nurses and midwifery personnel for every 100,000 population in the period 2000–10.

In *Water: At What Cost? The State of the World's Water 2016*, WaterAid reported that 42·2% of the population does not have access to safe water.

Religion

According to the Pew Research Center's Forum on Religion & Public Life, in 2010 the population was an estimated 63% Christian (mainly Eastern Orthodox but also Catholics, in the south) and 37% Muslim (mainly Sunnis, along the coast and in the north).

Culture

Press

In 2008 there were three government newspapers, one published three times a week and the others once a week. In Sept. 2001 the government closed down the country's eight independent newspapers. In the 2017 *World Press Freedom Index*, compiled by Reporters Without Borders, Eritrea ranked 179th out of the 180 countries covered. A number of journalists have been jailed.

Tourism

There were 107,000 non-resident visitors in 2011, up from 84,000 in 2010.

World Heritage Sites

Asmara: a Modernist City of Africa was inscribed on the UNESCO World Heritage List in 2017.

Diplomatic Representatives

Of Eritrea in the United Kingdom (96 White Lion St., London, N1 9PF)
    Ambassador: Estifanos Habtemariam Ghebreyesus.

Of the United Kingdom in Eritrea (66–68 Mariam Ghimbi St., Zip Code 174, PO Box 5584, Asmara)
    Ambassador: Ian Richards.

Of Eritrea in the USA (1708 New Hampshire Ave., NW, Washington, D.C., 20009)
    Ambassador: Vacant.
    Chargé d'Affaires a.i.: Berhane Gebrehiwet Solomon.

Of the USA in Eritrea (179 Alaa St., POB 211, Asmara)
    Ambassador: Vacant.
    Chargé d'Affaires a.i.: Natalie E. Brown.

Of Eritrea to the United Nations
    Ambassador: Vacant.
    Chargé d'Affaires a.i.: Amanuel Giorgio.

Of Eritrea to the European Union
    Ambassador: Negassi Kassa Tekle.

Further Reading

Connel, D., *Against All Odds: a Chronicle of the Eritrean Revolution.* 1993

Henze, Paul, *Eritrea's War: Confrontation, International Response, Outcome, Prospects.* 2001

Mengisteab, Kidane, *Anatomy of an African Tragedy: Political, Economic and Foreign Policy Crisis in Post-Independence Eritrea.* 2005

Negash, Tekeste and Tronvoll, Kjetil, *Brothers at War: Making Sense of the Eritrean–Ethiopian War.* 2001

Wrong, Michaela, *I Didn't Do It For You: How the World Betrayed a Small African Nation.* 2005

Estonia

Eesti Vabariik (Republic of Estonia)

Capital: Tallinn
Population projection, 2020: 1·30m.
GNI per capita, 2017: (PPP$) 28,993
HDI/world rank, 2017: 0·871/30
Internet domain extension: .ee

Key Historical Events

There is evidence of human habitation from around 11,000 BC. Remnants of a 'comb' pottery culture from 5000 BC show the arrival of the ancestors of the Eestii, one of the first known peoples to inhabit the Baltic's eastern shores and the forerunners of modern Estonians. Before the arrival of Christianity, animism was widespread and the cult of Tharapita (or Taara), a god of war, was popular in northern Estonia and the island of Saaremaa.

The failed Danish invasion of Saaremaa in 1206 under the Bishop of Lund marked the first attempt at the Christianization of Estonia. German invasions began in 1208 with the capture of Otepää in the southeast. Christianization came with Bishop Albert and his Sword Brothers, a military order established in 1202 that became the Livonian Order. Livonia (including southern Estonia) fell to them in 1217. Valdemar II of Denmark invaded the north in 1219, establishing Tanin Lidna (later Tallinn) at Reval on the Gulf of Finland. Danish forces had prevailed against indigenous forces by 1227 and took Saaremaa (Ösel).

In 1238 Wilhelm of Modena, the papal legate, negotiated the re-establishment of Danish power in the north after its seizure by the Sword Brothers, who shared the rest of the land with the prince-bishops of Ösel-Wiek and Dorpat (Tartu). The eastward expansion of the Sword Brothers was checked in 1242 at Lake Peipus by Alexander Nevsky, Prince of Novgorod.

Coastal Swedes arrived from the mid-13th century and a German merchant class emerged in the towns. In the St George's Night Uprising, beginning on 23 April 1343 and lasting until 1345, Estonians rebelled against Danish rule. The peasant army appealed to Swedish Finland for help but was defeated by the Danish vice-regents, who called on the Livonian Order. In 1346 Denmark's Valdemar IV sold his share of Estonia to the Teutonic Knights, who gave control to the Livonian Order.

The Reformation reached Estonia's semi-autonomous cities in the 1520s but met resistance from the Livonian Order. In 1558 Tsar Ivan IV demanded taxes from the bishopric of Dorpat (Tartu) as a pretext to invading the Livonian Confederation and gaining access to the Baltic Sea. The weakened Livonian Order disbanded in 1561. The treaties ending the Livonian War, which ran for 25 years, saw the division of Estonia between Sweden, Denmark and the Kingdom of Poland–Lithuania.

By 1600 Sweden, repelling the incursions of Muscovy, had strengthened its hold over Estland. Sweden's Gustavus Adolphus attempted to build a Reformist Baltic empire, winning all of Estonia in 1629 and reducing the power of German landowners while defending the country from Polish and Russian attacks. He also made education available to the peasants and established a university at Tartu. In 1645 the Danes ceded Ösel to the Swedes. Estonian territories were badly affected by the Great Famine of 1695–97, when over 70,000 people (around 20% of the population) died.

Russian ambitions to establish a Baltic base and Danish resentment of Swedish hegemony led to the Great Northern War (1700–21). Swedish forces won a string of victories under Charles XII, routing Peter the Great's army at Narva in 1700. However, Charles's over-ambitious attack on Poland led to a Swedish collapse. Peter seized Ingria (where he built St Petersburg) and ravaged Livonia. The Swedish defeat at Poltava in 1709 led to Estonia passing to Russia by the 1721 Treaty of Nystad.

Estonia remained dominated by German aristocrats after the reversal of Swedish land seizures and the reinforcement of serfdom. Estonian nationalism emerged in the mid-19th century despite Russian attempts to contain it. Baltic autonomy was severely curtailed, with the Russian language imposed in education and public administration, and Russian nationals parachuted into high office.

After nationalist success in the municipal elections of 1904, many Estonians joined the all-Russia workers' strikes of 1905, which were brutally suppressed. In the ensuing anti-landlord violence, about a fifth of the country's German-owned manors were destroyed by ethnic Estonians. Nicholas II's subsequent October Manifesto allowed for the establishment of political parties in Estonia, giving renewed momentum to the nationalist movement.

After the overthrow of the monarchy in 1917, Russia's provisional government amalgamated Estonia and Estonian-speaking northern Livonia. As the First World War continued into 1918, German forces pushed the Russians eastwards leading to their retreat from Estonia. In the brief period after the Soviet withdrawal and before the arrival of the German army, the Estonian Rescue Committee declared independence on 24 Feb. 1918. However, German troops took Tallinn the following day and the subsequent German occupation lasted until Nov.

The German withdrawal preceded Bolshevik attempts to regain control. However, a defensive campaign, referred to as the Estonian War of Independence, ejected the Russians in May 1919. The Treaty of Tartu on 2 Feb. 1920 saw Russia acknowledge Estonian independence.

In March 1934 this regime was, in turn, overthrown by a quasi-fascist coup. The secret protocol of the Soviet–German agreement of Aug. 1939 assigned Estonia to the Soviet sphere of interest. An ultimatum in June 1940 saw the formation of the Estonian Soviet Socialist Republic but a German occupation lasted from June 1941–Sept. 1944. An attempt to secure national independence quickly crumbled and the return to Soviet control saw the loss of 2,200 sq. km of Estonian territory to Pskov Oblast. There followed a Sovietization programme that lasted until the mid-1980s.

However, with crises emerging all over the Soviet Union, the Estonian Supreme Soviet unilaterally declared a sovereign republic in Nov. 1988. Pro-independence protests were brutally suppressed in Riga and Vilnius (in Latvia and Lithuania respectively) in 1990 on Kremlin orders but a popular referendum in Estonia the following year saw 77·8% vote in favour of independence. As Moscow was reeling from the August Coup of 1991, the Estonian Supreme Council passed a new independence resolution recognized by Moscow on 6 Sept. 1991. Estonia was admitted to the Council of Europe in 1993 and all Russian troops were withdrawn by Aug. 1994, although a sizeable Russian population remains (around a third of the total). Estonia became a member of NATO in March 2004 and the European Union in May 2004.

Territory and Population

Estonia is bounded in the west and north by the Baltic Sea, east by Russia and south by Latvia. There are 1,521 offshore islands, of which the largest are Saaremaa and Hiiumaa, but only 12 are permanently inhabited. Area, 45,227 sq. km (17,462 sq. miles). The census population in Dec. 2011 was 1,294,455 (693,929 females), giving a density of 27·6 per sq. km. In Jan. 2018 the population was estimated at 1,319,133.

The UN gives a projected population for 2020 of 1·30m.

In 2010, 69·5% of the population lived in urban areas. Of the whole population, Estonians accounted for 68·7% in 2011, Russians 24·8% and Ukrainians 1·7%. The capital is Tallinn (2011 population, 393,222 or 31·5%). Other large towns are Tartu (97,600), Narva (58,663), Pärnu (39,728) and Kohtla-Järve (37,201). In 2011 there were 15 counties, 47 cities and 193 rural municipalities.

The official language is Estonian.

Social Statistics

2015 registered births, 13,907; deaths, 15,243. Rates (per 1,000 population): birth, 10·6; death, 11·6. There were 6,629 registered abortions in 2015, including 4,889 legally induced abortions. Expectation of life in 2014 was 72·3 years for males and 81·5 for females. The annual population growth rate in the period 2010–14 was –0·3%. The suicide rate was 18·7 per 100,000

© Springer Nature Limited 2020
Palgrave Macmillan (ed.), *The Statesman's Yearbook 2020*,
https://doi.org/10.1057/978-1-349-95940-2_69

population in 2012. Infant mortality in 2015 was 2·5 per 1,000 births. In 2015 total fertility rate was 1·6 births per woman.

Climate

Because of its maritime location Estonia has a moderate climate, with cool summers and mild winters. Average daily temperatures in 2008: Jan. −1·5°C; July 17·0°C. Rainfall is heavy, 600–800 mm per year, and evaporation low.

Constitution and Government

A draft constitution drawn up by a constitutional assembly was approved by 91·1% of votes cast at a referendum on 28 June 1992. Turnout was 66·6%. The constitution came into effect on 3 July 1992. It defines Estonia as a 'democratic state guided by the rule of law, where universally recognized norms of international law are an inseparable part of the legal system.' It provides for a 101-member National Assembly (*Riigikogu*) elected for four-year terms. There are 12 electoral districts with eight to 12 mandates each. Candidates may be elected: a) by gaining more than 'quota', i.e. the number of votes cast in a district divided by the number of its mandates; b) by standing for a party which attracts for all of its candidates more than the quota, in order of listing; c) by being listed nationally for parties which clear a 5% threshold and eligible for the seats remaining according to position on the lists. The head of state is the *President*, elected by the Riigikogu for five-year terms. Presidential candidates must gain the nominations of at least 20% of parliamentary deputies. If no candidate wins a two-thirds majority in any of three rounds, the Speaker convenes an electoral college, composed of parliamentary deputies and local councillors. At this stage any 21 electors may nominate an additional candidate. The electoral college elects the President by a simple majority.

Citizenship requirements are two years residence and competence in Estonian for existing residents. For residents immigrating after 1 April 1995, five years qualifying residence is required.

National Anthem

'Mu isamaa, mu õnn ja rõõm' ('My native land, my pride and joy'); words by J. V. Jannsen, tune by F. Pacius (same as Finland).

Government Chronology

Heads of State since independence.

Chairman of the Supreme Council	
1991–92	Arnold Rüütel

Presidents	
1992–2001	Lennart Georg Meri
2001–06	Arnold Rüütel
2006–16	oomas Hendrik Ilves
2016–	Kersti Kaljulaid

Prime Ministers since independence. (IERSP (Isamaaliit) = Pro Patria Union; Kesk = Estonian Centre Party; KMÜ-K = Estonian Coalition Party; Rahvarinne = Popular Front of Estonia; RE (Reformierakond) = Estonian Reform Party; ResP = Union for the Republic-Res Publica; RK Isamaa = National Coalition Party Pro Patria; n/p = non-partisan)

1990–92	Rahvarinne	Edgar Savisaar
1992	n/p	Tiit Vähi
1992–94	RK	Isamaa Mart Laar
1994–95	n/p	Andres Tarand
1995–97	KMÜ-K	Tiit Vähi
1997–99	KMÜ-K	Mart Siimann
1999–2002	IERSP	Mart Laar
2002–03	RE	Siim Kallas
2003–05	ResP	Juhan Parts
2005–14	RE	Andrus Ansip
2014–16	RE	Taavi Rõivas
2016–	Kesk	Jüri Ratas

Recent Elections

Parliamentary elections were held on 3 March 2019; turnout was 63·7%. The Estonian Reform Party (Reform) won 34 of 101 seats (with 28·9% of the total votes); Estonian Centre Party (Kesk), 26 seats (23·1%); the Conservative People's Party of Estonia (EKRE), 19 seats (17·8%); Pro Patria (Isamaa), 12 seats (11·4%); Social Democratic Party (SDE), 10 (9·8%). Five other parties failed to win seats.

In 2007 Estonia became the first country to use internet voting at a national election, when it did so for the parliamentary election in March of that year.

On 3 Oct. 2016 Kersti Kaljulaid was elected president, winning 81 votes in the 101-seat parliament. Two previous rounds held at the electoral college had failed to produce a clear winner.

European Parliament

Estonia has six representatives. At the May 2014 elections turnout was 36·5% (43·9% in 2009). Reform won 2 seats with 24·3% of the vote (political affiliation in European Parliament: Alliance of Liberals and Democrats for Europe); Kesk, 1 with 22·4% (Alliance of Liberals and Democrats for Europe); IRL, 1 with 13·9% (European People's Party); SDE, 1 with 13·6% (Progressive Alliance of Socialists and Democrats). One independent was elected, with 13·2% (Greens/European Free Alliance).

Current Government

President: Kersti Kaljulaid; b. 1969 (sworn in 10 Oct. 2016).

In Feb. 2019 the coalition government comprised:

Prime Minister: Jüri Ratas; b. 1978 (Kesk; in office since 23 Nov. 2016).

Minister of Culture: Indrek Saar (SDE). *Defence:* Jüri Luik (IRL). *Economic Affairs and Infrastructure:* Kadri Simson (Kesk). *Education and Research:* Mailis Reps (Kesk). *Entrepreneurship and Information Technology:* Rene Tammist (SDE). *Environment:* Siim Kiisler (IRL). *Finance:* Toomas Tõniste (IRL). *Foreign Affairs:* Sven Mikser (SDE). *Health and Labour:* Riina Sikkut (SDE). *Interior:* Katri Raik (SDE). *Justice:* Urmas Reinsalu (IRL). *Public Administration:* Janek Mäggi (Kesk). *Rural Affairs:* Tarmo Tamm (Kesk). *Social Protection:* Kaia Iva (IRL).

Government Website: http://www.valitsus.ee

Current Leaders

Kersti Kaljulaid

Position
President

Introduction
When she was sworn in as president in Oct. 2016, Kersti Kaljulaid became the first woman and the youngest person to hold the post. A non-partisan consensus candidate, she had served in the European Court of Auditors since 2004.

Early Life
Kersti Kaljulaid was born on 30 Dec. 1969 in Estonia's second city, Tartu. She graduated in biology from the University of Tartu in 1992, before embarking on a career in commerce. She held a variety of positions in the telecommunications and banking sectors and in 1999 returned to university to study for a master's degree in business. She was subsequently recruited as an economic adviser to then prime minister, Mart Laar, of the Pro Patria Union party. Kaljulaid joined the party in 2001 and a year later went to work for a subsidiary of the state energy company, quickly rising to become its director.

When Estonia joined the European Union in 2004 Kaljulaid was appointed a representative in the European Court of Auditors in Luxembourg, a posting that required her to leave Pro Patria Union. She remained at that court until 2016. After several failed attempts that year to elect a president, Estonia's *Riigikogu* (parliament) agreed to bring in a political outsider. Kaljulaid was proposed and won majority support from the chamber to replace two-term president Toomas Hendrik Ilves.

Career in Office
The office of president is largely ceremonial. Kaljulaid has described her key duty as to 'be present whenever things are getting complicated'. Little known

in the wider country, she has stated her desire to engage people around Estonia and focus on domestic issues. She has also met Ukraine's President Petro Poroshenko, a move widely seen as showing support for sanctions on Russia.

Jüri Ratas

Position
Prime Minister

Introduction
Jüri Ratas took office as prime minister in Nov. 2016 after a period of domestic political turbulence. A businessman and former mayor of Tallinn, Ratas is a member of the centre-left, pro-Russia Estonian Centre Party, which had long been in opposition.

Early Life
Jüri Ratas was born in the capital, Tallinn, on 2 July 1978. He attended Tallinn Nomme Gymnasium until 1996 before graduating in business administration from Tallinn University of Technology (TUT). He undertook further studies in economics at TUT and law at the University of Tartu, alongside work as a market analyst and insurance salesman.

In 2000 Ratas joined the Estonian Centre Party, an offshoot of the Popular Front of Estonia, which during the late 1980s was a major force in the independence movement. In early 2002 he became adviser to former prime minister and mayor of Tallinn, Edgar Savisaar. Appointed deputy mayor of Tallinn in April 2003, Ratas was responsible for transport and utilities. He was then elected mayor in 2005.

Ratas entered the national parliament as a member of the opposition in 2007, ending his tenure as mayor. He served as a vice-president in parliament, although his party remained outside successive ruling coalitions. The party has strong support from Estonia's ethnic Russian population and has controversially forged links with Vladimir Putin's United Russia party.

Ratas was elected leader of the Centre Party in Oct. 2016 after Edgar Savisaar stepped down. After Prime Minister Taavi Rõivas lost a parliamentary confidence vote the following month, Ratas led his party into a coalition with the Social Democratic Party and Pro Patria and Res Publica Union. Ratas was subsequently sworn in as premier on 23 Nov. 2016.

Career in Office
Ratas indicated that he would maintain existing foreign and security policy, focused on EU and NATO allegiance, while attempting to pursue a working relationship with neighbouring Russia. Nonetheless, in March 2017 a contingent of British troops arrived in Estonia as part of a NATO mission to deter potential Russian aggression in the Baltic states.

In elections in March 2019 the centre-right Reform Party remained the largest parliamentary group followed by Ratas's Centre Party, prompting both to start seeking potential coalition partners. Ratas declined an offer by Reform to enter into talks and instead controversially began courting the right-wing Conservative People's Party, reversing an earlier undertaking not to do so.

Defence

The President is the head of national defence. Conscription is eight to 11 months for men and voluntary for women. Conscientious objectors may opt for 16 months civilian service instead.

Defence expenditure in 2013 totalled US$480m. (US$379 per capita), representing 2·0% of GDP.

The Estonian Defence Forces (EDF) regular component is divided into the Army, the Air Force and the Navy. The country's reserve force, the Estonian Defence League, has 15,500 members and together with its affiliated organizations more than 24,500 volunteers in total.

Army

The Estonian Land Forces has two infantry brigades, one being the primary military unit in the north of the country and the other the primary military unit in the south. The total number of personnel in the Army in 2011 was 5,300 (2,500 conscripts). There is also a Border Guard.

Navy

The Navy consists of the Naval Staff (Naval HQ), the Naval Base, and the Mine Countermeasures (MCM) Squadron. The total number of personnel in the Navy in 2011 was 200 including a platoon-sized conscript unit. Estonia, Latvia and Lithuania have established a joint naval unit 'BALTRON' (Baltic Naval Squadron), with bases at Tallinn in Estonia, Liepāja, Riga and Ventspils in Latvia, and Klaipėda in Lithuania.

Air Force

The Air Force consists of an Air Force Staff, Air Force Base and Air Surveillance Wing. The total number of personnel in the Air Force in 2011 was 200.

International Relations

Estonia became a member of NATO on 29 March 2004 and of the EU on 1 May 2004. Estonia held a referendum on EU membership on 14 Sept. 2003, in which 66·9% of votes cast were in favour of accession, with 33·1% against.

Economy

Agriculture contributed 4% of GDP in 2012, industry 29% and services 67%.

According to the anti-corruption organization Transparency International, Estonia ranked equal 18th in the world in a 2018 survey of the countries with the least corruption in business and government. It received 73 out of 100 in the annual index.

Overview

Estonia is a gateway for trade with the Nordic countries, especially Sweden and Finland, which each took 16% of Estonian exports in 2016. Latvia is the next most important export market at 9%. When Estonia gained independence in 1991 it was among the most competitive of the former Soviet bloc countries, boasting the highest per capital income, strong infrastructure and high education levels compared to its neighbours.

The cornerstones of economic reform were the introduction of a new currency, tight budgetary control, privatization programmes and trade liberalization. Since independence, Estonia has been among the fastest-growing of those countries that acceded to the European Union in 2004, its performance driven in large part by strong domestic demand and buoyant exports.

The economy began to slow in 2007 and fell into recession as the global financial crisis took hold. GDP contracted by 14·7% in 2009 and unemployment rose. Despite this, the government persevered with efforts to join the eurozone (which it did on 1 Jan. 2011), making a fiscal adjustment of nearly 9% of GDP in 2009. Growth, supported by rising exports, was restored in 2010 and measured 7·6% in 2011. It then averaged 2·5% per year in the five years to 2016. However, the trade balance has weakened since 2013, with robust private consumption fuelling rising imports.

Unemployment has declined since 2010, falling from a high of 16·7% that year to 6·8% in 2016. Government debt is among the lowest in the EU at 9·5% of GDP in 2016. In the medium term, the economy must weather any regional fallout from ongoing disputes between Russia and Ukraine. Meanwhile, rising labour costs may put pressure on the country's long-term competitiveness.

Currency

On 1 Jan. 2011 the *euro* (EUR) replaced the *kroon* (EEK) as the legal currency of Estonia at the irrevocable conversion rate of 15·6466 krooni to one euro. Foreign exchange reserves were US$1,768m. in July 2005, gold reserves 8,000 troy oz and total money supply was 42,396m. krooni. Inflation was 10·6% in 2008 but has since fallen, and was 0·1% in 2016 and 3·4% in 2017.

Budget

Budgetary central government revenue and expenditure in €1m. for calendar years:

	2009	2010	2011
Revenue	4,414	4,269	4,595
Expenditure	4,305	4,386	4,546

Tax revenue provided €2,555m. krooni in 2011; social benefits (€1,702m. krooni) were the main item of expenditure. There is a flat income tax rate of 21%.

Estonia registered a budget deficit in 2017 of 0·4% of GDP and of 0·3% in 2016. There was a surplus of 0·1% in 2015. The required target set by the EU is a budget deficit of no more than 3%.

VAT is 20%.

Performance

Estonia suffered particularly badly in the global downturn with the economy shrinking by 14·7% in 2009. However, it has since recovered and grew by 1·9% in 2015, 3·5% in 2016 and 4·9% in 2017. Total GDP in 2017 was US$25·9bn.

Banking and Finance

A central bank, the Bank of Estonia, was re-established in 1990 (*Governor*, Ardo Hansson). The Estonian Investment Bank was established in 1992 to provide financing for privatized and private companies. As of 30 June 2011 there were seven licensed credit institutions and 11 affiliated branches of foreign credit institutions in Estonia. The four largest institutions control 89% of the market. Total assets of Estonian credit institutions as of 30 June 2011 were €19,105m. The Estonian Banking Association was founded in 1992. It has 12 member banks that represent approximately 98% of the Estonian banking sector's assets.

Gross external debt amounted to US$20,224m. in June 2012.

In 2013 Estonia received US$950m. worth of foreign direct investment, down from US$1·5bn. in 2012.

A stock exchange opened in Tallinn in 1996.

Energy and Natural Resources

In 2011, 25·9% of energy consumption came from renewables (wind power, solar power, hydro-electric power, tidal power, geothermal energy and biomass), compared to the European Union average of 13·0%. A target of 25% had been set by the EU in 2009 for 2020. Estonia became the first EU member country to exceed its target.

Environment

Estonia's carbon dioxide emissions from the consumption of energy in 2011 were the equivalent of 4·3 tonnes per capita. Estonia's greenhouse gas emissions fell by 45·8% between 1990 and 2012, mainly owing to the decline of polluting industries from the Soviet era.

Electricity

Estonia is a net electricity exporter. In 2010 installed capacity was 3·1m. kW; production in 2012 was 12·0bn. kWh. Consumption per capita was 7,240 kWh in 2010. In 2012, 81% of electricity was produced by burning oil shale. The introduction of renewable sources has in part reduced the importance of waste-intensive oil shale in electricity production. In 2012 the share of electricity generated from renewable sources was 15·2% in total electricity consumption, compared to 12·7% in 2011. Production of hydro and wind energy increased about 20% compared to 2011. Although Estonia still exports large quantities of electricity, exports in 2012 fell nearly 6% compared to 2011.

Oil and Gas

Oil shale deposits were estimated at 4,814m. tonnes in 2010. A factory for the production of gas from shale and a pipeline from Kohtla-Järve supplies shale gas to Tallinn, and exports to St Petersburg. Natural gas is imported from Russia.

Minerals

Oil shale is the most valuable mineral resource. Production volume fell from 21m. tonnes in 1990 to 12m. tonnes in 2006 before rising again to 15m. tonnes in 2010. Peatlands occupy about 22% of Estonia's territory; there are extensive deposits, with production of peat for fuels and fertilizers totalling 399,300 tonnes in 2010. Phosphorites and super-phosphates are found and refined. Lignite (7·93m. tonnes in 2010), sand (1·80m. cu. metres of construction sand in 2010), gravel (1·43m. cu. metres of construction gravel in 2010), limestone (1·17m. cu. metres of construction limestone in 2010), clay and dolomite are mined.

Agriculture

Farming employed 4·3% of the population in 2010. In the same year there were 19,613 holdings (55,748 in 2001). In 2010 there were 640,000 ha. of arable land and 3,000 ha. of permanent crops. Total agricultural output in 2011 was valued at €811·6m., including: animal production €387·8m.; crop production, €336·3m.; agricultural services and other non-agricultural production, €86·5m.

Output of main agricultural products (in 1,000 tonnes) in 2011: wheat, 360; barley, 295; potatoes, 165; rapeseed, 144; oats, 63; rye, 31.

In 2011 there were 365,700 pigs, 238,300 cattle, 83,900 sheep and 1,973,300 chickens.

Livestock products, 2011: meat, 81,000 tonnes; milk, 693,000 tonnes; eggs, 184m. units.

Forestry

In 2015, 2·23m. ha. were covered by forests (53% of the total land area), which provide material for sawmills, furniture, and the match and pulp industries, as well as wood fuel. Private, municipal and state ownership of forests is allowed. In 2011 the annual timber cut was 7·11m. cu. metres.

Fisheries

In 2010 the Estonian fishing fleet numbered 947 vessels of 17,300 gross tonnes. The total catch in 2015 was 73,199 tonnes.

Industry

Important industries are engineering, metalworking, food products, wood products, furniture and textiles. In 2015 manufacturing accounted for 16·0% of GDP.

Labour

The workforce in 2010 totalled 686,800, of whom 570,900 were employed. The average monthly gross wage in the fourth quarter of 2011 was €865. The unemployment rate in Dec. 2018 was 4·2% (down from 5·8% in 2017 as a whole).

Retirement age was 63 years for men and 61 years for women in 2012 although the female retirement age has increased gradually since then and is now 63. Since Jan. 2017 the retirement age for both sexes is being increased gradually to reach 65 years in 2026.

International Trade

Imports and Exports

The following table shows the value of Estonia's foreign trade (in €1m.):

	Imports (c.i.f.)	Exports (f.o.b.)
2010	9,268·3	8,743·0
2011	12,726·8	12,003·4
2012	14,096·5	12,521·1
2013	13,904·8	12,288·8
2014	13,775·5	12,082·6

Principal imports are electrical equipment, mineral products, agricultural products and food preparations, mechanical appliances and transport equipment; principal exports are electrical equipment, mineral products, agricultural products and food preparations, food and products thereof, and miscellaneous manufactured articles.

Main import suppliers in 2014: Finland, 15·3%; Germany, 11·5%; Sweden, 10·8%; Latvia, 8·5%; Lithuania, 8·3%. Main export markets, 2014: Sweden, 18·0%; Finland, 15·3%; Latvia, 10·7%; Russia, 9·8%; Lithuania, 5·3%.

Communications

Roads

At the end of 2015 there were 16,597 km of national roads, of which 1,609 km were main roads. In Dec. 2015 there were 676,596 registered passenger cars in use, plus 101,770 lorries, 4,770 buses, 29,053 motorcycles and 16,462 mopeds. There were 1,392 road accidents with casualties in 2015 with 67 persons killed and 1,758 injured.

Rail

Length of railways in 2015 was 2,146 km (1,524 mm gauge), of which 918 km were operational public railways and 132 km were electrified. In 2015, 6·6m. passengers and 28·0m. tonnes of freight were carried.

Civil Aviation

There is an international airport at Tallinn (Lennart Meri International Airport), which handled 2·0m. passengers (99% on international flights) and over 19,400 tonnes of freight and mail in 2014. 87% of passengers and 44% of freight and mail were carried on scheduled flights. There were 30,750 commercial flights in 2014. Estonian-based airlines carried 771,300 passengers in 2014 (98% on international flights). The national carrier Estonian Air ceased operations and declared bankruptcy in Dec. 2015. The airline was 97·3% state-owned; in 2014 it carried 553,147 passengers (96% on scheduled flights). Estonian Air operated year-round services in 2014 to Amsterdam, Brussels, Copenhagen, Kyiv, Moscow, Oslo, St Petersburg, Stockholm, Trondheim and Vilnius, plus a number of seasonal routes.

Shipping

In 2015, 10·1m. passengers visited Estonian ports by international transport with 84% of them travelling between Estonia and Finland. 492,900 cruise passengers arrived by sea and 2·3m. passengers were transported on the main domestic ship routes. In 2015 Estonian ports handled 35m. tonnes of cargo. The most frequently handled group of goods in Estonian ports was refined petroleum products (15·1m. tonnes). Sea container transportation through ports totalled 209,100 TEUs (twenty-foot equivalent units). In Jan. 2014 there were 27 ships of 300 GT or over registered, totalling 270,000 GT.

Telecommunications

In 2011 there were 470,500 landline telephone subscriptions (equivalent to 351·0 per 1,000 inhabitants) and 1,863,000 mobile phone subscriptions (or 1,389·8 per 1,000 inhabitants). In 2011, 76·5% of the population were internet users. In March 2012 there were 448,000 Facebook users. In 2000 the Estonian parliament voted to guarantee internet access to its citizens.

Social Institutions

Out of 178 countries analysed in the 2017 *Fragile States Index*—a list published jointly by the Fund for Peace and *Foreign Policy* magazine—Estonia was ranked the 36th least vulnerable to conflict or collapse. The index is based on 12 indicators of state vulnerability across social, political and economic categories.

Justice

A post-Soviet criminal code was introduced in 1992. There is a three-tier court system with the State Court at its apex, and there are both city and district courts. The latter act as courts of appeal. The State Court is the final court of appeal, and also functions as a constitutional court. There are also administrative courts for petty offences. Judges are appointed for life. City and district judges are appointed by the President; State Court judges are elected by Parliament.

In 2014, 37,787 crimes were recorded; there were 12 murders and one attempted murder. In Jan. 2015, 2,921 persons were in penal institutions (222 per 100,000 of national population). In 2015 the World Justice Project *Rule of Law Index*, which provides data on how the rule of law is experienced by the general public across eight categories, ranked Estonia 18th of 102 countries for criminal justice and 12th for civil justice.

The death penalty was abolished for all crimes in 1998.

Education

Adult literacy rate in 2009 was estimated at 99·8% (99·8% for both males and females). There are nine years of comprehensive school starting at age six, followed by three years secondary school. In 2010–11 there were 545 general education schools: 68 primary, 253 basic and 224 secondary/upper secondary. Of these, 454 were Estonian-language, 31 non Estonian-language and 60 mixed-language. There were 43 schools for children with special needs. The total number of pupils at basic school level in general education was 112,600 in 2010–11, with 33,300 in secondary education. At the start of the 2010–11 academic year there were 69,100 higher education students studying at six public universities, three private universities, ten state higher schools and 12 private higher schools; two vocational educational institutions also provide higher education.

In 2010 public expenditure on education came to 5·7% of GDP and 12·7% of total government spending.

According to the OECD's 2015 PISA (Programme for International Student Assessment) study, 15-year-olds in Estonia rank third among OECD and other major countries and cities in science, sixth in reading and ninth in mathematics, making it the best performing European country overall. The three-yearly study compares educational achievement of pupils in over 70 countries.

Health

Estonia had 61 hospitals (21 private) in 2013, up from 49 hospitals (17 private) in 2003. There were 7,394 hospital beds in 2013. In Dec. 2013 there were 4,395 doctors, 1,190 dentists, 825 dental assistants and 7,428 nurses.

In *Water: At What Cost? The State of the World's Water 2016*, WaterAid reported that 0·4% of the population does not have access to safe water.

Welfare

In 2012 there were 0·4m. pensioners. The average monthly pension in the third quarter of 2012 was €279·40. An official poverty line was introduced in 1993 (then 280 krooni—equivalent to €17·90—per month). Persons receiving less than the subsistence level (€76·70 per month in 2012) are entitled to state benefit. Unemployment allowance was €65·41 a month in 2012.

Religion

There is freedom of religion in Estonia and no state church, although the population was traditionally seen as Lutheran. The Estonian Orthodox Church owed allegiance to Constantinople until it was forcibly brought under Moscow's control in 1940; a synod of the free Estonian Orthodox Church was established in Stockholm. Returning from exile, it registered itself in 1993 as the Estonian Apostolic Orthodox Church. By an agreement in 1996 between the Moscow and Constantinople Orthodox Patriarchates, there are now two Orthodox jurisdictions in Estonia. According to the Pew Research Center's Forum on Religion & Public Life, an estimated 59·6% of the population in 2010 had no religious affiliation and 39·9% were Christian. There was also a small Muslim minority. Among Christians, 51% in 2010 were Lutherans and 45% Orthodox.

Culture

World Heritage Sites

Estonia has two sites on the UNESCO World Heritage List: the Historic Centre (Old Town) of Tallinn (1997 and 2008) and the Struve Geodetic Arc (2005). The Arc is a chain of survey triangulations spanning from Norway to the Black Sea that helped establish the exact shape and size of the earth and is shared with nine other countries.

Press

In 2014 there were ten daily newspapers (combined circulation of 178,000) and 27 non-dailies (302,000). *The Baltic Times* is an English-language weekly covering news from Estonia, Latvia and Lithuania.

Tourism

In 2011, 1,808,000 non-resident tourists and 918,000 Estonians stayed in holiday accommodation. Of the foreign tourists most were from Finland (841,000), followed by Russia (203,000), Germany (104,000), Sweden (86,000) and Latvia (85,000).

Festivals

Festivals include: International Folklore Festival, BALTICA, which is staged every three years; Festival of Baroque Music; Jazz festival, JAZZKAAR; Pärnu International Documentary and Anthropology Film Festival and the Viljandi Folk Music Festival. Estonia's Song Festival, which was first held in 1869, is held every five years and is next scheduled to take place in 2024.

Baltoscandal, an international theatre festival that takes place every two years, celebrated its 15th staging in July 2018.

Diplomatic Representatives

Of Estonia in the United Kingdom (44 Queen's Gate Terrace, London, SW7 5PJ)
Ambassador: Tiina Intelmann.

Of the United Kingdom in Estonia (Wismari 6, 15098 Tallinn)
Ambassador: Theresa Bubbear.

Of Estonia in the USA (2131 Massachusetts Ave., NW, Washington, D.C., 20036)
Ambassador: Jonatan Vseviov.

Of the USA in Estonia (Kentmanni 20, 15099 Tallinn)
Ambassador: Vacant.
Chargé d'Affaires a.i.: Elizabeth Horst.

Of Estonia to the United Nations
Ambassador: Sven Jürgenson.

Of Estonia to the European Union
Permanent Representative: Kaja Tael.

Further Reading

Statistical Office of Estonia. *Statistical Yearbook.*
Ministry of the Economy. *Estonian Economy.* Annual
Hood, N., *et al.*, (eds) *Transition in the Baltic States.* 1997

Kasekamp, Andres, *A History of the Baltic States.* 2010
Kolsto, Pal, *National Integration and Violent Conflict in Post-Soviet Societies: The Cases of Estonia and Moldova.* 2002
Lieven, A., *The Baltic Revolution: Estonia, Latvia, Lithuania and the Path to Independence.* 2nd ed. 1994
Misiunas, R.-J. and Taagepera, R., *The Baltic States: Years of Dependence 1940–1990.* 2nd ed. 1993
O'Connor, Kevin, *The History of the Baltic States.* 2003
Plakans, Andrejs, *A Concise History of the Baltic States.* 2011
Smith, David J., Purs, Aldis, Pabriks, Artis and Lane, Thomas, (eds) *The Baltic States: Estonia, Latvia and Lithuania.* 2002
Taagepera, R., *Estonia: Return to Independence.* 1993
National Statistical Office: Statistical Office of Estonia, Tatari 51, 10134 Tallinn.
Website: http://www.stat.ee

Eswatini

Umbuso weSwatini (Kingdom of Eswatini)

Capitals: Mbabane (Administrative), Lobamba (Legislative)
Population projection, 2020: 1·44m.
GNI per capita, 2017: (PPP$) 7,620
HDI/world rank, 2017: 0·588/144=
Internet domain extension: .sz

Key Historical Events

Khoisan hunter-gatherers were the earliest inhabitants of Eswatini (formerly known as Swaziland); their rock-art can be found across the Mpumalanga Hills, which form the border of present-day Eswatini and South Africa. The region was colonized by Bantu-speaking groups from around AD 400, notably the Kashian tribe from central Africa. Nguni-speaking clans reached southern Mozambique during the 15th century. Their descendants included the Ngwane, who occupied the north bank of the Pongola river in present-day Eswatini during the 18th century. In the 1820s chief Sobhuza Dlamini I consolidated a kingdom of diverse peoples in the Ezulwini valley, which by the time of his death in 1839 had evolved into the Swazi state.

Over the next 25 years his son, Mswati Dlamini II, defended the kingdom against Zulu expansionism and pushed north and west into South Africa's Transvaal region. Weslyan missionaries reached Eswatini in 1844 and Dutch settlers followed; Mswati granted territory to the Ohrigstad Afrkaners in 1846. By 1852 Mswati had established relations with the British lieutenant-governor of Natal and persuaded him to keep the Zulu threat at bay. The Swazi state became increasingly cohesive and secure, underpinned by a network of royal villages that were commanded by loyal princes. As a reward for assisting British forces defeat Sekhukhune, King of the Bapedi people, the British government recognized Swazi independence in the conventions of 1881 and 1884 with the Government of the South African Republic. The death of King Mbandzeni in 1889 and increasing European interest in mineral exploration in the area led to Eswatini being administered, but not annexed, by Transvaal from 1894.

Following the Boer War in 1902 Eswatini came under British control. Sobhuza II reigned from 1921 to 1982 and managed to return around 40% of the territory to the traditional system of land tenure. He was only officially recognized as king in 1967. Swaziland (officially renamed Eswatini in 2018) became independent on 6 Sept. 1968. Sobhuza II repealed the 1968 constitution in 1973, dissolved parliament and assumed personal rule. When he died in 1982 power was transferred to Queen Regent Dzeliwe, followed by Queen Regent Ntombe. On 25 April 1986 Sobhuza's son, Mswati III, was installed as king. During the early 1990s protests by pro-democracy activists precipitated the first parliamentary elections in 1993, but most ministers were royal appointees rather than elected members. Sporadic pro-democracy protests have continued, notably in the commercial capital Manzini in 2007, but King Mswati remains one of the world's few absolute monarchs.

Territory and Population

Swaziland is bounded in the north, west and south by South Africa, and in the east by Mozambique. The area is 17,364 sq. km (6,704 sq. miles). Population (2017 census, provisional), 1,093,238 (562,127 females); density, 63·0 per sq. km.

The UN gives a projected population for 2020 of 1·44m.

In 2011, 21·3% of the population were urban. The country is divided into four regions: Hhohho, Lubombo, Manzini and Shiselweni.

Main urban areas: Mbabane, the administrative capital (60,281 inhabitants in 2007); Manzini; Big Bend; Mhlume; Nhlangano.

The population is 84% Swazi and 10% Zulu. The official languages are Swazi and English.

Social Statistics

2008 estimates: births, 35,000; deaths, 18,000. Estimated rates, 2008 (per 1,000 population): births, 29·9; deaths, 15·6. As a result of the impact of AIDS, expectation of life declined sharply. It was 59 years in 1990–95, but by 2000–05 was down to 45·9 years for females and 45·6 years for males. However, it has now started to rise again and in 2013 was 48·3 years for females and 49·6 years for males. Eswatini was one of only two countries where life expectancy at birth for males in 2013 was higher than for females (the other being Mali). In 2013, 27·4% of all adults between 15 and 49 were infected with HIV—the highest rate in any country. In 2010, 23% of Swazi children were orphans. In Sept. 2001 King Mswati III told the teenage girls of the country to stop having sex for five years as part of the country's drive to reduce the spread of HIV. Annual population growth rate, 2000–08, 1·0%. Infant mortality, 2010, 55 per 1,000 live births; fertility rate, 2008, 3·5 births per woman.

Climate

A temperate climate with two seasons. Nov. to March is the wet season, when temperatures range from mild to hot, with frequent thunderstorms. The cool, dry season from May to Sept. is characterized by clear, bright sunny days. Mbabane, Jan. 68°F (20°C), July 54°F (12·2°C). Annual rainfall 56" (1,402 mm).

Constitution and Government

The reigning King is **Mswati III** (b. 1968; crowned 25 April 1986), who succeeded his father, King Sobhuza II (reigned 1921–82). The King rules in conjunction with the Queen Mother (his mother, or a senior wife). Critics of the King or his mother run the risk of arrest. Political parties are banned.

A new constitution was signed into law on 26 July 2005 and came into force in Jan. 2006. There is a *House of Assembly* of 65 members, 55 of whom are elected each from one constituency (*inkhundla*) and ten appointed by the King; and a *House of Senators* of 30 members, ten of whom are elected by the House of Assembly and 20 appointed by the King. Elections are held in two rounds, the second being a run-off between the five candidates who come first in each constituency.

There is also a traditional *Swazi National Council* headed by the King and Queen Mother at which all Swazi men are entitled to be heard.

National Anthem

'Nkulunkulu mnikati wetibusiso temaSwati' ('O Lord our God bestower of blessings upon the Swazi'); words by A. E. Simelane, tune by D. K. Rycroft.

Recent Elections

In parliamentary elections held on 18 Aug. and 21 Sept. 2018, 59 independent candidates were elected with ten more chosen and appointed by King Mswati III. 30 candidates were subsequently assigned to senatorial posts in the Swazi legislature. Of these, ten were elected by parliament and 20 were appointed by the King. Political parties in Eswatini have been banned under the *tinkhundla* electoral system since 1978.

Current Government

In Feb. 2019 the cabinet comprised:

Prime Minister: Ambrose Mandvulo Dlamini; b. 1968 (sworn in 29 Oct. 2018).

Deputy Prime Minister: Paul Dlamini.

Minister for Agriculture: Jabulani Mabuza. *Commerce, Industry and Trade:* Manqoba Khumalo. *Economic Planning and Development:* Tambo Gina. *Education and Training:* Lady Howard Mabuza. *Finance:* Neal Reijkenberg. *Foreign Affairs and International Co-operation:* Thuli Dladla. *Health:* Lizzy Nkosi. *Home Affairs:* Princess Lindiwe. *Housing and Urban Development:* Prince Simelane. *Information, Communications and Technology:* Princess Sikhanyiso. *Justice and Constitutional Affairs:* Pholile Dlamini. *Labour and Social Security:* Makhosi Vilakati. *Natural Resources and Energy:* Peter Bhembe. *Public Service:* Christian Ntshangase. *Public Works and Transport:* Chief Ndlaluhlaza Ndwandwe. *Sports, Culture and*

Youth: Harries Madze Bulunga. *Tinkhundla Administration and Development:* David Ngcamphalala. *Tourism and Environmental Affairs:* Moses Vilakati.

Government Website: http://www.gov.sz

Current Leaders

Mswati III

Position

King

Introduction

Mswati came to the throne in 1986. Effectively an absolute monarchy, he has received domestic and international criticism during his reign for his suppression of political opposition, for economic mismanagement and for the rapid increase in cases of HIV and AIDS. In April 2018 he announced that the country was changing its name from Swaziland to Eswatini.

Early Life

Mswati was born on 19 April 1968 in Manzini to one of the wives of King Sobhuza II and given the name Makhosetive (King of All Nations). Sobhuza's death in 1982 left a power vacuum that led to several years of infighting between various queens regent, crown princes and members of Liqoqo (the traditional advisory body which wielded significant power over the crown). In Oct. 1985 Makhosetive's mother dismissed several leading Liqoqo figures and recalled her son from his schooling in England. Makhosetive was crowned as Mswati III in April 1986.

Career in Office

Among Mswati's first acts as King was to dissolve the Liqoqo. Popular discontent grew at the prohibition on opposition political parties and Mswati's increasingly autocratic rule, leading to the establishment of the illegal People's United Democratic Movement (Pudemo). In 1990 Mswati agreed to open dialogue on the nation's political future. The National Assembly was directly elected for the first time in 1993 and Mswati announced plans for a new constitution the following year.

With little progress having been made by 1996, Mswati established a constitutional commission. Pudemo continued to co-ordinate opposition, criticizing the King for filling the commission with his conservative supporters and boycotting the National Assembly elections of Oct. 1998. In 2000 Pudemo leader Mario Masuku demanded an end to the state of emergency called 27 years earlier and was arrested for sedition. He was imprisoned pending his trial which collapsed in 2002. On his release he stated his belief that government could only be reformed when the monarchy was 'wiped out'.

In 2001 the constitutional commission reported back, providing the framework for the writing of a new constitution but asserting that the majority of the population did not favour the formation of new parties. In Dec. 2002, amid declining relations with the judiciary, six court of appeal judges resigned in protest at the King's use of rule by decree. The judges claimed that Mswati's repeal of several court decisions was unconstitutional. The crisis gave renewed impetus to the opposition alliance who called for a series of mass strikes. A new draft constitution was presented to the King in 2003, introducing a bill of rights but maintaining the executive role of the monarchy and the ban on political parties. Having been adopted by parliament and signed by the King in 2005, the constitution came into force in Jan. 2006.

Eswatini has one of the highest AIDS rates in the world. In Oct. 2001 Mswati ordered that all virgins should abstain from sex for five years or face a fine. The following month Mswati made a gift of a cow in recompense for taking an 18 year-old bride, Zena Mahlangu. Mahlangu's mother accused aides of the King of kidnapping her daughter and undertook legal proceedings to secure her return. Although the case collapsed, it received international attention and highlighted the growing challenges to Mswati's autocratic style.

Opposition groups boycotted the Sept. 2008 elections and were critical of the lavish celebrations of Mswati's 40th birthday, coupled with the 40th anniversary of Eswatini's independence.

Pudemo leader Masuku, who had again been detained under anti-terror laws in Nov. 2008, was released in Sept. 2009 vowing to continue campaigning for democracy. In Sept. 2010 around 50 pro-democracy activists, including Masuku, were arrested by police as they prepared for a protest march through the capital, Mbabane. Non-party parliamentary elections in Sept. 2013 made little change to the political composition of the House of Assembly.

In 2012 the International Monetary Fund reiterated its warnings that Eswatini's budget problems were reaching crisis point, and in June 2014 the USA excluded Eswatini from a preferential trade programme offering duty-free access to the US market for its failure to meet eligibility criteria on human rights. Since then, despite ongoing economic mismanagement by the political elite and dire state of the public finances, the government has continued to resist popular and international demands for reforms.

In Aug. 2016 Mswati assumed the chair of the Southern African Development Community at the regional organization's annual summit of heads of state and government in Mbabane despite protests from within Eswatini and abroad.

Parliamentary elections in Aug. and Sept. 2018 returned 55 non-partisan members to the House of Assembly with a further ten appointed by Mswati.

Defence

Army Air Wing

There are two Israeli-built Arava transports with weapon attachments for light attack duties.

Economy

Agriculture accounted for 10·1% of GDP in 2014, industry 38·2% and services 51·7%.

At the core of Swazi society is Tibiyo Taka Ngwane. Created in 1968 by Royal Charter, Tibiyo is a national development fund that operates outside the government and falls directly under the King, who holds it in trust for the nation. Its money derives from its stake in virtually every sector of Swazi commerce and industry.

Overview

Despite Eswatini's strong economic ties with South Africa—which is by far the leading trading partner—its economic growth has lagged behind other members of the Southern African Customs Union (SACU). Growth slowed from 2·9% in 2013 to 1·7% in 2015, largely owing to a drought that hurt agricultural production, a weaker mining sector and subdued economic prospects in South Africa. A fall in revenue, coupled with increased public spending, have generated higher fiscal deficits and a growing public debt (the ratio to GDP reaching 17·4% in 2015).

SACU revenues accounted for around 60% of total government income and 25% of GDP in the financial year 2008–09 but collapsed in 2010–11 when the South African economy contracted. This, along with reduced expenditure on essential infrastructure and poverty alleviation plus unbudgeted wage increases for civil servants and politicians in 2010, sparked a serious fiscal crisis. The central bank reported a fall in national reserves to US$666m. and in 2011 the government failed to satisfy the criteria for IMF and African Development Bank loans. In Aug. 2011 South Africa made an emergency loan of R2·4bn. (US$350m.), demanding in return that the Swazi currency be pegged to the rand.

Despite its classification as a low middle-income economy, 63% of the population lived below the poverty line in 2013. About 70% of the population is employed in subsistence agriculture. There has been some progress over the past three decades in the fight against HIV—the overall incidence rate having declined from 3·1% in 2010 to 2·2% in 2013 and 1·9% in 2015—but the 26% rate among 15–49-year-olds is among the highest in the world. Other problems include a high unemployment rate (28·1% in 2016—although some estimates put the real figure at nearer 40%). Reducing dependency on SACU transfers is essential to boosting international competitiveness, while improving the poor business environment is also key to spurring development.

Currency

The unit of currency is the *lilangeni* (plural *emalangeni*) (SZL) of 100 *cents* but Eswatini remains in the Common Monetary Area and the South African rand is legal tender. Inflation was 7·8% in 2016 and 6·2% in 2017. In July 2005 foreign exchange reserves were US$291m. and total money supply was 1,229m. emalangeni.

Budget

The fiscal year begins on 1 April. Total revenue in 2010–11 came to 7,260m. emalangeni and total expenditure to 10,347m. emalangeni.

There is a sales tax of 14%.

Performance

The economy grew by 0·4% in 2015, 1·4% in 2016 and 1·6% in 2017. Total GDP in 2017 was US$4·4bn.

Banking and Finance

The central bank and bank of issue is the Central Bank of Eswatini (*Governor*, Majozi Sithole), established in 1974. In 2015 there were three commercial banks (First National Bank, Nedbank and Standard Bank), one development bank (Swaziland Development & Savings Bank, which is 100% owned by the Eswatini government) and one building society (Swaziland Building Society).

Foreign debt totalled US$616m. in 2010, representing 17·2% of GNI.

In 1990 Swaziland Stock Brokers was established to trade in stocks and shares for institutional and private clients. A fully-fledged stock exchange, the Swaziland Stock Exchange, was inaugurated in 1999.

Energy and Natural Resources

Environment

Eswatini's carbon dioxide emissions from the consumption of energy were the equivalent of 0·7 tonnes per capita in 2011.

Electricity

Installed capacity was an estimated 0·2m. kW in 2011. Production was 654m. kWh in 2011; total consumption was 1,460m. kWh. Eswatini imports over half of its electricity needs from South Africa.

Minerals

Output (in tonnes): coal (2010), 146,000; crushed stone (2012), 308,440 cu. metres. Eswatini's diamond mine closed down in 1996 (1996 production, 75,000 carats) and its asbestos mine in 2000 (2000 production, 12,690 tonnes).

The oldest known mine (iron ore) in the world, dating back to 41,000 BC, was located at the Lion Cavern Site on Ngwenya Mountain.

Agriculture

There were approximately 175,000 ha. of arable land and 15,000 ha. of permanent cropland in 2013. Production of principal crops (2013 estimates, in 1,000 tonnes): sugarcane, 5,473; maize, 119; grapefruit, 48; oranges, 42; pineapples, 35; potatoes, 8; bananas, 6; tomatoes, 5.

Livestock (2013 estimates): cattle, 620,000; goats, 270,000; sheep, 36,000; pigs, 35,000; chickens, 4m.

Livestock products, 2013 estimates (in 1,000 tonnes): milk, 40; meat, 27.

Forestry

Forests covered 0·59m. ha. in 2015, or 34% of the land area. In 2011 timber production was 1·41m. cu. metres.

Fisheries

Estimated total catch, 2015, 65 tonnes, exclusively from inland waters.

Industry

Most industries are based on processing agricultural products and timber. Footwear and textiles are also manufactured, and some engineering products.

Labour

The labour force in 2013 was 446,000 (349,000 in 2003). 58·9% of the population aged 15–64 was economically active in 2013. In the same year 22·3% of the population was unemployed.

International Trade

Eswatini has a customs union with South Africa and receives a *pro rata* share of the dues collected.

Imports and Exports

Trade in US$1m.:

	2002	2003	2004	2005	2006
Imports f.o.b.	1,027·0	1,540·2	1,715·3	1,949·4	1,960·7
Exports f.o.b.	1,078·5	1,666·8	1,806·2	1,965·5	1,975·7

Main import products are motor vehicles, machinery, transport equipment, foodstuffs, petroleum products and chemicals; main export commodities are soft drink concentrates, sugar, wood pulp and cotton yarn. By far the most significant trading partner is South Africa. In 2005, 88·3% of imports came from South Africa; 74·6% of exports went to South Africa in 2005.

Communications

Roads

The road network covers around 8,300 km. There were 52,200 passenger cars in use in 2007 plus 41,800 lorries and vans and 8,100 buses and coaches. There were 235 fatalities in road accidents in 2007.

Rail

In 2005 the system comprised 301 km of route (1,067 mm gauge). There are north and south connections to South Africa's rail system, and a link in the northeast with Mozambique and the port of Maputo. In 2009, 4m. tonnes of freight were transported.

Civil Aviation

There is an international airport at Manzini (Matsapha). A new airport, King Mswati III International Airport—also at Manzini—was inaugurated in March 2014 and received its first flights in Oct. 2014. The national carrier is Swaziland Airlink, which had direct flights from Manzini to Johannesburg in 2012. The unrelated Airlink also operated on the same route in 2012.

Telecommunications

In 2013 there were an estimated 46,000 main (fixed) telephone lines; mobile phone subscriptions numbered 805,000 in 2012 (65·4 per 100 persons). In 2013 an estimated 24·7% of the population were internet users.

Social Institutions

Out of 178 countries analysed in the 2017 *Fragile States Index*—a list published jointly by the Fund for Peace and *Foreign Policy* magazine—Eswatini was ranked the 42nd most vulnerable to conflict or collapse. The index is based on 12 indicators of state vulnerability across social, political and economic categories.

Justice

The constitutional courts practice Roman-Dutch law. The judiciary is headed by the Chief Justice. There is a High Court and various Magistrates and Courts. A Court of Appeal with a President and three Judges deals with appeals from the High Court. There are 16 courts of first instance. There are also traditional Swazi National Courts.

The population in penal institutions in March 2012 was 3,411 (284 per 100,000 of national population).

Education

In 2007 there were 232,572 primary school pupils with 7,169 teaching staff. The pupil/teacher ratio has decreased from 40/1 in the 1970s to 32/1. About half the children of secondary school age attend school. There are also private schools. In 2007 there were 83,049 pupils in secondary schools with 4,358 teaching staff. Many secondary and high schools teach agricultural activities.

There were 5,692 students in higher education in 2006 with 462 academic staff. The University of Eswatini, with its main campus at Kwaluseni, was founded in 1982 and has an enrolment of over 5,000 students.

Rural education centres offer formal education for children and adult education geared towards vocational training. The adult literacy rate in 2008 was 87%.

In 2006 public expenditure on education came to 7·9% of GNI and 24·4% of total government spending.

Health

In 2005 there were 400 health institutions, of which nine were hospitals and 19 were health centres. In 2009 there were two physicians for every 10,000 population, 160 nurses and midwives per 10,000 and four dentists for every 10,000.

In *Water: At What Cost? The State of the World's Water 2016*, WaterAid reported that 25·9% of the population does not have access to safe water.

Religion

In 2010 the population was an estimated 88·1% Christian (mainly Protestant) according to the Pew Research Center's Forum on Religion & Public Life. Most of the remainder of the population is religiously unaffiliated.

Culture

Press

In 2008 there were two daily newspapers: *The Times of Swaziland* (English-language with a circulation of 22,000 in 2008), founded in 1897, and *The Swazi Observer* (English, 15,000).

Tourism

In 2011 there were 1,328,000 non-resident visitor arrivals (including tourists and same-day visitors), down slightly from 1,343,000 in 2010.

Festivals

The annual Umhlanga (Reed Dance) takes place in Aug. or early Sept. in honour of the Queen Mother. Bush Fire is a festival of music and performing arts held in the Malkerns Valley south of Mbabane in May.

Diplomatic Representatives

Of Eswatini in the United Kingdom (20 Buckingham Gate, London, SW1E 6LB)
    High Commissioner: Christian Muzie Nkambule.

Of the United Kingdom in Eswatini (High Commission in Mbabane closed in Aug. 2005)
    High Commissioner: Nigel Casey, MVO (resides in Pretoria, South Africa).

Of Eswatini in the USA (1712 New Hampshire Ave., NW, Washington, D.C., 20009)
    Ambassador: Njabuliso Busisiwe Sikhulile Gwebu.

Of the USA in Eswatini (Corner of MR 103 and Cultural Center Drive, Ezulwini, PO Box D202, The Gables, H106, Mbabane)
    Ambassador: Lisa Peterson.

Of Eswatini to the United Nations
    Ambassador: Melusi Martin Masuko.

Of Eswatini to the European Union
    Ambassador: Sibusisiwe Mngomezulu.

Further Reading

Booth, Alan R., *Historical Dictionary of Swaziland.* 2000
Gillis, D. Hugh, *The Kingdom of Swaziland: Studies in Political History.* 1999
Matsebula, J. S. M., *A History of Swaziland.* 3rd ed. 1992
National Statistical Office: Central Statistical Office, POB 456, Mbabane.
Website: http://www.swazistats.org.sz

Ethiopia

Ye-Ityoppya Federalawi Dimokrasiyawi Ripeblik (Federal Democratic Republic of Ethiopia)

Capital: Addis Ababa
Population projection, 2020: 112·76m.
GNI per capita, 2017: (PPP$) 1,719
HDI/world rank, 2017: 0·463/173
Internet domain extension: .et

Key Historical Events

From as early as 3000 BC Egyptian Pharaohs referred to northern Ethiopia as the Land of Punt, rich in precious resources including gold, myrrh and ivory. The region was in contact with southern Arabia by around 2000 BC, with settlers bringing Semitic languages and stone-building techniques. Early in the 1st century AD a prosperous and advanced civilization arose in the northern highlands, centred on Aksum. Christianity reached Aksum in the 4th century AD when King Ezana was converted by Frumentius of Tyre. At its height in the 6th century AD the Aksumite empire controlled much of the Red Sea coast and traded with the Mediterranean powers, as well as Persia and India.

Between the 8th–10th centuries the declining Aksumite realm shifted southwards, while northern Ethiopia increasingly came under Arabian influence. Christianity held sway in the highlands and was central to the culture of the post-Aksumite Zagwe kingdom, founded in 1137. The Zagwe were ousted around 1270 by Yekuno Amlak, an Amharic warrior who restored the Solomonic dynasty which claimed descent from Aksum, King Solomon and the Queen of Sheba. The kingdom expanded to the south, particularly under Zara Yaqob (ruled 1434–68).

Portuguese mariners reached the Red Sea in the early 1500s and a diplomatic mission arrived in Ethiopia in 1508. Faced with raids from neighbouring Islamic states, Emperor Lebna Dengel sought an alliance with the Portuguese who, in 1543, assisted in defeating Ahmad ibn Ibrahim al Ghazi, the conqueror of much of southern and eastern Ethiopia. The Solomonic monarchy was reinstated in 1632 by Emperor Fasidas, who established a new capital at Gondar. The coastal provinces came largely under Ottoman rule.

Tigray and Amhara experienced sporadic civil wars until the emergence of Lij Kasa in the 19th century. Crowned Emperor Tewodros II in 1855, he set about unifying the country although his efforts to end the slave trade led to tensions with local rulers. Following disagreements with Britain, Tewodros arrested several British officials including the consul. Britain responded by sending 12,000 troops to Ethiopia under Robert Napier. When Napier overwhelmed the fortress at Magdala, Tewodros committed suicide, igniting civil war.

The opening of the Suez Canal in 1869 intensified the regional scramble for influence among the European powers. At the same time Ethiopia faced armed incursions from Egypt and the Madhists in Sudan. Menelik II, ruler of Shoa in central Ethiopia, increased his power base with Italian support and seized control of Ethiopia in 1889. He renounced Italian claims to Ethiopia and defeated the Italian army at Adwa in 1896 before founding a new capital at Addis Ababa. Menelik II centralized authority and developed the country's infrastructure. He was succeeded in 1913 by his grandson, Lij Iyasu, who was deposed three years later in favour of Empress Zawaditu, with Ras Tafari Makonnen as regent and heir apparent. Following Empress Zawaditu's death in 1930 Ras Tafari became emperor as Haile Selassie I, claiming direct descent from King Solomon and the Queen of Sheba.

Although Ethiopia was recognized as independent in 1923, the League of Nations was unable to prevent Benito Mussolini from launching a second Italian invasion from Eritrea on 3 Oct. 1935. When Addis Ababa was captured in May 1936 Haile Selassie fled to Britain, only returning when Allied forces defeated the Italians in 1941. He brought in social and political reforms and established a National Assembly. In 1950 Eritrea, an Italian colony under British military administration since 1941, was handed over to

Ethiopia. A secessionist movement, the Eritrean Peoples' Liberation Front (EPLF), began a guerrilla war for independence. Following famine and economic decline, a military government (the Dirgue) assumed power on 12 Sept. 1974 under Lieut. Col. Mengistu Haile Mariam. It deposed Haile Selassie (who was murdered in prison in 1975), abolished the monarchy and mounted an agricultural collectivization programme.

In 1977 Somalia invaded Ethiopia and took control of the Ogaden region. After a counter offensive, with Soviet and Cuban support, the area was recaptured. Droughts in the late 1970s and early 1980s led to a devastating famine, which received international attention in 1984 when the death toll had already reached 200,000. War-torn Tigray and Eritrea were again in conflict in 1989. In 1991 the Ethiopian People's Revolutionary Democratic Front (EPRDF), led by Meles Zenawi, defeated the Ethiopian army, forcing Mengistu to flee to Zimbabwe. In July 1991 a conference of 24 political groups, called to appoint a transitional government, agreed a democratic charter. Eritrea seceded and became independent on 24 May 1993.

In 1994 a new constitution established a bicameral legislature and a judicial system. Meles Zenawi was elected prime minister in May 1995 with Negasso Gidada as president. The ongoing conflict with Eritrea flared up again in 1999 and thousands were killed before a peace deal was brokered in June 2000. Economic progress raised hopes of higher living standards until three successive years of drought left food resources seriously depleted. Widespread malnutrition was alleviated by international aid. Meles's EPRDF won contested elections in May 2005, paving the way for his third five-year stint as prime minister.

In July 2008 the UN Security Council voted to end its Ethiopian–Eritrean peacekeeping mission. Zenawi won a fourth term as premier in May 2010 after the EPRDF dominated parliamentary elections. When he died in Aug. 2012, Hailemariam Desalegn succeeded him. By early 2016 Ethiopia was again faced with the impact of severe drought. In Oct. 2016 a state of emergency was declared—the first since the EPRDF seized power in 1991—amid a climate of civil unrest and anti-government protests. By the following month over 11,000 people had been detained under its terms. It was lifted in Aug. 2017.

In July 2018 Ethiopia's Prime Minister Abiy Ahmed and Eritrean President Issaias Afewerki issued a joint declaration formally ending their countries' border conflict. Full diplomatic relations were restored and the joint border was reopened to people, goods and services.

Territory and Population

Ethiopia is bounded in the northeast by Eritrea, east by Djibouti and Somalia, south by Kenya and west by South Sudan and Sudan. It has a total area of 1,127,127 sq. km. The secession of Eritrea in 1993 left Ethiopia without a coastline. An Eritrean–Ethiopian agreement of July 1993 gives Ethiopia rights to use the Eritrean ports of Assab and Massawa.

The first census was carried out in 1984: population, 42,616,876 (including Eritrea). The 2007 census population was 73,750,932 (36,533,802 females); density, 65·4 per sq. km. The United Nations population estimate for 2007 was 81,000,000. Ethiopia is Africa's second most populous country, after Nigeria. It is also the world's most populous landlocked country although its overall population is not even among the ten largest. In 2007, 83·9% of the population lived in rural areas.

The UN gives a projected population for 2020 of 112·76m.

Ethiopia has 11 administrative divisions—nine states (Afar, Amhara, Benshangul/Gumaz, Gambella, Harari, Oromia, the Peoples of the South, Somalia and Tigre) and two cities (Addis Ababa and Dire Dawa).

The population of the capital, Addis Ababa, was 2,739,551 in 2007. Other large towns (2007 populations): Dire Dawa, 233,224; Nazret, 220,212; Mekele, 215,914; Gonder, 207,044.

There are seven major ethnic groups (in % of total population in 2007): Oromo, 35%; Amhara, 27%; Somali, 6%; Tigrinya, 6%; Sidamo, 4%; Gurage, 3%; Welaita, 2%. The *de facto* official language is Amharic (which uses its own alphabet). Oromo is also widely spoken. In total there are around 80 local languages.

Social Statistics

Births, 2008 estimate, 3,086,000; deaths, 954,000. Rates per 1,000 population, 2008 estimates: births, 38·2; deaths, 11·8. Expectation of life at birth in 2013 was 62·0 years for males and 65·3 years for females. Annual population growth rate, 2000–08, 2·6%; infant mortality, 2010, 68 per 1,000 live births; fertility rate, 2008, 5·3 births per woman. Ethiopia has made some of the best progress in recent years in reducing child mortality. The number of deaths per 1,000 live births among children under five was reduced from 205 in 1990 to 64 in 2013.

Climate

The wide range of latitude produces many climatic variations between the high, temperate plateaus and the hot, humid lowlands. The main rainy season lasts from June to Aug., with light rains from Feb. to April, but the country is very vulnerable to drought. Addis Ababa, Jan. 59°F (15°C), July 59°F (15°C). Annual rainfall 50" (1,237 mm). Harar, Jan. 65°F (18·3°C), July 64°F (17·8°C). Annual rainfall 35" (897 mm). Massawa, Jan. 78°F (25·6°C), July 94°F (34·4°C). Annual rainfall 8" (193 mm).

Constitution And Government

A 548-member constituent assembly was elected on 5 June 1994; turnout was 55%. The EPRDF gained 484 seats. On 8 Dec. 1994 it unanimously adopted a new federal constitution which became effective on 22 Aug. 1995. It provided for the creation of a federation of nine regions based (except the capital and the southern region) on a predominant ethnic group. These regions have the right of secession after a referendum. The *President*, a largely ceremonial post, is elected for a six-year term by both chambers of parliament (renewable once only). The lower house is the 547-member *House of People's Representatives*; the upper house the 153-member *House of the Federation*.

National Anthem

'Yazegennat keber ba-Ityop yachchen santo' ('In our Ethiopia our civic pride is strong'); words by D. M. Mengesha, tune by S. Lulu Mitiku.

Recent Elections

Parliamentary elections were held on 24 May 2015. The Ethiopian People's Revolutionary Democratic Front (EPRDF) won 501 seats. The EPRDF's allies took 46 seats: the Somali People's Democratic Party 24, the Benishangul Gumuz People's Democratic Party 9, the Afar National Democratic Party 8, the Gambella People's Unity Democratic Movement 3, the Argoba People Democratic Organization 1 and the Harari National League 1. Opposition parties failed to win any seats. Turnout was 93·2%.

Mulatu Teshome Wirtu was unanimously elected president on 7 Oct. 2013 at the joint session of the two houses of the parliament. Outgoing president Girma Wolde-Giyorgis was constitutionally barred from running.

Current Government

President: Sahle-Work Zewde; b. 1950 (sworn in 25 Oct. 2018).

In Feb. 2019 the government comprised:

Prime Minister: Abiy Ahmed; b. 1976 (sworn in 2 April 2018).

Deputy Prime Minister: Demeke Mekonnen.

Minister of Agriculture: Omer Husen. *Culture and Tourism:* Hirut Kassaw. *Defence:* Aisha Mohammed. *Education:* Tilaye Gete. *Finance and Economic Development:* Ahmed Shide. *Foreign Affairs:* Workneh Gebeyehu. *Health:* Amir Aman. *Innovation and Technology:* Getahun Mekuria. *Labour and Social Affairs:* Ergoge Tesfaye. *Mines and Petroleum:* Samuel Hurka. *Peace:* Muferiat Kamil. *Planning and Development Commission:* Fitsum Assefa. *Revenue:* Adanech Abebe. *Science and Higher Education:* Hirut Woldemariam. *Trade and Industry:* Fetlework Gebregziabher. *Transport:* Dagmawit Moges. *Urban Development and Construction:* Jantrar Abay. *Water, Irrigation and Energy:* Sileshi Bekele. *Women, Children and Youth:* Yalem Tsegaye. *Attorney General:* Berhanu Tsegay.

Government Website: http://www.ethiopia.gov.et

Current Leaders

Abiy Ahmed

Position
Prime Minister

Introduction
Having been elected leader of the ruling Ethiopian People's Revolutionary Democratic Front (EPRDF) in late March 2018, Abiy Ahmed became prime minister on 2 April 2018. He is the country's first ethnic Oromo head of state in recent history.

Early Life
Abiy Ahmed was born on 23 April 1976 in Beshasha in the Oromia region, the son of mixed Christian and Muslim parents. After graduating in computer engineering, he received a master's degree in transformational leadership and change from Greenwich University in London, UK, studied at the International Leadership Institute in Addis Ababa, took another master's degree in business administration from Addis Ababa's Leadstar College of Management and Leadership and a doctorate in conflict resolution from the Institute for Peace and Security Studies at Addis Ababa University.

Ahmed's military career included service in the People's Democratic Organization (OPDO), the Ethiopian National Defense Force, the UN Assistance Mission for Rwanda (UNAMIR) and the Eritrean border war. Having achieved the rank of lieutenant-colonel, he retired from the military in 2010.

As a politician in OPDO, Ahmed was elected in 2010 to the House of People's Representatives where he focused on reconciling Muslim and Christian communities in the Jimma zone. In Oct. 2015 he became minister of science and technology and the following year was appointed deputy president of the Oromia region, when he addressed issues of land-grabbing and displaced people. Having become chairman of OPDO in Feb. 2018 and then chairman of the EPRDF (of which OPDO is a constituent partner), his election as prime minister by the House of People's Representatives on 2 April was a formality.

Career in Office
Given his mixed Christian and Muslim heritage and his Oromo background, together with his command of the Tigrayan language, it was hoped that Ahmed might be a catalyst for ethnic and religious reconciliation in the country. His immediate domestic priorities included ending the state of emergency (in June 2018) that had seen the detention of hundreds of people, tackling corruption and addressing a weak businesses climate and transportation infrastructure. In foreign policy he achieved an early breakthrough as diplomatic overtures towards President Afewerki of neighbouring Eritrea secured an end to the territorial dispute and state of war existing between their two countries since 1998. Furthermore, in Oct. Ahmed's government signed a peace agreement with the separatist Ogaden National Liberation Front, ending a 34-year rebellion.

Defence

In 2013 defence expenditure totalled US$351m. (US$4 per capita), representing 0·8% of GDP.

As at 31 May 2016 Ethiopia had 8,332 personnel serving in UN peacekeeping operations (the largest contingent of any country), mainly in Sudan.

Army

The strength of the Army was 135,000 in 2011. There are four military regional commands (Northern, Western, Eastern and Central) and one functional (support) command.

Air Force

Personnel numbered 3,000 in 2011. There were 26 combat-capable aircraft in 2011, including MiG-21s and Su-27s, and 18 attack helicopters.

International Relations

A border dispute between Ethiopia and Eritrea broke out in May 1998. Eritrean troops took over the border town of Badame after a skirmish between Ethiopian police units and armed men from Eritrea. Ethiopia maintained that Badame and Sheraro, a nearby town, had always been part of Ethiopia and called Eritrea's action an invasion. An agreement ending hostilities was signed in June 2000, followed by a peace accord in Dec. A buffer zone was created to separate the armies but tensions still arose from time to time, notably in late 2005 following a further dispute between the two countries over Badame. There were also border skirmishes in June 2016. Then, in July 2018, the leaders of the two countries signed a joint declaration formally ending the border conflict.

Economy

Agriculture accounted for 48·8% of GDP in 2012, industry 10·1% and services 41·1%.

Overview

Ethiopia is among the poorest countries in the world, with economic development stalled by frequent droughts, conflict with Eritrea from the late 1990s until 2018 and the global financial crisis. Nonetheless, it is among the fastest growing economies in sub-Saharan Africa.

Growth averaged 10·6% from 2006–17, while those living below the poverty line fell from 39% in 2006–07 to 29% in 2011–12 and 24% in 2014. The agriculture, construction and services sectors are the main contributors to growth, which has also been spurred by increasing levels of public investment and private consumption. The current account deficit narrowed from 10·2% of GDP in 2014–15 to 6·4% in 2017–18.

Donor assistance increased significantly under the IMF–World Bank Indebted Poor Countries Initiative. The country also qualified for debt relief under the Multilateral Debt Relief Initiative. The government hopes to achieve middle-income status for the country by 2025. To this end, there have been significant advances in the provision of universal primary education, as well as in addressing millennium development goals for child mortality, access to sanitary water and gender parity in primary schooling.

Nonetheless, political disruption, a weak private sector and limited competitiveness pose key challenges to poverty reduction and maintaining growth momentum, according to the World Bank.

Currency

The *birr* (ETB), of 100 *cents*, is the unit of currency. The birr was devalued in Oct. 1992. In April 2005 total money supply was 24,297m. birr. Foreign exchange reserves were US$1,444m. in May 2005. Inflation was 44·4% in 2008—the second highest rate in the world for that year behind Zimbabwe. It has since fallen, and was 7·3% in 2016 and 9·9% in 2017.

Budget

The fiscal year ends on 7 July. Budgetary central government revenue and expenditure in 1m. birrs:

	2008–09	2009–10	2010–11
Revenue	47,749	60,382	77,455
Expenditure	41,073	48,247	54,516

Principal sources of revenue in 2010–11: taxes on international trade and transactions, 22,973m. birrs; grants, 21,433m. birrs; taxes on income, profits and capital gains, 12,414m. birrs. Main items of expenditure by economic type in 2010–11: subsidies, 27,732m. birrs; use of goods and services, 10,820m. birrs; compensation of employees, 6,979m. birrs.

VAT of 15% was introduced in 2003.

Performance

After the economy contracted by 2·1% in 2003 there was a recovery with growth of 11·7% in 2004. This strong performance has continued since with real GDP growth of 10·4% in 2015, 8·0% in 2016 and 10·9% in 2017. Ethiopia was Africa's fastest-growing economy in 2014 and 2015. It also ranked among Africa's top half-dozen performing economies every year between 2004 and 2014 and is one of the world's fastest-growing non-oil producing economies. Total GDP was US$80·6bn. in 2017.

Banking and Finance

The central bank and bank of issue is the National Bank of Ethiopia (founded 1964; *Governor*, Yinager Dessie). The country's largest bank is the state-owned Commercial Bank of Ethiopia. The complete monopoly held by the bank ended with deregulation in 1994, but it still commands about 90% of the market share. There are eight other banks.

In 2010 external debt totalled US$7,147m., equivalent to 24% of GNI.

Energy and Natural Resources

Environment

Carbon dioxide emissions from the consumption of energy were the equivalent of 0·1 tonnes per capita in 2011.

The *Climate Change and Environmental Risk Atlas 2014* produced by Maplecroft, a risk analytics company, ranked Ethiopia as the country facing the tenth highest economic and social risk from climate change by 2025.

Electricity

Installed capacity in 2011 was around 2·0m. kW. Production in 2011 was 5·16bn. kWh. Hydro-electricity accounted for 99% of generation in 2011, but following the opening of a new wind farm (at the time the largest in Africa) at Ashegoda in 2013 dependence on hydro-power is expected to decline. Consumption per capita was 58 kWh in 2011. In 2016, 43% of the population had access to electricity compared to only 13% in 2000. The Grand Ethiopian Renaissance Dam, construction of which is expected to be completed by 2022, will nearly quadruple electricity generation capacity.

Oil and Gas

The Calub gas field in the southeast of Ethiopia had proven reserves of 25bn. cu. metres in 2013.

Minerals

Gold and salt are produced. Lege Dembi, an open-pit gold mine in the south of the country, has proven reserves of over 62 tonnes and produces more than five tonnes a year.

Agriculture

Small-scale farmers make up about 85% of Ethiopia's population. In 2011, 35·7% of total land area was agricultural, of which 40·8% was arable and 3·1% occupied by permanent crops.

Coffee is by far the most important source of rural income. Main agricultural products (2013, in 1,000 tonnes): maize, 6,674; sorghum, 4,338; wheat, 4,039; sugarcane, 2,750 (estimate); barley, 1,933; sweet potatoes, 1,355; yams, 1,192. Teff (*Eragrastis abyssinica*) and durra are also major products.

Livestock, 2012: cattle, 54·0m.; sheep, 25·5m.; goats, 24·1m.; asses, 6·7m.; horses, 1·9m.; camels, 916,000; chickens, 50·4m.

Forestry

In 2015 forests covered 12·50m. ha., representing 11% of the land area. Ethiopia is Africa's leading roundwood producer, with removals totalling 105·54m. cu. metres in 2011.

Fisheries

The catch in 2015 was 45,519 tonnes, entirely from inland waters.

Industry

Most public industrial enterprises are controlled by the state. Industrial activity is centred around Addis Ababa. Processed food, cement, textiles and drinks are the main commodities produced. Industrial production accounted for 10·1% of GDP in 2012, including 3·6% from manufacturing.

Labour

The estimated labour force in 2010 was 41,310,000 (52% males), up from 28,996,000 in 2000. Coffee provides a livelihood to a quarter of the population.

Ethiopia had 0·65m. people living in slavery according to the Walk Free Foundation's 2013 *Global Slavery Index*, the fifth highest total of any country.

International Trade

Imports and Exports

Goods imports were US$14,899·1m. in 2013 (US$11,912·9m. in 2012) and goods exports US$4,076·9m. (US$2,891·3m. in 2012).

Principal imports in 2013 were machinery and transport equipment (33·0%), manufactured goods and chemicals; main exports in 2013 were food, animals and beverages (52·3%), crude materials and animal and vegetable oils, and mineral fuels and lubricants.

The leading import supplier in 2010 was China (24·0%), followed by Saudi Arabia and India; the leading export destination in 2010 was Germany (11·4%), followed by China and Somalia.

Communications

Roads

There were 44,359 km of roads in 2007. Passenger cars in use in 2007 numbered 70,900 (one per 1,000 inhabitants) and there were also 149,000 lorries and vans, and 17,100 buses and coaches. In 2007 there were 2,517 deaths in road accidents.

Rail

The original Ethio-Djibouti Railway has a length of 781 km (metre gauge), but much of the route is abandoned. There are still passenger services from Dire Dawa, Ethiopia's second largest city, to Djibouti. However, there have not been services between Addis Ababa and Dire Dawa for many years. A new line, the 756 km Addis Ababa–Djibouti Railway, linking Ethiopia and Djibouti has been built by China Civil Engineering Construction Corporation. It became operational on a trial basis in Oct. 2016 and was officially opened on 1 Jan. 2018. Passenger-km travelled in 2005 came to 145m. and freight tonne-km to 118m. A new 16·9 km light rail system was inaugurated in Addis Ababa in Sept. 2015. A second line opened a month later, bringing the total length up to 31·6 km.

Civil Aviation

There are international airports at Addis Ababa (Bole) and Dire Dawa. There are plans to build a new international airport near Addis Ababa that would be able to serve up to 70m. passengers a year. The national carrier is the state-owned Ethiopian Airlines, which in 2013 served 79 international and 18 domestic destinations. In the same year it carried 5,594,000 passengers (4,916,000 on international flights). In 2012 Addis Ababa (Bole) handled 7,511,465 passengers and 153,395 tonnes of freight.

Shipping

In Jan. 2014 there were 17 ships of 300 GT or over registered, totalling 313,000 GT.

Telecommunications

The state-owned Ethio Telecom is the sole telecommunications service provider. There were 908,900 fixed telephone lines in 2010 (11·0 per 1,000 inhabitants). Mobile phone subscribers numbered 6·52m. in 2010. There were 7·5 internet users per 1,000 inhabitants in 2010. Fixed internet subscriptions totalled 74,600 in 2009 (0·9 per 1,000 inhabitants). Ethiopia's internet penetration rate is one of the lowest in Africa. In June 2012 there were 599,000 Facebook users.

Social Institutions

Out of 178 countries analysed in the 2017 *Fragile States Index*—a list published jointly by the Fund for Peace and *Foreign Policy* magazine—Ethiopia was ranked the 15th most vulnerable to conflict or collapse. The index is based on 12 indicators of state vulnerability across social, political and economic categories.

Justice

The legal system is based on the Justinian Code. A new penal code came into force in 1958 and Special Penal Law in 1974. Codes of criminal procedure, civil, commercial and maritime codes have since been promulgated. Provincial and district courts have been established, and High Court judges visit the provincial courts on circuit. The Supreme Court at Addis Ababa is presided over by the Chief Justice. The death penalty is in force; there was one execution in 2007 but none since.

The population in penal institutions in 2011–12 was approximately 111,000 (128 per 100,000 of national population). Ethiopia was ranked 61st of 102 countries for criminal justice and 98th for civil justice in the 2015 World Justice Project *Rule of Law Index*, which provides data on how the rule of law is experienced by the general public across eight categories.

Education

The adult literacy rate in 2007 was 39·0%. Primary education commences at seven years and continues with optional secondary education at 13 years. Up to the age of 12, education is in the local language of the federal region. In 2007 there were 12·17m. pupils at primary schools and 3·43m. pupils at secondary schools. During the period 1990–95 only 19% of females of primary school age were enrolled in school but this had increased to 62% by 2006. There were 32 universities in 2012, with many having just opened in the previous few years—there were only two as recently as the early 1990s. There were 210,456 students in tertiary education in 2007 and 8,355 academic staff.

In 2007 public expenditure on education came to 5·5% of GNI and 23·3% of total government spending.

Health

In 2009 there were 2,152 physicians, 20,109 nurses, 1,379 midwives and 661 pharmacists. In *Water: At What Cost? The State of the World's Water 2016*, WaterAid reported that 42·7% of the population does not have access to safe water (the tenth highest percentage of any nation). Ethiopia ranked as the country with the fourth largest number of people living without access to safe water (42·3m. in 2015).

Religion

According to estimates by the Pew Research Center's Forum on Religion & Public Life, 62·8% of the population in 2010 were Christians, 34·6% were Muslims and 2·6% folk religionists. Among the Christians, 69% in 2010 were Ethiopian Orthodox and 30% Protestants. The predominant church in the country is the Ethiopian Orthodox Tewahedo Church. However, the proportion of Orthodox Christians has been gradually declining over the past 30 years and the proportion of Protestants steadily rising. The Head of all Archbishops and Patriarch of the Ethiopian Orthodox Tewahedo Church is Abune Mathias (enthroned 3 March 2013). In Feb. 2019 there was one cardinal in the Roman Catholic Church.

Culture

World Heritage Sites

There are nine sites in Ethiopia that appear on the UNESCO World Heritage List. They are (with the year entered on list): the Rock-hewn Churches at Laibela (1978), 11 monolithic 13th century churches; Simien National Park (1978); Fasil Ghebbi, Gondar Region (1979), a 16th century fortress city; Aksum (1980), the capital of the ancient Kingdom of Aksum, containing tombs and castles dating from the first millennium AD; the Lower Valley of the Awash (1980), an important palaeontological site; the Lower Valley of the Omo (1980), where *Homo gracilis* was discovered; Tiya (1980), a group of archaeological sites south of Addis Ababa; Harar Jugol (2006), a fortified historic town; and the Konso Cultural Landscape (2011), an area of stone walled terraces and fortified settlements in the Konso highlands.

Press

In 2008 there were three paid-for daily newspapers with a combined circulation of 92,000 and 54 paid-for non-dailies. In the 2013 *World Press Freedom Index* compiled by Reporters Without Borders, Ethiopia was ranked 137th out of 179 countries.

Tourism

In 2011 there were 523,000 international tourist arrivals (excluding same-day visitors), up from 330,000 in 2006; tourist spending (excluding passenger transport) totalled US$1,998m. in 2011, up from US$639m. in 2006.

Calendar

The Ethiopian calendar is based on the ancient Coptic calendar; the year has 13 months (12 months with 30 days and one month with five or six, depending on the leap-year). It begins on 11 or 12 Sept. (Gregorian) and is seven or eight years behind the Gregorian calendar.

Diplomatic Representatives

Of Ethiopia in the United Kingdom (17 Prince's Gate, London, SW7 1PZ)
   Ambassador: Dr Hailemichael Aberra Afework.

Of the United Kingdom in Ethiopia (Comoros St., PO Box 858, Addis Ababa)
   Ambassador: Dr Alastair McPhail, CMG, OBE.

Of Ethiopia in the USA (3506 International Drive, NW, Washington, D.C., 20008)
   Ambassador: Kassa Teklebrhan Gebrehiwet.

Of the USA in Ethiopia (1014 Entoto Rd, Addis Ababa)
Ambassador: Michael Raynor.

Of Ethiopia to the United Nations
Ambassador: Taye Atske Selassie.

Of Ethiopia to the European Union
Ambassador: Teshome Toga Chanka.

Further Reading

Araia, G., *Ethiopia: the Political Economy of Transition.* 1995

Bigsten, Arne, Shimeles, Adebe and Kebede, Bereket, (eds) *Poverty, Income Distribution and Labour Markets in Ethiopia.* 2005

Crummey, Donald, *Land and Society in the Christian Kingdom of Ethiopia: From the Thirteenth to the Twentieth Century.* 2000

Henze, Paul B., *Layers of Time: A History of Ethiopia.* 2000

Marcus, H. G., *A History of Ethiopia.* 1994

Negash, Tekeste and Tronvoll, Kjetil, *Brothers at War: Making Sense of the Eritrean–Ethiopian War.* 2001

Pankhurst, Richard, *The Ethiopians.* 1999

Woodward, Peter, *The Horn of Africa: Politics and International Relations.* 2002

National Statistical Office: Central Statistical Office, Addis Ababa.

Website: http://www.csa.gov.et

Fiji

Matanitu Tugalala o Viti (Republic of Fiji)

Capital: Suva
Population projection, 2020: 925,000
GNI per capita, 2017: (PPP$) 8,324
HDI/world rank, 2017: 0·741/92=
Internet domain extension: .fj

Key Historical Events

Fiji was first settled by Melanesians around 1,500 BC. They travelled east in double-hulled canoes from settlements in present-day Papua New Guinea and the Solomon Islands. Their Lapita culture, an agriculturalist and partially mobile maritime way of life, is thought to have originated in southeast Asia. Remains of canoes made from indigenous Fijian trees found in Tonga point to long-standing trade links across the western Pacific.

The Dutch seafarer Abel Tasman reached Fiji in 1643, describing 12 islands and reefs. The English explorer James Cook passed by in 1774 and the archipelago was recorded in detail by Capt. Bligh after the mutiny of the *Bounty* in 1789. From about 1810 merchants visited the islands in search of sandalwood and beche-de-mer and by 1835 the first missionaries had arrived. Levuka, on the island of Ovalu, was established as a port by 1840 and Rotuma island, to the north, served as a whaling station.

The increasing availability of weapons sparked inter-tribal conflicts and by the mid-19th century a single clan (centred on the island of Bau) dominated, led by Nauvilou and then his nephew Cakobau. A convert to Christianity, Cakobau agreed to British demands that Fiji become a Crown dependency in 1874. Rotuma island was added to the territory in 1881. The first governor, Arthur Gordon, sought to protect traditional ways of life while encouraging sugar plantations and importing thousands of indentured workers from India. By 1916, when the scheme ended, more than 60,000 Indian workers had arrived. They began to demand more political and commercial influence in the 1920s. Calls for independence gained momentum during the 1960s, with much debate over the future form of government and land rights for ethnic Fijians.

Fiji gained independence within the Commonwealth on 10 Oct. 1970. In the general election of 12 April 1987 a left-wing coalition came to power with the support of the Indian population who outnumbered the indigenous Fijians by 50% to 44%. However, it was overthrown in a military coup. A month later, Fiji declared itself a Republic and Fiji's Commonwealth membership lapsed. In 1990 a new coalition restored civilian rule, but made it impossible for Fijian Indians to hold power before a rapprochement with Indian leaders led to an agreement to restore multi-racial government in 1998. Fiji meanwhile rejoined the Commonwealth in 1997.

A coup was staged in May 2000 under the leadership of George Speight, a failed businessman. His main aim was to exclude Indians from government. However, an interim administration was appointed in July 2000 to rule for 18 months and Speight and many of his supporters were subsequently arrested. On 5 Dec. 2006 Fiji suffered its fourth coup in less than 20 years when Commodore Frank Bainimarama ousted Prime Minister Laisenia Qarase, placing him under house arrest. Bainimarama assumed the powers of president and prime minister, although he subsequently restored his predecessor, Ratu Josefa Iloilo, to the presidency.

Against a backdrop of international pressure to schedule democratic elections, Iloilo repealed the constitution in April 2009. He appointed himself head of state and named Bainimarama as premier, while also imposing martial law. Bainimarama lifted martial law in Jan. 2012. A new constitution was promulgated in Sept. 2013, paving the way for elections 12 months later that returned Bainimarama as prime minister. Fiji was readmitted to the Commonwealth the same month.

Territory and Population

Fiji comprises 332 islands and islets (about one-third are inhabited) lying between 15° and 22° S. lat. and 174° E. and 178° W. long. The largest is Viti Levu, area 10,429 sq. km (4,027 sq. miles); followed by Vanua Levu, 5,556 sq. km (2,145 sq. miles). The island of Rotuma (47 sq. km, 18 sq. miles), about 12° 30' S. lat., 178° E. long., was added to the colony in 1881. Total area, 18,272 sq. km (7,055 sq. miles). Total population (2017 census), 884,887 (females, 436,292). In 2012 Fijians were estimated at 60% of the population (up from an estimated 54% in 2002), Indians 34% (down from an estimated 41% in 2002) and others 6%. Population density (2017), 48·4 per sq. km; 55·9% of the population lived in urban areas in 2017.

The UN gives a projected population for 2020 of 925,000.

The population of the capital, Suva (including Nasinu), was 185,913 at the 2017 census. Other large towns are Lautoka (71,573), Nadi (71,048) and Nausori (57,882).

English, Fijian and Hindustani are all official languages.

Social Statistics

2009 estimates: births, 19,000; deaths, 6,000. Rates, 2009 estimates (per 1,000 population): birth, 22; death, 7. Annual population growth rate, 2005–10, 0·9%. Life expectancy at birth in 2013 was 67·0 years for males and 73·0 years for females. Infant mortality, 2010, 15 per 1,000 live births; fertility rate, 2013, 2·6 births per woman.

Climate

A tropical climate, but oceanic influences prevent undue extremes of heat or humidity. The S. E. Trades blow from May to Nov., during which time nights are cool and rainfall amounts least. Suva, Jan. 80°F (26·7°C), July 73°F (22·8°C). Annual rainfall 117" (2,974 mm).

Constitution and Government

Parliament was reopened in Oct. 2001, having been suspended following a coup in May 2000. In 2006 another coup brought Commodore Frank Bainimarama to power but on 9 April 2009 the court of appeal declared his government illegal and he stood down. The next day the president repealed the constitution and assumed all governing power. The court was disbanded and Bainimarama's government restored. In March 2012 he disbanded the Great Council of Chiefs, which had existed in name only since April 2007 when Bainimarama suspended its operations. It had previously been responsible for appointing the president and 14 members of the Senate.

A new constitution received presidential assent on 6 Sept. 2013 and came into immediate effect. It was drawn up by the government itself after proposals from an independent Constitutional Committee were rejected.

The new constitution established a single-chamber 50-seat *Parliament* as the country's supreme authority, elected every four years by proportional representation from a single national constituency. It eliminated race-based electoral rolls and race-based seat quotas. The voting age was reduced from 21 to 18. The executive authority of the State is vested in the *President*, who is appointed by Parliament. The presidential term of office is three years and may be renewed once.

The constitution permits citizens to take multi-citizenship but in order to stand for Parliament, candidates must have Fijian-only citizenship. Communal land ownership by indigenous Fijians is expressly protected and the teaching of iTaukei and Fiji Hindi languages is compulsory in primary schools. An Accountability and Transparency Commission was also established to hold public officials to account.

A Bill of Rights included in the constitution was criticized by Amnesty International, not least for a clause granting immunity to those responsible for the 2006 coup.

National Anthem

'Meda Dau Doka' ('God Bless Fiji'); words and tune by M. Prescott.

© Springer Nature Limited 2020
Palgrave Macmillan (ed.), *The Statesman's Yearbook 2020*,
https://doi.org/10.1057/978-1-349-95940-2_72

Recent Elections

Parliamentary elections took place on 14 Nov. 2018. Incumbent Prime Minister Frank Bainimarama's FijiFirst Party won 27 of the 51 seats with 50·0% of votes cast, followed by the Social Democratic Liberal Party with 21 (39·9%) and the National Federation Party with 3 (7·4%). Turnout was 71·3%.

Jioji Konrote was re-elected president by parliament unopposed on 31 Aug. 2018.

Current Government

President: Jioji Konrote; b. 1947 (FijiFirst; sworn in 12 Nov. 2015 and re-elected 31 Aug. 2018).

In Feb. 2019 the government comprised:

Prime Minister, and Minister for iTaukei Affairs and Sugar Industry: Commodore Frank Bainimarama; b. 1954 (sworn in 5 Jan. 2007, then briefly ousted from 9–12 April 2009).

Attorney General and Minister for Economy, Civil Service and Communications: Aiyaz Sayed-Khaiyum. *Industry, Trade, Tourism, Local Government, Housing and Community Development:* Premila Devi Kumar. *Agriculture, Rural and Maritime Development, Waterways and Environment:* Mahendra Reddy. *Defence, National Security and Foreign Affairs:* Inia Seruiratu. *Education, Heritage and Arts:* Rosy Akbar. *Employment, Productivity and Industrial Relations, Youth and Sports:* Parveen Kumar. *Fisheries:* Semi Koroilavesau. *Forestry:* Osea Naiqamu. *Health and Medical Services:* Ifereimi Waqainabete. *Infrastructure, Transport, Disaster Management and Meteorological Services:* Jone Usamate. *Lands and Mineral Resources:* Ashneel Sudhakar. *Women, Children and Poverty Alleviation:* Mereseini Vuniwaqa.

Government Website: http://www.fiji.gov.fj

Current Leaders

Jioji Konrote

Position
President

Introduction
A retired army major-general with a background in diplomacy, Jioji Konrote became president in Nov. 2015. He was re-elected for a second term in Aug. 2018.

Early Life
Jioji Konrote was born on 26 Dec. 1947 on the island of Rotuma. After finishing high school, he enlisted in the army in May 1966. He received military training in both New Zealand and Australia, where he attended the Australian College of Defence and Strategic Studies and the Australian Defence Force Academy. In 1996 he became a Fellow at the latter institution, while in 2000 he completed a programme in national and international security at the Kennedy School of Government at Harvard in the USA.

Earlier, in 1974, he had spent a year with the British Army Far East Land Forces, serving as platoon commander in Hong Kong, and from 1986 took part in United Nations peacekeeping operations in Lebanon as part of the UN Interim Force (UNIFIL). In 1990 he was appointed vice-commander of UNIFIL and in 1999 served as force commander.

In 2000 Konrote was named permanent secretary for home affairs and immigration in Fiji, a role he retained until 2002. He then served as high commissioner to Australia and non-resident high commissioner to Singapore. At Fiji's parliamentary elections in 2006, he won the Rotuman Communal Constituency and was appointed minister of state for immigration and ex-servicemen, a position he held until Dec. 2006 when Laisenia Qarase's government was overthrown in a military coup.

Konrote joined the newly-established FijiFirst party ahead of the 2014 parliamentary election and, having won a seat, he took up the role of minister for employment opportunities, productivity and industrial relations in Sept. of that year. In this office he oversaw the introduction of a minimum wage. However, in 2015 he resigned his parliamentary positions so as to contest the first presidential election since the new constitution was promulgated in 2013, standing as the FijiFirst candidate.

Career in Office
At the parliamentary vote to elect the president on 12 Oct. 2015, Konrote received 31 votes to the 14 garnered by his opponent, Ratu Epeli Ganilau, and became the first Seventh-day Adventist and ethnic minority occupant of the office. He was sworn in on 12 Nov. 2015.

Josaia Voreqe Bainimarama

Position
Prime Minister

Introduction
Josaia Voreqe (commonly known as Frank) Bainimarama, former military commander of Fiji, became prime minister after leading a coup in Dec. 2006 against the incumbent, Laisenia Qarase. Previously a Qarase ally, Bainimarama had been a key figure in defeating a coup attempt by George Speight in 2000 and installing Qarase to the premiership. However, Bainimarama's relationship with Qarase deteriorated in 2006. He appointed himself as president before relinquishing that position to become prime minister.

Early Life
An ethnic Fijian, Bainimarama was born on 27 April 1954 on Bau Island and educated at the Marist Brothers High School. He enlisted in the navy in July 1975 and received his first command post in the early 1980s. He was promoted to lieutenant commander in Feb. 1986 and then served with the Multinational Force and Observers peacekeeping force in the Sinai Peninsula until returning to Fiji in Sept. 1987. He was appointed commander of the navy in Oct. 1988.

During his term as commander Bainimarama undertook extensive training, including in maritime surveillance, in disaster management and in exclusive economic zone management. He became acting chief of staff in Nov. 1997, and was promoted to the rank of commodore and appointed commander of the armed forces in March 1999.

In May 2000 George Speight led a coup with the declared aim of promoting Fijian nationalism and excluding ethnic Indians from government. Prime Minister Chaudhry was deposed and when President Mara fled, Bainimarama declared martial law. On 30 May he appointed an interim military government and appointed Laisenia Qarase as prime minister on 4 July. On 6 July the interim government responded to a military mutiny by signing an accord with Speight granting him immunity from prosecution. On 13 July it installed Iloilo as president, together with a pro-Speight vice-president, Jope Seniloli.

On 27 July the interim government revoked Speight's immunity, with Bainimarama claiming that the accord had been signed under duress. Speight and 369 others were arrested. On 2 Nov. pro-Speight soldiers mutinied in Suva, forcing Bainimarama to flee. The mutiny was quelled and Bainimarama accused a former prime minister, Sitiveni Rabuka, of involvement. He persisted in attempts to prove the involvement of Rabuka and other alleged conspirators and vehemently opposed Prime Minister Qarase's proposals in 2006 to offer amnesty to the rebels.

In Oct. 2006 Qarase attempted unsuccessfully to replace Bainimarama as commander of the armed forces while he was out of the country. Bainimarama then staged a coup on 5 Dec. 2006, with the support of senior military figures. Claiming he wanted to end corruption and stop racial divisions threatening national unity, he dismissed Qarase's government and appointed himself acting president. He placed government ministries under the control of their chief executive officers and appointed Jona Senilagakali as acting prime minister. International pressure forced Bainimarama to return the presidency to Iloilo on 4 Jan. 2007 and on 5 Jan. he replaced Senilagakali as interim prime minister.

Career in Office
Bainimarama's political legitimacy has since come under intense scrutiny domestically and internationally. Australia and New Zealand called for him to relinquish power and refused visas to members of his government. At home political opponents and leading institutions, including the influential Methodist Church, condemned the coup alleging human rights abuses although subsequent talks in Feb. 2007 led the Church to declare its support for the interim government. Internationally, particularly within the Pacific islands region, pressure continued to mount. In Feb. 2007 Bainimarama promised to work towards democratic elections, but initially would not commit to a time-frame. Then, in Oct. 2007 at the Pacific Islands Forum annual summit in Tonga, he agreed to hold a general election by March 2009.

However, in July 2008 he reneged on this commitment on the grounds that electoral reforms could not be completed in time.

Having briefly reimposed a state of emergency from Sept.–Oct. 2007 he claimed the following month to have foiled a plot to assassinate him. On 9 April 2009 Bainimarama stood down following a court of appeal judgment that his government was illegal. However, President Iloilo reinstated the cabinet on 12 April for another five years after having dismissed the judiciary and annulled the constitution.

In Sept. 2009 the Commonwealth suspended Fiji's membership and cut off all aid because of the country's lack of progress in re-establishing democracy. Bainimarama incurred further diplomatic reproach in Nov. that year when he accused Australia and New Zealand of interfering in Fiji's internal affairs and expelled their high commissioners.

In Sept. 2011 the Bainimarama government introduced a controversial decree severely restricting the rights of trade unions to strike in any industry designated by the authorities and nullifying existing collective bargaining agreements. However, in an apparently more liberal move, he announced the lifting of martial law in Jan. 2012 and set the stage for consultations on a new constitution and democratic elections. His subsequent agreement to schedule elections for Sept. 2014 led Australia and New Zealand to restore diplomatic ties in July 2012. In Sept. 2013 the government unveiled its new constitution, described by Bainimarama as a blueprint for democracy and a new beginning for the island nation despite generating scepticism from opponents at home and abroad. In March 2014 Bainimarama stood down as army commander and in Sept. that year his FijiFirst Party won the first parliamentary elections to be held since the 2006 coup. He was subsequently reappointed as prime minister and Fiji was reinstated as a full member of the Commonwealth. In a cabinet reshuffle in Sept. 2016 he took over the foreign affairs portfolio from Ratu Inoke Kubuabola who became defence minister. Further parliamentary elections in Nov. 2018 returned his FijiFirst Party to power with a majority 27 of the 51 assembly seats.

One of the strongest cyclones ever recorded in the southern hemisphere hit Fiji in Feb. 2016, causing extensive damage and killing more than 40 people.

Defence

In 2013 defence expenditure totalled US$58m. (US$65 per capita), representing 1·4% of GDP.

Army
Personnel in 2011 numbered 3,200 including 300 recalled reserves. There is an additional reserve force of around 6,000.

Navy
A small naval division of the armed forces numbered 300 in 2011.

Economy

Agriculture accounted for 11·4% of GDP in 2014, industry 18·2% and services 70·4%.

Overview
The main sources of foreign exchange are tourism, sugar exports and remittances from abroad, despite attempts to diversify the economy. Gold, silver and limestone mining are also important and there is a well-developed service sector.

At independence in 1970 sugar accounted for 70% of export earnings. In 1973 the government brought all sugar milling activities under the control of the Fiji Sugar Corporation, but the public company has operated at a loss since 2006. It is estimated that over 20% of the population still depend on the sugar industry for work, although its share of export earnings is declining.

Economic growth has been sluggish for several decades, in large part the result of internal political turmoil. It contracted by 1·8% in 2000 following a military coup in May of that year. After a further coup in late 2006 growth shrank by 0·9% in 2007, while tourist arrivals fell by 6% and the business climate deteriorated. The global financial crisis then combined with adverse weather conditions and weak domestic investment to cause a further economic contraction in 2009.

However, between 2011 and 2015 GDP growth averaged 3·6% per year, supported by sound macroeconomic policies including income tax cuts and low interest rates. Growth slowed to 0·4% in 2016 though, with the cost of damage from Cyclone Winston put at 28% of GDP—agriculture and forestry were the hardest hit sectors. Unemployment has persistently hovered around 9% and there has been a significant exodus of skilled workers. Also, some 28% of the population lives below the national poverty line. Continued structural reform is vital to achieving long-term fiscal stability, maintaining sustainable broad-based growth and reducing vulnerability to external shocks.

Currency
The unit of currency is the *Fiji dollar* (FJD) of 100 *cents*. In June 2005 total money supply was $F1,082m., foreign exchange reserves were US$397m. and gold reserves 1,000 troy oz. Inflation was 3·9% in 2016 and 3·4% in 2017. The Fiji dollar was devalued by 20% in both Jan. 1998 and April 2009.

Budget
Revenues in 2015 (provisional) totalled $F2,800·8m. and expenditures $F1,880·1m.

VAT of 10% was introduced in 1992 (increased to 12·5% in 2003 and 15% in 2011, but reduced to 9% from 1 Jan. 2016).

Performance
The economy grew by 3·8% in 2015, 0·7% in 2016 and 3·0% in 2017. Total GDP in 2017 was US$5·1bn.

Banking and Finance
The financial system in Fiji comprises the central bank, banking, insurance and superannuation industries, non-bank financial institutions (NBFIs), restricted foreign exchange dealers and money changers, and the South Pacific Stock Exchange.

The central bank and bank of issue is the Reserve Bank of Fiji (*Governor,* Ariff Ali). Total assets at 31 Dec. 2007 were $F1,170m.

Total assets of commercial banks were $F3,957m. at the end of 2007. Total assets for the Fiji National Provident Fund (the sole player in the superannuation industry) at 31 Dec. 2007 were $F3,437m. Non-regulated financial institutions include the Fiji Development Bank, Housing Authority and Unit Trust of Fiji. Their assets totalled $F738m. in Dec. 2007.

Foreign debt was US$387m. in 2007.

The South Pacific Stock Exchange is based in Suva.

Energy and Natural Resources

Environment
Carbon dioxide emissions from the consumption of energy in 2011 were the equivalent of 1·6 tonnes per capita.

Electricity
The Fiji Electricity Authority is responsible for the generation, transmission and distribution of electricity in most of the country. It operates 13 power stations, three of which are operated on hydro-power, and one 10 MW wind farm. The largest energy project is one of hydro-electricity that is capable of generating 70% of the main island's electric needs. Two rural hydro schemes have been completed, one private generating 100 kW and the other—operated by the Authority—producing 800 kW.

Installed capacity in 2011 was estimated at 215,000 kW. Production in 2011 was 835m. kWh with consumption per capita 962 kWh.

Minerals
The main gold-mine normally accounts for about a twelfth of the country's exports. Gold has for many years been one of Fiji's main exports. However, after an extended closure in 2006–07 gold production in 2007 was only 77 kg, valued at $F2·55m. Bauxite is also mined.

Agriculture
In 2013 there were an estimated 165,000 ha. of arable land and 85,000 ha. of permanent crops. Production figures for 2013 (in 1,000 tonnes): sugarcane, 1,610; coconut, 185; taro, 87; cassava, 74; sweet potatoes, 9; rice, 6; pineapples, 6; ginger, 5. Ginger is becoming increasingly important.

Livestock (2013 estimates): cattle, 312,000; goats, 252,000; pigs, 147,000; chickens, 5m. Products, 2013 (in 1,000 tonnes): chicken meat, 17; beef and veal (estimate), 7; pork and pork products (estimate), 4; eggs, 7. Total production of milk (estimate) was 61,000 tonnes in 2013.

Forestry

Forests covered 1·02m. ha.—56% of the land area—in 2015. Roundwood production in 2011 was 482,000 cu. metres.

Fisheries

The catch in 2011 was 41,236 tonnes, of which 38,555 tonnes came from sea fishing.

Industry

The main industries are tourism, sugar, fish, mineral water, garments and gold which in 2007 accounted for 12·6%, 3·4%, 1·9%, 1·9%, 1·8% and 0·5% of GDP respectively.

Output, 2007 (in tonnes): sugar, 240,000; cement, 144,000; flour, 52,677; animal feed, 37,820; coconut oil, 9,657; soap, 5,556; soft drinks, 213·4m. litres; beer, 19·0m. litres; cigarettes, 401m. units.

Labour

The labour force in 2013 was 345,000 (314,000 in 2003). 57·2% of the population aged 15–64 was economically active in 2013. In the same year 8·3% of the population was unemployed.

International Trade

The Tax Free Factory/Tax Free Zone Scheme was introduced in 1987 to stimulate investment and encourage export-oriented businesses.

Imports and Exports

In 2009 imports (c.i.f.) totalled US$1,437·0m. and exports (f.o.b.) US$628·7m. Chief exports are clothing and apparel, sugar, gold, prepared and preserved fish, beverages, and cereal and cereal preparations.

In 2009 the chief import sources (in US$1m.) were: Singapore (397·7); Australia (317·8); New Zealand (228·2). The chief export markets (in US$1m.) were: Singapore (103·1); Australia (100·0); United Kingdom (94·4).

Communications

Roads

The road network covers some 7,500 km. There were a total of 94,400 passenger cars and 48,000 lorries and vans in 2007. In 2006, 89 fatalities were caused by road accidents.

Rail

Fiji Sugar Cane Corporation runs 600 mm gauge railways at four of its mills on Viti Levu and Vanua Levu, totalling 597 km.

Civil Aviation

There are international airports at Nadi and Suva. The national carrier is Fiji Airways (51% government-owned). In 2013 it provided services to Australia, Hong Kong, New Zealand, USA and a number of Pacific island nations. In 2012 Nadi handled 1,856,667 passengers (1,602,216 on international flights).

Shipping

The three main ports are Suva (which handled 3,859,000 tonnes of cargo in 2013), Lautoka and Levuka. In Jan. 2014 there were 20 ships of 300 GT or over registered, totalling 25,000 GT. The inter-island shipping fleet is made up of private and government vessels.

Telecommunications

In 2013 there were 70,725 main (fixed) telephone lines and mobile phone subscriptions numbered 930,406 (105·6 per 100 persons). There were 148·2 internet users per 1,000 inhabitants in 2010. In 2009 there were 24·7 fixed broadband subscriptions per 1,000 inhabitants and 8·3 mobile broadband subscriptions per 1,000 inhabitants. In Dec. 2011 there were 163,000 Facebook users.

Social Institutions

Out of 178 countries analysed in the 2017 *Fragile States Index*—a list published jointly by the Fund for Peace and *Foreign Policy* magazine—Fiji was ranked the 76th most vulnerable to conflict or collapse. The index is based on 12 indicators of state vulnerability across social, political and economic categories.

Justice

An independent Judiciary is guaranteed under the constitution. A High Court has unlimited original jurisdiction to hear and determine any civil or criminal proceedings under any law. The High Court also has jurisdiction to hear and determine constitutional and electoral questions including the membership of the House of Representatives. The Chief Justice of Fiji is appointed by the President after consultation with the Prime Minister. The substantive Chief Justice was removed from office following the Dec. 2006 military coup and was replaced by an Acting Chief Justice in Jan. 2007, who was made permanent in Dec. 2008. Following the abolition of the constitution and the dismissal of all judges in April 2009, the Chief Justice was reappointed to his post in May 2009.

Fiji's Court of Appeal, of which the Chief Justice is *ex officio* President, is formed by three specially appointed Justices of Appeal, appointed by the President after consultation with the Judicial and Legal Services Commission. Generally, any person convicted of an offence has a right of appeal from the High Court of Appeal. The final appellant court is the Supreme Court. Most matters coming before the Superior Courts originate in Magistrates' Courts.

The population in penal institutions in Nov. 2012 was 1,537 (174 per 100,000 of national population). The death penalty, which was last used in 1964, was abolished in Feb. 2015.

Police

In 2008 the Royal Fiji Police Force had a total strength of 2,655 established officers, 60 support staff and 1,600 Special Constables.

Education

Total enrolment (2009): pre-primary schools, 9,149; primary schools, 129,444 (with 5,173 teachers); secondary schools, 67,072 (with 4,273 teachers); teacher training, 633 (with 88 teachers); technical/vocational education, 2,387 (with 391 teachers). In 2005 special schools had 1,007 pupils and 103 teachers. There were 721 primary schools, 172 secondary schools, 17 special schools, 4 teacher training schools and 69 technical/vocational schools in 2009. In 2005 there were 531 pre-primary schools.

Fiji has three universities: the University of the South Pacific, established in 1968 and with its main campus in Suva, which serves 12 countries in the South Pacific region; the University of Fiji, established in 2004; and Fiji National University, formed in 2010 as a result of a merger between six institutions—one of which was originally established in 1885.

In 2005 public expenditure on education came to 6·2% of GDP.

Health

In 2007 there were 25 public hospitals with 1,727 beds, two private hospitals, 76 health centres and 101 nursing stations. There were 318 doctors, 196 dental staff and 1,820 nurses.

Through its national health service system, the government continues to provide the bulk of health services both in the curative and public health programmes.

In *Water: At What Cost? The State of the World's Water 2016*, WaterAid reported that 4·3% of the population does not have access to safe water.

Religion

In 2010 the population was 64·4% Christian according to estimates by the Pew Research Center's Forum on Religion & Public Life, with 27·9% Hindu and 6·3% Muslim. Among Christians, 84% in 2010 were Protestants and 15% Catholics.

Culture

World Heritage Sites

There is one UNESCO site in Fiji: the Levuka Historical Port Town (2013), an outstanding example of late 19th century Pacific port settlements.

Press

In 2008 there were three national dailies with a combined circulation of 40,000.

Tourism

There were 693,000 foreign tourists in 2014 (excluding same-day visitors), up from 658,000 in 2013.

Diplomatic Representatives

Of Fiji in the United Kingdom (34 Hyde Park Gate, London, SW7 5DN)
High Commissioner: Jitoko Cakacakabalavu Tikolevu.

Of the United Kingdom in Fiji (47 Gladstone Rd, Suva)
High Commissioner: Melanie Hopkins.

Of Fiji in the USA (1707 L St., Suite 200, NW, Washington, D.C., 20036)
Ambassador: Ratu Naivakarurubalavu Solo Mara.

Of the USA in Fiji (158 Princes Rd, Tamavua, Suva)
Ambassador: Vacant.
Chargé d'Affaires a.i.: Michael Goldman.

Of Fiji to the United Nations
Ambassador: Satyendra Prasad.

Of Fiji to the European Union
Ambassador: Deo Saran.

Further Reading

Bureau of Statistics. *Annual Report; Current Economic Statistics*. Quarterly
Reserve Bank of Fiji. *Quarterly Review*
Belshaw, Cyril S., *Under the Ivi Tree: Society and Economic Growth in Rural Fiji.* 2004
Kelly, John D. and Kaplan, Martha, *Represented Communities: Fiji and World Decolonization.* 2001
Lal, B. J., *Broken Waves: a History of the Fiji Islands in the Twentieth Century.* 1992
Robertson, Robert and Sutherland, William, *Government by the Gun: Fiji and the 2000 Coup.* 2002
National Statistical Office: Bureau of Statistics, POB 2221, Government Buildings, Suva.
Website: http://www.statsfiji.gov.fj

Finland

Suomen Tasavalta—Republiken Finland (Republic of Finland)

Capital: Helsinki
Population projection, 2020: 5·58m.
GNI per capita, 2017: (PPP$) 41, 002
HDI/world rank, 2017: 0·920/15
Internet domain extension: .fi

Key Historical Events

Finland's first inhabitants moved northwards at the end of the Ice Age. Further waves of settlement came in 4000 BC and 1000 BC and social groups began to develop. During the Viking era Finland's location on the trade route between Russia and Sweden brought prosperity and conflict in equal measure, with attacks made on Finnish trading posts by the Swedes and the Danes.

In the 12th century economic and religious rivalry between Sweden and Russia centred on Finland. The defeat of Birger Jarl in 1240 marked the end of the Swedish incursions but efforts at strengthening the Swedish presence in areas it already held were intensified. By 1323 Russia was forced to recognize a boundary marking off those parts of Finland that were under Swedish control including all of western and southern Finland. Finland remained a duchy of Sweden until 1581.

In the 18th century Russian forces conquered the southeast territory. The rest of the country was ceded to Russia by the treaty of Hamina in 1809 when Finland became an autonomous grand duchy, retaining its laws and institutions but owing allegiance to the tsar.

Throughout the 19th century Finland remained in Russia's shadow while building on its status as a grand duchy. By the 1880s Finland had its own army. This proved too much for the Russian military, who feared that moves towards Finnish separatism would make more difficult their task of defending the long western border. With the appointment of Gen. Bobrikov as governor general in 1898 a start was made on bringing Finland back into the imperial fold. The army was put under Russian command, the Russian language was made compulsory for the civil service and for schools and decision-making reverted to the tsar's appointees. In June 1904 Bobrikov was assassinated and, as the Russian revolutionary movement gathered pace, the Marxists won an absolute majority in parliamentary elections. It was a short-lived victory but the far-left held its popular appeal.

Civil War

Following the Russian Revolution, on 6 Dec. 1917 Finland declared independence. This was recognized by the Russian Bolsheviks on 31 Dec. By now, however, the left- and right-wing parties were in open conflict. In Jan. 1918 the Whites (the government forces) took the western, Russian-controlled province of Ostrobothnia while the Reds (supported by the Bolsheviks) seized power in the south. At the end of Jan. the Reds staged a coup and the Whites were forced to abandon Helsinki, relocating to Vaasa. But government forces, led by Gen. Gustaf Mannerheim and aided by German troops, prevailed.

A new constitution by which a German prince, Friedrich Karl, would become regent was abandoned with the collapse of Germany at the end of the First World War. In the summer of 1919 Finland became a republic with K. J. Ståhlberg as its first president.

Throughout the 1920s and early 1930s class antagonism inherited from the civil war remained the dominant political issue. As a conciliatory measure the Social Democrats were brought into government and the party formed a minority government in 1926–27. In the early 1930s fascism entered domestic politics with the emergence of the Lapua Movement. After an unsuccessful coup attempt in 1932 the movement was banned. Finland was hit by the pre-war depression but cushioned by the dominant role of agriculture in the Finnish economy.

Winter War

As Europe was anticipating German aggression, the Finns were more fearful of Moscow's territorial demands. Outnumbered and outmatched in arms and equipment, their hopes were pinned on foreign involvement. When this failed to materialize, there was no option but to concede all the Russians demanded, including the Karelian Isthmus. The 1940 treaty, which ended the Winter War, required the resettlement of 12% of the Finnish population. Fearing worse to come from the Soviet Union, Helsinki opened up contacts with the Germans, allowing transit for military traffic in return for food and armaments.

There followed the German invasion of Russia, a campaign which Mannerheim, justifying active participation, described as a 'holy war' to restore Finnish borders. Having achieved this objective, the Finns wanted out, a desire which became all the more determined as the German advance ground to a halt at Stalingrad. But there was no basis for a settlement and the Finns could only wait for the inevitable Russian counter-attack. When it came, retreating Germans took revenge by devastating everything in their path.

Having fought first against Russia then against Germany, the country emerged from the Second World War defeated, demoralized and in political disarray. The terms of the 1944 armistice included the surrender of one-twelfth of Finnish territory and reparations in goods valued at US$300m.

Revered as a national hero by the right, Mannerheim became president. Carl Enckell, a close associate for many years, took charge of foreign affairs while Juho Paasikivi was appointed premier. The 1945 election confirmed Paasikivi and Enckell in their jobs and a cabinet was formed giving roughly equal representation to the social democrats, communists and the farmers' party. When Mannerheim, who had turned 78 and ailing fast, was persuaded to stand down in mid-term of his presidency, Paasikivi was the obvious successor.

A peace treaty with Russia signed in Feb. 1947 confirmed what had already been agreed by the 1944 armistice. Finland lost 12% of her border territory to the Soviet Union, including the country's second largest city, Viipuri, and the port and province of Petsamo on the Arctic coast. With a large part of the province of Karelia taken over by the Russians, the frontier was moved back from a distance of only 31 km from Leningrad to a new line 180 km from the former Russian capital; 400,000 people had to be resettled. The Åland Islands were to remain demilitarized and limitations were imposed on the size of the Finnish armed forces and its weaponry.

Pacifying Russia

An 'invitation' to negotiate a mutual assistance agreement suggested that only an administration answerable to Moscow would satisfy the Russians. Paasikivi argued that the interests of the Soviet Union on her northwestern border (the only part of Finland that really mattered to the Russian military) could best be served by a sovereign Finland whose sympathetic relations with her eastern neighbour precluded her territory being used as a platform for attack. Skilfully, this shifted the emphasis away from Russian ambitions for making Finland an ally towards the prospect of the two countries entering into a joint security arrangement. Finland promised to defend herself against an attack from Germany or an allied state, to confer with Russia in case of war or threat of war and, if necessary, to accept Russian aid. Great play was made of Finland's ambition 'to remain outside the conflicting interests of the great powers'.

The popular view in Europe was that Finland was as much under the control of Moscow as any of the communist satellites. Paasikivi tried to counteract this impression by reacting decisively to any hint of a threat to his authority. When in 1948 there were rumours that the communists were planning to seize power, he dismissed the powerful minister of internal affairs, Yrjö Leino. But the president was hyper-sensitive to Moscow's needs for reassurances of Finnish good faith. The press was told to tone down criticism of the Soviet Union. Most of the nation's productive capacity had survived the war, and the export demand for wood products was strong. But paying off reparations meant a transfer of resources to the engineering industry. All this had to be achieved without a share in Marshall Aid, though US loans totalling US$150m. were channelled in other ways. With skilled labour in short supply, wages and prices climbed steeply. In 1948 prices were eight times their pre-war level.

In the summer of 1949 the communists disrupted industry with a series of strikes, splitting the trade union movement and raising fears of an imminent

© Springer Nature Limited 2020
Palgrave Macmillan (ed.), *The Statesman's Yearbook 2020*,
https://doi.org/10.1057/978-1-349-95940-2_73

coup. Paasikivi promptly replaced the social democrat government with one formed by the agrarians under the leadership of Urho Kekkonen. Like Paasikivi, Kekkonen worked hard to establish good personal relations with the USSR. In 1952 he put up a plan for 'a neutral alliance between the Scandinavian countries', which 'would remove even the theoretical threat of an attack ... via Finland's territory'. In reality, a Scandinavian alliance, neutral or otherwise, was impracticable since Denmark and Norway had only recently joined NATO. But the gain to Kekkonen was approval from the Soviet Union.

Defending Neutrality

In 1955, two years after the death of Stalin had brought the first signs of an easing in the cold war, Finland negotiated the return of the Porkkala base near Helsinki, which had been leased to the Soviet Union for 50 years. This meant the departure of the last Soviet troops on Finnish territory. That same year Finland joined the United Nations but stayed out of the latest formation of Soviet defence, the Warsaw Pact. In 1956 Kekkonen succeeded Paasikivi as president. A succession of weak governments consolidated presidential power and confirmed Kekkonen as the only leader capable of handling the Russians.

His first move was to assert his country's freedom of action, by suggesting that Finland might come to a deal with the European Community. In response, the Soviet Union activated article 2 of the 1948 Treaty by demanding consultation on measures to ensure the defence of their frontiers. It was the most serious challenge yet to Finnish neutrality. It had been said that article 2 could be acted upon only when both parties agreed that a threat existed; it came as a shock to realize that a unilateral declaration of interest by the stronger partner was sufficient to start the process of military consultation. If the Soviet claim went uncontested Finnish independence would be seen as a sham.

Western observers expected the worst; nothing less than military bases on Finnish soil would satisfy Moscow. But Kekkonen called successfully for a postponement of military talks in favour of discussions aimed at reassuring the Kremlin that Finland would remain true to her foreign policy. This was accompanied by a warning that if military consultations went ahead there would be a war scare in Scandinavia, possibly leading to counter-measures by the West. When the Soviet Union backed down Kekkonen was feted as the country's saviour. He was elected for a second six-year term by an overwhelming majority on the first round of voting.

In 1981 the ailing Kekkonen was replaced by Mauno Koivisto. At first he adopted the foreign policy of his predecessor but with the collapse of the Soviet Union at the end of the 1980s he was able to move Finland towards closer ties with Western Europe. Koivisto played a major role in dismantling the 1948 Treaty and in the early 1990s fostered close relations with the EU. A referendum held in 1995 paved the way for Finland to join the EU.

In 2000 Tarja Halonen of the Social Democratic Party became Finland's first female president and won a further term in 2006. She was replaced in 2012 by Sauli Niinistö, the country's first conservative head of state since the 1950s.

Territory and Population

Finland, a country of lakes and forests, is bounded in the northwest and north by Norway, east by Russia, south by the Baltic Sea and west by the Gulf of Bothnia and Sweden. At the most recent ten-yearly census on 31 Dec. 2010 the population was 5,375,276. Finland has used a register-based method of calculating the population since 1990. The areas, populations and population density estimates of Finland and its regions on 31 Dec. 2016 (Swedish names in brackets) were as follows:

Regions	Area (sq. km)[1]	Population	Population per sq. km
Ahvenanmaa (Åland)	1,554	29,489	19·0
Etelä-Karjala (Södra Karelen)	5,327	129,865	24·4
Etelä-Pohjanmaa (Södra Österbotten)	13,444	190,910	14·2
Etelä-Savo (Södra Savolax)	14,257	147,194	10·3
Kainuu (Kajanaland)	20,198	73,959	3·7
Kanta-Häme (Egentliga Tavastland)	5,199	172,720	33·2
Keski-Pohjanmaa (Mellersta Österbotten)	5,020	68,780	13·7

(continued)

Regions	Area (sq. km)[1]	Population	Population per sq. km
Keski-Suomi (Mellersta Finland)	16,703	276,031	16·5
Kymenlaakso (Kymmenedalen)	5,149	175,511	34·1
Lappi (Lappland)	92,676	179,223	1·9
Päijät-Häme (Päijänne-Tavastland)	5,124	201,228	39·3
Pirkanmaa (Birkaland)	12,587	512,081	40·7
Pohjanmaa (Österbotten)	7,754	180,945	23·3
Pohjois-Karjala (Norra Karelen)	17,761	162,986	9·2
Pohjois-Pohjanmaa (Norra Österbotten)	36,816	411,856	11·2
Pohjois-Savo (Norra Savolax)	16,770	246,653	14·7
Satakunta	7,820	220,398	28·2
Uusimaa (Nyland)	9,098	1,655,624	182·0
Varsinais-Suomi (Egentliga Finland)	10,664	477,677	44·8
Total	*303,919*	*5,513,130*	*18·1*

[1]Excluding inland water area which totals 34,548 sq. km.

The semi-autonomous province of the **Åland Islands** (Ahvenanmaa) occupies a special position as a demilitarized area and is 91% Swedish-speaking. **Åland** elects a 30-member parliament (*Lagting*), which in turn elects the provincial government (*Landskapsstyrelse*). It has a population of 28,354. The capital is Mariehamn (Maarianhamina).

End of year	Urban[1]	Semi-urban[2]	Rural	Total	Percentage urban
1800	46,600	—	786,100	832,700	5·6
1900	333,300	—	2,322,600	2,655,900	12·5
1950	1,302,400	—	2,727,400	4,029,800	32·3
1970	2,340,300	—	2,258,000	4,598,300	50·9
1980	2,865,100	—	1,922,700	4,787,800	59·8
1990	2,846,220	803,224	1,349,034	4,998,500	56·9
2000	3,167,668	898,860	1,114,587	5,181,115	61·1
2005	3,294,777	896,181	1,064,622	5,255,580	62·7
2006	3,327,207	913,614	1,036,134	5,276,955	63·1
2007	3,444,620	852,225	1,003,639	5,300,484	65·0
2008	3,616,471	837,892	871,951	5,326,314	67·9
2009	3,644,491	851,259	855,677	5,351,427	68·1

The classification urban/rural has been revised as follows: [1]Urban—at least 90% of the population lives in urban settlements, or in which the population of the largest settlement is at least 15,000. [2]Semi-urban—at least 60% but less than 90% live in urban settlements, or the population of the largest settlement is more than 4,000 but less than 15,000.

The population on 31 Dec. 2009 by language spoken: Finnish, 4,852,209; Swedish, 290,392; Sami, 1,789; other languages, 207,037.

The UN gives a projected population for 2020 of 5·58m.

The principal towns with estimated resident populations, 31 Dec. 2017, are (Swedish names in brackets):

Helsinki (Helsingfors)—capital	643,272
Espoo (Esbo)	279,044
Tampere (Tammerfors)	231,853
Vantaa (Vanda)	223,027
Oulu (Uleåborg)	201,810
Turku (Åbo)	189,669
Jyväskylä	140,188

(continued)

Lahti	119,573
Kuopio	118,209
Pori (Björneborg)	84,587
Kouvola	84,196
Joensuu	76,067
Lappeenranta (Villmanstrand)	72,909
Hämeenlinna (Tavastehus)	67,662
Vaasa (Vasa)	67,392
Seinäjoki	62,676
Rovaniemi	62,420
Mikkeli (St Michel)	54,261
Kotka	53,539
Salo	52,984
Porvoo (Borgå)	50,159
Lohja (Lojo)	46,785
Hyvinkää (Hyvinge)	46,739
Järvenpää	42,572
Nurmijärvi	42,159
Rauma (Raumo)	39,620
Kirkkonummi (Kyrkslätt)	39,170
Tuusula (Tusby)	38,646
Kajaani (Kajana)	37,239
Kerava (Kervo)	35,554
Savonlinna (Nyslott)	34,664
Nokia	33,322
Kaarina (St Karins)	33,009
Ylöjärvi	32,878
Kangasala	31,437
Vihti (Vichtis)	29,054
Riihimäki	29,021
Raasepori (Raseborg)	27,851
Imatra	27,269
Raahe	25,001

In 2009, 68·1% of the population lived in urban areas. Nearly one-fifth of the total population lives in the Helsinki metropolitan region.

Finnish and Swedish are the official languages. Three Sami languages are spoken in Lapland.

Social Statistics

Statistics in calendar years:

	Living births	Of which outside marriage	Still-born	Marriages	Deaths (exclusive of still-born)	Emigration
2011	59,961	24,498	161	28,408	50,585	12,660
2012	59,943	24,695	161	28,878	51,707	13,845
2013	58,134	24,488	149	25,119	51,472	13,893
2014	57,232	24,516	163	24,462	52,186	15,486
2015	55,472	24,575	172	24,708	52,492	16,305

In 2015 the rate per 1,000 population was: births, 10; deaths, 10; marriages, 5; infant deaths (per 1,000 live births), 1·7. Annual population growth rate, 2005–15, 0·4%. In 2014 the suicide rate per 100,000 population was 22·2 among men and 6·8 among women, giving Finland one of the highest suicide rates in Europe. Life expectancy at birth, 2014, 78·2 years for males and 83·9 years for females. The most popular age range for marrying in 2014 was 25–29 for females and 30–34 for males. Fertility rate, 2015, 1·7 births per woman. Finland legalized same-sex marriage in March 2017. In 2014 Finland received 3,651 asylum applications, equivalent to 0·7 per 1,000 inhabitants.

UNICEF reported that 10·9% of children in Finland in 2014 lived in relative poverty (living in a household in which disposable income—when adjusted for family size and composition—is less than 60% of the national median income), the fourth lowest rate in the world. Finland was ranked third in a global gender gap index of 145 countries compiled by the World Economic Forum for its *Global Gender Gap Report 2015*. The annual index considers economic, political, education and health criteria.

Climate

A quarter of Finland lies north of the Arctic Circle. The climate is severe in winter, which lasts about six months, but mean temperatures in the south and southwest are less harsh, 21°F (–6°C). In the north, mean temperatures may fall to 8·5°F (–13°C). Snow covers the ground for three months in the south and for over six months in the far north. Summers are short but quite warm, with occasional very hot days. Precipitation is light throughout the country, with one third falling as snow, the remainder mainly as rain in summer and autumn. Helsinki (Helsingfors), Jan. 30·2°F (–1·0°C), July 68·4°F (20·2°C). Annual rainfall 27·9" (708·7 mm).

Constitution and Government

Finland is a republic governed by the constitution of 1 March 2000 (which replaced the previous constitution dating from 1919). Although the president used to choose who formed the government, under the new constitution it is the responsibility of parliament to select the prime minister. The government is in charge of domestic and EU affairs with the president responsible for foreign policy 'in co-operation with the government'.

Parliament consists of one chamber (*Eduskunta*) of 200 members chosen by direct and proportional election by all citizens of 18 or over. The country is divided into 15 electoral districts, with a representation proportional to their population. Every citizen over the age of 18 is eligible for parliament, which is elected for four years, but can be dissolved sooner by the president.

The *President* is elected for six years by direct popular vote. In the event of no candidate winning an absolute majority, a second round is held between the two most successful candidates.

National Anthem

'Maamme'/'Vårt land' ('Our land'); words by J. L. Runeberg, tune by F. Pacius (same as Estonia).

Government Chronology

(KESK = Centre Party; KOK = National Coalition Party; ML = Agrarian League; SDP = Social Democratic Party; SFP = Swedish People's Party; SKDL = Finnish People's Democratic League; VL = Liberal League; n/p = non-partisan)

Presidents of the Republic

1944–46	military	Carl Gustaf Emil Mannerheim
1946–56	KOK	Juho Kusti Paasikivi
1956–82	ML/KESK	Urho Kaleva Kekkonen
1982–94	SDP	Mauno Henrik Koivisto
1994–2000	SDP	Martti Oiva Kalevi Ahtisaari
2000–12	SDP	Tarja Kaarina Halonen
2012–	KOK	Sauli Väinämö Niinistö

Prime Ministers

1944–46	KOK	Juho Kusti Paasikivi
1946–48	SKDL	Mauno Pekkala
1948–50	SDP	Karl-August Fagerholm
1950–53	ML	Urho Kaleva Kekkonen
1953–54	VL	Sakari Severi Tuomioja
1954	SFP	Ralf Johan Gustaf Törngren
1954–56	ML	Urho Kaleva Kekkonen
1956–57	SDP	Karl-August Fagerholm

(*continued*)

1957	ML	Väinö Johannes Sukselainen
1957–58	n/p	Berndt Rainer von Fieandt
1958	n/p	Reino Iisakki Kuuskoski
1958–59	SDP	Karl-August Fagerholm
1959–61	ML	Väinö Johannes Sukselainen
1961–62	ML	Martti Juhani Miettunen
1962–63	ML	Ahti Kalle Samuli Karjalainen
1963–64	n/p	Reino Ragnar Lehto
1964–66	ML/KESK	Johannes Virolainen
1966–68	SDP	Kustaa Rafael Paasio
1968–1970	SDP	Mauno Henrik Koivisto
1970	n/p	Teuvo Ensio Aura
1970–71	KESK	Ahti Kalle Samuli Karjalainen
1971–72	n/p	Teuvo Ensio Aura
1972	SDP	Kustaa Rafael Paasio
1972–75	SDP	Taisto Kalevi Sorsa
1975	n/p	Keijo Antero Liinamaa
1975–77	KESK	Martti Juhani Miettunen
1977–79	SDP	Taisto Kalevi Sorsa
1979–81	SDP	Mauno Henrik Koivisto
1982–87	SDP	Taisto Kalevi Sorsa
1987–91	KOK	Harri Hermanni Holkeri
1991–95	KESK	Esko Tapani Aho
1995–2003	SDP	Paavo Tapio Lipponen
2003	KESK	Anneli Tuulikki Jäätteenmäki
2003–10	KESK	Matti Taneli Vanhanen
2010–11	KESK	Mari Johanna Kiviniemi
2011–14	KOK	Jyrki Tapani Katainen
2014–15	KOK	Cai-Göran Alexander Stubb
2015–	KESK	Juha Petri Sipilä

Recent Elections

In presidential elections held on 28 Jan. 2018 incumbent Sauli Niinistö (ind. but supoprted by the National Coalition Party and the Christian Democrats) received 62·7% of votes cast, ahead of Pekka Haavisto (Green League) with 12·4%, Laura Huhtasaari (Finns Party) with 6·9%, Paavo Väyrynen (ind.) 6·2% and Matti Vanhanen (Centre Party) 4·1%. There were three other candidates. Turnout was 66·7%.

At the elections for the 200-member parliament on 19 April 2015, turnout was 70·1%. The Centre Party (KESK) won 49 seats with 21·1% of the votes cast (35 seats in 2011), the Finns Party (PS) 38 with 17·7% (39 seats in 2011), the KOK 37 with 18·2% (44 seats in 2011), the Social Democratic Party (SDP) 34 with 16·5% (42), the Green League (VIHR) 15 with 8·5% (10), the Left Alliance (VAS) 12 with 7·1% (14), the Swedish People's Party (SFP) 9 with 4·9% (9) and the Christian Democrats (KD) 5 with 3·5% (6). One representative from the province of Åland was also elected.

European Parliament

Finland has 13 representatives. At the May 2014 elections turnout was 41·0% (40·3% in 2009). KOK won 3 seats with 22·6% of votes cast (political affiliation in European Parliament: European People's Party); KESK, 3 with 19·7% (Alliance of Liberals and Democrats for Europe); the Finns Party, 2 with 12·9% (European Conservatives and Reformists); SDP, 2 with 12·3% (Progressive Alliance of Socialists and Democrats); VIHR, 1 with 9·3% (Greens/European Free Alliance); VAS, 1 with 9·3% (European United Left/Nordic Green Left); SFP, 1 with 6·8% (Alliance of Liberals and Democrats for Europe).

Current Government

President: Sauli Niinistö; b. 1948 (National Coalition Party; sworn in 1 March 2012).

Following the elections of April 2015 a three-party coalition was formed consisting of the Centre Party (KESK), the Finns Party (PS) and the National Coalition Party (KOK). In June 2017 following Jussi Halla-aho's election as its leader the Finns Party split in two. The New Alternative faction (Uv) remained in the coalition government while the Finns Party went into opposition. In Feb. 2019 the caretaker government comprised:

Prime Minister: Juha Sipilä; b. 1961 (KESK; sworn in 29 May 2015).

Deputy Prime Minister and Minister of Finance: Petteri Orpo (KOK). *Foreign Affairs:* Timo Soini (Uv). *Foreign Trade and Development:* Anne-Mari Virolainen (KOK). *Justice:* Antti Häkkänen (KOK). *Interior:* Kai Mykkänen (KOK). *Defence:* Jussi Niinistö (Uv). *Local Government and Public Reforms:* Anu Vehviläinen (KESK). *Education:* Sanni Grahn-Laasonen (KOK). *European Affairs, Culture and Sport:* Sampo Terho (Uv). *Agriculture and Forestry:* Jari Leppä (KESK). *Transport and Communications:* Anne Berner (KESK). *Economic Affairs:* Mika Lintilä (KESK). *Employment:* Jari Lindström (Uv). *Social Affairs and Health:* Pirkko Mattila (Uv). *Family Affairs and Social Services:* Annika Saarikko (KESK). *Housing, Energy and the Environment:* Kimmo Tiilikainen (KESK).

Government Website: http://www.valtioneuvosto.fi

Current Leaders

Sauli Niinistö

Position
President

Introduction
Sauli Niinistö became president in March 2012, the first member of the conservative National Coalition Party (KOK) to hold the post since 1956. A fiscal conservative, he has maintained Finland's membership stance within the European Union, advocating restraint on financial bailout packages to partner countries and on further expansion.

Early Life
Born on 24 Aug. 1948 in Salo, Sauli Niinistö graduated in law from the University of Turku in 1974 before establishing his own law firm in Salo. In 1977 he was elected to Salo's municipal council, where he served until 1992. In 1987 he entered the national parliament as a member of the KOK, becoming chairman of the committee on constitutional law in 1993. He was elected leader of the KOK in 1994.

In the coalition government led by social democrat Paavo Lipponen, he served as justice minister from 1995–96 and as finance minister from 1996–2003. Between 1995 and 2001 he was also deputy prime minister. As finance minister he tackled recession by cutting social spending and taxes, and took Finland into the single European currency in 1999. He was chair of the European Democratic Union (EDU) grouping from 1998 and became honorary president of the European's People Party (EPP), following its merger with the EDU in 2002.

After standing down as KOK leader in 2001, Niinistö left parliament in 2003 to become vice-chairman of the board of directors of the European Investment Bank, a post he held until 2007. In 2006 he unsuccessfully challenged for the Finnish presidency, narrowly losing to incumbent Tarja Halonen. He re-entered parliament in 2007 and served as speaker from 2007–11, supporting measures for administrative reform.

In the wake of the economic turmoil in Europe amid the global financial crisis, he advocated continuing Finnish membership of the EU but was sceptical on further expansion and critical of the financial bailouts proposed for struggling member states. In 2012 he again contested the presidency, arguing for fiscal discipline and measures to help young people into employment. He was elected in the second round, winning 63% of the vote to beat Pekka Haavisto of the Green League.

Career in Office
Niinistö took office on 1 March 2012, promising to use the presidency to consolidate Finland's place within the EU while strengthening relations with the USA and China. His chief domestic challenges arose from economic uncertainty, a growing youth unemployment rate and an ageing population. Internationally, he has sought to address instability in the eurozone and to maintain good relations with Russia.

Following the resignation of Jyrki Katainen as prime minister, Niinistö appointed the new KOK leader, Alexander Stubb, in his place in June 2014. However, parliamentary elections in April 2015 heralded a new coalition government, and in May Niinistö swore in Juha Sipilä, the KESK party leader, as the new premier. In May 2017 Niinistö declared that he would stand again for the presidency in 2018 and he was duly re-elected at the end of Jan. with 63% of the popular vote.

Juha Sipilä

Position
Prime Minister

Introduction
Juha Sipilä was sworn in as prime minister on 29 May 2015. The leader of the liberal, agrarian Centre Party (KESK), he headed a coalition with the New Alternative faction (the more moderate wing of the far-right populist Finns Party that remained as a junior partner in the government after the party split in June 2017) and the National Coalition Party (KOK). A successful businessman who made his fortune during the information technology (IT) boom of the 1990s, Sipilä made the overhaul of the fragile economy his priority. However, having failed to progress planned social and healthcare reforms, his government resigned on 8 March 2019 but continued in a caretaker capacity pending fresh elections scheduled for 14 April.

Early Life
Juha Sipilä was born on 25 April 1961 in Veteli, in Finland's rural west. He gained his first—and, until his entry into parliament, only—experience in party politics during his time as a student, working for the Finnish Centre Youth. He began his career with Lauri Kuokkanen Ltd, a technology company and later joined Solitra Oy, based in Oulu, which has developed a reputation as a hub for technological innovation. Becoming the company's CEO in 1992 and its majority shareholder in 1994, he oversaw a rapid rise in the company's value before negotiating its sale in 1997. In 1995 he founded private equity finance company Fortel Invest, specializing in advanced technology. After a period at the helm of Elektrobit, an IT company, he returned to lead Fortel Invest until his entry into parliament as representative of the Oulu constituency in 2011.

In June 2012 Sipilä was elected chairman of KESK, which was then in opposition to a coalition led by Jyrki Katainen (who was replaced by Alexander Stubb in 2014). In his campaigning for the April 2015 parliamentary election, Sipilä pledged to prioritize economic growth, highlighting the 'bio-eonomy' as a driver for employment. He argued that investment in the sector could create 200,000 new jobs over the coming decade. He also declared his support for spending cuts and a wage freeze to restore Finland's competitiveness and end a three-year recession. In the election KESK won 49 of the 200 available seats, ahead of the eurosceptic Finns Party (38), KOK (37) and the Social Democrats (34).

Career in Office
Sipilä made restoring economic growth, boosting competitiveness and reducing public debt the focus of his tenure, with ambitious plans to make Finland a leader in new bio-technologies. Turbulence in Western relations with Russia, a major trading partner of Finland, represented a significant challenge to Sipilä, who opposed Finnish entry into NATO. Nonetheless, Finland and NATO signed an agreement on cyber defence co-operation in Feb. 2017. The following June the coalition government survived a confidence vote in parliament after hard-liners in the Finns Party left the coalition. However, in March 2019 Sipilä's failure to push through social and health reforms prompted the resignation of his government and the scheduling of fresh parliamentary elections.

In Aug. 2017 Finland suffered its first terror attack as a Moroccan Islamist asylum seeker killed two people and wounded several others in a knife attack in the city of Turku.

At the end of 2017 the country celebrated a century of independence as a democratic state.

Defence

Conscript service is 6–12 months. Total strength of trained and equipped reserves is about 490,000 (to be 350,000).

In 2013 defence expenditure totalled US$3,814m. (US$724 per capita), representing 1·4% of GDP.

Army

The Army consists of one armoured training brigade, three readiness brigades, three infantry training brigades, three jaeger regiments, one artillery brigade, three brigade artillery regiments, two air defence regiments, one engineer regiment (including ABC school), three brigade engineer battalions,

one signals regiment, four brigade signals battalions and a reserve officer school. Total strength of 37,700 (26,000 conscripts).

Border Guard

This comes under the purview of the ministry of the interior, but is militarily organized to participate in the defence of the country. It is in charge of border surveillance and border controls. It is also responsible for conducting maritime search and rescue operations. The Border Guard's mobilization force can be utilized for border security tasks if needed. If necessary in the interests of defence capability, the border troops or parts thereof may be attached to the Defence Forces. Personnel, 2011, 2,800 (professional) with a potential mobilizational force of 12,000.

Navy

The Navy operates along the coast and the archipelago. A total of about 1,800 officers, officer specialists and warrant officers, military personnel and civilians work in the Navy. Every year close to 3,400 conscripts, of which approximately 30 are women volunteers, do their military service in the Navy.

Air Force

Personnel (2012), 4,200 (1,500 conscripts). Equipment included 62 F-18 Hornets.

Economy

Agriculture accounted for 3·0% of GDP in 2013, industry 26·9% and services 70·1%.

According to the Berlin-based organization Transparency International, Finland ranked equal third in a 2018 survey of countries with the least corruption in business and government. It received 85 out of 100 in the corruption perceptions index.

Overview

GDP growth in 2015 was recorded at 0·0%, following three years of contractions averaging 0·9% per annum prompted by a downturn in the information and communications technology (ICT) industry, falling demand for paper and pulp (among the country's major exports) and increased wages. In 2016 the economy expanded by 1·9% as Finland saw positive growth for the first time since 2011.

The economy, once based on basic metals and forestry, has evolved to become a leading force in knowledge-based, high-technology production. It is one of the world's leading ICT producers. The country's legal framework provides effective protection of intellectual property, while open market policies encourage entrepreneurship and innovation.

Finland was ranked eighth in the World Economic Forum's *Global Competitiveness Index Report* in 2014–15. The emergence of venture capital financing in the 1990s created opportunities for high-risk technology startups. Research and development expenditure made up about 3·2% of GDP in 2014, one of the highest levels among the OECD countries.

Finland joined the European Union in 1995 and subsequently adopted the euro as its currency. Growth prior to the 2008 global financial crisis was well above the eurozone average, but the country experienced the worst recession of any euro nation in 2009. Exports, on which the country is heavily reliant, declined by 20% and there was a sharp drop in investment. GDP fell by 8·3% in 2009 and unemployment rose from 6·5% to over 8%. By 2015 unemployment was over 9%. Geopolitical tensions to Finland's east and a rapidly ageing population present potential long-term threats to growth.

Currency

On 1 Jan. 1999 the *euro* (EUR) became the legal currency in Finland at the irrevocable conversion rate of 5·94573 marks to one euro. The euro, which consists of 100 cents, has been in circulation since 1 Jan. 2002. On the introduction of the euro there was a 'dual circulation' period before the mark ceased to be legal tender on 28 Feb. 2002.

Inflation rates (based on OECD statistics):

2008	2009	2010	2011	2012	2013	2014	2015	2016	2017
3·9%	1·6%	1·7%	3·3%	3·2%	2·2%	1·2%	−0·2%	0·4%	0·8%

Foreign exchange reserves were US$7,002m. in Sept. 2009 and gold reserves were 1·58m. troy oz. Total money supply was €62,585m. in Aug. 2009.

Budget

Revenue and expenditure for the calendar years 2012–16 in €1m:

	2012	2013	2014	2015	2016
Revenue	50,437	52,591	53,225	53,377	52,012
Expenditure	53,446	54,587	54,234	53,700	54,419

Of the total revenue in 2016, 35% derived from value added tax, 25% from income and property tax, 14% from excise duties, 6% from net loans, 6% from other taxes and similar revenue and 14% from miscellaneous sources. Of the total expenditure, 2016, 24% went to health and social security, 12% to education and culture, 5% to agriculture and forestry, 5% to defence, 5% to transport and communication and 49% to other expenditure.

VAT is 24% (reduced rates, 14% and 10%).

At the end of Dec. 2016 the central government debt totalled €102,350m.

Finland's budget deficit in 2017 was 0·7% of GDP (1·7% in 2016 and 2·8% in 2015). The required target set by the EU is a budget deficit of no more than 3%.

Performance

GDP growth rates (based on OECD statistics):

2008	2009	2010	2011	2012	2013	2014	2015	2016	2017
0·7%	−8·3%	3·0%	2·6%	−1·4%	−0·8%	−0·6%	0·1%	2·5%	2·8%

Total GDP was US$251·9bn. in 2017.

Banking and Finance

The central bank is the Bank of Finland (founded in 1811), operating under the guarantee and supervision of parliament. The Bank is a member of the European System of Central Banks. As a member of the euro area, the Bank issues euro banknotes and coins in Finland by permission of the European Central Bank. The *Governor* is Olli Rehn.

The most important groups of banking institutions in Aug. 2017 were:

	Number of institutions	Number of branches[1]	Deposits (€1m.)	Loans (€1m.)
Commercial banks	9	78	22,632	45,474
Savings banks	24	183	7,161	8,076
Co-operative banks	195	521	46,993	55,102
Foreign banks	16	232	40,564	37,354

[1]Dec. 2016.

The three largest banks are Nordea Bank Finland, Pohjola Bank and Danske Bank. In 2016, 81% of the population between the ages of 16 and 89 were using online banking (one of the highest percentages of any country).

Gross external debt amounted to US$594,188m. in June 2012.

In 2012 Finland received US$4·2bn. worth of foreign direct investment (up from US$2·5bn. in 2011).

There is a stock exchange in Helsinki.

Energy and Natural Resources

In 2011, 31·8% of energy consumption came from renewables (wind power, solar power, hydro-electric power, tidal power, geothermal energy and biomass), compared to the European Union average of 13·0%. A target of 38% has been set by the EU for 2020.

Environment

Finland's carbon dioxide emissions from the consumption of energy in 2011 were the equivalent of 9·8 tonnes per capita. An *Environmental Performance Index* compiled in 2016 ranked Finland first in the world, with 90·7%. The index examined various factors in nine areas—agriculture, air quality, biodiversity and habitat, climate and energy, fisheries, forests, health impacts, water and sanitation, and water resources.

Electricity

Installed capacity was 16·7m. kW in 2011. Production was 73,481m. kWh. in 2011 (51% thermal and 17% hydro-electric). Consumption per capita in 2011 was an estimated 16,206 kWh. In 2011 there were four nuclear reactors, which contributed 32% of production. In May 2002 parliament approved the construction of a fifth reactor, on the island of Olkiluoto, which was scheduled to become operational in 2009. However, a number of problems have now delayed the start of electricity production until at least 2019.

Water

Finland has abundant surface water and groundwater resources relative to its population and level of consumption. The total groundwater yield is estimated to be 10–30m. cu. metres a day, of which some 6m. is suitable for water supplies. Approximately 15% of this latter figure is made use of at the present time.

Minerals

Notable of the mines are Pyhäsalmi (zinc–copper), Pahtavaara (gold ore), Hitura (nickel) and Keminmaa (chromium). In 2008 the metal content (in tonnes) of the output of zinc ore was 27,800; of copper ore, 13,300; of nickel ore, 4,000; of chromium ore and concentrate, 614,500.

Agriculture

The cultivated area covers only 8% of the land, and of the economically active population 4·1% were employed in agriculture and forestry in 2016. In 2015 there were 2·27m. ha. of arable land. This arable area was divided into 50,999 farms. The distribution of this area by the size of the farms was: less than 5 ha. cultivated, 2,076 farms; 5–20 ha., 16,421 farms; 20–50 ha., 17,114 farms; 50–100 ha., 10,377 farms; over 100 ha., 5,011 farms.

Agriculture accounted for 1·7% of exports and 3·1% of imports in 2015.

The principal crops (area in 1,000 ha., yield in 1,000 tonnes) were in 2015:

Crop	Area	Yield
Barley	512·5	1,569·0
Wheat	248·8	992·1
Oats	306·5	979·6
Potatoes	22·1	532·1
Hay	85·7	322·1

The total area under cultivation in 2015 was 2,273,304 ha. Approximately 8·3% of all agricultural land is used for organic farming. Production of dairy butter in 2015 was 54,655 tonnes; and of cheese, 88,356 tonnes.

Livestock (2015): pigs, 1,235,200; cattle, 914,700; reindeer, 191,000; horses, 75,000 (including trotting and riding horses, and ponies); poultry, 12,020,600.

Forestry

Forests covered 22·22m. ha. in 2015, or 73% of the total land area. Growing stock was 2,320m. cu. metres in 2015 (1,851m. cu. metres coniferous and 469m. cu. metres broadleaved). Timber production in 2015 was 59·28m. cu. metres. Finland is one of the largest producers of roundwood in Europe. Finland's per capita consumption of roundwood is the highest in the world, at 11·7 cu. metres per person in 2015.

Fisheries

The catch in 2015 was 182,872 tonnes, of which 153,396 tonnes came from sea fishing. In 2012 there were 178 food fish production farms in operation, of which 63 were freshwater farms. Their total production amounted to 12,659 tonnes. In addition there were 105 fry-farms and 202 natural food rearers, most of these in fresh water.

Industry

The leading companies by market capitalization in Finland in March 2019 were: Nokia, a communications and information technology company (US$35·7bn.); Sampo, an insurance company (US$29·2bn.); and Kone, an industrial engineering company (US$25·7bn.).

Forests are still Finland's most crucial raw material resource, although the metal and engineering industry has long been Finland's leading branch of manufacturing, both in terms of value added and as an employer. In 2012 there were 25,983 establishments in industry (of which 22,599 were manufacturing concerns) with 343,093 personnel (of whom 316,722 were in manufacturing). Gross value of industrial production in 2012 was €124,731m., of which manufacturing accounted for €111,310m.

Labour

In 2015 the labour force was 2,689,000 (52% males). Of this total, 73·8% of the economically active population worked in services (including 15·2% in trade and restaurants) and 13·4% in manufacturing. In Dec. 2018 unemployment was 6·7% (down from 8·6% in 2017 as a whole).

International Trade

At the start of the 1990s a collapse in trade with Russia led to the worst recession in the country's recent history. Today, exports to Russia are about 11% of the total.

Imports and Exports

In 1960 the wood and paper industry dominated exports with 69% of the total, but today the electronics industry/metal and engineering industry sector is the largest export sector.

Imports and exports for calendar years, in €1m.:

	2012	2013	2014	2015
Imports	59,517	58,407	57,769	54,493
Exports	56,878	56,048	55,973	53,880

Use of Goods	Imports 2015
Intermediate goods	36%
Investment goods	22%
Energy	14%
Durable consumer goods	8%
Other	20%

Industry	Exports 2015
Metal, engineering, electronics	48%
Forest industry	21%
Chemical industry	19%
Other	12%

Region	Imports 2015	Exports 2015
European Union	62%	59%
Other Europe	15%	12%
Developing countries	18%	17%
Other countries	5%	12%

Trade with principal partners in 2015 was as follows (in €1m.):

	Imports	*Exports*
Belgium	1,208	1,523
Brazil	569	475
China	4,003	2,534
Denmark	1,742	946
Estonia	1,552	1,579
France	2,064	1,501
Germany	8,285	7,501
Italy	1,459	1,264
Japan	653	1,085
Netherlands	3,537	3,557

(continued)

	Imports	*Exports*
Norway	1,020	1,565
Poland	1,413	1,416
Russia	5,981	3,157
South Korea	530	753
Spain	1,169	931
Sweden	6,189	5,523
UK	1,729	2,776
USA	2,031	3,762

Communications

Roads

At 1 Jan. 2015 there were 78,071 km of public roads, of which 50,884 km were paved. At the end of 2015 there were 3,257,581 registered cars, 142,020 lorries, 418,870 vans and pick-ups, 16,856 buses and coaches and 11,718 special automobiles. Road accidents caused 126 fatalities in 2015.

Rail

In 2015 the total length of the line operated was 5,923 km (3,262 km electrified), all of it owned by the State. The gauge is 1,524 mm. In 2013, 69·3m. passengers and 36·4m. tonnes of freight were carried. There is a metro (21 km) and tram/light rail network (117 km) in Helsinki.

Civil Aviation

The main international airport is at Helsinki (Vantaa), and there are also international airports at Turku, Tampere, Rovaniemi and Oulu. The national carrier is Finnair. Scheduled traffic of Finnish airlines covered 177m. km in 2012. The number of passengers in 2012 was 10·6m. and the number of passenger-km 24,953m.; the air transport of freight and mail amounted to 711·7m. tonne-km. Helsinki-Vantaa handled 12,611,187 passengers in 2009 (10,238,302 on international flights) and 122,107 tonnes of freight and mail. Oulu is the second busiest airport, handling 688,860 passengers in 2009, and Tampere-Pirkkala the third busiest, with 628,105 in 2009.

In the World Economic Forum's *Global Competitiveness Report 2017–2018* Finland ranked fifth for quality of air transport infrastructure.

Shipping

In Jan. 2014 there were 126 ships of 300 GT or over registered, totalling 1,564,000 GT. The Finnish-controlled fleet comprised 119 vessels of 1,000 GT or over in July 2014, of which 73 were under the Finnish flag and 46 under foreign flags.

Finland had 9,649 km of navigable rivers in 2013 and 125 km of navigable canals. Timber floating is still practised; in 2010 bundle floating was about 0·5m. tonnes.

Finland was ranked fifth in the World Economic Forum's *Global Competitiveness Report 2017–2018* for the quality of its port facilities.

Telecommunications

In 2012 mobile phone subscriptions numbered 9,320,000 (1,723·2 per 1,000 persons). In the same year there were 890,000 main (fixed) telephone lines.

In 2013 there were 123·6 wireless broadband subscriptions per 100 inhabitants and 30·8 fixed broadband subscriptions per 100. In March 2012 there were 2·1m. Facebook users. In 2010 Finland became the first country to grant its citizens a legal right to broadband internet.

According to the World Economic Forum's *Global Information Technology Report 2010–11* Finland is ranked third in the world in exploiting global information technology developments.

Social Institutions

According to the 2017 Fragile States Index—a list published jointly by the Fund for Peace and *Foreign Policy* magazine—Finland was ranked as the state least vulnerable to conflict or collapse. The Index is based on 12 indicators of state vulnerability across social, political and economic categories.

Justice

The lowest court of justice is the District Court. In most civil cases a District Court has a quorum of three legally qualified members. In criminal cases as well as in some cases related to family law the District Court has a quorum with a chair and three lay judges. In the preliminary preparation of a civil case and in a criminal case concerning a minor offence, a District Court is composed of the chair only. From the District Court an appeal lies to the courts of appeal in Turku, Vaasa, Kuopio, Helsinki, Kouvola and Rovaniemi. The Supreme Court sits in Helsinki. Appeals from the decisions of administrative authorities are in the final instance decided by the Supreme Administrative Court, also in Helsinki. Judges can be removed only by judicial sentence. Two functionaries, the Chancellor of Justice and the Ombudsman or Solicitor-General, exercise control over the administration of justice. The former acts also as counsel and public prosecutor for the government; the latter is appointed by Parliament.

At the end of 2014 the daily average number of prisoners was 3,097 of which 239 were women. The number of convictions in 2011 was 269,867, of which 23,594 carried a penalty of imprisonment. 8,519 of the prison sentences were unconditional. In 2015 the World Justice Project *Rule of Law Index*, which provides data on how the rule of law is experienced by the general public across eight categories, ranked Finland first of 102 countries for criminal justice and 10th for civil justice.

Education

Number of institutions, teachers and students (Sept. 2014):

Primary and Secondary Education

	Number of institutions		Teachers[1]	Students
First-level Education	}		}		366,563[2]
(Lower sections of the comprehensive schools, grades I–VI)	}		}		
Second-level Education	}	3,005	}	53,882	279,600
(Upper sections of the comprehensive schools, grades VII–IX, and upper secondary general schools)	}		}		
Vocational Education		157		15,916	321,736[3]

[1]Data for teachers refers to 2013.
[2]Including pre-primary education (11,424 pupils) in comprehensive schools.
[3]2014 average.

Tertiary Education

In 2014 polytechnic education was provided at 26 polytechnics with 138,682 students and 5,473 teachers[1]. In 2013, 29·3% of the population aged 15 years or over had been through tertiary education.

[1]Data refer to full-time equivalent of teaching personnel.

University Education

Universities with the number of teachers and students in 2014:

	Founded[1]	Teachers[2]	Students	
			Total	Women
Universities				
Helsinki	1640	4,165	34,833	22,131
Turku (Swedish)	1918	682	6,139	3,565
Turku (Finnish)	1922	1,822	16,788	10,145
Tampere	1925	1,068	15,134	9,791
Jyväskylä	1934	1,469	13,057	7,880
Oulu	1958	1,657	14,822	7,143
Vaasa	1968	279	5,387	2,803
Itä-Suomi	2010	1,506	15,752	9,747
Aalto	2010	2,778	18,343	5,844

(continued)

	Founded[1]	Teachers[2]	Students	
			Total	Women
Lapland	1979	296	4,349	3,032
Universities of Technology				
Tampere	1965	1,118	8,804	1,887
Lappeenranta	1969	583	5,004	1,402
Schools of Economics and Business Administration				
Helsinki (Swedish)	1909	125	2,433	1,101
Universities of Art				
Taideyliopisto	2013	393	1,985	1,110
National Defence University	1993	250	929	33
Total		18,190	163,759	87,614

[1]Year when the institution was founded regardless of status at the time.
[2]Includes teaching and research personnel (full-time equivalent).

Adult Education

Adult education provided by educational institutions in 2013:

Type of institution	Participants[1]
General education institutions	1,682,138
Vocational education institutions	343,233
Polytechnics	17,734
Universities	45,249
Other	111,321
Total	2,199,675

[1]Participants are persons who have attended adult education courses run by educational institutions in the course of the calendar year. The same person may have attended a number of different courses and has been recorded as a participant in each of them.

In 2012 public expenditure on education came to 6·1% of GDP and 12·2% of total government spending.

The adult literacy rate in 2014 was almost 100%.

Although education is only compulsory until 16, 93% of pupils stay on at school to 18.

Health

In 2013 there were 21,404 physicians, 5,069 dentists and 26,049 hospital beds. In 2012, 21% of males and 14% of females aged 15 and over smoked on a daily basis. The average Finnish adult consumed 12·3 litres of pure alcohol a year in the period 2008–10.

In 2013 Finland spent 9·1% of its GDP on health.

Welfare

The Social Insurance Institution administers old-age pensions (to all persons over 65 years of age and disabled younger persons) and health insurance. There is also a system of special assistance for resident immigrants over 65. In 2012 the full national pension was €608·63 per month for a single person and €539·85 for persons living with a spouse or partner from the age of 65. The national pension is supplemented with a guarantee pension, which in 2012 resulted in a minimum pension in total of €713·73 a month.

The total cost of social security amounted to €63,223m. in 2013. Of this €30,570m. (48%) was spent on old age and disability, €15,223m. (24%) on health, €8,331m. (13%) on family allowances and child welfare, €4,5976m. (7%) on unemployment and €4,502m. (7%) on general welfare purposes and administration. Out of the total expenditure, 34·6% was financed by employers, 28·0% by the State, 19·4% by local authorities, 12·5% by the insured and 5·5% by other sources.

Religion

Liberty of conscience is guaranteed to members of all religions. National churches are the Lutheran National Church and the Greek Orthodox Church of Finland. The Lutheran Church is divided into nine dioceses (Turku being the archiepiscopal see) and some 460 parishes. The Greek Orthodox Church is divided into three bishoprics (Kuopio being the archiepiscopal see) and 27 parishes, in addition to which there are a monastery and a convent. Percentage of the total population at the end of 2009: Lutherans, 79·9; Greek Orthodox, 1·1; others, 1·3; not members of any religion, 17·7.

Culture

World Heritage Sites

There are seven UNESCO sites in Finland: Old Rauma harbour (inscribed in 1991); the sea fortress of Suomenlinna (1991); the old church of Petäjävesi (1994); Verla groundwood and board mill (1996); the Bronze Age burial site of Sammallahdenmäki (1999); the Kvarken Archipelago and High Coast (2000 and 2006), shared with Sweden; and the Struve Geodetic Arc (2005). The Arc is a chain of survey triangulations spanning from Norway to the Black Sea that helped establish the exact shape and size of the earth and is shared with nine other countries.

Press

Finland had 235 newspapers in 2014, of which 46 were dailies (45 paid-for and one free) and 189 non-dailies. The total circulation of all newspapers in 2014 was 2·2m. In the same year Finland had 175 newspaper online editions. There were 2,471 registered periodicals in 2014. The bestselling newspapers in 2014 were *Helsingin Sanomat* (average daily circulation, 285,223 copies), *Ilta-Sanomat* (110,226) and *Aamulehti* (106,842). In 2014 a total of 10,352 book titles were published.

In the 2013 *World Press Freedom Index* compiled by Reporters Without Borders, Finland was ranked first out of 179 countries.

Tourism

In 2014 a total of 2,731,200 foreign visitors stayed at accommodation establishments (down from 2,796,839 in 2013), including 615,116 from Russia, 299,589 from Sweden, 248,308 from Germany and 180,562 from the United Kingdom.

Major international tourist attractions include Uspensky Cathedral, Helsinki Cathedral and Suomenlinna (all in Helsinki). Helsinki's churches and Santa Park in Rovaniemi are particularly popular among foreigners, who account for the majority of their visitors.

Festivals

Major music festivals include the Lakeside Blues Festival in Järvenpää, Pori Jazz Festival, Kaustinen Folk Music Festival, Ankkarock in Vantaa, Provinssirock in Seinäjoki, Ruisrock on the island of Ruissalo and Savonlinna Opera Festival. Other main festivals are the Helsinki Festival Week, the Maritime Festival in Kotka, Tampere Theatre Festival and Seinäjoki's Tango Festival.

Diplomatic Representatives

Of Finland in the United Kingdom (38 Chesham Pl., London, SW1X 8HW)
Ambassador: Päivi Luostarinen.

Of the United Kingdom in Finland (Itäinen Puistotie 17, 00140 Helsinki)
Ambassador: Tom Dodd.

Of Finland in the USA (3301 Massachusetts Ave., NW, Washington, D.C., 20008)
Ambassador: Kirsti Helena Kauppi.

Of the USA in Finland (Itäinen Puistotie 14, Helsinki 00140)
Ambassador: Robert Frank Pence.

Of Finland to the United Nations
Ambassador: Kai Jürgen Mikael Sauer.

Of Finland to the European Union
Permanent Representative: Marja Rislakki.

Further Reading

Statistics Finland. *Statistical Yearbook of Finland* (from 1879).—*Bulletin of Statistics* (1971–2015).

Constitution Act and Parliament Act of Finland. 1999

Suomen valtiokalenteri—Finlands statskalender (State Calendar of Finland). Annual

Finland in Figures. Annual

Jussila, Osmo, Hentila, Seppo and Nevakivi, Jukka, *From Grand Duchy to a Modern State: A Political History of Finland since 1809.* 2000

Kirby, D. G., *A Concise History of Finland.* 2006

Klinge, M., *A Brief History of Finland.* 1987

Lewis, Richard D., *Finland, Cultural Lone Wolf.* 2004

Pesonen, Pertti and Riihinen, Olavi, *Dynamic Finland: The Political System and the Welfare State.* 2004

Raunio, Tapio and Tiilikainen, Teija, *Finland in the European Union.* 2003

Singleton, F., *A Short History of Finland.* 2nd ed. 1998

National Statistical Office: Statistics Finland, Työpajankatu 13, 00580 Helsinki.
Website: http://www.stat.fi

France

République Française (French Republic)

Capital: Paris
Population projection, 2020: 65·72m.
GNI per capita, 2017: (PPP$) 39,254
HDI/world rank, 2017: 0·901/24
Internet domain extension: .fr

Key Historical Events

The Dordogne has evidence of Mousterian industry from 40,000 BC and of Cro-Magnon man of the Upper Paleolithic period. With the end of the Ice Age, agricultural settlement appeared around 7000 BC. By the beginning of the 8th century BC, Celtic tribes from Central Europe were inhabiting the Rhône valley of Gaul (now France) while the Greeks were building cities such as Massalia (Marseille) along the Mediterranean coast. The Romans crossed the Alps into southern France in 121 BC and Gaul was conquered by Julius Caesar in 52 BC. The country benefited from protected trade routes and from Roman infrastructure, speech and government. Roman rule was consolidated by the reign of Augustus at the end of the 1st century AD. But the Empire was threatened by Germanic ('barbarian') incursions from the north and east. Many of these tribes were assimilated as *foederati* (treaty nations) into the Gallo-Roman Empire but they assumed authority in their domains as Roman government receded in the 4th and 5th centuries. After the repulse of Attila and his Huns in 451, the Salian Franks emerged as the strongest of the Germanic tribes—their leader, Merovius, was the progenitor of the Merovingian dynasty that ruled France until the beginning of the 8th century.

On the death of Merovius's grandson, Clovis, the kingdom was divided between his three sons. The Merovingians remained in power for two centuries but their rule, weakened by internecine warfare, gave way to the Carolingian dynasty in 751. Having extended his empire over Germany and Italy, Charlemagne was crowned emperor of the West by the Pope in 800. He moved his seat of government to Aix-la-Chapelle (Aachen) where he presided over a revival of learning and education.

Charlemagne died in 814 and his empire was fought over by his grandsons before the 843 Treaty of Verdun officially split the territories. Charles le Chauve (823–77) inherited the western territories, an area roughly corresponding to modern day France. But by 912 Vikings had settled in Rouen, having laid siege to Paris. Further threats came from Muslim Saracens in the south and Hungarian Magyars in the east. The Carolingians struggled to keep their power for another century but they were weakened by unrest and disunity. In 987 Hugh Capet, the duke of the Franks, ousted the legitimate claimant to the throne, Charles of Lorraine, and appointed himself king. To control a diverse country, power was centralized on Paris.

Between 1150 and 1300 France underwent a period of economic expansion, though the 12th century also saw the Holy Land crusades and the expulsion of the Jews, followed by the bloody Albigensian Crusade against the heretical Cathars of Languedoc in 1209. The last Capetian king, Charles IV, died in 1328 (leaving only daughters) and the Capetian dynasty gave way to the House of Valois. However, King Edward III of England disputed Philippe de Valois's claim to the French throne, prompting the start of the Hundred Years War (1337–1453). With his son the Black Prince, Edward III's successful invasion led to the Treaty of Brétigny in 1360, which ceded Aquitaine to England. Edward renounced all claims to the French throne but the warfare continued until Charles V (ruled 1364–80) won back most of their territories.

In 1415 Henry V of England, with the backing of the Burgundians, defeated the French at Agincourt. He married the daughter of Charles IV and obtained the right of succession to the French throne. The war continued between his son Henry VI and the dauphin Charles (VI) who enlisted the help of Joan of Arc (Jeanne d'Arc). After leading a series of successful campaigns against the English, she was captured, tried as a heretic by a court of Burgundian ecclesiastics and burnt at the stake in Rouen in 1431. Nevertheless, French successes continued and eventually the English were driven from all their French possessions except Calais.

Rising Power

The reign of Louis XI (1461–83) saw a change from a medieval social system to a more modern state. Provincial governments were set up in major cities and nobles wielding independent power were crushed. In 1494 Charles VIII, encouraged to pursue his claim to the crown of Naples by Ludovico Sforza, duke of Milan, invaded Italy. The speed of his advance shocked the Italian cities into an alliance to expel his army. The appearance of Spanish power in Naples began the Habsburg-Valois wars that used Italy as a battlefield until the Peace of Cateau-Cambrésis in 1559. François I is considered the first Renaissance French king. He patronized some of Italy's greatest artists, commissioning palaces such as the Château de Chambord and rebuilding the Louvre and Château de Fontainebleau. To finance his cultural interests and his military failures in Italy—he was captured by Spanish forces at the Battle of Pavia in 1525—François imposed huge tax rises, severely straining the French economy.

From 1562–98 the Wars of Religion raged in France between the Protestant Huguenots and the Spanish-supported Catholic League. The civil war reached its peak with the 1572 St Bartholomew's Day massacre, in which 20,000 Huguenots were killed, before ending with Henry of Navarre's conversion to Catholicism. He did not abandon his Huguenot roots, however, and the 1598 Edict of Nantes guaranteed Protestants political and religious rights.

After Henry's assassination in 1610 the young Louis XIII took the throne with his mother, Marie de Médicis, acting as regent. Between 1624–42 Cardinal Richelieu held the reins of government and set about establishing absolute royal power in France, with the suppression of Protestant influences. This policy was continued for the next 20 years by his successor Cardinal Mazarin. On Mazarin's death Louis XIV (1643–1715) was able to govern alone. Louis, the 'Sun King', attempted to impose a centralized absolutism, gathering the aristocracy around him and thus denying it traditional regional power. The king formally revoked the Edict of Nantes, Protestant churches were destroyed and religious minorities persecuted. His successor, Louis XV, married Maria, the daughter of the deposed king of Poland, who drew France into the War of the Polish Succession. Further costly military disasters followed including the Seven Years' War, in which France lost her colonies in India, North America and the West Indies.

When Louis XVI succeeded to the throne in 1774, financial crises caused by prolonged military failure coupled with a succession of bad harvests led to grain riots in 1787–88 in Paris, Lyon, Nantes and Grenoble. The subsequent reforms were rejected by the aristocracy (*les privilégiés*), the upper ranks of the clergy (the First Estate) and the majority of the nobility (the Second Estate), who feared a reduction in their tax-levying privileges. Meanwhile, Louis XVI supported the American colonies in their struggle for independence from Britain, a policy that was financially disastrous and also did much to disseminate revolutionary and democratic ideals in France.

Revolution

The French Revolution erupted in 1789 when the Third Estate (*les non-privilégiés*) assumed power in the National Assembly and overthrew the government. Riots broke out across France, culminating in the storming of the Bastille in Paris on 14 July 1789. A new Legislative Assembly was formed and although the moderate Girondins held power at the start, the more extreme followers of Danton, Robespierre and Marat—the Jacobins—seized power and in 1792 declared a republic.

On 21 Jan. 1793 Louis XVI was guillotined in the Place de la Révolution. After his death a reign of terror led by Maximilien Robespierre followed in which thousands of people were guillotined. Despite the efforts of the royalists to re-establish a monarchy, in 1795 the 'Directory of Five' was appointed to run the country. As one of these five, Paul Barras had been responsible for the promotion of a young Corsican, Napoleon Bonaparte, to the rank of general. Over four years, Napoleon commanded the French troops in a series of successful campaigns against the Austrians and the British. On his return to Paris, he found the Directory in disarray and in 1799 overthrew the government and declared himself first consul. Napoleon immediately faced a hostile coalition of England, Austria and Russia. In 1805 he defeated

© Springer Nature Limited 2020
Palgrave Macmillan (ed.), *The Statesman's Yearbook 2020*,
https://doi.org/10.1057/978-1-349-95940-2_74

Austria and Russia at the Battle of Austerlitz but the British naval victory at the Battle of Trafalgar earlier the same year gave Britain maritime supremacy. Napoleon's best troops were bogged down supporting his brother Joseph in the Peninsula War in Spain and his success at Borodino, Russia in 1812 was followed by the army's forced retreat from Moscow during the harsh winter months. The Prussian army retaliated at Leipzig, entered France and forced the surrender of Paris in March 1814. Napoleon abdicated at Fontainebleau on 20 April 1814 and retired to Elba. But when Louis XVIII returned from exile in England later that year, Napoleon left Elba to attempt to recover his empire. He marched north towards Paris, gathering support on the way. But his defeat in 1815 at Waterloo by the Allies led by the duke of Wellington ended his 'Hundred Days' reign. He was exiled to the island of St Helena where he died in 1821.

Second Empire

The monarchy was restored with the Bourbon family. A revolution in 1830 brought Louis Philippe, son of the duke of Orléans, to the throne as a constitutional monarch. This 'July Monarchy' was overthrown in 1848 and superseded by the Second Republic, with Louis Napoleon (nephew of Napoleon I) elected president. In 1852 he took the title of Emperor Napoleon III, and hence began the Second Empire. However, the defeat of France in the Franco-Prussian War (1870–71) led to Napoleon being deposed and the proclamation of the Third Republic in 1870. After a four-month siege, Paris capitulated in Jan. 1871. By Sept. 1873 the occupying troops had gone but Alsace and Lorraine had been lost and French politics, embittered by the Dreyfus Affair (1894–1906), in which forged evidence resulted in a Jewish general staff captain being falsely imprisoned for spying, went from crisis to crisis.

An entente cordiale was established between France and Britain in 1904, putting an end to colonial rivalry and paving the way for future co-operation. In 1905 the Church was separated from the State, a measure to counteract ecclesiastical influence over education.

European War

Although Paris was saved from occupation during the First World War, ten departments were overrun and four long years of trench warfare followed. The tide began to turn against Germany in 1916 with the Battle of the Somme, the French stand at Verdun and the arrival of the Americans in 1917; the Armistice was finally signed on 11 Nov. 1918. By the end of the war France had lost a total of 1·3m. men. The main thrust of France's efforts to rebuild her defences after the First World War was concentrated on the 'Maginot Line'—a supposedly impregnable barrier running along the German frontier, but which was sidestepped by the advancing German forces in 1939. Demoralized French troops, unable to resist the German advance, were forced to retreat towards Dunkerque (Dunkirk). The French government capitulated and a pro-German government presided over by Marshal Pétain (a hero of the Battle of Verdun) was established at Vichy. A truce was signed with Germany agreeing German occupation in the northern third of the country and collaborationist government control in the south. Gen. Charles de Gaulle established the Forces Françaises Libres (Free French Forces) and declared the Comité National Français to be the true French government-in-exile with its headquarters first in London and then in Algiers. With help from the Resistance in France, in Aug. 1944 de Gaulle returned at the head of the allied armies and liberated Paris. An armistice with Germany was signed in March 1945.

In Oct. 1946 the Fourth Republic, institutionally similar to the Third Republic, was established but during prolonged wrangling over the form of the new constitution Gen. de Gaulle retired. Despite frequent changes of government and defeat in Indo-China, France achieved economic recovery. In 1957 a European common market was established of which France, West Germany, Italy and the Benelux countries were founder members.

Fifth Republic

From 1954–62 France was embroiled in a war of independence with Algeria that split public and political opinion. In 1958 de Gaulle prepared a new constitution and was persuaded to return first as prime minister and then, by popular election, as the first president of the newly declared Fifth Republic. The new constitution greatly enhanced the power of the president. The politics of the early Fifth Republic was dominated by the centre-right, with a succession of parties (including the Union of Democrats for the Republic, Union of Democrats for the V Republic, Union for the New Republic, Union for the French Republic-Democratic Union of Labour) working to a Gaullist agenda. There was an emphasis on national independence, government involvement in the economy and broadly conservative social policies.

In 1962 Algeria gained independence. De Gaulle continued to preside over a period of relative stability and economic growth but serious student riots in Paris in 1968 precipitated reforms to the authoritarian system of education. The students were joined by workers wanting better pay and conditions. The National Assembly was dissolved and, although the Gaullists were returned to power in the new election, de Gaulle's referendum proposing decentralization was defeated and in 1969 he resigned. Georges Pompidou, who had been de Gaulle's prime minister, succeeded him. Pompidou attempted to consolidate de Gaulle's legacy by concentrating on economic reform. When he died in office in 1974 he was succeeded by Valéry Giscard d'Estaing who continued right-wing policies, eventually precipitating a swing to the left. In 1981 the Socialist leader François Mitterrand was elected president. He immediately implemented widespread social reforms but a deep recession in 1983 forced him to take a series of unpopular deflationary measures.

When the ailing Mitterrand's term of office expired in 1995, Jacques Chirac was elected president with Alain Juppé as prime minister. After the Socialists won an assembly majority in 1997, Juppé resigned making way for the Socialist leader Lionel Jospin to take over as prime minister. The right- and left-wing *cohabitation* lasted five years until Jospin retired after a disastrous result in the first round presidential elections. Chirac's second electoral success was consolidated by the moderate right taking an assembly majority in the 2002 legislative elections.

In Oct. 2005 the death of two youths of African origin led to several days of rioting in immigrant ghettoes, prompting the government to declare a state of emergency, which was lifted in Jan. 2006. In May 2007 Nicolas Sarkozy was elected president. In 2009 he led France back into NATO's integrated military command after a 43-year absence. François Hollande was elected president in May 2012 to end 17 years of centre-right rule. During his tenure, the government undertook a programme of austerity against a backdrop of difficult economic conditions. In Jan. 2015 France's social cohesion was strained after Islamist jihadist gunmen killed 17 people in Paris. Jihadists then claimed responsibility for further co-ordinated terror attacks in Nov. 2015, in which 130 people were killed in Paris, and in July 2016, when 84 people died in Nice. In response, the government declared a state of emergency that was extended in Dec. 2016 to July 2017. It was ended in Nov. 2017 and replaced with a new security law.

Despite a growing populist challenge to the governmental order in Europe that gave impetus to the presidential election campaign of right-wing Front National candidate Marine Le Pen, the second round of polling in May 2017 resulted in a victory for Emmanuel Macron heading En Marche!, a social liberal and centrist political movement that he founded in 2016.

Territory and Population

France is bounded in the north by the English Channel *(La Manche)*, northeast by Belgium and Luxembourg, east by Germany, Switzerland and Italy, south by the Mediterranean (with Monaco as a coastal enclave), southwest by Spain and Andorra, and west by the Atlantic Ocean. The total area of metropolitan France is 543,965 sq. km. More than 14% of the population of Paris are foreign and 19% are foreign born.

The population was 58,518,395 at the census of 1999 and 64,027,784 on 1 Jan. 2014 (density, 117·7 persons per sq. km).

The UN gives a projected population for 2020 of 65·72m.

In 2011, 85·9% of the population lived in urban areas.

The growth of the population has been as follows:

Census	Population
1801	27,349,003
1861	37,386,313
1901	38,961,945
1921	39,209,518
1931	41,834,923
1946	40,506,639
1954	42,777,174
1962	46,519,997
1968	49,778,540
1975	52,655,802
1982	54,334,871

(continued)

Census	Population
1990	56,615,155
1999	58,518,395
2006[1]	61,399,733
2011[2]	63,070,344
2012[2]	63,375,971
2013[2]	63,697,865
2014[2]	64,027,784
2015[2,3]	64,343,948

[1]First recorded figure using the new 'rolling census' method of calculating the population that came into effect in Jan. 2004.
[2]Calculated using the 'rolling census' method.
[3]Provisional.

In 2012 there were 5·60m. people of foreign extraction in France (8·8% of the population). The largest groups of foreigners in 2012 were Algerians (748,000), Moroccans (692,000) and Portuguese (599,000). France's Muslim population, at an estimated 5m.–6m., is the highest in Europe.

Controls on illegal immigration were tightened in July 1991. Automatic right to citizenship for those born on French soil was restored in 1997 by the new left-wing coalition government. New immigration legislation, which came into force in 1998, brought in harsher penalties for organized traffic in illegal immigrants and extended asylum laws to include people whose lives are at risk from non-state as well as state groups. It also extended nationality at the age of 18 to those born in France of non-French parents, provided they have lived a minimum of five years in France since the age of 11.

In Jan. 2016 France's 22 former metropolitan regions were reconfigured into 13 new regions. Their chief towns, areas and recorded populations (Jan. 2014 figures) were as follows:

Regions	Area (sq. km)	Population	Chief town
Auvergne-Rhône-Alpes	69,711	7,820,966	Lyon
Bourgogne (Burgundy)-Franche-Comté	47,784	2,820,623	Dijon
Bretagne (Brittany)	27,208	3,276,543	Rennes
Centre-Val de Loire	39,151	2,577,435	Orléans
Corse (Corsica)	8,680	324,212	Ajaccio
Grand Est	57,433	5,554,645	Strasbourg
Hauts-de-France	31,813	6,006,156	Lille
Île-de-France	12,012	12,027,565	Paris
Normandie	29,906	3,335,645	Rouen
Nouvelle-Aquitaine	84,060	5,879,144	Bordeaux
Occitanie	72,724	5,730,753	Toulouse
Pays de la Loire	32,082	3,690,659	Nantes
Provence-Alpes-Côte d'Azur	31,400	4,983,438	Marseille

The 13 regions are divided into 96 metropolitan *départements,* which in 2015 consisted of 36,529 communes.

Populations of the largest cities (in descending order of size) in 2013:

	Population
Paris	2,229,621
Marseille	855,393
Lyon	500,715
Toulouse	458,298
Nice	342,295
Nantes	292,718
Strasbourg	275,718
Montpellier	272,084
Bordeaux	243,626
Lille	231,491

(*continued*)

	Population
Rennes	211,373
Reims	182,592
Le Havre	172,074
Saint-Étienne	172,023
Toulon	163,760
Grenoble	160,215
Dijon	153,003
Nîmes	150,564
Angers	150,125
Villeurbanne	147,192
Le Mans	144,244
Aix-en-Provence	141,545
Clermont-Ferrand	141,463
Brest	139,386
Limoges	135,098
Tours	134,803
Amiens	132,699
Perpignan	120,959
Metz	118,634
Besançon	116,952
Boulogne-Billancourt	116,794
Orléans	114,375
Mulhouse	112,063
Rouen	110,755
Saint-Denis	109,343
Caen	107,229
Argenteuil	106,817
Montreuil	104,139
Nancy	104,072

The largest agglomerations in 2011 were: Paris, with a population of 10,516,110 (including Argenteuil, Aulnay-sous-Bois, Boulogne-Billancourt, Créteil, Montreuil, Nanterre, Saint-Denis, Versailles and Vitry-sur-Seine); Lyon, 1,567,537 (including Vénissieux and Villeurbanne); Marseille–Aix-en-Provence, 1,560,921; Lille, 1,018,809 (including Roubaix and Tourcoing); Nice, 943,665; Toulouse, 892,115; Bordeaux, 851,071; Nantes, 597,879; Toulon, 556,920; Douai–Lens, 508,070.

France (including its overseas territories) has nine national parks, 45 regional nature parks and 164 national nature reserves.

Languages

The official language is French. Breton and Basque are spoken in their regions. The *Toubon* legislation of 1994 seeks to restrict the use of foreign words in official communications, broadcasting and advertisements (a previous such decree dated from 1975). The Constitutional Court has since ruled that imposing such restrictions on private citizens would infringe their freedom of expression.

Social Statistics

Statistics for calendar years (mainland France):

	Births	Deaths	Marriages	Divorces
2008	796,044	532,131	258,739	129,379
2009	793,420	538,116	245,151	127,578
2010	802,224	540,469	245,334	130,621
2011	792,996	534,795	231,100	129,602
2012	790,290	559,227	239,840	125,217
2013	781,621	558,408	225,784	121,849

Live birth rate (2011) was 12·5 per 1,000 population; death rate, 8·5; marriage rate, 3·7; divorce rate, 2·1. The number of births has fallen to the lowest total since the 1990s and the birth rate to the lowest since the First

World War. 52·9% of births in 2009 were outside marriage. In 2009 the average age at first marriage was 31·7 years for males and 29·8 years for females. Abortions were legalized in 1975; there were an estimated 209,300 in 2009. Life expectancy at birth, 2009, 77·7 years for males and 84·4 years for females. Annual population growth rate, 2005–10, 0·6%. In 2012 the suicide rate per 100,000 population was 15·1 (males, 24·9; females, 7·0). Infant mortality, 2010, three per 1,000 live births; fertility rate, 2013, 2·0 births per woman. In 2013 France received 60,234 asylum applications (35,404 in 2008), the third highest total after Germany and the USA. France legalized same-sex marriage in May 2013. UNICEF reported that 17·7% of children in France in 2014 lived in relative poverty (living in a household in which disposable income—when adjusted for family size and composition—is less than 60% of the national median income), compared to 9·2% in Denmark (the world's lowest rate).

Climate

The northwest has a moderate maritime climate, with small temperature range and abundant rainfall; inland, rainfall becomes more seasonal, with a summer maximum, and the annual range of temperature increases. Southern France has a Mediterranean climate, with mild moist winters and hot dry summers. Eastern France has a continental climate and a rainfall maximum in summer, with thunderstorms prevalent. Paris, Jan. 37°F (3°C), July 64°F (18°C). Annual rainfall 22·9" (573 mm). Bordeaux, Jan. 41°F (5°C), July 68°F (20°C). Annual rainfall 31·4" (786 mm). Lyon, Jan. 37°F (3°C), July 68°F (20°C). Annual rainfall 31·8" (794 mm).

Constitution and Government

The Constitution of the Fifth Republic, superseding that of 1946, came into force on 4 Oct. 1958. It consists of a preamble, dealing with the Rights of Man, and 89 articles.

France is a decentralized republic, indivisible, secular, democratic and social; all citizens are equal before the law (Art. 1). National sovereignty resides with the people, who exercise it through their representatives and by referendums (Art. 3). Constitutional reforms of July 1995 widened the range of issues on which referendums may be called. Political parties carry out their activities freely, but must respect the principles of national sovereignty and democracy (Art. 4).

A constitutional amendment of 4 Aug. 1995 deleted all references to the 'community' (communauté) between France and her overseas possessions, representing an important step towards the constitutional dismantling of the former French colonial empire.

The head of state is the President, who must be a French citizen, have attained the age of 18 years and be qualified to vote. The President sees that the Constitution is respected; ensures the regular functioning of the public authorities, as well as the continuity of the state; is the protector of national independence and territorial integrity (Art. 5). As a result of a referendum held on 24 Sept. 2000 the President is elected for five years by direct universal suffrage (Art. 6). Previously the term of office had been seven years. The President appoints (and dismisses) a Prime Minister and, on the latter's advice, appoints and dismisses the other members of the government (Council of Ministers) (Art. 8); presides over the Council of Ministers (Art. 9); may dissolve the National Assembly, after consultation with the Prime Minister and the Presidents of the two Houses (Art. 12); appoints to the civil and military offices of the state (Art. 13). In times of crisis, the President may take such emergency powers as the circumstances demand; the National Assembly cannot be dissolved during such a period (Art. 16).

Parliament consists of the National Assembly and the Senate. The National Assembly is elected by direct suffrage by the second ballot system (by which candidates winning 50% or more of the vote in their constituencies are elected, candidates winning less than 12·5% are eliminated and other candidates go on to a second round of voting); the Senate is elected by indirect suffrage (Art. 24). Since 1996 the National Assembly has convened for an annual nine-month session. It comprises 577 deputies, elected by a two-ballot system for a five-year term from single-member constituencies (including 11 constituencies for French residents abroad).

The Senate comprises 348 senators (343 prior to the elections of Sept. 2011) elected for six-year terms (one-half every three years) by an electoral college in each Department or overseas dependency, made up of all members of the Departmental Council or its equivalent in overseas dependencies, together with all members of Municipal Councils within that area. The President of the Senate deputizes for the President of the Republic in the event of the latter's incapacity. Senate elections were last held on 24 Sept. 2017.

The Constitutional Council is composed of nine members whose term of office is nine years (non-renewable), one-third every three years; three are appointed by the President of the Republic, three by the President of the National Assembly, three by the President of the Senate; in addition, former Presidents of the Republic are, by right, life members of the Constitutional Council (Art. 56). It oversees the fairness of the elections of the President (Art. 58) and Parliament (Art. 59), and of referendums (Art. 60), and acts as a guardian of the Constitution (Art. 61). Its President is Laurent Fabius (appointed 8 March 2016).

The Economic, Social and Environmental Council advises on Government and Private Members' Bills (Art. 69). It comprises representatives of employers', workers' and farmers' organizations in each Department and Overseas Territory.

Constitutional amendments of 25 March 2003 and 1 March 2005 added provisions for European Union arrest warrants and allowed for a referendum on the European Union constitution.

Ameller, M., L'Assemblée Nationale. 1994

Duhamel, O. and Mény, Y., Dictionnaire Constitutionnel. 1992

Local Government

The traditional system of centralized government was overhauled in 1982 to provide local government with greater power. There are three basic layers of local government: régions (of which there are 13), départements (of which there are 96) and communes (which number more than 36,000). Paris, Lyon and Marseille each have special status.

Régions

Mainland France comprises 13 régions, which are principally responsible for economic development, town and country planning and education. Government is through regional councils, with members elected every six years. The council works with an economic and social committee, which includes representatives from business and commerce, trade unions, voluntary bodies and other organizations. The council elects a president every three years.

Départements

Government at the department level is principally concerned with health and social welfare, rural capital works, highways and the administration of secondary education colleges. A prefect, appointed by the government, oversees the work of the department administration. Decision-making rests with a general council, with members elected every six years. Each department is divided into cantons to serve as electoral constituencies. The council elects a chairman who holds executive power.

Communes

These municipalities can vary greatly in size. Around 80% of communes have fewer than 1,000 citizens. As a result, smaller communes will often group themselves together, either as urban communities (communautés urbaines) or as associations called syndicats intercommunaux. Municipal government consists of a decision-making municipal council and a mayor, elected by the council, who wields executive power and also acts as the state's representative. The size of a municipal council is dependent on the size of the commune and members are elected every six years. The council oversees management in areas such as schools and the environment. In addition, the mayor has jurisdiction in security, public health and crime, as well as responsibility for registering births, deaths and marriages.

National Anthem

'La Marseillaise'; words and tune by C. Rouget de Lisle.

Government Chronology

(CD = Democratic Centre; CNIP = National Centre of Independents and Peasants; DL = Liberal Democracy; En Marche! = On the Move!; FNRI = National Federation of Independent Republicans; La République en Marche! = Republic on the Move!; LR = The Republicans; MRP = People's Republican Movement; PR = Republican Party; PS = Socialist Party; Rad. = Radical Party; RPR = Rally for the Republic; SFIO = French Section of the Workers International; UDF = Union for the French Democracy; UDR = Union of Democrats for the Republic; UDSR = Democratic and Social

Union of the Resistance; UDT = Democratic Union of Labour; UDVe = Union of Democrats for the V Republic; UMP = Union for a Popular Movement; UNR = Union for the New Republic; UNR-UDT = Union for the French Republic-Democratic Union of Labour; n/p = non-partisan)

Presidents of the French Republic since the Second World War.

| 1947–54 | SFIO | Vincent Auriol |
| 1954–59 | CNIP | René Coty |

With the advent of the Fifth Republic the power of the president gained at the expense of the prime minister.

1959–69	UNR, UNR-UDT, UDVe, UDR	Charles de Gaulle
1969	CD	Alain Poher
1969–74	UDR	Georges Pompidou
1974	CD	Alain Poher
1974–81	FNRI, PR-UDF	Valéry Giscard d'Estaing
1981–95	PS	François Mitterrand
1995–2007	RPR,UMP	Jacques Chirac
2007–12	UMP	Nicolas Sarkozy
2012–17	PS	François Hollande
2017–	En Marche!; La République en Marche!	Emmanuel Macron

Heads of Government since 1944.
Chairmen of the Provisional Government of the French Republic

1944–46	n/p	Charles de Gaulle
1946	SFIO	Félix Gouin
1946	MRP	Georges Bidault
1946–47	SFIO	Léon Blum

Chairmen of the Council of Ministers

1947	SFIO	Paul Ramadier
1947–48	MRP	Robert Schuman
1948	Rad.	André Marie
1948	MRP	Robert Schuman
1948–49	Rad.	Antoine Henri Queuille
1949–50	MRP	Georges Bidault
1950	Rad.	Antoine Henri Queuille
1950–51	UDSR	René Pleven
1951	Rad.	Antoine Henri Queuille
1951–52	UDSR	René Pleven
1952	Rad.	Edgar Faure
1952–53	CNIP	Antoine Pinay
1953	Rad.	René Mayer
1953–54	CNIP	Joseph Laniel
1954–55	Rad.	Pierre Mendès France
1955–56	Rad.	Edgar Faure
1956–57	SFIO	Guy Mollet
1957	Rad.	Maurice Bourgès-Maunoury
1957–58	Rad.	Félix Gaillard
1958	MRP	Pierre Pflimlin
1958–59	UNR	Charles de Gaulle

Prime Ministers

1959–62	UNR	Michel Debré
1962–68	UNR,UNR-UDT, UDVe	Georges Pompidou
1968–69	UDVe, UDR	Maurice Couve de Murville

(continued)

1969–72	UDR	Jacques Chaban-Delmas
1972–74	UDR	Pierre Messmer
1974–76	UDR	Jacques Chirac
1976–81	n/p, UDF	Raymond Barre
1981–84	PS	Pierre Mauroy
1984–86	PS	Laurent Fabius
1986–88	RPR	Jacques Chirac
1988–91	PS	Michel Rocard
1991–92	PS	Édith Cresson
1992–93	PS	Pierre Bérégovoy
1993–95	RPR	Édouard Balladur
1995–97	PR	Alain Juppé
1997–2002	PS	Lionel Jospin
2002–05	DL, UMP	Jean-Pierre Raffarin
2005–07	UMP	Dominique de Villepin
2007–12	UMP	François Fillon
2012–14	PS	Jean-Marc Ayrault
2014–16	PS	Manuel Valls
2016–17	PS	Bernard Cazeneuve
2017–	LR	Édouard Philippe

Recent Elections

At the first round of presidential elections on 23 April 2017 Emmanuel Macron of En Marche! ('On the Move!') gained the largest number of votes (24·0% of those cast) against ten opponents. His nearest rivals were the leader of the National Front, Marine Le Pen, who came second with 21·3% of votes cast, the candidate of Les Républicains ('The Republicans'), François Fillon, with 20·0%, and Jean-Luc Mélenchon, of La France Insoumise ('France Unbowed'), with 19·6%. In the second round of voting, held on 7 May 2017, Macron was elected president with 66·1% of votes cast against 33·9% for Le Pen. Turnout was 74·6% in the second round (77·8% in the first round).

Elections to the National Assembly were held on 11 and 18 June 2017. The election was won by La République en Marche! ('Republic on the Move!') along with its Presidential Majority allies with a total of 350 seats, providing Macron with an absolute parliamentary majority. La République en Marche! (LREM) won 308 of the 577 available seats; Les Républicains (LR), 113; the Democratic Movement (MoDem), 42; the Socialist Party (PS), 29; the Union of Democrats and Independents (UDI), 18; La France Insoumise (LFI), 17; Miscellaneous left (DVG), 12; the French Communist Party (PCF), 10; the National Front (FN), 8; Miscellaneous right (DVD), 6; regionalists, 5; Radical Party of the Left (PRG), 3; and others, 6.

Following the indirect election held on 24 Sept. 2017, the Senate was composed in March 2018 of (by group, including affiliates): Les Républicains, 146; the Socialist and Republican group, 78; the Centrist Union, 50; La République en Marche!, 21; the Democratic and Social European Rally, 21; Communist, Republican, Citizen and Ecologist, 15; The independents, and Republic and Territories group, 11; unattached, 6. In Oct. 2017 Gérard Larcher (UMP; since May 2015 Les Républicains) was re-elected *President* of the Senate for a three-year term (having previously held the post in 2008–11 and 2014–17).

Evans, Jocelyn and Ivaldi, Gilles, *The 2017 French Presidential Elections: A Political Reformation*. 2018

European Parliament

France has 74 representatives. At the May 2014 elections turnout was 42·4% (40·6% in 2009). Front National won 24 seats with 24·9% of votes cast (political affiliation in European Parliament: non-attached); UMP, 20 with 20·8% (European People's Party); PS/PRG, 13 with 14·0% (Progressive Alliance of Socialists and Democrats); Democratic Movement/Union of Democrats and Independents, 7 with 9·9% (Alliance of Liberals and Democrats for Europe); Europe Ecology, 6 with 8·9% (Greens/European Free Alliance); FG/Alliance of the Overseas, 4 with 6·6% (European United Left/Nordic Green Left). One of the Front National MEPs quit the party two days after the election and joined Europe of Freedom and Direct Democracy.

Current Government

President: Emmanuel Macron; b. 1977 (La République en Marche!; sworn in 14 May 2017).

In Feb. 2019 the government comprised:

Prime Minister: Édouard Philippe; b. 1970 (Les Républicains; sworn in 15 May 2017).

Minister of State: François de Rugy (also *Minister of Ecological and Inclusive Transition*).

Minister of Justice and Keeper of the Seals: Nicole Belloubet. *Europe and Foreign Affairs:* Jean-Yves Le Drian. *Armed Forces:* Florence Parly. *Solidarity and Health:* Agnès Buzyn. *Economy and Finance:* Bruno Le Maire. *Labour:* Muriel Pénicaud. *National Education and Youth:* Jean-Michel Blanquer. *Public Action and Accounts:* Gérald Darmanin. *Interior:* Christophe Castaner. *Higher Education, Research and Innovation:* Frédérique Vidal. *Territorial Cohesion and Relations with Local Authorities:* Jacqueline Gourault. *Overseas France:* Annick Girardin. *Culture:* Franck Riester. *Agriculture and Food:* Didier Guillaume. *Sports:* Roxana Maracineanu. *Minister in the Office of the Prime Minister, in Charge of Relations with Parliament:* Marc Fesneau.

President of the National Assembly: Richard Ferrand.

Government Website: http://www.gouvernement.fr

Current Leaders

Emmanuel Macron

Position

President

Introduction

Emmanuel Macron was elected president on 7 May 2017. He founded En Marche!, a centrist party, in 2016 and was previously the minister of economy, industry and digital affairs in the Socialist government. Promising fundamental change for the country, he defeated Marine Le Pen of the far-right Front National in the second round of the presidential poll.

Early Life

Macron was born on 21 Dec. 1977 in Amiens. He studied philosophy at Paris Nanterre University and obtained his master's degree in public affairs from the Paris Institute of Political Studies. In 2004 he graduated from the elite École Nationale d'Administration, before beginning work as an inspector of finances with France's state auditing and supervisory body. In 2007 he served on the Attali Commission, set up by then President Sarkozy and charged with devising a scheme to spur economic growth in the country. He then left the civil service in 2008 to take up a position as an investment banker at Rothschild & Cie Banque. While there, he was involved in corporate negotiations for Nestlé's €9bn. purchase of Pfizer's baby-food business.

In 2006 he joined the Socialist Party and in 2012 was appointed deputy secretary-general in François Hollande's presidential staff, in which role he was involved in the implementation of a high-profile tax credit scheme offered to businesses. In 2014 he was appointed minister of economy, industry and digital affairs, where he pushed through several business-friendly reforms, including the so-called Macron law of 2015.

Disillusioned with the ruling administration, Macron founded En Marche! in April 2016. He resigned as a minister in Aug. and declared his presidential candidacy in Nov. that year. Despite never having previously run for election, Macron quickly gained impressive support as he pledged a rebalancing of the French political system away from the traditional left- and right-wing parties. He led with 24·0% of the vote after the first round of voting on 23 April 2017 and won the run-off against Marine Le Pen of the Front National by 66·1% to 33·9% on 7 May.

Career in Office

Macron has championed free market, pro-business policies in a bid to boost the economy and reduce the public deficit, while raising spending on defence and the intelligence services to curb the threat from Islamist extremism. Strongly pro-European, he has advocated creating a new EU Commissioner with responsibility for the eurozone, and also suggested a policy of monitoring foreign investments in strategic EU sectors in order to protect the EU's dominance in those areas.

In June 2017 Macron's La République en Marche! movement (previously En Marche!) and its allies won 350 of 577 seats, giving the president an absolute parliamentary majority. However, his approval rating fell steeply through 2018, reflecting voter disaffection with his plans for radical economic policy changes (particularly labour, benefit and pension reforms, prompting widespread strike action), public expenditure cuts, a high-profile scandal concerning violent behaviour by his bodyguard and his perceived indifference to social issues. Although his government survived two parliamentary no-confidence motions in July, his administration has been seriously challenged since Nov. by the so-called 'yellow vest' populist movement, which has organized weekly mass demonstrations, often violent, in support of greater economic justice that were still continuing as of the end of Feb. 2019.

Macron has meanwhile been active in European Union affairs and on the wider international stage, making numerous bilateral trips abroad and attending multilateral gatherings.

Édouard Philippe

Position

Prime Minister

Introduction

Édouard Philippe became prime minister on 15 May 2017. He was appointed by President Emmanuel Macron despite hailing from the rival moderate right-wing Les Républicains. He was mayor of Le Havre from 2010–17 and had represented the 7th constituency of Seine-Maritime in the National Assembly since 2012.

Early Life

Philippe was born on 28 Nov. 1970 and grew up in Rouen. He graduated from Sciences Po in 1992 and the École Nationale d'Administration in 1997. He then worked as a lawyer for the Supreme Court until 2002.

In 2001 he entered front-line politics as deputy mayor of Le Havre and a year later, under the leadership of former prime minister Alain Juppé, he took a senior post in the newly-formed Union for a Popular Movement party, the precursor of Les Républicains. However, when Juppé was banned from elected office in 2004, Philippe entered the private sector and joined the American law firm Debevoise & Plimpton LLP in 2005.

From 2007 he worked for state nuclear group Areva as head of public affairs, then for law firm Wilhelm & Associés, and was also elected mayor of Le Havre. In June 2012 he entered the National Assembly.

Although Philippe was a spokesperson for Juppé's failed candidacy in the 2017 presidential elections, he was appointed prime minister following Macron's victory. After several resignations from his initial government in the wake of a political scandal, in July 2017 he secured a vote of parliamentary confidence allowing him to govern with a majority government.

Career in Office

With Macron having pledged to disrupt France's traditional left–right political divide, Philippe has sought to seek right-of-centre support for the president's reformist agenda, including plans to tackle public debt, improve the country's standing as a pro-business investment destination, execute a new immigration plan and bring in labour reforms.

Defence

The President of the Republic is the supreme head of defence policy and exercises command over the Armed Forces. He is the only person empowered to give the order to use nuclear weapons. He is assisted by the Council of Ministers, which studies defence problems, and by the Defence Council and the Restricted Defence Committee, which formulate directives.

Legislation of 1996 inaugurated a wide-ranging reform of the defence system over 1997–2002, with regard to the professionalization of the armed forces (brought about by the ending of military conscription and consequent switch to an all-volunteer defence force), the modification and modernization of equipment and the restructuring of the defence industry. In 2013 defence expenditure totalled US$52,352m. (equivalent to US$794 per capita). Defence spending as a proportion of GDP was 1·9% in 2013 (compared to the NATO target of 2%).

In Nov. 2010 France and the UK signed a Defence and Security Cooperation Treaty providing for the creation of a rapid reaction force, with troops from both nations called up as required after a joint political decision. Aircraft carriers may be jointly used under certain circumstances and there will be joint training exercises, pooling of resources for the maintenance and logistics of the A400M transport aircraft, and joint work on several other projects. The treaty provides for collaboration and co-operation through shared facilities to maintain the safety of the two countries' independent nuclear deterrents. As part of the requirements under the treaty, a joint Anglo/French Hydrodynamics Research Facility is being developed at Valduc in France. Known as the EPURE facility, it is replacing existing facilities in both countries. A new Technology Development Centre is also being built at Aldermaston in the UK.

France rejoined NATO as a full member in April 2009, having withdrawn from its integrated military structure in 1966. In 2014 French military personnel were stationed in a number of countries outside France including the Central African Republic, Chad, Côte d'Ivoire, Djibouti, Gabon, Mali, Senegal and the United Arab Emirates. Then President Hollande withdrew the last combat troops from Afghanistan in Dec. 2012.

Conscription was for ten months, but France officially ended its military draft on 27 June 2001 with a reprieve granted to all conscripts (barring those serving in civil positions) on 30 Nov. 2001. Active military personnel totalled 222,200 in 2012.

Nuclear Weapons

Having carried out its first nuclear test in 1960, there have been 210 tests in all. The last French test was in 1996 (this compares with the last UK test in 1991 and the last US test in 1993). The nuclear arsenal consisted of approximately 300 warheads in Jan. 2017 according to the Stockholm International Peace Research Institute. In 2008 France announced a 33% reduction in the airborne component of its nuclear forces.

Army

The Army comprises the Logistic Force (CFLT), based in Montlhéry with two logistic brigades, and the Land Force Command (CFAT), based in Lille. Apart from the Franco-German brigade (consisting of units from both the French Army and German Army), in 2013 there were 11 brigades, each made up of between four and seven battalions, including one airmobile brigade.

Personnel numbered (2013) 119,050 including 12,800 marines and a Foreign Legion of 7,300. There were 16,000 army reservists in 2013. Equipment levels in 2013 included 254 main battle tanks and 346 helicopters.

Gendarmerie

The paramilitary police force exists to ensure public security and maintain law and order, as well as participate in the operational defence of French territory as part of the armed forces. On 1 Jan. 2009 budgetary responsibility for the Gendarmerie was transferred from the ministry of defence to the ministry of the interior. It consisted in 2013 of 103,400 personnel. It comprises a departmental gendarmerie, a mobile gendarmerie and specialized formations including the Republican Guard, the Air Force and Naval Gendarmeries, and an anti-terrorist unit.

Navy

The missions of the Navy are to provide the prime element of the French independent nuclear deterrent through its force of strategic submarines; to assure the security of the French offshore zones; to contribute to NATO's missions; and to provide on-station and deployment forces overseas in support of French territorial interests and UN commitments. French territorial seas and economic zones are organized into two maritime districts (with headquarters in Brest and Toulon).

The strategic deterrent force comprises four nuclear-powered strategic-missile submarines of the *Triomphant* class (*Le Triomphant*, *Le Téméraire*, *Le Vigilant* and *Le Terrible*, which entered service in 1997, 1999, 2004 and 2010 respectively). The three older vessels in the *Triomphant* class have been upgraded so that they will be able to carry M51 ballistic missiles. *Le Terrible* was equipped to carry the missiles from its outset.

The principal surface ship is the 40,000-tonne nuclear-powered aircraft carrier *Charles de Gaulle*, which was launched at Brest in 1994 and commissioned in May 2001. Other vessels include three amphibious assault ships, 12 destroyers and eleven frigates. There are also six *Rubis* class nuclear-powered submarines.

The naval air arm, *Aviation Navale*, numbered some 6,500 personnel in 2013. Operational aircraft include Super-Étendard nuclear-capable strike aircraft and maritime Rafale combat aircraft. A small Marine force of 1,600 *Fusiliers Marins* provides assault groups.

Personnel in 2013 numbered 37,850, including 2,200 strategic nuclear forces. There were 5,500 reserves in 2013.

Air Force

Created in 1934, the Air Force was reorganized in 1994. The Treaty on Conventional Armed Forces in Europe imposes a ceiling of 800 combat aircraft. In 2013 there were 325 combat aircraft, 141 transport aircraft and 120 aircraft for training purposes.

Personnel (2013) 47,550. Air Force reserves in 2013 numbered 4,750.

International Relations

At a referendum in Sept. 1992 to approve the ratification of the Maastricht treaty on European Union of 7 Feb. 1992, 12,967,498 votes (50·8%) were cast for and 12,550,651 (49·2%) against. On 29 May 2005 France became the first European Union member to reject the proposed EU constitution, with 54·7% of votes cast in a referendum against the constitution and only 45·3% in favour.

France is the focus of the *Communauté Francophone* (French-speaking Community) which formally links France with many of its former colonies in Africa. A wide range of agreements, both with members of the Community and with other French-speaking countries, extend to economic and technical matters, and in particular to the disbursement of overseas aid.

Economy

Agriculture accounted for 1·7% of GDP in 2014, industry 19·4% and services 78·9%.

France gave US$11·3bn. in international aid in 2017, equivalent to 0·43% of GNI (compared to the UN target of 0·7%).

Overview

France has one of the eurozone's largest economies, but GDP growth has lagged behind other major European countries since 2008 as the economy has struggled with structural costs and high unemployment. Services are the main contributor to growth, although in manufacturing France is a global leader in the automotive, aerospace and railway sectors and is a major player in the cosmetics and luxury item industries. It is the sixth largest exporter of goods and fourth largest exporter of services in the world, with most of the country's exports going to other European countries. According to the World Tourism Organization, France is also the most popular tourist destination in the world, with 86·9m. international arrivals in 2017, supporting an industry that contributes 9·7% to annual GDP.

The election of independent centrist Emmanuel Macron as president in May 2017 heralded the introduction of a pro-business government strategy to promote employment and economic growth. His government intends to reduce the share of public spending in GDP by 3 percentage points over five years to make room for tax cuts. These include a gradual reduction of the corporate income tax rate from 33% to 25% and cuts in capital income, wealth and residency taxes. The government took some measures to reduce public spending in 2017–18, including reductions in housing subsidies and public sector employment costs, and plans to lower real public spending growth to less than 0·5% annually over the period 2018–22. In Dec. 2018, against a backdrop of sometimes violent popular protests by the so-called 'yellow vests', Macron promised tax cuts, and an increase in the minimum wage, and urged businesses to provide year-end bonuses. Protests continued into early 2019, although the number of participants dwindled from their peak of over 300,000 in Nov. 2018.

GDP growth had averaged 2% annually from 2003–07, driven by private consumption resulting from a steady increase in real disposable income. The global financial crisis forced the economy into recession in 2008. Following four successive quarters of contraction, France emerged from the downturn in the second quarter of 2009 but GDP declined by 2·9% for the year as a whole. Policy responses included a fiscal stimulus package, comprising temporary investment expenditures and tax breaks, and measures to recapitalize banks to support liquidity. However, the eurozone debt crisis, shrinking private investment, loss of competitiveness and rising unemployment undermined recovery. The economy grew at around 2% in 2010–11 but stagnated in 2012–14, averaging 0·6% per year. Between 2010 and 2014 foreign direct investment averaged 0·8% of GDP per year. Growth of 1·3% in 2016 was the highest since 2011, driven by higher export demand, a depreciating euro and lower oil prices. It was followed by growth of 1·4% the following year. Nonetheless, private consumption growth has declined as higher inflation has eaten into domestic disposable income. The years of low-level growth and high spending put pressure on public finances. The government deficit increased from 3·3% of GDP in 2008 to 7·5% in 2009, before falling to 3·6% in 2015 and 3·4% in 2016. Public debt increased from 68·2% of GDP in 2008 to 90·6% in 2012 (prompting international rating agency Standard & Poor's to strip France of its triple-A credit status), 95·6% in 2014 and 96·1% in 2015. However, with one of the highest tax burdens in the eurozone (47·9% of GDP in 2015), the authorities then embarked upon a programme of expenditure reduction that won support from the IMF. Aiming to achieve a zero deficit, the then Socialist government laid out plans for cuts worth €50bn. over the period 2014–17, with the bulk of the savings expected to come from local government.

Labour force participation is particularly low and structural unemployment high. Government-supported jobs and labour market reforms have aided employment growth, although continued rises in the minimum wage have hindered further job creation. Having reached a low of 7·6% in March 2008, nemployment rose steeply owing to the global economic downturn and stood at 10·4% in 2015. The IMF suggested that fostering job creation, especially for the young, the low-skilled and senior workers, would aid efforts to boost growth and competitiveness, safeguard fiscal sustainability and reduce welfare pending. It was hoped that new labour reforms rolled out in 2018—including changes to the complex governance surrounding workers' representation and substantial investment in training—would yield positive outcomes in regard to inclusiveness and less-skilled workers. The jobless rate reaching a ten-year low of 8·8% in the final months of 2018.

The state still plays a pivotal role in many economic sectors, notably services. However, efforts have been made to liberalize the economy and increase competition through the Macron Law that entered into force in Aug. 2015. Measures to address the ageing population problem are key to long-term rowth. The average legal retirement age across the OECD countries is between 63 and 64, but in France most people stop working before they are 60. Only 45% of people over 55 were employed in 2012, compared to the OECD average of 54%. Major pension reforms were passed in 2010 aimed at gradually increasing the etirement age from 60 to 62 years.

Business confidence reached its highest level since 2011 in Sept. 2017. However, France still faces economic challenges. Although initially predicted to exceed 3% (the maximum threshold authorized by the EU), France's deficit fell just short of that limit in early 2018 but was expected to rise in 2019 as a result of tax reforms and slowing growth.

Currency

On 1 Jan. 1999 the *euro* (EUR) became the legal currency in France at the irrevocable conversion rate of 6·55957 francs to one euro. The euro, which consists of 100 cents, has been in circulation since 1 Jan. 2002. On the introduction of the euro there was a 'dual circulation' period before the franc ceased to be legal tender on 17 Feb. 2002.

Foreign exchange reserves were US$26,170m. in Sept. 2009 and gold reserves 78·30m. troy oz. Total money supply was €431,879m. in Aug. 2009. Inflation rates (based on OECD statistics):

2008	2009	2010	2011	2012	2013	2014	2015	2016	2017
3·2%	0·1%	1·7%	2·3%	2·2%	1·0%	0·6%	0·1%	0·3%	1·2%

Franc Zone

13 former French colonies (Benin, Burkina Faso, Cameroon, Central African Republic, Chad, the Comoros, the Republic of the Congo, Côte d'Ivoire, Gabon, Mali, Niger, Senegal and Togo), the former Spanish colony of Equatorial Guinea and the former Portuguese colony of Guinea-Bissau are members of a Franc Zone, the CFA (*Communauté Financière Africaine*). The Comoros uses the Comorian franc. The *franc CFA* is pegged to the euro at a rate of 655·957 francs CFA to one euro. The franc CFP *(Comptoirs Français du Pacifique)* is the common currency of French Polynesia, New Caledonia, and Wallis and Futuna. It is pegged to the euro at 119·3317422 francs CFP to the euro.

Budget

General government revenues in 2015 (provisional) were €1,166bn. and expenditures €1,238bn. Principal sources of revenue in 2015 (provisional) were: social contributions, €413bn.; taxes on goods and services, €255bn.; taxes on income, profits and capital gains, €250bn. Main items of

expenditure by economic type in 2015 (provisional): social benefits, €567bn.; compensation of employees, €282bn.; use of goods and services, €112bn.

In 2017 tax revenues were 46·2% of GDP (the highest percentage of any developed country).

France's budget deficit in 2017 was 2·7% of GDP (3·5% in 2016 and 3·6% in 2015). The required target set by the EU is a budget deficit of no more than 3%.

VAT was raised from 19·6% to 20% on 1 Jan. 2014. There are reduced rates of 10%, 5·5% and 2·1%.

In 2015 the top rate of income tax was 45·0% and corporate tax was 33·3%.

Performance

Real GDP growth rates (based on OECD statistics):

2008	2009	2010	2011	2012	2013	2014	2015	2016	2017
0·1%	−2·8%	1·9%	2·2%	0·4%	0·6%	1·0%	1·0%	1·1%	2·3%

The real GDP growth rate in 2018 according to INSEE, the French National Institute for Statistics and Economic Studies, was 1·6%. Total GDP in 2017 was US$2,582·5bn.

Banking and Finance

The central bank and bank of issue is the Banque de France (*Governor*, François Villeroy de Galhau, appointed 2015), founded in 1800, and nationalized on 2 Dec. 1945. The Governor is appointed for a six-year term (renewable once) and heads the nine-member Council of Monetary Policy.

The National Credit Council, formed in 1945 to regulate banking activity and consulted in all political decisions on monetary policy, comprises 51 members nominated by the government; its president is the minister for the economy; its vice-president is the governor of the Banque de France.

In 2008 there were 722 banks and other credit institutions, including 304 financial companies, 290 commercial banks and 104 mutual or co-operative banks. Four principal deposit banks were nationalized in 1945, the remainder in 1982. The banking and insurance sectors underwent a flurry of mergers, privatizations, foreign investment, corporate restructuring and consolidation in 1997, in both the national and international fields. The largest banks in March 2014 by assets were BNP Paribas (US$2,460·30bn.) and Crédit Agricole (US$2,107·28bn.). In March 2014 the largest banks by market capitalization were BNP Paribas (US$69·96bn.) and Société Générale (US$34·45bn.).

The former state banks, the Caisses d'Épargne, became co-operative savings banks in 1999 although the group remains partly state-owned. There is a state-owned postal bank, La Banque Postale. Deposited funds are centralized by a non-banking body, the Caisse des Dépôts et Consignations, which finances a large number of local authorities and state-aided housing projects, and carries an important portfolio of transferable securities.

Gross external debt totalled US$4,838,186m. in June 2012.

France attracted US$42·9bn. worth of foreign direct investment in 2015, up from US$15·2bn. in 2014 but down from a record US$63·5bn. in 2007. At the end of 2015 foreign direct investment stocks totalled US$772,030m.

There is a stock exchange (*Bourse*) in Paris; it is a component of Euronext, which was created in Sept. 2000 through the merger of the Paris, Brussels and Amsterdam bourses.

Energy and Natural Resources

In 2011, 11·5% of energy consumption in mainland France came from renewables (wind power, solar power, hydro-electric power, tidal power, geothermal energy and biomass), compared to the European Union average of 13·0%. A target of 23% has been set by the EU for 2020.

Environment

France's carbon dioxide emissions from the consumption of energy in 2011 were the equivalent of 5·7 tonnes per capita. An *Environmental Performance Index* compiled in 2016 ranked France 10th of 180 countries, with 88·2%. The index examined various factors in nine areas—agriculture, air quality, biodiversity and habitat, climate and energy, fisheries, forests, health impacts, water and sanitation, and water resources.

Electricity

EDF is responsible for power generation and supply. It was privatized in Nov. 2005 when the government sold a 15·5% stake in the company. Installed capacity was 131·4m. kW in 2011. Electricity production in 2011: 561·96bn. kWh, of which 78·7% was nuclear. Hydro-electric power contributes about 8·9% of total electricity output. Consumption per capita in 2011 was 7,946 kWh. In 2011 France was the world's biggest exporter of electricity, with 65·9bn. kWh. EDF is Europe's leading electricity producer, generating 628·2bn. kWh in 2011.

France, not rich in natural energy resources, is at the centre of Europe's nuclear energy industry. In 2012 there were 58 nuclear reactors in operation—more than in any other country in the world apart from the USA—with a generating capacity of 63,130 MW. France has the highest percentage of its electricity generated through nuclear power of any country.

Oil and Gas

In 2011, 6·6m. bbls of crude oil were produced. The greater part came from the Parentis oilfield in Landes in the southwest of the country. Reserves in 2014 totalled 90m. bbls. The importation and distribution of natural gas is the responsibility of Engie, a company formed as GDF Suez in July 2008 following a merger between Gaz de France and fellow utility group Suez, and renamed in April 2015. The French government has a 25·5% stake in Engie.

Production of natural gas (2011) was 627m. cu. metres. Natural gas reserves were 9·7bn. cu. metres in 2014.

Minerals

France is a significant producer of nickel, uranium, iron ore, bauxite, potash, pig iron, aluminium and coal. Société Le Nickel extracts in New Caledonia and is the world's third largest nickel producer.

France's last coal mine closed in April 2004. Production of other principal minerals and metals, in 1,000 tonnes (2011): salt, 5,430; aluminium, 334.

Agriculture

France has the highest agricultural production in Europe. In 2007 the agricultural sector employed about 1,020,000 people, down from 2,038,000 in 1988 and over 6m. in the mid-1950s. Agriculture accounts for 10·4% of exports and 8·3% of imports.

In 2007 there were 507,000 holdings (average size 54 ha.), down from over 1m. in 1988. There were 1,176,000 tractors and 80,000 harvester-threshers in 2005. Although the total number of tractors has been declining steadily in recent years, increasingly more powerful ones are being used. In 2005, 497,000 tractors in use were of 80 hp or higher, compared to 96,000 in 1979.

Of the total area of France (54·9m. ha.), the utilized agricultural area comprised 29·27m. ha. in 2009. 18·26m. ha. were arable, 9·87m. ha. were grassland and 1·06m. ha. were under permanent crops including vines (0·84m. ha.).

Area under cultivation and yield for principal crops:

	Area (1,000 ha.)			Production (1,000 tonnes)		
	2006	2007	2008	2006	2007	2008
Wheat	5,246	5,239	5,492	35,364	32,764	39,002
Sugar beets	379	393	349	29,871	33,230	30,306
Maize	1,465	1,484	1,702	12,775	14,357	15,819
Barley	1,667	1,699	1,799	10,401	9,474	12,171
Potatoes	158	158	156	6,363	7,183	6,808
Rapeseed	1,406	1,619	1,421	4,144	4,691	4,719
Triticale[1]	331	324	343	1,694	1,450	1,821
Sunflower seeds	645	520	630	1,440	1,311	1,608

[1]Cross between wheat and rye.

Production of principal fruit crops (in 1,000 tonnes) as follows:

	2006	2007	2008
Grapes	6,777	6,019	5,664
Apples	2,081	2,144	1,940

(continued)

	2006	2007	2008
Peaches and nectarines	395	365	301
Melons	301	242	274
Pears	226	203	156
Plums and sloes	234	249	147

Total fruit and vegetable production in 2008 was 13,732,900 tonnes. Other important vegetables include tomatoes (714,683 tonnes in 2008), carrots (556,517 tonnes), sweetcorn (479,718 tonnes) and cauliflowers (392,648 tonnes). France is the world's leading producer of sugar beets. Total area under cultivation and yield of grapes from the vine (2008): 813,496 ha.; 5·7m. tonnes. Wine production (2010): 44,470,000 hectolitres. France was the second largest wine producer in the world in 2010 (16·9% of the world total) after Italy. Consumption in France has declined dramatically in recent times, from nearly 120 litres per person in 1966 to 53 litres per person in 2008.

In 2008 France set aside 583,800 ha. (2·1% of its agricultural land) for the growth of organic crops, compared to the EU average of 4·1% in 2007. Livestock (2008, in 1,000): cattle, 19,887; pigs, 14,801; sheep, 8,171; goats, 1,228; horses, 420; chickens (estimate), 175,000; turkeys, 25,253; ducks, 22,848. Livestock products (2008, in 1,000 tonnes): pork and pork products, 2,259; beef and veal, 1,496; lamb and mutton, 130; eggs, 11,618m. units. Milk production, 2008 (in 1,000 hectolitres): cow, 235,410; goat, 5,673; sheep, 2,442. Cheese production, 2008, 1,861,000 tonnes. France is the second largest cheese producer in the world after the USA.

Source: SCEES/Agreste

Forestry

Forestry is France's richest natural resource. In 2015 forests covered 16·99m. ha. (31% of the land area). Of the total area under forests 88% was naturally regenerated forest in 2015 and 12% planted forest. In 1990 the area under forests had been 14·44m. ha. Growing stock was 2,935m. cu. metres in 2015 (1,892m. cu. metres broadleaved and 1,043m. cu. metres coniferous). Timber production in 2011 was 55·04m. cu. metres.

Fisheries

In 2011 there were 7,209 fishing vessels (down from 8,165 in 2006). Catch in 2015 was 485,342 tonnes, of which 484,155 tonnes were from marine waters. Imports of fishery commodities were valued at US$5,949m. in 2010 (the fifth highest of any country) and exports at US$1,613m.

Industry

The leading companies by market capitalization in France in March 2019 were: Total, an integrated oil company (US$168·0bn.); L'Oreal, a cosmetics and beauty company (US$134·2bn.); and Sanofi, a pharmaceuticals company (US$94·9bn.).

Chief industries: steel, chemicals, textiles, aircraft, machinery, electronic equipment, tourism, wine and perfume. In 2008 industry accounted for 20% of GDP, with manufacturing contributing 12%.

Industrial production (in 1,000 tonnes): distillate fuel oil (2007, including Monaco), 34,392; cement (2008), 21,443; crude steel (2007), 19,252; rolled steel (2006), 17,437; petrol (2007, including Monaco), 16,479; pig iron (2006), 13,013; residual fuel oil (2007, including Monaco), 11,441; jet fuel (2007, including Monaco), 5,536. France is one of the biggest producers of mineral water, with 12,159m. litres in 2005. In 2005 soft drinks production was 4,777m. litres, beer production 1,720m. litres and cigarette production 46·5bn. units.

Engineering production (in 1,000 units): cars (2009), 1,819; commercial vehicles (2009), 228; car tyres (2007), 54,000.

Labour

The labour force in 2013 was 30,031,000 (28,330,000 in 2003). 70·9% of the population aged 15–64 was economically active in 2013.

A new definition of 'unemployed' was adopted in Aug. 1995, omitting persons who had worked at least 78 hours in the previous month. The unemployment rate was 8·9% in Dec. 2018 (down from 9·4% in 2017 as a whole), compared to the European Union average of 7·3%. The rate among the under 25s is more than double the overall national rate, at 25·7% in the fourth quarter of 2015 (compared to 19·9% for the European Union as a whole).

Conciliation boards (*conseils de prud'hommes*) mediate in labour disputes. They are elected for five-year terms by two colleges of employers and employees. In 2010 strikes cost France 316 days per 1,000 employees.

In Jan. 2018 the minimum wage (SMIC) was raised to €9·88 an hour (€1,498·47 per month for a 35-hour week). The minimum retirement age was lowered from 65 to 60 by then President Mitterrand in 1983. In Nov. 2010 then President Sarkozy signed a bill to increase it gradually to 62 by 2018, although the increase was fast-tracked to 2017. A five-week annual holiday is statutory.

In March 2005 the National Assembly voted by 350 to 135 to amend the working hours law restricting the legal working week to 35 hours, introduced by the former Socialist government between 1998–2000. Employees can, in agreement with their employer, work up to 48 hours per week. There is no change in the legal working week: any increased hours are on a voluntary basis. The maximum number of overtime hours was increased from 180 to 220 per year in Dec. 2004. To encourage the working of longer hours, payment of overtime work is now exempt from individual income tax, social contributions and social taxes (since 1 Oct. 2007).

France had 9,000 people living in slavery according to the Walk Free Foundation's 2013 *Global Slavery Index*.

International Trade

Imports and Exports

Goods imports in 2014 totalled US$659,872·1m. (US$671,253·6m. in 2013) and goods exports US$566,656·2m. (US$567,987·7m. in 2013).

Principal imports in 2014 were machinery and transport equipment (33·1%), manufactured articles (14·7%), mineral fuels and lubricants (14·6%), chemicals (14·1%) and manufactured goods (12·1%); main exports in 2014 were machinery and transport equipment (38·4%), chemicals (17·8%), food, animals and beverages (12·2%), manufactured articles (11·6%) and manufactured goods (11·0%).

The leading import supplier in 2010 was Germany (17·3%), followed by China (8·2%), Belgium (7·8%), Italy (7·5%) and Spain (6·2%); the leading export destination in 2010 was Germany (16·2%), followed by Italy (8·1%), Belgium (7·5%), Spain (7·4%) and the UK (6·7%).

Trade Fairs

Paris ranked as the world's most popular convention city in 2016 according to the International Congress and Convention Association. Paris hosted 196 international association meetings that year.

Communications

Roads

In 2007 there were 951,125 km of road, including 11,010 km of motorway and 9,115 km of highways and main roads. France has the longest road network in the EU. Around 90% of all freight is transported by road. In 2007 there were 30·70m. passenger cars (498 per 1,000 inhabitants), 6·27m. lorries and vans, and 83,000 buses and coaches. Road passenger traffic in 2007 totalled 775bn. passenger-km. In 2007 there were 4,620 road deaths, down from 8,445 in 1997.

Rail

In 1938 all the independent railway companies were merged with the existing state railway system in a Société Nationale des Chemins de Fer Français (SNCF), which became a public industrial and commercial establishment in 1983. Legislation came into effect in 1997 which vested ownership of the railway infrastructure (track and signalling) in a newly established public corporation, the Réseau Ferré de France (RFF/French Rail Network). The RFF is funded by payments for usage from the SNCF, government and local subventions and authority capital made available by the state derived from the proceeds of privatization. The SNCF remains responsible for maintenance and management of the rail network. The legislation also envisages the establishment of regional railway services which receive funds previously given to the SNCF as well as a state subvention. These regional bodies negotiate with SNCF for the provision of suitable services for their area. SNCF is the most heavily indebted and subsidized company in France.

In 2010 the RFF-managed network totalled 29,473 km of track (15,424 km electrified). High-speed inOui (formerly TGV) lines link Paris to the west, southwest, southeast and east of France, and north from Paris and Lille to the Channel Tunnel (Eurostar) and to Brussels in Belgium. The high-speed TGV line appeared in 1981; it had 2,024 km of track in 2015. TGV

began to be rebranded as inOui from July 2017. Services from London through the Channel Tunnel began operating in 1994. Rail passenger traffic in 2011 totalled 86·1bn. passenger km and freight tonne-km came to 23·2bn.

The Paris transport network consisted in 2014 of 220 km of metro (302 stations), 115 km of regional express railways and 104 km of tramway. Outside Paris and the Île-de-France region there are metros in Lille (45 km), Lyon (31 km), Marseille (22 km), Rennes (9 km) and Toulouse (28 km), and tram/light railway networks in Angers (12 km), Aubagne (3 km), Bordeaux (44 km), Brest (14 km), Caen (16 km), Clermont-Ferrand (14 km), Dijon (19 km), Grenoble (35 km), Le Havre (13 km), Le Mans (15 km), Lille (22 km), Lyon (62 km), Marseille (12 km), Montpellier (63 km), Mulhouse (16 km), Nancy (11 km), Nantes (44 km), Nice (9 km), Orléans (18 km), Reims (11 km), Rouen (18 km), Saint-Étienne (12 km), Strasbourg (59 km), Toulouse (11 km), Tours (15 km) and Valenciennes (18 km).

France was ranked fifth for rail infrastructure in the World Economic Forum's *Global Competitiveness Report 2017–2018*.

Civil Aviation

The main international airports are at Paris (Charles de Gaulle), Paris (Orly), Nice-Côte d'Azur, Lyon (Saint Exupéry), Marseille-Provence, Beauvais-Tillé, Toulouse (Blagnac), Nantes (Atlantique), Bordeaux (Mérignac) and Lille (Lesquin). The national airline, Air France, was 54·4% state-owned but merged in Oct. 2003 with the Dutch carrier KLM to form Air France-KLM. In the process the share owned by the French state fell to 44·2%. In Dec. 2004 the government sold off a further 18·4% to reduce its stake to 25·8%, and in the meantime the government's share has come down still further to 17·6%. In 2013 Air France-KLM carried 77·3m. passengers and 1·3m. tonnes of cargo on board its 552 aircraft. The second largest airline in terms of passenger numbers is HOP!, a regional subsidiary of Air France. In 2012 Charles de Gaulle airport handled 61,611,934 passengers (56,201,242 on international flights) and 2,150,950 tonnes of freight. Only Heathrow and Dubai handled more international passengers in 2012. Orly was the second busiest airport in 2012, handling 27,232,263 passengers (16,141,733 on international flights). Orly was also the second busiest for freight, with 106,372 tonnes in 2012.

In April 2003 Air France announced that Concorde, the world's first supersonic jet which began commercial service in 1976, would be permanently grounded from Oct. 2003.

Shipping

In Jan. 2014 there were 220 ships of 300 GT or over registered, totalling 6,029,000 GT. Of the 220 vessels registered, 79 were passenger ships, 47 oil tankers, 51 general cargo ships, 28 container ships, 13 liquid gas tankers and there were two bulk carriers. The French-controlled fleet comprised 275 vessels of 1,000 GT or over in July 2014, of which 154 were under foreign flags and 121 under the French flag. The chief ports are Marseille, Le Havre, Dunkerque, Calais and Saint-Nazaire.

France has extensive inland waterways. Canals are administered by the public authority France Navigable Waterways (VNF). There were 8,501 km of navigable rivers and canals in 2012. Total traffic on inland waterways in 2014 was 65·5m. tonnes.

Telecommunications

France Télécom, the country's largest telecommunications operator, was founded in 1988 and rebranded as Orange on 1 July 2013. The state has a 13·45% stake directly along with a further 9·60% indirectly through Bpifrance Participations (a public investment bank). In 2013 there were 39·1m. main (fixed) telephone lines. In 2012 mobile phone subscriptions numbered 62·3m. (973·8 per 1,000 persons). The largest operators are Orange, with a 38% share of the market, and SFR, with a 30% share. There were 24·2m. fixed internet subscriptions and 33·1m. wireless broadband subscriptions in 2013. In March 2012 there were 23·5m. Facebook users (37% of the population).

Social Institutions

Out of 178 countries analysed in the 2017 *Fragile States Index*—a list published jointly by the Fund for Peace and *Foreign Policy* magazine—France was ranked the 20th least vulnerable to conflict or collapse. The index is based on 12 indicators of state vulnerability across social, political and economic categories.

Justice

The system of justice is divided into two jurisdictions: the judicial and the administrative. Within the judicial jurisdiction are common law courts including 473 lower courts (*tribunaux d'instance*, 11 in overseas departments), 181 higher courts (*tribunaux de grande instance*, 5 *tribunaux de première instance* in the overseas territories) and 454 police courts (*tribunaux de police*, 11 in overseas departments).

The *tribunaux d'instance* are presided over by a single judge. The *tribunaux de grande instance* usually have a collegiate composition, but may be presided over by a single judge in some civil cases. The *tribunaux de police*, presided over by a judge on duty in the *tribunal d'instance*, deal with petty offences (*contraventions*); correctional chambers (*chambres correctionelles*, of which there is at least one in each *tribunal de grande instance*) deal with graver offences (*délits*), including cases involving imprisonment up to five years. Correctional chambers normally consist of three judges of a *tribunal de grande instance* (a single judge in some cases). Sometimes in cases of *délit*, and in all cases of more serious *crimes*, a preliminary inquiry is made in secrecy by one of 569 examining magistrates (*juges d'instruction*), who either dismisses the case or sends it for trial before a public prosecutor.

Within the judicial jurisdiction are various specialized courts, including 191 commercial courts (*tribunaux de commerce*), composed of tradesmen and manufacturers elected for two years initially, and then for four years; 271 conciliation boards (*conseils de prud'hommes*), composed of an equal number of employers and employees elected for five years to deal with labour disputes; 437 courts for settling rural landholding disputes (*tribunaux paritaires des baux ruraux*, 11 in overseas departments); and 116 social security courts (*tribunaux des affaires de sécurité sociale*).

When the decisions of any of these courts are susceptible of appeal, the case goes to one of the 35 courts of appeal (*cours d'appel*), composed each of a president and a variable number of members. There are 104 courts of assize (*cours d'assises*), each composed of a president who is a member of the court of appeal, and two other magistrates, and assisted by a lay jury of nine members. These try crimes involving imprisonment of over five years. The decisions of the courts of appeal and the courts of assize are final. However, the Court of Cassation (*cour de cassation*) has discretion to verify if the law has been correctly interpreted and if the rules of procedure have been followed exactly. The Court of Cassation may annul any judgment, following which the cases must be retried by a court of appeal or a court of assizes.

The administrative jurisdiction exists to resolve conflicts arising between citizens and central and local government authorities. It consists of 36 administrative courts (*tribunaux administratifs*, of which eight are in overseas departments and territories) and 15 administrative courts of appeal (*cours administratives d'appel*, of which eight are in overseas departments and territories). The Council of State is the final court of appeal in administrative cases, though it may also act as a court of first instance.

Cases of doubt as to whether the judicial or administrative jurisdiction is competent in any case are resolved by a *Tribunal de conflits* composed in equal measure of members of the Court of Cassation and the Council of State. In 1997 the government restricted its ability to intervene in individual cases of justice.

Penal code

A revised penal code came into force on 1 March 1994, replacing the *Code Napoléon* of 1810. Penal institutions consist of: (1) *maisons d'arrêt*, where persons awaiting trial as well as those condemned to short periods of imprisonment are kept; (2) punishment institutions – (a) central prisons (*maisons centrales*) for those sentenced to long imprisonment, (b) detention centres for offenders showing promise of rehabilitation, and (c) penitentiary centres, establishments combining (a) and (b); (3) hospitals for the sick. Special attention is being paid to classified treatment and the rehabilitation and vocational re-education of prisoners including work in open-air and semi-free establishments. Juvenile delinquents go before special judges in 139 (11 in overseas departments and territories) juvenile courts (*tribunaux pour enfants*); they are sent to public or private institutions of supervision and re-education.

A new post of Defender of Rights (*Défenseur des droits*) was created in March 2011 as a successor to the Ombudsman (*Médiateur*). The current Defender of Rights is Jacques Toubon.

Capital punishment was abolished in Aug. 1981. The population of penal establishments in metropolitan France in Sept. 2013 was 62,443 (98 per 100,000 of national population). In 2015 the World Justice Project *Rule of Law Index*, which provides data on how the rule of law is experienced by the general public across eight categories, ranked France 22nd of 102 countries for criminal justice and 19th for civil justice.

Elliott, Catherine, Jeanpierre, Eric and Vernon, Catherine, *French Legal System*. 2nd ed. 2006

Weston, M., *English Reader's Guide to the French Legal System*. 1991

Education

The primary, secondary and higher state schools constitute the 'Université de France'. Its Supreme Council of 84 members has deliberative, administrative and judiciary functions, and as a consultative committee advises respecting the working of the school system; the inspectors-general are in direct communication with the Minister. For local education administration France is divided into 25 academic areas, each of which has an Academic Council whose members include a certain number elected by the professors or teachers. The Academic Council deals with all grades of education. Each is under a Rector, and each is provided with academy inspectors, one for each department.

Compulsory education is provided for children of 6–16. The educational stages are as follows:

1. Non-compulsory pre-school instruction for children aged 2–5, to be given in infant schools or infant classes attached to primary schools.

2. Compulsory elementary instruction for children aged 6–11, to be given in primary schools and certain classes of the *lycées*. It consists of three courses: preparatory (one year), elementary (two years) and intermediary (two years). Children with special needs are cared for in special institutions or special classes of primary schools.

3. Lower secondary education (*Enseignement du premier cycle du second degré*) for pupils aged 11–15, consists of four years of study in the *lycées* (grammar schools), *Collèges d'Enseignement Technique* (CES) or *Collèges d'Enseignement Général* (CEG).

4. Upper secondary education (*Enseignement du second cycle du second degré*) for pupils aged 15–18: (1) *Long, général* or *professionel* provided by the *lycées* and leading to the *baccalauréat* or to the *baccalauréat de technicien* after three years; and (2) *Court*, professional courses of three, two and one year are taught in the *lycées d'enseignement professionel*, or the specialized sections of the *lycées*, CES or CEG.

The following table shows the number of schools in 2006–07 and the numbers of teaching staff and pupils in 2007:

	Number of schools	Teaching staff	Pupils
Nursery	17,410	141,476	2,594,074
Primary	38,257	216,654	4,105,628
Secondary	11,410	490,955	5,940,366

Higher education is provided by the state free of charge in universities and in special schools, and by private individuals in the free faculties and schools. Legislation of 1968 redefined the activities and workings of universities. Bringing several disciplines together, 780 units for teaching and research (*UER—Unités d'Enseignement et de Recherche*) were formed which decided their own teaching activities, research programmes and procedures for checking the level of knowledge gained. In 1984 they were reclassified as units for training and research (*UFR—Unités de Formation et de Recherche*). They and the other parts of each university must respect the rules designed to maintain the national standard of qualifications. The UFRs form the basic units of the 78 state universities in mainland France and three national polytechnic institutes (with university status), which are grouped into 25 administrative Académies. Private universities include seven Catholic universities, in Angers, Lille, Lyon, Paris, Rennes, Toulouse and La Roche-sur-Yon in the Vendée department. There were 2,179,505 students in higher education in 2007.

Outside the university system, higher education (academic, professional and technical) is provided by over 400 schools and institutes, including the 177 *Grandes Écoles*, which are highly selective public or private institutions offering mainly technological or commercial curricula. These have an annual output of about 20,000 graduates, and in 2013–14 there were also 83,500 students in preparatory classes leading to the *Grandes Écoles*; 255,000 students were registered in the *sections de techniciens supérieurs* and 179,400 in the *écoles d'ingénieurs*.

The adult literacy rate is at least 99%.

In 2010 public expenditure on education came to 5·7% of GNI and represented 10·4% of total government expenditure.

Health

Ordinances of 1996 created a new regional regime of hospital administration and introduced a system of patients' records to prevent abuses of public health benefits. In 2007 there were 972 public and 1,800 private health care establishments with 316,551 and 174,925 beds respectively. There were 208,191 physicians, 41,444 dentists, 483,380 nurses, 70,498 pharmacists and 17,483 midwives in 2007.

In 2008 France spent 11·2% of its GDP on health (the highest percentage in the EU), with public spending amounting to 77·8% of the total.

In 2009, 33% of the population aged 15 and over were smokers. The average French adult consumed 12·2 litres of pure alcohol a year in the period 2008–10, less than half the annual average of 50 years earlier.

Welfare

An order of 4 Oct. 1945 laid down the framework of a comprehensive plan of Social Security and created a single organization which superseded the various laws relating to social insurance, workmen's compensation, health insurance, family allowances, etc. All previous matters relating to Social Security are dealt with in the Social Security Code, 1956; this has been revised several times. The Chamber of Deputies and Senate, meeting as Congress on 19 Feb. 1996, adopted an important revision of the Constitution giving parliament powers to review annually the funding of social security (previously managed by the trade unions and employers' associations), and to fix targets for expenditure in the light of anticipated receipts.

In 2008 the welfare system accounted for €601bn., representing 31% of GDP. The Social Security budget had a deficit of some €20·2bn. in 2009.

Contributions

The general social security contribution (CSG) introduced in 1991 was raised by 4% to 7·5% in 1997 by the government of Lionel Jospin in an attempt to dramatically reduce the deficit on social security spending, effectively almost doubling the CSG. All wage-earning workers or those of equivalent status are insured regardless of the amount or the nature of the salary or earnings. The funds for the general scheme are raised mainly from professional contributions, these being fixed within the limits of a ceiling and calculated as a percentage of the salaries. The calculation of contributions payable for family allowances, old age and industrial injuries relates only to this amount; on the other hand, the amount payable for sickness, maternity expenses, disability and death is calculated partly within the limit of the 'ceiling' and partly on the whole salary. These contributions are the responsibility of both employer and employee, except in the case of family allowances or industrial injuries, where they are the sole responsibility of the employer.

Self-employed Workers

From 17 Jan. 1948 allowances and old-age pensions were paid to self-employed workers by independent insurance funds set up within their own profession, trade or business. Schemes of compulsory insurance for sickness were instituted in 1961 for farmers, and in 1966, with modifications in 1970, for other non-wage-earning workers.

Social Insurance

The orders laid down in Aug. 1967 ensure that the whole population can benefit from the Social Security Scheme; at present all elderly persons who have been engaged in the professions, as well as the surviving spouse, are entitled to claim an old-age benefit.

Sickness Insurance refunds the costs of treatment required by the insured and the needs of dependants.

Maternity Insurance covers the costs of medical treatment relating to the pregnancy, confinement and lying-in period; the beneficiaries being the insured person or the spouse.

Disability Insurance is divided into three categories: (1) those who are capable of working; (2) those who cannot work; (3) those who, in addition, are in need of the help of another person. According to the category, the pension rate varies from 30 to 50% of the average salary for the last ten years, with additional allowance for home help for the third category.

Old-Age Pensions for workers were introduced in 1910. Over the period 2003–08 the duration a private sector wage-earner or standard civil servant had to work in order to qualify for a pension was raised from 37½ years to 40 years. As a result, standard public sector workers were required to contribute for the same period as private sector workers. The contribution

period rose to 41 years in 2012 and thereafter was scheduled to increase in line with rises in life expectancy, so maintaining the ratio of pension payment period to contribution period. Pensions are payable at 60 to anyone with at least 25% insurance coverage. A pension worth 50% of the adjusted average salary is provided to those who have paid a full 40 years (160 quarters) worth of insurance. The pension is proportionately reduced for coverage less than 160 quarters (or less than 150 quarters for those claiming their pension before 2004). The exception is the special retirement plan for which employees of several state-owned companies (notably the SNCF) and organizations including the military and the police are eligible, allowing them to claim a full pension after 37½ years' contribution. A law was passed in Nov. 2010 to raise the minimum retirement age from 60 to 62 by 2017 (its initial target of 2018 amended in Nov. 2011 as part of a package of austerity measures), with the fully pensionable retirement age rising from 65 to 67. However, in June 2012 the Hollande government lowered the minimum retirement age back to 60 years for people who have worked 41 years, to be financed by an increase in pension contributions.

There is also an allowance payable to low-income pensioners, who also receive an old-age supplement at 65. A child's supplement, worth 10% of the pension, is awarded to those who have three or more children. Citizens who do not qualify for a pension may be allowed to claim an old-age special allowance.

Family Allowances

A controversial programme of means-testing for Family Allowance was introduced in 1997. The Family Allowance benefit system comprises: (a) Family allowances proper, equivalent to 25·5% of the basic monthly salary for two dependent children, 46% for the third child, 41% for the fourth child, and 39% for the fifth and each subsequent child; a supplement equivalent to 9% of the basic monthly salary for the second and each subsequent dependent child more than ten years old, and 16% for each dependent child over 15 years. (b) Family supplement for persons with at least three children or one child aged less than three years. (c) Ante-natal grants. (d) Maternity grant is equal to 260% of basic salary. Increase for multiple births or adoptions, 198%; increase for birth or adoption of third or subsequent child, 457%. (e) Allowance for specialized education of children with disabilities. (f) Allowance for orphans. (g) Single parent allowance. (h) Allowance for opening of school term. (i) Allowance for accommodation, under certain circumstances. (j) Minimum family income for those with at least three children. Allowances (b), (g), (h) and (j) only apply to those whose annual income falls below a specified level.

Workmen's Compensation

The law passed by the National Assembly on 30 Oct. 1946 forms part of the Social Security Code and is administered by the Social Security Organization. Employers are invited to take preventive measures. The application of these measures is supervised by consulting engineers (assessors) of the local funds dealing with sickness insurance, who may compel employers who do not respect these measures to make additional contributions; they may, in like manner, grant rebates to employers who have in operation suitable preventive measures. The injured person receives free treatment, the insurance fund reimburses the practitioners, hospitals and suppliers chosen freely by the injured. In cases of temporary disablement, the daily payments are equal to half the total daily wage received by the injured. In case of permanent disablement, the injured person receives a pension, the amount of which varies according to the degree of disablement and the salary received during the past 12 months.

Unemployment Benefits vary according to circumstances (full or partial unemployment) which are means-tested.

Ambler, J. S. (ed.) *The French Welfare State: Surviving Social and Ideological Change.* 1992

Religion

A law of 1905 separated church and state. A survey conducted by the French Institute of Public Opinion in 2010 estimated that some 64% of the population was Roman Catholic, 28% non-religious/atheist, 3% Protestant and 5% belonged to other religions. In Feb. 2019 there were seven cardinals. The Catholic Church had 13,822 diocesan priests in 2011, down from 18,528 in 2001. There are generally estimated to be about 5m.–6m. Muslims in France. France has the third largest Jewish population, after Israel and the USA.

Culture

World Heritage Sites

There are 44 sites under French jurisdiction that appear on the UNESCO World Heritage List. They are (with year entered on list): Mont-Saint-Michel and its Bay, the Versailles Palace and Park, the church and hill at Vézelay, Burgundy (all 1979 and 2007); the prehistoric sites and decorated grottoes of the Vézère Valley (Dordogne) and Chartres Cathedral (both 1979); Fontainebleau Palace and Park, Amiens Cathedral, and the Roman and Romanesque monuments of Arles (all 1981); Fontenay's Cistercian Abbey and Orange's Roman theatre and Arc de Triomphe (both 1981 and 2007); from the Great Saltworks of Salins-les-Bains to the Royal Saltworks of Arc-et-Senans, Franche-Comté (1982 and 2009); the Place Stanislas, Place de la Carrière and Place d'Alliance in Nancy and the Gulf of Porto (the Gulf of Girolata, Scandola Nature Reserve and the Calanche of Piana) in Corsica (both 1983); the Church of Saint-Savin-sur-Gartempe in Nouvelle-Aquitaine (1983 and 2007); the Pont du Gard Roman aqueduct, Languedoc (1985 and 2007); Strasbourg, Grande-Île and *Neustadt* (1988 and 2017); the Banks of the Seine and Reims's Notre Dame Cathedral, Abbey of Saint-Remi and Tau Palace (both 1991); Bourges Cathedral (1992); Avignon's historic centre (1995); the Canal du Midi, Languedoc (1996); the Historic Fortified City of Carcassonne (1997); Lyon's historic sites and the route of Santiago de Compostela (both 1998); Saint-Émilion Jurisdiction (1999); the Loire Valley between Sully-sur-Loire and Chalonnes-sur-Loire (2000); Provins, the Town of Medieval Fairs (2001); the city of Le Havre (2005); the historic centre of Bordeaux (2007); fortifications of Vauban and the lagoons of New Caledonia: reef diversity and associated ecosystems (both 2008); the Episcopal City of Albi, Languedoc and the Pitons, cirques and remparts of Réunion (both 2010); the Causses and the Cévennes, Mediterranean agro-pastoral cultural landscapes (2011); Nord-Pas de Calais Mining Basin (2012); Decorated Cave of Pont d'Arc, known as Grotte Chauvet-Pont d'Arc, Ardèche (2014); Champagne Hillsides, Houses and Cellars and Climats, terroirs of Burgundy (both 2015); Taputapuātea (2017); and Chaîne des Puys—Limagne fault tectonic area (2018).

France shares the Pyrénées–Mount Perdu site (1997 and 1999) with Spain; the Belfries of Belgium and France (1999 and 2005) with Belgium; the Preshistoric Pile dwellings around the Alps (2011) with Austria, Germany, Italy, Slovenia and Switzerland; and the Architectural Work of Le Corbusier, an Outstanding Contribution to the Modern Movement (2016), with Argentina, Belgium, Germany, India, Japan and Switzerland.

Press

There were 118 daily papers in 2014 (84 paid-for—of which 23 national—and 34 free). The leading dailies are: *Ouest-France* (average circulation, 732,000), *Le Figaro* (average circulation, 325,000), *Le Monde* (average circulation, 299,000), *Sud Ouest, La Voix du Nord, Le Parisien, L'Équipe* and *Le Dauphiné Libéré*. The *Journal du Dimanche* is the only national Sunday paper. In 2014 total average daily press circulation was 8·9m. copies. The daily newspaper websites with the highest number of unique monthly visitors are *Le Figaro* (9,036 in Dec. 2014) and *Le Monde* (7,899 in Dec. 2014). A total of 72,139 book titles were published in 2012 (70,109 in 2011).

Tourism

There were 82,700,000 foreign tourists in 2016; tourism receipts were US$54·5bn. France is the most popular tourist destination in the world. In 2012, 83·4% of tourists were from elsewhere in Europe and 7·8% from the Americas. Most visitors come from Germany, the UK, Belgium/Luxembourg, Italy, the Netherlands and Switzerland. As at 1 Jan. 2014 there were 1,245,600 beds at 17,100 tourist hotels.

Festivals

Religious Festivals
Ascension Day (40 days after Easter Sunday), Assumption of the Blessed Virgin Mary (15 Aug.) and All Saints Day (1 Nov.) are all public holidays.

Cultural Festivals
The Grande Parade de Montmartre, Paris (1 Jan.); the Carnival of Nice (Feb.–March); the Fête de la Victoire (8 May), celebrates victory in World War Two; the May Feasts take place in Nice regularly throughout May; the prestigious Cannes Film Festival, which has been running since 1946, lasts two weeks in mid-May; the Fête de la Musique (21 June); the Avignon Festival is a celebration of theatre that attracts average attendances of 140,000 each year and runs for most of July; Bastille Day (14 July) sees celebrations, parties and fireworks across the country. The Festival International d'Art Lyrique, focusing on classical music, opera and ballet, takes place in Aix-en-Provence every July. There are annual festivals of opera at Orange (July–Aug.) and baroque music at Ambronay (Sept.–Oct.). Celtic music and dance is celebrated at the Festival Interceltique de Lorient (Aug.). The biggest pop and rock festivals are Eurockéennes in Belfort (July), Les Vieilles Charrues in Carhaix (July), Rock en Seine in Paris (Aug.) and La Route du Rock in Saint-Malo (Aug.).

Diplomatic Representatives

Of France in the United Kingdom (58 Knightsbridge, London, SW1X 7JT)
    Ambassador: Jean-Pierre Jouyet.

Of the United Kingdom in France (35 rue du Faubourg St Honoré, 75383 Paris Cedex 08)
    Ambassador: Edward Llewellyn, OBE.

Of France in the USA (4101 Reservoir Rd, NW, Washington, D.C., 20007)
    Ambassador: Gérard Roger Araud.

Of the USA in France (2 Ave. Gabriel, 75382 Paris Cedex 08)
    Ambassador: Jamie D. McCourt.

Of France to the United Nations
    Ambassador: François Delattre.

Of France to the European Union
    Permanent Representative: Philippe Léglise-Costa.

Departments and Collectivities Overseas

Départements (DOM) et collectivités d'outre-mer (COM)

General Details

These fall into two main categories: *Overseas Departments and Regions* (French Guiana, Guadeloupe, Martinique, Mayotte, Réunion) and *Overseas Collectivities* (French Polynesia, St Barthélemy, St Martin, St Pierre and Miquelon, Wallis and Futuna). In addition there are two *Sui Generis Collectivities* (New Caledonia, Southern and Antarctic Territories) and one *Minor Territory* (Clipperton Island).

Overseas Departments and Regions

Départements et régions d'outre-mer

French Guiana

Guyane Française

Beginning as a settlement in 1604, French Guiana became a French possession in 1817 and assumed overseas department status in 1946. The territory is situated on the northeast coast of Latin America, bounded in the northeast by the Atlantic Ocean, west by Suriname, and south and east by Brazil. It includes Devil's Island (once a convict settlement), Royal Island and St Joseph, and has an area of 85,534 sq. km. The population in Jan. 2013 was 244,118; density: 2·9 per sq. km. In 2010, 76·2% lived in urban areas. 58% of the population is of African descent. Chief towns are Cayenne (the capital), Saint-Laurent-du-Maroni and Kourou. The official language is French.

The French government is represented by a *Prefect*. In Dec. 2015 French Guiana's political structure was overhauled, with the former *General Council* and *Regional Council* combined into a single *Assembly* comprising 51 members.
    Prefect: Patrice Faure.
    President of the Assembly of French Guiana: Rodolphe Alexandre.

The euro is the official currency. Principal crops are cassava, bananas and rice. Forests (99% of the land area) are rich in timber. Other important products include rum, rosewood essence and beer. The base of the European Space Agency (ESA) is located near Kourou and has been operational since 1979.

Primary education is free and compulsory. The University of Guiana was created on 1 Jan. 2015 after the University of the French West Indies and Guiana separated into two distinct institutions. In 2010 an estimated 84% of the population was Christian (predominantly Roman Catholic) according to the Pew Research Center's Forum on Religion & Public Life.

Guadeloupe

The islands were discovered by Columbus in 1493. The Carib inhabitants resisted Spanish attempts to colonize but, apart from short periods of British occupancy, Guadeloupe has been a French possession since 1635 and became an overseas department in 1946. It has a total area of 1,630 sq. km. The two main islands, Basse-Terre (to the west) and Grande-Terre (to the east), are joined by a bridge over a narrow channel. Adjacent to these are the islands of Marie-Galante (to the southeast), La Désirade (to the east), and the Îles des Saintes (to the south). The islands of St Martin and St Barthélemy seceded in Feb. 2007 and became separate overseas collectivities. The population in Jan. 2013 was 402,119. In 2010, 98·4% lived in urban areas. Basse-Terre is the seat of government, while larger Pointe-à-Pitre is the main economic centre and port. French is the official language, but Creole is spoken by the vast majority.

The French government is represented by an appointed *Prefect*. Guadeloupe is administered by a *Departmental Council* and a *Regional Council*.

Prefect: Philippe Gustin.

President of the Departmental Council: Josette Borel-Lincertin.

President of the Regional Council: Ary Chalus.

The euro is the official currency. Tourism is the chief economic activity.

The main agricultural product is sugarcane. Other industries are sugar refining, food processing, rum distilling and cement production.

Education is free and compulsory from six to 16 years. The University of the French West Indies, with campuses in Guadeloupe and Martinique, was created on 1 Jan. 2015 after the University of the French West Indies and Guiana separated into two distinct institutions. In 2010 an estimated 96% of the population was Christian (predominantly Roman Catholic) according to the Pew Research Center's Forum on Religion & Public Life.

Martinique

Discovered by Columbus in 1502, Martinique was a French colony from 1635 apart from brief periods of British occupation. In March 1946 it became an overseas department. Situated in the Lesser Antilles between Dominica and St Lucia, the island occupies an area of 1,128 sq. km. The population in Jan. 2013 was 385,551; density, 342 per sq. km. In 2010, 89·0% lived in urban areas. The capital and main port is Fort-de-France. Other towns are Le Lamentin, Le Robert, Schoelcher, Le François and Sainte-Marie. French is the official language but the majority of people speak Creole.

The French government is represented by a *Prefect*. In Dec. 2015 Martinique's political institutions were reconfigured, with the former *General Council* and *Regional Council* combined into a single *Assembly* comprising 51 members.

Prefect: Franck Robine.

President of the Assembly of Martinique: Claude Lise.

The euro is the official currency. Agriculture and tourism are important to the economy. The main crops are sugarcane and bananas. Forests cover about 46% of the land area providing timber. Other industries include food processing, chemical engineering, cement production, rum distilling and oil refining.

Education is compulsory between the ages of six and 16 years. The University of the French West Indies, with campuses in Martinique and Guadeloupe, was created on 1 Jan. 2015 after the University of the French West Indies and Guiana separated into two distinct institutions. In 2010 an estimated 83% of the population were Roman Catholics according to the Pew Research Center's Forum on Religion & Public Life.

Mayotte

Mayotte was a French colony from 1843 until 1914 when it was attached, with the other Comoros islands, to the government-general of Madagascar. The Comoro group was granted administrative autonomy within the French Republic and became an overseas territory. When the other three islands voted to become independent in 1974, Mayotte voted against and remained a French dependency. In 1976 it became a territorial collectivity and in July 2001 a departmental collectivity, which was denounced by the Comoros state as it claims Mayotte. In March 2003 it became an overseas collectivity and then an overseas department on 31 March 2011.

Mayotte, southeast of the Comoros, had a total population at the 2017 census of 256,518; density, 686 persons per sq. km. The whole territory covers 374 sq. km. It consists of a main island (363 sq. km) containing the chief town, Mamoudzou; and the smaller island of Pamanzi (11 sq. km) lying

2 km to the east containing the old capital of Dzaoudzi. The spoken language is Shimaoré (akin to Comorian, an Arabized dialect of Swahili), but French remains the official, commercial and administrative language. The island is administered by a directly elected *Departmental Council*. The French government is represented by an appointed *Prefect*. Executive powers were transferred from the prefect to the president of the General Council (the predecessor of the Departmental Council) in March 2004.

Prefect: Dominique Sorain.

President of the Departmental Council: Soibahadine Ibrahim Ramadani.

The euro is the official currency. Mayotte is the world's second largest producer of ylang-ylang essence. Important cash crops include cinnamon, ylang-ylang, vanilla and coconut. The main food crops are bananas and cassava. The commercial port is situated at Longoni. In 2010 an estimated 99% of the population was Muslim (predominantly Sunni) according to the Pew Research Center's Forum on Religion & Public Life.

Réunion

The island of Réunion (formerly Île Bourbon) became an overseas department in March 1946, having been a French possession since 1638. It lies in the Indian Ocean, about 880 km east of Madagascar and 210 km southwest of Mauritius. It has an area of 2,512 sq. km. The population in Jan. 2013 was 835,103; density, 332 per sq. km. In 2010, 94·0% lived in urban areas. The capital is Saint-Denis; other large towns are Saint-Paul, Saint-Pierre and le Tampon.

French is the official language, but Creole is also spoken.

Réunion is administered by a directly elected *Departmental Council* and by a *Regional Council*. The French government is represented by an appointed *Prefect*.

Prefect: Amaury de Saint-Quentin.

President of the Departmental Council: Cyrille Melchior.

President of the Regional Council: Didier Robert.

Owing to its geographical location, Réunion was, by two hours, the first territory to introduce the euro as the official currency on 1 Jan. 2002. Tourism is a major source of revenue. Main agricultural products are sugarcane, pineapples and bananas. Forests cover about 35% of the land area. Major industries are electricity generation and sugar production. Other activities include food processing, chemical engineering, printing and the production of perfume, textiles, leathers, tobacco, wood and construction materials.

The Université de La Réunion has six sites in Saint-Denis, Saint-Pierre and le Tampon. According to the Pew Research Center's Forum on Religion & Public Life, in 2010 an estimated 80% of the population was Roman Catholic. Réunion has one site of the UNESCO World Heritage List: its Pitons, cirques and remparts (inscribed in 2010). The site covers 40% of the island.

Overseas Collectivities

Collectivités d'outre-mer

French Polynesia

Territoire de la Polynésie Française

French protectorates since 1843, these islands in the south Pacific were annexed to France in 1880–82, opted in 1958 for overseas territory status and became an overseas collectivity in 2003. The total land area, comprising 121 volcanic islands and coral atolls (76 inhabited), is 3,521 sq. km. The population in 2017 was 275,918; density, 78 per sq. km. The official languages are French and Tahitian.

The islands are administratively divided into the:

Windward Islands (Îles du Vent), comprising Tahiti, Mooréa, Maiao (Tubuai Manu), Mehetia and Tetiaroa;

Leeward Islands (Îles sous le Vent), comprising Raiatéa, Tahaa, Huahine, Bora-Bora and Maupiti, together with four small atolls;

Marquesas Islands, six of the 12 being inhabited;

Austral or Tubuai Islands, a 1,300 km chain of volcanic islands (five inhabited) and reefs;

Tuamotu and Gambier Islands, comprising the Tuamotu Islands (76 atolls with 53 inhabited) and the sparsely populated Gambier Islands.

The Windward and Leeward Islands together are called the Society Archipelago (Archipel de la Société). The capital is Papeete on Tahiti. The Mururoa and Fangataufa atolls were ceded to France in 1964 and used for nuclear tests from 1966–96.

Under the 1984 constitution, French Polynesia is administered by a *Council of Ministers*, whose President is chosen by the directly-elected

Territorial Assembly from among its own members. The French government is represented by a *High Commissioner*.

High Commissioner: René Bidal.

President: Édouard Fritch.

The unit of currency is the franc CFP (XPF).

Agriculture accounts for only 2% of GDP, but important products are copra and the nono fruit, which has medicinal value. Polynesia has an exclusive fisheries zone of 5·0m. sq. km, one of the largest in the world. Pearl production is the second largest industry after tourism. Other industries include food and drink products, cosmetics, clothing and jewellery, furniture-making and metalwork.

The University of French Polynesia was formed from the Tahitian campus of the now-defunct French University of the Pacific (UFP) in 1999. In 2010 there were approximately 110,000 Protestants (about 40% of the population) and also around 110,000 Roman Catholics according to the Pew Research Center's Forum on Religion & Public Life.

French Polynesia has one site on the UNESCO World Heritage List: Taputapuātea, an area including two forested valleys, a portion of lagoon and coral reef and a strip of open ocean (inscribed on the list in 2017).

St Barthélemy

Saint-Barthélemy

There is evidence of habitation dating to 1000 BC. Columbus had visited the island in 1493 before the French settled in 1648. It came under Swedish rule in 1784, later prospering as a free port apart from a brief period of British ascendancy in 1801–02. The French regained control in 1878 and it was administered by Guadeloupe until seceding on 22 Feb. 2007 to become an overseas collectivity. The island has an area of 21 sq. km and is situated 200 km northwest of Guadeloupe. The population at 1 Jan. 2015 was 9,625. The capital is Gustavia. There is a *Territorial Council*, which is elected by popular vote every five years and which elects a *President*. The French government appoints a *Prefect*.

Prefect: Sylvie Feucher.

President of the Territorial Council: Bruno Magras.

St Martin

Saint-Martin

Sighted by Columbus in 1493, St Martin was settled by the Dutch in 1631. The Spanish claimed dominion in 1633 but by 1648 the island was divided between Dutch and French interests. The French part of the island was administered by Guadeloupe until it seceded on 22 Feb. 2007 to become an overseas collectivity (encompassing several neighbouring islets including Île Tintamarre). St Martin is situated 300 km southeast of Puerto Rico. The French-run part covers roughly the northern two-thirds while the southern third (Sint Maarten) is an autonomous country within the Kingdom of the Netherlands. The French area is 53 sq. km; population at 1 Jan. 2015 was 35,684. Marigot is the capital. There is a *Territorial Council*, elected by popular vote every five years. The council elects a *President* and the French government appoints a *Prefect*.

Prefect: Sylvie Feucher.

President of the Territorial Council: Daniel Gibbs.

St Pierre and Miquelon

Saint-Pierre et Miquelon

The only remaining fragment of the French possessions in North America, the archipelago was settled from France in the 17th century. It was a French colony from 1816 until 1976, an overseas department until 1985, and is now an overseas collectivity. The archipelago consists of two islands off the south coast of Newfoundland, with a total area of 242 sq. km, comprising the Saint-Pierre group (26 sq. km) and the Miquelon-Langlade group (216 sq. km). The population at 1 Jan. 2013 was 6,057. Approximately 90% of the population lives on Saint-Pierre. The chief town is St Pierre. The official language is French. The overseas collectivity is administered by a directly-elected *Territorial Council*. The French government is represented by a *Prefect*.

Prefect: Thierry Devimeux.

President of the Territorial Council: Stéphane Lenormand.

The euro is the official currency. The islands, being mostly barren rock, are unsuited for agriculture, but some vegetables are grown. The main industry is fish processing.

Primary education is free. The dominant religion is Roman Catholicism.

Wallis and Futuna

Wallis et Futuna

French dependencies since 1842, the inhabitants of these islands narrowly voted in 1959 in favour of overseas territory status, which took effect from July 1961. In March 2003 Wallis and Futuna became an overseas collectivity. The two groups of islands in the central Pacific have a total area of 274 sq. km. The population in 2018 was 11,562. The Îles de Hoorn lie 255 km northeast of Fiji and consist of Futuna (64 sq. km) and uninhabited Alofi (51 sq. km). The Wallis Archipelago lies another 160 km further northeast, with an area of 159 sq. km. It comprises the main island of Uvéa (60 sq. km) and neighbouring uninhabited islands, with a surrounding coral reef. The capital is Mata-Utu on Uvéa. Wallisian and Futunian are distinct Polynesian languages. A *Prefect* represents the French government, assisted by a directly-elected *Territorial Assembly* and by a *Territorial Council*, comprising the three traditional chiefs and three nominees of the Prefect agreed by the Territorial Assembly. There are three districts: Singave and Alo (both on Futuna), and Wallis; in each, tribal kings exercise customary powers assisted by ministers and district and village chiefs.

Prefect: Thierry Queffelec.

President of the Territorial Assembly: David Vergé.

The unit of currency is the franc CFP (XPF). The chief agricultural products are bananas, coconuts, copra, cassava, yams and taro. There are ports at Mata-Utu (Wallis) and Leava (Futuna).

The South Pacific University Institute for Teacher Training has three colleges: in Wallis and Futuna, French Polynesia and Nouméa (New Caledonia), where it is headquartered. Almost all of the population is Roman Catholic.

Sui Generis Collectivities

Collectivités sui generis

New Caledonia

Nouvelle-Calédonie

From the 11th century Melanesians settled in the islands that now form New Caledonia and dependencies. Capt. James Cook was the first European to arrive on Grande Terre on 4 Sept. 1774. The first European settlers (English Protestants and French Catholics) came in 1840. In 1853 New Caledonia was annexed by France and used as a penal colony. Nickel was discovered in 1863 and mining provoked revolt among the Kanak (Melanesian) tribes. During the Second World War, New Caledonia was used as a military base by the USA. Having fought for France during the war, the Kanaks were awarded citizenship in 1946. Together with most of its former dependencies, New Caledonia was made an overseas territory in 1958. It became a territorial collectivity under the 1998 Nouméa Accord and a *sui generis* collectivity (one that does not conform to the normal administrative structure) in March 2003. A referendum on independence was held in Nov. 2018, but 56·4% of votes cast were in favour of remaining part of France and only 43·6% of New Caledonia becoming an independent country.

The territory comprises Grande Terre (New Caledonia mainland) and various outlying islands, all situated in the southwest Pacific (Melanesia) with a total land area of 18,575 sq. km. It has the second biggest coral reef in the world. The 2014 census population was 268,767, giving a density of 14·5 per sq. km. The main ethnic groups are the native Kanaks and the Europeans (mostly French). There are also Wallisians and Futunians, Tahitians and Vietnamese and smaller minorities. The capital is Nouméa.

There are four main islands (or groups of):

Grande Terre: area, 16,372 sq. km (about 400 km long, 50 km wide). A central mountain range separates a humid east coast and a drier temperate west coast. The east coast is predominantly Melanesian; the Nouméa region predominantly European; and the rest of the west coast is of mixed population.

Loyalty Islands: 100 km east of New Caledonia, consisting of Maré, Lifou, Uvéa and Tiga with a total area of 1,981 sq. km.

Isle of Pines: a tourist and fishing centre 50 km to the southeast of Nouméa, with an area of 152 sq. km.

Bélep Archipelago: about 50 km northwest of New Caledonia, with an area of 70 sq. km.

The remaining islands are very small and have no permanent inhabitants.

New Caledonia has a remarkable diversity of Melanesian languages (29 vernacular), divided into four main groups (Northern, Central, Southern and Loyalty Islands). In March 2003 New Caledonia became a *sui generis* collectivity with specific status endowed with wide autonomy. Its institutions comprise the Territorial Congress (or 'congress'), government, economic and social council (CES), the customary senate and customary councils. The congress is made up of 'Councillors of New Caledonia' from the provincial assemblies. The president is elected by majority vote of all members.

In elections to the Territorial Congress on 11 May 2014 the anti-separatist L'Avenir Ensemble won 13 of 54 seats, Union Calédonienne 9, Le Rassemblement-UMP 7, Union pour la Calédonie dans la France 6, Construisons Notre Nation Arc en Ciel 6, Union Nationale pour l'indépendance 6 and Une Province Pour Tous 2. Five other parties won a seat each. Turnout was 70·0%.

High Commissioner: Thierry Lataste.
President of the Government: Philippe Germain.
President of the Congress: Gaël Yanno.

The unit of currency is the *franc CFP* (XPF).

A wide range of minerals has been found in New Caledonia including: nickel, copper and lead, gold, chrome, gypsum and platinum metals. The chief agricultural products are beef, pork, poultry, coffee, copra, maize, fruit and vegetables. Aquaculture (consisting mainly of saltwater prawns) provides New Caledonia's second highest source of export income after nickel.

In 2011 there were 36,048 pupils at primary schools and 33,672 at secondary schools; and there were 235 public schools and 121 private schools. In 1999 the New Caledonia campus of the former French University of the Pacific (UFP) became the University of New Caledonia (UNC). According to estimates by the Pew Research Center's Forum on Religion & Public Life, in 2010 the population was 51% Roman Catholic and 32% Protestant. New Caledonia has one site on the UNESCO World Heritage List: its lagoons-reef diversity and associated ecosystems (inscribed in 2008), some of the most extensive in the world.

Southern and Antarctic Territories

Terres Australes et Antarctiques Françaises

The Territory of the TAAF was created in 1955. It comprises the Kerguelen and Crozet archipelagoes, the islands of Saint-Paul and Amsterdam (formerly Nouvelle Amsterdam) and the Scattered Islands group, all in the southern Indian Ocean, plus Terre Adélie. It has been classified as a *sui generis* collectivity (one that does not conform to the normal administrative structure) since 2007. The Scattered Islands were incorporated into the TAAF in Feb. 2007. Since April 1997 the administration has had its seat in Saint-Pierre, Réunion; before that it was in Paris. The Administrator is assisted by a consultative council that meets twice yearly in Paris; its members are nominated by the government for five years. The 15-member Polar Environment Committee, which in 1993 replaced the former Consultative Committee on the Environment (est. 1982), meets at least once a year to discuss all problems relating to the preservation of the environment.

The French Institute for Polar Research and Technology was set up to organize scientific research and expeditions in Jan. 1992. The staff of the permanent scientific stations of the TAAF forms the only population.

Prefect: Evelyne Decorps.

Amsterdam and **Saint-Paul Islands** Situated 38–39° S. lat., 77° E. long. Amsterdam, with an area of 54 sq. km was discovered in 1522 by Magellan's companions; Saint-Paul, lying about 100 km to the south, with an area of 7 sq. km, was probably discovered in 1559 by Portuguese sailors. Both were first visited in 1633 by the Dutch explorer, Van Diemen, and were annexed by France in 1843. They are both extinct volcanoes. The only inhabitants are at Base Martin de Vivies (est. 1949 on Amsterdam Island), including several scientific research stations, a hospital, communication and other facilities. Crayfish are caught commercially on Amsterdam.

Crozet Islands Situated 46° S. lat., 50–52° E. long.; consists of five larger and 15 tiny islands, with a total area of 505 sq. km. The western group includes Apostles, Pigs and Penguins islands; the eastern group, Possession and Eastern islands. The archipelago was discovered in 1772 by Marion Dufresne, whose first mate, Crozet, annexed it for Louis XV. A meteorological and scientific station at Base Alfred-Faure on Possession Island was built in 1964.

Kerguelen Islands Situated 48–50° S. lat., 68–70° E. long.; consists of one large and 85 smaller islands, and over 200 islets and rocks, with a total area of 7,215 sq. km of which Grande Terre occupies 6,675 sq. km. It was discovered in 1772 by Yves de Kerguelen, but was effectively occupied by France only in 1949. Port-aux-Français has several scientific research stations. Reindeer, trout and sheep have been acclimatized.

Scattered Islands Situated in the Indian Ocean around Madagascar between 11–22° S. lat., 39–54° E. long., comprising Bassas da India, Europa Island, the Glorieuses Islands, Juan de Nova Island and Tromelin Island. Formerly French minor territories, the islands—which have a total area of 39 sq. km—were incorporated into the TAAF in Feb. 2007. Sovereignty of individual islands is disputed, with the Comoros, Madagascar, Mauritius and the Seychelles all making claims. The islands are designated as nature reserves and support meteorological stations, military garrisons and radio stations. About 12,000 tonnes of guano are mined annually on Juan de Nova Island.

Terre Adélie Comprises that section of the Antarctic continent between 136° and 142° E. long., south of 60° S. lat. The ice-covered plateau has an area of about 432,000 sq. km, and was discovered in 1840 by Dumont d'Urville. A research station is situated at Base Dumont d'Urville, which is maintained by the French Institute for Polar Research and Technology.

Minor Territories

Dépendances

Clipperton Island

Île Clipperton

In the 18th century the island was the hideout of a pirate, John Clipperton, for whom it was named. In 1855 it was claimed by France, and in 1897 by Mexico. It was awarded to France by international arbitration in 1935. Clipperton Island is a Pacific atoll, 3 km long, some 1,120 km southwest of the coast of Mexico. It covers an area of 7 sq. km and is uninhabited. The island is administered by the Minister of Overseas France. The island is occasionally visited by tuna fishermen.

Further Reading

France

Institut National de la Statistique et des Études Économiques: *Annuaire statistique de la France* (from 1878); *Bulletin mensuel de statistique* (monthly); *Documentation économique* (bi-monthly); *Économie et Statistique* (monthly); *Tableaux de l'Économie Française* (biennially, from 1956); *Tendances de la Conjoncture* (monthly).

Agulhon, M., and Nevill, A., *The French Republic, 1879–1992.* 1993

Ardagh, John, *France in the New Century: Portrait of a Changing Society.* 1999

Ardant, P., *Les Institutions de la Ve République.* 1992

Bell, David, *Presidential Power in Fifth Republic France.* 2000.—*Parties and Democracy in France: Parties under Presidentialism.* 2000

Brouard, Sylvain, Appelton, Andrew M. and Mazur, Amy G. (eds) *The French Fifth Republic at Fifty: Beyond Stereotypes.* 2008

Chafer, Tony and Sackur, Amanda, (eds) *French Colonial Empire and the Popular Front.* 1999

Cole, Alistair, Meunier, Sophie and Tiberj, Vincent, (eds) *Developments in French Politics 5.* 2013

Cubertafond, A., *Le Pouvoir, la Politique et l'État en France.* 1993

Culpepper, Pepper D., Hall, Peter A. and Palier, Bruno, (eds) *Changing France: The Politics that Markets Make.* 2008

Drake, Helen, *Contemporary France.* 2011

L'État de la France. Annual

Fenby, Jonathan, *The History of Modern France: From the Revolution to the Present Day.* 2015

Friend, Julius W., *The Long Presidency: France in the Mitterrand Years, 1981–95.* 1999

Gaffney, John, *France in the Hollande Presidency.* 2015

Gildea, R., *France since 1945.* 1996

Guyard, Marius-François, (ed.) *Charles de Gaulle: Mémoires.* 2000

Hollifield, J. F. and Ross, G., *Searching for the New France.* 1991

Jack, A., *The French Exception.* 1999

Jackson, Julian, *A Certain Idea of France: The Life of Charles De Gaulle.* 2018

Jones, C., *The Cambridge Illustrated History of France.* 1994

Kedward, Rod, *France and the French: A Modern History.* 2007

Kepel, Gilles, *Terror in France: The Rise of Jihad in the West.* 2017

Knapp, Andrew, *Parties and the Party System in France: A Disconnected Democracy?* 2004

Lacouture, Jean, *Mitterrand: Une histoire de Français.* 2 vols. 1999

Lewis-Beck, Michael S., *The French Voter: Before and After the 2002 Elections.* 2004

MacLean, Mairi, *The Mitterrand Years: Legacy and Evaluation.* 1999

McMillan, J. F., *Twentieth-Century France: Politics and Society in France, 1898–1991.* 2nd ed. [of *Dreyfus to De Gaulle*]. 1992

Milner, Susan and Parsons, Nick, (eds) *Reinventing France: State and Society in the 21st Century.* 2004

Noin, D. and White, P., *Paris.* 1998

Pedder, Sophie, *Revolution Française: Emmanuel Macron and the Quest to Reinvent a Nation.* 2018

Popkin, J. D., *A History of Modern France.* 1994

Price, Roger, *A Concise History of France.* 1993

Raymond, Gino G., *The Sarkozy Presidency: Breaking the Mould?* 2013

Sowerwine, Charles, *France since 1870.* 2nd ed. 2009

Stevens, Anne, *Government and Politics of France.* 2003

Tiersky, Ronald, *Mitterrand in Light and Shadow.* 1999.—*François Mitterrand: The Last French President.* 2000

Tippett-Spirtou, Sandy, *French Catholicism.* 1999

Zeldin, T., *The French.* 1997

(Also see specialized titles listed under relevant sections, above.)

National Statistical Office: Institut National de la Statistique et des Études Économiques (INSEE), 75582 Paris Cedex 12. *Director-General:* Jean-Luc Tavernier.

Website: https://www.insee.fr

Departments and Collectivities Overseas

Aldrich, R. and Connell, J., *France's Overseas Frontier: Départements et Territoires d'Outre-Mer.* 1992

Gabon

République Gabonaise (Gabonese Republic)

Capital: Libreville
Population projection, 2020: 2·15m.
GNI per capita, 2017: (PPP$) 16,431
HDI/world rank, 2017: 0·702/110=
Internet domain extension: .ga

Key Historical Events

The earliest inhabitants of Gabon were pygmy hunter-gatherers; Baka pygmies continue to inhabit the northern forests, while the Babongo remain in parts of the southeast. Bantu-speaking farmers originating in present-day Cameroon migrated south and east across the African continent from around 500 BC, leaving evidence of pottery and tools at Njole in central Gabon. Later Bantu migrations from the north included the Mpongwe in the 15th century and the Fang in the 18th century.

Portuguese mariners reached Equatorial Africa in 1472. The name Gabon derives from the Portuguese for a hooded coat, which the estuary of the Komo river apparently resembled. Settlement was slow to develop compared with the islands of São Tomé, Príncipe and Bioko, where sugar plantations were established. However, Portuguese and Dutch trade with the Vili group grew in the 17th century, with iron tools, cloth and tobacco exchanged for ivory, timber, rubber and, increasingly, slaves. The Ogooué river delta became a hub for Portuguese merchants trading with local Orungu chieftains for slaves from the interior, who were shipped mainly to Brazil and Cuba. The Mpongwe also profited from trade (including slaves) with Europeans around the Komo estuary.

By the early 19th century the British and French were vying for control of trade in the Gulf of Guinea. In 1839 Capt. Bouët-Willaumez negotiated treaties with two Mpongwe chiefs to end the slave trade and accept French sovereignty over their land. The current capital, Libreville, was founded by freed slaves in 1849 on the Komo estuary. Over the next two decades French agents made treaties with all of the coastal clans and from 1875 turned their attention inland.

Expeditions along the Ogooué river were led by Savorgnan de Brazza, who founded Franceville in 1880. In 1886 he established French Congo, which included Gabon and much of the present-day Republic of the Congo. The land rights of indigenous groups were denied and the region's resources depleted. Borders with German Cameroon and Spanish Guinea were fixed in the late 1890s and in 1910 Gabon became one of the four territories comprising French Equatorial Africa.

Conditions improved markedly after the Second World War, when the territory was incorporated into the French Fourth Republic with its own assembly and representation in Paris. Investment in infrastructure, industry, agriculture, education and health care invigorated the economy. Following the collapse of the Fourth Republic in 1958, Gabon became an autonomous republic within the French Community. Léon Mba, a prominent member of the Fang ethnic group and former mayor of Libreville, became the first prime minister under the new constitution of 1959 and president following independence on 17 Aug. 1960.

In Feb. 1964 Mba was toppled by the military in a bloodless coup, but was reinstated shortly afterwards with French assistance. His death in March 1967 ushered in Omar Bongo, the vice-president. Within months Bongo had established the Gabonese Democratic Party (PDG) as the sole political party. The economy developed steadily as minerals—including oil, manganese and uranium—were extracted. The stable political scene facilitated foreign investment in infrastructure and education, although freedoms were suppressed.

Financial difficulties emerged in the late 1970s caused by an over-reliance on petroleum and high interest rates on foreign loans. Bongo was also dogged by allegations of corruption and the misuse of public funds throughout the 1980s. Reports in 1989 that he and his associates had amassed vast personal fortunes, combined with the poor economic outlook and news of the break-up of Eastern Europe's autocratic regimes, spurred protests in Libreville in Jan. 1990. Bongo agreed to legalize opposition parties and in March 1991 the National Assembly adopted a constitution restoring a multi-party system.

Bongo narrowly won the presidential election in Dec. 1993, although opposition candidates alleged fraud. In the 1996 legislative election the PDG secured a landslide and Bongo was returned to the presidency in 1998 and 2005. His death in a Spanish hospital in June 2009 forced a presidential election that attracted 18 candidates. When Ali Bongo Ondimba was announced the winner, opposition leaders André Mba Obame and Pierre Mamboundou protested that the poll had been fixed to ensure dynastic succession. Unrest ensued in Libreville and Port-Gentil.

In 2010 Gabon signalled a shift in geopolitical focus away from France by announcing deals with India and Singapore for major infrastructure projects.

Territory and Population

Gabon is bounded in the west by the Atlantic Ocean, north by Equatorial Guinea and Cameroon and east and south by the Republic of the Congo. The area covers 267,667 sq. km, including 10,000 sq. km of inland waters. Its population at the 2013 census was reported as 1,811,079. United Nations estimate, 2013, 1·82m.; density, 7 per sq. km. In 2011, 86·4% of the population were urban.

The UN gives a projected population for 2020 of 2·15m.

The capital is Libreville (703,940 inhabitants, 2013 census), other large towns (2013 census) being Port-Gentil (136,462), Franceville (110,568), Owendo (79,300) and Oyem (60,685).

Provincial areas, populations and capitals:

Province	Area in sq. km	Population 2013 census	Capital
Estuaire	20,740	895,689	Libreville
Haut-Ogooué	36,547	250,799	Franceville (Masuku)
Moyen-Ogooué	18,535	69,287	Lambaréné
Ngounié	37,750	100,838	Mouila
Nyanga	21,285	52,854	Tchibanga
Ogooué-Ivindo	46,075	63,293	Makokou
Ogooué-Lolo	25,380	65,771	Koulamoutou
Ogooué-Maritime	22,890	157,562	Port-Gentil
Woleu-Ntem	38,465	154,986	Oyem

The largest ethnic groups are the Fangs (25%) in the north and the Bapounou (24%) in the south. There are some 40 smaller groups. French is the official language.

Social Statistics

2008 estimates: births, 39,000; deaths, 14,000. Estimated rates, 2008 (per 1,000 population): births, 27·3; deaths, 9·7. Annual population growth rate, 2000–08, 2·0%. Expectation of life at birth, 2013, 62·4 years for males and 64·5 years for females. Infant mortality, 2010, 54 per 1,000 live births; fertility rate, 2008, 3·3 births per woman.

Climate

The climate is equatorial, with high temperatures and considerable rainfall. Mid-May to mid-Sept. is the long dry season, followed by a short rainy season, then a dry season again from mid-Dec. to mid-Feb., and finally a long rainy season once more. Libreville, Jan. 80°F (26·7°C), July 75°F (23·9°C). Annual rainfall 99" (2,510 mm).

© Springer Nature Limited 2020
Palgrave Macmillan (ed.), *The Statesman's Yearbook 2020*,
https://doi.org/10.1057/978-1-349-95940-2_75

Constitution and Government

On 21 March 1997 the government presented to the Parliament legislation aimed at reforming the constitution in a number of key areas: notably, the bill mandated the creation of a Vice-President of the Republic, the extension of the presidential term of office from five to seven years, and the transformation of the Senate into an Upper Chamber of Parliament. Gabon has a bicameral legislature, consisting of a 143-member *National Assembly* (with members elected by direct, popular vote to serve five-year terms) and a 102-member *Senate* (elected for six-year terms in single-seat constituencies by local and departmental councillors). However, the Senate is due to be reduced to 52 members after elections scheduled for 2020. At a referendum on electoral reform on 23 July 1995, 96·5% of votes cast were in favour; turnout was 63·5%. The 1991 constitution provides for an executive *President* directly elected for a five-year term (renewable once only). In July 2003 Gabon's parliament approved an amendment to the constitution that allows the president to seek re-election indefinitely. The head of government is the *Prime Minister*, who appoints a Council of Ministers.

National Anthem

'La concorde' ('The Concord'); words and tune by G. Damas Aleka.

Recent Elections

Presidential elections were held on 27 Aug. 2016. Ali Bongo Ondimba was re-elected with 49·8% of votes cast against 48·2% for Jean Ping. There were eight other candidates. Violence broke out in the capital following the announcement of Bongo's re-election. Ping lodged a challenge to the result in the constitutional court but the court validated Bongo's narrow victory.

Elections for the National Assembly were held on 6 and 27 Oct. 2018. The Gabonese Democratic Party (PDG) won 95 of 143 seats, the Democrats took 9, the Restoration of Republican Values 6, the Social Democrats of Gabon 5 and the Heritage and Modernity Rally 4. A further eight parties took nine seats in total, with six going to independents. Nine seats remained vacant. Turnout was 58·6% in the first round. The poll was boycotted by Jean Ping, the main opposition leader who narrowly lost the 2016 presidential election.

Senate elections were held on 13 Dec. 2014. The PDG won 81 of 102 seats; Circle of Liberal Reformers, 7; Social Democrat Party, 2. Independents claimed seven seats and the remaining three went to minor parties. The results for two seats were nullified by the Constitutional Court. As at March 2019 these seats remained vacant.

Current Government

President: Ali Bongo Ondimba; b. 1959 (PDG; sworn in 16 Oct. 2009).

Vice-President: Pierre-Claver Maganga Moussavou.

In Feb. 2019 the Council of Ministers comprised:

Prime Minister: Julien Nkoghe Bekale; b. 1958 (PDG; sworn in 15 Jan. 2019).

Ministers of State: Régis Immongault Tatangani (also *Minister of Housing and Urban Development*); Guy-Bertrand Mapangou (also *Minister of Forests and Environment, in Charge of Sustainable Development*); Denise Mekam'ne Edzidzie (also *Minister of Health, Social Protection and National Solidarity*); Alain-Claude Bilie-By-Nze (also *Minister of Sport, Recreation, Culture and Handicrafts*); Michel Menga M'Essone (also *Minister of National Education, in Charge of Civic Education*); Francis Nkea Nzigue (also *Minister of Relations with Constitutional Institutions*); Rose Christiane Ossouka Raponda (also *Minister of National Defence and Territorial Security*); Lambert Noël Matha (also *Minister of Interior, Local and Territorial Administration, and Decentralization, in Charge of Citizenship and Immigration*); Jean-Fidèle Otandault (also *Minister of Budget and Public Accounts*); Edgard Anicet Mboumbou Miyakou (also *Minister of Justice and Human Rights, and Keeper of the Seals*); Jean de Dieu Moukagni Iwangou (also *Minister of Higher Education, Scientific Research, and Technology Transfers*).

Minister of Agriculture, Livestock and Food, in Charge of the Implementation of the Seed Programme: Biendi Maganga Moussavou. *Civil Service, Innovation, Public Administration and Labour:* Madeleine Berre. *Commerce, and Small and Medium-Sized Enterprises and Industries:* David Mbadinga. *Communication, Digital Economy and Posts:* Guy-Maixent Mamiaka. *Economy, Forecasting, Development Programming, and Promotion of Private Investment and Public–Private*

Partnerships: Jean-Marie Ogandaga. *Employment, Youth, Professional Training and Insertion, and Government Spokesperson:* Nanette Longa. *Family, Women's Decade and Equal Opportunities:* Estelle Ondo. *Fisheries and the Sea:* Prisca Nlend-Koho. *Foreign Affairs, International Co-operation, Regional Integration, La Francophonie and Gabonese Abroad:* Abdu Razzaq Guy Kambogo. *Industry and National Entrepreneurship:* Carmen Ndaot. *Infrastructure and Public Works:* Arnauld Calixte Engandji Alandji. *Petroleum, Gas and Hydrocarbons:* Pascal Houagni Ambouroue. *Tourism:* Marie Rosine Itsana. *Transport and Logistics:* Justin Ndoundangoye. *Water, Energy, Industrialization and Mining:* Emmanuel Norbert Tony Ondo Mba. *Minister in Charge of Economic Reforms and Development Planning:* Alexis Boutamba Mbina.

Government Website (French only): http://www.gouvernement.ga

Current Leaders

Ali Bongo Ondimba

Position
President

Introduction
Ali Bongo Ondimba was elected president in Aug. 2009 following the death of his father, Omar Bongo Ondimba (president from 1967–2009). Ali Bongo served as minister of foreign affairs under his father, as well as a deputy of the National Assembly, minister of defence and vice-president of the ruling Gabonese Democratic Party (PDG). He was controversially re-elected in Aug. 2016.

Early Life
Ali Bongo Ondimba is the oldest son of Omar Bongo, the country's longest-serving president. He was born Alain-Bernard Bongo in Feb. 1959 in Brazzaville, Republic of the Congo. His mother, Gabonese singer Josephine Kama (later Patience Dabany), was 15 at the time of his birth.

The family moved to Gabon in 1960, just after its independence from France. Alain-Bernard spent most of his youth in France, studying at a protestant primary school in Cévennes and then the Catholic College Notre-Dame de Sainte-Croix, on the outskirts of Paris. In 1973 Albert-Bernard Bongo and Alain-Bernard Bongo changed their names to Omar and Ali-Ben, taking the second name Ondimba as part of their conversion to Islam. Ali graduated in law from the Sorbonne before returning to Gabon in 1981. He went straight into the upper ranks of the PDG, presided over by his father.

In 1983 Ali Bongo was elected a member of the PDG central committee and in 1984 became his father's personal spokesman. In 1989 he was appointed minister of foreign relations, replacing his cousin Martin Bongo, who had been minister since 1976. At the 1990 elections Bongo was returned as representative for the province of Haut-Ogooué. Since the constitution of 1991, which allowed for multi-party politics, also set a minimum age of 35 for a minister, Bongo was replaced at the department of foreign relations. Bongo was re-elected to represent Haut-Ogooué in 1996 and again in 2006. In 1999 he returned to the cabinet as minister for defence. He became party vice-president in 2003 and in 2005 helped run his father's election campaign. After Omar Bongo died in Spain in June 2009, Bongo put himself at centre stage to run for the presidency in new elections in Aug. that year.

In competition against 17 opponents, he won 42% of the vote. As with previous elections, the results were contested amid allegations of government electoral fraud and bribery. Thousands took to the streets in the capital, Libreville, and in the second city, Port-Gentil. A recount was held and the result upheld by the Supreme Court. Six newspapers were suspended for criticism of the government.

Career in Office
Bongo's first act as president was to reinstate Paul Biyoghé Mba as head of the cabinet and to cut down the number of ministers, having pledged to slash government expenditure. Ministers underwent curbs on privileges and were subject to pay cuts. In Nov. 2009 Bongo travelled to Paris to meet the then French president Nicolas Sarkozy and in Dec. 2009 he made a state visit to the Vatican and Pope Benedict XVI.

Bongo pledged to fight corruption. Nonetheless, Transparency International and other NGOs have pushed for investigations into the Bongo family's finances.

In Dec. 2010 parliament adopted a controversial constitutional amendment allowing the president to extend his mandate in the case of an emergency. In early 2011 Bongo's main rival in the 2009 election, André Mba Obame, took refuge in the United Nations compound in Libreville. Mba Obame claimed to have been the rightful winner of the presidential poll, in response to which Bongo banned his party. In National Assembly elections in Dec. 2011 the PDG retained its substantial parliamentary majority. In Feb. 2012 Bongo appointed Raymond Ndong Sima as prime minister following Biyoghé Mba's resignation. Following local elections in Dec. 2013 he replaced Ndong Sima with Daniel Ona Ondo, who then served until Sept. 2016 when he was replaced by Emmanuel Issoze-Ngondet, previously the foreign minister.

In Nov. 2014 anti-government protests were sparked by a French writer's controversial book questioning Bongo's legitimacy and accusing him of falsifying his birth certificate. There was further discontent the following month, prompting violence in which three people were killed by security forces amid numerous arrests according to opposition claims. In Sept. 2015 Bongo conducted a cabinet reshuffle in an apparent attempt to dampen anti-government sentiment. He was re-elected to the presidency in Aug. 2016, although his narrow victory sparked further violent protests in the capital. The election was, according to several international observer bodies, fraught with irregularities. Opposition leader Jean Ping refused to accept the result and accused Ali Bongo's government of crimes against humanity before the International Criminal Court. He subsequently rejected the government's proposed draft changes to Gabon's constitution in Nov. 2017 as autocratic and liable to violate the principle of separation of powers. In parliamentary elections in Oct. 2018, the PDG retained its majority in the National Assembly with 98 of the 143 seats.

Julien Nkoghe Bekale

Position
Prime Minister

Introduction
Following a failed military coup in Jan. 2019, President Ali Bongo Ondimba appointed Julien Nkoghe Bekale as the new prime minister.

Early Life
Nkoghe Bekale was born in the capital, Libreville, on 23 Aug. 1958. A member of the Gabonese Democratic Party, he held several ministerial posts under both President Ali Bongo and his father, Omar Bongo, including those for oil, gas and hydrocarbons, transport and equipment, and labour and employment. In Jan. 2019, amid growing tensions around Ali Bongo's fitness to hold office after he suffered a stroke, disgruntled army officers launched a coup in Libreville. After it failed, Ali Bongo sought to shore up his domestic support by announcing Nkoghe Bekale as premier. The appointment represented a return to a tradition begun by Bongo's father of choosing prime ministers from the Fang, Gabon's largest ethnic group.

Career in Office
Nkoghe Bekale took office on 12 Jan. 2019, replacing Emmanuel Issoze-Ngondet, who had served since 2016. He faces the considerable challenge of reviving the economy in a country where one-third of the population lives below the poverty line.

Defence

In 2013 military expenditure totalled US$263m. (US$161 per capita), representing 1·4% of GDP.

Army

Total strength (2011) is 3,200 and includes a Presidential Guard. There is also a paramilitary Gendarmerie of 2,000. France maintains some 750 Army personnel in Gabon.

Navy

There is a small naval flotilla, about 500 strong in 2011, which operates seven patrol and coastal combatants.

Air Force

Personnel (2011) 1,000. There were 14 combat-capable aircraft in 2011 (including eight Mirage 5s) and seven helicopters.

Economy

Agriculture accounted for 3·9% of GDP in 2014, industry 57·5% and services 38·6%.

Gabon's 'shadow' (black market) economy is estimated to constitute approximately 47% of the country's official GDP.

Overview

The economy is dominated by the oil industry, which generates over 40% of GDP and 80% of exports annually. However, production has declined since 1997 and reserves are expected to run dry by 2025. The government aims to achieve emerging-market status by 2025 through a programme of economic diversification, increased private and public investment, and improved governance.

Gabon's GDP growth is above the average for sub-Saharan Africa and per capita income is among the highest in the region. In 2009 the economy shrank by 1·5% but over the following six years growth averaged more than 5·5% per annum. Inflation averaged 2·1% annually over that period. Although designated a middle-income country by the World Bank, income equality is marked. Some 20% of the population accounts for 90% of income and a third of the population live beneath the poverty line—Gabon had aimed for a reduction in poverty to 13·5% by 2015 in line with the UN's Millennium Goals. There is also consistently high unemployment, which ran at 19·7% in 2014.

The main non-oil pillars of the economy are logging and manganese mining (Gabon being the world's second largest producer of the mineral). The country also has potentially vast iron ore deposits, although attempts to secure investment for exploration have faltered.

Currency

The unit of currency is the *franc CFA* (XAF) with a parity of 655·957 francs CFA to one euro. Foreign exchange reserves were US$466m. in June 2005 and total money supply was 416,653m. francs CFA. Gold reserves were 13,000 troy oz in July 2005. Inflation was 2·1% in 2016 and 2·7% in 2017.

Budget

In 2008 revenue totalled 2,078·1bn. francs CFA and expenditure 1,296·3bn. francs CFA. Oil revenues accounted for 65·5% of total revenue in 2008; current expenditure accounted for 69·9% of total expenditure.

The standard rate of VAT is 18% (reduced rate, 10%).

Performance

The economy grew by 3·9% in 2015, 2·1% in 2016 and 0·5% in 2017. Total GDP in 2017 was US$14·6bn.

Banking and Finance

The Banque des Etats de l'Afrique Centrale (*Governor*, Abbas Mahamat Tolli) is the bank of issue. In 2016 there were nine commercial banks. The largest bank is BGFIBank, with assets in 2011 of US$4·5bn. Other major banks are Banque Internationale pour le Commerce et l'Industrie du Gabon and Union Gabonaise de Banque.

In 2010 foreign debt amounted to US$2,331m., representing 20·3% of GNI.

Energy and Natural Resources

Environment

Gabon's carbon dioxide emissions from the consumption of energy in 2011 were the equivalent of 3·4 tonnes per capita.

Electricity

Installed capacity was 0·4m. kW in 2011. Production totalled 1·77bn. kWh in 2011 (54% thermal and 46% hydro-electric). Consumption per capita was 1,110 kWh in 2011.

Oil and Gas

Proven oil reserves (2012), 2·0bn. bbls. Production, 2012, 12·3m. tonnes. There were proven natural gas reserves of 28bn. cu. metres in 2013. Natural gas production (2011) was 166m. cu. metres.

Minerals

There are an estimated 200m. tonnes of manganese ore and 850m. tonnes of iron ore deposits. Gold, zinc and phosphates also occur. Output, 2010: manganese ore, 3·20m. tonnes.

Agriculture

The agricultural area was an estimated 5·16m. ha. in 2013. There were an estimated 325,000 ha. of arable land in 2013 and 170,000 ha. of permanent crops. 4,000 ha. were equipped for irrigation in 2013.

The major crops (estimated production, 2013, in 1,000 tonnes) are: cassava, 315; sugarcane, 280; plantains, 272; yams, 210; taro, 65; maize, 45; groundnuts, 24; palm fruit oil, 21; rubber, 21; bananas, 17.

Livestock (2014 estimates): 220,000 pigs; 215,000 sheep; 110,000 goats; 38,500 cattle; 3m. chickens.

In 2013 an estimated 37,700 tonnes of meat, 2,500 tonnes of eggs and 2,500 tonnes of fresh milk were produced.

Forestry

Forests covered 23·0m. ha. in 2015, or 89% of the total land area. Of the total area under forests 56% in 2015 was primary forest and 44% other naturally regenerated forest. Timber production in 2011 was 4·47m. cu. metres.

Since 2002 a tenth of the country has been transformed into 13 national parks covering nearly 30,000 sq. km.

Fisheries

The catch in 2011 was an estimated 32,000 tonnes, mainly from marine waters.

Industry

Most manufacturing is based on the processing of food (particularly sugar), timber and mineral resources, cement and chemical production and oil refining. Production figures in 1,000 tonnes: residual fuel oil (2007), 356; cement (2006), 260; distillate fuel oil (2007), 260; petrol (2007), 56; beer (2003), 75·4m. litres; soft drinks (2005), 60·7m. litres.

Labour

The labour force in 2013 was 628,000 (472,000 in 2003). 62·5% of the population aged 15–64 was economically active in 2013. In the same year 20·3% of the population was unemployed. There is a 40-hour working week.

Gabon had 14,000 people living in slavery according to the Walk Free Foundation's 2013 *Global Slavery Index*.

International Trade

The government retains the right to participate in foreign investment in oil and mineral extraction.

Imports and Exports

Merchandise imports in 2009 totalled US$2,500·9m. (US$2,563·1m. in 2008) and merchandise exports US$5,356·0m. (US$9,565·9m. in 2008).

Principal imports include machinery and transport equipment, food and live animals, chemicals and related products, and iron and steel; exports are dominated by petroleum and petroleum products, with cork and wood also important.

The leading import supplier in 2009 was France (32·9%), followed by Belgium and the USA; the leading export destination in 2009 was the USA (59·0%), followed by China and Spain.

Communications

Roads

Gabon has some 10,000 km of roads. In 2010 there were about 195,000 registered vehicles. There were 252 deaths in road accidents in 2010.

Rail

The 669 km standard gauge Transgabonais railway runs from the port of Owendo to Franceville. Total length of railways, 2011, 810 km. In 2011 passenger-km travelled came to 118m. and freight tonne-km to 2,417m.

Civil Aviation

There are international airports at Libreville (Léon Mba Airport), Port-Gentil and Franceville (Masuku); scheduled internal services link these to a number of domestic airfields. Libreville, the main airport, handled 839,571 passengers and 18,268 tonnes of freight in 2012. In 2012 scheduled airline traffic of Gabonese-based carriers flew 2·6m. km; passenger-km totalled 115m. in the same year. Gabon Airlines was established in July 2006 as a successor to the bankrupt national carrier Air Gabon, but it ceased operations in 2011.

Shipping

In Jan. 2014 there were 11 ships of 300 GT or over registered, totalling 6,000 GT. Owendo (near Libreville), Mayumba and Port-Gentil are the main ports. Rivers are an important means of inland transport.

Telecommunications

In 2010 there were 30,400 landline telephone subscriptions (equivalent to 20·2 per 1,000 inhabitants) and 1,610,000 mobile phone subscriptions (or 1,069·4 per 1,000 inhabitants). Fixed internet subscriptions totalled 22,200 in 2010 (14·7 per 1,000 inhabitants).

Social Institutions

Out of 178 countries analysed in the 2017 *Fragile States Index*—a list published jointly by the Fund for Peace and *Foreign Policy* magazine— Gabon was ranked the 88th least vulnerable to conflict or collapse. The index is based on 12 indicators of state vulnerability across social, political and economic categories.

Justice

There are *Tribunaux de grande instance* at Libreville, Port-Gentil, Lambaréné, Mouila, Oyem, Franceville (Masuku) and Koulamoutou, from which cases move progressively to a central Criminal Court, Court of Appeal and Supreme Court, all three located in Libreville. Civil police number about 900. The death penalty was abolished in Feb. 2010.

Education

The adult literacy rate in 2009 was estimated at 87·7% (91·4% among males and 84·1% among females). Education is compulsory between 6–16 years. There were 317,946 pupils in primary education in 2011 and 146,080 in secondary general education.

In 2009 there was one university at Libreville (the Omar Bongo University) and one university of science and technology at Franceville (Masuku). In 2004 a university of health sciences (previously part of the Omar Bongo University) was created in Libreville.

In 2005 total expenditure on education came to 8·6% of GDP.

Health

In 2013 there were 536 physicians, 7,574 nursing personnel, 86 dentistry personnel and 167 pharmaceutical personnel. In 2006 there were 20 hospital beds per 10,000 inhabitants.

In *Water: At What Cost? The State of the World's Water 2016*, WaterAid reported that 6·8% of the population does not have access to safe water.

Religion

According to the Pew Research Center's Forum on Religion & Public Life, 76·5% of the population in 2010 was Christian and 11·2% Muslim, with 6·0% followers of folk religions; of the Christians, 69% were Catholics and 31% Protestants.

Culture

World Heritage Sites

Gabon has one site on the UNESCO World Heritage List: the ecosystem and relict cultural landscape of Lopé-Okanda (inscribed on the list in 2007), an area of rainforest and savannah containing the remains of Neolithic and Iron Age settlements.

Press

In 2008 there was one government-controlled daily newspaper (*L'Union*) with a circulation of 20,000. In the 2010 *World Press Freedom Index*, compiled by Reporters Without Borders, Gabon was ranked 107th out of 178 countries.

Tourism

358,000 non-resident tourists arrived at Libreville airport in 2008, up from 169,000 in 2001.

Festivals

Gabao Hip Hop Festival takes place in Libreville in June.

Diplomatic Representatives

Of Gabon in the United Kingdom (27 Elvaston Pl., London, SW7 5NL)
Ambassador: Aichatou Sanni Aoudou.

Of the United Kingdom in Gabon
Ambassador: Rowan James Laxton (resides in Yaoundé, Cameroon).

Of Gabon in the USA (2034 20th St., NW, Washington, D.C., 20009)
Ambassador: Michael Moussa-Adamo.

Of the USA in Gabon (Sablière, BP 4000, Libreville)
Ambassador: Joel Danies.

Of Gabon to the United Nations
Ambassador: Michel Xavier Biang.

Of Gabon to the European Union
Ambassador: Vacant.
Chargé d'Affaires a.i.: Marie Yolande Nzeh Ellang.

Further Reading

Barnes, J. F. G., *Gabon: Beyond the Colonial Legacy.* 1992
Gardinier, David E., *Historical Dictionary of Gabon.* 3rd ed. 2006
National Statistical Office: Direction Générale de la Statistique, BP 2119, Libreville.
Website (French only): http://www.stat-gabon.org

The Gambia

Republic of The Gambia

Capital: Banjul
Population projection, 2020: 2·29m.
GNI per capita, 2017: (PPP$) 1,516
HDI/world rank, 2017: 0·460/174
Internet domain extension: .gm

Key Historical Events

Stone circles thought to have been constructed by ancestors of the Jola people are estimated to date from AD 600. Kingdoms of Mandinka-speaking people were established near the Gambia River from around 1100. State-building by the Jolof and Serer groups gathered pace from around 1400. Portuguese mariners entered the Gambia River in 1455 but the first permanent European settlement was founded by traders from the Baltic Duchy of Courland (Latvia) in 1651. English and French merchants subsequently vied for control of the region (Senegambia). The British Captain, Alexander Grant, established Bathurst (Banjul) as a garrison in 1816 and it was controlled from the Freetown Colony (Sierra Leone). The Gambia became an independent member of the British Commonwealth on 18 Feb. 1965 and an independent republic on 24 April 1970.

Sir Dawda Jawara served as the country's first president until he was ousted by the military in 1994. Yahya Jammeh seized power and was elected president under a new constitution in 1996. He won further terms in 2001, 2006 and 2011. In Oct. 2013 he announced The Gambia's withdrawal from the Commonwealth. After losing the presidential election in Dec. 2016 to Adama Barrow, Jammeh went into exile after initially refusing to cede power. Barrow was sworn into office in Jan. 2017.

Territory and Population

The Gambia takes its name from the River Gambia, and consists of a strip of territory never wider than 10 km on both banks. It is bounded in the west by the Atlantic Ocean and on all other sides by Senegal. The area is 10,690 sq. km, including 2,077 sq. km of inland water. Census population, 2013: 1,857,181, giving a density of 215·6 per sq. km. In 2011, 58·9% of the population were urban.

The UN gives a projected population for 2020 of 2·29m.

The largest ethnic group is the Mandingo, followed by the Wolofs, Fulas, Jolas and Sarahuley. The country is administratively divided into eight local government areas (LGAs).

The eight LGAs, with their areas, populations and chief towns are:

Division	Area in sq. km	2013 census population	Chief town
Banjul	12	31,054	Banjul
Basse	2,070	237,220	Basse Santa Su
Brikama	1,764	688,744	Brikama
Janjangbureh	1,428	125,204	Janjangbureh
Kanifeng	76	377,134	Kanifeng
Kerewan	2,255	220,080	Kerewan
Kuntaur	1,467	96,703	Kuntaur
Mansakonko	1,618	81,042	Mansakonko

The official language is English.

Social Statistics

2008 estimates: births, 61,000; deaths, 19,000. Estimated birth rate in 2008 was 36·8 per 1,000 population; estimated death rate, 11·3. Annual population growth rate, 2000–08, 3·0%. Expectation of life, 2013, was 57·5 years for males and 60·2 for females. Fertility rate, 2008, 5·1 births per woman; infant mortality, 2010, 57 per 1,000 live births.

Climate

The climate is characterized by two very different seasons. The dry season lasts from Nov. to May, when precipitation is very light and humidity moderate. Days are warm but nights quite cool. The SW monsoon is likely to set in with spectacular storms and produces considerable rainfall from July to Oct., with increased humidity. Banjul, Jan. 73°F (22·8°C), July 80°F (26·7°C). Annual rainfall 52" (1,295 mm).

Constitution and Government

The 1970 constitution provided for an executive *President* elected directly for renewable five-year terms. The President appoints a *Vice-President* who is the government's chief minister. The single-chamber *National Assembly* has 58 members (53 elected by universal adult suffrage for a five-year term and five appointed by the President).

A new constitution took effect in Jan. 1997 and thereby created the Second Republic. Under this, a ban on political parties imposed in 1994 was lifted. Members of the ruling Military Council resigned from their military positions before joining the Alliance for Patriotic Reorientation and Construction (APRC).

National Anthem

'For The Gambia, our homeland'; words by V. J. Howe, tune traditional.

Recent Elections

Presidential elections were held on 1 Dec. 2016. Adama Barrow (Coalition 2016) was elected with 43·3% of votes cast against 39·6% for incumbent Yahya Jammeh (Alliance for Patriotic Reorientation and Construction) and 17·1% for Mamma Kandeh (Gambia Democratic Congress).

Parliamentary elections were held on 6 April 2017. The United Democratic Party won 31 seats with 37·5% of the votes cast; the Gambia Democratic Congress, 5 (17·4%); the Alliance for Patriotic Reorientation and Construction, 5 (15·9%); the National Reconciliation Party, 5 (6·3%); the People's Democratic Organisation for Independence and Socialism, 4 (8·4%); the People's Progressive Party, 2 (2·5%); ind., 1 (9·6%). Turnout was 42·8%.

Current Government

President, C.-in.-C. of the Armed Forces Adama Barrow; b. 1965 (Coalition 2016; inaugurated in Dakar, Senegal, on 19 Jan. 2017).

In March 2019 the government comprised:

Vice-President: Isatou Touray.

Minister of Agriculture: Lamin N. Dibba. *Basic and Secondary Education:* Claudiana Cole. *Finance and Economic Affairs:* Mambury Njie. *Fisheries, Water Resources and National Assembly Matters:* James Gomez. *Foreign Affairs, International Co-operation and Gambians Abroad:* Mamadou Tangara. *Forestry, Environment, Climate Change and Natural Resources:* Lamin B. Dibba. *Health and Social Welfare:* Dr Isatou Touray. *Higher Education, Research, and Science and Technology:* Badara Joof. *Information and Communication Infrastructure:* Ebrima Sillah. *Interior:* Ebrima M. Mballow. *Lands and Regional Government:* Alhajie Musa Drammeh. *Petroleum and Energy:* Fafa Sanyang. *Tourism and Culture:* Hamat Bah. *Trade, Regional Integration, Industry and Employment:* Amadou Sanneh. *Works, Transport and Infrastructure:* Lamin Jobe. *Youth and Sports:* Hadrammeh Sidibeh. *Attorney General and Minister of Justice:* Aboubacarr Marie Tambadou. *Secretary General and Head of the Civil Service:* Ebrima O. Camara. *Secretary to the Cabinet:* Ebrima S. Ceesay.

Office of the President: http://www.statehouse.gm

© Springer Nature Limited 2020
Palgrave Macmillan (ed.), *The Statesman's Yearbook 2020*,
https://doi.org/10.1057/978-1-349-95940-2_76

Current Leaders

Adama Barrow

Position
President

Introduction
Adama Barrow took office as president on 19 Jan. 2017, succeeding Yahya Jammeh who had governed since 1994.

Early Life
Barrow was born on 16 Feb. 1965 near Basse. After schooling in Banjul, he started in business and moved to the UK in the early 2000s, where he worked as a security guard in London to finance his studies in property management. On returning to The Gambia in 2006 he founded his own estate agency.

In Sept. 2016 Ousainou Darboe, head of the United Democratic Party (UDP) of which Barrow was treasurer, was jailed. Barrow succeeded him as leader but resigned in Nov. to lead a coalition of opposition parties (including the UDP) in the presidential elections. He emphasized his support for an independent judiciary and a free press.

In the elections in Dec. 2016 Barrow gained 43·3% of the vote against 39·6% for Jammeh, who refused to accept the result and triggered a constitutional crisis. On 18 Jan. 2017, a day before Barrow's scheduled inauguration, parliament extended Jammeh's term of office. Barrow was nonetheless sworn in at The Gambia's embassy in Senegal's capital, Dakar, the next day. The threat of military intervention by the Economic Community of West African States to uphold the results of the election forced Jammeh to leave The Gambia on 21 Jan. and Barrow returned to the country from Senegal on 26 Jan.

Career in Office
On coming to power, Barrow promised to limit leaders' time in office. He also pledged to stimulate the country's weak economy. In April 2017 the UDP emerged from parliamentary elections with an absolute majority, taking 31 of the 53 seats and inflicting a heavy defeat on Jammeh's Alliance for Patriotic Reorientation and Construction.

In a cabinet reshuffle in June 2018 Barrow appointed former foreign minister Ousainou Darboe as vice-president, replacing Fatoumata Tambajang, while Mamadou Tangara assumed the foreign affairs portfolio and Mambury Njie became finance minister.

Earlier, in Feb. 2018, Gambia was readmitted as a member of the Commonwealth, having previously withdrawn its membership from the grouping in 2013.

Defence

The Gambian National Army, 800 strong, has two infantry battalions, one engineer squadron and one company of presidential guards. The marine unit of the Army consisted in 2011 of approximately 70 personnel operating seven patrol boats.

Defence expenditure totalled an estimated US$6m. in 2011 (approximately US$4 per capita), representing around 0·5% of GDP.

Economy

Agriculture contributed 17·8% of GDP in 2016, industry 13·4% and services 68·8%.

Overview

The country has few natural resources and remittance inflows from Gambians abroad are crucial to the economy. The Gambia continues to struggle with high debt, even after meeting the requirements of the Heavily Indebted Poor Countries Initiative in Dec. 2007. In 2015 interest payments consumed over 30% of government revenues.

Tourism and agriculture are key drivers of the economy, with the latter accounting for a significant amount of foreign exchange earnings. Agriculture, dominated by groundnut cultivation, provides over 80% of employment. However, a drought in 2011 and poor harvest in 2014—in addition to an Ebola virus outbreak in neighbouring countries—resulted in a sharp contraction in GDP growth and tourist arrivals. A stronger performance in the tourism sector subsequently supported a recovery in 2015 but social indicators remain poor, with the country ranked 175th out of 188 on the United Nations Human Development Index for 2014.

Currency

The unit of currency is the *dalasi* (GMD), of 100 *butut*. The Gambia—along with Ghana, Guinea, Liberia, Nigeria and Sierra Leone—hopes to adopt a new common currency, the *eco*, by 2020. Inflation was 7·2% in 2016 and 8·0% in 2017. Foreign exchange reserves were US$90m. in July 2005. Total money supply in June 2005 was 3,256m. dalasis.

Budget

2013 revenues were 5,951·8m. dalasis (tax revenue, 76·4%) and expenditures 8,678·4m. dalasis (current expenditure, 73·2%).

VAT at 15% was introduced on 1 Jan. 2013.

Performance

Real GDP grew by 5·9% in 2015, 0·4% in 2016 and 4·6% in 2017. Total GDP was US$1·0bn. in 2017.

Banking and Finance

The Central Bank of The Gambia (founded 1971; *Governor*, Bakary Jammeh) is the bank of issue. There were 14 licensed banks in 2010. Foreign debt totalled US$470m. in 2010, representing 63·3% of GNI.

Energy and Natural Resources

Environment

Carbon dioxide emissions from the consumption of energy in 2011 were the equivalent of 0·2 tonnes per capita.

Electricity

Installed capacity was an estimated 74,000 kW in 2011. Production was approximately 256m. kWh in 2011; consumption per capita in 2011 was around 147 kWh.

Oil and Gas

Although The Gambia is not currently an oil-producing country, there is ongoing exploration both onshore and offshore.

Minerals

Heavy minerals, including ilmenite, zircon and rutile, have been discovered in Sanyang, Batokunku and Kartong areas.

Agriculture

In 2011, 60·8% of total land area was agricultural of which 73·2% was arable and 0·8% occupied by permanent crops. Groundnuts is the only export crop of financial significance, with cotton also exported on a limited scale. Major products (2013, in 1,000 tonnes) are: groundnuts, 94; millet, 94; rice, 70; maize, 33; sorghum, 30; cassava, 12 (estimate).

Livestock (2013): 436,000 cattle; 267,000 goats; 110,000 sheep; 1·3m. chickens (estimate).

Forestry

In 2015 forests covered 0·49m. ha., or 49% of the land area. Timber production in 2011 was 816,000 cu. metres.

Fisheries

The total catch in 2012 was 36,062 tonnes (mainly saltwater fish).

Industry

Labour

The labour force in 2010 totalled 751,000 (52·1% males). Around 70% of the economically active population are engaged in agriculture. There were 14,000 people living in slavery according to the Walk Free Foundation's 2013 *Global Slavery Index*.

International Trade

Imports and Exports

Merchandise imports in 2013 totalled US$350·2m. (US$380·0m. in 2012) and merchandise exports US$106·2m. (US$118·8m. in 2012).

Principal imports in 2013 were food, animals and beverages (32·3%), mineral fuels and lubricants, and machinery and transport equipment; main exports in 2013 were manufactured goods (64·9%), food, animals and beverages, and machinery and transport equipment.

The leading import supplier in 2010 was Côte d'Ivoire (19·7%), followed by Brazil and China; the leading export destination in 2009 was Senegal (26·8%), followed by Guinea and Guinea-Bissau.

Communications

Roads

There were 3,920 km of roads in 2015, of which 818 km were primary roads. In total 854 km of roads were paved in 2015. Number of vehicles (2007): 8,800 passenger cars; 2,600 lorries and vans.

Civil Aviation

There is an international airport at Banjul (Yundum), which handled 313,173 passengers and 1,247 tonnes of freight in 2009. The Gambia has not had a national carrier since Gambia Bird ceased operations in Dec. 2014.

Shipping

The chief port is Banjul. In Jan. 2014 there was one ship of 300 GT or over registered, totalling 9,000 GT.

Telecommunications

In 2010 there were 48,800 landline telephone subscriptions (equivalent to 28·2 per 1,000 inhabitants) and 1,478,300 mobile phone subscriptions (or 855·3 per 1,000 inhabitants). There were 92·0 internet users per 1,000 inhabitants in 2010.

Social Institutions

Out of 178 countries analysed in the 2017 *Fragile States Index*—a list published jointly by the Fund for Peace and *Foreign Policy* magazine—The Gambia was ranked the 37th most vulnerable to conflict or collapse. The index is based on 12 indicators of state vulnerability across social, political and economic categories.

Justice

Justice is administered by a Supreme Court consisting of a chief justice and puisne judges. The High Court has unlimited original jurisdiction in civil and criminal matters. The Supreme Court is the highest court of appeal and succeeds the judicial committee of the Privy Council in London. There are Magistrates Courts in each of the divisions plus one in Banjul and two in nearby Kombo St Mary's Division—eight in all. There are resident magistrates in provincial areas. There are also Muslim courts, district tribunals dealing with cases concerned with customary law, and two juvenile courts.

The death penalty was abolished in 1993 but restored in 1995. It was used in 2012—for the first time since 1985—when nine prisoners were executed. However, there have been no executions since then. The population in penal institutions in Dec. 2012 was approximately 1,000 (56 per 100,000 of national population).

Education

The adult literacy rate in 2008 was 45%. In 2007 there were 218,341 pupils with 5,341 teaching staff at primary schools and 101,670 pupils with 4,475 teachers at secondary schools. Higher education institutes include The University of The Gambia, which was founded in 1999, and The Gambia College. In 2008 there were 6,000 students and 400 academic staff in tertiary education.

In 2009 public expenditure on education came to 3·8% of GDP.

Health

In 2005 there were eight hospital beds per 10,000 inhabitants. In the period 2007–13 there were 1·1 physicians per 10,000 inhabitants, 8·7 nursing and midwifery personnel for every 10,000 and 0·3 dentistry personnel per 10,000.

In *Water: At What Cost? The State of the World's Water 2016*, WaterAid reported that 9·8% of the population does not have access to safe water.

Religion

In 2010 an estimated 95·1% of the population was Muslim (mainly Sunnis) and 4·5% Christian according to the Pew Research Center's Forum on Religion & Public Life.

Culture

World Heritage Sites

The Gambia has two sites on the UNESCO World Heritage List: James Island and Related Sites (inscribed on the list in 2003), containing important evidence of early Afro-European encounters and the slave trade; and the Stone Circles of Senegambia (added in 2006; shared with Senegal), a collection of 93 stone circles, tumuli and burial mounds from between the 3rd century BC and the 16th century AD.

Press

In 2008 there were three daily newspapers—the *Daily Observer*, *The Point* and the government-owned *Gambia Daily.*

Tourism

Tourism is The Gambia's biggest foreign exchange earner. In 2012 there were 157,000 non-resident charter tourists (excluding same-day visitors).

Diplomatic Representatives

Of The Gambia in the United Kingdom (92 Ledbury Rd, London, W11 2AH)
High Commissioner: Francis R. Blain.

Of the United Kingdom in The Gambia (48 Atlantic Rd, Fajara, PO Box 507, Banjul)
High Commissioner: Sharon Wardle.

Of The Gambia in USA (5630 16th St., NW, Washington, D.C., 20011)
Ambassador: Dawda Fadera.

Of the USA in The Gambia (Kairaba Ave., Fajara, PMB19, Banjul)
Ambassador: Vacant.

Chargé d'Affaires a.i.: Shelly Seaver.

Of The Gambia to the United Nations
Ambassador: Lang Yabou.

Of The Gambia to the European Union
Ambassador: Teneng Mba Jaiteh.

Further Reading

Gailey, Harry A., *Historical Dictionary of The Gambia.* 1999

Hughes, A. and Perfect, D., *A Political History of The Gambia, 1816–1994.* 2006

National Statistical Office: The Gambia Bureau of Statistics, Kanifing Institutional Layout, Serekunda, P. O. Box 3504, Serekunda.

Website: http://www.gbos.gov.gm

Georgia

Sakartvelos Respublika (Republic of Georgia)

Capital: Tbilisi
Population projection, 2020: 3·90m.
GNI per capita, 2017: (PPP$) 9,186
HDI/world rank, 2017: 0·780/70=
Internet domain extension: .ge

Key Historical Events

By the 1st millennium BC the Diakhi (Taokhi) and the Qolha (Colchis) tribal groups had developed bronze casting. A two-state confederation emerged as early as the 6th century BC, with Colchis (Egrisi) in the west and Kartli (Iberia) in the east. The Greeks established Black Sea colonies from the 6th century BC, including Phasis (present-day Poti), Gyenos (Ochamchire) and Dioscuras (Sukhumi). Parnavaz I ruled a united Kartli (or Georgia) from his citadel of Armaztsikhe from *c.* 302–237 BC.

The Romans under Pompey attacked Kartli in 65 BC, defeating King Artag and establishing a client state. In the first half of the 2nd century AD Kartli grew under Parsman II. Rome, realizing its value as an ally against Parthia (Iran), recognized Kartli's extended borders. In 298 the Sassanid Iranians acknowledged Roman jurisdiction over Kartli-Iberia and recognized King Mirian III (284–361), who adopted Christianity as the state religion. Christianity brought close ties with Rome's successor, Byzantium, though Persia controlled Kartli for much of the 4th–6th centuries.

Tbilisi fell to an Arab army in 645 but Kartli retained considerable autonomy under local Arab rulers. In 813 the Armenian prince Ashot I of the Bagrationi family took control of Georgia, beginning nearly a millennium of Bagratid rule. Bagrat V (1027–72) united west and east and David IV ('the Builder', 1099–1125) presided over a golden age, repulsing the Seljuk Turks and disseminating Georgian influence in the Caucasus.

The Mongols invaded in 1236 and the Turkic conqueror Timur destroyed Tbilisi in 1386. Turkish dominance was sealed when the Byzantine Empire collapsed. By the 18th century the Bagratids had regained autonomy under nominal Persian rule. In 1762 Herekle II took control of the eastern regions of Kartli and Kakhetia, reducing the powers of the Georgian nobility. Herekle opened channels with Russia to gain protection from the Turks, though Russo-Turkish rivalry soon afflicted Georgia. After the Persians sacked Tbilisi in 1795 Herekle again sought Russian protection, leading to annexation.

In 1801 Tsar Alexander I abolished the kingdom of Kartli-Kakhetia (Eastern Georgia). Western Georgia (Imeretia) was annexed in 1804 and the Georgian Orthodox Church lost its autocephalous status in 1811. Russification intensified in the second half of the 19th century but a national liberation movement emerged in the 20th century, with Russia declaring martial law in 1905 following peasant revolts and general strikes. Revolutionaries split between the gradualist Mensheviks and the radical Bolsheviks (led by Ioseb Jugashvili, later Joseph Stalin).

The Caucasus became a major battleground in 1915 when Russia invaded Turkey. In May 1918 Georgia declared independence under the protection of Germany (to prevent invasion by the Turks). Lenin gave recognition in May 1920 and the Menshevik-dominated government redistributed swathes of aristocratic landholdings. In 1921 the Bolshevik Red Army invaded Georgia. From 1922–36 Georgia was part of the Transcaucasian Soviet Federated Socialist Republic within the USSR. In 1936 the republic was divided into Armenia, Azerbaijan and Georgia.

Over 500,000 Georgians served in the Red Army in the Second World War and the autonomy of the Georgian Orthodox Church was restored in 1943. Stalin oversaw forced urbanization and industrialization and although he and Lavrentiy Beria (chief of secret police) were Georgians, Georgia suffered greatly under his regime. Criticism of Stalin in Georgia gained momentum under Gorbachev's *glasnost* policy of the late 1980s. In 1972 Eduard Shevardnadze took control of the Georgian Communist Party. His clearout of officials prompted dissident nationalists (led by the academic, Zviad Gamsakhurdia) to warn of Russification. In 1978 leaders of the Abkhazian Autonomous Republic threatened to secede from Georgia. Shevardnadze took steps to diffuse the crisis, including an affirmative action programme for ethnic Abkhaz. When Shevardnadze became Soviet foreign minister in 1985 his successor, Jumber Patiashvili, removed some of the Shevardnadze appointees, forcing reformist leaders underground.

In April 1989 Soviet troops broke up peaceful demonstrations in Tbilisi and 20 Georgians were killed. Following the 'April Tragedy' Shevardnadze was sent to restore calm. Multi-party elections in Oct. 1990 saw Gamsakhurdia's Round Table/Free Georgia coalition win a solid majority. Supported by a referendum, parliament declared independence and declined to participate in the Commonwealth of Independent States.

In May 1991 Gamsakhurdia was elected president but the National Guard joined the opposition. When fighting in central Tbilisi in late Dec. forced Gamsakhurdia to flee to Chechnya, a military council took control and invited Shevardnadze to return in March 1992. Post-Soviet Georgia was dogged by separatism, especially in South Ossetia and Abkhazia. Relations with Russia were strained by its support for these insurgencies. In 1990 Gamsakhurdia had removed South Ossetia's autonomous status. When the South Ossetian regional legislature attempted to unite with Russian North Ossetia, Georgian forces invaded. Thousands died and tens of thousands were displaced before Yeltsin mediated a ceasefire in July 1992.

In Abkhazia the ethnic Abkhaz population feared cultural annihilation while the Georgian majority resented disproportionate allocation of political and administrative positions to the Abkhaz. In July 1992 the Abkhazian Supreme Soviet voted to separate from Georgia. In Aug. 1992 the National Guard seized the Abkhazian capital, Sukhumi. Hundreds died and refugees fled to Russia and other parts of Georgia. The Abkhazian government requested Russian intervention, retaking Sukhumi and forcing the Georgian army out in 1993. A ceasefire began in early 1994. When Gamsakhurdia invaded Mingrelia (his home region where he had retained support) Shevardnadze asked for Russian military assistance. Defeated, Gamsakhurdia committed suicide in Jan. 1994.

Opposition to Shevardnadze's increasingly corrupt rule grew in the late 1990s, despite advantageous relations with the West and a US$3bn. Baku-Tbilisi-Ceyhan oil pipeline deal. In Nov. 2003 Shevardnadze resigned after opposition forces, alleging electoral fraud, stormed parliament. Following the 'Rose Revolution' Mikheil Saakashvili became president in Jan. 2004. Saakashvili's presidency was dominated by diplomatic sparring with Russia over Russian interference in Abkhazia and South Ossetia. Relations reached a new low in the months following Saakashvili's re-election in Jan. 2008. In March Abkhazia's separatist government requested the UN to recognize the region's independence and in April 2008 Moscow announced closer ties with both regions. In Aug. Saakashvili sent troops into South Ossetia to attack separatist forces. Russia claimed its citizens were under attack and responded by sending in several thousand troops. A week of fierce fighting was brought to an end by a French-brokered peace deal, with Russia recognizing independence for both South Ossetia and Abkhazia. Moscow was subsequently accused of delaying its troop withdrawal. Adjara, another autonomous region, was brought under Tbilisi's control with the ejection of its populist leader, Aslan Abashidze, in 2004.

In 2010 the constitution was amended to reduce the powers of the president in favour of those of the prime minister and parliament. The changes came into effect in 2013, with the election of Giorgi Margvelashvili as president in succession to Saakashvili. The government signed an association agreement with the European Union the following year. Also in 2014 relations with Russia became strained again after Moscow signed a strategic partnership agreement with Abkhazia, followed by an 'alliance and integration' treaty with South Ossetia in March 2015. South Ossetia held a presidential election and a referendum on a proposed change of name to South Ossetia-Alania in 2017 as part of a bid to ultimately accede to the Russian Federation.

Palgrave Macmillan (ed.), *The Statesman's Yearbook 2020*,
https://doi.org/10.1057/978-1-349-95940-2_77

Territory and Population

Georgia is bounded in the west by the Black Sea and south by Turkey, Armenia and Azerbaijan. Area, 69,700 sq. km (26,900 sq. miles). Its census population in 2014 was 3,713,804 (excluding Abkhazia and South Ossetia-Alania); density (excluding Abkhazia and South Ossetia-Alania), 65·0 per sq. km. 2014 population including estimates for Abkhazia and South Ossetia-Alania: 4,008,068.

The UN gives a projected population for 2020 of 3·90m.

In 2012, 53·2% of the population lived in urban areas. The capital is Tbilisi (2014 census population: 1,062,282). Other principal towns (with 2014 census population figures in brackets): Batumi (152,839), Kutaisi (147,635), Rustavi (125,103). After Russian-backed Abkhaz forces and their allies took Sukhumi in 1993, non-Abkhaz residents were ejected from the region. Sukhumi's population fell from 121,000 in 1991 to an estimated 64,500 in 2011.

Georgians accounted for 86·8% of the 2014 census population; others included 6·3% Azerbaijanis, 4·5% Armenians and 0·7% Russians.

Georgian is the official language. Armenian, Russian and Azeri are also spoken.

Social Statistics

Births, 2011, 58,014; deaths, 49,818. Rates, 2011: birth, 12·9 per 1,000 population; death, 11·1 per 1,000. Annual population growth rate, 2005–10, –0·4%. Life expectancy, 2013, 70·5 years for males and 77·8 years for females. Infant mortality, 2010, 20 per 1,000 live births; fertility rate, 2013, 1·8 births per woman.

Climate

The Georgian climate is extremely varied. The relatively small territory covers different climatic zones, ranging from humid sub-tropical zones to permanent snow and glaciers. In Tbilisi summer is hot: 25–35°C. Nov. sees the beginning of the Georgian winter and the temperature in Tbilisi can drop to –8°C; however, average temperature ranges from 2–6°C.

Constitution and Government

A new constitution of 24 Aug. 1995 defines Georgia as a presidential republic with federal elements. The head of state is the *President*, elected by universal suffrage for not more than two five-year terms. The 150-member *Supreme Council* is elected for four-year terms, with 73 members elected in single-seat constituencies and 77 by proportional representation. There is a 5% threshold.

Amendments limiting the power of the president in favour of the prime minister were passed in Oct. 2010 and came into force after Giorgi Margvelashvili was sworn in as president in Nov. 2013. The prime minister now has executive authority over domestic and foreign policy. The president remains head of state but no longer has the right to initiate laws, introduce a budget or hold an office in a political party.

National Anthem

'Tavisupleba' ('Freedom'); words by Dawit Magradse, tune by Zakaria Paliashvili.

Recent Elections

In the first round of presidential elections held on 28 Oct. 2018 Salome Zourabichvili (ind.) won 38·6% of the vote against Grigol Vashadze (United National Movement) with 37·7%, Davit Bakradze (European Georgia) with 11·0%, Shalva Natelashvili (Georgian Labour Party) with 3·7%, David Usupashvili (Development Movement) with 2·3% and Zurab Japaridze (Girchi) also with 2·3%. 19 other candidates won less than 2% of the vote each. Zourabichvili won the second round run-off on 28 Nov. 2018 with 59·5% against Vashadze with 40·5%. Turnout was 46·8% in the first round and 56·5% in the second round.

At parliamentary elections held on 8 and 30 Oct. 2016 the ruling Georgian Dream coalition won 115 of the 150 seats (with 48·7% of the party list vote). The United National Movement won 27 seats (27·1% of the party list vote); the Alliance of Patriots of Georgia 6 seats (5·0%); Industry Will Save Georgia–Our Fatherland 1 seat (0·8%). Turnout was 51·6%.

Current Government

President: Salome Zourabichvili; b. 1952 (ind.; sworn in 16 Dec. 2018).

In Feb. 2019 the government comprised:

Prime Minister: Mamuka Bakhtadze; b. 1982 (Georgian Dream; sworn in 20 June 2018).

Vice Prime Ministers: Giorgi Gakharia (also *Minister of Internal Affairs*); Maya Tskitishvili (also *Minister of Regional Development and Infrastructure*).

Minister of Defence: Levan Izoria. *Economy and Sustainable Development:* Giorgi Kobulia. *Education, Science, Culture and Sport:* Mikheil Batiashvili. *Environment Protection and Agriculture:* Levan Davitashvili. *Finance:* Ivane Machavariani. *Foreign Affairs:* David Zalkaliani. *Internally Displaced Persons from the Occupied Territories, Labour, Health and Social Affairs:* Davit Sergeenko. *Justice:* Thea Tsulukiani.

Minister of State for Reconciliation and Civic Equality: Ketevan Tsikhelashvili.

Office of the President: https://www.president.gov.ge

Current Leaders

Salome Zourabichvili

Position
President

Introduction
Salome Zourabichvili became president in Dec. 2018. She served in the French diplomatic service for nearly 30 years before entering the Georgian political arena. She is the country's first female president.

Early Life
Salome Zourabichvili was born in Paris, France, on 18 March 1952. Her parents were Georgian émigrés who fled their homeland in the aftermath of the 1921 Soviet annexation. The family maintained strong political and social ties to the local Georgian community, with her father, brother and cousin each serving as chairman of the Georgian diasporic association in Paris.

Zourabichvili graduated from the Institut d'Études Politiques de Paris (Science Po) in 1972, before being awarded a master's degree by New York's Columbia University School of International and Public Affairs in the USA in 1973. The following year she began her career in the French foreign service. Over the next three decades she held diplomatic positions both within France and abroad, including posts at the United Nations Permanent Mission in New York, the Western European Union in Brussels, the French ministry of defence and embassies in Italy, the USA and Chad. In 2003 she was appointed France's ambassador to Georgia.

Zourabichvili entered Georgian politics in 2004, when she was granted citizenship and appointed the country's first female minister of foreign affairs. She held the post for one year, during which time she negotiated the withdrawal of Russian military bases from Georgian territory. In 2006 she formed a new party, the Way of Georgia, which she led for four years before endorsing Georgian Dream, a coalition opposition group. Having won a parliamentary seat in 2016, she successfully ran for the presidency in 2018 as an independent with the backing of Georgian Dream. She was sworn into office on 16 Dec. 2018.

Career in Office
Zourabichvili's ultimate aim is to secure the reunification of the Georgian state. She has promised to protect minority language rights in Abkhazia, a separatist Georgian territory under increasing Russian influence. She also plans to further Georgia's presence on the international stage, with the end goal of joining the European Union and NATO.

Mamuka Bakhtadze

Position
Prime Minister

Introduction
Mamuka Bakhtadze was elected prime minister on 20 June 2018, following the resignation of Giorgi Kvirikashvili. He has stated that education is his government's priority focus.

Early Life
Bakhtadze was born on 9 June 1982 and graduated in management and microeconomics from the Tbilisi State University. He then undertook further

studies at other institutions, including the Georgian Technical University, Lomonosov Moscow State University and the INSEAD Business School. After initially working in the hospitality industry, he was general director of the Georgian International Energy Corporation from 2010 to 2012 and then in 2013 became director of the Georgian Railway LLC. In Nov. 2017 he entered government as the minister of finance.

Career in Office
After Kvirikashvili's resignation in June 2018, Bakhtadze was nominated as his successor by the ruling Georgian Dream party. His appointment was confirmed on 20 June by parliamentary vote. He has stated his intention to move Georgia closer to the West, with a view to joining the European Union and NATO—both to bolster the nation's economic standing and to boost security in light of a Russian presence in the disputed territories of Abkhazia and South Ossetia-Alania. However, hopes of accession to the EU rest on improving Georgia's record on civil and labour rights and environmental standards.

Defence

The total strength of the Armed Forces consisted of 20,655 personnel in 2011. Conscription was abolished in June 2016 by the then minister of defence Tina Khidasheli, but was restored in Feb. 2017 by her successor Levan Izoria. The UN peacekeeping mission (United Nations Observer Mission in Georgia, or UNOMIG, which was established in Aug. 1993) ended in June 2009 owing to a lack of consensus among Security Council members on mandate extension. Following the collapse of the USSR in 1991 Russia maintained two bases in Georgia with some 4,000 personnel. The last Russian troops left Georgia in Nov. 2007. However, several thousand soldiers returned in Aug. 2008 when Moscow responded to Georgia's military attack on separatist forces in South Ossetia. Despite a subsequent withdrawal, some forces remain as part of a 'buffer zone' around South Ossetia and Abkhazia.

Georgia hopes to join NATO, although its bid to become a member is fiercely opposed by Russia. In Sept. 2014 the Substantial NATO-Georgia Package (SNGP)—a partnership aimed at strengthening military co-operation and improving Georgia's defence capabilities—was agreed. NATO has monitored Georgia's progress in implementing SNGP reforms in order to assess the country's suitability for membership.

Defence expenditure in 2013 totalled US$389m. (US$85 per capita), representing 2·3% of GDP.

Army

The Army totalled 17,800 (3,800 conscripts) in 2011. In addition there were 1,600 active reservists in the National Guard and 6,300 Ministry of the Interior troops. A paramilitary border guard exists, estimated at 5,400.

Navy

The former Navy was absorbed into the Coast Guard in 2009. In 2011 it had 17 patrol and coastal combatants. The headquarters are at the Black Sea port of Poti.

Air Force

Personnel, 2011, 1,310 (290 conscripts). There were 12 combat-capable aircraft in 2011 (Su-25 fighter-bombers).

Economy

Agriculture accounted for 9·2% of GDP in 2014, industry 24·4% and services 66·4%.

Georgia's 'shadow' (black market) economy is estimated to constitute approximately 62% of the country's official GDP, one of the highest percentages of any country in the world.

Overview

Georgia is a small, lower-income transition economy. After independence in 1991, civil war and the loss of markets in the former Soviet Union led to economic collapse, with exports declining by 90% and output falling by 70%. Political tensions, declining living standards and low tax revenues undermined the funding of basic services. Progress towards macroeconomic stabilization in the late 1990s was then disrupted by internal fragmentation, drought and the 1998 financial crisis in Russia. IMF-supported programmes from 2001–04 aided growth recovery and price stability.

Prudent macroeconomic policies and structural reforms, notably a privatization programme, helped achieve average annual growth of 6·1% and single-digit inflation between 2003 and 2012. Reforms improved infrastructure and the business environment and strengthened public finances. However, growth has been capital-intensive, resulting in relatively high unemployment, which stood at 14·6% in 2013, although it had declined to 12·0% by 2015. Some 55% of the workforce is employed in agriculture—mainly subsistence farming, which contributes minimally to GDP.

Georgia's economy grew by 2·9% in 2015 and 2·7% in 2016, driven by construction and other non-tradable sectors, as well as an expanding tourism industry. Investment exceeded 30% of GDP in 2016. However, a decline in exports widened the current account deficit from 12% of GDP in 2015 to 12·4% in 2016—foreign direct investment financed nearly 90% of the deficit. As a result, external debt increased from 107% of GDP in 2015 to 111% in 2016.

Poverty in Georgia has gradually declined, with 20·1% of the population living below the national poverty line in 2015 according to the Asian Development Bank—the fourth lowest figure in central and west Asia. Increased social spending has helped raise the average incomes of the poorest 40% of the population so that only 3·9% was living on less than US$1·90 (PPP) per day in 2016.

A key macroeconomic challenge is to improve fiscal sustainability, while poverty reduction is over-reliant on an upsurge in private sector employment growth. The government aims to improve internal and regional market connectivity to enhance private sector competitiveness and access to economic opportunities. It also seeks to strengthen public sector management, encourage small and medium enterprise development and increase infrastructure investment.

Currency

The unit of currency is the *lari* (GEL) of 100 *tetri*, which replaced coupons at 1 lari = 1m. coupons on 25 Sept. 1995. Inflation was at 15,606% in 1994 and 163% in 1995, although it is much more under control now and in fact there was deflation of 2·1% in 2016 and 6·0% in 2017. There was then inflation of 3·1% in 2014 and 4·0% in 2015. Gold reserves are negligible. Total money supply was 882m. laris in July 2005.

Budget

Consolidated government revenues in 2011 totalled 7,251m. laris and expenditures 7,449m. laris. Tax revenue accounted for 84·6% of total revenues; social security and welfare accounted for 20·8% of total expenditures, and economic services 15·2%.

VAT is 18%.

Performance

The economy grew by 2·9% in 2015, 2·8% in 2016 and 5·0% in 2017. Total GDP was US$15·2bn. in 2017 (excluding Abkhazia and South Ossetia-Alania).

Banking and Finance

The *President* of the Central Bank is Koba Gvenetadze. In 2005 there were 19 commercial banks. Two foreign banks had representative offices. The largest bank is Bank of Georgia, with a 36% market share by assets.

In 2010 external debt totalled US$9,238m., equivalent to 80% of GNI.

Energy and Natural Resources

Environment

Carbon dioxide emissions from the consumption of energy were the equivalent of 1·3 tonnes per capita in 2011.

Electricity

The many fast-flowing rivers provide an important hydro-electric resource. Installed capacity was around 4·4m. kW in 2011. Production in 2011 was 10·75bn. kWh (76% hydro-electric); consumption per capita in 2011 was 2,352 kWh.

Oil and Gas

Output (2011) of crude petroleum, 0·4m. bbls. A 930 km long oil pipeline from an offshore Azerbaijani oilfield in the Caspian Sea across Azerbaijan and Georgia to a new oil terminal at Supsa, near Poti, on the Black Sea Coast started pumping oil in early 1999; the US$600m. pipeline allowed Georgia to create 25,000 new jobs. However, Georgia is still heavily dependent on

Russia for natural gas. Accords for the construction of a second oil pipeline through Georgia were signed in Nov. 1999, to take oil from Azerbaijan to Turkey via Georgia. Work on the pipeline began in Sept. 2002 and it was officially opened in May 2005. Natural gas production was 5·8m. cu. metres in 2011.

A gas pipeline from Baku through Georgia to Erzurum in Turkey was commissioned in June 2006.

Minerals
Manganese deposits are calculated at 250m. tonnes. Other important minerals are barytes, clays, gold, diatomite shale, agate, marble, alabaster, iron and other ores, building stone, arsenic, molybdenum, tungsten and mercury.

Agriculture
Agriculture plays an important part in Georgia's economy, contributing 12·8% of GDP in 2006. In 2013 there were an estimated 451,000 ha. of arable land and 160,000 ha. of permanent crops. Approximately 433,000 ha. were equipped for irrigation in 2013.

Output of main agricultural products (in 1,000 tonnes) in 2013: maize, 364; potatoes, 297; grapes, 223; tangerines, mandarins, clementines and satsumas, 107; wheat, 81; tomatoes, 75; apples, 69; watermelons, 66; hazelnuts, 40; barley, 35. Livestock, 2013: cattle, 1,212,000; sheep, 688,000; pigs, 204,000; chickens (estimate), 6m. Livestock products, 2013 estimates (in 1,000 tonnes): meat, 48; milk, 611; eggs, 28.

Forestry
There were 2·82m. ha. of forest in 2015, or 41% of the total land area. Timber production in 2011 was 838,000 cu. metres.

Fisheries
The catch in 2012 was 12,070 tonnes, down from over 100,000 tonnes in the late 1980s before the break-up of the Soviet Union.

Industry
Industry accounted for 21·2% of GDP in 2008. Production, 2008 unless otherwise specified (in 1,000 tonnes): cement, 1,351; flour, 218; refined sugar (2006), 123; footwear, 28,290 pairs; beer, 62·5m. litres; spirits (2007), 2·6m. litres; cigarettes, 5,156m. units.

Labour
The labour force in 2013 was 2,417,000 (2,259,000 in 2003). 69·3% of the population aged 15–64 was economically active in 2013. In the same year 14·6% of the population was unemployed.

Georgia had 16,000 people living in slavery according to the Walk Free Foundation's 2013 *Global Slavery Index*.

International Trade

Imports and Exports
Merchandise imports in 2014 totalled US$8,596·3m. (US$8,025·2m. in 2013) and merchandise exports US$2,861·2m. (US$2,908·4m. in 2013).

Principal imports in 2014 were machinery and transport equipment (28·4%), mineral fuels and lubricants, and manufactured goods; main exports in 2014 were food, animals and beverages (28·4%), machinery and transport equipment, and manufactured goods.

The leading import supplier in 2010 was Turkey (17·3%), followed by Ukraine and Azerbaijan; the leading export destination in 2010 was Azerbaijan (15·4%), followed by Turkey and the USA.

Communications

Roads
There were 20,329 km of roads in 2007 (94·1% hard-surfaced). Passenger cars in use in 2007 numbered 416,300, and there were also 51,500 lorries and vans and 42,800 buses and coaches. In 2007 there were 737 road deaths.

Rail
Total length in 2011 was 1,262 km (1,225 km of 1,524 mm gauge and 37 km of 900 mm gauge), all of which was electrified. In 2011 railways carried 20·1m. tonnes of freight and 3·3m. passengers. There is a metro system in Tbilisi.

Civil Aviation
The main airport is Tbilisi International Airport. The main Georgian carrier is Georgian Airways. In 2007 it had flights to Amsterdam, Athens, Dubai, Frankfurt, Kyiv, Minsk, Moscow, Paris, Tel Aviv and Vienna. In 2009 Tbilisi handled 702,596 passengers (714,976 in 2008) and 12,245 tonnes of freight.

Shipping
In Jan. 2014 there were 48 ships of 300 GT or over registered, totalling 110,000 GT. The principal port is Poti, which handled 7·9m. tonnes of cargo in 2013 (6·1m. tonnes of cargo in 2009). Georgia is a 'flag of convenience' country.

Telecommunications
In 2011 there were 1,342,400 landline telephone subscriptions (equivalent to 310·1 per 1,000 inhabitants) and 4,430,600 mobile phone subscriptions (or 1,023·5 per 1,000 inhabitants). There were 269·0 internet users per 1,000 inhabitants in 2010. Fixed internet subscriptions totalled 176,500 in 2009 (40·4 per 1,000 inhabitants). In March 2012 there were 908,000 Facebook users.

Social Institutions

Out of 178 countries analysed in the 2017 *Fragile States Index*—a list published jointly by the Fund for Peace and *Foreign Policy* magazine—Georgia was ranked the 79th most vulnerable to conflict or collapse. The index is based on 12 indicators of state vulnerability across social, political and economic categories.

Justice
The population in penal institutions in April 2013 (excluding Abkhazia and South Ossetia) was 10,202 (225 per 100,000 of national population). The death penalty was abolished in 1997. Georgia was ranked 35th of 102 countries for criminal justice and 26th for civil justice in the 2015 World Justice Project *Rule of Law Index*, which provides data on how the rule of law is experienced by the general public across eight categories.

Education
In 2005 there were 1,214 public pre-primary schools with 6,883 teachers for 76,416 pupils. In 2005–06 there were 2,744 public and private schools with 74,300 teachers and 634,700 pupils (326,600 at primary level and 308,100 at secondary). In 2005–06 there were 171 higher education institutions with 144,300 students and 11,280 academic staff; the largest is Tbilisi State University with 35,000 students in 2005–06. Adult literacy rate in 2009 was estimated at 99·7%.

Public spending on education in 2007 came to 2·6% of GNI and 7·8% of total government expenditure.

Health
Georgia had 13,600 hospital beds in 2009. In 2009 there were 20,609 physicians and 12,933 nurses; there were 1,269 dentistry personnel in 2006.

Welfare
In 2005 there were 549,900 old age and 352,200 other pensioners.

Religion

The Georgian Orthodox Church has its own organization under Catholicos (Patriarch) Ilia II who is resident in Tbilisi. According to estimates by the Pew Research Center's Forum on Religion & Public Life, in 2010 there were 3·8m. Orthodox and 500,000 Muslims (both Shias and Sunnis), plus small numbers of Catholics.

Culture

World Heritage Sites
Georgia has three sites on the UNESCO World Heritage List: City-Museum Reserve of Mtskheta (inscribed on the list in 1994), churches of the former Georgian capital; Gelati Monastery (1994 and 2017); and Upper Svaneti (1996), a mountainous area of medieval villages.

Press
In 2008 there were ten dailies with a combined circulation of 45,000, as well as 73 other papers.

Tourism

Investment in tourism has increased substantially in recent years, and large numbers of hotels have been built. In 2014 there were 5,516,000 non-resident visitors, up from 1,500,000 in 2009 and only 368,000 in 2004.

Diplomatic Representatives

Of Georgia in the United Kingdom (4 Russell Gdns, London, W14 8EZ)
Ambassador: Tamar Beruchashvili.

Of the United Kingdom in Georgia (51 Krtsanisi St., 0114 Tbilisi)
Ambassador: Justin McKenzie Smith.

Of Georgia in the USA (1824–1826 R St., NW, Washington, D.C., 20009)
Ambassador: David Bakradze.

Of the USA in Georgia (11 George Balanchine St., 0131 Tbilisi)
Ambassador: Vacant.
Chargé d'Affaires a.i.: Ross Wilson.

Of Georgia to the United Nations
Ambassador: Kaha Imnadze.

Of Georgia to the European Union
Ambassador: Natalie Sabanadze.

Abkhazia

Area, 8,600 sq. km; population (2011), 240,705. Capital, Sukhumi. The territory (ancient Colchis) saw the establishment of a West Georgian kingdom in the 4th century and became a Russian protectorate in 1810. Its status as an Autonomous Republic, within Georgia, was confirmed in 1930 (and again in 1995 by the Georgian Constitution).

In July 1992 the Abkhazian parliament declared sovereignty and the restoration of its 1925 constitution. Fighting broke out as Georgian forces moved into Abkhazia but they were driven out by Sept. 1993. In May 1994 Georgian and Abkhazian delegates under Russian auspices signed an agreement to deploy Russian troops as a peacekeeping force. In Nov. 1994 parliament adopted a new constitution proclaiming Abkhazian sovereignty and parliamentary elections were held in Nov. 1996. Neither the constitution nor the elections were recognized by the Georgian government or the international community. Further fighting flared up between rival militia forces in 1998 until a ceasefire was declared. In March 2008 Abkhazia appealed to the UN to have its independence recognized. Following fighting between Russian and Georgian forces in Aug. 2008, after Tbilisi had sent troops into South Ossetia, Russia confirmed its recognition of Abkhazia as an independent state. In Nov. 2014 Abkhazia signed an agreement on 'alliance and strategic partnership' with Russia—a move that the government in Georgia considered a step towards Russian annexation of the disputed territory.

In presidential elections held in Aug. 2014 Raul Khadjimba took 50·6% of the vote ahead of Aslan Bzhania with 35·9%, but the USA, the European Union and Georgia refused to recognize the poll.

President: Raul Khadjimba (since Sept. 2014).
Prime Minister: Valery Bganba (since Sept. 2018).

The unit of currency is the Russian *rouble*. The republic has coal, electric power, building materials and light industries. All agricultural land is owned by the state and private ownership is forbidden under still prevailing Soviet-era regulations.

Adjara

Area, 2,900 sq. km; census population (2014): 333,953. Density, 115 per sq. km. Capital, Batumi. Bounded by Turkey to the south, Adjara fell under Turkish rule in the 17th century and was annexed to Russia (rejoining Georgia) after the Berlin Treaty of 1878. In July 1921 the territory was constituted as an Autonomous Republic within the Georgian SSR, a status later confirmed by the Georgian Constitution of 1995. In Jan. 2004 the Adjaran leader refused to acknowledge the central government of President Mikheil Saakashvili and, fearing a Georgian invasion, declared a state of emergency. Saakashvili imposed direct rule over Adjara. Elections to the *Supreme Council*, Adjara's parliament, were held in Oct. 2012. Georgian Dream won 13 of 21 seats with 57·6% of the vote and Saakashvili's United National Movement 8 with 36·9%. The last Russian troops left the military base in Batumi in Nov. 2007.

Chairman of the Supreme Council: Davit Gabaidze (since Nov. 2016).
Prime Minister: Tornike Rizhvadze (since July 2018).

Adjara specializes in sub-tropical agricultural products, including tea, citruses, bamboo, eucalyptus and tobacco.

There is an airport, port and shipyard at Batumi. Industries include oil refining, food-processing and canning, clothing, building materials and pharmaceuticals.

South Ossetia-Alania

Area, 3,900 sq. km; population (2015), 53,532, including Ossetians, Georgians, Russians and Armenians. Capital, Tskhinvali. The UN High Commission for Refugees reported that some 30,000 people were displaced within South Ossetia as a result of the 2008 Russo-Georgian conflict. Populated by Ossetians from across the Caucasus (North Ossetia) from the 13th century, the region was absorbed within the Georgian SSR in 1922. Formerly an Autonomous Region, its administrative autonomy was abolished by the Georgian Supreme Soviet in Dec. 1990.

Fighting broke out in 1990 between insurgents wishing to unite with North Ossetia and Georgian forces. Russian peacekeeping troops moved into a buffer zone between South Ossetia and Georgia pending negotiations and an OSCE force was deployed from 1992. In Nov. 1996 Lyudvig Chibirov was elected president. Though maintaining a commitment to independence, he reached agreement with the Georgian government that neither force nor sanctions should be applied. Then in July 2003 his successor asked Russian president Vladimir Putin to let South Ossetia join the Russian Federation. However, then Georgian president Mikheil Saakashvili sought to revive the authority of the Georgian government and in Aug. 2008 sent troops against the region's separatist forces. Russian mobilization led to a week of fierce fighting and Moscow subsequently recognized South Ossetian independence. The Kremlin signed an 'alliance and integration' treaty with South Ossetia in March 2015, regarded as a further step towards the region ultimately acceding to the Russian Federation. In 2017 South Ossetia changed its name to South Ossetia-Alania after the move won approval in a referendum in 2015.

Presidential elections were held in April 2017 and parliamentary elections in June 2014, but the results were not recognized by Georgia, NATO or the European Union.

President: Anatoly Bibilov (since April 2017).
Prime Minister: Erik Pukhayev (since May 2017).

Main industries are mining, timber, electrical engineering and building materials.

Further Reading

Georgia

Areshidze, Irakly, *Democracy and Autocracy in Eurasia: Georgia in Transition.* 2007

Coppieters, Bruno and Legvold, Robert, (eds) *Statehood and Security: Georgia after the Rose Revolution.* 2005

Gachechiladze, R., *The New Georgia: Space, Society, Politics.* 1995

Jones, Stephen, *Georgia: A Political History since Independence.* 2012

Mikaberidze, Alexander, *Historical Dictionary of Georgia.* 2007

Nodia, Ghia and Scholtbach, Alvaro Pinto, *The Political Landscape of Georgia: Political Parties, Achievements, Challenges, and Prospects.* 2007

Pelkmans, Mathijs, *Defending the Border: Identity, Religion, and Modernity in the Republic of Georgia.* 2006

Rayfield, Donald, *Edge of Empires: A History of Georgia.* 2012

Suny, R. G., *The Making of the Georgian Nation.* 2nd ed. 1994

Wheatley, Jonathan, *Georgia from National Awakening to Rose Revolution: Delayed Transition in the Former Soviet Union.* 2005

National Statistical Office: National Statistics Service of Georgia, 30 Tsotne Dadiani Str., 0180 Tbilisi.

Website: http://www.geostat.ge

Germany

Bundesrepublik Deutschland (Federal Republic of Germany)

Capital: Berlin
Seats of government: Berlin, Bonn
Population projection, 2020: 82·54m.
GNI per capita, 2017: (PPP$) 46,136
HDI/world rank, 2017: 0·936/5
Internet domain extension: .de

Key Historical Events

From the 8th century BC the Celtic peoples inhabited most of present-day Germany but by about 500 BC Germanic tribes had pushed their way north and settled in the Celtic lands. The expanding Roman Empire established its boundaries along the Rhine and the Danube rivers but attempts to move further east had to be abandoned after the Roman provincial Governor Varius was defeated in AD 9 by the Germanic forces under Arminius. For the next thousand years the towns of Trier, Regensburg, Augsburg, Mainz and Cologne, founded by the Romans, formed the main centres of urban settlement. Christianity was introduced under Emperor Constantine and the first bishopric north of the Alps was established in Trier in AD 314.

At the start of the 5th century the Huns forced the indigenous Saxons north, towards Britain. However, the Franks, who came from the lowlands and were to become the founders of a German state, gradually asserted themselves over all the other Germanic people. Towards the end of the 5th century a powerful Rhenish state was founded under King Clovis, a descendant of Merovech (Merovius), a Salian Frankish king. The Merovingian dynasty eventually gave way to the Carolingians, whose authority was strengthened by papal support.

Charlemagne succeeded to the throne in 768, founding what was later known as the First Reich (Empire). The Franks continued to thrive until their influence stretched from Rome to the North Sea and from the Pyrenees to the River Elbe. The Pope crowned Charlemagne emperor on Christmas Day 800, creating what was to become known as the Holy Roman Empire. But the empire was too unwieldy to survive Charlemagne. On his death in 814 it began to break up. The Treaty of Verdun in 843 divided the French and German people for the first time, creating a Germanic Central Europe and a Latin Western Europe. The first king of the newly formed eastern kingdom was Ludwig the German and under him a specific German race and culture began to take shape. The last of Charlemagne's descendants died in 911 and with it the Carolingian dynasty. Power shifted, via Conrad I, duke of Franconia, to Henry I, duke of Saxony. Henry's son Otto the Great crushed the power of the hereditary duchies and by making grants of land to the Church he strengthened ties with Rome. His coronation as emperor of the Romans in 962 was the first to associate German kingship with the office of the Holy Roman Emperor.

Over two centuries, powerful dynasties emerged to threaten the emperor. After an intense feud the Hohenstaufens (of Swabia) gained supremacy over the Guelfs (the counts of Bavaria; later denoting anti-imperial loyalties and the papal faction) and managed to keep the upper hand for well over a century. Frederick Barbarossa, descended from both dynasties, led several expeditions to subjugate Italy and died on the Third Crusade. The Knights of the Teutonic Order set about converting Eastern Europe to Christianity and by the 14th century they had conquered much of the Baltic. By controlling the lucrative grain trade Germany grew rich.

Habsburg Rule

The Golden Bull of 1356 established the method for electing an emperor by setting up an Electoral College composed of seven princes or *electors*. Three of these were drawn from the church (the archbishops of Cologne, Mainz and Trier), and four from the nobility (the king of Bohemia, the duke of Saxony, the margrave of Brandenburg and the count palatine of the Rhine), all of whom had the right to build castles, mint their own coinage, impose taxes and act as judges. The title of Holy Roman Emperor nearly always went to an outsider and increasingly to members of the Austrian Habsburg dynasty. In 1273 Count Rudolph IV was the first Habsburg to be crowned king of the Germans. The Great Schism of 1378–1417, which resulted in rival popes holding court in Rome and Avignon, effectively ended the church's residual power over German affairs.

The Hundred Years War between France and England benefited the growing number of Free Imperial Cities along the German trading routes. Merchants and craftsmen organized themselves into guilds, wresting control of civic life away from the nobility and laying the foundations for a capitalist economy. Founded as a defence and trading league at Lübeck, the Hanseatic League combated piracy and established Germanic economic and political domination of the Baltic and North Sea. German communities were founded in Scandinavia and along the opposite coast as far as Estonia.

In the 14th century the bubonic plague wiped out a quarter of the German population. Rather than put the onus on their own tradesmen returning from Asia, it was the Jews, living in tightly-knit segregated communities, who were blamed. Excluded from guilds and trades they took to money lending, an occupation forbidden to Christians, and one which engendered envy and suspicion.

In 1273 Count Rudolph IV was the first Habsburg to be crowned king of the Germans. Over two centuries the Habsburg dynasty became increasingly powerful, retaining the title of Holy Roman Emperor from 1432 until its abolition nearly four centuries later. Succeeding to the title in 1493 Maximilian I gained the Netherlands by his marriage to Mary of Burgundy and control of Hungary and Bohemia by other marital alliances. Spain was added to the Habsburg dominions by the marriage of Maximilian's son, Philip, to Joanna the Mad.

Reformation

In the early part of the 15th century the unpopularity of the church was linked to the corrupt sale of indulgences. Land taxes were levied to pay for St Peter's Church and other sacred buildings in Rome. In 1517 an Augustinian monk named Martin Luther, professor of theology at the University of Wittenberg, made his famous protest with 95 Theses or arguments against indulgences. This open attack on the Church of Rome marked the beginning of the Reformation. Luther challenged the power of the pope, the privileged position of the priests and the doctrine of transubstantiation that had always been at the heart of Catholic dogma. But for the death of Maximilian I in 1519 and the subsequent power struggle for the title of Holy Roman Emperor, Luther might well have been executed as a heretic.

Following Maximilian's death, Francis I of France staked a claim to the succession in an attempt to avoid the concentration of power that would result in the election of the Habsburg candidate, Charles I of Spain. To placate the electors of Germany, the pope named Luther's patron, Frederick the Wise of Saxony, as a compromise candidate. This gained Luther only a temporary reprieve as, after much intrigue, the king of Spain was elected. Although Luther was excommunicated in 1520, he had the right to a hearing before an Imperial Diet (court). This was convened at Worms and although he was branded an outlaw and his books were ordered to be burned, he was given haven in Wartburg Castle where he translated the Bible into German. Thanks to the revolutionary system of printing invented by Johannes Gutenberg, Luther's ideas spread quickly throughout Germany. His doctrine of 'justification by faith alone', with its apparent invitation to resist the authority of the church, was one of the main causes of the Peasants' War of 1524–25 that led to wholesale destruction of monasteries and castles. To the surprise of the rebels, Luther aligned himself with the authorities and the uprising was crushed. The Reformation thus gained political authority. By 1555 so many of the small independent German states had joined the Protestant cause that Charles V admitted defeat and abdicated, retiring to a monastery in Spain. His brother Ferdinand succeeded him and signed the Peace of Augsburg. This agreement gave the secular rulers of each state the right to decide on religious practices (*cuius regio, eius religio*), so dividing Germany between Catholics and Lutherans.

© Springer Nature Limited 2020
Palgrave Macmillan (ed.), *The Statesman's Yearbook 2020*,
https://doi.org/10.1057/978-1-349-95940-2_78

Thirty Years War

Martin Luther died in 1546. The Catholics then launched a Counter-Reformation following the church reforms agreed at the Council of Trent. Bavaria's annexation of the mostly Protestant free city of Donauwörth in 1608 led to the formation of the Protestant Union, an armed alliance under the leadership of the Palatinate. The Catholic League was set up by the Bavarians the following year. Rudolf II, who reigned as emperor for 36 years, chose Prague as his power base, thus weakening his authority over his more distant territories. After he was deposed in 1611 a series of dynastic and religious conflicts set in train the Thirty Years' War. The countryside was laid waste, towns were pillaged and mass slaughter reduced the population by as much as a third. Although the Catholics were the early victors, Denmark and Sweden as well as Catholic France (who preferred the Protestants to the Habsburgs) backed the Protestants while Spain supported the Catholics. After repeated attempts to end the war, the Peace of Westphalia (signed in 1648) brought peace but deprived the emperor of much of his authority. Power was divided between 300 principalities and over 1,000 other territories.

In the 17th and 18th centuries the German princes consolidated their power. The Hanoverian branch of the Welf family inherited the British Crown in 1714; a royal union that was to last until 1837.

Meanwhile, the Habsburgs were struggling to hold on to the title of Holy Roman Emperor. The Turks reached Vienna in 1683 but after they were repulsed, the Austrians pushed eastwards and began to build up an empire in the Balkans. This left their western borders vulnerable where the French, who had long regarded the Rhine as the natural limit of their territory to their east, annexed Alsace and Strasbourg in 1688 and 1697. To the north, the presence of Brandenburg-Prussia under the Hohenzollern family was beginning to be felt. Throughout the 18th century Prussia was built up into a powerful independent state with its capital in Berlin. Strong militarism and a strict class-dominated society helped Prussia to become a major European power. When Frederick the Great came to the throne in 1740, he softened his country's military image by introducing reforms and by creating a cultured life at his court. His main preoccupation, however, continued to be expansion by force. His annexation of Silesia (under an old Brandenburg claim) provoked the Habsburgs to retaliate and, backed by Russia and France, they launched the Seven Years' War. Frederick had only the tacit support of Hanover and Britain to fall back on and, within three years, the Prussian armies were seriously overextended. But Frederick engineered a dramatic change in his fortunes by swelling the ranks of his armies with fresh recruits and in 1772, helped by the collapse of the alliance between Austria and Russia, he annexed most of Poland.

Unification

Revolutionary France had expanded east and when the left bank of the Rhine fell under French control during the War of the First Coalition of 1792–97 the way was paved for the unification of Germany. After Napoleon Bonaparte defeated Austria in 1802 he redrew the map of Germany. All but a few of the free German cities and all the ecclesiastical territories were stripped of their independence. In their place he created a series of buffer states. Bavaria, Württemberg and Saxony were raised to the status of kingdoms, with Baden and Hesse-Darmstadt as duchies. In 1806 the Holy Roman Empire was ended. The Habsburgs promoted themselves from archdukes to emperors of Austria and set about consolidating their position in the Balkans. After the defeat of Prussia and the occupation of Berlin by Napoleon, the country was forced to sign away half its territory. In the aftermath, Prussia abolished serfdom and allowed the cities their own municipal governments. Prussia played a critical role in the defeat of Napoleon at Waterloo in 1815. The Congress of Vienna, which met to determine the structure of post-Napoleon Europe, established Prussian dominance in German affairs. Westphalia and the Rhineland were added to its territories and although there were still 39 independent states, much of Napoleon's original vision for the reorganization of the Holy Roman Empire was ratified. A German Confederation was established, each state was represented in the Frankfurt-based Diet and Austria held the permanent right to the presidency with Prussia holding the vice-presidency.

The dominant political forces in Germany after the Congress of Vienna were conservative but the rapid advance of the industrial revolution brought about the emergence of a new social order, with wage-earning workers and a growing bourgeoisie. The workers were quick to agitate for better working conditions and the middle classes for political representation. Adding to the social unrest was the peasant class, whose poor living standards were made worse by the failed harvests of the late 1840s. By 1848 violence had erupted

all over Europe, forcing the Prussian king to allow elections to the National Assembly in Frankfurt. Although this presented an opportunity for the electorate to introduce liberal social reforms, the middle class members of the Assembly blocked all radical measures. When armed rebellions broke out in 1849, the National Assembly was disbanded and the Prussian army, backed by other German kingdoms and principalities, seized power. From the 1850s, Prussia was in an unassailable position. Realizing the importance of industrial might, Prussia became the driving force for creating a single German market.

Bismarck

In 1862 Wilhelm I appointed Otto von Bismarck as chancellor. Although a leading member of the Junker class, he set about introducing widespread reforms. In order to unite the liberal and conservative wings, he backed the demands for universal male suffrage and, in return for the Chancellor's support for a united Germany, the liberals supported his plans for modernizing the army. Bismarck persuaded Austria to back him in a war against Denmark, which resulted in the recapture of Schleswig and Holstein, and in a subsequent row with Austria over the spoils (the Seven Years' War) Austria was crushed by the superior strength of Prussian arms and military organization. Austria was forced out of German affairs and the previously neutral Hanover and Hesse-Kassel joined the other small German states under Prussia to form a North German Confederation. Bismarck still needed to bring the southern German states into the fold and, in 1870, he rallied all the German states to provoke a war with France. The outcome of the Franco-Prussian War of 1870–71 was the defeat of France and the creation of a united Germany (including the long disputed provinces of Alsace and Lorraine). Wilhelm I of Prussia was named kaiser and the empire was dubbed the Second Reich, commemorating the revival of German imperial tradition after a hiatus of 65 years.

At home, Bismarck continued with his liberal reforms. Uniform systems of law, currency, banking and administration were introduced nationwide, restrictions on trade and labour movements were lifted and the cities were given civic autonomy. These measures were designed to contain the liberals while he set about trying to undermine the influence of the Catholic Church. Although he forced the Catholics to support his agricultural policies designed to protect the interests of the Junker landowners, he had to back down on other issues. Despite the introduction of welfare benefits, opposition to Bismarck grew with the formation of the Social Democratic Party (SPD) in 1870.

Meanwhile, Bismarck was competing with Britain and France in the acquisition of colonies in Africa and the Pacific. In Germany he managed a political balancing act, on one hand creating an alliance of the three great imperial powers of Germany, Russia and Austria and on the other a Mediterranean alliance with Britain to prevent Russia from expanding into the Balkans. When Wilhelm I died in 1888, he was succeeded by his son, Friedrich III, who died after only a few months, and then by his grandson Kaiser Wilhelm II, a firm believer in the divine right of kings. After dismissing Bismarck from office in 1890, he appointed a series of 'yes men' to run his government, thereby seriously undermining the strength and stability that had been built up under Bismarck in the previous decade. Britain had long been an ally of Germany, bound by the ties of dynasty and common distrust of France but after the Kaiser came out in open support of the South African Boers, with whom Britain was in conflict, relations between the two countries plummeted and the European arms race accelerated. Bismarck's juggling of alliances collapsed and Europe was divided into two hostile camps. On one side, Germany was allied once more with Austria (who needed help in propping up her collapsing Eastern Empire) and with Italy. On the other, France and Russia, united in common mistrust of the German-speaking nations, drew Britain closer to them. The European war that was brewing was set in motion in 1914 when a Bosnian nationalist assassinated the Austrian Archduke Franz Ferdinand at Sarajevo. Austria sent a threatening memo falsely accusing Serbia of causing the assassination. This led Russia to mobilize in defence of her Slavic neighbours. Seeing this as an excuse to strike first, Germany attacked France. Belgium's neutrality (which had been guaranteed by Britain) was violated when the German armies marched through on their way to France and Britain declared war on Germany in 1914.

First World War

The German generals miscalculated the strength of the resistance from France and Russia. They had counted on a quick victory and when this did not happen, they were fighting on two fronts. A new form of warfare emerged with the digging of trenches all along Northern France and Belgium. The injury and loss of life suffered by both sides during the next four years was to devastate an entire generation of young men all over Europe. In 1917 the United States entered the war and although the Bolshevik revolution in Russia that same year gained Germany a reprieve, allowing the transfer of vast numbers of troops from the eastern to western fronts, the respite was short-lived. Troops returning from Russia agitated against the war. At the same time, the German lines were weakened by over-extension. On 8 Aug. 1918 the German defences were finally broken. In 1916 the Kaiser had handed over military and political power to Generals Paul von Hindenburg and Erich Ludendorff. As the threat of defeat came closer and in an attempt to minimize the potential damage of a harsh peace treaty, Ludendorff left peace negotiations to a parliamentary delegation. He felt they would be more likely to gain lenient terms and this might serve to nip a possible Bolshevik-style revolution in the bud. Two months of frenzied political activity followed which resulted in the abdication of the Kaiser and the announcement of a new German republic. The First World War ended on 11 Nov. 1918.

The Elections that followed confirmed the Social Democratic Party as the new political force in Germany. Friedrich Ebert, leader of the SPD, was made president, with Philipp Scheidemann as chancellor. In 1919 a new constitution was drawn up at Weimar and a republican government under Chancellor Ebert attempted to restore political and economic stability. But the Treaty of Versailles had exacted painful losses. The rich industrial regions of Saarland and Alsace-Lorraine were ceded to France and Upper Silesia was given to a resurrected Poland. A Polish corridor to the sea effectively cut off East Prussia from the rest of the country and all Germany's overseas colonies were confiscated. The Rhineland was declared a demilitarized zone and the size of the armed forces was severely limited. The German economy was burdened with a heavy reparation bill.

Feeling betrayed by what they saw as a harsh settlement, the German military fostered the 'stab in the back' excuse for failure, which was readily accepted by a disillusioned public. Scheidemann was forced to resign and in the elections of 1920 the SPD withdrew altogether, leaving power in the hands of minorities drawn from the liberal and moderate conservative parties. When, in 1923, reparation payments were withheld, France occupied the industrial region of the Ruhr. Passive resistance brought production to a halt and inflation ruined the middle class as the currency became worthless. Although the Weimar Republic seemed bound to fail, a new chancellor, Gustav Stresemann, ended passive resistance in the Ruhr and negotiated loans from the United States to help rebuild Germany's economy.

Rise of Hitler

By Oct. 1924 the currency was re-established at more or less its former value. Near full employment and general prosperity followed. Scheidemann went on to serve as foreign secretary when he re-established Germany as a world power. Reparation payments were scaled down and more US aid was negotiated. Even with the ailing and aged Hindenburg elected president, the German Republic seemed secure.

The National Socialist German Workers' Party was founded in 1918. Its first leader, a locksmith named Anton Drexler, was soon ousted by Adolf Hitler, a former soldier from Austria whose fanaticism had been fed by defeat in 1918. The party attracted political extremists and misfits whose views mixed the extremes of right- and left-wing opinion.

Putting his followers into uniform as the Brown Shirts or Storm Troopers (SA), Hitler led a failed *Putsch* in Bavaria in 1923. He was arrested and convicted of high treason. He served only nine months of his sentence and emerged having used his time in prison to write his political manifesto, *Mein Kampf*. Initially, sales of *Mein Kampf* were negligible and Hitler's views were treated as something of a joke. Only the power of his personality, and Joseph Goebbels's propaganda skills, sustained the National Socialists on the German political scene.

The recession of the late 1920s proved fertile ground for Hitler's ideas, which began to appeal to wounded national pride and seemed to offer an attractive solution to the growing economic crisis. Elections were held in 1930 and the Nazi party gained an astonishing 6·4m. votes, becoming the country's second largest party.

The young, the unemployed and the impoverished middle classes were Hitler's main supporters but it was the decision of the right-wing traditionalists to back Hitler in order to gain control over his supporters that gave him respectability. Financial support from leading industrialists and giant corporations followed, enabling the Nazi party to fight a strong campaign in the 1932 presidential elections. Hindenburg, backed by the SPD and other democratic parties, scraped a victory. Appointed chancellor, Heinrich

Brüning introduced a series of economic reforms, negotiated the end of reparation payments and regained Germany's right to arms equality. But his attempt to introduce land reform lost him the support of the landowners, who undermined his efforts to make the Republic work. Two short-term chancellors followed—Franz von Papen and Gen. Kurt von Schleicher. In 1932 one inconclusive election followed another. Hitler, greatly helped by a campaign of terror by his storm troopers, won increased support. Von Papen, who plotted to persuade Hindenburg to declare Hitler chancellor, mistakenly believed that his party's majority in the Reichstag would enable him to retain control. Hitler was sworn in as chancellor on 30 Jan. 1933.

No sooner had Hitler assumed power than he set about destroying all opposition, stepping up the campaign of terror, which was now backed by the apparatus of the state. He was greatly helped by Hermann Göring who, as Prussian minister of the interior, had control of the police. A month later, the Reichstag was burned down and Hindenburg was obliged to declare a state of emergency, giving Hitler the excuse to silence his opponents legally. Hitler was now the country's dictator, declaring himself president of the Third Reich in 1934.

Race to War

Hitler's policies embraced a theory of Aryan racial supremacy by which, during the following decade, millions of Jews, gypsies, and other non-Aryan 'undesirables' were persecuted, used as slave labour, shipped off to concentration camps, murdered and their assets confiscated. Hitler's expansionism led to his annexation of Austria (the *Anschluss*) and German-speaking Czechoslovakia (the Sudetenland) in 1938. The following year he declared all of Bohemia-Moravia a German protectorate and invaded Poland, attempting to restore the authority exercised there by Prussia before 1918. After the invasion of Czechoslovakia, Britain and France signed an agreement with Germany sacrificing Czech national integrity in return for what they believed would be world peace. Interpreting this as a sign of weakness, Hitler ordered the invasion of Poland, signed a non-aggression pact with Russia and expected a similar collapse of resistance on the part of other western powers. However, by now Britain and France had realized that the Munich agreement was a humiliating sham and that Hitler's invasion of Poland on 1 Sept. 1939 meant that he would pursue his expansionist policy of *Lebensraum* ('living space'). Two days after German tanks rolled into Poland, Britain and France declared war on Germany and the Second World War began.

Germany was well prepared for conflict and to begin with the war went well for Hitler. The fall of Poland was quickly followed by the defeat of the Low Countries and in 1940 France was forced to sign an armistice with Germany and to set up a puppet government in Vichy. Hitler bombarded Britain from the air but held back from invasion. Instead, he turned to the east, subduing the Balkans and, in 1941, planned an invasion of the Soviet Union. In Dec. 1941, after Hitler's Japanese allies attacked the United States naval base at Pearl Harbor, America declared war on the Axis powers. By this time, Germany was hopelessly overextended. Defeat in North Africa, in May 1943, was followed by the halt of the German advance on Russia. The Allies invaded France in June 1944, liberating Paris in Aug. while Russian troops advanced from the east. Hitler was faced with certain defeat but refused to surrender, ordering the German people to defend every square inch of German territory to the death. On 30 April 1945, as Soviet forces marched into Berlin, Hitler committed suicide in his bunker. Germany surrendered unconditionally on 7 May 1945, bringing the Third Reich to an end.

Post-War Period

The Allied forces occupied Germany—the UK, the USA and France holding the west and the USSR the east. By the Berlin Declaration of 5 June 1945 each was allocated a zone of occupation. The zone commanders-in-chief together made up the Allied Control Council in Berlin. The area of Greater Berlin was also divided into four sectors.

At the Potsdam Conference of 1945 northern East Prussia was transferred to the USSR. It was also agreed that, pending a final peace settlement, Poland should administer the areas east of the rivers Oder and Neisse, with the frontier fixed on the Oder and Western Neisse down to the Czechoslovak frontier.

By 1948 it had become clear that there would be no agreement between the occupying powers on the future of Germany. Accordingly, the western allies united their zones into one unit in March 1948. In protest, the USSR withdrew from the Allied Control Council, blockaded Berlin until May 1949, and consolidated control of eastern Germany, establishing the German Democratic Republic (East Germany).

A People's Council appointed in 1948 drew up a constitution for the German Democratic Republic (GDR) that came into force in Oct. 1949, providing for a communist state of five Länder with a centrally planned economy. In 1952 the government marked the division between its own territory and that of the Federal Republic of Germany (West Germany), with a three-mile cordon fenced along the frontier. Berlin was closed as a migration route by the construction of a concrete boundary wall in 1961. In 1953 there were popular revolts against food shortages and the pressure to collectivize. In 1954 the government eased economic restraints, the USSR ceased to collect reparation payments, and sovereignty was granted. The GDR signed the Warsaw Pact in 1955. Socialist policies were stepped up in 1958, leading to flight to the West of skilled workers.

Meanwhile, a constituent assembly met in Bonn in Sept. 1948. A Basic Law, which came into force in May 1949, created the Federal Republic of Germany. The occupation forces retained some powers, however, and the Republic did not become a sovereign state until 1955 when the Occupation Statute was revoked.

The Republic consisted of the states of Schleswig-Holstein, Hamburg, Lower Saxony, Bremen, North Rhine-Westphalia, Hessen, Rhineland-Palatinate, Baden-Württemberg, Bavaria and Saarland, together with West Berlin.

The first chancellor, Konrad Adenauer (1949–63), was committed to the ultimate reunification of Germany and refused to acknowledge the German Democratic Republic. It was not until 1972 that the two German states signed an agreement of mutual recognition and intent to co-operate, forged by West German Chancellor Willy Brandt.

The most marked feature of post-war West Germany was rapid population and economic growth. Immigration from the German Democratic Republic, about 3m. since 1945, stopped when the Berlin Wall was built in 1961; however, there was a strong movement of German-speaking people from German settlements in countries of the Soviet bloc. Industrial growth also attracted labour from Turkey, Yugoslavia, Italy and Spain.

Reunification

The Paris Treaty, which came into force in 1955, ensured the Republic's contribution to NATO and NATO forces were stationed along the Rhine in large numbers, with consequent dispute about the deployment of nuclear missiles on German soil. Even before sovereignty, the Republic had begun negotiations for a measure of European unity, and joined in creating the European Coal and Steel Community in 1951 and the European Economic Community in 1957. In Jan. 1957 the Saarland was returned to full German control. In 1973 the Federal Republic entered the UN.

In the autumn of 1989 movements for political liberalization in the GDR and reunification with the Federal Republic of Germany gathered strength. Erich Honecker and other long-serving Communist leaders were dismissed in Oct.–Nov. The Berlin Wall was breached on 9 Nov. Following the reforms in the GDR in Nov. 1989 the Federal Chancellor Helmut Kohl issued a plan for German confederation. The ambassadors of the four wartime allies met in Berlin in Dec. After talks with Chancellor Kohl on 11 Feb. 1990, Soviet General Secretary Mikhail Gorbachev said the USSR would raise no objection to German reunification. The Allies agreed a formula for reunification talks to begin after the GDR elections on 18 March. On 18 May the Federal Republic of Germany and the GDR signed a treaty extending the Federal Republic's currency, together with its economic, monetary and social legislation, to the GDR as of 1 July. On 23 Aug. the *Volkskammer* (the parliament of the GDR) by 294 votes to 62 'declared its accession to the jurisdiction of the Federal Republic as from 3 Oct. according to article 23 of the Basic Law', which provided for the Länder of pre-war Germany to accede to the Federal Republic. On 12 Sept. the Treaty on the Final Settlement with Respect to Germany was signed by the Federal Republic of Germany, the GDR and the four wartime allies: France, the USSR, the UK and the USA.

The single most important event in German post-war history took place on 3 Oct. 1990 with the reunification of the Federal Republic and the former GDR. That it happened at all was remarkable enough but that it was achieved without major social and political disruption was a huge tribute to the strength of a still young democracy. That is not to say that reunification has been trouble free. Notwithstanding the injection of billions of Deutsche Marks of public subsidy which transformed the infrastructure and restored urban areas, the easterners found the transition from communism to capitalism more painful than they had anticipated. Part of the problem was the adoption of the Deutsche Mark which, by virtue of its strength as an international currency, inspired confidence but at the same time made it harder for export markets in central and Eastern Europe to afford to buy

German. The collapse of much traditional industry in the east was hastened by wage equalization deals, pushing up labour costs.

The Federal Assembly (*Bundestag*) moved from Bonn to the renovated *Reichstag* in Berlin in 1999. As a psychological factor, the government move to Berlin was calculated to do much to bring eastern Germany back into the centre of national life as an equal part of the country. Gerhard Schröder served as chancellor from 1998 until 2005, when he was replaced by Angela Merkel of the Christian Democratic Union. She headed a 'grand coalition' of the Christian Democratic Union and the Social Democratic Party until securing a further term in 2009 with the Free Democratic Party as coalition partners. Her second term was dominated by instability within the eurozone but she secured a third term in Dec. 2013, following parliamentary elections in Sept., again leading a 'grand coalition' with the Social Democrats. In 2015 Germany was the focal point of a European refugee crisis. The country had received over 300,000 new asylum applications by migrants arriving from outside the European Union by the end of Oct., most of whom were fleeing Syria's civil war.

Territory and Population

Germany is bounded in the north by Denmark and the North and Baltic Seas, east by Poland, east and southeast by the Czech Republic, southeast and south by Austria, south by Switzerland and west by France, Luxembourg, Belgium and the Netherlands. Area: 357,582 sq. km. Population (2011 census), 80,219,695 (51·2% female) including Germans abroad. Population estimate, 31 Dec. 2017: 82,792,351; density 232 per sq. km. Of the total population in 2014, 65,223,097 lived in the former Federal Republic of Germany (excluding West Berlin) and 15,974,440 in the six new states of the former German Democratic Republic (including 3,469,849 in Berlin). In 2010, 73·8% of the population lived in urban areas. There were 40.22m. households in 2014 of which 40·8% were single-person. Germany has an ageing population. The proportion of the population over 60 has been steadily rising, and that of the under 20s steadily declining. By the mid-1990s the number of over 60s had surpassed the number of under 20s and now stands at 26·6% of the total population.

The UN gives a projected population for 2020 of 82·54m.

On 14 Nov. 1990 Germany and Poland signed a treaty confirming Poland's existing western frontier and renouncing German claims to territory lost as a result of the Second World War.

The capital is Berlin; the Federal German government moved from Bonn to Berlin in 1999.

The Federation comprises 16 *Bundesländer* (states). Area and population:

Bundesländer	Area in sq. km	Population (in 1,000) 1987 census	Population (in 1,000) Dec. 2017 estimate	Density per sq. km (2017)
Baden-Württemberg (BW)	35,748	9,286	11,023	308
Bavaria (BY)	70,542	10,903	12,997	184
Berlin (BE)[1]	891	—	3,613	4,055
Brandenburg (BB)[2]	29,654	—	2,504	84
Bremen (HB)	419	660	681	1,624
Hamburg (HH)	755	1,593	1,831	2,424
Hessen (HE)	21,116	5,508	6,243	296
Lower Saxony (NI)	47,710	7,162	7,963	167
Mecklenburg-West Pomerania (MV)[2]	23,294	—	1,611	69
North Rhine-Westphalia (NW)	34,112	16,712	17,912	525
Rhineland-Palatinate (RP)	19,858	3,631	4,074	205
Saarland (SL)	2,571	1,056	994	387

(continued)

Bundesländer	Area in sq. km	Population (in 1,000) 1987 census	Population (in 1,000) Dec. 2017 estimate	Density per sq. km (2017)
Saxony (SN)[2]	18,450	—	4,081	221
Saxony-Anhalt (ST)[2]	20,454	—	2,223	109
Schleswig-Holstein (SH)	15,804	2,554	2,890	183
Thuringia (TH)[2]	16,202	—	2,151	133

[1]1987 census population of West Berlin: 2,013,000.
[2]Reconstituted in 1990 in the Federal Republic.

On 31 Dec. 2014 there were 8,152,968 resident foreigners, including 1,527,118 Turks, 674,152 Poles, 574,530 Italians, 355,343 Romanians, 328,564 Greeks and 263,347 Croats. In 2016 Germany received 745,545 asylum applications (of which 722,370 first time applications), up from 28,018 in 2008. The main countries of origin in 2016 were Syria (36%) and Albania (12%). Tighter controls on entry from abroad were applied as from 1993. In 2013, 109,145 persons were naturalized, of whom 27,986 were from Turkey. In 2014 there were a record 914,241 emigrants and 1,464,724 immigrants (the highest number since 1992). In 2008 emigration exceeded immigration for the first time since the reunification of Germany in 1990. New citizenship laws were introduced on 1 Jan. 2000, whereby a child of non-Germans will have German citizenship automatically if the birth is in Germany, if at the time of the birth one parent has made Germany his or her customary legal place of abode for at least eight years, and if this parent has had an unlimited residence permit for at least three years. Previously at least one parent had to hold German citizenship for the child to become a German national. The coalition agreement of Nov. 2013 between the Christian Democratic Union and the Social Democratic Party introduced the provision that children born in Germany to foreign parents after 1990 will be allowed to hold dual citizenship.

Populations of the 80 towns of over 100,000 inhabitants in Dec. 2016 (in 1,000):

Town (and Bundesland)	Population (in 1,000)	Ranking by population
Aachen (NW)	245·0	30
Augsburg (BY)	290·0	23
Bergisch Gladbach (NW)	111·3	71
Berlin (BE)	3,574·8	1
Bielefeld (NW)	333·5	18
Bochum (NW)	364·9	16
Bonn (NW)	322·1	19
Bottrop (NW)	117·4	66
Braunschweig (NI)	248·7	27
Bremen (HB)	565·7	11
Bremerhaven (HB)	113·0	70
Chemnitz (SN)	246·4	29
Cologne/Köln (NW)	1,075·9	4
Cottbus (BB)	100·4	80
Darmstadt (HE)	157·4	52
Dortmund (NW)	585·8	8
Dresden (SN)	547·2	12
Duisburg (NW)	499·8	15
Düsseldorf (NW)	613·2	7
Erfurt (TH)	211·1	38
Erlangen (BY)	110·2	74
Essen (NW)	583·1	9
Frankfurt am Main (HE)	736·4	5
Freiburg im Breisgau (BW)	227·6	33
Fürth (BY)	125·4	59
Gelsenkirchen (NW)	262·5	25

(continued)

Town (and Bundesland)	Population (in 1,000)	Ranking by population
Göttingen (NI)	119·2	65
Hagen (NW)	188·3	41
Halle (ST)	238·0	32
Hamburg (HH)	1,810·4	2
Hamm (NW)	179·6	43
Hanover (NI)	532·9	13
Heidelberg (BW)	159·9	50
Heilbronn (BW)	123·8	63
Herne (NW)	156·8	53
Hildesheim (NI)	101·7	79
Ingolstadt (BY)	133·6	57
Jena (TH)	110·3	73
Karlsruhe (BW)	310·0	21
Kassel (HE)	199·1	40
Kiel (SH)	247·4	28
Koblenz (RP)	113·6	69
Krefeld (NW)	226·8	34
Leipzig (SN)	571·1	10
Leverkusen (NW)	163·1	49
Lübeck (SH)	216·7	35
Ludwigshafen am Rhein (RP)	166·6	46
Magdeburg (ST)	238·1	31
Mainz (RP)	213·5	36
Mannheim (BW)	304·8	22
Moers (NW)	103·9	76
Mönchengladbach (NW)	260·9	26
Mülheim a. d. Ruhr (NW)	170·9	45
Munich/München (BY)	1,464·3	3
Münster (NW)	311·8	20
Neuss (NW)	152·9	54
Nuremberg/Nürnberg (BY)	511·6	14
Oberhausen (NW)	211·4	37
Offenbach am Main (HE)	124·6	60
Oldenburg (NI)	165·7	47
Osnabrück (NI)	164·1	48
Paderborn (NW)	148·7	55
Pforzheim (BW)	123·5	64
Potsdam (BB)	171·8	44
Recklinghausen (NW)	114·0	68
Regensburg (BY)	148·6	56
Remscheid (NW)	110·6	72
Reutlingen (BW)	115·0	67
Rostock (MV)	207·5	39
Saarbrücken (SL)	179·7	42
Salzgitter (NI)	103·7	77
Siegen (NW)	101·9	78
Solingen (NW)	158·9	51
Stuttgart (BW)	628·0	6
Trier (RP)	110·1	75
Ulm (BW)	124·0	61
Wiesbaden (HE)	277·6	24
Wolfsburg (NI)	123·9	62
Wuppertal (NW)	352·4	17
Würzburg (BY)	126·0	58

The official language is German. Minor orthographical amendments were agreed in 1995. An agreement between German-speaking countries on 1 July 1996 in Vienna provided for minor orthographical changes and established a Commission for German Orthography in Mannheim. There have been objections within Germany, particularly in the North, and many *Bundesländer* are to decide their own language programmes for schools. Generally, both old and new spellings are acceptable.

Social Statistics

Calendar years:

	Marriages	Live births	Of these to single parents	Deaths	Divorces
2010	382,047	677,947	225,472	858,768	187,027
2011	377,816	662,685	224,744	852,328	187,640
2012	387,423	673,544	232,383	869,582	179,147
2013	373,655	682,069	237,562	893,825	169,833
2014	385,952	714,927	250,074	868,356	166,199

The annual number of births declined every year between 1997 and 2006 before rising in 2007, but it then fell again and the 2011 figure was a post-war low. Of the 373,655 marriages in 2013, 27,660 involved a foreign male and 33,519 involved a foreign female. The average age of bridegrooms in 2013 was 37·8 years, and of brides 34·7. The average first-time marrying age for men was 33·6 and for women 30·9.

Rates (per 1,000 population), 2014: birth, 8·8; death, 10·7; marriage, 4·8; divorce, 2·1; infant mortality (2013), 3·3 per 1,000 live births; stillborn rate, 3·7 per 1,000 live births. Life expectancy, 2013: men, 78·8 years; women, 83·4. Suicide rates, 2010, per 100,000 population, 12·3 (men, 18·6; women, 6·1). Annual population growth rate, 2001–11, –0·3%; fertility rate, 2013, 1·4 births per woman (one of the lowest rates in the world). Same-sex marriage became legal in Oct. 2017.

Since 1 Aug. 2001 same-sex couples have been permitted to exchange vows at registry offices. The law also gives them the same rights as heterosexual couples in inheritance and insurance law.

UNICEF reported that 15·1% of children in Germany in 2014 lived in relative poverty (living in a household in which disposable income—when adjusted for family size and composition—is less than 60% of the national median income), compared to 9·2% in Denmark (the world's lowest rate).

Climate

Oceanic influences are only found in the northwest where winters are quite mild but stormy. Elsewhere a continental climate is general. To the east and south, winter temperatures are lower, with bright frosty weather and considerable snowfall. Summer temperatures are fairly uniform throughout. Berlin, Jan. 31°F (–0·5°C), July 66°F (19°C). Annual rainfall 22·5" (563 mm). Cologne, Jan. 36°F (2·2°C), July 66°F (18·9°C). Annual rainfall 27" (676 mm). Dresden, Jan. 30°F (–0·1°C), July 65°F (18·5°C). Annual rainfall 27·2" (680 mm). Frankfurt, Jan. 33°F (0·6°C), July 66°F (18·9°C). Annual rainfall 24" (601 mm). Hamburg, Jan. 31°F (–0·6°C), July 63°F (17·2°C). Annual rainfall 29" (726 mm). Hanover, Jan. 33°F (0·6°C), July 64°F (17·8°C). Annual rainfall 24" (604 mm). Munich, Jan. 28°F (–2·2°C), July 63°F (17·2°C). Annual rainfall 34" (855 mm). Stuttgart, Jan. 33°F (0·6°C), July 66°F (18·9°C). Annual rainfall 27" (677 mm).

Constitution and Government

The Basic Law (*Grundgesetz*) was approved by the parliaments of the participating *Bundesländer* and came into force on 23 May 1949. It is to remain in force until 'a constitution adopted by a free decision of the German people comes into being'. The Federal Republic is a democratic and social constitutional state on a parliamentary basis. The federation is constituted by the 16 *Bundesländer* (states). The Basic Law decrees that the general rules of international law form part of the federal law. The constitutions of the *Bundesländer* must conform to the principles of a republican, democratic and social state based on the rule of law. Executive power is vested in the *Bundesländer*, unless the Basic Law prescribes or permits otherwise. Federal law takes precedence over state law.

Legislative power is vested in the *Bundestag* (Federal Assembly) and the *Bundesrat* (Federal Council). The Bundestag is currently composed of 709 members and is elected in universal, free, equal and secret elections for a term of four years. A party must gain 5% of total votes cast in order to gain representation in the Bundestag, although if a party has three candidates

elected directly, they may take their seats even if the party obtains less than 5% of the national vote. The electoral system combines relative-majority and proportional voting; each voter has two votes, the first for the direct constituency representative, the second for the competing party lists in the *Bundesländer*. There are 299 constituencies and therefore 598 directly elected members. Starting with the 2013 poll, further seats are allocated after the election in two phases. In each *Bundesland*, seats are allocated to party lists proportionate to their share of second votes, together with any 'overhang' seats (resulting from a party's surplus of directly elected seats over seats proportionate to its share of second votes). This prevents a party suffering any negative effect from gaining a lower share of second votes than its share of directly elected seats. In a second step, to ensure the parties' shares of seats in the *Bundestag* are proportionate to their vote at federal level, parties receive additional seats to balance 'overhang' mandates held by other parties. The Bundesrat consists of 69 members appointed by the governments of the *Bundesländer* in proportions determined by the number of inhabitants. Each *Bundesland* has at least three votes.

The Head of State is the Federal *President*, who is elected for a five-year term by a *Federal Convention* specially convened for this purpose. This Convention consists of all the members of the Bundestag and an equal number of members elected by the *Bundesländer* parliaments in accordance with party strengths, but who need not themselves be members of the parliaments. No president may serve more than two terms. Executive power is vested in the Federal government, which consists of the Federal *Chancellor*, elected by the Bundestag on the proposal of the Federal President, and the Federal Ministers, who are appointed and dismissed by the Federal President upon the proposal of the Federal Chancellor.

The Federal Republic has exclusive legislation on: (1) foreign affairs; (2) federal citizenship; (3) freedom of movement, passports, immigration and emigration, and extradition; (4) currency, money and coinage, weights and measures, and regulation of time and calendar; (5) customs, commercial and navigation agreements, traffic in goods and payments with foreign countries, including customs and frontier protection; (6) federal railways and air traffic; (7) post and telecommunications; (8) the legal status of persons in the employment of the Federation and of public law corporations under direct supervision of the Federal government; (9) trade marks, copyright and publishing rights; (10) co-operation of the Federal Republic and the *Bundesländer* in the criminal police and in matters concerning the protection of the constitution, the establishment of a Federal Office of Criminal Police, as well as the combating of international crime; (11) federal statistics.

In the field of finance the Federal Republic has exclusive legislation on customs and financial monopolies and concurrent legislation on: (1) excise taxes and taxes on transactions, in particular, taxes on real estate acquisition, incremented value and on fire protection; (2) taxes on income, property, inheritance and donations; (3) real estate, industrial and trade taxes, with the exception of the determining of the tax rates.

Federal laws are passed by the Bundestag and after their adoption submitted to the Bundesrat, which has a limited veto. The Basic Law may be amended only upon the approval of two-thirds of the members of the Bundestag and two-thirds of the votes of the Bundesrat.

Staatshandbuch Bund. Annual

National Anthem

'Einigkeit und Recht und Freiheit' ('Unity and right and freedom'); words by H. Hoffmann, tune by J. Haydn.

Government Chronology

Federal Republic of Germany (prior to reunification).

Chancellors since 1949 (CDU = Christian Democratic Union; FDP = Free Democratic Party; SPD = Social Democratic Party)

1949–63	CDU	Konrad Adenauer
1963–66	CDU	Ludwig Erhard
1966–69	CDU	Kurt Georg Kiesinger
1969–74	SPD	Willy Brandt
1974	FDP	Walter Scheel
1974–82	SPD	Helmut Schmidt
1982–90	CDU	Helmut Kohl

German Democratic Republic = Presidents of the Republic (1949–60) then Leaders of the Council of State. (LDPD = Liberal Democratic Party of Germany; SED = Socialist Unity Party of Germany)

1949	LDPD	Johannes Dieckmann
1949–60	SED	Willhelm Pieck
1960	LDPD	Johannes Dieckmann
1960–73	SED	Walter Ulbricht
1973	SED	Friedrich Ebert
1973–76	SED	Willi Stoph
1976–89	SED	Erich Honecker
1989	SED	Egon Krenz
1989–90	LDPD	Manfred Gerlach

Federal Republic of Germany.

Chancellors since reunification. (CDU = Christian Democratic Union; FDP = Free Democratic Party; SPD = Social Democratic Party; n/p = non-partisan)

1990–98	CDU	Helmut Kohl
1998–2005	SPD	Gerhard Schröder
2005–	CDU	Angela Merkel

Presidents since 1949.

1949–59	FDP	Theodor Heuss
1959–69	CDU	Karl Heinrich Lübke
1969–74	SPD	Gustav Heinemann
1974–79	FDP	Walter Scheel
1979–84	CDU	Karl Carstens
1984–94	CDU	Richard von Weizsäcker
1994–99	CDU	Roman Herzog
1999–2004	SPD	Johannes Rau
2004–10	CDU	Horst Köhler
2010	SPD	Jens Böhrnsen (acting)
2010–12	CDU	Christian Wulff
2012	CSU	Horst Seehofer (acting)
2012–17	n/p	Joachim Gauck
2017–	SPD	Frank-Walter Steinmeier

Recent Elections

On 12 Feb. 2017 Frank-Walter Steinmeier was elected Federal President by the Federal Convention with 931 votes, against 128 for Christoph Butterwegge and three other candidates. There were 103 abstentions.

Bundestag elections were held on 24 Sept. 2017. The Christian Democratic Union/Christian Social Union of Chancellor Angela Merkel (CDU/CSU; the CSU is a Bavarian party where the CDU does not stand) won 246 seats with 32·9% of votes cast (311 with 41·5% in 2013); the Social Democratic Party (SPD) won 153 with 20·5% (193 seats with 25·7%); Alternative for Germany (AfD), which was only formed in Feb. 2013, 94 with 12·6% (no seats and 4·7% in 2013); the Free Democratic Party (FDP), 80 with 10·7% (no seats and 4·8% in 2013); the Left Party (Linke), 69 with 9·2% (64 with 8·6%); and Alliance '90/the Greens (Grüne), 67 with 8·9% (63 with 8·4%). Turnout was 76·2% (71·5% in 2013).

European Parliament

Germany has 96 representatives. At the May 2014 elections turnout was 48·1% (43·3% in 2009). The CDU/CSU won 34 seats—CDU 29 and CSU 5—with 35·3% of votes cast (political affiliation in European Parliament: European People's Party); the SPD, 27 with 27·3% (Progressive Alliance of Socialists and Democrats); Alliance '90/the Greens, 11 with 10·7% (Greens/European Free Alliance); the Left Party, 7 with 7·4% (European Left/Nordic Green Left); AfD, 7 with 7·0% (European Conservatives and Reformists); FDP, 3 with 3·4% (Alliance of Liberals and Democrats for Europe); Free Voters, 1 with 1·5% (Alliance of Liberals and Democrats for Europe); Pirate Party, 1 with 1·4% (Greens/European Free Alliance); Animal Protection Party, 1 with 1·2% (European United Left/Nordic Green Left); National Democratic Party of Germany, 1 with 1·0% (non-attached); Family Party, 1 with 0·7% (European Conservatives and Reformists); Ecological Democratic Party, 1 with 0·6% (Greens/European Free Alliance); the PARTEI, 1 with 0·6% (non-attached).

Current Government

Federal President: Frank-Walter Steinmeier; b. 1956 (SPD; since 19 March 2017).

Chancellor: Angela Merkel; b. 1954 (CDU; sworn in 22 Nov. 2005, and re-elected in Sept. 2009, Sept. 2013 and March 2018). In Feb. 2019 the cabinet comprised:

Vice Chancellor and Minister of Finance: Olaf Scholz (SPD). *Defence:* Ursula von der Leyen (CDU). *Economic Affairs and Energy:* Peter Altmaier (CDU). *Economic Co-operation and Development:* Gerd Müller (CSU). *Education and Research:* Anja Karliczek (CDU). *Environment, Nature Conservation and Nuclear Safety:* Svenja Schulze (SPD). *Family Affairs, Senior Citizens, Women and Youth:* Franziska Giffey (SPD). *Food and Agriculture:* Julia Klöckner (CDU). *Foreign Affairs:* Heiko Maas (SPD). *Health:* Jens Spahn (CDU). *Interior:* Horst Seehofer (CSU). *Justice and Consumer Protection:* Katarina Barley (SPD). *Labour and Social Affairs:* Hubertus Heil (SPD). *Transport and Digital Infrastructure:* Andreas Scheuer (CSU). *Head of the Federal Chancellery and Minister for Special Tasks:* Helge Braun (CDU).

President of the Bundestag: Wolfgang Schäuble (CDU; elected Oct. 2017).

Government Website: http://www.bundesregierung.de

Current Leaders

Frank-Walter Steinmeier

Position
President

Introduction
Frank-Walter Steinmeier was elected president in Feb. 2017. A former leader of the Social Democratic Party (SPD), he twice served as foreign minister under federal Chancellor Angela Merkel.

Early Life
Steinmeier was born in Detmold, North Rhine-Westphalia, on 5 Jan. 1956. He undertook his military service from 1974–76 before studying law and political science at the Justus-Liebig University in Giessen. After completing a doctorate in law, he began working for the Chancellery of Lower Saxony and by 1992 was director of the personal office of the prime minister of the Bundesland, Gerhard Schröder. Steinmeier was subsequently Schröder's chief of staff when the latter served as federal Chancellor between 1998 and 2005.

When Merkel succeeded Schröder in 2005, she appointed Steinmeier as foreign minister in a grand coalition between his SPD and her Christian Democratic Union (CDU). He was the first SPD politician to hold the office since Willy Brandt relinquished the post in 1969.

Steinmeier developed a good working relationship with Merkel despite their differing views on Russia—he favoured his party's more diplomatic *Ostpolitik* approach to Moscow. Steinmeier's first period as foreign minister ended in 2009 when he became the SPD's candidate for the federal chancellorship. Despite the party's worst electoral showing since the Second World War, he was subsequently chosen to lead the party in opposition.

He was reappointed foreign minister in 2013 and enjoyed high approval ratings. In Jan. 2017 he resigned the post for a second time, this time to run for the presidency. He was elected with the support of 931 out of 1,260 members in the Federal Convention on 12 Feb. 2017 and was sworn in on 19 March 2017.

Career in Office
While largely a ceremonial role, the president's office nonetheless commands a high profile that Steinmeier used early in his tenure to criticize the conduct of the newly-elected populist US leader, Donald Trump. In the *Bundestag* elections in Sept. 2017, the ruling CDU and its SPD coalition partner both suffered damaging losses, prompting a long period of political deadlock.

Steinmeier had the potential options of reappointing incumbent Chancellor Angela Merkel to lead a minority CDU administration or dissolving the *Bundestag* and calling new elections until both parties reached an agreement in Feb. 2018 (subsequently endorsed by their respective memberships by early March) to renew their previous coalition pact.

Angela Merkel

Position
Chancellor

Introduction
Angela Merkel became Germany's first female chancellor in Nov. 2005. Her appointment followed federal elections that failed to give a parliamentary majority to either her party, the Christian Democrats (CDU), or the Social Democrats (SPD) of incumbent Gerhard Schröder. Despite her initial success in re-energizing Germany's economy, global turmoil in financial markets led to recession in 2008, which highlighted differences in her CDU–SPD coalition over the appropriate policy response. She was nevertheless returned as chancellor following the elections of Sept. 2009. In her second term economic concerns at home and abroad remained centre-stage. She was sworn in for a third term in Dec. 2013, again at the head of a CDU–SPD coalition after elections in Sept. While addressing weak economic growth in the eurozone remained a priority, from 2015 Merkel's attention was focused increasingly on the impact of the foreign refugee and migrant crisis in Germany and across the European Union as a whole, and the concurrent rise of right-wing, anti-immigrant sentiment among voters. In the federal elections in Sept. 2017, the CDU remained the largest party but lost over 60 seats, heralding four months of political wrangling before Merkel reached agreement with the SPD in Feb. 2018 to renew the previous coalition pact. Despite considerable reservations, the deal was endorsed by both party memberships by early March. In Oct. 2018 Merkel confirmed that she was willing to remain as chancellor until the federal polls scheduled for 2021, but announced that she was stepping down as leader of the CDU from Dec. when the post was up for biennial election.

Early Life
Angela Dorothea Kasner was born on 17 July 1954 in Hamburg, West Germany, the daughter of a Lutheran pastor and a teacher. Later in 1954 her father received a pastorship in East Germany (GDR) and the family moved to Templin, where Merkel was educated before studying physics at the University of Leipzig from 1973–78. Having married Ulrich Merkel in 1977, she continued her studies at the Academy of Sciences in East Berlin, receiving a doctorate in 1986.

Following the fall of the Berlin Wall in Nov. 1989 and the democratic elections in the GDR on 18 March 1990, Merkel became a member of the East German Christian Democratic Union (CDU). She was elected to the *Bundestag* in the first post-unification general elections in Dec. 1990, representing the united CDU, and was appointed to Chancellor Helmut Kohl's cabinet as minister for women and youth—a position she held until being promoted to minister for the environment in 1994.

Merkel lost office in 1998 when the CDU was defeated in federal elections but later that year was appointed secretary-general of the party. A funding scandal implicating the party's chairman, Wolfgang Schäuble, then Kohl himself then thrust Merkel into the political limelight. She criticized Kohl (who was later stripped of his CDU honorary chairmanship) and was elected party president in April 2000.

Unable to garner sufficient support to challenge Chancellor Schröder in the 2002 federal elections, Merkel ceded that role to Edmund Stoiber, leader of the CDU's sister party, the Bavarian Christian Social Union (CSU). Following Stoiber's narrow defeat, Merkel became leader of the conservative opposition in the *Bundestag*.

In May 2005 Merkel won the CDU/CSU nomination to challenge Schröder in the Sept. 2005 elections, in which the CDU/CSU won 35·2% of the vote to the SPD's 34·2%. A deal for a grand coalition was eventually reached whereby Merkel became chancellor and the SPD took eight of the 14 cabinet posts.

Career in Office
Merkel won plaudits for brokering an EU budget deal between France and Britain within weeks of becoming chancellor. However, countering the sluggish German economy and delivering health care and tax reforms were more challenging. Nevertheless, by Aug. 2006 she had claimed a reduction in the budget deficit and lower unemployment, and in the first half of 2007 the public sector recorded a surplus for the first time since unification.

Meanwhile, Merkel was instrumental in facilitating agreement on a new draft treaty streamlining the EU's institutional structure and decision-making process (which, officially concluded as the Treaty of Lisbon in Dec. 2007, eventually entered into force in Dec. 2009).

In March 2008 she became the first German head of government to address the Israeli parliament during a visit marking the 60th anniversary of the founding of Israel.

As the global financial crisis began to bite in 2008, Germany's economy slipped into recession and the government made €500bn. available in loan guarantees and capital to bolster the banking system. Merkel remained unconvinced about the wisdom of the huge economic stimulus packages unveiled by many of her EU partners but she did endorse a co-ordinated recovery package agreed at an EU summit in Dec. that year.

The CDU was the largest German party in the elections to the European Parliament in June 2009 and increased its majority in the federal elections in Sept. In Oct. Merkel was sworn in as chancellor for a second term leading a new centre-right coalition with the Free Democratic Party (FDP).

Meanwhile, the growing debt crisis in the eurozone led to large bailout packages for some partner states, which Merkel reluctantly endorsed. This proved unpopular with the German public, prompting CDU losses in regional elections in several states. She nevertheless strived to build a political consensus on containing Europe's debt problems. She helped negotiate a treaty change proposing greater fiscal union in the eurozone and also, in 2012, a rescue strategy for struggling eurozone economies (through the European Stability Mechanism) in return for stricter budgetary discipline.

In contrast to Merkel's controversial backing for the 2003 US-led invasion of Iraq, her government abstained in the United Nations Security Council vote in March 2011 sanctioning NATO military intervention to protect civilians against the Gaddafi regime in Libya.

Following the disaster in Japan at the Fukushima nuclear power plant, the German government announced in May 2011 that all of Germany's nuclear power stations would be phased out by 2022 in a transition to solar and wind power generation.

Merkel secured a further term as chancellor after the CDU/CSU won the federal elections in Sept. 2013 with 41·5% of the vote. However, without an overall parliamentary majority or the option of renewing the partnership with the FDP (which failed to gain any representation) she forged another coalition with the SPD following several weeks of negotiation. She was sworn in at the head of a new CDU-led government, which included six SPD ministers, in Dec.

In Oct. 2013, following earlier revelations about the worldwide covert electronic surveillance activities of the US National Security Agency (NSA), Merkel expressed her anger to then US President Barack Obama over reports that the NSA had tapped her mobile phone.

In Oct. 2014 Merkel recorded an almost 80% approval rating despite increasing criticism, both at home and abroad, of her economic policies. There were calls for more stimulation of domestic consumption and public investment in the hope of preventing deflation in the still fragile eurozone. Her decision to introduce a national minimum wage for the first time from Jan. 2015 also attracted concern among some economic think tanks. On the international stage, she took the lead among EU countries in criticizing Russian interference in the affairs of Ukraine during 2014.

In 2015 Merkel's attentions were increasingly drawn to the escalating refugee and migrant influx into the EU from predominantly Middle Eastern and African countries and its impact on EU free movement conventions and border controls. Initially adopting an open-door approach, she insisted in Aug. that Germany could cope with the record numbers aiming to reach her country. However, in the wake of opposition from within her own conservative ranks and a public backlash against asylum seekers following sex attacks on German women in some cities during New Year celebrations, she promised in Jan. 2016 to reduce the number of migrant entrants and to make deportation easier. The depth of populist disaffection was further reflected in the poor showing of the CDU in several state elections in 2016, aggravated by a series of security incidents in July and a more serious Islamist terror attack in Berlin in Dec. that left 12 people dead and many more injured. Having announced in Nov. that she planned to stand for a fourth term as chancellor in elections in 2017, Merkel pledged at her party's annual conference the following month—where she was re-elected as leader—that she would never repeat her open-door refugee policy and called for a ban on the Muslim burqa dress code in Germany wherever legally possible. At the same time she promised to defend the European Union in the wake of the earlier British referendum decision in June 2016 to initiate a withdrawal from EU membership.

The CDU and SPD both suffered substantial losses in the elections in Sept. 2017, losing ground to the far-right, anti-immigration Alternative for Germany, which resulted in an unusually fragmented parliament. The SPD, which recorded a record-low vote, initially ruled out a continuation of the existing coalition, heralding a potential political crisis. Talks between the CDU and the FDP and Greens collapsed in Nov., but the SPD were enticed back into negotiations with Merkel and in Jan. 2018 the parties announced that they would launch formal talks on a new coalition government, despite considerable misgivings among rank and file SPD members. Agreement on a new pact was nevertheless reached in Feb. and subsequently endorsed by both parties. However, policy divisions between the CDU and its CSU sister party and squabbling within the coalition government, particularly over the simmering issue of refugee migration, undermined Merkel's authority over the course of the year. In Oct. she announced her intention to see out her current term as chancellor, but she relinquished the CDU leadership in Dec.

Defence

Germany officially ended its compulsory military service on 1 July 2011. In July 1994 the Constitutional Court ruled that German armed forces might be sent on peacekeeping missions abroad. Germany has increased the number of professionals available for military missions abroad and sent troops to Afghanistan as part of the international alliance against terrorism in the aftermath of 11 Sept. 2001. The first time that German armed forces were deployed in this way since the Second World War, the move provoked controversy in Germany. In 2014 there were 3,200 German troops abroad. In addition to those in Afghanistan (nearly half of all German troops deployed abroad) there were German peacekeepers in various parts of the world including the Horn of Africa/Indian Ocean, Kosovo, Mali and Turkey. There have also been German troops in Lithuania since early 2017 as part of a multinational NATO battalion deployed in the country. Since 2001 women have been allowed to serve in all branches of the military on the same basis as men.

The total strength of the *Bundeswehr* (Federal Defence Forces of Germany) in Oct. 2012 was 195,893, including 7,132 in the vocational training service. In 2013 defence expenditure totalled US$44,201m. (US$545 per capita), representing 1·2% of GDP (compared to the NATO target of 2%). As a proportion of GDP, defence spending has halved since the reunification of Germany in 1990. In the early 1960s it had exceeded 4% of GDP.

Arms Trade

Germany is the world's fifth largest exporter after the USA, Russia, China and France, with 5·6% of the global major weapons total over the period 2012–16.

Army

The Army is organized in the Army Forces Command. The equipment of the former East German army is in store. Total strength was 70,062 in Oct. 2012. In Feb. 2017 Germany signed an agreement with Romania and the Czech Republic whereby the latter two countries would each contribute a brigade to a German-led multinational division. The move followed an earlier agreement between the Netherlands and Germany, under which two Dutch army units came under the command of the German army beginning in 2014.

The Territorial Army is organized into five Military Districts, under three Territorial Commands. Its main task is to defend rear areas and remains under national control even in wartime.

Navy

The Navy Command, formed in 2012 from a merger of the Navy Office, Naval Staff and Fleet Command, has its headquarters in Rostock.

In 2011 the fleet included four attack submarines, seven destroyers and 11 frigates. The main naval bases are at Wilhelmshaven, Kiel, Eckernförde and Warnemünde.

The Naval Air Arm, 2,200 strong in 2011, is organized into two wings and includes eight combat-capable aircraft (Orions) and 22 Lynx helicopters.

Personnel in Oct. 2012 numbered 15,852.

Air Force

The high command of the German Air Force is the Air Force Command, formed in 2013 through the merger of the Air Force Office, the German Air Staff and the Air Force Forces Command. Personnel in Oct. 2012 was 33,449. In 2017 the Air Force had 39 Eurofighter jets ready for action, 26 Tornado Jets and 12 Tiger attack helicopters.

Economy

Services accounted for 69·0% of GDP in 2014, industry 30·3% and agriculture 0·7%. Manufacturing's share of total GDP was 22·6%.

According to the anti-corruption organization Transparency International, Germany ranked equal 11th in the world in a 2018 survey of the countries with the least corruption in business and government. It received 80 out of 100 in the annual index.

In terms of total aid given, Germany was the second most generous country in the world in 2017 after the USA, donating US$25·0bn. in international aid in the course of the year. This represented 0·67% of GNI.

Overview

Germany has Europe's largest economy and is the world's second largest exporter of manufactured goods, behind China. The principal manufacturing sectors are the motor and chemical industries, with telecommunications an increasingly important growth area. However, the country's heavy dependence on exports (with an exports-to-GDP ratio of 47·2% in 2017) leaves it vulnerable to global slowdowns and recessions.

The economy is described as a 'social market' in that it embraces enlightened company management and social welfare. Companies are managed on the 'stakeholder' concept (meaning that they are responsible not only to their shareholders but also to employees, customers, suppliers and local communities), although this system is changing in response to globalization and the ending of large cross-shareholdings by companies and banks.

West Germany's post-Second World War economic miracle (*Wirtschaftswunder*) was marked by prudent fiscal and monetary policy, the growth of a globally competitive manufacturing sector and good industrial relations. However, the reunification of Germany in 1989 proved costly for the more prosperous West Germans. Relatively low growth in the post-unification years was attributed to weaknesses in the labour market and the high cost of restructuring the economy of the former East Germany. GDP growth, which had averaged 4·5% per annum in the 1960s, had slowed to less than 1% in the first five years of the 2000s, the lowest in the eurozone alongside Italy.

There was a resurgence in 2006, but the global financial crisis put renewed strain on the economy and the government was required to intervene in the markets on several occasions. In Oct. 2008 the finance ministry agreed a €50bn. plan to rescue Hypo Real Estate, one of the country's biggest banks. In Jan. 2009 the government announced a €50bn. stimulus package of public investment and tax cuts aimed at halting a descent into severe recession, alongside a €100bn. fund to underwrite fresh credit to companies starved of new loans. Having experienced an overall contraction in 2009 and limited annual expansion thereafter, the economy moved up a gear in 2017, with growth of 2·2%—the highest rate since 2011, driven in part by recovery among eurozone trading partners that boosted exports and investment. The construction sector was also buoyed by the housing needs of immigrants, while higher incomes and low interest rates increased domestic housing demand. In addition, the government stepped up spending on transport infrastructure and schools.

The financial crisis had seen an increase in public debt from 65% of GDP in 2007 to 84% in 2014, before dropping to 80% in 2015, 76·3% in 2016, 72·4% in 2017 and 59·8% in 2018. Having achieved a balanced budget in 2008 (for the first time since 1969), Germany's budget deficit reached 4·2% of GDP in 2010. This was above the 3% target set by the European Union's Stability and Growth Pact, but the deficit has since stayed below that ceiling. In June 2010 Chancellor Merkel announced €80bn. worth of expenditure cuts, including lower welfare and unemployment benefits, reduced defence spending (by some 10% by 2015) and a tax on air travel. These measures aimed to reduce the structural deficit from 2·5% of GDP in 2010 to 0·35% by 2016 (as required by an amendment to the constitution) and to 'set an example' for the rest of Europe. As a result of these structural reforms, Germany achieved a balanced budget in 2014 and the deficit fell to 0·7% in 2015. In 2017 the government recorded a budget surplus of almost €37bn., the highest since German reunification, although it fell to €11·2bn. in 2018.

Labour market reforms prompted by the global financial crisis saw joblessness fall to post-unification lows of 4·1% in 2016, 3·7% in 2017 and 3·4% in 2018. Female labour market participation is increasing and more women work longer hours, reflecting in part improved childcare provision.

Among the challenges the economy faces are risks related to the impact of the UK's exit from the European Union, which it is feared may disrupt the sourcing of inputs in key German industries, including automotive production and chemicals. On the other hand, some international businesses have announced an intention to transfer their bases away from the UK to Germany. Moreover, steps to implement reforms to the EU's single market and to establish a more comprehensive banking union in the eurozone could strengthen confidence in the euro and boost Germany's attractiveness as an investment destination.

Currency

On 1 Jan. 1999 the *euro* (EUR) became the legal currency in Germany at the irrevocable conversion rate of 1·95583 DM (Deutsche Mark) to one euro. The euro, which consists of 100 cents, has been in circulation since 1 Jan. 2002. It was still possible to make cash transactions in German marks until 28 Feb. 2002, although formally the mark had ceased to be legal tender on 31 Dec. 2001.

Foreign exchange reserves were US$37,492m. in Sept. 2009 and gold reserves were 109·56m. troy oz. Only the USA, with 261·50m. troy oz, had more in Sept. 2009. Total money supply was €934,352m. in Aug. 2009.

Inflation rates (based on OECD statistics):

2008	2009	2010	2011	2012	2013	2014	2015	2016	2017
2·8%	0·2%	1·1%	2·5%	2·1%	1·6%	0·8%	0·1%	0·4%	1·7%

The inflation rate in 2018 according to Destatis, the Federal Statistical Office, was 1·9%.

Budget

After winning the 2009 election, Chancellor Merkel's CDU agreed upon a coalition agreement with the liberal FDP based on major tax cuts. In June 2011 the government announced plans to introduce tax cuts worth up to €10bn. within two years. In the space of ten years corporate taxes were cut from 51·6% in 2000 to 29·8% in 2010, a drop of almost 22%.

VAT is (since 1 Jan. 2007) 19% (reduced rate, 7%). The federal government and the *Bundesländer* each receive 42·5% of income tax and the local authorities 15%. Corporation tax is equally split between the federal government and the *Bundesländer*. In 2014 the federal government received approximately 53·5% of VAT, the *Bundesländer* around 44·5% and the local authorities about 2%.

Budget for 2014 (in €1m.):

	All public authorities	Federal portion
Revenue	*Current*	
Taxes	1,091,349	229,065
Economic activities	28,983	9,520
Interest	14,015	8,748
Current allocations and subsidies	570,994	30,733
Other receipts	61,839	14,725
minus equalising payments	544,346	21,304
Total	1,222,834	341,488
Revenue	*Capital*	
Sale of assets	11,100	2,831
Capital transfers	23,527	437
Repayment of loans	8,283	1,894
Public sector borrowing	889	–
*minus*equalising payments	21,028	78
Total	22,772	5,084
Total revenues	*1,245,605*	*346,572*
Expenditure	*Current*	
Staff	254,939	46,330
Materials	338,204	28,546
Interest	56,735	33,906
Current allocations and subsidies	1,043,128	224,387
minus equalising payments	544,346	21,304
Total	1,148,659	311,865

Expenditure	*Capital*	
Construction	34,422	7,395
Acquisition of property	12,651	1,947
Capital transfers	44,637	17,664
Loans	7,664	1,036
Acquisition of shares	11,249	4,424
Repayments in the public sector	1,436	20
minus equalising payments	21,028	78
Total	91,030	32,408
Total expenditures	*1,239,689*	*344,273*

In 2017 Germany registered a budget surplus of 1·0% of GDP. There were also surpluses of 0·9% in 2016 and 0·8% in 2015. The required target set by the EU is a budget deficit of no more than 3%. In 2014 Germany balanced the federal budget for the first time since 1969.

Performance

Real GDP growth rates (based on OECD statistics):

2008	2009	2010	2011	2012	2013	2014	2015	2016	2017
0·8%	−5·6%	3·9%	3·7%	0·7%	0·6%	2·2%	1·5%	2·2%	2·5%

Germany had four quarters of negative growth from the second quarter of 2008 but emerged from recession in the second quarter of 2009. The real GDP growth rate in 2018 according to Destatis, the Federal Statistical Office, was 1·5%. Total GDP in 2017 was US$3,677·4bn., the fourth highest in the world.

Banking and Finance

The Deutsche Bundesbank (German Federal Bank) is the central bank and bank of issue. Its duty is to protect the stability of the currency. It is independent of the government but obliged to support the government's general policy. Its Governor is appointed by the government for eight years. The *President* is Jens Weidmann. Its assets were €671,259m. in Dec. 2010. The largest private banks are the Deutsche Bank, Commerzbank, Dresdner Bank and DZ Bank. In April 2001 Dresdner Bank accepted a takeover offer from Allianz, the country's largest insurance company. Commerzbank in turn agreed to buy Dresdner Bank from Allianz in Aug. 2008. In June 2005 Italy's UniCredit finalized an agreement to acquire HypoVereinsbank in Europe's biggest cross-border banking takeover.

In 2014 there were 1,990 credit institutes, including 296 credit banks, 416 savings banks and 1,050 credit unions. They are represented in the wholesale market by nine public sector *Landesbanken*. Total assets of banks, 2014, €7,853,364m. Savings deposits were €617,002m. in 2014. In 2011 approximately 44% of the German population were using online banking.

A single stock exchange, the Deutsche Börse, was created in 1992, based on the former Frankfurt stock exchange in a union with the smaller exchanges in Berlin, Bremen, Düsseldorf, Hamburg, Hanover, Munich and Stuttgart. Frankfurt processes 90% of equities trading in the country.

Gross external debt amounted to US$5,617,751m. in June 2012.

Germany attracted US$34·7bn. worth of foreign direct investment in 2017.

Gull, L., *et al., The Deutsche Bank, 1870–1995.* 1996

Energy and Natural Resources

In 2011, 12·3% of energy consumption came from renewables (wind power, solar power, hydro-electric power, tidal power, geothermal energy and biomass), compared to the European Union average of 13·0%. A target of 18% has been set by the EU for 2020.

Environment

Carbon dioxide emissions from the consumption of energy were the equivalent of 9·6 tonnes per capita in 2011. Germany is the world leader in recycling. In 2012 an estimated 65% of all municipal waste was recycled or composted.

Electricity

Installed capacity in 2011 was 123·80m. kW. In 2011 there were nine nuclear reactors in operation. Production of electricity was 512·72bn. kWh in 2011, of which about 17% was nuclear. There is a moratorium on further nuclear plant construction, and the SPD–Green coalition government agreed in 2000 to begin phasing out nuclear power, with the final plant closure scheduled for 2022. After the CDU/CSU–FDP coalition came to power following the Sept. 2009 election this date was extended to 2036. However, in the wake of Japan's nuclear incidents in March 2011, Chancellor Angela Merkel suspended the extension and temporarily shut down seven of Germany's oldest reactors. As a result, by 2014 nuclear power accounted for only 15·8% of electricity production (down from approximately 30% in 1992). Renewables accounted for 26·2% of electricity production in 2014 (up from just 4% in 1992) and lignite (brown coal) 25·4% (down from 29% in 1992). Renewables overtook lignite in 2014 to become the leading source for the first time. The quantity of electricity produced from lignite in 2013 was the highest since the reunification of Germany. Electricity consumption per capita was 7,297 kWh in 2011. In 2000 Veba and Viag merged to form E.ON, which became the world's largest private energy service provider. Germany is the second largest exporter of electricity in the world (after France), with 54·8bn. kWh in 2011.

Oil and Gas

The chief oilfields are in Emsland (Lower Saxony). In 2014, 2·05m. tonnes of crude oil were produced. Natural gas production was 9·0bn. cu. metres in 2012. Natural gas reserves were 100bn. cu. metres in 2012; crude petroleum reserves were 276m. bbls in 2011.

Wind

Germany is one of the world's largest wind-power producers. By the end of 2014 there were 24,867 wind turbines with a total rated power of 38,115 MW, ranking Germany third behind China and the USA. Production of wind-generated electricity in 2014 totalled 57·4bn. kWh.

Minerals

The main production areas are: North Rhine-Westphalia (for coal, iron and metal smelting-works), Central Germany (for lignite) and Lower Saxony (Salzgitter for iron ore; the Harz for metal ore).

Production (2012, in 1,000 tonnes): lignite, 185,432; salt, 14,445; hard coal, 10,770. In 2015 proved coal reserves were 36·2bn. tonnes (almost exclusively lignite). Germany is the world's largest lignite producer and the fourth largest salt producer after China, the USA and India.

Agriculture

In 2014 there were 11·87m. ha. of arable land. Sown areas in 2014 (in 1,000 ha.) included: wheat, 3,219·7; corn for silage, 2,092·6; barley, 1,573·7; rape, 1,394·2; rye and maslin, 629·9; maize, 481·3; triticale, 432·3; sugar beets, 372·5; grassland, 347·1; potatoes, 244·8. Crop production, 2014 (in 1,000 tonnes): corn for silage, 99,204; sugar beets, 29,748; wheat, 27,785; potatoes, 11,607; barley, 11,563; rapeseed, 6,247; maize, 5,142; rye and maslin, 3,854; triticale, 2,972.

In 2014, 6·3% of agricultural land was farmed organically in Germany. Organic food sales for Germany in 2011 were valued at €6·6bn. (the second highest in the world behind the USA).

In 2014 there were 286,800 farms, of which 26,300 were under five ha. and 35,400 over 100 ha. In 2013 there were 1,020,500 people working in the agricultural sector, of whom 505,600 were household members and 515,000 hired labourers (314,300 of them seasonal); 303,900 were full-time workers.

Wine production was 920·2m. litres in 2014.

Livestock, Nov. 2014 (in 1,000): pigs, 28,339·0; beef cattle, 12,742·2; dairy cows, 4,295·7; sheep, 1,600·8; horses, donkeys and mules (2013), 461·3 (estimate); poultry on farms (2013), 177,333·1. Livestock products (2014, in 1,000 tonnes): milk, 32,395; meat, 6,671; cheese, 2,472; eggs, 11,557m. units.

Forestry

Forest area in 2015 was 11·42m. ha., of which about half was owned by the State. Timber production was 54·36m. cu. metres in 2014. In recent years depredation has occurred through pollution with acid rain.

Fisheries

The total catch in 2015 was 261,744 tonnes (240,395 tonnes from marine waters). In 2010 the fishing fleet consisted of 1,766 vessels totalling 68,200 GT. Total employment in the German fleet in 2010 was about 1,640. Imports of fishery commodities were valued at US$5,305m. in 2012 and exports at US$2,710m.

Industry

The leading companies by market capitalization in Germany in March 2019 were: SAP, a software and computer services company (US$138·9bn.); Siemens, an engineering conglomerate (US$112·5bn.); and Bayer, a chemical and pharmaceutical company (US$104·6bn.).

In 2013 a total of 3,629,666 businesses were registered.

Manufacturing accounted for 22·6% of GDP in 2014, compared to 15·3% for the European Union as a whole. Output of major industrial products, 2014 unless otherwise indicated (in 1,000 tonnes): gas oil and diesel oil (2012), 46,015; crude steel, 42,943; hot-rolled steel products, 36,449; cement, 31,717; pig iron, 27,945; petrol and aviation fuel, 19,599; plastics, 17,103; paper, 10,635; fuel oil (2012), 8,319; flour, 5,812; jet fuels (2012), 5,216; sulphuric acid, 2,024; nitrogenous fertilizers, 1,351; synthetic fibre, 336; passenger cars, 5,584,000 units; household dishwashing machines (2010), 3,024,000 units; refrigerators, 2,315,000 units; bottles, 9,092m. units; TV sets, 180,000 units; beer, 8,428m. litres; soft drinks, excluding milk-based beverages (2013), 24,717m. litres.

Labour

Retirement age was traditionally 65 years, but is being raised gradually to 67 in a process that started at the beginning of 2012 and is to continue through to 2029. In 2014 the workforce was 44·67m., of whom 42·58m. were working and 2·09m. (0·90m. females) were unemployed. In 2014, 89·7% of those working were employees and 10·3% self-employed (including those helping family members). Of the total workforce in 2014 the year average for the number of employees (provisional) in the main industries was as follows: 7,202,000 in manufacturing industries; 5,327,000 in wholesale and retail trade, and the repair of motor vehicles and motorcycles; 4,449,000 in human health and social work activities (2010); 2,741,000 in public administration and defence (2010); 2,535,000 in administrative and support service activities (2010); 2,123,000 in education (2010); 1,960,000 in transport and storage; 1,932,000 in construction; 1,836,000 in professional, scientific and technical activities (2010); 1,531,000 in the hotel and catering industries; 1,084,000 in information and communications; 1,045,000 in banking and insurance. In Oct. 2015 there were 612,236 job vacancies.

The standardized unemployment rate was 3·3% in Dec. 2018—the second lowest in the European Union (down from 3·8% in 2017 as a whole and 4·6% in 2015). Unemployment in 2017 was at its lowest level since the reunification of Germany in 1990. Youth unemployment (under 25) is—at just 7·3% in Dec. 2014—the lowest in the European Union, helped by the fact that a quarter of employers provide formal apprenticeship schemes for young people. Long-term unemployment is particularly high, with 47·4% of the labour force in 2010 having been out of work for more than a year. In Jan. 2005 the number of people out of work had reached 5m., the highest total since the 1930s, although by Oct. 2010 it had fallen to below 3m. as Germany made a strong recovery from the recession. The gross annual earnings of full-time employees in the industry and services sector amounted to an average of €46,575 per person in 2014. A national minimum wage of €8·50 per hour was introduced for the first time in Jan. 2015.

Germany had 11,000 people living in slavery according to the Walk Free Foundation's 2013 *Global Slavery Index*.

International Trade

In 2014 Germany had a record trade surplus of €216·9bn. for the year.

Imports and Exports

Trade in €1m.:

	2011	2012	2013	2014
Imports	902,523	905,925	898,164	916,636
Exports	1,061,225	1,095,766	1,093,115	1,133,540

Main import sources in 2014 (trade figures in €1m.): Netherlands, 88,137; China, 79,349; France, 67,552; USA, 48,600; Italy, 48,487; UK, 42,295; Belgium, 39,863; Poland, 39,761; Switzerland, 39,329; Russia, 38,403. Main export markets in 2014 (trade figures in €1m.): France,

102,067; USA, 96,077; UK, 84,067; China, 74,504; Netherlands, 73,145; Austria, 56,234; Italy, 54,481; Poland, 47,544; Switzerland, 46,270; Belgium, 42,221.

Distribution of imports and exports by commodities in 2014 (in €1m.) includes: finished goods, 618,117 and 955,385; semi-finished goods, 75,699 and 61,517; foodstuffs, 61,617 and 54,283; raw materials, 101,025 and 17,385; alcohol and tobacco, 10,424 and 10,033; live animals, 1,601 and 1,278.

Germany is the third largest trading nation in the world after China and the USA. In 2003 it took over from the USA as the world's leading exporter but was in turn overtaken by China in 2009. The USA is now the second largest exporter and Germany the third largest, with 7·9% of global merchandise exports in 2014. Germany also ranks third for imports, with 6·4% of global merchandise imports in 2014.

Trade Fairs

Berlin ranked as the fourth most popular convention city in 2016 according to the International Congress and Convention Association. Berlin hosted 176 international association meetings that year. Germany has a number of major annual trade fairs, among the most important of which are Internationale Grüne Woche Berlin (International Green Week Berlin—Exhibition for the Food Industry, Agriculture and Horticulture), held in Berlin in Jan.; Ambiente (for high quality consumer goods and new products), held in Frankfurt in Feb.; ITB Berlin (International Tourism Exchange), held in Berlin in March; CeBit (World Business Fair for Office Automation, Information Technology and Telecommunications), held in Hanover in March; Hannover Messe (the World's Leading Fair for Industry, Automation and Innovation), held in Hanover, in April; Internationale Funkausstellung Berlin (Your World of Consumer Electronics), held in Berlin in late Aug./early Sept.; and Frankfurter Buchmesse (Frankfurt Book Fair) held in Frankfurt in Oct. Hanover's trade fair site is the largest in Europe and Frankfurt's the second largest.

Communications

Roads

In 2014 the total length of the road network was 230,377 km, including 12,917 km of motorway *(Autobahn)*, 39,389 km of federal highways and 86,210 km of secondary roads. The motorway network is the largest in Europe. On 1 Jan. 2015 there were 53,715,600 motor vehicles, including: passenger cars, 44,403,100; lorries, 2,701,300; buses, 77,500; motorcycles, 4,145,400. In 2013, 9,306m. passengers were transported by scheduled road transport services. There were 302,435 accidents in 2014 resulting in injuries to passengers. Road casualties in 2014 totalled 392,912, with 389,535 injured and 3,377 killed. In 2014 there were 4·2 fatalities per 100,000 population.

Rail

Legislation of 1993 provides for the eventual privatization of the railways, but the state-owned Deutsche Bahn still dominates the market. On 1 Jan. 1994 West German Bundesbahn and the former GDR Reichsbahn were amalgamated as the Deutsche Bahn, a joint-stock company in which track, long-distance passenger traffic, regional passenger traffic, goods traffic and railway stations/services are run as five separate administrative entities. These were intended after 3–5 years to become companies themselves, at first under a holding company, and ultimately independent. In 2013 the total length of railway track was 37,860 km (nearly all 1,435 mm gauge track). 2,613m. passengers were carried in 2013 and 365·0m. tonnes of freight in 2014.

There are metros in Berlin (152 km), Hamburg (101 km), Munich (101 km) and Nuremberg (35 km), and tram/light rail networks in over 50 cities.

Civil Aviation

Lufthansa, the largest carrier, was set up in 1953 and was originally 75% state-owned. The government sold its final shares in 1997. Other airlines include Condor, Eurowings and TUIfly. Air Berlin, which at the time was Germany's second largest airline, ceased operations in Oct. 2017. In 2012 the airlines of the Lufthansa Group carried 103m. passengers (20m. on long-haul flights); revenue passenger-km totalled 204·8bn. In 2014 civil aviation had 768 aircraft over 20 tonnes and 790 helicopters.

In 2014 there were 104·82m. passenger arrivals and 104·32m. departures. Main international airports: Berlin (Schönefeld), Berlin (Tegel), Bremen, Cologne-Bonn, Düsseldorf, Frankfurt am Main, Frankfurt (Hahn), Hamburg (Fuhlsbüttel), Hanover, Leipzig, Munich, Nuremberg and Stuttgart. Secondary airports in terms of passenger numbers include Dortmund, Dresden, Karlsruhe, Münster and Weeze (Niederrhein).

In 2014 Frankfurt am Main handled 59·55m. passengers and 2,164,000 tonnes of freight. It is the busiest airport in Europe in terms of freight handled. Munich was the second busiest German airport in terms of passenger traffic in 2014 (39·68m.) but fourth for freight. Leipzig was the second busiest in 2014 for freight, with 908,000 tonnes, but only 13th for passenger traffic.

Shipping

At 31 Dec. 2015 the mercantile marine comprised 351 ocean-going vessels of 10·30m. GT. Sea-going ships in 2014 carried 300·1m. tonnes of cargo. The busiest port, Hamburg, handled 126·0m. tonnes of cargo in 2014, ranking it third in Europe behind Rotterdam and Antwerp. Hamburg is Europe's second busiest container port after Rotterdam. Navigable rivers and canals had a total length of 7,728 km in 2013. The inland waterways fleet on 31 Dec. 2014 included 842 motor freight vessels totalling 1·11m. tonnes and 362 tankers of 689,341 tonnes. 228·5m. tonnes of freight were transported in 2014.

Telecommunications

Telecommunications were deregulated in 1989. On 1 Jan. 1995, three state-owned joint-stock companies were set up: Deutsche Telekom, Postdienst and Postbank. The partial privatization of Deutsche Telekom began in Nov. 1996; in 2016 the German government held only 14·5% of shares directly, and a further 17·5% indirectly through the government bank KfW.

In 2010 there were 45·6m. main (fixed) telephone lines, down from 54·8m. in 2005. Mobile phone subscriptions numbered 104·6m. in 2010 (1,270·4 per 1,000 persons), up from 79·3m. in 2005. O2, Telekom and Vodafone are the largest providers. Germany had 67·4m. internet users in Dec. 2011. The fixed broadband penetration rate in Dec. 2010 was 31·9 subscribers per 100 inhabitants. In March 2012 there were 22·1m. Facebook users (27% of the population).

Social Institutions

Out of 178 countries analysed in the 2017 *Fragile States Index*—a list published jointly by the Fund for Peace and *Foreign Policy* magazine—Germany was ranked the 14th least vulnerable to conflict or collapse. The index is based on 12 indicators of state vulnerability across social, political and economic categories.

Justice

Justice is administered by the federal courts and by the courts of the *Bundesländer*. In criminal procedures, civil cases and procedures of non-contentious jurisdiction the courts on the state level are the local courts *(Amtsgerichte)*, the regional courts *(Landgerichte)* and the courts of appeal *(Oberlandesgerichte)*. Constitutional federal disputes are dealt with by the Federal Constitutional Court *(Bundesverfassungsgericht)* elected by the Bundestag and Bundesrat. The *Bundesländer* also have constitutional courts. In labour law disputes the courts of the first and second instance are the labour courts and the *Bundesland* labour courts, and in the third instance the Federal Labour Court *(Bundesarbeitsgericht)*. Disputes about public law in matters of social security, unemployment insurance, maintenance of war victims and similar cases are dealt with in the first and second instances by the social courts and the *Bundesland* social courts and in the third instance by the Federal Social Court *(Bundessozialgericht)*. In most tax matters the finance courts of the *Bundesländer* are competent, and in the second instance the Federal Finance Court *(Bundesfinanzhof)*. Other controversies of public law in non-constitutional matters are decided in the first and second instance by the administrative and the higher administrative courts *(Oberverwaltungsgerichte)* of the *Bundesländer*, and in the third instance by the Federal Administrative Court *(Bundesverwaltungsgericht)*.

The death sentence was abolished in the Federal Republic of Germany in 1949 and in the German Democratic Republic in 1987.

The population in penal institutions at 31 March 2014 was 54,007 (of which 6% women), including 1,953 prisoners serving life sentences. In 2013, 5,961,662 crimes were recorded by the police (6,750,613 in 1993). There were 585 intentional homicides recorded in 2013, down from 859 in 2003. In 2015 the World Justice Project *Rule of Law Index*, which provides data on how the rule of law is experienced by the general public across eight categories, ranked Germany 12th of 102 countries for criminal justice and fifth for civil justice.

Education

Education is compulsory for children aged six to 15, although between the ages of 15 and 18 young people are obliged to pursue at least part-time vocational secondary education. After the first four (or six) years at primary school *(Grundschulen)* children attend secondary general *(Hauptschulen)*, intermediate *(Realschulen)*, grammar *(Gymnasien)*, or comprehensive schools *(Integrierte Gesamtschulen)*. The secondary general school certificate is awarded at the end of five or six years. The intermediate school is positioned between the secondary general school and the grammar school. It gives pupils a more comprehensive general education and normally encompasses six years of schooling. Grammar school traditionally lasted nine years but there has generally been a move towards reducing this to eight years (although some *Bundesländer* are either retaining the nine-year system or reverting to it owing to the unpopularity of the eight-year system). Entry to higher education is by the final Grammar School Certificate *(Abitur—Higher School Certificate)*. There are also schools for children with physical disabilities and those with other special needs *(Sonderschulen)*.

In 2013–14 there were 1,329 kindergartens with 27,696 pupils and 2,740 teachers; 15,749 primary schools with 2,708,400 pupils and 191,689 teachers; 3,191 special schools with 343,343 pupils and 70,647 teachers; 4,248 secondary general schools with 651,309 pupils and 45,557 teachers; 2,399 intermediate schools with 1,015,160 pupils and 63,934 teachers; 3,124 grammar schools with 2,329,990 pupils and 178,629 teachers; 1,666 comprehensive schools with 835,227 pupils and 67,392 teachers; 1,782 schools with different courses of education with 453,930 pupils and 40,371 teachers. Private schools exist but are less common than in many other countries. The proportion of pupils at private schools rose from 4·8% to 8·8% between 1992 and 2014.

In 2013–14 there were 664,659 working teachers, of whom 72% were female.

The adult literacy rate is at least 99%.

In 2010 public expenditure on education came to 5·1% of GDP and represented 10·7% of total government expenditure.

Vocational education is provided in part-time, full-time and advanced vocational schools *(Berufs-, Berufsaufbau-, Berufsfach- and Fachschulen,* including *Fachschulen für Technik* and *Schulen des Gesundheitswesens)*. Occupation-related, part-time vocational training of six to 12 hours per week is compulsory for all (including unemployed) up to the age of 18 years or until the completion of the practical vocational training. Full-time vocational schools comprise courses of at least one year. They prepare for commercial and domestic occupations as well as specialized occupations in the field of handicrafts. Advanced full-time vocational schools are attended by pupils over 18. Courses vary from six months to three or more years.

In 2013–14 there were 8,833 full- and part-time vocational schools with 2,530,586 students and 122,424 teachers.

Higher Education

In the winter term of the 2014–15 academic year there were 425 institutes of higher education *(Hochschulen)* with 2,694,579 students, including 107 universities with 1,702,326 students; 74 teacher training colleges, theological seminaries and schools of art (62,469 students); 215 technical colleges (895,701); and 29 colleges of public administration (34,083). Only 428,064 students (15·9%) were in their first year. In 2014 undergraduate tuition fees at all universities in Germany were abolished (although in some *Bundesländer* this had already happened in previous years). However, they may still charge registration fees. Tuition fees for international students from outside the European Union have been reintroduced at some universities in the meantime.

Health

In Dec. 2013 there were 357,252 doctors, 69,730 dentists and 49,288 pharmacists. There were 1,996 hospitals in 2013 with 500,671 beds (62·1 for every 10,000 people). In 2012 Germany spent 10·8% of its GDP on health, with public spending amounting to 75·6% of the total. In 2013 total expenditure on health came to €314·9bn.

Welfare

Social Health Insurance (introduced in 1883). Wage-earners and apprentices, salaried employees with an income below a certain limit and social insurance pensioners are compulsorily insured within the state system. Voluntary insurance is also possible.

Benefits: medical treatment, medicines, hospital and nursing care, maternity benefits, death benefits for the insured and their families, sickness payments and out-patients' allowances. Economy measures of Dec. 1992 introduced prescription charges related to recipients' income.

As part of a series of measures to tackle a funding shortfall in the health service, a patient charge of €10 was introduced from Jan. 2004, payable for the first visit only per quarter to a doctor.

70·29m. persons were insured in 2014 (30·85m. compulsorily). A total of €182,746m. was paid to beneficiaries in 2013.

Accident Insurance (introduced in 1884). Those insured are all persons in employment or service, apprentices and the majority of the self-employed and the unpaid family workers.

Benefits in the case of industrial injuries and occupational diseases: medical treatment and nursing care, sickness payments, pensions and other payments in cash and in kind, surviving dependants' pensions.

Number of insured in 2013, 64·22m.; number of current pensions, 917,265. A total of €10,884m. was paid to beneficiaries in 2013.

Workers' and Employees' Old-Age Insurance Scheme (introduced in 1889). All wage-earners and salaried employees, the members of certain liberal professions and—subject to certain conditions—self-employed craftsmen are compulsorily insured. The insured may voluntarily continue to insure when no longer liable to do so or increase the insurance.

Benefits: measures designed to maintain, improve and restore the earning capacity; pensions paid to persons incapable of work, old age and surviving dependants' pensions.

Number of current pensions in July 2014, 25·01m. (including old age pensions, 17·63m.; pensions to widows and widowers, 5·32m.). A total of €259,345m. was paid to beneficiaries in 2013.

There are also special retirement and unemployment pension schemes for miners and farmers, assistance for war victims and compensation payments to members of German minorities in East European countries expelled after the Second World War and persons who suffered damage because of the war or in connection with the currency reform.

Family Allowances

€33·47bn. were dispensed to 8·83m. recipients (13·8% foreigners) in 2014 on behalf of 14·53m. children. Paid child care leave is available for three years to mothers or fathers.

Unemployment Allowances

In 2014 a total of 0·95m. persons were receiving unemployment benefit and 6·10m. basic cost-of-living benefit for jobseekers. Total expenditure on these and similar benefits was €60·77bn. in 2014. Unemployment assistance was abolished in Jan. 2005 and replaced with a so-called 'Unemployment benefit II'. This benefit is no longer tied to the former income of the recipient but is around the same flat-rate level as the social assistance benefit.

Public Welfare

In 2013, €27·44bn. were distributed to 2,693,000 recipients (1,354,000 women).

Public Youth Welfare

For supervision of foster children, official guardianship, assistance with adoptions and affiliations, social assistance in juvenile courts, educational assistance and correctional education under a court order. A total of €35·35bn. was spent on recipients in 2013.

Pension Reform

A major reform of the German pension system became law in 2001. The changes entail a cut in the value of the average state pension from 70% to approximately 67% of average final earnings by 2030. There will be incentives in the form of tax concessions and direct payments to encourage individuals to build up supplementary provision by contributing up to 4% of their earnings into private-sector personal pensions. In the long term these could supply up to 40% of overall pension income, with 60% coming from the state as opposed to 85% prior to the changes.

The retirement age is being increased gradually from 65 to 67 in a process that started in Jan. 2012. By 2023 Germans will only be eligible for a state pension at the age of 66 and by 2029 at the age of 67. The coalition agreement of Nov. 2013 introduces changes so that workers who have contributed to pensions for 45 years will be able to retire at the age of 63 rather than 65.

Religion

In 2013 there were 24,171,000 Roman Catholics in 11,085 parishes, 23,040,000 Protestants in 14,412 parishes; and in 2014, 100,437 Jews with 71 rabbis and 100 synagogues. The Federal Office for Migration and Refugees estimated in 2015 that there were between 4·4m. and 4·7m. Muslims resident in Germany, a number exceeded in the EU only in France.

There are seven Roman Catholic archbishoprics (Bamberg, Berlin, Cologne, Freiburg, Hamburg, Munich and Freising, Paderborn) and 20 bishoprics. Chairman of the German Bishops' Conference is Reinhard Marx, Archbishop of Munich and Freising. A concordat between Germany and the Holy See dates from 10 Sept. 1933. In April 2005 Cardinal Joseph Ratzinger, former archbishop of Munich and Freising, was elected Pope as Benedict XVI. In Feb. 2013 he became the first Pope to resign in 600 years, citing age and declining health as the reasons for his decision. There were eight cardinals in Feb. 2019.

The Evangelical (Protestant) Church (EKD) consists of 22 member-churches comprising nine Lutheran Churches, 11 United-Lutheran-Reformed Churches and two Reformed Churches. Its organs are the Synod, the Church Conference and the Council under the chairmanship of Heinrich Bedford-Strohm. The Free Evangelical Church (BFeG) has some 480 communities.

Culture

World Heritage Sites

Germany has 44 sites on the UNESCO World Heritage List (date of inscription on the list in brackets): Aachen Cathedral (1978), begun in the 8th century under Charlemagne; Speyer Cathedral (1981), founded in 1030 and constructed in the Romanesque style; Würzburg Residence, with the Court Gardens and Residence Square (1981), an 18th century Baroque palace; Pilgrimage Church of Wies (1983), an 18th century Baroque-Rococo church; Castles of Augustusburg and Falkenlust at Brühl (1984), early examples of 18th century Rococo architecture; St Mary's Cathedral and St Michael's Church at Hildesheim (1985 and 2008), Romanesque constructions from the 11th century; Roman Monuments in Trier (1986), a Roman colony from the 1st century, and the Cathedral of St Peter and Church of Our Lady; Hanseatic City of Lübeck (1987), founded in the 12th century; Palaces and Parks of Potsdam and Berlin (1990, 1992 and 1999), an eclectic mix of 150 buildings covering 500 hectares built between 1730 and 1916; Abbey and Altenmünster of Lorsch (1991), an example of Carolignian architecture; Mines of Rammelsberg and Historic Town of Goslar (1992 and 2008), with a well-preserved historic centre; Town of Bamberg (1993), the country's biggest intact historical city core; Maulbronn Monastery Complex (1993), a former Cistercian abbey over 850 years old; Collegiate Church, Castle, and Old Town of Quedlinburg (1994), capital of the East Franconian German Empire; Völklingen Ironworks (1994), a preserved 19th/20th centuries ironworks; Messel Pit Fossil site (1995), containing important fossils from 57m.–36m. BC; Cologne Cathedral (1996 and 2008), a Gothic masterpiece begun in 1248; Bauhaus and its sites in Weimar and Dessau (1996 and 2017), buildings of the influential early 20th century architectural movement; Luther Memorials in Eisleben and Wittenberg (1996), including his birthplace, baptism church and religious sites; Classical Weimar (1998), a cultural epicentre during the 18th and early 19th centuries; Museumsinsel (Museum Island), Berlin (1999), including Altes Museum, Bodemuseum, Neues Museum and Pergamonmuseum; Wartburg Castle (1999), dating from the feudal period and rebuilt in the 19th century—Luther translated the New Testament here; Garden Kingdom of Dessau-Wörlitz (2000), an 18th century landscaped garden in the Enlightenment style; Monastic Island of Reichenau (2000), on Lake Constance, incorporating medieval churches and the remains of an 8th century Benedictine monastery; Zollverein Coal Mine Industrial Complex in Essen (2001), a 20th century mining complex with modernist buildings; Upper Middle Rhine Valley (2002), a 65 km-stretch of one of Europe's most important historical transport conduits; Historic Centres of Stralsund and Wismar (2002), Hanseatic towns; Town Hall and Roland on the Marketplace of Bremen (2004); Old Town of Regensburg with Stadtamhof (2006); the Berlin Modernism Housing Estates (2008); the Fagus Factory in Alfeld (2011), a landmark in the development of modern architecture and industrial design; the Margravial Opera House Bayreuth (2012), a stunning illustration of Baroque theatre architecture; Bergpark Wilhelmshöhe (2013), a monumental water display in Kassel dominated by a giant statue of Hercules; Carolingian Westwork and Civitas Corvey (2014), a rural site

located along the Weser River that illustrates one of the most important Carolingian architectural expressions; Speicherstadt and Kontorhaus District with Chilehaus (2015), two densely built urban areas in the centre of Hamburg; the Caves and Ice Age Art in the Swabian Jura (2017), a site in southern Germany featuring some of the oldest figurative art worldwide; the Archaeological Border complex of Hedeby and the Danevirke (2018), a site containing the remains of a trading town dating back to the 1st and early 2nd millennia BC; and Naumburg Cathedral (2018), an outstanding testimony to medieval art and architecture.

Germany and Poland are jointly responsible for Muskauer Park/Park Mużakowski (2004), a landscaped park astride the Neisse river. Germany and the United Kingdom share the Frontiers of the Roman Empire sites (1987, 2005 and 2008), which contain the border line of the Roman Empire at its greatest extent in the 2nd century AD. Ancient and Primeval Beech Forests of the Carpathians and Other Regions of Europe (2007 and 2017) are shared with Albania, Austria, Belgium, Bulgaria, Croatia, Italy, Romania, Slovakia, Slovenia, Spain and Ukraine. The Wadden Sea, the largest unbroken system of intertidal sand and mud flats in the world (2009 and 2014), is shared with Denmark and the Netherlands. The Prehistorical Pile dwellings around the Alps (2011) are shared with Austria, France, Italy, Slovenia and Switzerland. The Architectural Work of Le Corbusier, an Outstanding Contribution to the Modern Movement (2016), is shared with Argentina, Belgium, France, India, Japan and Switzerland.

Press

The daily press is mainly regional. The daily with the highest circulation is the tabloid *Bild* (2·22m. copies per day in the fourth quarter of 2014, down from 3·03m. in the fourth quarter of 2009). In 2014 the total circulation figures for the 349 German daily newspapers came to 16·3m. The total circulation of daily newspapers in Germany is the highest in Europe. The leading daily newspaper websites are *Bild.de* (17·3m. unique monthly visitors in Dec. 2014), *die Welt* (9·0m.), *Süddeutsche.de* (5·8m.) and *ZEIT ONLINE* (5·7m.). There were 659 newspaper online editions in 2014. In 2015 a total of 89,506 book titles were published, down from a record 96,479 in 2007.

Tourism

In 2014 there were 51,865 places of accommodation with 3,563,595 beds (including 13,270 hotels with 1,095,075 beds). 32,999,000 foreign visitors and 127,791,000 tourists resident in Germany spent a total of 424,062,000 nights in holiday accommodation. The most visited city is Berlin with 11,871,000 overnight visitors in 2014; Bavaria is the most visited *Bundesland* with 32,462,000 (6,594,000 visited Munich). In 2014 the Netherlands was the country of origin of the largest number of overnight visitors (4,238,000), ahead of Switzerland (2,778,000) and the UK (2,415,000). In 2014 tourism brought in €32·6bn. Expenditure by German travellers in foreign countries for 2014 was €70·3bn.

Festivals

The Munich Opera Festival takes place annually in June–July, and the Wagner Festspiele (the Wagner Festival) in Bayreuth is held from late July to the end of Aug. The Oberammergau Passion Play, which takes place every ten years, was last held in 2010. Karneval (Fasching in some areas), in Jan./Feb./March, is a major event in the annual calendar in cities such as Cologne, Munich, Düsseldorf and Mainz. The annual Berlin Film Festival (Berlinale) takes place over a two-week period in Feb. Oktoberfest, Munich's famous folk and beer festival which was first held in 1810, takes place each year in late Sept. and early Oct. and regularly attracts 7m. visitors. The biggest rock and pop festivals are Rock am Ring, Nürburg (June); Rock im Park, Nuremberg (June); and Hurricane, Scheessel (June).

Diplomatic Representatives

Of Germany in the United Kingdom (23 Belgrave Sq./Chesham Pl., London, SW1X 8PZ)
Ambassador: Dr Peter Wittig.

Of the United Kingdom in Germany (Wilhelmstrasse 70–71, 10117 Berlin)
Ambassador: Sir Sebastian Wood, KCMG.

Of Germany in the USA (4645 Reservoir Rd, NW, Washington, D.C., 20007)
Ambassador: Emily Margarethe Haber.

Of the USA in Germany (Pariser Platz 2, 10117 Berlin)
  Ambassador: Richard A. Grenell.

Of Germany to the United Nations
  Ambassador: Christoph Heusgen.

Of Germany to the European Union
  Permanent Representative: Reinhard Silberberg.

Baden-Württemberg

Key Historical Events

The *Bundesland* is a combination of former states. Baden (the western part of the present *Bundesland*) became a united margravate in 1771, after being divided as Baden-Baden and Baden-Durlach since 1535; Baden-Baden was predominantly Catholic, and Baden-Durlach predominantly Protestant. The margrave became an ally of Napoleon, ceding land west of the Rhine and receiving northern and southern territory as compensation. In 1805 Baden became a grand duchy and in 1806 a member state of the Confederation of the Rhine, extending from the Main to Lake Constance. In 1815 it was a founder-state of the German Confederation. A constitution was granted by the grand duke in 1818, but later rulers were less liberal and there was revolution in 1848, put down with Prussian help. The Grand Duchy was abolished and replaced by a *Bundesland* in 1919.

In 1949 Baden was combined with Württemberg to form three states; the three joined as one in 1952.

Württemberg, having been a duchy since 1495, became a kingdom in 1805 and joined the Confederations as did Baden. A constitution was granted in 1819 and the state remained liberal. In 1866 the king allied himself with Austria against Prussia, but in 1870 joined Prussia in war against France. The monarchy came to an end with the abdication of William II in 1918, and Württemberg became a state of the German Republic. In 1945 the state was divided between Allied occupation authorities but the divisions ended in 1952.

Territory and Population

Baden-Württemberg comprises 35,748 sq. km, with a population (at 31 Dec. 2017) of 11,023,425 (5,546,084 females; 5,477,341 males).

The *Bundesland* is divided into four administrative regions, nine urban and 35 rural districts, and numbers 1,101 communes.

The capital is Stuttgart, with a population (31 Dec. 2017) of 632,743.

Social Statistics

Statistics for calendar years:

	Live births	Marriages	Divorces	Deaths
2014	95,632	50,571	20,350	100,663
2015	100,269	52,627	19,917	108,066
2016	107,489	54,553	19,683	106,633
2017	107,375	54,591	18,362	109,120

Constitution and Government

Baden-Württemberg is a merger of Baden, Württemberg-Baden and Württemberg-Hohenzollern, which were formed after 1945. The merger was approved by a plebiscite held on 9 Dec. 1951, when 70% of the population voted in its favour. It has six votes in the Bundesrat.

Recent Elections

At the elections of 13 March 2016, turnout was 70·4%. The Greens won 47 seats with 30·3% of the vote, the Christian Democrats 42 with 27·0%, the Alternative for Germany 23 with 15·1%, the Social Democrats 19 with 12·7% and the Free Democrats 12 with 8·3%.

Current Government

Baden-Württemberg is governed by the Greens and the Christian Democrats (CDU).

Winfried Kretschmann (Greens) is *Prime Minister.*
Government Website: http://www.baden-wuerttemberg.de

Economy

Performance

GDP in 2017 was €493,265m., which amounted to 15·1% of Germany's total GDP. Industries *(Produzierendes Gewerbe)* provided 39·3% of GDP in 2017 (39·4% in 2000). Real GDP growth in 2017 was 3·4%. Service enterprises accounted for 60·3% of GDP in 2017.

Banking and Finance

There is a stock exchange in Stuttgart. Turnover of shares and bonds in 2017 was €80·7bn.

Energy and Natural Resources

Agriculture

Area and yield of the most important crops:

	Area (in 1,000 ha.)			Yield (in 1,000 tonnes)		
	2015	2016	2017	2015	2016	2017
Sugar beet	14·2	15·6	20·6	954·7	1,207·5	1,814·0
Wheat	237·4	227·9	217·2	1,798·3	1,502·1	1,686·1
Barley	151·5	144·4	140·3	940·2	879·0	948·0
Potatoes	4·7	5·4	5·0	173·8	197·4	221·8
Oats	20·1	18·4	19·8	93·8	84·1	89·6
Rye	10·2	9·3	8·2	54·2	51·8	44·1

Livestock in May 2018 (in thousands): cattle, 961·7 (including dairy cows, 338·8); pigs, 1,736·5; sheep (Nov. 2017) 213·3; poultry (2016), 5,436·1.

Forestry

Total area covered by forests is 13,525 sq. km or 37·8% of the total area.

Industry

Baden-Württemberg is one of Germany's most industrialized states. In 2017, 8,364 establishments (with 20 or more employees) employed 1,288,353 persons; of these, 318,283 were employed in machine construction; 238,328 in car manufacture; 168,246 in the manufacture of computer, electronic and optical products and of electrical equipment; 21,264 in the textile and clothing industry.

Labour

Economically active persons totalled 5,850,000 at the 1%-EU-sample survey of 2017: 5,293,000 were employees and 557,000 were self-employed (including family workers); 2,028,000 were engaged in power supply, mining, manufacturing and building; 1,369,000 in commerce and transport; 62,000 in agriculture and forestry; 2,391,000 in other industries and services. There were 174,000 unemployed in 2017, a rate of 3·9%.

International Trade

Imports and Exports

Total imports (2017): €170,794m. Total exports: €201,463m., of which €104,733m. went to the EU. Automotive exports totalled €45,719m. and machinery exports €41,283m.

Communications

Roads

On 1 Jan. 2017 there were 27,423 km of 'classified' roads, comprising 1,054 km of Autobahn, 4,231 km of federal roads, 10,043 km of first-class and 12,095 km of second-class highways. Motor vehicles, at 1 Jan. 2017, numbered 7,832,035, including 6,410,321 passenger cars, 8,784 buses, 345,941 lorries, 370,430 tractors and 664,475 motorcycles.

Civil Aviation

The largest airport in Baden-Württemberg is at Stuttgart, which in 2017 handled 10,942,000 passengers and 36,173 tonnes of freight. There are two further airports, Karlsruhe/Baden-Baden and Friedrichshafen.

Shipping

The harbour in Mannheim is the largest in Baden-Württemberg. In 2017 it handled 9·6m. tonnes of freight, compared to 7·3m. tonnes in Karlsruhe.

Social Institutions

Justice

There are a constitutional court *(Staatsgerichtshof)*, two courts of appeal, 17 regional courts, 108 local courts, a *Bundesland* labour court, nine labour courts, a *Bundesland* social court, eight social courts, a finance court, a higher administrative court *(Verwaltungsgerichtshof)* and four administrative courts.

Education

In 2016–17 there were 2,590 primary schools (Grund- und Werkreal-/Hauptschulen) with 26,437 teachers and 413,330 pupils; 562 special schools with 11,635 teachers and 49,339 pupils; 510 intermediate schools with 13,637 teachers and 219,116 pupils; 459 high schools with 22,282 teachers and 304,599 pupils; 58 Freie Waldorf schools with 1,749 teachers and 23,304 pupils. Other general schools had 612 teachers and 8,209 pupils in total; there were also 790 vocational schools with 428,746 pupils. There were 50 universities of applied sciences (Hochschulen für angewandte Wissenschaft) with 121,414 students in winter term 2017–18.

In the winter term 2017–18 there were nine universities (Freiburg, 24,354 students; Heidelberg, 28,477; Hohenheim, 9,196; Karlsruhe, 24,725; Konstanz, 11,077; Mannheim, 12,012; Stuttgart, 26,000; Tübingen, 27,318; Ulm 10,461); six teacher training colleges with 24,330 students; five colleges of music and three colleges of fine arts with a total of 4,441 students.

Health

In 2017 the 265 hospitals in Baden-Württemberg had 56,780 beds and treated 2,159,922 patients. The average occupancy rate was 77·0%.

Religion

In 2011, 35·8% of the population were Roman Catholics and 31·9% were Protestants.

Culture

Tourism

In 2017, 21,627,664 visitors spent a total of 52,932,457 nights in Baden-Württemberg. Only Bavaria of the German *Bundesländer* recorded more overnight stays.

Bavaria

Bayern

Key Historical Events

Bavaria was ruled by the Wittelsbach family from 1180. The duchy remained Catholic after the Reformation, which made it a natural ally of Austria and the Habsburg Emperors.

The present boundaries were set during the Napoleonic wars, and Bavaria became a kingdom in 1806. Despite the granting of a constitution and parliament, radical feeling forced the abdication of King Ludwig I in 1848. Maximilian II was followed by Ludwig II who allied himself with Austria against Prussia in 1866, but was reconciled with Prussia and entered the German Empire in 1871. In 1918 the King Ludwig III abdicated. The first years of republican government were filled with unrest, attempts at the overthrow of the state by both communist and right-wing groups culminating in an unsuccessful coup by Adolf Hitler in 1923.

The state of Bavaria included the Palatinate from 1214 until 1945, when it was taken from Bavaria and added to the Rhineland. The present *Bundesland* of Bavaria was formed in 1946. Munich became capital of Bavaria in the reign of Albert IV (1467–1508) and remains capital of the *Bundesland*.

Territory and Population

Bavaria has an area of 70,542 sq. km. There are seven administrative regions, 25 urban districts, 71 rural districts, 179 unincorporated areas and 2,056 communes, 982 of which are members of 311 administrative associations (as of 31 Dec. 2017). The population (31 Dec. 2017) numbered 12,997,204 (6,438,503 males; 6,558,701 females).

The capital is Munich, with a population (31 Dec. 2017) of 1,456,039.

Social Statistics

Statistics for calendar years:

	Live births	Marriages	Divorces	Deaths
2014	113,935	62,327	24,463	124,129
2015	118,228	65,128	24,247	133,536
2016	125,689	66,324	24,134	129,552
2017	125,191	66,790	22,599	133,902

Constitution and Government

The Constituent Assembly, elected on 30 June 1946, passed a constitution on the lines of the democratic constitution of 1919, but with greater emphasis on state rights; this was agreed upon by the Christian Social Union (CSU) and the Social Democrats (SPD). Bavaria has six seats in the Bundesrat. The CSU replaces the Christian Democratic Party in Bavaria.

Recent Elections

At the Diet elections on 14 Oct. 2018 the Christian Social Union lost its absolute majority by only winning 85 of 205 and so fell below the 5% threshold for gaining seats Turnout was 72·4%.

Current Government

The *Prime Minister* is Markus Söder (CSU).
Government Website (Germany only): http://www.bayern.de

Economy

Performance

Real GDP growth in 2017 was 2·8%, up from 1·7% in 2016.

Energy and Natural Resources

Agriculture

Area and yield of the most important products:

	Area (in 1,000 ha.)			Yield (in 1,000 tonnes)		
	2015	2016	2017	2015	2016	2017
Wheat	548·5	534·6	520·3	4,272·8	3,913·4	3,955·0
Sugar beet	49·9	59·6	71·1	3,365·9	4,766·1	6,567·7
Barley	350·1	328·3	327·9	2,247·1	2,152·7	2,260·8
Potatoes	40·0	40·2	41·7	1,415·2	1,832·5	1,856·3
Rye and maslin	35·4	35·4	33·5	186·8	206·5	170·8
Oats	23·8	21·8	25·7	113·2	101·9	114·3

Livestock, March 2017 unless otherwise indicated: 3,148,057 cattle (including 1,196,711 dairy cows); 91,300 horses (2013); 3,303,400 pigs; 268,400 sheep; 11,277,121 poultry (2016).

Industry

On 30 Sept. 2017, 7,408 establishments (with 20 or more employees) employed 1,294,760 persons; of these, 227,235 were employed in the manufacture of machinery and equipment, 205,425 in the manufacture of motor vehicles, 119,774 in the manufacture of electrical equipment, 112,990 in the manufacture of food products and 106,725 in the manufacture of metal products.

Labour

Economically active persons totalled 6,590,000 at the 1% sample survey of the microcensus of 2013. Of the total, 5,793,000 were employees, 739,000 were self-employed, 59,000 were unpaid family workers; 2,066,000 worked in power supply, mining, manufacturing and building; 1,642,000 in commerce, hotels and restaurants, and transport; 130,000 in agriculture and forestry; 2,752,000 in other services.

Communications

Roads

There were, on 1 Jan. 2018, 41,877 km of 'classified' roads, comprising 2,515 km of Autobahn, 6,049 km of federal roads, 14,471 km of first-class and 18,842 km of second-class highways. Number of motor vehicles on 1 Jan. 2018 was 9,972,076, including 7,845,761 passenger cars, 465,408 lorries, 14,203 buses and 926,882 motorcycles.

Civil Aviation

Munich airport handled 44,535,372 passengers (34,720,954 on international flights) and 378,694 tonnes of freight in 2017. Nuremberg handled 4,160,568 (3,129,102 on international flights) and 5,952 tonnes of freight in 2017. Memmingen handled 1,176,456 passengers (1,174,678 on international flights) and 23 tonnes of freight in 2017.

Social Institutions

Justice

There are a constitutional court (Verfassungsgerichtshof), three courts of appeal, 22 regional courts, 73 local courts, two Bundesland labour courts, 11 labour courts, a Bundesland social court, seven social courts, two finance courts, a higher administrative court (Verwaltungsgerichtshof) and six administrative courts. In Sept. 2018 the supreme court of Bavaria (Bayerisches Oberstes Landesgericht) was re-introduced after having been abolished in June 2006.

Education

In 2016–17 there were 3,309 primary schools with 43,921 teachers and 635,164 pupils; 351 special schools with 9,069 teachers and 53,669 pupils; 373 intermediate schools with 15,212 teachers and 224,845 pupils; 429 high schools with 25,458 teachers and 323,457 pupils; 229 part-time vocational schools with 8,930 teachers and 280,167 pupils, including 47 special part-time vocational schools with 1,130 teachers and 13,228 pupils; 850 full-time vocational schools with 5,810 teachers and 68,939 pupils including 467 schools for public health occupations with 2,393 teachers and 30,545 pupils; 350 advanced full-time vocational schools with 2,256 teachers and 25,367 pupils; 181 vocational high schools (Berufsoberschulen and Fachoberschulen) with 4,103 teachers and 59,128 pupils.

In 2017–18 there were 12 universities with 245,270 students (Augsburg, 20,035; Bamberg, 12,663; Bayreuth, 12,964; Eichstätt, 5,132; Erlangen-Nuremberg, 38,669; Munich, 50,527; Passau, 12,742; Regensburg, 20,792; Würzburg, 27,987; the Technical University of Munich, 40,196; University of the Federal Armed Forces, Munich (Universität der Bundeswehr), 3,260; the college of politics, Munich, 303), and three philosophical-theological colleges with 510 students in total (Neuendettelsau, 149; Munich, 361). There were also five colleges of music, two colleges of fine arts and one college of television and film, with 3,583 students in total; 33 vocational colleges (Fachhochschulen) with 134,280 students including one for the civil service (Bayerische Beamtenfachhochschule) with 5,250 students.

Welfare

In Dec. 2017 there were 49,060 persons receiving benefits of all kinds.

Religion

In 2011, 53·7% of the population were Roman Catholics and 20·2% were Protestants.

Culture

Tourism

In June 2017 there were 12,027 places of accommodation (with ten beds or more) providing beds for 557,336 people. In 2017 they received 37,278,748 guests of whom 9,379,696 were foreigners. They stayed an average of 2·5 nights each, totalling 94,368,996 nights (19,126,297 nights stayed by foreign visitors).

Festivals

Oktoberfest, Munich's famous folk and beer festival, takes place each year from the penultimate Saturday in Sept. through to the first Sunday in Oct. (extended to 3 Oct. if the last Sunday of the festival falls on 1 or 2 Oct.). There were 6·3m. visitors at the 185th Oktoberfest in 2018.

Berlin

Key Historical Events

After the end of World War II, Berlin was divided into four occupied sectors, each with a military governor from one of the victorious Allied Powers (the USA, the Soviet Union, Britain and France). In March 1948 the USSR withdrew from the Allied Control Council and in June blockaded West Berlin until May 1949. In response, the allies flew food and other supplies into the city in what became known as the Berlin Airlift. On 30 Nov. 1948 a separate municipal government was set up in the Soviet sector which led to the political division of the city. In contravention of the special Allied status agreed for the city, East Berlin became 'Capital of the GDR' in 1949 and thus increasingly integrated into the GDR as a whole. In West Berlin, the formal authority of the western allies lasted until 1990.

On 17 June 1953 the protest by workers in East Berlin against political oppression and economic hardship was suppressed by Soviet military forces. To stop refugees, the east German government erected the Berlin Wall to seal off West Berlin's borders on 13 Aug. 1961.

The Berlin Wall was breached on 9 Nov. 1989 as the regime in the GDR bowed to the internal pressure which had been building for months. East and West Berlin were amalgamated on the reunification of Germany in Oct. 1990.

With the move of the national government, the parliament (Bundestag), and the federal organ of the Bundesländer (Bundesrat) in 1999, Berlin once again became a capital city.

Territory and Population

The area is 891 sq. km. Population, 31 Dec. 2017, 3,613,495 (1,837,228 females). In Dec. 2014 the population included 496,518 foreign nationals.

Social Statistics

Statistics for calendar years:

	Live births	Marriages	Divorces	Deaths
2011	33,075	12,544	7,930	31,380
2012	34,678	13,222	7,267	32,218
2013	35,038	12,963	6,628	37,792
2014	37,368	13,373	6,405	32,314

Constitution and Government

According to the constitutions of Sept. 1950 and Oct. 1995, Berlin is simultaneously a Bundesland of the Federal Republic and a city. It is governed by a House of Representatives (of at least 130 members); executive power is vested in a Senate, consisting of the Governing Mayor, two Mayors and not more than eight senators. Since 1992 adherence to the constitution has been watched over by a Constitutional Court.

Although a proposed merger between Berlin and Brandenburg was rejected in a 1996 referendum, a number of joint institutions have been established on the basis of 20 state treaties.

Berlin has four seats in the Bundesrat.

Recent Elections

At the elections of 18 Sept. 2016 turnout was 66·9%. The Social Democratic Party (SPD) won 38 seats with 21·6% of votes cast; the Christian Democratic Union (CDU) 31, with 17·6%; the Left, 27 with 15·6%; the Greens, 27 with 15·2%; the Alternative for Germany, 25 with 14·2%; Free Democratic Party, 12 with 6·7%.

Current Government

The Governing Mayor is Michael Müller (SPD).
Government Website: http://www.berlin.de

Economy

GDP in 2014 was €117,271m. Berlin's real GDP growth in 2014 was 2·2%.

Industry

In Sept. 2014 there were 730 industrial concerns (20 or more employees) employing 93,532 people. The main industries were: food and animal feed, manufacture of electrical and optical equipment, and machine construction.

Labour
Economically active persons totalled 1,823,400 at the 1%-sample survey of the microcensus of 2014. There were on average 202,927 persons registered unemployed in 2014. The unemployment rate in 2014 was 11·1%.

Communications

Roads
On 1 Jan. 2014 there were 5,437·4 km of roads (245·7 km of 'classified' roads, made up of 76·7 km of Autobahn and 169·0 km of federal roads). In Jan. 2014, 1,352,600 motor vehicles were registered, including 1,154,100 passenger cars, 82,800 lorries, 2,100 buses and coaches, and 100,300 motorcycles. There were 132,717 road accidents in 2014, with 14,736 injured persons.

Civil Aviation
238,332 flights were made from Berlin's two airports—Tegel and Schönefeld—in 2014, carrying a total of 27,948,453 passengers.

Social Institutions

Justice
There are a court of appeal *(Kammergericht)*, a regional court, nine local courts, a *Bundesland* labour court, a labour court, a *Bundesland* social court, a social court, a higher administrative court, an administrative court and a finance court.

Education
In Sept. 2014 there were 330,232 pupils attending schools. There were 433 primary schools with 156,999 pupils, 165 integrated secondary schools with 84,494 pupils, 113 grammar schools with 75,529 pupils, 77 special schools with 8,993 pupils and ten *Freie Waldorf* schools with 4,217 pupils. In the winter semester 2014–15 there were 12 universities, five arts colleges and 30 technical colleges. There were a total of 171,263 students (49·5% female) in higher education.

Health
In 2014 there were 80 hospitals with 20,021 beds, 8,681 doctors and 30,229 medical personnel.

Religion
In Dec. 2012 membership and number of places of worship for major religions was as follows:

Religion	Members	Places of Worship
Protestant	641,316[1]	296
Roman Catholic	326,508	108
Jewish	11,137	8
Muslim	249,230[1]	130[1]

[1]2011.

Culture

Tourism
In 2014 (provisional) Berlin had 809 places of accommodation (with ten or more beds) providing 135,246 beds. 11,871,000 visitors (including 4,520,000 foreigners) spent 28,689,000 nights in Berlin (including at campsites).

Brandenburg

Key Historical Events
Brandenburg surrounds the capital city of Germany, Berlin, but in 1996 the people of the state voted against the recommendations of the Berlin House of Representatives and the Brandenburg State Parliament that the two states should merge. The state capital, Potsdam, is the ancient city of the Emperor Frederic II 'The Great' who transformed the garrison town of his father Frederic I 'The Soldier' into an elegant city.

Territory and Population
The area is 29,654 sq. km. Population, 31 Dec. 2017, 2,504,040 (1,268,069 females). There are four urban districts, 14 rural districts and 419 communes (31 Dec. 2013).

The capital is Potsdam, with a population (31 Dec. 2017) of 175,710.

Social Statistics
Statistics for calendar years:

	Live births	Marriages	Divorces	Deaths
2011	18,279	12,115	5,344	27,851
2012	18,482	12,505	5,031	28,403
2013	18,355	12,245	5,003	29,678
2014	19,339	12,812	4,887	28,990

Constitution and Government
The *Bundesland* was reconstituted on former GDR territory on 14 Oct. 1990. Brandenburg has four seats in the Bundesrat and following the 2009 election 19 in the Bundestag.

At a referendum on 14 June 1992, 93·5% of votes cast were in favour of a new constitution guaranteeing direct democracy and the right to work and housing.

Although a proposed merger between Brandenburg and Berlin was rejected in a 1996 referendum, a number of joint institutions have been established on the basis of 20 state treaties.

Recent Elections
At the Diet elections on 14 Sept. 2014 the Social Democrats (SPD) won 30 seats with 31·9% of the vote; the Christian Democrats (CDU) 21, with 23·0%; the Left 17, with 18·6%; the Alternative for Germany 11, with 12·2%; the Greens 6, with 6·2%; the Brandenburg United Citizens' Movement/Free Voters 3, with 2·7%. Turnout was 47·9%.

Current Government
The *Prime Minister* is Dietmar Woidke (SPD).

Since 2009 Brandenburg has had a 'red–red' coalition between the SPD and the former communist Left Party.
Government Website: http://www.brandenburg.de

Economy

Performance
GDP in 2014 was €61·9bn.; real GDP growth was 0·9%.

Energy and Natural Resources

Electricity
Power stations in Brandenburg produced 38,342m. kWh in 2013.

Agriculture
Area and yield of the most important crops:

	Area (in 1,000 ha.)			Yield (in 1,000 tonnes)		
	2012	2013	2014	2012	2013	2014
Wheat	135·2	140·4	159·6	760·3	1,008·9	1,208·8
Rye	210·4	236·9	184·5	974·1	1,188·7	954·6
Sugar beet	9·3	8·6	9·2	572·1	517·6	701·2
Barley	86·1	80·0	88·2	423·3	487·0	617·9
Rape	127·5	131·4	134·6	402·7	519·6	573·4
Potatoes	8·6	8·9	9·8	315·5	311·8	420·9

Livestock on 3 May 2014: cattle, 569,318 (including 164,986 dairy cows); horses, donkeys and mules (March 2010), 17,892; pigs, 786,275; sheep (Nov. 2014), 77,500; poultry (March 2013), 10,693,600.

Industry
In 2014, 1,200 establishments (20 or more employees) in the mining and manufacturing industries employed 99,432 persons. The main areas were: the food and animal feed industry; manufacture of chemical products; and metal production and treatment. There were 4,804 establishments in the building industry in 2014, employing an estimated 34,167 persons.

Labour
In 2014 at the 1%-sample of the microcensus, 1,281,800 persons were economically active. In 2014 there were on average 124,628 unemployed persons (9·4%).

Communications

Roads
On 1 Jan. 2014 there were 1,629,582 registered vehicles including 1,343,315 passenger cars, 117,610 lorries and 110,192 motorcycles. There were 79,286 accidents in 2014 with 8,419 injured persons.

Social Institutions

Education
In 2014–15 there were 977 schools providing general education (including special schools) with 241,434 pupils and 93 vocational schools with 34,431 pupils.

In the winter term 2014–15 there were four universities and eight colleges with 49,762 students.

Health
In 2014 there were 56 hospitals with 15,290 beds, 4,533 doctors and 20,848 medical personnel.

Religion

In 2011, 16·8% of the population were Protestants and 3·1% were Roman Catholics.

Culture

Tourism
In July 2014 there were 1,634 places of accommodation (with ten or more beds), including 435 hotels—providing a total of 84,576 beds—and 169 campsites. 4,400,436 visitors (388,662 foreign) spent a total of 11,935,669 nights (including camping) in Brandenburg in 2014.

Bremen

Freie Hansestadt Bremen

Key Historical Events

The state is dominated by the city of Bremen and its port, Bremerhaven. In 1815, when it joined the German Confederation, Bremen was an autonomous city and Hanse port with important Baltic trade. In 1827 the expansion of trade inspired the founding of Bremerhaven on land ceded by Hanover at the confluence of the Geest and Weser rivers. Further expansion followed the founding of the Nord-deutscher Lloyd Shipping Company in 1857. Merchant shipping, associated trade and fishing were dominant until 1940 but there was diversification in the post-war years. In 1939 Bremerhaven was absorbed by the Hanoverian town of Wesermünde. The combined port was returned to the jurisdiction of Bremen in 1947.

Territory and Population

The area of the *Bundesland*, consisting of the two urban districts and ports of Bremen and Bremerhaven, is 419·4 sq. km. Population, 31 Dec. 2017, 681,032 (336,665 males; 344,367 females).

The capital, Bremen, had a population of 565,719 at 31 Dec. 2016 and Bremerhaven had a population of 113,034.

Social Statistics

Statistics for calendar years:

	Live births	Marriages	Divorces	Deaths
2013	5,749	2,619	1,404	7,890
2014	6,211	2,800	1,382	7,437
2015	6,509	2,708	1,393	7,811
2016	7,136	2,676	1,419	7,732

Constitution and Government

Political power is vested in the 83-member House of Burgesses *(Bürgerschaft)* which appoints the executive, called the *Senate*. Bremen has three seats in the Bundesrat.

Recent Elections

At the elections of 10 May 2015 the Social Democratic Party won 30 seats with 32·8% of votes cast; the Christian Democratic Union 20 with 22·4%; the Greens 14 with 15·1%; the Left 8 with 9·5%; the Free Democratic Party 6 with 6·6%; the Alternative for Germany 4 with 5·5%; and Citizens in Rage 1 with 3·2%. Turnout was 50·1%.

Current Government

The *Burgomaster* is Carsten Sieling (SPD).
Government Website: http://www.bremen.de

Energy and Natural Resources

Agriculture
Agricultural area comprised (2015) 12,214 ha. Livestock includes: 9,765 cattle, of which 3,739 dairy cows (2016); 916 horses (2010); 3,467 laying hens (2016).

Industry

In 2016, 135 establishments (50 or more employees) employed 48,082 persons; of these, 23,164 were employed in the production of vehicles including 1,044 ship- and boatbuilding; 3,716 in production of metal products; 4,239 in machine construction; 2,759 in repair, maintenance, installation of machines including 484 in repair and maintenance of ships and boats; 1,549 in fish processing; 1,168 in coffee and tea processing.

Labour
Economically active persons totalled 326,000 at the microcensus of 2017. Of the total, 295,000 were employees including 14,000 trainees, 29,000 self-employed; 98,000 in commerce, trade and communications, 69,000 in production industries, 157,000 in other industries and services.

Communications

Roads
On 1 Jan. 2018 there were 116 km of 'classified' roads, of which 80 km were Autobahn and 34 km federal roads. Registered motor vehicles on 1 Jan. 2017 numbered 334,378 including 290,188 passenger cars, 18,075 lorries, 445 buses, 3,357 tractors and 20,446 motorcycles.

Civil Aviation
Bremen airport handled 2,540,084 passengers in 2017.

Shipping
Vessels entered in 2017, 7,656 of 329,097,000 GT; cleared, 5,976 of 247,465,000 GT. Sea traffic, 2017, incoming 37,105,000 tonnes; outgoing, 37,078,000 tonnes.

Social Institutions

Justice
There are a constitutional court *(Staatsgerichtshof)*, a court of appeal, a regional court, three local courts, a *Bundesland* labour court, two labour courts, a *Bundesland* social court, a finance court, a higher administrative court and an administrative court.

Education
In 2017 there were 294 schools of general education with 5,343 teachers and 65,479 pupils; 39 vocational schools (part-time and full-time) with 22,305 pupils; 28 advanced vocational schools (including institutions for the training of technicians) with 2,888 pupils; six schools for public health occupations with 872 pupils. In 2017 there were 25 special schools with 514 pupils.

In the winter term 2017–18, 18,736 students were enrolled at the University of Bremen and 1,262 at the Jacobs University Bremen. In addition to the universities there were seven other colleges in 2017–18 with 17,112 students.

Religion

In 2011, 39·7% of the population were Protestants and 12·2% were Roman Catholics.

Culture

Tourism
In 2017 there were 119 places of accommodation (with ten beds or more) providing 14,787 beds. Of the 1,329,820 visitors 19% were from abroad.

Hamburg

Freie und Hansestadt Hamburg

Key Historical Events
Hamburg was a free Hanse town owing nominal allegiance to the Holy Roman Emperor until 1806. In 1815 it became part of the German Confederation, sharing a seat in the Federal Diet with Lübeck, Bremen and Frankfurt. During the Empire it retained its autonomy. By 1938 it had become the third largest port in the world and its territory was extended by the cession of land (three urban and 27 rural districts) from Prussia. After World War II, Hamburg became a *Bundesland* of the Federal Republic with its 1938 boundaries.

Territory and Population
Total area, 755·1 sq. km (2017), including the islands Neuwerk and Scharhörn. Population (31 Dec. 2017), 1,830,584 (897,207 males; 933,377 females). The *Bundesland* forms a single urban district (*Stadtstaat)* with seven administrative subdivisions.

Social Statistics
Statistics for calendar years:

	Live births	Marriages	Divorces	Deaths
2012	17,696	6,774	3,446	17,012
2013	18,137	6,746	3,199	17,258
2014	19,039	6,142	3,265	16,780
2015	19,768	6,422	3,190	17,565

Constitution and Government
The constitution of 6 June 1952 vests the supreme power in the House of Burgesses *(Bürgerschaft)* of 121 members. The executive is in the hands of the Senate, whose members are elected by the Bürgerschaft. Hamburg has three seats in the Bundesrat.

Recent Elections
The elections of 15 Feb. 2015 had the following results: Social Democrats, 58 seats with 45·7% of votes cast; Christian Democrats, 20 with 15·9%; the Greens, 15 with 12·2%; the Left, 11 (8·5%); the Free Democratic Party, 9 (7·4%); the Alternative for Germany, 8 (6·1%). Turnout was 56·6%.

Current Government
The *First Mayor* is Peter Tschentscher (SPD).
Government Website: http://www.hamburg.de

Energy and Natural Resources

Agriculture
The agricultural area comprised 14,444 ha. in 2013.
  Livestock (May 2016) includes: 6,501 cattle, of which 1,145 dairy cows; 2,964 horses (March 2013); 2,881 sheep (March 2013); 2,664 poultry (March 2013).

Industry
In Sept. 2015, 433 establishments (with 20 or more employees) employed 85,622 persons; of these, 26,506 were employed in manufacturing transport equipment (including motor vehicles, aircraft and ships), 12,566 in manufacturing machinery, 9,787 in manufacturing electrical and optical equipment, 4,837 in manufacturing chemical products and 3,821 in the mineral oil industry.

Labour
Economically active persons totalled 912,000 at the 1%-sample survey of the microcensus of 2015. Of the total, 796,000 were employees and 116,000 were self-employed or unpaid family workers; 296,000 were engaged in commerce and transport, 144,000 in power supply, mining, manufacturing and building, 1,000 in agriculture and forestry, 471,000 in other industries and services.

Communications

Roads
In 2015 there were 3,928 km of roads, including 81 km of Autobahn and 109 km of federal roads. Number of motor vehicles (1 Jan. 2016), 879,843 of which 761,655 were passenger cars, 52,285 lorries, 1,714 buses, 55,535 motorcycles and 4,578 other motor vehicles.

Civil Aviation
Hamburg airport handled 15,583,546 passengers and 17,559 tonnes of freight in 2015.

Shipping
Hamburg is the largest sea port in Germany.

Vessels		2013	2014	2015
Entered:	Number	9,681	9,138	8,735
	Tonnage (gross)	250,591,979	258,591,421	260,940,664
Cleared:	Number	9,723	9,096	8,741
	Tonnage (gross)	250,575,600	257,248,571	259,744,450

Social Institutions

Justice
There are a constitutional court *(Verfassungsgericht)*, a court of appeal *(Oberlandesgericht)*, a regional court *(Landgericht)*, eight local courts *(Amtsgerichte)*, a *Bundesland* labour court, a labour court, a *Bundesland* social court, a social court, a finance court, a higher administrative court and an administrative court.

Education
In 2014–15 there were 382 schools of general education (not including the *Internationale Schule*) with 182,680 pupils; 31 special schools with 4,957 pupils; 46 part-time vocational schools with 36,545 pupils; 35 schools with 3,761 pupils in manual instruction classes; 44 full-time vocational schools with 4,918 pupils; six economic secondary schools with 1,206 pupils; two technical *Gymnasien* with 273 pupils; one pedagogical *Gymnasium* with 306 pupils; 20 advanced vocational schools with 5,398 pupils; 40 schools for public health occupations with 4,024 pupils; and 16 technical superior schools with 1,087 pupils.
  In the winter term 2015–16 there were four universities with 45,075 students; one technical university with 7,283 students; one college of music and one college of fine arts with 2,173 students in total; one university of the *Bundeswehr* (Helmut Schmidt University) with 2,298 students; 12 professional colleges with a total of 40,394 students.

Health
In 2015 there were 51 hospitals with 12,175 beds, 12,197 doctors and 1,979 dentists.

Religion
In 2011, 28·7% of the population were Protestants and 10·2% were Roman Catholics.

Culture

Tourism
At Dec. 2015 there were 344 places of accommodation with 57,919 beds. Of the 6,276,613 visitors in 2015, 22·3% were foreigners.

Hessen

Key Historical Events
The *Bundesland* consists of the former states of Hesse-Darmstadt and Hesse-Kassel, and Nassau. Hesse-Darmstadt was ruled by the Landgrave Louis X from 1790. He became grand duke in 1806 with absolute power, having dismissed the parliament in 1803. However, he granted a constitution and bicameral parliament in 1820. Hesse-Darmstadt lost land to Prussia in the Seven Weeks' War of 1866, but retained its independence, both then and as a state of the German Empire after 1871. In 1918 the grand duke abdicated and the territory became a state of the German Republic. In 1945 areas west of the Rhine were incorporated into the new *Bundesland* of Rhineland-Palatinate, areas east of the Rhine became part of the *Bundesland* of Greater Hesse.

Hesse-Kassel was ruled by the Landgrave William IX from 1785 until he became Elector in 1805. In 1807 the Electorate was absorbed into the Kingdom of Westphalia (a Napoleonic creation), becoming independent again in 1815 as a state of the German Confederation. In 1831 a constitution and parliament were granted but the Electors remained strongly conservative.

In 1866 the Diet approved alliance with Prussia against Austria; the Elector nevertheless supported Austria. He was defeated by the Prussians and exiled and Hesse-Kassel was annexed to Prussia. In 1867 it was combined with Frankfurt and some areas taken from Nassau and Hesse-Darmstadt to form a Prussian province (Hesse-Nassau). In 1801 Nassau west of the Rhine passed to France; Napoleon also took the northern state in 1806. The remnant of the southern states allied in 1803 and three years later they became a duchy. In 1866 the duke supported Austria against Prussia and the duchy was annexed by Prussia as a result. In 1944 the Prussian province of Hesse-Nassau was split in two: Nassau and Electoral Hesse, also called Kurhessen. The following year these were combined with Hesse-Darmstadt as the *Bundesland* of Greater Hesse which became known as Hessen.

Territory and Population

Area, 21,116 sq. km. There are three administrative regions with five urban and 21 rural districts and 426 communes. Population, 31 Dec. 2017, was 6,243,262 (3,081,636 males; 3,161,626 females).

The capital is Wiesbaden, with a population (31 Dec. 2017) of 278,654.

Social Statistics

Statistics for calendar years:

	Live births	Marriages	Divorces	Deaths
2012	51,607	27,721	14,334	61,857
2013	52,185	26,894	13,180	63,893
2014	54,631	28,009	13,149	61,183
2015	56,889	28,833	12,834	66,534

Constitution and Government

The constitution was put into force by popular referendum on 1 Dec. 1946. Hessen has five seats in the Bundesrat.

Recent Elections

At the Diet elections on 28 Oct. 2018 the Christian Democratic Union (CDU) won 40 of 137 seats with 27·0% of votes cast, the Greens 29 with 19·8%, the Social Democratic Party (SPD) 29 with 19·8%, the Alternative for Germany (AfD) 19 with 13·1%, Free Democratic Party (FDP) 11 with 7·5% and the Left 9 with 6·3%. Turnout was 67·3%.

Current Government

The cabinet is headed by *Prime Minister* Volker Bouffier (CDU). There is currently a CDU–Green Party coalition.

Government Website (German only): http://www.hessen.de

Economy

Performance

In 2015 the price-adjusted growth of the gross domestic product at market prices (GDP) was 1·7% in comparison with the previous year. The total amount at current prices was €263·4bn. in 2015. The GDP (at current prices) per person engaged in labour productivity was €78,790 in 2015 (€76,685 in 2014).

Energy and Natural Resources

Electricity

Electricity production in 2014 (provisional) was 13,103m. kWh (gross) and 12,409m. kWh (net). Total electricity consumption in 2014 was 34,740m. kWh (provisional).

Oil and Gas

Gas consumption in 2014 was 57,289m. kWh (provisional). All gas was imported from other parts of Germany.

Agriculture

Area and yield of the most important crops:
Area (in 1,000 ha.) Yield (in 1,000 tonnes)

	Area (in 1,000 ha.)			Yield (in 1,000 tonnes)		
	2013	2014	2015	2013	2014	2015
Wheat	169·0	167·2	165·8	1,401·7	1,398·5	1,318·4
Sugar beet	13·6	13·4	11·5	959·7	1,156·1	822·2
Barley	81·8	88·7	86·4	532·1	572·1	576·3
Rape	63·9	63·4	55·6	252·3	282·2	213·0
Potatoes	4·3	4·2	3·7	163·6	188·6	132·9
Rye	19·7	15·2	13·9	120·0	93·8	82·7
Oats	9·8	9·0	9·8	51·5	47·8	42·3

Livestock, Nov. 2015: cattle, 458,981 (including 145,218 dairy cows); horses, donkeys and mules (March 2013), 32,800; pigs, 599,900; sheep, 113,500; poultry (March 2013), 2·39m.

Industry

In Sept. 2015, 1,406 establishments (with 50 or more employees) employed 364,498 persons; of these, 57,985 were employed in the chemical industry; 52,001 in motor vehicle manufacture; 39,801 in machine construction; 28,832 in production of metal products.

Labour

Economically active persons totalled 3,050,000 at the 1% sample survey of the microcensus in 2015. Of the total, 2,706,000 were employees, 328,000 self-employed, 15,000 unpaid family workers; 837,000 were engaged in commerce, transport, hotels and restaurants, 734,000 in power supply, mining, manufacturing and building, 31,000 in agriculture and forestry, and 1,448,000 in other services.

Communications

Roads

On 1 Jan. 2015 there were 16,097 km of 'classified' roads, comprising 987 km of Autobahn, 3,015 km of federal highways, 7,165 km of first-class highways and 4,930 km of second-class highways. Motor vehicles licensed on 1 Jan. 2015 totalled 4,159,474, including 3,483,965 passenger cars, 5,755 buses, 188,240 lorries, 142,716 tractors and 318,507 motorcycles.

Civil Aviation

Frankfurt/Main airport is one of the most important freight airports in the world. In 2015, 468,153 aeroplanes took off and landed, carrying 61,040,613 passengers, 2,030,861 tonnes of air freight and 83,718 tonnes of air mail.

Shipping

Frankfurt/Main harbour and Hanau harbour are the two most important harbours. In 2015, 7·5m. tonnes of goods were imported into the *Bundesland* and 2·7m. tonnes were exported.

Social Institutions

Justice

There are a constitutional court *(Staatsgerichtshof)*, a court of appeal, nine regional courts, 44 local courts, a *Bundesland* labour court, seven labour courts, a *Bundesland* social court, seven social courts, a finance court, a higher administrative court *(Verwaltungsgerichtshof)* and five administrative courts.

Education

In 2015 there were 1,212 primary schools with 225,446 pupils (including *Förderstufen*); 149 intermediate schools with 43,456 pupils; 19,237 teachers in the primary and intermediate schools; 233 special schools with 5,843 teachers and 22,619 pupils; 181 high schools with 11,328 teachers and 144,814 pupils; 232 *Gesamtschulen* (comprehensive schools) with 13,227 teachers and 179,395 pupils; 115 part-time vocational schools with 108,753 pupils; 266 full-time vocational schools with 59,112 pupils; 120 advanced vocational schools with 16,354 pupils; 9,538 teachers in the vocational schools.

In the winter term 2015–16 there were four universities (Frankfurt/Main, 45,379 students; Giessen, 28,198; Marburg/Lahn, 26,062; Kassel, 24,168); one technical university in Darmstadt (26,503); two private scientific colleges (3,964); 20 universities of applied sciences (87,547); two Roman Catholic theological colleges and four Protestant theological colleges with a total of 764 students; one college of music and two colleges of fine arts with 1,737 students in total.

Religion
In 2012 the churches in Hessen reported 2,333,000 Protestants and 1,472,000 Roman Catholics.

Culture

Press
In 2012 there were 70 newspapers published in Hessen with a combined circulation of 1·2m.

Tourism
In 2015, 14·3m. visitors stayed 32·2m. nights in Hessen.

Lower Saxony

Niedersachsen

Key Historical Events
The *Bundesland* consists of the former states of Hanover, Oldenburg, Schaumburg-Lippe and Brunswick. It does not include the cities of Bremen or Bremerhaven. Oldenburg, Danish from 1667, passed to the bishopric of Lübeck in 1773; the Holy Roman Emperor made it a duchy in 1777. As a small state of the Confederation after 1815 it supported Prussia, becoming a member of the Prussian Zollverein (1853) and North German Confederation (1867). The grand duke abdicated in 1918 and was replaced by an elected government.

Schaumburg-Lippe was a small sovereign principality. As such it became a member of the Confederation of the Rhine in 1807 and of the German Confederation in 1815. Surrounded by Prussian territory, it also joined the Prussian-led North German Confederation in 1867. Part of the Empire until 1918, it then became a state of the new republic.

Brunswick, a small duchy, was taken into the Kingdom of Westphalia by Napoleon in 1806 but restored to independence in 1814. In 1830 the duke, Charles II, was forced into exile and replaced in 1831 by his more liberal brother, William. The succession passed to a Hanoverian claimant in 1913 but the duchy ended with the Empire in 1918.

As a state of the republican Germany, Brunswick was greatly reduced under the Third Reich. Its boundaries were restored by the British occupation forces in 1945.

Hanover was an autonomous Electorate of the Holy Roman Empire whose rulers were also kings of Great Britain from 1714 to 1837. From 1762 they ruled almost entirely from England. After Napoleonic invasions Hanover was restored in 1815. A constitution of 1819 made no radical change and had to be followed by more liberal versions in 1833 and 1848. Prussia annexed Hanover in 1866; it remained a Prussian province until 1946. On 1 Nov. 1946 all four states were combined by the British military administration to form the *Bundesland* of Lower Saxony.

Territory and Population
Lower Saxony has an area of 47,710 sq. km, and is divided into eight urban districts, 38 rural districts and 971 communes. Population, on 31 Dec. 2017, was 7,962,775 (3,931,876 males; 4,030,899 females).

The capital is Hanover, with a population (31 Dec. 2017) of 535,061.

Social Statistics
Statistics for calendar years:

	Live births	Marriages	Divorces	Deaths
2011	61,280	37,645	18,953	85,489
2012	61,478	38,947	17,806	87,040
2013	62,879	37,405	17,307	90,569
2014	66,406	38,792	16,776	87,571

Constitution and Government
The *Bundesland* Niedersachsen was formed on 1 Nov. 1946 by merging the former Prussian province of Hanover with Brunswick, Oldenburg and Schaumburg-Lippe. Lower Saxony has six seats in the Bundesrat.

Recent Elections
At the Diet elections on 15 Oct. 2017 the Social Democratic Party won 55 of 137 seats, receiving 36·9% of votes cast (up from 32·6% in 2013), the Christian Democratic Union 50 with 33·6% (down from 36·0% in 2015), the Greens 12 with 8·7%, the Free Democrats 11 with 7·5% and the Alternative for Germany 9 with 6·2%. Turnout was 63·1%.

Current Government
The *Prime Minister* is Stephan Weil (SPD).
Government Website: http://www.niedersachsen.de

Economy

Banking and Finance
179 credit institutions were operating in 2014. Deposits totalled €51,576m.

Energy and Natural Resources

Electricity
Electricity production in 2014 was 41,438m. kWh.

Agriculture
Area and yield of the most important crops:

	Area (in 1,000 ha.)			Yield (in 1,000 tonnes)		
	2012	2013	2014	2012	2013	2014
Sugar beet	108	97	101	7,695	6,322	8,435
Potatoes	104	103	105	4,803	4,405	5,046
Wheat	378	402	410	2,839	3,481	3,661
Barley	183	171	177	1,173	1,198	1,343
Rye	133	151	135	860	1,095	955
Oats	13	12	10	72	60	49

Livestock, May 2015 unless otherwise indicated: cattle, 2,632,442 (including 851,962 dairy cows); horses, donkeys and mules, 70,811 (March 2010); pigs, 8,826,900 (Nov. 2014); sheep, 170,100 (Nov. 2014); poultry 56,609,004 (March 2010).

Industry
In Sept. 2014, 3,569 establishments employed 530,126 persons; of these 59,512 were employed in machine construction.

Labour
Economically active persons totalled 3,794,000 in 2014. Of the total, 3,406,000 were employees, 364,000 self-employed, 23,000 unpaid family workers; 1,017,000 were engaged in power supply, mining, manufacturing and building, 981,000 in commerce and transport, 95,000 in agriculture and forestry, and 1,702,000 in other industries and services.

Communications

Roads
At 1 Jan. 2015 there were 28,068 km of 'classified' roads, comprising 1,444 km of Autobahn, 4,683 km of federal roads, 8,242 km of first-class and 13,699 km of second-class highways. Number of motor vehicles, 1 Jan. 2015, was 5,384,978 including 4,451,016 passenger cars, 254,989 lorries, 7,726 buses, 238,376 tractors and 403,383 motorcycles.

Rail
In 2014, 51·7m. tonnes of freight came into the *Bundesland* by rail and 41·3m. tonnes left by rail.

Civil Aviation
66,099 planes landed at Hanover airport in 2014, which saw 2,644,954 passenger arrivals and 2,621,477 departures. 7,284 tonnes of freight (including post) left by air and 7,896 tonnes (including post) came in.

Social Institutions

Justice
There are a constitutional court *(Staatsgerichtshof)*, three courts of appeal, 11 regional courts, 80 local courts, a *Bundesland* labour court, 15 labour courts, a *Bundesland* social court, eight social courts, a finance court, a higher administrative court and seven administrative courts.

Education
In 2014–15 there were 1,739 primary schools with 282,988 pupils; 425 post-primary schools with 42,790 pupils; 260 secondary schools with 55,261 pupils; 444 secondary modern schools with 104,357 pupils; 257 grammar schools with 222,565 pupils; 37 co-operative comprehensive schools with 42,877 pupils; 91 integrated comprehensive schools with 64,022 pupils; and 311 special schools with 29,257 pupils.

In the winter term 2014–15 there were seven universities (Göttingen, 28,544 students; Hanover, 25,249; Hildesheim, 6,882; Lüneburg, 8,912; Oldenburg, 13,237; Osnabrück, 12,679; Vechta, 4,866); two technical universities (Braunschweig, 18,319; Clausthal, 4,823); the medical college of Hanover (3,334); the veterinary college in Hanover (2,392); 14 colleges with 58,410 students; two colleges of music and fine arts with a total of 2,484 students and two colleges of public administration with 1,084 students.

Health
In 2014 there were 30,944 doctors and 196 hospitals with 5·4 beds per 1,000 population.

Religion
In 2013, 48·0% of the population were Protestants and 17·6% were Roman Catholics.

Culture

Tourism
In 2014, 13,080,201 guests spent 40,423,767 nights in Lower Saxony.

Mecklenburg-West Pomerania

Mecklenburg-Vorpommern

Key Historical Events
Pomerania was at one time under Swedish control while Mecklenburg was an independent part of the German Empire. The two states were not united until after the Second World War, and after a short period when it was subdivided into three districts under the GDR, it became a state of the Federal Republic of Germany in 1990. The people of the region speak a dialect known as Plattdeutsch (Low German). The four main cities of this state are Hanseatic towns from the period when the area dominated trade with Scandinavia. Rostock on the North Sea coast became the home of the GDR's biggest shipyards.

Territory and Population
The area is 23,294 sq. km. It is divided into two urban districts, six rural districts and 783 communes. Population on 31 Dec. 2017 was 1,611,119 (816,246 females). It is the most sparsely populated of the German *Bundesländer*, with a population density of 69 per sq. km in 2017.

The capital is Schwerin, with a population (31 Dec. 2017) of 95,797.

Social Statistics
Statistics for calendar years:

	Live births	Marriages	Divorces	Deaths
2009	13,014	10,493	3,221	18,342
2010	13,337	10,751	3,238	18,738
2011	12,638	10,400	3,407	18,572
2012	12,715	10,713	3,276	18,912

Constitution and Government
The *Bundesland* was reconstituted on former GDR territory in 1990. It has three seats in the Bundesrat.

Recent Elections
At the Diet elections of 4 Sept. 2016 the Social Democrats (SPD) won 26 seats with 30·6% of the vote; the Alternative for Germany (AfD), 18 with 20·8%; the Christian Democratic Union (CDU), 16 with 19·0%; the Left Party, 11 with 13·2%. Turnout was 61·6%.

Current Government
The *Prime Minister* is Manuela Schwesig (SPD).
Government Website: http://www.mecklenburg-vorpommern.eu

Energy and Natural Resources

Agriculture
Area and yield of the most important crops:

	Area (in 1,000 ha.)			Yield (in 1,000 tonnes)		
	2010	2011	2012	2010	2011	2012
Wheat	350·3	352·3	362·1	2,465·1	2,350·2	2,695·6
Sugar beet	24·6	27·6	26·2	1,296·9	1,719·7	1,575·6
Barley	119·1	118·4	126·8	870·5	644·8	855·1
Rape	252·0	204·9	198·2	1,011·7	558·0	780·6
Potatoes	13·9	13·6	12·8	434·1	473·3	476·3
Rye	62·8	70·5	82·2	277·5	301·7	451·4

Livestock in 2012: cattle, 544,558 (including 177,857 dairy cows); horses (2010), 13,869; pigs, 864,005; sheep, 69,200; poultry (2010), 8,722,482.

Fisheries
Sea catch, 2011: 19,575 tonnes (5,735 tonnes frozen, 13,840 tonnes fresh). Freshwater catch, 2012: 542 tonnes. Fish farming, 2012: 656 tonnes.

Industry
In 2012 there were 679 enterprises (with 20 or more employees) employing 57,292 persons.

Labour
763,900 persons (358,300 females) were employed at the 1%-sample survey of the microcensus (2012 average at the place of residence), including 391,600 white-collar workers, 247,600 manual workers and 68,100 self-employed and family assistants. 28,400 persons were employed as officials. Employment by sector (2012 average at the place of work): public and private services, 256,800; trade, guest business, transport and communications, 190,500; financing, leasing and services for enterprises, 115,800; manufacturing, 76,900; construction, 55,000; agriculture, forestry and fisheries, 23,000; mining, energy and water resources, 10,900; total, 729,000.

Communications

Roads
In 2012 there were 10,010 km of 'classified' roads, comprising 554 km of Autobahn, 1,993 km of federal roads, 3,309 km of first-class and 4,154 km of second-class highways. Number of motor vehicles at 1 Jan. 2013 was 988,768, including 820,717 passenger cars, 70,940 lorries and 57,420 motorcycles.

Shipping
There is a lake district of some 555 lakes greater than 0·1 sq. km. The ports of Rostock, Stralsund and Wismar are important for shipbuilding and repairs. In 2012 the cargo fleet consisted of 192 vessels (including eight tankers) of 2,718,000 GT. Marine freight traffic in 2012 totalled 25,670,000 tonnes.

Social Institutions

Justice
There are a court of appeal *(Oberlandesgericht)*, four regional courts *(Landgerichte)*, 21 local courts *(Amtsgerichte)*, four labour courts, four social courts, a finance court and two administrative courts.

Education
In 2012 there were 568 schools with 134,876 pupils, including 49,368 pupils in primary schools, 62,912 in secondary schools and 13,914 candidates for the school-leaving examination; and 8,655 pupils in special needs schools.

There are universities at Rostock and Greifswald with (in 2012–13) 26,798 students and 6,442 academic staff, and six institutions of equivalent status with 13,108 students and 1,561 academic staff.

Religion
In 2012 the Evangelical Lutheran Church of Mecklenburg had 186,700 adherents, 194 pastors and 266 parishes. The Pomeranian Evangelical Church had 90,000 adherents, 106 pastors and 176 parishes in 2012. Roman Catholics numbered 53,800, with 31 priests and 40 parishes.

Culture

Tourism
In July 2012 there were 3,063 places of accommodation (with nine or more beds; excluding camping places) providing a total of 290,166 beds. 6,993,178 guests stayed an average of 4·0 nights each in 2012 (excluding camping places).

North Rhine-Westphalia

Nordrhein-Westfalen

Key Historical Events
Historical Westphalia consisted of many small political units, most of them absorbed by Prussia and Hanover before 1800. In 1807 Napoleon created a Kingdom of Westphalia for his brother Joseph. This included Hesse-Kassel, but was formed mainly from the Prussian and Hanoverian lands between the rivers Elbe and Weser.

In 1815 the kingdom ended with Napoleon's defeat. Most of the area was given to Prussia, with the small principalities of Lippe and Waldeck surviving as independent states. Both joined the North German Confederation in 1867. Lippe remained autonomous after the end of the Empire in 1918; Waldeck was absorbed into Prussia in 1929.

In 1946 the occupying forces combined Lippe with most of the Prussian province of Westphalia to form the *Bundesland* of North Rhine-Westphalia. On 1 March 1947 the allied Control Council formally abolished Prussia.

Territory and Population
The *Bundesland* comprises 34,112 sq. km. It is divided into five administrative regions, 22 urban districts, 31 rural districts and 396 communes. Population, 31 Dec. 2017, 17,912,134 (9,124,555 females; 8,787,579 males).

The capital is Düsseldorf, with a population (31 Dec. 2017) of 617,280.

Social Statistics
Statistics for calendar years:

	Live births	Marriages	Divorces	Deaths
2014	155,102	82,322	39,489	192,913
2015	160,468	85,045	38,312	204,352
2016	173,276	87,060	37,650	202,251
2017	171,984	86,475	35,778	204,842

Constitution and Government
Since Oct. 1990 North Rhine-Westphalia has had six seats in the Bundesrat.

Recent Elections
At the Diet elections on 14 May 2017 the Christian Democratic Union won 72 of 199 seats with 33·0% of votes cast, the Social Democratic Party 69 (31·2%), the Free Democratic Party 28 (12·6%), the Alternative for Germany 16 (7·4%) and the Greens 14 (6·4%). Turnout was 65·2%.

Current Government
North Rhine-Westphalia is governed by the Christian Democratic Union (CDU) and the Free Democratic Party.

Prime Minister: Armin Laschet (CDU).
Government Website: https://www.land.nrw

Economy
North Rhine-Westphalia has the highest GDP of any German *Bundesland* (€691·5bn. in 2017). Foreign direct investment is also higher than in any other *Bundesland*.

Budget
The predicted total revenue for 2017 was €72,706m. and the predicted total expenditure was €72,707m.

Energy and Natural Resources

Agriculture
Area and yield of the most important crops:

	Area (in 1,000 ha.)			Yield (in 1,000 tonnes)		
	2015	2016	2017	2015	2016	2017
Sugar beet	47·8	48·4	61·0	3,768·6	3,626·2	5,411·5
Wheat	279·1	268·6	265·0	2,449·5	2,161·3	2,098·3
Potatoes	28·5	31·0	31·1	1,453·7	1,457·2	1,627·0
Barley	150·8	152·1	145·5	1,239·6	1,085·2	1,057·0
Rye	16·6	16·6	16·9	117·9	100·4	97·7
Oats	7·0	7·3	7·8	41·1	38·8	38·6

Livestock, May 2017: cattle, 1,423,617 (including 416,374 dairy cows); pigs, 7,239,500; sheep (Nov. 2017), 138,900; poultry (March 2016), 13,560,407.

Industry
In Sept. 2017, 10,144 establishments (with 20 or more employees) employed 1,228,302 persons: 284,640 were employed in metal production and manufacture of metal goods; 199,875 in machine construction; 123,439 in manufacture of office machines, computers, electrical and precision engineering and optics; 105,945 in the chemical industry; 108,876 in production of food and tobacco; and 82,849 in motor vehicle manufacture. 73·6% of the workforce is now employed in the services sector. Of the total population, 8·6% were engaged in industry.

Labour
Economically active persons totalled 8,657,000 at the 1%-sample survey of the microcensus of 2017. Of the total, 7,822,000 were employees, 813,000 self-employed and 21,000 unpaid family workers; 2,221,000 were engaged in power supply, mining, manufacturing, water supply and building, 2,316,000 in commerce, hotel trade and transport, 66,000 in agriculture, forestry and fishing, and 4,054,000 in other industries and services.

Communications

Roads
There were (1 Jan. 2018) 29,531 km of 'classified' roads, comprising 2,224 km of Autobahn, 4,448 km of federal roads, 13,089 km of first-class and 9,770 km of second-class highways. Number of motor vehicles (1 Jan. 2018): 11,721,774, including 9,950,324 passenger cars, 621,293 lorries, 16,563 buses and 833,009 motorcycles.

Civil Aviation
In 2017, 107,377 aircraft landed at Düsseldorf, bringing 12,327,365 incoming passengers; and 64,383 aircraft landed at Cologne-Bonn, bringing 6,178,514 incoming passengers.

Social Institutions

Justice
There are a constitutional court *(Verfassungsgerichtshof)*, three courts of appeal, 19 regional courts, 129 local courts, three *Bundesland* labour courts, 30 labour courts, one *Bundesland* social court, eight social courts, three finance courts, a higher administrative court and seven administrative courts.

Education
In Oct. 2016 there were 2,812 primary schools *(Grundschulen)* with 43,553 teachers and 632,693 pupils; 404 elementary schools and lower secondary schools (Volks- und Hauptschulen) with 8,840 teachers and 88,101 pupils; 504 special schools *(Förderschulen Grund-/Hauptschule/Förderschulen Realschule/Gymnasium)* with 17,156 teachers and 76,883 pupils; 538 intermediate schools *(Realschulen)* with 15,050 teachers and 235,524 pupils; 513 comprehensive schools *(PRIMUS-Schulen/Sekundarschulen/ Gesamtschulen/Gemeinschaftsschulen/Freie Waldorfschulen)* with 31,095

teachers and 369,451 pupils; 626 high schools (*Gymnasien*) with 40,566 teachers and 527,499 pupils; 306 vocational schools (*Berufsschulen*) with 347,280 pupils; 230 vocational high schools (*Berufliche Gymnasien*) with 37,671 pupils; 325 specialized vocational schools (*Berufsfachschulen*) with 109,257 pupils; 202 full-time vocational schools (*Fachoberschulen*) leading up to vocational colleges with 21,142 pupils; 273 advanced full-time vocational schools with 51,048 pupils; 389 schools for public health occupations (*Schulen des Gesundheitswesens*) with 12,109 teachers and 48,749 pupils; 53 training colleges with 1,710 teachers and 22,978 pupils.

In the winter term 2017–18 there were 15 universities (Bielefeld, 25,000 students; Bochum, 42,569; Bonn, 37,439; Cologne, 51,686; Dortmund, 33,862; Düsseldorf, 35,232; Duisburg-Essen, 42,676; Münster, 44,583; Paderborn, 20,132; Siegen, 19,352; Witten/Herdecke, 2,409; Wuppertal, 21,864; the Technical University of Aachen, 45,282; Fernuniversität at Hagen, 64,360; German Police University/DHPol, 367); German Sport University in Cologne, 5,318; three Roman Catholic and two Protestant theological colleges with a total of 388 students. There were also four colleges of music and five colleges of fine arts with 7,387 students in total and 44 *Fachhochschulen* (vocational colleges) with 249,438 students.

Health
In 2017 there were 344 hospitals in North Rhine-Westphalia with 118,506 beds, which had an average occupancy rate of 76·9%.

Religion
In 2011, 40·9% of the population were Roman Catholics and 26·9% were Protestants.

Culture

Tourism
In Dec. 2017 there were 5,227 places of accommodation (ten beds or more) providing 323,470 beds altogether. In 2017, 23,279,062 visitors (5,271,430 foreigners) spent 51,509,458 nights in North Rhine-Westphalia.

Rhineland-Palatinate

Rheinland-Pfalz

Key Historical Events
The *Bundesland* was formed from the Rhenisch Palatinate and the Rhine valley areas of Prussia, Hesse-Darmstadt, Hesse-Kassel and Bavaria.

From 1214 the Palatinate was ruled by the Bavarian house of Wittelsbach, with its capital as Heidelberg. In 1797 the land west of the Rhine was taken into France, and Napoleon divided the eastern land between Baden and Hesse. In 1815 the territory taken by France was restored to Germany and allotted to Bavaria. The area and its neighbours formed the strategically important Bavarian Circle of the Rhine. The rule of the Wittelsbachs ended in 1918 but the Palatinate remained part of Bavaria until the American occupying forces detached it in 1946. The new *Bundesland*, incorporating the Palatinate and other territory, received its constitution in April 1947.

Territory and Population
Rhineland-Palatinate has an area of 19,858 sq. km. It comprises 12 urban districts, 24 rural districts and 2,293 other communes. Population (at 31 Dec. 2017), 4,073,679 (2,062,556 females).

The capital is Mainz, with a population (31 Dec. 2017) of 215,110.

Social Statistics
Statistics for calendar years:

	Live births	Marriages	Divorces	Deaths
2012	31,169	20,242	9,724	44,404
2013	31,989	19,223	9,377	45,532
2014	33,427	19,627	9,022	44,307
2015	34,946	20,341	8,835	46,777

Constitution and Government
The constitution of the *Bundesland* Rheinland-Pfalz was approved by the Consultative Assembly on 25 April 1947 and by referendum on 18 May

1947, when 579,002 voted for and 514,338 against its acceptance. It has four seats in the Bundesrat.

Recent Elections
At the elections of 13 March 2016 the Social Democratic Party won 39 seats with 36·2% of votes cast, the Christian Democrats 35 with 31·8%, the Alternative for Germany 14 with 12·6%, the Free Democrats 7 with 6·2% and the Greens 6 with 5·3%. Turnout was 70·4%.

Current Government
The cabinet is headed by *Prime Minister* Malu Dreyer (SPD). There is currently an SPD–Free Democrats–Green Party coalition.
Government Website (limited English): http://www.rlp.de

Energy and Natural Resources

Agriculture
Area and yield of the most important products:

	Area (1,000 ha.)			Yield (1,000 tonnes)		
	2013	2014	2015	2013	2014	2015
Sugar beet	17·5	18·0	14·9	1,234·2	1,517·8	907·7
Wheat	120·5	119·9	117·6	927·9	855·8	862·1
Barley	71·5	78·0	79·2	445·3	469·9	500·2
Potatoes	7·9	7·3	7·2	286·3	285·2	244·8
Rye	15·3	10·7	10·1	102·9	70·0	67·2
Oats	5·9	5·8	4·8	29·1	27·6	22·8
Wine	61·9	62·4	62·3	5,725·0[1]	6,054·5[1]	5,894·5[1]

[1] 1,000 hectolitres.

Livestock (2015, in 1,000): cattle, 359·5 (including dairy cows, 118·1); horses, donkeys and mules, 19·0 (2013); pigs, 192·0; sheep, 66·2; poultry, 14·9 (2013).

Forestry
Total area covered by forests in Dec. 2015 was 8,339·0 sq. km, or 42·3% of the total area.

Industry
In 2015, 2,244 establishments (with 20 or more employees) employed 291,082 persons; of these 47,721 were employed in the chemical industry; 38,912 in machine construction; 37,658 in metal production and manufacture of metal goods; 25,766 in motor vehicle manufacture; 18,191 in production of food.

Labour
Economically active persons totalled 1,998,600 in 2015. Of the total, 1,795,900 were employees, 192,900 were self-employed, 9,800 were unpaid family workers; 551,800 were engaged in power supply, mining, manufacturing and building, 513,500 in commerce, transport, communication, hotels and restaurants, 34,400 in agriculture and forestry, and 898,800 in other industries and services.

Communications

Roads
In 2016 there were 18,384 km of 'classified' roads, comprising 877 km of Autobahn, 2,881 km of federal roads, 7,248 km of first-class and 7,378 km of second-class highways. Number of motor vehicles, 1 Jan. 2016, was 2,947,349, including 2,410,786 passenger cars, 133,226 lorries, 5,275 buses, 145,578 tractors and 238,034 motorcycles.

Social Institutions

Justice
There are a constitutional court *(Verfassungsgerichtshof)*, two courts of appeal, eight regional courts, 47 local courts, a *Bundesland* labour court, five labour courts, a *Bundesland* social court, four social courts, a finance court, a higher administrative court and four administrative courts.

Education

In 2015 there were 974 primary schools with 10,289 teachers and 135,614 pupils; 423 secondary schools with 21,152 teachers and 265,163 pupils; 132 special schools with 3,115 teachers and 14,578 pupils; 137 vocational and advanced vocational schools with 5,753 teachers and 122,215 pupils.

In higher education, in the winter term 2015–16 there were the University of Mainz (33,017 students), the University of Koblenz-Landau (15,757 students), the University of Kaiserslautern (14,242 students), the University of Trier (13,551 students), the *Deutsche Universität für Verwaltungswissenschaften* in Speyer (402 students), the *Wissenschaftliche Hochschule für Unternehmensführung* (Otto Beisheim Graduate School) in Vallendar (1,083 students), the Roman Catholic Theological College in Trier (273 students) and the Roman Catholic Theological College in Vallendar (346 students). There were also nine *Fachhochschulen* with 39,941 students and four *Verwaltungsfachhochschulen* with 2,847 students.

Religion

In 2015, 41·8% of the population were Roman Catholics and 28·2% Protestants.

Culture

Tourism
In 2015, 3,282 places of accommodation provided 148,230 beds for 7,684,980 visitors.

Saarland

Key Historical Events

Long disputed between Germany and France, the area was occupied by France in 1792. Most of it was allotted to Prussia at the close of the Napoleonic wars in 1815. In 1870 Prussia defeated France and when, in 1871, the German Empire was founded under Prussian leadership, it was able to incorporate Lorraine. This part of France was the Saar territory's western neighbour so the Saar was no longer a vulnerable boundary state. It began to develop industrially, exploiting Lorraine coal and iron.

In 1919 the League of Nations took control of the Saar until a plebiscite of 1935 favoured return to Germany. In 1945 there was a French occupation, and in 1947 the Saar was made an international area, but in economic union with France. In 1954 France and Germany agreed that the Saar should be a separate and autonomous state, under an independent commissioner. This was rejected by referendum and France agreed to return Saarland to Germany; it became a *Bundesland* of the Federal Republic on 1 Jan. 1957.

Territory and Population

The Saarland has an area of 2,571 sq. km (including a mutual area with Luxembourg). It comprises six rural districts and 52 communes. Population, 31 Dec. 2017, 994,187 (487,895 males; 506,292 females).

The capital is Saarbrücken, with a population (31 Dec. 2017) of 180,966.

Social Statistics

Statistics for calendar years:

	Live births	Marriages	Divorces	Deaths
2014	7,328	4,702	2,133	12,529
2015	7,511	4,861	2,131	13,427
2016	8,215	4,980	2,209	12,897
2017	8,313	4,698	2,037	13,275

Constitution and Government

The Saarland has three seats in the Bundesrat. Ten politicians from the Saarland were elected to the Bundestag.

Recent Elections

At the elections to the Saar Diet of 26 March 2017 the Christian Democrats (CDU) won 24 of 51 seats with 40·7% of votes cast; the Social Democrats (SPD) 17, with 29·6%; the Left 7, with 12·9%; the Alternative for Germany (AfD) 3, with 6·2%. Turnout was 69·7%.

Current Government

Since 2012 Saarland has been governed by a coalition of Christian Democrats (CDU) and Social Democrats (SPD). The *Prime Minister* is Tobias Hans (CDU).
Government Website (German only): http://www.saarland.de

Energy and Natural Resources

Electricity
In 2017 electricity production for public power supply was 4,383 GWh. End-user consumption totalled 6,385 GWh in 2017.

Oil and Gas
5,856m. kWh of gas was used in 2017.

Agriculture
The cultivated area (2017) occupied 110,374 ha. or 42·9% of the total area.
Area and yield of the most important crops:

	Area (in 1,000 ha.)			Yield (in 1,000 tonnes)		
	2015	2016	2017	2015	2016	2017
Wheat	9·9	—	9·2	64·4	52·6	55·0
Barley	4·7	4·5	4·3	26·6	24·5	22·8
Rye	2·9	3·0	2·7	15·6	13·3	14·2
Oats	1·9	1·5	2·0	8·1	5·8	7·3
Potatoes	0·1	0·1	0·1	3·6	2·6	3·7

Livestock, May 2017: cattle, 47,166 (including 14,139 dairy cows); pigs, 4,257; sheep, (Nov. 2017) 5,651; horses (March 2016), 5,064; poultry (March 2016), 166,145.

Forestry
The forest area (2017: 85,608 ha.) comprises 33·3% of the total (257,110 ha.).

Industry

In June 2018, 226 establishments (with 50 or more employees) employed 82,567 persons; of these 18,188 were engaged in manufacturing of motor vehicles, parts and accessories, 18,268 in machine construction, 9,983 in iron and steel production, 2,542 in steel construction and 1,803 in electrical engineering. Two blast furnaces and eight steel furnaces produced 4·6m. tonnes of pig iron and 6·5m. tonnes of crude steel in 2017. Coal mining ended in June 2012.

Labour
Economically active persons totalled 478,000 at the 1%-sample survey of the microcensus of 2017. Of the total, 433,000 were employees and 45,000 self-employed; 141,000 were engaged in power supply, mining, manufacturing and building, 113,000 in commerce and transport and 224,000 in other industries and services.

Communications

Roads
At 1 Jan. 2018 there were 2,048 km of classified roads, comprising 240 km of Autobahn, 309 km of federal roads, 872 km of first-class and 626 km of second-class highways. Number of registered motor vehicles, 1 Jan. 2018, 747,138, including 629,613 passenger cars, 34,965 lorries, 1,161 buses, 18,260 tractors and 59,963 motorcycles.

Shipping
In 2017, 2,479 ships docked in Saarland ports, bringing 3·8m. tonnes of freight. In the same year 2,479 ships left the ports, carrying 1·1m. tonnes of freight.

Social Institutions

Justice
There are a constitutional court *(Verfassungsgerichtshof)*, a regional court of appeal, a regional court, ten local courts, a *Bundesland* labour court, three labour courts, a *Bundesland* social court, a social court, a finance court, a higher administrative court and an administrative court.

Education
In 2017–18 there were 162 primary schools with 31,509 pupils; 37 special schools with 3,314 pupils; three *Realschulen* and *Erweiterte Realschulen* with 1,106 pupils; 60 *Gemeinschaftsschulen* with 28,282 pupils; two evening *Gemeinschaftsschulen* with 216 pupils; one *Gesamtschule* with 828 pupils;

35 high schools with 24,628 pupils; four *Freie Waldorfschulen* with 1,238 pupils; one evening high school with 133 pupils; one Saarland College with 100 pupils; 37 part-time vocational schools with 17,118 pupils; year of commercial basic training: 58 institutions with 2,618 pupils; 13 advanced full-time vocational schools and schools for technicians with 2,970 pupils; 39 full-time vocational schools with 3,038 pupils; 36 *Fachoberschulen* (full-time vocational schools leading up to vocational colleges) with 4,691 pupils; nine business and technical grammar schools with 1,669 pupils; 36 schools for public health occupations with 3,385 pupils. The number of pupils attending the vocational schools amounted to 35,489.

The Saarland has a range of six different institutions in the university sector. In the winter term 2017–18 the total number of students reached 31,370. There was the University of the Saarland with 16,441 students; one academy of fine art with 486 students; one academy of music with 427 students; one university of applied science (public administration) with 445 students; one university of applied science (business, engineering, technology and social science) with 5,970 students; and one university of applied science (health care and prevention) with 7,601 students.

Health

In 2017 the 23 hospitals in the Saarland contained 6,495 beds and treated 285,185 patients. The average occupancy rate was 85·4%. There were also 16 out-patient and rehabilitation centres that treated 29,641 patients in 2017. On average they were using 83·3% of their capacity.

Religion

In 2011, 62·3% of the population were Roman Catholics and 19·1% were Protestants.

Culture

Tourism
In 2017, 18,856 beds were available in 259 places of accommodation (of nine or more beds). 1,064,947 guests spent 3,088,723 nights in the Saarland, staying an average of 2·9 days each.

Saxony

Freistaat Sachsen

Key Historical Events

The former kingdom of Saxony was a member state of the German Empire from 1871 until 1918, when it became the state of Saxony and joined the Weimar Republic. After the Second World War it was one of the five states in the German Democratic Republic until German reunification in 1990. It has been home to much of Germany's cultural history. In the 18th century, the capital of Saxony, Dresden, became the cultural capital of northern Europe, earning the title 'Florence of the North', and the other great eastern German city, Leipzig, was a lively commercial city with strong artistic trends. The three cities of Dresden, Chemnitz and Leipzig formed the industrial heartland of Germany which, after World War II, was the manufacturing centre of the GDR.

Territory and Population

The area is 18,450 sq. km. It is divided into three self-administered cities, ten rural districts and 426 communes. Population on 31 Dec. 2017 was 4,081,308 (2,071,094 females; 2,010,214 males).

The capital is Dresden, with a population (31 Dec. 2017) of 551,072.

Social Statistics

Statistics for calendar years:

	Live births	Marriages	Divorces	Deaths
2012	34,686	18,348	7,104	51,315
2013	34,800	17,323	7,272	52,936
2014	35,935	17,883	6,928	51,159
2015	36,466	18,541	7,007	54,467

Constitution and Government

The *Bundesland* was reconstituted as the Free State of Saxony on former GDR territory in 1990. It has four seats in the Bundesrat.

Recent Elections

At the Diet elections of 31 Aug. 2014 the Christian Democratic Union won 59 of 126 seats, with 39·4% of the vote; the Left, 27, with 18·9%; the Social Democratic Party, 18, with 12·4%; the Alternative for Germany, 14, with 9·7%; the Greens, 8, with 5·7%. Turnout was 49·2%. The success of the anti-euro (although not at the time anti-EU) Alternative for Germany, which was only founded in 2013, gave the party its first ever seats in a German state parliament.

Current Government

The *Prime Minister* is Michael Kretschmer (CDU).
Government Website: http://www.sachsen.de

Energy and Natural Resources

Agriculture
Area and yield of the most important crops:

	Area (in 1,000 ha.)			Yield (in 1,000 tonnes)		
	2013	2014	2015	2013	2014	2015
Fodder	308·0	311·0	302·7	2,339·3	3,083·1	2,431·4
Wheat	191·8	194·9	196·8	1,343·3	1,716·6	1,562·7
Barley	116·3	114·9	118·8	652·6	884·5	868·1
Potatoes	6·5	6·9	6·4	181·8	339·0	255·4
Rye	44·1	35·1	33·4	242·0	208·5	168·3
Grain maize	15·6	18·5	19·0	128·2	182·0	151·0

Livestock in May 2015 (in 1,000): cattle, 508 (including dairy cows, 193); pigs, 654; sheep (Nov. 2015), 69.

Industry

In July 2015, 1,357 establishments (with 50 or more employees) employed 228,695 persons.

Labour
The unemployment rate was 8·2% in 2015.

Communications

Roads
On 1 Jan. 2015 there were 566·6 km of autobahn and 2,473·3 km of main roads. There were 2,505,640 registered motor vehicles, including 2,094,414 passenger cars, 233,164 lorries and tractors and 159,232 motorcycles.

Civil Aviation
Leipzig/Halle airport handled 2,328,341 passengers in 2014. Dresden airport handled 1,756,459 passengers in 2014.

Social Institutions

Education
In 2015–16 there were 826 primary schools (*Grundschulen*) with 131,991 pupils and 8,394 teachers; 340 secondary schools (*Mittelschulen*) with 103,762 pupils and 8,791 teachers; 155 grammar schools (*Gymnasien*) with 95,417 pupils and 8,107 teachers; and 156 high schools (*Förderschulen*) with 18,745 pupils and 3,316 teachers. There were six *Freie Waldorfschulen* (private) with 1,785 pupils and 146 teachers; 259 professional training schools with 99,389 students and 5,778 teachers; 11 adult education colleges with 2,172 students and 169 teachers. In 2015–16 there were six universities with 81,011 students, 12 polytechnics with 28,376 students, six art schools with 2,935 students and two management colleges with 959 students; in 2015–16 there were a total of 113,281 students in higher education institutions.

Health
In 2015 there were 78 hospitals with 25,825 beds. There were 16,930 doctors and 3,969 dentists.

Religion

In 2014, 19·4% of the population belonged to the Evangelical Church and 3·7% were Roman Catholic.

Culture

Tourism

In 2015 there were 121,666 beds in 2,152 places of accommodation. There were 7,405,916 visitors during the year.

Saxony-Anhalt

Sachsen-Anhalt

Key Historical Events

Saxony-Anhalt has a short history as a state in its own right. Made up of a patchwork of older regions ruled by other states, Saxony-Anhalt existed between 1947 and 1952 and then, after reunification in 1990, it was re-established. Geographically, it lies at the very heart of Germany and despite the brevity of its federal status, the region has some of the oldest heartlands of German culture.

Territory and Population

The area is 20,454 sq. km. It is divided into three self-administered cities, 11 rural districts and 222 communes. Population on 31 Dec. 2017 was 2,223,081.

The capital is Magdeburg, with a population (31 Dec. 2017) of 238,478.

Social Statistics

Statistics for calendar years:

	Live births	Marriages	Divorces	Deaths
2012	16,888	10,707	4,620	30,321
2013	16,797	10,083	4,220	31,385
2014	17,064	10,146	4,199	30,830
2015	17,415	10,575	4,109	32,369

Constitution and Government

The *Bundesland* was reconstituted on former GDR territory in 1990. It has four seats in the Bundesrat.

Recent Elections

At the Diet election on 13 March 2016 the CDU received 29·8% of votes cast giving them 30 seats, the Alternative for Germany 24·2% (24), the Left 16·3% (17 seats), the Social Democrats 10·6% (11) and the Greens 5·2% (5). Turnout was 61·1%.

Current Government

The *Prime Minister* is Reiner Haseloff (CDU).
Government Website: http://www.sachsen-anhalt.de

Energy and Natural Resources

Agriculture
Area and yield of the most important crops:

	Area (in 1,000 ha.)			Yield (in 1,000 tonnes)		
	2013	2014	2015	2013	2014	2015
Cereals	574·4	562·0	563·2	4,128·3	4,533·2	3,863·1
Sugar beet	44·1	46·4	33·1	2,590·6	3,701·3	2,340·5
Potatoes	12·8	13·1	12·6	525·9	712·2	584·2
Maize	19·6	18·4	17·6	145·5	180·3	151·2

Livestock in 2015 (in 1,000): cattle, 349·3 (including dairy cows, 125·7); pigs, 1,183·8; sheep, 76·6.

Industry

In 2015, 1,458 establishments (with 20 or more employees) employed 132,877 persons; of these, 60,591 were employed in basic industry, 39,656 in the capital goods industry and 20,616 in the food industry. Major sectors are extraction of metal, metalworking and metal articles; the nutrition industry; mechanical engineering; and the chemical industry.

Labour

Economically active persons totalled 1,041,000 in 2015. Of the total, 951,300 were employees and 89,700 self-employed; 290,500 were engaged in mining, manufacturing and building, 261,800 in commerce and transport, 17,100 in agriculture and forestry, and 471,600 in other industries and services.

Communications

Roads
At 1 Jan. 2015 there were 624 km of motorways, 2,298 km of main and 4,054 km of local roads. At 1 Jan. 2015 there were 1,423,417 registered motor vehicles, including 1,189,962 passenger cars, 95,488 lorries, 2,133 buses and 85,230 motorcycles.

Social Institutions

Education
In 2015–16 there were 875 schools with 188,245 pupils. In 2015 there were ten universities and institutes of equivalent status with 54,954 students.

Religion

In 2011, 13·9% of the population were Protestants and 3·5% were Roman Catholics.

Culture

Tourism
1,012 places of accommodation provided 60,169 beds in Dec. 2015. There were 3,143,256 visitors during the year.

Schleswig-Holstein

Key Historical Events

The *Bundesland* is formed from two states formerly contested between Germany and Denmark. Schleswig was a Danish dependency ruled since 1474 by the King of Denmark as Duke of Schleswig. He also ruled Holstein, its southern neighbour, as Duke of Holstein, but he did so recognizing that it was a fief of the Holy Roman Empire. As such, Holstein joined the German Confederation in 1815.

Disputes between Denmark and the powerful German states were accompanied by rising national feeling in the duchies, where the population was part-Danish and part-German. There was war in 1848–50 and in 1864, when Denmark surrendered its claims to Prussia and Austria. Following her defeat of Austria in 1866 Prussia annexed both duchies.

North Schleswig (predominantly Danish) was awarded to Denmark in 1920. Prussian Holstein and south Schleswig became the present *Bundesland* in 1946.

Territory and Population

The area of Schleswig-Holstein is 15,804 sq. km. It is divided into four urban and 11 rural districts and 1,112 communes. The population (31 Dec. 2017) numbered 2,889,821(1,416,535 males; 1,473,286 females).

The capital is Kiel, with a population (31 Dec. 2017) of 247,943.

Social Statistics

Statistics for calendar years:

	Live births	Marriages	Divorces	Deaths
2009	21,923	16,345	7,286	31,014
2010	22,578	16,456	7,389	31,201
2011	21,331	16,019	7,431	30,981
2012	22,003	16,384	7,113	31,441

Constitution and Government

The *Bundesland* has four seats in the Bundesrat.

Recent Elections

At the elections of 7 May 2017 the Christian Democrats won 25 of the 73 available seats with 32·0% of votes cast, the Social Democrats 21 with 27·2%, the Greens 10 with 12·9%, the Free Democrats 9 with 11·5%, the Alternative for Germany 5 with 5·9% and the South Schleswig Voters' Association 3 with 3·3%. Turnout was 64·2%.

Current Government

The *Prime Minister* is Daniel Günther (b. 1973; CDU).

Following the election of May 2017 the right-leaning CDU, the right-of-centre FDP and the Greens formed a 'Jamaica coalition' (the traditional colours of the three parties—black, yellow and green—being the same as the Jamaican flag).

Government Website: http://www.schleswig-holstein.de

Energy and Natural Resources

Agriculture

Area and yield of the most important crops:

	Area (in 1,000 ha.)			Yield (in 1,000 tonnes)		
	2009	2010	2011	2009	2010	2011
Wheat	196	208	211	1,861	1,843	1,679
Sugar beet	7	7	9	476	463	645
Barley	75	52	50	613	407	296
Potatoes	5	5	5	222	190	185
Rye	29	20	19	211	121	104
Oats	7	4	7	43	18	35

Livestock, Nov. 2012: 1,127,567 cattle (including 388,303 dairy cows); 43,584 horses (March 2010); 1,550,100 pigs; 194,000 sheep; 3,075,226 poultry (March 2010).

Fisheries

In 2012 the yield of small-scale deep-sea and inshore fisheries was 29,614 tonnes. The catch was valued at €52·3m. in 2012.

Industry

In Sept. 2012, 1,230 mining, quarrying and manufacturing establishments (with 20 or more employees) employed 121,500 persons; of these, 26,295 were employed in machine construction; 21,685 in food and related industries; 7,643 in electrical engineering; 4,605 in shipbuilding (except naval engineering).

Labour

Economically active persons totalled 1,379,000 in 2012. Of the total, 1,212,000 were employees, 167,000 were self-employed or unpaid family workers; 375,000 were engaged in commerce and transport, 298,000 in power supply, mining, manufacturing and building, 34,000 in agriculture and forestry, and 672,000 in other industries and services.

Communications

Roads

There were (1 Jan. 2012) 9,891 km of 'classified' roads, comprising 533 km of Autobahn, 1,559 km of federal roads, 3,675 km of first-class and 4,124 km of second-class highways. In Jan. 2013 the number of motor vehicles was 1,839,039 including 1,517,779 passenger cars, 97,955 lorries, 2,525 buses, 50,840 tractors and 136,835 motorcycles.

Shipping

The Kiel Canal *(Nord-Ostsee-Kanal)* is 98·7 km long; in 2012, 34,879 vessels of 166m. GT passed through it.

Social Institutions

Justice

There are a court of appeal, four regional courts, 22 local courts, a *Bundesland* labour court, five labour courts, a *Bundesland* social court, four social courts, a finance court, an upper administrative court and an administrative court.

Education

In 2012–13 there were 544 primary schools *(Grundschulen)* with 6,758 teachers and 101,085 pupils; 92 lower secondary schools *(Hauptschulen)* with 270 teachers and 4,031 pupils; 148 intermediate secondary schools *(Realschulen)* with 918 teachers and 16,729 pupils; 107 grammar schools *(Gymnasien)* with 6,771 teachers and 88,275 pupils; 188 comprehensive schools *(Gesamtschulen* and *Gemeinschaftsschulen)* with 5,850 teachers and 70,486 pupils; 230 other schools (including special schools) with 4,454 teachers and 30,569 pupils; 323 vocational schools with 4,910 teachers and 95,834 pupils.

In the winter term of the academic year 2011–12 there were 31,989 students at the three universities (Kiel, Flensburg and Lübeck) and 22,673 students at 11 further education colleges.

Religion

In 2011, 51·4% of the population were Protestants and 6·0% were Roman Catholics.

Culture

Tourism

4,024 places of accommodation provided 175,230 beds in 2012 for 5,366,252 visitors.

Thuringia

Thüringen

Key Historical Events

Thuringia with its capital Erfurt is criss-crossed by the rivers Saale, Werra and Weisse Elster and dominated in the south by the mountains of the Thuringian Forest. Martin Luther spent his exile in Eisenach where he translated the New Testament into German while he lived in protective custody in the castle. Weimar became the centre of German intellectual life in the 18th century. In 1919 Weimar was the seat of a briefly liberal Republic. Only ten miles from Weimar lies Buchenwald, the site of a war-time Nazi concentration camp, which is now a national monument to the victims of fascism.

Territory and Population

The area is 16,202 sq. km. Population on 31 Dec. 2017 was 2,151,205 (1,086,201 females); density, 133 per sq. km. It is divided into six urban districts, 17 rural districts and 849 communes.

The capital is Erfurt, with a population (31 Dec. 2017) of 212,988.

Social Statistics

Statistics for calendar years:

	Live births	Marriages	Divorces	Deaths
2012	17,342	10,105	4,275	27,141
2013	17,426	9,578	4,240	27,593
2014	17,887	9,666	4,033	26,957
2015	17,934	9,734	3,995	28,830

Constitution and Government

The *Bundesland* was reconstituted on former GDR territory in 1990. It has four seats in the Bundesrat.

Recent Elections

At the Diet elections of 14 Sept. 2014 the Christian Democrats (CDU) won 34 of 91 seats, with 33·5% of the vote; the Left 28, with 28·2%; the Social Democrats (SPD) 12, with 12·4%; the Alternative for Germany (AfD) 11, with 10·6%; and the Greens 6, with 5·7%. Turnout was 52·7%.

Current Government

The *Prime Minister* is Bodo Ramelow (Left Party).

Following the election of Sept. 2014 the Left formed a coalition government with the SPD and the Greens. For the first time since the fall of the Berlin Wall more than 25 years ago the former communist Left Party now leads a German state government.

Government Website (German only): http://www.thueringen.de

Energy and Natural Resources

Agriculture

Area and yield of the most important crops:

	Area (in 1,000 ha.)			Yield (in 1,000 tonnes)		
	2013	2014	2015	2013	2014	2015
Wheat	226·2	229·1	229·2	1,711·2	1,884·7	1,654·2
Barley	102·1	99·9	99·7	668·4	762·1	672·1
Sugar beet	7·7	8·6	6·9	447·8	664·8	422·4
Potatoes	2·0	2·0	1·8	58·3	95·5	67·6
Rye	14·9	10·9	9·4	101·9	81·4	60·2
Oats	3·7	3·8	3·7	15·8	15·5	13·4

Livestock, 3 Nov. 2015: 342,423 cattle (including 110,849 dairy cows); 8,606 horses (2010); 802,200 pigs; 123,700 sheep; 2,842,804 poultry (2010).

Industry

In 2015, 1,790 establishments (with 20 or more employees) employed 170,836 persons; of these, 81,202 were employed by producers of materials and supplies, 55,317 by producers of investment goods, 7,916 by producers of durables and 26,401 by producers of non-durables.

Labour

Economically active persons totalled 1,031,000 in 2015, including 495,000 professional workers, 370,000 manual workers and 96,000 self-employed. 336,000 were engaged in production industries, 249,000 in commerce, transport and communications, 19,000 persons in agriculture and forestry, and 427,000 in other sectors. The unemployment rate in 2015 was 7·7%.

Communications

Roads

At 1 Jan. 2016 there were 521 km of motorways, 1,519 km of federal roads, 4,262 km of first- and second-class highways and 3,293 km of district highways. Number of registered motor vehicles, Jan. 2016: 1,430,610, including 1,167,684 private cars, 100,348 lorries, 2,224 buses, 56,679 tractors and 94,345 motorcycles.

Social Institutions

Education

In 2015–16 there were 451 primary schools with 65,370 pupils, 210 core curriculum schools with 45,394 pupils, 100 grammar schools with 52,983 pupils and 81 special schools with 7,062 pupils; there were 48,996 pupils in technical and professional education, and 1,356 in professional training for people with disabilities; there were 12 universities and colleges with 50,163 students enrolled.

Health

In 2015 there were 44 hospitals with 16,017 beds. There were 9,160 doctors (one doctor per 237 population).

Welfare

2015 expenditure on social welfare was €602m.

Religion

In 2014, 491,939 persons were Protestant and 169,083 persons were Roman Catholic. In 2015, 732 were Jewish.

Culture

Tourism

In July 2015 there were 1,265 places of accommodation (with nine or more beds). There were 3,710,400 visitors who stayed 9,762,800 nights in 2015.

Further Reading

Germany

Statistisches Bundesamt. *Statistisches Jahrbuch für die Bundesrepublik Deutschland; Wirtschaft und Statistik* (monthly, from 1949).

Ardagh, J., *Germany and the Germans*. 3rd ed. 1995

Balfour, M., *Germany: the Tides of Power.* 1992

Bark, D. L. and Gress, D. R., *A History of West Germany, 1945–1991.* 2nd ed. 1993

Betz, H. G., *Postmodern Politics in Germany.* 1991

Blackbourn, D. and Eley, G., *The Peculiarities of German History.* 1985

Bulmer, Simon and Paterson, William E., *Germany and the European Union: Europe's Reluctant Hegemon.* 2018

Carr, W. and Allinson, M., *A History of Germany, 1815–2002.* 5th ed. 2010

Childs, D., *Germany in the 20th Century.* 1991.—*The Stasi: The East German Intelligence and Security Service.* 1999

Crawford, Alan and Czuczka, Tony, *Angela Merkel: A Chancellorship Forged in Crisis.* 2013

Dennis, M., *The German Democratic Republic: Politics, Economics and Society.* 1987

Fulbrook, Mary, *A Concise History of Germany.* 1991.—*The Divided Nation: A History of Germany, 1918–1990.* 1992.—*The Fontana History of Germany: 1918–1990 The Divided Nation.* 1994.—*German National Identity After the Holocaust.* 1999.—*Interpretation of the Two Germanies, 1945–1997.* 1999

Fulbrook, Mary, (ed.) *Twentieth-Century Germany: Politics, Culture and Society, 1918–1990.* 2001

Glees, A., *Reinventing Germany: German Political Development since 1945.* 1996

Green, Simon, Hough, Dan, Miskimmon, Alister and Timmins, Graham, *The Politics of the New Germany.* Revised ed. 2007

Green, Stephen, *Reluctant Meister: How Germany's Past is Shaping its European Future.* 2014

Heneghan, Tom, *Unchained Eagle: Germany After the Wall.* 2000

Huelshoff, M. G., *et al.*, (eds) *From Bundesrepublik to Deutschland: German Politics after Reunification.* 1993

Kitchen, Martin, *A History of Modern Germany: 1800 to the Present.* 2011

Langewiesche, Dieter, *Liberalism in Germany.* 1999

Lees, Charles, *Party Politics in Germany.* 2005

Loth, W., *Stalin's Unwanted Child—The Soviet Union, the German Question and the Founding of the GDR.* 1998

MacGregor, Neil, *Germany: Memories of a Nation.* 2014

Maier, C. S., *Dissolution: The Crisis of Communism and the End of East Germany.* 1997

Maull, Hanns W., *German Foreign Policy Since Reunification.* 2005

Merkl, Peter H. (ed.) *The Federal Republic of Germany at Fifty: The End of a Century of Turmoil.* 1999

Miskimmon, Alister, Paterson, William E. and Sloam, James, (eds) *Germany's Gathering Crisis: The 2005 Federal Election and the Grand Coalition.* 2008

Müller, Jan-Werner, *Another Country: German Intellectuals, Unification and National Identity.* 2000

Nicholls, A. J., *The Bonn Republic: West German Democracy, 1945–1990.* 1998

Novotná, Tereza, *How Germany Unified and the EU Enlarged.* 2015

Orlow, D., *A History of Modern Germany, 1871 to the Present.* 7th ed. 2011

Padgett, Stephen, Paterson, William E. and Zohlnhöfer, Reimut, (eds) *Developments in German Politics 4.* 2014

Pulzer, P., *German Politics, 1945–1995.* 1995

Sarotte, Mary Elise, *The Collapse: The Accidental Opening of the Berlin Wall.* 2014

Schulze, Hagen, *Germany: A New History.* 2001

Schweitzer, C.-C., Karsten, D., Spencer, R., Cole, R. T., Kommers, D. P. and Nicholls, A. J. (eds) *Politics and Government in Germany, 1944–1994: Basic Documents.* 2nd ed. 1995

Sereny, Gitta, *The German Trauma: Experiences and Reflections, 1938–99.* 2000

Sinn, G. and Sinn, H.-W., *Jumpstart: the Economic Reunification of Germany.* 1993

Smyser, W. R., *The Economy of United Germany: Colossus at the Crossroads.* 1992.—*From Yalta to Berlin: The Cold War Struggle over Germany.* 1999

Speirs, Ronald and Breuilly, John, (eds) *Germany's Two Unifications: Anticipations, Experiences, Responses.* 2005

Taylor, Frederick, *The Downfall of Money: Germany's Hyperinflation and the Destruction of the Middle Class.* 2013

Thompson, W. C., *et al.*, *Historical Dictionary of Germany.* 1995

Turner, Barry, *The Berlin Airlift: The Relief Operation that Defined the Cold War.* 2017

Turner, H. A., *Germany from Partition to Reunification.* 2nd ed. [of *Two Germanies since 1945*]. 1993

Watson, A., *The Germans: Who Are They Now?* 2nd ed. 1995

Watson, Peter, *The German Genius: Europe's Third Renaissance, the Second Scientific Revolution and the Twentieth Century.* 2010

Wende, Peter, *History of Germany.* 2004
Other more specialized titles are listed under CONSTITUTION AND GOV-
ERNMENT *and* BANKING AND FINANCE, *above.*
National library: Deutsche Nationalbibliothek, Deutscher Platz 1, 04103
Leipzig; Adickesallee 1, 60322 Frankfurt am Main; Deutsches
Musikarchiv, Gärtnerstrasse 25–32, 12207 Berlin. *Director General:*
Elisabeth Niggemann.
National Statistical Office: Statistisches Bundesamt, 65189 Wiesbaden, Gus-
tav Stresemann Ring 11. *President:* Georg Thiel.
Website: http://www.destatis.de

Baden-Württemberg

Statistical Information: Statistisches Landesamt Baden-Württemberg (70158
Stuttgart) publishes: *Statistisches Monatsheft* (monthly); *Statistisches
Taschenbuch* (latest issue 2016).
Website (German only): http://www.statistik-bw.de
State libraries: Württembergische Landesbibliothek, Konrad-Adenauer-Str.
8, 70173 Stuttgart. Badische Landesbibliothek Karlsruhe, Erbprinzenstr.
15, 76133 Karlsruhe.

Bavaria

Statistical Information: Bayerisches Landesamt für Statistik und Datenverarbeitung, Nürnberger Str. 95, 90762 Fürth. It publishes: *Statistisches
Jahrbuch für Bayern.* 1894 ff.—*Bayern in Zahlen.* Monthly (from Jan.
1947).—*Zeitschrift des Bayerischen Statistischen Landesamts.* July
1869–1943; 1948 ff.—*Beiträge zur Statistik Bayerns.* 1850 ff.—
Statistische Berichte. 1951 ff.—*Kreisdaten.* 1972 ff.—*Gemeindedaten.*
1973 ff.
State library: Bayerische Staatsbibliothek, Ludwigstr. 16, 80539 Munich.

Berlin

Statistical Information: The Amt für Statistik Berlin-Brandenburg
(Behlertstrasse 3a, 14467 Potsdam) was created in Jan. 2007 through
the merger of the Statistisches Landesamt Berlin and the Landesbetrieb
für Datenverarbeitung und Statistik Land Brandenburg. It is the main
source for the statistics above on Berlin and publishes: *Statistisches
Jahrbuch* (from 1867): *Zeitschrift für amtliche Statistik Berlin-Branden-
burg* (six a year from 2007).—*100 Jahre Berliner Statistik* (1962).
Website (German only): http://www.statistik-berlin-brandenburg.de
Kempe, Frederick, *Berlin 1961: Kennedy, Krushchev, and the Most Danger-
ous Place on Earth.* 2011
Large, David Clay, *Berlin.* 2000
Read, A., and Fisher, D., *Berlin, Biography of a City.* 1994
Richie, Alexandra, *Faust's Metropolis: A History of Berlin.* 1999
Taylor, R., *Berlin and its Culture.* 1997
Till, Karen, E., *The New Berlin: Memory, Politics, Place.* 2005
State library: Zentral- und Landesbibliothek, Blücherplatz 1, 10961 Berlin.

Brandenburg

Statistical office: The Amt für Statistik Berlin-Brandenburg (Behlertstrasse
3a, 14467 Potsdam) was created in Jan. 2007 through the merger of the
Landesbetrieb für Datenverarbeitung und Statistik Land Brandenburg
and the Statistisches Landesamt Berlin. It is the main source for the
statistics above on Brandenburg and publishes *Statistisches Jahrbuch
Land Brandenburg* (since 1991).
Website (German only): http://www.statistik-berlin-brandenburg.de

Bremen

Statistical Information: Statistisches Landesamt Bremen (An der Weide
14–16, 28195 Bremen), founded in 1850. Its current publications
include: *Statistisches Jahrbuch Bremen* (from 1992).—*Statistische
Mitteilungen* (from 1948).—*Statistische Monatsberichte*
(1954–2004).—*Statistische Hefte* (2005–09).—*Statistische Berichte*
(from 1956).—*Statistisches Handbuch Bremen (1950–60, 1961;
1960–64, 1967; 1965–69, 1971; 1970–74, 1975; 1975–80, 1982;
1981–85, 1987).—Bremen im statistischen Zeitvergleich 1950–1976.*
1977.—*Bremen in Zahlen* (from 1975).
Website (German only): http://www.statistik.bremen.de
State and University Library: Bibliotheksstrasse, 28359 Bremen.

Hamburg

Statistical Information: Statistisches Amt für Hamburg und Schleswig-
Holstein (Standort Hamburg, Steckelhörn 12, 20457 Hamburg).

Publications: *Statistische Berichte, Statistisches Jahrbuch, NORD.
regional, Statistik informiert spezial.*
Website (German only): http://www.statistik-nord.de
Hamburger Sparkasse, *Hamburg: von Altona bis Zollspieker.* 2002
Hamburgische Gesellschaft für Wirtschaftsförderung mbH, *Hamburg.* 1993
Klessmann, E., *Geschichte der Stadt Hamburg.* 7th ed. 1994
Kopitzsch, F. and Brietzke, D., *Hamburgische Biografie, Personenlexikon.*
Vol. 1. 2001
Kopitzsch, F. and Tilgner, D., *Hamburg Lexikon.* 1998
Landesbetrieb Geoinformation und Vermessung, *Hamburg in Luftaufnahmen
und Karten 1964–2012.* 2013
Möller, I., *Hamburg.* 2nd ed. 1999
Schubert, D. and Harms, H., *Wohnen am Hafen.* 1993
Schütt, E. C., Die Chronik Hamburgs. 1991
State library: Staats- und Universitätsbibliothek, Carl von Ossietzky, Von-
Melle-Park 3, 20146 Hamburg.

Hessen

Statistical Information: The Hessisches Statistisches Landesamt, Rheinstr.
35–37, 65175 Wiesbaden). Main publications: *Hessen kompakt*
(annual).—*Staat und Wirtschaft in Hessen* (bimonthly).—*Statistische
Berichte.—Hessische Gemeindestatistik* (annual, 1980 ff.).
Website (German only): http://www.statistik.hessen.de
State library: Hochschul- und Landesbibliothek RheinMain, Rheinstr.
55–57, 65185 Wiesbaden.
Website (limited English): http://www.hs-rm.de/bibliothek

Lower Saxony

Statistical Information: Landesamt für Statistik Niedersachsen, Postfach
910764, 30427 Hannover. Main publications are: *Statistische
Monatshefte Niedersachsen* (from 1947).—*Statistische Berichte Nieder-
sachsen.—Statistisches Taschenbuch Niedersachsen 2014* (biennial).
Website (German only): http://www.statistik.niedersachsen.de
State libraries: Niedersächsische Staats- und Universitätsbibliothek, Platz
der Göttinger Sieben 1, 37073 Göttingen; Gottfried Wilhelm Leibniz
Bibliothek-Niedersächsische Landesbibliothek, Waterloostr. 8, 30169
Hanover.

Mecklenburg-West Pomerania

Statistical office: Statistisches Amt Mecklenburg-Vorpommern, Postfach
120135, 19018 Schwerin.
Main publications are: *Statistische Hefte Mecklenburg-Vorpommern* (since
1991); *Gemeindedaten Mecklenburg-Vorpommern* (since 1999; elec-
tronic); *Statistische Berichte* (since 1991; various); *Statistisches
Jahrbuch Mecklenburg-Vorpommern* (since 1991); *Statistische
Sonderhefte* (since 1992; various).
Website (German only): http://www.statistik-mv.de

North Rhine-Westphalia

Statistical Information: Information und Technik Nordrhein-Westfalen
(IT NRW) (Mauerstr. 51, 40476 Düsseldorf) was founded in 1946 as
the Landesamt für Datenverabeitung und Statistik Nordrhein-Westfalen
by amalgamating the provincial statistical offices of Rhineland and
Westphalia. It was renamed on 1 Jan. 2009. IT NRW publishes (from
1949): *Statistisches Jahrbuch Nordrhein-Westfalen.* More than 550 other
publications yearly.
Website (German only): http://www.it.nrw.de
Bundesland Library: Universitätsbibliothek, Universitätsstr. 1, 40225
Düsseldorf.

Rhineland-Palatinate

Statistical Information: Statistisches Landesamt Rheinland-Pfalz (Mainzer
Str., 14–16, 56130 Bad Ems). Its publications include: *Statistisches
Jahrbuch Rheinland-Pfalz* (since 1948); *Statistische Monatshefte Rheinland-Pfalz* (since 1958); *Rheinland-Pfalz heute* (since 1973); *Statistik
von Rheinland-Pfalz* (from 1946 to 2004), then renamed *Statistische
Bände* (since 2004) 409 vols. to date; *Kreisfreie Städte und Landkreise*
(since 2004); *Rheinland-Pfalz—ein Ländervergleichin Zahlen*
(2005–13); *Die Wirtschaft in Rheinland-Pfalz* (since 2007).
Website (German only): http://www.statistik.rlp.de

Saarland

Statistical Information: Landesamt für Zentrale Dienste, Statistisches Amt Saarland (Virchowstrasse 7, 66119 Saarbrücken). The most important publications are: *Statistisches Jahrbuch Saarland* (annual).—*Saarland in Zahlen* (special issues).—*Einzelschriften zur Statistik des Saarlandes* (special issues).

Website (German only): http://www.statistik.saarland.de

Saxony

Statistical office: Statistisches Landesamt des Freistaates Sachsen, Postfach 1105, 01911 Kamenz. It publishes *Statistisches Jahrbuch des Freistaates Sachsen* (since 1990).

Saxony-Anhalt

Statistical office: Statistisches Landesamt Sachsen-Anhalt, Postfach 20 11 56, 06012 Halle. It publishes *Statistisches Jahrbuch des Landes Sachsen-Anhalt* (since 1991).

Schleswig-Holstein

Statistical Information: Statistisches Amt für Hamburg und Schleswig-Holstein (Fröbelstr. 15–17, 24113 Kiel). Publications: *Statistisches Taschenbuch Schleswig-Holstein* (1954–2003).—*Statistisches Jahrbuch Schleswig-Holstein,* since 1951.—*Statistische Monatshefte Schleswig-Holstein* (1949–2003).—*Statistische Berichte,* since 1947.—*Beitrage zur historischen Statistik Schleswig-Holstein,* 1967.

Website (German only): http://www.statistik-nord.de

Handbuch Schleswig-Holstein. 35th ed. 2010

Ibs, Jürgen, (ed.) *Historischer Atlas Schleswig-Holstein: Vom Mittelalter bis 1867.* 2004

Lange, Ulrich, (ed.) *Historischer Atlas Schleswig-Holstein: seit 1945.* 1999

Momsen, Ingwer, (ed.) *Historischer Atlas Schleswig-Holstein: 1867 bis 1945.* 2001

State library: Schleswig-Holsteinische Landesbibliothek, Kiel, Schloss.

Thuringia

Statistical information: Thüringer Landesamt für Statistik (Postfach 900163, 99104 Erfurt; Europaplatz 3, 99091 Erfurt). Publications: *Statistisches Jahrbuch Thüringen,* since 1993. *Kreiszahlen für Thüringen,* since 1995. *Gemeindezahlen für Thüringen,* since 1998. *Thüringen-Atlas,* since 1999. *Statistische Monatshefte Thüringen,* since 1994. *Statistische Berichte,* since 1991. *Faltblätter,* since 1991.

Website (German only): http://www.statistik.thueringen.de

State library: Thüringer Universitäts- und Landesbibliothek, Jena.

Ghana

Republic of Ghana

Capital: Accra
Population projection, 2020: 30·73m.
GNI per capita, 2017: (PPP$) 4,096
HDI/world rank, 2017: 0·592/140
Internet domain extension: .gh

Key Historical Events

Hunter gatherers inhabited Ghana from 8000 BC. There was animal husbandry and agriculture from 1500 BC, with iron technology developing from 100 BC. A centuries-long migration from the north was led by the Guan who moved south from present-day Burkina Faso. The northern Dagomba and Mamprusi kingdoms traded with western Sudanese counterparts from the 12th century, coming under the influence of Islam. In the early 15th century gold and kola nuts from the forested south were exchanged for goods from the savannah regions at towns including Begho.

Portuguese navigators reached Edina (Elmina) on the coast in 1472 and traded with Akan-speaking clans including the Denkyira and Asante. The Portuguese built the São Jorge fort in 1482 and named the region Costa da Mina (Gold Coast). Centred on Tafo and Kumasi, Asante power grew from the 16th century through the supply of gold, ivory, timber and, increasingly, slaves. By the 18th century around 5,000 slaves were shipped annually from European-controlled fortresses on the Gold Coast to plantations in the Caribbean and North America.

After Dutch forces captured Elmina from the Portuguese in 1642, the Dutch West India Company vied with rivals from Britain, Denmark, Sweden and Prussia for control of maritime trade. More than 40 fortresses built along the coast over the next 150 years were frequently attacked.

Britain became the dominant European power on the Gold Coast in the 19th century, focusing trade on timber, ivory and other natural resources. British forces clashed with the expanding Asante kingdom, ruled by Osei Bonsu (1800–24) and then Osei Yaw Akoto (1824–34), until peace was declared in 1831. This gave Britain control over the coastal provinces in return for Asante access to maritime trade. Disputes over control of the gold trade reignited in the 1860s. In 1874 British forces captured Kumasi and proclaimed the Gold Coast Colony, governed from Accra. Following the exile of the Asante king, the British annexed his kingdom and the Northern Territories in Jan. 1902, establishing boundaries with French West Africa.

Mining, agriculture and infrastructure developed with British rule, notably under the governorship of Frederick Guggisberg (1919–27). In the 1930s an educated middle class pushed for inclusion in the colony's administration. While the United Gold Coast Convention sought a gradual shift away from colonial rule after the Second World War, others demanded more rapid change. The Convention People's Party (CPP), formed in 1949 and led by Dr Kwame Nkrumah, campaigned for 'positive action', including strikes, boycotts and civil disobedience.

A new constitution, enacted in 1951, paved the way for legislative elections in which Nkrumah won a seat while serving a three-year jail sentence. Once released, he was a key figure in the parliamentary struggle that led to independence. On 6 March 1957 Ghana became the first independent African nation south of the Sahara, joining the Commonwealth on 1 July 1960, with Nkrumah as president.

In 1966 Nkrumah's regime was overthrown by the military who ruled until 1969 until handing over to a civilian regime under a new constitution. The armed forces seized power again in 1972. In 1979 the Supreme Military Council was toppled in a coup led by Flight-Lieut. J. J. Rawlings. The new government permitted scheduled elections that resulted in victory for Dr Hilla Limann and the People's National Party. However, in Dec. 1981 Rawlings led another coup and established the Provisional National Defence Council to rule.

A pluralist democratic constitution was approved by referendum in April 1992. Rawlings was elected president later that year as a member of the centre-left National Democratic Congress (NDC). He was re-elected in 1996.

John Kufuor, of the centre-right New Patriotic Party, became president in Dec. 2000, defeating John Atta Mills of the NDC. During his second term, Kufuor announced the discovery of substantial offshore oil reserves. He was then succeeded in Jan. 2009 by John Atta Mills, who died in 2012 and was replaced by John Mahama. Nana Akufo-Addo took over the presidency after defeating Mahama in the election of Dec. 2016.

Territory and Population

Ghana is bounded west by Côte d'Ivoire, north by Burkina Faso, east by Togo and south by the Gulf of Guinea. The area is 238,533 sq. km; the 2010 census population was 24,658,823 giving a density of 103·4 persons per sq. km.

The UN gives a projected population for 2020 of 30·73m.

In 2011, 52·2% of the population were urban. An estimated 3m. Ghanaians lived abroad in 2006.

Ghana is divided into 16 regions (ten at the time of the 2010 census):

Regions	Area (sq. km)	Population, census 2010	Capital
Ashanti	24,389	4,780,380	Kumasi
Brong-Ahafo[1]	39,557	2,310,983	Sunyani
Central	9,826	2,201,863	Cape Coast
Eastern	19,323	2,633,154	Koforidua
Greater Accra	3,245	4,010,054	Accra
Northern[2]	70,384	2,479,461	Tamale
Upper East	8,842	1,046,545	Bolgatanga
Upper West	18,476	702,110	Wa
Volta[3]	20,570	2,118,252	Ho
Western[4]	23,921	2,376,021	Sekondi-Takoradi

[1]In Feb. 2019 Brong-Ahafo was divided into three new regions: Bono Region (capital: Sunyani), Bono East Region (capital: Techiman) and Ahafo Region (capital: Goaso). [2]In Feb. 2019 Northern was divided into three new regions: Northern (capital: Tamale), Savannah (capital: Damongo) and North East (capital: Nalerigu). [3]In Feb. 2019 Volta was divided into two new regions: Volta Region (capital: Ho) and Oti (capital: Dambai). [4]In Feb. 2019 Western was divided into two new regions: Western Region (capital: Takoradi) and Western North (capital: Sefwi-Wiaso).

In 2010 the capital, Accra, had a population of 1,848,614. Other major cities are Kumasi, Tamale, Sekondi-Takoradi and Ashiaman.

About 42% of the population are Akan. Other tribal groups include Moshi (23%), Ewe (10%) and Ga-Adangme (7%). About 75 languages are spoken; the official language is English.

Social Statistics

2008 estimates: births, 756,000; deaths, 259,000. Rates, 2008 estimates (per 1,000 population): births, 32·4; deaths, 11·1. 2013 life expectancy, 60·2 years for men and 62·1 for women. Infant mortality, 50 per 1,000 live births (2010). Annual population growth rate, 2000–08, 2·2%; fertility rate, 2008, 4·0 births per woman.

Climate

The climate ranges from the equatorial type on the coast to savannah in the north and is typified by the existence of well-marked dry and wet seasons. Temperatures are relatively high throughout the year. The amount, duration and seasonal distribution of rain is very marked, from the south, with over 80" (2,000 mm), to the north, with under 50" (1,250 mm). In the extreme north, the wet season is from March to Aug., but further south it lasts until Oct. Near Kumasi, two wet seasons occur, in May and June and again in Oct., and this is repeated, with greater amounts, along the coast of Ghana. Accra, Jan. 80°F (26·7°C), July 77°F (25°C). Annual rainfall 29" (724 mm). Kumasi, Jan. 77°F (25°C), July 76°F (24·4°C). Annual rainfall 58" (1,402 mm). Sekondi-Takoradi, Jan. 77°F (25°C), July 76°F (24·4°C). Annual rainfall 47" (1,181 mm). Tamale, Jan. 82°F (27·8°C), July 78°F (25·6°C). Annual rainfall 41" (1,026 mm).

Constitution and Government

After the coup of 31 Dec. 1981, supreme power was vested in the Provisional National Defence Council (PNDC), chaired by Flight-Lieut. Jerry John Rawlings.

A new constitution was approved by 92·6% of votes cast at a referendum on 28 April 1992. The electorate was 8,255,690; turnout was 43·8%. The constitution sets up a presidential system on the US model, with a multi-party parliament and an independent judiciary. The *President* is elected by universal suffrage for a four-year term renewable once.

The unicameral *Parliament* has 275 members, elected for a four-year term in single-seat constituencies.

National Anthem

'God bless our Homeland, Ghana'; words by the government, tune by P. Gbeho.

Government Chronology

Heads of State since 1960. (CPP = Convention People's Party; NDC = National Democratic Congress; NPP = New Patriotic Party; PNP = People's National Party; n/p = non-partisan)

President of the Republic		
1960–66	CPP	Kofi Kwame Nkrumah
Chairmen of the National Liberation Council		
1966–69	military	Joseph Arthur Ankrah
1969	military	Akwasi Amankwaa Afrifa
Presidential Commission		
1969–70		Akwasi Amankwaa Afrifa (chairman), John Willie Kofi Harlley, Albert Kwesi Ocran
Presidents of the Republic		
1970–72	n/p	Edward Akufo-Addo
Chairman of the National Redemption Council		
1972–75	military	Ignatius Kutu Acheampong
Chairmen of the Supreme Military Council		
1975–78	military	Ignatius Kutu Acheampong
1978–79	military	Frederick Kwasi Akuffo
Chairman of the Armed Forces Revolutionary Council		
1979	military	Jerry John Rawlings
President of the Republic		
1979–81	PNP	Hilla Limann
Chairman of the Provisional National Defence Council		
1981–93	military	Jerry John Rawlings
Presidents of the Republic		
1993–2001	NDC	Jerry John Rawlings
2001–09	NPP	John Agyekum Kufuor
2009–12	NDC	John Atta Mills
2012–17	NDC	John Dramani Mahama
2017–	NPP	Nana Akufo-Addo

Recent Elections

Presidential elections were held on 7 Dec. 2016. Nana Akufo-Addo of the New Patriotic Party (NPP) won 53·8% of the vote and incumbent president John Dramani Mahama of the National Democratic Congress (NDC) 44·4%. Consequently a second round was not required. There were five other candidates. Turnout was 68·6%. In parliamentary elections held simultaneously the NPP won 171 of 275 seats and the NDC 104.

Current Government

President: Nana Akufo-Addo; b. 1944 (NPP; sworn in 7 Jan. 2017).
   Vice-President: Mahamudu Bawumia.
   In Feb. 2019 the government comprised the following:
   Senior Minister: Yaw Osafo-Maafo.
   Minister for Aviation: Kofi Adda. *Business Development:* Ibrahim Mohammed Awal. *Chieftaincy and Religious Affairs:* Kofi Dzamesi. *Communications:* Ursula Owusu-Ekuful. *Defence:* Dominic Nitiwul. *Education:* Matthew Opoku Prempeh. *Employment and Social Welfare:* Ignatius Baffour Awuah. *Energy:* John Peter Amewu. *Environment, Science and Technology:* Kwabena Frimpong-Boateng. *Finance:* Ken Ofori-Atta. *Fisheries and Aquaculture:* Elizabeth Naa Afoley Quaye. *Food and Agriculture:* Owusu Afriyie Akoto. *Foreign Affairs and Regional Integration:* Shirley Ayorkor Botchway. *Gender, Children and Social Protection:* Cynthia Morrison. *Health:* Kwaku Agyemang-Manu. *Information:* Kojo Oppong Nkrumah. *Inner Cities and Zongo Development:* Mustapha Abdul-Hamid. *Interior:* Ambrose Dery. *Justice and Attorney-General:* Gloria Akuffo. *Lands and Natural Resources:* Kwaku Asomah-Cheremeh. *Local Government and Rural Development:* Hajia Alima Mahama. *Monitoring and Evaluation:* Anthony Akoto Osei. *National Security:* Albert Kan-Dapaah. *Parliamentary Affairs:* Osei Kyei Mensah Bonsu. *Planning:* George Yaw Gyan-Baffour. *Railways Development:* Joe Ghartey. *Regional Reorganization and Development:* Dan Botwe. *Roads and Highways:* Kwasi Amoako-Atta. *Sanitation and Water Resources:* Cecilia Dapaah. *Special Development Initiatives:* Mavis Hawa Koomson. *Tourism, Arts and Culture:* Catherine Afeku. *Trade and Industry:* Alan John Kyerematen. *Transport:* Kweku Ofori Asiamah. *Works and Housing:* Samuel Atta Akyea. *Youth and Sports:* Isaac Kwame Asiamah. *Minister of State in the Office of the President:* Rockson Bukari. *Minister of State in the Office of the Vice-President:* Boniface Abubakar Siddique.

Current Leaders

Nana Akufo-Addo

Position
President

Introduction
Nana Akufo-Addo became president after winning the presidential election in Dec. 2016, after several previous unsuccessful attempts.

Early Life
Nana Akufo-Addo was born on 29 March 1944 in Accra, into a family that included three members of Ghana's founding fathers (nationalists known as the 'Big Six'). He studied in England at Lancing College, West Sussex, before attending New College, Oxford, to read politics, philosophy and economics from 1962, although he did not complete the course. He subsequently graduated in economics from the University of Ghana in 1967, before returning to England to begin his legal education. In July 1975 he was called to the Ghanaian bar, co-founding his own legal firm in 1979.

Akufo-Addo joined the People's Movement for Freedom and Justice in the 1970s. In 1992 he switched allegiance to the newly-founded New Patriotic Party (NPP) and was elected three times as a member of parliament for the Abuakwa South constituency between 1996 and 2004. He also put his name forward to be the party's presidential candidate in 1998 but lost out to John Kufuor. Between 2001 and 2007 he held several roles in Kufuor's administration, including attorney-general, minister for justice and foreign minister.

Akufo-Addo ran unsuccessfully as the NPP's presidential candidate in 2008 and 2012 (on the latter occasion challenging the result until the Supreme Court ruled in John Mahama's favour). At his third attempt in 2016 he secured 53·8% of the vote and assumed office on 7 Jan. 2017.

Career in Office
Akufo-Addo was faced with the task of stimulating the weak economy, which had necessitated support from the International Monetary Fund in 2015 in the form of a three-year US$918m. extended credit facility. The NPP also promised to create jobs for young people. In an effort to curb corruption, Akufo-Addo said he would establish a special prosecutor's office, with powers to prosecute without the authority of the attorney-general.

Defence

Defence expenditure totalled US$306m. in 2013 (US$12 per capita), representing 0·6% of GDP. Between 2012 and 2013 Ghana increased its defence spending by 129%, the largest rise of any country that year.

Army

Total strength (2011), 11,500.

Navy

The Navy, based at Sekondi and Tema, numbered 2,000 in 2011.

Air Force

The main air base is at Accra. Personnel strength (2011), 2,000; there were 13 combat-capable aircraft although their serviceability was in doubt.

Economy

Agriculture accounted for 22·4% of GDP in 2014, industry 27·7% and services 49·9%.

Overview

One of Africa's biggest borrowers, Ghana completed the IMF and World Bank's Heavily Indebted Poor Countries (HIPC) scheme in 2004, paving the way for debt cancellation by major donors. Foreign direct investment averaged 8·1% of GDP per year between 2009 and 2015. In 2011 a US$3bn. financing agreement was reached with the China Development Bank to encourage further growth and investment. Public debt stood at 49·4% of GDP in 2013.

Growth averaging 5–6% per year from the mid-1980s resulted from careful macroeconomic management and an increase in exports. Over the period 2010–14 it averaged 8·6% per year, driven by increased private and public investment in road-building, agricultural upgrading and extractive industries. A privatization programme began in 1988, with over 100 state-owned enterprises becoming more than 200 privately-owned companies. Privatization has raised over US$900m., with the Ashanti Goldfields sell-off alone worth more than US$400m. Only South Africa among sub-Saharan African nations has raised more from privatization.

Oil production, which started in Dec. 2010, led to Ghana being among the world's fastest-growing economies in 2011, registering a 14% increase. However, in 2015 the value of gold and oil—which together constituted over 50% of exports—fell by 8% and 47% respectively. Tourism, meanwhile, reached its highest level in 2015 (over 1m. arrivals), while remittances totalled US$4·9bn.

Currency

The monetary unit is the *cedi* (GHS) of 100 *pesewas*. It was introduced in July 2007 and is equal to 10,000 old cedi (GHC). Inflation rose from 15·5% in 2014 to 17·2% in 2015, to 17·5% in 2016 to 12·4 in 2017. In July 2011 foreign exchange reserves were US$4,345m., total money supply was ₵15,260m. and gold reserves totalled 281,000 troy oz.

Budget

In 2011 budgetary central government revenue totalled ₵12,935m. and expenditure ₵12,646m. Principal sources of revenue in 2011 were: taxes on goods and services, ₵3,549m.; taxes on income, profits and capital gains, ₵3,193m. Main items of expenditure by economic type in 2011: compensation of employees, ₵4,855m.; grants, ₵3,092m.

VAT is 12·5%.

Performance

Real GDP growth was 7·9% in 2010 and 14·0% in 2011—the highest rate of growth for any Sub-Saharan African country that year. 2011 had been Ghana's first full year as an oil-producing country. The economy continued to expand strongly in 2012 and 2013, although it slowed to 4·0% in 2014. In 2016 the growth rate of 3·7% was the lowest since 1994. Growth in 2017 was 8·4%. Total GDP was US$47·3bn. in 2017.

Banking and Finance

The Bank of Ghana (*Governor*, Ernest Kwamina Yedu Addison) was established in 1957 as the central bank and bank of issue. At Dec. 2010 its total assets were ₵11,230·7m. There were 27 licensed commercial banks in 2010 plus three state-owned development banks and some 100 rural banks.

Foreign investment is actively encouraged with the Ghana Free Zone Scheme offering particular incentives such as full exemption of duties and levies on all imports for production and exports from the zones, full exemption on tax on profits for ten years and no more than 8% after ten years. It is a condition of the scheme that at least 70% of goods made within the zones must be exported. Within 18 months of the scheme being set up in 1995, 50 projects had been registered.

There is a stock exchange in Accra.

Energy and Natural Resources

Environment

Ghana's carbon dioxide emissions from the consumption of energy in 2011 were the equivalent of 0·4 tonnes per capita.

Electricity

Installed capacity was 2·2m. kW in 2011. Production (2011) 11·4bn. kWh, approximately 67% of which was from two hydro-electric stations operated by the Volta River Authority—Akosombo and Kpong. A third hydro-electric station, the Bui hydro project, was brought onstream in 2013. Consumption per capita was 433 kWh in 2011. Production is becoming more dependent on gas—the 678-km West Africa Gas Pipeline bringing gas flows from Nigeria resumed operations in March 2010 following a year-long suspension. Ghana has one of the highest electricity penetration rates in sub-Saharan African countries, at 72% in 2011.

Oil and Gas

Ghana is pursuing the development of its own gas fields and plans to harness gas at the North and South Tano fields located off the western coast. Natural gas reserves, 2013, totalled 23bn. cu. metres. Oil reserves in 2011 were 660m. bbls. The Jubilee oil field, 60 km offshore, was discovered in 2007 and led to Ghana becoming the world's newest oil producer in Dec. 2010.

Minerals

Gold is one of the mainstays of the economy; Ghana ranks second only to South Africa among African gold producers. Production in 2010 was an estimated 101,000 kg. There are also large reserves of bauxite, diamonds and manganese. In 2010 estimated diamond production was 334,000 carats; manganese, 1·53m. tonnes; bauxite, 595,000 tonnes.

Agriculture

Agriculture is largely subsistence-based. Agriculture employed 53·6% of the total labour force in 2013. There were an estimated 4·7m. ha. of arable land in 2013 and 2·7m. ha. of permanent cropland.

Production of main food crops (2014 unless otherwise indicated, in 1,000 tonnes): cassava, 16,524; yams, 7,119; plantains (2013), 3,675; palm fruit oil, 2,443; maize 1,762; taro, 1,299; cocoa beans (2013), 835; oranges (2013), 663; pineapples (2013), 637; rice (paddy), 604. Cocoa is the main cash crop. Ghana is the second largest cocoa bean producer in the world after Côte d'Ivoire, and the second largest producer of yams after Nigeria.

Livestock, 2014: goats, 6·04m.; sheep, 4·34m.; cattle, 1·66m.; pigs, 682,000; chickens, 68·5m.

Forestry

There were 9·34m. ha. of forest in 2015, or 41% of the total land area. Reserves account for some 30% of the total forest lands. Timber production in 2011 was 40·27m. cu. metres.

Fisheries

In 2012 total catch was 364,949 tonnes, of which 274,949 tonnes came from sea fishing.

Industry

Ghana's industries include mining, lumbering, light manufacturing and food processing.

Labour

In 2013 the number of economically active persons totalled 14·04m. Females constituted 51·7% of the labour force in 2013. The unemployment rate was 5·2% in 2013.

Ghana had 0·18m. people living in slavery according to the Walk Free Foundation's 2013 *Global Slavery Index*.

International Trade

Imports and Exports

Goods imports were US$12,787·2m. in 2013 (US$13,578·1m. in 2012) and good exports US$12,643·9m. (US$15,761·2m. in 2012).

Principal imports in 2013 were machinery and transport equipment (39·5%), manufactured goods, and food, animals and beverages; main exports in 2013 were gold (42·4%), mineral fuels and lubricants, and food, animals and beverages.

The leading import supplier in 2010 was the USA (13·7%), followed by China and France; the leading export destination in 2010 was South Africa (53·5%), followed by the United Arab Emirates and the Netherlands.

Communications

Roads

In 2005 there were 57,614 km of roads, including 11,177 km of highways, main and national roads. About 14·9% of all roads are paved. A Road Sector Strategy and Programme to develop the road network ran from 1995 to 2000. There were 493,800 passenger cars in use in 2007, 158,400 lorries and vans, and 121,100 buses and coaches. Motorcycles and mopeds numbered 149,100.

Rail

Total length of railways in 2006 was 953 km of 1,067 mm gauge, all in the south of the country. In 2010 a US$6bn. deal was signed with China National Machinery Import & Export Corp. to construct a railway linking Kumasi (the northernmost point of the existing network) with Paga in the north of the country on the border with Burkina Faso. In 2006 railways carried 1·6m. tonnes of freight and 2·3m. passengers.

Civil Aviation

There is an international airport at Accra (Kotoka), which handled 2,424,153 passengers (1,726,051 on international flights) in 2012. As well as domestic flights, in 2010 there were direct international services connecting Accra with more than 20 destinations.

Shipping

The chief ports are Tema and Takoradi. In 2013, 11·5m. tonnes of cargo were handled at Tema and 5·4m. tonnes at Takoradi. There is inland water transport on Lake Volta. In Jan. 2014 there were 13 ships of 300 GT or over registered, totalling 27,000 GT. The Volta, Ankobra and Tano rivers provide 168 km of navigable waterways for launches and lighters.

Telecommunications

Ghana Telecom was privatized in 1996. There were 277,900 fixed telephone lines in 2010 (11·4 per 1,000 inhabitants). Mobile phone subscribers numbered 17·44m. in 2010. There were 85·5 internet users per 1,000 inhabitants in 2010. Fixed internet subscriptions totalled 92,700 in 2009 (3·9 per 1,000 inhabitants). In June 2012 there were 1·3m. Facebook users.

Social Institutions

Out of 178 countries analysed in the 2017 *Fragile States Index*—a list published jointly by the Fund for Peace and *Foreign Policy* magazine—Ghana was ranked the 71st least vulnerable to conflict or collapse. The index is based on 12 indicators of state vulnerability across social, political and economic categories.

Justice

The Courts are constituted as follows:

Supreme Court

The Supreme Court consists of the Chief Justice who is also the President, and not less than four other Justices of the Supreme Court. The Supreme Court is the final court of appeal in Ghana. The final interpretation of the constitution is entrusted to the Supreme Court.

Court of Appeal

The Court of Appeal consists of the Chief Justice with not less than five other Justices of the Appeal court and such other Justices of Superior Courts as the Chief Justice may nominate. The Court of Appeal is duly constituted by three Justices. The Court of Appeal is bound by its own previous decisions and all courts inferior to the Court of Appeal are bound to follow the decisions of the Court of Appeal on questions of law. Divisions of the appeal court may be created, subject to the discretion of the Chief Justice.

High Court of Justice

The Court has jurisdiction in civil and criminal matters as well as those relating to industrial and labour disputes including administrative complaints. The High Court of Justice has supervisory jurisdiction over all inferior Courts and any adjudicating authority and in exercise of its supervisory jurisdiction has power to issue such directions, orders or writs including writs or orders in the nature of *habeas corpus*, *certiorari*, *mandamus*, prohibition and *quo warranto*. The High Court of Justice has no jurisdiction in cases of treason. The High Court consists of the Chief Justice and not less than 12 other judges and such other Justices of the Superior Court as the Chief Justice may appoint.

Under the Provisional National Defence Council which ruled from 1981 to 2001 public tribunals were established in addition to the traditional courts of justice.

The population in penal institutions in Aug. 2013 was 14,021 (54 per 100,000 of national population). In 2015 the World Justice Project *Rule of Law Index*, which provides data on how the rule of law is experienced by the general public across eight categories, ranked Ghana 40th of 102 countries for criminal justice and 34th for civil justice.

Education

Schooling is free and compulsory, and consists of six years of primary, three years of junior secondary and three years of senior secondary education. In 2006–07 there were 3·37m. pupils in primary schools with 105,257 teachers; and 1·13m. pupils with 67,005 teachers in junior secondary schools. University education is free. In 2007 there were 140,017 students in tertiary education and 4,011 academic staff. Adult literacy in 2008 was 66%. In 1970 adult literacy was just 31%.

In 2005 public expenditure on education came to 5·5% of GNI.

Health

In the period 2006–13 there were ten doctors per 100,000 population and 93 nursing and midwifery personnel per 100,000. An estimated 270,000 people were living with HIV in 2015.

Ghana has been one of the most successful countries in reducing undernourishment in the past 20 years. Between 1994 and 2014 the proportion of undernourished people declined from 27% of the population to under 5%. In *Water: At What Cost? The State of the World's Water 2016*, WaterAid reported that 11·3% of the population does not have access to safe water.

Religion

In 2010 the population was 74·9% Christian according to estimates by the Pew Research Center's Forum on Religion & Public Life, with 15·8% Hindu and 4·9% folk religionist. Protestants constituted 81% of Christians in 2010 and Catholics 17%. In Feb. 2019 the Roman Catholic Church had one cardinal.

Culture

World Heritage Sites

Ghana has two sites on the UNESCO World Heritage List: Forts and Castles, Volta, Greater Accra, Central and Western Regions (inscribed on the list in 1979), Portuguese trading posts built between 1482 and 1786 along the coast; Asante Traditional Buildings (1980), the remains of the Asante civilization that peaked in the 18th century.

Press

There were 12 paid-for daily newspapers in 2008 with a combined circulation of 210,000 plus 95 paid-for non-dailies.

Tourism

There were 1,093,000 non-resident tourists in 2014, spending US$1·0bn.

Diplomatic Representatives

Of Ghana in the United Kingdom (13 Belgrave Sq., London, SW1X 8PN)
High Commissioner: Papa Owusu-Ankomah.

Of the United Kingdom in Ghana (Julius Nyerere Link, off Gamel Abdul Nasser Ave., PO Box 296, Accra)
High Commissioner: Iain Walker.

Of Ghana in the USA (3512 International Drive, NW, Washington, D.C., 20008)
Ambassador: Barfour Adjei-Barwuah.

Of the USA in Ghana (24, 4th Circular Rd, Cantonments, Accra)
Ambassador: Stephanie S. Sullivan.

Of Ghana to the United Nations
Ambassador: Martha Ama Akyaa Pobee.

Of Ghana to the European Union
Ambassador: Harriet Sena Siaw-Boateng.

Further Reading

Aryeetey, Ernest and Kanbur, Ravi, (eds) *The Economy of Ghana: Analytical Perspectives on Stability, Growth and Poverty.* 2008

Boafo-Arthur, Kwame, (ed.) *Ghana: One Decade of the Liberal State.* 2007

Carmichael, J., *Profile of Ghana.* 1992.—*African Eldorado: Ghana from Gold Coast to Independence.* 1993

Gocking, Roger S., *The History of Ghana.* 2005

Talton, Benjamin, *Politics of Social Change in Ghana: The Konkomba Struggle for Political Equality.* 2010

Tettey, Wisdom, Puplampu, Korbia P. and Berman, Bruce J. (eds) *Critical Perspectives in Politics and Socio-Economic Development in Ghana.* 2003

National Statistical Office: Ghana Statistical Service, P. O. Box GP 1098, Ministry of Finance and Economic Planning (MoFEP) Head Office Building, Accra.

Website: http://www.statsghana.gov.gh

Greece

Elliniki Dimokratia (Hellenic Republic)

Capital: Athens
Population projection, 2020: 11·10m.
GNI per capita, 2017: (PPP$) 24,648
HDI/world rank, 2017: 0·870/31
Internet domain extension: .gr

Key Historical Events

The land that is now Greece was first inhabited between 2000–1700 BC by tribes from the North. This period was followed by the Mycenaean Civilization which was overthrown by the Dorians at the end of the 12th century BC. Its dominant citadels were at Tiryns and Mycenae. What little is known about this period is from stories such as those by Homer written in the 9th or 8th century BC.

The following period, known as the Greek Dark Ages, ended by the 6th century BC when the *polis*, or city state, was formed. Built mainly on coastal plains, the two principal cities were Sparta and Athens. With government based on consensus of a ruling class, and rich in theatre, art and philosophy, the *polis* was the pinnacle of the Greek Classical Age. It was the era of Euripides, Theusidades and Socrates. With strong trade links, Greece also had territories in Southern Italy, Sicily, Southern France and Asia Minor.

Two Persian invasions in the 5th century were checked at Marathon (490 BC) and Thermopylae (480 BC) where Spartans held off a great force of Persian soldiers. In 431 BC rivalry between the dominant city states erupted into the Peloponnesian War. In 404 BC Sparta defeated Athens, but in the next century Sparta itself fell to Thebes (371 BC).

Led by Philip II of Macedon, the Macedonians defeated the city states in 338 BC. The *poleis* were forced to unify under his rule. With Plato and Aristotle active at this time, the latter serving as a tutor to Philip's son Alexander, this was a period of cultural enrichment. When Philip was assassinated in 336 BC, Alexander, then aged of 20, succeeded him. He spent the next 13 years on a relentless campaign to expand the Macedonian territories. The Greek Empire stretched to the edge of India and encompassed most of the known civilized world.

Following Alexander's death in 323 BC, the empire gradually disintegrated. By the end of the 2nd century AD, the Romans had defeated the Macedonians and Greece was incorporated into the Roman Empire. It remained in Roman hands until it became part of the Byzantine Empire in the 4th century AD. A population of Greek-speaking Christians had its power base in Constantinople.

Over the next six centuries Greece was invaded by Franks, Normans and Arabs but remained part of the Byzantine Empire. Following the Empire's decline in the 11th century, Greece was incorporated into the Ottoman Empire in 1460. Apart from a period under Venetian control between 1686–1715, Greece was part of Turkey until the Greek War of Independence.

Greece broke away from the Ottoman Empire in the 1820s and was declared a kingdom under the protection of Great Britain, France and Russia. Many Greeks were left outside the new state but Greece's area increased by 70%, the population growing from 2·8m. to 4·8m., after the Treaty of Bucharest (1913) recognized Greek sovereignty over Crete.

King Constantine opted for neutrality in the First World War, while Prime Minister Venezelos favoured the Entente powers. This National Schism led to British and French intervention which deposed Constantine on 11 June 1917. When his son Alexander died on 25 Oct. 1920, he returned and reigned until 1922. He was forced to abdicate by a coup after defeat by Turkey and the loss of Smyrna. The Treaty of Lausanne (1923) recognized Smyrna as Turkish with Eastern Thrace and the islands of Imvros and Tenedos, all of which had been ceded to Greece by the 1920 Treaty of Sevres. An exchange of Christian and Muslim populations followed. Resistance to Italian demands brought Greece into the Second World War when Germany had to come to the aid of the hard-pressed Italians. Athens was occupied on 27 April 1941. The occupation lasted until 15 Oct. 1944.

Shortly before the German withdrawal the leading communist resistance movement established a provisional government to supplant the monarchy and the existing government-in-exile. British attempts to oversee a coalition government between the communists and royalist groups collapsed in Dec. 1944. Two months of fierce fighting saw the communists claim most of the country bar Athens and Salonika, before the uprising was suppressed by the British. The communists boycotted the general election of March 1946, which returned a royalist government. When the king was restored to the throne in Sept. 1946 the communists responded with a guerrilla war. The Greek army, heavily backed by the USA, defeated the insurgents and the civil war came to an end in Oct. 1949, with 50,000 dead and around half a million people displaced.

The late 1950s saw the emergence of the Left, capitalizing on the movement for union with Cyprus and unease over NATO membership (1952). A military coup in 1967 led to the authoritarian rule of the 'Colonels' headed by George Papadopoulos. A republic was declared on 29 July 1973.

Papadopoulos was ousted by Brigadier-General Demetrios Ioannidis, head of the military police, who returned some civil powers but kept much power for himself. In 1974 an Athens-supported coup attempt against Cyprus's President Makarios led to a Turkish invasion of the island and the establishment of the 'Turkish Republic of Northern Cyprus'. Ioannidis's government fell and Konstantinos Karamanlis returned from 13 years in exile to head a civilian government of national unity. The monarchy was abolished by a referendum on 8 Dec. 1974 and a new constitution the following year established a parliamentary republic with an executive president. The 1981 election brought Andreas Papandreou to power at the head of a socialist government. Earlier that year Greece had become the tenth member of the EU. Re-elected in 1985, Papandreou imposed economic austerity to combat inflation and soaring budgets but industrial unrest and evidence of widespread corruption led to his fall and a succession of weak governments. Papandreou returned to power in Oct. 1993 but ill-health forced his resignation two years later. His successor Constantinos Simitis took a more pro-European stance, instituting economic reforms to prepare the way for entry into European Monetary Union (EMU).

Kostas Karamanlis led the Conservative New Democracy party to power in 2004, ending over a decade of rule by Pasok. In the same year Athens hosted the Olympic Games. Karamanlis won a second term in Sept. 2007. In March 2008 his government blocked Macedonia's accession to NATO because of a long-running dispute about Macedonia's name. Greece already had a constituent province called Macedonia.

Crippled by the global financial crisis of 2008–09, Greece threatened to default on its public debt. EU partners agreed to guarantee a potential €110bn. bailout in return for a swathe of austerity measures that prompted a series of general strikes in 2010 and 2011. By late 2011 the crisis had deepened amid fears that the entire eurozone could be destabilized. In Oct. 2011 eurozone leaders agreed to a 50% write-off of Greek debt in return for additional austerity measures.

The Greek prime minister, George Papandreou, resigned in Nov. 2011 after widespread criticism of his plan to put the rescue package to a referendum. A national unity government under Lucas Papademos was established ahead of elections held in May 2012. In Feb. 2012 the economy received a further €130bn. bailout from the EU and IMF. After the inconclusive May elections, a further round of polling the following month resulted in Antonis Samaras becoming prime minister at the head of a left–right coalition. Samaras oversaw a new wave of austerity measures while in Sept. 2013 his government launched a crackdown against the far-right Golden Dawn party, which had grown in popularity since the onset of the financial crisis. Opponents of Golden Dawn accused it of involvement in serious criminal activity.

In Feb. 2014 the unemployment rate reached a record high of 28%. Three months later the anti-austerity Coalition of the Radical Left (Syriza) emerged as the leading Greek party at elections for the European Parliament. With Karolos Papoulias due to stand down as Greek state president in March 2015 and parliament failing to elect a replacement in Dec. 2014, there was a snap general election in Jan. 2015. Syriza repeated its European success at the national level, winning the largest number of seats and forming a coalition

© Springer Nature Limited 2020
Palgrave Macmillan (ed.), *The Statesman's Yearbook 2020*,
https://doi.org/10.1057/978-1-349-95940-2_81

with the Independent Greeks party. Syriza leader Alexis Tsipras became prime minister and the following month his government negotiated an extension of Greece's financial bailout agreement with its eurozone and IMF creditors in return for implementing further reforms and dropping key anti-austerity election pledges.

Territory and Population

Greece is bounded in the north by Albania, North Macedonia and Bulgaria, east by Turkey and the Aegean Sea, south by the Mediterranean and west by the Ionian Sea. The total area is 131,958 sq. km (50,949 sq. miles), of which the islands account for 25,026 sq. km (9,663 sq. miles).

The population was 10,815,197 according to the census of March 2011 (5,512,404 females and 5,302,703 males), giving a density of 82·0 per sq. km. This excludes the population of the Monastic Republic of Mount Athos. As well as 9,903,268 Greek nationals, there were 199,101 citizens of other European Union countries in Greece in March 2011, plus 708,003 citizens of other countries and 4,825 stateless persons or people with no specified citizenship. The estimated population on 1 Jan. 2015 was 10,858,018. Estimates of the total number of Greeks living outside Greece vary from 3m. to 7m.

The UN gives a projected population for 2020 of 11·10m.

In 2011, 61·7% of the population lived in urban areas. In 2011 the former administrative system of 13 regions, 54 prefectures and 1,033 municipalities and communities was replaced by seven decentralized administrations, 13 regions and 325 municipalities. The autonomous monastic community of Mount Athos retained its status.

Areas and populations of the decentralized administrations according to the 2011 census:

Decentralized administrations	Area (sq. km)	Population	Capital
Aegean	9,122	508,206	Piraeus
Attica	3,808	3,827,624	Athens (Athinai)
Crete	8,336	623,065	Heraklion
Epirus and Western Macedonia	18,654	620,545	Ioannina
Macedonia and Thrace	32,969	2,490,051	Thessaloniki
Mount Athos[1]	336	1,811	Karyai
Peloponnese, Western Greece and the Ionian Islands	29,147	1,465,554	Patras
Thessaly and Central Greece	29,586	1,280,152	Larissa

[1]Autonomous monastic community.

The largest cities (2011 census populations) are Athens (the capital), 3,168,036 (including the municipalities of Piraeus, Peristeri and Kallithea); Thessaloniki, 806,396; Patras, 195,265; Heraklion, 157,452; Larissa, 144,651; Volos, 130,094; Acharnai, 100,723.

The Monastic Republic of **Mount Athos** (or Agion Oros, i.e. 'Holy Mountain'), the easternmost of the three prongs of the peninsula of Chalcidice, is a self-governing community composed of 20 monasteries. The peninsula is administered by a Council of four members and an Assembly of 20 members, one deputy from each monastery. The constitution of 1927 gives legal sanction to the Charter of Mount Athos, drawn up by representatives of the 20 monasteries on 20 May 1924, and its status is confirmed by the 1952 and 1975 constitutions. Women are not permitted to enter. Population, 2011, 1,811.

The modern Greek language had two contesting literary standard forms, the archaizing *Katharevousa* ('purist'), and a version based on the spoken vernacular, 'Demotic'. In 1976 Standard Modern Greek was adopted as the official language, with Demotic as its core.

Social Statistics

2009: 117,933 live births; 108,316 deaths; 59,212 marriages; 13,163 divorces (2008); 505 still births. 2009 rates: birth (per 1,000 population), 10·5; death, 9·6; marriage, 5·3; divorce, 1·2 (2008). Average annual population growth rate, 2005–10, 0·2%. In 2012 the suicide rate per 100,000 population was 3·8 (men, 6·3; women, 1·3). Expectation of life at birth, 2014, 78·0 years for males and 83·8 years for females. In 2005 the most

popular age range for marrying was 25–29 for females and 30–34 for males. Infant mortality, 2009, 3·2 per 1,000 live births; fertility rate, 2005, 1·2 births per woman (one of the lowest rates in the world). Greece was ranked 87th in a gender gap index of 145 countries compiled by the World Economic Forum for its *Global Gender Gap Report 2015*. The annual index considers economic, political, education and health criteria. Only 7·6% of live births in 2012 were outside of marriage, compared to 40·2% in the European Union as a whole. In 2014 Greece received 9,450 asylum applications (up from 8,220 in 2013), equivalent to 0·8 per 1,000 inhabitants. In 2010, 90% of all illegal immigrants into the European Union entered through Greece.

Climate

Coastal regions and the islands have typical Mediterranean conditions, with mild, rainy winters and hot, dry, sunny summers. Rainfall comes almost entirely in the winter months, though amounts vary widely according to position and relief. Continental conditions affect the northern mountainous areas, with severe winters, deep snow cover and heavy precipitation, but summers are hot. Athens, Jan. 48°F (8·6°C), July 82·5°F (28·2°C). Annual rainfall 16·6" (414·3 mm).

Constitution and Government

Greece is a presidential parliamentary democracy. A new constitution was introduced in June 1975 and was amended in March 1986, April 2001 and May 2008. The 300-member *Chamber of Deputies* is elected for four-year terms by proportional representation. There is a 3% threshold. Extra seats are awarded to the party which leads in an election. The Chamber of Deputies elects the head of state, the *President*, for a five-year term.

National Anthem

'Imnos eis tin Eleftherian' ('Hymn to Freedom'); words by Dionysios Solomos, tune by N. Mantzaros.
   (Same as Cyprus.)

Government Chronology

(EEK = National Unionist Party; EK = Center Union; EPEK = National Progressive Center Union; ERE = National Radical Union; ES = Hellenic Union; FDK = Liberal Democratic Center; KF = Liberal Party; LK = People's Party; ND = New Democracy; Pasok = Panhellenic Socialist Movement; Syriza = Coalition of the Radical Left; n/p = non-partisan)

Presidents since 1973.		
1973	n/p	Georgios C. (George) Papadopoulos
1973–74	military	Phaidon D. Gizikis
1974–75	n/p	Michail D. Stasinopoulos
1975–80	ND	Konstantinos D. Tsatsos
1980–85	ND	Konstantinos G. Karamanlis
1985–90	n/p	Christos A. Sartzetakis
1990–95	ND	Konstantinos G. Karamanlis
1995–2005	n/p	Konstantinos (Kostis) Stephanopoulos
2005–15	Pasok	Karolos G. Papoulias
2015–	ND	Prokopis Pavlopoulos
Prime Ministers since 1945.		
1945	military	Nikolaos Plastiras
1945	military	Petros Voulgaris
1945	EEK	Panagiotis Kanellopoulos
1945–46	KF	Themistoklis P. Sophoulis
1946	n/p	Panagiotis Poulitsas
1946–47	LK	Konstantinos S. Tsaldaris
1947	n/p	Dimitrios E. Maximos
1947	LK	Konstantinos S. Tsaldaris
1947–49	KF	Themistoklis P. Sophoulis
1949–50	n/p	Alexandros N. Diomidis
1950	LK	Ioannis G. Theotokis
1950	KF	Sophoklis E. Venizelos

(continued)

1950	EPEK	Nikolaos Plastiras
1950–51	KF	Sophoklis E. Venizelos
1951–52	EPEK	Nikolaos Plastiras
1952	n/p	Dimitrios Kiousopoulos
1952–55	ES	Alexandros L. Papagos
1955–58	ES, ERE	Konstantinos G. Karamanlis
1958–61	ERE	Konstantinos G. Karamanlis
1961–63	ERE	Konstantinos G. Karamanlis
1963	ERE	Panagiotis Pipinelis
1963	n/p	Stilianos Mavromichalis
1963	EK	Georgios A. Papandreou, Sr
1963–64	n/p	Ioannis Paraskevopoulos
1964–65	EK	Georgios A. Papandreou, Sr
1965	EK	Georgios T. Athanasiadis-Novas
1965	n/p	Elias I. Tsirimokos
1965–66	FDK	Stephanos C. Stephanopoulos
1966–67	n/p	Ioannis Paraskevopoulos
1967	ERE	Panagiotis Kanellopoulos
1967	n/p	Konstantinos V. Kollias
1967–73	military	Georgios C. (George) Papadopoulos
1973	n/p	Spiros V. Markezinis
1973–74	n/p	Adamantios Androutsopoulos
1974–80	ND	Konstantinos G. Karamanlis
1980–81	ND	Georgios I. Rallis
1981–89	Pasok	Andreas G. Papandreou
1989	ND	Tzannis P. Tzannetakis
1989–90	n/p	Xenophon E. Zolotas
1990–93	ND	Konstantinos K. Mitsotakis
1993–96	Pasok	Andreas G. Papandreou
1996–2004	Pasok	Costantinos G. (Kostas) Simitis
2004–09	ND	Konstantinos A. (Kostas) Karamanlis
2009–11	Pasok	George Papandreou
2011–12	n/p	Lucas Papademos
2012	n/p	Panagiotis Pikrammenos (interim)
2012–15	ND	Antonis Samaras
2015	Syriza	Alexis Tsipras
2015	n/p	Vassiliki Thanou-Christophilou (interim)
2015–	Syriza	Alexis Tsipras

Recent Elections

Prokopis Pavlopoulos (New Democracy) was elected president by the 300-member parliament on 18 Feb. 2015, receiving 233 votes in the fourth round of voting against Nikos Alivizatos with 30; there were 32 abstentions. Parliament had failed to elect Stavros Dimas, who had stood as the sole candidate, in three previous rounds of voting.

Snap parliamentary elections were held on 20 Sept. 2015 owing to prime minister Alexis Tsipras's resignation in Aug. Turnout was 56·6%. Seats gained (and % of vote): Syriza (Coalition of the Radical Left), 145 with 35·5% of the vote (149 with 36·3% at the election of Jan. 2015); New Democracy (ND), 75 and 28·1% (76 and 27·8% in Jan. 2015); Golden Dawn, 18 and 7·0% (17 and 6·3% in Jan. 2015); PASOK-DIMAR (Panhellenic Socialist Movement-Democratic Left), 17 and 6·3% (13 and 4·7% in Jan. 2015); Communist Party, 15 and 5·6% (15 and 5·5% in Jan. 2015); The River, 11 and 4·1% (17 and 6·0% in Jan. 2015); Independent Greeks, 10 and 3·7% (13 and 4·7% in Jan. 2015); Union of Centrists, 9 and 3·4% (none with 1·8% in Jan. 2015).

European Parliament

Greece has 21 representatives. At the May 2014 elections turnout was 58·2% (52·6% in 2009). Syriza won 6 seats with 26·6% of votes cast (political affiliation in European Parliament: European United Left/Nordic Green Left); ND, 5 with 22·7% (European People's Party); Golden Dawn, 3 with 9·4% (non-attached); Olive Tree–Democratic Alignment (Pasok), 2 with

8·0% (Progressive Alliance of Socialists and Democrats); The River, 2 with 6·6% (Progressive Alliance of Socialists and Democrats); Communist Party, 2 with 6·1% (non-attached); Independent Greeks, 1 with 3·5% (European Conservatives and Reformists).

Current Government

President: Prokopis Pavlopoulos; b. 1950 (ND; sworn in 13 March 2015).

In Feb. 2019 the coalition government comprised:

Prime Minister: Alexis Tsipras; b. 1974 (Syriza; sworn in 21 Sept. 2015, having previously held office from Jan.–Aug. 2015).

Deputy Prime Minister, and Minister of Economy and Development: Yannis Dragasakis.

Minister of Interior: Alexis Charitsis. *Citizen Protection:* Olga Gerovasili. *Digital Policy, Telecommunications and Media:* Nikos Pappas. *National Defence:* Adm. Evangelos Apostolakis. *Education, Research and Religious Affairs:* Kostas Gavroglou. *Labour, Social Solidarity and Social Security:* Effie Achtsioglou. *Foreign Affairs:* Georgios Katrougalos. *Justice, Transparency and Human Rights:* Michalis Kalogirou. *Finance:* Euclid Tsakalotos. *Health:* Andreas Xanthos. *Administrative Reform:* Mariliza Xenogiannakopulou. *Culture and Sport:* Myrsini Zorba. *Environment and Energy:* Giorgos Stathakis. *Infrastructure and Transport:* Christos Spirtzis. *Migration Policy:* Dimitris Vitsas. *Shipping and Island Policy:* Fotis Kouvelis. *Agricultural Development and Food:* Stavros Arachovitis. *Tourism:* Elena Kountoura.

Office of the Prime Minister: http://www.primeminister.gr

Current Leaders

Prokopis Pavlopoulos

Position
President

Introduction

Prokopis Pavlopoulos was sworn in as president on 13 March 2015. A veteran pro-European conservative, his nomination to the post by the recently-elected radical-left Syriza party was considered a bid to secure cross-party support for government attempts to renegotiate the terms of its EU financial bailout.

Early Life

Prokopis Pavlopoulos was born on 10 July 1950 in the city of Kalamata. He began legal studies at the University of Athens in 1968, a year after a coup had brought a military junta to power. When democracy was restored in 1974, Pavlopoulos became secretary to the new president, Michail Stasinopoulos, whom he had befriended during the latter's house arrest imposed by the junta. Pavlopoulos continued his studies at the Université de Paris II, France, receiving a doctorate in public law in 1977.

On completion of his military service in 1979, Pavlopoulos began an academic career at the Athens University Law School, becoming professor of public law in 1989. After serving briefly in the 1989–90 national unity government of Xenophon Zolotas, he was appointed legal adviser to President Konstantinos Karamanlis. Pavlopoulos entered parliament as a New Democracy MP in 1996 and was re-elected in 2000. With the victory of New Democracy at the 2004 legislative elections, Pavlopoulos was named minister of the interior, a post expanded in the wake of the 2007 general elections to incorporate the public order ministry.

When the sovereign debt crisis brought Greece to the brink of bankruptcy, Pavlopoulos voted against the first memorandum of international financial aid to Greece in 2010, although he later endorsed the deal. His initial opposition was crucial to his eventual nomination for president by Alexis Tsipras, the leader of Syriza who came to power after a snap parliamentary election on 25 Jan. 2015. On 18 Feb. 2015 Pavlopoulous was elected to a five-year presidential term, winning 233 votes in the 300-seat chamber.

Career in Office

Although performing a largely ceremonial role, the president was challenged with easing the tense diplomatic relations between the Tsipras government and the EU and IMF over the financial bailout programme that Greece eventually exited after eight years in Aug. 2018.

Alexis Tsipras

Position
Prime Minister

Introduction

Alexis Tsipras was sworn in as prime minister on 26 Jan. 2015 following a snap parliamentary election. As leader of the Coalition of the Radical Left (Syriza), he came to power pledging to reverse (but later accepted) the policies of austerity imposed upon Greece by its European Union and International Monetary Fund creditors in the wake of the global financial and eurozone public debt crises. The country's youngest prime minister since 1865, Tsipras is also the vice president of the Party of the European Left (an association of democratic socialist and communist political parties). He resumed the premiership following further elections in Sept. 2015.

Early Life

Alexis Tsipras was born in Athens on 28 July 1974. Politically active from an early age, he joined the Young Communists Society and at the age of 16 organized a sit-in at his school in protest at education reforms. He read civil engineering at the capital's National Technical University, at which he also completed a postgraduate degree in urban planning.

On leaving university he began working as a civil engineer, while also pursuing his political ambitions. In 1999 he was elected to lead the youth wing of the radical left Synapsismos party (which later merged into Syriza), and in 2004 joined its central political committee with responsibility for education and young people. After running for mayor of Athens in 2006 (coming third, with 10·5% of the vote), Tsipras was elected president of Synapsismos in 2008, although he did not gain leadership of Syriza until he entered parliament as a representative for an Athens district after the 2009 election.

In May 2010 Lucas Papademos's coalition government announced the imposition of austerity measures in order to secure a loan of €110bn. from the European Commission, European Central Bank and IMF. Popular anger with the terms of the agreement led to a sharp increase in support for Syriza, which in the rerun legislative election of 2012 gained 26·9% of the vote, only narrowly losing to New Democracy (which took 29·7%).

The failure of parliament to elect a new president in Dec. 2014 led to a snap election of the legislature on 25 Jan. 2015, from which Syriza emerged with 149 of 300 available seats. Two seats short of an overall majority, Tsipras formed a governing coalition with the populist right-wing Independent Greeks.

Career in Office

On taking office Tsipras and his then finance minister, Yanis Varoufakis, entered into crisis meetings with European finance ministers in Brussels. An agreement on 20 Feb. 2015 extended the loan programme for four months, temporarily averting the possibility of Greece's exit from the eurozone and a run on its banks. However, the deal included few of the concessions sought by the new prime minister.

In June 2015 Tsipras called for a referendum on bailout terms offered by the European Commission, the IMF and the European Central Bank. On 5 July, 61·3% of voters decided against the terms, rejecting proposals described by the prime minister as 'humiliating'. Tsipras subsequently negotiated a new deal with the creditors that included a rescue package worth up to €86bn. in exchange for reforms to Greece's economy, welfare system and further privatization of state assets. It was passed by parliament on 14 July. Varoufakis, noted for his opposition to the bailout, resigned as finance minister in July and was replaced by Euclid Tsakalotos.

Tsipras announced his resignation as prime minister on 20 Aug. 2015 and called a snap election following a rebellion by a number of disaffected Syriza members. Following Syriza's victory at the election held in Sept., Tsipras returned to the premiership and formed a new anti-austerity government with the Independent Greeks. The government subsequently won a parliamentary vote of confidence in Oct. that year by 155 votes to 144.

In May 2016 Greece's eurozone partners agreed a further tranche of loans to help meet pending debt repayments, but nevertheless imposed continuing unpopular austerity conditions, including privatizations. Against a political background of declining voter approval of the government, in Nov. that year Tsipras dismissed those hard-line ministers who objected to more economic retrenchment in an extensive cabinet reshuffle, while retaining Tsakalotos as finance minister. In July 2017 the IMF approved—in principle—another €1·6bn. support arrangement, dependent on assurances from Greece's European partners on debt sustainability and provided that implementation

of the country's economic programme to rebalance the budget remained on track. Also in July 2017, Greece sold its first government bonds on international markets in three years, while in Feb. 2018, with the economy slowly recovering, Fitch international credit rating agency raised its assessment of the country's financial stability. Furthermore, in Aug. Greece completed its financial bailout obligations, ending eight years of imposed austerity and economic oversight by the EU and IMF.

Despite some friction with the Independent Greeks, Tsipras's government again won a parliamentary vote of confidence in June 2018 (by 153 votes to 127) and, following a cabinet reshuffle in Aug. and the resignation in Oct. of the foreign minister, Tsipras additionally assumed responsibility for the foreign affairs portfolio.

In June 2018 Greece signed an historic agreement with the Former Yugoslav Republic of Macedonia to change the latter's official name to North Macedonia with the aim of resolving a longstanding dispute. Panos Kammenos—the defence minister and leader of the Independent Greeks—resigned from the coalition government in Jan. 2019 over a disagreement about the proposed North Macedonia name change, leaving Syriza with a minority in the parliament. Tsipras subsequently won a parliamentary vote of confidence by 151 votes to 148.

Like several of its southeast European neighbours, Greece has been confronted by an ongoing refugee and migrant crisis, emanating particularly from the civil war in Syria.

Defence

Conscription is nine months for the Army and 12 months for the Navy and the Air Force. A national defence policy was adopted in 2011 that emphasized deterrence, internal co-operation and enhanced situational awareness, as well as primary security tasks.

In 2013 defence expenditure totalled US$5,681m., with spending per capita US$527. The 2013 expenditure represented 2·3% of GDP (the second highest percentage in the EU and above the NATO target of 2%).

Army

Total Army strength (2012) 86,150 (around 44% conscripts). There is also a National Guard of 33,000 reservists whose role is internal security.

Navy

In 2012 the Hellenic Navy included eight diesel submarines, 13 frigates and five corvettes. Main bases are at Salamis, Patras and Soudha Bay (Crete). Personnel in 2012 totalled 19,000 (including 2,300 conscripts).

Air Force

The Hellenic Air Force (HAF) had a strength (2012) of 26,600 (including 4,550 conscripts). There were 277 combat-capable aircraft including A-7s, F-4s, F-16s and Mirage 2000s. The HAF is organized into Tactical, Air Defence, Air Support and Air Training Commands.

Economy

Agriculture accounted for 4% of GDP in 2012, industry 14% and services 82%.

Greece's 'shadow' (black market) economy is estimated to constitute approximately 27% of the country's official GDP.

In 2016 Greece gave US$314m. in international aid.

Overview

Greece has a small, service-led economy in which the state still plays a prominent role despite the introduction of privatization programmes from 1998 to meet European Union membership criteria. Up to the early 1990s the state had held around 70% of all industrial assets.

Greece's real GDP grew strongly between 1995–2007, by nearly 4% per year on average, outstripping both EU and OECD average rates. The economy benefited substantially from EU aid in that period, equal to 3·3% of annual GDP, and was further boosted by spending on the 2004 Olympic Games staged in Athens. Tourism was, and remains, an important revenue earner.

However, prompted by the global financial crisis, real GDP contracted by over 4% in 2009 and the country fell into prolonged recession (with nominal GDP falling by almost 22% between 2008 and 2014). The government deficit was 15·6% of GDP in 2009 while public debt, at 129·3% of GDP, was the highest in the eurozone. In early 2009 the government announced a public sector wage freeze and a surcharge on higher income earners. Its credit rating was downgraded in Dec. 2009. The same month, incumbent prime minister George Papandreou outlined proposals to further reduce public spending and to counter rampant tax evasion.

In early 2010 the government pledged to reduce the budget deficit to 8·7% by the end of the year. A US$11·2bn. austerity plan was passed in March 2010, including US$6·5bn. in savings through rises in sales tax, lower holiday bonuses to civil servants and a pension freeze. Public anger over the measures resulted in a succession of general strikes while concerns over Greek finances contributed to a fall in the value of the euro.

In April 2010 the government requested a financial bailout from the EU and IMF, arguing that high interest rates for Greece prohibited further market borrowing. The following month they agreed to provide up to €110bn. over three years. In return, Greece promised yet deeper spending cuts and greater revenue raising efforts, prompting further unrest. Nonetheless, the government was unable to meet its pledged targets in 2010, recording a budget deficit of 10·3% with debt standing at 144·9% of GDP. Following renewed fears that the government was set to default, eurozone leaders together with the IMF and private lenders agreed to provide a further €109bn. in July 2011. In Nov. that year an emergency coalition government led by Lucas Papademos was formed with a mandate to complete bailout and debt-cutting talks as a preliminary to a general election.

The victory secured by Alexis Tsipras's far-left anti-austerity Syriza party in the Jan. 2015 elections brought renewed fears of a Greek exit from the eurozone. Following lengthy deliberations between eurozone finance ministers, a bailout extension, without significant concessions, was granted in Feb. 2015 that was scheduled to expire in June. In March 2015 the authorities issued €1·3bn. in three-month bonds in order to meet a payment due to the IMF that month. However, in June that year, Greece missed a repayment of €1·5bn., making it the first developed economy to fall into arrears with the organization.

After several tumultuous years of recession or minimal growth, the economy showed significant signs of improvement in 2017 despite political uncertainties and policy constraints imposed by the eurozone. GDP grew by 2·7% in 2017 after a contraction of 0·2% in 2016, although it remains far below pre-crisis levels. Exports thrived—led by tourism and non-oil goods—while industrial production also picked up, increasing consumer and investor confidence. Also in 2017, the IMF approved in principle a €1·6bn. stand-by arrangement for Greece, equivalent to 55% of its special drawing rights (SDR) quota. The authorities have also loosened capital restrictions imposed in the summer of 2015 in an attempt to boost private consumption and improve the investment climate.

Nonetheless, unemployment and spare capacity continue to be high. Moreover, non-performing loans remain a significant problem, with Greek banks tasked by the European Central Bank with reducing such debts by 40% by the end of 2019. In 2017 the rate of extreme poverty was recorded at nearly 36%, with unemployment measured 20·8% in the same year. Despite encouraging signs of growth, the recovery remains fragile. Maintaining sustainable fiscal policy and reform momentum is key to a long-term upsurge, while improvements in relations with Greece's northern neighbours offers hope of improving investment and trade conditions.

Currency

In June 2000 EU leaders approved a recommendation for Greece to join the European single currency, the euro, and on 1 Jan. 2001 the *euro*(EUR) became the legal currency at the irrevocable conversion rate of 340·750 drachmas to 1 euro. The euro, which consists of 100 cents, has been in circulation since 1 Jan. 2002. On the introduction of the euro there was a 'dual circulation' period before the drachma ceased to be legal tender on 28 Feb. 2002.

Inflation rates (based on OECD statistics):

2008	2009	2010	2011	2012	2013	2014	2015	2016	2017
4·2%	1·3%	4·7%	3·1%	1·0%	−0·9%	−1·4%	−1·1%	0·0%	1·1%

Foreign exchange reserves were US$116m. in Sept. 2009 (US$17,726m. in 1999) and gold reserves 3·61m. troy oz. Total money supply in Aug. 2009 was €97,507m.

Budget

Central government revenue in 2011 totalled €86,000m. (€87,607m. in 2010) and expenditure €109,398m. (€111,651m. in 2010). Of the revenue in 2011,

€44,447m. came from taxes. Of the expenditure in 2011, €46,382m. went on social benefits.

Greece had a budget surplus in 2017 and in 2016 of 0·8% and of 0·9% of GDP respectively (following a deficit of 5·6% in 2015). The required target set by the EU is a budget deficit of no more than 3%.

VAT was raised from 23% to 24% in June 2016. There are reduced rates of 13% and 6%.

Performance

Real GDP growth rates (based on OECD statistics):

2008	2009	2010	2011	2012	2013	2014	2015	2016	2017
−0·3%	−4·3%	−5·5%	−9·1%	−7·3%	−3·2%	0·7%	−0·4%	−0·2%	1·5%

Up until 2007 Greece had recorded economic growth above the EU average every year since 1996. Total GDP in 2017 was US$200·3bn.

Banking and Finance

The central bank and bank of issue is the Bank of Greece. Its *Governor* is Yannis Stournaras. In July 2013 there were 27 credit institutions incorporated in Greece. Total assets of credit institutions in May 2013 was €422,093m. The largest banks are National Bank of Greece, EFG Eurobank Ergasias, Alpha Bank and Piraeus Bank. In June 2012 gross external debt amounted to US$526,151m. Foreign direct investment was US$2·6bn. in 2013.

There is a stock exchange in Athens.

Energy and Natural Resources

In 2011, 11·6% of energy consumption came from renewables (wind power, solar power, hydro-electric power, tidal power, geothermal energy and biomass), compared to the European Union average of 13·0%. A target of 18% has been set by the EU for 2020.

Environment

Carbon dioxide emissions from the consumption of energy in 2011 were the equivalent of 8·6 tonnes per capita in 2011. An *Environmental Performance Index* compiled in 2016 ranked Greece 21st of 180 countries, with 85·8%. The index examined various factors in nine areas—agriculture, air quality, biodiversity and habitat, climate and energy, fisheries, forests, health impacts, water and sanitation, and water resources.

Electricity

Installed capacity in 2011 was 16·5m. kW. A national grid supplies the mainland, and islands near its coast. Power is produced in remoter islands by local generators. Total production in 2011 was 59·4bn. kWh; consumption per capita in 2011 was 5,636 kWh. 86% of electricity was produced in 2011 by thermal power stations (mainly using lignite) and the rest was from hydro-electric and geothermal generation.

Oil and Gas

Output of crude petroleum, 2011, 0·7m. bbls; proven reserves, 2014, 10m. bbls. The oil sector plays a critical role in the Greek economy, accounting for more than 70% of total energy demand. Supply is mostly imported but oil prospecting is intensifying. Natural gas was introduced in Greece in 1997 through a pipeline from Russia, and an additional source of supply is liquefied natural gas from Algeria. In 2011 natural gas production ran to 7·7m. cu. metres.

Minerals

Greece produces a variety of ores and minerals, including in 2006 (with production, in tonnes): bauxite (2,162,900); gypsum and anhydrite (865,216 in 2005); pumice (850,000); magnesite (crude) (463,277); aluminium (164,800); caustic magnesia (68,065 in 2005); nickel ore (21,670); zinc (16,414); silver (25,900 kg); marble (250,000 cu. metres). There is little coal, and the lignite is of indifferent quality (66·31m. tonnes in 2007). Salt production (2005), 198,024 tonnes.

Agriculture

In 2012 there were 2·54m. ha. of arable land and 1·14m. ha. of permanent crops.

The Greek economy was traditionally based on agriculture, with small-scale farming predominating. However, there has been a steady shift towards industry and although agriculture still employs nearly 17% of the population, it accounted for only 4% of GDP in 2007. Nevertheless, prior to the accession of the ten new member countries in May 2004 Greece had a higher percentage of its population working in agriculture than any other European Union member country. Agriculture accounts for 33% of exports and 18% of imports.

Production (2014, in 1,000 tonnes):

Olives	2,284
Maize	2,170
Wheat	1,651
Tomatoes[1]	1,040
Grapes[1]	957
Seed cotton[2]	920
Oranges[1]	806
Peaches and nectarines[1, 2]	666
Potatoes	642
Watermelons[1]	620
Sugar beets	525
Cotton seed[2]	470
Barley	395
Olive oil	382

[1]2013. [2]Estimate.

Livestock (2014, in 1,000): 9,072 sheep, 4,387 goats, 1, 046 pigs, 659 cattle, 35,194 poultry (estimate). Livestock products, 2013 estimates (in 1,000 tonnes): milk, 1,850; meat, 430; cheese, 216.

Forestry
Area covered by forests in 2015 was 4·05m. ha., or 32% of the total land area. Timber production in 2011 was 1·74m. cu. metres.

Fisheries
Total catch in 2012 was 62,431 tonnes, mainly from sea fishing. In 2012 the fishing fleet consisted of 16,249 vessels totalling 80,783 GT (down from 17,568 totalling 90,386 GT in 2007). Imports of fishery commodities were valued at US$706m. in 2011 and exports at US$842m.

Industry

The leading companies by market capitalization in Greece in March 2019 were: Alpha Bank (US$4·1bn.); National Bank of Greece (US$3·4bn.); and Hellenic Petroleum (US$2·9bn.).

Manufacturing accounted for 9·4% of GDP in 2014, compared to 15·3% for the European Union as a whole. Greece's performance is hampered by the proliferation of small, traditional, low-tech firms, often run as family businesses. Food, drink and tobacco processing are the most important sectors, but there are also some steel mills and several shipyards. Shipping is of prime importance to the economy. In addition, there are major programmes under way in the fields of power, irrigation and land reclamation.

The six largest divisions accounted for 79·3% of the total value of sales of manufactured products in 2013. Total value of sales of manufactured products, by division of economic activity:

Industry groups	Value of sales in €1m. (2013)
Coke and refined petroleum products	14,802·7
Food products	7,315·5
Basic metals	2,953·2
Chemicals and chemical products	1,804·3
Beverages	1,305·9
Rubber and plastic products	1,231·6
Fabricated metal products except machinery and equipment	1,002·8
Basic pharmaceutical products and pharmaceutical preparations	887·0
Paper and paper products	857·1

(continued)

Industry groups	Value of sales in €1m. (2013)
Electrical equipment	803·7
Manufacturing total (including others)	36,654·3
Mining and quarrying total	450·2

Labour
The labour force in 2013 was 5,008,000 (4,935,000 in 2003). 68·1% of the population aged 15–64 was economically active in 2013. In the same year 27·2% of the population was unemployed. In 2014 there was a monthly minimum wage of €683·76, down from €876·62 in 2012. The 'official' retirement age is 67, although on average Greek men retire at 63 and women at 59. In 2013 only 36% of Greeks between the ages of 55 and 64 were in employment. Unemployment was 18·0% in Dec. 2018 (down from 21·5% in 2017 as a whole and 23·6% in 2016). Youth unemployment—those under 25—is particularly high, at 48·6% in Oct. 2015 (although it was 60·5% in Feb. 2013). Greece has the highest rate of self-employed people in the European Union, at 36·8% of total employment in 2012.

International Trade
There are disputes with Turkey over Cyprus, oil rights under the Aegean and ownership of uninhabited islands close to the Turkish coast.

Imports and Exports
Goods imports were US$62,180·6m. in 2014 (US$61,148·1m. in 2013) and goods exports US$35,755·4m. (US$36,261·6m. in 2013).

Principal imports in 2014 were mineral fuels and lubricants (34·3%), machinery and transport equipment, chemicals, food, animals and beverages, and manufactured goods; main exports in 2014 were mineral fuels and lubricants (38·4%), food, animals and beverages, manufactured goods, chemicals, and machinery and transport equipment.

The leading import supplier in 2010 was Germany (10·5%), followed by Italy, Russia, China and the Netherlands; the leading export destination in 2010 was Germany (10·9%), followed by Italy, Cyprus, Bulgaria and Turkey.

Communications

Roads
There were 116,631 km of roads in 2005, including 868 km of motorway, 9,299 km of national roads and 30,864 km of secondary roads. Number of motor vehicles in 2005: 4,303,129 passenger cars (388 per 1,000 inhabitants), 1,186,483 trucks and vans, 1,124,172 motorcycles and 26,829 buses. There were 1,612 road deaths in 2007. With 14·4 deaths per 100,000 population in 2007, Greece has among the highest death rates in road accidents of any industrialized country.

Rail
In 2011 the state network, Hellenic Railways (OSE), totalled 2,554 km, of which 1,782 km were of standard 1,435 mm gauge and 772 km were of narrow gauge (1,000 mm and 600 mm). Railways carried 3·2m. tonnes of freight and 15·3m. passengers in 2012. A 52 km long metro opened in Athens in 2000.

Civil Aviation
The main international airports at Athens (Spata 'Eleftherios Venizelos'), Heraklion ('Nikos Kazantzakis') and Thessaloniki ('Macedonia'). The airport at Spata opened in 2001. The national carrier, Olympic Airlines, ceased operations in Sept. 2009 and Olympic Air, the new airline formed from its privatization, commenced flights that month. In Oct. 2013 Olympic Air was acquired by Aegean Airlines, the largest Greek airline in terms of the number of passengers carried. Apart from the international airports there are a further 25 provincial airports. 5·70m. passengers were carried in 2005, of whom 2·90m. were on domestic and 2·80m. on international flights. Olympic Airlines operates routes from Athens to all important cities of the country, Europe, the Middle East and USA. In 2006 Athens airport (Spata) handled 15,079,708 passengers (9,611,095 on international flights).

Shipping
In Jan. 2014 there were 1,081 ships of 300 GT or over registered, totalling 43·32m. GT. Of the 1,081 vessels registered, 435 were oil tankers, 271 bulk

carriers, 255 passenger ships, 71 general cargo ships, 30 container ships and 19 liquid gas tankers. The Greek-controlled fleet comprised 4,147 vessels of 1,000 GT or over in July 2014, of which 3,328 were under foreign flags and only 819 under the Greek flag.

There is a canal (opened 9 Nov. 1893) across the Isthmus of Corinth (about 7 km). The principal port is Piraeus, which handled 40,192,000 tonnes of cargo in 2013 (8,806,000 tonnes in 2008). Other seaports are Thessaloniki, Patras, Volos, Igoumenitsa and Heraklion.

Telecommunications
In 2012 there were 5,461,000 main (fixed) telephone lines. In the same year mobile phone subscriptions numbered 13,360,000 (1,201·0 per 1,000 persons). In 2013, 59·8% of the population aged 16–74 were internet users. There were 24·1 fixed broadband subscriptions per 100 inhabitants in 2012. In March 2012 there were 3·6m. Facebook users.

Social Institutions

Out of 178 countries analysed in the 2017 *Fragile States Index*—a list published jointly by the Fund for Peace and *Foreign Policy* magazine—Greece was ranked the 52nd least vulnerable to conflict or collapse. The index is based on 12 indicators of state vulnerability across social, political and economic categories.

Justice
Judges are appointed for life by the President after consultation with the judicial council. Judges enjoy personal and functional independence. There are three divisions of the courts—administrative, civil and criminal—and they must not give decisions which are contrary to the Constitution. Final jurisdiction lies with a Special Supreme Tribunal.

The population in penal institutions in Jan. 2012 was 12,479 (111 per 100,000 of national population). The death penalty was abolished for all crimes in 2004. 21·0% of prisoners had yet to receive a trial according to 2014 estimates by the International Centre for Prison Studies. In 2015 the World Justice Project *Rule of Law Index*, which provides data on how the rule of law is experienced by the general public across eight categories, ranked Greece 42nd of 102 countries for criminal justice and 35th for civil justice.

Education
Public education is provided in nursery, primary and secondary schools, starting at 5½–6½ years of age and free at all levels. Estimated adult literacy rate, 2009, 97·2% (male 98·3%; female 96·1%).

In 2005–06 there were 5,715 nursery schools with 11,461 teachers and 143,401 pupils; 5,753 primary schools with 58,376 teachers and 639,685 pupils; 3,308 high schools (lycea) with 62,149 teachers and 569,887 pupils; 660 secondary technical, vocational and ecclesiastic schools with 16,066 teachers and 123,436 students. In 2006 there were 653,003 students in tertiary education with 28,863 academic staff.

In 2005 public expenditure on education came to 3·5% of GNI and 9·2% of total government spending.

Health
Doctor and hospital treatment within the Greek national health system is free, but patients have to pay 25% of prescription charges. Those living in remote areas can reclaim a proportion of private medical expenses. In 2011 there a total of 53,773 hospital beds. In 2005 there were 55,556 doctors and 13,438 dentists. In 2007 Greece spent 9·6% of its GDP on health. In 2008, 46·3% of Greek adult males and 33·5% of females smoked on a daily basis. Greece has among the highest smoking rates of any country.

Welfare
The majority of employees are covered by the Social Insurance Institute, financed by employer and employee contributions. Benefits include pensions, medical expenses and long-term disability payments. Social insurance expenditure in 2010 totalled €53,855m.

The basic pension is available to men aged 67 with at least 10,000 days of contributions and women aged 67 with at least 4,500 days. Men and women aged 62 qualify if they have 12,000 days of contributions. Men and women aged 61 and 6 months can claim if they only have 10,500 days but including at least 7,500 in arduous work. The basic pension is calculated on the length of the insurance period and on pensionable earnings in the last five years. A reduced early pension is available to men aged 62 with 10,000 days of contributions and women aged 62 with 4,500 days of contributions. The minimum pension for a single person is €487 per month and the maximum is €2,374.

Religion

Greek Orthodoxy is the state religion. The primate of the Greek Orthodox Church is Archbishop Ieronymos II of Athens and All Greece (b. 1938). According to the Pew Research Center's Forum on Religion & Public Life, an estimated 88·3% of the population in 2010 was Orthodox. Muslims constituted 5·4% of the population in 2010 and people with no religious affiliation 6·2%. There are also small numbers of Protestants and Catholics.

Culture
World Heritage Sites
Greece has 18 sites on the UNESCO World Heritage List: the Temple of Apollo Epicurius at Bassae (1986); the archaeological site of Delphi (1987); The Acropolis, Athens (1987); Mount Athos (1988); Meteora (1988); the Paleochristian and Byzantine monuments of Thessaloniki (1988); the Archaeological Site of Epidaurus (1988); the Medieval City of Rhodes (1988); the archaeological site of Olympia (1989); Mystras (1989); Delos (1990); the monasteries of Daphni, Hossios Luckas and Nea Moni of Chios (1990); the Pythagoreion and Heraion of Samos (1992); the archaeological site of Vergina (1996); the archaeological sites of Mycenae and Tiryns (1999); the historical sites on the Island of Patmos (1999); the old town of Corfu (2007); and the Archaeological Site of Philippi (2016).

Press
There were 45 daily newspapers published in 2008 (41 paid-for and four free) with a combined daily circulation of 1,447,000. The papers with the highest circulation are the free *City Press* and *Metro*.

Tourism
Travel and tourism is Greece's biggest industry, in 2016 accounting for 18·6% of GDP. In 2014 there were a record 22,033,462 foreign tourists (of which 2,459,228 came from Germany, 2,089,529 from the United Kingdom and 1,534,565 from Bulgaria) excluding cruise passenger arrivals, up from 17,919,580 in 2013 and 15,517,622 in 2012. There were 403,792 hotel rooms and 779,118 hotel beds in 2015.

Festivals
Independence Day is celebrated on 25 March. The Athens and Epidaurus Festival is the leading arts festival and takes place from May to Oct. Thessaloniki International Film Festival occurs in Nov./Dec.

Diplomatic Representatives

Of Greece in the United Kingdom (1A Holland Park, London, W11 3TP)
    Ambassador: Dimitris Caramitsos-Tziras.

Of the United Kingdom in Greece (1 Ploutarchou St., 106 75 Athens)
    Ambassador: Kate Smith, CMG.

Of Greece in the USA (2217 Massachusetts Ave., NW, Washington, D.C., 20008)
    Ambassador: Theocharis Lalacos.

Of the USA in Greece (91 Vasilissis Sophias Ave., 101 60 Athens)
    Ambassador: Geoffrey R. Pyatt.

Of Greece to the United Nations
    Ambassador: Maria Theofili.

Of Greece to the European Union
    Permanent Representative: Andreas Papastavrou.

Further Reading

Clogg, Richard, *A Concise History of Greece.* 3rd ed. 2013
Couloumbis, Theodore A., Kariotis, Theodore and Bellou, Fotini, (eds) *Greece in the Twentieth Century.* 2003
Dimitrakopoulos, Dionyssis G. and Passas, Argyris G. (eds) *Greece in the European Union.* 2004

Doumanis, Nicholas, *A History of Greece.* 2009

Jougnatos, G. A., *Development of the Greek Economy, 1950–91: an Historical, Empirical and Econometric Analysis.* 1992

Legg, K. R. and Roberts, J. M., *Modern Greece: A Civilization on the Periphery.* 1997

Mitsopoulos, Michael and Pelagidis, Theodore, *Understanding the Crisis in Greece: From Boom to Bust.* Revised ed. 2012

Mudde, Cas, *SYRIZA: The Failure of the Populist Promise.* 2016

Palaiologos, Yannis, *The 13th Labour of Hercules: Inside the Greek Crisis.* 2014

Pettifer, J., *The Greeks: the Land and the People since the War.* 1994

Veremis, T., *The Military in Greek Politics: From Independence to Democracy.* 1997

Woodhouse, C. M., *Modern Greece: a Short History.* Rev. ed. 1991

National Statistical Office: National Statistical Service; 46 Pireos & Eponiton str., 185 10 Piraeus.

Website: http://www.statistics.gr

Grenada

Capital: St George's
Population projection, 2020: 109, 000
GNI per capita, 2017: (PPP$) 12,864
HDI/world rank, 2017: 0·772/75
Internet domain extension: .gd

Key Historical Events

Carib Indians inhabited Grenada when it was sighted by Christopher Columbus in 1498. The Caribs prevented European settlement until French forces landed in 1654. The British took control of Grenada in 1783 and established sugar plantations using African slave labour. Eric Gairy led a violent uprising of impoverished plantation workers in 1951 and became the island's dominant political figure in the lead-up to independence on 7 Feb. 1974. He was ousted by a leftist coup on 13 March 1979. The army took control on 19 Oct. 1983 after a power struggle led to the killing of the prime minister, Maurice Bishop. At the request of a group of Caribbean countries, Grenada was invaded by US-led forces on 25–28 Oct. On 1 Nov. a state of emergency was imposed which ended later in the year with the restoration of the 1973 constitution.

In Sept. 2004 some 90% of the country's buildings were damaged by Hurricane Ivan, prompting a national disaster to be declared. In 2013 Keith Mitchell became prime minister in succession to Tillman Thomas, having previously held the office from 1995 to 2008.

Territory and Population

Grenada is the most southerly island of the Windward Islands with an area of 344 sq. km (133 sq. miles); the state also includes the Southern Grenadine Islands to the north, chiefly Carriacou (58·3 sq. km) and Petite Martinique. The total population at the 2011 census was 106,667 (53,898 males); density, 310 per sq. km.

The UN gives a projected population for 2020 of 109,000.

In 2011, 39·7% of the population were urban. The Borough of St George's, the capital, had 36,823 inhabitants in 2011 (provisional). 52% of the population is Black, 40% of mixed origins, 4% Indian and 1% White.

The official language is English. A French-African patois is also spoken.

Social Statistics

Births, 2008 estimates, 2,000; deaths, 600. Rates per 1,000 population, 2008 estimates: birth, 19·4; death, 6·1. Life expectancy, 2013: 70·3 years for males; 75·3 years for females. Infant mortality, 2010, nine per 1,000 live births. Annual population growth rate, 2000–08, 0·3%; fertility rate, 2008, 2·3 births per woman.

Climate

A tropical climate with a dry season from Jan. to May when days are warm and nights quite cool. In the wet season there is very little difference between day and night temperatures. On the coast, annual rainfall is about 60" (1,500 mm) but it is as high as 150–200" (3,750–5,000 mm) in the mountains. Average temperature, 27°C.

Constitution and Government

The head of state is the British sovereign, represented by an appointed *Governor-General.* There is a bicameral legislature, consisting of a 13-member *Senate,* appointed by the Governor-General, and a 15-member *House of Representatives,* elected by universal suffrage. Members of both houses serve five-year terms.

National Anthem

'Hail Grenada, land of ours'; words by I. M. Baptiste, tune by L. A. Masanto.

Recent Elections

At the elections of 13 March 2018 for the House of Representatives the ruling New National Party won all 15 seats for the second consecutive time, with 58·9% of the votes cast, against 40·5% for the National Democratic Congress, who failed to win any seats. Turnout was 73·7%.

Current Government

Governor-General: Dame Cécile La Grenade.

In Feb. 2019 the government comprised:

Prime Minister, and Minister for National Security, Public Administration, Home Affairs, Information and Communication Technology, Finance, Planning, Economic Development and Physical Development: Keith Mitchell; b. 1946 (New National Party; since 20 Feb. 2013, having previously held office from June 1995 to July 2008).

Minister for Agriculture and Lands: Yolande Bain-Horsford. *Carriacou and Petite Martinique Affairs, Local Government and Legal Affairs:* Kindra Maturine-Stewart. *Climate Resilience, the Environment, Forestry, Fisheries, Disaster Management and Information:* Simon Stiell. *Education, Human Resource Development and Religious Affairs:* Emmalin Pierre. *Foreign Affairs and Labour:* Peter David. *Health, Social Security and International Business:* Nickolas Steele. *Infrastructure Development, Public Utilities, Energy, Transport and Implementation:* Gregory Bowen. *Social Development, Housing and Community Development:* Delma Thomas. *Tourism and Civil Aviation:* Clarice Modeste-Curwen. *Trade, Industry, Co-operative and CARICOM Affairs:* Oliver Joseph. *Youth Development, Sports, Culture and Arts:* Norland Cox. *Attorney General:* Darshan Ramdhani.

Government Website: http://www.gov.gd

Current Leaders

Keith Mitchell

Introduction

Keith Mitchell, leader of the New National Party (NNP), was sworn in as prime minister in Feb. 2013, having previously served as premier over three terms from June 1995 to July 2008. He retained office following parliamentary elections in March 2018.

Early Life

Keith Claudius Mitchell was born on 12 Nov. 1946 in St George's, Grenada. He graduated in mathematics and chemistry from the University of the West Indies in Barbados in 1971. After briefly teaching he continued his studies, first in Barbados then in the USA where he gained a PhD from the American University in Washington, D.C. From 1977–83 he was professor of mathematics at Howard University in Washington, D.C. and acted as a statistical consultant to US government agencies and private corporations.

In 1984 he returned to Grenada and entered parliament for the ruling NNP. He served as minister of works, communications and public utilities from 1984 until the NNP lost power in 1989. When the NNP returned to power in 1995, he became prime minister.

Career in Office

In his first term, Mitchell diversified the agriculture-reliant economy by expanding the offshore banking sector. In 1999 he became the first Grenadian prime minister to win two consecutive terms as premier and to claim all 15 parliamentary seats at an election.

In 2000 Mitchell established a Truth and Reconciliation Commission to confront lingering tensions arising from Grenada's 'Revolutionary Years' of 1976–83. In 2001 the country was placed on a blacklist of international money-laundering and tax havens compiled by the G7-founded Financial Action Task Force (FATF). Mitchell's government duly revoked more than 20 offshore banking licences and strengthened financial regulations. Grenada was removed from the FATF blacklist in 2003. In the same year, Mitchell secured a new term in office.

In 2004 and 2005 hurricanes Ivan and Emily killed 40 in Grenada and damaged housing and infrastructure. Mitchell responded by calling on the UN to set up a special fund for small countries in crisis. In 2005 he renewed diplomatic relations with Beijing. When the NNP was comprehensively defeated by the National Democratic Congress (NDC) at the general election of June 2008, winning only four of 15 available seats, Mitchell was succeeded as premier by Tillman Thomas.

He remained as head of the NNP and in Feb. 2013 led the party to a repeat of its 1999 electoral performance, winning every parliamentary seat. His priority has been to tackle the stagnant economy and high unemployment. He aimed to deepen Grenada's involvement with CARICOM and has defended his track record of heavy government support for cricket in particular.

Mitchell retained the premiership following the NNP's landslide victory in legislative elections in March 2018.

In a constitutional referendum in Nov. 2018, the proposed amendment to replace the London-based Judicial Committee of the Privy Council by the Caribbean Court of Justice as the country's final court of appeal was rejected.

Defence

Royal Grenada Police Force
Modelled on the British system, the 730-strong police force includes an 80-member paramilitary unit and a 30-member coastguard.

Economy

Agriculture accounted for 7·4% of GDP in 2016, industry 14·5% and services 78·1%.

Overview
Grenada has transitioned since the 1990s from an agricultural economy to a service-based one. In 2004 Hurricane Ivan caused devastation amounting to almost 150% of GDP. Another hurricane the following year prompted the government to launch a medium-term reform package to tackle the large public debt, alleviate poverty and promote sustainable growth. This was supported by the International Monetary Fund's Poverty Reduction and Growth Facility arrangement.

Against the backdrop of the global economic downturn, fiscal performance deteriorated from 2008, reflecting high capital expenditure and shortfalls in grants from, among others, the European Union. GDP contracted in 2009 and 2010 as a result of weak performance in the construction sector and tourism (the largest earner of foreign currency), along with falling remittances.

A fragile recovery began in 2011, with GDP growth of 0·4% stemming principally from an improvement in tourism and agriculture. Momentum then gathered pace and in the five years from 2013 to 2017 average annual growth exceeded 4·3%, propelled by greater export demand from the USA and declining global energy prices. As the government continued to struggle with high public debt, the IMF extended its Growth Facility arrangement in June 2014. Debt subsequently declined from 108% of GDP in 2014 to 72% of GDP by the end of 2017.

Long-term prosperity relies on continued debt management, as well as addressing high current account deficits, unemployment and a vulnerable financial sector.

In June 2018, the World Bank announced that it had approved $30 million to support Grenada in its transition to a 'blue economy'—one that seeks to bolster its economy through the sustainable use of ocean resources.

Currency
The unit of currency is the *East Caribbean dollar* (XCD). Foreign exchange reserves were US$100m. in July 2005 and total money supply was EC$380m. There was inflation of 1·7% in 2016 and 0·9% in 2017.

Budget
In 2015 (provisional) revenue was EC$622·4m. and expenditure EC$669·8m. Income tax has been abolished. VAT of 15% (reduced rate, 10%) was introduced on 1 Feb. 2010.

Performance
Real GDP growth was 6·4% in 2015, 3·7% in 2016 and 5·1% in 2017. Total GDP in 2017 was US$1·1bn.

Banking and Finance
Grenada is a member of the Eastern Caribbean Central Bank. The *Governor* is Timothy Antoine. The Grenada Co-operative Bank, established in 1932, is the only local bank. In 2013 it had assets of EC$629·0m. There is a Grenada Development Bank, which assists in the economic development of the country.

External debt amounted to US$525m. in 2007.

Grenada is affiliated to the Eastern Caribbean Securities Exchange in Basseterre, St Kitts and Nevis.

Energy and Natural Resources

Environment
Grenada's carbon dioxide emissions from the consumption of energy in 2011 were the equivalent of 2·5 tonnes per capita.

Electricity
Installed capacity in 2011 was an estimated 50,000 kW. Production in 2011 was 204m. kWh, with consumption per capita 1,941 kWh.

Agriculture
There were about 3,000 ha. of arable land in 2013 and 4,000 ha. of permanent crops. Principal crop production (2013 estimates, in 1,000 tonnes): sugar-cane, 7; coconuts, 6; bananas, 3; mangoes and guavas, 2; grapefruit, 2; avocados, 2. Nutmeg, corn, pigeon peas, citrus, root-crops and vegetables are also grown.

Livestock (2013 estimate): sheep, 13,000; goats, 7,000; cattle, 5,000; pigs, 3,000.

Forestry
In 2015 the area under forests was 17,000 ha., or 50% of the total land area.

Fisheries
The catch in 2012 was 2,258 tonnes, entirely from marine waters.

Industry

Main products are wheat flour, soft drinks, beer, animal feed, rum and cigarettes.

Labour
In 2008 the labour force numbered 47,600, of whom 35,700 persons were employed. Unemployment was 24·9% in 2008.

International Trade

Imports and Exports
Merchandise imports totalled US$281·8m. in 2009 and merchandise exports US$30·5m. in 2008.

Principal imports include machinery and transport equipment, food and live animals, and manufactures of metals; principal exports include nutmeg, mace and cardamom, machinery and transport equipment, and fish and shellfish.

The leading import supplier in 2009 was the USA (31·9%), followed by Trinidad and Tobago and the UK; the leading export destinations in 2008 were the USA and Dominica (both 16·4%), followed by St Lucia.

Communications

Roads
There are about 1,050 km of paved roads.

Civil Aviation
The main airport is Maurice Bishop International Airport (MBIA), at St George's. Union Island and Carriacou have smaller airports. In 2010 there were direct flights from MBIA to Antigua, Barbados, Frankfurt, London, Miami, Porlamar (in Venezuela), Puerto Rico, St Vincent, Tobago, Toronto and Trinidad. MBIA handled 353,649 passengers in 2012 (293,933 on international flights) and 1,846 tonnes of freight.

Shipping
The main port is at St George's; the port has the capacity to handle cargo and cruise passengers in two distinct areas.

Telecommunications

There were 28,400 fixed telephone lines in 2010 (271·5 per 1,000 inhabitants). Mobile phone subscribers numbered 121,900 in 2010. There were 334·6 internet users per 1,000 inhabitants in 2010. Fixed internet subscriptions totalled 10,900 in 2009 (104·8 per 1,000 inhabitants).

Social Institutions

Out of 178 countries analysed in the 2017 *Fragile States Index*—a list published jointly by the Fund for Peace and *Foreign Policy* magazine—Grenada was ranked the 56th least vulnerable to conflict or collapse. The index is based on 12 indicators of state vulnerability across social, political and economic categories.

Justice

The Grenada Supreme Court, situated in St George's, comprises a High Court of Justice, a Court of Magisterial Appeal (which hears appeals from the lower Magistrates' Courts) and an Itinerant Court of Appeal (to hear appeals from the High Court). Grenada was one of ten countries to sign an agreement in Feb. 2001 establishing a Caribbean Court of Justice (CCJ) to replace the British Privy Council as the highest civil and criminal court. In the meantime the number of signatories has risen to 12. The court was inaugurated at Port of Spain, Trinidad on 16 April 2005. However, Grenada has not yet accepted the CCJ as its final court of appeal. For police *see* DEFENCE, *above*.

The population in penal institutions in 2012 was 441 (equivalent to 424 per 100,000 of national population). 52·3% of prisoners had yet to receive a trial according to 2014 estimates by the International Centre for Prison Studies.

Education

Adult literacy was an estimated 98·6% in 2014. In 2007 there were 13,733 pupils in primary schools (871 teaching staff) and 13,060 pupils (642 teaching staff) in secondary schools. The Grenada National College was established in 1988. There is also a branch of the University of the West Indies.

Health

In the period 2005–12 there were seven physicians per 10,000 inhabitants, two dentists per 10,000 persons, and 38 nursing and midwifery personnel per 10,000. Over the same period there were 35 hospital beds per 10,000 inhabitants. In 2010 government expenditure on health was 8·2% of total government spending.

In *Water: At What Cost? The State of the World's Water 2016*, WaterAid reported that 3·4% of the population does not have access to safe water.

Religion

According to the Pew Research Center's Forum on Religion & Public Life, half of the population in 2010 was Catholic and half Protestant.

Culture

Press

In 2008 there were five weekly newspapers and several others that were published irregularly.

Tourism

In 2013 there were 116,456 non-resident tourist arrivals by air and 197,309 cruise passenger arrivals. There were 144 cruise ship calls in 2013.

Diplomatic Representatives

Of Grenada in the United Kingdom (The Chapel, Archel Rd, London, W14 9QH)

Acting High Commissioner: Samuel Sandy.

Of the United Kingdom in Grenada

High Commissioner: Janet Douglas, CMG (resides in Bridgetown, Barbados).

Of Grenada in the USA (1701 New Hampshire Ave., NW, Washington, D.C., 20009)

Ambassador: Vacant.

Chargé d'Affaires a.i.: Dianne Charmaine Perrotte.

Of the USA in Grenada

Ambassador: Linda S. Taglialatela (resides in Bridgetown, Barbados).

Of Grenada to the United Nations

Ambassador: Keisha A. McGuire.

Of Grenada to the European Union

Ambassador: Cheryl J. Augustine-Kanu.

Further Reading

Steele, Beverley A., *Grenada: A History of its People.* 2003

Guatemala

República de Guatemala (Republic of Guatemala)

Capital: Guatemala City
Population projection, 2020: 17·91m.
GNI per capita, 2017: (PPP$) 7,278
HDI/world rank, 2017: 0·650/127=
Internet domain extension: .gt

Key Historical Events

Archaeological evidence suggests hunter-gatherers lived along Guatemala's Pacific coast and in the highlands from least 6500 BC. Maize was being cultivated from around 3500 BC and by 2000 BC villages had been established in the Pacific lowlands and along the Antigua Valley. Monte Alto, close to Guatemala's Pacific coast, became a centre of the region's first complex culture from around 1500 BC. It featured giant stone sculptures, stelae and altars.

To the north, in the Petén basin, Mayan tribes experimented with new crops. They established trade routes to the coast and developed elaborate raised causeways, terraces and temple-pyramids. El Mirador was an early settlement (from around 600 BC), which paved the way for city states such as Tikal, Yaxha and Uaxactun. As complex religious, political and economic hubs, they supported populations of more than 100,000. At its height during the classic period (AD 250–900), the Mayan civilization stretched from northern Guatemala to present-day Honduras, Belize and Mexico's Yucatan peninsula. It then collapsed during the 9th century, probably as a result of a series of severe droughts and soil degradation.

Mayan groups moved south to the highlands and established rival states–notably K'iche', K'umarcaaj and Kaqchiquels. Spanish forces reached Guatemala in 1524, three years after Hernán Cortés had defeated the Aztec Empire at Tenochtitlán (Mexico City). Leading a heavily armed force of 600, Pedro de Alvarado defeated K'iche' warriors near Quetzaltenango and sacked the capital, K'umarcaaj. Spanish troops initially allied with the Kaqchiquels and established a base at Tecpan, close to their capital, Iximché. However, relations later soured and by 1540 most of Guatemala's Mayan tribes had been overcome by Alvarado's forces. The K'iche' of Rabinal (Alta Verapaz) fared better under the Dominican friar Bartolome de las Casas, who had previously been granted the title Protector of the Indians. From 1543 the Captaincy General of Guatemala controlled much of central America from Antigua, which became one of the New World's largest and wealthiest cities before suffering severe earthquake damage during the 18th century.

Independence movements broke out across the Spanish colonies following the Peninsula War (1807–14). Guatemala, which then included Belize, Chiapas, Honduras and El Salvador, declared independence on 15 Sept. 1821, three weeks after Mexico had won freedom from Spain. It formed part of the Confederation of Central America from 1823 with its capital in Guatemala City. In 1840 Francisco Morazan, a Honduran general, was toppled by Rafael Carrera, a conservative who restored many of the privileges of the colonial period. A revolution in 1871 brought Rufino Barrios to power, who brought in sweeping reforms to the Catholic church and the aristocracy before he was killed during an attempted invasion of El Salvador in 1885. In 1898 another strongman president, Manuel Estrada Cabrera, came to power and remained in office until 1920.

The overthrow of the right-wing dictator Jorge Ubico in 1944 opened a decade of left-wing activity, which alarmed the USA. In 1954 the leftist regime of Jacobo Arbenz Guzmán was overthrown by a CIA-supported coup. A series of right-wing governments failed to produce stability while the toll in terms of lives and human rights prompted thousands of refugees to flee to Mexico. Elections to a National Constituent Assembly were held on 1 July 1984, and a new constitution was promulgated in May 1985.

Amid violence and assassinations, the presidential election in Dec. that year was won by Marco Vinicio Cerezo Arévalo. On 14 Jan. 1986 Cerezo's civilian government was installed—the first for 16 years. Violence continued, however, and there were frequent reports of torture and killings by right-wing 'death squads'. The presidential and legislative elections of Nov. 1995 saw

the return of open politics for the first time in over 40 years. Meanwhile the Guatemalan Revolutionary Unit (URNG) declared a ceasefire. On 6 May and 19 Sept. 1996 the government agreed reforms to the military, internal security, judicial and agrarian institutions.

A ceasefire was concluded in Oslo (Norway) on 4 Dec. 1996 and a final peace treaty was signed 25 days later. In Nov. 1999 the country's first presidential elections took place since the end of the 36-year-long civil war, which had claimed over 200,000 lives. A UN mission that was set up to monitor the peace process was wound up in 2014, but persistently high levels of deprivation, crime and human rights violations prompted the establishment of the International Commission Against Impunity in Guatemala (CICIG) two years later to identify and dismantle powerful clandestine armed groups.

Territory and Population

Guatemala is bounded on the north and west by Mexico, south by the Pacific ocean and east by El Salvador, Honduras and Belize, and the area is 108,889 sq. km (42,042 sq. miles). In March 1936 Guatemala, El Salvador and Honduras agreed to accept the peak of Mount Montecristo as the common boundary point.

The population at the last census, in 2002, was 11,237,196. The estimated population in 2012 was 15,073,400; density, 138 per sq. km.

The UN gives a projected population for 2020 of 17·91m.

In 2011, 49·9% of the population were urban. There are four recognized ethnic groups: Maya (the native people of the country); Ladino (people of mixed European and indigenous ancestry); Garifuna (a mix of African, Arawak and Carib); Xinca (also native people of the region but not descendants from the Maya). The Maya, Xinca and Garifuna are all officially considered indigenous groups, with Mayans making up the vast majority of the indigenous population. In 2012, 40% of the population identified themselves as indigenous. 51% speak Spanish, the official language of Guatemala, with the remainder speaking one or a combination of the 23 Indian dialects.

Guatemala is administratively divided into 22 departments, each with a governor appointed by the president. Area and population, 2012 estimates:

Departments	Area (sq. km)	Population
Alta Verapaz	8,686	1,147,600
Baja Verapaz	3,124	277,400
Chimaltenango	1,979	630,600
Chiquimula	2,376	379,400
El Progreso	1,922	160,800
Escuintla	4,384	716,200
Guatemala City	2,126	3,207,600
Huehuetenango	7,400	1,174,000
Izabal	9,038	423,800
Jalapa	2,063	327,300
Jutiapa	3,219	444,400
Petén	35,854	662,800
Quetzaltenango	1,951	807,600
Quiché	8,378	985,700
Retalhuleu	1,858	311,200
Sacatepéquez	465	323,300
San Marcos	3,791	1,044,700
Santa Rosa	2,955	353,300
Sololá	1,061	450,500
Suchitepéquez	2,510	529,100
Totonicapán	1,061	491,300
Zacapa	2,690	225,100

In 2010 Guatemala City, the capital, had an estimated population of 2,584,000. Other major towns are Mixco, Villa Nueva, Quetzaltenango, Petapa and Escuintla.

Social Statistics

Births, 2006, 368,399; deaths, 69,756. 2006 rates per 1,000 population: birth, 28·4; death, 5·4. Life expectancy, 2007: male 66·7 years; female 73·7. Annual population growth rate, 2005–10, 2·5%. Infant mortality, 2010, 25 per 1,000 live births; fertility rate, 2008, 4·1 births per woman.

Climate

A tropical climate, with little variation in temperature and a well-marked wet season from May to Oct. Guatemala City, Jan. 63°F (17·2°C), July 69°F (20·6°C). Annual rainfall 53" (1,316 mm).

Constitution and Government

A new constitution, drawn up by the Constituent Assembly elected on 1 July 1984, was promulgated in June 1985 and came into force on 14 Jan. 1986. In 1993, 43 amendments were adopted, reducing *inter alia* the President's term of office from five to four years. The President and Vice President are elected by direct election (with a second round of voting if no candidate secures 50% of the first-round votes) for a non-renewable four-year term. The unicameral *Congreso de la República* comprises 158 members, elected partly from constituencies and partly by proportional representation to serve four-year terms.

National Anthem

The national anthem has no official name but is referred to by Guatemalans as 'Himno Nacional' ('National Hymn'); words by J. J. Palma, tune by R. Alvárez.

Government Chronology

Heads of State since 1944. (CAO = Organized Aranista Central; DCG = Guatemalan Christian Democracy; FCN–Nación = National Convergence Front; FRG = Guatemalan Republican Front; GANA = Grand National Alliance; MAS = Solidarity Action Movement; MLN = National Liberation Movement; PAN = National Advancement Party; PAR = Revolutionary Action Party; PID = Democratic Institutional Party; PP = Patriotic Party; PR = Revolutionary Party; PRDN = National Democratic Reconciliation/Redemption Party; UNE = National Union of Hope; n/p = non-partisan

Military Junta		
1944–45		Maj. Francisco Javier Arana; Capt. Jacobo; Arbenz Guzmán; Jorge Toriello Garrido
Presidents		
1945–51	PAR	Juan José Arévalo Bermejo
1951–54	PAR	Jacobo Arbenz Guzmán
1954	military	Carlos Enrique Díaz de León
Military Juntas		
1954		Col. Elfego Hernán Monzón Aguirre; Col. José Ángel Sánchez; Col. José Luis Cruz Salazar; Col. Carlos Enrique Díaz de León; Col. Mauricio Dubois
1954		Col. Carlos Castillo Armas; Col. Mauricio Dubois; Maj. Enrique Trinidad Oliva; Col. Elfego Hernán Monzón Aguirre; Col. José Luis Cruz Salazar
Presidents		
1954–57	military	Carlos Castillo Armas
1957–58	military	Guillermo Flores Avendaño
1958–63	PRDN	José Ramón Ydígoras Fuentes
1963–66	military	Alfredo Enrique Peralta Azurdia
1966–70	PR	Julio César Méndez Montenegro
1970–74	military, MLN	Carlos Manuel Arana Osorio

(*continued*)

1974–78	military, MLN/PID	Kjell Eugenio Laugerud García
1978–82	military, PID/PR/ CAO	Fernando Romeo Lucas García
1982–83	military	José Efraín Ríos Montt
1983–86	military	Óscar Humberto Mejía Víctores
1986–91	DCG	Marco Vinicio Cerezo Arévalo
1991–93	MAS	Jorge Antonio Serrano Elías
1993–96	n/p	Ramiro de León Carpio
1996–2000	PAN	Álvaro Enrique Arzú Yrigoyen
2000–04	FRG	Alfonso Antonio Portillo Cabrera
2004–08	GANA	Óscar Rafael Berger Perdomo
2008–12	UNE	Álvaro Colom Caballeros
2012–15	PP	Otto Pérez Molina
2015–16	n/p	Alejandro Maldonado Aguirre (acting)
2016–	FCN-Nacion	Jimmy Morales

Recent Elections

In the first round of presidential elections on 6 Sept. 2015 Jimmy Morales of the Frente de Convergencia Nacional (FCN–Nación, National Convergence Front) won with 23·8% of the vote. Sandra Torres of the Unidad Nacional de la Esperanza (UNE, National Unity of Hope) took 19·8% and Manuel Baldizón of the Libertad Democrática Renovada (LIDER, Renewed Democratic Party) 19·6%. 11 other candidates received less than 7% of the vote each. Turnout was 71·2%. In the second round run-off on 25 Oct. 2015 Morales won with 67·4% of the vote against Torres with 32·6%. Turnout was 56·3%.

Congressional elections were held on 6 Sept. 2015. The Libertad Democrática Renovada won 44 seats with 19·1% of the vote; Unidad Nacional de la Esperanza 36 with 14·8%; Todos (All) 18 with 9·7%; Partido Patriota (PP, Patriotic Party) 17 with 9·4%; and Frente de Convergencia Nacional 11 with 8·8%. Eight other parties and coalitions won seven seats or fewer. Turnout was 71·1%.

Current Government

President: Jimmy Morales; b. 1969 (FCN–Nación; since 14 Jan. 2016).
Vice President: Jafeth Cabrera.
In Feb. 2019 the government comprised:
Minister of Agriculture, Livestock and Food: Mario Méndez Montenegro. *Communications, Infrastructure and Housing:* José Benito Ruiz. *Culture and Sport:* José Luis Chea Urruela. *Defence:* Brig.-Gen. Luis Miguel Ralda Moreno. *Economy:* Acisclo Valladares. *Education:* Óscar Hugo López Rivas. *Energy and Mines:* Luis Chang. *Environment and Natural Resources:* Alfonso Alonzo. *Foreign Affairs:* Sandra Jovel. *Interior:* Enrique Degenhart. *Labour:* Aura Leticia Teleguario. *Public Finance:* Julio Héctor Estrada. *Public Health and Social Assistance:* Carlos Soto Menegazzo. *Social Development:* Carlos Velásquez Monge.
Government Website (Spanish only): http://www.guatemala.gob.gt

Current Leaders

Jimmy Morales
Position
President

Introduction
Jimmy Morales was sworn in as president on 14 Jan. 2016. Prior to running for office, he was a comic actor best known for his role in a long-running television series. He was nominated for the presidency by the National Convergence Front, a party founded in 2008 by former members of the Guatemalan armed forces. Morales's campaign capitalized on public disenchantment at endemic corruption amongst the ruling elite.

Early Life

Morales was born James Ernesto Morales Cabrera on 18 March 1969 in a working class neighbourhood of Guatemala City. Raised an evangelical Christian, he graduated in business administration from the University of San Carlos.

He first came to the attention of the public when he and his brother, Sammy, launched a weekly sketch show that eventually spun off into several films and tours. In 2011 he entered the race to become mayor of the city of Mixco but finished a distant third. In March 2013 he was elected secretary-general the National Convergence Front, which had failed to win a seat in previous congressional elections. In 2015 he was nominated as the party's presidential candidate.

Morales ran on an anti-corruption ticket, declaring that he alone among the candidates was 'neither corrupt nor a thief'. His position strengthened in April 2015 when a corruption scandal in the customs agency led to mass protests and, ultimately, the resignation and impeachment of President Otto Pérez Molina. A self-declared 'Christian nationalist', Morales also appealed to conservative voters by opposing abortion (which remains illegal in the country except in extreme circumstances) and same-sex marriage.

Nonetheless, it was to widespread surprise that he claimed the largest share of the vote (23·8%) in the first round of presidential voting on 6 Sept. 2015. In the run-off on 25 Oct. against the former first lady, Sandra Torres, he received 67·4% of the ballot.

Career in Office

In the interim period between winning the election and taking office in Jan. 2016, Morales made a tour of Central America and visited Guatemalan migrants' advocacy groups in the USA. Despite his election rhetoric, Morales' tenure became embroiled in 2017 in scandal arising from alleged campaign finance irregularities by the FCN–Nación. He has since sought to block investigations by a United Nations-backed anti-corruption commission, including by revoking its mandate in Aug. 2018. The Constitutional Court has ruled against Morales, but the Congress has resisted opposition demands that his immunity from prosecution be lifted.

Morales has meanwhile courted favour with US President Donald Trump's administration by reaffirming Guatemala's diplomatic support for Taiwan ahead of China and by recognizing Jerusalem as Israel's capital (making Guatemala only the second country after the USA to do so).

In April 2018 voters in a referendum in Guatemala (in a very low turnout) approved the filing of a claim with the International Court of Justice demanding sovereignty over half of Belize's territory. Belize is expected to hold a similar referendum in due course on the historical dispute.

Defence

In 2013 defence expenditure totalled US$256m. (US$18 per capita), representing 0·5% of GDP.

Army

The Army numbered (2011) 13,400 and is organized in 15 military zones. It includes a special forces brigade. There is a paramilitary national police of 19,000 including 2,500 treasury police.

Navy

The Navy was (2011) 900-strong of whom 650 were marines. Main bases are Santo Tomás de Castilla (on the Atlantic Coast) and Puerto Quetzal (Pacific).

Air Force

There is an Air Force with nine combat-capable aircraft in 2011, although their serviceability was in doubt. Strength in 2011 was 870.

International Relations

In 2018 Guatemala's electorate voted in favour of filing a claim with the International Court of Justice demanding sovereignty over 53% of Belize.

Economy

In 2011 agriculture accounted for 11·8% of GDP, industry 29·3% and services 58·9%.

Overview

Guatemala has the largest economy in Central America but also one of the highest levels of income inequality. Despite strong growth (GDP expanded by 4·1% in 2015), 59·3% of the population lived below the poverty line in 2014. Coffee, sugar and bananas are the main exports, although a series of natural disasters in 2011 and 2012 cost the country an estimated US$1·8bn.

The Central American Free Trade Agreement has contributed to growth, while tourism is becoming an increasingly important sector. Large petroleum and zinc deposits have been largely unexploited, and organized crime (which deprived the country of the equivalent of 7·7% of GDP in 2011 according to the World Bank) is a major issue.

Currency

The unit of currency is the *quetzal* (GTQ) of 100 *centavos*, established on 7 May 1925. In July 2005 foreign exchange reserves were US$3,685m., total money supply was Q.30,083m. and gold reserves were 221,000 troy oz. Inflation was 4·4% in both 2016 and 2017.

Budget

Budgetary central government revenue in 2013 totalled Q.48,997m. (Q.45,681m. in 2012) and expenditure was Q.54,268m. (Q.51,171m. in 2012). VAT is 12%.

Performance

Real GDP growth was 4·1% in 2015, 3·1% in 2016 and 2·8% in 2017. Total GDP in 2017 was US$75·6bn.

Banking and Finance

The Banco de Guatemala is the central bank and bank of issue (*President*, Julio Roberto Suárez Guerra). In 2015 there were 17 licensed banks and 14 financial societies. Foreign debt was US$14,349m. in 2010, representing 35·9% of GNI.

There are two stock exchanges.

Energy and Natural Resources

Environment

Carbon dioxide emissions from the consumption of energy in 2011 were the equivalent of 0·9 tonnes per capita.

Electricity

Installed capacity in 2011 was 2·6m. kW. Production, 2011, 8·15bn. kWh. Consumption per capita in 2011 was 577 kWh.

Oil and Gas

In 2014 crude petroleum reserves were 83m. bbls; output in 2011 was 4·3m. bbls.

Minerals

There are deposits of gold, silver and nickel.

Agriculture

There were 1·00m. ha. of arable land in 2013 and 1·03m. ha. of permanent crops. 338,000 ha. were equipped for irrigation in 2013. Output, 2013 (in 1,000 tonnes): sugarcane, 26,335; bananas, 3,307; maize, 1,795; palm fruit oil (estimate), 1,480; melons and watermelons, 649; potatoes, 516; palm oil (estimate), 402; natural rubber, 356; tomatoes, 318; coffee, 249. Guatemala is one of the largest producers of essential oils (citronella and lemongrass). Livestock (2013): cattle, 3·42m.; pigs, 2·77m.; sheep, 581,500; horses (estimate), 130,000; goats, 113,300; chickens (estimate), 36m.

Forestry

In 2015 the area under forests was 3·54m. ha., or 33% of the total land area. Timber production in 2011 was 19·26m. cu. metres.

Fisheries

In 2015 the total catch was 21,798 tonnes, mainly from sea fishing.

Industry

Manufacturing contributed 20% of GDP in 2007. The principal industries are food and beverages, tobacco, chemicals, hides and skins, textiles, garments and non-metallic minerals. Cement production in 2007 was an estimated 2,500,000 tonnes; raw sugar production was 2,015,000 tonnes in 2005.

Labour

The labour force in 2013 was 6,628,000 (4,595,000 in 2003). 69·7% of the population aged 15–64 was economically active in 2013. In the same year 3·0% of the population was unemployed.

Guatemala had 13,000 people living in slavery according to the Walk Free Foundation's 2013 *Global Slavery Index*.

International Trade

In 2004 Guatemala signed the Central America-Dominican Republic-United States Free Trade Agreement (CAFTA-DR), along with Costa Rica, the Dominican Republic, El Salvador, Honduras, Nicaragua and the USA. The agreement entered into force for Guatemala on 1 July 2006.

Imports and Exports

Goods imports were US$18,263·2m. in 2014 (US$17,504·0m. in 2013) and goods exports US$10,890·7m. (US$10,065·3m. in 2013).

Principal imports in 2014 were machinery and transport equipment (22·4%), mineral fuels and lubricants, and manufactured goods; main exports in 2014 were food, animals and beverages (38·7%), manufactured articles, and crude materials and animal and vegetable oils.

The leading import supplier in 2010 was the USA (37·1%), followed by Mexico and China; the leading export destination in 2010 was the USA (38·8%), followed by El Salvador and Honduras.

Communications

Roads

In 2012 there were 16,293 km of roads, of which 44·6% were paved. There is a highway from coast to coast via Guatemala City. The Pacific Highway and the Pan-American Highway run from the Mexican to the Salvadorean frontier. Vehicles in use in 2007 numbered 1,558,100.

Rail

Ferrovías Guatemala (a subsidiary of Railroad Development Corporation, which secured a 50-year concession to upgrade Guatemala's decrepit rail network in 1997) operated 322 km of railway in 2007, with six locomotives carrying 40,000 tonnes of freight. However, after a contractual dispute with the government, the company suspended its operations in Sept. 2007 and no trains have run since then.

Civil Aviation

There are international airports at Guatemala City (La Aurora) and Flores. In 2013, 59,078 domestic flights and 40,505 international flights arrived at and departed from La Aurora; the international flights carried 2,107,670 passengers. Aviateca is Guatemala's flag carrier. It became a subsidiary of TACA Airlines (since merged with and rebranded to Avianca) in 1989.

Shipping

The chief ports on the Atlantic coast are Puerto Barrios and Santo Tomás de Castilla: on the Pacific coast, Puerto Quetzal and Champerico. Santo Tomás de Castilla, Guatemala's busiest port, handled 6·0m. tonnes of cargo in 2013.

Telecommunications

The government own and operate the telecommunications services. There were 1·50m. fixed telephone lines in 2010 (104·1 per 1,000 inhabitants). Mobile phone subscribers numbered 18·07m. in 2010. There were 105·0 internet users per 1,000 inhabitants in 2010. In Dec. 2011 there were 1·7m. Facebook users.

Social Institutions

Out of 178 countries analysed in the 2017 *Fragile States Index*—a list published jointly by the Fund for Peace and *Foreign Policy* magazine—Guatemala was ranked the 57th most vulnerable to conflict or collapse. The index is based on 12 indicators of state vulnerability across social, political and economic categories.

Justice

Justice is administered in a Constitution Court, a Supreme Court, six appeal courts and 28 courts of first instance. Supreme Court and appeal court judges are elected by Congress. Judges of first instance are appointed by the Supreme Court.

The death penalty was abolished for civilian cases in 2017 but still exists for military offences. There were two executions in 2000, but none since. There were 4,520 homicides in 2016, down from a peak of 6,498 in 2009.

A new National Civil Police force under the authority of the Minister of the Interior was created in 1996. It was 16,500-strong in 2011. There is also a Treasury Police, with 2,500 personnel in 2011.

The population in penal institutions in Aug. 2013 was 16,336 (105 per 100,000 of national population). Guatemala was ranked 95th of 102 countries for criminal justice and 97th for civil justice in the 2015 World Justice Project *Rule of Law Index*, which provides data on how the rule of law is experienced by the general public across eight categories.

Education

In 2007 there were 2,448,976 pupils at primary schools and 864,154 pupils at secondary level. The adult literacy rate in 2008 was 74%. There is one state university—the University of San Carlos of Guatemala (Universidad de San Carlos de Guatemala), founded in 1676—as well as several private universities. In 2006 there were 112,215 students and 3,843 academic staff in tertiary education.

In 2007 public expenditure on education came to 3·1% of GNI.

Health

Guatemala had 4,969 public sector doctors and 12,514 nursing staff in 2005. There were 66 hospitals with 8,270 beds (6·4 per 10,000 inhabitants) in 2006.

In *Water: At What Cost? The State of the World's Water 2016*, WaterAid reported that 7·2% of the population does not have access to safe water.

Welfare

A comprehensive system of social security was outlined in a law of 30 Oct. 1946.

Religion

In 2010 there were an estimated 8·37m. Roman Catholics, 5·13m. Protestants and 0·20m. other Christians according to the Pew Research Center's Forum on Religion & Public Life. A further 0·59m. people had no religious affiliation.

Culture

World Heritage Sites

There are three UNESCO sites in Guatemala: Tikal National Park (inscribed on the list in 1979); Antigua Guatemala (1979); and the Archaeological Park and Ruins of Quiriguá (1981).

Press

In 2008 there were nine paid-for daily newspapers, the main ones being *Nuestro Diario* and *Prensa Libre*.

Tourism

There were 2,142,000 non-resident visitors in 2014 (up from 2,000,000 in 2013 and 1,951,000 in 2012).

Diplomatic Representatives

Of Guatemala in the United Kingdom (1st Floor & Suite 1, 2nd Floor, 105a Westbourne Grove, London, W2 4UW)
    Ambassador: Acisclo Valladares Molina.

Of the United Kingdom in Guatemala (Edificio Torre Internacional, Nivel 11, 16 Calle 0-55, Zona 10, Guatemala City)
    Ambassador: Carolyn Davidson.

Of Guatemala in the USA (2220 R. St., NW, Washington, D.C., 20008)
    Ambassador: Manuel Alfredo Espina Pinto.

Of the USA in Guatemala (7–01 Avenida de la Reforma, Zone 10, Guatemala City)
    Ambassador: Luis E. Arreaga.

Of Guatemala to the United Nations
  Ambassador: Jorge Skinner-Klée.

Of Guatemala to the European Union
  Ambassador: José Alberto Briz Gutiérrez.

Further Reading

Benson, Peter and Fischer, Edward F., *Broccoli and Desire: Global Connections and Maya Struggles in Post-War Guatemala.* 2006

Jonas, Susanne, *Of Centaurs and Doves: Guatemala's Peace Process.* 2001

Sanford, Victoria, *Buried Secrets: Truth and Human Rights in Guatemala.* 2003

National Statistical Office: Instituto Nacional de Estadística, 8a calle 9–55, Zona 1, Guatemala City.

Website (Spanish only): http://www.ine.gob.gt

Guinea

République de Guinée (Republic of Guinea)

Capital: Conakry
Population projection, 2020: 13·75m.
GNI per capita, 2017: (PPP$) 2,067
HDI/world rank, 2017: 0·459/175
Internet domain extension: .gn

Key Historical Events

In 1888 Guinea became a French protectorate, in 1893 a colony, and in 1904 a constituent territory of French West Africa. Forced labour and other colonial depredations ensued, although a form of representation was introduced in 1946. The independent Republic of Guinea was proclaimed on 2 Oct. 1958, after the territory of French Guinea had decided to leave the French community. Guinea became a single-party state. In 1980 the armed forces staged a coup and dissolved the National Assembly. Following popular disturbances a multi-party system was introduced in April 1992.

In 2000 fierce fighting broke out between Guinean government troops and rebels, believed to be a mix of Guinean dissidents and mercenaries from Liberia and Sierra Leone. More than 250,000 refugees were caught up in what the United Nations High Commissioner for Refugees described as the world's worst refugee crisis. In 2003 the governments of Guinea, Liberia and Sierra Leone reached a deal on measures to secure mutual borders and to fight insurgency.

In 2008 President Lansana Conté died after 24 years of authoritarian rule. Power fell to the military, who appointed Capt. Moussa Dadis Camara as president. Camara promised presidential elections in Jan. 2010 and parliamentary elections in March 2010. In Sept. 2009 the army opened fire on an opposition rally, killing at least 150 people. The European Union, African Union and USA imposed sanctions the following month, the UN set up an enquiry into the incident and in Feb. 2010 the International Criminal Court condemned the massacre as a crime against humanity. After surviving an attempted assassination in Dec. 2009, Camara agreed to recuperate abroad while rule fell to his deputy, Gen. Sekouba Konaté. Konaté appointed Jean-Marie Doré as interim prime minister to oversee a return to civilian rule.

In Nov. 2010 Alpha Condé of the Rally of the Guinean People (RPG) was elected president. In July 2011 he survived an attack by forces led by a former military chief. Parliamentary elections—the first since 2002—were held in Sept. 2013. The RPG claimed victory although the opposition refused to recognize the result and international observers complained of voting irregularities.

Territory and Population

Guinea is bounded in the northwest by Guinea-Bissau and Senegal, northeast by Mali, southeast by Côte d'Ivoire, south by Liberia and Sierra Leone, and west by the Atlantic Ocean.

The area is 245,857 sq. km (94,926 sq. miles). In 2014 the census population was 10,523,261 (density 42·8 per sq. km).

The UN gives a projected population for 2020 of 13·75m.

The capital is Conakry. In 2011, 35·9% of the population were urban.

Guinea is divided into seven administrative regions and the governorate of Conakry (national capital). These are in turn divided into 34 administrative regions. The major divisions (with their areas in sq. km) are: Boké, 31,186; Conakry (special zone—national capital), 450; Faranah, 35,581; Kankan, 72,156; Kindia, 28,873; Labé, 22,869; Mamou, 17,074; Nzérékoré, 37,668.

The main towns are Conakry (census population, 2014, 1,660,973), Nzérékoré, Kankan, Kindia, Manéah and Siguiri.

The ethnic composition is Fulani (38·6%), Malinké (or Mandingo, 23·2%), Susu (11·0%), Kissi (6·0%), Kpelle (4·6%) and others (16·6%).

The official language is French.

Social Statistics

2008 estimates: births, 390,000; deaths, 108,000. Rates, 2008 estimates (per 1,000 population): births, 39·6; deaths, 11·0. Infant mortality, 2010, 81 per 1,000 live births. Life expectancy, 2013, 55·3 years for males and 56·9 for females. Annual population growth rate, 2000–08, 2·0%; fertility rate, 2008, 5·4 births per woman.

Climate

A tropical climate, with high rainfall near the coast and constant heat, but conditions are a little cooler on the plateau. The wet season on the coast lasts from May to Nov., but only to Oct. inland. Conakry, Jan. 80°F (26·7°C), July 77°F (25°C). Annual rainfall 172" (4,293 mm).

Constitution and Government

There is a 114-member *National Assembly*, 38 of whose members are elected for five-year terms on a first-past-the-post system, and the remainder from national lists by proportional representation. It was dissolved following the military coup of Dec. 2008, but reinstated after parliamentary elections held in Sept. 2013 (the first in 11 years).

On 11 Nov. 2001 a referendum was held in which 98·4% of votes cast were in favour of President Conté remaining in office for a third term, requiring an amendment to the constitution (previously allowing a maximum two presidential terms). The referendum, which also increased the presidential mandate from five to seven years, was boycotted by opposition parties.

National Anthem

'Peuple d'Afrique, le passé historique' ('People of Africa, the historic past'); words anonymous, tune by Fodeba Keita.

Recent Elections

On 11 Oct. 2015 Guinea held only its second democratic presidential elections since independence in 1958. Alpha Condé was re-elected president with 57·9% of the vote against Cellou Dalein Diallo with 31·4% and Sidya Touré with 6·0%. Five other candidates took less than 2% of the vote each. Turnout was 68·4%. Outbreaks of violence were reported during the campaign phase of the election, and at least three people died in clashes between rival groups. Despite a European Union monitoring delegation citing 'massive deficiencies' ahead of polling, it did state in its post-election report that the process was valid.

Much-delayed parliamentary elections (the first since 2002) took place on 28 Sept. 2013. President Alpha Condé's Rally of the Guinean People (RPG) gained 53 out of 114 seats, Union of Democratic Forces of Guinea (UFDG) 37, Union of Republican Forces (UFR) 10, Party of Hope for National Development (PEDN) 2 and Union for the Progress of Guinea (UPG) 2. Ten other parties won one seat each. Opposition leaders denounced the official results as fraudulent.

Current Government

President and Minister of National Defence: Alpha Condé; b. 1938 (Rally of the Guinean People/RPG; sworn in 21 Dec. 2010 and re-elected 11 Oct. 2015).

In Feb. 2019 the cabinet comprised:

Prime Minister: Ibrahima Kassory Fofana; b. 1954 (Guinea For All; since 24 May 2018).

Minister of State at the Presidency in Charge of Defence: Mohamed Diané. *Minister of State, and Minister of Justice and Keeper of the Seals:* Cheick Sako. *Minister of State, and Minister of Hotels, Tourism and Handicrafts:* Thierno Ousmane Diallo. *Minister of State, Minister in the Presidency and Special Adviser to the President, and Minister of Industry and*

© Springer Nature Limited 2020
Palgrave Macmillan (ed.), *The Statesman's Yearbook 2020*,
https://doi.org/10.1057/978-1-349-95940-2_84

Small and Medium Enterprises: Tibou Camara. *Minister of State, and Minister of Transport:* Aboubacar Sylla. *Minister of State, and Minister of Health:* Edouard Niankoye Lamah.

Minister of Territorial Administration and Decentralization: Bouréma Condé. *Foreign Affairs and Guineans Abroad:* Mamadi Touré. *Planning and Economic Development:* Kanny Diallo. *Economy and Finance:* Mamadi Camara. *National Unity and Citizenship:* Kalifa Gassama Diaby. *Public Works:* Moustapha Naité. *Energy and Water Resources:* Cheick Taliby Sylla. *Higher Education and Scientific Research:* Abdoulaye Yéro Baldé. *Mines and Geology:* Abdoulaye Magassouba. *Cities and Land Management:* Ibrahima Kourouma. *Sports, Culture and Historical Heritage:* Sanoussy Bantama Sow. *Youth and Youth Employment:* Mouctar Diallo. *Posts, Telecommunications and Digital Economy:* Moustapha Mamy Diaby. *Public Service, State Reform and Administrative Reform:* Billy Nankouma Doumbouya. *Budget:* Ismael Dioubaté. *Security and Civil Protection:* Alpha Ibrahima Keira. *Commerce:* Aboubacar Barry. *Social Affairs and Promotion of Women and Children:* Diaby Mariama Sylla. *National Education and Literacy:* Mory Sangare. *Technical Education, Vocational Training, Employment, Labour and Government Spokesperson:* Lansana Komara. *Co-operation and African Integration:* Djenè Keita. *Agriculture:* Mariama Camara. *Environment, Water and Forests:* Oyé Guilavogui. *Fisheries, Aquaculture and Maritime Economy:* Frédéric Loua. *Information and Communication:* Amara Somparé. *Livestock:* Roger Patrick Millimono. *Minister in Charge of Hydrocarbons:* Diakaria Coulibaly. *Minister in Charge of Investments and Public–Private Partnership:* Gabriel Curtis.

Office of the President (French only): http://www.presidence.gov.gn

Current Leaders

Alpha Condé
Position
President

Introduction
Alpha Condé was sworn in as Guinea's first democratically elected president on 21 Dec. 2010. His election was marred by violence and allegations of fraud but it marked a break with half a century of authoritarian rule. He was returned for a second term in Oct. 2015, although the opposition challenged the result of the poll.

Early Life
Born in Boké, French Guinea on 4 March 1938, Alpha Condé was educated in Paris at the Institut d'Études Politiques de Paris and the Sorbonne. He earned a PhD in public law before teaching at the Université Paris 1 Panthéon-Sorbonne and the School of Post, Telephone and Telecommunications.

In the 1950s Condé was heavily involved with the Fédération des Étudiants d'Afrique Noire en France, campaigning for Guinea's independence from France. After independence in 1958, Condé remained in France and became a vocal opponent of the then president, Ahmed Sékou Touré, and the one party system. Touré had Condé sentenced to death *in absentia* in 1970 for his opposition. In 1977 Condé co-founded the National Democratic Movement (NDM), a party that evolved into the Rally of the Guinean People (RPG) that Condé currently heads.

Condé returned to Guinea in 1991 and ran for the presidency in 1993 in the nation's first multi-party elections, losing to the incumbent president, Gen. Lansana Conté. In 1998 he again lost out to Conté, who gained 51·7% of the vote. Condé was then arrested along with other opposition leaders, accused of attempting to destabilize the government. Despite international pressure, Condé was imprisoned without trial for 20 months. In Sept. 2000 he was sentenced to five years in prison but was pardoned by Conté in May 2001 on condition that he withdraw from politics. Condé left for France soon after but returned to Guinea in July 2005.

He initially supported the National Council for Democracy and Development (CNDD) and Capt. Moussa Dadis Camara, who seized power in a military coup in Dec. 2008. However, he soon called for a return to civilian rule and free elections. In Feb. 2010 he announced his candidature for the June 2010 presidential elections. Condé was placed second with 20·7% of the vote in the first round but won the delayed run-off with 52·5% of the vote. His victory was confirmed on 3 Dec. 2010 by the Supreme Court, two weeks after the provisional results were challenged by his opponent, Cellou Dalein Diallo.

Career in Office
Nine days after being sworn into office, Condé announced that in an attempt to break the links with the previous regimes and to address the high unemployment rate among young graduates, all civil servants in the offices of the president and prime minister would be replaced. Condé was expected to review the country's mining contracts, reform the military, increase public access to basic amenities and form a Truth, Justice and Reconciliation Commission to investigate human rights abuses and reconcile ethnic divisions. Long-delayed parliamentary elections took place in Sept. 2013 but were marred by ethnic and religious disorder. Condé's RPG won the most seats, although not an outright majority, and the Supreme Court upheld the results despite an appeal from the opposition.

In 2014 Guinea was faced with a public health crisis as the worst-ever Ebola epidemic engulfed several West African countries. New cases were sporadically reported in 2015 before the World Health Organization declared the emergency at an end in Jan. 2016.

Condé was re-elected for a second and final presidential term in Oct. 2015, again defeating Cellou Dalein Diallo. Opposition parties had earlier called for a postponement of the vote on account of alleged anomalies in the electoral roll but the electoral commission rejected their demand. Continuing unrest led to violent opposition protests in Conakry in Aug. 2016 against the government, prompting a meeting between Condé and Diallo in Sept. at which they agreed to maintain regular exchanges. In Aug. 2017, against a backdrop of simmering ethnic and regional tensions, opposition supporters again demonstrated in Conakry demanding that Condé honour an earlier agreement to organize local elections. To boost the economy, the government announced in Sept. 2017 that it had concluded a US$20bn. loan from China in exchange for long-term mineral concessions, and in Oct. reached an initial agreement with the International Monetary Fund on a programme of reforms that would qualify for an extended credit facility arrangement.

In Jan. 2017 Condé was elected to the year-long chairmanship of the African Union.

Defence

There is selective conscription for two years. Defence expenditure totalled an estimated US$42m. in 2011 (approximately US$4 per capita), representing around 1% of GDP.

Army
The Army strength (2011) was 8,500. There are also three paramilitary forces: People's Militia (7,000), Gendarmerie (1,000) and Republican Guard (1,600) although only 2,600 are active.

Navy
A small force of around 400 (2011) operates from bases at Conakry and Kakanda.

Air Force
Personnel (2011) 800. There were three fighter aircraft in 2011 (MiG-21s), although their serviceability was in doubt, and four attack helicopters.

Economy

In 2014 agriculture accounted for 20·1% of GDP, industry 37·6% and services 42·3%.

Overview
Guinea is rich in natural resources, with around 27% of the world's bauxite reserves as well as large gold and diamond deposits. Mining and the processing of agricultural products are pillars of the economy, and there is potential for hydro-electric power.

Guinea achieved strong growth in the 1990s on the back of tight fiscal policies, low inflation and favourable commodity prices. Subsequent poor performance in the 2000s has stemmed from a weak policy framework, a fall in commodity export prices, the knock-on effect of conflicts in neighbouring countries, and persistent domestic political instability.

An economic stabilization programme launched in 2011 introduced a new mining code aimed at attracting foreign investment. Guinea completed its Enhanced Heavily Indebted Poor Countries Initiative programme in Sept. 2012, paving the way for multilateral debt relief. A subsequent agreement with Paris Club creditor nations reduced its total debt from 65·9% of GDP in 2011 to 19·0% in 2012.

Weaknesses in governance, particularly corruption, and poor electricity supply remain challenges to long-term development. According to the International Fund for Agricultural Development, rural poverty was around 63% in 2012, compared to 30% among the urban population.

Currency

The monetary unit is the *Guinean franc* (GNF). Guinea—along with The Gambia, Ghana, Liberia, Nigeria and Sierra Leone—hopes to adopt a new common currency, the *eco*, by 2020. Inflation was 8·2% in 2016 and 8·9% in 2017. Foreign exchange reserves were US$95m. in Dec. 2005 and total money supply was 1,394·2bn. Guinean francs.

Budget

The fiscal year is the calendar year. Revenue for 2013 was 8,544bn. Guinean francs and expenditure 10,785bn. Guinean francs.

VAT is 18%.

Performance

Real GDP growth was 3·8% in 2015, 10·5% in 2016 and 8·2% in 2017. Total GDP in 2017 was US$10·5bn.

Banking and Finance

In 1986 the Central Bank (*Governor*, Lounceny Nabe) and commercial banking were restructured, and commercial banks returned to the private sector. There were 14 commercial banks in 2014. There is an Islamic bank.

Foreign debt was US$2,923m. in 2010, representing 69·1% of GNI.

Energy and Natural Resources

Environment

Guinea's carbon dioxide emissions from the consumption of energy in 2011 were the equivalent of 0·1 tonnes per capita.

Electricity

In 2011 installed capacity was 436,000 kW. Production was approximately 878m. kWh in 2011; consumption per capita was estimated at 79 kWh.

Minerals

Mining accounted for 23% of state revenue in 2007. Guinea has the world's largest bauxite reserves, possessing nearly a third of the global total, and is the fifth largest producer. Output (2012): bauxite, 17,400,000 tonnes; alumina, 150,000 tonnes; gold, 14,790 kg. Diamond production in 2012, 267,000 carats. Guinea has the world's largest unexploited reserves of iron ore. There are also deposits of chrome, copper, granite, lead, manganese, molybdenum, nickel, platinum, uranium and zinc.

Agriculture

Subsistence agriculture supports about 70% of the population. There were around 2·2m. ha. of arable land in 2007 and 670,000 ha. of permanent crops. The chief crops (production, 2008, in 1,000 tonnes) are: rice, 1,534; cassava, 1,122; maize, 952; plantains (2007 estimate), 436; millet (2007 estimate), 323; groundnuts, 316; sugarcane (2007 estimate), 283; sweet potatoes (2007), 200; mangoes and guavas (2007 estimate), 165; bananas (2007 estimate), 160; cocoyams and taro, 105; pineapples, 102.

Livestock (2008): cattle, 4·15m.; goats, 1·53m.; sheep, 1·28m.; pigs, 82,000; chickens (2007 estimate), 18m.

Forestry

The area under forests in 2015 was 6·36m. ha., or 26% of the total land area. In 2011, 12·66m. cu. metres of roundwood were cut.

Fisheries

In 2012 the total catch was 132,233 tonnes, almost entirely from sea fishing.

Industry

Manufacturing accounted for 6·6% of GDP in 2014. Cement, corrugated and sheet iron, beer, soft drinks and cigarettes are produced.

Labour

In 2010 the labour force was 4,092,000 (54·8% males). The agricultural sector employs 80% of the workforce.

Guinea had 82,000 people living in slavery according to the Walk Free Foundation's 2013 *Global Slavery Index*.

International Trade

Imports and Exports

Imports and exports for calendar years in US$1m.:

	2004	2005	2006	2007	2008
Imports c.i.f.	955·0	1,647·8	1,063·9	1,281·5	1,835·5
Exports f.o.b.	628·7	795·7	770·5	1,059·0	1,430·5

In 2008 main import sources (in US$1m.) were: Netherlands (377·6); France (185·4); UK (144·3). Main export markets in 2008 (in US$1m.) were: France (349·8); Switzerland (278·4); Russia (151·3).

Principal imports in 2008 (in US$1m.) were: mineral fuels, lubricants and related materials (605·0); machinery and transport equipment (538·6); manufactured goods (233·3). Principal exports in 2008 (in US$1m.) were: aluminium ores and concentrates, including alumina (734·5); gold (458·0); printed matter (112·7). Guinea ranks among the world's largest exporters of bauxite.

Communications

Roads

In 2008 there were 6,758 km of roads, 35·4% of which were asphalted. In 2011 there were 299,200 vehicles in use.

Rail

A railway connects Conakry with Kankan (662 km) although much of it has been closed since 1995. A line 144 km long linking Conakry and Fria, where there is a bauxite mine and aluminium plant, opened in 1960 and a third line opened in 1973 links bauxite deposits at Sangaredi with Port Kamsar (134 km). There are two further railway used by the bauxite industry, running from Tougué to Dabola (130 km) and from Débéle to Conakry (102 km).

Civil Aviation

There is an international airport at Conakry (Gbessia). In 2010 there were scheduled flights to Abidjan, Bamako, Banjul, Bissau, Brussels, Casablanca, Dakar, Freetown, Monrovia, Nouakchott and Paris, as well as domestic services. In 2006 there were 103,200 air arrivals and 153,800 departures plus 9,600 passengers in transit. A total of 8·53m. tonnes of air freight were handled in 2006.

Shipping

There are ports at Conakry and for bauxite exports at Kamsar.

Telecommunications

There were 18,000 fixed telephone lines in 2010 (1·8 per 1,000 inhabitants). Mobile phone subscribers numbered 3·49m. in 2009. There were 9·6 internet users per 1,000 inhabitants in 2010.

Social Institutions

Out of 178 countries analysed in the 2017 *Fragile States Index*—a list published jointly by the Fund for Peace and *Foreign Policy* magazine—Guinea was ranked the 12th most vulnerable to conflict or collapse. The index is based on 12 indicators of state vulnerability across social, political and economic categories.

Justice

There are *tribunaux du premier degré* at Conakry and Kankan, and a *juge de paix* at Nzérékoré. The High Court, Court of Appeal and Superior Tribunal of Cassation are at Conakry. The death penalty, which had not been used since 2001, was abolished in 2016.

The population in penal institutions in 2012 was approximately 2,600 (25 per 100,000 of national population). The International Centre for Prison Studies estimated in 2014 that 65·0% of prisoners had yet to receive a trial.

Education

In 2009 adult literacy was estimated at 39·5%. In 2007 there were 1,317,791 pupils with 29,049 teaching staff in primary schools; and 530,590 pupils with

13,907 teaching staff in secondary schools. In 2006 there were 42,711 students and 1,439 academic staff in tertiary education.

Besides French, there are eight official languages taught in schools: Fulani, Malinké, Susu, Kissi, Kpelle, Loma, Basari and Koniagi.

In 2005 public expenditure on education came to 1·7% of GNI.

Health

In 2006 there were 35 hospitals. There were (2006) 689 doctors, 109 pharmacists and 279 midwives. The Ebola outbreak of 2014–15 resulted in 2,536 deaths.

In *Water: At What Cost? The State of the World's Water 2016*, WaterAid reported that 23·2% of the population does not have access to safe water.

Religion

In 2010, 84·4% of the population was Muslim and 10·9% Christian according to estimates by the Pew Research Center's Forum on Religion & Public Life. Most Muslims in Guinea are Sunnis and most Christians are Catholics. In Feb. 2019 there was one cardinal in the Roman Catholic Church.

Culture

World Heritage Sites

Guinea shares one site with Côte d'Ivoire on the UNESCO World Heritage List: Mount Nimba Strict Nature Reserve (inscribed on the list in 1981 and 1982). The dense forested slopes are home to viviparous toads and chimpanzees among other fauna.

Press

In 2008 there were two daily newspapers (circulation 25,000).

Tourism

In 2012, 96,000 non-resident tourists arrived at Conakry airport.

Diplomatic Representatives

Of Guinea in the United Kingdom (2nd Floor, 239 Marylebone Rd, London, NW1 5QT)
  Ambassador: Alexandre Cécé Loua.

Of the United Kingdom in Guinea (Villa 1, Residence 2000, Corniche Sud, Conakry)
  Ambassador: Catherine Inglehearn.

Of Guinea in the USA (2112 Leroy Pl., NW, Washington, D.C., 20008)
  Ambassador: Kerfalla Yansane.

Of the USA in Guinea (Transversale 2, Ratoma, Conakry)
  Ambassador: Vacant.
  Chargé d'Affaires a.i.: Hugues Ogier.

Of Guinea to the United Nations
  Ambassador: Fatoumata Kaba.

Of Guinea to the European Union
  Ambassador: Ousmane Sylla.

Further Reading

National Statistical Office: Direction Nationale de la Statistique, BP 221, Conakry.
Website (French only): http://www.stat-guinee.org

Guinea-Bissau

Republica da Guiné-Bissau (Republic of Guinea-Bissau)

Capital: Bissau
Population projection, 2020: 2·00m.
GNI per capita, 2017: (PPP$) 1,552
HDI/world rank, 2017: 0·455/177
Internet domain extension: .gw

Key Historical Events

Portugal was the major power in the area throughout the colonial period. In 1974, after the Portuguese revolution, Portugal abandoned the struggle to keep Guinea-Bissau and independence was formally recognized on 10 Sept. 1974. In 1975 Cape Verde also became independent but the two countries remained separate sovereign states. On 14 Nov. 1980 a coup d'état was in part inspired by resentment in Guinea-Bissau over the privileges enjoyed by Cape Verdians. Guineans obtained a more prominent role under the new government. In May 1984 a new constitution was approved based on Marxist principles but after 1986 there was a return to private enterprise in an attempt to solve critical economic problems and to lift the country out of poverty. A year-long civil war broke out in 1998 between army rebels and the country's long-time ruler. Neighbouring Senegal and Guinea sent troops in to aid the government. In May 1999 President João Bernardo Vieira was ousted in a military coup led by former chief of staff Gen. Ansumane Mané, whom the president had dismissed in 1998. Following the coup Mané briefly headed a military junta before National Assembly speaker Malam Bacaï Sanhá took power as acting president. After presidential elections in Nov. 1999 and Jan. 2000 Kumba Ialá gained the presidency in a landslide victory. Marking a change towards a democratic future in Guinea-Bissau's politics, Ialá rejected a demand made by the outgoing junta for special consultative status following the elections. Kumba Ialá was overthrown in a coup in Sept. 2003 led by army chief of staff Gen. Veríssimo Correia Seabra. Vieira returned from exile to win the 2005 presidential election but was murdered in March 2009 by a group of soldiers following the assassination of his rival Batista Tagme Na Waie, the Army Chief of Staff. Malam Bacaï Sanhá became president in July 2009. In July and Aug. 2011 Prime Minister Carlos Gomes Júnior survived popular calls for his resignation amid spiralling food prices. In Jan. 2012 Sanhá died after a long illness. After the first round of polls two months later to find a successor, the military staged a coup, deposing the interim president and detaining the front-runner in the election. Manuel Serifo Nhamadjo was installed as head of a transitional government promising to oversee new elections within a year.

Territory and Population

Guinea-Bissau is bounded by Senegal in the north, the Atlantic Ocean in the west and by Guinea in the east and south. It includes the adjacent archipelago of Bijagós. Area, 36,125 sq. km (13,948 sq. miles). 2009 census population, 1,520,830 (783,196 females); density, 42·1 per sq. km. In 2011, 30·2% of the population were urban.

The UN gives a projected population for 2020 of 2·00m.

The area, population, and chief town of the capital and the eight regions:

Region	Area in sq. km	Population (2009 census)	Chief town
Bissau City	78	387,909	—
Bafatá	5,981	210,007	Bafatá
Biombo	840	97,120	Quinhámel
Bolama	2,624	34,563	Bolama
Cacheu	5,175	192,508	Cacheu

(continued)

Region	Area in sq. km	Population (2009 census)	Chief town
Gabú	9,150	215,530	Gabú
Oio	5,403	224,644	Farim
Quinara	3,138	63,610	Fulacunda
Tombali	3,736	94,939	Catió

The largest ethnic group are the Balanta (nearly a third of the population), Fulani, Manjaco and Mandinga. Portuguese remains the official language, but Crioulo is spoken throughout the country.

Social Statistics

2008 births (estimates), 65,000; deaths, 27,000. Estimated rates per 1,000 population, 2008: births, 41·2; deaths, 17·2. Annual population growth rate, 2000–08, 2·4%. Life expectancy, 2013: male, 52·8 years; female, 55·8. Infant mortality, 2010, 92 per 1,000 live births; fertility rate, 2008, 5·7 births per woman.

Climate

The tropical climate has a wet season from June to Nov., when rains are abundant, but the hot, dry Harmattan wind blows from Dec. to May. Bissau, Jan. 76°F (24·4°C), July 80°F (26·7°C). Annual rainfall 78" (1,950 mm).

Constitution and Government

A new constitution was promulgated on 16 May 1984 and has been amended five times since, most recently in 1996. The Revolutionary Council, established following the 1980 coup, was replaced by a 15-member Council of State, while in April 1984 a new National People's Assembly was elected comprising 150 representatives elected by and from the directly-elected regional councils for five-year terms. The sole political movement was the *Partido Africano da Independência da Guiné e Cabo Verde* (PAIGC), but in Dec. 1990 a policy of 'integral multi-partyism' was announced, and in May 1991 the National Assembly voted unanimously to abolish the law making the PAIGC the sole party. The *President* is Head of State and Government and is elected for a five-year term. The *National Assembly* now has a maximum of 102 members who are elected for four-year terms.

In the wake of the coup of April 2012 the military junta suspended the constitution and dissolved parliament (although it was resumed in Nov. 2012), and defied international demands for the constitution's restoration.

National Anthem

'Sol, suor, o verde e mar' ('Sun, sweat, the green and the sea'); words and tune by A. Lopes Cabral.

Recent Elections

In the first round of presidential elections held on 13 April 2014 José Mário Vaz (African Party for the Independence of Guinea and Cabo Verde/PAIGC) took 40·9% of votes cast, ahead of Nuno Gomes Nabiam (ind.) with 24·8%, Paulo Gomes (ind.) with 10·4%, Abel Incanda (Party for Social Renewal/PRS) with 7·0%, Mamadú Iaia Djaló (New Democracy Party/PND) with 4·5% and Ibraima Sory Djaló (National Reconciliation Party/PRN) with 3·1%. Seven other candidates each received less than 3% of the votes cast. Turnout was 89·3%. A second round run-off between José Mário Vaz and Nuno Gomes Nabiam took place on 18 May 2014. Vaz was elected president with 61·9% of the vote, against Nabiam with 38·1%. Turnout for the second round was 78·2%.

At the parliamentary elections on 10 March 2019 turnout was 84·7%. The PAIGC won 35·2% of the vote (47 of 102 seats), the Movement for a Democratic Alternative G-15 21·1% (27 seats), the PRS 21·1% (21 seats)

© Springer Nature Limited 2020
Palgrave Macmillan (ed.), *The Statesman's Yearbook 2020*,
https://doi.org/10.1057/978-1-349-95940-2_85

and the Assembly of the People United 8·5% (5 seats). Two other parties took one seat each.

Current Government

President: José Mário Vaz; b. 1957 (African Party for the Independence of Guinea and Cabo Verde/PAIGC; since 23 June 2014).

In Feb. 2019 the government comprised:

Prime Minister, and Minister of Economy and Finance: Aristides Gomes; b. 1954 (Republican Party for Independence and Development/PRID; since 16 April 2018, having previously been prime minister from Nov. 2005–April 2007).

Minister of Administrative Reform, Public Service and Labour: Fernando Gomes. *Agriculture and Rural Development:* Nicolau dos Santos. *Education, Higher Education, Youth, Culture and Sport:* Camilo Simões Pereira. *Energy, Industry and Natural Resources:* António Serifo Embaló. *Fisheries:* Adiatu Djaló Nandinga. *Foreign Affairs, Co-operation and Communities:* João Ribeiro Có. *Homeland Freedom Fighters:* Aristides Ocante da Silva. *Interior:* Edmundo Mendes. *Justice and Human Rights:* Iaia Djaló. *National Defence:* Eduardo Costa Sanhá. *Public Health, Family and Social Cohesion:* Maria Inácia Có Sanhá. *Public Works, Construction and Urban Affairs:* António Óscar Barbosa. *Social Communication:* Victor Gomes Pereira. *Territorial Administration:* Ester Fernandes. *Trade, Tourism and Crafts:* Vicente Fernandes. *Transport and Communications:* Mamadú Serifo Jaquité. *Minister in the Presidency in Charge of Parliamentary Affairs:* Agnelo Regala.

Current Leaders

José Mário Vaz

Position
President

Introduction
José Mário Vaz became president on 23 June 2014, completing the country's return to civilian rule after a military coup had deposed the previous government in 2012. He is a member of the African Party for the Independence of Guinea and Cabo Verde (PAIGC), which has its origins in the armed struggle against colonial Portuguese rule.

Early Life
José Mário Vaz was born on 10 Dec. 1957 in Calequisse in the northwest of what was then Portuguese Guinea. In 1982 he began training at the Banco de Portugal. In 2004 he was elected mayor of Bissau, a position he held until his appointment as finance minister in 2009.

A military coup on 12 April 2012 ousted the interim president, Raimundo Pereira, and halted the election process to find a permanent successor to Malam Bacaï Sanhá, who had died in office. Vaz took exile in Portugal but returned in Feb. 2013 and was promptly detained on charges of embezzlement relating to a multi-million dollar aid donation from Angola to Guinea-Bissau. He maintained his innocence, describing the accusations as politically motivated.

Following the coup, the European Union, IMF and other donors withdrew aid. Two years of economic decline prompted a return to democratic government and, after numerous postponements, a presidential election was held on 13 April 2014. Vaz comprehensively defeated his closest challenger, the military-backed Nuno Gomes Nabiam, in a run-off five weeks later.

Career in Office
Vaz campaigned on a pledge to revive the country's impoverished economy, increase investment in agriculture and bring stability to the notoriously volatile political system. In Sept. 2014 it was announced that he had sacked the head of the country's armed forces and leader of the 2012 coup, Gen. Antonio Indjai, replacing him with Gen. Biague Na Ntan, head of the presidential guard.

Vaz dismissed the government led by Domingos Simões Pereira, a political rival, in Aug. 2015 following disagreements over issues including the use of aid money. Two months of discord ensued within the PAIGC before the president named a new government by decree in mid-Oct. under the leadership of Carlos Correia, a former prime minister, in an effort to restore a fragile political consensus. However, political instability continued throughout 2016 as Vaz dismissed the Correia administration in May 2016, naming Baciro Djá as the new prime minister, and then dissolved Djá's

government in Nov. that year. His subsequent appointment of Umaro Sissoco Embaló, a brigadier general, as the new premier did not have the majority backing of the PAIGC leadership and Embaló submitted his resignation in Jan. 2018. His replacement, Artur Silva, held office for only two and a half months until April when Vaz installed Aristides Gomes, a former premier in 2005–07, as the new head of government and also economy and finance minister.

Defence

There is selective conscription. In 2012 defence expenditure totalled US$26m., with spending per capita US$16. The 2012 expenditure represented 2·9% of GDP.

Army

Army personnel in 2011 numbered around 4,000 although numbers are reducing. There is a paramilitary Gendarmerie 2,000 strong. Equipment in 2011 included ten main battle tanks (Soviet T-34s).

Navy

The naval flotilla, based at Bissau, numbered an estimated 350 in 2011.

Air Force

Formation of a small Air Force began in 1978. Personnel (2011) 100 with one utility helicopter but no aircraft.

Economy

In 2012 agriculture accounted for 38·7% of GDP; followed by commerce, 18·5%; food processing, 11·3%; public administration services, 7·9%; transport and telecommunications, 5·0%.

Guinea-Bissau featured among the ten most corrupt countries in the world in a 2018 survey of 180 countries carried out by the anti-corruption organization Transparency International.

Overview

Guinea-Bissau is one of the poorest countries in the world. In 2014 it was among the bottom 10% of nations on the United Nations Human Development Index. Since gaining independence from Portugal in 1974, its development has been hindered by political instability. Civil war from 1998–99 and a series of military coups further undermined the economic and social infrastructure. In 2015 it was reported that 69% of the population lived in poverty.

Agriculture—particularly cashew nut production—accounts for 77% of exports, leaving the economy vulnerable to adverse weather conditions. Economic growth during the global downturn from 2008 was robust, despite lower prices for cashews and falling remittances. However, a military coup in April 2012 caused a sharp fall in cashew exports as well as declines in industry and construction, resulting in a 2·2% drop in GDP that year. Cashew exports in 2015 totalled 170,000 tonnes against a backdrop of a 25% increase in the commodity price.

External debt levels have remained stable following a debt relief programme jointly administered by the IMF and World Bank in 2010. The external debt-to-GDP ratio averaged below 25% from 2010–14. The IMF further extended its credit facility to Guinea-Bissau in July 2015 following an emergency loan in Nov. 2014.

Guinea-Bissau continues to depend heavily on donor support, with pledges amounting to US$1·5bn. in 2015. The dismissal of the government in Aug. 2015 and the resulting political upheaval have further undermined the economy's mid- to long-term outlook.

Currency

In May 1997 Guinea-Bissau joined the French Franc Zone, and the *peso* was replaced by the franc CFA at 65 pesos = one franc CFA. The *franc CFA* (XOF) has a parity rate of 655·957 francs CFA to one euro. Foreign exchange reserves were US$96m. in June 2005 and total money supply was 58,030m. francs CFA. There was inflation of 10·4% in 2008 but then deflation of 1·6% in 2009. More recently there was deflation of 1·5% in 2016 but then inflation of 1·1% in 2017.

Budget

Revenue in 2014 was 98·0bn. francs CFA; expenditure totalled 111·9bn. francs CFA.

Performance

Real GDP growth was 6·1% in 2015, 6·3% in 2016 and 5·9% in 2017. Total GDP in 2017 was US$1·3bn.

Banking and Finance

The bank of issue and the central bank is the regional Central Bank of West African States (BCEAO). The *Governor* is Tiémoko Meyliet Koné. There are four other banks (Banco da Africa Occidental; Banco Internacional de Guiné-Bissau; Caixa de Crédito de Guiné; Caixa Económica Postal).

In 2010 external debt totalled US$1,095m., equivalent to 124·8% of GNI.

Energy and Natural Resources

Environment

Carbon dioxide emissions from the consumption of energy in 2011 were the equivalent of 0·3 tonnes per capita. An *Environmental Performance Index* compiled in 2016 ranked Guinea-Bissau 155th of 180 countries, with 48·2%. The index examined various factors in nine areas—agriculture, air quality, biodiversity and habitat, climate and energy, fisheries, forests, health impacts, water and sanitation, and water resources.

The *Climate Change and Environmental Risk Atlas 2014* produced by Maplecroft, a risk analytics company, ranked Guinea-Bissau as the country facing the second highest economic and social risk from climate change by 2025.

Electricity

Installed capacity in 2011 was estimated at 27,000 kW. Production was about 33m. kWh in 2011; consumption per capita was an estimated 20 kWh.

Minerals

Mineral resources are not exploited. There are estimated to be 200m. tonnes of bauxite and 112m. tonnes of phosphate.

Agriculture

Agriculture employs 80% of the labour force. There were an estimated 300,000 ha. of arable land in 2013 and 250,000 ha. of permanent crops. The main crop is rice: production, 210,000 tonnes in 2013. Other important crops (2013 estimates, in 1,000 tonnes): cashew nuts, 135; palm fruit oil, 81; plantains, 51; coconuts, 43; groundnuts, 41. Livestock (2013 estimates): goats, 750,000; cattle, 670,000; sheep, 470,000; pigs, 460,000; chickens, 2m.

Forestry

The area covered by forests in 2015 was 1·97m. ha., or 70% of the total land area. In 2011, 2·77m. cu. metres of roundwood were cut.

Fisheries

Total catch in 2015 came to an estimated 6,700 tonnes, almost entirely from sea fishing.

Industry

Manufacturing accounted for 8·0% of GDP in 2009 and is limited to small and medium-scale enterprises that largely produce for the domestic market. The main industrial activities are the processing of agricultural products and the production of beer and soft drinks.

Labour

The labour force in 2010 was 648,000 (52·7% males). Guinea-Bissau had 12,000 people living in slavery according to the Walk Free Foundation's 2013 *Global Slavery Index*.

International Trade

Imports and Exports

Imports in 2013 totalled 136,187m. francs CFA (129,817m. francs CFA in 2012) and exports 98,070m. francs CFA (78,595m. francs CFA in 2012). Main imports in 2013 were: food and beverages, 38·6%; refined petroleum products, 15·0%; transport equipment, 8·3%. Cashew nuts represented 83·6% of exports in 2013. Leading import suppliers are Portugal and Senegal. India is by far the largest export market, with China and Vietnam also important export destinations.

Communications

Roads

In 2009 there were about 4,400 km of roads, of which 10% were paved. In 2008 there were 42,200 passenger cars in use (27 per 1,000 inhabitants in 2007) and 9,300 lorries and vans.

Civil Aviation

There is an international airport serving Bissau (Osvaldo Vieira). In 2010 there were scheduled flights to Conakry, Dakar, Lisbon and Praia.

Shipping

The main port is Bissau; minor ports are Bolama, Cacheu and Catió.

Telecommunications

There were an estimated 5,000 fixed telephone lines in 2010 (3·3 per 1,000 inhabitants) and 402,000 mobile phone subscriptions in 2011 (or 259·8 per 1,000 inhabitants). There were 24·5 internet users per 1,000 inhabitants in 2010. Fixed internet subscriptions totalled 699 in 2009 (0·5 per 1,000 inhabitants).

Social Institutions

Out of 178 countries analysed in the 2017 *Fragile States Index*—a list published jointly by the Fund for Peace and *Foreign Policy* magazine—Guinea-Bissau was ranked the 16th most vulnerable to conflict or collapse. The index is based on 12 indicators of state vulnerability across social, political and economic categories.

Justice

The death penalty was abolished for all crimes in 1993.

Education

Adult literacy was estimated at 52·2% in 2009 (male, 66·9%; female, 38·0%). In 2006 there were 269,287 pupils at primary schools (4,327 teachers), 55,176 at secondary schools (1,480 teachers) and 3,689 students in tertiary education.

Health

In 2006 there was one national hospital, seven regional hospitals and 26 prefectorial hospitals. In 2007 there were seven hospital beds per 10,000 inhabitants. In 2009 there were 124 physicians, 1,042 nursing and midwifery personnel, 13 dentistry personnel and 21 pharmaceutical personnel.

In *Water: At What Cost? The State of the World's Water 2016*, WaterAid reported that 20·7% of the population does not have access to safe water.

Religion

In 2010 there were an estimated 680,000 Muslims, 470,000 followers of folk religions and 300,000 Christians according to the Pew Research Center's Forum on Religion & Public Life.

Culture

Press

There are no daily newspapers. In 2008 there were six non-daily papers, which had a combined weekly circulation of 10,000 copies.

Tourism

In 2014 there were 36,000 international tourist arrivals (excluding same-day visitors).

Diplomatic Representatives

Of Guinea-Bissau in the United Kingdom
   Ambassador: Vacant (resides in Paris).

Of the United Kingdom in Guinea-Bissau
   Ambassador: George Hodgson (resides in Dakar, Senegal).

Of Guinea-Bissau in the USA
   Currently closed.

Of the USA in Guinea-Bissau
Ambassador: Tulinabo S. Mushingi (resides in Dakar, Senegal).

Of Guinea-Bissau to the United Nations
Ambassador: Vacant.
Chargé d'Affaires a.i.: Maria Antonieta Pinto Lopes D'Alva.

Of Guinea-Bissau to the European Union
Ambassador: Apolinário Mendes de Carvalho.

Further Reading

Barry, Boubacar-Sid, Creppy, Edward G. E., Gacitua-Mario, Estanislao and Wodon, Quentin, *Conflict, Livelihoods, and Poverty in Guinea-Bissau.* 2007

Forrest, J. B., *Lineages of State Fragility: Rural Civil Society in Guinea-Bissau.* 2003

National Statistical Office: Instituto Nacional de Estadística e Censos (INEC), CP 06 Bissau.

Website (Portuguese only): http://www.stat-guinebissau.com

Guyana

Co-operative Republic of Guyana

Capital: Georgetown
Population projection, 2020: 791,000
GNI per capita, 2017: (PPP$) 7,447
HDI/world rank, 2017: 0·654/125=
Internet domain extension: .gy

Key Historical Events

Recent archaeological evidence suggests the Berbica river valley in present-day Guyana was the site of intensive agriculture dating back at least 1,500 years. As well as hosting Arawak settlements, it was also inhabited by Carib and Warau groups. Christopher Columbus reached the coastal area in 1498, with Amerigo Vespucci and Alonso de Ojeda leading exploration of the Essequibo river the following year. Dutch seafarers established a trading post on the lower Essequibo in 1616 and formed the Dutch West India Company in 1621, setting up plantations—initially tobacco, then sugar—and trading with local Amerindians.

A second settlement, Berbice, was founded in 1627, followed by Demerara in 1741. Many Amerindians succumbed to infections carried by Europeans, and slaves were shipped from West Africa to work on the plantations during the 18th century. The Dutch held off various incursions by British, French and Spanish forces, but eventually ceded control of the three colonies to the British in 1814. Sixteen years later the colonies were merged to form British Guiana, the boundaries of which were demarcated by the German explorer, Robert Hermann Schomburgk. A border dispute with Venezuela rumbled on until 1899, when an international tribunal handed 94% of the territory to British Guiana, although further disagreements with Venezuela and Suriname subsequently flared up. The abolition of slavery in the British Empire in 1834 led plantation owners to seek indentured labourers from India, China and Portugal—with 340,000 coming from India alone between 1835 and 1918.

In the 1890s disgruntled Portuguese settlers established the Reform Association, which demanded greater participation in Guyana's affairs. In 1905 anger about poor pay and working conditions by Georgetown's dock-workers sparked riots across the capital. The trade union movement gathered momentum after the First World War. In 1928 a legislative council, with members appointed by the British government, was established and the colony has since become the headquarters of several major regional institutions, including CARICOM.

The independence struggle gathered pace after the Second World War, spearheaded by the leftist People's Progressive Party (PPP), established by Cheddi Jagan in 1950. Following the granting of universal suffrage, the PPP dominated a colony-wide election in 1953 and formed a government under a British-appointed chief executive. However, tensions mounted swiftly and in Oct. that year Britain suspended the constitution, sent in troops and installed an interim administration. When the constitution was restored in 1957 the PPP was divided on ethnic lines, with Jagan leading an Indo-Guyanese faction. Forbes Burnham's Afro-Guyanese group split from the PPP to form the more moderate People's National Congress (PNC), which absorbed the United Democratic Party two years later.

Guyana was granted full autonomy in 1961, although Britain retained control over defence matters. Political and ethnic rioting erupted in that year and again in 1963, devastating swathes of Georgetown. Guyana became a member of the Commonwealth in 1966 with Burnham as the first prime minister (and, later, president). The government nationalized many industries and forged ties with the USSR. Economic troubles mounted in the 1970s as debt rose and commodity prices fell. In 1985 Burnham died and was replaced by Desmond Hoyte, who oversaw some economic reform before Jagan returned to power in 1992.

After Jagan died in 1997 his wife, Janet, became president. She was succeeded in 1999 by the finance minister, Bharrat Jagdeo. In the general election of Nov. 2011 the ruling PPP/Civic again emerged victorious, but with a reduced majority. Donald Ramotar was elected president in succession to Jagdeo, advocating inter-ethnic tolerance. He was in turn succeeded by David Granger in May 2015, bringing to an end 23 years of PPP rule.

Territory and Population

Guyana is situated on the northeast coast of Latin America on the Atlantic Ocean, with Suriname on the east, Venezuela on the west and Brazil on the south and west. Area, 214,999 sq. km (83,013 sq. miles). In 2012 the census population was 746,955; density 3·5 per sq. km.

The UN gives a projected population for 2020 of 791,000.

Guyana has the highest proportion of rural population in South America, with only 28·7% living in urban areas in 2011. Ethnic groups by origin: 40% Indian, 29% African, 20% mixed race and 11% Amerindian. The capital is Georgetown (2012 provisional census population, 24,849; urban agglomeration, 118,363); other towns are Linden, New Amsterdam, Anna Regina and Corriverton.

Venezuela demanded the return of the Essequibo region in 1963 (nearly 75% of the area of Guyana). It was finally agreed in March 1983 that the UN Secretary-General should mediate, but the dispute is ongoing. There is also an ongoing unresolved claim by Suriname for the return of a triangle of uninhabited rainforest between the New River and the Courantyne River, near the Brazilian border. In Sept. 2007 the UN settled a long-standing maritime boundary dispute between Guyana and Suriname. The coastal area off both countries is believed to hold significant oil and gas deposits.

The official language is English.

Social Statistics

2009 estimates: births, 14,000; deaths, 5,000. Rates, 2009 estimates (per 1,000 population): birth, 18; death, 6. Life expectancy at birth in 2013: male 63·6 years and female 68·9 years. Annual population growth rate, 2005–10, 0·7%. Infant mortality, 2010, 25 per 1,000 live births; fertility rate, 2013, 2·5 births per woman. Guyana has among the highest suicide rates of any country, at 34·8 per 100,000 inhabitants in 2012 (a rate of 50·8 among males although only 18·3 among females).

Climate

A tropical climate, with rainy seasons from April to July and Nov. to Jan. Humidity is high all the year but temperatures are moderated by sea-breezes. Rainfall increases from 90" (2,280 mm) on the coast to 140" (3,560 mm) in the forest zone. Georgetown, Jan. 79°F (26·1°C), July 81°F (27·2°C). Annual rainfall 87" (2,175 mm).

Constitution and Government

A new constitution was promulgated in Oct. 1980. There is an *Executive Presidency* and a *National Assembly.* The president is elected by simple majority vote as the designated candidate of a party list in parliamentary elections; there are no term limits. The National Assembly has 69 members who serve five-year terms (65 directly elected, plus three non-elected ministers and the Speaker).

National Anthem

'Dear land of Guyana'; words by A. L. Luker, tune by R. Potter.

Recent Elections

David Granger and the coalition of A Partnership for National Unity and Alliance for Change (APNU+AFC) won the presidential and parliamentary elections of 11 May 2015. In the presidential election David Granger received 207,200 votes (50·3% of the vote) and incumbent president Donald Ramotar of the People's Progressive Party/Civic (PPP/C) received 202,694 (49·2%). The APNU+AFC won 33 seats in the parliamentary election,

© Springer Nature Limited 2020
Palgrave Macmillan (ed.), *The Statesman's Yearbook 2020*,
https://doi.org/10.1057/978-1-349-95940-2_86

followed by the PPC/C with 32. Four other parties contested the poll but did not win any seats.

Current Government

President: David Granger; b. 1945 (APNU+AFC; sworn in 16 May 2015).
In Feb. 2019 the government comprised:

Prime Minister and First Vice President, and Minister of Governance: Moses Nagamootoo; b. 1947 (APNU+AFC; sworn in 20 May 2015).

Second Vice President and Minister of Foreign Affairs: Carl Barrington Greenidge. *Third Vice President and Minister of Public Security:* Khemraj Ramjattan. *Fourth Vice President and Minister of Indigenous People's Affairs:* Sydney Allicock. *Attorney General and Minister of Legal Affairs:* Basil Williams. *Agriculture:* Noel Holder. *Business and Tourism:* Dominic Gaskin. *Citizenship:* Winston Felix. *Communities:* Ronald Bulkan. *Education:* Nicolette Henry. *Finance:* Winston Jordan. *Natural Resources:* Raphael Trotman. *Public Health:* Volda Lawrence. *Public Infrastructure:* David Patterson. *Public Telecommunications:* Catherine Hughes. *Social Cohesion:* George Norton. *Social Protection:* Amna Ally. *Minister of State:* Joseph Harmon. *Minister of the Presidency Responsible for the Public Service:* Rupert Roopnarine.

Guyanese Parliament: http://parliament.gov.gy

Current Leaders

David Granger

Position

President

Introduction

David Granger was sworn in as president on 16 May 2015 after his A Partnership for National Unity (APNU)–Alliance for Change (AFC) coalition won a one-seat majority at the general election.

Early Life

Granger was born on 15 July 1945 in Georgetown and was educated at Queen's College, where he was a member of the Cadet Corps. In 1965 he joined the Guyana Defence Force (GDF) as an officer cadet. A year later he was commissioned as a second lieutenant. Rising through the ranks, he held a number of positions including planning officer for the establishment of the Guyana National Service (1973–75) and the Guyana People's Militia (1976–77). He also headed various military delegations to Brazil, Cuba, Germany, Guinea, South Korea and Yugoslavia. In 1979 he was appointed commander of the GDF and was later promoted to the rank of brigadier. In 1990 he became national security adviser to the president, serving in that role until his retirement from the military in 1994.

In 2011 Granger stood as the People's National Congress–Reform candidate at the Nov. presidential polls, but was defeated by Donald Ramotar of the People's Progressive Party/Civic (PPP/C). On 16 Jan. 2012 he was elected leader of the opposition in the National Assembly. At early elections called by Ramotar on 11 May 2015, the APNU and AFC won 33 of 65 National Assembly seats. Despite allegations by the PPP/C that the elections were rigged, Granger took office five days later and ended the PPP/C's 23-year domination of the executive.

Career in Office

Granger's administration pledged to introduce anti-money laundering legislation, to set up a constitutional reform committee and to tackle the high levels of crime. His other challenges included countering the country's racially divisive politics, cracking down on corruption, and fighting drug and human trafficking. More positively, his government foresees an economic windfall from the recent discovery and planned exploitation of substantial oil reserves in Guyanese waters, which has prompted ambitious infrastructure planning.

Defence

In 2013 defence expenditure totalled US$35m. (US$48 per capita), representing 1·2% of GDP. The army, navy and air force are combined in a 1,100-strong Guyana Defence Force.

Army

The Guyana Army had (2011) a strength of 1,400 including 500 reserves. There is a paramilitary Guyana People's Militia approximately 1,500 strong.

Navy

The Coast Guard is an integral part of the Guyana Defence Force. In 2011 it had 100 personnel and five patrol and coastal combatants.

Air Force

The Air Command has no combat-capable aircraft. It was equipped in 2011 with two light aircraft and three helicopters. Personnel (2011) 100.

Economy

In 2013 agriculture, fishing and forestry accounted for 16·5% of GDP, followed by mining and quarrying 15·8%, trade and hotels 12·6%, and transport and communications 10·0%.

Overview

The economy grew by an annual average of 4% from 2008–15, compared to just over 2% between 2000 and 2007, and GDP per capita increased from US$1,710 in 1990 to US$4,127 in 2015 in real terms. Mining and agriculture have driven growth, supported by a more stable exchange rate, reduced inflation and closer co-operation with international organizations. Nonetheless, agriculture's relative importance is declining, its contribution to GDP having fallen from 30·8% in 2002 to 19·6% in 2015. The service sector meanwhile contributed 58·7% to GDP in 2015.

Expansion in the manufacturing and construction sectors, coupled with favourable external conditions and high foreign direct investment inflows, have further aided growth. Debt relief from the Inter-American Development Bank (which cancelled US$470m. of debt in 2007) and other international donors has resulted in a significant decline in the government's debt-to-GDP ratio, from 135·7% in 1998 to 48·6% in 2015.

Main exports include sugar, gold, diamonds, bauxite, shrimp, timber and rice. The unemployment rate remains high, particularly among the young, and a shortage of skilled labour persists. Guyana has been a member of CARICOM since 1973 and entered the CARICOM Single Market and Economy in 2006.

The country launched a Low Carbon Development Strategy in 2010 to protect its forests while promoting economic development and combating climate change. Protecting the environment, managing the effects of rising sea levels, improving governance, raising the economic prospects of the young and curbing crime are keys to future sustained growth.

Currency

The unit of currency is the *Guyana dollar* (GYD) of 100 *cents*. Inflation was 0·8% in 2016 and 2·0% in 2017. Foreign exchange reserves were US$223m. in July 2005 and total money supply was G$35·3bn.

Budget

Revenues in 2013 totalled G$174,695m. (current revenue, 94·8%) and expenditures G$195,825m. (current expenditure, 72·9%).

VAT of 16% was introduced in 2007. It was then lowered to 14% in Feb. 2017.

Performance

There was real GDP growth of 3·1% in 2015, 3·4% in 2016 and 2·1% in 2017. Total GDP was US$3·7bn. in 2017.

Banking and Finance

The bank of issue is the Bank of Guyana (*Governor*, Gobind Ganga), established 1965. There are five commercial banks and three foreign-owned. At Dec. 2009 the total assets of commercial banks were G$253,760m. Savings deposits were G$130,764m.

In 2010 external debt totalled US$1,354m., equivalent to 52·8% of GNI.

Energy and Natural Resources

Environment

Guyana's carbon dioxide emissions from the consumption of energy were the equivalent of 2·3 tonnes per capita in 2011.

Electricity

Capacity in 2011 was 0·3m. kW. In 2011 production was 910m. kWh and consumption per capita 1,151 kWh. Guyana is rich in hydro-electric potential. There are plans to build a hydro-electric power station at Amaila Falls in central Guyana.

Minerals

Placer gold mining commenced in 1884, and was followed by diamond mining in 1887. In 2012 output of bauxite was 2,210,000 tonnes and of gold 13,643 kg.

Agriculture

In 2007 Guyana had an estimated 420,000 ha. of arable land and 30,000 ha. of permanent crops. Agricultural production, 2007 unless otherwise indicated (in 1,000 tonnes): sugarcane, 3,099; rice (2009), 360; coconuts, 70; cassava, 20; maize (estimate), 8; pumpkins and squash (estimate), 7; oranges (estimate), 6; bananas, 6; green beans, 5; mangoes and guavas, 4.

Livestock (2008 estimate): sheep, 130,000; cattle, 110,000; goats, 79,000; pigs, 13,500; chickens, 20m. Livestock products, 2009: meat, 29,000 tonnes; milk, 33m. litres; eggs, 19m. units.

Forestry

In 2015 the area under forests totalled 16·53m. ha. (84% of the land area). Timber production in 2011 was 1·35m. cu. metres.

Fisheries

Fish landings in 2015 came to 36,558 tonnes, almost exclusively from sea fishing.

Oil and Gas

Since 2015 oil exploration has revealed reserves of around 2bn. bbls in the waters around the country. It is hoped that Guyana will be producing some 120,000 bbls per day by 2020, potentially rising to 750,000 bbls per day by 2025, potentially quadrupling the country's GDP.

Industry

The main industries are agro-processing (particularly sugar and rice) and mining (notably gold and bauxite). Production: sugar (2009), 233,736 tonnes; flour (2008), 29,425 tonnes; rum (2008), 14·2m. litres; beer (2008), 8·2m. litres; soft drinks (2006), 4,050,000 cases; clothes (2008), 1,256,000 items; footwear (2008), 25,901 pairs; margarine (2008), 1,528,121 kg; edible oil (2005), 928,500 litres; paint (2008), 2,488,667 litres; sawnwood (2007), 74,000 cu. metres.

Labour

In 2010 the estimated economically active population was 342,000 (66% males).

International Trade

Imports and Exports

Merchandise imports in 2014 totalled US$1,744·9m. (US$1,866·3m. in 2013) and merchandise exports US$1,147·5m. (US$1,375·9m. in 2013).

Principal imports in 2014 were mineral fuels and lubricants (30·8%), machinery and transport equipment, and food, animals and beverages; main exports in 2014 were food, animals and beverages (49·3%), gold, and crude materials and animal and vegetable oils.

The leading import supplier in 2010 was the USA (28·1%), followed by Trinidad and Tobago; the leading export destination in 2010 was the USA (21·8%), followed by Canada.

Communications

Roads

There are approximately 4,000 km of roads. In 2008 there were 44,700 passenger cars in use, plus 28,100 lorries and vans, and 37,100 motorcycles and mopeds.

Rail

There is a government-owned railway in the North West District, while the Guyana Mining Enterprise operates a standard gauge railway of 133 km from Linden on the Demerara River to Ituni and Coomacka.

Civil Aviation

There is an international airport at Georgetown (Cheddi Jagan International Airport), which handled 438,532 passengers in 2009. In 2010 there were direct flights to Antigua, Barbados, Miami, New York, Port of Spain, St Kitts and the British Virgin Islands.

Shipping

The major port is Georgetown; there are two other ports. In Jan. 2014 there were 18 ships of 300 GT or over registered, totalling 25,000 GT. There are ferry services across the mouths of the Demerara, Berbice and Essequibo rivers.

Telecommunications

In 2011 there were 152,600 landline telephone subscriptions (equivalent to 201·8 per 1,000 inhabitants) and 518,800 mobile phone subscriptions (or 686·2 per 1,000 inhabitants). In 2013 there were 36,900 fixed internet subscriptions (46·1 per 1,000 inhabitants). In March 2012 there were 124,000 Facebook users.

Social Institutions

Out of 178 countries analysed in the 2017 *Fragile States Index*—a list published jointly by the Fund for Peace and *Foreign Policy* magazine—Guyana was ranked the 79th least vulnerable to conflict or collapse. The index is based on 12 indicators of state vulnerability across social, political and economic categories.

Justice

The law, both civil and criminal, is based on the common and statute law of England, save that the principles of the Roman–Dutch law have been retained for the registration, conveyance and mortgaging of land.

The Supreme Court of Judicature consists of a Court of Appeal, a High Court and a number of courts of summary jurisdiction. Guyana was one of ten countries to sign an agreement in Feb. 2001 establishing a Caribbean Court of Justice to replace the British Privy Council as the highest civil and criminal court having ended appeals to the Privy Council when it gained independence in 1970. In the meantime the number of signatories has risen to 12. The court was inaugurated at Port of Spain, Trinidad on 16 April 2005 at which point it replaced the Guyana Court of Appeal as the country's final court of appeal.

The population in penal institutions in Oct. 2011 was 1,962 (260 per 100,000 of national population).

Education

In 2011–12 there were 442 pre-primary schools with 1,601 teachers for 25,543 pupils; 436 primary schools with 3,635 teachers for 88,106 pupils; and 276 general secondary schools and secondary departments of primary schools with 3,535 teachers for 75,399 pupils. In 2012 there were 8,857 students at university level.

Adult literacy in 2015 was estimated to be 87·5% (female, 89·2%; male, 85·8%). An OECD report published in 2005 showed that Guyana loses a greater proportion of its graduates (83%) to OECD member countries than any other non-OECD member.

In 2012 total expenditure on education came to 3·2% of GDP and 10·3% of total government spending.

Health

In 2006–07 there were 35 hospitals (seven private), 135 health centres and 207 health posts. There were 1,836 hospital beds in 2006–07. There were 5·1 physicians per 10,000 inhabitants in 2007 and 9·9 nurses per 10,000 inhabitants.

Religion

In 2010 the population was an estimated 66·0% Christian according to the Pew Research Center's Forum on Religion & Public Life, with Hindus constituting 24·9% and Muslims 6·4%.

Culture

Press

In 2008 there were three daily newspapers (the state-owned *Guyana Chronicle* and the privately-owned *Kaieteur News* and *Stabroek News*) with a combined average daily circulation of 32,000.

Tourism

177,000 non-resident overnight tourists arrived at Timehri airport in 2012 (157,000 in 2011).

Festivals

There are a number of Christian, Hindu and Muslim festivals throughout the year.

Diplomatic Representatives

Of Guyana in the United Kingdom (3 Palace Court, Bayswater Rd, London, W2 4LP)
High Commissioner: Frederick Hamley Case.

Of the United Kingdom in Guyana (44 Main St., Georgetown)
High Commissioner: Greg Quinn.

Of Guyana in the USA (2490 Tracy Pl., NW, Washington, D.C., 20008)
Ambassador: Sheikh Riyad David Insanally.

Of the USA in Guyana (100 Young and Duke Streets, Kingston, Georgetown)
Ambassador: Vacant.
Chargé d'Affaires a.i.: Terry Steers-Gonzalez.

Of Guyana to the United Nations
Ambassador: Rudolph Michael Ten-Pow.

Of Guyana to the European Union
Ambassador: David Hales.

Further Reading

Braveboy-Wagner, J. A., *The Venezuela-Guyana Border Dispute: Britain's Colonial Legacy in Latin America.* 1984

Daly, V. T., *A Short History of the Guyanese People.* 3rd. ed. 1992

Gafar, John, *Guyana: From State Control to Free Markets.* 2003

Seecoomar, Judaman, *Democratic Advance and Conflict Resolution in Post-Colonial Guyana.* 2006

National Statistical Office: Bureau of Statistics, 57 High Street, Kingston, P. O. Box 1070, Georgetown.

Website: http://www.statisticsguyana.gov.gy

Haiti

République d'Haïti (Republic of Haiti)

Capital: Port-au-Prince
Population projection, 2020: 11·37m.
GNI per capita, 2017: (PPP$) 1,665
HDI/world rank, 2017: 0·498/168=
Internet domain extension: .ht

Key Historical Events

In the 16th century, Spain imported large numbers of African slaves whose descendants now populate the country. The colony subsequently fell under French rule. In 1791 a slave uprising led to the 13-year-long Haitian Revolution. In 1801 Toussaint Louverture, one of the leaders of the revolution, succeeded in eradicating slavery. He proclaimed himself governor-general for life over the whole island. He was captured and sent to France, but Jean-Jacques Dessalines, one of his generals, led the final battle that defeated Napoleon's forces. The newly named Haiti declared its independence on 1 Jan. 1804, becoming the first independent black republic in the world. Ruled by a succession of self-appointed monarchs, Haiti became a republic in the mid-19th century. From 1915 to 1934 Haiti was under United States occupation.

A corrupt regime was dominated by François Duvalier (widely known as Papa Doc) from 1957 to 1964 when he was succeeded by his son, Jean-Claude Duvalier (Baby Doc). He fled the country on 7 Feb. 1986. After a period of military rule, Father Jean-Bertrand Aristide was elected president in Dec. 1990.

On 30 Sept. 1991 President Aristide was deposed by a military junta and went into exile. Under international pressure, parliament again recognized Aristide as president in June 1993. However, despite a UN led naval blockade, the junta showed no sign of stepping down. 20,000 US troops moved into Haiti on 19 Sept. in an uncontested occupation. President Aristide returned to office on 15 Oct. 1994 and on 1 April 1995 a UN peacekeeping force (MANUH) took over from the US military mission. Aristide was succeeded by René Préval who was generally assumed to be a stand-in for his predecessor. Jean-Bertrand Aristide subsequently won the presidential elections held in Nov. 2000. In Dec. 2001 there was an unsuccessful coup led by former police and army officers. After armed rebels took control of the north of the country President Aristide stood down in Feb. 2004 and fled into exile.

After a period of interim government, René Préval was elected president for a second time in 2006. In July 2009 the World Bank and IMF cancelled US$1·2bn. (80%) of the national debt. In Jan. 2010 an earthquake of magnitude 7·0 hit the capital, Port-au-Prince, and its surrounding region, killing at least 217,000 people, displacing over 1m. and seriously undermining Haiti's economic prospects.

Territory and Population

Haiti is bounded in the east by the Dominican Republic, to the north by the Atlantic and elsewhere by the Caribbean Sea. The area is 27,065 sq. km (10,450 sq. miles). The Île de la Gonâve, some 64 km long, lies in the gulf of the same name. Among other islands is La Tortue, off the north peninsula. At the last census, in 2003, the population was 8,373,750. The United Nations population estimate for 2003 was 8,977,000. On 1 July 2009 the official population estimate was 9,923,243, giving a density of 341 per sq. km. In 2011, 53·6% of the population were urban.

The UN gives a projected population for 2020 of 11·37m.

Areas, populations and chief towns of the ten departments:

Department	Area (in sq. km)	2009 estimated population	Chief town
Artibonite	4,887	15,71,020	Gonaïves
Centre	3,487	6,78,626	Hinche
Grande Anse	1,912	4,25,878	Jérémie
Nippes	1,268	3,11,497	Miragoâne
Nord	2,115	9,70,495	Cap Haïtien
Nord-Est	1,623	3,58,277	Fort-Liberté
Nord-Ouest	2,103	6,62,777	Port-de-Paix
Ouest	4,983	36,64,620	Port-au-Prince
Sud	2,654	7,04,760	Les Cayes
Sud-Est	2,034	5,75,293	Jacmel

The capital is Port-au-Prince (2009 estimated population, 875,978; urban agglomeration, 2,296,386); the other main cities are Gonaïves (228,725 in 2009) and Cap Haïtien (155,505). Most of the population is of African or mixed origin.

The official languages are French and Créole. Créole is spoken by all Haitians; French by only a small minority.

Social Statistics

2009 estimates: births, 266,000; deaths, 89,000. Rates, 2009 estimates (per 1,000 population): birth, 27; death, 9. Annual population growth rate, 2005–10, 1·5%. Expectation of life at birth, 2013, 61·2 years for males and 65·0 years for females. Infant mortality, 2010, 70 per 1,000 live births; fertility rate, 2013, 3·1 births per woman.

Climate

A tropical climate, but the central mountains can cause semi-arid conditions in their lee. There are rainy seasons from April to June and Aug. to Nov. Hurricanes and severe thunderstorms can occur. The annual temperature range is small. Port-au-Prince, Jan. 77°F (25°C), July 84°F (28·9°C). Annual rainfall 53" (1,321 mm).

Constitution and Government

A new constitution was signed off by then President Martelly in June 2012, replacing one promulgated in 1987. The 2012 constitution had received parliamentary backing in May 2011 but was not written into law until after a year of legal wrangling. Among its provisions is the relegalization of dual citizenship, which had been criminalized under the 1987 constitution. Haitians living abroad, who are responsible for remittances equivalent to 20% of GDP, have the right to own land in Haiti and to stand for political office (with the exceptions of the presidency, premiership, as a senator or a member of the Chamber of Deputies).

The constitution also established a permanent constitutional court to mediate in disputes between parliament and the executive, as well as an electoral council to oversee free and fair elections. Women are required to hold at least 30% of government posts.

There is a bicameral legislature (a 119-member *Chamber of Deputies* with direct elections for four-year terms and a 30-member *Senate* with direct

© Springer Nature Limited 2020
Palgrave Macmillan (ed.), *The Statesman's Yearbook 2020*,
https://doi.org/10.1057/978-1-349-95940-2_87

elections for six-year terms and a third of the membership renewed every two years) and an executive *President*, directly elected for a five-year term.

National Anthem

'La Dessalinienne' ('The Dessalines Song'); words by J. Lhérisson, tune by N. Geffrard.

Recent Elections

Presidential elections were held on 20 Nov. 2016. Jovenel Moïse was elected with 55·6% of the vote, against Jude Célestin with 19·6%, Jean-Charles Moïse 11·0% and Maryse Narcisse 9·0%. There were 23 other candidates. Turnout was 18·1%.

Elections for the Chamber of Deputies were held on 9 Aug. 2015 and 25 Oct. 2015 with a further round also scheduled to take place on 27 Dec. 2015 but this was similarly postponed. Partial results following the second round gave the Haitian Tèt Kale Party 26 seats, Truth 13, Convention for Democratic Unity/Konvansyon Inite Demokratik 7, Struggling People's Organization 7, Fanmi Lavalas 6, Haiti in Action 6 and Patriotic Unity 4. A further 14 parties took 23 seats in total.

Elections for a third of the seats in the Senate were held on 20 Nov. 2016 and 29 Jan. 2017. The Haitian Tèt Kale Party won six seats, and Haiti in Action, Bouclier, National Consortium of Haitian Political Parties and Union of Haitian Patriots one seat each.

Current Government

President: Jovenel Moïse; b. 1968 (Haitian Tèt Kale Party; sworn in 7 Feb. 2017).

In Feb. 2019 the government comprised:

Prime Minister: Jean-Henry Céant; b. 1956 (Renmen Ayiti; sworn in 16 Sept. 2018).

Minister of Agriculture, Natural Resources and Rural Development: Jobert C. Angrand. *Commerce and Industry:* Ronell Gilles. *Culture and Communication:* Jean-Michel Lapin. *Defence:* Enol Joseph. *Economy and Finance:* Ronald Décembre. *Education and Vocational Training:* Pierre Josué Agénor Cadet. *Environment:* Jouthe Joseph. *Foreign Affairs and Worship:* Bocchit Edmond. *Haitians Living Abroad:* Mamatha Irène Ternier. *Interior and Territorial Communities:* Jean-Marie Reynaldo Brunet. *Justice and Public Security:* Jean Roudy Aly. *Planning and External Co-operation:* Jean Claudy Pierre. *Public Health and Population:* Dr Marie Gréta Roy Clément. *Public Works, Transport and Communications:* Fritz Caillot. *Social Affairs and Labour:* Elise Gelin. *Tourism:* Marie-Christine Stephenson. *Women's Affairs and Women's Rights:* Evelyne Sainvil. *Youth, Sport and Civic Action:* Edwing Charles.

Office of the Prime Minister (French only): http://primature.gouv.ht

Current Leaders

Jovenel Moïse

Position
President

Introduction
Jovenel Moïse, a businessman, became president in Feb. 2017 in succession to Michel Martelly.

Early Life
Jovenel Moïse was born on 26 June 1968 in Trou-du-Nord in the Nord-Est department. After studying political science at the Université Quisqeya, he moved to Port-de-Paix in 1996 to set up in business. His early commercial interests included an automotive parts company and a banana plantation.

A leading proponent of regional development, he joined the Chamber of Commerce and Industry of the Northwest, as well as the Chamber of Commerce and Industry of Haiti. In 2001 he was a leading figure in the establishment of a clean water distribution centre covering the Nord-Ouest and Nord-Est regions. In 2002 he established a banana exporting business and in 2008 he co-founded a company tasked with increasing regional electrification. He was also integral to the creation of the nation's first agricultural free trade zone, generating thousands of new jobs.

The incumbent president, Michel Martelly, chose Moïse as the Haitian Tèt Kale Party's candidate for the 2015 presidential race. Moïse ran on a platform of economic recovery driven by the agricultural sector. He won the first round election in Oct. that year but there followed an investigation into allegations of electoral fraud. Despite accusations of money laundering, he won a delayed rerun poll in Nov. 2016, claiming 55·7% of the vote against 26 opponents. However, voter turnout was low at 18·1%.

Career in Office
Sworn in on 7 Feb. 2017, Moïse was faced with the challenge of leading the recovery of a country still suffering the impact of a devastating earthquake in 2010 as well as the more recent effects of Hurricane Matthew in Oct. 2016. He pledged to retain many of the policies set out by Martelly, with a focus on health care access, energy reform and job creation, while also reforming the constitution and the civil service and improving the business and investment climate. Violent street protests broke out in Sept. 2017 after the Senate passed a finance bill containing controversial tax increases.

In Aug. 2018 Moïse nominated Jean-Henry Céant as the new prime minister, replacing Jack Guy Lafontant who resigned in July following further protests in Port-au-Prince in response to the government's attempt (subsequently reversed) to raise fuel prices by about 40%.

Defence

After the restoration of civilian rule in 1994 the armed forces and police were disbanded and an Interim Public Security Force formed, although this was later also dissolved. In 1995 a new police force—Police Nationale d'Haiti (PNH)—was recruited from former military personnel and others not implicated in human rights violations. The PNH currently has about 2,000 members.

In the period 2002–12 annual defence expenditure is estimated to have averaged US$8m.

Army

The Army was disbanded in 1995 but plans were announced in 2011 to revive it. In 2013 a first batch of recruits returned from training in Ecuador. However, despite reporting to the ministry of defence they do not carry weapons.

Navy

There is a small Coast Guard, which was created in 1996 and is a specialized unit of the PNH.

Air Force

The Air Force was disbanded in 1995.

Economy

Trade and restaurants contributed 26·9% to GDP in 2010–11; followed by agriculture and forestry, 23·8%; finance and real estate, 11·3%; and services, public administration and defence, 11·3%.

Overview

Haiti is the poorest country in the western hemisphere, reflecting decades of mismanagement and corruption. The economy has been characterized by macroeconomic instability, rampant inflation and susceptibility to external shocks such as natural disasters. It is also highly dependent on international aid and remittances from the diaspora. Social and environmental indicators are poor. Real per capita GDP declined on average by 0·7% between 1970 and 2010 and stood at only US$846 in 2014.

Economic performance in the opening decade of the 21st century had suggested some progress, with inflation falling and GDP recording modest growth. However, grounds for optimism were then undermined, firstly by a devastating earthquake in 2010 and then by Hurricane Matthew in 2016. Boosted by post-earthquake reconstruction, GDP had grown by 5·6% in 2010–11 after a 5·4% contraction in 2009–10. Inflation receded to single-digit levels and the external economic position strengthened. However, Haiti's subsequent annual growth had slowed to 1·5% in 2016 and—in large measure the result of a poorly performing agricultural sector and increased public expenditure to meet post-Hurricane Matthew reconstruction needs—to 1·2% in 2017, while internal revenues reached only 12·9% of GDP.

Haiti faces significant challenges to foster long-term growth and fight poverty. 70% of Haitians live on less than US$2 per day, and 50% on less than US$1. Joblessness and underemployment affect 60% of the population, while the informal sector sustains 80% of those employed.

Currency

The unit of currency is the *gourde* (HTG) of 100 *centimes*. Inflation was 13·4% in 2016 and 14·7% 2017. In July 2005 foreign exchange reserves were US$74m. and total money supply was 19,263m. gourdes.

Budget

The fiscal year begins on 1 Oct. In 2012–13 revenues were 75,855m. gourdes and expenditures 100,208m. gourdes.

Performance

Although the earthquake of Jan. 2010 and the fragile global economic situation led to the economy contracting by 5·5% in 2010, it has since recovered and there were growth rates of 1·2% in 2015, 1·5% in 2016 and 1·2% in 2017. Total GDP in 2017 was US$8·4bn. Haiti is the country fourth most reliant on remittances from abroad, accounting for 29·2% of total GDP in 2017.

Banking and Finance

The Banque Nationale de la République d'Haïti is the central bank and bank of issue (*Governor*, Jean Baden Dubois). In 2010 there were nine commercial banks. The largest banks are Société Générale Haitienne de Banque SA (Sogebank) and Unibank.

In 2010 foreign debt totalled US$492m., equivalent to 7·3% of GNI.

Energy and Natural Resources

Environment

Carbon dioxide emissions from the consumption of energy in 2011 were the equivalent of 0·2 tonnes per capita.

The *Climate Change and Environmental Risk Atlas 2014* produced by Maplecroft, a risk analytics company, ranked Haiti as the country facing the fourth highest economic and social risk from climate change by 2025.

Electricity

Installed capacity was 0·3m. kW in 2011. Production in 2011 was 718m. kWh, with consumption per capita 72 kWh. Power cuts are common.

Minerals

Until the supply was exhausted in the 1970s, a small quantity of bauxite was mined.

Agriculture

There were an estimated 1·0m. ha. of arable land in 2012 and 280,000 ha. of permanent crops. Irrigation is used in some areas and in 2009 covered 97,000 ha. The main crops are (2012 production estimates, in 1,000 tonnes): sugarcane, 1,200; sweet potatoes, 543; yams, 298; cassava, 295; bananas, 270; plantains, 267. Livestock (2012 estimates): goats, 2·0m.; cattle, 1·5m.; pigs, 1·0m.; horses, 500,000; chickens, 5·7m.

Forestry

The area under forests in 2015 was 0·10m. ha., or 4% of the total land area. In 2011, 2·29m. cu. metres of roundwood were cut.

Fisheries

The total catch in 2011 was 16,520 tonnes, of which 96% was from marine waters.

Industry

Manufacturing is largely based on the assembly of imported components: toys, sports equipment, clothing, electronic and electrical equipment. Textiles, steel, soap, chemicals, paint and shoes are also produced. Many jobs were lost to other Central American and Caribbean countries during the 1991–94 trade embargo, after President Aristide was deposed.

Labour

In 2010 the labour force was 4,161,000 (53·0% males). The unemployment rate in 2009 was around 70%.

Haiti had 0·21m. people living in slavery according to the Walk Free Foundation's 2013 *Global Slavery Index*.

International Trade

Imports and Exports

In 2012 imports totalled US$2,679·4m. (provisional); exports, US$785·0m. (provisional). The leading imports are manufactured goods, food, machinery and transport equipment, fuel and raw materials. The main exports are wearing apparel, essential oils, mangoes, cocoa and coffee. The USA is by far the leading trading partner. The Dominican Republic provided 37% of imports in 2012 and the USA 25%. The USA accounted for 84% of exports in 2012 and Canada 4%.

Communications

Roads

Total length of roads was estimated at 3,500 km in 2013, although most of the network was in a poor state of repair.

Civil Aviation

There is an international airport at Port-au-Prince. There are also scheduled flights from Cap Haïtien to the Turks and Caicos Islands. Tortug'Air, Haiti's former flag carrier, ceased operations in 2015. In 2010 there were international flights to Cayenne, Curaçao, Fort de France, Fort Lauderdale, Higuero (Dominican Republic), Miami, Montreal, New York, Orlando, Panama City, Paris, Pointe-à-Pitre, Providenciales (Turks and Caicos Islands), Sint Maarten, San Juan (Puerto Rico), Santiago (Dominican Republic) and Santo Domingo. In 2012 Port-au-Prince handled 1,341,833 passengers (1,225,474 on international flights).

Shipping

Port-au-Prince and Cap Haïtien are the principal ports, and there are nine minor ports.

Telecommunications

The state telecommunications agency is Teleco. There were 108,300 fixed telephone lines in 2009 (11 per 1,000 inhabitants). Mobile phone subscribers numbered 3·65m. in 2009. There were 83·7 internet users per 1,000 inhabitants in 2010. In Dec. 2011 there were 295,000 Facebook users.

Social Institutions

Out of 178 countries analysed in the 2017 *Fragile States Index*—a list published jointly by the Fund for Peace and *Foreign Policy* magazine—Haiti was ranked the 11th most vulnerable to conflict or collapse. The index is based on 12 indicators of state vulnerability across social, political and economic categories.

Justice

The Court of Cassation is the highest court in the judicial system. There are four Courts of Appeal and four Civil Courts. Judges are appointed by the President. The legal system is based on Napoleonic civil law.

The population in penal institutions in Aug. 2013 was 9,936 (96 per 100,000 of national population). The International Centre for Prison Studies estimated in 2014 that 72·8% of prisoners had yet to receive a trial.

Education

The adult literacy rate in 2006 was an estimated 48·7% (53·4% among males and 44·6% among females). Education is divided into nine years 'education fondamentale', followed by four years to 'Baccalaureate' and university/ higher education. The school system is based on the French system and instruction is in French and Créole. About 20% of education is provided by state schools; the remaining 80% by private schools, including Church and Mission schools. Approximately 15% of household spending per child goes on education.

In 2010–11 there were 13,599 primary schools with 2,210,221 pupils and 3,477 secondary schools with 624,095 pupils.

There are a state university, several private universities and an Institute of Administration and Management.

In 2010 total expenditure on education came to 2·7% of GDP.

Health

There were four physicians, nursing and midwifery personnel per 10,000 population in 2011. Much of the health care infrastructure was destroyed in the earthquake of Jan. 2010. There were 44 health institutions (government and mixed) operating in May 2010.

In *Water: At What Cost? The State of the World's Water 2016*, WaterAid reported that 42·3% of the population does not have access to safe water.

Religion

According to estimates by the Pew Research Center's Forum on Religion & Public Life, 86·9% of the population in 2010 was Christian and 10·6% had no religious affiliation; of the Christians, 65% were Catholics and 34% Protestants. The Roman Catholic Church comprises two ecclesiastical provinces, each headed by an archbishop. In Feb. 2019 there was one Roman Catholic cardinal. Voodoo was recognized as an official religion in 2003.

Culture

World Heritage Sites

Haiti has one site on the UNESCO World Heritage List: National History Park—Citadel, Sans-Souci, Ramiers (inscribed on the list in 1982), 19th century monuments to independence.

Press

There were two paid-for daily newspapers in 2008 with a combined circulation of 23,000.

Tourism

In 2014 there were 465,174 stopover tourists (419,736 in 2013); cruise passenger arrivals in 2014 numbered 662,403 (643,634 in 2013).

Diplomatic Representatives

Of Haiti in the United Kingdom (21 Bloomsbury Way, London, WC1A 2TH).
    Ambassador: Vacant.
    Chargé d'Affaires a.i.: Laurent Pierre Prosper.

Of the United Kingdom in Haiti (Entre 73 et 75 Delmas, Port-au-Prince)
    Ambassador: Sharon Campbell (resides in Santo Domingo, Dominican Republic).

Of Haiti in the USA (2311 Massachusetts Ave., NW, Washington, D.C., 20008)
    Ambassador: Paul Getty Altidor.

Of the USA in Haiti (Tabarre 41, Blvd du 15 Octobre, Port-au-Prince)
    Ambassador: Michele J. Sison.

Of Haiti to the United Nations
    Ambassador: Denis Regis.

Of Haiti to the European Union
    Ambassador: Antonio Rodrigue.

Further Reading

Girard, Philippe, *Haiti: The Tumultuous History—From Pearl of the Caribbean to Broken Nation.* 2010
Heinl, Robert & Nancy, revised by Michael Heinl, *Written in Blood.* 1996
Nicholls, D., *From Dessalines to Duvalier: Race, Colour and National Independence in Haiti.* 3rd ed. 1996
Pierre, Hyppolite, *Haiti, Rising Flames from Burning Ashes: Haiti the Phoenix.* 2006
Quinn, Kate and Sutton, Paul, (eds) *Politics and Power in Haiti.* 2013
Shamsie, Yasmine and Thompson, Andrew S. (eds) *Haiti: Hope for a Fragile State.* 2006
Thomson, I., *Bonjour Blanc: a Journey through Haiti.* 1992
Weinstein, B. and Segal, A., *Haiti: the Failure of Politics.* 1992
Wucker, Michele, *Why the Cocks Fight: Dominicans, Haitians, and the Struggle for Hispaniola.* 2000
National library: Bibliothèque Nationale, 193 Rue du Centre, Port-au-Prince.
National Statistical Office: Institut Haïtien de Statistique et d'Informatique (IHSI), 1 Angle rue Joseph Janvier et Blvd Harry Truman, HT6110 Port-au-Prince.
Website (French only): http://www.ihsi.ht

Honduras

República de Honduras (Republic of Honduras)

Capital: Tegucigalpa
Population projection, 2020: 9·72m.
GNI per capita, 2017: (PPP$) 4,215
HDI/world rank, 2017: 0·617/133
Internet domain extension: .hn

Key Historical Events

Discovered by Columbus in 1502, Honduras was ruled by Spain until independence in 1821. Political instability was endemic throughout the 19th and most of the 20th century. The end of military rule seemed to come in 1981 when a general election gave victory to the more liberal and non-military party, PLH (Partido Liberal de Honduras). However, power remained with the armed forces. Internal unrest continued into the 1990s with politicians and military leaders at loggerheads, particularly over attempts to investigate violations of human rights. In Oct. 1998 Honduras was devastated by Hurricane Mitch, the worst natural disaster to hit the area in modern times. In June 2009 President Manuel Zelaya was deposed in a military coup, leading to international condemnation and the suspension of aid. A presidential poll was held in Nov. 2009, with Porfirio Lobo Sosa of the National Party emerging victorious after Zelaya's refusal to recognize the election. The following month Congress rejected proposals to return Zelaya to power and in Jan. 2010 Porfirio Lobo was sworn in as Zelaya went into exile.

Territory and Population

Honduras is bounded in the north by the Caribbean, east and southeast by Nicaragua, west by Guatemala, southwest by El Salvador and south by the Pacific Ocean. The area is 112,492 sq. km (43,433 sq. miles). In 2013 the census population was 8,303,771 (4,251,456 females), giving a density of 73·8 per sq. km. In 2011, 52·2% of the population lived in urban areas.

The UN gives a projected population for 2020 of 9·72m.

The chief cities and towns are (2013 census populations): Tegucigalpa, the capital (996,658), San Pedro Sula (598,519), La Ceiba (176,212), Choloma (163,818), El Progreso (114,934), Comayagua (92,883), Choluteca (86,179), Danlí (64,976), La Lima (62,903), Villanueva (62,711).

Areas and 2013 populations of the 18 departments:

Department	Area (in sq. km)	Population
Atlántida	4,372	436,252
Choluteca	3,923	437,618
Colón	4,360	309,926
Comayagua	8,249	493,466
Copán	5,124	371,057
Cortés	3,242	1,562,394
El Paraíso	7,489	444,507
Francisco Morazán	8,619	1,508,906
Gracias a Dios	16,997	90,795
Intibucá	3,123	232,553
Islas de la Bahía	236	62,557
La Paz	2,525	198,926
Lempira	4,228	321,179
Ocotepeque	1,630	146,430
Olancho	23,905	520,761
Santa Bárbara	5,024	421,337
Valle	1,665	174,511
Yoro	7,781	570,595

The official language is Spanish. The Spanish-speaking population is of mixed Spanish and Amerindian descent (87%), with 6% Amerindians.

Social Statistics

2009 estimates: births, 201,000; deaths, 37,000. Rates, 2009 estimates (per 1,000 population): birth, 27; death, 5. 2013 life expectancy, 71·5 years for men and 76·2 for women. Annual population growth rate, 2005–10, 1·7%. Infant mortality, 2010, 20 per 1,000 live births; fertility rate, 2013, 3·0 births per woman. Abortion is illegal.

Climate

The climate is tropical, with a small annual range of temperature but with high rainfall. Upland areas have two wet seasons, from May to July and in Sept. and Oct. The Caribbean Coast has most rain in Dec. and Jan. and temperatures are generally higher than inland. Tegucigalpa, Jan. 66°F (19°C), July 74°F (23·3°C). Annual rainfall 64" (1,621 mm).

Constitution and Government

Under the Constitution which came into force in 1982 and was amended in 1995 the *President* was elected for a single four-year term, with members of the *National Congress* (total 128 seats) and municipal mayors elected simultaneously on a proportional basis, according to combined votes cast for the Presidential candidate of their party.

In March 2009 the then president, Manuel Zelaya, proposed a referendum to approve an assembly to revise the constitution. His opponents feared that he was seeking changes to allow him to stand for re-election and a constitutional crisis culminated in a military coup and Zelaya's exile to Costa Rica. However, in April 2015 the Supreme Court controversially invalidated the constitutional clauses restricting the President to a single four-year term.

National Anthem

'Tu bandera es un lampo de cielo' ('Your flag is a splendour of sky'); words by A. C. Coello, tune by C. Hartling.

Recent Elections

Presidential and parliamentary elections took place on 26 Nov. 2017. In the presidential elections incumbent Juan Orlando Hernández (National Party, PNH) won 43·0% of votes cast against 41·4% for Salvador Nasralla (Opposition Alliance against Dictatorship—an alliance of Liberty and Refoundation and the Innovation and Unity Party, Libre–PINU) and 14·7% for Luis Orlando Zelaya (Liberal Party, PLH). There were six other candidates. Although the constitution permits only one four-year term Juan Orlando Hernández's re-election was authorized by the Supreme Court, leading to widespread protests against alleged electoral fraud. Turnout was 57·5%. In National Congress elections held on the same day the National Party won 61 of 128 seats, Liberty and Refoundation 30, Liberal Party 26, Innovation and Unity Party 4 and Honduran Patriotic Alliance 4, with Democratic Unification Party, the Christian Democratic Party and the Anti-Corruption Party taking one seat each.

Current Government

In Feb. 2019 the government consisted of:

President: Juan Orlando Hernández; b. 1968 (PNH; sworn in 27 Jan. 2014 and re-elected in Nov. 2017).

Presidential Delegates: Rossana Guevara; Ricardo Antonio Álvarez Arias; Lorena Herrera.

Minister of Agriculture and Livestock: Mauricio Guevara. *Communications and Government Strategy:* Christa Castro. *Defence:* Fredy Díaz Zelaya. *Economic Development:* Arnaldo Castillo. *Education:* Marcial Solís. *Energy, Natural Resources, Environment and Mines:* José Antonio Galdámes.

Finance: Isabel Rocío Tábora. *Foreign Relations:* María Dolores Agüero. *Health:* Dr Octavio Sánchez. *Human Rights:* Karla Cueva. *Justice, Interior and Decentralization:* Rigoberto Chang Castillo. *Labour and Social Security:* Carlos Madero. *Security:* Julián Pacheco. *Social Inclusion and Development:* Miguel Zúñiga. *Co-ordinator in the Presidential Ministry:* Jorge Ramón Hernández Alcerro. *Minister of the Presidency:* Ricardo Cardona. *Office of the President:* http://www.presidencia.gob.hn

Current Leaders

Juan Orlando Hernández

Position
President

Introduction
Juan Orlando Hernández was sworn in as president on 27 Jan. 2014. Leader of the conservative National Party, he assumed power in a country racked by poverty and political instability. He was re-elected controversially at the end of 2017.

Early Life
Hernández, popularly known as JOH, was born in Gracias in the west of the country on 28 Oct. 1968. He studied law at the Universidad Nacional Autónoma de Honduras and holds a master's degree from the State University of New York, USA. Leader of the student body during his time at university in Honduras, he was first elected to the National Congress in 1997 representing the department of Lempira.

The National Party took 71 of 128 seats in the parliamentary elections of 29 Nov. 2009 and Hernández was appointed president of the Congress in Jan. 2010. In this role he enacted legislation creating a special military police force to patrol the most dangerous districts of the country's largest cities. He left the post in June 2013 to focus on his presidential campaign.

Hernández campaigned on a platform of law and order—Honduras has one of the world's highest murder rates. In the election held on 24 Nov. 2013 he won 36·9% of the vote against 28·8% for Xiomara Castro, the candidate of the leftist Libre party, which was formed in the wake of her husband Manuel Zelaya's removal from power in 2009. Castro refused to recognize the result, claiming electoral fraud.

Career in Office
Parliamentary elections held at the same time as the presidential vote saw Hernández inherit a Congress divided between the National Party, Liberal Party and the recently-founded Libre and Anti-Corruption parties. He stated that his priorities were to alleviate poverty, tackle corruption and reduce violent crime. In his inaugural speech, he urged the USA to continue to support Honduras's counter-narcotics operations and in June 2014 the US government announced extra aid for programmes to combat gang violence.

In April 2015 the Supreme Court annulled constitutional legislation in force since 1982 that had banned presidents from seeking re-election. Although changing the single-term limit attracted widespread criticism from the opposition, in Nov. 2016 Hernández announced his intention to run for office again. Following the elections in Nov. 2017 Hernández claimed a narrow victory, but the leftist opposition candidate, Salvador Nasralla, contested the vote count as fraudulent. The Supreme Electoral Tribunal nevertheless declared Hernández the winner in mid-Dec.

A new international mission charged with tackling endemic corruption in Honduras was launched in Feb. 2016.

In Nov. 2018 a US court charged Hernández's brother with smuggling cocaine in the USA.

Defence

Conscription was abolished in 1995. In 2013 defence expenditure totalled US$177m. (US$21 per capita), representing 0·9% of GDP.

Army

In 2011 the Army numbered 8,300. A new 2,000-strong Military Police for Public Order was established in 2013.

Navy

The Navy, numbering 1,400 in 2011 including 830 marines, operates 17 patrol and coastal combatants.

Air Force

There were 19 combat-capable aircraft in 2011 (A-37B Dragonfly and F-5E/ F Tiger II fighters). Total strength was (2011) 2,300 personnel.

Economy

Manufacturing accounted for 17·4% of GDP in 2012, followed by trade and hotels 16·5%, finance and real estate 16·0% and services 13·6%.

Overview

Honduras is a lower-middle income country with a diversified economy based on international trading of manufactured and agricultural goods. It is one of the poorest countries in Latin America with weak social indicators, and is highly susceptible to external shocks and natural disasters.

GDP fell by 0·5% annually for three years after Hurricane Mitch (1998) ruined many small-scale farmers with knock-on damage to banking. Debt relief from the Enhanced Heavily Indebted Poor Countries Initiative, Paris Club creditors, the Multilateral Debt Relief Initiative and Inter-American Development Bank saw external debt, which was measured at 80·8% in 1999, fall dramatically in the following decade and stood at 37·6% in 2017. In the ten years to 2017 annual average growth of 3·2% was above the Latin American average of 2·0%, although GDP per capita averaged only $2,138 against the Latin American average of $8,488. Inequality levels are among the highest in Latin America, with the wealthiest 10% of the population consuming about 45% of output while about 66% live below the poverty line (one in five in extreme poverty). With the highest homicide rate in the world in 2014, crime cost the country nearly 6·5% of GDP that year.

The US recession of 2008–09 resulted in a decline in remittances, foreign direct investment and *maquilas* (re-export business). As a result of domestic political instability following a military-backed coup, along with the global economic downturn, GDP growth fell by 2·1% in 2009. Growth then averaged 3·7% between 2010 and 2017, spurred by lower oil prices, the strengthening of the US economy and buoyant private investment, while a robust government fiscal programme in 2014 saw the public sector deficit fall from 7·6% in 2013 to 4·3% the following year. Credit rating agency Moody's revised Honduras's government bond rating in May 2015 from stable to positive, echoing the more positive economic outlook. Nonetheless, corruption, widespread poverty and lack of transparency in governmental operations remain impediments to long-term, inclusive growth.

Currency

The unit of currency is the *lempira* (HNL) of 100 *centavos*. In July 2005 foreign exchange reserves were US$2,164m., total money supply was 19,865m. lempiras and gold reserves were 21,000 troy oz. Inflation was 2·7% in 2016 and 3·9% in 2017.

Budget

In 2015 budgetary central government revenues were 88,226m. lempiras (including taxes, 79,855m. lempiras) and expenditures 93,238m. lempiras (including compensation of employees, 38,187m. lempiras).

There is a sales tax of 15%.

Performance

The economy grew by 3·8% in both 2015 and 2016, and 4·8% in 2017. Total GDP in 2017 was US$23·0bn.

Banking and Finance

The central bank of issue is the Banco Central de Honduras (*President*, Wilfredo Cerrato). It had total assets in Dec. 2013 of US$5·1bn. The Central American Bank for Economic Integration (CABEI) has its head office in Tegucigalpa. In 2014 there were 17 private and two state-owned banks. The largest banks are Banco Ficohsa and Banco Atlántida.

In 2010 external debt totalled US$4,168m., representing 28·2% of GNI. There are stock exchanges in Tegucigalpa and San Pedro Sula.

Energy and Natural Resources

Environment
Carbon dioxide emissions from the consumption of energy in 2011 were the equivalent of 1·0 tonnes per capita.

Electricity
Installed capacity was 1·7m. kW in 2011 (0·5m. kW hydro-electric). Production in 2011 was 7·13m. kWh (40% hydro-electric); consumption per capita (2011) was 892 kWh.

Minerals
Output in 2006: zinc, 37,646 tonnes; lead, 11,775 tonnes; silver, 55,036 kg. Small quantities of gold are mined, and there are also deposits of tin, iron, copper, coal, antimony and pitchblende.

Agriculture
There were around 1·02m. ha. of arable land in 2012 and 0·46m. ha. of permanent crops. Legislation of 1975 provided for the compulsory redistribution of land, but in 1992 the grounds for this were much reduced, and a 5-ha. minimum area for land titles was abolished. Members of the 2,800 co-operatives set up in 1975 received individual shareholdings which can be broken up into personal units. Since 1992 women may have tenure in their own right. The state monopoly of the foreign grain trade was abolished in 1992. In 1996 the Agricultural Incentive Program was created (Ley de Incentivo Agrícola, LIA) which involves the redistribution of land for agricultural development.

Estimated crop production in 2012 (in 1,000 tonnes): sugarcane, 5,861; bananas, 765; maize, 524; palm oil, 398; melons and watermelons, 396; coffee, 300; oranges, 285.

Livestock (2013 estimates): cattle, 2·77m.; pigs, 487,000; horses, 182,000; mules, 70,000; chickens, 44·5m.

Forestry
In 2015 forests covered 4·59m. ha., or 41% of the total land area. In 2011, 9·03m. cu. metres of roundwood were cut.

Fisheries
Shrimp and lobster are important catches. The total catch in 2015 was approximately 10,800 tonnes, almost entirely from sea fishing.

Industry

Agriculture, particularly coffee and bananas, dominates the economy. Industry is small-scale and local. Output (in 1,000 tonnes): cement (2012), 1,730; sugar (2010), 429; wheat flour (2013), 369; paper and paperboard (2013 estimate), 75; wood based panels (2013), 30,000 cu. metres; plywood (2013), 29,000 cu. metres.

Labour

The labour force in 2013 was 3,275,000 (2,413,000 in 2003). 64·5% of the population aged 15–64 was economically active in 2013. In the same year 3·9% of the population was unemployed.

International Trade

In 2004 Honduras signed the Central America-Dominican Republic-United States Free Trade Agreement (CAFTA-DR), along with Costa Rica, the Dominican Republic, El Salvador, Guatemala, Nicaragua and the USA. The agreement entered into force for Honduras on 1 April 2006.

Imports and Exports
Imports in 2009 were valued at US$5,954m. and exports at US$2,628m.

Main imports are machinery and transport equipment, mineral fuels and lubricants, and chemicals. Main exports are food and live animals (of which coffee accounts for some 46% by value), manufactured articles, and machinery and transport equipment. Principal import suppliers, 2009: USA, 36·0%; Guatemala, 10·6%; Mexico, 6·6%; El Salvador, 6·1%. Principal export markets, 2009: USA, 47·7%; El Salvador, 7·0%; Germany, 6·5%; Guatemala, 6·4%.

Communications

Roads
Honduras is connected with Guatemala, El Salvador and Nicaragua by the Pan-American Highway. There are some 14,000 km of roads, of which about 21% are paved. In 2007 there were 487,700 passenger cars in use, 31,500 buses and coaches, 165,200 lorries and vans, and 94,400 motorcycles and mopeds.

Rail
The small government-run railway was built to serve the banana industry and is confined to the northern coastal region and does not reach Tegucigalpa. Much of the network is now out of service and in 2012 only 62 km of 914 mm gauge railway were operational. In 2013 the government signed an agreement with China to conduct a feasibility study for the construction of an inter-oceanic railway, connecting the seaports of Amapala in the south and Puerto Castilla in the north. It is hoped that construction of the railway will boost trade considerably.

Civil Aviation
There are four international airports: San Pedro Sula (Ramón Villeda) and Tegucigalpa (Toncontín) are the main ones, plus Roatún and La Ceiba, with over 80 smaller airstrips in various parts of the country. In addition to domestic flights and services to other parts of Central America and the Caribbean, there were flights in 2010 to Atlanta, Fort Lauderdale, Houston, Miami, New Orleans, New York, Philadelphia and Toronto. In 2012 San Pedro Sula handled 769,516 passengers (700,892 on international flights) and 15,775 tonnes of freight, and Tegucigalpa handled 581,740 passengers (466,956 on international flights) and 3,674 tonnes of freight.

Shipping
The largest port is Puerto Cortés on the Atlantic coast. There are also ports at Henecán (on the Pacific) and Puerto Castilla and Tela (northern coast). In Jan. 2014 there were 281 ships of 300 GT or over registered, totalling 299,000 GT. Honduras is a 'flag of convenience' country.

Telecommunications
In 2011 there were 609,200 landline telephone subscriptions (equivalent to 78·6 per 1,000 inhabitants) and 8,062,200 mobile phone subscriptions (or 1,039·7 per 1,000 inhabitants). There were 110·9 internet users per 1,000 inhabitants in 2010. Fixed internet subscriptions totalled 72,400 in 2009 (9·7 per 1,000 inhabitants). In Dec. 2011 there were 1·1m. Facebook users.

Social Institutions

Out of 178 countries analysed in the 2017 *Fragile States Index*—a list published jointly by the Fund for Peace and *Foreign Policy* magazine—Honduras was ranked the 68th most vulnerable to conflict or collapse. The index is based on 12 indicators of state vulnerability across social, political and economic categories.

Justice
Judicial power is vested in the Supreme Court, with nine judges elected by the National Congress for four years; it appoints the judges of the courts of appeal, and justices of the peace.

There were 5,150 homicides in 2016, equivalent to 57 per 100,000 people—the third highest rate in the world. However, the rate did fall every year from 2011 to 2016.

The population in penal institutions in Jan. 2013 was 12,263 (153 per 100,000 of national population). The International Centre for Prison Studies estimated in 2014 that 54·0% of prisoners had yet to receive a trial. Honduras was ranked 101st of 102 countries for criminal justice and 80th for civil justice in the 2015 World Justice Project *Rule of Law Index*, which provides data on how the rule of law is experienced by the general public across eight categories.

Education

Adult literacy in 2007 was 83·6% (male, 83·7%; female, 83·5%). Education is free, compulsory (from 6 to 15 years) and secular. There is a high drop-out rate after the first years in primary education. In 2015 there were 229,396 children in pre-primary schools (11,077 teaching staff); 1,154,139 children in primary schools (39,599 teaching staff); 637,727 pupils in secondary schools (39,613 teaching staff). There were an estimated 148,000 students in tertiary education in 2007–08 and 5,000 academic staff. The leading institution of higher learning is the National Autonomous University of Honduras (Universidad Nacional Autónoma de Honduras), founded in 1847, in Tegucigalpa.

In 2013 government spending on education came to 5·9% of GDP.

Health

In 2013 there were 7,283 physicians. There were 28 public hospitals in 2010 and seven hospital beds per 10,000 inhabitants in 2012.

In *Water: At What Cost? The State of the World's Water 2016*, WaterAid reported that 8·8% of the population does not have access to safe water.

Religion

In 2010 there were an estimated 3·82m. Roman Catholics and 2·78m. Protestants according to the Pew Research Center's Forum on Religion & Public Life, with a further 790,000 people not having any religious affiliation. In Feb. 2019 there was one cardinal.

Culture

World Heritage Sites

Honduras has two sites on the UNESCO World Heritage List: Maya Site of Copán (inscribed on the list in 1980), a centre of the Mayan civilization abandoned in the early 10th century; and Río Plátano Biosphere Reserve (1982), one of the few remains of the Central American rain forest.

Press

Honduras had six national daily papers in 2008, with a combined circulation of 200,000.

Tourism

In 2012 a record 895,000 non-resident tourists arrived by air (excluding same-day visitors), up from 871,000 in 2011 and 863,000 in 2010.

Festivals

There are a number of festivals and religious celebrations held throughout the year in Honduras. The Fiesta de San Isidro is a week-long carnival held in May every year to honour the city's patron saint.

Diplomatic Representatives

Of Honduras in the United Kingdom (4th Floor, 136 Baker St., London, W1U 6UD)
Ambassador: Ivan Romero-Martínez.

Of the United Kingdom in Honduras (embassy in Tegucigalpa closed in Dec. 2003)
Ambassador: Thomas Carter (resides in Guatemala City).

Of Honduras in the USA (3007 Tilden St., NW, Suite 4M, Washington, D.C., 20008)
Ambassador: Marlon Ramsses Tábora Muñoz.

Of the USA in Honduras (Av. La Paz, Tegucigalpa)
Ambassador: Vacant.
Chargé d'Affaires a.i.: Heide B. Fulton.

Of Honduras to the United Nations
Ambassador: Mary Elizabeth Flores.

Of Honduras to the European Union
Ambassador: Roberto Ochoa Madrid.

Further Reading

Banco Central de Honduras. *Honduras en Cifras 2015–17.* Online only
Euraque, Darío A., *Reinterpreting the Banana Republic: Region and State in Honduras, 1870–1972.* 1997
Loker, William M., *Changing Places: Environment, Development and Social Change in Rural Honduras.* 2004
Meyer, H. K. and Meyer, J. H., *Historical Dictionary of Honduras.* 2nd ed. 1994
National Statistical Office: Instituto Nacional de Estadísticas, Lomas del Guijarro, Edificio Plaza Guijarro, 5to piso, Tegucigalpa, M.D.C.
Website (Spanish only): http://www.ine.gob.hn

Hungary

Magyarország

Capital: Budapest
Population projection, 2020: 9·62m.
GNI per capita, 2017: (PPP$) 25,393
HDI/world rank, 2017: 0·838/45
Internet domain extension: .hu

Key Historical Events

Records date back to 9 BC, when the Romans subdued the Celts to establish Pannonia. From the 5th century both Romans and Celts retreated before attacks from the Huns who were followed by the Avars in the 7th century and the Magyars in the 9th. It was then that the name *On ogur* ('ten arrows') was adopted for the country that was to become Hungary. The founding date of Hungary is put at 896 after which Árpád, leader of one of the Magyar tribes, forged a dynasty which ruled Hungary until 1301. Forays into Italy, Germany, the Balkans and Spain ended after the Magyars were defeated by Holy Roman Emperor Otto I at the battle of Lechfeld in 955, and the Ostmark (Austria) was returned to Germanic control.

In seeking a truce with Otto I, the Árpád leader Géza invited him to send Catholic missionaries into Hungary. He had his son István (Stephen) crowned as King of Hungary and replaced the tribal structure with a system of counties (*megye*), administered by royal officials. A disputed succession led to intervention by the Holy Roman Emperor who established temporary suzerainty over Hungary. By the end of the 11th century, Slovakia, Carpathian Ruthenia and Transylvania were all under the crown of St Stephen. In a struggle for control of the ports on the Adriatic, Venice and Hungary went to war on 21 occasions between 1115–1420.

Andrew III, the last Árpád monarch, could do little to hold the country together against the opposition of feuding nobles. His death in 1301 led to a seven-year interregnum, after which, with two exceptions, Hungary was ruled by foreign kings. Linked to the Árpáds through marriage, Charles Robert of Anjou was elected to the throne. His primary task was to restore royal authority over the nobles. An economic boom coincided with Hungary becoming the leading gold producer in Europe and trade links with European neighbours were fostered.

Ottoman Threat

His successors had to contend with the growing power of the Ottoman Empire. Assaults on Hungary increased after the fall of Constantinople in 1453, but in 1456 János Hunyadi, acting as military regent, broke the siege of Belgrade to keep the Turks at bay for another 70 years.

Rival magnates reacted to Hunyadi's death from the plague in 1456 by trying to wipe out the omnipotent Hunyadi clan, but in 1457 the Diet appointed his 15-year-old son Matthias Corvinus as king. Matthias was an enlightened despot. He built up one of Europe's finest libraries—destroyed a century later by the Ottomans—and encouraged writers and artists, many of whom were Italian, to come and work in Hungary. The heirless Matthias was succeeded in 1490 by Bohemia's ruler Vladislav, or King Ulászló II (1490–1516), known as 'Rex Bene', because 'dobre', or 'good' was his reply to almost everything. He managed to repel a Habsburg invasion of Hungary but indulged the nobles with disproportionate powers and relied heavily on foreign financing. Vladislav II was succeeded in 1516 by his son Louis II, who held both the Hungarian and Bohemian thrones. A ten-year-old, he could do little to discourage the onslaught of the Turks, to whom Belgrade was lost in 1521. The Hungarians were defeated by the Turks under Suleiman II at the battle of Mohács on 29 Aug. 1526. Louis was killed in battle and Hungary lost its independence, not to be regained until 1918.

Hungary was partitioned, the largest section going to the Turks, royal Hungary to the Habsburgs and Transylvania, though theoretically autonomous, becoming a vassal state of the Ottomans. The Transylvanians were at constant war with the Habsburgs, who in turn fought the Ottomans. The economy along with the Magyar language declined and much agricultural land, mainly the Hungarian Plain, went to waste.

The Treaty of Vienna of 1606 was meant to set peaceful boundaries, but was soon violated. A series of costly territorial struggles culminated in the Ottoman siege of Vienna in 1683. Repelled by the Habsburgs, it marked a turning point for the Turks who, by 1699, had ceded most of their Hungarian territory. The Habsburgs became hereditary rulers pursuing a policy of divide and rule which led to anti-Habsburg risings. The second, under Ferenc Rákóczi, the last independent prince of Transylvania, united both nobles and peasants, and lasted from 1703–11. It was concluded by the signing of the Peace of Szatmár, in which the Habsburgs guaranteed political freedom for the three 'nations'—the ethnic Magyar, Saxon and Székelys groups. State education, introduced by Maria Theresa and Joseph II, led to greater Germanization.

Challenge to Habsburg Rule

Power was concentrated on the Magyar nobility, descendants of the Árpád royal line, who owned vast estates and were exempt from land tax. In March 1848 the Hungarian Diet renounced Viennese rule and legislated for a sovereign Magyar state, which was approved by Emperor Ferdinand. However, what began peacefully soon deteriorated as national minorities such as the Croats, the Romanians, Serbs and Slovaks demanded the same rights. In the War of Independence, heavy fighting broke out between the Hungarians and the Austrians, the Hungarians being led by Lajos Kossuth (1802–94).

When Emperor Franz Joseph I took the throne in 1848, the Hungarians refused to recognize him. This provoked an Austrian invasion, which was repelled, and in Feb. 1849 the diet in Debrecen declared Hungary an independent republic under Kossuth's leadership. Franz Joseph reacted by accepting the assistance of Tsar Nicholas I of Russia in suppressing the revolution. The Magyars chose to surrender to the Russians rather than the Austrians but the aftermath of the war witnessed mass executions and imprisonment of rebel factions. Kossuth escaped into exile. Direct rule was imposed from Vienna.

Dual Monarchy

Having lost territory to Sardinia in 1859 and to Prussia in 1866, Austria recognized the need for a compromise with Hungary. What became known as the 'Ausgleich' created a dual monarchy to preside over the Austro-Hungarian Empire. Hungary gained internal autonomy but while the Ausgleich profited Magyars and Austro-Germans it did little to benefit national minorities.

Bosnia and Herzegovina were annexed in 1908, which outraged Serbia, but Austria tried a number of tricks to prevent retaliation including the Zagreb Treason Trial of 1909, when evidence was produced of a Serb-Croat conspiracy to bring down the Habsburgs. It was the Czech professor and future president Tomáš Masaryk who proved the evidence to be fake.

On 28 June 1914 the heir to the Habsburg throne, Archduke Franz Ferdinand, and his wife were shot in Sarajevo by a Bosnian Serb. Austria-Hungary declared war on Serbia a month later, precipitating the First World War. The Entente of France, Britain and Russia united against the Central Powers of Germany and Austria-Hungary, with other nations soon joining in one or other alliance. By the Treaty of Versailles, the territories of Hungary and Austria were reduced drastically. Hungary became a republic in Nov. 1918, with Mihály Károlyi as president. Transylvania was handed over to Romania. New countries including Czechoslovakia and Yugoslavia were created, all of which gained former Hungarian territory.

On 21 March 1919, Károlyi was replaced by the Bolshevik leader, Béla Kun, who was in power for 133 days. His downfall was brought about by a non-communist revolutionary movement fighting to regain Slovakia and Romania. The Allies persuaded Romania to retreat, and Hungary's borders were finalized by the Treaty of Trianon on 4 June 1920. Two-thirds of Hungary's territory and over half of the population were assigned to neighbouring countries.

In 1919 the Hungarian Kingdom was restored under Count Miklós Horthy, who ruled as regent and appointed a chiefly aristocratic government. Despite Horthy's efforts to amend the Trianon treaty, Hungary's boundaries remained unchanged until the Second World War. Germany and Italy backed

© Springer Nature Limited 2020
Palgrave Macmillan (ed.), *The Statesman's Yearbook 2020*,
https://doi.org/10.1057/978-1-349-95940-2_89

the 'Vienna awards' of Nov. 1938 which restored to Hungary southern Slovakia and southern Subcarparthian Ruth, and in Aug. 1940, Transylvanian and Romanian territory. Hitler's support, including favourable trading terms, drew Hungary into fighting with Germany against the Soviet army in 1941, a tactical error which led to enormous losses.

In March 1944 the Germans occupied Hungary. Horthy was forced to abdicate and Hitler appointed a government of Ferenc Szálasi and his fascist Arrow Cross movement. Large-scale deportation of Jews and political dissidents began. Around 400,000 Jews are estimated to have been murdered. With civilian and military losses, almost a million Hungarians died in the war.

Soviet Rule
With the Soviets as the occupying power, post-war Communist rule was established in 1948–49 after a three-year multi-party democracy which the Communists conspired to undermine. Mátyás Rákosi and his Hungarian Workers' Party headed a dictatorship which went unchallenged until 1953, the year of Stalin's death. In July of that year Rákosi was ousted by reformers led by Imre Nagy. Appointed prime minister, Nagy began what he called 'the new stage in building socialism', which entailed industrial and economic reforms and the restoration of human rights. But disagreements within the Soviet leadership gave an advantage to Rákosi who was still general secretary of the Workers' Party. Nagy was forced out of office in April 1955.

On 23 Oct. 1956 a student-led demonstration demanded democratic reforms and Nagy's reinstatement as prime minister. Soviet troops fired into crowds trying to occupy the radio station. The next day Imre Nagy was reappointed prime minister but was unable to quell the riots. Revolutionary committees were set up and there was a general strike to promote the three aims of the revolution: national independence, a democratic political structure and the protection of social benefits. All of this, along with armed rebels in the capital, put pressure on the hard-liners in the party to accept reform.

A ceasefire, called by Nagy on 28 Oct., was honoured and Soviet troops retreated from Budapest. A multi-party democracy was announced, and the State Security Authority abolished. Even so, there were continuing demands for a clean sweep of all Stalinist-Rákosist ministers and total Soviet withdrawal. Nagy believed that such a transition should occur gradually and peacefully, but when he voiced the nation's support for neutrality and a withdrawal from the Warsaw pact, it was a step too far for Moscow. János Kádár was encouraged to form a counter-government with Soviet military backing. The Soviet Army marched into Budapest on 4 Nov., crushing all resistance.

Soviet hopes that Nagy would resign after this resounding defeat and support Kádár were disappointed. Kádár returned from Moscow on 7 Nov. after the heaviest fighting was over, to be confronted by a less than compromising nation. The renamed Hungarian Socialist Workers' Party declared all Oct. events as a counter-revolution, and began a series of revenge attacks. Nagy was hanged on 16 June 1958 along with several of his reformist associates. Many opponents of the regime were deported to labour camps in the Soviet Union and over 200,000 people fled the country.

Gradual Reform
János Kádár was party leader from 1956–89, and prime minister in the years 1956–58 and 1961–65. In the early '60s Kádár made a gradual shift towards liberalization. After the wave of executions, a distinction was made between political crime and mere error, and people were no longer required to be active in the party in order to succeed professionally. Trade unions were allowed to play a more active role, as was the press, so long as the government was not openly criticized.

The now-recognized need to loosen state control of the economy gave rise to the New Economic Mechanism (NEM) in 1968, which relaxed price controls, acknowledged the profit motive, improved manufacturing quality and shifted the emphasis from heavy to light industry. Subsidies were reduced and enterprise encouraged. Growing demands for a more open market economy coincided with the first signs of a weakening of the Soviet system. A group of Hungarian dissidents were sufficiently encouraged by the liberal trend in Moscow to form the Hungarian Democratic Forum. Led by their secretary general, Imre Pozsgay, they produced a manifesto 'Turn and Reform' which argued for a total overhaul of the economy.

The subsequent debate reopened divisions between hard-liners and reformists, and throughout the country there were demonstrations and strikes. The conservative old school of the Hungarian Socialist Workers' Party was gradually phased out by the reformists. A committee was set up to investigate the events of 1956, which concluded that it had been a popular uprising and not a counter-revolution. This called for the ceremonial reburial of Imre Nagy's remains on 16 June 1989, an event attended by a quarter of a million people who gathered in Heroes' Square, Budapest.

Post Communism
When prime minister Miklós Németh opened the borders with Austria, the flood of refugees from East Germany precipitated the fall of the Berlin wall. Multi-party democracy was enshrined in law in Sept. 1989 and Hungary ceased to be a People's Republic on 23 Oct. A unicameral National Assembly was formed and the first free elections took place on 25 March 1990. Of the 386 members elected to the National Assembly, only 21 had ever served in parliament before, and of the six successful parties, three were entirely new. The Hungarian Democratic Forum (MDF) and Alliance of Free Democrats advocated democracy, political pluralism, a market economy and a 'return' to Europe. The MDF came out ahead but having failed to secure a majority, formed a coalition with the Independent Smallholders' Party and the Christian Democratic People's Party.

A largely inexperienced government set about economic reform while trying to contain trade and budget deficits and high inflation. Social unrest prompted the government to slow down its privatization programme which proved popular with the electorate until they realized that the economy was stalling. In 1993 Iván Szabó became finance minister and adopted much stricter policies, cutting social budgets and devaluing the forint. This again led to domestic hardship. Unemployment, a hitherto unknown phenomenon, grew to over 12%. A nostalgia for a Communist past where jobs, housing and benefits were secure was perceptible in voting patterns at the 1994 elections.

Although the MDF's 'shock tactic' policies were praised by the West, and attracted foreign investment, the electorate opted for an updated version of the Hungarian Socialist Party (MSzP). Former Communist and leader Gyula Horn touted the party as one free of ideological limitations, playing down the traditional left and promising a higher standard of living along with continued economic reform under the guidance of László Bekesy, finance minister of the former Communist government. Horn became prime minister of a coalition led by the Alliance of Free Democrats (SzDSz) and the MSzP. Economic reforms were put back on the agenda but the government moved cautiously in an effort to carry public opinion.

The 1998 elections produced another coalition led by Viktor Orbán of the Federation of Young Democrats (later called Fidesz). He was succeeded in May 2002 by Péter Medgyessy, the Socialists' candidate, who formed a coalition with the SzDSz. In June 2002 revelations that Medgyessy had worked as a counter-intelligence agent for the communist regime highlighted the transitional problems for former Eastern Bloc nations. Hungary became a member of NATO in 1999 and of the EU on 1 May 2004. The economy was hit by the global economic downturn in 2008 and by the overspill from the subsequent euro crisis. A series of austerity measures came into force from 2009 when Hungary accepted emergency funding from the IMF. János Áder became president in May 2012 after his predecessor, Pál Schmitt, resigned following allegations of plagiarism involving a doctoral dissertation he had written 20 years earlier. Viktor Orbán became prime minister for a second time following elections in 2010, and his ruling Fidesz party was returned to power in April 2014 and again in April 2018 in elections criticized on both occasions by international monitors.

Territory and Population
Hungary is bounded in the north by Slovakia, northeast by Ukraine, east by Romania, south by Croatia and Serbia, southwest by Slovenia and west by Austria. The area of Hungary is 93,030 sq. km (35,919 sq. miles), including 690 sq. km (266 sq. miles) of inland waters.

At the census of 1 Oct. 2011 the population was 9,937,628 (52·5% females). In Jan. 2018 the population was estimated at 9,778,371.

The UN gives a projected population for 2020 of 9·62m.

68·9% of the population was urban in 2010; population density, Oct. 2011, 107·6 per sq. km. Hungary's population has been falling at such a steady rate since 1980 that its 2017 population was the same as that in the mid-1950s.

Although the 2011 census suggested that 3·1% of the population were Roma (up from 1·9% in 2001), most estimates put the figure at between 5–10%. Other ethnic minorities, 2011: Germans, 1·3%; Romanians, 0·3%; Slovaks, 0·3%; Croatians, 0·2%. A law of 1993 permits ethnic minorities to set up self-governing councils. There is a worldwide Hungarian diaspora of about 4·7m. (including 1·5m. in the USA and Canada; 1·4m. in Romania;

0·5m. in Slovakia; 0·3m. in Serbia, mainly in Vojvodina; 0·2m. in Israel; 0·2m. in Ukraine; 0·1m. in Brazil; 0·1m. in Germany). In total, 2·5m. Hungarians live in neighbouring countries.

Hungary is divided into 19 counties (*megyék*) and the capital, Budapest, which has county status.

Area (in sq. km) and population (in 1,000) of counties and chief towns:

Counties	Area	2011 population	Chief town	2011 population
Bács-Kiskun	8,445	520	Kecskemét	111
Baranya	4,430	386	Pécs	156
Békés	5,631	360	Békéscsaba	62
Borsod-Abaúj-Zemplén	7,247	686	Miskolc	168
Csongrád	4,263	417	Szeged	168
Fejér	4,359	426	Székesfehérvár	101
Győr-Moson-Sopron	4,089	448	Győr	130
Hajdú-Bihar	6,211	547	Debrecen	211
Heves	3,637	309	Eger	57
Jász-Nagykún-Szolnok	5,582	387	Szolnok	73
Komárom-Esztergom	2,265	305	Tatabánya	68
Nógrád	2,544	202	Salgótarján	37
Pest	6,393[1]	1,217[2]	Budapest	1,729
Somogy	6,036	316	Kaposvár	66
Szabolcs-Szatmár-Bereg	5,937	559	Nyíregyháza	120
Tolna	3,703	230	Szekszárd	34
Vas	3,336	257	Szombathely	79
Veszprém	4,613	353	Veszprém	62
Zala	3,784	282	Zalaegerszeg	59
Budapest	525	1,729	(has county status)	—

[1]Excluding area of Budapest.
[2]Excluding population of Budapest.

The official language is Hungarian. 84·6% of the population have Hungarian as their mother tongue. Ethnic minorities have the right to education in their own language.

Social Statistics

2011: births, 88,049; deaths, 128,795; marriages, 35,812; divorces, 23,335. There were 2,422 suicides in 2011. Rates (per 1,000 population), 2011: birth, 8·8; death, 12·9; marriage, 3·6; divorce, 2·3. Population growth rate, 2009, –0·2%. The suicide rate, at 24·6 per 100,000 population in 2009, is one of the highest in the world (although it has fallen since the mid-1980s when it was over 44 per 100,000). Expectation of life at birth, 2011, 70·9 years for males and 78·2 years for females. Infant mortality, 2010, 5 per 1,000 live births. Fertility rate, 2011, 1·2 births per woman.

Climate

A humid continental climate, with warm summers and cold winters. Precipitation is generally greater in summer, with thunderstorms. Dry, clear weather is likely in autumn, but spring is damp and both seasons are of short duration. Budapest, Jan. 32°F (0°C), July 71°F (21·5°C). Annual rainfall 25" (625 mm). Pécs, Jan. 30°F (–0·7°C), July 71°F (21·5°C). Annual rainfall 26·4" (661 mm).

Constitution and Government

On 18 Oct. 1989 the National Assembly approved by an 88% majority a constitution which abolished the People's Republic, and established Hungary as an independent, democratic, law-based state.

In April 2011 parliament passed proposals for a new constitution, known as the 'Easter constitution', by a vote of 263 to 44 (with one abstention).

It came into force on 1 Jan. 2012. Two of the three main opposition parties refused to vote in protest at what critics claimed were attacks by the ruling Fidesz party on the rights of various minority groups, including those with mental illness, the gay and lesbian community, and pro-abortion bodies. The constitution's preamble emphasizes Hungary's Christian heritage while other clauses restrict the voting rights of those with 'limited mental ability'. It defines marriage as a union of a man and a woman, and stipulates that the life of a foetus should be protected from conception. The German government subsequently warned that such clauses strained compatibility with EU law. The constitution also states Hungary's 'responsibility for the destiny of Hungarians living outside her borders', limits the jurisdiction of the constitutional court, reduces the number of parliamentary ombudsmen and determines that the national debt should be no more than 50% of the previous year's GDP except in exceptional circumstances. In Jan. 2012 the EU Commission requested clarification from Hungary on several aspects of the constitution, including curbs on the independence of the central bank that could violate EU law. In a referendum held in Oct. 2016, 98% of votes cast were against EU plans to compel member states to accept quotas of migrants. However, turnout was beneath the legally required 50% threshold.

The head of state is the *President*, who is elected for five-year terms by the National Assembly.

The single-chamber *National Assembly* currently has 199 members (386 prior to the elections of April 2014). It is elected for four-year terms. A *Constitutional Court* was established in Jan. 1990 to review laws under consideration.

National Anthem

'Isten áldd meg a magyart' ('God bless the Hungarians'); words by Ferenc Kölcsey, tune by Ferenc Erkel.

Government Chronology

(Fidesz-MPP = Fidesz-Hungarian Civic Party; Fidesz-MPSz = Fidesz-Hungarian Civic Alliance; FKgP = Independent Party of Smallholders, Agrarian Workers and Citizens; MDF = Hungarian Democratic Forum; MDP = Hungarian Workers' Party; MKP = Hungarian Communist Party; MSzMP = Hungarian Socialist Workers' Party; MSzP = Hungarian Socialist Party; SzDSz = Alliance of Free Democrats; n/p = non-partisan)

Presidents since 1946.

1946–48	FKgP	Zoltán Tildy
1948–50	MDP	Árpád Szakasits
1950–52	MDP	Sándor Rónai
1952–67	MSzMP	István Dobi
1967–87	MSzMP	Pál Losonczi
1987–88	MSzMP	Károly Németh
1988–89	MSzMP	Bruno Ferenc Straub
1989–90	MSzP	Mátyás Szűrös
1990–2000	SzDSz	Árpád Göncz
2000–05	n/p	Ferenc Mádl
2005–10	n/p	László Sólyom
2010–12	Fidesz-MPSz	Pál Schmitt
2012	Fidesz-MPSz	László Kövér (acting)
2012–	Fidesz-MPSz	János Áder

Prime Ministers since 1946.

1946–47	FKgP	Ferenc Nagy
1947–48	FKgP	Lajos Dinnyés
1948–52	MDP	István Dobi
1952–53	MDP	Mátyás Rákosi
1953–55	MDP	Imre Nagy
1955–56	MDP	András Hegedüs
1956	MDP	Imre Nagy

(*continued*)

1956–58	MSzMP	János Kádár
1958–61	MSzMP	Ferenc Münnich
1961–65	MSzMP	János Kádár
1965–67	MSzMP	Gyula Kállai
1967–75	MSzMP	Jenő Fock
1975–87	MSzMP	György Lázár
1987–88	MSzMP	Károly Grósz
1988–90	MSzP	Miklós Németh
1990–93	MDF	József Antall
1993–94	MDF	Péter Boross
1994–98	MSzP	Gyula Horn
1998–2002	Fidesz-MPP	Viktor Orbán
2002–04	n/p (MSzP)	Péter Medgyessy
2004–09	MSzP	Ferenc Gyurcsány
2009–10	n/p	Gordon Bajnai
2010–	Fidesz-MPSz	Viktor Orbán

Leaders of the Communist Party, 1945–89.

General Secretary of MKP/MDP	
1945–53	Mátyás Rákosi
First Secretaries of MDP/MSzMP	
1953–56	Mátyás Rákosi
1956	Ernő Gerő
1956–88	János Kádár
1988–89	Károly Grósz
Collective Chairmanship of MSzMP	
1989	Rezső Nyers; Miklós Németh; Károly Grósz; Imre Pozsgay

Recent Elections

János Áder was re-elected president by the National Assembly on 13 March 2017. In the first round (in which a two-thirds majority was required) he received 131 votes against 44 for László Majtényi, with 24 abstentions. In the second round—in which only a simple majority was needed—he won with 131 against 39 for Majtényi.

In the Hungarian parliamentary elections on 8 April 2018 the alliance of Fidesz-Hungarian Civic Alliance and the Christian Democratic People's Party (Fidesz-MPSz and KDNP) won 133 of 199 seats; Movement for a Better Hungary (Jobbik) 26; the alliance of the Hungarian Socialist Party and Dialogue for Hungary (MSzP-Párbeszéd) 20; the Democratic Coalition (DK) 9; Politics Can Be Different (LMP) 8; Together 1; National Self-Government of Germans in Hungary 1; ind. 1. Turnout was 69·7%.

European Parliament

Hungary has 21 representatives. At the May 2014 elections turnout was 29·0% (36·3% in 2009). The alliance of Fidesz and the Christian Democratic People's Party (Fidesz and KDNP) won 12 seats with 51·5% of votes cast (political affiliation in European Parliament: European People's Party); Jobbik, 3 with 14·7% (non-attached); the MSzP, 2 with 10·9% (Progressive Alliance of Socialists and Democrats); Democratic Coalition, 2 with 9·7% (Progressive Alliance of Socialists and Democrats); the alliance of Together 2014 and Dialogue for Hungary, 1 with 7·2% (Greens/European Free Alliance); Politics Can Be Different, 1 with 5·0% (Greens/European Free Alliance).

Current Government

President: János Áder; b. 1959 (Fidesz-MPSz; in office since 10 May 2012).
   Prime Minister: Viktor Orbán; b. 1963 (Fidesz-MPSz; sworn in 29 May 2010 for a second time and re-elected in May 2014 and May 2018, having previously held office from 1998–2002).
   In Feb. 2019 the government comprised:

Deputy Prime Ministers: Mihály Varga (also *Minister of Finance*); Sándor Pintér (also *Minister of Interior*); Zsolt Semjén (for *Hungarian Communities Abroad*).
   Minister of Agriculture and Rural Development: István Nagy. *Defence:* Tibor Benkő. *Foreign Affairs and Trade:* Péter Szijjártó. *Human Resources:* Miklós Kásler. *Justice:* László Trócsányi. *National Innovation and Technology:* László Palkovics. *Minister in the Prime Minister's Office:* Gergely Gulyás. *Minister of the Prime Minister's Cabinet Office:* Antal Rogán. *Ministers without Portfolio:* Andrea Bártfai-Mager; János Süli.
   Government Website: http://www.kormany.hu/en

Current Leaders

János Áder

Position
President

Introduction
János Áder was elected president by parliament on 2 May 2012 to serve a five-year term in the largely ceremonial role. He took over from László Kövér, who had held the post in a caretaker capacity after Pál Schmitt resigned on 2 April 2012. He was re-elected on 13 March 2017.

Early Life
János Áder was born on 9 May 1959 in Csorna. He graduated in law from Eötvös Loránd University (ELTE) in Budapest in 1983. From 1986–90 he was a researcher at the Sociological Research Institute of the Hungarian Academy of Sciences. He joined Fidesz (Federation of Young Democrats) at the party's inception in 1988 and took part in the 'round table' talks in 1989 that led to the end of communist single-party rule. Áder managed Fidesz's 1990 election campaign and was himself elected a member of parliament, retaining his seat until 2009.

From 1990–92 he served as deputy leader of the party's parliamentary group before being appointed chair of the national steering committee of Fidesz. In 1994 he led the party's election campaign, a role he repeated in 1998. He served as Fidesz's vice president from 1995–97 until his appointment as deputy parliamentary speaker.

From June 1998 until May 2002 Áder was parliamentary speaker and also held his party's vice presidency from 1999–2000. From 2002–06 he led Fidesz's parliamentary group while it was in opposition. In 2006 he returned as the deputy speaker of parliament, holding the post until 2009, when he became a member of the European Parliament. As an MEP, Áder demonstrated himself a Fidesz-Hungarian Civic Alliance (as it was by then called) party loyalist by voting along party lines on 98% of issues. In 2011 a number of domestic laws that Áder helped draft were ratified, including controversial reforms of the electoral system and the judiciary that critics argued infringed judicial independence.

On 16 April 2012 Áder was nominated by Prime Minister Orbán for the national presidency following Pál Schmitt's resignation over allegations of plagiarism in regard to his doctoral thesis. Áder resigned as an MEP and gave up his Fidesz-Hungarian Civic Alliance party membership in preparation for taking on the post. His election to office on 2 May 2012 was assured by Fidesz-Hungarian Civic Alliance's two-thirds majority in parliament. He formally assumed the presidency on 10 May.

Career in Office
As an Orbán ally and former member of Fidesz-Hungarian Civic Alliance, Áder's appointment was strongly attacked by those who questioned his adherence to the constitutional impartiality of the presidential office. In Feb. 2014 he signed a law to upgrade a nuclear power plant for which the government had approved a controversial financing deal with Russia.
   Áder was re-elected by parliament in the second round of voting on 13 March 2017.

Viktor Orbán

Position
Prime Minister

Introduction
Viktor Orbán previously served as Hungary's prime minister from 1998 until 2002. A lawyer, in 1988 he co-founded the Federation of Young

Democrats–Fidesz. A prominent pro-democracy campaigner during the communist era, as president of Fidesz he led the party to victory at the 1998 general election. He became head of a coalition government and, as prime minister, campaigned for Hungary to join the European Union (EU). He became prime minister for a second time in May 2010 following the landslide victory of Fidesz-Hungarian Civic Alliance in the April general election, and was re-elected in May 2014 and May 2018.

Early Life

Orbán was born on 31 May 1963 in Székesfehérvár. After his schooling he did military service from 1981–82. In 1987 he graduated in law from Hungary's ELTE University and worked for two years as a sociological researcher.

In March 1988 he helped set up Fidesz, serving as its chief spokesman until Oct. 1989. During this period he attended Imre Nagy's reburial in Budapest and made a widely publicized speech calling for free elections and the removal of Soviet troops from Hungarian soil. During the summer of 1989 he was involved with the Opposition Roundtable negotiations that sought to resolve key issues on Hungary's future. Later in the year he took up a political philosophy research scholarship at Oxford University's Pembroke College.

Having won a parliamentary seat at Hungary's first post-communist free elections in early 1990, Orbán led the Fidesz parliamentary group. In May 1993 he became party president and from 1994–98 was the leader of various government committees preparing for European integration. An advocate of close ties with the USA, in 1996 he helped found the Committee for Political Co-operation of the New Atlantic Initiative. In addition in the 1990s he held several prominent posts in the Liberal International.

At the elections of 1998 Fidesz won 28% of the vote, and 14 more seats that the Socialists who gained 32%. Orbán was able to form a coalition in alliance with the Independent Party of Smallholders and the Hungarian Democratic Forum. He was sworn in as prime minister on 6 July 1998.

Gaining entry into the EU dominated Orbán's tenure. Hungary, Poland and the Czech Republic were considered the frontline nations likely to secure earliest entry, but plans for integration in 2003 faltered as the individual nations struggled to satisfy EU criteria. Orbán campaigned vigorously to ensure entry for Hungary was not delayed, arguing the irrelevancy of the state of other East European economies.

Orbán stood down as party president in Jan. 2000 in order to concentrate on the premiership. Later in the year he visited Romania for the first time after an industrial accident in which Romanian waste devastated several Hungarian rivers strained relations between the two countries.

Relations with other East European nations came under scrutiny in 2001 when Orbán commented that the Hungarian economy would require an influx of several million workers. He suggested ethnic Hungarians returning from abroad would be targeted to boost employment, as laid out in the draft Status Law. This was regarded by some observers as an attempt to assure West European nations that there would not be a worker deluge from the East.

Orbán lost the premiership in April 2002 after a narrow defeat at the general elections. Unable to secure a majority, the new government was formed by a Socialist-Alliance of Free Democrats coalition, led by Péter Medgyessy.

Career in Office

Following a comprehensive win for Fidesz-Hungarian Civic Alliance (as Fidesz is now known) in the general election of April 2010 in which it claimed a two-thirds majority, Orbán took office as prime minister on 29 May. Having campaigned on a platform of tax cuts and job creation, he faced major challenges to meet his targets in light of the country's weak financial position.

In April 2011 the Fidesz-controlled parliament passed a revised and controversial new constitution, the legitimacy and democratic basis of which were questioned by the main opposition parties who boycotted the vote. The opposition was similarly critical of further legislation approved by parliament in Dec. that year and deemed to entrench the power of the Fidesz administration. In particular, one law demoted the status of the central bank and handed more control over monetary policy to the government, and another reduced the number of parliamentary members and redrew electoral boundaries.

Having previously decried the financial rescue package negotiated by the preceding government with the IMF in 2008, Orbán announced in Nov. 2011 that he would reopen talks with the IMF and the EU for a precautionary credit line in the light of Hungary's continuing financial and economic woes. EU and IMF opposition to the law affecting the central bank initially stalled negotiations but they resumed in mid-2012 following fears of an economic default by Hungary and some relaxation by the government of its measures to centralize power. However, in Sept. that year Orbán rejected stern IMF conditions and said he would pursue an alternative course. Subsequent

economic data indicated that Hungary came out of recession in the first quarter of 2013, which Orbán claimed was a vindication of his policy stance.

In April 2012 Pál Schmitt had resigned as state president after being stripped of his university doctorate for alleged plagiarism. The following month parliament elected János Áder, another Orbán loyalist, in his place.

In Jan. 2013 the constitutional court ruled against an amendment to the electoral law that had been passed by parliament the previous Nov. and which critics had deemed favourable to Fidesz by restricting voter rights. However, in March 2013 parliament approved a further constitutional change curbing legal checks on the executive, and in June Orbán's government proposed new constitutional provisions restricting political campaigning and the rights of religious groups. In response to criticism from the EU, the proposals were redrafted in Aug. but opposition groups continued to maintain that the constitution was anti-democratic.

Orbán was re-elected in April 2014 after his Fidesz-Hungarian Civic Alliance won 133 of 199 seats in parliamentary elections. There has since been increasing domestic protest over alleged government corruption, Orbán's centralization of political power and an unpopular proposed tax on online profits. Among EU states and the USA, there has also been growing disquiet concerning Orbán's authoritarianism and commitment to democracy, particularly given his assertion that Hungary should become an 'illiberal state' such as Russia and China. In Feb. 2015 his party lost its two-thirds majority in parliament in a by-election, and suffered a further by-election setback to the far-right Jobbik party in April.

Orbán adopted a tough stance against the growing influx of mainly Syrian migrants into the European Union in 2015 and 2016, erecting fencing on Hungary's border with Serbia to deter the flow. His refusal to participate in mandatory EU migrant quotas was backed in a national referendum in Oct. 2016.

In April 2017 parliament approved controversial legislation imposing conditions on the operation of foreign universities in Hungary (perceived particularly as an attack on the liberal Central European University), while in June another law similarly introduced limitations on foreign non-governmental organizations. Both measures were seen by Orbán's opponents as attacks on bodies critical of the government and were criticized by the European Union and the USA.

Orbán was returned for a further term as premier following a Fidesz election victory in April 2018 marked by 'intimidating and xenophobic rhetoric, media bias and opaque campaign financing' according to observers from the Organization for Security and Co-operation in Europe.

In July 2018 the European Commission referred Hungary to the European Court of Justice for non-compliance with EU asylum and migration legislation and in Sept. the European Parliament condemned Hungary as a 'systemic threat' to democracy and the rule of law.

Defence

The Hungarian Defence Force is the national defence force. It has two branches: the Hungarian Ground Force (including a riverine element) and the Hungarian Air Force. The President of the Republic is C.-in-C. of the armed forces.

Conscription was abolished in 2004.

In 2013 defence expenditure totalled US$1,100m. (US$111 per capita), representing 0·8% of GDP. In 1985 defence expenditure had represented 6·8% of GDP.

Army

The strength of the Army was (2011) 9,911 with 35,2000 reserves. Equipment in 2011 included 30 main battle tanks. There is an additional force of 12,000 border guards.

Air Force

The Air Force had a strength (2011) of 5,039. There were 14 combat-capable aircraft in 2011 (Saab Gripens) and 12 attack helicopters (Mi-24s).

International Relations

Hungary held a referendum on EU membership on 12 April 2003, in which 83·8% of votes cast were in favour of accession, with 16·2% against, although turnout was only 45·6%. It became a member of the EU on 1 May 2004. In 2000 Hungary introduced a visa requirement for Russians entering the country as one of the conditions for EU membership.

Hungary has had a long-standing dispute with Slovakia over the Gabčíkovo-Nagymaros Project, involving the building of dam structures in both countries for the production of electric power, flood control and improvement of navigation on the Danube as agreed in a treaty signed in 1977 between Hungary and Czechoslovakia. In late 1998 Slovakia and Hungary signed a protocol easing tensions between the two nations and settling differences over the dam.

Economy

Agriculture accounted for 4·6% of GDP in 2013, industry 30·1% and services 65·3%.

Overview

Hungary is defined as a high-income country with per capita income of US$14,225 in 2017. The economy underwent market liberalization in the 1990s in one of the smoothest transitions away from communism among the former Eastern Bloc nations. Hungary became a member of the Organisation for Economic Co-operation and Development in 1995, the World Trade Organization a year later and the European Union in 2004.

Since the mid-1990s the majority of state assets have been privatized and the private sector now accounts for over 80% of GDP. By 1998 Hungary had attracted nearly half of all foreign direct investment in Central Europe. However, growth slowed from 2005 and was further weakened by a fiscal consolidation package in mid-2006. In the wake of the global financial crisis that began in 2008, Hungary experienced declining exports and reduced domestic consumption. As a result it entered one of the worst recessions in its history, recording a 6·6% contraction of the economy in 2009. In Oct. 2008 the country reached an agreement with the International Monetary Fund, EU and World Bank for a rescue package worth US$25bn. aimed at restoring financial stability and investor confidence. From 2011 the economy showed signs of recovery, and GDP growth then averaged 2·3% annually up to 2017.

The fiscal deficit was equivalent to 2·3% of GDP in 2017, down from 5·2% in 2011—reflecting government spending restraints (notably in the local government sector) and the implementation of structural reforms for savings. There was also an increase in tax revenues between 2011 and 2017 (Hungary's 27% VAT rate being the highest in the world). Although total external debt fell from 136% of GDP in 2011 to around 103% in 2017, the debt burden remains among the highest in the region.

Currency

A decree of 26 July 1946 instituted a new monetary unit, the forint (HUF) of 100 fillér. The forint was made fully convertible in Jan. 1991 and moves in a 15% band against the euro either side of a central rate of €1=282·4 forints. There was inflation of 0·4% in 2016 and 2·4% in 2017. Foreign exchange reserves were US$42,988m. in Sept. 2009 and gold reserves 99,000 troy oz. Total money supply in Aug. 2009 was 5,930·4bn. forints.

Budget

Budgetary central government revenue and expenditure (in 1bn. forints):

	2009	2010	2011
Revenue	7,780·9	7,880·9	10,407·1
Expenditure	8,725·9	8,998·4	9,511·7

Principal sources of revenue in 2011: taxes on goods and services, 3,853·5bn. forints; taxes on income, profits and capital gains, 1,706·1bn. forints; grants, 629·0bn. forints. Main items of expenditure by economic type in 2011: grants, 2,908·6bn. forints; compensation of employees, 1,461·3bn. forints; use of goods and services, 1,169·2bn. forints. There is a flat income tax rate of 15%.

Hungary's budget deficit in 2017 was 2·2% of GDP (2016, 1·6%; 2015, 1·9%). The required target set by the EU is a budget deficit of no more than 3%.

VAT is 27% (reduced rates, 18% and 5%). Hungary has the highest rate of VAT of any country.

Performance

The economy grew by 3·4% in 2015, 2·2% in 2016 and 4·0% in 2017. Total GDP was US$139·1bn. in 2017.

Banking and Finance

In 1987 a two-tier system was established. The National Bank (*Governor*, György Matolcsy) remained the central state financial institution. It is responsible for the operation of monetary policy and the foreign exchange system. In Dec. 2009 the Hungarian financial system comprised 40 credit institutions, 140 co-operatives, 266 financial enterprises, 25 investment enterprises, 36 investment funds, 37 insurance companies, 20 pension funds and 37 health-related funds. They are all supervised by the Hungarian Financial Supervisory Authority (HFSA).

The largest bank is OTP Bank Rt. (the National Savings Bank plc), with assets in 2009 of 6,566bn. forints. Other leading banks are K+H (Hungarian Commercial and Credit Bank) and MKB (Hungarian Foreign Trade Bank). A law of June 1991 sets capital and reserve requirements, and provides for foreign investment in Hungarian banks. Permission is needed for investments of more than 10%.

In June 2012 gross external debt totalled US$203,265m.

Foreign direct investment was US$3·1bn. in 2013, down from US$14·0bn. in 2012. At the end of 2013 foreign direct investment stocks totalled US$111·0bn.

The Hungarian International Trade Bank opened in London in 1973. In 1980 the Central European International Bank was set up in Budapest with seven western banks holding 66% of the shares.

A stock exchange was opened in Budapest in June 1990.

Energy and Natural Resources

In 2011 an estimated 8% of energy consumption came from renewables (wind power, solar power, hydro-electric power, tidal power, geothermal energy and biomass), compared to the European Union average of 13%. A target of 13% has been set by the EU for 2020.

Environment

Hungary's carbon dioxide emissions from the consumption of energy in 2011 were the equivalent of 5·2 tonnes per capita.

Electricity

Installed capacity in 2011 was 9·7m. kW, about a fifth of which is nuclear. There is a 2,000 MW nuclear power station at Paks with four reactors. Two further reactors at Paks are planned, potentially to come online in 2025 and 2027 respectively. In 2011 Hungary produced 36·0bn. kWh of electricity and 14·7bn. kWh were imported. Hungary is a net importer of electricity. Total consumption in 2011 was 42·6bn. kWh; consumption per capita in the same year was 4,264 kWh.

Oil and Gas

Oil and natural gas are found in the Szeged basin and Zala county. Oil production in 2011 was 4·4m. bbls. Natural gas production in 2011 was 2·7bn. cu. metres; proven reserves were 8bn. cu. metres in 2013. However, Hungary relies on Russia for almost all of its oil and much of its gas.

Minerals

Production in 1,000 tonnes: lignite (2010), 9,113; bauxite (2009), 317.

Agriculture

Agricultural land was collectivized in 1950. It was announced in 1990 that land would be restored to its pre-collectivization owners if they wished to cultivate it. A law of April 1994 restricts the area of land that may be bought by individuals to 300 ha., and prohibits the sale of arable land and land in conservation zones to companies and foreign nationals. Today, although 90% of all cultivated land is in private hands, most farms are little more than smallholdings. In 2009 the agricultural area was 5·78m. ha. (equivalent to 64% of the total land area); arable land constituted 4·59m. ha.

Agricultural production has dropped drastically since 1989. Production figures (2011, in 1,000 tonnes): maize, 8,089 (6,747 in 1989); wheat, 4,130 (6,509 in 1989); vegetables (excluding potatoes), 1,600; sunflower seeds, 1,368; barley, 989; sugar beets, 771 (5,277 in 1989); potatoes, 564; fruit, 542.

Livestock has also drastically decreased since 1989 from 7·7m. pigs to 3·2m. by 2010, from 1·6m. cattle to 0·7m., and from 2·1m. sheep to 1·2m. Thus the pig stock, cattle stock and sheep stock have all declined to levels not seen in more than fifty years.

The north shore of Lake Balaton, Villány and the Tokaj area are important wine-producing districts. Wine production in 2010 was 176m. litres.

Forestry

The forest area in 2015 was 2·07m. ha., or 23% of the land area. Timber production in 2011 was 6·23m. cu. metres.

Fisheries

There are fisheries in the rivers Danube and Tisza and Lake Balaton. In 2015 total catch was 9,937 tonnes, exclusively from inland fishing.

Industry

The leading companies by market capitalization in Hungary in May 2018 were: OTP Bank Rt., US$10·9bn.; and MOL Magyar Olaj-és Gázipari Rt (Hungarian Oil and Gas Plc), US$8·0bn.

Manufacturing output grew by an average of 7·7% annually between 1992 and 2000 although it slowed between 2001 and 2007, with annual average growth of 5·2%, and contracted by 1·0% in 2008.

Production, 2009 unless otherwise indicated, in 1,000 tonnes: rolled steel products (2007), 103,347; cement (2007), 3,552; distillate fuel oil, 3,428; crude steel (2007), 2,232; plastics, 1,325; petrol (2007), 1,322; fertilizers, 825; alumina (2006), 270; residual fuel oil (2007), 200; refrigerators and freezers, 2,430,092 units; radio sets, 2,341,000 units; beer, 651·2m. litres.

Labour

In 2009 out of an economically active population of 4,202,600 there were 3,781,900 employed persons, of which 3,309,900 were employees. Among the employed persons in 2009, 64·2% worked in services, 31·2% in industry and construction, and 4·6% in agriculture. Average gross monthly wages of full-time employees in 2009: 199,837 forints. Minimum monthly wage, 2017, 127,650 forints (up 15% from 111,000 forints in 2016). There were a total of 6,474 working days lost to strike action in 2009, down from 25,004 in 2008. The unemployment rate was 3·7% in Nov. 2018 (down from 4·2% in 2017 as a whole and 5·1% in 2016). Long-term unemployment is particularly high, with 50·6% of the labour force in 2010 having been out of work for more than a year. In 2012 Hungary was one of only three OECD countries (the others being Ireland and the UK) in which the share of 15–24 year-olds who were unemployed or inactive and neither in education nor training was higher for the native rather than foreign-born population.

The normal retirement age is 63 years and 6 months but is increasing gradually to 65 for both men and women by 2022.

Hungary had 36,000 people living in slavery according to the Walk Free Foundation's 2013 *Global Slavery Index*.

International Trade

Imports and Exports

Imports and exports for calendar years in US$1m.:

	2006	2007	2008	2009	2010
Imports c.i.f.	76,978·5	94,659·7	108,784·7	77,272·4	87,432·1
Exports f.o.b.	74,055·4	94,590·9	108,211·2	82,571·8	94,748·7

Hungary's foreign trade was expanding at a very fast rate until the global economic downturn of 2008–09, with the value of both its imports and its exports increasing fourfold between 1997 and 2007.

Machinery and transport equipment accounted for 46·0% of imports and 57·5% of exports in 2010, and manufactured goods 12·4% of imports and 9·3% of exports.

In 2010, 24·0% of imports came from Germany and 25·1% of exports went to Germany. Russia was the second biggest supplier of imports in 2010 (7·8% of the total) and Italy the second biggest market for exports (5·5%). In 2010, 3·6% of exports went to Russia, down from 13·1% in 1992.

Communications

Roads

In 2007 there were 195,719 km of roads, including 1,157 km of motorways, 6,745 km of main roads and 23,280 km of secondary roads; 37·7% of roads were paved. Passenger cars numbered 3,012,200 in 2007; lorries and vans, 829,800; motorcycles and mopeds, 135,900; and buses and coaches, 17,900. In 2007 there were 20,635 road accidents with 1,232 fatalities.

Rail

In 2011 the rail network was 7,896 km in length; 115·6m. passengers were carried that year. Rail Cargo Hungaria carried 29·1m. tonnes of freight in 2012. There is a metro in Budapest (38·2 km), and tram/light rail networks in Budapest (332·0 km), Debrecen, Miskolc and Szeged.

Civil Aviation

Budapest airport (Ferihegy) handled 8,095,367 passengers in 2009 (all on international flights) and 54,355 tonnes of freight. Malév, the former national carrier, ceased operations in Feb. 2012. The largest Hungarian airline is now Wizz Air, which started flying in 2004 and is Central and Eastern Europe's largest low-cost carrier.

Shipping

Hungary had 1,691 km of navigable rivers in 2014 and 173 km of navigable canals; 7·8m. tonnes of freight were carried on inland waterways in 2014.

Telecommunications

In 2013 there were 2,978,000 main (fixed) telephone lines. In the same year mobile phone subscriptions numbered 11,590,000 (1,164·3 per 1,000 persons). Matav, the privatized former national telephone company, still has more than 80% of the fixed line market. 72·6% of the population aged 16–74 were internet users in 2013. There were 22·9 fixed broadband subscriptions per 100 inhabitants in 2012. In March 2012 there were 3·8m. Facebook users.

Social Institutions

Out of 178 countries analysed in the 2017 *Fragile States Index*—a list published jointly by the Fund for Peace and *Foreign Policy* magazine—Hungary was ranked the 44th least vulnerable to conflict or collapse. The index is based on 12 indicators of state vulnerability across social, political and economic categories.

Justice

The administration of justice is the responsibility of the Procurator-General, elected by Parliament for six years. There are 111 local courts, 20 labour law courts, 20 county courts, six district courts and a Supreme Court. Criminal proceedings are dealt with by the regional courts through three-member councils and by the county courts and the Supreme Court in five-member councils. A new Civil Code was adopted in 1978 and a new Criminal Code in 1979.

Regional courts act as courts of first instance; county courts as either courts of first instance or of appeal. The Supreme Court acts normally as an appeal court, but may act as a court of first instance in cases submitted to it by the Public Prosecutor. All courts, when acting as courts of first instance, consist of one professional judge and two lay assessors, and, as courts of appeal, of three professional judges. Local government Executive Committees may try petty offences.

Regional and county judges and assessors are elected by the appropriate local councils; members of the Supreme Court by Parliament.

The Office of Ombudsman was instituted in 1993. He or she is elected by parliament for a six-year term, renewable once.

There are also military courts of the first instance. Military cases of the second instance go before the Supreme Court.

The death penalty was abolished in Oct. 1990.

The population in penal institutions in June 2013 was 18,388 (186 per 100,000 of national population). There were 80,618 convictions of adults and 6,283 of juvenile offenders in 2009. Of 394,034 crimes registered in 2009, 23,914 were against the person (including 138 homicides). Hungary was ranked 33rd of 102 countries for criminal justice and 47th for civil justice in the 2015 World Justice Project *Rule of Law Index*, which provides data on how the rule of law is experienced by the general public across eight categories.

Education

Adult literacy rate in 2013 was estimated at more than 99%. Education is free and compulsory from five to 16. Primary schooling ends at 14; thereafter education is continued at secondary, secondary technical or secondary vocational schools, which offer diplomas entitling students to apply for higher education, or at vocational training schools which offer tradesmen's diplomas. Students at the latter may also take the secondary school diploma examinations after two years of evening or correspondence study. Optional religious education was introduced in schools in 1990.

In 2010–11 there were: 4,358 kindergartens with 30,359 teachers and 338,162 children; 3,306 primary schools with 73,565 teachers and 758,566 pupils; and 2,617 secondary schools (including vocational schools) with 48,953 teachers and 662,808 pupils (of which 578,301 were full-time). 361,347 students were enrolled in tertiary education at 69 institutions in 2010–11 (240,727 full-time).

In 2011 total expenditure on education came to 4·7% of GDP and 9·3% of total government spending.

Health
In 2009 there were 30,276 doctors, 4,920 dentists, 54,352 nurses and mid-wives and (2006) 5,364 pharmacists. While there is an excess supply of doctors, there are too few nurses and wages for both groups are exceptionally low. In 2009 there were 175 hospitals with 71,489 beds. Spending on health accounted for 7·3% of GDP in 2009.

Welfare
In 1998 the Hungarian parliament decided to place the financial funds of health and pension insurance under government supervision. The self-governing bodies which had previously been responsible for this were dissolved. Medical treatment is free. Patients bear 15% of the cost of medicines. Sickness benefit is 75% of wages, old age pensions 60–70%. In 2010, 1·9trn. forints was spent on pensions and pension-like benefits for 2·94m. recipients. Family benefits totalled 2·2% of GDP in 2009. On a monthly basis in 2010, 1·2m. families were receiving family allowance and child care allowance was being paid for 178,532 children.

Religion
According to the Pew Research Center's Forum on Religion & Public Life, an estimated 81·0% of the population in 2010 was Christian and 18·6% had no religious affiliation. Of the Christians, 73% in 2010 were Catholics and 26% Protestants. The Roman Catholic primate of Hungary is Péter Erdő, Archbishop of Esztergom-Budapest, installed in Jan. 2003. The Roman Catholic Church comprises four ecclesiastical provinces and nine suffragan dioceses. In Feb. 2019 the Roman Catholic Church had one cardinal.

Culture

World Heritage Sites
Sites under Hungarian jurisdiction which appear on UNESCO's World Heritage List are (with year entered on list): Budapest, and specifically the Banks of the Danube and the Buda Castle Quarter (1987 and 2002); Hollókő (1987), a preserved settlement developed during the 17th and 18th centuries; Millenary Benedictine Monastery of Pannonhalma and its Natural Environment (1996), first settled by Benedictine monks in 996; Hortobágy National Park (1999), a large area of plains and wetlands in eastern Hungary; Pécs (Sopianae) Early Christian Cemetery (2000), a series of decorated tombs dating from the 4th century; Tokaj Wine Region Historic Cultural Landscape (2002), a thousand-year-old wine-producing area.

Hungary also shares two UNESCO sites: the Caves of Aggtelek and Slovak Karst (1995, 2000 and 2008), a complex of 712 temperate-zone karstic caves, is shared with Slovakia; the Cultural Landscape of Fertö/Neusiedlersee (2001), an area that has acted as a meeting place for different cultures for 8,000 years, is shared with Austria.

Press
In 2014 there were 31 daily newspapers with a combined circulation of 1,210,000. The most widely read newspapers are the free tabloid *Metropol* and the paid-for tabloid *Blikk*. A total of 12,841 book titles were published in 2009 in 36·02m. copies.

Tourism
In 2011, 3,822,000 non-resident tourists and 4,199,000 domestic tourists stayed in holiday accommodation (3,462,000 and 4,011,000 respectively in 2010).

The main countries of origin of non-resident tourists in 2011 were: Germany (542,000), Austria (295,000), the UK (221,000) and Romania (216,000).

Festivals
The Budapest Spring Festival, comprising music, theatre, dance etc., takes place in March. The Balaton Festival is in May, Miskolc Opera Festival in June, the Szeged Open-Air Theatre Festival in July–Aug., and the Sziget music festival in Budapest in mid-Aug. The flower carnival in Debrecen, a five-day celebration of flowers, music and dance, culminates on 20 Aug. (St Stephen's Day).

Diplomatic Representatives

Of Hungary in the United Kingdom (35 Eaton Pl., London, SW1X 8BY)
    Ambassador: Kristóf Szalay-Bobrovniczky.

Of the United Kingdom in Hungary (Füge Utca 5–7, Budapest 1022)
    Ambassador: Iain Lindsay, OBE.

Of Hungary in the USA (1500 Rhode Island Ave., NW, Washington, D.C., 20005)
    Ambassador: László Szabó.

Of the USA in Hungary (Szabadság Tér 12, Budapest 1054)
    Ambassador: David B. Cornstein

Of Hungary to the United Nations
    Ambassador: Katalin Bogyay.

Of Hungary to the European Union
    Permanent Representative: Olivér Várhelyi.

Further Reading

Central Statistical Office. *Statisztikai Évkönyv.* Annual since 1871.—*Magyar Statisztikai Zsebkönyv.* Annual.—*Statistical Yearbook.—Statistical Handbook of Hungary.—Monthly Bulletin of Statistics.*

Bozóki, A., *et al.,* (eds) *Post-Communist Transition: Emerging Pluralism in Hungary.* 1992

Burawoy, M. and Lukács, J., *The Radiant Past: Ideology and Reality in Hungary's Road to Capitalism.* 1992

Cartledge, Bryan, *The Will to Survive: A History of Hungary.* 2011

Cox, T. and Furlong, A. (eds) *Hungary: the Politics of Transition.* 1995

Geró, A., *Modern Hungarian Society in the Making: the Unfinished Experience*; translated from Hungarian. 1995

Halpern, László and Wyplosz, Charles, (eds) *Hungary: Towards a Market Economy.* 2011

Kontler, László, *A History of Hungary.* 2002

Körösényi, András, *Government and Politics in Hungary.* 1999

Lendvai, Paul, *The Hungarians: A Thousand Years of Victory in Defeat.* 2004

Mitchell, K. D. (ed.) *Political Pluralism in Hungary and Poland: Perspectives on the Reforms.* 1992

Molnár, Miklós, *A Concise History of Hungary.* 2001

Rose-Ackerman, Susan, *From Elections to Democracy: Building Accountable Government in Hungary and Poland.* 2007

Schiemann, John W., *The Politics of Pact-Making: Hungary's Negotiated Transition to Democracy in Comparative Perspective.* 2005

Sugar, Peter F., *A History of Hungary.* 1990

Székely, István and Newbery, David M. G., *Hungary: An Economy in Transition.* 2008

Vardy, Steven B., *Historical Dictionary of Hungary.* 1997

National library: Széchényi Library, Budavári Palota 'F' épület, 1827 Budapest.

National Statistical Office: Központi Statisztikai Hivatal/Central Statistical Office, Keleti Károly u. 5/7, H-1024 Budapest.

Website: http://portal.ksh.hu

Iceland

Lyðveldið Ísland (Republic of Iceland)

Capital: Reykjavík
Population projection, 2020: 343,000
GNI per capita, 2017: (PPP$) 45,810
HDI/world rank, 2017: 0·935/6
Internet domain extension: .is

Key Historical Events

Scandinavia's North Atlantic outpost was first settled in 874. According to the *Landnámabók* or 'book of settlements', the first to land was Ingólfr Arnarson, who came from Norway to live on the site of present-day Reykjavík. He was followed by some 400 migrants, mainly from Norway but also from other Nordic countries and from Norse settlements in the British Isles.

A ruling class was soon formed by chieftains, known as the *godar*. In 930 they established the first ever democratic National Assembly, the *Alþingi* (Althing). Primarily an adjudicating body, it also served as a legislature and as a fair, a marriage mart and as a national celebration in which a large proportion of the Icelandic population participated for two weeks each June. The first notable event in its history occurred in 1000 when, by majority decision, Christianity was adopted as Iceland's official religion. Despite the change, the *godar* remained politically important and some of them were ordained. Bishoprics were established at Skálholt in 1056 and at Hólar in 1106. It was not until the 1800s, after the bishoprics were united, that Reykjavík became the new episcopal see, making it the leading community.

Trade flourished with homespun woollen cloth as the chief export, although certain materials such as grain and timber had to be imported. Iceland's only indigenous wood, birchwood, which grew in abundance yet proved unsuitable for building, later became valuable in making charcoal.

In the mid-13th century there were power struggles between the *godar*. With the 'Old Treaty' of 1262, the *godar* were persuaded to swear allegiance to the king of Norway, bringing Iceland under Norwegian rule but leaving it with internal autonomy. When Norway was joined with Denmark in 1380, Iceland still retained the Althing as well as its own code of law.

In the 14th century, the expansion of fishing to satisfy European demand stimulated agriculture and other basic industries. Iceland's newfound prosperity encouraged trade between the Icelandic fisherman and traders in Bergen, Norway. English traders in Bergen were keen to bypass Norwegian importers and instead began trading directly with Iceland. The Danish were largely unsuccessful in preventing this and it was not until the 16th century, when the English turned to the North American fishing grounds, that hostilities ceased.

Iceland's economic progress was checked when birchwood became depleted. Coupled with over-grazing, this led to soil erosion and put an end to crop growth. Further troubles came in the 15th century when Iceland fell victim to the Black Death, on two occasions losing around half of the population.

With the advent of Lutheranism in the first half of the 16th century, Iceland resisted Denmark's efforts to impose the Reformation on their North Atlantic possession. The bishoprics of Skálholt and Hólar were eventually overcome in 1550, marking the consolidation of Danish power over Iceland. In 1602 a royal decree gave all foreign trading rights in Iceland exclusively to Danish merchants. This restriction, which lasted until 1787, virtually ended Iceland's contacts with England and Germany, their one-time trading partners. Absolutism in Denmark and Norway under King Frederick III was recognized by Iceland in 1662, further strengthening external rule, and after economic hardship in the 18th century (in the 1780s famine killed one-fifth of the population) Iceland's reduced status was confirmed. When Norway split from Denmark in 1814 there were no similar calls for secession from Iceland.

Home Rule

In the 1830s a Danish consultative assembly was formed in which Iceland was given two seats. Denmark's transition to a system of representative democratic government after Frederick VII relinquished absolute power in 1848 did not extend to Iceland. After failures to reach agreement over the country's status, the Althing decided that 1874, the year that marked a thousand years of settlement, should be chosen as the year when it gained a new constitution. This was to provide the Althing with legislative if not executive control. During this period Iceland's economy continued to fare badly. With soil erosion still a problem, the strains of population growth forced mass emigration to North America. Around 15,000 emigrants left Iceland between 1870 and 1914. In 1904, after several decades of pressure for autonomy and, from 1901 onwards, support from the governing Danish Liberal party, Iceland finally achieved home rule.

Economic progress was led by modernization of the fishing industry and an expanded labour force. In 1916 a national trade unions organization was established and a process of urbanization began as the population moved towards the coastal fishing villages. Educational reform brought the introduction of compulsory education and in 1911, the establishment of the University of Iceland at Reykjavík.

In 1918 Iceland became a separate state under the Danish crown, with only foreign affairs remaining under Danish jurisdiction. The following decades were overshadowed by the influence of the 1930s' depression and the Spanish Civil War in 1936, the latter bringing an end to the lucrative fish trade with Spain.

In 1944 Iceland declared independence since Denmark was then occupied by Nazi Germany. The termination of the union was little more than a formality, the German invasion of Denmark in 1940 having effectively ended that country's responsibility for Iceland's foreign relations.

Iceland was occupied peacefully by Britain in 1940 but US troops took over a year later. They improved roads and docks, built an airport and paid high wages. An American request for a long-term lease on three military bases was reviewed sympathetically. But the continuing presence of American forces somehow gave the lie to the independence so recently celebrated. The answer was for Iceland to join NATO. Objections to the American-run Keflavík airbase were gradually withdrawn and in 1951 a defence agreement with the United States allowed for an increase in the number of troops brought in 'to defend Iceland and ... to ensure the security of the seas around the country'. Greater integration with Europe came with joining the European Free Trade Association in 1970.

Fish remained central to the economy, accounting for 90% of the export trade. But there were worries about over-dependence on a single product and concern that other nations were taking too large a share of the Icelandic catch. In 1948 the demarcation of new fishing zones was made subject to Icelandic jurisdiction. Two years later one mile was added to the three-mile offshore zone which Iceland had administered since 1901. This was just acceptable to other fishing nations but when, in 1958, the limit was extended to 12 miles, Britain sent naval vessels to protect trawlers from harassment and arrest. This was the first Cod War, a cat-and-mouse game between the British navy and coastguard patrols which continued to 1961. At that point Britain and West Germany, the other fishing nation involved in the dispute, accepted the 12-mile zone on condition that if Iceland intended to widen her jurisdiction still further she had to give six months' notice of her intention and, if challenged, refer her claims to the International Court of Justice at The Hague.

In 1971, however, the government fulfilled its promise to do something about over-fishing by unilaterally extending the offshore zone to 50 miles. Despite a clear contravention of treaty commitment, Iceland gained sympathy as the tiny nation fighting the giants. Also in Iceland's favour was the move by Britain and members of the European Community to extend their jurisdiction over the continental shelf. A law officially expanding the Icelandic fishery limits to 50 miles came into force on 1 Sept. 1972. However, a second Cod War began shortly after as British and German trawlers continued to fish within the new zone. Hostility intensified, with the Icelandic Coast Guard deploying net cutters to prevent the ships securing their catch. An agreement was signed on 8 Nov. 1973 confining British trawlers to specific areas within the 50 mile catch zone, and limiting their annual catch to 130,000 tonnes.

This agreement expired in Nov. 1975, after which Iceland declared the ocean up to 200 miles from its coast to be under Icelandic authority, and a third Cod War began. When the talks reached stalemate in Dec. 1976, British vessels were nevertheless banned from Icelandic waters. In 2006 the country undertook its first commercial whale hunt after a 21-year moratorium. The government took control of the country's three leading banks in late 2008 and requested help from the IMF in a bid to stabilize the near-bankrupt economy amid the global economic crisis. In April 2010 a volcanic explosion produced an ash cloud that paralysed the European air industry for several weeks.

Territory and Population

Iceland is an island in the North Atlantic, close to the Arctic Circle. Area, 102,819 sq. km (39,698 sq. miles).

There are eight regions:

Region	Inhabited land (sq. km)	Mountain pasture (sq. km)	Waste-land (sq. km)	Total area (sq. km)	Population (1 Jan. 2018)
Capital area	1,266	716	—	1,982	222,484
Southern Peninsula					25,770
West	5,011	3,415	275	8,701	16,257
Western Fjords	4,130	3,698	1,652	9,470	6,994
Northland West	4,867	5,278	2,948	13,093	7,195
Northland East	9,890	6,727	5,751	22,368	30,453
East	16,921	17,929	12,555	21,991	12,791
South				25,214	26,506
Iceland	42,085	37,553	23,181	102,819	348,450

Of the population of 317,630 in 2010, 20,428 were domiciled in rural districts and 297,202 (93·6%) in towns and villages (of over 200 inhabitants). Population density (2010), 3·1 per sq. km.

The UN gives a projected population for 2020 of 343,000.

The population is predominantly Icelandic. On 1 Jan. 2010 foreigners numbered 21,701 (9,583 Polish, 1,536 Lithuanian, 1,033 German, 884 Danish, 624 Latvian, 619 Portuguese, 603 Filipinos, 534 UK, 520 Thai, 499 US).

The capital, Reykjavík, had on 1 Jan. 2013 a population of 118,918; other towns were: Kópavogur, 31,719; Hafnarfjörður, 26,800; Akureyri, 17,963; Keflavík og Njarðvík, 14,153; Garðabær, 11,421; Mosfellsbær, 8,651; Akranes, 6,612; Selfoss, 6,510; Seltjarnarnes, 4,322; Vestmannaeyjar, 4,219; Grindavík, 2,856; Ísafjörður, 2,624; Sauðárkrókur, 2,575; Álftanes, 2,392; Egilsstaðir, 2,303; Hveragerði, 2,288; Húsavík, 2,228; Borgarnes, 1,759; Höfn í Hornafirði, 1,690.

The official language is Icelandic.

Social Statistics

Statistics for calendar years:

	Live births	Still-born	Marriages	Divorces	Deaths	Infant Deaths	Net immigration
2006	4,415	13	1,752	516	1,903	6	5,255
2007	4,560	7	1,797	526	1,943	9	5,132
2008	4,835	11	1,704	560	1,987	12	1,144
2009	5,027	12	1,480	550	2,002	12	-4,835

2009 rates per 1,000 population: births, 15·8; deaths, 6·3. 64·4% of births are to unmarried mothers, the highest percentage in Europe. Population growth rate, 2009, –0·5%. In 2009 the most popular age range for marrying was 30–34 for males and 25–29 for females. Iceland legalized same-sex marriage in July 2010. Life expectancy, 2009: males, 79·7 years; females, 83·3. Infant mortality, 2009, 2·4 per 1,000 live births (one of the lowest rates in the world); fertility rate, 2009, 2·2 births per woman. Iceland was ranked first in a gender gap index of 145 countries compiled by the World Economic Forum for its *Global Gender Gap Report 2015*. The annual index considers economic, political, education and health criteria.

UNICEF reported that 10·0% of children in Iceland in 2014 lived in relative poverty (living in a household in which disposable income—when adjusted for family size and composition—is less than 60% of the national median income), the second lowest rate in the world

Climate

The climate is cool temperate oceanic and rather changeable, but mild for its latitude because of the Gulf Stream and prevailing S.W. winds. Precipitation is high in upland areas, mainly in the form of snow. Reykjavík, Jan. 31·1°F (–0·5°C), July 51·1°F (10·6°C). Annual rainfall, 2009: 28·1" (713 mm).

Constitution and Government

The present constitution came into force on 17 June 1944 and has been amended four times since, most recently on 24 June 1999. The President is elected by direct, popular vote for a period of four years (no term limits).

The *Alþingi* (parliament) is elected for four-year terms in accordance with the electoral law of 1999, which provides for an *Alþingi* of 63 members. The country is divided into a minimum of six and a maximum of seven constituencies. There are currently six constituencies: Northwest (10 seats); Northeast (10 seats); South (10); Southwest (11); Reykjavík north (11); and Reykjavík south (11).

National Anthem

'Ó Guð vors lands' ('Oh God of Our Country'); words by M. Jochumsson, tune by S. Sveinbjörnsson.

Government Chronology

Presidents since 1944.

1944–52	Sveinn Björnsson
1952–68	Ásgeir Ásgeirsson
1968–80	Kristján Eldjárn
1980–96	Vigdís Finnbogadóttir
1996–2016	Ólafur Ragnar Grímsson
2016–	Guðni Thorlacius Jóhannesson

Prime Ministers since 1944. (AF = People's Party; FSF = Progressive Party; SF = Social Democratic Alliance; SSF = Independence Party; VG = Left-Green Movement)

1944–47	SSF	Ólafur Thors
1947–49	AF	Stefán Jóhann Stefánsson
1949–50	SSF	Ólafur Thors
1950–53	FSF	Steingrímur Steinthórsson
1953–56	SSF	Ólafur Thors
1956–58	FSF	Hermann Jónasson
1958–59	AF	Emil Jónsson
1959–63	SSF	Ólafur Thors
1963–70	SSF	Bjarni Benediktsson
1970–71	SSF	Jóhann Hafstein
1971–74	FSF	Ólafur Jóhannesson
1974–78	SSF	Geir Hallgrímsson
1978–79	FSF	Ólafur Jóhannesson
1979–80	AF	Benedikt Gröndal
1980–83	SSF	Gunnar Thoroddsen
1983–87	FSF	Steingrímur Hermannsson
1987–88	SSF	Þorsteinn Pálsson
1988–91	FSF	Steingrímur Hermannsson
1991–2004	SSF	Davíð Oddsson
2004–06	FSF	Halldór Ásgrímsson
2006–09	SSF	Geir Haarde
2009–13	SF	Jóhanna Sigurðardóttir
2013–16	FSF	Sigmundur Davíð Gunnlaugsson
2016–17	FSF	Sigurður Ingi Jóhannsson
2017	SSF	Bjarni Benediktsson
2017–	VG	Katrín Jakobsdóttir

Recent Elections

In presidential elections held on 25 June 2016, Guðni Jóhannesson won 39·1% of the vote against Halla Tómasdóttir with 27·9%, Andri Snær Magnason with 14·3% and former prime minister and central bank governor Davíð Oddsson with 13·7%. There were five other candidates. Turnout was 75·7%.

In the parliamentary election held on 28 Oct. 2017 the Independence Party (SSF) won 16 of the 63 seats with 25·2% of the votes cast, the Left-Green Movement (VG) 11 with 16·9%, the Progressive Party (FSF) 8 with 10·7%, the Social Democratic Alliance (SF) 7 with 12·1%, the Centre Party (MF) 7 with 10·9%, the Pirate Party (which supports civil rights, direct democracy and participation, reform of copyright and patent law, and freedom of information) 6 with 9·2%, the People's Party (FF) 4 with 6·9% and the Reform Party (Viðreisn) 4 with 6·7%. Turnout was 81·2%.

Current Government

President: Guðni Thorlacius Jóhannesson; b. 1968 (ind.; sworn in 1 Aug. 2016).

In Feb. 2019 the coalition government of the Left-Green Movement, the Independence Party and the Progressive Party comprised:

Prime Minister: Katrín Jakobsdóttir; b. 1976 (Left-Green Movement; sworn in 30 Nov. 2017).

Minister of Education, Science and Culture: Lilja Dögg Alfreðsdóttir. *Environment and Natural Resources:* Guðmundur Ingi Guðbrandsson. *Finance and Economic Affairs:* Bjarni Benediktsson. *Fisheries and Agriculture:* Kristján Þór Júlíusson. *Foreign Affairs:* Guðlaugur Þór Þórðarson. *Health:* Svandís Svavarsdóttir. *Justice:* Sigríður Ásthildur Andersen. *Social Affairs and Equality:* Ásmundur Einar Daðason. *Tourism, Industry and Innovation:* Þórdís Kolbrún Reykfjörð Gylfadóttir. *Transport and Local Government:* Sigurður Ingi Jóhannsson.

Government Offices of Iceland Website: http://www.government.is

Current Leaders

Guðni Thorlacius Jóhannesson

Position
President

Introduction
Guðni Thorlacius Jóhannesson, an academic, was elected president on 26 June 2016, having stood as an independent candidate. The presidency is the first public office that Jóhannesson has held.

Early Life
Jóhannesson was born in Reykjavík on 26 June 1968 but moved to the UK to study history and political science at the University of Warwick. He subsequently received a master's degree from the University of Oxford and a doctorate from Queen Mary University of London. He then began lecturing in history in the UK and at the University of Iceland, Reykjavík.

Jóhannesson's decision to run for the presidency came in 2016 after the leaked *Panama Papers* implicated many senior Icelandic officials, including members of the then prime minister's family, in corruption and money laundering. Jóhannesson exploited a seam of anti-establishment sentiment and won the presidency with 39·1% of the vote in June 2016. He succeeded Ólafur Ragnar Grímsson, who had been Iceland's head of state for 20 years.

Career in Office
The presidency is a largely ceremonial role but Jóhannesson's high approval ratings give him a significant voice in public life. Among his first tasks was to oversee negotiations to form a government following the legislative elections of Oct. 2016, in which no grouping had managed to secure a majority. In Dec. 2016 he charged Bjarni Benediktsson of the Independence Party with forming a new coalition that took office in Jan. 2017. However, Benediktsson resigned the following Sept. and the ensuing snap elections in Oct. were again indecisive. Subsequently, Jóhannesson asked Katrín Jakobsdóttir of the Left-Green Movement to form a new administration and she took office as prime minister at the head of a new coalition with the Independence Party and the Progressive Party at the end of Nov. that year.

Katrín Jakobsdóttir

Position
Prime Minister

Introduction
Katrín Jakobsdóttir was appointed prime minister on 30 Nov. 2017. She replaced Bjarni Benediktsson to become the country's fourth premier in two years. A former minister of education, Jakobsdóttir is chair of the Left-Green Movement and heads a broad coalition.

Early Life
Jakobsdóttir was born on 1 Feb. 1976 in Reykjavík. She graduated from the University of Iceland in 1999 in Icelandic and French, and received a master's degree in Icelandic literature from the same university in 2004. She comes from a family that includes several prominent figures in Icelandic political, academic and literary circles.

From 1999 to 2007 she had various jobs in the print and broadcast media (including at the public broadcaster RUV) as well as teaching and lecturing. In 2003 she became deputy chair of the Left-Greens and from Feb. 2009 to May 2013 served as minister of education, science and culture, and of Nordic co-operation.

Jakobsdóttir participated in several delegations, including in 2017 to the Council of Europe Parliamentary Assembly, and from 2014–16 she served as deputy chair of the European Union–Iceland joint Parliamentary Committee. Following indecisive elections in Oct. 2017 President Guðni Jóhannesson tasked Jakobsdóttir with forming a government, and she subsequently negotiated a coalition with the Independence Party and the Progressive Party.

Career in Office
Jakobsdóttir faced two initial challenges. The first was political instability resulting from low public trust in politics following a series of scandals, among them revelations from the *Panama Papers* (exposing the secret wealth of prominent figures in offshore tax havens). The second was her thin coalition majority, representing 33 seats in Iceland's 63-member parliament (*Alþingi*). Also, the coalition agreement with the Independence Party included keeping former prime minister and party leader Benediktsson as finance minister, which prompted criticism among some Left-Green members. Jakobsdóttir has pledged to invest in public services (notably health care, education and transport) to sustain Iceland's economic recovery and to support gender equality and gay rights.

Defence

Iceland possesses no armed forces. Under the North Atlantic Treaty, US forces were stationed for many years in Iceland as the Iceland Defence Force. In Sept. 2006 an agreement was signed between USA and Iceland, withdrawing all US forces from the island.

Navy

There is a paramilitary coastguard of 120.

Economy

Agriculture accounted for 7·8% of GDP in 2012, industry 23·6% and services 68·6%.

According to the anti-corruption organization Transparency International, Iceland ranked equal 13th in a 2017 survey of countries with the least corruption in business and government. It received 77 out of 100 in the annual index.

Overview

The economy experienced rapid growth in the mid-1990s as a result of privatization and deregulation, and per capita income doubled in the two decades to 2007. GDP expanded by more than 20% between 2003 and 2008. However, this vigorous expansion left the economy with large macroeconomic imbalances and high dependency on foreign financing. With financial sector assets amounting to over 1,000% of GDP and gross external indebtedness equivalent to roughly 550% of GDP by the end of 2007, the global credit squeeze hit the domestic financial markets hard. In Oct. 2008 all three of the country's major banks were nationalized to stabilize the financial system. The following month the IMF approved a US$2·1bn. loan, supplemented by US$3bn. in loans from Iceland's neighbours, to support the króna. The key interest rate reached a record high of 18%. In Jan. 2009 the government collapsed following political turmoil prompted by the crisis.

A rebound in consumption and investment saw growth resume in 2011 and GDP expanded by an annual average of 3·5% between 2012 and 2016. In 2017 the rate was 4·0%, driven by unprecedented growth in tourism (by 24·4% that year), strong consumption, falling unemployment, rising real wages and inflation stabilization. Unemployment fell to 2·8% in 2017 from 3% in 2016. However, the fiscal balance narrowed from a surplus of 12·4% of GDP in 2016 to 1·7% in 2017. Meanwhile, Iceland had paid back the loan granted by the IMF ahead of schedule (in Oct. 2015) and financial regulation was also strengthened.

The external debt-to-GDP ratio had fallen from its peak of 960% during the 2009 financial crisis to 95% in 2017 and the Central Bank decided in March to lift most of the restrictions on foreign exchange transactions and the cross-border movement of domestic and foreign currency that had been in place for nearly nine years. Nonetheless, given its small size, the economy remains subject to high volatility.

Currency

The unit of currency is the *króna* (ISK) of 100 *aurar* (singular: *eyrir*). Foreign exchange markets were deregulated on 1 Jan. 1992. The króna was devalued 7·5% in June 1993. There was inflation of 1·7% in 2016 and 1·8% in 2017. Foreign exchange reserves were US$3,263m. and gold reserves 64,000 troy oz in Sept. 2009. Total money supply in April 2008 was 420,423m. kr. Note and coin circulation in 2009 was 28,958m. kr.

Budget

Budgetary central government revenue and expenditure (in 1bn. kroner):

	2012	2013	2014
Revenue	544	588	686
Expenditure	614	616	662

Principal sources of revenue in 2014 were: taxes on goods and services, 232bn. kr.; taxes on income, profits and capital gains, 204bn. kr.; social contributions, 73bn. kr. Main items of expenditure by economic type in 2014: grants, 200bn. kr.; compensation of employees, 135bn. kr.; use of goods and services, 104bn. kr.

The standard rate of VAT was lowered from 25·5% to 24% as of 1 Jan. 2015. There is a reduced rate of 11%.

Performance

Real GDP growth was 4·5% in 2015, 7·4% in 2016 and 4·0% in 2017. In 2012 GDP per capita was US$44,389. Total GDP was US$23·9bn. in 2017.

Banking and Finance

The Central Bank of Iceland (founded 1961; *Governor*, Már Guðmundsson) is responsible for note issue and carries out the central banking functions. There were five commercial banks and 12 savings banks operating in 2010. On 31 Dec. 2009 the accounts of the Central Bank balanced at 1,178,082m. kr. Gross external debt amounted to US$106,359m. in June 2012.

There is a stock exchange in Reykjavík.

Energy and Natural Resources

Iceland is aiming to become the world's first 'hydrogen economy' by 2050; its buses started to convert to fuel cell-powered vehicles in late 2003. Ultimately it aims to run all its transport and even its fishing fleet on hydrogen produced in Iceland.

Environment

Iceland's carbon dioxide emissions from the consumption of energy in 2011 were the equivalent of 11·5 tonnes per capita. An *Environmental Performance Index* compiled in 2016 ranked Iceland second in the world behind Finland, with 90·5%. The index examined various factors in nine areas—agriculture, air quality, biodiversity and habitat, climate and energy, fisheries, forests, health impacts, water and sanitation, and water resources.

Electricity

The installed capacity of public electrical power plants in 2011 totalled 2,669,000 kW; installed capacity of hydro-electric plants was 1,884,000 kW. Electricity production totalled 17,211m. kWh in 2011. Virtually all of Iceland's electricity is produced from hydro-power and geothermal energy. Consumption per capita in 2011 was 53,442 kWh (the highest in the world).

Agriculture

Of the total area, around 86% is unproductive, but only about 1·3% is under cultivation, which is largely confined to hay and potatoes. In 2009 the total hay crop was 2,105,238 cu. metres; the crop of potatoes, 9,500 tonnes; of tomatoes, 1,481 tonnes; and of cucumbers, 1,452 tonnes. Livestock (2009): sheep, 469,429; horses, 77,158; cattle, 73,498 (dairy cows, 26,489); pigs, 3,818; poultry, 61,095. Livestock products (2009): lamb and mutton, 8,841 tonnes; poultry, 7,146 tonnes; pork, 6,375 tonnes; beef, 3,761 tonnes. Consumption of dairy products (2013): milk, 122,914 tonnes; cheese, 5,706 tonnes; butter and dairy margarines, 2,045 tonnes.

Forestry

In 2015 forests covered 49,000 ha. (equivalent to less than 0·5% of the total land area). Of the total area under forests 22% was naturally regenerated forest in 2015 and 78% planted forest.

Fisheries

Fishing is of vital importance to the economy. Fishing vessels in 2009 numbered 1,582 with a gross tonnage of 158,253. Total catch (in tonnes) in 2012: 1,453,911; 2013: 1,366,802, 2014: 1,081,842; 2015: 1,317,145. Virtually all the fish caught is from marine waters. Iceland has received international praise for its management system, which aims to avoid the overfishing that has decimated stocks in other parts of the world. Commercial whaling was prohibited in 1989, but recommenced in 2006. In 2009 fisheries accounted for 6·3% of GDP, down from 16·8% in 1996. The per capita consumption of fish and fishery products is the second highest in the world, after that of the Maldives.

Industry

Production, 2009, in 1,000 tonnes: aluminium, 813·9; ferro-silicon, 135·8. 132,438 tonnes of cement were sold in 2007.

Labour

In 2014 the labour force was 199,000 (173,000 in 2004). 82·1% of the population aged 15–64 was economically active in 2014. The female labour force participation rate is the highest of any industrialized country, at 84·2% in 2014. Agriculture and fishing employed 4·7% of the economically active population in 2014, industry 18·3% and services 77·0%. Iceland has a very high employment rate among older workers, with 55·3% of the population aged 65–69 in 2014 still working. The unemployment rate in Dec. 2018 was 2·6% (down slightly from 2·8% in 2017 as a whole and 3·0% in 2016).

International Trade

The economy is heavily trade-dependent.

Imports and Exports

Total value of imports (c.i.f.) and exports (f.o.b.) in 1m. kr.:

	2005	2006	2007	2008	2009
Imports	313,855	432,106	429,469	514,739	446,128
Exports	194,355	242,740	305,096	466,860	500,855

Main imports, 2009 (in 1m. kr.): industrial supplies, 140,178 (of which primary, 6,335; processed, 133,844); capital goods (except for transport), 94,279; consumer goods, 68,936; fuels and lubricants, 54,464. Main exports, 2009 (in 1m. kr.): industrial supplies, 225,654; food and beverages, 198,490; transport equipment, 33,449 (of which aeroplanes, 22,583); capital goods (except for transport), 19,159.

Value of trade with principal countries for three years (in 1,000 kr.):

	2007		2008		2009	
	Imports (c.i.f.)	Exports (f.o.b.)	Imports (c.i.f.)	Exports (f.o.b.)	Imports (c.i.f.)	Exports (f.o.b.)
Belgium	6,725,400	4,997,700	6,809,500	7,214,100	6,871,900	9,208,600
Brazil	526,400	263,300	1,635,600	575,800	18,298,000	391,300
Canada	7,583,100	1,463,800	5,313,800	2,201,400	8,584,800	2,293,600
China	21,601,800	2,375,900	34,110,300	10,276,900	22,161,800	11,728,300
Denmark	31,660,900	10,080,300	37,695,700	14,642,500	32,453,600	13,512,300
France	12,201,000	7,827,300	12,157,300	14,287,300	8,635,700	17,575,100
Germany	51,582,500	40,815,000	52,819,200	52,777,400	36,847,100	56,403,200
Ireland	7,193,000	23,077,400	5,547,900	1,350,300	6,821,100	15,228,400
Italy	14,550,000	1,991,200	14,411,700	3,647,500	12,299,800	5,106,100
Japan	20,161,600	12,775,600	19,130,900	20,453,000	15,317,300	9,304,500
Netherlands	24,012,800	64,885,800	31,234,400	160,477,500	38,506,200	153,981,700
Nigeria	1,300	3,720,800	200	5,442,900	300	10,187,500
Norway	19,682,300	11,565,000	57,644,400	20,344,800	57,865,600	29,066,700
Poland	7,305,500	1,909,400	7,072,600	3,545,200	5,257,600	5,321,200
Portugal	1,012,200	7,560,000	1,154,700	8,791,700	1,088,800	8,804,700
Spain	5,694,200	14,158,800	6,020,800	17,861,000	5,455,900	24,130,500
Sweden	42,848,300	2,214,400	46,277,000	3,912,700	35,937,700	4,000,800
Switzerland	8,555,200	3,856,600	16,314,300	4,271,000	12,241,000	6,609,300
UK	22,875,100	40,333,800	22,467,500	54,189,000	20,298,400	63,970,400
USA	57,558,600	16,049,700	41,353,800	25,720,100	30,972,200	19,402,900

Communications

Roads

On 1 Jan. 2009 the length of the public roads (including roads in towns) was 12,888 km. Of these 7,829 km were main and secondary roads and 5,059 km were provincial roads. Total length of surfaced roads was 4,566 km. A ring road of 1,400 km runs just inland from much of the coast; about 80% of it is smooth-surfaced. Motor vehicles registered at the end of 2009 numbered 238,149, of which 207,226 were passenger cars (643 per 1,000 inhabitants) and 30,923 lorries and vans; there were also 9,420 motorcycles. There were 15 fatal road accidents in 2009 with 17 persons killed.

Civil Aviation

Icelandair is the national carrier, serving 27 destinations in Europe and 16 in North America. In 2011 it carried 1·7m. passengers. The second largest airline is the low-cost carrier WOW air. The main international airport is at Keflavík (Leifsstöd), with Reykjavík for flights to the Faroe Islands, Greenland and domestic services. Keflavík handled 2,112,014 passengers in 2011 (of which 412,440 transit passengers) and 36,628 tonnes of freight.

Shipping

In Jan. 2014 there were five ships of 300 GT or over registered, totalling 5,000 GT.

Telecommunications

The number of telephone main lines was 168,023 in 2013; mobile phone subscriptions, 356,264 (more than the population of Iceland and equivalent to 1,081 subscriptions per 1,000 population). In 2013, 96·6% of the population (the highest percentage in the world) were internet users. In the same year there were 74·7 mobile broadband subscriptions per 100 inhabitants and 35·2 fixed broadband subscriptions per 100 inhabitants. In March 2012 there were 210,000 Facebook users.

Social Institutions

According to the 2017 *Fragile States Index*—a list published jointly by the Fund for Peace and *Foreign Policy* magazine—Iceland was ranked as the country eighth least vulnerable to conflict or collapse. The index is based on 12 indicators of state vulnerability across social, political and economic categories.

Justice

In 1992 jurisdiction in civil and criminal cases was transferred from the provincial magistrates to eight new district courts, separating the judiciary from the prosecution. From the district courts there is an appeal to the Supreme Court in Reykjavík, which has eight judges. The population in penal institutions in Sept. 2013 was 152 (47 per 100,000 of national population).

Education

Primary education is compulsory and free from 6–16 years of age. Optional secondary education from 16 to 19 is also free. In 2009 there were 42,929 pupils in primary schools, 26,364 in secondary schools (22,262 on day courses) and 17,738 tertiary-level students (13,888 on day courses). Some 10·6% of tertiary-level students study abroad.

There are seven universities and nine specialized institutions at tertiary level in Iceland. A total of 19,135 students were enrolled in universities in 2011. Universities (with total students, 2011): University of Iceland (founded 1911 and merged with Iceland University of Education in 2008), Reykjavík, 13,919; Reykjavík University, 2,468; University of Akureyri, 1,493; Bifröst University, 431; Iceland Academy of Arts, 414; Agricultural University of Iceland, 238; Hólar University College, 172.

In 2009 public sector spending on education was 7·8% of GDP.

The adult literacy rate is at least 99%.

Health

In 2012 there were 32 hospital beds per 10,000 population. There were 1,121 doctors and surgeons in 2011, plus 2,765 nurses, 357 pharmacists and 283 dentists. In the same year there were 3·5 doctors per 1,000 inhabitants. Iceland has one of the lowest alcohol consumption rates in Europe, at an average of 7·1 litres of alcohol per adult per year in the period 2008–10. Iceland spent 7·6% of its GDP on health in 2011.

Welfare

The main body of social welfare legislation is consolidated in six acts:
(i) The social security legislation *(a)* health insurance, including sickness benefits; *(b)* social security pensions, mainly consisting of old age pension, disablement pension and widows' pension, and also children's pension; *(c)* employment injuries insurance.
(ii) The unemployment insurance legislation, where daily allowances are paid to those who have met certain conditions.

(iii) The subsistence legislation

This is controlled by municipal government.

(iv) The tax legislation

Prior to 1988 children's support was included in the tax legislation. Since 1988 family allowances are paid directly to all children age 0–15 years. The amount is increased with the second child in the family, and children under the age of seven get additional benefits. Single parents receive additional allowances.

(v) The rehabilitation legislation

(vi) Child and juvenile guidance

Health insurance covers the entire population. Citizenship is not demanded and there is a six-month waiting period. Most hospitals are both municipally and state run, a few solely state run and all offer free medical help. Medical treatment out of hospitals is partly paid by the patient; the same applies to medicines, except medicines of lifelong necessary use, which are paid in full by the health insurance. Dental care is partly paid by the state for children under 17 years old and also for old age and disabled pensioners. Sickness benefits are paid to those who lose income because of periodical illness.

The pension system is composed of the public social security system and some 90 private pension funds. The social security system pays basic old age and disablement pensions of a fixed amount regardless of past or present income, as well as supplementary pensions to individuals with low present income. The pensions are index-linked, i.e. are changed in line with changes in wage and salary rates in the labour market. In the public social security system, entitlement to old age and disablement pensions at the full rates is subject to the condition that the beneficiary has been resident in Iceland for 40 years at the age period of 16–67. For shorter periods of residence, the benefits are reduced proportionally. Entitled to old age pension are all those who are 67 years old, and have been residents in Iceland for three years of the age period of 16–67. Old age and disablement pension are of equally high amount; in the year 2009 the total sum was 351,528 kr. for an individual. Married pensioners receive double the basic pension. Pensioners with little or no other income are entitled to an income supplement; in 2009 the maximum annual income supplement was 1,155,513 kr.

The employment injuries insurance covers medical care, daily allowances, disablement pension and survivors' pension and is applicable to practically all employees.

Religion

The national church, the Evangelical Lutheran, is endowed by the state. There is complete religious liberty. The affairs of the national church are under the superintendence of a bishop. In 2010, 251,487 persons (79·2% of the population) were members of it (93·2% in 1980). 16,497 persons (5·2%) belonged to Lutheran free churches. 39,310 persons (12·4%) belonged to other religious organizations and 10,336 persons (3·3%) did not belong to any religious community.

Culture

World Heritage Sites

There are two UNESCO sites in Iceland: Þingvellir National Park (2004), located on an active volcanic site; and Surtsey (2008), an island formed by volcanic eruptions in 1963–67.

Press

In 2008 there were four daily newspapers (two paid-for and two free) and 20 non-daily newspapers. Combined circulation was 336,459 (of which dailies accounted for 278,154 and non-dailies 58,305). Iceland has the highest circulation rates of daily newspapers in the world, at 817 per 1,000 adult inhabitants in 2008.

In 2008, 1,637 volumes of books and booklets were published.

Tourism

There were 1,289,139 visitors in 2015—more than double the number in 2011 and treble the number in 2006; revenue from foreign tourists amounted to 208,351m. kr. in 2015. Overnight stays in hotels and guest houses in 2015 numbered 4,108,890 (of which foreign travellers, 3,613,046; Icelanders, 495,844). Tourism accounted for 31·0% of foreign exchange earnings in 2015.

Festivals

Iceland's national day is celebrated on 17 June. The Reykjavík Arts Festival, an annual programme of international artists and performers, is held every May–June. Iceland Airwaves, an annual music festival in Reykjavík, takes place in Oct. There is also a folk festival in March, a blues festival at Easter and a jazz festival in Aug.

Diplomatic Representatives

Of Iceland in the United Kingdom (2A Hans St., London, SW1X 0JE)
    Ambassador: Stefán Haukur Jóhannesson.

Of the United Kingdom in Iceland (Laufásvegur 31, 101 Reykjavík)
    Ambassador: Michael Nevin.

Of Iceland in the USA (2900 K St., NW, Suite 509, Washington, D.C., 20007)
    Ambassador: Geir Hilmar Haarde.

Of the USA in Iceland (Laufásvegur 21, IS-101 Reykjavík)
    Ambassador: Vacant.
    Chargé d'Affaires a.i.: Jill Esposito.

Of Iceland to the United Nations
    Ambassador: Bergdís Ellertsdóttir.

Of Iceland to the European Union
    Ambassador: Gunnar Pálsson.

Further Reading

Statistics Iceland, *Landshagir* (Statistical Yearbook of Iceland) (1991–2015).—*Iceland in Figures.*

Central Bank of Iceland. *Monetary Bulletin* (four a year).—*The Economy of Iceland.*

Bergmann, Eirikur, *Iceland and the International Financial Crisis.* 2014

Boyes, Roger, Meltdown *Iceland.* 2009

Byock, Jesse, *Viking Age Iceland.* 2001

Karlsson, G., *The History of Iceland.* 2000

Smiley, Jane, (ed.) *The Sagas of Icelanders: A Selection.* 2002

Thorhallsson, Baldur, (ed.) *Iceland and European Integration: On the Edge.* 2004

National library: Landsbókasafn Íslands—Háskólabókasafn, Arngrímsgata 3, 107 Reykjavík.

National Statistical Office: Statistics Iceland, Bogartúni 21a, IS-150 Reykjavík.

Website: http://www.hagstofa.is

Central Bank of Iceland: Kalkofnsvegi 1, 150 Reykjavik.

Website: http://www.sedlabanki.is

India

Bharat (Republic of India)

Capital: New Delhi
Population projection, 2020: 1,383·20m.
GNI per capita, 2017: (PPP$) 6, 353
HDI/world rank, 2017: 0.640/130
Internet domain extension: .in

Key Historical Events

The valley of the Indus and its tributaries is divided today between India and Pakistan. Some 7,000 years ago the valley was one of the cradles of civilization. From the Indus Valley, Dravidian peoples spread agriculture and fixed settlements across India, arriving in the far south by about 4,000 years ago. The Indus Valley Harappan civilization, a Bronze Age culture, flourished from around 2300 to 1500 BC and had links with western Asian civilizations in Iran. The two great cities of the Harappan civilization—Mohenjo-Daro and Harappa—were in what is now Pakistan, but Harappan culture also thrived in northwestern India. Writing, fine jewellery and textile production, town planning, metalworking and pottery were the hallmarks of an advanced urban society, which collapsed for reasons unknown.

Another Bronze Age civilization existed in the Ganges Valley. With links to southeastern Asia, a rice-growing rural economy supported a number of city-states. Around 1500 BC a pastoral people, the Aryans, invaded the Indus Valley from Iran and Central Asia. Their arrival completed the destruction of the Harappan civilization and shifted the balance of power in the subcontinent to the Ganges Valley.

The Aryans took over northern and central India, merging their culture with that of the Dravidians. The caste system, still a feature of Indian society, dates back to the Dravidians, but the languages of northern and central India, and the polytheistic religion that is now followed by the majority of the inhabitants of the subcontinent, are both Aryan in origin. From these two cultures, a Hindu civilization emerged.

By 800 BC a series of Hindu kingdoms had developed in the Ganges Valley. This region gave birth to one of the world's great religions: Buddhism. Prince Gautama, the Buddha (*c.* 563–483 BC), renounced a life of wealth to seek enlightenment. His creed of non-violence was spread throughout India and, later, southeastern Asia. However, Buddhism was partly instrumental in destroying Magdalha, the most powerful of ancient states of the Ganges Valley.

Magdalha was ruled by the Nanda dynasty in the 4th century BC. In 321 BC the Nandas were replaced by the Mauryans under Chandragupta Maurya (reigned 321–297 BC). Chandragupta conquered most of northern India before his ascetic death from self-imposed starvation. His grandson, Ashoka, ruled an empire that stretched from the Deccan to Afghanistan from *c.* 272–*c.* 231, but he is mainly remembered for his enthusiasm for Buddhist pacifism. Attacked by enemies who did not share this creed, the Mauryan empire collapsed soon after Ashoka's death.

To the west, the Indus Valley had passed to the Persian Empire by the 5th century BC and then fell to Alexander the Great. After Alexander's death in 323 BC, Greek influences continued to be felt in the northwest of the subcontinent where an Indo-Greek civilization flourished for at least 200 years. This was brought to an end by nomadic invasions from Central Asia between the 1st and 5th centuries AD. By then, India had been divided into many small warring states, most of them short-lived.

Empire Building

Two strong states emerged briefly to reunite much of India: the Gupta empire and the Harsa empire. The Gupta empire was founded in the Ganges Valley by Chandragupta I (reigned *c.* 320–30). His warrior son, Samudragupta (reigned *c.* 330–80), won most of north India, but the empire was destroyed by succession disputes and a Hun invasion in the middle of the 5th century. The Harsa empire was the personal creation of a Buddhist convert, Harsa (reigned 606–47), who briefly ruled most of the north of the subcontinent.

With his death, his empire fell apart and India was once more divided into many rival kingdoms.

Although no Hindu state managed to unite India, the Hindu religion and culture proved powerful influences throughout the region. The agents of Hinduism were not kings or soldiers but merchants. By about 500 BC Sri Lanka was within the Hindu sphere of influence. Over the next 800 years Hindu kingdoms were established in Cambodia, Java, Myanmar, Sumatra and Thailand. From the 4th century BC, Indian merchants also spread Buddhism through southeastern Asia. The great Hindu kingdoms flourished far beyond the subcontinent. The most splendid were the Khmer kingdom based on Angkor Wat in Cambodia and the maritime kingdom of Sriwijaya, based in Sumatra.

While Indian religion and culture spread south and east, an invasion from the west threatened to change the subcontinent. In 713 a Muslim army conquered Sind. For the next 300 years, Islamic rulers were largely confined to what is now Pakistan, but in 1000 a raid by the ruler of Ghazni (now in Afghanistan) overran the Punjab. During the 11th and 12th centuries the Hindu states of the Ganges Valley were toppled by Muslim invaders.

The principal Islamic state of India, following the Muslim conquest of northern India, was the sultanate of Delhi. This powerful state was founded by Qutb-ud-Din Aybak (reigned *c.* 1208–10), a former slave, who united the Indus and Ganges valleys and founded the Mu'izzi dynasty. Under the short-lived Khaljis dynasty, the sultanate became the leading power in India, largely owing to the military prowess of Sultan 'Ala-ud-Din Khalji (reigned 1296–1316). But by 1388, following the inept rule of the three sultans of the Tughluq dynasty, the sultanate had ceased to be important.

The Delhi sultanate was eventually replaced in the north by the Mughal Empire, which was founded by Babur (reigned 1526–30), a descendant of Timur and Genghis Khan. Akbar the Great (reigned 1556–1605) extended the Mughal Empire, conquering Baluchistan, Gujarat, Bengal, Orissa, Rajasthan, Afghanistan and Bihar. In his campaign against Gujarat, Akbar marched his army 800 km (500 miles) in only 11 days. His grandson, Shah Jahan (reigned 1628–58), a pleasure-seeking ruler, is remembered for constructing the Taj Mahal as a memorial to his favourite wife.

The decline of the Mughal Empire began under Shah Jahan's son, Aurangzeb I (reigned 1658–1707). Aurangzeb persecuted Hindus with a vengeance. Inter-community violence and wars against Hindu states weakened the empire. Throughout the 18th century, disputed successions and fears of assassination diverted the Mughal emperors. By the close of the 18th century the last emperor was nominal ruler of the environs of Delhi.

The main Hindu state of the subcontinent from the 14th century to the 17th century was the kingdom of Vijayanagar, which occupied most of southern India. Harihara I (reigned 1336–54), who had been governor of part of central India for the Mughal emperor, rebelled and established his own kingdom. Under Devaraya II (reigned 1425–47), Vijayanagar included virtually all of southern India and much of Sri Lanka. This kingdom reached its zenith under Krsnadevaraya (reigned 1509–29). He encouraged good relations with the Portuguese who had founded trading posts on his shores. Vijayanagar collapsed in civil wars (1614–46).

The Bahmani sultanate of the Deccan was an Islamic state, which dominated central India from the mid-14th century until the 16th century. This state was founded by 'Ala-ud-Din Hasan Bahmani Shah (reigned 1347–58), the local governor for the sultan of Delhi who rebelled against Delhi and established his own dynasty. For a time the Bahmani sultanate was the most powerful state in central India, but defeats at the hands of the kingdom of Vijayanagar in the 15th century weakened the Bahmani sultans. On the death of the last Bahmani sultan in 1518 the kingdom was divided by the provincial governors into small states.

European Influence

By the 16th century European traders were established along India's coasts. The first to arrive were the Portuguese in 1498. In 1510 the Portuguese took Goa, which was to remain the centre of the fragmented possessions of Portuguese India until 1962. The creation of the (English) East India Company in 1600 heralded the beginning of what was to become the British

Palgrave Macmillan (ed.), *The Statesman's Yearbook 2020*,
https://doi.org/10.1057/978-1-349-95940-2_91

Indian Empire. Forts were established on the coast in 1619 and in 1661 England took possession of Bombay.

Initially, the Europeans were only interested in trade but they soon became involved in local politics, in particular, the disputed successions that bedevilled Indian states. Portugal and England were not alone in attempting to establish outposts in India. The Dutch were active in the 17th century but were effectively eliminated from the competition before 1759, when Britain took Chinsura, the headquarters of Dutch administration in India. Two small Danish colonies lasted from 1618 until 1858. However, the main threat to British rule in India was France. Although the East India Company controlled parts of Bengal and the Ganges Valley, France was supreme in the Deccan where French forces, and Indian rulers allied to France, held sway over an area twice the size of France itself.

In the 1750s Britain and France fought out their European wars overseas. The defeat of French forces, and France's Indian allies, at the battle of Plassey (1757), by British forces led by Robert Clive (1725–74), confirmed British rule in Bengal and Bihar and ejected France from the Deccan. Henceforth, France was restricted to five small coastal possessions.

The Maratha state was the major power in central and southern India in the 17th and 18th centuries. This empire was founded by Sivaji (1627–80), who built the state between 1653 and 1660. The Hindu Sivaji came into conflict with the fanatical Muslim Mughal emperor Aurangzeb, who imprisoned Sivaji. After his famous escape from captivity, concealed in a fruit basket, Sivaji made himself emperor of his Maratha state in 1674. This pious monarch ruled competently, establishing an efficient administration, but by the time of his grandson, Shahu (reigned 1707–27), the power of the Maratha emperors had been eclipsed by that of their hereditary chief minister, the Peshwa. In 1727 the Peshwa Baji Rao I (reigned 1720–40) effectively replaced the emperor and established his own dynasty. Baji Rao made the Maratha state the strongest in India. His descendant, Baji Rao II (reigned 1795–1817), raised a weakened state against the British and was crushed. He was the last important Indian monarch outside British influence.

East India Company
In the first half of the 19th century, wars against Sind (1843) and the Sikhs in Punjab (1849) extended the borders of British India. By the middle of the 19th century about 60% of the subcontinent was controlled by the East India Company. The remaining 40% was divided between about 620 Indian states, which were, in theory, still sovereign and ruled by their own maharajas, sultans, nawabs and other monarchs, each advised by a British resident. The Indian states ranged from large entities the size of European countries (such as Hyderabad, Baroda, Mysore and Indore) to tiny states no bigger than an English parish.

British rule brought land reform in the areas controlled by the East India Company. The traditional patterns of land holdings was broken up and private land ownership was introduced. This had the unintended result of concentrating ownership in the hands of a small number of powerful landlords. As a result, landless peasants and dispossessed princes united in their opposition to British rule. In 1857 a mutiny by soldiers of the East India Company quickly spread into full-scale rebellion. Throughout India those who resented the speed and nature of the changes brought about by British rule made one final attempt to eject the occupiers. The Indian Mutiny took 14 months to put down.

After the Mutiny the British government replaced the East India Company as the ruler of an Indian colonial empire (1858), and the modernization of India began apace. Emphasis was placed on building up an Indian infrastructure, particularly roads and railways. The participation of Indians within the civil administration, the construction of a vast national railway system and the imposition of the English language did much to forge a national identity overriding the divisions of local state and caste. But in deference to British manufacturers industry in India remained backward. In 1877 the Indian Empire was proclaimed and Queen Victoria became Empress of India (Kaiser-i-Hind).

Growing Nationalism
The (Hindu-dominated) Indian National Congress (often referred to simply as Congress) first met in 1885, and in 1906 the rival Muslim League was founded. Demands for Home Rule grew in the early years of the 20th century, and nationalist feeling was fuelled when British troops fired on a nationalist protest meeting—the Amritsar Massacre (1919).

Realizing that change was inevitable, the British government reformed the administration in 1919 and 1935. The creation of an Indian federation removed many of the differences between the Crown territories and the Indian states and granted an Indian government limited autonomy. The pace of reform was, however, too slow for popular opinion.

In 1920 Congress began a campaign of non-violence and non-cooperation with the British colonial authorities, led in its struggle by the charismatic figure of Mahatma Gandhi (1869–1948). The British authorities were forced to concede Gandhi's moral influence but he himself was opposed by the traditional rulers of the Indian states, whose own positions were at risk.

By the start of the Second World War (1939–45), relations between the Hindu and Muslim communities in India had broken down, with the Muslims demanding a separate independent Islamic state, later, Pakistan. During the war, Assam and other northeastern areas were faced with the threat of a Japanese invasion. Although many Indians served in the Allied forces during the war, a minority supported Japan as a possible liberator.

In 1945 Britain had neither the will nor the resources to maintain the Indian Empire. But while Britain accepted independence, religious tension made partition inevitable. In 1947 the sub-continent was divided between India, a predominantly Hindu state led by Jawaharlal (Pandit) Nehru (1889–1964) of Congress, and Pakistan, a Muslim state led by Mohammad Ali Jinnah (1876–1948) of the Muslim League. The rulers of the Indian states were entitled to choose their allegiance while British Crown territories were assigned to either India or Pakistan.

Partitions
Partition brought enormous upheaval. More than 70m. Hindus and Muslims became refugees as they trekked across the new boundaries. Many thousands were killed in intercommunal violence. The Muslim ruler of the large, mainly Hindu, southern Indian state of Hyderabad, declared independence and the adherence of his state to India was only achieved through Indian military intervention. The Hindu ruler of mainly Muslim Kashmir opted to join India, against the wishes of his people. Elsewhere the border remained disputed in many places. Tension increased when Gandhi was assassinated by a Hindu fundamentalist (1948). In 1950 India became a republic.

Tension between India and Pakistan erupted into war in 1947–49 when the two countries fought over Kashmir. The region was divided along a ceasefire line, although neither side recognized this as an international border. India and Pakistan went to war again over Kashmir in 1965 and again in 1971 when Bangladesh (formerly East Pakistan) gained its independence as a result of Indian military intervention. Indian forces saw action in 1961 when Indian troops invaded and annexed Portuguese India and in 1962 in a border war with China. France had already ceded its small enclaves to India in 1950 and 1955. In 1975 India annexed the small Himalayan kingdom of Sikkim.

Despite its involvement in several wars, India assumed joint leadership of the non-aligned world. Pandit Nehru, premier from 1947 to 1964, was briefly succeeded by Lal Bahadur Shastri. In 1966 Nehru's daughter Indira Gandhi (1917–84) became premier. Under her leadership, India continued to assert itself as a regional power and the rival of Pakistan. Although non-aligned, India developed close relations with the Soviet Union.

In 1971 Gandhi's government abolished the titles, pensions and privileges guaranteed to the Indian princes at independence as compensation for merging their states into India. India was wracked by local separatism and communal unrest. From 1975 to 1977 Gandhi imposed a state of emergency. Her actions split Congress, allowing Morarji Desai (1896–1995) of the Janata Party to form India's first non-Congress administration. However, his coalition soon shattered and a wing of Congress, led by Gandhi, was returned to power in 1980.

Violence in Sikh areas, fanned by demands by militant Sikhs for an independent homeland (called Khalistan) increased tensions. In 1984 Gandhi ordered that the Golden Temple in Amritsar be stormed after it had been turned into a storehouse for weapons by Sikh extremists. Soon afterwards, she was assassinated by her Sikh bodyguards.

Indira Gandhi was succeeded as premier by her son, Rajiv (1944–91), during whose period of office India became involved in Sri Lanka, supporting the central government against the separatist Tamil Tigers movement. Rajiv Gandhi was assassinated by a Tamil Tiger suicide bomber during the 1991 election campaign.

Recent Politics

By 1989 personality clashes and separatist tendencies had shattered the unity of the once all-powerful Congress. Regional parties and Hindu nationalist parties came to the fore and, since 1989, when Rajiv Gandhi left office, coalitions have held office. Seven prime ministers have led India since 1989: the longest periods have been enjoyed by Manmohan Singh (premier from 2004–14), Atal Bihari Vajpayee (premier in 1996 and again from 1998–2004) and P. V. Narasimha Rao (who led a coalition from 1991 to 1996). The right-wing Hindu nationalist Bharatiya Janata Party (BJP) has joined most of these coalitions. Support for the BJP increased following violence between Hindus and Muslims over a campaign, begun in 1990, to build a Hindu temple on the site of a mosque in the holy city of Ayodhya.

Since the fall of the Soviet Union (1991), India has retreated from state ownership and protectionism. Privatization has been accompanied by an economic revolution that has seen the development of high tech industries. At the same time, India has become a nuclear power. Although India exploded its first nuclear device in 1974, tests in 1998 confirmed the nation's capability to deliver these weapons.

There have been more than 40,000 deaths related to the Kashmir insurgency since its outbreak in 1988. Negotiations with Pakistan over the future of the disputed territory began in July 1999. Hopes of avoiding further violence were set back in Dec. 2001, in an attack on the Indian parliament by suicide bombers. 13 people died. Although no group claimed responsibility, Kashmiri separatists were blamed. However, Pakistani President Pervez Musharraf's subsequent crackdown on militants helped to bring the two countries back from the brink of war. Tension between India and Pakistan increased following an attack on an Indian army base in Indian-occupied Kashmir on 14 May 2002. The attack, which killed 31 people, was linked to Islamic terrorists infiltrating the Kashmir valley from Pakistan. It drew widespread criticism of President Musharraf for failing to combat terrorism in the disputed region. In Feb. 2002, 58 Hindu pilgrims returning from Ayodhya were killed when their train was set on fire following a confrontation with a Muslim crowd at Godhra in Gujarat. The incident led to three months of intermittent communal rioting, during which at least 800 Muslims died in attacks by Hindus. In Sept. 2010 the Allahabad High Court ruled that the holy site should be divided between Hindus and Muslims.

Relations between India and Pakistan cooled again in Aug. 2003 when 50 people were killed by terrorist bombings in Mumbai (Bombay). The two countries then embarked on a new phase of peace negotiations. In May 2004 India elected Manmohan Singh as its first Sikh prime minister. The peace process was set back when unidentified terrorists killed over 200 people and injured 700 more in a series of co-ordinated train bombings in Mumbai on 11 July 2006. In July 2007 Pratibha Patil became the country's first female president. In Dec. 2008 peace talks were temporarily suspended, a month after nearly 200 people died when gunmen launched a series of attacks on buildings in Mumbai's tourism and financial district. India claimed that Pakistani-based militants were responsible. The only surviving gunman from the attacks was executed in Nov. 2012.

In Sept. 2013 the gang rape and murder of a female student in Delhi prompted protests across the country. At the general election in May 2014 the BJP regained power from Congress, with Narendra Modi as prime minister.

Territory and Population

India is bounded in the northwest by Pakistan, north by China (Tibet), Nepal and Bhutan, east by Myanmar, and southeast, south and southwest by the Indian Ocean. The far eastern states and territories are almost separated from the rest by Bangladesh. The area is 3,287,263 sq. km (land area, 2,973,190 sq. km; water area, 314,073 sq. km). A Sino-Indian agreement of 7 Sept. 1993 settled frontier disputes dating from the war of 1962. Population, 2011 census: 1,210,854,977. 51·5% of the population was male and 48·5% female. Density, 407·3 persons per sq. km. There are also 20m. Indians and ethnic Indians living abroad, notably in Malaysia, the USA, Saudi Arabia, the UK and South Africa. 68·8% of the population was rural in 2011. Goa is the most urban state, at 62·2% in 2011; and Himachal Pradesh the most rural, at 90·0% in 2011.

The UN gives a projected population for 2020 of 1,383·20m.

By 2050 India is expected to have a population of 1·66bn. It is projected to overtake China as the world's most populous country around 2024.

Area and population of states and union territories (2011 census):

States	Area in sq. km	Population	Density per sq. km
Andhra Pradesh (AP)	275,045	84,580,777	308
Arunachal Pradesh (AC)	83,743	1,383,727	17
Assam (AS)	78,438	31,205,576	398
Bihar (BI)	94,163	104,099,452	1,106
Chhattisgarh (CG)	135,191	25,545,198	189
Goa (GO)	3,702	1,458,545	394
Gujarat (GU)	196,024	60,439,692	308
Haryana (HA)	44,212	25,351,462	573
Himachal Pradesh (HP)	55,673	6,864,602	123
Jammu and Kashmir (JK)	222,236	12,541,302	56
Jharkhand (JH)	79,714	32,988,134	414
Karnataka (KA)	191,791	61,095,297	319
Kerala (KE)	38,863	33,406,061	860
Madhya Pradesh (MP)	308,245	72,626,809	236
Maharashtra (MH)	307,713	112,374,333	365
Manipur (MN)	22,327	2,855,794	128
Meghalaya (ME)	22,429	2,966,889	132
Mizoram (MZ)	21,081	1,097,206	52
Nagaland (NA)	16,579	1,978,502	119
Odisha (formerly Orissa) (OD)	155,707	41,974,218	270
Punjab (PB)	50,362	27,743,338	551
Rajasthan (RJ)	342,239	68,548,437	200
Sikkim (SI)	7,096	610,577	86
Tamil Nadu (TN)	130,058	72,147,030	555
Tripura (TR)	10,486	3,673,917	350
Uttar Pradesh (UP)	240,928	199,812,341	829
Uttarakhand (formerly Uttaranchal) (UK)	53,483	10,086,292	189
West Bengal (WB)	88,752	91,276,115	1,028
Union Territories			
Andaman and Nicobar Islands (AN)	8,249	380,581	46
Chandigarh (CH)	114	1,055,450	9,258
Dadra and Nagar Haveli (DN)	491	343,709	700
Daman and Diu (DD)	112	243,247	2,172
Delhi (DL)	1,483	16,787,941	11,320
Lakshadweep (LK)	32	64,473	2,015
Puducherry (formerly Pondicherry) (PY)	479	1,247,953	2,605

On 2 June 2014 India's 29th state, Telangana, came into existence. It was previously one of three regions of Andhra Pradesh.

Urban agglomerations with populations over 2m., together with their core cities at the 2011 census:

	State/Union Territory	Urban agglomeration	Core city
Mumbai (Bombay)	Maharashtra	18,394,912	12,442,373
Delhi	Delhi	16,349,831	11,034,555
Kolkata (Calcutta)	West Bengal	14,035,959	4,496,694
Chennai (Madras)	Tamil Nadu	8,653,521	4,646,732

(continued)

	State/Union Territory	Urban agglomeration	Core city
Bengaluru (Bangalore)	Karnataka	8,520,435	8,443,675
Hyderabad[1]	Andhra Pradesh	7,674,689	6,731,790
Ahmedabad	Gujarat	6,361,084	5,577,940
Pune (Poona)	Maharashtra	5,057,709	3,124,458
Surat	Gujarat	4,591,246	4,467,797
Jaipur	Rajasthan	3,046,163	3,046,163
Kanpur	Uttar Pradesh	2,920,496	2,765,348
Lucknow	Uttar Pradesh	2,902,920	2,817,105
Nagpur	Maharashtra	2,497,870	2,405,665
Ghaziabad	Uttar Pradesh	2,375,820	1,648,643
Indore	Madhya Pradesh	2,170,295	1,964,086
Coimbatore	Tamil Nadu	2,136,916	1,050,721
Kochi	Kerala	2,119,724	602,046
Patna	Bihar	2,049,156	1,684,222
Kozhikode	Kerala	2,028,399	431,560

[1]Now located in Telangana, which was created in 2014.

Smaller urban agglomerations and cities with populations over 250,000 (with 2011 census populations, in 1,000):

Agartala (TR)	400
Agra (UP)	1,760
Ahmadnagar (MH)	380
Aizawl (MZ)	293
Ajmer (RJ)	551
Akola (MH)	426
Aligarh (UP)	911
Allahabad (UP)	1,212
Alwar (RJ)	341
Amravati (MH)	647
Amritsar (PB)	1,184
Anand (GU)	288
Anantapur (AP)	341
Arrah (BI)	261
Asansol (WB)	1,243
Aurangabad (MH)	1,193
Baharampur (WB)	304
Barddhaman (WB)	347
Bareilly (UP)	986
Bathinda (PB)	286
Begusarai (BI)	252
Belgaum (KA)	610
Bellary (KA)	410
Bhagalpur (BI)	412
Bharatpur (RJ)	253
Bhavnagar (GU)	606
Bhilai (CG)	1,064
Bhilwara (RJ)	359
Bhiwandi (MH)	736
Bhopal (MP)	1,886
Bhubaneswar (OD)	885
Bihar Sharif (BI)	297
Bijapur (KA)	327
Bikaner (RJ)	644
Bilaspur (CG)	454
Bokaro Steel City (JH)	564

(continued)

Brahmapur (OR)	357
Chandigarh (CH)	1,026
Chandrapur (MH)	320
Cherthala (KE)	456
Cuttack (OD)	663
Darbhanga (BI)	308
Davangere (KA)	435
Dehra Dun (UK)	706
Dewas (MP)	290
Dhanbad (JH)	1,196
Dhule (MH)	376
Dindigul (TN)	293
Durgapur (WB)	581
Eluru (AP)	251
Erode (TN)	522
Etawah (UP)	257
Faizabad (UP)	257
Faridabad Complex (HA)	1,414
Farrukhabad (UP)	291
Firozabad (UP)	604
Ganganagar (RJ)	250
Gaya (BI)	476
Gorakhpur (UP)	695
Gulbarga (KA)	543
Guntur (AP)	670
Gurgaon (HA)	902
Guwahati (AS)	962
Gwalior (MP)	1,118
Habra (WB)	300
Hapur (UP)	263
Hardwar (UK)	311
Hisar (HA)	307
Hubli-Dharwad (KA)	944
Ichalkaranji (MH)	325
Imphal (MN)	419
Ingraj Bazar (WB)	314
Jabalpur (MP)	1,269
Jalandhar (PB)	874
Jalgaon (MH)	460
Jalna (MH)	286
Jammu (JK)	657
Jamnagar (GU)	601
Jamshedpur (JH)	1,339
Jhansi (UP)	548
Jodhpur (RJ)	1,138
Junagadh (GU)	319
Kadapa (AP)	345
Kakinada (AP)	443
Kannur (KE)	1,641
Karimnagar (AP)[1]	297
Karnal (HA)	302
Kayamkulam (KE)	428
Khammam (AP)[1]	262
Kharagpur (WB)	300
Kolhapur (MH)	562
Kollam (KE)	1,111
Korba (CG)	365
Kota (RJ)	1,002

(continued)

Kottayam (KE)	357
Kurnool (AP)	484
Latur (MH)	383
Ludhiana (PB)	1,619
Madurai (TN)	1,466
Malappuram (KE)	1,699
Malegaon (MH)	577
Mangalore (KA)	624
Mathura (UP)	457
Maunath Bhanjan (UP)	279
Meerut (UP)	1,421
Moradabad (UP)	888
Morbi (GU)	252
Muzaffarnagar (UP)	496
Muzaffarpur (BI)	397
Mysore (KA)	991
Nanded (MH)	550
Nashik (MH)	1,562
Navsari (GU)	283
Nellore (AP)	559
Nizamabad (AP)[1]	311
Noida (UP)	637
Palakkad (KE)	294
Panipat (HA)	445
Parbhani (MH)	307
Patiala (PB)	446
Puducherry (PY)	657
Purnea (BI)	313
Raipur (CG)	1,124
Rajahmundry (AP)	477
Rajkot (GU)	1,391
Ramagundam (AP)[1]	252
Rampur (UP)	349
Ranchi (JH)	1,120
Ranippettai (TN)	264
Ratlam (MP)	274
Rohtak (HA)	374
Rourkela (OD)	552
Sagar (MP)	370
Saharanpur (UP)	705
Salem (TN)	917
Sambalpur (OD)	266
Sangli-Miraj (MH)	514
Santipur (WB)	290
Satna (MP)	283
Shahjahanpur (UP)	348
Shiliguri (WB)	706
Shillong (ME)	355
Shimoga (KA)	323
Sholapur (MH)	952
Sonipat (HA)	293
Srinagar (JK)	1,264
Surendranagar (GU)	254
Thanjavur (TN)	291
Thiruvananthapuram (KE)	1,680
Thrissur (KE)	1,861
Tiruchirapalli (TN)	1,023
Tirunelveli (TN)	498

Tirupati (AP)	462
Tiruppur (TN)	963
Tumkur (KA)	302
Tuticorin (TN)	412
Udaipur (RJ)	475
Ujjain (MP)	515
Vadodara (GU)	1,822
Varanasi (UP)	1,432
Vasai-Virar (MH)	1,222
Vellore (TN)	485
Vijayawada (AP)	1,477
Visakhapatnam (AP)	1,728
Warangal (AP)[1]	753
Yamunanagar (HA)	383

[1]Part of Telangana since June 2014.

(continued)

Social Statistics

Many births and deaths go unregistered. The Registrar General's data suggests a birth rate for 2009 of 22·5 per 1,000 population and a death rate of 7·3, which would indicate in a year approximately 27·2m. births and 8·8m. deaths. The growth rate is, however, slowing, and by 2010 had dropped to 1·4%, having been over 2% in 1991. Expectation of life at birth, 2013, 64·7 years for males and 68·3 years for females. In 2010, 50% of the population was aged under 25.

Many marriages and divorces go unregistered. A marriage can be registered under either of the two Marriage Acts: the Hindu Marriage Act 1955; or the Special Marriage Act 1954. To be eligible for marriage the minimum age limit is 21 for males and 18 for females. However, a survey carried out in 2005–06 found that 44·5% of women aged 20–24 had been married before the legal age of 18 (which has applied since 1978). Population growth rate, 2001–11, 17·64% (the lowest since 1941–51). Infant mortality, 2009, 50 per 1,000 live births; fertility rate, 2013, 2·5 births per woman. India was ranked 108th in a gender gap index of 145 countries compiled by the World Economic Forum for its *Global Gender Gap Report 2015*. The annual index considers economic, political, education and health criteria. Child deaths (under the age of five) fell from 123 per 1,000 in 1990 to 64 per 1,000 in 2009.

Climate

India has a variety of climatic sub-divisions. In general, there are four seasons. The cool one lasts from Dec. to March, the hot season is in April and May, the rainy season is June to Sept., followed by a further dry season until Nov. Rainfall, however, varies considerably, from 4" (100 mm) in the N.W. desert to over 400" (10,000 mm) in parts of Assam.

Range of temperature and rainfall: New Delhi, Jan. 57°F (13·9°C), July 88°F (31·1°C). Annual rainfall 26" (640 mm). Chennai, Jan. 76°F (24·4°C), July 87°F (30·6°C). Annual rainfall 51" (1,270 mm). Cherrapunji, Jan. 53°F (11·7°C), July 68°F (20°C). Annual rainfall 432" (10,798 mm). Darjeeling, Jan. 41°F (5°C), July 62°F (16·7°C). Annual rainfall 121" (3,035 mm). Hyderabad, Jan. 72°F (22·2°C), July 80°F (26·7°C). Annual rainfall 30" (752 mm). Kochi, Jan. 80°F (26·7°C), July 79°F (26·1°C). Annual rainfall 117" (2,929 mm). Kolkata, Jan. 67°F (19·4°C), July 84°F (28·9°C). Annual rainfall 64" (1,600 mm). Mumbai, Jan. 75°F (23·9°C), July 81°F (27·2°C). Annual rainfall 72" (1,809 mm). Patna, Jan. 63°F (17·2°C), July 90°F (32·2°C). Annual rainfall 46" (1,150 mm).

On 26 Dec. 2004 an undersea earthquake centred off the Indonesian island of Sumatra caused a huge tsunami that flooded coastal areas in southern India resulting in 16,000 deaths. In total there were more than 225,000 deaths in 14 countries.

Constitution and Government

The Constitution was passed by the Constituent Assembly on 26 Nov. 1949 and came into force on 26 Jan. 1950. It has since been amended 101 times.

India is a republic and comprises a Union of 29 States and seven Union Territories. Each State is administered by a Governor appointed by the President for a term of five years while each Union Territory is administered by the President through a Lieut.-Governor or an administrator appointed by him. The head of the Union (head of state) is the *President* in whom all executive power is vested, to be exercised on the advice of ministers responsible to Parliament. The President, who must be an Indian citizen at least 35 years old and eligible for election to the House of the People, is elected by an electoral college of all the elected members of Parliament and of the state legislative assemblies, holds office for five years and is eligible for re-election. There is also a *Vice-President* who is *ex officio* chairman of the Council of States.

There is a *Council of Ministers* to aid and advise the President; this comprises Ministers who are members of the Cabinet and Ministers of State and deputy ministers who are not. A Minister who for any period of six consecutive months is not a member of either House of Parliament ceases to be a Minister at the expiration of that period. The *Prime Minister* is appointed by the President; other Ministers are appointed by the President on the Prime Minister's advice.

Parliament consists of the President, the *Council of States (Rajya Sabha)* and the *House of the People (Lok Sabha)*. The Council of States, or the Upper House, normally consists of 245 members; in Feb. 2019 there were 225 elected members, 12 members nominated by the President and eight vacancies. The election to this house is indirect; the representatives of each State are elected by the elected members of the Legislative Assembly of that State. The Council of States is a permanent body not liable to dissolution, but one-third of the members retire every second year. The House of the People, or the Lower House, normally consists of 545 members—543 directly elected on the basis of adult suffrage from territorial constituencies in the States and the Union territories, and two nominated members of the Anglo-Indian Community. In March 2010 the Council of States approved a bill that would reserve a third of seats in the House of the People (and in each state legislature) for women. The bill is yet to go before the lower house, where it requires two-thirds support to become law. In March 2015 in the House of the People there were 543 elected members but no nominated members. Unless sooner dissolved it continues for a period of five years from the date appointed for its first meeting; in emergency, Parliament can extend the term by one year.

State Legislatures

For every State there is a legislature which consists of the Governor, and (a) two Houses, a Legislative Assembly and a Legislative Council, in the States of Andhra Pradesh, Bihar, Jammu and Kashmir, Karnataka, Madhya Pradesh (where it is provided for but not in operation), Maharashtra, Telangana and Uttar Pradesh, and (b) one House, a Legislative Assembly, in the other States. Every Legislative Assembly, unless sooner dissolved, continues for five years from the date appointed for its first meeting. In emergency the term can be extended by one year. Every State Legislative Council is a permanent body and is not subject to dissolution, but one-third of the members retire every second year. Parliament can, however, abolish an existing Legislative Council or create a new one, if the proposal is supported by a resolution of the Legislative Assembly concerned.

Fundamental Rights

Two chapters of the constitution deal with fundamental rights and 'Directive Principles of State Policy'. 'Untouchability' is abolished, and its practice in any form is punishable. The fundamental rights can be enforced through the ordinary courts of law and through the Supreme Court of the Union. The directive principles cannot be enforced through the courts of law; they are nevertheless fundamental in the governance of the country.

Citizenship

Under the Constitution, every person who was on the 26 Jan. 1950 domiciled in India and (a) was born in India or (b) either of whose parents was born in India or (c) who has been ordinarily resident in the territory of India for not less than five years immediately preceding that date became a citizen of India. Special provision is made for migrants from Pakistan and for Indians resident abroad. The right to vote is granted to every person who is a citizen of India and who is not less than 18 years of age on a fixed date and is not otherwise disqualified.

Parliament

Parliament and the state legislatures are organized according to the following schedule (figures show distribution of seats in March 2015 for the Lok Sabha, the Rajya Sabha and the State Legislatures):

| | Parliament | | State Legislatures | |
| | | | Legislative | Legislative |
	House of the People (Lok Sabha)	Council of States (Rajya Sabha)	Assemblies (Vidhan Sabhas)	Councils (Vidhan Parishads)
Union Territores States:				
Andhra Pradesh	25	11	175	58[1]
Arunachal Pradesh	2	1	60	—
Assam	14	7	126	—
Bihar	40	16	243	75
Chhattisgarh	11	5	90	—
Goa	2	1	40	—
Gujarat	26	11	182	—
Haryana	10	5	90	—
Himachal Pradesh	4	3	68	—
Jammu and Kashmir	6	4	89[2,3]	34[4]
Jharkhand	14	5	82[5]	—
Karnataka	28	12	225[5]	75
Kerala	20	9	141[5]	—
Madhya Pradesh	29	11	231[5]	—
Maharashtra	48	18	289[5]	78
Manipur	2	1	60	—
Meghalaya	2	1	60	—
Mizoram	1	1	40	—
Nagaland	1	1	60	—
Odisha	21	10	147	—
Punjab	13	7	117	—
Rajasthan	25	10	200	—
Sikkim	1	1	32	—
Tamil Nadu	39	18	235[5]	—
Telangana	17	7	120[5]	36
Tripura	2	1	60	—
Uttar Pradesh	80	31	404[5]	100
Uttarakhand	5	2	70	—
West Bengal	42	15	295[5]	—
Union Territories:				
Andaman and Nicobar Islands	1	—	—	—
Chandigarh	1	—	—	—
Dadra and Nagar Haveli	1	—	—	—
Daman and Diu	1	—	—	—
Delhi	7	3	70	—
Lakshadweep	1	—	—	—
Puducherry	1	1	30	—

(continued)

	Parliament		State Legislatures	
	House of the People (Lok Sabha)	Council of States (Rajya Sabha)	Legislative Assemblies (Vidhan Sabhas)	Legislative Councils (Vidhan Parishads)
Union Territores States:				
Nominated by the President under Article 80 (1) (a) of the Constitution	—	12	—	—
Total	543	241	4,131[6]	456[1]

[1]Includes eight nominated members.
[2]Includes two nominated members.
[3]Excludes 24 seats for Pakistan-occupied areas of the State which are in abeyance.
[4]Excludes seats for the Pakistan-occupied areas.
[5]Includes one nominated member.
[6]Includes 11 nominated members.

The number of seats allotted to the scheduled castes and the scheduled tribes in the House of the People is 84 and 47 respectively. Of the 4,120 elective seats in the state Legislative Assemblies, 570 are reserved for the scheduled castes and 532 for the scheduled tribes.

Language

The Constitution provides that the official language of the Union shall be Hindi in the Devanagari script. Hindi is spoken by over 30% of the population. It was originally provided that English should continue to be used for all official purposes until 1965. But the Official Languages Act 1963 provides that, after the expiry of this period of 15 years from the coming into force of the Constitution, English might continue to be used, in addition to Hindi, for all official purposes of the Union for which it was being used immediately before that day, and for the transaction of business in Parliament. According to the Official Languages (Use for official purposes of the Union) Rules 1976, an employee may record in Hindi or in English without being required to furnish a translation thereof in the other language and no employee possessing a working knowledge of Hindi may ask for an English translation of any document in Hindi except in the case of legal or technical documents.

The 58th amendment to the Constitution (26 Nov. 1987) authorized the preparation of a constitution text in Hindi.

The following 22 languages are included in the Eighth Schedule to the Constitution: Assamese, Bengali, Bodo, Dogri, Gujarati, Hindi, Kannada, Kashmiri, Konkani, Maithili, Malayalam, Manipuri, Marathi, Nepali, Odia, Punjabi, Sanskrit, Santhali, Sindhi, Tamil, Telugu, Urdu. Hindu has by far the most the most native speakers, followed by Bengali, Telugu, Marathi, Tamil and Urdu. It is estimated that over 850 different languages are spoken throughout the country.

Mohanty, Biswaranjan, *Constitution, Government and Politics in India.* 2009

National Anthem

'Jana-gana-mana' ('Thou art the ruler of the minds of all people'); words and tune by Rabindranath Tagore.

Government Chronology

Prime Ministers since 1947. (BJP = Bharatiya Janata Party; BLD = Indian People's Party/Bharatiya Lok Dal; INC = Indian National Congress (a.k.a. Indian Congress Party); INC(i) = Indian National Congress-Indira Gandhi faction; JD = People's Party/Janata Dal; JD(s) = Janata Dal-Chandra Shekhar faction; JP = People's Party/Janata Dal; UPA = United Progressive Alliance)

1947–64	INC	Jawaharlal Nehru
1964	INC	Gulzarilal Nanda
1964–66	INC	Lal Bahadur Shastri
1966	INC	Gulzarilal Nanda
1966–77	INC	Indira Gandhi

(*continued*)

1977–79	JP	Morarji Desai
1979–80	JP/BLD	Charan Singh
1980–84	INC(i)	Indira Gandhi
1984–89	INC(i)	Rajiv Gandhi
1989–90	JD	Vishwanath Pratap Singh
1990–91	JD(s)	Chandra Shekhar
1991–96	INC(i)	Pamulaparti Venkata Narasimha Rao
1996	BJP	Atal Bihari Vajpayee
1996–97	JD	Haradanahalli Dodde Deve Gowda
1997–98	JD	Inder Kumar Gujral
1998–2004	BJP	Atal Bihari Vajpayee
2004–14	INC, UPA	Manmohan Singh
2014–	BJP	Narendra Modi

Presidents of the Union since 1950.

1950–62	Rajendra Prasad
1962–67	Sarvepalli Radhakrishnan
1967–69	Zakir Husain
1969–74	Varahgiri Venkata Giri
1974–77	Fakhruddin Ali Ahmed
1977–82	Neelam Sanjiva Reddy
1982–87	Zail Singh
1987–92	Ramaswamy Iyer Venkataraman
1992–97	Shankar Dayal Sharma
1997–2002	Kocheril Raman Narayanan
2002–07	Avul Pakir Jainulabdeen Abdul Kalam
2007–12	Pratibha Patil
2012–17	Pranab Mukherjee
2017–	Ram Nath Kovind

Recent Elections

Presidential elections were held on 17 July 2017. Ram Nath Kovind (Bharatiya Janata Party) was elected by federal and state legislators, with 702,044 votes (65·7%), against 367,314 (34·3%) for former Speaker of the *Lok Sabha* Meira Kumar.

Parliamentary elections were held in nine phases between 7 April and 12 May 2014. They were the largest elections ever to be held in the world, with 814·5m. eligible voters. Turnout was a record 66·4%. The Bharatiya Janata Party (BJP)-led National Democratic Alliance (NDA) took 336 seats, thereby achieving the biggest win since the government of Rajiv Gandhi came to power in 1984; the ruling United Progressive Alliance (UPA) only won 58 seats. The BJP gained 282 seats, with the INC—the main party in the UPA—winning 44. The All India Anna Dravida Munnetra Kazhagam (AIADMK) won 37 seats, the All India Trinamool Congress (TMC) 34, Biju Janata Dal (BJD) 20, Shiv Sena (SHS) 18, Telugu Desam Party (TDP) 16, Telangana Rashtra Samithi (TRS) 11, and the Communist Party of India (Marxist) (CPM) and YSR Congress Party (YSRCP) 9 seats each. Other parties and independents won the remaining 63 seats.

Wallace, Paul, (ed.) *India's 2014 Elections: A Modi-led BJP Sweep.* 2015

Current Government

President: Ram Nath Kovind; b. 1945 (sworn in 25 July 2017).
Vice-President: Venkaiah Naidu.
In Feb. 2019 the government was composed as follows:
Prime Minister and Minister of Personnel, Public Grievances and Pensions, Atomic Energy, and Space: Narendra Modi; b. 1950 (BJP; since 26 May 2014).
Minister of Home Affairs: Rajnath Singh (BJP). *External Affairs:* Sushma Swaraj (BJP). *Finance, and Corporate Affairs:* Arun Jaitley (BJP). *Road Transport and Highways, Shipping, Water Resources, River Development and Ganga Rejuvenation:* Nitin Jairam Gadkari (BJP). *Commerce and Industries, and Civil Aviation:* Suresh Prabhu (BJP). *Statistics and Programme Implementation:* D. V. Sadananda Gowda (BJP). *Drinking Water and Sanitation:* Uma Bharati (BJP).*Consumer Affairs, Food and Public Distribution:* Ram Vilas

Paswan (Lok Janshakti Party). *Women and Child Development:* Maneka Gandhi (BJP). *Chemicals and Fertilizers, and Parliamentary Affairs:* Ananth Kumar (BJP). *Law and Justice, and Electronics and Information Technology:* Ravi Shankar Prasad (BJP). *Health and Family Welfare:* Jagat Prakash Nadda (BJP). *Heavy Industries and Public Enterprises:* Anant Geete (SHS). *Food Processing Industries:* Harsimrat Kaur Badal (Shiromani Akali Dal). *Rural Development, Panchayati Raj, and Mines:* Narendra Singh Tomar (BJP). *Steel:* Chaudhary Birender Singh (BJP). *Tribal Affairs:* Jual Oram (BJP). *Agriculture and Farmers' Welfare:* Radha Mohan Singh (BJP). *Social Justice and Empowerment:* Thawar Chand Gehlot (BJP). *Textiles, and Information and Broadcasting:* Smriti Irani (BJP). *Science and Technology, Earth Sciences, and Environment, Forest and Climate Change:* Harsh Vardhan (BJP). *Human Resource Development:* Prakash Javadekar (BJP). *Petroleum and Natural Gas, and Skill Development and Entrepreneurship:* Dharmendra Pradhan (BJP). *Railways, and Coal:* Piyush Goyal (BJP). *Defence:* Nirmala Sitharaman (BJP). *Minority Affairs:* Mukhtar Abbas Naqvi (BJP).

Speaker of the Lok Sabha: Sumitra Mahajan.

Office of the Prime Minister of India: http://www.pmindia.gov.in

Current Leaders

Ram Nath Kovind

Position
President

Introduction
Ram Nath Kovind, a lawyer by profession, was chosen as president on 17 July 2017. He is the second Dalit (formerly known as an untouchable in India's caste system) to hold the post.

Early Life
Kovind was born on 1 Oct. 1945 in Paraunkh, in the state of Uttar Pradesh. He studied law and commerce at Kanpur University, joining the Bar Council of Delhi in 1971. He was called up to the Delhi High Court in 1977, and from 1980–93 acted as Union government standing counsel in the Supreme Court.

Kovind entered politics when he was elected to represent Uttar Pradesh in the *Rajya Sabha* (the upper house of parliament) in April 1994. He had joined the Hindu-nationalist Bharatiya Janata Party (BJP) three years earlier. He served in parliament for two terms, until March 2006, during which time he sat on various committees overseeing home affairs, fossil fuels, caste and tribal welfare, and law and justice. He also championed education projects in rural areas, including in Uttarakhand and Uttar Pradesh. In Oct. 2002 he joined the Indian delegation to the United Nations and addressed the General Assembly. He also served as governor of Bihar from 2015–17.

Career in Office
On 19 June 2017 Amit Shah, the president of the BJP, nominated Kovind for the role of national president. Kovind stood as the National Democratic Alliance (NDA) candidate, resigning as governor of Bihar in order to be eligible. He won the election on 17 July with an overwhelming majority, beating fellow Dalit candidate Meira Kumar, who stood for the United Progressive Alliance (UPA).

In Dec. 2017 Kovind spoke out against the stigma associated with mental illnesses and warned of a looming mental health epidemic.

Narendra Modi

Position
Prime Minister

Introduction
Narendra Modi took office in May 2014 following the landslide victory of his Hindu-nationalist Bharatiya Janata Party (BJP) in national elections. He is the first Indian prime minister to have been born after independence. He previously served as chief minister of Gujarat from 2001–14 and is the parliamentary representative for Varanasi.

Early Life
Modi was born in Sept. 1950 in Gujarat into a low caste family. He began his adult working life in his uncle's canteen. At the age of eight he had come into contact with the Rashtriya Swayamsevak Sangh (RSS), a movement set on transforming India into a Hindu state. He was inducted as an RSS junior cadet and subsequently became a full-time campaigner and, in 1978, regional organizer. From 1975–77 he was forced underground when the RSS was

banned, during which time he helped print anti-government tracts and wrote a book entitled *The Struggles of Gujarat*.

In 1978 he completed a distance-learning degree from Delhi University and in 1983 received a master's in political science from Gujarat University. The RSS assigned Modi to the BJP in 1985 and in 1988 he was elected an organizing secretary of the BJP's Gujarat unit. By 1998 he was the BJP's general secretary.

He became chief minister of Gujarat in 2001 when his predecessor resigned for health reasons. He was elected to the post in 2002 and then re-elected in 2007 and 2012. In this role he focused on economic development and improving infrastructure, electricity distribution and agricultural production. He launched the Gujarat International Finance Tec-City project and hosted 'Vibrant Gujarat' summits, although critics argued that his policies had little impact on human development indicators. He was widely criticized for his actions during the 2002 Gujarat communal riots, but a legal case against him and his government for complicity in the anti-Muslim violence was dismissed in 2013.

In the same year Modi was elected chairman of the BJP election campaign committee for the 2014 elections and named as the party's prime ministerial candidate. After successfully contesting the election, he was sworn in on 26 May.

Career in Office
Modi is a polarizing figure, with a strong record in economic policy and good governance but divisive in terms of Hindu–Muslim relations. On assuming office he cut the cabinet from the 70 ministers of the former administration to 45. In Aug. 2014 he scrapped the bureaucratic Planning Commission, which had laid out five-year national economic plans, and replaced it with a new think tank, the National Institution for Transforming India. In Dec. he launched a part-privatization of state enterprises and forced through legislation to raise the foreign ownership cap on insurance companies from 26% to 49% (his first major legislative reform). However, despite the BJP's electoral success at national level, opposition to Modi's political philosophy and reformist agenda has been evident in some state-level polling.

Modi was particularly visible and active at international level in 2014 and 2015, seeking to forge closer economic and trading links through numerous state visits, including to Bhutan, Brazil, Nepal, Japan, the USA, Australia, Sri Lanka, France, Germany, Canada, China, South Korea, Bangladesh and Russia. Despite his surprise meeting with Pakistan's prime minister Nawaz Sharif in Dec. 2015, relations between the two neighbours have remained frosty and sporadic military clashes have continued over the disputed state of Kashmir. However, in June 2017 both India and Pakistan became full members of the Shanghai Cooperation Organisation, which aims to promote closer defence, economic and cultural co-operation within the intergovernmental grouping and to strengthen confidence and good neighbourly relations. However, relations between the two neighbours have remained frosty and sporadic military clashes have continued over the disputed state of Kashmir, escalating most recently in Feb. 2019. In Aug. 2017 India withdrew troops from a disputed Himalayan border area, easing a simmering stand-off with China.

In Sept. 2016 millions of workers took strike action to protest low wages and the government's economic reforms. Further public resentment was generated in Nov. that year as Modi abruptly announced the withdrawal of large denomination bank notes from the financial system in a crackdown on corruption and illegal cash holdings. Nonetheless, opinion polls conducted in 2017 confirmed Modi's enduring voter popularity with consistently high approval ratings. In July 2018 his government survived a parliamentary no-confidence motion by a large majority, but the BJP lost three key state elections in Rajasthan, Chhattisgarh and Madhya Pradesh in Dec.

Modi was again active on the international stage in 2018, seeking to further defuse border tensions with China at an informal summit with President Xi Jinping while bolstering relations with Russia, France and several Middle Eastern countries. In Oct. India also concluded a US$5bn. purchase of a Russian air defence missile system in a deal interpreted as a response to China's growing regional influence.

In Sept. 2018 the Supreme Court in Delhi struck down two colonial-era laws that had criminalized adultery and homosexual acts.

Defence

The Supreme Command of the Armed Forces is vested in the president. As well as armed forces of 1,325,000 personnel in 2011, there are 1,301,000 active paramilitary forces including 208,000 members of the Border Security Force based mainly in the troubled Jammu and Kashmir region. Military service is voluntary but, under the amended constitution, it is regarded as a fundamental duty of every citizen to perform National Service when called upon. Defence expenditure totalled US$36,297m. in 2013 (US$30 per capita), representing 1·8% of GDP. As at 31 May 2016 India had 7,692 personnel serving in UN peacekeeping operations (the second largest contingent of any country, after Ethiopia).

In the period 2012–16 India's spending on major weapons was the highest of any country, accounting for 13·0% of the global total. In Sept. 2003 India announced that it would be buying 66 Hawk trainer fighter jets; 24 were received directly from BAE Systems, with the last arriving in Nov. 2009, and 42 are being manufactured in India. A further agreement was signed in July 2010 ensuring India would receive an additional 57 aircraft.

In 2003 India agreed to pay US$1·1bn. for three of Israel's sophisticated Phalcon airborne early-warning radar systems, the first of which was delivered in 2009. In 2008 negotiations began to purchase two more. The military took delivery in 2012 of the first of three Brazilian-made Embraer 145 Airborne Early Warning and Control Aircraft. In Jan. 2013 the Indian Defence Research and Development Organisation announced that the government was to spend a further US$1·1bn. developing a complementary Airborne Warning and Control System.

Nuclear Weapons

India's first nuclear test was in 1974. Its most recent tests were a series of five carried out in May 1998. According to the Stockholm International Peace Research Institute, India's nuclear arsenal was estimated to consist of 130–140 nuclear warheads in Jan. 2018. India, which is known to have a nuclear weapons programme, has not signed the Comprehensive-Nuclear-Test-Ban-Treaty, which is intended to bring about a ban on any nuclear explosions. In 2006 the USA and India announced a civil nuclear co-operation initiative. Under the terms of the deal, India was exempted from a ban on nuclear energy sales that had previously covered non-signatories of the international non-proliferation treaty, of which India is one. In return India agreed to open up 14 of its 22 nuclear installations to international inspections. The agreement was signed in Oct. 2008.

Army

The Army is organized into six commands covering different areas, which in turn are subdivided into sub-areas, plus a training command.

The strength of the Army in 2013 was 1·1m. There are four 'RAPID' divisions, 17 infantry divisions, 12 mountain divisions, three armoured divisions and three artillery divisions. Each division consists of several brigades. Officers are trained at the Indian Military Academy, Dehra Dun (Uttarakhand). Army reserves number 300,000 with a further 500,000 personnel available as a second-line reserve force. There is a volunteer Territorial Army of 40,000 (with a further 120,000 reservists). There are numerous paramilitary groups including the Rashtriya Rifles (numbering 65,000), the Indo-Tibetan Border Police (36,300), the State Armed Police (450,000), the Civil Defence (500,000 reservists), the Central Industrial Security Force (134,100) and the ministry of home affairs Assam Rifles (63,900). An Army Aviation Corps was established in 1986.

Navy

The Navy has three commands; Eastern (at Visakhapatnam), Western (at Mumbai) and Southern (at Kochi and Port Blair), the latter a training and support command. The fleet is divided into two elements, Eastern and Western; and well-trained, all-volunteer personnel operate a mix of Soviet and western vessels. In May 2003 India held joint naval exercises with Russia in the Arabian Sea for the first time since the collapse of the Soviet Union.

The principal ship is the aircraft carrier INS *Vikramaditya*, formerly *Admiral Gorshkov*, purchased from Russia in 2004 and commissioned in Nov. 2013. In 2003 India approved the construction of an indigenous aircraft carrier, INS *Vikrant*, but delays have meant that completion is unlikely before 2023. The fleet also includes one nuclear-powered attack submarine, 13 other attack submarines, and 24 destroyers and frigates. India's first nuclear-powered *Arihant*-class submarine, INS *Arihant*, began sea trials in Dec. 2014 and was commissioned in Aug. 2106. The Naval Air Arm was 7,000-strong in 2013; equipment includes 40 combat aircraft. Main bases are at Mumbai (main dockyard), Goa, Visakhapatnam and Kolkata on the sub-continent and Port Blair in the Andaman Islands.

Naval personnel in 2013 numbered 58,350 including 7,000 Naval Air Arm and 1,200 marines.

Air Force

Units of the IAF are organized into five operational commands—Central at Allahabad, Eastern at Shillong, Southern at Thiruvananthapuram, South-Western at Gandhinagar and Western at Delhi. There is also a training command and a maintenance command. The air force had 127,200 personnel in 2013.

Equipment includes more than 850 combat aircraft. Major combat types include Su-30s, MiG-21s, MiG-27s, MiG-29s, *Jaguars* and Mirage 2000s. Air Force reserves numbered 140,000 in 2013.

Economy

Agriculture accounted for 18·0% of GDP in 2013 (down from 55% in 1950), industry 30·7% (up from 15% in 1950) and services 51·3% (up from 30% in 1950).

Since the late 1990s a divide has become increasingly pronounced between the south and west, where a modern economy is booming in cities such as Bangalore, Hyderabad and Chennai, and the poorer and politically volatile areas in the north and east.

Overview

With the world's seventh largest economy, India's growth and development has been striking since the turn of the 21st century. A 2015 report compiled by the Centre for Economics and Business Research projected that the country will have the world's third largest economy by 2022, behind only China and the USA. The report also predicted that India will overtake China in the second half of the 21st century to become the world leader.

The diverse economy incorporates a broad range of modern industries, services and agriculture along with traditional village farming and handicrafts. The service sector is the bedrock of an economy that boasts globally-recognized companies in pharmaceuticals, steel and information technology. India has also capitalized on its large, educated and English-speaking population to become an international centre for outsourcing services, particularly to the USA. Nonetheless, the World Bank estimated that 44·3% of the nation's workforce remained employed in the agricultural sector in 2017, although in 2015–16 gross value added rates in that sector were estimated at 1·2% compared to 8·9% for the services industry.

After independence, a broad but lacklustre industrial base was built behind a tariff wall. But from the late 1980s the country began to open up to the global economy. Industrial licensing (determining how much entrepreneurs could manufacture) was abolished and trade barriers were lowered after the country joined the World Trade Organization in 1995. Foreign direct investment rose from almost nothing in the early 1990s to US$8bn. in 2005 and US$47bn. in 2008, before averaging out at US$30·9bn. annually from 2009–14. It then rose to US$44bn. in 2015—second only to China among the ten largest Asian economies.

Economic growth was robust from 2003, averaging 7·7% per year through to 2014, while the poverty rate declined from 37·2% in 2004–05 to 21·9% in 2011–12 (although the Asian Development Bank reported that it remained at this latter level in 2015). GDP growth slowed in 2008 as a result of the global downturn (prompting the World Bank to approve four loans to the government worth US$4·3bn. in Sept. 2009), but the economy began to recover in mid-2009, led by domestic demand and investment in infrastructure. Growth faltered again between 2012 and 2014 as global liquidity strictures highlighted India's macroeconomic imbalances and structural weaknesses. The *rupee* also experienced the greatest depreciation among major Asian currencies during 2012–13 and fell by a further 2% in 2014 and 5% in 2015. Nonetheless, growth then averaged a buoyant 7·6% annually from 2014 to 2016, the result of higher wages and an increase in private consumption. Additionally, after coming to power in 2014 the Modi government introduced a series of economic reforms—including agricultural and subsidy measures.

In July 2017 the government introduced the Goods and Services Tax (GST)—India's largest indirect tax reform, which replaced dozens of state and central taxes with a national tax. Ahead of implementation, businesses ran down their inventories, resulting in a fall in manufacturing and a temporary downturn. However, the Organisation for Economic Co-operation and Development (OECD) predicted that the GST would boost corporate productivity, investment and growth in the long term.

Following disruptions including a controversial currency exchange initiative in Nov. 2016 and the GST roll-out in 2017, growth slowed to 6·7% in 2017, although it rebounded to 7·7% in the first quarter of 2018. Meanwhile, headline inflation averaged 3·6% in 2017–18, a 17-year low, reflecting low food prices on a return to normal monsoon rainfall and agriculture sector reforms, subdued domestic demand and currency appreciation. But, with demand recovering and international oil prices rising, it rose to 4·9% in May 2018 (above the mid-point of the Reserve Bank of India's headline target) while the current account deficit widened to 1·9% of GDP in 2017–18. Large general government fiscal deficits and debt remain key macroeconomic challenges.

India is expected to overtake China as the world's most populous country by 2024. It has the world's largest youth population but, according to the OECD, over 30% of its young people are not in employment, education or training. India also continues to suffer from low GDP per capita, while almost 25% of the population still lives below the poverty line. Moreover, about one-third of the world's population living on under US$ 1·90 per day live in India. Economic inequalities are striking, with the richest 1% of the population owning 53% of the country's wealth, and there is a wide discrepancy in labour force participation rates between men and women, standing at 75·7% and 31·1% respectively in the period 2015–16.

The short-term macroeconomic outlook is broadly favourable, although the economy is vulnerable to further increases in oil prices, tighter global financial conditions and spillover risks from international trade conflicts, as well as rising regional geopolitical tensions. Domestic risks include tax revenue short-falls related to continued GST implementation issues and delays in addressing the growing budget deficit and implementing structural reforms.

Currency

The unit of currency is the *Indian rupee* (INR) of 100 *paise*. Since July 2010 the Indian rupee has been represented by the symbol ₹. Foreign exchange reserves were US$261,247m. in Aug. 2009 and gold reserves 11·50m. troy oz. Inflation rates (based on IMF statistics):

2008	2009	2010	2011	2012	2013	2014	2015	2016	2017
9·1%	10·6%	9·5%	9·5%	10·0%	9·4%	5·8%	4·9%	4·5%	3·6%

India's 2009 inflation rate was the highest since 1998. The official exchange rate was abolished on 1 March 1993; the rupee now has a single market exchange rate and is convertible. The pound sterling is the currency of intervention. Total money supply in July 2009 was ₹12,133·0bn.

Budget

Budgetary central government revenues in 2012–13 (fiscal year beginning 1 April 2012) totalled ₹12,558bn.; expenditures totalled ₹16,076bn.

Principal sources of revenue in 2012–13 were: taxes on income, profits and capital gains, ₹5,631bn.; taxes on goods and services, ₹3,266bn.; taxes on international trade and transactions, ₹1,867bn. Main items of expenditure by economic type in 2012–13 were: grants, ₹6,242bn.; subsidies, ₹3,697bn.; interest, ₹3,128bn.

A Goods and Services Tax (GST) was introduced on 1 July 2017, with four rates: 28%, 18%, 12% and 5%.

Performance

India has one of the fastest-growing economies in Asia. Real GDP growth rates (based on IMF statistics):

2008	2009	2010	2011	2012	2013	2014	2015	2016	2017
3·9%	8·5%	10·3%	6·6%	5·5%	6·4%	7·4%	8·2%	7·1%	6·7%

Total GDP in 2017 was US$2,597·5bn. In 2014 India received US$70·4bn. in remittances from abroad—the most of any country.

Banking and Finance

The Reserve Bank, the central bank for India, was established in 1934 and started functioning on 1 April 1935 as a shareholder's bank; it became a nationalized institution on 1 Jan. 1949. It has the sole right of issuing currency notes. The *Governor* is Shaktikanta Das. The Bank acts as adviser to the government on financial problems and is the banker for central and state governments, commercial banks and some other financial institutions. It manages the rupee public debt of central and state governments and is the custodian of the country's exchange reserve.

Scheduled commercial banks are categorized in five different groups according to their ownership and/or nature of operation: the State Bank of India and its six associates; 19 nationalized banks; regional rural banks; foreign banks; and other scheduled commercial banks (in the private sector). Total deposits in commercial banks, March 2007, stood at ₹26,970,000m. The State Bank of India acts as the agent of the Reserve Bank for transacting government business as well as undertaking commercial functions. There

were 33 state co-operative banks in 2015–16 and 370 central co-operative banks in 2013–14. In 2017 India received US$39·9bn. worth of foreign direct investment. FDI inflows in 2015 were more than 12 times the level of 2000.

External debt totalled US$290,282m. in 2010 (US$120,222m. in 2005), equivalent to 16·9% of GNI.

There are stock exchanges in Ahmedabad, Chennai, Delhi, Kolkata, Mumbai and 18 other centres.

Energy and Natural Resources

Environment

India's carbon dioxide emissions from the consumption of energy in 2011 accounted for 5·5% of the world total (the third highest after China and the USA). However, this was equivalent to just 1·5 tonnes per capita, well below the global average and the lowest figure for any major industrial country. An *Environmental Performance Index* compiled in 2016 ranked India 141st of 180 countries, with 53·6%. The index examined various factors in nine areas—agriculture, air quality, biodiversity and habitat, climate and energy, fisheries, forests, health impacts, water and sanitation, and water resources.

Electricity

Installed capacity in Dec. 2012 was 211·0m. kW. In April 2018 the last of India's 597,464 inhabited villages gained access to electricity. Production of electricity in 2011–12 was 973·1bn. kWh, of which 86·0% came from thermal stations, 10·7% from hydro-electric stations and 3·3% from nuclear stations. In Feb. 2014 there were 21 nuclear reactors in use. An additional six reactors were under construction. Electricity consumption per capita in 2009–10 was 779 kWh. Electricity demand exceeds supply, making power surges and cuts frequent. According to the 2011 census 67% of households had electricity, up from 56% in 2001; 93% of urban households had electricity in 2011 compared to 55% of rural households.

Oil and Gas

Oil and Natural Gas Corporation Ltd and Oil India Ltd are the only producers of crude oil. Production 2012, 42·0m. tonnes. The main fields are in Assam and Gujarat and offshore in the Gulf of Cambay (the Mumbai High field). India imports 70% of its annual oil requirement. There were proven reserves of 5·7bn. bbls in 2012. Oil refinery capacity, 2011, was 4·3m. bbls daily. Natural gas production in 2012 was 40·2bn. cu. metres with 1·3trn. cu. metres of proven reserves.

Wind

India is one of the world's largest wind power producers, with 37·2bn. kWh in 2014. Total installed capacity amounted to 25,088 MW in 2015 (the fourth highest after China, the USA and Germany).

Minerals

The coal industry was nationalized in 1973. Production, 2014, 567·0m. tonnes; in the same year proven reserves were estimated at 126bn. tonnes. Production of other minerals in 2014 (in 1,000 tonnes): iron ore, 129,800; lignite, 27,000; salt, 17,000; bauxite, 21,000; chromite, 3,540; manganese ore, 2,570; aluminium, 3,800; silver, 303,339 kg; gold, 1,560 kg. Other important minerals are lead, zinc, limestone, apatite and phosphorite, dolomite, magnesite and uranium. Value of mineral production (excluding atomic minerals), 2012–13, ₹1,721,666·5m. (2011–12, ₹1,754,974·8m.).

Agriculture

The farming year runs from July to June through three crop seasons: kharif (monsoon), rabi (winter) and summer. In 2013 there were an estimated 157m. ha. of arable land and 13m. ha. of permanent cropland. An estimated 67m. ha. were equipped for irrigation in 2013. The average size of holdings for the whole of India is estimated at 1·4 ha. In 2009–10 there were 610,020 co-operative societies with a total membership of 249·4m.

Agricultural production, 2013 (in 1,000 tonnes): sugarcane, 341,200; rice, 159,200; wheat, 93,510; potatoes, 45,344; bananas, 27,575; maize, 23,290; onions, 19,299; seed cotton, 18,913; tomatoes, 18,227; mangoes and guavas, 18,002; aubergines, 13,444; cottonseed, 12,293; soybeans, 11,948; coconuts, 11,930; millet, 10,910; groundnuts, 9,472; chick-peas, 8,833; cabbages, kale, etc., 8,534; cauliflowers and broccoli, 7,887; rapeseed, 7,820. Jute is grown in West Bengal (70% of total yield), Bihar and Assam: total yield, 1,976,000 tonnes. India is the world's leading producer of a number of agricultural crops, including mangoes, millet, bananas and chick-peas. It is also the biggest exporter of rice.

The tea industry is important, with production concentrated in Assam, West Bengal, Tamil Nadu and Kerala. India is the world's second largest tea producer after China. The 2012 crop was 1,126,300 tonnes; exports in 2012, 208,300 tonnes, valued at US$680m.

Livestock (2013 estimates): cattle, 189·0m.; goats, 134·0m.; buffaloes, 109·4m.; sheep, 63·8m.; pigs, 10·1m.; horses, 628,000; camels, 380,000; donkeys, 300,000; chickens, 709m. There are more cattle and buffaloes in India than in any other country.

Forestry

The lands under the control of the state forest departments are classified as 'reserved forests' (forests intended to be permanently maintained for the supply of timber, etc., or for the protection of water supply, etc.), 'protected forests' and 'unclassed' forest land. In 2015 the total forest area was 70·68m. ha. (24% of the land area). Main types are teak and sal. About 16% of the area is inaccessible, of which about 45% is potentially productive. In 2011, 331·97m. cu. metres of roundwood were produced, making India the second largest producer after the USA (9·5% of the world total in 2011).

Fisheries

Total catch in 2015 was 4,843,388 tonnes (3,497,284 tonnes marine, 1,346,104 tonnes inland). Fishing provides a livelihood for over 14m. people, contributing about 1% of total GDP and 4·6% of the GDP from the agriculture sector. 541,701 tonnes of fish were exported in 2007–08.

Industry

The leading companies by market capitalization in India in May 2018 were: Tata Consultancy Services, a software and computer services company (US$98·4bn.), Reliance Industries, a chemical production company (US$93·1bn.); and HDFC Bank (US$77·6bn.).

The information technology industry has become increasingly important; its contribution to GDP rose from 1·2% in 1998–99 to 5·2% by 2007–08. The National Association of Software and Services Companies (NASSCOM) estimated that in 2007–08 the IT industry registered a growth rate of 28% and revenues of US$52bn. (up from US$40bn. in 2006–07).

There is expansion in petrochemicals, based on the oil and associated gas of the Mumbai High field, and gas reserves offshore in the Krishna Godavari basin and the Bassein field, and onshore in Andhra Pradesh, Assam and Gujarat.

In 2006–07 there were an estimated 12·8m. micro and small enterprises, accounting for about 39% of the gross value of output in the manufacturing sector.

Industrial production (2006–07, in 1,000 tonnes): cement, 154,746; distillate fuel oil (2007–08), 59,032; finished steel, 50,196; sugar, 24,187; nitrogenous and phosphate fertilizers, 16,153; residual fuel oil (2007–08), 15,804; petrol (2005–06), 10,502; jet fuel (2007–08), 9,107; kerosene (2005–06), 9,078; sulphuric acid, 7,156; paper and paperboard, 6,129; pig iron, 4,550; caustic soda, 1,929; jute goods (2003–04), 1,424. Other products (2006–07): 8,436,186 motorcycles, mopeds and scooters; 3,171,000 diesel engines; 1,238,737 cars; 520,000 commercial vehicles; 85·8bn. cigarettes.

Labour

The labour force in 2013 was 487,882,000 (442,357,000 in 2003). 56·4% of the population aged 15–64 was economically active in 2013. In the same year 3·6% of the population was unemployed. India's working-age population is set to overtake that of China to become the world's largest around 2025.

India had 13·96m. people living in slavery according to the Walk Free Foundation's 2013 *Global Slavery Index*, the highest total of any country.

Companies

The total number of companies registered as at 31 March 2015 was 1,459,278, of which 1,022,011 were active. Of the active companies at 31 March 2015, 1,015,601 (952,490 private companies and 63,111 public companies) were limited by shares. Of those companies limited by shares, 1,417 were government companies and 1,014,184 were non-government companies.

Most active companies in March 2015 were in business services (25%), manufacturing (21%), trading (15%), construction (11%), real estate and renting (7%), and community, personal and social services (6%). A total of 3,314 foreign companies were doing business in India as at 31 March 2015. In 2014–15, 64,395 new companies were registered, of which 64,109 were registered as companies limited by shares, 264 as companies limited by guarantees and 22 as unlimited companies.

International Trade

Imports and Exports

Trade (in US$1m.):

	Imports	Exports
2010	350,029·4	220,408·5
2011	462,402·8	301,483·3
2012	488,976·4	289,564·8
2013	466,045·6	336,611·4
2014	459,369·5	317,544·6

The main trading partners were as follows in 2010 (in US$1m.):

Countries	Value of imports
China	41,249·1
UAE	30,907·5
Switzerland	22,197·7
Saudi Arabia	20,374·1
USA	19,096·3
Australia	12,061·2
Germany	11,444·7
Iran	11,078·3
Nigeria	10,257·6
Korea (Republic of)	9,922·3
Indonesia	9,695·3
Kuwait	9,021·9
Japan	8,265·1
Hong Kong	7,772·5
Belgium	7,445·6
Iraq	7,291·5
Singapore	7,263·1
South Africa	6,912·2
Qatar	6,141·8
Malaysia	5,995·9

Countries	Value of exports
UAE	27,412·3
USA	23,587·4
China	17,440·0
Hong Kong	9,508·3
Singapore	9,066·2
Netherlands	6,572·9
UK	6,436·4
Germany	5,989·5
Belgium	5,025·9
France	4,903·0
Japan	4,805·1
Indonesia	4,557·1
Saudi Arabia	4,483·7
Italy	4,187·7
Brazil	3,669·6
South Africa	3,650·1
Korea (Republic of)	3,634·5
Malaysia	3,555·3
Sri Lanka	3,305·1
Bangladesh	3,016·1

In 2010 the main import suppliers (percentage of total trade) were: China, 11·8%; United Arab Emirates, 8·8%; Switzerland, 6·3%; Saudi Arabia,

5·8%; USA, 5·5%. Main export markets in 2010 were: United Arab Emirates, 12·4%; USA, 10·7%; China, 7·9%; Hong Kong, 4·3%; Singapore, 4·1%.

The value of the chief imports and exports in 2014 are shown in the following table (in US$1m.):

Imports	Value
Mineral fuels and lubricants	176,925·4
Machinery and transport equipment	74,776·5
Manufactured goods	59,539·2
Chemicals	48,052·0
Crude materials and animal and vegetable oils	35,644·4
Manufactured articles	14,756·2
Food, animals and beverages	8,036·6
Exports	Value
Manufactured goods	76,837·5
Mineral fuels and lubricants	62,347·0
Machinery and transport equipment	48,578·9
Manufactured articles	42,297·3
Chemicals	37,117·7
Food, animals and beverages	33,158·2
Crude materials and animal and vegetable oils	13,781·0

Communications

Roads
In March 2011 there were 3,790,342 km of roads of which 2,341,480 km were surfaced. Roads are divided into six main administrative classes, namely: national highways (70,934 km in length as at March 2011), state highways, other public works department (PWD) roads, *Panchayati Raj* roads, urban roads and project roads. The national highway system is linked with the UN Economic and Social Commission for Asia and the Pacific international highway system. The state highways are the main trunk roads of the states, while the other PWD roads and *Panchayati Raj* roads connect subsidiary areas of production and markets with distribution centres, and form the main link between headquarters and neighbouring districts.

In 2006 there were 11,526,000 passenger cars, 64,743,000 motorcycles and scooters, 992,000 buses and coaches, and 4,436,000 lorries and vans. In 2007 there were 476,219 road accidents resulting in 114,444 deaths.

Rail
The Indian railway system is government-owned (under the control of the Railway Board). There are 17 zones, as follows:

Zone	Headquarters	Year of creation
Central	Mumbai	1951
Southern	Chennai	1951
Western	Mumbai	1951
Eastern	Kolkata	1952
Northern	Delhi	1952
North Eastern	Gorakhpur	1952
South Eastern	Kolkata	1955
North East Frontier	Guwahati	1958
South Central	Secunderabad	1966
East Central	Hajipur	2002
East Coast	Bhubaneswar	2002
North Central	Allahabad	2002
North Western	Jaipur	2002
South East Central	Bilaspur	2002
South Western	Hubli	2002
West Central	Jabalpur	2002
Metro Railway, Kolkata	Kolkata	2010

The total length of the Indian railway network was 64,460 km in March 2011 (19,607 electrified), with the Northern zone having the longest network,

at 6,968 km. Work on India's first high-speed rail project, linking Ahmedabad and Mumbai, began in Sept. 2017.

The Konkan Railway (760 km of 1,676 mm gauge) linking Roha and Mangalore opened in 1996. It is operated as a separate entity.

Principal gauges are 1,676 mm (55,188 km) and 1 metre (6,809 km), with networks also of 762 mm and 610 mm gauge (2,463 km).

Passenger-km travelled in 2009–10 came to 903·5bn. and revenue earning freight tonne-km to 600·5bn. Revenues (2009–10), ₹871,047m.; expenses, ₹829,154m.

There are metros in Ahmedabad (6 km), Bangalore (42 km), Chennai (28 km), Delhi (252 km), Gurgaon (12 km), Hyderabad (30 km), Jaipur (10 km), Kochi (18 km), Kolkata (27 km), Luckow (9 km), Mumbai (11 km) and Noida (30 km).

Civil Aviation
The main international airports are at Chennai, Delhi (Indira Gandhi), Kolkata, Mumbai and Thiruvananthapuram, with some international flights from Ahmedabad, Amritsar, Bangalore, Calicut, Goa and Hyderabad. Air transport was nationalized in 1953 with the formation of two Air Corporations: Air India for long-distance international air services, and Indian Airlines for air services within India and to adjacent countries. Indian (as Indian Airlines became in 2005) merged into Air India in Feb. 2011. Both domestic and international air transport have been opened to private companies, the largest of which are IndiGo (a low-cost carrier and India's largest airline by market share), Jet Airways and SpiceJet (also a low-cost carrier). All operational airports handled a total of 116·9m. passengers (87·1m. domestic and 29·8m. international) in the year to 31 March 2008. Total aircraft movements reached 1·31m. and freight volumes increased to over 1·7m. tonnes.

In 2010 Air India operated direct flights to Africa (Johannesburg); to Mauritius; to Europe (Frankfurt, İstanbul, London, Moscow, Munich, Paris and Vienna); to western Asia (Abu Dhabi, Dammam, Dubai, Jeddah and Riyadh); to east Asia (Hong Kong, Osaka, Shanghai, Singapore and Tokyo); and to North America (New York, Toronto and Washington, D.C.). Indian operated international flights in 2010 to Bangkok, Dubai, Kabul, Kathmandu, Kuwait, Muscat and Yangon (Rangoon).

In 2007 Mumbai was the busiest airport, handling 25·2m. passengers, followed by Delhi, with 23·3m. passengers. They were ranked the world's 55th and 61st busiest airports respectively for the year 2006. Both airports were privatized in 2006, with extensive modernization.

Shipping
In Jan. 2014 there were 603 ships of 300 GT or over registered, totalling 8·42m. GT. Of the 603 vessels registered, 312 were general cargo ships, 108 oil tankers, 95 bulk carriers, 61 passenger ships, 14 liquid gas tankers and 13 container ships. The Indian-controlled fleet comprised 648 vessels of 1,000 GT or over in July 2014, of which 502 were under the Indian flag and 146 under foreign flags.

Cargo traffic of major ports for fiscal years, in 1,000 tonnes:

Port	2011–12	2012–13	2013–14
Chennai	55,707	53,404	51,105
Cochin (Kochi)	20,091	19,845	20,886
Jawaharlal Nehru (Nhava Sheva)	65,730	64,488	62,333
Kamarajar (Ennore)	14,956	17,885	27,337
Kandla	82,501	93,619	87,005
Kolkata and Haldia	43,248	39,928	41,386
Mormugao	39,001	17,738	11,739
Mumbai	56,186	58,038	59,184
New Mangalore	32,941	37,036	39,365
Paradip	54,254	56,552	68,003
V. O. Chidambaranar (Tuticorin)	28,105	28,260	28,642
Visakhapatnam	67,420	59,038	58,504

The busiest container port is Jawaharlal Nehru, which handled 4·2m. TEUs (twenty-foot equivalent units) in 2013.

There are about 3,700 km of major rivers navigable by motorized craft, of which 2,000 km are used. Canals, 4,300 km, of which 900 km are navigable by motorized craft.

Telecommunications

The telephone system is in the hands of the Telecommunications Department, except in Delhi and Mumbai, which are served by a public corporation. In 2010 there were 35·1m. main (fixed) telephone lines. Mobile phone subscriptions numbered 752·2m. in Dec. 2010 (623·9 per 1,000 persons), more than double the number just two years earlier and treble the number three years earlier. The number of fixed line subscribers has been gradually falling since 2005. India's largest mobile phone operator is Bharti Airtel, with a 22·8% market share in July 2014, ahead of Vodafone and Idea Cellular. Bharat Sanchar Nigam Limited (generally known as BSNL) is the largest landline provider, with a 63·8% market share in July 2014, ahead of Mahanagar Telephone Nigam Limited (generally known as MTNL) and Bharti Airtel. An estimated 12·6% of the population were internet users in 2012. In March 2012 there were 45·0m. Facebook users.

Social Institutions

Out of 178 countries analysed in the 2017 *Fragile States Index*—a list published jointly by the Fund for Peace and *Foreign Policy* magazine—India was ranked the 72nd most vulnerable to conflict or collapse. The index is based on 12 indicators of state vulnerability across social, political and economic categories.

Justice

All courts form a single hierarchy, with the Supreme Court at the head, which constitutes the highest court of appeal. Immediately below it are the High Courts and subordinate courts in each state. Every court in this chain administers the whole law of the country, whether made by Parliament or by the state legislatures.

The states of Andhra Pradesh (in common with Telangana), Assam (in common with Arunachal Pradesh, Mizoram and Nagaland), Bihar, Chhattisgarh, Gujarat, Himachal Pradesh, Jammu and Kashmir, Jharkhand, Karnataka, Kerala, Madhya Pradesh, Maharashtra (in common with Goa and the Union Territories of Daman and Diu, and Dadra and Nagar Haveli), Manipur, Meghalaya, Odisha, Punjab (in common with the state of Haryana and the Union Territory of Chandigarh), Rajasthan, Sikkim, Tamil Nadu (in common with the Union Territory of Puducherry), Tripura, Uttar Pradesh, Uttarakhand and West Bengal each have a High Court. There is a separate High Court for Delhi. For the Andaman and Nicobar Islands the Calcutta High Court, for Puducherry the Madras High Court and for Lakshadweep the High Court of Kerala are the highest judicial authorities. The Allahabad High Court has a Bench at Lucknow, the Bombay High Court has Benches at Nagpur, Aurangabad and Panaji, the Gauhati High Court has Benches at Aizwal, Itanagar and Kohima, the Madhya Pradesh High Court has Benches at Gwalior and Indore and the Rajasthan High Court has a Bench at Jaipur. Below the High Court each state is divided into a number of districts under the jurisdiction of district judges who preside over civil courts and courts of sessions. There are a number of judicial authorities subordinate to the district civil courts. On the criminal side magistrates of various classes act under the overall supervision of the High Court.

In Oct. 1991 the Supreme Court upheld capital punishment by hanging. In Nov. 2012 India carried out its first execution since 2004. There were no executions in 2014, one in 2015 but then none again in 2016, 2017 or 2018.

The population in penal institutions in Dec. 2012 was 385,135 (30 per 100,000 of national population). 67·6% of prisoners had yet to receive a trial according to 2014 estimates by the International Centre for Prison Studies. In 2015 the World Justice Project *Rule of Law Index*, which provides data on how the rule of law is experienced by the general public across eight categories, ranked India 44th of 102 countries for criminal justice and 88th for civil justice.

Police

The states control their own police forces. The Home Affairs Minister of the central government co-ordinates the work of the states. The Indian Police Service provides senior officers for the state police forces. The Central Bureau of Investigation functions under the control of the Cabinet Secretariat.

The cities of Ahmedabad, Bangalore, Chennai, Delhi, Hyderabad, Kolkata, Mumbai, Nagpur and Pune have separate police commissionerates.

Education

Adult literacy was 62·8% in 2006 (75·2% among males and 50·8% among females). Of the states and territories, Kerala and Mizoram have the highest rates.

Educational Organization

Education is the concurrent responsibility of state and Union governments. In the Union Territories it is the responsibility of the central government. The Union government is also directly responsible for the central universities and all institutions declared by parliament to be of national importance; the promotion of Hindi as the federal language and co-ordinating and maintaining standards in higher education, research, science and technology. Professional education rests with the ministry or department concerned. There is a Central Advisory Board of Education to advise the Union and the State governments on any educational question which may be referred to it.

School Education

The school system has four stages: primary, middle, secondary and senior secondary.

Primary education is imparted either at independent primary (or junior basic) schools or primary classes attached to middle or secondary schools. The period of instruction varies from four to five years and the medium of instruction is in most cases the mother tongue of the child or the regional language. Free primary education is available for all children. Legislation for compulsory education has been passed by some state governments and Union Territories but it is not practicable to enforce compulsion when the reasons for non-attendance are socio-economic. There are residential schools for country children. The period for the middle stage varies from two to three years. In 2005, 47·2% of children who enrolled in the first grade went on to finish the eighth grade. In the same year it was estimated that 42m. children aged 6–14 were not attending school. In Aug. 2009 legislation was passed making education free and compulsory for all children between the ages of six and 14.

School statistics for 2014–15:

Type of recognized institution	No. of institutions	No. of students on rolls	No. of teachers
Primary schools	847,118	130,501,000	2,670,396
Upper primary schools	425,094	67,165,000	2,559,769
Secondary schools	135,335	38,301,000	1,346,888
Senior secondary schools	109,318	23,501,000	1,984,711

Higher Education

Higher education is given in arts, science or professional colleges, universities and all-India educational or research institutions. The majority of universities act as affiliating bodies for colleges; they are responsible for course content, examinations and awarding degrees although the teaching is conducted at the college. In 2005–06 there were 19,753 higher education institutions, comprising: 350 universities, institutions deemed to be universities and institutions of national importance; 12,751 general education colleges (including arts, science and commerce colleges); 5,179 professional education colleges (including engineering, technology, architecture, medical and teacher training colleges); and 1,473 other institutions (including research institutions). Total enrolment in tertiary education in 2017 was 33,374,107, of which 16,053,706 were women.

Adult Education

The Directorate of Adult Education, established in 1971, is the national resource centre.

There is also a National Literacy Mission.

Expenditure

Total budgeted central expenditure on revenue account of education and other departments for 2013–14 was estimated at ₹465,143m. Total public expenditure on education during the Tenth (2002–07) Plan, ₹438,250m. (₹138,250m. on secondary and higher education, ₹300,000m. on elementary education and literacy). In 2013 total expenditure on education came to 3·8% of GDP and 14·1% of total government spending.

Health

Medical services are primarily the responsibility of the states. The Union government has sponsored major schemes for disease prevention and control which are implemented nationally.

Health spending accounted for 3·9% of GDP in 2011. General government expenditure on health that year represented 30·5% of total expenditure on health and 8·2% of total government expenditure. In 2013 there were 35,416 government hospitals. There were seven hospital beds per 10,000 inhabitants in 2011. In the same year India had 7·4 physicians for every 10,000 population, 17·1 nursing and midwifery personnel per 10,000 population and 1·0 dentistry personnel per 10,000.

In 2015, 15·2% of the population were undernourished (compared to 21·6% in 1995). In *Water: At What Cost? The State of the World's Water 2016*, WaterAid reported that 5·9% of the population does not have access to safe water. India ranked as the country with the greatest number of people living without access to safe water (75·8m. in 2015). In 2011–12, 21·9% of the population lived below the poverty line, compared to 38·9% in 1987–88.

Approximately 2·5m. Indians are HIV-infected, a number only exceeded in South Africa and Nigeria.

Religion

India is a secular state; any worship is permitted, but the state itself has no religion. The principal religions in 2011 were: Hindus, 966m. (80% of the population); Muslims, 172m. (14%); Christians, 28m.; Sikhs, 21m.; Buddhists, 8m.; Jains, 4m. In addition to having the largest Hindu population of any country, India has the third highest number of Muslims, after Indonesia and Pakistan. In Feb. 2019 the Roman Catholic Church had four cardinals.

Culture

World Heritage Sites

There are 37 sites under Indian jurisdiction that appear on the UNESCO World Heritage List. They are (with year entered on list): Ajanta Caves (1983); Ellora Caves (1983); Agra Fort (1983); Taj Mahal (1983); Sun Temple, Konârak (1984); Monuments at Mahabalipuram (1984); Kaziranga National Park (1985); Manas Wildlife Sanctuary (1985); Keoladeo National Park (1985); Churches and Convents of Goa (1986); Monuments at Khajuraho (1986); Monuments at Hampi (1986); Fatehpur Sikri (1986); Monuments at Pattadakal (1987); Elephanta Caves (1987); Great Living Chola Temples (1987 and 2004); Sundarbans National Park (1987); Nanda Devi National Park (1988 and 2005); Buddhist Monuments at Sanchi (1989); Humayan's Tomb, Delhi (1993); Qutb Minar and its Monuments, Delhi (1993); Mountain Railways of India (1999, 2005 and 2008); Mahabodhi Temple Complex at Bodh Gaya (2002); the Rock Shelters of Bhimbetka (2003); Champaner-Pavagadh Archaeological Park (2004); the Chhatrapati Shivaji Terminus—formerly Victoria Terminus—in Mumbai (2004); the Red Fort Complex, Delhi (2007); Jantar Mantar, Jaipur (2010); the Western Ghats mountain chain (2012); the Hill Forts of Rajasthan (2013); Great Himalayan National Park Conservation Area (2014); Rani-ki-Vav (the Queen's Stepwell) at Patan, Gujarat (2014); the Archaeological Site of Nalanda *Mahavihara* (Nalanda University) at Nalanda, Bihar (2016); Khangchendzonga National Park (2016); the Historic City of Ahmedabad (2017); and Victorian Gothic and Art Deco Ensembles of Mumbai (2018). The Architectural Work of Le Corbusier, an Outstanding Contribution to the Modern Movement (2016), is shared with Argentina, Belgium, France, Germany, Japan and Switzerland.

Press

There were 99,660 registered publications in March 2014 (up from 73,146 in March 2009), with a total circulation of 450·6m. In 2011 there were 4,397 dailies with a total circulation of 175·70m. (up from 162·35m. in 2010). India's circulation of paid-for dailies overtook that of China in 2008 to become the highest of any country; in 2014 it totalled 264·3m. Hindi papers have the highest number and circulation, followed by English and Urdu. The newspaper with the highest circulation is the *Dainik Bhaskar,* a Hindi-language paper (daily average of 3·6m. copies in 2014 and a readership of 13·8m.). The English-language paper with the highest circulation is *The Times of India*, with a daily average of 3·4m. copies in 2014 (although its readership is much larger than that of the *Dainik Bhaskar,* at 21·7m.). *Dainik Jagran* has the third highest circulation, with a daily average of 3·1m. copies in 2014 and a readership of 16·6m.

Tourism

In 2012 there were 6,578,000 non-resident overnight tourists. Of the non-resident overnight tourists in 2011, 34% were from Europe, 21% from the Americas and 19% from East Asia and the Pacific. Tourist receipts amounted to US$18·3bn. in 2012.

Calendar

The Indian National Calendar, adopted in 1957, is dated from the Saka era (Indian dynasty beginning AD 78). It uses the same year-length as the Gregorian calendar (also used for administrative and informal purposes) but begins on 22 March. Local and religious variations are also used.

Festivals

Independence Day is celebrated on 15 Aug. The Hindu festival of Diwali or Deepavali ('festival of lights') is held over five days between mid-Oct. and mid-Nov. Clay lamps are lit to symbolize the triumph of good over evil and firework displays take place. The biggest rock music festival is the Independence Rock Festival (Oct.) in Mumbai. The International Film Festival of India takes place in Nov.–Dec. in Goa.

Diplomatic Representatives

Of India in the United Kingdom (India House, Aldwych, London, WC2B 4NA)
   High Commissioner: Ruchi Ghanashyam.

Of the United Kingdom in India (Shantipath, Chanakyapuri, New Delhi 110021)
   High Commissioner: Sir Dominic Asquith, KCMG.

Of India in the USA (2107 Massachusetts Ave., NW, Washington, D.C., 20008)
   Ambassador: Navtej Singh Sarna.

Of the USA in India (Shantipath, Chanakyapuri, New Delhi 110021)
   Ambassador: Kenneth I. Juster.

Of India to the United Nations
   Ambassador: Syed Akbaruddin.

Of India to the European Union
   Ambassador: Gaitri Issar Kumar.

States and Territories

The Republic of India is composed of the following 29 States and seven centrally administered Union Territories:

State	Capital	State	Capital
Andhra Pradesh	Hyderabad	Manipur	Imphal
Arunachal Pradesh	Itanagar	Meghalaya	Shillong
Assam	Dispur	Mizoram	Aizawl
Bihar	Patna	Nagaland	Kohima
Chhattisgarh	Raipur	Odisha	Bhubaneswar
Goa	Panaji	Punjab	Chandigarh
Gujarat	Gandhinagar	Rajasthan	Jaipur
Haryana	Chandigarh	Sikkim	Gangtok
Himachal Pradesh	Shimla	Tamil Nadu	Chennai
Jammu and Kashmir	Srinagar	Telangana	Hyderabad
Jharkhand	Ranchi	Tripura	Agartala
Karnataka	Bangalore	Uttar Pradesh	Lucknow
Kerala	Thiruvananthapuram	Uttarakhand	Dehra Dun
Madhya Pradesh	Bhopal	West Bengal	Kolkata
Maharashtra	Mumbai		

Union Territories

Andaman and Nicobar Islands; Chandigarh; Dadra and Nagar Haveli; Daman and Diu; Delhi; Lakshadweep; Puducherry.

Andhra Pradesh

Constituted a separate state on 1 Oct. 1953, Andhra Pradesh has an area of 160,205 sq. km and a population (2011 census) of 49,386,799. It was split in two on 2 June 2014 with Telangana—occupying 114,840 sq. km in the northwest of Andhra Pradesh—becoming India's youngest state. The principal language is Telugu.

Andhra Pradesh has a bicameral legislature. The *Legislative Assembly* consists of 175 members and the *Legislative Council* of 50 members. The capital is Hyderabad (shared with Telangana), although geographically it is located in Telangana. The *de facto* capital is Vijayawada.

At the State Assembly elections held in April and May 2014 the Telugu Desam Party won 117 seats, the Yuvajana Sramika Rythu Congress Party 70, Telangana Rashtra Samithi 63, the Indian National Congress 21 and the Bharatiya Janata Party 9. Six other parties received a total of 14 seats.

Governor: E. S. L. Narasimhan (took office in Dec. 2009).

Chief Minister: Nara Chandrababu Naidu (took office in June 2014, having previously been chief minister from Sept. 1995–May 2004).

In 2011, 92·2% of households used electricity for lighting. Crude oil is refined at Visakhapatnam. The Krishna-Godavari basin has oil and gas on land and off-shore. In 2008–09, 1,524m. cu. metres of natural gas were produced from onshore fields. The state is an important producer of asbestos and barytes. The Cuppadah basin is a major source of uranium and other minerals. Major crops are bananas, pulses, foodgrains, rice, oil seeds and sugarcane. Fish production in 2012–13 totalled 1,808,000 tonnes (the largest of any Indian state). The main industries are textile manufacture, sugar-milling, machine tools, electronic equipment, heavy electrical machinery, aircraft parts and paper-making. India's major shipbuilding yards are at Visakhapatnam.

In March 2011 there were 238,001 km of roads of which 155,579 km were surfaced. There were 3,703 route-km of railway as at March 2016. A new Hyderabad airport (Rajiv Gandhi International Airport, located at Shamshabad) opened in March 2008. The chief port is Visakhapatnam, which handles about 60m. tonnes of cargo annually.

In 2011, 67·7% of the population were literate (75·6% of males and 59·7% of females). At the 2011 census Hindus accounted for 88·5% of the population; Muslims, 9·6%; Christians, 1·3%.

Arunachal Pradesh

Statehood was achieved in Dec. 1986. Arunachal Pradesh has an area of 83,743 sq. km and a population (2011 census) of 1,383,727. The state is mainly tribal. The official languages are English and Hindi, but there are also some 50 tribal dialects. The capital is Itanagar.

The *Legislative Assembly* has 60 members.

At the State Assembly elections held in April 2014 the Indian National Congress won 42 seats; the Bharatiya Janata Party 11; the People's Party of Arunachal 5; ind. 2.

Governor: B. D. Mishra (took office in Oct. 2017).

Chief Minister: Pema Khandu (took office in July 2016).

In 2011, 65·7% of households used electricity for lighting. Oil and gas production in 2008–09 was 102,400 tonnes of crude oil and 30m. cu. metres of gas. Coal reserves are estimated at 90·23m. tonnes; dolomite, 154·13m. tonnes; limestone, 409·35m. tonnes. In 2009 there were 17 medium and 2,526 small industries, 76 craft or weaving centres and 25 sericulture demonstration centres. Industries include coal, textiles, jute, iron and steel, chemicals, tea and leather.

In March 2011 there were 21,555 km of roads of which 14,336 km were surfaced.

In 2011, 67·0% of the population were literate (73·7% of males and 59·6% of females). At the 2011 census Christians accounted for 30·3% of the population; Hindus, 29·0%; Buddhists, 11·8%; Muslims, 2·0%; other religions, 27·0%.

Assam

Assam, which achieved full independent statehood in Jan. 1972, is in northeast India, almost separated from central India by Bangladesh. The area of the state is 78,438 sq. km. Population (2011 census), 31,205,576. The principal language is Assamese. The capital is Dispur.

The state has a unicameral legislature of 126 members.

In the elections of April 2016 the Bharatiya Janata Party (BJP) took 60 of 126 seats, Indian National Congress (INC) 26, Asom Gana Parishad (AGP) 14, All India United Democratic Front (AIUDF) 13, Bodoland People's Front (BPF) 12 and ind. 1.

Governor: Jagdish Mukhi (took office in Oct. 2017).

Chief Minister: Sarbananda Sonowal (took office in May 2016).

In 2011, 37·0% of households used electricity for lighting and 61·8% used kerosene. Assam produces about 16% of India's crude oil. Coal production (2012–13), 605,000 tonnes. The state also has limestone, refractory clay, dolomite and corundum. Over three-quarters of the workforce is engaged in agriculture. Assam produces 50% of India's tea. In 2017 there were 792 registered tea estates. Over 72% of the cultivated area is under food crops, of which the most important is rice. Fish production in 2012–13 totalled 254,000 tonnes. Sericulture and hand-loom weaving, both silk and cotton, are important home industries together with the manufacture of brass, cane and bamboo articles. 17% of workers are employed in the tea industry. The main heavy industry is petrochemicals; there are four oil refineries in the region. There were 1,859 factories in 2007–08 employing 134,300 people.

In March 2011 there were 241,789 km of roads of which 37,816 km were surfaced. The route-km of railways in 2015–16 was 2,443 km. Daily scheduled flights connect the principal towns with the rest of India.

In 2011, 73·2% of the population were literate (78·8% of males and 67·3% of females). At the 2011 census Hindus accounted for 61·5% of the population; Muslims, 34·2%; Christians, 3·7%.

Bihar

The state includes the ethnic areas of North Bihar, Santhal Pargana and Chota Nagpur. In 1956 some areas of Purnea and Manbhum districts were transferred to West Bengal. In 2000 the state of Jharkhand was taken from the mineral-rich southern region of Bihar, substantially reducing the state's revenue-earning power. The area of Bihar is 94,163 sq. km. Population (2011 census), 104,099,452. The capital is Patna. Hindi, Urdu and Maithili are all official languages.

Bihar has a bicameral legislature. The *Legislative Assembly* has 243 elected members, and the Council 75.

In elections held in Oct. and Nov. 2015 the Rashtriya Janata Dal won 80 of 243 seats; the Janata Dal (United), 71; Bharatiya Janata Party, 53; Indian National Congress, 27; Communist Party of India (Marxist–Leninist) Liberation, 3; the Lok Jan Shakti Party, 2; the Rashtriya Lok Samta Party, 2; Hindustani Awam Morcha (Secular), 1; ind., 4.

Governor: Lalji Tandon (took office in Aug. 2018).

Chief Minister: Nitish Kumar (took office for a third time in Feb. 2015).

In 2011 only 16·4% of households used electricity for lighting (the lowest proportion of any state) and 82·4% used kerosene. The state has deposits of bauxite, mica, glass sand and salt. The irrigated area was 4·92m. ha. in 2008–09 of a total area of 9·42m. ha. Production (2009–10): rice, 3·63m. tonnes; wheat, 4·56m.; total foodgrains, 10·15m. Other major food crops are maize and pulses. Fish production in 2012–13 totalled 400,000 tonnes. Iron, steel and aluminium are produced and there is an oil refinery. Other important industries are heavy engineering, machine tools, fertilizers, electrical engineering and fruit processing.

In March 2011 there were 130,642 km of roads of which 57,198 km were surfaced. In 2015–16 the state had 3,731 route-km of railway line. There are airports at Patna and Gaya.

In 2011, 63·8% of the population were literate—the lowest rate of any Indian state (73·4% of males and 53·3% of females). At the 2011 census Hindus accounted for 82·7% of the population; Muslims, 16·9%.

Chhattisgarh

Created from 16 mainly tribal districts of Madhya Pradesh, the state became the twenty-sixth state of India on 1 Nov. 2000. Chhattisgarh has an area of 135,191 sq. km. Population (2011 census), 25,545,198. The principal language is Hindi.

The council of ministers consists of 15 cabinet ministers and eight ministers of state. The capital is Raipur.

At elections in Nov. 2018 the Indian National Congress (INC) won 68 seats, the Bharatiya Janata Party (BJP) 15, the Janta Congress Chhattisgarh (J) 5 and the Bahujan Samaj Party (BSP) 2.

Acting Governor: Anandiben Patel (since Aug. 2018).

Chief Minister: Bhupesh Baghel (took office in Dec. 2018).

In 2011, 75·3% of households used electricity for lighting. Chhattisgarh is India's largest producer of coal. Production in 2012–13 was 117·83m. tonnes. The state has extensive mineral resources including tin ore, iron ore, dolomite and bauxite. There are also significant deposits of limestone, copper ore, rock phosphate, corundum, tin and manganese ore. Deobhog in the Raipur district has deposits of diamonds. Around 80% of the population are engaged in agriculture. 5·8m. ha. of land is agricultural. The great plains of Chhattisgarh produce 10,000 varieties of rice. Other crops include maize, millet, groundnuts, soybeans and sunflower. More than 25% of the land in Chhattisgarh is double cropped. Fish production in 2012–13 totalled 256,000 tonnes.

In March 2011 there were 93,965 km of roads of which 64,078 km were surfaced. There were 1,213 route-km of railway at March 2016.

In 2011, 71·0% of the population were literate (81·5% of males and 60·6% of females). At the 2011 census Hindus accounted for 93·3% of the population; Muslims, 2·0%; Christians, 1·9%.

Goa

The coastal area was captured by the Portuguese in 1510 and the inland area was added in the 18th century. In Dec. 1961 Portuguese rule was ended and Goa incorporated into the Indian Union as a Territory together with Daman and Diu. Goa was granted statehood on 30 May 1987. Daman and Diu remained Union Territories. Goa has a coastline of 105 km. The area is 3,702 sq. km. Population (2011 census), 1,458,545. Marmagao is the largest town. The capital is Panaji. The languages spoken are Konkani (the official language), Marathi, Kannada, Hindi and English.

There is a *Legislative Assembly* of 40 members.

In the elections of Feb. 2017 the Indian National Congress (INC) took 17 of 40 seats, Bharatiya Janata Party (BJP) 13, Maharashtrawadi Gomantak (MAG) 3, Goa Forward Party (GFP) 3 and Nationalist Congress Party (NCP) 1. Three seats went to independents.

Governor: Mridula Sinha (took office in Aug. 2014).

Chief Minister: Manohar Parrikar (took office in March 2017).

Goa had a per capita annual income of ₹192,652 in 2011–12, the highest of any Indian state.

Goa receives most of its power supply from Maharashtra and Karnataka. In 2011, 96·9% of households used electricity for lighting. Mineral resources include bauxite, ferro-manganese ore and iron ore, all of which are exported. Agriculture is the main occupation. Leading crops are rice, pulses, ragi, mango, cashew and coconuts. Manufacturing include automotive components, electronic goods, fertilizers, footwear, nylon fishing nets, pesticides, pharmaceuticals, ready-made clothing, shipbuilding and tyres.

In March 2011 there were 10,627 km of roads of which 7,531 km were surfaced. There is an airport at Dabolim. There are seaports at Panaji, Marmagao and Margao.

In 2011, 87·4% of the population were literate (92·8% of males and 81·8% of females). At the 2011 census Hindus accounted for 66·1% of the population; Christians, 25·1%; Muslims, 8·3%.

Gujarat

The Gujarati-speaking areas of India were part of the Moghul empire, coming under Mahratta domination in the late 18th century. At independence the area now forming Gujarat became part of Bombay State. In 1960 Bombay State was divided and the Gujarati-speaking areas became Gujarat. The area is 196,024 sq. km and the population (2011 census) 60,439,692; Gujarati and Hindi in the Devanagari script are the official languages.

Gujarat has a unicameral legislature, the *Legislative Assembly*, which has 182 elected members. The capital is Gandhinagar.

In elections held in Dec. 2017 the Bharatiya Janata Party retained power with a reduced majority, winning 99 seats against 77 for the Indian National Congress, with ind. and others winning six seats.

Governor: Om Prakash Kohli (took office in July 2014).

Chief Minister: Vijay Rupani (took office in Aug. 2016).

In 2011, 90·4% of households used electricity for lighting. There are large crude oil and gas reserves. Chief minerals produced are limestone, lignite, bauxite, quartz and silica, bentonite, crude china clay, dolomite and fire clay. Principal crops are wheat, rice, pulses, cotton, tobacco and groundnuts. Fish production in 2012–13 totalled 788,000 tonnes. Gujarat ranks among India's most industrialized states. Principal industries are textiles, general and electrical engineering, automobiles, oil refining, fertilizers, petrochemicals, machine tools, automobiles, heavy chemicals, pharmaceuticals, dyes, sugar, soda ash, cement, man-made fibres, salt, sulphuric acid, paper and paperboard.

In March 2011 there were 156,188 km of roads of which 141,565 km were surfaced. The route-km of railways in 2015–16 was 5,259 km. Sardar Vallabhbhai Patel International Airport at Ahmedabad is the main airport. The largest port is Kandla, which is India's busiest in terms of cargo traffic. There are 40 other ports.

In 2011, 79·3% of the population were literate (87·2% of males and 70·7% of females). At the 2011 census Hindus accounted for 88·6% of the population; Muslims, 9·7%.

Haryana

The state of Haryana, created in 1966, was formed from the Hindi-speaking parts of the state of Punjab. Delhi is an enclave on its eastern boundary. The state has an area of 44,212 sq. km and a population (2011 census) of 25,351,462. The principal language is Hindi.

The state has a unicameral legislature with 90 members. The capital (shared with Punjab) is Chandigarh.

In the elections of Oct. 2014 the Bharatiya Janata Party won 47 seats, the Indian National Lok Dal 19, the Indian National Congress 15, the Haryana Janhit Congress 2, and ind. and others 7.

Governor: Satyadev Narayan Arya (took office in Aug. 2018).

Chief Minister: Manohar Lal Khattar (took office in Oct. 2014).

In 2011, 90·5% of households used electricity for lighting. Minerals include placer gold, barytes, tin and rare earths. Agriculture employs over 80% of the working population; leading crops are rice, wheat, pulses, cotton, sugar and oilseeds. Haryana produces a surplus of wheat and rice. Fish production in 2012–13 totalled 111,000 tonnes. Haryana has a large market for consumer goods in neighbouring Delhi. The main industries are cotton textiles, agricultural machinery and tractors, woollen textiles, scientific instruments, glass, cement, paper and sugar milling, cars, tyres and tubes, motorcycles, bicycles, steel tubes, engineering goods, electrical and electronic goods. An oil refinery at Panipat includes a diesel hydro desulphurization plant.

In March 2011 there were 41,729 km of roads of which 37,701 km were surfaced. In 2015–16 the state had 1,711 route-km of railway line. The main stations are at Ambala and Kurukshetra. There is no airport within the state but Delhi is on its eastern boundary.

In 2011, 76·6% of the population were literate (85·4% of males and 66·8% of females). At the 2011 census Hindus accounted for 87·5% of the population; Muslims, 7·0%; Sikhs, 4·9%.

Himachal Pradesh

Thirty small hill states were merged to form the Territory of Himachal Pradesh in 1948; the state of Bilaspur was added in 1954 and parts of the Punjab in 1966. The whole territory, a Himalayan region of hill-tribes, rivers and forests, became a state in 1971. The area of the state is 55,673 sq. km and the population (2011 census) 6,864,602. Principal languages are Hindi and Pahari.

There is a unicameral *Legislative Assembly* with 68 members. The capital is Shimla, population (2011 census) 171,640.

Elections were held in Nov. 2017. The opposition Bharatiya Janata Party won 44 seats; Indian National Congress, 21; Communist Party of India (Marxist), 1; ind., 2.

Governor: Acharya Dev Vrat (took office in Aug. 2015).

Chief Minister: Jai Ram Thakur (took office in Dec. 2017).

In 2011, 96·8% of households used electricity for lighting. The state has a hydro-power potential of 23,000 MW. Of this only 29% has been harnessed. The Nathpa Jhakri project is India's largest hydro-electric power plant incorporating a 28 km power tunnel. The state has rock salt, slate, gypsum, limestone, barytes, dolomite, pyrites, copper, gold and sulphur. However, Himachal Pradesh supplies only 0·2% of the national mineral output. Main agricultural crops are seed potatoes, off season vegetables, wheat, maize, rice, hops and flowers, and fruits such as apples, peaches, apricots, kiwi fruit and strawberries.

In March 2011 there were 47,963 km of roads of which 33,247 km were surfaced. There is a railway line from Chandigarh to Shimla. Route-km in 2015–16 was 296 km. There are airports at Bhuntar near Kullu, at Jubbarhatti near Shimla and at Gaggal in Kangra district.

In 2011, 83·8% of the population were literate (90·8% of males and 76·6% of females). At the 2011 census Hindus accounted for 95·2% of the population; Muslims, 2·2%; Buddhists, 1·2%; Sikhs, 1·2%.

Jammu and Kashmir

The state of Jammu and Kashmir was created in 1846 at the close of the First Sikh War. With the Indian Independence Act 1947, all states had to accede to India or Pakistan. Kashmir asked for standstill agreements with both. Pakistan agreed, but India wanted further discussion. Meantime the state was subject to armed attack from Pakistan. The Maharajah acceded to India on 26 Oct. 1947. India approached the UN in Jan. 1948, and the conflict ended by ceasefire in Jan. 1949. The major part of the state remained with India after territory in the north and west went to Pakistan. Hostilities between the two countries broke out in 1965 and again in 1971. Notwithstanding bilateral agreements—the Tashkent Declaration (Jan. 1966) and the Simla Agreement (July 1972)—and pledges by both sides to find a peaceful solution, the issue remains unresolved and intermittent violence between nationalistic factions has continued with varying intensity. In May 2018 a truce was declared—the first since 2000—to mark Ramadan but did not hold. The area is 222,236 sq. km and the population (2011 census) 12,541,302. Srinagar is the summer and Jammu the winter capital. The official language is Urdu.

There is a bicameral legislature; the *Legislative Council* has 36 members and the *Legislative Assembly* 89. There was a period of Governor's rule in 1977, and since then Governor's rule has been imposed in 1986, 1990, 2002, 2008–09, 2015, 2016 and again in 2018. In Dec.2018 the state was placed under President's rule for the third time.

Elections to the State Assembly were held in Nov.–Dec. 2014. The pro-self-rule People's Democratic Party won 28 of the 87 seats, Bharatiya Janata Party 25, Jammu and Kashmir National Conference 15, Indian National Congress 12, Jammu and Kashmir People's Conference 2 and other parties 4, with independent candidates taking 3 seats.

Governor: Satya Pal Malik (took office in Aug. 2018).

Chief Minister: Vacant.

In 2011, 85·1% of households used electricity for lighting. Minerals include coal, bauxite and gypsum. About 80% of the population is engaged in agriculture. Rice, wheat and maize are the major cereals. Traditional handicrafts are silk spinning, wood-carving, papier mâché and carpet-weaving.

In March 2011 there were 26,980 km of roads of which 14,178 km were surfaced. There were 298 km of railways in the state in 2015–16. There are airports at Srinagar, Jammu and Leh.

The proportion of literate people was 68·7% in 2011 (78·3% of males and 58·0% of females). The majority of the population, except in Jammu, are Muslims, making it the only Indian state to have a Muslim majority. At the 2011 census Muslims accounted for 68·3% of the population; Hindus, 28·4%; Sikhs, 1·9%.

Jharkhand

The state was carved from Bihar to become the twenty-eighth state of India on 15 Nov. 2000. Jharkhand has an area of 79,714 sq. km. Population (2011 census), 32,988,134. The principal language is Hindi.

After the region was taken from Bihar it was decided that the capital would be Ranchi. The legislative assembly has 81 members.

In elections held in Nov.–Dec. 2014 the Bharatiya Janata Party won 37 seats; Jharkhand Mukti Morcha, 19; Jharkhand Vikas Morcha (Prajatantrik), 8; Indian National Congress, 6; All Jharkhand Students Union, 5; and other parties, 6.

Governor: Draupadi Murmu (took office in May 2015).

Chief Minister: Raghubar Das (took office in Dec. 2014).

In 2011, 45·8% of households used electricity for lighting and 53·1% used kerosene. Jharkhand is rich in minerals, including 90% of the country's cooking coal deposits, 40% of its copper, 37% of known coal reserves and 2% of iron ore. Jharkhand is India's second largest producer of coal. Production in 2012–13 was 111·00m. tonnes. Annually the state mines 18·0m. tonnes of iron ore, 2·0m. tonnes of bauxite and 0·4m. tonnes of copper ore. India's largest steel plant is at Bokaro.

In March 2011 there were 23,903 km of roads of which 16,379 km were surfaced. Route-km of railways 2015–16, 2,394 km.

In 2011, 67·6% of the population were literate (78·5% of males and 56·2% of females). At the 2011 census Hindus accounted for 67·8% of the population; Muslims, 14·5%; Christians, 4·3%.

Karnataka

Constituted as Mysore under the States Reorganization Act 1956 to bring together the Kannada-speaking people distributed over five states, the state was renamed Karnataka in 1973. The area is 191,791 sq. km, and its population (2011 census) 61,095,297. Kannada is the language of administration and is spoken by 66% of the people.

Karnataka has a bicameral legislature. The *Legislative Council* has 75 members. The *Legislative Assembly* consists of 225 members. The capital is Bangalore.

At state elections in May 2018 the BJP won 104 seats; the INC 78; the Janata Dal (Secular) 37. Two seats were won by other parties and one independent was elected. Two seats were vacant.

Governor: Vajubhai Rudabhai Vala (took office in Sept. 2014).

Chief Minister: H. D. Kumaraswamy (took office for a second time in May 2018).

In 2011, 90·6% of households used electricity for lighting. Karnataka is an important source of gold and silver. The state produces 84% of India's gold. Reserves of limestone, high-grade iron ore and manganese are also found. Karnataka is one of only two states in India producing magnesite. It is also the largest producer of chromite. Agriculture is the main occupation of more than three-quarters of the population. The main food crops are rice, sorghum and ragi. The state grows about 70% of the national coffee crop. Much of the world's sandalwood oil is processed in the state. Fish production in 2012–13 totalled 526,000 tonnes. Sericulture is an important cottage industry giving employment, directly or indirectly, to about 2·7m. persons.

Karnataka had 281,773 km of roads in March 2011 of which 179,099 km were surfaced. There were 3,281 route-km of railway in 2015–16. There are international airports at Bangalore and Mangalore. Mangalore is a deep-water port for the export of mineral ores.

In 2011, 75·6% of the population were literate (82·9% of males and 68·1% of females). At the 2011 census Hindus accounted for 84·0% of the population; Muslims, 12·9%; Christians, 1·9%.

Kerala

The state of Kerala was created in 1956, bringing together the Malayalam-speaking areas. Kochi (Cochin), a safe harbour, was an early site of European trading in India. The state has an area of 38,863 sq. km and a population of 33,406,061 (2011 census). Languages spoken are Malayalam, Tamil and Kannada.

The state has a unicameral legislature of 141 members. The capital is Thiruvananthapuram.

At the elections of May 2016 the Left Democratic Front (LDF), led by the Communist Party of India (Marxist), won 91 out of 140 seats. The United Democratic Party (UDF), led by Indian National Congress, took 47 seats, with one seat going to the National Democratic Alliance (NDA). The remaining seat was won by an independent.

Governor: Palanisamy Sathasivam (took office in Sept. 2014).

Chief Minister: Pinarayi Vijayan (took office in May 2016).

In 2011, 94·4% of households used electricity for lighting. The chief agricultural products are rice, tapioca, coconut, arecanut, cashew nuts, oil-seeds, pepper, sugarcane, rubber, tea, coffee and cardamom. About 98% of Indian black pepper and about 95% of Indian rubber is produced in Kerala. Fish production in 2012–13 totalled 680,000 tonnes. Industries include rubber, tea, coffee, chemicals and coir.

In March 2011 there were 201,220 km of roads of which 110,359 km were surfaced. The state had 1,045 route-km of railway in 2015–16. There are airports at Kozhikode, Kochi and Thiruvananthapuram. Cochin Port (Kochi) is one of India's major ports.

Kerala has the highest literacy rate of any Indian state, with 93·9% of the population being literate in 2011 (96·0% of men and 92·0% of women). At the 2011 census Hindus accounted for 54·7% of the population; Muslims, 26·6%; Christians, 18·4%.

Madhya Pradesh

The state was formed in 1956 to bring together the Hindi-speaking districts of central India. The present capital, Bhopal, was the centre of a Muslim princely state from 1723. In 2000, 16 mainly tribal districts were taken from Madhya Pradesh to form Chhattisgarh. The state has an area of 308,245 sq. km, making it the second largest state in the country (after Rajasthan). Population (2011 census), 72,626,809. Hindi, Marathi, Urdu and Gujarati are spoken. In April 1990 Hindi became the sole official language.

Madhya Pradesh is one of the nine states for which the Constitution provides a bicameral legislature, but the Vidhan Parishad or Upper House (to consist of 90 members) has yet to be formed. The Vidhan Sabha or Lower House has 231 members. The capital is Bhopal.

At the election in Nov. 2018 the Indian National Congress (INC) won 114 seats (58 in 2013) and the Bharatiya Janata Party (BJP) won 109 seats (165 in 2013). The Bahujan Samaj Party (BSP) won two seats and the Samajwadi Party (SP) one seat. Independents took four seats.

Governor: Anandiben Patel (took office in Jan. 2018).

Chief Minister: Kamal Nath (took office in Dec. 2018).

Madhya Pradesh is rich in low-grade coal suitable for power generation, and also has potential for hydro-electric energy. In 2011, 67·1% of households used electricity for lighting. Madhya Pradesh is India's only diamond producer. Other minerals include, coal, limestone, copper ore (Madhya Pradesh is India's largest copper ore producer), manganese ore, iron ore and bauxite. The creation of Chhattisgarh, previously known as the 'rice bowl' of Madhya Pradesh, had serious implications for the state. Agriculture is the mainstay of the state's economy and 76·8% of the people are rural. Madhya Pradesh is the chief source in India of best-quality teak. The major industries are steel, aluminium, paper, cement, motor vehicles, ordnance, textiles and heavy electrical equipment.

In March 2011 there were 197,293 km of roads of which 119,921 km were surfaced. The main rail route linking northern and southern India passes through Madhya Pradesh. Route length (2015–16), 5,000 km. There are domestic airports at Bhopal, Gwalior, Indore and Khajuraho.

In 2011, 70·6% of the population were literate (80·5% of males and 60·0% of females). At the 2011 census Hindus accounted for 90·9% of the population; Muslims, 6·6%.

Maharashtra

The Bombay Presidency region grew in the early 17th century from a collection of British East India Company trading posts. The island of Bombay was a Portuguese possession until it came under English control in 1661. In 1960 the Bombay Reorganization Act divided Bombay State between Gujarati and Marathi areas, the latter becoming Maharashtra. The state has an area of 307,713 sq. km. The population in 2011 was 112,374,333. The official language is Marathi.

Maharashtra has a bicameral legislature. The *Legislative Council* has 78 members. The *Legislative Assembly* has 288 elected members and one member nominated by the Governor to represent the Anglo–Indian community. The capital is Mumbai (formerly known as Bombay).

At the elections held in Oct. 2014 the Bharatiya Janata Party won 122 of the 288 seats, Shiv Sena 63, the Indian National Congress 42, the Nationalist Congress Party 41, and ind. and others 20.

Governor: Chennamaneni Vidyasagar Rao (took office in Aug. 2014).

Chief Minister: Devendra Fadnavis (took office in Oct. 2014).

At 32,508·98 MW in Dec. 2013, Maharashtra's installed power capacity is the largest in India. In 2011, 83·9% of households used electricity for lighting. Mumbai High (India's largest offshore oil field) produced 12·11m. tonnes of crude oil in 2007–08 and 16·7bn. cu. metres of natural gas in 2008–09. The main crops are rice, wheat, jowar, bajra and pulses. Fish production in 2012–13 totalled 586,000 tonnes. Industry is concentrated in Mumbai, Nashik, Pune and Thane. The main products are chemicals, food products, textiles, electrical and non-electrical machinery and petroleum.

In March 2011 there were 410,521 km of roads of which 339,794 km were surfaced. Maharashtra has the longest road network of any Indian state. There were 5,745 route-km of railway line in 2015–16. The main airport is Mumbai. There are also airports at Nagpur, Pune and Aurangabad. Maharashtra has a coastline of 720 km. Mumbai is the major port.

The number of literate people, according to the 2011 census, was 82·5m. (82·9%, 89·9% of males and 75·5% of females). At the 2011 census Hindus accounted for 79·8% of the population; Muslims, 11·5%; Buddhists, 5·8%; Jains, 1·3%.

Manipur

Manipur became a state on 21 Jan. 1972. It has an area of 22,327 sq. km and a population (2011 census) of 2,855,794. There are about 30 tribes and sub-tribes falling into two main groups of Nagas and Kukis. Manipuri and English are the official languages.

Manipur has a *Legislative Assembly* of 60 members, of which 19 are from reserved tribal constituencies. The capital is Imphal.

Elections were held in March 2017. The Indian National Congress party won 28 seats; Bharatiya Janata Party, 21; Naga People's Front, 4; National People's Party, 4; All India Trinamool Congress, 1; Lok Janshakti Party, 1. An independent also took one seat.

Governor: Najma Heptulla (took office in Aug. 2016).

Chief Minister: Nongthombam Biren Singh (took office in March 2017).

In 2011, 68·3% of households used electricity for lighting. Chromite is the only significant mineral resource. Rice is the principal crop; with wheat, maize and pulses. Fruit and vegetables include pineapples, oranges, bananas, mangoes, pears, peaches and plums. The main forest products are teak, jurjan and pine. There are also large areas of bamboo and cane. Manipur is one of the least industrialized states of India. Location, limited infrastructure and insufficient power hold back industrial development. Larger-scale industries include the manufacture of bicycles and TV sets, sugar, cement, starch, vegetable oil and glucose.

In March 2011 Manipur had 19,133 km of roads of which 8,140 km were surfaced. A railway links Karong with the Assamese railway system. There is an airport at Imphal.

In 2011, 79·9% of the population were literate (86·5% of males and 73·2% of females). At the 2011 census Hindus accounted for 41·4% of the population; Christians, 41·3%; Muslims, 8·4%; other religions, 8·9%.

Meghalaya

The state was inaugurated on 2 April 1970. Its status was that of a state within the State of Assam until 21 Jan. 1972 when it became a fully-fledged state of the Union. The area is 22,429 sq. km and the population (2011 census) 2,966,889. The main languages of the state are Khasi, Garo and English.

Meghalaya has a unicameral legislature. The *Legislative Assembly* has 60 seats. The capital is Shillong.

In elections held in Feb. 2018 the Indian National Congress won 21 seats; National People's Party, 19; United Democratic Party, 6; People's Democratic Front, 4; Bharatiya Janata Party, 2; Hill State People's Democratic Party, 2. Smaller parties and independents won four seats and one seat remained vacant.

Governor: Tathagata Roy (took office in Aug. 2018).

Chief Minister: Conrad Sangma (took office in March 2018).

In 2011, 60·9% of households used electricity for lighting. The state produces coal, sillimanite (95% of India's total output), limestone, fire clay, dolomite, feldspar, quartz and glass sand. Over 70% of the people depend on agriculture. Principal crops are rice, maize, potatoes, cotton, oranges, ginger, tezpata, areca nuts, jute, mesta, bananas and pineapples. Forest products are one of the state's chief resources. Apart from agriculture the main source of employment is the extraction and processing of minerals; there are also important timber processing mills and cement factories.

In March 2011 there were 11,984 km of roads of which 7,072 km were surfaced. The main airport serving the state is at Guwahati, 21 km across the state border in Assam but only 124 km from Shillong.

In 2011, 75·5% of the population were literate (77·2% of males and 73·8% of females). At the 2011 census Christians accounted for 74·6% of the population; Hindus, 11·5%; Muslims, 4·4%; other religions, 9·4%.

Mizoram

On 21 Jan. 1972 the former Mizo Hills District of Assam was created a Union Territory. A long dispute between the Mizo National Front (originally Separatist) and the central government was resolved in 1986. Mizoram became a state in July 1986. The area is 21,081 sq. km and the population (2011 census) 1,097,206. The main languages are Mizo and English.

Mizoram has a unicameral *Legislative Assembly* with 40 seats. The capital is Aizawl.

In the elections of Nov. 2018 the Mizo National Front won 26 seats; the Zoram People's Movement, 8; the Indian National Congress, 5; the Bharatiya Janata Party, 1.

Governor: Jagdish Mukhi (since March 2019).

Chief Minister: Zoramthanga (took office in Dec. 2018, having previously been chief minister from Dec. 1998–Dec. 2008).

In 2011, 84·2% of households used electricity for lighting. About 60% of the people are engaged in agriculture. Principal crops in 2007–08 were bananas, turmeric, ginger, passion fruit, oranges, squash and rice. Handloom weaving and other cottage industries are important.

In March 2011 Mizoram had 9,810 km of roads of which 7,001 km were surfaced. There is a metre-gauge rail link at Bairabi, 130 km from Aizawl. Lengpui Airport, Aizawl is connected by air with Kolkata, Guwahati and Imphal.

In 2011, 91·6% of the population were literate (93·7% of males and 89·4% of females). At the 2011 census Christians accounted for 87·2% of the population; Buddhists, 8·5%; Hindus, 2·8%; Muslims, 1·4%.

Nagaland

The state was created in 1961. Nagaland has an area of 16,579 sq. km and a population (2011 census) of 1,978,502. The official language is English; Nagamese, a variant language form of Assamese and Hindi, is the most widely spoken language.

The *Legislative Assembly* has 60 members. The capital is Kohima.

At the elections to the State Assembly in Feb. 2018 the Naga People's Front won 27 seats; Nationalist Democratic Progressive Party won 17 seats; Bharatiya Janata Party, 12; National People's Party, 2; Janata Dal (United), 1; ind., 1.

Governor: Padmanabha Acharya (took office in July 2014).

Chief Minister: Neiphiu Rio (took office in March 2018).

In 2011, 81·6% of households used electricity for lighting. Oil has been located in three districts. Reserves are estimated at 600m. tonnes. Other minerals include: coal, limestone, marble, chromite, magnesite, nickel, cobalt, chromium, iron ore, copper ore, clay, glass sand and slate. 90% of the people depend on agriculture.

In March 2011 there were 34,146 km of roads of which 15,470 km were surfaced.

In 2011, 80·1% of the population were literate (83·3% of males and 76·7% of females). At the 2011 census Christians accounted for 87·9% of the population; Hindus, 8·8%; Muslims, 2·5%.

Odisha

Odisha, known as Orissa until Sept. 2011, was divided between Mahratta and Bengal rulers when occupied by the British East India Company. It became a province in 1936 and a state in 1950. In Oct. 1999 Odisha was hit by a devastating cyclone which resulted in more than 10,000 deaths. The area of the state is 155,707 sq. km, and its population (2011 census) 41,974,218. The principal and official language is Odia.

The *Legislative Assembly* has 147 members. The capital is Bhubaneswar.

At the state elections held in April 2014 the Biju Janata Dal won 117 seats (with 43·4% of the vote); the INC, 16 (25·7%); the BJP, 10 (18·0%); the Samata Kranti Dal, 1 (0·4%); and the Communist Party of India (Marxist), 1 (0·4%). Two independents were elected.

Governor: Ganeshi Lal (took office in May 2018).

Chief Minister: Naveen Patnaik (took office in March 2000).

In 2011, 43·0% of households used electricity for lighting and 55·3% used kerosene. Odisha is India's leading producer of chromite, graphite, bauxite, dolomite, fire-clay, iron ore, manganese ore, limestone, quartz-quartzite and iron ore. The cultivation of rice is the principal occupation of about 80% of the workforce. Turmeric is cultivated in the uplands of the districts of Ganjam, Phulbani and Koraput. Fish production in 2012–13 totalled 410,000 tonnes. In 2011 there were 1,492,471 handicrafts and cottage industries in operation, 59,079 small-scale industries and 334 large and medium industries in operation.

In March 2011 there were 258,836 km of roads of which 58,719 km were surfaced. In 2015–16 there were 2,572 route-km of railway. There is an airport at Bhubaneswar. The busiest port is Paradip.

The percentage of literate people in the population in 2011 was 73·5% (males, 82·4%; females, 64·4%). At the 2011 census Hindus accounted for 93·6% of the population; Christians, 2·8%; Muslims, 2·2%; other religions, 1·4%.

Punjab

The Punjab was constituted an autonomous province of India in 1937. In 1947 it was partitioned between India and Pakistan as East and West Punjab. In 1966 the state was constituted as a Punjabi-speaking state. An area comprising 47,000 sq. km and an estimated (1967) population of 8·5m. was shared between the new state of Haryana and the Union Territory of Himachal Pradesh. The existing capital of Chandigarh was made joint capital of Punjab and Haryana. The area of the state is 50,362 sq. km, with a population (2011 census) of 27,743,338. The official language is Punjabi.

Punjab has a unicameral legislature, the *Legislative Assembly*, of 117 members. The capital is Chandigarh.

Legislative Assembly elections were held in Feb. 2017. The Indian National Congress (INC) won 77 seats, the Aam Aadmi Party (AAP) won 20, Shiromani Akali Dal (SAD) 15, the Bharatiya Janata Party (BJP) 3 and the Lok Insaaf Party (LIP) 2.

Governor: V. P. Singh Badnore (took office in Aug. 2016).

Chief Minister: Amarinder Singh (took office in March 2017).

In 2011, 96·6% of households used electricity for lighting. About 75% of the population depends on agriculture. Leading crops are wheat, potatoes, rice, kinnow, mangoes, grapes, pears, peaches, lemons, sugarcane and oil-seeds. Agriculture in Punjab is more advanced and mechanized than in most other parts of India. The chief manufactures are metals, textiles yarn, sports goods, hand tools and sugar. There is also an oil refinery.

In March 2011 there were 84,193 km of roads of which 76,612 km were surfaced. Punjab has an extensive rail system, served by the Northern Railway. Route-km (2015–16), 2, 269 km. The main airport is Amritsar's Sri Guru Ram Das Jee International Airport.

In 2011, 76·7% of the population were literate (81·5% of males and 71·3% of females). At the 2011 census Sikhs accounted for 57·7% of the population; Hindus, 38·5%; Muslims, 1·9%; Christians, 1·3%.

Rajasthan

The state is in the largely desert area formerly known as Rajputana. In 1818 Rajputana became a British protectorate over a group of princely states including Jaipur, Jodhpur and Udaipur. After independence the Rajput princes were replaced by a single state government. Rajasthan is the largest Indian state in size, with an area of 342,239 sq. km. Population (2011 census), 68,548,437. The main languages are Rajasthani and Hindi.

There is a unicameral legislature, the *Legislative Assembly*, having 200 members. The capital is Jaipur.

At the election in Dec. 2018 the Indian National Congress (INC) won 99 seats; the Bharatiya Janata Party (BJP), 73; the Bahujan Samaj Party, 6; the Rashtriya Loktantrik Party, 3; the Communist Party of India (Marxist), 2; the Bharatiya Tribal Party, 2; Rashtriya Lok Dal, 1; ind., 13.

Governor: Kalyan Singh (took office in Sept. 2014).

Chief Minister: Ashok Gehlot (took office in Dec. 2018, having previously been chief minister from Dec. 1998–Dec. 2003 and Dec. 2008–Dec. 2013).

In 2011, 67·0% of households used electricity for lighting. The state is the sole producer of garnet and jasper in India, and the leading producer of zinc, calcite, gypsum and asbestos. Other minerals include lead (80% of India's production), feldspar (70% of the country's production), fluorite (59%), barytes (53%) and kaolin (44%). Principal crops are pulses, wheat, rice and cotton. The Indira Gandhi Nahar Canal is India's largest irrigation project. Chief manufactures are textiles, dyeing, printing cloth, cement, glass and sugar. The state is a major textile centre and is the leading producer of polyester and viscose yarns in India.

In March 2011 there were 241,318 km of roads of which 194,979 km were surfaced. In 2015–16 there were 5,893 route-km of railway. There are airports at Jaipur (Sanganer Airport), Jodhpur, Kota and Udaipur. Sanganer has been upgraded to receive international flights.

In 2011, 67·1% of the population were literate (80·5% of males and 52·7% of females). At the 2011 census Hindus accounted for 88·5% of the population; Muslims, 9·1%; Sikhs, 1·3%.

Sikkim

A small Himalayan independent kingdom between Nepal and Bhutan, Sikkim was ruled by the 14th-century Namgyal dynasty. In 1950 a treaty was signed with the government of India, declaring Sikkim an Indian Protectorate. In 1975 the king was deposed after political unrest. Following a referendum, Sikkim became an Indian state. The area of the state is 7,096 sq. km. Population (2011 census), 610,577. The capital is Gangtok.

The Assembly has 32 members. English is the principal language and the official language of the government. Lepcha, Bhutia, Nepali and Limboo are also official languages.

At the State Assembly elections in April 2014 the Sikkim Democratic Front (SDF) won 22 of 32 seats and Sikkim Krantikari Morcha (SKM) 10.

Governor: Ganga Prasad (took office in Aug. 2018).

Chief Minister: Pawan Kumar Chamling (took office in Dec. 1994).

There are four hydro-electric power stations. In 2011, 92·5% of households used electricity for lighting. Copper, zinc and lead are mined. Main crops are apples, barley, buckwheat, cardamom, ginger, maize, mandarin oranges, millet, potatoes, rice and wheat. Tea is also grown. Sericulture produces about 180 kg of silk per annum. Small-scale industries include cigarettes, distilling, tanning, fruit preservation, carpets and watchmaking.

There were 4,630 km of roads in March 2011 of which 4,119 km were surfaced. Sikkim has the shortest road network of any Indian state. The nearest railhead is at Shiliguri (115 km from Gangtok). The nearest airport is at Bagdogra (128 km from Gangtok), linked to Gangtok by helicopter service.

In 2011, 82·2% of the population were literate (87·3% of males and 76·4% of females). At the 2011 census Hindus accounted for 57·8% of the population; Buddhists, 27·4%; Christians, 9·9%; Muslims, 1·6%; other religions, 3·3%.

Tamil Nadu

By 1801 the whole of the area from the Northern Circars to Cape Comorin (with the exception of certain French and Danish settlements) had been brought under British rule and was known as the Madras Presidency. After independence there were a number of boundary exchanges between Tamil Nadu and Andhra Pradesh, Orissa, Karnataka and Kerala. In Aug. 1968 the state was named Tamil Nadu. State area, 130,058 sq. km. Population (2011 census), 72,147,030. Tamil is the principal language and was adopted as the state language in 1958.

There is a unicameral legislature; the *Legislative Assembly* has 235 members. The capital is Chennai (formerly known as Madras).

At elections held in May 2016 the All India Anna Dravida Munnetra Kazhagam (AIADMK) won 134 seats, against 89 for the Dravida Munnetra Kazhagam (DMK), 8 for the Indian National Congress (INC) and 1 for the Indian Union Muslim League (IUML).

Governor: Banwarilal Purohit (took office in Oct. 2017).

Chief Minister: Edappadi K. Palaniswami (took office in Feb. 2017).

In 2011, 93·4% of households used electricity for lighting. The state has magnesite, lignite, bauxite, limestone, manganese, fireclay and feldspar. The land is a fertile plain watered by rivers flowing east from the Western Ghats. The staple food crops grown are paddy, maize, jowar, bajra, pulses and millets. Important commercial crops are sugarcane, oilseeds, cotton, tobacco, coffee, rubber and pepper. Forest products include timber, teak, wattle, sandalwood, pulp wood and sapwood. Fish production in 2012–13 totalled 620,000 tonnes. The biggest industrial project is Salem steel plant. Tamil Nadu produces around 70% of India's leather and 40% of its cotton textiles. Other important industries are automobile products, chemicals, agricultural and food processing, biotechnology and computer software.

In March 2011 there were 192,339 km of roads of which 158,473 km were surfaced. In 2015–16 there were 4,027 route-km of railway in Tamil Nadu. There are airports at Chennai, Coimbatore, Tiruchirapalli and Madurai. Chennai is an international airport and the main centre of airline routes in south India. Chennai, Kamarajar (at Ennore) and Tuticorin are the chief ports.

At the 2011 census, 80·3% of the population were literate (86·8% of males and 73·9% of females). At the 2011 census Hindus accounted for 87·6% of the population; Christians, 6·1%; Muslims, 5·9%. In 2015, 4·68m. foreign tourists visited Tamil Nadu (making it the most visited Indian state).

Telangana

Telangana became India's 29th state on 2 June 2014 after it split from Andhra Pradesh. Under the terms of the Andhra Pradesh Reorganization Act, the two states will share a capital city—Hyderabad—for ten years. The area is 114,840 sq. km. Population (2011), 35,193,978. The main languages spoken are Telugu and Urdu. There is a *Legislative Assembly* of 120 members and a *Legislative Council* of 40 members.

At the state elections held in Dec. 2018 Telangana Rashtra Samithi took 88 of the 119 elected seats (with 46·9% of the vote); the INC, 19 (28·4%); the All India Majlis-e-Ittehad-ul Muslimeen, 7 (2·7%); Telegu Desam Party, 2 (3·5%); the BJP, 1 (7·1%); the All India Forward Bloc, 1 (0·8%). One independent was elected.

Governor: E. S. L. Narasimhan (since June 2014).

Chief Minister: Kalvakuntla Chandrashekar Rao (took office in June 2014).

In 2010–11, 69·9% of rural homes had electricity. Mineral resources include coal, limestone, dolomites, quartz and feldspar. Agriculture is the state's main occupation, and leading crops are cereals, rice, cotton and pulses. Important industries include construction, mining and quarrying. Manufacturing is also significant with pharmaceuticals, granite, food processing and steel being produced. Hyderabad is one of the country's largest IT hubs, and a number of companies including Microsoft, Google and Facebook run their Indian operations from the city.

In 2012–13 there were 89,756 km of roads of which 60,613 km were surfaced. In 2015–16 there were 1,737 route-km of railway. There is one international airport at Hyderabad.

In 2011, 66·5% of the population were literate (75·0% of men and 57·9% of women). At the 2011 census Hindus comprised 85·1% of the population that now constitutes Telangana (including Hyderabad); Muslims, 12·7%; Christians, 1·3%.

Tripura

Tripura is a Hindu state of great antiquity having been ruled by the Maharajahs for 1,300 years before its accession to the Indian Union in 1949. With the reorganization of states on 1 Sept. 1956 Tripura became a Union Territory. The Territory was made a State in 1972. It has an area of 10,486 sq. km. Population, 3,673,917 (2011 census). The official languages are Bengali and Kokborok.

The *Legislative Assembly* has 60 members. The capital is Agartala.

The Bharatiya Janata Party won the Legislative Assembly elections in Feb. 2018 with 35 seats; the Communist Party of India (Marxist) took 16; the Indigenous People's Front of Tripura, 8.

Governor: Kaptan Singh Solanki (took office in Aug. 2018).

Chief Minister: Biplab Kumar Deb (took office in March 2018).

In 2011, 68·4% of households used electricity for lighting. The state has natural gas reserves of 31bn. cu. metres. The main crops are rice, wheat, jute, mesta, potatoes, oilseeds and sugarcane. Small industries include aluminium utensils, rubber, saw-milling, soap, piping, fruit canning, handloom weaving and sericulture.

Tripura had 33,772 km of roads in March 2011 of which 14,203 km were surfaced. There is a railway between Kumarghat and Kalkalighat (Assam). Route-km in 2015–16, 193 km. There are one airport (Agartala) and three airstrips.

In 2011, 87·8% of the population were literate (92·2% of males and 83·2% of females). At the 2011 census Hindus accounted for 83·4% of the population; Muslims, 8·6%; Christians, 4·4%; Buddhists, 3·4%.

Uttar Pradesh

On independence the states of Rampur, Banaras and Tehri-Garwhal were merged with the United Provinces of Agra and Oudh. In 1950 the name of the United Provinces was changed to Uttar Pradesh. In 2000 Uttaranchal (officially renamed Uttarakhand on 1 Jan. 2007) was taken from the northern, mainly mountainous, region of Uttar Pradesh. Since the formation of Uttarakhand in 2000 the area of Uttar Pradesh is 240,928 sq. km (previously 294,411 sq. km). Population (2011 census), 199,812,341. Uttar Pradesh has the highest population of any of the Indian states. If Uttar Pradesh were a separate country it would have the fifth highest population in the world (after China, India, the USA and Indonesia). The sole official language has been Hindi since April 1990.

Uttar Pradesh has had an autonomous system of government since 1937. There is a bicameral legislature. The *Legislative Council* has 100 members; the *Legislative Assembly* has 404 (one of which is nominated). The capital is Lucknow.

Elections were held in Feb.–March 2017. The Bharatiya Janata Party won 312 seats; Samajwadi Party, 47; Bahujan Samaj Party, 19; Apna Dal (Sonelal), 9; Indian National Congress, 7; Suheldev Bharatiya Samaj Party, 4; Nishad Party, 1; Rashtriya Lok Dal, 1. Independents took three seats.

Governor: Ram Naik (took office in July 2014).

Chief Minister: Ajay Mohan Bisht ('Yogi Adityanath') (took office in March 2017).

In 2011, 36·8% of households used electricity for lighting and 61·9% used kerosene. Minerals include magnesite, granite, dolomite, coal, marble, limestone, bauxite, uranium and silica sand. Uttar Pradesh is India's largest producer of foodgrains. The state is also one of India's main producers of sugar and potatoes. Fish production in 2012–13 totalled 450,000 tonnes. Important industries include cement, vegetable oils, textiles, cotton yarn, jute and glassware. In 2007–08 there were 10,717 registered factories employing 751,165 workers.

In March 2011 there were 390,256 km of roads of which 297,674 km were surfaced. Lucknow is the main junction of the northern rail network. Route-km in 2015–16, 9,077 km. The main airports are at Lucknow, Kanpur, Varanasi, Allahabad, Agra and Gorakhpur.

In 2011, 118·4m. people were literate (69·7%, 79·2% of males and 59·3% of females). At the 2011 census Hindus accounted for 79·7% of the population; Muslims, 19·3%.

Uttarakhand

The state was taken from Uttar Pradesh and became the twenty-seventh state of India on 9 Nov. 2000. It is located on the northern border of the Indian subcontinent. The Chinese suppression of revolt in Tibet in 1959 saw a rapid influx of Tibetan exiles to the region. The Indo–Chinese conflict of 1962 initiated a modernization programme throughout the Indian Himalayas with the development of roads and communication networks. From the 1970s Uttar Pradesh's hill districts called for separation from the state. On 1 Aug. 2000 the Uttar Pradesh Reorganisation Bill was passed, allowing for a separate state, called Uttaranchal (officially renamed Uttarakhand on 1 Jan. 2007), to incorporate 12 of these hill districts and, controversially, the lowland area of Udham Singh Nagar. Uttarakhand has an area of 53,483 sq. km. Population (2011 census), 10,086,292. The principal languages are the Hindi dialects of Garhwali and Kumaoni.

The Legislative Assembly has 70 members. The interim capital and seat of government is at Dehra Dun.

State assembly elections were held in Feb. 2017. The Bharatiya Janata Party (BJP) won 57 seats; the Indian National Congress (INC), 11; ind., 2.

Governor: Baby Rani Maurya (took office in Aug. 2018).

Chief Minister: Trivendra Singh Rawat (took office in March 2017).

In 2011, 87·0% of households used electricity for lighting. There are deposits of limestone, gypsum, iron ore, graphite and copper. Agriculture supports approximately 50% of the population. Subsistence farming is the norm, as only 9% of the land is cultivable. Tourism is by far the most important industry. Other industries include horticulture, floriculture, fruit-processing and medicine production.

In March 2011 there were 49,277 km of roads of which 26,664 km were surfaced. In 2015–16 there were 340 route-km of railway. There are airports at Dehra Dun and Udham Singh Nagar.

In 2011, 79·6% of the population were literate (88·3% of males and 70·7% of females). At the 2011 census Hindus accounted for 83·0% of the population; Muslims, 14·0%; Sikhs, 2·3%.

West Bengal

Bengal was under the overlordship of the Moghul emperor and ruled by a Moghul governor (*nawab*) who declared himself independent in 1740. Following conflict with the British East India Company, he was defeated by British forces in 1757 who subsequently installed their own *nawab* in 1760. At partition in 1947 the East (Muslim) chose to join what was then East Pakistan (now Bangladesh), leaving West Bengal as an Indian frontier state promoting a flow of non-Muslim Bengali immigrants from the East. The total area of West Bengal is 88,752 sq. km. Population (2011 census), 91,276,115. The principal language is Bengali.

The *Legislative Assembly* has 295 seats (294 elected and one nominated). The capital is Kolkata (formerly known as Calcutta).

In elections held in April and May 2016 the All India Trinamool Congress won 211 of 294 seats, the Indian National Congress 44, the Communist Party of India (Marxist) 26, the Bharatiya Janata Party 3, Gorkha Janmukti Morcha 3, the Revolutionary Socialist Party 3, ind. 1 and others 3.

Governor: Keshari Nath Tripathi (took office in July 2014).

Chief Minister: Mamata Banerjee (took office in May 2011).

In 2011, 54·5% of households used electricity for lighting. Coal production (2012–13) 10.36m. tonnes. Foodgrains include rice, wheat and pulses. Other principal crops are potatoes, sugarcane, oilseeds and jute. Tea is also produced. Fish production totalled 1,490,000 tonnes in 2012–13. Leading industries are chemicals, fertilizers, jute, medicines, pharmaceuticals, steel, sugar and tea. Small industries are important, employing some 2m. persons in 2007.

In March 2011 there were 299,209 km of roads of which 115,534 km were surfaced. The route-km of railways within the state was 4,135 km in 2015–16. There are two airports. The main airport is Kolkata's Netaji Subhas Chandra Bose International Airport. Kolkata is the chief port. West Bengal has about 800 km of navigable canals.

In 2011, 77·1% of the total population were literate (males, 82·7%; females, 71·2%). At the 2011 census Hindus accounted for 70·5% of the population; Muslims, 27·0%; other religions, 2·4%.

Andaman and Nicobar Islands

The Andaman and Nicobar Islands are administered by the President of the Republic of India acting through a Lieut.-Governor. There is a 30-member Pradesh Council. The seat of administration is at Port Blair, connected to Kolkata (1,255 km away) and Chennai (1,190 km) by steamer service that calls about every ten days. There are air services from Kolkata and Chennai. In March 2011 there were 1,156 km of paved roads and 230 km of other roads. The population (2011 census) was 380,581. In 2011, 86·1% of households used electricity for lighting. Literacy (2011 census), 86·3% (90·1% of males and 81·8% of females). At the 2011 census Hindus accounted for 69·5% of the population; Christians, 21·3%; Muslims, 8·5%.

Lieut.-Governor: Devendra Kumar Joshi (took office in Oct. 2017).

The **Andaman Islands** lie in the Bay of Bengal, 193 km from Cape Negrais in Myanmar. Five large islands grouped together are called the Great Andamans, and to the south is the island of Little Andaman. There are a total of 572 islands. The population of the Andaman Islands (including about 400–450 aboriginals) was 343,125 in 2011. The Great Andaman group, densely wooded, contains hardwood and softwood and supplies the match and plywood industries. Coconut, coffee and rubber are cultivated. The islands are slowly being made self-sufficient in paddy and rice. Fishing is also important.

The **Nicobar Islands** are situated to the south of the Andamans, 121 km from Little Andaman. There are 19 islands, seven uninhabited; total area, 1,841 sq. km. The chief islands are Great Nicobar, Camotra with Nancowrie and Car Nicobar. Nancowrie Harbour is between the islands of Camotra and Nancowrie. The population numbered 36,819 in 2011. The Nicobarese and Shompen tribes are in the majority. Coconut and areca nut are the main items of trade.

Chandigarh

The city of Chandigarh and the area surrounding it was constituted a Union Territory in 1966. Population (2011), 1,055,450. It serves as the joint capital of Punjab and the state of Haryana. The city will eventually be the capital of just the Punjab; joint status is to last while a new capital is built for Haryana.

In 2011, 98·4% of households used electricity for lighting. There is some cultivated land and some forest (27·5% of the territory). In March 2011 there were 2,284 km of roads, all with paved surfaces.

In 2011, 86·4% of the population were literate (90·5% of males and 81·4% of females). At the 2011 census Hindus accounted for 80·8% of the population; Sikhs, 13·1%; Muslims, 4·9%.

Administrator: V. P. Singh Badnore (took office in Aug. 2016).

Dadra and Nagar Haveli

Formerly Portuguese, the territories of Dadra and Nagar Haveli were occupied in July 1954 and a pro-India administration was formed. The territories became a centrally administered Union Territory in 11 Aug. 1961. Area

491 sq. km; population (census 2011), 343,709. There is an Administrator appointed by the government of India. The capital is Silvassa. 78·82% of the population is tribal. Languages used are dialects classified under Bhilodi (91%), Bhilli, Gujarati, Marathi and Hindi.

Administrator: Praful Patel (took office in Dec. 2016).

In 2011, 95·2% of households used electricity for lighting. Farming is the chief occupation and 21,015 ha. were under net crop in 2007–08. The tribal peoples have exclusive right to collect minor forest produce from the reserved forest area for domestic use. 92 sq. km of reserved forest was declared a wildlife sanctuary in 2000. There is no heavy industry. Industrial estates for small and medium scales have been set up at Piparia, Masat and Khadoli.

In March 2011 there were 808 km of road of which 806 km were surfaced. Although there are no railways in the territory the line from Mumbai to Ahmedabad runs through Vapi, 18 km from Silvassa. The nearest airport is at Mumbai, 180 km from Silvassa.

Literacy was 77·7% of the population at the 2011 census (86·5% of males and 65·9% of females). At the 2011 census Hindus accounted for 93·9% of the population; Muslims, 3·8%; Christians, 1·5%.

Daman and Diu

Daman (Damão) and the island of Diu were Portuguese until 1961 when the territories were occupied by India and incorporated into the Indian Union; they were administered as one unit with Goa, to which they were attached until May 1987 when Goa became a state.

The territory has an area of 112 sq. km and a population of 243,247 at the 2011 census. Daman has an area of 72 sq. km; Diu, 40 sq. km. Daman is the capital of the territory. The main language spoken is Gujarati.

Administrator: Praful Patel (took office in Aug. 2016).

In 2011, 99·1% of households used electricity for lighting. The main activities are tourism, fishing and toddy palm (preparing palm tree sap for consumption). In Daman there is rice-growing, some wheat and dairying. Diu has tourist beaches, grows coconuts and pearl millet, and processes salt. In March 2011 there were 236 km of roads, all with paved surfaces.

In 2011, 87·1% of the population were literate (91·5% of males and 79·6% of females). At the 2011 census Hindus accounted for 90·5% of the population; Muslims, 7·9%; Christians, 1·2%.

Delhi

Delhi became a Union Territory on 1 Nov. 1956 and was designated the National Capital Territory in 1995. Delhi has an area of 1,483 sq. km. Its population (2011 census) is 16,787,941. Under the New Delhi Municipal Act 1994 New Delhi Municipal Council is nominated by central government.

Elections for the 70-member Legislative Assembly were held in Feb. 2015. The Aam Aadmi Party (AAP) won 67 seats and the Bharatiya Janata Party (BJP) 3.

Lieut.-Governor: Anil Baijal (took office in Dec. 2016).

Chief Minister: Arvind Kejriwal (took office in Feb. 2015).

In 2011, 99·1% of households used electricity for lighting. There are deposits of kaolin (china clay), quartzite and fire clay. The modern city is the largest commercial centre in northern India. The largest single industry is the manufacture of garments. Some traditional handicrafts such as ivory carving and handwoven textiles still flourish.

In March 2011 there were 29,648 km of roads of which 20,962 km were surfaced. Five national highways pass through the city. Delhi has three main railway stations. Delhi's metro system opened in 2002. As of 2014 it incorporated five lines plus an Airport Express service. Total length: 193 km, serving 140 stations. There is a 40-km long electric ring railway. Indira Gandhi International Airport operates international flights.

The proportion of literate people to the total population was 86·3% at the 2011 census (91·0% of males and 80·9% of females). At the 2011 census Hindus accounted for 81·7% of the population; Muslims, 12·9%; Sikhs, 3·4%.

Delhi publishes many of India's major daily newspapers, including *The Times of India*, *Hindustan Times* and *The Hindu* (in English); and *Navbharat Times* and *Hindustan* (in Hindi).

Lakshadweep

The territory consists of an archipelago of 36 islands (ten inhabited), about 300 km off the west coast of Kerala. It was constituted a Union Territory in 1956 as the Laccadive, Minicoy and Amindivi Islands, and renamed in Nov. 1973. The total area of the islands is 32 sq. km. Population (2011 census), 64,473, nearly all Muslims. The language is Malayalam, but the language in Minicoy is Mahl. Headquarters of administration, Kavaratti on Kavaratti Island.

In 2011, 99·7% of households used electricity for lighting. Supplies of potable water is problematic in most of the islands. Rain water harvesting schemes have been introduced as well as desalination plants. There are several small factories processing fibre from coconut husks. The major industry is fishing. The principal catches are tuna and shark. The staple products are copra and fish; coconut is the only major crop.

There is an airport on Agatti Island. The islands are also served by ship from the mainland and have helicopter inter-island services. There are two catamaran-type inter-island ferries. In March 2011 the islands had 190 km of roads, all with paved surfaces.

In 2011, 92·3% of the population were literate (96·1% of males and 88·3% of females). At the 2011 census Muslims accounted for 96·6% of the population; Hindus, 2·8%.

Administrator: Farooq Khan (took office in Sept. 2016).

Puducherry

Formerly the chief French settlement in India, Puducherry (known as Pondicherry until 2006) was founded by the French in 1673. Administration was transferred to India in Nov. 1954. In May 1963 Pondicherry became a Union Territory. The total area of Puducherry is 479 sq. km. Total population (2011 census), 1,247,953. The principal languages spoken are Tamil, Telugu, Malayalam, French and English.

Puducherry is governed by a Lieut.-Governor, appointed by the President, and a Council of Ministers responsible to a Legislative Assembly.

In the elections of May 2016 the Indian National Congress won 15 seats, followed by the All Indian National Congress with 8 seats, the All India Anna Dravida Munnetra Kazhagam 4 seats and the Dravida Munnetra Kazhagam 2 seats. One seat went to an independent candidate.

Lieut.-Governor: Kiran Bedi (took office in May 2016).

Chief Minister: V. Narayanasamy (took office in June 2016).

In 2011, 97·7% of households used electricity for lighting. The main food crop is rice. Principal cash crops are sugarcane and groundnuts. Manufacturing includes textiles, sugar, cotton yarn, spirits and beer, potassium chlorate, rice bran oil and vehicle parts,

In March 2011 there were 2,740 km of road of which 2,404 km were surfaced. Puducherry is connected by rail to Viluppuram Junction in Tamil Nadu. Route-km in 2015–16, 22 km. The nearest main airport is Chennai.

In 2011, 86·6% of the population were literate (92·1% of males and 81·2% of females). At the 2011 census Hindus accounted for 87·3% of the population; Christians, 6·3%; Muslims, 6·1%.

Further Reading

India

Adeney, Katherine and Wyatt, Andrew, *Contemporary India*. 2010

Bhagwati, Jagdish and Panagariya, Arvind, *Why Growth Matters: How Economic Growth in India Reduced Poverty and the Lessons for Other Developing Countries*. 2013

Bhambhri, C. P., *The Political Process in India, 1947–91*. 1991

Bose, S. and Jalal, A. (eds) *Nationalism, Democracy and Development: State and Politics in India*. 1997

Brown, J., *Modern India: The Origins of an Asian Democracy*. 2nd ed. 1994

Drèze, Jean and Sen, Amartya, *An Uncertain Glory: India and its Contradictions*. 2013

Fernandes, Edna, *Holy Warriors: A Journey into the Heart of Indian Fundamentalism*. 2007

Gandhi, Rajmohan, *Gandhi: The Man, His People and the Empire*. 2007

Guha, Ramachandra, *India After Gandhi: The History of the World's Largest Democracy*. 2007—*India Before Gandhi*. 2013—*Gandhi 1914–1948: The Years That Changed the World*. 2018

Gupta, S. P., *Globalisation, Economic Reforms and Employment Strategy in India.* 2007

Hajari, Nisid, *Midnight's Furies: The Deadly Legacy of India's Partition.* 2015

Hardgrave, Robert L. and Kochanek, Stanley A., *India: Government and Politics in a Developing Nation.* 7th ed. 2007

Jaffrelot, C. (ed.) *L'Inde Contemporain de 1950 à nos Jours.* 1996

James, L., *Raj: The Making and Unmaking of British India.* 1997

Jha, Raghbendra, *Facets of India's Economy and Her Society.* 2 vols. 2018

Joshi, V. and Little, I. M. D., *India's Economic Reforms, 1991–2000.* 1996

Kamdar, Mira, *Planet India: The Turbulent Rise of the World's Largest Democracy.* 2007

Kapur, Akash, *India Becoming: A Portrait of Life in Modern India.* 2012

Keay, John, *India: A History.* 2000

Khan, Yasmin, *The Great Partition: The Making of India and Pakistan.* 2007.—*India at War: The Subcontinent and the Second World War.* 2015

Khilnani, S., *The Idea of India.* 1997

King, R., *Nehru and the Language Politics of India.* 1997

Metcalf, Barbara D. and Metcalf, Thomas R., *A Concise History of India.* 2001

Mohan, C. Raja, *Crossing the Rubicon: The Shaping of India's New Foreign Policy.* 2003

New Cambridge History of India. 2nd ed. 5 vols. 1994–96

Nilekani, Nandan, *Imagining India: The Idea of a Renewed Nation.* 2009

Panagariya, Arvind, *India: The Emerging Giant.* 2008

Paul, T. V., *The India-Pakistan Conflict: An Enduring Rivalry.* 2005

Raghavan, Srinath, *India's War: The Making of Modern South Asia, 1939–1945.* 2016

Rajadhyaksha, Niranjan, *The Rise of India: Its Transformation from Poverty to Prosperity.* 2006

Robb, Peter, *A History of India.* 2nd ed. 2011

Roberts, Adam, *Superfast Primetime Ultimate Nation: The Relentless Invention of Modern India.* 2017

SarDesai, D. R., *India: The Definitive History.* 2008

Sharma, Mihir, *Restart: The Last Chance for the Indian Economy.* 2015

Tseng, Wanda and Cowen, David, *India's and China's Recent Experience with Reform and Growth.* 2007

Tully, Mark, *India: The Road Ahead.* 2011

Vohra, R., *The Making of India: A Historical Survey.* 1997

Von Tunzelmann, Alex, *Indian Summer: The Secret History of the End of an Empire.* 2007

National library: Belvedere, Kolkata 700027. *Director General:* Dr Arun Kumar Chakraborty.

National Statistical Office: Ministry of Statistics and Programme Implementation, Computer Centre, East Block-10, RK Puram, New Delhi 110066. *Minister of Statistics and Programme Implementation:* D. V. Sadananda Gowda.

Website: http://mospi.nic.in

Other more specialized titles are listed under CONSTITUTION AND GOVERNMENT *and* RECENT ELECTIONS *above.*

Jammu and Kashmir

Behera, Navnita Chadha, *Demystifying Kashmir.* 2007

Hewitt, Vernon, *Towards the Future: Jammu and Kashmir in the 21st Century.* 2001

Punjab

Singh, Khushwant, *A History of the Sikhs.* 2 vols. 2007

Indonesia

Republik Indonesia (Republic of Indonesia)

Capital: Jakarta
Population projection, 2020: 272·22m.
GNI per capita, 2017: (PPP$) 10,846
HDI/world rank, 2017: 0·694/116=
Internet domain extension: .id

Key Historical Events

The Indonesian archipelago was populated from the north from around 3000 BC. Indian scholars described the Dvipantera civilization of Java and Sumatra as early as 200 BC and Indian-influenced Hindu kingdoms began to appear in the west of the archipelago from the 1st century AD. Small maritime trading settlements evolved into Srivijaya, a Buddhist Malay kingdom centred on southeast Sumatra. The Srivijaya empire controlled trade between India and China through the Melaka strait and by the late 7th century it had expanded to encompass much of Sumatra, the Malay peninsula and western Java. Other Indianized kingdoms developed in central Java, including Mataram (8th–10th centuries) and Mahayana (9th century).

Power shifted to east Java, culminating in the Majapahit empire (founded by Wijaya in 1293 and developed by Gaja Mada), which controlled much of present-day Indonesia. Islam was brought to northern Sumatra by Arab merchants from the 7th century but spread only gradually until the rise of the sultanate of Melaka from the early 15th century. The north Javanese coastal kingdoms that converted to Islam competed with the Majapahit empire, contributing to its decline by the early 16th century.

Portuguese forces, led by Afonso de Albuquerque, having conquered the sultanate of Melaka in 1511 attempted to control the spice trade, although local powers including Aceh (north Sumatra) and Makassar (Sulawesi) competed by opening new routes. Dutch mariners arrived in west Java in 1596 and Jan Pietersoon Coen established a base on Java (Batavia, which became Jakarta) in 1619. The capture of Melaka in 1641 heralded 150 years of Dutch control of the spice trade through its United East India Company (VOC).

Following the VOC's collapse at the end of the 18th century and after a short period of British rule under Thomas Stamford Raffles, the Dutch state took control of the archipelago. The Anglo-Dutch Treaty of 1824 delineated the border between British Malaya and the Dutch East Indies. Between 1825–50 the Dutch suppressed a rebellion on Java, initially led by Prince Diponegoro, and partly fuelled by opposition to the 'Cultivation System' whereby locals had to devote a percentage of their land to cultivating government-approved export crops. The Sarekat Islam (Islamic Union), founded in 1912, was the country's first major nationalist movement. In March 1942 Japanese forces invaded and began to dismantle the Dutch power base. The Indonesian nationalist leaders Sukarno and Mohammad Hatta worked with the Japanese occupiers whilst pushing for independence. On 17 Aug. 1945, two days after Japan's surrender, Sukarno and Hatta proclaimed an independent republic with Sukarno as its president, although the Netherlands did not concede unconditional sovereignty until 27 Dec. 1949.

In 1960 President Sukarno dismissed parliament after a dispute over the government's budget and dissolved political parties. In their place he set up the National Front and the Provisional People's Consultative Assembly. On 11–12 March 1966 the military commanders under the leadership of Lieut.-Gen. Suharto seized executive power, leaving President Sukarno as head of state. The Communist party, which had twice attempted to overthrow the government, was outlawed. On 22 Feb. 1967 Sukarno handed over all his powers to Gen. Suharto. Re-elected president at five-year intervals, on the final occasion on 10 March 1998, Suharto presided over a booming economy but one that was characterized by corruption and cronyism.

These weaknesses became apparent in 1997 when a failure of economic confidence spread from Japan across Asia. By May 1998 food prices had trebled and riots broke out in Jakarta. The risk of society fragmenting along ethnic and religious lines was emphasized by the sufferings of the Chinese community. President Suharto was forced to stand down on 21 May 1998 and was succeeded by his vice-president, Bacharuddin Jusuf Habibie, who promised political and economic reforms. Continuing protest centred on the Suharto family, which still exercised control over large parts of the economy. In Aug. 1999 Timor-Leste, the former Portuguese colony that Indonesia invaded in 1975, voted for independence, a move that was eventually approved by the Indonesian parliament after violent clashes between independence supporters and pro-Indonesian militia groups. It gained independence on 20 May 2002.

Abdurrahman Wahid was elected president by the People's Consultative Assembly in Oct. 1999. He oversaw some reform and economic growth but was forced to step down amid allegations of corruption on 29 Jan. 2001. His vice-president, Megawati Sukarnoputri, took control and assumed the presidency on 23 July 2001. In Oct. 2002 around 200 people died in a car-bomb explosion outside a nightclub in Bali. Jemaah Islamiyah, an extremist group with alleged links to Al-Qaeda, was implicated.

Indonesia's first direct presidential election took place in Sept. 2004 when Susilo Bambang Yudhoyono beat Megawati in a run-off vote. On 26 Dec. 2004 northwest Sumatra was hit by a devastating tsunami. The death toll in Indonesia was put at 166,000, mostly in Aceh. However, the disaster revived the peace process, initiated in late 2002, between the government and the separatist Free Aceh Movement (GAM). Accords signed in Helsinki, Finland in Aug. 2005 created a framework for a military stand-down on both sides.

In Oct. 2014 Joko Widodo succeeded Yudhoyono as president.

Territory and Population

Indonesia, with a land area of 1,910,931 sq. km (737,615 sq. miles), consists of 17,504 islands (6,000 of which are inhabited) extending about 3,200 miles east to west through three time-zones (East, Central and West Indonesian Standard time) and 1,250 miles north to south. The largest islands are Sumatra, Java, Kalimantan (Indonesian Borneo), Sulawesi (Celebes) and Papua, formerly West Papua (the western part of New Guinea). Most of the smaller islands except Madura and Bali are grouped together. The two largest groups of islands are Maluku (the Moluccas) and Nusa Tenggara (the Lesser Sundas). On the island of Timor, Indonesia is bounded in the east by Timor-Leste.

Population at the 2010 census was 237,641,326; density, 124·4 per sq. km. Indonesia has the fourth largest population in the world, after China, India and the USA. In 2011, 44·6% of the population were urban.

The UN gives a projected population for 2020 of 272·22m.

Area, population and chief towns of the provinces, autonomous regions and major islands:

	Area (in sq. km)	Population (2010 census)	Chief town	Population (2010 census)
Bali	5,780	3,890,757	Denpasar	788,589
Nusa Tenggara Barat	18,572	4,500,212	Mataram	402,843
Nusa Tenggara Timur	48,718	4,683,827	Kupang	336,239
Bali and Nusa Tenggara	73,070	13,074,796		
Banten	9,663	10,632,166	Serang	577,785
DKI Jakarta[1]	664	9,607,787	Jakarta	9,607,787
Jawa Barat	35,378	43,053,732	Bandung	2,394,873

(continued)

© Springer Nature Limited 2020
Palgrave Macmillan (ed.), *The Statesman's Yearbook 2020*,
https://doi.org/10.1057/978-1-349-95940-2_92

	Area (in sq. km)	Population (2010 census)	Chief town	Population (2010 census)
Jawa Tengah	32,801	32,382,657	Semarang	1,555,984
Jawa Timur	47,800	37,476,757	Surabaya	2,765,487
Yogyakarta[1]	3,133	3,457,491	Yogyakarta	388,627
Java	129,439	136,610,590		
Kalimantan Barat	147,307	4,395,983	Pontianak	554,764
Kalimantan Selatan	38,744	3,626,616	Banjarmasin	625,481
Kalimantan Tengah	153,565	2,212,089	Palangkaraya	220,962
Kalimantan Timur	204,534	3,553,143	Samarinda	727,500
Kalimantan Utara[1]	—	—	Tanjung Selor	30,486
Kalimantan	544,150	13,787,831		
Maluku	46,914	1,533,506	Ambon	331,254
Maluku Utara	31,983	1,038,087	Ternate	185,705
Papua[2]	319,036	2,833,381	Jayapura	256,705
Papua Barat[2]	97,024	760,422	Manokwari	187,726
Maluku and Papua	494,957	6,165,396		
Gorontalo	11,257	1,040,164	Gorontalo	180,127
Sulawesi Barat	16,787	1,158,651	Mamuju	336,973
Sulawesi Selatan	46,717	8,034,776	Makassar	1,338,663
Sulawesi Tengah	61,841	2,635,009	Palu	336,532
Sulawesi Tenggara	38,068	2,232,586	Kendari	289,966
Sulawesi Utara	13,852	2,270,596	Manado	410,481
Sulawesi	188,522	17,371,782		
Aceh[2]	57,956	4,494,410	Banda Aceh	223,446
Bangka-Belitung	16,424	1,223,296	Pangkalpinang	174,758
Bengkulu	19,919	1,715,518	Bengkulu	308,544
Jambi	50,058	3,092,265	Jambi	531,857
Kepulauan Riau	8,202	1,679,163	Tanjung Pinang	187,359
Lampung	34,624	7,608,405	Bandar Lampung	881,801
Riau	87,024	5,538,367	Pekanbaru	897,767
Sumatera Barat	42,013	4,846,909	Padang	833,562
Sumatera Selatan	91,592	7,450,394	Palembang	1,455,284
Sumatera Utara	72,981	12,982,204	Medan	2,097,610
Sumatra	480,793	50,630,931		

[1]Kalimantan Utara, consisting of four regencies and one city formerly in Kalimantan Timur, was established in Oct. 2012. [2]Province with special status.

The capital, Jakarta, had an estimated population of 9·61m. in 2010. Other major cities (2010 census population in 1m.): Surabaya, 2·77; Bandung, 2·39; Bekasi, 2·33; Medan, 2·10; Tangerang, 1·80; Depok, 1·74; Semarang, 1·52.

Indonesia has around 600 ethnic groups, of which the principal ones are the Acehnese, Bataks and Minangkabaus in Sumatra, the Javanese and Sundanese in Java, the Madurese in Madura, the Balinese in Bali, the Sasaks in Lombok, the Menadonese, Minahasans, Torajas and Buginese in Sulawesi, the Dayaks in Kalimantan, the Irianese in Papua and the Ambonese in the Moluccas. There were an estimated 6·5m. Chinese residents in 2005.

Indonesian (Bahasa Indonesia) is the official language. In spite of the Dutch presence in Indonesia for over 300 years, the language has no official status. Some older Indonesians still speak Dutch and some university students, notably those studying law, often have to study Dutch texts.

Social Statistics

Estimated births, 2008, 4,222,000; deaths, 1,434,000. 2008 estimated birth rate, 18·6 per 1,000 population; death rate, 6·3. Life expectancy in 2013 was 68·8 years for men and 72·9 for women. Annual population growth rate, 2000–08, 1·3%. Infant mortality, 2010, 27 per 1,000 live births; fertility rate, 2008, 2·2 births per woman. Indonesia was ranked 92nd in a gender gap index of 145 countries compiled by the World Economic Forum for its *Global Gender Gap Report 2015*. The annual index considers economic, political, education and health criteria.

Climate

Conditions vary greatly over this spread of islands, but generally the climate is tropical monsoon, with a dry season from June to Sept. and a wet one from Oct. to April. Temperatures are high all the year and rainfall varies according to situation on lee or windward shores. Jakarta, Jan. 78°F (25·6°C), July 78°F (25·6°C). Annual rainfall 71" (1,775 mm). Padang, Jan. 79°F (26·1°C), July 79°F (26·1°C). Annual rainfall 177" (4,427 mm). Surabaya, Jan. 79°F (26·1°C), July 78°F (25·6°C). Annual rainfall 51" (1,285 mm).

On 26 Dec. 2004 an undersea earthquake centred off Sumatra caused a huge tsunami that flooded large areas along the coast of northwestern Indonesia resulting in 166,000 deaths. In total there were more than 225,000 deaths in 14 countries.

Constitution and Government

The constitution originally dates from Aug. 1945 and was in force until 1949; it was restored on 5 July 1959.

The political system is based on *pancasila*, in which deliberations lead to a consensus. There is a 560-member *Dewan Perwakilan Rakyat* (House of People's Representatives), with members elected for a five-year term by proportional representation in multi-member constituencies. An upper house, the *Dewan Perwakilan Daerah* (House of Regional Representatives), has 132 members elected by single non-transferable vote to serve five-year terms. The two chambers together form the *Majelis Permusyawaratan Rakyat* (People's Consultative Assembly). The constitution was changed on 10 Aug. 2002 to allow for direct elections for the president and the vice-president.

There is no limit to the number of presidential terms. Although predominantly a Muslim country, the constitution protects the religious beliefs of non-Muslims.

National Anthem

'Indonesia, tanah airku' ('Indonesia, our native land'); words and tune by W. R. Supratman.

Government Chronology

Presidents since 1949. (Golkar = Party of the Functional Groups; PD = Democratic Party; PDIP = Indonesian Democratic Party–Struggle; PKB = National Awakening Party; PNI = Indonesian National Party)

1949–67	PNI	(Ahmed) Sukarno
1967–98	Golkar	(Mohamed) Suharto
1998–99	Golkar	Bacharuddin Jusuf Habibie
1999–2001	PKB	Abdurrahman Wahid
2001–04	PDIP	Megawati Sukarnoputri
2004–14	PD	Susilo Bambang Yudhoyono
2014–	PDIP	Joko Widodo

Recent Elections

Elections to the House of People's Representatives were held on 9 April 2014. The Indonesian Democratic Party–Struggle (PDIP) won with 109 of 560 seats (18·9% of the vote), ahead of the Party of the Functional Groups (Golkar) with 91 (14·7%), the Great Indonesia Movement Party (Gerindra) 73 (11·8%), the Democratic Party 61 (10·2%), the National Mandate Party 49 (7·6%), the National Awakening Party 47 (9·0%), the Prosperous Justice Party 40 (6·8%), the United Development Party 39 (6·5%), the Nasdem Party 35 (6·7%) and the People's Conscience Party 16 (5·3%). Two other parties contested the election but failed to win any seats.

In the presidential election of 9 July 2014 Joko Widodo (PDIP) won 53·2% of the vote against Prabowo Subianto (Gerindra) with 46·8%. Turnout was 69·6%.

Current Government

President: Joko Widodo; b. 1961 (PDIP; sworn in 20 Oct. 2014).

Vice-President: Jusuf Kalla.

In Feb. 2019 the cabinet was composed as follows:

Co-ordinating Ministers: (Maritime Affairs) Luhut Binsar Pandjaitan; *(Political, Legal and Security Affairs)* Wiranto; *(Economic Affairs)* Darmin Nasution; *(Human Development and Culture)* Puan Maharani.

Minister of Administrative and Bureaucratic Reform: Asman Abnur. *Agriculture:* Amran Sulaiman. *Co-operatives, and Small and Medium Enterprises:* Anak Agung Gede Ngurah Puspayoga. *Communication and Information Technology:* Rudiantara. *Defence:* Ryamizard Ryacudu. *Education and Culture:* Muhadjir Effendy. *Energy and Mineral Resources:* Archandra Tahar. *Environment and Forestry:* Siti Nurbaya Bakar. *Finance:* Sri Mulyani Indrawati. *Foreign Affairs:* Retno Marsudi. *Health:* Nila F. Moeloek. *Home Affairs:* Tjahjo Kumolo. *Industry:* Airlangga Hartanto. *Justice and Human Rights:* Yasonna Laoly. *Land and Spatial Planning:* Sofyan Djalil. *Manpower:* Hanif Dhakiri. *Maritime Affairs and Fisheries:* Susi Pudjiastuti. *National Development Planning:* Bambang Brodjonegoro. *Public Works and Housing:* Basuki Hadimuljono. *Religious Affairs:* Lukman Hakim Saifuddin. *Research, Technology and Higher Education:* Muhammad Nasir. *Social Affairs:* Idrus Marham. *State-Owned Enterprises:* Rini M. Soemarno. *Tourism:* Arief Yahya. *Trade:* Enggartiasto Lukita. *Transportation:* Budi Karya Sumadi. *Villages, Disadvantaged Regions and Transmigration:* Eko Putro Sandjojo. *Women's Empowerment and Child Protection:* Yohana S. Yambise. *Youth and Sport:* Imam Nahrawi. *State Secretary:* Pratikno. *Chief of Staff of the Presidency:* Gen. Moeldoko. *Attorney General:* Muhammad Prasetyo.

Office of the President (Indonesian only): http://www.presidenri.go.id

Current Leaders

Joko Widodo

Position

President

Introduction

Joko Widodo was elected president in July 2014. A businessman who became mayor of the capital, Jakarta, he is the country's first head of state from outside the military or political elite. He entered office promising an ambitious programme of reforms.

Early Life

Joko Widodo (widely known as Jokowi) was born on 21 June 1961 in Solo, central Java. He grew up in a poor neighbourhood before graduating in forestry from Gadya Madha University in Yogyakarta in 1985. He then worked at a state-owned paper producer in Aceh and for a furniture-making firm before establishing his own company, PT Rakabu, manufacturing furniture and flooring for export. The firm expanded during the 1990s and by 2002 he headed the local branch of the Indonesian Furniture Entrepreneurs Association.

This provided a springboard into the political arena. In 2005 Widodo won Solo's mayoral election, representing the centre-left Indonesian Democratic Party—Struggle (PDIP). His accessible personal style proved popular and, having secured improvements to the city's health care and education systems, he won a second term in 2010 by a landslide. It raised his national profile and in 2012 he was persuaded to stand for the mayorship of Jakarta.

After winning election to the post, he set out to reform the capital's notoriously corrupt and inefficient administration. He also won plaudits for his work to set up a universal health care system and for tackling persistent flooding problems. In March 2014 he was nominated as the PDIP's presidential candidate, and took an early lead in the opinion polls over his chief rival, Prabowo Subianto.

Widodo pledged to boost Indonesia's economic performance (setting an annual growth target of 7%), to crack down on public-sector corruption and waste, to improve the education and health care sectors, and to invest in national infrastructure. In the wake of contentious results of the election on 9 July 2014, both he and Prabowo declared victory, prompting the outgoing president, Susilo Bambang Yudhoyono, to appeal for calm. On 22 July Indonesia's election commission confirmed Widodo as the victor, with 53·2% of the vote, although Prabowo maintained that the election was flawed and undemocratic.

Career in Office

In spite of his lack of experience in national politics and his minority parliamentary support, Widodo vowed to take a tough line on corruption and nepotism, to strengthen Indonesia's infrastructure and to improve relations with neighbouring countries. Within three months of taking office he had abolished fuel subsidies amounting to US$18bn., with the intention of redirecting the finances towards education, health care and schemes to alleviate poverty. Despite several stimulus packages, the economy has been sluggish in view of weak external demand for commodities, delayed infrastructure spending and tight monetary policy, but his administration has sought to improve the business and investment environment by easing regulation and offering tax incentives. Having maintained high voter approval ratings, Widodo announced in Aug. 2018 that he would run for presidential re-election in polls scheduled for April 2019. He chose Ma'ruf Amin, a senior conservative Muslim cleric, as his running mate.

Indonesia's hard-line approach to drug trafficking led to the execution of several foreign nationals in early 2015, in turn prompting the recall by Australia, Brazil and the Netherlands of their respective ambassadors in protest. Meanwhile, Islamist jihadist extremists have claimed responsibility for several terror attacks in Jakarta in 2016 and 2017, and in Surabaya in May 2018.

In Sept. 2018 a powerful earthquake and resulting tsunami hit Sulawesi and its provincial capital of Palu, killing many hundreds of people.

Defence

In 2013 defence expenditure totalled US$8,366m. (up from US$6,524m. in 2012), with spending per capita US$33. The 2013 expenditure represented 0·9% of GDP.

Army

Army strength in 2011 was estimated at 233,000 with a strategic reserve (KOSTRAD) of 40,000 and further potential mobilizable reserves of 400,000.

There is a paramilitary police some 280,000 strong; and a part-time local auxiliary force, KAMRA (People's Security), which numbers around 40,000.

Navy

The Navy in 2011 numbered about 45,000, including some 20,000 marines and around 1,000 in Naval Aviation. Combatant strength in 2011 included two diesel submarines (although their serviceability was in doubt) and 11 frigates.

The Navy's principal command is split between the Western Fleet, at Teluk Ratai (Jakarta), and the Eastern Fleet, at Surabaya.

Air Force

Personnel (2011) 24,000. There were 69 combat-capable aircraft, including F-5s, F-16s, Su-27s and Su-30s.

Economy

Manufacturing accounted for 24·3% of GDP in 2011, followed by agriculture, fishing and forestry 14·7%, trade and hotels 13·8%, and mining and quarrying 11·9%.

Overview

Indonesia is rated a lower-middle income country after a significant rise in gross national income per capita from US$560 in 2000 to US$3,374 in 2015. It is the world's fourth most populous nation, has the eighth largest economy in term of GDP (PPP) and the largest in southeast Asia, and is a member of the G20. Indonesia was one of only three G20 members (along with China and India) to maintain economic growth during the global financial crisis that began in 2008 (although at a significantly slower pace than the other two). The economy depends on domestic demand, government spending and the regulation of prices of a range of basic goods including oil and gas, rice and electricity.

Indonesia has been one the world's fastest developing countries since the early 2000s, with average annual growth of 5·3% per year between 2001 and 2015. However, the lack of a solid export base has hindered expansion, particularly in view of decelerating demand from China and low commodities prices in 2015. Private consumption remains the cornerstone of the economy, supported by a strong labour market with real wage growth and improving consumer confidence.

The government introduced a 20-year development plan for the period 2005–25, with the 2015–20 phase focusing on infrastructure development and improving education and health care. The government has also aimed to rationalize subsidies and improve tax collection.

Although the poverty rate halved between 1999 and 2015 to 11·2%, some 28·6m. people remained below the poverty line in 2015, with approximately 40% of the population clustered around the line—a situation exacerbated by the failure of employment growth to match the rise in population. Moreover, inequality in Indonesia is high compared to its neighbours. Public services are inadequate by middle-income standards and the country measures poorly against a number of health- and infrastructure-related indicators. Other threats to long-term growth include inter-ethnic tensions and high levels of corruption in the government and public and private sectors.

Currency

The monetary unit is the *rupiah* (IDR) notionally of 100 *sen* (although *sen* are not used in practice). Inflation rates (based on IMF statistics):

2008	2009	2010	2011	2012	2013	2014	2015	2016	2017
9·8%	5·0%	5·1%	5·3%	4·0%	6·4%	6·4%	6·4%	3·5%	3·8%

In Aug. 2009 foreign exchange reserves were US$55,440m., gold reserves were 2·35m. troy oz and total money supply was 490,111bn. rupiahs.

Budget

The fiscal year used to start 1 April but since 2001 has been the calendar year. In 2015 general government revenues (provisional) totalled 1,742,000bn. rupiah (of which taxes 1,387,000bn. rupiah) and expenditures 1,712,000bn. rupiah. Main items of expenditure by economic type in 2015 (provisional): compensation of employees, 607,000bn. rupiah; use of goods and services, 396,000bn. rupiah; subsidies, 188,000bn. rupiah.

The standard rate of VAT is 10%.

Performance

Real GDP growth rates (based on IMF statistics):

2008	2009	2010	2011	2012	2013	2014	2015	2016	2017
7·4%	4·7%	6·4%	6·2%	6·0%	5·6%	5·0%	4·9%	5·0%	5·1%

The Asian economic crisis of 1997 affected Indonesia more than any other country, leading to a recession in 1998 when the economy shrank by 13·1%. In 2017 total GDP was US$1,015·5bn.

Banking and Finance

The Bank Indonesia, successor to De Javasche Bank established by the Dutch in 1828, was made the central bank of Indonesia on 1 July 1953. Its *Governor* is Perry Warjiyo. It had an original capital of 25m. rupiahs, a reserve fund of 18m. rupiahs and a special reserve of 84m. rupiahs. In Jan. 2000 independent auditors declared that the bank was technically bankrupt. In response the IMF stated that future loans would probably depend on recapitalization and an internal reorganization.

In Oct. 2011 there were 120 commercial banks, of which four were state-owned and 116 were private (90 private national banks and 26 regional development banks). The leading banks are Bank Mandiri (with assets of US$25·6bn. in June 2005), Bank Central Asia and Bank Rakyat Indonesia. All state banks are authorized to deal in foreign exchange.

The government owns one Savings Bank, Bank Tabungan Negara, and 1,000 Post Office Savings Banks. There are also over 3,500 rural and village savings banks and credit co-operatives. At least 16 banks closed in the wake of the 1997 financial crisis.

Foreign debt was US$179,064m. in 2010, representing 26·1% of GNI.

Indonesia attracted US$22,580m. worth of foreign direct investment in 2014, up from US$18,817m. in 2013.

There is a stock exchange in Jakarta.

Energy and Natural Resources

Environment

Indonesia's carbon dioxide emissions from the consumption of energy in 2011 were the equivalent of 1·8 tonnes per capita. An *Environmental Performance Index* compiled in 2016 ranked Indonesia 107th of 180 countries, with 65·9%. The index examined various factors in nine areas—agriculture, air quality, biodiversity and habitat, climate and energy, fisheries, forests, health impacts, water and sanitation, and water resources.

Electricity

In 2011 installed capacity was estimated at 39·9m. kW, with production totalling 182·38bn. kWh (12·42bn. kWh hydro-electric). Consumption per capita was 748 kWh in 2011.

Oil and Gas

The importance of oil in the economy is declining. The 2013 output of crude oil was 42·7m. tonnes, its lowest total since 1970. Proven reserves in 2013 totalled 3·7bn. bbls. With domestic demand having surpassed production, Indonesia became a net importer of oil in 2005.

Natural gas production, 2015, was 75·0bn. cu. metres with 2·8trn. cu. metres of proven reserves. In 2001 a 640-km gas pipeline linking Indonesia's West Natuna field with Singapore came on stream.

Minerals

The high cost of extraction means that little of the large mineral resources outside Java is exploited; however, there is copper mining in Papua, nickel mining and processing on Sulawesi, and aluminium smelting in northern Sumatra. Open-cast coal mining has been conducted since the 1890s, but since the 1970s coal production has been developed as an alternative to oil. Reserves are estimated at 28,000m. tonnes. Coal production (2007), 178·9m. tonnes. Other minerals: bauxite (2008), 1,152,000 tonnes; copper (2006), 818,000 tonnes (metal content); salt (2005 estimate), 680,000 tonnes; nickel (2006), 150,000 tonnes (metal content); tin (2006), 117,500 tonnes (metal content); silver (2011 estimate), 310 tonnes; gold (2011 estimate), 96 tonnes.

Agriculture

There were approximately 23·5m. ha. of arable land in 2012 and 22·0m. ha. of permanent crops. 6·72m. ha. were equipped for irrigation in 2012. Production (2012, in 1,000 tonnes): rice (paddy), 69,056; sugarcane, 28,700; palm oil, 26,900; cassava, 24,177; coconuts, 19,400; maize, 19,387; palm kernels, 6,560; bananas, 6,189; natural rubber, 3,040. Indonesia is the world's largest producer of coconuts and palm oil, and one of the largest producers of nutmeg.

Livestock (2013): goats, 18·58m.; cattle, 16·61m.; sheep, 14·56m.; pigs, 8·25m.; buffaloes, 1·48m.; chickens, 1·79bn.; ducks, 51m. Only China and the USA have more chickens.

Forestry

In 2015 the area under forests was 91·01m. ha., or 53% of the total land area. The annual loss of 684,000 ha. between 2010 and 2015 was exceeded during the same period only in Brazil. In 2011, 118·00m. cu. metres of roundwood were cut.

Fisheries

In 2015 total catch was 6,485,320 tonnes (the second highest of any country after that of China), of which 6,028,260 tonnes were sea fish. Aquaculture production totalled 2,304,828 tonnes in 2010, the fourth highest in the world. About 90% of the country's total fish production is consumed domestically. Imports of fishery commodities were valued at US$402m. in 2011 and exports at US$3·18bn.

Industry

The largest companies in Indonesia by market capitalization in March 2015 were: Bank Central Asia (US$27·7bn.); Astra International, an automobile company (US$26·6bn.); and Bank Rakyat Indonesia (US$24·8bn.).

There are shipyards at Jakarta Raya, Surabaya, Semarang and Ambon. There are textile factories, large paper factories, match factories, automobile and bicycle assembly works, large construction works, tyre factories, glass factories, caustic soda and other chemical factories. Production (2007, in 1,000 tonnes): cement, 35,033; distillate fuel oil, 11,828; residual fuel oil, 9,538; petrol, 8,363; fertilizers, 7,923; paper and paperboard, 7,223; kerosene, 6,894; raw sugar, 2,814; plywood, 4·2m. cu. metres; 464,800 cars and commercial vehicles (2009); 296bn. cigarettes (2010).

Labour

The labour force in 2013 numbered 122,125,000, up from 103,424,000 in 2003. 70·0% of the population aged 15–64 was economically active in 2013. Women constituted 38·0% of the workforce in 2013. In the same year 6·3% of the population was unemployed.

Indonesia had 0·21m. people living in slavery according to the Walk Free Foundation's 2013 *Global Slavery Index*.

International Trade

Since 1992 foreigners have been permitted to hold 100% of the equity of new companies in Indonesia with more than US$50m. part capital, or situated in remote provinces.

Pressure on Indonesia's currency and stock market led to an appeal to the IMF and World Bank for long-term support funds in Oct. 1997. A bailout package worth US$38,000m. was eventually agreed on condition that Indonesia tightened financial controls and instituted reforms, including the establishment of an independent privatization board, liberalizing foreign investment, cutting import tariffs and phasing out export levies.

Imports and Exports

Imports and exports in US$1m.:

	2006	2007	2008	2009	2010
Imports c.i.f.	61,066	74,473	129,244	96,829	135,663
Exports f.o.b.	100,799	114,101	137,020	116,510	157,779

Principal import items: machinery and transport equipment, basic manufactures and chemicals. Principal export items: gas and oil, forestry products, manufactured goods, rubber, coffee, fishery products, coal, copper, tin, pepper, palm products and tea. Indonesia is the world's largest exporter of both palm oil and tin. Main import suppliers, 2017: China, 21·9%; Singapore, 10·8%; Japan, 9·0%. Main export markets, 2017: China, 13·7%; USA, 10·6%; Japan, 10·5%.

Communications

Roads

In 2006 there were 324,150 km of classified roads (27,668 km of highways or main roads), of which 54% was surfaced. Motor vehicles, 2005: passenger cars, 5,494,034; buses and coaches, 1,184,918; trucks and vans, 2,920,828; motorcycles, 28,556,498. There were 11,451 fatalities in road accidents in 2005.

Rail

In 2005 the national railways totalled 6,482 km of 1,067 mm gauge, comprising 3,012 km on Java (of which 565 km electrified), 1,348 km on Sumatra and 2,122 km which was non-operational. Passenger-km travelled in 2008 came to 18·5bn. and freight tonne-km to 5·5bn.

Civil Aviation

Garuda Indonesia is the state-owned national flag carrier. Merpati Nusantara Airlines, its domestic subsidiary, suspended all services in Feb. 2014 owing to cashflow issues. There are international airports at Jakarta (Sukarno-Hatta), Denpasar (on Bali), Medan (Sumatra), Pekanbaru (Sumatra), Ujung Pandang (Sulawesi), Manado (Sulawesi), Solo (Java) and Surabaya Juanda (Java). Jakarta is the busiest airport, in 2012 handling 57,772,762 passengers (42,660,093 domestic passengers, 11,286,687 on international passengers and 3,285,982 direct transit passengers) and 634,751 tonnes of freight. It was the world's ninth busiest airport in 2012 in terms of overall passenger numbers. In 2012 scheduled airline traffic of Indonesia-based carriers flew 466·8m. km; passenger-km totalled 82·9bn. in the same year.

Shipping

Indonesia's busiest port is Tanjung Priok, which serves the Jakarta area and has a container terminal. In 2013 cargo traffic at Tanjung Priok totalled 58·4m. tonnes. The national shipping company Pelayaran Nasional Indonesia (PELNI) maintains inter-island communications. In Jan. 2014 there were 2,483 ships of 300 GT or over registered, totalling 9·06m. GT. Of the 2,483 vessels registered, 1,315 were general cargo ships, 472 oil tankers, 297 passenger ships, 186 container ships, 176 bulk carriers and 37 liquid gas tankers.

Telecommunications

In 2013 there were 30,723,000 main (fixed) telephone lines; in the same year mobile phone subscriptions numbered 313,227,000 (1,253·6 per 1,000 persons). The number of mobile phone subscriptions more than doubled between 2008 and 2013. 15·8% of the population were internet users in 2013, up from 6·9% in 2009. In March 2012 there were 43·5m. Facebook users.

Social Institutions

Out of 178 countries analysed in the 2017 *Fragile States Index*—a list published jointly by the Fund for Peace and *Foreign Policy* magazine—Indonesia was ranked the 85th least vulnerable to conflict or collapse. The index is based on 12 indicators of state vulnerability across social, political and economic categories.

Justice

There are around 250 district courts of first instance, 20 high courts of appeal and a Supreme Court of Justice (Mahkamah Agung) for the whole of Indonesia in Jakarta. Religious sharia courts with limited jurisdiction are also in place to handle civil cases between Muslim spouses.

The current legal system is a mixture of 'adat' (customary) law, Dutch colonial law and the national law that was brought in following independence in 1945. As in Dutch civil law, the rule of precedence does not apply.

The present criminal law has been in force since 1915 and is codified and based on European penal law. The death penalty is still in use; there were four executions in 2016 but none in 2017 or 2018.

The population in penal institutions in Dec. 2012 was 144,332 (59 per 100,000 of national population). The International Centre for Prison Studies estimated in 2014 that 31·9% of prisoners had yet to receive a trial. Indonesia was ranked 75th of 102 countries for criminal justice and 83rd for civil justice in the 2015 World Justice Project *Rule of Law Index*, which provides data on how the rule of law is experienced by the general public across eight categories.

Education

Adult literacy in 2008 was 92·2%. In 2007 there were 29,796,705 pupils and 1,583,589 teaching staff at primary schools, and 18,716,929 pupils and 1,434,874 teachers at secondary schools. There were 3,755,187 students in higher education in 2007 and 265,527 academic staff. The University of Indonesia in Jakarta, founded in 1849, is the leading institution in the tertiary sector. Other prominent institutions include the Gadjah Mada University (Universitas Gadjah Mada) in Yogyakarta, the Parahyangan Catholic University (Universitas Katolik Parahyangan) in Bandung, the Bandung Institute of Technology (Institut Teknologi Bandung) and the Bogor Agricultural Institute (Institut Pertanian Bogor).

In 2007 public expenditure on education came to 3·6% of GNI and 17·5% of total government spending.

Health

In 2012 there were 2·0 physicians per 10,000 inhabitants, and 13·8 nursing and midwifery personnel per 10,000. There were six hospital beds per 10,000 inhabitants in 2010. In 2012 Indonesia spent 3·0% of its GDP on health.

In *Water: At What Cost? The State of the World's Water 2016*, WaterAid reported that 12·6% of the population does not have access to safe water. Indonesia ranked as the country with the sixth largest number of people living without access to safe water (32·3m. in 2015).

Welfare

There are currently no unemployment benefits or family allowance programmes. Establishments with at least ten employees (or a monthly payroll of 1m. rupiahs or more) are obliged to contribute towards old-age, sickness and maternity benefits for employees with contracts of more than three months.

Religion

Indonesia has six officially recognized religions: Islam, Catholicism, Protestantism, Buddhism, Hinduism and Confucianism. In 2010 there were an estimated 209·1m. Muslims according to the Pew Research Center's Forum on Religion & Public Life (making Indonesia the country with the largest Muslim population). There were also 13·9m. Protestants in 2010, 7·2m. Catholics, 4·1m. Hindus and 1·7m. Buddhists. As a proportion of the total population in 2010, 87·2% were Muslims, 9·9% Christians, 1·7% Hindus and 0·7% Buddhists. In Feb. 2019 there was one cardinal.

Culture

World Heritage Sites

There are eight UNESCO World Heritage sites in Indonesia (the first four inscribed in 1991): Borobudur Temple Compounds, Ujung Kulon National Park, Komodo National Park, Prambanan Temple Compounds, Sangiran Early Man Site (1996), Lorentz National Park (1999), the Tropical Rainforest Heritage of Sumatra (2004) and Cultural Landscape of Bali Province (2012), the *Subak* System as a Manifestation of the *Tri Hita Karana* Philosophy.

Press

In 2014 there were a total of 653 newspapers (of which 431 were dailies and 222 non-dailies), with a total circulation of 10,994,000.

Tourism

In 2010 there were 7,003,000 international tourist arrivals (excluding same-day visitors), up from 6,324,000 in 2009 and 5,002,000 in 2005. The main countries of origin of non-resident tourists in 2010 were: Singapore (1,129,000), Malaysia (1,035,000), Australia (731,000) and China (422,000).

Festivals

Independence from the Dutch is celebrated on 17 Aug. with musical and theatrical performances, carnivals and sporting events. The military parades on Armed Forces Day (5 Oct.) and women are celebrated on Kartini Day (21 April) in memory of Raden Ajeng Kartini, a symbol of female emancipation. In Bali the Hindu new year is marked by a day of silence, Nyepi, followed by a day of feasting. Muslim, Hindu, Buddhist and Christian festivals are marked throughout the country.

Diplomatic Representatives

Of Indonesia in the United Kingdom (30 Great Peter St., London, SW1P 2HW)
  Ambassador: Dr Rizal Sukma.

Of the United Kingdom in Indonesia (Jl Patra Kuningan Raya Blok L5-6, Jakarta 12950)
  Ambassador: Moazzam Malik.

Of Indonesia in the USA (2020 Massachusetts Ave., NW, Washington, D.C., 20036)
  Ambassador: Budi Bowoleksono.

Of the USA in Indonesia (Medan Merdeka Selatan 2-5, Jakarta)
  Ambassador: Joseph R. Donovan, Jr.

Of Indonesia to the United Nations
  Ambassador: Dian Triansyah Djani.

Of Indonesia to the European Union
  Ambassador: Yuri Octavian Thamrin.

Further Reading

Central Bureau of Statistics. *Statistical Yearbook of Indonesia.—Monthly Statistical Bulletin: Economic Indicator.*
Cribb, R., *Historical Dictionary of Indonesia.* 1993.
Cribb, R. and Brown, C., *Modern Indonesia: a History since 1945.* 1995
Day, Tony, (ed.) *Identifying with Freedom: Indonesia after Suharto.* 2007
Elson, R. E., *Suharto; a Political Biography.* 2001
Forrester, Geoff and May, R. J., (eds) The Fall of Soeharto. 1999
Friend, Theodore, *Indonesian Destinies.* 2003
Glassburner, Bruce, (ed.) *The Economy of Indonesia: Selected Readings.* 2007
Holt, Claire, (ed.) Culture and Politics in Indonesia. 2007
Kingsbury, Damien, *The Politics of Indonesia.* 3rd ed. 2005
Ricklefs, M. C., *A History of Modern Indonesia since c. 1200.* 4th ed. 2008
Roberts, Christopher B., Habir, Ahmad D. and Sebastian, Leonard C., (eds) Indonesia's Ascent: Power, Leadership, and the Regional Order. 2015
Schwarz, Adam, *A Nation in Waiting: Indonesia's Search for Stability.* Revised ed. 1999
Schwarz, Adam and Paris, Jonathan, (eds) The Politics of Post-Suharto Indonesia. 1999
Vatikiotis, Michael R. J., *Indonesian Politics under Suharto: The Rise and Fall of the New Order.* 3rd ed. 1999
National Statistical Office: Central Bureau of Statistics, Jl. Dr. Sutomo 6–8, Jakarta, 10710.
Website: http://www.bps.go.id

Iran

Jomhuri-e-Eslami-e-Iran (Islamic Republic of Iran)

Capital: Tehran
Population projection, 2020: 83·59m.
GNI per capita, 2017: (PPP$) 19,130
HDI/world rank, 2017: 0·798/60=
Internet domain extension: .ir

Key Historical Events

Neolithic farmers established settlements in the Zagros mountains, in the west of modern Iran, from 6000 BC. From around 2700 BC the southwestern region of Khuzestan was inhabited by Elamite societies, a formative influence on the first Persian empire, established by Cyrus the Great in 550 BC. His Achaemenian dynasty lasted until around 320 BC and was ruled from Persepolis. Persia was subsequently controlled by the Parthian and Sassanian dynasties, during which the Zoroastrian religion took hold. Arabians arriving in the 7th century AD spread the Islamic faith. Their armies defeated the Sassanians at Nahavand in 641, ushering in a period of control by Arab caliphs and, from the 10th century, Seljuk Turks. Persia came under the control of Ghengis Khan's Mongol armies in the 1220s and was then ruled by Timur from 1370.

The Safavid dynasty (1502–1736) was founded by Shah Ismail, who restored internal order and established the Shia sect of Islam as the state religion. The dynasty reached its zenith in the reign of Shah Abbas I (1587–1628), during which Esfahan became the Persian capital. In 1779, following the death of Mohammad Karim Khan Zand, Agha Mohammad Khan, a leader of the Qajars (a Turkmen tribe from modern Azerbaijan), attempted to reunify Persia. He regained Persian control over much of the Caucasus and established his capital at Tehran.

The Qajars fought with an expansionist Russia during the early 1800s and in 1828 Fath Ali Shah was forced to sign the Treaty of Turkmanchai, acknowledging Russian sovereignty over present-day Armenia and Azerbaijan. The reign of Naser o-Din Shah (1848–96) saw a period of modernization and the increasing influence of the Russian and British empires in Persia, which continued after the adoption of the first constitution and the establishment of a National Assembly in Aug. 1906. The discovery of oil in Khuzestan province in 1908 led to further British and Russian jockeying for control in the region.

Following a bloodless coup in 1921, Reza Khan began his rise to power. He was crowned Reza Shah Pahlavi on 12 Dec. 1925 and set about a programme of reforms, encouraging the development of industry, education and a modern infrastructure. Responding to Iran's support for Germany in the Second World War, the Allies occupied the country and forced Reza Shah to abdicate in favour of his son, Muhammad Reza Shah, who was sworn in on 17 Sept. 1941.

The British-controlled oil industry was nationalized in March 1951 in line with the policy of the National Front Party, whose leader, Dr Muhammad Mussadeq, became prime minister in April 1951. He was opposed by the Shah, who fled the country until Aug. 1953, when Mussadeq was deposed in an Anglo-American sponsored monarchist coup. The Shah's policy, which included the redistribution of land to small farmers and the enfranchisement of women, was opposed by Shia religious scholars. Despite economic growth, unrest was caused by the Shah's repressive measures and his extensive use of the *Savak* (secret police). The opposition, led by Ayatollah Ruhollah Khomeini, the Shia Muslim spiritual leader who had been exiled in 1965, was increasingly successful. Following intense civil unrest in Tehran, the Shah left Iran with his family on 17 Jan. 1979 (and died in Egypt on 27 July 1980).

The Ayatollah Khomeini returned from exile on 1 Feb. 1979, the Shah's government resigned and parliament dissolved itself on 11 Feb. Following a referendum in March, an Islamic Republic was proclaimed. The Constitution gave supreme authority to a religious leader (*wali faqih*), a position held by Ayatollah Khomeini until his death in 1989. Ayatollah Ali Khamenei then became the nation's supreme leader. In Sept. 1980 border fighting with Iraq escalated into full-scale war. A UN-arranged ceasefire came into effect on 20 Aug. 1988, and in Aug. 1990, following Iraq's invasion of Kuwait, Iraq offered peace terms and began the withdrawal of troops from Iranian soil. 30,000 political opponents of the regime are believed to have been executed shortly after the end of the war.

In 1997 the election of Mohammad Khatami as president signalled a shift away from Islamic extremism. A clampdown on Islamic vigilantes who were waging a violent campaign against Western 'decadence' was evidence of a cautiously liberal integration of the constitution. However, the conservative faction led by Ayatollah Ali Khamenei retained considerable power, including the final say on defence and foreign policy.

In July 1999 riot police fought pitched battles with pro-democracy students in Tehran in the worst unrest since the 1979 revolution. Islamic leaders remain divided on the degree of overlap between politics and religion.

The election of Mahmoud Ahmadinejad as president in June 2005 was seen by some analysts as signalling a return to the extreme conservatism that preceded Khatami's tenure. Ahmadinejad's anti-Israeli rhetoric caused international concern. Under his leadership, Iran recommenced uranium conversion research. Despite Tehran's insistence that the research programme was for peaceful purposes only, increasing international disquiet culminated with the International Atomic Energy Agency reporting Iran to the UN Security Council in Feb. 2006. In April 2006 President Ahmadinejad announced that Iran had successfully enriched uranium.

The country witnessed an upsurge of civil unrest in June 2009 following a disputed presidential election in which the incumbent president, Mahmoud Ahmadinejad, was declared the victor by a large majority. Further international sanctions followed Iran's testing of medium- and longer-range missiles as concern grew over the nature of its nuclear programme. In June 2013 Hassan Rouhani was elected president, prompting hopes of a more conciliatory approach from Tehran. After prolonged negotiations, in July 2015 Iran agreed a deal with the international community that saw the country scale back its nuclear facilities in return for the lifting of sanctions. However, following a change of government in the USA, President Donald Trump announced in May 2018 that he was withdrawing the USA from the nuclear accord and reintroducing punitive sanctions on Iran.

Territory and Population

Iran is bounded in the north by Armenia, Azerbaijan, the Caspian Sea and Turkmenistan, east by Afghanistan and Pakistan, south by the Gulf of Oman and the Persian Gulf, and west by Iraq and Turkey. It has an area of 1,628,771 sq. km (628,872 sq. miles) including inland waters, but a vast portion is desert. Census population in 2016 (provisional): 79,926,270. Population density: 49 per sq. km. The population was 71·3% urban in 2011.

The UN gives a projected population for 2020 of 83·59m.

In 2015 Iran had 979,400 refugees, mainly from Afghanistan. Only Turkey, Pakistan and Lebanon have more refugees.

The areas, populations and capitals of the provinces *(ostan)* are:

Province	Area (sq. km)	Census Oct. 2011	Census Sept. 2016	Capital
Alborz	5,122	2,412,513	2,712,400	Karaj
Ardabil	17,800	1,248,488	1,270,420	Ardabil
Azarbayejan, East	45,651	3,724,620	3,909,652	Tabriz
Azarbayejan, West	37,411	3,080,576	3,265,219	Orumiyeh
Bushehr	22,743	1,032,949	1,163,400	Bushehr
Chahar Mahal and Bakhtyari	16,328	895,263	947,763	Shahr-e-Kord
Esfahan	107,018	4,879,312	5,120,850	Esfahan

(continued)

Province	Area (sq. km)	Census Oct. 2011	Census Sept. 2016	Capital
Fars	122,608	4,596,658	4,851,274	Shiraz
Gilan	14,042	2,480,874	2,530,696	Rasht
Golestan	20,367	1,777,014	1,868,819	Gorgan
Hamadan	19,368	1,758,268	1,738,234	Hamadan
Hormozgan	70,697	1,578,183	1,776,415	Bandar-e-Abbas
Ilam	20,133	557,599	580,158	Ilam
Kerman	180,726	2,938,988	3,164,718	Kerman
Kermanshah	25,009	1,945,227	1,952,434	Kermanshah
Khuzestan	64,055	4,531,720	4,710,509	Ahvaz
Kohgiluyeh and Boyer Ahmad	15,504	658,629	713,052	Yasuj
Kordestan	29,137	1,493,645	1,603,011	Sanandaj
Lorestan	28,294	1,754,243	1,760,649	Khorramabad
Markazi	29,127	1,413,959	1,429,475	Arak
Mazandaran	23,842	3,073,943	3,283,582	Sari
North Khorasan	28,434	867,727	863,092	Bojnurd
Qazvin	15,567	1,201,565	1,273,761	Qazvin
Qom	11,526	1,151,672	1,292,283	Qom
Razavi Khorasan	118,851	5,994,402	6,434,501	Mashhad
Semnan	97,491	631,218	702,360	Semnan
Sistan and Baluchestan	181,785	2,534,327	2,775,014	Zahedan
South Khorasan	95,385	662,534	768,898	Birjand
Tehran	13,692	12,183,391	13,267,637	Tehran
Yazd	129,285	1,074,428	1,138,533	Yazd
Zanjan	21,773	1,015,734	1,057,461	Zanjan

At the 2016 census the provisional populations of the principal cities were:

	Population
Tehran	8,693,706
Mashhad	3,001,184
Esfahan	1,961,260
Karaj	1,592,492
Shiraz	1,565,572
Tabriz	1,558,693
Qom	1,201,158
Ahvaz	1,184,788
Kermanshah	946,651
Orumiyeh	736,224
Rasht	679,995
Zahedan	587,730
Hamadan	554,406
Kerman	537,718
Yazd	529,673
Ardabil	529,374
Bandar-e-Abbas	526,648
Arak	520,944
Eslamshahr	448,129
Zanjan	430,871
Sanandaj	412,767
Qazvin	402,748

(continued)

	Population
Khorramabad	373,416
Gorgan	350,676
Sari	309,820
Shahriar	309,607
Qods	309,605
Kashan	304,487
Malard	281,027
Dezful	264,709
Nishabur	264,375
Babol	250,217

The official language is Farsi or Persian. Azerbaijani is the second most widely spoken language, primarily in the northwest. Other languages spoken include Kurdish and Luri in the west, Gilaki and Mazandarami in the north, and Baluchi in the southeast. There are more Azerbaijani speakers in Iran than in Azerbaijan. Most Iranians are Persians, not Arabs. Only around 2% of the population are Arabs.

Social Statistics

2007–08 births, 1,286,716; deaths, 412,735. Rates (2007–08, per 1,000 population): birth, 18·1; death, 5·8. Expectation of life at birth, 2013, 76·1 years for females and 72·2 years for males. Infant mortality, 2010, 22 per 1,000 live births. Annual population growth rate, 2005–10, 1·1%; fertility rate, 2013, 1·9 births per woman. Iran has had one of the largest reductions in its fertility rate of any country in the world over the past quarter of a century, having had a rate of 4·8 births per woman in 1990. Iran was ranked 141st in a gender gap index of 145 countries compiled by the World Economic Forum for its *Global Gender Gap Report 2015*. The annual index considers economic, political, education and health criteria. 2·3% of Iran's adult population are dependent on opiates—the second highest rate in world behind Afghanistan.

Climate

Mainly a desert climate, but with more temperate conditions on the shores of the Caspian Sea. Seasonal range of temperature is considerable, as is rain (ranging from 2" in the southeast to 78" in the Caspian region). Winter is normally the rainy season for the whole country. Abadan, Jan. 54°F (12·2°C), July 97°F (36·1°C). Annual rainfall 8" (204 mm). Tehran, Jan. 36°F (2·2°C), July 85°F (29·4°C). Annual rainfall 10" (246 mm).

Constitution and Government

The Constitution of the Islamic Republic was approved by a national referendum in Dec. 1979. It was revised in 1989 to expand the powers of the presidency and eliminate the position of prime minister. It gives supreme authority to the *Spiritual Leader* (*wali faqih*), a position which was held by Ayatollah Khomeini until his death on 3 June 1989. Ayatollah Seyed Ali Khamenei was elected to succeed him on 4 June 1989. Following the death of the previous incumbent, Ayatollah Ali Khamenei was proclaimed the *Source of Knowledge (Marja e Taghlid)* at the head of all Shia Muslims in Dec. 1994.

The 86-member *Assembly of Experts* was established in 1982. It is popularly elected every eight years. Its mandate is to interpret the constitution and select the Spiritual Leader. Candidates for election are examined by the *Council of Guardians*.

The *Islamic Consultative Assembly* has 290 members, elected for a four-year term in single-seat constituencies. All candidates have to be approved by the 12-member *Council of Guardians*.

The *President* of the Republic is popularly elected for not more than two 4-year terms plus a third non-consecutive term and is head of the executive; he appoints Ministers subject to approval by the *Islamic Consultative Assembly (Majlis)*. The president is Iran's second highest-ranking official.

Legislative power is held by the *Islamic Consultative Assembly*, directly elected on a non-party basis for a four-year term by all citizens aged 17 or over. A new law passed in Oct. 1999 raised the voting age from 16 to 17, thus depriving an estimated 1·5m. young people from voting. Two-thirds of the electorate is under 30. Voting is secret but ballot papers are not printed; electors must write the name of their preferred candidate themselves. Five seats are reserved for religious minorities. All legislation is subject to approval by the *Council of Guardians* who ensure it is in accordance with the Islamic code and with the Constitution. The Spiritual Leader appoints six members, as does the judiciary.

National Anthem

'Sar zad az ofogh mehr-e khavaran' ('Rose from the horizon the affectionate sun of the East'); words by a group of poets, tune by Dr Riahi.

Government Chronology

Spiritual Leaders of the Islamic Republic since 1980.

1980–89	Ayatollah Seyed Ruhollah Mousavi Khomeini
1989–	Ayatollah Seyed Mohammad Ali Hoseyn Khamenei

Heads of State since 1941.
Emperor (Shah)

1941–79	Mohammad Reza Pahlavi

Leader of the Revolution (Rahbar-e Enqelab)

1979–80	Ayatollah Seyed Ruhollah Mousavi Khomeini

President of the Republic

1980–81	Abolhasan Bani-Sadr

Interim Presidential Commission

1981	

President of the Republic

1981	Mohammad Ali Rajai

Interim Presidential Commission

1981	

Presidents of the Republic

1981–89	Hojatoleslam Seyed Mohammad Ali Hoseyn Khamenei

1989–97	Hojatoleslam Ali Akbar Hashemi Rafsanjani
1997–2005	Hojatoleslam Seyed Mohammad Khatami
2005–13	Mahmoud Ahmadinejad
2013–	Hojatoleslam Hassan Rouhani

Recent Elections

Presidential elections were held on 19 May 2017, in which Hassan Rouhani was re-elected with 57·1% of the vote ahead of Ebrahim Raisi with 38·3%, Mostafa Mir-Salim with 1·2% and Mostafa Hashemitaba with 0·5%. Turnout was 73·1%.

Elections to the Islamic Consultative Assembly were held on 26 Feb. and 29 April 2016. The reformist supporters of President Hassan Rouhani won 143 of 290 seats, with hard-liners taking 86. Independents won 61 seats.

Elections to the Assembly of Experts were held on 26 Feb. 2016. 52 of the 88 available seats went to reformist-backed candidates.

Current Government

Spiritual Leader (wali faqih): Ayatollah Seyed Ali Khamenei; b. 1939 (since 4 June 1989).

In Feb. 2019 the cabinet was composed as follows:

President: Hassan Rouhani; b. 1948 (sworn in 3 Aug. 2013 and re-elected 19 May 2017).

First Vice-President: Es'haq Jahangiri.

Head of the Presidential Office: Mahmoud Vaezi.

Vice-President and Head of Administrative and Recruitment Organization: Jamshid Ansari. *Vice-President and Head of Atomic Energy Organization:* Ali Akbar Salehi. *Vice-President and Head of Cultural Heritage, Handicrafts and Tourism Organization:* Ali Asghar Mounesan. *Vice-President for Economic Affairs:* Mohammad Nahavandian. *Vice-President and Head of the Environmental Protection Organization:* Isa Kalantari. *Vice-President for Legal Affairs:* Laaya Joneidi. *Vice-President and Head of Martyrs and Veterans Affairs Foundation:* Seyed Mohammad-Ali Shahidi. *Vice-President for Parliamentary Affairs:* Hossein-Ali Amiri. *Vice-President and Head of the Planning and Budget Organization:* Mohammad Bagher Nobakht. *Vice-President for Science and Technology Affairs:* Sorena Sattari. *Vice-President for Women and Family Affairs:* Massoumeh Ebtekar.

Minister of Agriculture Jihad: Mahmoud Hojjati. *Co-operatives, Labour and Social Welfare:* Mohammad Shariatmadari. *Culture and Islamic Guidance:* Abbas Salehi. *Defence:* Brig.-Gen. Amir Hatami. *Economic Affairs and Finance:* Farhad Dejpasand. *Education:* Mohammad Bathaei. *Energy:* Reza Ardakanian. *Foreign Affairs:* Mohammad Javad Zarif. *Health and Medical Education:* Hassan Qazizadeh Hashemi. *Industry, Mines and Trade:* Reza Rahmani. *Information and Communications Technology:* Mohammad Javad Azari Jahromi. *Intelligence:* Mahmoud Alavi. *Interior:* Abdolreza Rahmani Fazli. *Justice:* Alizera Avaei. *Oil:* Bijan Namdar Zanganeh. *Roads and Urban Development:* Mohammad Eslami. *Science, Research and Technology:* Mansour Gholami. *Youth and Sports:* Masoud Soltanifar. *Chief of Staff in the President's Office:* Mahmoud Vaezi Joz.

Presidency Website: http://www.president.ir

Current Leaders

Ayatollah Seyed Ali Khamenei
Position
Spiritual Leader (wali faqih)

Introduction
Seyed Ali Khamenei succeeded Ayatollah Khomeini as Iran's supreme spiritual leader on the latter's death in June 1989, having previously served from 1981 as the third president of the Islamic Republic.

Early Life
Khamenei was born in Mashhad on 17 July 1939. He attended theological colleges in Qom, where he was a pupil of Ayatollah Khomeini, and Mashhad. From 1963 he was involved with the Islamic opposition to the regime of the Shah, for which he spent three years in prison and a year in exile. Active in the Islamic revolution of 1979, Khamenei was appointed to the Revolutionary Council and became deputy minister of defence. He was also leader of the Friday congregational prayers in Tehran from mid-1980 and, from Aug. 1981, was appointed secretary-general of the Islamic Republican Party (IRP), dissolved in 1987.

Career in Office
On 2 Oct. 1981, as the IRP candidate, Khamenei was the first cleric to be elected as president, with 95% of the popular vote. Ayatollah Khomeini had previously barred the clergy from the office. He succeeded Mohammad Ali Radjai who had been assassinated in Aug. In Aug. 1985 he was re-elected, again overwhelmingly, for a second four-year term. He was injured in a bomb blast in June 1986. On the death of Khomeini, Khamenei was elected to succeed him on 4 June 1989 by an Assembly of Experts. Previously a middle-ranking cleric (Hojatoleslam), he assumed the title of Ayatollah, a constitutional precondition of appointment to the Islamic republic's spiritual leadership. In Dec. 1994 he was proclaimed the Marja e Taghlid (Source of Knowledge) at the head of all Shia Muslims.

The standoff between then President Khatami's reformist government and the hard-line conservative Council of Guardians reached a critical point in the run-up to the Feb. 2004 parliamentary elections. The Council's disqualification of over 2,000 reformist candidates provoked threats of resignations in government and boycott in the electorate. Khamenei intervened in Jan. 2004 on state television, calling for review of the Council's decisions and backing the 83 Majlis deputies whose candidacies had been rejected. However, over a third of the Majlis's deputies resigned in protest on 1 Feb. 2004 and in the subsequent election religious conservatives regained parliamentary control.

Khamenei subsequently presided over a serious decline in relations with Western powers over Iran's uranium enrichment activities, the confrontational foreign policy stance of the then hard-line Islamic state president, Mahmoud Ahmadinejad, and Iran's support for the Assad regime in Syria's civil war. Iran's alleged ambitions to acquire nuclear weapons incurred damaging international economic sanctions but Khamenei maintained the country's right to nuclear technology for peaceful purposes. Ahmadinejad had first been elected as state president in June 2005 and was formally endorsed by Khamenei. Furthermore, Khamenei upheld his disputed re-election in June 2009, dismissing calls for the poll to be rerun and endorsing the ensuing violent security crackdown on opposition to the regime.

However, he increasingly distanced himself from the president during the latter's second and final term of office, criticizing Ahmadinejad's economic stewardship, which saw a dramatic fall in the value of the currency, and also his inflammatory rhetoric. The election in June 2013 of Hassan Rouhani, a reformist cleric, as the new president heralded an easing of friction with the West as Rouhani, with Khamenei's presumed (if sceptical) endorsement, promptly oversaw the negotiation of an interim agreement in Nov. that year with the six-nation group of the USA, Russia, China, UK, Germany and France limiting Iran's uranium enrichment activities in return for sanctions relief. A comprehensive accord was reached in July 2015, although Khamenei maintained that the nuclear deal did not signal a rapprochement with the USA or any change in Iran's regional policies in the Middle East. Furthermore, the USA's subsequent withdrawal from the accord in May 2018 and reimposition of damaging sanctions on Iran reignited simmering tensions, and in Aug. he rejected US President Donald Trump's offer of dialogue and banned any future talks.

In Dec. 2017 Khamenei had also denounced the US president's recognition of the holy city of Jerusalem as the capital of Israel., while in Jan. 2018 he blamed the USA and UK for directing street protests that erupted the previous month in towns and cities across Iran against economic mismanagement and corruption by the clerical regime.

Hassan Rouhani

Position
President

Introduction
Hassan Rouhani became president in Aug. 2013 and was re-elected in May 2017. A reformist and pragmatic cleric, he sought to improve relations with Western states with the aim of easing economic sanctions against Iran. However, apparent progress in 2015 with the conclusion of a comprehensive international accord on the suspension of Iran's nuclear development aspirations was derailed in 2018 by hardline US President Donald Trump's withdrawal from the agreement and reimposition of sanctions on the Islamic Republic.

Early Life
Hassan Rouhani was born Hassan Fereydoun on 12 Nov. 1948 in Sorkheh, near Semnan, Iran. He was educated at Semnan and Qom seminaries from 1960, before studying judicial law at Tehran University from 1969–72. In the 1990s he earned a master's degree in law and a doctorate in constitutional law from Scotland's Glasgow Caledonian University.

From the mid-1960s Rouhani supported the growing Islamist movement in Iran and criticised the Shah's government. In 1977 he joined Ruhollah Khomeini in exile in France but returned to Iran after the fall of the Shah and was elected to parliament in 1980. He held key posts during the Iran–Iraq war, including head of the executive committee of the High Council for War Support from 1986–88, commander of national air defence from 1985–91 and deputy to the second-in-command of the joint chiefs of staff from 1988–89. He also served on the Supreme Defence Council from 1983–88.

In 1989 he was appointed secretary of the Supreme National Security Council, serving until 2005, and was also Supreme Leader Ayatollah Khamenei's council representative. He was national security adviser to President Rafsanjani from 1989–97 and to President Khatami from 2000–05. From 2003–05 he led the team negotiating with Western states

and the International Atomic Energy Agency over Iran's controversial nuclear development programme, agreeing to more inspections and the suspension of uranium enrichment—a deal subsequently dropped by President Ahmadinejad who was in office from 2005–13.

Concurrent with his security and foreign policy posts, Rouhani served on legal and religious bodies. In 1991 he joined the Expediency Council, which adjudicates in legislative disputes, and became head of its political, social and security commission. In 1998 he joined the Assembly of Experts, which appoints and supervises Iran's Supreme Leader, serving as head of its political and social committee from 2001–06 and resuming the post in 2013. He also served as deputy speaker of parliament from 1996–2000.

In 2013 Rouhani contested the June presidential election, pledging to improve Iran's international relations, negotiate an easing of economic sanctions and rescue the economy. He also promised civil reforms to increase freedom and openness. Although criticized by some for his links with the establishment and previous suppression of dissent, he nonetheless won support from moderates and conservatives and gained victory in the first round of voting.

Career in Office
Rouhani swiftly renewed negotiations over Iran's nuclear capability, agreeing an interim deal in Nov. 2013 with the permanent UN Security Council members, plus Germany, that saw a suspension of some sanctions pending further talks. A comprehensive accord was finally reached in July 2015 and was described by Rouhani, who struck a more conciliatory tone than supreme leader Ayatollah Khamenei, as a political, technical and legal victory for Iran. In Jan. 2016 the USA and European Union began lifting sanctions after the UN officially confirmed that the Iranian government was fulfilling its nuclear commitments. However, new US President Donald Trump adopted a more confrontational policy towards Iran in 2017, imposing fresh sanctions in response to an Iranian medium-range ballistic missile test in Jan., declining in Oct. to certify the 2015 nuclear accord to the US Congress and seeking to ban inward travel to the USA by residents of Iran. In May 2018 Trump announced the USA's formal withdrawal from the nuclear accord and subsequently reintroduced more punitive sanctions against Iran in Aug. and Nov.

From June 2014 Rouhani offered Iran's support to the Iraqi government in its efforts to resist an extremist insurgency by Islamic State Sunni militants. Relations with Saudi Arabia, however, further deteriorated over the two countries' opposing stance on civil conflict in Yemen and the sacking of the Saudi embassy in Tehran by Iranian protesters in Jan. 2016 following the execution of a prominent Shia Muslim cleric by the Saudi authorities. Meanwhile, Iran's support for President Assad's regime in the Syrian civil war was reconfirmed in Dec. 2016 when Rouhani said that Iran would continue to co-operate with Russia 'until the ultimate goal of eradicating terrorism and restoring peace and full security to the region is achieved'.

On the domestic front Rouhani's opponents pointed to a lack of progress on social reforms and civil rights. However, in parliamentary elections in Feb. and April 2016, moderate and reformist candidates supportive of the president made significant gains against religious conservatives and hard-liners, and in May 2017 Rouhani was re-elected to the presidency with 57% of the popular vote. The following month Islamic State jihadists claimed responsibility for co-ordinated terror attacks on the parliament and a shrine in Tehran.

Despite Rouhani's electoral victory, his reformist image was seriously weakened at the end of 2017 by major street protests across Iran over economic grievances and regime corruption, which prompted violent clashes with security forces. In the wake of the USA's reimposition of sanctions, there were more street protests in June 2018 over rising prices, the rapidly sinking value of the currency and the ongoing cost of Iranian military involvement in Syria and in the civil war in Yemen. In Aug. Rouhani's embattled government was further undermined by parliament's impeachment of the then finance minister, Massoud Karbasian, amid the mounting economic crisis. Discontent among Iran's Arab population was also evidenced by a mass shooting in Sept. at a military parade in the city of Ahvaz by suspected Arab nationalists that killed 25 people.

In Jan. 2016 Rouhani had met Pope Francis, the head of the Roman Catholic Church, in the Vatican and the two leaders stressed 'the importance of inter-religious dialogue'.

Defence

18 months' military service is compulsory (ten months in the case of university graduates). In 2013 defence spending totalled US$17,749m., with spending per capita US$222. The 2013 expenditure represented 4·1% of GDP

(down from 5·2% in 2012). The UN Security Council passed a number of resolutions imposing sanctions on Iran in the late 2000s banning the purchase of conventional arms and missile technology.

Iran has on a number of occasions successfully tested Shahab-3 medium-range ballistic missiles, initially with a range of 1,300 km, and most recently in Sept. 2009 an upgraded version that reportedly has a range of 2,000 km. In Nov. 2008, and again in Dec. 2009, it tested a new missile, the Sajil, which also reportedly has a range of 2,000 km. Unlike the Shahab-3, the Sajil is a solid fuel missile.

Nuclear Weapons

Although Iran is a member of the Non-Proliferation Treaty (NPT), there have been widespread and long-standing international concerns that its nuclear programme includes a military dimension. In Nov. 2011 IAEA inspectors reported that Iran was carrying out research 'relevant to the development of a nuclear explosive device'. Tehran maintains that its nuclear development programme is solely for civilian use but the UN Security Council has pressed for Iran to end uranium enrichment until its peaceful intentions are confirmed. In June 2013 the election of Hassan Rouhani as president led to talks over the country's nuclear activities and a partial lifting of sanctions. In July 2015 Iran and the five permanent members of the UN Security Council—China, France, Russia, the UK and the USA—plus Germany agreed the Joint Comprehensive Plan of Action, under which Tehran pledged to downgrade the centrifuges in use in its two uranium enrichment facilities and reduce its uranium stockpile in return for the easing of international sanctions. It must also allow IAEA inspectors to access any site deemed suspicious within 24 days. After concerted progress by the Iranian government towards meeting these conditions, sanctions were lifted in Jan. 2016.

Army

Strength (2011), 350,000 (about 220,000 conscripts). Reserves are estimated to be around 350,000, made up of ex-service volunteers.

Revolutionary Guard (Pasdaran Inqilab)

Numbering some 125,000, the Guard is divided between ground forces (around 100,000), naval forces (some 20,000) and marines (5,000). It controls the Basij, a volunteer 'popular mobilization army', which can number 1m. strong on mobilization.

Navy

In 2011 the fleet included 23 submarines (15 tactical) and six corvettes. Personnel numbered 18,000 in 2011 including 2,600 in Naval Aviation and 2,600 marines.

The Naval Aviation wing operated 22 aircraft and some 30 helicopters in 2011.

The main naval bases are at Bandar-e-Abbas, Bushehr and Chah Bahar.

Air Force

In 2011 there were 336 combat-capable aircraft including US F-14 Tomcat, F-5B Freedom Fighter, F-5E Tiger II and F-4D/E Phantom II fighter-bombers, and a number of Su-24 strike aircraft.

Strength (2011), 30,000 personnel (12,000 air defence).

Economy

Agriculture accounted for 9·0% of GDP in 2013, industry 40·2% and services 50·8%. Manufacturing's share of total GDP was 11·7%.

Overview

Iran is an upper-middle income country and has the second largest economy in the Middle East and North Africa (after Saudi Arabia). The economy is driven by a large hydrocarbons sector, although agriculture, manufacturing, financial services and small-scale private sector service companies also have a significant presence. Iran ranks second in the world in terms of natural gas reserves and fourth in proven crude oil reserves, on which government revenues remain over-reliant.

Between 2000 and 2005 GDP grew by an average annual rate of 5·5% as a result of high oil prices and strong private sector growth. In 2008 the country experienced a slowdown owing to a decline in oil revenues, but recovered in 2010 on the back of buoyant agricultural production. A tightening of sanctions by the USA then prompted the economy to contract in both 2012 and 2013. Growth resumed in 2014 after a partial lifting of sanctions in response to the accession of the comparatively moderate Hassan

Rouhani to the presidency and the prospect of progress in nuclear limitation talks. The inflation rate declined from nearly 35% in 2013 to 9·1% in 2016, in line with the easing of sanctions and the tightening of monetary policy by the Central Bank of Iran.

With crude oil, gas and related products accounting for over 70% of total export receipts, strong current account surpluses were recorded from 2011–14, when oil prices were high. Iran has managed to weather the price collapse that began in 2014, but unemployment has remained stubbornly high, measuring 11·3% in 2016.

In July 2015 Iran and the five permanent members of the UN Security Council plus Germany agreed on a plan to limit Iran's nuclear development programme in return for a lifting of sanctions. The Iranian economy then bounced back sharply in 2016 with growth of 12·5% following a contraction of 1·6% in 2015. Despite the dominance of hydrocarbons, there are some signs of dynamism in the non-oil sectors as well. The external and budget balances improved in 2016 and Iran's current account surplus witnessed a strong boost owing to the robust growth in oil exports. Poverty was estimated to have fallen from 13·1% to 8·1% between 2009 and 2013 (US$5·5 a day line in 2011 PPP).

The authorities have adopted a comprehensive market-based reform strategy, as reflected in the government's 20-year vision document and the sixth five-year development plan for the 2016–21 period. The government must also tackle the question of how best to boost non-oil sector growth, including improving the business environment and the efficiency of labour markets.

Currency

The unit of currency is the *rial* (IRR) of which $10 = 1$ *toman*. Total money supply in April 2008 was 440,095bn. rials. Inflation rates (based on IMF statistics) for fiscal years:

2008	2009	2010	2011	2012	2013	2014	2015	2016	2017
25·3%	10·8%	12·3%	21·5%	30·6%	34·7%	15·6%	11·9%	9·1%	9·6%

Budget

The financial year runs from 21 March. Revenues in 2008–09 totalled 948,745bn. rials and expenditures 923,015bn. rials. Petroleum and natural gas revenues accounted for 73·5% of all revenues and taxes 19·0%. Current expenditure accounted for 65·8% of all expenditures.

Performance

Real GDP growth rates (based on IMF statistics):

2008	2009	2010	2011	2012	2013	2014	2015	2016	2017
−0·1%	0·0%	5·7%	3·1%	−7·7%	−0·3%	3·2%	−1·6%	12·5%	3·7%

The effects of Western sanctions resulted in the economy contracting in 2012 for the first time since 1994, but positive growth in 2014 brought an end to two years of recession. Total GDP in 2017 was US$439·5bn.

Banking and Finance

The Central Bank is the note issuing authority and government bank. Its *Governor* is Abdolnasser Hemati. All other banks and insurance companies were nationalized in 1979, and reorganized into new state banking corporations. In April 2000 the government announced that it would permit the establishment of private banks for the first time since the revolution in 1979, ending the state monopoly on banking. The first private bank since the revolution came into existence in Aug. 2001 with the creation of Bank Eghtesad Novin (Modern Economic Bank). Several more private banks have opened in the meantime. In 2011 the banking sector comprised 26 institutions, including four large former public banks that had been privatized in 2008 and 2009.

Iran's external debt amounted to US$12,570m. in 2010 (equivalent to 4·1% of GNI), down from US$21,879m. in 2005 (equivalent to 11·6%).

A stock exchange reopened in Tehran in 1992.

Energy and Natural Resources

Environment

Iran's carbon dioxide emissions from the consumption of energy in 2011 accounted for 7·6 tonnes per capita. An *Environmental Performance Index* compiled in 2016 ranked Iran 105th of 180 countries, with 66·3%. The index examined various factors in nine areas—agriculture, air quality, biodiversity and habitat, climate and energy, fisheries, forests, health impacts, water and sanitation, and water resources.

Electricity

Total installed capacity in 2011–12 was 65·2m. kW; production (2011–12), 240·06bn. kWh (including 227·43bn. kWh thermal and 12·06bn. kWh hydro-electric). Consumption per capita in 2011–12 was 3,116 kWh. Iran's first civilian nuclear power plant has been built by Russia at Bushehr. It reached full capacity in Aug. 2012 and became operational in Sept. 2013. In Nov. 2014 Iran and Russia signed a deal to build two new nuclear reactors at Bushehr.

Oil and Gas

Oil is Iran's chief source of revenue. The main oilfields are in the Zagros Mountains where oil was first discovered in 1908. Oil companies were nationalized in 1979 and operations of crude oil and natural gas exploitation are now run by the National Iranian Oil Company, which is the world's third largest oil company in terms of output after Saudi Arabia's Aramco and Russia's Gazprom. Iran produced 234·2m. tonnes of oil in 2017 (5·3% of the world total oil output), up from the 2016 figure of 216·8m. tonnes. Output in 2013 (169·6m. tonnes) was the lowest annual total since 1990. Production peaked at 303·2m. tonnes in 1974. The low figure in 2013 came as Iran's biggest customers—all in Asia—cut their imports amid tightening Western sanctions. In 2017 Iran had reserves amounting to 157·2bn. bbls. In 1999 the most important discovery in more than 30 years was made, with the Azadegan oilfield in the southwest of the country being found to have reserves of approximately 26bn. bbls. In 2009 revenue from oil exports amounted to US$56bn. Iran depends on oil for some 86% of its exports, but domestic consumption has been increasing to such an extent that it is now as high as exports.

Iran has 17·2% of proven global gas reserves. Natural gas reserves in 2017 were 33·2trn. cu. metres. Natural gas production was 223·9bn. cu. metres in 2017, the third highest in the world. In Dec. 1997 the first natural gas pipeline linking Iran with the Caspian Sea via Turkmenistan was opened. The 200-km line links gas fields in western Turkmenistan to industrial markets in northern Iran.

Minerals

Production (in 1,000 tonnes), 2012: iron ore, 24,000; gypsum, 15,000; salt, 3,000; coal, 1,300; bauxite, 820; copper, 260; aluminium, 230; chromite, 190; zinc, 105; manganese, 70; crushed stone and marble, 27. It was announced in Feb. 2003 that uranium deposits had been discovered in central Iran. In Nov. 2003 the International Atomic Energy Agency announced that Iran had admitted to enriching uranium at an electric plant outside Tehran.

Agriculture

There were an estimated 17·71m. ha. of arable land in 2012 and 1·95m. ha. of permanent crops. Around 9·6m. ha. were equipped for irrigation in 2012. Estimated crop production (2012, in 1,000 tonnes): wheat, 13,800; tomatoes, 6,000; potatoes, 5,400; watermelons, 3,800; rice (paddy), 2,400; grapes, 2,150; apples, 1,700. Livestock (2013 estimates): 50·2m. sheep; 22·1m. goats; 8·7m. cattle; 1·6m. asses; 927m. chickens.

Forestry

Approximately 6% of Iran was forested (10·69m. ha.) in 2015, much of it in the Caspian region. Timber production in 2011 was 706,000 cu. metres.

Fisheries

In 2015 the total catch was 637,779 tonnes, of which 549,732 tonnes came from sea fishing and 88,047 tonnes from inland fishing.

Industry

Major industries: petrochemical, automotive, food, beverages and tobacco, textiles, clothing and leather, wood and fibre, paper and cardboard, chemical products, non-metal mining products, basic materials, machinery and equipment, copper, steel and aluminium. The textile industry uses local cotton and silk; carpet manufacture is an important industry. The country's steel industry is the largest in the Middle East.

Industry produced 38·2% of GDP in 2014, including 11·8% from manufacturing. Manufacturing grew by 6·7% in 2014. Of those in employment in 2014, 33·8% worked in industry. In 2010 there were 15,310 establishments employing 1,240,385 persons in manufacturing industries.

Labour

The labour force numbered 26,643,000 in 2013, up from 22,262,000 in 2003. 47·2% of the population aged 15–64 was economically active in 2013. Women constituted 18·3% of the workforce in 2013. In the same year 12·9% of the population was unemployed.

Iran had 65,000 people living in slavery according to the Walk Free Foundation's 2013 *Global Slavery Index*.

International Trade

There had been a limit on foreign investment, but legislation of 1995 permits foreign nationals to hold more than 50% of the equity of joint ventures with the consent of the Foreign Investment Board.

Imports and Exports

In 2011–12 (provisional) merchandise imports totalled US$56,500m. and exports US$95,500m. Main imports: machinery and motor vehicles, iron and steel, chemicals, pharmaceuticals and food. Main exports: oil, carpets, pistachios, leather and caviar. Crude oil exports (2011): 2,537,000 bbls a day. Oil exports account for more than 80% of hard currency earnings. Carpet exports are the second largest hard currency earner. Main import suppliers, 2011–12: United Arab Emirates, 31·9%; China, 12·0%; South Korea, 7·7%. Main export markets in 2011–12: China, 16·7%; Iraq, 15·3%; United Arab Emirates, 13·3%.

Communications

Roads

In 2006 the total length of roads was 174,301 km, of which 1,429 km were motorways, 27,256 km main roads, 41,129 km secondary regional roads and 104,487 km other local roads. In 2007 there were 920,100 passenger cars; 862,600 motorcycles and mopeds; 179,700 vans and lorries; 4,900 buses and coaches. In 2006 there were 165,130 road accidents resulting in 6,380 deaths.

Rail

The State Railways totalled 8,217 km in 2011, of which 148 km were electrified. The railways carried 28·6m. passengers in 2011 and 33·1m. tonnes of freight. An isolated 1,676 mm gauge line (94 km) in the southeast provides a link with Pakistan Railways. A rail link to Turkmenistan was opened in May 1996. A link between Khaf in the northeast of the country and Herat in Afghanistan is being built and was scheduled for completion in early 2019. Metro systems have been opened in Tehran in 1999, Mashhad in 2011, and Esfahan and Tabriz in 2015.

Civil Aviation

There are international airports at Tehran (Mehrabad), Shiraz and Bandar-e-Abbas. Tehran is the busiest airport, in 2014 handling 13,617,094 passengers. The Imam Khomeini International Airport, construction of which began in 1977 before being halted in 1979, was inaugurated in Feb. 2004. The first flight arrived at the airport in May 2004 but it was then shut down by Iran's Revolutionary Guard, citing breaches of security by the foreign operators. The state-owned IranAir is the flag-carrying airline. In 2012 scheduled airline traffic of Iranian-based carriers flew 105·4m. km; passenger-km totalled 13·6bn. in the same year.

Shipping

In Jan. 2014 there were 328 ships of 300 GT or over registered, totalling 2·79m. GT. Of the 328 vessels registered, 226 were general cargo ships, 41 bulk carriers, 25 container ships, 18 oil tankers and 18 passenger ships. The Iranian-controlled fleet comprised 204 vessels of 1,000 GT or over in July 2014, of which 133 were under foreign flags and 71 under the Iranian flag. The principal port is Bandar-e-Abbas, which handled 73,421,000 tonnes of cargo in 2013 (27,048,000 tonnes loaded and 46,373,000 tonnes discharged).

Telecommunications

In 2013 Iran had 29,689,000 main (fixed) telephone lines (383·3 per 1,000 population). In the same year mobile phone subscriptions numbered 65,246,000 (842·5 per 1,000 population). The number of mobile phone subscriptions more than doubled between 2007 and 2013. In 2013 there were 4,351,202 fixed broadband subscriptions, more than double the number in 2011.

Social Institutions

Out of 178 countries analysed in the 2017 *Fragile States Index*—a list published jointly by the Fund for Peace and *Foreign Policy* magazine—Iran was ranked the 49th most vulnerable to conflict or collapse. The index is based on 12 indicators of state vulnerability across social, political and economic categories.

Justice

A legal system based on Islamic law (*Sharia*) was introduced by the 1979 constitution. A new criminal code on similar principles was introduced in Nov. 1995. The President of the Supreme Court and the public Prosecutor-General are appointed by the Spiritual Leader. The Supreme Court has 16 branches and 109 offences carry the death penalty. To these were added economic crimes in 1990. The population in penal institutions in Dec. 2012 was 217,000 (284 per 100,000 of national population). There were 275 executions in 2018. Executions are frequently held in public. The International Centre for Prison Studies estimated in 2014 that 25·1% of prisoners had yet to receive a trial. In 2015 the World Justice Project *Rule of Law Index*, which provides data on how the rule of law is experienced by the general public across eight categories, ranked Iran 60th of 102 countries for criminal justice and 40th for civil justice.

Police

Women rejoined the police force in 2003 for the first time since the 1979 revolution.

Education

Adult literacy in 2012 was 84·3%. Most primary and secondary schools are state schools. Elementary education in state schools and university education is free; small fees are charged for state-run secondary schools. In 2012 there were 415,539 children in pre-primary schools, 5,746,859 pupils at primary schools and 7,118,357 pupils at secondary schools.

In 2012 there were 4,404,614 students at institutions of higher education. The number of students in higher education doubled between 2005 and 2012, with the percentage of the population enrolled in tertiary education increasing from 3·1 to 5·9 over the same period. The University of Tehran, established in 1851 and with university status since 1934, is the largest and oldest institute of tertiary education in Iran. Other leading universities include Sharif University of Technology, in Tehran, and Esfahan University of Technology. The Islamic Azad University, with more than 100 branches across Iran and in other countries, is the world's largest private university system.

In 2012 public expenditure on education came to 3·6% of GDP and represented 16·1% of total government expenditure.

Health

In the period 2005–12 there were nine physicians per 10,000 inhabitants and 14 nursing and midwifery personnel per 10,000. Over the same period there were 17 hospital beds per 10,000 inhabitants. In 2011 health spending represented 4·6% of GDP.

In *Water: At What Cost? The State of the World's Water 2016*, WaterAid reported that 3·8% of the population does not have access to safe water.

Welfare

The official retirement ages are 60 years (men) or 55 (women) with at least 20 years of contributions; age 50 (men) or 45 (women) with at least 30 years of contributions; and at any age with at least 35 years of contributions or between 20 and 25 years of work in an unhealthy or physically demanding natural environment. The pension is equal to 3·33% of the insured's average earnings during the last 24 months multiplied by the number of years of contributions, up to 35 years. The minimum old-age pension is 6,089,070 rials a month (the minimum wage of an unskilled labourer).

Religion

The official religion is the Shia branch of Islam. In 2009 approximately 90–95% of the population were adherents according to the Pew Research Center's Forum on Religion & Public Life, with most of the remainder of the population being Sunnis. However, adult attendance at Friday prayers is low compared to other Muslim countries, with some analysts putting the figure as only 2%, and Islam plays a smaller role in public life today than it did even in the mid-2000s.

Culture

World Heritage Sites

There are 23 UNESCO World Heritage sites in Iran: Tchogha Zanbil (inscribed on the list in 1979), the ruins of the holy city of the kingdom of Elam founded around 1250 BC; Persepolis (1979), the palace complex founded by Darius I in 518 BC and capital of the Achaemenid empire (the first Persian empire); Meidan Imam (1979), the square built in Esfahan by Abbas I in the early 17th century, which is bordered on all sides by monumental buildings linked by a series of arcades; Takht-e Soleyman (2003), a Sasanian royal residence with important Zoroastrian religious architecture and decoration; Bam and its Cultural Landscape (2004 and 2007), a fortified medieval town where 26,000 people lost their lives in the earthquake of 2003; Pasargadae (2004), the first dynastic capital of the great multicultural Achaemenid Empire in Western Asia; Soltaniyeh (2005), the capital of the Ilkhamid dynasty that stands as a monument to Persian and Islamic architecture; Bisotun (2006), an ancient town on the trade route that linked the Iranian high plateau with Mesopotamia; the Armenian Monastic Ensembles (2008), three monastic buildings dating back to the 7th century; Shushtar Historical Hydraulic System (2009), a homogeneous hydraulic system, designed globally and completed in the 3rd century AD; Sheikh Safi al-din Khanegah and Shrine Ensemble in Ardabil (2010), a spiritual retreat built in the Sufi tradition between the 16th and 18th centuries; Tabriz Historic Bazaar Complex (2010), one of the most complete examples of the traditional commercial and cultural system of Iran; the Persian Garden (2011), a collection of nine gardens selected from various regions of Iran; Gonbad-e Qabus (2012), a 53-metre high tomb built in AD 1006 for Qabus Ibn Voshmgir and the only remaining evidence of Jorjan, a former hub of science and arts in the Muslim world; Masjed-e Jamé of Esfahan (2012), the 'Friday Mosque' complex, a stunning example of the evolution of mosque architecture over 12 centuries starting in AD 841; Golestan Palace (2013), an 18th century masterpiece of the Qajar era; Shahr-i Sokhta (2014), the remains of the 'Burnt City', which represent the emergence of the first complex societies in eastern Iran; cultural landscape of Maymand (2015), a small and self-contained valley within Iran's central mountains; Susa (2015), a group of artificial archaeological mounds in the lower Zagros mountains; the Persian Qanat (2016), eleven qanats consisting of rest areas for workers, watermills and water reservoirs; Lut Desert (2016), a sub-tropical area located in the southeast of the country; the Historic City of Yazd (2017), a traditional city located in the middle of the Iranian plateau; and Sassanid Archaeological Landscape of Fars Region (2018), an area consisting of eight archaeological sites situated in the southeast of Fars Province.

Press

In 2008 there were 183 paid-for daily newspapers and more than 3,300 non-dailies. Approximately 80% of the Iranian press is printed in Farsi; much of the remaining 20% is in English or Arabic. In the 2013 *World Press Freedom Index* compiled by Reporters Without Borders, Iran ranked 174th out of 179 countries.

Tourism

There were 3,354,000 non-resident visitors in 2011 (1,402,000 in 2001), spending US$2,574m.

Calendar

The Iranian year is a solar year starting on varying dates between 19 and 22 March. The current solar year is 1398 (21 March 2019 to 20 March 2020). The Islamic *hegira* (AD 622, when Mohammed left Makkah for Madinah) year 1440 corresponds to 11 Sept. 2018–30 Aug. 2019, and is the current lunar year.

Festivals

Iran celebrates Revolution Day on 11 Feb. to mark the anniversary of the overthrow of the Shah in 1979. Nowruz (New Year's Day) falls on 21 March while Constitution Day is on 5 Aug. The feast of Shab-e Yelda, held to mark the longest night of the year, is in Dec.

Diplomatic Representatives

Of Iran in the United Kingdom (16 Princes Gate, London, SW7 1PT).
Ambassador: Hamid Baeidinejad.

Of the United Kingdom in Iran (198 Ferdowsi Ave., Tehran 11316-91144).
Ambassador: Rob Macaire.

The USA does not have diplomatic relations with Iran, but Iran has an Interests Section in the Pakistani embassy (1250 23rd St., Washington, D.C., 20037) and the USA has an Interests Section in the Swiss embassy in Tehran.

Of Iran to the United Nations
Ambassador: Vacant.
Chargé d'Affaires a.i.: Eshagh Al Habib.

Of Iran to the European Union
Ambassador: Peiman Seadat.

Further Reading

Abrahamian, Ervand, *Khomeinism: Essays on the Islamic Republic.* 1993.— *A History of Modern Iran.* 2008

Adib-Moghaddam, Arshin, *Iran in World Politics: The Question of the Islamic Republic.* 2010

Alizadeh, Parvin, (ed.) *The Economy of Iran: The Dilemma of an Islamic State.* 2001

Amanat, Abbas, *Iran: A Modern History.* 2017

Amuzegar, J., *Iran's Economy Under the Islamic Republic.* 1992

Ansari, Ali M., *Modern Iran Since 1921: The Pahlavis and After.* 2003

Axworthy, Michael, *A History of Iran: Empire of the Mind.* 2010.—*Revolutionary Iran: A History of the Islamic Republic.* 2013

Buchan, James, *Days of God: The Revolution in Iran and Its Consequences.* 2012

The Cambridge History of Iran. 7 vols. 1968–91

Coughlin, Con, *Khomeini's Ghost: Iran Since 1979.* 2009

Daniel, Elton L., *The History of Iran.* 2008

Daneshvar, P., *Revolution in Iran.* 1996

Ehteshami, A., *After Khomeini: the Iranian Second Republic.* 1994

Ehteshami, A. and Zweiri, M., *Iran and the Rise of its Neoconservatives: The Politics of Tehran's Silent Revolution.* 2007

Fuller, G. E., *Centre of the Universe: Geopolitics of Iran.* 1992

Gheissari, Ali, (ed.) *Contemporary Iran: Economy, Society, Politics.* 2009

Gheissari, Ali and Nasr, Vali, *Democracy in Iran: History and the Quest for Liberty.* 2009

Goodarzi, Jubin, *Syria and Iran: Diplomatic Alliance and Power Politics in the Middle East.* 2006

Hunter, S. T., *Iran after Khomeini.* 1992

Jett, Dennis, *The Iran Nuclear Deal: Bombs, Bureaucrats, and Billionaires.* 2017

Kamrava, M., *Political History of Modern Iran: from Tribalism to Theocracy.* 1993

Kinzer, Stephen, *All the Shah's Men: an American Coup and the Roots of Middle East Terror.* 2003

Martin, Vanessa, *Creating an Islamic State: Khomeini and the Making of a New Iran.* 2000

Mir-Hosseini, Ziba, *Islam and Gender: The Religious Debate in Contemporary Iran.* 1999

Moazami, Behrooz, *State, Religion, and Revolution in Iran, 1796 to the Present.* 2013

Modaddel, M., *Class, Politics and Ideology in the Iranian Revolution.* 1992

Moin, Baqer, *Khomeini: Life of the Ayatollah.* 1999

Omid, H., *Islam and the Post-Revolutionary State in Iran.* 1994

Polk, William R., *Understanding Iran.* 2009

Pollack, Kenneth M., *Unthinkable: Iran, the Bomb, and American Strategy.* 2013

Rahnema, A. and Behdad, S. (eds) *Iran After the Revolution: the Crisis of an Islamic State.* 1995

Rostami-Povey, Elaheh, *Iran's Influence: A Religious-Political State and Society in its Region.* 2010

Takeyh, Ray, *Hidden Iran: Paradox and Power in the Islamic Republic.* 2006

Wright, Robin, (ed.) *The Iran Primer: Power, Politics, and U.S. Policy.* 2010

National Statistical Office: Statistical Centre of Iran, Dr Fatemi Avenue, Tehran 1414663111, Iran.

Website: http://www.amar.org.ir

Iraq

Jumhouriya al 'Iraqia (Republic of Iraq)

Capital: Baghdad
Population projection, 2020: 41·50m.
GNI per capita, 2017: (PPP$) 17,789
HDI/world rank, 2017: 0·685/120
Internet domain extension: .iq

Key Historical Events

Around 3000 BC the Sumerian culture flourished in Mesopotamia—the part of the Fertile Crescent between and around the Tigris and Euphrates rivers. Incursions from Semitic peoples of the Arabian Peninsula led to Akkadian supremacy after the victory of Sargon the Great (*c.* 2340 BC). The Sumerian cities, such as Ur, reasserted their independence until 1700 BC, when King Hammurabi established the first dynasty of Babylon. Hammurabi and his son, Samsu-iluna, presided over the political and cultural apogee of Babylon. Babylonia was challenged by the Anatolian Hittites, who sacked Babylon in 1595 BC. A weakened Babylonia fell to the Kassites from the Zagros mountains, who held sway for over 400 years. The power-vacuum in northern Babylonia was filled by the Hurrian kingdom of Mitanni until Assyria's dominance in the 13th century BC. The Semitic Assyrians built an empire that stretched from Tarsus on the Mediterranean to Babylon, which they sacked in 1240 BC.

Elamite invasions in the 12th century BC allowed the establishment of a second Babylonian dynasty—Isin, or Pashe—but the assertiveness of its king, Nebuchadnezzar I, provoked Assyrian retaliation. Assyrian control of Babylonia was regained but tempered by massive immigration of Aramaeans from Upper Mesopotamia and Syria. Nevertheless, the Assyrians achieved considerable imperial expansion under Ashurnasirpal II in the early ninth century BC. Assyrian decline and revival was repeated in the eighth century. Babylon was recaptured in 729 BC and most of the Fertile Crescent, from the Nile Delta to the Persian Gulf, was subjugated. However, the empire soon crumbled after the death of the great King Ashurbanipal in 627 BC. Revolts in Babylonia were led by the Chaldeans, who had settled in the south from the ninth century. An alliance of old enemies—the Medes and the Scythians—ravaged the Assyrian Empire and in 612 BC, the capital, Nineveh, fell to the Medes.

Babylonia, known at this time as Chaldea, assumed control of much of the Fertile Crescent. In 586 BC, Nebuchadnezzar II conquered Phoenicia and Judah, destroying Jerusalem and deporting 15,000 Judaeans as labourers for Babylon. This Babylonian revival withered under his successors, who were defeated by Achaemenid Persia. Cyrus the Great captured Babylon in 539 BC. His rule was strengthened by his self-association with the Babylonian throne and by his religious tolerance; the Babylonian deity Bel-Marduk was restored and the Temple of Jerusalem rebuilt. Xerxes I (485–465 BC) styled himself the Persian Emperor and seized the Bel-Marduk statue, provoking several Babylonian rebellions.

Alexander

The last of the Achaemenids, Darius III, was defeated at the Battle of Gaugamela (near Mosul) in 331 BC by Alexander the Great of Macedon, who established the Hellenistic Age of the Near East. Having assumed the Persian throne, he died at Babylon in 323 BC. His empire was split in four; Seleucus took control of Mesopotamia and Persia and declared himself king in 305 BC. Babylon was soon eclipsed by a new capital at Seleucia on the Tigris and was abandoned during the third century. Parthia, Bactria and Anatolia were lost by Seleucus's successors until Antiochus III (223–187 BC) reasserted his lordship over the lost provinces. However, his foray into Greece was repulsed by Rome, which forced a heavy indemnity on the Seleucid Empire. Rapid territorial losses to Rome, Ptolemaic Egypt and local rebellions led to a Parthian invasion of Babylonia in 129 BC.

The Parthian Empire, with its winter capital at Ctesiphon on the Tigris, reached its territorial zenith under Mithridates II (123–88 BC), who defeated Armenia and repelled the Scythians. Though a looser political unit than the Seleucid state, Mithridates's empire was a conscious inheritor of the great traditions—Persian, Babylonian and Hellenistic—in culture, language and symbolism. Intrigue over its nominal vassal, Armenia, brought Parthia into conflict with Rome. At Carrhae the Parthians inflicted a crushing defeat on a Roman army under Crassus in 53 BC. Several wars followed until Vologases I achieved a settlement with Emperor Nero over the Armenian buffer-state in AD 63. Dynastic disputes bedevilled Parthia and its vassal kingdoms. The invasion of Armenia by Osroes I (AD 109–129) sparked a Roman invasion in AD 113 under Trajan, who annexed Armenia and occupied most of Mesopotamia. Roman control ended after Trajan's death but Vologases IV was forced to cede western Mesopotamia to Rome. However, Mesopotamia remained a battleground, with Emperor Severus invading in AD 195 and looting Ctesiphon, further weakening the Parthian state. In AD 224 Artabanus IV, the last of the Parthian kings, was defeated by Ardashir (Artaxerxes), ruler of Persia and founder of the Sassanid Dynasty.

The Sassanian Persians emulated the Achaemenids and attempted to regain their empire, leading to inevitable conflict with Rome. Ardashir's son, Shapur I, continued his father's expansion in the east and attacked Rome's Levantine provinces. Syria and Armenia were overrun and the Roman Emperor Valerian captured at Edessa in 259. Shapur II (309–379) consolidated Sassanid power, defeating threats from Arabia and Central Asia and wresting control of the Tigris and Armenia from the Romans. The religious policies of the Zoroastrian Sassanids fluctuated from tolerance to persecution. Khosrau I (531–579) revived imperial expansion; his grandson, Khosrau II, was restored to the throne by the Byzantine Emperor Maurice, who was rewarded with Armenia and northeastern Mesopotamia. However, Khosrau retook Mesopotamia after Maurice's murder, beginning a Persian rampage through the Byzantine East. The sack and pillage of Jerusalem provoked Emperor Heraclius, who struck the Persian heartland. In 627 Heraclius entered Ctesiphon and destroyed the palace of Khosrau, who was murdered. Sassanid Persia, exhausted by conflict with Rome, quickly fell to the Arab invasion.

Led by Sa'd ibn Abi Waqqas, the Arab forces of Islam defeated the Sassanians at the Battle of Al-Qadisiyyah (*c.* 636) on the Euphrates and at Nahavand, western Iran, in 642. By 639 most of Iraq (*Erak,* 'lower Iran'), comprising the centre and south of modern republic, had been conquered; as had Al-Jazirah ('The Island'), the area north of Tikrit. Mass Arab immigration saw the establishment of garrison towns at Kufa (near Babylon) and Basra and later at Mosul. After the first four caliphs, the Caliphate effectively became hereditary under the Ummayads, based at Damascus. However, their rule was disputed, especially in Iraq. The death of Ali's second son, Husayn, at Karbala in 680 left a body of opposition, the Shias, or 'partisans' of Ali. Iraq was controlled by a governor and, from the 690s, Arabic became the language of administration.

Rise of Baghdad

In 743 civil war came to the Caliphate. Having failed to resolve the tensions between rival Arab military groups, the Umayyads succumbed to the rebellion of the Abbasids, who called for a return to strong Islamic leadership. In 750 the last Ummayad caliph, Marwan II, was deposed by Abu al-'Abbas (As-Saffah), supported by Iranian and Iraqi Shias. However, As-Saffah installed himself as caliph, rejecting a Shia imam. In 754 he was succeeded by his brother Al-Mansur, who moved the capital to Baghdad on the Tigris. This move symbolized the end of the hegemony of Syrian and Yemeni Arabs over the Caliphate. Nevertheless, an overburdened Iraq provided numerous threats to Abbasid authority; Al-Mansur had to quell Shia revolts in Iraq in 763. Caliph Al-Mu'tasim moved his capital to Samarra in 836 to remove his Turkic Mamluk soldiers from Baghdad. The suppression of the Zanj Revolt (869–879) of African slaves around Basra prompted the return to Baghdad.

Rapid political fragmentation in the 930s broke the Caliphate. The Shia Buyids took Iraq in 946, depriving the Abbasid caliphs of temporal power. From the 970s, Egypt was ruled by a rival caliphate, the Ismaili Fatimids. Baghdad was taken by the Seljuk Turks under Toghrül, the Sultan of Iran, in 1055. Despite the Seljuk territories fragmenting after Malik Shah I died in 1092, Iraq remained under Seljuk authority until the Mongol invasion.

© Springer Nature Limited 2020
Palgrave Macmillan (ed.), *The Statesman's Yearbook 2020,*
https://doi.org/10.1057/978-1-349-95940-2_94

In 1258 Baghdad was sacked by the Mongol Hulagu Khan; the city was ravaged, its people slaughtered and its Grand Library destroyed. The sack ended the Abbasid Caliphate and Baghdad's role as a major cultural centre. Hulagu established the Il-Khanid Dynasty of Iran. Buddhism and Nestorian Christianity flourished under the patronage of Hulagu's successors until the conversion of Khan Ghazan to Sunni Islam in 1292. The Il-Khanate fragmented in the 1330s and Iraq was ruled by the Mongol Jalayirids.

Ottoman Rule

In 1401 Baghdad was sacked by Timur (also known as Tamburlaine), the greatest Central Asian warrior of the period. His death in 1405 allowed the Black Sheep Turkmen (Kara Koyunlu) to overthrow their Jalayirid masters. However, their rapid expansion ended in defeat in 1466 at the hands of the White Sheep Turkmen (Ak Koyunlu). Rivalry with the Ottoman Turks in Anatolia weakened the White Sheep Turkmen, who were forced to withdraw from Iraq by the Turkic Safavid rulers of Iran. Shah Ismail I took Baghdad in 1509 and made Shi'ism the state religion. However, Iraq soon fell to the Sunni Ottomans, with Sultan Suleyman the Magnificent taking Baghdad in 1534. Shah Abbas reclaimed Iraq for Iran in 1603, brutally suppressing a major Kurdish rebellion in 1610. Ottoman authority was reimposed by Sultan Murad IV, who led his army into Baghdad in 1638.

The Ottomans treated Iraq as a buffer state against Iran and allowed Kurdish and Bedouin tribes to dominate. Mamluks asserted their power in Iraq until 1831, when Baghdad was devastated by flooding. Serious administrative reform (*tanzimat*) came in 1869 with the appointment of Midhat Pasha as governor of Baghdad, with great improvements in the army, the law and education. The Young Turks revolution of 1908 gave Iraq limited political representation.

British Mandate

Anglo-German rivalry led to a British invasion of southern Iraq in Nov. 1914. Although Basra fell in 1915, the British suffered a major defeat at Al-Kut in 1916. Nevertheless, Baghdad was taken in March 1917. After the First World War the Allies entrusted Iraq to Britain under the Sykes-Picot Agreement, which protected British oil interests in the region. The State of Iraq became a League of Nations mandate under British Control in Nov. 1920. Rebellions in Kurdish and southern areas were suppressed. A Hashemite monarchy was installed, under Amir Faysal ibn Husayn from Mecca, a wartime ally, and an indigenous army created. The monarchy was supported by a plebiscite in 1921. Kurdish-dominated Mosul province—vital for its massive oil reserves—was granted to Iraq by the League of Nations in 1925. Britain's mandate ended in 1932. Rebellions followed in Kurdish areas, led by Mustafa Barzani until he fled to the USSR in 1945. Rejecting the partition of Palestine, Iraq went to war with Israel in 1948, leading to the emigration of 120,000 Iraqi Jews.

The monarchy was overthrown in a military coup on 14 July 1958. King Faisal II and Nuri al Said, the prime minister, were killed. A republic was established, controlled by a military-led Council of Sovereignty under Gen. Abdul Karim Qassim. In 1963 Qassim was overthrown and Gen. Abdul Salam Aref was made president, with a partial return to a civilian government. But on 17 July 1968 a successful coup was mounted by the Pan-Arabist Ba'ath Party. Gen. Ahmed Al Bakr became president, prime minister, and chairman of a newly established nine-member Revolutionary Command Council. In July 1979 Saddam Hussein, the vice-president and a Sunni Muslim, assumed the presidency, having persuaded the ailing Al Bakr to resign. Saddam promptly carried out a purge of the party, resulting in 22 executions.

The 1979 Iranian Revolution was perceived as a threat to the delicate Sunni-Shia balance in Iraq. In Sept. 1980 Iraq invaded Iran, ostensibly over territorial rights in the Shatt-al-Arab waterway. The war claimed over a million lives and saw the use of chemical weapons by the Iraqi army. The al-Anfal campaign (1986–89) countered Kurdish rebellions, killing 182,000 Kurds. Chemical weapons were prominent, most notably at Halabja, where 5,000 died in one day. A UN-arranged ceasefire took place on 20 Aug. 1988 and UN-sponsored peace talks continued in 1989. On 15 Aug. 1990 Iraq accepted the pre-war border and withdrew troops from Iranian soil.

1991 War

On 2 Aug. 1990 Iraqi forces invaded and rapidly overran Kuwait, on the pretext of alleged Kuwaiti 'slant-drilling' across the Iraqi border (drilling at an angle and taking oil that the Iraqis maintained was rightfully theirs). The UN Security Council voted to impose economic sanctions on Iraq until it withdrew from Kuwait and the USA sent a large military force to Saudi Arabia. Further Security Council resolutions included authorization for the use of military force if Iraq did not withdraw by 15 Jan. 1991. On the night of 16–17 Jan. coalition forces (US and over 30 allies) began an air attack on strategic targets in Iraq. A land offensive followed on 24 Feb. The Iraqi army was routed and Kuwait City was liberated on 28 Feb. Iraq agreed to the conditions of a provisional ceasefire, including withdrawal from Kuwait. Subsequent Kurdish and Shia rebellions were brutally suppressed.

In June 1991 UNSCOM, the United Nations Special Commission, conducted its first chemical weapons inspection in Iraq. In Sept. a UN Security Council resolution permitted Iraq to sell oil worth US$1,600m. to pay for food and medical supplies. In Oct. the Security Council voted unanimously to prohibit Iraq from all nuclear activities. Imports of materials used in the manufacture of nuclear, biological or chemical weapons were banned, and UN weapons inspectors received wide powers to examine and retain data throughout Iraq.

In Aug. 1992 the USA, UK and France began to enforce air exclusion zones over southern and northern Iraq in response to the government's persecution of Shias and Kurds. Following Iraqi violations of this zone and incursions over the Kuwaiti border, US, British and French forces made air and missile attacks on Iraqi military targets in Jan. 1993. On 10 Nov. 1994 Iraq recognized the independence and boundaries of Kuwait. In the first half of 1995 UN weapons inspectors secured information on an extensive biological weapons programme. At the beginning of Sept. 1996 Iraqi troops occupied the town of Erbil in a Kurdish haven in support of the Kurdish Democratic Party faction which was at odds with another Kurdish faction, the Patriotic Union of Kurdistan. On 3 Sept. 1996 US forces fired missiles at targets in southern Iraq and extended the no-fly area northwards to the southern suburbs of Baghdad.

Weapons Inspections

Relations with the USA deteriorated still further in 1997 when Iraq refused co-operation with UN weapons inspectors. The USA and the UK threatened retaliatory action and a renewal of hostilities looked probable until late Feb. 1998 when Kofi Annan, the UN Secretary General, forged an agreement in Baghdad allowing for 'immediate, unconditional and unrestricted access' to all suspected weapons sites. In Aug. 1998 Saddam Hussein engineered another stand-off with the UN arms inspectors, demanding a declaration that Iraq had rid itself of all weapons of mass destruction. This was refused by the UN chief inspector. In Nov. all UN personnel left Iraq as the USA threatened air strikes unless Iraq complied with UN resolutions. Russia and France urged further diplomatic efforts, but on 16 Dec. the USA and Britain launched air and missile attacks aimed at destroying Saddam Hussein's suspected arsenal of nuclear, chemical and biological weapons.

In Feb. 2000 the UN Security Council nominated Sweden's Hans Blix to head the new arms inspectorate to Iraq but he was refused entry into the country. In Feb. 2001 the USA and Britain launched a further series of air attacks on military targets in and around Baghdad. A new UN Security Council resolution was passed in May 2002. Constituting the biggest change since the introduction in 1966 of a UN-administered Oil-for-Food scheme to alleviate the suffering among the civilian population, the new resolution limited import restrictions to a number of specific sensitive goods. In Nov. 2002 the UN Security Council adopted Resolution 1441, holding Iraq in 'material breach' of disarmament obligations. Weapons inspectors, under the leadership of Hans Blix, returned to Iraq four years after their last inspections, but US and British suspicion that the Iraq regime was failing to comply led to increasing tension, resulting in the USA, the UK and Spain reserving the right to disarm Iraq without the need for a further Security Council resolution. Other Security Council members, notably China, France, Germany and Russia, opposed the proposed action.

Fall of Saddam

On 20 March 2003 US forces, supported by the UK, began a war aimed at 'liberating Iraq'. UK troops entered Iraq's second city, Basra, on 6 April. On 9 April 2003 American forces took control of central Baghdad, effectively ending Saddam Hussein's rule. Widespread looting and disorder followed the capital's fall. The bloodless capture of Tikrit, Saddam Hussein's hometown, on 14 April marked the end of formal Iraqi resistance. An interim government was planned until democratic elections could be held. On 22 May the UN Security Council voted to lift economic sanctions against Iraq and to support the US and UK occupation 'until an internationally recognized, representative government is established by the people of Iraq'. Only Syria opposed the resolution by boycotting the session. A 25-man Iraqi-led governing council (IGC) met in Baghdad for the first time in July 2003.

Resistance to the occupying forces increased from late summer. Bomb attacks in Aug. targeted the UN's Baghdad office, killing the UN special representative. Ayatollah Mohammed Baqr al-Hakim, the most senior Shia cleric in Iraq, was assassinated with 100 others in Najaf. Saddam Hussein was captured by American forces at Al-Dawr, near Tikrit, on 13 Dec. 2003. His trial for crimes against humanity, war crimes and genocide began in July 2004. In Feb. 2004 over 100 Kurds were killed in attacks in Erbil and the Shia community suffered 270 deaths in Baghdad and Karbala. In May 2004 accusations surfaced of abuse of Iraqi prisoners by American and British soldiers.

On 30 Jan. 2005 the first democratic elections to a Transitional National Assembly were won by the Shia-dominated United Iraqi Alliance. Jalal Talabani became the country's new president on 6 April 2005, and on 3 May 2005 Iraq's first democratically elected government under Prime Minister Ibrahim al-Jaafari was sworn in. In Oct. 2005 a new federal constitution was approved in a nationwide referendum (although without the support of the Sunni community) and the trial of former dictator Saddam Hussein for mass murder opened in Baghdad. In Dec. 2005 a general election for a new parliament was won by the United Iraqi Alliance. In April 2006 after months of deadlock Nouri al-Maliki was appointed prime minister.

Insurgent violence meanwhile continued, with militant groups from throughout the region—including al-Qaeda—wielding heavy influence. Nobody can be certain how many Iraqis have been killed since the start of the US-led invasion in March 2003. Estimates vary from 188,600 (to Dec. 2016) by Iraq Body Count on the basis of media reports through to about 600,000 in a John Hopkins University study of 2006 funded by the Massachusetts Institute of Technology based on interviews of households. In Nov. 2006 Saddam Hussein was sentenced to death. His execution on 30 Dec. 2006 drew mixed reaction both in Iraq and abroad.

In Jan. 2007 President Bush announced a 'troop surge' in Iraq, with 21,500 extra troops to be deployed to assist the Iraqi army in fighting insurgents and al-Qaeda forces. 4,000 US troops were stationed in Al-Anbar province, with the remainder sent to Baghdad. Iraqi forces gradually took control of internal security, initially in Basra (Al-Basrah) province from Dec. 2007 and then in Al-Anbar from Sept. 2008. UK combat operations ended in April 2009 and in June US troops withdrew from Iraqi towns and cities. The last US troop convoys left Iraq in Dec. 2011, in accordance with the US-Iraq Status of Forces Agreement of 2008. Sectarian conflict subsequently escalated, with Nouri al-Maliki's Shia-dominated government incurring the wrath of Sunni militant groups, including the jihadist Islamic State of Iraq and Syria (later renamed Islamic State).

In 2014 Islamic State-led Sunni insurgents took control of several key towns including Mosul, the country's second city, and in June declared a caliphate in territory under their control. However, subsequent retaliatory action by a US-led military coalition, together with Iraqi and Kurdish forces, dislodged the Islamic State's presence in the country by the end of 2017.

No political grouping had achieved a majority in parliamentary elections in April 2014, and in Sept. Haider al-Abadi replaced al-Maliki as prime minister at the head of a new broad-based coalition government. Then, after months of deadlock following the elections in May 2018, Adil Abdul-Mahdi, a consensus candidate with support across the political spectrum, was nominated as prime minister and formed a new government in Oct.

Territory and Population

Iraq is bounded in the north by Turkey, east by Iran, southeast by the Persian Gulf, south by Kuwait and Saudi Arabia, and west by Jordan and Syria. In April 1992 the UN Boundary Commission redefined Iraq's border with Kuwait, moving it slightly northwards in line with an agreement of 1932. Area, 434,128 sq. km. Population, 1997 census, 22,046,244; density, 50·8 per sq. km. 2018 estimate, 38,124,182, density 87·8 per sq. km. In 2009, 69·0% of the population lived in urban areas. Around 4·4m. Iraqis protected and assisted by the Office of the United Nations High Commissioner for Refugees are displaced within the country. In 2014 Iraqis

dropped to the ninth largest refugee group with just 377,700 living abroad (down from 1,873,500 in 2008), mainly in Syria and to a lesser extent Jordan.

The UN gives a projected population for 2020 of 41·50m.

The areas, populations and capitals of the governorates:

Governorate	Area (sq. km)	Population 1997 census	Population 2018 estimate	Capital
Al-Anbar	138,501	1,023,776	1,771,656	Ar-Ramadi
Babil (Babylon)	6,468	1,181,751	2,065,042	Al-Hillah
Baghdad	734	5,423,964	8,126,755	Baghdad
Basra (Al-Basrah)	19,070	1,556,445	2,908,491	Basra
Dahuk	6,553	402,970	1,292,535	Dahuk
Dhi Qar	12,900	1,184,796	2,095,172	An-Nasiriyah
Diyala	19,076	1,135,223	1,637,226	Ba'qubah
Erbil	14,471	1,095,992	1,854,778	Erbil
Karbala	5,034	594,235	1,218,732	Karbala
Kirkuk[1]	10,282	753,171	1,597,876	Kirkuk
Maysan	16,072	637,126	1,112,673	Al-Amarah
Al-Muthanna	51,740	436,825	814,371	As-Samawah
An-Najaf	28,824	775,042	1,471,592	An-Najaf
Ninawa (Nineveh)	37,323	2,042,852	3,729,998	Mosul
Al-Qadisiyah	8,153	751,331	1,291,048	Ad-Diwaniyah
Salah ad-Din	24,751	904,432	1,595,235	Tikrit
As-Sulaymaniyah[2]	17,023	1,362,739	2,162,000	As-Sulaymaniyah
Wasit	17,153	783,614	1,378,723	Al-Kut

[1]Also known as At-Ta'mim.
[2]Includes the governorate of Halabja, established in 2014.

The most populous cities are Baghdad (the capital), with an estimated population of 6,150,000 in 2011, Mosul and Basra. Other large cities include Erbil, Karbala, Kirkuk, An-Najaf and As-Sulaymaniyah.

The population is approximately 80% Arab, 17% Kurdish (mainly in the north of the country) and 3% Turkmen, Assyrian, Chaldean or other. Shia Arabs (predominantly in the south of the country) constitute approximately 60% of the total population and Sunni Arabs (principally in the centre) 20%.

The official language is Arabic. Other languages spoken are Kurdish (official in Kurdish regions), Assyrian and Armenian.

Social Statistics

2008 estimates: births, 940,000; deaths, 177,000; marriages, 171,000. Birth and death rates, 2008 estimates (per 1,000 population): births, 31·2; deaths, 5·9. Life expectancy at birth, 2007, was 64·2 years for men and 71·8 years for women. Annual population growth rate, 2000–08, 2·5%. Infant mortality, 2008: 36 per 1,000 live births. Fertility rate, 2008: 4·1 births per woman. Estimated maternal mortality rate per 10,000 live births, 2005: 30.

Climate

The climate is mainly arid, with limited and unreliable rainfall and a large annual range of temperature. Summers are very hot and winters are cold. Baghdad, Jan. 50°F (10°C), July 95°F (35°C). Annual rainfall 6" (140 mm). Basra, Jan. 55°F (12·8°C), July 92°F (33·3°C). Annual rainfall 7" (175 mm). Mosul, Jan. 44°F (6·7°C), July 90°F (32·2°C). Annual rainfall 15" (384 mm).

Constitution and Government

Until the fall of Saddam Hussein, the highest state authority was the Revolutionary Command Council (RCC) but some legislative power was given to the 220-member *National Assembly*. The only legal political grouping was the National Progressive Front (founded 1973) comprising the Arab Socialist

Renaissance (Ba'ath) Party and various Kurdish groups, but a law of Aug. 1991 legalized political parties provided they were not based on religion, race or ethnicity.

In July 2003 a 25-man Iraqi-led governing council met in Baghdad for the first time since the US-led war in an important staging post towards full self-government. The temporary Coalition Provisional Authority was dissolved on 28 June 2004. Power was handed over to the interim Iraqi government which assumed full sovereign powers for governing Iraq. It became a transitional government after elections in Jan. 2005. The 275-member Transitional National Assembly approved a draft new constitution on 29 Aug. 2005. It was approved in a nationwide referendum held on 15 Oct., with 78·6% of votes cast in favour. Shias and Kurds generally supported the constitution. Most Sunnis opposed it because of its reference to federalism and the risk that Iraq could ultimately break up, as Iraq's oil resources are in the Shia and Kurdish areas. The constitution states that Iraq is a democratic, federal, representative republic and a multi-ethnic, multi-religious and multi-sect country. Islam is the official religion of the state and a basic source of legislation. Elections were held in Dec. 2005 for the new 275-member *Council of Representatives*. In Dec. 2009 the number of seats was increased from 275 to 325 ahead of the March 2010 elections. It was increased to 328 ahead of the April 2014 elections and further to 329 ahead of the May 2018 elections.

National Anthem

'Mawtini' ('My Homeland'); words by I. Touqan, tune by M. Fuliefil.

Recent Elections

In parliamentary elections to the permanent Iraqi National Assembly held on 12 May 2018 the Forward (Saairun) alliance won 54 of 329 seats, ahead of the Conquest (al-Fatah) alliance with 47 seats, the Victory (Nasr) alliance with 42, the Kurdistan Democratic Party and the State of Law Coalition with 25 seats each, the National (al-Wataniya) coalition with 21, the National Wisdom Movement with 19, the Patriotic Union of Kurdistan with 18 and the Arab Decision Alliance with 14. The remaining 64 seats went to smaller parties and coalitions.

Fuad Masum was elected president by parliament in a second round of voting on 24 June 2014, gaining 211 votes against 17 for Hussein Musawi out of a total of 269 votes cast.

Current Government

President: Barham Salih; b. 1960 (sworn in 2 Oct. 2018).

In Feb. 2019 the government consisted of:

Prime Minister: Adil Abdul-Mahdi; b. 1942 (sworn in 25 Oct. 2018).

Minister of Agriculture: Saleh al-Hassani. *Communication:* Naim al-Rubaye. *Culture, Tourism and Antiquities:* Vacant. *Defence:* Vacant. *Displacement and Migration:* Vacant. *Education:* Vacant. *Electricity:* Luay al-Khatteeb. *Finance:* Fuad Hussein. *Foreign Affairs:* Mohammed Ali al-Hakeem. *Health:* Alaa al-Alwani. *Higher Education and Scientific Research:* Vacant. *Housing and Reconstruction:* Bangin Rekani. *Industry:* Salih Absullah Jabouri. *Interior:* Vacant. *Justice:* Vacant. *Labour and Social Affairs:* Basem al-Rubaye. *Oil:* Thamir Ghadhban. *Planning:* Vacant. *Trade:* Mohammed Hashim. *Transport:* Abdullah Luaibi. *Water Resources:* Jamal al-Adili. *Youth and Sports:* Ahmed Riyadh.

Government Website: http://www.cabinet.iq

Current Leaders

Barham Salih

Position
President

Introduction
Barham Salih became president of Iraq on 2 Oct. 2018 after an historic free vote by parliament. With wide-ranging experience in government, he secured support as an advocate of Iraqi unity.

Early Life
Barham Salih was born on 2 Sept. 1960 in the city of As-Sulaymaniyah. He joined the Patriotic Union of Kurdistan (PUK) in 1976, and in 1979 was arrested twice by the ruling Ba'athist regime and sent to prison where he was interrogated and tortured. Once released, he moved to the UK as a political émigré.

Salih graduated in civil engineering and construction from Cardiff University in the UK in 1983, and received his doctorate from the University of Liverpool in 1987. Following the first Gulf War and the liberation of Iraqi Kurdistan, Salih was elected to the leadership of the PUK and moved to the USA, where he ran the PUK office. In 2004 he became deputy prime minister of the interim Iraqi government. Between 2009 and 2012 he was prime minister of the Kurdistan regional government.

In Sept. 2017 Salih left the PUK to form a new opposition party, the Coalition for Democracy and Justice. However, he rejoined the PUK to contest the Oct. 2018 presidential election, which he won by 219 votes to 22.

Career in Office
Salih is faced with the challenge of consolidating Iraq's political institutions. Following the widespread destruction and displacement of people resulting from four years of conflict with the jihadist Islamic State, reconstruction is a priority. Saleh has promised to fund infrastructure projects, including a new deep-water port and a rail network. He has made it clear that he does not want Iraq to be burdened by US sanctions against Iran and has sought exemptions to import vital Iranian gas.

Adil Abdul-Mahdi

Position
Prime Minister

Introduction
Adil Abdul-Mahdi was sworn in as prime minister on 25 Oct. 2018. He was a consensus candidate with broad support from most Sunni political forces, as well as Kurdish leaders and the Iranian and US governments.

Early Life
Abdul-Mahdi was born on 1 Jan. 1942 in Baghdad, the son of a prominent Shia cleric and minister. He graduated in economics from Baghdad University in 1963. Politically active from a young age, he earned a reputation as a leading critic of Saddam Hussein.

Abdul-Mahdi joined the Iraqi civil service and worked at the foreign ministry until 1969, when, following death threats over his political activities, he fled to France. He studied economics at the International Institute for Public Administration in Paris and received a master's degree in political economy from the University of Poitiers in 1972.

After several years working at economic research institutes, he moved to Syria and then Lebanon. Returning to France in the early 1980s, he maintained links with Iraq's political scene. Along with other exiles, he joined the Supreme Islamic Iraqi Council, a powerful Shia organization with close links with Iran.

Returning to Iraq after the fall of Saddam Hussein in 2003, Abdul-Mahdi joined the transitional government. He briefly served as finance minister in Ayad Allawi's administration and managed to persuade some international creditors to write off Iraq's debt.

Following the country's first multi-party election in Jan. 2005, Abdul-Mahdi became vice president under Ibrahim al-Jaafari and then Nouri al-Maliki. In Feb. 2007 he survived an assassination attempt that killed ten people. Following his resignation in 2011, he was appointed oil minister in the government of Haider al-Abadi but resigned that post in 2016.

After months of deadlock in the wake of the May 2018 parliamentary elections, where two Shia-led blocs won most seats, President Barham Salih nominated Abdul-Mahdi as prime minister. He succeeded in forming a new government and was sworn in on 25 Oct. 2018.

Career in Office
In his inaugural address, Abdul-Mahdi pledged to prioritize delivering security, water and electricity to all Iraqis. His first action was to move the government out of Baghdad's highly secure Green Zone for the first time since 2003. However, his administration faces formidable challenges, including widespread corruption, high unemployment, dilapidated public services (power cuts and water shortages having sparked riots in Basra in 2018) and ongoing security issues relating to the Jihadist Islamic State group.

Defence

Following the downfall of Saddam Hussein, recruitment began in July 2003 for a new professional army run by the US military. Saddam Hussein's forces numbered 400,000 at their peak. In Nov. 2008 Iraq's parliament approved a plan that saw the last American troops leave the country in Dec. 2011.

However, US redeployment began again in June 2014 to counter Islamic State forces. In 2013 military expenditure totalled US$16,897m. (US$530 per capita), representing 7·2% of GDP.

Army

In 2011 personnel numbered an estimated 193,000. In July 2004 the Civil Defense Corps (23,100 personnel in April 2004) was disbanded and converted into a National Guard. It was in turn merged into the Army in Jan. 2005.

Navy

A 3,600-strong (2011) Iraqi Navy (initially called the Coastal Defense Force) has been re-established since the 2003 war. It began operations in Oct. 2004.

Air Force

An Iraqi Air Force (initially called the Army Air Corps) has been reconstructed since 2003. There were a total of 5,050 personnel in 2011. Equipment in 2011 included three combat-capable aircraft.

Economy

In 2011 oil and gas accounted for about 60% of GDP.

Overview

The economy faces serious challenges following decades of dictatorship, international sanctions and war. The economy has weathered declining oil prices since 2014 and the Islamic State (IS)-led insurgency. After average annual GDP increases of 7·8% between 2009 and 2013, the economy grew by just 0·7% in 2014. Growth in 2016 of 13·1% was the highest since 2012. Despite government efforts to prioritize expenditure, low oil revenue and high humanitarian and security spending saw the budget deficit reach 13·5% of GDP in 2015, while the current account returned a deficit of 6·1% of GDP that year from a surplus of 2·7% in 2014.

After the military victory of the US-led coalition in 2003, GDP declined by 41%, but in Nov. 2004 the Paris Club of creditor countries agreed to write off 80% of Iraq's external debt. However, private consumption and investment have since remained restrained, owing to the unstable security and political situation and a poor business environment. The non-oil economy contracted by almost 14% in 2015, following a 5% decrease the previous year.

The population remains extremely vulnerable to the current security problems and reduction in oil prices. The poverty rate, as estimated by the Iraqi government, reached 22·5% in 2014; in IS-affected governorates, the direct impact of economic, social and security disruptions is estimated to have doubled the rate to 41·2%.

Currency

From 15 Oct. 2003 a new national currency, the new *Iraqi dinar* (NID), was introduced to replace the existing currencies in circulation in the south and north of the country. Inflation rates (based on IMF statistics) for fiscal years:

2008	2009	2010	2011	2012	2013	2014	2015	2016	2017
2·7%	−2·2%	2·4%	5·6%	6·1%	1·9%	2·2%	1·4%	0·5%	0·1%

Budget

In 2012 (provisional) revenues were ID119,400bn. (crude oil export revenue, 91·6%) and expenditures ID109,400bn. (current expenditure, 69·3%).

Performance

Real GDP growth rates (based on IMF statistics):

2008	2009	2010	2011	2012	2013	2014	2015	2016	2017
8·2%	3·4%	6·4%	7·5%	13·9%	7·6%	0·7%	2·5%	13·1%	−2·1%

Total GDP in 2017 was US$197·7bn.

Banking and Finance

All banks were nationalized in 1964. Following the Gulf War in 1991 the formation of private banks was approved, although they were prohibited from conducting international transactions. A new post-Saddam banking law in Oct. 2003 authorized private banks to process international payments, remittances and foreign currency letters of credit. The Trade Bank of Iraq has been established as an export credit agency to facilitate trade financing. The independent Central Bank of Iraq is the sole bank of issue; its *Governor* is Ali Mohsin Ismail. All domestic interest rates were liberalized on 1 March 2004.

The Iraq Stock Exchange opened in Baghdad in June 2004 as the successor to the former Baghdad Stock Exchange.

Energy and Natural Resources

Environment

Iraq's carbon dioxide emissions from the consumption of energy accounted for 3·9 tonnes per capita in 2011.

Electricity

Installed capacity was 17·0m. kW in 2011. Production in 2011 was 54·24bn. kWh, with consumption per capita 1,932 kWh.

Oil and Gas

Proven oil reserves in 2017 totalled 148·8bn. bbls, the fifth highest in the world. Iraq's oil production in 2017 totalled 221·5m. tonnes, the highest annual total ever. In June 2015 production reached 4m. bbls per day for the first time, with the oil sector being largely unaffected by the security situation as Iraq's main oil fields and most of the export infrastructure are located in the south of the country, away from Islamic State-controlled areas. The sector provides 95% of government revenue.

In 2017 Iraq had natural gas reserves of 3·5trn. cu. metres.

Minerals

Output of minerals, 2012: sand and gravel, 23·2m. tonnes (estimate); limestone, 5·0m. tonnes; gypsum, 1·4m. tonnes; phosphate rock, 450,000 tonnes; salt, 143,000 tonnes.

Agriculture

There were around 3·43m. ha. of arable land in 2012 and 0·23m. ha. of permanent crops. An estimated 3·53m. ha. were equipped for irrigation in 2012. Production (2012 estimates, in 1,000 tonnes): wheat, 2,400; tomatoes, 1,100; dates, 650; potatoes, 560; cucumbers and gherkins, 505; barley, 500.

Livestock (2013 estimates): sheep, 8·3m.; cattle, 2·8m.; goats, 1·6m.; asses, 380,000; chickens, 38m.

Forestry

In 2015 forests covered 0·83m. ha., representing 2% of the land area. Of the total area under forests 98% was naturally regenerated forest and 2% planted forest. Timber production in 2011 was 177,000 cu. metres.

Fisheries

Catches in 2015 totalled 27,296 tonnes, of which 22,848 tonnes were from inland waters.

Industry

Iraq remains under-developed industrially. Production figures (2011, in 1,000 tonnes): residual fuel oil, 13,621; cement (estimate), 10,000; distillate fuel oil, 6,365; petrol, 3,226; kerosene, 2,258; jet fuel, 308.

Labour

In 2011 the labour force was 7·9m. (72% of working age males and 13% of working age females). The state employs nearly two-thirds of the workforce. Unemployment was officially put at 12% in Feb. 2012.

Iraq had 28,000 people living in slavery according to the Walk Free Foundation's 2013 *Global Slavery Index*.

International Trade

Imports and Exports

In 2007 imports amounted to US$18,289m. and exports to US$39,590m. Manufactures and food are the main import commodities. Crude oil is the main export commodity. Imports and exports have both increased significantly since the Saddam era. In Oct. 2012 oil exports totalled 81·3m. bbls, their highest level in more than 30 years.

Communications

Roads

In 2012 there were 59,623 km of roads (up from 40,988 km in 2007). Vehicles in use in 2006 included 785,000 passenger cars, 1,345,000 lorries and vans, and 112,000 buses and coaches. In 2005 there were 1,789 road accident deaths.

Rail

In 2005 railways comprised 2,032 km of 1,435 mm gauge route. Passenger-km travelled in 2014 came to 99m. and freight tonne-km to 249m.

Civil Aviation

In 2000 there were international flights for the first time since the 1991 Gulf War, with air links being established between Iraq and Egypt, Jordan and Syria. Since 2003 the two international airports at Baghdad and Basra have undergone post-war reconstruction. Major domestic airports are at Mosul, Kirkuk and Erbil. In May 2010 the government dissolved the state airline, Iraqi Airways, owing to a legal dispute with Kuwait dating back to the Iraqi invasion in 1990. It began flying again in 2012 and now serves a number of destinations in Europe, the Middle East and Asia.

Shipping

In Jan. 2014 there were three ships of 300 GT or over registered, totalling 18,000 GT. The Iraqi-controlled fleet comprised 12 vessels of 1,000 GT or over in July 2014, of which ten were under foreign flags and two under the Iraqi flag. A 565-km canal was opened in 1992 between Baghdad and the Persian Gulf for shipping, irrigation, the drainage of saline water and the reclamation of marsh land. Iraq has three oil tanker terminals at Basra, Khor Al-Amaya and Khor Al-Zubair. Its single deep-water port is at Umm Qasr.

Telecommunications

There were 1·72m. fixed telephone lines in 2010 (55·6 per 1,000 inhabitants). In the same year mobile phone subscriptions numbered 23·26m. (75·1 per 1,000 inhabitants). Mobile phones were banned during the Saddam Hussein era. Fixed internet subscriptions totalled just 270 in 2010. In March 2012 there were 1·6m. Facebook users.

Social Institutions

According to the 2017 *Fragile States Index*—a list published jointly by the Fund for Peace and *Foreign Policy* magazine—Iraq was ranked as the country 10th most vulnerable to conflict or collapse. The index is based on 12 indicators of state vulnerability across social, political and economic categories.

Justice

The Iraqi Constitution of 2005 provided for a judiciary comprised of a Higher Judicial Council (to oversee federal judicial affairs), a Supreme Court, a Court of Cassation and other federal courts including the Central Criminal Court. There is also a Judiciary Oversight Commission.

The death penalty was introduced for serious theft in 1992; amputation of a hand for theft in 1994. It is believed that during the Saddam era there were hundreds of executions annually. The death penalty was suspended in April 2003 after the fall of Saddam, but reinstated in Aug. 2004. There were at least 43 judicial executions in 2018, down from at least 125 in 2017 and at least 88 in 2016. However, there have also been widespread reports of extrajudicial executions since the emergence of Islamic State. The population in penal institutions in June 2012 was 37,014 (110 per 100,000 of national population). 41·5% of prisoners had yet to receive a trial according to 2014 estimates by the International Centre for Prison Studies.

Police

A new post-war Iraqi Police Service has been established since 2003 and numbered about 325,000 in Oct. 2011. The personnel includes both former officers who have been retrained and new recruits. There is also a 45,000-strong paramilitary Iraqi Federal Police and a 31,000-strong Oil Police.

Education

Primary education became compulsory in 1976. Primary school age is 6–11. Secondary education is for six years, of which the first three are termed intermediate. The medium of instruction is Arabic; Kurdish is used in primary schools in northern districts.

In 2005 there were 92,769 pre-primary school children with 5,981 teaching staff; 4·43m. primary school children with 215,795 teaching staff; and 1·75m. secondary school pupils with 93,219 teaching staff. Adult literacy rate was an estimated 78·1% in 2009 (male, 86·3%; female, 69·9%). There were 424,908 students and 19,231 academic staff in tertiary education in 2005.

Health

In 2014 there were 30,131 physicians, 7,891 dentistry personnel, 8,609 pharmaceutical personnel and 63,850 nurses and midwifery personnel. There were 14 hospital beds per 10,000 inhabitants in 2014.

In *Water: At What Cost? The State of the World's Water 2016*, WaterAid reported that 13·4% of the population does not have access to safe water.

Religion

The constitution proclaims Islam the state religion, but also stipulates freedom of creed and religious practices. In 2010 the population was 99·0% Muslim according to the Pew Research Center's Forum on Religion & Public Life; there were also an estimated 270,000 Christians. In Feb. 2019 there was one cardinal. *See also* TERRITORY AND POPULATION *above*.

Culture

World Heritage Sites

Iraq has five UNESCO World Heritage sites: Hatra (inscribed in 1985), a large fortified city of the Parthian (Persian) Empire; Ashur (Qal'at Sherqat) (2003), the first capital and the religious centre of the Assyrians from the 14th to the 9th centuries BC; Samarra Archaeological City (2007), the site of the capital of the former Abbasid Empire; Erbil Citadel (2014), an imposing occupied mound in Erbil created by many generations of people living and rebuilding on the same spot; and the Ahwar of Southern Iraq: Refuge of Biodiversity and the Relict Landscape of the Mesopotamian Cities (2016), made up of three archaeological sites and four wetland marsh areas in southern Iraq.

Press

In 2008 several hundred daily and weekly publications appeared regularly, the most popular of which, *Al-Sabah* ('The Morning'), had an average circulation of 50,000.

Tourism

In 2010 there were 1,518,000 foreign tourists, up from 864,000 in 2008.

Diplomatic Representatives

Of Iraq in the United Kingdom (21 Queens Gate, London, SW7 5JE)
Ambassador: Dr Salih Husain Ali.

Of the United Kingdom in Iraq (International Zone, Baghdad)
Ambassador: Jonathan Wilks, CMG.

Of Iraq in the USA (3421 Massachusetts Ave., NW, Washington, D.C., 20008)
Ambassador: Fareed Mustafa Kamil Yasseen.

Of the USA in Iraq (Al-Kindi St., International Zone, Baghdad)
Ambassador: Douglas Silliman.

Of Iraq to the United Nations
Ambassador: Mohammed Hussein Bahr Aluloom.

Of Iraq to the European Union
Ambassador: Jawad Khadim Jawad Al-Chlaihawi.

Kurdistan

The Kurdistan Region of Iraq ('Iraqi Kurdistan') is the only area of Kurdistan to be recognized officially as an autonomous federal entity. After decades of insurgency, Iraq granted limited independence in 1970. *De facto* independence was established following the Kurdish uprising at the end of the first Gulf war in 1991. This led to the creation of the Kurdistan Regional Government by the Iraqi Kurdistan Front a year later. Self-governance was disrupted in 1994 by civil war between the Kurdistan Democratic Party and the Patriotic Union of Kurdistan. Rival administrations were set up in As-

Sulaymaniyah and Erbil. Peace was restored in Sept. 1998 with the signing of a US-mediated agreement. The region was acknowledged officially in the 2005 Iraqi constitution and power-sharing began in 2006. On 25 Sept. 2017 over 93% of voters expressed support for independence from Iraq in a non-binding referendum. Kurdish leaders suggested it gave them a mandate to press the Baghdad government for full independence.

Area, 40,643 sq. km. The region comprises four governorates, As-Sulaymaniyah, Dahuk, Erbil and Halabja, and claims territory in other Kurdish areas.

The unified government is based at the capital, Erbil.

President: Vacant.

Prime Minister: Nechirvan Idris Barzani.

Oil exports began in 2009. A pipeline from Kurdistan to Ceyhan in Turkey was completed in 2013. Oil reserves have been estimated to total 45bn. bbls.

There are airports at As-Sulaymaniyah and Erbil.

Further Reading

Iraq

Aburish, S. K., *Saddam Hussein: The Politics of Revenge.* 2000

Allawi, Ali A., *The Occupation of Iraq: Winning the War, Losing the Peace.* 2007

Anderson, Liam and Stansfield, Gareth, *The Future of Iraq: Dictatorship, Democracy or Division?* 2004

Blix, Hans, *Disarming Iraq: The Search for Weapons of Mass Destruction.* 2004

Butler, R., *Saddam Defiant: The Threat of Weapons of Mass Destruction and the Crisis of Global Security.* 2000

Cockburn, Patrick, *The Rise of Islamic State: ISIS and the New Sunni Revolution.* 2015

Dodge, Toby, *Iraq: From War to a New Authoritarianism.* 2013

Herring, Eric and Rangwala, Glen, *Iraq in Fragments: The Occupation and its Legacy.* 2006

Mackey, Sandra, *The Reckoning: Iraq and the Legacy of Saddam Hussein.* 2002

Marr, Phebe, *The Modern History of Iraq.* 2003

Polk, William R., *Understanding Iraq: The Whole Sweep of Iraqi History, from Genghis Khan's Mongols to the Ottoman Turks to the British Mandate to the American Occupation.* 2006

Shahid, Anthony, *Night Draws Near: Iraq's People in the Shadow of America's War.* 2005

Sluglett, Marion Farouk and Sluglett, Peter, *Iraq Since 1958: From Revolution to Dictatorship.* 3rd ed. 2001

Stansfield, Gareth, *Iraq: People, History, Politics.* 2007

Stiglitz, Joseph E. and Bilmes. Linda J., *The Three Trillion Dollar War: The True Cost of the Iraq Conflict.* 2008

Tripp, Charles, *A History of Iraq.* 3rd ed. 2007

Weiss, Michael and Hassan, Hassan, *ISIS: Inside the Army of Terror.* 2015

National Statistical Office: Central Organization of Statistics & Information Technology, Baghdad.

Website: http://cosit.gov.iq

Ireland

Éire

Capital: Dublin
Population projection, 2020: 4·89m.
GNI per capita, 2017: (PPP$) 53,754
HDI/world rank, 2017: 0·938/4
Internet domain extension: .ie

Key Historical Events

Ireland was first inhabited around 7500 BC by Mesolithic hunter-gatherers who travelled across the land bridge that connected southwest Scotland with the northern part of Ireland (it was submerged around 6700 BC). Farmers from the Middle-East arrived in Ireland around 3500 BC. Their elaborate graves are also a feature of Neolithic communities in Brittany and the Iberian peninsula. From the sixth century BC, the island was invaded by waves of Celtic tribes from central Europe, including the Gaels, who established pastoral communities within massive stone forts. By AD 200 the Gaels dominated the island, though there was no central control: society was based on a complex structure of hundreds of small kingdoms. The Romans, who dominated much of northern Europe, never reached Ireland. The Gaels traded with other Celtic peoples and sent raiding parties to form settlements in Scotland (Dál Riata) and west Wales.

Christian missionaries reached Ireland during the 3rd century AD. St Patrick, born on the west coast of Britain, was consecrated as a bishop in Gaul and lived and preached in Ireland from *c.* 432 until his death *c.* 465. Monasteries were founded and, in an overwhelmingly agrarian society, they became important centres of learning and the dissemination of the written word. In contrast to much of northern Europe, ravaged by fragmentary forces following the collapse of the Roman Empire, Christianity found a haven in Ireland. Later, Irish missionaries took Celtic Christianity to Britain and continental Europe. By the 5th century AD there were five leading Gaelic kingdoms, which roughly correspond to the latter-day provinces of Ulster, Leinster, Munster and Connacht (the fifth kingdom occupied land in the modern counties of Meath and Westmeath). Each kingdom was dominated by one or two families—the Uí Néill clan was especially powerful in the north and east. The south (Munster) was dominated by the Eóganachta family.

Nordic Invasion

Viking longboats first appeared off the Irish coast in the late seventh century. 795 saw a full-scale Viking invasion, which heralded more than two hundred years of Scandinavian influence. The Vikings were great traders and established the first towns along the east and south coasts—the towns of Wexford, Waterford, Cork and Limerick became prosperous centres of manufacturing and commerce. Dublin, said to be founded in 841 by the Norse king Thurgesius, became a key outpost in a Viking diaspora stretching as far as Sicily and Russia. Gaelic kings made military alliances with the Viking settlers to support their struggles with neighbouring dynasties. In 976 the warrior Brian Boru (Bóruma) became king of Munster following a series of victories against the powerful Eóganachta. Following Boru's defeat of the Leinster groups and their Norse allies at Clontarf in 1014 he seemed destined to be the first high king of all Ireland, but was murdered shortly after his famous victory.

In the mid-12th century the Pope gave his blessing to an expedition of Anglo-Normans to Ireland. They were sent by the English King Henry II, who had been approached for military support by the deposed king of Leinster, Dermot MacMurrough (Díarmait Mac Murchada). Returning to Ireland in 1169 with Norman barons and Welsh mercenaries, MacMurrough recovered part of his former territories and captured Dublin. Richard de Clare (Strongbow), a powerful Norman invader, became MacMurrough's heir after marrying his daughter. During the 13th century various Anglo-Norman adventurers began to establish themselves in Ireland. Dublin Castle was built in 1204 on the site of a Norse fort and the first parliament sat there in 1264. After his decisive defeat of English forces at the Battle of Bannockburn

in 1314, Edward Bruce, the brother of Robert Bruce, king of Scotland, dreamed of establishing a Celtic kingdom. In 1315 he landed in Ulster and attempted to overthrow the English. Within a year he controlled most of Ireland north of Dublin, but his troops left a trail of destruction and soon lost support. Bruce was defeated and killed at Dundalk in 1317 by a Norman-Irish army reinforced from England under orders from King Edward II.

The descendants of the Anglo-Norman settlers were gradually identified with the native Irish, whose language, habits, and laws they adopted. To counteract this, the Anglo-Irish Parliament passed the Statute of Kilkenny in 1366, decreeing heavy penalties against all who allied themselves with the Irish. This statute, however, remained inoperative; although Richard II went to Ireland in 1394 and 1399 to reassert royal authority, he failed to achieve any practical result. During the subsequent Wars of the Roses in England the authority of the English crown became limited to the Pale, a coastal district around Dublin.

King Edward IV, of the House of York, came to the English throne in 1461 and appointed Gerald (Gearóid Mór) FitzGerald, 8th earl of Kildare as viceroy of Ireland. The FitzGeralds were wealthy Yorkists, well-connected to a network of Anglo-Norman and Gaelic families. Gearóid Mór wielded considerable power, and managed to hold onto it even after the return of the Lancastrians in 1485. He was eventually replaced in 1494 by Sir Edward Poynings, who, representing English interests, brought in legislation providing for the reduction of the power of the Anglo-Irish lords. The Poynings Laws removed the legal rights of the Irish parliament to legislate independently.

Henry VII reappointed Gearóid Mór as viceroy in 1496. For the next 38 years the FitzGeralds (Geraldines) ruled Ireland from Maynooth Castle, paying deference to the English crown. Henry VIII was determined to centralize power and reduce the influence of provincial magnates. He introduced the Reformation to Ireland in 1537 and began to dissolve the monasteries with little resistance.

Ulster Rebellion

Elizabeth I, through her deputy in Ireland, Sir Henry Sidley, removed the Irish chiefdoms from their positions of power. An uprising in Munster in the early 1570s was quickly suppressed and only Ulster now provided a stumbling block to Tudor domination. It was from Ulster that Hugh O'Neill and Red Hugh O'Donnell launched an open rebellion. In 1598 O'Neill ambushed and defeated a government force of over 4,000 at the Battle of Yellow Ford near Armagh. Spoken of as 'Prince of Ireland', his ambitions were thwarted by the arrival of 20,000 troops under Lord Mountjoy in 1600. Reinforcements of Spanish soldiers in 1601 were insufficient and O'Neill left for the Continent with his followers in the 1607 'Flight of the Earls'.

The Earls' lands were seized by the English crown and in 1609 Ulster-Scottish and English settlers were invited to colonize. Swathes of land were cleared of farms and woodland, and 23 walled new towns were created, including Belfast. By the early 1620s the Anglo-Scottish population of Ulster was more than 20,000. English politics in the 1630s was dominated by struggles between the crown and parliament (the Puritans) and the Irish in Ulster took advantage, rebelling against the planters in late 1641 in a series of attacks in which thousands of Protestants were killed. The following year Owen Roe O'Neill, who had fled to Spain with his uncle Hugh in 1607, returned to Ireland and led the Confederate forces. A provisional government was established at Kilkenny and by the end of 1642 O'Neill controlled the whole island apart from Dublin and parts of Ulster.

Victory for the English parliamentarians under Oliver Cromwell and the execution of Charles I in 1649 had a profound impact on Ireland. Cromwell was determined to avenge the 1641 massacre of the Ulster planters. With his New Model Army, he stormed Drogheda and murdered its garrison of 2,000. Wexford fell, and by 1652 all of Ireland was in Cromwellian hands. Hundreds of thousands of acres of land were confiscated and given to a new wave of Protestant settlers.

Following the restoration of the English monarchy in 1660, Catholics in Ireland hoped to be rewarded for their former loyalty, but Charles II restored only a small number of Catholic estates. King James II, however, was a

© Springer Nature Limited 2020
Palgrave Macmillan (ed.), *The Statesman's Yearbook 2020*,
https://doi.org/10.1057/978-1-349-95940-2_96

declared Catholic and under his viceroy in Ireland, Richard Talbot, earl of Tyrconnel, Catholics were advanced to positions of state and placed in control of the military. Protestant power was on the wane in England and the Protestant aristocracy invited William of Orange (the Dutch husband of James II's daughter Mary) to claim the English crown. James II fled to France, then travelled to Ireland with French soldiers. They moved north, aiming to subjugate Protestant Ulster. In the spring of 1689 only the walled towns of Derry/Londonderry and Enniskillen remained in Protestant hands. Derry/Londonderry was besieged, but it held out for 15 weeks until the arrival of William's forces, which defeated James at the Battle of the Boyne. The Jacobites retreated to Limerick, where they negotiated the Treaty of Limerick of 1691. Catholics were permitted some religious freedom, and the restoration of their lands. However, the treaty was not honoured by the English parliament and 11,000 Irish Jacobites set sail to join the French army.

Religious Divide
The defeat of the Catholic cause was followed by more confiscation of land and the introduction of the Penal Laws which prevented Catholics from buying freehold land, holding public office or bearing arms. During the American revolution, fear of a French invasion led Irish Protestants to form the Protestant Volunteer army. Led by Henry Grattan, they used their military strength to extract concessions from Britain. Trade concessions were granted in 1779 and the Poynings Laws repealed three years later. However, Catholics continued to be denied the right to hold political office.

The principles of the French Revolution found their most powerful expression in Ireland in the Society of United Irishmen, which, led by the Protestant lawyer Theobald Wolfe Tone, mounted a rebellion in 1798. Without the expected French assistance, the rebellion was crushed by crown troops led by Gen. Lake. The British prime minister, William Pitt, was convinced that the 'Irish problem' could be solved by the abolition of the Irish parliament, legislative union with Britain and Catholic emancipation. The first two goals were achieved in 1801, but the opposition of George III and British Protestants prevented the enactment of the Catholic Emancipation act until 1829, when it was accomplished largely through the efforts of Daniel O'Connell.

After 1829 the Irish representatives in the British Parliament, led by O'Connell, sought a repeal of the Act of Union. Calls for land reforms were drowned out by a disastrous potato famine. Between 1845–49 a blight wiped out the potato crop, the staple food of the Irish population and resulted in mass starvation. Of a population of 8·5m. almost 1m. died and over 1m. emigrated, mostly to the United States. Irish Catholics in the United States formed the secret Fenian movement, dedicated to achieving full Irish independence.

Home Rule Campaign
Charles Parnell, a Home Rule League MP, came to the fore of the nationalist movement in 1877 as president of the Home Rule Confederation of Great Britain. Parnell led parliamentary obstruction in response to the House of Lords' rejection of limited land reform in Ireland. Parnell's Irish Land League saw limited gains in Gladstone's 1881 Land Act but Parnell, voicing continuing discontent, was imprisoned in Dublin. His release in 1882 and the subsequent Kilmainham Treaty, granting more concessions to tenants, was seen by London as the quickest solution to an increasingly anarchic Ireland.

The Home Rule Party, led by Parnell, brought down the Conservative government at Westminster by voting with the Liberals, allowing William Gladstone to form a government in 1886. Gladstone attempted to resolve the 'Irish problem' by introducing a Home Rule Bill—seen as Parnell's greatest achievement—which would give the Irish Parliament the right to appoint the executive of Ireland. However, Home Rule was greatly opposed in Ulster and England and failed at Westminster in 1886 and 1893. Parnell's domination of Irish politics came to end with the disclosure of his affair with Kitty O'Shea—an English woman of aristocratic background—in 1890. After Gladstone rejected him, he lost control of the Irish parliamentarians and was condemned by the Catholic clergy.

During the 1880s a new pride in traditional Irish culture took root, symbolized by the establishment of the Gaelic Athletic Association in 1884 and the Gaelic League in 1893, which successfully campaigned for the return of the Irish language to the school curriculum. Though not political organizations, they provided a link between the conservative Catholic church and the Fenians (nationalists). In 1905 the Irish political leader and journalist Arthur Griffith founded Sinn Féin ('we ourselves') to promote Irish economic welfare and achieve complete political independence. However, at the time the dominant nationalist group remained the Home Rule party of John Redmond.

A Home Rule Bill was finally passed in 1914 but the act was suspended for the duration of the First World War. Redmond pledged the support of Ireland to the British war effort, which angered some nationalists. The Irish Republican Brotherhood (IRB) plotted a rebellion while Britain was at war, soliciting German support. On Easter Monday 1916 the IRB seized the General Post Office in Dublin and Patrick Pearse read out the proclamation of the Republic of Ireland. Though the Easter Rising was over in under a week, the emotional impact was heightened when the British executed 16 of the rebel leaders. Sinn Féin, linked in the Irish public's mind with the rising, scored a dramatic victory in the parliamentary elections of 1918. Its members refused to take their seats in Westminster, declared the *Dáil Éireann* ('Diet of Ireland') and proclaimed the Irish republic. The British outlawed Sinn Féin and the Dáil, which went underground and associated military groups including the Irish Republican Army (IRA) engaged in guerrilla warfare against the local authorities representing the Union. The British sent police reinforcements (the Black and Tans) who further inflamed the situation.

Civil War
A new Home Rule Bill was passed in 1920, establishing two parliaments, one in Belfast and the other in Dublin. The Unionists of the six counties accepted this scheme, and a Northern Parliament was duly elected in May 1921. Sinn Féin rejected the plan, but in autumn 1921 British Prime Minister Lloyd George negotiated with Griffith and Michael Collins of the Dáil a treaty granting Catholic Ireland dominion status within the British Empire. Collins managed to gain approval in the Dáil by a slim majority. The Republicans in the Dáil, led by Éamon de Valera, rejected the treaty, which had divided Ireland and fell short of full independence. A brutal civil war ensued; Collins, who had assumed command of the army, was assassinated in Aug. 1922 by anti-treaty rebels. The treaty supporters emerged as victors and the Irish Free State was established in Jan. 1922. William Cosgrave became the first prime minister and his Fine Gael party led for ten years. In 1932 de Valera, leader of the Fianna Fáil party, became prime minister (*taoiseach*). Five years later he brought in a new constitution establishing the sovereign nation of Ireland and abolishing the oath of allegiance sworn by Irish parliamentarians to the British crown.

Independence
Ireland remained neutral in the Second World War, though in the harsh economic conditions of the time tens of thousands of people emigrated to Britain for work and many thousands joined the war effort. In 1948 Prime Minister John Costello demanded total independence from Britain and reunification with the six counties of Northern Ireland. Independence came the following year and in 1955 the Republic of Ireland was admitted to the United Nations, but nothing came of the claim to the six Ulster counties under British rule. Economic relations between the Republic and Northern Ireland improved in the 1950s and '60s, though both decades were marked by large-scale emigration from the Republic, chiefly to the United States. Trouble in the North flared up in the late '60s over Catholic demands for civil rights and equality in the allocation of housing. Confrontation between the two religious communities intensified and in 1969 British troops were deployed to keep the peace. The British military soon lost the confidence of the Catholic community, the IRA increased its activity and more violence ensued. In 1972 the Unionist government in Belfast resigned and direct rule from London was imposed.

On 1 Jan. 1973 the Republic of Ireland became a member state of the European Economic Community. Jack Lynch led Fianna Fáil into power in 1977, though over the next decade there were party splits while general elections were held against a backdrop of soaring unemployment. Emigration increased, especially among young people, reaching a peak of 44,000 in 1989 under Charles Haughey's premiership. The 1990s were marked by an economic upturn, buoyed by EU subsidies and foreign investment. The legalization of divorce in 1995 symbolized the Irish Republic's embrace of modern European values. In the north, a ceasefire between the IRA and Protestant militias in 1994 formed the basis for the signing of the Good Friday Agreement in April 1998. On 2 Dec. 1999 the Irish constitution was amended to remove the articles laying claim to Northern Ireland. Prime Minister Bertie Ahern, who came to power in the 1997 general election, took Ireland into the single European currency in Jan. 2002. In Oct. 2002 the Northern Irish Assembly was suspended for the fourth time in its history over allegations of IRA spying at the Northern Ireland Office. Direct rule from London was subsequently reimposed.

In May 2007 a devolved Northern Ireland government replaced direct rule from London. The following month Ahern won a third term in office but resigned 11 months later in the face of a personal financial scandal. In

Oct. 2008 Ireland became the first Western European nation to fall into recession as the global financial crisis took hold. Meanwhile, the following year a report by the Irish Child Abuse Commission criticized senior figures within the Irish Catholic Church for their handling of sexual abuse allegations.

In Nov. 2010 Ireland received an EU–IMF bailout and the government implemented a programme of austerity. In March 2011, 13 years of Fianna Fáil rule ended and Enda Kenny became prime minister. There were subsequent major social developments as limited access to abortion was legalized in July 2013 and same-sex marriage was approved in a referendum in May 2015.

Territory and Population

The Republic of Ireland lies in the Atlantic Ocean, separated from Great Britain by the Irish Sea to the east, and bounded in the northeast by Northern Ireland (UK). In 2011, 62·3% of the population lived in urban areas. The population at the 2011 census was 4,588,252 (2,315,553 females), giving a density of 67·0 persons per sq. km. The census population in 2011 was the highest figure since 1851 when the census recorded a population of 5·11m. The census population in 2016 was 4,761,865.

The UN gives a projected population for 2020 of 4·89m.

The capital is Dublin (Baile Átha Cliath). Town populations, 2011: Greater Dublin, 1,110,627; Cork, 198,582; Limerick, 91,454; Galway, 76,778; Waterford, 51,519.

Counties and Cities[1]	Area in ha[2]	Population, 2011		
		Males	Females	Totals
Province of Leinster				
Carlow	89,655	27,431	27,181	54,612
Dublin City	11,758	257,303	270,309	527,612
Dun Laoghaire-Rathdown	12,638	98,567	107,694	206,261
Fingal	45,467	134,488	139,503	273,991
Kildare	169,540	104,658	105,654	210,312
Kilkenny	207,289	47,788	47,631	95,419
Laois	171,990	40,587	39,972	80,559
Longford	109,116	19,649	19,351	39,000
Louth	82,613	60,763	62,134	122,897
Meath	234,207	91,910	92,225	184,135
Offaly	200,117	38,430	38,257	76,687
South Dublin	22,364	129,544	135,661	265,205
Westmeath	183,965	42,783	43,381	86,164
Wexford	236,685	71,909	73,411	145,320
Wicklow	202,662	67,542	69,098	136,640
Total of Leinster	1,980,066	1,233,352	1,271,462	2,504,814
Province of Munster				
Clare	345,004	58,298	58,898	117,196
Cork City	3,953	58,812	60,418	119,230
Cork	746,042	198,658	201,144	399,802
Kerry	480,689	72,629	72,873	145,502
Limerick City[3]	2,087	27,947	29,159	57,106
Limerick[3]	273,504	67,868	66,835	134,703
North Tipperary[4]	204,627	35,340	34,982	70,322
South Tipperary[4]	225,845	44,244	44,188	88,432
Waterford City[5]	4,103	22,921	23,811	46,732
Waterford[5]	181,556	33,543	33,520	67,063
Total of Munster	2,467,410	620,260	625,828	1,246,088
Province of Connacht				
Galway City	5,057	36,514	39,015	75,529
Galway	609,820	88,244	86,880	175,124
Leitrim	159,003	16,144	15,654	31,798

(continued)

Counties and Cities[1]	Area in ha[2]	Population, 2011		
		Males	Females	Totals
Mayo	558,605	65,420	65,218	130,638
Roscommon	254,819	32,353	31,712	64,065
Sligo	183,752	32,435	32,958	65,393
Total of Connacht	1,771,056	271,110	271,437	542,547
Province of Ulster (part of)				
Cavan	193,177	37,013	36,170	73,183
Donegal	486,091	80,523	80,614	161,137
Monaghan	129,508	30,441	30,042	60,483
Total of Ulster (part of)	808,776	147,977	146,826	294,803
Total	7,027,308	2,272,699	2,315,553	4,588,252

[1]Cities were previously known as County Boroughs.
[2]Area details provided by Ordnance Survey.
[3]Limerick City Council and Limerick County Council merged in 2014.
[4]North Tipperary County Council and South Tipperary County Council merged in 2014 to create Tipperary County Council.
[5]Waterford City Council and Waterford County Council merged in 2014.

The official languages are Irish (the national language) and English; according to the 2011 census, Irish is spoken by 1·77m. persons in the Republic of Ireland aged three years and over (1·66m. in 2006). It is a compulsory subject at school.

Social Statistics

Statistics for five calendar years[1]:

	Births	Marriages	Deaths
2008	75,173	22,187	28,274
2009	75,554	21,627	28,380
2010	75,174	20,594	27,961
2011	74,033	19,855	28,456
2012	71,674	20,713	29,186

[1]Data for births and deaths are by year of occurrence; data for marriages are by year of registration.

2012 rates (per 1,000 population): birth, 15·6; death, 6·4; marriage, 4·5. Annual population growth rate, 2005–10, 1·5%. Expectation of life at birth, 2011, 78·3 years for males and 82·8 years for females.

In 2009 the suicide rate per 100,000 population was 11·8 (men, 19·0; women, 4·7). Infant mortality in 2010, three per 1,000 live births; fertility rate (2013), 2·0 births per woman. At a referendum on 25 May 2018 on repealing the eighth amendment to the constitution effectively restricting legal abortion only to those cases in which the mother's life was at risk, 66·4% of votes were in favour of the proposal.

Earlier, at a referendum on 24 Nov. 1995 on the legalization of civil divorce, 818,842 votes were in favour and 809,728 against, while at a further referendum on 22 May 2015 on the legalization of same-sex marriage, 1,201,607 votes were in favour and 734,300 against; it became legal in Nov. 2015.

Immigration peaked at 151,100 in 2006–07. For the year ended April 2012 preliminary figures show the estimated number of immigrants to be 52,700 while emigrants totalled 87,100 in the same period (including 46,500 Irish nationals). In 2012 Ireland received 956 asylum applications, the lowest annual total since 1995.

Climate

Influenced by the Gulf Stream, there is an equable climate with mild south-west winds, making temperatures almost uniform over the whole country. The coldest months are Jan. and Feb. (39–45°F, 4–7°C) and the warmest July and Aug. (57–61°F, 14–16°C). May and June are the sunniest months, averaging 5·5 to 6·5 hours each day, but over 7 hours in the extreme southeast. Rainfall is lowest along the eastern coastal strip. The central parts vary between 30–44" (750–1,125 mm), and up to 60" (1,500 mm) may be experienced in low-lying areas in the west. Dublin, Jan. 40°F (4°C), July 59°F (15°C). Annual rainfall 30" (750 mm). Cork, Jan. 42°F (5°C), July 61°F (16°C). Annual rainfall 41" (1,025 mm).

Constitution and Government

Ireland is a sovereign independent, democratic republic. Its parliament exercises jurisdiction in 26 of the 32 counties of the island of Ireland. The first Constitution of the Irish Free State came into operation on 6 Dec. 1922. Certain provisions which were regarded as contrary to the national sentiments were gradually removed by successive amendments, with the result that at the end of 1936 the text differed considerably from the original document. On 14 June 1937 a new constitution was approved by Parliament and enacted by a plebiscite on 1 July 1937. This constitution came into operation on 29 Dec. 1937. Under it the name Ireland (Éire) was restored. In its original form the Irish Constitution provided that the territory of Ireland comprised the whole island, and thus included that of Northern Ireland. This position was modified by referendum in 1998 following the Good Friday Agreement of that year. The former territorial claim has now been replaced with a statement that, while it is the aspiration of the Irish nation to unite the peoples of the island and the current territory of Ireland is not final, unification shall not take place without the consent of majorities in both jurisdictions.

The head of state is the *President*, whose role is largely ceremonial, but who has the power to refer proposed legislation which might infringe the Constitution to the Supreme Court.

The *Oireachtas* or National Parliament consists of the President, a House of Representatives (*Dáil Éireann*) and a Senate (*Seanad Éireann*). The *Dáil*, consisting of 158 members, is elected by adult suffrage on the Single Transferable Vote system in constituencies of three, four or five members. Of the 60 members of the Senate, 11 are nominated by the *Taoiseach* (Prime Minister), six are elected by the universities and the remaining 43 are elected from five panels of candidates established on a vocational basis, representing the following public services and interests: (1) national language and culture, literature, art, education and such professional interests as may be defined by law for the purpose of this panel; (2) agricultural and allied interests, and fisheries; (3) labour, whether organized or unorganized; (4) industry and commerce, including banking, finance, accountancy, engineering and architecture; (5) public administration and social services, including voluntary social activities. The electing body comprises members of the *Dáil*, Senate, county boroughs and county councils.

A maximum period of 90 days is afforded to the Senate for the consideration or amendment of bills sent to that House by the *Dáil*, but the Senate has no power to veto legislative proposals.

No amendment of the Constitution can be effected except with the approval of the people given at a referendum.

National Anthem

'Amhrán na bhFiann' ('The Soldier's Song'); words by P. Kearney, tune by P. Heeney and P. Kearney.

Government Chronology

(FF = Fianna Fáil; FG = Fine Gael; L = Labour; n/p = non-partisan)

Presidents since 1938.

1938–45	FF	Douglas Hyde
1945–59	FF	Séan Thomas O'Kelly
1959–73	FF	Éamon de Valera
1973–74	FF	Erskine Hamilton Childers
1974–76	FF	Cearbhall O'Dalaigh
1976–90	FF	Patrick John Hillery
1990–97	n/p	Mary Terese Robinson
1997–2011	FF	Mary Patricia McAleese
2011–	L	Michael Daniel Higgins

Prime Ministers since 1932.

1932–48	FF	Éamon de Valera
1948–51	FG	John Aloysius Costello

1951–54	FF	Éamon de Valera
1954–57	FG	John Aloysius Costello
1957–59	FF	Éamon de Valera
1959–66	FF	Séan Francis Lemass
1966–73	FF	John (Jack) Mary Lynch
1973–77	FG	Liam Thomas Cosgrave
1977–79	FF	John (Jack) Mary Lynch
1979–81	FF	Charles James Haughey
1981–82	FG	Garret Michael FitzGerald
1982	FF	Charles James Haughey
1982–87	FG	Garret Michael FitzGerald
1987–92	FF	Charles James Haughey
1992–94	FF	Albert Reynolds
1994–97	FG	John Gerard Bruton
1997–2008	FF	Bartholomew (Bertie) P. Ahern
2008–11	FF	Brian Cowen
2011–17	FG	Enda Kenny
2017–	FG	Leo Varadkar

Recent Elections

A general election was held on 26 Feb. 2016: Fine Gael (FG) won 50 seats with 25·5% of first preference votes (in 2011, 76 seats); Fianna Fáil (FF) 44 with 24·3% (20); Sinn Féin 23 with 13·8% (14); Labour Party (L), 7 with 6·6% (37); Anti-Austerity Alliance–People Before Profit, 6; Independents 4 Change, 4; Social Democrats, 3; Green Party, 2; ind., 19. Turnout was 65·2%.

Following elections to the Senate in April 2016, FG held 19 of the 60 seats, FF had 14, Sinn Féin had 7, L had 5, Green Party had 1 and independents held 14 seats.

Presidential elections took place on 26 Oct. 2018. Michael D. Higgins (ind.) was re-elected with 55·8% of the vote, ahead of Peter Casey (ind.) with 23·3%, Seán Gallagher (ind.) 6·4%, Liadh Ní Riada (Sinn Féin) 6·4%, Joan Freeman (ind.) 6·0% and Gavin Duffy (ind.) 2·2%. Turnout was 43·9%.

European Parliament

Ireland has 11 representatives. At the May 2014 elections turnout was 51·0% (58·6% in 2009). Fine Gael won 4 seats with 22·3% of votes cast (political affiliation in European Parliament: European People's Party); Sinn Féin, 3 with 19·5% (European United Left/Nordic Green Left); Fianna Fáil, 1 with 22·3% (European Conservatives and Reformists). Three independents were elected, with 19·8% (one with Alliance of Liberals and Democrats for Europe, one with Greens/European Free Alliance and one with Progressive Alliance of Socialists and Democrats).

Current Government

President: Michael D. Higgins (b. 1941; L), elected out of seven candidates on 27 Oct. 2011 and inaugurated 11 Nov. 2011.

In Feb. 2019 the government was composed as follows:

Taoiseach (Prime Minister) and Minister for Defence: Leo Varadkar; b. 1979 (FG; sworn in 14 June 2017).

Tánaiste (Deputy Prime Minister) and Minister for Foreign Affairs and Trade, with Special Responsibility for Brexit: Simon Coveney (b. 1972; FG). *Finance, and Public Expenditure and Reform:* Paschal Donohoe (b. 1974; FG). *Education and Skills:* Joe McHugh (b. 1971; FG). *Justice and Equality:* Charles Flanagan (b. 1956; FG). *Business, Enterprise and Innovation:* Heather Humphreys (b. 1963; FG). *Health:* Simon Harris (b. 1986; FG). *Agriculture, Food and the Marine:* Michael Creed (b. 1963; FG). *Communications, Climate Action and Environment:* Richard Bruton (b. 1953; FG). *Transport, Tourism and Sport:* Shane Ross (b. 1949; ind.). *Children and Youth Affairs:* Katherine Zappone (b. 1953; ind.). *Rural and Community Development:* Michael Ring (b. 1953; FG). *Employment and Social Protection:* Regina Doherty (b. 1971; FG). *Housing, Planning and Local Government:* Eoghan Murphy (b. 1982; FG). *Culture, Heritage and the Gaeltacht:* Josepha Madigan (b. 1970; FG).

There were 19 Ministers of State as at Feb. 2019.

Attorney General: Séamus Woulfe.

Government Website: http://www.gov.ie

(continued)

Current Leaders

Michael D. Higgins

Position
President

Introduction
Michael Daniel Higgins took office as president on 11 Nov. 2011. Prior to his appointment he was the head of the Labour Party. He initially stated that he would only serve one presidential term, but subsequently stood successfully for re-election in Oct. 2018, winning about 56% of the vote. He has published several volumes of poetry.

Early Life
Known popularly as Michael D., Higgins was born on 18 April 1941 in Limerick and raised in Co. Clare, in the west of Ireland. After working as a clerk he enrolled as a mature student at Galway University in 1962, where he would later lecture in sociology and politics. He undertook further studies at Manchester University in the UK and at the University of Indiana, USA.

Having twice stood unsuccessfully for election to the Dáil as a Labour Party candidate, Higgins was appointed to the Senate by Taoiseach Liam Cosgrave in 1973. He was elected to the Dáil in 1981 but lost his seat in Nov. 1982 following the collapse of the governing coalition. Known as a radical, he served as mayor of Galway from 1982–83, a position he again held from 1991–92. Re-elected to parliament in 1987, he retained his Galway West seat until opting not to stand at the 2011 election.

Having previously opposed Labour's entry into the ruling coalition, Higgins accepted the post of minister of the arts and culture in 1993. During his four years in the post he repealed the controversial Section 31, which allowed censorship over media coverage of the Troubles in Northern Ireland. He also oversaw the establishment of the Irish-language broadcaster, TG4.

Higgins was a vocal opponent of the 2003 Iraq War and has campaigned for human rights in Somalia, Chile, Nicaragua, Gaza and Cambodia. At the 2011 presidential election he defeated Seán Gallagher, a well-known entrepreneur, and Martin McGuinness, a former commander of the IRA and later deputy leader of the Northern Irish power-sharing assembly.

Career in Office
While campaigning for the largely ceremonial post, Higgins pledged to promote justice and equality as the country emerged from economic crisis. During his first term in office, the Irish Republic in May 2015 became the first country to legalize same-sex marriage by popular vote, and in May 2018 voters in a referendum opted to repeal a provision in the constitution banning abortion.

In April 2014 he made the first official state visit to Britain, including an address to the Westminster parliament, by an Irish president and in Dec. he completed a week-long visit to China.

He was re-elected as president in Oct. 2018.

Leo Varadkar

Position
Prime Minister

Introduction
Leo Varadkar became prime minister in June 2017 following the resignation of Enda Kenny. He is notable for being the country's youngest-ever prime minister, as well as the world's fourth openly gay head of government.

Early Life
Varadkar was born on 18 Jan. 1979 in Dublin and joined Fine Gael while still at secondary school. He studied law for a short period at Trinity College, Dublin, before switching to medicine and graduating in 2003. At university, he was an active member of Young Fine Gael and the Youth of the European People's Party.

He stood unsuccessfully as a candidate at local elections in 1999 and five years later was chosen as a replacement councillor in the Fingal County Council. In 2007 he became a member of the *Dáil Éireann* and served as spokesperson for enterprise, trade and employment until 2010.

In 2011 Varadkar became minister for transport, tourism and sport in the coalition government with Labour. He organized the Gathering initiative,

intended to boost tourism through events that celebrated Irish culture and by appealing to the Irish diaspora (numbering some 70m.). Following a cabinet reshuffle in 2014 he was named minister for health, and then minister for social protection from 2016–17. As health minister he faced criticism for diverting €35m. away from the mental health budget.

In 2015, a few months prior to Ireland legalizing same-sex marriage, Varadkar declared his sexuality. On 2 June 2017 he became leader of Fine Gael, replacing Enda Kenny who had resigned from the post, and took over as prime minister 12 days later.

Career in Office
Having inherited the thorny issue of the UK's impending withdrawal from the European Union and its implications for Ireland and its borders, Varadkar has continued to emphasize his government's commitment to free movement and trade with Northern Ireland. He has also overseen two national referendums in which voters opted in May 2018 to repeal a provision in the Irish constitution banning abortion and in Oct. approved the decriminalization of blasphemy as an offence in Irish law.

Defence

The President of Ireland is the supreme commander of the Irish Defence Forces. Military command and administrative powers in relation to the Defence Forces are exercisable by the Government through and by the Minister for Defence. The Defence Acts, as amended, provides the legislative basis for the Defence Forces (Óglaigh na hÉireann). The Act and associated Defence Force Regulations set out the guiding principles under which the Defence Forces operate.

The Defence Forces comprise the Permanent Defence Force (the regular Army, the Air Corps and the Naval Service) and the Reserve Defence Force (comprising a First Line Reserve of members who have served in the Permanent Defence Force, a second-line Army Reserve and a second-line Naval Reserve).

The total strength of the Permanent Defence Force in Dec. 2011 was 9,438 (including 565 women) and the total strength of the Reserve Defence Force was 5,220. In Dec. 2011, 529 Defence Forces personnel were involved in 11 peace-support missions throughout the world.

Defence expenditure in 2013 totalled US$1,197m. (US$251 per capita), representing 0·5% of GDP.

Army

The Army strength in Dec. 2011 was 7,650 personnel with 4,995 reservists. The Army currently provides the deployable military capabilities for overseas peace support, crisis management and humanitarian operations augmented by personnel from the Air Corps and Naval Service.

Navy

The Naval Service is based at Haulbowline in Co. Cork. The strength in Dec. 2011 was 997 with 225 reservists. It operates eight offshore patrol vessels.

Air Corps

The Air Corps has its headquarters at Casement Aerodrome, Baldonnel, Co. Dublin. As the air component of the Defence Forces, the Air Corps provides air support capabilities to the other components in carrying out their roles. The Air Corps strength in Dec. 2011 was 791 personnel. The Corps operates 17 fixed-wing aircraft and ten helicopters.

International Relations

On 12 June 2008 Ireland became the first European Union member to reject the Treaty of Lisbon when it held a national referendum in which 53·4% of votes cast were against the reform treaty and only 46·6% in favour. Turnout was 53·1%. However, at a second referendum on 2 Oct. 2009, the treaty was approved by 67·1% to 32·9% (turnout, 59·0%). Parliamentary ratification followed on 23 Oct. 2009.

Economy

Agriculture accounted for 1·4% of GDP in 2013, industry 26·1% and services 72·5%.

According to the anti-corruption organization Transparency International, Ireland ranked equal 18th in a 2018 survey of countries with the least corruption in business and government. It received 73 out of 100 in the annual index.

Overview

Ireland is a high-income OECD nation. In the decade to 2008 it experienced rapid growth fuelled by a housing and credit boom, but the global financial crisis sent the economy into recession in 2008 and 2009 and again in 2011 and 2012. However, by 2014 Ireland had bounced back to become the fastest-growing country in the European Union.

In Sept. 2008 the government moved to stabilize the domestic financial system with a €400bn. plan to protect all deposits, bonds and debts in six banks and building societies for two years. By Feb. 2009 the state had nationalized Anglo Irish Bank and provided emergency funding to Allied Irish Banks and the Bank of Ireland. In Nov. 2010, following widespread concerns in the EU over the Irish government's ability to service its banking sector's debts, the country accepted an €85bn. bailout from the EU, with the IMF providing €22·5bn. The government undertook a programme of austerity and tax rises to cut the budget deficit, amounting to some €25bn. (or 16% of output) between 2008 and 2013. Ireland exited the bailout programme in Dec. 2013, becoming the first eurozone country to do so. In Feb. that year the government negotiated a deal with the European Central Bank to extend the bailout period of the Anglo Irish Bank from ten to 40 years, so reducing borrowing needs by €20bn. over ten years.

GDP grew by 8·8% in 2014, driven by robust exports and a low corporation tax rate of 12·5%. Nonetheless, slow recovery in other eurozone economies and in the UK—Ireland's primary trading partners—threatened to restrain further export-led growth. However, domestic demand continued to increase through 2015 and into 2016, despite high levels of private and public debt significantly above the EU average.

Between 2015 and 2018 the economy experienced some of the most rapid growth in the European Union, driven by strong domestic demand and rising employment. Various multinational corporations relocated their headquarters and intellectual property to Ireland in 2015, resulting in a surge in GDP growth to 25·0%. This was followed by more modest expansions of 4·9% in 2016 and 7·2% in 2017.

Unemployment fell from above 15% in 2010 to 5·4% in late 2018. However, the country also lost almost 25% of its young people to emigration in the period 2009–15, highlighting the danger of high levels of youth joblessness to the country's future prospects. Meanwhile, the still unclear terms of the UK's exit from the European Union, with potentially significant impacts on the border arrangements between the Irish Republic and Northern Ireland, also pose a potential threat to long-term prosperity.

Currency

On 1 Jan. 1999 the *euro* (EUR) became the legal currency in Ireland at the irrevocable conversion rate of 0·787564 Irish pounds to 1 euro. The euro, which consists of 100 cents, has been in circulation since 1 Jan. 2002. On the introduction of the euro there was a 'dual circulation' period before the Irish pound ceased to be legal tender on 9 Feb. 2002.

Inflation rates (based on OECD statistics):

2008	2009	2010	2011	2012	2013	2014	2015	2016	2017
3·1%	−1·7%	−1·6%	1·2%	1·9%	0·5%	0·3%	0·0%	−0·2%	0·3%

The Central Bank has the sole right of issuing legal tender notes; token coinage is issued by the Minister for Finance through the Bank. Gold reserves were 176,000 troy oz in Sept. 2009 and foreign exchange reserves US$574m. Total money supply was €83,181m. in Aug. 2009.

Budget

Current revenue and expenditure (in €1m.):

Current revenue	2013	2014
Capital taxes	647	918
Corporation tax	4,270	4,614
Customs duties	246	270
Excise duties	4,791	4,991
Income tax	15,758	17,157
Local property tax	318	491
Motor tax receipts	100	—
Stamp duties	1,340	1,687
Value-added tax	10,336	11,153

(*continued*)

Current revenue	2013	2014
Non-tax revenue	2,676	2,966
Total	40,482	44,248
Current expenditure		
Agriculture, food and the marine	1,041	1,010
Education and skills	8,332	8,290
Health	13,745	13,354
Jobs, enterprise, and innovation	338	322
Justice and equality	2,215	2,196
Social protection	20,235	19,768
Transport, tourism and sport	756	685
Other	4,323	4,876
Gross current voted total	50,986	50,501
Less: Receipts	10,994	11,319
Net total	39,992	39,182

VAT is 23·0% (reduced rates of 13·5%, 9·0% and 4·8%).

Ireland's budget deficit in 2017 was 0·2% of GDP (2016, 0·5%; 2015, 1·9%). The required target set by the EU is a budget deficit of no more than 3%.

Performance

Real GDP growth rates (based on OECD statistics):

2008	2009	2010	2011	2012	2013	2014	2015	2016	2017
−4·4%	−5·1%	1·9%	3·7%	0·2%	1·3%	8·8%	25·0%	4·9%	7·2%

During the late 1990s Ireland had the fastest-growing economy in the European Union, with real GDP growth of 10·9% in 1997 and growth averaging 9·0% between 1995 and 1999. In Jan. 2016 new legislation reducing the tax rates on 'intangible assets' came into force in Ireland. As a consequence, a number of large multinational firms transferred their capital assets, financial activities and patents to the country for apparent corporate tax avoidance purposes. This explains the spike in the economic growth rate for 2015 to 25·5%, which in reality was not as significant as the GDP indicators suggested. Total GDP in 2017 was US$333·7bn.

Banking and Finance

In Oct. 2010 a new Central Bank of Ireland was created with a single fully-integrated structure and a unitary board—the Central Bank Commission. This replaced the boards of the Central Bank and Financial Services Authority of Ireland and the Irish Financial Services Regulatory Authority.

The Board of Directors of the Central Bank of Ireland consists of a Governor, appointed for a seven-year term by the President on the advice of the government, three *ex officio* directors (Director-General of Central Bank, Head of Financial Regulation and Secretary-General of Department of Finance) and between six and eight other directors, all appointed by the Minister for Finance. The *Governor* is Philip R. Lane. In 2009 the Bank's profit was €933·81m.; €745·47m. was paid to the Exchequer.

As at Nov. 2010, 420 credit institutions (including branches) were registered with the Central Bank. Ireland's largest banks are Bank of Ireland (with assets of US$142·3bn. in 2014) and AIB (assets of US$112·1bn. in 2014).

At Sept. 2010 total assets of within-the-State offices of all credit institutions amounted to €1,312bn.

Gross external debt totalled US$2,123,300m. in June 2012.

Ireland was one of the top five recipients of foreign direct investment in 2015, attracting US$100·5bn. that year. At the end of 2015 FDI stocks totalled US$435·5bn.

There is a stock exchange in Dublin.

Energy and Natural Resources

In 2011, 6·7% of energy consumption came from renewables (wind power, solar power, hydro-electric power, tidal power, geothermal energy and biomass), compared to the European Union average of 13·0%. A target of 16% has been set by the EU for 2020.

Environment

Ireland's carbon dioxide emissions from the consumption of energy in 2011 were the equivalent of 7·8 tonnes per capita.

Electricity

Installed capacity in 2011 was 8·8m. kW. In 2011 Ireland produced 27·7bn. kWh of electricity. Total consumption in 2011 was 28·1bn. kWh and consumption per capita 6,223 kWh.

Oil and Gas

Oil accounts for 56% of primary energy demand in Ireland while gas makes up 25% of demand. Over 0·6m. sq. km of the Irish continental shelf has been designated an exploration area for oil and gas; at the furthest point the limit of jurisdiction is 520 nautical miles from the coast. In the offshore there is a vast Continental Shelf in which a number of major basins and troughs have been identified. In March 2012 Providence Resources announced the discovery of a large oil field located 50 km off the Cork coast. Providing a flow in excess of 3,500 bbls per day, it is the first commercially viable oil field in Irish waters.

Natural gas reserves in 2014 totalled 10bn. cu. metres. Output in 2011 was 332m. cu. metres and consumption 4·8bn. cu. metres. 91% of natural gas supplies for the Irish Market are imported through the two sub-sea interconnectors connecting Ireland with Scotland and the remaining 9% is supplied from the Kinsale Head gas field, about 50 km off the south coast of Ireland. Deliveries from the Corrib gas field, about 80 km off the west coast, began in Dec. 2015.

Natural gas transmission and distribution is currently carried out by Gas Networks Ireland, a business division of Ervia (formerly known as Bord Gáis Éireann, meaning 'Gas Board of Ireland'). The gradual liberalization of the Irish gas market, which started in July 2004, was completed in July 2007 when domestic as well as business users became free to select any licensed natural gas supplier.

Peat

The country has very little indigenous coal, but possesses large reserves of peat, the development of which is handled largely by Bord na Móna (Peat Board). The Board owns 77 ha. of peatlands, representing 7·5% of total peatlands in Ireland. With peat as a finite resource the Board is pursuing a policy of sustainability with no new bogs being brought into production. In 2011–12 the Board produced 3·6m. tonnes of milled peat for use in three milled peat electricity generating stations. 202,000 tonnes of briquettes were produced for sale to the domestic heating market. Bord na Móna also produced 1·9m. cu. metres of horticultural peat, mainly for export.

Minerals

Ireland has three zinc-lead mines, which in 2009 produced a combined total of 357,000 tonnes of zinc in concentrate and 43,000 tonnes of lead in concentrate, together with some silver (in lead). Ireland is Europe's leading zinc mine producer (36% of European output in 2009) and ranks tenth in the world for total zinc production. Gross value of metal production (lead and zinc) in Ireland in 2009 was €314m. Production of gypsum is significant (400,000 tonnes in 2009). Aggregate production in 2009 was an estimated 65m. tonnes. In June 2010, 37 companies held 514 prospecting licences; a total of €20·2m. was spent on exploration in 2009. The main target is base metals but there is also interest in gold.

Agriculture

The Central Statistics Office's *Quarterly National Household Survey* showed that in the quarter of March–May 2012 there were 87,100 people whose primary source of income was from agriculture, forestry and fisheries. In 2010 a total of 272,016 people worked on farms on a regular basis, working the equivalent of 168,387 full-time jobs. There were 139,860 farm holdings in Ireland, almost all of which were family farms. Average farm size was 32·7 ha. The land area of Ireland is 6·9m. ha., of which 4·6m. ha. were used for agriculture in 2011.

Agriculture, fisheries and forestry represented 2·5% of gross value added in 2010 (provisional). More than 80% of the agricultural area is devoted to pasture, hay and grass silage (3·74m. ha.), 10% to rough grazing (0·45m. ha.) and 8% to crop production (0·37m. ha.). In 2011 beef and milk production accounted for 57% of goods output at producer prices.

In 2011: barley accounted (in ha.) for 180,600; wheat, 94,200; oats, 21,400; oilseed rape, 12,400; potatoes, 10,400. Production figures in 2011 (in 1,000 tonnes) were: barley, 1,412; wheat, 669; potatoes, 420; oats, 148; oilseed rape, 28.

Goods output at producer prices including changes in stock for 2011 was estimated at €6·3bn.; operating surplus (aggregate income) was €2·4bn. Direct income payments, financed or co-financed by the EU, amounted to €1·8bn. It is estimated that net subsidies (subsidies on products plus subsidies on production less taxes on products and taxes on production) represented 76% of aggregate income. Livestock figures in 2010 were: 6,606,585 cattle; 5,078,952 sheep; 1,518,332 pigs; 11,025,441 poultry.

Forestry

Total forest area in 2015 was 0·75m. ha. (11% of total land area). Timber production in 2011 was 2·64m. cu. metres.

Fisheries

In 2012 approximately 11,100 people were engaged full- or part-time in the sea fishing industry; at the end of the same year the fishing fleet consisted of 2,217 vessels. The quantities and values of fish landed in 2009 were: wet fish, 139,960 tonnes, value €98·8m.; shellfish, molluscs and crustaceans, 19,825 tonnes, value €57·6m. Total quantity (2009): 159,785 tonnes; total value, €156·4m. The main types of fish caught in 2009 were mackerel (40,150 tonnes), horse mackerel (37,092 tonnes) and herring (15,552 tonnes). More than 98% of fish caught is from sea fishing.

Industry

The leading companies by market capitalization in Ireland in May 2018 were: Medtronic, a medical technology supplier (US$116bn.); Accenture, a global professional services company (US$101bn.); and Allergan, a pharmaceutical product manufacturer and developer (US$52·1bn.).

The census of industrial production for 2011 gives the following details of the values (in €1m.) of gross and net output for the principal manufacturing industries.

	Gross output	Net output
Beverages	2,338	1,418
Wood and wood products, except furniture	601	209
Printing and reproduction of recorded media	902	638
Chemicals and chemical products	3,492	2,207
Rubber and plastic products	1,120	485
Other non-metallic mineral products	1,117	446
Fabricated metal products, except machinery and equipment	1,216	619
Computer, electronic and optical products	8,924	4,950
Electrical equipment	675	243
Machinery and equipment n.e.c.	2,154	1,145
Other manufacturing	8,125	5,762
Food products, tobacco, coke and refined petroleum products, transport equipment and furniture	21,815	9,580
Basic pharmaceutical products and preparations; basic metals	38,277	30,806
Total, including others (all industries)	92,765	59,469

Labour

The total labour force in 2008 was 2,239,600, of whom 126,700 were out of work. The unemployment rate in April and May 2001 was just 3·7%, down from 17·1% in Sept. 1985. However, it rose sharply as a consequence of the global economic crisis, peaking at 15·1% in Nov. 2011 and again in Feb. 2012. It has gradually declined since then and in Dec. 2018 was 5·3% (down from 6·7% in 2017 as a whole and 8·4% in 2016). It has now fallen to levels not seen since 2008. Of those at work in 2008, 1,246,400 were employed in the services sector, 492,000 in the industrial sector and 113,800 in the agricultural sector. Employment rose by approximately 40% between 1998 and 2008. In 2001 there were only 69,400 unemployed people, down from 226,000 in 1987, although this figure has risen steadily back up since then and in 2009 exceeded the 1987 total, with 264,600 unemployed. Ireland, along with the UK and Sweden, decided to open its labour market to nationals of the new EU member states in May 2004. Poles in particular went to Ireland following the EU expansion and by 2011 were the largest ethnic minority ahead of UK nationals; there were 122,585 Polish citizens in Ireland at the time of the 2011 census. In 2012 Ireland was one of only three OECD countries (the others being Hungary and the UK) in which the share of 15–24 year-olds who were unemployed or inactive and neither in education nor training was higher for the native rather than foreign-born population. On 1 Jan. 2016 the minimum hourly wage was raised to €9·15 from €8·65. The normal retirement age is 65 years.

International Trade

Imports and Exports

Value of imports and exports of merchandise for calendar years (in €1m.):

	2008	2009	2010	2011	2012
Imports	57,585	45,061	45,763	48,302	49,125
Exports	86,394	85,804	89,703	91,228	91,860

The values of the chief imports and total exports are shown in the following table (in €1m.):

	Imports		Exports	
	2011	2012	2011	2012
Animal and vegetable oils and waxes	248	251	54	55
Beverages and tobacco	806	862	1,177	1,209
Chemicals	10,415	10,265	56,031	55,060
Live animals and food	5,018	5,590	7,874	8,132
Machinery and transport equipment	12,414	12,559	10,370	10,448
Manufactured articles	6,013	6,067	10,231	10,848
Manufactured goods	3,712	3,712	1,658	1,689
Mineral fuels and lubricants	6,946	7,126	1,354	1,647
Raw materials	725	693	1,764	1,733

Ireland is one of the most trade-dependent countries in the world. However, export levels have fallen slightly since the peak in 2002, when merchandise exports amounted to €93·7bn., generating a trade surplus of €38·0bn. (although the record trade surplus, of €43·9bn., was in 2010). In 2012 merchandise imports from other European Union countries accounted for 61·4% of total imports while merchandise exports to other EU countries accounted for 59·0% of total exports.

Import and export totals for Ireland's top ten trading partners in 2011 and 2012 (€1m.):

	Imports		Exports	
	2011	2012	2011	2012
Belgium	1,166	956	13,227	13,620
China	2,571	2,760	1,502	1,565
France	1,994	1,905	4,951	4,379
Germany	3,694	3,437	6,285	7,490
Italy	775	783	2,992	2,669
Netherlands	2,434	2,334	3,123	3,304
Spain	667	659	3,049	2,774
Switzerland	762	957	3,686	5,070
United Kingdom	16,685	16,424	14,267	15,171
United States of America	5,907	6,408	21,601	18,157

Communications

Roads

At 31 Dec. 2012 there were 95,811 km of public roads, consisting of 5,515 km of National Primary Roads (including 1,187 km of motorway), 2,716 km of National Secondary Roads, 11,607 km of Regional Roads and 78,773 km of Local Roads.

Number of licensed motor vehicles at 31 Dec. 2011: private cars, 1,887,810; public service vehicles, 33,405; goods vehicles, 320,966; agricultural and industrial vehicles, 71,677; motorcycles, 36,582; other vehicles, 74,716. In 2011 a total of 186 people were killed in road accidents.

Rail

The total length of railway open for traffic in 2009 was 1,919 km (52 km electrified), all 1,600 mm gauge. A massive investment in public transport infrastructure is taking place in Ireland. The second National Development Plan that ran from Jan. 2007 to Dec. 2013 allowed for €12·9bn. to be invested in public transport, particularly in the Greater Dublin area.

Railway statistics for years ending 31 Dec.	2011	2012
Passengers (journeys)	37,400,000	36,900,000
Revenue (€1)	185,800,000	186,800,000
Operational costs (€1)	364,600,000	355,700,000

A light railway system was launched in Dublin in 2004.

Civil Aviation

Aer Lingus and Ryanair are the two major airlines operating in Ireland.

Aer Lingus was founded in 1936 as a State-owned enterprise. Its principal business is the provision of passenger and cargo services to the UK, Europe and North America with some flights to Morocco and the United Arab Emirates. It was privatized in 2006 and was bought in 2015 by International Airlines Group (IAG), the owner of British Airways. Ryanair began operations in 1985 and now operates to over 180 destinations (some seasonal only) in the UK and Europe as well as Morocco. In the year ended 31 March 2012 Ryanair carried 75·8m. passengers (all on international flights); revenue passenger-km totalled 94·3bn. Since 2007 Ryanair has been the airline carrying the highest number of international scheduled passengers. In addition to Aer Lingus and Ryanair, there are 13 other independent air transport operators.

The two busiest airports (Dublin and Cork) are operated by the Dublin Airport Authority plc; Shannon, the third busiest, used to be as well but has been a publicly owned commercial airport operated and run by the Shannon Airport Authority plc since the beginning of 2013. In 2012 Dublin handled 19·1m. passengers (an increase of 1·9% on 2011) and 111,069 tonnes of freight and mail; Cork handled 2·3m. passengers (decrease of 0·9%); Shannon handled 1·4m. passengers (decrease of 14·2%).

Shipping

In Jan. 2014 there were 36 ships of 300 GT or over registered, totalling 189,000 GT. Total cargo traffic passing through the country's ports amounted to 47,483,000 tonnes in 2014. The busiest port is Dublin, which handled 21·1m. tonnes of cargo in 2014.

Inland Waterways

The principal inland waterways open to navigation are the Shannon Navigation (270 km), which includes the Shannon-Erne Waterway (Ballinamore/Ballyconnell Canal), and the Grand Canal and Barrow Navigation (249 km). Merchandise traffic has now ceased and navigation is confined to pleasure craft operated either privately or commercially. The Royal Canal (146 km) from Dublin to Mullingar (53 km) was reopened for navigation in 1995.

Telecommunications

The Minister for Communications, Climate Action and Environment, a member of the government, has overall policy responsibility for the development of the sector. The core policy objective is to contribute to sustained macro-economic growth and competitiveness, and ensure that Ireland is best placed to avail of the emerging opportunities provided by the information and knowledge society.

Ireland's telecommunications sector has been fully liberalized with effect from 1 Dec. 1998 when the last remaining elements of Telecom Éireann's (the forerunner of today's eir) exclusive privilege were removed. All elements of the market are now open to competition from other licensed operators. The largest mobile phone operators in terms of subscribers are Vodafone Ireland and Three Ireland.

eir—Operational Information

The dominant operator in the telecommunications sector is eir (previously Telecom Éireann and then eircom plc). Telecom Éireann was a statutory body set up under the Postal and Telecommunications Services Act 1983. In 1996, 20% of the State's holding was sold to KPN/Telia, a Dutch–Swedish consortium, who had an option of a further 15%, which was taken up in July 1999. In 1998 the government concluded an Employee Share Ownership Scheme under which 14·9% of the company was to be made available to employees and also held an Initial Public Offer (IPO) of shares in the company in July 1999. In Oct. 1999 the newly privatized Telecom Éireann became eircom plc. Eircom was rebranded as eir in Sept. 2015

The level of network digitalization is 100%. In 2013 there were 4,755,000 mobile phone subscriptions (1,027·6 per 1,000 population) and 2,034,000 fixed telephone subscriptions. In 2013, 78·3% of the population aged 16–74 were internet users. In the same year there were 67·2 mobile broadband subscriptions per 100 inhabitants and 24·2 fixed broadband subscriptions per 100 inhabitants. In March 2012 there were 2·1m. Facebook users.

Social Institutions

Out of 178 countries analysed in the 2017 *Fragile States Index*—a list published jointly by the Fund for Peace and *Foreign Policy* magazine— Ireland was ranked the joint sixth least vulnerable (along with Australia) to conflict or collapse. The index is based on 12 indicators of state vulnerability across social, political and economic categories.

Justice

The Constitution provides that justice shall be administered in public in Courts established by law by Judges appointed by the President on the advice of the government. The jurisdiction and organization of the Courts are dealt with in the Courts (Establishment and Constitution) Act 1961, the Courts (Supplemental Provisions) Acts 1961–91, and the Courts and Court Officers Acts 1995–2002. These Courts consist of Courts of First Instance and a Court of Final Appeal, called the Supreme Court. The Courts of First Instance are the High Court with full original jurisdiction and the Circuit and the District Courts with local and limited jurisdictions. A judge may not be removed from office except for stated misbehaviour or incapacity and then only on resolutions passed by both Houses of the Oireachtas. Judges of the Supreme Court and High Court are appointed from among practising barristers or solicitors of not less than 12 years standing or by the elevation of an existing member of the judiciary. Judges of the Circuit Court are appointed from among practising barristers or solicitors of not less than ten years standing or a County Registrar who has practised as a barrister or solicitor for not less than ten years before being appointed to that post or by the elevation of a District Court Judge. Judges of the District Court are appointed from among practising barristers or solicitors of not less than ten years standing.

The Supreme Court, which consists of the Chief Justice (who is *ex officio* an additional judge of the High Court) and seven ordinary judges, may sit in two Divisions and has appellate jurisdiction from all decisions of the High Court. The President may, after consultation with the Council of State, refer a bill, which has been passed by both Houses of the Oireachtas (other than a money bill and certain other bills), to the Supreme Court for a decision on the question as to whether such bill or any provision thereof is repugnant to the Constitution.

The High Court, which consists of a President (who is *ex officio* an additional Judge of the Supreme Court) and 31 ordinary judges (or 32 when a High Court Judge is appointed as a Commissioner of the Law Reform Commission, as is currently the case), has full original jurisdiction in and power to determine all matters and questions, whether of law or fact, civil or criminal. In all cases in which questions arise concerning the validity of any law having regard to the provisions of the Constitution, the High Court alone exercises original jurisdiction. The High Court on Circuit acts as an appeal court from the Circuit Court.

The Court of Criminal Appeal consists of the Chief Justice or an ordinary Judge of the Supreme Court, together with either two ordinary judges of the High Court or the President and one ordinary judge of the High Court. It deals with appeals by persons convicted on indictment where the appellant obtains a certificate from the trial judge that the case is a fit one for appeal, or, in case such certificate is refused, where the court itself, on appeal from such refusal, grants leave to appeal. The decision of the Court of Criminal

Appeal is final, unless that court, the Attorney-General or the Director of Public Prosecutions certifies that the decision involves a point of law of exceptional public importance, in which case an appeal is taken to the Supreme Court.

The Offences against the State Act 1939 provides in Part V for the establishment of Special Criminal Courts. A Special Criminal Court sits without a jury. The rules of evidence that apply in proceedings before a Special Criminal Court are the same as those applicable in trials in the Central Criminal Court. A Special Criminal Court is authorized by the 1939 Act to make rules governing its own practice and procedure. An appeal against conviction or sentence by a Special Criminal Court may be taken to the Court of Criminal Appeal. On 30 May 1972 Orders were made establishing a Special Criminal Court and declaring that offences of a particular class or kind (as set out) were to be scheduled offences for the purposes of Part V of the Act, the effect of which was to give the Special Criminal Court jurisdiction to try persons charged with those offences.

The High Court exercising criminal jurisdiction is known as the Central Criminal Court. It consists of a judge or judges of the High Court, nominated by the President of the High Court. The Court tries criminal cases which are outside the jurisdiction of the Circuit Court.

The Circuit Court consists of a President (who is *ex officio* an additional judge of the High Court) and 33 ordinary judges. The country is divided into eight circuits. The jurisdiction of the court in civil proceedings is subject to a financial ceiling, save by consent of the parties, in which event the jurisdiction is unlimited. In criminal matters it has jurisdiction in all cases except murder, treason, piracy, rape, serious and aggravated sexual assault and allied offences. The Circuit Court acts as an appeal court from the District Court. The Circuit Court also has jurisdiction in the Family Law area such as divorce.

The District Court, which consists of a President and 54 ordinary judges, has summary jurisdiction in a large number of criminal cases where the offence is not of a serious nature. In civil matters the Court has jurisdiction in contract and tort (except slander, libel, seduction, slander of title and false imprisonment) where the claim does not exceed €6,348·69; in proceedings founded on hire-purchase and credit-sale agreements, the jurisdiction is also €6,348·69. The District Court also has jurisdiction in Family Law matters such as maintenance, custody, access and the issuing of barring orders. The District Court also has jurisdiction in a large number of licensing (intoxicating liquor) matters.

All criminal cases, except those of a minor nature, and those tried in the Special Criminal Court, are tried by a judge and a jury of 12. Generally, a verdict need not be unanimous in a case where there are not fewer than 11 jurors if ten of them agree on the verdict.

In 2009 the police force, the Garda Síochána, had a total staff of 14,547. There were 284,485 crimes recorded in 2009, of which 87 homicide offences. The National Juvenile Office received 23,952 referrals relating to 18,519 individual children during 2009. The population in penal institutions in May 2011 was 4,495 (100 per 100,000 of national population).

Education

Education is compulsory from six to 16 years of age. In 2014 net public expenditure on education came to 4·2% of GDP and 18·7% of total government spending. The adult literacy rate is at least 99%.

Elementary Elementary education is free and was given in 3,286 national schools (including special schools) in 2013–14. The total number of pupils on rolls in 2013–14 was 536,317, including pupils in special schools; the number of teachers of all classes was 32,828 in 2013–14. The total expenditure for first level education during the financial year ended 31 Dec. 2011 was €3,080·9m.

Special Special provision is made for children with disabilities in special schools which are recognized on the same basis as primary schools, in special classes attached to ordinary schools and in certain voluntary centres where educational services appropriate to the needs of the children are provided. Integration of children with disabilities in ordinary schools and classes is encouraged wherever possible, if necessary with special additional support. Special schools (2013–14) numbered 141 with 7,755 pupils. There were also 3,421 pupils enrolled in 585 special classes within mainstream schools. There is a National Education Officer for travelling children.

Secondary　Voluntary secondary schools are under private ownership and are conducted in most cases by religious orders. These schools receive grants from the State and are open to inspection by the Department of Education. The number of recognized secondary schools during the school year 2013–14 was 373, and the number of pupils in attendance was 188,791. There were 25,626 teachers across all secondary education in 2013–14.

Vocational Education Committee schools provide courses of general and technical education. Pupils are prepared for State examinations and for entrance to universities and institutes of further education. The number of vocational schools during the school year 2013–14 was 256 and the number of full-time students in attendance was 88,247. These schools are controlled by the local Vocational Education Committees; they are financed mainly by State grants and also by contributions from local rating authorities and Vocational Education Committee receipts. These schools also provide adult education facilities for their own areas.

Comprehensive and Community Schools　Comprehensive schools which are financed by the State combine academic and technical subjects in one broad curriculum so that pupils may be offered educational options suited to their needs, abilities and interests. Pupils are prepared for State examinations and for entrance to universities and institutes of further education. The number of comprehensive and community schools during the school year 2013–14 was 94 and the number of students in attendance was 56,137. These schools also provide adult education facilities for their own areas and make facilities available to voluntary organizations and to the adult community generally.

The total current expenditure from public funds for second level and further education for the financial year ended 31 Dec. 2011 was €2,995·3m.

Third Level Education　The third level education system funded by the State comprises the university sector, the technological sector and colleges of education—these are autonomous and self-governing. In addition there are a number of independent private colleges offering third level qualifications.

Ireland has a binary system of higher education, designed to ensure maximum flexibility and responsiveness to the needs of students and to the wide variety of social and economic requirements. However, within each sector, a diversity of institutions offer differing types and levels of programmes. The Universities are essentially concerned with undergraduate and postgraduate programmes, together with basic and applied research. The main work of the Institutes of Technology is in undergraduate programmes, with a smaller number of post-graduate programmes and a growing involvement in research. Numbers in third level education have expanded dramatically since the mid-1960s, from 21,000 full-time students in 1965 to 169,254 in 2013–14.

The total current expenditure from public funds on third level education during the financial year ended 31 Dec. 2011 was €1,661·7m.

There are seven universities in the Republic of Ireland. These are: NUI, Galway; NUI, Maynooth; University College Cork; University College Dublin; Trinity College, Dublin; University of Limerick; and Dublin City University. Four of the universities (NUI Galway, NUI Maynooth, UCC and UCD) are constituent universities of the National University of Ireland. The National University of Ireland also has a number of recognized colleges, including the Royal College of Surgeons in Ireland, National College of Art and Design and Shannon College of Hotel Management.

The Irish higher education university system offers degree programmes—at bachelor, master's and doctorate level—in the humanities, social sciences, scientific, technological and social sciences, and in the medical area. Typically teaching at undergraduate level is by way of a programme of lectures supplemented by tutorials and, where appropriate, practical demonstration and laboratory work. Master's degrees are usually taken by course work, research work or some combination of both. Doctoral degrees are awarded on the basis of research. Institutions award their own degrees using external examiners to ensure consistency of standards. The institutions also have continuing and some distance education programmes and also engage in research work.

There are 14 Institutes of Technology. They are Dublin Institute of Technology, Athlone IT, IT Blanchardstown, Cork IT, IT Carlow, Dundalk IT, Dun Laoghaire Institute of Art, Design and Technology, Letterkenny IT, Galway-Mayo IT, Limerick IT, IT Sligo, IT Tallaght, IT Tralee and Waterford IT.

HETAC (the Higher Education and Training Awards Council) was established on 11 June 2001, under the Qualifications (Education and Training) Act 1999. It is the successor to the National Council for Educational Awards (NCEA) and is the qualifications awarding body for third level education and training institutions outside the university sector. The Qualifications (Education and Training) Act 1999 extended autonomy to allow Institutes of Technology to apply to HETAC for delegation of authority to make their own awards. Delegation of authority also allows institutes to validate their own programmes subject to the policies and criteria determined by HETAC and within the parameters of the National Framework of Qualifications.

Initial teacher education is provided by the Colleges of Education (primary teacher education) and the Universities (post-primary teacher education).

Health

Health boards are responsible for administering health services in Ireland. There are currently ten health boards established: three area health boards located in the eastern region under the guidance of the Eastern Regional Health Authority (ERHA) and seven regional health boards covering the rest of the country. Each health board is responsible for the provision of health and social services in its area. The boards provide many of the services directly and they arrange for the provision of other services by health professionals, private health service providers, voluntary hospitals and voluntary/community organizations.

A health service reform programme is currently being implemented which will result in the most significant structural changes in the Irish health services in recent decades. The existing health boards will be replaced by a single Health Service Executive (HSE) with four regional administrative areas. A Health Information and Quality Authority (HIQA) will also be established.

Everybody ordinarily resident in Ireland has either full or limited eligibility for the public health services.

A person who satisfies the criteria of a means test receives a medical card, which confers Category 1 or full eligibility on them and their dependants. This entitles the holder to the full range of public health and hospital services, free of charge, i.e. family doctor, drugs and medicines, hospital and specialist services as well as dental, aural and optical services. Maternity care and infant welfare services are also provided.

The remainder of the population has Category 2 or limited eligibility. Category 2 patients receive public consultant and public hospital services subject to certain charges. Persons in Category 2 are liable for a hospital in-patient charge of €80 per night up to a maximum of €800 in any 12 consecutive months. Persons in Category 2 are liable for a charge of €100 if they attend the Accident and Emergency Department of a hospital or receive out-patient services without a letter from a General Practitioner.

The Long Term Illness Scheme entitles persons to free drugs and medicines, which are prescribed in respect of 15 specific illnesses. The needs of individuals with significant or ongoing medical expenses are met by a range of other schemes, which provide assistance towards the cost of prescribed drugs and medicines. The *Drug Payment Scheme* was introduced on 1 July 1999 and replaced the Drug Cost Subsidisation Scheme (DCSS) and the Drug Refund Scheme (DRS). Under this scheme no individual or family will have to pay more than €134 in any calendar month for approved prescribed drugs, medicines and appliances for use by the person or his/her family in that month.

Services for People with Disabilities: The Department of Health and Children provides, through the health boards and the Eastern Regional Health Authority, a wide range of services for people with disabilities. These include day care, home support, therapy services, training, employment, sheltered work and residential respite care. The following allowances and grants for eligible people with disabilities come under the aegis of the Department of Health and Children and are administered by the health boards and the Eastern Regional Health Authority:

Disability Allowance—payable to persons (including long-term residents in institutions) who have an injury, disease, illness or disability that substantially restricts their capacity to work. The maximum rate is €198·00 per week.

Blind Welfare Allowance—provides supplementary financial support to unemployed blind persons who are not maintained in an institution and who are in receipt of a Department of Social, Community and Family Affairs payment, such as Disability Allowance, Blind Pension or Old Age Pension.

Domiciliary Care Allowance (DCA)—a payment for a child aged under 16 with a severe disability, who requires ongoing care and attention, substantially over and above the care and attention usually required by a child of the same age. The maximum rate of DCA is €309·50 per month.

Carer's Support Grant—an annual payment of €1,700 (per person cared for) to help carers obtain respite care.

Universal Social Charge—a health contribution payable by those with a gross income of more than €13,000 per year. Those who are either a medical card holder or aged 70 or over and whose income for the year is €60,000 or less pay a reduced rate.

In 2011 there were 51 publicly funded acute hospitals in operation. The average number of in-patient beds available for use over the year was 10,849. Average length of stay for in-patients was 5·7 days. There were 104,392 wholetime equivalent numbers employed in the public health services at 31 Dec. 2011. Of these 8,331 were medical/dental staff, 16,217 were health and social care professionals and 35,902 were nursing staff. In 2011 Ireland spent 8·0% of its GDP on health.

In *Water: At What Cost? The State of the World's Water 2016*, WaterAid reported that 2·1% of the population does not have access to safe water.

Welfare

The Department of Employment Affairs and Social Protection is responsible for the day-to-day administration and delivery of social welfare schemes and services through a network of local, regional and decentralized offices. The Department's local delivery of services is structured on a regional basis. There are a total of seven regions, with offices in Waterford, Cork, Galway, Longford, Sligo and two in the Dublin area.

There are, in addition, three statutory agencies under the aegis of the Department:

—*the Pensions Board*, which has the function of promoting the security of occupational pensions, their development and the general issue of pensions coverage.

—*the Citizens Information Board*, which has the function of ensuring that all citizens have easy access to the highest quality of information, advice and advocacy on social services.

—*Office of the Pensions Ombudsman*, which investigates and decides complaints and disputes involving occupational pension schemes and Personal Retirement Savings Accounts (PRSAs). The Ombudsman is independent of the Minister and the Department in the performance of his functions.

A programme of significant reform has taken place in the Department including developments such as: the transfer of the General Register Office to the Department of Social Protection in Jan. 2008; the transfer of the Community Welfare Service from the Health Service Executive to the Department in Oct. 2011; and the integration of FÁS Employment and Community Employment Services into the operations of the Department of Social Protection in Jan. 2012.

The following schemes and services have also transferred to the Department of Social Protection: the Rural Social Scheme; the Community Services Programme; Domiciliary Care Allowance; and the Redundancy and Insolvency Scheme.

In 2010 social welfare expenditure accounted for 13·5% of GDP.

Social Welfare Schemes

The social welfare supports can be divided into three categories:

—*Social Insurance (Contributory)* payments made on the basis of a Pay Related Social Insurance (PRSI) record. Such payments are funded by employers, employees and the self-employed. Any deficit in the fund is met by Exchequer subvention.

—*Social Assistance (Non Contributory)* payments made on the basis of satisfying a means test. These payments are financed entirely by the Exchequer.

—*Universal payments* such as Child Benefit or Free Travel, which do not depend on PRSI or a means test.

State Pension (Contributory)

The State Pension (Contributory) is available to those aged 66 who have social insurance coverage beginning before 56 years of age.

People who reached pension age before 6 April 2002 must have 156 qualifying paid contributions (a total of three years although they do not have to be consecutive). This means that to be eligible people must have actually paid full-rate contributions.

People who reached pension age on or after 6 April 2002 but before 6 April 2012 need to have 260 paid contributions (effectively five years contributions although they need not be consecutive). However, anyone who paid voluntary contributions on or before 6 April 1997 only needs to have 156 paid contributions providing they have a yearly average of at least 20 contributions.

People who reach (or reached) pension age on or after 6 April 2012 will need to have 520 paid contributions (ten years paid contributions). In this case, not more than 260 of the 520 contributions may be voluntary contributions. However, anyone who paid voluntary contributions on or before 6 April 1997 and has a yearly average of ten contributions may also meet the requirements. They will need to have a total of 520 contributions, but only 156 need to be compulsory paid contributions.

There is also a means-tested non-contributory pension available to citizens aged 66 or older with limited means.

The Social Welfare and Pensions Act 2011 made a number of changes to the qualifying age for state pensions. The qualifying age rose to 66 from 1 Jan. 2014, and will rise to 67 in 2021 and 68 in 2028. For recipients born on or after 1 Jan. 1948 the minimum qualifying state pension age is 66; for recipients born on or after 1 Jan. 1955 the minimum qualifying state pension age is 67; for recipients born on or after 1 Jan. 1961 the minimum qualifying state pension age is 68.

The *Social Welfare Appeals Office (SWAO)* is an independent office responsible for determining appeals against decisions on social welfare entitlements.

Religion

According to the census of population taken in 2011 the principal religious professions were as follows:

	Leinster	Munster	Connacht	Ulster (part of)	Total
Roman Catholics	2,047,241	1,087,159	474,661	252,274	3,861,335
Church of Ireland (including Protestants)	75,374	28,782	11,851	13,032	129,039
Muslims	33,690	9,778	4,545	1,191	49,204
Orthodox	33,504	7,374	2,872	1,473	45,223
Other Christian religion n.e.c.	27,058	8,766	3,709	1,628	41,161
Presbyterians	10,830	2,709	1,586	9,475	24,600
Apostolic or Pentecostal	10,544	2,023	891	585	14,043
Other stated religions	50,955	19,016	7,403	3,548	80,922
Not stated or no religion	215,618	80,481	35,029	11,597	342,725

Eamon Martin (b. 1961) is the Archbishop of Armagh and Primate of All Ireland. In Feb. 2019 there was one cardinal.

The Church of Ireland did not divide when Ireland was partitioned in the 1920s. Around 35% of its members live in the Republic of Ireland with 65% in Northern Ireland.

Culture

World Heritage Sites

There are two UNESCO sites in Ireland: Archaeological Ensemble of the Bend of the Boyne (inscribed in 1993), the three principal sites of the Brú na Bóinne Complex, a major centre of prehistoric megalithic art; Skellig Michael (1996), a monastic complex on a craggy island from the 7th century.

Press

In 2014 there were nine dailies and seven Sunday newspapers (all in English) with a combined circulation of 1,202,000. There were 60 newspaper online editions in 2014.

Tourism

Total number of overseas tourists in 2014 was 7,105,000 (a 6·3% increase from 2013). In 2014 earnings from all visits to Ireland, including cross-border visits, amounted to €3,931m. 42% of visits in 2014 were from Great Britain. Irish residents made 6,579,000 visits abroad in 2013 (a 0·3% decrease on 2012).

Festivals

Ireland's national holiday, St Patrick's Day (17 March), is celebrated annually. Among the most popular festivals are Clonmel Junction arts festival (July), Galway Arts Festival (July), Ballyshannon Folk and Traditional Festival in Co. Donegal (July–Aug.), Fleadh Cheoil na hEireann (national festival of music) in Co. Cavan (Aug.), Dublin Theatre Festival and Dublin Fringe Festival (Sept.–Oct.), Wexford Opera Festival (Oct.) and Cork Jazz Festival (Oct.).

Diplomatic Representatives

Of Ireland in the United Kingdom (17 Grosvenor Pl., London, SW1X 7HR)
  Ambassador: Adrian O'Neill.

Of the United Kingdom in Ireland (29 Merrion Rd, Ballsbridge, Dublin 4)
  Ambassador: Robin Barnett, CMG.

Of Ireland in the USA (2234 Massachusetts Ave., NW, Washington, D.C., 20008)
  Ambassador: Daniel Gerard Mulhall.

Of the USA in Ireland (42 Elgin Rd, Ballsbridge, Dublin 4)
  Ambassador: Vacant.
  Chargé d'Affaires a.i.: Reece Smyth.

Of Ireland to the United Nations
  Ambassador: Geraldine Byrne Nason.

Of Ireland to the European Union
  Permanent Representative: Declan Kelleher.

Further Reading

Central Statistics Office. *National Income and Expenditure* (annual), *Statistical Yearbook of Ireland* (annual), *Census of Population Reports* (quin-quennial), *Census of Industrial Production Reports* (annual), *Vital Statistics* (annual and quarterly), *Trade Statistics* (monthly).

Adshead, Maura and Tonge, Jonathan, *Politics in Ireland: Convergence and Divergence in a Two-Polity Island.* 2009
Ardagh, J., *Ireland and the Irish: a Portrait of a Changing Society.* 1994
Bartlett, Thomas, *Ireland: a History.* 2010
Casey, Ciarán, *Policy Failures and the Irish Economic Crisis.* 2018
Chubb, B., *Government and Politics in Ireland.* 3rd ed. 1992
Cronin, Mike, *A History of Ireland.* 2001
Cronin, Mike, Gibbons, Luke and Kirby, Peadar, (eds) *Reinventing Ireland: Culture, Society and the Global Economy.* 2002
Delanty, G. and O'Mahony, P., *Rethinking Irish History: Nationalism, Identity and Ideology.* 1997
Foster, R. F., *The Oxford Illustrated History of Ireland.* 1991
Gallagher, Michael and Marsh, Michael, (eds) *How Ireland Voted 2016: The Election that Nobody Won.* 2016
Garvin, T., *1922: The Birth of Irish Democracy.* 1997
Harkness, D., *Ireland in the Twentieth Century: a Divided Island.* 1995
Kirby, Peadar, *The Celtic Tiger in Collapse.* 2nd ed. 2010
Kostick, C., *Revolution in Ireland – Popular Militancy 1917–1923.* 1997
Laffan, Brigid and O'Mahony, Jane, *Ireland and the European Union.* 2008
Lalor, Brian, (ed.) *The Encyclopedia of Ireland.* 2003
Lynch, David J., *When the Luck of the Irish Ran Out: The World's Most Resilient Country and its Struggle to Rise Again.* 2010
O'Beirne Ranelagh, John, *A Short History of Ireland.* 3rd ed. 2012
O'Malley, Eoin, *Contemporary Ireland.* 2011
O'Sullivan, Michael J., *Ireland and the Global Question.* 2006
Patterson, Henry, *Ireland Since 1939: The Persistence of Conflict.* 2006.—*Ireland's Violent Frontier: The Border and Anglo–Irish Relations During the Troubles.* 2013
Vaughan, W. E. (ed.) *A New History of Ireland.* 6 vols. 1996
Wyndham, Andrew Higgins, (ed.) *Re-Imagining Ireland.* 2006
National Statistical Office: Central Statistics Office, Skehard Road, Cork.
Website: http://www.cso.ie

Israel

Medinat Israel (State of Israel)

Capital: Jerusalem
Population projection, 2020: 8·71m.
GNI per capita, 2017: (PPP$) 32, 711
HDI/world rank, 2017: 0·903/22=
Internet domain extension: .il

Key Historical Events

A settled agricultural community by 6000 BC, the oasis of Jericho is possibly the world's oldest continuously inhabited settlement. Canaan—probably derived from 'Land of Purple', from the purple sea snail dye—described the Eastern Mediterranean coast and hinterland from the 3rd millennium BC. As part of the Fertile Crescent, it became an important caravan route between Egypt and Mesopotamia. 'Canaanite' has come to be associated with the Semitic group of languages and peoples of the pre-Classical Levant.

In the reign of Pharaoh Pepi I (*c.* 2313–2279 BC), Canaan was invaded five times by Egyptian forces. Egyptian authority collapsed in the 17th century, marking the end of the Middle Kingdom. Egyptian control was re-established with the reunification of Egypt in the 16th century. Thutmose III (1479–1425 BC), campaigning against the Mitanni Kingdom in Syria, defeated a Canaanite coalition at the Battle of Megiddo, subjugating Canaan and deporting thousands to Egypt. Egyptian power was challenged by the Hittites of Anatolia until Ramesses II concluded a peace treaty (the first recorded in the world) with the Hittite King Hattusilis III in 1258 BC, setting the border in northern Canaan.

The Israelite (or Hebrew) group occupied the hills of southern Canaan by the late 13th century. Around 1200 BC the Eastern Mediterranean littoral was attacked by the 'Sea Peoples' (probably including the Philistines), who destroyed coastal cities and settled on the coastal plain. The Israelite kingdom was formed from tribes supposedly returned from captivity in Egypt. In the late 11th century, Saul became king but it was his successor, David, who greatly expanded the Israelite state over most of southern Canaan. With Hittite and Egyptian power at low ebb, David conquered the trans-Jordanian states of Ammon, Edom and Moab, subjected Aram (lower Syria) to vassalage and made Jerusalem his capital. After the reign of Solomon (mid-10th century), who built the Temple of Jerusalem, the kingdom split into two: Judah in the south and the more populous Israel, centred on Samaria, in the north.

Having refused to pay tribute, Israel was conquered by Assyria's Sargon II in 722 BC and many of its people were deported; subsequent inhabitants of the Assyrian province of 'Samerina' became known as Samaritans, a mixed race of Israelites and immigrants from Mesopotamia and Persia. Sargon also besieged Jerusalem but was distracted by a Babylonian uprising. The resurgent Babylonians conquered Judah in 586 BC, having destroyed Philistia in 605 to clear access to Egypt. Nebuchadnezzar II had taken Jerusalem the previous year, deporting much of the Judaean (Jewish) nobility to Babylon. Having conquered Babylon in 539 BC, Cyrus II of Persia allowed the return of the Jews to Jerusalem, as Persian vassals, and the rebuilding of the Temple. Persia's defeat by Alexander the Great of Macedon brought the region, by then known as Palestine (derived from Philistia), under Hellenistic control. The Hellenistic period saw an influx of Arab groups, including the Nabataeans, who replaced the Edomites south of the Dead Sea.

Roman Rule

A revolt against the religious intolerance of the Seleucid King Antiochus IV began in 167 BC, led by Judas Maccabaeus, who established the Hasmonean Dynasty in Judaea. Relations with the Samaritans, who also followed the Torah (the first five books of the Hebrew bible), deteriorated when the Hasmonean King John Hyrcanus destroyed the Samaritan Temple at Mount Gerizim in 128 BC. The entire region was conquered for Rome by Pompey in 67 BC; Judaea, including Samaria, was administered as a client kingdom. After the Parthian invasion of Judaea in 40 BC, an Idumaean, Herod, was installed by Rome as king of Judaea. On Herod's death in 4 BC, the kingdom was split amongst three of his sons, who ruled as tetrarchs. Herod's grandson, Herod Agrippa, was granted a reunited Judaea by Emperor Claudius in AD 41, as a reward for supporting Claudius's claim to the imperial throne. However, Herod Agrippa was assassinated in AD 44 and Judaea placed under a Roman procurator. Jewish resentment against loss of autonomy grew until the Great Jewish Revolt (AD 66–73), which was brutally suppressed. Jerusalem was destroyed and hundreds of thousands were massacred or sold into slavery.

Jewish rebellions across the East in 115 (the Kitos War) were quickly suppressed. Emperor Hadrian's attempts to enforce cultural uniformity across the Empire included rebuilding Jerusalem as Aelia Capitolina and forbidding Jewish custom. Simon Bar Kokhba, supported by the Sanhedrin (Jewish sages), led a major revolt in AD 132 and established a Jewish government in Jerusalem. However, Roman armies prevailed in 135, with the death of around half a million Jews. Hadrian reacted to the rebellion by suppressing Judaism, banning Jews from Aelia Capitolina, deporting large numbers as slaves and renaming the province Syria Palaestina; the province was split in three around 390.

Christianity

Under the Christian Byzantine Empire, Palestine became a centre of Christianity (Jerusalem was recognized as a patriarchate in 451), bringing pilgrims and prosperity. It also received lavish imperial patronage, such as Constantine's Church of the Holy Sepulchre (*c.* 326). The Samaritans made a bid for independence in 529 but were crushed by Justinian I and the Ghassanid Arabs. Persecuted by Christians, Jews and later by Muslims, Samaritan numbers dwindled over the following centuries. Byzantine administration of Palestine ended temporarily during the Persian occupation of 614–28; Jerusalem was sacked, its churches burned and the city turned over to the Jews. A spectacular campaign in 628, led by Emperor Heraclius, forced the Persians to cede Palestine and Syria. However, Byzantine rule ended permanently after the Arabs conquered the region; Jerusalem was taken in 638.

The Arabs retained the existing system of administration in the provinces of Jund Filastine (the south) and Jund Urdunn (the north). Taxes and restrictions on religious practice and office-holding imposed on non-Muslims caused large-scale conversions. The Ummayad caliphs moved the capital to Damascus and built the Dome of the Rock on the site of the Jewish Temple in Jerusalem in the 690s. The Christian and Jewish communities of Palestine were partly administered by their own religious leaders. Under the Ummayads' successors, the Abbasids, the capital moved to Baghdad in 762, drawing Asian trade away from Palestine. Fragmentation of the Caliphate in the 9th century saw Egyptian independence under the Tulunids, who seized Palestine and Syria in 878. Although Palestine was retaken in 906 for the Caliphate, in 935 it again fell to Egypt, this time under the Ikhshid Dynasty and, in 970, to its successors, the Fatimids.

Crusades

1070 saw the arrival of the Seljuk Turks, who rapidly overran the Byzantine East. Seljuk restrictions on Christian pilgrimage led to the European Crusader invasions of Palestine and Syria in the 12th century. Having been wrested from the Seljuks by the Fatimids in 1098, Jerusalem was taken the following year by a Crusader army, which massacred the population. Baldwin, count of Edessa, became king of Jerusalem in 1100. Responding to Crusader threats to Mecca (Makkah), Saladin (Salah ad-Din), the Kurdish sultan of Egypt, recaptured Jerusalem in 1187, bringing Palestine under the Ayyubid Dynasty. A treaty in 1192 with Richard I of England allowed Christian pilgrimage to Jerusalem and secured the rump Crusader states along the coast. A treaty of 1229 gave much of Palestine (the Kingdom of Jerusalem) to the Holy Roman Emperor, Frederick II, though Jerusalem was destroyed by Central Asian Khwarezmians in 1244, on behalf of the Ayyubids. The fall of Acre (Akko) to the Mamluks, rulers of Egypt, in 1291 ended Crusader rule in the Holy Land.

Under Mamluk suzerainty, Palestine was administered by Muslim emirates. Economic decline was exacerbated by the arrival of the Black Death in

© Springer Nature Limited 2020
Palgrave Macmillan (ed.), *The Statesman's Yearbook 2020*,
https://doi.org/10.1057/978-1-349-95940-2_97

1351. Although the Mamluk sultanate successfully held off Mongol invasions, Palestine fell to the Ottomans in 1516, bringing it (as part of the Damascus-Syria province) and most of the Islamic world under the rule of Turkish İstanbul. Suleyman the Magnificent rebuilt Jerusalem's walls in 1537.

Zionism

Palestine was briefly invaded in 1799 by Napoleon Bonaparte of France, who had occupied Egypt. Muhammad Ali, the renegade Ottoman viceroy of Egypt, invaded Palestine and Syria in 1831, defeating the Ottoman army. However, British intervention at Beirut, on behalf of the sultan, forced the viceroy's withdrawal to Egypt. Jews from central and Eastern Europe arrived in Palestine from the 1880s as part of a nascent Zionist movement. In 1897 the first Zionist Congress met in Basle, Switzerland. Attempts were made in vain to gain the approval of Sultan Abdul Hamid II for Jewish settlement. However, by 1914, about 85,000 Jews were living in Palestine, many on agricultural collectives (*kibbutz*), in part funded by Western Europe's Jewry. Tel Aviv (originally called Ahuzat Bayit 'homestead') was founded by Jews in 1909 as a dormitory settlement for workers in Jaffa.

Britain, France and Russia declared war on the Ottoman Empire in Nov. 1914, in retaliation for its co-operation with Germany. Having repelled Ottoman attacks on the Suez Canal, British forces invaded Ottoman Palestine, seizing Rafah in Jan. 1917. Two abortive attacks on Gaza were followed by British-led success at Beersheba in Oct. 1917, leading to the fall of Gaza in Nov. and Jerusalem in Dec. The British won a major victory at Megiddo in Sept. 1918, effectively ending Ottoman rule in Palestine. The British were granted Palestine and Transjordan as mandates under the League of Nations, established in 1919 at the Versailles Peace Conference.

Britain supported a 'national home' for the Jews in Palestine, as laid out in the Balfour Declaration of 1917. Jewish immigration, though limited by the British authorities, increased in the 1920s. Land ownership disputes aggravated Jewish-Arab relations, leading to paramilitary communal attacks. While Transjordan was granted independence in 1928, proposals for an Arab–Jewish partition in Palestine were rejected. In 1936 an Arab strike degenerated into insurrection—the 'Great Uprising' or 'Great Revolt'— under the leadership of Amin al-Husayni, the Grand Mufti of Jerusalem. The revolt was suppressed by the British by 1939, aided informally by the Jewish paramilitary *Haganah*. Al-Husayni fled to Germany, where he declared *jihad* on the Allies during the Second World War. The Italian air force bombed Haifa and Tel Aviv in 1940. Some Jewish groups, such as the Lehi, fought the British during the war on account of the British ban on Jewish immigration to Palestine.

Arab Israeli Wars

In 1947 the United Nations intervened, recommending partition of Palestine and an international administration for Jerusalem. The plan was accepted by the Jewish Agency (not representative of all Jewish groups) but rejected by the Palestinian Arab leadership; inter-communal war followed. On 14 May 1948 the British Government terminated its mandate and the Jewish leaders proclaimed the State of Israel. No independent Arab state was established in Palestine. Instead the neighbouring Arab states invaded Israel on 15 May 1948. The Jewish state defended itself successfully, and the ceasefire in Jan. 1949 left Israel with one-third more land than had been originally assigned by the UN.

In 1956 Israel was subject to international criticism for its involvement in the Suez Crisis. When Egypt nationalized the Suez Canal, France and the UK resorted to military action. Under the premiership of David Ben-Gurion, Israel joined forces with the European powers and agreed to lead an initial attack on the Egyptian-controlled Gaza Strip and the Sinai Peninsula. The plan was that the UK and France would offer to intervene in the conflict and reoccupy the areas. Nasser's expected refusal of the offer would be the pretext for an invasion that would reclaim the Canal. The Israeli incursions began in late Oct. 1956 but amid widespread international condemnation, most damagingly from the USA, the three nations were forced into a humiliating withdrawal by Dec. Nasser promoted the affair as a victory for pan-Arabism.

In 1967, following some years of uneasy peace, local clashes on the Israeli–Syrian border were followed by Egyptian mass concentration of forces on the borders of Israel. Israel struck out at Egypt on land and in the air on 5–9 June 1967. Jordan joined in the conflict which spread to the Syrian borders. By 11 June the Israelis had occupied the Gaza Strip and the Sinai peninsula as far as the Suez Canal in Egypt, West Jordan as far as the Jordan valley and the heights east of the Sea of Galilee, including the Syrian city of Quneitra, which was destroyed during the conflict.

A further war broke out on 6 Oct. 1973 when Egyptian and Syrian offensives were launched. Following UN Security Council resolutions a ceasefire came into force on 24 Oct. In Sept. 1978 Egypt and Israel agreed on frameworks for peace in the Middle East. A treaty was signed in Washington on 26 March 1979 whereby Israel withdrew from the Sinai Desert in two phases; part one was achieved on 26 Jan. 1980 and the final withdrawal was completed on 26 April 1982.

In June 1982 Israeli forces invaded Lebanon. On 16 Feb. 1985 the Israeli forces started a withdrawal, leaving behind an Israeli trained and equipped Christian Lebanese force to act as a buffer against Muslim Shia or Palestinian guerrilla attacks.

Peace Process

In 1993, following declarations by Prime Minister Yitzhak Rabin recognizing the Palestine Liberation Organization (PLO) as representative of the Palestinian people, and by Yasser Arafat, leader of the PLO, renouncing terrorism and recognizing the State of Israel, an agreement was signed in Washington providing for limited Palestinian self-rule in the Gaza Strip and Jericho. The treaty marked the end of six years of violent opposition to the Israeli occupation in what is known as the first *intifada*, during which over 2,000 Palestinians and 150 Israelis were killed. Negotiations on the permanent status of the West Bank and Gaza began in 1996. On 4 Nov. 1995 Yitzhak Rabin was assassinated by a Jewish religious extremist. In the subsequent election, a right-wing coalition led by Binyamin Netanyahu took office. Peace talks with the Palestinians then stalled. In Oct. 1998 Israel accepted partial withdrawal from the West Bank on condition that the Palestinians cracked down on terrorism. The following month, 2% of the West Bank was handed over to Palestinian control. Further moves were put on hold after the collapse of the Netanyahu coalition and the announcement of early elections.

In Sept. 1999 Ehud Barak provided the first evidence that the Middle East peace process was back on track by releasing nearly 200 Palestinian prisoners and by handing over 430 sq. km of land on the West Bank. In May 2000 Israel completed its withdrawal from south Lebanon, 22 years after the first invasion. By Oct. 2000 violence had broken out again between Israelis and Palestinians, fuelled by the conflict over control of Jerusalem, with terrorist acts a daily occurrence, leading to heavy casualties on both sides. This second *intifada* ended in 2005. With peace talks stalled once again, Barak called for a nationwide vote of confidence by putting himself up for re-election as prime minister. Defeated by the right-wing Ariel Sharon in Feb. 2001, he retired from politics. As violence escalated, in Dec. 2001 Israel ended all contact with Yasser Arafat, besieging his compound at Ramallah and putting him under virtual house arrest. Israeli incursions into Palestinian-controlled areas of the West Bank and the Gaza Strip, and suicide attacks by Palestinians, continued unabated in early 2002 with heavy loss of life. In June 2002 Israel began constructing a barrier to cut off the West Bank, with the aim of shielding the country from suicide bombers. Arafat died on 11 Nov. 2004 and was succeeded by Mahmoud Abbas in Jan. 2005. In Feb. 2005 Israeli prime minister Ariel Sharon and Mahmoud Abbas agreed to a 'cessation of hostilities' between the two peoples, a move which encouraged hopes of a resumption of the peace process. In Aug. 2005 Israeli troops and police evicted the 8,500 Jewish settlers from the Gaza Strip in accordance with an agreement between Israel and the Palestinians. This was the first time Israel had withdrawn from Palestinian land captured in the 1967 war.

In July 2006, after Hizbollah forces in Lebanon had captured two Israeli soldiers, Israel launched a large-scale military campaign against Lebanon with a series of bombing raids, destroying large parts of the civilian infrastructure.

In Dec. 2008 Israel began a military assault on Gaza aimed at destroying Hamas strongholds responsible for rocket and mortar attacks on Israeli targets. Three weeks of air and ground operations resulted in many Palestinian civilian deaths and the destruction of much of Gaza's civilian infrastructure. Israel's action was widely criticized, particularly after the bombardment of the UN's relief and works headquarters. The UN Security Council called for an immediate ceasefire, with all members voting in favour of the motion bar the USA.

In Feb. 2009 Binyamin Netanyahu returned as prime minister after a ten-year gap, following elections in which Likud and other right-wing parties prevailed. In May the following year relations with Turkey were strained when Israeli personnel killed nine Turkish pro-Palestinian activists aboard ships carrying aid supplies attempting to break the blockade of Gaza. In Oct. 2011 a high-profile prisoner exchange saw Hamas release one captured Israeli soldier in return for over 1,000 Palestinian prisoners.

Israeli troops clashed with Syrian forces in May 2013 as Syria's civil war encroached on the Golan Heights. Israel also launched air and land strikes against targets in Gaza in July and Aug. of 2014 after an upsurge in attacks by militant Palestinian groups. Following inconclusive parliamentary elections in March 2015, Netanyahu formed a new Likud-led coalition of right-wing parties in May.

Territory and Population

The area of Israel, including the Golan Heights (1,154 sq. km) and East Jerusalem, is 22,072 sq. km (8,522 sq. miles), of which 21,643 sq. km (8,357 sq. miles) are land. The population in Dec. 2016 was 8,628,600 (6,446,100 Jews, 1,797,300 Arabs—a fifth of the population—and 385,200 others), including East Jerusalem, the Golan Heights and Israeli settlers in the West Bank but excluding 250,000 illegal foreign workers and African migrants. Population density, 391 per sq. km.

The UN gives a projected population for 2020 of 8·71m.

In 2011, 91·9% of the population lived in urban areas.

Jewish population by place of origin as of 2011: former USSR, 644,900; Morocco, 151,300; North America and Oceania, 93,900; Romania, 86,200; Ethiopia, 74,000; Iraq, 61,200; Poland, 49,500; Iran, 48,700.

The Jewish Agency, which, in accordance with Article IV of the Palestine Mandate, played a leading role in establishing the State of Israel, continues to organize immigration.

Israel is administratively divided into six districts:

District	Area (sq. km)	Population estimate, 2017	Chief town
Northern	4,473	1,425,700	Nazareth
Haifa	866	1,013,900	Haifa
Central	1,294	2,157,500	Ramia
Tel Aviv	172	1,406,400	Tel Aviv
Jerusalem[1]	653	1,108,900	Jerusalem
Southern	14,185	1,272,100	Beersheba

[1]Includes East Jerusalem.

A further 325,500 people lived in Judaea and Samara (roughly corresponding to the West Bank) in 2011.

On 23 Jan. 1950 the Knesset proclaimed Jerusalem the capital of the State and on 14 Dec. 1981 extended Israeli law into the Golan Heights. Population estimates of the main towns (Dec. 2017): Jerusalem, 901,302; Tel Aviv/Jaffa, 443,939; Haifa, 281,087; Rishon le-Ziyyon, 249,860; Petach Tikva, 240,357; Ashdod, 222,883.

The official languages are Hebrew and Arabic.

Social Statistics

2008 births, 156,923; deaths, 39,484; marriages, 50,038; divorces, 13,488. 2008 crude birth rate per 1,000 population of Jewish population, 20·4; Non-Jewish: Muslims, 28·5; Christians, 16·5; Druzes, 21·0. Crude death rate per 1,000 (2008), Jewish, 6·2; Muslims, 2·5; Christians, 4·7; Druzes, 3·0. Infant mortality rate per 1,000 live births (2005–09), 4·0 (Jewish, 2·9; Muslims, 7·5; Christians, 2·3; Druzes, 5·2). Life expectancy, 2013, 79·9 years for males and 83·6 for females. Average annual population growth rate, 2005–10, 2·3%. Fertility rate, 2008, 2·8 births per woman. There were 16,892 immigrants in 2011, up from 13,699 in 2008 but down from 199,516 in 1990 and 176,100 in 1991 following the fall of communism in Eastern Europe and the break-up of the former Soviet Union.

Climate

From April to Oct., the summers are long and hot, and almost rainless. From Nov. to March, the weather is generally mild, though colder in hilly areas, and this is the wet season. Jerusalem, Jan. 12·8°C, July 28·9°C. Annual rainfall, 657 mm. Tel Aviv, Jan. 17·2°C, July 30·2°C. Annual rainfall, 803 mm.

Constitution and Government

Israel is an independent sovereign republic, established by proclamation on 14 May 1948.

Israel does not have a written constitution. In 1950 the Knesset (*Parliament*), which in 1949 had passed the Transition Law dealing in general terms with the powers of the Knesset, President and Cabinet, resolved to enact from time to time basic laws, which eventually, taken together, would form the constitution. The 12 fundamental laws that have been passed are: the Knesset (1958), Israel Lands (1960), the President (1964), the State Economy (1975), the Army (1976), Jerusalem, capital of Israel (1980), the Judicature (1984), the State Comptroller (1988), Human Dignity and Liberty (1992), Freedom of Occupation (1994), the Government (2001) and Referendum (2014).

The *President* (head of state) is elected by the Knesset by secret ballot by a simple majority; his term of office is seven years. He may only serve for one term.

The Knesset, a one-chamber Parliament, consists of 120 members. It is elected for a four-year term by secret ballot and universal direct suffrage. Under the system of election introduced in 1996, electors vote once for a party and once for a candidate for Prime Minister. To be elected Prime Minister, a candidate must gain more than half the votes cast, and be elected to the Knesset. If there are more than two candidates and none gain half the vote, a second round is held 15 days later. The Prime Minister forms a cabinet (no fewer than eight members and no more than 18) with the approval of the Knesset.

National Anthem

'Hatikvah' ('The Hope'); words by N. H. Imber; folk-tune.

Government Chronology

Prime Ministers since 1948. (Avoda = Labour Party; Herut = Freedom Movement; Kadima = 'Forward'; Likud = 'Consolidation'; Mapai = Israeli Workers' Party)

1948–53	Mapai	David Ben-Gurion
1953–55	Mapai	Moshe Sharett
1955–63	Mapai	David Ben-Gurion
1963–69	Mapai	Levi Eshkol
1969–74	Avoda	Golda Meir
1974–77	Avoda	Yitzhak Rabin
1977–83	Herut/Likud	Menahem Begin
1983–84	Herut/Likud	Yitzhak Shamir
1984–86	Avoda	Shimon Peres
1986–92	Likud	Yitzhak Shamir
1992–95	Avoda	Yitzhak Rabin
1995–96	Avoda	Shimon Peres
1996–99	Likud	Binyamin Netanyahu
1999–2001	Avoda	Ehud Barak
2001–06	Likud, Kadima	Ariel Sharon
2006–09	Kadima	Ehud Olmert
2009–	Likud	Binyamin Netanyahu

Recent Elections

In the parliamentary (Knesset) elections on 17 March 2015, Likud won 30 of 120 seats with 23·4% of votes cast, the Zionist Union 24 (18·7%), the Joint List (an alliance of four Arab-dominated parties) 13 (10·5%), Yesh Atid 11 (11·8%), Kulanu 10 (7·5%), Jewish Home 8 (6·7%), Shas 7 (5·7%), Yisrael Beiteinu 6 (5·1%), United Torah Judaism 6 (5·0%) and Meretz 5 (3·9%). Turnout was 72·4%.

In a parliamentary vote for the presidency on 10 June 2014, Reuven Rivlin was elected in the second round with 63 votes against Meir Sheetrit with 53. Three other candidates had participated in the first round.

Current Government

President: Reuven Rivlin; b. 1939 (since 24 July 2014).

In Feb. 2019 the coalition government consisted of the following:

Prime Minister, and Minister of Defence, and Health: Binyamin Netanyahu; b. 1949 (Likud; since 31 March 2009, having previously held office from June 1996–July 1999).

Minister of Agriculture and Rural Development: Uri Yehuda Ariel (Jewish Home). *Communications:* Ayoob Kara (Likud). *Construction and Housing:* Yifat Shasha-Biton (Kulanu). *Culture and Sport:* Miri Regev (Likud). *Economy and Industry:* Eli Cohen (Kulanu). *Education, and Diaspora Affairs:* Naftali Bennett (Jewish Home). *Finance:* Moshe Kahlon (Kulanu). *Immigration and Absorption:* Yoav Gallant (Likud). *Internal Affairs, and Development of the Negev and Galil:* Aryeh Machluf Deri (Shas). *Jerusalem Affairs and Heritage, and Environmental Protection:* Zeev Elkin (Likud). *Justice:* Ayelet Shaked (Jewish Home). *Labour, Welfare and Social Services:* Haim Katz (Likud). *National Infrastructure, Energy and Water:* Yuval Steinitz (Likud). *Public Security, Strategic Affairs, and Information:* Gilad Erdan (Likud). *Regional Co-operation:* Tzachi Hanegbi (Likud). *Religious Services:* Yitzhak Vaknin (Shas). *Science, Technology and Space:* Ofir Akunis (Likud). *Social Equality:* Gila Gamliel (Likud). *Tourism:* Yariv Levin (Likud). *Transportation and Road Safety, and Intelligence, and Foreign Affairs (acting):* Yisrael Katz (Likud).

Israeli Parliament: http://main.knesset.gov.il

Current Leaders

Binyamin Netanyahu

Position

Prime Minister

Introduction

Following the general election of 10 Feb. 2009, right-wing Likud party leader Binyamin Netanyahu, who had previously been premier from 1996–99, formed a broad but politically volatile coalition government consisting of centre-right, centre-left and far-right parties. The next election was held in Jan. 2013 amid a continuing stalemate over the status of the Palestinians, further controversial Israeli settlement building in occupied territories, concerns over the nuclear capability of Iran and civil war in neighbouring Syria. The poll resulted in an alliance of the Likud and Yisrael Beiteinu parties, headed by Netanyahu, becoming the largest parliamentary grouping and heading a broad coalition from March that year with the centrist Yesh Atid, the far-right Jewish Home and the liberal Hatnuah party. Following the break-up of the coalition in Dec. 2014 and early elections in March 2015, Netanyahu formed a new multi-party coalition administration in May and has since remained the dominant political figure.

Early Life

Binyamin Netanyahu was born on 21 Oct. 1949 in Tel Aviv. After military service, he studied in the USA at the Massachusetts Institute of Technology and Harvard. Having worked in business consultancy, he then joined the Israeli diplomatic service in Washington, D.C. in 1982 and served as Israel's ambassador to the UN from 1984–88.

In 1988 Netanyahu was elected to the Knesset for Likud and named deputy foreign minister. From 1991–92 he served as deputy minister in the Prime Minister's Office before succeeding Yitzhak Shamir in 1993 as Likud chairman and leader of the opposition. Sceptical of the Sept. 1993 Oslo Accords, Netanyahu oversaw a slim victory at the elections of May 1996. However, he was defeated in 1999 by Labour's Ehud Barak and subsequently lost the Likud leadership to Ariel Sharon.

Netanyahu returned to politics in 2002 as foreign minister and in 2003 took the finance portfolio in Sharon's cabinet. In Aug. 2005 he resigned over the Gaza disengagement plan, but in Dec. he regained the Likud leadership and became opposition leader following the Kadima party's victory in the 2006 elections.

At the Feb. 2009 elections Netanyahu's Likud and its right-wing coalition partners won the majority of the vote.

Career in Office

Netanyahu's primary challenges on taking office were the economic downturn, the continuing crisis with the Palestinians and concerns over Iran's nuclear ambitions.

In June 2009 he expressed for the first time his acceptance of a two-state solution for Israel and Palestine, provided that the Palestinian state was demilitarized and recognized Israel as the state of the Jewish people. However, substantive progress in the peace process has remained elusive, particularly over the divisive issue of Jewish settlement building in the West Bank and East Jerusalem, which has undermined all attempts at meaningful dialogue.

Tensions were heightened in 2011 as Palestinian President Abbas confirmed in Sept. that he was applying for formal United Nations recognition of Palestinian independent statehood in defiance of Israel and the USA. In Nov. 2012 the UN General Assembly voted overwhelmingly to recognize Palestine's enhanced status as a non-member observer state, in response to which the Netanyahu government announced that Israel would extend Jewish settlement-building in the West Bank. The US government sought to revive peace negotiations but in April 2014, following a reconciliation between the rival Hamas and Fatah Palestinian factions holding sway in Gaza and the West Bank respectively, Netanyahu suspended further talks. In July and Aug. that year, a major military confrontation between Israel and Hamas erupted as Israeli forces launched air and ground assaults on Gaza in response to Hamas rocket attacks on Israeli border settlements. The conflict resulted in over 2,000 civilian deaths in Gaza before an Egyptian-brokered ceasefire. Tensions festered through the rest of the year, fuelled by a rash of small-scale Palestinian attacks on Israeli targets and also controversial legislation in Nov. by the Netanyahu government officially defining Israel as the nation state of the Jewish people. Several European countries were meanwhile edging towards recognition of Palestinian statehood and considering sanctions against continued Israeli settlement building. In Sept. 2015 Israeli–Palestinian tensions were again fuelled as the Palestinian president declared himself no longer bound by past peace agreements with Israel during a speech to the UN General Assembly. There followed a spate of shooting and stabbing attacks in Oct. and Nov. that year by Palestinians against Jewish citizens in Israel and the West Bank.

In Sept. 2009 Netanyahu had stated that Iran posed a threat to world peace and that it had to be prevented from acquiring nuclear weapons. He also condemned the then Iranian president's denial of the Holocaust. Such antagonism fuelled speculation about possible pre-emptive Israeli military action against Iran. Following the election of a more moderate president in June 2013, Iran reached a conditional agreement in Nov. with the major Western countries, Russia and China to freeze aspects of its nuclear development programme in return for an easing of sanctions. A comprehensive plan of action was signed in July 2015 but Netanyahu criticized the deal, and its US supporters, and continued to stress that Iran remains a threat to Israel's security.

Israel's relations with Turkey were severely undermined in 2010 by its military assault in May on a convoy of ships bringing aid to the Gaza Strip in defiance of the Israeli blockade, in which nine Turkish nationals were killed. The incident led in Sept. 2011 to the suspension of all defence links and the expulsion of the Israeli ambassador. However, both countries reached an agreement in June 2016 to normalize relations.

In Feb. 2011, in response to mounting concern over political turmoil in Egypt, Netanyahu said that Israel would review its security arrangements if Egypt reneged on the 1979 bilateral peace treaty. In Sept. that year bilateral relations came under further strain as an Egyptian crowd stormed the Israeli embassy in Cairo, prompting an airlift of diplomats and their dependents out of the country. Similarly mindful of the escalation of civil war in Syria and its potential security implications, Israel reportedly launched a bombing raid on an unspecified target near Damascus in Jan. 2013. In Jan. 2015 further confrontation between Israel and Hizbollah threatened when the radical Lebanese Shia militia fired missiles at Israeli military vehicles near the Lebanese border, killing two soldiers.

In Dec. 2014 Netanyahu dismissed the justice minister, Tzipi Livni, and finance minister, Yair Lapid, claiming disloyalty, which prompted the collapse of the coalition and scheduling of early elections for 17 March 2015. The poll again returned an array of disparate political and religious groupings and after seven weeks of negotiations Netanyahu formed a five-party right-wing coalition. In May 2016, in an attempt to broaden the government's thin parliamentary majority, Netanyahu concluded a deal with Yisrael Beiteinu, whose hard-line nationalist leader Avigdor Lieberman became defence minister in place of Moshe Ya'alon in an enlarged six-party administration.

In Dec. 2016, in an unprecedented US diplomatic move, President Obama's administration refused to veto a UN Security Council resolution demanding an end to Israeli settlement building in the West Bank and East Jerusalem, which prompted a furious denunciation from Netanyahu and some senior US politicians. However, the inauguration of new US President Donald Trump in Jan. 2017 restored a more supportive US stance towards the Israeli government. The following month Netanyahu made an official visit to the White House and also steered a bill through the Knesset retroactively legalizing the construction of contentious Jewish settlements on privately-owned Palestinian land in the West Bank despite broad international condemnation. Then, in a significant symbolic step on 6 Dec., Trump announced that the USA would recognize Jerusalem as Israel's capital—in defiance of Palestinian claims and a consequent violent backlash—in a move greeted by Netanyahu as 'historic' for which Israel was 'profoundly grateful'. Netanyahu's hawkish stance towards Iran was also reinforced in May 2018 when President Trump withdrew the USA from the 2015 multilateral nuclear accord and reimposed punitive sanctions on the Islamic republic.

In July 2018 the Knesset passed controversial legislation declaring Israel to be the nation state of the Jewish people and no longer recognizing Arabic as an official language.

Meanwhile, strains in the already fragile coalition government were aggravated in Nov. 2018 when the worst Palestinian–Israeli clashes since 2014 prompted Netanyahu to agree a truce with Hamas militants in Gaza, leading to the resignation of defence minister Avigdor Lieberman of Yisrael Beiteinu in protest. Netanyahu assumed the defence portfolio himself as another coalition partner, Jewish Home, backtracked from threats to bring down his administration. The prime minister's personal popularity among Israeli voters was also at risk from ongoing investigations into alleged bribery, fraud and breach of trust, sufficient evidence of which had been gathered by early Dec. for the police to recommend that charges could be brought. In Jan. 2019 Netanyahu called early elections for April in what some critics claimed was a bid to head-off the corruption charges.

Defence

Conscription (for Jews and Druze only) is three years (usually four years for officers; 24 months for women). Israel is one of the few countries with female conscription. A law passed in March 2014 ended the wholesale army exemptions granted to ultra-Orthodox seminary students. Following further legislation passed in Nov. 2015 extending draft exemptions it is now expected to be implemented in 2023. The Israel Defence Force is a unified force, in which army, navy and air force are subordinate to a single chief-of-staff. The Minister of Defence is *de facto* C.-in-C.

Defence expenditure in 2013 totalled US$15,163m., representing 6·0% of GDP (compared to over 30% in the early 1970s). Expenditure per capita in 2013 was US$1,967, a figure exceeded only by Oman and Saudi Arabia.

Nuclear Weapons

Israel has an undeclared nuclear weapons capability. Although known to have a nuclear bomb, it pledges not to introduce nuclear testing to the Middle East. According to the Stockholm International Peace Research Institute, the nuclear arsenal was estimated to have about 80 warheads in Jan. 2018. Israel is one of three countries not to have signed the Nuclear Non-Proliferation Treaty (the others being India and Pakistan).

Army

Strength (2011) 133,000 (conscripts 107,000). There are also 500,000 reservists available on mobilization. In addition there is a paramilitary border police of about 8,000.

Navy

The Navy, tasked primarily for coastal protection and based at Haifa, Ashdod and Eilat, includes three small diesel submarines and three corvettes.

Naval personnel in 2011 totalled about 9,500 (including a Naval Commando of 300) of whom 2,500 are conscripts. There are also 10,000 naval reservists available on mobilization.

Air Force

The Air Force (including air defence) has a personnel strength (2011) of 34,000, with 440 combat aircraft, all jets, of Israeli and US manufacture including F-15s and F-16s, and 77 attack helicopters. There were 55,000 Air Force reservists in 2011.

Economy

Services account for about 82% of GDP, industry 16% and agriculture 2%.

Overview

Israel has a diversified economy with a rapidly expanding technology sector, but possesses limited natural resources. Although significant natural gas reserves were discovered off Israel's Mediterranean coast in 2009, the country remains dependent on imports of petroleum, coal and food. Main exports include high-technology equipment, cut diamonds and pharmaceuticals.

Until the 1990s traditional industries, including the textile and garments sectors, benefited from protectionist policies, but have since been overshadowed by the technology sector, which over the past two decades has become the bedrock of the economy. The 1990s saw strong growth bolstered by the dot-com internet boom and innovative government incentive schemes. However, during 2001–02 Israel suffered its worst recession in 50 years as a result of the second Palestinian *intifada*. The economy then rebounded, averaging 5% annual growth between 2004 and 2007 owing to improved internal security, strong external demand and sound financial and macroeconomic policies. Israel's technological expertise, skilled labour force and high living standards have attracted significant foreign investment, which averaged 3·1% of GDP annually from 2009–15.

The economy showed resilience through the global financial crisis and the 2011 Arab Spring, in large part as a result of prudent fiscal policy and diverse trade ties. Growth averaged 3·9% between 2010 and 2015, driven by higher exports, private consumption and investment.

The discovery of natural gas should ensure a reduction in fuel imports in the longer term. The Tamar gas field, which came on stream in March 2013, and the Leviathan field, expected to start production in late 2019, have estimated combined reserves of 821bn. cu. metres.

Reducing the high public debt, which stood at around 64·8% of GDP in 2015, is a key challenge, while the poverty rate remains among the highest among the OECD countries. Israel has also experienced rapid house inflation in recent years, posing risks to long-term stability.

Currency

The unit of currency is the *shekel* (ILS) of 100 *agorot*. Foreign exchange reserves were US$58,426m. in Sept. 2009. Gold reserves have been negligible since 1998. Total money supply in Nov. 2008 was 83,131m. shekels.

Inflation rates (based on OECD statistics):

2008	2009	2010	2011	2012	2013	2014	2015	2016	2017
4·6%	3·3%	2·7%	3·5%	1·7%	1·6%	0·5%	−0·6%	−0·5%	0·2%

Budget

Central government revenue totalled 320,233m. shekels in 2011 (299,726m. shekels in 2010) and expenditure 358,284m. shekels (338,122m. shekels in 2010). Taxes constituted 66·4% of revenues in 2011 and social contributions 17·3%; use of goods and services accounted for 26·4% of expenditures and compensation of employees 24·3%.

The standard rate of VAT was raised from 17% to 18% in June 2013, before being lowered to 17% again in Oct. 2015.

Performance

Real GDP growth rates (based on OECD statistics):

2008	2009	2010	2011	2012	2013	2014	2015	2016	2017
3·3%	1·3%	5·5%	5·6%	2·2%	4·3%	3·9%	2·5%	4·0%	3·4%

Total GDP was US$350·9bn. in 2016.

Banking and Finance

The Bank of Israel was established by law in 1954 as Israel's central bank. Its Governor is appointed by the President on the recommendation of the Cabinet for a five-year term. The *Governor* is Amir Yaron. As part of a government scheme several banks were privatized in the years 1993–2006.

In 2014 there were 15 commercial banks (of which the largest are Bank Hapoalim, Bank Leumi le-Israel and Israel Discount Bank), four foreign banks, six credit card companies, one financial institution and two joint service companies. The three major banks hold over 70% of total assets of the banking system.

Gross external debt amounted to US$95,263m. in June 2012.

There is a stock exchange in Tel Aviv.

Energy and Natural Resources

Environment

Carbon dioxide emissions from the consumption of energy in 2011 accounted for 10·0 tonnes per capita.

Electricity

Installed capacity in 2011 was 14·0m. kW. Electric power production amounted to 59·65bn. kWh in 2011; consumption per capita was 7,348 kWh in 2011.

Oil and Gas

In 2009 large quantities of natural gas were discovered off the coast of Israel that are expected to meet the country's needs for 40 years and potentially allow Israel to become energy self-sufficient. Production from the Tamar gas field began in 2013. In 2010 the reserves totalled 238bn. cu. metres. Crude petroleum reserves in 2011 were 2m. bbls.

Minerals

The most valuable natural resources are the potash, bromine and other salt deposits of the Dead Sea. Production figures in 2013 (in 1,000 tonnes): potash, 2,155; phosphate rock, 1,600; salt, 442; lime, 300.

Agriculture

There were about 286,000 ha. of arable land in 2013 and 95,000 ha. of permanent crops. Farmers rely on reclaimed water for irrigation, as Israel treats 86% of its domestic wastewater and recycles it for agricultural use. Production, 2013 unless otherwise indicated (in 1,000 tonnes): potatoes (2014), 628; tomatoes, 421; carrots and turnips, 292; chillies and green peppers, 244; grapefruit, 211; maize (2014), 164; clementines, mandarins, satsumas and tangerines, 161; melons and watermelons, 134; wheat (2014), 126; apples, 118; cucumbers and gherkins, 101.

Livestock (2013): 540,000 sheep; 465,000 cattle; 177,000 pigs (estimate); 100,000 goats; 40m. chickens.

Types of rural settlement: (1) the *Kibbutz* and *Kvutza* (communal collective settlement), where all property and earnings are collectively owned and work is collectively organized (117,700 people lived in 267 *Kibbutzim* in 2005). (2) The *Moshav* (workers' co-operative smallholders' settlement) which is founded on the principles of mutual aid and equality of opportunity between the members, all farms being equal in size (213,600 in 402 *Moshavim* in 2005). (3) The *Moshav Shitufi* (co-operative settlement), which is based on collective ownership and economy as in the *Kibbutz,* but with each family having its own house and being responsible for its own domestic services (17,000 in 40 *Moshavim Shitufi'im* in 2005). (4) Other rural settlements in which land and property are privately owned and every resident is responsible for his own well-being. In 2005 there were a total of 240 non-cooperative villages with a population of 159,400.

Forestry

In 2015 forests covered 0·17m. ha. or 8% of the total land area. Timber production was 27,000 cu. metres in 2011.

Fisheries

Catches in 2013 totalled 1,983 tonnes, mainly from marine waters.

Industry

The leading company by market capitalization in Israel in May 2018 was Teva Pharmaceutical Industries Ltd (US$19·6bn.).

Products include chemicals, metal products, textiles, tyres, diamonds, paper, plastics, leather goods, glass and ceramics, building materials, precision instruments, tobacco, foodstuffs, electrical and electronic equipment.

Labour

The economically active workforce was 3,738,000 in 2014 (53% males). 71·0% of the population aged 15–64 was economically active in 2014. Unemployment was 4·3% in Dec. 2018 (up slightly from 4·2% in 2017 as a whole and down from 4·8% in 2016).

International Trade

Imports and Exports

Goods imports were US$72,311·8m. in 2014 (US$71,995·0m. in 2013) and goods exports US$68,965·0m. (US$66,781·2m. in 2013).

Principal imports in 2014 were machinery and transport (29·2%), manufactured goods, and mineral fuels and lubricants; main exports in 2014 were manufactured goods (34·9%), chemicals, and machinery and transport equipment.

The leading import supplier in 2013 was the USA (11·3%), followed by China and Germany; the leading export destination in 2013 was the USA (26·2%), followed by Hong Kong and the UK.

Communications

Roads

There were 17,870 km of paved roads in 2007, including 344 km of motorway. Motor vehicles in use in 2007 totalled 1,805,400 passenger cars, 362,200 lorries and vans, 94,800 motorcycles and mopeds, and 21,300 buses and coaches. There were 398 fatalities as a result of road accidents in 2007.

Rail

There were 1,079 km of standard gauge line in 2011. 35·9m. passengers and 6·2m. tonnes of freight were carried in 2011. Israel's first high-speed rail service, linking Jerusalem with Tel Aviv's Ben Gurion Airport, opened in Sept. 2018. A link to the centre of Tel Aviv is currently under construction. One of the smallest metro systems in the world (1,800 metres) was opened in Haifa in 1959. A tram system in Jerusalem opened in Aug. 2011.

Civil Aviation

There are international airports at Tel Aviv (Ben Gurion), Eilat (J. Hozman), Haifa and Ovda. Tel Aviv is the busiest airport, in 2012 handling 13,133,992 passengers (12,400,479 on international flights) and 285,813 tonnes of freight. The flag carrier is El Al, which in 2010 flew to nearly 40 destinations worldwide. In 2005 scheduled airline traffic of Israeli-based carriers flew 97·9m. km and carried 4,382,200 passengers. In 2010 services were also provided by another Israeli airline, Arkia, and by around 50 international carriers.

Shipping

Israel has three commercial ports—Haifa, Ashdod and Eilat. In Jan. 2014 there were 12 ships of 300 GT or over registered, totalling 280,000 GT.

Telecommunications

In 2011 there were 3·5m. main (fixed) telephone lines. In the same year mobile phone subscriptions numbered 9·2m. (1,219·8 per 1,000 persons). There were 25·8 fixed broadband subscriptions per 100 inhabitants in 2009 and 62·5 mobile broadband subscriptions per 100 inhabitants. In 2009, 74·5% of households had a computer and 66·3% of households had internet access at home. In March 2012 there were 3·5m. Facebook users.

Social Institutions

Out of 178 countries analysed in the 2017 *Fragile States Index*—a list published jointly by the Fund for Peace and *Foreign Policy* magazine— Israel was ranked the joint 69th most vulnerable (along with Colombia) to conflict or collapse. The index is based on 12 indicators of state vulnerability across social, political and economic categories.

Justice

Law

Under the Law and Administration Ordinance, 5708/1948, the first law passed by the Provisional Council of State, the law of Israel is the law which was obtaining in Palestine on 14 May 1948 in so far as it is not in conflict with that Ordinance or any other law passed by the Israel legislature and with such modifications as result from the establishment of the State and its authorities.

Capital punishment was abolished in 1954, except for support given to the Nazis and for high treason.

The law of Palestine was derived from Ottoman law, English law (Common Law and Equity) and the law enacted by the Palestine legislature, which to a great extent was modelled on English law.

Civil Courts

Municipal courts, established in certain municipal areas, have criminal jurisdiction over offences against municipal regulations and bylaws and certain specified offences committed within a municipal area. Magistrates courts, established in each district and sub-district, have limited jurisdiction in both civil and criminal matters. District courts, sitting at Jerusalem, Tel Aviv and

Haifa, have jurisdiction, as courts of first instance, in all civil matters not within the jurisdiction of magistrates courts, and in all criminal matters, and as appellate courts from magistrates courts and municipal courts. The 14-member Supreme Court has jurisdiction as a court of first instance (sitting as a High Court of Justice dealing mainly with administrative matters) and as an appellate court from the district courts (sitting as a Court of Civil or of Criminal Appeal).

In addition, there are various tribunals for special classes of cases. Settlement Officers deal with disputes with regard to the ownership or possession of land in settlement areas constituted under the Land (Settlement of Title) Ordinance.

Religious Courts

The rabbinical courts of the Jewish community have exclusive jurisdiction in matters of marriage and divorce, alimony and confirmation of wills of members of their community and concurrent jurisdiction with the civil courts in all other matters of personal status of all members of their community with the consent of all parties to the action.

The courts of the several recognized Christian communities have a similar jurisdiction over members of their respective communities.

The Muslim religious courts have exclusive jurisdiction in all matters of personal status over Muslims who are not foreigners, and over Muslims who are foreigners, if under the law of their nationality they are subject in such matters to the jurisdiction of Muslim religious courts.

Where any action of personal status involves persons of different religious communities, the President of the Supreme Court will decide which court shall have jurisdiction, and whenever a question arises as to whether or not a case is one of personal status within the exclusive jurisdiction of a religious court, the matter must be referred to a special tribunal composed of two judges of the Supreme Court and the president of the highest court of the religious community concerned in Israel.

The population in penal institutions in Dec. 2012 was 17,279 (223 per 100,000 of national population).

Education

The adult literacy rate is more than 97%. There is free and compulsory education from five to 18 years. There is a unified state-controlled elementary school system with a provision for special religious schools. The standard curriculum for all elementary schools is issued by the ministry of education with a possibility of adding supplementary subjects comprising not more than 25% of the total syllabus.

In 2013–14 there were 455,558 Hebrew pupils and 110,656 Arab pupils in the pre-primary education and day care centres. In primary schools in 2015–16 there were 741,033 Hebrew children and 260,426 Arab children. There were 64,064 Hebrew teachers and 20,464 Arab teachers in primary education in 2015–16. In secondary education there were 515,835 Hebrew pupils and 197,024 Arab pupils in 2015–16, with 27,312 Hebrew teachers and 8,238 Arab teachers. In special education there were 215,318 pupils in 2015–16. In post-secondary education, such as colleges, universities and vocational institutions, there were 268,164 pupils.

The Hebrew University of Jerusalem, founded in 1925, comprises faculties of the humanities, social sciences, law, science, medicine and agriculture. In 2018 it had approximately 23,500 students. The Technion–Israel Institute of Technology in Haifa had 14,000 students. The Weizmann Institute of Science in Rehovoth, founded in 1949, had approximately 1,000 students in 2018.

Tel Aviv University had approximately 30,000 students in 2018. The religious Bar-Ilan University at Ramat Gan, opened in 1965, had approximately 17,000 students, the Haifa University had approximately 18,000 students and the Ben Gurion University had approximately 20,000 students.

In 2008 public expenditure on education came to 5·9% of GDP and accounted for 13·7% of total government spending.

Health

In 2010 there were 121 hospitals. There were 60 hospital beds per 10,000 inhabitants in 2007. There were 25,138 physicians, 7,726 dentists, 4,958 pharmacists and 42,609 nurses and midwives in 2006. In 2009 health spending represented 7·5% of GDP.

Welfare

The National Insurance Law of 1954 provides for old-age pensions, survivors' insurance, work-injury insurance, maternity insurance, family allowances and unemployment benefits. In 2013 recipients of allocations from the National Insurance Institute included (monthly averages): child allowances, 1,088,251 families for 2,628,500 children; old age pensions, 733,686; general disability allowance, 222,641; birth grant, 169,711; long-term care benefit, 156,621.

Religion

Religious affairs are under the supervision of a special ministry, with departments for the Christian and Muslim communities. The religious affairs of each community remain under the full control of the ecclesiastical authorities concerned: in the case of the Jews, the Ashkenazi and Sephardi Chief Rabbis, in the case of the Christians, the heads of the various communities, and in the case of the Muslims, the Qadis. The Druze were officially recognized in 1957 as an autonomous religious community.

According to the Pew Research Center's Forum on Religion & Public Life, in 2010 there were an estimated 5·6m. Jews, 1·4m. Muslims, 230,000 people with no religious affiliation and 150,000 Christians.

The Chief Rabbis are David Lau (Ashkenazi) and Yitzhak Yosef (Sephardi).

Culture

World Heritage Sites

There are nine UNESCO sites in Israel. Masada and the old city of Acre were both inscribed in 2001. Masada was built as a palace complex and fortress by Herod the Great. It was the site of the mass suicide of about 1,000 Jewish patriots in the face of a Roman army in the 1st century AD and is a symbol of the ancient kingdom of Israel. The port city of Acre preserves remains of its medieval Crusader buildings beneath the existing Muslim fortified town dating from the 18th and 19th centuries. The White City of Tel Aviv—the Modern Movement (2003) is an example of early 20th century town planning, based on the plan of Sir Patrick Geddes. The Biblical Tels, a series of prehistoric settlement mounds with biblical connections, and the Incense Route, four Nabatean towns along the spice and incense trail, were added to the list in 2005. The Bahá'i Holy Places in Haifa and the Western Galilee (2008) is a complex of buildings including the Shrine of Bahá'u'lláh in Acre and the Shrine of the Báb in Haifa that are visited as part of the Bahá'i pilgrimage. Sites of Human Evolution at Mount Carmel: the Nahal Me'arot/Wadi el-Mughara Caves (2012) is an archaeological site displaying 500,000 years of human evolution with evidence of burials, early stone architecture and the transition from a hunter-gathering lifestyle to agriculture and animal husbandry. Caves of Maresha and Bet-Guvrin in the Judean Lowlands as a Microcosm of the Land of the Caves (2014) is situated under the former towns of Maresha and Bet Guvrin and contains some 3,500 underground chambers, which served as baths, places of worship and hideaways. Necropolis of Bet She'arim: A Landmark of Jewish Renewal (2015) consists of a series of catacombs that are a treasury of artworks and inscriptions in Greek, Aramaic, Hebrew and Palmyrene.

Press

In 2012 there were 11 daily newspapers with an estimated combined circulation of 1·1m. The most widely read paper is the free *Israel Hayom*, which was only launched in 2007.

Tourism

In 2011 there were 2,820,000 tourist arrivals (excluding same-day visitors), up from 2,803,000 in 2010. The main countries of origin of non-resident tourists in 2011 were the USA (21%), followed by Russia (13%) and France (10%). 86% of all tourist arrivals in 2011 were by air and 14% were by land border crossings.

Calendar

The Jewish year 5779 corresponds to 10 Sept. 2018–29 Sept. 2019; 5780 corresponds to 30 Sept. 2019–18 Sept. 2020.

Diplomatic Representatives

Of Israel in the United Kingdom (2 Palace Green, London, W8 4QB)
Ambassador: Mark Regev.

Of the United Kingdom in Israel (192 Hayarkon St., 6340502 Tel Aviv)
Ambassador: David Quarrey.

Of Israel in the USA (3514 International Drive, NW, Washington, D.C., 20008)
Ambassador: Ron Dermer.

Of the USA in Israel (14 David Flusser St., 9378322 Jerusalem)
  Ambassador: David Melech Friedman.

Of Israel to the United Nations
  Ambassador: Danny Danon.

Of Israel to the European Union
  Ambassador: Aharon Leshno-Yaar.

Palestinian Territories

Population projection, 2020: 5·33m.
GNI per capita, 2017: (PPP$) 5,055
HDI/world rank, 2017: 0·686/119
Internet domain extension: .ps

Key Historical Events

After Israel declared independence on 14 May 1948, Arab League troops invaded the former British Mandate for Palestine. The first Arab–Israeli War (known in Israel as the War of Independence) ended with an armistice in July 1949. Under its terms 77% of Palestine came under Israeli control (56% had been allocated by the UN Partition Plan of 1947). Around 700,000 Palestinians were displaced to the West Bank, the Gaza Strip or to neighbouring countries. Up to 150,000 Palestinians remained in Israel. Gaza came under Egyptian control and in April 1950 the West Bank and East Jerusalem were annexed into Jordan.

Border clashes were frequent in the early 1950s. When Egypt nationalized the Suez Canal in July 1956 Israeli troops occupied Gaza and the Sinai Peninsula until the arrival of UN Emergency Forces. Fatah (the Palestine National Liberation Movement) emerged in Gaza in the late 1950s, led by Yasser Arafat and Khalil al-Wazir. It became the leading faction in the Palestine Liberation Organization (PLO), launched by the Arab League in 1964.

Guerrilla attacks by Fatah on Israel began in Jan. 1965. Tensions between Egypt and Israel rose in 1967 when UN forces withdrew. Israel's pre-emptive strike on Egyptian air bases ignited the Six Day War on 5 June, culminating in Israeli control of the West Bank, Gaza Strip and Golan Heights. In Nov. 1967 the UN stated that Israel should withdraw its forces from the territories occupied during the war in return for peace with its Arab neighbours. However, the PLO refused to accept Israel's right to exist. Following the Yom Kippur war in 1973, the possibility of a settlement was lost when radical factions broke from the PLO. In Oct. 1974 the Arab League recognized the PLO as the 'sole, legitimate representative of the Palestinian people'.

When Israel and Egypt signed the Camp David Accords in Sept. 1978, Israel withdrew from Sinai. Plans for Palestinian autonomy in Gaza and the West Bank excluded the PLO and were rejected by Palestinians, while Israel made clear its intention to maintain a military presence in the Occupied Territories and expand Jewish settlements in the West Bank.

Israel's invasion of southern Lebanon in June 1982 ended the PLO's presence there. The 88-day siege of Beirut forced 10,000 militia into Yemen, Sudan and other Arab countries. Arafat established new headquarters in Tunisia. In Nov. 1988, almost a year after the first Palestinian *intifada* (uprising) against Israel began, the PLO declared a Palestinian state. Arafat also recognized Israel's right to exist and renounced terrorism, paving the way for the 1993 Oslo Accords.

After the Israeli prime minister, Yitzhak Rabin, recognized the PLO an agreement was signed in Washington providing for limited Palestinian self-rule (through the Palestinian National Authority) in the Gaza Strip and part of the West Bank. The six-year *intifada* ended, during which over 2,000 Palestinians and 150 Israelis were killed.

In Nov. 1995 Rabin was assassinated by a Jewish extremist. Under an agreement of 1995 the Israeli army withdrew from six of the seven largest Palestinian towns in the West Bank and from 460 smaller towns and villages. The rest of the West Bank stayed under Israeli control with further withdrawals at six-month intervals. Negotiations on the permanent status of the West Bank and Gaza began in May 1996.

After elections in 1996, a right-wing coalition under Binyamin Netanyahu approved plans for an expansion of Jewish settlement in the West Bank. In Oct. 1998 Israel accepted partial withdrawal from the West Bank on condition that the Palestinians cracked down on terrorism. The following month, 2% of the West Bank was handed over.

Netanyahu's defeat by Ehud Barak in elections in 1999 improved relations with the PLO. In March 2000 Arafat accepted plans for expanded self-rule in the West Bank, involving the transfer of another 6% of the area to the Palestinian Authority. However, by Oct. 2000 a second *intifada* had begun, fuelled by conflict over control of Jerusalem. When talks stalled, Barak went to the polls in Feb. 2001 but was defeated by Ariel Sharon. Amid escalating violence, in Dec. 2001 Israel broke off contact with Arafat, putting him under virtual house arrest.

Violence on both sides continued in 2002 with heavy loss of life. In March 2002 the UN endorsed a Palestinian state for the first time. In June 2002 Israel began constructing a barrier cutting off the West Bank to shield against suicide bombers. Arafat died in Nov. 2004 and was succeeded by Mahmoud Abbas. In Feb. 2005 Sharon and Abbas agreed to cease hostilities. In Aug. 2005 Israel evicted 8,500 Jewish settlers from Gaza.

In Jan. 2006 Palestinian legislative elections were won by Change and Reform (Hamas), which does not recognize Israel and has called for its destruction. Western aid was thus suspended. In Dec. 2006, after deadlock between Fatah and Hamas over forming a national unity government, Abbas called new elections. Tensions between Fatah and Hamas peaked in June 2007, with Hamas seizing control of the Gaza Strip while the West Bank remained under Fatah. Abbas established a new government, recognized by Fatah and Israel but not by Hamas, under the premiership of Salam Fayyad.

In Dec. 2008 Israel began an assault in Gaza aimed at destroying Hamas strongholds responsible for attacks on Israeli targets. The international community called for a ceasefire amid concerns over the high civilian death toll and infrastructural damage. On 13 Jan. 2009 the UN headquarters in Gaza was bombed by Israeli forces. Israel apologized, claiming its forces were attacked by militants taking refuge there. On 18 Jan. Israel and Hamas announced unilateral ceasefires. An estimated 1,300 Palestinians and 13 Israelis were killed during the three-week offensive, and 50,000 displaced.

In May 2011 Mahmoud Abbas and Khaled Meshaal, leaders of Fatah and Hamas respectively, agreed that a joint caretaker administration should hold power until Palestinian elections, although the elections have been repeatedly delayed. That year, the Palestinian National Authority's attempts to gain UN recognition for the 'State of Palestine' failed. However, Palestine was accepted as a member of UNESCO in Oct. 2011 and in Nov. 2012 the UN General Assembly granted the territory 'non-member observer state' status.

In June 2014 a Fatah and Hamas unity government took office. Over the following months Israel launched air and land attacks to remove missile launching sites and tunnel systems before an Egyptian-brokered ceasefire came into force in Aug.

The Vatican recognized Palestinian statehood in May 2015, but in Dec. 2017 US President Donald Trump acknowledged the disputed city of Jerusalem as the capital of Israel in a controversial reversal of long-standing international policy.

Territory and Population

The 2007 census population of the Palestinian territory was 3,767,126 (2,895,683 in 1997). Estimate, 2018: 4,854,013. In 2011, 74·4% of the population were urban. Life expectancy at birth, 2014, was 74·9 years for females and 71·0 years for males. The UN gives a projected population for 2020 of 5·33m. In 2012 the infant mortality rate was 20·6 per 1,000 live births. The fertility rate in 2012 was 4·1 births per woman. Agricultural production, 2008 estimates, in 1,000 tonnes: cucumbers and gherkins, 208; tomatoes, 208; olives, 86; potatoes, 69; aubergines, 60; grapes, 55; pumpkins and squash, 51. Total fish catch in 2005 for the Palestinian Territories was 1,805 tonnes. In 2011 there were 95,725 children in pre-primary education, 411,268 primary school pupils, 705,627 pupils at secondary level and 213,973 tertiary level students. 97·4% of the Palestinian population in 2007 were Muslims and 1·2% Christians.

The West Bank has an area of 5,655 sq. km; the 2007 census population was 2,350,583, in addition to 275,000 Jewish settlers and 10,000 troops deployed there. Estimate, 2018: 2,921,170. By 2009 the number of Jewish settlers had risen above 300,000. In 2006 there was a Palestinian diaspora of 5·0m. The birth rate in 2016 was estimated at 28·5 per 1,000 population and the death rate 3·7 per 1,000. In 2014 there were 160,863 vehicles registered. There were 50 hospitals in 2014.

The Gaza Strip has an area of 365 sq. km; the 2007 census population was 1,416,543. Estimate, 2018: 1,932,843. The seven-week Israel–Gaza conflict of July–Aug. 2014 left up to 500,000 Palestinians internally displaced. Two months after the ceasefire, more than 100,000 people were still homeless. The population doubled between 1990 and 2005. While the population is still growing, the rate of increase has slowed in the meantime. The chief town is Gaza itself. Over 98% of the population are Arabic-speaking Muslims. In 2005, 81·0% of the population lived in urban areas. Crude birth rate in 2016 was 35·8 per 1,000 population. The death rate was estimated at 3·3 per 1,000 population. In 2014 there were 83,652 vehicles registered. There were 30 hospitals in 2014. Gaza International Airport, at the southern edge of the Gaza Strip, opened in Nov. 1998.

Constitution and Government
In April 1996 the Palestinian Council removed from its Charter all clauses contrary to its recognition by Israel, including references to armed struggle as the only means of liberating Palestine, and the elimination of Zionism from Palestine. The *President* is directly elected and heads the executive organ, the Palestinian National Authority, one fifth of whose members he appoints, while four fifths are elected by the *Legislative Council*. The latter comprises 132 members (88 until 2005), of which 66 members are chosen by district voting and the other 66 by proportional representation. The 2007 Election Law passed by President Mahmoud Abbas during a period of emergency rule introduced proportional representation for all seats. Hamas claimed the reforms were illegal as they were not ratified by the Legislative Council. The Palestinian Authority was created by agreement of the PLO and Israel as an interim instrument of self-rule for Palestinians living on the West Bank and Gaza Strip. The failure of the PLO and Israel to strike a permanent status agreement has resulted in the Authority retaining its powers. It is entitled to establish ministries and subordinate bodies, as required to fulfil its obligations and responsibilities. It possesses legislative and executive powers within the functional areas transferred to it in the 1995 Interim Agreement. Its territorial jurisdiction is restricted to Areas A and B in the West Bank and approximately two-thirds of the Gaza Strip.

Following an Israeli-Palestinian agreement on customs duties and VAT in Aug. 1994 the Palestinians set up their own customs and immigration points into Gaza and Jericho. Israel collects customs dues on Palestinian imports through Israeli entry points and transfers these to the Palestinian treasury.

A special committee is working on drafting a new Palestinian constitution. In March 2003 parliament approved the creation of the position of prime minister. Yasser Arafat nominated Mahmoud Abbas, the PLO Secretary General, to be the first premier. The president may dismiss the prime minister but parliament has to approve any new government.

There is a Palestinian *Economic Council for Development and Reconstruction*.

Recent Elections
Legislative Council elections were held on 25 Jan. 2006. Change and Reform (Hamas) won 74 seats; Fatah Movement, 45; Popular Front for the Liberation of Palestine, 3; the Alternative, 2; Independent Palestine, 2; Third Way, 2; ind. and others, 4. Turnout was 74·6%.

Presidential elections were held on 9 Jan. 2005. Mahmoud Abbas was elected president by 67·4% of votes cast, ahead of Mustafa Barghouti with 21·0%. There were five other candidates.

Current Government
President of the Palestinian National Authority: Mahmoud Abbas (Fatah); b. 1935 (since Jan. 2005).

Prime Minister of the Palestinian National Authority: Mohammad Shtayyeh (Fatah); b. 1958 (since March 2019).

Office of the President: http://president.ps

International Relations
The Palestinian National Council unilaterally declared Palestine an independent state in 1988. In 2011 President Mahmoud Abbas of the Palestinian National Authority submitted an application for membership of the United Nations. Membership requires the backing of two-thirds of member states, including all five of the permanent members of the Security Council. As of March 2018, 136 member states of the United Nations—70·5% of the total—recognized Palestine, but only two of the Security Council members did (China and Russia). In addition, the Holy See also recognizes Palestine. Palestine was granted 'non-member observer state' status in the UN in Nov. 2012.

Economy

Overview
Following the outbreak of the second *intifada* in Sept. 2000, conditions in the Palestinian Territories deteriorated rapidly. Revival followed the appointment of a new caretaker government in the West Bank in 2007, with growth accelerating strongly in 2009, driven by donor assistance, increased 'tunnel activity' (shadow economic relations with neighbouring Egypt) and a relaxation of the Israeli blockade of Gaza.

However, growth subsequently slowed significantly, and in 2013 the economy was estimated to have contracted by 4·4%. The economic slowdown created fiscal pressures on the Palestinian Authority, undermining the provision of public services, with a higher than expected budget deficit and lower external donor support recorded in 2014. However, a revival in construction activity in the Gaza Strip and a surge in household consumption financed by bank loans in the West Bank boosted GDP growth, which averaged 4% in both 2015 and 2016. Despite this pick-up in growth, a quarter of the population lives in poverty, with unemployment hovering around 27%. Israel's restrictions on movement of goods and people stand in the way of developing a more dynamic private sector to create the conditions for sustainable growth.

Currency
Israeli currency is in use.

Performance
The total GDP of the West Bank and the Gaza Strip was US$14·5bn. in 2017.

Banking and Finance
Banking is regulated by the Palestine Monetary Authority. Palestine's leading bank is Arab Bank. A securities exchange, the Palestine Securities Exchange, opened in Nablus in Feb. 1997.

Budget
Budgetary central government revenue totalled US$3,134·8m. in 2011 and expenditure US$3,153·5m.

Energy and Natural Resources

Forestry
In 2015 forests covered 9,000 ha. or 2% of the total land area.

Communications

Telecommunications
There were 403,025 landline telephone subscriptions in 2013 (equivalent to 93·2 per 1,000 inhabitants) and 3,190,000 mobile phone subscriptions (or 737·4 per 1,000 inhabitants). In 2012, 43·4% of the population were internet users. In March 2012 there were 915,000 Facebook users.

Social Institutions

Justice
The Palestinian police consists of some 15,000; they are not empowered to arrest Israelis, but may detain them and hand them over to the Israeli authorities. There were three executions in 2016 and six in 2017, but none in 2018. All of the executions carried out in 2017 were in the Hamas-controlled Gaza Strip.

Education
Adult literacy was 94·6% in 2009 (97·4% among males and 91·7% among females).

Culture

Tourism
In 2013, 545,000 non-resident tourists stayed in hotels and similar accommodation (up from 490,000 in 2012).

World Heritage Sites
The Birthplace of Jesus: Church of the Nativity and the Pilgrimage Route, Bethlehem was the first Palestinian site added to the UNESCO World Heritage List (2012). The Church of the Nativity is considered to be the oldest continuously operating Christian church in the world. The Land of Olives and Vines—Cultural Landscape of Southern Jerusalem, Battir was

also inscribed on the list (2014). Hebron/Al-Khalil Old Town was inscribed on the list in 2017. The centre of interest of the town was the Al-Ibrahimi Mosque/the tomb of the Patriarchs, now a place of pilgrimage.

Further Reading

Israel

Central Bureau of Statistics. *Statistical Abstract of Israel.* (Annual)—*Statistical Bulletin of Israel.* (Monthly)

Beitlin, Y., *Israel: a Concise History.* 1992

Black, Ian, *Enemies and Neighbours: Arabs and Jews in Palestine and Israel, 1917–2017.* 2017

Bregman, Ahron, *History of Israel.* 2002.—*Cursed Victory: A History of Israel and the Occupied Territories.* 2014

Freedman, R. (ed.) *Israel Under Rabin.* 1995

Garfinkle, A., *Politics and Society in Modern Israel: Myths and Realities.* 1997

Gelvin, James L., *The Israel-Palestine Conflict: One Hundred Years of War.* 2005

Gilbert, Martin, *Israel: A History.* 1998

Hoffman, Bruce, *Anonymous Soldiers: The Struggle for Israel, 1917–1947.* 2015

Kershner, Isabel, *Barrier: The Seam of the Israeli-Palestinian Conflict.* 2005

Pfeffer, Anshel, *Bibi: The Turbulent Life and Times of Benjamin Netanyahu.* 2018

Sachar, H. M., *A History of Israel: From the Rise of Zionism to Our Time.* 3rd ed. 2007

Segev, T., *1949: The First Israelis.* 1986

Shavit, Ari, *My Promised Land: The Triumph and Tragedy of Israel.* 2013

Shulman, David, *Dark Hope: Working for Peace in Israel and Palestine.* 2007

Smith, Charles D., *Palestine and the Arab-Israeli Conflict.* 8th ed. 2013

Thomas, Baylis, *How Israel Was Won: A Concise History of the Arab–Israeli Conflict (1900–1999).* 2000

Wasserstein, Bernard, *Israel and Palestine: Why They Fight and Can They Stop?* 2003

Other more specialized titles are entered under PALESTINIAN TERRITORIES.

National library: The Jewish National and University Library, Edmond Safra Campus, Givat Ram, PO Box 39105, Jerusalem 91390.

National Statistical Office: Central Bureau of Statistics, Prime Minister's Office, POB 13015, Jerusalem 91130.

Website: http://www.cbs.gov.il

Palestinian Territories

Black, Ian, *Enemies and Neighbours: Arabs and Jews in Palestine and Israel, 1917–2017.* 2017

Bregman, Ahron, *Cursed Victory: A History of Israel and the Occupied Territories.* 2014

Chehab, Zaki, *Inside Hamas: The Untold Story of the Militant Islamic Movement.* 2007

Gelvin, James L., *The Israel-Palestine Conflict: One Hundred Years of War.* 2005

Hilal, Jamil, *Where Now for Palestine?: The Demise of the Two-State Solution.* 2007

Kershner, Isabel, *Barrier: The Seam of the Israeli-Palestinian Conflict.* 2005

Kimmerling, B. and Migdal J. S., *Palestinians: the Making of a People.* 1994.—*The Palestinian People: A History.* 2003

Mishal, Shaul and Sela, Avraham, *The Palestinian Hamas: Vision, Violence, and Coexistence.* 2006

Pappe, Ilan, *A History of Modern Palestine: One Land, Two Peoples.* 2003.—*The Forgotten Palestinians: A History of the Palestinians in Israel.* 2011

Peleg, Ilan and Waxman, Dov, *Israel's Palestinians: The Conflict Within.* 2011

Rubin, B., *Revolution Until Victory? The Politics and History of the PLO.* 1994

Segev, T., *One Palestine, Complete.* 2000

Smith, Charles D., *Palestine and the Arab-Israeli Conflict.* 8th ed. 2013

Stendel, O., *The Arabs in Israel.* 1996

Wasserstein, Bernard, *Israel and Palestine: Why They Fight and Can They Stop?* 2003

Statistical office: Palestinian Central Bureau of Statistics.

Website: http://www.pcbs.gov.ps

Italy

Repubblica Italiana (Italian Republic)

Capital: Rome
Population projection, 2020: 59·13m.
GNI per capita, 2017: (PPP$) 35,299
HDI/world rank, 2017: 0·880/28
Internet domain extension: .it

Key Historical Events

Excavations at Isernia have uncovered remains of Palaeolithic Neanderthal man that date back 70,000 years. New Stone Age settlements have been found across the Italian peninsula and at the beginning of the Bronze Age there were several Italic tribes, including the Ligurians, Veneti, Apulians, Siculi and the Sardi. The Etruscans were established in Italy by around 1200 BC. Their highly civilized society flourished between the Arno and Tiber valleys, with other important settlements in Campania, Lazio and the Po valley. The Etruscans were primarily navigators and travellers competing for the valuable trading routes and markets with the Phoenicians and Greeks. During the 8th century BC the Greeks had begun to settle in southern Italy and presented a challenge to Etruscan domination of sea trade routes. Greek settlements were established along the southern coast, on the island of Ischia in the Bay of Naples and in Sicily where the Corinthians founded the city of Syracuse. These colonies were known as *Magna Graecia* and flourished for six centuries. Magna Graecia eventually succumbed to the growing power of Rome where the impact of the Hellenic culture had already been felt.

According to legend, Rome was founded on 21 April 753 BC by Romulus (a descendant of Aeneas, a Trojan) who, after killing his twin brother, Remus, declared himself the first king of Rome. The Etruscan dynasty of Tarquins gained control in 616 BC and expanded Roman agriculture and trade to rival the Greeks. The Romans overthrew the Tarquins in 510 BC and the first Roman Republic was born.

With the Republic came the establishment of the 'Roman Code', a collection of principles of political philosophy that enshrined the sovereign rights of Roman citizens. The early Roman Senate was dominated by a few patrician families, who held a monopoly on public office with the *equites* (the highest class of non-noble rich).

With the exception of the Greek city-states, Italy was unified by the Romans, who then set their sights on the Mediterranean, controlled by Carthage. Between 264–146 BC Carthage and Rome fought three wars (the Punic Wars) for supremacy of the Mediterranean trade routes. At the start Carthage was the more powerful, with a colonial empire that stretched as far as Morocco and included Sicily, Corsica, Sardinia and parts of Spain. Rome was also inexperienced in maritime war. In 218 BC the second Punic War started when Hannibal crossed the Alps and marched south, defeating the Romans in a series of battles in Italy. Without taking Rome itself, he crossed over to Zama in North Africa where he was finally defeated by Scipio in 202 BC. But by the end of the third Punic War in 146 BC the destruction of Carthage was total and Macedonian Greece was added to Rome's provinces. Rome incorporated Spain into her colonies and became the dominant power in the Mediterranean.

This dominance of trade routes led to great riches for Rome and the ensuing corruption among the upper ruling classes gave rise to social unrest. Sulla, a patrician general, marched on Rome in 82 BC, took the city in a bloody coup and instituted a new constitution. Nine years later Spartacus, an escaped slave, led 70,000 of his fellow slaves in a rampage throughout the peninsula. Out of the ensuing chaos, Julius Caesar emerged as leader. He had already conquered Gaul and declared southern Britain a part of Rome in 54 BC. His disregard for the Senate led to his legions being disbanded but he remained popular and returned to Rome a hero. His strength and charisma led to his assassination by members of the Senate on the Ides of March 44 BC. After his death, various rival successors fought to gain control, including Mark Anthony (Marcus Antonius), Marcus Junius Brutus and Gaius Cassius.

But it was Caesar's nephew Octavian, having defeated Mark Anthony in 31 BC, who was crowned the first emperor of Rome in 27 BC, assuming the title Augustus.

Roman Domination

Augustus reigned for 45 years. With the aid of a professional army and an imperial bureaucracy he established the *Pax Romana* while extending the empire and disseminating its laws and civic culture. The arts thrived with writers, dramatists and philosophers such as Cicero, Plautus, Terence, Virgil, Horace and Ovid developing Latin into an expressive and poetic language. In 100 BC Rome itself had more than 1·5m. inhabitants and the Roman Empire was a unified diversity of many races and creeds. It had more than 100,000 km of paved roads, a complex of sophisticated aqueducts, and an efficient army and administrative system.

In AD 14 Augustus was succeeded by his stepson, Tiberius, who ruled in an era that saw the rise of Christianity. Successive emperors tried to suppress the new religion which spread quickly throughout the empire. The deranged Emperor Nero, who came to power in AD 54, intensified persecution of the Christians and was accused of setting Rome on fire. His death in AD 68 brought the Julio-Claudian dynasty to a close and, after a period of instability, Vespasian, the son of a provincial civil servant, took the throne and began some of the most ambitious building projects the Empire had seen. He started the Colosseum (completed by his son Titus) and the Arco di Tito (where the Via Sacra joins the Forum).

In AD 98 the Senate elected Trajan as emperor. Beginning a century of successful rule by the Antonine dynasty, he expanded the empire with the conquests of Dacia (Romania), Mesopotamia, Persia, Syria and Armenia. By the end of his reign the Roman Empire stretched from the Persian Gulf to Britain, from the Caspian Sea to Morocco and from the Sahara to the Danube. Trajan was responsible for several great architectural projects. A huge column depicting his Dacian campaigns served as his tomb in Rome. Trajan's successor, Hadrian, continued this programme of huge constructions, including Hadrian's Wall in Britain. After his death in 138, his tomb was converted into the fortress of Castel Sant'Angelo on the banks of the Tiber.

Under pressure from Teutonic tribes along the Danube and as a result of the increasingly strong influence of the Eastern religions, Rome began to lose control of its empire at the start of the 3rd century. In 306 Constantine became emperor. After he converted to Christianity in 313 his Edict of Milan established Rome as the headquarters of the Christian religion. A new building programme of Christian cathedrals and churches began throughout Italy. At the same time, Constantine cultivated the wealthy eastern regions of the Empire and, in 324, he moved his capital to Constantinople (now İstanbul). The decline of the Roman Empire continued when, after the death of Constantine, two brothers, Valens and Valentian, divided the Empire. The west and east gradually became alienated, separated by invaders, language and religious interpretation. 'Rome' endured in the east as the Byzantine Empire, the most powerful medieval state in the Mediterranean.

Fall of Rome

The western half of the Roman Empire, having embraced Christianity as the state religion, came under repeated attacks from Central European ('Barbarian') tribes. The Germanic Vandals had cut off Rome's corn supplies from North Africa, and the Visigoths, a Teutonic tribe, controlled the northern Mediterranean coast and northern Italy. In 452 Attila the Hun, from the steppes of Central Asia, invaded and forced the people of northeastern Italy onto a lagoon haven that became Venice. Rome was captured and sacked in 455 by the Vandals and in 476 a Germanic mercenary captain, Odovacar, deposed Romulus Augustus, the last of the Western Roman Emperors. This date is generally accepted as the end of the Roman Empire in the West.

In 493 Odovacar was succeeded by Theodoric, an Ostrogoth who had acquired a taste for Roman culture. Theodoric ruled from Ravenna and by the time he died in 527 he had managed to restore peace to Italy. On his death, Italy was reconquered by an emperor of the Eastern Roman Empire, Justinian, who together with his wife Theodora laid the foundations of the

Byzantine period. Although the Lombards drove back the Justinian conquest, Byzantine emperors managed to retain control of parts of southern Italy until the 11th century.

In the mid-5th century Attila the Hun had been persuaded not to attack Rome by Pope Leo I ('The Great'). This and a document known as the 'Donation of Constantine' secured the Western Roman Empire for the Catholic Church. In 590 Gregory I became pope and set about an extensive programme of reforms, including improved conditions for slaves and the distribution of free bread in Rome. He oversaw the Christianization of Britain, repaired Italy's network of aqueducts and created the foundations for Catholic services and rituals and church administration.

The invasion of Italy by the Lombards began before Gregory became pope and, although they eventually penetrated as far south as Spoleto and Benevento, they were unable to take Rome. They settled around Milan, Pavia and Brescia and abandoned their own language and customs in favour of the local culture. However, they were sufficiently threatening to cause the pope to invite the Franks under King Pepin to invade. In 756 the Franks overthrew the Lombards and established the Papal States (which survived until 1870). Pepin issued his 'Donation of Pepin', which gave the land still controlled by the Byzantine Empire to Pope Stephen II, proclaiming him and future popes the heirs of the Roman emperors. Pepin's son, Charlemagne, succeeded him and was crowned emperor on Christmas Day 800 by Pope Leo III in St Peter's Basilica in Rome. The installation of a 'Roman' emperor in the West—what was to become the Holy Roman Empire—endorsed the separation between Rome and Byzantium and moved the seat of European political power north of the Alps.

After Charlemagne's death it proved impossible to keep the enormous Carolingian Empire intact. In the period of anarchy that followed, many small independent rival states were established while in Rome the aristocratic families fought over the Papacy. Meanwhile, southern Italy was prospering under Muslim rule. By 831 Muslim Arabs had invaded Sicily and made Palermo their capital. Syracuse fell to them in 878. They created a Greek style civilization with Muslim philosophers, physicians, astronomers, mathematicians and geographers. Cotton, sugarcane and citrus fruits appeared for the first time in Italy and taxes were lowered. Hundreds of mosques were built and all over the region centres of academic and medical learning sprang up. Southern Italy lived harmoniously under Arab influence for more than 200 years while the north remained unsettled. After the collapse of the Carolingian Empire, warfare broke out between local rulers, forcing many people to take refuge in fortified hill towns. In 962 Otto I, a Saxon, was crowned Holy Roman Emperor, the first of a succession of Germanic emperors that was to continue until 1806.

At the beginning of the 11th century the Normans began to enter southern Italy in great numbers, where they had originally been recruited to fight the Arabs. Establishing themselves in Apulia and Calabria, they assimilated much of the eastern culture, co-existing peacefully with the Arabs. The architecture of churches and cathedrals built during this period shows the merging of the two cultural and religious influences. Roger II of Sicily (reigned 1112–54), nephew of the adventurer Robert Guiscard, extended Norman Hauteville power over southern Italy and his navy was dominant in the Mediterranean. He presided over a famous court of scholars and artists, many from the Muslim world, making Palermo a model of tolerance and learning.

North South Divide

Meanwhile, the delicate relationship between the Holy Roman Empire based in the north of Europe and the Papacy in the south was maintained by a common desire to recapture the Holy Land from the Muslims. Crusades were launched, mostly from the northern states, but achieved little. Germanic claims to the southern territories grew and after Frederick I (known as Barbarossa) was crowned Holy Roman Emperor in 1155, he married off his son Henry to the heir to the Norman throne in Sicily. Frederick II, Barbarossa's grandson, came to the throne of Sicily as a child in 1197 and was crowned Holy Roman Emperor in 1220. An enlightened and tolerant ruler, he was known as '*Stupor Mundi*' ('Wonder of the World'). An accomplished warrior, he valued scholarship and the Arab culture and allowed Muslims and Jews freedom to follow their own religions. He founded the University of Naples in 1224 with the intention of producing a generation of administrators for his kingdom and moved the court of the Holy Roman Empire to the newly built octagonal masterpiece, Castel del Monte, in Apulia.

During this period a new middle class emerged; with the seat of government so far south, some of the northern cities began to free themselves from feudal control and set themselves up as autonomous states under the protection of either the pope or the emperor. Milan, Cremona, Bologna, Florence, Pavia, Modena, Parma and Lodi were the most important of these new states, each dominated by a powerful family, exercising governmental power in the form of *signorie*. These states functioned autonomously within larger regional areas: Veneto, Lombardy, Tuscany, the Papal States and the Southern Kingdom. In 1265 Charles of Anjou (a Frenchman who had beheaded Frederick II's grandson) was crowned king of Sicily. Greatly increased taxes, especially on rich landowners, made him unpopular despite his programme of road building, reform of the monetary system, improvement of the ports and the opening of silver mines. In 1282 an uprising known as the Sicilian Vespers was sparked by a French soldier assaulting a Sicilian woman. As a consequence of the opposition to the French in southern Italy, Palermo declared itself an independent republic while supporting the Spaniard Peter of Aragon as king. By 1302 the Anjou dynasty had established itself in Naples.

Plague

The Black Death (La Peste), the deadly plague that swept throughout Europe towards the end of the 13th century, ravaged the populations of the major cities, which were already struggling with famine after years of war. Despite this, the strength of the northern and central Italian city-states was increasing. The rival maritime republics of Venice and Genoa had their own fleets. Venice had added the ports of Dalmatia, the Peloponnese and Cyprus to its possessions and Genoa's influence stretched as far as the Black Sea. Meanwhile, the pope and the Church turned their crusading zeal from the East towards European heretics. Pope Boniface, elected in 1294, came from Italian nobility and was determined to safeguard the interests of his own family. He claimed papal supremacy in worldly and spiritual affairs with his Papal Bull (*Unam Sanctam*) in 1302.

Meanwhile, a rival Papacy had appeared in Avignon, where John XXII was based. Rome had lost most of her former glory and had become little more than a battleground for the power struggles between the Orsini and Colonna families. The Papal claim to be temporal rulers of Rome was under threat and the Papal States began to fall apart. The period 1305–77, when seven successive popes ruled in Avignon, became known as the 'Babylonian Captivity'. In 1377 Pope Gregory XI returned to Rome after Cardinal Egidio d'Albornoz managed to restore the Papal States with his Egidian Constitutions. Rome was in such a ruined state that Gregory was obliged to set up his court in the Vatican, which was fortified and protected by the proximity of the Castel Sant'Angelo. Gregory died a year later and the Roman cardinals elected one of their own, Urban VI, as his successor. Urban's unpopularity was such that the French cardinals rebelled, electing their own pope, Clement VII, who set up his rival claim in Avignon. Yet another rival pope set himself in Pisa and thus began the Great Schism that would separate the papacy from Rome for nearly half a century.

Renaissance

In 1418 the Great Schism was brought to an end by the Council of Constance and Rome began to recapture her previous glory. Italy was at the forefront of the Renaissance, a flowering of artistic and intellectual humanist expression in the city-states. After the Peace of Lodi in 1454, the powerful ruling families—among others the Medici in Florence, the Gonzaga in Mantua and the d'Este in Ferrara—were at leisure to sponsor the Renaissance and Rome became again the centre of Italian political, cultural and intellectual life. In Florence the Signoria was taken over by a wealthy merchant, Cosimo de Medici. His nephew, Lorenzo Il Magnifico, became one of the great patrons of the arts. Feudal lords like Lorenzo de Medici frequently switched allegiance between the popes and the emperors, becoming wealthy bankers and captains of adventure in the process. Having defeated its arch-rival, Genoa, in 1381, Venice grew enormously, transforming its commercial maritime empire into a territorial empire that stretched almost to Milan.

The peace was shattered in 1494 by the invasion of Charles VIII, king of France. Encouraged to pursue his claim to the crown of Naples by Ludovico Sforza, duke of Milan, Charles shocked the Italian cities into an alliance to expel his army. As cities competed to become the richest and most cultured, a Dominican monk, Girolamo Savonarola, preached against humanism in Florence. He persuaded Charles VIII to overthrow the Medici family and declare a Florentine republic. Although he was eventually excommunicated, hanged and burned at the stake, Savonarola exerted a lasting influence on Florentine politics. The Venetian expansion, through diplomatic and military guile, had alienated Venice's neighbours, who formed in 1508 the League of Cambrai, which came close to eradicating the Venetian Republic.

The appearance of Spanish power in Naples began the Habsburg-Valois wars that used Italy as a battlefield until the Peace of Cateau-Cambrésis in 1559. These Italian Wars radically altered the political landscape of the peninsula, leaving Spain dominant in Italy. Florence's time as a republic was brief. The Emperor Charles V, who had sacked Rome in 1527, reinstated the Medici, who went on to rule Florence for the next 210 years.

By the second half of the 16th century, the Church of Rome was obliged to respond to the rise of the Protestant movement (the Reformation), inspired in Germany by Martin Luther. During the Counter-Reformation, the Inquisition, backed by Catholic Spain, was used to suppress heresy. Spain succeeded in dominating Italy during the second half of the 16th century but when Charles II (the last of the Spanish Habsburgs) died in 1700, the War of the Spanish Succession saw Italy become a prize for the dominant European powers. Italy was divided amongst the Austrian Habsburgs, the Spanish Bourbons, Savoy and the independent states. The papacy became less influential, the Jesuits were expelled from Portugal, France and Spain and, thanks to intermarriage between many of the ruling houses of Europe and new trading laws, many national barriers were broken down. The 18th century Age of Enlightenment gave Italy some of its greatest thinkers and writers as well as liberal legal reforms.

Unification

In 1796 Napoleon Bonaparte invaded Italy and declared an Italian Republic under his personal rule. In creating a single political entity, he laid the basis for modern Italy. The Congress of Vienna, which met after the defeat of Napoleon in 1815, reinstated Italy's former rulers. Secret societies, made up of disillusioned middle class intellectuals, fought for a new constitution to reunify the country. One such was founded in 1830 by a Genoan, Giuseppe Mazzini. His 'Young Italy' was committed to liberating the country from foreign dominance and to establishing a unified state under a republican government, a campaign that came to be known as *Il Risorgimento*. During the 1830s and 1840s Mazzini instigated a series of unsuccessful uprisings until he was exiled. By 1848 revolutionary uprisings were taking place all over Europe and the Italian Nationalist movement was gaining ground. Two supporters of the Nationalist cause, Cesare Balbo and Count Camillo Benso di Cavour, advocated an Italian constitution and a bicameral legislature.

As nationalist feeling increased, Giuseppe Garibaldi, whose terrorist activities for Young Italy had obliged him to flee to South America, returned to Italy and allied himself with the Italian National Society. Cavour, the prime minister of Sardinia-Piedmont, attempted to remove Austria from Italy with French help but it was not until Garibaldi and 1,000 volunteers (the Red Shirts) took Sicily and Naples from the Bourbons in 1860 that unification became a real possibility. Garibaldi handed over these kingdoms to Victor Emmanuel II, king of Sardinia-Piedmont. This was to the relief of Cavour, who had feared that Garibaldi might institute a rival republican government in the south. Although Italy was declared a kingdom in 1861 under Victor Emmanuel II, the country was still not unified. Venice was in the hands of the Austrians while France held Rome. In 1866 the Italians took the Veneto from the Prussians and in 1870 Rome was recaptured from the French. Only the Papal troops resisted the advance of the Italian army in 1870 and Pope Pius IX refused to recognize the Kingdom of Italy. In retaliation, the government stripped the pope of his temporal powers. Thus Italy was fully unified.

Twentieth Century

The turn of the 20th century saw popular support fluctuate between left-wing socialist and right-wing imperialist political parties. When the First World War broke out in 1914, Italy remained neutral although the State was associated with the British, French and Russian allies while the Papacy declared for Catholic Austria. In 1919 Benito Mussolini founded the Italian Fascist Party, whose black shirts and Roman salutes were to become the symbols of aggressive nationalism in Italy for the next two decades. In the elections of 1921 the Fascist Party won 35 of the 135 seats in the Italian parliament. A year later, Mussolini raised a militia of 40,000 'Black Shirts' and marched on Rome to 'liberate' it from the socialists. In 1922 the king asked Mussolini to form a government. His Fascist party won the elections of 1924 and Mussolini assumed the title *Il Duce*. By the end of 1925 Mussolini had expelled all opposition parties from parliament and gained control of the trade unions. Four years later, he signed a pact with Pope Pius XI declaring Catholicism the sole religion of Italy and recognizing the Vatican as an independent state. In return, the pope finally recognized the United Kingdom of Italy.

Mussolini's aggressive foreign policy resulted in disputes with Greece over Corfu and military campaigns in the Italian colony of Libya. In 1935 Italy invaded Abyssinia (now Ethiopia) and captured Addis Ababa. The newly formed League of Nations condemned this action and imposed sanctions. In the face of international isolation, Mussolini formed an alliance with the German dictator, Adolf Hitler, and in 1936 the Rome-Berlin Axis was formed. Having annexed Albania in April 1939, Italy entered the Second World War in June 1940. Mussolini's armies invaded Greece from Albania in Oct. 1940 but were repelled, forcing Hitler to invade Yugoslavia and Greece in April 1941. This diversion of German troops has been seen as a critical factor in the ultimate failure of the invasion of the USSR, delayed from May to June 1941. The Italian colonies of East Africa were lost in 1941 and Italian forces in North Africa surrendered in May 1943. The Allied armies landed in Sicily in July 1943 and, in the face of diminishing popular support for fascism and Hitler's refusal to assign more troops to the defence of Italy, the king led a coup against Mussolini and had him arrested. In the 45 days that followed, Italy exploded in a series of uprisings against the war. The king signed an armistice with the Allies and declared war on Germany but Nazi troops had already overrun northern Italy. The Germans rescued Mussolini from prison and installed him as a puppet ruler. In 1945 after trying to flee the country, Mussolini was recaptured by Italian partisans and shot. After the Italian Resistance suffered huge losses against the Germans, the allies liberated northern Italy in May 1945.

Post-War Period

In the years following the end of the Second World War, Italy's political forces attempted to regroup. The Marshall Plan, America's post-war aid programme, exerted considerable political and economic influence. The constitutional monarchy was abolished in 1946 by referendum and a republic was formed with a president (elected for a seven-year term by an electoral college), a two-chamber parliament and a separate judiciary. Initially the newly formed Christian Democrats under Alcide De Gasperi were in power with both the Communist Party and the Socialist Party, participating in a series of coalition governments until they were both excluded by De Gasperi in 1947. More than 300 separate political factions have struggled for power throughout the post-war era and no government has lasted longer than four years. Despite this instability, the war-damaged Italian economy began to pick up in the early 1950s. The industrialized northern regions thrived while the less industrialized south remained underdeveloped. The Cassa per il Mezzogiorno (a state fund for the South) was founded to try to redress the balance but with limited success.

In 1957 Italy became a founder member of the European Economic Community (EEC). The rapid growth of the motor industry, most notably Fiat in Turin, saw huge migrations of peasants from the south to work in the factories. By the mid-1960s the Communist Party, which had been gradually increasing its share of the poll at each election, had more card carrying members than the Christian Democrats but without participating in government. Social unrest was commonplace and in 1969 a series of strikes, demonstrations and riots followed on the heels of unrest elsewhere in Europe. Various terrorist groups were active including the extreme left-wing socialist group, the Red Brigade, founded in 1970. Right-wing neo-fascist terrorists were also in action, and in the less developed south, the Mafia, a loose coalition of crime 'families', flourished. Most of Italy's social, economic and political structures were manipulated by these unofficial organizations.

In 1963 Aldo Moro, a Christian Democrat, was appointed prime minister (a post he held until 1968) and invited the Socialists into his government. By the 1970s he was working towards a compromise to allow the Communists to enter government when he was captured, held hostage and finally murdered by the Red Brigade in 1978. This national outrage prompted the government to appoint Carabinieri Gen. Carlo Alberto dalla Chiesa to wipe out the terrorist groups. He instituted a system of *pentiti* (informants) who, in return for collaboration, would receive greatly reduced prison sentences. In 1980 he was asked to expand his area of operations to include the Mafia but was assassinated in Palermo a few months later. Throughout the 1970s Italy experienced radical social and political change. The country was divided into regional administrative areas with their own elected governments. Divorce became legal, women's rights were expanded (Italian women only achieved full suffrage after the Second World War) and abortion was legalized. In 1983 the minority Christian Democratic government handed the premiership to the Socialists under Bettino Craxi.

Italy was well on its way to becoming one of the world's leading economic powers but the 1990s brought fresh crises in the economic and political arenas. Unemployment and inflation rose sharply which, combined with a huge national debt and unstable lira, led to instability. On the political front, the Communist Party split with the hard-liners forming the

Rifondazione Communista, led by Fausto Bernotti, while the more moderate members set up the Democratic Party of the Left. In early 1992 the arrest of a Socialist Party worker on charges of accepting bribes in exchange for public works contracts sparked off Italy's largest ever political corruption scandal. Investigations into '*Tangentopoli*' ('kick-back city') implicated thousands of politicians, public officials and businessmen. Former Prime Minister Bettino Craxi was forced to resign as party secretary after he came under investigation for bribery. Allied to Italy's humiliating exit from Europe's Exchange Rate Mechanism (ERM), the old political establishment was driven out of office. In the April 1992 elections, the Christian Democrat share of the vote dropped by 5% while the Lega Nord (the Northern League), under Umberto Bossi, took 9% of the vote on an anti-corruption, federalist platform. Oscar Luigi Scalfaro was elected president on a promise to set about reforming electoral laws and clearing up the Tangentopoli scandal. Investigations into corruption continued, despite reprisals from the Mafia. Craxi was convicted *in absentia* while Giulio Andreotti, who was prime minister three times between 1972 and 1992, was brought to trial in 1995 on charges of dealing with the Sicilian Mafia.

In the 1994 elections a right-wing coalition was elected. The Freedom Alliance, including the neo-fascist National Alliance and the federalist Northern League, was led by Silvio Berlusconi, a multi-millionaire media tycoon. Berlusconi lost his majority when the Northern League withdrew after nine months. Under mounting criticism for his failure to disassociate himself from his business interests and after receiving a vote of no confidence, Berlusconi resigned. After leaving the Freedom Alliance, the Northern League became more fanatical, advocating a 'Northern Republic of Padania', a separation of the rich northern regions from the poorer southern ones. The 1996 elections brought to power the centre-left 'Olive Tree' alliance with Romano Prodi as prime minister. Prodi aimed to balance the budget and create a stable political environment. He gained his first objective with a succession of economic measures that prepared the way for Italy's entry into EMU.

Prodi was succeeded by Massimo D'Alema in 1998 who, in turn, was replaced by Giuliano Amato in 2000. By the time of the 2001 elections Berlusconi's popularity had revived and he formed a new centre-right coalition. He introduced the first major constitutional reforms in 55 years, allowing the nation's 20 regions increased responsibility for their own tax, education and environmental programmes.

Berlusconi's tenure was dogged by questions over his private business interests. In Oct. 2002 parliament passed new criminal reform legislation that critics claimed was partly designed to allow Berlusconi to escape charges of corruption. He nonetheless stood trial in May 2003 on corruption charges related to his business dealings in the 1980s but the trial was halted the following month when the new law granted the prime minister immunity from prosecution. The legislation was declared void by the constitutional court in Jan. 2004 and his trial resumed three months later, culminating in his acquittal in Dec. 2004.

The proposed EU constitution was approved by parliament in April 2005, shortly before Berlusconi's government collapsed after a poor showing in regional elections. He was then asked by the president to form a new government but was beaten by Prodi in the general election of April 2006. The following month Giorgio Napolitano was elected president. Prodi resigned in Feb. 2007 when his foreign policy failed to gain Senate backing but resumed his premiership after winning confidence votes in both the upper and lower houses.

In early 2008 Prodi's coalition split when a minor partner withdrew its support. Despite surviving a vote of no confidence in the lower house, Prodi lost a similar vote in the Senate. Parliament was dissolved in Feb. 2008 and Prodi was asked to remain as caretaker prime minister ahead of a general election in April 2008, in which Silvio Berlusconi was returned to power.

The economy was in a parlous state as the global financial crisis deepened. Berlusconi responded by imposing austerity measures but faced several votes of confidence as the economy continued to falter and revelations emerged about his private life. With the IMF warning that the country needed to reduce its public debt, Berlusconi resigned in Nov. 2011 following an impasse in parliament over a new austerity package. He was replaced by Mario Monti, a technocrat charged with restoring economic stability. Monti introduced an austerity programme before his government collapsed in Dec. 2012.

Parliamentary elections in Feb. 2013 resulted in deadlock until April when Giorgio Napolitano was re-elected president and appointed Enrico Letta of the Democratic Party (PD) as prime minister. Letta was replaced as premier in Feb. 2014 by Matteo Renzi, also of the PD, who headed up a new, broad-based coalition. Renzi resigned in Dec. 2016 after constitutional reforms that he championed were rejected in a referendum. He was succeeded by his PD ally Paolo Gentiloni. However, he likewise resigned after elections in March 2018 led to a hung parliament and the establishment in June of a populist and Eurosceptic coalition government headed by Giuseppe Conte, a little-known academic and jurist.

Territory and Population

Italy is bounded in the north by Switzerland and Austria, east by Slovenia and the Adriatic Sea, southeast by the Ionian Sea, south by the Mediterranean Sea, southwest by the Tyrrhenian Sea and Ligurian Sea and west by France.

The area is 301,308 sq. km. Populations at successive censuses (in 1,000) were as follows:

10 Feb. 1901	33,778
10 June 1911	36,921
1 Dec. 1921	37,856
21 April 1931	41,043
21 April 1936	42,399
4 Nov. 1951	47,516
15 Oct. 1961	50,624
24 Oct. 1971	54,137
25 Oct. 1981	56,557
20 Oct. 1991	56,778
21 Oct. 2001	56,996
9 Oct. 2011	59,434

Population in 2011, 59,433,744 (30,688,237 females). Dec. 2017 estimate, 60,483,973; density: 201 per sq. km.

The UN gives a projected population for 2020 of 59·13m.

In 2011, 68·6% of the population lived in urban areas.

The following table gives area and population of the Autonomous Regions (censuses 2001 and 2011):

Regions	Area in sq. km	Resident pop. census, 2001	Resident pop. census, 2011	Density per sq. km, 2011
Piedmont (Piemonte)	25,387	4,214,677	4,363,916	172
Valle d'Aosta[1]	3,261	119,548	126,806	39
Lombardy (Lombardia)	23,861	9,032,554	9,704,151	407
Trentino-Alto Adige[1]	13,606	940,016	1,029,475	76
Bolzano (Bozen)	7,398	462,999	504,643	68
Trento	6,207	477,017	524,832	85
Veneto	18,407	4,527,694	4,857,210	264
Friuli-Venezia Giulia[1]	7,862	1,183,764	1,218,985	155
Liguria	5,416	1,571,783	1,570,694	290
Emilia Romagna	22,453	3,983,346	4,342,135	196
Tuscany (Toscana)	22,987	3,497,806	3,672,202	160
Umbria	8,464	825,826	884,268	105
Marche	9,401	1,470,581	1,541,319	159
Lazio	17,232	5,112,413	5,502,886	320
Abruzzi	10,832	1,262,392	1,307,309	121
Molise	4,461	320,601	313,660	71
Campania	13,671	5,701,931	5,766,810	424

(continued)

Regions	Area in sq. km	Resident pop. census, 2001	Resident pop. census, 2011	Density per sq. km, 2011
Puglia	19,541	4,020,707	4,052,566	209
Basilicata	10,073	597,768	578,036	58
Calabria	15,222	2,011,466	1,959,050	130
Sicily (Sicilia)[1]	25,832	4,968,991	5,002,904	195
Sardinia (Sardegna)[1]	24,100	1,631,880	1,639,362	68

[1]With special statute.

Communes of more than 100,000 inhabitants, with population resident at the census of 9 Oct. 2011:

Rome (Roma)	2,617,175
Milan (Milano)	1,242,123
Naples (Napoli)	962,003
Turin (Torino)	872,367
Palermo	657,561
Genoa (Genova)	586,180
Bologna	371,337
Florence (Firenze)	358,079
Bari	315,933
Catania	293,902
Venice (Venezia)	261,362
Verona	252,520
Messina	243,262
Padua (Padova)	206,192
Trieste	202,123
Taranto	200,154
Brescia	189,902
Prato	185,456
Reggio di Calabria	180,817
Modena	179,149
Parma	175,895
Perugia	162,449
Reggio nell'Emilia	162,082
Livorno	157,052
Ravenna	153,740
Cagliari	149,883
Foggia	147,036
Rimini	139,601
Salerno	132,608
Ferrara	132,545
Sassari	123,782
Monza	119,856
Siracusa (Syracuse)	118,385
Latina	117,892
Pescara	117,166
Forli	116,434
Bergamo	115,349
Trento	114,198
Vicenza	111,500
Terni	109,193
Giugliano in Campania	108,793
Bolzano (Bozen)	102,575
Novara	101,952
Ancona	100,497
Piacenza	100,311
Andria	100,052

The official and by far the most widely spoken language is Italian. In 2011 there were 798,000 native Romanian speakers, 477,000 native Arabic speakers and 380,000 native Albanian speakers. In Jan. 2010, 7·0% of the population was foreign-born.

In addition to Sicily and Sardinia, there are a number of other Italian islands, the largest being Elba (363 sq. km), and the most distant Lampedusa, which is 205 km from Sicily but only 113 km from Tunisia.

Social Statistics

Vital statistics (and rates per 1,000 population), 2008: births, 576,659 (9·6); deaths, 585,126 (9·8). Marriages in 2007, 250,360 (4·2); divorces in 2006, 49,534 (0·8). Infant mortality rate, 2010 (up to one year of age): three per 1,000 live births. Expectation of life, 2007: females, 84·0 years; males, 78·1. In 2010, 20·3% of the population was over 65—one of the highest percentages in the world.

Annual population growth rate, 2010–15, –0·1%; fertility rate, 2008, 1·4 births per woman. With only 17·7% of births being to unmarried mothers in 2007 (albeit up from 8·1% in 1995), Italy has one of the lowest rates of births out of marriage in Europe.

In 2006 there were 3,701 suicides; 76·8% were men.

At 1 Jan. 2007 there were 2,938,922 foreigners living in Italy, up from 2,670,514 a year earlier. In 2005, 53,931 people emigrated from Italy and there were 304,960 immigrants into the country (compared to 440,301 immigrants in 2003). Since 1992 Italy has experienced net immigration every year, although for most of the 20th century up until the mid-1960s it saw mass emigration. Italy received 122,960 asylum applications in 2016 (up from 17,335 in 2012). The most common country of origin is Nigeria, responsible for 22% of all applications in 2016.

Climate

The climate varies considerably with latitude. In the south, it is warm temperate, with little rain in the summer months, but the north is cool temperate with rainfall more evenly distributed over the year. Florence, Jan. 47·7°F (8·7°C), July 79·5°F (26·4°C). Annual rainfall 33" (842 mm). Milan, Jan. 38·7°F (3·7°C), July 73·4°F (23·0°C). Annual rainfall 38" (984 mm). Naples, Jan. 50·2°F (10·1°C), July 77·4°F (25·2°C). Annual rainfall 36" (935 mm). Palermo, Jan. 52·5°F (11·4°C), July 78·4°F (25·8°C). Annual rainfall 35" (897 mm). Rome, Jan. 53·4°F (11·9°C), July 76·3°F (24·6°C). Annual rainfall 31" (793 mm). Venice, Jan. 43·3°F (6·3°C), July 70·9°F (21·6°C). Annual rainfall 32" (830 mm).

Constitution and Government

The Constitution dates from 1948. Italy is 'a democratic republic founded on work'. Parliament consists of the *Chamber of Deputies* and the *Senate.* The Chamber is elected for five years by universal and direct suffrage and consists of 630 deputies. The Senate is elected for five years on a regional basis by electors over the age of 25, each Region having at least seven senators. The total number of senators is 321, of which 315 are directly elected. The Valle d'Aosta is represented by one senator only and Molise by two. The President of the Republic can nominate five senators for life from eminent persons in the social, scientific, artistic and literary spheres. The President may become a senator for life. The *President* is elected in a joint session of Chamber and Senate, to which are added three delegates from each Regional Council (one from the Valle d'Aosta). A two-thirds majority is required for the election, but after a third indecisive scrutiny the absolute majority of votes is sufficient. The President must be 50 years or over; term of office, seven years. The Speaker of the Senate acts as the deputy President. The President can dissolve the chambers of parliament, except during the last six months of the presidential term.

There is a *Constitutional Court* that consists of 15 appointed judges, five each by the President, Parliament (in joint session) and the highest law and administrative courts. The Court can decide on the constitutionality of laws and decrees, define the powers of the State and Regions, judge conflicts between the State and Regions and between the Regions, and try the President and Ministers.

The revival of the Fascist Party is forbidden. Direct male descendants of King Victor Emmanuel are excluded from all public offices and have no right to vote or to be elected; their estates are forfeit to the State. For 56 years they were also banned from Italian territory until the constitution was changed in 2002 to allow them to return from exile.

Italy's electoral law passed in 1948 (and in effect from 1946) allowed for a proportional representation system. It later underwent significant reforms after the passing of the so-called *Matarellum* law in 1993, following approval by referendum. Under these reforms, around three-quarters of Chamber and Senate seats were elected by a first-past-the-post system, the remainder by proportional representation. No party could present more than one candidate in each constituency. There were further extensive reforms in 2005 under the terms of the *Porcellum* law. This introduced a modified proportional representation system on the basis of party and coalition lists (as opposed to individual candidates). However, in 2013 the constitutional court declared aspects of the *Porcellum* law unconstitutional. A new law—the *Italicum* law—was passed in 2015, signalling another overhaul. Dealing with elections to the Chamber of Deputies, it provides for a proportional representation system comprising two rounds of voting based on party lists. It includes a majority-assuring mechanism, whereby the largest party receives a 'majority bonus'. The country is divided into 100 constituencies, each electing between three and nine deputies. Parties designate a list of candidates, each of whom may stand in between one and ten constituencies. In the first round, voters choose a single party's 'head of list' candidate plus up to two more named candidates from the same party. Any party passing a 3% threshold is duly assigned seats. Should any party receive over 40% of the vote, they are automatically attributed a minimum of 340 seats, granting a parliamentary majority without recourse to a second round. However, where no party reaches 40%, a second round is held two weeks later in which electors choose between the two leading parties. The winning party is granted 340 seats, with the remainder distributed on a proportional basis.

National Anthem

'Fratelli d'Italia' ('Brothers of Italy'); words by G. Mameli, tune by M. Novaro, 1847.

Government Chronology

(DC = Christian Democrats; DS = Democrats of the Left-Party of the European Socialism; FI = Forza Italia; PA = Action Party; PD = Democratic Party; PdL = People of Freedom; PLI = Italian Liberal Party; PRI = Italian Republican Party; PSDI = Italian Democratic Socialist Party; PSI = Italian Socialist Party; Ulivo = Olive Tree; n/p = non-partisan)

Presidents of the Italian Republic since 1946.

1946–48	PLI	Enrico De Nicola
1948–55	PLI	Luigi Einaudi
1955–62	DC	Giovanni Gronchi
1962–64	DC	Antonio Segni
1964–71	PSDI	Giuseppe Saragat
1971–78	DC	Giovanni Leone
1978–85	PSI	Sandro Pertini
1985–92	DC	Francesco Cossiga
1992–99	DC	Oscar Luigi Scalfaro
1999–200	n/p	Carlo Azeglio Ciampi
2006–15	DS, n/p	Giorgio Napolitano
2015–	n/p	Sergio Mattarella

Presidents of the Council of Ministers (Prime Ministers) since 1944.

1944–45	n/p	Ivanoe Bonomi
1945	PA	Ferruccio Parri
1945–53	DC	Alcide De Gasperi
1953–54	DC	Giuseppe Pella
1954	DC	Amintore Fanfani
1954–55	DC	Mario Scelba
1955–57	DC	Antonio Segni
1957–58	DC	Adone Zoli
1958–59	DC	Amintore Fanfani
1959–60	DC	Antonio Segni
1960	DC	Fernando Tambroni
1960–63	DC	Amintore Fanfani
1963	DC	Giovanni Leone
1963–68	DC	Aldo Moro

1968	DC	Giovanni Leone
1968–70	DC	Mariano Rumor
1970–72	DC	Emilio Colombo
1972–73	DC	Giulio Andreotti
1973–74	DC	Mariano Rumor
1974–76	DC	Aldo Moro
1976–79	DC	Giulio Andreotti
1979–80	DC	Francesco Cossiga
1980–81	DC	Arnaldo Forlani
1981–82	PRI	Giovanni Spadolini
1982–83	DC	Amintore Fanfani
1983–87	PSI	Benedettino Craxi
1987	DC	Amintore Fanfani
1987–88	DC	Giovanni Giuseppe Goria
1988–89	DC	Ciriaco De Mita
1989–92	DC	Giulio Andreotti
1992–93	PSI	Giuliano Amato
1993–94	n/p	Carlo Azeglio Ciampi
1994–95	FI	Silvio Berlusconi
1995–96	n/p	Lamberto Dini
1996–98	n/p	Romano Prodi
1998–2000	DS	Massimo D'Alema
2000–01	n/p	Giuliano Amato
2001–06	FI	Silvio Berlusconi
2006–08		Ulivo Romano Prodi
2008–11	PdL	Silvio Berlusconi
2011–13	n/p	Mario Monti
2013–14	PD	Enrico Letta
2014–16	PD	Matteo Renzi
2016–18	PD	Paolo Gentiloni
2018–	n/p	Giuseppe Conte

Recent Elections

Parliamentary elections were held on 4 March 2018. Matteo Salvini's centre-right coalition won 265 of 630 seats in the Chamber of Deputies (including the League with 125 seats), the Five Star Movement 227, Matteo Renzi's centre-left coalition 122 (including the Democratic Party, 112), and Free and Equal 14. The Associative Movement Italians Abroad and the South American Union Italian Emigrants gained one seat each. Turnout was 72·9%. In the Senate, Salvini's coalition won 137 of 315 seats (including the League, 58), the Five Star Movement 112, Renzi's coalition 60, and Free and Equal four. Again, the Associative Movement Italians Abroad and the South American Union Italian Emigrants took one seat each.

Sergio Mattarella was elected president by an assembly of lawmakers and regional representatives on 31 Jan. 2015, winning 665 votes to Ferdinando Imposimato's 127 with 46 for Vittorio Feltri and 17 for Stefano Rodotà in the fourth round of voting after three earlier rounds had failed to produce a clear result.

European Parliament

Italy has 73 representatives. At the May 2014 elections turnout was 57·2% (65·1% in 2009). The Democratic Party won 31 seats with 40·8% of votes cast (political affiliation in European Parliament: Progressive Alliance of Socialists and Democrats); the Five Star Movement, 17 with 21·2% (Europe of Freedom and Direct Democracy); Forza Italia, 13 with 16·8% (European People's Party); the Northern League, 5 with 6·2% (non-attached); alliance of New Centre-Right, Union of the Centre and Populars for Italy, 3 with 4·4% (European People's Party); the Other Europe, 3 with 4·0% (European United Left/Nordic Green Left); South Tyrolean People's Party, 1 with 0·5% (European People's Party).

Current Government

President: Sergio Mattarella; b. 1941 (sworn in 3 Feb. 2015).
In Feb. 2019 the coalition government comprised:
President of the Council of Ministers (Prime Minister): Giuseppe Conte; b. 1964 (ind.; sworn in 1 June 2018).

(*continued*)

Secretary of the Council of Ministers: Giancarlo Giorgetti.

Vice-Presidents of the Council of Ministers: Luigi Di Maio (also *Minister of Economic Development, Labour and Social Policy*); Matteo Salvini (also *Minister of Interior*).

Minister of Agriculture, Food and Forestry: Gian Marco Centinaio. *Cultural Heritage and Tourism:* Alberto Bonisoli. *Defence:* Elisabetta Trenta. *Education, Universities and Research:* Marco Bussetti. *Environment, and Protection of Land and Sea:* Sergio Costa. *Finance:* Giovani Tria. *Foreign Affairs:* Enzo Moavero Milanese. *Health:* Giulia Grillo. *Infrastructure and Transport:* Danilo Toninelli. *Justice:* Alfonso Bonafede. *Ministers without Portfolio:* Giulia Bongiorno (for *Public Administration*); Lorenzo Fontana (for *Family and Disability*); Riccardo Fraccaro (for *Parliamentary Relations and Direct Democracy*); Paolo Savona (for *European Affairs*); Erika Stefani (for *Regional Affairs*); Barbara Lezzi (for *the South*).

Speaker of the Chamber of Deputies: Roberto Fico.

Government Website (Italian only): http://www.governo.it

Current Leaders

Sergio Mattarella

Position

President

Introduction

Sergio Mattarella was sworn in as president in Feb. 2015. Having previously held a number of cabinet posts, he co-founded the centre-left Democratic Party (PD) in 2007. Prior to becoming president, he served for four years as a judge at the constitutional court.

Early Life

Mattarella was born on 23 July 1941 in Palermo, Sicily. His father was a politician who co-founded the Christian Democrats (DC). His brother, Piersanti, was a prominent member of the party and president of Sicily's regional government before being assassinated in 1980 by the Mafia.

In 1964 Mattarella graduated in law from La Sapienza University in Rome. Having taught at the University of Palermo's law faculty and joined the Palermo Bar Association in 1967, he entered frontline politics following his brother's murder. He was elected to the Chamber of Deputies in 1983 as a member of the DC, retaining his seat until 2008.

After a period as minister for parliamentary affairs, he served as minister of education from 1989–90, whereupon he was elected party vice-secretary before resigning to become editor of the party newspaper, *Il Popolo*. When the DC was dissolved in 1994, on the back of a wide-ranging corruption scandal, Mattarella helped found a successor party, the Italian People's Party (PPI). When the PPI fostered closer ties with Silvio Berlusconi's Forza Italia party, Mattarella resigned in protest from his post on *Il Popolo*, although he retained his party membership.

In 1998 he became deputy prime minister in the government of Massimo D'Alema. He was minister of defence from 1999–2001, during which time conscription was abolished. He kept the defence portfolio for a further year after D'Alema was succeeded by Giuliano Amato. In 2007 he was one of the founders of the PD and in 2011 parliament ratified his appointment as a constitutional judge.

Career in Office

In 2015 Mattarella was nominated for the presidency by then Prime Minister Matteo Renzi and endorsed by the PD. He was elected on 31 Jan. with 665 of 1,009 parliamentary and regional representative votes after four rounds of voting, overtaking the early front-runner, Ferdinando Imposimato. Mattarella is the first Sicilian to hold the largely ceremonial role. He has stated that nations must be united 'to defeat whoever wants to drag us into a new age of terror'.

In Dec. 2016, having lost a referendum on proposed controversial constitutional reforms, Renzi resigned as prime minister and Mattarella appointed Paolo Gentiloni, previously the foreign minister, as his successor.

Legislative elections in March 2018 resulted in a hung parliament, although Eurosceptic and anti-establishment parties won more than half of the overall vote. Gentiloni consequently resigned and, after weeks of party wrangling, Mattarella swore in Giuseppe Conte, a non-political lawyer, as prime minister at the head of a fragile coalition government comprising the populist left-wing Five Star Movement and the nationalist League.

Giuseppe Conte

Position

Prime Minister

Introduction

Giuseppe Conte took office as prime minister in June 2018 following an inconclusive general election and three-months of political deadlock. A law professor from southern Italy, he had no prior political experience before his selection as a compromise candidate by the two largest parties.

Early Life

Conte was born in Volturara Appula, near Foggia, on 8 Aug. 1964. He graduated in law from the Sapienza University of Rome in 1988 and during the 1990s worked as a lecturer in law at the Libera Università Maria SS. Assunta, a private Catholic University in Rome. He also worked at the University of Sassari, Sardinia, and established a law practice in Rome.

In 2013 Conte was elected as a member of the Bureau of Administrative Justice by the Chamber of Deputies, part of the lower house of the Parliament. A legal consultant to Rome's chamber of commerce, Conte also lectured in public administration law at LUISS University in Rome and Florence University.

In early 2018 Conte was approached by the leader of the anti-establishment Five Star Movement, Luigi di Maio, as a potential ministerial candidate in the event of victory in the March general election. After the inconclusive polling and three months of political wrangling, Conte emerged as a compromise prime ministerial candidate for the Five Star Movement and the election's other nominal victor, the hard-right League led by Matteo Salvini. Conte was eventually asked by President Sergio Mattarella to succeed Paolo Gentiloni as premier and form a new government. He was sworn in on 1 June 2018.

Career in Office

Conte's cabinet comprised an uneasy alliance of Five Star Movement and League members, alongside independent economists and financial experts. He has pledged to streamline Italy's bureaucratic administration, but the coalition's programme of increased public spending while reducing taxes is ambitious given Italy's towering public debt and the troubled banking sector.

Defence

Head of the armed forces is the Defence Chief of Staff. Conscription was abolished at the end of 2004 with the military becoming all-professional from 2005. In Aug. 1998 the government voted to allow women into the armed forces.

In 2013 defence expenditure totalled US$25,229m. (US$410 per capita), representing 1·2% of GDP (compared to the NATO target of 2%).

Army

Strength (2011) 107,500. Equipment includes 120 *Leopard*, 300 *Centauro* and 200 *Ariete* tanks. There are 38,300 Army reserves.

The paramilitary Carabinieri (police force with military status) number 106,700.

Navy

The principal ships of the Navy are the aircraft carriers *Giuseppe Garibaldi* and *Cavour*, commissioned in 1985 and 2008 respectively. The combatant forces also include six diesel submarines, four destroyers and 12 frigates. The Naval Air Arm, 2,200 strong, operates 16 combat aircraft and 50 helicopters.

Main naval bases are at La Spezia, Brindisi, Taranto and Augusta. The personnel of the Navy numbered 33,000 in 2011. There were 3,800 naval reservists.

Air Force

The Air Force has four Commands: air squadron; training; logistics; operations.

Air Force strength in 2011 was about 43,000. There were 247 combat aircraft in operation in 2011 including Typhoons and Tornados.

Economy

Agriculture accounted for 2% of GDP, industry 24% and services 74% in 2012.

Italy's 'shadow' (black market) economy is estimated to constitute approximately 17% of the country's official GDP.

Italy gave US$5·9bn. in international aid in 2017, equivalent to 0·30% of GNI (compared to the UN target of 0·7%).

Overview

The Italian economy is among the eurozone's largest but has suffered from weak growth since the late 1990s. Its main sectors are tourism, fashion, engineering, chemical and automotive manufacturing and food production. A diversified industrial sector exists mainly in the north, driven by small- and medium-sized enterprises (many of which are family-owned) producing high-quality consumer goods. Italy has the eighth largest export economy in the world and its main trading partners in 2015 were Germany (which accounted for 12% of exports), France (10%) and the USA (8%). Foreign direct investment averaged 0·7% of GDP between 2009 and 2015, ranking Italy 10th among global investors, but was nevertheless well behind other leading European countries.

Over the decade to 2015 the economy recorded average annual growth of 0·7% as investment concerns, high unemployment and low consumption weakened productivity. The economy was smaller in 2015 than in 2000, with GDP per capita declining over that period by 16·3%. In the decade leading up to the global financial crisis, Italy lost significant market share in world trade as a result of its specialization in slow-growing sectors of world demand, comparatively weak foreign direct investment and low investment in research and development. The economy contracted by 5·5% in 2009 as the country entered its worst recession since the Second World War. Italy struggled to emerge from the downturn and a second contraction that began in mid-2011 lasted through to 2014 when GDP increased by 0·2%. Subsequent growth rates of 0·8% and 1·0% were recorded in 2015 and 2016 respectively, before a 1·6% rise in 2017 buoyed by a spike in business investment as companies took advantage of generous tax incentives. However, this figure was still below the eurozone's average of 2·5%.

There is a stark divide between the richer, industrialized north that boasts some of the highest incomes in Europe and the less developed, welfare-dependent, agricultural south (known as the *Mezzogiorno*). This gap was magnified by the global financial crisis and exacerbated by the growth of the shadow economy (particularly in the agricultural and construction sectors), which has been estimated to be worth around 20% of GDP annually.

Public debt stood at a record 132·7% of GDP in 2015, burdening Italy with funding requirements of €450bn. In the same year the government deficit was recorded at 2·6% of GDP, before declining to 2·4% by 2018. The 2018 budget repealed a VAT increase planned for the year and extended tax incentives for business investment and real estate improvements. It also introduced lower social security contributions for young people hired on a permanent basis, while allocating resources for raising civil servants' wages. The country has one of the most restrictive labour markets in Europe, leading to structural unemployment. The jobless rate peaked in Nov. 2014 at a record 13·0% (compared to the then eurozone average of 11·5%) but had declined to 11·4% by Nov. 2015 (against the eurozone's 10·5%). In 2017 the employment rate increased by 1·2%, while unemployment stood at 11·2%. Youth unemployment remains one of the highest in Europe and has been increasing steadily since about 2005, peaking at over 44% in the second quarter of 2015 (the highest level since the late 1970s) before falling to 34·8% in 2018.

In Dec. 2016 a referendum on constitutional reform brought down Prime Minister Matteo Renzi's administration. The resulting political instability compounded the ongoing crisis in the banking sector, spurred by high levels of non-performing loans (NPLs). According to the European Banking Authority, around 17% of all loans issued by Italian banks were non-performing in 2016, with the third largest Italian bank—Banca Monte dei Paschi di Siena—holding €45bn. worth. The government earmarked €20bn. (1·2% of GDP) to deal with banking sector vulnerabilities, leading to a significant reduction in NPLs by mid-2017.

With low birth rates and a rising proportion of people over 65, Italy faces one of the greatest challenges from population ageing of any country in the Organisation for Economic Co-operation and Development. The ageing society, together with ongoing eurozone financial difficulties, low productivity, high unemployment, weak competitiveness and a growing regional divide, are all expected to constrain Italy's medium-term growth prospects. Quota-driven immigration is a further brake on economic activity. The implementation of planned structural reform is necessary to support business

expansion and attract foreign investment, which is historically low owing to complex bureaucracy and inconsistent enforcement of regulations, and to secure a durable, long-term recovery.

Currency

On 1 Jan. 1999 the *euro* (EUR) became the legal currency in Italy at the irrevocable conversion rate of 1,936·27 lire to 1 euro. The euro, which consists of 100 cents, has been in circulation since 1 Jan. 2002. On the introduction of the euro there was a 'dual circulation' period before the lira ceased to be legal tender on 28 Feb. 2002.

Inflation rates (based on OECD statistics):

2008	2009	2010	2011	2012	2013	2014	2015	2016	2017
3·5%	0·8%	1·6%	2·9%	3·3%	1·2%	0·2%	0·1%	−0·1%	1·3%

In Sept. 2009 gold reserves were 78·83m. troy oz and foreign exchange reserves US$35,474m. Total money supply in Aug. 2009 was €711,993m.

Budget

In 2011 central government revenues totalled €595·17bn. (€591·83bn. in 2010) and expenditures €655·81bn. (€654·26bn. in 2010). Principal sources of revenue in 2011: social security contributions, €211·97bn.; taxes on income, profits and capital gains, €191·98bn.; taxes on goods and services, €132·44bn. Main items of expenditure by economic type in 2011: social benefits, €302·95bn.; grants, €118·47bn.; compensation of employees, €98·39bn.

Italy's budget deficit in 2017 was 2·4% of GDP (2016, 2·5%, 2015, 2·6%). The required target set by the EU is a budget deficit of no more than 3%.

VAT was increased from 21% to 22% in Oct. 2013. There are reduced of 10%, 5% and 4%.

The public debt totalled €1,988,363m. at 31 Dec. 2012.

Performance

Real GDP growth rates (based on OECD statistics):

2008	2009	2010	2011	2012	2013	2014	2015	2016	2017
−1·0%	−5·5%	1·6%	0·7%	−2·9%	−1·7%	0·2%	0·8%	1·0%	1·6%

According to the National Institute of Statistics, the real GDP growth rate was 0·9% in 2018. Total GDP was US$1,934·8bn. in 2017.

Banking and Finance

The bank of issue is the Bank of Italy (founded 1893). It is owned by public-sector banks. Its *Governor* (Ignazio Visco) is nominated by the government for a six-year term, renewable once. In 1991 it received increased responsibility for the supervision of banking and stock exchange affairs, and in 1993 greater independence from the government.

The number of banks has gradually been declining in recent years, from 1,176 in 1990 to 807 (32,818 branches) in 2007. Of these, 439 were mutual banks and 39 were co-operative banks. Italy's largest bank in terms of assets is UniCredit (until May 2008 known as UniCredito Italiano). In June 2005 UniCredito Italiano finalized an agreement to acquire Germany's Hypo-Vereinsbank in Europe's biggest cross-border banking takeover. In 2006 it had Italian assets of €282bn. (€752bn. including assets from its German and Eastern European operations). In Aug. 2006 Italy's second and third largest banks, Banca Intesa and Sanpaolo IMI, agreed to merge. The merger was approved in Dec. 2006, creating the largest Italian bank, Intesa Sanpaolo, with assets of €541bn.

The 'Amato' law of July 1990 gave public sector banks the right to become joint stock companies and permitted the placing of up to 49% of their equity with private shareholders. In 1999 the last state-controlled bank was sold off.

On 31 Dec. 2005 banks had total deposits of €690,746m.

Gross external debt totalled US$2,356,371m. in June 2012.

Italy attracted US$17·1bn. worth of foreign direct investment in 2017, down from a record US$43·8bn. in 2007.

Legislation reforming stock markets came into effect in Dec. 1990. In 1996 local stock exchanges, relics of pre-unification Italy, were closed, and stock exchange activities concentrated in Milan.

Energy and Natural Resources

In 2011, 11·5% of energy consumption came from renewables (wind power, solar power, hydro-electric power, tidal power, geothermal energy and biomass), compared to the European Union average of 13·0%. A target of 17% has been set by the EU for 2020.

Environment

Italy's carbon dioxide emissions from the consumption of energy in 2011 were the equivalent of 6·7 tonnes per capita.

Electricity

In 2011 installed capacity was 118,443 MW and the total power generated was 301·8bn. kWh (75·5% thermal and 15·8% hydro-electric). Consumption per capita was 5,733 kWh in 2011. Italy has four nuclear reactors in permanent shutdown, the last having closed in 1990. Plans to build a series of new reactors were proposed in 2008, but were subsequently abandoned following a referendum in 2011 in which 94% of votes cast were against the construction of new nuclear plants.

Oil and Gas

Oil production, 2012, 5·4m. tonnes. Proven oil reserves in 2012 were 1·4bn. bbls. In 2012 natural gas production was 7·8bn. cu. metres with proven reserves of 100bn. cu. metres.

Minerals

Output in 2013 included: sand and gravel, 102·4m. tonnes; crushed and broken stone, 63·8m. tonnes; limestone for lime and cement, 24·7m. tonnes; silica sand, 13·9m. tonnes; feldspar (estimate), 4·7m. tonnes; pozzolan (estimate), 4·0m.; salt, 2·9m. tonnes. Italy is the world's second largest producer of feldspar, after Turkey.

Agriculture

In 2012, 833,400 persons were employed in agriculture, of whom 242,100 were female. The agricultural area totalled 13,630,000 ha. in 2013. Italy had 6,827,000 ha. of arable land in 2013 and 2,260,000 ha. of permanent crops. There were 1,621,000 agricultural holdings in 2010, down from 2,154,000 in 2000. In 2012 organic crops were grown in an area covering 1·17m. ha., representing 8·6% of all agricultural land.

Food and live animals accounted for 5·7% of exports and 7·1% of imports in 2010.

Output of principal crops (in 1,000 tonnes) in 2013: grapes, 8,010; maize, 7,900; wheat, 7,312; tomatoes, 5,321; olives, 2,941; apples, 2,217; sugar beets, 2,159; oranges, 1,701; rice, 1,433; peaches and nectarines, 1,402; potatoes, 1,272; barley, 876.

Wine production in 2010 totalled 48,525,000 hectolitres (18·4% of the world total) making Italy the world's largest wine producer. Wine consumption has declined considerably in recent times, from more than 110 litres per person in 1966 to 50·1 litres per person in 2008.

Livestock, 2013: pigs, 8,561,683; sheep, 7,181,828; cattle, 5,846,672; goats, 975,858; buffaloes, 402,659; horses, 393,915; chickens (estimate), 136m. Livestock products, 2013 (in 1,000 tonnes): cow's milk, 10,398; sheep's milk, 384; buffalo's milk, 195; pork and pork products, 1,652; poultry meat, 1,215; beef and veal, 842; cheese (estimate), 1,243; butter, 98; eggs, 710.

Forestry

In 2015 forests covered 9·30m. ha. or 32% of the total land area. Timber production was 7·74m. cu. metres in 2011.

Fisheries

In 2012 the fishing fleet comprised 12,783 vessels of 165,619 GT. The catch in 2015 was 196,988 tonnes, of which more than 98% were from marine waters. Imports of fishery commodities were valued at US$6,211m. in 2012 and exports at US$775m.

Industry

The leading companies by market capitalization in Italy in May 2018 were: Eni, an integrated oil and gas company (US$70·7bn.); Intesa Sanpaolo, a banking group (US$63·1bn.); and Enel, an electricity and gas company (US$61·6bn.).

In 2007 industry accounted for 28% of GDP, with manufacturing contributing 18%.

Industrial products (in tonnes): cement (2008), 43·0m.; distillate fuel oil (including San Marino; 2007), 41·1m.; crude steel (2007), 32·0m.; petrol (including San Marino; 2007), 21·4m.; residual fuel oil (including San Marino; 2007), 17·4m.; pig iron (2006), 11·5m.; lime (2005), 5·9m.; polyethylene (2014), 751,000.

Motor vehicle production in 2009 totalled 843,239 units (661,100 cars). In 2007, 1·34m. fridge-freezers and 9·83m. washing and drying machines were produced. In 2014 Italy produced 22,891m. litres of soft drinks, 12,550m. litres of mineral water and 1,352m. litres of beer.

Labour

The labour force in 2013 was 25,474,000 (24,007,000 in 2003). 63·9% of the population aged 15–64 was economically active in 2013. Of those in employment in 2013, 69·4% worked in services, 27·2% in industry and 3·4% in agriculture. In that year 41·8% of the labour force was female. 47·1% of the labour force had a secondary education as the highest level and 18·8% had a tertiary education. Unemployment stood at 10·3% in Dec. 2018 (down from 11·2% in 2017 as a whole). Long-term unemployment is particularly high, with 48·5% of the labour force in 2010 having been out of work for more than a year. In 2014 the pensionable retirement age was 62 years and 3 months for women employed in the private sector and 66 years and 3 months for men and for women in the public sector. The pensionable retirement age is gradually increasing and in 2018 was 66 years and 7 months for both men and women. This was set to increase to 67 for both sexes from 1 Jan. 2019. However, the new government that took office in June 2018 is aiming to reverse proposed increases in the retirement age.

Italy had 8,000 people living in slavery according to the Walk Free Foundation's 2013 *Global Slavery Index*.

International Trade

Imports and Exports

The following table shows the value of Italy's foreign trade (in US$1bn.):

	2006	2007	2008	2009	2010
Imports c.i.f.	442·6	511·8	561·0	414·8	486·6
Exports f.o.b.	417·2	500·2	541·8	406·5	447·5

Principal import suppliers, 2010 (US$1m.): Germany, 77,464; France, 40,323; China, 38,135; Netherlands, 25,957; Spain, 22,051. Principal export markets, 2010 (US$1m.): Germany, 57,809; France, 51,515; USA, 26,832; Spain, 25,707; UK, 23,722.

Imports/exports by category, 2010 (in US$1bn.):

	Imports	Exports
Beverages and tobacco	4·6	7·2
Chemicals and related products	65·7	51·2
Food and live animals	34·8	25·5
Inedible crude materials, excluding fuels	20·1	5·8
Machinery and transport equipment	132·6	159·0
Manufactured goods and articles	121·9	161·6
Mineral fuels and lubricants	92·1	21·8
Other products	14·8	13·1

Communications

Roads

Roads totalled 175,430 km in 2005, of which 6,542 km were motorways, 21,524 km were highways and main roads, and 147,364 km were regional and provincial roads. In 2005 there were 47,104,048 motor vehicles, including: passenger cars, 34,882,476 (594 per 1,000 inhabitants); buses and coaches, 96,477; vans and trucks, 3,982,001. There were 5,426 fatalities in road accidents in 2005.

Rail

The length of state-run railway (*Ferrovie dello Stato*) in 2011 was 16,726 km (11,925 km electrified). Italy's first section of high-speed railway opened in

1981; by 2009 the total length had reached 923 km. In 2011 the railways carried 522·9m. passengers and 46·1m. tonnes of freight. There are metros in Milan (76·0 km), Rome (38·0 km), Naples (29·8 km), Turin (9·6 km), Genoa (5·3 km) and Catania (3·8 km), and tram/light rail networks in Bergamo, Cagliari, Florence, Genoa, Messina, Milan, Naples, Padua, Perugia, Rome, Sassari, Trieste, Turin and Venice. A driverless automated metro system opened in Brescia in March 2013.

Civil Aviation

There are major international airports at Bologna (G. Marconi), Genoa (Cristoforo Colombo), Milan (Linate and Malpensa), Naples (Capodichino), Pisa (Galileo Galilei), Rome (Leonardo da Vinci/Fiumicino), Turin (Caselle) and Venice (Marco Polo). A number of other airports have a small selection of international flights. Alitalia commenced operations in Jan. 2009 as a privately-owned company (25%-owned by Air France-KLM), having taken over the name, landing rights and significant assets of the former national carrier (also Alitalia, which went bankrupt in 2008) and having merged with rival airline Air One. In Dec. 2014 the Abu Dhabi-based Etihad Airways purchased a 49% stake in Alitalia. There are a number of other Italian airlines, notably Air Italy. In 2013 the Alitalia group carried 23,993,486 passengers. In 2012 Rome (Fiumicino) airport handled 36,980,157 passengers (24,925,722 on international flights) and 143,172 tonnes of freight. Milan Malpensa was the second busiest for passengers, handling 18,522,760 (14,773,460 on international flights), but the busiest for freight, with 414,318 tonnes.

Shipping

In Jan. 2014 there were 777 ships of 300 GT or over registered, totalling 17·39m. GT. Of the 777 vessels registered, 267 were passenger ships, 243 oil tankers, 133 general cargo ships, 94 bulk carriers, 24 liquid gas tankers and 16 container ships. The Italian-controlled fleet comprised 1,003 vessels of 1,000 GT or over in July 2014, of which 525 were under the Italian flag and 478 under foreign flags. The chief ports are Trieste (which handled 56,586,000 tonnes of cargo in 2013), Genoa (49,541,000 tonnes in 2013) and Livorno (27,953,000 tonnes in 2013). Gioia Tauro, the busiest container port, handled 3·7m. TEUs (twenty-foot equivalent units) in 2013.

Telecommunications

In May 1999 Olivetti bought a controlling stake in the telephone operator Telecom Italia, and in July 2001 Pirelli, backed by the Benetton clothing empire, in turn paid €7bn. (US$6·1bn.) to take over control of Telecom Italia. In 2014 mobile phone subscriptions numbered 94,200,000, equivalent to 1,542·5 per 1,000 persons. TIM (Telecom Italia Mobile) is the largest operator, with a 34% share of the market, just ahead of Vodafone Italia, which has a 33% share. There were 20,570,000 main (fixed) telephone lines in 2014. 62·0% of the population were internet users in 2014. There were 235·3 fixed broadband subscriptions per 1,000 inhabitants in 2014. In March 2012 there were 20·9m. Facebook users.

Social Institutions

Out of 178 countries analysed in the 2017 *Fragile States Index*—a list published jointly by the Fund for Peace and *Foreign Policy* magazine—Italy was ranked the 37th least vulnerable to conflict or collapse. The index is based on 12 indicators of state vulnerability across social, political and economic categories.

Justice

Italy has one court of cassation, in Rome, and is divided for the administration of justice into 29 appeal court districts, subdivided into 164 tribunal *circondari* (districts). There are also 93 first degree assize courts and 29 assize courts of appeal. For civil business, besides the magistracy above mentioned, *Giudici di pace* have jurisdiction in petty plaints.

2,818,834 crimes were reported in 2012. In Aug. 2013 there were 64,835 persons in prison (including persons imprisoned by San Marino). In 1947 the re-established democracy rewrote the Legislative Order; the constitution of the Italian Republic abolished the death penalty sanctioned in 1930 by Codice Penale, commonly known as Codice Rocco. Although the death penalty was abolished for ordinary crimes in 1947, it was not until 1994 that it was abolished for all crimes.

Italy was ranked 25th of 102 countries for criminal justice and 36th for civil justice in the 2015 World Justice Project *Rule of Law Index*, which provides data on how the rule of law is experienced by the general public across eight categories.

Education

Five years of primary and five years of secondary education are compulsory from the age of six. In 2005–06 there were 24,845 pre-school institutions with 1,662,139 children and 140,687 teachers (state and non-state schools); 18,218 primary schools with 2,790,254 pupils and 293,091 teachers (state and non-state schools); 7,886 compulsory secondary schools (*scuole secondarie primo grado*) with 1,764,230 pupils and 211,093 teachers (state and non-state schools); and 6,565 higher secondary schools with 2,691,713 pupils and 305,383 teachers (state and non-state schools).

Higher secondary education is subdivided into classical (*ginnasio* and classical *liceo*), scientific (scientific *liceo*), language lyceum, professional institutes and technical education: agricultural, industrial, commercial, technical, nautical institutes, institutes for surveyors, institutes for girls (five-year course) and teacher-training institutes (five-year course).

In 2005–06 there were 98 universities (79 state and 19 non-state), of which two are universities of Italian studies for foreigners, three specialized universities (commerce; education; Roman Catholic), three polytechnical university institutes; seven specialized university institutes (architecture; bio-medicine; modern languages; naval studies; oriental studies; social studies; teacher training). In 2005–06 there were 1,823,886 university students and 61,097 academic staff. Europe's first university was founded in 1088 in Bologna.

Estimated adult literacy rate, 2009, 98·9% (male 99·2%; female 98·6%).

In 2008 public expenditure on education came to 4·6% of GDP and 9·4% of total government spending.

Health

In 2013 there were 199,474 hospital beds (331·2 per 100,000 population). There were 165,384 curative care beds in 2013, 24,506 rehabilitative care beds and 9,584 long-term care beds. There were 246,834 physicians, 28,566 dentists and 59,580 pharmacists in 2008; and 379,213 nursing and midwifery personnel in 2009. In 2009 Italy spent 9·5% of its GDP on health.

Welfare

Social expenditure is made up of transfers which the central public departments, local departments and social security departments make to families. Payment is principally for pensions, family allowances and health services. Expenditure on subsidies, public assistance to various classes of people and people injured by political events or national disasters are also included.

In 2014 the minimum retirement age was 66 years and 3 months for men and for women in the public sector and 62 years and 3 months for women employed in the private sector. Since then it has risen gradually to 66 years and 7 months in 2018. In order to receive this 'old-age pension', social security contributions must have been made for at least 20 years (five years if the claimant is aged 70 or older). The age restriction does not apply in the case of men who started making contributions before 1 Jan. 1996 with 42 years and 10 months of pension contributions, and women with 41 years and 10 months. Pensions accounted for 15·4% of GDP in 2009.

Public pensions are indexed to prices; 23,257,480 pensions were paid in 2005, with payments totalling €214,881·3m. (including 16,875,341 private sector, with payments totalling €152,483·5m.). The average annual pension in 2005 was €9,239. Social contributions in 2005 totalled €184,642m.

Religion

The treaty between the Holy See and Italy of 11 Feb. 1929, confirmed by article 7 of the Constitution of the republic, lays down that the Catholic Apostolic Roman Religion is the only religion of the State. Other creeds are permitted, provided they do not profess principles, or follow rites, contrary to public order or moral behaviour.

The appointment of archbishops and of bishops is made by the Holy See; but the Holy See submits to the Italian government the name of the person to be appointed in order to obtain an assurance that the latter will not raise objections of a political nature. In Feb. 2019 there were 44 cardinals.

According to the Pew Research Center's Forum on Religion & Public Life, in 2010 there were an estimated 50·3m. Roman Catholics, 7·5m. people with no religious affiliation, 2·2m. Muslims, 800,000 Protestants and 500,000 other Christians.

Culture

Milan hosted Expo 2015 under the theme 'Feeding the Planet, Energy for Life' from 1 May to 31 Oct. 2015.

Matera is one of two European Capitals of Culture for 2019. The title attracts large European Union grants.

World Heritage Sites

There are 54 UNESCO sites in Italy (the most of any country): the Rock Drawings in Valcamonica near Brescia (inscribed in 1979); Santa Maria delle Grazie with 'The Last Supper' by Leonardo da Vinci (1980); San Paolo Fuori le Mura Historic Centre of Florence (1982); Venice and its Lagoon (1987); Piazza del Duomo, Pisa (1987 and 2007); Historic Centre of San Gimignano (1990); I Sassi di Matera (1993); Vicenza, the City of Palladio and the Villas of the Veneto (1994 and 1996); Historic Centre of Siena (1995); Historic Centre of Naples (1995); Ferrara and its Po Delta (1995 and 1999); Crespi d'Adda (1995); Castel del Monte (1996); Trulli of Alberobello (1996); Early Christian Monuments and Mosaics of Ravenna (1996); Historic Centre of the City of Pienza (1996); The 18th-Century Royal Palace at Caserta with the Park, the Aqueduct of Vanvitelli and the San Leucio Complex (1997); Residences of the Royal House of Savoy (1997); Botanical Garden (Orto Botanico), Padua (1997); Cathedral, Torre Civica and Piazza Grande, Modena (1997); Archaeological Areas of Pompeii, Ercolano and Torre Annunziata (1997); Villa Romana del Casale (1997); Su Nuraxi di Barumini (1997); Portovenere, Cinque Terre and the Islands (Palmaria, Tino and Tinetto) (1997); The Costiera Amalfitana (1997); Archaeological Area of Agrigento (1997); Cilento and Vallo di Diano National Park (1998); Historic Centre of Urbino (1998); Archaeological Area and the Patriarchal Basilica of Aquileia (1998); Villa Adriana (1999); Aeolian Islands (2000); Assisi (2000); the City of Verona (2000); Villa d'Este, Tivoli (2001); the Late Baroque Towns of the Val di Noto (2002); Monte San Giorgio (2003); Sacri Monti of Piedmont and Lombardy (2003); Val d'Orcia (2004), part of the agricultural hinterland of Siena; the Etruscan Necropolises of Cerveteri and Tarquinia (2004); Syracuse and the Rocky Necropolis of Pantalica (2005); Genoa (2006), featuring the Strade Nuove and the system of the Palazzi dei Rolli; Mantua and Sabbioneta (2008); the Dolomites (2009); the Longobards in Italy, Places of Power, 568–774 AD, comprising seven groups of important buildings throughout the country (2011); the Medici Villas and Gardens in Tuscany (2013); Mount Etna (2013); Vineyard Landscape of Piedmont: Langhe-Roero and Monferrato (2014); Arab–Norman Palermo and the Cathedral Churches of Cefalú and Monreale (2015); and Ivrea, industrial city of the 20th century (2018).

The Historic Centre of Rome, the properties of the Holy See in that city enjoying extraterritorial rights (1980 and 1990), is shared with Vatican City State. Ancient and Primeval Beech Forests of the Carpathians and Other Regions of Europe (2007 and 2017) are shared with Albania, Austria, Belgium, Bulgaria, Croatia, Germany, Romania, Slovakia, Slovenia, Spain and Ukraine. The Rhaetian Railway in the Albula/Bernina Landscapes (2008) is shared with Switzerland. The Prehistoric Pile dwellings around the Alps (2011) are shared with Austria, France, Germany, Slovenia and Switzerland. The Venetian Works of Defence between the 16th and 17th Centuries: *Stato da Terra*—Western *Stato da Mar* (2017) are shared with Croatia and Montenegro.

Press

In 2011 there were 97 paid-for dailies with a combined circulation of 4·3m. copies and ten free dailies with a combined circulation of 1·7m. copies. Several of the papers are owned or supported by political parties. The church and various economic groups exert strong right of centre influence on editorial opinion. Most newspapers are regional but *Corriere della Sera* (which has the highest circulation of any Italian newspaper), *La Repubblica*, *Il Sole 24 Ore*, *La Gazzetta* and *La Stampa* are the most important of those papers that are nationally circulated. In 2011 there were 101 newspaper online editions.

Tourism

In 2010, 43·6m. international tourists visited Italy (43·2m. in 2009); receipts from tourism in 2010 were US$38·8bn. (US$40·2bn. in 2009). Only France, the USA, China and Spain received more foreign tourists in 2010.

Festivals

One of the most traditional festivals in Italy is the Carnival di Ivrea which lasts for a week in late Feb. or early March. Among the famous arts festivals is the Venice Film Festival in Sept. Venice also plays host, in the ten days before Ash Wednesday, to a large carnival. Major music festivals are the Maggio Musicale Fiorentino in Florence (May–June), the Ravenna Festival (June–July), the Spoleto Festival (June–July), the Rossini Opera Festival at Pesaro (Aug.) and the Verona Arena Opera Festival (June–Aug.). The biggest rock festival is the Italia Wave Love Festival in Livorno (known as the Arezzo Wave Festival until 2007), which is held in July, while the largest jazz festival is the Umbria Jazz Festival, also in July. Until 2010 Europe's largest reggae festival, Rototom Sunsplash, was held at Osoppo, in Tuscany. However, it was forced to relocate to Spain after the Italian authorities accused the festival and its organizers of facilitating the use of drugs.

Diplomatic Representatives

Of Italy in the United Kingdom (14 Three Kings' Yard, Davies St., London, W1K 4EH)
    Ambassador: Raffaele Trombetta.

Of the United Kingdom in Italy (Via XX Settembre 80/a, 00187 Rome)
    Ambassador: Jill Morris, CMG.

Of Italy in the USA (3000 Whitehaven St., NW, Washington, D.C., 20008)
    Ambassador: Armando Varricchio.

Of the USA in Italy (Via Vittorio Veneto 119/a, 00187 Rome)
    Ambassador: Lewis M. Eisenberg.

Of Italy to the United Nations
    Ambassador: Maria Angela Zappia.

Of Italy to the European Union
    Permanent Representative: Maurizio Massari.

Further Reading

Istituto Nazionale di Statistica. *Annuario Statistico Italiano.—Compendio Statistico Italiano* (Annual).—*Italian Statistical Abstract* (Annual).—*Bollettino Mensile di Statistica* (Monthly).

Baldoli, Claudia, *A History of Italy.* 2009

Bufacchi, Vittorio and Burgess, Simon, *Italy since 1989.* 1999

Burnett, Stanton H. and Mantovani, Luca, *The Italian Guillotine: Operation 'Clean Hands' and the Overthrow of Italy's First Republic.* 1999

Cotta, Maurizio and Verzichelli, Luca, *Political Institutions of Italy.* 2007

Di Scala, S. M., *Italy from Revolution to Republic: 1700 to the Present.* 1995

Doumanis, Nicholas, *Italy: Inventing the Nation.* 2001

Duggan, Christopher, *A Concise History of Italy.* 1994.—*The Force of Destiny: A History of Italy Since 1796.* 2007

Emmott, Bill, *Good Italy, Bad Italy: Why Italy Must Conquer Its Demons to Face the Future.* 2012

Foot, John, *Modern Italy.* 2003

Frei, M., *Italy: the Unfinished Revolution.* 1996

Furlong, P., *Modern Italy: Representation and Reform.* 1994

Gilbert, M., *Italian Revolution: the Ignominious End of Politics, Italian Style.* 1995

Gilmour, David, *The Pursuit of Italy: A History of a Land, its Regions and their Peoples.* 2011

Ginsborg, Paul, *Italy and its Discontents, 1980–2001.* 2002.—*A History of Contemporary Italy: Society and Politics, 1943–1988.* 2003

Gundie, S. and Parker, S., (eds) *The New Italian Republic: from the Fall of the Berlin Wall to Berlusconi.* 1995

Hearder, H., *Italy: A Short History.* 1990

Leonardi, Roberto, *Government and Politics of Italy.* 2017

Plant, Margaret, *Venice: Fragile City 1797–1997.* 2002

Putnam, R., *et al.*, *Making Democracy Work: Civic Traditions in Modern Italy.* 1993

Richards, C., *The New Italians.* 1994

Smith, D. M., *Modern Italy: A Political History.* 1997

Volcanasek, Mary L., *Constitutional Politics in Italy.* 1999

National library: Biblioteca Nazionale Centrale, Vittorio Emanuele II, Viale Castro Pretorio, Rome.

National Statistical Office: Istituto Nazionale di Statistica (ISTAT), 16 Via Cesare Balbo, 00184 Rome. *President:* Giorgio Alleva.

Website: http://www.istat.it

Jamaica

Capital: Kingston
Population projection, 2020: 2·91m.
GNI per capita, 2017: (PPP$)7,846
HDI/world rank, 2017: 0·732/97
Internet domain extension: .jm

Key Historical Events

Jamaica was discovered by Columbus in 1494 and was occupied by the Spaniards from 1509 until 1655 when the island was captured by the English. In 1661 a representative constitution was established consisting of a governor, privy council, legislative council and legislative assembly. The slavery introduced by the Spanish was augmented as sugar production increased in value and extent in the 18th century. The plantation economy collapsed with the abolition of the slave trade in the late 1830s. The 1866 Crown Colony government was introduced with a legislative council. In 1884 a partially elective legislative council was instituted. Women were enfranchised in 1919. By the late 1930s, demands for self-government increased. The constitution of Nov. 1944 introduced a freely-elected house of representatives of 32 members, a legislative council (the upper house) of 15 members, and an executive council. In 1958 Jamaica joined with Trinidad, Barbados, the Leeward Islands and the Windward Islands to create the West Indies Federation. In 1959 internal self-government was achieved. Jamaica withdrew from the West Indies Federation in 1961 and became an independent state within the British Commonwealth in 1962.

Power alternated between the Jamaica Labour Party and the People's National Party. The latter held power from 1989 until 2007, with Portia Simpson-Miller becoming the country's first female premier in 2006. In May 2010 a state of emergency was declared after the death of dozens of people in an operation to arrest one of the country's leading drug lords, Christopher 'Dudus' Coke. He was subsequently captured and extradited to the USA.

Territory and Population

Jamaica is an island in the Caribbean Sea about 150 km south of Cuba. The area is 10,991 sq. km (4,244 sq. miles). The population at the census of April 2011 was 2,697,983, distributed on the basis of the 13 parishes of the island as follows: Kingston and St Andrew, 662,426; St Catherine, 516,218; Clarendon, 245,103; Manchester, 189,797; St James, 183,811; St Ann, 172,362; St Elizabeth, 150,205; Westmoreland, 144,103; St Mary, 113,615; St Thomas, 93,902; Portland, 81,744; Trelawny, 75,164; Hanover, 69,533. 2011 density: 245 per sq. km. There is a worldwide Jamaican diaspora of more than 2m.

The UN gives a projected population for 2020 of 2·91m.

Chief towns (in 1,000), 2011: Kingston (metropolitan area), 585; Portmore, 182; Spanish Town, 147; Montego Bay, 110; May Pen, 62.

In 2011, 52·1% of the population were urban. The population is about 92% of African ethnic origin. The official language is English. Patois, a combination of English and African languages, is widely spoken.

Social Statistics

Vital statistics (2006): births, 46,277 (17·4 per 1,000 population); deaths, 16,317 (6·1); marriages, 23,181 (8·7); divorces, 1,768 (0·7). There were 17,100 emigrants in 2006, mainly to the USA. Expectation of life at birth, 2007, 68·3 years for males and 75·1 years for females. Annual population growth rate, 2008–10, 0·3%; infant mortality, 2010, 20 per 1,000 live births; fertility rate, 2008, 2·4 births per woman.

Climate

A tropical climate but with considerable variation. High temperatures on the coast are usually mitigated by sea breezes, while upland areas enjoy cooler and less humid conditions. Rainfall is plentiful over most of Jamaica, being heaviest in May and from Aug. to Nov. The island lies in the hurricane zone. Kingston, Jan. 76°F (24·4°C), July 81°F (27·2°C). Annual rainfall 32" (800 mm).

Constitution and Government

Under the constitution of Aug. 1962 the Crown is represented by a Governor-General appointed by the Crown on the advice of the Prime Minister. The Governor-General is assisted by a Privy Council of six appointed members. The Legislature comprises the *House of Representatives* and the *Senate.* The Senate consists of 21 senators appointed by the Governor-General, 13 on the advice of the Prime Minister, eight on the advice of the Leader of the Opposition. The House of Representatives (increased from 60 to 63 members for the 2011 election) is elected by universal adult suffrage for a period not exceeding five years. Electors and elected officials must be Jamaican or Commonwealth citizens resident in Jamaica for at least 12 months before registration.

National Anthem

'Eternal Father, bless our land'; words by H. Sherlock, tune by R. Lightbourne.

Recent Elections

In parliamentary elections held on 25 Feb. 2016 the opposition Jamaica Labour Party took (JLP) 32 of the 63 seats with 50·1% of votes cast (up from 21 in 2011) and the People's National Party (PNP) 31 with 49·7% (down from 42 in 2011). Turnout was 48·4%.

Current Government

Governor-General: Sir Patrick Allen.

In Feb. 2019 the cabinet comprised:

Prime Minister, and Minister of Defence, and Economic Growth and Job Creation: Andrew Holness; b. 1972 (JLP; sworn in 3 March 2016).

Minister of Culture, Gender, Entertainment and Sports: Olivia 'Babsy' Grange. *Education, Youth and Information:* Ruel Reid. *Energy, Science and Technology:* Andrew Wheatley. *Finance and Public Service:* Nigel Clarke. *Foreign Affairs and Foreign Trade:* Kamina Johnson Smith. *Health:* Christopher Tufton. *Industry, Commerce, Agriculture and Fisheries:* Audley Shaw. *Justice:* Delroy Chuck. *Labour and Social Security:* Shahine Robinson. *Local Government and Community Development:* Desmond McKenzie. *National Security:* Horace Chang. *Tourism:* Edmund Bartlett. *Transport and Mining:* Robert Montague. *Attorney General:* Marlene Malahoo. *Ministers without Portfolio:* Michael Henry; J. C. Hutchinson; Karl Samuda; Daryl Vaz; Fayval Williams.

Cabinet Website: http://www.cabinet.gov.jm

Current Leaders

Andrew Holness

Position
Prime Minister

Introduction
Andrew Holness took office as prime minister for a second time on 3 March 2016. His first term had been brief, having been appointed following the resignation of Bruce Golding on 23 Oct. 2011 only to suffer defeat at the polls just two months later. He is the leader of the Jamaica Labour Party (JLP).

Early Life

Holness was born in Spanish Town, in the south of the island, on 22 July 1972. He studied at the University of the West Indies, where he received a master's degree in development studies. On leaving university he worked for a voluntary organization based in Kingston, before accepting a job as personal assistant to the then JLP leader, Edward Seaga.

In 1997 Holness was elected to parliament representing the constituency of Saint Andrew West Central. He was made opposition spokesperson on land and development in 1999, a position he held for three years before taking over the portfolio for housing. In 2005 he moved to education and when the JLP returned to power after an 18-year hiatus in 2007 he was asked to lead that ministry.

When Bruce Golding resigned over his handling of the extradition of Jamaican drug lord Christopher Coke to the USA in 2011, Holness became the country's youngest ever prime minister and the first to have been born post-independence. Although his party suffered a landslide defeat at the ballot box on 29 Dec. 2011, he remained leader in opposition.

After a campaign dominated by economic issues, the JLP was narrowly returned to power in elections held on 25 Feb. 2016 with 32 seats against 31 for the People's National Party. Juliet Holness, the prime minister's wife, was among those elected to parliament.

Career in Office

With the previous government having pursued austerity policies to meet the conditions of a 2013 IMF loan, Holness promised to tackle unemployment, grow the economy by turning Jamaica into the 'Silicon Valley of the Caribbean' and invest in education and health care. He promptly set up a new ministry of economic growth and job creation under his direction, and in Nov. 2016 the IMF approved a new US$1,640m. loan to support ongoing economic reform. Despite allegations of corruption against the JLP in 2017, the party slightly increased its majority in the House of Representatives in Oct. that year following by-elections in three constituencies.

Defence

In 2013 defence expenditure totalled US$129m. (US$44 per capita), representing 0·8% of GDP.

Army

The Jamaica Defence Force consists of a Regular and a Reserve Force. Total strength (Army, 2009): 3,377, including 877 reservists.

Navy

The Coast Guard, numbering 250 in 2009 including 60 reservists, operates nine patrol craft based at Port Royal and Pedro Cays.

Air Force

The Air Wing of the Jamaica Defence Force was formed in July 1963 and has since been expanded and trained successively by the British Army Air Corps and Canadian Air Force personnel. There are no combat aircraft. Personnel (2009), 156 (including 16 reservists).

Economy

In 2012 agriculture accounted for 6·7% of GDP, industry 21·0% and services 72·3%.

Overview

Jamaica has a small and open upper-middle income economy that is dominated by the service sector. Tourism—the biggest source of employment—proved resilient during the global financial crisis, with visitor arrivals increasing in 2009 and averaging an annual 5% increase year-on-year from 2010–14. Leading commodity exports are alumina, bauxite, bananas, sugar, rum and coffee. The agricultural sector rebounded well from the damage caused by Tropical Storm Nicole in 2010.

The economy grew by 1·4% in 2011 after recording negative growth between 2008 and 2010, and averaged an increase of just over 0·5% from 2012–14. Prior to that there had been four decades of negligible growth. The national debt represented 140% of GDP in 2015, while unemployment stood at 13·5% and youth unemployment at 30·3%. Joblessness among women is roughly double that of men. Remittances from workers abroad accounted for 16·9% of GDP in 2015. Rural poverty, political instability and high levels of crime pose significant obstacles to long-term growth.

Ongoing government reform programmes have received international support, including a four-year IMF Extended Fund Facility worth US$932m. (signed off in 2013), and funding from the World Bank and the Inter-American Development Bank which is worth over US$500m. In 2015 Jamaica was ranked 58th of 189 countries for ease of doing business by the World Bank Group—a 27-place year-on-year rise.

Currency

The unit of currency is the *Jamaican dollar* (JMD) of 100 *cents*. The Jamaican dollar was floated in Sept. 1990. Inflation was 22·0% in 2008 but has since fallen, and was 2·3% in 2016 and 4·4% in 2017. Foreign exchange reserves were US$2,423m. in July 2005 and total money supply was J$68,141m.

Budget

General government revenue (provisional) in 2015–16 totalled J$551bn. (taxes, J$446bn.) and expenditure J$500bn. (compensation of employees, J$192bn.; interest, J$133bn.).

There is a General Consumption Tax of 16·5%.

Performance

After suffering major economic difficulties with negative growth in 1996, 1997 and 1998, Jamaica's economy recovered slightly, with growth reaching 2·9% in 2006. However, there was again negative growth in 2008, of –0·8%, in 2009, of –3·4%, and in 2010, of –1·4%. In 2011 the economy experienced another slight recovery, growing by 1·4%, before contracting by 0·5% in 2012. Jamaica then came out of recession and the economy grew by 0·9% in 2015, 1·5% in 2016 and 0·7% in 2017. Total GDP was US$14·8bn. in 2017.

Banking and Finance

The central bank and bank of issue is the Bank of Jamaica. The *Governor* is Brian Wynter.

In 2016 there were six commercial banks, two merchant banks and three building societies. Total assets of commercial banks at March 2006 were J$385,759·5m.; deposits were J$255,315·4m.

Foreign debt was US$13,865m. in 2010, representing 104·2% of GNI.

There is a stock exchange in Kingston, which participates in the regional Caribbean exchange.

Energy and Natural Resources

Environment

In 2011 carbon dioxide emissions from the consumption of energy were the equivalent of 3·4 tonnes per capita.

Electricity

The Jamaica Public Service Company Limited is the public supplier. Total installed capacity was 0·8m. kW in 2011. Production in 2011 totalled 5·10bn. kWh; consumption per capita in 2011 was 1,851 kWh.

Oil and Gas

There is an oil refinery in Kingston.

Minerals

Jamaica ranks among the world's largest producers of bauxite. Ceramic clays, marble, silica sand and gypsum are also commercially viable. Production in 2014 (in tonnes): bauxite ore, 9·7m.; limestone, 2·1m.; sand and gravel, 2·1m.; gypsum, 45,201.

Agriculture

In 2012 there were an estimated 120,000 ha. of arable land and 100,000 ha. of permanent crops.

2012 production (in 1,000 tonnes): sugarcane, 1,475; coconuts (estimate), 315; yams, 145; oranges, 92; pumpkins and squash, 52; bananas, 47; sweet potatoes, 42; plantains, 36.

Livestock (2013 estimates): goats, 520,000; pigs, 210,000; cattle, 170,000; chickens, 13·5m. Livestock products, 2012 estimates (in tonnes): pork and pork products, 9,500; beef and veal, 5,800; goat meat, 1,100; poultry meat, 102,200.

Forestry

Forests covered 0·34m. ha. in 2015, or 31% of the total land area. Timber production was 693,000 cu. metres in 2011.

Fisheries

Catches in 2015 totalled 17,025 tonnes, almost exclusively from sea fishing.

Industry

Alumina production, 2005, 4·1m. tonnes. Output of other products (2007 unless otherwise indicated, in tonnes): cement (2005), 844,840; residual fuel oil, 473,000; distillate fuel oil, 190,000; wheat flour (2013), 133,000; sugar (2013), 116,110; petrol, 104,000; molasses (2008), 62,654; rum (2008), 26·5m. litres. In 2005 industry accounted for 33·1% of GDP, with manufacturing contributing 13·6%.

Labour

The labour force in 2013 was 1,291,000 (1,202,000 in 2003). 67·8% of the population aged 15–64 was economically active in 2013. In the same year 15·0% of the population was unemployed.

International Trade

Imports and Exports

Value of imports and domestic exports for calendar years (in US$1m.):

	2006	2007	2008	2009	2010
Imports c.i.f.	5,041·4	6,747·6	8,465·4	5,064·3	5,225·2
Exports f.o.b.	1,988·8	2,224·0	2,438·8	1,316·0	1,327·6

Principal imports in 2010 (US$1m.): mineral fuels and lubricants, 1,585·6; food and live animals, 812·9; machinery and transport equipment, 795·2; chemicals and related products, 699·1; manufactured goods, 587·1.

Principal exports in 2010 (US$1m.): inedible crude materials (excluding fuels), 555·7; mineral fuels and lubricants, 282·0; food and live animals, 208·9; beverages and tobacco, 103·9; chemicals, 83·8.

Main import suppliers, 2010 (US$1m.): USA, 1,875·1; Venezuela, 732·8; Trinidad and Tobago, 721·0; China, 242·9. Main export markets, 2010 (US$1m.): USA, 659·1; Canada, 163·4; UK, 83·9; Norway, 68·5.

Communications

Roads

In 2007 the island had 22,121 km of roads, including 44 km of motorway and 4,922 km of main roads. In 2006 there were 373,700 passenger cars in use and 29,100 motorcycles and mopeds. There were 350 fatalities in traffic accidents in 2007.

Rail

Passenger traffic ceased in 1992, but restarted in 2011. However, it closed again in Aug. 2012 as a result of the service suffering heavy losses. Freight transport continues on a limited basis, mainly for carrying bauxite to docks.

Civil Aviation

International airlines operate through the Norman Manley and Sangster airports at Palisadoes and Montego Bay. Sangster International is the busiest for passenger traffic, handling 3,378,000 passengers in 2006–07. Norman Manley airport is busier for freight, handling 16,136 tonnes of freight in 2006 but only 1,715,078 passengers. Air Jamaica, originally set up in conjunction with BOAC and BWIA in 1966, became a new company, Air Jamaica (1968) Ltd. In 1969 it began operations as Jamaica's national airline. It was acquired in May 2010 by Caribbean Airlines, the national airline of Trinidad and Tobago, but the name Air Jamaica has been retained. In 2006 scheduled airline traffic of Jamaica-based carriers flew 52m. km and carried 1,527,000 passengers.

Shipping

In Jan. 2014 there were 16 ships of 300 GT or over registered, totalling 153,000 GT. Kingston handled 12·0m. tonnes of cargo in 2013 (down from 19·0m. tonnes in 2011).

Telecommunications

In 2011 there were 272,100 landline telephone subscriptions (equivalent to 98·9 per 1,000 inhabitants) and 2,974,700 mobile phone subscriptions (or 1,081·2 per 1,000 inhabitants). There were 261·0 internet users per 1,000 inhabitants in 2010. Fixed internet subscriptions totalled 114,600 in 2009 (42·0 per 1,000 inhabitants). In Dec. 2011 there were 684,000 Facebook users.

Social Institutions

Out of 178 countries analysed in the 2017 *Fragile States Index*—list published jointly by the Fund for Peace and *Foreign Policy* magazine—Jamaica was ranked the 62nd least vulnerable to conflict or collapse. The index is based on 12 indicators of state vulnerability across social, political and economic categories.

Justice

The Judicature comprises a Supreme Court, a court of appeal, resident magistrates' courts, petty sessional courts, coroners' courts, a traffic court and a family court which was instituted in 1975. The Chief Justice is head of the judiciary. Jamaica was one of ten countries to sign an agreement in Feb. 2001 establishing a Caribbean Court of Justice to replace the British Privy Council as the highest civil and criminal court. In the meantime the number of signatories has risen to 12. The court was inaugurated at Port of Spain, Trinidad on 16 April 2005 but Jamaica has yet to accept it as its final court of appeal.

In 2012 there were 1,099 murders, down from the record high of 1,683 in 2009. The rate of 40 per 100,000 persons in 2012 (62 per 100,000 in 2009) is around nine times that of the USA and ranks among the highest in the world. The death penalty is permitted but has not been used since 1988.

The population in penal institutions in Sept. 2013 was 4,201 (152 per 100,000 of national population). Jamaica was ranked 45th of 102 countries for criminal justice and 52nd for civil justice in the 2015 World Justice Project *Rule of Law Index*, which provides data on how the rule of law is experienced by the general public across eight categories.

Education

Adult literacy was an estimated 86·4% in 2009 (91·1% among females but only 81·2% among males).

Education is free in government-operated schools. Enrolment in 2007 in primary institutions was 310,000; in secondary institutions, 257,000; and in tertiary institutions (2008), 61,000.

The University of the West Indies, which was founded in 1948 and has its main campus at Kingston, is the oldest, fully regional institution of higher learning in the Commonwealth Caribbean. In 2006 there were two public universities and two private universities as well as six teacher training colleges, five community colleges, and several technical/vocational training institutes and specialist colleges. Large numbers of educated Jamaicans have left the island over the past 30 years, but in the early part of the 21st century there are signs that young professionals are increasingly returning to Jamaica. However, 72% of Jamaican graduates live in OECD member countries.

In 2005 public expenditure on education came to 5·6% of GNI and 8·8% of total government spending.

Health

In 2012 Jamaica had 17 hospital beds per 10,000 people. In the period 2000–10 there were 8·5 physicians for every 10,000 population, 16·5 nursing and midwifery personnel per 10,000 population and 0·8 dentistry personnel per 10,000.

In *Water: At What Cost? The State of the World's Water 2016*, WaterAid reported that 6·2% of the population does not have access to safe water.

Welfare

The official retirement age is 65 years (men) or 60 years (women). The old-age pension is made up of a basic benefit of J$900 a week (reduced to J$675 a week with annual average contributions of between 26 and 38 weeks; J$450 with 13 weeks to 25 weeks), plus an earnings-related benefit of J$0·06 a week for every J$13 of employer-employee contributions paid during the working lifetime.

Jamaica's social welfare projects also cover disability and survivor benefits, sickness and maternity, and work injury. Jamaica has no unemployment programmes.

Religion

Freedom of worship is guaranteed under the Constitution. The main Christian denominations are Anglican, Baptist, Roman Catholic, Methodist, Church of God, United Church in Jamaica and the Cayman Islands (Presbyterian-Congregational-Disciples of Christ), Moravian, Seventh-day

Adventist, Pentecostal, Salvation Army and Quaker. Pocomania is a mixture of Christianity and African survivals. Non-Christians include Hindus, Jews, Muslims, Bahá'i followers and Rastafarians.

Culture

Press

In 2008 there were three daily newspapers with a combined circulation of 115,000.

Tourism

In 2011 there were a record 1,951,752 non-resident overnight tourists, and 1,125,481 cruise passenger arrivals (down from a peak of 1,336,994 in 2006).

World Heritage Sites

Jamaica has one site on the UNESCO World Heritage List: Blue and John Crow Mountains (2015), a forested and mountainous region in the southeast of Jamaica.

Diplomatic Representatives

Of Jamaica in the United Kingdom (1–2 Prince Consort Rd, London, SW7 2BZ)
High Commissioner: Seth George Ramocan.

Of the United Kingdom in Jamaica (PO Box 575, 28 Trafalgar Rd, Kingston 10)
High Commissioner: Asif Ahmad, CMG.

Of Jamaica in the USA (1520 New Hampshire Ave., NW, Washington, D.C., 20036)
Ambassador: Audrey Patrice Marks.

Of the USA in Jamaica (142 Old Hope Rd, Kingston 6)
Ambassador: Vacant.
Chargé d'Affaires a.i.: Eric Khant.

Of Jamaica to the United Nations
Ambassador: Courtenay Rattray.

Of Jamaica to the European Union
Ambassador: Sheila Sealy Monteith.

Further Reading

Planning Institute of Jamaica. *Economic and Social Survey, Jamaica.* Annual.—*Survey of Living Conditions.* Annual

Statistical Institute of Jamaica. *Statistical Abstract.* Annual.—*Demographic Statistics.* Annual.—*Production Statistics.* Annual

Hart, R., *Towards Decolonisation: Political, Labour and Economic Developments in Jamaica 1938–1945.* 1999

Henke, H. W. and Mills, D., *Between Self-Determination and Dependency: Jamaica's Foreign Relations 1972–1989.* 2000

National library: National Library of Jamaica, 12 East Street, Kingston.

National Statistical Office: Statistical Institute of Jamaica (STATIN), 7 Cecelio Ave., Kingston 10.

Website: http://statinja.gov.jm

Japan

Nihon (or Nippon) Koku (Land of the Rising Sun)

Capital: Tokyo
Population projection, 2020: 126·50m.
GNI per capita, 2017: (PPP$) 38,986
HDI/world rank, 2017: 0·909/19
Internet domain extension: .jp

Key Historical Events

When the last ice sheets covered much of Asia, the sea level fell low enough for a land bridge to appear between Japan and the Asian mainland. This route was taken by hunter-gatherers from Asia who crossed into previously uninhabited Japan. By 10,000 BC the first pottery was produced in Japan and there was some cultivation. Rice was introduced, probably from Korea, by about 400 BC, and the use of metals around a century later, but agriculture and fixed settlements were confined to the south for a long period. During this time waves of migrants came from mainland Asia, bringing with them skills and technologies, including the Chinese characters for writing.

Religion, too, came from China: both Buddhism and Confucianism entered Japan, the former gaining a large following. In time traditional beliefs consolidated into Shintoism, which became the national religion. But, until the first millennium AD, there was no Japanese nation, although the legends of Japan tell us otherwise. According to myth, the first Japanese emperor was Jimmu around 600 BC, said to be a descendant of the sun goddess, Amaterasu.

In the first century BC, another wave of migrants entered Japan from Korea. The first Japanese state appeared in the central region of Honshu in the 7th century. This state soon controlled most of the west and centre of the island. In 710 the first permanent Japanese capital was established in Nara by Empress Genmei. In 794 the seat of power moved to Heian-kyo (present-day Kyoto).

Following the court and government tradition of China, Japan cut itself off from the outside world. As the imperial office became increasingly religious the day-to-day power passed into the hands of powerful nobles, such as the Fujiwara clan. Fujiwara Yoshifusa (804–872) was a powerful regent of Japan from 857 until his death, and by the 11th century the Fujiwaras were unchallenged rulers of the country. In the 12th century, however, Japan entered into a period of anarchy. The country passed under the control of barons, the *daimyo*, who exercised power through the warrior class known as the *samurai*.

Shogun

The anarchy ended when Taira Kiyamori seized power and made himself dictator. A civil war, the Gempei War, followed (1180–85). When Taira was defeated, power passed to Minamoto Yoritomo (1147–99), a distant descendant of the imperial family. Yoritomo established a new office, the *shogun*. For the next 700 years Japan was ruled by a military dictator, the shogun, while the emperor lived reclusively as a religious and national symbol.

At first the shogunate was seated in Kamakura, near modern Tokyo. Nine shoguns ruled during the Kamakura epoch (1185–1333) although latterly the Kamakura shogun was a puppet of the Hojo clan. In 1274 and 1281 Mongol attempts to invade Japan were unsuccessful: in 1281 the invasion was thwarted by a sudden typhoon that became known as the 'divine wind' (kami-kaze).

In 1334 a brief restoration of power to the emperor was ended by Ashikaga Takauji (1305–58), who established a strong military government. Subsequent members of the Ashikaga family ruled as shoguns based in Kyoto. Eventually this system, too, collapsed into anarchy, the victim of the ambitions of rival warlords. From 1467 to 1603 Japan suffered the Fighting Principalities (*Sengokujidai*). It was when the country was at its weakest that another powerful outside influence began to exert itself.

From 1543 Portuguese traders and missionaries arrived on the southern and western coasts. At first, trade was welcomed. Christianity, too, made converts after the Spanish Jesuit missionary St Francis Xavier landed in Japan in 1549. Along with western ideas and religion, the Portuguese, and later the Dutch, brought firearms. Three warlords in turn used western

weapons to seize power and reunite the country. The last of this trio was Tokugawa Ieyasu (1542–1616), who held power from 1600. Ieyasu ordered the nobles to destroy their fortifications, except their principal residences, and encouraged the arts and learning as a preferred alternative to warfare.

Isolation

As the true rulers of Japan until 1869, the Tokugawa shogunate established itself at Edo (present-day Tokyo). They ruled harshly, subduing the warring lords by holding members of their families hostages. The Tokugawa perceived foreign influences as unsettling and a danger to their supremacy. For this reason, they decreed that Japan should become a closed society. In 1636 Japanese were forbidden to emigrate. Europeans were expelled, except for a single Dutch trading post in Nagasaki, which after 1639 became Japan's only contact with the outside world. Christianity was suppressed and the ownership of firearms, except by the central authorities, was made illegal. Japan entered 220 years of self-imposed isolation.

Cut off from outside influences, Japan gained stability and a strong sense of national identity. Yet this isolation came at a price. In 1853 a US fleet led by Commodore Matthew C. Perry appeared off the Japanese coast. Japan was forced to open up to international trade through the threat of invasion. Other western nations followed the American example. Japan was thrust into a modern world for which it was ill suited. The voices for reform grew and the Tokugawa shogunate, humiliated by Perry's mission, collapsed. Reformers seized Kyoto and parts of the west, but they needed a national symbol to legitimize their rule. In 1869 the shadowy figure of the emperor was called out of his cloistered life. His city, Edo, had by then been renamed Tokyo, meaning 'eastern capital'. The emperor surprised the country by his zeal for modernization which led to a period of rapid reform and transformed Japan into a modern nation.

But while a constitution was introduced, the resemblance to a western democracy was skin deep. Though the peasants were freed from serfdom, power remained in the hands of the nobility. Priority was given to developing industry and modern technology. Japan's rise as an industrial state began.

Rise of the Military

Much emphasis was given to modernizing the armed forces. A revitalized Japan defeated China in the First Sino-Japanese War in 1894–95 and gained Taiwan. In 1900 Japan intervened alongside the western powers against the Boxer Rebellion in China. An even greater shock was Japan's victory against Russia in 1903–04 in a war over Korea and Manchuria. Having contained Russian land forces in Manchuria, the Japanese decisively defeated the Russian Baltic Fleet in the Tsushima Strait. Russia's influence in the region faded and Japan received half of Sakhalin and the Kurile Islands. Later, with Russia removed from the scene, Japan annexed Korea (1910) and took control of parts of Manchuria.

In 1902 Japan made an alliance with Britain. To emphasize Japan's western credentials, Tokyo entered the First World War against Germany in 1914. Japanese forces took the German island colonies in the north and central Pacific and received these archipelagoes as a League of Nations Trust Territory in 1919. But greater rewards for their efforts in the war had been expected and Tokyo's disillusion with the west began. The collapse of world trade at the end of the 1920s brought hardship and helped the rise of political extremism and nationalism.

Japan began a phase of aggressive expansionism. In 1931 Japan invaded Manchuria and, two years later, installed the deposed last emperor of China as puppet emperor of Manchukuo. From 1932 Japanese forces entered various coastal and border areas of China, and in 1937 there was a full-scale war with China. Japanese forces took Shanghai in 1937, Guangzhou in 1938 and Nanjing in 1940. By the end of 1940 Japan had occupied French Indochina and formed a triple alliance (or Axis) with Nazi Germany and Fascist Italy.

Pearl Harbor

Under premier Gen. Tojo Hideki (1884–1948), Japan attacked the US fleet in Pearl Harbor, Hawaii in Dec. 1941. This action brought the United States into

© Springer Nature Limited 2020
Palgrave Macmillan (ed.), *The Statesman's Yearbook 2020*,
https://doi.org/10.1057/978-1-349-95940-2_100

the Second World War (1939–45) and ranged Japan against forces that were superior in size and technology. Nevertheless, the war was initially in Japan's favour. Japanese forces swept through the Pacific and into Malaya and the Dutch East Indies (now Indonesia). The speed of Japan's ruthless advance overwhelmed the Allied powers as British and American positions were surrendered. The tide turned with the American victory at Midway in late 1942, but by the time Germany surrendered in May 1945 Japanese forces were still in control of large areas of the Pacific and Southeast Asia. In Aug. 1945 US planes dropped atomic bombs on the Japanese cities of Hiroshima and Nagasaki, devastating the two cities and causing more than 200,000 deaths. The emperor Hirohito (1926–89) surrendered.

The war had cost Japan dearly. Not only had two cities suffered the horror of atomic warfare, but many more Japanese had died in combat. Nearly 2m. Japanese were abandoned in China, most of whom were shipped to Siberia as prisoners. Japan was to be reformed by the occupying US forces under Gen. MacArthur. In 1945 Shintoism, which had become associated with aggressive nationalism, ceased to be the state religion. In the following year, the emperor renounced his divinity.

A new liberal constitution was introduced in 1946. Japan signed a peace treaty in 1951 at San Francisco and the American occupation of Japan ended in April 1952 when the country regained its independence. A separate peace treaty was concluded later between Japan and China. There was, however, no agreement with the Soviet Union, which, at American behest, had declared war against Japan in the closing days of the Second World War. Soviet forces occupied Sakhalin and the Kurile islands to which Japan still lays claim.

The new Japan remained a monarchy, albeit one in which the emperor was a figurehead. Japan renounced war and the threat or use of force, but retained 'Self Defence Forces'. Japanese cities and industry were rebuilt. An astonishing economic recovery was led by an aggressive export policy. Huge investment in new technology gave the country a dominant position in many industries including motor vehicles, shipbuilding, electrical goods, electronics and computers. Japan grew to be the world's second biggest economy. This success is owed, in part, to the protection of domestic markets.

The power of Japanese industry was reflected in the political power of a small number of major corporations. From 1955 until 1993 the political scene was dominated by the centre-right pro-business Liberal Democrats (LDP). However, a series of major financial scandals broke the party's monopoly and coalition governments followed. Since 2000 the LDP has resumed its largely dominant role in government, although the Democratic Party of Japan was briefly in power from 2009–12.

In recent years, Japan has shown more confidence in international relations. The country is a major aid donor to developing countries. In 1992 the Diet (parliament) approved the involvement of Japanese military personnel and equipment in UN peacekeeping missions. For the first time since the end of the Second World War, parliament approved the creation in 2006 of the country's first defence ministry and in 2015 passed a law allowing Japanese troops to fight overseas. The move came amid rising tensions with China over disputed claims to several islands in the South China Sea.

Despite having one of the world's biggest economies, Japan has faced major economic problems in recent decades, driven by heavy international debt and domestic deflation. In 2011 its economy was overtaken by China's as the world's second largest.

In March 2011 a huge offshore earthquake and a resulting tsunami devastated large areas of the northeast of Japan, causing between US$120bn. and US$235bn. of damage and killing over 10,000 people. The disaster also caused extensive damage to the Fukushima nuclear plant.

In June 2017 parliament passed legislation allowing Emperor Akihito to abdicate.

Territory and Population

Japan consists of four major islands, Honshu, Hokkaido, Kyushu and Shikoku, and many small islands, with an area of 377,971 sq. km. Census population of 1 Oct. 2015: 127,094,745 (128,057,352 in 2010), of which 61,841,738 males (62,327,737 in 2010) and 65,253,007 females (65,729,615 in 2010). Population density (land area only) in 2015 was 336 per sq. km (351 per sq. km in 2010).

The UN gives a projected population for 2020 of 126·50m. The population started to decline in 2010; the UN projects that by 2050 it will only be 107m.

In 2011, 67·0% of the population lived in urban areas. Foreigners registered on 31 Dec. 2014 were 2,121,831: including 654,777 Chinese, 501,230 South Koreans, 217,585 Filipinos, 175,410 Brazilians, 99,865 Vietnamese, 51,256 Americans, 47,978 Peruvians, 43,081 Thais, 42,346 Nepalese, 30,210 Indonesians, 24,524 Indians, 15,262 British, 11,802 Pakistanis and 598 stateless persons. In 2014 Japan accepted 11 asylum seekers (out of more than 5,000 applications), up from just six in 2013.

Japanese overseas, Oct. 2013, 1,258,263; of these 412,639 lived in the USA, 135,078 in China, 81,981 in Australia, 67,148 in the UK, 62,349 in Canada, 59,270 in Thailand, 56,217 in Brazil, 37,393 in Germany, 36,719 in South Korea, 32,579 in France and 31,038 in Singapore.

The official language is Japanese.

A law of May 1997 'on the promotion of Ainu culture' marked the first official recognition of the existence of an ethnic minority in Japan. The Ainu were recognized as a people in their own right through a resolution passed by parliament in June 2008.

Japan is divided into 43 prefectures, one metropolis (Tokyo), one territory (Hokkaido) and two urban prefectures (Kyoto and Osaka). The populations and chief cities are:

Prefecture	Census pop. 2015	Chief city
Aichi	7,483,128	Nagoya
Akita	1,023,119	Akita
Aomori	1,308,265	Aomori
Chiba	6,222,666	Chiba
Ehime	1,385,262	Matsuyama
Fukui	786,740	Fukui
Fukuoka	5,101,556	Fukuoka
Fukushima	1,914,039	Fukushima
Gifu	2,031,903	Gifu
Gumma	1,973,115	Maebashi
Hiroshima	2,843,990	Hiroshima
Hokkaido	5,381,733	Sapporo
Hyogo	5,534,800	Kobe
Ibaraki	2,916,976	Mito
Ishikawa	1,154,008	Kanazawa
Iwate	1,279,594	Morioka
Kagawa	976,263	Takamatsu
Kagoshima	1,648,177	Kagoshima
Kanagawa	9,126,214	Yokohama
Kochi	728,276	Kochi
Kumamoto	1,786,170	Kumamoto
Kyoto	2,610,353	Kyoto
Mie	1,815,865	Tsu
Miyagi	2,333,899	Sendai
Miyazaki	1,104,069	Miyazaki
Nagano	2,098,804	Nagano
Nagasaki	1,377,187	Nagasaki
Nara	1,364,316	Nara
Niigata	2,304,264	Niigata
Oita	1,166,338	Oita
Okayama	1,921,525	Okayama
Okinawa	1,433,566	Naha
Osaka	8,839,469	Osaka
Saga	832,832	Saga
Saitama	7,266,534	Saitama
Shiga	1,412,916	Otsu
Shimane	694,352	Matsue
Shizuoka	3,700,305	Shizuoka
Tochigi	1,974,255	Utsunomiya
Tokushima	755,733	Tokushima
Tokyo	13,515,271	Tokyo
Tottori	573,441	Tottori
Toyama	1,066,328	Toyama
Wakayama	963,579	Wakayama

(continued)

Prefecture	Census pop. 2015	Chief city
Yamagata	1,123,891	Yamagata
Yamaguchi	1,404,729	Yamaguchi
Yamanashi	834,930	Kofu

The leading cities, with population in 2015 (in 1,000), are:

Akashi	293
Akita	316
Amagasaki	453
Aomori	288
Asahikawa	340
Chiba	972
Fuchu	260
Fujisawa	424
Fukui	266
Fukuoka	1,539
Fukushima	294
Fukuyama	465
Funabashi	623
Gifu	407
Hachioji	578
Hakodate	266
Hamamatsu	798
Higashiosaka	503
Himeji	536
Hirakata	404
Hiratsuka	258
Hiroshima	1,194
Ibaraki	280
Ichihara	275
Ichikawa	482
Ichinomiya	381
Iwaki	350
Kagoshima	600
Kakogawa	267
Kanazawa	466
Kashiwa	414
Kasugai	307
Kawagoe	351
Kawaguchi	578
Kawasaki	1,475
Kitakyushu	961
Kobe	1,537
Kochi	337
Koriyama	335
Koshigaya	337
Kumamoto	741
Kurashiki	477
Kurume	305
Kyoto	1,475
Machida	432
Maebashi	336
Matsudo	483
Matsuyama	515
Mito	271
Miyazaki	401
Morioka	298
Nagano	378

(continued)

Nagaoka	275
Nagasaki	430
Nagoya	2,296
Naha	319
Nara	360
Niigata	810
Nishinomiya	488
Oita	478
Okayama	719
Okazaki	381
Osaka	2,691
Otsu	341
Sagamihara	721
Saitama	1,264
Sakai	839
Sapporo	1,952
Sasebo	255
Sendai	1,082
Shimonoseki	269
Shizuoka	705
Suita	374
Takamatsu	421
Takasaki	371
Takatsuki	352
Tokorozawa	340
Tokushima	259
Tokyo	9,273
Toyama	419
Toyohashi	375
Toyonaka	395
Toyota	423
Tsu	280
Utsunomiya	519
Wakayama	364
Yamagata	254
Yao	269
Yokkaichi	311
Yokohama	3,725
Yokosuka	407

The Tokyo conurbation, with a population in 2010 of 36·9m., is the largest in the world, having overtaken New York around 1970.

Social Statistics

Statistics (in 1,000) for calendar years:

	2010	2011	2012	2013	2014
Births	1,071	1,051	1,037	1,030	1,004
Deaths	1,197	1,253	1,256	1,268	1,273

Birth rate in 2013, 8·1 per 1,000 population (1947: 34·3); death rate, 10·0. Marriage rate in 2015 (per 1,000 persons), 5·1; divorce rate, 1·8. In 2015 the mean age at first marriage was 31·1 for males and 29·4 for females. The infant mortality rate per 1,000 live births, 2·1 (2013), is one of the lowest in the world. In 2012 only 2·0% of births were outside marriage. Life expectancy at birth was 86·8 years for women and 80·5 years for men in 2014. Japan's life expectancy is the highest of any sovereign country. The World Health Organization's *World Health Statistics 2014* put the Japanese in second place in a 'healthy life expectancy' list, with an expected 75 years of healthy life for babies born in 2012. Japan has the oldest population of any country and a very quickly ageing population, stemming from a sharply declined fertility rate and one of the highest life expectancies in the world. The total fertility rate was 1·43 births per woman in 2013 (compared to a low of 1·26 in 2005 but 1·91 in 1975 and 3·65 in 1950). In 2014, 26·0% of the population was aged 65 or over (compared to 10% in 1985); by around 2039 it is expected that one in three will be over 65. Japan had an estimated 60,000 centenarians (52,000 women) in Oct. 2014.

There were 23,121 suicides in 2015, when suicide became the leading cause of deaths for people aged between 15 and 39. The rate among women is one of the highest in the world.

UNICEF reported that 18·2% of children in Japan in 2014 lived in relative poverty (living in a household in which disposable income—when adjusted for family size and composition—is less than 60% of the national median income), compared to 9·2% in Denmark (the world's lowest rate).

Climate

The islands of Japan lie in the temperate zone, northeast of the main monsoon region of southeast Asia. The climate is temperate with warm, humid summers and relatively mild winters except in the island of Hokkaido and northern parts of Honshu facing the Sea of Japan. There is a month's rainy season in June–July, but the best seasons are spring and autumn, although Sept. may bring typhoons. Tokyo, Jan. 5·8°C, July 25·4°C. Annual rainfall 1,467 mm. Hiroshima, Jan. 5·3°C, July 26·9°C. Annual rainfall 1,541 mm. Nagasaki, Jan. 6·8°C, July 26·6°C. Annual rainfall 1,960 mm. Osaka, Jan. 5·8°C, July 27·2°C. Annual rainfall 1,306 mm. Sapporo, Jan. –4·1°C, July 20·5°C. Annual rainfall 1,128 mm.

Constitution and Government

The Emperor is **Akihito** (b. 23 Dec. 1933), who succeeded his father, Hirohito on 7 Jan. 1989 (enthroned, 12 Nov. 1990); married 10 April 1959, to Michiko Shoda (b. 20 Oct. 1934). *Offspring:* Crown Prince Naruhito (Hironomiya; b. 23 Feb. 1960); Prince Akishino (Akishinomiya; b. 30 Nov. 1965); Princess Sayako (Norinomiya; b. 18 April 1969). Prince Naruhito married Masako Owada (b. 9 Dec. 1963) 9 June 1993. *Offspring:* Princess Aiko (b. 1 Dec. 2001). Prince Fumihito (henceforth to adopt his new title Prince Akishino) married Kawashima Kiko (b. 11 Sept. 1966) 29 June 1990. *Offspring:* Princess Mako (23 Oct. 1991); Princess Kako (29 Dec. 1994); Prince Hisahito (6 Sept. 2006). Princess Sayako married Yoshiki Kuroda (b. 17 April 1965) 15 Nov. 2005 and gave up her imperial title in doing so as required by law. The succession to the throne is fixed upon the male descendants. Prince Hisahito was the first male born into the imperial family since 1965. The 1947 constitution supersedes the Meiji constitution of 1889. In it the Japanese people pledge themselves to uphold the ideas of democracy and peace. The Emperor is the symbol of the unity of the people. Sovereign power rests with the people. The Emperor has no powers related to government. Fundamental human rights are guaranteed.

Legislative power rests with the *Diet*, which consists of the *House of Representatives* (Shugi-in), elected by men and women over 18 years of age (the age limit was lowered from 20 in June 2015) for a four-year term, and an upper house, the *House of Councillors* (Sangi-in) of 242 members (96 elected by party list system with proportional representation according to the d'Hondt method and 146 from prefectural districts), one-half of its members being elected every three years. The number of members has been reduced in recent years. There had been 252 members until 2001 and 247 members from 2001 until elections of July 2004.

The number of members in the House of Representatives was reduced from 500 to 480 in 2000 and again to 475 in 2013 and further to 465 in 2017, of whom 289 are elected from single-seat constituencies and 176 by proportional representation on a base of 11 regions. There is a 2% threshold to gain one of the latter seats. Donations to individual politicians are to be supplanted over five years by state subsidies to parties.

A new electoral law passed in Oct. 2000 gives voters a choice between individual candidates and parties when casting ballots for the proportional representation seats in the *House of Councillors*.

National Anthem

'Kimigayo' ('The Reign of Our Emperor'); words 9th century, tune by Hayashi Hiromori. On 9 Aug. 1999 a law on the national flag and the national anthem was enacted. The law designates the Hinomaru and 'Kimigayo' as the national flag and national anthem of Japan. The 'Kimi' in 'Kimigayo' indicates the Emperor who is the symbol of the State and of the unity of the people, deriving his position from the will of the people with whom resides

sovereign power; 'Kimigayo' depicts the state of being of the country as a whole.

Government Chronology

Prime ministers since 1945. (DPJ = Democratic Party of Japan; JNP = Japan New Party; JSP = Japan Socialist Party; Jt = Liberal Party; LDP = Liberal Democratic Party; Mt = Democratic Party; SDP = Social Democratic Party; SSt = Renewal Party; n/p = non-partisan)

1945	military	Kantaro Suzuki
1945	military	Naruhito Kigashi-Kuni
1945–46	n/p	Kijuro Shidehara
1946–47	Jt	Shigeru Yoshida
1947–48	JSP	Tetsu Katayama
1948	Mt	Hitoshi Ashida
1948–54	Jt	Shigeru Yoshida
1954–56	LDP	Ichiro Hatoyama
1956–57	LDP	Tanzan Ishibashi
1957–60	LDP	Nobusuke Kishi
1960–64	LDP	Hayato Ikeda
1964–72	LDP	Eisaku Sato
1972–74	LDP	Kakuei Tanaka
1974–76	LDP	Takeo Miki
1976–78	LDP	Takeo Fukuda
1978–80	LDP	Masayoshi Ohira
1980	LDP	Masayoshi Ito
1980–82	LDP	Zenko Suzuki
1982–87	LDP	Yasuhiro Nakasone
1987–89	LDP	Noboru Takeshita
1989	LDP	Sosuke Uno
1989–91	LDP	Toshiki Kaifu
1991–93	LDP	Kiichi Miyazawa
1993–94	JNP	Morihiro Hosokawa
1994	SSt	Tsutomu Hata
1994–96	SDP	Tomiichi Murayama
1996–98	LDP	Ryutaro Hashimoto
1998–2000	LDP	Keizo Obuchi
2000	LDP	Michio Aoki
2000–01	LDP	Yoshiro Mori
2001–06	LDP	Junichiro Koizumi
2006–07	LDP	Shinzo Abe
2007–08	LDP	Yasuo Fukuda
2008–09	LDP	Taro Aso
2009–10	DPJ	Yukio Hatoyama
2010–11	DPJ	Naoto Kan
2011–12	DPJ	Yoshihiko Noda
2012–	LDP	Shinzo Abe

Recent Elections

Elections to the House of Representatives were held on 22 Oct. 2017. The coalition between the ruling Liberal Democratic Party (LDP, Jiminto) and the Komeito party won 313 seats (with 49·7% of the single-seat constituency vote); the opposition Constitutional Democratic Party of Japan (CDP, Rikken Minshuto) 55 seats (8·8%); Party of Hope (Kibo no To) 50 (20·6%); Japanese Communist Party (JCP, Nihon Kyosanto) 12 (9·0%); Nippon Ishin no Kai 11 (3·2%); Social Democratic Party (SDP, Shakai Minshuto) 2 (1·1%). Independents took 22 seats. Turnout was 53·7%. Although the Constitutional Democratic Party of Japan was only formed less than a month before the election it is now the largest opposition party.

Elections to 121 seats of the House of Councillors were held on 10 July 2016. The LDP gained 56 seats, DPJ 32, Komeito party (the LDP's junior partner in the ruling coalition) 14, Initiatives from Osaka 7, Japanese

Communist Party 6, and ind. and others 6. As a result the LDP held 121 seats, DPJ 49, Komeito party 25, Japanese Communist Party 14, Initiatives from Osaka 12, and ind. and others 21. The LDP-Komeito party coalition held 146 of the 242 seats.

Pekkanen, Robert J., Reed, Steven R., Scheiner, Ethan and Smith, Daniel, (eds) *Japan Decides 2017: The Japanese General Election*. 2018

Current Government

Prime Minister: Shinzo Abe; b. 1954 (LDP; sworn in 26 Dec. 2012 and re-elected in Nov. 2017, having previously held office from Sept. 2006–Sept. 2007).

Following resounding election victories for the Liberal Democratic Party in the 2012, 2014 and 2017 parliamentary elections, in Feb. 2019 the coalition government consisting of the Liberal Democratic Party and the Komeito party comprised:

Deputy Prime Minister: Taro Aso (also *Minister of Finance, Minister of State for Financial Services, and Minister in Charge of Overcoming Deflation*).

Minister of Internal Affairs and Communications, and Minister of State for the Social Security and Tax Number System: Masatoshi Ishida. *Justice:* Takashi Yamashita. *Foreign Affairs:* Taro Kono. *Education, Culture, Sports, Science and Technology, and Minister in Charge of Education Rebuilding:* Masahiko Shibayama. *Health, Labour and Welfare, and Working-Style Reform:* Takumi Nemoto. *Agriculture, Forestry and Fisheries:* Takamori Yoshikawa. *Economy, Trade and Industry, Economic Co-operation with Russia, Minister of State for the Nuclear Damage Compensation and Decommissioning Facilitation Corporation, and Minister in Charge of Industrial Competitiveness and the Response to the Economic Impact caused by the Nuclear Accident:* Hiroshige Seko. *Land, Infrastructure, Transport and Tourism, and Minister in Charge of Water Cycle Policy:* Keiichi Ishii. *Environment, and Minister of State for the Nuclear Emergency Preparedness:* Yoshiaki Harada. *Defence:* Takeshi Iwaya. *Chief Cabinet Secretary, Minister in Charge of Mitigating the Impact of US Forces in Okinawa, and Minister in Charge of the Abduction Issue:* Yoshihide Suga. *Reconstruction, and Minister in Charge of Comprehensive Policy Co-ordination for Revival from the Nuclear Accident at Fukushima:* Hiromichi Watanabe. *Chairperson of the National Public Safety Commission, Minister of State for Disaster Management, and Minister in Charge of Building National Resilience:* Junzo Yamamoto. *Promoting Dynamic Engagement of All Citizens, Minister in Charge of Administrative Reform, Civil Service Reform, and Territorial Issues, and Minister of State for Okinawa and Northern Territories Affairs, Consumer Affairs and Food Safety, Measures for Declining Birthrate, and Ocean Policy:* Mitsuhiro Miyakoshi. *Minister of State for 'Cool Japan' Strategy, Intellectual Property Affairs, Science and Technology Policy, and Space Policy, and Minister in Charge of Information Technology Policy:* Takyua Hirai. *Minister of State for Economic and Fiscal Policy, and Minister in Charge of Social Security Reform, and Trans-Pacific Partnership and Japan-US Trade Negotiations:* Toshimitsu Motegi. *Minister of State for Regional Revitalization, Regulatory Reform, and Gender Equality, and Minister in Charge of Women's Empowerment, and Regional Revitalization:* Satsuki Katayama. *Minister in Charge of the Tokyo Olympic and Paralympic Games:* Yoshitaka Sakurada.

Speaker of the House of Representatives: Tadamori Oshima.

Office of the Prime Minister: http://www.kantei.go.jp

Current Leaders

Shinzo Abe

Position
Prime Minister

Introduction
Shinzo Abe, who first served as prime minister from 2006–07, became president of the Liberal Democratic Party (LDP) for the second time in Sept. 2012. He was sworn in as premier for a second spell after leading the party to victory at the Dec. 2012 parliamentary elections. A conservative from a prominent political family, Abe has consistently argued for Japan to take a more assertive role on the world stage and he started his second term promising to boost the economy and to defend Japanese interests. Relations with China, however, became increasingly strained in 2013, while the economy slipped back into recession towards the end of 2014. Abe nonetheless comfortably won further parliamentary elections in Dec. 2014 and in Oct. 2017 that he had called ahead of schedule to reinforce his mandate.

Early Life
Abe was born on 21 Sept. 1954 in Nagato, Yamaguchi Prefecture. He is the son of Shintaro Abe, a former secretary-general of the centre-right LDP. Shinzo Abe graduated in political science from Seikei University in 1977 before undertaking further study at the University of Southern California. Returning to Japan in 1979 he took up employment at Kobe Steel Ltd and entered the political scene in 1982 as executive assistant to his father, who was minister for foreign affairs in the government of Yasuhiro Nakasone.

In elections for the house of representatives in July 1993 Abe won the seat in Yamaguchi Prefecture that had been held by his father (who died in 1991), although the ruling LDP lost its overall majority for the first time since 1955 and was replaced by an eight-party alliance headed by Morihiro Hosokawa. Appointed to the House of Representatives' committee on foreign affairs, Abe also served as director of the LDP's social affairs division, where he focused on pensions and social security against the backdrop of deep recession. The economy began to revive in 1999 after the government, led by the LDP's Keizo Obuchi, spent more than US$1trn. on public works and other programmes to stimulate growth.

In 2000 Abe was appointed deputy chief cabinet secretary in the second cabinet of Prime Minister Yoshiro Mori. In the wake of the 11 Sept. attacks in the USA, Abe led the parliamentary campaign for co-operation with the US-led 'war on terror', securing widespread support after initial opposition. In 2002 he accompanied Junichiro Koizumi, leader of the LDP and prime minister since April 2001, to Pyongyang to attend landmark summit talks with the North Korean leader, Kim Jong Il. Abe won plaudits for his tough stance with North Korea over the repatriation of Japanese nationals who had been abducted by North Koreans in the 1970s and 1980s.

He became secretary-general of the LDP in 2003. Following the party's landslide victory in the Sept. 2005 general election, he was appointed chief cabinet secretary and was central to the government's reform programme. During Koizumi's final parliamentary session the LDP passed 82 of its 91 proposed bills, including provision for the staged controversial privatization of the postal service. On 20 Sept. 2006 Abe was elected to succeed Koizumi, who had stepped down as leader of the LDP in accordance with party rules. Six days later Abe was elected prime minister with 339 of 475 votes in the lower house and a majority in the upper house.

Career in Office
Abe pledged to continue Koizumi's economic reforms and to work to improve relations with China. He announced a 30% cut in his pay as a 'good model' for cutting government spending. His visits to China and South Korea within weeks of taking office demonstrated an assertive approach in international affairs. He also made it clear that he intended to pursue his predecessor's goals of revising Japan's pacifist constitution and securing a permanent seat on the UN Security Council.

However, his premiership went into meltdown in May 2007 when his minister of agriculture, Toshikatsu Matsuoka, committed suicide shortly before facing questions over a financial scandal. The LDP fared badly at elections to the upper house in July 2007 and Abe's position was further weakened when the new agriculture minister, Norihiko Akagi, resigned. He appointed a new cabinet in Aug. but another agriculture minister, Takehiko Endo, resigned after being linked to a separate financial scandal.

Abe faced stern parliamentary opposition to his anti-terrorism bill, which included provision for Japanese logistical support to the USA in Afghanistan. His failure to win passage for the law was widely believed to have influenced his decision to resign on 12 Sept. 2007. Health concerns were also cited, and he subsequently received treatment for ulcerative colitis.

He was replaced as prime minister and LDP president by Yasuo Fukuda but retained his seat in the House of Representatives. After the LDP went into opposition in 2009, he argued for measures to strengthen the existing social order and ease restrictions on defence institutions. He also called for increased government investment in the economy, especially the technology sector.

In Sept. 2012 Abe was reappointed as LDP president and in Nov. 2012, as opposition leader, secured a promise of early elections in return for supporting a government finance bill. In the subsequent Dec. 2012 general election, the LDP secured an outright majority in coalition with Komeito. Abe was sworn in on 26 Dec. 2012. As in his first term, Japan's economy and continuing regional tensions, notably with China, were dominant issues in his first year of office. On the economic front, exports grew strongly as a result of the weak currency, so boosting Abe's recovery plan. In Nov. 2013 he announced the phasing out of the long-established system of agricultural subsidies for rice growers, heralding a free market for the country's staple food. His political position was strengthened when the LDP-Komeito coalition won an outright victory in the elections to the House of Councillors in July 2013, giving him control over both branches of the Diet.

Meanwhile, a long-standing sovereignty dispute with China over islands in the East China Sea degenerated further. In Nov. 2013 China declared an 'air defence identification zone' over a swathe of the sea area, including the islands, prompting a defiant response from both Japan and the USA. The following month Abe's government approved plans to significantly boost Japan's defence spending over a five-year period under a new national security strategy. He also visited the Yasukuni Shrine, a memorial to Japan's war dead, which provoked condemnation from China and South Korea, as well as criticism from the USA. In another controversial move, in July 2014 his government approved moves to change Japan's post-war pacifist security policy to allow its armed forces to engage in combat overseas. The legislation was passed in July 2015, prompting domestic and international protest.

Against a backdrop of continuing economic difficulties and despite a major cabinet reshuffle in Sept. 2014, Abe sought to bolster his political authority by calling a parliamentary election two years early in Dec. 2014. With the opposition Democratic Party of Japan in disarray, the LDP-Komeito party coalition comfortably retained its majority, taking 326 of 475 seats in the House of Representatives. Following the LDP's victory in the House of Councillors in July 2016, Abe enjoyed a commanding majority in both legislative houses. The LDP also agreed to extend its leader's maximum term from six years to nine, further enhancing the prime minister's powerful position. In Aug. that year the government approved a further 28trn. yen (US$275bn.) stimulus to boost the economy.

Political and diplomatic attention in Japan in 2017 was firmly focused on a series of nuclear and ballistic missile tests conducted by North Korea. Abe again called early elections for Oct. as he sought a new mandate to confront the communist regime's increasing regional military threat. The LDP-Komeito coalition maintained its majority with 313 of the 465 assembly seats and Abe promised 'strong counter measures' against Japan's hostile neighbour. In Sept. 2018 Abe won a third consecutive term as LDP leader, winning almost 70% of the votes in a ballot of party and parliamentary members.

In April 2015 Abe had become the first Japanese prime minister to address a joint sitting of the US Congress, expressing repentance over Japan's role in the Second World War, and also the first, in Dec. 2016, to visit Pearl Harbor, the attack on which drew the USA into the conflict in 1941.

Defence

Japan has renounced war as a sovereign right and the threat or the use of force as a means of settling disputes with other nations. Its troops had not previously been able to serve abroad, but in 1992 the House of Representatives voted to allow up to 2,000 troops to take part in UN peacekeeping missions. A law of Nov. 1994 authorizes the Self-Defence Force to send aircraft abroad in rescue operations where Japanese citizens are involved. Following the attacks on New York and Washington of 11 Sept. 2001, legislation was passed allowing Japan's armed forces to take part in operations in the form of logistical support assisting the US-led war on terror. The legislation permits troops to take part in limited overseas operations but not to engage in combat. In May 2003 parliament passed a series of measures in response to North Korea's nuclear programme. Central government won increased control over the military which now has greater freedom to requisition civilian property in the event of attack.

In Jan. 1991 Japan and the USA signed a renewal agreement under which Japan pays 40% of the costs of stationing US forces and 100% of the associated labour costs. US forces in Japan totalled 40,180 in 2011 (mostly marines and air force personnel), around 60% of which are based on the island of Okinawa. The USA has more troops in Japan than in any other foreign country.

Total armed forces in 2011 numbered 247,750.

In 2013 defence expenditure totalled US$50,977m. (US$401 per capita), representing just 1·0% of GDP.

Army

The 'Ground Self-Defence Force' is organized in five regional commands and in 2011 had a strength of 151,600. Equipment in 2011 included 806 main battle tanks.

Navy

The 'Maritime Self-Defence Force' is tasked with coastal protection and defence of the sea lanes to 1,000 nautical miles range from Japan. The main elements of the fleet are organized into four escort flotillas based at Yokosuka, Kure, Sasebo, Maizuru and Ominato. The submarines are based at Yokosuka and Kure.

Personnel in 2011 numbered 45,500. The combatant fleet, all home-built, includes 18 diesel submarines, 29 destroyers and 15 frigates. Japan's biggest warship since the Second World War, the *Izumo*, was unveiled in Aug. 2013. Officially a destroyer, sea trials began in Sept. 2014 and it entered service in March 2015. The Air Arm operated 95 combat aircraft in 2011. Air Arm personnel was estimated at 9,800 in 2011.

Air Force

An 'Air Self-Defence Force' was inaugurated on 1 July 1954. Its equipment includes (2011) F-15 *Eagles*, F-4E *Phantoms* and Mitsubishi F-2 fighters.

Strength (2011) 47,100 operating 371 combat aircraft.

Economy

In 2011 services accounted for 73% of GDP, industry 26% and agriculture 1%.

According to the anti-corruption organization Transparency International, Japan ranked equal 18th in the world in a 2018 survey of the countries with the least corruption in business and government. It received 73 out of 100 in the annual index.

Japan was the fourth most generous country in the world in 2017 after the USA, Germany and the UK, donating US$11·5bn. in international aid in the course of the year. This was equivalent to 0·23% of GNI (compared to the UN target of 0·7%).

Overview

Following China's rapid growth in recent decades, Japan now has the world's third largest economy, having had the second largest up to 2010. It is a major provider of global aid, capital and credit. The traditional corporate system of *keiretsu* (closely knit production chains linking manufacturers, suppliers and distributors) has been gradually eroded. Japan ranks fourth among OECD countries for expenditure on research and development, with spending equalling 3·3% of GDP in 2015.

From 1973 until 1991, Japan's economy grew at an average rate of more than 4% per year. Lax monetary policies, however, caused an unsustainable bubble economy and in its aftermath there was deflation, static wages and declining investment. Over the two decades to 2015 yearly growth averaged below 1%. Exports were the principal driving force of expansion (their share of GDP rising from 10·6% to 17·6%) before momentum shifted to domestic demand and private investment.

Global financial turmoil saw the economy experience six consecutive quarters of contraction in 2008 and 2009, with a collapse in overseas demand compounded by a strong *yen* (which by mid-2012 was 24% higher than in 2007 in real terms). Difficulties were accentuated by a reliance on manufactured exports, notably cars and consumer technology products. The economy emerged from recession in the first quarter of 2010 on a rebound in exports and a fiscal stimulus, but contracted again in 2011 after a major earthquake and subsequent tsunami caused massive damage valued at 3·5% of GDP (with reconstruction estimated to have cost 25·5trn. yen by 2015). Nonetheless, by 2013 per capita income exceeded its 2007 pre-financial crisis level.

Foreign direct investment (FDI) had nearly tripled between 1998 and 2002, and reached record levels in 2008 before turning negative in 2010 and 2011 and averaging only 0·1% of GDP between 2011 and 2014. Inward FDI was ranked 21st among the 35 countries of the Organisation for Economic Co-operation and Development (OECD) as of 2016. Earlier, there had been a trade deficit in 2011 for the first time in 31 years before the economy began to recover in 2012, led by reconstruction activity, industrial production and private consumption. By Nov. 2017 unemployment measured 2·7%—its lowest level since 1993.

The IMF has attributed the strengthening of the economy to reforms in labour and product markets, bank restructuring and corporate efforts to eliminate excess capacity and debt. However, while the traditional system of lifetime employment, which has limited labour market adaptability, is slowly being replaced by more flexible contracts, the number of low-paid temporary workers has risen substantially. Social inequality and relative poverty have widened as a result, with temporary workers (of which 60% are women) receiving less social protection and training.

Between 2002 and Jan. 2018 Japan acceded to Economic Partnership Agreements with 14 countries and the Association of South East Asian Nations. In March 2018 Japan signed the Comprehensive and Progressive Agreement for Trans-Pacific Partnership, an international free trade agreement that the government hopes will prompt domestic industrial reforms. The Long-Term Trade Agreement had meanwhile led to Japan becoming China's most important trading partner in the late 1970s, with Japan relying on China for its oil. However, since the adoption of market policies in China, domestic demand for energy has increased rapidly, constraining the export market and causing friction between the two countries. Expanding its international ties has been a priority of the Chinese government, leading to Japan's relative decline as a major trading partner. Nevertheless, China took 19% of Japanese exports in 2017 (less than the USA at 19·3%) and became the leading source of Japan's imports, accounting for 26%.

Economic growth stood at 1% in 2018, with record corporate profits and labour shortages driving business investment. Consumer price inflation was measured at around 1%. The unemployment rate was 2·5%, while the ratio of job openings to applicants had risen to its highest level since 1974. However, exports declined in the third quarter of 2018 in the context of weaker world trade growth.

Gross public debt (the highest in the world) had reached 243% of GDP in 2013 and remained high at 226% of GDP in 2018, while government revenues stood at 30·7% of GDP in 2016, among the lowest in the OECD. The government ran a deficit of 3% of GDP in 2018. To offset the impact of a hike in the consumption tax from 8% to 10% scheduled for Oct. 2019, the government has put in place plans for a temporary increase in public spending and a cut in taxes on cars and housing in fiscal year 2019–20.

The banking system has been strengthened by tighter regulation, although bank profitability remains low by OECD standards. Nonetheless, the system was relatively well insulated from the global financial crisis as a result of its low exposure to toxic securities and bad debts. In 2018 domestic credit growth slowed, although lending by regional banks to small enterprises continued to grow rapidly and indirect overseas investments via investment trusts remained strong.

In 2012 incumbent prime minister Shinzo Abe proposed a range of economic reforms, popularly labelled 'Abenomics', based on the 'three arrows' of fiscal spending, monetary easing and structural reforms. In Jan. 2013 the government revealed a 10·3trn. *yen* package to boost growth and a further 3·5trn. *yen* stimulus followed in 2014. He won re-election in 2014 and 2017, although by 2018 his Liberal Democratic Party's leadership contest (which he won) highlighted concerns over the persistently high public debt, stagnation of household incomes and the unevenness of economic gains.

Japan has the world's most aged and fastest-ageing population, with the proportion of elderly people increasing by 17 percentage points between 1980 and 2014. In 2016 more than a quarter of the population was over 65. It is one of the few OECD countries where the working-age population started declining in the early 2000s. The mandatory retirement age of 60 has put further pressure on public finances as social spending more than doubled between 1990 and 2013, with many economists arguing for abolition of the mandatory retirement age.

Currency

The unit of currency is the *yen* (JPY). Inflation rates (based on OECD statistics):

2008	2009	2010	2011	2012	2013	2014	2015	2016	2017
1·4%	−1·4%	−0·6%	−0·3%	0·0%	0·3%	2·8%	0·8%	−0·1%	0·5%

Japan's foreign exchange reserves totalled US$1,179,004bn. in Dec. 2015—second only to those of China. Gold reserves in Dec. 2015 were 26·13m. troy oz. In Dec. 2015 the currency in circulation consisted of 98,430,000m. yen Bank of Japan notes and 4,690,000m. yen coins.

Budget

Ordinary revenue and expenditure for fiscal year 2015 balanced at 96,342,000m. yen.

The general account budget for fiscal year 2016 set expenditure and revenue at 96,721,800m. yen. Of the proposed revenue (in yen) 57,604,000m. was to come from taxes and stamps, 34,432,000m. from public bonds and 4,685,800m. from other sources. Main items of expenditure

(in yen): social security, 31,973,800m.; local government, 15,281,100m.; redemption of national debt, 13,716,100m.; interest payments, 9,896,100m.; public works, 5,973,700m.; education and science, 5,358,000m.; defence, 5,054,100m.

The estimated 2013 budgets of the prefectures and other local authorities forecast a total revenue of 101,099,835m. yen, to be made up partly by local taxes and partly by government grants and local loans.

Consumption tax was increased from 5% to 8% with effect from 1 April 2014.

Performance

Real GDP growth rates (based on OECD statistics):

2008	2009	2010	2011	2012	2013	2014	2015	2016	2017
−1·1%	−5·4%	4·2%	−0·1%	1·5%	2·0%	0·4%	1·4%	1·0%	1·7%

In 2017 total GDP was US$4,872·1bn., the third highest in the world after the USA and China, which replaced Japan as the second largest economy in 2010.

Banking and Finance

The Nippon Ginko (Bank of Japan), founded 1882, finances the government and the banks, its function being similar to that of a central bank in other countries. The Bank undertakes the management of Treasury funds and foreign exchange control. Its *Governor* is Haruhiko Kuroda (appointed March 2013). Its gold bullion and cash holdings at 31 March 2016 stood at 651,246m. yen.

In Sept. 2015 there were 114 domestically licensed banks of which five were city banks, 105 regional banks and four trust banks. Financial institutions for small business in Feb. 2016 numbered 265 credit depositories and 153 credit co-operatives. There were also 255 securities companies in Feb. 2016. From 1999 a number of important mergers were announced in the banking sector, most notably that of the Industrial Bank of Japan, Dai-Ichi Kangyo and Fuji Bank, which in Sept. 2000 created Mizuho Financial Group—at the time the world's biggest bank in terms of assets, at over 135,000bn. yen (US$1·3trn.). In Jan. 2006 the Mitsubishi Tokyo Financial Group and UFJ Holdings merged to create the Bank of Tokyo–Mitsubishi UFJ, with assets of 190,000bn. yen (US$1·6trn.) and in Oct. 2007 the newly created Japan Post Bank (now part of the Japan Post Group handling postal, banking and insurance services through the post office network) became the world's largest bank by assets, at US$3·1trn. (although by March 2013 its ranking had fallen considerably and its assets had declined to US$2·1trn.). As at March 2016 there were 24,126 post offices in the country.

Gross external debt amounted to US$3,092,027m. in June 2012.

Foreign direct investment was US$10·4bn. in 2017, down from a record US$24·4bn. in 2008.

There are five stock exchanges, the largest being in Tokyo.

Energy and Natural Resources

Environment

Japan's carbon dioxide emissions from the consumption of energy 2011 accounted for 3·7% of the world total and were equivalent to 9·4 tonnes per capita. An *Environmental Performance Index* compiled in 2016 ranked Japan 39th of 180 countries, with 80·6%. The index examined various factors in nine areas—agriculture, air quality, biodiversity and habitat, climate and energy, fisheries, forests, health impacts, water and sanitation, and water resources.

Electricity

Japan is poor in energy resources, and nuclear power generation has been important in reducing dependence on foreign supplies. However, following the March 2011 earthquake and Fukushima disaster all of the 54 reactors in operation before the earthquake—with a capacity of 48,960 MW—were shut for safety checks. The last one was shut down in May 2012, but two months later one of three reactors at Ohi became the first reactor to be restarted since the disaster. When the last of the reactors was taken offline for maintenance in May 2012 it left Japan without nuclear power for the first time since 1970. Scheduled maintenance and safety fears meant that in Sept. 2013 Japan again had no reactors in use. However, one of the reactors at the Sendai nuclear power plant in southwest Japan was reactivated in Aug. 2015 with the second one following two months later. In 2010 nuclear reactors produced approximately 26% of electricity. During the 1990s nuclear power was the main source of electricity but natural gas now accounts for the largest share. Total installed generating capacity was 292·1m. kW in 2011. Electricity produced in 2011 was 1,051,251m. kWh. Consumption per capita in 2011 was 8,257 kWh.

Oil and Gas

Output of crude petroleum, 2008, was 985,680 kilolitres, almost entirely from oilfields on the island of Honshu, but 234·4m. kilolitres of crude oil had to be imported. Output of natural gas, 2008, 3,735m. cu. metres; with reserves (2013) of 21bn. cu. metres.

Minerals

Production in tonnes: zinc (2006), 7,169; copper (2013), 3,031; lead (2006), 777; iron (2005), 736; silver (2006), 11,463 kg; gold (2008), 6,868 kg. Output of other minerals (2014, in 1,000 tonnes): limestone, 148,008; quartzite, 9,496; gypsum, 4,674; dolomite, 3,446; silica sand, 2,932; coal (estimate), 1,200; salt (2012), 1,052.

Agriculture

Total agricultural output in 2014 was valued at 8,364bn. yen. The number of agricultural workers has dropped from 13·4m. in 1960 (30·2% of the total workforce) to 2·3m. in 2014 (3·6%). In 2011, 12·5% of land was agricultural (4·56m. ha., down from 6·09m. ha. in 1961), of which 93·3% was arable and 6·7% permanent crops. In 2015 there were 1·33m. farm households engaged in commercial farming.

Rice is the staple food, but its consumption is declining. Rice cultivation accounted for 1,575,000 ha. in 2014 and output (in 1,000 tonnes) was 8,439.

Production in 2014 (in 1,000 tonnes) of sugar beets was 3,567; potatoes, 2,456; cabbage, 1,480; Japanese radishes, 1,452; onions, 1,169; sugarcane, 1,159; Chinese cabbage, 914; sweet potatoes, 887; wheat, 852; tomatoes, 740; carrots, 633; lettuce, 578; cucumbers, 549; aubergines, 323; spinach, 257.

Fruit production, 2014 (in 1,000 tonnes): mandarins, 875; apples, 816; Asian pears, 271; grapes, 189.

Livestock (2014): 9·54m. pigs, 3·96m. cattle, 17,000 goats (estimate), 16,000 horses (estimate), 13,300 sheep (estimate) and 311m. chickens (estimate). Livestock products, 2014 (in 1,000 tonnes): milk, 7,334; broiler meat, 1,946; pork, 1,264; beef, 501; eggs, 2,502.

Forestry

Forests covered 24·96m. ha. in 2015, or 69% of the land area. Of the total area under forests 20% was primary forest in 2015, 39% other naturally regenerated forest and 41% planted forest. Timber production was 18·37m. cu. metres in 2011.

Fisheries

The catch in 2011 was 3,775,545 tonnes. More than 99% of fish caught are from marine waters. Japan is the second largest importer of fishery commodities (after the USA), with imports in 2011 totalling US$17·34bn.

Industry

The leading companies by market capitalization in Japan in May 2017 were: Toyota Motor Corporation (US$171·9bn.); Nippon Telegraph and Telecom Corp., a telecommunications services company (US$92·2bn.); and Mitsubishi UFJ Financial Group, Inc. (US$83·9bn.).

The industrial structure is dominated by corporate groups (*keiretsu*) either linking companies in different branches or linking individual companies with their suppliers and distributors.

Japan's industrial capacity, 2014, numbered 202,410 plants of all sizes, employing 7·40m. production workers.

Output in 2016 (unless otherwise indicated) included: watches and clocks, 268·89m.; refrigerators, 20·98m.; personal computers, 4·81m.; radio sets (2005), 1·77m.; flat panel television sets, 0·77m. The chemical industry ranks fourth in shipment value after machinery, metals and food products. Production, 2008, included (in tonnes): sulphuric acid, 7·23m.; caustic soda (2005), 3·89m.; ammonium sulphate, 1·41m.; compound fertilizers, 1·23m. A total of 9,630,000 motor vehicles were manufactured in Japan in 2013. It was the world's largest vehicle producer until 2009 when China overtook it both on the number of cars and vehicles overall. Japan is now the second largest producer of passenger cars (8,189,000 in 2013).

The leading companies by market capitalization in Japan in May 2018 were: Toyota Motor Corporation (US$200·7bn.); Nippon Telegraph and Telecom Corp., a telecommunications services company (US$96·1bn.); and Mitsubishi UFJ Financial Group, Inc. (US$86·2bn.).

The industrial structure is dominated by corporate groups (*keiretsu*) either linking companies in different branches or linking individual companies with their suppliers and distributors.

Japan's industrial capacity, 2014, numbered 202,410 plants of all sizes, employing 7·40m. production workers.

Output in 2016 (unless otherwise indicated) included: watches and clocks, 268·89m.; refrigerators, 20·98m.; personal computers, 4·81m.; radio sets (2005), 1·77m.; flat panel television sets, 0·77m. The chemical industry ranks fourth in shipment value after machinery, metals and food products. Production, 2008, included (in tonnes): sulphuric acid, 7·23m.; caustic soda (2005), 3·89m.; ammonium sulphate, 1·41m.; compound fertilizers, 1·23m. A total of 9,630,000 motor vehicles were manufactured in Japan in 2013. It was the world's largest vehicle producer until 2009 when China overtook it both on the number of cars and vehicles overall. Japan is now the second largest producer of passenger cars (8,189,000 in 2013).

Output, in 1,000 tonnes, 2009: crude steel, 87,534; pig iron, 66,943; cement (2008), 62,810; ordinary rolled steel, 62,024.

2007 production (in 1,000 tonnes): distillate fuel oil, 55,300; petrol, 42,801; residual fuel oil, 29,545; kerosene, 18,783.

In 2008 paper production was 18·83m. tonnes; paperboard, 11·80m. tonnes.

Output of woven fabrics, 2008, 1,554m. sq. metres. Output of cotton yarn, 2007, 71,669 tonnes; and of cotton woven fabrics (2008), 327m. sq. metres. Output, 2007, 3,870 tonnes of woollen yarns and (2008) 61m. sq. metres of wool fabrics. Output, 2008, of synthetic woven fabrics, 1,008m. sq. metres; rayon woven fabrics, 36m. sq. metres; silk fabrics, 14m. sq. metres.

3,213m. litres of beer were produced in 2008–09; 13,649m. litres of soft drinks and mineral water in 2003; 878,000 tonnes of sugar in 2008–09.

Shipbuilding orders in 2005 totalled 8,698,000 GRT. In 2007, 17,240,220 GRT were launched of which 5,284,893 GRT were tankers.

Labour

The labour force in 2013 was 65,559,000, down from 66,934,000 in 2003. 74·9% of the population aged 15–64 was economically active in 2013. Of those in employment in 2013, 69·1% worked in services, 25·8% in industry and 3·7% in agriculture. In that year 42·6% of the labour force was female. In Dec. 2018 unemployment stood at 2·4%, down from a record high of 5·7% in July 2009. The youth unemployment rate in 2013 was the lowest in the industrialized world, at just 6·9%. Long-term unemployment rose from 26·6% of the labour force between 16 and 64 having been out of work for more than a year in 2001 to 39·4% in 2011. The declining population means that the United Nations expects the working-age population in 2050 to be lower than it was in the 1950s. Retirement age is being raised progressively from 60 years to reach 65 by 2025.

Japan had 80,000 people living in slavery according to the Walk Free Foundation's 2013 *Global Slavery Index*.

International Trade

Imports and Exports

Trade (in US$1m.):

	2007	2008	2009	2010
Imports	622,243	762,534	551,985	694,059
Exports	714,327	781,412	580,719	769,774

In 2011 merchandise imports exceeded exports for the first time since 1980. In 2013 Japanese imports accounted for 4·4% of the world total imports, and exports 3·8% of the world total exports.

Main import suppliers, 2010 (US$1m.): China, 153,203; USA, 69,115; Australia, 45,097; Saudi Arabia, 35,972; UAE, 29,341; South Korea, 28,601; Indonesia, 28,283; Malaysia, 22,701; Qatar, 21,748; Thailand, 21,017. Main export markets, 2010 (US$1m.): China, 149,451; USA, 120,338; South Korea, 62,361; Hong Kong, 42,312; Thailand, 34,191; Singapore, 25,230; Germany, 20,290; Malaysia, 17,641; Netherlands, 16,338; Indonesia, 15,926.

Imports/exports by category, 2010 (in US$1bn.):

	Imports	Exports
Chemicals and related products	60·8	78·4
Food and live animals	52·9	4·0
Inedible crude materials, excluding fuels	55·6	10·9
Machinery and transport equipment	161·5	458·0
Manufactured goods	58·8	99·8
Mineral fuels and lubricants	199·1	13·0
Miscellaneous manufactured articles	84·5	58·4
Other products	20·9	47·3

The importation of rice was prohibited until the emergency importation of 1m. tonnes from Australia, China, Thailand and the USA in 1993–94 to offset a poor domestic harvest. The prohibition was lifted in line with WTO agreements. Until 2000 rice imports had limited access; the market is now fully open.

Communications

Roads
The total length of roads (including urban and other local roads) was 1,196,217 km at 1 April 2008. There were 54,736 km of national roads of which 49,756 km were paved. In 2006, 79·2% of all roads were paved. Motor vehicles, at 31 March 2010, numbered 78,693,000, including 40,419,000 passenger cars and 6,362,000 trucks. In 2007 there were 5,353,648 new vehicle registrations. In 2009 there were 4,914 road deaths (10,679 in 1995).

The world's longest undersea road tunnel, spanning Tokyo Bay, was opened in Dec. 1997. The Tokyo Bay Aqualine, built at a cost of 1·44trn. yen (US$11·3bn.), consists of a 4·4 km (2·7 mile) bridge and a 9·4 km tunnel that allows commuters to cross the bay in about 15 minutes.

Rail
The first railway was completed in 1872, between Tokyo and Yokohama (29 km). Most railways are of 1,067 mm gauge, but the high-speed 'Shinkansen' lines are standard 1,435 mm gauge. In April 1987 the Japanese National Railways was reorganized into seven private companies, the Japanese Railways (JR) Group—six passenger companies and one freight company. Total length of railways in 2008–09 was 27,343 km, of which the JR had 19,987 km and other private railways 7,356 km. In 2014–15 the JR carried 9,088m. passengers (other private, 14,512m.); railway freight transport totalled 43·4m. tonnes. An undersea tunnel linking Honshu with Hokkaido was opened to rail services in 1988.

There are metros in Tokyo (two metro systems, total 304·1 km in 2008), Fukuoka (29·8 km), Hiroshima (18·4 km), Kobe (30·6 km), Kyoto (28·8 km), Nagoya (89·1 km), Osaka (137·8 km), Sapporo (48·0 km), Sendai (14·8 km) and Yokohama (40·4 km). There are over 40 electric light railways and tram networks in 14 cities.

Japan was ranked second only to Switzerland for quality of rail infrastructure in the World Economic Forum's *Global Competitiveness Report 2017–2018*.

Civil Aviation
The main international airports are at Fukuoka, Hiroshima, Kagoshima, Nagoya, Naha, Niigata, Osaka (Kansai International), Sapporo, Sendai and two serving Tokyo—at Narita (New Tokyo International) and Haneda (Tokyo International). The principal airlines are Japan Airlines (JAL) and All Nippon Airways. In Jan. 2010 JAL filed for bankruptcy protection after making a single-quarter loss of nearly 100bn. yen, prompting a restructuring of the company. In fiscal year 2014 Japanese companies carried 95·20m. passengers on domestic services and 16·04m. passengers on international services. In fiscal year 2015 JAL carried 32,114,322 domestic and 8,080,676 international passengers while All Nippon Airways carried 38,429,874 domestic and 8,167,951 international passengers.

In 2015 Narita handled 37,328,213 passengers (mainly on international flights) and 2,035,968 tonnes of freight (making it the eighth busiest airport in the world for freight). Tokyo Haneda was mainly used for domestic flights until the opening in 2010 of a dedicated international terminal in conjunction with the completion of a fourth runway allowed the number of international flights serving the airport to increase considerably; in 2015 it handled 75,316,718 passengers, making it the fifth busiest airport in the world.

Shipping
In Jan. 2014 there were 2,536 ships of 300 GT or over registered, totalling 15·14m. GT. Of the 2,536 vessels registered, 1,021 were general cargo ships, 704 oil tankers, 376 bulk carriers, 275 passenger ships, 158 liquid gas tankers and two container ships. The Japanese-controlled comprised 4,149 vessels of 1,000 GT or over in July 2014. Only 702 of the 4,149 vessels in July 2014 were flying the Japanese flag. The busiest ports are Nagoya (208,241,000 freight tons handled in 2013), Chiba, Yokohama, Kitakyushu and Kobe.

Coastguard
The 'Japan Coast Guard' consists of one main headquarters, 11 regional headquarters, 71 offices, 61 stations, seven vessel traffic service centres, 14 air stations, one transnational organized crime strike force station, one special security station, one special rescue station, one national strike team station, one hydrographic observatory and 5,284 aids-to-navigation facilities. It controlled 62 large patrol vessels, 38 medium patrol vessels, 30 small patrol vessels, 238 patrol craft, 13 hydrographic service vessels, one large firefighting boat, seven lighthouse tenders, three training boats and 63 special guard and rescue boats in the financial year 2017. Personnel numbered 13,744. The 'Japan Coast Guard' aviation service includes 26 fixed-wing aircraft and 48 helicopters.

Telecommunications
Telephone services have been operated by private companies (NTT and others) since 1985. In 2013 there were 1,176·3 mobile phone subscriptions per 1,000 inhabitants and 479·9 fixed telephone subscriptions per 1,000 population. There were 289·0 fixed broadband subscriptions per 1,000 inhabitants in 2013 and 1,205·4 mobile broadband subscriptions per 1,000. In 2013, 86·3% of the population aged 15–74 were internet users. In March 2012 there were 7·7m. Facebook users (only 6% of the population).

Social Institutions

Out of 178 countries analysed in the 2017 *Fragile States Index*—a list published jointly by the Fund for Peace and *Foreign Policy* magazine—Japan was ranked the 23rd least vulnerable to conflict or collapse. The index is based on 12 indicators of state vulnerability across social, political and economic categories.

Justice
The Supreme Court is composed of the Chief Justice and 14 other judges. The Chief Justice is appointed by the Emperor, the other judges by the Cabinet. Every ten years a justice must submit himself to the electorate. All justices and judges of the lower courts serve until they are 70 years of age.

Below the Supreme Court are eight regional higher courts, district courts in each prefecture (four in Hokkaido) and the local courts.

The Supreme Court is authorized to declare unconstitutional any act of the Legislature or the Executive which violates the Constitution.

Jury trials were reintroduced in Aug. 2009 for the first time since the Second World War.

In 2012, 2,015,347 penal code offences were reported, including 1,030 homicides. The death penalty is authorized; there were three executions in 2016, four in 2017 and 15 in 2018. The population in penal institutions in Dec. 2014 was 60,486 (48 per 100,000 population—compared to the global average of 144 per 100,000 population). In 2015 the World Justice Project *Rule of Law Index*, which provides data on how the rule of law is experienced by the general public across eight categories, ranked Japan 16th of 102 countries for criminal justice and 14th for civil justice.

Education
Education is compulsory and free between the ages of six and 15. Almost all national and municipal institutions are co-educational. In May 2015 there were 11,674 kindergartens with 101,000 full-time teachers and 1,403,000 pupils; 20,601 elementary schools with 417,000 teachers and 6,543,000 pupils; 10,484 lower secondary schools with 254,000 teachers and 3,465,000 pupils; 4,939 upper secondary schools with 235,000 teachers and 3,319,000 pupils; 346 junior colleges with 8,000 teachers and 132,000 pupils; and 57 colleges of technology with 4,000 teachers and 58,000 pupils. There were also 1,114 special needs schools (81,000 teachers, 138,000 pupils).

Japan has seven main state universities: Tokyo University (1877); Kyoto University (1897); Tohoku University, Sendai (1907); Kyushu University, Fukuoka (1910); Hokkaido University, Sapporo (1918); Osaka University

(1931); and Nagoya University (1939). In addition, there are various other state and municipal as well as private universities. In May 2015 there were 779 universities overall with 2,860,000 students and 183,000 full-time teaching staff.

In 2011 expenditure on education came to 3·8% of GDP and 9·7% of total government spending.

The adult literacy rate is at least 99%.

According to the OECD's 2015 PISA (Programme for International Student Assessment) study, 15-year-olds in Japan rank second among OECD and other major countries and cities in science, fifth in mathematics and eighth in reading. The three-yearly study compares educational achievement of pupils in over 70 countries.

Health

Hospitals on 1 Oct. 2014 numbered 8,493 with 1,568,261 beds; the bed provision of 123·4 per 10,000 population was one of the highest in the world. Physicians in 2014 numbered 308,651; dentists, 102,534. In 2011 Japan spent 10·1% of its GDP on health, with public spending accounting for 81·9% of total expenditure on health and private spending 18·1%. A survey carried out in May 2012 found that 21·1% of Japanese were smokers (32·7% of males but only 10·4% of females).

Welfare

There are various types of social security schemes in force, such as health insurance, unemployment insurance and age pensions. The old age pension system in Japan is made up of a two-tiered public benefit. The first tier of the public pension is the basic pension which is payable from age 65 with 25 years' contributions. To receive the full benefit amount, 40 years' contributions to the system are necessary. There is an earnings floor for contributions at approximately 28% of average earnings. The monthly premium of the National Pension is uniformly fixed (15,040 yen in fiscal year 2013). The full basic pension was a flat amount of 772,800 yen per annum in fiscal year 2014, paid in two-monthly instalments. A reduced early pension is available between the ages 60–64, while pensions may also be deferred up to age 70.

14 weeks maternity leave is statutory.

Social security expenditure in fiscal year 2013 was 110,657bn. yen (amounting to 869,300 yen per person), including 53,610bn. yen on pension benefits and 19,963bn. on medical insurance.

Religion

All religious teachings are forbidden in public schools. In Dec. 2012 Shintoism claimed 100·94m. adherents, Buddhism 85·14m. These figures overlap as many Japanese follow both religions. Christians numbered 1·91m. In Feb. 2019 there was one cardinal.

Culture

World Heritage Sites

Japan has 22 sites on the UNESCO World Heritage List (date of inscription on the list in brackets): the Buddhist Monuments in the Horyu-ji Area (1993); Himeji-jo (1993); Yakushima (1993); Shirakami-Sanchi (1993); the Historic Monuments of Ancient Kyoto (Kyoto, Uji and Otsu Cities) (1994), including 13 of Kyoto's Buddhist temples, three Shinto shrines and one castle—temples include Byōdo-in, Daigo-ji, Enryaku-ji, Ginkaku-ji, Kinkaku-ji, Kiyomizu-dera, Kōzan-ji, Ninna-ji, Nishi Hongan-ji, Ryōan-ji, Saihō-ji, Tenryū-ji and Tō-ji; the Historic Villages of Shirakawa-go and Gokayama (1995); Hiroshima Peace Memorial (Genbaku Dome) (1996); Itsukushima Shinto Shrine (1996); the Historic Monuments of Ancient Nara (1998), including five Buddhist temples—Tōdai-ji, Kōfuku-ji, Gango-ji, Yakushi-ji and Tōshōdai-ji—and three listed shrines—Kasuga Taisha, Kasuga Yama Primeval Forest and the remains of Heijō-kyō Palace; Shrines and Temples of Nikko (1999); Gusuku Sites and Related Properties of the Kingdom of Ryukyu (2000); Sacred sites and pilgrimage routes in the Kii mountain range (2004); marine and land ecosystems at Shiretoko (2005); the Iwami Ginzan Silver Mine and its cultural landscape (2007); Hiraizumi—temples, gardens and archaeological sites representing the Buddhist Pure Land (2011); Ogasawara Islands (2011); the stratovolcano, Fujisan, generally known as Mount Fuji (2013); Tomioka Silk Mill and Related Sites (2014); Sites of Japan's Meji Industrial Revolution: Iron and Steel, Shipbuilding and Coal Mining (2015); the Sacred Island of Okinoshima and Associated Sites in the Munakata Region (2017); and Hidden Christian Sites in the Nagasaki Region (2018). The Architectural Work of Le Corbusier, an Outstanding Contribution to the Modern Movement (2016), is shared with Argentina, Belgium, France, Germany, India and Switzerland.

Press

In 2014 daily newspapers numbered 104 with aggregate circulation of 45.45m. including four major English-language newspapers. The newspapers with the highest circulation are *Yomiuri Shimbun* (daily average of 9·2m. copies in 2014) and *Asahi Shimbun* (daily average of 6·8m. copies in 2014). They are also the two most widely read newspapers in the world. Japan has one of the highest circulation rates of daily newspapers in any country. There were 75 newspaper online editions in 2014. In the 2013 *World Press Freedom Index* compiled by Reporters Without Borders, Japan was ranked 53rd out of 179 countries.

In 2013, 82,589 new book titles were published.

Tourism

In 2012 there were 8,358,000 foreign visitors (up from 6,219,000 in 2011 although down from 8,611,000 in 2010). Of the foreign visitors in 2011, 77% were from elsewhere in East Asia and the Pacific, 12% from the Americas and 9% from Europe. Tourist receipts amounted to US$16·2bn. in 2012.

Festivals

Japan has a huge number of annual festivals, among the largest of which are the Sapporo Snow Festival (Feb.); Hakata Dontaku, Fukuoka City (May); the Sanja Festival of Asakusa Shrine, Tokyo (May); the Tanabata Festival in Hiratsuka City (July) and Sendai City (Aug.); the Nebuta Festival in Aomori City (Aug.); and Jidai Matsuri, Kyoto (Oct.). Leading rock and pop festivals include Fuji Rock Festival, Naeba (July); Rising Sun Rock Festival, Otaru (Aug.); and Summer Sonic, Chiba and Osaka (Aug.).

Diplomatic Representatives

Of Japan in the United Kingdom (101–104 Piccadilly, London, W1J 7JT)
Ambassador: Koji Tsuruoka.

Of the United Kingdom in Japan (1 Ichiban-cho, Chiyoda-ku, Tokyo 102-8381)
Ambassador: Paul Madden, CMG.

Of Japan in the USA (2520 Massachusetts Ave., NW, Washington, D.C., 20008)
Ambassador: Shinsuke Sugiyama.

Of the USA in Japan (10–5, Akasaka 1-chome, Minato-ku, Tokyo)
Ambassador: William F. Hagerty IV.

Of Japan to the United Nations
Ambassador: Koro Bessho.

Of Japan to the European Union
Ambassador: Kazuo Kodama.

Further Reading

Statistics Bureau of the Prime Minister's Office (up to 2000) and Statistics Bureau of the Ministry of Internal Affairs and Communications (from 2001): *Statistical Yearbook* (from 1949).—*Statistical Handbook* (from 1958).—*Monthly Statistics of Japan* (from 1947–2006; online only since 2006 as *Japan Monthly Statistics*).—*Historical Statistics* (from 1868–2002)

Economic Planning Agency (up to 2000) and Economic and Social Research Institute (from 2001) of the Cabinet Office: *Economic Survey* (annual), *Economic Statistics* (monthly), *Economic Indicators* (monthly)

Ministry of International Trade and Industry (up to 2000) and the Ministry of Economy, Trade and Industry (from 2001): *Foreign Trade of Japan* (annual)

Allinson, G. D., *Japan's Postwar History.* 1997

Argy, V. and Stein, L., *The Japanese Economy.* 1996

Bailey, P. J., *Post-war Japan: 1945 to the Present.* 1996

Beasley, W. G., *The Rise of Modern Japan: Political, Economic and Social Change Since 1850.* 3rd ed. 2000

Buruma, Ian, *Inventing Japan: 1853–1964.* 2003

The Cambridge Encyclopedia of Japan. 1993

Cambridge History of Japan. Vols. 1–5. 1990–93

Campbell, A., (ed.) *Japan: an Illustrated Encyclopedia.* 1994

Clesse, A., et al., (eds) *The Vitality of Japan: Sources of National Strength and Weakness.* 1997

Henshall, K. G., *A History of Japan: From Stone Age to Superpower.* 3rd ed. 2012

Kingston, Jeff, *Contemporary Japan: History, Politics and Social Change Since the 1980s.* 2010

McCargo, Duncan, *Contemporary Japan.* 3rd ed. 2012

McClain, James, *Japan: A Modern History.* 2001

McGregor, Richard, *Asia's Reckoning: China, Japan and the Fate of US Power in the Pacific Century.* 2017

Morton, W. Scott and Olenik, J. Kenneth, *Japan: Its History and Culture.* 2004

Murphy, R. Taggart, *Japan and the Shackles of the Past.* 2014

Pekkanen, Robert J., Reed, Steven R. and Scheiner, Ethan, (eds) *Japan Decides 2014.* 2015

Perren, R., *Japanese Studies From Pre-History to 1990.* 1992

Schirokauer, C., *Brief History of Japanese Civilization.* 1993

Stockwin, J., *Dictionary of the Modern Politics of Japan.* 2003

Takao, Yasuo, *Reinventing Japan: From Merchant Nation to Civic Nation.* 2008

Woronoff, J., *The Japanese Economic Crisis.* 2nd ed. 1996

Yoda, Tomiko, *Japan After Japan: Social and Cultural Life from the Recessionary 1990s to the Present.* 2006

A more specialized title is listed under RECENT ELECTIONS, *above.*

National library: The National Diet Library, 1-10-1 Nagata-cho, Chiyoda-ku, Tokyo 100-8924.

National Statistical Office: Statistics Bureau, Ministry of Internal Affairs and Communications, 19-1 Wakamatsu-cho, Shinjuku-ku, Tokyo 162-8668. *Director-General of the Statistical Survey Department, Statistics Bureau:* Masato Chino.

Website: http://www.stat.go.jp

Jordan

Al-Mamlaka Al-Urduniya Al-Hashemiyah (Hashemite Kingdom of Jordan)

Capital: Amman
Population projection, 2020: 10·21m.
GNI per capita, 2017: (PPP$) 8,288
HDI/world rank, 2017: 0·735/95=
Internet domain extension: .jo

Key Historical Events

Egyptian control was established over Semitic Amorite tribes in the Jordan valley in the 16th century BC. However, Egypt's conflict with the Hittite Empire allowed the development of autonomous kingdoms such as Edom, Moab, Gilead and Ammon (centred on modern Amman). The Israelites settled on the east bank of the Jordan in the 13th century and crossed into Canaan. David subjugated Moab, Edom and Ammon in the 10th century but the Assyrians wrested control in the 9th century, remaining until 612 BC. Nabataea expanded in the south during the Babylonian and Persian periods until conquered for Rome by Pompey in the 1st century BC. After Trajan's campaign of AD 106, the Jordan area was absorbed as Arabia Petraea.

Rome (later Byzantium) and Sassanid Persia clashed over the area but a Muslim army under Khalid ibn al-Walid defeated Byzantium in 636 at the Yarmuk River. After the fall of the Umayyad Caliphate in 750, the centre of power moved from Damascus to Baghdad. The principality of Oultre Jourdain, established by the Christian crusader kingdom of Jerusalem in the early 12th century, was destroyed by Saladin in 1187. The Mamluk Empire held power until the advent of the Turkish Ottoman Empire in the 16th century.

The Arabs of the Ottoman Damascus province rebelled with British support in 1916. The Hashemite Prince Faisal ibn Husayn took Aqaba in 1917 and the British took Amman and Damascus in 1918. The First World War victors decreed two mandates—British Palestine and French Syria. Britain created the Transjordan Emirate in 1922, ruled semi-autonomously by Faisal's brother, Abdullah. Full independence was achieved on 25 May 1946 as the Hashemite Kingdom of Transjordan (Jordan from 1949).

Transjordan declared war on the Israeli state in May 1948, taking the West Bank and East Jerusalem, an occupation supported only by Britain. Palestinian resistance to the annexation culminated in King Abdullah's assassination in 1951. Talal, his son and successor, was deemed mentally unfit in 1952 and Hussein Bin Talal was installed in 1953. After an attempted coup in 1957, instigated by West Bank Palestinians, King Hussein banned political parties and ended Palestinian representation. A brief union with Iraq, ruled by his cousin, ended after an Iraqi republican coup in 1958. Hussein turned to Britain and the USA for military and financial support.

Fatah and the Palestine Liberation Organization (PLO) maintained terrorist attacks on Israel from Jordan, provoking Israeli retaliation in the West Bank. Despite secret co-operation with Israel over containing the Palestinians, Hussein allied with Syria and Egypt in the war of June 1967. Israel repelled Jordanian forces from the West Bank, moving the *de facto* border to the River Jordan. This devastated the Jordanian economy but removed Palestinian opposition to the Hashemite regime. However, Jordan's relations with the Palestinians deteriorated; in Sept. 1970 four airliners were destroyed by Palestinian extremists in the Jordanian desert. Jordan, with US and British assistance, repelled a Syrian invasion and evicted the PLO. Relations with Israel also worsened from 1977 with the Jewish settlement programme in the West Bank.

On 31 July 1988 Hussein dissolved Jordan's legal and administrative ties with the West Bank in reaction to the *intifada*, which he saw as a threat to his regime. Elections in 1989 led the way to the suspension of martial law—in place from 1967–91. Hussein, constrained by Jordan's economic and political ties with Iraq, refused to abandon Saddam Hussein in the 1991 Gulf War, creating a rift with Jordan's Western partners. Multi-party elections were held in 1993, giving Hussein parliamentary support. He signed a peace treaty with Israel in 1994. In Jan. 1999 Hussein replaced as crown prince his brother, Hassan, with his son, Abdullah, who succeeded on his father's death a month later.

In Jan. 2011 large-scale protests across much of the Arab world demanding political reform spread to Jordan. Subsequent parliamentary elections in Jan. 2013 were boycotted by the main opposition Islamic Action Front. From Sept. the following year Jordan, along with four other Arab states, took part in US-led air strikes against Islamic State (IS) militants in Syria. In Feb. 2015 IS released a video that it claimed showed a Jordanian air force pilot being burned alive. Jordan responded by intensifying its air strikes.

Territory and Population

Jordan is bounded in the north by Syria, east by Iraq, southeast and south by Saudi Arabia and west by Israel. It has an outlet to an arm of the Red Sea at Aqaba. Its area is 88,794 sq. km (including 540 sq. km inland water). The 2015 census population was 9,531,712, giving a density of 108·0 per sq. km.

The UN gives a projected population for 2020 of 10·21m.

In 2011, 78·6% of the population lived in urban areas. Populations of the 12 governorates:

Governorate	2015 census
Ajloun	176,080
Amman	4,007,526
Aqaba	188,160
Balqa	491,709
Irbid	1,770,158
Jerash	237,059
Karak	316,629
Ma'an	144,082
Madaba	189,192
Mafraq	549,948
Tafilah	96,291
Zarqa	1,364,878

The largest towns are (2015 census population): Amman, the capital, 1,812,059; Zarqa, 635,160; Irbid, 502,714.

At the end of 2016 Jordan's population included 685,000 refugees, most of whom were from neighbouring Syria. At 88 refugees per 1,000 inhabitants in Dec. 2016, Jordan has the second highest number of refugees compared to the national population of the host country (after Lebanon).

The official language is Arabic.

Social Statistics

Births (est.), 2008, 180,000; deaths, 20,000. Rates, 2008 per 1,000 population: birth (est.), 31; death (est.), 4. Annual population growth rate, 2008–10, 2·2%. Life expectancy at birth in 2013; 72·3 years for men, 75·6 for women. Infant mortality, 2010, 18 per 1,000 live births; fertility rate, 2008, 3·1 births per woman.

Climate

Predominantly a Mediterranean climate, with hot dry summers and cool wet winters, but in hilly parts summers are cooler and winters colder. Those areas below sea-level are very hot in summer and warm in winter. Eastern parts have a desert climate. Amman, Jan. 46°F (7·5°C), July 77°F (24·9°C). Annual rainfall 13·4" (340·6 mm). Aqaba, Jan. 61°F (16°C), July 89°F (31·5°C). Annual rainfall 1·4" (36·7 mm).

© Springer Nature Limited 2020
Palgrave Macmillan (ed.), *The Statesman's Yearbook 2020*,
https://doi.org/10.1057/978-1-349-95940-2_101

Constitution and Government

The Kingdom is a constitutional monarchy headed by H. M. King **Abdullah Bin Al Hussein II**, born 30 Jan. 1962, married H. M. Queen Rania (Rania Al Yassin, b. 31 Aug. 1970) on 10 June 1993. He succeeded on the death of his father, H. M. King Hussein, on 7 Feb. 1999. *Sons:* Hussein, b. 28 June 1994; Hashem, b. 30 Jan. 2005; *daughters:* Iman, b. 27 Sept. 1996; Salma, b. 26 Sept. 2000.

The Constitution ratified on 8 Dec. 1952 provides that the Cabinet is responsible to Parliament. It was amended in 1954, 1958, 1960, 1973, 1974, 1976, 1984, 2011 and 2016. The legislature consists of a *Senate* of 65 members appointed by the King and a *House of Representatives* of 130 members (15 are reserved for women) elected by universal suffrage. Nine seats are reserved for Christians, and three for Circassians or Chechens. A law of 1993 restricts each elector to a single vote.

The lower house was dissolved in 1976 and elections postponed because no elections could be held in the West Bank under Israeli occupation. Parliament was reconvened on 9 Jan. 1984. By-elections were held in March 1984 and six members were nominated for the West Bank, bringing Parliament to 60 members. Women voted for the first time in 1984. On 9 June 1991 the King and the main political movements endorsed a national charter which legalized political parties in return for the acceptance of the constitution and monarchy. Movements linked to, or financed by, non-Jordanian bodies are not allowed.

National Anthem

'Asha al Malik' ('Long Live the King'); words by A. Al Rifai, tune by A. Al Tanir.

Government Chronology

Kings since 1946.

1946–51	Abdullah Bin Al Hussein Al Hashimi I
1951–52	Talal Bin Abdullah Al Hashimi
1953–99	Hussein Bin Talal Al Hashimi
1999–	Abdullah Bin Al Hussein Al Hashimi II

Recent Elections

Elections to the House of Representatives were held on 20 Sept. 2016 after the King dissolved the parliament in May 2016. Independents, mostly loyal to King Abdullah, won 114 of the 130 seats. The Islamic Action Front (the political wing of the Muslim Brotherhood) and its allies won 16 seats. 20 women were also elected, up from 18 in the outgoing legislature. Turnout was 36·0%.

Current Government

In Feb. 2019 the government consisted of:

Prime Minister and Minister of Defence: Omar Razzaz; b. 1970 (ind.; took office on 5 June 2018).

Deputy Prime Minister: Rajai Muasher (also *Minister of State*).

Minister of Agriculture, and Environment: Ibrahim Subhi Al-Shehadeh. *Awqaf and Islamic Affairs:* Abdul Nasser Abul Bassal. *Culture, and Youth:* Mohammed Suleiman. *Energy and Mineral Resources:* Hala Zawati. *Finance:* Izzidine Kanakrieh. *Foreign Affairs and Expatriate Affairs:* Ayman Safadi. *Health:* Ghazi Mansour Al-Zabin. *Industry, Trade and Supply:* Tareq Hammouri. *Information and Communications Technology:* Muthana Gharaibeh. *Interior:* Samir Mubaidin. *Justice, and Education and Higher Education and Scientific Research (acting):* Bassam Samir Talhouni. *Labour:* Samir Murad. *Planning and International Co-operation:* Mary Qawar. *Political and Parliamentary Affairs:* Musa Maaytah. *Public Works and Housing:* Falal Abdullah Al-Amoush. *Social Development:* Basma Mousa Ishaqat. *Tourism and Antiquities:* Lina Annab. *Transport, and Municipal Affairs:* Walid Masri. *Water and Irrigation:* Raed Muzaffar Abu Al-Saud.

Minister of State for Administrative and Institutional Development, and Minister of Tourism (acting): Majd Mohammad Shweikeh. *Minister of State*

for Investment Affairs: Muhannad Shehadeh. *Minister of State for Legal Affairs:* Abu Yamin. *Minister of State for Media Affairs:* Jumana Ghunaimat. *Government Website:* http://www.jordan.gov.jo

Current Leaders

Abdullah Bin Al Hussein II

Position
King

Introduction
Abdullah came to the throne of the Hashemite Kingdom in Feb. 1999 on the death of his father, Hussein Bin Talal. He had been declared Crown Prince and heir by his father the previous month, replacing his uncle, Prince Hassan, who had served in that capacity since 1965. Abdullah has maintained the moderate regional policies of his late father. He has aimed to reconcile the domestically unpopular 1994 peace agreement with Israel and friendly relations with the USA with the need to appease Jordan's more militant Arab neighbours and its own large Palestinian population. Following the wave of discontent that swept across the Arab world from 2011, he faced popular demands for democratic reform and has conceded limited constitutional changes in an effort to maintain political stability.

Early Life
Born in Amman on 30 Jan. 1962, Abdullah was educated in England and the USA. In 1980 he enrolled in the Royal Military Academy Sandhurst, England and then attended Oxford University and Georgetown University in Washington, D.C., for studies in international relations. He subsequently rose through the ranks of Jordan's armed forces to become Major-Gen. in May 1998.

Career in Office
Abdullah became Crown Prince on 25 Jan. 1999 after King Hussein had rescinded the 1965 constitutional amendment in favour of his younger brother Hassan. Two weeks later Hussein died and Abdullah assumed the throne. Consistent with the policy of his father, Abdullah has deterred Islamic militancy (particularly the activities of the radical Palestinian Hamas group), while extending economic liberalization. He revived the privatization programme, oversaw Jordan's admission to the World Trade Organization and concluded a free trade accord with the USA.

Abdullah has supported the wider Arab-Israeli peace process and maintains a close affinity with the USA. He also backs Palestinian statehood in the West Bank, a policy that takes account of Jordan's large Palestinian population. He made early overtures towards Jordan's moderate Arab neighbours, visiting Egypt, Saudi Arabia, Oman and the United Arab Emirates in the first few months of his reign, and also tried to forge closer relations with Syria, a traditional antagonist. In 2003 Abdullah backed the US intervention in Iraq, a decision not wholly popular with Jordanian citizens. The subsequent insurgency in Iraq spilled over into Jordan in Nov. 2005 in co-ordinated suicide bomb attacks apparently perpetrated by an Iraqi wing of the al-Qaeda terrorist network. Nevertheless, in Aug. 2008 Abdullah became the first leader of an Arab state to visit Iraq since the 2003 US invasion in a move signifying a rapprochement across the confessional Sunni-Shia divide and also growing international confidence in the Iraqi government.

Although Abdullah retains the power to rule by decree, there is an elected Chamber of Deputies to which a large majority of non-partisan candidates loyal to the King were returned in polling in Nov. 2007. Abdullah subsequently appointed Nader Dahabi as the new prime minister, replacing Marouf Al Bakhit who had been in office since Nov. 2005. In Nov. 2009 the King unexpectedly dissolved the Chamber only halfway through its four-year term and called for early elections. No official reason was given, but the assembly had reportedly been accused of inaction and inept handling of legislation. Abdullah appointed Samir Zaid Al Rifai as the new prime minister in Dec. that year and a new electoral law was introduced in May 2010. Fresh parliamentary elections were held in Nov. 2010, despite a boycott by the opposition Islamic Action Front, and the poll returned mainly pro-government candidates to the 120-member Chamber, provoking street protests.

Jordan was not immune from the anti-government disaffection across much of the Arab world from early 2011. Although on a lesser scale than in some neighbouring countries, the protests prompted Abdullah to appoint new prime ministers in Feb. and Oct. 2011 and in April and Oct. 2012, charged with balancing political reform against establishment concerns over the increasing influence of the Islamist opposition. Following changes to the electoral law in mid-2012 that increased the number of seats for political parties, in Oct. the King announced that parliamentary elections would be held in Jan. 2013. The Islamic Action Front, dissatisfied with the scope of the changes, boycotted the poll, which returned a pro-government majority.

In March 2013 a fresh administration led by incumbent prime minister, Abdullah Ensour, took office. However, Jordan's economic outlook remained precarious, with large fiscal and external deficits necessitating continued dependence on foreign support and the additional burden of an unprecedented refugee influx from neighbouring war-torn Syria. In May 2016 Abdullah dissolved parliament and appointed Hani Al Mulki as interim prime minister ahead of fresh elections (held under proportional representation) in Sept., which were again won overwhelmingly by pro-monarchy loyalists. Al Mulki formed a new government later that month but with no substantive ministerial changes. From Sept. 2014 Jordan took part in Western-led air offensives against Islamic State in Syria because of concerns about the threat that the jihadist movement posed to Jordanian security. Similarly, from March 2015, Jordan joined Saudi Arabia in an air campaign against Houthi rebels in Yemen.

In Dec. 2017 the Jordanian government condemned US President Donald Trump's recognition of Jerusalem as the capital of Israel and transfer of the US embassy to the city as a violation of international law and the United Nations Charter. Abdullah stated that the decision would have 'dangerous repercussions on the stability and security of the region' and would obstruct efforts to resume Arab–Israeli peace talks.

In June 2018 Abdullah dismissed Hani Al Mulki as prime minister as his government's proposals to cut subsidies and raise new taxes to address Jordan's struggling economy provoked hostile public protests. Al Mulki was replaced as premier by Omar Razzaz, a former World Bank economist, with a remit to reform the tax system.

Defence

Defence expenditure in 2013 totalled US$1,216m. (US$188 per capita), representing 3·6% of GDP.

Army

Total strength (2011) 88,000. In addition there were 60,000 army reservists, a paramilitary Public Security Directorate of approximately 10,000 and a civil militia 'People's Army' of approximately 35,000.

Navy

The Royal Jordanian Navy numbered an estimated 500 in 2011 and operates 17 patrol and coastal combatants, all based at Aqaba.

Air Force

Strength (2011) 12,000 personnel, 115 combat-capable aircraft (including F-5Es, F-16As and Mirage F1s) and some 25 attack helicopters.

International Relations

A 46-year-old formal state of hostilities with Israel was brought to an end by a peace agreement on 26 Oct. 1994.

Economy

Services accounted for 66·4% of GDP in 2014, industry 29·8% and agriculture 3·8%.

Overview

Jordan is an upper-middle income country but it has few natural resources (aside from potash and phosphate) and suffers from a shortage of water, fertile land and oil. Between 2000 and 2009 the economy grew on average by 7·1% per year, led by a favourable external environment and the expansion of the manufacturing and construction sectors. However, annual growth declined to an average of 3·1% between 2011 and 2015.

Around 84% of the population lived in cities in 2015; the population is one of the youngest among middle income countries, with 38% aged under 14. Services accounted for over 75% of employment and 66% of GDP in 2014. Jordan has one of the most open economies in the Middle East and is well integrated with its neighbours. Remittances from abroad are also important.

Since the early 2000s, the government has focused on liberalization and privatization and implementing structural reforms to the health, education and tax systems. However, declining gas supplies from Egypt in 2012 forced Jordan towards more expensive alternatives, worsening the fiscal position. In addition, the conflict in Syria since 2011 has resulted in a mass influx of refugees, putting pressure on public services.

Long-term development has suffered as funds planned for capital expenditures have been diverted to meet current operating costs. In 2012 an IMF stand-by arrangement worth US$2bn. was granted to stabilize the financial markets. Nevertheless, Jordan remains highly vulnerable to fluctuations in world oil and food prices. Further reforms are needed to address the country's high unemployment, dependency on remittances, and the knock-on effects of regional instabilities.

Currency

The unit of currency is the *Jordan dinar* (JOD), usually written as JD, of 1,000 *fils*, pegged to the US dollar since 1995 at a rate of one dinar = US$1·41. There was deflation of 0·8% in 2016 and inflation of 3·3% in 2017. Foreign exchange reserves were US$5,601m. and gold reserves 411,000 troy oz in July 2005. Total money supply in May 2005 was JD 3,487m.

Budget

In 2011 budgetary central government revenues totalled JD 5,413·8m. and expenditures JD 6,047·1m. Principal sources of revenue in 2011: taxes on goods and services, JD 2,033·1m.; grants, JD 1,215·0m.; taxes on income, profits and capital gains, JD 667·5m. Main items of expenditure by economic type in 2011: compensation of employees, JD 2,863·2m.; social benefits, JD 1,097·3m.; subsidies, JD 947·9m.

There is a sales tax of 16%. There is a reduced rate of 8%.

Performance

Total GDP was US$40·1bn. in 2017. Real GDP grew by 2·4% in 2015, 2·0% in 2016 and 2·0% in 2017.

Banking and Finance

The Central Bank of Jordan was established in 1964 (*Governor*, Ziad Fariz). In 2015 there were 13 national commercial banks, eight foreign banks and three national Islamic banks. The largest bank is Arab Bank Group, with assets in Dec. 2013 of US$46·4bn.

Foreign debt was US$7,822m. in 2010, representing 27·9% of GNI.

There is a stock exchange in Amman (Amman Financial Market).

Energy and Natural Resources

Environment

Carbon dioxide emissions from the consumption of energy in 2011 accounted for 2·8 tonnes per capita.

Electricity

Installed capacity was 3·7m. kW in 2011. Production (2011) 14·65bn. kWh; consumption per capita was 2,421 kWh. Nuclear power is seen as the solution to meeting the country's growing energy needs. Construction of its first research reactor was approved in Aug. 2013 and completed in Dec. 2016. Two commercial reactors are planned, with construction expected to be completed by 2022.

Oil and Gas

Natural gas reserves in 2013 totalled 6bn. cu. metres, with production (2011) 160m. cu. metres. Jordan relies heavily on oil from other Arab countries, importing around 96% of its energy needs.

Minerals

Phosphate ore production in 2009 was 5·28m. tonnes; potash, 1·20m. tonnes.

Agriculture

The country east of the Hejaz Railway line is largely desert; northwestern Jordan is potentially of agricultural value and an integrated Jordan Valley project began in 1973. In 2012, 96,400 ha. were equipped for irrigation. In 2012 there were 214,400 ha. of arable land and 85,900 ha. of permanent crops.

Production in 2012 (in 1,000 tonnes): tomatoes, 616; aubergines, 178; cucumbers and gherkins, 156; olives, 156; potatoes, 142; watermelons, 109.

Livestock (2013 estimates): 2·25m. sheep; 795,000 goats; 69,000 cattle; 13,500 camels; 9,000 asses; 27m. chickens. Total estimated meat production was 235,000 tonnes in 2012; milk, 310,000 tonnes.

Forestry

Forests covered 0·10m. ha. in 2015, or 1% of the land area. In 2011, 314,000 cu. metres of roundwood were cut.

Fisheries

Fish landings in 2014 totalled 873 tonnes, mainly from inland waters.

Industry

The largest company by market capitalization in Jordan in April 2015 was Arab Bank (US$5·5bn.).

The number of industrial establishments in 2006 was 20,214, employing 174,368 persons. Production, 2007 (in 1,000 tonnes) includes: cement, 4,051; distillate fuel oil, 1,292; residual fuel oil, 1,215; fertilizers, 831; phosphoric acid, 480.

Labour

The labour force in 2013 was 1,717,000 (1,294,000 in 2003). 43·6% of the population aged 15–64 was economically active in 2013. In the same year 12·6% of the population was unemployed.

Jordan had 13,000 people living in slavery according to the Walk Free Foundation's 2013 *Global Slavery Index*.

International Trade

Imports and Exports

Imports (c.i.f.) in 2010 totalled US$15,262m. and exports (f.o.b.) US$7,023m. Major exports are phosphate, potash, fertilizers, foodstuffs, pharmaceuticals, clothes, cement, fruit and vegetables, textiles and plastics.

Principal imports in 2010 were from: Saudi Arabia, 19·8%; China, 10·8%; Germany, 6·1%; USA, 5·6%. Main exports in 2010 were to: Iraq, 16·0%; USA, 13·2%; India, 11·1%; Saudi Arabia, 9·4%. In 2000 Jordan became the first Arab country to sign a free trade agreement with the USA.

Communications

Roads

Total length of roads, 2007, 7,768 km, of which 3,206 km were main roads. In 2007 there were 536,700 passenger cars (94 per 1,000 inhabitants), 2,800 motorcycles and mopeds, 17,200 coaches and buses, and 230,800 lorries and vans. There were 992 deaths in road accidents in 2007 (388 in 1992).

Rail

The 1,050 mm gauge Hedjaz Jordan Railway (HJR) runs from the Syrian border to Amman. HJR controls 496 km of track but much of it is out of use. The Aqaba Railway Corporation (ARC) leases a section of track (169 km) south of Menzil from HJR for freight traffic and owns a 115 km stretch from Batn el Ghul to the port town of Aqaba. Passenger-km travelled in 2010 came to 0·5m. Freight tonne-km travelled amounted to 353m. on ARC in 2009 and 0·4m. on HJR in 2008.

Civil Aviation

The Queen Alia International airport is at Zizya, 30 km south of Amman. There are also international flights from Amman's second airport. Queen Alia International handled 6,250,048 passengers in 2012 (6,190,911 on international flights) and 96,855 tonnes of freight. Royal Jordanian is the national carrier; the government owns 60·3% of its shares. In 2012 scheduled airline traffic of Jordan-based carriers flew 65·8m. km; passenger-km totalled 8·2bn. in the same year.

Shipping

In Jan. 2014 there were ten ships of 300 GT or over registered, totalling 63,000 GT. The main port is Aqaba, which handled 16·3m. tonnes of foreign cargo in 2013.

Telecommunications

In 2011 there were 465,400 landline telephone subscriptions (equivalent to 73·5 per 1,000 inhabitants) and 7,482,600 mobile phone subscriptions (or 1,182·0 per 1,000 inhabitants). In 2000 the government sold a 40% stake in Jordan Telecommunications Company (Jordan Telecom) to France Télécom. In 2006 France Télécom (rebranded as Orange in 2013) became the majority shareholder when it purchased a further 11% of Jordan Telecom from the government. Jordan Telecom's monopoly on fixed-line services ended on 1 Jan. 2005. In 2011, 34·9% of the population were internet users. In March 2012 there were 2·2m. Facebook users.

Social Institutions

Out of 178 countries analysed in the 2017 *Fragile States Index*—a list published jointly by the Fund for Peace and *Foreign Policy* magazine—Jordan was ranked the 71st most vulnerable to conflict or collapse. The index is based on 12 indicators of state vulnerability across social, political and economic categories.

Justice

The legal system is based on Islamic law (Sharia) and civil law, and administers justice in cases of civil, criminal or administrative disputes. The constitution guarantees the independence of the judiciary. Courts are divided into three tiers: regular courts (courts of first instance, magistrate courts, courts of appeal, Court of Cassation/High Court of Justice); religious courts (Sharia courts and Council of Religious Communities); special courts (e.g. police court, military councils, customs court, state security court).

The death penalty is authorized; there were 15 executions in March 2017 although no executions took place in 2018. The population in penal institutions in 2011 was 6,066 (95 per 100,000 of national population). In 2015 the World Justice Project *Rule of Law Index*, which provides data on how the rule of law is experienced by the general public across eight categories, ranked Jordan 34th of 102 countries for criminal justice and 31st for civil justice.

Education

Adult literacy in 2007 was 91·1% (male, 95·7%; female, 88·4%). Basic primary and secondary education is free and compulsory. In 2006–07 there were 1,267 kindergartens (1,259 private) with 4,834 teachers and 93,236 pupils; 2,996 basic schools (706 private) with 66,075 teachers and 1,294,075 pupils; 1,268 secondary schools (160 private) with 17,771 teachers and 184,663 pupils; and 27 vocational schools with 3,581 teachers and 31,432 pupils. In 2006–07 there were ten state and 15 private universities.

The ministry of education received 9·9% of central government budget allocations in 2010 (9·5% in 2009).

Health

There were 26,019 physicians, 23,651 nursing and midwifery personnel, 6,806 dentistry personnel and 12,076 pharmaceutical personnel in 2015. In 2007 there were a total of 11,029 hospital beds in 103 hospitals.

In *Water: At What Cost? The State of the World's Water 2016*, WaterAid reported that 3·1% of the population does not have access to safe water.

Welfare

There are numerous government organizations involved in social welfare projects. The General Union of Voluntary Societies finances and supports the Governorate Unions, voluntary societies, and needy individuals through financial and in-kind aid. There are also 240 day care centres run by non-governmental organizations.

Religion

According to the Pew Research Center's Forum on Religion & Public Life, in 2010 an estimated 97·2% of the population were Muslims (mainly Sunnis) and 2·2% Christians (mainly Orthodox).

Culture

World Heritage Sites

There are five sites on the World Heritage List: the rose-red rock-carved city of Petra and Quseir Amra (both entered on the list in 1985); Um er-Rasas (2004); the Wadi Rum protected area (2011); and Baptism Site 'Bethany Beyond the Jordan' (2015). Petra is over 2,000 years old and contains more than 800 monuments, some built but most carved out of the natural rock. Quseir Amra is the best preserved of Jordan's 'desert castles' and is noted for its frescoes. Um er-Rasas (Kastron Mefa'a) is an archaeological site largely unexcavated, containing remains from the Roman, Byzantine and Early Muslim periods. The Wadi Rum protected area features a varied desert landscape with rock carvings and inscriptions that trace the evolution of human thought and the early development of the alphabet. Baptism Site 'Bethany Beyond the Jordan' is an archaeological site believed to be the location where Jesus of Nazareth was baptized by John the Baptist.

Press

In 2008 there were seven paid-for daily newspapers with a combined circulation of 270,000 and 23 paid-for non-dailies.

Tourism

In 2014 there were 3,990,000 non-resident tourists (excluding same-day visitors), up from 3,945,000 in 2013 although down from 4,162,000 in 2012.

Diplomatic Representatives

Of Jordan in the United Kingdom (6 Upper Phillimore Gdns, London, W8 7HA)
Ambassador: Omar Barakat Mnawer Al Nahar.

Of the United Kingdom in Jordan (PO Box 87, Abdoun, Amman 11118)
Ambassador: Edward Oakden, CMG.

Of Jordan in the USA (3504 International Drive, NW, Washington, D.C., 20008)
Ambassador: Dina Khalil Tawfiq Kawar.

Of the USA in Jordan (Al Umawyeen St., Abdoun, Amman 11118)
Ambassador: Vacant.
Chargé d'Affaires a.i.: Paul Malik.

Of Jordan to the United Nations
Ambassador: Sima Sami Bahous.

Of Jordan to the European Union
Ambassador: Yousef R. Bataineh.

Further Reading

Department of Statistics. *Statistical Yearbook.—Jordan in Figures*
Central Bank of Jordan. *Monthly Economic and Monetary Developments*
Dallas, R., *King Hussein, The Great Survivor.* 1998
George, Alan, *Jordan: Living in the Crossfire.* 2006
Lucas, Russell E., *Institutions and the Politics of Survival in Jordan: Domestic Responses to External Challenges, 1988–2001.* 2006
Rogan, E. and Tell, T., (eds) *Village, Steppe and State: the Social Origins of Modern Jordan.* 1994
Salibi, Kamal, *The Modern History of Jordan.* 1998
National Statistical Office: Department of Statistics, P. O. Box 2015, Amman.
Website: http://www.dos.gov.jo

Kazakhstan

Qazaqstan Respūblīkasy (Republic of Kazakhstan)

Capital: Astana
Population projection, 2020: 18·78m.
GNI per capita, 2017: (PPP$) 22,626
HDI/world rank, 2017: 0·800/58=
Internet domain extension: .kz

Key Historical Events

Neolithic settlements in Kazakhstan date from at least 4000 BC. The Botai culture, which developed along the Ishim River, shows evidence of the domestication of horses and pottery decorated with geometric patterns. Later Bronze Age cultures included the Afanasievo and Andronovo cultures. From around 1000 BC various nomadic Indo-European and Uralic-speaking peoples, including the Alans, Budini, Huns, Madjars and Scythians, inhabited the Central Asian steppes.

Turkic nomads became increasingly dominant and established kingdoms (Kaganat) including that of the Ashina clan (in AD 502) and the Turgesh (AD 704). Parts of southern Kazakhstan came under the influence of the Persian Samanid dynasty in the 9th century. Genghis Khan's Mongol Hordes overran Central Asia from 1221 and retained power in the region under his second son, Chagatai, until 1334.

In 1458 descendants of Genghis Khan's eldest son, Jochi, founded the Kazakh khanate. It expanded in the early 16th century during the reign of Kassym Khan, who instituted the first code of laws in 1520. The khanate was formed of three groups known as *Juzes:* the Major *Juz*—broadly occupying Kazakhstan's southern and eastern territories; the Middle *Juz*—located in central and northern districts; and the Minor *Juz*—in the western steppes stretching to the Caspian Sea. Each *Juz* consisted of several tribal confederations, mainly comprising herders who moved with their flocks to higher pastures during summer.

The Kazakh khanate began to decline from the mid-17th century amid divisions among ruling clans and encroachment from neighbouring kingdoms, including the Uzbeks to the south. Russian traders established a settlement at Guriev (Atyraū) in 1640, and in 1730 Abulkhair, Khan of the Minor *Juz*, sought protection from the Russian Empire, paving the way for Russian expansion through Orenburg where a fort was founded in 1743.

By 1822 the authority of the Kazakh Khans in the Middle *Juz* had been removed. By the end of the century all of present-day Kazakhstan had come under Russian control, known as the Governor-Generalship of Russian Turkestan and the Steppes. Many of the 400,000 migrants to the territory settled in Semirechye (Zhetysu) province in the east, and more Russian and European settlers moved to western and southern areas following the completion of the trans-Aral railway between Orenburg and Tashkent in 1906. Kazakh resentment towards the Russian Empire led to several uprisings against settlers and military garrisons in 1916.

Following the Russian revolution in 1917, the authority of the Soviet government was extended to these regions. The Khan of Khiva was deposed in Feb. 1920, and the Kyrghyz Autonomous Soviet Socialist Republic was set up. In the autumn of 1924 the Soviets of the Turkestan, Bokhara and Khiva Republics decided to redistribute their territories on a nationality basis. The redistribution was completed in May 1925, when the new states of Uzbekistan, Turkmenistan and Tajikistan were accepted into the USSR as Union Republics. The remaining districts of Turkestan populated by Kazakhs were united with Kazakhstan, which was established as an Autonomous Soviet Socialist Republic in 1925

Soviet leader Stalin's first five-year plan, launched in 1929, prioritized the collectivisation of agriculture, which in the Kazakh Soviet Socialist Republic meant a rapid and at times brutal shift from a semi-nomadic herding tradition to cultivating grain. A famine from 1930–33 killed an estimated 1·5m. people. During the 1930s and 1940s the Kazakh Republic became a centre for exiled and deported people, including around 400,000 Volga Germans. Several of the Soviet Union's notorious labour camps were located in the territory. Under Khrushchev in the 1950s and 1960s agriculture was

further expanded and industrial sites were developed alongside the Republic's coal, oil, gas and uranium reserves.

Independence was declared on 16 Dec. 1991 when Kazakhstan joined the Commonwealth of Independent States. Nursultan Nazarbayev became president, and legislation has since been introduced to award him privileges for life. In 1997 the country's capital was moved from Alma Ata to Astana. Over 1m. of the country's ethnic Russians and Germans have returned to their homelands since the end of the first decade of this century. In April 2015 Nazarbayev consolidated his grip on power, winning a further term in office with almost 98% of votes cast.

Territory and Population

Kazakhstan is bounded in the west by the Caspian Sea and Russia, in the north by Russia, in the east by China and in the south by Uzbekistan, Kyrgyzstan and Turkmenistan. With an area of 2,724,900 sq. km (1,052,090 sq. miles) it is the world's largest landlocked country. The population at the census of Feb. 2009 was 16,009,597 (density of 5·9 per sq. km), of whom Kazakhs accounted for 63·1% and Russians 23·7%. There are also Uzbeks, Ukrainians, Uigurs, Tatars, Germans and smaller minorities. Estimate, Jan. 2018: 18,157,078. In 2009 the population was 51·7% female; it was 58·8% urban in 2011. During the 1990s some 1·5m. people left Kazakhstan—mostly Russians and Germans returning to their homelands. In 2008 around 4m. ethnic Kazakhs were living abroad.

The UN gives a projected population for 2020 of 18·78m.

Kazakhstan's administrative divisions consist of 14 provinces and three cities as follows, with area and population:

	Area (sq. km)	Population (July 2017 estimate)
Almaty[1]	223,600	2,003,063
Almaty City	700	1,772,779
Aqmola[2]	146,200	737,443
Aqtöbe	300,600	851,339
Astana City	700	1,006,570
Atyraū[3]	118,600	613,880
Batys Qazaqstan	151,300	643,874
Bayqonyr (city)	(6,700)	—[4]
Mangghystaū	165,600	650,509
Pavlodar	124,800	755,847
Qaraghandy	428,000	1,381,501
Qostanay	196,000	876,833
Qyzylorda	226,000	777,730
Shyghys Qazaqstan	283,200	1,386,208
Shymkent City[5]	1,200	1,001,871[6]
Soltüstik Qazaqstan	98,000	560,553
Turkistan[7]	116,100	2,899,853
Zhambyl[8]	144,300	1,116,384

[1]Formerly Alma-Ata.
[2]Formerly Tselinograd and then Akmola.
[3]Formerly Gurev.
[4]As the space base of Bayqonyr is under Russian administration, its 6,700 sq. km and estimated 39,000 inhabitants are excluded from overall Kazakhstan figures. The lease was extended until 2050 in 2004.
[5]Formerly part of Ongtüstik Qazaqstan.
[6]June 2018 estimate.
[7]Formerly Ongtüstik Qazaqstan.
[8]Formerly Dzhsmbul.

In Dec. 1997 the capital was moved from Almaty to Aqmola, which was renamed Astana in May 1998 (the name of the province remained as

© Springer Nature Limited 2020
Palgrave Macmillan (ed.), *The Statesman's Yearbook 2020*,
https://doi.org/10.1057/978-1-349-95940-2_102

Aqmola). Astana has a population of 1,006,570 (July 2017 estimate). Other major cities, with July 2017 population estimates: Almaty (1,772,779); Shymkent (932,415); Qaraghandy (501,129).

The official languages are Kazakh and Russian; Russian is more widely spoken.

Social Statistics

2007: births, 321,963; deaths, 158,297; marriages, 146,379; divorces, 36,107. Rates, 2007 (per 1,000 population): birth, 20·8; death, 10·2; marriage, 9·5; divorce, 2·3. Suicides in 2007 numbered 4,168 (rate of 26·9 per 100,000 population). Annual population growth rate, 2010–15, 1·6%. Expectation of life at birth, 2007, 59·1 years for males and 71·2 years for females. Infant mortality, 2010, 29 per 1,000 live births; fertility rate, 2008, 2·3 births per woman.

Climate

The climate is generally fairly dry. Winters are cold but spring comes earlier in the south than in the far north. Almaty, Jan. –4°C, July 24°C. Annual rainfall 598 mm.

Constitution and Government

Relying on a judgement of the Constitutional Court that the 1994 parliamentary elections were invalid, President Nazarbayev dissolved parliament on 11 March 1995 and began to rule by decree. A referendum on the adoption of a new constitution was held on 30 Aug. 1995. The electorate was 8·8m.; turnout was 80%. 89% of votes cast were in favour. The Constitution thus adopted allowed the President to rule by decree and to dissolve parliament if it holds a no-confidence vote or twice rejects his nominee for Prime Minister. It established a parliament consisting of a 39-member Senate (two selected by each of the elected assemblies of Kazakhstan's 16 principal administrative divisions plus seven appointed by the president); and a lower house (*Majlis*) of 77 (67 popularly elected by single mandate districts, with ten members elected by party-list vote). The constitution was amended in Oct. 1998 to provide for a seven-year presidential term. It was amended again in May 2007 to lift the term-limit clause on the president, reduce the presidential term to five years with effect from 2012, oblige the president to consult with parliament when choosing a prime minister and adopt proportional representation for the lower house. The amendment also raised from seven to 15 the number of senators appointed by the president (increasing the total number of senators to 47) and from 77 to 107 the number of lower house deputies (with 98 elected by proportional representation from party lists and nine elected by the Assembly of the People of Kazakhstan—a body comprising the various ethnic groups in the country, which itself is appointed by the president). In June 2010 parliament approved an amendment to the constitution giving President Nazarbayev the title 'Leader of the Nation' and with it a wide range of privileges after the end of his presidential term.

A Constitutional Court was set up in Dec. 1991 and a new constitution adopted on 28 Jan. 1993, but President Nazarbayev abolished the Constitutional Court in 1995. In June 2000 a bill to provide President Nazarbayev with life-long powers and privileges was passed into law.

National Anthem

'Mening Qazaqstan' ('My Kazakhstan'); words by Z. Nazhimedenov and N. Nazarbayev, tune by S. Kaldayakov.

Government Chronology

Presidents since 1991.

1991–	Nursultan Abishuly Nazarbayev

Recent Elections

At the presidential election of 26 April 2015 Nursultan Nazarbayev was re-elected with 97·7% of votes cast against two other candidates.

National Assembly elections were held on 20 March 2016. President Nursultan Nazarbayev's Nur Otan (Light of the Fatherland) Party took 84 of the 98 seats with 82·2% of votes cast, the Democratic Party of Kazakhstan Ak Zhol (Bright Path) 7 with 7·2% and the Communist People's Party of Kazakhstan 7 with 7·1%. Turnout was 77·1%. International

observers noted the lack of genuine opposition and the restriction of fundamental civil rights.

Current Government

President: Nursultan Nazarbayev; b. 1940 (elected in 1991 and re-elected in 1999, 2005, 2011 and 2015).

In Feb. 2019 the government comprised:

Prime Minister: Askar Mamin; b. 1965 (since 21 Feb. 2019—acting until 25 Feb. 2019).

First Deputy Prime Minister and Minister of Finance: Alikhan Smailov.

Deputy Prime Ministers: Zhenis Kassymbek; Gulshara Abdykalikova.

Minister of Agriculture: Saparkhan Omarov. *Culture and Sport:* Arystanbek Mukhamediuly. *Defence:* Nurlan Yermekbayev. *Digital Development, Defence and Aerospace Industry:* Askar Zhumagaliyev. *Education and Science:* Kulyash Shamshidinova. *Energy:* Kanat Bozumbayev. *Foreign Affairs:* Beibut Atamkulov. *Healthcare:* Yelzhan Birtanov. *Industry and Infrastructure Development:* Roman Sklyar. *Information and Social Development:* Dauren Abayev. *Internal Affairs:* Yerlan Turgumbayev. *Justice:* Marat Beketayev. *Labour and Social Protection:* Berdybek Saparbayev. *National Economy:* Ruslan Dalenov.

Government Website: http://www.government.kz

Current Leaders

Nursultan Abishuly Nazarbayev

Position
President

Introduction

Nursultan Nazarbayev, leader of the Nur Otan (Light of the Fatherland) Party, was first elected president of Kazakhstan in 1991, leading the country to independence after the collapse of the USSR. He has sought to exploit the nation's rich mineral resources although much of the population remains poor. He has also sought close ties with southern regional neighbours as well as Russia, China and the West. His autocratic regime, however, has been widely accused of intolerance of any opposition, as well as corruption and human rights abuses.

Early Life

Nursultan Nazarbayev was born on 6 July 1940 in Chemolgan in the Almaty region and graduated in engineering in 1967. Having joined the Soviet Communist Party in 1962, he became secretary of the party's regional committee in 1977 and rose through the ranks to the central committee. In 1984 he was appointed chairman of the Republic's council of ministers and became a full member of the Politburo five years later. In the same year Nazarbayev was named first secretary of the Kazakh Communist party. In April 1990 he was chosen by the Supreme Soviet as president of the Republic of Kazakhstan.

Career in Office

Nazarbayev spoke out in support of Soviet leader Mikhail Gorbachev during a coup attempt in Moscow on Aug. 1991. Nevertheless, Kazakhstan seceded from the USSR in Dec. 1991 to join the Commonwealth of Independent States (CIS). In the same month Nazarbayev's position as head of state was consolidated in presidential elections.

In 1992 Nazarbayev secured Kazakhstan's membership of the UN and of the Conference on Security and Co-operation in Europe (the precursor of the OSCE). Despite parliamentary opposition, he implemented a series of economic reforms, including privatization. He sought close co-operation with his CIS partners and signed treaties on strategic arms reduction and nuclear non-proliferation and an agreement on economic and military co-operation with Russia. His term of office was also extended by referendum to 2000 amid accusations of increasing authoritarianism.

In 1997 Nazarbayev announced the transfer of the national capital from Almata to Aqmola (renamed Astana in 1998). He then won presidential elections brought forward to Jan. 1999 with 79·8% of the vote, but earned international criticism for the disqualification of the leading opposition figure, Akezhan Kazhegeldin, from the polls. Kazhegeldin was accused of corruption, went into exile and was sentenced *in absentia* to ten years imprisonment. Parliamentary elections held later in the year were criticized by the OSCE.

In 2000 the government passed constitutional amendments granting Nazarbayev wide-ranging influence once he has retired from office. In

June 2001 Kazakhstan joined the Shanghai Cooperation Organisation (along with China, Russia, Kyrgyzstan, Uzbekistan and Tajikistan) to bolster regional co-operation in economics and against ethnic and religious activism. In the aftermath of the 11 Sept. attacks on Washington and New York in 2001, Nazarbayev met the then US President George W. Bush to consolidate relations between the two countries. In Nov. that year he purged his government of founding members of Democratic Choice, a group seeking to reduce presidential powers. Leading Democratic Choice figures were subsequently imprisoned on disputed charges, as were journalists critical of his regime.

In June 2003 the then prime minister, Imangali Tasmagambetov, resigned in protest at land reforms allowing private ownership for the first time in the nation's history. Nazarbayev's Otan Party (the predecessor of the Nur Otan Party) won a majority of National Assembly seats in parliamentary elections in 2004, and on 4 Dec. 2005 he was re-elected president with 91% of the votes cast. There was some movement towards further democratization. Kazakhstan also ratified two international covenants on civil, political, economic and cultural rights. However, the political opposition remained sceptical in the light of parliament's vote in May 2007 to allow Nazarbayev to stay in office for an unlimited number of terms and the legislative elections later in the year that returned all the seats to his Nur Otan Party. Moreover, in mid-2010 parliament approved legislation giving Nazarbayev the title of 'Leader of the Nation' and granting him additional powers including immunity from prosecution. In Jan. 2010 Kazakhstan became the first former Soviet state to chair the OSCE, despite widespread reservations about Nazarbayev's commitment to democracy.

After almost a decade of average annual growth of around 10%, Kazakhstan's economy started to slow markedly in 2008 in the wake of the global credit crisis. This prompted Nazarbayev in Oct. that year to announce a US$10bn. injection of reserves from the National Fund (established in 2000 to accumulate revenues from the expanding oil and gas sector) into the economy, with a further US$5bn. in support for struggling local banks.

Nazarbayev secured a further term in the presidential elections of April 2011, taking 96% of the vote. In Nov. he brought forward the date of parliamentary elections to Jan. 2012, at which his Nur Otan Party was again dominant. In Sept. 2012 Karim Massimov resigned as prime minister to join the presidential office as chief of staff and Nazarbayev appointed Serik Akhmetov in his place at the head of a largely unchanged cabinet. However, Massimov was reinstated as premier in April 2014 when Akhmetov resigned.

On 1 Jan. 2015 the Eurasian Economic Union officially came into force, facilitating the free movement of trade, services and capital between Kazakhstan, Russia, Belarus and Armenia and superseding the former Eurasian Economic Community customs union.

At early presidential elections held in April 2015 Nazarbayev extended his mandate, defeating two other pro-government candidates with 97·7% of the vote. Then in March 2016 his Nur Otan Party again won the parliamentary polling.

In Sept. 2016 Nazarbayev dismissed Massimov as prime minister, replacing him with Bakhytzhan Sagintayev and announcing a minor cabinet reshuffle.

In Jan. 2017 Nazarbayev proposed a number of constitutional amendments that were approved by the National Assembly in March. The key reform provided for the transfer of some presidential powers to the legislature and the government in an apparent move to redistribute political responsibilities and to genuinely democratize the autocratic system.

Defence

Defence expenditure in 2013 totalled US$2,318m. (US$131 per capita), representing 1·1% of GDP. Conscription is held twice a year with males aged 18–27 years drafted for 12 months' military service. Kazakhstan was intending to switch to a fully professional army in 2016, but as of Feb. 2019 there were no firm plans to end conscription.

Nuclear Weapons

When Kazakhstan gained independence from the USSR in 1991 it became the world's fourth largest nuclear power. However, all the weapons systems were returned to Russia unilaterally and Kazakhstan's nuclear infrastructure was dismantled.

Army

Personnel, 2011, 30,000. Paramilitary units: Presidential Guard (2,000), Government Guard (500), Internal Security Troops (approximately 20,000), State Border Protection Forces (approximately 9,000).

Navy

A 3,000-strong Navy was established in 2003. In 2009 it was equipped with 14 inshore patrol craft.

Air Force

In 2011 there were 12,000 personnel (including Air Defence) with 162 combat-capable aircraft, including MiG-29, MiG-31 and Su-27 interceptors and Su-24 and Su-25 strike aircraft.

International Relations

In Jan. 1995 agreements were reached for closer integration with Russia, including the combining of military forces, currency convertibility and a customs union.

In 1998 President Nazarbayev signed major treaties with Russia and China, Kazakhstan's neighbours to the north, west and east, in the hope of improving relations with both countries.

Economy

Agriculture accounted for 4·7% of GDP in 2014, industry 35·9% and services 59·4%.

Overview

Kazakhstan has large natural resources but is over-reliant on its extractive industries. Its oil reserves are the ninth largest in the world, and hydrocarbon output constituted nearly 18% of GDP in 2015. The country is also of strategic geographical importance, offering road and rail links between the large and fast-growing markets of China and southern Asia and those of Russia and Western Europe, along with port facilities on the Caspian Sea.

From 2002–13 GDP growth averaged 7·5% per year, driven by foreign investment in the oil industry together with expansion in the construction and financial sectors. However, Kazakhstan has been severely affected by lower oil prices since 2014, the slowdown in China's growth momentum and Russia's deteriorating economic outlook. GDP growth slowed from 4·3% in 2014 to 1·2% in 2015. Nonetheless, the incidence of poverty fell from 46·7% in 2001 to 2·7% in 2015.

Despite progress toward a more transparent, less-regulated and more market-driven business environment, the economy faces long-term challenges, including poor governance, weak infrastructure, underdeveloped institutions and insufficient incentives for capital and technological investment.

Currency

The unit of currency is the *tenge* (KZT) of 100 *tiyn*, which was introduced on 15 Nov. 1993 at 1 tenge = 500 roubles. It became the sole legal tender on 25 Nov. 1993. The tenge was devalued by 18% in Feb. 2009 and 19% in Feb. 2014. In Aug. 2015 Kazakhstan allowed the tenge to float freely. Inflation rates (based on IMF statistics):

2008	2009	2010	2011	2012	2013	2014	2015	2016	2017
17·1%	7·3%	7·1%	8·3%	5·1%	5·8%	6·7%	6·7%	14·6%	7·4%

Inflation was running at nearly 1,880% in 1994, but has since dropped dramatically. In July 2005 foreign exchange reserves were US$6,953m. and gold reserves amounted to 1·88m. troy oz. Total money supply was 876,981m. tenge in June 2005.

Budget

In 2014 revenues were 7,364·5bn. tenge and expenditures 7,791·9bn. tenge. Tax revenue accounted for 69·5% of revenues in 2014; social security accounted for 19·9% of expenditures, education 17·4% and health 11·0%.

VAT is 12%.

Performance

Real GDP growth rates (based on IMF statistics):

2008	2009	2010	2011	2012	2013	2014	2015	2016	2017
3·3%	1·2%	7·3%	7·5%	5·0%	6·0%	4·3%	1·2%	1·1%	4·0%

Total GDP in 2017 was US$$159·4bn.

Banking and Finance

The central bank and bank of issue is the National Bank (*Governor*, Yerbolat Dossayev). In 2013 there were 38 banks. As at 1 Dec. 2013 assets of the banks amounted to 15,109bn. tenge. The largest banks are Kazkommertsbank (KKB), Halyk Bank and BTA Bank. Foreign banks are banned from operating unless formed under subsidiaries incorporated within the country. However, as at 2013 there were 17 foreign-majority owned banks. External debt was US$118,723m. in 2010, representing 94·3% of GNI.

Energy and Natural Resources

Environment

Carbon dioxide emissions from the consumption of energy in 2011 were the equivalent of 12·0 tonnes per capita.

Electricity

Installed capacity was an estimated 18·7m. kW in 2011. Output in 2011 was 86·6bn. kWh. Consumption per capita was 5,478 kWh in 2011.

Oil and Gas

Proven oil reserves in 2012 were 30·0bn. bbls. The onshore Tengiz field has estimated oil reserves between 6bn. and 9bn. bbls; the onshore Karachaganak field has oil reserves of 2bn. bbls, and gas reserves of 600bn. cu. metres. Output in 2012 of oil, 81·3m. tonnes; natural gas, 19·7bn. cu. metres with proven reserves of 1·3trn. cu. metres. The first major pipeline for the export of oil from the Tengiz field was opened in March 2001, linking the Caspian port of Atyraū with the Russian Black Sea port of Novorossiisk. In Sept. 1997 Kazakhstan signed oil agreements with China worth US$9·5bn.; although only a small portion of that investment ever materialized. However, a 962-km oil pipeline linking Atasu in Kazakhstan and Alashankou in China opened in Dec. 2005. Oil and gas investment by foreign companies is now driving the economy. In 1997 oil production sharing deals were concluded with two international consortia to explore the North Caspian basin and to develop the Karachaganak gas field. A huge new offshore oilfield in the far north of the Caspian Sea, known as Kashagan, was discovered in early 2000. The field could prove to be the largest find in the last 30 years, and estimates suggest that it may contain 50bn. bbls of oil. In 2013 the Chinese state-owned oil and gas company, China National Petroleum Corporation, acquired an 8·3% stake in the field. Commercial production began in Sept. 2013, but ceased after only a few weeks owing to leaks of poisonous gas. Production resumed in Oct. 2016 with a daily output of 90,000 bbls.

It is believed that there may be as much as 14bn. tonnes of oil and gas reserves under Kazakhstan's portion of the Caspian Sea.

Minerals

Kazakhstan is extremely rich in mineral resources, including coal, bauxite, cobalt, vanadium, iron ores, chromium, phosphates, borates and other salts, copper, lead, manganese, molybdenum, nickel, tin, gold, silver, tungsten and zinc. Production figures (2013), in tonnes: coal, 112·88m.; iron ore, 25·23m.; lignite, 6·69m.; bauxite, 5·19m.; copper, 440,300; zinc, 361,500; uranium, 22,500; silver, 963·8; gold, 42·6. Kazakhstan overtook Canada as the world's largest producer of uranium in 2009 and now produces around 40% of the annual world total.

Agriculture

Kazakh agriculture has changed from primarily nomad cattle breeding to production of grain, cotton and other industrial crops. In 2011 agriculture accounted for 5% of GDP. There were 22·9m. ha. of arable land and 75,000 ha. of permanent crops in 2012. 2·1m. ha. were equipped for irrigation in 2012.

Kazakhstan is noted for its livestock, particularly its sheep, from which excellent quality wool is obtained. Livestock (2013): 15·2m. sheep (33·6m. in 1993), 5·9m. cattle (9·6m. in 1993), 2·4m. goats, 1·8m. horses, 0·9m. pigs and 33·2m. chickens.

Output of main agricultural products (in 1,000 tonnes) in 2013: wheat, 9,841; potatoes, 3,126; barley, 1,491; watermelons, 1,155; tomatoes, 706; onions, 525; maize, 520.

Forestry

Forests covered 3·31m. ha. in 2015, or 1% of the land area. In 2011, 345,000 cu. metres of timber were cut.

Fisheries

Catches in 2015 totalled 41,489 tonnes, exclusively freshwater fish.

Industry

Kazakhstan was heavily industrialized in the Soviet period, with non-ferrous metallurgy, heavy engineering and the chemical industries prominent. Industrial output was valued at 16,852bn. tenge in 2012, up from 15,929bn. tenge in 2011. Production, 2007 unless otherwise indicated (in 1,000 tonnes) includes: cement (2008), 5,837; crude steel, 4,784; distillate fuel oil, 4,295; wheat flour (2010), 3,754; pig iron, 3,240; petrol, 2,633; residual fuel oil, 2,584; ferroalloys, 1,713; cotton woven fabrics (2008), 42m. sq. metres; leather footwear (2008), 532,000 pairs; TV sets (2008), 326,374 units.

Labour

The labour force in 2013 was 9,198,000 (7,756,000 in 2003). 78·6% of the population aged 15–64 was economically active in 2013. In the same year 5·2% of the population was unemployed.

Kazakhstan had 47,000 people living in slavery according to the Walk Free Foundation's 2013 *Global Slavery Index*.

International Trade

In Jan. 1994 an agreement to create a single economic zone was signed with Kyrgyzstan and Uzbekistan. Since Jan. 1992 individuals and enterprises have been able to engage in foreign trade without needing government permission, except for goods 'of national interest' (fuel, minerals, mineral fertilizers, grain, cotton, wool, caviar and pharmaceutical products) which may be exported only by state organizations.

In Jan. 2010 Kazakhstan joined a customs union, together with Russia and Belarus, which was superseded by the Eurasian Economic Union in Jan. 2015.

Imports and Exports

In 2010 imports (c.i.f.) were valued at US$24,023·6m. and exports (f.o.b.) at US$57,244·1m. In 2010, 22·8% of imports came from Russia, 16·5% from China, 7·6% from Germany and 6·6% from Italy. Main export markets in 2010 were China, 17·7%; Italy, 16·7%; France, 7·7%; Netherlands, 7·3%. Main imports, 2010 (US$1m.): machinery and transport equipment, 9,727; manufactured goods, 4,346; chemicals and related products, 2,858; and mineral fuels, lubricants and related materials, 2,380. Main exports, 2010 (US$1m.): mineral fuels, lubricants and related materials, 41,033; manufactured goods, 7,430; inedible crude materials (except fuels), 3,085; and chemicals and related materials, 2,510.

Communications

Roads

In 2007 there were 93,123 km of roads, of which 23,507 were highways, main or national roads. Passenger cars in use in 2007 numbered 2,183,100, and there were also 359,200 lorries and vans, 83,400 buses and coaches, and 45,200 motorcycles and mopeds. There were 4,365 fatalities as a result of road accidents in 2007.

Rail

In 2012 there were 14,319 km of 1,520 mm gauge railways. Two new lines of a combined 1,202 km opened in 2014. Passenger-km travelled in 2009 came to 14·9bn. and freight tonne-km to 197·3bn. The first section of a metro in Almaty, covering 8·6 km, opened in 2011. Eventually it is expected to reach 45 km in length.

Civil Aviation

The national carrier is Air Astana, which carried 3,770,000 passengers in 2014. There are international airports at Almaty and Astana.

Shipping

There is one large port, Aktau. In Jan. 2014 there were 11 ships of 300 GT or over registered, totalling 59,000 GT.

Telecommunications

There were 4·01m. fixed telephone lines in 2010 (250·3 per 1,000 inhabitants). Mobile phone subscribers numbered 19·77m. in 2010. There were 182·0 internet users per 1,000 inhabitants in 2009. Fixed internet subscriptions totalled 846,900 in 2010 (52·8 per 1,000 inhabitants). In March 2012 there were 452,000 Facebook users.

Social Institutions

Out of 178 countries analysed in the 2017 *Fragile States Index*—a list published jointly by the Fund for Peace and *Foreign Policy* magazine—Kazakhstan was ranked the joint 65th least vulnerable (along with Suriname) to conflict or collapse. The index is based on 12 indicators of state vulnerability across social, political and economic categories.

Justice

Jury trials for serious offences were introduced in Jan. 2007. In 2009, 121,667 crimes were reported, of which 1,638 homicides or attempted homicides. The population in penal institutions in Jan. 2013 was 48,684 (295 per 100,000 of national population). In 2015 the World Justice Project *Rule of Law Index*, which provides data on how the rule of law is experienced by the general public across eight categories, ranked Kazakhstan 58th of 102 countries for criminal justice and 53rd for civil justice.

Education

In 2007, 330,897 children were attending pre-school institutions, there were 947,807 pupils at primary schools, 1,874,213 pupils at secondary schools and 772,600 students in tertiary education. Adult literacy rate is more than 99%.

In 2007 public government expenditure on education came to 3·2% of GNI.

Health

There were 913 hospitals in 2012. The provision of hospital beds was 81 per 10,000 inhabitants in 2007. There were 57,514 physicians, 5,612 dentists, 113,098 nurses and midwives and 14,048 pharmacists in 2006.

In *Water: At What Cost? The State of the World's Water 2016*, WaterAid reported that 7·1% of the population does not have access to safe water.

Welfare

In 1998 the former social insurance system was replaced by mandatory individual accounts. Pension contributions are 10% of employees' monthly income. The basic state old-age pension is 40% of the monthly minimum wage. There were 1·7m. old-age pensioners in 2006.

Religion

In 2010 there were an estimated 11·3m. Muslims according to the Pew Research Center's Forum on Religion & Public Life (70·4% of the population), with the main minorities being Orthodox Christians (3·4m.), Catholics (380,000) and Protestants (310,000). A further 670,000 people had no religious affiliation.

Culture

World Heritage Sites

Kazakhstan has five sites on the UNESCO World Heritage List: the Mausoleum of Khoja Ahmed Yasawi (inscribed on the list in 2003), an excellent and well preserved example of late 14th century Timurid architecture; Petroglyphs within the Archaeological Landscape of Tamgaly (2004), a concentration of some 5,000 rock carvings; and Saryarka-Steppe and the Lakes of Northern Kazakhstan (2008), 450,344 ha. of wetlands that contain the Naurzum State Nature Reserve and the Korgalzhyn State Nature Reserve and are of outstanding importance for migratory water birds. Shared with China and Kyrgyzstan, Silk Roads: the Routes Network of Chang'an–Tianshan Corridor (2014) is a 5,000-km section of the extensive Silk Roads network stretching from Chang'an/Luoyang in China to the Zhetysu region in present-day Kazakhstan. Shared with Kyrgyzstan and Uzbekistan, Western Tien-Shan (2016) is a transnational property located in one of the largest mountain ranges in the world.

Press

There were 1,900 newspapers and magazines in 2008. The leading newspapers are the Kazakh-language *Egemen Kazakhstan* and the Russian-language *Kazakhstanskaya Pravda*.

Tourism

In 2010 there were 3,393,000 non-resident tourists, up from 3,118,000 in 2009. There were 1,460 hotels in 2010.

Diplomatic Representatives

Of Kazakhstan in the United Kingdom (125 Pall Mall, London, SW1Y 5EA)
  Ambassador: Erlan Abilfayizuly Idrissov.

Of the United Kingdom in Kazakhstan (62 Kosmonavtov St., Renco Building, 6th Floor, Astana 010000)
  Ambassador: Michael Gifford.

Of Kazakhstan in the USA (1401 16th St., NW, Washington, D.C., 20036)
  Ambassador: Erzhan Kazykhanov.

Of the USA in Kazakhstan (Rakhymzhan Koshkarbayev Ave., No. 3, Astana)
  Ambassador: Vacant.
  Chargé d'Affaires a.i.: Theodore J. Lyng.

Of Kazakhstan to the United Nations
  Ambassador: Kairat Umarov.

Of Kazakhstan to the European Union
  Ambassador: Aigul Kuspan.

Further Reading

Cummings, Sally, *Kazakhstan: Power and the Elite.* 2005

Nazpary, J., *Post-Soviet Chaos: Violence and Dispossession in Kazakhstan.* 2001

Olcott, Marta Brill, *Kazakhstan: Unfilled Promise.* 2001

National Statistical Office: Agency of Kazakhstan on Statistics, House of Ministries, 4th entry, Astana 010000, Kazakhstan.

Website: http://www.stat.gov.kz

Kenya

Jamhuri ya Kenya (Republic of Kenya)

Capital: Nairobi
Population projection, 2020: 53·49m.
GNI per capita, 2017: (PPP$) 2,961
HDI/world rank, 2017: 0·590/142
Internet domain extension: .ke

Key Historical Events

Aboriginal hunter-gatherers—possibly ancestors of the Okiek who live on the Rift Valley's Mau escarpment—were Kenya's earliest inhabitants. Cushitic-speaking cattle-herders migrated south from the horn of Africa from around 1500 BC, followed by Nilo-Saharan pastoralists and, from early in the first millennium AD, Bantu-speaking farmers from western Cameroon settled. Prominent Bantu groups include the Kikuyu, the Kamba, the Luhya and the Meru, while speakers of Nilotic languages include the Luo, Maasai, Samburu and Turkana. Muslim seafarers from the Arabian peninsula (Oman) established trading settlements along the Kenyan coast from the seventh century, with thriving ports like Lamu and Mombasa developing a distinctive African-Arabic 'Swahili' culture.

The Portuguese explorer Vasco da Gama reached Mombasa in 1498, heralding two centuries of Portuguese influence in coastal Kenya, centred on Mombasa and the island of Kilwa (now southern Tanzania). Skirmishes with Venetian merchants and Omani Arabs occurred frequently; the capture of Mombasa's Fort Jesus in 1698 paved the way for Omani control over the coastal strip and parts of the interior. Clove plantations were established in the 18th century and trade in slaves and ivory increased, particularly after 1840 when Sayyid bin Sultan moved his capital from Muscat to Zanzibar.

British merchants were increasingly active in coastal Kenya during the 19th century, notably through the British India Steam Navigation Company, founded in 1856 by William Mackinnon. Following the Berlin Conference in 1885, the British government appointed Mackinnon to administer their new East African dependency, leased from the Sultan of Zanzibar and centred on Mombasa. In 1895 the British declared the region the East Africa Protectorate and the following year work began on a railway connecting Mombasa with Kisumu on Lake Victoria. 30,000 labourers from British India worked on the line, which was completed in 1902 and spearheaded the development of tea and coffee plantations and big-game hunting in the Kenyan highlands.

The outpost of Nairobi grew quickly, becoming capital of the protectorate in 1905 and, from 1920, capital of the colony of Kenya. African resentment at the loss of land rights and the exclusively white-representative colonial legislative council was voiced by leaders such as Jomo Kenyatta. In 1952 the Mau Mau uprising began when Kikuyu militants attacked politicians and raided settler farms. A state of emergency was declared and the British administration fought a violent counter-insurgency over the next eight years, detaining tens of thousands without trial, often in appalling conditions. The number of casualties is disputed, with official figures claiming 11,000 but some estimates running to more than 150,000. In 1960 the British administration announced a plan for transition to African majority rule. The following year Kenyatta was freed and reinstated as president of the pro-independence Kenya African National Union (KANU) party.

Full internal self-government was achieved in 1962 and in Dec. 1963 Kenya became independent, with Kenyatta elected president of the new republic the following year. Ethnic unrest ignited in 1969 after the assassination of Tom Mboya, a high-profile Luo government minister. On the death of Kenyatta in Aug. 1978, Daniel T. arap Moi, the vice-president, became acting president. He was elected to the role outright in 1979 and again in 1983 (having survived an attempted coup the previous year), 1988, 1992 and 1997.

In 1982 Kenya became a one-party state but multi-party elections were reintroduced in 1992, paving the way for the first genuinely competitive election since 1963. At the 2002 polls the opposition united behind Mwai Kibaki. He won a landslide victory against Moi's successor as KANU leader,

Uhuru Kenyatta, to become the first non-KANU president of independent Kenya.

In Nov. 2005 a new draft constitution was rejected amid criticism that it gave the president too much power. In Dec. 2007 Kibaki claimed victory in a disputed presidential election that prompted a wave of civil unrest in which 1,500 were killed. In Feb. 2008 Kibaki and the opposition leader, Raila Odinga, agreed a power-sharing deal. In March 2013 Uhuru Kenyatta won the election for the presidency. An appeal by Odinga, his chief rival, was rejected by the Supreme Court.

Territory and Population

Kenya is bounded by South Sudan and Ethiopia in the north, Uganda in the west, Tanzania in the south and Somalia and the Indian Ocean in the east. The total area is 581,313 sq. km. The 2009 census gave a population of 38,610,097 (19,417,639 females); density, 66 per sq. km. In 2009, 70·2% of the population were rural. In 2006 more than 30,000 Somali refugees entered Kenya to escape the fighting that escalated in Somalia the course of the year.

The UN gives a projection population for 2020 of 53·49m.

Kenya is divided into seven provinces and one national capital area (Nairobi). The land areas, populations and capitals are:

Province	Sq. km	Census 2009	Capital	Census 2009
Rift Valley	173,868	10,006,805	Nakuru	286,411
Eastern	159,891	5,668,123	Embu	35,736
Nyanza	16,162	5,442,711	Kisumu	259,258
Central	13,176	4,383,743	Nyeri	63,626
Western	8,360	4,334,282	Kakamega	69,502
Coast	83,603	3,325,307	Mombasa	915,101
Nairobi	684	3,138,369	—	—
North-Eastern	126,902	2,310,757	Garissa	110,383

Other large towns (2009): Eldoret (252,061), Ruiru (236,961), Kikuyu (190,208), Thika (136,576).

Most of Kenya's 38·61m. people belong to 13 tribes, the main ones including Kikuyu (about 22% of the population), Luhya (14%), Luo (13%), Kalenjin (12%), Kamba (11%), Gusii (6%), Meru (5%) and Mijikenda (5%). There is a large Somali minority, numbering over 2·4m. at the time of the 2009 census.

Swahili and English are both official languages, but people belonging to the different tribes have their own language as their mother tongue.

Social Statistics

2008 births (estimates), 1,503,000; deaths, 451,000. Estimated birth rate in 2008 was 38·8 per 1,000 population; estimated death rate, 11·6. Annual population growth rate, 2000–08, 2·6%. Expectation of life at birth in 2007 was 53·2 years for males and 54·0 years for females. Infant mortality, 2010, 55 per 1,000 live births. Fertility rate, 2008, 4·9 births per woman. In 2005, 46% of Kenyans lived below the poverty line (down from 52% in 1997).

Climate

The climate is tropical, with wet and dry seasons, but considerable differences in altitude make for varied conditions between the hot, coastal lowlands and the plateau, where temperatures are very much cooler. Heaviest rains occur in April and May, but in some parts there is a second wet season in Nov. and Dec. Nairobi, Jan. 65°F (18·3°C), July 60°F (15·6°C). Annual rainfall 39" (958 mm). Mombasa, Jan. 81°F (27·2°C), July 76°F (24·4°C). Annual rainfall 47" (1,201 mm).

© Springer Nature Limited 2020
Palgrave Macmillan (ed.), *The Statesman's Yearbook 2020,*
https://doi.org/10.1057/978-1-349-95940-2_103

Constitution and Government

A new constitution was approved in a referendum on 4 Aug. 2010 with 66·9% of votes cast in favour. Under its terms, the *President* and *Parliament* will have five-year fixed terms. The president may not serve more than two terms. To be elected president, a candidate must secure at least 50% of votes cast, with at least a quarter coming from more than half of the county constituencies. The old 46 local government districts were restructured into 47 counties, with each county having a governor and a senator. Senators sit in a newly created 68-member upper house, providing the country with a bicameral legislature following the elections of March 2013. The *National Assembly*, the lower house, is made up of 350 members following the election with 290 directly elected, 47 women, 12 nominated plus the Speaker (up from 224 previously, with 210 directly elected, 12 appointed plus the Speaker and the Attorney General). The *Senate* consists of 47 elected senators, 20 nominated senators plus the Speaker. Each county assembly must return at least one female MP. Parliament has the power to vet key appointments previously appointed by order of the president. The constitution also provides for a supreme court (the highest court in the land) backed by a court of appeals. Judges are subject to review by a judicial appointments panel.

National Anthem

'Ee Mungu nguvu yetu' ('Oh God of all creation'); words by a collective, tune traditional.

Government Chronology

President since 1964. (DP = Democratic Party; KANU = Kenya African National Union; NARC = National Rainbow Coalition; PNU = Party of National Unity; TNA = The National Alliance)

1964–78	KANU	Jomo Kenyatta
1978–2002	KANU	Daniel arap Moi
2002–13	NARC/DP, PNU	Mwai Kibaki
2013–	TNA	Uhuru Kenyatta

Recent Elections

In presidential elections held on 8 Aug. 2017 Uhuru Kenyatta of the Jubilee Party of Kenya received 54·3% of votes cast and Raila Odinga of the Orange Democratic Movement (ODM) 44·7%. There were six other candidates. However, on 1 Sept. the Supreme Court annulled the election claiming that irregularities and illegalities were committed in favour of Kenyatta. The Court initially announced that the election would be rerun on 17 Oct. although this was later put back to 26 Oct. Incumbent Uhuru Kenyatta then received 98·3% and Raila Odinga 1·0% of votes cast after the latter's supporters boycotted the vote. Turnout was 38·8%.

National Assembly elections also held on 4 March 2013 were the first after the passing of the new constitution in 2010. Uhuru Kenyatta's Jubilee alliance won 167 seats (of which TNA won 89); Raila Odinga's Coalition for Reforms and Democracy (CORD) alliance, 141 (of which ODM won 96); Musalia Mudavadi's Amani coalition, 24 (of which UDF won 12); and the Eagle coalition, 2. Unaffiliated parties and independent candidates obtained 15 seats. In elections to the Senate (which was established under the new constitution) the same day the Jubilee coalition obtained 30 of 67 seats; CORD coalition, 28; Amani coalition, 6; and the Alliance Party of Kenya (APK), 3.

Current Government

President: Uhuru Kenyatta; b. 1961 (TNA; sworn in 9 April 2013 and re-elected 26 Oct. 2017).

Deputy President: William Ruto.

In Feb. 2019 the government comprised:

Cabinet Secretary for Agriculture and Irrigation: Mwangi Kiunjuri. *Defence:* Raychelle Omamo. *Devolution and Arid and Semi-Arid Lands:* Eugene Wamalwa. *East African Community:* Adan Mohammed. *Education:* Amina Mohammed. *Energy:* Charles Keter. *Environment and Forestry:* Keriako Tobiko. *Foreign Affairs and International Trade:* Monica Juma. *Health:* Sicily Kariuki. *Industry, Trade and Co-operatives:* Peter Munya.

Information, Communication and Technology: Joseph Mucheru. *Interior:* Fred Matiang'i. *Labour and Social Protection:* Ukur Yattani. *Lands:* Farida Karoney. *Petroleum and Mining:* John Munyes. *Public Service, Youth and Gender Affairs:* Margaret Kobia. *Sports and Heritage:* Rashid Achesa. *Tourism and Wildlife:* Najib Balala. *Transport and Infrastructure Development:* James Macharia. *Treasury and Planning:* Henry Rotich. *Water and Sanitation:* Simon Chelgui.

Office of the President: http://www.president.go.ke

Current Leaders

Uhuru Kenyatta

Position
President

Introduction
Uhuru Kenyatta, son of Kenya's first president, won a disputed election in March 2013 to become the nation's fourth president. Although deadly protests and alleged fraud committed in his favour led the Kenyan Supreme Court to annul the Aug. 2017 election, Kenyatta was re-elected for a second term in Oct. 2017 after a fresh vote.

Early Life
Kenyatta was born in Oct. 1961 in Nairobi. His father, Jomo, became president three years later. Uhuru attended St Mary's School in Nairobi and in 1985 graduated in political science and economics from Amherst College in Massachusetts, USA.

He began his political career in 1997 when he was elected chairman of his hometown branch of the ruling party, the Kenya African National Union (KANU). In the same year he ran for the parliamentary seat of Gatundu South, losing to Moses Muhia. Kenyatta was appointed chairman of the Kenya Tourism Board in 1999 by then President Daniel arap Moi.

In 2001 he was nominated for a parliamentary seat by Moi and was appointed minister for local government. He was Moi's preferred choice to succeed him as president and ran as the KANU candidate in the 2002 presidential election, losing by a large margin to Mwai Kibaki. In 2005 Kenyatta defeated Nicholas Biwott to become chairman of KANU.

Kenyatta withdrew from the 2007 presidential election and threw his support behind former rival Kibaki's re-election. In 2010 he was named as a suspect by the International Criminal Court (ICC) in relation to the violence that swept the nation in the aftermath of the election, which Kibaki won and the opposition disputed. Specifically, Kenyatta was accused of organizing attacks against members of groups who supported Kibaki's rival, Raila Odinga.

Kenyatta was appointed minister of local government by Kibaki in 2008 and subsequently held the posts of deputy prime minister and minister of trade. In 2009 he became minister of finance. In 2012 he took over The National Alliance (TNA), which formed a coalition with the United Republican Party of William Ruto to oppose Raila Odinga's Coalition for Reforms and Democracy in the 2013 presidential election.

Career in Office
Five days after polling on 4 March 2013, Kenyatta was declared president. Odinga unsuccessfully lodged a formal challenge with the Supreme Court, claiming the election was fraudulent. Kenyatta's new cabinet comprised only 18 ministers, significantly less than its predecessor, and included six women, notably Amina Mohamed as foreign minister and Raychelle Omamo as minister of defence.

Kenyatta faced the prospect of carrying out his duties while on trial at the ICC accused of crimes against humanity for his alleged part in the violence that left over 1,200 dead following the 2007 election. As he awaited his trial he maintained his innocence and contested the evidence against him. In Dec. 2014 the prosecution case was controversially withdrawn. Nonetheless, the allegations left relations with the international community strained and weakened his authority domestically.

In Sept. 2013 nearly 70 people were killed, including Kenyatta's nephew, in a four-day terrorist attack and siege by Somali Islamist extremists at a shopping mall in Nairobi. In a further incident in April 2015 militants killed abound 150 people in an assault on a university in Garissa in the east of the country. In Nov. that year Kenyatta announced a new government structure, increasing the number of ministries and departments, which was prompted by claims of corruption in the administration and saw six cabinet secretaries sacked.

In presidential elections in Aug. 2017, Kenyatta again claimed victory with 54% of the vote over Odinga, who disputed the result prompting street protests and violence. The following month the Supreme Court overturned the result and ordered a rerun of the poll in Oct. Kenyatta nevertheless won decisively as the opposition boycotted the vote amid Odinga's continued denunciation of electoral fraud and official corruption.

Defence

In 2013 defence expenditure totalled US$975m. (US$22 per capita), representing 2·1% of GDP.

Army

Total strength (2011) 20,000. In addition there is a paramilitary Police General Service Unit of 5,000.

Navy

The Navy, based in Mombasa, consisted in 2011 of 1,620 personnel (including 120 marines).

Air Force

An air force, formed on 1 June 1964, was built up with RAF assistance. Personnel (2011) 2,500, with 38 combat-capable aircraft.

International Relations

In Nov. 1999 a treaty was signed between Kenya, Tanzania and Uganda to create a new East African Community as a means of developing East African trade, tourism and industry and laying the foundations for a future common market and political federation.

Economy

Agriculture contributed 29·5% of GDP in 2013, industry 19·9% and services 50·6%.

Overview

In the period 2012–16 GDP growth averaged 5·5% annually, driven by the industrial and agricultural sectors and aided by improving political stability that saw largely peaceful elections in 2013. However, after the results of the Aug. 2017 presidential election were nullified by the Supreme Court and the rerun in Oct. was again controversially won by incumbent Uhuru Kenyatta there were fears of renewed instability with knock-on effects for the economy.

As of 2016 inflation had been kept low at 6·3% by strong monetary policy and relatively stable exchange rates. Meanwhile, increased remittances boosted foreign exchange reserves. Kenya has the third largest banking sector in Africa. Private sector lending growth accelerated from 7·7% in 2012 to 17·4% in 2013, although it had dropped back to 3·3% by early 2017. In 2013 the International Monetary Fund extended a credit facility programme that distributed US$750m. to reinforce foreign reserves, thus reducing the fiscal deficit and lowering public debt.

Nonetheless, the economy has been held back by long-standing political uncertainty that has seen it underperform relative to its sub-Saharan neighbours and to its own potential. Other risks to growth include rising interest rate payments, increasing import prices and consistently low export demand. The government also faces challenges from external security threats and energy supply bottlenecks.

Currency

The monetary unit is the *Kenya shilling* (KES) of 100 *cents*. The currency became convertible in May 1994. The shilling was devalued by 23% in April 1993. Inflation was 6·3% in 2016 and 8·0% in 2017. Foreign exchange reserves were US$1,653m. in July 2005, total money supply was K Sh 222,558m. and gold reserves were 1,000 troy oz.

Budget

In 2014–15 revenues totalled K Sh 1,204,800m. and expenditures K Sh 1,556,500m. Tax revenue accounted for 83·5% of revenues; current expenditure accounted for 67·8% of expenditures. The fiscal year ends on 30 June.

VAT is 16%.

Performance

Real GDP growth was 5·7% in 2015, 5·9% in 2016 and 4·9% in 2017. Total GDP in 2017 was US$74·9bn.

Banking and Finance

The central bank and bank of issue is the Central Bank of Kenya (*Governor*, Patrick Njoroge). There are 43 banks, two non-banking financial institutions and a couple of building societies. The largest banks are Barclays Bank of Kenya, Equity Bank and Kenya Commercial Bank.

Foreign debt was US$8,400m. in 2010, representing 26·9% of GNI.

There is a stock exchange in Nairobi.

Energy and Natural Resources

Environment

Kenya's carbon dioxide emissions from the consumption of energy in 2011 were the equivalent of 0·3 tonnes per capita.

Electricity

Installed generating capacity was 1·80m. kW in 2011, mostly provided by hydro-power from power stations on the Tana river with some from oil-fired power stations and by geothermal power. Kenya is the largest producer of geothermal energy in Africa. Total production in 2011 was 7·85bn. kWh, with consumption per capita 187 kWh. In 2016, 56% of the population had access to electricity (up from 19% in 2010).

Oil and Gas

Oil was discovered in the northwest of the country in March 2012. It was announced in 2015 that production would begin in 2022.

Minerals

Production, 2014 (in 1,000 tonnes): soda ash, 410; galvanized steel (estimate), 285; salt, 223. Other minerals include gold, raw soda, diatomite, garnets, titanium and vermiculite.

Agriculture

As agriculture is possible from sea-level to altitudes of over 2,500 metres, tropical, sub-tropical and temperate crops can be grown and mixed farming is pursued. In 2012 there were around 5·6m. ha. of arable land and 530,000 ha. of permanent crop land. 103,000 ha. were equipped for irrigation in 2012. Four-fifths of the country is range-land producing mainly livestock products and the wild game that is a major tourist attraction.

Tea, coffee and horticultural products—particularly flowers—are all major foreign exchange earners.

Kenya is the world's third largest producer of tea. The production is high quality tea, raised in near-perfect agronomic conditions. In 2012 production was 369,400 tonnes.

Coffee output in 2013 was 39,800 tonnes, although production now has halved since the late 1980s. Other major agricultural products (2012, in 1,000 tonnes): sugarcane, 5,823; maize, 3,600; potatoes, 2,915; mangoes and guavas, 2,782; bananas, 1,394; cassava, 893; sweet potatoes, 860.

Livestock (2013 estimates): goats, 30·0m.; cattle, 19·5m.; sheep, 18·5m.; camels, 3·1m.; pigs, 360,000; chickens, 32·5m.

Forestry

Forests covered 4·41m. ha. in 2015 (8% of the land area). There are coniferous, broad-leaved, hardwood and bamboo forests. Timber production was 27·55m. cu. metres in 2011.

Fisheries

Catches in 2015 totalled 165,135 tonnes, of which 156,468 tonnes were freshwater fish (mostly from Lake Victoria). Marine fishing has not reached its full potential, despite a coastline of 640 km. Fish landed from the sea totals less than 10,000 tonnes annually, but there is an estimated potential of 150,000 tonnes in tuna and similar species.

Industry

In 2006 industry accounted for 18·8% of GDP, with manufacturing contributing 11·5%. In 2010 there were 2,096 manufacturing firms; 305,078 persons were employed in manufacturing in June 2009. The main areas of employment are food products, coke and refined petroleum products, beverages, printing and reproduction of recorded media, chemicals and chemical products, rubber and plastics products, and basic metals. Production (2014) included (in tonnes): cement, 5,883,000; wheat flour, 988,733; sugar, 592,697; maize meal, 571,173; animal feeds, 539,550.

Labour

The labour force in 2013 was 16,969,000 (12,574,000 in 2003). 67·8% of the population aged 15–64 was economically active in 2013. In the same year 9·1% of the population was unemployed.

Kenya had 37,000 people living in slavery according to the Walk Free Foundation's 2013 *Global Slavery Index*.

International Trade

Imports and Exports

Imports (c.i.f.) in 2010 totalled US$12,092·9m. and exports (f.o.b.) US$5,169·1m. The gap between imports and exports has widened considerably since 2005, when imports (c.i.f.) totalled only US$5,846·2m. but exports (f.o.b.) were US$3,419·9m. Principal imports in 2010 (US$1m.): machinery and transport equipment, 3,841; mineral fuels, lubricants and related materials, 2,670; manufactured goods, 1,775. Leading exports in 2010 (US$1m.): food and live animals, 2,096; manufactured goods, 626; inedible crude materials (except fuels), 613. Tea constituted 22·5% of Kenya's exports in 2010. Main import suppliers, 2010: China, 12·6%; United Arab Emirates, 21·1%; India, 10·8%. Main export markets, 2010: Uganda, 12·7%; UK, 9·8%; Tanzania, 8·1%.

Communications

Roads

In 2013 there were 160,886 km of roads (11,197 km paved). There were, in 2007, 562,400 passenger cars in use, 210,900 vans and lorries, 180,800 motorcycles and mopeds, and 20,100 buses and coaches. There were 2,893 fatalities as a result of road accidents in 2007.

Rail

In 2006 there were 2,064 km of railways (metre gauge). Most of the network (1,918 km, including non-operational sections) is managed by Rift Valley Railways (Kenya) Ltd. In 2008–09, 4·4m. passengers and 1·6m. tonnes of freight were carried. The Magadi Railway Co. Ltd manages a 146 km stretch of line from Manzi to Konza to carry soda ash for export through Mombasa. A new railway line from Mombasa to Nairobi has been constructed with Chinese assistance. Passenger services began in June 2017 and freight services in Jan. 2018.

Civil Aviation

There are international airports at Nairobi (Jomo Kenyatta International) and Mombasa (Moi International). The national carrier, Kenya Airways, is operated under a public-private partnership with the Kenyan government owning a 48·9% share, KQ Lenders Co. owning 38·1% and Dutch airline KLM 7·8%. In 2013 it carried 3,693,000 passengers (2,808,000 on international flights), serving 58 international and four domestic destinations. In 2010 Jomo Kenyatta International handled 5,484,771 passengers and Moi International 1,271,078.

Shipping

The main port is Mombasa, which handled 22·3m. tonnes of cargo in 2013; container traffic totalled 894,000 TEUs (twenty-foot equivalent units) in 2013. A new port is being developed at Lamu, which by the late 2020s is expected to be larger than the port at Mombasa. In Jan. 2014 there were five ships of 300 GT or over registered, totalling 3,000 GT.

Telecommunications

Kenya had 283,500 landline telephone subscribers in 2011, or 6·8 per 1,000 persons. Since 1999 the government has been introducing measures to liberalize the telecommunications sector that have led to massive price reductions and improved services. In 2011 mobile phone subscribers numbered 26,980,800. The main mobile providers are Safaricom and Airtel Kenya. There were 209·8 internet users per 1,000 inhabitants in 2010. Fixed internet subscriptions totalled 8,300 in 2009 (0·2 per 1,000 inhabitants). In June 2012 there were 1·4m. Facebook users.

Social Institutions

Out of 178 countries analysed in the 2017 *Fragile States Index*—a list published jointly by the Fund for Peace and *Foreign Policy* magazine— Kenya was ranked the 22nd most vulnerable to conflict or collapse. The

index is based on 12 indicators of state vulnerability across social, political and economic categories.

Justice

The courts of Justice comprise the Supreme Court, Court of Appeal and the High Court, beneath which are specialized courts, magistrates courts and Kadhis (Islamic) courts. The Chief Justice is the president of the Supreme Court, which also comprises the Deputy Chief Justice and five other judges. Only the Supreme Court can hear and determine any case challenging the election of the president. The Court of Appeal, comprising at least 12 judges, is based in Nairobi and in the course of its Appellate duties visits Mombasa, Kisumu, Nakuru, Nyeri and Eldoret. The High Court, with full jurisdiction in both civil and criminal matters, comprises the Chief Justice and not fewer than 11 but not more than 50 puisne judges. There are 15 High Court stations in the country. Kadhis courts are established in areas of concentrated Muslim populations: Mombasa, Nairobi, Malindi, Lamu, Garissa, Kisumu and Marsabit.

There were 63,476 recorded crimes in 2008; the prison population was approximately 52,000 in Oct. 2012 (121 per 100,000 of national population). Kenya was ranked 89th of 102 countries for criminal justice and 73rd for civil justice in the 2015 World Justice Project *Rule of Law Index*, which provides data on how the rule of law is experienced by the general public across eight categories.

Education

The adult literacy rate in 2008 was 87%. Free primary education was introduced in 2003. In 2007 there were 1,691,093 children in pre-primary schools with 76,323 teaching staff, 6,687,510 pupils were in primary schools with 146,796 teaching staff and 2,729,040 pupils in secondary schools with 102,449 teaching staff. There were 139,524 students in higher education in 2007.

In 2015 public expenditure on education came to 5·3% of GDP and 16·7% of total government spending.

Health

In 2013 there were 8,682 physicians, 37,907 nursing and midwifery personnel, 1,045 dentistry personnel and 2,202 pharmaceutical personnel. There were 1·5 hospitals per 100,000 population in 2013. In the period 2006–12 Kenya had a provision of 14 hospital beds per 10,000 population. Free medical service for all children and adult out-patients was launched in 1965.

In *Water: At What Cost? The State of the World's Water 2016*, WaterAid reported that 36·8% of the population does not have access to safe water. Kenya ranked as the country with the ninth largest number of people living without access to safe water (17·2m. in 2015).

Religion

In 2010 there were 24·2m. Protestants according to the Pew Research Center's Forum on Religion & Public Life, 9·0m. Catholics, 3·9m. Muslims and 0·7m. folk religionists. A further 1·0m. people did not have any religious affiliation. In Feb. 2019 there was one Roman Catholic cardinal.

Culture

World Heritage Sites

Kenya has seven sites on the UNESCO World Heritage List: Mount Kenya National Park/Natural Forest (1997 and 2013), including the second highest peak in Africa; Lake Turkana National Parks (1997 and 2001), a breeding ground for Nile crocodiles and hippopotami; Lamu Old Town (2001), the oldest and best-preserved Swahili settlement in East Africa; the Sacred Mijikenda Kaya Forests (2008), 11 separate forest sites containing the remains of numerous fortified villages; Fort Jesus, Mombasa (2011), a 16th century Portuguese fort; the Kenya Lake System in the Great Rift Valley (2011), consisting of three lakes that are home to numerous threatened bird species; and Thimlich Ohinga Archaeological Site (2018), a dry-stone walled settlement in the Lake Victoria region.

Press

In 2010 there were eight paid-for daily papers with a total average daily circulation of 310,000 plus 15 paid-for non-dailies. The most widely read paper is the English-language *Daily Nation*.

Tourism

In 2014 there were 1,261,000 non-resident tourists (down from a high of 1,750,000 in 2011). Receipts from tourism in 2014 amounted to US$1,833m., down from a record US$2,004m. in 2012. Tourism has suffered as a consequence of attacks by Al-Shabaab militants from neighbouring Somalia in retaliation for Kenya's military intervention.

Diplomatic Representatives

Of Kenya in the United Kingdom (45 Portland Pl., London, W1B 1AS)
High Commissioner: Vacant.

Of the United Kingdom in Kenya (Upper Hill Rd, PO Box 30465-00100, Nairobi)
High Commissioner: Nic Hailey.

Of Kenya in the USA (2249 R. St., NW, Washington, D.C., 20008)
Ambassador: Robinson Njeru Githae.

Of the USA in Kenya (United Nations Ave., Gigiri, Nairobi)
Ambassador: Robert F. Godec.

Of Kenya to the United Nations
Ambassador: Lazarus Amayo.

Of Kenya to the European Union
Ambassador: Jacob Thuranira Kaimenyi.

Further Reading

Anderson, David, *Histories of the Hanged: The Dirty War in Kenya and the End of Empire*. 2005

Elkins, Caroline, *Britain's Gulag*. 2005; US title: *Imperial Reckoning: The Untold Story of the End of Empire in Kenya*. 2005

Haugerud, A., *The Culture of Politics in Modern Kenya*. 1995

Kyle, Keith, *The Politics of the Independence of Kenya*. 1999

Miller, N. N., *Kenya: the Quest for Prosperity*. 2nd ed. 1994

Murunga, Godwin R. and Nasong'o, Shadrack W., *Kenya: The Struggle for Democracy*. 2007

Ogot, B. A. and Ochieng, W. R. (eds) *Decolonization and Independence in Kenya, 1940–93*. 1995

Throup, David and Hornsby, Charles, *Multi-Party Politics in Kenya*. 1999

National Statistical Office: Kenya National Bureau of Statistics, PO Box 30266—00100 GPO, Nairobi.

Website: http://www.knbs.or.ke

Kiribati

Ribaberikin Kiribati (Republic of Kiribati)

Capital: Bairiki (Tarawa)
Population projection, 2020: 122,000
GNI per capita, 2017: (PPP$) 3,042
HDI/world rank, 2017: 0·612/134=
Internet domain extension: .ki

Key Historical Events

The islands that now constitute Kiribati were first settled by early Austronesian-speaking peoples long before the 1st century AD. Fijians and Tongans arrived about the 14th century and subsequently merged with the older groups to form the traditional I-Kiribati Micronesian society and culture. The Gilbert and Ellice Islands were proclaimed a British protectorate in 1892 and annexed at the request of the native governments as the Gilbert and Ellice Islands Colony on 10 Nov. 1915. On 1 Oct. 1975 the Ellice Islands severed constitutional links with the Gilbert Islands and took on a new name, Tuvalu. The Gilberts achieved full independence as Kiribati in 1979. Internal self-government was obtained on 1 Nov. 1976 and independence on 12 July 1979 as the Republic of Kiribati.

Territory and Population

Kiribati (pronounced Kiribahss) consists of three groups of coral atolls and one isolated volcanic island, spread over a large expanse of the Central Pacific with a total land area of 811 sq. km (313 sq. miles). It comprises **Banaba** or Ocean Island (6 sq. km), the 16 **Gilbert Islands** (280 sq. km), the eight **Phoenix Islands** (29 sq. km) and eight of the 11 **Line Islands** (496 sq. km), the other three Line Islands (Jarvis, Palmyra Atoll and Kingman Reef) being uninhabited dependencies of the USA. The capital is the island of Bairiki in Tarawa. The gradual rise in sea levels in recent years is slowly reducing the area of the islands. Most of the land is less than 3 metres above sea level.

Population, 2015 census, 110,136 (56,040 females); density, 136 per sq. km.

The UN gives a projected population for 2020 of 122,000.

In 2011, 44·0% of the population lived in urban areas.

All 17 Gilbert Islands (including Banaba, which is 600 km west of the other Gilbert Islands), Kanton (or Abariringa) in the Phoenix Islands and three atolls in the Line Islands (Teraina, Tabuaeran and Kiritimati—formerly Washington Island, Fanning Island and Christmas Island respectively) are inhabited; their census populations in 2015 were as follows:

Tarawa[1]	63,017
North Tarawa	6,629
South Tarawa	56,388
Kiritimati[2]	6,456
Abaiang[1]	5,568
Tabiteuea[1]	5,261
North Tabiteuea	3,955
South Tabiteuea	1,306
Abemama[1]	3,262
Butaritari[1]	3,224
Marakei[1]	2,799
Nonouti[1]	2,743
Tabuaeran[2]	2,315
Beru[1]	2,051

(*continued*)

Makin[1]	1,990
Maiana[1]	1,982
Nikunau[1]	1,789
Teraina[2]	1,712
Onotoa[1]	1,393
Aranuka[1]	1,125
Tamana[1]	1,104
Kuria[1]	1,046
Arorae[1]	1,011
Banaba (Ocean Is.)[1]	268
Kanton[3]	20

[1]Island in the Gilbert Islands.
[2]Island in the Line Islands.
[3]Island in the Phoenix Islands.

The remaining 12 atolls have no permanent population; the seven Phoenix Islands comprise Birnie, Rawaki (formerly Phoenix), Enderbury, Manra (formerly Sydney), Orona (formerly Hull), McKean and Nikumaroro (formerly Gardner), while the others are Malden and Starbuck in the Central Line Islands, and Millennium Island (formerly Caroline), Flint and Vostok in the Southern Line Islands. The population is almost entirely Micronesian.

Social Statistics

2005 estimates: births, 2,460; deaths, 810. Rates, 2005 estimates (per 1,000 population): births, 26·6; deaths, 8·7. Infant mortality rate (2010), 39 per 1,000 live births; life expectancy (2005), 61·0 years. Annual population growth rate, 2000–05, 1·8%; fertility rate, 2008, 3·1 births per woman.

Climate

The Line Islands, Phoenix Islands and Banaba have a maritime equatorial climate, but the islands further north and south are tropical. Annual and daily ranges of temperature are small; mean annual rainfall ranges from 50" (1,250 mm) near the equator to 120" (3,000 mm) in the north. Typhoons are prevalent (Nov.–March) and there are occasional tornadoes. Tarawa, Jan. 83°F (28·3°C), July 82°F (27·8°C). Annual rainfall 79" (1,977 mm).

Constitution and Government

Under the constitution founded on 12 July 1979 the republic has a unicameral legislature, the *House of Assembly* (Maneaba ni Maungatabu), comprising 46 members, 44 of whom are elected by popular vote, and two (the Attorney-General *ex officio* and a representative from the Banaban community) appointed for a four-year term. The *President* is both Head of State and government.

National Anthem

'Teirake kain Kiribati' ('Stand up, Kiribatians'); words and tune by U. Ioteba.

Recent Elections

The last House of Assembly elections were held on 30 Dec. 2015 and 7 Jan. 2016. Following the election, Boutokaan Te Koaua (BTK; 'Pillars of Truth') had 26 seats in the House of Assembly and the Tobwaan Kiribati Party/TKP 19.

On 9 March 2016 Taneti Maamau (Tobwaan Kiribati Party/TKP) was elected president with 60·0% of the vote, defeating Rimeta Beniamina who took 38·6% and Tianeti Ioane with 1·5%.

Palgrave Macmillan (ed.), *The Statesman's Yearbook 2020*,
https://doi.org/10.1057/978-1-349-95940-2_104

Current Government

President, and Minister for Foreign Affairs and Immigration: Taneti Maamau; b. 1960 (since 11 March 2016).

In Feb. 2019 the government comprised:

Vice President, and Minister of Women, Youth and Social Affairs: Kourabi Nenem.

Minister for Commerce, Industry and Co-operatives: Atarake Nataara. *Education:* David Collins. *Environment, Lands and Agricultural Development:* Alexander Tebao. *Finance and Economic Development:* Teuea Toatu. *Fisheries and Marine Resources Development:* Tetabo Nakara. *Health and Medical Services:* Vacant. *Information, Communications, Transport and Tourism Development:* Willie Tokataake. *Internal Affairs:* Kobebe Taitai. *Justice:* Natan Teewe. *Labour and Human Resources Development:* Ruateki Tekaiara. *Line and Phoenix Islands Development:* Mikarite Temari. *Public Works and Utilities:* Tauanei Marea.

Office of the President: http://www.president.gov.ki

Current Leaders

Taneti Maamau

Position
President

Introduction
Taneti Maamau became president on 11 March 2016. He is a member of the Tobwaan Kiribati Party.

Early Life
Born on 16 Sept. 1960, Maamau comes from Onotoa and studied at the University of the South Pacific before taking a master's degree at the University of Queensland, Australia. He completed his thesis—on industrialization and trade policies in India—in 2003.

He has been a member of parliament for several decades. In the mid-1990s President Teburoro Tito appointed him permanent secretary at the ministry of finance and economic development, a post he held for several years. During the presidency of Anote Tong from 2003–16, Maamau was part of the opposition that advocated greater government transparency and campaigned to establish a system of committees to scrutinize the government executive, especially in relation to health spending.

Following the 2015–16 general election that resulted in the Boutokaan Te Koaua party receiving the most seats, two opposition parties—Karikirakean Tei-Kiribati and Maurin Kiribati—formed a new coalition, the Tobwaan Kiribati Party. In Feb. 2016 Maamau was nominated as its presidential candidate and campaigned on promises to focus on domestic policies. He won the election with 60% of the vote and was sworn in on 11 March 2016.

Career in Office
Maamau's principal challenges include strengthening the economy, ensuring transparency of government and working with the international community to address the impact of climate change on Kiribati.

Economy

Agriculture accounted for 24·3% of GDP in 2012, industry 5·8% and services 69·9%.

Overview

Kiribati is one of the least developed of the Pacific island nations and possesses few natural resources. Its economy depends on revenues from the sale of fishing licences derived from its Exclusive Economic Zone, its Revenue Equalization Reserve Fund (RERF, created using pre-1979 revenues accrued from phosphate mining), passport fees, foreign aid (including remittances from native seamen abroad) and tourism. The economy has a narrow production base, with exports limited to coconut, copra, seaweed and fish (from which around 80% of households make a living). The public sector accounts for nearly 80% of employment.

Kiribati was badly hit by the global financial crisis through a fall in remittances and a decline in the value of the RERF and Kiribati Provident Fund (the government-owned pension asset fund). Following two years of contraction, the economy began recovery in the second half of 2010, due in part to copra subsidies and increased civil servant wages. Growth averaged 2·9% per year from 2011–14, largely driven by increased revenue from fishing licences and construction projects funded by development partners. In the period 2015–17 average growth rose slightly to just over 3% per year.

Limited resources and geographic isolation make transport and communications costly. The country is also extremely vulnerable to climate change and rising sea levels. However, recent studies suggest that marine resources offer a viable route to a long-term sustainable economy.

Currency

The currency in use is the Australian *dollar*. There was inflation of 1·9% in 2016 and 0·4% in 2017.

Budget

Foreign financial aid, mainly from the UK and Japan, has amounted to 25–50% of GDP in recent years. Budgetary central government revenues in 2011–12 totalled $A135·4m. and expenditures $A105·4m.

Performance

The economy grew by 10·3% in 2015, 1·1% in 2016 and 3·1% in 2017. Total GDP in 2017 was US$196m.

Banking and Finance

ANZ Bank (Kiribati) Ltd is 25% government-owned and 75% owned by ANZ Bank. In Sept. 2009 deposits totalled $A47·2m. There is also a Development Bank of Kiribati and a network of village lending banks and credit institutions.

Energy and Natural Resources

Environment

Carbon dioxide emissions from the consumption of energy were the equivalent of 0·6 tonnes per capita in 2011.

Electricity

Installed capacity (2011 estimate), 6,000 kW; production (2011), 24m. kWh.

Agriculture

In 2012 there were about 2,000 ha. of arable land and 32,000 ha. of permanent crops. Copra and fish represent the bulk of production and exports. The principal tree is the coconut; other food-bearing trees are the pandanus palm and the breadfruit. The only vegetable which grows in any quantity is a coarse calladium (alocasia) with the local name 'bwabwai', which is cultivated in pits; taro and sweet potatoes are also grown. Coconut production (2012 estimate), 170,000 tonnes; bananas, 7,000 tonnes; taro, 1,800 tonnes. Principal livestock, 2013 estimates: pigs, 13,500; chickens, 610,000.

Forestry

There were 12,000 ha. of forest in 2015, or 15% of the total land area.

Fisheries

Fishing licence fees provide key sources of income. Total catches in 2015 amounted to 145,832 tonnes, exclusively from sea fishing. Fish landings doubled between 2011 and 2015.

Industry

Industry is concentrated on fishing and handicrafts.

Labour

The economically active population classified as cash workers (not including village workers engaged in subsistence activities) totalled 13,133 in 2005. In 2005, 52·9% of cash workers were employed in public administration, 11·2% in transport and communication, 9·0% in retail trade, and 7·1% in agriculture and fishing. 6·1% of the labour force were unemployed in 2005; the unemployment rate in 2005 including village workers was 64·5%.

International Trade

Imports and Exports

Total imports (2009), US$68·1m.; exports (2005), US$3·6m. Main import sources in 2009: Australia, 29·4%; Fiji, 25·8%; France, 6·9%; USA, 6·8%. Main export markets in 2005: Free zones, 33·3%; Australia, 22·2%; Fiji, 16·7%; Hong Kong, 8·3%. Principal exports: copra, seaweed, fish; imports: foodstuffs, machinery and equipment, manufactured goods and fuel.

Communications

Roads
There are some 810 km of roads, of which about 130 km are sealed. There were 9,600 cars, 4,320 trucks and vans and 2,080 motorcycles in 2008.

Civil Aviation
The national airline is the state-owned Air Kiribati. In 2010 there were scheduled services from Tarawa (Bonriki) to Fiji as well as domestic flights linking the main islands of Kiribati.

Shipping
The main port is at Betio (Tarawa). Other ports of entry are Banaba, English Harbor and Kanton. There is also a small network of canals in the Line Islands. In Jan. 2014 there were 100 ships of 300 GT or over registered, totalling 349,000 GT. Kiribati is a 'flag of convenience' country.

Telecommunications
In 2011 there were 8,461 main (fixed) telephone lines and 13,788 mobile phone subscriptions. There were 90 internet users per 1,000 inhabitants in 2010.

Social Institutions

Justice
Kiribati's police force is under the command of a Commissioner of Police who is also responsible for prisons, immigration, fire service (both domestic and airport) and firearms licensing. There are a Court of Appeal and High Court, with judges at all levels appointed by the President.

The population in penal institutions in Oct. 2012 was 118 (equivalent to 114 per 100,000 of national population).

Education
In 2010 there were 9,823 pupils and 368 teachers at primary schools and 4,359 pupils in general secondary education with 206 teachers. There is a regional campus of the University of the South Pacific on Tarawa. Other post-secondary institutions include a teacher training college, a marine training centre, a fisheries training centre, a school of nursing and a technical institute.

Health
The government maintains free medical and other services. In 2013 there were 22 physicians, 501 nursing and midwifery personnel, 27 dentistry personnel and 15 pharmaceutical personnel. There are a national referral hospital in South Tarawa and three other hospitals. In 2005 there were 15 hospital beds per 10,000 inhabitants.

In *Water: At What Cost? The State of the World's Water 2016*, WaterAid reported that 33·1% of the population does not have access to safe water.

Religion
In 2010 an estimated 50% of the population were Roman Catholics according to the Pew Research Center's Forum on Religion & Public Life and 40% Kiribati Protestants; there are also small numbers of Seventh-day Adventists, Latter-day Saints (Mormons) and Bahá'ís.

Culture

World Heritage Sites
Kiribati has one site on the UNESCO World Heritage List: Phoenix Islands Protected Area (inscribed on the list in 2010).

Press
In 2008 there were three newspapers with a combined circulation of 4,000.

Tourism
In 2011, 5,264 non-resident tourists—excluding same-day visitors—arrived by air at Tarawa and Kiritimati (the two most populous islands).

Diplomatic Representatives

Of Kiribati in the United Kingdom
Acting High Commissioner: Makurita Baaro (resides in Kiribati).
Honorary Consul: Michael Ravell Walsh (The Great House, Llanddewi Rhydderch, Monmouthshire, NP7 9UY).

Of the United Kingdom in Kiribati
High Commissioner: Melanie Hopkins (resides in Suva, Fiji).

Of Kiribati in the USA and to the United Nations
Ambassador: Teburoro Tito.

Of the USA in Kiribati
Ambassador: Vacant.
Chargé d'Affaires a.i.: Michael Goldman (resides in Suva, Fiji).

Further Reading

Tearo, T., *Coming of Age*. 1989
National Statistical Office: Kiribati Statistics Office, PO Box 67, Bairiki.
Website: http://www.mfed.gov.ki/statistics

Korea, North

Chosun Minchu-chui Inmin Konghwa-guk (Democratic People's Republic of Korea)

Capital: Pyongyang
Population projection, 2020: 25·84m.
GDP per capita, 2015: US$648
Internet domain extension: .kp

Key Historical Events

The Korean peninsula was first settled by tribal peoples from Manchuria and Siberia who provided the basis for the modern Korean language. By 3000 BC agriculture-based communities had emerged. The earliest known colony in the region was established at Pyongyang in the 12th century BC. Among the most prominent agricultural communities was Old Choson, which by 194 BC had evolved into a league of tribes ruled by Wiman or 'Wei Man'. His realm was taken over by the Han empire of China in 108 BC and replaced by four Chinese colonies.

The rest of the peninsula evolved into tribal states; Puyo in the north and Chin south of the Han River. Chin was itself split into three tribal states (Mahan, Chinhan and Pyonhan); these states then evolved into three rival kingdoms (Koguryo, Paekche and Silla). Three powerful figures, King T'aejo (AD 53–146) of Koguryo, King Koi (AD 234–86) of Paekche and King Naemul (AD 356–402) of Silla, established hereditary monarchies while powerful aristocracies developed from tribal chiefdoms.

With China's support Silla conquered the other two kingdoms; Paekche in 660 and Koguryo in 668. In 676 Silla drove out the Chinese and gained complete control of the peninsula. Survivors from Koguryo established Parhae, under the leadership of Tae Cho-yong, in the northern region. After a period of conflict with Silla, Parhae grew into a prosperous state in its own right before being taken over by northern nomadic peoples. In Silla an absolute monarchy replaced the council of nobles (its former decision making body) with a central administrative body called the chancellery (*Chipsabu*), thus undermining aristocratic power. Meanwhile, the capital Kumsong (now Kyongju in South Korea) was developed. The state was divided into administrative units by province (*chu*), prefecture (*kun*), and county (*hyon*), and five provincial capitals prospered as cultural centres. Avatamsaka Buddhism was the dominant religion.

Divisions within the aristocracy in the 8th century led to the restoration of the Council of Nobles and the overthrow of the monarchy. Forced to pay taxes to powerful provincial families and central government, the peasants rebelled. Two provincial leaders, Kyonhwon and Kungye, established the Later Paekche (892) and Later Koguryo (901) as rivals to Silla.

National Unity

The powerful leader Wang Kon founded Koryo (now Kaesong, North Korea) in 918, and established a unified kingdom in the Korean peninsula in 936. Three chancelleries and the royal secretariat formed the supreme council of state and governed the kingdom. Koryo's leaders were then largely aristocratic, and the political system greatly favoured those in the top five tiers of the nine hierarchical levels. That the military was not eligible for any hierarchical position above the second level and received little land, led to a military coup in 1170. Gen. Ch'oe Ch'ung-hon established a military regime which held power for the next sixty years. Zen Buddhism and the allied ideology of Confucianism had grown but were suppressed under the Ch'oe regime. Many monks fled to the mountains, where they formed what became Korean Buddhism, the *Chogye*.

In 1231 the Mongols invaded Koryo but were resisted by the Ch'oe leaders for nearly three decades, until a peasant uprising saw the Ch'oe overthrown. A power-sharing agreement between the rebels and the Mongols came into force in 1258. Despite some interference from the Mongols, Koryo retained its identity as a unified state. Conflict between the aristocracy and the bureaucratic class led to a rebellion. With the help of the Ming dynasty in China and supported by government officials, Gen. Yi Song-gye seized power in 1392. A new system of land distribution ended the Koryo dynasty.

Gen. Yi named the state Choson, designating Hanyang (now Seoul, South Korea) as the capital. Buddhism was dropped in favour of a new Chinese-influenced Confucian ethical system and the state was governed by a hereditary aristocracy (the *yangban*), who controlled all aspects of Korean society. In 1420 the Hall of Worthies (*Chiphyonjon*) was established for scholars, and after 1443 the Korean phonetic alphabet (*hangul*) was adopted. Later in the period, a centralized yangban government was formed and the country divided into eight administrative regions, with standardized laws and a central decision-making and judicial body.

In 1592 Japan, newly unified under the command of Toyotomi Hideyoshi, sent an army to Korea supposedly as part of an invasion of China. Korea's naval forces, under Admiral Yi Sun-shin, were able to repel the invaders. Swelling anti-Japanese sentiment prompted Koreans from all hierarchical divisions to fight in the war alongside troops dispatched from Ming China. However, Japanese forces did not withdraw completely until Toyotomi's death in 1598, leaving Korea in ruins.

Despite joint efforts by China and Korea to stem the advances of the nomadic Manchu in the early 17th century, Seoul was captured in 1636. The Manchu established the Ch'ing dynasty several years later and demanded tribute from Korea.

During the 17th and 18th centuries, advances in irrigation increased the output of rice, tobacco and ginseng. By the late 18th century many Korean scholars had turned to Roman Catholicism, leading to government suppression of Christianity in a bid to preserve the dominance of Confucianism. However, European priests maintained strong links in the country.

Japanese Influence

In the 19th century, a succession of monarchs yet to attain the age of majority undermined national stability. In 1864 Taewon'gun, the father of the child-king Kojong, took power and pursued a programme of controversial political reform that increasingly isolated Korea from the outside world. When Taewon'gun was eventually forced to step down, Korea came under pressure from Japan to open up its ports. Nervous of growing Japanese influence, China placed troops in Korea following a failed coup attempt by pro-Taewon'gun forces. There followed a trade agreement which greatly benefited Chinese commercial interests. Further treaties with France, Germany, Russia, the UK and the USA followed in the 1880s. As foreign influence increased, Korea's ruling elite divided between moderates and radicals. The radicals carried out a coup in 1884 but were quickly defeated by Chinese troops. An agreement to maintain a balance of power in the region was signed by Japan and China the following year.

As modernization gathered pace, government spending increased, adding to the burden of reparations payments to Japan. The peasants turned to *Tonghak* ('Eastern Learning'), a new religion established by an old yangban scholar and based on traditional beliefs. A Tonghak rebellion in 1894 caused China to send in troops. Japan responded by sending its own forces and war broke out. By the following year Japan had secured control of the peninsula.

Korea declared neutrality at the outbreak of war between Japan and Russia in 1904 but was pressured by Japan into allowing use of Korean territory. Japan achieved victory in 1905 and made Korea a protectorate. An unsuccessful appeal to the international peace conference at The Hague further undermined relations between Japan and Korea. Anti-Japanese guerrilla fighters in the southern provinces were active during 1908–09 but were crushed the following year when Korea was annexed by Japan.

Japan established a government in Korea and implemented a programme designed to supplant the Korean identity. There were restrictions on freedom of speech, press and assembly while the language and history of Japan were taught in schools. Many Koreans were dispossessed as Japan built new transport and communications infrastructures. After the Japanese suppressed a mass demonstration in 1919, independence leaders set up a provisional government in Shanghai and named Syngman Rhee as president. Hoping to calm dissent, Japan lifted certain press restrictions and replaced the gendarmerie with an ordinary police force, but uncompromising colonial rule remained in place.

© Springer Nature Limited 2020
Palgrave Macmillan (ed.), *The Statesman's Yearbook 2020*,
https://doi.org/10.1057/978-1-349-95940-2_105

Korea became a market for Japanese goods and attracted much capital investment but at the expense of agriculture, leading to a long-term shortage of rice. Tokyo reimposed military rule in 1931 when war broke out between Japan and China. Magazines, newspapers and academic organizations operating in the Korean language were banned and hundreds of thousands of Koreans were made to fight in the Japanese army or work in Japanese mines and factories to support Japan in the Second World War. The provisional government, having moved from Shanghai to Chungking in southwest China, declared war on Japan in Dec. 1941. An army of Korean resistance fighters joined the Allied forces in China and fought with them until the Japanese surrender in 1945.

Korea Divided

Korea was promised independence by China, Britain and the USA at the Cairo conference of 1943 but at the end of the war, after Japan's collapse, Korea was divided along the 38th Parallel. A planned four-way power share in Korea, involving Britain and the Republic of China, was abandoned after US troops took control of the south of the country while the USSR occupied the north. The Soviet forces helped to establish a Communist-led provisional government under Kim Il-sung. As relations between the USA and the Soviet Union worsened, trade ceased between the two zones.

General elections in Korea were proposed by the United Nations in Sept. 1947. However, a commission to oversee voting was denied entry by Soviet troops. Rhee was elected in the South while the North appointed Kim Il-sung as leader. In 1948 the southern Republic of Korea (with Seoul as the capital) and the northern Democratic People's Republic of Korea (with Pyongyang as capital) were formally recognized.

Soviet and US troops left the peninsula in 1949 and war broke out between the North and South in June 1950. A US-led UN force under Gen. Douglas MacArthur entered South Korea and pushed back the North Korean forces. The UN pressed on into North Korea and established a commission for the reunification. China, which at that point had no representation in the United Nations, entered the war adding 1·2m. troops to the North Korean side. Peace negotiations began in 1951 and a new international boundary and demilitarized zone were declared in 1953. The USA offered South Korea financial support and signed a mutual security pact with Rhee, who had been reluctant to accept the division of the country. The issue of prisoner returns, particularly of North Koreans unwilling to return to the communist state, remained a point of contention. The war left 4m. people dead or injured.

In the aftermath, Kim set about tightening his grip on his country. He established a dictatorship based on a personality cult and introduced his philosophy of *Juche*, by which the country was to develop without any help from outside. Industrialization and military spending gathered pace in the late 1950s and the 1960s despite North Korea's international isolation. However, by the late 1970s North Korea had fallen far behind its southern neighbour and a period of stagnation began.

Kim maintained close relations with China and the Soviet Union, although his allegiance wavered between the two as Sino-Soviet relations deteriorated in the 1960s. When the Soviet Union collapsed in 1990–91, North Korea went into an economic crisis that included widespread famine. Attempts to improve relations with South Korea in the early 1990s faltered over the North's alleged nuclear capacity although in 1994 North Korea agreed to shut down controversial reactors in return for aid and oil. Kim died in 1994 and power passed to his son, Kim Jong-il.

Under the younger Kim the economy collapsed to subsistence level although spending on the military remained high. In 1997 the UN World Food Programme estimated that 2m. North Koreans faced starvation. More than 5% of the population starved to death during the 1990s. In 2000 Kim received South Korean President Kim Dae-jung as relations between the North and South appeared to be thawing. The two leaders agreed that reunification was the eventual aim of both Koreas but relations again deteriorated in 2002 after a naval battle in the Yellow Sea between North and South forces killed four South Korean and around 30 North Korean sailors. Kim Jong-il blamed the USA and South Korea for the attack. South Korean President Kim Dae-jung suspended rice shipments to the North and demanded an apology.

Relations with the USA worsened during 2002 and 2003 after the USA claimed that North Korea had a secret nuclear programme. US president George W. Bush accused North Korea of forming part of what he called the 'Axis of Evil' along with Iraq and Iran. North Korea subsequently reactivated a nuclear plant and demanded the withdrawal of inspectors from the UN International Atomic Energy Agency. Pyongyang claimed it had been forced to reopen the reactor in response to US plans for a pre-emptive nuclear strike. North Korea then announced its withdrawal from the nuclear non-proliferation treaty, although it denied any intention to produce nuclear weapons. Many observers suggested Kim carried out these manoeuvres to pressurize the USA into direct talks with a view to signing a mutual non-aggression pact. North Korea's nuclear programme has in turn unsettled relations with regional neighbours including South Korea and Japan. In Feb. 2005 North Korea publicly admitted for the first time that it possessed nuclear weapons. On 9 Oct. 2006 it conducted its first nuclear test, carrying out an underground explosion. In Feb. 2007 at talks between North Korea, South Korea, Japan, Russia, China and the USA, Pyongyang agreed to close its chief nuclear reactor in return for fuel aid. In Oct. 2007 it agreed to close a further three installations and was scheduled to surrender its nuclear stockpile in 2008. However, Pyongyang missed a Dec. 2007 deadline to disclose full details of all of its nuclear facilities.

In Oct. 2007 North and South Korea issued a joint declaration calling for a permanent peace on the peninsula to replace the armistice in place since the end of the Korean War. However, relations soon deteriorated and at the end of 2008 Pyongyang accused Seoul of fostering hostility. The South accused the North of testing long-range missile technology in April 2009 and a month later North Korea walked out of international talks aimed at ending its nuclear programme. In May 2010 an international report concluded that North Korea had been responsible for the sinking of a South Korean ship two months earlier. A collapse in trading and diplomatic relations followed.

In Dec. 2011 it was announced that Kim Jong-il had died of a heart attack. State-run television called on the public to support his son, Kim Jong-un, as 'the great successor'. Kim Jong-un has overseen an accelerated programme of ballistic and nuclear missile testing, prompting widespread international condemnation and renewed sanctions. Nonetheless, in Jan. 2018 talks were held between North and South Korea for the first time in two years and a joint team was sent to the Winter Olympic Games held the following month. Then in March 2018 US president Donald Trump announced his willingness to meet Kim.

Territory and Population

North Korea is bounded in the north by China, east by the Sea of Japan (East Sea of Korea), west by the Yellow Sea and south by South Korea, from which it is separated by a demilitarized zone of 1,262 sq. km. Its area is 122,762 sq. km.

The census population in 2008 was 24,052,231; density 195·9 per sq. km. In 2011, 60·3% of the population were urban.

The UN gives a projected population for 2020 of 25·84m.

The area, 2008 census population (in 1,000) of the provinces and Pyongyang (directly governed city):

	Area in sq. km	Population	Chief Town
Chagang	16,968	1,300	Kanggye
North Hamgyong[1]	17,570	2,327	Chongjin
South Hamgyong	18,970	3,066	Hamhung
North Hwanghae[2]	9,262	2,114	Sariwon
South Hwanghae	8,002	2,310	Haeju
Kangwon[3]	11,152	1,478	Wonsan
North Pyongan[4]	12,191	2,729	Sinuiju
South Pyongan	12,330	4,052	Pyongsong
Pyongyang (directly governed city)	2,000	3,255	—
Yanggang	14,317	719	Hyesan

[1]Area and population include Rason directly governed city.
[2]Area and population include Kaesong industrial region.
[3]Area and population include Kumgangsan tourist region.
[4]Area and population include Sinuiju special administrative region.

Pyongyang, the capital, had a 2008 census population of 2,581,076. Other large towns (census, 2008): Hamhung (703,610); Chongjin (614,892); Sinuiju (334,031).

The official language is Korean.

Social Statistics

2008 estimated births, 327,000; deaths, 238,000. 2008 estimated birth rate, 13·7 per 1,000 population; death rate, 10·0. Annual population growth rate, 2000–08, 0·5%. Marriage is discouraged before the age of 32 for men and 29 for women. Life expectancy at birth, 2013, was 66·4 years for men and 73·4 years for women. Infant mortality, 2010, 26 per 1,000 live births; fertility rate, 2008, 1·9 births per woman. North Korea has the highest suicide rate of any independent country, at 39·5 per 100,000 inhabitants in 2012 (a rate of 41·0 among males and 38·1 among females).

Climate

There is a warm temperate climate, though winters can be very cold in the north. Rainfall is concentrated in the summer months. Pyongyang, Jan. 18°F (−7·8°C), July 75°F (23·9°C). Annual rainfall 37" (916 mm).

Constitution and Government

North Korea adopted a new constitution in April 2009 that formalized *songun* or 'military first' politics as a guiding principle of state but dropped the word 'communism'. The Constitution provides for a 687-seat *Supreme People's Assembly* elected every five years by universal suffrage. Citizens of 17 years and over can vote and be elected. The government consists of the *Administration Council* directed by the Central People's Committee.

In 1998, four years after the death of Kim Il-sung, the title of president was abolished. On the death of Kim Jong-il on 19 Dec. 2011 his son and designated successor, Kim Jong-un (b. 1983), assumed the role of 'Supreme Leader'.

About 3m. people are affiliated with the ruling party, the Korean Workers' Party. There are also the puppet religious Chongu and Korean Social Democratic Parties and various organizations combined in a Fatherland Front.

National Anthem

'A chi mun bin na ra i gang san' ('Shine bright, o dawn, on this land so fair'); words by Pak Se Yong, tune by Kim Won Gyun.

Recent Elections

Elections to the Supreme People's Assembly were held on 10 March 2019. Only the list of the Democratic Front for the Reunification of the Fatherland (led by the Korean Workers' Party) was allowed to participate. 687 deputies were elected unopposed.

Current Government

Supreme Leader, Commander of the Korean People's Army, First Secretary of the Workers' Party of Korea and First Chairman of the National Defence Commission: Kim Jong-un.

In Feb. 2019 the government comprised:

Prime Minister: Pak Pong-ju; b. 1939 (appointed 1 April 2013).

Vice Prime Ministers: Im Chol-ung; Ko In-ho (also *Minister of Agriculture*); Ro Tu-chol (also *Chairman of the State Planning Commission*); Ri Mu-yong; Kim Tok-hun; Ri Ju-o; Ri Ryong-nam; Jon Kwang-ho; Tong Jong-ho.

Minister of Atomic Energy Industry: Wang Chang-uk. *Chemical Industry:* Jang Kil-ryong. *Coal Industry:* Mun Myong-hak. *Commerce:* Kim Kyong-nam. *Construction and Building Materials Industry:* Pak Hun. *Culture:* Pak Chun-nam. *Electric Power Industry:* Kim Man-su. *Electronics Industry:* Kim Jae-song. *External Economic Affairs:* Kim Yong-jae. *Finance:* Ki Kwang-ho. *Fisheries:* Song Chun-sop. *Food and Consumer Goods Industries:* Jo Yong-chol. *Food Procurement and Administration:* Mun Ung-jo. *Foreign Affairs:* Ri Yong-ho. *Forestry:* Han Ryong-guk. *General Education:* Kim Sung-du. *Higher Education:* Thae Hyong-chol. *Labour:* Jong Yong-su. *Land and Environment Protection:* Kim Kyong-jun. *Land and Maritime Transport:* Kang Jong-gwan. *Light Industry:* Cho Il-ryong. *Machine-Building Industry:* Ri Jong-guk. *Metallurgical Industry:* Kim Chung-gol. *Mining Industry:* Ri Hak-chol. *Oil Industry:* Pae Hak. *Physical Culture and Sports:* Kim Il-Guk. *Post and Telecommunications:* Kim Kwang-chol. *Public Health:* Jang Jun-sang. *Railways:* Jang Hyok. *State*

Construction Control: Kwon Song-ho. *State Natural Resources Development:* Ri Chun-sam. *Urban Management:* Kang Yong-su.

President, Supreme People's Assembly Presidium: Kim Yong-nam. *Vice Presidents:* Yang Hyong-sop, Kim Yong-dae.

In addition there is one minister who is not in the cabinet. *Minister of the People's Armed Forces:* Gen. No Kwang-chol.

In practice the country is ruled by the Korean Workers' (i.e. Communist) Party, which elects a Central Committee that in turn appoints a Politburo. *Government Website:* http://www.korea-dpr.com

Current Leaders

Kim Jong-un
Position
Supreme Leader

Introduction
Kim Jong-un was named Supreme Commander of North Korea's military in Dec. 2011 after the death of his father, Kim Jong-il. Officially, Kim is a member of a triumvirate—with Premier Pak Pong-ju and President of the Supreme People's Assembly Presidium Kim Yong-nam—that heads the executive branch of government. However, it is widely understood that Kim, like his late father, yields absolute power over the state, party and army.

Early Life
Kim Jong-un was born in 1983 or 1984. He was educated in Switzerland and at the Kim Il-sung Military University. In 2009 he was given a mid-level position within the National Defence Commission and became clear favourite to take over from his father when he was appointed a four-star *Daejang* (General) of the People's Army on 27 Sept. 2010, despite his lack of experience. A day later he was given the post of vice-chairman of the Central Military Commission of the Workers' Party.

In the months before Kim Jong-il's death, Kim accompanied him to public events, apparently in preparation for assuming the leadership. Following his father's sudden death, Kim was proclaimed as 'the great successor' by the North Korean media before his appointment as Supreme Commander of the Army on 30 Dec. 2011.

Career in Office
There was initial optimism within the international community that the new administration might be open to reform. However, a moratorium on missile tests, brokered with the USA in Feb. 2012 in return for food aid, was broken when North Korea unsuccessfully tested a long-range rocket in April. Another rocket was then successfully test-launched in Dec. 2012, prompting condemnation from the international community. Meanwhile, Kim had been named First Secretary of the ruling Workers' Party and First Chairman of the National Defence Commission in April 2012 and in July had assumed the highest military rank of marshal.

In March 2013 the UN imposed new sanctions in response to North Korea's third nuclear test the previous month. Pyongyang reacted by threatening pre-emptive nuclear strikes against South Korea and the USA and the following month announced the resumption of operations at the Yongbyon nuclear enrichment complex. It also withdrew its participation in the Kaesong industrial park run jointly with South Korea, although this decision was reversed in Sept.

In Dec. 2013 Kim had his uncle and former political mentor, Jang Song-taek, executed for alleged treason and corruption.

In 2014 and the first half of 2015 North Korea continued to conduct missile tests, including, it was claimed, from a submarine for the first time. The consequent friction with the USA was further soured amid mutual allegations of internet cyber-attacks stemming from the distribution of a controversial US comedy cinema film depicting Kim's assassination. Tensions with South Korea also escalated from Aug. 2015 following an artillery confrontation along the border over the South's propaganda broadcasts across the demilitarized zone, and high-level talks in Dec. to defuse the standoff ended without agreement. In Jan. 2016 the North claimed that it had conducted its fourth nuclear test (the detonation of a hydrogen bomb for the first time) since 2006 and then carried out its fifth test in Sept., incurring more international condemnation—including from China—and further UN sanctions.

Also in 2016, Kim presided at the first Korean Workers' Party's congress since 1980 in May in a perceived move to further reinforce his political dominance.

Hostile exchanges between Kim and the new US president, Donald Trump, escalated through 2017 as North Korea persisted with provocative missile tests over the Sea of Japan, claiming that it had attained the capability to target the USA, and conducted its sixth and largest nuclear test to date in Sept., again incurring more punitive UN sanctions. However, in an unexpected development in Jan. 2018, delegates from North and South Korea held talks for the first time in two years and the North agreed to participate in the winter Olympic Games being hosted by the South in Feb. The apparent thaw in relations was reinforced in April as Kim and his South Korean counterpart, Moon Jae-in, met in the demilitarized zone and agreed to work together to end the state of war existing between the two states since 1953. Then, in June, Kim and US President Trump met in Singapore for a historic summit at which they jointly agreed that North Korea would work towards denuclearization of the Korean peninsula in exchange for US security guarantees and sanctions relief. However, despite the initial optimism, progress on disarmament had stalled by the end of the year as Kim continued the North's nuclear programme and the US maintained its diplomatic and economic pressure on his regime

Defence

The Supreme Commander of the Armed Forces is Kim Jong-un. Military service is compulsory at the age of 17 for periods of 5–12 years in the Army, 5–10 years in the Navy and 3–4 years in the Air Force, followed by obligatory part-time service in the Pacification Corps to age 40. Total armed forces troops were estimated to number 1,190,000 in 2013, up from 840,000 in 1986. Around 70% of the troops are located along or near the demilitarized zone between North and South Korea.

Defence expenditure in 2012 totalled an estimated US$3·5bn. in 2012, which is believed to equate to approximately 22% of GDP.

In 1998 North Korea tested a medium-range nuclear-capable Taepo Dong-1 missile. It has also developed a shorter-range Nodong ballistic missile in addition to Scud B and Scud C missiles, and been developing a longer-range inter-continental ballistic missile, the two- or three-stage Taepo Dong-2, which experts believe could reach outlying American territories. In March 2014 Pyongyang is known to have tested its medium-range Nodong ballistic missile and in June 2016 successfully launched a medium-range Hwasong-10 missile, with the US military base at Guam theoretically within its range. Two months later it launched a Pukkuksong-1 missile, its first successful test of a solid fuel rocket. Then in Sept. 2016, three Nodong missiles were fired into the Sea of Japan. In 2017 several intercontinental ballistic missiles were test-fired, notably a Hwasong-14 missile in July, which it is believed could reach Alaska, and a Hwasong-12 missile in Sept. that was fired over Japan and into the Pacific Ocean. The latter's journey of 3,700 km (2,300 miles) represented Pyongyang's longest missile flight to date. Then, in Nov. 2017 a new Hwasong-15 missile was launched amid claims from the North Korean government that it could hit any target in the USA. Persistent international condemnation has failed to deter the regime's military ambitions.

Nuclear Weapons

North Korea was for many years suspected of having a secret nuclear weapons programme, and in Oct. 2002 it revealed that it had developed a nuclear bomb in violation of an arms control pact agreed with the USA in 1994. North Korea has not signed the Comprehensive Nuclear-Test-Ban-Treaty but did ratify the Nuclear Non-Proliferation Treaty (the international agreement limiting the spread of nuclear weapons) in 1985 before withdrawing in 2003; it is the only country to have done so. In Feb. 2005 it declared that it had manufactured nuclear weapons and stated that it would not re-enter multilateral negotiations on its disarmament. It carried out its first test of a nuclear weapon in Oct. 2006. In July 2007 Pyongyang closed the Yongbyon nuclear complex in return for international aid and in Oct. pledged to disable a further three facilities, ahead of surrendering its nuclear stockpile in 2008. However, Pyongyang missed a Dec. 2007 deadline to give a full account of all of its nuclear facilities although it eventually did so in June 2008, when it also destroyed Yongbyon's cooling tower. Further dismantling of its nuclear facilities was postponed after the USA refused to remove North Korea from its list of state sponsors of terrorism until Pyongyang produced verification of its nuclear downgrading. North Korea was removed from the list in Oct. 2008 and pledged to resume dismantling the Yongbyon reactor.

In April 2009 North Korea was accused by South Korea and the UN of testing long-range nuclear missile technology. North Korea responded by walking out of international talks to wind up its nuclear programme. The following month Pyongyang claimed it had successfully completed underground nuclear tests. In June the UN imposed new sanctions, with Pyongyang stating its intent to weaponize plutonium supplies. A 'miniaturized' nuclear device was tested underground at the Punggye-ri test site in Feb. 2013, prompting new UN sanctions the following month. Pyongyang subsequently threatened pre-emptive nuclear strikes against South Korea and the USA and in April 2013 announced plans to revive the Yongbyon reactor. In Nov. 2013 the International Atomic Energy Agency reported activity at the complex consistent with this aim and in Sept. 2015 the North Korean authorities announced the facility had resumed 'normal operations'. In Jan. 2016 Pyongyang claimed to have carried out a successful underground hydrogen bomb test. While the declaration was regarded as a provocation by the international community, there was widespread scepticism as to its veracity. A further nuclear detonation (believed to be the most powerful yet conducted by Pyongyang) was carried out at Punggye-ri test site in Sept. 2016. In Sept. 2017 Pyongyang carried out its most powerful nuclear test to date—which it claimed was a hydrogen bomb for use on intercontinental ballistic missiles—resulting in a 5·7-magnitude earth tremor in the northeast of the country.

Army

One of the world's biggest, the Army was estimated at 1,020,000 personnel in 2011 with 600,000 reserves. There is also a paramilitary worker-peasant Red Guard of some 5·7m. reservists and a ministry of public security force of 189,000 including border guards.

Equipment includes some 3,500 T-34, T-54/55, T-62 and Type-59 main battle tanks.

Navy

In 2011 the Navy, principally tasked to coastal patrol and defence, included 72 tactical submarines, three frigates, and 383 patrol and coastal combatants. Personnel in 2011 totalled about 60,000.

Air Force

The Air Force had a total of 603 combat-capable aircraft and 110,000 personnel in 2011. Combat-capable aircraft include J-5/6/7s (Chinese built versions of MiG-17/19/23s), MiG-23s, MiG-29s, Su-7s and Su-25s.

Economy

Agriculture is estimated to account for approximately 25% of GDP, industry 60% and services 15%.

In 2012 North Korea received approximately US$126m. in foreign aid.

North Korea featured among the ten most corrupt countries in the world in a 2018 survey of 180 countries carried out by the anti-corruption organization Transparency International.

Overview

Economic progress in North Korea has been impeded by all-powerful state bureaucracy and control, and by a reluctance to depart from Marxist-Stalinist dogma. International aid agencies estimate that food shortages caused by natural disasters and economic mismanagement have resulted in up to 2m. deaths since the mid-1990s.

Punitive international sanctions over North Korea's nuclear development programme have meanwhile led to a greater economic reliance on neighbouring China, which accounts for four-fifths of its trade. In June 2011 it was announced that special economic zones at Rason and on the islands of Hwanggumpyong and Wihwa would be developed in co-operation with China, an idea long promoted by the government.

Despite the impediments, North Korea's economy grew at its fastest pace this century in 2016 according to estimates from South Korea's central bank. GDP expanded by 3·9%, following a contraction in 2015 as a result of drought and low commodity prices. The expansion, driven by the mining and energy sector, marked the biggest annual increase since a 6·1% gain in 1999. Mining and manufacturing accounted for 33·2% of GDP in 2016.

The North Korean government continues to stress its goal of improving the overall standard of living, but has taken few steps to achieve that aim. In 2016 the regime called two mass mobilizations—one totalling 70 days and another 200 days—to spur increased production and complete construction projects. Pyongyang's five-year economic strategy was released in May

2016, although continued tight state control is expected to nullify necessary economic reforms.

Currency

The monetary unit is the *won* (KPW) of 100 *chon*. Banknotes were replaced by a new issue in July 1992. Exchanges of new for old notes were limited to 500 won. In Nov. 2009 the government readjusted the value of the won, with 100 old won worth one new won. Officially the won trades at 135 per US dollar but unofficially it can sometimes trade at up to 3,000 per dollar. North Korea has periodically suffered from high inflation rates since 2000. Following a failed currency reform in Nov. 2009 the inflation rate soared, peaking at an estimated monthly rate of 496% in March 2010.

Budget

Estimated revenue, 2007, US$3·2bn.; expenditure, US$3·3bn.

Performance

The economy is estimated to have shrunk by 1·1% in 2015 but then grown by 3·9% in 2016 according to the Bank of Korea. In 2012 real GDP growth was put at 1·3%. GDP per head was put at US$696 in 2014, or less than a fortieth of that of South Korea.

Banking and Finance

The bank of issue is the Central Bank of the Democratic People's Republic of Korea (*President*, Kim Chon-gyun). Other banks include the Foreign Trade Bank of the Democratic People's Republic of Korea, First Credit Bank and Daedong Credit Bank.

Energy and Natural Resources

Environment

Carbon dioxide emissions from the consumption of energy in 2011 were the equivalent of 2·7 tonnes per capita.

Electricity

Installed capacity was an estimated 9·5m. kW in 2011 (approximately 61% hydro-electric). Production in 2011 was 21·63bn. kWh. Consumption per capita was 878 kWh in 2011. In Feb. 2003 North Korea reactivated its nuclear reactor at Yongbyon that had been dormant since 1994. It was again shut down in July 2007 in exchange for economic aid and political concessions following negotiations with China, Japan, Russia, South Korea and the USA. In April 2009 it was reactivated again following United Nations condemnation of a controversial long-range rocket launch.

Oil and Gas

Oil wells went into production in 1957. An oil pipeline from China came on stream in 1976. China's supplies account for up to 90% of North Korea's oil consumption.

Minerals

North Korea is rich in minerals. Estimated reserves in tonnes: coal, 11,990m.; manganese, 6,500m.; iron ore, 3,300m.; uranium, 26m.; zinc, 12m.; lead, 6m.; copper, 2·15m. 23·9m. tonnes of coal were mined in 2007, 6·5m. tonnes of lignite in 2007, 5m. tonnes of iron ore in 2006, 500,000 tonnes of salt in 2006 and 12,000 tonnes of copper in 2006. 2006 production of silver was 20 tonnes; gold, 2,000 kg.

Agriculture

In 2012 there were approximately 2·35m. ha. of arable land and 230,000 ha. of permanent crop land. An estimated 3·05m. persons were economically active in agriculture in 2011.

In 2012 the total area equipped for irrigation was around 1·46m. ha., making possible two rice harvests a year. The technical revolution in agriculture (nearly 95% of ploughing, etc., is mechanized) has considerably increased the yield of wheat (sown on an estimated 60,000 ha. in 2013). Areas harvested of other major crops (2013 estimates): rice (paddy), 664,000 ha.; maize, 520,000 ha.; soybeans, 305,000 ha. Production (2012 estimates, in 1,000 tonnes): rice, 2,681; maize, 2,000; potatoes, 1,800; apples, 785; cabbages, kale, etc., 700.

Livestock, 2013 estimates: goats, 3·60m.; pigs, 2·26m.; cattle, 590,000; sheep, 170,000; 18m. chickens.

A chronic food shortage has led to repeated efforts by UN agencies to stave off famine. In Jan. 1998 the UN launched an appeal for US$378m. for food for North Korea, the largest ever relief effort mounted by its World Fund Programme.

Forestry

Forest area in 2015 was 5·03m. ha. (42% of the land area). Timber production was 7·53m. cu. metres in 2011.

Fisheries

In 2015 total catch was an estimated 220,000 tonnes, of which 98% were sea fish.

Industry

Industries were intensively developed by the Japanese occupiers, notably cotton spinning, hydro-electric power, cotton, silk and rayon weaving, and chemical fertilizers. Production: cement (2007), 6·1m. tonnes; crude steel (2007), 1·23m. tonnes; pig iron (2007), 900,000 tonnes. The suspension of economic assistance from the former Soviet Union following its break-up in 1990 caused a great shock to the North Korean economy. A shortage of coking coal, electric power and timber led to the virtual collapse of industrial production. Manufacturing was estimated to have accounted for 22% of GDP in 2012.

Labour

The labour force in 2013 was 15,206,000 (14,048,000 in 2003). 82·7% of the population aged 15–64 was economically active in 2013. In the same year 4·1% of the population was unemployed.

International Trade

Joint ventures with foreign firms have been permitted since 1984. A law of Oct. 1992 revised the 1984 rules: foreign investors may now set up wholly-owned facilities in special economic zones, repatriate part of profits and enjoy tax concessions. In Jan. 2012 foreign debt was estimated at US$20bn. The USA imposed sanctions in Jan. 1988 for alleged terrorist activities. From June 1995 to May 2010 South Korean businesses and individuals were permitted to make investments and set up branch offices in North Korea. However, following the sinking of its warship *Cheonan* in March 2010, South Korea imposed trade restrictions on the North that banned all inter-Korean economic exchanges with the exception of the joint industrial park at Kaesong.

Imports and Exports

Trade figures for 2013 (excluding inter-Korean trade): imports, US$4·12bn.; exports, US$3·22bn. In 2006 China was the biggest import supplier (27%), followed by South Korea (16%) and Thailand (9%); in 2007 South Korea was the main export destination (45%), ahead of China (35%) and Thailand (5%). Leading export commodities are minerals, textiles, metallurgical products, agricultural and fishery products, and armaments. Main import categories are petroleum, machinery and equipment, coking coal, textiles and grain.

Communications

Roads

There were 25,554 km of road in 2006. The first of two planned cross-border roads between the two Koreas opened in Feb. 2003. Private car ownership is rare.

Rail

Rail transport is provided by Korean State Railways. There is an extensive network of standard gauge lines totalling over 6,000 km and a network of 762 mm narrow gauge lines covering some 350 km. Main lines cover around 2,500 km. In June 2000 it was agreed to start consultations to restore the railway from Sinuiju, on the North Korean/Chinese border, to Seoul by rebuilding an 8 km long stretch from Pongdong-ni to Changdan, on the North Korean/South Korean border, and a 12 km long stretch in South Korea. Two passenger trains crossed the border between North and South Korea on 17 May 2007 (one northbound and one southbound), completing the first cross-border journey in more than 50 years. Regular freight services between the two Koreas were resumed in Dec. 2007 but usage is very limited.

There are a metro and two tramways in Pyongyang.

Civil Aviation

There is an international airport at Pyongyang (Sunan). There were flights in 2010 to Bangkok, Beijing, Shenyang and Vladivostok. The national carrier is Air Koryo.

Shipping

The leading ports are Chongjin, Wonsan and Hungnam. Pyongyang is connected to the port of Nampo by railway and river. In Jan. 2014 there were 208 ships of 300 GT or over registered, totalling 572,000 GT.

The biggest navigable river is the Yalu, on the border between North Korea and China.

Telecommunications

There were 1·18m. main (fixed) telephone lines in 2013. A mobile phone service was introduced in Dec. 2008 four years after a previous service had been shut down without explanation. In 2013 there were 2·42m. subscribers (972 for every 10,000 inhabitants). It was only in 2013 that the number of mobile phone subscriptions surpassed the number of fixed telephone subscriptions.

Social Institutions

Out of 178 countries analysed in the 2017 *Fragile States Index*—a list published jointly by the Fund for Peace and *Foreign Policy* magazine—North Korea was ranked the 30th most vulnerable to conflict or collapse. The index is based on 12 indicators of state vulnerability across social, political and economic categories.

Justice

The judiciary consists of the Supreme Court, whose judges are elected by the Assembly for three years; provincial courts; and city or county people's courts. The procurator-general, appointed by the Assembly, has supervisory powers over the judiciary and the administration; the Supreme Court controls the judicial administration.

In May 2011 some 150,000–200,000 political prisoners were being held at a number of detention camps in the country. North Korea does not divulge figures on its use of the death penalty; however, Amnesty International 'received reports of executions and death sentences but could not independently verify the information' during 2017. In 2013 people were reportedly executed for offences including cannibalism, corruption, embezzlement, attempting to escape to China, pornography and watching banned videos from South Korea.

Education

Free compulsory universal technical education lasts 11 years: one pre-school year, four years primary education starting at the age of six, followed by six years secondary. In 2008, 2·18m. pupils attended pre-primary or primary schools and 2·47m. pupils were at secondary school. There were also 437,000 students in tertiary education in 2008.

The adult literacy rate in 2008 was 100%.

Health

Medical treatment is free. In 2011 there were 68,393 physicians, and 100,768 nursing and midwifery personnel. Over the period 2005–12 there were 132 hospital beds per 10,000 population. Expenditure on health came to an estimated 3·5% of GDP in 2006.

North Korea has been one of the least successful countries in the battle against undernourishment in the past 20 years. The proportion of undernourished people rose from 27% of the population in 1993 to 42% in 2013.

Religion

The state-sanctioned philosophy of *Juche* is the only government-recognized ideology, to the point of excluding all other religions. *Juche* means 'self-reliance' in Korean. Although the official North Korean line is that it is an atheistic philosophy, many observers maintain that is a religion. There are small numbers of Buddhists, Cheondoists and Christians. Persecution of Christians is considered to be more severe than in any other country.

Culture

World Heritage Sites

There are two UNESCO sites in North Korea: the Complex of Koguryo Tombs (2004); and the Historic Monuments and Sites in Kaesong (2013).

Press

There were three national daily newspapers and 12 regional dailies in 2008 with a combined circulation of 4·5m. The party newspaper is *Nodong* (or *Rodong*) *Sinmun* (Workers' Daily News). In the 2013 *World Press Freedom Index* compiled by Reporters Without Borders, North Korea ranked 178th out of 179 countries.

Tourism

A 40-year ban on non-Communist tourists was lifted in 1986. In 2014 there were approximately 100,000 foreign tourists. On 19 Nov. 1998 North Korea received its first tourists from South Korea, on a cruise and tour organized by the South Korean firm Hyundai.

Calendar

A new yearly calendar was announced on 9 July 1997 based on Kim Il-sung's birthday on 15 April 1912. Thus 1912 became *Juche* year 1; 2019 is *Juche* 108.

Diplomatic Representatives

Of North Korea in the United Kingdom (73 Gunnersbury Ave., London, W5 4LP)
Ambassador: Choe Il.

Of the United Kingdom in North Korea (Munsu-Dong Compound, Pyongyang)
Ambassador: Colin Crooks, LVO.

The USA does not have diplomatic relations with North Korea, but the Swedish Embassy in North Korea provides limited consular services to US citizens while North Korea is represented in the USA through its mission to the United Nations.

Of North Korea to the United Nations
Ambassador: Kim Song.

Of North Korea to the European Union
Ambassador: Vacant.

Further Reading

Bechtol, Bruce, *North Korea and Regional Security in the Kim Jong-un Era.* 2014

Becker, Jasper, *Rogue Regime: Kim Jong Il and the Looming Threat of North Korea.* 2005

Cha, Victor D, *The Impossible State: North Korea, Past and Future.* 2012

Cha, Victor D. and Kang, David C., *Nuclear North Korea: A Debate on Engagement Strategies.* 2003

Cumings, Bruce, *North Korea: Another Country.* 2004

Harrison, S., *Korean Endgame: A Strategy for Reunification and US Disengagement.* 2002

Hassig, Ralph and Oh, Kongdan, *The Hidden People of North Korea: Everyday Life in the Hermit Kingdom.* 2009

Hunter, H., *Kim Il-Song's North Korea.* 1999

Jager, Sheila Miyoshi, *Brothers at War: The Unending Conflict in Korea.* 2013

Kleiner, J., *Korea: a Century of Change.* 2001

Lankov, Andrei, *The Real North Korea: Life and Politics in the Failed Stalinist Utopia.* 2013

Myers, B. R., *The Cleanest Race: How North Koreans See Themselves and Why It Matters.* 2010

Oh, K. and Hassig, R. C., *North Korea Through the Looking Glass.* 2000

O'Hanlon, Michael E. and Mochizuki, Mike, *Crisis on the Korean Peninsula: How to Deal with a Nuclear North Korea.* 2003

Sigal, L. V., *Disarming Strangers: Nuclear Diplomacy with North Korea.* 1999

Smith, H., *et al.*, (eds) *North Korea in the New World Order.* 1996

Tudor, Daniel and Pearson, James, *North Korea Confidential: Private Markets, Fashion Trends, Prison Camps, Dissenters and Defectors.* 2015

National Statistical Office: Central Statistics Bureau, Pyongyang.

Korea, South

Daehan Minguk (Republic of Korea)

Capital: Seoul
Population projection, 2020: 51·51m.
GNI per capita, 2017: (PPP$) 35,945
HDI/world rank, 2017: 0·903/22=
Internet domain extension: .kr

Key Historical Events

The Korean peninsula was first settled by tribal peoples from Manchuria and Siberia who provided the basis for the modern Korean language. By 3000 BC agriculture-based communities had emerged. The earliest known colony in the region was established at Pyongyang in the 12th century BC. Among the most prominent agricultural communities was Old Choson, which by 194 BC had evolved into a league of tribes ruled by Wiman or 'Wei Man', a leader widely held to have defected from China, although he may have been a native of the Choson region. His realm was taken over by the Han empire of China in 108 BC and replaced by four Chinese colonies.

The rest of the peninsula developed into tribal states; Puyo in the north and Chin south of the Han River. Chin was itself split into three tribal states (Mahan, Chinhan and Pyonhan); these states then evolved into three rival kingdoms, Koguryo, Paekche, and Silla. Three powerful figures, King T'aejo (AD 53–146) of Koguryo, King Koi (AD 234–86) of Paekche and King Naemul (AD 356–402) of Silla, established hereditary monarchies while powerful aristocracies developed from tribal chiefdoms.

With China's support Silla conquered the other two kingdoms; Paekche in 660 and Koguryo in 668. In 676 Silla drove out the Chinese and gained complete control of the peninsula. Survivors from Koguryo established Parhae, under the leadership of Tae Cho-yong, in the northern region. After a period of conflict with Silla, Parhae grew into a prosperous state in its own right before being taken over by northern nomadic peoples. In Silla an absolute monarchy replaced the council of nobles (its former decision making body) with a central administrative body called the chancellery (*Chipsabu*), thus undermining aristocratic power. Meanwhile, the capital Kumsong (now Kyongju in South Korea) was developed. The state was divided into administrative units by province (*chu*), prefecture (*kun*), and county (*hyon*), and five provincial capitals prospered as cultural centres. Avatamsaka Buddhism was the dominant religion.

Divisions within the aristocracy in the 8th century led to the restoration of the Council of Nobles and the overthrow of the monarchy. Forced to pay taxes to powerful provincial families and central government, the peasants rebelled. Two provincial leaders, Kyonhwon and Kungye, established the Later Paekche (892) and Later Koguryo (901) as rivals to Silla.

National Unity

The powerful leader Wang Kon founded Koryo (now Kaesong, North Korea) in 918, and established a unified kingdom in the Korean peninsula in 936. Three chancelleries and the royal secretariat formed the supreme council of state and governed the kingdom. Koryo's leaders were then largely aristocratic, and the political system greatly favoured those in the top five tiers of the nine hierarchical levels. That the military was not eligible for any hierarchical position above the second level and received little land, led to a military coup in 1170. Gen. Ch'oe Ch'ung-hon established a military regime which held power for the next 60 years. Zen Buddhism and the allied ideology of Confucianism had grown popular but were suppressed under the Ch'oe regime. Many monks fled to the mountains, where they formed what became Korean Buddhism, the *Chogye*.

In 1231 the Mongols invaded Koryo but were resisted by the Ch'oe leaders for nearly three decades, until a peasant uprising saw the Ch'oe overthrown. A power-sharing agreement between the rebels and the Mongols came into force in 1258. Despite some interference from the Mongols, Koryo retained its identity as a unified state. The aristocracy established seats of power throughout the country, encouraging peasants to seek protection as serfs. This, however, led to reduced tax revenues and when the government did not have sufficient resources to reward its bureaucratic class, a rebellion ensued. Led by General Yi Song-gye, and with the help of the Ming dynasty in China, government officials seized power in 1392 and established a new system of land distribution, thus ending the Koryo dynasty.

Gen. Yi named the state Choson, designating Hanyang (now Seoul, South Korea) as the capital. Buddhism was dropped in favour of a new Chinese-influenced Confucian ethical system and the state was governed by a hereditary aristocracy (the *yangban*), who controlled all aspects of Korean society. In 1420 the Hall of Worthies (*Chiphyonjon*) was established for scholars, and after 1443 the Korean phonetic alphabet (*hangul*) developed. Later in the period, a centralized yangban government was formed and the country divided into eight administrative regions, with standardized laws and a central decision-making and judicial body.

In 1592 Japan, newly unified under the command of Toyotomi Hideyoshi, sent an army to Korea supposedly as part of an invasion of China. Korea's naval forces, under Admiral Yi Sun-shin, were able to repel the invaders. Swelling anti-Japanese sentiment prompted Koreans from all hierarchical divisions to fight in the war alongside troops dispatched from Ming China. However, Japanese forces did not withdraw completely until Toyotomi's death in 1598, leaving Korea in ruins.

Despite joint efforts by China and Korea to stem the advances of the nomadic Manchu in the early 17th century, Seoul was captured in 1636. The Manchu established the Ch'ing dynasty several years later and demanded tribute from Korea.

During the 17th and 18th centuries, Korea's agriculture developed as irrigation improved and rice, tobacco and ginseng became increasingly important crops. By the late 18th century many Korean scholars had turned to Roman Catholicism, leading to government suppression of Christianity in a bid to preserve the dominance of Confucianism. However, European priests maintained strong links in the country.

Japanese Influence

In the 19th century, a succession of monarchs yet to attain the age of majority undermined national stability. In 1864 Taewon'gun, the father of the child-king Kojong, took power and pursued a programme of controversial political reform that increasingly isolated Korea from the outside world. When Taewon'gun was eventually forced to step down, Korea came under pressure from Japan to open up its ports. Nervous of growing Japanese influence, China placed troops in Korea following a failed coup attempt by pro-- Taewon'gun forces. There followed a trade agreement which greatly benefited Chinese commercial interests. Further treaties with France, Germany, Russia, the UK and the USA followed in the 1880s. As foreign influence increased, Korea's ruling elite divided between moderates and radicals. The radicals carried out a coup in 1884 but were quickly defeated by Chinese troops. An agreement to maintain a balance of power in the region was signed by Japan and China the following year.

As modernization gathered pace, government spending increased, adding to the burden of reparations payments to Japan. The peasants turned to *Tonghak* ('Eastern Learning'), a new religion established by an old yangban scholar and based on traditional beliefs. A Tonghak rebellion in 1894 caused China to send in troops. Japan responded by sending its own forces and war broke out. By the following year Japan had secured control of the peninsula.

Korea declared neutrality at the outbreak of war between Japan and Russia in 1904 but was pressured by Japan into allowing use of Korean territory. Japan achieved victory in 1905 and made Korea a protectorate. An unsuccessful appeal to the international peace conference at The Hague further undermined relations between Japan and Korea. Anti-Japanese guerrilla fighters were active in the southern provinces during 1908–09 but were crushed the following year when Korea was annexed by Japan.

Japan established a government in Korea and implemented a programme designed to supplant the Korean identity. There were restrictions on freedom of speech, press and assembly and the language and history of Japan was taught in schools at the expense of those of Korea. Many Koreans were dispossessed of their land as Japan built new transport and communications infrastructures. When the Japanese brutally suppressed a 2m.-strong

© Springer Nature Limited 2020
Palgrave Macmillan (ed.), *The Statesman's Yearbook 2020*,
https://doi.org/10.1057/978-1-349-95940-2_106

demonstration in 1919, independence leaders established a provisional government in Shanghai and named Syngman Rhee as president. Hoping to calm dissent, Japan lifted certain press restrictions and replaced the gendarmerie with an ordinary police force, but uncompromising colonial rule remained in place.

Korea became a market for Japanese goods and attracted much capital investment but at the expense of agriculture, leading to a long-term shortage of rice. Tokyo reimposed military rule in 1931 when war broke out between Japan and China and attempted to quash all manifestations of a separate Korean identity over the following decade. Magazines, newspapers and academic organisations operating in the Korean language were banned. Hundreds of thousands of Koreans were made to fight in the Japanese army, or work in Japanese mines and factories in order to support Japan's military efforts during the Second World War. The provisional government, having moved from Shanghai to Chungking in southwest China, declared war on Japan in Dec. 1941. An army of Korean resistance fighters joined the Allied forces in China and fought with them until the Japanese surrender in 1945.

Korea Divided

Korea was promised independence by China, Britain and the USA at the Cairo conference of 1943 but at the end of the war, after Japan's collapse, Korea was divided in two along the 38° Parallel. Initially the USA and the USSR had agreed informally to a four-way power share in Korea, involving Britain and the Republic of China. However, in order to hasten a Japanese surrender, US troops controlled the south of the country while the USSR took command of the north. The Soviet forces helped to establish a Communist-led provisional government under Kim Il Sung. As relations between the USA and the Soviet Union worsened, trade ceased between the two zones, causing economic hardship because industry was concentrated in the north and agriculture in the south.

In Sept. 1947 the United Nations urged elections in both sectors. However, a commission to oversee voting in the North was denied entry by Soviet troops. Rhee was elected in the South while the North appointed Kim Il Sung as leader. In 1948 the southern Republic of Korea (with Seoul as the capital) and the northern Democratic People's Republic of Korea (with Pyongyang as capital) came into being.

Soviet and US troops left the peninsula in 1949 and war broke out between the North and South in June 1950. A US-led UN force under Gen. Douglas MacArthur entered South Korea and pushed back the North Korean forces. The UN pressed on into North Korea and established a commission for the reunification and rehabilitation of Korea. China, which at that point had no representation in the United Nations, entered the war and contributed 1·2m. troops to the North Korean side. Peace negotiations began in 1951 and a new international boundary and demilitarized zone were declared in 1953. The USA offered South Korea financial support and signed a mutual security pact with Rhee, who had been reluctant to accept the division of the country. The issue of prisoner returns, particularly of North Koreans unwilling to return to the communist state, remained a point of contention. The war left 4m. people dead or injured.

Traditionally an agricultural region, South Korea faced severe economic problems after partition. Limited resources, war damage and a flood of refugees from North Korea all pointed towards economic disaster, and the country became dependent on foreign aid, particularly from the USA.

The authoritarian rule of President Rhee, marred by corruption, received widespread condemnation. The elections of 1960 were blighted by violence and fraud and when the police shot 125 students during a demonstration, the government was forced to step down. Rhee was exiled. Subsequent leaders failed to solve the country's problems and in May 1961 Gen. Park Chung-hee led a military coup. As leader of the Democratic Republican Party, he was elected president in 1963, 1967 and, following a constitutional amendment to allow a third term in office, 1971.

Park's government was powerful and efficient, reviving the economy through the development of manufacturing for export and attracting increased foreign investment, especially from America. In 1972 Park proclaimed martial law and abolished the National Assembly. In 1979 he was assassinated and the country collapsed into chaos. Chun Doo-hwan became leader in 1980 in another military coup and, as leader of the Democratic Justice Party (DJP), revived the National Assembly.

In 1983 a South Korean passenger jet strayed into Soviet airspace and was shot down with the loss of all 269 lives on board. The incident increased tensions significantly between Moscow and Washington.

Popular dissatisfaction with the South Korean government grew throughout the decade and a new constitution in 1987 stipulated that the president be elected by popular vote and his term of office reduced to five years.

Roh Tae-woo was elected president in 1988 as leader of the DJP and later of the Democratic Liberal Party. Fighting rising inflation, he established diplomatic relations with China and the Soviet Union and developed a better relationship with opposition parties in his own country. North and South Korea met several times during the 1980s in a bid to improve relations. In 1991 the two countries signed a treaty of non-aggression, with each country promising not to interfere in the internal affairs of the other.

In 1992 Kim Young-sam, the former opposition leader who had merged his party with Roh's, became the first civilian to be elected president since the Korean War. He launched an anti-corruption campaign and continued to pursue closer relations with North Korea. During the financial crisis that affected East Asia in 1997 South Korea was forced to ask the International Monetary Fund for help, though it largely avoided long-term economic damage and remains one of Asia's most affluent countries.

In Dec. 1997 Kim Dae-jung, a pro-democracy dissident during the years of military dictatorship, was elected president. Kim forged a 'sunshine policy' aimed at closer ties with the North and received the Nobel peace prize for his efforts. The two Koreas subsequently undertook a series of joint commercial and infrastructural projects. Constitutionally disqualified from standing for the presidency again in 2002, Kim was replaced by Roh Moo-hyun who continued the 'sunshine policy', despite North Korea's deteriorating relationship with the USA.

In Oct. 2007 South and North Korea jointly called for a permanent peace on the peninsula to replace the armistice in place since the end of the Korean War. However, diplomatic and trading relations subsequently deteriorated markedly, reflecting South Korean and the wider international community's concerns over the threat to regional security from the North's nuclear weapon and long-range missile technology development.

In presidential elections in Dec. 2012 Park Geun-hye of the conservative Saenuri Party (and daughter of the former president Park Chung-hee) became South Korea's first female leader. However, in the face of a corruption scandal and widespread public disenchantment, she was suspended from office in Dec. 2016 after parliament voted for her impeachment. Moon Jae-in was elected to succeed her in May 2017. Despite rising tensions with North Korea throughout 2017, Seoul and Pyongyang sent a joint team to the Winter Olympic Games in Feb. 2018.

Territory and Population

South Korea is bounded in the north by the demilitarized zone (separating it from North Korea), east by the Sea of Japan (East Sea), south by the Korea Strait (separating it from Japan) and west by the Yellow Sea. The area is 100,222 sq. km. The population at the census of 1 Nov. 2015 was 51,069,375; density, 509·6 per sq. km (one of the highest in the world). In 2011 the urban population was 83·3%.

The UN gives a projected population for 2020 of 51·51m.

The official language is Korean. In July 2000 the Korean government introduced a new Romanization System for the Korean Language to romanize Korean words into English.

Area of the eight provinces, one special autonomous province, six metropolitan cities and one special city in 2015 plus their populations:

Province	Area (in sq. km)	Population (in 1,000)
Busan[1]	768	3,449
Chungcheongbuk	7,405	1,589
Chungcheongnam	8,192	2,108
Daegu[1]	884	2,466
Daejeon[1]	540	1,538
Gangwon	16,866	1,518
Gwangju[1]	501	1,503
Gyeonggi	10,170	12,479
Gyeongsangbuk	19,030	2,680
Gyeongsangnam	10,533	3,335
Incheon[1]	1,032	2,890
Jeju[2]	1,849	606
Jeollabuk	8,067	1,834
Jeollanam	12,252	1,799
Sejong	465	204

(continued)

Province	Area (in sq. km)	Population (in 1,000)
Seoul[3]	605	9,904
Ulsan[1]	1,060	1,167

[1]Metropolitan city.
[2]Special autonomous province.
[3]Special city.

Cities with over 500,000 inhabitants (census 2015):

Seoul	9,904,312
Busan	3,448,737
Incheon	2,890,451
Daegu	2,466,052
Daejeon	1,538,394
Gwangju	1,502,881
Suwon	1,194,313
Ulsan	1,166,615
Changwon	1,059,241
Goyang	990,073
Yongin	971,327
Seongnam	948,757
Bucheon	843,794
Cheongju	833,276
Ansan	747,035
Jeonju	658,172
Cheonan	629,062
Namyangju	629,061
Hwaseong	608,725
Anyang	585,177
Gimhae	534,124
Pohang	511,804

Social Statistics

2008: births, 465,900; deaths, 246,100; marriages, 327,700; divorces, 116,500. Rates per 1,000 population in 2008: birth, 9·7; death, 5·1; marriage, 6·8; divorce, 2·4. In 2012 only 2·1% of births were outside marriage, one of the lowest rates in the world. South Korea has among the highest suicide rates of any country, at 36·6 per 100,000 inhabitants in 2012 (a rate of 49·9 among males although only 23·4 among females). Expectation of life at birth, 2007, 82·4 years for females and 75·8 for males. Life expectancy had been 47 in 1955 and 62 in 1971. Infant mortality, 2010, four per 1,000 live births. The fertility rate in 2013 was 1·3 births per woman (the joint lowest rate in the world), down from 6·3 per woman in the period 1955–60. Annual population growth rate, 2005–10, 0·5%. In 2009 the average age of first marriage was 31·6 for men and 28·7 for women.

South Korea has one of the most rapidly ageing populations in the world, partly owing to an ever-decreasing birth rate. In 2009, 10·7% of the population were over 65, up from 2·9% in 1960. There were 16·92m. households in 2009, with on average 2·8 members per household. According to the UN Human Development Report 2009, South Korea has an emigration rate of 3·1%; North America is the main destination, with 50·3% of South Korean migrants living there. Within South Korea, there are 551,200 foreign migrants, representing 1·2% of the total population. UNICEF reported that 11·5% of children in South Korea in 2014 lived in relative poverty (living in a household in which disposable income—when adjusted for family size and composition—is less than 60% of the national median income), the fifth lowest rate in the world.

Climate

The country experiences continental temperate conditions. Rainfall is concentrated in the period April to Sept. and ranges from 40" (1,020 mm) to 60" (1,520 mm). Busan, Jan. 36°F (2·2°C), July 76°F (24·4°C). Annual rainfall 56" (1,407 mm). Seoul, Jan. 23°F (−5°C), July 77°F (25°C). Annual rainfall 50" (1,250 mm).

Constitution and Government

The 1988 constitution provides for a *President*, directly elected for a single five-year term, who appoints the members of the *State Council* and heads it, and for a *National Assembly* (*Gukhoe*), of 300 members, directly elected for four years (246 from constituencies and 54 from party lists in proportion to the overall vote). The current constitution created the Sixth Republic. The minimum voting age is 20.

National Anthem

'Aegukga' ('A Song of Love for the Country'); words anonymous, tune by Ahn Eaktay.

Government Chronology

Heads of State of South Korea since 1948. (DJP = Democratic Justice Party; DLP = Democratic Liberal Party; DP = Democratic Party; DPK = Democratic Party of Korea; DRP = Democratic Republican Party; GNP = Grand National Party; LP = Liberal Party; MDP = Millennium Democratic Party; NCNP = National Congress for New Politics; NDP = New Democratic Party; NFP = Saenuri Party; NKP = New Korea Party; UD = Uri Party; n/p = non-partisan)

Presidents		
1948–60	LP	Syngman Rhee
1960–62	DP, NDP	Yun Po-sun
Chairman of the Supreme Council for National Reconstruction		
1962–63	military	Park Chung-hee
Presidents		
1963–79	DRP	Park Chung-hee
1979–80	DRP	Choi Kyu-hah
1980–88	military, DJP	Chun Doo-hwan
1988–93	DJP, DLP	Roh Tae-woo
1993–98	DLP, NKP	Kim Young-sam
1998–2003	NCNP, MDP	Kim Dae-jung
2003–08	MDP, UD	Roh Moo-hyun
2008–13	GNP, NFP	Lee Myung-bak
2013–16	NFP	Park Geun-hye
2016–17	n/p	Hwang Kyo-ahn (acting)
2017–	DPK	Moon Jae-in

Recent Elections

Presidential elections were held on 9 May 2017. Moon Jae-in of the Democratic Party of Korea (formerly the Minjoo Party of Korea) won with 41·1% of votes cast, ahead of Hong Jun-pyo of the Liberty Korea Party (formerly the Saenuri Party) with 24·0% and 11 other candidates. Turnout was 77·2%.

Elections to the National Assembly were held on 13 April 2016. Turnout was 58·0%. The Minjoo Party of Korea won 123 of 300 seats (110 from first-past-the-post constituencies and 13 from proportional party lists); the Saenuri Party 122 (105 from first-past-the-post constituencies and 17 from proportional party lists); the People's Party 38; and the Justice Party 6. 11 seats went to independents. Presidential elections were scheduled to take place on 9 May 2017.

Current Government

President: Moon Jae-in; b. 1953 (Democratic Party of Korea/DPK; sworn in 10 May 2017).

In March 2019 the cabinet comprised:

Prime Minister: Lee Nak-yon; b. 1951 (Democratic Party of Korea/DPK; sworn in 31 May 2017).

Deputy Prime Ministers: Yoo Eun-he (also *Minister of Education*); Hong Nam-ki (also *Minister of Economy and Finance*).

Minister of Agriculture, Food and Rural Affairs: Lee Gae-ho. *Culture, Sport and Tourism:* Park Yang-woo. *Employment and Labour:* Lee Jae-kap. *Environment:* Kim Eun-kyung. *Foreign Affairs:* Kang Kyung-wha. *Gender Equality and Family:* Jin Sun-mee. *Health and Welfare:* Park Neung-hoo.

Interior and Safety: Chin Young. *Justice:* Park Sang-ki. *Land, Infrastructure and Transport:* Choi Jeong-ho. *National Defence:* Jeong Kyeong-doo. *Oceans and Fisheries:* Moon Seong-hyeok. *Science and ICT:* Cho Dong-ho. *Small and Medium-Sized Businesses, and Startups:* Park Young-sun. *Trade, Industry and Energy:* Sung Yun-mo. *Unification:* Kim Yeon-chul.

National Assembly Speaker: Moon Hee-sang.

Government Website: http://www.korea.net

Current Leaders

Moon Jae-in

Position

President

Introduction

Moon Jae-in, a former aide to President Roh Moo-hyun, unsuccessfully contested the 2012 presidential election before winning the snap election of 9 May 2017.

Early Life

Moon Jae-in was born on 24 Jan. 1953 in Geoje. He became active in student politics while studying law at Kyunghee University, and was arrested and expelled for leading a protest against the dictatorship of President Park Chung-hee. He completed his mandatory military service between 1975 and 1978 before passing his Bar exams. As a human rights lawyer in the 1980s, he grew close to Roh Moo-hyun through their involvement in pro-democracy protests. Moon joined Roh's administration in 2008 as an aide, eventually becoming chief of staff.

Moon won a seat in the National Assembly in April 2012. Later that year he was nominated as the candidate of the then Democratic United Party (renamed the Democratic Party of Korea the following year) to contest the presidential election but was narrowly defeated by Park Geun-hye. Following the March 2017 impeachment of Park amid corruption allegations, Moon once again stood as a presidential candidate. He pledged to adopt a softer approach to North Korea but a less conciliatory one towards the USA. Moon won the election on 9 May with 41·1% of the vote and was sworn in the following day.

Career in Office

Moon was expected to challenge the economic dominance of the *chaebol* (business conglomerates). He also argued for more transparent government, and pledged to move the president's office to the Gwanghwamun district of Seoul that bore witness to the protests against President Park.

On the international stage, he faced the challenge of rebalancing relations with the USA and with North Korea against the backdrop of Pyongyang's continued nuclear and ballistic missile tests and regional military threat. However, the new year heralded an unexpected rapprochement between the two Koreas and, initially, between the North and the USA. In April and Sept. 2018 Moon met his North Korean counterpart, Kim Jong-un, and agreed to work together to end the state of war existing between the two states since 1953 and to denuclearize the Korean peninsula. However, despite the optimism generated by a summit between Kim and US President Donald Trump in June, progress on disarmament had stalled by the end of the year as Kim continued the North's nuclear programme and the US maintained its diplomatic and economic pressure on his regime.

Defence

Peacetime operational control, which had been transferred to the United Nations Command (UNC) under a US general in July 1950 after the outbreak of the Korean War, was restored to South Korea on 1 Dec. 1994. In the event of a new crisis, operational control over the Korean armed forces will revert to the Combined Forces Command (CFC). Conscription is 21 months in the Army, 23 months in the Navy and 24 months in the Air Force. In Sept. 2007 it was announced that the length of conscription will be gradually reduced and that conscientious objectors will be allowed to choose community service in place of military service. In 2004 the USA and South Korea agreed to the redeployment of 12,500 US personnel in three phases that would continue until 2008. In April 2008 the number of troops had been reduced to 28,000 (mainly army and air force personnel) from 37,000 in 2002. The number of US troops in South Korea has remained unchanged since then.

In 2013 defence expenditure totalled US$31,846m. (US$651 per capita), representing 2·5% of GDP.

Army

Strength (2011) 522,000. Paramilitary Civilian Defence Corps, 3·0m. The armed forces reserves numbered 4·5m.

Navy

In 2011 the Navy had a substantial force of 68,000, including 27,000 marine corps troops. In 2011 the fleet included 23 submarines, two cruisers, six destroyers, 12 frigates, 30 corvettes and 80 fast-attack craft. Naval Aviation operated eight combat-capable aircraft. The naval headquarters are at Gyeryong.

Air Force

In 2011 the Air Force had a strength of 65,000 personnel and 390 combat-capable aircraft (F-4s, F-5s, F-15s and F-16s).

International Relations

Defections to South Korea from North Korea totalled 1,397 in 2014 compared to a record 2,914 in 2009.

South Korea's foreign policy is predominantly directed towards maintaining regional security in light of its volatile relationship with neighbouring North Korea. Eventual reunification of the two states remains a long-term goal.

Economy

Agriculture accounted for 2·5% of GDP in 2013, industry 38·4% and services 59·3%.

In 2017 South Korea gave US$2·2bn. in international aid. In terms of a percentage of GNI, however, it was one of the least generous major industrialized countries, giving just 0·14%.

Overview

South Korea used to have a centrally planned economy and its GDP per capita in the 1960s was comparable to that in some of the poorest countries in Africa. However, market reforms over the ensuing decades saw the economy record remarkable levels of growth, driven largely by export-oriented manufacturing. The World Bank ranked South Korea the world's 11th largest economy in 2016, measured by GDP.

The 1997 Asian financial crisis exposed weaknesses in the country's development model and led to a severe recession in 1998. High debt-to-equity ratios, heavy foreign borrowing and an undisciplined financial sector with a significant amount of non-performing loans weighed heavily on the economy. Nonetheless, there was average annual growth of 5·8% from 1999 to 2007. In 2008 the global financial crisis saw exports slump and capital leave the country at a higher rate than at the height of the Asian crisis. GDP growth declined to 2·8% in 2008 and 0·7% in 2009 (the slowest rate since 1998), but recovered robustly in 2010, recording a 6·5% rise—one of the earliest rebounds in the OECD.

Annual GDP growth averaged 2·8% between 2012 and 2017. However, future growth prospects have been impacted by a deterioration in relations with China, the country's main trading partner, following the South's decision to accept the deployment of a US anti-missile system on its territory in response to North Korean nuclear tests.

Output growth fell below 3% in 2018, reflecting a slowdown in fixed investment and employment, and the unemployment rate reached 4% for the first time since 2010. Also, a 16·4% hike in the minimum wage in 2018 and restructuring in manufacturing negatively affected the labour market. Core inflation meanwhile fell to 1%, reflecting sluggish domestic demand, government measures to reduce the cost of education and healthcare and a cut in the consumption tax on cars.

The government aims to address weaker domestic demand through a fiscal stimulus, with spending budgeted to increase by 9·7% in 2019. In addition, it is seeking to boost public employment by 34% over the period 2017–22.

The ageing population poses long-term problems for the economy, with 6·8m. people (13·6% of the population) aged over 65 in 2016. South Korea is expected to have the second oldest population in the OECD by 2050 and has one of the lowest fertility rates in the world. The government has committed to medium-term fiscal consolidation in a bid to address these demographic challenges. Meanwhile almost half of the elderly live in relative poverty, a rate that is the eighth highest in the OECD.

An improvement in relations with North Korea may have positive economic implications. However, trends towards trade protectionism are a concern, with South Korea—as a major supplier of intermediate goods to China—vulnerable to higher import barriers on Chinese exports to the USA.

Currency

The unit of currency is the *won* (KRW). Inflation rates (based on OECD statistics):

2008	2009	2010	2011	2012	2013	2014	2015	2016	2017
4·7%	2·8%	2·9%	4·0%	2·2%	1·3%	1·3%	0·7%	1·0%	1·9%

Foreign exchange reserves were US$240,915m. in Aug. 2009 (US$51,963m. in 1998) and gold reserves 463,000 troy oz. Total money supply in June 2009 was 103,242bn. won.

Budget

In 2011 central government revenue was 287,404bn. won and expenditure 251,895bn. won. Principal sources of revenue in 2011: taxes on income, profits and capital gains, 87,161bn. won; taxes on goods and services, 71,519bn. won. Main items of expenditure by economic type in 2011: grants, 101,234bn. won; social benefits, 45,837bn. won.

VAT is 10%.

Performance

Real GDP growth rates (based on OECD statistics):

2008	2009	2010	2011	2012	2013	2014	2015	2016	2017
2·8%	0·7%	6·5%	3·7%	2·3%	2·9%	3·3%	2·8%	2·9%	3·1%

Total GDP in 2017 was US$1,530·8bn.

Banking and Finance

The central bank and bank of issue is the Bank of Korea (*Governor*, Lee Ju-yeol). There are four major financial groups—Woori Finance Holdings (assets in May 2014 of US$309·7bn.), Shinhan Financial Group (US$295·0bn.), Hana Financial Group (US$279·7bn.) and KB Financial Group (US$276·5bn.). Specialized banks include the National Agricultural Co-operative Federation (NACF), Korea Development Bank and Industrial Bank of Korea. Foreign-owned banks operating in South Korea include ABN AMRO, Bank of America, Bank of Tokyo-Mitsubishi UFJ, Deutsche Bank and Hongkong and Shanghai Banking Corporation. The use of real names in financial dealings has been required since 1994.

Gross external debt amounted to US$418,607m. in June 2012, up from US$399,249m. in June 2011.

In 2017 South Korea attracted US$17·1bn. in foreign direct investment, up from US$12·1bn. in 2016.

There is a stock exchange in Seoul.

Energy and Natural Resources

Environment

South Korea's carbon dioxide emissions from the consumption of energy in 2011 were the equivalent of 13·3 tonnes per capita.

Electricity

Installed capacity in 2011 was 84·7m. kW. Electricity generated (2011) was 522,839m. kWh (including: thermal, 358,505m. kWh; nuclear, 154,723m. kWh; hydro-electric, 7,831m. kWh). There were 21 nuclear reactors in use in 2011. Consumption per capita in 2011 was 10,738 kWh.

Oil and Gas

South Korea is the world's fifth largest importer of crude oil and second largest importer of liquefied natural gas (LNG). Domestic oil and gas production is negligible. In 2009 total gross petroleum imports amounted to 3·1m. bbls per day; daily consumption was 2·2m. bbls. Three of the world's ten largest oil refineries are in South Korea. In 2009 consumption of natural gas totalled 34·09bn. cu. metres. South Korea has no international gas pipeline connections and all imports are delivered by LNG tankers.

Minerals

Output, 2008, included (in tonnes): limestone, 82·25m.; anthracite coal, 2·77m.; salt, 0·38m.; iron ore, 0·37m.; silver, 1,462; gold, 38.

Agriculture

Cultivated land was 1·74m. ha. in 2009, of which 1·01m. ha. were rice paddies; the area of dry field was 727,000 ha. As at Dec. 2009 the farming population was 3·12m. and there were 1·20m. farm households. 1·76m. people were employed in agriculture, forestry and fishing in Sept. 2010. There were 243,662 tractors in 2007. Food and live animals accounted for 0·7% of exports and 3·7% of imports in 2007.

Production (2008, in 1,000 tonnes): rice, 6,919; cabbage, 2,902; onions, 1,540; watermelons, 857; tangerines, mandarins and clementines, 636; potatoes, 605; apples, 471; pears, 471; persimmons, 431; tomatoes, 408; chillies and green peppers, 386; cucumbers and gherkins, 384; garlic, 375; grapes, 334.

Livestock in 2008 (in 1,000): pigs, 9,153; cattle, 2,894; goats, 266; chickens, 120,000.

Livestock products in 2008 (in 1,000 tonnes): pork 1,056; beef, 246; poultry meat, 542; milk, 2,204; eggs, 595.

Forestry

Forest area was 6·18m. ha. in 2015 (64% of the land area). Of the total area under forests 56% was primary forest in 2015, 14% other naturally regenerated forest and 30% planted forest. Timber production was 6·15m. cu. metres in 2011.

Fisheries

The fish catch totalled 1,670,385 tonnes in 2012 (almost entirely from sea fishing). Imports of fishery commodities were valued at US$3,935m. in 2011 and exports at US$2,012m.

Industry

The leading companies by market capitalization in South Korea in May 2018 were: Samsung Electronics Company Ltd (US$325·9bn.); SK Hynix, a memory chipmaker (US$56·8bn.); and Hyundai Motor (US$31·6bn.).

Manufacturing industry is concentrated primarily on oil, petrochemicals, chemical fibres, construction, iron and steel, mobile phones, cement, machinery, chips, shipbuilding, automobiles and electronics. Tobacco manufacture is a semi-government monopoly. Industry is dominated by giant conglomerates (*chaebol*). There were 5·78m. businesses in 2016 including: 1,376,775 in wholesale and retail trades, 1,174,997 in real estate activities, 811,260 in hotels and restaurants, 534,918 in transport and communications, 502,662 in manufacturing and 384,861 in construction. The leading *chaebol* are Samsung, LG, Hyundai and SK Group.

New shipbuilding orders stood at 6·45m. gross tonnage (176 vessels) at Jan. 2018 (second only to China).

Labour

In Sept. 2010 the population of working age was 40·68m.; the economically active population was 24·91m. (14·51m. males and 10·40m. females) including 16·44m. persons employed in services, 5·85m. in construction, manufacturing and mining, and 1·76m. in agriculture, fisheries and forestry. 5·61m. persons were self-employed in Sept. 2010. Unemployment was 3·8% in Dec. 2018—one of the lowest rates in the industrialized world. Long-term unemployment is particularly low, with only 0·3% of the labour force in 2010 having been out of work for more than a year. An annual legal minimum wage is set by the Minimum Wage Act (enforced from 1988), which applies to all industries. In Jan. 2018 it was increased to 7,530 won per hour and 60,240 won per eight-hour day.

A five-day working week for smaller companies has being gradually phased in; small businesses with between five and 20 employees did not have to introduce the shorter working week until July 2011. Workers in South Korea put in among the longest hours in the industrialized world. In 2013 workers put in an average of 2,079 hours.

A minimum retirement age of 60 has been introduced after a law was passed in April 2013. Employers can no longer specify a retirement age under 60, although it is still be possible for employees to retire early if they wish.

South Korea had 10,000 people living in slavery according to the Walk Free Foundation's 2013 *Global Slavery Index.*

International Trade

Total external foreign debt was US$381,100m. in 2008. In May 1998 the government removed restrictions on foreign investment in the Korean stock market. It also began to allow foreign businesses to engage in mergers and acquisitions. From July 1998 foreigners were allowed to buy plots of land for both business and non-business purposes. Since Aug. 1990 South Korean businesses and individuals have been permitted to make investments and set up branch offices in North Korea, on an approval basis.

Imports and Exports

Imports (c.i.f.) and exports (f.o.b.) for calendar years in US$1m.:

	2006	2007	2008	2009	2010
Imports	309,379·5	356,841·0	435,271·4	323,081·7	425,094·2
Exports	325,457·2	371,477·1	422,003·5	363,531·1	467,730·2

Leading import sources in 2010 (US$1m.) were: China, 71,526; Japan, 64,269; USA, 40,610; Saudi Arabia, 26,773. The principal export markets in 2010 (US$1m.) were: China, 117,167; USA, 50,115; Japan, 28,274; Hong Kong, 25,308.

Imports/exports by category, 2010 (in US$1bn.):

	Imports	Exports
Chemicals and related products	41·0	49·2
Food and live animals	16·3	3·9
Inedible crude materials, excluding fuels	30·6	5·6
Machinery and transport equipment	123·3	264·8
Manufactured goods	56·1	60·7
Mineral fuels and lubricants	122·6	32·5
Miscellaneous manufactured articles	31·5	46·9
Other products	3·7	4·1

Rice imports were prohibited until 1994 but following the GATT Uruguay Round the rice market opened to foreign imports in 1995.

Communications

Roads

In 2017 there were 101,870 km of roads, comprising 4,717 km of expressways, 13,847 km of highways and 16,809 km of local roads; 92·8% of roads (94,549 km) were paved. In 2017 there were 18,034,540 registered motor cars and 4,407,845 vans and freight vehicles.

The first of two planned cross-border roads between the two Koreas opened in Feb. 2003.

Rail

In 2009 Korail's system totalled 3,380 km of 1,435 mm gauge (including 240 km of high speed railways). In 2009 passenger-km travelled came to 31·3bn. and freight tonne-km to 9·3bn. In June 2000 it was agreed to start consultations to restore the railway from Seoul to Sinuiju, on the North Korean/Chinese border, by rebuilding a 12 km long stretch from Munsan, in South Korea, to Jangdan, on the South Korean/North Korean border, and an 8 km long stretch in North Korea.

Two passenger trains crossed the border between North and South Korea on 17 May 2007 (one northbound and one southbound), completing the first cross-border journey in more than 50 years. Freight services between the two Koreas were resumed in Dec. 2007 but usage is very limited.

There is an extensive metro system in Seoul and smaller ones in Busan, Daegu, Daejeon, Gwangju and Incheon.

Civil Aviation

There are international airports at Seoul (Incheon and Gimpo), Busan (Gimhae), Jeju, Daegu, Cheongju, Muan and Yangyang. Incheon airport, 50 km to the west of Seoul and built on reclaimed land made up of four small islands, opened in March 2001 and is the largest airport in Asia. Incheon handled about 57·8m. passengers in 2016, while Jeju handled 29·7m., Gimpo 25·0m. and Gimhae 14·9m.

The national carrier is Korean Air, which in Sept. 2018 owned 167 aircraft and operated scheduled flights to 125 cities in 44 countries. In 2017 Korean Air carried 26·8m. passengers (18·8m. on international flights) and 1·7m. tons of freight. The other main Korean carrier is Asiana Airlines, which was established in 1988.

Shipping

Major seaports are Busan, Incheon, Gunsan, Mokpo, Yeosu, Pohang, Donghae, Jeju, Masan, Ulsan, Daesan and Kwangyang. In 2017 South Korean ports handled 1·57 tons of cargo (4·1% higher than in 2016); non-container cargo totalled 1·09bn. tons while container freight reached 274·2m. TEUs (twenty-foot equivalent units). The busiest port is Busan, which handled 400·5m. tons of cargo in 2017.

Telecommunications

In 2014 mobile phone subscriptions numbered 57,290,356 (1,157·1 per 1,000 persons). The largest operator, SK Telecom, has 49% of the market share for smartphone subscriptions, ahead of KT with 31%. There were 29,481,226 main (fixed) telephone lines in 2014.

In 2014, 84·3% of the population were internet users. In March 2012 there were 6·4m. Facebook users.

Social Institutions

Out of 178 countries analysed in the 2017 *Fragile States Index*—a list published jointly by the Fund for Peace and *Foreign Policy* magazine—South Korea was ranked the 25th least vulnerable to conflict or collapse. The index is based on 12 indicators of state vulnerability across social, political and economic categories.

Justice

Judicial power is vested in the Supreme Court, High Courts, District Courts and Family Court, as well as the Administrative Court and Patent Court. The single six-year term Chief Justice is appointed by the President with the consent of the National Assembly. The other 13 Justices of the Supreme Court are appointed by the President with the consent of the National Assembly, upon the recommendation of the Chief Justice, for renewable six-year terms; the Chief Justice appoints other judges. There has been an unofficial moratorium on executions since 1998—the death penalty was last used in Dec. 1997. In Dec. 2009 there were 2,468 judges, 1,699 prosecutors and 11,016 registered private attorneys.

In 2008 there were 2·19m. recorded offences; the most serious offences (including murder, rape, theft and assault) numbered 439,000. The population in the 50 penal institutions in Jan. 2010 was 47,514 (98 per 100,000 of national population); 5·4% were females and 3·2% foreigners. South Korea was ranked 13th of 102 countries for criminal justice and seventh for civil justice in the 2015 World Justice Project *Rule of Law Index*, which provides data on how the rule of law is experienced by the general public across eight categories.

Education

The Korean education system consists of a six-year elementary school, a three-year middle school, a three-year high school and college and university (two to four years). Elementary education for 6–11 year olds and middle school education are compulsory. Mandatory middle school education began in 2002.

In 2017 the total number of schools was 20,815, with 6,445,561 students and 490,993 staff. There were 9,029 kindergartens with 694,631 pupils and 53,808 teachers; 6,040 primary schools with 2,674,227 pupils and 184,358 teachers; 3,213 middle schools with 1,381,334 pupils and 109,130 teachers; and 2,360 high schools with 1,669,669 pupils and 134,754 teachers. In 2017 there were 430 tertiary education institutions (with 3,437,309 students and 90,902 teachers), including 189 universities with 2,050,619 students and 66,795 teachers. In 2016, 70% of 25 to 34-year-olds had attained tertiary education, up from 29% in 1995.

According to Organisation for Economic Co-operation and Development figures, total South Korean expenditure on primary to tertiary education in 2015 came to 5·8% of GDP (of which 4·4% was public expenditure and 1·4% private). 1·8% was dedicated to tertiary education. Overall education spending in 2015 was 0·8 percentage points above the OECD average. The adult literacy rate is at least 99%.

Health

In 2009 there were 2,666 hospitals with 403,932 beds. There were 111,694 physicians in 2014 (22·3 per 10,000 population), plus 283,897 nursing and midwifery personnel, 22,952 dentistry personnel and 32,645 pharmaceutical personnel. There is a dual health care delivery system that incorporates both traditional Korean and Western medicine. In 2009 there were 11,705 oriental clinics, 158 oriental hospitals and 8,694 oriental hospital beds.

In 2008 South Korea spent 6·5% of its GDP on health, with public spending accounting for 55·3% of total expenditure on health and private spending 44·7%.

Welfare

In 2006, 12·8m. persons were covered by the National Pension System introduced in 1988. Employers and employees should make contributions amounting to 4·5% of the standard monthly income respectively, based on the employees' earned income. The Scheme covers old age pensions, disability pensions and survivors' pensions.

Under a system of unemployment insurance introduced in July 1995, workers laid off after working at least six months for a member employer are entitled to benefits averaging 50% of their previous wage for a period of 90 up to 240 days.

Religion

Traditionally, Koreans have lived under the influence of shamanism, Buddhism (introduced AD 372) and Confucianism, which was the official faith from 1392 to 1910. Catholic converts from China introduced Christianity in the 18th century, but a ban on Roman Catholicism was not lifted until 1882. The Anglican Church was introduced in 1890 and became an independent jurisdiction in 1993 under the Archbishop of Korea. According to the Pew Research Center's Forum on Religion & Public Life, in 2010 estimated affiliations of the main religions were: Buddhism, 11,050,000; Protestantism, 8,560,000; Roman Catholicism, 5,270,000. People with no religious affiliation numbered 22,350,000 in the same year, equivalent to 46·4% of the population. In Feb. 2019 there were two Roman Catholic cardinals.

Culture

World Heritage Sites

There are 13 sites in South Korea that appear on the UNESCO World Heritage List. They are (with year entered on list): the Sokkuram Grotto and Pulguksa Temple (1995), the Temple of Haeinsa (1995), Chongmyo Shrine (1995), Changdeokgung Palace, Seoul (1997), Hwaseong Fortress, Suwon (1997), the dolmens of Gochang, Hwasun and Ganghwa (2000), Gyeongju historic area (2000), Jeju volcanic island and lava tubes (2007), the Royal Tombs of the Joseon Dynasty (2009), the Historic Villages of Hahoe and Yangdong (2010), Namhansanseong (2014), Baekje Historic Areas (2015) and Sansa, Buddhist Mountain Monasteries in Korea (2018).

Press

There were 324 daily newspapers in 2012. With 10·9m. paid daily newspaper subscriptions in 2012, South Korea has the fifth highest newspaper circulation among developed countries. The most widely read dailies are *Chosun Ilbo* (average daily circulation of 1·8m. per issue in 2013), *JoongAng Ilbo* (1·3m. copies) and *Dong-A Ilbo* (907,000 copies). Newspaper online editions had 847,000 unique monthly visitors in 2010.

Tourism

A record 9,795,000 foreign nationals visited South Korea in 2011 (up from 8,798,000 in 2010 and 6,023,000 in 2005). The leading countries of origin of non-resident tourists in 2011 were: Japan (3,289,000), mainland China (2,220,000), the USA (662,000), Taiwan (428,000) and the Philippines (337,000). 12,694,000 South Koreans travelled abroad in 2011 (up from 12,488,000 in 2010 and 10,080,000 in 2005). In Nov. 1998 the first South Korean tourists to visit North Korea went on a cruise and tour organized by the South Korean firm Hyundai.

Festivals

Korean New Year or Seollal is celebrated on the first day of the lunar calendar and generally falls on the same date as the Chinese New Year. Other traditional festivals include the festival for the first full moon of the year known as Daeboreum; Dano or Surit-nal (spring festival) which is held on the fifth day of the fifth month of the lunar calendar; and Chuseok (harvest festival) on the 15th day of the eighth month. The biggest music festivals are the Tongyeong International Music Festival (March), specializing in Western and Asian classical music, and the Pentaport Rock Festival in Incheon (July).

Diplomatic Representatives

Of the Republic of Korea in the United Kingdom (60 Buckingham Gate, London, SW1E 6AJ)
 Ambassador: Park Enna.

Of the United Kingdom in the Republic of Korea (Sejong-daero, 19-gil 24, Jung-gu, Seoul 04519)
 Ambassador: Simon Smith.

Of the Republic of Korea in the USA (2450 Massachusetts Ave., NW, Washington, D.C., 20008)
 Ambassador: Cho Yoon-je.

Of the USA in the Republic of Korea (188 Sejong-daero, Jongno-gu, Seoul 03141)
 Ambassador: Harry B. Harris, Jr.

Of the Republic of Korea to the United Nations
 Ambassador: Cho Tae-yul.

Of the Republic of Korea to the European Union
 Ambassador: Kim Hyoung-zhin.

Further Reading

National Bureau of Statistics. *Korea Statistical Yearbook*

Bank of Korea. *Annual Reports*

Castley, R., *Korea's Economic Miracle*. 1997

Cumings, B., *Korea's Place in the Sun: A Modern History*. 1997

Jager, Sheila Miyoshi, *Brothers at War: The Unending Conflict in Korea*. 2013

Jwa, Sung-Hee, *The Rise and Fall of Korea's Economic Development: Lessons for Developing and Developed Economies*. 2017

Kang, M.-H., *The Korean Business Conglomerate: Chaebol Then and Now*. 1996

Kim, D.-H. and Tat, Y.-K., (eds) *The Korean Peninsula in Transition*. 1997

Kim, Myung Oak and Jaffe, Sam, *The New Korea: An Inside Look at South Korea's Economic Rise*. 2010

Lie, John, *Han Unbound: The Political Economy of South Korea*. 2000

Mosler, Hannes, Lee, Eun-Jeung, Kim, Hak-Jae, (eds) *The Quality of Democracy in Korea: Three Decades after Democratization*. 2017

Simons, G., *Korea: the Search for Sovereignty*. 1995

Smith, H., *Industry Policy in Taiwan and Korea in the 1980s*. 2000

Song, P.-N., *The Rise of the Korean Economy*. 3rd ed. 2003

Tennant, R., *A History of Korea*. 1996

Uttam, Jitendra, *The Political Economy of Korea: Transition, Transformation and Turnaround*. 2014

National Statistical Office: Statistics Korea, Government Complex Daejeon, 189 Cheongsa-ro, Seo-gu, Daejeon 35208. *Commissioner:* Hwang Soo-kyeong.

Website: http://kostat.go.kr

Kuwait

Dowlat al Kuwait (State of Kuwait)

Capital: Kuwait
Population projection, 2020: 4·30m.
GNI per capita, 2017: (PPP$) 70,524
HDI/world rank, 2017: 0·803/56
Internet domain extension: .kw

Key Historical Events

Northern Kuwait formed part of ancient Mesopotamia and there is evidence of settlement during the Ubaid prehistoric period. For instance, fragments of a reed boat preserved in bitumen tar at As-Sabiyah have been dated to around 5,000 BC. Settlements along the bay of Kuwait and on the island of Failaka were part of the Bronze Age Dilmun civilization, which flourished and controlled trade in the Persian Gulf between 4,000 BC and 1,800 BC. After 600 BC the coastal settlements came under Babylonian rule. Alexander the Great's arrival in the region in the third century BC paved the way for a period of Hellenistic influence, including a settlement on Failaka founded by Nearchus (one of Alexander's officers). The area was part of the Sassanid Empire from the third century AD to the seventh century, and known as Maishan.

The Bani Khaled clan moved into the area from central Arabia from the 14th century, establishing fishing and pearling villages on the bay of Kuwait. A small fort, known as Al Kout, was constructed in 1613. Other clans, notably the al-Sabah, profited when nearby Basra came under Persian control in 1775 and expanded to become a major port on the lucrative trade route between the Mediterranean and India. Kuwait was ostensibly under Ottoman control, administered from Basra, for much of the 19th century. In 1899 Sheikh Mubarak signed a treaty with Britain that offered his support for British interests in return for naval protection.

Crude oil, discovered in vast quantities beneath the desert in 1938 by the British–US Kuwait Oil Company, fuelled Kuwait's transformation after the Second World War. Made the capital of an independent country on 19 June 1961, Kuwait City expanded rapidly, drawing in hundreds of thousands of migrants to work in the oil industry and the myriad services that supplied it.

Kuwait supported Iraq during the Iran–Iraq war in the 1980s. However, on 2 Aug. 1990 Iraqi forces invaded the country, having accused Kuwait of stealing Iraqi oil from a field straddling the border between the two countries. Following the expiry of the date set by the United Nations for Iraq's withdrawal, an air offensive was launched by coalition forces, followed by a land attack on 24 Feb. 1991. Although led by the USA, the coalition personnel came from over 30 countries, including Saudi Arabia, the United Kingdom, Egypt and Syria. Iraqi forces were routed and Kuwait City was liberated on 26 Feb. The Amir and his cabinet returned from exile in Saudi Arabia the following month. On 10 Nov. 1994 Iraq recognized the independence and boundaries of Kuwait.

Kuwait holds around 7% of the world's oil reserves, with oil exports, increasingly shipped to East Asia, accounting for about half of GDP. Compared with elsewhere in the region, Kuwait has done little to diversify its economy. This partly reflects its strong fiscal position, but acrimonious relations between the ruling al-Sabah family and the elected parliament have also hindered reforms. Mass protests have become more frequent since the 2011 'Arab Spring', including a series of demonstrations in late 2012 over proposed changes to electoral boundaries. Tribal and liberal groups emerged as the main winners of the parliamentary election in July 2013, with minority Shia MPs losing more than half of their seats.

Territory and Population

Kuwait is bounded in the east by the Persian Gulf, north and west by Iraq and south and southwest by Saudi Arabia, with an area of 17,818 sq. km. In 1992–93 the UN Boundary Commission redefined Kuwait's border with Iraq, moving it slightly northwards in conformity with an agreement of 1932. The population at the 2011 census was 3,065,850; density, 172 per

sq. km. In 2011, 98·4% of the population were urban. In June 2017 the population was estimated at 4,437,590, of which 69·5% were non-Kuwaitis.

The UN gives a projected population for 2020 of 4·30m.

The country is divided into six governorates: the capital (comprising Kuwait City, Kuwait's nine islands and territorial and shared territorial waters) (2011 census population, 326,513); Farwaniya (818,571); Hawalli (672,910); Ahmadi (588,068); Jahra (400,975); Mubarak al-Kabir (258,813). The capital city is Kuwait, with an estimated population in 2010 (metropolitan area) of 2,102,000. Other major cities are Hawalli, Qalib ash-Shuyukh and as-Salimiya.

The Neutral Zone (Kuwait's share, 2,590 sq. km), jointly owned and administered by Kuwait and Saudi Arabia from 1922 to 1966, was partitioned between the two countries in May 1966, but the exploitation of the oil and other natural resources continues to be shared.

Over 78% speak Arabic, the official language. English is also used as a second language.

Social Statistics

Births, 2008, 54,571; deaths, 5,701. The birth rate in 2009 was 21·9 per 1,000 population and death rate 2·3 per 1,000 population (one of the lowest in the world). Expectation of life at birth, 2013, was 73·5 years for males and 75·5 years for females. Infant mortality, 2010, ten per 1,000 live births. Annual population growth rate, 2005–10, 5·3%.

Fertility rate, 2008, 2·2 births per woman. Kuwait has had one of the largest reductions in its fertility rate of any country in the world over the past 30 years, having had a rate of 7·2 births per woman in 1975. It was ranked 117th in a gender gap index of 145 countries compiled by the World Economic Forum for its *Global Gender Gap Report 2015*. The annual index considers economic, political, education and health criteria.

Climate

Kuwait has a dry, desert climate which is cool in winter but very hot and humid in summer. Rainfall is extremely light. Kuwait, Jan. 56°F (13·5°C), July 99°F (36·6°C). Annual rainfall 5" (125 mm).

Constitution and Government

The ruler is HH Sheikh Sabah al-Ahmed al-Jaber al-Sabah, the 15th Amir of Kuwait, who succeeded on 29 Jan. 2006. *Crown Prince:* Sheikh Nawwaf al-Ahmed al-Sabah (b. 1937). The present constitution was approved and promulgated on 11 Nov. 1962.

In 1990 the *National Council* was established, consisting of 50 elected members and 25 appointed by the Amir. It was replaced by a *National Assembly* or *Majlis al-Umma* in 1992, consisting at the time of 50 elected members. It now has 65 members, of whom 50 are elected. The franchise extends to Kuwaiti citizens who are 21 or older, with the exception of those who are serving in the armed forces and citizens who have been naturalized for fewer than 30 years. In May 1999 the cabinet approved a draft law giving women the right to vote and run for parliament. However, in Dec. 1999 parliament rejected the bill allowing women to vote by a margin of 32 to 20. Women were granted the right to vote and run for office in May 2005 when parliament voted in favour of amending the election law by a margin of 35 votes to 23. Women were eligible to stand for election and to vote in a council by-election held in April 2006 and in the full parliamentary election held in June 2006.

Executive authority is vested in the *Council of Ministers*.

National Anthem

'Watanil Kuwait salemta lilmajdi, wa ala jabeenoka tali ossaadi,' ('Kuwait, my fatherland! May you be safe and glorious! May you always enjoy good fortune!'); words by Moshari al-Adwani, tune by Ibrahim Nassar al-Soula.

Government Chronology

Amirs since 1950.

1950–65	Sheikh Abdullah al-Salem al-Sabah
1965–77	Sheikh Sabah al-Salem al-Sabah
1977–2006	Sheikh Jaber al-Ahmed al-Jaber al-Sabah
2006–	Sheikh Sabah al-Ahmed al-Jaber al-Sabah

Recent Elections

Parliamentary elections were held on 26 Nov. 2016. Opposition candidates won 24 of 50 seats in the National Assembly. Turnout was around 70%.

Current Government

In Feb. 2019 the government comprised:

Prime Minister: Sheikh Jaber Mubarak al-Hamad al-Sabah; b. 1942 (sworn in 4 Dec. 2011).

First Deputy Prime Minister: Sheikh Nasser Sabah al-Hamad al-Sabah (also *Minister of Defence*).

Deputy Prime Ministers: Sheikh Sabah Khaled al-Hamad al-Sabah (also *Minister of Foreign Affairs*); Lieut.-Gen. Sheikh Khaled al-Jarrah al-Sabah (also *Minister of the Interior*); Anas Khaled al-Saleh (also *Minister of State for Cabinet Affairs*).

Minister of Finance: Nayef Falah al-Hajraf. *Social Affairs and Labour, and Minister of State for Economic Affairs:* Hind Subaih Barrak al-Subaih. *Commerce and Industry, and Minister of State for Youth Affairs:* Khaled Nasser Abdullah al-Roudhan. *Information:* Mohammad Nasser al-Jabri. *Health:* Dr Bassel Humoud Hamad al-Sabah. *Oil, and Electricity and Water:* Bakheet Shibeeb al-Rasheedi. *Education, and Higher Education:* Hamid Mohammad al-Azmi. *Public Works, and Minister of State for Municipal Affairs:* Hussam Abdullah al-Roumi. *Justice, and Awqaf and Islamic Affairs:* Fahad Mohammad al-Afasi. *Minister of State for Housing Affairs and Service Affairs:* Jinan Mohsin Ramadan. *Minister of State for National Assembly Affairs:* Adel Musaed al-Kharafi.

Government Website: http://www.e.gov.kw

Current Leaders

Sheikh Sabah al-Ahmed al-Jaber al-Sabah

Position
Amir

Introduction
Sheikh Sabah became Amir of Kuwait in Jan. 2006, ending a brief constitutional crisis in the wake of the death of Sheikh Jaber. As foreign minister for over 40 years, Sheikh Sabah oversaw the positioning of Kuwait as a key Western ally in the Gulf, allowing the USA to use the country as a launch pad for its invasion of Iraq in 2003. He has faced increasing calls for greater democratization.

Early Life
Sabah al-Ahmed al-Jaber al-Sabah was born in 1929 in Kuwait, then a British protectorate. He is the fourth son of Sheikh Ahmed al-Jaber al-Sabah, the founder of modern Kuwait and its leader from 1921–50. Educated at al Mubarakya School and by tutors, Sheikh Sabah became a member of the central committee municipality council in 1954. He also served as a member of the building and construction council at a time when the Amir, Sheikh Abdullah al-Salem al-Sabah, was pumping much of the state's new oil wealth into an ambitious public works programme.

From 1956–62 Sheikh Sabah chaired the printing and publishing authority and was then appointed minister of information in the first post-independence cabinet. He was promoted to foreign minister in 1963 and headed Kuwait's inaugural delegation to the UN later that year. He presided over a generally low-profile, neutralist foreign policy. Palestinian rights received strong support; Fatah was founded in Kuwait.

On 16 Feb. 1978 Sheikh Sabah was appointed deputy prime minister while keeping the foreign affairs portfolio. A broadly pro-Iraqi orientation

was adopted during the early stages of the Iran–Iraq War and Kuwait became a member of the Gulf Co-operation Council. After Iraq's invasion of Kuwait in 1990, Sheikh Sabah joined other government members in exile in Saudi Arabia. The al-Sabahs' flight caused resentment among those left behind in Kuwait but post-liberation elections and the creation of a National Assembly in 1992 were well received. In 1996 Sheikh Sabah joined the Supreme Council of Planning.

The increasingly frail Sheikh Jaber issued a decree separating the posts of crown prince and prime minister on 13 July 2003 and appointed Sheikh Sabah as premier. Endowed with considerable executive powers, he continued the reforms begun by the Amir, appointing the first woman minister and promoting religious tolerance in schools. After the death of Sheikh Jaber in Jan. 2006, the 76-year old crown prince, Sheikh Saad al-Abdullah al Salim al-Sabah, was deemed too ill to take the Amir's oath of office. He was voted out of office by parliament on 24 Jan. 2006 and the cabinet nominated Sheikh Sabah to take over. He was sworn in on 29 Jan. 2006.

Career in Office
Sheikh Sabah promised to speed up reforms promoting greater economic transparency, full political rights for women and democratic elections. Women had their first opportunity to vote in April 2006 in a municipal election, and were also allowed to stand as candidates in the parliamentary elections in June that year although none were successful. However, two women ministers were included in a new cabinet appointed in March 2007. In March 2008 Sheikh Sabah dissolved parliament and called fresh elections in May, in which Islamists won 30 of the 50 National Assembly seats. Women candidates were again unsuccessful. A year later he dissolved parliament again when the cabinet resigned on 16 March 2009 to prevent questioning of the Amir's nephew, Prime Minister Sheikh Nasser Muhammad al-Ahmad al-Sabah, on charges of misuse of public funds. Sheikh Nasser was reappointed prime minister following elections held on 16 May 2009 in which four women candidates were returned as parliamentary members for the first time.

Reflecting the political disaffection that spread across much of the Arab world from early 2011, there were demonstrations calling for reforms in Kuwait in March. The cabinet again resigned, but Sheikh Nasser was reinstated once more and in May formed a new administration with no changes to key personnel. However, after a crowd stormed parliament in Nov. in protest at alleged high-level corruption, Sheikh Nasser stood down again. The Amir accepted his resignation and appointed Sheikh Jaber Mubarak al-Hamad al-Sabah as the new prime minister. In Feb. 2012 Sheikh Jaber also resigned, but his administration was promptly reinstated with no changes to key ministries other than defence.

Islamists won a majority of seats in the Feb. 2012 elections but the Constitutional Court annulled the results in June. The Amir called for new elections in Dec. that year while issuing a decree in Oct. amending the electoral law. The opposition claimed that the law favoured government candidates, prompting violent street protests. The Dec. poll was boycotted by the opposition and was further undermined by a low voter turnout. In June 2013 the Constitutional Court again intervened to dissolve parliament, heralding further elections the following month in which liberals made some gains at the expense of minority Shia candidates. Political tensions persisted in 2014 and 2015 as the government revoked citizenship from opponents calling for reform and those associated with extremist groups, and also maintained a policy of tight media control. In June 2015 a suspected Sunni suicide attack on a Shia mosque killed 27 people and injured many more. Earlier, in April, the government reintroduced compulsory military service.

Parliamentary hostility to government spending cuts prompted the Amir to dissolve the National Assembly in Oct. 2016, although fresh elections the following month saw opposition candidates win almost half of the seats in a high voter turnout. In Dec. the incumbent prime minister formed a new government, but with most key cabinet portfolios unchanged. Meanwhile, speculation about who will succeed the ageing Amir has continued to increase.

From March 2015 Kuwait participated in air strikes by a Saudi-led coalition against Houthi rebels in Yemen, while in Jan. 2016 Kuwaiti relations with Iran were downgraded in response to that country's widening regional rift with Saudi Arabia and the other Gulf states. In July 2017 Kuwait ordered the expulsion of the Iranian ambassador and other diplomats for alleged links to a terrorist cell, further increasing tensions between the two countries.

Defence

In Sept. 1991 the USA signed a ten-year agreement with Kuwait to store equipment, use ports and carry out joint training exercises. In March 2013, 15,000 US troops were stationed in Kuwait. Compulsory military service for males was reintroduced in 2015, having been suspended in 2001, and was implemented in 2017.

In 2013 defence expenditure totalled US$4,427m., with spending per capita US$1,642. The 2013 expenditure represented 2·6% of GDP.

Army

Strength (2011) 11,000. In addition there is a National Guard of around 6,600.

Navy

Personnel in 2011 numbered an estimated 2,000, including 500 Coast Guard personnel.

Air Force

From a small initial combat force the Air Force has grown rapidly, although it suffered heavy losses after the Iraqi invasion of 1990–91. Equipment includes F/A-18 *Hornet* strike aircraft and British Aerospace *Hawks*. Personnel strength was (2011) 2,500, with 66 combat-capable aircraft and 16 attack helicopters.

Economy

Agriculture accounted for 0·4% of GDP in 2014, industry 64·3% and services 35·3%.

Overview

Kuwait has experienced major fluctuations in GDP since the global financial crisis. After a near 5% contraction in 2009, there was growth of nearly 11% in 2011 and 8% in 2012 owing to a surge in oil production before the rate fell to an average of 0·7% per year between 2013 and 2015. The oil and gas industry annually accounts for over 60% of nominal GDP, 95% of exports and 80% of government revenue, rendering Kuwait's economy more oil-dependent than most of its Gulf neighbours. Falling oil prices in 2015 resulted in the first budget deficit since the turn of the century.

Progress in transforming the country into a regional trade and finance hub has been slow. However, the financial services, tourism, warehousing and real estate sectors are expanding in response to increased incentives for foreign investors. A US$130bn. economic development plan includes the construction of Silk City at Subiya and a vast port complex on Bubiyan Island to the north of Kuwait City, intended as a gateway to both Kuwait and Iraq.

The government aims to reduce social welfare and public spending by improving efficiency within the public sector. There are also moves to lower the number of foreign workers by 100,000 a year over the decade to 2022, although the indigenous labour force currently lacks the skills needed to replace them.

Currency

The unit of currency is the *Kuwaiti dinar* (KWD), usually written as KD, of 1,000 *fils*. Inflation was 3·5% in 2016 and 1·5% in 2017. Foreign exchange reserves were US$7,544m. in July 2005, monetary gold reserves were 2·54m. troy oz and total money supply was KD 3,581m.

Budget

The fiscal year begins on 1 April. Budgetary central government revenue and expenditure (in KD 1m.):

	2009–10	2010–11	2011–12
Revenue	17,473	21,239	29,944
Expenditure	10,269	13,109	15,879

Oil accounts for 85% of government revenues. Main items of expenditure by economic type in 2011–12 (in KD 1m.): compensation of employees, 3,786; subsidies, 3,535; use of goods and services, 2,130.

Performance

The economy grew by 10·9% in 2011 and 7·9% in 2012. However, real GDP growth has since slowed and was only 2·2% in 2016 before shrinking by 3·3% in 2017. Total GDP in 2017 was US$120·1bn.

Banking and Finance

The *Governor* of the Central Bank is Dr Mohammad al-Hashel. There is also the Kuwait Finance House. In 2016 there were 11 domestic commercial banks, including five Islamic banks. In addition, 12 foreign banks had branches in Kuwait in 2016. In March 2016 the combined assets of banks operating in Kuwait totalled KD 36,167m. Foreign banks were not permitted until 2005.

There is a stock exchange, linked with those of Bahrain and Oman.

Energy and Natural Resources

Environment

Kuwait's carbon dioxide emissions from the consumption of energy accounted for 38·7 tonnes per capita in 2011.

Electricity

Installed capacity was 14·8m. kW in 2011. Production in 2011 was 57·5bn. kWh; consumption per capita was 18,388 kWh.

Oil and Gas

Oil production in 2017, 146·0m. tonnes. Kuwait had reserves in 2017 amounting to 101·5bn. bbls. Most of the oil is in the Great Burgan area (reserves of approximately 70bn. bbls), comprising the Burgan, Maqwa and Ahmadi fields located south of Kuwait City. Natural gas production was 17·4bn. cu. metres in 2017, with 1·7trn. cu. metres of proven reserves.

Water

The country depends upon desalination plants. Fresh mineral water is pumped and bottled at Rawdhatain. Underground brackish water is used for irrigation, street cleaning and livestock. Production, 2014, 164,694m. gallons (145,035m. gallons fresh, 19,659m. gallons brackish). Consumption, 2014, 163,181m. gallons (145,221m. gallons fresh, 17,960m. gallons brackish).

Agriculture

There were an estimated 10,600 ha. of arable land in 2013 and 7,000 ha. of permanent crops. Production of main crops, 2013 (in 1,000 tonnes): tomatoes, 73; cucumbers and gherkins, 53; potatoes, 47; dates, 31; chillies and green peppers, 28; onions, 21; maize, 20; pumpkins and squash, 16.

Livestock (2013): sheep, 517,000; goats, 150,000; cattle, 25,000; chickens, 44m.

Forestry

Forests covered 6,000 ha. in 2015, or 0·4% of the land area.

Fisheries

The total catch in 2012 was 4,030 tonnes, exclusively from sea fishing. In the space of a month in 2001 more than 2,000 tonnes of dead fish were washed ashore. Some experts claimed the cause was the alleged pumping of raw sewage into the Gulf while others attributed it to waste from the oil industry. Shrimp fishing was important, but has declined since the 1990–91 war through oil pollution of coastal waters. Before the discovery of oil, pearls were at the centre of Kuwait's economy, but today pearl fishing is only on a small scale.

Industry

The leading companies by market capitalization in Kuwait in May 2018 were: National Bank of Kuwait (US$15·0bn.); Kuwait Finance House, a banking group (US$10·9bn.); and Kuwait Projects, an investment service provider (US$1·1bn.).

Industries, apart from oil, include boat building, fishing, food production, petrochemicals, gases and construction. Production figures in 2011 unless otherwise indicated (in 1,000 tonnes): distillate fuel oil, 10,872; residual fuel oil, 9,766; kerosene, 5,912; liquefied petroleum gas, 4,428; jet fuel, 2,538; cement (2012 estimate), 2,250; petrol, 2,206.

Labour

The labour force in 2013 was 1,899,000 (1,051,000 in 2003). 70·1% of the population aged 15–64 was economically active in 2013. In the same year 3·2% of the population was unemployed. Approximately 80% of nationals work for the government, with around 95% of private jobs being filled by expatriates. In March 2013 the government announced its intention to reduce by a million the number of foreign workers over a period of ten years.

International Trade

Kuwait, along with Bahrain, Oman, Qatar, Saudi Arabia and the United Arab Emirates entered into a customs union in Jan. 2003.

Imports and Exports

Imports (c.i.f.) were valued at US$24,840m. in 2008 and exports (f.o.b.) at US$87,457m. Oil accounts for 92% of revenue from exports. In 2008 the leading import suppliers were China, the USA and Japan; the main export markets were Japan, South Korea and India.

Communications

Roads

In 2012 the road network covered 7,180 km. There were 750,600 passenger cars in use in 2007 (282 per 1,000 inhabitants), 573,200 lorries and vans, and 27,300 buses and coaches. In 2014 there were 99,047 road accidents involving injury with 461 fatalities.

Civil Aviation

There is an international airport (Kuwait International). The national carrier is the state-owned Kuwait Airways. Kuwait's first low-cost airline, Jazeera Airways, began operations in Oct. 2005. In 2012 scheduled airline traffic of Kuwait-based carriers flew 57·7m. km; passenger-km totalled 11·1bn. in the same year. Kuwait International airport handled 8,967,413 passengers in 2012 and 184,784 tonnes of freight.

Shipping

The port of Kuwait formerly served mainly as an entrepôt, but this function is declining in importance with the development of the oil industry. The largest oil terminal is at Mina Ahmadi. Three small oil ports lie to the south of Mina Ahmadi: Mina Shuaiba, Mina Abdullah and Mina al-Zor. In Jan. 2014 there were 43 ships of 300 GT or over registered (including 18 oil tankers), totalling 2·33m. GT.

Telecommunications

In 2010 Kuwait had 519,000 landline telephone subscriptions (equivalent to 173·6 per 1,000 inhabitants) and 3,979,000 mobile phone subscriptions (or 1,330·1 per 1,000 inhabitants). In 2011, 74·2% of the population were internet users. In the same year 66·9% of households had a computer and 62·0% of households had internet access at home. In March 2012 there were 899,000 Facebook users.

Social Institutions

Out of 178 countries analysed in the 2017 *Fragile States Index*—a list published jointly by the Fund for Peace and *Foreign Policy* magazine—Kuwait was ranked the 53rd least vulnerable to conflict or collapse. The index is based on 12 indicators of state vulnerability across social, political and economic categories.

Justice

In 1960 Kuwait adopted a unified judicial system covering all levels of courts. These are: Courts of Summary Justice, Courts of the First Instance, Supreme Court of Appeal, Court of Cassation and a Constitutional Court. Islamic Sharia is a major source of legislation. The death penalty is in force and was used in Jan. 2017, when seven executions were carried out, for the first time since 2013. There were no executions in 2018. The population in penal institutions in 2010 was 4,179 (137 per 100,000 of national population). The International Centre for Prison Studies estimated in 2014 that 10·0% of prisoners had yet to receive a trial.

Education

Education is free and compulsory from six to 14 years. In 2007 there were 211,576 pupils in primary schools with 22,016 teaching staff, and 247,233 pupils in secondary schools with 26,050 teaching staff. In 2006 there were 37,521 students in tertiary education and 1,986 academic staff. There are two state-supported higher education institutions, Kuwait University and the Public Authority for Applied Education and Training. There were approximately 28,000 students at Kuwait University in 2009. There are also a number of private universities and colleges, a teacher training college, a music academy and several Quranic schools. The Arab Open University, which opened in Nov. 2002, is based in Kuwait and has branches in several other Middle Eastern countries. There were more than 28,000 enrolments across its campuses in eight countries in 2015. Adult literacy rate in 2007 was 94%. In 2005 public expenditure on education came to 4·7% of GDP and accounted for 12·7% of total government spending.

Health

Medical services are free to all residents. In 2011 there were 15 public general and specialized hospitals, with a provision of 5,276 beds (17 per 10,000 population). There were 4,840 doctors (18 per 10,000 population), 810 dentists, 9,940 nurses and midwives and 1,340 pharmacists in 2005.

In *Water: At What Cost? The State of the World's Water 2016*, WaterAid reported that 1·0% of the population does not have access to safe water.

Religion

In 2010 there were 2·0m. Muslims according to estimates by the Pew Research Center's Forum on Religion & Public Life (of whom approximately two-thirds to three-quarters Sunnis and the rest Shias), plus 390,000 Christians and 230,000 Hindus.

Culture

Press

In 2008 there were 17 daily newspapers, with a combined circulation of 630,000. Formal press censorship was lifted in Jan. 1992.

Tourism

There were 5,729,000 non-resident visitors in 2012 (up from 4,482,000 in 2007), bringing revenue of US$780m.

Diplomatic Representatives

Of Kuwait in the United Kingdom (2 Albert Gate, London, SW1X 7JU)
   Ambassador: Khaled al-Duwaisan, GCVO.

Of the United Kingdom in Kuwait (Arabian Gulf St., Dasman, Kuwait)
   Ambassador: Michael Davenport, MBE.

Of Kuwait in the USA (2940 Tilden St., NW, Washington, D.C., 20008)
   Ambassador: Salem Abdulla al-Jaber al-Sabah.

Of the USA in Kuwait (Al-Masjed al-Aqsa St., Bayan, Plot 14, Kuwait)
   Ambassador: Lawrence R. Silverman.

Of Kuwait to the United Nations
   Ambassador: Mansour Ayyad al-Otaibi.

Of Kuwait to the European Union
   Ambassador: Jasem Mohamed Albudaiwi.

Further Reading

Al-Yahya, M. A., *Kuwait: Fall and Rebirth.* 1993
Boghardt, Lori Plotkin, *Kuwait Amid War, Peace and Revolution: 1979–1991 and New Challenges.* 2007
National Statistical Office: Kuwait Central Statistics Bureau, Al Sharq, Arabian Gulf Street, Kuwait City.
Website: http://www.csb.gov.kw

Kyrgyzstan

Kyrgyz Respublikasy (Kyrgyz Republic)

Capital: Bishkek
Population projection, 2020: 6·30m.
GNI per capita, 2017: (PPP$) 3,255
HDI/world rank, 2017: 0·672/122
Internet domain extension: .kg

Key Historical Events

The remains of Neolithic settlements discovered in the Chui Valley in northern Kyrgyzstan date back to at least 3000 BC. During the second millennium BC semi-nomadic groups from central Siberia known as the Andronovo settled the area. They herded cattle, horses and Bactrian camels—moving with the seasons between the valleys and lakesides and the higher pastures of the Tien Shan mountains. To the south, in the Ferghana valley around present-day Osh and Djalal-Abad and through to Tajikistan and Uzbekistan, the Chush Bronze Age culture was more sedentary and agricultural.

From around 1000 BC various nomadic Indo-European and Uralic-speaking peoples, including the Alans, Budini, Huns, Madjars and Scythians (Sakas), inhabited the Central Asian steppes and mountains. Kyrgyzstan's ancient tracks and passes through the Tien Shan and Pamir-Altai mountain ranges formed part of the fabled Silk Route linking the cultures of the Mediterranean, northern Europe, Anatolia and East Asia.

Turkic nomads became increasingly dominant in the region and established kingdoms (Kaganat) from the sixth century, including the Turgesh, Karluks and Uighurs. Genghis Khan's Mongol Hordes overran Central Asia from 1221 and retained power in the region under his second son, Chagatai, until 1334. Parts of present-day Kyrgyzstan came under the influence of the Timurid dynasty from the late 14th century; Timur saw himself as an heir to Genghis Khan. Turkic-speaking Kyrgyz tribes migrated into the region in the 16th century from northwestern Mongolia. Groups located to the north of the Tien Shan mountains tended to maintain semi-nomadic traditions, while those in the valleys to the south were more likely to be settled farmers. Islamic influences from Persia were centred on Osh.

The 17th and 18th centuries saw frequent battles between Kyrgyz, Kalmyk, Manchu and Uzbek tribes. The Khanate of Koquand held sway across the Ferghana valley from 1709 to 1876, when it was annexed by the Russian Empire. Diplomatic ties had been established between Atake Baatyr of northern Kyrgyzstan and Catherine the Great in 1775. Russian and Ukrainian settlers arrived in increasing numbers, along with Uighurs and Dungan from the east fleeing persecution. Competition for farming and herding and resentment about compulsory military service led to numerous rebellions—notably the Andijan Uprising in 1898 and a revolt across several regions by Kyrgyz, Kazakh and Uighur groups in 1916.

In the brutal military crackdown that followed, thousands were killed and many others fled to Chinese Turkestan. The Kyrgyz continued their resistance after the 1917 Russian Revolution, when Kyrgyzstan became part of Soviet Turkestan. In 1924 Kirghizia (encompassing the territory of modern Kyrgyzsthan) was established as a district within the Russian Soviet Federated Socialist Republic and two years later it was declared a Soviet autonomous republic. During Stalin's collectivization from 1929, Kyrgyz pastoralists were forcibly settled on collective and state farms. Many responded by slaughtering their livestock and moving to Xinjiang, China. The 1930s, 1940s and 1950s were characterized by wide-scale Russian and Ukrainian migration and the steady development of Soviet education, housing, agriculture and mining. The capital, Bishkek, was renamed Frunze. With the collapse of the Soviet Union, the republic asserted its claim to sovereignty in 1990 and declared independence in Sept. 1991. Askar Akayev became president in 1990 and subsequently expanded presidential powers. Kyrgyzstan became a member of the Commonwealth of Independent States in Dec. 1991.

Incursions into Kyrgyz territory by Islamic rebels and border skirmishes in the Ferghana Valley have been ongoing threats. Allegations of government corruption and disputed parliamentary elections in Feb. 2005 led to widespread popular protests. The Supreme Court declared the elections void and Kurmanbek Bakiyev was appointed prime minister and acting president. Akayev, in exile in Russia, resigned as president in April 2005. Bakiyev was confirmed as president by winning the elections held in July 2005. The doubling of household utility costs in Jan. 2010 sparked a further wave of protests that resulted in Bakiyev stepping down in April 2010 and Roza Otunbayeva, previously foreign minister, heading an interim government until Almazbek Atambayev took office as president in Dec. 2011. Atambayev was in turn replaced in Nov. 2017 by Sooronbek Jeenbekov.

Territory and Population

Kyrgyzstan is situated on the Tien-Shan mountains and bordered in the east by China, west by Kazakhstan and Uzbekistan, north by Kazakhstan and south by Tajikistan. Area, 199,945 sq. km (77,199 sq. miles). Population (census 2009), 5,362,793 (51·3% females); density, 27 per sq. km. In 2009, 65·9% of the population lived in rural areas. In Jan. 2018 the population was estimated at 6,256,700.

The UN gives a projected population for 2020 of 6·30m.

The republic comprises seven provinces (Batken, Djalal-Abad, Issyk-Kul, Naryn, Osh, Talas and Chu) plus the city of Bishkek, the capital (formerly Frunze; 2018 estimated population, 987,600). Other large towns (with 2018 estimates) are Osh (260,000), Djalal-Abad (107,500), Karakol (formerly Przhevalsk, 74,900), Tokmak (63,200), Uzgen (58,800), Balykchy (47,500) and Karabalta (46,100).

The Kyrgyz are of Turkic origin and formed 69·2% of the population in 2008; the rest included Uzbeks (14·5%), Russians (8·7%) and Dungans (1·2%).

The official languages are Kyrgyz and Russian. After the break-up of the Soviet Union, Russian was only the official language in provinces where Russians are in a majority. However, in May 2000 parliament voted to make it an official language nationwide, mainly in an attempt to stem the ever-increasing exodus of skilled ethnic Russians. The Cyrillic alphabet is still used although the reintroduction of the Roman alphabet (in use 1928–40) remains a source of political debate.

Social Statistics

2009 births, 135,494; deaths, 35,898; marriages (2006), 43,760. Rates, 2009 (per 1,000 population): birth, 26·4; death, 7·0; infant mortality (per 1,000 live births, 2010), 33. Life expectancy, 2007, 63·9 years for males and 71·4 for females. In 2006 the most popular age for marrying was 20–24 for females and 25–29 for males. Annual population growth rate, 2010–15, 1·6%; fertility rate, 2008, 2·5 births per woman.

Climate

The climate varies from dry continental to polar in the high Tien-Shan, to sub-tropical in the southwest (Fergana Valley) and temperate in the northern foothills. Bishkek, Jan. 9°F (–13°C), July 70°F (21°C). Annual rainfall 14·8" (375 mm).

Constitution and Government

A new constitution was adopted in June 2010 after it won overwhelming support in a referendum following the ousting of the incumbent president, Kurmanbek Bakiyev, in April 2010. The referendum was held two weeks after ethnic violence between Kyrgyz and Uzbek groups killed up to 2,000 and left 400,000 displaced. Nonetheless, international observers deemed the vote fair. Turnout was put at 72·2%, with 90·5% of votes cast in favour.

Under the terms of the constitution, greater power is invested in parliament at the expense of the presidency. The president is allowed to serve a maximum of one six-year term and cannot seek re-election, although the office does retain its power of veto and has the authority to appoint heads of various state institutions. The unicameral parliament (*Jogorku Kenesh*) is comprised of 120 seats, with no single party allowed to hold more than 65. Political parties cannot be constituted on religious or ethnic grounds and members of the armed forces, the judiciary and the police are banned from party membership.

National Anthem

'Ak möngülüü aska yoolor, talaalar' ('High mountains, valleys and fields'); words by D. Sadykov and E. Kuluev, tune by N. Davlyesov and K. Moldovasanov.

Recent Elections

Presidential elections were held on 15 Oct. 2017. Former prime minister Sooronbay Jeenbekov won with 54·7% of the vote, ahead of Omurbek Babanov (also a former prime minister) with 33·7% and Adakhan Madumarov with 6·5%. There were eight other candidates. Turnout was 55·9%. The election was considered to be the first genuinely competitive poll to be held in Central Asia.

Parliamentary elections were held on 4 Oct. 2015 in which 38 of 120 seats were won by the Social Democratic Party of Kyrgyzstan, 28 by Ata-Zhurt (Fatherland), 18 by the Kyrgyzstan Party, 13 by Onuguu–Progress, 12 by Bir Bol and 11 by Ata Meken. Turnout was 57·6%.

Current Government

In Feb. 2019 the government comprised:

President: Sooronbay Jeenbekov; b. 1958 (Social Democratic Party of Kyrgyzstan; since 24 Nov. 2017).

Prime Minister: Muhamedkaliy Abulgaziyev; b. 1968 (ind.; sworn in 20 April 2018).

First Vice Prime Minister: Kubatbek Boronov. *Vice Prime Ministers:* Zamirbek Askarov; Altynay Omurbekova; Zhenish Razakov.

Minister of Agriculture, Land Reclamation and Food Industry: Nurbek Murashev. Culture, *Information and Tourism:* Azamat Zhamankulov. *Economy:* Oleg Pankratov. *Education and Science:* Gulmira Kudaiberdieva. *Emergency Situations:* Nurbolot Mirzammedov. *Finance:* Baktygul Jeenbaeva. *Foreign Affairs:* Chingiz Aidarbekov. *Health:* Kosmosbek Cholponbaev. *Internal Affairs:* Kashkar Dzhunushaliev. *Justice:* Marat Jamankulov. *Labour and Social Development:* Ulukbek Kochkorov. *Transport and Roads:* Zhamshitbek Kalilov. *Chief of Staff of the Government:* Shamilbek Asymbekov.

Office of the President (Kyrgyz and Russian only): http://www.president.kg

Current Leaders

Sooronbay Jeenbekov

Position
President

Introduction
Sooronbay Jeenbekov was sworn in as president on 24 Nov. 2017. He previously served as prime minister and was regarded as the favoured candidate of the former president, Almazbek Atambayev.

Early Life
Jeenbekov was born on 16 Nov. 1958 in Biy-Myra in the Osh region of Kyrgyzstan. He graduated in zoological engineering from the Kyrgyz Academy of Agriculture and in 2003 took a degree in accounting from the National Agrarian University. After a period teaching, he became a livestock specialist and then chairman of a collective farm. His political career began in 1993 when he became a parliamentary deputy. He became minister of agriculture, water resources and the processing industry in 2007, and then served as governor of Osh region before his appointment as prime minister in April 2016.

Jeenbekov stepped down as premier in Aug. 2017 to contest the Oct. presidential election. As the candidate of the Social Democratic Party of Kyrgyzstan, he won 54·7% of the vote, while his closest rival, Omurbek Babanov, claimed 33·7%, thus avoiding the need for a run-off. Although the presidential transition was peaceful by Kyrgyz standards, the Organization for Security and Co-operation in Europe nonetheless observed that 'pressures on voters and vote-buying remain a concern'.

Career in Office
Jeenbekov pledged to combat corruption and to reform the health and education systems, as well as to overhaul the electricity sector. However, in Jan. 2018 a prominent opposition politician was sentenced to a long prison term for alleged corruption but claimed that the charges against him were fabricated by a repressive government.

In April 2018 Prime Minister Sapar Isakov, who had been appointed in Aug. 2017, lost a parliamentary confidence vote and resigned, relinquishing the premiership to Muhamedkaliy Abulgaziyev, an independent.

On the foreign stage, Jeenbekov has agreed a programme with President Nursultan Nazarbayev of Kazakhstan to resolve border control issues and bilateral differences within the Eurasian Economic Union, and is also expected to target better relations with other regional neighbours including Turkey and China.

Defence

Conscription is for 12 months. Defence expenditure in 2013 totalled US$102m. (US$18 per capita), representing 1·4% of GDP. The USA opened a military base in Kyrgyzstan in 2001 to aid the war in Afghanistan against the Taliban. The base was scheduled to close by the end of Aug. 2009 after an eviction notice was served on 20 Feb. 2009 giving the US military 180 days to vacate the site. However, on 23 June 2009 the Kyrgyz and US governments agreed a new deal that allowed a one-year extension of the lease. The base closed when a further lease expired in June 2014. In Sept. 2003 Kyrgyzstan also agreed to allow Russia to open an air force base in the country.

Army

Personnel, 2011, 8,500. In addition there are 5,000 border guards, 3,500 interior troops and a National Guard of 1,000.

Air Force

Personnel, 2011, 2,400, with 33 combat-capable aircraft (mainly MiG-21 fighters) and two attack helicopters.

Economy

Agriculture accounted for 17·1% of GDP in 2014, industry 27·8% and services 55·1%.

Overview

After independence in 1991, Kyrgyzstan suffered from the loss of Soviet economic support. The country was plagued by nepotism and corruption during the post-independence rule of President Akayev (1990–2005). In 2010 the power of the president was constitutionally curtailed, but wealth inequality nonetheless has remained endemic and exacerbates simmering ethnic tensions.

There has been under-investment in infrastructure and social services and the economy is classed as low-income. The country has also suffered as a result of the global financial crisis, internal political unrest and inflated food prices. GDP per capita stood at US$1,038 in 2016, although the poverty rate had fallen marginally from 33·7% in 2010 to 32·1% by 2015.

Mining annually brings in over 25% of government revenues and over 40% of all export earnings. When gold mining was temporarily reduced in the country's largest mine at Kumtor (responsible for some 60% of the country's industrial output) in 2012, GDP contracted by 0·9% despite robust growth in non-gold sectors.

The government has set about reforming the agricultural sector which employs the vast majority of workers, establishing a land reform programme, a rural bank and an agricultural advisory service to help boost investment and productivity. Long-term challenges include reducing over-reliance on the Kumtor mine, cutting energy imports, reforming the education, health care and social protection systems, and providing the framework for improved governance.

Currency

On 10 May 1993 Kyrgyzstan introduced its own currency unit, the *som* (KGS), of 100 *tyiyn*, at a rate of 1 som = 200 roubles. Inflation was 24·5% in 2008, and more recently 0·4% in 2016 and 3·2% in 2017. Gold reserves totalled 83,000 troy oz in July 2005, foreign exchange reserves US$509m. and total money supply 13,884m. soms.

Budget

Budgetary central government revenue totalled 69,021·5m. soms in 2011 and expenditure 62,184·3m. soms. Tax revenues in 2011 were 46,125·2m. soms. Main items of expenditure by economic type in 2011 were: compensation of employees (16,124·2m. soms) and use of goods and services (14,092·6m. soms).

VAT is 12%.

Performance

The economy expanded strongly in 2013, growing by 10·9%, but has since slowed and grew by 4·3% in 2016 and 4·6% in 2017. Total GDP in 2017 was US$7·6bn. According to World Bank data for 2017, Kyrgyzstan is the country second most reliant on remittances from abroad (behind Tonga), accounting for 32·9% of total GDP.

Banking and Finance

The central bank and bank of issue is the National Bank (*Chair*, Tolkunbek Abdygulov). There were 25 commercial banks at Sept. 2016.

Foreign debt was US$3,984m. in 2010, representing 89·2% of GNI.

There is a stock exchange in Bishkek.

Energy and Natural Resources

Environment

Kyrgyzstan's carbon dioxide emissions from the consumption of energy were the equivalent of 1·6 tonnes per capita in 2011.

Electricity

Installed capacity was an estimated 3·9m. kW in 2011. Production in 2011 was 15·16bn. kWh, of which 93·3% hydro-electric; consumption per capita was 2,288 kWh. Kyrgyzstan exports electricity to Russia and to other neighbouring countries.

Oil and Gas

Output of oil, 2011, 0·7m. bbls; natural gas, 2011, 27m. cu. metres.

Minerals

In 2009 lignite production totalled 535,000 tonnes and hard coal production 67,000 tonnes. Gold is also mined. Output in 2009 (gold content) was 16,950 kg. Gold is by far the country's leading mineral commodity in terms of value. One gold mine, the Kumtor mine, accounts for nearly 12% of the country's annual GDP.

Agriculture

Kyrgyzstan is famed for its livestock breeding, in particular the small Kyrgyz horse. In 2014 there were 4,918,778 sheep, 1,458,377 cattle, 910,246 goats, 432,972 horses and 4m. chickens. Yaks are bred as meat and dairy cattle, and graze on high altitudes unsuitable for other cattle. Crossed with domestic cattle, hybrids give twice the yield of milk.

There were 1·28m. ha. of arable land in 2013 and 75,300 ha. of permanent crops.

Principal crops include wheat, barley, corn and vegetables. Fodder crops for livestock are grown, particularly lucerne; also sugar beets, cotton, tobacco and medicinal herbs. Sericulture, fruit, grapes and vegetables are major branches.

Output of main agricultural products (in 1,000 tonnes) in 2013: potatoes, 1,332; wheat, 819; maize, 568; barley, 310; watermelons, 196; sugar beets, 195; tomatoes, 195; onions, 152; apples (estimate), 143; carrots and turnips, 137; cabbages, kale, etc., 109. Livestock products, 2013, in 1,000 tonnes: beef and veal, 99; lamb and mutton (estimate), 44; milk, 1,408; eggs (estimate), 24.

Forestry

In 2015 forests covered 637,000 ha., or 3% of the land area. Timber production in 2011 was 46,000 cu. metres.

Fisheries

The catch in 2015 was 31 tonnes, entirely from freshwater fishing.

Industry

Industrial enterprises include food, timber, textile, engineering, metallurgical, oil and mining. There are also sugar refineries, tanneries, cotton and wool-cleansing works, flour-mills and a tobacco factory. In 2014 industry accounted for 27·8% of GDP, with manufacturing contributing 15·9%. Output was valued at 171,108·9m. soms in 2014.

Production, 2014 unless otherwise indicated: cement, 1,727,500 tonnes; fuel oil, 51,000 tonnes; carpets (2012), 10,300 sq. metres; footwear (2012), 714,000 pairs.

Labour

The labour force in 2013 was 2,677,000 (2,172,000 in 2003). 70·9% of the population aged 15–64 was economically active in 2013. In the same year 8·3% of the population was unemployed.

Kyrgyzstan had 16,000 people living in slavery according to the Walk Free Foundation's 2013 *Global Slavery Index*.

International Trade

Imports and Exports

Imports (c.i.f.) were valued at US$4,072m. in 2008 and exports (f.o.b.) at US$1,618m.

In 2008 main import sources (in US$1m.) were: Russia (1,492); China (728); Kazakhstan (377). Main export markets in 2008 (in US$1m.) were: Switzerland (445); Russia (186); Uzbekistan (167).

Principal imports in 2008 (in US$1m.) were: machinery and transport equipment (646); manufactured goods (514); food (401). Principal exports in 2008 (in US$1m.) were: gold (464); articles of apparel and clothing accessories (99); non-metallic mineral manufactures (90).

Communications

Roads

There were 34,000 km of roads in 2007. Passenger cars in use in 2007 numbered 229,700 (44 per 1,000 inhabitants). There were 1,252 road accident fatalities in 2007.

Rail

In the north a railway runs from Lugovaya through Bishkek to Rybachi on Lake Issyk-Kul. Towns in the southern valleys are linked by short lines with the Ursatyevskaya–Andizhan railway in Uzbekistan. Total length of railway, 2011, 417 km. Passenger-km travelled in 2011 came to 83m. and freight tonne-km to 798m.

Civil Aviation

The main international airport is at Bishkek (Manas). The national carrier is Air Kyrgyzstan, founded in 2001 as Altyn Air. In 2012 scheduled airline traffic of Kyrgyz-based carriers flew 5·0m. km; passenger-km totalled 522·9m. in the same year.

Telecommunications

In 2010 there were 489,100 landline telephone subscriptions (equivalent to 91·7 per 1,000 inhabitants) and 5,275,500 mobile phone subscriptions (or 989·0 per 1,000 inhabitants). Fixed internet subscriptions totalled 68,900 in 2010 (12·9 per 1,000 inhabitants).

Social Institutions

Out of 178 countries analysed in the 2017 *Fragile States Index*—a list published jointly by the Fund for Peace and *Foreign Policy* magazine—Kyrgyzstan was ranked the joint 65th most vulnerable (along with Tanzania) to conflict or collapse. The index is based on 12 indicators of state vulnerability across social, political and economic categories.

Justice

The population in penal institutions in Jan. 2012 was 9,828 (181 per 100,000 of national population). The new constitution that came into force in Jan. 2007 abolished the death penalty. In 2015 the World Justice Project *Rule of Law Index*, which provides data on how the rule of law is experienced by the general public across eight categories, ranked Kyrgyzstan 84th of 102 countries for criminal justice and 77th for civil justice.

Education

In 2008–09 there were 72,000 children in pre-primary education (3,000 teaching staff), 392,000 pupils in primary education (16,000 teaching staff), an estimated 679,000 pupils in secondary education (51,000 teaching staff) and 17,000 university level lecturers for 294,000 students. There were 54 higher educational institutions in 2015. Kyrgyz National University had approximately 22,000 students in 2010. Adult literacy was 99·2% in 2009.

In 2005 public expenditure on education came to 4·9% of GDP.

Health

In 2006 there were 12,710 physicians, 1,017 dentists and 30,824 nurses and midwives. In 2009 there were 122 hospitals with 25,975 beds.

In *Water: At What Cost? The State of the World's Water 2016*, WaterAid reported that 10·0% of the population does not have access to safe water.

Welfare

In Dec. 2007 there were 529,000 pensioners.

Religion

In 2010 there were an estimated 4·69m. Muslims (mainly Sunnis) and 610,000 Christians (mainly Orthodox) according to the Pew Research Center's Forum on Religion & Public Life. There were 1,784 mosques, 359 Christian congregations, one synagogue and one Buddhist temple in 2008.

Culture

World Heritage Sites

There are three sites in Kyrgyzstan that appear on the UNESCO World Heritage List. Sulaiman-Too Sacred Mountain in the Fergana Valley was inscribed in 2009. Situated at the crossroads of important routes on the Central Asian Silk Roads system, Sulaiman-Too is the site of numerous ancient places of worship and caves with petroglyphs. Shared with China and Kazakhstan, Silk Roads: the Routes Network of Chang'an–Tianshan Corridor (2014) is a 5,000 km section of the extensive Silk Roads network stretching from Chang'an/Luoyang in China through the northeast of present-day Kyrgyzstan to the Zhetysu region in what is now Kazakhstan. Shared with Kazakhstan and Uzbekistan, Western Tien-Shan (2016) is a transnational property located in one of the largest mountain ranges in the world.

Press

There were three national daily newspapers in 2008, with a combined circulation of 40,000.

Tourism

In 2010 there were 1,316,000 non-resident tourists, down from 2,147,000 in 2009. This was as a consequence of the political upheaval in April 2010 and the ethnic conflict that ensued.

Diplomatic Representatives

Of Kyrgyzstan in the United Kingdom (Ascot House, 119 Crawford St., London, W1U 6BJ)
Ambassador: Gulnara Iskakova.

Of the United Kingdom in Kyrgyzstan (21 Erkindik Blvd, Office 404, Bishkek 720040)
Ambassador: Robin Ord-Smith, MVO.

Of Kyrgyzstan in the USA (2360 Massachusetts Ave., NW, Washington, D.C., 20008)
Ambassador: Kadyr M. Toktogulov.

Of the USA in Kyrgyzstan (171 Prospekt Mira, Bishkek 720016)
Ambassador: Donald Lu.

Of Kyrgyzstan to the United Nations
Ambassador: Otunbaev Bolot Isakovich.

Of Kyrgyzstan to the European Union
Ambassador: Asein Isaev.

Further Reading

Abazov, Rafis, *Historical Dictionary of Kyrgyzstan.* 2004
Anderson, J., *Kyrgyzstan: Central Asia's Island of Democracy?* 1999
Marat, Erica, *The Tulip Revolution: Kyrgyzstan One Year After.* 2006
National Statistical Office: National Statistical Committee of the Kyrgyz Republic, 374 Frunze Street, Bishkek City 720033.
Website: http://www.stat.kg

Laos

Sathalanalath Pasathipatai Pasasonlao (Lao People's Democratic Republic)

Capital: Vientiane
Population projection, 2020: 7·16m.
GNI per capita, 2017: (PPP$) 6,070
HDI/world rank, 2017: 0·601/139
Internet domain extension: .la

Key Historical Events

Neolithic settlements were established in upland areas of present-day Laos by around 2000 BC. Migrants from southern China introduced rice cultivation and trade in iron ore and manufactured goods. Thousands of large stone vessels containing ceramics and burial goods on the Xieng Khoung plateau in central Laos are testament to the society's wealth and sophistication. From around 300 BC the Hindu-influenced Funan Kingdom held sway across parts of southern and central Laos, as well as much of present-day Cambodia. Trading links with India, China and the Middle East developed and strengthened under the Funan.

During the sixth century AD a rival kingdom, Chenla, rose in southern Laos (modern Champassak province). Over the next 300 years its influence spread across Cambodia and northern Thailand. The colonization of Cambodia's coastal regions in the eighth century by Javanese mariners forced Khmer-speaking clans inland, including to southern and central Laos. The crowning of Jayavarman II as a *deva-raja* (god-king) in AD 802 heralded a long period of regional Khmer domination centred on Angkor. Tai peoples originating in southern China settled in growing numbers in northern Laos from the ninth century. Several independent city states were united in the mid-14th century by Chao Fa Ngum, founder of Lan Xang ('land of a million elephants'). The kingdom encompassed a wide area either side of the Mekong River, with its capital at Luang Prabang.

In the mid-16th century King Saya Setthathirat transferred the capital to Viang Chan (Vientiane), which boosted trade. Under Suriya Vongsa's 57-year reign the Lan Xang reached its zenith. Viang Chan developed into a centre of Buddhist learning, while trade links were established with Europe through the Dutch East India Company. However, the kingdom's influence waned in the 18th century as divisions emerged in Luang Prabang and Champassak, while Siam—led by Gen. Taksin—became increasingly powerful. By 1779 all three Lao kingdoms had surrendered to Siamese armies and came under Bangkok's control.

The Lao frequently rebelled against Siamese dominance, most notably under King Anouvong in 1827–28. Eventually captured and imprisoned in Bangkok, he nevertheless became a national hero. Siamese rule was reinstated but by the 1880s it was being undermined by French expansion in the region. In 1863 France had established a protectorate in Cambodia and in 1893 French gunboats threatened Bangkok, eventually gaining control of Lao territories to the east of the Mekong. Vientiane was reinstated as the administrative centre, although real power lay in Hanoi, the capital of French Indochina. Investment in infrastructure and institutions was greatest in Vietnam and Cambodia while Laos remained a relative backwater.

In 1945, after French authority had been suppressed by the Japanese, an independence movement known as Lao Issara (Free Laos) set up a government. However, it collapsed the following year with the return of French rule. Under a new constitution of 1947 Laos became a constitutional monarchy under the Luang Prabang dynasty and in 1949 became an independent sovereign state within the French Union.

An almost continuous state of war began in 1953 between the Royal Lao Government, supported by US bombing campaigns and Thai mercenaries, and the Patriotic Front Pathet Lao, backed by North Vietnamese troops. Peace talks resulted in an agreement on 21 Feb. 1973 providing for the formation of a provisional national unity coalition government and the withdrawal of foreign troops. However, after Communist victories in neighbouring Vietnam and Cambodia in April 1975, the Pathet Lao effectively took over the running of the whole country. On 29 Nov. 1975 King Savang Vatthana abdicated and the People's Congress proclaimed the People's Democratic Republic of Laos on 2 Dec. 1975.

After decades of isolationism, the authorities responded to the collapse of the Soviet Union by cautiously embracing economic reform and forging international ties. In 1995 the USA ended its aid embargo and two years later Laos joined the Association of South East Asian Nations. In 2005 the USA normalized trade relations with the country and a stock market was opened in Vientiane in 2011. Having applied to join the World Trade Organization in 1997, Laos became a member in Feb. 2013.

Territory and Population

Laos is a landlocked country of 236,800 sq. km (91,428 sq. miles) bordered on the north by China, the east by Vietnam, the south by Cambodia and the west by Thailand and Myanmar. Apart from the Mekong River plains along the border of Thailand, the country is mountainous, particularly in the north, and in places densely forested.

The 2015 census population was 6,492,228 (3,237,458 females); density, 27·4 per sq. km. In 2011, 34·3% of the population lived in urban areas.

The UN gives a projected population for 2020 of 7·16m.

There are 17 provinces and one prefecture. Administrative centres and populations (2015 census) are as follows:

Province	Administrative centre	Population (in 1,000)
Attopeu	Samakhi Xai	139·6
Bokeo	Ban Houei Xai	179·2
Bolikhamxai	Paksan	273·7
Champassak	Pakse	694·0
Houa Phan	Xam Neua	289·4
Khammouane	Thakhek	392·1
Luang Namtha	Luang Namtha	175·8
Luang Prabang	Luang Prabang	431·9
Oudomxai	Muang Xai	307·6
Phongsali	Phongsali	178·0
Salavan	Salavan	397·0
Savannakhet	Shanthabouli	969·7
Sayabouri	Sayabouri	381·4
Sekong	Sekong	113·0
Vientiane	Phonghong	419·1
Vientiane[1]	Vientiane	820·9
Xieng Khouang	Phonsavanh	244·7
Xaisomboun	Anouvong	85·2

[1]Prefecture.

The capital and largest town is Vientiane, with a population (2015 census) of 620,157. Other important towns are Savannakhet, Pakse, Luang Prabang and Phonsavanh.

The population is divided into three groups: about 67% Lao-Lum (Valley-Lao); 17% Lao-Theung (Lao of the mountain sides); and 7% Lao-Sung (Lao of the mountain tops), who comprise the Hmong and Yao (or Mien). Lao is the official language. French and English are spoken.

Social Statistics

2009 estimates: births, 141,000; deaths, 37,000. Rates, 2009 estimates (per 1,000 population): birth, 23; death, 6. Infant mortality (per 1,000 live births, 2010), 42. Life expectancy, 2013: 66·9 years for men and 69·7 for women.

Annual population growth rate, 2005–10, 2·0%. Fertility rate, 2013, 3·0 births per woman.

Climate

A tropical monsoon climate, with high temperatures throughout the year and very heavy rains from May to Oct. Vientiane, Jan. 70°F (21·1°C), July 81°F (27·2°C). Annual rainfall 69" (1,715 mm).

Constitution and Government

In Aug. 1991 the National Assembly adopted a new constitution. The head of state is the President, elected by the National Assembly, which consists of 149 members.

Under the constitution the People's Revolutionary Party of Laos (PPPL) remains the 'central nucleus' of the 'people's democracy'; other parties are not permitted. The PPPL's Politburo comprises 11 members, including Bounnhang Vorachit (PPPL, *President*).

National Anthem

'Xatlao tangtae dayma lao thookthuana xeutxoo sootchay' ('For the whole of time the Lao people have glorified their Fatherland'); words by Sisana Sisane, tune by Thongdy Sounthonevichit.

Recent Elections

The Eighth Legislature of the National Assembly elected Bounnhang Vorachit as president on 20 April 2016. Thongloun Sisoulith was elected prime minister on the same day.

There were parliamentary elections on 20 March 2016 in which 149 members were elected from a total of 210 candidates. Candidates needed support from a local authority or mass organization to run for office, with election committees approving candidacies. Turnout was 97·9%.

Current Government

President: Bounnhang Vorachit; b. 1938 (PPPL; since 20 April 2016).
  Vice President: Phankham Viphavanh.
  In Feb. 2019 the government consisted of:
  Prime Minister: Thongloun Sisoulith; b. 1945 (PPPL; since 20 April 2016).
  Deputy Prime Ministers: Bounthong Chitmany; Sonexay Siphandone; Somdy Duangdy (also *Minister of Finance*).
  Minister of Agriculture and Forestry: Lien Thikeo. *Education and Sports:* Sengdeuan Lachanthaboun. *Energy and Mines:* Khammany Inthirath. *Foreign Affairs:* Saleumxay Kommasith. *Health:* Bounkong Sihavong. *Home Affairs:* Khammanh Sounvileuth. *Industry and Commerce:* Khemmani Pholsena. *Information, Culture and Tourism:* Bosengkham Vongdara. *Justice:* Xaysi Santivong. *Labour and Social Welfare:* Khampheng Saysompheng. *National Defence:* Lieut.-Gen. Chansamone Chanyalath. *Natural Resources and Environment:* Sommad Pholsena. *Planning and Investment:* Souphanh Keomixay. *Posts and Telecommunications:* Thansamy Kommasith. *Public Security:* Maj.-Gen. Vilay Lakhamfong. *Public Works and Transport:* Bounchanh Sinthavong. *Science and Technology:* Boviengkham Vongdara. *Minister at the Presidential Office:* Khammeung Phongthady. *Ministers at the Prime Minister's Office:* Souvanpheng Bouphanouvong; Alounkeo Kittkhoun; Phet Phomphiphak; Bounkeuth Sangsomsak; Chaleun Yiapaoher.
  National Assembly Website (limited English): http://www.na.gov.la

Current Leaders

Bounnhang Vorachit

Position
President

Introduction
Bounnhang Vorachit became president on 20 April 2016. He had earlier been appointed general secretary of the dominant People's Revolutionary Party of Laos (PPPL) in Jan. 2016, having previously served as prime minister and vice president. Bounnhang's election to the presidency by a National Assembly vote was widely interpreted as a continuation of the political status quo.

Early Life
Bounnhang Vorachit was born on 15 Aug. 1938 in the district of Thapangthong, in the southern province of Savannakhet. He studied economics and politics in Vietnam before joining the revolutionary communist movement in Laos.

He served for ten years from 1982 as the governor of Savannakhet, and as mayor of Vientiane from 1993 until 1996. He subsequently enjoyed a steady ascent through the ranks of the PPPL, serving as deputy prime minister from 1996 to 2001 and then as prime minister. On 8 June 2006 he was named vice president, a position he held until his promotion to the presidency in 2016.

He was appointed leader of the PPPL at its five-year Congress in Jan. 2016. Then in April the National Assembly elected him as the country's new president with more than two-thirds of votes cast. He leads a 77-member central committee and an 11-person politburo.

Career in Office
Speaking at his inauguration, he pledged to pursue 'peaceful international policies, unity, friendship and co-operation'. He took charge of an economy enjoying strong growth on the back of heavy Chinese investment, although a visit by Bounnhang to Vietnam suggested that he intended to pursue a balance between Laos's two main traditional allies. Among his first tasks as president was to manage Laos's chairmanship of the Association of South East Asian Nations (ASEAN).

Defence

Military service is compulsory for a minimum of 18 months. Defence expenditure in 2013 totalled US$21m. (US$3 per capita), representing 0·2% of GDP.

Army

There are four military regions. Strength (2011) about 25,600. In addition there are local defence forces totalling over 100,000.

Navy

There is an Army Marine Section of about 600 personnel (2011).

Air Force

There are no combat-capable aircraft or armed helicopters. Personnel strength, 3,500 in 2011.

Economy

In 2014 agriculture accounted for 27·7% of GDP, industry 31·4% and services 40·9%.

Overview

Laos, with a lower-middle income economy and gross national income per capita of US$1,600 in 2014, has been one of the fastest-growing countries in the East Asia and Pacific region in this century. The economy expanded by an average of 7% per year in the decade from the mid-2000s—boosted by abundant natural resources, including water, minerals and forestry. Construction, power generation and service sectors have also performed well, while regional integration has boosted tourism and attracted foreign investment. As a consequence, the fiscal and trade deficits are predicted to steadily narrow by 2020.

Laos has made good progress on a number of Millennium Development Goals, including addressing poverty and hunger and improving education and health provision. However, the decline in the poverty rate has been slower than in several regional neighbours. Furthermore, the unpredictable macroeconomic environment remains a challenge to long-term prosperity.

Currency

The unit of currency is the *kip* (LAK). Inflation was 128·4% in 1999 but has since fallen steeply and was 0·0% in 2009. It was 1·6% in 2016 and 0·8% in 2017. Foreign exchange reserves were US$199m. in March 2005 and gold reserves were 117,000 troy oz. Total money supply was 1,364·1bn. kip in Feb. 2005.

Budget

The fiscal year begins on 1 Oct. Budgetary central government revenues in 2014–15 were 23,868bn. kip (taxes, 66·3%) and expenditures 17,462bn. kip (compensation of employees, 50·2%).

VAT is 10%.

Performance

Real GDP growth was 7·3% in 2015, 7·0% in 2016 and 6·9% in 2017. Total GDP in 2017 was US$16·9bn.

Banking and Finance

The central bank and bank of issue is the State Bank (*Governor*, Sonexay Sithphaxay). In Dec. 2010 there were four state-owned commercial banks, nine private banks, two joint venture banks and 11 branches of foreign banks; assets totalled 27,897bn. kip. External debt was US$5,559m. in 2010, representing 79·0% of GNI.

A stock exchange opened in Vientiane in Jan. 2011.

Energy and Natural Resources

Environment

In 2011 carbon dioxide emissions from the consumption of energy were the equivalent of 0·2 tonnes per capita.

Electricity

Total installed capacity in 2011 was 2·8m. kW of which around 2·6m. kW was hydro-electric. In 2011 production was 3,802m. kWh (about 87% hydro-electric). Consumption per capita in 2011 was an estimated 388 kWh; approximately 2,020 kWh were exported.

Minerals

Production in 2009 (in tonnes): gypsum (estimate), 775,000; lignite (2010), 502,000; coal (2010), 212,000; refined copper (estimate), 68,000; salt (estimate), 35,000.

Agriculture

In 2010, 71·3% of those in employment were engaged in agriculture. There were an estimated 1·49m. ha. of arable land in 2013 and 169,000 ha. of permanent crop land. The chief products (2014 unless otherwise indicated, in 1,000 tonnes) are: rice, 4,002; sugarcane, 1,840; cassava, 1,630; maize, 1,412; bananas (2013 estimate), 402; melons and watermelons (2013 estimate), 120; coffee (2013 estimate), 89; sweet potatoes, 80; groundnuts, 59; pineapples (2013 estimate), 50.

Livestock (2013): pigs, 2·95m.; cattle, 1·71m.; buffaloes, 1·19m.; chickens, 31m.

Livestock products (2013 estimates, in 1,000 tonnes): pork and pork products, 65; beef and veal, 30; poultry, 29; milk, 7; eggs, 17.

Forestry

Forests covered 18·76m. ha. in 2015, or 81% of the land area. They produce valuable woods such as teak. Timber production, 2011, 6·79m. cu. metres.

Fisheries

The catch in 2015 was 62,636 tonnes, entirely from inland waters.

Industry

In 2014 industry accounted for 31·4% of GDP, with manufacturing contributing 8·9%. The garment sector is the largest manufacturing employer and is heavily dependent on exports.

Labour

The labour force in 2013 was 3,297,000 (2,569,000 in 2003). 80·6% of the population aged 15–64 was economically active in 2013. In the same year 1·3% of the population was unemployed.

Laos had 50,000 people living in slavery according to the Walk Free Foundation's 2013 *Global Slavery Index*.

International Trade

Since 1988 foreign companies have been permitted to participate in Lao enterprises.

Imports and Exports

Merchandise imports were US$3,055m. in 2012 and exports US$2,071m. Leading imports are consumer goods, food, fuel, machinery and equipment, and vehicles and spare parts. Leading exports are coffee and other agricultural products, copper, electricity, garments, gold, rattan, tin, and wood and wood products. The main import suppliers are Thailand, China, Vietnam and South Korea; the leading export markets are Thailand, China, Vietnam and Japan.

Communications

Roads

In 2006 there were 29,811 km of roads, of which 13·5% were paved. In 2007 there were 12,800 passenger cars (two per 1,000 inhabitants), 109,000 lorries and vans, 6,400 buses and coaches, and 506,500 motorcycles and mopeds. There were 5,198 traffic accidents with 608 fatalities in 2006. A bridge over the River Mekong, providing an important north-south link, was opened in 1994.

Rail

A 3·5 km stretch of railway from Nongkhai, on the Thai bank of the Mekong River, across the Thai–Lao Friendship Bridge to Thanaleng in Laos was opened in 2009.

Civil Aviation

There are four international airports at Vientiane (Wattay), Pakse, Savannakhet and Luang Prabang. The national carrier is Lao Airlines, which in 2018 operated domestic services and international flights to Bangkok, Busan, Changsha, Changzhou, Chiang Mai, Guangzhou, Hanoi, Ho Chi Minh City, Jinghong, Kunming, Phnom Penh, Seoul and Siem Reap. In 2006 scheduled airline traffic of Laos-based carriers flew 4m. km, carrying 327,000 passengers (81,000 on international flights).

Shipping

The River Mekong and its tributaries are an important means of transport. In Jan. 2013 there were two ships of 300 GT or over registered, totalling 15,000 GT.

Telecommunications

In 2011 there were 107,600 landline telephone subscriptions (equivalent to 17·1 per 1,000 inhabitants) and 5,480,900 mobile phone subscriptions (or 871·6 per 1,000 inhabitants). In 2011, 9·0% of the population were internet users. In March 2012 there were 156,000 Facebook users.

Social Institutions

Out of 178 countries analysed in the 2017 *Fragile States Index*—a list published jointly by the Fund for Peace and *Foreign Policy* magazine—Laos was ranked the 59th most vulnerable to conflict or collapse. The index is based on 12 indicators of state vulnerability across social, political and economic categories.

Justice

Criminal legislation of 1990 established a system of courts and a prosecutor's office. Polygamy became an offence.

Education

In 2007 there were 891,807 pupils in primary schools with 29,604 teaching staff, and 403,833 pupils and 17,110 teaching staff at secondary level.

There are eight teacher training institutes (four teacher training colleges and four teacher training schools) and one college of Pali. In June 1995 the National University of Laos (NUOL) was established by merging nine existing higher education institutes and a centre of agriculture. NUOL comprises faculties in agriculture, pedagogy, political science, economics and management, forestry, engineering and architecture, medical science, humanities and social science, science, and literature. In 2007 there were 75,003 students in higher education and 3,030 academic staff.

Adult literacy was 84·7% in 2015 (90·0% among males and 79·4% among females).

In 2007 public expenditure on education came to 3·6% of GNI and 15·8% of total government spending.

Health

In 2010–11 there were 23 tertiary and secondary care hospitals, 130 district-level hospitals and 860 primary health care centres. Laos had eight hospital beds per 10,000 population in 2010. There were 1,160 physicians in 2012 plus 225 dentistry personnel, and 5,581 nursing and midwifery personnel.

In *Water: At What Cost? The State of the World's Water 2016*, WaterAid reported that 24·3% of the population does not have access to safe water.

Religion

In 2010 there were an estimated 4·1m. Buddhists and 1·9m. folk religionists according to the Pew Research Center's Forum on Religion & Public Life. There is also a small Christian minority. In Feb. 2019 there was one cardinal.

Culture

World Heritage Sites

Laos has two sites on the UNESCO World Heritage List: the Town of Luang Prabang (inscribed on the list in 1995), a unique blend of Lao and European colonial architecture; and Vat Phou and Associated Ancient Settlements within the Champasak Cultural Landscape (2001), including a Khmer era Hindu temple complex.

Press

In 2008 there were six paid-for national dailies with a combined circulation of 25,000.

Tourism

There were 2,140,000 non-resident tourists in 2012 (up from 1,142,000 in 2007); revenue from tourism amounted to US$461m.

Festivals

The national day is celebrated on 2 Dec. The Boun Bang Fai (Rocket Festival) takes place at the beginning of the rainy season in May and is thought to have originated in the pre-Buddhist fertility rites and ceremonies to induce the coming of the rains. It is celebrated with parades, songs and dances and homemade bottle rockets and also coincides with the Visakha Puja festival that commemorates the life of Buddha.

Diplomatic Representatives

Of Laos in the United Kingdom (49 Porchester Terrace, London, W2 3TS)
Ambassador: Sayakane Sisouvong.

Of the United Kingdom in Laos (Rue Yokkabat, Phonexay, Saysettha District, Vientiane)
Ambassador: Hugh Evans.

Of Laos in the USA (2222 S. St., NW, Washington, D.C., 20008)
Ambassador: Mai Sayavongs.

Of the USA in Laos (Ban Somvang Thai, Thadeua Rd, km 9, Hatsayfong, Vientiane)
Ambassador: Rena Bitter.

Of Laos to the United Nations
Ambassador: Khiane Phansourivong.

Of Laos to the European Union
Ambassador: Khamkheuang Bounteum.

Further Reading

Lao Statistics Bureau. *Statistical Yearbook.* Annual.

Evans, Grant, *A Short History of Laos: The Land in Between.* 2002

Stuart-Fox, M., *Laos: Politics, Economics and Society.* 1986—*History of Laos.* 1997

National Statistical Office: Ministry of Planning and Investment, Lao Statistics Bureau, Sitrannuea Village, Sikhodthabong District, Vientiane.

Website: http://www.lsb.gov.la

Latvia

Latvijas Republika (Republic of Latvia)

Capital: Riga
Population projection, 2020: 1·89m.
GNI per capita, 2017: (PPP$) 25,002
HDI/world rank, 2017: 0·847/41=
Internet domain extension: .lv

Key Historical Events

The name Latvia derives from *latvis*, a 'forest clearer'. Human inhabitation dates from around 9000 BC and the Balts (or proto-Balts) probably arrived around 2000 BC. In addition to the Finnic predecessors of the Estonians and Livs, four Baltic tribal groups emerged during the Iron Age: the Couronians (Kurši), Selonians (Sēļi), Semigallians (Zemgaļi) and Latgallians (Latgaļi). Linguistic evidence points to the habitation of central Latvia by Latgallians and Lithuanians while coastal areas were populated by Couronians, Semigallians, Selonians and Prussians. The north of the country, occupied mainly by Finnic Livs, was separated by sparsely inhabited areas, which accounts for the lack of cultural mixing between the ethnic groupings.

Scandinavian settlements were established after AD 650, disappearing abruptly around 850. In the 10th century the Baltic tribes came under attack from Varangians (Swedish Vikings), attracted in part by amber which was traded up the Daugava River to Russia and south to Byzantium. Slavic incursions from the east were hampered by primeval forest and marshes.

The region was transformed by German colonization in the 13th century. The Archbishop of Bremen ordered the Christian conquest of the Eastern Baltic sending his nephew Albert, who founded Riga in 1201 and became its bishop. He also created the Sword Brothers (or Livonian Order), a small military order that carved out a feudal state ruled mainly by German aristocracy. It subdued Livonia (southern Estonia and northeastern Latvia), Courland and Zemgale, forming the Livonian Confederation. In 1237 the weakened Sword Brothers were incorporated as an autonomous order into the Order of the Teutonic Knights, which completed the conquest of modern-day Latvia. Riga joined the Hanseatic League in 1282.

The Teutonic Knights were defeated in 1410 at the Battle of Grünwald (Tannenberg) by a Polish–Lithuanian army. Russian Tsar Ivan IV invaded in 1558 in an attempt to gain access to the Baltic Sea. The Livonian War ended with the disbandment of the Livonian Order and the partition of Livonia in 1561. The north went to Lithuania, while Courland became a Lithuanian fief. During the early 17th century Latvia was a theatre of war between Sweden and the Commonwealth of Lithuania–Poland. In 1605 the small hussar army of Jan Karol Chodkiewicz destroyed a much larger Swedish force at the Battle of Kircholm (Salaspils), near Riga. However, Sweden had taken control of Livonia by 1621 and its empire in the Baltic did not end until the signing of the Treaty of Nystad in 1721. The Livonian territory of Vidzeme passed to Russia which acquired Latgale (Latgallia) in 1772 from Poland, and Courland in 1795.

The German landowners remained within the Russian Empire, bolstered by unification with other Germans in the Baltic. The abolition of serfdom in 1817 created new tensions between the Latvian and German communities, though there were German elements who supported land reform which duly arrived in 1847. Nascent Latvian nationalism in the 1860s prompted the Russian authorities to centralize power away from the German aristocracy. Tensions between the communities erupted during the 1905 Russian Revolution when attacks on hundreds of German settlements precipitated a wave of German emigration.

After the German occupation of 1915 demands for the creation of a Latvian state grew until the 1917 Russian Revolution. Soviet rule was proclaimed in Dec. 1917 but was overthrown when the Germans reinvaded in Feb. 1918, with Russia ceding its claims on Latvia by the Treaty of Brest-Litovsk. After the armistice, Latvia declared independence but the Soviets reasserted power following the German withdrawal in Dec. 1918. The Soviets were again overthrown between May–Dec. 1919 by combined British naval and German military forces and a democratic government was established.

In the wake of economic depression, the democratic regime fell in a May 1934 coup when Prime Minister Kārlis Ulmanis dissolved parliament and, in 1936, merged his office with that of the president. When the secret protocol of the Soviet–German agreement of 23 Aug. 1939 assigned Latvia to the Soviet sphere of interest, most of the ancient Baltic German community emigrated. Formal annexation came in 1940 and over 15,000 Latvians were deported to Siberia. The German occupation of 1941–45 caused the deaths of over 90,000 Latvians, mostly Jews. Violent resistance to Soviet reoccupation led to the deportation of another 43,000 Latvians to Siberia and substantial Soviet immigration followed.

The Latvian Supreme Soviet declared sovereignty in July 1989 and on 4 May 1990, having declared the 1940 Soviet occupation illegal, re-established the 1922 constitution. This was annulled by Soviet President Mikhail Gorbachev, sparking violent protest and police crackdowns. Following a referendum, independence was declared on 21 Aug. 1991 and recognized in Sept. by the USSR. With independence, issues of ethnic identity came to the fore, with the large Russian minority initially disadvantaged by new citizenship and language laws (later repealed). President Vaira Vīķe-Freiberga was elected as the former Communist bloc's first female president in 1999. Latvia became a member of NATO and the European Union in 2004.

From March–Dec. 2004 Indulis Emsis was prime minister, becoming the EU's first Green Party premier. Latvia suffered badly during the global economic crisis, prompting popular protests and an IMF bailout in Dec. 2008. The government imposed swingeing austerity measures to stabilize the economy and in June 2013 its application to join the eurozone in Jan. 2014 was accepted by the European Commission.

Territory and Population

Latvia is situated in northeastern Europe. It is bordered by Estonia on the north and by Lithuania on the southwest, while on the east there is a frontier with the Russian Federation and to the southeast with Belarus. Territory, 64,559 sq. km (larger than Denmark, the Netherlands, Belgium and Switzerland), including 2,402 sq. km of inland waters. Population (2011 census), 2,070,371; density, 32·1 per sq. km. In Jan. 2018 the population was estimated at 1,934,379.

The UN gives a projected population for 2020 of 1·89m.

In 2010, 67·7% of the population were urban. Major ethnic groups in 2011: Latvians 62·1%, Russians 26·9%, Belarusians 3·3%, Ukrainians 2·2%, Poles 2·2%, Lithuanians 1·2%. There are also Jews, Roma, Germans and smaller minorities.

There are 110 municipalities (*novadi*) and nine republican cities (*republikas pilsētas*). The capital is Riga (658,640, or nearly a third of the country's total population, at the 2011 census); other principal towns, with 2011 populations, are Daugavpils (93,312), Liepāja (76,731), Jelgava (59,511), Jurmala (50,840) and Ventspils (38,750).

The official language is Latvian. Latgalian is also spoken.

Social Statistics

2010: births, 19,219 (rate of 8·6 per 1,000 population); deaths, 30,040 (13·4 per 1,000 population); marriages, 9,290 (4·1 per 1,000 population); divorces, 4,930 (2·2 per 1,000 population); infant mortality, 5·7 per 1,000 live births (2010). In 2007 life expectancy was 67·1 years for males but 77·1 years for females. In 2005 the most popular age range for marrying was 25–29 for males and 20–24 for females. The annual population growth rate in the period 2000–05 was –0·6%. Fertility rate, 2011, 1·2 births per woman (the joint lowest rate in the world). The suicide rate was 22·9 per 100,000 population in 2009 (rate among males, 40·0). In 2005 there were 1,886 immigrants and 2,450 emigrants.

© Springer Nature Limited 2020
Palgrave Macmillan (ed.), *The Statesman's Yearbook 2020*,
https://doi.org/10.1057/978-1-349-95940-2_110

2014–16	Vienotība	Laimdota Straujuma
2016–19	ZZS	Māris Kučinskis
2019–	Vienotība	Arturs Krišjānis Kariņš

Climate

Owing to the influence of maritime factors, the climate is relatively temperate but changeable. Average temperatures in Jan. range from –2·8°C in the western coastal town of Liepāja to –6·6°C in the inland town of Daugavpils. The average summer temperature is 20°C.

Constitution and Government

The Declaration of the Renewal of the Independence of the Republic of Latvia dated 4 May 1990, and the 21 Aug. 1991 declaration re-establishing *de facto* independence, proclaimed the authority of the Constitution *(Satversme)*. The Constitution was fully reinstituted as of 6 July 1993, when the fifth Parliament *(Saeima)* was elected.

The head of state in Latvia is the *President*, elected by parliament for a period of four years and for a maximum of two terms.

The highest legislative body is the one-chamber parliament comprised of 100 deputies and elected in direct, proportional elections by citizens 18 years of age and over. Deputies serve for four years and parties must receive at least 5% of the national vote to gain seats in parliament.

In a referendum on 3 Oct. 1998, 53% of votes cast were in favour of liberalizing laws on citizenship, which would simplify the naturalization of the Russian-speakers who make up nearly a third of the total population and who were not granted automatic citizenship when Latvia regained its independence from the former Soviet Union in 1991. Around half of the 650,000 ethnic Russians in Latvia have not taken out Latvian citizenship. Ethnic Russians who are not Latvian citizens do not have the right to vote. A seven-member *Constitutional Court* was established in 1996 with powers to invalidate legislation not in conformity with the constitution. Its members are appointed by parliament for ten-year terms.

Executive power is held by the *Cabinet of Ministers*.

National Anthem

'Dievs, svētī Latviju' ('God, bless Latvia'); words and tune by Kārlis Baumanis.

Government Chronology

(JL = New Era; LC = Latvian Way; LTF = Latvian Popular Front; LZP = Latvian Green Party; LZS = Latvian Farmers' Union; TB/LNNK = For Fatherland and Freedom/LNNK; TP = People's Party; Vienotība = Unity; ZZS = Union of Greens and Farmers; n/p = non-partisan)

Heads of State since 1990.

Chairman of the Supreme Council/Head of State		
1990–93	n/p, LC	Anatolijs Gorbunovs
Presidents		
1993–99	LZS	Guntis Ulmanis
1999–2007	n/p	Vaira Vīķe-Freiberga
2007–11	n/p	Valdis Zatlers
2011–15	ZZS	Andris Bērziņš
2015– ZZS	(LZP)	Raimonds Vējonis

Prime Ministers since 1990.

1990–93	LTF	Ivars Godmanis
1993–94	LC	Valdis Birkavs
1994–95	LC	Māris Gailis
1995–97	n/p	Andris Škēle
1997–98	TB/LNNK	Guntars Krasts
1998–99	LC	Vilis Krištopāns
1999–2000	TP	Andris Škēle
2000–02	LC	Andris Bērziņš
2002–04	JL	Einars Repše
2004	ZZS (LZP)	Indulis Emsis
2004–07	TP	Aigars Kalvītis
2007–09	LC	Ivars Godmanis
2009–14	JL, Vienotība	Valdis Dombrovskis

(continued)

Recent Elections

In indirect presidential elections held on 3 June 2015 Raimonds Vējonis of the Green Party won in the fifth round of voting. Three other candidates had contested the poll. Incumbent president Andris Bērziņš had announced in April that he would not seek a second term.

Parliamentary elections were held on 6 Oct. 2018. The pro-Russia Social Democratic Party 'Harmony' (Sociāldemokrātiskā Partija 'Saskaņa') won 23 seats with 19·8% of the votes cast; Who Owns the State? (Kam pieder Valsts?), 16 seats with 14·2%; the New Conservative Party (Jaunā Konservatīvā Partija), 16 with 13·6%; Development/For! (Attīstībai/Par!), 13 seats with 12·0%; National Alliance (Nacionālā Apvienība), 13 seats with 11·0%; Union of Greens and Farmers (Zaļo un Zemnieku savienība/ZZS; comprises Latvian Farmers' Union and Latvian Green Party), 11 with 9·9%; New Unity (Jaunā Vienotība), 8 with 6·7%. Turnout was 54·6%.

European Parliament

Latvia has eight representatives. At the May 2014 elections turnout was 30·2% (53·7% in 2009). Unity won 4 seats with 46·2% of votes cast (political affiliation in European Parliament: European People's Party); National Alliance, 1 with 14·2% (European Conservatives and Reformists); Social Democratic Party 'Harmony', 1 with 13·0% (Progressive Alliance of Socialists and Democrats); Union of Greens and Farmers, 1 with 8·3% (Europe of Freedom and Direct Democracy); Latvian Russian Union (Latvijas Krievu savienība), 1 with 6·4% (Greens/European Free Alliance).

Current Government

President: Raimonds Vējonis; b. 1966 (LZP; sworn in 8 July 2015).

In Feb. 2019 the five-party coalition government comprised:

Prime Minister: Arturs Krišjānis Kariņš; b. 1964 (New Unity; took office on 23 Jan. 2019).

Deputy Prime Minister and Minister of Defence: Artis Pabriks; *Deputy Prime Minister and Minister of Justice:* Jānis Bordāns.

Minister for Agriculture: Kaspars Gerhards. *Culture:* Dace Melbārde. *Defence:* Raimonds Bergmanis. *Economics:* Ralfs Nemiro. *Education and Science:* Ilga Šuplinska. *Environment and Regional Development:* Juris Pūce. *Finance:* Jānis Reirs. *Foreign Affairs:* Edgars Rinkēvičs. *Health:* Ilze Viņķele. *Interior:* Sandis Ģirģens. *Justice:* Dzintars Rasnačs. *Transport:* Tālis Linkaits. *Welfare:* Ramona Petraviča.

Office of the President: http://www.president.lv

Current Leaders

Raimonds Vējonis

Position
President

Introduction
Raimonds Vējonis first entered parliament in 2002 and served as minister of environment and of defence before becoming president on 8 July 2015.

Early Life
Vējonis was born on 15 June 1966 in the Pskov Oblast of Russia. He developed an early interest in environmentalism following an accident on a collective farm that left his grandfather blinded by chemicals. Having graduated in biology from the University of Latvia in 1989, he went on to earn a master's degree in environmental engineering from the same university in 1995 after teaching for a time in the town of Madona. An early recruit to the Latvian Green Party, he was a member of the Madona city council from 1990–93. In 1996 he became director of the Greater Riga regional environmental board, a position he kept until 2002.

Career in Office
From Nov. 2002 Vējonis became engaged in frontline politics as he was appointed minister of environmental protection and regional development in the government of the then premier Einars Repše. The following year he was named minister of the environment in a cabinet reorganization, before

reverting to the previous title in 2011. After a spell out of government, he was named minister of defence in 2014 by then prime minister Laimdota Straujuma. In this post he adopted a tougher policy stance towards Russia in the face of perceived aggression from Moscow.

Having been nominated as a presidential candidate by parliament, Vējonis succeeded Andris Bērziņš following his election on 3 June 2015. He was the first European Union head of state to come from a green party. He emphasized the need for reinforcing national security and strengthening Latvia's armed forces while maintaining the country's political neutrality on the international stage. He also acknowledged the difficulty of improving relations with Russia while Moscow maintains a hostile regional stance towards neighbouring Ukraine. In Dec. 2015 Vējonis strongly advocated the need to secure an agreement at the United Nations climate change summit in Paris, which concluded with a landmark agreement on limiting the increase in global average temperature.

Following the parliamentary elections in Oct. 2018, Vējonis asked Jānis Bordāns to form a new government. When Bordāns failed to reach an agreement Vējonis nominated Aldis Gobzems, but negotiations with other parties also failed. Eventually Krišjānis Kariņš of New Unity took office as prime minister in Jan. 2019 at the head of a five-party coalition.

Krišjānis Kariņš
Position
Prime Minister

Introduction
Krišjānis Kariņš became prime minister in Jan. 2019, leading a broadly centre-right coalition consisting of five liberal and conservative parties.

Early Life
Kariņš was born in Wilmington, Delaware, in the USA on 13 Dec. 1964. He graduated in linguistics from Pennsylvania University in 1988 and was awarded a doctorate in the same subject in 1996. He then moved to Latvia, where he set up a frozen food company.

In 2002 he became a member of the Latvian *Saeima* and helped to create the New Era party. In Dec. 2007 he was appointed minister of economics. In May 2009 Kariņš entered the European Parliament as a member of the European People's Party and joined the committee on industry, research and energy. He helped drive forward a new EU directive on the prevention of money laundering and terrorist financing that was adopted by the European Parliament on 19 April 2018.

In Aug. 2011 Kariņš's New Era party was subsumed into the centre-right Unity party. In 2018 he was chosen as Unity's candidate for the premiership ahead of the Oct. general election and, following an inconclusive result at the poll, President Raimonds Vējonis invited Kariņš in Jan. 2019 to form a new government. He was sworn in after securing agreement on a five-party coalition.

Career in Office
Taking office following the collapse of the ABLV bank—one of the largest private banks in the Baltic states—Kariņš faced the immediate challenge of restoring equilibrium to the financial sector and addressing the issue of money laundering. On defence, Kariņš has expressed enthusiastic support for NATO in the face of Russia's muscular foreign policy. He is expected to initiate reform of both the judicial and the healthcare systems, as well as seeking to access EU funding to regenerate the nation's science and research base.

Defence

The National Armed Forces (NAF) were created in 1994 and comprise the Land Forces, which are based on an infantry brigade and the National Guard, the Naval Forces, the Air Forces, the Logistic Command, the Training Doctrine Command and the National Defence Academy. Compulsory military service was abolished in Jan. 2007.

In 2013 defence expenditure totalled US$300m. (US$138 per capita), representing 1·0% of GDP.

Army

The Land Forces were 1,137 strong in 2011. There is a National Guard reserve numbering 10,666 in 2011.

Navy

The Naval Forces, based at Riga and Liepāja, numbered 485 in 2011 (including a Coast Guard). Latvia, Estonia and Lithuania have established a

joint naval unit 'BALTRON' (Baltic Naval Squadron), with bases at Liepāja, Riga and Ventspils in Latvia, Tallinn in Estonia and Klaipēda in Lithuania.

Air Force

Personnel numbered 284 in 2011. There are no combat-capable aircraft.

International Relations

Latvia held a referendum on EU membership on 20 Sept. 2003, in which 67·4% of votes cast were in favour of accession, with 32·6% against. It became a member of NATO on 29 March 2004 and the EU on 1 May 2004.

Economy

Services accounted for 72·8% of GDP in 2013, industry 23·8% and agriculture 3·4%.

Overview

With Latvia's transition from communism in the early 1990s, the economy suffered from raw material and energy shortages, the loss of Soviet export markets and weak international competitiveness. After independence, market reforms were introduced including privatization of state assets, price liberalization, land reform and the establishment of a local currency and an independent central bank.

After joining the European Union in May 2004 growth accelerated to double-digit figures, driven by private sector capital inflows and EU funding. However, by mid-2006 the economy showed signs of overheating, inflation rose and the current account deficit peaked at over 20% of GDP. In 2008 the global financial crisis led to a slowdown in lending driven by the withdrawal of funds from foreign banks. In Dec. that year Latvia accepted a US$9·5bn. IMF-led bailout programme, causing widespread social turmoil and the resignation of the ruling coalition in Feb. 2009.

A new coalition government agreed a series of spending cuts, including significant reductions in public sector pay and pensions to meet IMF targets to reduce the budget deficit. The economy contracted by more than 14% in 2009 and unemployment was the highest in the EU at nearly 21%. However, the economy emerged from recession in the first quarter of 2010 and fiscal adjustment measures brought the deficit down from 9·7% in 2009 to 1·5% of GDP by 2014. International reserves meanwhile rose above pre-crisis levels, while wage and price cuts, along with productivity growth, improved competitiveness and reduced external imbalances. Unemployment had fallen to 8% by Feb. 2018. Nonetheless, poverty rates are among the highest in Europe. After robust growth of 6·2% in 2011, the annual rate averaged 2·8% from 2012 to 2016. In 2017 it was recorded at 3·4%, driven by higher exports, strengthened business investment, greater private consumption, and EU funding.

Latvia has historically faced challenges in its tax administration—the informal sector's share in the economy is around 25%, far exceeding the OECD average of 14%—and in Dec. 2017 the World Bank and the European Commission committed to assisting the country make reforms.

Currency

On 1 Jan. 2014 the *euro* (EUR) replaced the *lats* (LVL) as the legal currency of Latvia at the irrevocable conversion rate of 0·702804 lats to one euro. Inflation, which reached a high of 109·2% in 1993, was 0·1% in 2016 and 2·9% in 2017. Gold reserves were 249,000 troy oz in July 2005, foreign exchange reserves US$2,076m. and total money supply 1,736m. lats.

Budget

The financial year is the calendar year. General government revenue in 2015 (provisional) totalled €8,702m. and expenditure €8,845m.

Principal sources of revenue in 2015 (provisional) were: taxes on goods and services, €2,991m.; social contributions, €2,111m. Main items of expenditure by economic type in 2015 (provisional): social benefits, €2,733m.; compensation of employees, €2,414m. There is a flat income tax rate of 24%.

Latvia reported a government deficit in 2017 of 0·6% of GDP, following a budget surplus of 0·1% in 2016 and a deficit of 1·4% in 2015. The required target set by the EU is a budget deficit of no more than 3%.

The standard rate of VAT is 21·0% (reduced rates, 12·0% and 5·0%).

Performance

In 2007 real GDP growth was 10·0%. However, having contracted by 3·5% in 2008 the economy shrank by 14·4% in 2009 and a further 3·9% in 2010. It has since recovered, with growth of 2·2% in 2016 and 4·5% in 2017. Latvia has the lowest GDP per capita of any of the ten countries that joined the EU in May 2004. Total GDP was US$30·3bn. in 2017.

Banking and Finance

The Bank of Latvia both legally and practically is a completely independent institution. Governor of the Bank and Council members are appointed by Parliament for office for six years (present *Governor*, Ilmārs Rimšēvičs). In 2010 there were 29 banks in Latvia, including nine foreign banks' branches. Latvia's banks have 11 branches abroad. Latvian banks' assets to GDP exceeded 170% at the end of 2010. The banking sector assets constitute almost 90% of Latvia's financial sector assets. Foreign debt was US$39,555m. in 2010, equivalent to 164·3% of GNI.

NASDAQ OMX Riga (formerly Riga Stock Exchange) is the only regulated secondary securities market in Latvia.

Energy and Natural Resources

In 2011, 33·1% of energy consumption came from renewables (wind power, solar power, hydro-electric power, tidal power, geothermal energy and bio-mass), compared to the European Union average of 13·0%. A target of 40% has been set by the EU for 2020.

Environment

Latvia's carbon dioxide emissions from the consumption of energy in 2011 were the equivalent of 3·7 tonnes per capita. Latvia's greenhouse gas emissions fell by 120·8% between 1990 and 2012, mainly owing to the decline of polluting industries from the Soviet era.

Electricity

Electricity production in 2011 totalled 6·09bn. kWh. Consumption per capita in 2011 was 3,540 kWh. 47% of electrical power produced in Latvia is generated in hydro-electric power stations. Installed capacity was 2·6m. kW in 2011.

Oil and Gas

Latvia produces virtually no oil and is dependent on imports, although the Latvian Development Agency estimates that there are 733m. bbls of offshore reserves in the Latvian areas of the Baltic Sea. Consumption of oil products was 1,488,000 tonnes in 2010. All Latvia's natural gas supplies are imported from Russia. Consumption in 2010 totalled 620m. cu. metres.

Minerals

Peat deposits extend over 645,000 ha. or about 10% of the total area, and it is estimated that total deposits in Jan. 2012 were 168m. tonnes. Peat output in 2011 (provisional) totalled 1,387,689 tonnes.

Production of other minerals in 2011 (provisional, in 1,000 tonnes): gravel, pebbles, shingle and flint, 5,642; silica and construction sand, 2,338; crushed stone for concrete aggregate, 2,051. Crude dolomite, clays, gypsum and limestone are also produced.

Agriculture

In 2010 there were 1·17m. ha. of arable land and 6,800 ha. of permanent crops (excluding strawberries). Field crops and dairy farming are the chief agricultural occupations. In 2010 there were 83,300 economically active agricultural holdings. 34% of holdings have fewer than 5 ha. of utilized agricultural land. There were 50,000 tractors, 6,500 grain combine harvesters and 1,500 potato combine harvesters in 2010. In 2010, 8·8% of the economically active population were employed in agriculture, forestry and fishing.

Output of crops (in 1,000 tonnes), 2010: wheat, 989; potatoes, 484; barley, 229; rapeseeds, 226; oats, 101; rye, 70; cabbage, 61; carrots, 34; apples, 10. Livestock, 2010: pigs, 390,000; cattle, 380,000; sheep, 77,000; poultry, 4·9m. Livestock products (2010, in 1,000 tonnes): meat, 80; milk, 835; eggs, 45.

Forestry

In 2015 Latvia's total forest area was 3·36m. ha., or 54% of the land area. Timber production in 2011 was 12·83m. cu. metres.

The share of the forest sector in gross industrial output is between 13 and 15%. Timber and timber products exports account for 37–38% of Latvia's total exports.

To provide the protection of forests there are three forest categories: commercial forests, 70·4%; restricted management forests, 18·6%; protected forests, 11·0%.

Fisheries

In 2015 the total catch was 81,532 tonnes (less than half of the 2010 total), almost exclusively saltwater fish. The Latvian fishing fleet numbered 758 vessels of 9,100 gross tonnes in 2011.

Industry

Industry accounted for 23·8% of GDP in 2013, with manufacturing contributing 12·6%.

Industrial output in 1,000 tonnes: cement (2011 estimate), 1,100; hot-rolled steel products (2012 estimate), 810; crude steel (2011), 568; sawnwood (2013), 3·35m. cu. metres; wood-based panels (2012), 1·01m. cu. metres; plywood (2012), 278,000 cu. metres; beer (2013), 151·3m. litres.

Labour

The total labour force (persons aged 15–74) in 2011 numbered 1,028,200. In 2011 there were 861,600 persons in employment in Latvia. The leading areas of activity were: wholesale and retail trade/repair of motor vehicles and motorcycles, 136,200; manufacturing, 114,400; education, 88,800. In 2011 women constituted 52% of the workforce. In 2011 there was a monthly minimum wage of 200 lats. Average gross monthly salary was 464 lats in 2011. The average gross monthly salary in the public sector in 2011 was 492 lats.

The unemployment rate in Dec. 2018 was 7·1% (down from 8·7% in 2017 as a whole and 9·6% in 2016).

International Trade

Imports and Exports

Imports (f.o.b.) were valued at US$16,782m. in 2013 and exports (f.o.b.) at US$13,317m. The leading imports in 2013 were machinery, mechanical appliances and electrical equipment (18·4%), mineral products (17·2%), chemical and allied industries (9·4%), and base metals and articles of base metal (8·7%). The main exports in 2013 were wood and wood products (15·9%), machinery, mechanical appliances and electrical equipment (15·6%), base metals and articles of base metal (10·5%), and prepared foodstuffs, beverages and tobacco (9·4%). Main import suppliers (2013): Lithuania, 20·4%; Germany, 11·6%; Poland, 9·9%; Russia, 8·4%; Estonia, 8·2%. Main export markets (2013): Lithuania, 17·2%; Estonia, 12·7%; Russia, 11·6%; Germany, 7·4%; Poland, 6·7%.

Communications

Roads

In 2014 there were 58,628 km of roads, including 20,150 km of state roads. Road passenger traffic in 2012 totalled 13,886m. passenger-km; freight transport totalled 13,670m. tonne-km in 2014. There were 3,728 road accidents in 2014 resulting in 212 deaths. Passenger cars in 2014 numbered 657,799 (331 per 1,000 inhabitants), in addition to which there were 83,205 lorries and tractors and 4,845 buses.

Rail

In 2014 there were 1,860 km of 1,520 mm gauge route (251 km electrified). In 2014, 57·0m. tonnes of cargo and 19·2m. passengers were carried by rail. The main groups of freight transported are oil and oil products, mineral fertilizers, ferrous metals and ferrous alloys.

Civil Aviation

There is an international airport at Riga. The national carrier is airBaltic (80·05% state-owned). Founded in 1995, it became Eastern Europe's first low-cost airline; in 2012 it carried 3·08m. passengers and operated scheduled services to 55 destinations. In 2010 Riga handled 4,663,692 passengers and 12,247 tonnes of freight.

Shipping

There are two major ports. Riga handled 41·1m. tonnes of cargo in 2014 and Ventspils 26·2m. tonnes. There is a smaller port at Liepāja. A total of 65·1m. tonnes were loaded at the three ports in 2014 and 9·1m. tonnes unloaded. In Jan. 2014 there were 22 ships of 300 GT or over registered, totalling 180,000 GT.

Telecommunications

Telecommunications are conducted by companies in which the government has a 51% stake, under the aegis of the state-controlled Lattelecom. There were 516,300 landline telephone subscriptions in 2011 (equivalent to 230·2 per 1,000 inhabitants) and 2,303,600 mobile phone subscriptions in 2009 (or 1,018·7 per 1,000 inhabitants). There were 684·2 internet users per 1,000 inhabitants in 2010. In 2009 there were 18·6 fixed broadband subscriptions per 100 inhabitants and 8·8 mobile broadband subscriptions per 100 inhabitants. In March 2012 there were 319,000 Facebook users.

Social Institutions

Out of 178 countries analysed in the 2017 *Fragile States Index*—a list published jointly by the Fund for Peace and *Foreign Policy* magazine—Latvia was ranked the 38th least vulnerable to conflict or collapse. The index is based on 12 indicators of state vulnerability across social, political and economic categories.

Justice

A new criminal code came into force in 1998. Judges are appointed for life. There are a Supreme Court, regional and district courts and administrative courts. The death penalty was abolished for all crimes in Jan. 2012, having previously been abolished for peacetime offences in 1999. In 2009, 56,748 crimes were reported; 10,855 people were convicted for offences (79 for intentional homicide). In Jan. 2013 there were 6,117 people in penal institutions, giving a prison population rate of 304 per 100,000 population.

Education

Adult literacy rate in 2009 was estimated at 99·8% (99·8% among both males and females). The former Soviet education system was restructured on the UNESCO model. Education begins with two years of compulsory attendance at pre-primary education institutions. From the age of six or seven education is compulsory for nine years in comprehensive schools. This may be followed by three years in secondary school or one to six years in art, technical or vocational schools. In 2011–12 there were 839 schools with 218,442 pupils.

State-financed education is available in Latvian and four national minority languages (Russian, Polish, Ukrainian and Belarusian), although the use of Latvian in the classroom is being increased. A bilingual curriculum had to be implemented by all minority primary schools from the start of the 2002–03 school year. Secondary schools started to implement minority education curricula with an increased Latvian-language component (60% of all teaching) from Sept. 2004. In 2011–12, 158,828 pupils were taught solely in Latvian, 58,087 received instruction in Russian and 1,527 in other minority languages.

In 2011–12 there were 34 state-recognized higher education institutions. Courses at state-financed universities are conducted in Latvian. A number of private educational institutions have languages of instruction other than Latvian.

Public expenditure on education in 2009 came to 5·6% of GDP and accounted for 12·1% of total government expenditure.

Health

At the end of 2010 there were 7,951 physicians and dentists, 10,024 nurses and 408 midwives. There were 67 hospitals in 2010 with a provision of 53 beds per 10,000 persons.

In *Water: At What Cost? The State of the World's Water 2016*, WaterAid reported that 0·7% of the population does not have access to safe water.

Welfare

The official retirement age was increased from 62 years to 62 years and 3 months from 1 Jan. 2014 for both men and women and is being increased gradually each year so that by 2025 it will be 65 years. In 2014 the minimum pension was just over the state social security allowance of €64·03 a month at €70·43. The minimum pension is increased by 1·1% for an insurance period of up to 20 years, by 1·3% for an insurance period of 20 to 30 years, 1·5% for an insurance period of 30 to 40 years and 1·7% for an insurance period of more than 40 years. In Dec. 2013 there were 580,800 pension recipients.

The government runs an unemployment benefit scheme in which the amount awarded is determined by the number of insurance contributions and the length of previous employment.

Religion

In order to practise in public, religious organizations must be licensed by the department of religious affairs attached to the ministry of justice. New sects are required to demonstrate loyalty to the state and its traditional religions over a three-year period. According to estimates by the Pew Research Center's Forum on Religion & Public Life, 990,000 people (43·8% of the population) had no religious affiliation in 2010. There were some 450,000 Protestants in the same year, 430,000 Catholics and 370,000 Orthodox Christians. In Feb. 2019 the Roman Catholic Church had one cardinal.

Culture

World Heritage Sites

Latvia has two sites on the UNESCO World Heritage List: the Historic Centre of Riga (inscribed on the list in 1997), a late-medieval Hanseatic centre; and the Struve Geodetic Arc (2005). The Arc is a chain of survey triangulations spanning from Norway to the Black Sea that helped establish the exact shape and size of the earth and is shared with nine other countries.

Press

Latvia had 12 daily paid-for newspapers in 2014 (six national paid-for dailies and six regional and local paid-for dailies). The leading newspapers in terms of readership in 2014 were *Latvijas Avīze* and *Diena*, both of which are in Latvian, and the Russian-language *Vesti Segodnya*.

Tourism

In 2010 there were 1,373,000 overnight non-resident tourists (1,323,000 in 2009). The main countries of origin of non-resident tourists in 2010 were Russia (189,000), Lithuania (182,000), Sweden (157,000) and Estonia (130,000).

Festivals

There is an annual Riga Opera Festival in June and the city also hosts the Lielais Kristaps National Film Festival in Sept.–Oct. The biggest music festival is Positivus Festival which takes place in July at Salacgrīva. The National Song Festival (held every five years) will next be held in 2023.

Diplomatic Representatives

Of Latvia in the United Kingdom (45 Nottingham Pl., London, W1U 5LY)
    Ambassador: Baiba Braže.

Of the United Kingdom in Latvia (5 J. Alunana ielā, Riga, LV 1010)
    Ambassador: Keith Shannon.

Of Latvia in the USA (2306 Massachusetts Ave., NW, Washington, D.C., 20008)
    Ambassador: Andris Teikmanis.

Of the USA in Latvia (Samnera Velsa iela 1, Riga, LV 1510)
    Ambassador: Nancy Bikoff Pettit.

Of Latvia to the United Nations
    Ambassador: Andrejs Pildegovičs.

Of Latvia to the European Union
    Permanent Representative: Sanita Pavļuta-Deslandes.

Further Reading

Central Statistical Bureau. *Statistical Yearbook of Latvia.—Latvia in Figures.* Annual.
Dreifeld, J., *Latvia in Transition.* 1997
Hood, N., *et al.,* (eds) *Transition in the Baltic States.* 1997
Kasekamp, Andres, *A History of the Baltic States.* 2010
Lieven, A., *The Baltic Revolution: Estonia, Latvia, Lithuania and the Path to Independence.* 2nd ed. 1994
Misiunas, R. J. and Taagepera, R., *The Baltic States: the Years of Dependence, 1940–90.* 2nd ed. 1993
O'Connor, Kevin, *The History of the Baltic States.* 2003
Plakans, Andrejs, *A Concise History of the Baltic States.* 2011
Smith, David J., Purs, Aldis, Pabriks, Artis and Lane, Thomas, (eds) *The Baltic States: Estonia, Latvia and Lithuania.* 2002
National Statistical Office: Central Statistical Bureau, Lācplēša ielā 1, 1301 Riga.
Website: http://www.csb.lv

Lebanon

Jumhouriya al-Lubnaniya (Republic of Lebanon)

Capital: Beirut
Population projection, 2020: 6·02m.
GNI per capita, 2017: (PPP$) 13, 312
HDI/world rank, 2015: 0·763/76
Internet domain extension: .lb

Key Historical Events

The Ottomans invaded Lebanon, then part of Syria, in 1516–17 and held nominal control until 1918. After 20 years' of French mandatory regime, Lebanon was proclaimed independent on 26 Nov. 1941. In early May 1958 the Muslim opposition to President Chamoun rose in insurrection and for five months the Muslim quarters of Beirut, Tripoli, Sidon and the northern Bekaa were in insurgent hands. On 15 July the US Government landed army and marines who re-established Government authority. Internal problems were exacerbated by the Palestinian problem. An attempt to regulate the activities of Palestinian fighters through the secret Cairo agreement of 1969 was frustrated both by the inability of the Government to enforce its provisions and by an influx of battle-hardened fighters expelled from Jordan in Sept. 1970. From March 1975 Lebanon was beset by civil disorder bringing the economy to a virtual standstill.

By Nov. 1976 large-scale fighting had been brought to an end by the intervention of the Syrian-dominated Arab Deterrent Force. Large areas of the country, however, remained outside governmental control, including West Beirut, which was the scene of frequent conflict between opposing militia groups. In March 1978 there was an Israeli invasion following a Palestinian attack inside Israel. Israeli troops eventually withdrew in June, but instead of handing over all their positions to UN Peacekeeping Forces, they installed Israeli-controlled Christian Lebanese militia forces in border areas. In June 1982 Israeli forces once again invaded, this time in massive strength, and swept through the country, eventually laying siege to and bombing Beirut. In Sept. Palestinian forces, together with the PLO leadership, evacuated Beirut. Israeli forces started a withdrawal on 16 Feb. 1985 but it was not until the end of 1990 that the various militias which had held sway in Beirut withdrew. A new Government of National Reconciliation was announced on 24 Dec. 1990. The dissolution of all militias was decreed by the National Assembly in April 1991, but the Shia Muslim militia Hizbollah was allowed to remain active. Following a 17-day Israeli bombardment of Hizbollah positions in April 1996, a US-brokered unsigned 'understanding' of 26 April 1996 guaranteed that Hizbollah guerrillas and Palestinian radical groups would cease attacks on civilians in northern Israel and granted Israel the right to self-defence. Hizbollah maintained the right to resist Israel's occupation of Lebanese soil. In May 2000 Israel completed its withdrawal from south Lebanon, 22 years after the first invasion.

On 14 Feb. 2005 former Prime Minister Rafiq al-Hariri was assassinated in a bomb attack, sparking international condemnation and mass public protests at the continued presence of 14,000 Syrian soldiers and intelligence agents in the country. By the end of April 2005 all Syrian troops had been withdrawn from Lebanon. In July 2006, after Hizbollah forces in Lebanon had captured two Israeli soldiers, Israel launched another military campaign against Lebanon, destroying large parts of the civilian infrastructure and killing more than 1,200 mainly civilian Lebanese. Following the resignation of five Shia Muslim cabinet ministers and the assassination of industry minister Pierre Gemayel in Nov. 2006 there were anti-government demonstrations in Beirut in which over 800,000 protesters—nearly a quarter of the population—demanded the resignation of Prime Minister Fouad Siniora.

In Nov. 2007 Siniora's cabinet assumed presidential powers in the wake of Emile Lahoud's resignation until parliament chose Michel Suleiman to fill the office in May 2008. Suleiman reappointed Siniora as premier. Diplomatic relations were established with Syria in Oct. 2008, the first time since both countries became independent. Following a general election in June 2009, Saad al-Hariri of the pro-Western 14 March Alliance formed a coalition government in Nov. However, in Jan. 2011 the coalition collapsed, and in June 2011 Najib Mikati took over as prime minister at the head of a Hizbollah-dominated government. That administration also collapsed in March 2013, with Mikati nominally retaining the premiership until Tammam Salam formed a workable coalition in Feb. 2014. Meanwhile, Lebanon saw 1m. refugees from neighbouring Syria cross the border to escape the civil war.

President Suleiman ended his term in office in May 2014, leading to a prolonged political deadlock before the Lebanese parliament finally elected a successor—Michel Aoun, a former army commander—in Oct. 2016 after 46 attempts. The following month Aoun named al-Hariri prime minister for the second time and he took office at the head of a new coalition government in Dec.

Territory and Population

Lebanon is mountainous, bounded on the north and east by Syria, on the west by the Mediterranean and on the south by Israel. The area is 10,201 sq. km (3,939 sq. miles). The last census was in 1932. In Dec. 2015 the population was estimated at 5·37m. (excluding non-registered Syrian refugees and Palestinian refugees residing in camps); density, 526 per sq. km. In 2011, 87·4% of the population were urban.

Around 1·1m. refugees have fled to Lebanon from Syria since the start of the civil war there in 2011. As of Dec. 2016 Lebanon had the largest concentration of refugees of any host country, at 169 refugees per 1,000 inhabitants.

The UN gives a projected population for 2020 of 6·02m.

Beirut (the capital) had an estimated population in 2015 of 2·2m. Other large towns are Tripoli, Sidon and Tyre.

The official language is Arabic. French and, increasingly, English are widely spoken in official and commercial circles.

Social Statistics

2008 estimates: births, 66,000; deaths, 29,000. Estimated rates, 2008 (per 1,000 population): births, 15·7; deaths, 7·0. Infant mortality was 19 per 1,000 live births in 2010; expectation of life (2013), 78·1 years for males and 82·3 for females. Annual population growth rate, 2000–08, 1·3%; fertility rate, 2008, 1·8 births per woman.

Climate

A Mediterranean climate with short, warm winters and long, hot and rainless summers, with high humidity in coastal areas. Rainfall is largely confined to the winter months and can be torrential, with snow on high ground. Beirut, Jan. 55°F (13°C), July 81°F (27°C). Annual rainfall 35·7" (893 mm).

Constitution and Government

The first Constitution was established under the French Mandate on 23 May 1926. It has since been amended in 1927, 1929, 1943 (twice), 1947 and 1990. It is based on a separation of powers, with a President, a single-chamber *National Assembly* elected by universal suffrage at age 21 in 12 electoral constituencies, and an independent judiciary. The President serves a six-year term, although in both 1995 and 2004 the terms of office of the then Presidents were extended from six to nine years through 'exceptional' constitutional amendments. The executive consists of the President and a Prime Minister and Cabinet appointed after consultation between the President and the National Assembly. A new electoral law passed in 2017 paved the way for a system of proportional representation

© Springer Nature Limited 2020
Palgrave Macmillan (ed.), *The Statesman's Yearbook 2020*,
https://doi.org/10.1057/978-1-349-95940-2_111

within 15 multi-member constituencies, while maintaining the tradition of agreed allocations of deputies for each religious community. By convention, the President is always a Maronite Christian, the Prime Minister a Sunni Muslim and the Speaker of the Assembly a Shia Muslim. In Aug. 1990, and again in July 1992, the National Assembly voted to increase its membership, and now has 128 deputies with equal numbers of Christians and Muslims (although Muslims make up a clear majority of the population).

National Anthem

'Kulluna lil watan lil 'ula lil 'alam' ('All of us for our country, flag and glory'); words by Rashid Nakhlé, tune by W. Sabra.

Government Chronology

Presidents since 1943.

1943–52	Béchara Khalil El-Khoury
1952–58	Camille Nemr Chamoun
1958–64	Fouad Abdallah Chehab
1964–70	Charles Alexandre Hélou
1970–76	Soleiman Kabalan Franjieh
1976–82	Elias Sarkis
1982–88	Amine Pierre Gemayel
1989	René Anis Moawad
1989–98	Elias Khalil Haraoui
1998–2007	Emile Geamil Lahoud
2007–08	Fouad Siniora (acting)
2008–14	Gen. Michel Suleiman
2014–16	Tammam Salam (acting)
2016–	Michel Aoun

Prime Ministers since 1943.

1943–45	Riyad as-Solh
1945	Abdulhamid Karame
1945–46	Abd' Rashin Sami as-Solh
1946	Saadi al-Munla
1946–51	Riyad as-Solh
1951	Hussein al-Oweini
1951–52	Abdullah Aref al-Yafi
1952	Abd Rashin Sami as-Solh
1952	Nazim al-Akkari
1952	Saeb Salam
1952	Abdullah Aref al-Yafi
1952–53	Amir Khalid Chehab
1953	Saeb Salam
1953–54	Abdullah Aref al-Yafi
1954–55	Abd Rashin Sami as-Solh
1955–56	Rashid Karame
1956	Abdullah Aref al-Yafi
1956–58	Abd Rashin Sami as-Solh
1958	Khalil al-Hibri
1958–60	Rashid Karame
1960	Ahmed Daouk
1960–61	Saeb Salam
1961–64	Rashid Karame
1964–65	Hussein al-Oweini
1965–66	Rashid Karame
1966	Abdullah Aref al-Yafi
1966–68	Rashid Karame

(continued)

1968–69	Abdullah Aref al-Yafi
1969–70	Rashid Karame
1970–73	Saeb Salam
1973	Amin al-Hafez
1973–74	Takieddin as-Solh
1974–75	Rashid as-Solh
1975	Nureddin Rifai
1975–76	Rashid Karame
1976–80	Sélim Ahmed Hoss
1980	Takieddin as-Solh
1980–84	Shafiq al-Wazzan
1984–87	Rashid Karame
1987–90	Sélim Ahmed Hoss
1990–92	Omar Karame
1992	Rashid as-Solh
1992–98	Rafiq al-Hariri
1998–2000	Sélim Ahmed Hoss
2000–04	Rafiq al-Hariri
2004–05	Omar Karame
2005	Najib Mikati
2005–09	Fouad Siniora
2009–11	Saad al-Hariri
2011–14	Najib Mikati
2014–16	Tammam Salam
2016–	Saad al-Hariri

Recent Elections

Much-delayed parliamentary elections were held on 6 May 2018. The Hizbollah-Amal alliance won 40 of 128 seats, the Free Patriotic Movement and its allies 29, the Future Movement and its allies 20, the Lebanese Forces and its allies 15 and the Progressive Socialist Party 9. Other parties won four seats or fewer. Turnout was 49·2%.

Indirect presidential elections were held in April 2014. A two-thirds majority must be achieved in order for a president to be elected in a first round of voting. As no candidate managed this in the first round of voting on 23 April or in four more rounds before the end of President Michel Suleiman's term on 25 May 2014, a sixth attempt was scheduled for 9 June. Eventually at the 46th attempt on 31 Oct. 2016 Michel Aoun was elected president, receiving 83 of 127 votes in parliament (easily securing the 50-percent-plus-one majority that was required).

Current Government

President: Michel Aoun; b. 1935 (Free Patriotic Movement; sworn in 31 Oct. 2016).

In Feb. 2019 the government comprised:

Prime Minister: Saad al-Hariri; b. 1970 (14 March Alliance, took office on 20 Dec. 2016, having previously been prime minister from Nov. 2009–June 2011).

Deputy Prime Minister: Ghassan Hasbani.

Minister of Agriculture: Hasan Lakkis. *Culture*: Muhammad Daoud. *Defence*: Elias Bou Saab. *Displaced Citizens*: Ghassan Atallah. *Economy and Commerce*: Mansour Bteich. *Education*: Akram Chehayeb. *Energy and Water*: Nada Boustani. *Environment*: Fadi Jreissati. *Finance*: Ali Hasan Khalil. *Foreign Affairs and Emigrants*: Gebran Bassil. *Health*: Jamil Jabaq. *Industry*: Wael Abou Faour. *Information*: Jamal Jarrah. *Interior*: Raya El Hassan. *Justice*: Albert Serhan. *Labour*: Camille Abousleiman. *Public Works and Transport*: Youssef Finianos. *Social Affairs*: Richard Kouyoumijan. *Telecommunications*: Mohamed Choucair. *Tourism*: Avedis Guidanian. *Youth and Sports*: Mohamad Fneich.

Office of the President (Arabic only): http://www.presidency.gov.lb

Current Leaders

Michel Aoun

Position
President

Introduction
Michel Aoun took office as president on 31 Oct. 2016, ending a two-and-a-half year political vacuum. A military leader during Lebanon's civil war, he has been a key figure on the political scene since returning from exile in 2005.

Early Life
Michel Aoun was born in Beirut's southern suburb of Haret Hreik on 18 Feb. 1935. A Maronite Christian, he enrolled in Beirut's military academy in 1955 and later graduated as an artillery officer in the Lebanese Army.

During the civil war that erupted in 1975, Aoun served as head of the Defence Brigade, which patrolled the Green Line separating east and west Beirut. Promoted to brigadier general in 1982, he commanded the largely Maronite Christian 8th Infantry Brigade, which recaptured southern and western Beirut from Syrian-backed Druze and Palestinian militias. In 1984 he was appointed general and four years later served as prime minister of the interim military government.

Aoun claimed the Taif Accords that ended Lebanon's civil war ceded too much control to Syria and he subsequently declared a 'war of liberation' in March 1989. However, his troops lost momentum against Syrian forces buoyed by US support following Syria's backing of the USA against Iraq in the first Gulf War. Having survived an assassination attempt, Aoun fled to Paris and remained in exile for the next 15 years.

He maintained popularity among Lebanese Christians and returned to Beirut in 2005 after the assassination of Prime Minister Rafiq al-Hariri prompted mass demonstrations calling for the removal of the Syrian army. In the parliamentary election that followed, Aoun was returned for the Free Patriotic Movement (FPM), which forged alliances with former opponents and, to the surprise of many, signed a memorandum of understanding with the militant Islamist Hizbollah group in 2006. As well as leading the FPM, Aoun spearheaded the Reform and Change bloc—the second largest grouping in parliament after the 2009 elections.

When President Michel Suleiman stepped down in May 2014 a political stalemate ensued. After 45 abortive attempts to elect a new president, a breakthrough occurred when former premier Saad al-Hariri agreed to back Aoun on the understanding that al-Hariri would be returned as premier. On 31 Oct. 2016 Aoun won parliamentary backing and was sworn in.

Career in Office
In a combative inaugural address, Gen. Aoun promised to defend Lebanon from terrorism, strengthen the military and take measures to enable over 1m. registered Syrian refugees in the country to return home.

Saad al-Hariri

Position
Prime Minister

Introduction
Saad al-Hariri, a Sunni Muslim, was appointed premier for the first time on 27 June 2009, after his pro-Western coalition, the 14 March Alliance, defeated a pro-Syrian, Hizbollah-led alliance in elections. However, in June 2011 he resigned amid political and sectarian divisions and then lived abroad until 2016. In Nov. that year Michel Aoun, whose election as president by parliament the previous month had ended a protracted political deadlock, turned to al-Hariri to form a new government. In May 2018 Hizbollah made significant gains in Lebanon's first legislative elections since 2009, although al-Hariri retained the premiership after winning the backing of the majority of parliamentarians.

Early Life
Al-Hariri was born on 18 April 1970, the son of former prime minister Rafiq al-Hariri. In 1992 he graduated in the USA with a business degree. After his father's assassination in 2005 he assumed the leadership of the Sunni Muslim Movement for the Future. Protesters demanded that Syrian forces withdraw from Lebanon and that a new independent government be formed. The pro-Syrian government of Omar Karami resigned on 13 April 2005, following the departure of the last Syrian troops. Al-Hariri meanwhile formed a wider anti-Syrian

coalition movement—the 14 March Alliance—that won control of parliament in elections in June that year and formed a government under Fouad Siniora as prime minister. However, Israel's military campaign against Hizbollah forces in 2006 aggravated Lebanon's fragile internal political balance.

Career in Office
Parliamentary elections were held in June 2009 and the 14 March Alliance won a majority of seats. In Sept. 2009 al-Hariri resigned as prime minister-designate when his proposed cabinet was rejected, but he was nevertheless reappointed by then President Michel Suleiman and formed a national unity government in Nov. However, the government then fell in Jan. 2011 when several Hizbollah ministers withdrew. He remained caretaker premier until June when his designated successor Najib Mikati finally formed a new administration. Al-Hariri subsequently left Lebanon and in 2012 Syria issued an arrest warrant against him for allegedly financing and arming forces opposed to President Assad. He spent the next few years living in France and Saudi Arabia before returning to Lebanon in Feb. 2016.

President Suleiman left office in May 2014, ushering in a prolonged political vacuum before parliament eventually elected a successor—Michel Aoun, a former army commander—in Oct. 2016. The following month Aoun named al-Hariri prime minister for the second time and he took office at the head of a new coalition government in Dec. In June 2017 Lebanon's rival parties agreed on a new electoral law introducing a proportional representation system and paving the way for proposed parliamentary elections in May 2018, and in Oct. the government passed the country's first budget since 2005.

In Nov. 2017, in speculative circumstances, al-Hariri announced his resignation as premier while in Saudi Arabia, but subsequently rescinded his decision in early Dec. following his return to Lebanon. He then secured a further term as premier following the May 2018 parliamentary elections—the first in nearly a decade—despite the advances made by Hizbollah and its allies.

Defence

There were 14,000 Syrian troops in the country in early 2005, but in March 2005 Lebanon and Syria agreed that the troops would be redeployed to the Bekaa Valley in the east of the country. They were subsequently all withdrawn from Lebanon. The United Nations Interim Force in Lebanon (UNIFIL), created in 1978, had a strength of 1,990 in June 2006. Following the conflict between Israel and Lebanon of July–Aug. 2006 the Security Council established UNIFIL II, a more powerful peacekeeping force deployed to maintain the ceasefire, support the Lebanese armed forces and aid humanitarian efforts. In Dec. 2017 UNIFIL II comprised 15,000 uniformed personnel from some 40 countries.

Conscription was reduced from 12 months to six in 2005, and was finally abolished in Feb. 2007.

Defence expenditure in 2012 totalled US$1,735m. (US$419 per capita), representing 4·2% of GDP.

Army

The strength of the Army was 57,000 in 2011 and includes a Presidential Guard and five special forces regiments. There is an internal security force, run by the ministry of the interior, some 20,000 strong.

Navy

A force of 1,100 personnel (2011) operate 11 patrol and coastal combatants. An additional seven inshore patrol craft are operated by customs.

Air Force

The Air Force had (2011) 1,000 personnel. Equipment in 2011 included four fighter aircraft and nine multi-role helicopters.

Economy

Agriculture accounted for 7·2% of GDP in 2014, industry 21·3% and services 71·5%.

Overview

Services contribute four-fifths of GDP, with the financial sector dominant. In 2015 the estimated asset-base of the banking sector was equivalent to 375% of GDP. Remittances are also vital, contributing US$7·4bn. in 2014. GDP expanded by 1·8% per year on average in the five years to 2016, while the fiscal deficit had reached US$4·9bn. by end of that year.

The economy has suffered as a result of ongoing regional unrest since 2011, especially the civil war in Syria, the Islamic State jihadist insurgency and civil discord in Yemen. The resulting influx of refugees has strained Lebanon's public services, jobs market and health care capacity. Yet despite a disruption in trade routes, tourism increased in 2016. Rising unemployment, especially among the young and unskilled, is a particularly pressing concern.

Currency
The unit of currency is the *Lebanese pound* (LBP) of 100 *piastres*. There was deflation of 0·8% in 2016 and inflation of 4·5% in 2017. In July 2005 foreign exchange reserves totalled US$10,627m., gold reserves were 9·22m. troy oz and total money supply was £Leb.3,005·7bn. The Lebanese pound has been pegged to the US dollar since Sept. 1999 at £Leb.1,507·5 = 1 US$.

Budget
The fiscal year is the calendar year.

In 2014 budgetary central government revenue totalled £Leb.14,467bn. and expenditure £Leb.18,812bn. Tax revenues in 2014 were £Leb.10,230bn. Main items of expenditure by economic type in 2014 were interest (£Leb.6,314bn.) and compensation of employees (£Leb.4,144bn.).

VAT of 10% was introduced in 2002. It was raised to 11% in 2018.

Performance
Total GDP was US$51·8bn. in 2017. Real GDP growth was 0·2% in 2015, 1·7% in 2016 and 1·5% in 2017.

Banking and Finance
The Bank of Lebanon (*Governor*, Riad Salameh) is the bank of issue. In Jan. 2008 there were 66 functioning banks (45 domestic and 21 foreign) of which 51 were commercial, 11 were investment and/or private and four were Islamic. Commercial bank deposits in May 2011 totalled US$110·5bn.

There is a stock exchange in Beirut (closed 1983–95).

Energy and Natural Resources

Environment
Lebanon's carbon dioxide emissions from the consumption of energy in 2011 accounted for 5·0 tonnes per capita.

Electricity
Installed capacity in 2011 was 3·2m. kW. Production in 2011 was 16·37bn. kWh and consumption per capita 3,842 kWh. Supply fails to meet demand and power cuts are frequent.

Minerals
There are no commercially viable deposits.

Agriculture
In 2013 there were around 132,000 ha. of arable land and 126,000 ha. of permanent crop land. Crop production (in 1,000 tonnes), 2013 estimates: potatoes, 412; tomatoes, 274; oranges, 163; wheat, 140; cucumbers and gherkins, 131; apples, 127; olives, 105; lemons and limes, 104.

Livestock (2013): goats, 550,000; sheep, 450,000; cattle, 80,500; pigs, 7,900; chickens, 59·5m.

Forestry
The forests of the past have been denuded by exploitation and in 2015 covered 0·14m. ha., or 13% of the total land area. Timber production was 26,000 cu. metres in 2011.

Fisheries
The catch in 2011 was an estimated 3,800 tonnes, mainly from sea fishing.

Industry
In 2014 industry accounted for 21·3% of GDP, with manufacturing contributing 9·3%. Manufactures include cement, flour, sulphuric acid and mineral water.

Labour
The labour force in 2013 was 1,628,000 (1,203,000 in 2003). 51·6% of the population aged 15–64 was economically active in 2013. In the same year 6·2% of the population was unemployed.

International Trade

Imports and Exports
Trade, 2010, in US$1m.: imports (c.i.f.), 17,970; exports (f.o.b.), 4,254. Main imports, 2010 (in US$1m.), were: machinery and transport equipment (4,100); mineral fuels, lubricants and related materials (3,674); manufactured goods (2,736). Main exports, 2010 (in US$1m.), were: gold (830); arms and ammunition (333); non-metallic mineral manufactures (273). In 2010 major import sources (in US$1m.) were: USA (1,919); China (1,639); Italy (1,394). Major export markets in 2010 (in US$1m.) were: Switzerland (503); UAE (419); France (349).

Communications

Roads
There were 6,970 km of roads in 2005, including 170 km of motorway. Registered vehicles in 2011 numbered 1,525,738. In 2007 there were 4,281 road accidents resulting in 487 deaths.

Rail
Railways are state-owned. There is 222 km of standard gauge track.

Civil Aviation
Beirut International Airport was served in 2010 by more than 40 airlines. It handled 5,960,414 passengers (5,913,225 on international flights) in 2012 and 84,911 tonnes of freight. The national airline is the state-owned Middle East Airlines. In 2012 scheduled airline traffic of Lebanese-based carriers flew 42·0m. km; passenger-km totalled 4·1bn. in the same year.

Shipping
Beirut is the largest port, followed by Tripoli, Jounieh and Saida (Sidon). In Jan. 2014 there were 33 ships of 300 GT or over registered, totalling 127,000 GT.

Telecommunications
In 2010 there were 887,800 landline telephone subscriptions (equivalent to 210·0 per 1,000 inhabitants) and 2,874,800 mobile phone subscriptions (or 680·0 per 1,000 inhabitants). In 2011, 52·0% of the population were internet users. In March 2012 there were 1·4m. Facebook users.

Social Institutions
Out of 178 countries analysed in the 2017 *Fragile States Index*—a list published jointly by the Fund for Peace and *Foreign Policy* magazine—Lebanon was ranked the 43rd most vulnerable to conflict or collapse. The index is based on 12 indicators of state vulnerability across social, political and economic categories.

Justice
The population in penal institutions in Dec. 2012 was 5,094 (118 per 100,000 of national population). The International Centre for Prison Studies estimated in 2014 that 66·2% of prisoners had yet to receive a trial. The death penalty is still in force. It was last used in 2004 when three people were executed. In 2015 the World Justice Project *Rule of Law Index*, which provides data on how the rule of law is experienced by the general public across eight categories, ranked Lebanon 62nd of 102 countries for criminal justice and 78th for civil justice.

Education
There are state and private primary and secondary schools. In 2007 there were 450,566 pupils with 32,412 teaching staff at primary schools; and 368,359 pupils with 40,919 teaching staff in secondary education. The Lebanese University, founded in 1951, is the only public university. Private universities include the American University of Beirut, founded in 1866 as the Syrian Protestant College; the Lebanese American University, established in 1924; and the Lebanese International University, established in 2001. There is a Lebanese Academy of Fine Arts, which is part of the University of Balamand. In 2007 there were 187,055 students in tertiary education and 21,778 academic staff. Adult literacy was 90% in 2007.

In 2007 public expenditure on education came to 2·7% of GNI and 9·6% of total government spending.

Health

There were 162 hospitals in 2008. The provision of hospital beds was 29 per 10,000 inhabitants in 2014. There were 9,876 doctors in 2007, and 4,316 dentists, 4,990 pharmacists and 1,699 nurses in 2008.

In *Water: At What Cost? The State of the World's Water 2016*, WaterAid reported that 1·0% of the population does not have access to safe water.

Religion

In 2010 an estimated 61·3% of the population were Muslims according to the Pew Research Center's Forum on Religion & Public Life (roughly similar numbers of Sunnis and Shias) and 38·3% Christians (mainly Catholics). Christians were in the majority at the time of the last census in 1932. In Feb. 2019 there were two cardinals.

Culture

World Heritage Sites

There are five UNESCO sites in Lebanon. Four were entered on the list in 1984: the ruins of Anjar, a city founded by the Muslim Arab caliph Walid I at the beginning of the 8th century; Baalbek, the most impressive ancient site in Lebanon and one of the most important Roman ruins in the Middle East; Byblos, the site of multi-layered ruins of one of the most ancient cities of Lebanon, dating back to Neolithic times; and Tyre, which has important archaeological remains, principally from Roman times. The Qadisha Valley and Bcharre district, inscribed in 1998, has been the site of monastic communities since the earliest years of Christianity. Its cedar trees, an example of which adorns the national flag, are survivors of a sacred forest.

Press

In 2009 there were 14 paid-for daily newspapers with a combined circulation of 244,000 and two free dailies. The newspapers with the highest circulation are *An-Nahar* and *As-Safir*.

Tourism

In 2012 there were 1,366,000 foreign tourists (excluding Syrians, Palestinians, students and same-day visitors), down from a record 2,168,000 in 2010.

Festivals

Major annual cultural events are the Al Bustan Festival of music, dance and theatre in Feb.–March; Hamra Festival in June; Baalbek International Festival, which reopened in 1997 after an absence of 23 years, in June–Aug.; Beiteddine Festival in July–Aug.; Tyre Festival; Byblos Festival; and the Beirut Film Festival.

Diplomatic Representatives

Of Lebanon in the United Kingdom (21 Kensington Palace Gdns, London, W8 4QN)
Ambassador: Rami Mortada.

Of the United Kingdom in Lebanon (Embassy Complex, Serail Hill, PO Box 11–471, Beirut)
Ambassador: Chris Rampling, MBE.

Of Lebanon in the USA (2560 28th St., NW, Washington, D.C., 20008)
Ambassador: Gabriel Issa.

Of the USA in Lebanon (PO Box 70-840, Antelias, Beirut)
Ambassador: Elizabeth H. Richard.

Of Lebanon to the United Nations
Ambassador: Amal Mudallali.

Of Lebanon to the European Union
Ambassador: Fadi Hajali.

Further Reading

Fisk, R., *Pity the Nation: Lebanon at War.* 3rd ed. 2001

Harris, William, *The New Face of Lebanon: History's Revenge.* 2005

Hirst, David, *Beware of Small States: Lebanon, Battleground of the Middle East.* 2010

Young, Michael, *The Ghosts of Martyrs Square: An Eyewitness Account of Lebanon's Life Struggle.* 2010

National library: Dar el Kutub, Parliament Sq., Beirut.

National Statistical Office: Kantary, Army St., Finance & Trade Building, 5th Floor, Beirut.

Website: http://www.cas.gov.lb

Lesotho

Muso oa Lesotho (Kingdom of Lesotho)

Capital: Maseru
Population projection, 2020: 2·32m.
GNI per capita, 2017: (PPP$) 3,255
HDI/world rank, 2017: 0·520/159=
Internet domain extension: .ls

Key Historical Events

Khoisan people were the earliest inhabitants of Lesotho; their rock-art at Liphofung cave is thought to date back several thousand years. Southern Africa's high plains were colonized by Bantu-speaking tribes from the north and west from around AD 500.

The Basotho nation was constituted in the 19th century under the leadership of Moshoeshoe, who brought together refugees from disparate groups scattered by Zulu expansionism in the region from around 1815. The first contact with European settlers came in 1833, when French missionaries obtained permission from Moshoeshoe to establish a base. Voortrekkers (early Boer pioneers) reached the territory in 1836 and signed a treaty of friendship with the Basotho the following year. Nevertheless, they declared a separate republic on Basotho land in 1843, which precipitated a series of territorial wars in the 1850s and 1860s. Moshoeshoe appealed for British protection, which was granted in 1868.

Boundary negotiations with the Voortrekkers were concluded in 1869, and resulted in tracts of Basotho land being ceded to the Orange Free State. In 1871 Basutoland was annexed to the Cape Colony, but a revolt by chief Moirosi in 1879 sparked disturbances that the Cape proved unable to manage. The Territory of Basutoland came under the direct control of the British government through the High Commissioner for South Africa in 1884. It was divided into seven administrative districts and ruled by a British Resident Commissioner from Maseru. He worked through a national assembly (Pitso) of hereditary chiefs under a paramount chief, the first of which was Lerothodi, son of King Moshoeshoe. Basutoland was still under British control when the Union of South Africa was founded in 1910. Plans to annex the colony were halted amid widespread local opposition to the South African National Party's apartheid policies.

In 1965 Basutoland achieved full internal self-government under King Moshoeshoe II, and on 4 Oct. 1966 it became an independent sovereign state as the Kingdom of Lesotho. Chief Leabua Jonathan, leader of the Basotho National Party and prime minister from 1965, suspended the constitution when the elections of 1970 were declared invalid. On 20 Jan. 1986, after a border blockade by the Republic of South Africa, Chief Jonathan was deposed in a bloodless military coup led by Maj.-Gen. Justin Lekhanya who granted significant powers to the king. King Moshoeshoe II was then deposed in Nov. 1990 and replaced by Letsie III.

Lekhanya was deposed in May 1991 and a democratic constitution was promulgated in April 1993. The elections in May 1998 were won by the ruling Lesotho Congress for Democracy. In Sept. 1998 an army mutiny prompted intervention from South Africa to support the government. Pakalitha Mosisili began a second five-year term as prime minister in 2002, a period that included the opening of the Lesotho Highlands Water Project, which supplies fresh water to South Africa, and two severe droughts. Mosisili was returned to power in elections in Feb. 2015 after the previous prime minister, Tom Thabane, fled to South Africa, accusing the military of trying to overthrow him. However, in June 2017 Mosisili lost early elections and Thabane resumed the premiership.

Territory and Population

Lesotho is an enclave within South Africa. The area is 30,355 sq. km (11,720 sq. miles).

The census in 2016 showed a total population of 2,007,201 (1,025,068 females); density, 66·1 per sq. km. In 2016 the population was 65·8% rural.

The UN gives a projected population for 2020 of 2·32m.

There are ten districts, all named after their chief towns, except Berea (chief town, Teyateyaneng). Area and population:

Region	Area (in sq. km.)	2016 census population
Berea	2,222	262,616
Butha-Buthe	1,767	118,242
Leribe	2,828	337,521
Mafeteng	2,119	178,222
Maseru	4,279	519,186
Mohale's Hoek	3,530	165,590
Mokhotlong	4,075	100,442
Qacha's Nek	2,349	74,566
Quthing	2,916	115,469
Thaba-Tseka	4,270	135,347

In 2016 the capital, Maseru, had a population of 330,760. Other major towns are: Maputsoe, 55,541; Mohale's Hoek, 40,040; Mafeteng, 39,754; Hlotse, 38,558; Botha-Bothe, 35,108; Quthing, 27,314; Teyateyaneng, 24,257.

The official languages are Sesotho and English.

The population is more than 98% Basotho. The rest is made up of Xhosas, plus some expatriate Europeans and Asians.

Social Statistics

2008 estimated births, 59,000; deaths, 35,000. Rates, 2008 estimates: birth (per 1,000 population), 28·9; death, 16·9. Annual population growth rate, 2000–08, 1·0%. Life expectancy has declined since 1990, largely owing to the huge number of people in the country with HIV, although it is now starting to rise again. It was 59·4 years in 1990 but fell to 43·7 in 2005. However, by 2013 it had risen gone back up to 49·4 years. Lesotho is also one of the few countries to have seen a rise in child and infant mortality since 1990. The number of deaths per 1,000 live births among children under five rose from 85 in 1990 to 114 in 2000 although it fell back to 100 in 2012. Similarly the infant mortality rate (the number of deaths per 1,000 live births among babies under one year of age) went up from 68 in 1990 to 80 in 2000 before falling back down to 74 in 2012. In 2013, 22·9% of all adults between 15 and 49 were infected with HIV—the second highest rate after Eswatini. Fertility rate, 2008, 3·3 births per woman.

Climate

A mild and temperate climate, with variable rainfall, but averaging 29" (725 mm) a year over most of the country. The rain falls mainly in the summer months of Oct. to April, while the winters are dry and may produce heavy frosts in lowland areas and frequent snow in the highlands. Temperatures in the lowlands range from a maximum of 90°F (32·2°C) in summer to a minimum of 20°F (–6·7°C) in winter.

Constitution and Government

Lesotho is a constitutional monarchy with the King as Head of State. Following the death of his father, Moshoeshoe II, **Letsie III** succeeded to the throne in Jan. 1996.

The 1993 constitution provided for a *National Assembly* comprising an elected 80-member lower house and a *Senate* of 22 principal chiefs and 11 members nominated by the King. For the elections of May 2002 a new voting system was introduced, increasing the number of seats in the National Assembly to 120, elected for a five-year term as before, but with 80 members in single-seat constituencies and 40 elected by proportional representation.

National Anthem

'Lesotho fatse la bontata rona' ('Lesotho, land of our fathers'); words by F. Coillard, tune by F.-S. Laur.

Recent Elections

Parliamentary elections were held on 3 June 2017. The All Basotho Convention won 48 of 120 seats, Democratic Congress 30, Lesotho Congress for Democracy 11, Alliance for Democrats 9, Movement for Economic Change 6, Basotho National Party 5 and Popular Front for Democracy 3. Five other parties won a single seat each and three seats remained vacant. Turnout was 46·4%.

Current Government

In Feb. 2019 the government comprised:

Prime Minister: Tom Thabane; b. 1939 (All Basotho Convention; sworn in 16 June 2017, having previously been prime minister from June 2012–March 2015).

Deputy Prime Minister and Minister of Parliamentary Affairs: Monyane Moleleki.

Minister of Agriculture and Food Security: Mahala Molapo. *Communications, Science and Technology:* Thesele 'Maseribane. *Defence and National Security:* Tefo Mapesela. *Development Planning:* Tlohelang Aumane. *Education and Training:* Ntoi Rapapa. *Energy and Meteorology:* Tsukutlane Au. *Finance:* Moeketsi Majoro. *Foreign Affairs and International Relations:* Lesego Makgothi. *Forestry, Range and Soil Conservation:* Leshoboro Mohlajoa. *Gender, Youth, Sport and Recreation:* Mahali Phamotse. *Health:* Nkaku Kabi. *Home Affairs:* Mokoto Hloaele. *Justice, Human Rights and Correctional Services:* Mokhele Moletsane. *Labour and Employment:* Keketso Rantšo. *Law and Constitutional Affairs:* Lebohang Hlaele. *Local Government and Chieftainship Affairs:* Litšoane Litšoane. *Mining:* Keketso Sello. *Police and Public Safety:* 'Mampho Mokhele. *Public Service:* Semano Sekatle. *Public Works and Transport:* Maliehe Prince Maliehe. *Small Business Development, Co-operatives and Marketing:* Chalane Phori. *Social Development:* 'Matebatso Doti. *Tourism, Environment and Culture:* Joang Molapo. *Trade and Industry:* Habofanoe Lehana. *Water:* Samonyane Ntsekele. *Minister in the Prime Minister's Office:* Temeki Tšolo.

The *College of Chiefs* settles the recognition and succession of Chiefs and adjudicates cases of inefficiency, criminality and absenteeism among them.

Government Website: http://www.gov.ls

Current Leaders

Tom Thabane

Position
Prime Minister

Introduction
Thomas Motsoahae Thabane became prime minister on 16 June 2017, heading a coalition government following snap parliamentary elections. Thabane previously held the post from June 2012 to March 2015, ending 14 years of Lesotho Congress for Democracy (LCD) rule. His priorities included tackling poverty, education, curbing violent crime, addressing corruption and promoting economic development.

Early Life
Born in 1939, Thabane worked in the ministry of health and education from 1970–72 and at the ministry of justice from 1972–76. In 1976 he became principal secretary for the interior and from 1978–83 was principal secretary for health. He then took over the foreign affairs portfolio until 1985 before serving a further year as principal secretary for the interior.

After the overthrow of Leabua Jonathan's government in Jan. 1986, Thabane served in the military administration that ruled for seven years. As secretary to the military council, he negotiated the return of political exiles and smoothed relations between the military government and civilian political groups. He was minister of foreign affairs, information and broadcasting in 1990 and 1991 and chaired the committee responsible for creating the constituent assembly that in turn paved the way for democratic multi-party elections.

From 1991–94 Thabane worked as a development consultant, based in South Africa. In 1995 he began a three-year term as special political adviser to the prime minister, Ntsu Mokhehle. From 1998–2006 he served variously as foreign minister, minister of home affairs and public safety, and minister of communications, science and technology in the government of Pakalitha Mosisili. However, in 2006 he broke with the ruling LCD to form the All Basotho Convention (ABC).

In 2012 elections, Mosisili's newly formed Democratic Congress was unable to form a coalition despite winning the most seats. The ABC agreed to enter government with the LCD and two smaller parties and Thabane became premier on 8 June 2012.

Career in Office
In June 2014 a political crisis developed as Thabane attempted to suspend parliament after being threatened with a no confidence vote. He fled to South Africa from Aug.–Sept., accusing the military of trying to stage a coup in favour of deputy prime minister Mothetjoa Metsing. Tensions were subsequently defused when early parliamentary elections were called.

Thabane's term as prime minister ended on 17 March 2015 following elections held the previous month, where he was succeeded by Mosisili and the Democratic Congress. In May 2015 he fled the country for a second time fearing assassination. He returned on 12 Feb. 2017. Owing to Lesotho's growing political instability and his cabinet's inability to contain a violent conflict between military and police forces, Mosisili lost a confidence vote in parliament on 1 March 2017. On 6 June 2017, following Lesotho's third parliamentary elections in five years, it was announced that the ABC had won 48 seats. Whilst not a clear majority, it secured Thabane's return as prime minister at the head of a coalition government.

Thabane pledged to end the political uncertainty, party splits and fragile coalitions that had resulted in failed governments. However, with an agenda of radical reforms, he was expected to face strong opposition despite his electoral victory. Just before his inauguration, his estranged wife, Lipolelo Thabane, was murdered, casting suspicion that her death was politically motivated.

His ambitious plans also included voluntary demilitarization, reforming the regional Southern African Development Community (SADC) to promote further regional economic integration and ending corruption. On 2 Dec. 2017 a seven-nation SADC peacekeeping force of over 250 soldiers was deployed to Lesotho, with a mandate to protect Thabane's government while taking action against renegade soldiers associated with the murder of a military chief. The force ended its mission in Nov. 2018 despite fears of further instability after its departure. Also that month the government launched a three-day 'multi-stakeholder' national dialogue in an attempt to resolve outstanding political conflicts.

Defence

South African and Batswanan troops intervened after a mutiny by Lesotho's armed forces in Sept. 1998. The foreign forces were withdrawn in May 1999.

The Royal Lesotho Defence Force has about 2,000 personnel. Defence expenditure totalled US$54m. in 2013 (US$28 per capita), representing 2·1% of GDP.

Economy

In 2014 agriculture accounted for 5·9% of GDP, industry 33·0% and services 61·1%.

Overview

Lesotho's economy is heavily integrated with that of South Africa. Its only significant natural resource is water, exported to South Africa via the Lesotho Highlands Water Project. Subsistence agriculture dominates, although the textiles sector also has a significant role in generating employment and exports. The economy is heavily dependent on Southern African Customs Union (SACU) receipts and workers' remittances. Lesotho is a member of the Common Monetary Area together with Eswatini, Namibia and South Africa.

Following several sluggish years, economic growth exceeded 4% in three consecutive years from 2006 to 2008 before slowing to 3·8% in 2009 as a result of the global slowdown. The crisis resulted in a fall in textile and diamond exports and a drop in SACU revenues and remittances. Growth then averaged 4·5% per annum between 2010 and 2015, driven largely by the construction sector. However, there is significant income inequality, with the rural population suffering from high youth unemployment and poverty. According to the United Nations *Human Development Report 2016*, 59·7%

of the population lived below the international poverty line of US$1·90 (PPP) per day.

Inflation has remained in single digits, but the economy is vulnerable to volatility in SACU revenues that finance up to 50% of the national budget. Long-term prosperity will depend on finding new growth engines, accelerating structural reforms and developing a more dynamic private sector.

Currency

The unit of currency is the *loti* (plural *maloti*) (LSL) of 100 *lisente*, at par with the South African rand, which is legal tender. Total money supply in July 2005 was 1,659m. maloti and foreign exchange reserves were US$539m. Inflation was 6·2% in 2016 and 5·3% in 2017.

Budget

The fiscal year is 1 April–31 March. Revenues in 2011–12 were 9,103m. maloti and expenditures 10,100m. maloti. Tax revenue accounted for 73·6% of revenues in 2011–12; current expenditure accounted for 85·5% of expenditures.

The standard rate of VAT is 15%.

Performance

Real GDP growth was 2·5% in 2015 and 3·1% in 2016 before contracting by 1·6% in 2017. Total GDP in 2017 was US$2·6bn.

Banking and Finance

The Central Bank of Lesotho (*Governor*, Rets'elisitsoe Adelaide Matlanyane) is the bank of issue, founded in 1982 to succeed the Lesotho Monetary Authority. There are four commercial banks (First National Bank of Lesotho, Lesotho Post Bank, Nedbank Lesotho and Standard Lesotho Bank). Gross national savings were estimated at 12·2% of GNI in 2010, compared to 25·8% of GNI in 2009. The decline in savings mainly reflected lower private sector savings as household disposable income fell during the year. Foreign debt was US$726m. in 2010, representing 28·4% of GNI.

Energy and Natural Resources

Environment

Lesotho's carbon dioxide emissions from the consumption of energy in 2011 were the equivalent of 0·2 tonnes per capita.

Electricity

Capacity (2011 estimate) 80,000 kW. Production in 2011 was 549m. kWh (all hydro-electric). Consumption in 2011 was 723m. kWh.

Minerals

Diamonds are the main product; 2009 output was 91,815 carats (up from 721 carats in 2002). The huge increase was owing to the start of commercial operations at Letseng Diamonds mine in 2004. Gravel and crushed rock production (2009 estimate), 300,000 cu. metres.

Agriculture

The chief crops were (2011 production estimates in 1,000 tonnes): potatoes, 112; maize, 73; wheat, 20; sorghum, 10. Soil conservation and the improvement of crops and pasture are matters of vital importance. In 2013 there were 248,000 ha. of arable land and an estimated 4,000 ha. of permanent crop land.

Livestock (2013): sheep, 1·41m.; goats, 839,000; cattle, 548,000; asses, 101,000; chickens, 367,000.

Forestry

In 2015 Lesotho's total forest area was 49,000 ha., or 2% of the land area. Timber production was 2·10m. cu. metres in 2011.

Fisheries

The catch in 2014 was 52 tonnes, exclusively from inland waters.

Industry

Important industries are food products, beverages, textiles and chemical products. In 2014 industry accounted for 33·0% of GDP, with manufacturing contributing 11·2%.

Labour

The labour force in 2013 was 871,000 (798,000 in 2003). 67·4% of the population aged 15–64 was economically active in 2013. In the same year 24·6% of the population was unemployed.

Lesotho had 15,000 people living in slavery according to the Walk Free Foundation's 2013 *Global Slavery Index*.

International Trade

Lesotho is a member of the Southern African Customs Union (SACU) with Botswana, Eswatini, Namibia and South Africa.

Imports and Exports

Trade, 2008, in US$1m.: imports (c.i.f.), 1,066; exports (f.o.b.), 245.

The principal imports in 2008 (in US$1m.) were: machinery and transport equipment (208); food (177); miscellaneous manufactured articles (152). The principal exports in 2008 (in US$1m.) were: machinery and transport equipment (100); miscellaneous manufactured articles (65); food (33).

South Africa accounted for 95% of imports in 2008 and 83% of exports. Other significant trading partners are Japan and Germany for imports and the USA for exports.

Communications

Roads

In 2009 the road network totalled about 6,550 km, of which around 1,220 km were paved. There were 75,000 motor vehicles in 2009 including 34,000 light vehicles, 21,000 medium vehicles and 13,000 minibuses. There were 402 deaths as a result of road accidents in 2007.

Rail

A branch line built by the South African Railways, one mile long, connects Maseru with the Bloemfontein–Natal line at Marseilles for transport of cargo.

Civil Aviation

There are direct flights from Maseru's Moshoeshoe International Airport to Johannesburg with the South African airline Airlink. A Lesotho-based airline, Maluti Sky, ceased operations in 2017.

Telecommunications

In 2010 there were 38,600 landline telephone subscriptions (equivalent to 17·8 per 1,000 inhabitants) and 987,400 mobile phone subscriptions (or 454·8 per 1,000 inhabitants). There were 38·6 internet users per 1,000 inhabitants in 2010.

Social Institutions

Out of 178 countries analysed in the 2017 *Fragile States Index*—a list published jointly by the Fund for Peace and *Foreign Policy* magazine—Lesotho was ranked the 62nd most vulnerable to conflict or collapse. The index is based on 12 indicators of state vulnerability across social, political and economic categories.

Justice

The legal system is based on Roman-Dutch law. The Lesotho High Court and the Court of Appeal are situated in Maseru, and there are Magistrates' Courts in the districts.

The population in penal institutions in 2012 was 2,564 (121 per 100,000 of national population).

Education

Education levels: pre-school, 3 to 5 years; first level (elementary), 6 to 12; second level (secondary or teacher training or technical training), 7 to 13; third level (university or teacher training college). Free primary education was introduced in 2000. Lesotho has the highest proportion of female pupils at secondary schools in Africa, with 56% in 2007. In 2006 there were 424,855 pupils in primary schools with 10,513 teaching staff, 93,996 pupils in secondary schools with 3,725 teaching staff and 8,500 students in higher education with 638 academic staff. The National University of Lesotho was established in 1975 at Roma; enrolment in 2006–07, 8,566 students. There are eight government-supported technical and vocational training institutions as well as a teacher training college, the Lesotho College of Education. The adult literacy rate in 2008 was 90% (among the highest in Africa).

In 2008 public expenditure on education came to 11·4% of GDP and 24·7% of total government spending (one of the highest percentages of any country).

Health

In 2011 there were 232 physicians, 20 dentists and 41 pharmacists. There were 13 hospital beds per 10,000 inhabitants in 2006.

In *Water: At What Cost? The State of the World's Water 2016*, WaterAid reported that 18·2% of the population does not have access to safe water.

Religion

A study by the Pew Research Center's Forum on Religion & Public Life estimated that there were 1·08m. Protestants in 2010 and 999,000 Catholics, with most of the remainder of the population being religiously unaffiliated. In Feb. 2019 was one Roman Catholic cardinal.

Culture

World Heritage Sites

Lesotho has one site on the UNESCO World Heritage List, shared with South Africa: Maloti-Drakensberg Park (added to the list in 2013), a transboundary site composed of the Sehlabathebe National Park in Lesotho and the uKhahlamba Drakensberg Park in South Africa.

Press

There were 14 non-daily newspapers and periodicals in 2008, but no dailies.

Tourism

In 2010 there were a record 425,870 non-resident visitors, up from 343,743 in 2009 and 293,073 in 2008.

Festivals

The Morija Arts & Cultural Festival is held annually at Morija, where missionaries first arrived in Lesotho in 1833.

Diplomatic Representatives

Of Lesotho in the United Kingdom (7 Chesham Pl., London, SW1X 8HN)
   Acting High Commissioner: Mosele Majoro.

Of the United Kingdom in Lesotho (High Commission in Maseru closed in 2005)
   High Commissioner: Nigel Casey, MVO (resides in Pretoria, South Africa).

Of Lesotho in the USA (2511 Massachusetts Ave., NW, Washington, D.C., 20008)
   Ambassador: Sankatana Gabriel Maja.

Of the USA in Lesotho (254 Kingsway Ave., Maseru 100)
   Ambassador: Rebecca E. Gonzales.

Of Lesotho to the United Nations
   Ambassador: Nkopane Raseeng Monyane.

Of Lesotho to the European Union
   Ambassador: Mpeo Mahase-Moiloa.

Further Reading

Bureau of Statistics. *Statistical Reports.* [Various years]
Haliburton, G. M., *A Historical Dictionary of Lesotho.* 1977
Machobane, L. B. B. J., *Government and Change in Lesotho, 1880–1966: A Study of Political Institutions.* 1990
Rosenberg, Scott, Weisfelder, Richard F. and Frisbie-Fulton, Michelle, (eds) *Historical Dictionary of Lesotho.* 2003
National Statistical Office: Bureau of Statistics, PO Box 455, Maseru 100.

Liberia

Republic of Liberia

Capital: Monrovia
Population projection, 2020: 5·10m.
GNI per capita, 2017: (PPP$) 667
HDI/world rank, 2017: 0·435/181
Internet domain extension: .lr

Key Historical Events

The Republic of Liberia was created on the Grain Coast for freed American slaves. In 1822 a settlement was formed near the spot where Monrovia now stands. On 26 July 1847 the state was constituted as the Free and Independent Republic of Liberia.

On 12 April 1980 President Tolbert was assassinated and his government overthrown in a coup led by Master-Sergeant Samuel Doe. At the beginning of 1990 rebel forces entered Liberia from the north and fought their way successfully southwards to confront President Doe's forces in Monrovia. The rebels comprised the National Patriotic Front of Liberia (NPFL) led by Charles Taylor, and the hostile breakaway Independent National Patriotic Front led by Prince Johnson. A peacekeeping force dispatched by the Economic Community of West African States (ECOWAS) disembarked at Monrovia on 25 Aug. 1990. On 9 Sept. President Doe was assassinated by Johnson's rebels. ECOWAS installed a provisional government led by Amos Sawyer. Charles Taylor declared himself president, as did the former vice-president, Harry Moniba. A succession of ceasefires was negotiated and broken. An ECOWAS-sponsored peace agreement was signed on 17 Aug. 1996 in Abuja, providing for the disarmament of all factions by the end of Jan. 1997 and the election of a president on 31 May 1997. By the end of Jan. 1997 some 20,000 out of approximately 60,000 insurgents had surrendered their arms. It is estimated that up to 200,000 people died in the civil war and up to 1m. were made homeless. Charles Taylor was elected president in July 1997. In Feb. 2002 Taylor declared a state of emergency after an attack by a group of rebels on the town of Kley, where thousands of refugees from Sierra Leone were encamped.

In Aug. 2003 the UN called for the immediate deployment of an ECOWAS peacekeeping force, to be replaced by a full UN force on 1 Oct. Nigerian peacekeepers arrived on 4 Aug. 2003. Taylor relinquished power to his vice-president, Moses Blah, and to a transitional government on 11 Aug. In Nov. 2005 Ellen Johnson-Sirleaf won presidential elections to become Africa's first elected female head of state. In May 2012 Charles Taylor received a 50-year prison sentence for war crimes from the UN-sponsored Special Court for Sierra Leone.

Territory and Population

Liberia is bounded in the northwest by Sierra Leone, north by Guinea, east by Côte d'Ivoire and southwest by the Atlantic Ocean. The total area is 97,036 sq. km. At the last census, in 2008, the population was 3,476,608; density, 36 per sq. km.

The UN gives a projected population for 2020 of 5·10m. Liberia's population has doubled since the mid-1990s.

In 2007, 59·5% of the population lived in urban areas. English is the official language spoken by 20% of the population. The rest belong in the main to three linguistic groups: Mande, West Atlantic and the Kwa. These are in turn subdivided into 16 ethnic groups: Bassa, Bella, Gbandi, Mende, Gio, Dey, Mano, Gola, Kpelle, Kissi, Krahn, Kru, Lorma, Mandingo, Vai and Grebo.

The population of Monrovia (the capital) was 970,824 in 2008 including its suburbs.

There are 15 counties, whose areas, populations and capitals are as follows:

County	Sq. km	2008 population	Chief town
Bomi	1,942	84,119	Tubmanburg
Bong	8,769	333,481	Gbarnga
Gbarpolu	9,685	83,388	Bepolu
Grand Bassa	7,932	221,693	Buchanan
Grand Cape Mount	5,160	127,076	Robertsport
Grand Gedeh	10,480	125,258	Zwedru
Grand Kru	3,894	57,913	Barclayville
Lofa	9,978	276,863	Voinjama
Margibi	2,615	209,923	Kakata
Maryland	2,296	135,938	Harper
Montserrado	1,908	1,118,241	Bensonville
Nimba	11,546	462,026	Saniquillie
River Cess	5,592	71,509	Cesstos City
River Gee	5,110	66,789	Fish Town
Sinoe	10,133	102,391	Greenville

Social Statistics

2008 births, estimate, 145,000; deaths, 40,000. 2008 rates (per 1,000 population), estimate: birth, 38·3; death, 10·5. Annual population growth rate, 2000–08, 3·7%. Life expectancy at birth (2013): 59·6 years for men and 61·5 years for women. Infant mortality in 2010 was at 74 per 1,000 live births. Fertility rate, 2008, 5·9 births per woman.

Climate

An equatorial climate, with constant high temperatures and plentiful rainfall, although Jan. to May is drier than the rest of the year. Monrovia, Jan. 79°F (26·1°C), July 76°F (24·4°C). Annual rainfall 206" (5,138 mm).

Constitution and Government

A constitution was approved by referendum in July 1984 and came into force on 6 Jan. 1986. Under it the *National Assembly* consisted of a 26-member *Senate* and a 64-member *House of Representatives*. For the elections of 2005 the number of seats in the Senate was increased to 30 and in 2010 a further nine seats were added to the House of Representatives, bringing the total to 73. The executive power of the state is vested in the *President*, who may serve up to two six-year terms.

National Anthem

'All hail, Liberia, hail!'; words by President Daniel Warner, tune by O. Luca.

Recent Elections

In the first round of presidential elections held on 10 Oct. 2017 George Weah of the Coalition for Democratic Change (CDC) received 38·4% of the vote, followed by Joseph Boakai of the Unity Party (UP) with 28·8% and Charles Brumskine of the Liberty Party with 9·6%. There were 17 other candidates. Turnout was 75·2%. With no candidate receiving an absolute majority a run-off had been scheduled to take place on 7 Nov. 2017 but was postponed after Charles Brumskine challenged the outcome. However, the Supreme Court confirmed the result and announced that the election would be rerun on 26 Dec. 2017. Weah won with 61·5% of the vote against Boakai with 38·5%. Turnout in the run-off was 55·8%.

In the elections to the House of Representatives also on 10 Oct. 2017 the CDC won 21 seats; UP, 20; the People's Unification Party, 5; the All Liberia Party, 3; the Liberal Party, 3; the Movement for Democracy and Reconstruction, 2. Six parties won one seat each and independents 13. Elections for half of the seats in the Senate were held on 20 Dec. 2014. As a result the UP held 8 of the 30 seats; the Congress for Democratic Change, 4; the National Patriotic Party, 4; and the Liberty Party, 3. Five parties held one seat each and independents also five with one seat vacant. The elections were scheduled to take place on 14 Oct. 2014 but were postponed by the Electoral Commission owing to an outbreak of Ebola virus disease earlier that year.

Current Government

President: George Weah; b. 1966 (Coalition for Democratic Change; sworn in 22 Jan. 2018).

In Feb. 2019 the government comprised:

Vice-President: Jewel Howard-Taylor.

Minister of Agriculture: Mogana S. Flomo, Jr. *Commerce and Industry:* Wilson K. Tarpeh. *Education:* Ansu D. Sonii. *Finance and Development Planning:* Samuel D. Tweh, Jr. *Foreign Affairs:* Gbehzohngar Findley. *Gender, Children and Social Protection (acting):* Alice Johnson-Howard. *Health and Social Welfare:* Dr Williamina Jallah. *Information, Culture and Tourism:* Eugene Lenn Nagbe. *Internal Affairs:* Varney A. Sirleaf. *Justice and Attorney General:* Musa F. Dean. *Labour:* Moses Y. Kollie. *Lands, Mines and Energy:* Gesler E. Murray. *National Defence:* Daniel Dee Ziankahn. *Posts and Telecommunications:* Cooper W. Kruah. *Public Works:* Mobutu Nyenpan. *Transport:* Samuel Wlue. *Youth and Sports:* D. Zeogar Wilson. *Minister of State for Presidential Affairs:* Nathaniel McGill. *Minister of State Without Portfolio:* Trokon A. Kpui.

Government Website: http://www.emansion.gov.lr

Current Leaders

George Weah

Position

President

Introduction

George Weah took office as president on 22 Jan. 2018. Prior to his political career, he was an internationally decorated professional footballer.

Early Life

George Tawlon Manneh Oppong Ousman Weah was born on 1 Oct. 1966 in Grand Kru County, one of Liberia's most underdeveloped areas. He was schooled in Monrovia and at the age of 15 began playing soccer for the Young Survivors youth club.

Weah signed for leading French football club AS Monaco in 1988 and then moved to Paris Saint-Germain four years later. In 1995 he transferred to AC Milan in Italy and helped them win the top Italian league title twice, in 1995 and 1999. In 2000 he played in the English Premier League for both Chelsea and Manchester City before joining Olympique de Marseille of France in 2001. His football career ended in Aug. 2003 after a period with Al-Jazira in the United Arab Emirates. During his career, Weah was named FIFA World Player of the Year in 1995, as well as African Footballer of the Year three times.

Heavily involved in humanitarian work, he became a UNICEF Goodwill Ambassador in April 1997. Liberia's civil war had ended in 1997, and in 2005 Weah ran unsuccessfully for the state presidency backed by a new political party, the Congress for Democratic Change. In 2011 he graduated in business management from DeVry University in Florida, USA. In the same year, he ran unsuccessfully for the vice-presidency but in 2014 was elected to the Senate for Montserrado County. In the second round of the 2017 national presidential election he defeated Joseph Boakai with more than 61% of the vote.

Career in Office

Weah's presidential victory marked Liberia's first peaceful democratic transition in over seven decades. He inherited one of the world's poorest economies, but stated his intention to eradicate corruption, reform the economy, combat illiteracy and improve living conditions. One of his first acts in office was to slash his own salary and benefits by 25%.

In Sept. 2018 the government banned 15 people, including former president Ellen Johnson Sirleaf's son, from leaving Liberia as part of a corruption investigation.

Defence

In June 2003 UN Secretary-General Kofi Annan called for an international peacekeeping force to restore peace after fighting broke out between government forces and Liberians United for Reconciliation and Democracy (LURD). An ECOWAS peacekeeping force of over 3,000 troops was deployed initially, but was replaced by the United Nations Mission in Liberia (UNMIL). UNMIL had 15,000 personnel at its peak but its mission ended in March 2018.

The Armed Forces of Liberia (AFL) were created in 2007 to replace the Liberian Army, which was demobilized in 1999. In 2009 there were approximately 2,100 troops. The AFL became operational in June 2013 when a Liberian platoon was deployed to Mali as part of the African-led International Support Mission in Mali (AFISMA).

Defence expenditure totalled US$13m. in 2011 (US$3 per capita), representing 0·8% of GDP.

Economy

Agriculture accounted for 39% of GDP in 2012, industry 16% and services 45%.

Overview

Liberia is one of the world's poorest countries and relies heavily on foreign aid despite possessing rich natural resources. Years of civil war and government mismanagement destroyed much of the economy's human and physical capital, especially in the capital city of Monrovia. However, with the country's transition towards democratically-elected government since the early years of the century, its economy has benefited from a period of post-war reconstruction.

In 2007, four years after the end of the second civil war, real GDP growth rose to 12·7%, supported by continued recovery in agriculture, mining and services. Growth then averaged 7% per year between 2008 and 2013, driven largely by commodities exports (principally iron ore and rubber). Foreign direct investment (FDI) has been strong in the iron ore and palm oil sectors, while construction activity has experienced rapid growth in the last decade. The agricultural and manufacturing sectors, however, have been hampered by low productivity and poor infrastructure.

An outbreak of the Ebola virus from March 2014 had a severe impact on economic and social progress, although the disease has been progressively contained. The related cost of healthcare provision strained government finances, while fear of an epidemic led to a slowdown in economic activity. GDP grew by only 0·7% in 2014 and flatlined in 2015 before contracting by 1·6% in 2016.

By the end of 2017 the economy showed signs of a resurgence, with GDP growth for the year estimated at 2·5%. This was largely driven by the recovery of the mining sector, which benefitted from a rise in global commodity prices. However, 2017 also saw a budget deficit equivalent to 7·4% of GDP. The government increased the general sales tax and petroleum storage surcharge, among other revenue measures, to contain it.

In the medium term, job creation, education, infrastructure rehabilitation and tackling corruption are key priorities. Slower global demand for commodities and weakened FDI inflows following the 2014 Ebola outbreak continue to pose challenges to the economic outlook.

Currency

US currency is legal tender. There is a *Liberian dollar* (LRD), in theory at parity with the US dollar. Between 1993 and March 2000 different notes were in use in government-held Monrovia and the rebel-held country areas, but on 27 March 2000 a set of new notes went into circulation to end the years of trading in dual banknotes. Inflation was 8·8% in 2016 and 12·4% in 2017. Total money supply was L$4,316m. in July 2005 and foreign exchange reserves were US$21m.

Budget

The fiscal year begins on 1 July. Revenue in 2010–11 was US$334·6m.; expenditure was US$423·2m. Tax revenue accounted for 80·5% of revenues in 2010–11; current expenditure accounted for 71·3% of expenditures.

Performance

There was zero real GDP growth in 2015. The economy contracted by 1·6% in 2016 and grew by 2·5% in 2017. Total GDP was US$2·2bn. in 2017.

Banking and Finance

The Central Bank of Liberia opened on 18 Oct. 1999. The *Governor* of the bank is Nathaniel Patray. There were nine banks in operation in March 2018. External debt was US$228m. in 2010, representing 28·3% of GNI.

Energy and Natural Resources

Environment

Liberia's carbon dioxide emissions from the consumption of energy were the equivalent of 0·2 tonnes per capita in 2011.

Electricity

Installed capacity in 2011 was estimated at 197,000 kW. Production in 2011 was approximately 353m. kWh. Consumption per capita in 2011 was about 87 kWh.

Minerals

2010 estimates: gold production 666 kg and diamond production 26,591 carats.

Agriculture

In 2007 the agricultural population was approximately 2·31m., of which about 853,000 were economically active. There were an estimated 385,000 ha. of arable land in 2007 and 215,000 ha. of permanent crops. Principal crops (2013 estimates) in 1,000 tonnes: cassava, 529; rice, 270; sugarcane, 265; palm fruit oil, 171; bananas, 131; natural rubber, 75; plantains, 47; palm oil, 42; taro, 28; sweet potatoes, 23. Coffee, cocoa and palm kernels are produced mainly by the traditional agricultural sector.

Livestock (2013 estimates): goats, 345,000; pigs, 292,000; sheep, 275,000; cattle, 42,000; chickens, 8m.

Livestock products (2013 estimates) in tonnes: meat, 33,000; milk, 800; eggs, 5,000.

Forestry

Forest area was 4·18m. ha. (43% of the land area) in 2015. In 2011, 7·74m. cu. metres of roundwood were cut. There are rubber plantations.

Fisheries

Fish landings in 2012 were an estimated 9,500 tonnes, mainly from sea fishing.

Industry

There are a number of small factories. Production of cement, cigarettes, soft drinks, palm oil and beer are the main industries.

Labour

In 2010 the labour force was 1,374,000 (52·3% males). Liberia had 30,000 people living in slavery according to the Walk Free Foundation's 2013 *Global Slavery Index.*

International Trade

Imports and Exports

Imports in 2013 were US$1,210m. and exports US$540m. Main import partners are Côte d'Ivoire, Japan and China. Principal export partners are China, France and Poland.

Main imports are food and live animals, petroleum and petroleum products, and machinery and transport equipment. Main exports are rubber, and logs and timber.

Communications

Roads

The road network totals around 10,000 km, much of it in extremely poor condition. In 2007 there were 7,400 passenger cars in use and 2,800 lorries and vans.

Rail

There is a total of 490 km single track. A 148 km freight line connects iron mines to Monrovia. There is a line from Bong to Monrovia (78 km). The railways were out of use for many years because of the civil wars but there is now some traffic, both freight and passenger. However, large sections of track have been dismantled.

Civil Aviation

There are two international airports (Roberts International and Sprigg Payne), both near Monrovia. In 2010 there were services to Abidjan, Accra, Addis Ababa, Banjul, Brussels, Casablanca, Conakry, Freetown, Lagos and Nairobi as well as internal flights.

Shipping

There are ports at Buchanan, Greenville, Harper and Monrovia. Over 4,000 vessels entered Monrovia in 2013. The Liberian government requires only a modest registration fee and an almost nominal annual charge and maintains no control over the operation of ships flying the Liberian flag. In Jan. 2014 there were 3,025 ships of 300 GT or over registered, totalling 128·85m. GT (a figure only exceeded by Panama's fleet). Of the 3,025 vessels registered, 984 were container ships, 825 oil tankers, 809 bulk carriers, 289 general cargo ships, 115 liquid gas tankers and three passenger ships.

Telecommunications

In 2009 Liberia had just 2,200 main (fixed) telephone lines, but there were 1,058,000 mobile phone subscribers. No other country had such a high ratio of mobile phone subscriptions to fixed telephone lines in 2009. There were an estimated 5·1 internet users per 1,000 inhabitants in 2009.

Social Institutions

Out of 178 countries analysed in the 2017 *Fragile States Index*—a list published jointly by the Fund for Peace and *Foreign Policy* magazine—Liberia was ranked the 27th most vulnerable to conflict or collapse. The index is based on 12 indicators of state vulnerability across social, political and economic categories.

Justice

Liberia is governed by a dual system of statutory law. The modern sector is regulated by Anglo-American common law with the indigenous sector following customary law based on unwritten tribal practices. Following a 2003 proposal by UNMIL (United Nations Mission in Liberia), which only left the country in March 2018, a scheme to rebuild the post-civil war justice system was introduced. However, reforms are progressing at a slow rate and the judiciary remains severely dysfunctional.

The International Centre for Prison Studies estimated in 2014 that 83·0% of prisoners had yet to receive a trial. In 2015 the World Justice Project *Rule of Law Index*, which provides data on how the rule of law is experienced by the general public across eight categories, ranked Liberia 92nd of 102 countries for criminal justice and 81st for civil justice.

The population in penal institutions in 2012 was 1,930 (46 per 100,000 of national population).

Education

Schools are classified as: (1) Public schools, maintained and run by the government; (2) Mission schools, supported by foreign Missions and subsidized by the government, and operated by qualified Missionaries and Liberian teachers; (3) Private schools, maintained by endowments and sometimes subsidized by the government.

Adult literacy in 2009 was estimated at 59·1%.

Health

In 2008 there were 51 physicians, 978 nursing and midwifery personnel, four dentistry personnel and 269 pharmaceutical personnel. The John F. Kennedy Memorial Hospital in Monrovia is the country's leading health care institution. The Ebola outbreak of 2014–15 resulted in 4,809 deaths.

In *Water: At What Cost? The State of the World's Water 2016*, WaterAid reported that 24·4% of the population does not have access to safe water.

Religion

In 2010 there were an estimated 3·4m. Christians (mainly Protestants) and 480,000 Muslims (mainly Sunnis) according to the Pew Research Center's Forum on Religion & Public Life.

Culture

Press

There were seven paid-for daily newspapers in 2008 with a combined circulation of 55,000, plus 24 paid-for non-dailies.

Diplomatic Representatives

Of Liberia in the United Kingdom (23 Fitzroy Sq., London, W1T 6EW)
Ambassador: Vacant.
Chargé d'Affaires a.i.: Famatta Morris Manu.

Of the United Kingdom in Liberia (Leone Compound, 12th St. Beach-side, Sinkor, Monrovia)
Ambassador: David Belgrove, OBE.

Of Liberia in the USA (5201 16th St., NW, Washington, D.C., 20011)
Ambassador: Lois Cheche Brutus.

Of the USA in Liberia (502 Benson St., Monrovia)
Ambassador: Christine A. Elder.

Of Liberia to the United Nations
Ambassador: Dee-Maxwell Saah Kemayah.

Of Liberia to the European Union
Ambassador: Isaac Wehyee Nyenabo.

Further Reading

Daniels, A., *Monrovia Mon Amour: a Visit to Liberia.* 1992
Ellis, Stephen, *The Mask of Anarchy: The Destruction of Liberia and the Religious Dimension of an African Civil War.* 1999
Sawyer, A., *The Emergence of Autocracy in Liberia: Tragedy and Challenge.* 1992
National Statistical Office: Liberia Institute of Statistics & Geo-Information Services, Statistics House, Capitol Hill, P. O. Box 629, Monrovia.
Website: http://www.lisgis.net

Libya

Dawlat Libya (State of Libya)

Capital: Tripoli
Population projection, 2020: 6·66m.
GNI per capita, 2017: (PPP$) 11,100
HDI/world rank, 2017: 0·706/108=
Internet domain extension: .ly

Key Historical Events

Libya's earliest inhabitants were the semi-nomadic Berbers, whose descendants still live throughout North Africa's Atlas Mountains. Phoenician merchants from the Levant began to settle in what is today Libya from around 1000 BC and founded Carthage in what is now Tunisia in 814 BC. Carthage became the leading port in the western Mediterranean, extending its influence over Libya and most of coastal North Africa for the next five centuries. The port of Oea (now Tripoli) was founded by Phoenicians around 500 BC. Greek traders settled in the Cyrenaica region (eastern Libya) in the seventh century BC, founding Cyrene in 630 BC. Roman settlements appeared in Libya in the third century BC, growing in importance following Rome's sacking of Carthage in 146 BC. The port of Leptis Magna was founded in Tripolitania in the first century AD, becoming a major centre of commerce until it fell to the Vandals early in the fifth century.

The first of several waves of Arab conquerors arrived in 630, spreading the Islamic faith, initially along the coastal fringes. Libya became part of the powerful Umayyad and Abbasid Caliphates, the latter centred on Baghdad where it reached its apotheosis under Harun al Rashid (786–809). From 971 until 1045 Libya, along with present-day Algeria and Tunisia, were ruled by the Zirid amirs who were loyal to the Fatimid Caliphs of the Nile Valley. Bedouin Arabs from the Nile Valley, known as the Banu Hilal, entered the region in around 1000 spreading Islam and the Arabic language throughout Libya over the next three centuries.

By the beginning of the 15th century the Libyan, or Barbary, coast had become infamous as a haven for pirates. Habsburg Spain occupied Tripoli in 1510 but it fell to Ottoman corsairs in 1551. Direct control from İstanbul was superseded by rule through local Turkish governors (known as beys). In 1711 Ahmed Karamanli, an Ottoman cavalry officer, seized power and declared Libyan independence. Direct Ottoman rule was re-established in 1835 when Sultan Mahmud II made Libya a province of the Sublime Ports.

On 29 Sept. 1911 Italy declared war on the ailing Ottoman Empire and occupied Tripoli four days later. Italian control was confirmed following the signing of the Treaty of Ouchy in 1912 but local resistance, particularly by the Sanusi Order in Cyrenaica, confined Italian power to the coastal cities of Tripoli, Benghazi, Tobruk and Derna.

During the Second World War the British army expelled the Italians and their German allies, placing Tripolitania and Cyrenaica under British military administration and Fezzan under French control. This continued under a UN directive until 1951 when Libya gained independence. The former Amir of Cyrenaica, Muhammad Idris al Senussi, was crowned king.

The discovery of oil in 1959 brought rapid economic growth but resentment grew as wealth remained in the hands of the elite. Idris was deposed in Sept. 1969 by a group of army officers, 12 of whom formed the Revolutionary Command Council which, chaired by Col. Muammar Gaddafi, proclaimed the Libyan Arab Republic. In 1977 the Revolutionary Command Council was superseded by a more democratic People's Congress, though Gaddafi remained head of state. Throughout the 1980s Libya found itself at odds with its neighbours while deteriorating relations with the USA and other Western countries culminated in the US bombing of Tripoli in April 1986, a punishment for Gaddafi's alleged support of international terrorism. A US trade embargo was also enforced that year.

In 1992 the UN imposed sanctions after Libya refused to surrender suspects in the 1988 bombing of a Pan Am flight over Lockerbie in Scotland. In April 1999 Libya handed over two suspects to face trial under Scottish law in the Netherlands. In Jan. 2001 Abdelbaset Ali Mohmed Al-Megrahi was found guilty of murder and sentenced to life imprisonment. The UN suspended sanctions in 1999 but they were not lifted formally until Sept. 2003. The USA lifted its remaining sanctions in Sept. 2004 after Col. Gaddafi pledged to end his weapons of mass destruction programme. Libya's auction of oil and gas exploration licences in Jan. 2005 led to the return of US energy companies and full diplomatic ties between the two countries were resumed in May 2006.

In Aug. 2009 Al-Megrahi was released from prison on compassionate grounds following a ruling by the Scottish courts. He was said to be suffering terminal cancer. His subsequent enthusiastic reception in Libya raised tensions with the USA.

In Feb. 2011 Gaddafi faced popular demands, originating in Benghazi and spreading to other cities, for him to step down. In March he began a military campaign to seize back the east of the country from insurgents. In response, the UN, with the backing of the Arab League, authorized a no-fly zone over the country and air strikes as required in an attempt to protect civilians. In May the International Criminal Court issued an arrest warrant for Gaddafi, citing his 'widespread and systematic attacks' on civilians. In Aug. rebel forces seized control of Tripoli and a National Transitional Council (NTC) became the *de facto* government as Gaddafi went into hiding. The following month, rebels launched a fresh assault on Gaddafi's home town of Sirte, one of the last remaining pockets of loyalist support. On 20 Oct. 2011 Gaddafi was found hiding in the city by National Transitional Council troops and killed. One of Gaddafi's sons, Mutassim Gaddafi, a senior army officer and security adviser, was also killed. The death of the Muammar Gaddafi brought an end to 42 years of violent rule and on 23 Oct. 2011 in Benghazi the NTC formally announced the liberation of the country.

In Aug. 2012 the NTC handed power to the General National Congress (GNC), which was itself supposed to be replaced in June 2014 by a newly-elected parliament. However, from Sept. 2014—and amid a climate of ongoing civil unrest—there were two competing governments: the National Salvation Government (appointed by the GNC and dominated by Islamist factions) in Tripoli and its internationally-recognized rival at that time, the new House of Representatives based in Tobruk. Then in Dec. 2015 a UN-brokered agreement was signed setting out plans for a new Government of National Accord (GNA) to serve as the sole legitimate government. In March 2016 the GNA moved its base from Tunis to Tripoli. However, despite previously granting a vote of confidence to the GNA, the House of Representatives subsequently voted against approving the new regime and co-operation between the two administrations had collapsed by early 2017. As of Feb. 2018 there remained two competing governments.

Territory and Population

Libya is bounded in the north by the Mediterranean Sea, east by Egypt and Sudan, south by Chad and Niger and west by Algeria and Tunisia. The area is 1,759,540 sq. km. The population at the 2006 census was 5,657,692; density, 3·2 per sq. km. Population estimate, Jan. 2012: 5,363,000. The United Nations population estimate for 2012 was 6,198,000. In 2011, 78·1% of the population lived in urban areas. The population is largely a mixture of Arab and Berber ethnicities. Among foreign residents the largest groups are from other African nations.

The UN gives a projected population for 2020 of 6·66m.

Libya is divided into 22 districts (*sha'biyat*). Capitals and populations (2006 census) are as follows:

	Capital	*Population*
Al Butnan	Tubruq (Tobruk)	157,747
Al Jabal al Akhdar	Al Bayda	206,180
Al Jabal al Gharbi	Gharyan	302,705
Al Jifarah	Al' Aziziyah	451,175
Al Jufrah	Hun	52,092
Al Kufrah	Al Jawf	48,328

(continued)

	Capital	Population
Al Marj	Al Marj	184,531
Al Marqab	Al Hums	427,886
Al Wahah	Ajdabiya	179,155
An Nuqat al Khams	Zuwarah	287,359
Ash Shati'	Birat	78,563
Az Zawiyah	Az Zawiyah	290,637
Benghazi	Benghazi	674,951
Darnah	Darnah	162,857
Ghat	Ghat	23,199
Misratah	Misratah	543,129
Murzuq	Murzuq	78,772
Nalut	Nalut	93,896
Sabha	Sabha	133,206
Surt	Surt	141,495
Tarabulus (Tripoli)	Tarabulus (Tripoli)	1,063,571
Wadi al Hayat	Awbari	76,258

The two largest cities are Tripoli, the capital (with an estimated population of 1,095,000 in 2010), and Benghazi (estimated population of 678,000 in 2010).

The official language is Arabic.

Social Statistics

Estimates, 2008: births, 147,000; deaths, 26,000. Estimated rates, 2008 (per 1,000 population): births, 23·3; deaths, 4·1. Life expectancy (2013), 73·5 years for men and 77·3 for women. Annual population growth rate, 2000–08, 2·0%; infant mortality, 2010, 13 per 1,000 live births; fertility rate, 2008, 2·7 births per woman.

Climate

The coastal region has a warm temperate climate, with mild wet winters and hot dry summers, although most of the country suffers from aridity. Tripoli, Jan. 52°F (11·1°C), July 81°F (27·2°C). Annual rainfall 16" (400 mm). Benghazi, Jan. 56°F (13·3°C), July 77°F (25°C). Annual rainfall 11" (267 mm).

Constitution and Government

Following the uprising in 2011 that culminated in the capture and killing of Libya's incumbent leader, Col. Gaddafi, the National Transitional Council (NTC)—formed in Feb. 2011—formally announced the country's 'liberation' in Oct. and appointed an executive committee to serve as the *de facto* interim government.

A panel to draft a new constitution was elected in Feb. 2014. Once the new constitution has won approval by referendum, parliamentary elections are required to be held within six months. However, as of Feb. 2018 the country remained riven by civil unrest and political instability.

National Anthem

'Libya, Libya, Libya'; words by Al Bashir Al Arebi, tune by Mohammed Abdel Wahab. Originally the Kingdom of Libya's national anthem from 1951–69, 'Libya, Libya, Libya' became the country's new national anthem following the death of Muammar Gaddafi in 2011.

Government Chronology

Leaders since 1951.

1951–69	(King) Muhammad Idris I al Senussi
1969–2011	Col. Muammar Abu Minyar Gaddafi (Chairman of the Revolutionary Command Council until 1977; General Secretary of the General People's Congress until 1979; *de facto* leader 1979–2011)

Chairman of the National Transitional Council

2011–12	Mustafa Abdul Jalil

Presidents of the General National Congress

2012–13	Mohamed Magariaf
2013	Juma Ahmad Atigha (acting)
2013–14	Nouri Abusahmain

President of the House of Representatives

2014–	Aguila Salah Issa (disputed)

Heads of Government since 2011.

Prime Ministers

2011	Mahmoud Jibril (interim)
2011	Ali Tarhouni (acting)
2011–12	Abdurrahim al-Keib (interim)
2012–14	Ali Zeidan
2014–	Abdullah al-Thanay (disputed)
2014–15	Omar al-Hasi (disputed)
2015–17	Khalifa al-Ghawi (disputed)
2016–	Fayez Serraj (disputed)

Recent Elections

Elections to the General National Congress (GNC) were held in July 2012. The National Forces Alliance won 39 seats, the Justice and Construction Party (the Muslim Brotherhood's political party in Libya) 17, the National Front Party 3, National Centrist Party 2, Union for Homeland 2 and Wadi Al-Hayah Gathering 2. 15 other parties won one seat each and 120 seats went to independents.

In June 2014 fresh elections intended to create a new parliament replacing the GNC took place. As political party lists were banned under the new electoral system, all candidates ran as independents. Nonetheless, the liberal faction held a majority over the Islamists in the new 200-seat 'House of Representatives'. However, in Nov. 2014 the Supreme Court declared the elections unconstitutional. Both a National Salvation Government (appointed by the GNC) and the House of Representatives have continued to claim legitimacy as Libya's legal government.

Current Government

Despite a UN-brokered deal in Dec. 2015 setting out plans for a new Government of National Accord (GNC), Libya still had two competing power centres in Feb. 2018—the House of Representatives (based in Tobruk since Aug. 2014, and supported by the Libyan National Army headed by Field Marshal Khalifa Haftar) and the GNC (based in Tripoli since March 2016). However, under a tentative agreement reached in July 2017, both sides committed to a ceasefire and to the holding of national elections 'as soon as possible'. Meanwhile, owing to the political fragmentation that followed the collapse of Muammar Gaddafi's regime, a third government—the National Salvation Government led by Khalifa al-Ghawi—had also competed for power and occupied Tripoli before being pushed out by forces loyal to the GNC, initially in March 2016 and then for a second time in March 2017.

Prime Minister of the UN-backed Government of National Accord: Fayez Serraj; b. 1960 (since April 2016).

Prime Minister of the House of Representatives: Abdullah al-Thanay; b. 1954 (since March 2014).

Current Leaders

Fayez Serraj
Position
UN-backed Prime Minister

Introduction

Fayez Serraj was named prime minister of the Government of National Accord (GNA), based in Tripoli, on 5 April 2016. His administration is recognized by the United Nations and the Western powers as Libya's only legitimate government, but it has struggled to assert its authority over much of the country and has been challenged by the rival elected House of Representatives—a largely powerless assembly but backed by the self-styled Libyan National Army headed by military strongman Khalifa Haftar, based in the eastern city of Tobruk.

Early Life

Fayez Serraj was born on 20 Feb. 1960 in Tripoli. His father was Moustafa Serraj, a cabinet minister under King Idriss.

A trained architect, Fayez Serraj worked in Libya's public sector before entering politics after Muammar Gaddafi was deposed in 2011. In July 2012 he was elected to the General National Congress, an interim legislative authority tasked with the transition to democracy. It was succeeded by the House of Representatives, to which Serraj was elected on 25 June 2014. The parliament fled to Tobruk after Tripoli was overrun by militias and a rival government, the new General National Congress (GNC), was established there on 8 Aug. 2014.

On 17 Dec. 2015 the UN-mediated Libyan Political Agreement was signed between the GNC and House of Representatives, according to which a Government of National Accord (GNA) headed by Serraj would take power. Having survived an assassination attempt on 9 Jan. 2016, Serraj travelled to Tripoli on 30 March. The following day it was reported that the GNA had seized control of the prime ministerial offices.

Career in Office

Serraj was tasked with leading the fight against Islamic State and paving the way for democratic elections. Other challenges included a banking crisis, a steep rise in the cost of living and the high number of people displaced by civil war. The GNA struggled to assert its authority across the country as the rival House of Representatives refused to endorse Serraj's administration, leading in March 2017 to violent clashes between GNA forces and rival militias in Tripoli. However, in talks hosted by the French president in July that year both sides committed to a conditional ceasefire and to the holding of early national elections, while in Dec. the UN said that it was 'intensively trying to establish the proper political, legislative and security conditions for elections to be held before the end of 2018'. In May 2018, at another summit hosted by France, the rival Libyan factions agreed to hold presidential and parliamentary elections by Dec. However, the initiative failed amid continuing militia violence, and in Nov. the UN presented a new plan at a conference in Palermo, Italy, proposing a national conference in early 2019 and the subsequent staging of elections.

Khalifa Haftar

Position

Rival Leader

Introduction

Once one of Col. Muammar Gaddafi's most trusted generals, Khalifa Haftar has since played a prominent role in first opposing the ousted Gaddafi regime and then the current rival administration based in Tripoli. A scourge of Islamist militants, he is a key player in the complex ongoing struggle for power and security in Libya.

Early Life

A member of the Ferjan tribe, Khalifa Haftar was born in Ajdabiya in 1943. After completing his secondary education in 1964, he joined the Benghazi Military University Academy, graduating in 1966. In 1969 he took part in the coup against King Idris which brought Gaddafi to power.

In 1987 Haftar and other Libyan officers were captured during the war against Chad. Having been disowned by Gaddafi, Haftar moved to Virginia in the USA, and helped to form the National Front for the Salvation of Libya. In March 1996 he took part in a failed coup against Gaddafi.

Haftar returned to Libya in 2011 during the civil war but failed to secure a suitable role for himself and resettled in the USA. Having subsequently returned, he assembled forces that assaulted Islamist militia in Benghazi in May 2014 and established his control over the east of the country. In March 2015 the House of Representatives (the Tobruk-based government) appointed Haftar commander of the Libyan National Army.

Career in Office

A divisive figure in Libya owing to his mixed record of both support for, and opposition to, the Gaddafi regime, Haftar wields considerable influence and enjoys widespread recognition from foreign governments, including Russia, Egypt and members of the European Union. He has been invited to high-level international peace talks and is seen as key to stabilizing the ongoing crisis of uncontrolled migration from North Africa to Europe.

Defence

Defence expenditure in 2013 was estimated US$4,771m. (US$795 per capita), representing 5·0% of GDP. The former Libyan Army effectively ceased to exist as an organized force in 2011 as the civil war escalated. Much of the equipment was damaged or destroyed during the conflict.

Economy

Petroleum, natural gas and mining contributed 67·8% to GDP in 2008; followed by public administration, defence and services, 6·8%; finance, insurance and real estate, 6·5%; and construction, 5·7%.

Libya featured among the ten most corrupt countries in the world in a 2018 survey of 180 countries carried out by the anti-corruption organization Transparency International.

Overview

Until the 2011 uprising that saw the overthrow of Col. Gaddafi, Libya had one of the highest GDP per capita rates in Africa at US$12,900. The country had enjoyed solid growth in the first decade of the century, supported by international investment. In 2003 UN sanctions were lifted after Libya admitted complicity in the 1988 Lockerbie bombing and in 2004 US sanctions were lifted after the country agreed to abandon its nuclear weapons programme.

After suffering recession in 2009 as a result of the global downturn following the financial crisis, there was subsequently a greater economic contribution from non-oil industries in the wake of increased government spending and the liberalization of the trade, tourism and service sectors. Following the 2011 revolution, GDP contracted by 67% but quickly rebounded, supported by an oil-financed consumption boom. The hydrocarbon sector accounted for about 96% of total fiscal revenue in 2013 (although only 2% of total employment). However, severe disruptions in production and exports, which began in mid-2013 as militant groups blockaded oil facilities, then reversed the post-revolution economic improvements. By 2014 GDP per capita had declined to US$6,600.

The economy remained in recession for a fourth consecutive year in 2016. Economic growth contracted by 3·0% that year, following shrinkage of 10·3% in 2015. A considerable decrease in oil production and a high degree of volatility in oil prices have affected both the current account and budget revenue. Moreover, the competing governments in Tripoli and Tobruk failed to approve budgets in 2016 and 2017. The central bank has continued to disburse funds for wages and essential subsidies, but the unemployment rate remains high, reaching 19·2% in 2016.

Immediate challenges include managing fiscal spending pressures while restoring and improving basic public services. A longer-term goal is to develop the framework and institutions for a more diversified market-based economy, broadening activity beyond the oil and gas sector. Establishing political stability is essential for development, while corruption and unemployment must also be addressed. Increases in the oil price and a recovery in crude production would offer some hope for the future.

Currency

The unit of currency is the *Libyan dinar* (LYD) of 1,000 *millemes*. The dinar was devalued 15% in Nov. 1994, and alongside the official exchange rate a new rate was applied to private sector imports. Foreign exchange reserves were US$29,315m. in June 2005. Total money supply in May 2005 was 11,552m. dinars. Inflation was 25·9% in 2016, rising to 28·5% in 2017.

Budget

In 2013 (provisional) revenues totalled 54,764m. dinars and expenditures 65,284m. dinars.

Performance

Total GDP in 2017 was US$51·0bn. The Libyan armed conflict resulted in the economy contracting by 66·7% in 2011. The country began to recover the following year, with real GDP growth of 124·7%—the highest percentage increase of any country in 2012. However, there was then negative growth of 36·8% in 2013, 53·0% in 2014 and 13·0% in 2015 as internal turmoil returned to the country. In 2016 the economy shrank again, by 7·4%, but it then grew by 64·0% in 2017.

Banking and Finance

A National Bank of Libya was established in 1955; it was renamed the Central Bank of Libya in 1972. All foreign banks were nationalized by Dec. 1970. In 1972 the government set up the Libyan Arab Foreign Bank. The Agricultural Bank was set up to give loans and subsidies to farmers and to assist them in marketing their crops. Following the popular uprising against Col. Gaddafi in 2011, international sanctions were imposed on the central bank and its subsidiaries. As of Feb. 2018 the competing governments in Tripoli and Tobruk each had their own Central Bank governors.

A stock exchange was opened in Tripoli in March 2007.

Energy and Natural Resources

Environment

Libya's carbon dioxide emissions from the consumption of energy in 2011 were the equivalent of 7·1 tonnes per capita. An *Environmental Performance Index* compiled in 2016 ranked Libya 119th of 180 countries, with 63·3%. The index examined various factors in nine areas—agriculture, air quality, biodiversity and habitat, climate and energy, fisheries, forests, health impacts, water and sanitation, and water resources.

Electricity

Installed capacity in 2011 was an estimated 8·9m. kW. Production was 27·61bn. kWh in 2011 (down from 32·75bn. kWh in 2010) and consumption per capita 4,517 kWh.

Oil and Gas

Oil accounts for 30% of Libya's GDP. Oil production in 2017 was 40·8m. tonnes, down from 71·1m. tonnes in 2012 but up from 20·1m. tonnes in 2016, the lowest since modern records began as the country continued to be embroiled in civil conflict. Proven reserves (2017) 48·4bn. bbls, the highest of any African country. Oil export revenues fell from US$60·2bn. in 2012 to US$9·3bn. in 2016.

Proven natural gas reserves totalled 1·4trn. cu. metres in 2017. Production (2017), 11·5bn. cu. metres.

Water

Since 1984 a US$20bn. project has been under way to bring water from aquifers underlying the Sahara to the inhabited coastal areas of Libya. This scheme, called the 'Great Man-Made River', is intended, on completion, to bring 6,000 cu. metres of water a day along some 5,000 km of pipes. Phase I was completed in Aug. 1991; Phase II of the project (covering the west of Libya) was completed in Sept. 1996 and work on Phase III was completed in 2009. The river is providing Libya's main centres of population with clean water as well as making possible the improvement and expansion of agriculture. The whole project is more than three-quarters complete.

Minerals

Iron ore deposits have been found in the south.

Agriculture

Only the coastal zone, which covers an area of about 17,000 sq. miles, is really suitable for agriculture. Of some 25m. acres of productive land, nearly 20m. are used for grazing and about 1m. for static farming. Agriculture employs around 17% of the workforce. The sub-desert zone produces the alfalfa plant. The desert zone and the Fezzan contain some fertile oases. In 2013 there were an estimated 1·7m. ha. of arable land and 0·3m. ha. of permanent crops. An estimated 0·5m. ha. were equipped for irrigation in 2013.

Cyrenaica has about 10m. acres of potentially productive land and is suitable for grazing. Certain areas are suitable for dry farming; in addition, grapes, olives and dates are grown. About 143,000 acres are used for settled farming; about 272,000 acres are covered by natural forests. The Agricultural Development Authority plans to reclaim 6,000 ha. each year for agriculture. In the Fezzan there are about 6,700 acres of irrigated gardens and about 297,000 acres are planted with date palms.

Production (2013 estimates, in 1,000 tonnes): potatoes, 295; watermelons, 216; tomatoes, 213; wheat, 200; olives, 187; onions, 183; dates, 170; barley, 97.

Livestock (2013 estimates): 7·2m. sheep; 2·6m. goats; 199,000 cattle; 58,000 camels; 35m. chickens.

Forestry

Forest area in 2015 was 0·22m. ha. (0·1% of the land area). In 2011, 1·08m. cu. metres of roundwood were cut.

Fisheries

The catch in 2012 totalled an estimated 35,000 tonnes, entirely from marine waters.

Industry

Industry employs nearly 30% of the workforce. Small-scale private sector industrialization in the form of partnerships is permitted. Output (in 1,000 tonnes): cement (2010 estimate), 7,000; residual fuel oil (2011), 2,011; distillate fuel oil (2011), 1,828; jet fuels (2011), 499.

Labour

The labour force in 2010 was 2,379,000 (72·0% males). Libya had 18,000 people living in slavery according to the Walk Free Foundation's 2013 *Global Slavery Index*.

International Trade

In 1986 the USA applied a trade embargo on the grounds of Libya's alleged complicity in terrorism. Many of the economic sanctions were suspended in April 2004, and in June 2006 Libya was removed from Washington's list of state sponsors of terror. In 1992 UN sanctions were imposed for Libya's refusal to deliver suspected terrorists for trial in the UK or USA, but these were formally lifted in 2003.

In 1989 Libya signed a treaty of economic co-operation with the four other Maghreb countries: Algeria, Mauritania, Morocco and Tunisia.

Libya applied for WTO membership in Dec. 2001 and accession negotiations began in 2004. However, they were suspended in Feb. 2011 after the Libyan civil war broke out.

Imports and Exports

In 2006 imports were valued at US$13·2bn. and exports at US$37·5bn. Some 80% of GDP derives from trade. Oil accounts for over 95% of exports. Main import suppliers in 2000 were Italy (24%), Germany (12%), Tunisia (9%) and the UK (7%); main export markets were Italy (33%), Germany (24%), Spain (10%) and France (5%).

Communications

Roads

In 2010 the road network covered about 34,000 km. In 2007 there were 1,388,200 passenger cars in use (225 per 1,000 inhabitants), plus 310,500 lorries and vans. There were 2,301 deaths as a result of road accidents in 2009, which at 38·6 per 100,000 inhabitants gave Libya one of the highest traffic-related death rates in the world.

Rail

Although there have not been any operational railways since 1965, some routes were under construction at the outbreak of the civil conflict in Feb. 2011. However, the projects were then abandoned. Talks were held in early 2013 between Chinese and Russian companies and the Libya Rail Implementation Authority when Libya was starting to show signs of a recovery. As Libya then became less stable the projects were again put on hold. However, talks with Russia resumed in early 2017.

Civil Aviation

The UN ban on air traffic to and from Libya enforced since April 1992 was lifted in April 1999 following the handing over for trial of two suspected Lockerbie bombers. The national flag carrier, Libyan Airlines, was grounded in March 2011 as a result of the Libyan revolution but has now resumed operations. However, in Dec. 2014 all Libya-based carriers were added to the EU aviation safety blacklist, which either banned or restricted Libyan airlines from operating in the European Union.

Shipping

In Jan. 2014 there were 20 ships of 300 GT or over registered, totalling 531,000 GT.

Telecommunications

There were 1·23m. fixed telephone lines in 2010 (193·3 per 1,000 inhabitants). Mobile phone subscribers numbered 9·53m. in 2009. There were 108·0 internet users per 1,000 inhabitants in 2009. Fixed internet subscriptions totalled 772,500 in 2009 (123·3 per 1,000 inhabitants). In June 2012 there were 560,000 Facebook users.

Social Institutions

Out of 178 countries analysed in the 2017 *Fragile States Index*—a list published jointly by the Fund for Peace and *Foreign Policy* magazine—Libya was ranked the 23rd most vulnerable to conflict or collapse. The index is based on 12 indicators of state vulnerability across social, political and economic categories.

Justice

The Civil, Commercial and Criminal codes are based mainly on the Egyptian model. Matters of personal status of family or succession matters affecting Muslims are dealt with in special courts according to the Muslim law. All other matters, civil, commercial and criminal, are tried in the ordinary courts, which have jurisdiction over everyone.

There are civil and penal courts in Tripoli and Benghazi, with subsidiary courts at Misratah and Darnah; courts of assize in Tripoli and Benghazi, and courts of appeal also in Tripoli and Benghazi.

The population in penal institutions in Jan. 2013 was 5,328 (81 per 100,000 of national population). The death penalty is in force; there were at least four executions in 2009 and 18 in 2010. However, there have been no judicial executions since 2010 although there have been widespread reports of extrajudicial executions. The International Centre for Prison Studies estimated in 2014 that 90·0% of prisoners had yet to receive a trial.

Education

In 2006 there were 755,338 primary school pupils and 732,614 secondary level pupils. In 2009 the government launched a five-year US$9bn. plan to reform higher education and scientific research through strengthening international ties and improving the information technology network as well as creating a National Authority for Scientific Research. In 2015 there were 14 accredited universities in Libya, of which 13 were state universities. The largest universities are Al Fateh University in Tripoli and Garyounis University in Benghazi. Adult literacy in 2009 was estimated at 88·9%.

Health

There were 13,095 physicians, 43,216 nursing and midwifery personnel, 4,583 dentistry personnel and 3,928 pharmaceutical personnel in 2014. Provision of hospital beds in 2006 was 37 per 10,000 population.

Religion

Islam is declared the State religion, but the right of others to practise their religion is provided for. In 2010 an estimated 96·6% of the population were Muslim (almost all Sunnis) according to the Pew Research Center's Forum on Religion & Public Life.

Culture

World Heritage Sites

Libya has five sites on the UNESCO World Heritage List: the Archaeological Site of Leptis Magna (inscribed on the list in 1982); the Archaeological Site of Sabratha (1982); the Archaeological Site of Cyrene (1982); the Rock-art Sites of Tadrart Acacus (1985); and the Old Town of Ghadamès (1986).

Press

In 2008 there were six daily newspapers with a combined circulation of 100,000. In the 2016 *World Press Freedom Index* compiled by Reporters Without Borders, Libya ranked 164th out of 180 countries.

Tourism

In 2007 there were 106,000 non-resident visitors, down from 125,000 in 2006.

Diplomatic Representatives

Of Libya in the United Kingdom (15 Knightsbridge, London, SW1X 7LY)
    Ambassador: Vacant.
    Chargé d'Affaires a.i.: Mohamed Elkoni.

Of the United Kingdom in Libya
    Ambassador: Frank Baker, CMG, OBE (resides in Tunis, Tunisia)

Of Libya in the USA (1460 Dahlia St., NW, Washington, D.C., 20012)
    Ambassador: Wafa M. T. Bughaigis.

Of the USA in Libya
    Currently closed.

Of Libya to the United Nations
    Ambassador: Vacant.
    Chargé d'Affaires a.i.: Elmahdi S. Elmajerbi.

Of Libya to the European Union
    Ambassador: Abdulhafed Gaddur.

Further Reading

Hehir, Aidan and Murray, Robert, (eds) *Libya, the Responsibility to Protect and the Future of Humanitarian Intervention.* 2013

Simons, G., *Libya: the Struggle for Survival.* 1993.—*Libya and the West: From Independence to Lockerbie.* 2004

St John, Ronald Bruce, *Libya: From Colony to Revolution.* 2011

Vandewalle, D. (ed.) *Qadhafi's Libya, 1969–1994.* 1995.—*A History of Modern Libya.* 2006.—*Libya Since 1969: Qadhafi's Revolution Revisited.* 2008

Liechtenstein

Fürstentum Liechtenstein (Principality of Liechtenstein)

Capital: Vaduz
Population projection, 2020: 39,000
GNI per capita, 2017: (PPP$) 97,336
HDI/world rank, 2017: 0·916/17=
Internet domain extension: .li

Key Historical Events

Liechtenstein is a sovereign state with a history dating back to 1342 when Count Hartmann III became ruler of the county of Vaduz. Additions were later made to the count's domains and by 1434 the territory reached its present boundaries. On 23 Jan. 1719 Emperor Charles VI constituted the two counties as the Principality of Liechtenstein. In 1862 the constitution established an elected diet. After the First World War, Liechtenstein was represented abroad by Switzerland. Swiss currency was adopted in 1921. On 5 Oct. 1921 a new constitution based on that of Switzerland extended democratic rights, but in March 2003 the people of Liechtenstein voted in a referendum to give their prince the power to govern without reference to elected representatives.

Territory and Population

Liechtenstein is bounded on the east by Austria and the west by Switzerland. Total area 160 sq. km (61·8 sq. miles). The population (Dec. 2016) was 37,810 (19,064 female), including 12,795 resident foreigners, giving a density of 236·3 per sq. km.

The UN gives a projected population for 2020 of 39,000.

The population of Liechtenstein is predominantly rural. The capital is Vaduz. Population of Schaan (2016), 5,992; Vaduz (2016), 5,407.

The official language is German.

Social Statistics

In 2011 there were 395 births and 248 deaths (rates of 10·9 per 1,000 population and 6·8 respectively). The annual population growth rate was 0·7% over the period 2007–12.

Climate

There is a distinct difference in climate between the higher mountains and the valleys. In summer the peaks can often be foggy while the valleys remain sunny and warm, while in winter the valleys can often be foggy and cold whilst the peaks remain sunny and comparatively warm. Vaduz, Jan. 0°C, July 20°C. Annual rainfall 1,090 mm.

Constitution and Government

Liechtenstein is a constitutional monarchy ruled by the princes of the House of Liechtenstein.

The reigning Prince is **Hans-Adam II**, b. 14 Feb. 1945; he succeeded his father Prince Francis Joseph, 13 Nov. 1989 (he exercised the prerogatives to which the Sovereign is entitled from 26 Aug. 1984); married on 30 July 1967 to Countess Marie Kinsky von Wchinitz und Tettau. *Offspring:* Hereditary Prince Alois (b. 11 June 1968), married Duchess Sophie of Bavaria on 3 July 1993 (*offspring:* Prince Joseph Wenzel, b. 24 May 1995; Marie Caroline, b. 17 Oct. 1996; Georg Antonius, b. 20 April 1999; Nikolaus Sebastian, b. 6 Dec. 2000); Prince Maximilian (b. 16 May 1969), married Angela Brown on 29 Jan. 2000 (*offspring:* Alfons, b. 18 May 2001); Prince Constantin (b. 15 March 1972), married Countess Marie Kálnoky de Köröspatak on 17 July 1999 (*offspring:* Moritz, b. 27 May 2003; Georgina, b. 23 July 2005; Benedikt, b. 18 May 2008); Princess Tatjana (b. 10 April 1973), married Philipp von Lattorff on 5 June 1999 (*offspring:* Lukas, b. 13 May 2000; Elisabeth, b. 25 Jan. 2002; Marie, b. 18 Jan. 2004; Camilla, b. 4 Nov. 2005;

Anna, b. 3 Aug. 2007; Sophie, b. 30 Oct. 2009; Maximilian, b. 17 Dec. 2011). The monarchy is hereditary in the male line.

The present constitution of 5 Oct. 1921 provided for a unicameral parliament (*Landtag*) of 15 members elected for four years, but this was amended to 25 members in 1988. Election is on the basis of proportional representation. The prince can call and dismiss the parliament, and following a referendum held on 16 March 2003, dismiss the government and veto bills. On parliamentary recommendation, he appoints the ministers. According to the constitution, the Government is a collegial body consisting of five ministers including the prime minister. Each minister has an Alternate who takes part in the meetings of the collegial Government if the minister is unavailable. Any group of 1,000 persons or any three communes may propose legislation (initiative). Bills passed by the parliament may be submitted to popular referendum. A law is valid when it receives a majority approval by the parliament and the prince's signed concurrence.

National Anthem

'Oben am jungen Rhein' ('Up above the young Rhine'); words by H. H. Jauch; tune, 'God save the Queen'.

Recent Elections

At the parliamentary elections on 5 Feb. 2017 the Progressive Citizens' Party (FBP) gained 9 seats (35·2% of votes cast); the Patriotic Union (VU), 8 (33·7%); the Independents, 5 (18·4%); the Free List (FL), 3 (12·6%). Turnout was 77·8%.

Current Government

Head of Government, and Minister for Finance and General Government Affairs: Adrian Hasler; b. 1964 (FBP; sworn in 27 March 2013).

In Feb. 2019 the cabinet comprised:

Deputy Head of Government and Minister for Infrastructure, Economic Affairs and Sports: Daniel Risch. *Foreign Affairs, Justice and Culture:* Aurelia Frick. *Home Affairs, Education and Environment:* Dominique Gantenbein. *Social Affairs:* Mauro Pedrazzini.

Princely House Website: http://www.fuerstenhaus.li

Current Leaders

Hans-Adam II

Position
Prince

Introduction
Hans-Adam II succeeded his father, Francis Joseph II, as Prince of Liechtenstein in 1989. A successful banker with a large personal fortune, in March 2003 he was granted extensive legal rights which effectively made him Europe's only absolute monarch. He handed day-to-day responsibility for running the country to his son, Crown Prince Alois, in 2004.

Early Life
Hans-Adam, whose full name is Johannes Adam Pius Ferdinand Alois Josef Maria Marko d'Aviano von und zu Liechtenstein, was born on 14 Feb. 1945. The eldest son of the ruling Prince Francis Joseph II, he was brought up with his three brothers and one sister in Vaduz castle. He was schooled in Austria and Vienna, worked for a short while at a London bank and studied at the St Gallen School of Economics and Social Sciences, graduating with a master's degree in 1969.

In 1970 he was named head of the Prince of Liechtenstein Foundation, a position he retained until 1984. In 1972 his father put him in charge of running the royal estate, during which time he won a reputation for sound management and an interest in the wider economic sphere. In Aug. 1984 Franz Joseph transferred much of his executive power to Hans-Adam, who formally acceded to the throne on his father's death in Nov. 1989.

© Springer Nature Limited 2020
Palgrave Macmillan (ed.), *The Statesman's Yearbook 2020*,
https://doi.org/10.1057/978-1-349-95940-2_115

Career in Office

Hans-Adam has striven to maintain Liechtenstein's strong economy, consolidating its position as an offshore financial centre. In 1990 he successfully concluded membership talks with the United Nations. A year later, despite having previously declared his support for European unity, he ruled out a bid for membership of the European Union.

In March 2003 Hans-Adam called a national referendum on constitutional amendments which would award him the right to dissolve the government, appoint judges and unilaterally veto legislation. In return he proposed that his right to rule by emergency decree would be reduced to six months, his entitlement to nominate government officials be terminated and that the future of the monarchy be subject to referendum. He threatened to leave for Vienna if the proposals were rejected, a move many Liechtensteiners feared would severely diminish the country's economic standing. Despite the presence of a strong pro-democracy group within Liechtenstein and the threat that the nation might lose its membership of the Council of Europe if the motion was passed, the reforms won 64·3% backing.

In Aug. 2004 Hans-Adam formally transferred responsibility for day to day affairs to his son, Alois. However, he reiterated he had no intention of abdicating the throne. In July 2012 voters rejected by a large margin a proposal to end the ruling prince's political power to veto the results of national referendums. In Nov. 2014 Liechtenstein celebrated the 25th anniversary of Hans-Adam's accession to the throne.

Economy

Liechtenstein is one of the world's richest countries with a well-diversified economy. Low taxes and bank secrecy laws have made Liechtenstein a successful financial centre.

Overview

Liechtenstein has a diversified and highly industrialized economy, and had the world's second highest GDP per capita ratio after Monaco in 2016, according to the United Nations. Industry and manufacturing comprise the largest sector, producing mainly capital- and research-intensive products and generating close to 40% of GDP. Much of the economy's wealth has been derived from its status as an offshore financial centre, with many international businesses establishing 'letter-box' offices in the state to take advantage of the 20% maximum tax rate.

Financial services account for over 30% of Liechtenstein's GDP and over 15% of employment, with around 90% of financial business conducted for non-residents. The country's earlier blacklisting by the OECD as an 'uncooperative tax haven' was removed in May 2009 after it committed to tackling money laundering. In 2015 Liechtenstein signed an agreement with the European Union to automatically exchange financial information in the case of tax disputes.

The country has limited natural resources and imports around 90% of its energy requirements. It has shared a common economic area with Switzerland since the conclusion of a customs treaty in 1923, after which it adopted the Swiss franc as the official currency. With its small domestic base, the economy has sought to capture foreign markets through global integration. Liechtenstein became a member of the European Free Trade Association in 1991, the European Economic Area in 1995 and the Schengen Area in 2011. As of 2015 around half of the workforce commuted into Liechtenstein from neighbouring countries daily.

Currency

Swiss currency has been in use since 1920 and became legal tender in 1924.

Budget

Budget (in 1,000 Swiss francs), 2011: revenue, 1,143,000; expenditure, 1,267,000. There is no public debt.

Performance

Real GDP growth was –5·0% in 2009. Total GDP in 2015 was US$6·3bn.

Banking and Finance

There were 16 banks in 2010. Combined total assets were 52,466·4m. Swiss francs in 2010.

Energy and Natural Resources

Electricity

In 2011 the consumption of electricity was 398,000 MWh (imported 326,000 MWh; produced in Liechtenstein 72,000 MWh).

Agriculture

In 2013 there were 3,567 ha. of agricultural land. In 2009, 1,005 ha. (26·9% of all agricultural land—the highest proportion of any sovereign country) was set aside for organic farming. The rearing of cattle on the Alpine pastures is highly developed. In 2009 there were 6,078 cattle (including 2,993 dairy cows), 3,963 sheep, 1,811 pigs, 495 horses and 452 goats. Total production of dairy produce in 2009 was 13,308 tonnes.

Forestry

In 2015 there were 7,000 ha. of forest (43% of the land area). Timber production in 2011 was 26,000 cu. metres.

Industry

Liechtenstein has a broadly diversified economic structure with a significant emphasis on industrial production. The most important branches of the heavily export-oriented industry are mechanical engineering, plant construction, manufacturing of precision instruments, dental technology and the food-processing industry.

Labour

The workforce was 32,435 in 2007, including employees commuting from abroad (16,242 in 2007). The farming population went down from 70% in 1930 to 1·1% in 2007. The rapid change-over led to the immigration of foreign workers (Austrians, Germans, Italians, Swiss).

International Trade

Liechtenstein has been in a customs union with Switzerland since 1923.

Imports and Exports

Value of the imports and exports of goods, excluding trade with and through Switzerland: imports, 2008, 2,461m. Swiss francs; exports, 2008, 4,245m. Swiss francs. Machinery, electronic goods and fabricated metals are both the leading imports and leading exports. Most trade is with other European countries.

Communications

Roads

There are 400 km of roads. Postal buses are the chief means of public transportation within the country and to Austria and Switzerland. There were 28,102 cars in 2013. There were 403 road accidents in 2012 (one fatal).

Rail

The 10 km of main railway passing through the country is operated by Austrian Federal Railways.

Telecommunications

Liechtenstein had 18,559 main telephone lines in 2012 and 36,080 mobile phone subscriptions. In 2009 there were 751·9 fixed broadband subscriptions per 1,000 inhabitants and 452·2 mobile broadband subscriptions per 1,000 inhabitants.

Social Institutions

Justice

The principality has its own civil and penal codes. The lowest court is the county court, *Landgericht*, presided over by one judge, which decides minor civil cases and summary criminal offences. The criminal court, *Kriminalgericht*, with a bench of five judges is for major crimes. Another court of mixed jurisdiction is the court of assizes (with three judges) for misdemeanours. Juvenile cases are treated in the Juvenile Court (with a bench of three judges). The superior court, *Obergericht*, and Supreme Court, *Oberster Gerichtshof*, are courts of appeal for civil and criminal cases (both with benches of five judges). An administrative court of appeal from government actions and the State Court determines the constitutionality of laws.

The death penalty was abolished in 1989. Some persons convicted by Liechtenstein are held in Austrian prisons.

Police

The principality has no army. In 2009 there were 88 police officers (excluding civilian staff, auxiliary police officers, village policemen and Swiss customs officers).

Education

In 2009 there were 16 primary, three upper, seven secondary and two grammar schools, with approximately 5,000 pupils and 640 teachers. There is a university, a music school and an art school.

Health

There is an obligatory sickness insurance scheme. In 2008 there was one hospital, but Liechtenstein has an agreement with the Swiss cantons of St Gallen and Graubünden and the Austrian Federal State of Vorarlberg that her citizens may use certain hospitals. In 2008 there were 87 physicians, 27 dentists and two pharmacies.

Religion

Religious affiliation at the 2010 census: Roman Catholic, 75·9%; Protestant, 8·5%; Muslim, 5·4%; other religion, 2·2%; no religion, 5·4%; not stated, 2·6%.

Culture

Press

In 2008 there were two daily newspapers (*Liechtensteiner Vaterland* and *Liechtensteiner Volksbatt*) with an estimated total circulation of 20,000.

Tourism

In 2014, 62,305 overnight tourists visited Liechtenstein.

Diplomatic Representatives

In 1919 Switzerland agreed to represent the interests of Liechtenstein in countries where it has diplomatic missions and where Liechtenstein is not represented in its own right. In so doing Switzerland always acts only on the basis of mandates of a general or specific nature, which it may either accept or refuse, while Liechtenstein is free to enter into direct relations with foreign states or to set up its own additional diplomatic missions.

Of the United Kingdom in Liechtenstein
Ambassador: Jane Owen (resides in Berne).

Of Liechtenstein to the USA (2900 K. St., NW, Washington, D.C., 20007)
Ambassador: Kurt Jäger.

Of the USA in Liechtenstein
Ambassador: Edward McMullen, Jr (resides in Berne).

Of Liechtenstein to the United Nations
Ambassador: Christian Wenaweser.

Of Liechtenstein to the European Union
Ambassador: Sabine Monauni.

Further Reading

Amt für Volkswirtschaft. *Statistisches Jahrbuch.* Vaduz
Rechenschaftsbericht der Fürstlichen Regierung. Vaduz. Annual, from 1922
Jahrbuch des Historischen Vereins. Vaduz. Annual since 1901
National library: Landesbibliothek, Vaduz
Beattie, David, *Liechtenstein: A Modern History.* 2004
National Statistical Office: Amt für Statistik, Äulestrasse 51, 9490 Vaduz.
Website (limited English): http://www.as.llv.li

Lithuania

Lithuania Lietuvos Respublika (Republic of Lithuania)

Capital: Vilnius
Population projection 2020: 2.85m.
GNI per capita, 2017: (PPP$) 28,314
HDI/world rank, 2017: 0.858/35=
Internet domain extension: .lt

Key Historical Events

Lithuania has been inhabited since the 10th millennium BC, with agriculture developing in the 3rd millennium BC. Baltic tribes settled in the area around 2000 BC. In the 13th century AD their lands came under threat from two German religious orders, the Teutonic Knights and the Livonian Brothers of the Sword, prompting several of the tribes to establish a defensive union. The union defeated the Livonians in 1236 and in 1250 its leader, Mindaugas, signed a peace treaty with the Teutonic Order.

In 1253 Lithuania was proclaimed a state, with Mindaugas its crowned head. In the second half of the 13th century the Grand Duchy of Lithuania suffered internal unrest and was repeatedly raided by the Turks and Mongols of the Golden Horde. In the 14th century, led by Grand Duke Gediminas, Lithuania repulsed the threat from the Golden Horde and expanded eastwards. Gediminas established relations with the Christian church while retaining pagan beliefs.

In 1386 Lithuania's ruler Jogaila married Jadwiga, queen of Poland, and became king of Poland. During the 14th century Lithuania was Christianized. Lithuania continued its expansion and by 1430 extended from the Baltic to the Black Sea. Lithuania and Poland were allied from 1447 and from 1501 they shared the same leader. In 1569 the Lublin Union legislated for a Lithuanian-Polish commonwealth. Polish culture was increasingly influential and Polish became the official state language in 1696. The constitution promulgated on 3 May 1791 is generally regarded as Europe's first national constitution (and the world's second after the USA). However, its democratic and egalitarian tone provoked Prussia and Russia.

During partitions of the Polish–Lithuanian Commonwealth by Russia, Prussia and Austria in 1772, 1793 and 1795, Lithuania was divided between Russia and Prussia. From 1795 Russia ruled most of Lithuania, including its capital, Vilnius. Uprisings were quelled in 1831 and 1863. In the second half of the 19th century, a cultural awakening interacted with an independence movement. On 5 Dec. 1905 at the Great Seimas (Congress) of Vilnius, Lithuanian representatives demanded political autonomy within the Russian Empire. The demand failed but in its aftermath pro-independence political parties were formed.

During the First World War Lithuania was occupied by Germany. Following the Russian revolution, heavy fighting occurred between Soviet Russian, German, Polish and Lithuanian forces in Feb. 1918. In Nov. 1918, after Germany's surrender, Lithuania declared full independence. In April 1919 the Soviets withdrew and the reformed Lithuanian government established a democratic republic. Lithuanian independence was recognized by the Treaty of Versailles later that year. Territorial disputes led to Lithuania supporting an uprising in the Memelland (under French jurisdiction from 1920) in Jan. 1923. In May 1924 Memelland became an autonomous part of Lithuania. There was also continued conflict with Poland over ownership of Vilnius. Following the establishment of a Polish-controlled mini-state around the city in 1922, Lithuania maintained a formal state of war with Poland.

In Dec. 1926 an internal coup deposed Lithuania's elected government and a non-democratic regime was installed. In 1938, under Polish pressure, diplomatic relations with Poland were restored. The secret protocol of the Soviet–German non-aggression pact of 1939 assigned the greater part of Lithuania to the Soviet sphere of influence. Soviet troops occupied Lithuania in June 1940 and it became part of the USSR on 3 Aug. 1940. Following the German invasion of the USSR in 1941, Lithuania was occupied by Germany. Lithuanian armed groups fought against or with German troops, according to

regional and ideological loyalties. Pogroms took place against the Jewish population, which had risen to 250,000 following influxes of refugees from Poland. In 1944 the USSR reclaimed Lithuania as a Soviet Republic, with the agreement of the USA and Britain. An estimated 350,000 Lithuanians were deported to Siberia. In 1949 the Soviets closed most Lithuanian churches. More deportations occurred in 1956, when Poles and Russians were encouraged to move to Vilnius.

In 1988 the Lithuanian Movement for Reconstruction (Sajudis) drew up a programme of democratic and national rights. In the same year the ruling communists relaxed anti-nationalist measures and legalized a multi-party system. On 11 March 1990 the newly elected Lithuanian Supreme Soviet declared independence, a move rejected by the USSR. Initially despatched to Vilnius to enforce conscription, Soviet army units occupied key buildings in the face of mounting popular unrest. On 13 Jan. 1991 the army fired on demonstrators. A referendum held in Feb. 1991 produced a 90·5% vote in favour of independence. The USSR recognized Lithuania's independence on 6 Sept. 1991, with all Russian troops withdrawn by Aug. 1993. The 1992 Lithuanian constitution provided for a presidency and Algirdas Brazauskas won the first presidential elections the following year. Lithuanian became the official language in Jan. 1995, prompting protests from some Polish and Russian speakers. Lithuania joined NATO on 29 March 2004 and became a member of the EU on 1 May 2004.

Territory and Population

Lithuania is bounded in the north by Latvia, east and south by Belarus, and west by Poland, the Russian enclave of Kaliningrad and the Baltic Sea. The total area is 65,300 sq. km (25,212 sq. miles), including 2,265 sq. km (875 sq. miles) of inland waters, and the population (2011 census) 3,043,429 (1,640,825 females); density, 48·3 per sq. km. In Jan. 2017 the population was estimated at 2,847,904.

The UN gives a projected population for 2020 of 2·85m.

In 2011, 67·1% of the population lived in urban areas. Of the 2011 census population, Lithuanians accounted for 84·2%, Poles 6·6%, Russians 5·8% (9·4% in 1989), Belarusians 1·2% and Ukrainians 0·5%.

There are ten counties (with capitals of the same name): Alytus; Kaunas; Klaipėda; Marijampolė; Panevėžys; Šiauliai; Tauragė; Telšiai; Utena; Vilnius.

The capital is Vilnius (2011 census population, 535,631). Other large towns are Kaunas (315,933 in 2011), Klaipėda (162,360), Šiauliai (109,328) and Panevėžys (99,690).

The official language is Lithuanian, but ethnic minorities have the right to official use of their language where they form a substantial part of the population. All residents who applied by 3 Nov. 1991 received Lithuanian citizenship, requirements for which are ten years' residence and competence in Lithuanian.

Social Statistics

2009: births, 36,682; deaths, 42,032; marriages, 20,542; divorces, 9,270; infant deaths, 181. Rates (per 1,000 population): birth, 11·0; death, 12·6; marriage, 6·2; divorce, 2·8. The population started to decline in 1993, a trend which is set to continue. Annual population growth rate, 2010–15, −1·3%. In 2014, 8,809 live births were registered to unmarried mothers and there were 5,231 legally induced abortions. Life expectancy at birth in 2007 was 65·9 years for males and 77·7 years for females. In 2006 the most popular age range for marrying was 25–29 for males and 20–24 for females. Infant mortality, 2010, five per 1,000 live births; fertility rate, 2008, 1·3 births per woman (one of the lowest rates in the world). In 2014 there were 36,621 emigrants and 24,294 immigrants.

Lithuania has one of the world's highest suicide rates, at 33·3 per 100,000 inhabitants in 2012 (a rate of 59·5 among males but only 10·9 among females). The male suicide rate is the highest in any country.

Climate

Vilnius, Jan. −2·8°C, July 20·5°C. Annual rainfall 520 mm. Klaipėda, Jan. −0·6°C, July 19·4°C. Annual rainfall 770 mm.

Constitution and Government

A referendum to approve a new constitution was held on 25 Oct. 1992. Parliament is the 141-member *Seimas*. Under a new electoral law passed in July 2000, 71 of the parliament's 141 members will defeat rivals for their seats if they receive the most votes in a single round of balloting. Previously they had to win 50% of the votes or face a run-off against the nearest competitor. The parliament's 70 other seats are distributed according to the proportional popularity of the political parties at the ballot box.

The *Constitutional Court* is empowered to rule on whether proposed laws conflict with the constitution or existing legislation. It comprises nine judges who serve nine-year terms, one third rotating every three years.

National Anthem

'Lietuva, tėvyne mūsų' ('Lithuania, our fatherland'); words and tune by V. Kurdirka.

Government Chronology

(LDDP = Democratic Labour Party of Lithuania; LDP = Liberal Democratic Party; LKP = Communist Party of Lithuania; LLS = Lithuanian Liberal Union; LSDP = Social Democratic Party of Lithuania; Sajūdis = 'Unity'/ Reform Movement of Lithuania; TS(LK) = Homeland Union (Conservatives of Lithuania); TS-LKD = Homeland Union-Lithuanian Christian Democrats; n/p = non-partisan)

Heads of State since 1990.

Chairman of the Supreme Council		
1990–92	Sajūdis	Vytautas Landsbergis
Chairman of the Seimas (Parliament)		
1992–93	LDDP	Algirdas Brazauskas
Presidents of the Republic		
1993–98	LDDP	Algirdas Brazauskas
1998–2003	n/p	Valdas Adamkus
2003–04	LDP	Rolandas Paksas
2004–09	n/p	Valdas Adamkus
2009–	n/p	Dalia Grybauskaitė
Prime Ministers since 1990.		
1990–91	LKP/LDDP	Kazimiera Prunskienė
1991	Sajūdis	Albertas Simenas
1991–92	Sajūdis	Gediminas Vagnorius
1992	n/p	Aleksandras Abišala
1992–93	LDDP	Bronislovas Lubys
1993–96	LDDP	Adolfas Šleževičius
1996	LDDP	Mindaugas Stankevičius
1996–99	TS(LK)	Gediminas Vagnorius
1999	TS(LK)	Rolandas Paksas
1999–2000	TS(LK)	Andrius Kubilius
2000–01	LLS	Rolandas Paksas
2001–06	LSDP	Algirdas Brazauskas
2006–08	LSDP	Gediminas Kirkilas
2008–12	TS-LKD	Andrius Kubilius
2012–16	LSDP	Algirdas Butkevičius
2016–	n/p	Saulius Skvernelis

Recent Elections

In the first round of presidential elections held on 11 May 2014, incumbent president Dalia Grybauskaitė won 45·9% of the vote, ahead of Zigmantas Balčytis with 13·6%, Artūras Paulauskas 12·0%, Naglis Puteikis 9·3%, Valdemar Tomaševski 8·2%, Artūras Zuokas 5·2% and Bronis Ropė 4·1%.

Turnout was 52·2%. In the run-off held on 25 May, Grybauskaitė was re-elected to a second term gaining 57·9% of votes against Balčytis with 40·1%. Turnout for the second round was 47·3%.

Parliamentary elections were held in two rounds on 9 and 23 Oct. 2016. The Lithuanian Peasant and Greens Union (LVŽS) won 54 of the 141 seats, of which 35 were in single-member constituencies and 19 through proportional representation; Homeland Union-Lithuanian Christian Democrats 31, of which 11 were in single-member constituencies and 20 through proportional representation; Social Democratic Party of Lithuania 17, of which 4 were in single-member constituencies and 13 through proportional representation; Liberals' Movement of the Republic of Lithuania 14; Electoral Action of Poles in Lithuania-Christian Families Alliance 8; Order and Justice 8; Labour Party 2; Anti-Corruption Coalition (LCP-LPP) 1; Lithuanian Green Party 1; Lithuanian List 1. Four seats went to independents.

European Parliament

Lithuania has 11 representatives. At the May 2014 elections turnout was 47·4% (21·0% in 2009). The Homeland Union-Lithuanian Christian Democrats won 2 seats with 17·4% of votes cast (political affiliation in European Parliament: European People's Party); Social Democratic Party of Lithuania, 2 with 17·3% (Progressive Alliance of Socialists and Democrats); Liberals' Movement of the Republic of Lithuania, 2 with 16·6% (Alliance of Liberals and Democrats for Europe); Order and Justice, 2 with 14·3% (Europe of Freedom and Direct Democracy); Labour Party, 1 with 12·8% (Alliance of Liberals and Democrats for Europe); Electoral Action of Poles in Lithuania, 1 with 8·1% (European Conservatives and Reformists); Lithuanian Peasant and Greens Union, 1 with 6·6% (Greens/European Free Alliance).

Current Government

President: Dalia Grybauskaitė; b. 1956 (ind.; in office since 12 July 2009).

Prime Minister: Saulius Skvernelis; b. 1970 (ind.; in office since 13 Dec. 2016).

In Feb. 2019 the coalition government comprised:

Minister of Agriculture: Giedrius Surplys. *Culture:* Liana Ruokytė-Jonsson. *Economy:* Virginijus Sinkevičius. *Education and Science:* Jurgita Petrauskienė. *Energy:* Žygimantas Vaičiūnas. *Environment:* Kęstutis Navickas. *Finance:* Vilius Šapoka. *Foreign Affairs:* Linas Antanas Linkevičius. *Heath:* Aurelijus Veryga. *Interior:* Eimutis Misiūnas. *Justice:* Elvinas Jankevičius. *National Defence:* Raimundas Karoblis. *Social Security and Labour:* Linas Kukuraitis. *Transport and Communications:* Rokas Masiulis.

Office of the Prime Minister: http://ministraspirmininkas.lrv.lt

Current Leaders

Dalia Grybauskaitė

Position
President

Introduction
Dalia Grybauskaitė was sworn in as the first female president of Lithuania on 12 July 2009 after a landslide election victory. She left her job as EU commissioner for financial programming and budget to stand as an independent candidate, backed by the incumbent centre-right government. Renowned as a tough negotiator and skilled economist, she took office during the worst economic crisis since the dissolution of the Soviet Union. Her re-election in May 2014, albeit with a reduced vote share, marked the first time in the country's history that a president had been returned for two consecutive terms.

Early Life
Grybauskaitė was born on 1 March 1956 in Vilnius, the then capital of the Lithuanian Soviet Socialist Republic, and went on to study political and economic science at Zhdanov University (now St Petersburg State University).

After graduating, Grybauskaitė returned to Lithuania and embarked on a career as a lecturer at the department of political economy at Vilnius Higher Party School, in which role she worked for seven years. She received her doctorate in economic sciences from the Moscow Academy of Social Sciences in 1988.

Following the dissolution of the USSR and Lithuanian independence, Grybauskaitė completed a special course for leaders at Georgetown University in Washington in 1991. She subsequently entered government, going on to head departments in the ministries of international economic relations and foreign affairs between 1991 and 1994. She was Lithuania's representative when it entered into the European Union Free Trade Agreement in 1993.

She continued her involvement with the EU in 1994, when she was appointed envoy extraordinary and minister plenipotentiary at the Lithuanian mission to the EU. She continued her diplomatic work when she moved to the Lithuanian embassy in the USA.

In 1999 Grybauskaitė was appointed vice-minister of finance and foreign affairs in the cabinet of Prime Minister Andrius Kubilius. In this role she was responsible for conducting negotiations with international institutions including the World Bank and the IMF. In 2001 she was made minister of finance in the government of Algirdas Brazauskas.

Lithuania acceded to the EU on 1 May 2004, with Grybauskaitė appointed EU commissioner responsible for managing the EU budget and embarking on an ambitious programme of reform. In 2005 she criticized the UK's presidency of the EU, stating that the 'main obstacle' to reaching agreement on budgetary reform was Britain's insistence that it retain its rebate.

On 26 Feb. 2009 Grybauskaitė ended months of speculation by announcing her intention to stand in the forthcoming presidential elections. A popular figure across party lines, her entry into the race rendered the election a foregone conclusion, with opposition candidates either withdrawing or remaining in the race only to develop support ahead of elections to the European parliament. In the event, Grybauskaitė gained 69·1% of the vote, against 11·8% for her nearest challenger, Algirdas Butkevičius.

Career in Office

Grybauskaitė's victory was broadly popular, with several media commentators comparing the optimism that her election inspired with that seen in the United States on the inauguration of President Obama. In her inaugural address she promised to invest in local government and to narrow the gap between rich and poor in Lithuanian society, although she supported austerity measures to reduce the long-term impact of the prevailing economic crisis. She has also said that the reinforcement of Lithuania's energy security was among her top priorities and that she would seek to secure the provision of extra funds from the EU to develop energy links with the West and reduce dependence on Russia.

In Dec. 2012, following parliamentary elections in Oct., Grybauskaitė approved Algirdas Butkevičius, the leader of the opposition Social Democrats and a former rival for the presidency, as prime minister at the head of a new coalition government. She won a second term as president by winning the elections of May 2014.

Despite her close association with the EU, Grybauskaitė had initially promised that greater integration into Europe would not come at the price of deteriorating bilateral relations with Russia and that she would adopt a less confrontational approach to issues of international relations. However, in the wake of Russian intervention in Ukraine and annexation of Crimea in 2014, she said in Aug. that year that Russia was 'practically in a war with Europe'.

On 1 Jan. 2015 she oversaw Lithuania's adoption of the euro. Following parliamentary elections in Oct. 2016, Grybauskaitė appointed Saulius Skvernelis—an independent nominated by the Lithuanian Peasant and Greens Union—as prime minister in Nov. at the head of a new coalition government.

Saulius Skvernelis
Position
Prime Minister

Introduction
Saulius Skvernelis, a former police commissioner, became prime minister in Dec. 2016.

Early Life
Born 23 July 1970 in Kaunas (when Lithuania was still a republic of the Soviet Union), Skvernelis graduated in mechanical engineering from Vilnius Technical University (now the Vilnius Gediminas Technical University) in 1994. He subsequently attended the Lithuanian police academy and began his law enforcement career in 1998. He initially worked as a traffic inspector, rising to become general commissioner of the national police force in 2011.

He was appointed minister for the interior in Nov. 2014, having been nominated by the Order and Justice party despite not being a member. However, at parliamentary elections in Oct. 2016 he led the populist Lithuanian Peasant and Greens Union—a move that forced his ministerial resignation. The Union

achieved unexpected success, claiming 22·5% of the vote nationally and 54 of 141 seats—making it the largest party in parliament and undermining the Social Democratic Party–Labour Party coalition that previously held power. The Peasants and Green Union entered into coalition with the Social Democrats, and Skvernelis was appointed prime minister by President Dalia Grybauskaitė on 22 Nov. 2016. He assumed office on 13 Dec.

Career in Office
Skvernelis pledged Lithuania's commitment to NATO and the EU, criticizing Russia's use of force on the international stage, and to build a fence on Lithuania's borders with Russia and Belarus to reinforce security and prevent illegal migration. He also supported US President Donald Trump's call for NATO to spend more on defence and promised to increase Lithuania's military budget by 2% by 2018, alongside increased spending on border controls and intelligence services. He aims to deter young people from emigrating by improving investment in rural areas and tackling corruption, but he has been accused by some opponents of being a puppet of Ramūnas Karbauskis, the businessman who funds the Peasant and Greens Union.

Defence

Conscription ended on 1 July 2009 but was reintroduced in 2015 in view of Russia's military intervention in Ukraine. Conscripts between the ages of 19–26 are subjected to nine months of service. In 2013 defence expenditure totalled US$355m. (US$101 per capita), representing 0·8% of GDP.

Army
The Land Forces numbered 8,200 in 2011 and included one rapid reaction brigade. Reserves numbered 6,700 in 2011 and there were also 4,700 active reservists in the National Defence Voluntary Forces. There was a paramilitary riflemen union numbering 9,600 and a state border guard service of 5,000 operates under the ministry of internal affairs.

A joint Polish/Lithuanian battalion (LITPOLBAT), which was a component of the EU's rapid reaction forces, was disbanded in 2007. However, it was replaced in 2016 with a Lithuanian/Polish/Ukrainian Brigade (LITPOLUKRBRIG).

Navy
In 2011 the Navy numbered 530 personnel (120 conscripts). It operates several vessels including four patrol and coastal combatants. Lithuania, Estonia and Latvia have established a joint naval unit 'BALTRON' (Baltic Naval Squadron), with bases at Klaipėda in Lithuania, Tallinn in Estonia, and Liepāja, Riga and Ventspils in Latvia.

In addition there is a 540-strong Coast Guard.

Air Force
The Air Force consisted of 980 personnel (plus 190 civilians) in 2011. There are no combat-capable aircraft.

The joint Baltic Regional Air Surveillance Network (BALTNET), established in co-operation between the air forces of Estonia, Latvia and Lithuania, has its co-ordination centre in Karmėlava in Lithuania.

International Relations

Lithuania held a referendum on EU membership on 10–11 May 2003, in which 91·0% of votes cast were in favour of accession, with 9·0% against. It became a member of NATO on 29 March 2004 and the EU on 1 May 2004.

Economy

Agriculture accounted for 3·9% of GDP in 2011, industry 31·0% and services 65·1%.

Overview
The economy has a strong export base. Core exports include mineral products (14·9% of total exports in 2017), machinery and equipment (8·8%), furniture and household items (7·3%), and electrical machinery and equipment (7%). In 2016, 61% of exports went to other European Union member states. Russia's share of Lithuanian exports declined from 30% in 1997 to 13% in 2016, although 21·6% of imports (mostly of energy) still came from Russia. GDP growth averaged 4·1% per year between 2010 and 2014, before falling prices for export products saw it decline to 2·0% in 2015 before rising to 2·3% in 2016. The economy picked up in 2017, with growth increasing to 3·9%.

Most state enterprises have been privatized and the government has maintained a stable macroeconomic policy while strengthening economic ties with other countries. It is a member of the World Trade Organization and joined the European Union in May 2004. It has attracted significant foreign investment from EU partners, particularly the Nordic countries.

Following the collapse of the Soviet Union, recession in the early years of transition to a market economy from a command structure was more pronounced in Lithuania than in other Baltic states, partly because its export sector had closer ties to the Russian market. From 1995 to 1998 the economy grew at a strong rate, but the country again fell into recession in 1999 following the 1998 Russian financial crisis. However, in 2000 Lithuania recovered and enjoyed one of the highest annual growth rates of any transition economy.

Thriving exports and domestic consumer demand ensured average growth of 8% per annum in the four years before the 2008 global financial crisis. Between 1998 and 2008 real per capita incomes rose from about two-fifths to two-thirds of the EU average. Meanwhile, unemployment fell from 17·4% in 2001 to a record low of 4·3% in 2007. However, the downturn prompted by the 2008 crisis was severe. A contraction in domestic demand was compounded by Lithuania's main export partners also falling into recession. The economy shrank by 14·8% in 2009, while unemployment surged to 18·3% by June 2010.

In the boom years a large structural deficit had been accumulated, putting public finances under strain during the crisis. With the currency fixed against the euro at that time, and lending from the international bond markets unforthcoming, the government implemented a package of austerity measures in Dec. 2009. Public spending was cut by 30%, public sector wages fell by between 20–30%, pensions were cut by up to 11%, VAT rose from 18% to 21%, corporate tax went from 15% to 20% and there were significant tax rises on alcohol and pharmaceuticals. The measures resulted in savings equivalent to 9% of GDP, negating the need to call on the assistance of the IMF, while the government deficit fell to 0·7% of GDP by 2014.

Ongoing uncertainty in the eurozone is the main threat to Lithuania's long-term economic prospects, particularly following the country's adoption of the euro in Jan. 2015. A further challenge is posed by tensions between Russia and several of its European neighbours.

Currency

On 1 Jan. 2015 the *euro* (EUR) replaced the *litas* (LTL) as the legal currency of Lithuania at the irrevocable conversion rate of 3·45280 litai to one euro. Inflation, which reached a high of 1,161% in the early 1990s, was just 0·7% in 2016. There was then inflation of 3·7% in 2017. Total money supply was 13,884m. litai in July 2005, foreign exchange reserves were US$3,411m. and gold reserves 186,000 troy oz.

Budget

Budgetary central government revenue and expenditure (in 1m. litai):

	2009	2010	2011
Revenue	17,487	19,032	20,724
Expenditure	21,691	22,423	23,091

Principal sources of revenue in 2011: taxes on goods and services, 11,859m. litai; grants, 4,419m. litai; taxes on income, profits and capital gains, 2,317m. litai. Main items of expenditure by economic type in 2011: grants, 6,395m. litai; compensation of employees, 5,106m. litai; social benefits, 3,369m. litai. There is a flat income tax rate of 15%.

Lithuania registered a budget surplus 0·5% of GDP in 2017. There was a surplus in 2016 (0·3%) and a deficit in 2015 (0·3%). The required target set by the EU is a budget deficit of no more than 3%.

VAT is 21% (reduced rates, 9% and 5%).

Performance

Between 2000 and 2006 growth averaged 7·0%. In 2007 and 2008 the economy continued to grow, by 11·1% and 2·6% respectively, although Lithuania was then one of the countries most affected by the economic crisis in 2009, with the GDP contracting by 14·8%. There was a slight recovery in 2010 when the economy grew by 1·6%. More recently real GDP growth was 2·0% in 2015, 2·3% in 2016 and 3·9% in 2017. Total GDP in 2017 was US$47·2bn.

Banking and Finance

The central bank and bank of issue is the Bank of Lithuania (*Governor*, Vitas Vasiliauskas). A programme to restructure and privatize the state banks was started in 1996. In 2007 there were 11 commercial banks and foreign bank branches, the central credit union of Lithuania and 66 credit unions in operation. The largest private bank in Lithuania is SEB Vilniaus bankas, which controls approximately 36% of the total banking assets in the country. In 2006 it was estimated that total assets of domestic commercial banks amounted to 59bn. litai.

Foreign debt amounted to US$29,602m. in 2010, up from US$11,433m. in 2005 and US$4,723m. in 2000. Lithuania's foreign debt in 2010 was equivalent to 83·0% of GNI (up from 42·0% in 2000).

A stock exchange opened in Vilnius in 1993. In Nov. 2007 its capitalization was €6·8bn. The trading turnover in 2006 was €1·6bn.

Energy and Natural Resources

In 2011, 20·3% of energy consumption came from renewables (wind power, solar power, hydro-electric power, tidal power, geothermal energy and biomass), compared to the European Union average of 13·0%. A target of 23% has been set by the EU for 2020.

Environment

Carbon dioxide emissions from the consumption of energy were the equivalent of 4·3 tonnes per capita in 2011.

Electricity

Installed capacity was estimated at 3·51m. kW in 2011; production was 4·82bn. kWh in 2011. A nuclear power station (with two reactors) in Ignalina was responsible for 70·2% of total output in 2007. At the time no other country had such a high percentage of its electricity generated through nuclear power. However, as a condition of entry into the European Union the government agreed to close down Ignalina. The process to close the first reactor began on 31 Dec. 2004. The whole facility was shut down on 31 Dec. 2009. Plans to build a successor near the old site are being reconsidered after 64·8% opposed the idea in a consultative referendum held in Oct. 2012. Prior to the closure of Ignalina, Lithuania was one of the countries most reliant on nuclear energy. Electricity consumption per capita in 2011 was 3,798 kWh.

Oil and Gas

Oil production started from a small field at Kretinga in 1990. Reserves were 12m. bbls in 2014. Oil production in 2011 was 0·8m. bbls. Lithuania relies on Russia for almost all of its oil and gas.

Minerals

Output of minerals in 2006 (1,000 cu. metres): dolomite, 1,600; limestone, 900; peat, 400. Quarrying of gravel, clay and sand totalled 8·7m. cu. metres in 2006.

Agriculture

In 2013 agriculture employed about 7·4% of the total number of employed persons. As of 1 June 2010 the average farm size was 13·8 ha.; the utilized agricultural land area was 2,890,928 ha. In 2012 there were 2,260,500 ha. of arable land and 31,800 ha. of permanent crops. In 2013, 95,500 persons were employed in agriculture.

Output of main agricultural products (in 1,000 tonnes) in 2013: wheat, 2,869; sugar beets, 967; barley, 687; rapeseed, 542; potatoes, 426; oats, 164; rye, 97; cabbage, 77. Value of agricultural production, 2013 (in 1m. litai), was 8,800·2 of which from individual farm holdings, 6,353·1; and from agricultural partnerships and enterprises, 2,447·1.

Livestock, as of 1 Jan. 2014 (in 1,000): cattle, 713·5 (of which dairy cows, 315·7); pigs, 754·6; sheep and goats, 113·4; horses, 22·2; poultry, 9,761·6.

Animal products, 2013 unless otherwise indicated (in 1,000 tonnes): meat (2012), 207·4; milk, 1,723·1; eggs, 772m. units.

Forestry

In 2015 forests covered 2·2m. ha., or 35% of the land area, and consist of conifers, mostly pine. Of the total area under forests 1% was primary forest in

2015, 73% other naturally regenerated forest and 26% planted forest. Timber production in 2011, 7·00m. cu. metres.

Fisheries

In 2011 the fishing fleet comprised 171 vessels of a combined 45,960 gross tonnes. Total catch in 2015 amounted to 85,144 tonnes (mainly from sea fishing), down from 187,513 tonnes in 2007 although up from 44,002 tonnes in 1997.

Industry

Industrial output in 2006 included (in 1,000 tonnes): petrol, 2,303; cement, 1,100; sulphuric acid, 730; sugar, 97; woollen fabrics, 22·5m. sq. metres; cotton fabrics, 20·4m. cu. metres; linen, 12·8m. sq. metres; television picture tubes, 1,240,000 units; TV sets, 711,300 units; bicycles, 330,000 units.

Labour

In 2013 the number of employed persons was 1·3m. (71·4% in private enterprises and 28·6% in the public sector). Employed population by activity (as a percentage): wholesale and retail trade, repair of motor vehicles and motorcycles, 17·6; manufacturing, 15·4; education, 9·7; construction, 7·7; transportation and storage, 7·3; human health and social work activities, 6·6; real estate activities, 1·2. Employment skills in 2013 included 41·0% with tertiary education and 55·0% with upper secondary and post-secondary non-tertiary education. There were a total of 3,080 working days lost to strike action in 2012 (31,601 in 2008, legal strikes did not take place in 2009–11 or in 2013). In 2013 average gross monthly earnings were 2,231·7 litai; legal minimum wage was 1,000 litai in 2013.

International Trade

Foreign investors may purchase up to 100% of the equity companies in Lithuania.

Individual laws on three free economic zones (namely the laws on Šiauliai, Klaipėda and Kaunas) have been cleared by Lithuania's Parliament, the Seimas.

Imports and Exports

Imports and exports for calendar years in US$1m.:

	2006	2007	2008	2009	2010
Imports c.i.f.	19,388·4	24,445·1	31,294·7	18,340·6	23,378·0
Exports f.o.b.	14,135·2	17,162·4	23,769·9	16,496·3	20,813·9

Leading import suppliers, 2006: Russia, 24·2%; Germany, 14·9%; Poland, 9·5%; Latvia, 4·8%. Principal export markets, 2006: Russia, 12·8%; Latvia, 11·1%; Germany, 8·6%; Estonia, 6·5%.

Main imports are machinery and apparatus, crude petroleum, road vehicles, and chemicals and chemical products. Main exports are mineral products, electrical equipment, textiles and textile articles, transport equipment, TV sets, chemical products and prepared foodstuffs.

Communications

Roads

In 2007 there were 80,715 km of roads (including 309 km of motorways), of which 28·6% were paved. There were 1,587,900 passenger cars in use in 2007 (470 per 1,000 inhabitants), plus 14,000 buses and coaches, 14,500 lorries and vans, and 35,300 motorcycles and mopeds. There were 6,448 traffic accidents in 2007, with 740 fatalities.

Rail

In 2011 there were 1,767 km of railway track in operation in Lithuania. The majority of rail traffic was diesel propelled, although 122 km of track was electrified. In 2011, 4·7m. passengers and 52·3m. tonnes of freight were carried.

Civil Aviation

The main international airport is based in the capital, Vilnius. Other international airports are at Kaunas and Palanga. FlyLAL–Lithuanian Airlines,

formerly Lithuania's largest airline, ceased operations in 2009. Air Lituanica, founded in 2013, was the national flag carrier until it ceased operations in May 2015. In 2015 a number of international airlines ran regular scheduled flights to Lithuania. Vilnius handled 1,308,065 passengers in 2009 and 4,336 tonnes of freight. Kaunas handled 456,698 passengers in 2009 and Palanga 105,195.

Shipping

The ice-free port of Klaipėda plays a dominant role in the national economy and Baltic maritime traffic. It handled 33,418,000 tonnes of cargo in 2013 (23,621,000 tonnes loaded and 9,797,000 tonnes discharged); container traffic totalled 403,000 TEUs (twenty-foot equivalent units) in 2013. A 412 ha. site at the port is dedicated a Free Economic Zone, which offers attractive conditions to foreign investors.

In Jan. 2014 there were 43 ships of 300 GT or over registered, totalling 370,000 GT.

Telecommunications

A majority stake in Lithuanian Telecom (the only fixed telephone service provider) was sold to the Finnish and Swedish consortium SONERA in 1998 and by Jan. 2003 the telecommunications market was fully liberalized. In 2010 there were 733,700 landline telephone subscriptions (equivalent to 220·8 per 1,000 inhabitants) and 4,891,000 mobile phone subscriptions (or 1,471·6 per 1,000 inhabitants). There were 621·2 internet users per 1,000 inhabitants in 2010. Fixed internet subscriptions totalled 636,000 in 2009 (190·3 per 1,000 inhabitants). In March 2012 there were 983,000 Facebook users.

Social Institutions

Out of 178 countries analysed in the 2017 *Fragile States Index*—a list published jointly by the Fund for Peace and *Foreign Policy* magazine—Lithuania was ranked the joint 30th least vulnerable (along with Mauritius) to conflict or collapse. The index is based on 12 indicators of state vulnerability across social, political and economic categories.

Justice

The general jurisdiction court system consists of the Supreme Court, the Court of Appeal, five county courts and 54 district courts. Specialized administrative courts were established in 1999. In 2006 there were 732 judges: 469 in district courts, 144 in county courts, 27 in the Court of Appeal, 34 in the Supreme Court, 43 in the administrative county courts and 15 in the High Administrative Court.

The population in penal institutions in Sept. 2015 was 7,810 (268 per 100,000 of national population). Lithuania's prison population rate is the highest in the European Union. In 2006 there were 294 murders. The death penalty was abolished for all crimes in 1998.

Education

Education is compulsory from seven to 16. In 2013 there were 93,569 children with (2012) 12,542 teaching staff in pre-primary schools, 109,028 pupils with (2012) 8,961 teachers in primary schools and 294,274 pupils with (2012) 36,649 teachers in secondary schools. There were 159,695 students in tertiary education in 2013 with (2012) 13,923 academic staff.

The adult literacy rate in 2009 was estimated at 99·7% (99·7% for both males and females).

In 2006 public expenditure on education represented 5·0% of GNI and 14·4% of total government expenditure.

Health

In 2006 there were 13,510 physicians, 2,249 dentists, 26,140 nurses and midwives and 2,184 pharmacists. There were 72 hospital beds per 10,000 population in 2014.

In *Water: At What Cost? The State of the World's Water 2016*, WaterAid reported that 3·4% of the population does not have access to safe water.

Welfare

The social security system is financed by the State Social Insurance Fund. In 2013, 616,801 persons were eligible for state social insurance old-age pensions (including anticipatory old-age pensions), 215,616 for work incapacity/disability pensions and 266,378 for widow's/widower's (including orphan's) pensions. In 2013 the average state social insurance old-age pension was 822 litai (monthly).

In 2014 the retirement age for men was 63 years and for women 61 years. Prior to 2012 the retirement age was 62 years and 6 months for men and 60 years for women. It is rising gradually for both sexes until men and women will both retire at 65 in 2026. The average number of persons entitled to the state social insurance old-age pension in 2013 was 598,700.

Religion

Under the Constitution, the state recognizes traditional Lutheran churches and religious organizations, as well as other churches and religious organizations if their teaching and rituals do not contradict the law. According to the Pew Research Center's Forum on Religion & Public Life, in 2010 there were an estimated 2·76m. Catholics and 170,000 Orthodox Christians; a further 330,000 people had no religious affiliation. In Feb. 2019 there was one cardinal.

Culture

World Heritage Sites

Lithuania has four sites (two shared) on the UNESCO World Heritage List: Vilnius Historic Centre (inscribed on the list in 1994) and Kernavė Archaeological Site (2004).

Lithuania shares the Curonian Spit (2000) with the Russian Federation as a UNESCO site. A sand-dune spit between Zelenogradsk, Kaliningrad Region, and Klaipėda, Lithuania, the Spit was subject to massive protective engineering in the 19th century. Lithuania also shares the Struve Geodetic Arc (2005). The Arc is a chain of survey triangulations spanning from Norway to the Black Sea that helped establish the exact shape and size of the earth and is shared with nine other countries.

Press

In 2014 there were 239 newspapers (ten paid-for dailies and 229 paid-for non-dailies). The papers with the highest readership are *Lietuvos rytas* and *Vakaro žinios*.

Tourism

In 2010 accommodation establishments received 1,552,900 guests (up from 1,325,600 in 2005), of whom 840,400 were foreigners (681,500 in 2005). The leading countries of origin of non-resident overnight visitors in 2010 were: Poland (135,900), Russia (105,900), Germany (105,800) and Belarus (71,400). Lithuania had 908 accommodation establishments in 2010 with 50,087 beds, including 342 hotels with 23,137 beds.

Festivals

The Lithuanian Song and Dance Celebration is held every four years, focusing international attention on the country's culture. There is also a Kaunas Jazz Festival and the Pažaislis Classical Music Festival (also in Kaunas). The main rock festivals are the summer festivals, Be2gether at Norviliškės near the Belarusian border and Rock Nights at Zarasai. Major film festivals include Cinema Spring in Vilnius and the Kaunas International Film Festival. The annual Klaipėda Sea Festival attracts nearly half a million visitors each year.

Diplomatic Representatives

Of Lithuania in the United Kingdom (Lithuania House, 2 Bessborough Gdns, London, SW1V 2JE)
Ambassador: Renatas Norkus.

Of the United Kingdom in Lithuania (Antakalnio str. 2, 10308 Vilnius)
Ambassador: Claire Lawrence.

Of Lithuania in the USA (2622 16th St., NW, Washington, D.C., 20009)
Ambassador: Rolandas Kriščiūnas.

Of the USA in Lithuania (Akmenų 6, 03106 Vilnius)
Ambassador: Anne Hall.

Of Lithuania to the United Nations
Ambassador: Audra Plepytė.

Of Lithuania to the European Union
Permanent Representative: Jovita Neliupšienė.

Further Reading

Department of Statistics to the Government. *Statistical Yearbook of Lithuania.* Annual. *Economic and Social Development in Lithuania.* Monthly.
Hood, N., *et al.*, (eds) *Transition in the Baltic States.* 1997
Kasekamp, Andres, *A History of the Baltic States.* 2010
Lane, Thomas, *Lithuania: Stepping Westward.* 2001
Lieven, A., *The Baltic Revolution: Estonia, Latvia, Lithuania and the Path to Independence.* 2nd ed. 1994
Misiunas, R. J. and Taagepera, R., *The Baltic States: the Years of Dependence, 1940–90.* 2nd ed. 1993
O'Connor, Kevin, *The History of the Baltic States.* 2003
Plakans, Andrejs, *A Concise History of the Baltic States.* 2011
Smith, David J., Purs, Aldis, Pabriks, Artis and Lane, Thomas, (eds) *The Baltic States: Estonia, Latvia and Lithuania.* 2002
Vardys, V. S. and Sedaitis, J. B., *Lithuania: the Rebel Nation.* 1997
National Statistical Office: Department of Statistics to the Government, Gedimino Pr. 29, LT 01 500 Vilnius.
Website: http://www.stat.gov.lt

Luxembourg

Grand-Duché de Luxembourg (Grand Duchy of Luxembourg)

Capital: Luxembourg
Population projection, 2020: 604,000
GNI per capita, 2017: (PPP$) 65,016
HDI/world rank, 2017: 0·904/21
Internet domain extension: .lu

Key Historical Events

Celtic tribes, with origins in the Danube basin, settled in the Ardennes hills and surrounding plains from at least 1000 BC. The Romans advanced north into the region (then part of Gaul) from around 50 BC and controlled much of it over the next five centuries from garrisons such as that at Trier. Frankish clans from the middle Rhine valley spread across present-day Luxembourg from around the 5th century AD and intermarried with the Gallo-Romans. Anglo-Saxon missionaries were active in the region during the 7th century, and a Benedictine monastery was founded at Echternach in 698. From the early 9th century the region was controlled by Charlemagne, the Roman Emperor in the West, who ruled from Hungary to the Atlantic Ocean. The empire's division, following the signing of the Treaty of Verdun in 843, enabled the rise of several feudal states, one of which became Luxembourg; the castle of Lutzilinburhurch was founded by Count Sigefroi in 963 on an outcrop overlooking the river Alzette.

Subsequent Counts of Luxembourg were influential in the wider European arena. From 1353, under Wenzel I, Luxembourg expanded to its greatest extent, covering four times the area of the present state. The House of Luxembourg subsequently went into decline and from 1443 was ruled by the Burgundians from their capital, Brussels. In 1477 Luxembourg became one of the 17 provinces of the Netherlands to come under Habsburg rule, initially under Maximilian of Austria and later under Charles of Ghent, who became the King of Spain in 1516 and Holy Roman Emperor in 1520. Luxembourg was ruled as part of the Spanish Netherlands for much of the next 200 years, although there were brief periods of French dominance under Louis XIV in the 1680s and 1690s. The transfer of the Spanish Netherlands to Austrian rule in 1715 heralded a period of relative tranquility for Luxembourg, which lasted until the territory was occupied by French revolutionary forces in the 1790s.

The 1815 Congress of Vienna made Luxembourg a grand duchy, which subsequently came under the jurisdiction of the house of Orange-Nassau, the ruling house of the Netherlands. At the same time it became part of the German Confederation. In 1839 the Walloon-speaking area was joined to Belgium, which had achieved independence in 1831, giving the Lëtzebuergesch-speaking provinces autonomy. At the London Conference of 1867 the European powers declared Luxembourg a neutral territory and in 1890 the union with the Netherlands was ended. Full independence was confirmed in the same year when Adolf of Nassau-Weilburg became grand duke, founding the present line of rulers.

Luxembourg was invaded and occupied by Germany in both the First and Second World Wars. In June 1942 the Grand Duchy staged a general strike against occupation. In 1948 a Benelux customs union formed by Belgium, the Netherlands and Luxembourg allowed for standardization of prices, taxes and wages and the free movement of labour among the three countries. Luxembourg joined NATO in 1949 and was one of six founding countries of the European Economic Community in 1957. On 24 Dec. 1999 Prime Minister Jean-Claude Juncker announced Grand Duke Jean's decision to abdicate the throne on 7 Oct. 2000. He was succeeded by Prince Henri who assumed the title of Grand Duke.

Territory and Population

Luxembourg has an area of 2,586 sq. km (999 sq. miles) and is bounded on the west by Belgium, south by France and east by Germany. A census took place on 1 Feb. 2011; the population was 512,353. On 1 Jan. 2013 the population was 537,039 (including 238,800 foreigners); density, 208 per sq. km. The percentage of foreigners living in Luxembourg has increased dramatically in recent years, from 26% in 1986 to 45% in 2013 (the highest percentage in the EU). The main countries of origin of foreigners living in Luxembourg are Portugal (88,200 in Jan. 2013), France (35,200) and Italy (18,300).

In 2011, 85·4% of the population were urban. The capital, Luxembourg, has (Jan. 2013) 103,641 inhabitants; Esch-sur-Alzette, the centre of the mining district, 31,898; Differdange, 22,769; Dudelange, 19,292; Pétange, 16,762; Sanem, 14,832; Hésperange, 14,027.

The UN gives a projected population for 2020 of 604,000.

Luxembourgish (Lëtzebuergesch) is spoken by most of the population, and since 1984 has been an official language with French and German.

Social Statistics

Statistics (figures in parentheses indicate births and deaths of resident foreigners):

	Births	Deaths	Marriages	Divorces
2007	5,477 (2,959)	3,886 (721)	1,969	1,106
2008	5,596 (3,126)	3,595 (612)	1,917	977
2009	5,638 (2,952)	3,655 (659)	1,739	1,052
2010	5,874 (2,845)	3,760 (711)	1,749	1,083

2010 rates per 1,000 population; birth, 11·6; death, 7·4; marriage, 3·5; divorce, 2·1. Nearly half of annual births are to foreigners. In 2013 the most popular age range for marrying was 30–34 for males and 25–29 for females. Life expectancy at birth in 2013 was 78·0 years for males and 83·0 years for females. Annual population growth rate, 2005–10, 2·1%. Infant mortality, 2010, two per 1,000 live births (one of the lowest rates in the world); fertility rate, 2013, 1·7 births per woman. In 2012 Luxembourg received 2,055 asylum applications.

Climate

In general the country resembles Belgium in its climate, with rain evenly distributed throughout the year. Average temperatures are Jan. 0·8°C, July 17·5°C. Annual rainfall 30·8" (782·2 mm).

Constitution and Government

The Grand Duchy of Luxembourg is a constitutional monarchy.

The reigning Grand Duke is **Henri**, b. 16 April 1955, son of the former Grand Duke Jean and Princess Joséphine-Charlotte of Belgium; succeeded 7 Oct. 2000 on the abdication of his father; married Maria Teresa Mestre 14 Feb. 1981. *Offspring:* Prince Guillaume, b. 11 Nov. 1981 (married Countess Stéphanie Marie Claudine Christine de Lannoy, b. 18 Feb. 1984, on 19 Oct. 2012); Prince Félix, b. 3 June 1984 (married Claire Lademacher, b. 21 March 1985, on 17 Sept. 2013; *offspring,* Amalia, b. 15 June 2014; Liam, b. 28 Nov. 2016); Prince Louis, b. 3 Aug. 1986 (married Tessy Antony, b. 28 Oct. 1985, on 29 Sept. 2006, divorced 17 Feb. 2017; *offspring,* Gabriel, b. 12 March 2006; Noah, b. 21 Sept. 2007); Princess Alexandra, b. 16 Feb. 1991; Prince Sébastien, b. 16 April 1992.

The constitution of 17 Oct. 1868 was revised in 1919, 1948, 1956, 1972, 1979, 1983, 1988 and more than 20 occasions since then.

The separation of powers between the legislature and the executive is not very strong, resulting in much interaction between the two bodies. Only the judiciary is completely independent.

The 12 cantons are divided into four electoral districts: the South, the East, the Centre and the North. Voters choose between party lists of candidates in multi-member constituencies. The parliament is the *Chamber of Deputies*, which consists of a maximum of 60 members elected for five years. Voting is compulsory for all citizens between the age of 18 and 75 (but not residents who are not citizens) and there is universal suffrage. Seats are allocated according to the rules of proportional representation and the principle of the smallest electoral quote. There is a *Council of State* of 21 members appointed by the Sovereign. Membership is for a maximum period of 15 years, with retirement compulsory at the age of 72. It advises on proposed laws and any other question referred to it.

The head of state takes part in the legislative power, exercises executive power and has a part in the judicial power. The constitution leaves to the sovereign the right to organize the government, which consists of a Minister of State, who is Prime Minister, and of at least three Ministers. Direct consultation by referendum is provided for in the Constitution.

National Anthem

'Ons Hemecht' ('Our Homeland'); words by M. Lentz, tune by J. A. Zinnen.

Government Chronology

Prime Ministers since 1937. (CSV = Christian Social Party; DP = Democratic Party)

1937–53	CSV	Pierre Dupong
1953–58	CSV	Joseph Bech
1958–59	CSV	Pierre Frieden
1959–74	CSV	Pierre Werner
1974–79	DP	Gaston Thorn
1979–84	CSV	Pierre Werner
1984–95	CSV	Jacques Santer
1995–2013	CSV	Jean-Claude Juncker
2013–	DP	Xavier Bettel

Recent Elections

Parliamentary elections took place on 14 Oct. 2018. The Christian Social People's Party (CSV) won 21 seats (with 28·3% of the vote), the Democratic Party (DP) 12 (16·9%), the Socialist Workers' Party (LSAP) 10 (17·6%), the Greens (Déi Gréng) 9 (15·1%), the Alternative Democratic Reform Party (ADR) 4 (8·3%), the Pirate Party 2 (6·4%) and the Left 2 (5·5%). Turnout was 89·7%.

European Parliament

Luxembourg has six representatives. At the May 2014 elections turnout was 90·0% (90·8% in 2009). CSV won 3 seats with 37·7% of votes cast (political affiliation in European Parliament: European People's Party); the Greens, 1 with 15·0% (Greens/European Free Alliance); DP, 1 with 14·8% (Alliance of Liberals and Democrats for Europe); LSAP, 1 with 11·8% (Progressive Alliance of Socialists and Democrats).

Current Government

In Feb. 2019 the three-party coalition government comprised:

Prime Minister, Minister of State, and of Communications and Media, Religious Affairs, Digitization, and Administrative Reform: Xavier Bettel; b. 1973 (DP; in office since 4 Dec. 2013).

Deputy Prime Minister, and Minister of Economy, and Health: Étienne Schneider. *Deputy Prime Minister, and Minister of Justice:* Félix Braz.

Minister of Agriculture, Viticulture and Rural Development, and Social Security: Romain Schneider. *Culture, and Housing:* Sam Tanson. *Defence, Mobility and Public Works, and Internal Security:* François Bausch. *Development Co-operation and Humanitarian Affairs, and Consumer Protection:* Paulette Lenert. *Environment, Climate and Sustainable Development:* Carole Dieschbourg. *Equality between Women and Men, and Home Affairs:* Taina Bofferding. *Family and Integration, and the Greater Region:* Corinne Cahen. *Finance:* Pierre Gramegna. *Foreign and European Affairs, and Immigration and Asylum:* Jean Asselborn. *Middle Classes, and Tourism:* Lex Delles. *National Education, Children and Youth, and Higher Education and Research:* Claude Meisch. *Public Service, and Relations with Parliament:* Marc Hansen. *Spatial Planning, and Energy:* Claude Turmes. *Sport, and Labour, Employment, and the Social and Solidarity Economy:* Dan Kersch. *Government Website:* http://www.gouvernement.lu

Current Leaders

Xavier Bettel

Position
Prime Minister

Introduction
Xavier Bettel became prime minister in Dec. 2013, taking over from Jean-Claude Juncker who had held the position for 18 years. A barrister and long-standing member of the centre-right Democratic Party (DP), he headed the first government since 1979 not to be led by the Christian Social Party (CSV). Following the parliamentary elections in Oct. 2018, in which the DP became the second largest party, Bettel formed a new coalition government that took office on 5 Dec.

Early Life
Bettel was born on 3 March 1973 in Luxembourg City. He graduated in public and European law from the University of Nancy, France, and undertook further studies in maritime law at Aristotle University in Thessaloniki, Greece. He entered parliament as a DP member in 1999 and qualified as a barrister in 2001.

Re-elected to parliament in 2004 and 2009, he served on its legal affairs committee and was chairman of the DP parliamentary group between 2009 and 2011. Also active in municipal politics, he was variously a councillor, alderman and mayor of Luxembourg City between 2011 and 2013.

In snap legislative elections in Oct. 2013 (prompted by a phone-tapping scandal that engulfed the ruling CSV in mid-2013), the DP, in coalition with the Socialist Workers' Party and the Greens, emerged as narrow victors. Bettel was charged with forming a government by Grand Duke Henri, and was sworn in as prime minister on 4 Dec. 2013.

Career in Office
Bettel pledged to cut the budget deficit and preserve Luxembourg's triple-A international credit rating by cutting public spending and raising VAT. The government promised not to introduce a wealth tax on individuals or an inheritance tax, but in Nov. 2014 it became embroiled in a controversy over tax concessions by the previous administration to multinational companies. As the country's first openly gay premier, Bettel was expected to promote socially liberal policies and in June 2014 he supported parliament's vote to legalize same-sex marriage. In June 2015 proposals to allow foreign residents to vote in national elections, to lower the voting age to 16 and to introduce term limits in government were all rejected in a constitutional referendum.

After the Oct. 2018 legislative elections, Bettel was reappointed as prime minister in Dec. heading a coalition of the DP, the the Socialist Workers' Party (LSAP) and Déi Gréng.

Defence

There is a volunteer light infantry battalion of (2009) 900, of which only the career officers are professionals. In recent years Luxembourg soldiers and officers have been actively participating in peacekeeping missions, mainly in the former Yugoslavia. There is also a Gendarmerie of 600. In 2000 the Gendarmerie and the police force merged to form the Police Grand-Ducale. NATO maintains a squadron of E-3A *Sentries*.

In 2013 defence expenditure totalled US$249m. (US$484 per capita), representing 0·4% of GDP.

Economy

Services accounted for 86% of GDP in 2012 and industry 14%.

According to the anti-corruption organization Transparency International, Luxembourg ranked equal ninth in the world in a 2018 survey of the countries with the least corruption in business and government. It received 81 out of 100 in the annual index.

Luxembourg gave US$424m. in international aid in 2017, which at 1·00% of GNI made it the second most generous developed country as a percentage of its gross national income, after Sweden. Luxembourg was one of only five industrialized countries to meet the UN target of 0·7%.

Overview

Luxembourg has a service-based economy dominated by the financial sector, which contributes over 33% of GDP annually. The country hosts Europe's largest investment fund industry and second largest money market sector. Other dynamic sectors include telecommunications, audio-visual and multi-media and air transport industries. Steel production has historically been an economic driver and the traditionally small industrial sector has diversified to include chemical, plastics, rubber and other manufactured products.

Given its large financial sector, Luxembourg was badly damaged by the global financial crisis. Gross investment decreased by 23% in 2009, two major banks were bailed out, three smaller banks failed and unemployment increased. This led to the economy's worst performance for 30 years, contracting by 5·4% in that year. However, despite a further shallow recession in 2012, a fiscal stimulus package then spurred annual average GDP growth of 3·2% over the period 2012–16.

Key challenges include reducing the economy's reliance on, and addressing vulnerabilities in, the financial sector, especially in the face of eurozone volatility.

Currency

On 1 Jan. 1999 the *euro* (EUR) became the legal currency in Luxembourg at the irrevocable conversion rate of 40·3399 Luxembourg francs to 1 euro. The euro, which consists of 100 cents, has been in circulation since 1 Jan. 2002. On the introduction of the euro there was a 'dual circulation' period before the Luxembourg franc ceased to be legal tender on 28 Feb. 2002. There was zero inflation in 2016 and inflation of 2·1% in 2017. Foreign exchange reserves were US$285m. in Sept. 2009 (none in 2002) and gold reserves 73,000 troy oz. Total money supply was €84,140m. in March 2009.

Budget

Budgetary central government revenue and expenditure for calendar years in €1m.:

	2009	2010	2011
Revenue	10,488·9	11,276·8	11,732·7
Expenditure	11,072·5	11,677·6	12,169·0

Principal sources of revenue in 2011: taxes on income, profits and capital gains, €4,978·0m.; taxes on goods and services, €4,822·4m. Main items of expenditure by economic type in 2011: grants, €5,483·1m; compensation of employees, €2,571·7m.

Luxembourg registered a budget surplus of 1·4% of GDP in 2017. There had been surpluses of 1·6% in 2016 and 1·3% in 2015. The required target set by the EU is a budget deficit of no more than 3%.

VAT is 17%, with reduced rates of 14%, 8% and 3%. Income taxes and business taxes have been reduced to preserve competitiveness in the international environment. The normal tax rate for companies at 1 Jan. 2013 was 29·2%, compared with 40·3% in 1996.

Performance

In terms of GDP per head, Luxembourg ranks among the richest countries in the world with a purchasing power parity (PPP) per capita GDP of 79,258 current international dollars in 2009. The economy grew by 2·9% in 2015, 3·1% in 2016 and 2·3% in 2017. Total GDP in 2017 was US$62·4bn.

Banking and Finance

Luxembourg's Central Bank (formerly the Monetary Institute) was established in July 1998 (*Director-General*, Gaston Reinesch). In March 2015 there were 143 banks, down from 155 in 2005 and 220 in 1995. German banks make up approximately 20% of all the banks and French banks around 10%. Total assets and liabilities in Dec. 2015 were €743·2bn. There is a stock exchange.

The financial sector accounts for 27% of gross value added. The total number of approved insurance companies in 2015 was 94, with reinsurance companies numbering 217.

Luxembourg's gross external debt amounted to US$2,197,354m. in June 2012.

Energy and Natural Resources

In 2011 just 2·9% of energy consumption came from renewables (wind power, solar power, hydro-electric power, tidal power, geothermal energy and biomass), compared to the European Union average of 13·0%. A target of 11% has been set by the EU for 2020.

Environment

Carbon dioxide emissions from the consumption of energy in 2011 were the equivalent of 23·1 tonnes per capita (compared to the European average of 7·1 tonnes per capita).

Electricity

Apart from hydro-electricity and electricity generated from fossil fuels, Luxembourg has no national energy resources. Installed capacity in 2011 was 1·7m. kW. Production was 3,717m. kWh in 2011 and consumption per capita 15,879 kWh.

Agriculture

The contribution of agriculture to the economy has been gradually declining over the years, with agriculture, forestry and fishing accounting for only 0·3% of gross domestic product in 2008. There were 4,950 workers engaged in agricultural work in 2013. In 2007 there were 2,303 farms with an average area of 63·4 ha.; 130,884 ha. were under cultivation in 2007.

Production, 2007 (in tonnes) of main crops: grassland and pasturage, 749,101; maize, 197,508; forage crops, 129,096; bread crops, 77,435; potatoes, 19,968; colza (rape), 18,302. Production, 2007 (in 1,000 tonnes) of meat, 26·8; milk, 274·2. In 2007–08, 142,000 hectolitres of wine were produced. Total tractors and other agriculture vehicles, 2008: 15,238.

Livestock (15 May 2007): 4,334 horses; 191,928 cattle; 83,255 pigs; 9,339 sheep.

Forestry

In 2015 there were 87,000 ha. of forests (34% of the total land area). In 2011, 261,000 cu. metres of roundwood were cut.

Industry

The largest companies by market capitalization in Luxembourg in April 2015 were Altice, a telecommunications company (US$28·1bn.); SES, a telecommunications company (US$18·6bn.); and Tenaris, a manufacturer and supplier of steel pipe products (US$16·9bn.).

In 2014 there were 4,480 industrial and construction enterprises, of which 3,523 were construction companies. Production, 2007 (in tonnes): rolled steel products, 2,933,000; steel, 2,858,000. The world's largest steel producer, ArcelorMittal, has its headquarters in Luxembourg. Created in June 2006 through the merger of Arcelor and Mittal Steel, it produces in excess of 100m. tonnes of steel annually and accounts for approximately 10% of world steel output. The steel industry mainly relies on imported ore.

Labour

The labour force in 2013 was 260,000 (195,000 in 2003). 68·7% of the population aged 15–64 was economically active in 2013. Of those in employment in 2013, 84·0% worked in services, 11·7% in industry and 1·4% in agriculture. In that year 44·2% of the labour force was female. 42·4% of the labour force had a secondary education as the highest level and 43·0% had a tertiary education. The government fixes a legal minimum wage.

Retirement is at 65. In Dec. 2018 the unemployment rate was 4·9% (down from 5·6% in 2017 as a whole and 6·3% in 2016). More than 150,000 people cross into Luxembourg every day from neighbouring France, Germany and Belgium to work, principally in the financial services industry.

International Trade

Imports and Exports

Imports in 2007 (provisional figures) totalled €16,262·2m. and exports €11,823·0m. In 2016 exports reached 228% of GDP. In 2007, 90·5% of imports were from other EU member countries and 85·9% of exports went to other EU member countries.

Principal imports and exports by standard international trade classification (provisional figures) in €1m.:

	Imports 2007	Exports 2007
Food and live animals	1,120·7	539·2
Beverages and tobacco	425·3	195·0
Crude materials, oils, fats and waxes	1,297·9	251·3

(continued)

	Imports 2007	Exports 2007
Mineral fuels and lubricants	2,076·4	91·9
Chemicals and related products	1,568·2	798·7
Manufactured goods in metals	1,250·8	1,821·1
Other manufactured goods classified chiefly by material	1,789·4	3,928·5
Machinery	2,547·1	2,136·0
Transport equipment	2,602·4	885·7
Other manufactured goods	1,583·9	1,175·6
Total	16,262·2	11,823·0

Trade with selected countries (provisional figures) in €1m.:

	Imports 2007	Exports 2007
Austria	137·8	243·1
Belgium	5,496·3	1,481·2
France	1,899·8	1,993·0
Germany	4,800·0	3,124·1
Italy	356·6	641·7
Netherlands	1,002·6	644·9
Poland	109·0	196·1
Spain	168·9	413·5
Sweden	112·9	172·7
UK	282·1	553·7
(Total EU)	14,722·7	10,154·4)
China	95·1	194·4
Switzerland	152·2	144·7
USA	623·2	298·7
Total (including others)	16,262·2	11,823·0

Trade Fairs

The *Foires Internationales de Luxembourg* occur twice a year, and there are a growing number of specialized fairs.

Communications

Roads

On 1 Jan. 2008 there were 2,894 km of roads of which 147 km were motorways. Motor vehicles registered at 1 Jan. 2008 numbered 394,917 including 321,520 passenger cars, 27,043 trucks, 1,455 coaches and 14,946 motorcycles. In 2009 there were 47 fatalities in road accidents.

Rail

In 2011 there were 275 km of railway (standard gauge) of which 262 km were electrified; passenger-km totalled 349m. in 2011.

Civil Aviation

Findel is the airport for Luxembourg. 1,643,000 passengers and 856,450 tonnes of freight were handled in 2007. The national carrier is Luxair, in which the state has a 39·05% stake directly along with a further 21·81% indirectly through the Banque et Caisse d'Epargne de l'Etat (State and Savings Bank). Cargolux has developed into one of the major international freight carriers. In 2006 scheduled airline traffic of Luxembourg-based carriers flew 93m. km, carrying 928,000 passengers (all on international flights).

Shipping

A shipping register was set up in 1990. In Jan. 2014 there were 59 ships of 300 GT or over registered, totalling 1·54m. GT.

Telecommunications

In 2013 there were 267,600 main (fixed) telephone subscriptions. Mobile phone subscriptions numbered 788,400 in 2013 (1,486·4 per 1,000 persons). In the same year 93·8% of the population aged 16–74 were internet users.

There were 80·6 mobile broadband subscriptions per 100 inhabitants in 2013 and 33·3 fixed broadband subscriptions per 100 inhabitants. In March 2012 there were 190,000 Facebook users.

Social Institutions

Out of 178 countries analysed in the 2017 *Fragile States Index*—a list published jointly by the Fund for Peace and *Foreign Policy* magazine—Luxembourg was ranked the 11th least vulnerable to conflict or collapse. The index is based on 12 indicators of state vulnerability across social, political and economic categories.

Justice

The Constitution makes the Courts of Law independent in performing their functions, restricting their sphere of activity, defining their limit of jurisdiction and providing a number of procedural guarantees. The Constitution has additionally laid down a number of provisions designed to ensure judges remain independent of persons under their jurisdiction, and to ensure no interference from the executive and legislative organs. All judges are appointed by Grand-Ducal order and are irremovable.

The judicial organization comprises three Justices of the Peace (conciliation and police courts). The country is, in addition, divided into two judicial districts—Luxembourg and Diekirch. District courts deal with matters such as civic and commercial cases. Offences which are punishable under the Penal Code or by specific laws with imprisonment or hard labour fall within the jurisdiction of the criminal chambers of District Courts, as the Assize Court was repealed by law in 1987. The High Court of Justice consists of a Supreme Court of Appeal and a Court of Appeal.

The judicial organization of the Grand Duchy does not include the jury system. A division of votes between the judges on the issue of guilt/innocence may lead to acquittal. Society before the Courts of Law is represented by the Public Prosecutor Department, composed of members of the judiciary directly answerable to the government.

In 1999 a new Administrative Tribunal, Administrative Court and Constitutional Court were established.

The population in penal institutions in Jan. 2013 was 656 (122 per 100,000 of national population).

Education

Education is compulsory for all children between the ages of four and 15 (including two years of pre-primary school attendance). In 2006–07 there were 13,672 children in pre-primary school (pre-nursery education, 3,671; nursery education, 10,001) with 1,227 teachers; 33,136 pupils in primary schools; 34,970 pupils in secondary schools. The University of Luxembourg, founded in 2003 and the only public university, had 6,287 students in 2014–15. In 2015 international students accounted for 45·9% of tertiary level enrolments. A number of foreign universities also have a campus in Luxembourg. In 2006–07, 7,222 students pursued university studies abroad.

In 2005 public expenditure on education came to 3·8% of GDP.

The adult literacy rate is at least 99%.

Health

In 2016 there were 1,683 doctors (505 GPs and 1,178 specialists) and 550 dentists. There were 12 hospitals and 2,746 hospital beds in 2016. In 2007 Luxembourg spent 7·1% of its GDP on health.

Welfare

The official retirement age is 65 years for both men and women. To be eligible, a pensioner must have paid 120 months contributions. The maximum old-age pension is €7,991·36 per month. The minimum pension, based on 40 years of coverage, is €1,726·13 per month. A minimum pension is paid with at least 20 years of coverage.

Unemployment benefit is 80% (85% if the insured has a dependent child) of the basis salary during the previous three months, up to 2·5 times the social minimum wage. Recent graduates receive 70% of the social minimum wage whereas self-employed persons receive 80% of the social minimum wage.

Religion

According to the Pew Research Center's Forum on Religion & Public Life, an estimated 64·7% of the population in 2010 were Roman Catholics and 27·5% had no religious affiliation. There are small Protestant,

Jewish, Greek Orthodox, Russian Orthodox and Muslim communities as well.

Culture

World Heritage Sites
Luxembourg has one site on the UNESCO World Heritage List: the City of Luxembourg—its Old Quarters and Fortifications (inscribed on the list in 1994).

Press
There were eight paid-for daily newspapers in 2008 with an average circulation of 117,000 and two free dailies with an average circulation of 127,000; there were also 15 non-dailies. The German-language *Luxemburger Wort* has the highest circulation, with an average of 72,000 copies in 2008. In the 2013 *World Press Freedom Index* compiled by Reporters Without Borders, Luxembourg was ranked fourth out of 179 countries.

Tourism
In 2010 there were 907,000 overnight tourists and 2,256,000 overnight stays; there were 7,751 hotel rooms in 2010. Tourists spent US$4,108m. in 2010 (excluding passenger transport). Camping is widespread; there were 739,000 overnight stays at campsites in 2010.

Festivals
The Festival International Echternach (May–June) and the Festival of Wiltz (June–July) are annual events. Both feature a variety of classical music, jazz, theatre and recitals.

Diplomatic Representatives

Of Luxembourg in the United Kingdom (27 Wilton Cres., London, SW1X 8SD)
Ambassador: Jean Alfred Olinger.

Of the United Kingdom in Luxembourg (5 Blvd Joseph II, L-1840 Luxembourg)
Ambassador: John Marshall.

Of Luxembourg in the USA (2200 Massachusetts Ave., NW, Washington, D.C., 20008)
Ambassador: Sylvie Lucas.

Of the USA in Luxembourg (22 Blvd Emmanuel Servais, L-2535 Luxembourg)
Ambassador: James Randolph Evans.

Of Luxembourg to the United Nations
Ambassador: Christian Braun.

Of Luxembourg to the European Union
Permanent Representative: Georges Friden.

Further Reading

STATEC. *Annuaire Statistique 2012.—Le Luxembourg en chiffres 2018*
Arblaster, Paul, *A History of the Low Countries.* 2005
Newcomer, J., *The Grand Duchy of Luxembourg: The Evolution of Nationhood, 963 AD to 1983.* 2nd ed. 1995
National library: 37 Boulevard Roosevelt, Luxembourg City, L-2450 Luxembourg.
National Statistical Office: Service Central de la Statistique et des Études Économiques (STATEC), CP 304, Luxembourg City, L-2013 Luxembourg.
Website: http://www.statec.public.lu

Madagascar

Repoblikan'i Madagasikara (Republic of Madagascar)

Capital: Antananarivo
Population projection, 2020: 27·69m.
GNI per capita, 2017: (PPP$) 1,358
HDI/world rank, 2017: 0·519/161
Internet domain extension: .mg

Key Historical Events

The island was settled by people of African and Indonesian origin when it was visited by the Portuguese explorer, Diego Diaz, in 1500. The island was unified under the Imérina monarchy between 1797 and 1861. A French protectorate was established in 1895. Madagascar became a French colony on 6 Aug. 1896 and achieved independence on 26 June 1960.

In Feb. 1975 Col. Richard Ratsimandrava, head of state, was assassinated. The 1975 constitution instituted a 'Democratic Republic' allowing for only one political party. After six months of anti-government unrest an 18-month transitional administration was agreed. A new constitution instituted the Third Republic in Sept. 1992.

Following the presidential election of Dec. 2001 the opposition candidate Marc Ravalomanana claimed victory, although the High Constitutional Court called for a run-off. On 22 Feb. 2002 Ravalomanana declared himself president and imposed a state of emergency. However, incumbent Didier Ratsiraka and his government set up a rival capital in Toamasina. In April 2002 both men agreed to a recount of votes to solve the dispute. Ravalomanana was declared president.

Re-elected in 2006, the suppression of political opponents led to an army mutiny against Ravalomanana in early 2009. As civil unrest increased, he resigned the presidency and handed power to the military which installed Andry Rajoelina, Ravalomanana's chief political rival, as president. In Aug. 2010 Ravalomanana was sentenced *in absentia* (he was living in exile in South Africa at the time) to life imprisonment for ordering the killing of opposition supporters.

A new constitution was promulgated in Dec. 2010 and in Nov. 2011 the South African Development Community brokered a deal to establish a unity government, including representatives from opposition parties, under Rajoelina's leadership. Long-delayed presidential elections held in Dec. 2013 were won by Hery Rajaonarimampianina after Rajoelina and Ravalomanana both agreed not to stand. In May 2015 the country entered a new period of constitutional turmoil as parliament attempted to impeach Rajaonarimampianina on charges of misrule, although the Constitutional Court declared the move invalid.

Territory and Population

Madagascar is situated 400 km (250 miles) off the southeast coast of Africa, from which it is separated by the Mozambique Channel. Its area is 587,041 sq. km (226,658 sq. miles), including 5,500 sq. km (2,120 sq. miles) of inland water. At the 1993 census the population was 12,092,157 (50·45% female); density, 20·6 per sq. km. The estimate for 2011 was 20,696,100; density, 35·6 per sq. km. 69·8% of the population lived in rural areas in 2010.

The UN gives a projected population for 2020 of 27·69m.

Regions	Area in sq. km	Population (2011 estimate)	Chief town
Alaotra Mangoro	31,948	973,200	Ambatondrazaka
Amoron'i Mania	16,141	677,500	Ambositra
Analamanga	16,911	3,173,100	Antananarivo
Analanjirofo	21,930	980,800	Fenoarivobe
Androy	19,317	695,400	Ambovombe
Anosy	25,731	636,600	Taolagnaro
Atsimo Andrefana	66,236	1,247,700	Toliary

(continued)

Regions	Area in sq. km	Population (2011 estimate)	Chief town
Atsimo Atsinanana	18,863	851,500	Farafangana
Atsinanana	21,934	1,204,000	Toamasina
Betsiboka	30,025	278,100	Maevatanana
Boeny	31,046	757,700	Mahajanga
Bongolava	16,688	433,400	Tsiroanomandidy
Diana	19,266	663,300	Antsiranana
Haute Matsiatra	21,080	1,136,300	Fianarantsoa
Ihorombe	26,391	295,900	Ihosy
Itasy	6,993	694,400	Miarinarivo
Melaky	38,852	274,400	Maintirano
Menabe	46,121	561,000	Morondava
Sava	25,518	929,300	Sambava
Sofia	50,100	1,181,600	Antsohihy
Vakinankaratra	16,599	1,708,700	Antsirabe
Vatovavy Fitovinany	19,605	1,342,100	Manakara

The indigenous population is of Malayo-Polynesian stock, divided into 18 ethnic groups of which the principal are Merina (24%) of the central plateau, the Betsimisaraka (13%) of the east coast and the Betsileo (11%) of the southern plateau. Foreign communities include Europeans (mainly French), Indians, Chinese, Comorians and Arabs.

Malagasy, French and (since 2007) English are all official languages.

Social Statistics

2008 estimates: births, 686,000; deaths, 176,000. Rates, 2008 estimates (per 1,000 population): births, 35·9; deaths, 9·2. Infant mortality, 2010 (per 1,000 live births), 43. Expectation of life in 2013 was 63·2 years for males and 66·2 for females. Annual population growth rate, 2000–08, 2·8%. Fertility rate, 2008, 4·7 births per woman.

Climate

A tropical climate, but the mountains cause big variations in rainfall, which is very heavy in the east and very light in the west. Antananarivo, Jan. 70°F (21·1°C), July 59°F (15°C). Annual rainfall 54" (1,350 mm). Toamasina, Jan. 80°F (26·7°C), July 70°F (21·1°C). Annual rainfall 128" (3,256 mm).

Constitution and Government

A new constitution was promulgated on 10 Dec. 2010, having won 74·2% support at a referendum held in Nov. 2010. However, the referendum was boycotted by the three main opposition parties and turnout was 52·6%. It reduced the minimum age requirement for the presidency from 40 years to 35 and demanded that presidential candidates should be resident in the country in the six months leading up to an election. The parliament is comprised of the *National Assembly* (151 members, directly elected for five-year terms) and the *Senate* (63 members, of whom 42 are indirectly elected and 21 are appointed for five-year terms).

National Anthem

'Ry tanindrazanay malala ô!' ('O our beloved Fatherland'); words by Pastor Rahajason, tune by N. Raharisoa.

Recent Elections

Presidential elections were held on 7 Nov. and 19 Dec. 2018. In the second round run-off, Andry Rajoelina won with 55·7% of the vote against Marc Ravalomanana with 44·3%. There were 34 further candidates in the first

© Springer Nature Limited 2020
Palgrave Macmillan (ed.), *The Statesman's Yearbook 2020*,
https://doi.org/10.1057/978-1-349-95940-2_118

round. Turnout was 54·2% in the first round and 48·1% in the run-off. In parliamentary elections held on 20 Dec. 2013, Party of Andry Rajoelina (the party supporting the outgoing interim president) won 49 of the 151 seats, Ravalomanana Movement 20 and Vondrona Politika 13. Independents won 25 seats and the remaining seats went to a number of smaller parties.

Current Government

President: Andry Rajoelina; b. 1974 (Young Malagasies Determined/TGV; sworn in 19 Jan. 2019).

In Feb. 2019 the government was composed as follows:

Prime Minister: Christian Ntsay; b. 1961 (ind.; since 6 June 2018).

Minister of Agriculture, Fisheries and Livestock: Lucien Fanomezantsoa Ranarivelo. *Communication and Culture:* Lalatiana Andriatongarivo Rakotondrazafy. *Economy and Finance:* Richard Randriamandranto. *Energy, Water and Hydrocarbons:* Vonjy Andriamanga. *Environment and Sustainable Development:* Alexandre Georget. *Foreign Affairs:* Naina Andriatsitohaina. *Higher Education and Scientific Research:* Madeleine Félicité Rejo Finena. *Industry, Trade and Handicrafts:* Landisoa Rakotomalala. *Interior and Decentralization:* Tianarivelo Razafimahefa. *Justice:* Jacques Randrianasolo. *Labour:* Gisèle Ranampy. *Mines and Strategic Resources:* Fidiniavo Ravokatra. *National Defence:* Gen. Léon Richard Rakotonirina. *National Education and Technical and Vocational Education:* Marie-Thérèse Volahaingo. *Population, Social Welfare and Women's Empowerment:* Lucien Irmah Naharimamy. *Post, Telecommunications and New Technologies:* Christian Ramarolahy. *Public Health:* Julio Rakotonirina. *Public Security:* Roger Rafanomezantsoa. *Spatial Planning, Housing and Public Works:* Hajo Andrianainarivelo. *Transport, Tourism and Meteorology:* Joël Randriamadranto. *Youth and Sports:* Tinoka Roberto.

Office of the President (French only): http://www.presidence.gov.mg

Current Leaders

Andry Rajoelina

Position

President

Introduction

Andry Rajoelina became president for the second time in Jan. 2019. From 2009–14 he was president of the High Transitional Authority (HTA), a provisional executive body established after he suspended parliament.

Early Life

Rajoelina was born in Antsirabe on 30 May 1974 into the wealthy family of a colonel in the Malagasy army. He rose to prominence as a disc jockey before setting up a TV and radio station and running an advertising company. His brash personality earned him the nickname TGV, after the French high-speed train. The initials went on to serve as the acronym for his political movement, Tanora malaGasy Vonona (Young Malagasies Determined). He harnessed his public profile to win the Antananarivo mayoral election in Dec. 2007.

In Dec. 2008 and Jan. 2009 Rajoelina's radio and TV networks were shut down by the government headed by President Marc Ravalomanana amid accusations of inciting civil disobedience. Rajoelina called a general strike, creating widespread disorder. This resulted in Ravalomanana stepping down in March 2009 under pressure from military chiefs, who immediately installed Rajoelina as his successor. He became the country's youngest president at 34 despite the prevailing constitution stipulating that presidential candidates must be at least 40 years of age.

Career in Office

Upon assuming office, Rajoelina suspended parliament and set up the HTA. The African Union (AU) denounced the change of government as a coup and suspended Madagascar's membership. Rajoelina's ascent to power was also condemned by the European Union and the USA.

In Aug. 2009 a power-sharing agreement was signed between the rival Rajoelina and Ravalomanana political camps with the aim of establishing a transitional unity government. However, disputes continued and in Dec. 2009 Rajoelina announced that he was abandoning the agreement. This prompted the AU to impose targeted sanctions against his administration in March 2010.

A referendum on a new constitution in Nov. 2010 was boycotted by the main opposition parties, which regarded the revision as an illegal attempt to consolidate Rajoelina's hold on power by lowering the age requirement for

the presidency from 40 to 35. 74% of participants voted in favour. At the same time, an attempted coup against Rajoelina failed as troops loyal to him arrested a group of dissident army officers.

Owing to pressure from the AU and the suspension of electoral funding from the European Union, neither Rajoelina nor Ravalonmanana contested the presidential elections held in 2013. However, Rajoelina remained head of the majority party. In Aug. 2018 he registered his candidacy for the presidency and campaigned for his Initiative for the Emergence of Madagascar (IEM). It included pledges to close the Senate to save money, to build universities, increase access to electricity, work towards agricultural self-sufficiency and increase security. In the subsequent election, Rajoelina faced Ravalomanana and emerged victorious in the run-off poll in Dec. with almost 56% of the vote. The result was contested by Ravalomanana, who alleged that it was fraudulent, but a constitutional court upheld the outcome and Rajoelina was inaugurated as president on 18 Jan. 2019.

Rajoelina has to overcome his long-term friction with Ravalomanana to avoid further political instability and make good on his electoral promise of being a president for the poor. His primary challenge is to boost the economy of one of the world's poorest countries, where three-quarters of the population lives in poverty.

Defence

There is conscription (including civilian labour service) for 18 months. Defence expenditure totalled US$72m. in 2013 (US$3 per capita), representing 0·7% of GDP.

Army

Strength (2011) approximately 12,500 and gendarmerie 8,100.

Navy

In 2011 the Navy had a strength of 500 (including some 100 marines).

Air Force

Personnel (2011) 500. There are no combat-capable aircraft.

Economy

In 2014 agriculture contributed 26·5% of GDP, industry 15·9% and services 57·6%.

Overview

Agriculture, fishing and forestry employ 80% of the workforce and together contributed over 25% of GDP in 2015. The country is rich in natural resources (notably cobalt, nickel and ilmenite) and mining is increasingly important.

However, a domestic political crisis saw tourism decline by 50% in 2009, and in 2010 the textile industry suffered a sharp contraction when its duty-free access to the US market ended. Parts of the country returned to a barter economy amid a decline into poverty for the great majority of the population. The country had failed to reach any of the United Nations' Millennium Development Goals by 2015.

Currency

In July 2003 then President Marc Ravalomanana announced that the *Ariary* (MGA) would become the official currency, replacing the *Malagasy franc* (MGFr). The Ariary became legal tender on 1 Aug. 2003 at a rate of 1 *Ariary* = 5 *Malagasy francs*. The Ariary is subdivided into five *Iraimbilanja*. In July 2005 foreign exchange reserves were US$435m. and total money supply was 1,324·0bn. ariarys. Inflation was 6·7% in 2016 and 8·3% in 2017.

Budget

Revenues totalled 2,402bn. ariarys in 2011 and expenditures 2,769bn. ariarys. Tax revenue accounted for 90·8% of revenues in 2011; current expenditure accounted for 78·0% of expenditures.

VAT is 20%.

Performance

Total GDP in 2017 was US$11·5bn. There was a recession in 2002 with the economy contracting by 12·4% as a result of the six-month long political crisis, but a recovery followed in 2003 and 2004 with real GDP growth of 9·8% and 5·3%. The economy grew by 3·1% in 2015 and 4·2% in both 2016 and 2017.

Banking and Finance

A Central Bank, the Banque Centrale de Madagascar, was formed in 1973, replacing the former Institut d'Émission Malgache as the central bank of issue. The *Governor* is Alain Hervé Rasolofondraibe. All commercial banking and insurance was nationalized in 1975 and privatized in 1988. Of the six other banks, the largest are the Bankin'ny Tantsaha Mpamokatra and the BNI—Crédit Lyonnais de Madagascar.

External debt was US$2,295m. in 2010, representing 26·6% of GNI.

Energy and Natural Resources

Environment

Madagascar's carbon dioxide emissions from the consumption of energy in 2011 were the equivalent of 0·1 tonnes per capita.

Electricity

Installed capacity was estimated at 0·5m. kW in 2011. Production in 2011 was 1,438m. kWh, with consumption per capita 66 kWh.

Oil and Gas

Several oil blocks both on land and offshore were discovered in 2005.

Minerals

Mining production in 2009 (estimates) included: ilmenite concentrate, 160,000; salt, 75,000 tonnes; chromite, 60,000 tonnes; graphite (2008 estimate), 5,000 tonnes. There have also been discoveries of precious and semi-precious stones in various parts of the country, in particular sapphires, topaz and garnets. Madagascar is believed to have the world's largest reserves of sapphires.

Agriculture

75–80% of the workforce is employed in agriculture. There were an estimated 3·5m. ha. of arable land in 2013 and 0·6m. ha. of permanent crops. Approximately 1·1m. ha. were equipped for irrigation in 2013. The principal agricultural products in 2013 were (1,000 tonnes): rice, 3,611; cassava, 3,115; sugarcane (estimate), 2,904; sweet potatoes (estimate), 1,095; maize, 381; bananas (estimate), 355; mangoes and guavas (estimate), 305; taro (estimate), 234; potatoes (estimate), 215; oranges (estimate), 87. Rice is produced on some 40% of cultivated land. Madagascar is the world's largest producer of vanilla.

Cattle breeding and agriculture are the chief occupations. There were, in 2013 (estimates), 10·0m. cattle, 1·5m. pigs, 1·5m. goats, 839,000 sheep and 27m. chickens.

Forestry

In 2015 the area under forests was 12·47m. ha., or 21% of the total land area. The forests contain many valuable woods, while gum, resins and plants for tanning, dyeing and medicinal purposes abound. Timber production was 13·38m. cu. metres in 2011.

Fisheries

The catch of fish in 2015 was 113,954 tonnes (mainly from marine waters).

Industry

Industry, hitherto confined mainly to the processing of agricultural products, is now extending to cover other fields.

Labour

The labour force in 2013 was 11,688,000 (8,182,000 in 2003). 89·7% of the population aged 15–64 was economically active in 2013. In the same year 3·6% of the population was unemployed.

Madagascar had 19,000 people living in slavery according to the Walk Free Foundation's 2013 *Global Slavery Index*.

International Trade

Imports and Exports

Trade, 2010, in US$1m.: imports (c.i.f.), 2,546; exports (f.o.b.), 1,082. Leading imports in 2010 (in US$1m.) were: machinery and transport equipment (752); manufactured goods (634); mineral fuels, lubricants and related materials (386). Leading exports in 2010 (in US$1m.) were: articles of apparel and clothing accessories (303); food and live animals (248); machinery and transport equipment (120).

In 2010 main import sources (in US$1m.) were: France (368); China (310); South Africa (197). Main export markets in 2010 (in US$1m.) were: France (359); Germany (79); China (57).

Communications

Roads

In 2012 there were 31,640 km of roads, 21·9% of which were paved. There were 146,300 passenger cars, 280,800 buses and coaches and 83,800 lorries and vans in 2008. 550 people died in road accidents in 2006.

Rail

In 2005 there were 854 km of railways, all metre gauge. In 2005, 100,000 passengers and 300,000 tonnes of freight were transported.

Civil Aviation

There are international airports at Antananarivo (Ivato) and Mahajanga (Amborovy). The national carrier is Air Madagascar, which is 90% state-owned. In 2013 it carried 539,000 passengers (303,000 on domestic flights), serving six international and 22 domestic destinations. In 2012 Antananarivo handled 890,632 passengers (586,532 on international flights) and 22,276 tonnes of freight.

Shipping

The main ports are Toamasina, Mahajanga, Antsiranana and Toliary. In Jan. 2014 there were seven ships of 300 GT or over registered, totalling 4,000 GT.

Telecommunications

In 2011 there were 130,100 landline telephone subscriptions (equivalent to 6·5 per 1,000 inhabitants) and 8,159,600 mobile phone subscriptions (or 382·8 per 1,000 inhabitants). There were 17·0 internet users per 1,000 inhabitants in 2010. Fixed internet subscriptions totalled 8,300 in 2009 (0·4 per 1,000 inhabitants). In June 2012 there were 233,000 Facebook users.

Social Institutions

Out of 178 countries analysed in the 2017 *Fragile States Index*—a list published jointly by the Fund for Peace and *Foreign Policy* magazine— Madagascar was ranked the 55th most vulnerable to conflict or collapse. The index is based on 12 indicators of state vulnerability across social, political and economic categories.

Justice

The Supreme Court and the Court of Appeal are in Antananarivo. In most towns there are Courts of First Instance for civil and commercial cases. For criminal cases there are ordinary criminal courts in most towns.

The population in penal institutions in June 2010 was 18,647 (93 per 100,000 of national population). 53·0% of prisoners had yet to receive a trial according to 2014 estimates by the International Centre for Prison Studies. In 2015 the World Justice Project *Rule of Law Index*, which provides data on how the rule of law is experienced by the general public across eight categories, ranked Madagascar 78th of 102 countries for criminal justice and 90th for civil justice. The death penalty, which was last used in 1958, was abolished in Jan. 2015.

Education

Education is compulsory from six to 14 years of age. In 2007 there were 78,743 teaching staff for 3,837,343 pupils in primary schools, 835,539 pupils at secondary level with 34,320 teaching staff and 58,313 students at tertiary level with 3,032 academic staff. Adult literacy rate in 2008 was 71%. In 2007 public expenditure on education came to 3·4% of GNI and 16·4% of total government spending.

Health

There were three hospital beds per 10,000 population in 2005. In 2012 there were 3,188 physicians, 4, 858 nursing and midwifery personnel, 181 dentistry personnel and six pharmaceutical personnel. In 2005 government expenditure on health came to 9·6% of total government spending.

In *Water: At What Cost? The State of the World's Water 2016*, WaterAid reported that 48·5% of the population does not have access to safe water—the sixth highest percentage of any nation.

Welfare

In 2006 social security accounted for 10·4% of government expenditure.

Religion

In 2010 there were an estimated 8·11m. Protestants and 7·26m. Catholics according to the Pew Research Center's Forum on Religion & Public Life, with folk religionists numbering 900,000 and 1·4m. people having no religious affiliation. In Feb. 2019 there was one cardinal.

Culture

World Heritage Sites

Tsingy de Bemaraha Strict Nature Reserve joined the UNESCO World Heritage List in 1990. The undisturbed forests, lakes and mangrove swamps are the habitat for rare and endangered lemurs and birds. The Royal Hill of Ambohimanga was added in 2001, a royal city and burial site and a symbol of Malagasy identity. The rainforests of Atsinanana, comprising six national parks in the eastern part of the island, were inscribed on the list in 2007.

Press

In 2008 there were 13 daily newspapers with a total circulation of 115,000.

Tourism

In 2011, 225,005 non-resident tourists arrived by air (excluding same-day visitors), up from 196,052 in 2010 although down from the peak of 375,010 in 2008.

Diplomatic Representatives

Of Madagascar in the United Kingdom (307a, 10 Greycoat Pl., London, SW1P 1SB)
  Ambassador: Andriniaina Bretino Raharinomena.

Of the United Kingdom in Madagascar (Ninth Floor, Tour Zital, Ravoninahitriniarivo St., Ankorondrano, Antananarivo 101)
  Ambassador: Phil Boyle.

Of Madagascar in the USA (2374 Massachusetts Ave., NW, Washington, D.C., 20008)
  Ambassador: Eric Andriamihaja Robson.

Of the USA in Madagascar (Lot 207A, Andranoro, Antehiroka, 105 Antananarivo)
  Ambassador: Vacant.
  Chargé d'Affaires a.i.: Stuart R. Wilson.

Of Madagascar to the United Nations
  Ambassador: Arisoa Lala Razafitrimo.

Of Madagascar to the European Union
  Ambassador: Jeannot Rakotomalala.

Further Reading

Banque des Données de l'État. *Bulletin Mensuel de Statistique*
Allen, P. M., *Madagascar.* 1995 (Allen 1995)
National Statistical Office: Institut National de la Statistique (INSTAT), BP 485 Anosy, Antananarivo 101.
Website (French only): http://www.instat.mg

Malaŵi

Dziko la Malaŵi (Republic of Malaŵi)

Capital: Lilongwe
Population projection, 2020: 20·28m.
GNI per capita, 2017: (PPP$) 1,064
HDI/world rank, 2017: 0·477/171
Internet domain extension: .mw

Key Historical Events

The area was dominated by the Twa and Fulani tribes until the 1st century AD when Bantu-speaking tribes made inroads. The explorer David Livingstone reached Lake Nyasa, now Lake Malaŵi, in 1859 and it was the land along the lake's western shore that became, in 1891, the British Protectorate of Nyasaland. In 1884 the British South Africa Company applied for a charter to trade. Pressure on land, the colour bar and other grievances generated Malaŵian resistance. In 1893 it was renamed the British Central African Protectorate. This became Nyasaland in 1907. By the mid-1940s a nationalist movement had emerged, spearheaded by the Nyasaland African Congress. In 1953 Nyasaland was joined with Southern Rhodesia (Zimbabwe) and Northern Rhodesia (Zambia) to form the Federation of Rhodesia and Nyasaland, under British control. This union was dissolved in 1963. Nyasaland was self-governing until on 6 July 1964 it became independent, adopting the name Malaŵi. In 1966 Malaŵi was declared a republic and Dr Hastings Banda became the first president, establishing a one party dictatorship which lasted for 30 years. In 1994 Malaŵi returned to multi-party democracy. One of the world's least developed countries, Malaŵi has suffered periodic drought, flooding and famine, most recently prompting the government in April 2016 to declare a state of emergency.

Territory and Population

Malaŵi lies along the southern and western shores of Lake Malaŵi (the third largest lake in Africa), and is otherwise bounded in the north by Tanzania, south by Mozambique and west by Zambia. Area (including the inland water areas of Lake Malombe, Chilwa, Chiuta and the Malaŵi portion of Lake Malaŵi, which total 24,208 sq. km), 118,484 sq. km (45,747 sq. miles).

Census population (2008), 13,077,160 (6,718,227 females); density, 138·7 per sq. km. The United Nations population estimate for 2008 was 14,271,000. In 2011, 20·3% of the population were urban.

The UN gives a projected population for 2020 of 20·28m.

Population of main towns (2008): Lilongwe, 674,448; Blantyre, 661,256; Mzuzu, 133,968; Zomba, 88,314. Population of the regions (2008): Northern, 1,708,930; Central, 5,510,195; Southern, 5,858,035.

The official languages are Chichewa, spoken by over 58% of the population, and English.

Social Statistics

2008 estimates: births, 597,000; deaths, 182,000. Estimated rates, 2008 (per 1,000 population): births, 40·2; deaths, 12·3. Annual population growth rate, 2000–08, 2·8%. Expectation of life at birth in 2013 was 55·1 years for males and 55·4 for females. Infant mortality, 2010, 58 per 1,000 live births; fertility rate, 2008, 5·5 births per woman.

Climate

The tropical climate is marked by a dry season from May to Oct. and a wet season for the remaining months. Rainfall amounts are variable, within the range of 29–100" (725–2,500 mm), and maximum temperatures average 75–89°F (24–32°C), and minimum temperatures 58–67°F (14·4–19·4°C). Lilongwe, Jan. 73°F (22·8°C), July 60°F (15·6°C). Annual rainfall 36" (900 mm). Blantyre, Jan. 75°F (23·9°C), July 63°F (17·2°C). Annual rainfall 45" (1,125 mm). Zomba, Jan. 73°F (22·8°C), July 63°F (17·2°C). Annual rainfall 54" (1,344 mm).

Constitution and Government

The *President* is head of state and head of government. Malaŵi was a one-party state, but following a referendum on 14 June 1993, in which 63% of votes cast were in favour of reform, a new constitution was adopted on 17 May 1994 which ended Hastings Banda's life presidency and provided for the holding of multi-party elections. At these Bakili Muluzi was elected president with 47·2% of votes cast, beating President Banda and two other opponents. There is a *National Assembly* of 193 members, elected for five-year terms in single-seat constituencies.

National Anthem

'O God Bless our Land of Malaŵi'; words and tune by M.-F. Sauka.

Recent Elections

At presidential elections of 20 May 2014 Peter Mutharika of the Democratic Progressive Party (DPP) won with 36·4% of the vote, ahead of Lazarus Chakwera of the Malaŵi Congress Party (MCP—until 1993 the only legal party) with 27·8%, incumbent president Joyce Banda of the People's Party (PP) with 20·2% and Atupele Muluzi of the United Democratic Front (UDF) with 13·7%. There were eight other candidates who all received less than 1% of the vote. Turnout was 70·7%.

At parliamentary elections held on the same day the DPP won 50 seats, the MCP 48, the PP 26 and the UDF 14. The Alliance for Democracy (AFORD) and Chipani cha Pfuko took one seat each, with independents winning the remaining 52 seats. One seat remained vacant.

Current Government

President and Minister of Defence: Peter Mutharika; b. 1940 (Democratic Progressive Party; sworn in 31 May 2014).

Vice President: Vacant.

The government consisted of the following in Feb. 2019:

Minister of Agriculture, Irrigation and Water Development: Joseph Mwanamvekha. *Civic Education, Culture and Community Development:* Everton Chimulirenji. *Education, Science and Technology:* Bright Msaka. *Finance, Economic Planning and Development:* Goodall Gondwe. *Foreign Affairs and International Co-operation:* Emmanuel Fabiano. *Gender, Children, Disability and Social Welfare:* Cecilia Chazama. *Health and Population:* Atupele Muluzi. *Homeland Security:* Nicholas Dausi. *Industry, Trade and Tourism:* Francis Kasaila. *Information and Communications Technology:* Henry Mussa. *Justice and Constitutional Affairs:* Samuel Tembeni. *Labour, Youth, Sports and Manpower Development:* Grace Chiumia. *Lands, Housing and Urban Development:* Jean Kalilani. *Local Government and Rural Development:* Kondwani Nankhumwa. *Natural Resources, Energy and Mining:* Aggrey Masi. *Transport and Public Works:* Jappie Mhango. *Attorney General:* Kalekeni Kaphale.

Government Website: http://www.malawi.gov.mw

Current Leaders

Peter Mutharika

Position
President

Introduction

Peter Mutharika was sworn into office on 31 May 2014 after being declared winner of a disputed presidential election. Although widely regarded as part

Palgrave Macmillan (ed.), *The Statesman's Yearbook 2020*,
https://doi.org/10.1057/978-1-349-95940-2_119

of the Democratic Progressive Party's old guard, owing to his familial ties to the late Bingu wa Mutharika, Mutharika has been keen to portray himself as a reformer.

Early Life

Arthur Peter Mutharika was born in Malaŵi's Thyolo district in 1940. He graduated in law from the University of London in the UK in 1965 and then attended Yale University in the USA, earning a master's degree and a doctorate in law (in 1966 and 1969, respectively). Unable to return to Malaŵi as his brother, Bingu wa Mutharika, was being targeted by the Malaŵi Young Pioneers (the paramilitary wing of the then dominant Malaŵi Congress Party), Mutharika undertook various advisory and teaching posts at universities around the world, including the University of Dar es Salaam in Tanzania and Washington University in the USA.

Returning to Malaŵi after the establishment of democratic elections, Mutharika advised his brother during his successful presidential re-election campaign in 2009 and also won a seat for himself in the National Assembly. Tipped as Bingu wa's successor, Mutharika was given charge of high profile portfolios, including justice and constitutional affairs, education, science and technology, and foreign affairs. In Aug. 2011 the governing body of the Democratic Progressive Party endorsed his candidacy for the 2014 presidential elections. This fuelled tensions with Vice President Joyce Banda and led to treason charges against Mutharika in March 2013 for allegedly plotting a coup to prevent Banda from taking power following Bingu wa's death a year earlier. Nonetheless, on 20 May 2014 Mutharika won the presidential election.

Career in Office

Mutharika's main challenges included cutting the country's dependence on international aid while maintaining national unity. His first budget, published in Sept. 2014, aimed to regain donor confidence and encourage political stability. However, popular discontent has since increased over high living costs, while his opponents have continued to criticize him for weak governance, for failing to act against widespread corruption and for ignoring security problems. Meanwhile, Malaŵi remains vulnerable to severe drought, famine and flooding, which had prompted his government in April 2016 to declare a state of emergency.

Despite his declining public support, Mutharika announced in Oct. 2016 his intention to stand for re-election at the next presidential polling scheduled for May 2019.

Defence

All services form part of the Army. Defence expenditure totalled US$25m. in 2013 (US$2 per capita), representing 0·7% of GDP.

Army

Personnel (2011) 5,300. In addition there is a paramilitary mobile police force totalling 1,500.

Navy

The small Navy, based at Monkey Bay on Lake Malaŵi, numbered 220 personnel in 2011.

Air Wing

The Air Wing acts as infantry support and numbered 200 in 2011 with no combat-capable aircraft.

Economy

Agriculture accounted for 30·8% of GDP in 2014, industry 15·7% and services 53·5%.

Overview

Malaŵi enjoyed solid annual GDP growth between 2006 and 2010, averaging 7·1% compared to 2% in 2005. This reflected improved government finances, a reform programme, strong mining revenues and healthy construction and manufacturing activity. However, between 2010 and 2015 weak agricultural returns, mismanaged macroeconomic policies (leading to the devaluation of the *kwacha* by 10% in 2011 and 34% in 2012) and stricter rules governing foreign exchange transactions hampered economic performance, with growth averaging 4·6% annually in that period. Corruption has also been a problem and in 2013 it was revealed that over US$30m. of

government money had gone missing. The contribution of uranium mining to GDP declined from 4·4% in 2013 to 0·2% in 2014 after production at the Kayelekera mine was halted following a fall in the commodity price.

Heavy dependence on agriculture (which accounted for over 28% of GDP in 2016 and 80% of foreign exchange earnings) makes the economy vulnerable to weather shocks and natural disasters. In Aug. 2006 the IMF's Heavily Indebted Poor Countries initiative redirected government spending towards farming programmes, boosting agricultural development. Tobacco, tea, cotton, coffee and sugar are the primary exports, with tobacco accounting for 80% of the total.

Social indicators are poor. In 2016 GNI per capita was US$1,140 (PPP) and Malaŵi has relied heavily on assistance from the World Bank, IMF and other international donors. However, education, environmental conditions and health care all show signs of improvement.

Challenges to long-term sustainability are numerous. Energy constraints mean that only 12% of the population have access to electricity, while a weak balance-of-payments threatens exchange rate and price stability and prospects for international tobacco consumption are uncertain.

Currency

The unit of currency is the *kwacha* (MWK) of 100 *tambala*. Foreign exchange reserves were US$119m. in June 2005, gold reserves 13,000 troy oz and total money supply was K.29,579m. In May 2012 Malaŵi ended its currency peg to the dollar and adopted a floating exchange rate regime, which led to the devaluing of the kwacha by 34%. Inflation, which was 83·1% in 1995, had been brought down to 7·4% by 2010 but more recently was 21·9% in 2015, 21·7% in 2016 and 12·2% in 2017.

Budget

The fiscal year runs from 1 July–30 June. In 2010–11 revenues were K.292·85bn. and expenditures K.312·78bn. Tax revenue accounted for 58·0% of revenues in 2010–11; current expenditure accounted for 68·2% of expenditures.

VAT is 16·5%.

Performance

Real GDP growth was 2·9% in 2015, 2·3% in 2016 and 4·0% in 2017. Total GDP was US$6·3bn. in 2017.

Banking and Finance

The central bank and bank of issue is the Reserve Bank of Malaŵi (founded 1964). The *Governor* is Daliso Kabambe. In 2014 there were 12 commercial banks.

Foreign debt was US$922m. in 2010, representing 18·5% of GNI.

There is a stock exchange in Blantyre.

Energy and Natural Resources

Environment

Carbon dioxide emissions from the consumption of energy in 2011 were the equivalent of 0·1 tonnes per capita.

Electricity

The Electricity Supply Commission of Malaŵi is the sole supplier. Installed capacity was 0·5m. kW in 2011. Production was estimated at 1,978m. kWh in 2011; consumption per capita was estimated at 127 kWh. Only 11% of the population has access to electricity and power cuts are frequent.

Oil and Gas

Malaŵi does not currently produce any oil or natural gas and imports all its fuel products. However, the government is currently undertaking oil exploration. In 2011 it issued exploration licences for six oil blocks, two of which overlap with the potentially oil-rich Lake Malaŵi. These efforts have been aided by foreign governments but have caused controversy among environmental groups because of the lake's proximity to Lake Malaŵi National Park, a UNESCO World Heritage Site.

Minerals

Mining operations have been limited to small-scale production of coal, limestone, rubies and sapphires, but companies are now moving in to start exploration programmes. Bauxite reserves are estimated at 29m. tonnes and there are proven reserves of clays, diamonds, glass and silica sands, gold, graphite, limestone, mercurate, phosphates, tanzanite, titanium and uranium.

Output in 2007: crushed stone, 226,351 tonnes; coal, 58,550 tonnes; limestone, 42,088 tonnes; gemstones, 3,710 kg.

Agriculture

Malaŵi is predominantly an agricultural country. Agricultural produce contributes 90% of export earnings. There were an estimated 3·8m. ha. of arable land in 2013 and 140,000 ha. of permanent crops. Maize is the main subsistence crop and is grown by over 95% of all smallholders. In 2016 a state of emergency was declared when drought led to food shortages that left an estimated 2·8m. people facing food insecurity.

Tobacco is the chief cash crop, employing 12% of the workforce and generating a quarter of tax earnings. Also important are groundnuts, cassava, millet and rice. There are large plantations which produce sugar, tea and coffee. Production (2013, in 1,000 tonnes): cassava, 4,814; potatoes, 4,536; maize, 3,640; sugarcane (estimate), 2,900; bananas (estimate), 387; groundnuts, 381; plantains (estimate), 363; pigeon peas, 288; dry beans, 189; seed cotton, 159; tobacco, 133; rice, 125.

Livestock in 2013: goats, 5·4m.; pigs, 2·8m.; cattle, 1·2m.; sheep, 256,000; chickens (estimate), 17m.

Forestry

In 2015 the area under forests was 3·15m. ha., or 33% of the total land area. Timber production in 2011 was 6·87m. cu. metres.

Fisheries

Landings in 2015 were 141,643 tonnes, entirely from inland waters. The annual catch has doubled since 2009, when it was 69,325 tonnes.

Industry

Manufactures includes agro-processing, textiles, footwear, clothing and building materials. In 2014 industry accounted for 15·7% of GDP, with manufacturing contributing 10·3%.

Labour

The labour force in 2010 was 6,708,000 (51·5% female). Approximately 80% of the economically active population in 2010 were engaged in agriculture.

Malaŵi had 0·11m. people living in slavery according to the Walk Free Foundation's 2013 *Global Slavery Index*.

International Trade

Imports and Exports

In 2010 imports (c.i.f.) amounted to US$2,173m. and exports (f.o.b.) US$1,066m.

Principal imports in 2010 (in US$1m.) were: chemicals and related products (532); machinery and transport equipment (515); manufactured goods (347). Principal exports in 2010 (in US$1m.) were: tobacco and tobacco products (585); uranium ores and concentrates (114); tea (81).

In 2010 major import sources (in US$1m.) were: South Africa (654); China (198); India (165). Major export markets in 2010 (in US$1m.) were: Belgium (133); Canada (118); Egypt (98).

Trade Fairs

The annual Malaŵi International Trade Fair takes place in Blantyre, the commercial capital.

Communications

Roads

The road network consisted of 24,929 km in 2008, of which 16·3% were paved. There were 53,300 passenger cars and 59,800 vans and trucks in 2007.

Rail

In 2005 Malaŵi Railways operated 797 km on 1,067 mm gauge, providing links to the Mozambican ports of Beira and Nacala. In 2009 passenger-km travelled came to 44m. and freight tonne-km to 47m.

Civil Aviation

The national carrier is Malawian Airlines, which is 49% owned by Ethiopian Airlines. It was founded in 2013 following the liquidation of the former flag carrier, Air Malawi. In 2012 scheduled airline traffic of Malaŵi-based carriers flew 3·7m. km; passenger-km totalled 207·5m. in the same year. The main international airport is Lilongwe (Lilongwe International Airport). The airport at Blantyre (Chileka) also has some international flights. Lilongwe handled 261,267 passengers in 2012 (198,620 on international flights) and 3,932 tonnes of freight.

Telecommunications

In 2011 there were 173,500 landline telephone subscriptions (equivalent to 11·3 per 1,000 inhabitants) and 3,855,800 mobile phone subscriptions (or 250·7 per 1,000 inhabitants). In 2011, 3·3% of the population were internet users. In June 2012 there were 140,000 Facebook users.

Social Institutions

Out of 178 countries analysed in the 2017 *Fragile States Index*—a list published jointly by the Fund for Peace and *Foreign Policy* magazine—Malaŵi was ranked the joint 44th most vulnerable (along with Burkina Faso) to conflict or collapse. The index is based on 12 indicators of state vulnerability across social, political and economic categories.

Justice

Justice is administered in the High Court and in the magistrates' courts. Traditional courts were abolished in 1994. Appeals from magistrates' courts lie to the High Court, and appeals from the High Court to Malaŵi's Supreme Court of Appeal.

The population in penal institutions in Dec. 2012 was 12,236 (76 per 100,000 of national population). In 2015 the World Justice Project *Rule of Law Index*, which provides data on how the rule of law is experienced by the general public across eight categories, ranked Malaŵi 48th of 102 countries for criminal justice and 50th for civil justice.

Education

The adult literacy rate in 2009 was estimated at 73·7% (80·6% among males and 67·0% among females). Fees for primary education were abolished in 1994. In 2007 the number of pupils in primary schools was 2,943,248 (44,048 teaching staff). The primary school course is of eight years' duration, followed by a four-year secondary course. In 2007 there were 574,003 pupils in secondary schools. English is taught from the 1st year and becomes the general medium of instruction from the 4th year.

The University of Malaŵi (consisting of four colleges and one polytechnic) had 6,257 students and 676 academic staff in 2007. A university at Mzuzu opened in 1998 and provides courses for secondary school teachers. In 2007 there were 6,458 students in higher education and 861 academic staff.

In 2009 public expenditure on education came to 2·8% of GDP.

Health

In 2009 there were 265 physicians, 4,812 nursing and midwifery personnel, 180 dentistry personnel and 221 pharmaceutical personnel. In 2007 there were 11 hospital beds per 10,000 inhabitants.

In *Water: At What Cost? The State of the World's Water 2016*, WaterAid reported that 9·8% of the population does not have access to safe water.

Religion

According to estimates by the Pew Research Center's Forum on Religion & Public Life, in 2010 the population was 82·7% Christian (mainly Protestants) and 13·0% Muslim.

Culture

World Heritage Sites

Malaŵi has two sites on the UNESCO World Heritage List: Lake Malaŵi National Park (inscribed on the list in 1984); and the Chongoni Rock-Art area (2006).

Press

There were two paid-for dailies and nine paid-for non-dailies in 2008. The two dailies are *The Nation* (average circulation of 15,000 copies daily in 2008); and *The Daily Times* (7,000 copies daily in 2008).

Tourism

There were 755,031 non-resident tourists in 2009 (excluding same-day visitors), up from 742,457 in 2008.

Diplomatic Representatives

Of Malaŵi in the United Kingdom (36 John St., London, WC1N 2AT)
  High Commissioner: Kenna Alewa Mphonda.

Of the United Kingdom in Malaŵi (off Convention Drive, PO Box 30042, Lilongwe 3)
  High Commissioner: Holly Tett.

Of Malaŵi in the USA (2408 Massachusetts Ave., NW, Washington, D.C., 20008)
  Ambassador: Edward Yakobe Sawerengera.

Of the USA in Malaŵi (Area 40, Plot 24, Kenyatta Rd, Lilongwe 3)
  Ambassador: Virginia E. Palmer.

Of Malaŵi to the United Nations
  Ambassador: Perks Ligoya.

Of Malaŵi to the European Union
  Ambassador: Tedson Aubrey Kalebe.

Further Reading

National Statistical Office. *Monthly Statistical Bulletin*
Ministry of Economic Planning and Development. *Economic Report*. Annual
Kalinga, Owen J. M., *Historical Dictionary of Malawi*. 4th ed. 2011
Sindima, Harvey J., *Malawi's First Republic: An Economic and Political Analysis*. 2002
National Statistical Office: National Statistical Office, POB 333, Zomba.
Website: http://www.nsomalawi.mw

Malaysia

Persekutuan Tanah Malaysia (Federation of Malaysia)

Capitals: Putrajaya (Administrative), Kuala Lumpur (Legislative and Financial)
Population projection, 2020: 32·87m.
GNI per capita, 2017: (PPP$) 26,107
HDI/world rank, 2017: 0·802/57
Internet domain extension: .my

Key Historical Events

Excavations at Niah in Sarawak, East Malaysia have uncovered evidence of human settlement from 38,000 BC (the oldest relic of *homo sapiens* in southeast Asia). There are numerous sites in the north of Peninsular Malaysia where evidence of hunter-gatherers has been dated to around 10,000 BC. These Hoabinhians were spread across the region from present-day Myanmar to southern China between 12,000 and 3,000 BC. After 3,000 BC Mon-Khmer speaking immigrants moved south into Peninsular Malaysia and introduced a more advanced Neolithic culture, engaging in simple farming. The indigenous people known as Orang Asli, who still live in the more remote, mountainous areas of the northern Malay Peninsula, are considered to be descendants of the Neolithic farmers. Indian traders first visited the Malay Peninsula in the 1st century BC and introduced political ideas, art forms and the Sanskrit language. Hinduism and Buddhism gained a foothold and were practised alongside traditional animist beliefs.

Various Hinduized city-states were established, one of which was located in Kedah. In the 7th century AD Kedah came under the control of the Hinduized Srivijaya empire, centred on Palembang in Sumatra. Srivijaya rule ended in the late 13th century when Sumatra fell to a Javan invasion, after which the king of Sukothai sent forces south into the Malay Peninsula. The Sumatran kingdom of Melayu next ruled over the southern part of the Peninsula, followed by the Madjapahit, the last Hindu empire of Java. In the mid-15th century Melaka emerged as the key trading port in the region—it was host to indigenous Malays, Sumatrans, Javans, Gujaratis, Arabs, Persians, Filipinos and Chinese—and grew rapidly in prosperity. A pattern of government was established in Melaka that became the basis of Malay identity and it was emulated by subsequent Malay kingdoms. Gujarati sailors introduced Islam to the region through Melaka in the 15th century. In 1511 the port was captured by the Portuguese navigator Alfonso de Albuquerque (who had seized Goa in western India the previous year), and who sought to dominate the route by which precious spices were shipped to Europe.

The sultan of Melaka fled to Johor and some of the Muslim mercantile elite relocated to Brunei in northwest Borneo. Sultanates also emerged in Pahang and Perak, which subsequently received large numbers of immigrants from Indonesian islands, notably Acehnese, Bugis and Minangkabau settlers, who displaced the Orang Asli from their coastal communities and drove them to the Malay Peninsula's interior. Conflict arose between the sultanates of Johor and Aceh and the Portuguese as they vied for control over the Straits of Melaka. In the late 16th century the northern Peninsular states of Kedah, Kelantan and Terengganu came under the control of the Thai state of Phetburi. The early 17th century saw the arrival of Dutch traders in the strait of Melaka. As part of the United Netherlands East India Company (Vereenigde Oostindische Compagnie, VOC) they made an alliance with Johor to besiege Melaka, capturing it in 1641. The Dutch brokered a peace deal between Aceh and Johor in the same year, ushering in an era of relative peace and prosperity for Johor under Laksamana Tun Abdul Jamil.

In the late 17th century the Malay Peninsula came under the influence of Bugis merchants from the Indonesian island of Sulawesi, who began settling in Selangor to trade in tin. The Bugis were formidable warriors, renowned for their navigational and commercial skills. By the 1740s they controlled many of the key shipping routes across the Indonesian archipelago and influenced all areas of government in Johor and the Riau archipelago, although Sultan Suliaman was permitted to remain as a figurehead.

British Influence

In the mid-18th century Johor and Melaka became entrepôts for the trade in tea between China and Europe. Ships owned by the British East India Company (EIC) began plying the Melaka straits in greater numbers. The British foothold in India allowed them to expand eastwards, and their control of India's poppy fields enabled them to dominate the lucrative opium trade. In 1786 Francis Light of the EIC leased the island of Penang from the Sultan Abdullah of Kedah who hoped the British would provide protection against attacks from Siam or Burma. Penang grew swiftly, luring trade away from Melaka (which remained in Dutch control) and Johor-Riau. The British sought to increase their control over the maritime route to China and Sir Thomas Stamford Raffles was ordered to establish an entrepôt in the southern reaches of the Melaka Straits. In 1819 he signed a treaty with Sultan Husein Syah of Johor and founded Singapore. Five years later the British formally acquired Melaka from the Dutch. From 1826 Penang, Singapore and Melaka were ruled by the British authorities in India under a joint administration known as the Straits Settlements. By 1831 the population of Singapore had reached 18,000 (a large proportion were Chinese immigrants) and the following year the port replaced Penang as the capital of the Straits Settlements. Meanwhile, the northern provinces of Kedah and Perak came under the influence of the Siamese Chakri dynasty.

The discovery of tin deposits at Larut (western Malay Peninsula) in the 1850s led to large-scale immigration by Chinese miners and labourers. They organized themselves into *hui* (brotherhoods), which eventually became powerful political and economic organizations. Vast profits could be made from tin and there were clashes between rival developers. At the same time, piracy was on the increase in the Melaka straits, and merchants asked the British to intervene and restore order. A series of agreements in 1874 introduced the British Residential system to Perak, Selangor and Sungei Ujung. In each region, a British Resident functioned as an adviser to the Malay Sultan on all aspects of administration apart from matters relating to the Islamic faith and Malay tradition.

Colonial Rule

In 1896 the three states and Pahang were grouped together as the Federated Malay States, presided over by a British Resident-General at Kuala Lumpur in the heart of the tin-mining district. By the end of the century, a British colonial infrastructure was taking shape in the form of public buildings, municipal services, rubber plantations and road and rail construction, which required a stream of cheap workers. Tamils from south India and Sri Lanka arrived as indentured (and later as licensed) labourers. Negotiations between the British and Siamese in the early years of the 20th century led to British control over the northern states of Kedah, Perlis, Kelantan and Terengganu. A rubber boom followed the expansion of the motor car industry in Europe and North America. Rubber plants, originally from the forests of Brazil and introduced to Malaysia in the 1880s, were planted in every state in Malaysia by 1908 and by 1913 rubber had eclipsed tin as the country's chief export.

Sabah, Sarawak and Brunei, which had come under the control of the North Borneo Chartered Company and was granted protectorate status in 1888, experienced slower economic development than British Malaya but gold, antimony and coal were mined and oil was discovered at Miri in 1910. The colony was hit hard by the global depression of 1929–31 and widespread unemployment in the mines and plantations caused the repatriation of Chinese and Indian workers. Rubber, tin and oil made Malaya a focus for Imperial Japan from early in the Second World War. When Pearl Harbor and Hong Kong came under attack from Japanese forces in Dec. 1941, other Japanese divisions came ashore at Kota Bharu and Miri. British forces retreated south to Singapore, but the 'impregnable' island capitulated within a few weeks, on 15 Feb. 1942. Japanese troops quickly took over from British colonial officers and controlled Malaya from Singapore (Shonan), meting out harsh treatment to the Chinese population. Thailand allied itself with Japan and was granted control of the northern Malay states in 1943.

Palgrave Macmillan (ed.), *The Statesman's Yearbook 2020*, https://doi.org/10.1057/978-1-349-95940-2_120

Post-War Period

Returning in 1946, the British reorganized the colony into the Malayan Union. The Malay elite, fearing an end to their privileges as a consequence of equal rights for Chinese and Indian subjects, campaigned via the United Malays National Organization (UMNO, led by Datuk Onn) to demand the continuation of the sultanates. The British were forced to compromise and established the Federation of Malaya in Feb. 1948, consisting of the nine Malay states, Melaka and Penang and administered by a High Commissioner in Kuala Lumpur. Within months the Federation was under attack by the Chinese-dominated Malayan Communist Party (MCP) which had grown during the Japanese occupation, when it controlled various anti-Japanese National Salvation Organizations. In 1950 the High Commissioner, Sir Henry Gurney, responded to guerrilla attacks by the MCP by putting Malaya on a war-footing, including tightening security, recruiting soldiers from other colonies and dispersing the Chinese squatter settlements that harboured the MCP. More than 500,000 Chinese were resettled by the mid-1950s. The Communist insurrection, known by the British as 'the Emergency', hastened the transition to Malayan independence and local elections were held in Penang in late 1951. Four years later the first federal-level election was won convincingly by the Alliance Party, a loose coalition of Malay, Chinese and Indian parties, led by Tuanku (Prince) Abdul Rahman. On 31 Aug. 1957 the Federation of Malaya became an independent state with Tuanku Abdul Rahman as the first prime minister.

The concept of Malaysia as a broader federation including Sabah, Sarawak, Singapore and the British protectorate of Brunei, was first suggested by Abdul Rahman in 1961. It was opposed by neighbouring Indonesia and the Philippines, but public support in Sabah and Sarawak led to Malaysia's formation in Sept. 1963, although Brunei declined to join. The new nation faced continuing hostility from Indonesia, led by Ahmed Sukarno, over the sovereignty of Borneo. Disagreements with Singapore's Prime Minister Lee Kuan Yew ended with Singapore declaring independence in 1965. Tension arose between the Chinese and Malay communities over the use of the Malay language and Malay fears about Chinese economic dominance. The 1969 elections were fought on the highly emotional issues of education and language. When the Alliance party failed to obtain a majority, rioting and serious inter-ethnic violence followed and an emergency government was set up, led by Deputy Prime Minister Abdul Razak. Parliamentary rule was restored in 1971 when Razak launched the New Economic Policy—a series of five-year plans to eradicate poverty and restructure society to improve ethnic relations, specifically by encouraging ethnic Malays, the *bumiputera*, to shift from subsistence agriculture into the mainstream economy.

Mahathir Mohamad was the first non-royal or non-aristocrat to become prime minister of Malaysia, winning the 1981 elections for the UMNO and leading the National Front coalition to further victories in 1986, 1990, 1995 and 1999. Mahathir shifted the economy away from dependence on commodities and towards manufacturing, services and tourism, aided by substantial Japanese and east Asian investment in manufacturing. The prolonged spell of economic growth and stability was broken by the 1997–98 recession but Mahathir refused to accept financial aid from the International Monetary Fund. In Sept. 1998 Mahathir dismissed Anwar Ibrahim, his finance minister, deputy prime minister and heir apparent. Anwar was found guilty of corruption charges in 1999 and sentenced to prison for six years. In 2002 Mahathir announced that he would resign from the presidency of UMNO and he stepped down as prime minister on 31 Oct. 2003, to be succeeded by Abdullah Ahmad Badawi. Badawi won a landslide victory in the March 2004 general elections for the National Front. In Sept. 2004 Anwar was unexpectedly released after being acquitted by the Federal Court. Najib Razak succeeded Badawi in 2009, winning re-election in 2013. However, he was implicated in a corruption scandal and was ousted when the National Front lost the May 2018 parliamentary elections to the opposition Alliance of Hope (Pakatan Harapan) headed by former premier Mahathir, who again became prime minister.

Territory and Population

The federal state of Malaysia comprises the 13 states and three federal territories of Peninsular Malaysia, bounded in the north by Thailand, and with the island of Singapore as an enclave on its southern tip; and, on the island of Borneo to the east, the state of Sabah (which includes the federal territory of the island of Labuan), and the state of Sarawak, with Brunei as an enclave, both bounded in the south by Indonesia and in the northwest and northeast by the South China and Sulu Seas.

The area of Malaysia is 330,345 sq. km (127,547 sq. miles), and the 2010 census population 28,334,135; density, 85·8 per sq. km. The estimated population in July 2018 was 32,385,000. Malaysia's national waters cover 515,256 sq. km. In 2011, 73·0% of the population lived in urban areas.

The UN gives a projected population for 2020 of 32·87m.

The growth of the population has been:

Year	Peninsular Malaysia	Sarawak	Sabah/ Labuan	Total Malaysia
1980	10,944,844	1,235,553	955,712	13,136,109
1991	14,131,723	1,642,771	1,788,926	17,563,420
2000	17,649,266	2,009,893	2,539,117	22,198,276
2010	22,569,345	2,471,140	3,293,650	28,334,135

The areas, populations and chief towns of the states and federal territories are:

Peninsular states	Area (in sq. km)	Population (2010, in 1,000)	Chief town	Population (2010, in 1,000)
Johor	19,210	3,348	Johor Bharu	497
Kedah	9,500	1,948	Alor Star	406
Kelantan	15,099	1,540	Kota Bharu	315
Kuala Lumpur[1]	243	1,675	Kuala Lumpur	1,589[1]
Melaka	1,664	821	Melaka	485
Negeri Sembilan	6,686	1,021	Seremban	556
Pahang	36,137	1,501	Kuantan	428
Perak	21,035	2,353	Ipoh	658
Perlis	821	232	Kangar	226
Pulau Pinang (Penang)	1,048	1,561	Penang (George Town)	800
Putrajaya[1]	46	72	Putrajaya	—
Selangor	8,108	5,462	Shah Alam	641
Terengganu	13,035	1,036	Kuala Terengganu	338
Other states				
Labuan[1]	91	87	Victoria	—
Sabah	73,631	3,207	Kota Kinabalu	452
Sarawak	124,450	2,471	Kuching	618

[1]Federal territory.

Other large cities are Seberang Perai, Kajang, Klang, Subang Jaya, Petaling Jaya and Selayang.

Putrajaya, a planned new city described as an 'intelligent garden city', became the administrative capital of Malaysia in 1999 and was created a federal territory on 1 Feb. 2001.

Malay (Bahasa Malaysia) is the official language of the country—54% of the population are Malays. The government promotes the use of the national language to foster national unity. However, the people are free to use their mother tongue and other languages. English is widely used in business. In Peninsular Malaysia, Chinese dialects and Tamil are also spoken. In Sabah there are numerous tribal dialects and Chinese (Mandarin and Hakka dialects predominate). In Sarawak, Mandarin and numerous tribal languages are spoken. In addition to Malays, 25% of the population are Chinese, 13% other indigenous ethnic groups, 7% Indians and 1% others. Malays and indigenous people, collectively known as *bumiputera* ('sons of the soil'), make up around two-thirds of the population.

Social Statistics

2007 estimated births, 481,000; deaths, 120,000. 2007 rates (per 1,000 population): birth, 18·1; death, 4·5. Life expectancy, 2007: males, 71·9 years; females, 76·6 years. Annual population growth rate, 2000–08, 1·9%.

Infant mortality, 2010, five per 1,000 live births; fertility rate, 2007, 2·3 births per woman. Today only 6% of Malaysians live below the poverty line, compared to 50% in the early 1970s. Malaysia was ranked 111th in a gender gap index of 145 countries compiled by the World Economic Forum for its *Global Gender Gap Report 2015*. The annual index considers economic, political, education and health criteria.

Climate

Malaysia lies near the equator between latitudes 1° and 7° North and longitudes 100° and 119° East. Malaysia is subject to maritime influence and the interplay of wind systems which originate in the Indian Ocean and the South China Sea. The year is generally divided into the South-East and the North-East Monsoon seasons. The average daily temperature throughout Malaysia varies from 21°C to 32°C. Humidity is high.

Constitution and Government

The Constitution of Malaysia is based on the Constitution of the former Federation of Malaya, but includes safeguards for the special interests of Sabah and Sarawak. It was amended in 1983. The Constitution provides for one of the Rulers of the Malay States to be elected from among themselves to be the *Yang di-Pertuan Agong* (Supreme Head of the Federation). He holds office for a period of five years. The Rulers also elect from among themselves a Deputy Supreme Head of State, also for a period of five years.

Supreme Head of State (Yang di-Pertuan Agong)
Sultan Abdullah Ri'ayatuddin al-Mustafa Billah Shah, b. 1959, acceded 31 Jan. 2019.

Sultan of Johor
Sultan Ibrahim Ismail ibni al-Marhum Sultan Iskandar, b. 1958, acceded 23 Jan. 2010.

Sultan of Kedah
Sultan Sallehuddin ibni al-Marhum Sultan Badlishah, b. 1942, acceded 12 Sept. 2017.

Sultan of Kelantan
Sultan Muhammad V (Tuanku Muhammad Faris Petra Ibni Sultan Ismail Petra), b. 1969, acceded 13 Sept. 2010 (but disputed by Tuanku Ismail Petra Sultan Yahya Petra—the previous sultan and his ailing father).

Yang Di-Pertuan Besar Negeri Sembilan
Tuanku Muhriz ibni al-Marhum Tuanku Munawir, b. 1948, acceded 29 Dec. 2008.

Sultan of Pahang
Sultan Abdullah Ri'ayatuddin al-Mustafa Billah Shah, b. 1959, acceded 15 Jan. 2019.

Sultan of Perak
Sultan Nazrin Muizzuddin Shah ibni al-Marhum Sultan Azlan Muhibuddin Shah, b. 1956, acceded 29 May 2014.

Raja of Perlis
Tuanku Syed Sirajuddin ibni al-Marhum Syed Putra Jamalullail, b. 1943, acceded 17 April 2000.

Sultan of Selangor
Sultan Sharafuddin Idris Shah Alhaj ibni al-Marhum Sultan Salahuddin Abdul Aziz Shah Alhaj, b. 1945, acceded 22 Nov. 2001.

Sultan of Terengganu
Sultan Mizan Zainal Abidin ibni al-Mahrum Sultan Mahmud al-Muktafi Billah Shah, b. 1962, acceded 15 May 1998.

Yang di Pertua Negeri Melaka
Tun Mohd Khalil bin Yaakob, b. 1937, appointed 4 June 2004.

Yang di-Pertua Negeri Pulau Pinang (Penang)
Tun Haji Abdul Rahman bin Haji Abbas, b. 1938, appointed 1 May 2001.

Yang di-Pertua Negeri Sabah
Tun Haji Juhar bin Haji Mahiruddin, b. 1953, appointed 1 Jan. 2011.

Yang di-Pertua Negeri Sarawak
Tun Abdul Taib Mahmud, b. 1936, appointed 1 March 2014.

The federal parliament consists of the *Yang di-Pertuan Agong* and two *Majlis* (Houses of Parliament) known as the *Dewan Negara* (Senate) of 70 members (26 elected, two by each state legislature; and 44 appointed by the *Yang di-Pertuan Agong*) and the *Dewan Rakyat* (House of Representatives) of 222 members plus the Speaker. Appointment to the Senate is for three years. The maximum life of the House of Representatives is five years, subject to its dissolution at any time by the *Yang di-Pertuan Agong* on the advice of his Ministers.

National Anthem

'Negaraku' ('My Country'); words collective, tune by Pierre de Béranger.

Government Chronology

Supreme Heads of State since 1957.

1957–60	Tuanku Abdul Rahman ibni al-Marhum
1960	Sultan Hisamuddin Alam Shah ibni al-Marhum
1960–65	Tuanku Syed Harun Petra ibni al-Marhum
1965–70	Sultan Ismail Nasiruddin Shah ibni al-Marhum
1970–75	Sultan Abdul Halim Muadzam Shah ibni al-Marhum
1975–79	Sultan Yahaya Petra ibni al-Marhum
1979–84	Sultan Ahmad Shah al-Mustain Billah ibni al-Marhum
1984–89	Sultan Mahmud Iskandar ibni al-Marhum
1989–94	Sultan Azlan Muhibuddin Shah ibni al-Marhum
1994–99	Tuanku Jaafar ibni al-Marhum
1999–2001	Sultan Salehuddin Abdul Aziz Shah ibni al-Marhum
2001–06	Tuanku Syed Sirajuddin ibni al-Marhum
2006–11	Sultan Mizan Zainal Abidin ibni al-Marhum Sultan Mahmud
2011–16	Sultan Abdul Halim Muadzam Shah ibni al-Marhum Sultan Badlishah
2016–19	Sultan Muhammad V ibni Sultan Ismail Petra
2019–	Sultan Abdullah Ri'ayatuddin al-Mustafa Billah Shah

Prime Ministers since 1957. (PPBM = Malaysian United Indigenous Party; UMNO = United Malays National Organization)

1957–59	UMNO	Tunku Abdul Rahman Putra
1959	UMNO	Tun Abdul Razak bin Hussein (acting)
1959–70	UMNO	Tunku Abdul Rahman Putra
1970–76	UMNO	Tun Abdul Razak bin Hussein
1976–81	UMNO	Hussein bin Onn
1981–2003	UMNO	Mahathir bin Mohamad
2003–09	UMNO	Abdullah bin Haji Ahmad Badawi
2009–18	UMNO	Najib Tun Razak
2018–	PPBM	Mahathir bin Mohamad

Recent Elections

Elections to the *Dewan Rakyat* and 12 state assemblies (except Sarawak) were held on 9 May 2018. The Alliance of Hope (PH; Pakatan Harapan) gained 113 seats, obtaining 50·9% of the votes cast (the predominant partner, the People's Justice Party, winning 49 seats). The ruling National Front coalition (BN; Barisan Nasional) won 79 seats, the Ideas of Prosperity coalition (GS; Gagasan Sejahtera) 18, the Sabah Heritage Party 8, independent candidates 3 and the United Sabah Alliance 1.

Current Government

In Feb. 2019 the government comprised:
Prime Minister: Mahathir Mohamad; b. 1925 (PPBM; took office on 10 May 2018 having previously been prime minister from July 1981–Oct. 2003).

Deputy Prime Minister, and Minister of Women, Family and Community Development: Wan Azizah Wan Ismail.

Minister of Agriculture and Agro-Based Industry: Salahuddin Ayub. *Communication and Multimedia:* Gobind Singh Deo. *Defence:* Mohamed Sabu. *Domestic Trade and Consumer Affairs:* Saifuddin Nasution Ismail. *Economic Affairs:* Mohamed Azmin Ali. *Education:* Mazlee Malik. *Energy, Technology, Science, Climate Change and Environment:* Yeao Bee Yin. *Entrepreneur Development:* Mohd Redzuan Yusof. *Federal Territories:* Khalid Abdul Samad. *Finance:* Lim Guan Eng. *Foreign Affairs:* Saifuddin Abdullah. *Health:* Dzulkefly Ahmad. *Home Affairs:* Muhyiddin Yassin. *Housing and Local Government:* Zuraida Kamaruddin. *Human Resources:* Kulasegaran Murugeson. *International Trade and Industry:* Ignatius Dorell

Leiking. *Primary Industries:* Teresa Kok Suh Sim. *Rural Development:* Rina Harun. *Tourism, Art and Culture:* Mohammadin Ketapi. *Transport:* Anthony Loke Siew Fook. *Water, Land and Natural Resources:* Xavier Jayakumar. *Works:* Baru Bian. *Youth and Sports:* Syed Saddiq Syed Abdul Rahman. *Ministers in the Prime Minister's Department:* Mujahid Yusof Rawa (*in Charge of Religious Affairs*); Liew Vui Keong (*in Charge of Law*); Waytha Moorthy Ponnusamy (*in Charge of National Unity and Social Wellbeing*). *Office of the Prime Minister:* http://www.pmo.gov.my

---

Current Leaders

Sultan Abdullah

Position

King (Yang di-Pertuan Agong)

Introduction

Sultan Abdullah Ri'ayatuddin Al-Mustafa Billah Shah came to the throne on 31 Jan. 2019, following the abdication of Sultan Muhammad V. As part of Malaysia's rotational monarchy, he is expected to rule for a five-year term. He is the hereditary ruler and sultan of the state of Pahang.

Early Life

Abdullah was born on 30 July 1959, the eldest son of Sultan Ahmad Shah of Pahang. He was educated in England and attended the Royal Military Academy, Sandhurst, from 1978–79, where he was made a second lieutenant. He continued his education at Worcester College, University of Oxford, and Queen Elizabeth College, London, from where he received a diploma in international relations and diplomacy.

On 1 July 1975 Abdullah was conferred the title Tengku Mahkota of Pahang. From 1979–84 he served as the Regent of Pahang when his father ascended the Malaysian throne. He served in the position again in Dec. 2016 when his father's health deteriorated. He has also worked as an adviser to several international sporting bodies, including the football governing body FIFA and the International Hockey Federation.

On 6 Jan. 2019 Sultan Muhammad V announced his unprecedented abdication as the country's ruler. Nine days later Abdullah became Sultan of Pahang following his father's own abdication as a result of ill health. On 24 Jan. Abdullah was elected king by the Conference of Rulers. He ascended to the throne on 31 Jan., assuming the regnal name Sultan Abdullah Ri'ayatuddin Al-Mustafa Billah Shah.

Career in Office

Abdullah's role is largely ceremonial. However, he took the throne as a new government moved to introduce wide-ranging institutional reforms. Consequently, his constitutional powers—which include the right to veto the appointment of key political positions, including the prime minister, and to grant pardons—may have greater than usual significance.

Mahathir Mohamad

Position

Prime Minister

Introduction

Mahathir Mohamad became the fourth prime minister of Malaysia in 1981, and went on to be Asia's longest-serving elected leader. He stepped down in 2003 but resumed the premiership once again in 2018 at the head of an opposition coalition.

Early Life

Mahathir Mohamad was born in the state of Kedah on 20 Dec. 1925. He was educated in Kedah and studied medicine in Singapore. Graduating in 1953, he returned to Malaya to serve as a government medical officer until 1957, when he went into private practice. He entered politics in the 1960s and was elected to parliament in 1964 as a member for the United Malays National Organization (UMNO). However, in 1969 he was expelled from the party for advocating preferential treatment for ethnic Malays.

Mahathir was readmitted to UMNO in 1970, becoming minister of education in 1974 and deputy prime minister in 1976. While retaining the deputy premiership, he was transferred to the ministry of trade in 1978 and subsequently led trade delegations abroad. In June 1981 he was elected party leader and became premier in July that year.

Career in Office

The first non-royal or non-aristocrat to become prime minister of Malaysia, Mahathir encouraged rapid industrialization. He promoted foreign investment and freer trade, aiming to achieve higher living standards. From reliance on raw materials exports, Malaysia's economy was driven towards manufacturing and tourism and grew on average by 7·3% annually between 1990 and 1999.

The Asian economic crisis prompted disagreements within UMNO, principally between Mahathir and the finance minister, Anwar Ibrahim. Mahathir turned away from foreign investment, taking a protectionist stance, and in 1998 he dismissed Anwar who was subsequently convicted of corruption and sodomy. The charges were widely disputed and the conduct of the trial attracted international criticism. Mahathir was accused of abusing the democratic process. However, he remained defiant, rejecting what he saw as the attempted imposition of Western values on the Islamic world.

Relations with Singapore were also at times strained. In 1998 Mahathir suggested that Singapore should not take its relationship with Malaysia for granted, given its dependency on Malaysia for water supplies, while Singapore's elder statesman Lee Kuan Yew criticized Mahathir's handling of the detention and trial of Anwar Ibrahim.

In June 2001 Mahathir also assumed the finance portfolio. Meanwhile, his outspoken leadership style was both criticized and admired in Malaysia. In June 2002 he attacked the ethnic Malays for failing to build on the privileges granted to help them reach the level of prosperity of the Chinese Malaysian community. He also angered Malay nationalists by insisting on the teaching of English as a core subject in schools despite the revival of the indigenous language, Bahasa Malaysia.

In a shock public broadcast in June 2002 Mahathir resigned as prime minister. He was persuaded to withdraw the resignation but reiterated that he would leave office in late 2003. His deputy, Abdullah Ahmad Badawi, was named as his successor. Mahathir's final months in office were dominated by attacks on Western values and perceived Jewish 'world power'. He stepped down as prime minister on 31 Oct. 2003.

In Sept. 2004 Anwar Ibrahim was released from prison. Mahathir would later defend his conduct in regard to Anwar by suggesting that the latter's imprisonment prevented Malaysia from having a homosexual leader in the future. In Dec. 2004 Mahathir expressed outspoken disapproval of Australia's desire to join the Association of South East Asian Nations. However, Badawi took a more accommodating approach and Mahathir became an increasingly vocal critic of his successor.

The situation escalated when Mahathir left UMNO in May 2008, citing Badawi's premiership as his reason and calling for the prime minister to step down. Mahathir rejoined UMNO on 4 April 2009, just days after Najib Razak (whom Mahathir seemed to support) succeeded Badawi as prime minister.

Mahathir's outspoken views focused on an array of targets. In 2014 he railed against the 'laziness' of Malays, especially in comparison to Chinese Malaysians, and expressed disapproval of the repeal of one of his own policies—the teaching of science and mathematics in English. He also commented on the disappearance of the Malaysia Airlines flight MH370 and suggested possible US Central Intelligence Agency involvement.

His opposition to Najib also became increasingly virulent. In 2015 Najib's involvement in a financial scandal gave Mahathir an opportunity to call for a 'people's power' movement in order to remove the premier. In Aug. that year he participated in a popular protest calling for the removal of the prime minister and leading to the release of a Malaysian Citizens' Declaration in early 2016, amid allegations that Najib had transferred huge sums of money from an investment firm to his personal account. Mahathir broke once more with UMNO in 2016 and in Sept. that year established the Malaysian United Indigenous Party, with himself as chairman.

In Jan. 2018 the opposition Alliance of Hope (Pakatan Harapan) announced Mahathir as its candidate for prime minister in the forthcoming general election. Wan Azizah Wan Ismail, Anwar Ibrahim's wife, was declared the deputy prime ministerial candidate, indicating that the desire to remove Najib from power was strong enough to unite two erstwhile political foes.

In the elections in May the Alliance of Hope won the majority of seats in parliament, ousting the ruling National Front coalition (Barisan Nasional) for the first time since Malaysia's independence in 1957. Mahathir was sworn in as premier (the world's oldest at the age of 92) and declared his intention to address the country's economic woes. He inherited a national debt of some 686bn. ringgit, although some estimates put it at over 1trn. ringgit. Although he effectively abolished the goods and service tax from June 2018 to fulfil a campaign promise, he announced in Oct. the possibility of new taxes and the sale of assets in order to reduce the debt level.

Internationally, he has remained an outspoken critic of Israel, arguing in late 2018 that Australia's planned move of embassy to Jerusalem from Tel Aviv could fuel the threat of terrorism and that the troubles in the Middle East were linked to 'the creation of Israel', prompting accusations of anti-Semitism.

Defence

The Constitution provides for the Head of State to be the Supreme Commander of the Armed Forces who exercises his powers in accordance with the advice of the Cabinet. Under their authority, the Armed Forces Council is responsible for all matters relating to the Armed Forces other than those relating to their operational use. The ministry of defence has established bilateral defence relations with countries within as well as outside the region. Malaysia is a member of the Five Powers Defence Arrangement with Australia, New Zealand, Singapore and the UK.

The Malaysian Armed Forces has participated in 25 UN peacekeeping missions in Africa, the Middle East, Indo-China and Europe.

In 2004 a lottery system was introduced which chose conscripts to serve three months of national service. This was abolished in 2018. In 2013 defence expenditure totalled US$5,000m. (US$169 per capita), representing 1·5% of GDP.

Army

Strength (2011) about 80,000. There is a paramilitary Police General Operations Force of 18,000 and a People's Volunteer Corps of 240,000 of which some 17,500 are armed.

Navy

The Royal Malaysian Navy is commanded by the Chief of the Navy from the integrated Ministry of Defence in Kuala Lumpur. The main base is at Lumut, with other bases at Kuantan, Labuan, Sandakan, Semporna, Sepanggar and Tanjung Pengelih. Further bases are under construction at Langkawi and Sejingkat. The peacetime tasks include fishery protection and anti-piracy patrols. In 2011 the fleet included two submarines, ten frigates and four corvettes. The two Scorpene-class submarines were jointly built by French and Spanish firms and were delivered in Sept. 2009 and July 2010 respectively. A Naval aviation squadron operates six helicopters.

Navy personnel in 2011 totalled 14,000 including 160 Naval Air personnel. There were 1,000 naval reserves.

In addition, there is a maritime enforcement agency some 4,500 strong and 2,100 marine police.

Air Force

Formed in 1958, the Royal Malaysian Air Force is equipped primarily to provide air defence and air support for the Army, Navy and Police. Its secondary role is to render assistance to government departments and civilian organizations.

Personnel (2011) totalled 15,000, with 67 combat-capable aircraft including F-5Es, MiG-29s and British Aerospace *Hawks*. There were 600 Air Force reserves.

Economy

In 2013 agriculture accounted for 9·1% of GDP, industry 39·9% and services 51·0%.

Overview

Malaysia's economy is classified as upper-middle income and is very open to trade and investment. Growing by 7% per year on average in the quarter-century to 2008, the economy developed from a dependency on tin, rubber and other raw materials in the 1970s to become a leading exporter of electrical appliances, electronic components, palm oil and natural gas. The electrical and electronics industry accounted for 43% of total exports in 2014.

In 1998 Malaysia was hit hard by currency and banking crises, shrinking the economy by 7·4%. The government sought to boost growth via spending on large infrastructure projects. When global recession cut export demand in 2001, the country managed to avoid recession by introducing a US$1·9bn.

fiscal stimulus package. The recovery subsequently moderated, with GDP and export growth both slowing. Although the financial system has remained sound, gross household debt increased by 12·3% to 89·1% of GDP between 2008 and 2015.

Owing to its openness, the economy is at risk from ongoing low growth in major advanced economies and from exposure to European banking frailty. Long-term sustainability depends on the implementation of labour reforms to boost productivity and competition. The government introduced a New Economic Model in 2010, designed to implement reforms by 2020 driven by private sector growth and underpinned by sustainability and more equable wealth distribution. In 2014 and 2015 the government rolled back fuel subsidies and implemented a goods and services tax. In March 2018 Malaysia and ten other countries bordering the Pacific (although not the USA) signed the Comprehensive and Progressive Agreement for Trans-Pacific Partnership.

The population living below the national poverty line (measured at US$8·50 per day at 2012 prices) declined from 50% in the 1960s to 0·6% in 2014, while those living in relative poverty fell from 49·3% in 1970 to 1·7% in 2012. Real wages for the lowest-earning 40% grew by an average of 6·3% per year from 2009 to 2012. Pockets of poverty nonetheless remain, particularly in the rural areas, and income inequality is relativity high compared to other developing economies.

Currency

The unit of currency is the Malaysian *ringgit* (RM) of 100 *sen*. For seven years it was pegged to the US dollar at 3·8 ringgit = 1 US$, but since the revaluation of the Chinese yuan on 21 July 2005 it has been allowed to operate in a managed float. Foreign exchange reserves were US$92,217m. and gold reserves 1·17m. troy oz in Sept. 2009. Inflation rates (based on IMF statistics):

2008	2009	2010	2011	2012	2013	2014	2015	2016	2017
5·4%	0·6%	1·7%	3·2%	1·7%	2·1%	3·1%	2·1%	2·1%	3·8%

Total money supply in April 2009 was RM179,274m.

Budget

Budgetary central government revenue and expenditure (in RM1m.):

	2013	2014	2015
Revenue	213,370	220,625	219,089
Expenditure	209,856	217,787	215,274

Taxes accounted for 75·5% of revenues in 2015; compensation of employees accounted for 32·5% of expenditures, grants 17·3% and use of goods and services 16·9%.

There are sales taxes of 10% and 6%.

Performance

Malaysia was badly affected by the Asian financial crisis, with the economy contracting by 7·4% in 1998. The country narrowly avoided a recession in 2001 but failed to do so in the global financial crisis of 2009. Real GDP growth rates (based on IMF statistics):

2008	2009	2010	2011	2012	2013	2014	2015	2016	2017
4·8%	−1·5%	7·5%	5·3%	5·5%	4·7%	6·0%	5·1%	4·2%	5·9%

Total GDP in 2017 was US$314·5bn.

Banking and Finance

The central bank and bank of issue is the Bank Negara Malaysia (*Governor*, Nor Shamsiah Mohd Yunus). In 2013 there were eight domestic commercial banks and 19 foreign-owned banks. Total deposits of commercial banks, finance companies and merchant banks at 31 Dec. 2005 were RM140·6bn. The largest commercial bank is Malayan Banking Berhad (Maybank), with assets in 2009 of RM238·3bn. The Islamic Bank of Malaysia began operations in July 1983. In Jan. 2006 there were 54 banks licensed by the Labuan Offshore Financial Services Authority (LOFSA).

External debt amounted to US$81,497m. in 2010, up from US$51,855m. in 2005 and US$41,765m. in 2000—this was equivalent to 35·4% of GNI, compared to 48·5% in 2000.

Malaysia attracted a record US$12,306m. worth of foreign direct investment in 2013, up from US$10,074m. in 2012.

There is a stock exchange at Kuala Lumpur, known as Bursa Malaysia.

Energy and Natural Resources

Environment
Malaysia's carbon dioxide emissions from the consumption of energy in 2011 were the equivalent of 6·8 tonnes per capita.

Electricity
Installed capacity in 2011 was 28·7m. kW. In 2011, 124,893m. kWh were generated (117,269m. kWh thermal and 7,624m. kWh hydro-electric). Consumption per capita in 2011 was 4,355 kWh.

Oil and Gas
Oil reserves, 2012, 3·7bn. bbls. Oil production, 2012, was 29·7m. tonnes. In 2012 exports of oil stood at 11·6m. tonnes. Natural gas reserves, 2012, 1·3trn. cu. metres. Production of natural gas in 2013 was 69·1bn. cu. metres. In April 1998 Malaysia and Thailand agreed to share equally the natural gas jointly produced in an offshore area (the Malaysian–Thailand Joint Development Area) which both countries claim as their own territory.

Minerals
In 2013 mining contributed 8·1% of GDP. Production in 2013 unless otherwise indicated (in tonnes): aggregate (2012), 110,339,000; limestone (2012), 36,580,000; sand and gravel, 35,552,000; iron ore (estimate), 6,900,000; coal, 2,893,962; silica sand, 1,243,660; kaolin, 293,480; ilmenite concentrate, 16,043; gold, 3,822 kg.

Agriculture
In 2013 agriculture contributed 9·1% of GDP. There were an estimated 954,000. ha. of arable land in 2013 and 6·60m. ha. of permanent crops. In 2013 approximately 380,000 ha. were equipped for irrigation. Production in 2013 (in 1,000 tonnes): palm fruit oil, 95,729; palm kernels, 4,859; rice, 2,604; rubber, 826; coconuts, 625; pineapples, 316; bananas, 290; watermelons, 227; tomatoes, 130; cabbages, kale, etc., 95. Livestock (2014): pigs, 1·83m.; cattle, 761,000; goats, 456,000; sheep, 140,000; buffaloes, 123,000; chickens, 293m. Oil palms account for 75% of Malaysia's agricultural area.

Forestry
In 2015 there were 22·20m. ha. of forests, or 68% of the total land area. Of the total area under forests 23% was primary forest in 2015, 68% other naturally regenerated forest and 9% planted forest. Timber production in 2011 was 20·69m. cu. metres.

Fisheries
Total catch in 2015 amounted to 1,491,974 tonnes, almost entirely from sea fishing. There were 31,503 licensed motorized fishing vessels in 2010, up 44% from 21,871 in 2005; non-motorized vessels fell from 170 to 89 in the same period.

Industry

The leading companies by market capitalization in Malaysia in May 2018 were: Malayan Banking Berhad (Maybank) (US$29·6bn.); Public Bank Berhad (US$23·3bn.); and Tenaga Nasional Berhad, an electric utility company (US$23·1bn.).

In 2013 industry accounted for 39·9% of GDP, with manufacturing contributing 22·8%. Production figures for 2012 (in 1,000 tonnes): cement, 21,726; distillate fuel oil (2007), 8,891; petrol (2007), 5,029; residual fuel oil (2007), 2,006; refined sugar, 1,595; wheat flour, 976; plywood, 4,232,000 cu. metres; radio sets, 28·4m. units; cigarettes, 26·1bn. units; TV sets, 13·1m. units; pneumatic tyres (2006), 9·2m. units.

Labour
In July 2015 the workforce was 14,225,800, of whom 13,765,900 were employed. Unemployment was 3·2% in July 2015 (2·8% in July 2014). It is estimated that Malaysia has some 2m. illegal workers.

Malaysia had 25,000 people living in slavery according to the Walk Free Foundation's 2013 *Global Slavery Index*.

International Trade

Privatization policy permits foreign investment of 25–30% generally; total foreign ownership is permitted of export-oriented projects.

Imports and Exports
In 2006 imports totalled US$124,144m. and exports US$160,842m. The trade surplus in 2006 was US$36·7bn., up from US$18·1bn. in 2002.

Main imports, 2006: electrical machinery, apparatus and appliances, 31·9%; manufactured goods, 11·6%; petroleum and petroleum products, 8·3%; chemicals and related products, 7·8%. Chief exports, 2006: electrical machinery, apparatus and appliances, 21·3%; office machines and computers, etc., 17·4%; telecommunications, sound recording and reproducing equipment, 9·0%; petroleum and petroleum products, 8·9%.

The principal import sources in 2006 were: Japan (13·2%); USA (12·5%); China (12·1%); Singapore (11·7%). The leading export markets were: USA (18·8%); Singapore (15·4%); Japan (8·9%); China (7·2%).

Communications

Roads
Total road length in 2012 was 180,882 km, of which 78·1% were paved. In 2006 there were 7,024,000 passenger cars in use, 60,000 buses and coaches, 836,600 lorries and vans, and 7,458,100 motorcycles and mopeds. There were 6,287 deaths as a result of road accidents in 2006, which at 24·1 per 100,000 people ranks among the highest rates in the world.

Rail
Length of route in 2011, 2,250 km, of which 350 km were electrified. The Malayan Railway carried 39·5m. passengers and 5·4m. tonnes of freight in 2010; the Sabah State Railway carried 594,000 passengers and 89,000 tonnes of freight in 2011. A railway from Kuala Lumpur to the international airport opened in 2002 and carried 3·9m. passengers in 2009. There are two metro systems in Kuala Lumpur with a combined length of 56 km.

Civil Aviation
There are a total of 19 airports of which five are international airports and 14 are domestic airports at which regular public air transport is operated. *International airports:* Kuala Lumpur, Penang, Kota Kinabalu, Kuching and Langkawi. *Domestic airports:* Johor Bharu, Alor Star, Ipoh, Kota Bharu, Kuala Terengganu, Kuantan, Melaka, Sandakan, Lahad Datu, Tawau, Labuan, Bintulu, Sibu and Miri. There are 39 Malaysian airstrips of which ten are in Sabah, 15 in Sarawak and 14 in peninsular Malaysia.

In 2017 more than 50 international airlines operated through Kuala Lumpur (KLIA-Sepang). Malaysia Airlines, the national airline, operates domestic flights within Malaysia and international flights to nearly 20 countries. In 2014 it suffered two disasters when one of its planes went missing in flight and another was shot down over Ukraine. Following these events its primary shareholder, Khazanah (the sovereign wealth fund that manages the commercial assets of the government), sought to buy out the 31% of shares it did not already own and to de-list the airline from the stock exchange. Its stated aim was to restructure the company and return it to profit before relisting it by 2020. A low-cost airline, AirAsia, began operations in Nov. 1996; its sister budget long-haul carrier, Air Asia X, started flying in Nov. 2007. Air Asia and its subsidiaries (AirAsia India, Indonesia AirAsia, Malaysia AirAsia, AirAsia Philippines and Thai AirAsia) now rank among Asia's half dozen largest airlines, total passenger numbers having doubled from 22·7m. to 45·6m. between 2009 and 2014. In 2012 scheduled airline traffic of Malaysian-based carriers flew 209·0m. km; passenger-km totalled 38·6bn. in the same year. In 2012 Kuala Lumpur handled 39,887,866 passengers (27,612,088 on international flights) and 702,226 tonnes of freight. Kota Kinabalu handled 5,848,135 passengers in 2012 and Penang 4,767,815.

Shipping
The major ports are Port Kelang, Pulau Pinang, Johor Pasir Gudang, Tanjung Beruas, Miri, Rajang, Pelabuhan Sabah, Port Dickson, Kemaman, Teluk Ewa, Kuantan, Kuching and Bintulu. Port Kelang, the busiest port, handled 198,928,000 tonnes of cargo in 2013; container throughput in 2013 was 10,350,000 TEUs (twenty-foot equivalent units), making it Malaysia's busiest container port. In Jan. 2014 there were 427 ships of 300 GT or over

registered, totalling 5·69m. GT. Of the 427 vessels registered, 168 were general cargo ships, 165 oil tankers, 31 liquid gas tankers, 27 container ships, 24 passenger ships and 12 bulk carriers. The Malaysian-controlled fleet comprised 320 vessels of 1,000 GT or over in July 2014, of which 226 were under the Malaysian flag and 94 under foreign flags.

Telecommunications

In 2013 there were 4,536,000 main (fixed) telephone lines. In the same year mobile phone subscriptions numbered 42,996,000 (1,446·9 per 1,000 persons). 67·0% of the population were internet users in 2013. In March 2012 there were 12·4m. Facebook users.

Social Institutions

Out of 178 countries analysed in the 2017 *Fragile States Index*—a list published jointly by the Fund for Peace and *Foreign Policy* magazine—Malaysia was ranked the 63rd least vulnerable to conflict or collapse. The index is based on 12 indicators of state vulnerability across social, political and economic categories.

Justice

The highest judicial authority and final court of appeal is the Federal Court. There are also two High Courts, one for Peninsular Malaysia and one for the States of Sabah and Sarawak, as well as a system of subordinate courts (comprising Magistrate Courts and Sessions Courts).

The Federal Court comprises the Chief Justice—the head of the Malaysian judiciary—the President of the Court of Appeal, the Chief Judges of the two High Courts and four other judges. It has jurisdiction to determine the validity of any law made by Parliament or by a State legislature and disputes between States or between the Federation and any State. It also has jurisdiction to hear and determine appeals from the High Courts.

There were at least nine executions in 2016 and at least four in 2017, but in Oct. 2018 a moratorium was imposed on the death penalty when Malaysia announced its intention to abolish capital punishment. The population in penal institutions in June 2013 was 39,144 (132 per 100,000 of national population). In 2015 the World Justice Project *Rule of Law Index*, which provides data on how the rule of law is experienced by the general public across eight categories, ranked Malaysia 30th of 102 countries for criminal justice and 37th for civil justice.

Education

School education is free; tertiary education is provided at a nominal fee. There are six years of primary schooling starting at age seven, three years of universal lower secondary, two years of selective upper secondary and two years of pre-university education.

In 2017 there were 3,084,630 pupils at primary schools with 264,648 teaching staff, 2,744,639 pupils with 231,106 teaching staff at secondary schools and 1,248,927 students in tertiary education and 89,839 academic staff at tertiary institutions.

Adult literacy was 92% in 2008.

In 2006 public expenditure on education came to 4·7% of GNI.

Health

In 2010 there were 1·2 physicians for every 1,000 population, 3·3 nursing and midwifery personnel per 1,000 population and 0·4 pharmaceutical personnel per 1,000. In 2013 there were 132 government hospitals, nine government special medical institutions and 214 private hospitals. In the same year there were 1,039 government health clinics and 6,801 private medical clinics. The government health care facilities had a total of 39,728 beds in 2013 and the private health care facilities 14,033 beds.

In *Water: At What Cost? The State of the World's Water 2016*, WaterAid reported that 1·8% of the population does not have access to safe water.

Welfare

The Malaysian social security system (SOCSO) administers and executes two types of scheme—the Employment Injury Insurance Scheme (which provides protection to employees who suffer from employment injury including occupational disease/illness) and the Invalidity Pension Scheme (which provides 24-hours coverage to employees against invalidity or death). There is no provision for entitlement for unemployment benefits. Under the Minimum Retirement Age Act 2012 the minimum retirement age for private sector workers is now 60, the same as for public sector employees.

Religion

Malaysia's multi-faith population is principally divided between Islam, Buddhism, Taoism, Hinduism and Christianity. Under the Federal constitution, Islam is the official religion of Malaysia but there is freedom of worship. A study by the Pew Research Center's Forum on Religion & Public Life estimated that in 2010 there were 18·1m. Muslims (almost exclusively Sunnis), 5·0m. Buddhists, 2·7m. Christians and 1·7m. Hindus. Of the Christians in 2010, 51% were Catholics and 48% Protestants. In Feb. 2019 there was one Roman Catholic cardinal.

Culture

World Heritage Sites

There are four sites in Malaysia that appear on the UNESCO World Heritage List: the Gunung Mulu National Park (inscribed on the list in 2000) with its limestone caves; Kinabalu Park/Mount Kinabalu (2000); the historic cities of Melaka and Georgetown (2008) in the Straits of Malacca; and the Archaeological Heritage of the Lenggong Valley (2012), one of the longest records of early man in a single locality and the oldest outside the African continent.

Press

In 2014 there were 25 daily newspapers (24 paid-for and one free) with a combined circulation of 2,758,000. The dailies with the highest circulation are the Chinese-language *Sin Chew Daily* and the Malay-language *Hairan Metro*.

Tourism

In 2014 a record 27,437,000 international tourists visited Malaysia (up from 25,715,000 in 2013); receipts from tourism in 2014 totalled US$22,595m. Most tourists in 2014 were from Singapore (13,933,000), Indonesia, China, Thailand and Brunei.

Festivals

National Day (31 Aug.) is celebrated in Kuala Lumpur at the Dataran Merdeka and marks Malaysia's independence. The Rainforest World Music Festival has been held annually in July in Kuching, Borneo since 1998.

Diplomatic Representatives

Of Malaysia in the United Kingdom (45–46 Belgrave Square, London, SW1X, 8QT)
  Acting High Commissioner: Mohd Suhaimi Jaafar.

Of the United Kingdom in Malaysia (Level 27, Menara Binjai, 2 Jalan Binjai, 50450 Kuala Lumpur)
  High Commissioner: Vicki Treadell, CMG, MVO.

Of Malaysia in the USA (3516 International Court, NW, Washington, D.C., 20008)
  Ambassador: Vacant.
  Chargé d'Affaires a.i.: Murni Abdul Hamid.

Of the USA in Malaysia (376 Jalan Tun Razak, Kuala Lumpur)
  Ambassador: Kamala Shirin Lakhdir.

Of Malaysia to the United Nations
  Ambassador: Dato' Muhammad Shahrul Ikram bin Yaakob.

Of Malaysia to the European Union
  Ambassador: Dato' Hasnudin bin Hamzah.

Further Reading

Department of Statistics: *Malaysia 2016: Statistical Handbook.—Yearbook of Statistics, Sabah* (2015).—*Yearbook of Statistics, Sarawak* (2016).—*Vital Statistics, Malaysia* (2015).
Prime Minister's Department: Economic Planning Unit. *Malaysian Economy in Figures.* Annual, 2016
BNM: Kuala Lumpur. *Bank Negara Malaysia, Annual Report.* 2015
Andaya, B. W. and Andaya, L. Y., *A History of Malaysia.* 2nd ed. 2001
Drabble, J., *An Economic History of Malaysia, c. 1800–1990.* 2001

Gomez, Edmund Terence, *Politics in Malaysia.* 2009
Kahn, J. S. and Wah, F. L. K., *Fragmented Vision: Culture and Politics in Contemporary Malaysia.* 1992
Stockwell, A. J., *The Making of Malaysia.* 2005
Swee-Hock, Saw, *Malaysia: Recent Trends and Challenges.* 2006

Wain, Barry, *Malaysian Maverick: Mahathir Mohamad in Turbulent Times.* 2nd ed. 2012
National Statistical Office: Department of Statistics, Block C6, Parcel C, Federal Government Administrative Centre, 62514 Putrajaya.
Website: http://www.statistics.gov.my

Maldives

Divehi Raajjeyge Jumhooriyyaa (Republic of the Maldives)

Capital: Malé
Population projection, 2020: 459,000
GNI per capita, 2017: (PPP$) 13,567
HDI/world rank, 2017: 0·717/101=
Internet domain extension: .mv

Key Historical Events

Divehi-speaking people (a language related to Sinhalese) have lived on the Maldives since at least AD 400. Visited by Middle Eastern merchants from around AD 1000, the archipelago became an Islamic sultanate in 1153. Portuguese explorers occupied the island of Malé (the modern capital) from 1558 until they were expelled by Muhammad Thakurufaanu Al-Azam in 1573. The Dutch, who replaced the Portuguese as the dominant power in Ceylon in the mid-1600s, controlled Maldivian affairs until 1796, although the sultanate held sway over local administration. Thereafter the Maldives came under British protection (formalized in an agreement in 1887) until complete independence was achieved on 26 July 1965. A republic was declared on 11 Nov. 1968.

Territory and Population

The republic, some 650 km to the southwest of Sri Lanka, consists of 1,192 low-lying (the highest point is 2·4 metres above sea-level) coral islands, grouped into 26 atolls. 199 are inhabited. Area 298 sq. km (115 sq. miles). In 2014 the census population was 402,071; density, 1,349 per sq. km.

The UN gives a projected population for 2020 of 459,000.

In 2011, 41·3% of the population lived in urban areas. Capital, Malé (2014 census population, 153,904).

The official and spoken language is Divehi.

Social Statistics

2006 births, 5,827; deaths, 1,084. Birth rate, 2006, per 1,000 population, 19·5; death rate, 3·6. Annual population growth rate, 2005–10, 1·8%. Life expectancy at birth in 2007 was 69·7 years for males and 72·7 years for females. Infant mortality, 2010, 14 per 1,000 live births; fertility rate, 2008, 2·0 births per woman. The Maldives has had the largest reduction in its fertility rate of any country in the world over the past quarter of a century, having had a rate of 6·1 births per woman in 1990. It has also made some of the best progress in recent years in reducing child mortality. The number of deaths per 1,000 live births among children under five was reduced from 94 in 1990 to 11 in 2012.

Climate

The islands are hot and humid, and affected by monsoons. Malé: average temperature 81°F (27°C), annual rainfall 59" (1,500 mm).

Constitution and Government

The present constitution, the country's sixth, came into effect on 7 Aug. 2008. Its provisions allowed for the Maldives' first multi-party polls and for the direct election of the president (who had previously been elected by the Citizens' *Majlis*). It also introduced a bill of rights and established a clearer separation of powers between parliament and the president. The constitution specifies that 'a non-Muslim may not become a citizen of the Maldives'.

National Anthem

'Gavmii mi ekuverikan matii tibegen kuriime salaam' ('In national unity we salute our nation'); words by M. J. Didi, tune by W. Amaradeva.

Recent Elections

At the presidential election held on 23 Sept. 2018 Ibrahim Mohamed Solih (Maldivian Democratic Party; MDP) won 58·4% of the vote against incumbent Abdulla Yameen (Progressive Party of Maldives; PPM) with 41·6%. Turnout was 89·2%.

Parliamentary elections were held on 22 March 2014. The Progressive Party of Maldives won 33 of 85 seats, Maldivian Democratic Party 26, Jumhooree Party 15, Maldives Development Alliance 5 and Adhaalath Party 1. Five seats went to independent candidates. The ruling Progressive Coalition—consisting of the Progressive Party of Maldives, Jumhooree Party and Maldives Development Alliance—secured a combined total of 53 seats.

Current Government

In Feb. 2019 the government consisted of:

President: Ibrahim Mohamed Solih; b. 1964 (Maldivian Democratic Party; in office since 17 Nov. 2018).

Vice President: Faisal Naseem.

Minister of Foreign Affairs: Abdullah Shahid. *Defence:* Mariya Ahmed Didi. *Home Affairs:* Sheikh Imran Abdulla. *Finance:* Ibrahim Ameer. *National Planning and Infrastructure:* Mohamed Aslam. *Higher Education:* Ibrahim Hassan. *Communication, Science and Technology:* Mohamed Maleeh Jamal. *Health:* Abdulla Ameen. *Education:* Aishath Ali. *Transport and Civil Aviation:* Aishath Nahula. *Arts, Culture and Heritage:* Yumna Maumoon. *Tourism:* Ali Waheed. *Economic Development:* Fayyaz Ismail. *Fisheries, Marine Resources and Agriculture:* Zaha Waheed. *Islamic Affairs:* Ahmed Zahir. *Housing and Urban Development:* Aminath Athifa. *Youth, Sports and Community Empowerment:* Ahmed Mahloof. *Gender, Family and Social Services:* Sidhatha Shareef. *Environment:* Hussain Rasheed Hassan. *Attorney General:* Ibrahim Riffath.

Office of the President: http://www.presidencymaldives.gov.mv

Current Leaders

Ibrahim Mohamed Solih

Position
President

Introduction
Ibrahim Mohamed Solih became president in Nov. 2018.

Early Life
Solih was born, one of 13 children, on 4 May 1964 on Hinnavaru Island, Lhaviyani Atoll. He is married to a cousin of former President Mohamed Nasheed.

Solih entered parliament in 1994 as representative for the Lhaviyani Atoll, after defeating a ruling party candidate at a time when the country had no opposition party. He was one of the founding members of the Maldivian Democratic Party (MDP) in 2003. Solih advocated parliamentary democracy from Malé while fellow MDP leaders in exile worked from Sri Lanka. He was part of the Special Majlis that drafted a new constitution in 2008 allowing multi-party democracy.

In 2011 Solih became leader of the MDP's parliamentary group following a coup that led to the ousting of President Mohamed Nasheed. Solih was selected as a presidential candidate by a coalition of opposition parties in the 2018 election, after former president Nasheed withdrew his candidacy. Solih contested the poll against Abdulla Yameen (half-brother of former President Maumoon Abdul Gayoom) who was bidding for a second five-year term. Yameen was widely expected to win, despite accusations of authoritarianism following the jailing of several opposition leaders (which had prompted the USA and European Union to threaten sanctions). Solih voiced his concerns about election rigging against a backdrop of further arrests of opposition politicians and a police search of the MDP's office on

© Springer Nature Limited 2020
Palgrave Macmillan (ed.), *The Statesman's Yearbook 2020*,
https://doi.org/10.1057/978-1-349-95940-2_121

the eve of voting. Against expectations, Solih went on to claim victory, winning 58.4% of the vote.

Career in Office
Solih assumed office on 17 Nov. 2018 pledging to end widespread corruption following alleged human rights abuses under his predecessor.

Defence

In 2008 military expenditure totalled US$43m. (US$111 per capita), representing 3·4% of GDP.

Economy

Fisheries accounts for approximately 7% of GDP, industry 15% and services 78%.

Overview

Compared to other countries in the region, the Maldives have high levels of human development and only moderate levels of poverty. The economy grew by 2·2% in 2015, down from 6·5% in 2014. Despite declining in the wake of the global financial crisis, tourism accounts for approximately 30% of total GDP and 60% of foreign exchange receipts each year. Fishing is the second largest industry. Economic diversification is hindered by a lack of cultivable land, mineral resources and skilled labour. Imports constituted 69% of GDP in 2014.

High levels of public spending caused a balance of payments crisis and in 2009 the IMF approved a stand-by credit arrangement while the government created new taxes to boost revenues. In 2011 a goods and services tax for tourists came into force, and a business profit tax followed in 2012.

With 80% of the Maldives below sea level, the effects of climate change pose serious long-term risks to the country and its economy. Environmental hazards and natural disasters pose a constant threat to the country.

Currency

The unit of currency is the *rufiyaa* (MVR) of 100 *laari*. Inflation was 0·8% in 2016 and 2·3% in 2017. Gold reserves were 2,000 troy oz in July 2005, foreign exchange reserves were US$218m. and total money supply was 3,163m. rufiyaa.

Budget

In 2012 budgetary central government revenue totalled 9,832·2m. rufiyaa; expenditure totalled 14,215·9m. rufiyaa. Tax revenue accounted for 68·3% of revenues in 2012; current expenditure accounted for 74·0% of expenditures.

Performance

After shrinking by 8·7% in 2005 as a consequence of the devastation wreaked by the tsunami, the economy rebounded spectacularly in 2006 with a real GDP growth rate of 19·6%, driven by the return of tourists, reconstruction efforts and new development. The economy grew by 2·2% in 2015, 4·5% in 2016 and 4·8% in 2017. Total GDP in 2017 was US$4·6bn.

Banking and Finance

The Maldives Monetary Authority (*Governor*, Ahmed Naseer), established in 1981, is endowed with the regular powers of a central bank and bank of issue. There is one domestic commercial bank (Bank of Maldives) and branches of four foreign banks.

External debt totalled US$1,229m. in 2010 and represented 86·6% of GNI.

There is a stock exchange in Malé.

Energy and Natural Resources

Environment

Carbon dioxide emissions from the consumption of energy were the equivalent of 2·7 tonnes per capita in 2011.

Electricity

Installed capacity was 78,000 kW in 2011. Production in 2011 was 274m. kWh; consumption per capita in 2011 was 824 kWh.

Minerals

Inshore coral mining has been banned as a measure against the encroachment of the sea.

Agriculture

There were approximately 3,000 ha. of arable land in 2011 and 3,000 ha. of permanent crops. Principal crops in 2011 (estimates, in 1,000 tonnes): bananas, 7; coconuts, 4. Various other types of fruit, vegetables, roots and tubers, and nuts are also produced.

Fisheries

The total catch in 2015 was 127,352 tonnes. The Maldives has the highest per capita consumption of fish and fishery products of any country in the world. In the period 2008–10 the average person consumed 158 kg (348 lb) a year, or more than eight times the average for the world as a whole.

Industry

The main industries are fishing, tourism, shipping, lacquerwork and garment manufacturing.

Labour

The labour force in 2013 was 190,000 (115,000 in 2003). 68·9% of the population aged 15–64 was economically active in 2013. In the same year 11·3% of the population was unemployed.

International Trade

Imports and Exports

In 2008 imports (c.i.f.) were valued at US$1,387·5m. and exports (f.o.b.) at US$126·4m. Tuna is the main export commodity. It is exported principally to Thailand, Sri Lanka and some European markets. Main import suppliers in 2008 were Singapore (21·3%), the UAE (18·0%), India (10·4%), Malaysia (7·7%) and Sri Lanka (5·9%). Leading export destinations were Thailand (49·0%), Sri Lanka (9·5%), France (8·8%), Italy (8·3%) and the UK (7·6%).

Communications

Roads

In 2007 there were 3,060 passenger cars in use (10 per 1,000 inhabitants), 26,780 motorcycles and mopeds, 2,870 lorries and vans, and 74 buses and coaches.

Civil Aviation

The former national carrier Air Maldives collapsed in April 2000 with final losses in excess of US$50m. The national airline is now Maldivian, which was founded in 2000 and initially operated domestic flights only. It began to serve international destinations in Asia in 2008. In 2010 there were international flights from Malé International Airport (now officially known as Velana International Airport) to Bangalore, Bangkok, Bologna, Colombo, Doha, Dubai, Düsseldorf, Frankfurt, Guangzhou, Kuala Lumpur, London, Milan, Moscow, Munich, Muscat, Paris, Rome, Singapore, Thiruvananthapuram and Zürich, as well as domestic services.

Shipping

In Jan. 2014 there were 28 ships of 300 GT or over registered, totalling 36,000 GT.

Telecommunications

There were 48,000 fixed telephone lines in 2010 (152·0 per 1,000 inhabitants). Mobile phone subscribers numbered 494,400 in 2010. There were 283·0 internet users per 1,000 inhabitants in 2010. Fixed internet subscriptions totalled 20,100 in 2009 (64·4 per 1,000 inhabitants). In March 2012 there were 120,000 Facebook users.

Social Institutions

Out of 178 countries analysed in the 2017 *Fragile States Index*—a list published jointly by the Fund for Peace and *Foreign Policy* magazine—the Maldives was ranked the joint 86th most vulnerable (along with Turkmenistan) to conflict or collapse. The index is based on 12 indicators of state vulnerability across social, political and economic categories.

Justice

Justice is based on the Islamic Sharia.

There were 994 sentenced inmates in penal institutions in 2012 (307 per 100,000 of national population). The Maldives has had a *de facto* moratorium on the death penalty for more than 60 years, but President Abdulla Yameen has repeatedly threatened to carry out executions since he came to power in 2013.

Education

Adult literacy in 2006 was 98%. In 2015 there were 213 government schools (60,525 pupils), 124 community schools (13,309 pupils) and 122 private schools (14,191 pupils) with a total of 8,817 teachers. In 2005 public expenditure on education came to 7·8% of GDP and 15·0% of total government spending.

Health

In 2011 there were 275 beds at the Indira Gandhi Memorial Hospital in Malé. In the same year there were also one private hospital, six regional public hospitals, 13 atoll hospitals and 132 health centres. In 2010 there were 525 physicians, 1,868 nursing and midwifery personnel, and 247 pharmaceutical personnel.

Religion

The State religion is Islam—adherence to it is legally required of citizens.

Culture

Press

In 2008 there were six paid-for daily newspapers and around 200 independent newspapers and periodicals in total.

Tourism

Tourism is the major foreign currency earner. There were a record 1,125,202 tourist arrivals in 2013 (958,027 in 2012), mainly from China, Germany, the United Kingdom and Russia. Tourist spending in 2013 totalled US$2,424m.

Diplomatic Representatives

Of the Maldives in the United Kingdom (22 Nottingham Pl., London, W1U 5NJ)
Ambassador: Vacant.
Chargé d'Affaires a.i.: Aishath Azeema.

Of the United Kingdom in the Maldives
Ambassador: James Dauris (resides in Colombo, Sri Lanka).

Of the Maldives in the USA and to the United Nations (800 Second Ave., Suite 400E, New York, NY 10017)
Ambassador: Ali Naseer Mohamed.

Of the USA in the Maldives
Ambassador: Alaina Teplitz (resides in Colombo, Sri Lanka).

Of the Maldives to the European Union
Ambassador: Ahmed Shiaan.

Further Reading

Gayoom, M. A., *The Maldives: A Nation in Peril.* 1998
Robinson, J. J., *The Maldives: Islamic Republic, Tropical Autocracy.* 2015
National Statistical Office: Ministry of Finance and Treasury, Ameenee Magu, Malé 20125.
Website: http://www.planning.gov.mv

Mali

République du Mali (Republic of Mali)

Capital: Bamako
Population projection, 2020: 20·28m.
GNI per capita, 2017: (PPP$) 1,953
HDI/world rank, 2017: 0·427/182
Internet domain extension: .ml

Key Historical Events

Mali's power reached its peak between the 11th and 13th centuries when its gold-based empire controlled much of the surrounding area. The country was annexed by France in 1904. As French Sudan it was part of French West Africa. The country became an autonomous state within the French Community on 24 Nov. 1958, and on 4 April 1959 joined with Senegal to form the Federation of Mali. The Federation achieved independence on 20 June 1960, but Senegal seceded on 22 Aug. and Mali proclaimed itself an independent republic on 22 Sept. There was an army coup on 19 Nov. 1968, which brought Moussa Traoré to power. Ruling the country for over 22 years, he wrecked the economy. A further coup followed in March 1991.

In Jan. 1991 a ceasefire was signed with Tuareg insurgents in the north and in April 1992 a national pact was concluded providing for a special administration for the Tuareg north.

Under President Alpha Oumar Konaré, two elections for the National Assembly were held. The first (April 1997) was cancelled by the constitutional court and the second, in July 1997, was boycotted by opposition parties. Amadou Toumani Touré, a former military ruler, won presidential elections held in April and May 2002. In July 2005 severe food shortages led to more than 1m. people facing starvation. In March 2012 Touré was ousted in a military coup. A civilian interim government was nominally established the following month, with Dioncounda Traoré installed as president. However, after allegations of a counter-coup by supporters of Touré, the military reasserted control in May. In Aug. a government of national unity was sworn in to oversee the transition to civilian government.

In May 2012 Tuareg and Islamic militant groups declared the northern Azawad region an independent Islamic state. In Sept. 2012 the government in Bamako agreed to host 3,000 ECOWAS troops in a bid to displace the rebels. The following month Mali was readmitted to the African Union, having been suspended following the March coup.

In Jan. 2013 President Traoré appealed to France for assistance after an escalation in militant operations. French forces quickly seized the cities of Gao and Tombouctou (Timbuktu), dislodging the rebels from their principal strongholds.

Territory and Population

Mali is bounded in the west by Senegal, northwest by Mauritania, northeast by Algeria, east by Niger and south by Burkina Faso, Côte d'Ivoire and Guinea. Its area is 1,248,574 sq. km (482,077 sq. miles) and it had a population of 14,528,662 at the 2009 census; density, 11·6 per sq. km. In 2011, 36·6% of the population were urban.

The UN gives a projected population for 2020 of 20·28m.

The areas, populations and chief towns of the regions are:

In 2009 the capital, Bamako, had a population of 1,810,000. The second largest town, Sikasso, had a population of 227,000 in 2009.

Region	Sq. km	2009 census population	Chief town
Gao[1]	170,572	542,304	Gao
Kayes	119,743	1,993,615	Kayes
Kidal	151,430	67,739	Kidal

(*continued*)

Region	Sq. km	2009 census population	Chief town
Koulikoro	95,848	2,422,108	Koulikoro
Mopti	79,017	2,036,209	Mopti
Ségou	64,821	2,338,349	Ségou
Sikasso	70,280	2,643,179	Sikasso
Tombouctou[2]	496,611	674,793	Tombouctou
Capital District	252	1,810,366	Bamako

[1] In 2012 the region of Ménaka was created from Ménaka Cercle, in the region of Gao. [2] In 2012 the region of Taoudénit was created from the northern part of Timbuktu Cercle, in the region of Tombouctou.

The Bambara, Khassonké, Malinké and Soninké, all of which belong to the broader Mandé group, make up 50% of the population; the other leading groups are the Fula (17%), Voltaic (12%), Songhai (6%), and Tuareg and Moor (10%). The official language is French; Bambara is spoken by about 68% of the population.

Social Statistics

2008 estimates: births, 541,000; deaths, 200,000. Rates, 2008 estimates (per 1,000 population): births, 42·6; deaths, 15·7. Infant mortality, 2010 (per 1,000 live births), 99. Expectation of life in 2013 was 55·1 years for males and 54·9 for females. Mali was one of only two countries where the life expectancy at birth for males in 2013 was higher than for females (the other being Eswatini). Annual population growth rate, 2000–08, 2·4%; fertility rate, 2008, 6·5 children per woman.

Climate

A tropical climate, with adequate rain in the south and west, but conditions become increasingly arid towards the north and east. Bamako, Jan. 76°F (24·4°C), July 80°F (26·7°C). Annual rainfall 45" (1,120 mm). Kayes, Jan. 76°F (24·4°C), July 93°F (33·9°C). Annual rainfall 29" (725 mm). Tombouctou, Jan. 71°F (21·7°C), July 90°F (32·2°C). Annual rainfall 9" (231 mm).

Constitution and Government

A constitution was approved by a national referendum in 1974; it was amended by the National Assembly on 2 Sept. 1981. The sole legal party was the *Union démocratique du peuple malien* (UDPM).

A national conference of 1,800 delegates agreed a draft constitution enshrining multi-party democracy in Aug. 1991, and this was approved by 99·76% of votes cast at a referendum in Jan. 1992. Turnout was 43%.

The *President* is elected for not more than two terms of five years.

There is a *National Assembly*, consisting of 147 deputies (formerly 116) plus 13 Malinese living abroad.

A *Constitutional Court* was established in 1994.

In May 2012 the rebel National Movement for the Liberation of Azawad (MNLA) and Ansar Dine, an Islamist militant group, declared Azawad—a region in the north covering over half of Mali's total land area—a breakaway Islamic state. The unilateral declaration went unrecognized by Bamako and the international community. Relations between the MNLA and Ansar Dine soon strained. By the end of June 2012 Ansar Dine had militarily defeated the MNLA to claim control of the region.

National Anthem

'A ton appel, Mali' ('At your call, Mali'); words by S. Kouyate, tune by B. Sissoko.

Recent Elections

Presidential elections were held on 29 July 2018 with the two leading candidates proceeding to a run-off. In the second round of voting, held on 12 Aug. 2018, incumbent Ibrahim Boubacar Keïta was re-elected president with 67·2% of votes cast against 32·8% for Soumaïla Cissé. Turnout was 42·7% in the first round and 34·5% in the second.

Parliamentary elections were held in two rounds on 24 Nov. and 15 Dec. 2013. The Rally for Mali (RPM) won 66 seats (11 in 2007), Union for the Republic and Democracy 17, Alliance for Democracy in Mali (ADEMA) 16, Alternative Forces for Renewal and Emergence 6, African Solidarity for Democracy and Independence 5, Convergence for the Development of Mali 5, National Congress for Democratic Initiative 4, Alliance for the Solidarity of Mali 3, Party for Economic and Social Development 3, Party for National Rebirth 3, Patriotic Movement for Renewal 3, Alliance for Democracy and Progress 2, Malian Union–African Democratic Rally 2, Movement for the Independence, Renaissance and Integration of Africa 2 and Social Democratic Convention 2. Four other parties won one seat each and four seats went to independents. President Keïta's party, the RPM, subsequently formed a coalition with ADEMA and a number of other small parties.

Current Government

President: Ibrahim Boubacar Keïta; b. 1945 sworn in 4 Sept. 2013 and re-elected 12 Aug. 2018).

Prime Minister: Soumeylou Boubèye Maïga; b. 1954 (sworn in 31 Dec. 2017).

In Feb. 2019 the government comprised:

Minister of Administrative Reform and Transparency: Safia Bolly. *Agriculture:* Nango Dembélé. *Culture:* N'Diaye Ramatoulaye Diallo. *Defence and Veterans' Affairs:* Tiémoko Sangaré. *Digital Economy and Communication:* Arouna Modibo Touré. *Economy and Finance:* Boubou Cissé. *Energy and Water:* Sambou Wagué. *Environment, Sanitation and Sustainable Development:* Keïta Aïda M'bo. *Foreign Affairs and International Co-operation:* Kamissa Camara. *Handicrafts and Tourism:* Nina Walet Intallou. *Health and Public Hygiene:* Samba Ousmane Sow. *Housing and Urban Development:* Mohamed Moustapha Sidibé. *Industrial Development:* Moulaye Ahmed Boubacar. *Infrastructure:* Traoré Seynabou Diop. *Innovation and Scientific Research:* Assétou Founè Samaké Migan. *Justice and Keeper of the Seals:* Tiéna Coulibaly. *Labour and Civil Service, in Charge of Institutional Relations:* Diarra Raky Talla. *Livestock and Fisheries:* Kane Rokia Maguiraga. *Malians Abroad and African Integration:* Yaya Sangaré. *Mines and Petroleum:* Lelenta Hawa Baba Bah. *National Education:* Abinou Témé. *Planning and Land Management:* Adama Tiémoko Diarra. *Promotion of Women, Family and Children:* Diakité Aïssata Traoré. *Religious Affairs and Worship:* Thierno Amadou Omar Hass Diallo. *Security and Civil Protection:* Brig.-Gen. Salif Traoré. *Social Cohesion, Peace and National Reconciliation:* Lassine Bouaré. *Solidarity and Humanitarian Action:* Hamadoun Konaté. *Sport:* Jean-Claude Sidibé. *Territorial Administration and Decentralization:* Mohamed Ag Erlaf. *Trade and Competition:* Al Hassan Ag Ahmed Moussa. *Transport:* Soumana Mory Coulibaly. *Youth and Citizenship Promotion:* Amadou Koïta.

Office of the Prime Minister (French only): http://www.primature.gov.ml

Current Leaders

Ibrahim Boubacar Keïta

Position
President

Introduction
Ibrahim Boubacar Keïta became president in Sept. 2013. He is a former prime minister and president of the National Assembly, as well as leader of the Rally for Mali (RPM), which he founded in 2001. He was re-elected for a further presidential term in Aug. 2018.

Early Life
Keïta, nicknamed 'IBK', was born in Jan. 1945 in Koutiala. He studied at the Lycée Janson-de-Sailly in Paris and the Lycée Askia-Mohamed in Bamako, before reading history, political science and international relations at the University of Dakar and University of Paris I. He worked as a researcher at the French National Centre for Scientific Research and taught Third World

politics at the University of Paris I. Returning to Mali in 1986, he worked with the European Development Fund and the non-governmental organization, Terre des Hommes.

In the 1990s Keïta founded the Alliance for Democracy (ADEMA) and was a key figure in ADEMA candidate Alpha Oumar Konaré's successful 1992 presidential campaign. Konaré subsequently appointed him ambassador to Côte d'Ivoire, Gabon, Burkina Faso and Niger, as well as minister of external affairs, Malians abroad and African integration. In 1994 Keïta was named prime minister and in the same year became president of ADEMA. In 2000 rifts emerged within the party and Keïta resigned both as premier and ADEMA leader. The following year he founded the RPM.

Keïta ran unsuccessfully for the presidency in 2002 but did win a seat in the National Assembly. He was subsequently elected its president. In 2007 he again lost out on the presidency but kept his seat in the assembly, serving on its commission for foreign affairs. He was also a member of the parliament of the Economic Community of West African States. In 2013 he entered the presidential race for the third time and defeated Soumaïla Cissé in a run-off in Aug. He was sworn in the next month.

Career in Office
Keïta's presidency followed an ECOWAS-supported interim government with its roots in a March 2012 military coup that ousted Amadou Toumani Touré as president. A key challenge for Keïta has been to address the tenuous security situation in the north, which has seen a rebellion by Tuareg separatists and militant Islamic groups. He has pushed forward plans to give greater independence to the regions, declaring that 'national reconciliation is our most pressing priority', but terror attacks have nonetheless continued in 2016 and 2017 despite a tentative peace agreement reached with Tuareg rebels in 2015. Keita was sworn in for his second term of office in Sept. 2018 following the presidential run-off election the previous month.

Defence

There is selective conscription for two years. In 2013 military expenditure totalled US$301m. (US$19 per capita), representing 2·6% of GDP.

A UN peacekeeping force, the United Nations Multidimensional Integrated Stabilization Mission in Mali (MINUSMA), has been deployed in the country since 1 July 2013 to restore stability in the north of the country following the Tuareg rebellion of early 2012.

Army

Strength in 2011 was an estimated 7,350. There are also paramilitary forces of 4,800.

Navy

There is a Navy of around 50 operating three patrol craft although their serviceability is in doubt.

Air Force

Personnel (2011) total 400. There were four combat-capable aircraft and four attack helicopters in 2011.

Economy

Agriculture accounted for 40·3% of GDP in 2014, industry 20·5% and services 39·2%.

Overview

The economy is heavily dependent on agriculture, which accounted for 38·3% of GDP in 2017 and provides income to some 80% of the population. Drought and conflict have increased the incidence of poverty, particularly in the rural areas where 90% of the country's poor reside.

In the 15 years from 1996, GDP growth averaged over 5% per year and macroeconomic stability was maintained during the global financial crisis from 2008. With political stability and security conditions broadly improving (despite persistent militant threats), growth accelerated to 7% in 2014, its highest level since 2003, and remained robust in 2015, 2016 and 2017 at 6·2%, 5·8% and 5·4%, respectively.

Inflation increased from −1·8% in 2016 to 1·8% in 2017 owing to higher food and international oil prices. A slight deterioration in the terms of trade (prompted by the higher oil costs as well as lower gold prices) saw the current external deficit (including grants) fall to 6·2% of GDP in 2017 from 7·2% in

2016. Public debt rose slightly to 31·8% of GDP in 2017, largely as a result of an increase in domestic debt from 7% in 2015 to 15% in 2017.

Despite the encouraging signs of growth and efforts to gradually restore the government's ability to provide basic social services, significant challenges remain. Long-term prosperity requires a lasting improvement in the security situation and expansive private sector development underpinned by investor confidence and increased transparency.

Currency

The unit of currency is the *franc CFA* (XOF), which replaced the Mali franc in 1984. It has a parity rate of 655·957 francs CFA to one euro. Total money supply in June 2005 was 573,692m. francs CFA and foreign exchange reserves were US$827m. There was deflation of 1·8% in 2016 and inflation of 1·8% in 2017.

Budget

Budgetary central government revenue and expenditure in 1bn. francs CFA:

	2011	*2012*	*2013*
Revenue	1,012	896	1,179
Expenditure	750	762	867

Principal sources of revenue in 2013 were: taxes on goods and services, 353bn. francs CFA; taxes on income, profits and capital gains, 258bn. francs CFA. Main items of expenditure by economic type in 2013 were: compensation of employees, 307bn. francs CFA; use of goods and services, 240bn. francs CFA.

VAT is 18%.

Performance

Real GDP growth was 6·2% in 2015, 5·8% in 2016 and 5·4% in 2017. Total GDP in 2017 was US$15·3bn.

Banking and Finance

The bank of issue and the central bank is the regional Central Bank of West African States (BCEAO). The *Governor* is Tiémoko Meyliet Koné. In 2015 there were 14 banks and three non-bank financial institutions.

External debt was US$2,326m. in 2010, representing 26·1% of GNI.

There is a stock exchange in Bamako.

Energy and Natural Resources

Environment

Carbon dioxide emissions from the consumption of energy were the equivalent of less than 0·1 tonnes per capita in 2011.

Electricity

Installed capacity in 2011 was 0·5m. kW. Production in 2011 was estimated at 1,702m. kWh, approximately 41% of it hydro-electric. Consumption per capita was an estimated 93 kWh in 2011.

Minerals

Gold (42,364 kg in 2009) is the principal mineral produced. There are also deposits of iron ore, uranium, diamonds, bauxite, manganese, copper, salt, limestone, phosphate, gypsum and lithium.

Agriculture

About 80% of the population depends on agriculture, mainly carried on by small peasant holdings. Mali is second only to Egypt among African cotton producers. In 2013 there were an estimated 6·41m. ha. of arable land and 150,000 ha. of permanent cropland. Production in 2013 included (in 1,000 tonnes): rice, 1,978; millet, 1,854; maize, 1,636; sorghum, 1,468; groundnuts, 515; oranges, 493; seed cotton, 440; watermelons, 372; sweet potatoes (estimate), 354; sugarcane, 336.

Livestock, 2013: goats, 18·22m.; sheep, 13·08m.; cattle, 9·72m.; camels, 960,000; asses, 920,000; horses, 507,000; chickens, 37m.

Approximately 380,000 ha. were equipped for irrigation in 2013.

Forestry

In 2015 forests covered 4·72m. ha., or 4% of the total land area. Timber production in 2011 was 5·85m. cu. metres.

Fisheries

In 2015, 92,480 tonnes of fish were caught (exclusively from inland waters).

Industry

The main industries are food processing, followed by cotton processing, textiles and clothes. Cement and pharmaceuticals are also produced.

Labour

The labour force in 2013 was 5,748,000 (3,310,000 in 2003). 67·0% of the population aged 15–64 was economically active in 2013. In the same year 8·1% of the population was unemployed.

Mali had 0·10m. people living in slavery according to the Walk Free Foundation's 2013 *Global Slavery Index*.

International Trade

Imports and Exports

The following table shows the value of Mali's foreign trade (in US$1m.):

	2006	*2007*	*2008*
Imports c.i.f.	1,819·8	2,184·8	3,338·9
Exports f.o.b.	1,526·1	1,440·6	1,918·3

Principal import commodities are machinery and equipment, foodstuffs, construction materials, petroleum and textiles. Principal export commodities are cotton and livestock (between them accounting for three-quarters of Mali's annual exports) and gold.

The main import suppliers are France and its former colonies (in particular Côte d'Ivoire), Western Europe and China. Main export markets are also France and its former colonies, Western Europe and China.

Communications

Roads

There were 18,912 km of roads in 2005, of which 19·0% were paved. In 2007 there were 87,000 passenger cars (seven per 1,000 inhabitants), 26,800 lorries and vans, and 10,000 motorcycles and mopeds.

Rail

Mali has a railway from Kayes to Koulikoro by way of Bamako, a continuation of the currently non-operational Dakar–Kayes line in Senegal; total length, 2005, 643 km (metre gauge). In 2005, 179,000 passengers and 1·7m. tonnes of freight were transported.

Civil Aviation

There is an international airport at Bamako (Senou), which handled 533,054 passengers (446,793 on international flights) and 7,538 tonnes of freight in 2012. In 2010 Air Mali operated direct flights to Abidjan, Accra, Conakry, Cotonou, Dakar, Kinshasa, Libreville, Lomé, Luanda, Madrid, Marseille, Niamey, Nouakchott, Ouagadougou, Paris and Pointe-Noire. Air Mali ceased operations in Dec. 2012. There were also flights in 2010 with foreign airlines to Abidjan, Addis Ababa, Algiers, Brazzaville, Casablanca, Conakry, Cotonou, Dakar, Johannesburg, Libreville, Lomé, Nairobi, Niamey, Nouakchott, Ouagadougou, Paris, Tripoli (Libya) and Tunis.

Shipping

For about seven months in the year small steamboats operate a service from Koulikoro to Tombouctou and Gao, and from Bamako to Kouroussa.

Telecommunications

In 2013 there were 126,000 fixed telephone lines; mobile phone subscriptions numbered 19,749,000 in the same year (129·1 per 100 persons). There were 27,677 fixed internet subscriptions in 2013. In June 2012 there were 141,000 Facebook users.

Social Institutions

Out of 178 countries analysed in the 2017 *Fragile States Index*—a list published jointly by the Fund for Peace and *Foreign Policy* magazine—Mali was ranked the 31st most vulnerable to conflict or collapse. The index is based on 12 indicators of state vulnerability across social, political and economic categories.

Justice

The Supreme Court was established at Bamako in 1969 with both judicial and administrative powers. The Court of Appeal is also at Bamako, at the apex of a system of regional tribunals and local *juges de paix*.

The population in penal institutions in Sept. 2011 was 5,817 (36 per 100,000 of national population). The International Centre for Prison Studies estimated in 2014 that 52·8% of prisoners had yet to receive a trial.

Education

The adult literacy rate in 2006 was 26%. In 2007 there were 1,510 teaching staff for 54,591 children in pre-primary schools, 33,230 teaching staff for 1,716,956 pupils in primary schools, 15,013 teaching staff for 533,849 secondary school pupils and 50,787 students in tertiary education with 976 academic staff. During the period 1990–95 only 19% of females of primary school age were enrolled in school but by 2007 this had risen to 56%.

In 2015 public expenditure on education came to 3·8% of GDP.

Health

In 2010 there was one hospital bed per 10,000 population. In the same year there were eight physicians for every 100,000 persons and 43 nurses and midwives per 100,000.

In *Water: At What Cost? The State of the World's Water 2016*, WaterAid reported that 23·0% of the population does not have access to safe water.

Religion

The state is secular, but predominantly Sunni Muslim. According to the Pew Research Center's Forum on Religion & Public Life, an estimated 3·2% of the population in 2010 were Christians and 2·7% folk religionists. In Feb. 2019 there was one Roman Catholic cardinal.

Culture

World Heritage Sites

Mali has four sites on the UNESCO World Heritage List: Old Towns of Djenné (inscribed on the list in 1988), a market centre established in 250 BC and an important Islamic centre in the 16th century—its buildings are all mudbrick, plastered annually with adobe; Tombouctou (1988), an important Islamic centre containing the Koranic Sankore University and the famous Djingareyber Mosque; the Cliff of Bandiagara (Land of the Dogons) (1989), for its natural and architectural wonders; and the Tomb of Askia (2004).

Press

In 2008 there were 12 daily newspapers with an estimated combined circulation of 40,000.

Tourism

There were 169,000 non-resident tourists in 2010; tourist revenue totalled US$296m. in the same year.

Diplomatic Representatives

Of Mali in the United Kingdom and to the European Union
    Ambassador: Sékou Dit Gaoussou Cissé (resides in Brussels)

Of the United Kingdom in Mali (Cité du Niger II, Bamako).
    Ambassador: Cat Evans

Of Mali in the USA (2130 R. St., NW, Washington, D.C., 20008)
    Ambassador: Mahamadou Nimaga

Of the USA in Mali (ACI 2000, Rue 243, Porte 297, Bamako)
    Ambassador: Vacant.
    Chargé d'Affaires a.i.: Gregory L. Garland.

Of Mali to the United Nations
    Ambassador: Issa Konfourou.

Further Reading

Bingen, R. James, *Democracy and Development in Mali.* 2000
English, Charlie, *The Storied City: The Quest for Timbuktu and the Fantastic Mission to Save its Past.* 2017
National Statistical Office: Direction National de la Statistique et de l'Informatique, BP 12 rue Archinard, Porte 233, Bamako.
Website (French only): http://www.instat-mali.org

Malta

Repubblika ta' Malta (Republic of Malta)

Capital: Valletta
Population projection, 2020: 434,000
GNI per capita, 2017: (PPP$) 34,396
HDI/world rank, 2017: 0·878/29
Internet domain extension: .mt

Key Historical Events

Neolithic settlements date from 5200 BC and the megalithic temples at Ġgantija on the island of Gozo, constructed around 3500 BC, are considered the second oldest man-made religious structures in the world. Subsequent Bronze Age settlements (the Tarxien Cemetery culture) show similarities with ones discovered on Sicily. Phoenicians, possibly from Tyre in modern-day Lebanon, began colonizing Malta during the 7th century BC.

The islands came under Carthaginian control from around 400 BC and were used as a naval base in the First Punic War. Part of the Roman Empire for almost 300 years from 218 BC, Malta prospered by exporting textiles. Visigoths seized power during the 5th century AD and Arab conquest in 870 led to the building of new settlements, including the future capital Mdina, as well as the creation of irrigation schemes.

Roger I, the Norman king of Sicily, seized power in 1090 and introduced Christianity, although Islam and the Arabic language continued to prosper. The islands remained subject to the rulers of Sicily, including the dynasties of Anjou and Aragon, until 1530. In that year, Charles V, King of Spain and Holy Roman Emperor, gave Malta to the Knights of St John, who had been forced out of Rhodes by Ottoman Turks in 1522. The knights were charged a yearly rent of a Maltese falcon.

The arrival of Napoleonic troops in 1798 heralded sweeping religious reforms but there was a popular uprising against rising taxes and other aspects of French control. The arrival of British naval forces precipitated a French retreat in 1800. The Maltese requested the protection of the British Crown in 1802 on condition that key rights and privileges be preserved. The Knights of St John attempted to regain control of the islands but Malta was annexed by the British in 1814 under the terms of the Treaty of Paris. It became an important staging post for naval and commercial shipping—it was headquarters of the Royal Navy's Mediterranean Fleet—and played a key role in the First World War, hosting a large garrison and the region's largest hospital. In 1921 Malta became self-governing, with power shared between British and Maltese ministers.

During 1940–41 the islands were hit by sustained German and Italian bombing that killed more than 300. After the Second World War the political scene was split between those who wanted full integration with Great Britain and those favouring independence. In a referendum in 1956 there was majority support for integration, although the results were deemed inconclusive owing to a boycott by the Nationalist Party. Changes to the constitution allied to Giorgio Borg Olivier's election as prime minister in 1962 paved the way for independence on 21 Sept. 1964.

Dom Mintoff's Malta Labour Party emerged victorious in the 1971 general election, Mintoff having previously served as premier from 1955–58. He ushered in an era of non-alignment, during which Malta forged ties with the Eastern Bloc, China and Libya (until a falling-out over oil rights). Playing off East against West, he secured greatly increased revenues for British use of Malta's military facilities in 1972. The island became a republic in 1974 and its British naval base closed in 1979. Moves towards European integration began in 1987 after the Nationalist Party's electoral success and on 1 May 2004 Malta joined the European Union.

Territory and Population

The three Maltese islands and minor islets lie in the Mediterranean 93 km (at the nearest point) south of Sicily and 288 km east of Tunisia. The area of Malta is 246 sq. km (94·9 sq. miles); Gozo, 67 sq. km (25·9 sq. miles) and the virtually uninhabited Comino, 3 sq. km (1·1 sq. miles); total area, 316 sq. km

(121·9 sq. miles). The census population in 2011 was 417,432 (Malta island, 386,057; Gozo and Comino, 31,375); density, 1,321 per sq. km. The estimated population at 31 Dec. 2017 was 475,701.

The UN gives a projected population for 2020 of 434,000.

In 2011, 94·8% of the population were urban. Chief town and port, Valletta, population 5,748 (2011 census). Other towns: Birkirkara, 21,749; Mosta, 19,750; St Paul's Bay, 16,395; Qormi, 16,394; Zabbar, 14,916.

The constitution provides that the national language and language of the courts is Maltese, but both Maltese and English are official languages. Italian is also spoken.

Social Statistics

2009: births, 3,713; deaths, 3,221; marriages, 2,353; emigrants, 9,708 (1,771 Maltese); immigrants, 8,147 (1,190 returning Maltese). 2009 rates per 1,000 population: birth, 9·4; death, 7·8; marriage, 5·7. Abortion is illegal, as was divorce until Oct. 2011. Parliament voted in July 2011 to legalize divorce following a vote in favour of the reform by 52·7% to 47·3% in a referendum held in May. Until then Malta had been one of only three countries still to outlaw divorce (the others being the Philippines and the Vatican). In 2013 the most popular age range for marrying was 25–29 for both males and females. Life expectancy at birth in 2013: 77·5 years for males and 82·0 years for females. Annual population growth rate, 2005–10, 0·5%. Infant mortality in 2010: five per 1,000 live births; fertility rate, 2013, 1·4 births per woman.

Climate

The climate is Mediterranean, with hot, dry and sunny conditions in summer and very little rain from May to Aug. Rainfall is not excessive and falls mainly between Oct. and March. Average daily sunshine in winter is six hours and in summer over ten hours. Valletta, Jan. 12·8°C (55°F), July 25·6°C (78°F). Annual rainfall 578 mm (23").

Constitution and Government

Malta is a parliamentary democracy. The constitution of 1964 provides for a *President*, a *House of Representatives* of members elected by universal suffrage and a Cabinet consisting of the Prime Minister and such number of Ministers as may be appointed. The Constitution makes provision for the protection of fundamental rights and freedom of the individual, and for freedom of conscience and religious worship, and guarantees the separation of executive, judicial and legislative powers. The House of Representatives currently has 68 members (65 directly elected members, the Speaker—who was designated from outside the parliament and became an *ex officio* member—and two additional members elected in accordance with the Constitution, each of whom serve five-year terms. Malta uses the single transferable vote system.

National Anthem

'Lil din l'art helwa, l'omm li tatna isimha' ('Guard her, O Lord, as ever Thou hast guarded'); words by Dun Karm Psaila, tune by Dr Robert Samut.

Recent Elections

At the elections of 3 June 2017 the electorate was 341,856; turnout was 92·1%. The Labour Party (LP; formerly the Malta Labour Party or MLP) gained 37 seats with 55·0% of votes cast; the Nationalist Force (NF; an electoral alliance between the Nationalist Party and the Democratic Party), 30 with 43·7%.

European Parliament

Malta has six representatives. At the May 2014 elections turnout was 74·8% (78·8% in 2009). The LP won 3 seats with 53·4% of votes cast (political affiliation in European Parliament: Progressive Alliance of Socialists and Democrats); and the NP 3 with 40·0% (European People's Party).

© Springer Nature Limited 2020
Palgrave Macmillan (ed.), *The Statesman's Yearbook 2020*,
https://doi.org/10.1057/978-1-349-95940-2_123

Current Government

President: Marie-Louise Coleiro Preca; b. 1958 (LP; sworn in 4 April 2014). In Feb. 2019 the government comprised:

Prime Minister: Joseph Muscat; b. 1974 (LP; sworn in 11 March 2013).

Deputy Prime Minister and Minister of Health: Christopher Fearne.

Minister of Economy, Investment and Small Business: Christian Cardona. *Education and Employment:* Evarist Bartolo. *Energy and Water:* Joe Mizzi. *Environment, Sustainable Development and Climate Change:* José Herrera. *European Affairs and Equality:* Helena Dalli. *Family, Children's Rights and Social Solidarity:* Michael Falzon. *Finance:* Edward Scicluna. *Foreign Affairs and Trade Promotion:* Carmelo Abela. *Gozo:* Justyne Caruana. *Home Affairs and National Security:* Michael Farrugia. *Justice, Culture and Local Government:* Owen Bonnici. *Tourism:* Konrad Mizzi. *Transport, Infrastructure and Capital Projects:* Ian Borg.

Government Website: http://www.gov.mt

Current Leaders

Marie-Louise Coleiro Preca

Position
President

Introduction
Marie-Louise Coleiro Preca was unanimously elected president by parliament in April 2014. She is scheduled to serve a five-year term.

Early Life
Coleiro Preca was born on 7 Dec. 1958 in Qormi. She graduated in international legal and humanistic studies from the University of Malta and went on to earn a doctorate in law.

Coleiro Preca joined the then Malta Labour Party (MLP) in the early 1980s and had various party roles before serving as its general secretary from 1982–91. She is the only woman to have held such a senior post in any major Maltese political party. She was also a member of the National Bureau of Socialist Youths, led the Women's Section of the party (1996–2001), was a founding member of the Ġużè Ellul Mercer Foundation (an educational organization) and published the MLP's now-defunct weekly newspaper.

In 1998 she was elected to parliament in a seat she has successfully defended at every subsequent election. While the MLP was in opposition, she served as shadow minister for social policy and as a member of the parliamentary permanent committee for social affairs. In 2008 she unsuccessfully contested the party leadership, losing out to Joseph Muscat.

Following the renamed Labour Party's triumph at the 2013 general election, she was appointed family and social solidarity minister. On 1 March 2014 Coleiro Preca accepted Prime Minister Muscat's invitation to become president and was sworn into office on 4 April 2014, having gained the approval of parliament.

Career in Office
The presidency is a largely ceremonial role but Coleiro Preca maintains a number of her former roles. She remains, for instance, in charge of the national strategy against poverty and the food aid programme. As president, she signed into law a controversial civil union bill shortly after taking office in April 2014 following its approval by parliament.

Joseph Muscat

Position
Prime Minister

Introduction
Joseph Muscat became prime minister in March 2013 and was returned for a second term of office in June 2017. A former member of the European Parliament (MEP), Muscat is considered a modernizer and centrist.

Early Life
Joseph Muscat was born on 22 Jan. 1974 in Pietà, Malta. In 1997 he graduated from the University of Malta with a master's degree in European studies, management and public policy. From 1997–99 he worked as a market intelligence manager, and from 2000–04 as an investment adviser. He was a journalist on the Malta Labour Party (MLP) radio station from 1992–96 and assistant head of news on its television channel from 1996–97.

He served as financial secretary of the Labour Youth Forum from 1994–97 and was its acting chairperson in 1997. He also served on the national executive of the MLP from 1994–2001 and, under Alfred Sant's Labour government, was a member of the national commission for fiscal morality from 1997–98.

After Labour returned to opposition, Muscat was the party's education spokesman between 2001–03. In 2003 he helped formulate the party's opposition to EU accession. When Malta joined the European Union in 2004, Muscat was elected as an MEP. In this capacity he served on the committee for economic and monetary affairs, advocating a reduction in mobile phone roaming charges. In 2006 he produced a report into new regulations for EU financial services. During this period he completed academic research into multinationals and small businesses in Malta, receiving his PhD from the UK's Bristol University in 2007.

In June 2008 Muscat successfully contested the leadership of the MLP after Alfred Sant resigned. Muscat surrendered his seat in the European Parliament in Oct. 2008 in favour of leading the opposition in Malta. He espoused a more inclusive brand of politics and abbreviated the party's name to the Labour Party (LP). Following gains at the 2009 European Parliamentary elections, he fought the 2013 general election on a platform of lower electricity charges, less bureaucracy, protection for whistle-blowers and reforms to reinvigorate the small business sector. He emerged from the polls on 9 March 2013 with a majority of nine seats.

Career in Office
Muscat took office on 11 March 2013. He has faced the challenge of building economic confidence at a time of continued financial uncertainty among Malta's European neighbours. He has also urged other EU countries to take more action to prevent boat tragedies in the Mediterranean waters around Malta in the wake of the increasing surge of foreign migrants trying to access southern Europe by sea from North Africa and the Middle East. The Labour Party retained power in parliamentary elections in June 2017, but repeated allegations of high-level corruption, aggravated by the murder of a prominent investigative journalist in Oct., have cast a shadow over Muscat's administration.

Defence

The Armed Forces of Malta (AFM) are made up of a Headquarters and three Regiments. In 2011 they had a strength of 1,954 personnel. An Emergency Volunteer Reserve Force was introduced in 1998 on a small scale (120 in 2011). There were also 53 individual reserves in 2011. In addition to infantry and light air defence artillery weapons, the AFM are equipped with helicopters, light fixed-wing and trainer aircraft. There is no conscription.

Apart from normal military duties, AFM are also responsible for Search and Rescue, airport security, surveillance of Malta's territorial and fishing zones, harbour traffic control and anti-pollution duties.

In 2013 defence expenditure totalled US$60m. (US$145 per capita), representing 0·6% of GDP.

Navy

There is a maritime squadron organized into five divisions that operated eight patrol and coastal combatants in 2011.

Air Force

The Air Wing, which mainly serves as a support branch of the ground forces and the maritime squadron, operates eight fixed-wing aircraft and five helicopters.

International Relations

Malta held a referendum on EU membership on 9 March 2003, in which 53·6% of votes cast were in favour of accession, with 46·4% against. It became a member of the EU on 1 May 2004.

Economy

Services accounted for 82·7% of GDP in 2014, industry 16·0% and agriculture 1·3%.

Overview

Malta has the smallest economy in the eurozone. After joining the European Union in 2004, GDP growth was stimulated by a public investment boom largely financed by EU grants. Fiscal policy was directed towards reducing the budget deficit, which had expanded to 56% of GDP by the late 1990s. By 2006 the government had brought the general deficit down to 2·5% of GDP, allowing Malta to join the eurozone on 1 Jan. 2008.

The global financial crisis led to a downturn from late 2008, with manufacturing and tourism the worst hit sectors. However, the economy rebounded strongly in 2010 and weathered the eurozone debt crisis better than many of its partners, supported by strong private consumption, a stable banking sector and growth in tourism and services exports. GDP growth between 2011 and 2015 averaged 3·8% per year. Unemployment fell to 5·8% in Jan. 2015, compared to a eurozone average of 11·4%, while fiscal adjustments saw the general government deficit stabilize at around 2·1% of GDP.

GDP growth was measured at 5·2% in 2016 and 6·7% in 2017. The gaming industry (lotteries, sports betting, etc.) served as a key driver of this expansion, accounting for more than 25% of nominal gross value added growth between 2012 and 2016 and becoming the third largest industry in the economy. In 2004 Malta had been the first EU country to regulate the gaming industry, which attracted investors.

The International Monetary Fund has identified developing infrastructure as a major factor in securing long-term growth.

Currency

On 1 Jan. 2008 the *euro* (EUR) replaced the *Maltese lira* (MTL) as the legal currency of Malta at the irrevocable conversion rate of Lm0·4293 to one euro. There was inflation of 0·9% in 2016 and 1·3% in 2017. Foreign exchange reserves stood at US$2,390m. in March 2005, gold reserves were 4,000 troy oz in May 2005 and total money supply was Lm1,413m. in July 2005.

Budget

In 2012 revenues were €2,738·0m. and expenditures €2,963·9m. Direct taxes accounted for 34·1% of revenues in 2012 and indirect taxes 33·6%; current expenditure accounted for 91·6% of expenditures.

Malta had a budget surplus in 2017 of 3·5% of GDP. There was a surplus in 2016 (0·9%) and a deficit in 2015 (1·0%) The required target set by the EU is a budget deficit of no more than 3%.

The standard rate of VAT is 18·0% (reduced rates, 7% and 5%).

Performance

Real GDP growth was 9·5% in 2015, 5·2% in 2016 and 6·7% in 2017. Total GDP in 2017 was US$12·5bn.

Banking and Finance

The Central Bank of Malta (*Governor*, Mario Vella) was founded in 1968. In 2014 there were 27 licensed credit institutions carrying out domestic and international banking activities. In addition 13 local financial institutions licensed in terms of the Financial Institutions Act 1994 also provide services that range from exchange bureau related business to merchant banking.

Gross external debt amounted to US$44,388m. in June 2012.

There is a stock exchange in Valletta.

Energy and Natural Resources

In 2011 just 0·4% of energy consumption came from renewables (wind power, solar power, hydro-electric power, tidal power, geothermal energy and biomass), compared to the European Union average of 13·0%. A target of 10% has been set by the EU for 2020.

Environment

Malta's carbon dioxide emissions from the consumption of energy in 2011 were the equivalent of 18·4 tonnes per capita.

Electricity

Installed electrical capacity was 571,000 kW in 2013. Production in 2011 was 2·2bn. kWh; consumption per capita was 5,146 kWh.

Oil and Gas

Malta's large offshore area, made up of geological extensions of southeast Sicily, east Tunisia and northwest Libya, contains significant hydrocarbon reserves.

Agriculture

Malta is self-sufficient in fresh vegetables, pork, poultry, eggs and fresh milk. The main crops are potatoes (the spring crop being the country's primary agricultural export), vegetables and fruits, with some items such as tomatoes serving as the main input in the local canning industry. Malta had 12,466 agricultural holdings in 2013, with 1,372 full-time farmers and 17,693 part-time. In 2013 there were 8,967 ha. of arable land and 1,264 ha. of permanent crops.

Agriculture contributes around 1·9% of GDP annually. 2014 production figures (in 1,000 tonnes): wheat (estimate), 16; tomatoes, 13; potatoes, 11; onions, 8; cauliflowers, 6; grapes, 5; cabbages, 4; lettuce, 4; watermelons, 4.

Livestock in 2014: pigs, 47,465; cattle, 14,883; sheep, 10,526; goats, 4,627; chickens (2013), 918,426.

Livestock products accounted for 34·7% of the total value of agricultural production in 2014.

Fisheries

In 2012 the fishing fleet comprised 1,043 vessels of 7,998 GT. Total catch in 2013 was 2,356 tonnes.

Industry

Besides manufacturing (food, clothing, chemicals, electrical machinery parts and electronic components and products), the mainstays of the economy are ship repair and shipbuilding, agriculture, small crafts units, tourism and the provision of other services such as the freeport facilities. The majority of state-aided manufacturing enterprises operating in Malta are foreign-owned or with foreign interests. The Malta Development Corporation is the government agency responsible for promoting investment, while the Malta Export Trade Corporation serves as a catalyst to the export of local products.

Labour

The labour force in 2013 was 187,000 (162,000 in 2003). 63·4% of the population aged 15–64 was economically active in 2013. 30·5% of the labour force in 2013 had a secondary education as the highest level and 23·7% had a tertiary education. Malta's unemployment rate in June 2017, at 4·0%, was the lowest on record.

International Trade

Imports are being liberalized. Marsaxlokk is an all-weather freeport zone for transhipment activities. The Malta Export Trade Corporation promotes local exports.

Imports and Exports

In 2010 imports (c.i.f.) amounted to US$4,245·8m. and exports (f.o.b.) US$3,357·5m.

Principal imports in 2010 (in US$1m.) were: machinery and transport equipment (1,923·1); food (480·6); chemicals and related products (465·1). Principal exports in 2010 (in US$1m.) were: machinery and transport equipment (2,029·7); miscellaneous manufactured articles (388·8); food and live animals (271·9).

Main import suppliers (in US$1m.) in 2010 were: Italy (985·0); UK (352·3); Germany (348·0); France (337·4). Main export markets in 2010 (in US$1m.) were: Singapore (495·2); USA (370·4); Hong Kong (344·4); Germany (311·2).

Trade Fairs

The Malta Trade Fairs Corporation organizes the International Fair of Malta (early July).

Communications

Roads

In 2016 there were 2,854 km of roads, including 111 km of arterial roads. 84·4% of roads are paved. Malta has one of the densest road networks in the world. Motor vehicles in use in 2007 included 203,900 passenger cars, 23,600 vans and lorries, 10,600 motorcycles and mopeds, and 690 buses and coaches. There were 1,209 casualties in traffic accidents in 2007, including 14 fatalities (equivalent to 3·4 fatalities per 100,000 population, giving Malta the lowest death rate in road accidents of any industrialized country).

Civil Aviation

The national carrier is Air Malta, which is 98% state-owned. In 2010 it carried 1·70m. passengers and flew from Malta to nearly 40 destinations in other European countries. In 2012 there were 32,286 aircraft movements at Malta International Airport. A total of 3,658,972 passengers and 16,487 tonnes of cargo were handled.

Shipping
There is a car ferry between Malta and Gozo. In Jan. 2014 there were 1,669 ships of 300 GT or over registered, totalling 46·34m. GT; Malta's fleet was the tenth largest in terms of the number of ships and the seventh largest on the basis of gross tonnage. Of the 1,669 vessels registered, 537 were bulk carriers, 507 oil tankers, 389 general cargo ships, 134 container ships, 66 passenger ships and 36 liquid gas tankers.

The Malta Freeport plays an important role in the economy as it is effectively positioned to act as a distribution centre in the Mediterranean.

Telecommunications
In 2013 there were 231,331 main (fixed) telephone lines; mobile phone subscriptions numbered 556,652 in 2013 (129·8 per 100 persons). There were 135,758 fixed internet subscriptions in 2012 and 149,788 wireless broadband subscriptions. In March 2012 there were 192,000 Facebook users.

Social Institutions
Out of 178 countries analysed in the 2017 *Fragile States Index*—a list published jointly by the Fund for Peace and *Foreign Policy* magazine—Malta was ranked the 26th least vulnerable to conflict or collapse. The index is based on 12 indicators of state vulnerability across social, political and economic categories.

Justice
There were 17,584 recorded offences committed in 2013, down from a peak of 18,578 in 2005.

In 2015 the total number of police officers was 2,162 of which 1,745 were male officers and 417 female.

Malta abolished the death penalty for all crimes in 2000.

Education
Adult literacy rate, 2005, 92·4% (male, 91·2%; female, 93·5%).

Education is compulsory between the ages of 5 and 16 and free in government schools from kindergarten to university. Kindergarten education is provided for three- and four-year old children. The primary school course lasts six years.

In 2015 there were 9,217 pre-primary school children with 743 teaching staff; 24,624 primary school children with 2,021 teaching staff; and 29,434 secondary school pupils with 3,915 teaching staff. At all levels there are state, Church and independent schools, with the state schools having the most pupils at each of the three levels.

The University of Malta, at Msida, was founded in 1769 and is the only university. It has some 11,500 students, including around 1,000 international students from more than 90 different countries. The Malta College of Arts, Science and Technology, founded in 2001, is a vocational education and training institution.

In 2008 public expenditure on education came to 5·9% of GDP.

Health
In 2006 there were 1,564 doctors, 190 dentists, 790 pharmacists and 2,411 nurses and midwives. There were seven hospitals (two private) with 1,833 beds in 2012. There are also eight health centres.

Welfare
Legislation provides a national contributory insurance scheme and also for the payment of non-contributory allowances, assistances and pensions. It covers the payment of marriage grants, maternity benefits, child allowances, parental allowances, disabled child allowance, family bonus, sickness benefit, injury benefits, disablement benefits, unemployment benefit, contributory pensions in respect of retirement, invalidity and widowhood, and non-contributory medical assistance, free medical aids, social assistance, a carers' pension and pensions for the visually impaired, disabled or severely disabled persons and the aged.

As of 2016 the statutory retirement age was 62 for both sexes. It is gradually rising and will be 65 for both sexes in 2026.

Religion
97% of the population belong to the Roman Catholic Church, which is established by law as the religion of the country, although full liberty of conscience and freedom of worship are guaranteed. In Feb. 2019 there was one cardinal.

Culture
Valletta was one of two European Capitals of Culture for 2018, along with Leeuwarden.

World Heritage Sites
Malta has three sites on the UNESCO World Heritage List (all inscribed on the list in 1980): Hal Saflieni Hypogeum, a prehistoric underground necropolis; the City of Valletta, a highly concentrated centre marked by the influences of Romans, Byzantines and Arabs and the Knights of St John; and the Megalithic Temples of Malta (reinscribed in 1992), seven temples on Malta and Gozo containing Bronze Age structures.

Press
In 2008 there were two English paid-for dailies (*The Times* and *The Malta Independent*) and two Maltese dailies (*In-Nazzjon* and *L-Orizzont*). There were seven paid-for non-dailies and six Sunday newspapers (three in English and three in Maltese).

Tourism
Tourism is a major component of the Maltese economy. In 2010 there were 1,336,000 staying foreign tourists, spending US$1,130m.; 31% of tourists in 2010 were from the UK and 16% from Italy. Cruise passenger visits totalled 491,201 in 2010 (more than double the 2000 total of 170,782).

Festivals
Major festivals include the Malta Song Festival; Carnival Festivals at Valletta (Feb.); History and Elegance Festival at Valletta (April); National Folk Singing; Malta International Arts Festival; Malta Jazz Festival; International Food and Beer Festival (June/July); Festa Season (June–Sept.); Malta International Choir Festival (Nov.).

Diplomatic Representatives
Of Malta in the United Kingdom (Malta House, 36–38 Piccadilly, London, W1J 0LE)
High Commissioner: Joseph Cole.

Of the United Kingdom in Malta (Whitehall Mansions, Ta' Xbiex Seafront, Ta' Xbiex, XBX 1026)
High Commissioner: Stuart Gill, OBE.

Of Malta in the USA (2017 Connecticut Ave., NW, Washington, D.C., 20008)
Ambassador: Keith Azzopardi.

Of the USA in Malta (Ta' Qali National Park, Attard, ATD 4000)
Ambassador: Vacant.
Chargé d'Affaires a.i.: Mark A. Shapiro.

Of Malta to the United Nations
Ambassador: Carmelo Inguanez.

Of Malta to the European Union
Permanent Representative: Daniel Azzopardi.

Further Reading

National Statistics Office (Lascaris, Valletta). *Regional Statistics Malta 2017 Edition.*

Department of Information (3 Castille Place, Valletta). *The Malta Government Gazette, Malta Information, Economic Survey, Acts of Parliament and Subsidiary Legislation, Laws of Malta, Constitution of Malta 1992.*

Central Bank of Malta. *Annual Reports.*

Chamber of Commerce (annual). *Trade Directory.*

Berg, W. G., *Historical Dictionary of Malta.* 1995

Pace, Roderick, *The European Union's Mediterranean Enlargement: Cyprus and Malta.* 2006

National Statistical Office: National Statistics Office, Lascaris, Valletta CMR 02.

Website: http://www.nso.gov.mt

Marshall Islands

Republic of the Marshall Islands

Capital: Majuro
Population projection, 2020: 53,000
GNI per capita, 2017: (PPP$) 5,125
HDI/world rank, 2017: 0·708/106
Internet domain extension: .mh

Key Historical Events

The Pacific archipelago was populated by emigrants from southeast Asia from around 2000 BC and first documented by Portuguese mariners in 1528. The islands owe their name to the English seafarer, John Marshall, who visited in 1788. They became part of the protectorate of German New Guinea in 1886 and administrative affairs were managed by private German and Australian interests. Japan seized control in 1914 and received a League of Nations mandate over the islands in 1919. The Marshall Islands were occupied by Allied forces in 1944 and became part of the UN Trust Territory of the Pacific Islands on 18 July 1947 (administered by the USA). On 21 Oct. 1986 the islands gained independence. A Compact of Free Association with the USA that came into force at the time was extended by 20 years in May 2004.

Territory and Population

The Marshall Islands lie in the North Pacific Ocean north of Kiribati and east of Micronesia, and consist of an archipelago of 31 coral atolls, five single islands and 1,152 islets strung out in two chains, eastern and western. Of these, 25 atolls and islands are inhabited. The land area is 181 sq. km (70 sq. miles). At the 2011 census the population was 53,158 (27,243 males); density, 294 per sq. km.

The UN gives a projected population for 2020 of 53,000.

The capital is Majuro (also known as Dalap-Uliga-Darrit) on Majuro Atoll (2011 population, 27,797) in the eastern chain. The largest atoll in the western chain is Kwajalein (2011 population, 11,408) containing the only other town, Ebeye. In 2011, 73·8% of Marshall Islanders lived on these two atolls. The two archipelagic island chains of Bikini and Enewetak are former US nuclear test sites; Kwajalein is now used as a US missile test range. The islands lay claim to the US territory of Wake Island. In 2011 the population was 72·1% urban. About 88% of the population are Marshallese, a Micronesian people.

English is universally spoken and is the official language. Two major Marshallese dialects from the Malayo-Polynesian family and Japanese are also spoken.

Social Statistics

2006 births, estimate, 1,576; deaths, 318. 2006 rates per 1,000 population, estimates: birth, 30·3; death, 6·1. Infant mortality rate, 2010, 22 per 1,000 live births. Life expectancy, 2008: male, 68·9 years; female, 73·0. Annual population growth rate, 1998–2008, 1·6%; fertility rate, 2008, 3·7 births per woman.

Climate

Hot and humid, with wet season from May to Nov. The islands border the typhoon belt. Jaluit, Jan. 81°F (27·2°C), July 82°F (27·8°C). Annual rainfall 161" (4,034 mm).

Constitution and Government

Under the constitution which came into force on 1 May 1979, the Marshall Islands form a republic with a *President* as head of state and government, who is elected for four-year terms by the parliament. The parliament consists of a 33-member *House of Assembly* (Nitijela), directly elected by popular vote for four-year terms. There is also a 12-member appointed *Council of Chiefs* (Iroij) which has a consultative and advisory capacity on matters affecting customary law and practice.

National Anthem

'Forever Marshall Islands'; words and tune by Amata Kabua.

Recent Elections

At the House of Assembly elections on 16 Nov. 2015, 33 non-partisan members were elected. Although candidates are officially non-partisan and their party affiliation may change after the elections, many of them belong either to the Kien Eo Am party/KEA ('Your Government') or the Aelon Kein Ad party/AKA ('Our Island'). An indirect presidential election was held on 27 Jan. 2016. The sole candidate Hilda Heine won with 24 votes.

Current Government

President: Hilda Heine; b. 1951 (ind.; took office on 28 Jan. 2016).
In Feb. 2019 the government comprised:
Minister in Assistance to the President, and Environment: David Paul. *Culture and Internal Affairs:* Amenta Matthew. *Education, Sports and Training:* Wilbur Heine. *Finance, Banking and Postal Services:* Brenson S. Wase. *Foreign Affairs and Trade:* John Silk. *Health and Human Services:* Kalani Kaneko. *Justice, Immigration and Labour:* Jack Ading. *Natural Resources and Commerce:* Alfred Alfred, Jr. *Transportation, Communication and Information Technology:* Thomas Heine. *Works, Infrastructure and Utilities:* Tony Muller.
Marshall Islands Parliament: https://rmiparliament.org

Current Leaders

Hilda C. Heine

Position
President

Introduction
Former education minister Hilda Heine was elected president in Jan. 2016, following the one-week tenure of Casten Nemra.

Early Life
Born on 6 April 1951 in Majuro Atoll, Hilda Heine studied at the University of Oregon, USA, and attained a master's degree in education from the University of Hawaii in 1974. She was a teacher and counsellor at Marshall Islands High School, Majuro, until 1982, and held administrative posts in education until 1990. From 1990–92 she served as president of the College of the Marshall Islands and from 1993–95 was secretary of education at the ministry of education in Majuro.

From 1995 she worked on a series of projects associated with the non-governmental Pacific Resources for Education and Learning (PREL), including initiatives to promote leadership in education. In 2000 she founded Women United Together Marshall Islands (WUTMI) to campaign for women's rights. From 2001–04 she worked as a researcher for PREL in Hawaii and in 2004 received her doctorate in education from the University of Southern California.

After serving as director for policy and capacity building for PREL, Hawaii from 2004–05, and as programme director at the Pacific Comprehensive Assistance Center, PREL, Hawaii from 2006–12, Heine successfully stood for the senatorial seat of Aur Atoll in 2012. The following year she was appointed minister of education. Following a closely-fought general election in Jan. 2016, coalition wrangling led to President Nemra losing a vote of no confidence after only a week in office. Heine was then elected to succeed him.

© Springer Nature Limited 2020
Palgrave Macmillan (ed.), *The Statesman's Yearbook 2020*,
https://doi.org/10.1057/978-1-349-95940-2_124

Career in Office

Heine took office on 28 Jan. 2016 and on 3 Feb. announced a state of emergency in response to a drought. Environmental problems are expected to feature prominently among her main challenges, alongside the need to further develop infrastructure, education and employment. In Nov. 2018 she narrowly survived a parliamentary no-confidence.

Defence

The Compact of Free Association gives the USA responsibility for defence in return for US assistance. In 2003 the US lease of Kwajalein Atoll, a missile testing site, was extended by 50 years.

Economy

Agriculture accounts for approximately 15% of GDP, industry 13% and services 72%.

Overview

Foreign aid contributes 70% of the Marshall Islands state budget. The main sources of revenue come from subsidies under the 1986 Compact of Free Association (COFA) with the USA (renegotiated in 2002 and 2003) and the leasing of land for US missile testing. The USA and Marshall Islands are jointly financing a trust fund for the people of the Islands that will provide an income stream beyond 2024 when COFA aid (worth some US$1·5bn. in direct assistance between 2004 and 2024) ends.

The economy experienced moderate growth in the early 2000s but contracted in 2008 and 2009 before a recovery from 2010–11. In 2017 GDP growth reached 2·5% owing to the strong performance of the fishing and construction sectors. Nonetheless, the economy is vulnerable to external shocks owing to its geographical isolation, narrow production base and reliance on foreign aid. Fiscal consolidation and structural reform to stimulate the private sector are needed to ensure long-term sustainability.

The government is attempting to develop the country's marine resources (fishing and aquaculture) as well as agriculture and tourism. Tourism, which employs around 10% of the labour force, offers potential for foreign exchange earnings. The services and banking sectors are relatively well developed and represent more than half of GDP, while industry contributes around one-third.

The government made cryptocurrency legal tender in May 2018 alongside the US dollar—making the Marshall Islands the first country in the world to fully embrace the digital economy. The government also hopes that the introduction of a traceable currency will counter the nation's reputation as a hub for money laundering.

Emigration and climate change constitute long-term challenges. Parts of the Islands are at risk of being engulfed by rising sea levels, with many of the atolls only one metre above the water level.

Currency

In March 2018 the government announced that a digital currency (the digital *Sovereign* or SOV) was to be introduced with equal status to the *US dollar* as official currency. The Marshall Islands thus became the first nation to adopt a cryptocurrency as legal tender. There was deflation of 1·5% in 2016 and then zero inflation in 2017.

Budget

Revenue in 2012–13 was US$90·2m.; expenditure was US$91·6m. Under the terms of the Amended Compact, which entered force in 2004 as a follow-up to the Compact of Free Association, the USA provides approximately US$70m. a year in aid. The fiscal year begins on 1 Oct.

Performance

Total GDP in 2017 was US$199m.; GDP per capita in 2012 was US$3,508. The economy grew by 2·0% in 2015, 3·6% in 2016 and 2·5% in 2017.

Banking and Finance

There are three banks: the Bank of Marshall Islands, the Marshall Islands Development Bank and the Bank of Guam.

Energy and Natural Resources

Electricity

Total installed capacity (2011 estimate), 17,000 kW. Production (2011 estimate), 114m. kWh.

Minerals

High-grade phosphate deposits are mined on Ailinglaplap Atoll. Deep-seabed minerals are an important natural resource.

Agriculture

A small amount of agricultural produce is exported: coconuts, tomatoes, melons and breadfruit. Other important crops include copra, taro, cassava and sweet potatoes. Pigs and chickens constitute the main livestock. In 2012 there were approximately 2,000 ha. of arable land and 7,000 ha. of permanent crop land.

Forestry

There were 13,000 ha. of forest in 2015, or 70% of the total land area.

Fisheries

Total catch in 2015 amounted to 89,714 tonnes (more than double the 2008 total). There is a commercial tuna-fishing industry with a processing plant on Majuro. Seaweed is cultivated. Fisheries offer some of the best opportunities for economic growth.

Industry

The main industries are copra, fish, tourism, handicrafts (items made from shell, wood and pearl), mining, manufacturing, construction and power.

Labour

In 2011 the employed workforce was 12,647. Approximately 60% of those in the working age population in 2011 were unemployed or not in the labour force. In 2007, 37% of employed people worked in the private sector. In the same year 35% of workers were employed in public administration, 18% in wholesale and retail trade, 12% in extra-territorial organizations and bodies and 8% in construction. Agriculture, hunting, forestry and fishing accounted for just 3%.

International Trade

The Amended Compact between the Marshall Islands and the USA is the major source of income, and accounts for about 70% of total GDP.

Imports and Exports

Imports (mainly oil) were US$133·3m. in 2009–10; exports, US$32·3m. By far the most important trading partner is the USA. Main imports are mineral fuels and lubricants, and machinery and transport equipment. Main exports are: copra, coconut, and chilled and frozen fish.

Communications

Roads

There are paved roads on major islands (Majuro, Kwajalein); roads are otherwise stone-, coral- or laterite-surfaced. In 2013 there were 1,917 cars and four-wheeled light vehicles, and 89 trucks and buses.

Civil Aviation

The main airport is Marshall Islands International Airport. There are also 29 outer island airstrips. In 2017 there were flights to Guam, Honolulu, Kiribati, Micronesia and Nauru as well as domestic services. The national carrier is Air Marshall Islands.

Shipping

Majuro is the main port. In Jan. 2014 there were 2,047 ships of 300 GT or over registered, totalling 88·70m. GT (a figure exceeded only by the fleets of Panama and Liberia). Of the 2,047 vessels registered, 796 were bulk carriers, 753 oil tankers, 245 container ships, 160 general cargo ships, 83 liquid gas tankers and ten passenger ships. The ship's register of the Marshall Islands is a flag of convenience register.

Telecommunications

In 2014 there were 2,361 main (fixed) telephone lines. There are a US satellite communications system on Kwajalein and two Intelsat satellite earth stations (Pacific Ocean). The National Telecommunications Authority provides domestic and international services. Mobile phone subscribers numbered 15,500 in 2014. An estimated 11·7% of the population were internet users in 2013.

Social Institutions

Justice

The Supreme Court is situated on Majuro. There are also a High Court, a District Court and 23 Community Courts. A Traditional Court deals with disputes involving land properties and customs.

Education

In 2008–09 there were 8,000 pupils enrolled in primary schools and 5,000 pupils in secondary schools. There is a College of the Marshall Islands and a subsidiary of the University of the South Pacific on Majuro. In 2016 public expenditure on education came to 20·5% of total government expenditure.

Health

There were two hospitals in 2015, with a total of 138 beds. In 2010 there were four doctors for every 10,000 people, and 17 nurses and midwives per 10,000. There were two dentists per 10,000 population in 2008.

In *Water: At What Cost? The State of the World's Water 2016*, WaterAid reported that 5·4% of the population does not have access to safe water.

Religion

The population is mainly Protestant (primarily the United Church of Christ). Other churches and denominations include Assemblies of God, Roman Catholics, Latter-day Saints (Mormons), Bukot Nan Jesus and Baptists.

Culture

World Heritage Sites

The Marshall Islands have one site on the UNESCO World Heritage List: Bikini Atoll (inscribed on the list in 2010), the site used by the US military to carry out 67 nuclear tests between 1946 and 1958.

Press

There is a weekly publication called *The Marshall Islands Journal*. Since 2007 it has also had an online edition.

Tourism

In 2011, 4,559 non-resident tourists (excluding same-day visitors) arrived by air.

Festivals

Custom Day and the Annual Canoe Race are the main festivals.

Diplomatic Representatives

Of the United Kingdom in the Marshall Islands
Ambassador: Melanie Hopkins (resides in Suva, Fiji).

Of the Marshall Islands in the USA (2433 Massachusetts Ave., NW, Washington, D.C., 20008)
Ambassador: Gerald M. Zackios.

Of the USA in the Marshall Islands (PO Box 1379, Majuro, MH 96960)
Ambassador: Karen Brevard Stewart.

Of the Marshall Islands to the United Nations
Ambassador: Amatlain Elizabeth Kabua.

Of the Marshall Islands to the European Union
Ambassador: Vacant.

Further Reading

Barker, Holly, *Bravo for the Marshallese: Regaining Control in a Post-Nuclear, Post-Colonial World.* 2003

National Statistical Office: Economic Policy, Planning and Statistics Office (EPPSO), Office of the President, PO Box 7, Majuro, MH 96960.

Website: http://rmi.prism.spc.int

Mauritania

Al-Jumhuriyah al-Islamiyah al-Muritaniyah (Islamic Republic of Mauritania)

Capital: Nouakchott
Population projection, 2020: 4·78m.
GNI per capita, 2017: (PPP$) 3,592
HDI/world rank, 2017: 0·520/159=
Internet domain extension: .mr

Key Historical Events

Mauritania became a French protectorate in 1903 and a colony in 1920. It achieved full independence on 28 Nov. 1960. Mauritania was made a one-party state in 1964.

The 1980s were marked by territorial disputes with Morocco and Senegal. Seizing power in 1984, Lieut.-Col. Maaouya Ould Sid'Ahmed Taya prepared the way for a new constitution allowing for a multi-party political system, which also gave extensive powers to the president. A coup attempt against Ould Taya failed in June 2003. But in Aug. 2005, while out of the country, he was overthrown in a bloodless coup by a group of army officers who set up a Military Council for Justice and Democracy. Under the leadership of Col. Ely Ould Mohammed Vall, the Council pledged to hold democratic elections within two years. In June 2006 a new constitution was approved, limiting the president to two 5-year terms. Sidi Mohamed Ould Cheikh Abdallahi won presidential elections in March 2007 but was ousted in a coup in Aug. 2008.

Territory and Population

Mauritania is bounded west by the Atlantic Ocean, north by Western Sahara, northeast by Algeria, east and southeast by Mali, and south by Senegal. The total area is 1,030,700 sq. km (398,000 sq. miles) of which 47% is desert. The population at the 2013 census was 3,537,368; density, 3·4 per sq. km. The United Nations population estimate for 2013 was 3,946,000. In 2011, 41·7% of the population lived in urban areas.

The UN gives a projected population for 2020 of 4·78m.

Area (in sq. km), population (2013 census) and chief towns of the Nouakchott Capital District and 12 regions:

Region	Area	Population	Chief town
Açâba	36,600	325,897	Kiffa
Adrar	215,300	62,658	Atar
Brakna	33,800	312,277	Aleg
Dakhlet Nouâdhibou	22,300	123,779	Nouâdhibou
Gorgol	13,600	335,917	Kaédi
Guidimaka	10,300	267,029	Sélibaby
Hodh ech-Chargui	182,700	430,668	Néma
Hodh el-Gharbi	53,400	294,109	Aïoun el Atrouss
Inchiri	46,800	19,639	Akjoujt
Nouakchott District[1]	1,000	958,399	Nouakchott
Tagant	95,200	80,962	Tidjikdja
Tiris Zemmour	252,900	53,261	Zouérate
Trarza	67,800	272,773	Rosso

[1]In 2014 Nouakchott District split into three new regions—Nouakchott Nord, Nouakchott Ouest and Nouakchott Sud.

Principal town (2013 census): Nouakchott, 958,399.

Mauritania was traditionally a nomadic country but since independence in 1960 there has been rapid urbanization, primarily as a result of a series of droughts.

It is estimated that around 40% of the population are Black Moors, 30% White Moors and 30% Black Africans of the Pulaar, Soninke and Wolof tribes.

Arabic is the official language. French no longer has official status. Pulaar, Soninke and Wolof are national languages.

Social Statistics

2008 estimates: births, 108,000; deaths, 33,000. 2008 rates, estimate (per 1,000 population): births, 33·6; deaths, 10·3. Expectation of life at birth in 2013 was 60·0 years for males and 63·1 for females. Annual population growth rate, 2000–08, 2·6%. Infant mortality, 2010, 75 per 1,000 live births; fertility rate, 2008, 4·5 births per woman.

Climate

A tropical climate, but conditions are generally arid, even near the coast, where the only appreciable rains come in July to Sept. Nouakchott, Jan. 71°F (21·7°C), July 82°F (27·8°C). Annual rainfall 6" (158 mm).

Constitution and Government

A referendum was held on 25 June 2006 to approve a new constitution. Turnout was 76·5%; 96·99% of votes cast were in favour.

The constitution imposes a limit of two five-year terms for a president, to be elected by popular vote. It also sets a maximum age of 75 for a president. The 157-member *National Assembly* is a unicameral legislature. The former *Senate* was abolished in 2017.

Following a coup d'état in Aug. 2008 a transitional government took power, headed by an 11-member High Council of State (all of whom came from the military). The junta retained the constitution and vowed to protect the country's democratic institutions. In April 2009 Gen. Mohamed Ould Abdel Aziz—the leader of the coup—stood down as head of government to run in the presidential elections of July 2009, which he won by a large margin.

National Anthem

'Bilada-l ubati-l hudati-l kiram' ('The Country of Fatherland is the Honorable Gift'); words anonymous, tune by Rageh Daoud.

Recent Elections

Presidential elections took place on 21 June 2014. Incumbent president Mohamed Ould Abdel Aziz was re-elected with 81·9% of the vote against Biram Dah Ebeid with 8·7%, Boydiel Ould Houmeid 4·5%, Ibrahim Moctar Sarr 4·4% and Lalla Meryem Mint Moulaye Idriss 0·5%. Turnout was 56·5%. The National Forum for Democracy and Unity (a coalition of opposition parties) boycotted the election.

Elections for the National Assembly were held on 1 and 15 Sept. 2018. The Union for the Republic (UPR) retained its majority in parliament, winning 89 seats of the 157 seats. Tawassoul won 14 seats. The remaining seats went to a number of smaller parties. Turnout in the first round was 73·4%.

Current Government

President: Gen. Mohamed Ould Abdel Aziz; b. 1956 (since 5 Aug. 2009).

Prime Minister: Mohamed Salem Ould Béchir; b. 1962 (Union for the Republic; in office since 29 Oct. 2018).

In Feb. 2019 the government comprised:

Minister of Justice: Dia Moctar Malal. *Foreign Affairs and Co-operation:* Ismail Ould Cheikh Ahmed. *National Defence:* Mohamed Ould Ghazouani. *Interior and Decentralization:* Ahmedou Ould Abdella. *Economic Affairs and Finance:* Mokhtar Ould Diay. *Islamic Affairs and Traditional Education:* Ahmed Ould Ehil Daoud. *Petroleum, Energy and Mines:*

© Springer Nature Limited 2020
Palgrave Macmillan (ed.), *The Statesman's Yearbook 2020*,
https://doi.org/10.1057/978-1-349-95940-2_125

Mohamed Ould Abdel Fattah. *Public Service, Labour and Modernization of the Administration:* Seyidna Aly Ould Mohamed Khouna. *Health:* Kane Boubacar. *Fisheries and Maritime Economy:* Yahya Ould Abdedayem. *Commerce, Industry and Tourism:* Khadija M'bareck Fall. *Housing, Urban Planning and Land Management:* Nani Ould Chrougha. *Rural Development:* Lamina Mint El Ghoutoub Ould Moma. *Infrastructure and Transport:* Amal Mint Mouloud. *Water and Sanitation:* Isselmou Ould Sid'El Mokhtar Ould Lehbib. *National Education and Vocational Training:* Naha Mint Hamdy Ould Moukness. *Higher Education, Scientific Research, and Information and Communications Technology:* Sidi Ould Salem. *Culture, Crafts, Relations with Parliament, and Government Spokesperson:* Sidi Mohamed Ould Maham. *Youth and Sports:* Djinda Ball. *Social Affairs, Children and Family:* Mariem Mint Bilal. *Environment and Sustainable Development:* Amédy Camara. *Secretary General of the Government:* Zeinebou Mint Ely Salem. *Office of the Prime Minister (French and Arabic only):* http://www.primature.gov.mr/index.php

Current Leaders

Gen. Mohamed Ould Abdel Aziz

Position
President

Introduction
Gen. Mohamed Ould Abdel Aziz was elected president of Mauritania in July 2009, having called elections after seizing power in a coup against his predecessor Sidi Mohamed Ould Cheikh Abdallahi in Aug. 2008. Aziz led the country at the head of a governing council until April 2009. He was returned for a second five-year term in June 2014 in an election boycotted by most opposition parties.

Early Life
Ould Abdel Aziz was born on 20 Dec. 1956 in Akjoujt, between Nouakchott and Atâr. He was born into the Oulad Bou Sbaa Berber-Arab tribe, from which a number of powerful Mauritanian figures have emerged. In 1977 he attended officer training at the Royal Military Academy in Meknès, Morocco. After a stint in the army, he returned to the Military Academy in 1980 to receive training in logistics.

From 1978 Mauritania had a string of *de facto* governments following the overthrow of the civilian president Ould Daddah. Aziz became a staff officer in 1982 and in 1984 was appointed aide-de-camp to Col. Maaouya Ould Sid'Ahmed Taya, the nation's *de facto* military leader. After further training at the École Militaire Inter-Arme (EMIA), Aziz attained the rank of captain and, at Ould Taya's request, established an elite presidential guard (BASEP).

In 1992 Aziz became the army chief of staff, continuing to serve Ould Taya. In 1998, by then a lieutenant colonel, he once again took charge of BASEP. After defeating coups in 2003 and 2004, for which he received the country's highest military award, Aziz was a leading figure in the 2005 coup that overthrew Ould Taya. Aziz emerged as a driving force for the restoration of civilian government and in March 2007 Ould Abdallahi was elected president in open elections.

Abdallahi named Aziz (still head of BASEP) commander of the armed forces, and even sent Aziz to meet King Mohammed of Morocco in an official state visit. In 2008 Aziz became a general. However, relations between the military and the civilian government grew strained as the economic situation deteriorated and Islamic political forces gained strength. The government began a curb of military power and in Aug. 2008 announced a restructuring of the military. In response, the army ousted Abdallahi. As head of a military-dominated interim council, Aziz announced new elections to be held in June 2009. In March 2009 Aziz announced his intention to run for president in the elections, rescheduled for July.

Career in Office
His assumption of office in Aug. 2009 was attacked by France (the former colonial power), the African Union (AU), the USA and Algeria. However, he was received warmly in neighbouring Morocco and in Libya.

The AU continued to impose sanctions in 2010, including a travel ban in AU countries for military personnel who had supported the coup and a seizure of their assets in AU banks. Aziz's electoral pledges included re-establishing civilian governance, improving national unity and consolidating republican institutions. In July 2010 his government adopted new anti-terrorism legislation to give security forces greater powers.

There were opposition demonstrations in May 2012 calling on Aziz to resign, and in Oct. he was wounded in a shooting incident, apparently by troops at a military checkpoint. Described officially as an accident, other sources claimed it was a coup attempt.

Parliamentary elections held over two rounds in Nov. and Dec. 2013 were boycotted by most opposition groups and resulted in a landslide victory for the ruling pro-Aziz Union for the Republic (UPR) and allied parties. In Jan. 2014 Aziz took office as chair of the African Union for a year-long term. In June that year he was also re-elected as state president with nearly 82% of the vote.

In Aug. 2017, in a controversial referendum boycotted by the opposition, voters endorsed Aziz's proposal to abolish the upper house of parliament—the indirectly-elected Senate that had previously rejected the president's plan in March—and replace it with regional law-making councils. Further parliamentary elections were held in Sept. 2018, in which the UPR remained the largest single party in terms of vote share and seats. The following month Aziz named Mohamed Salem Ould Béchir as prime minister following the resignation of Yahya Ould Hademine.

Defence

Conscription is authorized for two years. Defence expenditure in 2013 totalled US$145m. (US$42 per capita), representing approximately 3% of GDP.

Army

There are six military regions. Army strength was 15,000 in 2011. In addition there was a Gendarmerie of about 3,000 and a National Guard of 2,000.

Navy

The Navy, some 620 strong in 2011, has bases at Nouâdhibou and Nouakchott.

Air Force

Personnel (2011), 250 with 15 aircraft (none combat-capable) and three helicopters.

Economy

In 2016 agriculture accounted for 27·4% of GDP, industry 30·0% and services 42·6%.

Overview

Mauritania is a developing economy with limited agrarian resources but extensive mineral deposits (especially gold and copper) and rich fishing grounds. Mining accounted for nearly 60% of exports and represented 20% of GDP in 2015. Fishing generated 7% of GDP in 2014. In Oct. 2013 the country took an important step towards protecting its fishery resources by signing a partnership agreement with the European Union.

Oil was discovered in 2001, with production in the country's main oilfield starting five years later. However, technical difficulties have resulted in output falling from 75,000 bbls per day in early 2006 to 5,100 by the end of 2015. Oil's contribution to GDP declined from 7·3% in 2008 to 2·0% in 2014 and deposits are expected to run out by 2025.

The economy was hit hard by the global recession in 2008, aggravated by a fuel crisis and a military coup that led to the suspension of donor assistance. However, despite a severe drought in 2011, GDP growth rebounded to average 4·1% per year from 2012–15. The business climate weakened though, with the country ranked 168th out of 193 nations in the World Bank's 2014 *Doing Business* report, down from 159th in 2012. While some progress has been made in alleviating poverty, it remains a significant problem. According to the United Nations *Human Development Index 2015*, Mauritania remained below the sub-Saharan average.

Long-term challenges include diversifying the economy away from mining and cutting dependence on food imports. The government must also aim to improve job security, with over half of all jobs considered vulnerable.

Currency

The monetary unit is the *ouguiya* (MRU), which is divided into five *khoums*. A new ouguiya was introduced on 1 Jan. 2018: 1 new ouguiya = 10 old ouguiya. Inflation was 1·5% in 2016 and 2·3% in 2017. Total money supply in April 2013 was 38,963m. ouguiya and gold reserves 12,000 troy oz. Foreign exchange reserves were US$813m. in Dec. 2016.

Budget

Revenues were 474·9bn. ouguiya in 2013 and expenditures 444·9bn. ouguiya.

The standard rate of VAT is 16%.

Performance

The economy grew by 0·4% in 2015, 1·8% in 2016 and 3·5% in 2017. Mauritania's total GDP in 2017 was US$5·0bn.

Banking and Finance

The Central Bank (created 1973) is the bank of issue (*Governor*, Abdel Aziz Ould Dahi). In 2010 there were ten commercial banks. Bank deposits totalled 35·2bn. ouguiya in 2009.

In 2010 external debt totalled US$2,461m., equivalent to 67·0% of GNI.

Energy and Natural Resources

Environment

In 2011 carbon dioxide emissions from the consumption of energy were the equivalent of 0·5 tonnes per capita.

Electricity

Installed capacity was estimated at 196,000 kW in 2011. Production in 2011 was 744m. kWh; consumption per capita was 232 kWh.

Oil and Gas

Oil was discovered off the coast of Mauritania in 2001. Production began in Feb. 2006. For the rest of 2006 production averaged 31,000 bbls a day but by 2012 it had declined to 7,000 bbls a day.

In Feb. 2018 the governments of Mauritania and Senegal signed an agreement pledging co-operation over the Greater Tortue Complex gas field, which straddles their maritime boundary. The Complex's reserves are estimated at 700bn. cu. metres, with production expected to begin in 2021.

Minerals

There are reserves of copper, gold, phosphate, gypsum, platinum and diamonds. Iron ore, 11·2m. tonnes of which were mined in 2006, accounts for about 69% of exports. Prospecting licences have also been issued for diamonds.

Agriculture

Only 1% of the country receives enough rain to grow crops, so agriculture is mainly confined to the south, in the Senegal River Valley. In 2007 the agricultural population numbered 1,598,000 of whom 674,000 were economically active. There were an estimated 450,000 ha. of arable land in 2007 and 12,000 ha. of permanent crops. Production (2006, in 1,000 tonnes): sorghum, 84; rice, 70; dates, 20; maize, 17; dry beans, 10 (estimate); dry peas, 10 (estimate); yams, 3 (estimate); millet, 2; potatoes, 2 (estimate).

Herding is the main occupation of the rural population and accounted for 11% of GDP in 2005. In 2006–07 there were 17·15m. sheep and goats; 1·37m. cattle; 1·35m. camels; 4·3m. chickens (estimate).

Forestry

There were 0·23m. ha. of forests in 2015, chiefly in the southern regions, where wild acacias yield the main product, gum arabic. In 2011, 1·88m. cu. metres of roundwood were cut.

Fisheries

Total catch in 2015 was 403,776 tonnes (more than double the 2008 total), of which 96% came from marine waters. Mauritania's coastal waters are among the world's most abundant fishing areas, earning it significant amounts of hard currency through licensing agreements. The fishing sector accounts for an estimated 20% of Mauritania's national budget.

Industry

Manufacturing accounted for 7·9% of GDP in 2012. Manufactures include fish processing, chemicals and plastics, building materials, and paper and packaging materials.

Labour

The labour force in 2013 was 1,242,000 (885,000 in 2003). 55·0% of the population aged 15–64 was economically active in 2013. In the same year 31·1% of the population was unemployed.

Slavery was only abolished in Mauritania in 1981, making it the last country where it was still being practised legally. Nonetheless, the practice remains widespread and there were 0·15m. people living in slavery according to the Walk Free Foundation's 2013 *Global Slavery Index*.

International Trade

In Feb. 1989 Mauritania signed a treaty of economic co-operation with the four other Maghreb countries—Algeria, Libya, Morocco and Tunisia.

Imports and Exports

In 2007 imports were valued at US$1,376·6m. and exports at US$1,302·4m. Main imports in 2007 were petroleum products (30·6% of total imports), foodstuffs and capital goods. Main exports in 2007 were iron ore (41·3% of total exports), oil and fish products. Main import suppliers in 2007 were France (15·9%), Brazil (6·0%), China (5·8%) and Belgium (4·5%). Principal export markets in 2006 were China (26·3%), Italy (11·8%), France (10·2%) and Belgium (6·8%).

Communications

Roads

There were about 11,066 km of roads in 2006, of which 26·8% were paved.

Rail

A 704 km railway links Zouérate with the port of Point-Central, 10 km south of Nouâdhibou, and is used primarily for iron ore exports. In 2008 it carried 11·1m. tonnes of freight and 100,000 passengers.

Civil Aviation

There are international airports at Nouakchott, Nouâdhibou and Néma. In 2012 scheduled airline traffic of Mauritania-based carriers flew 2·0m. km; passenger-km totalled 160·8m. in the same year. Mauritania Airlines International, founded in 2010, is the national flag carrier.

Shipping

The major ports are at Point-Central (for mineral exports), Nouakchott and Nouâdhibou.

Telecommunications

In 2013 there were 54,000 active fixed telephone subscriptions and 3,988,000 active mobile phone subscriptions (102·5 per 100 persons). In the same year an estimated 6·2% of the population were internet users.

Social Institutions

Out of 178 countries analysed in the 2017 *Fragile States Index*—a list published jointly by the Fund for Peace and *Foreign Policy* magazine—Mauritania was ranked the 28th most vulnerable to conflict or collapse. The index is based on 12 indicators of state vulnerability across social, political and economic categories.

Justice

There are courts of first instance at Nouakchott, Atar, Kaédi, Aïoun el Atrouss and Kiffa. The Appeal Court and Supreme Court are situated in Nouakchott. Islamic jurisprudence was adopted in 1980.

The population in penal institutions in 2012 was 1,602 (45 per 100,000 of national population).

Education

Basic education is compulsory for all children between the ages of six and 14. In 2007 there were 483,776 pupils and 11,379 teaching staff in primary schools, 102,130 secondary level pupils with 3,843 teaching staff and 11,794 tertiary level students with (2006) 353 academic staff. The University of Nouakchott, founded in 1981, is the leading tertiary education institution. Adult literacy rate in 2008 was 57%.

Public expenditure on education came to 2·8% of GNI in 2006.

Health

In 2006 there were four hospital beds per 10,000 persons. There were 445 physicians, 93 dentistry personnel, and 2,303 nursing and midwifery personnel in 2009.

In *Water: At What Cost? The State of the World's Water 2016*, WaterAid reported that 42·1% of the population does not have access to safe water.

Religion

Over 99% of Mauritanians are Sunni Muslim, mainly of the Qadiriyah sect.

Culture

World Heritage Sites

Mauritania has two sites on the UNESCO World Heritage List: Banc d'Arguin National Park (inscribed on the list in 1989), a coastal park of dunes and swamps; and the Ancient Ksour of Ouadane, Chinguetti, Tichitt and Oualata (1996), Islamic trading and religious centres in the Sahara.

Press

In 2008 there were four daily newspapers with a circulation of 9,000.

Tourism

There were 29,000 foreign tourists in 2007–08; spending by tourists in 2007 totalled US$39m.

Diplomatic Representatives

Of Mauritania in the United Kingdom (Carlyle House, 235–237 Vauxhall Bridge Rd, London, SW1V 1EJ)
    Ambassador: Dr Isselkou Ahmed Izid Bih Neye.

Of the United Kingdom in Mauritania
    Ambassador: Thomas Reilly (resides in Rabat, Morocco).

Of Mauritania in the USA (2129 Leroy Pl., NW, Washington, D.C., 20008)
    Ambassador: Mohamedoun Daddah.

Of the USA in Mauritania (No. 350, Avenue Al Quds, Nouadhibou Road, Nouakchott)
    Ambassador: Michael J. Dodman.

Of Mauritania to the United Nations
    Ambassador: Sidi Mohamed Taleb Amar.

Of Mauritania to the European Union
    Ambassador: Abdallahi Bah Nagi Kebd.

Further Reading

Belvaud, C., *La Mauritanie.* 1992
National Statistical Office: Office National de la Statistique, BP240, Nouakchott.
Website (French only): http://www.ons.mr

Mauritius

Republic of Mauritius

Capital: Port Louis
Population projection, 2020: 1·27m.
GNI per capita, 2017: (PPP$) 20,189
HDI/world rank, 2017: 0·790/65
Internet domain extension: .mu

Island	Area in sq. km	2011 census population
Mauritius	1,865	1,196,383
Rodrigues	104	40,434
Outer Islands	71	274
Total	2,040	1,237,091

Key Historical Events

The uninhabited, volcanic Indian Ocean island of Mauritius was visited by Middle Eastern and Malay seafarers from the ninth century and documented by Portuguese mariners between 1507 and 1512. In 1598 the Dutch admiral, Wybrand van Warwyck, established a settlement and named the island after Prince Maurice of Nassau—the *stadthouder*, or military chief, of Holland and Zeeland. The colony proved a useful staging post as the Dutch developed trade links with India, Southern Africa and the East Indies, but it was abandoned in favour of the Cape Colony in 1710. By then the Dutch settlers had cleared tracts of forest, introduced new species and, as of 1662, had caused the extinction of the island's iconic flightless bird, the dodo.

French traders, who had established settlements in Madagascar, Bourbon (Réunion) and Rodrigues, landed on Mauritius in 1715 and renamed it Ile de France. Mahé de La Bourdonnais, who arrived in 1735, began cultivating sugarcane using East African slave labour. He developed Port Louis as the capital of the island and several other French possessions to the east. British forces took control of Ile de France in 1810 and it became an important link in a secure shipping route between Britain and India. While English was adopted as the language of education, French cultural influences persisted.

Following the abolition of slavery in 1835, hundreds of thousands of indentured labourers were transported from India. By 1850 the island was the British Empire's largest producer of sugarcane but workers faced harsh conditions. Malaria, cholera and rabies were widespread and cyclones frequently destroyed housing and crops. Mauritius acquired its first elected legislative council in 1885, although voting restrictions ensured the plantation owners remained dominant. Although the indentured labour system was abolished in 1910, working conditions were slow to improve. In 1936 the Mauritian Labour Party (MLP), founded by Dr Maurice Cure, began to organize protests and strikes on the plantations.

A new constitution in 1947 paved the way for internal self-government ten years later. In 1958 the MLP, led by Dr Seewoosagur Ramgoolam, won the first elections under universal suffrage. Full independence was achieved after Ramgoolam led the MLP, allied to the Independence Forward Bloc and the Muslim Action Committee, to victory at the 1967 election. On 12 March 1968 Mauritius became independent within the British Commonwealth and Ramgoolam was sworn in as the first prime minister.

In the 1970s and 1980s sugar exports declined and the country became a centre for textile production and upmarket tourism. Mauritius achieved republic status in March 1992 and secured a seat on the United Nations Security Council for the first time in 2000.

Navin Ramgoolam (son of Dr Seewoosagur Ramgoolam) served as prime minister between 1995 and 2000 and won further terms at the head of the Social Alliance in 2005 and 2010. He oversaw a period of economic expansion driven by tourism, international finance and business outsourcing. He was succeeded as premier in 2014 by Sir Anerood Jugnauth, who had previously served as prime minister from 1983–95 and 2000–03. He was also president from 2003 until 2012.

Territory and Population

Mauritius, the main island, lies 800 km (500 miles) east of Madagascar. Rodrigues is 560 km (350 miles) to the east. The outer islands are Agalega and the St Brandon Group. Area and population:

Port Louis is the capital (128,851 inhabitants in 2010). Other towns: Beau Bassin-Rose Hill, 110,687; Vacoas-Phoenix, 106,404; Curepipe, 84,487; Quatre Bornes, 77,495. In 2010, 58·3% of the population were rural. July 2017 population estimate: 1,264,887.

The UN gives a projected population for 2020 of 1·27m.

The majority of the population are Indo-Mauritians (people of Indian descent). The Afro-Mauritians are the other major group, and there are also Sino-Mauritians (of Chinese origin) and Franco-Mauritians (descendants of French settlers). Mauritius has no indigenous population.

The official language is English, although French is widely used. Creole and Bhojpuri are vernacular languages.

Social Statistics

2007: births, 17,034 (rate of 13·5 per 1,000 population); deaths, 8,498 (6·7 per 1,000); marriages, 11,547 (9·2 per 1,000); divorces, 1,302 (1·0 per 1,000). In 2007 the suicide rate was 15·7 per 100,000 population among men and 4·7 per 100,000 among women. Population growth rate in 2007 was 0·65%. In 2007 the most popular age range for marrying was 25–29 for males and 20–24 for females. Life expectancy at birth in 2007 was 69·1 years for males and 75·8 for females. Infant mortality, 2010, 13 per 1,000 live births; fertility rate, 2007, 2·0 births per woman.

Climate

The sub-tropical climate is humid. Most rain falls in the summer. Rainfall varies between 40" (1,000 mm) on the coast to 200" (5,000 mm) on the central plateau, though the west coast only has 35" (875 mm). Mauritius lies in the cyclone belt, whose season runs from Nov. to April, but is seldom affected by intense storms. Port Louis, Jan. 73°F (22·8°C), July 81°F (27·2°C). Annual rainfall 40" (1,000 mm).

Constitution and Government

The present constitution came into effect on 12 March 1968 and was amended on 12 March 1992. The head of state is the *President*, elected by a simple majority of members of the National Assembly. The role of *President* is largely a ceremonial one.

The 69-seat *National Assembly* consists of 62 elected members (three each for the 20 constituencies of Mauritius and two for Rodrigues) and seven additional seats in order to ensure a fair and adequate representation of each community within the Assembly. The government is headed by the *Prime Minister* and a Council of Ministers. Elections are held every five years on the basis of universal adult suffrage.

National Anthem

'Glory to thee, Motherland'; words by J. G. Prosper, tune by P. Gentille.

Recent Elections

Parliamentary elections were held on 10 Dec. 2014. The Alliance of the People/Alliance Lepep (consisting of the Militant Socialist Movement, the Mauritian Social Democrat Party and the Muvman Liberater) won 51 seats with 49·8% of votes cast, followed by the Alliance of

Palgrave Macmillan (ed.), *The Statesman's Yearbook 2020*,
https://doi.org/10.1057/978-1-349-95940-2_126

Unity and Modernity (consisting of the Mauritius Labour Party and the Mauritian Militant Movement) with 16 seats (38·5% of votes cast) and the Rodrigues People's Organisation with two seats (1·1%). Turnout was 74·1%.

Current Government

Acting President: Barlen Vyapoory (Militant Socialist Movement; since 23 March 2018).

Vice President: Vacant.

In Feb. 2019 the cabinet was composed as follows:

Prime Minister, and Minister of Home Affairs, External Communications and National Development Unit, and Finance and Economic Development: Pravind Kumar Jugnauth; b. 1961 (Militant Socialist Movement; sworn in 23 Jan. 2017).

Minister Mentor, Minister of Defence and Minister for Rodrigues: Sir Anerood Jugnauth.

Deputy Prime Minister, and Minister of Energy and Public Utilities: Ivan Collendavelloo. *Vice Prime Minister, and Minister of Local Government and Outer Islands, and Gender Equality, Child Development and Family Welfare:* Fazila Jeewa-Daureeawoo.

Minister of Agro-Industry and Food Security: Mahen Kumar Seeruttun. *Arts and Culture:* Prithvirajsing Roopun. *Business, Enterprise and Co-operatives:* Soomilduth Bholah. *Civil Service and Administrative Affairs:* Eddy Boissézon. *Education and Human Resources, Tertiary Education and Scientific Research:* Leela Devi Dookun-Luchoomun. *Financial Services and Good Governance:* Dharmendar Sesungkur. *Foreign Affairs, Regional Integration and International Trade:* Vishnu Lutchmeenaraidoo. *Health and Quality of Life:* Dr Mohammad Anwar Husnoo. *Housing and Lands:* Mahen Jhugroo. *Industry, Commerce and Consumer Protection:* Ashit Kumar Gungah. *Justice, Human Rights and Institutional Reforms, and Attorney General:* Maneesh Gobin. *Labour, Industrial Relations, Employment and Training:* Soodesh Satkam Callichurn. *Ocean Economy, Marine Resources, Fisheries, Shipping and Outer Islands:* Premdut Koonjoo. *Public Infrastructure and Land Transport:* Nandcoomar Bodha. *Social Integration and Economic Empowerment:* Alain Wong. *Social Security, National Solidarity, Environment and Sustainable Development:* Etienne Sinatambou. *Technology, Communication and Innovation:* Yogida Sawmynaden. *Tourism:* Anil Kumarsingh Gayan. *Youth and Sports:* Stephan Toussaint.

Government Website: http://www.govmu.org

Current Leaders

Pravind Jugnauth

Position
Prime Minister

Introduction
Pravind Jugnauth assumed office on 23 Jan. 2017 after his father, Anerood Jugnauth, resigned the premiership after decades at the forefront of national political life. Anerood Jugnauth's decision to appoint his son as his successor received widespread criticism, with the leader of the opposition (and former prime minister) Navin Ramgoolam claiming that the Jugnauth family was turning the island nation into a 'banana republic'.

Early Life
Pravind Jugnauth was born on 25 Dec. 1961 in Vacoas-Phoenix. He graduated in law from the University of Buckingham in the UK, then studied for a master's degree in the same subject at Aix-Marseille University in France. He worked for a short time as a barrister in the UK.

Jugnauth first gained political office in 1996 as a councillor in Vacoas-Phoenix. By 1999 he was deputy leader of his father's Militant Socialist Movement (MSM) and in 2000 he was appointed minister of agriculture. He subsequently became leader of the MSM and held various ministerial portfolios including finance, technology, communications and innovation. He also served as deputy and vice prime minister.

He became embroiled in controversy after purchasing a private clinic from his sister in 2010 while minister of finance. An investigation into the sale concluded that the government had overpaid for the facility and had also purchased certain buildings that did not actually exist. Jugnauth was initially found guilty of corruption but his conviction was overturned on appeal.

Career in Office
On taking office, Jugnauth faced domestic and international condemnation given the apparent nepotistic nature of his appointment. In June 2017 the United Nations General Assembly voted to refer a controversial colonial dispute between Mauritius and the United Kingdom over territorial control of the Chagos Islands in the Indian Ocean to the International Court of Justice. The ICJ hearing began in Sept. 2018, at which the UK government apologized for the eviction of the islanders in the 1970s to make way for a US military base but disputed the court's right to issue an opinion on the question of sovereignty.

Defence

The Police Department is responsible for defence. Its strength was (2008) 8,000. In addition there is a special mobile paramilitary force of approximately 1,400, a Coast Guard of about 700 and a helicopter unit of about 100.

Defence expenditure totalled US$83m. in 2013 (US$63 per capita), representing 0·7% of GDP.

Economy

Agriculture accounted for 3·7% of GDP in 2014, industry 22·3% and services 74·0%.

Overview

After 2000 the economy was hit badly by the loss of long-standing preferential trading agreements for its sugar and textiles industries. Nonetheless, sugarcane production remains important, occupying 90% of cultivable land and accounting for 15% of total exports, despite a reduction in output in 2015. Also, the revised Cotonou Agreement signed with the European Union in 2010 has restored some of the sector's trading privileges.

The government has sought to diversify the economy, which remained resilient in the wake of the 2008 global financial crisis. Annual GDP growth averaged 4% between 2007 and 2015, among the highest rates in Africa. Over two-thirds of GDP is now generated by the services sector; financial services alone had attracted over US$1bn. worth of investment by 2012, and tourism is also important.

The country benefits from advanced digital infrastructure and state-of-the-art telecommunications. Over 32,000 companies are located on the island, taking advantage of government incentives and the geographical proximity to India. Fishing and fish processing are emerging industries that offer potential for future growth.

Mauritius was ranked the 15th freest country in the world in the 2016 Heritage Foundation Index, having slipped from eighth place in 2013.

Currency

The unit of currency is the *Mauritius rupee* (MUR) of 100 *cents*. There are Bank of Mauritius notes, cupro-nickel coins, nickel-plated steel coins and copper-plated steel coins. Inflation was 1·0% in 2016 and 3·7% in 2017. In July 2005 foreign exchange reserves were US$1,365m. and gold reserves totalled 62,000 troy oz. Total money supply was Rs 22,646m. in June 2005.

Budget

Budgetary central government revenue in 2012 was Rs 75,047m. (Rs 70,432m. in 2011); expenditure was Rs 71,509m. (Rs 72,147m. in 2011). Principal sources of revenue, 2012: taxes on goods and services, Rs 47,511m.; taxes on income, profits and capital gains, Rs 14,634m.; grants, Rs 2,398m. Main items of expenditure in 2012 were: grants, Rs 25,228m.; compensation of employees, Rs 20,871m.; interest, Rs 10,129m. Since 2015 the fiscal year, which was previously the calendar year, has run from 1 July–30 June.

VAT is 15%.

Performance

Real GDP growth was 3·6% in 2015 and 3·8% in 2016 and 2017. Total GDP in 2017 was US$13·3bn. Thanks to tourism, financial services and the traditional industries of sugar and textiles, Mauritius is now one of Africa's richest and most developed countries.

Banking and Finance

The Bank of Mauritius (founded 1967) is the central bank. The *Governor* is Yandraduth Googoolye. In 2015 there were 23 banks and one development bank. Since 2005 there has been no distinction between onshore and offshore banks. Non-bank financial intermediaries are the Post Office Savings Bank, the State Investment Corporation Ltd, the Mauritius Leasing Company, the National Mutual Fund, the National Investment Trust and the National Pension Fund. Other financial institutions are the Mauritius Housing Company and the Development Bank of Mauritius. External debt was US$1,916m. at June 2015. There is also a stock exchange in Port Louis.

Energy and Natural Resources

Environment
Carbon dioxide emissions from the consumption of energy were the equivalent of 3·7 tonnes per capita in 2011.

Electricity
Installed capacity was 0·74m. kW in 2011. Production (2011) was 2·73bn. kWh. Consumption per capita in 2011 was 2,211 kWh.

Agriculture
57,081 ha. were planted with sugarcane in 2014; yield in 2014 was 4,044,422 tonnes. Main secondary crops (2014, in 1,000 tonnes): potatoes, 19; pineapples, 11; tomatoes, 11; bananas, 9; tea, 8; pumpkins and squash, 8; cucumbers, 7; onions, 6. In 2012 there were an estimated 76,000 ha. of arable land and 4,000 ha. of permanent cropland; in 2014, 17,183 ha. were irrigated.

Livestock, 2014: cattle, 6,041; goats and sheep, 29,280; pigs, 17,511.

Livestock products (2014) in tonnes: beef and veal, 2,001; pork and pork products, 557; milk, 5,000; eggs, 11,500.

Forestry
The total forest area was 39,000 ha. in 2015 (19% of the land area). In 2011 timber production totalled 11,000 cu. metres.

Fisheries
The catch in 2015 totalled 15,505 tonnes, exclusively sea fish.

Industry

Manufacturing includes: sugar, textile products, footwear and other leather products, diamond cutting, jewellery, furniture, watches and watchstraps, sunglasses, plastic ware, chemical products, electronic products, pharmaceutical products, electrical appliances, ship models and canned food. There were six sugar mills in 2010 producing 452,473 tonnes of sugar. Production figures for other leading commodities in 2010: beer and stout, 36·8m. litres; animal feeds, 175,250 tonnes; molasses, 145,752 tonnes.

Labour
The labour force in 2013 was 588,000 (535,000 in 2003). 64·6% of the population aged 15–64 was economically active in 2013. In the same year 8·0% of the population was unemployed.

International Trade

Imports and Exports
Imports in 2010 were valued at Rs 135,394m. and exports at Rs 69,556m. In 2010 imports valued at Rs 30,239m. came from India, Rs 18,027m. from China, Rs 11,393m. from South Africa and Rs 10,992m. from France. Exports valued at Rs 13,542m. went to the UK in 2010, Rs 10,376m. to France, Rs 6,229m. to the USA and Rs 4,052m. to Spain.

Major imports in 2010 included machinery and transport equipment, Rs 27,451m.; mineral fuels, lubricants and related products, Rs 25,929m.; manufactured goods (paper, textiles, iron and steel), Rs 25,901m.; food and live animals, Rs 24,006m. Major exports (2010) included articles of apparel and clothing, Rs 23,004m.; fish and fish preparations, Rs 7,782m.; sugar, Rs 7,740m.; textile yarns, fabrics and finished articles, Rs 1,899m.

Communications

Roads
In 2007 there were 75 km of motorway, 962 km of main roads and 991 km of secondary and other roads. In 2007 there were 144,400 passenger cars, 142,600 motorcycles and mopeds, 40,900 lorries and vans, and 4,000 buses and coaches. In 2007 there were 140 deaths as a result of road accidents.

Civil Aviation
In 2012, 2,690,869 passengers were handled at Sir Seewoosagur Ramgoolam International Airport. The national carrier is Air Mauritius, which is partly state-owned. In 2013 it carried 1,318,000 passengers (1,196,000 on international flights).

Shipping
A free port was established at Port Louis in Sept. 1991. In 2013 Port Louis handled 6,761,000 tonnes of cargo. In Jan. 2014 there were six ships of 300 GT or over registered, totalling 61,000 GT.

Telecommunications
In 2012 there were 349,100 main (fixed) telephone lines; mobile phone subscriptions numbered 1,486,000 in 2012 (119·9 per 100 persons). Communication with other parts of the world is by satellite and microwave links. In 2013, 39·0% of the population were internet users. In June 2012 there were 324,000 Facebook users.

Social Institutions

Out of 178 countries analysed in the 2017 *Fragile States Index*—a list published jointly by the Fund for Peace and *Foreign Policy* magazine—Mauritius was ranked the joint 30th least vulnerable (along with Lithuania) to conflict or collapse. The index is based on 12 indicators of state vulnerability across social, political and economic categories.

Justice
There is an Ombudsman. The death penalty was abolished for all crimes in 1995.

The population in penal institutions in Jan. 2013 was 2,663 (202 per 100,000 of national population).

Education
The adult literacy rate in 2009 was estimated at 87·9% (90·6% among males and 85·3% among females). Primary and secondary education is free, primary education being compulsory. Almost all children aged 5–11 years attend schools. In 2008 there were 114,007 pupils in 286 primary schools and 112,995 pupils in 175 secondary schools in the island of Mauritius, and 5,015 pupils in 13 primary schools and 3,508 in six secondary schools in Rodrigues. In 2007, 3,945 teachers were enrolled for training at the Mauritius Institute of Education.

In 2007–08 there were 7,794 students and 487 academic staff at the University of Mauritius.

In 2007–08 total expenditure on education came to 3·2% of GDP and 12·7% of total government spending.

Health
In 2013 there were 351 dentists, 3,879 nurses and midwives, 460 pharmacists and 2,046 physicians. There were 4,271 hospital beds in 2013 with a provision of 35 beds per 10,000 inhabitants.

In *Water: At What Cost? The State of the World's Water 2016*, WaterAid reported that 0·1% of the population does not have access to safe water.

Religion
In 2010 an estimated 56·4% of the population were Hindus according to the Pew Research Center's Forum on Religion & Public Life, with 25·3% Christians (mainly Catholics) and 16·7% Muslims. In Feb. 2019 there was one Roman Catholic cardinal.

Culture

World Heritage Sites
Mauritius has two sites on the UNESCO World Heritage List: Aapravasi Ghat (inscribed on the list in 2006), the site where the modern indentured labour diaspora began; and Le Morne cultural landscape (2008), a rugged mountain jutting into the Pacific Ocean that was used by runaway slaves (maroons) as a shelter in the 18th and 19th centuries.

Press
In 2008 there were four daily papers with a combined circulation of 110,000, plus 16 non-dailies.

Tourism

In 2010 there were 934,827 visitors (including 605,401 from Europe and 226,207 from other African countries), bringing in US$1,227m. in tourist revenue.

Festivals

Independence Day is marked by an official celebration at the Champ de Mars racecourse on 12 March. The Hindu festival of Cavadee is celebrated by the Tamil community at the beginning of the year; the major three-day Hindu festival of Maha Shivarati takes place around Feb./March. Other Hindu festivals include Diwali and Ganesh Chaturhi, which is celebrated around Aug./Sept. The Spring Festival is celebrated on the eve of the Chinese New Year; Ougadi, the Telegu new year, is celebrated in March; the Tamil new year, Varusha Pirappu, takes place in April. Muslim festivals include Eid al-Fitr and Eid al-Adha. On 9 Sept. pilgrims visit the grave of the 19th century missionary Père Laval who is regarded as a national saint.

Diplomatic Representatives

Of Mauritius in the United Kingdom (32–33 Elvaston Pl., London, SW7 5NW)
  High Commissioner: Girish Nunkoo.

Of the United Kingdom in Mauritius (7th Floor, Cascades Building, Edith Cavell St., PO Box 1063, Port Louis)
  High Commissioner: Keith Allan.

Of Mauritius in the USA (1709 N. St., NW, Washington, D.C., 20036)
  Ambassador: Sooroojdev Phokeer.

Of the USA in Mauritius (4th Floor, Rogers House, John Kennedy Ave., Port Louis)
  Ambassador: David Reimer.

Of Mauritius to the United Nations
  Ambassador: Jagdish Dharamchand Koonjul.

Of Mauritius to the European Union
  Ambassador: Haymandoyal Dillum.

Further Reading

Central Statistical Information Office. *Bi-annual Digest of Statistics.*
Bowman, L. W., *Mauritius: Democracy and Development in the Indian Ocean.* 1991
Tang, Vanessa T., Shaw, Timothy M. and Holden, Merle G. (eds), *Development and Sustainable Growth of Mauritius.* 2018
National Statistical Office: Central Statistics Office, LIC Building, President John Kennedy St., Port Louis.
Website: http://statsmauritius.govmu.org

Mexico

Estados Unidos Mexicanos (United Mexican States)

Capital: Mexico City
Population projection, 2020: 133·87m.
GNI per capita, 2017: (PPP$) 16,944
HDI/world rank, 2017: 0·774/74
Internet domain extension: .mx

Key Historical Events

The first settlers of the New World arrived in Alaska from Asia about 15,000 years ago. From about 2000 BC the people of Ancient Mexico began to settle in villages and to cultivate maize and other crops. From about 1000 BC the chief tribes were the Olmec on the Gulf Coast, the Maya in the Yucatán peninsula and modern day Chiapas, the Zapotecs and Mixtecs in Oaxaca, the Tarascans in Michoacán and the Toltecs in central Mexico. One of the largest and most powerful cities in ancient Mexico was Teotihuacán, which in the 6th century AD was one of the six largest cities in the world. By the time the Spanish *conquistadores* arrived in 1519, the dominant people were the Mexica, more commonly known as the Aztecs, whose capital Tenochtitlán became Mexico City after the conquest.

Hernán Cortés landed on the Gulf Coast in 1519 and by 1521 his small band of Spaniards, assisted by an army of indigenous peoples, had destroyed the Aztec state. The land conquered by Cortés was named New Spain, and was ruled by the Spanish Crown for three centuries. The new colony was the personal property of the King, whose representative, the Viceroy, was charged with extracting the maximum income for the Crown. The mainstays of the colonial economy were silver and land. Rich silver mines were discovered and large estates (*haciendas*) were formed. Spain controlled trade with the colonies and discouraged manufacturing to maximize profits for the King. Acapulco became Spain's sole port for trade with Asia.

One early result of the Conquest was a collapse of the indigenous population caused by social dislocation and European diseases. In 1520 the native population was probably 20m. By 1540 it had fallen to 6·5m. and by 1650 the figure was just over 1m.

The beginning of the end of Spanish rule came on 16 Sept. 1810 when the parish priest of Dolores, Miguel Hidalgo y Costilla, called for independence (the 'grito de Dolores') and led a popular army against the Spaniards. Hidalgo's revolution failed as did that of the insurrectionary José María Morelos y Pavón. Independence from Spain was declared in the Plan of Iguala on 24 Feb. 1821 when Agustín de Iturbide proclaimed himself Emperor of Mexico. He ruled for two years.

There followed half a century of coups and counter coups. Spain invaded Tampico in 1829. Texas declared secession in 1836. The Mexican dictator Antonio López de Santa Anna marched north but was defeated by the Texans. France invaded Veracruz in 1838 (the 'Pastry War'). In 1846 the USA declared war on Mexico. The war was ended in 1848 by the Treaty of Guadalupe which forced Mexico to cede a huge swathe of its territory to the USA. Liberals and conservatives fought the War of the Reform from 1858–61. The liberal government of Benito Juárez abolished the *fueros* (clerical and military privileges) and hereditary titles, confiscated the church's lands and attempted far-reaching land reform. This was followed by the French Intervention (1862–67), which installed the Habsburg Archduke Maximilian of Austria as Emperor of Mexico. The French were resisted stubbornly by President Juárez but the republicans were forced into the resource-poor and sparsely populated north. Napoleon III withdrew his troops from Mexico in 1867 despite a pledge to support Maximilian, allowing the republicans to take back the country virtually unopposed. Asserting Mexico's independence, Juárez ordered the execution of Maximilian.

From 1876–1910, a period known as the *porfiriato*, Mexico was ruled (with one interlude from 1880–84) by Gen. Porfirio Díaz. Díaz imposed a degree of stability and order. He encouraged foreign investment, which funded a rapid expansion of the railways and an export-led economic boom. The economy faltered in the first decade of the 20th century. Díaz was deposed in 1911 by Francisco Madero, whose Plan of San Luís Potosí launched the Mexican Revolution.

Madero was deposed and assassinated in 1913. There followed a civil war fought by the armies of Venustiano Carranza, Pancho Villa and Emiliano Zapata. A new constitution was written in 1917. Zapata was ambushed and killed in 1919 and Carranza was assassinated in 1920. Villa retired the same year but was assassinated in 1923.

In the 1920s Mexico was ruled by Alvaro Obregón and Plutarco Elías Calles. Obregón's assassination in 1928 led to the formation of the Natural Revolutionary Party (PRN), later the Institutional Revolutionary Party (PRI), which ruled Mexico for the rest of the century. Lázaro Cárdenas was president from 1934–40. He nationalized the oil industry and accelerated the distribution of land to the peasantry. The election of Miguel Alemán in 1946 was opposed unsuccessfully by the last military rebellion in Mexico's history. Alemán's pro-business administration began a long period of relative economic prosperity, the 'Mexican Miracle'.

However, by the late 1960s the Mexican economic and political system was under increasing strain. An uprising led by students ended in a bloody massacre in the Tlatelolco district of Mexico City in 1968. Successive PRI presidents made gestures towards democratization and effective opposition gradually developed. Financial and economic problems in the 1980s increased the pressure on the political system. The crisis came in 1988 when the PRI candidate, Carlos Salinas de Gortari, defeated Cuauhtémoc Cárdenas, son of the former president and candidate of the Democratic Revolutionary Party (PRD), in a rigged election. Salinas took Mexico into the North American Free Trade Agreement (NAFTA) with the USA and Canada in 1992. Salinas's choice as the PRI's presidential candidate, Luís Donaldo Colosio, was assassinated in Tijuana on 23 March 1994. He was replaced by Ernesto Zedillo. In the same year the Zapatista National Liberation Army (EZLN) led an uprising in Chiapas, which is ongoing.

In 2000 Vicente Fox Quesada of the National Action Party (PAN) was elected to the presidency. Fox attempted to address two key issues: Mexico's economic and financial weakness and illegal migration to the USA. However, the PRI majority in Congress blocked Fox's fiscal reforms and the Bush administration in the USA was unwilling to support Fox's proposal to liberalize immigration. In the 2006 presidential elections the conservative Felipe Calderón and the socialist Andrés Manuel López Obrador both claimed victory. Calderón was finally declared the winner more than two months after the election, but in Nov. López Obrador proclaimed himself the 'legitimate' president. Nevertheless, Calderón was sworn in as scheduled in Dec. 2006. The PRI returned to power when Enrique Peña Nieto was elected president in 2012. US President Donald Trump pledged during his 2016 election campaign to build a wall along the US–Mexican border to deter illegal immigration and to make Mexico pay for it, but Peña Nieto strongly resisted any such suggestion.

Territory and Population

Mexico is bounded in the north by the USA, west and south by the Pacific Ocean, southeast by Guatemala, Belize and the Caribbean Sea, and northeast by the Gulf of Mexico. It comprises 1,964,375 sq. km (758,464 sq. miles), including uninhabited islands (5,127 sq. km) offshore.

Population at recent censuses: 2000, 97,483,412; 2005, 103,263,388; 2010, 112,336,538 (57,481,307 females). Population density (2010), 57·2 per sq. km. Dec. 2012 population estimate, 115,639,915. 78·1% of the population were urban in 2011.

The UN gives a projected population for 2020 of 133·87m.

Area, population and capitals of Ciudad de México and the 31 states:

© Springer Nature Limited 2020
Palgrave Macmillan (ed.), *The Statesman's Yearbook 2020*,
https://doi.org/10.1057/978-1-349-95940-2_127

	Area (Sq. km)	Population (2010 census)	Capital
Ciudad de México	1,486	8,851,080	Mexico City
Aguascalientes	5,618	1,184,996	Aguascalientes
Baja California	71,446	3,155,070	Mexicali
Baja California Sur	73,922	637,026	La Paz
Campeche	57,924	822,441	Campeche
Chiapas	73,289	4,796,580	Tuxtla Gutiérrez
Chihuahua	247,455	3,406,465	Chihuahua
Coahuila de Zaragoza	151,563	2,748,391	Saltillo
Colima	5,625	650,555	Colima
Durango	123,451	1,632,934	Victoria de Durango
Guanajuato	30,608	5,486,372	Guanajuato
Guerrero	63,621	3,388,768	Chilpancingo de los Bravo
Hidalgo	20,847	2,665,018	Pachuca de Soto
Jalisco	78,599	7,350,682	Guadalajara
México	22,357	15,175,862	Toluca de Lerdo
Michoacán de Ocampo	58,643	4,351,037	Morelia
Morelos	4,893	1,777,227	Cuernavaca
Nayarit	27,815	1,084,979	Tepic
Nuevo Léon	64,220	4,653,458	Monterrey
Oaxaca	93,793	3,801,962	Oaxaca de Juárez
Puebla	34,290	5,779,829	Heroica Puebla de Zaragoza
Querétaro Arteaga	11,684	1,827,937	Santiago de Querétaro
Quintana Roo	42,361	1,325,578	Chetumal
San Luis Potosí	60,983	2,585,518	San Luis Potosí
Sinaloa	57,377	2,767,761	Culiacán Rosales
Sonora	179,503	2,662,480	Hermosillo
Tabasco	24,738	2,238,603	Villahermosa
Tamaulipas	80,175	3,268,554	Ciudad Victoria
Tlaxcala	3,991	1,169,936	Tlaxcala de Xicohténcatl
Veracruz-Llave	71,820	7,643,194	Xalapa-Enríquez
Yucatán	39,612	1,955,577	Mérida
Zacatecas	75,539	1,490,668	Zacatecas
Total	1,959,248	112,336,538	

The *de facto* official language is Spanish, the mother tongue of over 93% of the population (2005), but there are some indigenous language groups (of which Náhuatl, Maya, Zapotec, Otomi and Mixtec are the most important) spoken by 6,011,202 persons over five years of age (census 2005).

The populations (2010 census) of the largest cities (250,000 and more) were:

Mexico City	8,555,272
Ecatepcec de Morelos	1,655,015
Guadalajara	1,495,182
Heroica Puebla de Zaragoza	1,434,062
Juárez	1,321,004
Tijuana	1,300,983

(continued)

León de los Aldama	1,238,962
Zapopan	1,142,483
Monterrey	1,135,512
Ciudad Nezahualcoyotl	1,104,585
Chihuahua	809,232
Naucalpan de Juárez	792,211
Mérida	777,615
San Luis Potosí	722,772
Aguascalientes	722,250
Hermosillo	715,061
Saltillo	709,671
Mexicali	689,775
Culiacán Rosales	675,773
Guadalupe	673,616
Acapulco de Juárez	673,479
Tlalnepantla	653,410
Cancún	628,306
Santiago de Querétaro	626,495
Chimalhuacan	612,383
Torreón	608,836
Morelia	597,511
Reynosa	589,466
Tlaquepaque	575,942
Tuxtla Gutiérrez	537,102
Durango	518,709
Toluca de Lerdo	489,333
Ciudad López Mateos	489,160
Cuautitlán Izcalli	484,573
Apodaca	467,157
Heroica Matamoros	449,815
San Nicolás de los Garza	443,273
Veracruz	428,323
Xalapa-Enríquez	424,755
Tonala	408,759
Mazatlán	381,583
Irapuato	380,941
Nuevo Laredo	373,725
Xico	356,352
Villahermosa	353,577
Escobedo	352,444
Celaya	340,387
Cuernavaca	338,650
Tepic	332,863
Ixtapaluca	322,271
Ciudad Victoria	305,155
Ciudad Obregón	298,625
Tampico	297,284
Villa Nicolás Romero	281,799
Ensenada	279,765
San Francisco Coacalco	277,959
Ciudad Santa Catarina	268,347
Uruapan	264,439
Gómez Palacio	257,352
Los Mochis	256,613
Pachuca de Soto	256,584
Oaxaca de Juárez	255,029
Soledad Díez Gutiérrez	255,015

Social Statistics

Statistics for calendar years:

	Births	Deaths	Marriages	Divorces
2005	2,567,906	495,240	595,713	70,184
2006	2,505,939	494,471	586,978	72,396
2007	2,655,083	514,420	595,209	77,255
2008	2,636,110	539,530	589,352	81,851
2009	2,577,214	564,673	558,913	84,302

Rates per 1,000 population, 2009: births, 18·0; deaths, 4·9. In 2013 the most popular age range for marrying was 20–24 for both males and females. Infant mortality was 14·7 per 1,000 live births in 2009. Life expectancy at birth in 2013 was 75·1 years for males and 79·8 years for females. Annual population growth rate, 2005–10, 1·8%. Fertility rate, 2013, 2·2 births per woman (less than half the number in the late 1970s). Much of the population still lives in poverty, with the gap between the modern north and the underdeveloped south constantly growing.

Climate

Latitude and relief produce a variety of climates. Arid and semi-arid conditions are found in the north, with extreme temperatures, whereas in the south there is a humid tropical climate, with temperatures varying with altitude. Conditions on the shores of the Gulf of Mexico are very warm and humid. In general, the rainy season lasts from May to Nov. Mexico City, Jan. 55°F (12·9°C), July 61°F (16·2°C). Annual rainfall 31" (787·6 mm). Guadalajara, Jan. 63°F (17·0°C), July 72°F (22·1°C). Annual rainfall 39" (987·6 mm). La Paz, Jan. 62°F (16·8°C), July 86°F (29·9°C). Annual rainfall 7" (178·3 mm). Mazatlán, Jan. 68°F (20·0°C), July 84°F (29·0°C). Annual rainfall 32" (822·1 mm). Mérida, Jan. 73°F (23·0°C), July 81°F (27·4°C). Annual rainfall 39" (990·0 mm). Monterrey, Jan. 58°F (14·3°C), July 83°F (28·1°C). Annual rainfall 23" (585·4 mm). Puebla de Zaragoza, Jan. 52°F (11·4°C), July 62°F (16·9°C). Annual rainfall 36" (900·8 mm).

Constitution and Government

A new constitution was promulgated on 5 Feb. 1917 and has occasionally been amended. Mexico is a representative, democratic and federal republic, comprising 31 states and a federal district, each state being free and sovereign in all internal affairs, but united in a federation established according to the principles of the Fundamental Law. The head of state and supreme executive authority is the *President*, directly elected for a non-renewable six-year term. The constitution was amended in April 2001, granting autonomy to 10m. indigenous peoples. The amendment was opposed both by the National Congress of Indigenous Peoples and Zapatista rebels who claimed it would leave many indigenous people worse off.

There is complete separation of legislative, executive and judicial powers (Art. 49). Legislative power is vested in a *Congress of the Union* of two chambers, a *Chamber of Deputies* and a *Senate*. The Chamber of Deputies consists of 500 members directly elected for three years, 300 of them from single-member constituencies and 200 chosen under a system of proportional representation. In 1990 Congress voted a new Electoral Code. This established a body to organize elections (IFE), an electoral court (TFE) to resolve disputes, new electoral rolls and introduce a voter's registration card. Priests were enfranchised in 1991.

The Senate comprises 128 members. In each of the 31 states and the Federal District the party coming first wins two seats and the party coming second wins one seat, making 96 in total. An additional 32 seats are filled through proportional representation from national party lists. Members of both chambers are not immediately re-eligible for election. Congress sits from 1 Sept. to 31 Dec. each year; during the recess there is a permanent committee of 15 deputies and 14 senators appointed by the respective chambers.

National Anthem

'Mexicanos, al grito de guerra' ('Mexicans, at the war-cry'); words by F. González Bocanegra, tune by Jaime Nunó.

Government Chronology

Presidents since 1940. (MORENA = National Regeneration Movement; PAN = National Action Party; PRI = Institutional Revolutionary Party)

1940–46	PRI	Manuel Ávila Camacho
1946–52	PRI	Miguel Alemán Valdés
1952–58	PRI	Adolfo Ruiz Cortines
1958–64	PRI	Adolfo López Mateos
1964–70	PRI	Gustavo Díaz Ordaz Bolaños
1970–76	PRI	Luis Echeverría Álvarez
1976–82	PRI	José López Portillo y Pacheco
1982–88	PRI	Miguel de la Madrid Hurtado
1988–94	PRI	Carlos Salinas de Gortari
1994–2000	PRI	Ernesto Zedillo Ponce de León
2000–06	PAN	Vicente Fox Quesada
2006–12	PAN	Felipe de Jesús Calderón Hinojosa
2012–18	PRI	Enrique Peña Nieto
2018–	MORENA	Andrés Manuel López Obrador

Recent Elections

In the presidential election 1 July 2018, Andrés Manuel López Obrador of the Movimiento Regeneración Nacional (National Regeneration Movement/MORENA) won 53·2% of the vote, Ricardo Anaya of the Partido Acción Nacional (National Action Party/PAN) 22·3%, José Antonio Meade of the ruling Partido Revolucionario Institucional (Institutional Revolutionary Party/PRI) 16·4%, Jaime Rodríguez Calderón (ind.) 5·2% and Margarita Zavala (ind.) 0·1%. Turnout was 63·4%. Some observers suggested that irregularities and violence tarnished the election.

Elections for the Congress of the Union were held on 1 July 2018. In elections to the Chamber of Deputies, the National Regeneration Movement won 191 of the 500 seats, the National Action Party 81, the Labor Party 61, the Socialist Encounter Party 56, the Institutional Revolutionary Party 45, the Citizens' Movement 27, the Party of the Democratic Revolution 21, the Ecologist Green Party of Mexico 16 and the New Alliance Party 2. In elections to the Senate the National Regeneration Movement won 55 seats, the National Action Party 23, the Institutional Revolutionary Party 13, the Party of the Democratic Revolution 8, the Social Encounter Party 8, the Citizens' Movement 7, the Ecologist Green Party of Mexico 7, the Labour Party 6 and the New Alliance Party 1.

Current Government

President: Andrés Manuel López Obrador; b. 1953 (National Regeneration Movement; sworn in 1 Dec. 2018).

In Feb. 2019 the government comprised:

Secretary of the Interior: Olga Sánchez Cordero. *Foreign Affairs:* Marcelo Ebrard Casaubón. *Finance and Public Credit:* Carlos Urzúa Macías. *Welfare:* María Luisa Albores. *Labour and Social Protection:* Luisa María Alcalde. *Economy:* Graciela Márquez Colín. *Health:* Jorge Alcocer Varela. *National Defence:* Luis Crescencio Sandoval. *Environment and Natural Resources:* Josefa González Blanco Ortiz Mena. *Energy:* Rocío Nahle García. *Agriculture and Rural Development:* Victor Villalobos. *Communication and Transport:* Javier Jiménez Espriú. *Civil Service:* Irma Eréndira Sandoval. *Agrarian, Territorial and Urban Development:* Román Meyer Falcón. *Public Education:* Esteban Moctezuma Barragán. *Tourism:* Miguel Torruco Marqués. *Culture:* Alejandra Frausto Guerrero. *Chief of Staff of the Presidency:* Alfonso Romo Garza.

President of the Chamber of Deputies: Porfirio Muñoz Ledo.

Presidency Website: http://www.presidencia.gob.mx

Current Leaders

Andrés Manuel López Obrador

Position
President

Introduction
Andrés Manuel López Obrador became president in 2018. He was previously mayor of Mexico City.

Early Life
López Obrador was born on 13 Nov. 1953 in Tabasco state, Mexico. He attended the National Autonomous University of Mexico in Mexico City between 1973 and 1976, studying public administration and political science.

In 1977 he became director of the National Indigenous Institute of Tabasco. In 1983 he was appointed head of the Institutional Revolutionary Party in Tabasco, but transferred his allegiance to the Democratic Current in 1986, which evolved into the Party of the Democratic Revolution (PRD). During this period his profile grew as he encouraged workers of the state oil organization, Pemex, to negotiate for better wages and other benefits.

López Obrador unsuccessfully contested the governorship of Tabasco in 1988 and 1994. Between 1996 and 1999 he was the PRD's president before being elected mayor of Mexico City in 2000. His tenure saw an extension of welfare programmes—particularly for the elderly, the disabled and single mothers—and various development and reconstruction projects, although he struggled to tackle the high crime rate. When impeachment charges were brought against him in 2004, there were protests supporting him in Mexico City before the case was dismissed the following year.

López Obrador ran in the 2006 presidential election after leaving the mayoral office but lost by a narrow margin. He was again unsuccessful in the 2012 election, prompting him to challenge the legality of the vote count. In 2014 he founded the left-wing National Regeneration Movement (MORENA) and successfully contested the next presidential poll on 1 July 2018.

Career in Office
López Obrador had capitalized on the unpopularity of his predecessor, Enrique Peña Nieto, whose tenure became mired in corruption allegations and he was sworn into office on 1 Dec. 2018. He must tackle rising violence and organized crime, particularly drug trafficking and associated homicides. On 5 Jan. 2019 he announced tax cuts and wage increases in a bid to promote business growth and boost productivity.

Defence

Conscription is for 12 months. In 2013 defence expenditure totalled US$5,775m. (US$50 per capita), representing 0·5% of GDP.

Army

Enlistment into the regular army is voluntary, but there is also one year of conscription (four hours per week) by lottery. Strength of the regular army (2011) 212,000. Reserve forces (National Military Service conscripts) numbered 87,344 in 2011. In addition there is a rural defence militia of 18,000.

Navy

The Navy is primarily equipped and organized for offshore and coastal patrol duties. It includes seven frigates. Naval Aviation, 1,250 strong, operated seven combat-capable aircraft in 2011.

Naval personnel in 2011 totalled 56,500, including Naval Aviation. In addition there were 19,500 marines.

Air Force

The Air Force had (2011) a strength of 11,750 with 76 combat-capable aircraft, including PC-7s and F-5Es.

Economy

Agriculture accounted for 3·3% of GDP in 2013, industry 34·5% and services 62·2%.

Overview

Mexico, an upper-middle income country with average gross per capita income in 2015 of US$10,058, has the second largest economy in Latin America (by GDP) after Brazil. The economy has traditionally benefited from its proximity to the USA, providing cheap labour for US firms. Mexico's share of US manufacturing imports increased from 10% in 2010 to 13% in 2015, aided by declining unit labour costs. However, a reliance on the US market (which absorbs 80% of all Mexican exports) leaves the country susceptible to any downturn in US economic fortunes. Bilateral trade doubled between 2003 and 2015, although the election in 2016 of Donald Trump as US president was expected to strain relations between the two nations, given his intention to erect a wall along their shared border and to seek financial recompense from the Mexican government. Nonetheless, there was little evidence of an immediate, large-scale economic impact over the course of 2017.

Mexico is the world's tenth largest producer of oil and is heavily dependent on the sector, which provides over 10% of state revenues annually. In Dec. 2013 the government announced plans to attract private investment into the industry, ending the state's 75-year monopoly in hydrocarbon production and distribution. Earthquakes and hurricanes in Aug. and Sept. 2017 briefly disrupted production.

The economy expanded by an annual average of 4·1% between 2010 and 2012 but growth has slowed since then, averaging 2·6% per year between 2013 and 2016. This was in part the result of weaknesses in industrial production in the USA, along with a reduction in oil production, financial market volatility and dwindling hydrocarbon revenues as a result of the global collapse in oil prices. Future significant expansion will require growth in private consumption and investment and a rebound in oil prices.

Nonetheless, public sector revenue in 2015 grew owing to a sharp increase in income taxes, reflecting the deferred impact of tax reforms enacted at the end of 2013. Public debt, meanwhile, grew from 43% of GDP in 2012 to over 58% in 2016. The current account deficit (measuring 4% of GDP in 2015) has been almost entirely covered by foreign direct investment inflows. Mexico also benefits from a flexible credit line with the IMF.

An ambitious structural reform agenda has been in place since 2012, bolstering expectations of a positive medium-term outlook. In particular, energy sector reforms have opened the hydrocarbons and electricity industries to private capital, while the telecommunications sector has been subjected to greater competition. The oil sector reforms allow for a boost in US–Mexican energy trade relations, but their success will also depend on rising oil prices and the maintenance of cordial relations between the two countries during the Trump presidency. In March 2018 Mexico and ten other countries bordering the Pacific (although not the USA) signed the Comprehensive and Progressive Agreement for Trans-Pacific Partnership.

Tackling poverty remains a significant challenge. Around 11% of the population lives below the poverty threshold as defined by the World Bank, while in 2015 the government estimated that 33% lived in 'moderate' poverty and 9% in 'extreme' poverty. Furthermore, there is a high degree of income inequality—the World Bank estimates that the richest 10% of the population earns over 40% of national income. According to the OECD, Mexico is second only to Chile in Latin America in terms of economic disparity between the extremely poor and extremely rich. Corruption, crime and the weak rule of law hamper growth prospects, with drug-related violence a particular concern.

Currency

The unit of currency is the *Mexican peso* (MXN) of 100 *centavos*. A new peso was introduced on 1 Jan. 1993: 1 new peso = 1,000 old pesos. The peso was devalued by 13·94% in Dec. 1994. Foreign exchange reserves were US$82,023m. and gold reserves 288,000 troy oz in Sept. 2009. Inflation rates (based on OECD statistics):

2008	2009	2010	2011	2012	2013	2014	2015	2016	2017
5·1%	5·3%	4·2%	3·4%	4·1%	3·8%	4·0%	2·7%	2·8%	6·0%

Total money supply in Aug. 2009 was 1,391·5bn. new pesos.

Budget

In 2013 revenues were 2,703·6bn. new pesos and expenditures 3,097·7bn. new pesos.

VAT is 16% (11% in the frontier region).

Performance

Real GDP growth rates (based on OECD statistics):

2008	2009	2010	2011	2012	2013	2014	2015	2016	2017
0·9%	−5·0%	5·1%	3·7%	3·4%	1·6%	2·8%	3·3%	2·6%	2·3%

In 2017 total GDP was US$1,149·9bn.

Banking and Finance

The Bank of Mexico, established 1 Sept. 1925, is the central bank of issue (*Governor*, Alejandro Díaz de León). It gained autonomy over monetary policy in 1993. Exchange rate policy is determined jointly by the bank and the Finance Ministry. Banks were nationalized in 1982, but in May 1990 the government approved their reprivatization. The state continues to have a majority holding in foreign trade and rural development banks. In 1999 Congress approved the removal of regulations limiting foreign holdings to 49%.

In 2007 there were 38 commercial banks (including seven development banks) and 81 representative offices of foreign banks. Mexico's largest banks are BBVA Bancomer with assets of US$85·0bn. in June 2009, followed by Banamex with assets of US$74·9bn. and Santander with assets of US$48·7bn. Most of Mexico's leading banks are now foreign-owned.

Foreign debt was US$200,081m. in 2010, representing 19·5% of GNI.

Mexico received US$29·7bn. worth of foreign direct investment in 2017, down from a record US$48·5bn. in 2013.

There is a stock exchange in Mexico City.

Energy and Natural Resources

Environment

Mexico's carbon dioxide emissions from the consumption of energy in 2011 were the equivalent of 3·9 tonnes per capita.

Electricity

Installed capacity, 2011, 61·6m. kW. Output in 2011 was 295·84bn. kWh and consumption per capita 2,474 kWh. In 2010 there were two nuclear reactors in operation.

Oil and Gas

Oil production in 2013, 141·8m. tonnes. Mexico had reserves in 2012 amounting to 11·4bn. bbls. Revenues from oil exports provide about a third of all government revenues. Natural gas production was 58·5bn. cu. metres in 2012 with 400bn. cu. metres in proven reserves.

Minerals

Output, 2014 unless otherwise specified (in 1,000 tonnes): iron ore, 16,628; lignite (2007), 10,456; salt, 10,251; gypsum and anhydrite, 5,495; coal (estimate), 4,733; sulphur, 603; copper, 515; barite (estimate), 420; zinc, 321; lead, 314; manganese, 235; feldspar, 151; silver, 2·3m. kg; gold, 32,808 kg. Mexico is the biggest producer of silver in the world.

Agriculture

In 2007 Mexico had an estimated 24·5m. ha. of arable land and around 2·4m. ha. of permanent cropland. There were 5·4m. ha. of irrigated land in 2006. There were 238,830 tractors and some 22,500 harvester-threshers in 2007. In 2007 agriculture, fishing and forestry contributed 3·6% of GDP. In 1992 the Mexican constitution was amended to permit the voluntary privatization of *ejidos*, communal land in which each member farms an independent plot, to combat the low productivity resulting from the fragmentation of farming units, some 58% of which were less than 5 ha. in 1991.

Sown areas, 2013 (in 1,000 ha.) included: maize, 7,096; beans, 1,755; sorghum, 1,689; sugarcane, 783; coffee beans, 700; wheat, 634; oranges, 321; barley, 297; mangoes and guavas, 199; coconuts (estimate), 176; soybeans, 157. Production in 2013 (in 1,000 tonnes): sugarcane, 61,182; maize, 22,664; sorghum, 6,308; oranges, 4,410; wheat, 3,357; tomatoes, 3,283; chillies and green peppers, 2,294; lemons and limes, 2,139; bananas, 2,128; mangoes and guavas, 1,902; potatoes, 1,630; avocados, 1,468; beans, 1,295; onions, 1,270.

Livestock (2013): cattle, 32·40m.; pigs, 16·20m.; goats, 8·66m.; sheep, 8·50m.; horses (estimate), 6·36m.; mules (estimate), 3·29m.; asses (estimate), 3·28m.; chickens, 524m. Production, 2013 (in 1,000 tonnes): beef and veal, 1,807; pork and pork products, 1,284; horse (estimate), 84; lamb and mutton, 58; goat meat, 40; chicken meat, 2,808; cow's milk, 10,966; goat's milk, 152; eggs, 2,516; cheese (estimate), 156; honey, 57.

Forestry

Forests extended over 66·04m. ha. in 2015, representing 34% of the land area, containing pine, spruce, cedar, mahogany, logwood and rosewood. There are 14 forest reserves (nearly 0·8m. ha.) and 47 national park forests of 0·75m. ha. Timber production was 43·71m. cu. metres in 2011.

Fisheries

The total catch in 2015 was 1,467,203 tonnes, of which 1,315,787 tonnes came from sea fishing.

Industry

The leading companies by market capitalization in Mexico in May 2018 were: América Móvil, S.A.B.. de C.V. (a mobile phone company), US$57·8bn.; Femsa (a beverages company), US$31·2bn; and Grupo de México, S.A.B.. de C.V. (metallurgical business), US$22·6bn.

In 2013 the manufacturing industry provided 17·5% of GDP. Output (in 1,000 tonnes): cement (2008), 37,139; petrol (2007), 21,563; distillate fuel oil (2007), 18,011; residual fuel oil (2007), 17,252; crude steel (2009), 13,957; sugar (2012–13), 6,975; pig iron (2009), 3,925; wheat flour (2012), 3,224; cigarettes (2012), 36·2bn. units; soft drinks (2012), 19,502·0m. litres; beer (2007), 8,051·0m. litres. Car production has increased from 994,000 in 1999 to 1,810,000 in 2012.

Labour

The labour force in 2013 was 54,476,000 (41,785,000 in 2003). 64·9% of the population aged 15–64 was economically active in 2013. Of those in employment in 2013, 62·4% worked in services, 23·6% in industry and 13·4% in agriculture. In the same year 37·2% of the labour force was female. In 2011, 45·0% of the labour force had a secondary education as the highest level and 23·3% had a tertiary education. Unemployment rate, Dec. 2018, 3·6% (up slightly from 3·4% in 2017 as a whole). The daily minimum wage for general workers at Jan. 2014 ranged from 63·77 new pesos to 67·29 new pesos.

Mexico had 0·1m. people living in slavery according to the Walk Free Foundation's 2013 *Global Slavery Index*.

International Trade

In Sept. 1991 Mexico signed the free trade Treaty of Santiago with Chile, envisaging an annual 10% tariffs reduction from Jan. 1992. The North American Free Trade Agreement (NAFTA), between Canada, Mexico and the USA, was signed on 7 Oct. 1992 and came into effect on 1 Jan. 1994. A free trade agreement was signed with Costa Rica in March 1994. Some 8,300 products were free from tariffs, with others to follow over ten years. The Group of Three (G3) free trade pact with Colombia and Venezuela came into effect on 1 Jan. 1995. A free trade agreement was signed with the European Union in 1999.

Imports and Exports

Trade for calendar years in US$1m.:

	2003	2004	2005	2006	2007
Imports c.i.f.	170,546	196,809	221,819	256,086	281,927
Exports f.o.b.	164,907	187,980	214,207	249,961	271,821

Of imports in 2007, 49·6% came from the USA, 10·6% from China, 5·8% from Japan, 4·5% from South Korea and 3·8% from Germany. Of exports in 2007, 82·2% went to the USA, 2·4% to Canada, 1·5% to Germany, 1·4% to Spain and 1·1% to Colombia.

The in-bond (*maquiladora*) assembly plants generate the largest flow of foreign exchange. Although originally located along the US border when the programme was introduced in the 1960s, they are now to be found in almost every state. In 2009 there were over 5,200 'foreign to Mexico' manufacturing companies, employing more than 1·6m. people. Manufactured goods account for 90% of trade revenues.

Communications

Roads

The total road length in 2007 was 360,075 km, of which 6,565 km were motorways, 40,631 km other main roads, 73,874 km secondary roads and 239,005 km other roads. In 2005 there were 14,074,669 passenger cars, 7,111,172 trucks and vans and 264,726 buses and coaches. There were 5,398 fatalities as a result of road accidents in 2007.

Rail

The National Railway, *Ferrocarriles Nacionales de México*, was split into four companies in 1995 as a preliminary to privatization. It ceased operations in 1999. The rail network comprises 26,717 km of 1,435 mm gauge. In 2010 railways carried 40·2m. passengers and 104·6m. tonnes of freight. There is a 202 km metro in Mexico City with 11 lines. There are light rail lines in Guadalajara (24 km) and Monterrey (32 km).

Civil Aviation

There are an international airport at Mexico City (Benito Juárez) and 55 other international and 29 national airports. A new international airport serving Mexico City was under construction and scheduled to open in 2020, but was abandoned following a referendum in Oct. 2018. Holding the referendum had been a key campaign promise of incoming president Andrés Manuel López Obrado, who had been elected in July 2018 and was to take office in Dec. of that year. Each of the larger states has a local airline which links it with main airports. The national carrier is Aeroméxico, which was privatized in 1988 and in 2014 carried 17,190,000 passengers (11,894,000 on domestic flights). The second largest carrier is Volaris, a low-cost carrier founded in 2004. Two former flag carriers, Aviacsa and Mexicana, both ceased operations in 2010 (in April and Aug. respectively). In 2012 Mexico City handled 29,491,553 passengers (19,678,042 on domestic flights). Cancún was the second busiest airport for passengers in 2012, with 14,555,184 (9,855,771 on international flights). Guadalajara handled 7,448,214 passengers (4,966,411 on domestic flights).

Shipping

Mexico's most important ports are Altamira and Veracruz on the Gulf coast, and Lázaro Cárdenas and Manzanillo on the Pacific coast. The busiest port is Lázaro Cárdenas, which handled 34·91m. tonnes of cargo in 2013 (17·96m. tonnes loaded and 16·95m. tonnes discharged).

In Jan. 2014 there were 65 ships of 300 GT or over registered, totalling 824,000 GT.

Telecommunications

Telmex (Teléfonos de México), a former state-run company privatized in 1991 and a wholly owned subsidiary of América Móvil, is the leading provider of fixed-line telephone services and broadband, with around 80% of the market. In 2011 there were 19,997,000 fixed telephone lines and 94,583,000 mobile phone subscribers (792·4 per 1,000 persons). The leading mobile phone operator is Telcel (part of América Móvil), which has about 70% of the market. In 2013 there were 13,539,000 fixed internet subscriptions and 16,865,000 wireless broadband subscriptions. In Dec. 2011 there were 31·0m. Facebook users.

Social Institutions

Out of 178 countries analysed in the 2017 *Fragile States Index*—a list published jointly by the Fund for Peace and *Foreign Policy* magazine—Mexico was ranked the 88th most vulnerable to conflict or collapse. The index is based on 12 indicators of state vulnerability across social, political and economic categories.

Justice

Magistrates of the Supreme Court are appointed for six years by the President and confirmed by the Senate; they can be removed only on impeachment. The courts include the Supreme Court with 21 magistrates, 12 collegiate circuit courts with three judges each and nine unitary circuit courts with one judge each, and 68 district courts with one judge each.

The penal code of 1 Jan. 1930 abolished the death penalty, except for the armed forces. Mexico abolished the death penalty for all crimes in Dec. 2005—the last execution had been in 1961.

There were a record 31,174 murders in 2017 (a rate of 25 per 100,000 population), up from 8,867 in 2007. The population in penal institutions in June 2013 was 246,226 (210 per 100,000 of national population). Following the collapse of the main Colombian drug cartels in the 1990s, Mexican cartels are estimated to control 70% of illicit foreign drugs entering the US market. In 2009, 9,616 people died in drug-related killings in Mexico.

Mexico was ranked 93rd of 102 countries for criminal justice and 82nd for civil justice in the 2015 World Justice Project *Rule of Law Index*, which provides data on how the rule of law is experienced by the general public across eight categories.

Education

Adult literacy was 93·4% in 2009 (male, 94·9%; female, 92·1%). Primary and secondary education is free and compulsory, and secular, although religious instruction is permitted in private schools.

In 2013 there were 4,772,612 children with 188,789 teaching staff in pre-primary schools, 14,837,204 pupils with 535,814 teachers in primary schools and 12,467,278 pupils with 694,325 teachers in secondary schools. There were 3,300,348 students in tertiary education in 2013 with 364,641 academic staff.

In 2006 public expenditure on education came to 4·8% of GDP and 22·0% of total government spending (the highest share in the OECD).

Health

There were 4,456 hospitals in 2015, with a total provision of 183,527 beds. In 2013 there were 256,281 physicians, 310,441 nursing and midwifery personnel, and 14,494 dentistry personnel. In 2008 Mexico spent 5·9% of its GDP on health. In 2006, 70% of Mexicans were considered overweight (one of the highest rates in the world) and 30% obese (having a body mass index over 30).

In *Water: At What Cost? The State of the World's Water 2016*, WaterAid reported that 3·9% of the population does not have access to safe water.

Welfare

As of 1 July 1997 all workers had to join the private insurance system, while the social insurance system was being phased out. At retirement, employees covered by the social insurance system before 1997 can choose to receive benefits from either the social insurance system or the private insurance system. The official retirement age is 65 years but to be eligible, a pensioner must have paid 1,250 weeks of contributions. The guaranteed minimum pension in 2011 was 2,095·99 new pesos.

Unemployment benefit exists under a labour law which requires employers to pay a dismissed employee a lump sum equal to three months' pay plus 20 days' pay for each year of service. Social security pays an unemployment benefit of between 75% and 95% of the old-age pension for unemployed persons aged 60 to 64.

Religion

In 2010 there were an estimated 96·3m. Roman Catholics according to the Pew Research Center's Forum on Religion & Public Life, giving Mexico the second largest Catholic population after Brazil. In Feb. 2019 there were seven cardinals. The Church is separated from the State, and the constitution of 1917 provided strict regulation of this and all other religions. In 1991 Congress approved an amendment to the 1917 constitution permitting the recognition of churches by the state, the possession of property by churches and the enfranchisement of priests. Church buildings remain state property. There were also an estimated 9·4m. Protestants and 2·0m. other Christians in 2010. A further 5·3m. people in 2010 were religiously unaffiliated.

Culture

World Heritage Sites

Mexico has 35 UNESCO World Heritage sites. They are (with year entered on list): the Sian Ka'an nature reserve; the historic centre of Mexico City and the canal and island network of Xochimilco; Puebla's historic centre; the pre-Hispanic city of Teotihuacán, now a major archaeological site; the Historic Centre of Oaxaca and archaeological site of Monte Alban; and Palenque—lying in the foothills of the Altos de Chiapas, the Maya ruins of Palenque are surrounded by waterfalls, rainforest and fauna (all 1987); the historic town of Guanajuato and adjacent disused silver mines; and the pre-Hispanic city of Chichen-Itza, Yucatan (both 1988); the historic centre of Morelia, on the southern Pacific coast (1991); the pre-Hispanic city of El Tajin, Veracruz (1992); the El Vizcaino whale sanctuary; the historic centre of Zacatecas, once a major silver mining centre; and the Sierra de San Francisco rock paintings (all 1993); the 14 early 16th-century monasteries on Popocatépetl, to the southeast of Mexico City (1994); the Maya town of Uxmal, Yucatán, with its preserved pyramids and sculptures; and the historic monuments zone of Querétaro (both 1996); the Hospicio (Hospice) Cabañas, Guadalajara (1997); the historic monuments zone of Tlacotalpan; and the archaeological zone of Paquimé, Casas Grandes in Chihuahua (both 1998); the historic fortified town of Campeche; and Xochicalco's archaeological monuments zone, Morelos state (both 1999); the Ancient Maya City of Calakmul, Campeche (2002 and 2014); the Franciscan Missions in the Sierra Gorda of Querétaro (2003); Luis Barragán House and Studio in Mexico City (2004); the islands and protected areas of the Gulf of California (2005 and 2007); the Agave landscape and ancient industrial facilities of Tequila (2006); the Central University City Campus of the Universidad Nacional Autónoma de México (2007); the Monarch Butterfly Biosphere Reserve (2008); the fortified town of San Miguel and Sanctuary of Jesús Nazareno de Atotonilco (2008); Camino Real de Tierra Adentro, also known as the Silver Route, between Mexico City and the USA; the Prehistoric Caves of Yagul and Mitla in the Central Valley of Oaxaca (both 2010); El Pinacate and Gran Desierto de Altar Biosphere Reserve (2013), a 714,566 ha. site comprising various desert and volcanic landforms; the Aqueduct of Padre Tembleque Hydraulic System (2015); Archipiélago de Revillagigedo (2016); and Tehuacán-Cuicatlán Valley: originary habitat of Mesoamerica (2018).

Press

In 2012 there were 510 daily newspapers with an estimated circulation of 6·4m. The three leading dailies are *El Gráfico* (average daily circulation of 641,000 in 2013), *Metro* (456,000) and *El Universal* (324,000).

Tourism

There were 21·45m. non-resident tourists in 2009 (excluding same-day visitors), making Mexico the tenth most popular tourist destination; spending amounted to US$11,275m. in 2009.

Diplomatic Representatives

Of Mexico in the United Kingdom (16 St George St., London, W1S 1FD)
    Ambassador: Julián Ventura Valero.

Of the United Kingdom in Mexico (Rio Lerma 71, Colonia Cuauhtémoc, 06500 Mexico City)

Ambassador: Corin Robertson.

Of Mexico in the USA (1911 Pennsylvania Ave., NW, Washington, D.C., 20006)
    Ambassador: Gerónimo Gutiérrez Fernández.

Of the USA in Mexico (Paseo de la Reforma 305, Colonia Cuauhtémoc, 06500 Mexico City)
    Ambassador: Vacant.
    Chargé d'Affaires a.i.: John S. Creamer.

Of Mexico to the United Nations
    Ambassador: Juan Ramón de la Fuente Ramírez.

Of Mexico to the European Union
    Ambassador: Mauricio Escanero.

Further Reading

Instituto Nacional de Estadística, Geografía e Informática. *Anuario Estadístico de los Estados Unidos Mexicanos. Mexican Bulletin of Statistical Information.* Quarterly.
Bethell, L. (ed.) *Mexico since Independence.* 1992
Castañeda, Jorge G., *Mañana Forever?: Mexico and the Mexicans.* 2011
Hamnett, Brian R., *A Concise History of Mexico.* 1999
Krauze, E., *Mexico, Biography of Power: A History of Modern Mexico, 1810–1996.* 1997
Levy, Daniel C., *Mexico: The Struggle for Democratic Development.* 2006
Mentinis, Mihalis, *Zapatistas: The Chiapas Revolt and What it Means for Radical Politics.* 2006
Philip, G. (ed.) *The Presidency in Mexican Politics.* 1991
Randall, Laura, *Changing Structure of Mexico: Political, Social and Economic Prospects.* 2005
Ruíz, R. E., *Triumphs and Tragedy: a History of the Mexican People.* 1992
Snyder, Richard, *Politics After Neoliberalism: Reregulation in Mexico.* 2006
Whiting, V. R., *The Political Economy of Foreign Investment in Mexico: Nationalism, Liberalism, Constraints on Choice.* 1992
National Statistical Office: Instituto Nacional de Estadística, Geografía e Informática (INEGI), Av. Héroe de Nacozari Sur 2301, Fracc. Jardines del Parque, CP 20276 Aguascalientes. *President:* Julio Santaella.
Website (Spanish only): http://www.inegi.org.mx

Micronesia

Federated States of Micronesia

Capital: Palikir
Population projection, 2020: 108,000
GNI per capita, 2017: (PPP$) 3,843
HDI/world rank, 2017: 0·627/131
Internet domain extension: .fm

Key Historical Events

Spain acquired sovereignty over the Caroline Islands in 1886 but sold the archipelago to Germany in 1899. Japan occupied the Islands at the beginning of the First World War and in 1921 they were mandated to Japan by the League of Nations. Captured by Allied Forces in the Second World War, the Islands became part of the UN Trust Territory of the Pacific Islands created on 18 July 1947 and administered by the USA. The Federated States of Micronesia came into being on 10 May 1979. American trusteeship was terminated on 3 Nov. 1986 by the UN Security Council and on the same day Micronesia entered into a 15-year Free Association with the USA. An amended 20-year Compact of Free Association was signed into law on 17 Dec. 2003, guaranteeing US$1·8bn. to Micronesia in grants for a government trust fund.

Territory and Population

The Federated States lie in the North Pacific Ocean between 137° and 163° E, comprising 607 islands with a total land area of 701 sq. km (271 sq. miles). The 2010 census population was 102,843; density, 147 per sq. km.

The UN gives a projected population for 2020 of 108,000.

In 2011, 22·8% of the population lived in urban areas.

The areas and populations of the four major groups of island states (east to west) are as follows:

State	Area (sq. km)	Population (2010 census)	Headquarters
Kosrae	110	6,616	Tofol
Pohnpei	345	36,196	Kolonia
Chuuk	127	48,654	Weno
Yap	119	11,377	Colonia

Kosrae consists of a single island. Its main town is Lelu (2,160 inhabitants in 2010). Pohnpei comprises a single island (covering 334 sq. km) and eight scattered coral atolls. Kolonia (6,074 inhabitants in 2010) was the national capital until 1989. The new capital, Palikir (6,647 inhabitants in 2010), lies approximately 10 km southwest in the Palikir valley. Chuuk consists of 542 islets in a 7,190 sq. km reef-fringed lagoon (36,152 inhabitants in 2010); the state also includes coral atolls (12,502 inhabitants in 2010), the most important being the Mortlock Islands. The chief town is Weno (13,856 inhabitants in 2010). Yap comprises a main group of four islands (covering 100 sq. km with 7,371 inhabitants in 2010) and 15 outer islands (4,006 inhabitants), the main ones being Ulithi and Woleai. Colonia is its chief town (3,126 inhabitants in 2010).

English is used in schools and is the official language. Trukese, Pohnpeian, Yapese and Kosrean are also spoken.

Social Statistics

2009 estimates: births, 2,800; deaths, 700. Rates, 2009 estimates (per 1,000 population): birth, 25; death, 6. Infant mortality rate (2010), 34 per 1,000 live births. 2013 life expectancy, 68·0 years for men and 69·9 years for women. Population growth rate, 2005–10, −0·5%; fertility rate, 2013, 3·3 births per woman.

Climate

Tropical, with heavy year-round rainfall, especially in the eastern islands, and occasional typhoons (June–Dec.). Kolonia, Jan. 80°F (26·7°C), July 79°F (26·1°C). Annual rainfall 194" (4,859 mm).

Constitution and Government

Under the Constitution founded on 10 May 1979, there is an executive presidency and a 14-member *National Congress*, comprising ten members elected for two-year terms from single-member constituencies of similar electorates, and four members elected one from each State for a four-year term by proportional representation. The *Federal President* and *Vice-President* first run for the Congress before they are elected by members of Congress for a four-year term.

National Anthem

'Patriots of Micronesia'; words anonymous, tune adapted from J. Brahms's 'Academic Festival Overture'.

Recent Elections

The last election for Congress was held on 5 March 2019. Only non-partisans were elected. Peter M. Christian was elected president by Congress on 11 May 2015.

Current Government

President: Peter M. Christian; b. 1947 (took office 11 May 2015).
Vice-President: Yosiwo P. George.
In Feb. 2019 the government comprised:
Secretary of Education: Kalwin Kephas. *Environment, Climate Change and Emergency Management:* Andrew Yatilman. *Finance and Administration:* Sihna Lawrence. *Foreign Affairs:* Lorin Robert. *Health and Social Affairs:* Magdalena Walter. *Justice:* Joses Gallen. *Resources and Development:* Marion Henry. *Transportation, Communications and Infrastructure:* Lukner Weilbacher. *Chief Public Defender:* Lorrie Johnson-Asher.
Government Website: http://www.fsmgov.org

Current Leaders

Peter M. Christian
Position
President

Introduction
Peter M. Christian was elected president of the Federated States of Micronesia (FSM) in May 2015 to serve a four-year term, having spent over 35 years in public service.

Early Life
Christian was born on 16 Oct. 1947 in Pohnpei, the administrative centre of Micronesia. From 1968 he studied at the University of Hawaii in Manoa as a recipient of the East-West Center Scholarship.

In 1979 he became the youngest of the 14 elected non-partisan senators in the new National Congress. During his time in Congress he variously advised or chaired committees responsible for resources and development, transportation and communication, and ways and means. He also served as speaker of the Congress from 2003–07. From 2003–04 he was chief negotiator for the Amended Compact of Free Association with the USA and chaired the FSM Task Force from 2007–08. This latter group oversaw the creation of the FSM Petroleum Corporation (PetroCorp) to manage the nation's energy

© Springer Nature Limited 2020
Palgrave Macmillan (ed.), *The Statesman's Yearbook 2020*,
https://doi.org/10.1057/978-1-349-95940-2_128

requirements and oversee the exit of the multinational Exxon Mobil Corporation from the country.

Having been re-elected as senator for Pohnpei in 2011, he subsequently announced his intention to run for president in 2015.

Career in Office

Christian came to office with Micronesia facing serious economic and environmental challenges. He signed up to the newly inaugurated SIDS Dock, an organization of small island developing nations—many of which are under threat from rising sea levels and increasingly frequent extreme weather events—backed by the United Nations to support efforts in climate change adaptation. He then attended the UN Paris Climate Change talks in Dec., urging the UN secretary-general to declare a global emergency.

In foreign relations, he has pursued close ties with Japan (which formerly governed the country) and has also established diplomatic relations with Kazakhstan. He has secured funding for an assortment of national projects from China, the United Arab Emirates-Pacific Partnership Fund and the UN Environmental Programme.

Economy

Overview

Following independence in 1986, the country signed a Compact of Free Association (COFA) with the USA, providing it with grants upon which it still relies heavily. From 1987 to 2003 these grants made up half of annual GDP, although a renegotiated COFA signed in 2003 and worth US$3·5bn. steadily lowers aid payments until 2023. The agreement included the creation of a trust fund in a bid to make Micronesia self-reliant, although the global downturn from 2008 led to lower financial returns than anticipated.

The economy had experienced flat or negative GDP growth from 2001–08. COFA-related spending cuts reduced public sector employment, stimulating migration to the USA (where citizens can work without a visa), while higher fuel and food import costs put further pressure on state finances.

GDP then grew by an annual average of 1·5% from 2009–12 before volatile inflation and an unfavourable business climate resulted in a contraction in 2013 and 2014. Growth resumed in 2015 and 2016 (by 3·9% and 2·9% respectively), driven by fisheries, retail trade and manufacturing (particularly new water bottling plants). In 2017 growth was measured at 2% and the state budget reached a surplus of 3·4% (up from 3·2% in 2016). Public debt was also relatively low, at 24·3% of GDP. Inflation was estimated at 0·5% in the same year.

Despite a small population and aid packages from the USA and Japan, Micronesia's unemployment rate is high (at around 20%) and some 40% of the population lives below the national poverty line. The private sector's share of the economy has remained unchanged at around 25% since the early 1990s and contributes little to GDP growth. Public sector economic activity is largely financed by international donors and is the largest source of employment. The islands have few commercially valuable mineral deposits. The potential for tourism is also limited owing to the country's isolated location, lack of adequate facilities and inadequate internal air and water transport infrastructure. However, remittances are significant and rising.

The medium-term outlook is fragile as a result of the stagnant private sector and heavy dependence on US assistance. The government is looking to China for economic support once US subsidies end in 2023.

Currency

US currency is used. Foreign exchange reserves were US$50m. and total money supply was US$23m. in June 2005. There was inflation of 0·5% in 2016 and 2017.

Budget

Under the terms of the Amended Compact, which entered force in 2004 as a follow-up to the Compact of Free Association, the USA provides approximately US$130m. a year in aid. Consolidated central government revenue (2013–14), US$216·7m.; expenditure, US$184·5m. The financial year runs from 1 Oct.–30 Sept.

Performance

In 2017 total GDP was US$336m.; real GDP grew by 3·9% in 2015, 2·9% in 2016 and 2·0% in 2017.

Banking and Finance

There are three commercial banks: Bank of Guam, Bank of Hawaii and Bank of the Federated States of Micronesia. There are also a Federated States of Micronesia Development Bank and a regulatory Banking Board.

Energy and Natural Resources

Electricity

Electricity production in 2011 was 66m. kWh.

Minerals

The islands have few mineral deposits except for high-grade phosphates.

Agriculture

Agriculture consists mainly of subsistence farming: coconuts, breadfruit, bananas, sweet potatoes and cassava. A small amount of crops are produced for export, including copra, tropical fruits, peppers and taro. Production (2008 estimates, in 1,000 tonnes): coconuts, 41; cassava, 12; sweet potatoes, 3; bananas, 2. Livestock (2008 estimates): pigs, 33,000; cattle, 14,000; goats, 4,000. In 2007 there were approximately 2,500 ha. of arable land and 18,000 ha. of permanent crops.

Forestry

The total forest area was 64,000 ha. in 2015 (92% of the land area).

Fisheries

In 2012 the catch amounted to 45,816 tonnes, almost entirely from marine waters. Fishing licence fees are a primary revenue source, making up around 15% of GDP.

Industry

The chief industries are construction, fish processing, tourism and handicrafts (items from shell, wood and pearl).

Labour

In 2007 just over half the labour force were government employees. In 2007, 41·7% of employees worked in public administration, 21·1% in wholesale and retail trade and repairs and 7·0% in transport, storage and communications. Agriculture, hunting, forestry and fishing accounted for 1·7% of employees. The unemployment rate was 16·2% in 2010.

International Trade

Imports and Exports

Total imports (c.i.f.) in 2007, US$142·7m.; exports (f.o.b.), US$16·2m. Main import suppliers, 2007: US mainland, 41·2%; Guam, 14·4%; Singapore, 8·7%. Main export markets, 2007: Guam, 22·5%; US mainland, 17·2%; Northern Mariana Islands, 4·3%. The main imports are mineral products, foodstuffs and beverages, machinery, mechanical and electrical appliances, animals and animal products, and vegetable products. Main exports: marine products, kava, handicrafts and souvenirs, citrus fruits and garments.

Communications

Roads

There are around 180 km of paved roads. In 2013 there were 9,002 registered motor vehicles.

Civil Aviation

There are international airports on Pohnpei, Chuuk, Yap and Kosrae. There were 12 operational airports and airfields in total in 2012. Services are provided by United Airlines. In 2013 there were international flights to Guam, Honolulu, Manila, the Marshall Islands and Palau in addition to domestic services.

Shipping

The main ports are Kolonia (Pohnpei), Colonia (Yap), Lepukos (Chuuk), Okat and Lelu (Kosrae). In Jan. 2014 there were nine ships of 300 GT or over registered, totalling 29,000 GT.

Telecommunications

There were an estimated 38,000 mobile phone subscriptions in 2009 (343·2 per 1,000 inhabitants) and 8,700 fixed telephone lines; in the same year there were an estimated 15,350 internet users.

Social Institutions

Out of 178 countries analysed in the 2017 *Fragile States Index*—a list published jointly by the Fund for Peace and *Foreign Policy* magazine—Micronesia was ranked the 80th most vulnerable to conflict or collapse. The index is based on 12 indicators of state vulnerability across social, political and economic categories.

Justice

There are a Supreme Court headed by the Chief Justice with two other judges, and a State Court in each of the four states with 13 judges in total.

Education

In 2007 there were 18,512 pupils in primary schools with 1,113 teaching staff; and 14,742 pupils in secondary schools. The College of Micronesia Pohnpei, initially founded as the Micronesian Teacher Education Center in 1963, is the only institute of higher education and now has campuses on all four major island groups, including the Fisheries and Maritime Institute on the Yap Islands.

Health

In 2006 there were 33 hospital beds per 10,000 population. There were 72 physicians, 13 dentists and 305 nursing staff in 2007.

In *Water: At What Cost? The State of the World's Water 2016*, WaterAid reported that 11·0% of the population does not have access to safe water.

Religion

The population is predominantly Christian. Yap is mainly Roman Catholic; Protestantism is prevalent elsewhere.

Culture

Tourism

In 2012 there were 38,263 foreign visitors, up from 35,378 in 2011 although down from 44,738 in 2010.

World Heritage Sites

Nan Madol: Ceremonial Centre of Eastern Micronesia was inscribed on the UNESCO World Heritage List in 2016.

Diplomatic Representatives

Of the United Kingdom in Micronesia
    Ambassador: Melanie Hopkins (resides in Suva, Fiji).

Of Micronesia in the USA (1725 N St., NW, Washington, D.C., 20036)
    Ambassador: Akillino Harris Susaia.

Of the USA in Micronesia (1286 U.S. Embassy Pl., Kolonia, Pohnpei, FM96941)
    Ambassador: Robert Riley.

Of Micronesia to the United Nations
    Ambassador: Jane J. Chigiyal.

Further Reading

Wuerch, W. L. and Ballendorf, D. A., *Historical Dictionary of Guam and Micronesia.* 1995
National Statistical Office: FSM Statistics Division, P. O. Box PS 253, Palikir, Pohnpei, FM 96941.

Moldova

Republica Moldova (Republic of Moldova)

Population projection, 2020: 4·02m.
GNI per capita, 2017: (PPP$) 5,554
HDI/world rank, 2017: 0·700/112
Internet domain extension: .md
Capital: Chişinău

Key Historical Events

In antiquity the territories that make up Moldova were inhabited by the Dacians. In 1359 the region was subsumed into the Principality of Moldavia, founded by Dragoş of Bedeu. From the 16th to 19th centuries Russia and the Ottoman Empire wrestled for influence. In 1812 the Treaty of Bucharest gave Russia control of eastern Moldavia, or Bessarabia (the area between the River Prut and the Dniester, which corresponds to much of present-day Moldova). The Ottomans ruled western Moldavia. In 1918 Romania absorbed Bessarabia, while the Soviet Union controlled the territory east of the Dniester from 1924. Bessarabia reverted from Romanian rule to become part of the Moldavian Socialist Republic within the USSR in 1940.

In Dec. 1991 Moldova became a member of the Commonwealth of Independent States, a decision ratified by parliament in April 1994. Fighting took place in 1992 between government forces and separatists in the (largely Russian and Ukrainian) area east of the River Nistru (Transnistria). An agreement signed by the presidents of Moldova and Russia on 21 July 1992 brought to an end the armed conflict and established a 'security zone' controlled by peacekeeping forces from Russia, Moldova and Transnistria. On 21 Oct. 1994 a Moldo-Russian agreement obliged Russian troops to withdraw from the territory of Moldova over three years but the agreement was not ratified by the Russian Duma. On 8 May 1997 an agreement between Transnistria and the Moldovan government to end the separatist conflict stipulated that Transnistria would remain part of Moldova as it was territorially constituted in Jan. 1990. In 1997 some 7,000 Russian troops were stationed in Transnistria. In the autumn of 1999 Ion Sturza's centre-right coalition collapsed, along with privatization plans for the wine and tobacco industries. In April 2001 a Communist, Vladimir Voronin, was elected president. In Aug. 2009 the Communist government fell to a coalition of four opposition parties after earlier disputed elections and a failure to elect a new president.

Territory and Population

Moldova is bounded in the east and south by Ukraine and on the west by Romania. The area is 33,848 sq. km (13,067 sq. miles). At the last census, in 2014, the population was 3,503,000 (52% female); density, 103 per sq. km.

The UN gives a projected population for 2020 of 4·02m.

In 2011, 47·7% of the population lived in urban areas. Main ethnic groups (2014, excluding predominantly Russian-speaking Transnistria): Moldovans 75%, Romanians 7%, Ukrainians 5%, Gagauz 4%, Russians 2%.

Apart from Chişinău, the capital (population of 532,513 in 2014), major towns are Tiraspol (estimated population of 133,807 in 2014), Bălţi (97,930 in 2014) and Bender (Tighina) (estimated population of 91,882 in 2014).

The official Moldovan language (i.e. Romanian) was written in Cyrillic prior to the restoration of the Roman alphabet in 1989. It is spoken by 62% of the population; the use of other languages (Russian, Gagauz) is safeguarded by the Constitution.

Social Statistics

2007: births, 37,973; deaths, 43,050. Rates, 2007 (per 1,000 population): births, 10·6; deaths, 12·0. In 2006 the most popular age at first marriage was 20–24 for both males and females. Life expectancy at birth in 2007 was 65·0 years for males and 72·6 years for females. Annual population growth rate, 2010–15, –0·1%. Infant mortality, 2010, 16 per 1,000 live births; fertility rate, 2008, 1·3 births per woman (one of the lowest rates in the world). In

2011, 17·5% of the population were classified as living below the national poverty line.

Climate

The climate is temperate, with warm summers, crisp, sunny autumns and cold winters with snow. Chişinău, Jan. –7°C, July 20°C. Annual rainfall 677 mm.

Constitution and Government

A declaration of republican sovereignty was adopted in June 1990 and in Aug. 1991 the republic declared itself independent. A new constitution came into effect on 27 Aug. 1994, which defines Moldova as an 'independent, democratic and unitary state'. At a referendum on 6 March 1994 turnout was 75·1%; 95·4% of votes cast favoured 'an independent Moldova within its 1990 borders'. The referendum (and the Feb. parliamentary elections) were not held by the authorities in Transnistria. In a further referendum on 4 June 1999, on whether to switch from a parliamentary system to a presidential one, turnout was 58% with the majority of the votes cast being in favour of the change.

Parliament (*Parlamentul*) has 101 seats and is elected for four-year terms. There is a 4% threshold for election; votes falling below this are redistributed to successful parties. The *President* is elected for four-year terms. The constitution was amended in 2000 to abolish direct presidential elections. However, in March 2016 the constitutional court ruled that the amendment was unconstitutional and reintroduced them. The first direct election in 20 years was held in Oct. 2016.

The 1994 constitution makes provision for the autonomy of Transnistria and the Gagauz (Gagauz Yeri) region. Work began in July 2003 on the drafting of a new constitution to resolve the conflict between Moldova and Transnistria. The proposal, known as the 'Kozak Plan', was drafted by Russia, and involved the creation of an asymmetric federal Moldovan state, with Moldova holding a majority and Transnistria being a minority part of the federation. The proposal also stipulated the presence of Russian troops in Transnistria for a transitional period but not later than 2020. It was, however, opposed by the European Union and the USA and subsequently rejected by Vladimir Voronin, the then Moldovan president.

Transnistria

In the predominantly Russian-speaking areas of Transnistria a self-styled 'Dniester Republic' was established in Sept. 1991, and approved by a local referendum in Dec. 1991. A Russo-Moldovan agreement of 21 July 1992 provided for a special statute for Transnistria and a guarantee of self-determination should Moldova unite with Romania. The population at the 2015 census was 475,665. Romanian here is still written in the Cyrillic alphabet. At a referendum on 24 Dec. 1995, 81% of votes cast were in favour of adopting a new constitution proclaiming independence.

On 17 June 1996 the Moldovan government granted Transnistria a special status as 'a state-territorial formation in the form of a republic within Moldova's internationally recognized border'.

At elections to the Supreme Council held on 29 Nov. 2015, which were not internationally recognized as legitimate, turnout was 48·3%. Renewal won 33 of 43 seats; Pridnestrovie Communist Party, 1. Independents won nine seats. In a referendum held on 17 Sept. 2006, 97·2% of votes cast were in favour of independence and possible future union with Russia, although no international organization or foreign country recognized the referendum. Elections for president were held on 11 Dec. 2016. Turnout was 59·2%. Vadim Krasnoselsky won 62·3% of the vote and incumbent Yevgeny Shevchuk 27·4%.

Following the Crimean crisis in early 2014 the president of the Transnistrian parliament, Mikhail Burla, requested that the Russian government pass a law that would allow the region's accession to the Russian Federation.

© Springer Nature Limited 2020

Palgrave Macmillan (ed.), *The Statesman's Yearbook 2020*,
https://doi.org/10.1057/978-1-349-95940-2_129

President

Vadim Krasnoselsky; b. 1970.

Gagauz Yeri

This was created an autonomous territorial unit by Moldovan legislation of 13 Jan. 1995. In 2014 the census population was 134,535. There is a 35-member *Popular Assembly* directly elected for four-year terms and headed by a *Governor*, who is a member of the Moldovan cabinet. At the elections of 20 Nov. and 4 Dec. 2016 independents took 28 seats, the Part of Socialists of the Republic of Moldova 5 and the Democratic Party of Moldova 1. One seat remained vacant.

Governor

Irina Vlah; b. 1974.

National Anthem

The Romanian anthem was replaced in 1994 by a traditional tune, 'Lîmbă noastră' ('Our Tongue'); words by Alexei Mateevici, tune by Alexandru Cristi.

Recent Elections

Presidential elections were held in two rounds on 30 Oct. and 13 Nov. 2016. In the first round Igor Dodon of the Party of Socialists of the Republic of Moldova received 48·0% of votes cast, Maia Sandu of Action and Solidarity 38·7%, Dumitru Ciubașenco of Our Party 6·0% and former prime minister Iurie Leancă of the European People's Party 3·1%. Five other candidates took less than 2% of the vote each and turnout was 49·2%. In the second round run-off, Igor Dodon received 52·1% of votes cast against Maia Sandu with 47·9%. Turnout in the second round was 53·4%.

Parliamentary elections were held on 24 Feb. 2019. The Party of Socialists of the Republic of Moldova won 34 seats with 31·2% of the vote, NOW Platform DA and PAS (an alliance of the Dignity and Truth Platform Party and the Party of Action and Solidarity) 27 with 26·8%, the Democratic Party of Moldova 30 with 23·6% and the Republican Socio-Political Movement Equality 7 with 8·3%. Turnout was 49·2%.

Current Government

In Feb. 2019 the government comprised:

President: Igor Dodon; b. 1975 (Party of Socialists of the Republic of Moldova; since 23 Dec. 2016).

Prime Minister: Pavel Filip; b. 1966 (Democratic Party of Moldova; since 20 Jan. 2016).

Deputy Prime Minister for European Integration: Iurie Leancă. *Deputy Prime Minister for Reintegration:* Cristina Lesnic.

Minister of Agriculture, Regional Development and Environment: Nicolae Ciubuc. *Economy and Infrastructure:* Chiril Gaburici. *Finance:* Octavian Armașu. *Foreign Affairs and European Integration:* Tudor Ulianovschi. *Justice:* Victoria Iftodi. *Interior:* Alexandru Jizdan. *Education, Culture and Research:* Monica Babuc. *Health, Labour and Social Protection:* Silvia Radu. *Defence:* Eugen Sturza.

Government Website: http://www.gov.md

Current Leaders

Igor Dodon

Position
President

Introduction
Igor Dodon became Moldova's president on 23 Dec. 2016, aiming to pursue a strongly pro-Russian agenda in the face of opposition from the largely pro-European Union government and parliament.

Early Life
Dodon was born in the rural village of Sadova in Moldova—then part of the USSR—on 18 Feb. 1975. He studied economics at Moldova's Agricultural State University and later received his doctorate from the Academy of Economics Studies. Before embarking on a political career, he worked as an assistant professor of economics.

His first political position was as associate minister of trade and economics in 2005. The following year he took over the full ministerial post, retaining the portfolio for three years. He also served as Zinaida Greceanîi's deputy prime minister from March 2008–Sept. 2009. After Greceanîi's electoral defeat in 2009, Dodon had a period out of the political limelight before making an unsuccessful run for the mayoralty of Chișinău in 2011. He subsequently left the Communist Party to join the Socialists, of whom he later became leader.

In Nov. 2016 he won the run-off poll in the first direct elections for the presidency in 20 years, having campaigned on a pro-Russian platform.

Career in Office
Dodon embarked on an official state visit to Russia within a month of taking office and vowed to overturn a pro-EU trade deal struck in 2014 after the country's next parliamentary election, scheduled for Feb. 2019. However, political wrangling with the government and legislature resulted in his temporary suspension as president by the Constitutional Court on several occasions between Oct. 2017 and Sept. 2018 for failing to swear in proposed government ministers and for vetoing a government bill aiming to restrict Russian news broadcasts.

Defence

Conscription is for 12 months (three months for higher education graduates). In 2018 it was announced that conscription would be gradually abolished. In 2013 military expenditure totalled US$24m. (US$7 per capita), representing 0·3% of GDP.

Russian troops remained in Transnistria after Moldova gained independence, but in Nov. 1999 the Organization for Security and Co-operation in Europe (OSCE) passed a resolution at its summit requiring Russia to withdraw its troops to Russia by Dec. 2002, unconditionally and under international observation. This deadline was extended to Dec. 2003 but around 1,500 Russian troops still remained in the region in early 2017 as part of a joint peacekeeping force. In Aug. 2017 the government of Moldova called on the United Nations to discuss the withdrawal of Russian peacekeepers from the region.

Army

Personnel, 2011, 3,231 (1,934 conscripts). In 2011 there was also a paramilitary Interior Ministry force of 2,379, riot police numbering 900 and combined forces reserves of 58,000.

Air Force

Personnel (including air defence), 2011, 826 (259 conscripts).

Economy

Agriculture accounted for 15·5% of GDP in 2014, industry 17·2% and services 67·3%.

Overview

Robust growth since the early 2000s, averaging 5% annually, has led to a significant overall decline in the poverty rate. Nevertheless, high unemployment, political instability, volatile commodity prices and the fragile global economy pose risks in the long term. Moldova's economy has historically been closely aligned to that of Russia—the main destination for Moldovan exports and the leading source of remittances—and consistently maintains a negative trade balance.

After poor performance throughout the 1990s, the economy began to recover in 2000. Growth was strong from 2000–07, averaging 5·7%, but the economy experienced a contraction in 2009 prompted by the global downturn. A rebound followed in 2010 driven by private domestic demand and buoyant agricultural exports, and the economy was among the fastest-growing in central and Eastern Europe into 2011. However, in 2012 it contracted again following a drought and weak external demand from the eurozone. Although a record harvest the following year helped restore momentum, Moldova faced yet another recession in 2015, followed by a further quick recovery in 2016 largely spurred by the services sector.

Currency

A new unit of currency, the *leu* (MDL), replaced the *rouble* in Nov. 1993. Inflation was 0·0% in 2009, down from a peak of 2,198% in the early 1990s. More recently it was 6·4% in 2016 and 6·6% in 2017. Foreign exchange reserves were US$506m. in July 2005. Total money supply in June 2005 was 6,523m. lei.

Budget

In 2011 budgetary central government revenue totalled 18,639m. lei and expenditure 18,702m. lei. Principal sources of revenue in 2011 were: taxes 15,053m. lei; grants, 1,565m. lei. Main items of expenditure by economic type in 2011: grants, 8,856m. lei; compensation of employees, 3,502m. lei.

VAT is 20% (reduced rates, 10% and 8%).

Performance

Moldova's economy contracted by 6·0% in 2009 at the height of the global downturn. More recently it contracted by 0·4% in 2015 before growing by 4·3% in 2016 and 4·5% in 2017.

Total GDP was US$8·1bn. in 2017 (excluding Transnistria). The private sector accounts for over 50% of official GDP.

Banking and Finance

The central bank and bank of issue is the National Bank (*Governor*, Octavian Armașu). At Aug. 2016 there were 11 licensed banks. In 2014 the banking sector experienced a crisis when the country's three largest lenders were defrauded of an estimated total of US$1bn. The banks were subsequently brought under government control and recapitalized, with significant knock-on effects for the economy as a whole. Foreign debt was US$4,615m. in 2010, representing 73·5% of GNI. There is a stock exchange in Chișinău.

Energy and Natural Resources

Environment

Moldova's carbon dioxide emissions from the consumption of energy in 2011 were the equivalent of 1·8 tonnes per capita.

Electricity

Installed capacity in 2011 was 503,000 kW. Production was 1·02bn. kWh in 2011; consumption per capita in 2011 was 1,174 kWh.

Minerals

There are deposits of lignite, phosphorites, gypsum and building materials.

Agriculture

There were 387,400 people employed in agriculture in 2008. Land under cultivation in 2008 was 2·5m. ha., of which 0·3m. ha. was accounted for by private subsidiary agriculture and 668,600 ha. by farms. In 2008 there were 1·82m. ha. of arable land and 303,000 ha. of permanent crops. The agricultural and food sector accounts for 38% of Moldova's total exports.

Output of main agricultural products (in 1,000 tonnes) in 2008: maize, 1,479; wheat, 1,286; sugar beets, 961; grapes, 636; sunflower seeds, 372; barley, 353; potatoes, 271.

Livestock (2008): 853,000 sheep and goats, 299,000 pigs, 232,000 cattle, 17m. chickens.

Livestock products, 2008 (in 1,000 tonnes): milk, 542; meat, 78; eggs, 541m. units.

Forestry

In 2015 forests covered 0·41m. ha., or 12% of the total land area. Timber production in 2011 was 352,000 cu. metres.

Fisheries

The catch in 2015 (exclusively freshwater fish) was an estimated 50 tonnes.

Industry

There are canning plants, wine-making plants, woodworking and metallurgical factories, a factory of ferro-concrete building materials, footwear, dairy products and textile plants. Manufacturing accounted for 14·8% of GDP in 2007. Production (in tonnes): cement (2011 estimate), 1,400,000; crude steel (2011), 320,600; flour (2007), 113,300; canned fruit and vegetables (2007), 94,000; granulated sugar (2007), 74,000; footwear (2007), 3·8m. pairs; 5·0bn. cigars and cigarettes (2007); wine (2008), 397·9m. litres.

Labour

The labour force in 2013 was 1,218,000 (1,472,000 in 2003). 46·0% of the population aged 15–64 was economically active in 2013. In the same year 5·1% of the population was unemployed.

Moldova had 33,000 people living in slavery according to the Walk Free Foundation's 2013 *Global Slavery Index*.

International Trade

Imports and Exports

Imports and exports for calendar years in US$1m.:

	2002	2003	2004	2005	2006
Imports f.o.b.	1,037·5	1,428·1	1,748·2	2,296·1	2,644·4
Exports f.o.b.	659·7	805·1	994·1	1,104·6	1,053·0

Chief import sources in 2006 were: Ukraine, 19·2%; Russia, 15·5%; Romania, 12·8%; Germany, 7·9%. Main export markets in 2006 were: Russia, 17·3%; Romania, 14·8%; Ukraine, 12·2%; Italy, 11·1%.

Moldova's leading imports are mineral products and fuel, machinery and equipment, chemicals and textiles. The main export commodity is wine, ahead of tobacco. Fruit and vegetables, textiles and footwear, and machinery are also significant exports.

Communications

Roads

There were 9,343 km of public roads in 2009 (94·3% hard surfaced). Registered passenger cars (including taxis) in 2008 numbered 366,351, there were 115,967 goods vehicles and 21,491 buses and minibuses. In 2005 there were 2,289 road accidents resulting in 391 deaths.

Rail

Total length in 2011 was 1,146 km of 1,524 mm gauge. Passenger-km travelled in 2011 came to 363m. and freight tonne-km to 1,172m.

Civil Aviation

The main Moldovan-based airline is Air Moldova, which in 2013 carried 527,000 passengers. In 2010 it flew to Athens, Bucharest, Frankfurt, İstanbul, Larnaca, Lisbon, London, Madrid, Milan, Moscow, Paris, Prague, Rome, St Petersburg, Verona and Vienna. In 2012 the airport at Chișinău handled 1,220,496 passengers (almost all on international flights) and 2,766 tonnes of cargo.

Shipping

There were 558 km of navigable waterways in 2013. In Jan. 2014 there were 140 ships of 300 GT or over registered, totalling 528,000 GT.

Telecommunications

There were 2,785,000 mobile phone subscriptions (772·8 per 1,000 inhabitants) in 2009 and 1,139,000 fixed telephone lines. In the same year there were 187,000 fixed broadband internet subscriptions and 80,000 mobile broadband subscriptions. In March 2012 there were 221,000 Facebook users.

Social Institutions

Out of 178 countries analysed in the 2017 *Fragile States Index*—a list published jointly by the Fund for Peace and *Foreign Policy* magazine—Moldova was ranked the 81st least vulnerable to conflict or collapse. The index is based on 12 indicators of state vulnerability across social, political and economic categories.

Justice

A total of 24,362 crimes were recorded in 2007. The population in penal institutions in Sept. 2007 was 8,130 (227 per 100,000 of national population). The death penalty was abolished for all crimes in 1995. In 2015 the World Justice Project *Rule of Law Index*, which provides data on how the rule of law is experienced by the general public across eight categories, ranked Moldova 82nd of 102 countries for criminal justice and 84th for civil justice.

Education

In 2007 there were 103,811 children and 10,517 teaching staff in pre-schools; 160,528 pupils and 9,876 teaching staff in primary schools; and 367,636 pupils and 30,376 teaching staff in secondary schools. There were 148,449 students (8,570 academic staff) in tertiary education in 2007. In 2006 there were 16 public and 15 private higher education institutions. Adult literacy rate in 2008 was 98%.

In 2007 public expenditure on education came to 7·3% of GNI and represented 19·8% of total government expenditure.

Health

In 2007 there were 83 hospitals with 21,892 beds, a provision of 61 per 10,000 inhabitants. In 2007 there were 12,733 physicians (11% private sector), 1,566 dentists, 20,868 nurses and 2,834 pharmacists (2006).

In *Water: At What Cost? The State of the World's Water 2016*, WaterAid reported that 11·6% of the population does not have access to safe water.

Welfare

There were 469,600 age pensioners and 169,800 other pensioners in 2008.

Religion

According to the Pew Research Center's Forum on Religion & Public Life, in 2010 the population was an estimated 95·5% Orthodox. There are two main Orthodox denominations. The larger Moldovan Orthodox Church is subordinate to the Russian Orthodox Church while the Bessarabian Orthodox Church is subordinate to the Romanian Orthodox Church.

Culture

World Heritage Sites

Moldova has one site on the UNESCO World Heritage List: the Struve Geodetic Arc (inscribed in 2005). The Arc is a chain of survey triangulations spanning from Norway to the Black Sea that helped establish the exact shape and size of the earth and is shared as a UNESCO site with nine other countries.

Press

In 2008 there were seven paid-for daily newspapers and 240 non-dailies. The dailies had a combined circulation of 303,000, with the most widely read being the Russian-language *Komsomolskaya Pravda v Moldove*.

Tourism

In 2010, 64,000 non-resident tourists stayed in holiday accommodation; 24% of tourists in 2010 were from Romania, 10% from Russia and 10% from Ukraine.

Diplomatic Representatives

Of Moldova in the United Kingdom (5 Dolphin Sq., Edensor Rd, London, W4 2ST)
Ambassador: Angela Ponomariov.

Of the United Kingdom in Moldova (18 Nicolae Iorga St., Chișinău MD-2012)
Ambassador: Lucy Joyce, OBE.

Of Moldova in the USA (2101 S St., NW, Washington, D.C., 20008)
Ambassador: Cristina Balan.

Of the USA in Moldova (103 Strada Alexei Matveevici, Chișinău MD-2009)
Ambassador: Dereck J. Hogan.

Of Moldova to the United Nations
Ambassador: Victor Moraru.

Of Moldova to the European Union
Ambassador: Eugen Caras.

Further Reading

King, C., *Post-Soviet Moldova: A Borderland in Transition.* 1997.—*The Moldovans: Romania, Russia, and the Politics of Culture.* 2000

Kolsto, Pal, *National Integration and Violent Conflict in Post-Soviet Societies: The Cases of Estonia and Moldova.* 2002

National Statistical Office: National Bureau of Statistics of Moldova, MD-2019, Chișinău mun., 106 Grenoble St.

Website: http://www.statistica.md

Monaco

Principauté de Monaco (Principality of Monaco)

Capital: Monaco
Population projection, 2020: 39,000
GDP per capita, 2015: US$163,394
Internet domain extension: .mc

Key Historical Events

Monaco's natural harbour was settled by Phoenicians, Greeks and Ligurians and later by Saracens. A fortress, built where the palace now stands, was captured by the Grimaldi family of Genoa in 1297. It was passed on through the male line until 1731, when control of Monaco passed to Louise Hippolyte, daughter of Antoine I and wife of Jacques de Goyon Matignon, who took the name of Grimaldi. The Principality was placed under the protection of the Kingdom of Sardinia by the Treaty of Vienna in 1815, and under that of France in 1861. Prince Rainier III succeeded his grandfather, Louis II, in 1949 and ruled the Principality until his death on 6 April 2005 when his son, Prince Albert II, inherited the throne.

Territory and Population

Monaco is bounded in the south by the Mediterranean and elsewhere by France (Department of Alpes Maritimes). The area is 2·03 sq. km (0·8 sq. miles), making it the second smallest sovereign country—only the Vatican City is smaller. The Principality is divided into four districts: Monaco-Ville, la Condamine, Monte-Carlo and Fontvieille. Population (2016 census), 37,308; giving a density of 18,378 persons per sq. km and making Monaco the world's most densely populated country. There were 8,378 Monegasques in 2016 (22·5%), 9,286 French (24·9%) and 8,172 Italian (21·9%).

The UN gives a projected population for 2020 of 39,000.

The population is 100% urban.

The official language is French.

Social Statistics

2008: births, 970; deaths, 545. 2005 marriages, 161; divorces, 69. Rates per 1,000 population, 2008: birth, 31·2; death, 17·5; marriage (2005), 5·0; divorce (2005), 2·1. Annual population growth rate, 1998–2008, 0·4%; fertility rate, 2008, 1·5 births per woman. Infant mortality per 1,000 live births (2010), 3.

Climate

A Mediterranean climate, with mild moist winters and hot dry summers. Monaco, Jan. 50°F (10°C), July 74°F (23·3°C). Annual rainfall 30" (758 mm).

Constitution and Government

On 17 Dec. 1962 a new constitution was promulgated which maintains the hereditary monarchy.

The reigning Prince is **Albert II**, b. 14 March 1958, son of Prince Rainier III, 1923–2005, and Grace Kelly, 1929–82. Prince Albert succeeded his father Rainier III, who died on 6 April 2005. He married Charlene Wittstock on 1 and 2 July 2011. *Offspring:* Crown Prince Jacques, b. 10 Dec. 2014; Princess Gabriella, b. 10 Dec. 2014.

Sisters of the Prince

Princess Caroline Louise Marguerite, b. 23 Jan. 1957; married Philippe Junot on 28 June 1978, divorced 9 Oct. 1980; married Stefano Casiraghi on 29 Dec. 1983 (died 3 Oct. 1990); married Prince Ernst of Hanover on 23 Jan. 1999. *Offspring:* Andrea, b. 8 June 1984; Charlotte, b. 3 Aug. 1986; Pierre, b. 5 Sept. 1987; Alexandra, b. 20 July 1999. Princess Stéphanie Marie Elisabeth, b. 1 Feb. 1965, married Daniel Ducruet on 1 July 1995, divorced 4 Oct. 1996;

married Adans López Peres on 12 Sept. 2003; divorced 24 Nov. 2004. *Offspring:* Louis, b. 26 Nov. 1992; Pauline, b. 4 May 1994; Camille, b. 15 July 1998.

Prince Rainier III renounced the principle of divine right. Executive power is exercised jointly by the Prince and a five-member *Council of Government*, headed by a Minister of State (a French citizen). A 24-member *National Council* is elected for five-year terms.

The constitution can be modified only with the approval of the National Council. Laws of 1992, 2003 and 2005 permit Monegasque women to give their nationality to their children.

National Anthem

'Principauté Monaco ma patrie' ('Principality of Monaco my fatherland'); words by T. Bellando de Castro, tune by C. Albrecht.

Recent Elections

In parliamentary elections held on 11 Feb. 2018 Priorité Monaco (Primo!) won 21 of 24 seats against 2 for Horizon Monaco; Union Monégasque won one seat. Turnout was 70·4%.

Current Government

Chief of State: Prince Albert II.

In Feb. 2019 the cabinet comprised:

Minister of State: Serge Telle; b. 1955 (sworn in 1 Feb. 2016).

Minister of External Relations and Co-operation: Gilles Tonelli. *Facilities, Environmental Affairs and Town Planning:* Marie-Pierre Gramaglia. *Finance and Economics:* Jean Castellini. *Interior:* Patrice Cellario. *Social Affairs and Health:* Didier Gamerdinger.

Government Website: http://www.monaco.gouv.mc

Current Leaders

Albert II

Position
Prince

Introduction
Albert II became ruler of Monaco on 6 April 2005 following the death of his father, Prince Rainier III, who had ruled the principality for 56 years. Albert II has maintained the status quo, upholding the low-tax regime that has made Monaco a haven for the super-rich.

Early Life
Albert Alexandre Louis Pierre Grimaldi was born in Monaco on 14 March 1958, the second child and only son of Prince Rainier III and Grace Kelly, a US cinema actress. He attended the Lycée Albert Ier, then the principality's sole secondary school, where he developed a passion for sport. Having received his baccalaureate diploma in 1976, Albert enrolled the following year at Amherst College in Massachusetts, USA, and graduated with a degree in political science in 1981. From Sept. 1981–April 1982 he served in the French Navy as a sub-lieutenant on the aircraft carrier *Jeanne d'Arc*. On 14 Sept. 1982 his mother was killed in a car crash in the mountains near Monaco. Subsequently, he became vice-president of the Princess Grace-USA Foundation, which grants scholarships to talented young musicians, actors and dancers. In the same year he also became president of the Monaco Red Cross.

During the mid-1980s Albert undertook work experience at an investment bank and an international law firm in New York, as well as the French luxury goods group, Moet-Hennessy, in Paris. Back in Monaco he chaired the principality's prestigious Yacht Club, the International Television Festival and Monaco's Athletic Federation. Albert also became increasingly involved in the Olympic movement, both as an administrator (as a member of the International Olympic Committee in 1985 and president of Monaco's

© Springer Nature Limited 2020
Palgrave Macmillan (ed.), *The Statesman's Yearbook 2020*,
https://doi.org/10.1057/978-1-349-95940-2_130

Olympic Committee in 1993) and competitor (in the principality's bobsleigh team at four Winter Olympics between 1988 and 2002).

During the 1990s he began to increase his involvement in the day-to-day administration of Monaco. In 1997 he organized the 700th anniversary celebrations of the Grimaldi family's control over the principality. He also assisted his father and the government in preparing reports that strongly denied allegations by French parliamentarians in 2000 that Monaco's lax policies had facilitated money laundering.

Long described in the press as the world's 'most eligible bachelor', Albert's unmarried status became a matter of political concern, casting doubt on the succession of the Grimaldi family and the independence of the principality. A change to the constitution was formulated in April 2002, however, allowing the throne to continue through the female line. On 31 March 2005 the Palace of Monaco announced that Albert would take over the duties of his father as Regent, after Prince Rainier III, who had been admitted to hospital, was no longer able to rule. Following the death of his father on 6 April 2005, he became Sovereign Prince of Monaco, and was enthroned on 12 July.

Career in Office

In his first public statement as Prince Albert II, he said that the death of his father, who had governed for 56 years, had left the people of the principality feeling orphaned and united in a profound sense of loss. He has retained the territory's famously low-tax regime and continued to develop tourism, as well as nurturing Monaco's precision engineering, fish canning, banking and pharmaceutical industries. In July 2011 he married Charlene Wittstock, a former Olympic swimmer for South Africa.

Economy

Overview

With sparse natural resources, Monaco's tiny economy is primarily geared towards tourism and finance. These together account for 95% of GDP. Tourism provides 15% of revenues, focused around Monte Carlo's casino and the Formula 1 motor racing Grand Prix hosted every May. Many foreign companies are attracted by low corporate taxes. Having been identified as a tax haven by the International Monetary Fund in 2003, Monaco was subsequently placed on the Organisation for Economic Co-operation and Development's blacklist of uncooperative tax havens. However, in 2009 it was delisted following its commitment to implement standards of transparency and effective exchange of information. In Oct. 2014 Monaco joined with 83 other nations to counter offshore tax avoidance and evasion in a multilateral convention.

Although not a member of the European Union, Monaco is closely associated with its economic structures, and EU states account for over 50% of its trade. Customs, postal services, telecommunications and banking are governed via an economic and customs union with France under EU rules. As a result, Monaco was exposed to the downturn in France and other European economies in the wake of the global financial crisis in 2008. Having fallen by 11·5% in 2009, GDP grew again by 2·5% in 2010, although the budget recorded a deficit of 1·9% of GDP that year. In 2013 growth surpassed pre-crisis levels, expanding by 9·3%, before moderating to an annual rise of 3·2% in 2016.

Living standards are high and per capita GDP is among the highest in the world—recorded at €72,091 in 2015.

Currency

On 1 Jan. 1999 the *euro* (EUR) replaced the French franc as the legal currency in Monaco at the irrevocable conversion rate of 6·55957 French francs to one euro. The euro, which consists of 100 cents, has been in circulation since 1 Jan. 2002. On the introduction of the euro there was a 'dual circulation' period before the franc ceased to be legal tender on 17 Feb. 2002.

Budget

Revenues in 2014 totalled €1,111·4m. and expenditures €1,085·7m.

Performance

In 2011 total GDP was US$6·1bn.

Banking and Finance

There were 36 banks in 2012 of which 18 were Monegasque banks.

Energy and Natural Resources

Electricity

More than 97% of the electricity consumed is imported from France. In 2010 electricity consumption totalled 552,993 MWh.

Oil and Gas

In 2016 a total of 66·1 GWh of natural gas were distributed by the Société Monégasque de l'Electricité et du Gaz, including 46·5 GWh to industries and 13·6 GWh to residents.

Industry

The main industry is tourism. There is some production of cosmetics, pharmaceuticals, glassware, electrical goods and precision instruments.

Labour

There were 49,610 persons employed in Jan. 2012. 45,442 worked in the private sector; 4,168 in the public sector. 32,401 French citizens worked in Monaco in 2012 (of which 29,778 in the private sector and 2,623 in the public sector).

International Trade

Imports and Exports

There is a customs union with France. Imports for 2012 totalled €761m.; exports, €696m. Main imports: pharmaceuticals, perfume, clothing, paper, synthetic and non-metallic products, and building materials.

Communications

Roads

There were 77 km of roads in 2007. In 2013 there were 41,055 vehicles. Monaco has the densest network of roads of any country in the world. In 2016, 7,151,831 people travelled by bus.

Rail

The 1·7 km of main line passing through the country are operated by the French National Railways (SNCF). In 2011, 5·45m. people arrived at or departed from Monaco railway station.

Civil Aviation

There are helicopter flights to Nice with Héli Air Monaco and Monacair. The nearest airport is at Nice in France.

Shipping

In 2014 a total of 182 liners put in to port in Monaco; 15,759 people embarked, 17,334 disembarked and 166,946 were in transit.

Telecommunications

There were 46,850 fixed telephone lines in 2013 (1,238·4 per 1,000 inhabitants). Mobile phone subscriptions numbered 35,464 in 2013. An estimated 90·7% of the population were internet users in 2013.

Social Institutions

Justice

The *Tribunal suprême* (Supreme Court) has final jurisdiction in constitutional affairs. In civil and criminal proceedings, judgements delivered by the jurisdictions of first instance may be appealed to and reviewed by the *Cour d'appel* (Court of Appeal) and the *Cour de révision* (Court of Review). In civil cases, small claims are adjudicated by a *Justice de paix* (Justice of the Peace) and larger claims by the *Tribunal de première instance* (Court of First Instance). Criminal cases are either heard in the *Tribunal de simple police* (Police Court), the *Tribunal de première instance* (Court of First Instance) sitting on penal matters or the *Tribunal correctionnel* (Criminal Court). There is no death penalty. 82·8% of prisoners had yet to receive a trial according to 2014 estimates by the International Centre for Prison Studies.

Police

In 2006 the police force (Sûreté Publique) comprised 517 personnel. Monaco has one of the highest number of police per head of population of any country in the world.

Education

In 2016, in the public sector, there were five pre-school institutions (*écoles maternelles*) with 689 pupils; four elementary schools with 1,372 pupils; four secondary schools with 2,288 pupils. There were 209 primary teachers and 392 secondary school teachers in total in 2016. In the private sector there were three pre-schools and three primary schools with 300 and 620 pupils respectively; and four secondary schools with 1,005 pupils. In 2005 the government allocated 5·2% of its total budget to education.

The International University of Monaco had 300 students in 2006.

Health

In 2011 Monaco had 250 doctors, 610 nursing and midwifery personnel, and 38 dentists. There were 13·8 hospital beds per 1,000 population in 2012—the highest provision of hospital beds of any country. General government expenditure on health in 2012 represented 18·8% of total government expenditure.

Religion

Around three-quarters of the resident population are Roman Catholic. Much of the rest of the population does not have any religious affiliation. There is one Roman Catholic archbishop.

Culture

Press

Monaco does not have a domestically-published daily newspaper. In 2008 there were two state weeklies: *Journal de Monaco* (published by the government) and *Monaco Hebdo*.

Tourism

In 2009, 264,540 foreign visitors (212,966 leisure and 51,574 business) spent a total of 778,451 nights in Monaco; the main visitors were French, followed by Italians and British. There were also 235,904 cruise ship passengers in 2009. There are three casinos run by the state, including the one at Monte Carlo.

Diplomatic Representatives

Of Monaco in the United Kingdom (7 Upper Grosvenor St., London, W1K 2LX)
Ambassador: Evelyne Genta.
British Consul-General (resident in France): Simon Taylor.
British Honorary Consul: Eric G. F. Blair.

Of Monaco in the USA (888 17th St., NW, Suite 500, Washington, D.C., 20006)
Ambassador: Maguy Maccario Doyle.

Of the USA in Monaco
Ambassador: Jamie D. McCourt (resides in Paris).

Of Monaco to the United Nations
Ambassador: Isabelle Picco.

Of Monaco to the European Union
Ambassador: Sophie Thevenoux.

Further Reading

Journal de Monaco. Bulletin Officiel. 1858 ff.
National Statistical Office: Institut Monégasque de la Statistique et des Etudes Economiques, 9 rue du Gabian, MC 98000 Monaco.
Website: http://www.monacostatistics.mc

Mongolia

Mongol Uls

Capital: Ulaanbaatar
Population projection, 2020: 3·21m.
GNI per capita, 2017: (PPP$) 10,103
HDI/world rank, 2017: 0·741/92=
Internet domain extension: .mn

Key Historical Events

Temujin became khan of Hamag Mongolia in 1190. Having united by conquest various Tatar and Mongolian tribes he was confirmed as 'Universal' ('Genghis', 'Chingiz') khan in 1206. The expansionist impulse of his nomadic empire (Beijing captured in 1215; Samarkand in 1220) continued after his death in 1227. Tamurlaine (died 1405) was the last of the conquering khans. In 1368 the Chinese drove the Mongols from Beijing, and for the next two centuries Sino-Mongolian relations alternated between war and trade. In 1691 Outer Mongolia accepted Manchu rule. The head of the Lamaist faith became the symbol of national identity, and his seat ('Urga', later Ulan Bator and since 1990 more commonly known as Ulaanbaatar) was made the Mongolian capital. When the Manchu dynasty was overthrown in 1911 Outer Mongolia declared its independence under its spiritual ruler and turned to Russia for support against China. Soviet and Mongolian revolutionary forces set up a provisional government in March 1921. On the death of the spiritual ruler a people's republic and new constitution were proclaimed in May 1924. With Soviet help Japanese invaders were fended off during the Second World War. The Mongols then took part in the successful Soviet campaign against Inner Mongolia and Manchuria. On 5 Jan. 1946 China recognized the independence of Outer Mongolia. Until 1990 sole power was in the hands of the (Communist) Mongolian People's Revolutionary Party (MPRP), but an opposition Mongolian Democratic Party, founded in Dec. 1989, achieved tacit recognition and held its first congress in Feb. 1990. Following demonstrations and hunger-strikes, on 12 March the entire MPRP Politburo resigned and political opposition was legalized.

The country's first democratic elections were held in 1992, with the first direct presidential election a year later. A state of emergency was declared in 2008 amid violent protests in Ulaanbaatar in response to claims of election-rigging by the MPRP government. By 2011 the economy was among the fastest-growing in the world on the back of a minerals boom.

Territory and Population

Mongolia is bounded in the north by the Russian Federation, and in the east and south and west by China. Area, 1,564,100 sq. km (603,900 sq. miles). Population (2010 census), 2,647,545. Density in 2010 was 1·7 per sq. km, making Mongolia the most sparsely populated country in the world. Dec. 2017 population estimate: 3,131,750. In 2011, 62·5% of the population were urban. More Mongolians live in China than in Mongolia (5·8m. according to China's 2010 census).

The UN gives a projected population for 2020 of 3·21m.

The population is predominantly made up of Mongolian peoples (78·8% Khalkh). There are a Turkic Kazakh minority (3·7% of the population) and 21 Mongol minorities.

The official language is Khalkh Mongol, which uses a modified Cyrillic alphabet.

The republic is administratively divided into 21 provinces *(aimag)* and the capital, Ulaanbaatar (Ulan Bator). The provinces are subdivided into 334 districts or counties *(suums)*.

Social Statistics

Births, 2005, 45,326; deaths, 16,480. 2001 rates: birth, 17·8 per 1,000 population; death, 6·5 per 1,000; marriage, 5·9 per 1,000; divorce, 0·6 per 1,000. Annual population growth rate, 2010–15, 1·9%. Infant mortality rate, 2010, 26 per 1,000 live births. Expectation of life in 2007 was 63·0 years for males and 69·6 for females. Fertility rate, 2008, 2·0 births per woman. Mongolia has had one of the most impressive reductions in its fertility rate of any country in the world over the past quarter of a century, having had a rate of 4·2 births per woman in 1990.

Climate

A very extreme climate, with six months of mean temperatures below freezing, but much higher temperatures occur for a month or two in summer. Rainfall is very low and limited to the months from mid-May to mid-Sept. Ulaanbaatar, Jan. −14°F (−25·6°C), July 61°F (16·1°C). Annual rainfall 8" (208 mm).

Constitution and Government

The constitution of 12 Feb. 1992 abolished the 'People's Democracy', introduced democratic institutions and a market economy and guarantees freedom of speech.

The *President* is directly elected for renewable four-year terms.

Since June 1992 the legislature has consisted of a single-chamber 76-seat parliament, the *Great Hural (Ulsyn Ich-Chural)*, which elects the Prime Minister.

National Anthem

'Darkhan manai khuvsgalt uls' ('Our sacred revolutionary country'); words by Tsendiyn Damdinsüren, tune by Bilegin Damdinsüren and Luvsanjamts Murjorj.

Recent Elections

At the parliamentary elections of 29 June 2016 the Mongolian People's Party (known as the Mongolian People's Revolutionary Party from 1924–2010) won 65 of the 76 available seats, the Democratic Party 9, the Mongolian People's Revolutionary Party 1 and ind. 1. Turnout was 74·3%.

In the first round of the presidential elections held on 26 June 2017 Khaltmaagiin Battulga (Democratic Party) won 38·6% of the vote, followed by former prime minister Miyeegombyn Enkhbold (Mongolian People's Party) with 30·7% and Sainkhuugiin Ganbaatar (Mongolian People's Revolutionary Party) with 30·6%. Turnout was 68·3%. As none of the three candidates secured an absolute majority a second round run-off was held on 7 July, which Battulga won with 55·2% of the valid votes against Enkhbold with 44·8%. Turnout in the run-off was 60·7%.

Current Government

President: Khaltmaagiin Battulga; b. 1963 (Democratic Party; sworn in 10 July 2017).

In Feb. 2019 the coalition government comprised:

Prime Minister: Ukhnaagiin Khurelsukh; b. 1968 (Mongolian People's Party; sworn in 4 Oct. 2017).

Deputy Prime Minister: Ulziisaikhan Enkhtuvshin.

Minister of Construction and Urban Development: Khavdislam Badelkhan. *Defence:* Nyamaa Enkhbold. *Education, Culture, Sciences and Sports:* Tsedenbal Tsogzolmaa. *Energy:* Tserenpil Davaasuren. *Environment and Tourism:* Chimed Tserenbat. *Finance:* Chimed Khurelbaatar. *Food, Agriculture and Light Industry:* Batjargal Batzorig. *Foreign Affairs:* Damdin Tsogtbaatar. *Health:* Davaajantsan Sarangerel. *Justice and Home Affairs:* Tsend Nyamdorj. *Labour and Social Protection:* Sodnom Chinzorig. *Mining and Heavy Industry:* Dolgorsuren Sumiyabazar. *Road and Transport Development:* Jadamba Bat-Erdene. *Head of Cabinet Secretariat:* Gombojav Zandanshatar.

Office of the President: http://www.president.mn

© Springer Nature Limited 2020
Palgrave Macmillan (ed.), *The Statesman's Yearbook 2020*,
https://doi.org/10.1057/978-1-349-95940-2_131

Current Leaders

Khaltmaagiin Battulga

Position
President

Introduction
A business tycoon, Khaltmaagiin Battulga was elected president in July 2017.

Early Life
Battulga was born on 3 March 1963 in Ulaanbaatar, studying at the city's school of fine arts from 1978 to 1982. Between 1982 and 1986 he was a member of the Union of Mongolian Artists. He also won fame for competing throughout the 1980s for Mongolia's national team in sambo, a Soviet martial art and combat sport.

In the 1990s and 2000s he held a number of senior executive roles with various businesses, including a real estate company that funded the building of the country's largest statue of Genghis Khan at a cost of US$4·1m. Battulga entered parliament in 2004, using his personal wealth to fund his campaigning. In 2008 he was appointed minister of transportation and in 2012 became minister of agriculture, a position he held until 2014.

Battulga was one of three candidates at the presidential election of 26 June 2017, representing the centre-right Democratic Party (DP). The outgoing president, Tsakhiagiin Elbegdorj, also of the DP, did not run because he had served the maximum two four-year terms. In the run-up to the first round, each of the three candidates was mired in corruption allegations and none won an outright majority, triggering a run-off for the first time since Mongolia began holding presidential elections in 1993. Battulga faced the parliament speaker Mieygombyn Enkhbold of the Mongolian People's Party on 7 July, winning with 55·2% of the vote.

Career in Office
Battulga was inaugurated on 10 July. He pledged to stabilize Mongolia's economy and lessen its dependence on China, which purchases 80% of Mongolian exports. He also faced a divided government and a parliament controlled by the Mongolian People's Party (MPP).

Ukhnaagiin Khurelsukh

Position
Prime Minister

Introduction
Ukhnaagiin Khurelsukh was elected prime minister on 4 Oct. 2017 following the collapse of the Mongolian People's Party (MPP) government led by Jargaltulga Erdenebat. A former military officer, Khurelsukh has been involved in Mongolian politics since the early 1990s, shortly after the country became a democracy.

Early Life
Khurelsukh was born on 14 June 1968 in Ulaanbaatar. He graduated in political studies from the National Defense University of Mongolia in 1989 and became an officer in the Mongolian Armed Forces. He entered politics two years later, joining the Central Committee of the Mongolian People's Revolutionary Party (MPRP), which had won the majority of seats in the country's first multi-party elections in July 1990. From 1994 he served as an adviser to the office of the MPRP caucus in the *Great Hural* (Parliament) before becoming the director of the party's youth development wing in 1996.

Khurelsukh was first elected as the member of parliament for Khentii Province in northeast Mongolia in 2000. Four years later he became a cabinet minister, initially for emergency management. He was elected leader of the MPRP in 2008, which reverted to its original name of the MPP in 2010. He served as Mongolia's deputy prime minister from 2014–15 and from 2016–17.

A reformist popular with younger voters, Khurelsukh mobilized against an MPP faction associated with former prime minister and defeated presidential candidate Miyeegombyn Enkhbold, and his resignation as deputy prime minister from the government led by Jargaltulga Erdenebat in Aug. 2017 precipitated its collapse. On 4 Oct. 2017 Khurelsukh was approved by parliament as the new prime minister, although only 47 of the 76 members voted.

Career in Office
In his inaugural address Khurelsukh promised to strengthen the economy and state institutions while fighting corruption. He added that he would focus on the development of mining, agriculture, energy, information technology and tourism. In Nov. 2018 he survived a parliamentary no-confidence vote, initiated by his own party, following weeks of public protests in Ulaanbaatar concerning a government embezzlement scandal.

Defence

Conscription is for one year for males aged 18–25 years. Defence expenditure in 2013 totalled US$133m. (US$41 per capita), representing 1·1% of GDP.

Army

Strength (2011) 8,900 (3,300 conscripts). There are a border guard of 6,000, 1,200 internal security troops and 300 Construction Troops.

Air Force

The Air Force had a strength of 800 in 2011 with three aircraft (none combat-capable) and 13 helicopters.

Economy

In 2012 agriculture accounted for 12·7% of GDP, industry 34·6% and services 52·7%.

Overview

Despite its nomadic and pastoral tradition, Mongolia has made substantial progress since the turn of the century towards creating a private sector-led, open economy. The country is rich in mineral resources, especially copper and gold. The mining sector has become increasingly important, making up 20% of GDP annually. Mongolia has also received significant international loans for the development of its energy and transport sectors.

The economy was nevertheless hit hard by the effects of the global financial crisis. Foreign direct investment fell 17% in 2012 to US$3·8bn. from US$4·6bn. in 2011. With minerals then accounting for 89% of total exports and with 93% of them destined for China, a sharp contraction in Chinese demand weakened overall growth. However, robust agricultural production and healthy performance in the construction, transportation and technology sectors helped Mongolia achieve growth of 11·6% in 2013, down from a high of 17·3% in 2011 although up from 7·3% in 2010. Growth had slowed by 2016, when it was only 1·2% as a result of declining exports, but further development of the mining sector saw the economy record a more solid performance in the first half of 2017. The poverty rate fell from 38·7% in 2010 to 27·4% in 2012, and continued to decline until 2016, when it returned to 2012 levels.

In a bid to improve macroeconomic stability, the government announced a fiscal consolidation plan in 2013. Nevertheless, with a substantial balance of payments deficit, Mongolia is vulnerable to changing conditions in the international economy. Additionally, structural challenges and a lack of export diversification hinder long-term growth.

Currency

The unit of currency is the *tugrik* (MNT) of 100 *möngö*. The tugrik was made convertible in 1993. In March 2005 foreign exchange reserves were US$276m. and gold reserves totalled 112,000 troy oz. Broad money supply totalled 11,186bn. tugriks in June 2016. Inflation, which reached a high of 268% in 1993, was just 0·5% in 2016. It rose to 4·6% in 2017.

Budget

In 2014 revenues were 6,145·1bn. tugriks and expenditures 7,031·4bn. tugriks; taxes accounted for 84·1% of revenue, and subsidies and transfers 30·3% of expenditure.

VAT is 10%.

Performance

The economy grew by 2·4% in 2015, 1·2% in 2016 and 5·1% in 2017. Total GDP in 2017 was US$11·5bn.

Banking and Finance

The Bank of Mongolia (*Governor*, Bayartsaikhan Nadmid) is the bank of issue. In 2013 there were 14 licensed banks, the largest being the Trade and Development Bank (TDB), Khan Bank and Golomt Bank.

External debt was US$2,444m. in 2010, representing 44·3% of GNI.

A stock exchange opened in Ulaanbaatar in 1992.

Energy and Natural Resources

Environment

In 2011 carbon dioxide emissions from the consumption of energy accounted for 2·7 tonnes per capita.

Electricity

Installed capacity was estimated at 0·9m. kW in 2011. Production, 2011, 4·54bn. kWh; consumption per capita in 2011 was 1,739 kWh. Mongolia imports electricity from Russia to meet increasing demand.

Minerals

There are large deposits of coal, chromium, cobalt, copper, emeralds, gold, iron, molybdenum, phosphates, tin, wolfram and fluorspar; production of the latter in 2011, 461,000 tonnes. There are major coal mines near Ulaanbaatar and Darhan. A huge gold and copper mine at Oyu Tolgoi began production in July 2013. In 2010 hard coal production was 19·44m. tonnes; lignite production, 5·72m. tonnes. Copper production, 2012, 121,660 tonnes; gold production, 2012, 5,995 kg.

Agriculture

The prevailing Mongolian style of life is pastoral nomadism. Livestock production comprises 79·5% of the total agricultural production. In 2013 there were 20·1m. sheep, 2·9m. cattle, 2·6m. horses and 321,000 camels. The number of goats rose from 5·6m. to 19·2m. between 1993 and 2013 as production of cashmere has increased along with the market economy. The winter of 2009–10 was extremely harsh, resulting in the loss of some 7·8m. animals, representing 17% of Mongolia's livestock. In spite of this, livestock outnumber humans by 14 to 1.

In 2007 there were around 851,000 ha. of arable land and 2,000 ha. of permanent crop land. In 2013 output of major crops was 368,000 tonnes of wheat and 192,000 tonnes of potatoes. Vegetables produced in 2013 included (in tonnes): carrots and turnips, 35,000; cabbages, kale, etc., 21,000; onions, 9,000. Livestock products, 2013 (in 1,000 tonnes): milk, 510; meat, 251. There were 48 tractors and seven harvester-threshers per 10,000 ha. of arable land in 2006.

Forestry

Forests, chiefly larch, cedar, fir and birch, occupied 12·55m. ha. in 2015 (8% of the land area). Timber production was 815,000 cu. metres in 2011.

Fisheries

The catch in 2012 was 61 tonnes, entirely from inland waters.

Industry

Industry is still small in scale and local in character. The food industry accounts for 25% of industrial production. The main industrial centre is Ulaanbaatar; others are at Darhan and Erdenet. Production figures (2014): cement, 411,300 tonnes; lime, 58,000 tonnes; bread, 30,200 tonnes; carpets, 743,600 sq. metres; sawnwood, 16,400 cu. metres.

Labour

The labour force in 2013 was 1,302,000 (1,024,000 in 2003). 65·6% of the population aged 15–64 was economically active in 2013. In the same year 5·0% of the population was unemployed.

International Trade

Imports and Exports

In 2006 imports (f.o.b.) were valued at US$1,356·7m. and exports (f.o.b.) at US$1,545·2m. Main exports, 2006: copper concentrate, 42·7%; gold, 18·1%; refined copper, 7·2%. Minerals account for over 80% of Mongolia's exports. Principal import suppliers in 2006: Russia, 36·9%; China, 27·2%; Japan, 6·6%; South Korea, 5·6%. Main export markets, 2006: China, 67·8%; Canada, 11·1%; USA, 7·7%; Russia, 2·9%. In the meantime China's share of Mongolia's exports has risen to over 80%. Mongolia sends a larger percentage of its total exports to China than any other country.

Communications

Roads

The total road network covers around 49,200 km, of which about 2,400 km are paved. Truck services run where there are no surfaced roads. Vehicles in use in 2007 included 110,200 passenger cars and 37,300 lorries and vans. In 2008 passenger transport totalled 1,215m. passenger-km and freight 782m. tonne-km. In 2007 there were 562 fatalities as a result of road accidents.

Rail

The Trans-Mongolian Railway (1,815 km of 1,520 mm gauge in 2011) connects Ulaanbaatar with the Russian Federation and China. There are spur lines to Erdenet and to the coal mines at Baganuur, Nalayh and Sharyn Gol and the fluorspar mine at Bor-Öndör. A separate line connects Choybalsan in the east with Borzaya on the Trans-Siberian Railway. In 2011, 3·8m. passengers and 18·4m. tonnes of freight were carried.

Civil Aviation

MIAT Mongolian Airlines operates internal services, and in 2010 flew from Ulaanbaatar to Beijing, Berlin, Moscow, Seoul and Tokyo. In 2012 scheduled airline traffic of Mongolian-based carriers flew 7·4m. km; passenger-km totalled 861·0m. in the same year. In 2012 Ulaanbaatar handled 1,096,649 passengers and 6,143 tonnes of freight.

Shipping

There is a steamer service on the Selenge River and a tug and barge service on Hövsgöl Lake.

Telecommunications

In 2013 there were 175,698 main (fixed) telephone lines; mobile phone subscriptions numbered 3,526,000 in 2013 (124·2 per 100 persons). An estimated 17·7% of the population were internet users in 2013. In March 2012 there were 459,000 Facebook users.

Social Institutions

Out of 178 countries analysed in the 2017 *Fragile States Index*—a list published jointly by the Fund for Peace and *Foreign Policy* magazine—Mongolia was ranked the joint 50th least vulnerable (along with Trinidad and Tobago) to conflict or collapse. The index is based on 12 indicators of state vulnerability across social, political and economic categories.

Justice

The Procurator-General is appointed, and the Supreme Court elected, by parliament for five years. There are also courts at province, town and district level. Lay assessors sit with professional judges. The death penalty, which had not been used since 2008, was abolished in 2017.

The population in penal institutions in Oct. 2012 was 8,193 (287 per 100,000 of national population). Mongolia was ranked 57th of 102 countries for criminal justice and 41st for civil justice in the 2015 World Justice Project *Rule of Law Index*, which provides data on how the rule of law is experienced by the general public across eight categories.

Education

Adult literacy was 98·3% in 2010 (male, 98·2%; female, 98·3%). Schooling begins at the age of seven. In 2007 there were 94,702 children in pre-primary education and 3,262 teaching staff; 239,262 pupils and 7,572 teaching staff in primary education; and 328,009 pupils and 16,605 teaching staff in secondary schools. There were 142,411 students in tertiary education in 2007 and 8,754 academic staff. In 2009 there were 151 tertiary education institutions (42 public and 109 private).

In 2007 public expenditure on education came to 5·2% of GNI.

Health

Over the period 2006–13 Mongolia had 27·6 physicians for every 10,000 inhabitants, 35·0 nursing and midwifery personnel for every 10,000 and 1·9 dentistry personnel per 10,000. In 2013 there were 2·5 public hospitals per 100,000 inhabitants. Mongolia had the equivalent of 68 hospital beds per 10,000 inhabitants in 2011.

In *Water: At What Cost? The State of the World's Water 2016*, WaterAid reported that 35·6% of the population does not have access to safe water.

Religion

Tibetan Buddhist Lamaism is the prevalent religion; the Dalai Lama is its spiritual head. In 2009 there were 457 registered places of worship; 239 of these were Buddhist, 161 Christian and 44 Muslim.

Culture

World Heritage Sites

Mongolia has five sites (two shared) on the UNESCO World Heritage List: the Orkhon Valley Cultural Landscape (inscribed on the list in 2004), an extensive area on both banks of the Orkhon River including the archaeological remains of Kharkhorum, the 13th and 14th century capital of Genghis Khan's vast Empire; the Petroglyphic Complexes of the Mongolian Altai (2011), numerous rock carvings and funerary monuments that date back to 11,000 BC; and Great Burkhan Khaldun Mountain and its surrounding sacred landscape (2015), believed to be the place of birth and burial of Genghis Khan. The fourth site falls under joint Mongolian and Russian jurisdiction: Uvs Nuur Basin (2003), an important saline lake system supporting a rich wildlife, especially the snow leopard and Asiatic ibex. Landscapes of Dauria (2017), an outstanding example of the Daurian Steppe eco-region, is shared with the Russian Federation.

Press

In 2008 there were 15 paid-for daily newspapers with a combined circulation of 61,000 and 115 paid-for non-dailies with a circulation of 197,000. The leading paid-for dailies are *Udriin Sonin* (Daily News) and *Onoodor*.

Tourism

In 2011 there were 458,000 non-resident visitors to Mongolia; visitor numbers have doubled since 2003 and trebled since 2000.

Diplomatic Representatives

Of Mongolia in the United Kingdom (7–8 Kensington Court, London, W8 5DL)
Ambassador: Tulga Narkhuu.

Of the United Kingdom in Mongolia (Peace Ave. 30, Bayanzurkh District, Ulaanbaatar 13381)
Ambassador: Philip Malone, LVO.

Of Mongolia in the USA (2833 M St., NW, Washington, D.C., 20007)
Ambassador: Yondon Otgonbayar.

Of the USA in Mongolia (Denver St. No. 3, 11th Micro District, Ulaanbaatar 14190)
Ambassador: Vacant.
Chargé d'Affaires a.i.: Manuel P. Micaller.

Of Mongolia to the United Nations
Ambassador: Sukhbold Sukhee.

Of Mongolia to the European Union
Ambassador: Khishigdelger Davaadorj.

Further Reading

State Statistical Office: *Statistical Yearbook* (now discontinued).—*National Economy of the MPR, 1924–1984: Anniversary Statistical Collection.* Ulaanbaatar, 1984

Akiner, S. (ed.) *Mongolia Today.* 1992

Becker, J., *The Lost Country.* 1992

Bruun, O. and Odgaard, O. (eds) *Mongolia in Transition.* 1996

Griffin, K. (ed.) *Poverty and the Transition to a Market Economy in Mongolia.* 1995

Hanson, Jennifer L., *Mongolia.* 2003

Rossabi, Morris, *Modern Mongolia: From Khans to Commissars to Capitalists.* 2005

National Statistical Office: Government Building-III, Bagatoiruu-44, Ulaanbaatar-11.

Website: http://www.nso.mn

Montenegro

Republika Crna Gora (Republic of Montenegro)

Capital: Podgorica
Population projection, 2020: 629,000
GNI per capita, 2017: (PPP$) 16,779
HDI/world rank, 2017: 0·814/50
Internet domain extension: .me

Key Historical Events

Montenegro emerged as a separate entity on the break-up of the Serbian Empire in 1355. Owing to its mountainous terrain, it was never effectively subdued by Turkey. It was ruled by Bishop Princes until 1851, when a royal house was founded. The Treaty of Berlin (1828) recognized the independence of Montenegro and doubled the size of the territory.

The assassination of Archduke Franz Ferdinand of Austria in Sarajevo on 28 June 1914 precipitated the First World War. In the winter of 1915–16 the Serbian army was forced to retreat to Corfu, where the government aimed at a centralized, Serb-run state. But exiles from Croatia and Slovenia wanted a South Slav federation. This was accepted by the victorious Allies as the basis for the new state. The Croats were forced by the pressure of events to join Serbia and Montenegro on 1 Dec. 1918. From 1918–29 the country was known as the Kingdom of the Serbs, Croats and Slovenes.

A constitution of 1921 established an assembly but the trappings of parliamentarianism could not bridge the gulf between Serbs and Croats. On 6 Jan. 1929 King Alexander I suspended the constitution and established a royal dictatorship, redrawing provincial boundaries without regard for ethnicity. In Oct. 1934 he was murdered by a Croat extremist while on an official visit to France.

During the regency of Prince Paul, the government pursued a pro-fascist line. On 25 March 1941 Paul was persuaded to adhere to the Axis Tripartite Pact. On 27 March he was overthrown by military officers in favour of the boy king Peter. Germany invaded on 6 April. Within ten days Yugoslavia surrendered; king and government fled to London. Resistance was led by a royalist group and the communist-dominated partisans of Josip Broz, nicknamed Tito. Having succeeded in liberating Yugoslavia, Tito set up a Soviet-type constitution but he was too independent for Russian leader Joseph Stalin, who sought to topple him. However, Tito made a *rapprochement* with the west and it was the Soviet Union under Khrushchev that had to extend the olive branch in 1956. Yugoslavia was permitted to evolve its 'own road to socialism'. Collectivization of agriculture was abandoned; and Yugoslavia became a champion of international 'non-alignment'. A collective presidency came into being with the death of Tito in 1980.

Dissensions in Kosovo between Albanians and Serbs, and in parts of Croatia between Serbs and Croats, reached crisis point after 1988. Fighting began in Croatia between Croatian forces and Serb irregulars from Serb-majority areas of Croatia. On 25 Sept. 1991 the UN Security Council imposed a mandatory arms embargo on Yugoslavia. Slovenia and Croatia declared their independence from the Yugoslav federation on 8 Oct., and on 15 Jan. 1992 the EU recognized both as independent states. Bosnia and Herzegovina was recognized on 7 April (and later Macedonia—now called North Macedonia—on 8 April 1993). On 27 April 1992 Serbia and Montenegro created a new Federal Republic of Yugoslavia.

On 30 May 1992, responding to further Serbian military activities in Bosnia and Croatia, the UN Security Council voted to impose sanctions. In mid-1992 NATO committed air, sea and eventually land forces to enforce sanctions and protect humanitarian relief operations in Bosnia. At a joint UN-EC peace conference on Yugoslavia held in London on 26–27 Aug. some 30 countries and all the former republics of Yugoslavia endorsed a plan to end the fighting in Croatia and Bosnia, install UN supervision of heavy weapons, recognize the borders of Bosnia and Herzegovina and return refugees. At a further conference at Geneva on 30 Sept. the Croatian and Yugoslav presidents agreed to make efforts to bring about a peaceful solution in Bosnia, although fighting continued. Following the Bosnian-Croatian-Yugoslav (Dayton) agreement all UN sanctions were lifted in Nov. 1995.

In July 1997 Slobodan Milošević switched his power base to become president of federal Yugoslavia. The former Yugoslav foreign minister, Milan Milutinović, succeeded Milošević as Serbian President. Meanwhile, in Montenegro, the pro-western Milo Đukanović succeeded a pro-Milošević president.

In 1998 unrest in Kosovo, with its largely Albanian population, led to a bid for outright independence. Violence flared resulting in what a US official described as 'horrendous human rights violations', including massive shelling of civilians and destruction of villages. US support for a degree of autonomy (short of independence), accepted in principle by President Milošević, lifted the immediate threat of NATO air strikes. Following further outbreaks of violence in early 1999, peace talks in Paris broke down without a settlement though subsequently Albanian freedom fighters accepted terms allowing them broad autonomy. The sticking point on the Serbian side was the international insistence on having 28,000 NATO-led peacemakers in Kosovo to keep apart the warring factions. Meanwhile, the scale of Serbian repression in Kosovo persuaded the NATO allies to take direct action. On the night of 24 March 1999 NATO aircraft began a bombing campaign against Yugoslavian military targets. Further Serbian provocation in Kosovo caused hundreds of thousands of ethnic Albanians to seek refuge in neighbouring countries. On 9 June after 78 days of air attacks NATO and Yugoslavia signed an accord on the Serb withdrawal from Kosovo, and on 11 June NATO's peacekeeping force, KFOR, entered Kosovo.

When the general election held on 24 Sept. 2000 resulted in a victory for the opposition democratic leader Vojislav Koštunica, President Milošević demanded a second round of voting. However, in the wake of a strike by coal miners and a mass demonstration in Belgrade when the parliament building was set on fire, Milošević accepted defeat on 6 Oct. He was arrested on 1 April 2001 after a 30-hour confrontation with the authorities. On 28 June he was handed over to the United Nations War Crimes Tribunal in the Hague to face charges of crimes against humanity. On 12 Feb. 2002 the trial of Milošević, on charges of genocide and war crimes in the Balkans over a period of nearly ten years, began at the International Criminal Tribunal in The Hague. Milošević defended himself and questioned the legitimacy of the court but died in March 2006 before his trial had ended.

On 14 March 2002 Montenegro and Serbia agreed to remain part of a single entity called Serbia and Montenegro, thus relegating the name Yugoslavia to history. The agreement was ratified in principle by the federal parliament and the republican parliaments of Serbia and Montenegro on 9 April 2002. The new union came into force on 4 Feb. 2003. Most powers in this loose confederation were divided between the two republics. After 4 Feb. 2006 Serbia and Montenegro had the right to vote for independence. Following a referendum held on 21 May 2006, Montenegro declared independence on 3 June and was recognized as such by Serbia on 15 June. Montenegro became the 192nd member state of the United Nations on 28 June 2006.

Territory and Population

Montenegro is a mountainous country that opens to the Adriatic in the southwest. It is bounded in the west by Croatia, northwest by Bosnia and Herzegovina, in the northeast by Serbia and in the southeast by Albania. The capital is Podgorica (2011 census population, 150,977), although some capital functions have been transferred to Cetinje, the historic capital of the former kingdom of Montenegro. Its area is 13,812 sq. km. Population at the 2011 census was 620,029; population density per sq. km, 44·9. The main ethnic groups in 2011 were: Montenegrins (44·98%); Serbs (28·73%); Bosniaks (8·65%); Albanians (4·91%). 61·5% of the population lived in urban areas in 2011. The estimated population at 30 June 2017 was 622,373.

The UN gives a projected population for 2020 of 629,000.

© Springer Nature Limited 2020
Palgrave Macmillan (ed.), *The Statesman's Yearbook 2020*,
https://doi.org/10.1057/978-1-349-95940-2_132

The official language is the Serbian language of the Ijekavian dialect. The Roman and Cyrillic alphabets have equal status.

Social Statistics

Statistics for calendar years:

	Live births	Deaths	Marriages	Divorces
2005	7,352	5,839	3,291	499
2006	7,531	5,968	3,462	470
2007	7,834	5,979	4,005	453
2008	8,258	5,708	3,445	460

Life expectancy, 2013, 72·5 years for men and 77·2 years for women. Infant mortality per 1,000 births (2010), 7.

Climate

Mostly a central European type of climate, with cold winters and hot summers. Podgorica, Jan. 2·8°C, July 26·5°C. Annual rainfall 1,499 mm.

Constitution and Government

The *President* is elected by direct vote to serve a five-year term. There is an 81-member single-chamber *National Assembly*, elected through a party list proportional representation system to serve four-year terms. The *Prime Minister* is nominated by the President and has to be approved by the National Assembly.

A referendum was held on 29 Feb.–1 March 1992 to determine whether Montenegro should remain within a common state, Yugoslavia, as a sovereign republic. The electorate was 412,000, of whom 66% were in favour. The then president, Milo Đukanović, had pledged a referendum on independence in May 2002, but this was postponed with the announcement of the creation of the new entity of Serbia and Montenegro, which came into being on 4 Feb. 2003.

Montenegro held a referendum on 21 May 2006 in which 55·5% voted for independence. The margin required for victory was 55·0%. Turnout was 86·6%.

Recent Elections

In presidential elections held on 15 April 2018 former president (from 1998–2002) and four-time prime minister Milo Đukanović of the Democratic Party of Socialists of Montenegro was elected with 53·9% of votes cast, defeating the independent candidate Mladen Bojanić with 33·4%, Draginja Vuksanović of the Social Democratic Party with 8·2% and four other candidates. Turnout was 63·9%.

Parliamentary elections were held on 16 Oct. 2016. The Democratic Party of Socialists of Montenegro (DPS CG) won 36 of 81 seats (with 41·4% of votes cast), the Democratic Front (consisting of New Serb Democracy, the Movement for Changes, the Democratic People's Party and the Workers' Party) 18 (20·3%), the Key Coalition 9 (11·1%), Democratic Montenegro 8 (10·0%), the Social Democratic Party 4 (5·2%), the Social Democrats 2 (3·3%), the Bosniak Party 2 (3·2%), Albanians Decisively 1 (1·3%) and the Croatian Civic Initiative 1 (0·5%). Turnout was 73·3%.

Current Government

President: Milo Đukanović; b. 1962 (DPS CG; sworn in 20 May 2018).
In Feb. 2019 the cabinet comprised:
Prime Minister: Duško Marković; b. 1958 (DPS CG; sworn in 28 Nov. 2016).
Deputy Prime Minister for Economic Policy and the Financial System: Milutin Simović (also *Minister of Agriculture and Rural Development*). *Deputy Prime Minister for the Political System, Interior and Foreign Policy:* Zoran Pažin (also *Minister of Justice and Acting Minister of European Affairs*). *Deputy Prime Minister for Regional Development:* Rafet Husović.
Minister of Culture: Aleksandar Bogdanović. *Defence:* Predrag Bošković. *Economy:* Dragica Sekulić. *Education:* Damir Šehović. *Finance:* Darko Radunović. *Foreign Affairs:* Srđan Darmanović. *Health:* Kenan Hrapović. *Human and Minority Rights:* Mehmed Zenka. *Interior:* Melvudin

Nuhodžić. *Labour and Social Welfare:* Kemal Purišić. *Public Administration:* Suzana Pribilović. *Science:* Sanja Damjanović. *Sports:* Nikola Janović. *Sustainable Development and Tourism:* Pavle Radulović. *Transport and Maritime Affairs:* Osman Nurković. *Minister without Portfolio:* Marija Vučinović.
Government Website: http://www.gov.me

Current Leaders

Milo Đukanović

Position
President

Introduction

Milo Đukanović, the head of the Democratic Party of Socialists of Montenegro (DPS CG), became president for a second time in May 2018. He has frequently led Montenegro since 1991, both as prime minister and president.

Early Life

Đukanović was born on 15 Feb. 1962 in Nikšić, graduating in economics from Veljko Vlahović University in 1986. As a high school student, he had joined the Yugoslav Communist League (that later became the DPS CG), of which his father was a prominent local branch member. Đukanović quickly rose through the League's ranks and was appointed prime minister on 15 Feb. 1991 by President Momir Bulatović (with the blessing of Serbian President Slobodan Milošević).

During his first premiership, Montenegro formally joined with Serbia to form the Federal Republic of Yugoslavia. In the 1991–95 Bosnian War he sanctioned attacks on Dubrovnik in Croatia and on assorted Bosnian towns, and oversaw the arrest of Bosnian refugees who were sent to Serb prison camps.

In 1997 Đukanović defeated Montenegro's incumbent president, Momir Bulatović, in elections tainted by allegations of irregularities. Đukanović was sworn in as president on 15 Jan. 1998 and in the same year was elected president of the DPS CG. As Yugoslavia found itself estranged from much of the international community under the stewardship of Milošević, Đukanović sought to maintain communications with the West. In Nov. 2002 he resigned as president to become prime minister for a second time (from Jan. 2003). In July 2003 Italian prosecutors linked him to an organised crime racket worth billions of euros, but the case was eventually dropped in April 2009.

Having been instrumental in the creation of the State Union of Serbia and Montenegro, Đukanović then steered Montenegro into a peaceful separation from Serbia on 3 Jun. 2006. In Nov. that year he retired as prime minister, endorsing Željko Šturanović as his successor, but returned to office in Feb. 2008 following Šturanović's resignation. His third stint as prime minister saw Montenegro become an official European Union candidate country on 17 Dec. 2010. It was also granted a NATO Membership Action Plan in Dec. 2009, leading ultimately to NATO accession on 5 June 2017.

Đukanović resigned again as prime minister in Dec. 2010 but returned to office for a fourth time in Dec. 2012. In Oct. 2015 widespread protests sought to secure his resignation as he was named 'Man of the Year in Organized Crime' by the Organized Crime and Corruption Project, a consortium of investigative centres. In the general elections of Oct. 2016 Russia allegedly attempted a coup against the Montenegrin government but failed. Đukanović abruptly stepped down, only to return to high office on the back of a landslide victory in the April 2018 presidential elections. He was sworn in as head of state on 20 May 2018.

Career in Office

As president for a second time, Đukanović's agenda is to take Montenegro into the European Union. To do so, he must align the country's foreign policy with that of the EU, while managing strong pro-Russian sympathies within his country. Domestically, he must strive to reduce organized crime by reforming the rule of law and eradicating corruption, nepotism and bureaucracy. Economic prosperity relies on lowering the unemployment rate, which stood at over 20% in 2018.

Defence

The all-professional Military of Montenegro was formed from part of the Armed Forces of Serbia and Montenegro when the two countries became independent in 2006.

Defence expenditure in 2013 totalled US$54m. (US$82 per capita), representing 1·2% of GDP.

Army

Strength (2011) 2,356. There are paramilitary forces numbering around 10,100.

Navy

Strength (2011) 402, with five patrol and coastal combatants.

Economy

In 2014 agriculture accounted for 10·0% of GDP, industry 17·7% and services 72·3%.

Overview

From its independence in 2006 until the onset of the global financial crisis two years later, Montenegro's economy experienced strong expansion. Real GDP growth averaged 9% annually from 2006–08, with tourism attracting large inflows of foreign direct investment and generating construction activity. The contribution of tourism to GDP rose from 15% in 2004 to over 22% in 2016, despite a temporary decline resulting from the financial crisis. In Dec. 2008 Montenegro applied to join the European Union and accession negotiations opened in 2012.

Although the global downturn had prompted a deep recession, there was a strong rebound after 2013 when GDP growth of 3·5% restored output to 2008 levels. Growth then averaged 2·6% from 2014 to 2016. According to the World Bank, the economy has good potential but is hindered by structural and fiscal vulnerabilities.

Currency

On 2 Nov. 1999 the pro-Western government decided to make the Deutsche Mark legal tender alongside the dinar. Subsequently it was made the sole official currency, and consequently the *euro* (EUR) became the currency of Montenegro on 1 Jan. 2002. There was deflation of 0·3% in 2016 but then inflation of 2·4% in 2017.

Budget

In 2013 revenues totalled €1,587·1m. and expenditures €1,605·3m.

VAT was raised from 19% to 21% as of Jan. 2018. The reduced rate remained at 7%.

Performance

Total GDP in 2017 was US$4·8bn. The economy grew by 3·4% in 2015, 2·9% in 2016 and 4·3% in 2017.

Banking and Finance

The Central Bank of Montenegro (*Governor*, Radoje Žugić) was established in Nov. 2000. Montenegro has 11 commercial banks. Foreign debt was US$1,554m. in 2010, representing 39·1% of GNI.

Energy and Natural Resources

Electricity

Electricity production in 2012 was 2,844,456 MWh.

Minerals

Lignite production in 2012 totalled 1,785,999 tonnes; bauxite production in 2011 was 158,614 tonnes.

Agriculture

In 2011 the cultivated area was 189,100 ha. Yields (2011, in 1,000 tonnes): potatoes, 180·1; grapes, 32·8; plums, 12·1; maize, 11·7; oranges and tangerines, 7·9; wheat, 2·4. Livestock (1 Dec. 2011, 1,000 head): poultry, 470; sheep, 209; cattle, 87; pigs, 21.

Forestry

Forest area in 2015 was 0·83m. ha., covering 62% of the total land area. Timber cut in 2011: 915,000 cu. metres.

Fisheries

In 2015 the catch amounted to 1,486 tonnes, of which 55% came from marine waters.

Environment

Carbon dioxide emissions from the consumption of energy in 2011 were the equivalent of 25·5 tonnes per capita.

Industry

Production (2012 unless otherwise indicated, in 1,000 tonnes): crude steel (2010), 130; wheat flour, 40; steel ingots, 20; bread, 17; cigarettes, 535m. units; beer, 41·7m. litres.

Labour

In 2011 there were 163,082 people in employment, including 37,820 in wholesale and retail trade, repair of vehicles, personal and household goods; 19,195 in public administration and defence, and compulsory social security; 14,368 in manufacturing. Average gross monthly wages for 2011 were €722. Unemployment rate in 2011 was 19·7%.

Communications

Roads

In 2013 there were 7,965 km of roads. Passenger-km in 2013 were 109m.; tonne-km of freight carried, 67m.

Rail

In 2009 there were 249 km of railway. 1·1m. passengers and 2m. tonnes of freight were carried in 2009.

Civil Aviation

The national carrier is Montenegro Airlines, which has flights to a number of cities throughout Europe. There are airports at Podgorica and Tivat, which handled 450,504 and 532,148 passengers in 2009 respectively.

Shipping

In Jan. 2014 there were four ships of 300 GT or over registered, totalling 45,000 GT.

Telecommunications

There were 1,159,000 mobile phone subscriptions in 2011 and an estimated 171,000 landline telephone subscriptions. In 2012, 55·0% of households had internet access. In March 2012 there were 293,000 Facebook users.

Social Institutions

Out of 178 countries analysed in the 2017 *Fragile States Index*—a list published jointly by the Fund for Peace and *Foreign Policy* magazine—Montenegro was ranked the 49th least vulnerable to conflict or collapse. The index is based on 12 indicators of state vulnerability across social, political and economic categories.

Justice

There are a Supreme Court, two High Courts, 15 Municipal Courts, two Commercial Courts, one Appellate Court and one Administrative Court. In 2011 the Supreme Court had 18 judges, the High Courts 54, the Municipal Courts 147, the Commercial Courts 22, the Appellate Court 12 and the Administrative Court 10.

Education

In 2011–12 there were: 108 pre-schools with 14,155 pupils and 841 teachers; 163 central primary schools with 69,461 pupils and 269 regional primary schools with 5,048 teachers; and 49 secondary schools with 31,914 pupils and 2,396 teachers. There were three universities in 2011 (one public and two private). A total of 25,313 students were enrolled at the universities and other higher education institutions at the beginning of the 2011–12 academic year, including 3,086 in postgraduate and doctoral studies.

Health

In 2011 there were eight general hospitals with 1,706 beds. A total of 66,451 patients were admitted in 2011.

In *Water: At What Cost? The State of the World's Water 2016*, WaterAid reported that 0·3% of the population does not have access to safe water.

Religion

The Serbian Orthodox Church is the official church in Montenegro. The Montenegrin Church was banned in 1922, but in Oct. 1993 a breakaway Montenegrin Church was set up under its own patriarch.

Culture

World Heritage Sites

There are four sites on the UNESCO World Heritage List: the Natural and Culturo-Historical Region of Kotor (inscribed on the list in 1979); and Durmitor National Park (1980 and 2005).

Montenegro shares the Stećci Medieval Tombstones Graveyards (2016) with Bosnia and Herzegovina, Croatia and Serbia. The Venetian Works of Defence between the 16th and 17th Centuries: *Stato da Terra*—Western *Stato da Mar* (2017) are shared with Croatia and Italy.

Press

In 2008 there were four daily newspapers with a combined circulation of 46,000.

Tourism

In 2010 there were 1,087,794 non-resident overnight tourist arrivals. The main countries of origin were: Serbia (314,836); Russia (150,194); Bosnia and Herzegovina (103,025); France (42,099).

Diplomatic Representatives

Of Montenegro in the United Kingdom (47 De Vere Gdns, London, W8 5AW)
    Ambassador: Borislav Banović.

Of the United Kingdom in Montenegro (Ulcinjska 8, Gorica C, 81000 Podgorica)
    Ambassador: Alison Kemp.

Of Montenegro in the USA (1610 New Hampshire Ave., Washington, D.C., 20009)
    Ambassador: Nebojša Kaludjerović.

Of the USA in Montenegro (Dzona Dzeksona 2, 81000 Podgorica)
    Ambassador: Judy Rising Reinke.

Of Montenegro to the United Nations
    Ambassador: Milica Pejanović-Đurišić.

Of Montenegro to the European Union
    Ambassador: Bojan Šarkić.

Further Reading

Fleming, Thomas, *Montenegro: The Divided Land.* 2002
Roberts, Elizabeth, *Realm of the Black Mountain: A History of Montenegro.* 2007
Stevenson, Francis Seymour, *A History of Montenegro.* 2002
National Statistical Office: Statistical Office of the Republic of Montenegro, IV Proleterske No. 2, 81000 Podgorica.
Website: http://www.monstat.org

Morocco

Mamlaka al-Maghrebia (Kingdom of Morocco)

Capital: Rabat
Population projection, 2020: 37·07m.
GNI per capita, 2017: (PPP$) 7,340
HDI/world rank, 2017: 0·667/123
Internet domain extension: .ma

Key Historical Events

Neolithic settlements in western North Africa date from around 6000 BC. Semi-nomadic Berber clans established a foothold in the region at the end of the second millennium BC. Phoenician and Carthaginian merchants founded coastal settlements in northern Morocco from around 500 BC. In the following centuries Roman traders established bases, including Tangier and Volubilis. Roman influence increased after the fall of Carthage in 146 BC and endured until the 5th century AD, when the region was attacked by the Vandals in AD 429 and Byzantines in AD 533.

An Arab invasion of Morocco in 682 made Islam the dominant religion although several Jewish colonies remained. The first Arab rulers established an independent Kingdom in 788 under Idris I and held sway until around 900, when Morocco fragmented into Arab and Berber tribal states. Conflict ensued with the Fatimids of Tunisia and the Umayidds of Andalusia until 1062, when the Almoravids of Marrakesh established a kingdom that stretched from Spain to Senegal.

Portuguese forces captured the port of Ceuta in 1415 and subsequently took most other Moroccan coastal towns, except Melilla and Larache which fell to Spain. The threat from Christian Portugal and Spain spurred resistance among Islamic families, culminating in the rise of Ahmed I al-Mansur, whose Sharifian dynasty unified the country between 1579 and 1603. Moors and Jews expelled from Spain settled in Morocco during this time and the country flourished.

The second Sharifian dynasty emerged in 1660 and by 1700 Moroccan forces had regained control of most ports. During the 18th and early 19th centuries the North African (Barbary) coast was notorious for piracy. The European powers vied to exploit Morocco's strategic position and resources as the century progressed, with French forces defeating Sultan Abd ar Rahman in 1844 and Spain invading in 1860.

As part of the Entente Cordiale, signed in 1904, Britain recognized Morocco as a French sphere of influence and Morocco was divided between France and Spain. In 1912 a Franco–Spanish agreement divided Morocco into four administrative areas: a French protectorate, the largest share of the territory, centred on Rabat; a Spanish protectorate with its capital at Tétouan; a Southern Protectorate of Morocco, administered as part of the Spanish Sahara; and the international zone of Tangier.

A revolt led by Abd al-Krim in the northern region of Rif in 1921 was crushed after five years. A nationalist movement gradually gained ground and an independence party, the Istiqlal, was formed during the Second World War. Facing growing disorder and nationalist revolts in its North African colonies, France relinquished control over Morocco in March 1956 and on 29 Oct. 1956 the international status of the Tangier Zone was abolished. Morocco became an independent kingdom on 18 Aug. 1957, with the Sultan taking the title Mohammed V.

Succeeding his father on 3 March 1961, King Hassan II tried to establish an elected House of Representatives but, following political unrest, he seized legislative and executive powers in June 1965. The country returned to partial democracy under a controversially amended constitution. Morocco annexed Western Sahara in 1975, which sparked a guerrilla war with Algerian-backed pro-independence forces (Polisario) that continued until 1991. The territory's status remains unresolved. Hassan II received plaudits for his work promoting peace in the Middle East but criticism for human rights abuses. Following his death in 1999 his son, Mohammed VI, introduced a more liberal economic and social regime but retains sweeping powers.

Territory and Population

Morocco is bounded by Algeria to the east and southeast, Mauritania to the south, the Atlantic Ocean to the northwest and the Mediterranean to the north. Excluding the Western Saharan territory claimed and retrieved since 1976 by Morocco, the area is 446,550 sq. km. The population at the 2014 census (including Western Sahara) was 33,848,242 (excluding Sahrawi refugees living in Algerian camps). Population density in 2014 (including Western Sahara), 48 per sq. km; density excluding Western Sahara, 75 per sq. km. At the 2014 census Western Sahara had a population of about 500,000 (excluding Sahrawi refugees living in Algerian camps). The Moroccan superficie is 710,850 sq. km. The population was 58·8% urban in 2011.

The UN gives a projected population for 2020 of 37·07m.

Morocco has 12 regions, which are subdivided into 62 provinces and 13 prefectures. Regions with their census populations in 2014 and capitals are:

Region	Population	Capital
Béni Mellal-Khénifra	2,520,776	Béni Mellal
Dakhla-Oued Eddahab[1]	142,955	Oued Eddahab
Drâa-Tafilalet	1,635,008	Errachidia
Fès-Meknès	4,236,892	Fès (Fez)
Grand Casablanca-Settat	6,861,739	Casablanca
Guelmim-Oued Noun	433,757	Guelmim
Laâyoune-Sakia Al Hamra[1]	367,758	Laâyoune
Marrakesh-Safi	4,520,569	Marrakesh (Marrakech)
Oriental	2,314,346	Oujda Angad
Rabat-Salé-Kénitra	4,580,866	Rabat
Sous-Massa	2,676,847	Agadir Ida-Outanane
Tangier-Tétouan-Al Hoceima	3,556,729	Tanger-Asilah (Tanger-Assilah)

[1]Dakhla-Oued Eddahab and Laâyoune-Sakia Al Hamra correspond roughly to Western Sahara.

The chief cities (with populations in 1,000, 2014) are as follows:

Casablanca	3,360
Fez	1,112
Tangier	948
Marrakesh	929
Salé	890
Rabat	578
Meknès	520
Oujda	494
Kénitra	431
Agadir	422
Tétouan	381
Safi	309

The official languages are Arabic, spoken by 65% of the population, and Berber (since July 2011). Berber languages, including Tachelhit (or Soussi), Tamazight and Tarafit (or Rifia), are spoken by about half the population. French (widely used for business), Spanish (in the north) and English are also spoken.

Social Statistics

2008 estimates: births, 645,000; deaths, 184,000. Estimated rates, 2008 (per 1,000 population): birth, 20·4; death, 5·8. Annual population growth rate, 2000–08, 1·2%. Life expectancy at birth in 2013 was 69·1 years for males and 72·7 years for females. Infant mortality, 2010, 30 per 1,000 live births; fertility rate, 2008, 2·4 births per woman.

Climate

Morocco is dominated by the Mediterranean climate which is made temperate by the influence of the Atlantic Ocean in the northern and southern parts of the country. Central Morocco is continental while the south is desert. Rabat, Jan. 55°F (12·9°C), July 72°F (22·2°C). Annual rainfall 23" (564 mm). Agadir, Jan. 57°F (13·9°C), July 72°F (22·2°C). Annual rainfall 9" (224 mm). Casablanca, Jan. 54°F (12·2°C), July 72°F (22·2°C). Annual rainfall 16" (404 mm). Marrakesh, Jan. 52°F (11·1°C), July 84°F (28·9°C). Annual rainfall 10" (239 mm). Tangier, Jan. 53°F (11·7°C), July 72°F (22·2°C). Annual rainfall 36" (897 mm).

Constitution and Government

The ruling King is **Mohammed VI**, born on 21 Aug. 1963, married to Salma Bennani on 21 March 2002; succeeded on 23 July 1999, on the death of his father Hassan II, who reigned 1961–99. *Offspring:* Hassan, b. 8 May 2003; Khadija, b. 28 Feb. 2007. The King holds supreme civil and religious authority, the latter in his capacity of Emir-el-Muminin or Commander of the Faithful. He resides usually at Rabat, but occasionally in one of the other traditional capitals, Fez (founded in 808), Marrakesh (founded in 1062), or at Skhirat.

In Feb. and March 2011, Morocco experienced popular protests echoing those occurring in other North African states. In response King Mohammed established a commission to bring about 'comprehensive constitutional reform'. It recommended that: the king select the prime minister from the party with the greatest parliamentary representation; the prime minister, not the king, be head of government and have the power to dissolve parliament; parliament have greater influence on civil rights, nationality issues and electoral law; women be guaranteed 'civic and social' equality with men; the Berber language become an official state language; and a reference to the king as 'sacred' be removed from the constitution. It also provides for the independence of the judiciary. On 1 July 2011 the reforms won 98·5% support in a referendum (turnout: 73·5%), although some opponents claimed electoral irregularities.

The new constitution came into effect on 29 July 2011, ahead of the parliamentary elections four months later. It replaced an earlier constitution that was approved in March 1972 and amended several times. The Kingdom of Morocco is a constitutional monarchy. Parliament consists of a House of Representatives composed of 395 deputies directly elected for five-year terms. A referendum on 13 Sept. 1996 established a second House of Councillors, which since 2011 has been composed of a minimum of 90 and a maximum of 120 indirectly elected members serving six-year terms, with one-third renewed every two years. The House of Councillors has power to initiate legislation, issue warnings of censure to the government and ultimately to force the government's resignation by a two-thirds majority vote.

An electoral code of March 1997 fixed voting at 20 and made enrolment on the electoral roll compulsory. In Dec. 2002 King Mohammed VI announced that the voting age was to be lowered from 20 to 18.

National Anthem

'Manbit al Ahrah, mashriq al anwar' ('Fountain of freedom, source of light'); words by Ali Squalli Houssaini, tune by Leo Morgan.

Government Chronology

Kings since 1955.

1955–61	Mohammed V ibn Yusuf (sultan from 1955–57)
1961–99	Hassan II ibn Mohammed
1999–	Mohammed VI ibn al-Hassan

Recent Elections

Elections to the House of Representatives took place on 7 Oct. 2016. The Islamist Parti de la Justice et du Développement (PJD/Party of Justice and Development) took 125 of 395 seats; Parti Authenticité et Modernité (PAM/Authenticity and Modernity Party) 102; Parti de l'Indépendance/Istiqlal (PI/Independence Party) 46; Rassemblement National des Indépendants (RNI/National Rally of Independents) 37; Mouvement Populaire (MP/Popular Movement) 27; Union Socialiste des Forces Populaires (USFP/Socialist Union of Popular Forces) 20; Union Constitutionnelle (UC/Constitutional Union) 19; Parti du Progrès et du Socialisme (PPS/Party of Progress and Socialism) 12; Mouvement Démocratique et Social (MDS/Democratic and Social Movement) 3; Fédération de la Gauche Démocratique (FGD/Federation of the Democratic Left) 2. Two other parties took one seat each. Turnout was 43%.

In indirect elections to the House of Councillors on 2 Oct. 2015 Istiqlal gained 24 of 120 seats, PAM 23, PJD 12, MP 10, RNI 8 and independents 8. The remaining seats went to 13 other parties.

Current Government

In Feb. 2019 the government comprised:

Prime Minister: Saadeddine Othmani; b. 1956 (Party of Justice and Development; in office since 5 April 2017).

Minister of State for Human Rights: Mustapha Ramid.

Minister of the Interior: Abdelouafi Laftit. *Foreign Affairs and International Co-operation:* Nasser Bourita. *Justice:* Mohamed Aujjar. *Endowments and Islamic Affairs:* Ahmed Toufiq. *Economy and Finance:* Mohamed Benchaaboun. *Agriculture, Marine Fisheries, Rural Development, and Waters and Forests:* Aziz Akhannouch. *National Planning, Urban Planning, Housing and Urban Policy:* Abdelahad Fassi-Fihri. *National Education, Vocational Training, Higher Education and Scientific Research:* Saïd Amzazi. *Industry, Investment, Trade and the Digital Economy:* Moulay El Alamy. *Infrastructure, Transport, Water and Logistics:* Abdelkader Amara. *Health:* Anas Doukkali. *Energy, Mines and Sustainable Development:* Aziz Rebbah. *Tourism, Air Transport, Crafts and Social Economy:* Mohamed Sajid. *Youth and Sports:* Rachid Talbi Alami. *Culture and Communication:* Mohamed Laaraj. *Solidarity, Women, Family and Social Development:* Bassima Hakkaoui. *Employment and Vocational Integration:* Mohamed Yatim. *Secretary General of the Government:* Mohamed Hajoui.

Office of the Prime Minister (French, Berber and Arabic only): http://www.pm.gov.ma

Current Leaders

Mohammed VI ibn al-Hassan

Position
King

Introduction
Mohammed VI ibn al-Hassan was crowned King in July 1999 after the death of his father, King Hassan II. Less austere than his father, he has promoted modest political reforms while retaining ultimate authority. He has also encouraged private investment in key economic sectors, although there is still widespread hardship and high unemployment.

Early Life
King Mohammed VI was born on 21 Aug. 1963 in Rabat, Morocco. In 1985 he graduated from the College of Law in the Rabat Mohammed V University. In 1987 he took a degree in political science and in 1993 was awarded a law doctorate from the French University of Nice-Sophia Antipolis.

Mohammed undertook his first official royal duty aged 11 and by the time he was 20 he had led a Moroccan delegation to the Franco-African conference and negotiated with the Organization of African Unity (now the African Union) over the Western Sahara conflict.

Appointed head of the general staff of the Royal Armed Forces in 1985, he succeeded to the throne in 1999.

Career in Office
Mohammed voiced support for developing a market economy and urged increased private sector investment. However, economic liberalization has not significantly alleviated Morocco's widespread poverty or reduced unemployment. Political power remained concentrated in the monarchy until protests in early 2011—reflecting disaffection across much of the Arab world—prompted Mohammed to cede constitutional reforms in July that year, with some of the monarchy's powers being transferred to parliament and the prime minister. In line with the new constitution, Mohammed was obliged to choose Abdelilah Benkirane as his premier following the victory of the

Islamist Party of Justice and Development (PJD) in parliamentary elections in Nov. 2011 and again in Oct. 2016. However, in March 2017, five months after Benkirane had failed to form a new coalition government, Mohammed dismissed him and appointed Saadeddine Othmani, also of the PJD, in his place from April. Growing popular unrest prompted Mohammed in Aug. 2018 to replace the economy and finance minister and urge more government action to address Morocco's economic and social problems and to boost investment.

In foreign policy, Mohammed has co-operated with the USA in its anti-terror initiatives since the Sept. 2001 attacks. Morocco has itself been targeted by terrorist violence, including co-ordinated suicide bombings in Casablanca in May 2003 and further incidents in 2007 and April 2011. Elsewhere, Mohammed has expressed support for Palestinian claims to their own independent state.

In 2002 the King came into conflict with Spain when Moroccan forces landed on the uninhabited island of Perejil (a Spanish possession since 1668) off the Moroccan coast. Spain launched a bloodless counter-assault before withdrawing its troops on the understanding that neither country would occupy the island. In Jan. 2006 Spain's then prime minister, Rodríguez Zapatero, became the first Spanish leader in 25 years to make an official visit to the enclaves of Melilla and Ceuta. However, a subsequent visit to the territories by Spain's then King Juan Carlos in Nov. 2007 was criticized by Mohammed, and tension arose again in Aug. 2010 following incidents near the Melilla border.

Saadeddine Othmani

Position
Prime Minister

Introduction
Saadeddine Othmani took office as the prime minister in April 2017. He succeeded Abdelilah Benkirane, who was dismissed as premier by King Mohammed VI in mid-March after five months of deadlock in inter-party negotiations following inconclusive elections to the House of Representatives in Oct. 2016. A member of the Party of Justice and Development (PJD), Othmani heads a broad coalition in parliament.

Early Life
Saadeddine Othmani was born on 16 Jan. 1956 in Inezgane, near Agadir, on Morocco's Atlantic coast. He was awarded a doctorate in medicine from the University of Casablanca in 1986 and later earned a diploma in psychiatry. He studied Islamic law alongside medicine and in 1999 received a degree in Islamic Studies from the University of Rabat. He has since published numerous academic articles and books on the subject.

Othmani, who began his professional career working in a psychiatric hospital, was first elected to parliament in 1997. He served on the House of Representatives foreign affairs committee between 2001 and 2002, and in 2004 was appointed to lead the PJD. After ceding the party leadership to Abdelilah Benkirane in July 2008, he served as deputy parliamentary Speaker between 2010 and 2011. In Jan. 2012 he was named minister of foreign affairs, holding the position until Oct. 2013.

The PJD emerged from parliamentary elections on 7 Oct. 2016 as the largest party, with 125 of 395 seats. Benkirane, who had been prime minister since 2011, was nonetheless unable to build a workable coalition. On 15 March 2017 Mohammed VI invoked his constitutional right to dismiss Benkirane as premier, inviting the less confrontational Othmani to try to form a government instead.

Career in Office
Within days of his appointment, Othmani succeeded in forming a broad but fragmented six-party coalition. He and his new ministers were sworn in on 5 April 2017. With a reputation as a consensus builder, he was tasked with maintaining the political stability that Morocco has njoyed, relative to its more volatile regional neighbours, in recent years. However, unrest has grown in the more marginalized areas of northern Morocco that resent the slow pace of economic development and political inclusion. Consequently, at the behest of the King, Mohamed Boussaid as dismissed as economy and finance minister and replaced by Mohamed Benchaaboun in Aug. 2018.

Defence

Compulsory national military service was abolished in 2006 before being reintroduced in 2019. Defence expenditure in 2013 totalled US$3,730m. (US$114 per capita), representing 3·5% of GDP.

Army

The Army is deployed in two commands: Northern Zone and Southern Zone. There is also a Royal Guard of 1,500. Strength in 2011 was an estimated 175,000 (100,000 conscripts). There are also a Royal Gendarmerie of 20,000, an Auxiliary Force of 30,000 and reserves of 150,000.

Navy

The Navy includes three frigates, 49 patrol and coastal combatants and six amphibious craft.

Personnel in 2011 numbered 7,800, including 1,500 marines. Bases are located at Casablanca, Agadir, Al Hoceima, Dakhla and Tangier.

Air Force

Personnel strength (2011) 13,000, with 72 combat-capable aircraft, including F-5s and Mirage F-1s.

International Relations

The land border between Morocco and Algeria has been closed since 1994 following a hotel bombing in Marrakesh in which Algeria was suspected of being involved.

Economy

Agriculture accounted for 13·0% of GDP in 2014, industry 29·4% and services 57·6%.

Overview

The coalition government formed at the start of 2012 in the aftermath of popular protests the previous year embarked on cutting public subsidies, reforming pensions and encouraging greater competition. Public service provision was also high on the agenda with a view to improving education and health care. However, while a programme of subsidy cuts was completed in 2014, delays in forming a new government following the Oct. 2016 elections have slowed other ongoing reforms.

Despite the regional unrest resulting from the Arab Spring, growth averaged almost 4% per year between 2011 and 2015. Trade is strongly focused on the European Union, a 2012 agreement between the EU and Morocco having abolished tariffs on a range of industrial goods.

Extreme poverty stands at only 0·3% but income inequality is stubbornly high, with 13·3% of the population living just above the poverty line. Agriculture remains a key industry along with fisheries and forestry. About 33% of the rural poor are employed in the informal agricultural sector. Despite record cereal production in 2015, the agricultural sector contracted by 10% in 2016 due mainly to poor rainfall. The economy as a whole grew by 1·1% in 2016. New industries—most importantly, the automotive and aeronautical sectors—have helped diversify the country's export base, although non-agricultural sectors recorded growth of only 3% in 2016.

Unemployment stood at 9·4% in 2016, although 38% of urban youth were jobless. The labour participation rate is among the lowest among developing economies, measuring below 50% in 2016. Long-term job creation requires an improvement in the general business environment.

Currency

The unit of currency is the *dirham* (MAD) of 100 *centimes*, introduced in 1959. Foreign exchange reserves were US$14,710m. in July 2005, gold reserves 708,000 troy oz and total money supply was DH353,598m. Inflation was 1·6% in 2016 and 0·8% in 2017.

Budget

Revenues in 2012 totalled DH228·0bn. and expenditures DH293·9bn. Tax revenue accounted for 88·0% of revenues; current expenditure accounted for 80·1% of total expenditures.

VAT is 20% (reduced rates, 14%, 10% and 7%).

Performance

Real GDP growth was 4·5% in 2015, 1·1% in 2016 and 4·1% in 2017. Total GDP in 2017 was US$109·1bn. (including Western Sahara).

Banking and Finance

The central bank is the Bank Al Maghrib (*Governor*, Abdellatif Jouahri), which had assets of DH226,667m. in Dec. 2011. The largest bank is Attijariwafa Bank, with assets of US$40·0bn. in Dec. 2011. Other leading banks are Banque Populaire and BMCE Bank. Morocco's external debt amounted to US$25,403m. in 2010 (equivalent to 28·1% of GNI), up from US$16,174m. in 2005.

There is a stock exchange in Casablanca.

Energy and Natural Resources

Environment
Carbon dioxide emissions from the consumption of energy in 2011 were the equivalent of 1·3 tonnes per capita.

Electricity
Installed capacity was 6·7m. kW in 2011. Production was 24·36bn. kWh (approximately 88% thermal) in 2011 and consumption per capita 904 kWh. Morocco aims to have over 40% of its electricity from renewables by 2020 following the opening of a new solar power station in Feb. 2016.

Oil and Gas
Natural gas reserves in 2013 were 1·4bn. cu. metres; output (2011), 60m. cu. metres. Offshore exploration for oil is currently under way.

Minerals
The principal mineral exploited is phosphate (Morocco has the largest reserves in the world), the output of which was 27·24m. tonnes in 2006. Other minerals (in tonnes, 2006) are: barytine, 628,400; salt, 506,700; zinc, 148,700; lead, 59,100; iron, 35,500; copper, 17,800; manganese, 4,815; silver, 246.

Agriculture
Agricultural production is subject to drought; an estimated 1·53m. ha. were equipped for irrigation in 2012. There were 8·05m. ha. of arable land in 2012 and 1·36m. ha. of permanent crops. Main land usage, 2013 (in 1,000 ha.): wheat, 3,204; barley, 1,967; olives, 922. Production in 2013 (in 1,000 tonnes): wheat, 6,934; barley, 2,723; sugar beets, 2,142; potatoes, 1,929; melons and watermelons, 1,312; tomatoes, 1,293; olives, 1,182; onions, 930; oranges, 759; tangerines, mandarins, clementines and satsumas, 664. Livestock, 2013: sheep, 19·96m.; goats, 6·24m.; cattle, 3·17m.; asses, 944,000; chickens (estimate), 185m. Livestock products, 2013 (in 1,000 tonnes): chicken meat, 560; beef and veal, 254; lamb and mutton, 118; eggs (estimate), 5,245; cow's milk, 2,290; goat's milk (estimate), 62; sheep's milk (estimate), 42.

Forestry
Forests covered 5·63m. ha. in 2015, or 13% of the total land area. Of the total area under forests 87·5% was naturally regenerated forest in 2015 and 12·5% planted forest. Timber production was 7·13m. cu. metres in 2011.

Fisheries
Total catch in 2015 was 1,364,643 tonnes (sea fish, 1,349,637 tonnes). Morocco's annual catch is the highest of any African country.

Industry

The leading companies by market capitalization in Morocco in May 2018 were Maroc Telecom, US$14·5bn.; and Attijariwafa Bank, US$10·0bn.

Manufacturing contributed 15·2% of GDP in 2012. Production in 1,000 tonnes (2014): cement, 15,710; gas oil and diesel oil, 2,275; fuel oil, 1,656; sugar, 480; petrol, 331; paper and paperboard (estimate), 156; olive oil (estimate), 137.

Labour
The labour force in 2013 was 12,256,000 (10,629,000 in 2003). 52·5% of the population aged 15–64 was economically active in 2013. In the same year 9·2% of the population was unemployed. Of those in employment in 2012, 39·4% worked in services, 39·2% in agriculture and 21·4% in industry. 26·9% of the labour force in 2012 was female.

Morocco had 51,000 people living in slavery according to the Walk Free Foundation's 2013 *Global Slavery Index*.

International Trade

Imports and Exports
Imports (c.i.f.) in 2010 were US$35,379m. and exports (f.o.b.) US$17,765m. Imports in 2006 included: machinery and transport equipment, 27·7%; mineral fuels, 21·6%; chemicals and related products, 9·7%; food and live

animals, 7·0%. Exports included: apparel and clothing accessories, 25·8%; machinery and transport equipment, 17·2%; chemicals and related products, 13·4%; fish and seafood, 9·3%. In the meantime motor vehicles have become the country's biggest export. Main import suppliers, 2006: France, 16·5%; Spain, 11·6%; Saudi Arabia, 6·8%; Italy, 6·4%. Main export markets, 2006: France, 28·4%; Spain, 20·8%; UK, 6·0%; Italy, 4·9%.

Communications

Roads
In 2007 there were 57,799 km of classified roads, including 813 km of motorways and 11,251 km of main roads. By 2010 the motorway network had been extended to 1,042 km. In 2007 freight transport totalled 697m. tonne-km. In 2007 there were 1,644,500 passenger cars in use, 525,300 lorries and vans and 22,800 motorcycles and mopeds. There were 58,924 road accidents in 2007 (3,838 fatalities).

Rail
In 2010 there were 2,109 km of railways, of which 1,284 km were electrified. Passenger-km travelled in 2009 came to 4·19bn. and freight tonne-km to 4·11bn. Construction began in 2011 of Morocco's first high-speed rail link, initially from Tangier to Kénitra and eventually to Casablanca. Test runs started in early 2017 before the rail link officially launched in Nov. 2018. There are plans to build 1,500 km of high-speed rail lines in the country. In 2003 the construction of two 38 km-long rail tunnels under the Straits of Gibraltar was agreed in principle with Spain. As of late 2016 a joint research committee was analysing the technological feasibility and economic viability of the project.

Civil Aviation
The national carrier is Royal Air Maroc, which in 2013 carried 5,856,000 passengers (5,170,000 on international flights). The major international airport is Mohammed V at Casablanca; there are eight other airports. Casablanca handled 7,186,331 passengers in 2012 (6,551,781 on international flights) and 50,567 tonnes of freight. Marrakesh (Menara) handled 3,373,475 passengers in 2012 and Agadir (Al Massira) 1,384,931.

Shipping
The busiest ports are Tanger Med (which handled 39,273,000 tonnes of cargo in 2014), Casablanca, Jorf Lasfar, Mohammedia and Safi. In Jan. 2014 there were 29 ships of 300 GT or over registered, totalling 252,000 GT.

Telecommunications
In 2013 there were 2,925,000 main (fixed) telephone lines; mobile phone subscriptions numbered 42,424,000 in 2013 (128·5 per 100 persons). The main telecommunication company is Maroc Telecom, which was privatized in 2001. Maroc Telecom's principal competitor is Méditel. 56·0% of the population were internet users in 2013. In June 2012 there were 4·6m. Facebook users.

Social Institutions

Out of 178 countries analysed in the 2017 *Fragile States Index*—a list published jointly by the Fund for Peace and *Foreign Policy* magazine—Morocco was ranked the 84th most vulnerable to conflict or collapse. The index is based on 12 indicators of state vulnerability across social, political and economic categories.

Justice
The legal system is based on French and Islamic law codes. There are a Supreme Court, 21 courts of appeal, 65 courts of first instance, 196 centres with resident judges and 706 communal jurisdictions for petty offences.

The population in penal institutions in Jan. 2013 was approximately 72,000 (220 per 100,000 of national population). On ascending to the throne in July 1999, King Mohammed VI pardoned and ordered the release of 7,988 prisoners and reduced the terms of 38,224 others. In 2015 the World Justice Project *Rule of Law Index*, which provides data on how the rule of law is experienced by the general public across eight categories, ranked Morocco 86th of 102 countries for criminal justice and 54th for civil justice.

Education
The adult literacy rate in 2009 was 56·1% (68·9% among males and 43·9% among females). Education in Berber languages has been permitted since

1994; Berber languages were officially added to the syllabus in 2003. Education is compulsory from the age of six to 15. In 2008–09 pre-primary schools had an estimated 33,000 teachers for 722,000 children and there were 145,000 teachers at primary schools for 3,851,000 pupils. In 2006–07 there were 2,173,000 pupils in secondary schools. There were 20,000 teaching staff at universities for 419,000 students in 2008–09. The University of al-Karaouine, founded in Fez in 859, is considered to be the oldest university in the world. There is an English-language university at Ifrane.

In 2008 public expenditure on education came to 5·6% of GDP.

Health

In 2006 there were 18,269 physicians, 3,473 dentists, 27,658 paramedical personnel and 8,002 pharmacists. There were 133 public hospitals in 2006 with about 27,000 beds.

In *Water: At What Cost? The State of the World's Water 2016*, WaterAid reported that 14·6% of the population does not have access to safe water.

Religion

Islam is the established state religion. 99% of the population are Sunni Muslims. There is also a small Catholic minority.

Culture

World Heritage Sites

Morocco has nine sites on the UNESCO World Heritage List: the Medina of Fez (inscribed on the list in 1981); the Medina of Marrakesh (1985); the Ksar of Ait-Ben-Haddou (1987); the Historic City of Meknès (1996); the Archaeological Site of Volubilis (1997 and 2008); the Medina of Tétouan (1997); the Medina of Essaouira/Magador (2001); the Portuguese City of Mazagan, now part of the city of El Jadida (2004); and Rabat, Modern Capital and Historic City (2012).

Press

In 2008 there were 33 paid-for daily newspapers. The leading dailies are the Arabic-language *Al-Massae, Assabah* and *Al-Ahdath al-Maghrebia* and the French-language *Le Matin du Sahara et du Maghreb*.

Tourism

In 2014 there were a record 10,283,000 non-resident tourists, up from 10,046,000 in 2013 and 9,375,000 in 2012. Tourist numbers increased every year between 2000 and 2014.

Diplomatic Representatives

Of Morocco in the United Kingdom (49 Queen's Gate Gdns, London, SW7 5NE)
Ambassador: Abdesselam Aboudrar.

Of the United Kingdom in Morocco (28 avenue S.A.R. Sidi Mohammed, Souissi 10105 (BP45), Rabat)
Ambassador: Thomas Reilly.

Of Morocco in the USA (1601 21st St., NW, Washington, D.C., 20009)
Ambassador: Lalla Joumala Alaoui.

Of the USA in Morocco (Km 5.7, Ave. Mohammed VI, Souissi, Rabat 10170)
Ambassador: Vacant.
Chargé d'Affaires a.i.: Stephanie Miley.

Of Morocco to the United Nations
Ambassador: Omar Hilale.

Of Morocco to the European Union
Ambassador: Ahmed Réda Chami.

Western Sahara

General Details

The Western Sahara was designated a non-decolonized territory by the United Nations in 1975, its borders having been marked as a result of agreements made between France, Spain and Morocco in 1900, 1904 and 1912. Since the mid-1970s, following Spain's administrative withdrawal and Mauritania's renunciation of its territorial claims, sovereignty over the area has been in dispute between Morocco and the Algerian-backed Polisario Front (Popular Front for the Liberation of the Saguia el Hamra and Rio de Oro), which proclaimed a government-in-exile of the Sahrawi Arab Democratic Republic in Feb. 1976. Morocco has resisted autonomy proposals by the UN, which has maintained a peacekeeping mission to the territory (the United Nations Mission for the Referendum in Western Sahara, or MINURSO) since 1991.

Approximate area, 264,300 sq. km. The UN gave an estimated population for 2015 of 573,000. Around 500,000 inhabitants are within Moroccan jurisdiction. Another estimated 100,000 Sahrawis live in refugee camps around Tindouf in southwest Algeria. The main towns are El-Aaiún (Laâyoune, the capital), Dakhla and Es-Semara.

The population is Arabic-speaking, and almost entirely Sunni Muslim.
President: Brahim Ghali.
Prime Minister: Mohamed Wali Akeik.

Rich phosphate deposits were discovered in 1963 at Bu Craa, but exploitation has been disrupted by guerrilla activity.

Further Reading

Morocco

Direction de la Statistique. *Annuaire Statistique du Maroc.—Conjoncture Économique.* Quarterly.—*Bulletin Officiel.* Weekly.
Bourqia, Rahma and Gilson Miller, Susan, (eds) *In the Shadow of the Sultan: Culture, Power and Politics in Morocco.* 2000
Pennell, C. R., *Morocco: From Empire to Independence.* 2003
National library: Bibliothèque Générale et Archives, 5 Avenue Ibn Batouta, BP 1003, Rabat.
National Statistical Office: Direction de la Statistique, Haut-Commissariat au Plan, BP 178, Rabat.
Website (French only): http://www.hcp.ma

Western Sahara

Sheley, Toby, *Endgame in the Western Sahara: What Future for Africa's Last Colony?* 2004

Mozambique

República de Moçambique (Republic of Mozambique)

Capital: Maputo
Population projection, 2020: 32·31m.
GNI per capita, 2017: (PPP$) 1,093
HDI/world rank, 2017: 0·437/180
Internet domain extension: .mz

Key Historical Events

San and Khoikhoi hunter-gatherers were the indigenous peoples of southern Africa, including present-day Mozambique. From around AD 400 the area was settled by Bantu-speaking farmers, thought to have originated from the borders of present-day Nigeria and Cameroon. The coastal site of Chibuene was occupied from around AD 600 and traded with other East African coastal settlements as well as the town of Manyikeni, gateway to the Great Zimbabwe civilization renowned for its ivory and gold. From the seventh century, Sofala became the region's principal port, with people and goods shipped along the Buzi River.

Seafarers from Arabia reached Sofala in the 11th century. It was seized by Sultan Suleiman Hassan of Kilwa (present-day Tanzania) in the 1180s and a 'Swahili' culture developed from a fusion of Persian, Omani Arab and Bantu people in port cities from Imhambane (in the south) to Mombasa. At its zenith in the 15th century the Kilwa Sultanate maintained outposts in Madagascar and controlled shipping routes to Arabia, Persia and India.

Portuguese explorer Pero da Covilha arrived at Sofala in 1489, having travelled overland disguised as an Arab merchant. His reports of the gold trade prompted further expeditions. Pero de Anaia established Fort São Caetana in 1505 as Portugal's second East African foothold. By the 1540s Portuguese mariners had established garrisons and trading posts at Mozambique Island, Sena and Tete. Attempts to control the gold trade gained momentum in the 1620s when Mavura, the new leader of Zimbabwe's Mutapa Empire, began ceding mineral rights to Portuguese prospectors.

A permanent settler community centred on several large estates (*prazos da coroa*) was administered from Goa, along with other Portuguese colonies around the Indian Ocean. The lucrative coastal trade continued to be hotly contested. Omani Arabs seized Fort Jesus on Mozambique Island in 1698, forcing Portuguese merchants south. In 1752 Portugal proclaimed Mozambique a separate colony and established a slave trade centred on Lourenço Marques (modern day Maputo). Over the next century hundreds of thousands of slaves were shipped to Brazil and to French sugar plantations in Mauritius and Réunion.

At the Congress of Berlin (1884–85) Portugal's claims to Mozambique, Angola and land linking them were questioned on grounds of lack of authority and unwillingness to end the slave trade. The current boundaries of Mozambique were agreed in a treaty with Britain in 1891. Authority increasingly shifted to large corporations, notably the Mozambique Company, Zambezia Company and Niassa Company. Railways were constructed and new plantations established using British funds and forced labour. Many southern Mozambicans worked in mines in neighbouring South Africa. During the 1930s Oliveira Salazar sought to strengthen Portugal's control of Mozambique, which led to the modernization and development of agriculture and industry. This led to waves of new settlers, numbering more than 200,000 by 1970.

Nationalist groups arose during the 1960s, with three banned organizations merging to form FRELIMO (Liberation Front of Mozambique), prompting a decade-long guerrilla war of independence. Following the April 1974 revolution in Portugal, FRELIMO took control and Mozambique became independent on 25 June 1975. The first president, Samora Machel, led a one-party state on Marxist lines, with Soviet backing. Within a year most Portuguese settlers had fled, leaving an inexperienced government and weak institutions. An armed insurgency, led by the anti-Communist Mozambican National Resistance (RENAMO), took hold, with backing from the then South African and Rhodesian governments. Civil war raged through the 1980s, killing hundreds of thousands of people and forcing more than 1m. to flee to neighbouring countries.

A peace treaty signed on 4 Oct. 1992 provided for all weapons to be handed over to the United Nations and all armed groups to be disbanded within six months. In 1994 the country held its first multi-party elections. Joaquim Chissano was re-elected president, serving until 2005 when he was succeeded by Armando Guebuza, who was in turn followed by Filipe Nyusi in 2015.

Territory and Population

Mozambique is bounded east by the Indian Ocean, south by South Africa, southwest by Eswatini, west by South Africa and Zimbabwe and north by Zambia, Malaŵi and Tanzania. It has an area of 799,380 sq. km (308,642 sq. miles) and a population, according to the 2017 census (provisional), of 28,861,863 (15,061,006 females), giving a density of 36·1 per sq. km. In 2011, 39·2% of the population were urban.

The UN gives a projected population for 2020 of 32·31m.

The areas, populations and capitals of the provinces are:

Province	Sq. km	2017 census (provisional)	Capital
Cabo Delgado	82,625	2,333,278	Pemba
Gaza	75,709	1,446,654	Xai-Xai
Inhambane	68,615	1,496,824	Inhambane
Manica	61,661	1,911,237	Chimoio
City of Maputo	347	1,101,170	—
Province of Maputo	26,011	2,507,098	Maputo
Nampula	81,606	6,102,867	Nampula
Niassa	129,056	1,865,976	Lichinga
Sofala	68,018	2,221,803	Beira
Tete	100,724	2,764,169	Tete
Zambézia	105,008	5,110,787	Quelimane

The capital is Maputo (2017 provisional population, 1,101,170). Other large cities (with 2017 provisional populations) are Matola (1,616,267), Nampula (743,125) and Beira (533,825).

The main ethnolinguistic groups are the Makua/Lomwe (52% of the population), the Tsonga/Ronga (24%), the Nyanja/Sena (12%) and Shona (6%).

Portuguese remains the official language, but vernaculars are widely spoken throughout the country. English is also widely spoken.

Social Statistics

2008 estimates: births, 877,000; deaths, 357,000. Estimated rates per 1,000 population, 2008: births, 39·2; deaths, 15·9. Infant mortality per 1,000 live births, 2010, 92. Life expectancy at birth, 2013, was 49·3 years for males and 51·0 years for females. Annual population growth rate, 2000–08, 2·6%; fertility rate, 2008, 5·1 births per woman.

Climate

A humid tropical climate, with a dry season from June to Sept. In general, temperatures and rainfall decrease from north to south. Maputo, Jan. 78°F (25·6°C), July 65°F (18·3°C). Annual rainfall 30" (760 mm). Beira, Jan. 82°F (27·8°C), July 69°F (20·6°C). Annual rainfall 60" (1,522 mm).

© Springer Nature Limited 2020
Palgrave Macmillan (ed.), *The Statesman's Yearbook 2020*,
https://doi.org/10.1057/978-1-349-95940-2_134

Constitution and Government

On 2 Nov. 1990 the People's Assembly unanimously voted in favour of a new constitution, which came into force on 30 Nov. This changed the name of the state to 'Republic of Mozambique', legalized opposition parties, provided for universal secret elections and introduced a bill of rights including the right to strike, press freedoms and *habeas corpus*. The head of state is the *President*, directly elected for a five-year term. Parliament is a 250-member *Assembly of the Republic*, elected for a five-year term by proportional representation.

National Anthem

'Pátria Amada' ('Beloved Motherland'); words and tune by J. Sigaulane Chemane.

Recent Elections

In the parliamentary elections of 15 Oct. 2014 the Liberation Front of Mozambique (FRELIMO) won 144 of the 250 seats with 55·9% of the vote, the Mozambican National Resistance (RENAMO) 89 with 32·5% and the Democratic Movement of Mozambique 17 with 8·4%. Turnout was 48·6%.

In the presidential election, also held on 15 Oct. 2014, Filipe Nyusi of FRELIMO took 57·0% of the vote against 36·6% for RENAMO's Afonso Dhlakama and 6·4% for Daviz Simango of the Democratic Movement of Mozambique. Turnout was 48·5%.

Current Government

President: Filipe Nyusi; b. 1959 (FRELIMO; sworn in 15 Jan. 2015).

In Feb. 2019 the government comprised:

Prime Minister: Carlos Agostinho do Rosário; b. 1954 (FRELIMO; sworn in 19 Jan. 2015).

Minister of Agriculture and Food Security: Higino Francisco Marrule. *Culture and Tourism:* Silva Armando Dunduro. *Defence:* Atanásio Salvador Mtumuke. *Economy and Finance:* Adriano Afonso Maleiane. *Education and Human Development:* Conceita Sortane. *Foreign Affairs and Co-operation:* José Condugua António Pacheco. *Gender, Children and Social Welfare:* Cidália Manuel Chaúque Oliveira. *Health:* Nazira Karimo Vali Abdula. *Industry and Commerce:* Ragendra de Sousa. *Interior:* Jaime Basílio Monteiro. *Justice, Constitutional Affairs and Religion:* Joaquim Veríssimo. *Labour, Employment and Social Security:* Vitória Dias Diogo. *Land, Environment and Rural Development:* Celso Ismael Correia. *Mineral Resources and Energy:* Ernesto Max Elias Tonela. *Public Works, Housing and Water Resources:* João Osvaldo Machatine. *Science and Technology, and Higher and Vocational Education:* Jorge Penicela Nhambiu. *Sea, Inland Waters and Fisheries:* Agostinho Salvador Mondlane. *State Administration and Civil Service:* Carmelita Rita Namashulua. *Transport and Communications:* Carlos Fortes Mesquita. *Veterans' Affairs:* Eusébio Lambo Gondiwa. *Youth and Sport:* Nyeleti Mondlane. *Chief of Staff in the President's Office:* Adelaide Anchia Amurane.

Government Website (Portuguese only): http://www.portaldogoverno.gov.mz

Current Leaders

Filipe Nyusi

Position
President

Introduction
Filipe Nyusi took office in Jan. 2015 as the fourth successive Liberation Front of Mozambique (FRELIMO) head of state.

Early Life
Filipe Nyusi was born on 9 Feb. 1959 in Namau, in the province of Cabo Delgado, to parents who were members of the FRELIMO movement. After fighting broke out in the mid-1960s, he became a refugee in Tanzania where he attended a FRELIMO school in Tunduru. In 1973 he received political and military training at its base in Nachingwea.

He then returned to Mozambique and completed his schooling before studying mechanical engineering at Brno University of Technology in what

was then Czechoslovakia. From 1992 he worked at Mozambique's ports and railways authority (CFM), and from 1993–95 he served as director of railways of the northern division (CFM-Norte). Between 1995 and 2007 he was its managing director. In 1999 he undertook postgraduate studies in management at the UK's Victoria University of Manchester (now the University of Manchester). In 2007 he was appointed to CFM's board of directors.

From 2008–14 Nyusi served as defence minister under President Guebuza. In Sept. 2012 he was elected to FRELIMO's central committee and in March 2014 entered the contest to be its presidential candidate. Regarded as a close ally of President Guebuza—in contrast to his main rival, former prime minister Luisa Diogo—Nyusi achieved an outright majority of 68% in the second round of voting.

In Sept. 2014, after the Mozambican National Resistance (RENAMO) had called off its low-level insurgency, campaigning got under way for the Oct. 2014 general elections. RENAMO and the Democratic Movement of Mozambique were the leading opposition parties. Nyusi campaigned on pledges to continue developing the oil and gas industries and address wealth disparity. In a closely fought race, he emerged the victor with 57% of the vote. Following the vote, opposition parties made allegations of electoral fraud; RENAMO boycotted the first sitting of parliament but promised not to resume violence.

Career in Office
Nyusi took office on 15 Jan. 2015. His cabinet appointments were regarded as a sign that he was distancing himself from his predecessor and tending more towards consensus politics. His principal challenges were to improve living standards for the general population and manage political discontent in order to avoid a return to unrest.

In April 2016 the IMF and other donors suspended funding to Mozambique in response to the government's failure to disclose debts of over US$1bn., after which Nyusi pledged to co-operate with an international audit. However, the country fell into default in early 2017 and macroeconomic instability has persisted owing to low foreign investment and fiscal constraints. By Oct. 2018 total public debt as a share of GDP reached 112%, the fourth highest level in Africa.

Also, long-standing tensions between FRELIMO and RENAMO had been reignited following the assassination in Oct. 2016 of Jeremias Pondeca, a member of the RENAMO delegation involved in ongoing, but still inconclusive, peace negotiations with the government. Meanwhile, terror attacks by Islamist jihadists since Oct. 2017 have posed a growing insurgent threat in the northern coastal province of Cabo Delgado.

Defence

The President of the Republic is C.-in-C. of the armed forces. Defence expenditure totalled US$75m. in 2013 (US$3 per capita), representing 0·5% of GDP. Conscription for both men and women is for two years.

Army
Personnel numbered around 9–10,000 in 2011.

Navy
Naval personnel in 2011 were believed to total 200.

Air Force
Personnel (2011) 1,000 (including air defence units). There were two attack helicopters although their serviceability was in doubt but no combat-capable aircraft.

Economy

Agriculture accounted for 26·6% of GDP in 2013, industry 18·7% and services 54·7%.

Overview

Following the end of civil war in 1992, political stability alongside fiscal and structural reform contributed to sound economic growth. Between 1993 and 2009 Mozambique had the fastest-growing non-oil economy in sub-Saharan Africa, increasing on average by 7·5% per year driven by public expenditure and burgeoning foreign direct investment in the minerals sector. Growth has remained strong, measuring 7·5% in 2014 and 6·6% in 2015. However, the country ranks close to the bottom of the Human Development Index, with more than half of the 24m. population living below poverty line.

In 2010 there was a major discovery of natural gas, although progress towards exploiting it has been delayed by prolonged negotiations with potential operators. However, once approved, the project has the potential to transform Mozambique into a major energy player. Longer-term challenges include diversifying the economy and improving education, health and infrastructure provision.

Natural disasters are an ongoing threat. Floods in Jan. and Feb. 2013 damaged crops and infrastructure, leading to inflation generated by rising food prices.

Currency

The unit of currency is the *new metical* (MZN) of 100 *centavos*, which replaced the *metical* (MZM) in July 2006. The currency was revalued at a rate of 1 new metical = 1,000 meticais. Inflation was 19·2% in 2016 and 15·3% in 2017. Foreign exchange reserves were US$979m. in July 2005 and total money supply was 18,258·3bn. meticais.

Budget

In 2011 revenues were 108,208m. meticais and expenditures 121,410m. meticais.

Performance

Until growth slowed considerably in 2016 and 2017 Mozambique had been one of Africa's fastest-expanding economies for some 20 years. There was real GDP growth of 6·6% in 2015, 3·8% in 2016 and 3·7% in 2017. Total GDP in 2017 was US$12·3bn.

Banking and Finance

Most banks had been nationalized by 1979. The central bank and bank of issue is the Bank of Mozambique (*Governor*, Rogério Zandamela) which hived off its commercial functions in 1992 to the newly founded Commercial Bank of Mozambique. It in turn merged in 2001 with Banco Internacional de Moçambique, which now trades as Millennium bim and is the country's largest bank. In July 2010 the Bank of Mozambique had external assets of US$2,105·0m. In 2008 there were 14 commercial banks, one microbank and six credit co-operatives. The Mozambique Stock Exchange opened in Maputo in Oct. 1999. By the late 1990s financial services had become one of the fastest-growing areas of the economy. Foreign debt was US$4,124m. in 2010, representing 43·8% of GNI.

Energy and Natural Resources

Environment

Carbon dioxide emissions from the consumption of energy in 2011 were the equivalent of 0·2 tonnes per capita.

Electricity

Installed capacity was 2·5m. kW in 2011. Production in 2011 was 16·83bn. kWh; consumption per capita was 547 kWh.

Oil and Gas

Since 2010 there have been prolific natural gas discoveries in the northern offshore Rovuma basin. In 2013 natural gas reserves were 2·8trn. cu. metres; output in 2011 was 3·4bn. cu. metres. Mozambique could potentially become one of the world's largest liquefied natural gas exporters. Both onshore and offshore foreign companies are prospecting for oil.

Minerals

There are deposits of apatite, bauxite, graphite, iron ore, pegamite, rubies, tantalite and tin. Other known reserves are: nepheline, syenite, magnetite, copper, garnet, kaolin, asbestos, bentonite, limestone, gold, titanium and tin. Mozambique also has extensive—largely unexploited—coal reserves. Output in 2005 (in 1,000 tonnes): aluminium, 554; sea salt (estimate), 80; bauxite, 10; coal, 3.

Agriculture

All land is owned by the state but concessions are given. There were an estimated 5·7m. ha. of arable land in 2013 and 0·3m. ha. of permanent crops.

Around 118,000 ha. were equipped for irrigation in 2013. Production in 1,000 tonnes (2013): cassava, 4,303; sugarcane, 3,166; sweet potatoes, 1,469; maize, 1,207; bananas, 570; tomatoes, 300. Livestock, 2013: 4·36m. goats; 1·77m. pigs; 1·65m. cattle; 250,000 sheep (estimate); 21m. chickens.

Forestry

In 2015 there were 37·94m. ha. of forests, or 48% of the land area, including eucalyptus, pine and rare hardwoods. In 2011 timber production was 18·20m. cu. metres.

Fisheries

The catch in 2015 was 286,587 tonnes (more than double the 2008 total), of which 193,567 tonnes were from sea fishing.

Industry

Although the country is overwhelmingly rural, there is some substantial industry in and around Maputo (steel, engineering, textiles, processing, docks and railways). A huge aluminium smelter, Mozal, was constructed in two phases—the last phase was completed in 2003. Production exceeds its theoretical annual capacity of 506,000 tonnes and is a focal point in the country's strategy of attracting foreign investment.

Labour

The labour force in 2013 was 12,105,000 (9,332,000 in 2003). 84·5% of the population aged 15–64 was economically active in 2013. In the same year 22·5% of the population was unemployed.

Mozambique had 0·17m. people living in slavery according to the Walk Free Foundation's 2013 *Global Slavery Index*.

International Trade

Imports and Exports

Imports (c.i.f.) totalled US$5,295m. in 2016 (US$7,908m. in 2015). Exports (f.o.b.) totalled US$3,352m. in 2016 (US$3,196m. in 2015).

Principal imports in 2016 were machinery and transport equipment (28·1%), mineral fuels and lubricants (19·2%) and manufactured goods classified chiefly by material (15·9%); main exports in 2016 were manufactured goods classified chiefly by material (29·9%), mineral fuels and lubricants (27·9%) and food, animals and beverages (14·5%). Main import suppliers in 2016: South Africa, 31·3%; China, 9·6%; Netherlands, 5·9%. Main export markets in 2016: Netherlands, 24·5%; South Africa, 19·8%; India, 12·4%.

Communications

Roads

In 2008 there were 29,323 km of roads, of which 17·9% were paved. There were 290,600 vehicles in 2008. There were 5,438 road accidents in 2008, with 1,529 fatalities. The flooding of early 2000 washed away at least one fifth of the country's main road linking the north and the south.

Rail

The railway system consists of three separate networks, with principal routes on 1,067 mm gauge radiating from the ports of Maputo, Beira and Nacala. Total length in 2009 was 3,116 km, mainly on 1,067 mm gauge with some 762 mm gauge lines, but only 1,929 km was operational. In 2009 passenger-km travelled on the Mozambique Ports and Railways network came to 164m. and freight tonne-km to 2,078m.

Civil Aviation

There are international airports at Maputo and Beira. The national carrier is the state-owned Linhas Aéreas de Moçambique (LAM), which in 2013 carried 684,000 passengers (462,000 on domestic flights). In the same year it served ten domestic and five international destinations. In 2012 Maputo handled 839,390 passengers (454,236 on international flights) and Beira 164,324 (105,467 on domestic flights).

Shipping

The principal ports are Maputo, Beira, Nacala and Quelimane. In Jan. 2014 there were ten ships of 300 GT or over registered, totalling 11,000 GT.

Telecommunications

There were 5,971,000 mobile phone subscribers in 2009 (260·8 per 1,000 inhabitants), up from just 51,000 in 2000. Fixed telephone lines numbered 82,400 in 2009, down from 87,400 in 2002. In 2009 there were 92,000 mobile broadband subscriptions and 12,500 fixed broadband internet subscriptions. There were 248,000 Facebook users in June 2012.

Social Institutions

Out of 178 countries analysed in the 2017 *Fragile States Index*—a list published jointly by the Fund for Peace and *Foreign Policy* magazine—Mozambique was ranked the 40th most vulnerable to conflict or collapse. The index is based on 12 indicators of state vulnerability across social, political and economic categories.

Justice

The 1990 constitution provides for an independent judiciary, *habeas corpus*, and an entitlement to legal advice on arrest. The death penalty was abolished in Nov. 1990.

The population in penal institutions in Oct. 2010 was 15,249 (65 per 100,000 of national population).

Education

The adult literacy rate in 2008 was 54%.

In 2007 there were 4,563,633 pupils with 70,389 teaching staff in primary schools; and 444,926 pupils with 12,064 teaching staff at secondary schools. Private schools and universities were permitted to function in 1990. There were 200,649 students and 14,235 academic staff in tertiary education in 2017. The largest higher education institution is the Eduardo Mondlane University, founded in 1962 and granted university status in 1968.

In 2006 public expenditure on education came to 5·8% of GNI and 21·0% of total government spending.

Health

In 2009 there were 50 hospitals, 435 health centres and 652 health posts. There were two psychiatric hospitals. In 2012 there were four doctors for every 100,000 population, 41 nurses and midwives for every 100,000 and six pharmaceutical personnel per 100,000. Private health care was introduced alongside the national health service in 1992.

In *Water: At What Cost? The State of the World's Water 2016*, WaterAid reported that 48·9% of the population does not have access to safe water—the fifth highest percentage of any nation.

Religion

According to estimates by the Pew Research Center's Forum on Religion & Public Life, in 2010 the population was 56·7% Christian and 18·0% Muslim; 7·4% were folk religionists and 17·9% religiously unaffiliated. Of the Christians in 2010, an estimated 51% were Catholics and 48% Protestants. In Feb. 2019 there were two cardinals.

Culture

World Heritage Sites

Mozambique has one site on the UNESCO World Heritage List: the Island of Mozambique (inscribed on the list in 1991), a Portuguese trading post with a style of architecture unchanged since the 16th century.

Press

There were two well-established daily newspapers in 2008 (*Notícias* and *Diário* in Maputo and Beira respectively) with a combined circulation of 13,000.

Tourism

Tourism is a potential growth area for the country. There were 1,661,000 non-resident overnight tourists in 2014 (1,886,000 in 2013).

Diplomatic Representatives

Of Mozambique in the United Kingdom (21 Fitzroy Sq., London, W1T 6EL)
    High Commissioner: Filipe Chidumo.

Of the United Kingdom in Mozambique (Ave. Vladimir Lenine 310, Maputo City, Maputo, PO Box 55)
    High Commissioner: NneNne Iwuji-Eme.

Of Mozambique in the USA (1525, New Hampshire Ave., NW, Washington, D.C., 20036)
    Ambassador: Carlos dos Santos.

Of the USA in Mozambique (Ave. Kenneth Kaunda 193, Maputo)
    Ambassador: H. Dean Pittman.

Of Mozambique to the United Nations
    Ambassador: António Gumende.

Of Mozambique to the European Union
    Ambassador: Berta Celestino Cossa.

Further Reading

Alden, Chris, *Mozambique and the Construction of the New African State: From Negotiations to Nation Building.* 2001
Cabrita, João M., *Mozambique: The Tortuous Road to Democracy.* 2001
Finnegan, W., *A Complicated War: the Harrowing of Mozambique.* 1992
Manning, Carrie L., *The Politics of Peace in Mozambique: Post-Conflict Democratization, 1992–2000.* 2002
Newitt, M., *A History of Mozambique.* 1996
Pitcher, M. Anne, *Transforming Mozambique: The Politics of Privatization, 1975–2000.* 2002
National Statistical Office: Instituto Nacional de Estatística, Av. Ahmed Sekou Touré, No. 21, Maputo.
Website (Portuguese only): http://www.ine.gov.mz

Myanmar

Pyidaunzu Thanmăda Myăma Nainngandaw (Republic of the Union of Myanmar)

Capitals: Naypyidaw/Pyinmana (Administrative and Legislative), Yangon/Rangoon (Commercial)
Population projection, 2020: 54·81m.
GNI per capita, 2017: (PPP$) 5,567
HDI/world rank, 2017: 0·578/148
Internet domain extension: .mm

Key Historical Events

Caves near Taunggyi in modern Myanmar's Shan State show evidence of Neolithic settlement dating to 9,000 BC. Copper was mined in the Shan hills from 1,500 BC and subsequent farming communities traded with Chinese kingdoms. Tibeto-Burman-speaking Pyu people began moving south from Yunnan (in present-day China) into the upper Irrawaddy valley from about 200 BC, eventually establishing several city states in central Myanmar. One of the most important was the Sri Ksetva kingdom, perhaps the earliest urban centre in southeast Asia. Extensive trade with India over centuries led to the rise of Buddhism. The Pyu calendar, forerunner of the famed Burmese calendar, is thought to date from AD 638.

During the seventh century Mon people began moving into the Bago and Yangon regions from present-day Thailand. From around 750 the Pyu city states came under repeated attack from the expanding Nanzhou kingdom, centred on Yunnan province. The city-state of Pagan grew in importance and Anawrahta Minsaw, who was crowned king in 1044, forged an empire that led to him being considered father of the Burmese nation. By the early 12th century the Pagan Empire encompassed the whole Irrawaddy Valley, held sway over parts of the Shan States and Arakan (Rakhine), and became a major power in the region alongside the Khmer Empire. However, uprisings by Mon and Shan peoples and attacks by Mongols (conquerors of Yunnan) led to Pagan's break-up by 1300 and ushered in a period of new, smaller fiefdoms including the Ava in central Myanmar and the prosperous Mon-speaking Hanthawaddy kingdom to the south.

Reunification came during the 15th century under the Toungoo dynasty, which rose from the Ava kingdom at a time when many Burmese-speaking migrants were arriving from the north. It reached its zenith under King Bayinnaung in the 1570s. A Mon rebellion in the south paved the way to a restoration of the Hanthawaddy kingdom in the 1750s and 1760s but its attempts to capture territory further north were thwarted by King Alaungpaya, whose Konbaung dynasty, centred on Mandalay, expanded Burmese control as far north as Assam (India) and into Siam (present-day Thailand).

Following the invasion of Assam, the British East India Company retaliated in defence of its interests and in 1826 drove the Burmese out of India. Territory was annexed in south Burma but the kingdom of Upper Burma, ruled from Mandalay, remained independent. A second war with Britain in 1852 ended with the British annexation of the Irrawaddy delta. In 1885 the British invaded and occupied Upper Burma and in 1886 all Burma became a province of the Indian Empire. There were violent uprisings in the 1930s and in 1937 Burma was separated from India and permitted some degree of self-government. Independence was achieved in 1948. In 1958 there was an army coup, and another in 1962 led by Gen. Ne Win, who installed a Revolutionary Council and dissolved parliament.

The Council lasted until March 1974 when the country became a one-party socialist republic. On 18 Sept. 1988 the armed forces seized power and set up the State Law and Order Restoration Council (SLORC). Subsequent civil unrest accounted for thousands of deaths. On 19 June 1989 the government changed the name of the country in English to the Union of Myanmar. Aung San Suu Kyi, leader of the opposition National League for Democracy (NLD), was put under house arrest in July 1989. Despite her continuing detention, her party won the 1990 election by a landslide but the military junta refused to accept the result. In 1992 Than Shwe became

national leader, beginning 19 years of hard-line rule until he stepped down in 2011. Aung San Suu Kyi was freed in July 1995 but was detained again on several further occasions before being released most recently in Nov. 2010.

In May 2008 the Irrawaddy delta suffered a cyclone that caused massive damage, claimed an estimated 145,000 lives and left 1m. people displaced. Nonetheless, the following week the government proceeded with a referendum on a new constitution, which it claimed secured 92% support. In Nov. 2010 the pro-government Union Solidarity and Development Party won the first elections for 20 years. Thein Sein became president, overseeing a transition towards civilian rule, although the military retained significant influence within government. Having dominated a series of by-elections in April 2012 (with Aung San Suu Kyi among those winning a seat in parliament), the NLD secured enough seats at the general election in Nov. 2015 to form the next government. Htin Kyaw became president on 1 April 2016, although Aung San Suu Kyi assumed the *de facto* leadership of the NLD administration.

Since 2012 there have been sporadic but increasing outbreaks of communal violence between Buddhists (the majority religious group) and Muslims. In March 2017 the UN Human Rights Council began an investigation into alleged human rights abuses by the military against the Rohingya Muslim minority. By Oct. 2017 an estimated 1m. Rohingya Muslims had fled to Bangladesh.

Territory and Population

Myanmar is bounded in the east by China, Laos and Thailand, and west by the Indian Ocean, Bangladesh and India. Three parallel mountain ranges run from north to south; the Western Yama or Rakhine Yama, the Bagu Yama and the Shaun Plateau. The total area of the Union is 676,590 sq. km (261,230 sq. miles), including 23,070 sq. km (8,910 sq. miles) of inland water. In 2014 the census population was 51,486,253; density, 78·8 per sq. km. In 2011, 34·3% of the population lived in urban areas.

The UN gives a projected population for 2020 of 54·81m.

The administrative capital is Naypyidaw (Pyinmana); its census population was 1,160,242 in 2014. The largest city is Yangon (Rangoon), with a population of 7,360,703 in 2014. Other leading towns are Mandalay (2014 population of 1,225,546), Bago (Pegu), Hpa-an (Pha-an), Taunggyi, Monywa and Myitkyina. In Nov. 2005 the government began relocating from Yangon to the new administrative and legislative capital, Pyinmana, subsequently renamed Naypyidaw. The move was completed in Feb. 2006.

Myanmar's constitution of 2008 established a new administrative order dividing the country into one union territory (Naypyidaw), one self-administered division (Wa), five self-administered zones (Danu, Kokang, Naga, Pa Laung and Pa-O), seven states (Chin, Kachin, Kayah, Kayin, Mon, Rakhine and Shan) and seven regions (Ayeyarwady, Bago, Magway, Mandalay, Sagaing, Taninthayi and Yangon).

Myanmar is inhabited by many ethnic nationalities. There are 135 national groups with the Bamars, comprising about 68% of the population, forming the largest group. The Shan and the Karen account for 9% and 7% of the population respectively. There are around 1m. stateless Rohingya (Muslims of South Asian descent, in a mainly Buddhist country), who are not recognized as an official ethnic group. Myanmar has more stateless people than any other country.

The official language is Burmese; English is also in use.

Social Statistics

2008 estimates: births, 1,020,000; deaths, 496,000. Estimated birth rate in 2008 was 21 per 1,000 population; estimated death rate, 10. Annual population growth rate, 2000–08, 0·8%. Life expectancy at birth, 2013, was 63·1 years for males and 67·2 years for females. Infant mortality, 2010, 50 per 1,000 live births; fertility rate, 2008, 2·3 births per woman. Abortion is illegal unless a woman's life is at risk.

Climate

The climate is equatorial in coastal areas, changing to tropical monsoon over most of the interior, but humid temperate in the extreme north, where there is a more significant range of temperature and a dry season lasting from Nov. to April. In coastal parts, the dry season is shorter. Very heavy rains occur in the monsoon months May to Sept. Yangon, Jan. 77°F (25°C), July 80°F (26·7°C). Annual rainfall 104" (2,616 mm). Sittwe, Jan. 70°F (21·1°C), July 81°F (27·2°C). Annual rainfall 206" (5,154 mm). Mandalay, Jan. 68°F (20°C), July 85°F (29·4°C). Annual rainfall 33" (828 mm).

Constitution and Government

In Nov. 1997 the country's ruling generals changed the name of the government to the *State Peace and Development Council* (SPDC). It nominally ceded power to an elected president in Feb. 2011 and was abolished a month later.

In May 2008 an army-drafted constitution won 92·5% support in a referendum. The constitution specified that multi-party elections should be scheduled for 2010; 25% of parliamentary seats were automatically allocated to the military. It called for the creation of a National Defence and Security Council, dominated by military appointments, with the power to suspend the constitution under certain circumstances. It also laid out rules that would ban opposition leader Aung San Suu Kyi from holding public office. The constitution was formally adopted on 30 May 2008. The previous constitution, dating from 3 Jan. 1974, had been suspended since 1988. Amendments to the Political Party Registration law in Oct. 2011 allow Aung San Suu Kyi to hold public office, although under the current constitution she was not eligible to become president following the elections that took place in Nov. 2015.

The 440-member lower chamber, the House of Representatives (*Pythu Hluttaw*), has 330 elected seats with 110 appointed and the 224-member upper chamber, the House of Nationalities (*Amyotha Hluttaw*), has 168 elected seats with 56 appointed. Parliament convened in Jan. 2011 for the first time since 1988.

National Anthem

'Gba majay Bma' ('We shall love Burma for ever'); words and tune by Saya Tin.

Recent Elections

In elections to the House of Representatives on 8 Nov. 2015 the National League for Democracy (NDL), led by Aung San Suu Kyi, won 255 of 330 elected seats. The ruling Union Solidarity and Development Party (USDP) won 30 seats, the Arakan National Party (ANP) 12 and the Shan Nationalities League for Democracy (SNLD) 12. A further 14 seats went to seven smaller parties and independent candidates, with seven vacant owing to insurgent activity. 110 seats are automatically reserved for the military. The results meant that the NDL had the parliamentary majority needed to elect its nominee to the presidency.

On 28 March 2018 parliament elected Win Myint as president, winning 403 of 636 votes. Myint Swe (211 votes) and Henry Van Thio (18) remained vice presidents.

Current Government

In Feb. 2019 the government comprised:
President: Win Myint; b. 1951 (in office since 30 March 2018).
First Vice President: Myint Swe. *Second Vice President:* Henry Van Thio.
State Counsellor and Minister of Foreign Affairs and of the President's Office: Aung San Suu Kyi; b. 1945 (in office since 6 April 2016).
Minister of Agriculture, Livestock and Irrigation: Aung Thu. *Border Affairs:* Lieut.-Gen. Ye Aung. *Commerce:* Than Myint. *Construction:* Han Zaw. *Defence:* Lieut.-Gen. Sein Win. *Education:* Myo Thein Gyi. *Electricity and Energy:* Win Khaing. *Ethnic Affairs:* Naing Thet Lwin. *Health and Sport:* Myint Htwe. *Home Affairs:* Lieut.-Gen. Kyaw Swe. *Hotels and Tourism:* Ohn Maung. *Industry:* Khin Maung Cho. *Information:* Pe Myint. *International Co-operation:* Kyaw Tin. *Labour, Immigration and Population:* Thein Swe. *Natural Resources and Environmental Conservation:* Ohn Win. *Planning and Finance:* Soe Win. *Religious Affairs and Culture:* Aung

Ko. *Social Welfare, Relief and Resettlement:* Win Myat Aye. *Transport and Communications:* Thant Sin Maung.
Office of the President: http://www.president-office.gov.mm

Current Leaders

Win Myint
Position
President

Introduction
Win Myint, a close ally of *de facto* leader Aung San Suu Kyi, became president of Myanmar in March 2018.

Early Life
Win Myint was born in the Ayeyawadi region in 1951. He studied geology in Yangon (formerly Rangoon) and went on to practise law, becoming a High Court advocate in 1985.

Win Myint took part in the 1988 anti-government revolt against Gen. Ne Win and was briefly imprisoned by the military junta. Upon his release, he ran as a National League for Democracy (NLD) candidate in the elections of 1990, winning a seat in his home region's Danubyu Township. However, he was not permitted to take up his seat as the military junta rendered the vote invalid. He joined the NLD's central executive committee in 2010.

In 2012 Win Myint won the parliamentary seat for the Pathein Township of Ayeyawadi, calling for greater government transparency. In 2015 he was re-elected to parliament and promoted to speaker in the House of Representatives. Buoyed by the NLD's strong parliamentary position, he used his powers to rein in military-backed politicians, including ensuring they complied with parliament's strict dress codes.

In March 2018 President Htin Kyaw resigned owing to poor health. Win Myint was one of the two vice-presidents eligible to be selected for the role, once he had resigned as speaker. In an election on 28 March he won well over half of the available parliamentary votes.

Career in Office
Win Myint's closeness to Aung San Suu Kyi led many to suspect that he would act as a mouthpiece for the former political prisoner and, despite his reputation as a wilful parliamentary speaker, he was expected to defer to her on major policy decisions. He took power as Myanmar faced global pressure to respond decisively to the humanitarian crisis surrounding displaced Rohingya Muslim minority refugees. The government's—and Aung San Suu Kyi's—apparent inaction over atrocities perpetrated against the Rohingyas prompted a damning report by the United Nations in Aug., accusing Myanmar's military leaders of genocide and crimes against humanity.

Defence

Military expenditure in 2013 totalled US$2,400m. (US$44 per capita), representing 4·2% of GDP. A law making conscription obligatory was introduced in 2010 but has not been implemented.

Army
The strength of the Army was reported to be about 375,000 in 2011. The Army is organized into 12 regional commands. There are three paramilitary units: People's Police Force (72,000), People's Militia (35,000) and People's Pearl and Fishery Ministry (approximately 250).

Navy
Personnel in 2011 totalled about 16,000 including 800 naval infantry.

Air Force
The Air Force is intended primarily for internal security duties. Personnel (2011) approximately 15,000 operating 136 combat-capable aircraft, including Chinese F-7s and A-5s.

Economy

In 2014 agriculture accounted for 27·8% of GDP, industry 34·5% and services 37·7%.

Overview

Myanmar has one of the least developed economies in the world, having suffered decades of stagnation, mismanagement and isolation under military rule. However, since the transition to an ostensibly civilian government in 2011, the economy has undergone a revival as it has begun to integrate into the world system. GDP is mainly derived from agriculture, forestry, livestock and fisheries, which consistently employ an estimated 70% of the labour force. The construction, manufacturing and service sectors have also seen strong expansion since 2011, driven by government investment, foreign direct investment (FDI) and increased tourist arrivals. In addition, Myanmar has abundant natural resources, including offshore oil and gas deposits, and is a major source of gems.

GDP grew by an average of 7·5% per annum between 2011 and 2014, led by the government's ambitious structural reform programme and by the relaxing of long-term EU and US sanctions from April 2012. Reforms focused on unifying multiple informal market exchange rates, reducing the fiscal deficit, increasing social spending and modernizing the financial system. FDI expanded rapidly after 2011 and was estimated by the government at US$5bn. in 2014, principally from mainland China, Thailand and Hong Kong. Growth continued through 2015–17, although at a slightly lower average of 6·4% per annum, spurred by a strong performance in the garment manufacturing sector. The poverty rate fell from 48% to 32% between 2005 and 2015.

Currency

The unit of currency is the *kyat* (MMK) of 100 *pyas*. Total money supply was K.1,742,810m. in June 2005. Foreign exchange reserves were US$691m. and gold reserves 231,000 troy oz in May 2005. Myanmar adopted a managed float for the kyat in April 2012, having had a fixed exchange rate for the previous 35 years. Inflation was 6·8% in 2016, rising to 4·0% in 2017. Since 1 June 1996 import duties have been calculated at a rate of US$1 = K.100.

Budget

In 2013–14 revenues were K.18,936bn. and expenditures K.21,601bn. Current revenue accounted for 96·6% of revenues in 2013–14; current expenditure accounted for 70·1% of expenditures. The fiscal year begins on 1 April.

Performance

Real GDP growth was 8·4% in 2013, 8·7% in 2014 and 7·0% in 2015. Myanmar's economic growth averaged 7·5% in the five years to 2015. Total GDP in 2017 was US$69·3bn.

Banking and Finance

The Central Bank of Myanmar was established in 1990. Its *Governor* is Kyaw Kyaw Maung. In 2010 there were four state banks (Myanma Economic Bank, Myanma Foreign Trade Bank, Myanma Agricultural and Rural Development Bank, and Myanma Investment and Commercial Bank) and 19 private banks. In Oct. 2014 Myanmar awarded licences to nine foreign banks, which were the first allowed to operate in the country for half a century. The state insurance company is the Myanmar Insurance Corporation. Deposits in state and private banks were K.903,722m. in 2006.

Before being delisted in Oct. 2006, Myanmar was the only country named in a report in June 2006 as failing to co-operate in the fight against international money laundering. The Financial Action Task Force on Money Laundering was set up by the G7 group of major industrialized nations.

Foreign debt was US$6,352m. in 2010.

A stock exchange officially opened for business in Yangon in 2016. It is Myanmar's third attempt to establish a proper stock exchange after two earlier ventures had been unsuccessful.

Energy and Natural Resources

Environment

Myanmar's carbon dioxide emissions from the consumption of energy in 2011 were the equivalent of 0·2 tonnes per capita.

Electricity

Total electricity generated was about 10·42bn. kWh in 2011–12; consumption per capita in 2011–12 was estimated at 199 kWh. Installed capacity was approximately 3·4m. kW in 2011–12.

Oil and Gas

Production (2012–13) of crude oil was 849,000 tonnes; natural gas (2012), 12·7bn. cu. metres. There were proven natural gas reserves of 200bn. cu. metres in 2012. It is believed that there may be huge reserves of both offshore oil and gas yet to be discovered. A 1,060-km gas pipeline from Kyaukphyu on Myanmar's west coast to Kunming in China opened in July 2013. An oil pipeline from Kyaukphyu to Kunming was inaugurated in Jan. 2015. The two pipelines will allow China to obtain oil and gas directly from the Middle East.

Minerals

Myanmar's mineral resources include antimony, coal, copper, lead, limestone, marble, precious stones (notably jade and rubies), tin, tungsten and zinc. Production (in tonnes unless otherwise indicated): hard coal (2007–08), 1,075,000; lignite (2007–08), 414,000; gypsum (2014), 104,994; copper (2014), 33,200; jade (2014), 16,684,386 kg; ruby, sapphire and spinel (2014), 2,237,228 kg. Myanmar ranks among the largest producers of rubies.

Agriculture

In 2007 there were 10·6m. ha. of arable land and 1·1m. ha. of permanent crops. 2·2m. ha. were irrigated in 2006–07. Production (2006–07, in 1,000 tonnes): rice, 30,435; sugarcane, 8,039; pulses, 4,198; maize, 1,114; groundnuts, 1,088; onions, 918; plantains (2008 estimate), 630; sesame seeds, 614; potatoes, 508. Opium output was an estimated 670 tonnes in 2014, down from 870 tonnes in 2013. Myanmar's opium production is second only to that of Afghanistan.

Livestock (2005–06): cattle, 12·15m.; pigs, 5·79m.; buffaloes, 2·71m.; sheep and goats, 2·44m.; chickens, 85m. In 2006–07 there were 12,000 tractors.

Forestry

Forest area in 2015 was 29·04m. ha., covering 44% of the total land area. The annual loss of 546,000 ha. between 2010 and 2015 was exceeded during the same period only in Brazil and Indonesia. Teak resources cover about 6m. ha. (15m. acres). In 2011, 43·03m. cu. metres of roundwood were cut.

Fisheries

In 2015 the total catch was an estimated 1,953,500 tonnes (56% from sea fishing). Aquaculture production totalled 852,791 tonnes in 2010.

Industry

Production in 1,000 tonnes (unless otherwise specified): cement (2007), 618; raw sugar (2007), 160; nitrogenous fertilizers (2007), 115; paper and paperboard (2007), 45; sawnwood (2007), 1·5m. cu. metres; cigarettes (2007), 2,755m. units; bricks (2005–06), 72·3m. units; bicycles (2007), 53,880 units.

Labour

The estimated labour force in 2013 was 31,670,000. Agriculture provides employment to two-thirds of the population. In Jan. 2013, 37% of the population was unemployed.

Myanmar had 0·38m. people living in slavery according to the Walk Free Foundation's 2013 *Global Slavery Index*, the ninth highest total of any country.

International Trade

In Aug. 1991 the USA imposed trade sanctions in response to alleged civil rights violations. A law of 1989 permitted joint ventures, with foreign companies or individuals able to hold 100% of the shares.

Imports and Exports

Since 1990, in line with market-oriented measures, firms have been able to participate directly in trade.

Imports in 2006–07 totalled K.16,835·0m. and exports K.30,026·1m. Main imports, 2006–07: mineral fuels, lubricants and related materials, 24·1%; machinery and transport equipment, 20·3%; manufactured goods, 19·6%; chemicals, 10·7%. Leading import suppliers in 2006–07 were Singapore, 35·2%; China, 24·9%; Thailand, 10·4%; Japan, 5·3%. Main exports in 2006–07: gas, 38·9%; pulses, 11·6%; timber, 9·8%; precious stones and pearls, 7·4%. Main export markets, 2006–07: Thailand, 45·1%; India, 14·0%; China, 11·8%; Hong Kong, 7·7%.

Communications

Roads

There were 27,000 km of roads in 2005, of which 11·9% were surfaced. In 2005 there were 194,411 passenger cars, 54,482 vans and lorries, 17,985 buses and coaches, and 640,313 motorcycles and mopeds. There were 1,638 deaths as a result of road accidents in 2007.

Rail

In 2005 there were 4,809 km of route on metre gauge. Passenger-km travelled in 2006–07 came to 5,307m. and freight tonne-km to 887m.

Civil Aviation

The flag carrier is Myanmar National Airlines (Myanma Airways until 2014). The main airport is Yangon International Airport. In 2010 there were international flights to Bangkok, Beijing, Guangzhou, Hanoi, Kolkata, Kuala Lumpur, Kunming, Singapore and Taipei. In 2012 scheduled airline traffic of Myanmar-based carriers flew 1·0m. km; passenger-km totalled 117·1m. in the same year.

Shipping

There are nearly 100 km of navigable canals. The Irrawaddy is navigable up to Myitkyina, 1,450 km from the sea, and its tributary, the Chindwin, is navigable for 630 km. The Irrawaddy delta has approximately 3,000 km of navigable water. The Salween, the Attaran and the G'yne provide about 400 km of navigable waters around Moulmein. In Jan. 2014 there were 47 ships of 300 GT or over registered, totalling 248,000 GT. Myanmar's largest port is Myanmar International Terminal Thilawa, 25 km from Yangon.

Telecommunications

In 2011 there were 521,100 landline telephone subscriptions (equivalent to 10·8 per 1,000 inhabitants) and 1,243,600 mobile phone subscriptions (or 25·7 per 1,000 inhabitants). In 2011, 1·0% of the population were internet users. Following decades of military rule, Myanmar has one of Asia's lowest phone penetration rates.

Social Institutions

Out of 178 countries analysed in the 2017 *Fragile States Index*—a list published jointly by the Fund for Peace and *Foreign Policy* magazine—Myanmar was ranked the 25th most vulnerable to conflict or collapse. The index is based on 12 indicators of state vulnerability across social, political and economic categories.

Justice

The highest judicial authority is the Chief Judge, appointed by the government. In mid-2007 there were 65,063 people (126 per 100,000 of national population) held in prisons. Amnesty International reported in 2007 that before the protests against the government resulting in hundreds more arrests there were around 1,150 political prisoners in the country's jails. In Oct. 2011 then President Thein Sein granted amnesty to more than 6,300 prisoners, although it was unclear how many of Myanmar's 2,100 political prisoners would be freed. In Jan. 2012, 651 prisoners were released, including political activists, student leaders and army dissidents.

Although Myanmar is considered a *de facto* abolitionist country, two executions were reported in 2016 in the self-administered division of Wa. In 2015 the World Justice Project *Rule of Law Index*, which provides data on how the rule of law is experienced by the general public across eight categories, ranked Myanmar 96th of 102 countries for criminal justice and 94th for civil justice.

Education

Education is free in primary, middle and vocational schools; fees are charged in senior secondary schools and universities. In 2007 there were 5,013,582 pupils at primary schools with 172,209 teaching staff; and 2,686,198 pupils at secondary schools with 81,943 teaching staff. In 2006–07 there were 1,055 monastic primary schools (permitted since 1992) with 152,548 pupils, 256 monastic middle schools with 22,992 pupils and two monastic high schools with 3,887 pupils. There were 507,660 students and 10,669 academic staff in tertiary education in 2007.

In higher education in 2005–06 there were 521,702 students enrolled at 35 universities of arts and sciences, including 413,902 at the University of Distance Education. There were also 59,503 students enrolled at vocational universities in 2005–06, with 16,216 studying computers, computer science and technology, 14,516 medicine, 12,079 economics, 6,286 education, 1,738 dentistry, 1,711 technology, 1,387 nursing, 1,287 agriculture, 1,231 pharmacy and 1,077 paramedical science.

The adult literacy rate was an estimated 92·0% in 2009.

In the period 1998–2007, 13% of central government expenditure was allocated to education.

Health

In 2006–07 there were 826 government hospitals with 43,128 beds. In 2006–07 there were 20,501 doctors (65% private), 21,075 nurses, 17,703 midwives and 1,732 dentists. Spending on health in 2005 amounted to 2·2% of GDP although only 10·6% came from the state. General government expenditure on health in 2005 totalled 1·1% of total government spending.

In *Water: At What Cost? The State of the World's Water 2016*, WaterAid reported that 19·4% of the population does not have access to safe water.

Welfare

In 2006–07 contributions to social security totalled (K.1m.) 3,697·9 (from employers, 2,311·2; from employees, 1,386·7). Benefits paid totalled 935·7, and included: medical care, 764·7; sickness, 77·5; maternity, 41·0; death, 36·0.

Religion

In 2010 an estimated 80·1% of the population—mainly Bamars, Shans, Mons, Rakhines and some Kayins—were Buddhists according to the Pew Research Center's Forum on Religion & Public Life. The Pew Research Center estimated that a further 7·8% were Christians (mainly Protestants), 5·8% were folk religionists, 4·0% Muslims and 1·7% Hindus (the last two being mainly people of Indian origin). In Feb. 2019 the Roman Catholic Church had one cardinal.

Culture

Press

There were six daily newspapers in 2008, with a combined circulation of 420,000. In 2013 the publication of private daily papers was permitted for the first time in nearly 50 years.

Tourism

In 2011 there were 391,000 non-resident tourists (193,000 in 2008); spending by tourists totalled US$293m. in 2011.

World Heritage Sites

There is one UNESCO site in Myanmar: Pyu Ancient Cities (2014), comprising the remains of three bricked, walled and moated cities. They reflect the Pyu Kingdoms that flourished between 200 BC and AD 900.

Diplomatic Representatives

Of Myanmar in the United Kingdom (19A Charles St., London, W1J 5DX)
Ambassador: Kyaw Zwar Minn.

Of the United Kingdom in Myanmar (80 Strand Rd, Box No. 638, Yangon)
Ambassador: Dan Chugg.

Of Myanmar in the USA (2300 S. St., NW, Washington, D.C., 20008)
Ambassador: Aung Lynn.

Of the USA in Myanmar (110 University Ave., Kamayut Township, Yangon)
Ambassador: Scot Marciel.

Of Myanmar to the United Nations
Ambassador: Hau Do Suan.

Of Myanmar to the European Union
Ambassador: Soe Lynn Han.

Further Reading

Aung San Suu Kyi, *Freedom from Fear and Other Writings.* 1991

Carey, P. (ed.) *Burma: The Challenge of Change in a Divided Society.* 1997

Cockett, Richard, *Blood, Dreams and Gold: The Changing Face of Burma.* 2015

Hiaing, Kyaw Yin, *Myanmar: Beyond Politics to Social Imperatives.* 2005

Lall, Marie, *Understanding Reform in Myanmar: People and Society in the Wake of Military Rule.* 2016

Metraux, Daniel A., *Burma's Modern Tragedy.* 2005

Myint, S., *Burma File: A Question of Democracy.* 2004

Rogers, Benedict, *Burma: A Nation at the Crossroads.* 2012

Schrank, Delphine, *The Rebel of Rangoon: A Tale of Defiance and Deliverance in Burma.* 2015

Seekins, Donald M., *Historical Dictionary of Burma.* 2006

Skidmore, Monique, *Burma at the Turn of the Twenty-First Century.* 2005

Smith, Martin, *Burma: Insurgency and the Politics of Ethnicity.* 1999

Steinberg, David I., *Burma: The State of Myanmar.* 2002

Thant Myint-U, *The Making of Modern Burma.* 2001.—*The River of Lost Footsteps: Histories of Burma.* 2007.—*Where China Meets India: Burma and the New Crossroads of Asia.* 2011

Tucker, Shelby, *Burma: The Curse of Independence.* 2001

Wade, Francis, *Myanmar's Enemy Within: Buddhist Violence and the Making of a Muslim 'Other'.* 2017

National Statistical Office: Ministry of National Planning and Economic Development, Yangon.

Website: http://www.csostat.gov.mm

Namibia

Republic of Namibia

Capital: Windhoek
Population projection, 2020: 2·70m.
GNI per capita, 2017: (PPP$) 9,387
HDI/world rank, 2017: 0·647/129
Internet domain extension: .na

Key Historical Events

Namibia was first settled by people from the Khoisan language group. The earliest, the nomadic San people, were followed about 2000 years ago by the pastoral Nama, who became dominant in the south. In the 9th century AD the Damara settled the central grasslands (known as Damaraland). Other clans followed and by the 19th century three Bantu peoples were established: the Herero in northeastern and central Namibia (Kaokoland); the Ovambo around the Kunene River in the north; and the Kavango people in the east. In the far east, the Barotse expanded from Zambia to settle the Caprivi Strip while the Tswana (from Botswana) settled the edges of the Kalahari desert.

European traders and settlers arrived in the late 18th century. Walvis Bay came under Dutch (1793) then British (1797) control, and European settlement began on the coast. In the 1830s the Oorlans, from South Africa, expanded into Nama and Damara territory, becoming dominant under the leadership of Jonker Afrikaner.

In 1884 the area then known as South West Africa became a German protectorate. From 1904–08 conflict between German troops and the Herero and Nama peoples saw the deaths of 80% of the Herero population and 50% of the Nama. In the aftermath, Germany introduced racial segregation and used forced labour for diamond mines. In 1915 the Union of South Africa occupied German South West Africa and on 17 Dec. 1920 the League of Nations entrusted the territory as a Mandate to the Union of South Africa. After the Second World War South Africa applied unsuccessfully to annex the territory, continuing to administer it in defiance of the UN. Indigenous opposition to South African rule intensified in the 1950s: the Ovamboland Peoples' Organization was founded in 1958 (known as the South West Africa Peoples' Organization, or SWAPO, from 1960) and the South West Africa National Union (SWANU) in 1959.

In 1968 the UN changed the territory's name to Namibia. Following widespread strikes in 1971–72, negotiations took place between South Africa and the UN and in 1973 a multi-racial advisory council was appointed in preparation for independence. However, attempts at organizing free elections failed. In 1988, after military defeat in Angola, South Africa withdrew. UN-supervised elections took place in Nov. 1989, delivering a victory for SWAPO. After independence on 21 March 1990, Namibia joined the Commonwealth.

In April 1990 Namibia joined the UN and in June 1990 the Organization of African Unity, forerunner of the African Union. In 2004 the country suffered major flooding. It continues to face a serious AIDS epidemic, with around 20% of adults infected, although in 2007 the rate fell for the first time.

Territory and Population

Namibia is bounded in the north by Angola and Zambia, west by the Atlantic Ocean, south and southeast by South Africa and east by Botswana. The Caprivi Strip (part of which is in the Zambezi Region and part in the Kavango East Region), about 300 km long, extends eastwards up to the Zambezi river, projecting into Zambia and Botswana and touching Zimbabwe. The area, including the Caprivi Strip and Walvis Bay, is 825,615 sq. km. South Africa transferred Walvis Bay to Namibian jurisdiction on 1 March 1994. 2011 census population, 2,113,077 (1,091,165 females); density 2·6 per sq. km. In 2011, 38·6% of the population were urban.

The UN gives a projected population for 2020 of 2·70m.

The largest ethnic group is the Ovambo (about half the population), followed by the Kavango, Damara and Herero. Since Aug. 2013 Namibia

has been administratively divided into 14 regions (previously 13). Area, population and chief towns of the 13 regions at the time of the 2011 census:

Region	Area (in sq. km)	Population	Chief town
Caprivi (Liambezi)[1]	14,785	90,596	Katima Mulilo
Erongo	63,539	150,809	Swakopmund
Hardap	109,781	79,507	Mariental
Karas[2]	161,514	77,421	Keetmanshoop
Kavango[3]	48,742	223,352	Rundu
Khomas	36,964	342,141	Windhoek
Kunene	115,260	86,856	Opuwo
Ohangwena	10,706	245,446	Eenhana
Omaheke	84,981	71,233	Gobabis
Omusati	26,551	243,166	Outapi
Oshana	8,647	176,674	Oshakati
Oshikoto	38,685	181,973	Tsumeb
Otjozondjupa	105,460	143,903	Grootfontein

[1]Renamed Zambezi in 2013.
[2]Renamed llKaras in 2013.
[3]Split into two new regions, Kavango East and Kavango West, in 2013.

Towns with populations over 10,000 (2011): Windhoek, 325,858; Rundu, 63,431; Walvis Bay, 62,096; Swakopmund, 44,725; Oshakati, 36,541; Rehoboth, 28,843; Katima Mulilo, 28,362; Otjiwarongo, 28,249; Ondangwa, 22,822; Okahandja, 22,639; Keetmanshoop, 20,977; Ongwediva, 20,260; Helao Nafidi, 19,375; Tsumeb, 19,275; Gobabis, 19,101; Grootfontein, 16,632; Lüderitz (renamed !Nami≠Nüs in 2013), 12,537; Mariental, 12,478.

English is the official language. Afrikaans and German are also spoken.

Social Statistics

Estimates, 2008: births, 59,000; deaths, 18,000. Estimated birth rate in 2008 was 27·6 per 1,000 population; estimated death rate, 8·6. Expectation of life, 2013: males, 61·7 years; females, 67·1. Annual population growth rate, 2000–08, 1·9%; infant mortality, 2010, 29 per 1,000 live births. The fertility rate dropped from 5·5 births per woman in 1994 to 3·4 births per woman in 2008.

Climate

The rainfall increases steadily from less than 50 mm in the west and southwest up to 600 mm in the Caprivi Strip. The main rainy season is from Jan. to March, with lesser showers from Sept. to Dec. Namibia is the driest African country south of the Sahara. The average temperature in Windhoek is 24°C in Jan. and 14°C in July.

Constitution and Government

On 9 Feb. 1990 with a unanimous vote the Constituent Assembly approved the Constitution which stipulated a multi-party republic, an independent judiciary and an executive *President* who may serve a maximum of two five-year terms. The constitution became effective on 12 March 1990 and was amended in 1999 to allow then President Sam Nujoma to stand for a third term in office. The bicameral legislature consists of a 104-seat *National Assembly* (increased for the 2014 election from 78 in 2009), 96 members of which are elected for five-year terms by proportional representation and up to eight appointed by the president by virtue of position or special expertise, and a 42-seat *National Council* consisting of three members from each Regional Council indirectly elected for five-year terms.

National Anthem
'Namibia, land of the brave'; words and tune by Axali Doeseb.

Recent Elections

Presidential and parliamentary elections held on 28 Nov. 2014 were the first in Africa to utilize electronic or e-voting. Hage Geingob (South West Africa People's Organization/SWAPO) was elected president with 86·7% of votes cast, followed by McHenry Venaani (Democratic Turnhalle Alliance/DTA) with 5·0%, Hidipo Hamutenya (Rally for Democracy and Progress/RDP) with 3·4% and Asser Mbai (National Unity Democratic Organization/NUDO) with 1·9%. There were five other candidates. Turnout was 71·8%. In the parliamentary elections SWAPO won 77 of the available 96 seats with 80·0% of the vote; DTA, 5 with 4·8%; RDP, 3 with 3·5%; All People's Party, 2 with 2·3%; United Democratic Front, 2 with 2·1%; NUDO, 2 with 2·0%; the Communist Party of Namibia, 2 with 1·5%; South West Africa National Union, 1 with 0·7%; United People's Movement, 1 with 0·7%; Republican Party, 1 with 0·7%.

Current Government

President: Hage Geingob; b. 1941 (SWAPO; sworn in 21 March 2015).
    Vice President: Nangolo Mbumba.
    In Feb. 2019 the government comprised:
    Prime Minister: Saara Kuugongelwa-Amadhila; b. 1967 (SWAPO; sworn in 21 March 2015).
    Deputy Prime Minister, and Minister of International Relations and Co-operation: Netumbo Nandi-Ndaitwah.
    Minister of Agriculture, Water and Forestry: Alpheus !Naruseb. *Defence:* Penda Ya Ndakolo. *Economic Planning:* Obeth Kandjoze. *Education, Arts and Culture:* Katrina Hanse-Himarwa. *Environment and Tourism:* Pohamba Shifeta. *Finance:* Calle Schlettwein. *Fisheries and Marine Resources:* Bernhard Esau. *Gender Equality and Child Welfare:* Doreen Sioka. *Health and Social Services:* Dr Bernhard Haufiku. *Higher Education, Training and Innovation:* Itah Murangi-Kandjii. *Home Affairs and Immigration:* Frans Kapofi. *Industrialization, Trade, and Small and Medium Enterprise Development:* Tjekero Tweya. *Information and Communication Technology:* Stanley Simataa. *Justice:* Sackeus Shanghala. *Labour, Industrial Relations and Employment Creation:* Erkki Nghimtina. *Land Reform:* Uutoni Nujoma. *Mines and Energy:* Tom Alweendo. *Poverty Alleviation:* Bishop Zephania Kameeta. *Presidential Affairs:* Immanuel Ngatjieko. *Public Enterprises:* Leon Jooste. *Safety and Security:* Gen. Charles Namoloh. *Sport, Youth and National Service:* Erastus Utoni. *Urban and Rural Development:* Peya Mushelenga. *Works and Transport:* John Mutorwa. *Attorney General:* Albert Kawana.
    Office of the Prime Minister: http://www.opm.gov.na

Current Leaders

Hage Geingob
Position
President

Introduction
Hage Geingob became president in March 2015. A former prime minister, he promised a programme of industrialization to combat poverty.

Early Life
Born on 3 Aug. 1941 in Otjiwarongo in what was then South West Africa, Hage Geingob was educated in Otavi. After qualifying as a teacher from the Augustineum Training College in 1961, he worked briefly as a primary school teacher before moving to Botswana. When his plans to travel farther afield and work with the African National Congress were thwarted, he remained in Botswana, serving as assistant representative of the South West Africa People's Organization (SWAPO) from 1963–64.
    From 1964 he studied in the USA, first at Temple University, Philadelphia and then at Fordham University, New York, graduating in 1970. He then gained a master's degree in international relations from The New School, New York. He also served as SWAPO representative at the United Nations and to the Americas from 1964–71 and was political affairs officer at the UN secretariat from 1972–75. Between 1975 and 1989 he was director of the UN Institute for Namibia, an establishment that trained civil servants and researched policy.

Having risen through the SWAPO ranks, in 1989 he returned to Namibia to head its successful election campaign. He served as chairman of the constituent assembly that drew up Namibia's constitution from Nov. 1989–March 1990, and then became Namibia's first prime minister (under President Sam Nujoma). In this post, he oversaw the development of the tourism industry and a related programme of nature conservation. After being replaced as prime minister in 2002, he served from 2003–04 as executive secretary of the intergovernmental Global Coalition for Africa.
    Having regained a seat in parliament in 2004, he became SWAPO's chief whip and, in 2007, its vice president. In 2008 he was named minister of trade and industry and in 2012 became prime minister for the second time. He fought the Nov. 2014 presidential election on a platform of industrialization and good governance, winning 87% of the vote.

Career in Office
Geingob signalled his intention to create new ministries to implement reform programmes. His main challenges included developing the economy so as to reduce poverty, while also combating corruption. However, economic growth has stalled since 2015 and political dissent was evident at the SWAPO congress in Nov. 2017. Nonetheless, Geingob was re-elected party president at the congress by a large margin.
    In Aug. 2018 he became chairperson of the Southern African Development Community for a one-year term.

Defence

In 2013 defence expenditure totalled US$458m. (US$210 per capita), representing 3·6% of GDP.

Army
Personnel (2011), 9,000. There is also a 6,000-strong paramilitary police force.

Navy
A force of around 200 (2011) is based at Walvis Bay.

Air Force
The Namibian Air Force, which was established in 2005, had 24 combat-capable aircraft in 2011.

Economy

Agriculture accounted for 6·9% of GDP in 2016, industry 31·3% and services 61·8%.

Overview
Mining accounts for over 12% of GDP annually and 50% of export earnings, yet employs only 8% of the working population. Rich in natural resources, the country is the world's fifth largest producer of uranium and also boasts large deposits of zinc, copper and diamonds. A flourishing mining sector allied to high government spending saw growth average 4% annually from 2001 to 2011 and reach 6·5% in 2014. However, weaker commodity prices and drought pushed GDP growth down to 5·3% in 2015.
    About 35% of national revenues come from the Southern African Customs Union (SACU), which pools and redistributes customs and excise duties generated by its member nations. 80% of Namibia's foreign investment comes from its main trading partner, South Africa, and the Namibian dollar is pegged to the South African rand. Consequently, the knock-on effects from a weaker South African economy were expected to result in a 1·75% decline in SACU revenues for 2015–16. The Namibian government is trying to diversify the economy by expanding the fishing and tourism industries and pursuing closer trading ties with the European Union and the USA.
    HIV is a major health problem, affecting 13·3% of the working population, while a lack of education and skills means the majority of people continue to rely on subsistence farming. The unemployment rate was 28·1% in 2014. The poverty rate remains especially acute in rural areas at around 27% compared to 9% in urban areas. The income of the richest 10% of the population was estimated at over five times that of the poorest 40% in 2015.

Currency

The unit of currency is the *Namibia dollar* (NAD) of 100 *cents*, introduced on 14 Sept. 1993 and pegged to the South African rand. The rand is also legal tender at parity. Inflation was 6·7% in 2016 and 6·1% in 2017. In May 2005 foreign exchange reserves were US$333m. Broad money supply totalled N$85,950m. in Dec. 2016.

Budget

The financial year runs from 1 April. In 2014–15 revenues were N$52,473m. and expenditures N$60,204m. Tax revenue constituted 93·8% of revenues in 2014–15; current expenditure accounted for 80·2% of expenditures.

VAT is 15%.

Performance

Real GDP growth was 6·1% in 2015 and 0·7% in 2016, before contracting by 0·8% in 2017; total GDP in 2017 was US$13·2bn.

Banking and Finance

The Bank of Namibia is the central bank. Its *Governor* is Ipumbu Wendelinus Shiimi. Assets in June 2010 were N$12,717·4m. Total assets of other depository corporations (First National Bank of Namibia, Standard Bank of Namibia, Nedbank Namibia, Bank Windhoek, Agribank of Namibia, National Housing Enterprise and the Namibia Post Office Savings Bank) were N$50,990·5m. in June 2010.

Total foreign debt was US$2·0bn. in Dec. 2009.

A stock exchange (NSE) is in operation in Windhoek.

Energy and Natural Resources

Environment

Carbon dioxide emissions from the consumption of energy were the equivalent of 1·5 tonnes per capita in 2011.

Electricity

Installed capacity in 2011 was 0·4m. kW. In 2011 electricity production was 1·6bn. kWh. Namibia also imports electricity to meet demand (2·4bn. kWh in 2011, mainly from South Africa). Consumption per capita in 2011 was 1,766 kWh.

Oil and Gas

Natural gas reserves in 2013 totalled 62bn. cu. metres.

Minerals

There are diamond deposits both inshore and off the coast, with production equally divided between the two. Some 1·5bn. carats of diamonds are believed to be lying in waters off Namibia's Atlantic coast. Namibia produced 1·7m. carats in 2013, exclusively of gem quality. Output in 2013 (in tonnes): salt, 717,612; zinc (metal content), 184,109; lead (estimate, metal content), 11,000; copper (metal content), 4,896; uranium (metal content), 4,323; silver (estimate, metal content), 45,100 kg; gold (metal content), 1,960 kg.

Agriculture

Namibia is essentially a stock-raising country, the scarcity of water and poor rainfall rendering crop-farming, except in the northern and northeastern parts, almost impossible. There were an estimated 800,000 ha. of arable land in 2007 and 5,000 ha. of permanent crops. There were 39 tractors per 10,000 ha. of arable land in 2006. Generally speaking, the southern half is suited for the raising of small stock, while the central and northern parts are more suited for cattle. Guano is harvested from the coast, converted into fertilizer in South Africa and most of it exported to Europe. In 2007 the agricultural population was an estimated 905,000, of which some 252,000 were economically active.

Principal crops (2013 estimates, in tonnes): maize, 40,000; millet, 25,000; grapes, 23,000; onions, 23,000; wheat, 15,000; potatoes, 12,000. Livestock (2013): 2·63m. cattle, 2·19m. sheep, 1·69m. goats, 5m. chickens (estimate). In 2013 an estimated 120,000 tonnes of milk and 80,000 tonnes of meat were produced.

Forestry

Forests covered 6·92m. ha. in 2015, or 8% of the land area. In 2011 timber production was 827,000 cu. metres.

Fisheries

Namibia has one of the most productive fishing grounds in the world. Fish processing is the fastest-growing sector of the economy. The catch in 2012 was 469,613 tonnes, of which more than 99% came from marine waters.

Industry

Of the estimated total of 400 undertakings, the most important branches are food production (accounting for 29% of total output), metals (13%) and wooden products (7%). The supply of specialized equipment to the mining industry, the assembly of goods from predominantly imported materials and the manufacture of metal products and construction material play an important part. Small industries (including home industries, textile mills, leather and steel goods) have expanded. Products manufactured locally include chocolates, beer, cement, leather shoes, delicatessen meats and game meat products.

Labour

Of 690,019 people in employment in 2013, 215,311 were engaged in agriculture, forestry and fishing; 79,391 in wholesale and retail trade; 57,668 in private households; 47,859 in construction; 41,797 in education; 36,767 in accommodation and food service activities; and 35,160 in administrative and support service activities. The unemployment rate in 2013 was 29·6%.

Namibia had 16,000 people living in slavery according to the Walk Free Foundation's 2013 *Global Slavery Index*.

International Trade

Export Processing Zones were established in 1995 to grant companies with EPZ status some tax exemptions and other incentives. The Offshore Development Company (ODC) is the flagship of the Export Processing Zone regime. The EPZ regime does not restrict; any investor (local or foreign) enjoys the same or equal advantages in engaging themselves in any choice of business (allowed by law).

Imports and Exports

In 2007 imports (c.i.f.) were valued at US$4,026·0m. and exports (f.o.b.) at US$4,040·3m. Exports in 2007 (in US$1m.) included diamonds (705), zinc (624), fish (432), uranium ores and concentrates (350), machinery and transport equipment (280), meat products (153). The largest import supplier in 2006 was South Africa with 82·4%; largest export markets: UK, 25·6%; South Africa, 24·6%.

Communications

Roads

In 2011 the road network covered 45,645 km. In 2008 there were 107,800 passenger cars in use and 117,400 lorries and vans. There were 368 deaths as a result of road accidents in 2007.

Rail

The Namibia system connects with the main system of the South African railways at Ariamsvlei. The total length of the line inside Namibia was 2,628 km of 1,065 mm gauge in 2005.

Civil Aviation

The national carrier is the state-owned Air Namibia, which in 2013 carried 458,000 passengers (381,000 on international flights). In the same year it served six domestic and nine international destinations. In 2012 the major airport, Windhoek's Hosea Kutako International, handled 814,890 passengers (764,384 on international flights). Eros is used mainly for domestic flights.

Shipping

Walvis Bay, the busiest port, handled 6,497,000 tonnes of cargo in 2013–14. There is a harbour at !Nami≠Nüs (formerly Lüderitz) which handles mainly fishing vessels. Merchant shipping totalled 3,000 GT in Jan. 2014.

Telecommunications

Telecom Namibia is the responsible corporation. In 2013 there were 183,000 main (fixed) telephone lines and 2,728,000 mobile phone subscriptions (118·4 per 100 persons). An estimated 13·9% of the population were internet users in 2013. In June 2012 there were 172,000 Facebook users.

Social Institutions

Out of 178 countries analysed in the 2017 *Fragile States Index*—a list published jointly by the Fund for Peace and *Foreign Policy* magazine—Namibia was ranked the 76th least vulnerable to conflict or collapse. The index is based on 12 indicators of state vulnerability across social, political and economic categories.

Justice

There are a Supreme Court, a High Court and a number of magistrates' and lower courts. An Ombudsman is appointed. Judges are appointed by the president on the recommendation of the Judicial Service Commission.

The population in penal institutions in Nov. 2011 was 4,314 (191 per 100,000 of national population).

Education

Literacy was an estimated 88·5% in 2009 (male, 88·9%; female, 88·1%). Primary education is free and compulsory. In 2007 there were 409,508 pupils at primary schools, 158,162 at secondary schools and (2006) 13,185 students at institutions of higher education.

In 2010 public expenditure on education came to 8·1% of GDP.

Health

There were 45 hospitals (11 private) and 296 health centres and clinics in 2005. In 2006 there were 33 hospital beds per 10,000 population. There were 774 physicians, 5,750 nursing and midwifery personnel, 90 dentistry personnel and 376 pharmaceutical personnel in 2007.

In *Water: At What Cost? The State of the World's Water 2016*, WaterAid reported that 9·0% of the population does not have access to safe water.

Religion

According to estimates by the Pew Research Center's Forum on Religion & Public Life, in 2010 the population was 97·5% Christian (mainly Protestants) with 1·9% not having any religious affiliation.

Culture

World Heritage Sites

Namibia has two sites on the UNESCO World Heritage List: a large collection of rock engravings at Twyfelfontein (added to the list in 2007); and Namib Sand Sea (2013), the only coastal desert in the world that includes extensive dune fields influenced by fog.

Press

There were four daily newspapers in 2008 with a combined circulation of 55,000.

Tourism

In 2011 there were 1,027,000 non-resident tourists who spent US$645m. Tourist numbers rose every year from 2003 to 2011.

Diplomatic Representatives

Of Namibia in the United Kingdom (6 Chandos St., London, W1G 9LU)
    High Commissioner: Linda Anne Scott.

Of the United Kingdom in Namibia (116 Robert Mugabe Ave., PO Box 22202, Windhoek)
    High Commissioner: Kate Airey, OBE.

Of Namibia in the USA (1605 New Hampshire Ave., NW, Washington, D.C., 20009)
    Ambassador: Vacant.
    Charge d'Affaires a.i.: Helena Elizabeth Gray.

Of the USA in Namibia (14 Lossen St., Windhoek)
    Ambassador: Lisa A. Johnson.

Of Namibia to the United Nations
    Ambassador: Neville Melvin Gertze.

Of Namibia to the European Union
    Ambassador: Kaire Munionganda Mbuende.

Further Reading

Kaela, L. C. W., *The Question of Namibia.* 1996
Melber, Henning, *Re-examining Liberation in Namibia: Political Cultures Since Independence.* 2003
Sparks, D. L. and Green, D., *Namibia: the Nation after Independence.* 1992
National Statistical Office: Namibia Statistics Agency, PO Box 2133, Windhoek.
Website: http://www.nsa.org.na/index.php

Nauru

Ripublik Naoero (Republic of Nauru)

Population projection, 2020: 11,000
GNI per capita, 2015: (PPP$) 12,058
Internet domain extension: .nr

Key Historical Events

Nauru was originally settled by Melanesians and Polynesians. Tradition holds that among the earliest settlers were castaways from another island, probably Kiribati. The name 'Nauru' is a European corruption of 'A-nao-ero', which means 'I am going to the beach to lay my bones'. The island has had little contact with its neighbours, enabling its distinctive language to survive. By the 18th century the society was organized into 12 matrilineal tribes, each headed by a different chief.

The island was discovered by a British captain, John Fearn, in 1798 but was avoided by most ships in subsequent decades because of the region's notoriety for piracy. In the 1830s European whaling ships began using Nauru as a supply port and European settlers arrived. Though small in number, they had a profound impact by introducing alcohol, firearms and disease. An escalation in tribal conflict resulted in a war from 1878–88, killing 500 people or one third of the population. Germany annexed the island in 1888 to protect its trading interests and in the early 1900s agreed a deal to allow the British Pacific Phosphate Company to mine newly discovered phosphates.

Nauru was surrendered to Australian forces in 1914. In 1920 its administration was formally passed to the UK under a League of Nations mandate but in practice Australia continued to run the island. Australia, Britain and New Zealand set up and jointly ran the British Phosphate Commission, which controlled the phosphate mining industry. During the Second World War Japanese forces occupied from 1942–45, deporting 1,200 Nauruans to Truk (now Chuuk, in present-day Micronesia) as forced labour. Only 737 of the deportees returned. In 1947 Nauru became a UN trust, with Australia, New Zealand and the UK as trustees.

On 31 Jan. 1968 the country gained independence. The government of President Hammer DeRoburt took over the phosphate industry, continuing to run it as a communal trust. Phosphate prices rose and the country enjoyed a boom throughout the 1970s, achieving one of the world's highest rates of GDP per capita. However, mismanagement of the revenues, poor investment decisions and a lack of political accountability led to problems when prices fell in 1988. In 1993 Australia and the UK paid US$73m. compensation for environmental damage during mining. Nauru developed an offshore banking industry in the 1990s but was accused of money-laundering by the international community. In the mid-1990s the economic crisis deepened with the collapse of the Bank of Nauru and in 2000 the OECD's financial watchdog (Financial Action Task Force on Money Laundering, or FATF) blacklisted the country. In 2001 Nauru agreed to hold detained asylum seekers on behalf of Australia and has subsequently relied heavily on Australian aid.

The 21st century has seen much political turmoil. During 2003 there were six changes of president and in Sept. 2004 President Ludwig Scotty declared a state of emergency. Following regulatory tightening of the offshore banking industry, Nauru was removed from the FATF blacklist in 2005. The island continues to face severe challenges, including a health crisis arising from having one of the world's highest obesity rates.

Territory and Population

Nauru is a coral island surrounded by a reef situated 0° 32' S. lat. and 166° 56' E. long. Area, 21·2 sq. km (8·2 sq. miles). At the 2011 census the population totalled 10,084 (5,105 males). Population density, 476 per sq. km.

The UN gives a projected population for 2020 of 11,000.

In 2011, 94% of the population were indigenous Nauruans. The *de facto* capital is Yaren.

Nauruan is the official language, although English is widely used for government purposes.

Social Statistics

2012 births, 366; deaths, 71. Annual population growth rate, 2003–13, 0·0%; fertility rate, 2013, 2·9 births per woman. Life expectancy at birth in the period 2011–13 was 64·9 years for females and 58·0 years for males.

Climate

A tropical climate, tempered by sea breezes, but with a high and irregular rainfall, averaging 82" (2,060 mm). Average temperature, Jan. 81°F (27·2°C), July 82°F (27·8°C). Annual rainfall 75" (1,862 mm).

Constitution and Government

A Legislative Council was inaugurated on 31 Jan. 1966. The constitution was promulgated on 29 Jan. 1968 and was amended on 17 May 1968. A 19-member Parliament (18 prior to the June 2013 election) is elected on a three-yearly basis.

National Anthem

'Nauru bwiema, ngabena ma auwe' ('Nauru our homeland, the country we love'); words by M. Hendrie, tune by L. H. Hicks.

Recent Elections

At the parliamentary elections of 9–11 July 2016, 19 non-partisan members were elected. On 11 July 2016 Baron Waqa was re-elected president by parliament by 16 votes to 2.

Current Government

In Feb. 2019 the government comprised:

President, Cabinet Chairman, Minister for the Public Service, Foreign Affairs and Trade, Climate Change, Police, Emergency Services, Commerce, Industry and Environment, Telecommunications, Naoero Postal Services Corporation, Nauru Phosphate Royalties Trust, and Cenpac Corporation: Baron Divavesi Waqa; b. 1959 (sworn in 11 June 2013).

Minister Assisting the President, Minister for Finance and Sustainable Development, Justice and Border Control, Multicultural Affairs, Eigigu Holdings Corporation, and Nauru Air Corporation: David Adeang. *RONPHOS, Nauru Rehabilitation Corporation, and Utilities Corporation:* Aaron Cook. *Home Affairs, Education and Youth, Land Management, and Health:* Charmaine Scotty. *Sports, Transport, Port Authority, Infrastructure Development, and Fisheries:* Lyn-Wannan Tawaki Kam.
Government Website: http://www.naurugov.nr

Current Leaders

Baron Divavesi Waqa

Position
President

Introduction
Baron Waqa was sworn in as president on 11 June 2013 after he was elected by parliament. In line with the constitution, he is both head of government and head of state. He was re-elected in July 2016.

Early Life
Baron Divavesi Waqa was born on 31 Dec. 1959. In 1981 he gained his teacher training certificate from the Nasinu Teachers College in Suva, the capital of Fiji. Five years later he graduated in education from the University of the South Pacific in Suva.

Waqa was first elected to parliament in the 2003 general election representing the constituency of Boe, a seat he has held in each subsequent

© Springer Nature Limited 2020
Palgrave Macmillan (ed.), *The Statesman's Yearbook 2020*,
https://doi.org/10.1057/978-1-349-95940-2_137

election. He was appointed minister of education in Ludwig Scotty's administration from May–Aug. 2003 and went on to hold the portfolios for health, education, telecommunications and public works in later governments.

Following his re-election to parliament in June 2013, Waqa defeated Roland Kun by 13 votes to 5 in a parliamentary ballot for the presidency.

Career in Office
Waqa's main challenge has been to tackle the failing economy, hit hard by the global financial crisis, and to arrest rising food and fuel prices. There has also been rioting and reported widespread abuse at Nauru's controversial detention centre for refugees attempting to reach Australia, prompting expressions of concern at the United Nations about conditions at the facility.

Economy

Overview
Nauru's economy was for a long time based on phosphate mining, although the depletion of deposits has seen GDP per capita recede since peaking in the 1970s and 1980s. The country is now largely dependent on external aid and imports owing to its narrow resource base. Attempts to diversify the economy into offshore banking during the 1990s proved unsuccessful and the country became a haven for money laundering, resulting in its blacklisting by international bodies until 2005. In 2001 Nauru signed an agreement with Australia to house asylum seekers on the island, generating revenues amounting to one-fifth of annual GDP before the agreement ended in 2008. However, in Sept. 2012 Australia reopened its asylum-seeker processing centre, which has become Nauru's largest private sector employer. GDP growth in 2014 was put at 10·0% by the Asian Development Bank, up from 4·5% the previous year. There was further uneven growth of 2·8% in 2015, 10·4% in 2016 and 4·0% in 2017.

In 2008 new phosphate contracts brought about the resumption of growth-driving exports. Nauru has also benefited from lucrative fishing-licence revenues. However, the long-term economic outlook depends on the diversification of the economy ahead of the complete exhaustion of phosphate reserves (estimated to be by the late 2040s). Further challenges include reducing public debt and promoting public and private investment.

Currency
The Australian dollar is in use.

Budget
The fiscal year is 1 July–30 June. Revenues in 2007 were $A17·8m. and expenditures $A21·8m.

Performance
Real GDP growth was 2·8% in 2015, 10·4% in 2016 and 4·0% in 2017; total GDP in 2017 was US$114m.

Banking and Finance
The Bank of Nauru is a state bank and there is a commercial bank, Hampshire Bank and Trust Inc.

Nauru was one of three countries named in a report in June 2005 as failing to co-operate in the fight against international money laundering. In Oct. 2005 Nauru was delisted and its formal monitoring was ended a year later. The Financial Action Task Force on Money Laundering was set up by the G7 group of major industrialized nations.

Energy and Natural Resources

Environment
Carbon dioxide emissions from the consumption of energy were the equivalent of 18·1 tonnes per capita in 2011.

Electricity
Installed capacity in 2011 was 5,000 kW; production was 23m. kWh in 2011.

Minerals
A central plateau contained high-grade phosphate deposits. The interests in the phosphate deposits were purchased in 1919 from the Pacific Phosphate Company by the UK, Australia and New Zealand. In 1967 the British Phosphate Corporation agreed to hand over the phosphate industry to Nauru for approximately $A20m. over three years. Nauru took over the industry in July 1969, and the profits from the mining meant that Nauru

had, for a brief period, one of the highest rates of GDP per capita in the world. However, production declined (from 1·67m. tonnes in 1985–86 to 162,000 tonnes in 2001–02) and the primary reserves were exhausted in 2003. Mining of a deeper layer of secondary phosphate began in 2006, and it is hoped that this development might resuscitate Nauru's ailing economy. Production was an estimated 84,000 tonnes in 2006. In May 1989 Nauru filed a claim against Australia for environmental damage caused by the mining. In Aug. 1993 Australia agreed to pay compensation of $A73m. In March 1994 New Zealand and the UK each agreed to pay compensation of $A12m.

Agriculture
In 2011 about 1,000 people were economically active in agriculture. In 2013 the crop of coconuts was an estimated 2,700 tonnes. Livestock (2013 estimates): pigs, 3,000; chickens, 5,000.

Fisheries
The catch in 2014 was 530 tonnes.

International Trade

Imports and Exports
Imports are food, building construction materials, machinery for the phosphate industry and medical supplies. Phosphates—formed from fossilized bird droppings and used for fertilizer—have traditionally accounted for virtually all of Nauru's exports, but the reserves are now largely depleted.

Imports, 2014, $A126·2m.; exports, $A16·5m. The leading import sources are Australia, Fiji and Japan; the main export markets are Japan, Australia South Korea and New Zealand.

Communications

Roads
There is a sealed road circling the island 19 km long, plus other roads running inland.

Civil Aviation
The only airport is Nauru International Airport. The national carrier, Nauru Airlines, is a wholly-owned government subsidiary. In 2017 it flew to Brisbane, Honiara, Majuro, Nadi, Pohnpei and Tarawa.

Shipping
Deep offshore moorings can accommodate medium-size vessels. Shipping coming to the island consists of vessels under charter to the phosphate industry or general purpose vessels bringing cargo by way of imports.

Telecommunications
There were 6,800 mobile phone subscriptions in 2012.

Social Institutions

Justice
The highest Court is the Supreme Court of Nauru. It is the Superior Court of record and has the jurisdiction to deal with constitutional matters in addition to its other jurisdiction. There is also a District Court which is presided over by the Resident Magistrate who is also the Chairman of the Family Court and the Registrar of Supreme Court. The laws applicable in Nauru are its own Acts of Parliament. A large number of British statutes and much common law has been adopted insofar as is compatible with Nauruan custom. The death penalty, which had not been used since Nauru became independent in 1968, was abolished in 2016.

Education
Attendance at school is compulsory between the age of six and 16. In 2007–08 there were 1,000 children in pre-primary schools with 40 teachers, 1,000 pupils in primary schools with 100 teachers and 1,000 pupils in secondary education with (2006–07) 30 teachers. There is a technical school and also a mission school. Scholarships are available for Nauruan children to receive secondary and higher education and vocational training in Australia and New Zealand.

In 2007 public expenditure on education came to an estimated 7·5% of total government spending.

Health

In 2008 there were ten physicians and 69 nursing and midwifery personnel.

Nauru has one of the highest percentages of overweight people of any country, with 77% of adults overweight or obese according to 2014 World Health Organization estimates.

In *Water: At What Cost? The State of the World's Water 2016*, WaterAid reported that 3·5% of the population does not have access to safe water.

Religion

In 2010 an estimated 79·0% of the population were Christians according to the Pew Research Center's Forum on Religion & Public Life, 8·1% folk religionists and 4·5% religiously unaffiliated.

Diplomatic Representatives

Of Nauru in the United Kingdom
Honorary Consul: Martin W. L. Weston (Romshed Courtyard, Underriver, Nr Sevenoaks, Kent, TN15 0SD).

Of the United Kingdom in Nauru
High Commissioner: David Ward (resides in Honiara, Solomon Islands).

Of Nauru in the USA and to the United Nations (801 Second Ave., New York, NY 10017)
Ambassador: Marlene Inemwin Moses.

Of the USA in Nauru
Ambassador: Vacant.
Chargé d'Affaires a.i.: Michael Goldman (resides in Suva, Fiji).

Further Reading

McDaniel, Carl N., *Paradise for Sale: Back to Sustainability.* 2000
National Statistical Office: Nauru Bureau of Statistics, Ministry of Finance, Government Offices, Yaren District.
Website: http://nauru.prism.spc.int

Nepal

Sanghiya Loktantrik Ganatantra Nepal (Federal Democratic Republic of Nepal)

Capital: Kathmandu
Population projection, 2020: 30·26m.
GNI per capita, 2017: (PPP$) 2,471
HDI/world rank, 2017: 0·574/149
Internet domain extension: .np

Key Historical Events

Nepal is an independent Himalayan republic located between India and the Tibetan region of China. From the 8th to the 11th centuries many Buddhists fled to Nepal from India, which had been invaded by Muslims. In the 18th century Nepal was a collection of small principalities and the three kingdoms of the Malla dynasty: Kathmandu, Patan and Bhadgaon. In central Nepal lay the principality of Gurkha (or Gorkha); its ruler after 1742 was Prithvi Narayan Shah, who conquered the small neighbouring states. Fearing his ambitions, in 1767 the Mallas requested armed support from the British East India Company. In 1769 these forces were withdrawn and Gurkha was then able to conquer the Malla kingdoms and unite Nepal as one state with its capital at Kathmandu. In 1846 the Rana family became the effective rulers of Nepal, establishing the office of prime minister as hereditary. In 1860 Nepal reached agreement with the British in India whereby Nepali independence was preserved and the recruitment of Gurkhas to the British army was sanctioned.

In 1950 the Shah royal family allied itself with Nepalis abroad to end the power of the Ranas. The last Rana prime minister resigned in Nov. 1951, the king having proclaimed a constitutional monarchy in Feb. 1951. A new constitution, approved in 1959, led to confrontation between the king and his ministers; it was replaced by one less liberal in 1962. In Nov. 1990 the king relinquished his absolute power. The Maoists abandoned parliament in 1996 and launched a 'people's war' in the aim of turning the kingdom into a republic. This resulted in over 13,000 deaths over a ten-year period.

In June 2001 the king and queen, along with six other members of the royal family, were shot dead by their son and heir to the throne, Crown Prince Dipendra, allegedly following a dispute over his choice of bride. Prince Dipendra then shot himself. The former monarch's younger brother, Gyanendra, was crowned king. In Nov. 2001 King Gyanendra declared a state of emergency and ordered troops to contain a fresh outbreak of Maoist violence. The government lifted the state of emergency in Aug. 2002. In Jan. 2003 the government and Maoist rebels reached a ceasefire agreement, seen as a first step towards bringing to an end the rebels' seven-year insurgency. In Feb. 2005 King Gyanendra dismissed his government and once more declared a state of emergency, taking control of the country and suspending democracy for three years. He lifted the state of emergency on 29 April 2005. In April 2006 he agreed to a return to parliamentary democracy after more than two weeks of unrest. On 21 Nov. 2006 a peace agreement was signed between the government and the country's Maoist rebels, bringing a formal end to the decade-long insurgency. In Dec. 2007 an agreement was made to abolish the monarchy and establish Nepal as a republic.

On 28 May 2008 the newly elected Constituent Assembly officially inaugurated the Federal Democratic Republic of Nepal, with Ram Baran Yadav as president, and began the process of creating a new constitution that was adopted in Sept. 2015. In April 2015 central Nepal was hit by an earthquake and several aftershocks that killed over 8,500 people and caused extensive damage.

Territory and Population

Nepal is bounded in the north by China (Tibet) and the east, south and west by India. Area 147,181 sq. km; 2011 census population, 26,494,504 (13,645,463 females); density 180·0 per sq. km. In 2011, 19·2% of the population were urban.

The UN gives a projected population for 2020 of 30·26m.

The country is divided into five developmental regions and 75 administrative districts. Area, population and administrative centres are:

Region	Sq. km	Population (2011)	Administrative centre
Central Region	27,410	9,656,985	Kathmandu
East Region	28,456	5,811,555	Dhankuta
West Region	29,398	4,926,765	Pokhara
Mid-West Region	42,378	3,546,682	Surkhet
Far West Region	19,539	2,552,517	Dipayal

Capital, Kathmandu; population (2011) 1,003,285. Other towns include (2011 census population): Pokhara, 264,991; Lalitpur, 226,728; Biratnagar, 204,949; Bharatpur, 147,777.

The indigenous people are of Tibetan origin with a considerable Hindu admixture. The Gurkha clan became predominant in 1559 and has given its name to men from all parts of Nepal. There are 18 ethnic groups. The official language is Nepalese but there are 20 new languages divided into numerous dialects.

Social Statistics

2008 estimates: births, 731,000; deaths, 185,000. Estimated rates per 1,000 population, 2008: births, 25·4; deaths, 6·4. Annual population growth rate, 2000–08, 2·1%. Expectation of life was 67·3 years for males and 69·6 years for females in 2013. Infant mortality, 2010, 41 per 1,000 live births; fertility rate, 2008, 2·9 births per woman.

Climate

Varies from cool summers and severe winters in the north to sub-tropical summers and mild winters in the south. The rainfall is high, with maximum amounts from June to Sept., but conditions are very dry from Nov. to Jan. Kathmandu, Jan. 10°C, July, 25°C. Average annual rainfall, 1,424 mm.

Constitution and Government

Following years of political turbulence an interim constitution was approved in Dec. 2006, effectively removing King Gyanendra as the head of the state.

On 23 Dec. 2007 the interim government declared the establishment of the Federal Democratic Republic of Nepal, with the abolition of the monarchy approved by parliament five days later. This change entered into force on 28 May 2008 at the first meeting of a 601-member Constituent Assembly. The Assembly was charged with drafting a new constitution but missed numerous deadlines. Elections to a new Assembly were then held in Nov. 2013 and, after further delays, a new constitution was adopted on 20 Sept. 2015 with the backing of 507 out of 598 members. It defines Nepal as a secular republic, divided into seven federal provinces (although at the time of promulgation, the provinces had yet to be named and their borders were provisional). It also tightens citizenship rights for any child whose father is not a Nepali citizen, enshrines equal rights for lesbian, gay, bisexual and transgender people, and abolishes the death penalty.

The Constitution created a bicameral federal parliament—in place since March 2018—comprising a *House of Representatives* of 275 members (165 of which are directly elected and the remainder filled by proportional representation) and a *National Assembly* of 59 members (with eight members from each of the seven provinces plus three appointed by the government).

The head of state is the *President*, who is elected for a five-year term by an 'electoral college' of the federal parliament and provincial assemblies.

© Springer Nature Limited 2020
Palgrave Macmillan (ed.), *The Statesman's Yearbook 2020*,
https://doi.org/10.1057/978-1-349-95940-2_138

National Anthem

'Sayaun thunga phoolka hami eutai mala Nepali' ('From hundreds of flowers, we are one garland Nepali'); words by Byakul Maila, tune by Ambar Gurung.

Recent Elections

In elections to the House of Representatives held on 26 Nov. and 7 Dec. 2017 the Communist Party of Nepal (Unified Marxist-Leninist) won 121 of the 275 seats, the Nepali Congress won 63, the Communist Party of Nepal (Maoist-Centre) 53, the Rastriya Janata Party Nepal 17 and the Federal Socialist Forum-Nepal 16. The five remaining seats were shared among other parties and independents. In Feb. 2018 Khadga Prasad Oli was appointed prime minister by President Bidhya Devi Bhandari.

Bidhya Devi Bhandari was elected Nepal's first female president by parliament on 28 Oct. 2015, gaining 327 votes to 214 for Kul Bahadur Gurung. She was re-elected for a second term in March 2018.

Current Government

President: Bidhya Devi Bhandari; b. 1961 (Communist Party of Nepal (Unified Marxist-Leninist); sworn in 29 Oct. 2015).

Vice President: Nanda Kishor Pun.

In Feb. 2019 the government comprised:

Prime Minister: Khadga Prasad Oli; b. 1952 (Communist Party of Nepal (Unified Marxist-Leninist); sworn in 15 Feb. 2018, having previously been prime minister from Oct. 2015 to Aug. 2016).

Deputy Prime Ministers: Ishwor Pokharel (also *Minister of Defence*); Upendra Yadav (also *Minister of Health and Population*).

Minister of Agricultural and Livestock Development: Chakrapani Khanal. *Communication and Information Technology:* Gokul Prasad Baskota. *Culture, Tourism and Civil Aviation:* Rabindra Prasad Adhikari. *Drinking Water:* Beena Magar. *Education, Science and Technology:* Girirajmani Pokharel. *Energy, Water Resources and Irrigation:* Barsaman Pun. *Federal Affairs and General Administration:* Lal Babu Pandit. *Finance:* Yuvaraj Khatiwada. *Foreign Affairs:* Pradeep Kumar Gyawali. *Forest and Environment:* Shakti Bahadur Basnet. *Home Affairs:* Ram Bahadur Thapa. *Industry, Commerce and Supplies:* Matrika Prasad Yadav. *Infrastructure and Transportation:* Raghubir Mahaseth. *Labour, Employment and Social Protection:*Gokarna Bista. *Land Management, Co-operatives and Poverty Alleviation:* Padma Kumari Aryal. *Law, Justice, and Parliamentary Affairs:* Bhanubhakta Dhakal. *Urban Development:* Mohammad Istiyak Rai. *Women, Children and Social Welfare Development:* Tham Maya Thapa. *Youth and Sports:* Jagat Bahadur Sunar.

Office of the Prime Minister and Council of Ministers: http://www.opmcm. gov.np

Current Leaders

Bidhya Devi Bhandari

Position

President

Introduction

Bidhya Bhandari became Nepal's first female president when she won a majority parliamentary vote on 28 Oct. 2015. She replaced Ram Baran Yadav in the largely ceremonial role, and is scheduled to hold office until 2020.

Early Life

Bidhya Devi Bhandari was born on 19 June 1961 in Bhojpur District in eastern Nepal to an influential local political family. She became involved in politics as a college student, joining the youth wing of the then Communist Party of Nepal (Marxist-Leninist) in 1979. She gained national attention at the 1994 general election when she defeated former prime minister and Nepali Congress leader Krishna Prasad Bhattarai in the Kathmandu constituency of her late husband, Madan Bhandari. He was a leading communist killed in an apparent accident less than a year earlier.

Bhandari was re-elected to the House of Representatives in 1999. She was actively involved in the 2006 demonstrations against then King Gyanendra that brought about the abolition of the monarchy and establishment of democracy in Nepal. In 2008 she contested a seat at the first

Constituent Assembly (CA) elections but failed to win election. She was, however, named vice-chair of the (renamed) Communist Party of Nepal (Unified Marxist-Leninist) or CPN-UML at the party convention in Feb. 2009, and retained the position at the next convention in 2014. In Nov. 2013 she became a member of the second CA under a new proportional representation system.

Bhandari was credited with ensuring a one-third quota for women in parliament as decreed in the new constitution. However, she came under fire from critics who questioned her support for legislation barring single mothers and women married to foreigners from passing citizenship to their children.

In 2015 she was nominated by the CPN-UML as its presidential candidate. At the parliamentary vote to appoint the president, she won 327 out of 549 votes with the support of 14 other political parties.

Career in Office

Bhandari claimed that her election was a first step towards assuring that the new constitutional 'guarantees of equality' were realized. Although her role is mainly ceremonial, she promised to use her presidency to continue to champion minority and women's rights.

In Aug. 2016 Bhandari swore in Pushpa Kamal Dahal of the Communist Party of Nepal (Maoist-Centre) as the new prime minister following his election by parliament. Dahal then resigned and was succeeded in June 2017 in a parliamentary vote by Sher Bahadur Deuba of the Nepali Congress before national elections in Nov.–Dec. returned Bhandari's CPN-UML as the largest party in a leftist alliance with the Communist Party of Nepal (Maoist-Centre) under the premiership from Feb. 2018 of Khadga Prasad Oli.

In March 2018 Bhandari was re-elected as president by the federal parliament and provincial assemblies.

Khadga Prasad Oli

Position

Prime Minister

Introduction

Khadga Prasad Oli, charismatic leader of the Communist Party of Nepal (Unified Marxist-Leninist; CPN-UML) and a key figure in the country's troubled transition from an absolute monarchy to a multi-party democracy, was elected prime minister for the first time on 11 Oct. 2015 under a new constitution adopted the previous month. His first term of office, however, ended with his resignation in July 2016 following the tabling of a non-confidence motion in his premiership. He was nevertheless reappointed on 15 Feb. 2018 in the wake of fresh parliamentary elections in Nov.–Dec. 2017.

Early Life

K. P. Oli was born on 22 Feb. 1952 in Terhathum, eastern Nepal. He attended Adarsha secondary school in Mechinagar, Jhapa province, and joined the local branch of the Communist Party of Nepal (CPN) in 1970. Three years later, having been promoted to chief of the Jhapa branch, he was arrested and imprisoned during a crackdown by the Panchayat regime—essentially a one-party state in which the king, Birendra Bir Bikram Shah, controlled all three branches of government as well as the civil service and military. Oli spent the next 14 years behind bars.

On his release in 1987, Oli became a key player in the CPN's pro-democracy campaign. In the multi-party general election of May 1991 that followed the dissolution of the Panchayat system, Oli was elected to parliament. He retained his seat in the 1994 election, in which the CPN-UML won the largest number of parliamentary seats, and was able to form a minority national government led by Man Mohan Adhikari. Oli served as home affairs minister until the minority government collapsed in Sept. 1995, sparking an insurgency by the Maoist faction of the CPN that ground on for a decade, causing over 15,000 deaths and forcing more than 100,000 people from their homes. By May 2002 conditions had deteriorated to the extent that a state of emergency was declared and parliament was dissolved.

Oli served as deputy prime minister and minister of foreign affairs in the interim government that was formed in Nov. 2006. In the subsequent Constituent Assembly election in April 2008, which brought about a parliamentary republic, Oli lost his seat to the representative of the CPN's Maoist faction. Nationally, the Maoist faction won an overwhelming victory, ostensibly ending the protracted civil war. Oli managed the CPN's international department from 2009 and was re-elected to parliament for the CPN-UML in the delayed Constituent Assembly election of Nov. 2013. In Feb. 2014 he became leader of the CPN-UML. Following the adoption of Nepal's controversial new constitution, Oli was elected premier on 11 Oct. 2015, securing 89 more votes than his Nepali Congress rival, Sushil Koirala.

Career in Office

Oli faced several severe challenges, including reconstruction and rehabilitation in the wake of the devastating April 2015 earthquake. Protests and ethnic unrest, linked to the new constitution that divides Nepal into seven federal states, led to violent clashes at the Indian border and costly blockades.

Oli announced his resignation as prime minister in July 2016 after the withdrawal of the Communist Party of Nepal (Maoist-Centre) from the coalition government and the subsequent tabling of a no-confidence motion against his premiership. Puspha Kamal Dahal of the Communist Party of Nepal (Maoist-Centre) succeeded him in early Aug.

Following parliamentary elections at the end of 2017 (in which a leftist alliance of communist parties won a majority of seats) and the subsequent resignation of Prime Minister Sher Bahadur Deuba of the Nepali Congress (who had been in office since June 2017), Oli was again sworn is as premier in Feb. 2018.

In July 2018 Oli signed a memorandum of understanding with China's President Xi Jinping on the construction of a trans-Himalayan rail link between their two countries.

Defence

Defence expenditure in 2013 totalled US$238m. (US$8 per capita), representing 1·2% of GDP.

Army

Strength (2011) 95,800, and there is also a 62,000-strong paramilitary police force (15,000 armed).

Air Force

The Army's air wing has no combat-capable aircraft. Personnel, 2011, 320.

Economy

Agriculture, forestry and fishing contributed 32·7% to GDP in 2012–13; followed by trade, restaurants and hotels, 15·3%; finance and real estate, 11·9%; and services, 9·7%.

Overview

Nepal is one of the poorest countries in the world, with per capita income of US$730 in 2014. Although civil conflict came to an end in 2006, delays in the implementation of a promised new constitution until 2015 have prolonged political instability and undermined long-term economic prospects. Foreign direct investment accounted for only around 0·1% of GDP in 2014, according to World Bank data, while devastating earthquakes in April and May 2015 further restrained economic growth.

Infrastructure is poor. There is limited energy capacity, road coverage is the lowest in southeast Asia, and hydro-electric power potential for domestic consumption and exports to neighbouring India remains largely untapped. In addition to resolving infrastructure deficiencies, other challenges to sustained growth include encouraging public and private investment, improving poor human development indicators, implementing regulatory reform and increasing stability in the financial sector.

Currency

The unit of currency is the *Nepalese rupee* (NPR) of 100 *paisas*. 50 *paisas* = 1 *mohur*. Inflation was 9·9% in 2016 and 4·5% in 2017. Foreign exchange reserves were US$1,478m. in July 2005 and gold reserves totalled 129,000 troy oz. Total money supply in March 2009 was NRs 177,682m.

Budget

Budgetary central government revenue totalled NRs 252,910m. in 2010–11 (NRs 216,250m. in 2009–10) and expenditure NRs 217,323m. (NRs 186,493m. in 2009–10). Main sources of revenue, 2010–11 (NRs 1m.): taxes, 181,255 (including: taxes on goods and services, 96,657; taxes on income, profits and capital gains, 43,121); grants, 49,327. Major items of expenditure by economic type, 2010–11 (NRs 1m.): grants, 90,074; compensation of employees, 59,472; use of goods and services, 27,133.

VAT is 15%.

Performance

Real GDP growth was 3·3% in 2015, 0·6% in 2016 and 7·9% in 2017. Nepal's total GDP in 2017 was US$24·5bn. Nepal is the country fifth most reliant on remittances from abroad, accounting for 28·3% of total GDP in 2017.

Banking and Finance

The Central Bank is the bank of issue (*Governor*, Chiranjibi Nepal). In July 2015 there were 30 commercial banks and 76 development banks.

External debt totalled US$3,702m. in 2010. As a proportion of GNI, external debt fell from 52·0% in 2000 to 23·4% in 2010.

There is a stock exchange in Kathmandu.

Energy and Natural Resources

Environment

Nepal's carbon dioxide emissions from the consumption of energy in 2011 were the equivalent of 0·1 tonnes per capita.

Electricity

Installed capacity was approximately 0·8m. kW in 2010–11, but Nepal has vast untapped hydro-power potential. Production in 2010–11 was 3·31bn. kWh (over 99% hydro-electric), with consumption per capita 147 kWh. Around a fifth of the electricity consumed has to be imported.

Minerals

Production (in tonnes), 2013–14: limestone, 3,371,071; coal, 8,051; talc, 5,703; clay, 18,070 cu. metres.

Agriculture

Agriculture is the mainstay of the economy, providing a livelihood for around 80% of the population and accounting for 35% of GDP. Agricultural land makes up 28·7% of the country's land area. In 2013 there were about 2·1m. ha. of arable land and 212,000 ha. of permanent crops. Crop production (2013, in 1,000 tonnes): rice, 4,505; sugarcane, 2,930; potatoes, 2,690; maize, 1,999; wheat, 1,727; millet, 306.

Livestock (2014): goats, 10·18m.; cattle, 7·24m.; buffaloes, 5·18m.; pigs, 1·19m.; sheep, 789,000; chickens, 48m.

Livestock products (2013 estimates, in 1,000 tonnes): meat, 347; milk, 1,770; eggs, 45.

Forestry

In 2015 the area under forests was 3·64m. ha., or 25% of the total land area. There are eight national parks, covering 1m. ha., five wildlife reserves (170,490 ha.) and two conservation areas (349,000 ha.). Timber production was 13·72m. cu. metres in 2011, mainly for use as fuelwood and charcoal. Expansion of agricultural land has led to widespread deforestation.

Fisheries

The catch in 2015 was an estimated 21,500 tonnes, exclusively from inland waters.

Industry

In 2008–09 manufacturing accounted for 6·8% of GDP. In 2006–07 there were 158 manufacturing establishments with 200 or more staff employing 71,409 people. Production (2007 unless otherwise stated): cement, 1,060,490 tonnes; raw sugar, 140,000 tonnes; soap (2005–06), 55,000 tonnes; jute fibres, 17,000 tonnes; paper and paperboard, 13,000 tonnes; tea, 12,200 tonnes; sawnwood, 630,000 cu. metres; plywood, 30,000 cu. metres; spirits and liqueurs (2007–08), 10·5m. litres; beer (2005–06), 26·0m. litres; cigarettes, 6,081m. units; clay bricks, 12·7m. units; shoes, 10m. pairs.

Labour

The labour force in 2013 was 15,201,000 (12,621,000 in 2003). 85·7% of the population aged 15–64 was economically active in 2013. In the same year 2·7% of the population was unemployed. Nepal had 0·26m. people living in slavery according to the Walk Free Foundation's 2013 *Global Slavery Index*.

International Trade

Imports and Exports

Imports (c.i.f.) in 2015 totalled US$6,612·1m. and exports (f.o.b.) US$660·2m. The main import suppliers in 2015 were: India (63·2%); China (11·9%); UAE (5·2%). The leading export markets in 2015 were: India (65·2%); USA (8·8%); Germany (3·8%).

Principal imports in 2015 were manufactured goods classified chiefly by material (22·8%), machinery and transport equipment (22·4%) and food, animals and beverages (14·3%); main exports in 2015 were manufactured goods classified chiefly by material including hand-knotted woollen carpets (47·2%) and food, animals and beverages (26·7%).

Communications

Roads

In 2006 there were 16,834 km of roads, of which 17% were paved.

Rail

51 km (762 mm gauge) connected Jayanagar on the North Eastern Indian Railway with Janakpur and Bijalpura. It shut down in 2014 but is expected to reopen during 2019 after conversion to 1,676 mm gauge.

Proposals for a 77 km long metro system in Kathmandu were submitted in 2012.

Civil Aviation

There is an international airport (Tribhuvan) at Kathmandu. The national carrier is the state-owned Nepal Airlines (formerly known as Royal Nepal Airlines). In 2010 it flew from Kathmandu to Bangkok, Delhi, Doha, Dubai, Hong Kong and Kuala Lumpur. In 2012 Kathmandu handled 4,444,529 passengers (2,854,933 on international flights) and 13,198 tonnes of freight. In 2012 scheduled airline traffic of Nepali-based carriers flew 6·4m. km; passenger-km totalled 608·1m. in the same year.

Telecommunications

In Dec. 2011 there were 845,542 main (fixed) telephone lines in Nepal and mobile phone subscribers numbered 13,354,000 (49·2 per 100 persons). An estimated 13·3% of the population were internet users in 2013. In March 2012 there were 1·4m. Facebook users.

Social Institutions

Out of 178 countries analysed in the 2017 *Fragile States Index*—a list published jointly by the Fund for Peace and *Foreign Policy* magazine—Nepal was ranked the 33rd most vulnerable to conflict or collapse. The index is based on 12 indicators of state vulnerability across social, political and economic categories.

Justice

The Supreme Court Act established a uniform judicial system, culminating in a supreme court of a Chief Justice and no more than six judges. Special courts to deal with minor offences may be established at the discretion of the government. The King previously had the power to appoint the Chief Justice, but this power passed to the prime minister under the temporary constitution signed in Dec. 2006. A new Civil Code entered force in Aug. 2018.

The death penalty was abolished in 1997. The population in penal institutions in Aug. 2012 was 14,936 (48 per 100,000 of national population). The International Centre for Prison Studies estimated in 2014 that 58·9% of prisoners had yet to receive a trial. In 2015 the World Justice Project *Rule of Law Index*, which provides data on how the rule of law is experienced by the general public across eight categories, ranked Nepal 56th of 102 countries for criminal justice and 87th for civil justice.

Education

The adult literacy rate in 2009 was estimated 59·1% (72·0% among males but only 46·9% among females).

In 2007 there were 4,515,059 pupils and 112,827 teaching staff in primary schools and 1,998,990 pupils in secondary schools with (in 2008) 56,294 teaching staff. There were 320,844 students in tertiary education in 2007 with 9,932 academic staff. The oldest and largest university in Nepal is Tribhuvan University, which was established in 1959.

In 2009 public expenditure on education came to 4·7% of GDP and 19·5% of total government spending.

Health

Over the period 2000–10 Nepal had two physicians per 10,000 population and five nurses and midwives per 10,000. There were 50 hospital beds per 10,000 people in the period 2006–12.

In *Water: At What Cost? The State of the World's Water 2016*, WaterAid reported that 8·4% of the population does not have access to safe water.

Religion

Nepal is a Hindu state. Hinduism was the religion of 80·7% of the people in 2010 according to estimates by the Pew Research Center's Forum on Religion & Public Life, with Buddhists comprising 10·3% and Muslims 4·6%. An estimated 3·7% of the population in 2010 were folk religionists. There is also a small Christian minority.

Culture

World Heritage Sites

Nepal has four sites on the UNESCO World Heritage List: Sagarmatha National Park (inscribed on the list in 1979); Kathmandu Valley (1979 and 2006); Royal Chitwan National Park (1984); and Lumbini, the Birthplace of the Lord Buddha (1997). Several of the heritage sites were severely damaged by the earthquake of April 2015, but have since been reopened to the public.

Press

In 2008 there were 298 daily newspapers, including the official English-language *Rising Nepal*, 25 bi-weeklies, 1,442 weeklies and 273 fortnightlies. Press censorship was relaxed in 1991, but following the imposition of a state of emergency in 2005 the press was subjected to total censorship.

Tourism

In 2012 there were a record 803,000 non-resident tourists (up from 736,000 in 2010 and 527,000 in 2007). In 2011, 32% of tourists came from South Asia, 29% from Europe and 27% from East Asia and the Pacific. Tourist receipts amounted to US$379m. in 2012.

Festivals

Hindu, Buddhist and traditional festivals crowd the Nepali lunar calendar. Dasain (Sept./Oct.) is the longest and most widely observed festival in Nepal. The 15 days of celebration include Dashami, when family elders are honoured. Tihar (Oct./Nov.) celebrates the Hindu goddess Laxmi. During the first three days crows, dogs and cows are worshipped, followed by the spirit, or self. It concludes with Bhai Tika ('Brother's Day'). Buddha Jayanti (May/June) remembers the birth, enlightenment and death of the Buddha. Sherpas gather at Tengboche Monastery near Mount Everest in May to observe Mani Rimdu with meditation, mask dances and Buddhist ceremonies.

Diplomatic Representatives

Of Nepal in the United Kingdom (12A Kensington Palace Gdns, London, W8 4QU)
    Ambassador: Durga Bahadur Subedi.

Of the United Kingdom in Nepal (Lainchaur, Kathmandu, POB 106)
    Ambassador: Richard Morris.

Of Nepal in the USA (2131 Leroy Pl., NW, Washington, D.C., 20008)
    Ambassador: Arjun Kumar Karki.

Of the USA in Nepal (Maharajgunj, Chakrapath, Kathmandu)
    Ambassador: Randy Berry.

Of Nepal to the United Nations
    Ambassador: Vacant.
    Chargé d'Affaires a.i.: Nirmal Raj Kafle.

Of Nepal to the European Union
    Ambassador: Lok Bahadur Thapa.

Further Reading

Central Bureau of Statistics. *Nepal in Figures.—Statistical Pocket Book.—Statistical Yearbook.*

Hutt, Michael, (ed.) *Himalayan 'People's War': Nepal's Maoist Rebellion.* 2004

Jha, Prashant, *Battles of the New Republic: A Contemporary History of Nepal.* 2014

Lawoti, Mahendra, *Towards a Democratic Nepal: Inclusive Political Institutions for a Multicultural Society.* 2005

Sanwal, D. B., *Social and Political History of Nepal.* 1993

Thapa, Deepak, *A Kingdom Under Siege: Nepal's Maoist Insurgency, 1996 to 2004.* 2005

Whelpton, John, *A History of Nepal.* 2005

National Statistical Office: Central Bureau of Statistics, National Planning Commission Secretariat, Kathmandu.

Website: http://www.cbs.gov.np

Netherlands

Koninkrijk der Nederlanden (Kingdom of the Netherlands)

Capital: Amsterdam
Seat of government: The Hague
Population projection, 2020: 17·18m.
GNI per capita, 2017: (PPP$) 47,900
HDI/world rank, 2017: 0·931/10
Internet domain extension: .nl

Key Historical Events

Flint tools found in the Maastricht area have been estimated to be 250,000 years old. The first definable culture (*c.* 3000 BC) was the Late Stone Age 'Funnel-neck Beaker' culture, named after the objects made by a people known for their monolithic burial monuments. The environment of the 'Low Countries' affected the behaviour of its earliest inhabitants, as demonstrated by the *terpen*—islands of earth and clay—built by the autochthonous Frisians (Frisii) *c.* 500 BC as protection from the sea.

The Romans encountered Celtic tribes to the west and south of the Rhine and Germanic tribes, such as the Frisii, to the north and east. In the 1st century BC Julius Caesar attested to the resistance of the Celtic Eburones and Aduatuci. Roman power beyond the Rhine was limited to isolated forts and client kingdoms.

In the 3rd century AD the stagnant Roman borders began to crumble as military posts were abandoned. Among the most prominent of the encroaching Germanic tribes were the Franks, who settled at first in Toxandria (modern Brabant). Like many 'barbarian' tribes, the Franks entered into agreements with Rome, settling and guarding the border region and assimilating Roman culture. The Frisians became important traders, holding strategic territory between the German (North) Sea and the Meuse and Rhine rivers. With the collapse of Roman government in Gaul and the Rhine in the 5th century, the Franks extended their power, centred on Austrasia (the central Rhine region). The spread of Christianity in the 7th century, first from the bishoprics of Arras, Tournai and Cambrai, assisted Frankish expansion into the northern Low Countries, where the missionary bishopric of Utrecht was established.

Viking raids on the North Sea coast devastated the flourishing Frisian economy. The Frisian trading centre of Dorestad was destroyed four times between 834–37 by raiders seeking Carolingian silver. Frisia came under Frankish domination during the reign of Pippin the Short, the founder of the Carolingian Empire.

The High Middle Ages saw the development of independent and semi-autonomous principalities, both secular and ecclesiastical. Great landlords established the large counties (Flanders, Hainault, Namur and Holland and Zeeland) and duchies (Brabant, Limburg and Guelders), increasing their authority and size through dynastic alliances and inheritance. The majority fell broadly under the authority of the German king, heirs to the Eastern Frankish realm, though the feudal relationship allowed the growth of a tradition of independence that became a defining characteristic of Dutch politics. The growth of population and its pressure on the land increased the need for land reclamation. Dykes were built from Friesland to Flanders to drain the bogs and marshes for pasturage and, later, agrarian use. The development of urban centres outside the feudal structure was encouraged by the strength of trade and the merchant classes.

The Burgundian era in the Low Countries was born of a series of dynastic matches, most importantly that of Duke Philip II (the Bold) of Burgundy and Margaret, Countess of Flanders and Artois in 1369. Their son, Philip III (the Good), brought most of the northern Low Countries under one lord by inheriting Brabant and Hainault-Holland in the 1430s as well as Luxembourg in 1443. Although the dukes attempted to rule through new centralized bodies, the Burgundian Low Countries were held in a personal union and did not constitute a state. The duke appointed *stadhouders* and governors to represent him in each of his territories. The summoning of the Estates in 1464 in Brugge (Bruges) represented the first parliamentary assembly in the Low Countries and the importance of the *Nederlands* in the Burgundian realm.

Burgundian Rule

The reign of Charles the Bold, or Rash (1467–77), saw the brief land connection of the realm (by the acquisition of Lorraine) and the first explicit attempt to create a unitary kingdom—an echo of the Middle Frankish Kingdom, Lotharingia. Charles failed in his bid to make himself regent of this kingdom in 1473 and his death at the Battle of Nancy left his domains to his daughter, Mary. The duchess was soon stripped of the Duchy of Burgundy by the French king and was forced to concede privileges to the provinces. Her marriage to Maximilian of Habsburg, the future Holy Roman Emperor, brought the Low Countries into personal union with Austria and, later, Spain. Mary's son, Philip the Handsome, inherited the Spanish throne through his wife, Joanna the Mad, forging a massive and disparate empire of kingdoms, principalities and lordships. Philip's son, Charles V, though born in Ghent, spent little time in the Low Countries after succeeding to the Spanish throne. They were administered by governors-general, normally taken from the ruler's family. Centralization, though consistently opposed, continued to be pressed on the inhabitants of the Low Countries. The 17 provinces were brought together formally in 1548 as the 'Burgundian *Kreis*' and the sovereign succession regulated by Pragmatic Sanction the following year. Brussels became the centre of government, being the location of the court and most organs of government.

Philip II (of Spain) imposed a new ecclesiastical hierarchy, sanctioned by papal bull in 1559, in an attempt to use the church as a centralizing force. The traditional resistance of the towns and provinces was given added fervour by the religious controversies attributable to the Reformation. Erasmus, a leading Dutch humanist, openly attacked the abuses and corruptions of the Church but rejected the theology of the reformers such as Martin Luther. However, the works of the radical Jean Calvin arrived in Antwerp in 1545, spreading throughout the region rapidly after their translation in 1560. Calvinism appealed to the intellectual middle classes, as well as the artisans, whose work ethic it extolled. The government focused its repressive efforts on the Anabaptists, whose refusal to swear allegiance to the prince was an affront to temporal and spiritual authority. The iconoclastic purges of 1566 provoked Philip to send the duke of Alba to restore his authority, thereby sparking full-scale revolt and the Eighty Years War (1568–1648).

The causes of the Dutch Revolt were numerous; religious tensions, resentment towards 'Spanish' authority, the heavy burden of taxes and absolutist government and the perceived desecration of traditional privileges were combined with years of hardship caused by climatic conditions and wars with France. However, in the earlier years of the revolt, the 'legitimate' *casus belli* claimed by the Dutch was the influence of 'evil advisers' around the prince—few openly rejected Philip's sovereignty. The *Geuzen*, an army of beggars, pillaging and pirating in the name of William of Orange, took the port of Brielle in 1572. This began the expulsion of Spanish authority from the northern provinces, a process completed by 1574.

The conversion of William (the Silent) to Calvinism in 1572, in response to his selection as stadtholder of Holland and Zeeland, was a political move to gain support for a united Netherlands of Catholics and Protestants. The 1576 Pacification of Ghent brought together predominantly Catholic and Protestant provinces in the face of bloody repression meted out by Alba's Council of Troubles (Council of Blood) and the notorious 'Spanish Fury' massacre in Antwerp. The mainly Catholic southern provinces were largely regained for Philip by the brilliant Alessandro Farnese, duke of Parma in 1578, forcing a 'closer union'—the Union of Utrecht—in the north in 1579, committed to resisting the Spanish. This marked the birth of the United Provinces of the Netherlands, or the 'Dutch Republic', with power concentrated in the hands of the stadtholders, nominally representing the hereditary prince. Philip's refusal to compromise led to his 'forfeiture of sovereignty' in the States-General Act of Abjuration in 1581, on the grounds of persistent tyranny.

The constitutional position of the Republic was unclear. The House of Orange was recognized as the traditional stadtholders of each province, though the lordship of the territories was tendered to both France and England in the 1580s. Maurice of Nassau, the son of William of Orange, was named stadtholder of Holland and Zeeland in 1587. Maurice's victories over Farnese came to be called the 'closing of the garden', giving the United Provinces the approximate borders it has maintained to the modern day. With recognition from England and France, the government negotiated the Twelve Year Truce in 1609 with Spain, which recognized the independence of the United Provinces.

The Calvinist church divided between the followers of two prominent clerics, Jacobus Arminius (the Remonstrants) and Franciscus Gomarus (the Contra-Remonstrants). The Arminians, championed by the elite of Holland and the towns, objected to the repressive orthodoxy of the Gomarists and demanded an inclusive reformed church to protect trade and foreign relations. The execution of the Remonstrant Johan van Oldenbarnvelt, the Advocate of Holland, signified the triumph of Maurice's Contra-Remonstrants and made permanent peace with Spain impossible. After initial Spanish success at Breda in 1621, Maurice's successor, Frederick Henry, turned the tide, taking Maastricht in the far south. Ending the persecution of the Remonstrants, Frederick Henry augmented the authority of his princely house, even earning an honorific royal title from the French King. Lasting peace with Spain was finally won at the 1648 Treaty of Münster, which formally recognized the Dutch Republic.

Independence and the Golden Age

The 17th century has traditionally been called the Golden Age of the Dutch. From the Twelve Year Truce, the Dutch economy expanded massively, principally through trade in the Baltic and with France, Iberia and the colonies of the West and East Indies. The United East Indies Company, chartered in 1602, held quasi-sovereign authority over its colonies in Sri Lanka, India and Indonesia. Dutch banking financed the northern European markets, chiefly through foreign government bonds. The increase of wealth stimulated the arts. Prosperous life in Dutch towns was painted by Jan Vermeer and Amsterdam's burghers by Rembrandt. Although Calvinism had been officially adopted, Catholics were left unmolested but public worship was prohibited.

After the death of Frederick Henry's bellicose son, William II, in 1650, the republic experienced its first 'stadtholderless' period when the prosperous province of Holland dominated the Netherlands. Relations with Republican England deteriorated because of the execution of Charles I, who was closely related to the House of Orange. More importantly, competition for trade and shipping between the two great maritime powers caused skirmishes in America and Europe and a series of Anglo-Dutch Wars, conducted at sea. The destruction of the English fleet at Chatham in 1667 destroyed relations with Charles II, who had supported Orangist interests in the Netherlands.

The House of Orange reassumed the leadership of the Netherlands when William III took the stadtholdership of Holland in 1672 and defeated the French and the English in naval encounters. The Dutch supported William in his invasion of England—the Glorious Revolution—in 1688, claiming the throne with his wife, Mary Stuart. His death without issue in 1702 heralded the second stadtholderless period, when the councillor pensionaries of Holland asserted the province's leadership. However, the oligarchic nature of government attracted little support, especially during Dutch humiliations at the hands of the French in the War of the Austrian Succession (1740–48). William IV of Orange was elected to all provinces in 1747, the House of Orange being seen as the natural leaders of the Dutch people.

Both William IV and William V resisted calls for a more relaxed rule. The Patriot Movement took advantage of the Dutch defeat in the Fourth Anglo-Dutch War of the 1780s to depose William V. However, Prussia's intervention restored the stadtholder and many Patriots fled to France, then on the brink of revolution.

Revolutionary France's invasion of Belgium (the Spanish Netherlands) in 1794 was soon extended to the United Provinces. William V fled to England and the Patriots, supported by the French, assumed control of government. The new 'Batavian Republic', styled after the supposedly original inhabitants, was in reality a protectorate of France. This truly republican period enabled political modernization, much of which has lasted to the modern day. An elected National Assembly was instituted (though the franchise was

retained by property owners only), with new electoral constituencies to replace the old provinces. Religious toleration was adopted, with all denominations awarded equal treatment. However, the economy declined, partly because of the seizure of the Dutch colonies in the name of William V by Great Britain, which had declared war on France.

Napoleon

The republic was ended in 1806 when Napoleon incorporated the Netherlands into his empire. He installed his brother, Louis, as king of Holland. Louis adopted the cause of his new subjects, frequently defying his brother's orders in favour of Dutch interests. Napoleon ended his brother's reign in 1810 and brought his kingdom under French rule. Gijsbert Karel van Hogendorp, who drew up the new constitution after the French withdrawal in 1813, led the opposition to France. The new constitution provided for a constitutional monarchy, with William V's son proclaimed king (William I), as demanded by the Congress of Vienna. The northern provinces were united with Belgium and Luxembourg under the Kingdom of the Netherlands.

William I saw the revival of the economy as the first priority. Using his personal resources as well as the treasury, he invested heavily in the re-establishment of Dutch shipping, especially to the restored colonies. Domestically, William was not so successful. In 1830 Belgium proclaimed its independence, rejecting a common identity with the predominantly Protestant north—the declaration of Dutch as the sole official language had alienated the French-speaking Walloons in Brussels. Though defeated by the Dutch army, the Belgians gained their independence in 1839 thanks to French and British intervention in 1832.

In response to the European revolutions of 1848, the king granted a liberal constitution. Support for the king was bolstered by the patriotic reaction in the northern provinces to the Belgian secession. The reintroduction of the Catholic hierarchy in 1853 won over a community which made up over a third of the population.

Dutch imperialism was consolidated in the second half of the 19th century. Having lost numerous colonies in the Americas, southern Africa and India, attention focused on the Indonesian archipelago. War with Aceh in northern Sumatra, famous for its piracy, was long and bloody but secured the archipelago for the Netherlands. The division of New Guinea was settled with Germany and Great Britain in 1875. Personal union with Luxembourg came to an end on the accession of Wilhelmina in 1890, barred by Salic Law from inheriting the Grand Duchy.

European War

In 1917 universal male suffrage was granted in return for the secular parties' acceptance of funding for religious schools, thus concluding the 30-year School Conflict. Female suffrage followed in 1922. Wilhelmina, though less active in government than her father, William III, strongly advocated neutrality in the conflicts of the early 20th century, keeping the Netherlands out of the First World War. The German Kaiser, Wilhelm II, was granted asylum in the Netherlands.

The inter-war years were a period of social and political continuity. The *zuilen* system expanded, cementing what has been described as a bourgeois consensus, though worldwide depression hit the Netherlands hard in the 1930s. In 1932 the IJsselmeer dam was completed, transforming the Zuider Zee, an inlet of the North Sea, into a freshwater lake, the IJsselmeer.

The neutrality of the Netherlands was not respected by Germany in the Second World War, despite assurances from Hitler after the invasion of Poland. Control of the Netherlands and Belgium was seen as essential to protect the industrial centres of the Ruhr and to gain broader access to the North Sea. The Dutch armed forces were overwhelmed within a week in May 1940. The queen and government went into exile in London. Persecution of the Jews began in Oct. 1941. The first transports left in July 1942, mostly to Auschwitz. 107,000 Dutch Jews died. Dutch resistance took the form of civilian sabotage and the hiding of Jews and *onkerduikers* ('underdivers')—underground military operatives.

The Netherlands saw some of the bitterest fighting near the close of the war when Allied troops made airborne incursions—Arnhem Bridge in Sept. 1944—to speed victory over Germany. By the end of the war the Dutch were on the brink of famine. The destruction of the economy and much of the infrastructure caused large-scale emigration. In 1947 the Netherlands accepted US$1bn. for reconstruction from the Marshall Plan and entered the Benelux Economic Union with Belgium and Luxembourg (fully established in 1958). The Netherlands abandoned its neutrality when it joined NATO in 1949, the year it granted Indonesia independence. Further changes to Dutch overseas possessions took place in 1954 under the *Statute for the Kingdom*, which gave the territories in the West Indies equal status. Dutch New Guinea (Irian Jaya) was ceded to Indonesia in 1963 and Suriname was given its independence in 1974.

Dutch politics saw several important changes in the post-war years, such as the introduction of proportional representation in elections. From the end of the war until 1958, a coalition of Catholic and labour parties held power, taking the Netherlands into the Korean War in 1950. The Netherlands was a founder member of the European Coal and Steel Community (ECSC) in 1951, which later merged with the European Economic Community (EEC).

The economy grew rapidly in the late 1950s when the welfare state was greatly expanded. Social unrest in the 1960s was led by youth and labour groups. Social changes in the '70s included the demise of the traditional *zuilen* and the creation of new political parties across religious divides; most notable of these was the Christian Democratic Appeal (CDA). Newspapers, the voice of the *zuilen*, disassociated themselves from religious denominations, becoming independent commercial enterprises. The decriminalization of personal cannabis use in the 1970s indicated a policy towards drug use and abuse that focused on rehabilitation (for hard drug users) as opposed to punishment. Vocal youth action was seen most clearly in the confrontations between the police and the *krakers*—squatters demanding affordable housing.

Opposition to nuclear weapons grew in the 1980s, sparked by the support given by Prime Minister Andreas van Agt to placing US cruise missiles on Dutch soil. In 1986 the pressures of the Netherlands' population density led to creation of the 12th province, Flevoland, from four polders reclaimed from the IJsselmeer.

The Netherlands joined the coalition forces in the 1991 Gulf War, providing two naval frigates. Serious flooding in Gelderland and the threat of worse to come led to the evacuation of 240,000 people from the province in 1995.

The Netherlands became the first country to legalize homosexual marriage and adoption, in 2001, and euthanasia, in 2002. In April 2002, Prime Minister Wim Kok's government resigned in the wake of a report that criticized Dutch inaction in preventing the massacre at Srebrenica in 1995. During the subsequent election campaign, the right-wing politician Pim Fortuyn was assassinated by an animal rights activist who opposed Fortuyn's anti-immigration policies.

The coalition government led by Jan Peter Balkenende, formed in July, collapsed in Oct., necessitating fresh elections. Balkenende formed a new government in May 2003. In 2005 the electorate voted in a referendum against adopting a proposed EU constitution. In June 2006 Balkenende's coalition again collapsed, although he remained head of a minority government until elections in Nov. In Feb. 2007, after months of negotiations, he was sworn in for a new tenure as premier, leading a centrist coalition of three parties. It collapsed in Feb. 2010 amid tensions over troop deployment in Afghanistan. The People's Party for Freedom and Democracy (VVD) emerged from elections in June 2010 with the most seats and formed a coalition, with Mark Rutte as prime minister, with the support of the far-right Freedom Party. In April 2012 Rutte resigned after the Freedom Party refused to back his austerity measures. However, after parliamentary elections in Sept. that year he headed a new coalition government of the VVD and the Labour Party and similarly formed another coalition in Oct. 2017 following further inconclusive elections the previous March.

In July 2014, 193 Dutch nationals were killed when a Malaysian Airlines jet travelling from Amsterdam was shot down over disputed territory in eastern Ukraine.

Territory and Population

The Netherlands is bounded in the north and west by the North Sea, south by Belgium and east by Germany. The area is 41,540 sq. km, of which 33,718 sq. km is land. Projects of sea-flood control and land reclamation (polders) by the construction of dams and drainage schemes have continued since 1920. More than a quarter of the country is below sea level.

The population was 13,060,115 at the last traditional census in 1971 and 17,181,084 on 1 Jan. 2018. Population growth in 2017, 0·6%.

The UN gives a projected population for 2020 of 17·18m.

Ongoing 'rolling' censuses have replaced the former decennial counts.

Area in 2012 and population, density and chief towns of the 12 provinces on 1 Jan. 2018:

	Land area 2012 (in sq. km)	Population 2018	Density 2018 per sq. km land area	Provincial capital
Groningen	2,325	582,944	251	Groningen
Friesland	3,340	647,268	194	Leeuwarden
Drenthe	2,639	492,100	186	Assen
Overijssel	3,324	1,151,501	346	Zwolle
Flevoland	1,415	411,670	291	Lelystad
Gelderland	4,970	2,060,103	415	Arnhem
Utrecht	1,383	1,295,484	937	Utrecht
Noord-Holland	2,665	2,831,182	1,062	Haarlem
Zuid-Holland	2,808	3,681,044	1,311	The Hague
Zeeland	1,784	382,304	214	Middelburg
Noord-Brabant	4,914	2,528,286	514	's-Hertogenbosch
Limburg	2,150	1,117,198	520	Maastricht
Total	33,718[1]	17,181,084	510	

[1]Totals do not add up because of rounding.

In 2011, 83·3% of the population lived in urban areas.

Population of municipalities with over 50,000 inhabitants on 1 Jan. 2018:

Alkmaar	108,470
Almelo	72,629
Almere	203,990
Alphen a/d Rijn	109,682
Amersfoort	155,226
Amstelveen	89,870
Amsterdam	854,047
Apeldoorn	161,156
Arnhem	157,223
Assen	67,708
Barneveld	57,339
Bergen op Zoom	66,354
Breda	183,448
Capelle a/d Ijssel	66,854
De Fryske Marren	51,742
Delft	102,253
Deventer	99,653
Doetinchem	57,382
Dordrecht	118,426
Ede	114,682
Eindhoven	229,126
Emmen	107,192
Enschede	158,261
Gooise Meren	57,337
Gouda	72,700
Groningen	202,810
Haarlem	159,709
Haarlemmermeer	147,282
The Hague (Den Haag)	532,561
Hardenberg	60,539
Heerenveen	50,192
Heerhugowaard	55,850
Heerlen	86,762
Den Helder	55,760

(*continued*)

Helmond	90,903
Hengelo	80,593
's-Hertogenbosch	153,434
Hilversum	89,521
Hoogeveen	55,677
Hoorn	72,806
Kampen	53,259
Katwijk	64,956
Krimpenerwaard	55,644
Lansingerland	61,155
Leeuwarden	122,415
Leiden	124,306
Leidschendam-Voorburg	74,947
Lelystad	77,389
Maastricht	122,723
Meierijstad	80,148
Midden-Groningen	60,953
Nieuwegein	62,426
Nijmegen	175,948
Nissewaard	84,593
Oosterhout	55,147
Oss	90,951
Pijnacker-Nootdorp	53,634
Purmerend	79,983
Rijkswijk	52,208
Roermond	57,761
Roosendaal	77,000
Rotterdam	638,712
Schiedam	77,907
Sittard-Geleen	92,956
Smallingerland	55,889
Stichtse Vecht	64,513
Súdwest Fryslân	89,594
Terneuzen	54,440
Tilburg	215,521
Utrecht	347,483
Veenendaal	64,918
Velsen	67,831
Venlo	101,192
Vlaardingen	72,050
Westland	107,492
Woerden	51,758
Zaanstad	154,865
Zeist	63,322
Zoetermeer	124,695
Zwolle	126,116

Urban agglomerations as at 1 Jan. 2015: Amsterdam, 1,122,748; Rotterdam, 1,020,076; The Hague, 662,787; Utrecht, 493,444; Eindhoven, 339,472; Leiden, 260,195; Dordrecht, 238,148; Tilburg, 234,662; Groningen, 219,260; Haarlem, 205,381; Heerlen, 200,136; Amersfoort, 181,543; Breda, 180,937; Nijmegen, 170,681; 's-Hertogenbosch, 170,023; Enschede, 158,553; Apeldoorn, 158,099; Arnhem, 153,802; Sittard-Geleen, 135,072; Zwolle, 123,861; Maastricht, 122,397; Leeuwarden, 107,691.

Dutch is the official language. Frisian, spoken as a first language by 2·2% of the population, is also recognized as an official language in the northern province of Friesland.

Social Statistics

Vital statistics for calendar years:

	Live births				
	Total	Outside marriage	Marriages	Divorces	Deaths
2007	181,336	71,559	72,485	31,983	133,022
2008	184,634	76,137	75,438	32,236	135,136
2009	184,915	80,036	73,477	30,779	134,235
2010	184,397	75,752	75,399	33,723	136,058
2011	180,060	75,196	71,572	33,755	135,741
2012	175,959	75,030	70,315	34,317	140,813

2012 rates per 1,000 population: birth, 10·8; death, 8·4. Annual population growth rate, 2007–12, 0·5%. In 2009 the suicide rate per 100,000 population was 9·3 (men, 13·1; women, 5·5). In 2012 the average age for marrying was 37·0 years for males and 33·8 for females. Expectation of life, 2012, was 79·2 years for males and 82·9 for females. Infant mortality, 2012, 3·7 per 1,000 live births; fertility rate, 2012, 1·8 births per woman. Percentage of population by age in 2010: 0–14 years, 17·7%; 15–64, 67·0%; 65 and over, 15·3%. The Netherlands received 11,590 asylum applications in 2011, down from 13,333 in 2010. In 2001 the Netherlands became the first country to legalize same-sex marriage.

Climate

A cool temperate maritime climate, marked by mild winters and cool summers, but with occasional continental influences. Coastal temperatures vary from 37°F (3°C) in winter to 61°F (16°C) in summer, but inland the winters are slightly colder and the summers slightly warmer. Rainfall is least in the months Feb. to May, but inland there is a well-defined summer maximum in July and Aug.

The Hague, Jan. 37°F (2·7°C), July 61°F (16·3°C). Annual rainfall 32·8" (820 mm). Amsterdam, Jan. 36°F (2·3°C), July 62°F (16·5°C). Annual rainfall 34" (850 mm). Rotterdam, Jan. 36·5°F (2·6°C), July 62°F (16·6°C). Annual rainfall 32" (800 mm).

Constitution and Government

According to the Constitution (promulgated 1815; last revision, 2005), the Kingdom consists of the Netherlands and its overseas countries and territories. Their relations are regulated by the 'Statute' for the Kingdom, which came into force on 29 Dec. 1954 and was revised on 10 Oct. 2010 in recognition of the dissolution of the Netherlands Antilles, by which Curaçao and Sint Maarten became (along with Aruba) independent countries within the Kingdom and Bonaire, Saba and Sint Eustatius became autonomous special municipalities. Each part enjoys full autonomy; they are united, on a footing of equality, for mutual assistance and the protection of their common interests.

The Netherlands is a constitutional and hereditary monarchy. The royal succession is in the direct female or male line in order of birth. The reigning King is **Willem-Alexander**, born 27 April 1967, son of Princess Beatrix Wilhelmina Armgard and Claus von Amsberg; married to Máxima Zorreguieta on 2 Feb. 2002 (born 17 May 1971); succeeded to the crown on 30 April 2013, on the abdication of his mother. *Offspring:* Catharina-Amalia, born 7 Dec. 2003 (heiress apparent); Alexia, born 26 June 2005; Ariane, born 10 April 2007.

Constitutional allowances are paid to King Willem-Alexander, Queen Máxima and Princess Beatrix. The estimated amounts for 2015 were: King Willem-Alexander, €5,318,000; Queen Máxima, €911,000; Princess Beatrix, €1,430,000.

Other Members of the Royal House

Princess Beatrix, born 31 Jan. 1938; *Prince Constantijn* (the King's brother), born 11 Oct. 1969, married to Laurentien Brinkhorst (*Princess Laurentien*) on 19 May 2001 (*offspring*: Eloise, born 8 June 2002; Claus-Casimir, born 21 March 2004; Leonore, born 3 June 2006); *Princess Margriet Francisca* (sister of Princess Beatrix), born in Ottawa, Canada, 19 Jan. 1943, married to *Pieter van Vollenhoven* on 10 Jan. 1967 (*sons*: Prince Maurits, born 17 April 1968; Prince Bernhard, born 25 Dec. 1969; Prince Pieter-Christiaan, born 22 March 1972; Prince Floris, born 10 April 1975). Names in italics represent members of the Royal House.

The central executive power of the State rests with the Crown, while the central legislative power is vested in the Crown and Parliament (the *States-General*), consisting of two Chambers. The upper *First Chamber* is composed of 75 members, elected by the members of the Provincial States. The 150-member *Second Chamber* is directly elected by proportional representation for four-year terms. Members of the States-General must be Netherlands subjects of 18 years of age or over. The Hague is the seat of the Court, government and Parliament; Amsterdam is the capital.

The *Council of State*, appointed by the Crown, is composed of a vice-president and not more than 28 members. The monarch is president, but the day-to-day running of the Council is in the hands of the vice-president. The Council has to be consulted on all legislative matters. The Sovereign has the power to dissolve either Chamber, subject to the condition that new elections take place within 40 days, and the new Chamber be convoked within three months. Both the government and the Second Chamber may propose bills; the First Chamber can only approve or reject them without inserting amendments. The meetings of both Chambers are public, although each of them may by a majority vote decide on a secret session. A Minister or Secretary of State cannot be a member of Parliament at the same time.

The Constitution can be revised only by a bill declaring that there is reason for introducing such revision and containing the proposed alterations. The passing of this bill is followed by a dissolution of both Chambers and a second confirmation by the new States-General by two-thirds of the votes. Unless it is expressly stated, all laws concern only the realm in Europe, and not the overseas parts of the kingdom.

National Anthem

'Wilhelmus van Nassaue' ('William of Nassau'); words by Philip Marnix van St Aldegonde, tune anonymous.

Government Chronology

Prime Ministers since 1940. (ARP = Anti-Revolutionary Party; CDA = Christian Democratic Appeal; KVP = Catholic People's Party; PvdA = Labour Party; VDB = Liberal Democratic League; VVD = People's Party for Freedom and Democracy)

1940–45	ARP	Pieter Sjoerds Gerbrandy
1945–46	VDB/PvdA	Willem Schermerhorn
1946–48	KVP	Louis Jozef Maria Beel
1948–58	PvdA	Willem Drees
1958–59	KVP	Louis Jozef Maria Beel
1959–63	KVP	Jan Eduard de Quay
1963–65	KVP	Victor Gérard Marie Marijnen
1965–66	KVP	Joseph Maria Laurens Theo (Jo) Cals
1966–67	ARP	Jelle Zijlstra
1967–71	KVP	Petrus Josephus Sietse (Piet) de Jong
1971–73	ARP	Barend Willem Biesheuvel
1973–77	PvdA	Johannes Marten (Joop) den Uyl
1977–82	CDA	Andreas Maria (Andries) van Agt
1982–94	CDA	Rudolphus Frans Marie (Ruud) Lubber
1994–2002	PvdA	Willem (Wim) Kok
2002–10	CDA	Jan Peter Balkenende
2010–	VVD	Mark Rutte

Recent Elections

Party affiliation in the First Chamber as elected on 26 May 2015: People's Party for Freedom and Democracy (VVD), 13 seats; Christian Democratic Appeal (CDA), 12; Democrats '66 (D66), 10; Party for Freedom (PVV), 9; Socialist Party (SP), 9; Labour Party (PvdA), 8; Green Left (GL), 4; Christian Union (CU), 3; Party for the Animals (PvdD), 2; Reformed Political Party (SGP), 2; 50Plus (50+), 2; Independent Group in the Senate, 1.

Elections to the Second Chamber were held on 15 March 2017. The VVD won 21·3% of the vote (33 of 150 seats), PVV 13·1% (20), CDA 12·4% (19), D66 12·2% (19), GL 9·1% (14), SP 9·1% (14), PvdA 5·7% (9), CU 3·4% (5), PvdD 3·2% (5), 50+ 3·1% (4), SGP 2·1% (3), Denk 2·1% (3) and Forum for Democracy (FvD) 1·8% (2). Turnout was 81·9%.

European Parliament

The Netherlands has 26 representatives. At the May 2014 elections turnout was 37·3% (36·8% in 2009). The CDA won 5 seats with 15·0% of votes cast (political affiliation in European Parliament: European People's Party); D66, 4 with 15·4% (Alliance of Liberals and Democrats for Europe); PVV, 4 with 13·3% (non-attached); VVD, 3 with 12·0% (Alliance of Liberals and Democrats for Europe); PvdA, 3 with 9·4% (Progressive Alliance of Socialists and Democrats); SP, 2 with 9·6% (European United Left/Nordic Green Left); GL, 2 with 6·9% (Greens/European Free Alliance); CU–SGP, 2 with 6·8% (European Conservatives and Reformists); PvdD, 1 with 4·2% (European United Left/Nordic Green Left).

Current Government

Following elections in March 2017 a coalition government of VVD, CDA, D66 and Christian Union was sworn in on 20 Oct. 2017. In Feb. 2019 it comprised:

Prime Minister and Minister of General Affairs: Mark Rutte; b. 1967 (VVD).

Deputy Prime Ministers: Carola Schouten (also *Minister of Agriculture, Nature and Food Quality*, Christian Union); Hugo de Jonge (also *Minister of Health, Welfare and Sport*, CDA); Kajsa Ollongren (also *Minister of Interior and Kingdom Affairs*, D66).

Minister of Defence: Ank Bijleveld (CDA). *Economic Affairs and Climate Policy:* Eric Wiebes (VVD). *Education, Culture and Science:* Ingrid van Engelshoven (D66). *Finance:* Wopke Hoekstra (CDA). *Foreign Affairs:* Stef Blok (VVD). *Infrastructure and Water Management:* Cora van Nieuwenhuizen (VVD). *Justice and Security:* Ferdinand Grapperhaus (CDA). *Social Affairs and Employment:* Wouter Koolmees (D66). *Ministers without Portfolio:* Bruno Bruins (VVD) (for *Medical Care*); Sander Dekker (VVD) (for *Legal Protection*); Sigrid Kaag (D66) (for *Foreign Trade and Development Co-operation*); Arie Slob (Christian Union) (for *Primary and Secondary Education and Media*); Mark Harbers (VVD) (for *Migration*).

Government Website: http://www.government.nl

Current Leaders

Mark Rutte

Position
Prime Minister

Introduction
Mark Rutte became prime minister in Oct. 2010, heading a coalition between his People's Party for Freedom and Democracy (VVD) and the Christian Democratic Appeal (CDA) with outside support of the Party for Freedom (PVV). His premiership ended an era of alternating Labour Party and Christian Democratic governments uninterrupted since 1918. He continued as prime minister as the VVD formed a new coalition with the Labour Party (PvdA) following elections in Sept. 2012, and he retained the premiership when the VVD again emerged the largest party in parliamentary elections in March 2017.

Early Life
Rutte was born in The Hague on 14 Feb. 1967 and read history at Leiden University. He served as national president of the VVD youth party from 1988–91. After graduating in 1992, he was employed by the Unilever group as a human resources manager.

Rutte became a member of the VVD's national board in 1993, resigning in 1997 to focus on his business career. He was a personnel manager at Unilever subsidiary Van den Bergh Nederland until 2000, when he was promoted to Unilever's corporate human resources group. In 2002 he became director of human resources for Unilever subsidiary IgloMora Group.

Rutte worked on the VVD candidate committee at the 2002 general election. Later that year he became state secretary for social affairs and employment in the coalition government. In 2003 he entered the House of Representatives and in 2004 was appointed state secretary for higher education and science.

Despite managing a disappointing VVD municipal election campaign, in May 2006 the party elected him 'lijstrekker' (effective leader). In June 2006 he resigned from Jan Peter Balkenende's cabinet. He won notable victories in televised debates ahead of the June 2010 general election, attracting praise for his stance on economic affairs. The VVD won the election and after months of coalition talks Rutte was appointed premier.

Career in Office

Rutte and the VVD negotiated a coalition agreement with the CDA and the right-leaning PVV. Rutte shared executive posts evenly between VVD and CDA politicians, giving the CDA the ministries of defence, the interior and finance. The PVV, whose popularity sprang from its stance on immigration, was given a stake in policy-making, although controversial leader Geert Wilders has since gone on trial twice for inciting hatred against Muslims.

Rutte pledged to cut the budget deficit from 6% to 0·9% of GDP by 2015, raise the retirement age from 65 to 66 and support nuclear power. He imposed funding cuts on universities, while immigration policy was also tightened, with a clamp-down on repeat asylum applications and low-skilled immigrants, and restrictions on the wearing of the Islamic burqa in public.

In Jan. 2011 Rutte won parliamentary approval to send personnel to Afghanistan (the Netherlands having previously withdrawn from involvement there) to train the Afghan police. In the same month he held talks with the then UK prime minister, David Cameron, on reactivating the EU's Service Directive to encourage free-market reforms in the European business community.

In April 2012 Rutte and his government resigned, having failed to secure parliamentary endorsement of austerity measures following the PVV's withdrawal of support for the coalition. He stayed in office in a caretaker capacity until elections in Sept. The VVD remained the largest party, with increased representation, and entered into a coalition with the PvdA in Nov. 2012.

Rutte's government was criticized through 2013 for its tight fiscal policy, which restrained growth and delayed the Netherlands' exit from recession. In June that year he stated that the EU goal of ever closer union in all policy areas was over and that his government wanted powers over social security, working conditions and media regulation to remain at the national level.

In July 2014 he led national mourning for 193 Dutch citizens who died aboard a Malaysian passenger airliner shot down over rebel-held territory in Ukraine's civil conflict zone.

Increasing support for far-right political opinion, fuelled by the European migrant crisis, together with the continuing economic malaise and voter hostility to a proposed EU–Ukraine association agreement contributed to a sharp decline in the government's standing in 2015 and 2016. However, the coalition survived two no-confidence votes in parliament over that period and in legislative elections in March 2017 the VVD was again returned as the largest party—despite losing seats—against a fragmented political background. Following protracted inter-party negotiations, a new, but fragile, centre-right VVD-led coalition government, excluding the PVV, was eventually sworn in on 26 Oct. that year.

In 2018 Rutte was faced with tensions in the coalition, scandals in his own party and widespread opposition to his controversial (and subsequently withdrawn) tax plans, prompting two parliamentary no-confidence motions in Feb. and again in Oct., which he nevertheless survived.

Defence

Conscription ended on 30 Aug. 1996.

The total strength of the armed forces in 2011 was 37,368. Reserves: 3,189. In 2013 defence expenditure totalled US$10,350m. (US$616 per capita), representing 1·3% of GDP (compared to the NATO target of 2%).

Army

Personnel in 2011 numbered 20,386. The core fighting element of the Army consists of a single element divided into two mechanized brigades and one airborne brigade. Some units in the Netherlands may be assigned to the UN as peacekeeping forces. The army is responsible for the training of these units. The 1st Netherlands Army Corps merged with a German corps to become 1 German/Netherlands Corps in 1995. It is based in Münster, Germany, and is a certified NATO Response Force. Then, between 2014 and 2016, two of the three Dutch combat brigades were integrated into German divisions.

There is a paramilitary Royal Military Constabulary, 5,911 strong in 2011. In addition there were 2,686 army reservists.

Navy

The principal headquarters and main base of the Royal Netherlands Navy is at Den Helder, with a minor base at Curaçao. Command and control in home waters is exercised jointly with the Belgian Naval Component (submarines excepted).

The combatant fleet includes four diesel submarines, four destroyers and two frigates. In 2011 personnel totalled 8,502 including 2,654 in the Royal Netherlands Marine Corps.

Air Force

The Royal Netherlands Air Force (RNLAF) had 8,030 personnel in 2011. It had 72 combat-capable aircraft in 2011 (F-16s) and 29 attack helicopters. All squadrons are operated by Tactical Air Command.

International Relations

On 1 June 2005 the Netherlands became the second European Union member after France to reject the proposed EU constitution, with 61·54% of votes cast in a referendum against the constitution and only 38·46% in favour.

The Hague is the seat of several international organizations, including the International Court of Justice.

Economy

Services accounted for 76% of GDP in 2012, industry 22% and agriculture 2%.

According to the anti-corruption organization Transparency International, the Netherlands ranked eighth in the world in a 2018 survey of the countries with the least corruption in business and government. It received 82 out of 100 in the annual index.

The Netherlands gave US$5·0bn. in international aid in 2017. This represented 0·6% of GNI.

Overview

The Dutch economy boasts one of the world's highest levels of average income as well as relatively low income inequality. Given its small domestic market, location at the heart of northwest Europe and favourable harbour facilities, the Netherlands is notably open and outward-looking. It is a leading donor of international aid with a commitment to poverty reduction in Africa. GDP growth averaged 1·9% annually in the three years to 2016.

Dutch sovereign bonds enjoy safe haven status given the country's sound fiscal policies, low interest rates and strong institutional framework. Although domestic investment is weak, a favourable tax environment for multinationals has attracted many foreign companies and significant investment inflows. The country also has one of the highest levels of labour productivity.

The Netherlands is the fifth largest exporter of goods in the world (exports of goods and services accounting for 80·8% of GDP in 2016) and boasts Europe's largest port in Rotterdam. Trade dependency is even greater because of the scarcity of industrial raw materials. Industry is geared towards processing, and re-exports now account for over half of the trade balance of goods compared to a third in 1995. Relative to Europe's bigger countries, manufacturing's share of GDP is small compared to the agricultural and service sectors. The Netherlands is a leader in horticulture and is a competitive meat and dairy product exporter.

The global financial crisis saw the economy fall into its worst recession for several decades, recording a 3·8% drop in 2009. Exports declined by 25% while domestic demand also contracted. State support was needed to save several financial institutions, with four of the five largest subject to restructuring programmes. Public debt meanwhile rose to 62·9% of GDP in 2010 and 70·8% in 2012 (reaching 75% by 2016).

Nonetheless, the Netherlands was to weather the crisis better than many of its European partners, with recovery linked to resurgent exports. In Oct. 2012 the government announced austerity measures totalling €16bn. (US$20·7bn.). Low consumer confidence, beginning in 2008, was cited as a major factor in the weak performance of the economy in the second half of 2012, when spending was affected by falling real wages and a 2% increase in VAT to 21%. Unemployment rose to 7·9% in Feb. 2014 while the budget deficit exceeded the European Union's 3% limit in both 2012 and 2013. Although the unemployment rate had fallen to 6·7% by 2016, the economy has remained susceptible to weaknesses in the eurozone to which around two-thirds of Dutch exports go. Trade with developing countries nevertheless tripled over the decade to 2016.

Despite a nominal 20% correction in house prices in 2008 and a decline of 27% in real terms, the real estate market has since stabilized; prices of owner-occupied houses were on average 3·4% higher in Oct. 2015 than in Oct. 2014. A long-term challenge is to tackle the debt-to-income ratio, which stood at 225·7% in 2016. Household indebtedness has also led to a reduction in consumption, which has in turn hampered investment and growth.

The welfare system and labour market institutions follow the German model, with extensive social security provisions and worker influence at the corporate level. The state's pension liabilities are thought to be unsustainable. To address the high health care costs of the ageing population, the Dec. 2012 Stability Programme update recommended improving cost effectiveness and merging homecare with municipal care.

Currency

On 1 Jan. 1999 the *euro* (EUR) became the legal currency in the Netherlands at the irrevocable conversion rate of 2·20371 guilders to 1 euro. The euro, which consists of 100 cents, has been in circulation since 1 Jan. 2002. On the introduction of the euro there was a 'dual circulation' period before the guilder ceased to be legal tender on 28 Jan. 2002.

Inflation rates (based on OECD statistics):

2008	2009	2010	2011	2012	2013	2014	2015	2016	2017
2·2%	1·0%	0·9%	2·5%	2·8%	2·6%	0·3%	0·2%	0·1%	1·3%

Gold reserves were 19·69m. troy oz in Sept. 2009 and foreign exchange reserves US$10,102m. Total money supply was €217,793m. in Aug. 2009.

Budget

In 2011 central government revenues totalled €245,790m. (€244,161m. in 2010) and expenditures €268,137m. (€266,882m. in 2010). Principal sources of revenue in 2011: social security contributions, €88,798m.; taxes on goods and services, €64,742m.; taxes on income, profits and capital gains, €61,929m. Main items of expenditure by economic type in 2011: social benefits, €128,942m.; grants, €75,625m.; compensation of employees, €19,722m.

The Netherlands had a budget surplus in 2017 of 1·2% of GDP. There was a government balance in 2016 and a budget deficit in 2015 (2·0%) The required target set by the EU is a budget deficit of no more than 3%.

VAT is 21·0% (reduced rate, 9·0%).

Performance

Real GDP growth rates (based on OECD statistics):

2008	2009	2010	2011	2012	2013	2014	2015	2016	2017
2·2%	−3·7%	1·3%	1·5%	−1·0%	−0·1%	1·4%	2·0%	2·1%	3·0%

The Netherlands experienced 26 consecutive years of economic growth before the recession of 2009. In 2017 total GDP was US$826·2bn.

Banking and Finance

The central bank and bank of issue is the Netherlands Bank (*President*, Klaas Knot), founded in 1814 and nationalized in 1948. Its Governor is appointed by the government for seven-year terms. In 2011 the capital amounted to €500m. There were 82 registered commercial banks in 2011. The largest bank in 2014 was ING Bank NV (assets of €1,481·6bn.), ahead of Rabobank and ABN Amro. In Oct. 2007 ABN Amro and a consortium led by the UK's Royal Bank of Scotland (and including Santander from Spain and the Belgian-Dutch company Fortis) agreed a merger worth US$98·5bn., representing Europe's largest banking takeover. The Dutch part of Fortis was nationalized in Oct. 2008 and its shares in ABN Amro were also transferred to the Dutch government. There is a stock exchange in Amsterdam; it is a component of Euronext, which was created in Sept. 2000 through the merger of the Amsterdam, Brussels and Paris bourses.

Gross external debt amounted to US$2,416,352m. in June 2012.

The Netherlands received US$72·6bn. worth of foreign direct investment in 2015, up from US$52·2bn. in 2014.

In Dec. 2011, 66·3% of internet users in the Netherlands were using online banking—the highest proportion of any country.

Energy and Natural Resources

In 2011, 4·3% of energy consumption came from renewables (wind power, solar power, hydro-electric power, tidal power, geothermal energy and biomass), compared to the European Union average of 13·0%. A target of 14% has been set by the EU for 2020.

Environment

Carbon dioxide emissions from the consumption of energy in 2011 were the equivalent of 14·4 tonnes per capita.

The Netherlands is one of the world leaders in recycling. In 2012, 50% of municipal waste was recycled or composted, with only 2% going to landfill.

Electricity

Installed capacity was 28·0m. kW in 2011. Production of electrical energy in 2011 was 112·80bn. kWh (92% thermal and 4% nuclear, with the remainder coming from biomass, wind and other sources); consumption per capita was 7,324 kWh. There was one nuclear reactor in operation in 2010.

Oil and Gas

Production of natural gas in 2012, 63·9bn. cu. metres. Reserves in 2012 were 1·0trn. cu. metres. The Groningen gas field in the north of the country is the largest in continental Europe. In 2011 crude oil production was 7·6m. bbls; reserves were 150m. bbls in 2014.

Minerals

In 2009, 6·0m. tonnes of salt were produced. Aluminium production in 2009 totalled 300,000 tonnes.

Agriculture

The Netherlands is one of the world's largest exporters of agricultural produce. There were 72,300 agricultural holdings in 2010. Food and live animals accounted for 12·1% of exports and 8·4% of imports in 2010. The agricultural sector (including forestry and fisheries) employs 2·5% of the workforce. In 2009 there were 1,054,700 ha. of arable land and 35,500 ha. of permanent crops. The total area of cultivated land in 2011 was 1,858,000 ha.: grassland and green fodder crops, 1,225,000 ha.; arable crops, 535,000 ha.; open ground horticulture, 89,000 ha.; glasshouse horticulture, 10,000 ha. In 2010, 212,000 people were employed in agriculture (of which family workers, 148,000; non-family workers, 64,000).

The yield of the more important arable crops, in 1,000 tonnes, was as follows:

Crop	2010	2011
Potatoes	6,843	7,333
Sugar beets	5,280	5,858
Wheat	1,370	1,175
Sown onions	1,252	1,582
Barley	204	205

Other major fruit and vegetable production in 2010 included (in 1,000 tonnes): tomatoes, 815; cucumbers, 435; carrots, 350; sweet peppers, 345; apples, 338; mushrooms, 240; pears, 195.

Cultivated areas of main flowers (2011) in 1,000 ha.: tulips, 11·9; lilies, 5·1. Total area of bulbs, 24,100 ha.

Livestock, 2011 (in 1,000) included: 12,429 pigs; 3,885 cattle; 1,088 sheep; 380 goats; 96,919 chickens.

Animal products in 2010 (in 1,000 tonnes) included: pork and pork products, 1,288; beef and veal, 388; poultry, 751; milk, 11,626; cheese, 753; butter, 133; hens' eggs, 631.

Forestry

Forests covered 0·38m. ha. in 2015, or 11% of the land area. In 2011, 982,000 cu. metres of roundwood were cut.

Fisheries

Total catch in 2015 was 384,476 tonnes (down from 555,606 tonnes in 2005), of which 382,572 tonnes were from marine waters. In 2012 the fishing fleet comprised 849 vessels of 145,451 GT.

Industry

In May 2018 the leading companies by market capitalization were: Royal Dutch Shell (Dutch/British), an oil and gas company (US$306·5bn.); Unilever (Dutch/British), a consumer goods firm (US$155·8bn.); and AIRBUS, an aircraft manufacturer (US$92·1bn.).

In 2011 there were 51,170 companies in the manufacturing industry (48% in textiles, paper, wood, furniture and miscellaneous industries; 20% basic metals and metal products; 11% electrical engineering and machinery; 9% food industry; 8% oil, chemicals, rubber and synthetics; 4% transport equipment). Total production value in 2010 was €270·4bn.

The largest industrial sectors by production value in 2010 were oil, chemicals, rubber and synthetics (37%); food industry (22%); textiles, paper, wood, furniture and miscellaneous industries (13%); and electrical engineering and machinery (13%). There were 809,000 employees (full-time equivalent) in manufacturing in 2008: textiles, paper, wood, furniture and other industry, 274,000; electrical engineering and machinery, 138,000; oil, chemicals, rubber and synthetics, 128,000; food industry, 117,000; basic metals and metal products, 112,000; transport equipment, 40,000.

Labour

The total labour force (15–65 years) in 2011 was 7,811,000 persons (3,492,000 women) of whom 419,000 (195,000 women) unemployed. Of the 7,392,000 employed persons, 5,709,000 were in permanent employment, 606,000 were in flexible employment and 1,077,000 were self-employed. Nearly a third of all 15–65-year-old women were working between 20 and 35 hours per week. By education level, the 2011 employed labour force included (in 1,000): primary education, 361; junior secondary education, 1,309; senior secondary education, 3,130; university education, 2,524 (bachelor, 1,639; master's or PhD, 885).

The unemployment rate was 3·6% in Dec. 2018, down from 4·9% in 2017 as a whole. Although the Netherlands has a very low unemployment rate, for every 100 people below the age of 65 who are active in the labour market, 35 are not. In 2010, 48·9% of the labour force was in part-time employment with 76·5% of all women employed working part-time.

In 2010 the average weekly working hours of employees were 34·4. In 2011 employees' average annual working hours totalled 1,379. Workers in the Netherlands put in among the shortest hours of any industrialized country.

Average annual earnings of employees in 2009 totalled €30,700 with average hourly earnings of €20·01. By type of employment hourly earnings in 2009 ranged from €12·47 in hotels and restaurants up to €33·57 in mineral extraction.

International Trade

On 5 Sept. 1944 and 14 March 1947 the Netherlands signed agreements with Belgium and Luxembourg for the establishment of a customs union. On 1 Jan. 1948 this union came into force and the existing customs tariffs of the Belgium–Luxembourg Economic Union and of the Netherlands were superseded by the joint Benelux Customs Union Tariff. It applied to imports into the three countries from outside sources, and exempted from customs duties all imports into each of the three countries from the other two.

Imports and Exports

In 2011 imports totalled €364,000m. (provisional), up from €332,000m. in 2010; exports, €405,000m. (provisional), up from €372,000m. in 2010.

Value of trade with major partners (in €1bn.):

Region/ Country	Imports 2010	Exports 2010	Imports 2011 (provisional)	Exports 2011 (provisional)
Europe	205	298	228	327
Belgium	32	41	36	49
France	14	32	17	36
Germany	59	90	61	97
Italy	7	19	8	20
Russia	14	6	17	6
UK	22	30	25	32
Africa	11	11	12	12
Americas	40	26	42	27
USA	25	17	24	17
Asia	74	32	79	34
China	31	5	31	7
Japan	9	3	10	3
Australia and Oceania	1	5	2	4

The main imports in 2011 (provisional) were (in €1bn.): machines and transport equipment, 103 (100 in 2010); mineral fuels, 79 (60); chemical products, 47 (51); manufactured goods, 39 (34); food and live animals, 32 (28); inedible raw materials except fuel, 16 (13). Main exports in 2011 (provisional) were (in €1bn.): machines and transport equipment, 112 (106 in 2010); chemical products, 71 (71); mineral fuels, 65 (51); food and live animals, 48 (45); manufactured goods, 37 (33); inedible raw materials except fuels, 21 (19). The Netherlands ranks second only behind the USA for the value of its agricultural exports.

Communications

Roads

In 2011 the total length of the Netherlands' road network was 139,235 km (including 2,658 km of motorways). Number of vehicles (2008): private cars, 7·39m.; trucks and vans, 1·07m.; motorcycles and mopeds, 1·37m. There were 750 fatalities as a result of road accidents in 2008, equivalent to 4·6 fatalities per 100,000 population (one of the lowest death rates in road accidents of any industrialized country).

The Netherlands was ranked fifth for its road infrastructure in the World Economic Forum's *Global Competitiveness Report 2017–18*.

Rail

Most rail services are operated by N.V. Nederlandse Spoorwegen. Route length in 2011 was 3,013 km. Passenger-km travelled in 2009 came to 16·32bn. Goods transported in 2010 totalled 36m. tonnes. There is a metro (44 km) and tram/light rail network (154 km) in Amsterdam and another in Rotterdam (76 km and 67 km). Tram/light rail networks operate in The Hague (128 km) and Utrecht (22 km).

Civil Aviation

There are international airports at Amsterdam (Schiphol), Rotterdam, Maastricht and Eindhoven. The Royal Dutch Airlines (KLM) was founded on 7 Oct. 1919. In Oct. 2003 it merged with Air France to form Air France-KLM, in which the French state owns a 17·6% stake.

Airport passenger traffic reached 53·9m. in 2011: Amsterdam handled 49·8m. passengers, Eindhoven 2·6m. and Rotterdam 1·1m. Amsterdam was the fourth busiest airport in Europe in 2011 on the basis of passenger numbers and the 14th busiest in the world. In 2011, 1·6m. tonnes of freight were transported via Dutch airports.

In the World Economic Forum's *Global Competitiveness Report 2017–2018* the Netherlands ranked fourth for quality of air transport infrastructure.

Shipping

In Jan. 2014 there were 879 ships of 300 GT or over registered, totalling 7,318,000 GT. Of the 879 vessels registered, 675 were general cargo ships, 66 oil tankers, 53 container ships, 39 passenger ships, 28 liquid gas tankers and 18 bulk carriers. The Dutch-controlled fleet comprised 891 vessels of 1,000 GT or over in July 2014, of which 635 were under the Dutch flag and 256 under foreign flags.

Total throughput at Rotterdam, the busiest port in the Netherlands and Europe and the sixth busiest in the world, was 440,464,000 tonnes in 2013 (down from a record 441,527,000 tonnes in 2012). Of the total cargo handled in 2013, 310,768,000 tonnes were incoming and 129,696,000 tonnes outgoing. Rotterdam is also the busiest container port in both the Netherlands and Europe; in 2013 it was the 11th busiest container port in the world, handling 11,664,000 TEUs (twenty-foot equivalent units). Rotterdam handles more than double the amount of cargo of Antwerp, Europe's second busiest port. The Amsterdam ports were the second busiest in the Netherlands in 2013, handling a record 95,753,000 tonnes of cargo.

There were 4,716 km of navigable canals in 2014 and 1,395 km of navigable rivers; 366·6m. tonnes of freight were carried on inland waterways in 2014.

The Netherlands was ranked first in the World Economic Forum's *Global Competitiveness Report 2017–2018* for the quality of its port facilities.

Telecommunications

In 2012 there were 7,182,000 main (fixed) telephone lines. In the same year mobile phone subscriptions numbered 19,717,000 (1,179·7 per 1,000 persons). 94·0% of the population aged 16–74 were internet users in 2013. There were 62·3 mobile broadband subscriptions per 100 inhabitants in 2013 and 40·1 fixed broadband subscriptions per 100 inhabitants. In March 2012 there were 5·8m. Facebook users.

Social Institutions

Out of 178 countries analysed in the 2017 *Fragile States Index*—a list published jointly by the Fund for Peace and *Foreign Policy* magazine—the Netherlands was ranked the 12th least vulnerable to conflict or collapse. The index is based on 12 indicators of state vulnerability across social, political and economic categories.

Justice

Justice is administered by the High Court (Court of Cassation), by five courts of justice (Courts of Appeal), by 19 district courts and by 61 cantonal courts. The Cantonal Court, which deals with minor offences, comprises a single judge; more serious cases are tried by the district courts, comprising as a rule three judges (in some cases one judge is sufficient); the courts of appeal are constituted of three and the High Court of five judges. All judges are appointed for life by the Sovereign (the judges of the High Court from a list prepared by the Second Chamber of the States-General). They can be removed only by a decision of the High Court.

At the district court the juvenile judge is specially appointed to try children's civil cases and at the same time charged with administration of justice for criminal actions committed by young persons between 12 and 18 years old, unless imprisonment of more than six months ought to be inflicted; such cases are tried by three judges.

The population in penal institutions in Sept. 2012 was 13,749 (82 per 100,000 of national population), down from 21,013 in July 2006 (128 per 100,000). Owing to the declining prison population, since Feb. 2010 some Belgian prison inmates have been accommodated at Tilburg prison in the Netherlands. There are now more prison guards in the Netherlands than prisoners. 1,193,000 crimes were recorded by the police in 2010 (1,402,000 in 2002).

In 2015 the World Justice Project *Rule of Law Index*, which provides data on how the rule of law is experienced by the general public across eight categories, ranked the Netherlands first of 102 countries for civil justice and 14th for criminal justice.

Police

The police force is divided into 25 regions. There is also a National Police Service which includes the Central Criminal Investigation Office, which deals with serious crimes throughout the country, and the International Criminal Investigation Office, which informs foreign countries of international crimes.

Education

Statistics for the academic year 2009–10:

	Schools/ institutions	Full-time pupils/students (in 1,000) Total
Primary education	6,895	1,548
Special primary education	311	43
Special schools	323	68
Secondary education	657	935
Senior secondary vocational education	71	522
Higher professional education	43	403
University education	13	233

University student enrolment by subject in 2009–10 (with total students): behaviour and society (49,600); economics (39,600); language and culture (32,300); health (31,500); engineering and technology (30,600); law (28,100); science (20,100); cross-sector programmes (3,200); university teacher-training courses (1,700).

In 2007 there were 29,104 Open University students and 752 staff. There are 12 study centres in the Netherlands and three support centres, plus six study centres in Belgium.

In 2006 public expenditure on education came to 5·4% of GNI and 12·0% of total government spending. The adult literacy rate is at least 99%.

Health

In 2014 there were 57,762 physicians, 3,635 pharmaceutical personnel, 177,818 nursing and midwifery personnel, and 8,596 dentistry personnel. There were 61,767 hospital beds in 2016, of which 54,424 were curative care beds.

The 1919 Opium Act (amended in 1928 and 1976) regulates the production and consumption of 'psychoactive' drugs. Personal use of cannabis is effectively decriminalized and the sale of soft drugs through 'coffee shops' is not prosecuted provided certain conditions are met.

Euthanasia became legal when the First Chamber (the Senate) gave its formal approval on 10 April 2001 by 46 votes to 28. The Second Chamber had voted to make it legal by 104 votes to 40 in Nov. 2000. The law came into effect on 1 April 2002. In 2007 euthanasia organizations recorded 2,120 instances of doctors helping patients to die. The Netherlands was the first country to legalize euthanasia. In 2007 the Netherlands spent 8·9% of its GDP on health.

Welfare

The General Old Age Pensions Act (AOW) entitles everyone to draw an old age pension from the age of 66, although this is to rise gradually to 67 by 2024. At 31 Dec. 2010 there were 2,881,000 persons entitled to receive an old age pension, and 98,000 a pension under the General Surviving Relatives Act; 1,932,000 parents were receiving benefits under the General Child Benefit Act. In 2011 there were 825,000 persons claiming incapacity benefits and 270,000 persons claiming benefits under the Unemployment Benefits Act.

Religion

Entire liberty of conscience is granted to the members of all denominations. The royal family belong to the Protestant Church in the Netherlands.

Population aged 12 years and over in 2009 was: Roman Catholics, 27%; Protestant Church in the Netherlands, 9%; Calvinist, 3%; other creeds, 10%; no religion, 44%. The Dutch Reformed Church merged with the Reformed Churches in the Netherlands and the Evangelical Lutheran Church in the Kingdom of the Netherlands in May 2004 to form the Protestant Church in the Netherlands—now the second largest church body in the country. The Roman Catholic Church has one archdiocese (of Utrecht) and six dioceses. In Feb. 2019 there were two Roman Catholic cardinals. The Old Catholic Church of the Netherlands has one Archbishop (of Utrecht), one Bishop (of Haarlem) and 26 parishes. There were 1·0m. Muslims in 2010 according to estimates by the Pew Research Center's Forum on Religion & Public Life; there were also small numbers of Hindus, Buddhists and Jews.

Source: Statistics Netherlands

Culture

Leeuwarden was one of two European Capitals of Culture for 2018, along with Valletta.

World Heritage Sites

The Kingdom of the Netherlands has ten sites on the UNESCO World Heritage List: Schokland and its surroundings (inscribed on the list in 1995); the defence line at Amsterdam (1996); the mill network at Kinderdijk-Elshout (1997); the historic area of Willemstad, the inner city and harbour in Curaçao (1997); the D. F. Wouda steam pumping station (1998); Droogmakerij de Beemster (Beemster Polder) (1999); the Rietveld Schröder house in Utrecht (2000); the Seventeenth-century canal ring area of Amsterdam inside the Singelgracht (2010); and Van Nellefabriek in Rotterdam (2014).

The Netherlands shares the Wadden Sea (2009 and 2014) with Denmark and Germany. It is the largest unbroken system of intertidal sand and mud flats in the world.

Press

In 2014 there were 30 daily newspapers with a combined circulation of 3,555,000. The most widely read daily is *De Telegraaf*, with an average daily circulation of 513,000 copies in 2014. There were 32 newspaper online editions in 2014, when there were 7,824,000 unique monthly visitors. In the 2013 *World Press Freedom Index* compiled by Reporters Without Borders, the Netherlands was ranked second out of 179 countries.

Tourism

Tourism is a major sector of the economy. In 2011 international tourist spending totalled €10,400m. A total of 11,299,000 non-resident tourists stayed in holiday accommodation in 2011 (up from 10,883,000 in 2010 and 9,921,000 in 2009).

Festivals

Floriade, a world-famous horticultural show, takes place every ten years and is the largest Dutch attraction, with 2·0m. people attending the 2012 festival. The Maastricht Carnival in April attracts many visitors. The Flower Parade from Noordwijk to Haarlem occurs in late April. Koningsdag on 27 April is a nationwide celebration of King Willem-Alexander's birthday. The Oosterparkfestival, a cultural celebration of that district of Amsterdam, runs for three days in the first week of May. Liberation Day is celebrated every five years on 5 May, with the next occurrence being in 2020. An international music festival, the Holland Festival, is held in Amsterdam throughout June each year and the Early Music Festival is held in Utrecht. The North Sea Jazz Festival, the largest in Europe, takes place in The Hague. Pinkpop, one of Europe's leading rock and pop festivals, is held at Landgraaf in May or June. Each year the most important Dutch and Flemish theatre productions of the previous season are performed at the Theatre Festival in Amsterdam and Antwerp (Belgium). The Holland Dance Festival is held every other year in The Hague and the Springdance Festival in Utrecht annually. Film festivals include the Rotterdam Film Festival in Feb., the Dutch Film Festival in Sept. and the International Documentary Film Festival of Amsterdam in Dec.

Diplomatic Representatives

Of the Netherlands in the United Kingdom (38 Hyde Park Gate, London, SW7 5DP)
Ambassador: Simon Smits.

Of the United Kingdom in the Netherlands (Lange Voorhout 10, 2514 ED The Hague)
Ambassador: Peter Wilson, CMG.

Of the Netherlands in the USA (4200 Linnean Ave., NW, Washington, D.C., 20008)
Ambassador: Hendrik Jan Jurriaan Schuwer.

Of the USA in the Netherlands (John Adams Park 1, 2244 BZ, Wassenaar, The Hague)
Ambassador: Peter Hoekstra.

Of the Netherlands to the United Nations
Ambassador: Karel J. G. van Oosterom.

Of the Netherlands to the European Union
Permanent Representative: Robert de Groot.

Overseas Countries and Territories

Landen en gebieden overzee
These fall into two categories: *Autonomous Countries within the Kingdom of the Netherlands* (Aruba, Curaçao and Sint Maarten) and *Autonomous Special Municipalities of the Netherlands* (Bonaire, Saba and Sint Eustatius). Following the dissolution of the Netherlands Antilles on 10 Oct. 2010, Curaçao and Sint Maarten became autonomous countries within the Kingdom of the Netherlands (a status held by Aruba since 1986) while Bonaire, Saba and Sint Eustatius were granted a status comparable to that of the municipalities within the Netherlands itself.

Autonomous Countries within the Kingdom of the Netherlands

Zelfstandige landen binnen het Koninkrijk der Nederlanden

Aruba

Discovered by Alonzo de Ojeda in 1499, Aruba was initially claimed for Spain and then acquired by the Dutch in 1634. From 1828 it formed part of the Dutch West Indies and from 1845 part of the Netherlands Antilles. In 1954 it achieved internal self-government and was constitutionally separated from the Netherlands Antilles from 1 Jan. 1986.

The island, with a tropical marine climate, lies in the southern Caribbean 32 km north of the Venezuelan coast and 68 km west of Curaçao. Area, 193 sq. km (75 sq. miles); estimated population, 104,000 (2015). Chief towns: Oranjestad, the capital, and San Nicolas. Languages: Dutch (official) and Papiamento (a creole language). Aruba has its own legislature, government, judiciary, civil service and police force. The Kingdom of the Netherlands is represented by a Governor appointed by the monarch. The unicameral legislature (Staten) has 21 members elected for a four-year term of office.

Governor: Alfonso Boekhoudt.
Prime Minister: Evelyn Wever-Croes.

The currency is the Aruban florin (AWG). There is an international airport (Reina Beatrix). Oranjestad has a container terminal and cruise ship port. The ports at Barcadera and San Nicolas service the offshore and energy sector and Aruba's oil refinery. In 2010 an estimated 81% of the population were Roman Catholics according to the Pew Research Center's Forum on Religion & Public Life.

Curaçao

Initially settled by Arawak Amerindians, the Dutch West India Company established a presence on Curaçao in 1634 and built the capital, Willemstad, on a natural harbour. The island became a regional commercial centre, which was integrated into the Dutch West Indies from 1828 and formed part of the Netherlands Antilles from 1845. Granted internal self-government in 1954, Curaçao became autonomous (except for defence and foreign affairs) within the Kingdom of the Netherlands in Oct. 2010 when the Netherlands Antilles was dissolved.

Curaçao lies around 100 km north of the Venezuelan coast. Area, 444 sq. km; estimated population, 157,000 (2015). Languages: Dutch, Papiamento (a creole language) and English. The head of state is the monarch of the Netherlands, represented by a Governor. The Prime Minister heads the Executive Council. The Staten (parliament) is comprised of 21 members elected by popular vote every four years.

Governor: Lucille George-Wout.
Prime Minister: Eugene Rhuggenaath.

The economy is reliant on oil refining, tourism and offshore finance. It is expected that the *Caribbean guilder* will eventually replace the *Netherlands Antillean guilder*. There is an international airport (Curaçao International Airport or Hato International Airport).

Around 73% of the population are Roman Catholics. The Historic Area of Willemstad, Inner City and Harbour was inscribed on the UNESCO World Heritage List in 1997.

Sint Maarten

The island was first settled in 1631 by the Dutch but attracted competition for control as a centre of salt mining from the British, French and Spanish. In 1648 it was divided by treaty in two, with the French administering the north (called St Martin) and the Dutch the south. In 1954 it was incorporated into the Netherlands Antilles and in Oct. 2010 became autonomous (except for defence and foreign affairs) within the Kingdom of the Netherlands.

Sint Maarten lies around 950 km northeast of the Venezuelan coast. Area, 34 sq. km; estimated population, 39,000 (2015). Philipsburg is the capital. Languages: Dutch and English (official), Papiamento (a creole language) and Spanish.

The head of state is the monarch of the Netherlands, represented by a Governor. The Prime Minister heads a Council of Ministers. The Staten (parliament) is comprised of 15 members elected by proportional representation every four years.

Governor: Eugene Holiday.

Prime Minister: Leona Marlin-Romeo.

Tourism is the mainstay of the economy. It is expected that the *Caribbean guilder* will eventually replace the *Netherlands Antillean* guilder. There is an international airport (Princess Juliana Airport). Around 33% of the population are Roman Catholics and 15% Pentecostals.

Autonomous Special Municipalities of the Netherlands

Bijzondere gemeenten van Nederland

Bonaire

Inhabited by Arawak Caquetios Indians by AD 1000, the island was settled from 1623 by the Dutch who were challenged by the Spanish until the Dutch established dominance in 1636. The British seized control from 1800–03 and also from 1807–16. After Nazi Germany invaded the Netherlands in 1940 Bonaire was used as an internment camp. The island became an Autonomous Special Municipality of the Netherlands when the Netherlands Antilles was dissolved in Oct. 2010.

Bonaire lies some 100 km north of the Venezuelan coast. Area, 288 sq. km; population, 17,408 (2013). The capital is Kralendijk. Dutch, English and Papiamento (a creole language) are the official languages. The mainstays of the economy are tourism and the salt industry. The US dollar replaced the Netherlands Antillean guilder as the legal currency in Jan. 2011. There is an international airport.

Lieut.-Governor: Edison Rijna.

Saba

Archaeological evidence suggests Saba was originally inhabited by Arawak or Carib Indans. Western colonization dates from 1640 when the Dutch West India Company sent a party of settlers. An English buccaneer, Thomas Morgan, then seized the island in 1664 and it served as a centre of piracy. The French, English and Dutch battled for dominance, with rum and sugar important revenue earners, until 1816 when the Dutch reclaimed the island. After the dissolution of the Netherlands Antilles in Oct. 2010, Saba became an Autonomous Special Municipality of the Netherlands.

Area, 13 sq. km; population, 1,991 (Jan. 2013). The capital is The Bottom. Dutch, English and Papiamento (a creole language) are the official languages. Roman Catholicism is the dominant religion. Tourism is increasingly important to the economy and fishing is also a major revenue earner. There is an airport, and a ferry service operates to and from Sint Maarten. The US dollar replaced the Netherlands Antillean guilder as the legal currency in Jan. 2011. The Saba University School of Medicine has been in operation since 1986.

Lieut.-Governor: Jonathan G. A. Johnson.

Sint Eustatius

The island was settled by a delegation from Zeeland, a province of the Netherlands, in 1636. From 1678 the Dutch West India Company was directly responsible for government. A free port from 1756, it became a focus of smuggling and a centre of sugar production. Having come under British and then French control, the island was transferred back to Dutch sovereignty in 1784. A referendum in Sint Eustatius in 2005 favoured remaining within the Netherlands Antilles (the only constituent territory to do so), but the island became an Autonomous Special Municipality of the Netherlands following the dissolution of the Antilles in Oct. 2010. In Feb. 2018 Sint Eustatius was placed under direct Dutch rule on grounds of corruption and neglect.

Area, 21 sq. km; population, 3,897 (Jan. 2013). The capital is Oranjestad. Dutch, English and Papiamento (a creole language) are the official languages. The US dollar replaced the Netherlands Antillean guilder as the legal currency in Jan. 2011. The government is the principal employer. The airport has scheduled flights from Sint Maarten and several other Caribbean islands. The University of Sint Eustatius School of Medicine received its charter in 1999.

Government Commissioner: Marcolino Franco.

Further Reading

Netherlands

Centraal Bureau voor de Statistiek. *Statistical Yearbook of the Netherlands.* From 1923/24.—*Statistisch Jaarboek.* From 1899/1924.—*CBS Select (Statistical Essays).* From 1980.—*Statistisch Bulletin.* From 1945; weekly.—*Maandschrift.* From 1944; monthly bulletin.—*90 Jaren Statistiek in Tijdreeksen* (historical series of the Netherlands 1899–1989)

Nationale Rekeningen (National Accounts). From 1948–50.—*Statistische onderzoekingen.* From 1977.—*Regionaal Statistisch Zakboek* (Regional Pocket Yearbook). From 1972

Staatsalmanak voor het Koninkrijk der Nederlanden. Annual from 1814

Staatsblad van het Koninkrijk der Nederlanden. From 1814

Staatscourant (State Gazette). From 1813

Andeweg, Rudy B. and Irwin, Galen A., *Governance and Politics of the Netherlands.* 4th ed. 2014

Arblaster, Paul, *A History of the Low Countries.* 2005

Blom, J. C. H. and Lamberts, E. (eds) *History of the Low Countries.* Revised ed. 2006

Cox, R. H., *The Development of the Dutch Welfare State: from Workers' Insurance to Universal Entitlement.* 1994

Gladdish, K., *Governing from the Centre: Politics and Policy-Making in the Netherlands.* 1991

National library: De Koninklijke Bibliotheek, Prinz Willem Alexanderhof 5, The Hague.

National Statistical Office: Centraal Bureau voor de Statistiek, Netherlands Central Bureau of Statistics, POB 24500, 2490 HA Den Haag.

Statistics Netherlands Website: http://www.cbs.nl

New Zealand

Aotearoa

Capital: Wellington
Population projection, 2020: 4·83m.
GNI per capita, 2017: (PPP$) 33,970
HDI/world rank, 2017: 0·917/16
Internet domain extension: .nz

Key Historical Events

The earliest settlers of New Zealand are thought to have come from eastern Polynesia, around the turn of the first millennium. Maori oral traditions point to discovery of the country by Kupe, who gave New Zealand its first name, Aotearoa, or 'Land of the Long White Cloud'. Oral tradition also refers to seven waka leaving a homeland known as Hawaiiki in a Great Fleet. The waka are still remembered in the names of significant tribal groupings and descent lines: *Aotea, Kurahaupo, Mataatua, Tainui, Takitimu, Te Arawa* and *Tokomaru.*

By Capt. James Cook's arrival in 1769, substantial settlements existed throughout the North Island, with smaller settlements in the South Island. Sporadic warfare was common as tribes, or 'iwi', fought for resources and status, or 'mana'.

The first recorded European contact was with Dutch explorer Abel Tasman in 1642. Believing the South Island to be the beginning of a mythical continent connected to Southern Africa, he bequeathed the name 'Staten Land'. A Dutch cartographer corrected Tasman, giving the name New Zealand to compliment the larger New Holland, as Australia was known at the time. Earlier on the same voyage Tasman had landed on an island off Australia which he named Van Diemen's Land, later called Tasmania.

Contact between Maori and Europeans, or 'Pakeha', followed Cook's journeys to New Zealand and mapping of the coastline, opening the way for sealing and whaling stations. Coastal trade grew throughout the first decades of the 19th century and trade routes were established between Maori and the new colony of New South Wales as early as the 1820s. The Maori adapted quickly to both a market economy—selling provisions, timber and flax—and to new technologies (notably the musket). Pakeha settlement in the decades following Cook's arrival was often on Maori terms and was used by Maori in the traditional pursuit of mana in the eyes of rivals and neighbours. Mission stations soon appeared: the Church Missionary Society established three stations in the Bay of Islands between 1814 and 1823, and were joined by a Wesleyan Missionary Society station in the Hokianga in the 1820s.

British Ascendancy

With greater contact both Maori and Pakeha saw the need to regulate Pakeha settlement. The Colonial Office in London appointed a Resident, James Busby, in 1833. In 1835, prompted by Busby, thirty-five chiefs signed a Declaration of Independence naming themselves the heads of state of a 'United Tribes of New Zealand'. Relations between Maori and Pakeha were formalized by the signing of the Treaty of Waitangi in 1840. In principle—or at least in the Maori text—this treaty guaranteed Maori chieftainship, or 'rangatiratanga', while granting governorship, or 'kawanatanga', to Queen Victoria. Until 1860 Maori outnumbered Pakeha but in practice—and in the English text—sovereignty was transferred, allowing greater British settlement and control.

Established in 1840, Auckland was chosen as the colony's capital by its first governor, Capt. William Hobson. Immigration was encouraged by the New Zealand Company with settlements at Wellington and Wanganui (1840), New Plymouth (1841), and Nelson (1842). Scottish immigrants founded Dunedin (1848); and Edward Gibbon Wakefield made plans for a model English settlement at Christchurch (1851). In 1852 representative government was established with a constitution providing for a House of Representatives and Legislative Council, as well as six provincial councils. The governor at the time, Sir George Grey, retained the right of veto and was responsible for 'Native' policy. At first, each provincial council exercised extensive powers. Their abolition in 1876 marked the beginnings of central government. The Legislative Council was disbanded in 1950 leaving New Zealand with a single-tier parliament.

Initially, voting—based on individual land ownership—excluded Maori who traditionally owned land collectively. Participation was extended to Maori in 1867 with four Maori seats. James Carroll, Apirana Ngata, Maui Pomare, and Peter Buck (Te Rangi Hiroa) were all prominent: Carroll was the first Maori to enter government. He was minister of native affairs and later acting prime minister.

Settlement was not always peaceful: war broke out in the 1840s and 1860s in the central and western North Island. British troops fought alongside local militia and friendly Maori, facing some of the earliest forms of trench and guerrilla warfare. The Native Land Court was set up in 1865 to determine the ownership of Maori land according to Pakeha law. Where Maori land and user rights existed communally, the Court sought to define parcels of land owned individually, thereby facilitating land sales.

Economic Boom

Land speculation fuelled an agricultural boom in the 1840s and 1850s providing the colony's first sustainable export commodity. New Zealand provided 8·6% of Britain's wool imports in 1861 and had 8·5m. sheep by 1867. The development of refrigerated shipping in the 1880s bolstered the pastoral economy through meat exports. Gold rushes in the 1860s and 1870s in Otago, the west coast of the South Island, and in Coromandel also contributed to the economy. Gold exports totalled £46m. by 1890. Wealth brought progress; the 1870s administrations of Julius Vogel and Harry Atkinson borrowed heavily to fund work schemes to encourage immigration and settlement. 1,100 miles of rail track were laid by 1879, and telegraphs linked all the main towns. The population doubled to 500,000 by 1881.

The 1880s saw the beginnings of party politics. A Liberal agenda, with policies of 'one man, one vote' and the compulsory purchase of large estates, was popular and succeeded in extending suffrage to all men. Robert Stout and John Ballance's leasehold land policies in the mid-1880s were also popular. A Liberal Party was formed in 1889 and, backed by unions and the landless, won the 1890 election with Ballance as its leader. The Conservatives formed the first genuine opposition. Richard John Seddon took over the Liberal leadership in 1892 and remained premier until his death in 1906. Among Liberal achievements were the Land and Income Tax Act 1891 and the Advance to Settlers Act 1894, which assisted 17,000 people by 1912. In 1893, New Zealand became the first country to extend the suffrage to women. Other reforms included William Pember Reeves's Industrial Conciliation and Arbitration Act of 1894 and one of the world's first national pension schemes.

In 1901 New Zealand declined the offer to join the Commonwealth of Australia and remained a British colony until 1907 when it gained Dominion status. Parliament remained subordinate to the British parliament until the adoption of the *Statute of Westminster 1931* in 1947, when New Zealand became fully sovereign with the British monarch as head of state. New Zealand annexed the Cook Islands in 1901, and was granted administration of Western Samoa at the Treaty of Versailles in 1918. It administered Samoa until the 1960s. New Zealand contributed around 100,000 soldiers in the First World War from a population of little more than a million; nearly 17,000 did not return. Nearly 9,000 New Zealanders died in the influenza epidemic spread by returning soldiers, with a Maori mortality rate six times that of Pakeha. In the Second World War around 200,000 New Zealanders joined Allied forces from a population of 1·6m.

Twentieth Century

Class-based political divisions intensified in the early twentieth century. Amid industrial unrest in 1912, the Liberal government fell to a vote of no confidence. Reform took power, introducing anti-union legislation. Strikes in Waihi, Wellington and Huntly were quelled. Reform governed until 1928, assisted at first by a wartime coalition with the Liberals, and then with tacit Liberal support. Policies broadly followed the dictates of farmers, creating a national Meat Board (1922) and Dairy Board (1923).

A United–Reform coalition (1931–35) coped with world recession. Employment reached 12%; the national income fell from an estimated £150m. to £90m., and the value of exports fell by 40%. To balance the budget, cuts were made to pensions, education, health and public works. In the absence of an unemployment benefit, men were sent to rural relief camps to work on low-capital, high-labour tasks. Measures such as a Reserve Bank and currency devaluation in 1933 helped farmers but did not address the broader social distress.

Welfare State

Michael Joseph (Micky) Savage's first Labour government (1935–49) reclaimed for New Zealand its title of social laboratory of the world. It introduced one of the world's most comprehensive social welfare systems—incorporating pensions, health, education and family benefits—and increased state housing; introduced state guaranteed prices for farm produce to protect farmers from international price fluctuations; and nationalized the Reserve Bank.

After 1936 rural support rallied around a National Party formed from remnants of the United–Reform coalition. Labour retained power with support of the four Maori seats, all held by the Ratana Party. The National Party won the 1949 election, promising to increase spending power and curb union power and economic controls. National retained power for most of the post-war boom years; brief Labour administrations under Walter Nash (1957–60) and Norman Kirk (1972–75) coincided with unfavourable economic conditions. Keith Holyoake's National government (1960–72) was concerned that Britain's anticipated entry to the EEC would damage New Zealand's exports to the UK. The Equal Pay Act (1972) challenged gender-based pay discrimination. A state-funded workplace injury compensation was set up.

Maori demands for recognition of the Treaty of Waitangi grew in the 1970s. The 1975 Land March saw tens of thousands march on parliament and the occupation of Bastion Point in 1977–78 centred on land compulsorily acquired by the government in 1951. Labour established the Waitangi Tribunal in 1975 to hear Maori claims of Treaty breaches. It lacked authority until 1985 when a Labour government made its powers retrospective to 1840. Tribunal recommendations have formed the basis for negotiations between the Crown and tribal authorities.

Britain's entry into the EEC in 1973 was a set-back for an economy dependent on exports to Britain. Robert Muldoon's National government (1975–84) introduced tariff protection, wage and price freezes, and increased borrowing for 'Think Big' public works. Muldoon won a narrow victory in the 1981 election following civil unrest during the 'Springbok' rugby tour. Riot police faced massive demonstrations as many New Zealanders opposed sporting links with the South African apartheid regime. The country found a new direction in the free market policies of David Lange's Labour government, which came to power in 1984. The economic direction of Roger Douglas, 'Rogernomics', radically altered the socio-economic landscape, reducing trade barriers and selling state assets to fund debt recovery.

In international affairs the Labour government introduced the New Zealand Nuclear Free Zone, Disarmament, and Arms Control Act 1987, declaring the country nuclear free. The legislation—supported by all political parties—led to the end of New Zealand's involvement in the ANZUS military agreement with Australia and the USA. In 1973 Australia and New Zealand tried to halt French nuclear testing in the Pacific through the International Court of Justice. New Zealand sent two frigates to Mururoa Atoll in protest. The 1985 bombing of the *Rainbow Warrior* in Auckland harbour by French secret service agents reopened the issue.

Wrangling over economic direction in the late 1980s led to Lange's resignation. He was replaced by Geoffrey Palmer in 1989, who in turn resigned shortly before the 1990 election. He was succeeded by Mike Moore. Labour lost the 1990 election to a National Party led by Jim Bolger who was determined on free market reforms. Social welfare reform, cuts in tertiary education funding and reform of accident compensation legislation cut back state intervention. The Employment Contracts Act (1991) outlawed compulsory union membership and introduced individual contracts, weakening union power. Jenny Shipley led a leadership coup in 1997 to become the country's first female prime minister, though not the first elected female prime minister. That landmark was achieved by Helen Clark who led the Labour Party to victory in the 1999 election. In 2008 John Key led National back to power.

Electoral reform in the 1990s saw New Zealand move from a first-past-the-post system to proportional representation under the mixed-member-proportional system (MMP). Despite the debacle of the first MMP election

in 1996 when a minor party (New Zealand First, formed by disgruntled National supporters) played National off against Labour for two months before forming a coalition with National, the system has provided greater representation for minorities.

Territory and Population

New Zealand lies southeast of Australia in the south Pacific, Wellington being 1,983 km from Sydney. There are two principal islands, the North and South Islands, besides Stewart Island, Chatham Islands and small outlying islands, as well as the territories overseas.

New Zealand (i.e. North, South and Stewart Islands) extends over 1,750 km from north to south. Area, excluding territories overseas, 267,707 sq. km. The main islands are: North Island, 114,154 sq. km; South Island, 150,416 sq. km; Stewart Island, 1,681 sq. km; Chatham Islands, 963 sq. km. The minor islands included within the geographical boundaries of New Zealand (but not within any local government area) are: Antipodes Islands, Auckland Islands, Bounty Islands, Campbell Island, Kermadec Islands, Snares Islands, Solander Island and Three Kings Islands. With the exception of meteorological station staff on Raoul Island in the Kermadec Group and Campbell Island there are no inhabitants.

The Kermadec Islands were annexed to New Zealand in 1887, have no separate administration and all New Zealand laws apply to them. Situation, 29° 10' to 31° 30' S. lat., 177° 45' to 179° W. long., 1,600 km NNE of New Zealand. The largest of the group is Raoul or Sunday Island, 29 sq. km, smaller islands being Macauley and Curtis, while Macauley Island is 5 km in circuit.

Growth in census population, exclusive of territories overseas:

	Total population	Average annual increase (%)
1858	115,461	—
1874	344,985	—
1878	458,007	7·33
1881	534,030	5·10
1886	620,451	3·06
1891	668,652	1·50
1896	743,214	2·13
1901[1]	815,862	1·90
1906	936,309	2·75
1911	1,058,313	2·52
1916[1]	1,149,225	1·50
1921	1,271,667	2·27
1926	1,408,140	2·06
1936[1]	1,573,812	1·13
1945[1, 2]	1,702,329	0·83
1951[1]	1,939,473	2·37
1956[1]	2,174,061	2·31
1961[1]	2,414,985	2·12
1966[1]	2,676,918	2·11
1971[1]	2,862,630	1·35
1976[1]	3,129,384	1·80
1981[1]	3,175,737	0·29
1986[1]	3,307,083	0·82
1991[1]	3,434,949	0·76
1996[1]	3,681,546	1·40
2001[1]	3,820,749	0·74
2006[1]	4,143,282	1·63
2013[1, 2]	4,353,198	0·71

[1]Excluding members of the Armed Forces overseas.
[2]The census of New Zealand is normally quinquennial, but the census falling in 1931 was abandoned as an act of national economy, the census due in 1941 was not taken until 25 Sept. 1945 owing to war conditions and the census due in 2011 was not taken until 5 March 2013 owing to the Christchurch earthquake of Feb. 2011.

The latest census took place on 5 March 2013. Of the 4,353,198 people counted, 4,242,048 were usually resident in the country and 111,150 were overseas visitors.

The usually-resident populations of the 11 regional councils, five unitary authorities and one special territorial authority (all data conforms with boundaries redrawn after the 1989 reorganization of local government) in 2006 and 2013:

| Local government region | Total population | | Percentage change |
	2006 census[1]	2013 census[1]	2006–13 (%)
Northland	148,470	151,689	2·2
Auckland[2]	1,304,961	1,415,550	8·5
Waikato	380,823	403,638	6·0
Bay of Plenty	257,379	267,741	4·0
Gisborne[2]	44,496	43,653	–1·9
Hawke's Bay	147,783	151,179	2·3
Taranaki	104,124	109,608	5·3
Manawatu-Wanganui	222,423	222,669	0·1
Wellington	448,959	471,315	5·0
Total North Island	3,059,421	3,237,048	5·8
Tasman[2]	44,625	47,157	5·7
Nelson[2]	42,888	46,437	8·3
Marlborough[2]	42,558	43,416	2·0
West Coast	31,326	32,148	2·6
Canterbury	521,832	539,433	3·4
Otago	193,803	202,470	4·5
Southland	90,876	93,339	2·7
Total South Island	967,908	1,004,397	3·8
Area outside region[3]	618	600	–2·9
Total New Zealand	4,027,947	4,242,048	5·3

[1]Totals do not add up because of rounding. [2]Unitary Authorities. [3]Special Territorial Authority—Chatham Islands.

The UN gives a projected population for 2020 of 4·83m.

In 2011, 86·2% of the population lived in urban areas. Density, 16 per sq. km (2013).

Resident populations of main urban areas at the 2006 census were as follows:

North Island	
Auckland	1,208,091
Gisborne	32,529
Hamilton	184,838
Kapiti	37,344
Napier	118,404
New Plymouth	49,281
Palmerston North	76,032
Rotorua	53,766
Tauranga	108,882
Wanganui	38,988
Wellington	397,974
Whangarei	49,080
South Island	
Christchurch	360,768
Dunedin	110,997
Invercargill	46,773
Nelson	56,364

Between 2006 and 2013 the number of people who identified themselves as being of European ethnicity rose from 64·8% to 70·0%. Pacific Island people made up 7·0% of the population in 2013 (6·6% in 2006); Asian ethnic groups went from 8·8% in 2006 to 11·1% in 2013. Permanent and long-term arrivals in 2009–10 totalled 82,106, including 15,691 from Australia, 15,340 from the UK, 6,924 from India, 5,951 from the People's Republic of China and 3,476 from the USA. Permanent and long-term departures in 2009–10 totalled 67,599, including 33,027 to Australia, 8,809 to the UK, 2,646 to the USA and 2,398 to the People's Republic of China.

Maori population: 1896, 42,113; 1936, 82,326; 1945, 98,744; 1951, 115,676; 1961, 171,553; 1971, 227,414; 1981, 279,255; 1986, 294,201; 1991, 324,000; 1996, 523,374; 2001, 526,281; 2006, 565,329; 2013, 598,602 (14·1% of the total population compared with 15·1% in 1996). In the 2013 census, 148,395 New Zealand residents (3·5%) said they could hold a conversation about everyday matters in Maori. In 2013, 21·3% of people of Maori ethnicity could hold a conversation about everyday matters in Maori.

From the 1970s organizations were formed to pursue Maori grievances over loss of land and resources. The Waitangi Tribunal was set up in 1975 as a forum for complaints about breaches of the Treaty of Waitangi, and in 1984 empowered to hear claims against Crown actions since 1840. Direct negotiations with the Crown have been offered to claimants and a range of proposals to resolve historical grievances launched for public discussion in Dec. 1994. These proposals specify that all claims are to be met over ten years with treaty rights being converted to economic assets. There have been four recent major treaty settlements: NZ$170m. each for Tainui and Ngai Tahu, the NZ$150m. Sealord fishing agreement and NZ$40m. for Whakatohea in the Bay of Plenty. The Maori Land Court has jurisdiction over Maori freehold land and some general land owned by Maoris under the Te Ture Whenua Maori Act 1993.

English, Maori and New Zealand Sign Language are the official languages. In 2006 New Zealand became the first country to declare sign language as an official language.

Social Statistics

Statistics for calendar years:

	Live births	Deaths	Marriages	Divorces
2008	64,343	29,188	21,948	9,713
2009	62,543	28,964	21,628	8,737
2010	63,897	28,438	20,940	8,874
2011	61,403	30,082	20,231	8,551
2012	61,178	30,099	20,521	8,785
2013	58,717	29,568	19,237	8,279

Birth rate, 2013, 13·1 per 1,000 population; death rate, 6·6 per 1,000 population; infant mortality rate, 4·4 per 1,000 live births. Annual population growth rate, 2011, 0·7%. In 2010 there were 522 suicides (380 males). Expectation of life, 2010–12: males, 79·3 years; females, 83·0. Fertility rate, 2013, 2·0 births per woman. New Zealand legalized same-sex marriage in Aug. 2013.

In 2013 there were 88,235 permanent and long-term immigrants (84,402 in 2012) and 80,328 permanent and long-term emigrants (87,593 in 2012).

Climate

Lying in the cool temperate zone, New Zealand enjoys very mild winters for its latitude owing to its oceanic situation, and only the extreme south has cold winters. The situation of the mountain chain produces much sharper climatic contrasts between east and west than in a north-south direction. Mean daily maximum temperatures and rainfall figures (monthly values for the period 1981–2010):

	Jan. (°C)	July (°C)	Annual rainfall (mm)
Auckland	23·1	14·7	1,212
Christchurch	22·7	11·3	618
Dunedin	18·9	10·0	738
Wellington	20·3	11·4	1,207

The highest temperature recorded in 2011 was 41·3°C, at Timaru on 6 Feb., and the lowest –10·2°C, at Manapouri on 26 July.

Constitution and Government

Definition was given to the status of New Zealand by the (Imperial) Statute of Westminster of Dec. 1931, which had received the antecedent approval of the New Zealand Parliament in July 1931. The Governor-General's assent was given to the Statute of Westminster Adoption Bill on 25 Nov. 1947.

The powers, duties and responsibilities of the *Governor-General* and the *Executive Council* are set out in Royal Letters Patent and Instructions thereunder of 11 May 1917. In the execution of the powers vested in him the Governor-General must be guided by the advice of the Executive Council.

At a referendum on 6 Nov. 1993 a change from a first-past-the-post to a proportional representation electoral system was favoured by 53·9% of votes cast.

Parliament is the *House of Representatives*, consisting of 120 members, elected by universal adult suffrage on the mixed-member-proportional system (MMP) for three-year terms. Citizens and permanent residents (someone who is entitled to live indefinitely in the country) who are aged 18 years and over are required to enrol to vote, but voting is not compulsory. Following the 2017 election there were 71 members from general electorate members (including seven representing Maori electorates) and 49 members selected from party lists. The seven Maori electoral districts cover the whole country. Maori and people of Maori descent are entitled to register either for a general or a Maori electoral district. As at Sept. 2014 there were 239,441 persons on the Maori electoral roll. Parliament made Maori an official language in 1985.

Angelo, Anthony H., *Constitutional Law in New Zealand.* 2011
Joseph, P. A. (ed.) *Essays on the Constitution.* 1995
McGee, D. G., *Parliamentary Practice in New Zealand.* 2nd ed. 1994
Palmer, Geoffrey and Palmer, Matthew, *Bridled Power: New Zealand's Constitution and Government.* 2004
Ringer, J. B., *An Introduction to New Zealand Government.* 1992

National Anthem

'God Defend New Zealand'; words by T. Bracken, tune by J. J. Woods. There is a Maori version, 'Aotearoa', words by T. H. Smith. The UK national anthem has equal status.

Government Chronology

Prime Ministers since 1940. (Lab = Labour; Nat = National)

1940–49	Lab	Peter Fraser
1949–57	Nat	Sidney Holland
1957	Nat	Keith Jacka Holyoake
1957–60	Lab	Walter Nash
1960–72	Nat	Keith Jacka Holyoake
1972	Nat	John Ross Marshall
1972–74	Lab	Norman Eric Kirk
1974	Lab	Hugh Watt (acting)
1974–75	Lab	Wallace Edward Rowling
1975–84	Nat	Robert David Muldoon
1984–89	Lab	David Lange
1989–90	Lab	Geoffrey Palmer
1990	Lab	Mike Moore
1990–97	Nat	Jim Bolger
1997–99	Nat	Jenny Shipley
1999–2008	Lab	Helen Clark
2008–16	Nat	John Key
2016–17	Nat	Bill English
2017–	Lab	Jacinda Ardern

Recent Elections

At general elections on 23 Sept. 2017 turnout was 79·8%. The ruling National Party won 56 seats with 44·4%; the Labour Party 46 with 36·9%; New Zealand First 9 with 7·2%; the Green Party 8 with 6·3%; ACT New Zealand 1 with 0·5%.

Current Government

Governor-General: Dame Patsy Reddy, GNZM, QSO, DStJ (b. 1954; sworn in 28 Sept. 2016).

In Feb. 2019 the coalition government of the Labour Party, New Zealand First and the Green Party consisted of:

Prime Minister, and Minister for Arts, Culture and Heritage, and National Security and Intelligence: Jacinda Ardern; b. 1980 (Labour Party; took office 26 Oct. 2017).

Deputy Prime Minister, Minister of Foreign Affairs, and Minister for State Owned Enterprises, and Racing: Winston Peters.

Minister of Agriculture, and Minister for Biosecurity, Food Safety, and Rural Communities: Damien O'Connor. *Corrections, and Tourism, and Minister for Crown-Maori Relations:* Kelvin Davis. *Defence, and Minister for Veterans:* Ron Mark. *Education, and State Services:* Chris Hipkins. *Energy and Resources, and Research, Science and Innovation, and Minister for Greater Christchurch Regeneration, and Government Digital Services:* Megan Woods. *Finance, and Minister for Sport and Recreation:* Grant Robertson. *Forestry, and Minister for Infrastructure, and Regional Economic Development:* Shane Jones. *Health:* Dr David Clark. *Housing and Urban Development, and Transport:* Phil Twyford. *Immigration, and Minister for Workplace Relations, and ACC (Accident Compensation Corporation):* Iain Lees-Galloway. *Internal Affairs, and Ministers for Children, and Seniors:* Tracey Martin. *Justice, and Minister for Courts, and Treaty of Waitangi Negotiations:* Andrew Little. *Local Government, and Minister for Maori Development:* Nanaia Mahuta. *Police, Fisheries, and Revenue, and Minister for Small Business:* Stuart Nash. *Attorney General, and Minister for Economic Development, the Environment, and Trade and Export Growth:* David Parker. *Minister for Building and Construction, and Ethnic Communities:* Jenny Salesa. *Minister for Social Development, and Disability Issues:* Carmel Sepuloni.

In addition there are eight ministers who are not in the cabinet: *Broadcasting, Communications and Digital Media, Civil Defence, Commerce and Consumer Affairs, and Customs:* Kris Faafoi. *Minister for the Community and Voluntary Sector, Whanau Ora, and Youth:* Peeni Henare. *Employment:* Willie Jackson. *Minister for Pacific Peoples:* Aupito William Sio. *Statistics, and Minister for Climate Change:* James Shaw. *Minister for Women:* Julie Anne Genter. *Conservation, and Minister for Land Information:* Eugenie Sage.

Office of the Prime Minister: http://www.dpmc.govt.nz

Current Leaders

Jacinda Ardern

Position
Prime Minister

Introduction
Jacinda Ardern was sworn in as prime minister on 26 Oct. 2017. The leader of the New Zealand Labour Party, she is her country's youngest prime minister since the mid-19th century.

Early Life
Jacinda Ardern was born on 26 July 1980 in Hamilton, on New Zealand's North Island. She joined the Labour Party at the age of 18. After graduating in communications studies from the University of Waikato in 2001, she worked as a researcher for a Labour member of parliament before joining the staff of then Prime Minister Helen Clark. In 2005 she moved to London, where she worked in the UK cabinet office and the department for business and enterprise. In 2007 she became president of the International Union of Socialist Youth.

Ardern first stood for parliament as Labour candidate for Waikato district in 2008. She lost the seat but entered parliament as a 'list candidate' (as - New Zealand's system of proportional representation ensures that a party's nationwide vote is reflected in its number of MPs). In 2011 and again in 2014 she was narrowly defeated in elections for the seat of Auckland Central, but was nonetheless returned to parliament.

In Feb. 2017 Ardern won a by-election in the Labour stronghold of Mount Albert in Auckland, and the following month was confirmed as Labour's deputy leader. When low poll ratings forced Andrew Little to resign as party leader on 1 Aug. that year, Ardern succeeded him unopposed.

Despite a turnaround in the polls under her leadership, Labour could only come second (with 46 seats) to the National Party (56) in the election of 23 Sept. 2017. The result left both sides vying to form a coalition with the centre-right New Zealand First, which Ardern succeeded in doing after weeks of negotiations. She also garnered support from the Green Party in the 120-seat parliament on a confidence and supply basis.

Career in Office

Ardern, who appointed Winston Peters of New Zealand First as her deputy prime minister, came to power promising a 'fairer New Zealand' with a focus on welfare and environmental issues. In June 2018 she had a baby, becoming only the second elected leader in modern history (after Benazir Bhutto in Pakistan in 1990) to give birth while in office.

Defence

The New Zealand Defence Force consists of three services: the Royal New Zealand Navy, the New Zealand Army and the Royal New Zealand Air Force. New Zealand forces serve abroad in Australia, Iraq and Singapore, and with UN peacekeeping missions.

Defence expenditure in 2013 totalled US$2,715m. (US$622 per capita), representing 1·5% of GDP.

Army

Personnel total in 2011: 4,905, plus reserves numbering 1,789.

Navy

The Navy includes two frigates. The main base and Fleet headquarters is at Auckland.

The Royal New Zealand Navy personnel totalled 2,161 uniformed plus 339 reserve personnel in 2011.

Air Force

Squadrons are based at RNZAF Base Auckland and RNZAF Base Ohakea. Flying training is conducted at Ohakea and Auckland. Ground training is carried out at RNZAF Base Woodbourne.

The uniform strength in 2011 was 2,607 with 186 reserves. There were six combat-capable aircraft.

Economy

Services contributed 19·7% to GDP in 2012–13; followed by finance and real estate, 17·2%; manufacturing, 13·1%; trade and hotels, 12·2%; transport and communications, 11·1%; agriculture, forestry and mining, 6·1%; and public administration and defence, 4·1%.

According to the anti-corruption organization Transparency International, New Zealand ranked second in a 2018 survey of the countries with the least corruption in business and government. It received 87 out of 100 in the annual index.

New Zealand gave US$450m. in international aid in 2017, equivalent to 0·23% of GNI (compared to the UN target of 0·7%).

Overview

Compared to most other OECD countries New Zealand has weathered the global climate of economic uncertainty since 2008 well, although public debt is a concern. Annual GDP growth in the five years to 2015 averaged 2·5%. Previously, the economy had grown every year from 1991 until 2007, although since the beginning of the century much of it was debt-financed. Unemployment rose from 3·7% in 2007 to 6·9% in 2012, thereafter falling to 5·4% in 2015. In March 2018 New Zealand and ten other countries bordering the Pacific (although not the USA) signed the Comprehensive and Progressive Agreement for Trans-Pacific Partnership.

New Zealand went into recession in 2008, the result of a severe drought and the end of a housing boom, exacerbated by the global financial crisis. However, a government stimulus package tied to fast-growing Asian markets and the robust Australian economy brought about a quick rebound.

The effects of the financial crisis, along with earthquakes in 2010 and 2011, saw net government debt increase from 5·5% of GDP in 2008 to 58% in 2015. From 2012 the economy was boosted by post-earthquake

reconstruction projects (although the country suffered further extensive quake damage in Nov. 2016). Tourism and dairy exports are important sources of revenue, with Australia and China the largest export markets. Prior to the 1980s the economy was one of the most regulated and protected in the developed world. Liberalization in the 1990s stalled towards the end of the century, with public ownership of commercial enterprises increasing in the following decade. The impact of low dairy prices on exports coupled with an end to the post-earthquake stimulus package presents challenges for the long term.

Currency

The monetary unit is the New Zealand dollar (NZD), of 100 cents. The total value of notes and coins on issue from the Reserve Bank in Sept. 2010 was NZ$3,979m. Inflation was 0·6% in 2016 and 1·9% in 2017. In Aug. 2009 foreign exchange reserves were US$11,783m. and total money supply was NZ$33,640m. Gold reserves are negligible.

Budget

The government fiscal year begins 1 July; the company and personal financial year begins on 1 April. Total central government revenue for 2014–15 was NZ$83,340m. (NZ$78,688m. in 2013–14). Central government expenditure in 2014–15 was NZ$80,821m. (NZ$78,598m. in 2013–14).

In 2014–15 tax revenue was NZ$69,267m. (NZ$64,312m. in 2013–14). Social benefits was the leading item of expenditure in 2014–15, at NZ$35,067m. (NZ$33,377m. in 2013–14).

There is a Goods and Services Tax (GST) of 15% (reduced rate, 9%).

Performance

There was real GDP growth of 4·2% in 2015, 4·1% in 2016 and 3·0% in 2017. Total GDP was US$205·9bn. in 2017.

Banking and Finance

The central bank and bank of issue is the Reserve Bank (*Governor*, Adrian Orr).

The financial system comprises a central bank (the Reserve Bank of New Zealand), registered banks and other financial institutions. Registered banks include banks from abroad, which have to satisfy capital adequacy and managerial quality requirements. Other financial institutions include the regional trustee banks, now grouped under Trust Bank, building societies, finance companies, merchant banks and stock and station agents. The number of registered banks in 2007 was 17, of which only two (TSB Bank Ltd and Kiwibank Ltd) were not wholly overseas-owned.

The primary functions of the Reserve Bank are the formulation and implementation of monetary policy to achieve the economic objectives set by the government, and the promotion of the efficiency and soundness of the financial system, through the registration of banks, and supervision of financial institutions.

On 30 June 2007 the assets of the Reserve Bank were NZ$21,095m. (including government securities totalling NZ$4,342m. and marketable securities totalling NZ$12,526m.).

Total overseas debt was NZ$246,462m. in June 2010.

The stock exchange in Wellington conducts on-screen trading, unifying the three former trading floors in Auckland, Christchurch and Wellington. There is also a stock exchange in Dunedin.

Energy and Natural Resources

Environment

New Zealand's carbon dioxide emissions from the consumption of energy were the equivalent of 8·8 tonnes per capita in 2011. An *Environmental Performance Index* compiled in 2016 ranked New Zealand 11th of 180 countries, with 88·0%. The index examined various factors in nine areas—agriculture, air quality, biodiversity and habitat, climate and energy, fisheries, forests, health impacts, water and sanitation, and water resources.

Electricity

On 1 April 1987 the former electricity division of the ministry of energy became a state-owned enterprise, the Electricity Corporation of N.Z. Ltd. In 1994 Transpower separated out from the company to operate the national grid. The remainder of ECNZ was subsequently divided in stages into four state-owned enterprises (Contact Energy, Genesis Power Limited, Meridian

Energy Limited and Mighty River Power Limited), causing a competitive wholesale electricity market to be established. Around 70% of the country's electricity is generated by renewable sources. Hydro-electric plants, mainly based in the South Island, account for some 55% with geothermal power, generated in the North Island, accounting for around 8%. The rest comes from natural gas (22%), coal, wind and landfill gas. Electricity generating capacity, 2011, 9·6m. kW. Consumption per capita was 10,081 kWh in 2011.

Electricity consumption statistics (in GWh) for years ended 31 March are:

	Residential	Commercial	Industrial	Total consumption
2003	11,723	7,734	15,431	34,889
2004	12,255	7,389	16,151	35,795
2005	12,161	7,975	16,190	36,326
2006	12,231	8,383	16,780	37,394

New Zealand also has 12 wind farms.

Oil and Gas
Crude oil production was 15m. bbls in 2011. New Zealand's annual crude petroleum imports are more than three times as much as its production. Proven reserves were 113m. bbls in 2011.

In 2013 proven natural gas reserves were 29·4bn. cu. metres. Output in 2011 was 3·8bn. cu. metres and consumption 3·7bn. cu. metres.

Minerals
Coal production in 2010 was 5·33m. tonnes. There were 16 opencast and five underground mines in operation that year, responsible for 75% and 25% of total coal production respectively.

While New Zealand's best known non-fuel mineral is gold (producing about 13·44 tonnes in 2009 worth NZ$662m.) there is also production of silver, ironsand, aggregate, limestone, clay, aluminium, dolomite, pumice, salt, serpentinite, zeolite and bentonite. In addition, there are resources or potential for deposits of titanium (ilmenite beach sands), platinum, sulphur, phosphate, silica and mercury.

Agriculture
About 54% of the land area in 2012 was suitable for agriculture and grazing. The total area of farmland in use in 2010 was 14,580,000 ha.; there were 11,302,000 ha. of grazing, arable, fodder and fallow land, 127,000 ha. of land for horticulture and 1,608,000 ha. of plantations of exotic timber. In 2007, 3·2% of land was arable and 0·2% permanent cropland.

The number of farm holdings as at 30 June 2012 was as follows:

Regional Council	Number of farms
Auckland	3,480
Bay of Plenty	4,785
Gisborne	1,236
Hawke's Bay	2,991
Manawatu-Wanganui	5,421
Northland	4,671
Taranaki	3,240
Waikato	9,900
Wellington	1,983
Total North Island	37,707
Canterbury	8,823
Marlborough	1,701
Nelson	93
Otago	3,681
Southland	3,699
Tasman	1,587
West Coast	738
Chatham Islands	39
Total South Island	20,361
Total New Zealand	58,071

Production of main crops (2011, in 1,000 tonnes): potatoes (estimate), 522; apples (estimate), 438; wheat (2011–12), 489; barley (2011–12), 439; grapes (estimate), 234; maize (2011–12), 211; pumpkins and squash (estimate), 141; tomatoes (estimate), 63; carrots and turnips (estimate), 55; cauliflower and broccoli (estimate), 37.

Livestock, 2010: sheep, 32·56m.; dairy cattle, 5·92m.; beef cattle, 3·95m.; deer, 1·12m.; pigs (2007), 367,000; goats (2007), 112,000; chickens (2010), 13·51m. Total meat produced in 2006–07 was 1·44m. tonnes (including 624,000 tonnes of beef and veal, and 573,000 tonnes of lamb and mutton). Meat industry products are New Zealand's second largest export income earner, accounting for about 12% of merchandise exports. New Zealand's main meat exports are beef, lamb and mutton. About 73% of lamb, 58% of mutton and 57% of beef produced in New Zealand in 2006–07 was exported overseas. The domestic market absorbs over 99% of the pigmeat and poultry produced in New Zealand. 54% of the world's exported sheepmeat comes from New Zealand.

Production of wool for the year 2006–07 was 216,300 tonnes. Milk production for 2010–11 totalled a record 17,339m. litres. In 2011 butter production totalled an estimated 385,000 tonnes and cheese production an estimated 311,000 tonnes.

Forestry
Forests covered 10·15m. ha. in 2015 (39% of New Zealand's land area). New planting was 12,000 ha. in 2011. Introduced pines form the bulk of the large exotic forest estate and among these radiata pine is the best multi-purpose tree, reaching log size in 25–30 years. Other species planted are Douglas fir and Eucalyptus species. Total roundwood production in 2006–07 was 20·04m. cu. metres. The table below shows production of rough sawn timber in 1,000 cu. metres for years ending 31 March:

	Indigenous			Exotic			All Species
	Rimu and Miro	Beech	Total (including others)	Radiata Pine	Douglas Fir	Total (including others)	Total
2004	5	8	16	3,992	178	4,206	4,222
2005	5	7	13	4,178	167	4,379	4,392
2006	0	0	12	4,038	156	4,222	4,234
2007	3	6	9	4,102	157	4,292	4,301

In 2006–07 forest industries consisted of approximately 264 sawmills, seven plywood and 11 veneer plants, and six fibreboard mills.

Production of wood pulp in the year ending 31 March 2007 amounted to 1,528,991 tonnes and of paper (including newsprint paper and paperboard) to 871,946 tonnes.

Fisheries
In 2012 the total catch was 440,683 tonnes, almost entirely from sea fishing. The total value of New Zealand's fisheries exports in 2012 was NZ$1,569m., of which frozen fish exports constituted NZ$259m.

Industry
Statistics of manufacturing industries (in NZ$1m.):

Production year	Salaries and wages paid	Closing stocks of raw materials	Closing stocks of finished goods	Sales	Purchases and other operating expenditure
2010–11	11,729	14,451	37,152	86,728	66,627
2011–12	12,107	16,124	40,447	91,261	71,331

The following is a statement of the value of the products (including repairs) of the principal industries for the year 2011–12 (in NZ$1m.):

Industry group	Salaries and wages paid	Closing stocks of raw materials	Closing stocks of finished goods	Sales	Purchases and other operating expenditure
Dairy and meat products	2,323	1,506	16,718	28,067	25,057
Seafood processing	308	364	1,093	1,857	1,303
Other food	1,018	1,012	2,255	7,023	5,276
Beverage, malt and tobacco	490	1,128	3,361	4,570	3,047
Textile and apparel	422	703	1,024	2,084	1,521
Wood products	1,252	1,216	2,815	7,396	5,721
Printing	443	237	156	1,661	1,009
Petroleum and coal products	134	3,102	3,437	7,986	6,662
Rubber, plastic and other chemical products	1,119	1,824	3,378	7,587	5,573
Non-metallic mineral products	435	279	893	2,461	1,737
Metal products	1,508	1,713	1,981	9,398	6,969
Transport equipment manufacturing	2,244	2,662	2,948	9,598	6,449
Furniture and other manufacturing	410	377	387	1,573	1,004

According to the World Bank's *Doing Business 2017* New Zealand is the easiest country both in which to do business and to start a business.

Labour

The labour force in 2013 was 2,398,000 (2,071,000 in 2003). 77·9% of the population aged 15–64 was economically active in 2013. Of those in employment in 2013, 73·0% worked in services, 20·2% in industry and 6·4% in agriculture. In that year 47·2% of the labour force was female. The unemployment rate in the fourth quarter of 2018 was 4·3%, down from 4·7% in 2017 as a whole. Long-term unemployment is low, with only 9·0% of the labour force in 2010 having been out of work for more than a year.

A minimum wage is set by the government annually. As of 1 April 2010 it was NZ$12·75 an hour; a new rate for those entering the labour market for the first time was introduced in April 2008—it was NZ$10·20 an hour in April 2010. In 2011 there were 12 work stoppages (31 in 2009 and 215 in 1986) with 4,850 person-days of work lost (14,088 in 2009 and 1,329,054 in 1986).

International Trade

In 1990 New Zealand and Australia completed the Closer Economic Relations Agreement (initiated in 1983), which provides for mutual free trade in goods.

Imports and Exports

Trade in NZ$1m. for recent years ending 30 June:

	Imports (c.i.f.)	Exports, including re-exports (f.o.b.)	Balance of merchandise trade
2009	46,139	43,028	−3,110
2010	40,079	40,669	590
2011	45,073	46,072	999
2012	47,451	46,688	−763

The principal imports for the 12 months ended 30 June 2012 were:

Commodity	Value (NZ$1m. c.i.f.)
Petroleum and products	8,366
Mechanical machinery and equipment	6,071
Vehicles, parts and accessories	4,882
Electrical machinery and equipment	3,948
Textiles and textile articles	2,116
Plastics and plastic articles	1,685
Optical, medical and measuring equipment	1,337
Iron or steel articles	1,247
Pharmaceutical products	1,109
Aircraft and parts	1,102

The principal exports for the 12 months ended 30 June 2012 were:

Commodity	Value (NZ$1m. f.o.b.)
Milk powder, butter and cheese	11,625
Meat and edible offal	5,114
Wood and articles of wood	3,060
Crude oil	2,023
Machinery and mechanical appliances	1,865
Fruit	1,587
Fish, crustaceans and molluscs	1,367
Wine	1,177
Electrical machinery, equipment and parts	1,162
Aluminium and aluminium articles	1,144

The principal import suppliers in 2011–12 (imports c.i.f., in NZ$1m.) were: China, 7,658; Australia, 7,240; USA, 4,695; Japan, 3,229; Singapore, 2,283; Germany, 2,076. The leading export destinations in 2011–12 (exports and re-exports f.o.b., in NZ$1m.) were: Australia, 10,460; China, 6,106; USA, 4,083; Japan, 3,387; South Korea, 1,556; UK, 1,443.

Communications

Roads

Total length of roads in 2007 was 93,748 km (65·4% paved), including 172 km of motorways. There were 10,893 km of highways, main or national roads. At 30 June 2008 motor vehicles licensed numbered 4,125,932, of which 2,788,938 were passenger cars and vans. In addition, there were 577,684 trailers and caravans, 519,992 commercial vehicles, and 130,213 motorcycles and mopeds. In 2007 there were 422 deaths in road accidents.

In 2008 there were 34,590 persons employed in road transport. Total expenditure on roads (including infrastructure) by the central government and local authorities combined amounted to NZ$1,751m. in 2008.

Rail

The national rail operator is KiwiRail. In 2008–09 KiwiRail rolling stock included 231 diesel, electric and shunting locomotives, 4,215 freight wagons, 50 passenger carriages and 16 non-passenger coaches.

In 1994 a 24-hour freight link was introduced between Auckland and Christchurch. In 2011, 4,128 km of 1,067 mm gauge railway was open for traffic (504 km electrified). In 2008–09 KiwiRail carried 4·0m. tonnes of freight and 12·4m. passengers. Total income in the financial year 2008–09 was NZ$636·6m. and total expense NZ$573·3m.

Civil Aviation

There are international airports at Wellington, Auckland and Christchurch, with Auckland International being the main airport. The national carrier is Air New Zealand, which was privatized in 1989 but then renationalized in 2001, although in the meantime the government has reduced its stake from 73% to 52%.

There were 4,499 aircraft registered in Dec. 2011. In 2011 there were 1,019,685 domestic and international aircraft movements. A total of

21,852,000 passenger-km were flown in 2010 by New Zealand-based carriers on scheduled services.

Shipping

In Jan. 2014 there were 26 ships of 300 GT or over registered, totalling 146,000 GT. The busiest port is Tauranga, which handled a record 19,736,000 tonnes of cargo in 2013–14 (up from 13,458,000 tonnes in 2008–09). Other major ports are Wellington, Lyttelton and Auckland.

Telecommunications

The predominant telecommunications service provider is Spark New Zealand (or 'Spark'), known as Telecom New Zealand until Aug. 2014. Telecom New Zealand had been formed in 1987 and privatized in 1990. The largest mobile phone operators are Vodafone New Zealand and Spark. In 2013 there were 1,850,000 main (fixed) telephone lines. In the same year active mobile phone subscriptions numbered 4,766,000 (1,057·8 per 1,000 persons). An estimated 82·8% of the population were internet users in 2013. There were 81·3 mobile broadband subscriptions per 100 inhabitants in 2013 and 29·2 fixed broadband subscriptions per 100 inhabitants. In Dec. 2011 there were 2·1m. Facebook users.

Social Institutions

Out of 178 countries analysed in the 2017 *Fragile States Index*—a list published jointly by the Fund for Peace and *Foreign Policy* magazine—New Zealand was ranked the joint ninth least vulnerable (along with Canada) to conflict or collapse. The index is based on 12 indicators of state vulnerability across social, political and economic categories.

Justice

The judiciary consists of the Supreme Court, the Court of Appeal, the High Court and District Courts. All exercise both civil and criminal jurisdiction. The Supreme Court replaced the Privy Council in London as the court of final appeal in 2004. Special courts include the Maori Land Court, the Maori Appellate Court, Family Courts, the Youth Court, Environment Court and the Employment Court. In March 2011 there were 8,755 sentenced inmates of whom 556 were women. Of inmates in 2011, 51·2% (some 4,483) identified themselves as Maori only compared to 33·7% who identified themselves as European only. There were an all-time low 365,185 recorded offences in 2012–13, compared to 394,522 in 2011–12 and 416,324 in 2010–11. The death penalty for murder was replaced by life imprisonment in 1961. In 2015 the World Justice Project *Rule of Law Index*, which provides data on how the rule of law is experienced by the general public across eight categories, ranked New Zealand eighth of 102 countries for criminal justice and ninth for civil justice.

The Criminal Injuries Compensation Act 1963, which came into force on 1 Jan. 1964, provided for compensation of persons injured by certain criminal acts and the dependants of persons killed by such acts. However, this has now been phased out in favour of the Accident Compensation Act 1982 except in the residual area of property damage caused by escapees. The Offenders Legal Aid Act 1954 provides that any person charged or convicted of any offence may apply for legal aid which may be granted depending on the person's means and the gravity of the offence etc. Since 1970 legal aid in civil proceedings (except divorce) has been available for persons of small or moderate means. The Legal Services Act 1991 brought together in one statute the civil and criminal legal aid schemes.

Police

The police are a national body maintained by the central government. In June 2012 there were 8,940 full-time equivalent sworn officers (17·7% female).

Ombudsmen

The office of Ombudsman was created in 1962. From 1975 additional Ombudsmen have been authorized. There are currently two. Ombudsmen's functions are to investigate complaints under the Ombudsman Act, the Official Information Act and the Local Government Official Information and Meetings Act from members of the public relating to administrative decisions of central, regional and local government. In 2011–12, 10,636 complaints and other contacts were received (a 22% increase on 2010–11) and 10,250 were completed.

Education

Education is compulsory between the ages of six and 16. Early childhood services are available for education and care for children from birth to six years of age. In 2009 there were 626 kindergartens and 485 play centres (24 licence exempt). In 2009 there were 39,346 and 15,498 children on the rolls respectively. There were also 464 *te kohanga reo* (providing early childhood education in the Maori language) with 9,288 children, and a number of other providers of early childhood care and education.

In 2009 there were 2,027 primary schools (including full primary, contributing primary and intermediate schools), with 434,810 pupils; the number of teachers was 27,640. A correspondence school for children in remote areas (*Te Kura*) and those otherwise unable to attend school had 6,076 pupils and 270 teachers.

In 2009 there were 336 secondary schools with 20,439 teachers and 273,409 pupils. There were also 149 composite schools with 2,500 teachers and 43,149 pupils.

There were 469,107 (including 43,457 international) enrolments in tertiary institutions in 2009. Of the international students in 2009, 30,946 were from Asia and 4,068 from Europe. The most popular subject areas studied in 2009 by domestic students were society and culture, management and commerce, health, and engineering related technologies. New Zealand has eight state-funded universities—the University of Auckland, Auckland University of Technology, University of Waikato (at Hamilton), Victoria University of Wellington, Massey University (at Palmerston North), the University of Canterbury (at Christchurch), the University of Otago (at Dunedin) and Lincoln University (near Christchurch). The number of students attending universities in 2009 was 154,866. 180,709 students were enrolled in institutes of technology and polytechnics in 2009.

In 2008–09 public expenditure on education came to 6·4% of GDP, representing 17·9% of total government spending. The universities are autonomous bodies. All state-funded primary and secondary schools are controlled by boards of trustees. Education in state schools is free for children under 19 years of age.

The adult literacy rate is at least 99%.

Health

In 2011 there were 14,330 practising doctors. In 2011–12 there were about 14·0m. general practitioner visits and 67·7m. prescription items were dispensed. There were 23 hospital beds per 10,000 population over the period 2005–12. In 2010 New Zealand spent 10·2% of its GDP on health; public expenditure on health in 2009–10 was NZ$16·5bn.

Welfare

On 1 April 1992 the Guaranteed Retirement Income Scheme (GRI) was replaced by the national superannuation scheme which is income-tested. Eligibility has been gradually increased to 65 years. Universal eligibility is available at 70 years. At 1 April 2012 a married, civil union or *de facto* couple received NZ$536·80 per week, a single person living alone NZ$348·92 per week.

Social Welfare Benefits

Benefits	Number of recipients, 2012	Total expenditure (NZ$1,000), 2012
New Zealand Superannuation	598,933	9,855,488
Domestic Purposes' Benefit	112,828	2,103,922
Invalids' Benefit	87,187	1,434,904
Unemployment	57,783	945,876
Sickness	60,361	924,546
Veterans' Pension	9,549	162,239
War Pension	17,697	148,579
Orphans' Benefit/Unsupported Child's Benefit	8,595	111,761
Widows' Benefit	6,082	81,778
Training	6,273	72,707
Total	*965,288*	*15,841,800*

Changes to the welfare system came into effect in July 2013 when three new benefits—jobseeker support, sole parent support and supported living payment—replaced most of the previous main benefits listed above.

Reciprocity with Other Countries
New Zealand has overseas social security agreements with the United Kingdom, the Netherlands, Greece, Ireland, Australia, Jersey and Guernsey, Denmark, Canada and a number of Pacific countries. The main purpose of these agreements is to encourage free movement of labour and to ensure that when a person has lived or worked in more than one country, each of those countries takes a fair share of the responsibility for meeting the costs of that person's social security coverage. New Zealand also pays people eligible for New Zealand Superannuation or veterans' pensions who live in the Cook Islands, Niue or Tokelau.

Religion
No direct state aid is given to any form of religion. According to the Pew Research Center's Forum on Religion & Public Life, in 2010 the population was an estimated 57·0% Christian with a further 36·6% being religiously unaffiliated and 2·1% Hindu. Of the Christians in 2010, an estimated 70% were Protestants and 25% Catholics. Anglicans are the largest denomination, with Roman Catholics second and Presbyterians third. For the Church of England the country is divided into seven dioceses, with a separate bishopric (Aotearoa) for the Maori. The Roman Catholic Church is divided into one Archdiocese (Wellington) and five suffragan dioceses. In Feb. 2019 there were two cardinals.

Culture
World Heritage Sites
There are three UNESCO World Heritage sites under New Zealand jurisdiction. Te Wahipounamu on South Island was listed in 1990; Tongariro National Park, on North Island, was listed in 1990 and 1993; the Sub-Antarctic Islands, consisting of the Auckland Islands, Antipodes Islands, Bounty Islands, Campbell Island and the Snares, were inscribed on the list in 1998.

Press
In 2014 there were 21 paid-for daily newspapers with a combined circulation of 519,000. *TheNew Zealand Herald,* published in Auckland, has the largest daily circulation, followed by *The Dominion Post* and *The Press*. In 2014 there were also three Sunday newspapers, with the *Sunday Star-Times* having the largest circulation. There were three paid-for non-dailies and 164 free non-dailies in 2014. In the 2016 *World Press Freedom Index* compiled by Reporters Without Borders, New Zealand ranked fifth out of 180 countries.

Tourism
There were a record 3,543,631 tourists in the year to March 2017 (2,617,930 in the year to March 2012) of whom 1,406,256 were from Australia, 404,384 were from China, 312,816 were from the USA and 222,784 were from the UK. Tourism receipts totalled NZ$22,848m. in 2010–11. Employment in tourism in 2010–11 totalled 188,100 (full-time equivalents), of whom 120,700 were directly employed in tourism and 67,400 indirectly.

Festivals
The biennial New Zealand Festival takes place in Wellington in Feb./March in even-numbered years. The biennial Christchurch Arts Festival takes place in July/Aug. in odd-numbered years.

Diplomatic Representatives
Of New Zealand in the United Kingdom (2nd Floor, New Zealand House, 80 Haymarket, London, SW1Y 4TQ)
High Commissioner: Sir Jerry Mateparae.

Of the United Kingdom in New Zealand (44 Hill St., Thorndon, Wellington 6011)
High Commissioner: Laura Clarke.

Of New Zealand in the USA (37 Observatory Cir., NW, Washington, D.C., 20008)
Ambassador: Timothy John Groser.

Of the USA in New Zealand (29 Fitzherbert Terr., PO Box 1190, Thorndon, Wellington)
Ambassador: Scott Brown.

Of New Zealand to the United Nations
Ambassador: Craig John Hawke.

Of New Zealand to the European Union
Ambassador: David Taylor.

Territories Overseas
Tokelau
Tokelau is some 500 km to the north of Samoa and comprises three atolls—Atafu, Fakaofo and Nukunonu. The land area is 10·1 sq. km. Population in 2016 was 1,499. Density (2016), 143 per sq. km.

Formal sovereignty over Tokelau was transferred by Britain to New Zealand in 1948. New Zealand legislation is extended to Tokelau only with its consent. In 1994 the Tokelau Administrator's powers were delegated to the *General Fono* (the national representative body), and when the *General Fono* is not in session, to the *Council of Faipule*. Legislation in 1996 gave the *General Fono* a power to make rules, including to impose taxes. Referendums on self-determination took place in Feb. 2006 and again in Oct. 2007, but both fell short of the two-thirds majority in favour needed to effect a change of status.

There are no political parties—in elections held between 23 and 31 Jan. 2017, 21 independents were elected to the *General Fono*.
Administrator: Ross Ardern.
Head of Government: Afega Gaualofa.

Coconuts (the source of copra) are the only cash crop. Pulaka, breadfruit, papayas, the screw-pine and bananas are cultivated as food crops. Livestock comprises pigs, poultry and goats.

Ross Dependency
The Ross Dependency comprises the territories between 160° E. long. and 150° W. long. and south of 60° S. lat. They were brought within New Zealand's jurisdiction in 1923. Laws for the Dependency are made periodically by regulations promulgated by the Governor-General of New Zealand.

The area is 400,000–450,000 sq. km and mostly ice-covered. In Jan. 1957 a New Zealand expedition under Sir Edmund Hillary established a base in the Dependency en route to the South Pole.

The main base—Scott Base, at Pram Point, Ross Island—is manned throughout the year with scientists and support staff, and is managed by a crown agency, Antarctica New Zealand, based in Christchurch.

Self-Governing Territories Overseas
The Cook Islands
The Cook Islands lie between 8° and 23° S. lat., and 156° and 167° W. long. A British protectorate from 1888, they were annexed as part of New Zealand in June 1901 and became a self-governing territory in free association with New Zealand in 1965. The Southern group of islands comprises Aitutaki, Atiu, Mangaia, Manuae and Te au-o-tu, Mauke (Parry Is.), Mitiaro and Rarotonga, while the Northern group consists of Manihiki (Humphrey), Nassau, Palmerston (Avarua), Penrhyn (Tongareva), Pukapuka (Danger), Rakahanga (Reirson) and Suwarrow (Anchorage). The collective area is 236·7 sq. km and the population at the census of 2016 was 14,802. Density (2016), 63 per sq. km. The capital is Avarua on Rarotonga.

At the Legislative Assembly elections held on 14 June 2018 the Democratic Party won 11 of the 24 seats, the Cook Islands Party ten seats and the One Cook Islands Movement one. Independents took two seats.
High Commissioner: Tessa Temata.
Prime Minister: Henry Puna.

The currency is the New Zealand dollar. There are four banks.

The exclusive economic zone seabed has some of the highest concentrations of manganese nodules (rich in cobalt and nickel) in the world. In 2015 forests made up 64% of total land area. Total fishing catch in 2014 was 3,843 tonnes.

Main exports are fish, pearls, and fruit and vegetables. Leading imports are petroleum and related minerals, food, and machinery and transport equipment.

There is an international airport at Rarotonga and domestic services are provided by Air Rarotonga. Two international shipping services connect Rarotonga with Auckland (in New Zealand), Samoa, Tonga and Niue. There were 11,500 mobile phone subscriptions in 2013 and 7,800 fixed telephone subscriptions.

In 2010 there were 24 early childhood education centres, 13 primary schools, four secondary schools, and 12 combined primary and secondary schools. There were 1,841 primary pupils with 123 teachers and 1,893 secondary pupils with 121 teachers in 2010. The Rarotonga Hospital is the largest hospital and the referral hospital for the outer islands.

Niue

Capt. James Cook sighted Niue in 1774 and called it 'Savage Island'. It is the largest uplifted coral island in the world. The area is 261 sq. km. The population at the census of 2011 was 1,613. Density (2011), 6 per sq. km. The capital is Alofi. Niue became a British Protectorate in 1900 and was annexed to New Zealand in 1901. Internal self-government was achieved in free association with New Zealand on 19 Oct. 1974.

At the Legislative Assembly (*Fono*) elections held on 6 May 2017, all 20 members returned were non-partisan.

High Commissioner: Kirk Yates.

Prime Minister: Sir Toke Talagi.

The main commercial crops of the island are coconuts, taro and yams. In 2015, 70% of the total land area was under forest. The total fishery catch in 2013 was 38 tonnes.

Commercial air services link Niue with New Zealand, Australia and Samoa. Niue launched its own mobile phone service in 2011.

The University of the South Pacific has a regional campus in Niue.

Further Reading

New Zealand

Statistics New Zealand. *New Zealand Official Yearbook* (1893–2012).—*Key Statistics: a Monthly Abstract of Statistics.—Profile of New Zealand.*

Belich, James, *Making Peoples: a History of the New Zealanders from Polynesian Settlement to the End of the Nineteenth century.* 1997.—*Paradise Reforged: A History of New Zealanders from the 1880s to the Year 2000.* 2002

Birks, Stuart and Chatterjee, Srikanta, *The New Zealand Economy: Issues & Policies.* 1997

Harland, B., *On Our Own: New Zealand in a Tripolar World.* 1992

Harris, P. and Levine, S. (eds) *The New Zealand Politics Source Book.* 3rd ed. 1999

Massey, P., *New Zealand: Market Liberalization in a Developed Economy.* 1995

Mein Smith, Philippa, *A Concise History of New Zealand.* 2005

Miller, Raymond, *Political Leadership in New Zealand.* 2006

Miller, Raymond, (ed.) *New Zealand Government & Politics.* 5th ed. 2009

Mulgan, Richard, *Politics in New Zealand.* Revised ed. 2004

Rowe, James E., *Economic Development in New Zealand.* 2005

Sinclair, Keith, (ed.) *The Oxford Illustrated History of New Zealand.* 2nd ed. revised. 1996

Sinclair, Keith, revised by Raewyn Dalziel, *A History of New Zealand.* 2001

Wood, G. A. and Rudd, Chris, *The Politics and Government of New Zealand: Robust, Innovative and Challenged.* 2004

For other more specialized titles see under CONSTITUTION AND GOVERNMENT above.

National Statistical Office: Statistics New Zealand, Statistics House, The Boulevard, Harbour Quays, PO Box 2922, Wellington 6140.

Website: http://www.stats.govt.nz

Nicaragua

República de Nicaragua (Republic of Nicaragua)

Capital: Managua
Population projection, 2020: 6·42m.
GNI per capita, 2017: (PPP$) 5,157
HDI/world rank, 2017: 0·658/124
Internet domain extension: .ni

Key Historical Events

There is evidence of settlement by Paleo-Indians in the region around 4000 BC. Spanish explorers, led by Gil González de Ávila, arrived in the west of present-day Nicaragua in 1523. They made contact with the Niquirano and the Chorotegano tribes, thought to have been linked to the Aztec civilization in Mexico, and the Chontal, who shared cultural traits with the Honduran Maya people. Government up to this point was through tribal monarchies and each grouping had distinct customs. In 1524 Francisco Hernández de Córdoba established Granada on Lake Nicaragua and León on Lake Managua. Many indigenous Indians were killed, died of introduced diseases or were enslaved. Estimates suggest the population fell from 1m. to less than 100,000.

In 1538 the Vice Royalty of New Spain was established, spanning Mexico and most of Central America. In 1570 present-day Nicaragua came under the authority of the Captaincy General of Guatemala. A conservative landholding elite developed around Granada, whilst León was associated with the colonial government. British pirates and adventurers took control of parts of the Mosquito Coast during the 17th century. After it declared independence from Spain in 1821, Nicaragua briefly came under the influence of the Mexican Empire, ruled by Agustín de Iturbide. From 1825–38 it was part of the Central American Federation, which unsuccessfully attempted to build a democratic union along US lines.

The 1840s and '50s saw escalating conflict between the elites of Conservative Granada and Liberal León. In 1855 the American mercenary, William Walker, arrived with 57 men to support the Liberal cause. Having defeated the national Nicaraguan army, he took Granada and proclaimed himself the country's ruler. However, his rule was short-lived and he was driven out of office by Honduran forces, with British assistance, two years later. There followed 30 years of relative stability under Conservative rule.

José Santos Zelaya's defeat of the Conservatives in 1893 led to a Liberal dictatorship, which became synonymous with economic decline. Civil war erupted in 1912, prompting the arrival of US forces. The Bryan–Chamarro Treaty of 1914 entitled the USA to a permanent option for a canal route through Nicaragua, a 99-year option for a naval base in the Bay of Fonseca on the Pacific coast and occupation of the Corn Islands on the Atlantic coast. The treaty was not abrogated until 1970 when the Corn Islands returned to Nicaragua.

The Somoza family dominated Nicaragua from 1933 to 1979. Imposing a brutal dictatorship, they plundered a large share of the national wealth. In 1962 the Sandinista National Liberation Front (FLSN; named after the murdered Liberal general, Augusto César Sandino, who fought against the US military presence in the 1920s) was formed to overthrow the Somozas. After 17 years of civil war the Sandinistas triumphed. On 17 July 1979 President Somoza fled into exile. The USA made efforts to unseat the revolutionary government by supporting the Contras (counter-revolutionary forces). It was not until 1988 that the state of emergency was lifted as part of the Central American peace process. Rebel anti-Sandinista activities had ceased by 1990 and the last organized insurgent group negotiated an agreement with the government in April 1994. In Oct. 1998 Hurricane Mitch devastated the country, killing 3,800. In Nov. 2006 presidential elections were won by Daniel Ortega of the FLSN, returning him to power after 16 years in opposition.

Territory and Population

Nicaragua is bounded in the north by Honduras, east by the Caribbean, south by Costa Rica and west by the Pacific. Area, 131,812 sq. km (121,428 sq. km dry land). The coastline runs 450 km on the Atlantic and 305 km on the Pacific. The census population in May 2005 was 5,142,098 (density, 39·0 per sq. km). Estimate, June 2017: 6,393,824. 57·6% of the population were urban in 2011.

The UN gives a projected population for 2020 of 6·42m.

15 administrative departments and two autonomous regions are grouped in three zones. Areas (in sq. km), populations at the 2005 census and chief towns:

	Area	Population	Chief town
Pacific Zone	18,429	2,778,257	
Carazo	1,050	166,073	Jinotepe
Chinandega	4,926	378,970	Chinandega
Granada	929	168,186	Granada
León	5,107	355,779	León
Managua	3,672	1,262,978	Managua
Masaya	590	289,988	Masaya
Rivas	2,155	156,283	Rivas
Central-North Zone	35,960	1,647,605	
Boaco	4,244	150,636	Boaco
Chontales	6,378	153,932	Juigalpa
Estelí	2,335	201,548	Estelí
Jinotega	9,755	331,335	Jinotega
Madriz	1,602	132,459	Somoto
Matagalpa	8,523	469,172	Matagalpa
Nueva Segovia	3,123	208,523	Ocotal
Atlantic Zone	67,039	716,236	
Atlántico Norte[1]	32,159	314,130	Puerto Cabezas
Atlántico Sur[1]	27,407	306,510	Bluefields
Río San Juan	7,473	95,596	San Carlos

[1]Autonomous region.

The capital is Managua with (2005 census population) 908,892 inhabitants. Other cities (2005 populations): León, 139,433; Chinandega, 95,614; Masaya, 92,598; Estelí, 90,294; Tipitapa, 85,948; Matagalpa, 80,228; Granada, 79,418; Ciudad Sandino, 72,501; Juigalpa, 42,763.

The population is of Spanish and Amerindian origins with an admixture of Afro-Americans on the Caribbean coast. The majority of the population is mestizo (mixed Amerindian and white) and white. There are also Blacks and Amerindians. The official language is Spanish.

Social Statistics

2008 estimates: births, 140,000; deaths, 27,000. Estimated rates (per 1,000 population), 2008: births, 24·6; deaths, 4·7. Annual population growth rate, 2000–08, 1·3%. 2013 life expectancy: male 71·8 years; female 77·9. Infant mortality, 2010, 23 per 1,000 live births; fertility rate, 2008, 2·7 births per woman. A law prohibiting abortion was passed in Nov. 2006.

Climate

The climate is tropical, with a wet season from May to Jan. Temperatures vary with altitude. Managua, Jan. 81°F (27°C), July 81°F (27°C). Annual rainfall 38" (976 mm).

Constitution and Government

A new constitution was promulgated on 9 Jan. 1987 and underwent reforms in 1995, 2000 and 2014. It provides for a unicameral 92-seat *National Assembly* comprising 90 members directly elected by proportional representation for a five-year term, together with one seat for the previous president and one seat for the runner-up in the previous presidential election. Citizens are entitled to vote at the age of 16.

The *President* and *Vice President* are directly elected for a five-year term commencing on 10 Jan. following their date of election. Amendments that came into force in Feb. 2014 ended restrictions on presidential re-election. Previously, the president could stand for a second term in office but not consecutively (although in Oct. 2009 the Supreme Court ruled in favour of a petition brought by President Daniel Ortega to remove the barrier against consecutive terms). Also abolished was the need for a minimum required vote to avoid a presidential run-off. Candidates leading after the first round of voting had previously required at least 40% of the vote (or 35% and a 5% margin over the second-placed candidate) to claim outright victory.

National Anthem
'Salve a ti, Nicaragua' ('Hail to thee, Nicaragua'); words by S. Ibarra Mayorga, tune by L. A. Delgadillo.

Recent Elections
Presidential and parliamentary elections took place on 6 Nov. 2016. In the presidential elections incumbent José Daniel Ortega Saavedra of the Sandinista National Liberation Front (FSLN) was elected with 72·4% of votes cast, defeating Maximino Rodríguez (15·0%) and four other candidates. At the parliamentary elections the Sandinista National Liberation Front won 70 seats, the Constitutionalist Liberal Party 13, the Independent Liberal Party 2 and the Nicaraguan Liberal Alliance 2 with three other parties each taking one seat. In addition two seats are reserved for 'special members' (specifically, the runner-up in the presidential election and the outgoing president).

Current Government
President: José Daniel Ortega Saavedra; b. 1945 (FSLN; in office since 10 Jan. 2007, having previously been president from Jan. 1985–April 1990).

Vice President: Rosario Murillo.

In Feb. 2019 the government comprised:

Minister of Agriculture and Forestry: Edward Francisco Centeno Gadea. *Defence:* Martha Elena Ruiz Sevilla. *Development, Industry and Commerce:* Orlando Solórzano Delgadillo. *Education:* Miriam Ráudez. *Energy and Mines:* Salvador Mansell Castrillo. *Environment and Natural Resources:* María José Corea Pérez. *Family:* Johana Vanessa Flores. *Finance and Public Credit:* Iván Acosta Montalván. *Foreign Affairs:* Denis Rolando Moncada Colindres. *Health:* Dr Sonia Castro González. *Interior:* Amelia Coronel Kinloch. *Labour:* Alba Luz Torrez Briones. *Transportation and Infrastructure:* Óscar Salvador Mojica Obregón. *Women:* Ángela Yadira Meza. *Minister in the Office of the President for Special Issues:* Moisés Omar Halleslevens Acevedo.

Nicaraguan Parliament (Spanish only): http://www.asamblea.gob.ni

Current Leaders

Daniel Ortega
Position
President

Introduction
An iconic figure of the Sandinista movement since the late 1970s, Daniel Ortega first served as president from 1985–90 and was elected to further five-year terms in Nov. 2006, Nov. 2011 and Nov. 2016.

Early Life
Ortega was born in Nov. 1945 in La Libertad, Chontales to a middle-class family who opposed the Somoza family's dictatorship. After briefly attending the University of Central America in Managua, Ortega joined the Sandinista National Liberation Front (FSLN) in 1963. In 1967 he was convicted of robbing a bank to raise money for arms. He was released in 1974 in exchange for FSLN-held hostages and spent a brief spell in Cuba.

He led the FSLN in Somoza Debayle's overthrow in 1979 and joined the governing junta. The Sandinistas dominated the junta and established a national constitution and democratic elections, which Ortega won in 1984. His first term was marked by conflict with the US-backed Contras, resulting in tens of thousands of deaths.

In the 1990 elections Ortega suffered a surprise defeat to a US-supported coalition of anti-Sandinista groups led by Violeta de Chamorro. Ortega retained the leadership of the FSLN but was again defeated at the 1996 elections. He survived several scandals, including allegations in 1998 by his step-daughter of sexual abuse, followed in 1999 by a furore over an immunity pact with then President Miguel Aleman, who was facing charges of corruption. Ortega made another unsuccessful bid for office in 2001.

His politics moderated, with him publicly apologizing for excesses during his first presidency and increasingly embracing Catholicism. Despite US opposition to his 2006 presidential candidacy he emerged victorious from the polls in Nov.

Career in Office
Ortega campaigned on a platform of 'unity and reconciliation', symbolized by his appointment of former Contra leader Jaime Morales as vice president. He also sought to reassure foreign investors and the private sector, many of whom feared further deterioration in US–Nicaraguan relations. He announced plans to address poverty, affecting 80% of the population, as well as soaring inflation, crippling interest payments on public debt, a national energy shortage and endemic corruption. In Nov. 2006 the FSLN came out in support of a strict anti-abortion law.

Ortega committed Nicaragua to the Bolivarian Alternative for the Americas (ALBA) while guaranteeing active membership of a free trade agreement with the USA (CAFTA). He pledged to maintain good relations with the USA while simultaneously strengthening links with Iran, Cuba and China. He also signed off a major natural gas deal with Bolivia. Venezuela pledged US$60m. in debt relief and donations for social development and helped establish a 40% Nicaraguan-owned and 60% Venezuelan-owned oil company, Albanic. In Oct. 2007 the Nicaraguan and Honduran governments accepted an International Court of Justice (ICJ) ruling settling a long-running territorial dispute between them. However, in Nov. 2010 a dispute with neighbouring Costa Rica over a river border area led to the deployment of security forces by both countries before the ICJ ruled in Costa Rica's favour in Dec. 2015. In a further territorial arbitration in March 2016, the ICJ ruled in Nicaragua's favour in a maritime border dispute with Colombia.

In 2008 doubts about Ortega's democratic credentials resurfaced and in municipal elections in Nov. that year opposition parties denounced the Sandinista victory as rigged. He also circumvented a constitutional barrier to his standing for re-election through a favourable Supreme Court ruling in Oct. 2010. In the Nov. 2011 presidential polls Ortega retained power with 63% of the vote, although international observers questioned the results. In 2013 the government proposed constitutional reforms extending Ortega's executive powers and permitting limitless presidential re-election. The amendments came into force in Feb. 2014, but opponents claimed that they posed a threat to democracy. In the next elections in Nov. 2016 Ortega won a third consecutive term, with his wife Rosario Murillo as his vice presidential running mate, while the FSLN comfortably maintained its parliamentary majority. Opponents again condemned the polls and the USA similarly expressed concern over the outcome.

From April 2018 Ortega was confronted by nationwide protests after he decreed cuts in pension payments. Although the pension measure was subsequently reversed, continuing opposition to his autocratic regime was met with violent repression by security forces.

Defence
In 2013 defence expenditure totalled US$85m. (US$15 per capita), representing 0·8% of GDP.

Army
The present-day National Army of Nicaragua was established in 1995. Strength (2011) around 10,000.

Navy
The Nicaraguan Navy was some 800 strong in 2011.

Air Force
The Air Force has been semi-independent since 1947. Personnel (2011) 1,200, with no combat-capable aircraft.

Economy

In 2012 agriculture accounted for 20·0% of GDP, industry 26·7% and services 53·3%.

Overview

Despite the global financial crisis that began in 2008, Nicaragua has maintained growth levels above the average in Latin America and the Caribbean. Owing to disciplined macroeconomic policies, combined with a steady expansion of exports and foreign direct investment, the economy grew by an average of 4·8% per year from 2010 to 2014. Furthermore, the country's macroeconomic stability has allowed the government to progress from crisis-control management towards pioneering policy strategies aimed at fighting long-term poverty.

Nonetheless, Nicaragua remains among the least developed countries in the Western hemisphere. Accessing basic services is a daily struggle for large sections of the population despite a gradual reduction in poverty and inequality levels in recent years.

Currency

The monetary unit is the *córdoba* (NIO), of 100 *centavos*, which replaced the córdoba oro in 1991 at par. Inflation was 19·8% in 2008, and more recently 3·5% in 2016 and 3·9% in 2017. In July 2005 Nicaragua had foreign exchange reserves of US$628m. In June 2005 total money supply was 4,746m. córdobas.

Budget

In 2011 budgetary central government revenues were 37,696m. córdobas and expenditures 32,823m. córdobas. Taxes accounted for 84·4% of revenues in 2011; compensation of employees accounted for 36·4% of expenditures.

The standard rate of VAT is 15%.

Performance

The economy grew by 4·8% in 2015, 4·7% in 2016 and 4·9% in 2017. Total GDP in 2017 was US$13·8bn.

Banking and Finance

The Central Bank of Nicaragua came into operation on 1 Jan. 1961 as an autonomous bank of issue, absorbing the issue department of the National Bank. The *President* is Leonardo Ovidio Reyes Ramírez. There were six private commercial banks in 2012.

In 2010 external debt totalled US$4,786m., equivalent to 76·9% of GNI. There is a stock exchange in Managua.

Energy and Natural Resources

Environment

Nicaragua's carbon dioxide emissions from the consumption of energy in 2011 were the equivalent of 0·9 tonnes per capita.

Electricity

Installed capacity in 2011 was 1·1m. kW. In 2011, 3·83bn. kWh were produced; consumption per capita in 2011 was 642 kWh.

Minerals

Production in 2011: gold, 6,395 kg; silver, 7,927 kg.

Agriculture

In 2012 there were an estimated 1·5m. ha. of arable land and 296,000 ha. of permanent cropland. Approximately 199,000 ha. were equipped for irrigation in 2012. Production (in 1,000 tonnes) in 2012: sugarcane, 6,718; maize (estimate), 471; rice (paddy) (estimate), 440; dry beans, 234; groundnuts (estimate), 200; coffee (estimate), 107; oranges (estimate), 100.

In 2013 there were an estimated 3·7m. cattle, 494,000 pigs, 269,000 horses and 21m. chickens. Livestock products (2013 estimates, in 1,000 tonnes): beef and veal, 134; chicken meat, 110; cows' milk, 765; eggs, 28.

Forestry

The forest area in 2015 was 3·11m. ha., or 26% of the land area. Timber production was 6·23m. cu. metres in 2011.

Fisheries

In 2015 the catch was 40,639 tonnes (40,033 tonnes from sea fishing).

Industry

In 2012 manufacturing accounted for 16·4% of GDP. Meat and fish is the dominant sector (around a fifth of output by value in 2012), followed by fabrics and apparel, processed food products and refined oil products. Beverages, dairy products and sugar are also important.

Labour

The labour force in 2013 was 2,599,000 (2,000,000 in 2003). 65·8% of the population aged 15–64 was economically active in 2013. In the same year 5·3% of the population was unemployed.

International Trade

In 2004 Nicaragua signed the Central America-Dominican Republic-United States Free Trade Agreement (CAFTA-DR), along with Costa Rica, the Dominican Republic, El Salvador, Guatemala, Honduras and the USA. The agreement entered into force for Nicaragua on 1 April 2006.

Imports and Exports

In 2010 imports (c.i.f.) were valued at US$4,190·8m. and exports (f.o.b.) at US$1,847·6m.

Main imports in 2010 (US$1m.): machinery and transport equipment, 915·3; mineral fuels and lubricants, 909·1; chemicals and related products, 756·9. Leading exports in 2010 (US$1m.): coffee, 341·5; beef, 307·7; seafood, 136·7.

Main import suppliers, 2010 (US$1m.): USA, 868·6; Venezuela, 742·9; China, 365·5. Leading export markets, 2010 (US$1m.): USA, 606·6; Venezuela, 248·6; El Salvador, 198·2.

Communications

Roads

Road length in 2007 was 20,333 km, of which 1,081 km were main roads. In 2007 there were 101,900 passenger cars (18 per 1,000 inhabitants), 7,700 buses and coaches, 179,900 lorries and vans and 61,200 motorcycles and mopeds. 522 fatalities were caused by road accidents in 2007.

Civil Aviation

In 2013 airports in Nicaragua handled 1,206,172 passengers. The main airport, Augusto C. Sandino International Airport at Managua, handled 1,108,933 passengers in 2009 (of which 963,715 on international flights). There were flights in 2013 from Managua to over 20 international and domestic destinations with a number of different airlines.

Shipping

In Jan. 2014 there were two ships of 300 GT or over registered, totalling 1,000 GT. The Pacific ports are Corinto (the largest), San Juan del Sur and Puerto Sandino through which pass most of the external trade. The chief eastern ports are El Bluff (for Bluefields) and Puerto Cabezas.

Telecommunications

In 2011 there were 288,000 fixed telephone lines; mobile phone subscriptions numbered 4,824,000 in 2011 (81·7 per 100 persons). In 2011, 10·6% of the population were internet users. In Dec. 2011 there were 664,000 Facebook users.

Social Institutions

Out of 178 countries analysed in the 2017 *Fragile States Index*—a list published jointly by the Fund for Peace and *Foreign Policy* magazine—Nicaragua was ranked the 74th most vulnerable to conflict or collapse. The index is based on 12 indicators of state vulnerability across social, political and economic categories.

Justice

The judicial power is vested in a Supreme Court of Justice at Managua, five chambers of second instance and 153 judges of lower courts.

The population in penal institutions in Dec. 2012 was 9,168 (153 per 100,000 of national population). Nicaragua was ranked 87th of 102 countries for criminal justice and 99th for civil justice in the 2015 World Justice Project

Rule of Law Index, which provides data on how the rule of law is experienced by the general public across eight categories.

Education

Adult literacy rate in 2005 was 78·0% (male, 78·1%; female, 77·9%). In 2007 there were 214,615 pre-primary schoolchildren (9,680 teachers), 952,964 primary school pupils (31,188 teachers) and 470,520 secondary school pupils (15,126 teachers). Nicaragua has a number of public and private universities. The largest university is the National Autonomous University of Nicaragua, established in 1812.

In 2010 public expenditure on education came to 4·5% of GDP.

Health

In 2011 there were 32 public hospitals. Nicaragua had a provision of nine hospital beds per 10,000 population in the period 2006–12. There were 5,495 physicians, 260 dentistry personnel, and 8,323 nursing and midwifery personnel in 2014.

In *Water: At What Cost? The State of the World's Water 2016*, WaterAid reported that 13·0% of the population does not have access to safe water.

Religion

The prevailing form of religion is Roman Catholicism (3·38m. adherents in 2010 according to estimates by the Pew Research Center's Forum on Religion & Public Life), but religious liberty is guaranteed by the Constitution. The Pew Research Center estimated that there were also 1·53m. Protestants in 2010 and 730,000 people with no religious affiliation. In Feb. 2019 the Roman Catholic Church had one cardinal.

Culture

World Heritage Sites

Nicaragua has two sites on the UNESCO World Heritage List: the Ruins of León Viejo (inscribed on the list in 2000), a 16th century Spanish settlement; and León Cathedral (2011), a Baroque and Neoclassical monument built between 1747 and the early 19th century.

Press

In 2008 there were seven paid-for daily newspapers in Nicaragua, with a total circulation of 175,000.

Tourism

In 2011 there were 1,060,000 non-resident tourists, spending US$378m.

Diplomatic Representatives

Of Nicaragua in the United Kingdom (Suite 31, Vicarage House, 58–60 Kensington Church St., London, W8 4DB)
    Ambassador: Guisell Morales-Echaverry.

Of the United Kingdom in Nicaragua (embassy in Managua closed in March 2004)
    Ambassador: Ross Denny (resides in San José, Costa Rica).

Of Nicaragua in the USA (1627 New Hampshire Ave., NW, Washington, D.C., 20009)
    Ambassador: Francisco Obadiah Campbell Hooker.

Of the USA in Nicaragua (Km. 5·5 Carretera Sur, Managua)
    Ambassador: Kevin K. Sullivan.

Of Nicaragua to the United Nations
    Ambassador: Jaime Hermida Castillo.

Of Nicaragua to the European Union
    Ambassador: Mauricio Lautaro Sandino Montes.

Further Reading

Baracco, Luciano, *Nicaragua: The Imagining of a Nation—From Nineteenth-Century Liberals to Twentieth-Century Sandinistas.* 2005
Horton, Lynn, *Peasants in Arms: War and Peace in the Mountains of Nicaragua, 1979–94.* 1998
National Statistical Office: Dirección General de Estadística y Censos, Managua.
Website (Spanish only): http://www.inide.gob.ni

Niger

République du Niger (Republic of Niger)

Capital: Niamey
Population projection, 2020: 24·07m.
GNI per capita, 2017: (PPP$) 906
HDI/world rank, 2017: 0·354/189
Internet domain extension: .ne

Key Historical Events

Niger has been settled for at least 6,000 years. Early cattle-herding and agricultural economies developed in the Sahara and by the 14th century the Hausa people had established city-states in the south of the region. Meanwhile Berbers dominated trade routes in the north, which came under the control of the Songhai Empire around 1515. After the fall of the Songhai Empire in the late 16th century the Bornu Empire expanded into the centre and east of the region, while the Hausa people retained the south and the Tuareg were prominent in the north. The Djerma people later became established in the southwest.

In the 19th century Fulani Muslims vied for power with the Hausas and Bornus. French forces took control of the region at the end of the century, creating the military district of Niger as part of the larger territory of Haut-Sénégal et Niger. Tuareg resistance led to a major uprising during the First World War, which was put down by combined French and British forces. France formally designated Niger as a colony in 1922.

Gradual decentralization of power began in 1946. Niger became an autonomous state in 1958 and on 3 Aug. 1960 it obtained independence, with Hamani Diori as its first president. Diori was deposed in a 1974 military coup and Lieut. (later Col.) Seyni Kountché took power. Kountché survived several coup attempts as he replaced the military government with civilians. He was succeeded in 1987 by Ali Seibou, whose National Movement for the Development of Society (MNSD), became Niger's only legal political party. A new constitution was approved in 1989 and in the early 1990s Seibou legalized opposition parties.

In 1990 conflict broke out in the north between government forces and the Tuaregs, who demanded autonomy. Relations with Libya deteriorated as the Niger government suspected its neighbour of encouraging the insurgency. In 1995 a ceasefire established land rights for the Tuaregs and formalized their relationship with government. The agreement has largely held despite sporadic conflict.

In July 1991 a constitutional conference removed Seibou's powers and established a transitional government under André Salifou. Multi-party elections were held in 1993 and, following victory for the Alliance of the Forces of Change, Mahamane Ousmane was elected president. However, the MNSD won back control of the National Assembly in 1995 and tensions mounted between President Ousmane and the government. In Jan. 1996 Ousmane was deposed in a military coup and replaced by Col. Ibrahaim Baré Mainassara (known as Baré).

Strict military rule was eventually relaxed and in July 1996 Baré claimed decisive victory in a disputed election. In April 1999 Baré was killed by his bodyguards and Major Daoude Wanké took power with military backing. Under international pressure, multi-party elections were held in Oct. 1999. Mamadou Tandja of the MNSD was elected president and his party won control of the National Assembly. The new National Assembly established amnesties for those involved in the 1996 and 1999 coups. In Dec. 2004 Mamadou Tandja won a second term as president, with Hama Amadou as prime minister.

Niger continues to suffer severe economic problems. In 2005 the government increased tax on basic goods (including food), leading to widespread protests and strikes until the government granted exemptions on some staples. Drought and locust infestations the previous year devastated harvests. After UN World Food Programme warnings that millions faced severe malnutrition, an international relief effort staved off the worst of the disaster but thousands still died of diseases associated with hunger and poverty.

In 2006 the International Court of Justice settled a land dispute with Benin by awarding Niger most of the river islands along the shared border. In April 2009 the government reached a peace agreement with the rebel Movement of Niger People for Justice after several years of troubles. The following month President Mamadou Tandja dismissed parliament and suspended the constitution after a constitutional court ruling against his attempt to hold a referendum on his running for a third presidential term. In Aug. 2009 the referendum, criticized for lacking legitimacy, supported Tandja's candidacy but elections in Oct. were boycotted by opponents. Tandja claimed a landslide victory but was removed from office in a coup in Feb. 2010, with power falling to a military junta. The presidential elections in Jan.–March 2011 signalled a peaceful return to democracy with outgoing President Salou Djibo heralding them as an example for Africa.

Territory and Population

Niger is bounded in the north by Algeria and Libya, east by Chad, south by Nigeria, southwest by Benin and Burkina Faso, and west by Mali. Area, 1,186,408 sq. km, with a population at the 2012 census of 17,138,707; density, 14·4 per sq. km. In 2011, 17·2% of the population were urban.

The UN gives a projected population for 2020 of 24·07m. Niger's population has more than doubled since the early 1990s.

The country is divided into the capital—Niamey, an autonomous district—and seven regions. Area, population and chief towns:

Regions	Sq. km	Population (2012 census)	Chief town	Population (2012 census)
Agadez	634,209	487,620	Agadez	110,497
Diffa	140,216	593,821	Diffa	39,960
Dosso	31,002	2,037,713	Dosso	58,671
Maradi	38,581	3,402,094	Maradi	267,249
Niamey	670	1,026,848	Niamey	978,029
Tahoua	106,677	3,328,365	Tahoua	117,826
Tillabéri	89,623	2,722,482	Tillabéri	22,774
Zinder	145,430	3,539,764	Zinder	235,605

The population is composed chiefly of Hausa (53%), Djerma-Songhai (21%), Fulani (10%), Tuareg (10%) and Kanuri-Manga (4%). The official language is French. Hausa, Djerma and Fulani are national languages.

Social Statistics

Estimates, 2008: births, 787,000; deaths, 219,000. Estimated birth rate in 2008 was 53·5 per 1,000 population (the highest in the world); estimated death rate, 14·9. Niger has one of the youngest populations of any country, with 73% of the population under the age of 30 and 49% under 15. Infant mortality, 2010, 73 per 1,000 live births. Annual population growth rate, 2000–08, 3·6%. Expectation of life at birth, 2013, 58·3 years for males and 58·6 for females. Fertility rate, 2012, 7·6 children per woman (the highest anywhere in the world). A UNICEF report published in 2014 revealed that 77% of women aged 20–49 had been married or in union before the age of 18, the highest percentage of any country.

Climate

Precipitation determines the geographical division into a southern zone of agriculture, a central zone of pasturage and a desert-like northern zone. The country lacks water, with the exception of the southwestern districts, which are watered by the Niger and its tributaries, and the southern zone, where there are a number of wells. Niamey, 95°F (35°C). Annual rainfall varies from 22" (560 mm) in the south to 7" (180 mm) in the Sahara zone. The rainy season lasts from May until Sept., but there are periodic droughts.

Constitution and Government

Following a coup in Feb. 2010 a military junta suspended the constitution and dissolved the cabinet. In March 2010 the military leadership announced it had formed a transitional government and promised to return Niger to democracy. In Oct. 2010 a new constitution received 90·2% support in a referendum; turnout was 52·7%. Establishing Niger as a secular state, it reimposes a limit of two five-year terms on the presidency (a provision abandoned in the constitution promulgated the previous year), prohibits members of the military from running for office and guarantees that the government will release data on national oil and mining revenues. Legislative power rests with the unicameral National Assembly of 171 members, elected by universal suffrage for a five-year term.

National Anthem

'Auprès du grand Niger puissant' ('By the banks of the mighty great Niger'); words by M. Thiriet, tune by R. Jacquet and N. Frionnet.

Recent Elections

In the first round of presidential elections held on 21 Feb. 2016 incumbent Mahamadou Issoufou won 48·4% of the votes, Hama Amadou (a former prime minister) 17·7%, Seyni Oumarou (a second former prime minister) 12·1% and Mahamane Ousmane (a former president) 6·3%. There were 11 other candidates. Turnout was 66·8%. In the run-off on 20 March 2016 Mahamadou Issoufou won 92·5% of the votes and Hama Amadou 7·5%. Turnout was 59·8%.

Parliamentary elections were also held on 21 Feb. 2016. The Nigerien Party for Democracy and Socialism (PNDS) won 75 seats; the Nigerien Democratic Movement for an African Federation (MODEN/FA), 25; the National Movement for the Development of Society (MNSD), 20; the Patriotic Movement for the Republic (MPR-JAMHURIYA), 13; the Nigerien Movement for Democratic Renewal–the Party for Socialism and Democracy in Niger (MNRD–PSDN), 6. 11 smaller parties each won five seats or fewer.

Current Government

President: Mahamadou Issoufou; b. 1952 (in office since 7 April 2011).
　　Prime Minister: Brigi Rafini; b. 1953 (in office since 7 April 2011).
　　In Feb. 2019 the government comprised:
　　Minister of State for Interior, Public Security, Decentralization and Traditional and Religious Affairs: Bazoum Mohamed. *Agriculture and Livestock:* Albadé Abouba.
　　Minister of Oil: Foumakoye Gado. *Finance:* Mamadou Diop. *Foreign Affairs, Co-operation, African Integration and Expatriate Affairs:* Kalla Ankourao. *Transport:* Mahamadou Karidjo. *Hydrology and Sanitation:* Issoufou Katambé. *National Defence:* Kalla Moutari. *Justice and Keeper of the Seals:* Marou Amadou. *Youth and Sports:* Moctar Kassoum. *Humanitarian Action and Disaster Management:* Magagi Laouan. *Communication:* Habi Mahamadou Salissou. *Employment, Labour and Social Protection:* Mohamed Ben Omar. *Planning:* Kané Aïchatou Boulama. *Trade and Promotion of the Private Sector:* Sadou Seydou. *Primary Education, Literacy, Promotion of National Languages and Civic Education:* Daouda Mamadou Marthé. *Lands, Urban Planning and Housing:* Waziri Maman. *Population:* Amadou Aïssata. *Higher Education, Research and Innovation:* Yahouza Sadissou. *Posts, Telecommunications and Digital Economy:* Sani Maïgochi. *Infrastructure:* Kadi Abdoulaye. *Mines:* Hassane Barazé Moussa. *Energy:* Amina Moumouni. *Public Health:* Dr Illiassou Maïnassara. *Professional and Technical Education:* Tidjani Idrissa Abdoulkadri. *Secondary Education:* Mohamed Sanoussi Elhadji Samro. *Cultural Renaissance, Arts and Social Modernization:* Assoumana Mallam Issa. *Tourism and Handicrafts:* Ahmed Boto. *Public Service and Administrative Reform:* Kaffa Rakiatou Christelle Jackou. *Youth Entrepreneurship:* Ibrahim Issifi Sadou. *Promotion of Women and Child Protection:* Elbak Adam Zeinabou. *Environment, Urban Sanitation and Sustainable Development:* Almoustapha Garba. *Community Development and Land Management:* Amani Abdou. *Industry:* Mallam Zaneidou Amirou. *Government Spokesperson:* Zakaria Abdourarahamane. *Minister in the Presidency:* Rhissa Ag Boula. *Minister in Charge of Relations with Institutions:* Barkaï Issouf.
　　Office of the President (French only): http://www.presidence.ne

Current Leaders

Mahamadou Issoufou

Position
President

Introduction
Mahamadou Issoufou was sworn in as president on 7 April 2011. The veteran opposition leader defeated rival candidate Seyni Oumarou, a former ally of deposed leader Mamadou Tandja, in a run-off on 12 March 2011. The election fulfilled a pledge by the military that it would reinstate civilian rule following the ousting of Tandja in a coup in 2010. Heading the Nigerien Party for Democracy and Socialism (PNDS), Issoufou has previously served as prime minister and as president of the National Assembly. He was re-elected in March 2016.

Early Life
Issoufou, an ethnic Hausa, was born in 1952 in Dan Daji, in the Tahoua department of central Niger. Trained as a mining engineer in France, Issoufou returned to Niger to work for French company Areva. From 1980 he was national director of mines for five years before becoming secretary-general of the Mining Company of Niger.

In Feb. 1993, at the country's first open elections, Issoufou was elected to parliament for the PNDS. Later that month he came third in presidential polling, marking the first of four failed election bids. He was appointed prime minister by the successful candidate, Mahamane Ousmane, in April 1993 but resigned in Sept. 1994 in protest at Ousmane's decree diminishing prime ministerial influence.

After parliamentary elections in 1995 had led to the establishment of a new coalition, Issoufou was appointed president of the National Assembly. Following a military coup in Jan. 1996 and subsequent flawed presidential elections, he spent intermittent periods under house arrest. He made two further unsuccessful bids for the presidency in 1999 and 2004.

In 2009 he was charged with misappropriating funds after the opposition called for a general strike to protest Mamadou Tandja's attempt at changing the constitution to secure a third term. Issoufou briefly fled the country but the ousting of Tandja and the establishment of a transitional junta allowed him to return to national politics. He gained 58% of the vote in the second round of presidential elections in March 2011, defeating Seyni Oumarou.

Career in Office
Issoufou pledged to secure a more equal distribution of the wealth from Niger's substantial uranium reserves. Among his first challenges was coping with the influx of refugees fleeing conflict in Libya and Côte d'Ivoire. An alleged assassination plot against him was then foiled in July 2011. In May 2013 there were simultaneous suicide bombings at a military barracks and a French-run uranium mining site in the north of the country by suspected Islamist militants.

Issoufou announced the formation of a new government in Aug. 2013 in an effort to reinforce internal political stability and security. Nonetheless, in Dec. that year thousands of protesters staged an anti-government rally, organized by a new coalition of opposition parties, over the failure to improve living standards. In Dec. 2015 Issoufou announced that the government had foiled another plot to overthrow him and that nine senior military personnel had been arrested. Opposition figures disputed the claim, however, and accused the government of trying to manipulate the political climate ahead of elections in Feb. and March 2016 that Issoufou won in a second round run-off. Despite claims that the result was fraudulent, the National Movement for the Development of Society agreed to join the government in Aug. 2016 following Issoufou's call to the country's opposition parties to form a national union administration.

Islamist extremist attacks in the Sahel region have continued to threaten Niger's political stability. In March 2017 the government declared a state of emergency in the west of the country and in July that year Niger and four other West African states agreed to form a regional military force to confront growing militancy.

Defence

Selective conscription for two years operates. Defence expenditure totalled US$70m. in 2012 (US$4 per capita), representing 1·1% of GDP.

Army

There are three military districts. Strength (2011) 5,200. There are additional paramilitary forces of 5,400.

Air Force

In 2011 the Air Force had 100 personnel. There are no combat-capable aircraft.

Economy

Agriculture accounted for 38·1% of GDP in 2012, industry 21·1% and services 40·8%.

Overview

Niger is among the poorest countries in the world, ranking 187th of 188 countries in the 2015 UN Human Development Index. Long-term GDP growth has been low and volatile, averaging 2·6% per year between 1980 and 2014 and failing to keep pace with population growth averaging 3·4% annually over the period. The economy is dominated by agriculture, uranium mining and development assistance, the last financing about 45% of the national budget. A democratically-elected government took office in April 2011 following an earlier military coup in 2010 and announced its intention to accelerate economic development and reduce corruption. GDP grew by over 11% in 2012 owing to new investment in oil production, higher uranium production and a good harvest. However, floods in the third quarter of 2012 caused extensive structural damage and loss of life, while the country has also been affected by insecurity in neighbouring Mali.

Currency

The unit of currency is the *franc CFA* (XOF) with a parity of 655·957 francs CFA to one euro. In June 2005 total money supply was 170,798m. francs CFA and foreign exchange reserves were US$177m. There was deflation of 0·2% in 2016 but then inflation of 2·4% in 2017.

Budget

In 2012 revenue totalled 729·3bn. francs CFA and expenditure 823·6bn. francs CFA.

Performance

The economy grew by 4·3% in 2015 and 4·9% in both 2016 and 2017. Total GDP in 2017 was US$8·1bn.

Banking and Finance

The regional Central Bank of West African States (BCEAO)—*Governor*, Tiémoko Meyliet Koné—functions as the bank of issue. There were ten banks operating in Feb. 2012.

In 2010 external debt totalled US$1,127m., equivalent to 20·5% of GNI. There is a stock exchange in Niamey.

Energy and Natural Resources

Environment

In 2011 Niger's carbon dioxide emissions from the consumption of energy were the equivalent of 0·1 tonnes per capita.

Electricity

Installed capacity was approximately 0·1m. kW in 2011. Production in 2011 amounted to 295m. kWh, with consumption per capita 55 kWh.

Minerals

Large uranium deposits are mined at Arlit and Akouta. Uranium production (2010), 4,198 tonnes. Niger's uranium production is the fifth largest in the world. Phosphates are mined in the Niger valley, and coal reserves are being exploited by open-cast mining (production of hard coal in 2011 was 246,011 tonnes). Salt production in 2011 was an estimated 30,000 tonnes.

Agriculture

There were an estimated 15·9m. ha. of arable land in 2013 and 100,000 ha. of permanent crops. About 100,000 ha. were equipped for irrigation in 2013. Production in 2013 (in 1,000 tonnes): millet, 2,922; cow peas, 1,790; onions, 1,448; sorghum, 1,320; groundnuts, 343; cabbages, kale, etc., 206; sugar-cane, 195; tomatoes, 189. Livestock (2013): goats, 14·3m.; cattle, 10·7m.; sheep, 10·7m.; camels, 1·7m.; asses, 1·7m.; chickens (estimate), 18m.

Forestry

There were 1·14m. ha. of forests in 2015 (1% of the land area). Timber production in 2011 was 10·79m. cu. metres, mainly for fuel.

Fisheries

There are fisheries on the River Niger and along the shores of Lake Chad. In 2011 the catch was 53,173 tonnes, exclusively from inland waters.

Industry

Some small manufacturing industries, mainly in Niamey, produce textiles, food products, furniture and chemicals. Output of cement in 2011 (estimate), 72,500 tonnes.

Labour

The estimated economically active population in 2009 totalled 4,803,000 (68% males). Agriculture, fisheries and forestry remains the largest sector of employment.

Niger had 0·12m. people living in slavery according to the Walk Free Foundation's 2013 *Global Slavery Index*.

International Trade

Imports and Exports

In 2008 imports (c.i.f.) were valued at US$1,247·5m. and exports at US$503·1m. Main imports in 2008: machinery and transport goods, 20·2%; petroleum and petroleum products, 15·2%; cereal and cereal preparations, 11·4%; medicinal and pharmaceutical products, 9·5%. Main exports in 2008: uranium ores and concentrates, 57·5%; livestock, 9·2%; textile fibres, 6·1%; cotton fabrics, 4·5%. Main import suppliers in 2008 (as % of total): France, 13·2; China, 12·6; USA, 7·6; Netherlands, 7·2. Main export destinations in 2008 (as % of total): France, 33·3; USA, 17·6; Nigeria, 11·8; Japan, 9·9.

Communications

Roads

In 2007 there were 18,949 km of roads including 3,912 km of paved roads. Niamey and Zinder are the termini of two trans-Sahara motor routes; the Hoggar–Aïr–Zinder road extends to Kano and the Tanezrouft–Gao–Niamey road to Benin. A 648 km 'uranium road' runs from Arlit to Tahoua. There were, in 2005, 57,732 passenger cars, 11,261 vans, 2,613 buses and 1,035 lorries. In 2007 there were 676 road accidents resulting in 265 fatalities.

Civil Aviation

There is an international airport at Niamey (Diori Hamani Airport), which handled 154,460 passengers in 2009 and 3,327 tonnes of freight. In 2010 there were international flights to Abidjan, Abuja, Accra, Algiers, Bamako, Casablanca, Cotonou, Dakar, Nouakchott, Ouagadougou, Paris and Tripoli (Libya) as well as domestic flights; nine airlines flew to Niamey in 2010.

Shipping

Sea-going vessels can reach Niamey (300 km inside the country) between Sept. and March.

Telecommunications

There were 100,500 fixed telephone subscriptions in 2012 (equivalent to 5·9 per 1,000 inhabitants) and 5,396,000 mobile phone subscriptions (or 314·5 per 1,000 inhabitants). In 2011, 1·3% of the population were internet users.

Social Institutions

Out of 178 countries analysed in the 2017 *Fragile States Index*—a list published jointly by the Fund for Peace and *Foreign Policy* magazine—Niger was ranked the 20th most vulnerable to conflict or collapse. The index is based on 12 indicators of state vulnerability across social, political and economic categories.

Justice

There are Magistrates' and Assize Courts at Niamey, Zinder and Maradi, and justices of the peace in smaller centres. The Court of Appeal is at Niamey.

The population in penal institutions in 2012 was 6,899 (42 per 100,000 of national population). 54·0% of prisoners had yet to receive a trial according to 2014 estimates by the International Centre for Prison Studies.

Education

Adult literacy in 2012 was 31%. In 2007 there were 31,131 teaching staff for 1,235,065 primary school pupils and 7,852 teaching staff for 213,991 secondary school pupils. There were 11,208 students in tertiary education (1,095 academic staff) in 2006. There is a university and an Islamic university.

In 2006 public expenditure on education came to 3·3% of GNI and 17·6% of total government spending.

Health

During the period 2000–09 there were three hospital beds per 10,000 inhabitants. There were 427 physicians, 28 dentists, 1,988 nurses, 500 midwives and 22 pharmacists in 2008.

In *Water: At What Cost? The State of the World's Water 2016*, WaterAid reported that 41·8% of the population does not have access to safe water.

Religion

According to the Pew Research Center's Forum on Religion & Public Life, in 2010 the population was an estimated 98·4% Muslim (nearly all Sunnis). There are also small numbers of Protestants and people with no religious affiliation.

Culture

World Heritage Sites

Niger has three sites on the UNESCO World Heritage List: the Aïr and Ténéré Natural Reserves (inscribed on the list in 1991), part of the largest protected area in Africa (7·7m. ha.); and the historic centre of Agadez (2013), a site containing numerous palatial and religious buildings. The W-Arly-Pendjari Complex (1996 and 2017), shared with Benin and Burkina Faso, is an area including the largest and most important continuum of terrestrial, semi-aquatic and aquatic ecosystems in the West African savannah belt.

Press

In 2008 there was one government-owned daily newspaper (*Le Sahel*) and 45 private non-daily newspapers.

Tourism

In 2012 there were 94,000 non-resident tourists; spending by tourists totalled US$86m. in 2011.

Diplomatic Representatives

Of Niger in the United Kingdom
    Ambassador: Ado Elhadji Abou (resides in Paris).

Of the United Kingdom in Niger
    Ambassador: Cat Evans (resides in Bamako, Mali).

Of Niger in the USA (2204 R. St., NW, Washington, D.C., 20008)
    Ambassador: Hassana Alidou.

Of the USA in Niger (BP 11201, Rue des Ambassades, Niamey)
    Ambassador: Eric P. Whitaker.

Of Niger to the United Nations
    Ambassador: Abdallah Wafy.

Of Niger to the European Union
    Ambassador: Ousmane Alhassane Abba.

Further Reading

Miles, W. F. S., *Hausaland Divided: Colonialism and Independence in Nigeria and Niger.* 1994
National Statistical Office: Institut National de la Statistique, 182 rue de la Sirba, BP 13416, Niamey.
Website (French only): http://www.stat-niger.org

Nigeria

Federal Republic of Nigeria

Capital: Abuja
Population projection, 2020: 206·15m.
GNI per capita, 2017: (PPP$) 5,231
HDI/world rank, 2017: 0·532/157
Internet domain extension: .ng

Key Historical Events

The earliest evidence of human settlement in Nigeria dates from 9000 BC and by 2000 BC its inhabitants were cultivating crops and domestic animals. However, the first organized society was of the Nok people, from around 800 BC to AD 200. Traces of Nok influence are visible in Nigerian art today, particularly in areas such as Igbo, Ukwe, Esie and Benin City. By AD 1000, Nok had given way to the Kanem, thanks to the trans-Saharan trade route that ran from West Africa to the Mediterranean.

In the 11th century northern Nigeria split into seven independent Hausa city-states, Biram, Daura, Gobir, Kano, Katsina, Rano and Zaria. By the 14th century, two states had developed in the south, Oyo and Benin, with the Igbo people of the southeast living in small village communities. South of the Hausa states and west of the Niger, the Ife flourished between the 11th and 15th centuries. The importance of the Ife civilization is evident today; all Yoruba states claim that their leaders are descended from the Ife as a way of establishing legitimacy, and its ritual is imitated in their modern public ceremonies.

Most of the north was held by the Songhai empire by the early 16th century, only to be taken later in the century by Kanem-Bornu, allowing the Hausa states to retain their autonomy. At the end of the 18th century, Fulani religious groups waged war in the north, merging states to create the single Islamic state of the Sokoto Caliphate.

In the late 15th century Portuguese navigators, following the demise of the spice trade, began to purchase slaves from middlemen in the region. They were followed by British, French and Dutch traders. Wealthy traders established towns such as Bonny, Owome and Okrika. Slave trading had a profound effect on Nigeria. From the 1650s until the 1860s, it caused a forced migration of around 3·5m. people. Within Nigeria itself, the defensive measures adopted to avoid enslavement led to the reinforcement of ethnic distinctions and of the north-south divide.

After the abolition of the slave trade in Britain in 1807, attempts to find a lucrative alternative and to discourage the predominance of slavery in Nigeria (other countries continued to trade in slaves until 1875) led to a large-scale campaign to encourage the production of palm oil for export. This itself caused the development of an internal slave trade, involving slaves in the collection and manufacture of palm fruits, as well as the transportation of the oil. The British also took over the mines at Jos at the expense of the livelihoods of independent tin producers. When heavy reliance on mining exports resulted in the neglect of agricultural work, Nigeria experienced its first food shortage.

Religious missions were active at this time, with Presbyterians, Methodists, Baptists and the Church Missionary Society (CMS) operating in Lagos, Abeokuta, Ibadan, Oyo and Ogbomosho. The CMS pioneered trade on the Niger by encouraging merchants to run steamboats, partially as a means of travel for the missionaries but also to ship goods.

In 1804 Usuman dan Fodio began a 'Holy war' to reform the practice of Islam in the north, conquering the Hausa city-states, though Kanem-Bornu retained its independence. However, by the late 19th century Kanem-Bornu's power was in decline. Usuman's son, Muhammed Bello, established a state centred at Sokoto, controlling most of northern Nigeria for the rest of the century. In the south, the Oyo region was troubled by civil wars, only brought to a close when the British intervened and the Oyo Empire collapsed. Britain took Lagos as its colony in 1861.

In 1879 Sir George Goldie gained all British firms trading on the Niger, and in the 1880s took over French companies trading there, signing treaties with African leaders and enabling Britain's domination of southern Nigeria in 1884–85. In 1887, Jaja, an African trader based in the Niger Delta, was deported following his fierce opposition to European competition. Goldie's firm received a British Royal Charter as the Royal Niger Company to administer the Niger River and north Nigeria, and this monopoly of trade on the river angered Africans and Europeans alike. The Royal Niger Company also lacked sufficient power to control north Nigeria. In 1900 its charter was revoked and British forces moved in, taking Sokoto in 1903. By 1906 Britain controlled Nigeria as the Colony (Lagos), the Protectorate of Southern Nigeria and the Protectorate of Northern Nigeria, amalgamating the regions in 1914 to establish the Colony and Protectorate of Nigeria. The administration was based on existing leadership systems. Yet the appointment of African officials failed to gain wide acceptance from Nigeria's people. The British governor made all major decisions, and the traditional authority of African rulers was weakened irreparably.

British dominance met with major resistance from the Nigerian people. In the south, the tribal Yoruba group, the Ijebu, fought against colonial rule in 1892, as did the Aro in the east and the Aniocha (both Igbo groups) in the west. There were also rebellions in the north. The British forces responded with brutality, destroying the homes of many Nigerians in order to secure their capitulation.

British colonial rule brought development in the transportation and communications systems and a shift towards cash crops. Western and Christian influences prevailed, including widespread use of the English language. This influence spread far more rapidly in the south, where British control had been secure over a longer period, and this added to the growing disparity between north and south. Nigerian forces helped defeat the German army in Cameroon during the First World War, involved in an arduous campaign until 1916.

Growing unrest and widespread anticolonialism became focused in the 1920s as demands for African representation increased. In 1923 Herbert Macaulay, grandson of the first Nigerian to be ordained, established the first Nigerian political party, the Nigerian National Democratic Party. In 1944 he united the party with several others to form the National Council of Nigeria and the Cameroons (NCNC). In response to this activity, the British attempted to quell demands for an end to colonial rule by granting some political reforms. In 1947 they announced a new constitution that they claimed would give traditional authorities a stronger voice. This met with resistance, and in 1951 the British agreed to form a new constitution that would provide for elected representation on a regional basis.

Three political parties developed, the National Council of Nigeria and the Cameroons (later the National Convention of Nigerian Citizens), largely supported by the Igbo, the Action Group, with mostly Yoruba membership, and the Northern People's Congress (NPC). When the constitution failed in 1952, a new one divided Nigeria into three regions, Eastern, Western and Northern, plus the federal territory of Lagos. In 1956 the Western and Eastern regions became self-governing, as did the Northern region in 1959.

In 1960 Nigeria declared independence. Elections failed to elect any one party by a majority, and the NPC and the NCNC formed a coalition government, with Abukar Tafawa Balewa (NPC) as prime minister. Nnamdi Azikiwe, who had helped Herbert Macaulay to establish the NCNC in 1944, was governor-general. When Nigeria became a republic in 1963 Azikiwe became president.

Continuing conflict between north and south undermined the new republic. In 1966 fighting culminated in a military coup that installed Maj.-Gen. Aguiyi-Ironsi, an Igbo, as head of a military government. Another coup later in the year placed Lieut.-Col. Yakubu Gowon in power and saw many northern Igbo massacred. In May 1967 the Igbo people of the south declared their region independent from the rest of the country, naming the breakaway republic Biafra. Civil war raged for three years until federal Nigeria triumphed at the price of 1m. dead and widespread famine and destruction.

This was followed by a period of relative prosperity as oil prices rose. Foreign interest and investment flourished but government overspending and high levels of corruption and crime led to social chaos. In the 1980s recession sent oil prices down, and Nigeria found itself struggling with major debt, rising inflation and mass unemployment.

Gowon's regime was overthrown in 1975 by Gen. Murtala Muhammed whose plans for a new capital to be built at Abuja drained the economy. He was assassinated in 1976, to be succeeded by Gen. Olusegun Obasanjo who

Palgrave Macmillan (ed.), *The Statesman's Yearbook 2020*,
https://doi.org/10.1057/978-1-349-95940-2_143

oversaw the transition to civilian rule, while juggling the need for Western aid with his support for African nationalist movements.

In 1979 elections brought Alhaji Shehu Shagari to power. Shagari's government came under popular attack for alleged corruption but he was re-elected in 1983, amidst rumours of voting irregularities. Under Shagari relations with the USA improved, heralded by a visit from President Jimmy Carter. However, dogged by worsening economic problems, Shagari was ousted in a military coup in 1983 and replaced by Gen. Muhammadu Buhari. Buhari's regime quickly fell out of favour with the public when it arrested not only the politicians blamed for the country's social and economic problems, but also journalists and academics.

A bloodless coup in 1985 brought to power Maj.-Gen. Ibrahim Babangida, who promulgated a new constitution with the aim of returning to civilian government. Babangida, however, clung to power and refused to accept electoral defeat in 1990, 1992 and 1993. Unrest eventually forced his resignation, but after just three months of rule by an interim leader, one of Babangida's long-term allies, Gen. Sani Abacha, became president and closed down all unions and political institutions. He extended his military rule for a further three years in 1995, proposing a return to civilian rule after this period. To this end five political parties were formed in 1996. However, the Abacha regime attracted international controversy when it executed writer Ken Saro-Wiwa and eight other human rights activists for alleged seditious political activity. Nigeria was suspended from the Commonwealth as a result. Further outrage followed with the arrest of former leader Obasanjo and the murder of the wife of leading political dissident, Chief Moshood Abiola, who had claimed victory at the presidential elections of 1993. Rioting and civil unrest broke out across Nigeria and Abacha's family was accused of siphoning off US$4bn. of national assets.

Abacha died in office in 1998. Maj.-Gen. Abdusalam Abubakar came to power and brought about a return to civilian rule, scrapping plans that would have extended Abacha's rule and releasing political prisoners. Abiola was scheduled to be freed as part of this process but died the day before his scheduled release. In Feb. 1999 Nigeria chose Obasanjo, the 62-year-old retired general and previous military leader, to be president.

This transition of power greatly improved Nigeria's international standing and the country was readmitted to the Commonwealth. However, tribal and religious conflict continued and fighting between the Igbo Christians and Hausa Muslims over the implementation of Islamic law has left thousands dead. Obasanjo's re-election in 2003 was accompanied by violence and rumours of ballot-rigging and bribery.

In July 2005 the Paris Club (an informal grouping of wealthy nations) wrote off around US$20bn. of Nigeria's debt. Assisted by high oil prices, Nigeria had paid off the remaining US$10bn. by April 2006, the first African nation to fully service its Paris Club debt. In April 2007 Umaru Yar'Adua won disputed presidential elections. In March 2008 Nigeria and Cameroon reached agreement on the long-running dispute over sovereignty of the Bakassi Peninsula.

In May 2010 Yar'Adua died and was succeeded by the vice president, Goodluck Jonathan, who won the presidential election of March 2011. In Dec. 2011 he declared a state of emergency following a spate of attacks by the Islamist militia group Boko Haram. Founded in 2002, the group intensified its attacks from 2009, principally focusing on Christians in the north of the country. In May 2013 the government sent troops into three northern states in a bid to contain the militias amid growing international concern that the organization might destabilize the entire Lake Chad basin region. In April 2014 the group kidnapped 200 girls from a boarding school in Chibok, prompting an international campaign to try and recover them, while in Aug. it announced a caliphate in the northeastern territories under its control, although the government in Abuja rejected the declaration. In Feb. 2015 Nigeria entered into an alliance with Cameroon, Chad and Niger to combat the further spread of Boko Haram's influence. Former military dictator Muhammadu Buhari became president in May 2015. He had defeated Goodluck Jonathan in elections two months earlier that were held up as a positive model to the rest of Africa.

Territory and Population

Nigeria is bounded in the north by Niger, east by Chad and Cameroon, south by the Gulf of Guinea and west by Benin. It has an area of 923,768 sq. km (356,667 sq. miles). For sovereignty over the Bakassi Peninsula *see* CAMEROON: Territory and Population. Census population, 2006, 140,431,790 (69,086,302 females); population density, 152·0 per sq. km. Nigeria is Africa's most populous country and the world's seventh most populous. The United Nations predicts that by 2050 it will be ranked third, after India and China. In 2011, 50·5% of the population were urban.

The UN gives a projected population for 2020 of 206·15m.

There were 36 states and a Federal Capital Territory (Abuja) in 2006. Area, population and capitals of these states:

State	Area (in sq. km)	Population (2006 census)	Capital
Adamawa	36,917	3,178,950	Yola
Bauchi	45,837	4,653,066	Bauchi
Benue	34,059	4,253,641	Makurdi
Borno	70,898	4,171,104	Maiduguri
Gombe	18,768	2,365,040	Gombe
Jigawa	23,154	4,361,002	Dutse
Kaduna	46,053	6,113,503	Kaduna
Kano	20,131	9,401,288	Kano
Katsina	24,192	5,801,584	Katsina
Kebbi	36,800	3,256,541	Birnin-Kebbi
Kogi	29,833	3,314,043	Lokoja
Kwara	36,825	2,365,353	Ilorin
Nassarawa	27,117	1,869,377	Lafia
Niger	76,363	3,954,772	Minna
Plateau	30,913	3,206,531	Jos
Sokoto	25,973	3,702,676	Sokoto
Taraba	54,473	2,294,800	Jalingo
Yobe	45,502	2,321,339	Damaturu
Zamfara	39,762	3,278,873	Gusau
Federal Capital Territory	7,315	1,406,239	Abuja
Total North	*730,885*	*75,269,722*	
Abia	6,320	2,845,380	Umuahia
Akwa Ibom	7,081	3,902,051	Uyo
Anambra	4,844	4,177,828	Awka
Bayelsa	10,773	1,704,515	Yenagoa
Cross River	20,156	2,892,988	Calabar
Delta	17,698	4,112,445	Asaba
Ebonyi	5,670	2,176,947	Abakaliki
Edo	17,802	3,233,366	Benin City
Ekiti	6,353	2,398,957	Ado Ekiti
Enugu	7,161	3,267,837	Enugu
Imo	5,530	3,927,563	Owerri
Lagos	3,345	9,113,605	Ikeja
Ogun	16,762	3,751,140	Abeokuta
Ondo	14,606	3,460,877	Akure
Osun	9,251	3,416,959	Oshogbo
Oyo	28,454	5,580,894	Ibadan
Rivers	11,077	5,198,716	Port Harcourt
Total South	*192,883*	*65,162,068*	

Abuja replaced Lagos as the federal capital and seat of government in Dec. 1991.

Estimated population of the largest cities, 2010:

Lagos	10,788,000
Kano	3,271,000
Ibadan	2,855,000
Abuja (capital)	2,010,000
Port Harcourt	1,807,000
Kaduna	1,476,000
Benin City	1,311,000
Ogbomosho	1,039,000
Onitsha	867,000
Aba	836,000
Maiduguri	827,000
Ilorin	788,000

Lagos is estimated to have overtaken Cairo in 2011 as Africa's most populous city.

There are about 250 ethnic groups. The largest linguistic groups are the Yoruba (17·5% of the total) and the Hausa (17·2%), followed by Igbo (13·3%), Fulani (10·7%), Ibibio (4·1%), Kanuri (3·6%), Egba (2·9%), Tiv (2·6%), Bura (1·1%), Edo (1·0%) and Nupe (1·0%). The official language is English, but 50% of the population speak Hausa as a *lingua franca*.

Social Statistics

2008 estimates: births, 6,050,000; deaths, 2,420,000. Rates, 2008 estimates (per 1,000 population): births, 40; deaths, 16. Infant mortality, 2010, 88 (per 1,000 live births). Annual population growth rate, 2005–10, 2·7%. Life expectancy at birth, 2013, was 52·2 years for males and 52·8 years for females. Fertility rate, 2008, 5·3 children per woman.

Climate

Lying wholly within the tropics, temperatures everywhere are high. Rainfall varies greatly, but decreases from the coast to the interior. The main rains occur from April to Oct. Lagos, Jan. 81°F (27·2°C), July 78°F (25·6°C). Annual rainfall 72" (1,836 mm). Ibadan, Jan. 80°F (26·7°C), July 76°F (24·4°C). Annual rainfall 45" (1,120 mm). Kano, Jan. 70°F (21·1°C), July 79°F (26·1°C). Annual rainfall 35" (869 mm). Port Harcourt, Jan. 79°F (26·1°C), July 77°F (25°C). Annual rainfall 100" (2,497 mm).

Constitution and Government

The constitution was promulgated on 5 May 1999, and entered into force on 29 May. Nigeria is a federation, comprising 36 states and a federal capital territory. The constitution includes provisions for the creation of new states and for boundary adjustments of existing states. The legislative powers are vested in a *National Assembly*, comprising a *Senate* and a *House of Representatives*. The 109-member Senate consists of three senators from each state and one from the federal capital territory, who are elected for a term of four years. The House of Representatives comprises 360 members, representing constituencies of nearly equal population as far as possible, who are elected for a four-year term. The *President* is elected for a term of four years and must receive not less than one-quarter of the votes cast at the federal capital territory. A president may not serve more than two consecutive four-year terms. In 2006 Olusegun Obasanjo sought to alter the constitution to allow him to run for a third term, but he failed to win backing for the amendment.

National Anthem

'Arise, O compatriots, Nigeria's call obey'; words by a collective, tune by B. Odiase.

Government Chronology

(APC = All Progressives Congress; NCNC = National Council of Nigeria and the Cameroons; NPN = National Party of Nigeria; PDP = People's Democratic Party; n/p = non-partisan)

Heads of State since 1963.

President of the Republic		
1963–66	NCNC	Benjamin Nnamdi Azikiwe
Heads of the Military Government		
1966	military	Johnson Aguiyi-Ironsi
1966–75	military	Yakubu Gowon
1975–76	military	Murtala Ramat Muhammed
1976–79	military	Olusegun Obasanjo
President of the Republic		
1979–83	NPN	Shehu Shagari
Head of the Federal Military Government		
1983–85	military	Muhammadu Buhari
Chairman of the Armed Forces Ruling Council, then Chairman of the National Defence and Security Council		
1985–93	military	Ibrahim Babangida

(continued)

Head of the Interim National Government		
1993	n/p	Ernest Shonekan
Chairmen of the Provisional Ruling Council		
1993–98	military	Sani Abacha
1998–99	military	Abdulsalam Abubakar
Presidents of the Republic		
1999–2007	PDP	Olusegun Obasanjo
2007–10	PDP	Umaru Yar'Adua
2010–15	PDP	Goodluck Jonathan
2015–	APC	Muhammadu Buhari

Recent Elections

Presidential elections held on 23 Feb. 2019 were won by Muhammadu Buhari, the incumbent president and candidate for All Progressives Congress (APC) party, with 55·6% of votes cast. He defeated Atiku Abubakar of the People's Democratic Party (PDP), who took 41·2%. There were a further 71 candidates. Turnout was 34·7%.

In elections to the House of Representatives also held on 23 Feb. 2019 the APC won 216 seats, PDP 114 and others 20. Ten seats were yet to be declared.

In Senate elections held on the same day, 64 seats went to the APC and 41 to the PDP. The Young Progressive Party won one seat and three seats were yet to be declared.

Hamalai, Ladi, Egwu, Samuel and Omotola, J. Shola, *Nigeria's 2015 General Elections*. 2017

Current Government

President and Minister of Petroleum Resources: Muhammadu Buhari; b. 1942 (APC; sworn in 29 May 2015).

Vice President: Yemi Osinbajo.

In Feb. 2019 the government comprised:

Minister of Agriculture: Audu Ogbeh. *Budget and National Planning:* Udoma Udo Udoma. *Communication:* Adebayo Shittu. *Defence:* Mansur Dan Ali. *Education:* Adamu Adamu. *Environment:* Ibrahim Usman Jibril. *Federal Capital Territory:* Muhammadu Bello. *Finance:* Zainab Ahmed. *Foreign Affairs:* Geoffrey Onyeama. *Health:* Isaac Adewole. *Industry, Trade and Investment:* Okechukwu Enelamah. *Information and Culture:* Lai Mohammed. *Interior:* Abdulrahman Dambazau. *Justice:* Abubakar Malami. *Labour and Employment:* Chris Ngige. *Mines and Steel Development:* Vacant. *Niger Delta:* Usani Uguru. *Power, Works and Housing:* Babatunde Fashola. *Science and Technology:* Ogbonaya Onu. *Transportation:* Rotimi Amaechi. *Water Resources:* Suleiman Adamu. *Women's Affairs:* Vacant. *Youth and Sports:* Solomon Dalong.

Ministers of State: Heineken Lokpobiri (for *Agriculture*); Hadi Sirika (for *Aviation*); Zainab Ahmed (for *Budget and National Planning*); Anthony Onwuka (for *Education*); Khadija Bukar Ibrahim (for *Foreign Affairs*); Osagie Ehanire (for *Health*); Stephen Ocheni (for *Labour and Employment*); Abubakar Bawa Bwari (for *Mines and Steel Development*); Claudius Omoleye Daramola (for *Niger Delta*); Ibe Kachikwu (for *Petroleum*); Mustapha Baba Shehuri (for *Power, Works and Housing*); Aisha Abubakar (for *Industry, Trade and Investment*).

Nigerian Parliament: http://www.nassnig.org

Current Leaders

Muhammadu Buhari

Position
President

Introduction
Muhammadu Buhari took office as president on 29 May 2015. A retired major-general in the Nigerian army, he previously spent two years as the country's head of state following a military coup on 31 Dec. 1983. His defeat of Goodluck Jonathan in the 2015 presidential election marked the first time that an incumbent Nigerian president had been defeated at the polls. However, his effectiveness in office has been disrupted by absences abroad for treatment for an undisclosed illness.

Early Life

Muhammadu Buhari was born on 17 Dec. 1942 in the northern state of Katsina. In 1961 he joined the army and in the course of his career underwent military training in the United Kingdom (1962–64), India (1973) and the USA (1979–80). In 1975, after participating in the military coup that replaced Yakubu Gowon with Murtala Muhammed, he was named military governor of what was then known as North-Eastern state. In the wake of Muhammed's assassination, he was appointed federal commissioner for petroleum resources by Olusegun Obasanjo.

Buhari returned to regular army duties with the restoration of civilian government in 1979. However, exasperation with the government's perceived mishandling of the economy led to another military coup in Dec. 1983 and the installation of Buhari as the country's head of state. Buhari's authoritarian regime was marked by economic austerity, heavy restrictions on imports, draconian drug laws, the breaking of ties with the IMF, a crackdown on dissent and also a wide-ranging campaign against corruption for which he maintains a reputation to this day. In Nigerian political life, 'Buharism' has become synonymous with the economic and social policies of that period. However, in Aug. 1985 he was ousted by the military and replaced with Ibrahim Babangida. In 1994 he was appointed executive chairman of the newly-formed Petroleum Trust Fund under Sani Abacha, a position he held until its disbandment in 1999.

In 2003 Buhari ran unsuccessfully for president against the incumbent, Olusegun Obasanjo of the People's Democratic Party (PDP). He was again defeated by the PDP candidate, Umaru Yar'Adua, in 2007, and in 2011 by Goodluck Jonathan (a result that led to several hundred deaths in widespread protests). In 2014 the All Progressives Congress nominated Buhari to contest the 2015 election against Jonathan. Buhari, a Muslim who counted on the strong support of the country's northern regions, campaigned on the promise of a tough stance against the extremist Islamist insurgency led by Boko Haram and the elimination of corruption. In an election declared clean by international observers, he gained 15·4m. votes against 12·9m. for Jonathan, who did not contest the result. Buhari was inaugurated on 29 May 2015.

Career in Office

On confirmation of his victory, Buhari called successfully for calm between supporters of the rival candidates. He promptly initiated an overhaul of the energy industry, splitting the state-owned Nigerian National Petroleum Corporation into two entities and announcing that he would serve as the country's petroleum resources minister. In Jan. 2016 he claimed that the Nigerian army had succeeded in degrading Boko Haram to the extent that the sect could 'no longer launch military style attacks as they had done in the past'. He again asserted in Dec. that year that the extremist group was facing imminent military defeat, but sporadic attacks continued through 2017 and 2018, along with other militant action against installations in the oil-producing Niger Delta. Furthermore, separatist sentiment in the former breakaway territory of Biafra resurfaced in Aug.–Sept. 2017 amid reports of repressive army operations.

Speculation about Buhari's health and capacity to govern increased in 2017 as he spent extended periods abroad for medical treatment between Feb. and Aug., leaving Vice President Yemi Osinbajo in charge. However, in April 2018 Buhari confirmed his intention to run for a further term. He was politically weakened in July as the APC lost its majority in the Senate amid a flood of party defections but he was nevertheless re-elected president in Feb. 2019.

Defence

In 2013 defence expenditure totalled US$2,143m., equivalent to US$12 per capita and representing 0·8% of GDP.

Army

Strength (2011) 62,000. Equipment in 2011 included 266 main battle tanks.

Navy

In 2011 the fleet included one German-built frigate and 21 patrol and coastal combatants. There is a small aviation element. Naval personnel in 2011 totalled 8,000. The main bases are at Apapa (Lagos) and Calabar.

Air Force

Personnel (2011) total 10,000 although the force has a very limited operational capacity. There were 55 combat-capable aircraft in 2011 including F-7s and Aero L-39s, but the serviceability of much of the equipment is in doubt. In addition there were nine attack helicopters in 2011.

Economy

Crude petroleum and mining contributed 36·8% to GDP in 2012; followed by agriculture, forestry and fishing, 32·6%; trade and hotels, 15·6%; and finance and real estate, 5·9%.

Overview

Since independence in 1960, political insecurity has hindered economic development and deterred foreign investment. GDP per capita is low, at approximately US$1,968 in 2017 according to World Bank figures, and unemployment was 7·0% that year. According to the United Nations, over 42·4% of the population lived in poverty in 2017.

Nonetheless, the economy has strong fundamentals and overtook South Africa's to become Africa's largest in 2014. Nigeria is also Africa's largest oil exporter and holds the continent's greatest reserves of natural gas. The oil and gas sector accounted for 95% of all export earnings, 80% of government revenue and approximately 9% of GDP in 2017, and was also among the pioneers in adopting and implementing the Extractive Industries Transparency Initiative (EITI) in 2011, which aims to improve governance in the hydrocarbon industry.

A ten-year rift with the International Monetary Fund ended with an agreement in Jan. 1999 on a Fund-monitored reform programme, including provisions for abolishing the dual exchange rate, ending subsidies on local fuel and expanding privatization. Between 2004 and 2007 there were wide-ranging reforms, particularly in the management of public finance, governance and the banking sector. External debt was also reduced following negotiations with international creditors to eradicate major arrears, with the result that foreign debt represented only 3% of GDP in 2014, although it had risen to 5·1% by 2017.

Since the beginning of the 21st century Nigeria has had one of the highest GDP growth rates in Sub-Saharan Africa. It averaged 10·2% annually between 2003 and 2010 although then only 5·2% between 2011 and 2014. The economy weathered the global financial crisis and also a 2009 domestic banking crisis resulting in part from countercyclical policies. A sovereign wealth fund (comprising a stabilization fund, an infrastructure fund and an inter-generational saving fund) was launched in Oct. 2011.

The collapse in global oil prices from 2014 had a significant impact on fiscal and external accounts. In 2015 exports dropped by 40%, pushing the current account deficit from a surplus of 0·2% of GDP to a deficit of 2·4%. Fuel shortages and security concerns compounded the situation and hindered private sector activity. GDP growth fell from 6·3% in 2014 to 2·7% in 2015 before Nigeria went into recession in 2016 as the economy shrank by 1·6%. In 2017 the government instituted an economic recovery plan and GDP growth staged a partial recovery, measuring 0·8%.

The economy continues to face a range of challenges. Despite growth in non-oil sectors—notably agriculture, trade and services—the outlook remains inextricably linked to the global oil price. The government aims to further diversify economic activity in the face of continued volatility and weak investment. However, security challenges and high levels of poverty and unemployment threaten longer-term prospects.

Currency

The unit of currency is the *naira* (NGN) of 100 *kobo*. It was devalued by 8% in Nov. 2014. In Feb. 2015 the central bank ceased weekly foreign exchange sales designed to support the currency, so effectively implementing a further *de facto* devaluation of the naira. In June 2016 the naira's peg to the dollar was removed and a flexible currency exchange regime was introduced in a bid to engineer a further devaluation. Foreign exchange reserves were US$44,786m. in May 2009 (US$7,100m. in 1998) and gold reserves were 687,000 troy oz. Inflation rates (based on IMF statistics):

2008	2009	2010	2011	2012	2013	2014	2015	2016	2017
11·6%	12·5%	13·7%	10·8%	12·2%	8·5%	8·0%	9·0%	15·7%	16·5%

In June 2009 total money supply was ₦4,247·6bn.

Budget

The financial year is the calendar year. 2011 budgetary central government revenue, ₦3,554m. (including taxes, 32·4%); expenditure, ₦3,794m. (including compensation of employees, 45·4%; use of goods and services, 17·7%).

VAT was raised from 5% to 10% in May 2007, but as a result of a general strike in protest against the increase was lowered back to 5% a month later.

Performance

Real GDP growth rates (based on IMF statistics):

2008	2009	2010	2011	2012	2013	2014	2015	2016	2017
7·2%	8·4%	11·3%	4·9%	4·3%	5·4%	6·3%	2·7%	−1·6%	0·8%

Before the discovery of oil in the early 1970s Nigeria's GDP per head was around US$200. By the early 1980s it had reached around US$800, but has now declined to some US$300. Total GDP in 2017 was US$375·8bn., making Nigeria Africa's largest economy.

Banking and Finance

The Central Bank of Nigeria (CBN) is the bank of issue (*Governor*, Godwin Emefiele).

In 2004 a major banking reform was announced, consolidating the existing institutions at the time (nearly 100) into 25 large universal banks. However, despite attempts to strengthen the banking sector, the financial condition of the banks deteriorated. Subsequently the CBN requested technical assistance from the IMF to strengthen the banking system. Another banking crisis in 2008 prompted a ₦600bn. bailout from the Central Bank to five of the leading banks: Intercontinental Bank, Oceanic International Bank (now Ecobank), Union Bank of Nigeria, Bank PHB (now Keystone Bank) and Afribank (now Skye Bank). More ambitious reforms took effect in Oct. 2010. In 2007 bank reserves at the CBN totalled ₦1,195bn. and CBN foreign assets amounted to ₦6,570bn.

Nigeria was one of three countries and territories named in a report in June 2005 as failing to co-operate in the fight against international money laundering. In June 2006 Nigeria was delisted and its formal monitoring was ended a year later. The Financial Action Task Force on Money Laundering was set up by the G7 group of major industrialized nations.

Foreign debt amounted to US$7,883m. in 2010, down from US$22,060m. in 2005 and US$31,355m. in 2000—this was equivalent to just 4·5% of GNI (down from 22·3% in 2005 and 77·9% in 2000).

Nigeria attracted US$5,609m. worth of foreign direct investment in 2013, down from a record US$8,915m. in 2011.

The Nigerian Stock Exchange is in Lagos.

Energy and Natural Resources

Environment

Nigeria's carbon dioxide emissions from the consumption of energy were the equivalent of 0·5 tonnes per capita in 2011.

The *Climate Change and Environmental Risk Atlas 2014* produced by Maplecroft, a risk analytics company, ranked Nigeria as the country facing the sixth highest economic and social risk from climate change by 2025.

Electricity

Installed capacity, 2011 estimate, 8·4m. kW. Production, 2011, 27·03bn. kWh (21% hydro-electric); consumption per capita was 165 kWh in 2011. Power cuts are frequent, with both businesses and homes having to rely on generators as demand for electricity far outweighs supply.

Oil and Gas

Nigeria's oil production is the largest of any African country and amounted to 95·3m. tonnes in 2017. Reserves in 2017 totalled 37·5bn. bbls. There are four refineries. Oil accounts for some 95% of Nigeria's export income and over three-quarters of government revenues. Most of Nigeria's oil wealth comes from onshore wells, but there are also large untapped offshore deposits.

Natural gas reserves, 2017, were 5·2trn. cu. metres; production, 47·2bn. cu. metres in 2017. In March 2007 the 678-km West Africa Gas pipeline was completed to supply natural gas to Benin, Ghana and Togo. After a series of delays resulting from vandalism and fuel quality problems, it was restarted in March 2010 and should help to reduce Nigeria's dependence on oil for government revenue.

Minerals

Production, 2014 estimates (in tonnes): limestone, 24·0m.; granite, 16m.; marble, 15m. There are large deposits of iron ore, coal (reserves estimate 245m. tonnes), lead and zinc. There are small quantities of gold and uranium. Lead production was an estimated 5,000 tonnes in 2009. Tin is also mined.

Agriculture

Of the total land mass, 75% is suitable for agriculture, including arable farming, forestry, livestock husbandry and fisheries. In 2012 an estimated 35m. ha. were arable and 6·7m. ha. permanent cropland. 0·29m. ha. were equipped for irrigation in 2012. Main food crops are millet and sorghum in the north, plantains and oil palms in the south, and maize, yams, cassava and rice in much of the country. The north is, however, the main food producing area. Cocoa is the crop that contributes most to foreign exchange earnings. Output, 2010 (in 1,000 tonnes): cassava, 42,533; yams, 37,328; maize, 7,677; sorghum, 7,141; millet, 5,170; rice, 4,473; groundnuts, 3,799; beans, 3,368; taro, 2,957; plantains, 2,676; sweet potatoes, 2,168. Nigeria is the biggest producer of yams, accounting for more than two-thirds of the annual world output. It is also the leading cassava and taro producer and the second largest sorghum producer.

Livestock, 2011: cattle, 18·87m.; goats, 65·65m.; pigs, 6·04m.; sheep, 37·42m.; chickens, 102m. Products (in 1,000 tonnes), 2011 estimates: beef and veal, 384; goat meat, 292; pork and pork products, 243; lamb and mutton, 172; poultry meat, 300; milk, 563; eggs, 636.

Forestry

There were 7·00m. ha. of forests in 2015, or 8% of the land area, down from 17·23m. ha. in 1990 and 13·14m. ha. in 2000. Timber production in 2011 was 73·02m. cu. metres.

Fisheries

The total catch in 2015 was 710,331 tonnes, of which 372,457 tonnes came from marine waters and 337,874 tonnes from inland waters.

Industry

The largest company by market capitalization in Nigeria in April 2015 was Dangote Cement, a diversified conglomerate (US$15·6bn.).

In 2009 manufacturing accounted for 4·2% of GDP. Production, in 1,000 tonnes: cement (2008 estimate), 5,000; residual fuel oil (2007), 1,002; distillate fuel oil (2007), 623; petrol (2007), 287; jet fuel (2007), 232; kerosene (2007), 98; paper and paperboard (2007 estimate), 19; cigarettes (2005), 1,813m. units; motorcycles (2005), 6,900 units. Also plywood (2007 estimate), 55,000 cu. metres.

Labour

The labour force in 2013 was 54,199,000 (41,222,000 in 2003). 56·2% of the population aged 15–64 was economically active in 2013. In the same year 7·5% of the population was unemployed.

Nigeria had 0·70m. people living in slavery according to the Walk Free Foundation's 2013 *Global Slavery Index*, the fourth highest total of any country.

International Trade

Imports and Exports

Imports (c.i.f.) in 2014 totalled US$46,532·3m. (US$44,598·2m. in 2013) and exports (f.o.b.) US$102,878·5m. (US$90,554·5m. in 2013). Principal imports in 2014 were: machinery and electronics, 23·2%; fuels, 16·3%; transportation, 11·9%; metals, 9·2%. In 2014 fuels amounted to 90·9% of exports by value.

In 2006 the main import suppliers were: USA, 15·7%; China, 13·8%; UK, 11·8%; Germany, 5·6%. Leading export destinations in 2006 were: USA, 45·0%; India, 9·3%; Spain, 8·0%; France, 5·7%.

Communications

Roads

The road network covered approximately 200,000 km in 2013, including 83,000 km of main roads. In 2007 there were 4,560,000 passenger cars in use and 3,040,000 motorcycles and mopeds. There were 17,797 road accidents with 9,390 fatalities in 2007.

Rail

In 2005 there were 3,505 route-km of track (1,067 mm gauge). There are plans to convert the entire network to 1,435 mm gauge. In Feb. 2013 passenger services between Lagos and Kano, Nigeria's two most populous cities, were resumed after a ten-year gap. A light rail system in Lagos is scheduled to open during 2022. Passenger-km travelled in 2008 came to 773m. and freight tonne-km to 41m.

Civil Aviation

Lagos (Murtala Muhammed) is the major airport, and there are also international airports at Abuja, Kano and Port Harcourt. After the former national carrier, Air Nigeria, ceased operations in 2012, the country's largest airline is now Arik Air. In 2012 Murtala Muhammed International Airport handled 7,186,595 passengers and 167,702 tonnes of freight.

Shipping

In Jan. 2014 there were 90 ships of 300 GT or over registered, totalling 445,000 GT. The principal ports are Lagos and Port Harcourt. There is an extensive network of inland waterways.

Telecommunications

There were 95,167,000 mobile phone subscriptions in 2011 (equivalent to 579·6 per 1,000 inhabitants) and 719,000 fixed telephone subscriptions (or 4·4 per 1,000 inhabitants). Nigeria has now surpassed South Africa as the continent's largest mobile phone market. The largest mobile phone company is MTN Nigeria Communications. In 2012, 32·8% of the population were internet users. In June 2012 there were 5·1m. Facebook users.

Social Institutions

Out of 178 countries analysed in the 2017 *Fragile States Index*—a list published jointly by the Fund for Peace and *Foreign Policy* magazine—Nigeria was ranked the joint 13th most vulnerable (along with Zimbabwe) to conflict or collapse. The index is based on 12 indicators of state vulnerability across social, political and economic categories.

Justice

The highest court is the Federal Supreme Court, which consists of the Chief Justice of the Republic, and up to 15 Justices appointed by the government. It has original jurisdiction in any dispute between the Federal Republic and any State or between States; and to hear and determine appeals from the Federal Court of Appeal, which acts as an intermediate appellate Court to consider appeals from the High Court.

High Courts, presided over by a Chief Justice, are established in each state. All judges are appointed by the government. Magistrates' courts are established throughout the Republic, and customary law courts in southern Nigeria. In each of the northern States of Nigeria there are the Sharia Court of Appeal and the Court of Resolution. Muslim Law has been codified in a Penal Code and is applied through Alkali courts. The northern province of Zamfara introduced *sharia*, or Islamic law, in Oct. 1999, as have the other 11 predominantly Muslim northern provinces in the meantime. The death penalty is in force and was used in 2013, when four people were executed, for the first time since 2006. There were then three executions in 2016 although none in 2017 or 2018.

The population in penal institutions in May 2013 was 54,144 (32 per 100,000 of national population). 69·3% of prisoners had yet to receive a trial according to 2014 estimates by the International Centre for Prison Studies. Nigeria was ranked 73rd of 102 countries for criminal justice and 62nd for civil justice in the 2015 World Justice Project *Rule of Law Index*, which provides data on how the rule of law is experienced by the general public across eight categories.

Education

The adult literacy rate was an estimated 60·8% in 2009. Free, compulsory education for nine years is provided for all children from the age of six. However, in 2010 a total of 10·5m. children were out of school. In 2006 there were 22·86m. pupils and 565,646 teaching staff in primary schools; 6·44m. pupils and 202,082 teaching staff in secondary schools; and (2005) 1·39m. students in tertiary education with 37,031 academic staff.

Among the leading institutions of higher education are Ahmadu Bello University in Zaria—Nigeria's largest university—with around 35,000 students, and the University of Ibadan—the country's oldest university—founded in 1948.

Health

In 2009 there were 41 doctors for every 100,000 population and two dentists for every 100,000. There were 161 nurses and midwives per 100,000 people in 2008 and 13 pharmaceutical personnel per 100,000.

Nigeria has made significant progress in the reduction of undernourishment in the past 25 years. In the period 2015 only 7% of the population was undernourished, one of the lowest rates in sub-Saharan Africa.

In *Water: At What Cost? The State of the World's Water 2016*, WaterAid reported that 31·5% of the population does not have access to safe water. Nigeria ranked as the country with the third largest number of people living without access to safe water (57·8m. in 2015).

An estimated 2·9m. people in Nigeria are living with HIV/AIDS, a total exceeded only in South Africa.

Religion

Muslims and Christians both constitute about 49% of the population; traditional animist beliefs are also widespread. Northern Nigeria is mainly Muslim; southern Nigeria is predominantly Christian and western Nigeria is evenly divided between Christians, Muslims and animists. Far more Nigerians consider their religion to be of prime importance rather than their nationality. In Feb. 2019 the Roman Catholic Church had three cardinals.

Culture

World Heritage Sites

The Sukur Cultural Landscape, a hilly area in Adamawa State (northeastern Nigeria), was entered on the UNESCO World Heritage list in 1999. Osun Sacred Grove is one of the last remnants of primary high forest in southern Nigeria and was inscribed in 2005.

Press

In 2008 there were 28 paid-for daily newspapers with a combined circulation of 510,000 and 61 paid-for weeklies. The dailies with the highest circulation figures are *The Sun* and *ThisDay*.

Tourism

In 2010 there were 1,555,000 international tourist arrivals, excluding same-day visitors (up from 1,414,000 in 2009); spending by tourists in 2010 totalled US$576m.

Diplomatic Representatives

Of Nigeria in the United Kingdom (Nigeria House, 9 Northumberland Ave., London, WC2N 5BX)
High Commissioner: George Adesola Oguntade.

Of the United Kingdom in Nigeria (Plot 1137, Diplomatic Drive, Central Business District, Abuja)
High Commissioner: Catriona Laing CB.

Of Nigeria in the USA (3519 International Court, NW, Washington, D.C., 20008)
Ambassador: Sylvanus Adiewere Nsofor.

Of the USA in Nigeria (Plot 1075, Diplomatic Drive, Central District, Abuja)
Ambassador: W. Stuart Symington.

Of Nigeria to the United Nations
Ambassador: Tijjani Muhammad Bande.

Of Nigeria to the European Union
Ambassador: Ahmed Inusa.

Further Reading

Forrest, T., *Politics and Economic Development in Nigeria*. 1993

Hill, Jonathan, *Nigeria Since Independence: Forever Fragile?* 2012

Maier, K., *This House Has Fallen: Midnight in Nigeria*. 2000

Miles, W. F. S., *Hausaland Divided: Colonialism and Independence in Nigeria and Niger*. 1994

Okafor, Victor Oguejiofor, *A Roadmap for Understanding African Politics*. 2006

Smith, Mike, *Boko Haram: Inside Nigeria's Unholy War*. 2015

A more specialized title is listed under RECENT ELECTIONS, *above*.

National Statistical Office: National Bureau of Statistics, Plot 762, Independence Ave., Central Business District, Garki, P.M.B. 127, Abuja.

Website: http://www.nigerianstat.gov.ng

North Macedonia

Republika Severna Makedonija (The Republic of North Macedonia)

Capital: Skopje
Population projection, 2020: 2·09m.
GNI per capita, 2017: (PPP$) 12,505
HDI/world rank, 2017: 0·757/80=
Internet domain extension: .mk

Key Historical Events

The history of North Macedonia can be traced to the reign of King Karan (808–778 BC), but the country was at its most powerful at the time of Philip II (359–336 BC) and Alexander the Great (336–323 BC). At the end of the 6th century AD Slavs began to settle in Macedonia. There followed a long period of internal fighting but the spread of Christianity led to consolidation and the creation of the first Macedonian Slav state, the Kingdom of Samuel, 976–1018. In the 14th century it fell to Serbia, and in 1355 to the Turks. After the Balkan wars of 1912–13 Turkey was ousted and Serbia received part of the territory, the rest going to Bulgaria and Greece. In 1918 Yugoslav Macedonia was incorporated into Serbia as South Serbia, becoming a republic in the Socialist Federal Republic of Yugoslavia. Claims to the historical Macedonian territory have long been a source of contention with Bulgaria and Greece. Macedonia (officially known as the former Yugoslav Republic of Macedonia until Feb. 2019 when it was renamed North Macedonia) declared its independence on 18 Sept. 1991. In April 1999 the Kosovo crisis which led to NATO air attacks on Yugoslavian military targets set off a flood of refugees into Macedonia, though subsequently most returned home.

In March 2001 there were a series of clashes between government forces and ethnic Albanian separatists near the border between Macedonia and Kosovo. As violence escalated Macedonia found itself on the brink of civil war. In May 2001 the new national unity government gave ethnic Albanian rebels a 'final warning' to end their uprising. As the crisis worsened, a stand-off within the government between the Macedonian and the ethnic Albanian parties was only resolved after the intervention of Javier Solana, the EU's foreign and security policy chief. A number of Macedonian soldiers were killed in clashes with the rebels, and following reverses in the military campaign the commander of the Macedonian army, Jovan Andrevski, resigned in June 2001. In Aug. 2001 a peace accord was negotiated.

In Feb. 2019 a festering diplomatic dispute with Greece was finally resolved as Macedonia changed its official name to North Macedonia, paving the way for its aspiring accession to the European Union and NATO.

Territory and Population

North Macedonia is bounded in the north by Serbia, in the east by Bulgaria, in the south by Greece and in the west by Albania. Its area is 25,713 sq. km, including 490 sq. km of inland water. According to the 2002 census final results, the population on 1 Nov. 2002 was 2,022,547. A census scheduled for 2011 was deferred following ethnic disputes. The main ethnic group are Macedonians, followed by Albanians, with smaller numbers of Turks, Roma, Serbs and Bosniaks. Ethnic Albanians predominate on the western side of North Macedonia. Population estimate, Dec. 2017, 2,075,301; density, 81 per sq. km. Minorities are represented in the Council for Inter-Ethnic Relations. In 2011, 59·4% of the population lived in urban areas.

The UN gives a projected population for 2020 of 2·09m.

North Macedonia is divided into 84 municipalities. The major cities (with Dec. 2016 population estimates) are: Skopje, the capital, 505,400; Kumanovo, 73,360; Bitola, 71,890; Prilep, 64,830; Tetovo, 56,080.

The official language is Macedonian, which uses the Cyrillic alphabet. Around 25% of the population speak Albanian.

Social Statistics

In 2011: live births, 22,770; deaths, 19,465; marriages, 14,736; divorces, 1,753; infant deaths, 172. Rates (per 1,000 population): live births, 11·1; deaths, 9·5; marriages, 7·2; divorces, 0·9. Infant mortality, 2011 (per 1,000 live births), 7·6. Expectation of life at birth in 2007 was 71·7 years for males and 76·5 years for females. Annual population growth rate, 2005–10, 0·2%. In 2012 the most popular age range for marrying was 25–29 for males and 20–24 for females. Fertility rate, 2011, 1·6 births per woman.

Climate

North Macedonia has a mixed Mediterranean-continental type climate, with cold moist winters and hot dry summers. Skopje, Jan. –0·4°C, July 23·1°C.

Constitution and Government

At a referendum held on 8 Sept. 1991 turnout was 74%; 99% of votes cast were in favour of a sovereign Macedonia. On 17 Nov. 1991 parliament promulgated a new constitution which officially proclaimed Macedonia's independence. This was replaced by a constitution adopted on 16 Nov. 2001 which for the first time included the recognition of Albanian as an official language. It also increased access for ethnic Albanians to public-sector jobs. In Feb. 2019 the country officially changed its name to North Macedonia.

The *President* is directly elected for five-year terms. Candidates must be citizens aged at least 40 years. The parliament is a 123-member single-chamber *Assembly* (*Sobranie*), elected by universal suffrage for four-year terms. There is a *Constitutional Court* whose members are elected by the assembly for non-renewable eight-year terms, and a *National Security Council* chaired by the President. Laws passed by the Assembly must be countersigned by the President, who may return them for reconsideration, but cannot veto them if they gain a two-thirds majority.

National Anthem

'Denes nad Makedonija se radja novo sonce na slobodata' ('Today a new sun of liberty appears over Macedonia'); words by V. Maleski, tune by T. Skalovski.

Recent Elections

Parliamentary elections were held on 11 Dec. 2016. The ruling Internal Macedonian Revolutionary Organization-Democratic Party for Macedonian National Unity (VMRO-DPMNE) won 51 of 120 seats with 39·4% of votes cast. The Social Democratic Union of Macedonia (SDSM) took 49 (37·9%), the Democratic Union for Integration (DUI) 10, the Besa Movement 5, the 'Alliance for the Albanians' coalition 3 and the Democratic Party of Albanians (DPA) 2. Turnout was 66·8%.

Presidential elections were held on 13 April 2014. Incumbent president Gjorgje Ivanov (VMRO-DPMNE) took 51·7% of the vote, Stevo Pendarovski (SDSM) 37·5%, Iljaz Halimi (DPA) 4·5% and Zoran Popovski (Citizens Option for Macedonia) 3·6%. In the run-off on 27 April Ivanov won with 55·3% against Pendarovski with 41·1%. Turnout was 48·9% in the first round and 54·4% in the second.

Current Government

President: Gjorgje Ivanov; b. 1960 (VMRO-DPMNE; sworn in 12 May 2009 and re-elected 27 April 2014).

Prime Minister: Zoran Zaev; b. 1974 (SDSM; sworn in 31 May 2017).

In Feb. 2019 the three-party coalition government was composed as follows:

Palgrave Macmillan (ed.), *The Statesman's Yearbook 2020*,
https://doi.org/10.1057/978-1-349-95940-2_144

Deputy Prime Minister for European Affairs: Bujar Osmani. *Deputy Prime Minister for Economic Affairs:* Koco Angjusev. *Deputy Prime Minister for Political Systems and Relations among Communities:* Hazbi Lika.

Minister of Agriculture, Forestry and Water Supply: Ljupco Nikolovski. *Culture:* Asaf Ademi. *Defence:* Radmila Sekerinska-Jankovska. *Economy:* Kreshnik Bekteshi. *Education and Science:* Arber Ademi. *Environment and Physical Planning:* Sadula Duraku. *Finance:* Dragan Tevdovski. *Foreign Affairs:* Nikola Dimitrov. *Health:* Venko Filipce. *Information Society and Public Administration:* Damjan Mancevski. *Interior:* Oliver Spasovski. *Justice:* Renata Deskoska. *Labour and Social Affairs:* Mila Carovska. *Local Government:* Suhejl Fazliu. *Transport and Communications:* Goran Sugareski. *Ministers without Portfolio:* Edmond Ademi; Aksel Ahmedovski; Zorica Apostolovska; Bardul Dauiti; Adnan Kjahil; Robert Popovski; Zoran Sapuric.

Government Website: http://www.vlada.mk

Current Leaders

Gjorgje Ivanov

Position
President

Introduction
Gjorgje Ivanov was sworn into office on 12 May 2009 after his election victory in April. Although his duties are largely ceremonial, he is supreme commander of the army and has decision-making powers on foreign policy and the judiciary.

Early Life
Gjorgje Ivanov was born on 2 May 1960 in Valandovo. He graduated in law in 1982, subsequently becoming an assistant and then associate law professor while completing his doctorate.

In 1999 Ivanov was made a professor of post-graduate studies at the University of Athens before joining the political science departments of the University of Bologna and the University of Sarajevo the following year. He returned to his alma mater in Skopje in 2001 to take up the post of director of political studies. In 2008 he received his political science professorship and was appointed as chair of the Macedonian Higher Education Accreditation Council.

The ruling conservative VMRO-DPMNE announced Ivanov as its presidential candidate for the 2009 election and in the second round of voting in April he won with 63% of the vote.

Career in Office
Ivanov pledged to continue Macedonia's campaign for membership of the European Union and NATO. In Dec. 2011 the International Court of Justice ruled against Greece's obstruction of Macedonia's bid to join the military alliance in their dispute over the country's name (*see* GREECE: Key Historical Events *on page* 547). He also aimed to diffuse ongoing tensions with Macedonia's ethnic Albanian minority. However, in March 2012 there were violent clashes between youths from both communities in Skopje.

In parliamentary elections in June 2011 Ivanov's VMRO-DPMNE was returned to office but without a majority. In Dec. 2012 differences over the state budget led the opposition Social Democratic Union of Macedonia (SDSM) to boycott parliamentary proceedings. The European Union, which said that there was a 'need for more inclusive and constructive politics', mediated between the government and opposition resulting in an agreement in March 2013 to end the stand-off. Meanwhile, an EU report in April acknowledged Macedonia's continued progress towards membership of the Union.

In April 2014 Ivanov was re-elected to a second term as president, taking 55% of the vote in a run-off, and the VMRO-DPMNE retained power in parliamentary polling. However, 2015 saw a further souring of relations between the VMRO-DPMNE and the SDSM, as well as a resurgence of inter-ethnic rivalry and violence.

From April 2016 public protests broke out against Ivanov and the government over Ivanov's efforts to block judicial investigations into officials and politicians facing criminal prosecution over a wiretapping scandal. Amid further prolonged political turmoil, parliamentary elections scheduled for June were postponed until Dec. that year, at which the VMRO-DPMNE narrowly remained the largest party, taking 51 of 120 seats but only two more than the opposition SDSM. Subsequent coalition negotiations between the VMRO-DPMNE and the leading

ethnic Albanian party failed, and Ivanov initially resisted asking the SDSM to try to form an alternative coalition. However, in May 2017 he mandated SDSM leader Zoran Zaev to establish a new administration, with Albanian backing, and the new government was sworn in on 1 June with a small parliamentary majority.

In June 2018 Macedonia signed an historic agreement with Greece to change the former's official name to North Macedonia with the aim of resolving a long-standing bilateral dispute and boosting the country's bids to join the EU and NATO. A subsequent referendum in Macedonia in Sept. on the agreement attracted only one-third of voters, although about 90% of them backed the change, and the following month the Macedonian parliament approved it.

Defence

The President is the C.-in-C. of the armed forces. Compulsory national military service was abolished in 2006. Total armed forces personnel numbered 8,000 in 2013. There is a paramilitary police force of 7,600.

Defence expenditure in 2012 totalled US$129m. (US$62 per capita), representing 1·3% of GDP.

The European Union's first ever peacekeeping force (EUFOR) officially started work in North Macedonia (then known as Macedonia) on 31 March 2003, replacing the NATO-led force that had been in the country since 2001. EUFOR left the country in Dec. 2003.

Army

The Army is the primary arm of the military. It is commanded by the minister of defence through the chief of the general staff. Equipment in 2013 included 31 main battle tanks and 11 armoured infantry fighting vehicles.

Navy

In 2013 the Marine Wing operated seven patrol and coastal combatants.

Air Force

The Air Wing had six aircraft and four attack helicopters in 2013.

International Relations

On 13 Sept. 1995 under the auspices of the UN, Macedonia (now North Macedonia) and Greece agreed to normalize their relations.

Economy

Agriculture accounted for 9·9% of GDP in 2016, industry 29·7% and services 60·4%.

Overview

Between 2004 and 2014 the economy grew by an annual average of 3·4%, reaching a high of 8·2% in 2005. The main export is chemicals, accounting for over 22% of trade revenue. The production of metals, textiles, wine and vegetables is also important.

Unemployment stood at 24·5% in the first quarter of 2016, although a large informal sector skews both employment and GDP statistics. Macroeconomic stability has been maintained by prudent monetary policies that keep the domestic currency pegged to the euro.

Currency

The national currency of North Macedonia is the *denar* (MKD), of 100 *deni*. Foreign exchange reserves were US$910m. in July 2005, gold reserves 197,000 troy oz and total money supply was 29,745m. denars. There was deflation of 0·2% in 2016 and inflation of 1·4% in 2017.

Budget

In 2011 revenues totalled 148,408m. denars and expenditures 159,992m. denars. Tax revenue accounted for 82·4% of revenues in 2011; current expenditure accounted for 86·9% of expenditures.

VAT is 18%.

Performance

In 2001 political turmoil in the country resulted in the economy contracting by 4·5%. There was then a slight recovery in 2002, with a growth rate of 0·9%. In the financial crisis of 2009 the economy contracted by 0·4%, but recovered to grow by 3·4% in 2010. More recently it grew by 3·9% in 2015,

2·9% in 2016 before slowing to zero in 2017. Total GDP in 2017 was US$11·3bn.

Banking and Finance

The central bank and bank of issue is the National Bank of North Macedonia. Its *Governor* is Anita Angelovska-Bezhoska (since May 2018). Privatization of the banking sector was completed in 2000. There were 16 banks in 2012. The three largest banks by total assets in Dec. 2012 were Komercijalna Banka (82·8bn. denars), Stopanska Banka (75·4bn. denars) and NLB Tutunska Banka (59·6bn. denars); between them they control more than half the assets of all banks in the country, which totalled 352·9bn. denars in Dec. 2012.

External debt was US$5,804m. in 2010, representing 65·1% of GNI.

A stock exchange opened in Skopje in 1996.

Energy and Natural Resources

Environment

North Macedonia's carbon dioxide emissions from the consumption of energy were the equivalent of 4·2 tonnes per capita in 2011.

Electricity

Installed capacity in 2011 was 1·6m. kW. Output in 2011: 6·76bn. kWh, of which 1·43bn. kWh were from hydro-electric plants. Consumption per capita was 4,485 kWh in 2011.

Oil and Gas

A 230-km long pipeline bringing crude oil to North Macedonia from Thessaloniki in Greece opened in July 2002. Built at a cost of over US$130m., it has the capacity to provide North Macedonia with 2·5m. tonnes of crude oil annually.

Minerals

North Macedonia is relatively rich in minerals, including lead, zinc, copper, iron, chromium, nickel, antimony, manganese, silver and gold. Output in 2009, unless otherwise indicated (in tonnes): lignite, 7,454,000; copper ore, 3,767,000; gypsum, 155,000; lead concentrate, 52,000; copper concentrate, 35,430; zinc concentrate, 32,000.

Agriculture

In 2015, 18% of employed persons were engaged in agriculture. In 2009, 9·5% of arable land were owned by agricultural enterprises and co-operatives and 90·5% by individual farmers. There were 53,600 tractors in use in 2007.

Crop production, 2013 (in 1,000 tonnes): grapes, 292; wheat, 259; potatoes, 191; cabbages, Brussels sprouts, etc., 157; chillies and green peppers, 152; maize, 135; tomatoes, 131; watermelons, 128; barley, 126; apples, 113. In 2014, 51,013 tonnes of wine were produced.

Livestock, 2014 (in 1,000): sheep, 740; cattle, 242; pigs, 165; horses, 19; chickens, 1,940. Livestock products, 2014 (in 1,000 tonnes): pork and pork products, 10; beef, 6; lamb and mutton, 5; poultry, 2; cow's milk, 387; sheep's milk, 36; eggs (total), 248m.

Forestry

Forests covered 1·00m. ha. in 2015 (40% of the land area), chiefly oak and beech. 597,000 cu. metres of timber were cut in 2011.

Fisheries

Total catch in 2012 was 249 tonnes, entirely from inland waters.

Industry

In 2013 there were 71,290 business entities, with the main sectors of activity as follows: wholesale and retail trade, and repair of motor vehicles and motorcycles, 25,429 entities; manufacturing, 7,918; transportation and storage, 6,095; professional, scientific and technical activities, 5,817. Manufacturing contributed 11·4% of GDP in 2013.

Labour

The labour force in 2013 was 946,000 (861,000 in 2003). 64·2% of the population aged 15–64 was economically active in 2013. The unemployment rate in 2013 was 29·0% (31·0% in 2012).

International Trade

Imports and Exports

In 2009 imports (c.i.f.) were valued at US$5,403m. and exports (f.o.b.) at US$2,692m.

Leading imports in 2009 (in US$1m.) were: manufactured goods (1,202); machinery and transport equipment (1,038); chemicals and related products (566). Leading exports in 2009 (in US$1m.) were: articles of apparel and clothing accessories (584); iron and steel (169); fruit and vegetables (143).

In 2009 major import sources (in US$1m.) were: Germany (518); Russia (495); Greece (439). Major export markets in 2009 (in US$1m.) were: Serbia (652); Germany (450); Greece (290).

Communications

Roads

In 2007 there were 221 km of motorways, 690 km of other main roads, 3,774 km of regional roads and 9,155 km of local roads. There were 248,800 passenger cars in use in 2007, plus 2,300 buses and coaches, and 26,600 lorries and vans. In the same year there were 4,037 road accidents with 173 fatalities.

Rail

In 2009 there were 699 km of railways (234 km electrified). 1·5m. passengers and 2·9m. tonnes of freight were transported in 2009. The former Macedonian Railways was reorganized in 2007 with two new entities being created—Macedonian Railways Infrastructure (PE Makedonski Železnici Infrastructure, or MŽ-I), which is responsible for the maintenance and operation of the infrastructure, and Macedonian Railways Transport (MŽ Transport AD, or MŽ-T), which is responsible for the operation of passenger and freight services.

Civil Aviation

There are international airports at Skopje and Ohrid. A new North Macedonia-based carrier, Aeromak, has been established to replace MAT Macedonian Airlines, the former flag carrier which ceased operations in 2009. In 2009 Skopje handled 602,298 passengers (658,366 in 2008) and 2,326 tonnes of freight. The much smaller airport at Ohrid handled 36,652 passengers in 2009 (44,413 in 2008).

Telecommunications

In 2011 there were 413,500 landline telephone subscriptions (equivalent to 200·3 per 1,000 inhabitants) and 2,257,100 mobile phone subscriptions (or 1,093·6 per 1,000 inhabitants). In 2011, 56·7% of the population were internet users. In 2002 the Hungarian firm Matav acquired a 51% stake in MakTel, the state monopoly telecommunications provider, in the most significant economic development in the country's history. The deal was worth €618·2m. (US$568·4m.) over two years. In March 2012 there were 880,000 Facebook users.

Social Institutions

Out of 178 countries analysed in the 2017 *Fragile States Index*—a list published jointly by the Fund for Peace and *Foreign Policy* magazine—North Macedonia (then called Macedonia) was ranked the 67th least vulnerable to conflict or collapse. The index is based on 12 indicators of state vulnerability across social, political and economic categories.

Justice

Courts are autonomous and independent. Judges are tenured and elected for life on the proposal of the *Judicial Council*, whose members are themselves elected for renewable six-year terms. The highest court is the Supreme Court. There are 27 courts of first instance and three higher courts.

The population in penal institutions in Sept. 2011 was 2,515 (122 per 100,000 of national population). North Macedonia (then called Macedonia) was ranked 51st of 102 countries for criminal justice and 38th for civil justice in the 2015 World Justice Project *Rule of Law Index*, which provides data on how the rule of law is experienced by the general public across eight categories.

Education

The adult literacy rate was estimated at 97·8% in 2014 (98·8% among males and 96·7% among females). Education is free and compulsory for nine years. In 2012 there were 19,785 children and 2,475 teaching staff in pre-primary schools, 107,278 pupils and 7,081 teachers in primary schools, and 186,149 pupils and 17,742 teachers in secondary schools. There were 60,682 students in tertiary education in 2013 with 3,430 academic staff. There are five public universities: Cyril and Methodius University at Skopje (the oldest and the largest university); St Clement of Ohrid University of Bitola; Goce Delchev University of Shtip; State University of Tetovo; University of Information Science and Technology 'St Paul the Apostle', at Ohrid. There are also several private universities.

Health

In 2013 there were 5,804 physicians, 1,705 dentistry personnel and 930 pharmaceutical personnel. There were 86 hospitals with 8,801 beds in 2014.

In *Water: At What Cost? The State of the World's Water 2016*, WaterAid reported that 0·6% of the population does not have access to safe water.

Welfare

In 2016 social assistance was paid to 29,215 households. In the same year there were 12,955 recipients of child care allowances, and 15,473 juveniles and 42,549 adults received social benefits. There were 311,500 pensioners in 2018.

Religion

North Macedonia is traditionally Orthodox but the church is not established and there is freedom of religion. A study by the Pew Research Center's Forum on Religion & Public Life estimated that there were 1·33m. Orthodox Christians in 2010 and 810,000 Muslims (mainly Sunni). In 1967 an autocephalous Orthodox church—the Macedonian Orthodox Church—split off from the Serbian Orthodox Church. Its head is the Archbishop of Ohrid and Macedonia, whose seat is at Skopje.

Culture

World Heritage Sites

North Macedonia has one site on the UNESCO World Heritage List: Ohrid Region with its Cultural and Historic Aspect and its Natural Environment (inscribed on the list in 1979 and 1980), a rich repository of Byzantine art and architecture.

Press

There were 12 daily newspapers in 2008 with a circulation of 295,000 copies. *Dnevnik* is the most popular with a daily circulation of 50,000 copies in 2008.

There are four news agencies in North Macedonia: the Macedonian Information Agency (national); and Macedonian Information Centre, Makfax and Net Press (privately owned). Net Press is exclusively an internet news agency.

Tourism

There were 261,696 foreign tourists in 2010, the highest total since 1991. The main countries of origin of non-resident tourists in 2010 were: Serbia (13·7%), Greece (10·3%), Turkey (7·7%) and Albania (6·5%).

Festivals

The main festivals are Days of Macedonian Music in Skopje (March), the Balkan Festival of Folk Songs and Dances in Ohrid (July), the Ohrid Summer Festival focusing on music and drama (July–Aug.) and the Skopje Jazz Festival (Oct.).

Diplomatic Representatives

Of North Macedonia in the United Kingdom (Suites 2·1 and 2·2, Buckingham Court, 75–83 Buckingham Gate, London, SW1E 6PE)
Ambassador: Aleksandra Miovska

Of the United Kingdom in North Macedonia (Todor Aleksandrov 165, 1000 Skopje)
Ambassador: Rachel Galloway.

Of North Macedonia in the USA (2129 Wyoming Ave., NW, Washington, D.C., 20008)
Ambassador: Vasko Naumovski.

Of the USA in North Macedonia (ul. Samoilova 21, 1000 Skopje)
Ambassador: Jess L. Baily.

Of North Macedonia to the United Nations
Ambassador: Vacant.
Chargé d'Affaires a.i.: Tanja Dinevska.

Of North Macedonia to the European Union
Ambassador: Agneza Rusi Popovska.

Further Reading

Danforth, L. M., *The Macedonian Conflict: Ethnic Nationalism in a Transnational World*. 1996
Phillips, John, *Macedonia: Warlords and Rebels in the Balkans.* 2004
Poulton, H., *Who Are the Macedonians?* 1996
National Statistical Office: State Statistical Office, Dame Gruev 4, Skopje.
Website: http://www.stat.gov.mk

Norway

Kongeriket Norge (Kingdom of Norway)

Capital: Oslo
Population projection, 2020: 5·45m.
GNI per capita, 2017: (PPP$) 68,012
HDI/world rank, 2017: 0·953/1
Internet domain extension: .no

Key Historical Events

The first settlers arrived at the end of the Ice Age, as the glaciers retreated north. Archaeological remains in Finnmark in the north and in Rogaland in the southwest of Norway date from between 9500 to 8000 BC and suggest coastal, hunting-fishing communities. By 2500 BC a new influx of settlers brought cattle and crop farming and gradually replaced the earlier hunting-fishing communities. Although there is little evidence of the impact of the bronze and iron ages on Norway as its people had not yet found ways to exploit their natural resources for trade, links with Roman-occupied Gaul in the first four centuries AD were strong. By the time of the collapse of the Roman Empire, tribal groups had started to develop and by AD 800 had each established their own legislative and adjudicatory assemblies, known as *thing*.

In the ninth century communities from the Vik, an area between the south coasts of Norway and Sweden, gave their name to the people collectively known as Vikings. The Norwegian Vikings sailed to the Atlantic islands, England, France, Scotland and Ireland, and also colonized Iceland. One of the many whose exploits were faithfully recorded by the saga writers was Eric the Red, who discovered Greenland. His son, Leif Erikson, voyaged across the Davis Strait, to America, becoming possibly the first European to do so.

The first steps towards centralized rule were taken by Harold Fairhair who extended his rule along the coastal region of Norway. Battles with rival chieftains culminated in about 900 when Harold was proclaimed king of the Norwegians. His successors were less assertive and by the mid-tenth century the country was effectively under the suzerainty of Harold Bluetooth, king of Denmark and Skåne. Bluetooth's grandson, Canute the Great, fought successfully to incorporate England into his North Sea Empire before setting his sights on Sweden. But the limitations of royal authority were shown on the death of Canute when the English, unchallenged, simply chose their own king while the Danish and Norwegian nobles decided that whichever of their own monarchs lived longest should take power in both countries, an agreement which for a time resulted in a Norwegian ruler for Denmark.

Viking Strength

The Viking's territorial expansion came to an end with the Norwegian King Harald Hardrada's defeat at the battle of Stamford Bridge in England in 1066. Supported by the English church, the Norwegian monarchy gained strength. By the 12th century the balance of power between the church and monarchy had become a source of civil conflict which was only resolved when Håkon IV became King in 1217. Thus began Norway's 'Golden Age' in which the unity of the kingdom was solidly established. Blood feuds were prohibited, a royal council was created, and primogeniture was introduced to secure the continuity of the monarchic line. Under Håkon's rule, both Greenland and Iceland ceded control to Norway. It was Håkon's son, Magnus VI, known as the Lawmender, who oversaw the codification of a national law system between 1274–76, elements of which have survived to this day. Under Erik II, Magnus's son, much of the royal power was divested to wealthy magnates. His succession by his brother Håkon V in 1299 marked a renewed effort to strengthen the monarchy and also a movement of political power to Oslo.

Union with Sweden came in 1319 with the coronation of Magnus VII, the son of Håkon's daughter and Duke Erik of Sweden. This was to last until 1355, when the Swedish crown passed to Magnus's son. Between 1349–50 Norway fell victim to the Black Death which killed around two-thirds of its population. The effects of this were to dramatically reduce the strength of the nobility and to undermine the cohesion of the government, as many official positions were taken up by Danes and Swedes. Newly vulnerable to the threat of encroachment by the Germans, the incentive for all three Scandinavian kingdoms to unite was strong. When the Danish king died in 1375 his widow, Margaret, claimed the throne on behalf of her five-year-old son, Olav. Acting for her son, Margaret became regent of Denmark and, on the death of Håkon, regent of Norway. Confirmed as regent of Denmark and Norway, Margaret defeated Albrecht, the German claimant to the Swedish throne, thus clearing the way to a Nordic union. With the death of her son in 1387 and unable to take the triple crown for herself, she nominated her five-year-old nephew, Erik of Pomerania, as king of all three countries. His election was formalized at Kalmar in 1397.

From 1450 the Norwegian government was based in Copenhagen and many administrative positions were taken by Germans and Danes. An attempt by the Norwegian council to gain independence in 1523 led to civil war between 1534–36 and the council's subsequent abolition. Norway was then to remain a province of Denmark, with limited control over internal affairs, until the 19th century.

In the Napoleonic Wars, Denmark and Norway were allied with Napoleon I. Napoleon's defeat at the battle of Leipzig in 1813 was followed by a successful attack on Denmark from Sweden which resulted in the Treaty of Kiel (Jan. 1814). With the signing of the treaty Norway was conceded to the Swedish throne and, despite Denmark's continued resistance, its newly written constitution came into force in Nov. 1814. Although the arrangement meant the regency and foreign policy were to be shared with Sweden, the new constitution gave Norway control over internal affairs, with a newly established political base at Christiania.

The economic damage of the Napoleonic Wars was remedied by the rapid expansion of the fishing industry and, from the 1850s onwards, agriculture. In the latter half of the century, the merchant navy grew to become the third largest in the world after the United States and Great Britain.

Independence

From the 1880s, successive steps towards self-government within the union culminated in a referendum in which the overwhelming majority of Norwegians voted for separation. In Oct. 1905 Oscar II renounced his title to the western provinces and a month later a Danish prince was confirmed as Håkon VII of free Norway. Reigning for 52 years, he was succeeded by his son.

At the outset of the First World War Norway declared its neutrality. This did not prevent the loss of almost half of its merchant navy and damage to the economy as a result of trade embargos. But despite the hardships of the 1930s' depression, industrial expansion continued.

From 1940 to 1944, during the Second World War, Norway was occupied by the Germans who set up a pro-German government under Vidkun Quisling. Apart from this wartime episode, the Labour Party held office, and the majority in the *Storting* (parliament), from 1935 to 1965. Norway's first postwar prime minister, Einar Gerhardsen, had spent four years in a concentration camp. He had been vice-chairman of Oslo city council until he became leader of the underground anti-Nazi movement in the early days of the occupation. As recently elected social democrat leader he was the natural choice to head the 1945 caretaker government.

The action needed to restore Norway's prosperity was self-evident: to make good the heavy losses in the merchant fleet; to increase the output of hydro-electricity; and to develop new industries. The chief worry for the social democrats was the likely impact of communists who had gained credit for leading the resistance. Talks on a possible merger of the parties were as unproductive as parallel negotiations in Denmark, but the electoral results of each party's going its own way were markedly different in the two countries. More confident of their purpose, the Norwegian social democrats took the electorate by storm, increasing their share of the popular vote in the 1945 election by close on 10%. Their advance gave them the one prize that eluded their colleagues everywhere else in Scandinavia—an absolute majority and the freedom to govern without always looking over their shoulder.

The government was supported wholeheartedly by the trade unions. In return for price controls and food subsidies which stabilized the cost of living for almost five years, and the guarantee of full employment, the unions

© Springer Nature Limited 2020
Palgrave Macmillan (ed.), *The Statesman's Yearbook 2020*,
https://doi.org/10.1057/978-1-349-95940-2_145

accepted compulsory arbitration for all wage disputes. Returned in 1949 with an increased majority, the social democrats were able to point to a rise in productivity and living standards well beyond that achieved by most other Western countries. But the general increase in world prices triggered by the Korean War meant that Norway had to pay much more for essential imports. The use of subsidies to counteract price increases reached its limit when they became the largest item in the national budget. In 1950 food prices were allowed to get closer to their market level and the cost of living started on an upward curve, leading to a 30% increase over three years. Industrial investment suffered a sharp cutback.

The social democrats held on to power until the mid-sixties when a centre right coalition took over led by Per Borten. By 1969 the social democrats had recovered much of their lost ground. The centre right coalition government struggled on with a majority of two until the EEC issue broke through the normally placid surface of Norwegian politics.

Although Norway's application for membership in the EEC in 1969 was successful, a referendum held in 1972 found more than 53% of voters opposed to joining. Norway had been a member of EFTA since that organization's foundation, and continued to sign up to a series of bilateral free-trade treaties with members of the EEC, but opposition to joining the EEC remained strong. On the inception of the EU in 1992, Norway, like its Scandinavian neighbours, applied for membership. But, again, a referendum was won by the anti-European lobby.

Norway's continued reluctance to join the EU hinges on its dependence on the export of petroleum and natural gas. Since the 1960s and the discovery of vast off-shore deposits, the oil and gas export industry has contributed to making Norway one of the world's richest economies.

In 2010 relations with China came under pressure when the Norwegian Nobel committee awarded its Peace Prize to Liu Xiaobo, a jailed dissident. In July 2011 an anti-immigration extremist set off a bomb at the prime minister's office in Oslo before carrying out a gun attack at a summer camp on the island of Utøya in Tyrifjorden, organized by the youth wing of the Labour Party. A total of 77 people were killed in the two attacks.

Territory and Population

Norway is bounded in the north by the Arctic Ocean, east by Russia, Finland and Sweden, south by the Skagerrak Straits and west by the Norwegian Sea. The total area of mainland Norway is 323,787 sq. km, including 19,539 sq. km of fresh water. Total coastline, including fjords, 25,148 km. There are more than 50,000 islands along the coastline. Exposed mountain (either bare rock or thin vegetation) makes up over 70% of the country. 25% of the land area is woodland and 4% tilled land.

In Nov. 2011 the population at Norway's first fully register-based census (including Svalbard) was 4,979,955 (2,494,777 males); density per sq. km, 16·3. Estimated population, 1 Jan. 2018, 5,295,619. With the exception of Iceland, Norway is the most sparsely populated country in Europe.

The UN gives a projected population for 2020 of 5·45m.

There are 18 counties (*fylke*). Land area, population and densities:

	Land area (sq. km)	Population (2011 census)	Population (2018 estimate)	Density per sq. km 2018
Østfold	3,888	278,014	295,420	76
Akershus	4,579	554,881	614,026	134
Oslo (City)	426	612,314	673,469	1,581
Hedmark	26,084	192,722	196,966	8
Oppland	23,784	187,019	189,870	8
Buskerud	13,796	264,742	281,769	20
Vestfold	2,147	236,120	249,058	116
Telemark	13,854	169,930	173,391	13
Aust-Agder	8,314	111,370	117,222	14
Vest-Agder	6,677	174,184	186,532	28
Rogaland	8,589	442,265	473,526	55
Hordaland	14,525	489,786	522,539	36
Sogn og Fjordane	17,676	108,124	110,230	6

(continued)

	Land area (sq. km)	Population (2011 census)	Population (2018 estimate)	Density per sq. km 2018
Møre og Romsdal	14,583	256,381	266,856	18
Trøndelag[2]	38,618	—	458,744	12
Nordland	36,079	237,856	243,335	7
Troms Romsa	24,866	158,147	166,499	7
Finnmark	45,762	73,694	76,167	2
Mainland total	304,248[1]	4,978,237	5,295,619	17

[1]117,471 sq. miles.
[2]Trøndelag was created from the amalgamation of Nord-Trøndelag and Sør-Trøndelag in 2018.

The Arctic territories of Svalbard and Jan Mayen have an area of 61,397 sq. km. Persons staying on Svalbard and Jan Mayen are registered as residents of their home Norwegian municipality.

At Jan. 2011, 79·2% of the population lived in urban areas.

Population of the principal urban settlements on 1 Jan. 2013:

Oslo	925,228
Bergen	247,731
Stavanger/Sandnes	203,771
Trondheim	169,972
Drammen	110,503
Fredrikstad/Sarpsborg	106,758
Porsgrunn/Skien	90,621
Kristiansand	58,662
Tønsberg	49,735
Ålesund	49,528
Moss	44,449
Sandefjord	41,934
Arendal	41,703
Haugesund	40,152
Bodø	38,973
Tromsø	32,774
Hamar	26,004
Halden	24,410
Larvik	23,523

The official language is Norwegian, which has two versions: Bokmål (or Riksmål) and Nynorsk (or Landsmål).

The Sami, the indigenous people of the far north, number some 40,000 and form a distinct ethnic minority with their own culture and language.

Social Statistics

Statistics for calendar years:

	Births	Still-born	Outside marriage	Deaths	Marriages	Divorces
2006	58,545	201	31,056	41,253	21,721	10,598
2007	58,459	241	31,849	41,954	23,471	10,280
2008	60,497	221	33,302	41,712	25,125	10,158
2009	61,807	215	34,038	41,449	24,582	10,235
2010	61,442	190	33,655	41,499	23,577	10,264

Rates per 1,000 population, 2010, birth, 12·6; death, 8·5; marriage, 4·8; divorce, 2·1. Average annual population growth rate, 2000–10, 0·86% (2010, 1·28%). In 2009 there were 573 suicides, giving a rate of 11·9 per 100,000 population (men, 17·3 per 100,000; women, 6·5).

Expectation of life at birth, 2010, was 78·9 years for males and 83·2 years for females. Infant mortality, 2010, 2·8 per 1,000 live births; fertility rate,

2010, 1·95 births per woman. 55% of births are to unmarried mothers. In 2009 the average age at marriage was 37·3 years for males and 33·8 years for females (33·8 years and 31·0 years respectively for first marriages). Norway legalized same-sex marriage in Jan. 2009.

At 1 Jan. 2011 the immigrant population totalled 600,922, including 60,610 from Poland, 34,108 from Sweden, 31,884 from Pakistan and 27,827 from Iraq. In 2010 Norway received 10,064 asylum applications. Most were from Eritrea (1,711), Somalia (1,397), Afghanistan (979) and Russia (628).

UNICEF reported that 10·2% of children in Norway in 2014 lived in relative poverty (living in a household in which disposable income—when adjusted for family size and composition—is less than 60% of the national median income), the third lowest rate in the world.

In the Human Development Index, or HDI (measuring progress in countries in longevity, knowledge and standard of living), Norway was ranked first in the 2015 rankings published in the annual Human Development Report. Norway was ranked second in a global gender gap index of 145 countries compiled by the World Economic Forum for its *Global Gender Gap Report 2015*. The annual index considers economic, political, education and health criteria.

Climate

There is considerable variation in the climate because of the extent of latitude, the topography and the varying effectiveness of prevailing westerly winds and the Gulf Stream. Winters along the whole west coast are exceptionally mild but precipitation is considerable. Oslo, Jan. 24·3°F (−4·3°C), July 61·5°F (16·4°C). Annual rainfall 30·0" (763 mm). Bergen, Jan. 34·3°F (1·3°C), July 57·7°F (14·3°C). Annual rainfall 88·6" (2,250 mm). Trondheim, Jan. 26°F (−3·5°C), July 57°F (14°C). Annual rainfall 32·1" (870 mm). Bergen has one of the highest rainfall figures of any European city. The sun never fully sets in the northern area of the country in the summer and even in the south the sun rises at around 3 a.m. and sets at around 11 p.m.

Constitution and Government

Norway is a constitutional and hereditary monarchy.

The reigning King is **Harald V**, born 21 Feb. 1937, married on 29 Aug. 1968 to Sonja Haraldsen. He succeeded on the death of his father, King Olav V, on 21 Jan. 1991. *Offspring:* Princess Märtha Louise, born 22 Sept. 1971 (married Ari Behn, b. 30 Sept. 1972, on 24 May 2002; *offspring,* Maud Angelica, b. 29 April 2003; Leah Isadora, b. 8 April 2005; Emma Tallulah, b. 29 Sept. 2008); Crown Prince Haakon Magnus, born 20 July 1973 (married Mette-Marit Tjessem Høiby, b. 19 Aug. 1973, on 25 Aug. 2001; *offspring,* Ingrid Alexandra, b. 21 Jan. 2004; Sverre Magnus, b. 3 Dec. 2005; *offspring* of Crown Princess Mette-Marit from previous relationship, Marius, b. 13 Jan. 1997). In 2016 the king and queen together received an annual personal allowance of 11·2m. kroner from the civil list, and the Crown Prince and Crown Princess together 9·3m. kroner. Princess Märtha Louise relinquished her allowance in 2002. Women have been eligible to succeed to the throne since 1990. There is no coronation ceremony. The royal succession is in direct male line in the order of primogeniture. In default of male heirs the King may propose a successor to the *Storting*, but this assembly has the right to nominate another, if it does not agree with the proposal.

The Constitution, voted by a constituent assembly on 17 May 1814 and modified at various times, vests the legislative power of the realm in the *Storting* (Parliament). The royal veto may be exercised; but if the same bill passes two Stortings formed by separate and subsequent elections it becomes the law of the land without the assent of the sovereign. The King has the command of the land, sea and air forces, and makes all appointments.

The 169-member Storting (increased from 165 for the 2005 election) is directly elected by proportional representation. The country is divided into 19 districts, each electing from 4 to 15 representatives.

The Storting, when assembled, divides itself by election into the *Lagting* and the *Odelsting*. The former is composed of one-fourth of the members of the Storting, and the other of the remaining three-fourths. Each Ting (the Storting, the Odelsting and the Lagting) nominates its own president. Most questions are decided by the Storting, but questions relating to legislation must be considered and decided by the Odelsting and the Lagting separately. In the event of the Odelsting and the Lagting disagreeing the bill is considered by the Storting in plenary sitting, with a majority of two-thirds of the votes required for a new law to be passed. The same majority is required for

alterations of the Constitution, which can only be decided by the Storting in plenary sitting. The Storting elects five delegates, whose duty it is to revise the public accounts. The Lagting and the ordinary members of the Supreme Court of Justice (the *Høyesterett*) form a High Court of the Realm (the *Riksrett*) for the trial of ministers, members of the *Høyesterett* and members of the Storting. The impeachment before the *Riksrett* can only be decided by the Odelsting.

The executive is represented by the King, who exercises his authority through the Cabinet. Cabinet ministers are entitled to be present in the Storting and to take part in the discussions, but without a vote.

National Anthem

'Ja, vi elsker dette landet' ('Yes, we love this land'); words by B. Bjørnson, tune by R. Nordraak.

Government Chronology

Prime Ministers since 1945. (AP = Labour Party; DNA = Norwegian Labour Party; H = Conservative Party; KrF = Christian People's Party; Sp = Center Party)

1945–51	DNA	Einar Henry Gerhardsen
1951–55	DNA	Oscar Fredrik Torp
1955–63	DNA	Einar Henry Gerhardsen
1963	H	John Fyrstenberg Lyng
1963–65	DNA	Einar Henry Gerhardsen
1965–71	Sp	Per Borten
1971–72	DNA	Trygve Martin Bratteli
1972–73	KrF	Lars Korvald
1973–76	DNA	Trygve Martin Bratteli
1976–81	DNA	Odvar Nordli
1981	DNA	Gro Harlem Brundtland
1981–86	H	Kåre Isaachsen Willoch
1986–89	DNA	Gro Harlem Brundtland
1989–90	H	Jan Peder Syse
1990–96	DNA	Gro Harlem Brundtland
1996–97	DNA	Thorbjørn Jagland
1997–2000	KrF	Kjell Magne Bondevik
2000–01	DNA	Jens Stoltenberg
2001–05	KrF	Kjell Magne Bondevik
2005–13	DNA, AP	Jens Stoltenberg
2013–	H	Erna Solberg

Recent Elections

At the elections for the Storting held on 11 Sept. 2017 the following parties were elected: the Norwegian Labour Party (DNA), winning 49 out of 169 seats with 27·4% of the vote; Conservative Party (H), 45 (25·0%); Progress Party (FrP), 27 (15·2%); Centre Party (Sp), 19 (10·3%); Socialist Left Party (SV), 11 (6·0%); Liberal Party (V), 8 (4·4%); Christian Democratic Party (KrF), 8 (4·2%); Green Party (MDG), 1 (3·2%); Red Party (R), 1 (2·4%). Turnout was 78·2%.

Current Government

In Feb. 2019 the Conservative–Progress–Liberal–Christian Democratic party coalition government comprised:

Prime Minister: Erna Solberg; b. 1961 (Conservative Party; sworn in 16 Oct. 2013).

Minister of Agriculture and Food: Olaug Vervik Bollestad (KrF). *Children and Families:* Kjell Ingolf Ropstad (KrF). *Climate and the Environment:* Ola Elvestuen (V). *Culture and Equality:* Trine Skei Grande (V). *Defence:* Frank Bakke-Jensen (H). *Digitalization:* Nikolai Astrup (H). *Education and Integration:* Jan Tore Sanner (H). *Elderly and Public Health:* Åse Michaelsen (FrP). *Finance:* Siv Jensen (FrP). *Fisheries:* Harald T. Nesvik (FrP). *Foreign Affairs:* Ine Marie Eriksen Søreide (H). *Health and Care Services:* Bent Høie (H). *International Development:* Dag Inge Ulstein (KrF). *Justice and Immigration:* Tor Mikkel Wara (FrP). *Labour and Social*

Affairs: Anniken Hauglie (H). *Local Government and Modernization:* Monica Mæland (H). *Petroleum and Energy:* Kjell-Børge Freiberg (FrP). *Public Security:* Ingvil Smines Tybring-Gjedde (FrP). *Research and Higher Education:* Iselin Nybø (V). *Trade and Industry:* Torbjørn Røe Isaksen (H). *Transport and Communications:* Jon Georg Dale (FrP). *Office of the Prime Minister:* http://www.regjeringen.no

Current Leaders

Erna Solberg

Position

Prime Minister

Introduction

Erna Solberg was appointed prime minister on 16 Oct. 2013. The leader of the Conservative Party since 2004, she formed a minority coalition with the anti-immigration Progress Party. She is the second woman, after Gro Harlem Brundtland, to have been elected to the office.

Early Life

Solberg was born in Bergen on 24 Feb. 1961. Politically active from a young age, she was appointed chair of the Bergen Conservative Youth organization in 1980 and headed the Bergen Conservative student association while at the city's university. Having graduated in 1986 with a doctorate in sociology, politics, statistics and social economics, she was elected to parliament in 1989.

Between 2001 and 2005, as part of the coalition government fronted by Christian Democrat Kjell Magne Bondevik, Solberg served as minister of local government and regional development. Her uncompromising stance on issues including immigration earned her the moniker 'Iron Erna'. In 2002 she became deputy leader of the Conservative Party and two years later succeeded Jan Petersen at its head. At the parliamentary elections of 2005 her party suffered its worst result since the Second World War, losing 15 of its 38 seats. Although it fared better in 2009, it remained the third largest party after Labour and the Progress Party.

Her election campaign in 2013 sought to downplay her stern reputation, focusing instead on promoting job security, health care and education. At the election on 9 Sept. the Conservative Party won 48 seats, only seven fewer than Labour and sufficient to form a minority coalition with the Progress Party. It was the first parliamentary election since anti-immigration extremist Anders Breivik, who had once been a Progress Party activist, killed 77 people in a gun attack in 2011, many of them young people attending a summer camp organized by the youth wing of the Labour Party on the island of Utøya.

Career in Office

Solberg led a fragile coalition. Having balked at joining a coalition including the Progress Party, the centrist Liberal and Christian Democratic parties entered into a separate agreement to provide parliamentary support in return for influence on policy-making. These tensions were evident in budget negotiations in late 2016 when the Liberals and Christian Democrats announced their withdrawal before an eventual agreement was secured that prevented a government collapse.

Solberg pledged to reduce Norway's dependence on its North Sea oil revenue—which has declined substantially since 2014 as a result of falling international oil prices, undermining consumer confidence and offshore investment—by promoting a more balanced economy. She also promised to privatize, in whole or in part, many companies in which the government holds a large stake.

The ruling coalition retained power with a narrow victory in the parliamentary elections in Sept. 2017 and Solberg claimed a new mandate as prime minister.

In Oct.–Nov. 2018 Norway hosted the North Atlantic Treaty Organization's largest military exercise staged since the end of the Cold War.

Defence

Conscription is for 19 months with a 12-month service obligation. In June 2013 Norway became the first European country to introduce mandatory military service for women, with effect from Jan. 2015. Total active armed forces personnel numbered 24,450 in 2011, including 7,500 in Central Support, Administration and Command.

In 2013 defence spending totalled US$7,523m. (US$1,593 per capita), representing 1·4% of GDP. Expenditure per capita was the highest of any European country in 2013.

Army

Strength (2011) 8,900 (including 4,400 conscripts). The Army had 52 main battle tanks in 2011 plus 390 armoured personnel carriers and 104 armoured infantry fighting vehicles.

Navy

The Royal Norwegian Navy is organized into the Fleet, Coast Guard and Naval Schools. Main naval combatants include six German-built Ula class submarines and five destroyers. The Coast Guard had 14 patrol and coastal combatants in 2011.

The personnel of the Navy totalled 3,900 in 2011, of whom 1,450 were conscripts. The main naval base is at Bergen (Håkonsvern), with a logistics base at Ramsund.

Air Force

The Royal Norwegian Air Force was established in 1944. There are seven airbases, ten air wings, two control and reporting centres, nine flying squadrons and two anti-aircraft units. Total strength (2011) is 3,650 personnel, including 850 conscripts. There were 63 combat-capable aircraft in 2011 including F-16A/Bs.

Home Guard

The Home Guard is organized in small units equipped and trained for special tasks. Service after basic training is one week a year. The Home Guard consists of the Land Home Guard (strength, 2011, 42,650 with reserves), Naval Home Guard (1,900) and Anti-Air Home Guard (1,450).

International Relations

In a referendum on 27–28 Nov. 1994, 52·2% of votes cast were against joining the EU. The electorate was 3,266,182; turnout was 88·9%.

Economy

Services accounted for 57% of GDP in 2012, industry 42% and agriculture 1%.

Transparency International, the anti-corruption organization, ranked Norway seventh in the world in a survey of the countries with the least corruption in business and government in 2018. It received 84 out of 100 in the annual index.

Norway gave US$4·13bn. in international aid in 2017, which at 0·99% of GNI made it the third most generous developed country as a percentage of its gross national income, after Sweden and Luxembourg. Norway was one of only five industrialized countries to meet the UN target of 0·7%.

Overview

Norway has one of the world's highest levels of GDP per capita and one of the lowest levels of income inequality. In 2018 it was the 15th largest oil producer and seventh largest gas producer in the world, with hydrocarbons accounting for 22% of GDP. The country is also well endowed with other natural resources, including hydro-power, fish, forests and minerals. Unemployment stood at 4·0% in late 2018.

The economy combines free market capitalism with an advanced welfare state. GDP growth slowed in 2008 as a result of lower oil prices and the global financial crisis, heralding a recession in 2009. Recovery then began in 2010 and in 2012 there was growth of 2·7%. However, lower oil production, weak private consumption and a reduction in oil prices from 2014 have since had a further restrictive effect. GDP expanded by only 1·1% in 2016, although there was a moderate rebound to 1·9% the following year spurred by improved conditions in the labour market and a rise in oil prices.

Since emerging as a major oil and gas exporter in the mid-1970s, Norway has run large fiscal surpluses. Fiscal guidelines, effective since the 2002 budget, hold the central government non-oil deficit to 4% of the assets of the Government Pension Fund–Global (a sovereign wealth fund) to which revenue from oil production is transferred. In 2011 Statoil (an international energy company in which the Norwegian government is the largest shareholder) made two large discoveries at the Skrugard oilfield and the Aldous/Avaldsnes oilfield, the latter representing one of the ten largest oil finds ever on the Norwegian continental shelf.

Household debt is among the highest in the OECD countries, reaching a record high in early 2018 of 101·6% of GDP. The housing market was at risk of overheating before prices stabilized in mid-2013, although they remain at high levels. Other significant policy concerns include how to finance pensions for an ageing population (although new pension regulations are being implemented gradually under the Flexible Retirement Act), declining investment in oil-related industries, a strained global trading environment and growing unemployment.

Currency

The unit of currency is the *Norwegian krone* (NOK) of 100 *øre*. After Oct. 1990 the krone was fixed to the ecu in the EMS of the EU in the narrow band of 2·25%, but it was freed in Dec. 1992. Inflation rates (based on OECD statistics):

2008	2009	2010	2011	2012	2013	2014	2015	2016	2017
3·8%	2·2%	2·4%	1·3%	0·7%	2·1%	2·0%	2·2%	3·6%	1·9%

Foreign exchange reserves were US$42,214m. in Aug. 2009. Gold reserves are negligible. On 30 Sept. 2011 the nominal value of notes and coins in circulation was 49,609m. kroner.

Budget

General government revenue in 2015 (provisional) totalled 1,722bn. kroner and expenditure 1,472bn. kroner.

Principal sources of revenue in 2015 (provisional) were: taxes on income, profits and capital gains, 486bn. kroner; taxes on goods and services, 367bn. kroner; social contributions, 326bn. kroner. Main items of expenditure by economic type in 2015 (provisional): social benefits, 530bn. kroner; compensation of employees, 462bn. kroner; use of goods and services, 206bn. kroner.

The standard rate of VAT is 25·0% (reduced rates of 15·0%, 12·0% and 11·11%).

Norway had a budget surplus in 2014 of 9·1% of GDP.

Performance

Real GDP growth rates (based on OECD statistics):

2008	2009	2010	2011	2012	2013	2014	2015	2016	2017
0·5%	−1·7%	0·7%	1·0%	2·7%	1·0%	2·0%	2·0%	1·2%	2·0%

Major oil discoveries on the Norwegian continental shelf coincided with the 1974 and 1979 oil shocks, resulting in a pronounced upswing in the mainland economy which lasted until the 1986 oil price collapse. Norway only began to recover from the subsequent slump in the economy in 1993. The strong performance of the Norwegian economy in 1993–98 lifted mainland GDP by 20%, but there was a significant slowdown in 1998 when the oil price collapsed at a time when the labour market was overheated. Norway's total GDP in 2017 was US$398·8bn.

Banking and Finance

Norges Bank is the central bank and bank of issue. Supreme authority is vested in the Executive Board consisting of seven members appointed by the King and the Supervisory Council consisting of 15 members elected by the Storting. The *Governor* is Øystein Olsen. Total assets and liabilities at 30 Sept. 2011 were 3,375,882m. kroner.

Norway's largest commercial bank is DNB bank (with assets at 31 Dec. 2010 of 1,862bn. kroner); the second largest bank is Nordea Bank Norge. There were 16 commercial banks in 2007 (with total assets of 1,799bn. kroner) and 121 savings banks (with total assets of 1,993bn. kroner).

In June 2012 gross external debt amounted to US$618,646m.

There is a stock exchange in Oslo.

Energy and Natural Resources

Environment

Norway's carbon dioxide emissions from the consumption of energy in 2011 were the equivalent of 8·9 tonnes per capita. An *Environmental Performance Index* compiled in 2016 ranked Norway 17th of 180 countries, with 86·9%. The index examined various factors in nine areas—agriculture, air quality, biodiversity and habitat, climate and energy, fisheries, forests, health impacts, water and sanitation, and water resources.

In 2016 there were 39 national parks on the mainland (total area, 31,295 sq. km), plus 194 landscape protected areas (17,234 sq. km) and 464 other areas with protected flora and fauna (387 sq. km).

Electricity

The potential total hydro-electric power was estimated at 205,937m. kWh in 2010. Installed electrical capacity in 2011 was 31·7m. kW, 94% of it hydro-electric. Production, 2011, was 128,067m. kWh (95% hydro-electric). Consumption per capita in 2011, at 25,299 kWh, was one of the highest in the world. In 1991 Norway became the first country in Europe to deregulate its energy market. Norway is a net exporter of electricity.

Oil and Gas

There are enormous oil reserves in the Norwegian continental shelf. In 1966 the first exploration well was drilled. Production of crude oil, 2017, 88·8m. tonnes (down from a peak of 162·5bn. tonnes in 2001). Norway ranks among the world's biggest oil exporters, with net oil exports of around 1·9m. bbls a day in 2010. It had proven reserves of 7·9bn. bbls in 2012. In March 1998 Norway announced that it would reduce its output for the year by 100,000 bbls per day as part of a plan to cut global crude production. In June 2001 the Norwegian government sold a 17·5% stake in Statoil, the last major state-owned oil company in Western Europe. It now owns 67% of the company. In Oct. 2007 Statoil and the oil and gas division of Norsk Hydro (a Norwegian energy and metals company) merged to form StatoilHydro, as a result creating the world's largest offshore oil and natural gas producer.

Output of natural gas, 2017, 123·2bn. cu. metres with proven reserves of 1·7trn. cu. metres in 2017. In 2017 Norway ranked as Europe's second largest natural-gas supplier, after Russia.

Minerals

Production in 2008 unless otherwise indicated (in tonnes): coal (2009), 2,640,000; aluminium, 1,368,000; ilmenite concentrate, 915,000; iron ore, 477,000; zinc, 145,469; nickel, 88,741; refined copper (2007), 34,212.

Agriculture

Norway is barren and mountainous. The arable area is in strips in valleys and around fjords and lakes.

In 2010 the agricultural area was 1,003,010 ha., of which 651,176 ha. were meadow and pasture, 145,818 ha. were sown to barley, 75,810 ha. to oats, 71,945 ha. to wheat and 13,207 ha. to potatoes. Production in 2010 (in 1,000 tonnes): hay, 2,659; barley, 541; wheat, 331; potatoes, 321; oats, 299.

Livestock, 2010 (provisional): 875,169 cattle (308,399 dairy cows), 919,046 sheep (one year and over), 97,318 pigs for breeding, 36,935 dairy goats, 3,891,109 hens, 150,000 silver fox, 105,000 blue and silver blue fox, 650,000 mink and 251,400 tame reindeer.

Forestry

In 2015 the total area under forests was 12·11m. ha., or 40% of the total land area. Growing stock was 1,157m. cu. metres in 2015 (841m. cu. metres coniferous and 316m. cu. metres broadleaved). In 2011, 10·29m. cu. metres of roundwood were cut.

Fisheries

The total number of fishermen in 2011 was 12,768, of whom 2,548 had another chief occupation. In 2011 the number of registered fishing vessels (all with motor) was 6,250.

The catch in 2011 totalled 2,298,903 tonnes, almost entirely from sea fishing. The catch of herring in 2011 totalled 633,103 tonnes, capelin 362,368 tonnes and cod 340,167 tonnes. 10,334 harp seals were caught in 2011. The catch of hooded seals was prohibited in 2007. Commercial whaling was prohibited in 1988, but recommenced in 1993: 533 whales were caught in 2011. Norway is the second largest exporter of fishery commodities, after China. In 2011 exports were valued at US$9·46bn.

Industry

The leading companies by market capitalization in Norway in May 2018 were: Equinor (formerly Statoil), (US$90·2bn.); Telenor Group, a telecommunications company (US$32·4bn.); and DNB, a financial services group (US$31·7bn.).

Industry is chiefly based on raw materials. Paper and paper products, industrial chemicals and basic metals are important export manufactures. In the following table figures are given for industrial establishments in 2009. The values are given in 1m. kroner.

Industries	Establishments	Number of employees	Gross value of production	Value added (in market prices)
Mining and quarrying	745	4,680	11,463	4,032
Food products	2,269	44,207	131,352	23,700
Beverages and tobacco	106	4,487	16,405	9,932
Textiles, clothing and leather	1,338	4,772	6,101	2,183
Wood and wood products	1,930	14,248	21,557	6,429
Paper and paper products	93	5,475	14,470	2,415
Printing and reproduction of recorded media	1,414	7,461	10,851	4,079
Refined petroleum products, chemicals and pharmaceuticals	316	13,443	108,196	23,464
Rubber, plastic and mineral products	1,389	15,887	33,734	10,608
Basic metals	163	10,515	47,753	3,638
Fabricated metal products	2,609	25,225	44,124	15,314
Computer and electrical equipment	822	16,841	38,587	13,563
Machinery and equipment	1,501	20,872	78,404	23,620
Ships, boats, and oil platforms	534	22,761	65,130	16,353
Other transport equipment	182	4,085	6,482	2,157
Furniture and other manufacturing industries	2,056	11,335	13,553	5,371
Repair and installation of machinery and equipment	2,117	17,307	33,856	11,765
Total	19,584	243,601	682,019	178,623

Labour

Norway has a tradition of centralized wage bargaining. Since the early 1960s the contract period has been for two years with intermediate bargaining after 12 months, to take into consideration such changes as the rate of inflation.

The labour force averaged 2,602,000 in 2010 (1,224,000 females). The total number of employed persons in 2010 averaged 2,508,000 (1,187,000 females), of whom 1,835,000 were in full-time employment, 667,000 in part-time employment and 6,000 working unspecified hours. Of those in employment in 2013, 77·2% worked in services, 20·4% in industry and 2·1% in agriculture. 43·0% of the labour force that year had a secondary education as the highest level and 38·8% had a tertiary education. In 2013, 34·6% of those in employment worked in the public sector.

The unemployment rate in Nov. 2018 was 3·8%, down from 4·2% in 2017 as a whole.

There were 12 work stoppages in 2010 (two in 2009): 500,009 working days were lost (180 in 2009).

International Trade

Imports and Exports

Total imports and exports in calendar years (in 1m. kroner):

	2006	2007	2008	2009	2010
Imports	411,755	468,918	504,481	430,363	466,810
Exports	782,943	795,366	953,154	717,965	792,575

Norway's trade surplus was 325,765m. kroner in 2010. Major import suppliers in 2010 (value in 1m. kroner): Sweden, 65,603·1; Germany, 57,461·5; China, 39,614·9; Denmark, 29,018·6; UK, 27,460·5; USA, 25,324·6. Imports from economic areas: EU, 295,667·6; Nordic countries, 108,068·6; OECD, 360,693·1.

Major export markets in 2010 (value in 1m. kroner): UK, 213,981·8; Netherlands, 94,720·9; Germany, 89,725·8; Sweden, 55,315·6; France, 50,532·8; USA, 39,368·0. Exports to economic areas: EU, 639,798·7; Nordic countries, 93,203·0; OECD, 721,729·5.

Principal imports in 2010 (in 1m. kroner): motor vehicles, 43,800·5 (including passenger cars and station wagons, 26,205·3); transport equipment excluding motor vehicles, 32,708·0; petroleum, petroleum products and related materials, 23,151·6; electrical machinery, apparatus and appliances, 22,784·0; metalliferous ores and metal scrap, 22,288·8; general industrial machinery and equipment, 21,925·9.

Principal exports in 2010 (in 1m. kroner): petroleum, petroleum products and related materials, 315,259·3 (including crude petroleum, 283,337·2); natural and manufactured gas, 188,010·4 (including natural gas, 163,970·3); fish, crustaceans and molluscs, and preparations thereof, 52,307·6; non-ferrous metals, 44,083·6 (including aluminium, 26,493·6); general industrial machinery and equipment, 18,423·9; chemical materials and products, 17,992·3.

Communications

Roads

In Jan. 2011 the length of public roads (including roads in towns) totalled 93,509 km. Total road length in Jan. 2011 included: national roads, 10,496 km; provincial roads, 44,281 km; local roads, 38,732 km. Number of registered motor vehicles, 2010, included: 2,308,548 passenger cars (including station wagons and ambulances), 397,279 vans, 254,674 tractors and special purpose vehicles, 168,904 mopeds, 146,592 motorcycles, 81,330 goods vehicles (including lorries), 48,432 combined vehicles and 20,348 buses. In 2010, 9,130 injuries were sustained in road accidents, with 208 fatalities. Norway has one of the lowest death rates in road accidents of any industrialized country, at 4·3 deaths per 100,000 people in 2010.

Rail

The length of state railways in 2010 was 4,169 km (2,566 km electrified). In 2009 passenger-km travelled came to 2,669m. and freight tonne-km to 2,804m. Sales and other operating income totalled 11,179m. kroner in 2010. There is a metro (104 km) and a tram network (146 km) in Oslo.

Civil Aviation

The main international airports are at Oslo (Gardermoen), Bergen (Flesland), Stavanger (Sola), Sandefjord (Torp) and Moss (Rygge). Norway's largest airline is SAS Norge, a subsidiary of Scandinavian Airlines (SAS). It was established in 2004 as SAS Braathens through the merger of the Norwegian part of SAS and Braathens, and was renamed SAS Norge in 2007. SAS Norge carries around 10m. passengers a year to 55 destinations. The second largest airline is the low-cost carrier Norwegian, which operates long-haul flights as well as services within Europe.

In 2010 Oslo (Gardermoen) handled 19,140,384 passengers (10,123,605 on international flights). Bergen is the second busiest airport for passenger traffic, with 5,189,714 passengers in 2010 (3,604,882 on domestic flights).

Shipping

The Norwegian International Ship Register was set up in 1987. In 2011, 507 ships were registered (390 Norwegian) totalling 13,590,000 GT. 206 tankers accounted for 6,917,000 GT. There were also 891 vessels totalling 1,996,000 GT on the Norwegian Ordinary Register. These figures do not include fishing boats, tugs, salvage vessels, icebreakers and similar special types of vessels. In Jan. 2011 Norway's merchant fleet represented 3·4% of total world tonnage. The busiest port is Bergen, which handled 51,814,000 tonnes of cargo in 2013. The warm Gulf Stream ensures ice-free harbours throughout the year.

Telecommunications

In 2013 there were 5,863,000 mobile phone subscriptions (equivalent to 1,162·7 per 1,000 inhabitants) and 1,237,000 fixed telephone subscriptions (or 245·2 per 1,000 inhabitants). In the same year 66·5% of the population aged 16–74 were internet users. In March 2012 there were 2·6m. Facebook users. Since 2000 the government has been reducing its interest in Telenor, the country's largest telecommunications operator, and in March 2004 lowered its stake to 54·0%.

Social Institutions

According to the 2017 *Fragile States Index*—a list published jointly by the Fund for Peace and *Foreign Policy* magazine—Norway was ranked as the country second least vulnerable to conflict or collapse. The index is based on 12 indicators of state vulnerability across social, political and economic categories.

Justice

The judicature is common to civil and criminal cases; the same professional judges preside over both. These judges are state officials. The participation of lay judges and jurors, both summoned for the individual case, varies according to the kind of court and kind of case.

The 96 city or district courts of first instance are in criminal cases composed of one professional judge and two lay judges, chosen by ballot from a panel elected by the local authority. In civil cases two lay judges may participate. These courts are competent in all cases except criminal cases where the maximum penalty exceeds six years imprisonment. In every community there is a Conciliation Board composed of three lay persons elected by the district council. A civil lawsuit usually begins with mediation by the Board which can pronounce judgement in certain cases.

The five high courts, or courts of second instance, are composed of three professional judges. Additionally, in civil cases two or four lay judges may be summoned. In serious criminal cases, which are brought before high courts in the first instance, a jury of ten lay persons is summoned to determine whether the defendant is guilty according to the charge. In less serious criminal cases the court is composed of two professional and three lay judges. In civil cases, the court of second instance is an ordinary court of appeal. In criminal cases in which the lower court does not have judicial authority, it is itself the court of first instance. In other criminal cases it is an appeal court as far as the appeal is based on an attack against the lower court's assessment of the facts when determining the guilt of the defendant. An appeal based on any other alleged mistakes is brought directly before the Supreme Court.

The Supreme Court *(Høyesterett)* is the court of last resort. There are 18 Supreme Court judges. Each individual case is heard by five judges. Some major cases are determined in plenary session. The Supreme Court may in general examine every aspect of the case and the handling of it by the lower courts. However, in criminal cases the Court may not overrule the lower court's assessment of the facts as far as the guilt of the defendant is concerned.

The Court of Impeachment *(Riksretten)* is composed of five judges of the Supreme Court and ten members of Parliament.

All serious offences are prosecuted by the State. The Public Prosecution Authority consists of the Attorney General, 18 district attorneys and legally qualified officers of the ordinary police force. Counsel for the defence is in general provided for by the State.

The population in penal institutions in Sept. 2013 was 3,649 (72 per 100,000 of national population). Norway was ranked second of 102 countries for civil justice and fourth for criminal justice in the 2015 World Justice Project *Rule of Law Index*, which provides data on how the rule of law is experienced by the general public across eight categories. It ranked second in the overall 2015 Index.

Education

Free compulsory schooling in primary and lower secondary schools was extended to ten years from nine, and the starting age lowered to six from seven, in July 1997. All young people between the ages of 16 and 19 have the statutory right to three years of upper secondary education. In 2010 there were 6,579 kindergartens (children up to six years old) with 277,139 children and 87,401 staff. There were 614,020 pupils at primary and lower secondary schools in 2010; 228,170 pupils at upper secondary schools; and 20,658 students at folk high schools and vocational schools.

There are eight universities: Oslo (founded 1811), with 27,341 students in 2007; Bergen (1948), with 14,057 students; Tromsø (1972), with 5,424 students; the Norwegian University of Science and Technology (1996, formerly the University of Trondheim and the Norwegian Institute of Technology), with 19,351 students; Stavanger (2005, formerly Stavanger University College), with 8,050 students; Norwegian University of Life Sciences (1859, university since 2005—formerly the Agricultural University of Norway), with 2,817 students; Agder (2007, formerly Agder University College), with 7,801 students; and Nordland (2011, formerly Bodø University College), with 5,700 students in 2011. There are also nine specialized university institutions, 21 state university colleges and a number of private colleges. In 2010 the universities had 93,768 students and the state university colleges 89,572 students. The University of Tromsø is responsible for Sami language and studies.

In 2009 public expenditure on education came to 7·2% of GDP and 15·8% of total government spending. The adult literacy rate is at least 99%.

Health

The health care system, which is predominantly publicly financed (mainly by a national insurance tax), is run on both county and municipal levels. Persons who fall ill are guaranteed medical treatment, and health services are distributed according to need. In Aug. 2008 there were 20,035 active physicians in Norway. On 31 Dec. 2009 there were 15,205 hospital beds (excluding those in psychiatric institutions). In 2012 Norway spent 9·3% of its GDP on health. In 2010, 19% of men and 19% of women aged 16–74 smoked on a daily basis.

Welfare

Expenditure on social assistance in 2009 totalled 4,642m. kroner. On 31 Dec. 2010 there were 663,799 old age pensioners (377,170 women) and 301,088 disability pensioners (170,959 women). Maternity leave is either for 44 weeks on 100% of previous salary or 54 weeks on 80% of previous salary; unused portions may pass to the father. In Dec. 2010, 33,433 children aged one to three received cash benefit (27% of all children between one and three years of age).

Religion

There is freedom of religion, the Church of Norway (Evangelical Lutheran), however, being the national church. Its clergy are nominated by the King. Ecclesiastically Norway is divided into 11 dioceses, 100 deaneries and 1,298 parishes. About 80% of Norwegians belong to the Church of Norway (which had 3,848,841 members in 2009) and approximately 68% of infants were baptised in the Church in 2009. There were 431,287 members of registered and unregistered religious and philosophical communities outside the Church of Norway in 2009, subsidized by central government and local authorities, including 234,772 Christians and 92,744 Muslims. The Roman Catholics are under a Bishop at Oslo, and Prelates at Tromsø and Trondheim.

Culture

World Heritage Sites

Norway's UNESCO heritage sites (with year listed) are: the 12–13th century wooden church in Sogn og Fjordane on the west coast, the Urnes Stave Church (1979), a testimony to the city's key role in the Hanseatic League trading route between the 14–16th centuries; the 58 wooden buildings in Bergen's wharf of Bryggen (1979); the wooden houses of the copper mining village of Røros (1980), active between the 17–20th centuries; the pre-historic Rock Drawings of Alta (1995) in the Alta Fjord, near the Arctic Circle, dating from 4200 to 500 BC; Vegaøyan—the Vega Archipelago (2004), a cluster of dozens of islands centred on Vega, just south of the Arctic Circle; the West Norwegian Fjords—Geirangerfjord and Nærøyfjord (2005); and Rjukan-Notodden Industrial Heritage Site (2015), comprising hydro-electric power plants, transmission lines, factories, transport systems and towns.

The Struve Geodetic Arc was inscribed in 2005. It is a chain of survey triangulations spanning from Norway to the Black Sea that helped establish the exact shape and size of the earth and is shared with nine other countries.

Press
There were 72 paid-for daily newspapers with a combined average daily circulation of 1·54m. in 2014, and 158 non-dailies with a circulation of 605,000. In 2012 there were 228 newspaper online editions, with 3·28m. unique monthly visitors. In the 2013 *World Press Freedom Index* compiled by Reporters Without Borders, Norway was ranked third out of 179 countries.

Tourism
In 2014 there were 30,306,594 guest nights in commercial accommodation (hotels, campsites, cabin villages and youth/family hostels), of which 22,152,158 by Norwegians and 8,154,436 by foreigners. In the same year there were 2,667,362 day visitors from cruises to Norwegian ports. The average length of a holiday in Norway was 7·6 days in 2014.

Festivals
The Bergen International Festival, Norway's oldest festival, is held annually in May/June and includes music, dance and theatre. The biennial Ibsen Festival (theatre) is held in Oslo in Aug./Sept. in even-numbered years. CODA (the Oslo International Dance Festival) runs for three weeks every Sept./Oct.

Diplomatic Representatives

Of Norway in the United Kingdom (25 Belgrave Sq., London, SW1X 8QD)
    Ambassador: Wegger Christian Strømmen.

Of the United Kingdom in Norway (Thomas Heftyes Gate 8, 0244 Oslo)
    Ambassador: Richard Wood.

Of Norway in the USA (2720 34th St., NW, Washington, D.C., 20008).
    Ambassador: Kåre Reidar Aas.

Of the USA in Norway (Morgedalsvegen 36, 0378 Oslo)
    Ambassador: Kenneth J. Braithwaite.

Of Norway to the United Nations
    Ambassador: Mona Juul.

Of Norway to the European Union
    Ambassador: Rolf Einar Fife.

Svalbard
General Details
An archipelago situated in the Arctic between 10° and 35° E. long. and between 74° and 81° N. lat. Total area, 61,022 sq. km (23,561 sq. miles). The main islands are Spitsbergen, Nordaustlandet, Edgeøya, Barentsøya, Prins Karls Forland, Bjørnøya, Hopen, Kong Karls Land and Kvitøya. Rival Dutch, British and Danish-Norwegian claims to sovereignty since the 17th century were eventually settled by a treaty in 1920 which recognized Norwegian control and in 1925 the archipelago was officially incorporated into the Kingdom of Norway.

The sparse population (2,394 in Jan. 2011) is predominantly Norwegian, but with some Russians and Poles. Coal mining is the principal industry. There are research and radio stations, and an airport near Longyearbyen (Svalbard Lufthavn).

Jan Mayen
This mountainous island of volcanic origin and partly covered by glaciers is situated at 71° N. lat. and 8° 30' W. long., 300 miles north-northeast of Iceland. Total area, 377 sq. km (146 sq. miles). Beerenberg, its highest peak, reaches 2,277 metres. Its present name derives from the Dutch whaling captain Jan Jacobsz May, who mapped the island in 1614. Subsequently established as a whaling base, the island was then abandoned in 1638 and remained uninhabited until 1921 when Norway established a radio and meteorological station. In 1929 Jan Mayen was officially proclaimed as incorporated into the Kingdom of Norway. Its relation to Norway was finally settled by law in 1930.

Bouvet Island
Bouvetøya
This uninhabited volcanic island, mostly covered by glaciers and situated at 54° 25' S. lat. and 3° 21' E. long., was discovered in 1739 by a French naval officer, Jean-Baptiste Loziert Bouvet, but a British sea captain claimed it for the British crown in 1825. In 1928 Britain waived its claim in favour of Norway, which had occupied it in 1927. A law in 1930 declared Bouvetøtya a Norwegian dependency. Area, 49 sq. km (19 sq. miles). Since 1977 there has been an automatic meteorological station on the island.

Peter I Island
Peter I Øy
This uninhabited island is situated at 68° 48' S. lat. and 90° 35' W. long. The first landing was made in 1929 by a Norwegian expedition which hoisted the Norwegian flag. In May 1931 Peter I Island was placed under Norwegian sovereignty and in March 1933 incorporated as a dependency. Area, 156 sq. km (60 sq. miles).

Queen Maud Land
Dronning Maud Land
That part of the Antarctic Continent from the border of Falkland Islands dependencies in the west to the border of the Australian Antarctic Dependency in the east (between 20° W. and 45° E.) came under Norwegian sovereignty in 1939, having previously been ownerless. It became a dependency in 1957.

Further Reading

Norway
Statistics Norway (formerly Central Bureau of Statistics). *Statistisk Årbok/ Statistical Yearbook of Norway* (now discontinued).—*Economic survey* (annual, from 1935; with English summary from 1952, now published in *Økonomiske Analyser*, annual).—*Historisk Statistikk; Historical Statistics.—Statistisk Månedshefte* (with English index)
Norges Statskalender (1816–2012).
Archer, Clive, *Norway and an Integrating Europe.* 2004
Danielsen, R., *et al., Norway: a History From the Vikings to Our Own Times.* 1994
Petersson, O., *The Government and Politics of the Nordic Countries.* 1994
Sejersted, Francis, *The Age of Social Democracy: Norway and Sweden in the Twentieth Century.* 2011
National library: The National Library of Norway, Henrik Ibsens gate 110, 0255 Oslo; Finsetveien 2, 8624 Mo i Rana.
National Statistical Office: Statistics Norway, Akersveien 26, 0177 Oslo.
Website: http://www.ssb.no

Svalbard
Greve, T., *Svalbard: Norway in the Arctic.* 1975
Hisdal, V., *Geography of Svalbard.* Rev. ed., 1984

Oman

Saltanat 'Uman (Sultanate of Oman)

Capital: Muscat
Population projection, 2020: 5·15m.
GNI per capita, 2015: (PPP$) 34,402
HDI/world rank, 2015: 0·796/52=
Internet domain extension: .om

Key Historical Events

The ancestors of present day Oman are believed to have arrived in two waves of migration, the first from Yemen and the second from northern Arabia. In the 9th century maritime trade flourished and Sohar became the greatest sea port in the Islamic world. In the early 16th century the Portuguese occupied Muscat. The Ya'aruba dynasty introduced a period of renaissance in Omani fortunes both at home and abroad, uniting the country and bringing prosperity; but, on the death in 1718 of Sultan bin Saif II, civil war broke out over the election of his successor. Persian troops occupied Muttrah and Muscat but failed to take Sohar which was defended by Ahmad bin Said, who expelled the Persians from Oman after the civil war had ended. In 1744 the Al bu Said family assumed power and has ruled to the present day. Oman remained largely isolated from the rest of the world until 1970 when Said bin Taimur was deposed by his son Qaboos in a bloodless coup.

Territory and Population

Situated at the southeast corner of the Arabian peninsula, Oman is bounded in the northeast by the Gulf of Oman and southeast by the Arabian Sea, southwest by Yemen and northwest by Saudi Arabia and the United Arab Emirates. There is an enclave at the northern tip of the Musandam Peninsula. An agreement of April 1992 completed the demarcation of the border with Yemen, and an agreement of March 1990 finalized the border with Saudi Arabia.

With a coastline of 1,700 sq. km from the Strait of Hormuz in the north to the borders of the Republic of Yemen, the Sultanate is strategically located overlooking ancient maritime trade routes linking the Far East and Africa with the Mediterranean.

The Sultanate of Oman occupies a total area of 309,500 sq. km and includes different terrains that vary from plain to highlands and mountains. The coastal plain overlooking the Gulf of Oman and the Arabian Sea forms the most important and fertile plain in Oman.

The **Kuria Muria** islands were ceded to the UK in 1854 by the Sultan of Muscat and Oman. On 30 Nov. 1967 the islands were retroceded to the Sultan of Muscat and Oman, in accordance with the wishes of the population. They are now commonly known as the **Halaniyat Islands**.

Population at the census of Dec. 2010, 2,773,479 (1,612,411 males); density 9·0 per sq. km. The population comprised 1,957,336 Omanis and 816,143 expatriates. Mid-2015 population: 4,159,102.

The UN gives a projected population for 2020 of 5·15m.

In 2011, 73·3% of the population lived in urban areas. The census population of the capital, Muscat, in 2010 was 775,878.

The official language is Arabic; English is in commercial use.

Social Statistics

2008 estimates: births, 61,000; deaths, 8,000. Estimated rates, 2008 (per 1,000 population): births, 22·0; deaths, 2·7. Expectation of life at birth, 2013, was 74·8 years for males and 79·0 years for females. Average annual population growth rate, 2000–08, 1·8%. Fertility rate, 2008, 3·0 births per woman, down from 7·8 in 1988.

Oman has achieved some of the most rapid advances ever recorded. Infant mortality declined from 200 per 1,000 live births in 1960 to eight per 1,000 live births in 2010, and as recently as 1970 life expectancy was just 40.

Climate

Oman has a desert climate, with exceptionally hot and humid months from April to Oct., when temperatures may reach 47°C. Light monsoon rains fall in the south from June to Sept., with highest amounts in the western highland region. Muscat, Jan. 28°C, July 46°C. Annual rainfall 101 mm. Salalah, Jan. 29°C, July 32°C. Annual rainfall 98 mm.

Constitution and Government

Oman is a hereditary absolute monarchy. The Sultan legislates by decree and appoints a Cabinet to assist him. The Basic Statute of the State was promulgated on 6 Nov. 1996.

The present Sultan is **Qaboos bin Said Al Said** (b. Nov. 1940). He does not have any children and has not publicly named an heir or a designated successor.

In 1991 a new consultative assembly, the *Majlis al-Shura*, replaced the former State Consultative Chamber. The Majlis consists of 85 elected members. It debates domestic issues, but has no legislative or veto powers. There is also an upper house, the *Majlis al-Dawla*, which consists of 85 appointed members; it too has advisory powers only.

In Dec. 2002 the Sultan of Oman extended voting rights to all citizens over the age of 21.

National Anthem

'Ya Rabbana elifidh lana jalalat al Saltan' ('O Lord, protect for us his majesty the Sultan'); words by Rashid bin Aziz, tune by Rodney Bashford.

Government Chronology

Sultans since 1932.

1932–70	Said bin Taimur Al Said
1970–	Qaboos bin Said Al Said

Recent Elections

The last elections to the *Majlis al-Shura* were on 25 Oct. 2015. No parties are allowed. 85 legislators were chosen for four-year terms from 590 candidates, including 20 women (although only one woman was elected).

Current Government

The Sultan is nominally Prime Minister and Minister of Foreign Affairs, Defence and Finance.

In Feb. 2019 the other Ministers were:

Deputy Prime Minister for Cabinet Affairs: Fahd bin Mahmud Al Said.

Minister Responsible for Defence Affairs: Sayyid Badr bin Saud bin Harib Al Busaidi. *Minister Responsible for Foreign Affairs:* Yusuf bin Alawi bin Abdallah. *Minister Responsible for Financial Affairs:* Darwish bin Ismail bin Ali Al Balushi.

Minister of Agriculture and Fisheries: Fuad bin Jaffer bin Mohammed Al Sajwani. *Awqaf and Religious Affairs:* Abdallah bin Muhammad bin Abdallah Al Salimi. *Civil Service:* Shaikh Khalid bin Omar bin Saeed Al Marhoon. *Commerce and Industry:* Ali bin Masoud bin Ali Al Sunaidi. *Education:* Madeeha bint Ahmed bin Nassir Al Shibaniyah. *Environment and Climate Change:* Mohammed Salem Al Tobi. *Health:* Ahmed bin Mohammed bin Obaid Al Sa'eedi. *Higher Education:* Rawya bint Saud Al Busaidi. *Housing:* Sheikh Saif bin Mohammed bin Saif Al Shabibi. *Information:* Abdulmunem Al Hasni. *Interior:* Sayyid Hamoud bin Faisal Al Busaidi. *Justice:* Shaikh Abdul Malik bin Abdullah Al Khalili. *Legal Affairs:* Abdullah bin Mohammed bin Saeed Al Saeedi. *Manpower:* Abdullah bin Nasser Al Bakri. *National Heritage and Culture:* Sayyid Haitham bin Tariq Al Said. *Oil and Gas:* Muhammad bin Hamad bin Seif Al Rumhi. *Regional*

Municipalities and Water Resources: Ahmed bin Abdullah bin Mohammed Al Sahi. *Social Development:* Shaikh Mohammed bin Saeed Al Kalbani. *Sport:* Shaikh Saad bin Mohammed Al Saadi. *Tourism:* Ahmed bin Nasser Al Mahrazi. *Transportation and Communications:* Ahmed bin Mohammed bin Salem Al Futaisi. *Diwan of the Royal Court:* Sayyid Khalid bin Hilal bin Saud Al Busaidi. *Royal Office:* Lieut.-Gen. Sultan bin Mohammed Al Nu'amani. *Minister of State and Governor of the Capital:* Sayyid Soud bin Hilal Al Busaidi. *Minister of State and Governor of Dhofar:* Sayyid Mohammed bin Sultan bin Hamoud Al Busaidi. *Secretary General of the Council of Ministers:* Shaikh Fadhjil bin Mohammed Al Harthi.
Government Website: http://www.oman.om

Current Leaders

Qaboos bin Said
Position
Sultan

Introduction
Qaboos has been the Sultan since 23 July 1970 when he deposed his father, Said bin Taimur. He has carried out an ambitious social and economic modernization programme, opening Oman to the outside world through accession to the League of Arab States, Gulf Co-operation Council and United Nations and pursuing a moderate regional foreign policy while preserving a long-standing political and military relationship with the United Kingdom. He is nominally prime minister, minister of defence, minister of foreign affairs, minister of finance and chairman of the central bank.

Early Life
Born in Salalah on 18 Nov. 1940, Qaboos attended a private school in England from the age of 16. In 1960 he went to the British Royal Military Academy at Sandhurst as an officer cadet. He subsequently served in the British army on operational duty and then studied in England before returning to Oman.

Career in Office
Concerned at his father's reactionary regime and inability to channel Oman's new oil wealth into the country's development, Qaboos led a coup in 1970. He then undertook a range of infrastructure projects, including the construction of roads, hospitals, schools, communications systems, and industrial and port facilities. He also abrogated his father's more extreme moralistic laws. A popular ruler, his regime has since remained stable despite periods of labour unrest, an alleged Islamist extremist plot in 2005 to overthrow the government and protests in 2011 demanding employment and political reform against a background of wider disaffection spreading across the Arab world.

Although the Sultan continues to legislate by decree, he is advised by an appointed Cabinet, an elected consultative assembly (*Majlis al-Shura*) and an appointed upper house (*Majlis al-Dawla*). In March 2004 Qaboos appointed Oman's first female Cabinet minister. In Feb. 2013 the government approved an increase in the minimum wage and limits on the employment of foreign workers to ease popular discontent at the level of unemployment.

In 2017 Oman's relations with some of its regional Gulf neighbours became strained over the sultanate's closeness to Iran and Qatar, perceived as hostile states by Saudi Arabia, the United Arab Emirates and Bahrain. Then in Oct. 2018 Binyamin Netanyahu made a surprise first state visit by an Israeli prime minister to Oman in 22 years.

There have been growing concerns over the ageing Sultan's health and absences abroad for treatment, in turn generating speculation about Oman's political future given the lack of an heir or designated successor.

Defence

Military expenditure in 2013 totalled US$9,246m. (US$2,931 per capita), representing 11·7% of GDP.

Army
Strength (2011) 25,000. In addition there are 6,400 Royal Household troops. A paramilitary tribal home guard numbers 4,000.

Navy
The main naval base is at Wudam. Naval personnel in 2011 totalled 4,200. There is a wholly separate Royal Yacht Squadron with 150 personnel in 2011.

Air Force
The Air Force, formed in 1959, had 54 combat-capable aircraft in 2011 including F-16s, *Jaguars* and British Aerospace *Hawks*.
Personnel (2011) 5,000.

Economy

Oil and natural gas (excluding petroleum products) contributed 52·2% to GDP in 2012; followed by manufacturing (including petroleum products), 10·1%; trade, restaurants and hotels, 8·1%; and finance and real estate, 7·6%.

Overview
Oman is a high-income country reliant on natural resources, mainly crude oil and natural gas. Oil accounted for more than one-third of GDP in 2017 and over 70% of government receipts and export earnings. However, oil reserves are expected to be severely depleted by 2030, although gas supplies are predicted to last longer.

Annual GDP growth averaged 4·9% from 2008 to 2016, but in 2017 the economy contracted by 0·3%. The general government debt-to-GDP ratio was 25% in 2000 but, on the back of buoyant oil prices, fell to around 5% in 2014 before accelerating to a record 40% in 2017. A combination of high state spending and reduced oil revenues is expected to see further debt increases in the short- to mid-term.

Oman Vision 2020 is a national programme of diversification, designed to reduce dependency on hydrocarbons and expand the manufacturing, tourism and services sectors. To this end, it envisages improving infrastructure and developing human resources with the aim of increasing the non-oil contribution to GDP to 81% by 2020.

Currency
The unit of currency is the *Rial Omani* (OMR). It is divided into 1,000 *baiza*. The rial is pegged to the US dollar. In July 2005 foreign exchange reserves were US$4,511m. and gold reserves totalled 1,000 troy oz (291,000 troy oz in April 2002). Total money supply was RO 1,067m. in May 2005. Inflation was 1·1% in 2016 and 1·6% in 2017.

Budget
In 2012 revenues were RO 14,080·3m. and expenditures RO 13,555·0m. Oil revenue accounted for 74·1% of revenues in 2012; current expenditure accounted for 64·7% of expenditures.

Performance
Real GDP growth was 4·7% in 2015 and 5·0% in 2016 before contracting by 0·9% in 2017. Total GDP in 2017 was US$72·6bn.

Banking and Finance
The bank of issue is the Central Bank of Oman, which commenced operations in 1975 (*President*, Tahir bin Salim bin Abdullah Al Amri). All banks must comply with BIS capital adequacy ratios and have a minimum capital of RO 20m. (minimum capital requirement for foreign banks established in Oman is RO 3m.). In 2015 there were nine local banks, two specialized banks, nine foreign commercial banks and two sharia-compliant banks. The largest bank is BankMuscat SAOG, with assets of US$25·3bn. in Dec. 2014.

Total foreign debt was US$3,472m. in 2005.

There is a stock exchange in Muscat, which is linked with those in Bahrain and Kuwait.

Energy and Natural Resources

Environment
Oman's carbon dioxide emissions from the consumption of energy in 2011 were the equivalent of 17·7 tonnes per capita.

Electricity
Installed capacity was 4·9m. kW in 2011. Production in 2011 was 21·35bn. kWh, with consumption per capita 7,060 kWh.

Oil and Gas

The economy is dominated by the oil industry. Oil in commercial quantities was discovered in 1964 and production began in 1967. Production in 2012 was 45·1m. tonnes and exports 37·5m. tonnes. Total proven reserves in 2012 were 5·5bn. bbls. It was announced in Aug. 2000 that two new oilfields in the south of the country had been discovered, with a potential combined daily production capacity of 12,200 bbls. Earlier in 2000 oil began to be pumped from two further recently-discovered oilfields.

Gas is likely to become the second major source of income for the country. Oman's proven natural gas reserves were 900bn. cu. metres in 2012. Natural gas production was 29·0bn. cu. metres in 2012.

Minerals

Production in 2009 (in 1,000 tonnes): sand and gravel, 77,114; limestone, 7,948; chromite, 636 (up from 19 in 2004); marble, 588; gypsum, 333; quartz, 198. The mountains of Oman are rich in mineral deposits; these include chromite, coal, asbestos, manganese, gypsum, limestone and marble.

Agriculture

Agriculture and fisheries are the traditional occupations of Omanis and remain important to the people and economy of Oman to this day. The country now produces a wide variety of fresh fruit, vegetables and field crops. The country is rapidly moving towards its goal of self-sufficiency in agriculture with the total area under cultivation standing at over 70,000 ha. and total output more than 1m. tonnes. This has not been achieved without effort. In a country where water is a scarce commodity it has meant educating farmers on efficient methods of irrigation and building recharge dams to make the most of infrequent rainfall. There were 37,700 ha. of arable land in 2013 and 30,800 ha. of permanent crops. In the same year 59,000 ha. were equipped for irrigation. In 2010, 5% of employed persons were engaged in agriculture.

The coastal plain (Batinah) northwest of Muscat is fertile, as are the Dhofar highlands in the south. In the valleys of the interior, as well as on the Batinah coastal plain, date cultivation has reached a high level. Agricultural products, 2013 (in 1,000 tonnes): dates, 308; tomatoes, 75; cucumbers and gherkins, 44; sorghum, 32. Livestock are raised in the south where there are monsoon rains. Camels (243,000 in 2013) are bred by the inland tribes. Other livestock, 2013: goats, 2·1m.; sheep, 548,000; cattle, 360,000; chickens (estimate), 4·6m.

Fisheries

The catch was 257,022 tonnes in 2015, exclusively sea fish.

Industry

Apart from oil production, copper smelting and cement production, there are light industries, mainly food processing and chemical products. The government gives priority to import substitute industries.

Labour

In 2013 the labour force totalled 1,985,000 with the unemployment rate standing at 7·9%. Males constituted 85·9% of the workforce in 2013. In 2014 there were 232,980 persons in government service and 197,510 Omanis in the private sector. The employment of foreign labour is being discouraged following 'Omanization' regulations of 1994. However, in 2014 expatriate workers totalled 1,570,132. Omanis constitute only 15% of private sector workers. Following the unrest of early 2011 the private sector monthly minimum wage for national workers was increased in Feb. 2011 from RO 140 to RO 200. There is no minimum wage for foreign workers.

International Trade

Oman, along with Bahrain, Kuwait, Qatar, Saudi Arabia and the United Arab Emirates entered into a customs union in Jan. 2003.

Imports and Exports

Imports and exports in US$1m.:

	2012	2013	2014	2015	2016
Imports c.i.f.	28,118	34,331	29,303	29,007	23,260
Exports f.o.b.	52,138	55,497	50,718	31,927	24,455

The United Arab Emirates is the main source of imports (37·0% in 2016) and China the leading export market (44·0% in 2016). In 2016 machinery and transport equipment accounted for 22·4% of Oman's imports and manufactured goods classified chiefly by material 20·0%. In 2015 crude oil exports made up 50% of total exports.

Communications

Roads

A network of adequate graded roads links all the main sectors of population, and only a few mountain villages are not accessible by motor vehicles. In 2005 there were about 42,300 km of roads (16,500 km paved) including 953 km of dual carriageway. In 2007 there were 453,400 passenger cars in use (174 per 1,000 inhabitants), 113,300 vans and lorries, and 26,400 buses and coaches. In 2007 there were 8,816 road accidents and 798 deaths.

Civil Aviation

The national airline is Oman Air, which in 2007 had 15 aircraft and served 26 destinations. Oman formerly had a 50% share in Gulf Air with Bahrain, but withdrew in May 2007. In 2009 Seeb International Airport (Muscat) handled 4,556,502 passengers (3,983,413 international) and 64,418 tonnes of freight.

Oman's two major airports, Muscat International and Salalah (mainly domestic flights), are both currently being upgraded and expanded.

Shipping

In Mutrah a deep-water port (named Mina Qaboos) was completed in 1974. In 2013 it handled 12·2m. tonnes of foreign cargo. In Jan. 2014 there were ten ships of 300 GT or over registered, totalling 20,000 GT.

Telecommunications

In 2013 there were 351,000 main (fixed) telephone lines in Oman; mobile phone subscriptions numbered 5,617,000 in 2013 (1,546·5 per 1,000 persons). An estimated 60% of the population were internet users in 2012. In March 2012 there were 422,000 Facebook users.

Social Institutions

Out of 178 countries analysed in the 2017 *Fragile States Index*—a list published jointly by the Fund for Peace and *Foreign Policy* magazine— Oman was ranked the 46th least vulnerable to conflict or collapse. The index is based on 12 indicators of state vulnerability across social, political and economic categories.

Justice

The population in penal institutions in 2013 was 1,300 (36 per 100,000 of national population). The death penalty is in force; there were two executions in 2015 but none in 2016, 2017 or 2018.

Education

Adult literacy was 87% in 2008. In 2015 there were 1,025 schools, up from just three when Qaboos bin Said became Sultan in 1970. The total number of pupils in state education in 2015 was 540,068 (450,966 in basic education and 89,102 in general education) with 56,586 teachers (50,504 in basic education and 6,082 in general education). Oman's first university, the Sultan Qaboos University, opened in 1986 and in 2015 there were 14,215 students. A number of private universities and colleges have opened in the meantime.

In 2006 public expenditure on education came to 4·2% of GNI and 31·1% of total government spending (the highest percentage of any country).

Health

In the period 2006–13 Oman had 22·2 physicians for every 10,000 inhabitants, 50·0 nursing and midwifery personnel for every 10,000 and 2·6 dentistry personnel per 10,000. In 2015 there were 49 hospitals with 4,998 beds. There were also 205 health centres.

In *Water: At What Cost? The State of the World's Water 2016*, WaterAid reported that 6·6% of the population does not have access to safe water.

Religion

In 2010, 85·9% of the population were Muslims according to estimates by the Pew Research Center's Forum on Religion & Public Life. Most Omanis are Ibadhis, a distinct branch of Islam that is neither Sunni nor Shia. The Pew Research Center estimated that 6·5% of the population were Christians in 2010 and 5·5% Hindus.

Culture

World Heritage Sites

The five sites on the UNESCO World Heritage List under Omani jurisdiction are (with the year entered on the list): Bahla Fort (1987); the archaeological sites of Bat, Al-Khutm and Al-Ayn, a collection of settlements and necropolises of the 3rd millennium BC (1988); the Frankincense Trail, a group of archaeological sites representing the production and distribution of frankincense (2000); the five ancient Aflaj irrigation systems (2006); and the Ancient City of Qalhat (2018). A sixth site, the Arabian Oryx Sanctuary, was removed from the list after the Omani government decided to reduce the size of the protected area by 90%.

Press

In 2008 there were seven daily newspapers with a combined circulation of 239,000.

Tourism

Non-resident tourists staying at hotels and similar establishments numbered 1,014,000 in 2011 (1,038,000 in 2010).

Festivals

National Day (18 Nov.); Spring Festival in Salalah (July–Aug.); Ramadan (April–May in 2020).

Diplomatic Representatives

Of Oman in the United Kingdom (167 Queen's Gate, London, SW7 5HE)
Ambassador: Sheikh Abdulaziz bin Abdullah bin Zahir Al Hinai.

Of the United Kingdom in Oman (PO Box 185, Mina Al Fahal 116, Muscat)
Ambassador: Hamish Cowell, CMG.

Of Oman in the USA (2535 Belmont Rd, NW, Washington, D.C., 20008)
Ambassador: Hunaina Sultan Ahmed Al Mughairy.

Of the USA in Oman (P.C. 115, Madinat Al Sultan Qaboos, Muscat)
Ambassador: Marc J. Sievers.

Of Oman to the United Nations
Ambassador: Khalifa Ali Issa Al Harthy.

Of Oman to the European Union
Ambassador: Najeem Bin Suleiman Al Abri.

Further Reading

Ghubash, Hussein, *Oman: The Islamic Democratic Tradition.* 2005
Manea, Elham, *Regional Politics in the Gulf: Saudi Arabia, Oman and Yemen.* 2005
Oman. A Country Study. 2004
Owtram, Francis, *A Modern History of Oman: Formation of the State since 1920.* 2002
National Statistical Office: National Centre for Statistics and Information, PO Box 848, Muscat 133.
Website: http://www.ncsi.gov.om

Pakistan

Islami Jamhuriya e Pakistan (Islamic Republic of Pakistan)

Capital: Islamabad
Population projection, 2020: 208·36m.
GNI per capita, 2017: (PPP$) 5,311
HDI/world rank, 2017: 0·562/150
Internet domain extension: .pk

Key Historical Events

The Neolithic settlement of Mehrgarh in Balochistan, western Pakistan dates from around 7000 BC. Continuously occupied for over 4,000 years, it was a precursor to the Indus Valley civilization, which flourished between 3300 and 1700 BC. Indus Valley settlements spread across much of present-day Pakistan and northwest India, from the Arabian Sea to the foothills of the Himalayas, centring on the cities of Mohenjo-Daro and Harappa. The civilization's decline coincided with the arrival of Indo-European-speaking tribes, including the Aryans, from central Asia. Taxila in northern Pakistan became a centre for the development of Vedic/Hindu culture from the 6th century BC.

Under the influence of the Persian Achaemenid Empire from around 550 BC, most of present-day Pakistan was ruled by Darius the Great from Persepolis after 515 BC. Alexander the Great, conqueror of the Persian Empire, invaded northern Pakistan in 326 BC but was superseded by the Maurya dynasty from around 300 BC. Its emperor, Ashoka the Great, ruled over central Asia and much of the Indian sub-continent between 273 and 232 BC. The Indus Valley came under Greco-Bactrian control from around 180 BC, bringing about a fusion of classical Greek culture and Buddhism. Invasions by Scythians and Parthians were followed by the arrival of the Yuechi from the steppes of western China. They established the Buddhist Kushan dynasty in the 1st century AD. Centred on Peshawar, it linked the Silk Road with the Arabian Sea and the Ganges Valley.

Arab settlers introduced Islam early in the 8th century. In 712 Muhammad ibn Qasim conquered Sindh province and incorporated it into the Umayyad Caliphate, ruled from Baghdad. Over the next three centuries the southern provinces of Multan and Balochistan were also absorbed. In 1005 Peshawar was conquered by the Turkic-Afghan warlord, Sultan Mahmud of Ghazni, who went on to take Punjab, Kashmir and Balochistan. The Ghaznavid Dynasty made Lahore one of its key cities—the easternmost outpost of Islam—though it was destroyed during Genghis Khan's Mongol invasion of 1219.

In the late 13th century northern and eastern Pakistan came under the influence of Islamic sultanates. Centred on Delhi, they gradually gained control of most of the Indian subcontinent. Timur-i Lang seized Persia, Afghanistan and western Pakistan in the 1380s, absorbing them into a vast central Asian empire. Babur, the founder of the Moghul dynasty in the early 16th century, initially made Kabul his capital, before power transferred to Lahore, Delhi and Agra. While most of the Indian sub-continent remained part of a united Moghul empire between the 16th and 19th centuries, the northwestern fringe was attacked by Persians in the 1730s and Sindh and Punjab were incorporated into Ahmad Shah Durrani's Afghan state from 1747.

The British, who established a protectorate in Bengal in 1757 and subsequently controlled much of the sub-continent, attempted to secure the anarchic northwest against Russian expansion in the first Afghan War (1838–42). Although Sindh and the Punjab were absorbed into British India in the 1840s, Balochistan and Afghanistan remained independent. Following Britain's failure to win these mountainous regions in the second Afghan War (1878–80), the North-West Frontier Province was created in 1901 as a semi-autonomous region.

Hindu–Muslim tensions escalated and in the 1930s the poet Muhammad Iqbal proposed a separate Muslim nation, an idea taken up by Muhammad Ali Jinnah, leader of the Muslim League. Following the League's victories in most of the majority-Muslim constituencies in the 1946 elections, the British agreed to the formation of East and West Pakistan under the 1947 Independence of India Act. Jinnah became West Pakistan's governor-general in the new capital, Karachi.

The partition of India saw 14m. people leaving their homes, with violence claiming 500,000 lives on both sides of the border. The signing over to India of Kashmir in Oct. 1947 was disputed by Pakistan. War broke out until a UN-brokered ceasefire and temporary border was agreed in 1949. In 1951 Pakistan's first prime minister, Liaquat Ali Kahn, was assassinated. The popularity of the Muslim League declined and Pakistan became increasingly unstable.

1958 saw the first of several periods of martial law, followed by the rule of Field Marshal Mohammad Ayub Khan (until 1969) and Gen. Agha Mohammad Yahya Khan (until 1971). Discontent in East Pakistan with the federal government led to calls by the Awami League for full autonomy. Following East Pakistan's declaration of independence as Bangladesh in March 1971, West Pakistan sent in troops, sparking civil war. Hundreds of thousands died and 10m. refugees fled to India. The surrender of Pakistan's forces to the Indian army in Dhaka on 16 Dec. 1971 cleared the way to an independent Bangladesh.

A new constitution in 1973 provided for a federal parliamentary government with a president and prime minister. Zulfiqar Ali Bhutto, representing the Pakistan People's Party (PPP), became premier. Considered by traditionalists to be insufficiently Islamic, in July 1977 Gen. Mohammad Zia ul-Haq led an army coup against Ali Bhutto, who was hanged for conspiracy to murder. His daughter, Benazir, led the PPP to victory in the elections in 1988 but was dismissed on charges of corruption and incompetence in 1990. Reinstated as prime minister following elections in 1993, President Farooq Leghari overthrew her administration in 1996.

Indo–Pakistani relations have foundered over Kashmir. In May 1998 Pakistan carried out five nuclear tests in the deserts of Balochistan in response to India's tests earlier in the month. US President Bill Clinton invoked sanctions but Pakistan carried out a sixth test. On 11 June, following India's example, Pakistan announced a unilateral moratorium on nuclear tests. On 12 Oct. 1999 Gen. Pervez Musharraf seized power in a coup, overthrowing the democratically-elected government of Nawaz Sharif after Sharif tried to dismiss Musharraf as army chief of staff. Sharif was convicted of corruption and sentenced to life imprisonment.

Negotiations with India over Kashmir began in July 1999. In May 2001 India ended its six-month long ceasefire but invited Pakistan for further talks, prompting hopes of avoiding more violence. Following the attacks on New York and Washington of 11 Sept. 2001 Pakistan found itself central to the war against terrorism. Neighbouring Afghanistan was believed to be sheltering Osama bin Laden and the USA persuaded Musharraf to allow its forces to use Pakistani air bases. In return the USA lifted its remaining sanctions. In Dec. 2001 suicide bombers attacked the Indian parliament. Although no-one claimed responsibility, the Indian authorities suspected Kashmiri separatists, heightening Indo-Pakistani tensions. Musharraf's subsequent crackdown on militants helped to reduce tension between the two countries.

An attack on an Indian army base in Indian-occupied Kashmir in May 2002, killing 31, was linked to terrorists infiltrating from Pakistan. Musharraf drew widespread criticism for failing to combat terrorism in the region. In Nov. 2003 Pakistan and India agreed to another ceasefire along Kashmir's Line of Control. Relations gradually improved and in April 2005 bus services resumed across the divided territory for the first time in 60 years.

In Oct. 2005 Pakistan-administered Kashmir was struck by an earthquake which killed 73,300 people and left 3m. homeless. In 2006 there was an upsurge in violence by tribal groups in Balochistan demanding greater autonomy. Bomb blasts rocked Karachi and Islamabad in early 2007 and 68 passengers were killed in an explosion on a train travelling between Lahore and New Delhi. Musharraf's decision to suspend the chief justice of the Supreme Court, Iftikhar Mohammad Chaudhry, for alleged abuse of power in March 2007 sparked riots in Karachi.

In July 2007 security forces stormed Islamabad's Red Mosque, considered to have close links with militant groups. At the end of a week-long siege, over 100 people were killed and 250 injured. In Oct. 2007 Musharraf won the

© Springer Nature Limited 2020
Palgrave Macmillan (ed.), *The Statesman's Yearbook 2020*,
https://doi.org/10.1057/978-1-349-95940-2_147

presidential election, though the Supreme Court refused to confirm the result until it had ruled on Musharraf's eligibility to stand while still head of the army. The court dismissed challenges to the result the following month. Meanwhile, fighting intensified in Waziristan, a stronghold of Islamic militant groups.

The assassination of Benazir Bhutto in Dec. 2007 ahead of elections in Jan. 2008 threw the already fragile political climate into turmoil. The election was rescheduled for Feb. when the leading opposition parties, including Bhutto's, won a resounding victory against pro-Musharraf parties and formed a coalition government. Musharraf's presidency was severely weakened as a result and he eventually resigned in Aug. 2008. In Sept. 2008 Asif Ali Zardari was elected his successor. His term in office has seen continued fighting between government forces and Islamic militant groups linked with several high-profile attacks including the Mumbai bombings of Nov. 2008 and an assault on the visiting Sri Lankan cricket team in March 2009. In Oct. 2009 the military launched an offensive against Taliban forces in the South Waziristan region, resulting in large numbers of deaths.

Flooding in Aug. 2010 killed 1,600 people and affected 20m. altogether. In May 2011 US special forces killed Osama bin Laden in the Pakistani town of Abbottabad. The operation was carried out in secret, raising tensions between Islamabad and Washington amid suspicions that figures within Pakistan had been providing refuge and support for bin Laden and his al-Qaeda network. In Oct. 2012 the Taliban earned international condemnation after shooting a 14-year-old girl, education activist Malala Yousafzai, as she made her way to school at Mingora in Khyber Pakhtunkhwa. The Taliban sparked renewed outrage in Dec. 2014 when almost 150 people—most of them children—died in an attack on a school in Peshawar. In June 2013 Nawaz Sharif became prime minister for an unprecedented third time after his Pakistan Muslim League-N won the previous month's parliamentary elections. However, in Aug. 2017 he was forced to resign over corruption charges. In July 2018 former international cricketer Imran Khan led his Pakistan Movement for Justice/Pakistan Tehreek-e-Insaf to electoral victory and took office as premier the following month.

In Feb. 2014 the former president, Pervez Musharraf, was put on trial for treason and legal proceedings were still ongoing as of March 2019.

Territory and Population

Pakistan is bounded in the west by Iran, northwest by Afghanistan, north by China, east by India and south by the Arabian Sea. The area (excluding the disputed area of Kashmir) is 796,096 sq. km (307,380 sq. miles), including 25,220 sq. km (9,740 sq. miles) of inland water. 2017 provisional census population (excluding the Pakistani-administered parts of Kashmir and Afghan refugees living in refugee villages), 207,776,954. In 2011, 36·2% lived in urban areas. There were 1·6m. refugees in mid-2016, mostly from Afghanistan, the second highest number in any country (after Turkey) and 10% of the global total.

The UN gives a projected population for 2020 of 208·36m.

The provisional census population of the principal cities in 2017 was as follows:

Karachi	14,916,456
Lahore	11,126,285
Faisalabad	3,204,726
Rawalpindi	2,098,231
Gujranwala	2,027,001
Peshawar	1,970,042
Multan	1,871,843
Hyderabad	1,734,309
Islamabad	1,009,832
Quetta	1,001,205

The country is divided into four provinces, two centrally administered areas and one federal territory (areas in sq. km): Balochistan (347,190)[1]; Khyber Pakhtunkhwa (101,741)[1]; Punjab (205,344)[1]; Sindh (140,914)[1]; Azad Kashmir (13,297)[2]; Gilgit-Baltistan (64,817)[2]; Islamabad Capital Territory (906)[3].
[1]Province.
[2]Centrally administered area.
[3]Federal territory.

English, the official language, is used in business, higher education and in central government; Urdu is the national language and the *lingua franca*, although only spoken as a first language by about 8% of the population. Around 48% of the population speak Punjabi.

Social Statistics

Estimates, 2008: births, 5,324,000; deaths, 1,224,000. Estimated birth rate in 2008 was 30·1 per 1,000 population; estimated death rate, 6·9. Infant mortality (per 1,000 live births), 70 (2010). Pakistan has the highest neonatal mortality rate of any country, at 46 per 1,000 live births in 2016. Formal registration of marriages and divorces has not been required since 1992. Expectation of life in 2013 was 65·7 years for men and 67·5 years for women. Annual population growth rate, 2000–08, 2·2%. Fertility rate, 2008, 4·0 births per woman. In 2013–14, 29·5% of Pakistanis were living below the national poverty line (down from 64·3% in 2001–02).

Climate

A weak form of tropical monsoon climate occurs over much of the country, with arid conditions in the north and west, where the wet season is only from Dec. to March. Elsewhere, rain comes mainly in the summer. Summer temperatures are high everywhere, but winters can be cold in the mountainous north. Islamabad, Jan. 50°F (10°C), July 90°F (32·2°C). Annual rainfall 36" (900 mm). Karachi, Jan. 61°F (16·1°C), July 86°F (30°C). Annual rainfall 8" (196 mm). Lahore, Jan. 53°F (11·7°C), July 89°F (31·7°C). Annual rainfall 18" (452 mm). Multan, Jan. 51°F (10·6°C), July 93°F (33·9°C). Annual rainfall 7" (170 mm). Quetta, Jan. 38°F (3·3°C), July 80°F (26·7°C). Annual rainfall 10" (239 mm).

Constitution and Government

Under the 1973 constitution, the *President* was elected for a five-year term by a college of parliamentary deputies, senators and members of the Provincial Assemblies. Parliament is bicameral, comprising a *Senate* of 104 members and a *National Assembly* of 342. In the *Senate*, each of the four provinces is allocated 14 seats, while the federally administered tribal areas and the federal capital are assigned eight and two seats respectively. In addition, each province is conferred four seats for technocrats and four for women. Two seats, one for technocrats and another for women, are reserved for the federal capital. The *National Assembly* is directly elected for five-year terms. 272 members are elected in single-seat constituencies, there are ten seats for non-Muslim minorities and 60 seats for women.

Following the 1999 coup Gen. Musharraf announced that the Constitution was to be held 'in abeyance' and issued a 'Provisional Constitution Order No. 1' in its place. In Aug. 2002 he unilaterally amended the constitution to grant himself the right to dissolve parliament.

During the period of martial law from 1977–85 the Constitution was also in abeyance, but not abrogated. In 1985 it was amended to extend the powers of the President, including those of appointing and dismissing ministers and vetoing new legislation until 1990. Legislation of 1 April 1997 abolished the President's right to dissolve parliament, appoint provincial governors and nominate the heads of the armed services.

Gen. Pervez Musharraf, Chief of the Army Staff, assumed the responsibilities of the chief executive of the country following the removal of Prime Minister Nawaz Sharif on 12 Oct. 1999. He formed a National Security Council consisting of six members belonging to the armed forces and a number of civilians with expertise in various fields. A Federal Cabinet of Ministers was also installed working under the guidance of the National Security Council. Also formed was the National Reconstruction Bureau, a think tank providing institutional advice and input on economic, social and institutional matters. The administration declared that it intended to first restore economic order before holding general elections to install a civilian government. The Supreme Court of Pakistan allowed the administration a three-year period, which expired on 12 Oct. 2002, to accomplish this task. Elections were held on 10 Oct. 2002. On 30 April 2002 a referendum was held in which 97·7% voted in favour of extending Musharraf's rule by a further five years. Turnout was around 50%. He amended the constitution in Aug. 2002 to formally extend his mandate by five years. The constitution was further amended in Dec. 2003 to enhance Musharraf's power and allow a vote of confidence in his presidency.

In March 2007 Musharraf announced his intention to stand for a five-year presidential term. The Supreme Court rejected his candidacy while opposition parties challenged his constitutional right to hold the presidency and head the military. In Sept. 2007 the Supreme Court's earlier judgement was overturned and the following month Musharraf was granted a further term of office by the national parliament and provincial assemblies. However, the Supreme Court refused to sanction the appointment until the surrounding legal questions had been resolved. In Nov. 2007 Musharraf suspended the constitution and imposed martial rule. Several prominent members of the judiciary and opposition leaders, including Benazir Bhutto and Imran Khan, were arrested or jailed. The Constitution was reinstated in Dec. but judicial freedom was severely compromised by the dismissal of senior court officials. Amendments were introduced to extend the military's power to try citizens and facilitate the arrest of political opponents. Following Musharraf's resignation in Aug. 2008, ousted Chief Justice Iftikhar Chaudry was reinstated in March 2009. The 2007 amendments to the constitution were subsequently revoked in July 2009 and in Aug. the Supreme Court ruled that Musharraf's actions had been illegal.

National Anthem

'Pak sarzamin shadbad' ('Blessed be the sacred land'); words by Abul Asr Hafeez Jaulandhari, tune by Ahmad G. Chaagla.

Government Chronology

Heads of State since 1947. (AL = Awami League; ML = Muslim League; PML = Pakistan Muslim League; PML-N = Pakistan Muslim League-Nawaz Sharif; PML-Q = Pakistan Muslim League (Quaid-e-Azam); PPP = Pakistan People's Party; RP = Republican Party; PTI = Pakistan Movement for Justice/Pakistan Tehreek-e-Insaf; n/p = non-partisan)

Governors-General

1947–48	ML	Mohammad Ali Jinnah
1948–51	ML	Khwaja Nazimaddin
1951–55	ML	Ghulam Mohammad
1955–56	military	Iskander Ali Mirza

Presidents of the Republic

1956–58	RP	Iskander Ali Mirza
1958–69	military	Mohammad Ayub Khan
1969–71	military	Agha Mohammad Yahya Khan
1971–73	PPP	Zulfiqar Ali Bhutto
1973–78	PPP	Fazal Elahi Chaudhry
1978–88	military	Mohammad Zia ul-Haq
1988–93	n/p	Ghulam Ishaq Khan
1993–97	PPP	Farooq Ahmed Khan Leghari
1998–2001	PML-N	Mohammad Rafiq Tarar
2001–08	military	Pervez Musharraf
2008	PML-Q	Mohammadmian Soomro (acting)
2008–13	PPP	Asif Ali Zardari
2013–18	PML-N	Mamnoon Hussain
2018–	PTI	Arif Alvi

Heads of Government since 1947.

Prime Ministers

1947–51	ML	Liaquat Ali Khan
1951–53	ML	Khwaja Nazimuddin
1953–55	ML	Mohammad Ali Bogra
1955–56	ML	Chaudhry Mohammad Ali
1956–57	AL	Huseyn Shaheed Suhrawardy
1957	ML	Ismail Ibrahim Chundrigar
1957–58	RP	Malik Firoz Khan Noon
1958–71		Military rule during which the post of prime minister was not occupied.
1973–77	PPP	Zulfikar Ali Bhutto
1977–85	military	Mohammad Zia ul-Haq (as Chief Martial Law Administrator)
1985–88	PML	Mohammad Khan Junejo
1988–90	PPP	Benazir Bhutto
1990–93	PML-N	Nawaz Sharif

(*continued*)

1993–96	PPP	Benazir Bhutto
1997–99	PML-N	Nawaz Sharif
1999–2002	military	Gen. Pervez Musharraf (as Chief Executive)
2002–04	PML-Q	Mir Zafarullah Khan Jamali
2004	PML-Q	Chaudhry Shujaat Hussain
2004–07	PML-Q	Shaukat Aziz
2008–12	PPP	Yousaf Raza Gilani
2012–13	PPP	Raja Pervez Ashraf
2013–17	PML-N	Nawaz Sharif
2017–18	PML-N	Shahid Khaqan Abbasi
2018–	PTI	Imran Khan

Recent Elections

Parliamentary elections were held on 25 July 2018. The Pakistan Movement for Justice/Pakistan Tehreek-e-Insaf (PTI, led by Imran Khan) gained 149 of the National Assembly's 342 elected seats and received 31·8% of votes cast; the Pakistan Muslim League (N) (PML-N, led by Shehbaz Sharif) won 82 seats and received 24·3%; the Pakistan People's Party (PPP, led by Bilawal Bhutto) gained 54 seats and received 13·0% of the vote; Muttahida Majlis-e-Amal (MMA) gained 15 seats with 4·8%; the Muttahida Qaumi Movement (MQM) won 7 seats with 1·4%. The remaining seats went to smaller parties and non-partisans. Turnout was 51·6%.

In indirect elections held on 4 Sept. 2018 Arif Alvi (PTI) was elected president by federal and provincial lawmakers, winning 353 votes against 185 for Fazlur Rehman (MMA) and 124 for Aitzaz Ahsan (PPP).

Current Government

President: Arif Alvi; b. 1949 (PTI; since 9 Sept. 2018).

In Feb. 2019 the government comprised:

Prime Minister: Imran Khan; b. 1952 (PTI; since 18 Aug. 2018).

Minister of Communications, and Postal Services: Murad Saeed. *Defence:* Pervez Khattak. *Defence Production:* Zubaida Jalal Khan. *Federal Education and Professional Training, and National History and Literary Heritage:* Shafqat Mehmood. *Finance, Revenue and Economic Affairs:* Asad Umar. *Foreign Affairs:* Shah Mehmood Qureshi. *Health:* Aamir Mehmood Kiani. *Housing and Works:* Tariq Bashir Cheema. *Human Rights:* Shireen Mazari. *Information and Broadcasting:* Fawad Chaudhry. *Information Technology and Telecommunication:* Khalid Maqbool Siddiqui. *Interprovincial Co-ordination:* Fahmida Mirza. *Kashmir Affairs and Gilgit Baltistan:* Ali Amin Khan Gandapur. *Law and Justice:* Farogh Naseem. *Maritime Affairs:* Syed Ali Haider Zaidi. *Narcotics Control:* Ali Muhammad Khan Mahar. *National Food Security and Research:* Sahibzada Muhammad Mehboob Sultan. *Petroleum:* Ghulam Sarwar Khan. *Planning, Development and Reform:* Makhdoom Khusro Bakhtiar. *Power:* Omar Ayub Khan. *Privatization and Aviation:* Muhammad Mian Soomro. *Railways:* Sheikh Rasheed Ahmad. *Religious Affairs:* Noor-ul-Haq Qadri. *Science and Technology:* Muhammad Azam Khan Swati. *Water Resources:* Muhammad Faisal Vawda.

Office of the President: http://www.president.gov.pk

Current Leaders

Arif Alvi

Position
President

Introduction
Arif Alvi, a founding figure of the Pakistan Movement for Justice (PTI) party, became president in 2018. He is a close ally of the prime minister, Imran Khan.

Early Life
Alvi was born in Karachi on 29 Aug. 1949. He studied dentistry in Lahore, becoming involved with the Jamaat-e-Islami Pakistan (JI) party as he protested against the regime of Mohammad Ayub Khan. Alvi then received US master's degrees from the University of Michigan and the University of the Pacific (in San Francisco) in 1975 and 1984, respectively.

He stood unsuccessfully as a JI candidate for the Sindh provincial assembly in 1979 but left the party in 1988. Eight years later, he joined with Imran Khan to found the PTI. In 1997 Alvi became president of the PTI in Sindh province, but again stood unsuccessfully for the provincial assembly that year and in 2002. From 2006 he was the PTI's acting secretary-general, standing down in 2013 before joining the National Assembly, representing a Karachi constituency. He held this seat through to the 2018 general election. In 2017 he was indicted on charges of having been involved in an attack on a television headquarters by PTI supporters three years earlier.

Following the PTI's success in the 2018 election, the new premier—Imran Khan—nominated Alvi as the party's candidate for the presidency. Alvi was duly elected on 4 Sept. and was sworn in five days later.

Career in Office
On assuming the presidency, Alvi cited constitutional immunity in relation to the allegations of the television station attack. He has expressed support for the majority Muslim population in the Indian state of Jammu and Kashmir, citing the right to 'self-determination', but has nonetheless emphasized his desire for cordial relations between India and Pakistan.

Imran Khan
Position
Prime Minister

Introduction
Following a successful career as captain of the Pakistan cricket team, Imran Khan led his party, the Pakistan Movement for Justice/Pakistan Tehreek-e-Insaf (PTI), to victory in the elections of July 2018 and assumed office as prime minister the following month.

Early Life
Khan was born in Lahore on 5 Oct. 1952. After attending Aitchison College in Lahore, he was educated in the UK at the Royal Grammar School, Worcester. He graduated in politics, philosophy and economics from Keble College, Oxford, in 1975. He played for Worcestershire County Cricket Club (1971–76) and Sussex County Cricket Club (1983–88) and then led the Pakistan cricket team to victory at the 1992 Cricket World Cup before retiring from the game. In 2009 he was inducted into the International Cricket Council Hall of Fame.

Apart from a spell as a media cricket commentator, he engaged in various philanthropic projects including founding the first cancer hospital in Pakistan. In April 2008 he established Namal technical college in Mianwali District as an associate college of the University of Bradford, of which he was vice-chancellor from 2005–14. He had earlier founded the PTI party in April 1996 and in 2013 was elected to parliament, with his party the second largest in the country. At the 2018 general election the PTI won the largest number of seats and defeated the ruling Pakistan Muslim League (N). Khan was sworn in as prime minister on 18 Aug. 2018.

Career in Office
As premier, Khan must confront an array of formidable challenges. While promising to tackle corruption and political patronage, he has faced accusations that the army helped to engineer his victory. Meanwhile, the national infrastructure (especially in energy) requires extensive development, with some areas lacking basic electrical power. In foreign policy, he must navigate the rivalries between the USA and China—both important allies (despite Khan's own opposition to US drone strikes against the Taliban in Pakistan's northern territories)—as well as seeking to diffuse long-term tensions with India. Friction over Kashmir again escalated in Feb. 2019 as an Islamist terror attack in the Indian-administered territory prompted engagements between Pakistani and Indian warplanes. Khan also faces military opposition to his desire for a more open border with Afghanistan. Domestically, he favours deregulation of the economy and a strong welfare state, although he must contend with a widening current account deficit and negotiations with the International Monetary Fund over a bailout loan.

Defence

A *Council for Defence and National Security* was set up in Jan. 1997, comprising the President, the Prime Minister, the Ministers of Defence, Foreign Affairs, Interior, Finance and the military chiefs of staff. The Council advised the government on the determination of national strategy and security priorities, but was disbanded in Feb. 1997. The Council was revived in Oct. 1999 following the change of government but was to have a wider scope and not restrict itself to defence matters.

Defence expenditure in 2013 totalled US$5,890m. (US$30 per capita), representing 2·5% of GDP. Expenditure is increasingly targeted at developing counter-insurgency capabilities as a result of the threat from Taliban forces along the border with Afghanistan.

As at 31 May 2016 Pakistan had 7,178 personnel serving in UN peace-keeping operations (the third largest contingent of any country, after Ethiopia and India).

Nuclear Weapons
Pakistan began a secret weapons programme in 1972 to reach parity with India, but was restricted for some years by US sanctions. The Stockholm International Peace Research Institute estimates that Pakistan possesses 140–150 nuclear warheads. In May 1998 Pakistan carried out six nuclear tests in response to India's tests earlier in the month. Pakistan, known to have a nuclear weapons programme, has not signed the Comprehensive Nuclear-Test-Ban-Treaty, which is intended to bring about a ban on any nuclear explosions. According to *Deadly Arsenals*, published by the Carnegie Endowment for International Peace, Pakistan has both chemical and biological weapon research programmes.

Army
Strength (2011) 550,000. There were also up to 304,000 personnel in paramilitary units: National Guard, Frontier Corps and Pakistan Rangers.

Most armoured equipment is of Chinese origin including over 2,400 main battle tanks. There is an aviation corps with fixed-wing aircraft and 42 attack helicopters in 2011.

Navy
In 2011 the combatant fleet included five French-built diesel submarines, three midget submarines for swimmer delivery and ten frigates. The Naval Air wing operated seven combat-capable aircraft in 2011.

The principal naval base and dockyard are at Karachi. There are secondary bases at Gwadar, Jiwani, Ormara and Pasni. Naval personnel in 2011 totalled 22,000 (including an estimated 1,400 marines and some 2,000 Marine Security Agency personnel).

Air Force
The Pakistan Air Force came into being on 14 Aug. 1947. It has its headquarters at Peshawar and is organized within three air defence sectors, in the northern, central and southern areas of the country. There is an Air Force Academy at Risalpur, which includes a College of Aeronautical Engineering.

Total strength in 2011 was 453 combat-capable aircraft and 70,000 personnel. Equipment included F-7s, Mirage IIIs, Mirage 5s, F-16s, Q-5s and JF-17s.

International Relations

Following Gen. Musharraf's coup in Oct. 1999, Pakistan was suspended from the Commonwealth's councils although the suspension was ended in May 2004. Pakistan was again suspended in Nov. 2007 after then President Musharraf declared emergency rule but it was readmitted in May 2008.

Economy

Agriculture accounted for 24·6% of GDP in 2016, industry 19·4% and services 56·0%.

Overview
Pakistan's service-based economy has significant growth potential. Boasting a strategic geographical location in Asia, a large population and diverse natural resources, there is untapped potential for trade. However, the country faces serious economic, governance and security challenges if it is to achieve its development goals. Frequent energy black-outs and water shortages regularly undermine production and state-run energy firms are notoriously inefficient. Rising expenditure has increased government debt, which stood at 64·8% of GDP in 2015, and the government has become dependent on foreign aid to compensate for low tax revenues. Inflation is persistently high, averaging 7% between 2003 and 2015.

Although growth in the agricultural sector has been falling since the 1980s, it contributes over 20% of GDP and accounts for over 42% of jobs. Pakistan is one of the world's largest producers of raw cotton, but historically textile exports have added little value. The official unemployment figure was 6% in 2014, although this does not take into account the significant informal economy.

In 2007–08 international oil and food prices rose sharply, with negative effects on Pakistan. A stabilization programme supported by the IMF was initiated in Nov. 2008 to avoid a default on debt payments. Severe flooding in July 2010 affected more than 20m. people and disrupted 500,000 ha. of cropped land. A US$451m. emergency assistance package was provided by the IMF. The World Bank estimated the damage at US$9·7bn. and committed US$1bn. towards recovery. In 2011 and 2014 more floods affected over 6m. people.

Although growth has been erratic since 2008, the country has avoided recession. Between 2010 and 2013 it averaged 3·4% per year, driven by buoyant service and manufacturing sectors and sound macroeconomic management. In May 2014 the IMF indicated that the government's reform programme was on track to deliver improvements in the balance of payments and increased central bank reserves. In addition, efforts to broaden the tax base have boosted revenues, although the revenue-to-GDP ratio has remained low, at around 11% in 2015.

To secure sustainable, long-term growth, the government needs to address political instability, structural problems in the energy sector, poor infrastructure and a volatile security situation, while also improving basic human development indicators.

Currency

The monetary unit is the *Pakistan rupee* (PKR) of 100 *paisas*. Gold reserves in Sept. 2009 were 2·10m. troy oz; foreign exchange reserves, US$10,418m. Inflation rates (based on IMF statistics):

2008	2009	2010	2011	2012	2013	2014	2015	2016	2017
12·0%	19·6%	10·1%	13·7%	11·0%	7·4%	8·6%	4·5%	2·9%	4·1%

The rupee was devalued by 3·65% in Sept. 1996, 8·5% in Oct. 1996 and 8·7% in Oct. 1997, and by 4·2% in June 1998 in response to the financial problems in Asia. In June 2008 total money supply was Rs3,359·3bn.

Budget

The financial year ends on 30 June. Budgetary central government revenues totalled Rs2,271·0bn. in 2010–11; expenditures totalled Rs3,219·2bn. in 2010–11. Taxes accounted for 73·9% of revenues in 2010–11; interest accounted for 26·6% of expenditures, and goods and services 19·7%.

There is a general sales tax of 17%.

Performance

Real GDP growth rates (based on IMF statistics):

2008	2009	2010	2011	2012	2013	2014	2015	2016	2017
5·0%	0·4%	2·6%	3·6%	3·8%	3·7%	4·1%	4·1%	4·6%	5·4%

Pakistan's total GDP in 2017 was US$305·0bn.

Banking and Finance

The State Bank of Pakistan is the central bank (*Governor*, Tariq Bajwa); it came into operation as the Central Bank on 1 July 1948 and was nationalized in 1974 with other banks. Private commercial bank licences were reintroduced in 1991.

The State Bank of Pakistan is the issuing authority of domestic currency, custodian of foreign exchange reserves and bankers for the federal and provincial governments and for scheduled banks. It also manages the rupee public debt of the federal and provincial governments. The National Bank of Pakistan acts as an agent of the State Bank where the State Bank has no offices of its own.

In Feb. 1994 the State Bank of Pakistan was granted more autonomy to regulate the monetary sector of the economy.

In Dec. 2011 there were 44 scheduled banks (31 Pakistani and 13 foreign) with 9,772 branches. Of the Pakistani banks in Dec. 2011 five were public sector commercial banks, four were specialized banks and 22 were domestic private banks. The largest bank is Habib Bank. Other leading banks are MCB Bank, National Bank of Pakistan, United Bank and Allied Bank.

In 2010 external debt totalled US$1,127m., equivalent to 31·3% of GNI.

There are stock exchanges in Islamabad, Karachi and Lahore.

Energy and Natural Resources

Environment

Pakistan's carbon dioxide emissions from the consumption of energy were the equivalent of 0·8 tonnes per capita in 2011.

Electricity

Installed capacity in 2011–12 was 22·80m. kW, of which 15·45m. kW was thermal, 6·56m. kW was hydro-electric and 0·79m. kW was nuclear. In 2010 there were two nuclear reactors in use. Production in 2011–12 was 95·09bn. kWh, of which 64% was thermal and 30% was hydro-electric. Pakistan has vast untapped hydro potential but at present supply fails to meet demand and power cuts are frequent. Consumption per capita in 2011–12 was 541 kWh.

Oil and Gas

Crude petroleum production in 2011 was 25m. bbls. Reserves in 2014 were 342m. bbls. Exploitation is mainly through government incentives and concessions to foreign private sector companies. Natural gas production in 2012 was 41·5bn. cu. metres with 600bn. cu. metres of proven reserves. The French oil company Total agreed a US$3bn. deal with the government in July 2003 for exploration in the Arabian Sea. Pakistan has to import more than 85% of its oil needs, mainly from Arab countries.

Water

Pakistan's Indus Basin irrigation system is the largest and oldest in the world. It includes a network of 43 independent canal systems and two storage reservoirs. Total length of main canals is 58,000 km which serve 35m. acres of cultivable land.

Currently three major surface water projects are under way, as are flood control schemes and programmes to check the problems of waterlogging and salinity.

Minerals

Production (tonnes, 2005): limestone, 14·86m.; coal, 3·37m.; rock salt, 1·65m.; gypsum, 552,496; fire clay, 253,501; dolomite, 199,653; chromite, 46,359; barytes, 42,087; china clay, 37,732; fuller's earth, 17,001; bauxite, 6,504. Other minerals of which useful deposits have been found are copper, magnesite, sulphur, marble, antimony ore, bentonite, celestite, fluorite, phosphate rock, silica sand and soapstone.

Agriculture

The north and west are covered by mountain ranges. The rest of the country consists of a fertile plain watered by five big rivers and their tributaries. Agriculture is dependent almost entirely on the irrigation system based on these rivers. There were 30·47m. ha. of arable land in 2013 and 810,000 ha. of permanent crops. In the same year an estimated 20·20m. ha. were equipped for irrigation.

Areas harvested, 2013: wheat, 8·66m. ha.; cotton lint, 2·81m. ha.; rice, 2·79m. ha.; seed cotton, 2·75m. ha.; sugarcane, 1·17m. ha.; maize, 1·17m. ha. Production, 2013 (1,000 tonnes): sugarcane, 67,460; wheat, 24,211; rice, 6,798; seed cotton, 6,243; maize, 4,944; cottonseed, 4,071; potatoes, 3,802; cotton lint, 2,172; onions, 1,661; mangoes and guavas, 1,659; oranges, 1,401; chick-peas, 751; apples, 606; tomatoes, 574; watermelons, 561.

A Land Reforms Act of 1977 reduced the upper limit of land holding to 100 irrigated or 200 non-irrigated acres. A new agricultural income tax was introduced in 1995, from which holders of up to 25 irrigated or 50 unirrigated acres are exempt. Of about 5m. farms, 12% are of less than 10 ha. Agriculture employs nearly half of the workforce.

Livestock, 2013 (in 1m.): goats, 64·9; cattle, 38·3; buffaloes, 33·6; sheep, 28·8; asses, 4·9; camels, 1·0; chickens, 785·0.

Livestock products, 2013 (in 1,000 tonnes): chicken meat, 907; buffalo meat, 825, beef and veal, 822; goat meat, 304; lamb and mutton, 163; buffalo's milk, 24,370; cow's milk, 13,897; goat's milk, 801; eggs (estimate), 661.

Forestry

The area under forests in 2015 was 1·47m. ha., some 2% of the total land area. Timber production in 2011 totalled an estimated 32·65m. cu. metres.

Fisheries

In 2015 the catch totalled 491,990 tonnes, mainly from marine waters.

Industry

The leading company by market capitalization in Pakistan in March 2015 was Oil & Gas Development Company Limited (OGDCL) (US$7·7bn.).

Industry is based largely on agricultural processing, with engineering and electronics. Government policy is to encourage private industry, particularly small businesses. The public sector, however, is still dominant in large industries. Steel, cement, fertilizer and vegetable ghee are the most valuable public sector industries.

Production in 1,000 tonnes (in 2006–07 unless otherwise stated): cement (2007 estimate), 21,000; raw sugar (2007), 4,355; distillate fuel oil, 3,697; residual fuel oil, 3,324; cotton yarn (2005–06), 2,547; petrol, 1,337; paper and paperboard (2007), 1,010; pig iron (2005–06), 768; clays, 358; coke, 326; soda ash (2005), 260; caustic soda, 242; woven cotton fabrics, 965m. sq. metres; bicycles, 486,350 items; tractors (2007), 54,610 items.

Labour

The labour force in 2013 was 63,649,000 (45,607,000 in 2003). 56·4% of the population aged 15–64 was economically active in 2013. In the same year 5·1% of the population was unemployed. Of those in employment in 2011, 45·1% worked in agriculture, 33·7% in services and 21·2% in industry.

Pakistan had 2·13m. people living in slavery according to the Walk Free Foundation's 2013 *Global Slavery Index*, the third highest total of any country.

International Trade

Most foreign exchange controls were removed in Feb. 1991. Tax exemptions are available for companies set up before 30 June 1995.

Imports and Exports

Trade in US$1m.:

	2005	2006	2007	2008	2009
Imports c.i.f.	25,097	29,826	32,594	42,327	31,584
Exports f.o.b.	16,050	16,933	17,838	20,279	17,555

Major imports in 2009 (as % of total value): petroleum and petroleum products, 26·2; machinery and transport equipment, 22·9; chemicals and related products, 16·9; manufactured goods, 10·6. Major exports in 2009: textile yarn, fabrics and finished articles, 37·1; clothing and apparel, 19·1; rice, 17·1; petroleum and petroleum products, 4·1.

Major import suppliers in 2009 (as % of total): China, 12·0; Saudi Arabia, 11·1; UAE, 10·6; Kuwait 5·7; USA, 5·7. Major export markets in 2009: USA, 18·3; UAE, 8·8; Afghanistan, 7·8; China, 5·7; UK, 5·4. In the meantime China has become the largest trading partner.

Communications

Roads

In 2006 there were 260,420 km of roads, of which 65·4% were paved. There are ten motorways providing links between Pakistan's major cities. These include the M-1 from Islamabad to Peshawar, the M-2 from Islamabad to Lahore, the M-4 from Faisalabad to Multan and the M-9 from Karachi to Hyderabad. In 2007 there were 1,440,100 passenger cars in use, 187,100 vans and lorries, 170,400 buses and coaches and 2,684,300 motorcycles. There were 10,466 road accidents involving injury in 2007, with 5,465 fatalities.

All traffic in Pakistan drives on the left. All cars must be insured and registered. Minimum age for driving: 18 years.

Rail

In 2011 Pakistan Railways had a route length of 7,791 km (of which 293 km electrified) mainly on 1,676 mm gauge, with some metre gauge line. Passenger-km travelled in 2011 came to 20·6bn. and freight tonne-km to 1·8bn.

Civil Aviation

There are international airports at Karachi, Islamabad, Lahore, Peshawar and Quetta.

The national carrier is the state-owned Pakistan International Airlines, or PIA. It operates scheduled services to 46 international and 24 domestic destinations. In 2006, 88,302,000 revenue-km were flown. The revenue passengers carried totalled 5·73m. in 2006 and revenue tonne-km came to 1,801m. Operating revenues of the corporation stood at Rs70,587m. in 2006 and operating expenditure at Rs79,164m.

Shipping

In Jan. 2014 there were ten ships of 300 GT or over registered, totalling 352,000 GT. The busiest port is Karachi. In 2013 cargo traffic totalled 41,350,000 tonnes (11,007,000 tonnes loaded and 30,343,000 tonnes discharged). There are also ports at Port Qasim, which handled 25,775,000 tonnes in 2013, and Gwadar.

Telecommunications

The telephone system is government-owned. In 2013 there were an estimated 6·4m. main (fixed) telephone lines. In the same year mobile phone subscriptions numbered an estimated 127·7m. An estimated 10·9% of the population were internet users in 2013. In March 2012 there were 6·4m. Facebook users.

Social Institutions

Out of 178 countries analysed in the 2017 *Fragile States Index*—a list published jointly by the Fund for Peace and *Foreign Policy* magazine—Pakistan was ranked the joint 17th most vulnerable (along with Burundi) to conflict or collapse. The index is based on 12 indicators of state vulnerability across social, political and economic categories.

Justice

The Federal Judiciary consists of the Supreme Court of Pakistan, which is a court of record and has threefold jurisdiction; original, appellate and advisory. There are four High Courts in Lahore, Peshawar, Quetta and Karachi. Under the Constitution, each has power to issue directions of writs of *Habeas Corpus, Mandamus, Certiorari* and others. Under them are district and sessions courts of first instance in each district; they have also some appellate jurisdiction. Below these are subordinate courts and village courts for civil matters and magistrates for criminal matters.

The Constitution provides for an independent judiciary, as the greatest safeguard of citizens' rights. There is an Attorney-General, appointed by the President, who has right of audience in all courts and the Parliament, and a Federal Ombudsman.

A Federal Sharia Court at the High Court level has been established to decide whether any law is wholly or partially un-Islamic. In Aug. 1990 a presidential ordinance decreed that the criminal code must conform to Islamic law (Sharia), and in May 1991 parliament passed a law incorporating it into the legal system.

538,048 crimes were reported in 2007 (399,558 in 2002). Execution of the death penalty for murder, in abeyance since 1986, was resumed in 1992. The first judicial execution in four years was carried out in Nov. 2012, although there have been frequent reports of extrajudicial executions since 2008. There were at least nine judicial executions in 2018. There were 10,556 murders in 2007 (9,396 in 2002). The population in penal institutions in Dec. 2012 was 74,944 (39 per 100,000 of national population). The International Centre for Prison Studies estimated in 2014 that 69·1% of prisoners had yet to receive a trial. In 2015 the World Justice Project *Rule of Law Index*, which provides data on how the rule of law is experienced by the general public across eight categories, ranked Pakistan 94th of 102 countries for criminal justice and 91st for civil justice.

Education

In 1998 the landmark National Education Policy (1998–2010) was launched with the aim of eradicating illiteracy and spreading basic education. The policy stressed vocational and technical education, disseminating a common culture based on Islamic ideology. The follow-up National Education Policy 2009 reinforced the position that education and training 'should enable the citizens of Pakistan to lead their lives according to the teachings of Islam'. In 2010 the constitution was amended by the addition of an article declaring: 'The state shall provide free and compulsory education to all children of the age of five to sixteen in such a manner as may be determined by law.' The adult literacy rate in 2008 was 54%. Adult literacy programmes are being strengthened.

In 2016 there were 19·35m. primary schools pupils (10·72m. male), 3·33m. high school pupils (1·91m. male) and 1·86m. students in tertiary education (1·02m. male). There are 70 public and 58 private universities of which Quaid-i-Azam University in Islamabad and the University of the Punjab in Lahore are considered to be the most prestigious.

Government expenditure on education came to 2·5% of GDP and 12·6% of total government spending in 2016.

Health

In the period 2006–12 Pakistan had six hospital beds per 10,000 population. There were 184,711 physicians, 94,766 nursing and midwifery personnel and 16,652 dentistry personnel in 2015.

In *Water: At What Cost? The State of the World's Water 2016*, WaterAid reported that 8·6% of the population does not have access to safe water. Pakistan ranked as the country with the tenth largest number of people living without access to safe water (16·1m. in 2015).

Welfare

The official retirement age is 60 (men), 55 (women) or 50 (miners). To qualify for a pension, 15 years of contributions are needed. In 2014 the minimum old age and survivor pension was Rs3,600 per month.

Medical services, provided mainly through social security facilities, cover cash and medical benefits such as general medical care, specialist care, medicines, hospitalization, maternity care and transportation.

Religion

Pakistan was created as a Muslim state. Around 85–90% of Muslims are Sunni and 10–15% Shia according to estimates by the Pew Research Center's Forum on Religion & Public Life. Religious groups: Muslims, 93%; Christians, 2%; Hindus, Parsees, Buddhists, Qadianis and others. Pakistan has the second highest number of Muslims, after Indonesia. There is a Minorities Wing at the Religious Affairs Ministry to safeguard the constitutional rights of religious minorities. In Feb. 2019 there was one cardinal.

Culture

There is a Pakistan National Council of the Arts, a cultural organization to promote art and culture in Pakistan and abroad.

World Heritage Sites

There are six sites under Pakistani jurisdiction which appear on the UNESCO World Heritage List. They are (with year entered on list): the archaeological ruins at Moenjodaro (1980), Taxila (1980), the Buddhist ruins at Tahkt-i-Bahi and the neighbouring city remains at Sahr-i-Bahlol (1980), Thatta (1981), the Fort and Shalimar Gardens in Lahore (1981) and Rohtas Fort (1997).

Press

In 2007 there were 400 paid-for dailies and 1,200 paid-for non-daily periodicals. Average combined circulation of all dailies in 2007 was 9,935,000. The most popular daily papers in 2008 were *Jang*, with a circulation of 450,000, and *Express*, with a circulation of 375,000. The most widely read English-language paper is *Dawn*, with an average daily circulation of 225,000 copies in 2008.

Tourism

In 2010 there were 906,800 non-resident tourists including 288,200 from the UK, 120,400 from the USA, 110,900 from Afghanistan, 46,200 from Canada and 43,700 from India. 54% of tourists in 2010 visited Punjab and 29% Sindh.

Festivals

Pakistan is rich in culture. Famous festivals include the Eid Festival, Eid-e-Milad un Nabi (Birthday of Prophet Muhammad), the Basnat Festival, Shab-e-Baraat Festival and the Independence Day Festival.

Diplomatic Representatives

Of Pakistan in the United Kingdom (35–36 Lowndes Sq., London, SW1X 9JN)
> *High Commissioner:* Sahebzada Ahmed Khan.

Of the United Kingdom in Pakistan (Diplomatic Enclave, Ramna 5, PO Box 1122, Islamabad)
> *High Commissioner:* Thomas Drew, CMG.

Of Pakistan in the USA (3517 International Court, NW, Washington, D.C., 20008)
> *Ambassador:* Aizaz Ahmad Choudhry.

Of the USA in Pakistan (Diplomatic Enclave, Ramna, 5, Islamabad)
> *Ambassador:* Vacant.
> *Charge d'Affaires a.i.:* Paul W. Jones.

Of Pakistan to the United Nations
> *Ambassador:* Maleeha Lodhi.

Of Pakistan to the European Union
> *Ambassador:* Naghmana Hashmi.

Further Reading

Federal Bureau of Statistics.—*Pakistan Statistical Yearbook.—Statistical Pocket Book of Pakistan.* (Annual)

Ahmed, A. S., *Jinnah, Pakistan and Islamic Identity: The Search for Saladin.* 1997

Ahsan, A., *The Indus Saga and the Making of Pakistan.* 1997

Akhtar, R., *Pakistan Year Book.*

Cohen, Stephen Philip, *The Idea of Pakistan.* 2006

Hajari, Nisid, *Midnight's Furies: The Deadly Legacy of India's Partition.* 2015

Jaffrelot, Christophe, (ed.) *A History of Pakistan and Its Origins.* Revised ed. 2004

Jalal, Ayesha, *The Struggle for Pakistan: A Muslim Homeland and Global Politics.* 2014

Jetly, Rajshree, *Pakistan in Regional and Global Politics.* 2009

Joshi, V. T., *Pakistan: Zia to Benazir.* 1995

Khan, Hamid, *Constitutional and Political History of Pakistan.* 2005

Lieven, Anatol, *Pakistan: A Hard Country.* 2011

Lodhi, Maleeha, *Pakistan: Beyond 'The Crisis State'.* 2011

Malik, Iftikhar H., *State and Civil Society in Pakistan: the Politics of Authority, Ideology and Ethnicity.* 1996.—*The History of Pakistan.* 2008

Paul, T. V., *The India-Pakistan Conflict: An Enduring Rivalry.* 2005

Rashid, Ahmed, *Pakistan on the Brink: The Future of Pakistan, Afghanistan and the West.* 2012

Riedel, Bruce, *Deadly Embrace: Pakistan, America, and the Future of Global Jihad.* 2011

Small, Andrew, *The China-Pakistan Axis: Asia's New Geopolitics.* 2015

Talbot, Ian, *Pakistan: A Modern History.* 1999

Wynbrandt, James, *A Brief History of Pakistan.* 2009

Zaidi, S. Akbar, *Issues in Pakistan's Economy.* 2005

Ziring, Lawrence, *Pakistan in the 20th Century: A Political History.* 2004

National library: National Library of Pakistan, Constitution Avenue, Islamabad.

National Statistical Office: Pakistan Bureau of Statistics, Statistics House Plot # 21, Mauve Area, G-9/1, Islamabad.

Website: http://www.pbs.gov.pk

Palau

Beluu er a Belau (Republic of Palau)

Capital: Melekeok
Population projection, 2020: 22,000
GNI per capita, 2017: (PPP$) 12,831
HDI/world rank, 2017: 0·798/60=
Internet domain extension: .pw

Key Historical Events

Spain acquired sovereignty over the Palau Islands in 1886 but sold the archipelago to Germany in 1899. Japan occupied the islands in 1914 and in 1921 they were mandated to Japan by the League of Nations. Captured by Allied Forces in 1944, the islands became part of the UN Trust Territory of the Pacific Islands created on 18 July 1947 and administered by the USA. Following a referendum in July 1978 in which Palauans voted against joining the new Federated States of Micronesia, the islands became autonomous from 1 Jan. 1981. A referendum in Nov. 1993 favoured a Compact of Free Association with the USA. Palau became an independent republic on 1 Oct. 1994.

Territory and Population

The archipelago lies in the western Pacific and has a total land area of 488 sq. km (188 sq. miles). It comprises 26 islands and over 300 islets. Only nine of the islands are inhabited, the largest being Babelthuap (396 sq. km), but most inhabitants live on the small island of Koror (18 sq. km) to the south. In Oct. 2006 the capital moved from Koror to Melekeok, a newly built town in eastern Babelthuap. The total population of Palau at the time of the 2015 census was 17,661 (9,433 males and 8,228 females), giving a density of 36·2 per sq. km. In 2015 approximately 73% of the population were Palauans.

The UN gives a projected population for 2020 of 22,000.

In 2011, 84·3% of the population lived in urban areas. Some 6,000 Palauans live abroad. The local language is Palauan; both Palauan and English are official languages.

Social Statistics

2012 births, 268; deaths, 164. Rates, 2012 (per 1,000 population): births, 12·7; deaths, 7·8; infant mortality (2012), 12 per 1,000 live births. Annual population growth rate, 2003–13, 0·6%. Expectation of life at birth, 2010: males, 61 years; females, 68. Fertility rate, 2013, 1·7 births per woman.

Climate

Palau has a pleasantly warm climate throughout the year with temperatures averaging 81°F (27°C). The heaviest rainfall is between July and Oct.

Constitution and Government

The Constitution was adopted on 2 April 1979 and took effect from 1 Jan. 1981. The Republic has a bicameral legislature, the *Olbiil Era Kelulau* (National Congress), comprising a 13-member *Senate* and a 16-member *House of Delegates* (one from each of the Republic's 16 states), both elected for a term of four years as are the *President* and *Vice-President*. Customary social roles and land and sea rights are allocated by a matriarchal 16-clan system.

National Anthem

'Belau loba klisiich er a kelulul' ('Palau is coming forth with strength and power'); words anonymous, tune Y. O. Ezekiel.

Recent Elections

In presidential elections held on 1 Nov. 2016 incumbent Tommy Remengesau, Jr won re-election with 51·3% of the vote, against 48·7% for Surangel Whipps, Jr. At legislative elections that were also held on 1 Nov. 2016 only non-partisans were elected.

Current Government

President: Tommy Remengesau, Jr; b. 1956 (in office since 17 Jan. 2013, having previously been president from Jan. 2001–Jan. 2009).

Vice-President and Minister of Justice: Raynold Oilouch.

In Feb. 2019 the cabinet consisted of:

Minister of Community and Cultural Affairs: Baklai Temengil. *Education:* Sinton Soalablai. *Finance:* Elbuchel Sadang. *Health:* Dr Emais Roberts. *Natural Resources, Environment and Tourism:* Flemming Umiich Sengebau. *Public Infrastructure, Industries and Commerce:* Charles Obichang. *Minister of State for Foreign Affairs:* Faustina K. Rehuher-Marugg.

Government Website: http://palaugov.org

Current Leaders

Tommy Remengesau, Jr

Position
President

Introduction
Tommy Remengesau, Jr first became president in Jan. 2001 and was re-elected in Nov. 2004. Out of office from 2009, he won a third term in the Nov. 2012 elections and a fourth in Nov. 2016. The US-educated career politician has prioritized improvements in basic services, higher levels of foreign investment and increasing environmental awareness.

Early Life
Tommy Esang Remengesau, Jr was born on 28 Feb. 1956 on the island of Koror, Palau, in the US-administered Trust Territory of the Pacific Islands (TTPI). The eldest son of Thomas O. Remengesau, Sr (who served as president from 1988–89), he graduated in criminal justice from Grand Valley State College in Michigan, USA in 1978. On his return to Palau, Remengesau began work at the *Olbiil Era Kelulau* (OEK), Palau's National Congress. In 1984 he became the youngest Palauan to be elected a senator in the OEK. Re-elected in 1988, he served on the committee on ways and means, playing a key role in reducing Palau's budget deficit and securing financial stability.

In 1992 Remengesau was elected vice-president and the following year Palauan voters approved a Compact of Free Association with the USA. With responsibility for the finance portfolio, Remengesau was credited with reforming the financial system and preparing the new sovereign state (established in 1994) for membership of the IMF and the World Bank Group. He won the 2000 presidential elections, claiming 52% of the vote against Peter Sugiyama.

Career in Office
Remengesau set out to reduce his country's dependence on the USA and announced plans to increase revenue from tourism. He pledged to achieve these aims while protecting the country's natural environment, particularly the coral reef, and preserving the island's resources. In 2006 he launched the Micronesia Challenge, which encouraged neighbouring countries to follow Palau's conservation commitments.

Remengesau began a new four-year term following the election of Nov. 2004, in which he claimed 66·5% of the vote against Polycarp Basilius. In Oct. 2006 the institutions of government began relocating to a new capital, Melekeok, in eastern Babelthuap. In 2008 Remengesau announced he would seek a seat in the Senate, having held the presidency for the maximum two

Palgrave Macmillan (ed.), *The Statesman's Yearbook 2020*,
https://doi.org/10.1057/978-1-349-95940-2_148

consecutive terms allowed by the constitution. However, his campaign was unsuccessful and he came 11th in the election. He was succeeded as president by Johnson Toribiong in Jan. 2009.

In April 2009 an investigation found that Remengesau was guilty of incorrectly filing the financial details of properties in which he had an interest. He was charged with 19 counts of violating Palau's code of ethics in 2002 and 2003, accusations he described as 'selective persecution'. In April 2010 Associate Justice Kathleen Salii fined Remengesau US$156,400, equivalent to an eighth of the amount initially recommended by prosecutor Michael Copeland.

Remengesau was elected to a further four-year term as president in Nov. 2012, having defeated Toribiong on a platform of encouraging foreign investment and improving services for grassroots communities. In 2014 he announced a ban on all commercial fishing in Palau's exclusive economic zone, creating a marine sanctuary to prevent over-exploitation. Standing against his brother-in-law, Surangel Whipps, Jr, in run-off elections in Nov. 2016, Remengesau was only narrowly returned for another presidential term with 51·3% of the vote.

Economy

Overview

The economy is dependent on tourism and foreign aid, which contributed about 50% and 25% of GDP respectively in 2015. The USA provides assistance under a Compact of Free Association, giving Washington responsibility for Palau's defence and security matters. US grants under the Compact are guaranteed until 2024 but, with their conclusion in sight, the IMF has stressed the importance of public deficit reduction policies and tax reforms as Palau's tax revenues are among the lowest in the Pacific region.

The global downturn caused a 20% decline in tourism arrivals in 2008–09 but the sector had rebounded strongly by 2012. However, overreliance on tourism, aid and imports, along with restrictions on foreign investment, pose risks to an otherwise favourable economic outlook supported by a strong and efficient banking sector.

Currency

US currency is used. There was deflation of 1·0% in 2016 and inflation of 0·9% in 2017.

Budget

The fiscal year begins on 1 Oct. Revenues for 2011–12 were US$94·2m. and expenditures US$94·6m. Grants accounted for 48·0% of revenues in 2011–12 and tax revenue 42·2%; current expenditure accounted for 80·7% of expenditures in 2011–12.

Performance

Total GDP in 2017 was US$292m. The economy grew by 10·1% in 2015 before experiencing zero growth in 2016 and contracting by 3·7% in 2017. In 2015 Palau's real GDP growth rate was one of the highest in the world, at 9·4%.

Banking and Finance

The National Development Bank of Palau is situated in Koror. Other banks include the Bank of Guam, the Bank of Hawaii and Bank Pacific.

Energy and Natural Resources

Electricity

Electricity production was approximately 96m. kWh in 2011; installed capacity was about 52,000 kW in 2011.

Agriculture

Subsistence farming is one of the major economic activities. In 2012 approximately 2,000 people were economically active in agriculture. Agricultural products include bananas, coconuts, copra, cassava, sweet potatoes, taro and yams. There were about 1,000 ha. of arable land in 2012 and 2,000 ha. of permanent crop land.

Forestry

Forests covered 0·04m. ha. in 2015, or 88% of the land area.

Fisheries

In 2012 the catch totalled an estimated 900 tonnes, mainly tuna.

Industry

There is little industry, but the principal activities are food-processing and boat-building.

Labour

In 2005 the total labour force numbered 10,203 (6,214 males and 3,989 females), of whom 9,777 were employed (5,982 males and 3,795 females).

International Trade

Imports and Exports

Imports (2011–12) US$135·6m.; exports (2011–12) US$20·9m. The main trading partner is Japan for exports and the USA for imports.

Communications

Roads

There were 146 km of roads in 2007 including the 85 km US-funded two-lane highway around Babelthuap, providing a link between the old capital of Koror and the new capital of Melekeok.

Civil Aviation

The main airport is on Koror (Roman Tmetuchl International Airport, near Airai). In 2010 there were scheduled flights to Guam, Manila, Seoul, Taipei and Yap (Micronesia). A new Palau-based carrier, Palau Airways, was founded in 2011 and launched scheduled passenger services between Koror and Taipei in May 2012, but it halted its operations in April 2013.

Shipping

There is a port at Malakal.

Telecommunications

In 2011 there were 6,916 main (fixed) telephone lines and 15,445 mobile phone subscribers.

Social Institutions

Justice

There are a Supreme Court and various subsidiary courts. The population in penal institutions in 2010 was 79 (378 per 100,000 national population).

Education

In 2013–14 there were 1,679 pupils at public elementary schools and 429 at private elementary schools. There were 643 pupils at public secondary schools in 2013–14 and 429 at private secondary schools. Palau Community College is a post-secondary vocational/academic institution. The adult literacy rate is more than 99%.

Health

There were 26 doctors, 117 nurses and one midwife in 2006 and five dentists and one pharmacist in 2007. Palau has the highest incidence of overweight or obese adults of any nation according to World Health Organization estimates in 2014, at 78·4%.

Religion

The majority of the population is Roman Catholic.

Culture

Press

There are three local newspapers—*Island Times*, *Tia Belau* and *Palau Horizon*—although none are published daily.

Tourism

Tourism is a major industry, particularly marine-based. There were 83,795 visitor arrivals in 2009 (down from a record 94,895 in 2004). Of the visitor arrivals in 2009, 68,329 were for tourist purposes. Visitors to Palau in 2009 included: 27,180 from Japan; 16,571 from the Republic of China; 13,193 from the Republic of Korea.

World Heritage Sites

Rock Islands Southern Lagoon was added to the UNESCO World Heritage List in 2012. It covers hundreds of large and small forested limestone islands, channels, tunnels, caves, arches and coves scattered within a marine lagoon protected by a barrier reef. The site is of exceptional aesthetic beauty and home to diverse and abundant marine life.

Diplomatic Representatives

Of Palau in the United Kingdom
  Honorary Consul: Q. Mohamed (Bankfoot Sq., Bankfoot St., Batley, West Yorkshire, WF17 5LH).

Of the United Kingdom in Palau
  Ambassador: Daniel Pruce (resides in Manila, Philippines).

Of Palau in the USA (1701 Pennsylvania Ave., NW, Suite 300, Washington, D.C., 20006)
  Ambassador: Hersey Kyota.

Of the USA in Palau (PO Box 6028, PW 96940, Koror)
  Ambassador: Amy J. Hyatt.

Of Palau to the United Nations and to the European Union
  Ambassador: Jeraldine Ebil Tudong.

Further Reading

National Statistical Office: 3rd Floor, Executive Building Ngerulmud, Palau 96939.
Website: http://palaugov.org/executive-branch/ministries/finance/budgetandplanning

Panama

República de Panamá (Republic of Panama)

Capital: Panama City
Population projection, 2020: 4·29m.
GNI per capita, 2017: (PPP$) 19,178
HDI/world rank, 2017: 0·789/66
Internet domain extension: .pa

Key Historical Events

Ceramic objects unearthed on Panama's Pacific coast suggest the area was settled from 2,500 BC. Maize cultivation began in southern Panama around 1,500 BC and by 300 BC it supported numerous large, permanent villages. Public architecture was in evidence by AD 500, along with pottery (Gran Cocle), gold ornaments and elaborate burial chambers. From AD 750 present-day Panama was widely settled by Chibchan, Chocoan and Cueva peoples, and there was trade with other groups across central America.

A Spanish adventurer, Rodrigo de Bastidas, explored the isthmus of Panama in 1501, followed by Christopher Columbus the following year. Nuestra Señora de la Asunción de Panamá (present-day Panama City) was founded in 1519. The first European settlement on the Pacific Ocean, it was a staging post for later Spanish conquests across central and south America. A part of the New Kingdom of Granada, from 1549 Panama was ruled by the *Audiencia* of Bogotá. It was a key port for shipping gold, silver and other treasures from the western fringe of South America to Spain.

In the late 1690s the isthmus saw an ill-fated attempt by the Kingdom of Scotland to establish a colony called New Caledonia. Poor planning, insufficient resources, a lack of opportunities for trade and crippling diseases led to the scheme's demise at the hands of Spanish forces in 1700. Panama was formally incorporated into the Viceroyalty of New Granada in 1739, which encompassed present-day Colombia, Ecuador and Venezuela.

An independence movement for New Granada was precipitated by the Napoleonic invasion of Spain in 1808. Antonio Nariño, who took part in an uprising at Bogotá in 1810, and Simón Bolívar became leading revolutionary figures. Bolívar's victory at Boyacá in 1819 was followed by the Spanish surrender of Cartagena in 1821. Panama was incorporated into the new independent Republic of Colombia, which included Venezuela and (from 1822) Ecuador under Bolívar's leadership. Rebellions against rule from Bogotá took place in 1830 and 1840, before the Bidlack-Mallarino Treaty of 1846 granted the USA rights to both build a railway across Panama (completed in 1855) and intervene militarily in the event of disturbances.

While Colombia was embroiled in the Thousand Day War (1899–1902) Panama again sought independence, with separatists such as José Agustín Arango favouring direct negotiation with the USA over plans for a Panama Canal. The USA chose to back the revolution and Panama declared independence on 3 Nov. 1903. A subsequent treaty granted the USA the use, occupation and control of a Canal Zone, with full sovereign rights in perpetuity. In return the USA guaranteed the independence of the republic. The Canal was opened on 15 Aug. 1914.

US domination of Panama provoked frequent anti-American protests. In 1968 Col. Omar Torrijos Herrera took power in a coup and attempted to negotiate a more advantageous treaty with the USA. Two new treaties between Panama and the USA were agreed in Aug. 1977 and signed in Sept. of the same year. One dealt with the operation and defence of the Canal until the end of 1999 and the other guaranteed permanent neutrality.

Torrijos vacated his position as chief of government in 1978 but remained head of the National Guard until his death in an air crash in 1981. Subsequently, Gen. Manuel Noriega, Torrijos's successor as head of the National Guard, became the strong man of the regime. His position was threatened by internal political opposition and economic pressure applied by the USA but in Oct. 1989 a US-backed coup attempt failed. On 15 Dec. Gen. Noriega declared a 'state of war' with the USA. On 20 Dec. the USA invaded. Gen. Noriega surrendered on 3 Jan. 1990. Accused of drug dealing, he was convicted by a court in Miami. All remaining US troops left the country when the Panama Canal was handed back to Panama at the end of 1999.

In a referendum in 2006, voters backed a US$5·2bn. plan to widen the Panama Canal, potentially doubling its capacity. The conservative retail tycoon Ricardo Martinelli won a landslide victory in the April 2009 presidential election, promising to take a tough stance on crime and rising prices.

Territory and Population

Panama is bounded in the north by the Caribbean Sea, east by Colombia, south by the Pacific Ocean and west by Costa Rica. The area is 75,001 sq. km. Population at the census of 2010 was 3,405,813 (1,693,229 females); density, 44·9 per sq. km. The population was 75·5% urban in 2011.

The UN gives a projected population for 2020 of 4·29m.

The largest towns (2010) are Panama City, the capital, on the Pacific coast (430,299) and its suburb San Miguelito (315,019). Other large towns are Las Cumbres, Tocumen, David, Arraiján and Colón.

The areas and populations of the nine provinces and the three province-level indigenous regions, plus their capitals, are:

Province	Sq. km	Census 2010	Capital
Bocas del Toro	4,601	125,461	Bocas del Toro
Chiriquí	6,477	416,873	David
Coclé	4,927	233,708	Penonomé
Colón	4,891	241,928	Colón
Darién[1]	11,866	48,378	La Palma
Emberá[2]	4,398	10,001	Cirilo Guainora
Herrera	2,341	109,955	Chitré
Kuna Yala[2]	2,393	33,109	El Porvenir
Los Santos	3,805	89,592	Las Tablas
Ngöbe-Buglé[2]	6,673	156,747	Chichica
Panamá[3, 4]	11,952	1,713,070	Panama City[3, 4]
Veraguas	10,677	226,991	Santiago

[1]Includes the indigenous sub-province of Kuna de Wargandí. [2]Indigenous region. [3]Includes the indigenous sub-province of Kuna de Madungandí. [4]Includes the province of Panamá Oeste, established in 2014.

The population is a mix of African, American, Arab, Chinese, European and Indian immigrants. The official language is Spanish.

Social Statistics

2006 births, 65,764; deaths, 14,358; marriages, 10,747; divorces, 2,866. Birth rate, 2006 (per 1,000 population), 20·0; death rate, 4·4. Annual population growth rate, 2010–15, 1·7%. Expectation of life at birth, 2007, was 73·0 years for males and 78·2 years for females. In 2006 the most popular age range for marrying was 25–29 for both males and females. Infant mortality, 2010, 17 per 1,000 live births; fertility rate, 2006, 2·4 births per woman.

Climate

Panama has a tropical climate, unvaryingly with high temperatures and only a short dry season from Jan. to April. Rainfall amounts are much higher on the north side of the isthmus. Panama City, Jan. 79°F (26·1°C), July 81°F (27·2°C). Annual rainfall 70" (1,770 mm). Colón, Jan. 80°F (26·7°C), July 80°F (26·7°C). Annual rainfall 127" (3,175 mm). Balboa Heights, Jan. 80°F (26·7°C), July 81°F (27·2°C). Annual rainfall 70" (1,759 mm). Cristóbal, Jan. 80°F (26·7°C), July 81°F (27·2°C). Annual rainfall 130" (3,255 mm).

Constitution and Government

The 1972 constitution, as amended in 1978, 1983, 1994 and 2004, provides for a *President*, elected for five years, two *Vice-Presidents* and a 72-seat *Legislative Assembly* (since reduced to 71 seats) to be elected for five-year

Palgrave Macmillan (ed.), *The Statesman's Yearbook 2020*,
https://doi.org/10.1057/978-1-349-95940-2_149

terms by a direct vote. As a result of the amendment of 2004 there has only been one *Vice-President* since the election of May 2009. To remain registered, parties must have attained at least 50,000 votes at the last election. A referendum held on 15 Nov. 1992 rejected constitutional reforms by 64% of votes cast. Turnout was 40%. In a referendum on 30 Aug. 1998 voters rejected proposed changes to the constitution which would allow for a President to serve a second consecutive term.

National Anthem

'Alcanzamos por fin la victoria' ('We achieve victory in the end'); words by J. de la Ossa, tune by Santos Jorge.

Government Chronology

(CD = Democratic Change; CNP = National Patriotic Coalition; PA = Arnulfist Party; PL = Liberal Party; PLN = National Liberal Party; PP = Panameñista Party; PR = Republican Party; PRA = Authentic Revolutionary Party; PRD = Democratic Revolutionary Party; n/p = non-partisan)

Heads of State since 1941.

Presidents of the Republic		
1941–45	n/p	Ricardo Adolfo de la Guardia Arango
1945–48	PL	Enrique Adolfo Jiménez Brin
1948–49	PL	Domingo Díaz Arosemena
1949	PL	Daniel Chanis Pinzón
1949–51	PRA	Arnulfo Arias Madrid
1951–52	PRA	Alcibíades Arosemena Quinzada
1952–55	CNP	José Antonio Remón Cantera
1955–56	CNP	Ricardo Manuel Arias Espinosa
1956–60	CNP	Ernesto de la Guardia Navarro
1960–64	PLN	Roberto Francisco Chiari Remón
1964–68	PLN	Marco Aurelio Robles Méndez
1968	PP	Arnulfo Arias Madrid
Chairmen of the Provisional Junta of Government		
1968–69	military	José María Pinilla Fábrega
1969–72	n/p	Demetrio Basilio Lakas Bahas
Presidents of the Republic		
1972–78	n/p	Demetrio Basilio Lakas Bahas
1978–82	n/p	Arístides Royo Sánchez
1982–84	n/p	Ricardo de la Espriella Toral
1984	n/p	Jorge Enrique Illueca Sibauste
1984–85	PRD	Nicolás Ardito Barletta Vallarino
1985–88	PR	Eric Arturo Delvalle Cohen-Henríquez
1989–94	PA	Guillermo David Endara Galimany
1994–99	PRD	Ernesto Pérez Balladares González
1999–2004	PA	Mireya Elisa Moscoso de Arias
2004–09	PRD	Martín Erasto Torrijos Espino
2009–14	CD	Ricardo Martinelli Berrocal
2014–	PP	Juan Carlos Varela Rodríguez
De facto rulers from 1968–89.		
1968–81	military	Omar Efraín Torrijos Herrera
1982–83	military	Rubén Darío Paredes del Río
1983–89	military	Manuel Antonio Noriega Moreno

Recent Elections

In the presidential election on 4 May 2014, Juan Carlos Varela of the Panameñista Party (PP) won 39·1% of the vote, against 31·4% for José Domingo Arias of the ruling Democratic Change (CD) and 28·1% for Juan Carlos Navarro of the Democratic Revolutionary Party (PRD). Four other candidates took less than 1% of the vote each. Turnout was 76·8%.

At the parliamentary elections, also held on 4 May 2014, the United for More Change coalition won 32 seats (with the CD taking 30 seats and the Nationalist Republican Liberal Movement—MOLIRENA 2); the PRD, 25;

the People First coalition, 13 (with the Panameñista Party taking 12 seats and the People's Party 1); independents, 1. Turnout was 69·2%.

Current Government

President: Juan Carlos Varela Rodríguez; b. 1963 (Panameñista Party; sworn in 1 July 2014).

Vice-President and Minister of Foreign Affairs: Isabel Saint Malo de Alvarado.

In Feb. 2019 the government comprised:

Minister of Interior: Carlos Rubio. *Economy and Finance:* Eyda Varela de Chinchilla. *Education:* Ricardo Pinzón. *Public Works:* Ramón Arosemena Crespo. *Health:* Miguel Mayo. *Labour and Workforce Development:* Zulphy Santamaría. *Commerce and Industry:*Néstor González. *Housing and Land Management:* Martín Sucre Champsaur. *Agricultural Development:* Eduardo Enrique Carles. *Social Development:* Michelle Muschett. *Canal Affairs:* Roberto Roy. *Security:*Jonattan Del Rosario. *Environment:* Emilio Sempris. *Minister of the Presidency:* Jorge González.

Office of the President (limited English): http://www.presidencia.gob.pa

Current Leaders

Juan Carlos Varela

Position

President

Introduction

Juan Carlos Varela Rodríguez was elected president in May 2014. His scheduled five-year term was expected to be dominated by efforts to tackle government corruption.

Early Life

Born in Panama City on 12 Dec. 1963 into one of the country's wealthiest families, he graduated in industrial engineering from Georgia Institute of Technology in the USA in 1985 and began working in politics in the 1990s. He was head of the Panameñista Party's election campaign for the state presidency in 1994 and became party president in 2006. He has also held senior posts within his family's Varela Hermanos drinks business.

In 2009 Varela was the Panameñista Party's presidential candidate but joined forces with rival contender Ricardo Martinelli of the Democratic Change party in order to secure the position of vice-president. He also served as foreign minister. Domestically, he was behind a popular programme that aimed to provide US$100 a month to those over the age of 70 who did not have alternative retirement income.

The relationship between Martinelli and Varela broke down in 2011 amid allegations of corruption. Varela denied receiving funds from bank accounts linked to an international gambling ring, instead accusing Martinelli of being behind the story in an attempt to derail Varela's presidential aspirations. Martinelli dismissed him as foreign minister after he refused to back a referendum to allow the president to serve consecutive terms. Varela subsequently became a staunch critic of Martinelli, accusing him of corruption and racketeering.

Career in Office

In May 2014 Varela won the race for the presidency, defeating José Domingo Arias of Martinelli's Democratic Change. Having campaigned on a platform of greater honesty and transparency in government, he was sworn in on 1 July and allied himself with the Democratic Revolutionary Party to secure majority congressional backing.

Bequeathed a Panama Canal expansion project that had already overrun its budget by US$1·6bn., Varela pushed back its completion deadline to 2016 (inaugurating the scheme in June). Meanwhile, he backed up his promise to fight corruption by suspending a Supreme Court judge following charges including money-laundering and illicit enrichment.

On the international stage, he oversaw the restoration of diplomatic relations with Venezuela in July 2014 after President Nicolás Maduro had cut ties with Panama in March that year on the grounds that the country was in an 'open conspiracy' with the USA against him. Varela also strongly opposed Colombia's decision to list Panama as a tax haven, a designation that allowed Bogotá to impose higher taxes on Colombian-held assets in the country. In June 2017 he announced that Panama was cutting its diplomatic ties with Taiwan in favour of the People's Republic of China.

Varela's government suffered a credibility blow in April 2016 when documents from a specialist Panamanian law firm, Mossack Fonseca, were leaked and revealed how prominent international clients have used offshore tax havens to hide their wealth. In response, Varela announced the creation of an international panel of experts to help improve transparency in Panama's offshore financial industry.

Defence

The armed forces were disbanded in 1990 and constitutionally abolished in 1994. Divided between both coasts, the National Maritime Service, a coast guard rather than a navy, numbered around 600 personnel in 2011. In addition there is a paramilitary police force of 11,000 and a paramilitary national air service of 400 with no combat-capable aircraft. In 2013 defence expenditure totalled US$637m. (US$179 per capita), representing 1·5% of GDP. For Police see JUSTICE below.

Economy

Agriculture accounted for 2·7% of GDP in 2016, industry 28·1% and services 69·2%.

Overview

Panama is an upper-middle income country in Latin America and has been one of the fastest-growing economies in the world since the turn of the century. The annual growth rate averaged 7·8% between 2006 and 2016, mainly driven by buoyant transportation, commerce and tourism sectors, as well as a developed financial services industry. The annual growth average over the period 2015–17 was 5·4%.

Given its geographical location between North and South America, Panama is strategically important for shipping and trade. Most of the country's economic activities are centred on its Canal and the Colón Free Zone, at the Canal's Atlantic entrance. 80% of GDP is derived from related sectors, including transportation, packaging, importing and exporting, and the country is a consistently attractive destination for foreign direct investment. Public investment is expected to decrease in the short term after completion of major infrastructure projects, such as the Canal expansion (which opened in June 2016) and the country's first metro line (which opened in 2014). Canal toll revenues in 2017 were put at US$2·2bn.

The poverty rate fell from 39·9% to 26·2% between 2007 and 2012, before a further decline to 14·1% by 2017; extreme poverty declined from 15·6% to 11·3% and then to 6·6% over those respective periods. However, many challenges remain, particularly in terms of wealth inequality. Nationally, extreme poverty is below 4% in urban areas but around 27% in rural areas, while in the indigenous people's regions poverty is recorded at over 70% and extreme poverty at above 40%. The public debt, meanwhile, surpassed US$37bn. in 2016.

The banking system is highly integrated with international markets. The national currency is pegged to the US dollar, making it vulnerable to global trends. Panama and the USA entered a Free Trade Agreement in June 2007, approved by the Panamanian National Assembly the following month and by the US Congress in Oct. 2011.

Currency

The monetary unit is the balboa (PAB) of 100 centésimos, at parity with the US dollar. The only paper currency used is that of the USA. US coinage is also legal tender. Inflation was 0·7% in 2016 and 0·9% in 2017. In July 2005 foreign exchange reserves were US$1,018m. and total money supply was 1,587m. balboas.

Budget

Revenues in 2013 were 9,628·7m. balboas (tax revenue, 50·5%) and expenditures also 9,628·7m. balboas (current expenditure, 54·9%).

VAT is 7%.

Performance

Real GDP growth was 5·8% in 2015, 5·0% in 2016 and 5·4% in 2017. Total GDP in 2017 was US$61·8bn.

Banking and Finance

There is no statutory central bank. Banking is supervised and promoted by the Superintendency of Banks (formerly the National Banking Commission); the Superintendent is Ricardo Fernández. Government accounts are handled through the state-owned Banco Nacional de Panama. In 2007 there were two other state banks, 39 banks operating under general licence, 34 under international licence and 11 as representative offices. In Aug. 2007 the combined assets of those banks operating under general and international licences totalled US$50,500m.; their combined deposits were US$36,500m.

Foreign debt was US$11,412m. in 2010, representing 45·8% of GNI.

There is a stock exchange in Panama City.

Energy and Natural Resources

Environment

Panama's carbon dioxide emissions from the consumption of energy in 2011 were the equivalent of 5·0 tonnes per capita.

Electricity

In 2011 capacity was 2·4m. kW. Production was 7·9bn. kWh in 2011 (52% hydro-electric and 48% thermal), with consumption per capita 2,118 kWh.

Minerals

Limestone, clay and salt are produced. There are known to be copper deposits.

Agriculture

In 2012 there were approximately 563,000 ha. of arable land and 185,000 ha. of permanent crops. Production in 2012 (in 1,000 tonnes): sugarcane, 2,264; bananas, 308; rice, 274; maize, 130; plantains, 105; pineapples, 100; palm fruit oil (estimate), 53; oranges, 45.

Livestock (2013): 1,727,000 cattle, 342,000 pigs, 115,000 horses (estimate) and 20m. chickens.

Livestock products (2013 estimates, in 1,000 tonnes): beef and veal, 85; pork and pork products, 34; poultry meat, 146; milk, 206; eggs, 26.

Forestry

Forests covered 4·62m. ha. in 2015 (62% of the land area). There are great timber resources, notably mahogany. Production in 2011 totalled 1·30m. cu. metres.

Fisheries

In 2015 the catch totalled 142,315 tonnes (mainly shrimp), almost entirely from sea fishing.

Industry

The main industry is agricultural produce processing. Other areas include chemicals and paper-making. Cement production (2008 estimate), 1,843,000 tonnes; sugar (2005), 157,280 tonnes.

Labour

The labour force in 2013 was 1,799,000 (1,414,000 in 2003). 69·9% of the population aged 15–64 was economically active in 2013. In the same year 4·1% of the population was unemployed.

International Trade

The Colón Free Zone, the largest free zone in the Americas, is an autonomous institution set up in 1953. More than 2,500 companies were operating there in 2007.

Imports and Exports

Imports and exports in US$1m.:

	2002	2003	2004	2005	2006
Imports f.o.b.	3,035·3	3,122·3	3,592·2	4,152·8	4,817·7
Exports f.o.b.	759·6	805·0	891·1	963·2	1,021·8

Main imports: machinery and apparatus, mineral fuels, chemicals and chemical products. Main exports: marine products, bananas, melons.

Chief import suppliers, 2006: USA, 27%; Curaçao, 10%; Costa Rica, 5%; Japan, 5%. Principal export markets, 2006: USA, 39%; Spain, 8%; Netherlands, 7%; Sweden, 6%.

Communications

Roads

In 2006 there were 13,365 km of roads, of which 34·1% were paved. The road from Panama City westward to the cities of David and Concepción and to the Costa Rican frontier, with several branches, is part of the Pan-American Highway. The Trans-Isthmian Highway connects Panama City and Colón. In 2007 there were 436,200 passenger cars, 174,500 lorries and vans and 20,100 buses and coaches. There were 425 road accident fatalities in 2007.

Rail

The 1,435 mm gauge Ferrocarril de Panama, which connects Panama City on the Pacific with Colón on the Atlantic along the bank of the Panama Canal, is the only operational railway. It provides both passenger and freight services, with one weekday passenger service in each direction. In 2012 the railway had the capacity to move 1,800 containers a day. A metro system opened in Panama City in April 2014.

Civil Aviation

There is an international airport at Panama City (Tocumén International). The national carrier is COPA, which flew to nearly 50 different destinations in 2010. In 2012 scheduled airline traffic of Panama-based carriers flew 134·8m. km; passenger-km totalled 14·5bn. in the same year. In 2005 Tocumén International handled 2,710,857 passengers and 100,063 tonnes of freight.

Shipping

Panama, a nation with a transcendental maritime career and a strategic geographic position, is the shipping world's preferred flag for ship registry. The Ship Registry System equally accepts vessels of local or international ownership, as long as they comply with all legal parameters. Ship owners also favour Panamanian registry because fees are low. The Panamanian merchant fleet is the largest in the world. In Jan. 2014 there were 6,971 ships of 300 GT or over registered, totalling 224·61m. GT (representing 21·1% of the world total). Of the 6,971 vessels registered, 2,686 were bulk carriers, 1,910 general cargo ships, 1,294 oil tankers, 719 container ships, 236 liquid gas tankers and 126 passenger ships.

All the international maritime traffic for Colón and Panama runs through the Canal ports of Cristóbal, Balboa and Manzanillo International.

Panama Canal

The Panama Canal Commission is concerned primarily with the operation of the Canal. In Oct. 2002 a new toll structure was adopted based on ship size and type. A referendum was held in Oct. 2006 on whether to expand the canal and double its capacity. The US$5·25bn. plan was approved by 78% of voters. The expansion work began in Sept. 2007 and the newly expanded canal was opened in June 2016.

Administrator of the Panama Canal Authority
Jorge Quijano.

Particulars of the ocean-going commercial traffic through the Canal are given as follows:

Fiscal year ending 30 Sept.	No. of vessels transiting	Cargo in long tons	Tolls revenue (in US$1)
2008	13,138	209,705,000	1,316,031,000
2009	12,849	197,896,000	1,436,810,000
2010	12,582	204,816,000	1,480,554,000

Most numerous transits by flag (fiscal year 2010): Panama, 2,636; Liberia, 1,989; The Bahamas, 849; Marshall Islands, 703; Hong Kong, 646.

Statistical Information: The Panama Canal Authority Corporate Communications Division

Annual Reports on the Panama Canal, by the Administrator of the Panama Canal

Rules and Regulations Governing Navigation of the Panama Canal. The Panama Canal Authority

Major, J., *Prize Possession: the United States and the Panama Canal, 1903–1979.* 1994

Telecommunications

Panama had 5,677,000 mobile phone subscriptions in 2009 (1,643·7 per 1,000 inhabitants) and 537,100 fixed telephone lines. There were 277·9 internet users per 1,000 inhabitants in 2009. In Dec. 2011 there were 896,000 Facebook users.

Social Institutions

Out of 178 countries analysed in the 2017 *Fragile States Index*—a list published jointly by the Fund for Peace and *Foreign Policy* magazine—Panama was ranked the 42nd least vulnerable to conflict or collapse. The index is based on 12 indicators of state vulnerability across social, political and economic categories.

Justice

The Supreme Court consists of nine justices appointed by the executive. There is no death penalty. The police force numbered 11,000 in 2011, and includes a Presidential Guard.

The population in penal institutions in Aug. 2013 was 15,126 (411 per 100,000 of national population). 62·5% of prisoners had yet to receive a trial according to 2014 estimates by the International Centre for Prison Studies. In 2015 the World Justice Project *Rule of Law Index*, which provides data on how the rule of law is experienced by the general public across eight categories, ranked Panama 90th of 102 countries for criminal justice and 61st for civil justice.

Education

Adult literacy was 94% in 2008. Elementary education is compulsory for all children from six to 14 years of age. In 2007 there were 446,176 pupils with 18,183 teaching staff at primary schools and 260,694 pupils with 16,847 teaching staff at secondary schools. In 2006 there were 130,838 students and 11,528 academic staff in tertiary education. The University of Panama (Universidad de Panamá), founded in 1935 in Panama City, is the leading higher education institution.

In 2008 public expenditure on education came to 3·8% of GDP.

Health

In 2014 there were 22 hospital beds per 10,000 persons. In the same year there were 6,179 physicians, 5,262 nursing and midwifery personnel, and 1,196 dentists.

In *Water: At What Cost? The State of the World's Water 2016*, WaterAid reported that 5·3% of the population does not have access to safe water.

Religion

80% of the population is Roman Catholic and 14% Protestant. The remainder of the population follow other religions (notably Islam). There is freedom of religious worship and separation of Church and State. Clergymen may teach in schools but may not hold public office. In Feb. 2019 there was one Roman Catholic cardinal.

Culture

World Heritage Sites

Panama has five sites on the UNESCO World Heritage List: the Fortifications on the Caribbean side of Panama: Portobelo-San Lorenzo (inscribed on the list in 1980); Darien National Park (1981); the Archaeological Site of Panamá Viejo and the Historic District of Panamá (1997 and 2003); and the Coiba National Park (2005).

Panama shares a UNESCO site with Costa Rica: the Talamanca Range-La Amistad Reserves (1983 and 1990), an important cross-breeding site for North and South American flora and fauna.

Press

In 2008 there were seven dailies with a combined circulation of 233,000.

Tourism

In 2011 there were 1,473,000 non-resident tourists (1,324,000 in 2010); spending by tourists totalled US$2,925m. in 2011 (US$2,552m. in 2010).

Festivals

Leading festivals include: the National Folkloric Festival, held annually (Sept.) in Guararé since 1949; the Panama Jazz Festival (Jan.); the International Fair of the Sea, held in Bocas del Toro province in Sept.; and the International Fair of Changuinola, also in Bocas del Toro in Sept.

Diplomatic Representatives

Of Panama in the United Kingdom (40 Hertford St., London, W1J 7SH)
  Ambassador: Daniel Eduardo Fábrega Venier.

Of the United Kingdom in Panama (Humboldt Tower, 4th Floor, Calle 53, Marbella, Panama City)
  Ambassador: Damion Potter.

Of Panama in the USA (2862 McGill Terr., NW, Washington, D.C., 20008)
  Ambassador: Emanuel Arturo Gonzalez-Revilla Lince.

Of the USA in Panama (Edificio 783, Avenida Demetrio Basilio Lakas, Panama City)
  Ambassador: Vacant.
  Chargé d'Affaires a.i.: Roxanne J. Cabral.

Of Panama to the United Nations
  Ambassador: Melitón Alejandro Arrocha Ruíz.

Of Panama to the European Union
  Ambassador: Miguel Verzbolovskis.

Further Reading

Statistical Information: The Controller-General of the Republic (Contraloria General de la República, Calle 35 y Avenida 6, Panama City) publishes an annual report and other statistical publications.

Harding, Robert C., *The History of Panama.* 2006

Lindsay-Poland, John, *Emperors in the Jungle.* 2003

McCullough, D. G., *The Path Between the Seas: The Creation of the Panama Canal, 1870–1914.* 1999

Sahota, G. S., *Poverty Theory and Policy: a Study of Panama.* 1990

Other titles are listed under Panama Canal, *above.*

National library: Biblioteca Nacional, Departamento de Información, Av. Balboa y Federico Boyd, Ciudad de Panama.

Website (Spanish only): http://www.contraloria.gob.pa

Papua New Guinea

Capital: Port Moresby
Population projection, 2020: 8·76m.
GNI per capita, 2017: (PPP$) 3, 403
HDI/world rank, 2017: 0·544/153
Internet domain extension: .pg

Key Historical Events

The region was settled by Asian peoples around 50, 000 years ago, when New Guinea was still part of the main Australian landmass. 10, 000 years ago, at the end of the last ice age, the waters of the Torres Straight cut off New Guinea from Australia, giving rise to separate development of the indigenous peoples. Plant-based agriculture developed about 9, 000 years ago in the New Guinea highlands. 2,500 years ago a large migration of Austronesian-speaking peoples settled the coastal areas. These communities developed animal husbandry, pottery and fishing and there is evidence of trade with the southeast Asian mainland. The rugged topography meant that contact between communities was limited and they retained their separate languages and customs. This heterogeneity continued down the centuries, so that today Papua New Guinea has an estimated 1,000 different cultural groups. Spanish and Portuguese explorers reached the island in the early 16th century and the Portuguese are thought to have introduced the kaukau (sweet potato), which became a staple crop. Spain laid claim to the western half of the island in 1545, naming it 'New Guinea' because of the supposed resemblance of its inhabitants to the people of Africa's Guinea coast.

From the late 18th century the British and Dutch competed for control of the island. In 1828 the Dutch claimed the western half as part of the Dutch East Indies, while the eastern half came under British influence. Following an abortive annexation attempt by Australian colonists, Britain declared a protectorate over the southern coast and islands adjacent to the eastern half of New Guinea on 6 Nov. 1884. Germany colonized the northern portion of the eastern half, along with New Britain, New Ireland and Bougainville, an arrangement formalized by the 1885 Anglo–German Agreement.

In 1888 Britain formally annexed the area under its control as British New Guinea and passed its administration to Australia in 1902. On 1 Sept. 1906 the Australian administration renamed it the Territory of Papua, Papua being a Malay word used to describe the Melanesian inhabitants' curly hair. The northeastern section of the island remained a German colony until the outbreak of the First World War in 1914, when Australian armed forces occupied it. For the next seven years it was under their administration and remained so after 1921, when it became a League of Nations mandated territory. In the Second World War, Allied and Japanese forces fought a prolonged military campaign on the island. It began with a Japanese victory at the Battle of Rabaul, New Britain in Feb. 1942 and continued throughout the war, with Japanese troops in occupation for much of the time until the Allies' victory in Aug. 1945.

In 1947 the northeastern part of the island became the UN Trust Territory of New Guinea, before merging in 1949 with the Territory of Papua to become the Territory of Papua New Guinea. A legislative council was established in 1953, succeeded by a house of assembly in 1964. On 1 Dec. 1973 Australia granted Papua New Guinea self-government. After a vigorous debate over questions of land-reform and citizenship, a constitution was passed and on 16 Sept. 1975 Papua New Guinea became fully independent. It also became a member of the Commonwealth, recognizing the British monarch as its own. In the same year the new state ignored a unilateral declaration of independence by the island of Bougainville and suppressed its campaign of civil disobedience. In 1988 an armed campaign by tribes claiming traditional land rights against the Australian owner of the massive Panguna copper field escalated into a civil war for Bougainville's secession. Fighting lasted nine years and cost an estimated 20,000 lives before a permanent truce was signed in April 1998. Bougainville gained autonomy in 2005 and is expected to hold a referendum on full independence in the future.

Political volatility caused frequent changes of government in Papua New Guinea during its first three decades of independence. In 2002, following violence in the general election, the electoral system was changed to encourage stable government. The deployment of Australian police on the island in 2003 caused resentment and from 2005, under a new agreement between the two governments, they operated in smaller numbers and with reduced powers. Despite its considerable mineral resources, the country's economy has stagnated in recent years; the difficulty of establishing land ownership has contributed to this, as has the need to protect the environment in what remains a largely subsistence culture. In 2006 the United Nations downgraded Papua New Guinea's status to least developed nation.

In 2011–12 Papua New Guinea experienced a leadership crisis between Sir Michael Somare and Peter O'Neill. In Aug. 2011, with Prime Minister Somare having been out of the country for five months on medical leave, the government declared the post vacant and O'Neill was elected by parliament, replacing acting prime minister Sam Abal. However, in Dec. the Supreme Court ruled the declaration and the election of O'Neill illegal. It also ordered the reinstatement of Somare. Although Somare and a new cabinet were sworn in, O'Neill refused to step down and the power struggle triggered a failed mutiny by rebel soldiers in Jan. 2012. Having the support of the civil service, the police, the defence force and most MPs, O'Neill remained effectively in control of the country. In May 2012 the Supreme Court once again ruled that Somare should be recognized as the legitimate prime minister. O'Neill's government subsequently ordered the arrest of the chief justice on charges of sedition. The prime minister's office was again declared vacant owing to Somare's continued absence. At the end of the month O'Neill was re-elected unopposed and sworn in as prime minister for the third time.

Territory and Population

Papua New Guinea extends from the equator to Cape Baganowa in the Louisiade Archipelago to 11° 40' S. lat. and from the border of West Irian to 160° E. long. with a total area of 462,840 sq. km. According to the 2011 census the population was 7,275,324 (3,772,864 males); density, 15·7 per sq. km.

The UN gives a projected population for 2020 of 8·76m.

In 2011, 12·6% of the population lived in urban areas (the second lowest percentage in the world). In 2011 population of Port Moresby (National Capital District) was 364,125. Other main towns are Lae, Madang, Mount Hagen, Wewak, Goroka and Kimbe. The areas, populations and capitals of the provinces are:

Provinces	Sq. km	Census 2011	Capital
Bougainville	9,384	249,358	Arawa
Central	29,998	269,756	Port Moresby
Chimbu	6,122	376,473	Kundiawa
East New Britain	15,274	328,369	Rabaul
East Sepik	43,426	450,530	Wewak
Eastern Highlands	11,157	579,825	Goroka
Enga	11,704	432,045	Wabag
Gulf	34,472	158,197	Kerema
Hela	10,498	249,449	Tari
Jiwaka	4,798	343,987	Banz
Madang	28,886	493,906	Madang
Manus	2,000	60,485	Lorengau
Milne Bay	14,345	276,512	Alotau
Morobe	33,705	674,810	Lae
National Capital District	240	364,125	Port Moresby
New Ireland	9,557	194,067	Kavieng
Oro	22,735	186,309	Popondetta
Southern Highlands	15,089	510,245	Mendi

(continued)

Provinces	Sq. km	Census 2011	Capital
West New Britain	20,387	264,264	Kimbe
West Sepik	35,820	248,411	Vanimo
Western	98,189	201,351	Daru
Western Highlands	4,299	362,850	Mount Hagen

Tok Pisin (or Pidgin, a creole of English), Hiri Motu and English are all official languages. Papua New Guinea has about 850 different languages, more than any other country.

Social Statistics

Estimates, 2008: births, 207,000; deaths, 52,000. Rates, 2008 estimates (per 1,000 population): births, 31·4; deaths, 7·9. Expectation of life at birth in 2013 was 60·4 years for males and 64·6 years for females. Annual population growth rate, 2000–08, 2·5%. Infant mortality, 2010, 47 per 1,000 live births; fertility rate, 2008, 4·1 births per woman.

Climate

There is a monsoon climate, with high temperatures and humidity the year round. Port Moresby is in a rain shadow and is not typical of the rest of Papua New Guinea. Jan. 82°F (27·8°C), July 78°F (25·6°C). Annual rainfall 40" (1,011 mm).

Constitution and Government

The constitution took effect on 16 Sept. 1975. The head of state is the British sovereign, who is represented by a *Governor-General*, nominated by parliament for six-year terms. A single legislative house, known as the *National Parliament*, is made up of 111 members: 89 district representatives and 22 provincial representatives (MPs). The members are elected by universal suffrage; elections are held every five years. All citizens over the age of 18 are eligible to vote and stand for election. Voting is by secret ballot and follows the limited preferential system. The *Prime Minister*, nominated by parliament and appointed by the Governor-General, selects ministers for the National Executive Council. The government cannot be subjected to a vote of no confidence in the first 18 months of office. The 20 provincial assemblies, comprising elected national MPs, appointed members and elected local government representatives, are headed by a Governor, normally the provincial representative in the National Parliament.

National Anthem

'Arise, all you sons of this land'; words and tune by T. Shacklady.

Recent Elections

Parliamentary elections were held between 24 June and 8 July 2017. Prime Minister Peter O'Neill's People's National Congress won 27 of 111 seats; the National Alliance Party 14; the Pangu Party 11; the United Resources Party 9; the Papua New Guinea Party 6; the People's Progress Party 5; the Social Democratic Party 3; the Triumph Heritage Empowerment Rural Party 3. A number of smaller parties each took one or two seats, with 14 going to independents. Four seats were yet to be declared.

Bob Dadae was elected governor-general by parliament on 1 Feb. 2017.

Current Government

Governor-General: Bob Dadae (since 28 Feb. 2017).

In Feb. 2019 the government comprised:

Prime Minister, Chairman of the National Executive Council, and Minister for Sports: Peter O'Neill; b. 1965 (People's National Congress; in office since 3 Aug. 2011).

Deputy Prime Minister and Treasurer: Charles Abel.

Minister for Agriculture and Livestock: Benny Allen. *Civil Aviation:* Alfred Manase. *Commerce and Industry:* Wera Mori. *Communication, Information Technology and Energy:* Sam Basil. *Correctional Services:* Roy Biyama. *Culture and Tourism:* Emil Tammur. *Defence:* Solan Mirisim. *Education:* Nick Kuman. *Environment, Conservation and Climate Change:* John Pundari. *Finance and Rural Development:* James Marape. *Fisheries:* Patrick Basa. *Foreign Affairs and Trade:* Rimbink Pato. *Forestry:* Douglas

Tomuriesa. *Health and HIV/AIDS:* Puka Temu. *Higher Education, Research, Science and Technology:* Pila Niningi. *Housing and Urbanization:* John Kaupa. *Immigration and Border Security:* Petrus Thomas. *Intergovernmental Relations:* Kevin Isifu. *Justice and Attorney General:* Davis Steven. *Labour and Industrial Relations:* Mehrra Kipefa. *Lands and Physical Planning, and Asia-Pacific Economic Co-operation Affairs:* Justin Tkatchenko. *Mining:* Johnson Tuke. *Petroleum:* Fabian Pok. *Planning and Monitoring:* Richard Maru. *Police:* Jelta Wong. *Public Enterprise and State Investment:* William Duma. *Public Service:* Elias Kapavore. *Religion, Youth and Community Development:* Soroi Eoe. *Transport:* Westly Nukundj. *Works and Implementation:* Michael Nali. *Minister assisting the Prime Minister on Bougainville Affairs, Sports and Constitutional Matters:* William Samb.

Parliament Website: http://www.parliament.gov.pg

Current Leaders

Peter O'Neill

Position

Prime Minister

Introduction

Peter O'Neill was elected by MPs to succeed Sir Michael Somare in Aug. 2011. After Somare refused to acknowledge the result, there were two rival administrations in late 2011. Having been confirmed in office, O'Neill, a businessman and former treasury minister, pledged to fight corruption and develop the nation's infrastructure and services.

Early Life

Born on 13 Feb. 1965 in Pangia District in the Southern Highlands Province, O'Neill graduated in accountancy and commerce from the University of Papua New Guinea in 1988. He practised as a chartered accountant before going into the real estate business. From 1993–97 he was executive chairman of Pangia Enterprises and from 1997–99 served as executive chairman of Pacific Finance, which managed state-owned enterprises including the PNG Banking Corporation and the National Provident Fund.

O'Neill came in for criticism when several of these public enterprises failed, though his supporters praised his financial management and efforts to improve transparency. In 1999 he became executive chairman of Remington Technologies and in 2002 was elected to parliament for the People's National Congress (PNC), representing the constituency of Ialibu-Pangia. From 2002–03 he served as minister for labour and industrial relations and from 2003–04 was minister for public service and leader of government business.

As head of the PNC, he led the opposition from 2004–07. In 2007 he was appointed minister for public service in Somare's National Alliance Party-led coalition government and from 2010–11 also took on the finance and treasury portfolios. In office, he supported the liquefied national gas projects undertaken in partnership with foreign companies. On 2 Aug. 2011, during Somare's prolonged absence from government for medical treatment, MPs from across the political spectrum elected O'Neill prime minister by 70 votes to 24.

Career in Office

O'Neill's early months were dominated by political instability as Somare challenged the legality of his election. In Dec. 2011 Somare formed a rival administration after the Supreme Court found in favour of the ex-incumbent. Somare's government was initially recognized by Governor-General Sir Michael Ogio but he later reversed his decision and declared O'Neill's premiership to be legitimate. By early 2012 O'Neill had gained widespread recognition, although Somare pursued his legal challenge. In May 2012 the Supreme Court ruled that Somare was still the country's legitimate leader. The chief justice was charged with sedition and a group of police blockaded parliament. However, given that Somare had missed three consecutive sessions of parliament, the prime minister's office was again declared vacant. Having been elected unopposed by 56 of the 109 members of parliament, O'Neill was sworn in as the country's prime minister for the third time on 31 May 2012.

In parliamentary elections held in June and July 2012, the PNC was returned as the largest party, effectively ending the year-long feud with Somare and his supporters. O'Neill promised to act against corruption and to manage a natural gas and minerals boom in the national interest. He faced demands to develop the education and health sectors and to improve the national infrastructure. In Nov. 2012 he proposed an amendment to the constitution (which was approved in Feb. 2013) to extend a ban on votes of no confidence from 18 to 30 months after a government is elected. In Jan. 2013 the People's Party announced that it would merge with the PNC, increasing O'Neill's parliamentary representation. Also that month he banned ministers and officials from travelling abroad on government business without approval, claiming that public money had been abused.

In July 2013 it was agreed that asylum seekers who had arrived by boat in Australia would be sent to a detention facility on Manus Island in Papua New Guinea for assessment and, if their cases were upheld, they would be resettled. In return, Australia promised to provide substantial aid. However, the detention facility was declared illegal by the Supreme Court in a ruling in April 2016 and in Aug. the Australian and Papuan governments agreed that it should be closed.

It was reported in Jan. 2014 that arrest warrants served against O'Neill and other ministers by the National Fraud and Anti-Corruption Directorate had been dismissed by a district court. O'Neill had brought an injunction against the warrants, claiming they were part of an opposition coup attempt. However, in June a further arrest warrant was issued after the Directorate accused O'Neill of authorizing fraudulent government payments, and in Nov. 2014 he was referred to a judicial tribunal over allegations of misconduct in office. Investigations into his conduct continued through 2015 as he remained dogged by scandals and in July 2016, following public protests and demands for his resignation, he faced a parliamentary vote of no confidence that he nevertheless survived.

Following a general election held in June and July 2017 and marked by violence, parliament re-elected O'Neill as prime minister by 60 votes to 46 on 2 Aug.

Defence

The Papua New Guinea Defence Force had a total estimated strength of 3,100 in 2011 consisting of land, maritime and air elements. The Land Element, the senior of the three services, had around 2,500 personnel in 2011. The Maritime Operations Element, with around 400 personnel in 2011, has four patrol boats and two landing craft. There is an Air Operations Element, 200 strong in 2011, but it does not possess any combat-capable aircraft.

Defence expenditure in 2013 totalled US$84m. (US$13 per capita), representing 0·5% of GDP.

Economy

Agriculture, forestry and fishing contributed 30·5% to GDP in 2011; followed by mining and quarrying, 18·1%; construction, 16·1%; and public administration, defence and services, 8·5%.

Overview
Papua New Guinea is among the poorest of the Pacific nations. Its economy relies on agriculture, forestry and fishing (which engages most of the labour force) and the minerals and energy extraction sector (accounting for the majority of export earnings and GDP).

Prudent macroeconomic management preceding the global downturn from 2009 saw annual GDP growth average 7·3% between 2008 and 2012. A significant driver of the economy is US energy giant ExxonMobil's liquefied natural gas extraction project, backed by US$19bn. of investment, which came online in 2014 ahead of schedule.

Improving public service delivery and transparency and accountability in public finances are fundamental to capitalizing on the country's rich natural resource base in order to bring about inclusive growth and address widespread, acute poverty.

Currency
The unit of currency is the *kina* (PGK) of 100 *toea*. The kina was floated in Oct. 1994. Foreign exchange reserves were US$543m. in July 2005, gold reserves 63,000 troy oz and total money supply was K2,765m. Inflation, which averaged 12·8% between 1995 and 2000, was 6·7% in 2016 and 5·4% in 2017.

Budget
In 2012 revenues totalled K9,704·7m. (tax revenue, 83·7%) and expenditures K10,044·1m. (current expenditure, 61·7%).

VAT is 10%.

Performance
Real GDP growth was 5·3% in 2015, 1·6% in 2016 and 2·5% in 2017. Total GDP in 2017 was US$21·1bn.

Banking and Finance
The Bank of Papua New Guinea (*Governor*, Loi Martin Bakani) assumed the central banking functions formerly undertaken by the Reserve Bank of Australia on 1 Nov. 1973. In 2010 there were four commercial banks: ANZ Papua New Guinea, Bank South Pacific, Maybank (PNG) Ltd and Westpac Papua New Guinea. They had combined assets of K18·3bn. at the end of 2010. There were also 22 savings and loan societies, eight finance companies and two microfinance institutions in 2010.

Foreign debt was US$5,882m. in 2010, representing 62·9% of GNI.

There is a stock exchange in Port Moresby.

Energy and Natural Resources

Environment
Carbon dioxide emissions from the consumption of energy in 2011 were the equivalent of 0·5 tonnes per capita.

Electricity
Installed capacity was an estimated 0·7m. kW in 2011. Production in 2011 was 3·53bn. kWh, around 28% of it hydro-electric. Consumption per capita was an estimated 503 kWh.

Oil and Gas
Natural gas reserves in 2012 were 400bn. cu. metres; output in 2011 was 158m. cu. metres. Crude oil production (2009), 16m. bbls. Oil comes predominantly from the Iagifu field in the Southern Highlands. There were 88m. bbls of proven oil reserves in 2011.

Minerals
In 2011 mining and quarrying produced 18·1% of GDP. Copper is the main mineral product. Gold, copper and silver are the other minerals produced in quantity. A nickel–cobalt mining scheme is also under development. The Misima open-pit gold mine was opened in 1989 but its resources were depleted by the end of 2001. The Porgera gold mine opened in 1990 with an expected life of 20 years. Major copper deposits in Bougainville have proven reserves of about 800m. tonnes; mining was halted by secessionist rebel activity. Copper and gold deposits in the Star Mountains of the Western Province are mined by Ok Tedi Mining Ltd at the Mt Fubilan mine. Production of gold commenced in 1984 and of copper concentrates in 1987. In 2011 Ok Tedi Mining Ltd produced 130,456 tonnes of copper and 13 tonnes of gold. Gold mining also began at Lihir in 1997. In 2012 total gold production was 59 tonnes; silver production in 2012 was 81 tonnes.

Agriculture
In 2013 there were an estimated 300,000 ha. of arable land and 700,000 ha. of permanent cropland. Minor commercial crops include pyrethrum, tea, peanuts and spices. Locally consumed food crops include sweet potatoes, maize, taro, bananas, rice and sago. Tropical fruits grow abundantly. There is extensive grassland. The sugar industry has made the country self-sufficient in this commodity while a beef-cattle industry is being developed.

Production (2012 estimates, in 1,000 tonnes): palm fruit oil, 2,050; coconuts, 1,210; bananas, 1,180; sweet potatoes, 580; yams, 345; sugarcane, 330; taro, 250; green maize, 231.

Livestock (2013 estimates): pigs, 2·0m.; cattle, 93,000; chickens, 4·4m.

Forestry
The forest area totalled 33·56m. ha. in 2015 (73% of the land area). 52% of forest area is primary forest. Timber production is important for both local consumption and export. Timber production was 10·01m. cu. metres in 2011.

Fisheries
Tuna is the major resource. In 2015 the fish catch was an estimated 235,100 tonnes (94% sea fish).

Industry

Secondary and service industries are expanding for the local market. The main industries are food processing, beverages, tobacco, timber products, wood and fabricated metal products. Industry accounted for 45·2% of GDP in 2006, with manufacturing contributing 6·1%. Production (2013): wood-based panels, 91,000 cu. metres; sawnwood (estimate), 82,000 cu. metres.

Labour

In 2012 the economically active population numbered 3·19m. persons. The rate of unemployment was 2·3%.

International Trade

Australian aid in 2014–15 amounted to $A450·6m. The 'Pactra II' agreement of 1991 established a free trade zone with Australia and protects Australian investments.

Imports and Exports

Goods imports were US$8,340·7m. in 2012 (US$6,105·5m. in 2011) and goods exports US$4,517·7m. (US$5,499·3m. in 2011).

Main imports in 2012 were machinery and transport equipment (42·4%), mineral fuels and lubricants, and manufactured goods; main exports in 2012 were crude materials and animal and vegetable oils (41·3%), manufactured goods, and food, animals and beverages. In 2014 Papua New Guinea began exporting liquefied natural gas, which is expected to have a huge impact on the economy.

The leading import source in 2012 was Australia (34·4%), followed by Singapore and China; the leading export market in 2012 was Australia (35·9%), followed by Japan and Germany.

Communications

Roads

The national road system comprises some 8,800 km and there are about 8,100 km of provincial roads, as well as district, local and other roads. However, much of the network is in poor condition. There were 38,200 passenger cars in use in 2007 and 11,300 lorries and vans.

Civil Aviation

Jacksons International Airport is at Port Moresby. The state-owned national carrier is Air Niugini, which carried 1·5m. passengers in 2013 (1·1m. on domestic flights). In 2010 there were scheduled international flights to Brisbane, Cairns, Hong Kong, Honiara, Manila, Nadi, Singapore, Sydney and Tokyo.

Shipping

In Jan. 2014 there were 66 ships of 300 GT or over registered, totalling 102,000 GT. The busiest port is Lae, which handled 3·5m. tonnes of cargo in 2013.

Telecommunications

In 2009 there were 133·7 mobile phone subscriptions for every 1,000 inhabitants and 8·9 fixed telephone lines per 1,000 inhabitants. In the same year there were an estimated 18·6 internet users per 1,000 inhabitants. In 2004 the government rejected a bid by a South African joint venture to acquire a 51% stake in the state-owned telecommunications company Telikom PNG.

Social Institutions

Out of 178 countries analysed in the 2017 *Fragile States Index*—a list published jointly by the Fund for Peace and *Foreign Policy* magazine—Papua New Guinea was ranked the 48th most vulnerable to conflict or collapse. The index is based on 12 indicators of state vulnerability across social, political and economic categories.

Justice

The judicial system consists of a Supreme Court, a National Court, and district and local courts. The Supreme Court sittings are usually held with three or five judges. The death penalty for wilful murder was abolished in 1970 but reintroduced in 1991, although there have not been any executions since 1954.

The population in penal institutions in Dec. 2010 was 4,268 (61 per 100,000 of national population).

Education

The education system has three levels: primary, secondary and tertiary. However, there are no legal provisions regarding either free or compulsory education. In 2008 there were 9,457 elementary and primary schools with 1,138,356 pupils and 33,082 teachers, 94,192 pupils in 208 secondary schools (3,700 teachers) and 30,181 students in institutes of vocational and similar education. There are six universities: the University of Papua New Guinea (UPNG), Port Moresby; the Papua New Guinea University of Technology, Lae; Divine Word University, Madang; Pacific Adventist University, Boroko; the University of Goroka; and the Papua New Guinea University of Natural Resources and Environment, Rabaul. In 2015 there were also 31 colleges, including eight nursing colleges and eight teachers' colleges.

Adult literacy rate was an estimated 60·1% in 2009 (63·6% among males and 56·5% among females).

Government expenditure on education totalled K2,155m. in 2013.

Health

In 2008 there were 392 medical officers, 123 dentists and 3,777 nurses and midwives. There were 36 hospitals and 698 clinics plus health centres in 2010.

In *Water: At What Cost? The State of the World's Water 2016*, WaterAid reported that 60·0% of the population does not have access to safe water—the highest percentage of any nation.

Religion

The Constitution provides for freedom of religion. In 2010 there were an estimated 4·69m. Protestants and 2·06m. Catholics according to the Pew Research Center's Forum on Religion & Public Life. In Feb. 2019 there was one Roman Catholic cardinal.

Culture

World Heritage Sites

There is one UNESCO site in Papua New Guinea: Kuk Early Agricultural Site (inscribed on the list in 2008).

Press

In 2008 there were two daily newspapers (the *Papua New Guinea Post-Courier* and the *National*) and a number of weeklies and monthlies. The *Papua New Guinea Post-Courier* is the oldest (1969) and most widely read, with a daily circulation of 30,000 (2007).

Tourism

In 2011 there were 165,000 non-resident tourists (excluding same-day visitors), up from 146,000 in 2010 and 126,000 in 2009.

Festivals

Alongside the major Christian festivals several cultural shows are held, in Enga (late July), at Mount Hagen (Western Highlands; late Aug.) and at Goroka (Eastern Highlands; mid-Sept.). The Tumbuan Mask Festival takes place at Rabaul (July) and the Hiri Moale Festival in Port Moresby (Sept.) was established to preserve the trading expeditions between the Motu-Koitabu people and the Erema (Kerema). Independence Day is celebrated on 16 Sept.

Diplomatic Representatives

Of Papua New Guinea in the United Kingdom (14 Waterloo Pl., London, SW1Y 4AR)
High Commissioner: Winnie Anna Kiap.

Of the United Kingdom in Papua New Guinea (Sec 411 Lot 1 and 2, Kiroki St., Waigani, National Capital District, Port Moresby)
High Commissioner: Keith Scott.

Of Papua New Guinea in the USA (1779 Massachusetts Ave., NW, Suite 805, Washington, D.C., 20036)
Ambassador: Vacant.
Chargé d'Affaires a.i.: Cephas Kayo.

Of the USA in Papua New Guinea (PO Box 1492, NCD, Douglas St., Port Moresby)
Ambassador: Catherine Ebert-Gray.

Of Papua New Guinea to the United Nations
Ambassador: Max Hufanen Rai.

Of Papua New Guinea to the European Union
  Ambassador: Joshua Kalinoe.

Bougainville

Bougainville, as part of New Guinea, became a United Nations Trust Territory in 1947 under the jurisdiction of Australia. The region declared independence in 1975 but the uprising was suppressed and the islands became part of the North Solomons Province of the newly independent Papua New Guinea. Conflict between separatists and Papua New Guinea began in 1989. Following a UN-brokered ceasefire in 1998 a peace agreement was signed in 2001, providing for an autonomous government and a referendum on full independence scheduled to take place in Oct. 2019.

Area, 9,300 sq. km (3,600 sq. miles); population (2011), 249,358. The autonomous region comprises Bougainville island, Buka island and several smaller island groups. The government is based at Buka but the capital city will eventually revert to the former capital, Arawa.

  President: John Momis.

Agriculture is the mainstay of the economy (major crops include cocoa and copra), but the region is still reliant on grants and donors. There is an airport at Buka.

Further Reading

Papua New Guinea

National Statistical Office. *Summary of Statistics.* Annual.—*Abstract of Statistics.* Quarterly.
Bank of Papua New Guinea. *Quarterly Economic Bulletin.*
Connell, John, *Papua New Guinea: The Struggle for Development.* 1997
Turner, A., *Historical Dictionary of Papua New Guinea.* 1995
Waiko, John Dademo, *Short History of Papua New Guinea.* 1993.—*Papua New Guinea: A History of Our Times.* 2003
National Statistical Office: National Statistical Office, PO Box 337, Waigani, National Capital District, Port Moresby.
Website: http://www.nso.gov.pg

Paraguay

República del Paraguay (Republic of Paraguay)

Capital: Asunción
Population projection, 2020: 7·07m.
GNI per capita, 2017: (PPP$) 8,380
HDI/world rank, 2017: 0·702/110=
Internet domain extension: .py

Key Historical Events

Paraguay was occupied by the Spanish in 1537 and became a Spanish colony as part of the Viceroyalty of Peru. The area gained its independence, as the Republic of Paraguay, on 14 May 1811. Paraguay was then ruled by a succession of dictators. A devastating war fought from 1865 to 1870 between Paraguay and a coalition of Argentina, Brazil and Uruguay reduced Paraguay's population from about 600,000 to 233,000. Further severe losses were incurred during the war with Bolivia (1932–35) over territorial claims in the Chaco inspired by the unfounded belief that minerals existed in the territory. A peace treaty by which Paraguay obtained most of the area her troops had conquered was signed in July 1938.

A new constitution took effect in Feb. 1968 under which executive power is discharged by an executive president. Gen. Alfredo Stroessner Matiauda was re-elected seven times between 1958 and 1988. Since then, Paraguay has had more or less democratic government. On 23 March 1999 Paraguay's vice president Luis Maria Argaña was assassinated. The following day, Congress voted to impeach President Raúl Cubas who was said to be implicated in the murder. He then resigned. The victory of Fernando Lugo of the Patriotic Alliance for Change in the April 2008 presidential election brought to an end the 61-year rule of the Colorado Party, at the time the world's longest-ruling party.

Territory and Population

Paraguay is bounded in the northwest by Bolivia, northeast and east by Brazil and southeast, south and southwest by Argentina. The area is 406,752 sq. km (157,042 sq. miles).

The 2002 census population was 5,163,198. Although a census was held in 2012 only 76% of the population was covered. According to international standards, the population census of a country should have a coverage of at least 90% for it to be valid. Population estimate 2014: 6,657,000 (3,360,000 males), giving a density of 16 per sq. km. In 2011, 62·1% lived in urban areas.

The UN gives a projected population for 2020 of 7·07m.

In 2014 the estimated population of the capital, Asunción, was 2,307,000 (metropolitan area). Other major cities are Ciudad del Este, San Lorenzo and Luque.

There are 17 departments and the capital city. Area and population (2010 estimates):

Department	Area in sq. km	Population
Asunción (city)[1]	117	518,200
Central	2,465	2,068,100
Alto Paraná	14,895	753,700
Itapúa	16,525	535,500
Caaguazú	11,474	480,800
San Pedro	20,002	357,300
Cordillera	4,948	276,900
Paraguari	8,705	239,600
Concepción	18,051	190,500
Guairá	3,846	197,000

(continued)

Department	Area in sq. km	Population
Canendiyú	14,667	183,700
Caazapá	9,496	151,300
Amambay	12,933	125,300
Misiones	9,556	117,000
Neembucú	12,147	83,800
Oriental	*159,827*	*6,278,700*
Presidente Hayes	72,907	103,400
Boquerón[2]	91,669	57,800
Alto Paraguay[3]	82,349	11,300
Occidental	*246,925*	*172,500*

[1]Capital district.
[2]Incorporates former department of Nueva Asunción.
[3]Incorporates former department of Chaco.

The population is mixed Spanish and Guaraní Indian. There are 89,000 unassimilated Indians of other tribal origin in the Chaco and the forests of eastern Paraguay. The official languages are Spanish and Guaraní: 24·8% of the population speak only Guaraní; 51·5% are bilingual (Spanish/Guaraní); and 7·6% speak only Spanish.

Mennonites, who arrived in three groups (1927, 1930 and 1947), are settled in the Chaco and eastern Paraguay. There are also Korean and Japanese settlers.

Social Statistics

2006 births, 112,659; deaths, 19,298. Rates, 2006 (per 1,000 population): birth, 18·7; death, 3·2. Annual population growth rate, 2000–05, 2·0%. Expectation of life, 2007: 69·6 years for males and 73·8 for females. Infant mortality, 2010, 21 per 1,000 live births; fertility rate, 2008, 3·0 births per woman.

Climate

A tropical climate, with abundant rainfall and only a short dry season from July to Sept., when temperatures are lowest. Asunción, Jan. 81°F (27°C), July 64°F (17·8°C). Annual rainfall 53" (1,316 mm).

Constitution and Government

On 18 June 1992 a Constituent Assembly approved a new constitution. The head of state is the *President,* elected for a non-renewable five-year term. Parliament consists of an 80-member *Chamber of Deputies,* elected from departmental constituencies, and a 45-member *Senate,* elected from a single national constituency.

National Anthem

'Paraguayos, república o muerte!' ('Paraguayans, republic or death!'); words by F. Acuña de Figueroa, tune by F. Dupuy.

Recent Elections

Parliamentary and presidential elections were held on 22 April 2018. Mario Abdo Benítez of the National Republican Association–Colorado Party (ANR–PC) was elected president with 49·0% of votes cast. Efraín Alegre of the Authentic Radical Liberal Party (PLRA) won 45·1% of the vote and Juan Bautista Ybáñez of the Paraguay Green Party 3·4%. There were seven other candidates who received less than 1% of the vote each. Turnout was 61·3%.

In the parliamentary elections the National Republican Association--Colorado Party (ANR–PC) won 42 seats in the Chamber of Deputies, the

Authentic Radical Liberal Party (PLRA) 17 seats, the Great Renewed National Alliance 13, the Beloved Fatherland Party 3, the Hagamos Party 2 and the National Encounter Party 2. Four other parties won one seat each. In the Senate the ANR–PC won 17 seats, the PLRA 13, the Guasú Front 6, the Beloved Fatherland Party 3, the Hagamos Party 2, the Progressive Democratic Party 2, the National Crusade Movement 1 and the National Union of Ethical Citizens 1.

Current Government

President: Mario Abdo Benítez; b. 1971 (ANR–PC; sworn in 15 Aug. 2018).
In Feb. 2019 the cabinet comprised:
Vice President: Hugo Velázquez Moreno.
Minister of Agriculture and Livestock: Denis Lichi. *Education and Science:* Eduardo Petta. *Finance:* Benigno López. *Foreign Affairs:* Luis Castiglioni. *Industry and Trade:* Liz Cramer. *Interior:* Juan Ernesto Villamayor. *Justice:* Julio Ríos. *Labour:* Carla Bacigalupo. *National Defence:* Bernardino Soto. *Public Health:* Dr Julio Mazzoleni. *Public Works:* Arnoldo Wiens. *Social Development:* Mario Varela. *Women's Affairs:* Nilda Romero.
Chief of Staff of the Presidency: Julio Ullón.
Office of the President (Spanish only): http://www.presidencia.gov.py

Current Leaders

Mario Abdo Benítez

Position
President

Introduction
A former senator, Abdo Benítez became president in Aug. 2018 following his election in April.

Early Life
Born on 10 Nov. 1971 in the capital, Asunción, Benítez joined the armed forces after finishing his schooling, becoming a paratrooper in the air force. In 1995 he graduated in marketing from the former Teikyo Post University (the Post University since 2004) in Connecticut, USA. Between 1998 and 2012 he worked in the asphalt industry. He entered politics in 2005 when he joined the Colorado Party's Republican National Reconstruction movement, becoming party vice-president in 2008. In 2013 he entered the Senate and two years later led the Senate's Colorado contingent.
Benítez has faced criticism for his links to the former military dictatorship of Gen. Alfredo Stroessner, his father having been Stroessner's private secretary. When Stroessner died in 2006, Abdo Benítez was a pallbearer at the funeral. He went on to establish the Colorado Party's Peace and Progress movement with the dictator's grandson. In Dec. 2017 he won the Colorado Party presidential primaries by defeating former minister of finance, Santiago Peña.

Career in Office
In the 2018 election race Abdo Benítez beat Efraín Alegre, candidate of the Authentic Radical Liberal Party, claiming 49·0% of the vote compared to 45·1%—the lowest victory margin since Paraguay's return to democracy. He took office on 15 Aug., pledging to work towards national unity, to improve judicial transparency, and to fight poverty and corruption. His inauguration came one week after thousands of people took part in street protests in Asunción against political graft.

Defence

The army, navy and air forces are separate services under a single command. The President of the Republic is the active C.-in-C. Conscription is for 12 months (two years in the navy).
In 2013 defence expenditure totalled US$364m. (US$55 per capita), representing 1·2% of GDP.

Army
Strength (2011) 7,600 (1,500 conscripts). In addition there is a paramilitary Special Police Force numbering 14,800 (4,000 conscripts).

Navy
Personnel in 2011 totalled 1,950 (or which 850 conscripts) including 900 marines (of which 200 conscripts) and 100 naval aviation.

Air Force
The air force had a strength of 1,100 in 2011 (200 conscripts). There were six combat-capable aircraft in 2011.

Economy

In 2012 agriculture accounted for 17·4% of GDP, industry 28·1% and services 54·5%.

Overview
Agriculture and foreign trade underpin the economy. The country is the world's sixth largest producer of soybeans and a major exporter of hydro-electric power. The economy experienced an average annual growth rate of 5% in the decade to 2015, including a leap of 14·0% in 2013 (its highest level since the 1970s), reflecting an improved fiscal outlook—on the back of restored confidence in public institutions, structural reform and debt reduction—and strong exports.
The growth rate has since fallen back slightly, averaging 4·0% from 2015–17, and—despite the adoption in 2013 of a limit on the authorized fiscal deficit of 1·5% of GDP—the deficit was recorded at 1·6% in 2017. Meanwhile, a focus on public development saw foreign debt double in the five years to 2017, although the country retained the lowest public debt ratio in Latin America in 2017 at 25·7% of GDP. In the same year, inflation measured 3·6%, down from 4·1% in 2016.
Paraguay had the lowest unemployment rate in the MERCOSUR (Southern Common Market) area in 2017, at 6·5%. Between 2009 and 2014 the proportion of Paraguayans living on less than US$4 per day (the regional poverty threshold) fell from 32·5% to 18·8%. However, lowering poverty and income inequality remain major challenges. A national development plan for 2014–30 is centred around three pillars: poverty reduction and social development, shared economic growth and the integration of Paraguay into international markets.

Currency
The unit of currency is the *guaraní* (PYG), notionally divided into 100 *céntimos*. In July 2005 total money supply was 4,733·6bn. guaranís and foreign exchange reserves were US$1,109m. Inflation was 4·1% in 2016 and 3·6% in 2017.

Budget
Budgetary central government revenue and expenditure in 1bn. guaranís:

	2009	2010	2011
Revenue	13,877·9	16,242·2	18,969·3
Expenditure	12,057·1	13,076·6	15,716·9

Principal sources of revenue in 2011: taxes on goods and services, 8,811·8bn. guaranís; taxes on income, profits and capital gains, 2,610·6bn. guaranís; taxes on international trade and transactions, 1,704·0bn. guaranís. Main items of expenditure by economic type in 2011: compensation of employees, 8,046·9bn. guaranís; grants, 2,534·6bn. guaranís; social benefits, 1,965·2bn. guaranís.
VAT is 10% (reduced rate, 5%).

Performance
The economy grew by 14·0% in 2013—the highest rate of any Latin American or Caribbean country that year. More recently, there was growth of 3·1% in 2015, 4·3% in 2016 and 4·8% in 2017. Total GDP in 2017 was US$29·7bn.

Banking and Finance
The Central Bank is a state-owned autonomous agency with the sole right of note issue, control over foreign exchange and the supervision of commercial banks (*President*, José Cantero Sienra). There is a Superintendencia de Bancos under Nelson Valiente Saucedo. In June 2010 there were 15 commercial banks, one of which was state-owned with three foreign-owned.
Foreign debt was US$4,938m. in 2010, representing 25·3% of GNI.
There is a stock exchange in Asunción.

Energy and Natural Resources

Environment
Paraguay's carbon dioxide emissions from the consumption of energy were the equivalent of 0·6 tonnes per capita in 2011.

Electricity
Installed capacity was 8·8m. kW in 2011. Output (2011), 57·63bn. kWh (almost exclusively hydro-electric); consumption per capita in 2011 was 1,750 kWh. Paraguay is the fourth largest exporter of electricity (after France, Germany and Canada), with 46·1bn. kWh in 2011.

Minerals
The country is poor in minerals. Limestone, gypsum, kaolin and salt are extracted. Deposits of bauxite, iron ore, copper, manganese and uranium exist. 2006 estimated output: kaolin, 66,000 tonnes; limestone, 16,000 tonnes.

Agriculture
In 2015, 20·1% of employed persons were engaged in agriculture. In 2013 there were an estimated 4·6m. ha. of arable land and 85,000 ha. of permanent crops.

Output (in 1,000 tonnes), 2012: soybeans, 4,345; sugarcane, 4,186; maize, 3,080; cassava, 1,686; wheat, 1,561; rice, 396; oranges, 230; palm fruit oil (estimate), 152; sorghum, 125; rapeseed, 111; watermelons (estimate), 110. *Yerba maté*, or strongly flavoured Paraguayan tea, continues to be produced but is declining in importance.

Livestock (2013): 13·38m. cattle, 11·98m. pigs, 448,000 sheep, 300,000 horses (estimate) and 16·91m. chickens.

Forestry
The area under forests in 2015 was 15·32m. ha., or 39% of the total land area. Timber production was 10·73m. cu. metres in 2011.

Fisheries
In 2011 the catch totalled an estimated 17,000 tonnes, exclusively from inland waters.

Industry

Paraguay is one of the least industrialized countries in Latin America. Industries include meat packing, sugar processing, cement, textiles, brewing, wood products and consumer goods. In 2012 industry accounted for 28·1% of GDP, with manufacturing contributing 11·6%.

Labour
The labour force in 2013 was 3,132,000 (2,485,000 in 2003). 73·4% of the population aged 15–64 was economically active in 2013. In the same year 5·0% of the population was unemployed.

Paraguay had 20,000 people living in slavery according to the Walk Free Foundation's 2013 *Global Slavery Index*.

International Trade

Imports and Exports
Trade in US$1m.:

	2003	2004	2005	2006	2007
Imports c.i.f.	2,227·5	3,097·4	3,714·9	5,878·8	5,844·7
Exports f.o.b.	1,241·5	1,625·7	1,687·8	1,906·4	2,784·7

Main imports in 2006: machinery and transport equipment, 46·9%; chemicals and chemical products, 12·2%; petroleum oils, 11·8%; metal tools, 2·6%. Main exports, 2006: soybeans, 23·0%; beef, 21·5%; maize, 8·7%; oilcake and other solid residues, 7·2%. Main import suppliers in 2006: China, 25·1%; Brazil, 19·0%; Argentina, 13·0%; USA, 6·0%. Main export markets, 2006: Uruguay, 22·0%; Brazil, 17·2%; Russia, 11·9%; Cayman Islands, 9·5%.

Communications

Roads
In 2012 there were 30,401 km of roads, of which 17·0% were paved. Passenger cars numbered 240,700 in 2007, and there were 248,100 lorries and vans, 12,800 buses and coaches, and 134,900 motorcycles and mopeds. There were 845 fatalities as a result of road accidents in 2007.

Rail
The President Carlos Antonio López (formerly Paraguay Central) Railway used to run from Asunción to Encarnación, on the Río Alto Paraná, with a length of 441 km (1,435 mm gauge), and connected with Argentine Railways over the Encarnación-Posadas bridge. However, most commercial operations ended in 1999.

Civil Aviation
There is an international airport at Asunción (Silvio Pettirossi). The main Paraguay-based carrier is TAM Airlines (formerly TAM Mercosur). In 2012 scheduled airline traffic of Paraguayan-based carriers flew 4·2m. km; passenger-km totalled 720·8m. in the same year. In 2014 Asunción (Silvio Pettirossi) handled 915,425 passengers (840,459 on international flights) and 10,954 tonnes of freight.

Shipping
Asunción, the chief port, is 1,500 km from the sea. In Jan. 2014 there were 24 ships of 300 GT or over registered, totalling 44,000 GT.

Telecommunications
In 2013 there were 437,643 main (fixed) telephone lines; mobile phone subscriptions numbered 7,053,000 in 2013 (103·7 per 100 persons). In the same year there were 115,772 fixed broadband subscriptions and 374 wireless broadband subscriptions. In March 2012 there were 1·0m. Facebook users.

Social Institutions

Out of 178 countries analysed in the 2017 *Fragile States Index*—a list published jointly by the Fund for Peace and *Foreign Policy* magazine—Paraguay was ranked the 80th least vulnerable to conflict or collapse. The index is based on 12 indicators of state vulnerability across social, political and economic categories.

Justice
The 1992 constitution confers a large measure of judicial autonomy. The highest court is the Supreme Court with nine members. Nominations for membership must be backed by six of the eight members of the Magistracy Council, which appoints all judges, magistrates and the electoral tribunal. The Council comprises elected representatives of the Presidency, Congress and the bar. There are special Chambers of Appeal for civil and commercial cases, and criminal cases. Judges of first instance deal with civil, commercial and criminal cases in six departments. Minor cases are dealt with by Justices of the Peace.

The Attorney-General represents the State in all jurisdictions, with representatives in each judicial department and in every jurisdiction.

The population in penal institutions in Sept. 2012 was 7,901 (118 per 100,000 of national population). 75·1% of prisoners had yet to receive a trial according to 2014 estimates by the International Centre for Prison Studies. The death penalty was abolished for all crimes in 1992.

Education
Adult literacy was 95% in 2007. Education is free and nominally compulsory. In 2012 there were 838,198 pupils at primary schools (with 34,694 teaching staff) and 631,003 at secondary level (with 34,286 teaching staff). There were 225,211 students in tertiary education in 2010. Paraguay's leading institute of higher education is the National University of Asunción (Universidad Nacional de Asunción), the country's oldest university, founded in 1889.

In 2007 public expenditure on education came to 4·0% of GDP and 11·9% of total government spending.

Health
In 2013 there were 2·4 public hospitals per 100,000 population. In the period 2006–12 Paraguay had a provision of 13 hospital beds per 10,000 population. In 2012 there were 12 physicians per 10,000 people, ten nurses and midwives per 10,000 population and two dentists for every 10,000.

In *Water: At What Cost? The State of the World's Water 2016*, WaterAid reported that 2·0% of the population does not have access to safe water.

Religion
Religious liberty was guaranteed by the 1967 constitution. Article 6 recognized Roman Catholicism as the official religion of the country. In 2010 there were 6·25m. Christians (of which about 92% Catholics and 7% Protestants)

according to estimates by the Pew Research Center's Forum on Religion & Public Life and 110,000 folk religionists.

Culture

World Heritage Sites
Paraguay has one site on the UNESCO World Heritage List: the Jesuit Missions of La Santísima Trinidad de Paraná and Jesús de Tavarangue (inscribed on the list in 1993).

Press
In 2008 there were eight daily newspapers with a combined circulation of 135,000.

Tourism
In 2011 there were 524,000 foreign tourists, spending US$281m.

Diplomatic Representatives

Of Paraguay in the United Kingdom (3rd Floor, 344 Kensington High St., London, W14 8NS)
  Ambassador: Genaro Vicente Pappalardo Ayala.

Of the United Kingdom in Paraguay (Edificio Citicenter, Piso 5, Ave. Mariscal López y Cruz del Chaco, Asunción)
  Ambassador: Matthew Hedges.

Of Paraguay in the USA (2209 Massachusetts Ave., NW, Washington, D.C., 20008)
  Ambassador: Germán Hugo Rojas Irgoyen.

Of the USA in Paraguay (1776 Mariscal López Ave., Asunción)
  Ambassador: Lee McClenny.

Of Paraguay to the United Nations
  Ambassador: Julio César Arriola Ramírez.

Of Paraguay to the European Union
  Ambassador: Rigoberto Gauto.

Further Reading

Gaceta Official, published by the Palace of Government, Asunción
Anuario Estadístico de la República del Paraguay (now discontinued).
Nickson, R. A. and Lambert, P. (eds) *The Transition to Democracy in Paraguay.* 1997
National library: Biblioteca Nacional, Calle de la Residenta, 820 c/ Perú, Asunción.
National Statistical Office: Naciones Unidas y Saavedra, Fernando de la Mora, Zona Norte.
Website (Spanish only): http://www.dgeec.gov.py

Peru

República del Perú (Republic of Peru)

Capital: Lima
Population projection, 2020: 33·31m.
GNI per capita, 2017: (PPP$) 11,789
HDI/world rank, 2017: 0·750/89
Internet domain extension: .pe

Key Historical Events

Hunter-gatherers lived in Peru from at least 9000 BC. Irrigation canals discovered recently in the Andean foothills of northern Peru date farming from around 3400 BC. The Chavin culture in central and northern Peru between 900 BC and 200 BC left monumental temples and intricate artwork across a wide area. The Paracas culture emerged on the southern coast in around 300 BC and evolved into the Nazca culture, famed for its exquisite textiles. Further north, the coastal Moche culture flourished between around 100 BC and AD 700, producing distinctive metalwork and pottery. The following centuries saw the rise of inland, Andean cultures and powerful city states such as Chancay, Sipan and Cajamarca.

The Inca civilization is thought to have its origins in a Quechua-speaking tribe that settled in the Cusco Valley from about 1200. By the mid-15th century, under Emperor Tupac Yupanqui (1471–93) and subsequently under Huayna Capac, the empire stretched along the Andes from Ecuador to Chile. The Inca's road network was an engineering masterpiece, as were the terraced fields and cities such as the famed Machu Picchu.

The Spanish adventurer, Francisco Pizarro, landed on the Ecuadorian coast in 1532 and moved south. Relations between the Spanish and the Incas quickly soured and Emperor Atahualpa was captured following the battle of Cajamarca. He was executed in 1533 and a year later Pizarro conquered the city of Cusco. Lima was founded in 1535 and in 1542 it became the seat of the Viceroyalty of Peru, which for a time had jurisdiction over all the Spanish colonies in South America. The Spanish conquistadors amassed vast wealth and power by controlling the trade in Andean gold and silver, while the Incas became increasingly marginalized. Revolts against Spanish rule occurred in the 1780s but concerted demands for independence came only after the French Revolution and Napoleon's conquest of Spain in 1808.

José de San Martin of Argentina (who had ended Spanish rule in Chile in 1818) and Simón Bolívar of Venezuela proclaimed Peruvian independence on 28 July 1821 but it was only confirmed in Dec. 1824, when Antonio José de Sucre defeated Spanish troops at Ayacucho. After independence Peru and its neighbours engaged in various territorial disputes. Chile's victory over Peru and Bolivia in the War of the Pacific (1879–83) resulted in Peru ceding the department of Tarapaca and the provinces of Tacna and Arica to Chile. Gen. Andrés Avelino Cáceres became president in 1885 and tried to breathe life into the crippled economy by encouraging foreign management of the railways and guano (fertilizer) exports.

A businessman, Augusto Leguía, who became president for four years in 1908, pushed through economic reforms. He became increasingly authoritarian during his second term of office (1919–30), and in 1924 Dr Victor Raúl Haya de la Torre founded the Alianza Popular Revolucionaria Americana (APRA), which called for radical reform. The party was banned by Leguía and then outlawed by his successor, Sanchez Cerro, during the 1930s. Peru sided with the Allies during the Second World War and in 1945 Luis Bustamante y Rivero was elected president, with APRA backing. Splits soon emerged and Manuel Odría led a military coup three years later. An inconclusive election in 1962 enabled Gen. Ricardo Pérez Godoy to seize power, although he was deposed in a coup led by Gen. Nicolás Lindley López a year later. There followed a period of civilian rule but the military staged yet another coup in 1968. In 1978–79 a constituent assembly drew up a new constitution, after which a civilian government was installed.

Peru was plagued by political violence between the early 1980s and the late 1990s with 69,000 people killed by Maoist Shining Path insurgents, the smaller Tupac Amaru Revolutionary Movement and government forces. On 5 April 1992 President Alberto Fujimori suspended the constitution, dissolved parliament and implemented drastic economic reforms to tackle rampant inflation. A new constitution was promulgated on 29 Dec. 1993. But while Peru enjoyed stability and economic growth, continuing autocratic rule put some politicians above the law. Embroiled in a bribery and corruption scandal, President Fujimori's discredited administration came to an end in Nov. 2000 when he resigned while out of the country.

A caretaker government under Valentín Paniagua presided over new presidential and congressional elections in April 2001. A new government led by President Alejandro Toledo took office in July 2001. The Toledo government consolidated Peru's return to democracy and presided over a period of strong economic growth, although great inequalities persisted. Alan García, who had been president for five years in the second half of the 1980s, narrowly won a run-off election in April 2006 and was sworn in as president for a second term in July 2006.

Territory and Population

Peru is bounded in the north by Ecuador and Colombia, east by Brazil and Bolivia, south by Chile and west by the Pacific Ocean. Area, 1,285,216 sq. km (including the area of the Peruvian part of Lake Titicaca).

In 2008 Peru lodged a claim with the International Court of Justice (ICJ) for a large area of Pacific waters extending from its territorial border with Chile and incorporating valuable fishing grounds. In Jan. 2014 the ICJ awarded Peru some 50,000 sq. km of additional waters, although many of the most lucrative fishing areas remain under Chilean jurisdiction. For an account of the border dispute with Ecuador, *see* ECUADOR: Territory and Population.

Census population, 2017, 29,381,884; density, 22·9 per sq. km. In 2011 the population was 77·3% urban.

The UN gives a projected population for 2020 of 33·31m.

The country is administratively divided into 25 regions and an autonomous province of Lima (with capitals): Amazonas (Chachapoyas), Ancash (Huaráz), Apurímac (Abancay), Arequipa (Arequipa), Ayacucho (Ayacucho), Cajamarca (Cajamarca), Callao (Callao), Cusco (Cusco), Huancavelica (Huancavelica), Huánuco (Huánuco), Ica (Ica), Junín (Huancayo), La Libertad (Trujillo), Lambayeque (Chiclayo), Lima (Huacho), Lima province (Lima), Loreto (Iquitos), Madre de Dios (Puerto Maldonado), Moquegua (Moquegua), Pasco (Cerro de Pasco), Piura (Piura), Puno (Puno), San Martín (Moyobamba), Tacna (Tacna), Tumbes (Tumbes), Ucayali (Pucallpa).

The largest cities (with 2017 census populations) are: Lima, 9,562,280; Arequipa, 1,002,846; Trujillo, 857,063; Chiclayo, 606,907; Piura, 460,876; Cusco, 428,450.

Mestizos (mixed Amerindian and White) account for about 47% of the population, Amerindians 32%, European descendants 18·5%, Afro-Peruvians 2%, and Asian Peruvians and others (mainly Chinese and Japanese) 0·5%.

The official languages are Spanish (spoken by 83·9% of the population in 2007), Quechua (13·2%) and Aymara (1·8%). There are more than 40 indigenous languages in total, but some in danger of extinction. Around 13% of the population speak one of the country's native languages as their mother tongue.

Social Statistics

2009 births (estimate), 604,000; 2009 deaths (estimate), 144,000. Rates per 1,000 population (2009): birth, 21; death, 5. Annual population growth rate, 2005–10, 1·1%; infant mortality, 2010, 15 per 1,000 live births. Life expectancy, 2013: males, 72·2 years; females, 77·6. Fertility rate, 2013, 2·4 births per woman.

Climate

There is a very wide variety of climates, ranging from tropical in the east to desert in the west, with perpetual snow in the Andes. In coastal areas, temperatures vary very little, either daily or annually, though humidity and

© Springer Nature Limited 2020
Palgrave Macmillan (ed.), *The Statesman's Yearbook 2020*,
https://doi.org/10.1057/978-1-349-95940-2_152

cloudiness show considerable variation, with highest humidity from May to Sept. Little rain is experienced in that period. In the Sierra, temperatures remain fairly constant over the year, but the daily range is considerable. There the dry season is from April to Nov. Desert conditions occur in the extreme south, where the climate is uniformly dry, with a few heavy showers falling between Jan. and March. Lima, Jan. 74°F (23·3°C), July 62°F (16·7°C). Annual rainfall 2" (48 mm). Cusco, Jan. 56°F (13·3°C), July 50°F (10°C). Annual rainfall 32" (804 mm). El Niño is the annual warm Pacific current that develops along the coasts of Peru and Ecuador. El Niño in 1982–83 resulted in agricultural production down by 8·5% and fishing output down by 40%. El Niño in 1991–94 was unusually long. El Niño in 1997–98 resulted in a sudden rise in the surface temperature of the Pacific by 9°F (5°C) and caused widespread damage and loss of life.

Constitution and Government

The 1980 constitution provided for a legislative *Congress* consisting of a *Senate* and a *Chamber of Deputies*, and an Executive formed of the President and a Council of Ministers appointed by him. Elections were to be every five years with the President and Congress elected, at the same time, by separate ballots.

On 5 April 1992 then President Alberto Fujimori suspended the 1980 constitution and dissolved Congress.

A referendum was held on 31 Oct. 1993 to approve the 12th constitution, including a provision for the president to serve a consecutive second term. 52·2% of votes cast were in favour. The constitution was promulgated on 29 Dec. 1993. In 2000 an amendment rescinded the right of the president to stand for two consecutive terms of office, although it is permitted to contest elections for non-consecutive terms.

Congress has 130 members, elected for a five-year term by proportional representation. All citizens over the age of 18 are eligible to vote. Voting is compulsory.

National Anthem

'Somos libres, seámoslo siempre' ('We are free, let us always be so'); words by J. De La Torre Ugarte, tune by J. B. Alcedo.

Government Chronology

Heads of State since 1945. (AP = Popular Action; APRA = American Popular Revolutionary Alliance; FDN = National Democratic Front; MDP = Pradista Democratic Movement/Peruvian Democratic Movement; NM-C90 = New Majority/Change 90; PAP = Peruvian Aprista Party; PNP = Peruvian Nationalist Party; PP = Peru Possible; PPK = Peruvians for Change; PR = Restorer Party; n/p = non-partisan)

President of the Republic		
1945–48	FDN	José Luis Bustamante y Rivero
Chairmen of the Military Junta of Government		
1948–50	military	Manuel Apolinario Odría Amoretti
1950	military	Zenón Noriega Agüero
Presidents of the Republic		
1950–56	PR	Manuel Apolinario Odría Amoretti
1956–62	MDP	Manuel Prado y Ugarteche
Junta of Government/Joint Command of the Armed Forces		
1962–63	military	Ricardo Pío Pérez Godoy, Nicolás Lindley López, Juan Francisco Torres Matos, Pedro Vargas Prada Peirano
Presidents of the Republic		
1963–68	AP	Fernando Belaúnde Terry
1968–75	military	Juan Francisco Velasco Alvarado
1975–80	military	Francisco Morales Bermúdez
1980–85	AP	Fernando Belaúnde Terry
1985–90	APRA	Alan Gabriel Ludwig García Pérez
1990–2000	NM-C90	Alberto Keinya Fujimori Fujimori
2000–01	AP	Valentín Paniagua Corazao
2001–06	PP	Alejandro Celestino Toledo Manrique

(continued)

2006–11	PAP	Alan Gabriel Ludwig García Pérez
2011–16	PNP	Ollanta Moisés Humala Tasso
2016–18	PPK	Pedro Pablo Kuczynski Godard
2018–	n/p	Martín Alberto Vizcarra Cornejo

Recent Elections

The first round of presidential elections were held on 10 April 2016. Keiko Fujimori of the Fuerza Popular (Popular Force) won 39·9% of the vote, followed by Pedro Pablo Kuczynski of Peruanos por el Kambio (Peruvians for Change) with 21·0%, Verónika Mendoza of Frente Amplio (Broad Front) with 18·8%, Alfredo Barnechea of Acción Popular (Popular Action) with 7·0% and former president Alan García of Alianza Popular (Popular Alliance) with 5·8%. There were five other candidates. In the second round run-off held on 5 June 2016, Kuczynski won with 50·1% of the vote against Fujimori with 49·9%. Turnout was 80·1%.

In congressional elections also held on 10 April 2016 Fuerza Popular won 73 of 130 seats, Frente Amplio 20, Peruanos por el Kambio 18, Alianza para el Progreso (Alliance for Progress) 9, Alianza Popular 5 and Acción Popular 5. Five other parties contested the poll but did not win any seats.

Current Government

President: Martín Vizcarra; b. 1963 (ind..; sworn in 23 March 2018).
    First Vice-President: Vacant.
    Second Vice-President: Mercedes Aráoz.
    In March 2019 the government comprised:
    President of the Council of Ministers (Prime Minister): Salvador del Solar; b. 1970 (ind.; sworn in 11 March 2019).
    Minister of Agriculture and Irrigation: Fabiola Muñoz. *Culture:* Ulla Holmquist. *Defence:* Gen. José Modesto Huerta. *Development and Social Inclusion:* Paola Bustamante Suárez. *Economy and Finance:* Carlos Oliva. *Education:* Flor Pablo Medina. *Energy and Mines:* Francisco Ísmodes. *Environment:* Lucía Ruiz Ostoic. *Foreign Affairs:* Néstor Popolizio. *Foreign Trade and Tourism:* Édgar Vásquez Vela. *Health:* Zulema Tomás. *Housing, Construction and Sanitation:* Carlos Bruce. *Interior:* Gen. (retd) Carlos Morán Soto. *Justice and Human Rights:* Vicente Zeballos. *Labour and Employment Promotion:* Sylvia Cáceres. *Production:* Rocío Ingred Barrios Alvarado. *Transport and Communication:* Edmer Trujillo. *Women and Vulnerable Populations:* Gloria Edelmira Montenegro Figueroa.
    Office of the President (Spanish only): https://www.presidencia.gob.pe

Current Leaders

Martín Vizcarra

Position
President

Introduction
Martín Vizcarra became president in March 2018 after his predecessor, Pedro Pablo Kuczynski, resigned over a vote-buying scandal.

Early Life
Vizcarra was born on 22 March 1963 in Lima. In 1984 he graduated from the National Engineering University and went on to study at Lima's ESAN Graduate School of Business. He worked as a manager in the construction industry for some eight years and briefly served as dean of an engineering school in Moquegua.

As a candidate for the American Popular Revolutionary Alliance, Vizcarra unsuccessfully contested the governorship of Moquegua in 2006. Two years later he organized protests to demand better remuneration for the region's mining community. In 2011 he was elected governor of Moquegua and was credited with overseeing an improvement in living standards during his term that ended in 2014.

In 2016 Vizcarra served as an adviser to Kuczynski, who defeated the Fuerza Popular candidate, Keiko Fujimori, in presidential elections. Vizcarra was named vice-president and assumed the transport and communication ministerial portfolio. However, a combination of natural disasters, bribery allegations and bureaucracy slowed work on several major construction projects, including Chinchero International Airport. Although he remained as vice-president, he resigned his ministerial post in May 2017 to become Peru's ambassador to Canada.

Meanwhile, Kuczynski became increasingly embroiled in corruption claims and resigned in late March 2018 ahead of impeachment proceedings. Vizcarra was sworn in as his successor on 23 March.

Career in Office

Vizcarra pledged to eradicate corruption from Peruvian politics. In April 2018 he took steps to create a more unified government by announcing a cabinet that won approval from Fuerza Popular after César Villaneuva was named prime minister. Then in July he called for a nationwide referendum to ban private funding for political campaigns, to bar the re-election of legislators and to create a bicameral congress. The vote took place in early Dec., despite congressional obstruction, and the proposals were approved with the exception of that for a bicameral legislature. In March 2019, in response to the government's declining approval ratings among voters, Vizcarra accepted Villanueva's resignation and named Salvador del Solar, a former actor and minister of culture, as the new premier at the head of a reshuffled cabinet.

Defence

Conscription was abolished in 1999. In 2013 defence expenditure totalled US$2,844m. (US$95 per capita), representing 1·3% of GDP.

Army

There are four military regions. In 2011 the Army comprised 74,000 personnel and 188,000 reserves. In addition there is a paramilitary national police force of 77,000 personnel.

Navy

The principal ship of the Navy until it was decommissioned in 2017 was the former Netherlands cruiser *Almirante Grau*, built in 1953. Other combatants include six diesel submarines (two in refit) and eight Italian-built frigates.

Callao is the main base, where the dockyard is located and most training takes place. There are a number of smaller bases, both on the coast and inland.

Naval personnel in 2011 totalled 24,000 including 1,000 Coast Guards, about 800 Naval Air Arm and 4,000 Marines.

Air Force

The operational force is divided into five regions—North, Lima, South, Central and Amazon.

In 2011 there were some 17,000 personnel and 78 combat-capable aircraft (including Cessna A-37s, Mirage 2000s and MiG-29s) and 18 attack helicopters.

Economy

Agriculture produced 7·4% of GDP in 2012, industry 36·8% and services 55·8%.

Overview

Peru is an upper-middle income country and was one of Latin America's fastest-growing economies in the decade to 2014. During this period, the average annual growth rate was 6·1%, while inflation—which averaged 2·9%—was the lowest in Latin America. The cycle of high growth and low inflation resulted from prudent macroeconomic policies, a programme of structural reform and favourable external conditions. Prior to the early 2000s Peru's growth had been slow, in part because of a spill-over from emerging market crises and commodity price weaknesses, along with high debt levels and hyperinflation dating back to the 1990s.

Economic growth has decelerated since 2014—averaging 3·3% annually between 2015 and 2017—as a consequence of deteriorating external conditions, a corresponding drop in domestic confidence and lower investment. In March 2018 Peru and ten other countries bordering the Pacific (although not the USA) signed the Comprehensive and Progressive Agreement for Trans-Pacific Partnership.

Prolonged growth saw the poverty rate fall from 55·6% in 2005 to 20·7% in 2016. The proportion of the population living below the official extreme poverty line also decreased in the same period, from 15·8% to 3·5%. Extreme poverty is now concentrated in a relatively small swathe of rural districts.

To achieve sustainable and balanced economic growth, the government aims to further develop infrastructure, promote employment and expand access to basic services such as education, health and social security. It also aims to continue to reduce extreme poverty (principally by developing the rural economy) while avoiding serious environmental degradation.

Currency

The monetary unit is the *nuevo sol* (PEN), of 100 *céntimos*, which replaced the *inti* in 1991 at a rate of 1m. intis = 1 nuevo sol. Inflation, which had been over 7,000% in 1990, was 3·6% in 2016 and 2·8% in 2017. Foreign exchange reserves were US$14,773m. in July 2005, gold reserves totalled 1·12m. troy oz and total money supply was 24,565m. nuevos soles.

Budget

Budgetary central government revenue and expenditure (in 1m. sols), year ending 31 Dec.:

	2012	*2013*	*2014*
Revenue	98,135	104,705	110,356
Expenditure	81,559	92,019	102,927

Principal sources of revenue in 2014 were: taxes on goods and services, 44,931m. sols; taxes on income, profits and capital gains, 40,157m. sols. Main items of expenditure by economic type in 2014 were: grants, 45,512m. sols; use of goods and services, 19,680m. sols.

In Dec. 2005 the World Bank approved a US$150m. loan to assist with the government decentralization process and enhance competitiveness.

VAT is 18%.

Performance

Peru's real GDP growth was above average for Latin America every year between 2002 and 2014 apart from 2004. The economy grew by 3·3% in 2015, 4·0% in 2016 and 2·5% in 2017. Total GDP in 2017 was US$211·4bn.

Banking and Finance

The bank of issue is the Banco Central de Reserva (*President*, Julio Velarde Flores), which was established in 1922. The government's fiscal agent is the Banco de la Nación. In 2013 Peru had 16 registered banks. The largest banks are Banco de Crédito del Perú (BCP), BBVA Continental, Scotiabank and Interbank. Legislation of April 1991 permitted financial institutions to fix their own interest rates and reopened the country to foreign banks. The Central Reserve Bank sets the upper limit.

External debt in 2010 totalled US$36,271m., equivalent to 24·6% of GNI.

In 2013 Peru received US$10,172m. of foreign direct investment, down from a record US$12,240m. in 2012. The total stock of FDI at the end of 2013 was US$73·6bn.

There are stock exchanges in Lima and Arequipa.

Energy and Natural Resources

Peru lays claim to 84 of the world's 114 ecosystems; 28 of its climate types; 19% of all bird species; 20% of all plant species; and 25 conservation areas (seven national parks, eight national reserves, seven national sanctuaries and three historic sanctuaries).

Environment

Peru's carbon dioxide emissions from the consumption of energy in 2011 were the equivalent of 1·4 tonnes per capita.

Electricity

In 2011 output was 39·22bn. kWh (21·57bn. kWh hydro-electric and 17·65bn. kWh thermal). Total generating capacity was 8·6m. kW in 2011. Consumption per capita in 2011 was 1,325 kWh.

Oil and Gas

Proven oil reserves at the end of 2012 amounted to 1·2bn. bbls. Output, 2012, 4·8m. tonnes. Natural gas reserves in 2012 were 400bn. cu. metres; output in 2012 more than quadrupled since 2007 to 12·9bn. cu. metres. Commercial development of the huge Camisea gas field began in late 2004. In June 2010 Peru became a net gas exporter.

Minerals

The mining and fuel sectors accounted for some 8·1% of GDP in 2005. Lead, copper, iron, silver, zinc and petroleum are the chief minerals exploited. Mineral production, 2013 (in 1,000 tonnes): iron, 6,788; zinc, 1,351; copper, 1,286; lead, 266; silver, 3·4; gold, 136,000 kg. 188,591 tonnes of coal were produced in 2013. Peru ranks as the world's third largest producer of copper, silver, tin and zinc.

Agriculture

There are four natural zones: the Coast strip, with an average width of 80 km; the Sierra or Uplands, formed by the coast range of mountains and the Andes proper; the Montaña or high wooded region which lies on the eastern slopes of the Andes; and the jungle in the Amazon Basin, known as the Selva. Legislation of 1991 permits the unrestricted sale of agricultural land. Workers in co-operatives may elect to form limited liability companies and become shareholders.

Production in 2013 (in 1,000 tonnes): sugarcane, 10,992; potatoes, 4,570; rice, 3,051; bananas and plantains, 2,354; maize, 1,670; cassava, 1,185; onions, 748; palm fruit oil, 567; mangoes and guavas, 461; pineapples, 439; grapes, 438.

Livestock, 2013: sheep, 12·4m.; alpacas and llamas (estimate), 5·6m.; cattle, 5·6m.; pigs, 3·1m.; goats, 1·9m.; chickens, 137m. Livestock products (in 1,000 tonnes), 2013 estimates: chicken meat, 1,203; beef and veal, 191; pork and pork products, 128; lamb and mutton, 35; milk, 1,832.

In 2013 there were an estimated 4·2m. ha. of arable land and 1·4m. ha. of permanent crops. About 2·6m. ha. were equipped for irrigation in 2013.

Coca, the raw material for cocaine, was cultivated in Dec. 2012 on approximately 60,400 ha., making Peru the country with the largest area of coca leaves.

Forestry

In 2015 the area covered by forests was 73·97m. ha., or 58% of the total land area. The forests contain valuable hardwoods; oak and cedar account for about 40%. In 2011 timber production was 8·92m. cu. metres.

Fisheries

Sardines and anchovies are caught offshore to be processed into fishmeal, of which Peru is the world's largest producer (with a 2009 output of 1,346,900 tonnes or 28% of world production). Total catch in 2015 was 4,824,050 tonnes, of which 99% was from sea fishing. In 2009 total exports of fishery commodities came to a value of US$2·21bn.

Industry

The leading company by market capitalization in Peru in May 2018 was Credicorp, a financial holding company (US$18·0bn.).

About 70% of industries are located in the Lima/Callao metropolitan area. Industry accounted for 36·8% of GDP in 2012, with manufacturing contributing 14·9%. Production (2007 unless otherwise indicated, in 1,000 tonnes): cement (2012 estimate), 9,500; distillate fuel oil, 3,063; prepared animal feeds (2012), 2,794; residual fuel oil, 2,693; petrol, 2,356; sugar (2012), 1,095; soft drinks (2013), 2,045·7m. litres; beer (2005), 797·0m. litres; cigarettes (2005), 1·5bn. units.

Labour

The labour force in 2014 totalled 16,396,400 (56% males). In 2014, 37·3% of those in employment were engaged in services, 24·9% in agriculture, forestry and fisheries, and 18·0% in commerce. In the same year 3·7% of the workforce was unemployed, down from 5·3% in 2004. On taking office in July 2011 the then president, Ollanta Humala, announced an immediate rise in the monthly minimum wage from 600 to 675 nuevos soles, with a further increase to 750 nuevos soles from Jan. 2012 (although this was subsequently postponed but did take effect from June 2012).

Peru had 82,000 people living in slavery according to the Walk Free Foundation's 2013 *Global Slavery Index*.

International Trade

An agreement of 1992 gives Bolivia duty-free transit for imports and exports through a corridor leading to the Peruvian Pacific port of Ilo from the Bolivian frontier town of Desaguadero, in return for Peruvian access to the Atlantic via Bolivia's roads and railways. In April 2006 Peru and the USA signed a free trade agreement that eliminates tariffs on each other's goods; it took effect in Jan. 2009.

Imports and Exports

The following table shows the value of Peru's foreign trade (in US$1m.):

	2007	*2008*	*2009*	*2010*
Imports c.i.f.	20,368·3	29,952·8	21,869·7	29,879·5
Exports f.o.b.	28,084·6	31,288·2	26,738·3	35,073·2

The principal import suppliers in 2009 were: USA, 19·8%; China, 14·9%; Brazil, 7·7%; Ecuador, 4·7%. The principal export markets in 2009 were: USA, 17·2%; China, 15·3%; Switzerland, 14·8%; Canada, 8·6%.

The leading imports in 2009 were machinery and transport equipment (34·8%), manufactured goods (15·9%), chemicals and related products (15·0%), and petroleum and petroleum products (13·6%). Leading exports in 2009 were gold (25·2%), copper, copper ores and concentrates (22·9%), petroleum and petroleum products (7·2%), and animal feeds (5·7%).

Communications

Roads

In 2006 there were 78,986 km of roads, of which 13·9% were paved. In 2007 there were 917,100 passenger cars, 480,900 lorries and vans and 44,400 buses and coaches. There were 67,155 road accidents involving injury in 2006 with 3,481 fatalities.

Rail

Total length (2008), 1,884 km on 1,435- and 914-mm gauges. Passenger-km travelled in 2005 came to 126m. and freight tonne-km to 1,101m. A mass transit system opened in Lima in 2003. Peru's first metro, also in Lima, opened in Jan. 2012.

Civil Aviation

There is an international airport at Lima (Jorge Chávez International). In 2010 there were direct international services to nearly 40 destinations from Lima. The main airline is LATAM Perú, which was founded in 1998 as LAN Perú. In 2012 scheduled airline traffic of Peruvian-based carriers flew 108·4m. km; passenger-km totalled 13·1bn. in the same year. In 2012 Jorge Chávez International handled 13,330,290 passengers (6,901,988 on international flights) and 293,675 tonnes of freight.

Shipping

In Jan. 2014 there were 17 ships of 300 GT or over registered, totalling 274,000 GT. Callao is the busiest port, handling 24,333,000 tonnes of cargo in 2013. There are also ports at Matarani, Paita and Salaverry.

Telecommunications

In 2010 there were 3,160,000 main (fixed) telephone lines; mobile phone subscriptions numbered 29,115,000 in 2010 (99·5 per 100 persons). In 2013, 39·2% of the population aged six and over were internet users. In March 2012 there were 8·2m. Facebook users.

Social Institutions

Out of 178 countries analysed in the 2017 *Fragile States Index*—a list published jointly by the Fund for Peace and *Foreign Policy* magazine—Peru was ranked the 75th least vulnerable to conflict or collapse. The index is based on 12 indicators of state vulnerability across social, political and economic categories.

Justice

The judicial system is a pyramid at the base of which are the justices of the peace who decide minor criminal cases and civil cases involving small sums of money. The apex is the Supreme Court with a president and 12 members; in between are the judges of first instance, who usually sit in the provincial capitals, and the superior courts.

The police had 95,789 personnel in 2008. The population in penal institutions in Dec. 2012 was 61,390 (202 per 100,000 of national population). Peru was ranked 79th of 102 countries for criminal justice and 86th for civil justice in the 2015 World Justice Project *Rule of Law Index*, which provides data on how the rule of law is experienced by the general public across eight categories.

Education

Adult literacy was 90% in 2007. Elementary education is compulsory and free between the ages of six and 16; secondary education is also free. In 2007 there were 1,204,022 children in pre-school education with 58,177 teaching staff, 3,993,965 pupils in primary schools with 179,743 teaching staff and 2,861,313 pupils in secondary schools with 158,890 teaching staff. There were 952,437 students in tertiary education in 2006. The leading higher education institute is the National University of San Marcos (Universidad Nacional Mayor de San Marcos), founded in 1551, making it the oldest both in the country and in South America.

In 2007 public expenditure on education came to 2·7% of GNI and 16·4% of total government spending.

Health

In the period 2006–12 Peru had 15 hospital beds per 10,000 population. In 2012 there were 113 doctors for every 100,000 population, 151 nurses and midwives for every 100,000 and 15 dentistry personnel per 100,000.

Peru has been one of the most successful countries in reducing under-nourishment in the past 20 years. Between 1995 and 2015 the proportion of undernourished people declined from 26·5% of the population to 7·5%.

In *Water: At What Cost? The State of the World's Water 2016*, WaterAid reported that 13·3% of the population does not have access to safe water.

Welfare

An option to transfer from state social security (IPSS) to privately-managed funds was introduced in 1993.

Religion

Religious liberty exists, but the Roman Catholic religion is protected by the State, and since 1929 only Roman Catholic religious instruction is permitted in schools, state or private. In 2010 an estimated 95·5% of the population were Christians according to the Pew Research Center's Forum on Religion & Public Life, with 3·0% having no religious affiliation. Of the Christians, 85% were Catholics and 13% Protestants. In Feb. 2019 there were two cardinals.

Culture

World Heritage Sites

There are 12 sites under Peruvian jurisdiction that appear on the UNESCO World Heritage List. They are (with the year entered on the list): the City of Cusco (1983), the Historic Sanctuary of Machu Picchu (1983), Chavin Archaeological Site (1985), Huascarán National Park (1985), Chan Chan Archaeological Zone (1986), Manú National Park (1987), Historic Centre of Lima (1988 and 1991), Río Abiseo National Park (1990 and 1992), Lines and Geoglyphs of Nasca and Pampas de Jumana (1994), the Historical Centre of the City of Arequipa (2000) and the Sacred City of Caral-Supe (2009). Shared with Argentina, Bolivia, Colombia, Ecuador and Chile, Qhapaq Ñan, Andean Road System (2014) is an extensive Inca communication, trade and defence network of roads covering 30,000 km.

Press

In 2008 there were 89 paid-for daily newspapers, of which 23 were national and 66 regional and local. The leading dailies are *Líbero* (with an average daily circulation in 2008 of 214,000), *Trome* (average daily circulation in 2008 of 213,000) and *El Comercio* (average daily circulation in 2008 of 199,000).

Tourism

There were 2,846,000 non-resident tourists in 2012, up from 1,916,000 in 2007; tourist spending in 2012 totalled US$3,074m., compared to US$2,007m. in 2007.

Festivals

The Lord of Tremors festival (the second part of March and the first week of April) renders homage to the image of Taitacha Temblores, the Lord of the Earthquakes, and demonstrates the fusion of Andean religions and Christianity; Fiesta de las Cruces (3 May) is celebrated across Peru as well as Spain and other parts of Hispanic America, and includes processions, folk music and dance; Inti Raymi (24 June), one of the biggest celebrations in Peru, celebrates the winter solstice and the Inca sun god; Corpus Christi (June) includes a traditional and colourful procession of saints and virgins; Virgin of the Carmen (second week of July) takes place in the small town of Paucartambo and includes a series of processions in honour of Mamacha Carmen, the patron saint of the mestizo population; All Saints Day (1–2 Nov.) is dedicated to the memory of the dead.

Diplomatic Representatives

Of Peru in the United Kingdom (52 Sloane St., London, SW1X 9SP)
   Ambassador: Juan Carlos Gamarra.

Of the United Kingdom in Peru (Torre Parque Mar, Piso 22, Avenida José Larco 1301, Miraflores, Lima)
   Ambassador: Kate Harrison.

Of Peru in the USA (1700 Massachusetts Ave., NW, Washington, D.C., 20036)
   Ambassador: Carlos José Pareja Ríos.

Of the USA in Peru (Avenida La Encalada Cdra 17, s/n Surco, Lima)
   Ambassador: Krishna R. Urs.

Of Peru to the United Nations
   Ambassador: Gustavo Meza-Cuadra Velásquez.

Of Peru to the European Union
   Ambassador: Gonzalo Gutiérrez Reinel.

Further Reading

Instituto Nacional de Estadística e Informática.—*Anuario Estadistico del Perú.*—*Perú: Compendio Estadístico.* Annual.—*Boletin de Estadistica Peruana.* Quarterly
Banco Central de Reserva. Monthly Bulletin.—*Renta Nacional del Perú.* Annual
Cameron, M. A., *Democracy and Authoritarianism in Peru: Political Coalitions and Social Change.* 1995
Carrion, Julio F., *The Fujimori Legacy: The Rise of Electoral Authoritarianism in Peru.* 2006
Daeschner, J., *The War of the End of Democracy: Mario Vargas Llosa vs. Alberto Fujimori.* 1993
Gorriti, Gustavo, (trans. Robin Kirk) *The Shining Path: A History of the Millenarian War in Peru.* 1999
Starn, Orin, *The Peru Reader: History, Culture, Politics.* 2005
National Statistical Office: Instituto Nacional de Estadística e Informática, Av. Gral. Garzón 654–658, Jesús María, Lima.
Website (limited English): http://www.inei.gob.pe

Philippines

Republika ng Pilipinas (Republic of the Philippines)

Capital: Manila
Population projection, 2020: 109·70m.
GNI per capita, 2017: (PPP$) 9,154
HDI/world rank, 2017: 0·699/113=
Internet domain extension: .ph

Key Historical Events

Pottery was being made on the Philippine archipelago from at least 3000 BC, probably by people of Malay origin, and metals were being worked by the first millennium BC. Merchants from south China reached the islands during the 10th century AD (Tang Dynasty), heralding centuries of Chinese trade with the region. Arab traders brought Islam from the Malay peninsula via Borneo and the Sulu archipelago in the late 13th century, and by the 15th century Islamic influence had spread as far north as Luzon. Most islanders lived in barangays, communities of 30–100 households based largely on kinship.

The Portuguese explorer, Ferdinand Magellan, landed at Samar on 16 April 1521 during his Spanish-financed expedition round the world. Subsequent expeditions consolidated Spanish control over the islands, which were named after Philip II of Spain in 1542. Manila was established by Miguel López de Legazpi in 1571 on the site of an existing Moro (Muslim Filipinos) settlement. By the end of the 16th century the Philippines had become a major trading centre with India, China and the East Indies. The islands came under Dutch control from around 1600.

The waning of the Spanish Empire during the 18th century saw a rise in the power base of the Jesuit orders, which caused resentment and stoked demands for independence. In 1896 revolution in the province of Cavite, led by Emilio Aguinaldo among others, spread through the major islands. However, in Dec. 1898, following the Spanish-American War, the Philippines were ceded to the United States. Aguinaldo fought a guerrilla campaign but was captured in 1901. The US granted the Philippines partial autonomy in 1916 and the Hare-Hawes-Cutting Act of 1932 set a timetable for full independence after a ten-year period of self-governance as a Commonwealth of the USA. Manuel Quezon was elected the first president in Sept. 1935.

In Dec. 1941 the islands were invaded by Japanese troops, who went on to take complete control in 1942. Quezon escaped to the USA and established a government-in-exile in Washington, D.C. Sergio Osmena succeeded Quezon in 1944 and returned to the Philippines with a US-backed liberation force in Oct. 1944. Manuel Roxas defeated Osmena in the election of April 1946, becoming president of the Republic of the Philippines when independence was achieved on 4 July 1946. The USA continued to play a key role in its former colony, particularly in economic policy. In return for assistance in rebuilding the country's war-torn infrastructure, the USA secured 99-year leases over several air and naval bases. Relations with neighbouring countries improved and in 1954 the Philippines joined the Southeast Asia Treaty Organization, precursor to the Association of South East Asian Nations (ASEAN).

Ferdinand Marcos was elected president in 1965 and re-elected four years later, although his rule became increasingly unpopular. In Sept. 1972 Marcos declared martial law and thousands of political opponents were arrested. In May 1980 Benigno Aquino, Jr, the leading opponent of Marcos, was released from prison to go to the USA for medical treatment. His assassination, on his return to the Philippines in 1983, led to growing US pressure for Marcos to restore democracy. In late 1985 he announced a snap presidential election. He was challenged by Aquino's widow, Corazón, who eventually emerged victorious from a controversial poll and was installed as president on 25 Feb. 1986. Marcos fled the country and a new constitution limiting the president to a single, six-year term in office was ratified in Feb. 1987.

More than twenty years of insurgency by the Moro National Liberation Front were ended by a peace agreement of 2 Sept. 1996, providing for a Muslim autonomous region in an area of Mindanao island. The rebellion left more than 120,000 people dead. In Oct. 2000 impeachment proceedings began against President Estrada who was alleged to have received more than US$10·8m. from gambling kickbacks. His impeachment trial collapsed in Jan. 2001 when he was forced from office by mass protests. Subsequently Estrada's supporters tried to overthrow his successor, Gloria Macapagal-Arroyo.

In Nov. 2001 the fragile peace between the government and Islamic militants was shattered. Since then violence has frequently erupted, notably in early 2005, when fighting on the southern island of Jolo left 90 dead and caused 12,000 people to flee. On 14 Feb. 2005 three bombs were detonated killing nine and injuring 130. In Feb. 2006 President Arroyo declared a week-long state of emergency after the military declared it had discovered a coup plot. A further coup attempt by renegade soldiers in Nov. 2007 was also foiled.

In June 2010 Benigno Aquino became president. In May 2012 Filipino naval vessels were involved in a stand-off with Chinese ships near a disputed reef in the South China Sea. In Dec. 2012 parliament introduced legislation allowing for the state to distribute contraception, despite fierce opposition from the Catholic church. Then in March 2014 the government signed a peace deal with the Moro Islamic Liberation Front, offering hope of an end to a civil conflict responsible for some 120,000 deaths over four decades. Nonetheless, there have been a number of subsequent skirmishes between government troops and the remnants of rebel forces.

Rodrigo Duterte was elected president in May 2016, having run a populist campaign centred around a pledge to spearhead a crackdown on the criminal drugs trade.

Territory and Population

The Philippines is situated between 21° 25' and 4° 23' N. lat. and between 116° and 127° E. long. It is composed of 7,100 islands and islets, 3,144 of which are named. Approximate land area, 300,076 sq. km (115,859 sq. miles). The largest islands (in sq. km) are Luzon (104,688), Mindanao (94,630), Samar (13,080), Negros (12,710), Palawan (11,785), Panay (11,515), Mindoro (9,735), Leyte (7,214), Cebu (4,422), Bohol (3,865) and Masbate (3,269). The census population in Aug. 2015 was 100,981,437; density, 336·5 per sq. km. In 2011, 49·1% of the population lived in urban areas.

The UN gives a projected population for 2020 of 109·70m.

The Philippines is divided into 17 regions, subdivided into 81 provinces. The areas of the regions (from north to south) and populations are:

Region	Sq. km	2015 census
Ilocos	12,840	5,026,128
Cordillera[1]	18,294	1,722,006
Cagayan Valley	26,838	3,451,410
Central Luzon	21,470	11,218,177
National Capital	636	12,877,253
Calabarzon	16,229	14,414,774
Mimaropa	27,456	2,963,360
Bicol	17,632	5,796,989
Western Visayas	20,794	4,477,247[2]
Central Visayas	15,896	6,041,903[2]
Eastern Visayas	21,432	4,440,150
Northern Mindanao	17,125	4,689,302
Davao	19,672	4,893,318
Soccskargen	18,433	4,545,276
Zamboanga Peninsula	14,811	3,629,783

(continued)

© Springer Nature Limited 2020
Palgrave Macmillan (ed.), *The Statesman's Yearbook 2020*,
https://doi.org/10.1057/978-1-349-95940-2_153

Region	Sq. km	2015 census
Muslim Mindanao[3]	12,695	3,781,387
Caraga	18,847	2,596,709

[1]Administrative region.
[2]The region of Negros Island (2015 census population of 4,414,131) was abolished in 2017 and divided up between Central Visayas and Western Visayas.
[3]Autonomous region.

City populations (2015 census, in 1,000) are as follows; all on Luzon unless indicated in parenthesis.

Quezon City[1]	2,936
Manila (the capital)[1]	1,780
Caloocan[1]	1,584
Davao (Mindanao)	1,325
Cebu (Cebu)	923
Taguig[1]	805
Antipolo	776
Pasig[1]	755
Zamboanga (Mindanao)	695
Cagayan de Oro (Mindanao)	676
Parañaque[1]	666
Dasmariñas	659
Valenzuela[1]	620
Bacoor	601
Las Piñas[1]	589
Makati[1]	583
San Jose del Monte	574
Bacolod (Negros)	562
Muntinlupa[1]	505
General Santos (Mindanao)	474
Calamba	454
Marikina[1]	451
Iloilo (Panay)	448
Pasay[1]	417
Angeles	412
Lapu-Lapu (Cebu)	408
Imus	404
Mandaluyong[1]	386
Malabon[1]	366
Mandaue (Cebu)	363
Rodriguez	361
Santa Rosa	354

[1]City within Metropolitan Manila. Population of Metro Manila in 2015, 12,877,253.

Filipino (based on Tagalog) is spoken as a mother tongue by only 29·3%; among the 76 other indigenous languages spoken, Cebuano is spoken as a mother tongue by 23·3% and Ilocano by 9·3%. English, which along with Filipino is one of the official languages, is widely spoken.

In 2013, 10·2m. Filipinos were living and working abroad (permanently and temporarily), including 3·5m. in the USA, 1·0m. in Saudi Arabia and 822,000 in the United Arab Emirates.

Social Statistics

Births, 2007, 1,749,878; deaths, 2007, 441,956. Divorce is illegal. Birth rate per 1,000 population (2007), 19·7; death rate (2007), 5·1. Expectation of life at birth, 2007, was 69·4 years for males and 73·9 years for females. Annual population growth rate, 2000–05, 2·2%. Infant mortality, 2010, 23 per 1,000 live births; fertility rate, 2008, 3·1 births per woman. Abortion is illegal.

Climate

Some areas have an equatorial climate while others experience tropical monsoon conditions, with a wet season extending from June to Nov. Mean temperatures are high all year, with very little variation. Manila, Jan. 77°F (25°C), July 82°F (27·8°C). Annual rainfall 83·3" (2,115·9 mm).

On 8 Nov. 2013 tropical cyclone Typhoon Haiyan hit the Philippines, killing an estimated 6,000 people and leaving hundreds of thousands more homeless. The cost of the damage was put at nearly US$13bn.

Constitution and Government

A new constitution was ratified by referendum in Feb. 1987 with the approval of 78·5% of voters. The head of state is the *President*, directly elected for a non-renewable six-year term.

Congress consists of a 24-member upper house, the *Senate* (elected for a six-year term from 'at large' seats covering the country as a whole, half of them renewed every three years), and a *House of Representatives* of 297 members. In the *House of Representatives* 238 members are directly elected for a three-year term and the rest are chosen from party and minority-group lists.

A campaign led by the president at the time, Fidel Ramos, to amend the constitution to allow him to stand for a second term was voted down by the Senate by 23 to one in Dec. 1996.

Bangsamoro

This is an autonomous Muslim-majority territory in the southern Philippines with a history of insurgency by the ethnic Moro people over land and religious disputes. It was previously known as the Autonomous Region in Muslim Mindanao until a two-stage plebiscite in Jan. and Feb. 2019 approved the ratification of legislation paving the way for the formal establishment of the Bangsamoro Autonomous Region in an effort to underpin a lasting peace. Pending the election of new regional government officials in 2022 the Bangsamoro Transition Authority, composed of 80 members, exercises executive and legislative powers.

Acting Chief Minister: Murad Ebrahim; b. 1948.

National Anthem

'Land of the Morning', lyric in English by M. A. Sane and C. Osias, tune by Julian Felipe; 'Lupang Hinirang', Tagalog lyric by the Institute of National Language.

Government Chronology

Presidents since 1946. (KBL = New Society Movement; Lakas-CMD = Lakas-Christian Muslim Democrats; LE-NUCD = People's Power-National Union of Christian Democrats; LMP = Struggle of the Philippine Masses; PDP–Laban = Philippine Democratic Party–People's Power; PL = Liberal Party; PN = Nacionalista Party; UNIDO = Nationalist Democratic Organization)

1946–48	PL	Manuel Roxas y Acuña
1948–53	PL	Elpidio Quirino y Rivera
1953–57	PN	Ramon Magsaysay y del Fierro
1957–61	PN	Carlos Polestico García
1961–65	PL	Diosdado Pañgan Macapagal
1965–86	PN, KBL	Ferdinand Emmanuel Edralin Marcos
1986–92	UNIDO	Corazón Cojuangco Aquino
1992–98	LE-NUCD	Fidel Valdez Ramos
1998–2001	LMP	Joseph Marcelo Ejercito Estrada
2001–10	Lakas-CMD	Gloria Macapagal-Arroyo
2010–16	PL	Benigno Aquino III
2016–	PDP–Laban	Rodrigo Roa Duterte

Recent Elections

In presidential elections of 9 May 2016 were won by Rodrigo Duterte (Philippine Democratic Party–People's Power) with 39·0% of votes cast, ahead of Mar Roxas (Liberal Party, PL) with 23·4% of the vote, Grace Poe (ind.) with 21·4%, Jejomar Binay (United Nationalist Alliance) with 12·7% and Miriam Defensor Santiago (People's Reform Party) 3·4%. Turnout was 81·5%.

Elections to the House of Representatives were held on 13 May 2013. 113 seats went to the PL and its allies (of which 111 to President Aquino's Liberal Party itself), 42 to the Nationalist People's Coalition, 24 to the National Unity Party, 17 to the Nacionalista Party, 14 to Lakas–CMD (Lakas–Christian Muslim Democrats) and 10 to the United Nationalist Alliance and its allies. The remaining seats went to independents and smaller parties.

Following senatorial elections held concurrently on 13 May 2013 the make-up of the Senate was: PN 5, United Nationalist Alliance 5, PL 4, Lakas–CMD 2, Nationalist People's Coalition 2, People's Reform Party 1, Philippine Democratic Party–People's Power 1, Struggle of Democratic Filipinos 1 and ind. 3.

Current Government

President: Rodrigo 'Rody' Duterte; b. 1945 (PDP–Laban; sworn in 30 June 2016).

Vice-President: Leni Robredo (sworn in 30 June 2016).

In March 2019 the government comprised:

Minister of Agrarian Reform: John Castriciones. *Agriculture:* Manny Piñol. *Budget and Management (acting):* Janet Abucl. *Education:* Leonor Briones. *Energy:* Alfonso Cusi. *Environment and Natural Resources:* Roy Cimatu. *Finance:* Carlos Dominguez III. *Foreign Affairs:* Teodoro Locsin, Jr. *Health:* Francisco Duque III. *Human Settlements and Urban Development:* Vacant. *Information and Communications Technology:* Gregorio Honasan II. *Interior and Local Government:* Eduardo Año. *Justice:* Menardo Ilasco Guevarra. *Labour and Employment:* Silvestre Bello III. *National Defence:* Delfin Lorenzana. *Public Works and Highways:* Mark Villar. *Science and Technology:* Fortunato de la Peña. *Social Welfare and Development:* Rolando Bautista. *Tourism:* Bernadette Romulo Puyat. *Trade and Industry:* Ramón López. *Transportation:* Arthur Tugade. *Executive Secretary:* Salvador Medialdea.

Government Website: http://www.gov.ph

Current Leaders

Rodrigo Duterte

Position
President

Introduction
Rodrigo Duterte took office on 30 June 2016, succeeding Benigno Aquino III. He has adopted a hard-line and controversial approach to fighting crime, particularly the drugs trade.

Early Life
Rodrigo 'Rody' Roa Duterte was born on 28 March 1945 in Maasin. He graduated in political science from the Lyceum of the Philippines University in 1968 and earned a law degree from San Beda College of Law in 1972. His career as a lawyer included a spell as prosecutor for Davao City from 1977–86. Following the revolution that overthrew Ferdinand Marcos in 1986, Duterte was appointed vice mayor of Davao City before assuming the mayoralty itself two years later. Interspersed with stints as a congressman and again as vice mayor, he served as mayor for a total of 22 years. During this period he won a reputation for effectively fighting crime and corruption.

In Nov. 2015 Duterte announced his presidential bid and on 9 May 2016 he secured a decisive victory at the polls winning 39·0% of the vote, well ahead of his closest rival.

Career in Office
Duterte's abrasive, populist style has attracted intense international criticism, yet he has remained a popular figure domestically. Vowing to replicate his anti-corruption and anti-crime initiatives at the national level, he has led an unrelenting crackdown on illegal drug dealers and users, earning him the nickname 'the Punisher'. He has called for the reimposition of capital punishment and voiced support for extra-judicial killings of suspects by the police and vigilante squads, resulting in thousands of deaths in his tenure to date. Critics have variously accused him of inciting violence, overstepping the law, disrespecting democratic freedoms and insulting various heads of states, ambassadors, the Catholic church, the media and human rights groups.

Duterte vowed to pursue an independent foreign policy, rejecting interference by foreign governments, notably the USA. He also expressed a desire for closer relations with China and Russia. Domestically, his challenges have included upholding his promise to introduce a federal form of government while maintaining economic growth, combating corruption and dealing with communist and militant Islamist insurgencies. In May 2017 he declared martial law in the southern island of Mindanao in response to extremist Islamist violence, and the crackdown was extended in July and again in Dec. for a further year. In Aug. 2017, in an apparent populist manoeuvre that nevertheless drew considerable criticism, Duterte approved legislation abolishing student tuition fees in state universities.

By Oct. 2018 Duterte was facing the first sustained fall in his presidential popularity ratings, mainly because of a controversial tax policy and consequent rises in the price of staple foods and fuel. Also, his political authority was dented by the courts as a judge rejected the petition in Sept. for the arrest of Antonio Trillanes, one of his fiercest opponents.

Defence

An extension of the 1947 agreement granting the USA the use of several Army, Navy and Air Force bases was rejected by the Senate in Sept. 1991. An agreement of Dec. 1994 authorizes US naval vessels to be repaired in Philippine ports. The Philippines is a signatory of the South-East Asia Collective Defence Treaty. The Armed Forces are organized into six unified commands, which are multi-service, regional entities.

Defence expenditure in 2013 totalled US$2,205m. (US$21per capita), representing 0·8% of GDP.

Army

Strength (2011) 86,000, with reserves totalling 100,000. The paramilitary Philippines National Police numbered 40,500 in 2011 with 40,000 reservists.

Navy

The Navy consists principally of ex-US ships completed in 1944 and 1945, and serviceability and spares are a problem. The modernization programme in progress has been revised and delayed, but the first 30 inshore patrol craft of US and Korean design have been delivered. The present fleet includes one ex-US frigate.

Navy personnel in 2011 was estimated at 24,000 including 8,300 marines.

Air Force

The Air Force had an estimated strength of 15,000 in 2011, with 24 combat-capable aircraft. There was one fighter squadron of Agusta S-211s.

Economy

Agriculture accounted for 9·7% of GDP in 2016, industry 30·8% and services 59·5%.

Overview

Market-oriented reforms have been implemented since the 1990s, with trade barriers dismantled and many industries deregulated. Most state industrial assets were privatized between 1992 and 1995 and monopolies were ended in the telecommunications, oil, civil aviation, shipping, water and power industries. Since the early 2000s, chronic public finance deficits have been reduced, tax collection has become more effective and VAT reform has been implemented (from 2006).

As of 2016 the Philippines was one of the fastest-growing economies in east Asia, with significant improvement in the country's macroeconomic fundamentals and a strong labour market. Growth averaged 6·2% per year from 2010–15, compared to an annual average of 4·5% from 2000–09. Growth benefited from strong private investment, solid domestic demand, low inflation and robust remittance inflows. Industry and services have been the main engines of growth, as agriculture continues to play a less important role following the devastating Typhoon Haiyan in Nov. 2013.

Public debt fell from 68·5% GDP in 2005 to around 45% in 2015. However, robust growth has only partially translated into poverty reduction; 25·2% of the population lived below the national poverty line in 2015, one of the highest levels in southeast Asia. Extreme poverty, measured against the international standard of US$1·90 a day, fell from 10·6% of the population in 2012 to 8·4% in 2015. The poorest segment of the population, meanwhile, reported faster growth in household income than the average figure, suggesting a gradual downward trend in income inequality.

In 2016 the government adopted a socio-economic agenda aimed at promoting greater transparency and accountability, improving the business environment, and continuing investment in education, skills and social assistance to the poor. However, against an uncertain political landscape, the government has attracted international criticism for controversial programmes such as its anti-drugs strategy, which may have detrimental knock-on effects for the economy.

Currency

The unit of currency is the *peso* (PHP) of 100 *centavos.* Inflation rates (based on IMF statistics):

2008	2009	2010	2011	2012	2013	2014	2015	2016	2017
9·3%	3·2%	4·1%	4·8%	3·0%	2·6%	3·6%	0·7%	1·3%	2·9%

Foreign exchange reserves were US$35,493m. in Aug. 2009 and gold reserves 5·08m. troy oz. Total money supply in Feb. 2008 was 836,709m. pesos.

Budget

Budgetary central government revenue and expenditure (in 1bn. pesos):

	2013	2014	2015[1]
Revenue	1,713	1,907	2,047
Expenditure	1,592	1,693	1,879

[1]Provisional.

Taxes accounted for 90·1% of revenues in 2014; compensation of employees accounted for 35·7% of expenditures, grants 20·3% and interest 19·1%.

VAT was introduced in 1988. The standard rate was raised from 10·0% to 12·0% in 2006.

Performance

Real GDP growth rates (based on IMF statistics):

2008	2009	2010	2011	2012	2013	2014	2015	2016	2017
4·2%	1·1%	7·6%	3·7%	6·7%	7·1%	6·1%	6·1%	6·9%	6·7%

The 2010 growth rate was the highest since democracy was restored to the Philippines in 1986 following the Marcos era. Total GDP in 2017 was US$313·6bn.

Banking and Finance

The Central Bank (*Governor*, Nestor A. Espenilla, Jr) issues the currency, manages foreign exchange reserves and supervises the banking system. At 31 Dec. 2013 there were 36 universal and commercial banks, 71 thrift banks, and 566 rural and co-operative banks. In Dec. 2013 the total number of banking institutions was 9,935, with total assets of 9,970,800m. pesos.

External debt amounted to US$72,337m. in 2010, up from US$58,304m. in 2000—this was equivalent to 36·2% of GNI (compared to 72·0% in 2000).

The financial crisis that struck southeast Asia in 1997 led to the floating of the peso in July of that year. It subsequently lost 36% of its value against the dollar.

There is a stock exchange in Manila.

Energy and Natural Resources

Environment

Carbon dioxide emissions from the consumption of energy in 2011 were the equivalent of 0·8 tonnes per capita.

The *Climate Change and Environmental Risk Atlas 2014* produced by Maplecroft, a risk analytics company, ranked the Philippines as the country facing the ninth highest economic and social risk from climate change by 2025.

Electricity

Total installed capacity was 16·2m. kW in 2011. Production was 69·21bn. kWh in 2011 (49·46bn. kWh thermal and 9·72bn. kWh hydro-electric). Consumption per capita was 728 kWh in 2011.

Oil and Gas

The largest natural gas field is the Camago-Malampaya gas field, discovered off the island of Palawan in 1992, with reserves initially put at 76bn. cu. metres but now increased to 85bn. cu. metres. The Philippines' total natural gas reserves in 2013 were 99bn. cu. metres.

Crude petroleum reserves were 139m. bbls in 2011.

Minerals

Mineral production in 2013 (in tonnes): coal, 10,731,900; salt, 992,640; nickel (mine output, nickel content), 464,000; silica sand, 428,580; copper (mine output, copper content), 90,861; chromite (gross weight), 35,281; silver, 40,043 kg; gold, 17,248 kg. Other minerals include iron ore, white clay, zinc, sand and gravel. Total value of mineral production, 2013, 157,087m. pesos.

Agriculture

Agriculture is still a mainstay of the economy, although its share of national output has halved since the late 1980s. In 2013 there were an estimated 5·59m. ha. of arable land and 5·35m. ha. of permanent crops. In 2014, 30·4% of the working population was employed in agriculture.

Output (in 1,000 tonnes) in 2013: sugarcane, 24,585; rice, 18,439; coconuts, 15,354; bananas, 8,646; maize, 7,377; pineapples, 2,459; cassava, 2,362; copra (estimate), 1,209. The Philippines is the second largest producer of coconuts.

Livestock, 2013: pigs, 11·84m.; goats, 3·69m.; buffaloes, 2·91m.; cattle, 2·50m.; chickens, 163·39m.; ducks, 10·14m.

Forestry

Forests covered 8·04m. ha. (27% of the land area) in 2015, up from 6·56m. ha. in 1990 and 7·03m. ha. in 2000. Of the total area under forests 10·7% was primary forest in 2015, 73·8% other naturally regenerated forest and 15·5% planted forest. Timber production was 16·12m. cu. metres in 2011.

Fisheries

The catch in 2015 was 2,151,502 tonnes (1,948,136 tonnes from marine waters).

Industry

The leading companies by market capitalization in the Philippines in May 2018 were: SM Investments, a shopping mall developer and operator (US$21·2bn.); and Ayala, a holding company (US$11·5bn.).

Leading sectors are foodstuffs, oil refining and chemicals. Production, 2013 unless otherwise indicated (in 1,000 tonnes): cement, 20,150; gas oil and diesel oil, 2,951; sugar, 2,366; fuel oil, 1,605; petrol, 1,255; paper and paperboard, 803; plywood (2012), 317,000 cu. metres.

Labour

The labour force in 2013 was 42,923,000 (34,721,000 in 2003). 67·0% of the population aged 15–64 was economically active in 2013. The unemployment rate in Oct. 2013 was 6·5%.

The Philippines had 0·15m. people living in slavery according to the Walk Free Foundation's 2013 *Global Slavery Index.*

International Trade

A law of June 1991 gave foreign nationals the right to full ownership of export and other firms considered strategic for the economy.

Imports and Exports

Imports (c.i.f.) in 2007 totalled US$57,995·7m. (US$54,078·0m. in 2006) and exports (f.o.b.) US$50,465·7m. (US$47,410·1m. in 2006).

Main imports: electronics and components, mineral fuels, lubricants and related materials, industrial machinery and equipment, telecommunications equipment and transport equipment. Principal exports: electronics, garments, machinery, transport equipment and apparatus, and processed foods. In 2001 electronics exports were worth US$21·4bn. and constituted 67% of all exports although this had shrunk to US$16·3bn. and 32% by 2007. In 1992 they had been worth just US$3bn.

Main sources of imports in 2007: USA, 14·0%; Japan, 12·4%; Singapore, 11·1%; China, 7·3%. Main export markets, 2007: USA, 17·0%; Japan, 14·5%; Hong Kong, 11·5%; China, 11·4%.

Communications

Roads

In 2013 roads totalled 216,612 km, including 32,227 km of national roads. In 2007 there were 937,600 passenger cars in use, 55,200 buses and coaches, 1,875,300 vans and lorries, and 2,647,500 motorcycles and mopeds. There were 6,240 road accidents involving injury in 2006 with 961 fatalities.

Rail

In 2005 the National Railways totalled 419 km (1,067 mm gauge). In 2008 passenger-km totalled 16m. There is a light metro railway in Manila.

Civil Aviation

There are international airports at Manila (Ninoy Aquino) and Cebu (Mactan International). In Sept. 1998 the Asian economic crisis that had started more than a year earlier forced the closure of the national carrier, Philippine Airlines, after it had suffered huge losses. However, it has since resumed its operations both internally and externally. In 2012 scheduled airline traffic of Philippine-based carriers flew 117·1m. km; passenger-km totalled 21·5bn. in the same year. Manila handled 31,878,935 passengers in 2012 (17,739,000 on domestic flights) and 460,135 tonnes of freight.

Shipping

The main ports are Cagayan de Oro, Cebu, Davao, Iloilo and Manila. Manila, the leading port, handled 45,068,000 tonnes of cargo in 2013. In Jan. 2014 there were 807 ships of 300 GT or over registered, totalling 4,588,000 GT. Of the 807 vessels registered, 388 were general cargo ships, 157 oil tankers, 143 passenger ships, 83 bulk carriers, 20 container ships and 16 liquid gas tankers.

Telecommunications

In 2013 there were 3,149,000 main (fixed) telephone lines. In the same year mobile phone subscriptions numbered 102,824,000 (1,045·0 per 1,000 persons). An estimated 36·2% of the population were internet users in 2012. In March 2012 there were 27·7m. Facebook users.

Social Institutions

Out of 178 countries analysed in the 2017 *Fragile States Index*—a list published jointly by the Fund for Peace and *Foreign Policy* magazine—the Philippines was ranked the 54th most vulnerable to conflict or collapse. The index is based on 12 indicators of state vulnerability across social, political and economic categories.

Justice

There is a Supreme Court which is composed of a chief justice and 14 associate justices; it can declare a law or treaty unconstitutional by the concurrent votes of the majority sitting. There is a Court of Appeals, which consists of a presiding justice and 50 associate justices. There are 15 regional trial courts, one for each judicial region, with a presiding regional trial judge in each of its 720 branches. Municipal trial courts and municipal circuit trial courts are found in the municipalities of the Philippines. If the court covers one municipality it is a municipal trial court; if it covers two or more municipalities it is a municipal circuit trial court. In Metropolitan Manila the equivalents are metropolitan trial courts, and in the cities outside Metropolitan Manila the courts are known as municipal trial courts in cities.

The Supreme Court may designate certain branches of the regional trial courts to handle exclusively criminal cases, juvenile and domestic relations cases, agrarian cases, urban land reform cases which do not fall under the jurisdiction of quasijudicial bodies and agencies and/or such other special cases as the Supreme Court may determine. The death penalty, abolished in 1987, was officially restored in Dec. 1993 as punishment for 'heinous crimes'. In Feb. 1999 a rapist was executed, the first incident of capital punishment in the Philippines since 1976. The death penalty was abolished again for all crimes in 2006.

In Oct. 2011 there were 140,000 police officers. Local police forces are supplemented by the Philippine Constabulary, which is part of the armed forces.

In 2014 the prison population was 120,076 (121 per 100,000 of national population). The International Centre for Prison Studies estimated in 2014 that 63·6% of prisoners had yet to receive a trial. In 2015 the World Justice Project *Rule of Law Index*, which provides data on how the rule of law is experienced by the general public across eight categories, ranked the Philippines 66th of 102 countries for criminal justice and 75th for civil justice.

Police

Since 1990 public order has been maintained completely by the Philippine National Police. Qualified Philippine Constabulary personnel were absorbed by the PNP or were transferred to branches or services of the Armed Forces of the Philippines.

Education

Public elementary education is free and schools are established in virtually all parts of the country. The majority of secondary and post-secondary schools are private. Formal education consists of an optional one to two years of pre-school education; six years of elementary education; four years of secondary education; and four to five years of tertiary or college education leading to academic degrees. Three-year post-secondary non-degree technical/vocational education is also considered formal education. In 2016 there were 2,119,579 children in pre-school institutions with 63,031 teaching staff; 14,293,635 pupils in primary schools with 493,084 teaching staff; 7,397,290 pupils in secondary schools with 314,482 teaching staff; and (2017) 3,589,484 students in tertiary education with 151,252 academic staff. President Duterte signed a law abolishing tuition fees at state universities from the start of the 2017–18 academic year.

Non-formal education consists of adult literacy classes, agricultural and farming training programmes, occupation skills training, youth clubs, and community programmes of instructions in health, nutrition, family planning and co-operatives.

In 2016–17 there were 1,943 higher education institutions, including 112 state universities and colleges, 107 local universities and colleges, and 1,710 private higher education institutions. The adult literacy rate in 2008 was 94%.

Public expenditure on education in 2009 came to 2·7% of GDP and was equivalent to 13·2% of total government spending.

Health

In 2009 there were 1,796 hospitals (1,075 private); there were 94,199 beds in 2008 (1·0 beds per 1,000 inhabitants). Over the period 2000–10 there were 115 physicians for every 100,000 population, 600 nursing and midwifery personnel per 10,000 population, 56 dentistry personnel per 10,000 and 61 pharmaceutical personnel per 10,000.

In *Water: At What Cost? The State of the World's Water 2016*, WaterAid reported that 8·2% of the population does not have access to safe water.

Welfare

The Social Security System (SSS) is a contributory scheme for employees. Benefit disbursements in 2014 included (in 1m. pesos): retirement, 56,086; death, 33,530; maternity, 4,416; disability, 3,763.

Religion

In 2010 an estimated 92·6% of the population were Christians according to the Pew Research Center's Forum on Religion & Public Life, with 5·5% Muslims and 1·5% folk religionists. Of the Christians, 87% were Catholics and 12% Protestants.

The Roman Catholic Church had three cardinals in Feb. 2019. There are 16 ecclesiastical provinces, each of which consists of an archdiocese and a number of suffragan dioceses and is overseen by an archbishop.

Culture

World Heritage Sites

The Philippines has six sites on the UNESCO World Heritage List: Tubbataha Reefs Natural Park (inscribed on the list in 1993 and 2009); the Baroque Churches of the Philippines (1993); the Rice Terraces of the Philippine Cordilleras (1995); the Historic Town of Vigan (1999); Puerto-Princesa Subterranean River National Park (1999); and Mount Hamiguitan Range Wildlife Sanctuary (2014).

Press

There were 28 daily newspapers in 2008, with a combined circulation of 3,870,000. The leading daily is *Remate*, with an average daily circulation of 620,000 in 2008.

Tourism

In 2012, 4,273,000 non-resident tourists brought revenue of US$4,963m.

Diplomatic Representatives

Of the Philippines in the United Kingdom (6–11 Suffolk St., London, SW1Y 4HG)
Ambassador: Antonio Manuel Lagdameo.

Of the United Kingdom in the Philippines (120 Upper McKinley Rd, McKinley Hill, Taguig City 1634, Manila)
Ambassador: Daniel Pruce.

Of the Philippines in the USA (1600 Massachusetts Ave., NW, Washington, D.C., 20036)
Ambassador: Jose Manuel Del Gallego Romualdez.

Of the USA in the Philippines (1201 Roxas Blvd, Ermita 1000, Manila)
Ambassador: Sung Kim.

Of the Philippines to the United Nations
Ambassador: Teodoro Lopez Locsin, Jr.

Of the Philippines to the European Union
Ambassador: José A. De Vega.

Further Reading

National Statistics Office. *Philippine Statistical Yearbook.*
Abinales, Patricio N., *State and Society in the Philippines.* 2005
Balisacan, Arsenio M. and Hill, Hal, (eds) *The Philippine Economy: Development, Policies, and Challenges.* 2003
Francia, Luis H., *A History of the Philippines: From Indios Bravos to Filipinos.* 2010
Hamilton-Paterson, J., *America's Boy: The Marcoses and the Philippines.* 1998
Hedman, Eva-Lotta, *In the Name of Civil Society: From Free Election Movements to People Power in the Philippines.* 2005
Hedman, Eva-Lotta and Sidel, John, (eds) *Philippine Politics and Society in the Twentieth Century: Colonial Legacies.* 2000
Larkin, J. A., *Sugar and the Origins of Modern Philippine Society.* 1993
Miller, Jonathan, *Duterte Harry: Fire and Fury in the Philippines.* 2018
National Statistical Office: NSO-CVEA Building, East Ave., Diliman, Quezon City, Manila 1101.
Website: http://psa.gov.ph

Poland

Rzeczpospolita Polska (Polish Republic)

Capital: Warsaw
Population projection, 2020: 37·94m.
GNI per capita, 2017: (PPP$) 26,150
HDI/world rank, 2017: 0·865/33
Internet domain extension: .pl

Key Historical Events

In the 7th and 8th centuries Slavic peoples first settled on the forest covered plains between the Odra and Vistula rivers. Poland takes its name from the Polanie ('plain dwellers'), whose ruler Mieszko I, first in line of the Piast dynasty, founded the Polish state in 966. Christianity came via Bohemia and Moravia to the Kraków region, and in 991 Mieszko I placed Poland under the Holy Roman See. His son and heir, Bolesław I the Brave (ruled 992–1025) continued his father's territorial expansionism until Poland's boundaries were much as they are today. He established an independent Polish Catholic Church in the year 1000 and was officially crowned the first king of Poland in 1024 with the support of Holy Roman Emperor Otto III. The growing power of the church stimulated economic activity ranging from the manufacture of parchment and glass to building and painting.

In the twelfth century, under the rule of Bolesław III, German infiltration and internecine struggles led to Bolesław's 1138 Testament which divided the kingdom between his three sons. Around this time, many Jewish immigrants from Western Europe were attracted by the offer of asylum. The General Charter of Jewish Liberties was published in 1264 by Bolesław V, the Duke of Kraków.

A series of Mongol invasions in 1241–42 laid waste much of Poland, and in 1308 the crusades of the Teutonic Knights captured Gdańsk, cutting off Poland's access to the sea. In 1320 Władysław I Łokietek (the Short) of Kraków reunited the majority of the Polish lands that had been divided in 1138 and was crowned king of a united Poland. His son Casimir III the Great (Kasimierz, ruled 1333–70) continued this work, and his reign brought prosperity and administrative efficiency. He negotiated a truce with the Teutonic Knights and fostered closer diplomatic relations with the neighbouring kingdoms of Bohemia and Hungary.

Casimir III was the last monarch in the Piast line, and when he died his nephew Louis of Anjou, simultaneously King Lajos I of Hungary, donned the Polish crown. His death led to a disjointed succession. After a brief civil war his eleven-year-old daughter Jadwiga married Jagiełło, the pagan Grand Duke of Lithuania, who converted to Catholicism. Their marital union in 1386 signalled the beginning of the Jagiełłonian dynasty which ruled over Lithuania and Poland, at the time the largest state in Europe. The Jagiełłonian period to 1572 is regarded as an economic and cultural 'golden age'. This joint, multi-ethnic power managed to quell opposition on its eastern and western fronts. Poland–Lithuania crushed the Tatars and in 1410 defeated an army of 27,000 Teutonic Knights at the Battle of Tannenberg. In 1454 the Polish–Teutonic war broke out. King Casimir IV (1427–92) led a successful campaign, taking control of Western Prussia. At the Peace of Toruń in 1466 Gdańsk was returned to the Polish crown. The city, granted autonomy in exchange for its efforts in the war, thrived on shipping trade with the Netherlands, Spain and England among others while the population outgrew that of Warsaw.

The link between Poland and Lithuania was further strengthened by the Union of Lublin in 1569, which was primarily signed to protect both parties from expansionist threats on the Eastern front from Russia's Tsar Ivan IV (the Terrible). Warsaw became the capital of the two kingdoms which were henceforth known as the Commonwealth of Poland–Lithuania.

The last Jagiełłonian, Zygmunt II, died in 1572, after which the nobility introduced an elective monarchy with powers limited by the Acta Henriciana, so called because the first elected king to whom it applied was Henri III de Valois. He was obliged to swear his allegiance to maintaining the elective monarchy, which consulted the nobles on tax and warfare, respected religious tolerance and held a bi-annual meeting of the Sejm, the bicameral assembly dating from 1493. In contrast to many other countries in Europe, the Commonwealth was sufficiently broadminded on religious issues to abide by the Statute of Toleration (1573), although Catholicism was still the official religion.

Polish Wars

During this period, many foreign leaders were elected, partly to neutralize external interests. In 1573 Catherine de Médicis of France organized the election of her third son, Henry, duke of Anjou, to the Polish crown. When he returned to France as king on his brother's death, he was succeeded by a Transylvanian, Prince István Bathory. He increased Poland–Lithuania's military strength—a necessity given Ivan the Terrible's bellicose claims. In campaigns throughout 1578–81 the latter was beaten with a huge loss of Russian lives, and the territories he had encroached upon were restored.

1587 marked the beginning of Vasa rule, with Swedish-born Sigismund III taking the throne. But his succession led to territorial claims from his native land. Disapproving of Sigismund's Catholic persuasion, Calvinist Sweden occupied Livonia and Pomerania. In alliance with Russia, King Karl X of Sweden mounted a full invasion of Poland–Lithuania, devastating Warsaw and Kraków. During the ensuing Polish–Swedish war of 1655–60, support for Poland–Lithuania came from the Netherlands and Denmark. The Poles fought back against the invaders, winning a major battle at Częstochowa, but were eventually defeated. King Jan Kazimiercz (John Casimir), the last in line of the Vasa dynasty, abdicated in 1668.

Hopes of salvation for the Commonwealth came with Jan III Sobieski's election to the throne in 1674. He fought off the Ottomans who were advancing onto Polish territory. But further invasions and wars weakened Poland. The Great Northern War of 1700–21 had Poland as the battleground for fierce fighting between Russia, Denmark–Norway and Saxony–Poland (also Prussia from 1715) on one side against Sweden on the other. Each of the warring factions occupied parts of Poland, which was also subject to internecine fighting. Russia played the dominant role in Polish affairs until Frederick II, king of an increasingly powerful Prussia, proposed the division of Poland between Russia, Prussia and Austria. The outcome was the first Partition of Poland, in 1772. Austria was awarded the Kingdom of Galicia–Lodomeria, with 2·5m. inhabitants. Russia took over an area with a population of over 1m. Prussia contented itself with 0·5m. new citizens, and the long-desired connection between Western Pomerania and East Prussia.

In 1791 Stanisław II, the last king of the remaining Poland–Lithuania, introduced a constitution which amounted to a bid for independence. The three surrounding superpowers nonetheless engaged in a second partition in 1793. A peasant uprising against Russian rule, led by Tadeusz Kościuszko, was crushed, along with Poland itself which lost control of all its territory to Austria, Prussia and Russia in the third partition (1795).

The territory remained a battleground, particularly during the Napoleonic wars. Napoleon established the Grand Duchy of Warsaw in 1807, which had a French-style constitution, but came under Saxon, and later Russian, administration. Polish legions, which fought on the French side against Prussia, incurred heavy losses. In 1815, when the victorious Allies redistributed the territory Napoleon had won, the 'Congress' Kingdom of Poland reappeared, this time under Russian rule, with the Tsar as its hereditary king.

Thereafter the Poles suffered by their colonizers' attempts to assimilate their culture. A series of uprisings against the Russians took place throughout the century. In the November Revolution of 1830 inexperienced military cadets were suppressed by Tsar Nicholas, who led a campaign of bloody reprisals. Around 8,000 Poles emigrated after this defeat—many of them intellectuals, and most headed for France. During the peasants' revolt in Galicia in 1846 up to 2,000 nobles were murdered and their land ravaged. There was a strong insurgent movement among the peasants, but in 1848 they failed once more to topple their oppressors, this time the Prussians.

The January Uprising against the Russians which began in 1863–64 and ended in the spring of 1865 again led to defeat. Wide-scale Russianization followed, though the abolition of serfdom marked a significant concession. As part of Bismarck's 'Kulturkampf'—the Germanization of the Prussian zones—German was introduced as the official language and Polish began to

© Springer Nature Limited 2020

Palgrave Macmillan (ed.), *The Statesman's Yearbook 2020*,
https://doi.org/10.1057/978-1-349-95940-2_154

be taught in schools as a foreign language. Anti-Semitism became rife, and pogroms were not unusual. Many Jewish and Gentile Poles fled.

The Habsburg-dominated part of Poland, Galicia, was more tolerant of Polish nationalism which centred on Kraków. At one point the Austrian prime minister, finance minister and foreign minister were all Polish. Newly formed parties began to gain ground, with the National Democrats under Roman Dmowski campaigning for autonomy and Józef Piłsudski's Socialists engaging in an underground struggle for independence. Piłsudski led an anti-Russian uprising in 1905, and was to take up arms against Russia in the First World War when Poland's territory again bore the brunt of much of the fighting between its three partitioners.

In 1917 a Polish National Committee, formed by Roman Dmowski in Paris, was recognized by the Allies. One of its members and US representative was the pianist Ignacy Jan Paderewski, who urged the Americans to support the cause for Polish independence. President Woodrow Wilson's 'Fourteen Points' for peace addressed the Polish issue, guaranteeing independence and access to the sea under point thirteen. A Polish army was formed in France in 1918. In Poland, Piłsudski set up the Polish legions and a rival government. Poland regained its independence under Piłsudski's leadership on 11 Nov. 1918.

But while the Paris Peace Conference recognized the republic, the question of its borders was highly contentious. Poland challenged Lithuania over Vilnius, the city changing hands more than once before the Second World War. Fighting also took place against Ukraine over the issue of Galicia. A war with Russia followed over the next two years, which Poland narrowly managed to win before signing the Soviet–Polish Peace Treaty in Riga in 1921. The Treaty established the borders between Russia, Ukraine and Belarus, the last two being swallowed up by the USSR the following year. Gdańsk was awarded the status of a free city, and the Polish Corridor was formed between German West and East Prussia and the rest of Germany.

Between the wars there were 16 palatinates, all centrally governed from Warsaw. The new republic was first headed by President Narutowicz, the representative of the left and centre parties, who served for only days before being assassinated by a right-wing fanatic, and replaced in 1922 by Stanisław Wojciechowski. A series of intra-party disputes and factionalisms led the way for Józef Piłsudski to mount a coup in May 1926, seizing the power he maintained under a dictatorship until his death in 1935.

Second World War

In foreign affairs Poland managed to maintain a balance between its two most intimidating neighbours, Germany and the USSR, signing a non-aggression pact with Germany in 1934. However, the Molotov-Ribbentrop non-aggression pact of Aug. 1939 secretly agreed to partition Poland between Germany and the Soviet Union in the event of war. British and French guarantees of Polish independence that had been agreed in April of the same year obliged them to declare war on Nazi Germany two days after Hitler's troops marched into Poland on 1 Sept. 1939.

The response of Britain and France signalled the start of the Second World War. The German army invaded Poland along the entire front from the Baltic Sea to Slovakia, annexing over half of the country within three weeks. Stalin's troops marched into Poland from the Eastern Front on 17 Sept., leaving the country occupied for most of the duration of the war. The Nazis undertook a policy of liquidation—not only of Jews and ethnic 'undesirables' but also of the intelligentsia, so as to avoid any possibility of a Polish leadership class. Many Polish children seen as racially pure were taken away from their parents to be brought up as Germans, while others were deported. A total of over 6m. Polish nationals, or 17% of the population, were killed in the war, half of them Jewish. Not all of the murders were attributable to the Nazis, however. In 1989 Soviet authorities finally admitted to having murdered 15,000 Polish officers in the Katyn Forest in May 1940. The Soviet secret service had been equally keen to obliterate potential opposition leaders.

Polish forces regrouped on Allied soil under a government-in-exile headed by Gen. Władysław Sikorski, first in Paris and then, after 1940, in London. In Poland an underground national army, the AK, was formed under Gen. Komorowski to fight against the occupiers and to organize resistance. After Germany's invasion of the USSR in 1941, Poland was occupied solely by Nazi forces. Many of the largest concentration camps were built on Polish soil, including Auschwitz near Kraków.

In 1943 the exiled prime minister Gen. Sikorski was killed in a plane crash. He was replaced by Stanisław Mikołajczyk of the Polish Peasants' Party. The same year saw a Jewish uprising in the Warsaw ghetto, and in 1944 there was a second rebellion against the Nazi occupation which lasted

for two months. The Red Army was on the threshold of Warsaw throughout the two month revolt, but did not intervene. 150,000 civilians and 18,000 members of the AK lost their lives with virtually the whole of the remaining urban population deported and 85% of the city destroyed. By the time of Warsaw's liberation in Jan. 1945, the Jewish population numbered 200. The decimated underground movement was forced to seek assistance from Moscow, and after a number of compromises the Soviets recognized the Polish Committee of National Liberation, or the 'Lublin Committee', which proclaimed itself the sole legal government when Lublin was liberated in July 1944.

Poland's post-war fate was decided by the Allies at the Yalta and Potsdam conferences. At Yalta, Stalin agreed that the Lublin government should be extended to include non-Communists from the exile government, a promise that he failed to keep. Stanisław Mikołajczyk and three other members joined the provisional cabinet in July 1945. Nonetheless, many Polish politicians left the country. The Potsdam conference set Poland's Western border along the Oder–Neisse line, with all former German territories east of these rivers handed to Poland. As a result, Poles and Germans had to be resettled.

The first post-war elections were held in Jan. 1947. The Stalinist Polish Workers' Party (PPR) managed to crush both official and underground opposition. A Communist-dominated coalition under the leadership of Władysław Gomułka, the 'Democratic Bloc', won over three-quarters of the votes. Bolesław Bierut, leader of the USSR-backed Polish Communist Party, was named president. Defeated, Stanisław Mikołajczyk fled the country. An independently minded politician, Gomułka entered into conflict with Stalin by opposing agricultural collectivization and by speaking out against the formation of Cominform (Communist Information Bureau) in 1947. As a result he was removed as Secretary General of the PPR in Sept. 1948. Expelled from the party in late 1949, he was put under house arrest in July 1951. In 1948 the Polish United Workers' Party (PZPR) was formed, with Bierut as first party secretary. The nationalization of industry, land expropriation and the restructuring of the economy to favour heavy industry, including arms production, were accompanied in 1952 by a Soviet-style constitution and the renaming of the country as the People's Republic of Poland. This 'Stalinization' also included political and religious suppression and persecution, which targeted the Catholic church in particular.

Post-War Reform

In 1955 Poland joined other Eastern bloc countries in signing the Warsaw Pact military treaty. Meanwhile, the planned economy was failing, leading to widespread public unrest as food prices spiralled. Workers' strikes and riots in Poznań in 1956 were brutally suppressed by the authorities resulting in the death of 53 people. At this time Gomułka, the opponent of Stalinism, gained popularity. Readmitted to the party in 1956, Gomułka was reinstated as first secretary of the Party.

He attempted to introduce reforms, winning public support for his pledges of a 'Polish way' to socialism. Gomułka cut the power of the secret police, halted agricultural collectivization and brought an end to attacks on the Catholic Church. However, the suppression of freedom of expression continued and the economy did not improve. Gomułka's popular appeal began to falter. Student riots sprang up throughout the 1960s. In the 'March events' of 1968, the campaign for intellectual freedom led to widespread student riots and a reactive Party campaign against intellectuals and Jews, many of whom were forced to flee abroad.

Unrest and dissatisfaction with the party remained. Increased food prices in Dec. 1970 resulted in riots and strikes in the shipyards of Gdańsk, Szczecin and Gdynia. These were met with armed opposition, the authorities firing into the masses and killing several demonstrators. Gomułka and other leaders subsequently resigned, although Gomułka at least had the satisfaction of procuring West Germany's recognition of the Oder–Neisse line as the official Western border of Poland in Dec. 1970.

Solidarity

Edward Gierek succeeded Gomułka as first secretary, and in the following years launched a reform programme which was chiefly financed by loans from Western banks. He was hoping for a Polish economic miracle, but lacked the will to push through the necessary reforms. Short-term rewards were not enough to overcome the problems of a failing infrastructure, economic mismanagement of successive governments and a faltering world economy following the 1973–74 world oil crisis. Further demonstrations took place in several cities in 1976 to protest at more food price increases, and in Radom a Workers' Defence Committee was founded. While the government expressed disapproval, it did not act against the Committee.

In 1978 the election of Karol Wojtyła, Cardinal of Kraków, as Pope John Paul II boosted Poland's national self-esteem, celebrated in his trip to his native country the following year. Nonetheless, increased meat prices in July 1980 led to more waves of strikes, rippling out from the Ursus tractor plant near Warsaw across the country, and culminating in the Lenin shipyards in Gdańsk, where the Solidarity (*Solidarność*) movement was born. The first independent trade union to be established in a communist country soon boasted a membership of 10m. Its leader, Lech Wałęsa, a shipyard electrician, set up a strike committee, the first of a succession across the country, and drew up a 21-point accord, demanding the right to strike and to form independent trade unions, the abolition of censorship, freedom of expression, the release of political prisoners and access to the media. Soviet and Polish communist efforts to curb Solidarity's popularity failed and the group was officially recognized after some government resistance.

The social unrest, coupled with failing health, led to Gierek's resignation in Sept. 1980. In Feb. 1981 Gen. Wojciech Jaruzelski, the defence minister, became prime minister. This brought the military into the political front line and in Dec. 1981 Jaruzelski imposed martial law. A Military Council of National Salvation was established and Solidarity was proscribed. Wałęsa was among the thousands of members who were arrested and imprisoned. Demonstrations and strikes provoked the government into even stricter controls with the banning of all independent trade unions, although martial law was dropped a year later.

New hope was given to Poland in 1983, by the Pope's second visit, and by the award of the Nobel Peace Prize to Lech Wałęsa. Economic difficulties continued throughout the 1980s, and when the government proposed unpopular economic reforms in 1987, support for Solidarity led to nationwide strikes during 1988. Jaruzelski was forced to embark on negotiations with Wałęsa and the Catholic Church. Agreement was reached in April 1989 and Solidarity was given legal status and freedom to fight the upcoming elections, whilst the previously ceremonial post of Presidency was vested with new legislative powers. In return, Solidarity agreed to compete for only 35% of the seats in the Sejm.

At the July 1989 elections Solidarity won virtually all the seats they contested but because of the 35% rule Jaruzelski was voted in as president. However, Solidarity refused to join the communists in a grand coalition and Jaruzelski had to appoint Tadeusz Mazowiecki, an official of Solidarity, to be Poland's first non-communist premier in over 40 years. Jaruzelski subsequently resigned.

The first round of presidential elections in Nov. 1990 pitted Lech Wałęsa against Tadeusz Mazowiecki. Wałęsa won 43% of the votes in the first round and 74% in the second round in Dec., when he was inaugurated. Mazowiecki resigned his premiership and was replaced by Jan Bielcki, whose government held office until Aug. 1991. Genuinely free parliamentary elections did not take place until Oct. 1991, when there was a surprisingly low electoral turnout. In the absence of a clear-cut winner, several parties combined to form a centre-right coalition headed by Jan Olszewski. Owing to disputes both within the party and with President Wałęsa, however, the government lasted only seven months. This factionalism and inability to make compromises was typical of Poland's early post-Communist years. The government formed under Hanna Suchocka, Poland's first female prime minister, fared no better.

As in other post-Communist states, the economic measures necessary for the transition to a profitable market economy were highly unpopular with the electorate, not least when industrial modernization led to unemployment. In 1990 the finance minister, Leszek Balcerowicz, had introduced a range of tight austerity measures, including price rises and currency devaluation in an attempt to stabilize the economy before opening it to market forces. The Polish economy prospered but Wałęsa's popular appeal diminished as his tenure progressed. His skills as Solidarity's leader revolved around his ability to speak for the common people, but in government his tone was often regarded as aggressive and his style of leadership autocratic. Solidarity's loyalties as a trade union were often incompatible with its responsibilities as a political party. The elections of 1993 saw the return of the left under Waldemar Pawlak of the Polish Peasants' Party. After a series of intra-party quarrels and accusations of corruption, Pawlak's premiership ended in Feb. 1995.

Western Integration

Pawlak was replaced by the Communist Józef Oleksy of the Democratic Left Alliance. The left gained further political clout when Wałęsa was ousted in the presidential elections of 1995 by Aleksander Kwaśniewski. Redundancies in the Gdańsk shipyards in 1997 saw a renewed outbreak of nationwide strikes. Revising its political agenda, Solidarity forged a coalition of 25 centre-right parties to create Solidarity Electoral Action. This party emerged as the strongest in the 1997 general election when Jerzy Buzek, a member of Solidarity since its inception, became prime minister. A new constitution came into effect, reducing the powers of the president and committing the country to a social market economy.

Kwaśniewski's communist heritage caused concern among many Western leaders, but he confirmed his intention to press for EU and NATO membership. Market reforms and privatization continued apace. In 1999, at a joint ceremony with Czech president Václav Havel, Kwaśniewski signed Poland into NATO. The following year Kwaśniewski secured a second term and in 2001 Buzek was succeeded by Leszek Miller. A former communist turned social democrat, Miller's key aim was to prepare Poland for entry into the EU. Facing a deteriorating economy, he cut the national debt by increases in taxation and spending cuts. On 1 May 2004 Poland became a member of the EU.

Lech Kaczyński succeeded Kwaśniewski in 2005, with his twin brother Jarosław Kaczyński, serving as prime minister in 2006–07. President Kaczyński was killed in April 2010 when his plane crashed over Russia on its way to a war memorial service. The head of the national bank, the entire command of the armed services and several senior government figures, MPs, clergy and academics also perished in the accident. Bronisław Komorowski succeeded Kaczyński as president.

In Oct. 2011 Donald Tusk of Civic Platform secured a further term as premier, having come to office in 2007. He resigned in Sept. 2014 to become president of the European Council and was replaced by Ewa Kopacz. Relations with Russia became strained in 2014, with Poland warning against increasing Russian militarism following the Kremlin's annexation of Crimea.

Territory and Population

Poland is bounded in the north by the Baltic Sea and Russia, east by Lithuania, Belarus and Ukraine, south by the Czech Republic and Slovakia and west by Germany. Poland comprises an area of 312,685 sq. km (120,728 sq. miles).

At the census of 31 March 2011 the population was 38,511,824, giving a density of 123·2 per sq. km. Population estimate, Dec. 2017: 38,433,558. In 2009, 61·0% of the population lived in urban areas.

The UN gives a projected population for 2020 of 37·94m.

The country is divided into 16 regions or voivodships (*wojewodztwo*), created from the previous 49 on 1 Jan. 1999 following administrative reform. Area (in sq. km) and census population (in 1,000) in 2011 (density per sq. km in brackets).

Voivodship	Area	Population	Density
Dolnośląskie	19,948	2,915	(146)
Kujawsko-Pomorskie	17,970	2,098	(117)
Lubelskie	25,122	2,176	(87)
Lubuskie	13,989	1,023	(73)
Łódzkie	18,219	2,539	(139)
Małopolskie	15,190	3,337	(220)
Mazowieckie	35,560	5,269	(148)
Opolskie	9,412	1,016	(108)
Podkarpackie	17,844	2,127	(119)
Podlaskie	20,186	1,202	(60)
Pomorskie	18,293	2,276	(124)
Śląskie	12,331	4,630	(376)
Świętokrzyskie	11,708	1,281	(109)
Warmińsko-Mazurskie	24,192	1,452	(60)
Wielkopolskie	29,826	3,447	(116)
Zachodniopomorskie	22,897	1,723	(75)

Population (in 1,000) of the largest towns and cities (2011 census):

Warsaw (Warszawa)	1,700·6
Cracow (Kraków)	757·6
Łódź	728·9
Wrocław	630·1

(*continued*)

Poznań	554·7
Gdańsk	460·3
Szczecin	410·1
Bydgoszcz	363·9
Lublin	349·1
Katowice	310·8
Białystok	294·0
Gdynia	249·1
Częstochowa	236·8
Radom	221·3
Sosnowiec	216·4
Toruń	205·0
Kielce	202·2
Gliwice	187·5
Zabrze	181·1
Rzeszów	179·4
Bytom	176·9
Olsztyn	174·6
Bielsko-Biała	174·5

The population is 94% Polish. Minorities at the 2011 census included 418,000 who stated that they were Silesians as a national-ethnic identification, 49,000 Germans, 37,000 Belarusians and 36,000 Ukrainians. There are an estimated 230,000 people in Poland of Kashubian ethnicity (direct descendants of an early Slavic tribe of Pomeranians). They generally declare Polish nationality and consider themselves both Poles and Kashubians.

There is a large Polish diaspora, some 53% in the USA.

The official language is Polish.

Social Statistics

2014 (in 1,000): births, 376·5; deaths, 376·5; marriages, 188·5; divorces, 65·8; infant deaths, 1·6. Rates (per 1,000 population): birth, 9·9; death, 9·9; marriage, 5·0; divorce, 1·7; infant mortality (per 1,000 live births), 4·2. A law prohibiting abortion was passed in 1993, but an amendment of Aug. 1996 permits it in cases of hardship or difficult personal situation. The most popular age range for marrying in 2014 was 25–29 for both males and females. Expectation of life at birth, 2014, was 73·8 years for males and 81·6 years for females. In 2014 there were 28,080 emigrants (including 10,266 to Germany) and 12,330 immigrants. According to the Ukrainian ministry of foreign affairs and Polish government estimates, around 1m. Ukrainian nationals have moved to Poland since fighting began in eastern Ukraine in 2014. Number of suicides, 2013, 6,215; the suicide rate per 100,000 population was 29·2 among males and 4·3 among females in 2013. Population growth rate, 2014, 0·0%; fertility rate, 2014, 1·3 births per woman (one of the lowest rates in the world).

Climate

Climate is continental, marked by long and severe winters. Rainfall amounts are moderate, with a marked summer maximum. Warsaw, Jan. 24°F (–4·3°C), July 64°F (17·9°C). Annual rainfall 18·3" (465 mm). Gdańsk, Jan. 29°F (–1·7°C), July 63°F (17·2°C). Annual rainfall 22·0" (559 mm). Kraków, Jan. 27°F (–2·8°C), July 67°F (19·4°C). Annual rainfall 28·7" (729 mm). Poznań, Jan. 26°F (–3·3°C), July 64°F (17·9°C). Annual rainfall 21·0" (534 mm). Szczecin, Jan. 27°F (–3·0°C), July 64°F (17·7°C). Annual rainfall 18·4" (467 mm). Wrocław, Jan. 24°F (–4·3°C), July 64°F (17·9°C). Annual rainfall 20·7" (525 mm).

Constitution and Government

The present Constitution was passed by national referendum on 25 May 1997 and became effective on 17 Oct. 1997. The head of state is the *President*, who is directly elected for a five-year term (renewable once). The President may appoint, but may not dismiss, cabinets.

The authority of the republic is vested in the *Sejm* (Parliament of 460 members), elected by proportional representation for four years by all citizens over 18. There is a 5% threshold for parties and 8% for coalitions, but seats are reserved for representatives of ethnic minorities even if their vote falls below 5%. 69 of the Sejm seats are awarded from the national lists of parties polling more than 7% of the vote. The Sejm elects a *Council of State* and a *Council of Ministers*. There is also an elected 100-member upper house, the *Senate*. The President and the Senate each has a power of veto which only a two-thirds majority of the Sejm can override. The President does not, however, have a veto over the annual budget. The *Prime Minister* is chosen by the President with the approval of the Sejm.

A *Political Council* consultative to the presidency consisting of representatives of all the major political tendencies was set up in Jan. 1991.

National Anthem

'Jeszcze Polska nie zginęła' ('Poland has not yet perished'); words by J. Wybicki, tune by M. Ogiński.

Government Chronology

First Secretaries of the Polish United Workers' Party (1943–90) and Presidents of the Republic (since 1990). (PiS = Law and Justice Party; PO = Civic Platform; PZPR = Polish United Workers' Party; SdRP = Social Democracy of the Republic of Poland; SLD = Democratic Left Alliance; n/p = non-partisan)

First Secretaries of PZPR	
1943–48	Władysław Gomułka
1948–52	Bolesław Bierut
1952–54	Hilary Minc
1954–56	Bolesław Bierut
1956	Edward Ochab
1956–70	Władysław Gomułka
1970–80	Edward Gierek
1980–81	Stanisław Kania
1981–89	Wojciech Jaruzelski (military)
1989–90	Mieczysław F. Rakowski

Presidents		
1989–90	n/p	Wojciech Jaruzelski
1990–95	Solidarność	Lech Wałęsa
1995–2005	SdRP/SLD	Aleksander Kwaśniewski
2005–10	PiS	Lech Kaczyński
2010–15	PO	Bronisław Komorowski
2015–	n/p	Andrzej Duda

Prime Ministers since 1945. (AWS = Solidarity Electoral Action; KLD = Liberal Democratic Congress; PC = Centre Alliance; PiS = Law and Justice Party; PO = Civic Platform; PPR = Polish Workers' Party; PPS = Polish Socialist Party; PSL = Polish Peasants' Party; PZPR = Polish United Workers' Party; RS AWS = Social Movement-Solidarity Electoral Action; SdRP = Social Democracy of the Republic of Poland; SLD = Democratic Left Alliance; UD = Democratic Union)

1945–47	PPS	Edward Osóbka-Morawski
1947–52	PPR, PZPR	Józef A. Z. Cyrankiewicz
1952–54	PZPR	Bolesław Bierut
1954–70	PZPR	Józef A. Z. Cyrankiewicz
1970–80	PZPR	Piotr Jaroszewicz
1980	PZPR	Edward Babiuch
1980–81	PZPR	Józef Pińkowski
1981–85	PZPR/military	Wojciech Jaruzelski
1985–88	PZPR	Zbigniew Messner
1988–89	PZPR	Mieczysław F. Rakowski
1989	PZPR	Czesław Kiszczak
1989–91	Solidarność, UD	Tadeusz Mazowiecki

(*continued*)

1991	KLD	Jan Krzysztof Bielecki
1991–92	PC	Jan Olszewski
1992	PSL	Waldemar Pawlak
1992–93	UD	Hanna Suchocka
1993–95	PSL	Waldemar Pawlak
1995–96	SdRP/SLD	Józef Oleksy
1996–97	SdRP/SLD	Włodzimierz Cimoszewicz
1997–2001	RS	AWS/AWS Jerzy Buzek
2001–04	SLD	Leszek Miller
2004–05	SLD	Marek Belka
2005–06	PiS	Kazimierz Marcinkiewicz
2006–07	PiS	Jarosław Kaczyński
2007–14	PO	Donald Tusk
2014–15	PO	Ewa Kopacz
2015–17	PiS	Beata Szydło
2017–	PiS	Mateusz Morawiecki

Recent Elections

Parliamentary elections were held on 25 Oct. 2015. The opposition Law and Justice Party (PiS) won 235 of 460 seats with 37·6% of the vote, ahead of the ruling Civic Platform (PO), with 138 seats and 24·1%; Kukiz' 15 (K'15), with 42 and 8·8%; Modern, with 28 and 7·5%; Polish People's Party (PSL), with 16 and 5·1%; German Minority (MN), with 1 and 0·2%. In winning 235 seats the PiS became the first party to achieve an absolute majority at a free election in Poland. In the Senate elections held on the same day, the Law and Justice Party won 61 of 100 seats, the Civic Platform 34 and the Polish People's Party 1; four seats went to independents. Turnout was 50·9%.

Presidential elections were held in two rounds on 10 and 24 May 2015. In the first round 11 candidates stood; turnout was 49·0%. Andrzej Duda of the PiS gained 34·8% of votes cast, Bronisław Komorowski (ind.) 33·8%, Paweł Kukiz (ind.) 20·8%, Janusz Korwin-Mikke of the Coalition for the Restoration of Freedom and Hope to the Republic 3·3% and Magdalena Ogórek (ind.) 2·4%. Other candidates obtained less than 2%. In the second round run-off Andrzej Duda was elected president with 51·5% of the vote against 48·5% for Bronisław Komorowski.

European Parliament

Poland has 51 representatives. At the May 2014 elections turnout was 23·8% (24·5% in 2009). The PO won 19 seats with 32·1% of votes cast (political affiliation in European Parliament: European People's Party); the PiS, 19 with 31·8% (European Conservatives and Reformists); the Democratic Left Alliance–Union of Labour, 5 with 9·4% (Progressive Alliance of Socialists and Democrats); the Congress of the New Right, 4 with 7·2% (non-attached); the PSL, 4 with 6·8% (European People's Party).

Current Government

President: Andrzej Duda; b. 1972 (ind.; since 6 Aug. 2015).

In Feb. 2019 the PiS-led government consisted of:

Prime Minister: Mateusz Morawiecki; b. 1968 (PiS; sworn in 11 Dec. 2017).

Deputy Prime Ministers: Piotr Gliński (also *Minister of Culture and National Heritage*); Jarosław Gowin (also *Minister of Science and Higher Education*); Beata Szydło.

Minister of Agriculture and Rural Development: Jan Krzysztof Ardanowski. *Digitization:* Marek Zagórski. *Energy:* Krzysztof Tchórzewski. *Entrepreneurship and Technology:* Jadwiga Emilewicz. *Environment:* Henryk Kowalcyk. *Family, Labour and Social Policy:* Elżbieta Rafalska. *Finance:* Teresa Czerwińska. *Foreign Affairs:* Jacek Czaputowicz. *Health:* Łukasz Szumowski. *Infrastructure and Construction:* Andrzej Adamczyk. *Interior and Administration:* Joachim Brudziński. *Investment and Economic Development:* Jerzy Kwieciński. *Justice:* Zbigniew Ziobro. *Maritime Economy and Inland Waterways:* Marek Gróbarczyk. *National Defence:* Mariusz Błaszczak. *National Education:* Anna Zalewska. *Sport and Tourism:* Witold Bańka. *Head of the Chancellery of the Prime Minister:* Beata Kempa.

Office of the Prime Minister: http://www.kprm.gov.pl

Current Leaders

Andrzej Duda

Position
President

Introduction
As the candidate of the right-leaning Law and Justice Party (PiS), Andrzej Duda defeated incumbent Bronisław Komorowski in a presidential election run-off held on 24 May 2015. He is a lawyer and former member of the European Parliament.

Early Life
Duda was born on 16 May 1972 in Kraków and studied law at the Jagiellonian University, where his parents were both professors. In 2001 he became an assistant professor in the university's department of administrative law. Four years later he was awarded his doctorate in law.

Duda joined the Freedom Party in the early 2000s but joined the PiS in 2005. From 2006 until 2010 in the government of Lech Kaczyński he was variously undersecretary of state at the ministry of justice and in the chancellery of the president as well as a member of the state tribunal (a constitutional court). In 2010 Duda failed in his bid to become mayor of Kraków but was elected to parliament in the 2011 elections. In 2014 he became a member of the European Parliament, where he held a eurosceptic line, before being announced as the PiS's presidential candidate.

In the first round of the 2015 presidential election, Duda came first with 34·8% of votes. In the second round he polled 51·5% to force Bronisław Komorowski from office after a single term.

Career in Office
Duda was sworn in on 6 Aug. 2015 and consolidated his position two months later when the PiS party won 51% of the seats in the parliamentary elections. Since taking office he has rejected the EU's proposals for a compulsory migrant quota. Also, wary of the threat from Russia, he has fostered closer ties with Poland's central and Eastern European neighbours and welcomed the deployment in April 2017 of NATO troops in the northeast of the country. On the domestic front, he signed a government bill in Jan. 2016 that ensured senior figures in the state media would be appointed and dismissed by the treasury minister, rather than the National Broadcasting Council. However, in 2017 he blocked some military appointments in defiance of the defence ministry and in July resisted the government's unpopular efforts to put the courts under political control, vetoing legislation (which was subsequently modified and approved by parliament in Dec.) that sought to limit judicial independence.

Following the resignation in early Dec. 2017 of Beata Szydło as prime minister, Duda asked Mateusz Morawiecki, her deputy and finance minister, to succeed her. The change was reportedly instigated by Jarosław Kaczyński, the ruling party's influential leader and a former prime minister.

In Feb. 2018 Duda signed controversial legislation making it illegal to accuse the Polish nation or state of complicity in the crimes of the Nazi Holocaust in the Second World War. Later, in Dec., and in response to nationwide protests and pressure from the European Union, he approved an amendment to an unpopular law passed in July forcing senior judges into retirement before the expiration of their constitutional terms. The law was widely viewed as a government-orchestrated purge of the judiciary.

Mateusz Morawiecki

Position
Prime Minister

Introduction
Mateusz Morawiecki, formerly deputy prime minister to Beata Szydło, was appointed premier in Dec. 2017. He also retained his portfolios as finance minister and minister of development.

Early Life
Morawiecki was born on 20 June 1968 in Wrocław. From an early age, he was involved in anti-communist activities—including printing and distributing underground Solidarity magazines, which led to arrests and beatings by the secret police. He began reading history at the University of Wrocław in 1992, then studied European law and economic integration at the University of Hamburg in Germany between 1995 and 1997. He also attended the

advanced executive programme at the Kellogg School of Management at Northwestern University in the USA. During this period he became fluent in both German and English.

In 1991 he took a job with an industrial firm before moving into publishing. After a subsequent internship at Deutsche Bank, he led banking and economic research at the University of Frankfurt before joining Bank Zachodni WBK in 1998, becoming its chief executive officer in 2007. His political career took off in 1998 when he served as deputy director of the Accession Negotiations Department in the Committee of European Integration, helping to negotiate Poland's accession to the European Union. In 2010 Morawiecki became economic adviser to the then prime minister Donald Tusk (of the liberal Civic Platform party). Then, in 2015, he was appointed minister of economic development in the conservative PiS administration. During his tenure as finance minister, Poland's economy enjoyed strong growth and falling unemployment.

Career in Office

Morawiecki's appointment as prime minister by President Andrzej Duda in Dec. 2017 was widely seen as an attempt to mollify the European Union over its opposition to controversial judicial reforms, as well as Poland's failure to follow EU policy over quotas for migrants and refugees. He was expected to continue his commitment to deregulation and to promote a conservative Catholic social agenda. After a cabinet reshuffle designed to further assuage EU criticisms, Morawiecki's government found itself at the centre of international scrutiny in Feb. 2018 as a law banning any association of the Polish state with the crimes committed by the Nazi Third Reich during its wartime occupation of Poland came into effect, causing friction in relations with the Israeli government.

Defence

Poland is divided into two military districts: Pomeranian (North) and Silesian (South). In 2013 defence expenditure totalled US$9,829m. (US$256 per capita), representing 1·9% of GDP.

Conscription ended on 1 Jan. 2010.

Army

Strength (2011) 46,900. In accordance with a programme of modernization of the armed forces, the strength has been gradually declining, from 230,000 in the socialist era in 1988 to 186,000 in 1995 and further to the current figure of under 50,000. In addition there were 14,100 border guards in 2011. Equipment in 2011 included 944 main battle tanks and 1,670 armoured infantry fighting vehicles.

Navy

The fleet comprises four ex-Soviet and one ex-Norwegian diesel submarines, two frigates, and six patrol and coastal combatants. There is a small Naval Aviation force.

Personnel in 2011 totalled 8,100 including 1,350 in Naval Aviation. Bases are at Gdynia, Hel, Świnoujście and Kolobrzeg.

Air Force

The Air Force had a strength (2011) of 17,200. There were 112 combat-capable aircraft in 2011 (including F-16s, MiG-29s and Su-22s). Since the end of the communist era in 1989, Poland has been steadily reducing its reliance on Russian-built aircraft.

International Relations

A treaty of friendship with Germany signed on 17 June 1991 renounced the use of force, recognized Poland's western border as laid down at the Potsdam conference of 1945 (the 'Oder–Neisse line') and guaranteed minority rights in both countries.

A referendum held on 8 June 2003 approved accession to the EU, with 77·4% of votes cast for membership and 22·6% against. Poland became a member of the EU on 1 May 2004.

Poland's Senate approved the European Union's Treaty of Lisbon on 2 April 2008, the day after the *Sejm* had done so. However, then President Lech Kaczyński did not ratify it until 12 Oct. 2009, following acceptance of the Treaty by Ireland in a referendum ten days earlier.

Economy

In 2011 trade, restaurants and hotels contributed 17·1% to GDP; followed by finance and real estate, 16·6%; manufacturing, 16·6%; services, 11·1%; construction, 6·2%; and transport and communications, 6·1%.

Overview

Having pursued a policy of economic liberalization since 1990, Poland has the largest economy in Central Europe according to World Bank statistics. Under the communist regime the economy had been heavily skewed towards industry but since 1990 the service sector has expanded, contributing 64% of GDP in 2014 (compared to industry's 33%). Most of the banking sector has been privatized, as have many large industries. An unspectacular yet solid growth performance since the transition has helped raise living standards, with per capita income levels increasing by 250% between 1993 and 2010.

In 1990 and 1991 the economy shrank by 11·5% and 7·0% respectively, although subsequent economic restructuring helped to achieve productivity gains. Total factor productivity grew at an estimated annual average of over 3% from 1994–2003, reflecting sound macroeconomic management combined with a raft of transition policies, including price liberalization and lower import barriers. After accession to the European Union in 2004 growth was buoyant, with exporters benefiting from EU market integration.

The unemployment rate meanwhile declined steadily (from 19·9% in 2002 to 7·1% in 2008) until the effects of the global financial crisis began to be felt. By Dec. 2012 it had risen to 10·4%. Joblessness has been highest where state farms once dominated (with agriculture still making up 11% of total employment but accounting for only 2·4% of GDP in 2016), while former industrial areas have proved more dynamic. By 2016 real wages had climbed by more than 10% since early 2008, while unemployment had fallen below the EU average to 5·5% by the end of that year.

Despite being hit by the financial crisis, Poland fared better than many of its neighbours and became the only EU country in 2009 to avoid recession. This was largely a result of the floating exchange rate regime, which limited imbalances, allied to effective policy responses. Real GDP growth fell to 4·2% in 2008, down from 7·0% in 2007. In response the central bank cut the seven-day reference interest rate from 5·0% to 4·25%. Output in the industrial sector fell by 4·4% in Dec. 2008 and manufacturing output fell by 3·9%, mirroring a slowdown in the export market. Exports contracted by 30% year-on-year in the first quarter of 2009 and foreign direct investment fell by 50%.

In April 2009 the government approached the IMF for US$20·5bn. from its flexible credit line to shore up borrowing needs in the face of the crisis. Real GDP growth rebounded to 5·0% in 2011, aided by the economy's large domestic market, stable private consumption and limited reliance on exports. However, tax cuts enacted in 2006 and 2007, combined with a counter-cyclical fiscal stimulus, saw the government deficit rise from 2% of GDP in 2007 to 7% in 2009, before falling to 2·4% by 2016.

Growth slowed to 1·6% in 2012 and 1·4% in 2013, reflecting uncertain prospects in the eurozone, a slowdown in exports (75% of which went to the EU) and lower public investment. However, it accelerated to over 3·3% per year on average between 2014 and 2016, propelled by increased domestic demand aided by a strong labour market and improved external conditions.

The IMF has stressed the need for continuing privatization and structural reforms to further strengthen the labour market and improve the business climate. Other priorities are to reduce public debt, which stood at 54·1% of GDP in 2016, and to insulate Poland from the effects of eurozone sovereign debt crises.

Currency

The currency unit is the *złoty* (PLN) of 100 *groszy*. A new złoty was introduced on 1 Jan. 1995 at 1 new złoty = 10,000 old złotys. Inflation rates (based on OECD statistics):

2008	2009	2010	2011	2012	2013	2014	2015	2016	2017
4·2%	3·8%	2·6%	4·2%	3·6%	1·0%	0·1%	−0·9%	−0·7%	2·1%

Inflation, in single figures since 1999, had been nearly 250% in 1990. The złoty became convertible on 1 Jan. 1990. In 1995 the złoty was subject to a creeping devaluation of 1·2% per month; it was allowed to float in a 14% (+/−7%) band from 16 May 1995. In April 2000 Poland introduced a floating exchange rate. Foreign exchange reserves were US$72,280m. and gold reserves 3·31m. troy oz in Sept. 2009. In July 2009 total money supply was 363,655m. złotys.

Budget

Budgetary central government revenue totalled 288,989m. złotys in 2013 (289,242m. złotys in 2012) and expenditure 346,365m. złotys (342,380m. złotys in 2012).

Principal sources of revenue in 2013 were: taxes on goods and services, 180,202m. złotys; taxes on income, profits and capital gains, 65,007m. złotys. Main items of expenditure by economic type in 2013: grants, 187,287m. złotys; compensation of employees, 55,683m. złotys.

Poland's budget deficit in 2017 was 1·4% of GDP (2016, 2·2%; 2015, 2·7%). The required target set by the EU is a budget deficit of no more than 3%.

VAT is 23·0% (reduced rates, 8% and 5%).

Performance

Real GDP growth rates (based on OECD statistics):

2008	2009	2010	2011	2012	2013	2014	2015	2016	2017
4·2%	2·8%	3·6%	5·0%	1·6%	1·4%	3·3%	3·8%	3·1%	4·8%

Poland was the only EU member country not to experience a recession in 2009 and the only one with positive growth. Total GDP in 2017 was US$524·5bn.

Banking and Finance

The National Bank of Poland (established 1945) is the central bank and bank of issue (*President*, Adam Glapiński). There were 67 commercial banks operating in 2011 and 574 co-operative banks. Poland's leading banks are PKO Bank Polski with assets of 156·5bn. złotys in Dec. 2009 and Bank Pekao (assets of 130·6bn. złotys in Dec. 2009).

Gross external debt amounted to US$331,790m. in June 2012.

In 2012 Poland received US$6·1bn. of foreign direct investment, down from US$20·6bn. in 2011. The total stock of FDI at the end of 2012 was US$235·1bn.

There is a stock exchange in Warsaw.

Energy and Natural Resources

In 2011, 10·4% of energy consumption came from renewables (wind power, solar power, hydro-electric power, tidal power, geothermal energy and biomass), compared to the European Union average of 13·0%. A target of 15% has been set by the EU for 2020.

Environment

Poland's carbon dioxide emissions from the consumption of energy in 2011 were the equivalent of 8·0 tonnes per capita.

Electricity

Installed capacity was 34·6m. kW in 2011. Production (2011) 163·55bn. kWh; consumption per capita was 4,144 kWh in 2011. Poland is a net exporter of electricity.

Oil and Gas

Total oil reserves (2011) amount to some 96m. bbls; natural gas reserves (2012), 100bn. cu. metres. Crude oil production was 4·6m. bbls in 2011; natural gas (2012), 4·2m. cu. metres. Poland is dependent on Russia for around 60% of its gas. The largest oil distributor is Polski Koncern Naftowy ORLEN SA, created by the merger of Petrochemia Płock and Centrala Produktów Naftowych.

Minerals

Poland is a major producer of coal (reserves of some 7,500m. tonnes), copper (26m. tonnes) and sulphur. Production (2012, in tonnes): coal, 79·9m.; brown coal, 64·3m.; salt, 4·1m.; copper, 427,064; silver, 1,149.

Agriculture

In 2014, 16·2% of the employed persons were engaged in agriculture. In 2014 there were 10·90m. ha. of arable land. There were 1·4m. farms in 2014; private farms accounted for 90·9% of the total area of agricultural land and state-owned farms for 9·1%. In 2013 agriculture, forestry and fishing contributed 2·9% of GDP.

Output in 2014 (in 1,000 tonnes): sugar beets, 13,489; wheat, 11,629; potatoes, 7,689; maize, 4,468; rapeseed, 3,276; barley, 3,275; apples, 3,195;

rye, 2,793; oats, 1,459; cabbage, 1,156; carrots, 823; onions, 651. Poland is the second largest producer of rye, after Russia.

Livestock, 2014: pigs, 11·72m.; cattle, 5·92m. (including cows, 2·48m.); sheep, 222,800; horses, 207,000; chickens, 121m.

Livestock products, 2013: pork and pork products, 1,775,000 tonnes; beef and veal, 386,000 tonnes; poultry meat, 1,694,000 tonnes; milk, 12,718,000 tonnes; cheese (including soft cheese), 823,000 tonnes; eggs, 558,000 tonnes.

In 2013 there were 1,436,100 tractors in use.

Forestry

In 2015 forest area was 9·44m. ha. (predominantly coniferous), or 31% of the land area. Timber production in 2011 was 37·18m. cu. metres.

Fisheries

The catch was 198,385 tonnes in 2012, of which 179,691 tonnes were sea fish. Imports of fishery commodities were valued at US$1,600m. in 2012 and exports at US$1,548m.

Industry

The leading companies by market capitalization in Poland in May 2018 were: PKO Bank (US$14·9bn.); PKN Orlen (US$10·4bn.); and Pgnig Group, an insurance company (US$10·3bn.).

In 2012 there were 177 state firms, 290,291 limited liability companies, 340,558 other companies and 17,155 co-operatives. Production in 2012 unless otherwise indicated (in 1,000 tonnes): cement, 15,919; distillate fuel oil, 12,139; crude steel, 8,539; nitrogenous fertilizers, 5,455; residual fuel oil, 4,630; petrol, 4,027; pig iron, 3,944; paper and paperboard, 3,822; plastics in primary forms, 2,615; nitric acid, 2,323; ammonia, 2,026 (in terms of pure nitrogen); sugar, 1,996; sulphuric acid, 1,693; soda ash, 1,116; paints and lacquers, 1,057; sulphur, 676; beer, 3,961m. litres; mineral water, 3,235m. litres; fruit and vegetable juice, 756m. litres; vodka, 103m. litres; cigarettes, 156bn. units; bricks, 473m. units; television receivers, 20,526,000 units; washing machines, 3,109,983 units; refrigerators and freezers, 2,220,651 units; cars, 540,000 units; telephone sets, 25,500 units; public transport vehicles, 4,000 units; tractors, 3,539 units.

Output of light industry in 2012: cotton woven fabrics, 25·3m. sq. metres; woollen woven fabrics, 2·6m. sq. metres; shoes, 35·7m. pairs.

Labour

In 2014 a total of 14,563,400 persons were in employment. As of Dec. 2014, 2,955,700 persons worked in industry, 2,176,600 in trade and repairs, 1,124,200 in education, 971,100 in public administration and defence, and compulsory social security, 827,300 in health and social work activities, 820,000 in construction, 743,700 in transportation and storage, and 588,700 in professional, scientific and technical activities. The unemployment rate increased steadily for several years peaking at 20·3% in the period Aug.–Oct. 2002 (more than double the EU average at the time). It has declined considerably since then and in Dec. 2018 stood at 3·5% (the lowest rate on record), down from 4·9% in 2017 as whole. Unemployment among the under 25s was 26·0% in the third quarter of 2011. Despite strong public opposition an amendment to the Act on Pensions was passed in 2012 increasing the retirement age to 67 for both men and women (having previously been 65 for men and 60 for women). Starting from Jan. 2013 the retirement age began to increase by three months every year and was set to reach 67 for men in 2020 and for women in 2040. However, in 2016 parliament voted to reverse the rise, which had been introduced under the previous government. The change took effect from Oct. 2017.

Poland had 0·14m. people living in slavery according to the Walk Free Foundation's 2013 *Global Slavery Index.*

International Trade

Imports and Exports

In 2014 imports (c.i.f.) totalled US$225·90bn.; exports (f.o.b.), US$222·34bn. The main imports in 2014 were machinery and transport equipment (33·8%); manufactured goods classified chiefly by material (17·5%); chemicals and related products (14·4%); mineral fuels, lubricants and related materials (10·5%); miscellaneous manufactured articles (10·5%). Leading exports were machinery and transport equipment (37·8%); manufactured goods classified chiefly by material (19·7%); miscellaneous manufactured articles (14·0%); food and live animals (10·8%); chemicals and related products (9·1%).

Main import suppliers, 2014: Germany, 22·0%; China, 10·4%; Russia, 10·3%; Italy, 5·6%; Netherlands, 3·8%. Main export markets, 2014: Germany, 26·3%; Czech Republic, 6·5%; United Kingdom, 6·4%; France, 5·6%; Italy, 4·5%. In 2014 trade with other European Union member countries accounted for 59·0% of Polish imports and 77·5% of Polish exports.

Communications

Roads
The total length of public roads at the end of 2012 amounted to 412,000 km of which hard surface roads accounted for 68% and motorways amounted to 1,365 km. The total number of registered motor road vehicles and road tractors amounted to 24·9m. as of 31 Dec. 2012, of which 18,744,000 passenger cars, 3,178,000 lorries, vans and road tractors, 99,900 buses, and 2,208 motorcycles and mopeds. In 2012 road transport totalled 20,012m. passenger-km and freight 233,310m. tonne-km. The number of persons killed in road accidents amounted to 3,577 in 2012, representing 9·3 deaths per 100,000 population. Poland has one of the highest death rates in road accidents in the European Union.

Rail
In 2011 there were 19,725 km of railways in use managed by Polish State Railways (11,817 km electrified). Over 98% is standard 1,435 mm gauge with the rest broad gauge (1,520 mm). In 2011 railways carried 184·6m. passengers and 140·5m. tonnes of freight. Passenger-km travelled in 2011 came to 15·7bn. and freight tonne-km to 37·2bn. An 11·1 km metro opened in Warsaw in 1995, extended by 2008 to 22·7 km. A second 32 km line is currently under construction. The initial 6·3 km of the line were opened in March 2015. The second phase of the project is due to be completed in late 2019 or early 2020. There are also 14 tram/light rail networks with a total length of 930 km.

Civil Aviation
The main international airport is at Warsaw (Frederic Chopin), with some international flights from Kraków (John Paul II Balice International), Bydgoszcz, Gdańsk, Katowice, Łódź, Poznań, Rzeszów, Szczecin and Wrocław. The national carrier is LOT-Polish Airlines (68% state-owned). It flew 107·7m. km in 2011, carrying 6,491,199 passengers (5,377,869 on international flights). In 2011 Warsaw handled 9,324,635 passengers (8,253,153 on international flights) and 60,625 tonnes of freight.

Shipping
The principal ports are Gdańsk, Szczecin, Świnoujście and Gdynia. The total volume of cargo traffic at all Polish seaports amounted to 58·8m. tonnes in 2012, including 24·4m. tonnes at Gdańsk and 13·2m. tonnes at Gdynia. The Polish maritime transport fleet carried 7·5m. tonnes of cargo and 642,200 passengers in 2012. At the end of 2012 the Polish maritime fleet comprised 110 ships totalling 3,045,000 DWT.

The total length of inland waterways at the end of 2012 was 3,659 km. In 2012 inland waterway transport totalled 24m. passenger-km and 815m. freight tonne-km.

Telecommunications
In 2014 mobile phone subscriptions numbered 56,905,306 (1,488·9 per 1,000 persons). In the same year there were 4,822,233 main (fixed) telephone lines. The privatization of Telekomunikacja Polska (TP SA), the former state telecom operator, was completed in 2001 with France Télécom (now Orange S.A.) purchasing a 49·8% stake in the company. This rose to 50·67% in June 2013. In April 2012 Telekomunikacja Polska was renamed Orange Polska in line with France Télécom's international branding. 66·6% of the population were internet users in 2014. In March 2012 there were 7·5m. Facebook users.

Social Institutions

Out of 178 countries analysed in the 2017 *Fragile States Index*—a list published jointly by the Fund for Peace and *Foreign Policy* magazine—Poland was ranked the 28th least vulnerable to conflict or collapse. The index is based on 12 indicators of state vulnerability across social, political and economic categories.

Justice
The penal code was adopted in 1969. Espionage and treason carry the severest penalties. For minor crimes there is provision for probation sentences and fines. In 1995 the death penalty was suspended for five years; it had not been applied since 1988. A new penal code abolishing the death penalty was adopted in June 1997.

In 2009 there were the following courts: one Supreme Court, one Supreme Administrative Court, 16 administrative courts of first instance, 11 appeal courts, 45 regional courts, 320 district courts, 68 family consultative centres and 35 juvenile institutions. Judges are appointed by the President of the Republic from candidatures proposed by the National Council of the Judiciary and have life tenure.

In 2014, 295,353 criminal sentences were passed. There were 578 ascertained homicides in 2014. The population in penal institutions in Dec. 2014 was 77,371 (201 per 100,000 of national population). Poland was ranked 15th of 102 countries for criminal justice and 22nd for civil justice in the 2015 World Justice Project *Rule of Law Index*, which provides data on how the rule of law is experienced by the general public across eight categories.

Education
Education from six to 18 is free and compulsory, although from 16 to 18 it may be part-time. Secondary education is then optional in general or vocational schools. In the 2009–10 school year there were: pre-primary schools, 17,444 with 994,138 pupils and 53,103 full-time equivalent teachers; primary schools, 13,972 with 2,235,018 pupils and 224,351 full-time equivalent teachers; lower secondary schools, 7,810 with 1,346,112 pupils and 104,755 full-time equivalent teachers; upper secondary schools, 10,709 with 1,770,013 pupils and 134,573 full-time equivalent teachers; post-secondary schools, 3,108 with 266,057 pupils and 8,210 full-time equivalent teachers; tertiary institutions, 563 with 1,918,793 students and 105,309 academic staff (excluding postgraduate and doctoral courses). In 2011, 39% of 25–34 year-olds had a tertiary qualification. Since the early 1990s there has been a boom in private higher education—in 2009–10 more than 30% of all students in higher education were at private colleges.

The adult literacy rate in 2008 was over 99%.

Religious (Catholic) instruction was introduced in all schools in 1990; for children of dissenting parents there are classes in ethics.

In 2009 total expenditure on education came to 5·8% of GDP and 11·5% of total government spending.

Health
Medical treatment is free and funded from public sources. Medical care is also available in private clinics. In 2009 there were 795 general hospitals with a total of 193,400 beds (including beds and incubators for newborn babies). 82,700 physicians, 12,100 dentists, 193,100 nurses, 24,200 pharmacists and 22,400 thousand midwives worked directly with patients within hospital and outpatient care in 2009. In Jan. 1999 reform of the health care system was inaugurated. All citizens can now choose their own doctor, who is paid by the public sector under the social security system. The share of health insurance paid mainly by employees, equalling 7·5% of the amount earned by them, is assigned for the financing of the health care system. In 2013 Poland spent 6·4% of its GDP on health, with 29·4% of health expenditure coming from private sources.

In *Water: At What Cost? The State of the World's Water 2016*, WaterAid reported that 1·7% of the population does not have access to safe water.

Welfare
All social security benefits are administered by the State Insurance Office and funded 45% by a payroll tax and 55% from the state budget. In 2010 social benefits totalling 198,479·6m. złotys were paid (including 170,879·5m. złotys for retirement pay and pensions, 7,830·1m. złotys for family benefits and supplements to the family benefits, nursing benefits and allowances, 7,213·9m. złotys for sick benefits, 3,038·2m. złotys for maternity benefits, 2,622·9m. złotys for unemployment benefits and 2,435·5m. złotys for funeral benefits). There were a total of 9,243,427 pensioners in 2010. Unemployment benefits are paid from a fund financed by a 3% payroll tax. It is indexed in various categories to the average wage and payable for 12 months.

A retirement pension is available to an insured person who fulfils the following conditions: has attained the retirement age dependent on gender, specific employment conditions or functions, and an appropriate contributory and non-contributory period. The basic retirement pay for people born before 1949 is defined by job seniority and wages in chosen work periods. For people who were born after 31 Dec. 1948 and who joined the Open Pension Fund (OPF), or who are not members of the OPF and who did not fulfil the requirements needed to obtain retirement pay under the previous rules, basic retirement pay depends on the capital that was built up in individual insurance accounts.

The retirement age was being raised gradually from 60 for men and 65 for women to 67 for both men and women, by 2020 and 2040 respectively. In Nov. 2016 parliament voted to overturn the rise, which had been approved by the previous administration in 2012.

Religion

State relations are regulated by laws of 1989 which guarantee religious freedom, grant the Catholic Church radio and TV programmes and permit it to run schools, hospitals and old age homes. The Church has a university (Lublin) and seminaries. On 28 July 1993 the government signed a Concordat with the Vatican regulating mutual relations. The religious capital is Gniezno. Its archbishop, Wojciech Polak (b. 1964), is the primate of Poland. Kazimierz Nycz was appointed archbishop of Warsaw on 1 April 2007. In Oct. 1978 Cardinal Karol Wojtyła, archbishop of Kraków, was elected Pope as John Paul II. In Feb. 2019 there were six cardinals.

Statistics of major churches as at Dec. 2009:

Church	Congregations	Clergy	Adherents
Roman Catholic	10,157	30,142	33,695,233
Uniate	134	74	55,000
Old Catholics	142	128	47,043
Polish Orthodox	225	390	504,150
Protestant (45 churches)	1,225	2,423	156,201
Muslim	19	33	2,667
Jewish	10	6	1,410
Jehovah's Witnesses	1,816	—	128,292

Culture

World Heritage Sites

There are 15 UNESCO World Heritage sites in Poland. They are: Kraków's Historic Centre (inscribed on the list in 1978), Poland's former capital; Wieliczka Salt Mine (1978, 2008 and 2013), a mine since the 13th century; Auschwitz Concentration Camp (1979), the German concentration camp and nearby Birkenau death camp; Historic Centre of Warsaw (1980), celebrating the 20th century reconstruction of the city's 18th century heart decimated during World War II; Old City of Zamość (1992), a 16th century town; Medieval Town of Toruń (1997); Castle of the Teutonic Order in Malbork (1997), a medieval brick castle; Kalwaria Zebrzydowska: the Mannerist Architectural and Park Landscape Complex and Pilgrimage Park (1999); Churches of Peace in Jawor and Świdnica (2001), Europe's biggest timber-framed religious buildings; Wooden Churches of Southern Little Poland (2003); the Centennial Hall in Wrocław (2006); and Tarnowskie Góry Lead-Silver-Zinc Mine and its Underground Water Management System (2017).

Poland and Belarus are jointly responsible for Belovezhskaya Pushcha/Białowieża Forest (1979, 1992 and 2014), in the Baltic/Black Sea region; Poland and Germany are jointly responsible for Muskauer Park/Park Mużakowski (2004), a landscaped park astride the Neisse river; and Poland and Ukraine are jointly responsible for the wooden *tserkvas* (churches) of the Carpathian region (2013), comprising 16 *tservkas* in the eastern fringe of Central Europe.

Press

In 2014 there were 36 daily newspapers with a combined daily circulation of 2,190,000. The most popular newspapers are *Fakt Gazeta*, *Super Express*, *Gazeta Wyborcza* and *Nasz Dziennik*. In 2011, 31,515 book titles were published.

Tourism

In 2011 there were 13,350,000 tourist arrivals, up from 12,470,000 in 2010 and 11,890,000 in 2009. The main countries of origin of non-resident tourists in 2011 were Germany (4,590,000), Ukraine (1,580,000), Belarus (1,220,000) and Lithuania (630,000).

Festivals

The International Chopin Festival at Duszniki Zdrój is held in Aug. and the Warsaw Autumn Festival takes place in Sept. Kraków Film Festival runs from May–June. Popular music festivals include Metalmania in Katowice (March), Open'er Festival in Gdynia (July), Przystanek Woodstock at Kostrzyn nad Odrą (July–Aug.), Off Festival at Mysłowice (Aug.) and Zaduszki Jazzowe (All Soul's Day Jazz Festival) in Kraków (Nov.).

Diplomatic Representatives

Of Poland in the United Kingdom (47 Portland Pl., London, W1B 1JH)
    Ambassador: Arkady Józef Rzegocki.

Of the United Kingdom in Poland (ul. Kawalerii 12, 00-468, Warsaw)
    Ambassador: Jonathan Knott.

Of Poland in the USA (2640 16th St., NW, Washington, D.C., 20009)
    Ambassador: Piotr Antoni Wilczek.

Of the USA in Poland (Aleje Ujazdowskie 29/31, 00-540 Warsaw)
    Ambassador: Georgette Mosbacher.

Of Poland to the United Nations
    Ambassador: Joanna Wronecka.

Of Poland to the European Union
    Permanent Representative: Vacant.
    Chargé d'Affaires a.i: Andrzej Sadoś.

Further Reading

Central Statistical Office, *Rocznik Statystyczny.* Annual—*Concise Statistical Yearbook of Poland*—*Statistical Bulletin.* Monthly
Biskupski, M. B., *The History of Poland.* 2000
Chodakiewicz, Marek Jan, *Poland's Transformation: A Work in Progress.* 2006
Kochanski, Halik, *The Eagle Unbowed: Poland and the Poles in the Second World War.* 2012
Lukowski, Jerzy and Zawadzki, Hubert, *A Concise History of Poland.* 2001
Prazmowska, Anita J., *History of Poland.* 2nd ed. 2011.—*Poland: A Modern History.* 2010
Ramet, Sabrina P., *The Catholic Church in Polish History.* 2017
Sikorski, R., *The Polish House: An Intimate History of Poland.* 1997; US title: *Full Circle.* 1997
Slay, B., *The Polish Economy: Crisis, Reform and Transformation.* 1994
Staar, R. F. (ed.) *Transition to Democracy in Poland.* 1993
Wedel, J., *The Unplanned Society: Poland During and After Communism.* 1992
Zając, Justyna, *Poland's Security Policy: The West, Russia, and the Changing International Order.* 2016
Zamoyski, Adam, *Poland: A History.* 2009
National library: Biblioteka Narodowa, al. Niepodległości 213, 02-086 Warsaw.
National Statistical Office: Central Statistical Office, Aleje Niepodległości 208, 00-925 Warsaw.
Website: http://www.stat.gov.pl

Portugal

República Portuguesa (Republic of Portugal)

Capital: Lisbon
Population projection, 2020: 10·22m.
GNI per capita, 2017: (PPP$) 27,315
HDI/world rank, 2017: 0·847/41=
Internet domain extension: .pt

Key Historical Events

The western fringe of the Iberian peninsula was inhabited from 8000 BC by Neolithic peoples known as Iberians. Celtic tribes settled in the north and west of the peninsula in the first millennium BC with Phoenician settlements in the southwest around Cádiz from around 800 BC. From 241 BC the Iberian peninsula came under the influence of Carthage, and then Rome after 206 BC. The Romans made their way north to what is now central Portugal and clashed with a Celtic federation, the Lusitanians. They resisted the Roman advance under their leader Viriathus until he was killed in 140 BC, after which the Romans were able to move north across the Douro river. In 25 BC Augustus founded Augustus Emirita (now Mérida) as the capital of Lusitania.

From AD 409, with the Roman Empire in decline, the Iberian Peninsula was invaded by Germanic tribes from central Europe, including the Suevi and Visigoths, who established Christian kingdoms. Southern Galicia was settled by the Suevi, who were converted to Christianity by St Martin of Braga in around AD 550. Following the arrival of Muslim armies in Iberia in 711, the southern part of what is now Portugal became part of the Muslim dominion of al-Andalus. The northern and western fringes of Iberia remained largely agrarian, poor and Christian.

From 850 the Christians began to push southward: the region between the rivers Minho and Douro became known as Territorium Portugualense and was ruled by Mumadona Dias after 931. Fernando I, King of Castile, drove the Muslims from the city of Viseu in 1058 and reconquered Coimbra in 1064. Fernando's successor, Afonso VI of Leon, set up his power base in the town of Braga. His daughter, Teresa, who was married to Henry of Burgundy, then governed Portugal as regent for their son, Afonso Henriques. Teresa eventually lost the support of many of the powerful local barons, who united behind Afonso and made him the first king of Portugal in 1139.

Muslim chroniclers refer to Afonso I as 'the cursed of Allah'. He crusaded southwards through the Muslim strongholds, capturing Lisbon in 1147. However, the Portuguese reconquest was not completed for 150 years, when Afonso III finally took Algarve in the far south. Afonso III established the first *Cortes* (government) at Leiria in 1254. Large swathes of the newly conquered lands were given over to the army and monastic orders to ensure their protection. Afonso's son, Dinis (1279–1325), became one of the most celebrated of the Burgundian dynasty. He established trade links with other European powers and in 1317 worked with a Genoese admiral to establish a navy. Dinis made the vernacular, rather than Latin, the official language and founded the first university in Lisbon in 1290.

The later kings of the House of Burgundy were entangled in various marriage alliances with neighbouring Castile. Fernando I (1367–83) inherited the Portuguese crown as a battle raged in Castile between King Pedro 'the Cruel' and his half-brother Enrique de Trastámara. Both sides attempted to garner support from outside the kingdom, with the English supporting Pedro (Peter) and his heirs and the French backing Enrique (Henry) and his supporters. Enrique eventually prevailed, being crowned Enrique II of Castile in 1369. The new king offered his support to Fernando, who accepted, and Castilian rule was duly established in Portugal.

After Fernando's heiress, Beatriz, married Juan I of Castile the nobility broadly supported Castilian rule but Portugal's coastal towns wanted independence and rebelled. Their choice for ruler was João of Avis, half brother of Fernando, who was declared King João I in 1384. A year later, with English support, the Portuguese defeated Juan I and his Castilian army at the battle of Aljbarrota. The Anglo–Portuguese alliance was cemented by King João's marriage in 1387 to Philippa of Lancaster, sister of England's future King Henry IV.

Empire Building

Having made peace with Spain, João turned his attention overseas. The capture of the town of Ceuta on the north African coast in 1415 was the beginning of an era of discovery by Portuguese mariners, spearheaded by João's third son Henry who became known as Henry the Navigator. He founded a school of navigation at Sagres and organized numerous expeditions along the west coast of Africa. Madeira and the Azores were also discovered and settled during this period.

Relations with Castile deteriorated in the reign of Afonso V (1438–81). Afonso married Juana, daughter of Enrique IV of Castile, and laid claim to the Castilian throne. The marriage of Fernando II and Isabella I of Castile and the merging of the powerful kingdoms of Aragon and Castile, weakened Afonso's claim. There were lengthy battles in the Zamora and Toro regions, which Afonso lost in 1476. Peace was made three years later by Afonso's heir, João II. Overseas explorations were resumed, and Portugal became a haven for tens of thousands of Jews fleeing persecution in Spain.

In 1487 Bartolomeu Dias rounded the southern cape of Africa, but the Portuguese crown rejected Christopher Columbus's proposal for finding a new westward route to the Indies. Backed instead by Fernando II and Isabella I of Castile, he reached the New World in 1492. The 1493 Treaty of Tordesillas gave the newly unified Spain all lands west of a vertical line drawn 370 degrees west of the Cabo Verde Islands. Land to the east, including Brazil, went to Portugal. In 1497, with backing from King Manuel I, Vasco da Gama set out to map a sea route to India. Indian spices were used for preserving food, in the preparation of medicines and in glues, perfumes, dyes and varnishes. The Portuguese built an administrative capital at Goa and by 1550 it was considered Portugal's second city.

Fortified trading posts were later established along the coast of East Africa and India, and commercial centres set up further east. The profits generated by the spice trade made Manuel I 'the Fortunate' one of the wealthiest rulers in Europe. No longer dependent on taxes, Manuel was able to rule independently. The *Cortes* did not meet between 1502–25 and the expulsion of the Jews in 1496 (a condition of Manuel's marriage to Princess Isabella of Castile, daughter of Isabella I) dealt a heavy blow to the economy.

In 1568 King Sebastião launched a disastrous crusade to eradicate Islam in the Maghreb. More than 10,000 Portuguese troops, including Sebastião, were killed by superior Moroccan forces. After the death of the elderly and childless Cardinal Henrique, the line of succession passed to the cardinal's nephew, Felipe II of Spain.

Spanish Rule

Felipe II annexed Portugal in 1580. The Spanish empire was at its height and Portuguese merchants saw commercial advantages in forming an alliance with Spain. Portugal was granted autonomy but this was gradually eroded. The Inquisition was established in Portugal and the ports of Lisbon and Porto (Oporto) were closed to English and Dutch ships, which then made their own way to the east and snatched control of the spice trade. The 'Spanish domination' of Portugal lasted for 60 years, though after 1621 Spain was considerably weakened by the cost of defending its empire against France and England. A rebellion in Catalonia spurred the Portuguese to stage their own revolution. They rallied round the duke of Bragança, who was crowned King João IV in 1640.

João IV was anxious to formalize new alliances with the other European powers. Spain's peace with France, set out in the 1659 Treaty of the Pyrenees, made João's successor, Afonso VI, anxious to strengthen Portugal's alliance with England. Thus, Catherine of Bragança was married to King Charles II in 1662. Her dowry included the right to trade with the Portuguese colonies and the cession of Bombay and Tangier. In return, England agreed to defend Portugal and its colonies. In the late 1600s gold and then diamonds were discovered in Brazil. Money poured into the Portuguese court, but the crown's wealth did little to enrich the nation. João V (1706–50) emulated

Louis XIV of France's lavish spending on ambitious building projects, including a gigantic convent-palace at Mafra.

Portuguese political development lagged behind that of many European states and it remained comparatively untouched by the Enlightenment until the Marquess of Pombal was made chief minister shortly after the great Lisbon earthquake in 1755. His methods were harsh and he made enemies quickly. His principal victims were the conservative Jesuits and the nobility with their vast array of privileges. Pombal is also credited with reforming the education system but ultimately his legacy was limited. When Maria I came to the throne in 1777, she immediately banished Pombal to his estates and rescinded many of his reforms.

After Louis XVI of France was guillotined in 1793, the new French Republic invaded Catalonia and the Basque provinces. Following these defeats, King Charles IV of Spain formed an alliance with Napoleon. In 1801 France and Spain demanded that Portugal abandon its alliance with Britain, open its ports to French and Spanish shipping and hand over some of its colonies to Spain. Portugal refused and a French army marched into Lisbon in 1807. King João VI and his family escaped to Brazil with the help of the British navy and the defence of Portugal was left in the hands of British Generals Wellesley and Beresford. The French were finally driven out of Portugal in 1811 and the British, as a reward, were granted free access to the Brazilian ports, a concession which damaged the Portuguese economy and stoked-up popular resentment.

After an army-backed revolution in Porto in 1820, an unofficial *Cortes* was set up to devise a new liberal constitution. The *Cortes* was to be a single chamber parliament elected by universal male suffrage, and feudal and clerical rights would be abolished. Returning from Brazil the following year, João VI accepted the new constitution. Brazil declared its independence, with Pedro IV (João's elder son) as emperor.

Following João's death in 1826, Pedro became king of Portugal in defiance of the Brazilian constitution. Forced to abdicate in favour of his daughter, Maria II, then aged seven, he chose his brother Miguel as her steward. Miguel seized the throne in 1828, defeating the liberals and repealing Pedro's constitution. Pedro IV returned to Portugal in 1832 to lead the liberals in the Miguelist Wars. Maria was eventually restored to the throne. The late 1850s saw improvements in the nation's infrastructure but by the start of the reign of Carlos I in 1889, Portugal's economy was in a poor way. Explorations in Africa strengthened Portugal's hold on Angola and Mozambique but the British refused to give up territory which would have linked the two colonies. Carlos attempted to end inefficiency and corruption, establishing a dictatorship in 1906 under the conservative João Franco. Amidst growing public discontent, Carlos and his eldest son Prince Luís Filipe were assassinated in 1908. Manuel II succeeded to the throne but in 1910 a republican revolution forced his abdication and flight to Britain.

In the First World War Portugal was at first neutral, then joined the Allies in 1916. The economy deteriorated further and in 1926 there was a military coup. Gen. Carmona became president. António de Oliveira Salazar was made finance minister in 1928 with a brief to reform the economy.

Dictatorship to Democracy

Salazar became prime minister in 1932. His *Estado Novo* (New State) had a strongly nationalist and dictatorial flavour. Political parties, unions and strikes were abolished and dissent was crushed by the notorious PIDE (Polícia Internacional e de Defesa do Estado) secret police force. Portugal was neutral in the Second World War but allowed the Allies to establish naval and air bases. After Goa was seized by India in 1961, Salazar was determined to cling on to the African territories. By 1968, over 100,000 Portuguese were fighting independence movements in Angola, Guinea-Bissau and Mozambique.

In 1968 Salazar suffered a stroke and was replaced by Marcello Caetano. Under Caetano repression was eased but the unpopular wars in Africa continued. In 1974, amid mounting public discontent, a group of officers formed the Movement of Armed Forces and toppled the government in a bloodless coup in April that year known as 'the Carnation Revolution'. Gen. António de Spínola was appointed head of the ruling military junta. The secret police force was abolished. All political prisoners were released; full civil liberties, including freedom of the press and of all political parties, were restored and, in 1975, Angola, Mozambique, São Tomé and Príncipe and Cabo Verde were granted independence. Timor-Leste was forcibly taken by Indonesia. Following an attempted revolt in late 1975, the military junta was dissolved and a Supreme Revolutionary Council ruled until a new constitutional government resumed the following year. During the late 1970s several

moderate, Socialist-dominated governments tried unsuccessfully to stabilize the country. In 1982 a centre-right coalition revised the constitution, reducing presidential power and the right of the military to intervene in politics. From 1983 to 1985 a coalition government under Socialist leader Mário Soares made progress in reducing the chaos and poverty that were the legacy of Salazar's long dictatorship.

In 1985 the centrist Social Democratic party under Aníbal Cavaco Silva won an undisputed majority in parliament. In 1986 Soares was elected to the presidency, and Portugal was admitted to the European Community. Political stability and economic reforms created a favourable business climate, especially for renewed foreign investment, and Portugal became one of the fastest-growing economies in Europe. The Socialists returned to power as a minority government after the 1995 parliamentary elections. Macao, Portugal's colony on the south coast of China, was handed back to China in 1999. Portugal joined the single European currency in 2001. In Jan. 2006 the centre-right candidate Aníbal Cavaco Silva was elected president, beginning a period of political 'cohabitation' alongside the Socialist prime minister, Jóse Sócrates. In March 2011, following an appeal to the EU for assistance to avoid a debt default, the government resigned.

Territory and Population

Mainland Portugal is bounded in the north and east by Spain and south and west by the Atlantic Ocean. The Atlantic archipelagoes of the Azores and of Madeira form autonomous but integral parts of the republic, which has a total area of 92,207 sq. km. Population (2011 census), 10,562,178 (5,515,578 females). In Dec. 2017 the population was estimated at 10,291,027, with the decline a consequence of emigration outstripping immigration and deaths exceeding births since the 2011 census was taken. There were 134,624 emigrants in 2014, the most in any single year.

Mainland Portugal is divided into five regions. At the 2011 census the regions, with their populations, were: North (3,689,682); Central (2,327,755); Lisbon (2,821,876); Alentejo (757,302); Algarve (451,006). Population of the Azores, 246,772; Madeira, 267,785. Density (2011), 114·5 per sq. km (North, 173; Central, 83; Lisbon, 940; Alentejo, 24; Algarve, 90; Azores, 106; Madeira, 334).

The UN gives a projected population for 2020 of 10·22m.

In 2011, 61·3% of the population lived in urban areas. The populations of the districts and Autonomous Regions (2011 census):

Areas	Population
North	*3,689,682*
Alto Trás-os-Montes	204,381
Ave	511,737
Cávado	410,169
Douro	205,902
Entre Douro e Vouga	274,859
Grande Porto	1,287,282
Minho-Lima	244,836
Tâmega	550,516
Central	*2,327,755*
Baixo Mondego	332,326
Baixo Vouga	390,822
Beira Interior Norte	104,417
Beira Interior Sul	75,028
Cova da Beira	87,869
Dão-Lafões	277,240
Médio Tejo	220,661
Oeste	362,540
Pinhal Interior Norte	131,468
Pinhal Interior Sul	40,705
Pinhal Litoral	260,942
Serra da Estrela	43,737
Lisbon	*2,821,876*
Grande Lisboa	2,042,477
Península de Setúbal	779,399

(continued)

Areas	Population
Alentejo	*757,302*
Alentejo Central	166,822
Alentejo Litoral	97,925
Alto Alentejo	118,410
Baixo Alentejo	126,692
Lezíria do Tejo	247,453
Algarve	*451,006*

In 2010 there were 443,055 foreign citizens with legal residency status, with the leading nationalities as follows: Brazil, 119,195; Ukraine, 49,487, Cabo Verde, 43,510; Romania, 36,830; Angola, 23,233; Guinea-Bissau, 19,304. Large numbers of immigrants have come to Portugal from Eastern Europe since 1999, mainly from Ukraine, Romania and Moldova.

The capital is Lisbon (Lisboa), with a population of 547,733 in 2011 (metropolitan area population, 2,821,876 in 2011). Other major cities are Porto, 237,591 in 2011 (metropolitan area population, 1,672,670 in 2011), Almada, Amadora, Braga, Funchal (in Madeira) and Vila Nova de Gaia.

The official language is Portuguese.

The Azores islands lie in the mid-Atlantic Ocean, between 1,200 and 1,600 km west of Lisbon. They are divided into three widely separated groups with clear channels between, São Miguel (759 sq. km) together with Santa Maria (97 sq. km) being the most easterly; about 160 km northwest of them lies the central cluster of Terceira (382 sq. km), Graciosa (62 sq. km), São Jorge (246 sq. km), Pico (446 sq. km) and Faial (173 sq. km); still another 240 km to the northwest are Flores (143 sq. km) and Corvo (17 sq. km), the latter being the most isolated and undeveloped of the islands. São Miguel contains over half the total population of the archipelago.

Madeira comprises the island of Madeira (745 sq. km), containing the capital, Funchal; the smaller island of Porto Santo (40 sq. km), lying 46 km to the northeast of Madeira; and two groups of uninhabited islets, Ilhas Desertas (15 sq. km), being 20 km southeast of Funchal, and Ilhas Selvagens (4 sq. km), near the Canaries.

Social Statistics

2012: births, 89,841; deaths, 107,612; marriages, 34,423; divorces, 25,380. Rates per 1,000 population in 2012: birth, 8·5; death, 10·2; marriage, 3·3; divorce, 2·4. Annual population growth rate, 2005–10, 0·2%. Expectation of life at birth, 2013, was 76·9 years for males and 82·9 years for females. Infant mortality in 2010 was three per 1,000 live births, down from 77 per 1,000 live births in 1960, representing the greatest reduction in infant mortality rates in Europe over the past half century. Fertility rate, 2013, 1·3 births per woman (the joint lowest in the world). Around one in five babies are born outside marriage, up from one in 14 in 1970. In 2009 the most popular age range for marrying was 25–29 for both males and females. Portugal legalized same-sex marriage in June 2010.

On 11 Feb. 2007 a national referendum was held on whether to decriminalize abortion up until the 10th week of pregnancy. Turnout was low at 44%; 59·3% of voters approved the motion. Despite results only having to be legally binding if the turnout exceeded 50%, parliament voted overwhelmingly in favour on 9 March 2007. In 1998 the same question had been put in another referendum. 51% voted against the motion; turnout was 32%.

In 2010 Portugal received 160 asylum applications.

Climate

Because of westerly winds and the effect of the Gulf Stream, the climate ranges from the cool, damp Atlantic type in the north to a warmer and drier Mediterranean type in the south. July and Aug. are virtually rainless everywhere. Inland areas in the north have greater temperature variation, with continental winds blowing from the interior. Lisbon, Jan. 52°F (11°C), July 72°F (22°C). Annual rainfall 27·4" (686 mm). Porto, Jan. 48°F (8·9°C), July 67°F (19·4°C). Annual rainfall 46" (1,151 mm).

Constitution and Government

Portugal is governed under the constitution of April 1976, amended in 1982, 1989, 1992, 1997, 2001, 2004 and 2005. The 1982 revision abolished the (military) Council of the Revolution and reduced the role of the President under it. Portugal is a sovereign, unitary republic. Executive power is vested in the *President*, directly elected for a five-year term (for a maximum of two consecutive terms). Political parties may support a candidate in presidential elections but not actually field a candidate. The President appoints a Prime Minister and, upon the latter's nomination, other members of the Council of Ministers.

The 230-member *National Assembly* is a unicameral legislature elected for four-year terms by universal adult suffrage under a system of proportional representation. Women did not have the vote until 1976.

National Anthem

'Herois do mar, nobre povo' ('Heroes of the sea, noble breed'); words by Lopes de Mendonça, tune by Alfredo Keil.

Government Chronology

(PS = Socialist Party; PSD = Social Democratic Party; UN = National Union; n/p = non-partisan)

Presidents since 1926.

1926–51	UN/military	António (Óscar de) Fragoso Carmona
1951–58	UN/military	Francisco (Higino de) Craveiro Lopes
1958–74	UN/military	Américo (de Deus Rodrigues) Thomaz
1974		National Salvation Junta (all military)
1974	military	António (Sebastião Ribeiro) de Spínola
1974–76	military	Francisco da Costa Gomes
1976–86	military, n/p	(António dos Santos) Ramalho Eanes
1986–96	PS	Mário (Alberto Nobre Lopes) Soares
1996–2006	PS	Jorge (Fernando Branco de) Sampaio
2006–16	PSD	Aníbal (António) Cavaco Silva
2016–	PSD	Marcelo (Nuno Duarte) Rebelo de Sousa

Prime Ministers since 1932.

1932–68	UN	António de Oliveira Salazar
1968–74	UN	Marcello (das Neves Alves) Caetano
1974	n/p	Adelino da Palma Carlos
1974–75	military	Vasco (dos Santos) Gonçalves
1975–76	military	José (Batista) Pinheiro de Azevedo
1976–78	PS	Mário (Alberto Nobre Lopes) Soares
1978	n/p	Alfredo (Jorge) Nobre da Costa
1978–79	n/p	Carlos (Alberto) da Mota Pinto
1980	PSD	Francisco (Manuel Lumbrales de) Sá Carneiro
1981–83	PSD	Francisco (José Pereira) Pinto Balsemão
1983–85	PS	Mário (Alberto Nobre Lopes) Soares
1985–95	PSD	Aníbal (António) Cavaco Silva
1995–2002	PS	António (Manuel de Oliveira) Guterres
2002–04	PSD	José Manuel Durão Barroso
2004–05	PSD	Pedro (Miguel de) Santana Lopes
2005–11	PS	José Sócrates (Carvalho Pinto de Sousa)
2011–15	PSD	Pedro (Manuel Mamede) Passos Coelho
2015–	PS	António (Luís Santos da) Costa

Recent Elections

At the presidential elections of 24 Jan. 2016 Marcelo Rebelo de Sousa (Social Democratic Party) won 52·0% of the vote, António Sampaio da Nóvoa (ind.) 22·9%, Marisa Matias (Left Bloc) 10·1%, Maria de Belém (ind.) 4·2%, Edgar Silva (Communist Party) 4·0%, Vitorino Silva (ind.) 3·3% and Paulo de Morais (ind.) 2·2%. Three other independent candidates took less than 1% of the vote each. Turnout was 48·7%.

At the parliamentary elections of 4 Oct. 2015 the Portugal Ahead alliance formed by the Social Democratic Party (PSD) and the CDS–People's Party (CDS–PP) won 102 seats (36·9% of votes cast); the Socialist Party (PS), 86 (32·3%); the Left Bloc, 19 (10·2%); the Democratic Unity Coalition (CDU), 17 (8·3%); the Social Democratic Party, 5 in Madeira and the Azores (1·5%); People–Animals–Nature (PAN), 1 (1·4%). Turnout was 55·9%.

European Parliament

Portugal has 21 representatives. At the May 2014 elections turnout was 33·8% (36·8% in 2009). The PS won 8 seats with 31·5% of votes cast (political affiliation in European Parliament: Progressive Alliance of Socialists and Democrats); the Portugal Alliance (PSD and CDS–PP), 7 with 27·7% (European People's Party); CDU, 3 with 12·7% (European United Left/Nordic Green Left); the Earth Party, 2 with 7·1% (Alliance of Liberals and Democrats for Europe); the Left Bloc, 1 with 4·6% (European United Left/Nordic Green Left).

Current Government

President: Marcelo Rebelo de Sousa; b. 1948 (PSD; sworn in 9 March 2016).
   In Feb. 2019 the coalition government comprised:
   Prime Minister: António Costa; b. 1961 (PS; sworn in 26 Nov. 2015).
   Minister of Agriculture, Forestry and Rural Development: Luís Capoulas Santos. *Culture:* Graça Fonseca. *Economy:* Pedro Siza Vieira. *Education:* Tiago Brandão Rodrigues. *Environment:* João Pedro Matos Fernandes. *Finance:* Mário Centeno. *Foreign Affairs:* Augusto Santos Silva. *Health:* Marta Temido. *Internal Administration:* Eduardo Cabrita. *Justice:* Francisca Van Dunem. *Labour, Solidarity and Social Security:* José António Vieira da Silva. *National Defence:* João Gomes Cravinho. *Planning and Infrastructure:* Pedro Marques. *Presidency, and Administrative Modernization:* Maria Manuel Leitão Marques. *Science, Technology and Higher Education:* Manuel Heitor. *Sea:* Ana Paula Vitorino.
   Government Website (Portuguese only): https://www.portugal.gov.pt

Current Leaders

Marcelo Rebelo de Sousa
Position
President

Introduction
A lawyer and centre-right politician, Marcelo Rebelo de Sousa has been best known in Portugal for his work as a political commentator on major TV networks. His election in 2016 to the largely ceremonial post of president came only months after the unexpected establishment of a Socialist-led coalition government.

Early Life
Marcelo Duarte Nuno Rebelo de Sousa was born in Lisbon on 12 Dec. 1948. He graduated in law from the University of Lisbon in 1971, specializing in administrative law. Active in the centre-right Social Democratic Party (PSD), he was first elected to the National Assembly in 1980, serving in the government led by Francisco Pinto Balsemão.
   Briefly minister of parliamentary affairs in the early 1980s, he turned to journalism following defeat in the 1983 election. He co-founded the *Expresso* newspaper with Pinto Balsemão, while also developing a reputation as a political commentator on radio. Elected leader of the PSD in 1996, de Sousa became the *de facto* leader of the opposition to the Socialist Party led by António Guterres. A centre-right coalition with the People's Party (PP) that began in 1998 proved short-lived, with de Sousa resigning a year later amid mounting tensions with the PP leader, Paulo Portas.
   Subsequently, de Sousa continued to work as a political commentator, appearing regularly on both public and private TV networks. He was meanwhile a professor of law at the Portuguese Catholic University and also taught at the New University of Lisbon. In Oct. 2015 he declared his intention to run for the presidency. He emerged victorious from the election on 24 Jan. 2016, taking 52·0% of the vote, well ahead of his centre-left rival, António Sampaio de Nóvoa.

Career in Office
De Sousa was sworn in as president on 9 March 2016. He promised to serve as a mediator between the opposing factions in parliament and to focus on improving the economy.

António Costa
Position
Prime Minister

Introduction
On 26 Nov. 2015 António Costa was appointed the first Communist-backed Socialist prime minister of Portugal since the Salazar dictatorship was overthrown in 1974. The lawyer and former mayor of Lisbon promised to 'turn the page on austerity'.

Early Life
António Costa was born on 17 July 1961 in Lisbon, the son of an eminent writer, Orlando da Costa. His mother was a journalist and women's rights advocate. He studied law at Lisbon University in the early 1980s and briefly practised as a solicitor. Elected to Lisbon's municipal council in 1982 for the Socialist Party, he developed his political profile and won a seat at the legislative elections of Oct. 1991.
   Costa was named minister of parliamentary affairs in the Socialist government of António Guterres, serving from 1997 until 1999. He was then justice minister until April 2002, after which a spell in the European Parliament followed from 2004–05. He returned to national politics as interior minister in José Sócrates's first government from March 2005, when he gained a reputation as a key ally of the prime minister. He left the interior ministry in May 2007 to contest Lisbon's mayoral election. Having won, he helped to reinvigorate the city as a tourist destination and to stabilize its finances. He was re-elected in 2009 and 2013.
   In Sept. 2014 Costa challenged António José Seguro for the Socialist Party leadership and subsequently won the election with 68% of the vote. The general election on 4 Oct. 2015 was closely fought, after which then President Aníbal Cavaco Silva asked a centre-right coalition of the Social Democratic Party and the CDS–People's Party to form a government despite not having a working majority. Costa—in alliance with the Communist, Green and Left Bloc parties—passed a vote of no confidence in the new government, toppling it within two weeks. Costa was then chosen by the president as the next premier and took office on 26 Nov. 2015.

Career in Office
Costa promised to temper the effects of the previous administration's austerity policies, raise the minimum wage, lift a freeze on pensions and cancel pay cuts for civil servants, while meeting the country's international commitments on its budget and debts. He has faced a tough challenge in keeping his fragile alliance united, particularly in the wake of the country's emergence from the €78bn. international financial bailout arranged in 2011 and EU demands for effective action to correct Portugal's excessive budget deficit.
   In 2017 Portugal suffered its most damaging wildfires in living memory, killing over 100 people. In Oct. criticism of the government's perceived weak response to the outbreaks prompted the replacement of the interior minister and also a no-confidence motion in parliament, which Costa survived by 122 votes to 105.

Defence

Conscription was abolished in Nov. 2004. Portugal now has a purely professional army.
   In 2013 defence expenditure totalled US$2,773m. (US$257 per capita), representing 1·3% of GDP.

Army
Strength (2011) 25,701. There are Army reserves totalling 210,000. Paramilitary forces include the National Republican Guard (26,100) and the Public Security Police (21,600).

Navy
In 2011 the combatant fleet comprised two German-built attack submarines, five frigates and seven corvettes. Naval personnel in 2011 totalled 9,715 including 1,563 marines. There were also 1,267 naval reserves.

Air Force
The Air Force in 2011 had a strength of 7,218. There were 43 combat-capable aircraft (mainly F-16s).

Economy

Services accounted for 76·0% of GDP in 2012, industry 21·8% and agriculture 2·2%.

Overview

Since the 1980s Portugal's economy has become increasingly dependent on services, which now account for around three-quarters of GDP annually. Low productivity, weak competitiveness and high corporate debt have meanwhile hindered growth and led to high fiscal imbalances. The country suffered badly as a result of the global recession from 2008 and the accompanying eurozone debt crisis. The economy recorded average annual growth of less than 1% in the period 2004–14 and in 2013 unemployment, at 16·5%, was among the highest in the eurozone.

In April 2011 the government applied to the European Commission for financial assistance to avoid a debt default. The Extended Fund Facility for Portugal was agreed the following month, providing €78bn. (US$116bn.) over three years, funded by the European Union, the European Central Bank and the International Monetary Fund (IMF). To meet the terms of the bailout, income tax rose from 24·5% to 28·5% with effect from Jan. 2013, with a resulting squeeze on living standards and reduced consumer spending. The government also undertook a 'fire sale' of €5bn. worth of state assets to foreign investors. This resulted, for instance, in the sale of 21% of the utility company Energias de Portugal and 25% of the state electricity grid.

The economy has since rebounded, recording real GDP growth of 2·8% in 2017 reflecting strong investment (particularly in construction), robust exports and stable domestic consumption. Tourism growth has also been strong, despite the sector facing capacity constraints. Unemployment fell from 10·1% in Dec. 2016 to 7·1% in April 2018, even as labour force participation was rising, owing to broad-based employment growth.

Inflation was measured at 2% year-on-year in June 2018 and the government deficit was under its target of 2% of GDP in 2017—its lowest level in 40 years. Nonetheless, the banking system remains fragile and persistent high levels of corporate and household debt, high unemployment, rising energy prices and uncertainties in the eurozone also still pose risks. To secure long-term prosperity, the IMF recommends an 8·5% annual increase in productivity investment, although the rate stood at only 4·9% in 2017.

Currency

On 1 Jan. 1999 the *euro* (EUR) became the legal currency in Portugal at the irrevocable conversion rate of 200·482 escudos to 1 euro. The euro, which consists of 100 cents, has been in circulation since 1 Jan. 2002. On the introduction of the euro there was a 'dual circulation' period before the escudo ceased to be legal tender on 28 Feb. 2002.

Inflation rates (based on OECD statistics):

2008	2009	2010	2011	2012	2013	2014	2015	2016	2017
2·7%	−0·9%	1·4%	3·6%	2·8%	0·4%	−0·2%	0·5%	0·6%	1·6%

Gold reserves were 12·30m. troy oz in Sept. 2009 and foreign exchange reserves US$774m. Total money supply was €52,659m. in Aug. 2009.

Budget

In 2011 central government revenues totalled €69,222m. and expenditures €75,387m. Taxes accounted for 53·0% of revenues in 2011 and social contributions 29·4%; social benefits accounted for 48·1% of expenditures and compensation of employees 21·1%.

Portugal's budget deficit in 2017 was 3·0% of GDP (2016, 2·0%; 2015, 4·4%). The required target set by the EU is a budget deficit of no more than 3%.

The standard rate of VAT is 23·0% (reduced rates, 13% and 6%).

Performance

Real GDP growth rates (based on OECD statistics):

2008	2009	2010	2011	2012	2013	2014	2015	2016	2017
0·2%	−3·0%	1·9%	−1·8%	−4·0%	−1·1%	0·9%	1·8%	1·9%	2·8%

In the years since Portugal joined the European Union its GDP per head has risen from being 53% of the EU average to 80% in 2010. Portugal's total GDP in 2017 was US$217·6bn.

Banking and Finance

The central bank and bank of issue is the Bank of Portugal, founded in 1846 and nationalized in 1974. Its *Governor* is Carlos Costa.

In 2006 there were 5,039 branches of banks and savings banks and 676 branches of agricultural credit co-operatives. Deposits in all monetary establishments totalled €146·7bn. in 2006. The largest Portuguese bank is the state-owned Caixa Geral de Depósitos, with assets of €111·1bn. in 2008. Other major banks are Banco Comercial Português, Banco Santander Totta and Banco Português de Investimento.

Gross external debt amounted to US$485,816m. in June 2012.

There are stock exchanges in Lisbon and Porto.

Energy and Natural Resources

In 2011, 24·9% of energy consumption came from renewables (wind power, solar power, hydro-electric power, tidal power, geothermal energy and biomass), compared to the European Union average of 13·0%. A target of 31% has been set by the EU for 2020.

Environment

Portugal's carbon dioxide emissions from the consumption of energy in 2011 were the equivalent of 4·9 tonnes per capita.

Electricity

Installed capacity was 19·9m. kW in 2011. Production in 2011 was 52·46bn. kWh; consumption per capita was 5,216 kWh.

Minerals

Portugal possesses considerable mineral wealth. Production in tonnes (2005): limestone, marl and calcite, 51,025,000; granite (2006), 27,489,000; marble, 752,000; salt, 597,945; kaolin, 164,072; copper, 89,541; tungsten, 816.

Agriculture

There were 274,563 agricultural holdings in 2007. The agricultural sector employs 11·6% of the workforce. In 2007 there were 1·08m. ha. of arable land and 796,000 ha. of permanent crops.

The following figures show the production (in 1,000 tonnes) of the chief crops:

Crop	2005	2006	2007
Cabbages, Brussels sprouts, etc.[1]	200	145	150
Carrots and turnips[1]	150	160	170
Fruits			
Oranges	218	234	211
Apples	252	258	247
Grapes	989	1,029	822
Pears	130	175	141
Lettuce and chicory[1]	95	100	100
Maize	511	535	605
Olive oil[2]	318	518	353
Olives	212	373	375[1]
Onions[1]	118	118	121
Potatoes	570	611	657
Rice	120	149	156
Sugar beets	605	320	254
Tomatoes	1,085	983	1,236
Wheat	82	250	102
Wine[2]	7,064	7,338	5,842

[1]Estimates.
[2]In 1,000 hectolitres.

Livestock (1,000 head):

	2005	2006	2007
Cattle	1,441	1,407	1,443
Goats	551	547	509
Pigs	2,344	2,295	2,374
Sheep	3,583	3,549	3,356
Poultry[1]	42,000	43,200	44,500

[1]Estimates.

Animal products in 2007 (1,000 tonnes): meat, 844·8; eggs, 121·6; cheese, 79·5; milk, 2,029m. litres.

Forestry

Forests covered 3·18m. ha. (35% of the land area) in 2015. Portugal is the world's largest producer of cork, averaging 157,000 tonnes annually. Timber production was 10·96m. cu. metres in 2011.

Fisheries

The fishing industry is important, although much less so than in the past, and the Portuguese eat more fish per person than in any other European Union member country (more than twice the EU average). The catch was 197,817 tonnes in 2012 (almost exclusively from marine waters). In the same year the fishing fleet consisted of 8,291 vessels totalling 100,670 GT. Imports of fishery commodities were valued at US$2,027m. in 2011 and exports at US$1,082m.

Industry

The leading companies by market capitalization in Portugal in May 2018 were: Galp Energia (US$17·0bn.); EDP Energias de Portugal, an electricity company (US$13·5bn.); and Jerónimo Martins, a food distribution group (US$10·3bn.).

In 2014 industry accounted for 21·5% of GDP, with manufacturing contributing 13·3%. Manufacturing output grew by 2·2% in 2014. Major industries are: chemicals; clothing, textiles and footwear; fish canning; food processing; metal working; oil refining; and wood pulp, paper and cork.

Labour

The labour force in 2013 was 5,397,000 (5,463,000 in 2003). 73·6% of the population aged 15–64 was economically active in 2013. Of those in employment in 2013, 68·5% worked in services, 24·9% in industry and 6·6% in agriculture. Employment is higher among foreign-born persons than among native-born persons, with 66·6% of the foreign-born population between 15 and 64 in employment compared to only 62·2% of the native-born population in the same age group. In Dec. 2018 the unemployment rate was 6·7%, down from 9·0% in 2017 as a whole. A minimum wage is fixed by the government. In 2011 the minimum wage was €485 a month. Retirement is at 65 years for men and 62 for women.

International Trade

Imports and Exports

In 2010 imports (c.i.f.) totalled US$75,573m. (US$69,985m. in 2009); exports (f.o.b.), US$48,744m. (US$43,397m. in 2009).

In 2010 main import sources (in US$1m.) were: Spain (23,557); Germany (10,460); France (5,466); Italy (4,292); Netherlands (3,866). Main export markets in 2010 (in US$1m.) were: Spain (12,917); Germany (6,262); France (5,729); UK (2,656); Angola (2,533).

Principal imports in 2010 (in US$1m.) were: machinery and transport equipment (22,828); manufactured goods (11,294); mineral fuels, lubricants and related materials (11,026); chemicals and chemical products (9,481); food (8,392). Principal exports in 2010 (in US$1m.) were: machinery and transport equipment (13,225); manufactured goods (10,871); miscellaneous manufactured articles including articles of apparel, clothing accessories and footwear (8,037); chemicals and chemical products (4,030); food (3,411).

Communications

Roads

In 2005 there were 2,613 km of motorways, 5,883 km of national roads, 4,406 km of secondary roads and 63,900 km of other roads. In 2006 the number of vehicles registered included 5,234,500 passenger cars, 535,300 motorcycles and mopeds, 119,000 lorries and vans and 29,700 buses and coaches. In 2007 there were 854 deaths in road accidents.

Rail

In 2011 total railway length was 2,794 km. Passenger-km travelled in 2011 came to 3·75bn. and freight tonne-km to 2·06bn. There is a metro (19 km) and tramway (94 km) in Lisbon. New light rail systems were opened in Porto in 2002 and Almada in 2007.

Civil Aviation

There are international airports at Portela (Lisbon), Pedras Rubras (Porto), Faro (Algarve) and Funchal (Madeira). The national carrier is the state-owned TAP-Air Portugal, with some domestic and international flights being provided by Portugália. In 2006 scheduled airline traffic of Portuguese-based carriers flew 171m. km, carrying 9,449,000 passengers (6,449,000 on international flights). In 2007 Lisbon handled 13,393,000 passengers (11,249,000 on international flights) and 82,645 tonnes of freight. Faro was the second busiest in terms of passenger traffic, with 5,471,000 passengers, and Porto was the second busiest for freight, with 31,991 tonnes.

Shipping

In Jan. 2014 there were 134 ships of 300 GT or over registered, totalling 1,144,000 GT. The main ports are Aveiro, Leixões, Lisbon, Sines and Setúbal. In 2014, 33·84m. tonnes of cargo were loaded at Portuguese ports and 46·31m. tonnes were unloaded.

Telecommunications

Portugal Telecom (PT) was formed from a merger of three state-owned utilities in 1994. It is now fully privatized. In 2013 there were 4,530,000 main (fixed) telephone lines. In the same year mobile phone subscribers numbered 11,991,000 excluding machine-to-machine subscriptions. 62·1% of the population aged 16–74 were internet users in 2013. There were 36·7 mobile broadband subscriptions per 100 inhabitants in 2013 and 23·8 fixed broadband subscriptions per 100 inhabitants. In March 2012 there were 4·2m. Facebook users.

Social Institutions

Out of 178 countries analysed in the 2017 *Fragile States Index*—a list published jointly by the Fund for Peace and *Foreign Policy* magazine—Portugal was ranked the 15th least vulnerable to conflict or collapse. The index is based on 12 indicators of state vulnerability across social, political and economic categories.

Justice

There are four judicial districts (Lisbon, Porto, Coimbra and Évora) divided into 58 circuits. In 2007 there were 335 courts, including 329 common courts of first instance. There are also six higher courts (five courts of appeal and a Supreme Court in Lisbon).

Capital punishment was abolished completely in the constitution of 1976.

The population in penal institutions in Nov. 2008 was 11,017 (104 per 100,000 of national population). Portugal was ranked 21st of 102 countries for criminal justice and 23rd for civil justice in the 2015 World Justice Project *Rule of Law Index*, which provides data on how the rule of law is experienced by the general public across eight categories.

Education

Adult literacy rate was an estimated 94·9% in 2009. Compulsory education has been in force since 1911.

In 2007 there were 263,887 children in pre-school establishments with 16,599 teaching staff, 753,646 pupils in primary schools with 64,274 teaching staff and 680,338 pupils in secondary schools with 92,965 teaching staff.

In 2006 public tertiary education institutions included 14 universities and a non-integrated university institution; 15 polytechnics and a number of polytechnic schools integrated in universities; 9 non-integrated nursing schools; 4 university-level military schools; and 5 polytechnic military schools. In the private sector there were 34 university level institutions and 66 polytechnics as well as a Catholic university. Portugal's oldest university is the University of Coimbra (Universidade de Coimbra), initially established in Lisbon in 1290; its largest is the University of Porto (Universidade do Porto), with 27,184 students in 2007–08. In 2007 there were 366,729 students in higher education with 36,069 academic staff.

Public expenditure on education came to 5·5% of GNI in 2006 (11·3% of total government expenditure).

Health

There were 200 hospitals in 2006 with 36,563 beds, and 378 clinics. In 2007 there were 37,904 doctors, 5,629 dentists, 10,117 pharmacists and 54,079 nurses. In 2007 Portugal spent 10·0% of its GDP on health.

Welfare

There were 1,991,991 old-age pensioners as at 31 Dec. 2012, plus 713,340 survivor pensioners and 277,113 disability pensioners. In 2012 there were 858,080 recipients of child benefit, 638,317 recipients of unemployment benefits, 496,228 recipients of sickness benefits and 167,063 recipients of initial parental benefits.

Pensions are available to men and women aged at least 66 years and 2 months with 15 years of contributions. Pensions are available at a younger age to workers in specified industries including mining, and the fisheries and maritime sectors. The minimum old-age pension is a fixed monthly amount depending on the number of calendar years of contributions. This ranges from €261·95 with up to 15 calendar years of contributions to €379·04 with at least 31 years. There is no maximum pension, but the amount may not exceed 92% of the reference earnings used for the pension calculation.

Religion

There is freedom of worship, both in public and private, with the exception of creeds incompatible with morals and the life and physical integrity of the people. A study by the Pew Research Center's Forum on Religion & Public Life estimated that there were 10·01m. Christians in 2010 (98% of which were Catholics) and 470,000 people with no religious affiliation. In Feb. 2019 there were four cardinals.

Culture

The Community of Portuguese-Speaking Countries (CPLP, comprising Angola, Brazil, Cabo Verde, Equatorial Guinea, Guinea-Bissau, Mozambique, Portugal, São Tomé and Príncipe and Timor-Leste) was founded in July 1996 with headquarters in Lisbon, primarily as a cultural and linguistic organization.

World Heritage Sites

(With year entered on list). In the Central Zone of the Town of Angra do Heroísmo in the Azores (1983) are the fortresses of San Sebastião and San Filipe, the latter built around 1590 on the orders of King Phillip II of Spain. The Monastery of the Hieronymites was built at the turn of the 16th century in Belém, Lisbon, while the capital's Tower of Belém was constructed as a monument to Vasco da Gama's explorations (1983 and 2008). The Monastery of Batalha (1983) near Leiria was built from 1388. The Convent of Christ in Tomar (1983) was originally built in 1160 as the centre of the Templar order. It was taken over by the Order of Christ in 1360 of which Henry the Navigator was made governor in 1418, and was greatly enriched in the 16th century. Other sites are the medieval walled Historic Centre of Évora (1988), the Gothic Cistercian 12th century Monastery of Alcobaça, north of Lisbon (1989), the Cultural Landscape of Sintra (1995), the Historic Centre of Porto (1996) and the Laurisilva of Madeira (1999), an area of biodiverse laurel forest. In 2001 two more sites were added: the Alto Douro Wine Region, famous for its port wine since the 18th century, and the Historic Centre of Guimarães, a town closely associated with the formation of Portuguese identity. The Landscape of the Pico Island Vineyard Culture followed in 2004. The Garrison Border Town of Elvas and its Fortifications (2012) houses the remains of an enormous war fortress, extensively fortified from the 17th to 19th centuries. It is the largest bulwarked dry ditch system in the world. The University of Coimbra–Alta and Sofia was added to the list in 2013. Situated on a hilltop, the university has grown and evolved over more than seven centuries.

The Prehistoric Rock Art Sites in the Côa Valley and Siega Verde (1998) is shared with Spain.

Press

There were 17 daily papers in 2014 (of which 14 were paid-for and three free), with a combined circulation of 904,000. There were nine national paid-for dailies in 2014 and five regional and local dailies. The most widely read newspapers are *Correio da Manhã* and *Jornal de Notícias*.

Tourism

In 2010, 6,831,600 non-resident tourists stayed in holiday accommodation (6,478,700 in 2009) including: 1,375,800 from Spain; 1,111,200 from the UK; 728,800 from Germany; 574,800 from France. There were 2,011 hotel establishments with 279,506 beds in 2010.

Festivals

Popular rock and pop music festivals include Rock in Rio in Lisbon (May), Optimus Alive at Oeiras (June), Super Bock Super Rock at Meco (July), Paredes de Coura Festival (Aug.), Festival Sudoeste at Zambujeria do Mar (Aug.) and the Jazz in August festival in Lisbon. Other music events are the Festival Músicas do Mundo that takes place in Sines (July), the Estoril Music Festival (July) and Sintra Music Festival (July). The Almada Theatre Festival takes place in Lisbon in July and the Festival Internacional de Cinema de Setúbal in June. Porto's most important festival, Festa de São João, takes place on 24 June.

Diplomatic Representatives

Of Portugal in the United Kingdom (11 Belgrave Sq., London, SW1X 8PP)
Ambassador: Manuel Lobo Antunes.

Of the United Kingdom in Portugal (Rua de São Bernardo 33, 1249-082 Lisbon)
Ambassador: Chris Sainty.

Of Portugal in the USA (2012 Massachusetts Ave., NW, Washington, D.C., 20036)
Ambassador: Domingos Teixeira de Abreu Fezas Vital.

Of the USA in Portugal (Ave. das Forças Armadas, 131, 1649-044, Lisbon)
Ambassador: George E. Glass.

Of Portugal to the United Nations
Ambassador: Francisco Duarte Lopes.

Of Portugal to the European Union
Permanent Representative: Nuno Brito.

Further Reading

Instituto Nacional de Estatística. *Anuário Estatístico de Portugal/Statistics Year-Book.—Estatísticas do Comércio Externo.* 2 vols. Annual from 1967

Birmingham, David, *A Concise History of Portugal.* 1993

Costa Pinto, António and Pequito Teixeira, Conceição (eds), *Political Institutions and Democracy in Portugal: Assessing the Impact of the Eurocrisis.* 2019

Maxwell, K., *The Making of Portuguese Democracy.* 1995

Page, Martin, *The First Global Village: How Portugal Changed the World.* 2002

Saraiva, J. H., *Portugal: A Companion History.* 1997

Wheeler, Douglas L., *Historical Dictionary of Portugal.* 2nd ed. 2002

National library: Biblioteca Nacional de Lisboa, Campo Grande 83, 1749-081 Lisbon.

National Statistical Office: Instituto Nacional de Estatística (INE), Avenida António José de Almeida, 1000-043 Lisbon.

Website: http://www.ine.pt

Qatar

Dawlat Qatar (State of Qatar)

Capital: Doha
Population projection, 2020: 2·79m.
GNI per capita, 2017: (PPP$) 116,818
HDI/world rank, 2017: 0·856/37
Internet domain extension: .qa

Key Historical Events

Qatar has rock carvings, inscriptions and fragments of pottery dating from 4000 BC. The early population was swelled by seasonal migration of Arab tribes and the peninsula became a centre for fishing and pearls. Commercial activity declined in the Roman era, when trade was concentrated in the Red Sea, but recovered in the 3rd century AD.

Islam was established in Qatar in the mid-7th century AD. During the Abbasid period (750–1258) Qatar enjoyed strong relations with the Caliphs in Baghdad. After briefly coming under Portuguese influence in the early 16th century, Qatar fell under Ottoman sovereignty. For the next four centuries it was nominally part of the Ottoman Empire, though considerable power remained with local tribal sheikhs.

Pearling and trading settlements were established along the coast in the 18th century, which also saw the rise of the Al Thani family who were originally from Saudi Arabia. In the mid-19th century Sheikh Mohammed bin Thani moved the family to the growing coastal town of Doha and established control of the surrounding region. Territorial disputes with the Al Khalifa family in neighbouring Bahrain led to a war in 1867 in which Doha was almost destroyed. The British intervened to recognize the Al Thani family as rulers of Qatar and in 1878 Sheikh Mohammed was succeeded by his son, Sheikh Qassim, who became the first Amir. With the collapse of the Ottoman Empire during the First World War, Qatar came under British rule. Under the treaties of 1916 and 1934 Qatar ceded Britain control over its external affairs in return for British military protection.

Oil was discovered in 1939 and, after a delay caused by the Second World War, exports began in 1949. In Dec. 1961 Qatar joined the Organization of the Petroleum Exporting Countries (OPEC). In 1968 British troops left Qatar and in 1970 Qatar adopted a constitution confirming the emirate as an absolute monarchy. It led negotiations to establish a union of Arab emirates but terms could not be agreed. On 3 Sept. 1971 Qatar assumed full independence under the rule of Sheikh Ahmad and joined the Arab League and the United Nations. In 1972 Sheikh Ahmad was ousted in a coup and chief minister Sheikh Khalifa bin Hamad Al Thani assumed power.

The discovery in 1971 of a large offshore oil field gave further impetus to the economy and Qatar rapidly developed a modern infrastructure, building up its health and education services. In 1981 it was a founder member of the Gulf Co-operation Council (GCC) and in 1988 established diplomatic relations with the USSR and the People's Republic of China. Qatar allied itself with Saudi Arabia on many regional and international issues and in 1991 joined the US-led international alliance against Iraq following the invasion of Kuwait.

In Jan. 1992 pressure for political reform culminated in demands from 50 prominent Qataris for a consultative assembly. On 27 June 1995 Amir Sheikh Khalifa was ousted by his son, Sheikh Hamad, who announced plans to introduce democratic reforms. In 1996 he survived an assassination attempt, part of an abortive attempt to restore his father to power. In 1996 the Arabic-language news agency Al-Jazeera was established in Doha, with the Amir's personal support and state financial backing. The station has won widespread respect and influence, despite pressure from some powers to tone down what is seen as an anti-West bias.

In 2001 a long-standing territorial dispute between Qatar and Bahrain was settled by the International Court of Justice, with Qatar recognizing Bahrain's sovereignty over the Hamar Islands in return for Bahrain renouncing claims on parts of mainland Qatar. In 2003 Qatar supported the UN-backed, American- and British-led invasion of Iraq, with Doha hosting the coalition headquarters.

In recent years Qatar's economy has grown rapidly. In 2003 a referendum was held to approve the country's constitution, which provides for a parliament with 30 elected and 15 appointed members. In the same year Qatar's first female minister, Sheikha Ahmad Al Mahmoud, was appointed.

Territory and Population

Qatar is a peninsula running north into the Persian Gulf. It is bounded in the south by Saudi Arabia. The territory includes a number of islands in the coastal waters of the peninsula, the most important of which is Halul, the storage and export terminal for the offshore oilfields. The area of Qatar is 11,586 sq. km. Population at the mini-census of April 2015, 2,404,776; density 207·6 per sq. km. In 2011, 95·9% of the population lived in urban areas.

The UN gives a projected population for 2020 of 2·79m.

Areas and populations of the eight municipalities:

Municipalities	Sq. km	2015 census population
Doha	243	956,457
Al Rayyan	2,511	605,712
Al Wakra	2,518	299,037
Al Khour	1,546	202,031
Al Shahaniya	3,299	187,571
Umm Salal	318	90,835
Al Daayen	249	54,339
Al Shamal	901	8,794

The capital is Doha, which is the main port, and had a census population in 2015 of 587,055. Other towns are Dukhan (the centre of oil production), Umm Said (the oil terminal of Qatar), Ruwais, Wakra, Al Khour, Umm Salal Mohammad and Umm Bab.

About 40% of the population are Arabs, 18% Indian, 18% Pakistani and 10% Iranian. Other nationalities make up the remaining 14%. Only about 10% of the working-age population are Qatari citizens.

The official language is Arabic.

Social Statistics

Births, 2008, 17,210; deaths, 1,942; marriages, 3,235; divorces, 939. 2008 rates per 1,000 population: births, 11·9; deaths, 1·3. Qatar's 2008 death rate was among the lowest in the world. Infant mortality, 2010 (per 1,000 live births), 7. Expectation of life in 2013 was 77·8 years for males and 79·5 for females. Annual population growth rate, 2000–08, 9·1% (the highest in the world). Fertility rate, 2008, 2·4 births per woman.

Climate

The climate is hot and humid. Doha, Jan. 62°F (16·7°C), July 98°F (36·7°C). Annual rainfall 2·5" (62 mm).

Constitution and Government

Qatar is ruled by an *Amir*. HH Sheikh Tamim bin Hamad Al Thani (b. 1980) assumed power after his father, HH Sheikh Hamad bin Khalifa Al Thani, KCMG, abdicated on 25 June 2013. The heir apparent was Sheikh Hamad's third son, Sheikh Jasim bin Hamad Al Thani (b. 1978), but in Aug. 2003 he named his fourth son, Sheikh Tamim bin Hamad Al Thani, as heir apparent instead.

Qatar's first written constitution was approved in June 2004 and came into force on 9 June 2005. Parliament is the unicameral *Advisory Council* (*Majlis Al-Shura*) consisting of 41 members who are appointed by the Amir for three-year terms.

© Springer Nature Limited 2020
Palgrave Macmillan (ed.), *The Statesman's Yearbook 2020*,
https://doi.org/10.1057/978-1-349-95940-2_156

National Anthem

'As-Salam Al-Amiri' ('Peace for the Amir'); words by Sheikh Mubarak bin Saïf al-Thani, tune by Abdul Aziz Nasser Obaidan.

Government Chronology

Amirs since 1971.

1971–72	Sheikh Ahmad bin Ali Al Thani
1972–95	Sheikh Khalifa bin Hamad Al Thani
1995–2013	Sheikh Hamad bin Khalifa Al Thani
2013–	Sheikh Tamim bin Hamad Al Thani

Current Government

Amir, Minister of Defence and C.-in-C. of the Armed Forces: HH Sheikh Tamim bin Hamad Al Thani; b. 1980.

Deputy Amir: Sheikh Abdullah bin Hamad Al Thani.

In Feb. 2019 the government comprised:

Prime Minister and Minister of Interior: Sheikh Abdullah bin Nasser bin Khalifa Al Thani; b. 1959 (in office since 26 June 2013).

Adviser to the Amir for Defence Affairs: Maj.-Gen. Hamad bin Ali Al Attiyah.

Deputy Prime Ministers: Ahmed bin Abdullah bin Zaid Al Mahmoud (also *Minister of State for Cabinet Affairs*); Khalid bin Mohamed Al Attiyah (also *Minister of State for Defence Affairs*); Sheikh Mohamed bin Abdulrahman Al Thani (also *Minister of Foreign Affairs*).

Minister of Administrative Development, Labour and Social Affairs: Issa Saad Al Jafali Al Nuaimi. *Awqaf and Islamic Affairs:* Ghaith bin Mubarak Al Kuwari. *Culture and Sports:* Salah bin Ghanem bin Nasser Al Ali. *Development Planning and Statistics:* Saleh Mohamed Salem Al Nabit. *Economy and Commerce:* Sheikh Ahmed bin Jassim bin Mohamed Al Thani. *Education and Higher Education:* Mohammed Abdul Wahed Ali Al Hammadi. *Energy and Industry:* Mohammed bin Saleh Al Sada. *Finance:* Ali Sherif Al Emadi. Al Thani. *Justice:* Hassan Lahdan Saqr Al Mohannadi. *Municipalities and Environment:* Mohamed bin Abdullah al Rumaihi. *Public Health:* Dr Hanan Mohamed Al Kuwari. *Transport and Communications:* Jassim Seif Ahmed Al Sulaiti.

Government Website: http://www.gov.qa/wps/portal

Current Leaders

Tamim bin Hamad bin Khalifa Al Thani

Position

Amir

Introduction

Sheikh Tamim bin Hamad bin Khalifa Al Thani became Amir on 25 June 2013 following the abdication of Sheikh Hamad bin Khalifa Al Thani, who had led Qatar since 1995.

Early Life

Sheikh Tamim was born on 3 June 1980 in Doha, the second son of Amir Sheikh Hamad and his second wife. Sheikh Tamin was educated in the UK and subsequently attended the Royal Military Academy, Sandhurst. Upon graduating in 1998 he was commissioned in the Qatari armed forces. He was named heir apparent in 2003, ahead of his older brother.

He has since served in a number of diverse roles, including president of the Qatar National Olympic Committee, deputy commander-in-chief of the Qatar Armed Forces, chair of the Supreme Education Council and chair of the Qatar Investment Authority, the country's sovereign wealth fund. He married Sheikha Jawaher bint Hamad bin Suhaim Al Thani in 2005 and Sheikha Anoud bint Mana Al Hajri in 2009.

Career in Office

In the first six months of his rule, Sheikh Tamim undertook a cabinet reshuffle that saw Hamad bin Jassim replaced as prime minister and foreign minister by Sheikh Abdullah bin Nasser bin Khalifa Al Thani and Khalid Al Attiyah respectively.

Economically, the government's long-term Vision 2030 programme has envisaged heavy investment in infrastructure largely related to the hosting of the 2022 football World Cup tournament. This includes a new metro system, museums, revamped roads and a new airport. However, international attention ahead of the 2022 tournament has put pressure on Sheikh Tamim to review Qatar's treatment of foreign workers and its human rights record, while the sharp decline in oil prices since mid-2014 has put an increasing strain on the public finances.

In regional affairs, Qatar adopted an active military role from 2014 in the Syrian security crisis against Islamic State jihadists and in the Saudi Arabian-led campaign against Houthi rebels in Yemen. However, relations soured with Saudi Arabia, the United Arab Emirates, Bahrain and Egypt, which broke off diplomatic relations and cut transport links with Qatar in June 2017, accusing the country of promoting international terrorism and aligning with Iran. Qatar subsequently re-established full diplomatic ties with Iran two months later.

In Dec. 2018 the government announced that it would withdraw Qatar from the Organization of the Petroleum Exporting Countries from Jan. 2019 after nearly 60 years of membership, citing its increasing emphasis on exploiting its huge gas resources.

Defence

Defence expenditure in 2011 totalled an estimated US$3,476m. (approximately US$1,880 per capita), representing around 2% of GDP.

Army

Personnel (2011) 8,500.

Navy

Personnel in 2011 totalled 1,800 including Marine Police; the base is at Doha.

Air Force

Personnel (2011) 1,500; equipment included 18 combat-capable aircraft and 13 multi-role helicopters.

Economy

Oil, natural gas and other mining contributed 38·6% to GDP in 2015; followed by finance and real estate, 17·8%; trade and hotels, 9·9%; and manufacturing (excluding oil and natural gas-related manufacturing), 9·7%.

Overview

Qatar, a member of the Gulf Co-operation Council, has one of the world's highest per capita income levels, at US$61,025 in 2017. Oil and natural gas exports are the keystones of the economy, contributing more than two-thirds of GDP, 80% of export earnings and 90% of government revenues in 2017. Proven oil reserves of 15bn. bbls should ensure current levels of production can be maintained until well into the 2030s, while reserves of natural gas (the third largest in the world) account for more than 5% of the global total.

After a rapid gas sector-led expansion (including double-digit real GDP growth every year between 2006 and 2011), the economy slowed to annual average growth of 4·4% between 2012 and 2014 and then 2·5% between 2015 and 2017. The government announced its intention to withdraw in Jan. 2019 from the Organization of the Petroleum Exporting Countries (OPEC), ostensibly in order to focus on the natural gas sector. With international energy prices declining from mid-2014, pressure has increased on the government to reduce reliance on the hydrocarbon sector. In particular, there has been major investment in construction and transport infrastructure, with a development plan incorporating publicly-funded projects for a national railway system and a new international airport and seaport. Investor interest has been further generated by Qatar's role as host of the 2022 football World Cup competition, aiming to boost the country's aspirations as a tourist hub.

Qatar has a substantial asset base, including significant foreign investments, and a sovereign wealth fund worth in excess of US$335bn. in 2017. A current account surplus equivalent to 3·8% of GDP in 2017 indicated a healthy mid-term economic outlook, despite the blockade imposed on Qatar by other Gulf Co-operation Council members (led by Saudi Arabia) and Egypt from 2017.

Currency

The unit of currency is the *Qatari riyal* (QAR) of 100 *dirhams*, introduced in 1973. Foreign exchange reserves were US$4,370m. in July 2005, gold reserves were 19,000 troy oz and total money supply was 19,159m. riyals. Inflation rates (based on IMF statistics):

2008	2009	2010	2011	2012	2013	2014	2015	2016	2017
15·1%	−4·9%	−2·4%	2·0%	1·8%	3·2%	3·4%	1·8%	2·7%	0·4%

Budget

The fiscal year is 1 April–31 March. Revenue (2013–14) 346,641m. riyals; expenditure, 231,663m. riyals.

Performance

In terms of GDP per head, Qatar ranks among the richest countries in the world with a purchasing power parity (PPP) per capita GDP of 77,568 current international dollars in 2009. Qatar has the highest density of dollar millionaires of any country, with 14% of households holding private wealth of at least US$1m. The country has been experiencing a period of rapid economic expansion, driven by rising oil prices and the increased exploitation of its natural gas reserves, the third largest in the world. Real GDP growth (based on IMF statistics):

2008	2009	2010	2011	2012	2013	2014	2015	2016	2017
17·7%	12·0%	18·1%	13·4%	4·7%	4·4%	4·0%	3·7%	2·1%	1·6%

Total GDP was US$167·6bn. in 2017.

Banking and Finance

The Qatar Monetary Agency, which functioned as a bank of issue, became the Central Bank in 1995 (*Governor*, Abdullah bin Saud Al-Thani). In Dec. 2014 there were 18 registered banks—seven national banks, four Islamic national banks and seven foreign banks. The largest bank is the Qatar National Bank, with assets in 2008 of US$41·8bn.

A stock exchange was established in Doha by the Amir's decree in 1995.

Energy and Natural Resources

Environment

Qatar's carbon dioxide emissions from the consumption of energy in 2011 were the equivalent of 44·1 tonnes per capita, among the highest in the world.

Electricity

Installed capacity was 7·8m. kW in 2011. Production was 30·73bn. kWh in 2011; consumption per capita was 16,081 kWh.

Oil and Gas

Proven reserves of oil (2017) 25·2bn. bbls. Output more than doubled between 2002 and 2012, rising from 37·4m. tonnes to 83·3m. tonnes.

The North Field, the world's biggest single reservoir of gas and containing 12% of the known world gas reserves, is half the size of Qatar itself. Development cost is estimated at US$25bn. In 2017 natural gas reserves were 24·9trn. cu. metres (the third largest after Iran and Russia); output more than doubled between 2008 and 2012, rising from 77·0bn. cu. metres to 157·0bn. cu. metres. Production in 2017 was 175·7bn. cu. metres.

Agriculture

An estimated 13,000 ha. were equipped for irrigation in 2013. There were approximately 13,000 ha. of arable land in 2013 and 3,000 ha. of permanent crops. Production (2013) in 1,000 tonnes: dates, 31; tomatoes, 12; pumpkins and squash, 7; aubergines, 3; cabbages, kale, etc., 2; onions, 2.

Livestock (2013): sheep, 400,000; goats, 236,000; camels, 68,000; cattle, 18,000; chickens (estimate), 9m. Livestock products, 2013 estimates (in 1,000 tonnes): meat, 23; milk, 24; eggs, 5.

Fisheries

The catch in 2015 totalled 15,203 tonnes, entirely from sea fishing.

Industry

The leading companies by market capitalization in Qatar in May 2018 were Qatar National Bank (US$36·4bn.); and Industries Qatar, a producer of petrochemicals, fertilizer and steel (US$18·3bn.).

Production (2005, in 1,000 tonnes): urea, 2,979; ammonia, 2,134; petrol, 1,656; butane, 1,075; cement, 1,049; distillate fuel oil, 926; jet fuel, 905; steel bars, 791; ethylene, 544; residual fuel oil, 418; polyethylene, 415. There is an industrial zone at Umm Said.

Labour

In 2011 the economically active population totalled 1,271,100. Males constituted 88% of the labour force in 2011; foreigners (particularly from South Asia) make up 94% of the workforce. Qatar has the lowest percentages of females in the workforce of any country.

International Trade

Qatar, along with Bahrain, Kuwait, Oman, Saudi Arabia and the United Arab Emirates entered into a customs union in Jan. 2003.

Imports and Exports

Imports in 2016 totalled US$32,060·1m. and exports US$57,310·5m. The main imports are machinery and equipment, consumer goods, food and chemicals. Main exports are petroleum and petroleum products (52%) and liquefied natural gas (35%). Qatar is by far the world's largest exporter of liquefied natural gas. Principal import suppliers in 2016: USA, 14·4%; China, 10·4%; Germany, 9·3%. Leading export markets, 2016: Japan, 19·1%; South Korea, 15·7%; India, 12·9%.

Communications

Roads

In 2007 there were about 7,790 km of roads. Vehicles in use in 2007 totalled 605,700. In 2007 there were 199 fatalities as a result of road accidents.

Civil Aviation

The flag carrier is Qatar Airways, which is state-owned and carried 18m. passengers in 2012–13. Qatar's airport is Hamad International Airport, which opened in April 2014 to replace the old Doha International Airport (where passenger numbers had quadrupled between 2003 and 2013).

Telecommunications

In 2013 there were an estimated 413,000 main (fixed) telephone lines; mobile phone subscribers numbered an estimated 3,310,000 in the same year. 69·3% of the population were internet users in 2012. In March 2012 there were 481,000 Facebook users.

Rail

A railways development programme includes a long distance passenger and freight rail project as well as various light rail schemes. Additionally, a metro is currently under construction in Doha and is scheduled to open in late 2019.

Social Institutions

Out of 178 countries analysed in the 2017 *Fragile States Index*—a list published jointly by the Fund for Peace and *Foreign Policy* magazine—Qatar was ranked the 33rd least vulnerable to conflict or collapse. The index is based on 12 indicators of state vulnerability across social, political and economic categories.

Justice

The judicial system is administered by the ministry of justice which comprises three main departments: legal affairs, courts of justice and land and real estate register. In 2004 a High Judicial Council was established to oversee the court system, which as a result of a new Judicial Authority Law that took effect at the same time comprises the Court of Cassation, the Court of Appeal and the Court of First Instance. The death penalty is in force but has not been used since 2003. The population in penal institutions in 2011 was approximately 1,150 (60 per 100,000 of national population).

All issues related to personal affairs of Muslims under Islamic Law embodied in the Holy Koran and Sunna are decided by Sharia Courts.

Education
Adult literacy rate was 94·7% in 2009. In 2013 there were 106,801 pupils at primary schools (45,399 public and 61,402 private) with 10,677 teaching staff and 79,006 pupils at secondary schools with 8,169 teaching staff. In the same year there were 20,902 students in tertiary education and 1,793 academic staff. Qatar University had 8,801 students in 2008 and 637 full-time academic staff in 2007–08. Education City, a campus built in the outskirts of Doha, houses branches of eight prestigious international universities along with the Qatar Faculty of Islamic Studies.

In 2005 public expenditure on education accounted for 19·6% of total government spending.

Health
Over the period 2006–12 Qatar had 12 hospital beds per 10,000 population. In 2014 there were 4,267 physicians, 12,381 nursing and midwifery personnel, 1,242 dentistry personnel and 2,023 pharmaceutical personnel.

Religion
The population is predominantly Muslim (primarily Sunnis), although there is a small Christian minority among expatriates.

Culture

World Heritage Sites
The walled coastal town of Al Zubarah was added to the UNESCO World Heritage List in 2013. It is designated as an archaeological site and flourished as a pearling and trading centre in the late 18th and 19th centuries, although it is now deserted.

Press
There are four Arabic language daily newspapers—*Al-Rayah*, *Al-Sharq*, *Al-Watan* and *Al-Arab*. *The Gulf Times*, *The Peninsula* and *Qatar Tribune* are English dailies. In 2008 the combined circulation was 115,000. *Qatar Chronicle*, launched in 2012, is an online news portal published on a daily basis in English and Arabic.

Tourism
In 2013 there were 2,611,000 international tourist arrivals (excluding same-day visitors), up from 2,346,000 in 2012.

Diplomatic Representatives

Of Qatar in the United Kingdom (1 South Audley St., London, WIK 1NB)
Ambassador: Yousef Ali Al-Khater.

Of the United Kingdom in Qatar (West Bay, Dafna Area, Onaiza Zone 66, Al Shabab St., PO Box 3, Doha, Qatar)
Ambassador: Ajay Sharma, CMG.

Of Qatar in the USA (2555 M St., NW, Washington, D.C., 20037)
Ambassador: Meshal bin Hamad Al Thani.

Of the USA in Qatar (22 February St., Doha)
Ambassador: Vacant.
Chargé d'Affaires a.i.: William Grant.

Of Qatar to the United Nations
Ambassador: Alya Ahmed Seif Al Thani.

Of Qatar to the European Union
Ambassador: Abdulrahman Mohammed Al Khulaifi.

Further Reading

Central Statistical Organization. *Annual Statistical Abstract.*
El-Nawawy, Mohammed and Iskandar, Adel, *Al-Jazeera: How the Free Arab News Network Scooped the World and Changed the Middle East.* 2002
National Statistical Office: Ministry of Development Planning and Statistics (MDPS), Doha, Qatar, P.O. Box 1855.
Website: http://www.qsa.gov.qa

Romania

România

Capital: Bucharest
Population projection, 2020: 19·39m.
GNI per capita, 2017: (PPP$) 22,646
HDI/world rank, 2017: 0·811/52
Internet domain extension: .ro

Key Historical Events

Neolithic peoples with links to Anatolia settled from 5000 BC at Lake Golovita, close to Romania's Black Sea coast. The subsequent Boian culture spread across the lower Danube valley by 3500 BC. Later, Indo European peoples, collectively known as the Thracians, entered the Carpathian-Balkan region. The Dacii (or Getae to the Greeks, who had established colonies on the western Black Sea coast by the 7th century BC) occupied much of present-day Romania. Dacian power grew under King Burebista (82–44 BC), attracting Roman attention. In AD 106 the Roman emperor Trajan succeeded in making the kingdom a frontier province.

Under Barbarian attack, in 271 Emperor Aurelian withdrew the Roman Army and administration south of the Danube to Dobrogea (Constanța), although much of Dacia remained in the Roman-Byzantine sphere through trade along the Danube. As Rome's influence waned, Dacia was populated between the 3rd and 9th centuries by tribes from the Steppes to the east, including Goths, Huns, Avars, Bulgars and Magyars. Magyar power was centred on Transylvania and for most of the 10th–13th centuries it was a Hungarian dependency. Mongol Invasion in 1241 was followed by the foundation of the feudal 'Danubian Principalities' of Wallachia and Moldavia in the late 13th and early 14th centuries. In 1415, under Prince Mircea, Wallachia became a vassal of the Ottoman Empire, although retaining some independence. Prince Vlad Țepeș (known as Dracula) ruled Wallachia from 1456–62 and Stephen the Great reigned in Moldavia from 1457–1504.

Following the Magyar defeat at the battle of Mohács in 1526, Transylvania came under Ottoman vassalage. Moldavia succumbed to Ottoman domination in 1538. Michael the Brave, ruler of Wallachia from 1593, defeated an Ottoman invasion in 1595 and conquered Transylvania four years later. In 1600 he briefly unified the three Romanian provinces. Several independent princes then ruled Transylvania in the 17th century until the Habsburgs expanded eastward in the 1680s. In 1686, through the Treaty of Vienna, Transylvania accepted Habsburg protection under Leopold I. In Wallachia, the late 17th century saw prolonged struggle against Ottoman rule, with Princes Cantacuzino and Brâncoveanu even negotiating with the Austrian and Russian Empires. The Ottomans responded by backing the suzerainty of the İstanbul-based Phanariots, whose rule included phases of corruption and enlightened reform. Prince Mavrocordat abolished serfdom in 1746. The treaty of Kuchuk Kainarji (1774) boosted Russian influence in Wallachia and Moldavia.

Phanariot rule ended in 1821, following a revolt led by Tudor Vladimirescu and the outbreak of the Greek War of Independence. Local princes were reinstated in Wallachia and Moldavia. The 1829 Treaty of Adrianople that concluded the Russo–Turkish war prompted Russian repression in the principalities. Transylvania remained under Habsburg influence until revolution in all three provinces in 1848, sparked by opposition to foreign rule and the power of local landowners (*boyars*). That year the Diet of Cluj voted for union between Transylvania and the other three provinces of Hungary. Support grew for the union of Moldavia and Wallachia. The election of Alexander Cuza as prince of both territories in 1859 paved the way for union as Romania in 1862, with Bucharest as its capital. In 1866 Carol of Hohenzollern was crowned and adopted a constitution based on that of Belgium. Romania was declared independent by the Treaty of Berlin of 1878.

Despite economic expansion, the peasantry remained downtrodden and rebelled in 1907. Romania joined the First World War on the allied side in 1916. Victory brought Transylvania (with large Hungarian and German populations), Bessarabia, Bucovina and Dobrudja into the union with the 'Old Kingdom'. The world recession then drew Romania into Germany's economic orbit. The fascist Iron Guard assassinated Liberal leader Ion G. Duca in 1933 and King Carol II became increasingly totalitarian. Following Nazi and Soviet annexations of Romanian territory in 1940, he abdicated in favour of his son Mihai. The fascist government of Ion Antonescu declared war on the USSR on 22 June 1941 but on 23 Aug. 1944 Mihai, with the backing of opposition parties, deposed Antonescu and switched sides.

The armistice of Sept. 1944 gave the Soviet army control of Romania. This, and the 'spheres of influence' diplomacy of the Allies, ensured Romania's communist future. Transylvania was restored to Romania (although it lost Bessarabia and Northern Bucovina), and large estates were broken up for the benefit of the peasantry. Following elections in Nov. 1946, marred by intimidation and fraud, Mihai was forced to abdicate and a People's Republic proclaimed. The communist leader, Gheorghe Gheorghiu-Dej, purged his fellow leaders in the early 1950s. Under Nicolae Ceaușescu, who became the centre of power in 1965, Romania took a relatively independent stand in foreign affairs while domestic repression and impoverishment increased.

In Dec. 1989 there were mass demonstrations, backed by the army, against the government. Ceaușescu fled the capital and the National Salvation Front (FSN) proclaimed itself the provisional government. Ceaușescu and his family were captured, secretly tried and, on 25 Dec., executed. A day later the FSN's Ion Iliescu became president, overseeing a reformist administration inhibited by its communist origins.

With the economy stalled, a four-party coalition led by Emil Constantinescu came to power in 1996. Iliescu returned as president in 2000 and in 2004 was replaced by Traian Băsescu. On 1 Jan. 2007 Romania joined the EU. An IMF-led bailout followed the global economic crisis of late 2008.

Territory and Population

Romania is bounded in the north by Ukraine, in the east by Moldova, Ukraine and the Black Sea, south by Bulgaria, southwest by Serbia and northwest by Hungary. The area is 238,391 sq. km. Population (2011 census), 20,121,641; density, 84·4 per sq. km. In 2011, 58·0% of the population lived in urban areas. Romania's population has been falling at such a steady rate since 1990 that its population at the time of the 2011 census was the same as that in the early 1970s. In Jan. 2018 the population was estimated at 19,523,621.

The UN gives a projected population for 2020 of 19·39m.

Romania is divided into 41 counties (*judeţ*) and the municipality of Bucharest (Bucureşti).

County	Area in sq. km	Population (2011 census)	Capital	Population (in 1,000) (2011)
Bucharest (Bucureşti)[1]	238	1,883,425	—	—
Alba	6,242	342,376	Alba Iulia	64
Arad	7,754	430,629	Arad	159
Argeş	6,826	612,431	Piteşti	155
Bacău	6,621	616,168	Bacău	144
Bihor	7,544	575,398	Oradea	196
Bistriţa-Năsăud	5,355	286,225	Bistriţa	75
Botoşani	4,986	412,626	Botoşani	107
Brăila	4,766	321,212	Brăila	180
Braşov	5,363	549,217	Braşov	253
Buzău	6,103	451,069	Buzău	115

(continued)

© Springer Nature Limited 2020
Palgrave Macmillan (ed.), *The Statesman's Yearbook 2020*,
https://doi.org/10.1057/978-1-349-95940-2_157

County	Area in sq. km	Population (2011 census)	Capital	Population (in 1,000) (2011)
Călăraşi	5,088	306,691	Călăraşi	65
Caraş-Severin	8,520	295,579	Reşiţa	73
Cluj	6,674	691,106	Cluj-Napoca	325
Constanţa	7,071	684,082	Constanţa	284
Covasna	3,710	210,177	Sf. Gheorghe	56
Dâmboviţa	4,054	518,745	Tîrgovişte	80
Dolj	7,414	660,544	Craiova	270
Galaţi	4,466	536,167	Galaţi	249
Giurgiu	3,526	281,422	Giurgiu	61
Gorj	5,602	341,594	Tîrgu Jiu	83
Harghita	6,639	310,867	Miercurea-Ciuc	39
Hunedoara	7,063	418,565	Deva	61
Ialomiţa	4,453	274,148	Slobozia	46
Iaşi	5,476	772,348	Iaşi	290
Ilfov[1]	1,583	388,738	—	—
Maramureş	6,304	478,659	Baia Mare	124
Mehedinţi	4,933	265,390	Drobeta-Turnu Severin	93
Mureş	6,714	550,846	Tîrgu Mureş	134
Neamţ	5,896	470,766	Piatra-Neamţ	85
Olt	5,498	436,400	Slatina	70
Prahova	4,716	762,886	Ploieşti	210
Sălaj	3,864	224,384	Zalău	56
Satu Mare	4,418	344,360	Satu Mare	102
Sibiu	5,432	397,322	Sibiu	147
Suceava	8,554	634,810	Suceava	92
Teleorman	5,790	380,123	Alexandria	45
Timiş	8,697	683,540	Timişoara	319
Tulcea	8,499	213,083	Tulcea	74
Vâlcea	5,765	371,714	Râmnicu Vâlcea	99
Vaslui	5,318	395,499	Vaslui	55
Vrancea	4,857	340,310	Focşani	79

[1]Bucharest municipality and surrounding localities of Ilfov cover 1,821 sq. km.

At the 2011 census the following ethnic minorities numbered over 25,000: Hungarians, 1,227,600 (mainly in Transylvania); Roma, 621,600; Ukrainians, 50,900; Germans, 36,000; Turks, 27,700. A *Council of National Minorities* made up of representatives of the government and ethnic groups was set up in 1993. The actual number of Roma is estimated to be nearer 2m. Romania has one of the largest Roma populations of any country.

The official language is Romanian.

Social Statistics

2010 (in 1,000): births, 212·2; deaths, 259·7; marriages, 115·8; divorces, 32·6. Rates, 2010 (per 1,000 population): live births, 9·9; deaths, 12·1; marriages, 5·4; divorces, 1·5. Infant mortality, 2010 (per 1,000 live births), 9·8. Expectation of life at birth, 2013, was 70·3 years for males and 77·5 years for females. In 2010 the most popular age range for marrying was 25–29 for males and 20–24 for females. Measures designed to raise the birth rate were abolished in 1990, and abortion and contraception legalized. The annual abortion rate, at approximately 41 per 1,000 women, ranks among the highest in the world. Population growth rate, 2010, –0·2%; fertility rate, 2013, 1·4 births per woman.

Climate

A continental climate with an annual average temperature varying between 8°C in the north and 11°C in the south. Bucharest, Jan. 27°F (–2·7°C), July 74°F (23·5°C). Annual rainfall 23·1" (579 mm). Constanţa, Jan. 31°F (–0·6°C), July 71°F (21·7°C). Annual rainfall 15" (371 mm).

Constitution and Government

A new constitution was approved by a referendum on 18–19 Oct. 2003. Turnout was 55·7%, and 89·7% of votes cast were in favour. The Constitution, which replaces the previous one from 1991, defines Romania as a republic where the rule of law prevails in a social and democratic state. Private property rights and a market economy are guaranteed. The new pro-European constitution was aimed at helping Romania achieve EU membership.

The head of state is the *President*, elected by direct vote for a maximum of two five-year terms. The president is not allowed to be affiliated with any political party while in office. The President appoints the *Prime Minister*, who then has to be approved by a vote in parliament. The President is empowered to veto legislation unless it is upheld by a two-thirds parliamentary majority. The National Assembly consists of a 329-member *Chamber of Deputies* and a 136-member *Senate*; both are elected for four-year terms from 43 constituencies through a proportional mixed member system. 18 seats in the Chamber of Deputies are reserved for ethnic minorities. There is a 3% threshold for admission to either house. Votes for parties not reaching this threshold are redistributed.

There is a *Constitutional Court*.

National Anthem

'Desteaptăte, Române, din somnul cel de moarte' ('Wake up, Romanians, from your deadly slumber'); words by A. Muresianu, tune by A. Pann.

Government Chronology

(ALDE = Alliance of Liberals and Democrats; FDSN = Democratic National Salvation Front; FSN = National Salvation Front; PCR = Romanian Communist Party; PD = Democratic Party; PDSR = Party of Social Democracy in Romania; PD-L = Democratic Liberal Party; PNL = National Liberal Party; PNTCD = National Peasant Party Christian Democratic; PSD = Social Democratic Party; n/p = non-partisan)

Heads of State since 1940		
King		
1940–47	Mihai I	
Presidents of the Presidium of the Grand National Assembly		
1947–52	PCR	Constantin Ion Parhon
1958	PCR	Anton Moisescu
1958–61	PCR	Ion Gheorghe Maurer
Chairmen of the Council of State		
1961–65	PCR	Gheorghe Gheorghiu-Dej
1965–67	PCR	Chivu Stoica
1967–74	PCR	Nicolae Ceauşescu
Presidents		
1974–89	PCR	Nicolae Ceauşescu
1989–96	PCR, n/p, FSN, FDSN, PDSR	Ion Iliescu
1996–2000	PNTCD	Emil Constantinescu
2000–04	PDSR, PSD	Ion Iliescu
2004–07	PD	Traian Băsescu
2007	PSD	Nicolae Văcăroiu (acting for Traian Băsescu)
2007–12	PD, PD-L	Traian Băsescu
2012	PNL	Crin Antonescu (acting for Traian Băsescu)
2012–14	PD-L	Traian Băsescu
2014–	n/p	Klaus Iohannis
Heads of Government since 1945.		
Chairmen of the Council of Ministers		
1945–52	PCR	Petru Groza
1952–55	PCR	Gheorghe Gheorghiu-Dej
1955–61	PCR	Chivu Stoica
1961–74	PCR	Ion Gheorghe Maurer

(continued)

1974–79	PCR	Manea Mănescu
1979–82	PCR	Ilie Verdeţ
1982–89	PCR	Constantin Dăscalescu
Prime Ministers		
1989–91	FSN	Petre Roman
1991–92	n/p	Theodor Stolojan
1992–96	n/p, PDSR	Nicolae Văcăroiu
1996–98	PNTCD	Victor Ciorbea
1998–99	PNTCD	Radu Vasile
1999–2000	n/p	Mugur Isărescu
2000–04	PDSR/PSD	Adrian Năstase
2004–08	PNL	Călin Popescu-Tăriceanu
2008–12	PD-L	Emil Boc
2012	n/p	Mihai-Răzvan Ungureanu
2012–15	PSD	Victor Ponta
2015	ALDE	Sorin Mihai Cîmpeanu (acting)
2015–17	n/p	Dacian Cioloş
2017	PSD	Sorin Grindeanu
2017–18	PSD	Mihai Tudose
2018–	PSD	Viorica Dăncilă

Recent Elections

Presidential elections were held in two rounds on 2 Nov. and 16 Nov. 2014. In the first round incumbent Prime Minister Victor Ponta of the Social Democratic Party (in alliance with the Conservative Party and the National Union for the Progress of Romania) (PSD-PC-UNPR) received 40·4% of votes cast, Klaus Iohannis of the National Liberal Party (in alliance with the Democratic Liberal Party) (PNL-PDL) 30·4% and Călin Popescu-Tăriceanu (ind.) 5·4%. There were 11 other candidates. Turnout was 53·2%. In the second round run-off, Iohannis won with 54·4% of the vote against 45·6% for Ponta; turnout was 64·1%.

In parliamentary elections held on 11 Dec. 2016 the Social Democratic Party (PSD) took 154 seats (45·5% of the vote) in the lower house and 67 (45·7% of the vote) in the Senate, the National Liberal Party (PNL) 69 seats (20·0%) and 30 (20·4%), the Save Romania Union (USR) 30 seats (8·9%) and 13 (8·9%), the Democratic Union of Hungarians in Romania (UDMR) 21 seats (6·2%) and 9 (6·2%), the Alliance of Liberals and Democrats (ALDE) 20 seats (5·6%) and 9 (6·0%), and the People's Movement Party (PMP) 18 seats (5·3%) and 8 (5·7%). 17 smaller parties won one seat each in the lower house. Turnout was 39·5%.

European Parliament

Romania has 32 representatives. At the May 2014 elections turnout was 32·4% (27·7% in 2009). The Social Democratic Union (consisting of the Social Democratic Party, the Conservative Party and the National Union for the Progress of Romania) won 16 seats with 37·6% of the vote (political affiliation in European Parliament: Progressive Alliance of Socialists and Democrats); PNL, 6 seats with 15·0% (European People's Party); PD-L, 5 with 12·2% (European People's Party); UDMR, 2 with 6·3% of the vote (European People's Party); the People's Movement Party, 2 with 6·2% of the vote (European People's Party). One independent was elected, with 6·8% of the vote (Alliance of Liberals and Democrats for Europe).

Current Government

President: Klaus Iohannis; b. 1959 (ind.; sworn in 21 Dec. 2014).

In Feb. 2019 the government comprised:

Prime Minister: Viorica Dăncilă; b. 1963 (PSD; sworn in 29 Jan. 2018).

Deputy Prime Ministers: Ana Birchall (also *Minister for Strategic Partnerships' Implementation*); Graţiela Leocadia Gavrilescu (also *Minister of Environment*); Paul Stănescu (also *Minister of Regional Development and Public Administration*); Viorel Ştefan.

Minister of Agriculture and Rural Development: Petre Daea. *Business Environment, Commerce and Entrepreneurship:* Ştefan-Radu Oprea. *Communications and Information Society:* Alexandu Petrescu. *Culture and National Identity:* Valer-Daniel Breaz. *Economy:* Niculae Bădălău. *Energy:* Anton Anton. *European Funds:* Rovana Plumb. *Foreign Affairs:* Teodor-Viorel

Meleşcanu. *Health:* Sorina Pintea. *Internal Affairs:* Carmen Daniela Dan. *Justice:* Tudorel Toader. *Labour and Social Justice:* Marius-Constantin Budăi. *National Defence:* Gabriel-Beniamin Leş. *National Education:* Ecaterina Andronescu. *Public Finance:* Eugen Orlando Teodorovici. *Relations with Parliament:* Viorel Ilie. *Research and Innovation:* Nicolae Hurduc. *Romanians Abroad:* Natalia-Elena Intotero. *Tourism:* Bogdan Gheorghe Trif. *Transport:* Lucian Şova. *Waters and Forests:* Ioan Deneş. *Youth and Sports:* Constantin-Bogdan Matei.

Government Website: http://www.gov.ro

Current Leaders

Klaus Iohannis

Position

President

Introduction

Klaus Iohannis became president on 21 Dec. 2014, having defeated the Social Democratic prime minister, Victor Ponta, in an election the previous month. He is the first president from Romania's ethnic German Protestant minority.

Early Life

Iohannis was born on 13 June 1959 in the city of Sibiu to parents of Transylvanian Saxon heritage. He graduated in physics from Babeş-Bolyai University in Cluj-Napoca in 1983 and became a physics teacher, working in several schools across Sibiu including an eight-year spell at Brukenthal Gymnasium, Romania's oldest German-speaking school. He left full-time teaching in 1997 and took up a position as a school inspector.

A member of the Democratic Forum of Germans in Romania since the 1989 revolution, Iohannis was elected to the party's leadership committee in 1998 and became head of its education commission. He was elected mayor of Sibiu in June 2000 and went on to serve four consecutive terms, overseeing the city's revitalization as a vibrant regional centre and tourist destination. It was named the European City of Culture in 2007 and Iohannis won praise for tackling long-standing corruption and attracting foreign investment.

Following the dismissal of Emil Boc's government in 2009, Iohannis was put forward as an independent prime ministerial candidate by four of the five political groups in parliament. However, the president, Traian Băsescu, refused to endorse him, instead instructing the economist Lucian Croitoru to form a government.

Iohannis joined the National Liberal Party in early 2013 and rose swiftly through its ranks, becoming leader in June 2014. Having helped to forge the Christian Liberal Alliance (ACL) with the centre-right Democratic Liberal Party, he was chosen as the ACL's candidate for the presidential election later in the year. His rival, Prime Minister Victor Ponta, was widely expected to win and took the lead in the first round of voting. However, there were widespread complaints about difficulties and delays experienced by Romanians living abroad as they tried to cast their votes, leading to criticism of the government and prompting the foreign minister to resign. In the second round of voting on 16 Nov. 2014, Iohannis took 54·4% of the vote on a 64% turnout, the highest for 14 years.

Career in Office

Iohannis promised to tackle corruption and build a fully independent judiciary, while favouring a pro-European foreign policy stance and stronger ties with Moldova. However, he inherited a weak economy and challenging fiscal situation, together with growing anti-government sentiment. In June 2015 Iohannis called upon Ponta to resign as prime minister after prosecutors named him in an inquiry into forgery, tax evasion and money laundering. Ponta eventually stood down in Nov. that year, following street protests prompted by a nightclub fire in which over 60 people died amid lax safety regulations. Iohannis then appointed Dacian Cioloş to head a technocratic government until parliamentary elections in Dec. 2016 that were won by the centre-left Social Democratic Party (PSD). Having rejected the nomination of Sevil Shhaideh, a female Muslim candidate, for the premiership Iohannis named Sorin Grindeanu, a social democrat and former communications minister, as prime minister-designate and his new government was approved by parliament in Jan. 2017. However, Grindeanu was ousted by parliament in a no-confidence vote in June after his government had adopted a controversial and unpopular decree decriminalizing certain official misconduct, following which Iohannis designated Mihai Tudose, previously the economy minister, as the new premier. Tudose then resigned in Jan. 2018 and, in a bid to end the political instability, Iohannis accepted PSD nominee Viorica Dăncilă as the country's first female prime minister.

Viorica Dăncilă
Position
Prime Minister

Introduction
Viorica Dăncilă was sworn in as Romania's first female prime minister on 29 Jan. 2018. A member of the Social Democratic Party (PSD), she came to power after the resignation of her fellow Social Democrat Mihai Tudose, becoming the country's third prime minister in seven months.

Early Life
Viorica Dăncilă was born on 16 Dec. 1963 in Roşiorii de Vede. In 1988 she graduated from the Petroleum & Gas University of Ploieşti. After briefly working as a teacher, she was an engineer at the oil and gas company Petrom SA from 1997 until 2009.

Dăncilă joined the PSD in 1996 and became the leader of the party's Women's Organization at the regional level in 2003. She entered the European Parliament as a representative of the PSD in 2009, a position to which she was re-elected in 2014. As acting chairwoman of the parliament's committee on women's rights and gender equality in 2015, she proposed legislation to protect women from domestic violence. In the same year, she was elected president of the PSD Women's Organization, in which capacity she introduced a reform to guarantee that at least 30% of candidates on the party's electoral lists were female.

Tudose was forced to resign on 15 Jan. 2018 amidst party infighting exacerbated by his controversial comments about Romania's ethnic Székely community. Two days later, the president of the PSD, Liviu Dragnea, nominated Dăncilă to succeed Tudose—a choice approved by Romania's president, Klaus Iohannis.

Career in Office
Dăncilă leads a centre-left coalition of the PSD and the Alliance of Liberals and Democrats (ALDE), which holds a narrow majority in both chambers of parliament. The government received a vote of confidence on 29 Jan. with the support of the Democratic Alliance of Hungarians in Romania (UDMR) and other members representing various national minorities.

A pro-European moderate, Dăncilă's election was welcomed by supporters as a victory for women's rights. However, critics have raised concerns over her independence from PSD president Dragnea, who is prevented from running for the premiership owing to a prior conviction for vote rigging.

In June 2018 her government survived a parliamentary no-confidence vote by 166 votes to four after the centrist opposition accused her ruling party of trying to weaken anti-corruption laws and institutions.

Defence

Compulsory national military service was abolished in 2006.

In 2013 defence expenditure totalled US$2,475m. (US$114 per capita), representing 1·3% of GDP.

Army
Strength (2011) 41,500. There is a joint reserve of 45,000. The ministry of the interior operates a paramilitary Border Guard (22,900 strong in 2011) and a Gendarmerie (around 57,000). In 2017 the Romanian government reached an agreement with Germany to integrate a Romanian army brigade into a division of the German army.

Navy
The fleet includes three destroyers and four corvettes. There is also a naval infantry force.

Personnel in 2011 totalled 6,900. There are naval bases at Brăila, Constanţa, Mangalia and Tulcea.

Air Force
The Air Force numbered 9,500 in 2011, with 70 combat-capable aircraft (MiG-21s and Romanian-built IAR-99s).

International Relations

At the European Union's Helsinki Summit in Dec. 1999 Romania, along with five other countries, was invited to begin full negotiations for membership in Feb. 2000. Romania joined the EU on 1 Jan. 2007. Romania became a member of NATO on 29 March 2004.

Economy

Agriculture accounted for 6·1% of GDP in 2013, industry 28·6% and services 65·3%.

Overview
The global financial crisis saw the economy contract by 7% in 2009 and the IMF provided a €20bn. bailout that demanded the introduction of a tough austerity programme. In 2010 reforms led to riots that brought about the downfall of Emil Boc's government. There were, however, signs of recovery with GDP growth of 2·3% in 2011 and 0·6% in 2012, and between 2013 and 2015 annual expansion averaged 3·4%—one of Europe's highest rates.

Entry into the European Union in 2007 drove modernization and reform programmes, particularly in financial services, public administration and tax collection. The energy sector has been opened up to greater competition, with state-owned companies seeking private sector investment. However, plans to adopt the euro have been suspended in light of ongoing eurozone instability.

The economy is weighted heavily towards banking—largely foreign-owned—and exports. However, the eurozone crisis allied to domestic political uncertainty has restricted export growth in the short to medium term. Reform of state-owned enterprises is considered key to long-term growth. Romania has one of the widest urban-rural poverty gaps in Europe, with the World Bank estimating that 70% of the population in rural areas live beneath the poverty line. Despite once being a 'breadbasket' for Europe, food imports have increased to compensate for the underdeveloped agricultural sector.

Currency
The monetary unit has since 1 July 2005 been the new leu, pl. new lei (RON) notionally of 100 bani, which replaced the leu (ROL) at a rate of one new leu = 10,000 lei. Foreign exchange reserves were US$41,571m. and gold reserves 3·34m. troy oz in Sept. 2009. There was deflation of 1·6% in 2016 and inflation of 1·3% in 2017. Total money supply was 64,201m. new lei in Aug. 2009.

Budget
Central government revenue and expenditure (in 1m. new lei) for calendar years:

	2009	2010	2011
Revenue	152,055	162,102	172,162
Expenditure	224,072	211,808	195,999

Romania's budget deficit in 2017 was 2·9% of GDP (2016, 2·9%; 2015, 0·7%). The required target set by the EU is a budget deficit of no more than 3%.

VAT is 19% (reduced rates, 9% and 5%). There is a flat income tax rate of 16%.

Performance
The economy grew by 3·9% in 2015, 4·8% in 2016 and 6·9% in 2017. Total GDP in 2017 was US$211·8bn.

Banking and Finance
The National Bank of Romania (founded 1880; nationalized 1946) is the central bank and bank of issue under the Minister of Finance. Its *Governor* is Dr Mugur Isărescu. In 2015 there were 36 credit institutions, seven of which were branches of foreign banks. The largest banks are the Romanian Commercial Bank (Banca Comercială Română), BRD Groupe Société Générale (formerly Romanian Development Bank/Banca Română pentru Dezvoltare) and Banca Transilvania. The Romanian Commercial Bank is part of Austria's Erste Group and BRD Groupe Société Générale part of France's Groupe Société Générale.

Foreign debt was US$121,505m. in 2010, representing 76·4% of GNI.

A stock exchange reopened in Bucharest in 1995.

Energy and Natural Resources

In 2011, 21·4% of energy consumption came from renewables (wind power, solar power, hydro-electric power, tidal power, geothermal energy and biomass), compared to the European Union average of 13·0%. A target of 24% has been set by the EU for 2020.

Environment

Romania's carbon dioxide emissions from the consumption of energy were the equivalent of 4·1 tonnes per capita in 2011.

Electricity

In 2011 installed capacity was approximately 20·5m. kW; output in 2011 was 62·22bn. kWh (24% hydro-electric and 19% nuclear). Consumption per capita in 2011 was 2,765 kWh. A nuclear power plant at Cernavodă began working in 1996. A second reactor became operational there in 2007.

Oil and Gas

Oil production in 2012 was 4·1m. tonnes, but with annual consumption of more than twice as much a large amount has to be imported. There were 0·6bn. bbls of proven oil reserves in 2012. Romania was the first country to start oil exploration, and in the late 1850s was the world's leading oil producer, with an output of 200 tonnes a year. Natural gas production in 2012 totalled 10·9bn. cu. metres with 100bn. cu. metres in proven reserves.

The oil company Petrom, Romania's largest company, was privatized in 2004 when the government sold a 51% stake to the Austrian oil and gas group OMV.

Minerals

The principal minerals are oil and natural gas, salt, lignite, iron and copper ores, bauxite, chromium, manganese and uranium. Output, 2005 (in 1,000 tonnes): lignite, 31,070; salt, 2,420; iron ore, 265; zinc, 14.

Agriculture

Romania has the biggest agricultural area in Eastern Europe after Poland. In 2013, 29·3% of the economically active population were engaged in agriculture. There were 13·91m. ha. of agricultural land in 2013 including 8·75m. ha. of arable land and 442,000 ha. of permanent crops. There were 181,000 ha. of irrigated land in 2013.

Production (2013, in 1,000 tonnes): maize, 11,348; wheat, 7,296; potatoes, 3,290; sunflower seeds, 2,196; barley, 1,542; cabbages, Brussels sprouts, etc., 1,159; sugar beets, 1,029; grapes, 992; tomatoes, 749.

Livestock, 2013 (in 1,000): sheep, 8,834; pigs, 5,234; cattle, 2,009; goats, 1,266; horses, 575; chickens, 80,136.

Forestry

Total forest area was 6·86m. ha. in 2015 (30% of the land area). Of the total area under forests 4% was primary forest in 2015, 88% other naturally regenerated forest and 8% planted forest. Timber production in 2011 was 14·36m. cu. metres.

Fisheries

The catch in 2015 totalled 9,307 tonnes (up from 2,688 tonnes in 2010 but down from 224,188 tonnes in 1987), of which 4,464 tonnes were from inland waters.

Industry

In 2013 industry accounted for 28·6% of GDP. Industrial output grew by 3·8% in 2013.

Output of main products (in 1,000 tonnes): cement (2006 estimate), 8,253; rolled steel (2007), 5,589; crude steel (2008), 5,035; distillate fuel oil (2007), 4,660; petrol (2007), 3,799; pig iron (2008), 2,945; hot-rolled steel products (2012 estimate), 2,700; lime (2006 estimate), 1,942; fertilizers (2012), 1,707; residual fuel oil (2007), 1,186; wheat flour (2012), 844; soda ash (2012 estimate), 430; paper and paperboard (2012), 402; caustic soda (2012), 256.

Labour

The labour force in 2013 was 9,521,000 (10,258,000 in 2003). 64·7% of the population aged 15–64 was economically active in 2013. In the same year 7·3% of the population was unemployed. The standard retirement age is 65 years for men and 60 for women. A minimum monthly wage was set in 1993; it was set at 670 new lei for full-time adult employees from 1 Jan. 2011. The average gross monthly wage was 1,845 new lei in 2009.

Romania had 24,000 people living in slavery according to the Walk Free Foundation's 2013 *Global Slavery Index*.

International Trade

Imports and Exports

Imports in 2007 were valued at US$69,946m. (US$24,003m. in 2003) and exports US$40,247m. (US$17,618m. in 2003). Principal imports are mineral fuels, machinery and transport equipment, and textiles; main export commodities are textiles, mineral products and chemicals.

Romania's main import sources in 2007 were: Germany (17·2%); Italy (12·8%); Hungary (6·9%); Russia (6·3%); France (6·3%). In 2007 Romania's main export markets were: Italy (17·2%); Germany (17·0%); France (7·7%); Turkey (7·0%).

Communications

Roads

There were 81,693 km of roads in 2008, of which 281 km were motorways, 16,318 km main and national roads and 65,094 km secondary and other roads. Passenger cars in 2005 numbered 3,363,800 (156 per 1,000 inhabitants). In 2007 there were 2,712 fatalities as a result of road accidents.

Rail

Length of standard gauge route in 2011 was 10,638 km, of which 4,031 km were electrified; there were 135 km of 1,524 mm gauge lines and four km of narrow gauge. Freight carried in 2011, 54·8m. tonnes; passengers, 53·5m. There is a metro (62·4 km) and tram/light rail network (338 km) in Bucharest, and tramways in 13 other cities.

Civil Aviation

Tarom (*Transporturi Aeriene Române*) is the 97·2% state-owned airline. In 2010 it provided domestic services and international flights to over 40 cities. The largest Romanian airline is Blue Air, a low-cost carrier founded in 2004. In 2016 it carried a record 3,590,129 passengers.

Bucharest's main airport is Henri Coandă International Airport, generally known by its former official name of Bucharest Otopeni International Airport. A second Bucharest airport, Aurel Vlaicu International, used to be the country's second busiest airport but since early 2012 caters exclusively for business air traffic. Outside of Bucharest the busiest airports are at Cluj-Napoca and Timişoara. Henri Coandă International handled 7,120,024 passengers in 2012 and 26,494 tonnes of freight; Timişoara handled 1,039,109 passengers in 2012, Cluj-Napoca 936,145 and Aurel Vlaicu International 424,016.

Shipping

In Jan. 2014 there were 18 ships of 300 GT or over registered, totalling 65,000 GT. The Romanian-controlled fleet comprised 82 vessels of 1,000 GT or over in July 2014, of which three were under the Romanian flag and 79 under foreign flags. The main ports are Constanţa and Constanţa South Agigea on the Black Sea and Galaţi, Brăila and Tulcea on the Danube. Romania had 1,647 km of navigable rivers in 2013 and 132 km of navigable canals.

Telecommunications

In 2013 there were 4,720,000 main (fixed) telephone lines. In the same year mobile phone subscribers numbered 22,910,000. The telecommunications sector was fully liberalized on 1 Jan. 2003, ending the monopoly of the Greek-controlled operator Romtelecom (now Telekom Romania). In 2013, 49·8% of the population aged 16–74 were internet users. In March 2012 there were 4·2m. Facebook users.

Social Institutions

Out of 178 countries analysed in the 2017 *Fragile States Index*—a list published jointly by the Fund for Peace and *Foreign Policy* magazine—Romania was ranked the 43rd least vulnerable to conflict or collapse. The index is based on 12 indicators of state vulnerability across social, political and economic categories.

Justice

The legal system is based on the Civil Code of Quebec, but also influenced by Napoleonic code. The judiciary is constitutionally independent. The High Court of Cassation and Justice is the highest judicial authority, with its judges appointed by the president after consultation with the Superior Council of the Magistracy (an elected professional body). There is also a Constitutional Court.

Day-to-day hearings are administered through a system of local courts and 41 county courts (and the Bucharest Municipal Court), whose judgements may be challenged in any one of 15 courts of appeal.

As a condition of EU accession and World Bank financing, Romania was subject to a Judicial Reform Project aimed at increasing the efficiency of the court system, improving transparency and reducing corruption. This included the implementation of four revised codes (the criminal code, civil code, criminal procedures code and civil procedures code).

The death penalty was abolished in Jan. 1990 and is forbidden by the 1991 constitution. The population in penal institutions in Sept. 2013 was 33,015 (155 per 100,000 of national population). In 2015 the World Justice Project *Rule of Law Index*, which provides data on how the rule of law is experienced by the general public across eight categories, ranked Romania 28th of 102 countries for both criminal justice and civil justice.

Education

Education is free and compulsory from the age of six. There is compulsory school attendance for ten years. Primary education comprises four years of study, secondary education comprises lower secondary education (organized in two cycles: grades 5th–8th in elementary schools and grades 9th–10th in high schools or vocational schools) and upper secondary education includes further education in high schools. Further secondary education is also available at *lycées*, professional schools or advanced technical schools.

In 2007 there were 648,862 children and 36,555 teaching staff in pre-primary schools; 917,829 pupils and 55,487 teaching staff in primary schools; and 1,954,077 pupils and 153,805 teaching staff in secondary schools.

In 2007 there were 928,175 students in tertiary education and 30,583 academic staff. There are 49 public higher education institutions in Romania—the oldest is Alexandru Ioan Cuza University in Iaşi (established in 1860) and the largest is Babeş-Bolyai University in Cluj-Napoca (41,690 students in 2015–16). There are also a number of private universities.

Adult literacy rate in 2009 was estimated at 97·7% (male 98·3%; female 97·0%).

In 2015 public expenditure on education came to 3·1% of GDP and 9·1% of total government spending.

Health

In 2006 there were 419 public hospitals with 141,225 beds; there were 45,815 physicians and 4,360 dentists in the public sector in 2006.

Welfare

In 2014 pensioners comprised 4,541,900 old age, survivors and early retirement, 736,271 social assistance, 701,000 disability and 508,791 retired farmers. These drew average monthly pensions ranging from 792,698 lei to 3,504,205 lei. In 2012 general government spending on social protection amounted to 33·8% of total general government expenditure.

Religion

The government officially recognizes 17 religions (which receive various forms of state support); the predominant one is the Romanian Orthodox Church. It is autocephalous, but retains dogmatic unity with the Eastern Orthodox Church. Its *Patriarch* is Daniel (enthroned 30 Sept. 2007). There are six metropolitanates, made up of archdioceses and dioceses, with a total of 13,527 parishes. In Feb. 2019 there was one cardinal.

Religious affiliation at the 2011 census included: Romanian Orthodox, 16,307,004 (about 81% of the population); Roman Catholic, 870,774; Protestant Reformed Church, 600,932; Pentecostal, 362,314; Greek Catholics, 150,593; Baptist, 112,850.

Culture

World Heritage Sites

Romania has eight sites on the UNESCO World Heritage List: the Danube Delta (inscribed on the list in 1991); the Villages with Fortified Churches in Transylvania (1993 and 1999); the Monastery of Horezu (1993); the Churches of Moldavia (1993); the Historic Centre of Sighişoara (1999); the Dacian Fortresses of the Orăştie Mountains (1999); and the Wooden Churches of Maramureş (1999). Ancient and Primeval Beech Forests of the Carpathians and Other Regions of Europe (2007 and 2017) are shared with Albania, Austria, Belgium, Bulgaria, Croatia, Germany, Italy, Slovakia, Slovenia, Spain and Ukraine.

Press

In 2014 there were 42 daily papers (40 paid-for and two free) with a combined circulation of 550,000. The most widely read newspapers are the paid-for *Click!* and *Libertatea* and the free *Adavarul de seara* and *Ring*.

Tourism

In 2009, 1,275,600 non-resident tourists stayed in holiday accommodation (down from 1,465,900 in 2008) including: 181,100 from Germany; 141,600 from Italy; 100,300 from France; 76,900 from Hungary.

Festivals

The George Enescu Festival of classical music is held every two years in Aug.–Sept. with concerts across Bucharest, Iaşi and Sibiu. The Peninsula/Félsziget rock festival takes place annually in July or Aug. in Târgu Mureş in Transylvania. Other notable events are the EUROPAfest of music in Bucharest (May), the International Romani Art Festival in Timişoara (July), Garana Jazz Festival at Poiana Lupului (July) and the Romanian National Theatre Festival in Bucharest (Oct.–Nov.).

Diplomatic Representatives

Of Romania in the United Kingdom (Arundel House, 4 Palace Green, London, W8 4QD)
  Ambassador: Sorin-Dan Mihalache.

Of the United Kingdom in Romania (24 Strada Jules Michelet, 010463 Bucharest)
  Ambassador: Andrew Noble.

Of Romania in the USA (1607 23rd St., NW, Washington, D.C., 20008)
  Ambassador: George Cristian Maior.

Of the USA in Romania (4–6, Dr Liviu Librescu Blvd, District 1, Bucharest)
  Ambassador: Hans Klemm.

Of Romania to the United Nations
  Ambassador: Ion Jinga.

Of Romania to the European Union
  Permanent Representative: Luminiţa Teodora Obodescu.

Further Reading

Comisia Nationala pentru Statistica. *Anuarul Statistic al României/Romanian Statistical Yearbook.* Annual.—*Revista de Statistica.* Monthly
Carey, Henry F., *Romania since 1989: Politics, Economics and Society.* 2004
Gallagher, T., *Romania after Ceauşescu; the Politics of Intolerance.* 1995
Papadimitriou, Dimitris and Phinnemore, David, *Romania and The European Union: From Marginalisation to Membership.* 2011
Phinnemore, David, (ed.) *The EU and Romania: Accession and Beyond.* 2006
National Statistical Office: Comisia Nationala pentru Statistica, 16 Libertatii Ave., sector 5, Bucharest.
Website: http://www.insse.ro

Russia

Rossiiskaya Federatsiya (Russian Federation)

Capital: Moscow
Population projection, 2020: 143·79m.
GNI per capita, 2017: (PPP$) 24,233
HDI/world rank, 2017: 0·816/49
Internet domain extension: .ru

Key Historical Events

Archaeological evidence points to the influence of Arabic and Turkic cultures prior to the 4th century AD. Avar, Goth, Hun and Magyar invasions punctuated the development of the East Slavs over the next five centuries, while trade with Germanic, Scandinavian and Middle Eastern regions began in the 8th century.

In 882 the Varangian prince Oleg of Novgorod took Kyiv and made it the capital of Kievan Rus, the first unified state of the East Slavs, uniting Finnish and Slavic tribes. During the 10th century, trade was extended between the Baltic and Black Seas, forming Kyiv's main economy. The Varangians, led by Rurik of Jutland, led attacks on Baghdad and Constantinople, subsequently establishing a trade link with the latter.

During the 13th century the area was invaded from the west by Teutonic Knights, Lithuanians and Swedes, and from the south by Mongol and Tatar tribes. In 1223 Genghis Khan's grandson, Batu Khan, conquered Kievan Rus. Despite the ruthless reign of the Mongols, trade flourished during the period and many cities were reinvigorated. The Mongols and Tatars created an ascendency known as the 'Golden Horde' around most of Western Russia and Central Asia and made Itil (near modern Astrakhan) the capital. Its dominance lasted until the 15th century when internal struggles finally forced the break-up of the empire.

Co-operation between Moscow's leader Ivan and the Mongol Öz Beg (ruled 1312–41), in addition to geographical advantages and natural resources, allowed Moscow to develop and prosper. The city was first consolidated under the Muscovite Grand Duke Ivan III (ruled 1462–1505), who adopted the Roman title of tsar and Byzantine ritual after marrying into Byzantine royalty. Ivan annexed the East Slavic regions, as well as Belarus and the Ukraine, conquered Novgorod in 1478 and opened up contacts with Western Europe.

The empire was strengthened and further expanded by his son Vasily III and reformed by Vasily's successor Ivan IV, a sickly and volatile ruler known as Ivan the Terrible (or 'Awesome', *Grozny*) who came to the throne at the age of 16 in 1547. Ivan's divisive and suppressive administration, *oprichnina*, led a reign of terror from 1566–72 in which thousands were executed (although it is believed that initially the Russian nobles, or boyars, had strong control over the throne and its direction, including local government reforms, a new law code and restrictions of hereditary rights). Ivan bolstered the military and led campaigns against the khanates of Kazan (1552), Astrakhan (1556) and the Crimea, extending Russia's territory towards Siberia and down to the Caspian Sea. But the costly war with Livonia (1558–82) drained Russia's resources. Ivan murdered his son in 1581 leaving a hereditary gap and a struggle for succession.

Russia was ruled nominally by Ivan's feeble-minded brother Fyodor I—in actuality by Fyodor's brother-in-law Boris Godunov, who succeeded Fyodor in 1598. But in 1601 False Dmitri claimed to be Ivan IV's son (Dmitri had died in 1591) and challenged Boris for the throne. With the backing of the boyars, the Cossacks and the Polish nobility, Dmitri succeeded Boris as tsar on the latter's death in 1605. There followed a chaotic period of instability as differing sides fought for control of the realm. The following year Dmitri was assassinated and the boyars crowned the rebel leader Vasily Shuysky in return for privileges. But soon a subgroup of boyars led by the Romanovs gave support to a second False Dmitri (a pretender to the throne who claimed to be Ivan IV's youngest son) in 1608, establishing a shadow government just outside Moscow. Shuysky turned to Sweden for help, bargaining away territory and triggering Poland's invasion of Muscovy and the siege of Smolensk (1609). Both governments collapsed and a coalition government was formed. A peace treaty signed with Sweden in 1617 lost Russia Novgorod in exchange for Baltic control, while an armistice with Poland began the following year.

Romanovs

With the Polish occupiers ejected from Moscow, Mikhail Fyodorovich Romanov, the first of a dynasty that would rule until 1917, became tsar of a country ruined by war and with regions occupied by Swedish, Polish or rebel forces. But by avoiding involvement in the Thirty Years' War, in which Sweden and Poland were embroiled, he managed to restore some stability and to strengthen Russia's holdings in the southern regions. His son Aleksey inherited the throne as a child. Unpopular measures implemented by Aleksey's adviser, Boris Ivanovich Morozov, including a crippling salt tax, led to a riot in 1648 and rebellion in Novgorod and Pskov. Eastern Ukraine was annexed, while the support of a Cossack rebellion against Polish rule in the Ukraine degenerated into a costly war with Sweden and Poland over Ukrainian, Baltic and Belorussian territory. Russia consequently lost the Baltic coast to Sweden in 1661 and later Belarus and parts of the Ukraine to Poland. Sophia succeeded Aleksey to the disputed throne in 1682, followed seven years later by her half brother Peter the Great.

The reign of Peter I (1689–1725) signalled a new era for Russia that broke so far with Muscovy tradition as to be seen as the birth of modern Russia. The empire was expanded and strengthened and there was increased trade with Western Europe. His modest upbringing and travels to the West gave Peter a novel pro-European stance. The capital was transferred from Moscow to the newly built St Petersburg (1712), as part of a Europeanization programme. Peter introduced radical structural changes to the Russian body politic, converting it into the Western European mould. The tsardom of Muscovy became the Empire of All the Russias and Peter became head of state as opposed to ruling patriarch. Administrative reforms divided Russia into eight main provinces, put the church under state control and introduced compulsory secular education for the nobility, although the rights of the peasantry were abolished and they were forced into serfdom. Peter expanded industry, created the navy, introduced army conscription and strengthened the southern border against the Crimean Tatars. He formed an alliance with Denmark, Poland and Saxony against Sweden, resulting in the Great Northern War (1700–21), which ended with Russia claiming Livonia in the Treaty of Nystad (1721). The expanded empire made Russia the leading Baltic power.

Catherine the Great

Despite Peter's rejection of hereditary rule in favour of appointing a successor, his choice was never named before his sudden death. The rest of the 18th century was marked by disputed succession. After Peter's death, his widow Catherine I was declared empress, though Peter's collaborator Prince Menshikov ruled in her name. A supreme privy council was established to distribute power; Peter's grandson, Peter II, ruled briefly before dying of smallpox. He was succeeded by Peter I's niece, Anna, the duchess of Courland (1730), then by her niece Anna Leopoldovna, before Peter I's daughter, Elizabeth, came to power in 1741 in a bloodless coup. During her 21-year reign, her father's reforms were consolidated and Western culture and literature flourished. She founded the University of Moscow and established the St Petersburg Academy of Arts. At the end of her reign Russia was involved in the Seven Years' War, occupying Berlin for a short time before Elizabeth's death in 1762. Russia's subsequent withdrawal saved Frederick the Great's Prussia from destruction.

Elizabeth's nephew, Peter III, proved an unpopular ruler. Childless, his politically ambitious wife, Catherine the Great, plotted to depose him, claiming the throne for herself soon after. Influenced by the Enlightenment, she attempted to implement legislative, educative and administrative reforms. But many of these, as well as the emancipation of the serfs, were blocked by the nobility. The imposed Russification of the Ukrainian, Polish and Baltic regions proved unpopular, while civil unrest led to the Pugachev Revolt (1773–75), in which peasants, Cossacks and workers rebelled against the aristocracy. Catherine's foreign policy was an aggressive expansion plan to the south and east to make Russia the leading European power at the expense of the Turks and Tatars. She forged a path through to the Mediterranean Sea to maximize maritime trade routes and developed close relations with Prussia and Austria with whom Poland was shared. But despite two wars with Turkey she failed to take Constantinople, as much an emotional as a political prize.

© Springer Nature Limited 2020
Palgrave Macmillan (ed.), *The Statesman's Yearbook 2020*,
https://doi.org/10.1057/978-1-349-95940-2_158

After Catherine's death in 1796, her son Paul's tyrannical rule led to his murder in 1801. His son Alexander I adopted more liberal policies in administration, science and education. War with France in 1805 led to a crushing defeat at Austerlitz, but when Napoleon invaded Russia in 1812 his army fell victim to the Russian winter. Alexander's death in 1825 provoked instability and uprisings which were quashed by military force. Russia was defeated by Britain, France and Turkey in the Crimean War (1853–56). Alexander II (ruled 1855–81), who followed Nicholas I (ruled 1825–55), implemented reforms, the most important of which was the partial emancipation of the serfs in 1861. Major judicial reform followed three years later and universal military service in 1874. But towards the end of his reign Alexander's increasingly conservative measures exacerbated the revolutionary mood of socialist-influenced university students and the peasantry. He was assassinated in 1881 and was succeeded by Alexander III (1881–94). Labour reforms introduced by Alexander III were harsh and restrictive and the peasants' lot failed to improve. The government's neglect of agricultural policy resulted in crop failure and widespread famine in 1891.

The Russian empire had expanded to the far reaches of Asia, to Afghanistan and into Central Europe. By the end of Alexander III's reign, only half the population spoke Russian or were members of the Orthodox Church.

Revolution

Nicholas II's reign (1894–1917) marked the end of Tsarist Russia. Like his father, he did little to improve social conditions for the masses, concentrating instead on military power. Industrial growth produced an unskilled urban working class whose living conditions fuelled revolutionary feeling. Socialism and Liberalism were also taking hold of the educated middle classes—doctors, teachers and engineers—as well as disaffected civil servants. In 1904 Nicholas embarked on and lost an unpopular war with Japan. The middle classes campaigned for a Legislative Assembly. In Jan. 1905 the priest, Georgy Gapon, led a protest of factory workers to St Petersburg's Winter Palace. Tsarist troops opened fire on the crowds killing over 100 people. Public outrage to 'Bloody Sunday' soon spread throughout the country. A general strike, paralysing most of Russia, led to violence between monarchists and insurgents well into 1907, while factions in the armed forces rebelled. Yielding to the pressure of the 1905 revolution, the tsar permitted the establishment of the first *Duma* (parliament), which convened in St Petersburg in 1906. But it lasted only 70 days. Violence continued into 1907.

In 1912 the two strands of the Social Democratic Workers' Party—the Bolsheviks (or majority) led by Vladimir Ilyich Ulyanov (Lenin), and the Mensheviks (or minority)—split, the Bolsheviks pursuing revolution, the Mensheviks evolutionary change. The outbreak of the First World War in 1914 temporarily unified Russians in the war effort. The tsar took command of the armed forces in 1915, leaving an authoritarian vacuum that allowed the tsarina and the influential adviser Grigori Rasputin to implement various unpopular ministerial changes. Rasputin was assassinated by disgruntled nobles in 1916. Depleting military resources and social unrest caused by hardship forced the end of the tsar's reign. A succession of anti-tsar demonstrations culminated in a mass protest in St Petersburg. Soldiers deserted, allying themselves with the workers, a pattern repeated throughout the country. A provisional government comprising Menshevik and Bolshevik elements was established and Tsar Nicholas abdicated on 2 March 1917. The Royal Family was executed in July 1918.

Tension between moderate Mensheviks and radical Bolsheviks intensified and in Oct. 1917 the Bolsheviks led by Lenin, newly returned from exile, seized control. The new government headed by Lenin, the Council of People's Commissars, created the Soviet constitution the following year. Russia was declared the Soviet Republic of Workers, Soldiers and Peasants and the capital was moved back to Moscow. Russia eventually withdrew from the First World War in 1918 but its forced acceptance of the unfavourable Brest-Litovsk treaty led many to abandon the government. Between 1918–21 a civil war raged between the Bolshevik Red Army, led by Lenin's ally Leon Trotsky, and the White Army, formed by former imperial officers, Cossacks, anti-communists and anarchists. The government imposed 'war communism'—forced labour and expropriation of business and food supplies—to support its cause, and eventually overcame the White Army. Lenin instituted the New Economic Policy (NEP) in 1921 to replace War Communism, reintroducing a monetary system and private ownership of small-scale industry and agriculture. In 1922 the Union of Soviet Socialist Republics was established comprising Russia, the Ukraine, Belarus and Transcaucasia. The Turkmen and Uzbek republics were added two years later, and the Tadzhik republic joined in 1929.

Stalin

On Lenin's death in 1924, Joseph Stalin (Ioseb Dzhugashvili) became general secretary of the Communist Party. Stalin rejected the 'state capitalism' of the NEP, which had failed to provide enough food for the urban workforce. From 1928 Stalin pursued a programme of industrialization and from 1933 agricultural collectivization, which cost the lives of 10m. peasants through famine or persecution. Constructing a personality cult for Lenin and himself, Stalin reasserted his absolute authority in massive purges; in 1934 and 1937 the NKVD (political police) eliminated millions of political dissidents.

Despite a non-aggression pact signed with Germany in Aug. 1939, the USSR was forced into the Second World War (termed the Great Patriotic War) in 1941 when the Nazi's Plan Barbarossa targeted Kyiv, Moscow and Leningrad for invasion. Up to 20m. Soviet lives were lost, almost 1m. in the battle of Stalingrad alone (1942–43). Expansion before and during the war created 15 aligned republics. Transcaucasia was divided into Armenia, Georgia and Azerbaijan, Kazakh and Kirghiz Soviet Socialist Republics were formed, and, along with Latvia, Lithuania, Estonia and Moldavia, were incorporated into the USSR. Following the war, Stalin managed to gain Western acceptance of a Soviet sphere of influence in Eastern Europe. The Baltic States and large tracts of land from neighbouring countries were annexed, while puppet regimes established Poland, Czechoslovakia, East Germany, Hungary, Bulgaria and Romania as satellites of Moscow.

The blockade of West Berlin (1948–49) and the Soviet detonation of an atomic bomb in Aug. 1949 were major factors in the escalation of the Cold War, waged indirectly in the Korean War (1950–53). On Stalin's death, Nikita Khrushchev reversed many of Stalin's policies and condemned his predecessor. In reaction to the famine in his native Ukraine, he developed the vast wheatfields in Kazakhstan. Relaxing control in the Eastern Bloc allowed for some liberalization although the Hungarian Uprising and the Poznań Riots in Poland (both 1956) were brutally suppressed and the Berlin Wall built in 1961. Relations with the Soviet Union's great ideological ally, China, collapsed over differences in interpretation of Marxist doctrine and Chinese opposition to Khrushchev's attempts at détente with the West (which came to be known as 'peaceful co-existence'). The Cuban Missile Crisis of 1962 intensified hostilities with the West and led the world to the brink of nuclear war. Khrushchev's perceived failure in the crisis, coupled with food shortages, led to widespread discontent. He was forced out of office in a 1964 coup led by Leonid Brezhnev, who ruled until 1982.

Soviet Reform

By the 1970s, Russia's international status had reached its zenith. Along with the USA, it was perceived as one of two global superpowers, despite relative economic stagnation. But Brezhnev kept a tight grip on the Eastern Bloc, introducing his 'Brezhnev Doctrine' which permitted the Soviet Union to intervene in the Eastern Bloc countries if Communist rule was ever threatened. In Aug. 1968 the USSR invaded Czechoslovakia to suppress an increasingly liberal regime. Relations with the West were further strained when the Soviets invaded Afghanistan in 1979. By the end of his tenure Brezhnev's failing health mirrored the country's economic decline. The domestic price of Brezhnev's obsessive pursuit of prominence in the space race was the failure of the agricultural and consumer-goods sectors and the decline of living standards. From his death in 1982, the country was led by his aides Yuri Andropov, a short-lived reformer, then Konstantin Chernenko.

When the latter died in 1985, Mikhail Gorbachev became general secretary of the Communist Party. He launched *perestroika*, a policy of economic and structural reform. *Glasnost* ('openness') extended civil liberties, including freedom of the press, and led to official rejection of Stalinist-style totalitarianism. The political system was overhauled, with electoral processes made more democratic and some free-market principles introduced. Gorbachev sought warmer relations with both Communist and Western governments and withdrew troops from Afghanistan in 1989. In a rejection of the 'Brezhnev Doctrine', throughout 1989 and 1990 Gorbachev refused to intervene as one Communist regime after another fell in the Eastern Bloc. Within the USSR, the republics demanded independence. Initially rejected, ethnic tensions arose between and within the republics, with heavy fighting in the Caucasus. Suppressed for so long, the newfound freedom also brought chaos and Gorbachev was blamed. Nonetheless, he won the first USSR presidential elections. Opposition parties were legalized soon after, although he was reluctant to open up the economy to privatization. An attempted coup in Aug. 1991 led to Gorbachev's house arrest for three days and though the coup failed, largely owing to Russian president Boris Yeltsin's intervention (elected June 1991), Gorbachev's leadership was on borrowed time. He resigned his party membership, dismantled the central committee and took KGB and military control away from the Communists. On Christmas Day 1991 Gorbachev resigned as Soviet president and the Soviet Union was dissolved.

Post-Soviet Era

A period of confrontation in 1992–93 between President Yeltsin and parliament climaxed when thousands of armed anti-Yeltsin demonstrators assembled on

3 Oct. 1993 and were urged to seize the Kremlin and television centre. On 4 Oct. troops took the parliament building by storm after a ten-hour assault in which 140 people died. Vice-President Rutskoi and Speaker Khasbulatov were arrested.

Boris Yeltsin was re-elected president in 1996. Many took this as a signal of confidence in the new, democratic Russia. But the reality was a state in which democratic institutions were weakened to the point of impotence by racketeering and bureaucratic dead-weight. Russia defaulted on its debt, the rouble halved in value, imports fell by 45% and oil revenues slumped. In Aug. 1998 the government freed the rouble, in effect devaluing it, imposed currency controls and froze the domestic debt market.

In Aug. 1999 Boris Yeltsin appointed as prime minister Vladimir Putin, a former KGB colonel and director of the KGB's successor organization, the FSB. On 31 Dec. 1999, Yeltsin resigned the presidency, nominating Putin as his interim successor, a job he retained after a clear-cut victory in the presidential election of March 2000. Under Putin, Russia continued the war with separatist Chechnya that began in Dec. 1994. In 2000 a programme of regional reform divided Russia's 89 regions into seven new districts run by Kremlin representatives.

Following the attacks on the USA in Sept. 2001, Putin made clear his support for the war on terrorism. In Oct. 2002 a group of Chechen rebels took control of a Moscow theatre and held hostage 800 people for three days before Russian troops stormed the building. An anaesthetic gas, used to combat the rebels, killed many of the hostages. The new relationship with the USA faltered as a result of the war with Iraq, which Russia opposed. Russia's vulnerability to terrorism was highlighted in Sept. 2004 when hostage takers seized a school in Beslan, in the Russian republic of North Ossetia. A three-day standoff ended with more than 350 people killed, nearly half of them children. Chechen rebels claimed responsibility for the siege.

In 2006 Russia temporarily cut off oil and gas links to Ukraine, Georgia and Belarus ostensibly over pricing disputes. As well as incurring the wrath of those governments immediately involved, the knock-on effects to pipeline flows throughout Europe prompted official protests. The future of Chechnya continues to be a thorn in Moscow's side. Relations with Georgia took a downturn in 2006 over Russia's implicit support for the breakaway Georgian region of South Ossetia. They reached a new low in Aug. 2008 when Russian and Georgian troops fought each other for a week following the Georgian government's military attack on separatist forces in the region.

Putin's human and civil rights records have come under increasing international scrutiny. In the aftermath of the Beslan siege, Putin assumed responsibility for nominating regional governors who had previously been directly elected. Restrictions on press freedom have been criticized as has the absence of a credible opposition and an independent judiciary. Particularly controversial was the imprisonment of Mikhail Khodorkovsky, a multibillion dollar businessman and Putin critic who was sentenced to nine years in 2005 amid claims that the prosecution was politically motivated. In 2006 there was widespread concern at Putin's new powers to monitor non-governmental organizations and potentially expel foreign-based groups, some of which Putin accused of being 'led by puppeteers from abroad'.

In March 2008 Dmitry Medvedev won the presidential election, from which Putin was constitutionally barred. Medvedev named Putin his prime minister in May 2008. At parliamentary elections in Dec. 2011 international observers recorded widespread abuses at the polls and Putin faced popular protests in several cities across the country. In March 2012 he regained the presidency for an extended six-year term and appointed Medvedev as premier.

Following the collapse of President Viktor Yanukovych's regime in Ukraine in Feb. 2014, pro-Russian forces seized control of the Crimea region. On 6 March the parliament of Crimea voted in favour of joining Russia, a proposal that received 97% support in a referendum in the peninsula ten days later. On 18 March Putin signed a bill absorbing Crimea into the Russian Federation, prompting economic sanctions by the USA and the European Union.

In Sept. 2015 Russia carried out its first air strikes in Syria, ostensibly aimed at Islamic State targets but supportive of President Assad's regime. Two months later Moscow imposed sanctions on Turkey after a Russian warplane was shot down by Turkish forces. At parliamentary elections in Sept. 2016 the ruling United Russia party extended its majority, with pro-Putin allies taking the remaining seats. In Nov. 2016 Russia became the focus of international scrutiny over allegations that the Kremlin authorized cyber meddling in the US presidential election won by Donald Trump.

Territory and Population

Russia is bounded in the north by various seas (Barents, Kara, Laptev, East Siberian) which join the Arctic Ocean, and in which is a fringe of islands, some of them large. In the east Russia is separated from the USA (Alaska) by the Bering Strait; the Kamchatka peninsula separates the coastal Bering and Okhotsk Seas. Sakhalin Island, north of Japan, is Russian territory. Russia is bounded in the south by North Korea, China, Mongolia, Kazakhstan, the Caspian Sea, Azerbaijan, Georgia, the Black Sea and Ukraine, and in the west by Belarus, Latvia, Estonia, the Baltic Sea and Finland. Kaliningrad (the former East Prussia) is an exclave on the Baltic Sea between Lithuania and Poland in the west. Russia's area is 17,075,400 sq. km and it has nine time zones (11 until March 2010). In 2007 Russia claimed control over 1·2m. sq. km of the Arctic Ocean bed, known to be rich in energy sources. Immediately disputed by the international community, the claim will require validation by the UN Commission on the Limits of the Continental Shelf. The 2010 census population was 142,856,536 density, 8·4 per sq. km. In Jan. 2018 the population was estimated at 144,530,031. Ethnicity in 2010 showed 80·9% were Russians, 3·9% Tatars, 1·4% Ukrainians, 1·2% Bashkir, 1·0% Chechens and 1·0% Chuvash.

In 2011, 73·2% of the population lived in urban areas.

The UN gives a projected population for 2020 of 143·79m.

Russia's population has been declining since the break-up of the Soviet Union and will continue to do so in the future. By 2050 its population is projected to be the same as it was in the late 1960s.

The two principal cities are Moscow (Moskva), the capital, with a 2010 census population of 11·50m. and St Petersburg (formerly Leningrad), with 4·88m. Moscow is the most populous agglomeration in Europe. Other major cities (with 2010 populations) are: Novosibirsk (1·47m.), Ekaterinburg (1·35m.), Nizhny Novgorod (1·25m.), Samara (1·16m.) and Omsk (1·15m.). In May 2000 President Putin signed a decree dividing Russia into seven federal districts (*okrug*), in the process creating a layer above the various federal subjects (*see* CONSTITUTION AND GOVERNMENT *below*). These, with their administrative centres and 2010 populations in brackets, are: Central (Moscow, 38·43m.), North-Western (St Petersburg, 13·62m.), Southern (Rostov-on-Don, 13·85m.), Volga (Nizhny Novgorod, 29·90m.), Ural (Ekaterinburg, 12·08m.), Siberian (Novosibirsk, 19·26m.) and Far-Eastern (Khaborovsk, 6·29m.). In Jan. 2010 then President Medvedev created a new North Caucasus federal district by splitting the Southern federal district in two. The 2010 population in the area that constitutes the North Caucasus federal district was 9·43m. Its administrative centre is Pyatigorsk. In March 2014, following Russia's annexation of Crimea, the Crimean federal district was created (with its administrative centre is Simferopol), making nine districts in total. However, most of the international community has refused to recognize the legitimacy of the annexation. In July 2016 the Crimean federal district was merged into the Southern federal district, making eight in total again.

The official federal language is Russian, although there are several other officially-recognized languages within individual administrative units.

Social Statistics

2008 births, 1,717,500; deaths, 2,081,000; marriages, 1,178,700; divorces, 703,400. Rates, 2008 (per 1,000 population): birth, 12·1; death, 14·7; marriage, 8·3; divorce, 5·0. At the beginning of the 1970s the death rate had been just 9·4 per 1,000 population. Death rates caused by alcohol abuse in 2009 were 77·0 males and 23·8 females per 100,000 population. Infant mortality, 2010 (per 1,000 live births), 9. There were 1,292,400 legal abortions in 2009. The annual abortion rate (34·2 per 1,000 women aged 15–49 in 2009) ranks among the highest in the world. The divorce rate is also among the highest in the world. The most popular age range for marrying in 2008 was 25–34 for males and 18–24 for females. Expectation of life at birth, 2012, was 64·6 years for males and 75·9 years for females. In 2012, 11% of Russians were living below the national poverty line. Annual population growth rate, 2000–10, –0·3%; fertility rate, 2008, 1·4 births per woman. The suicide rate in 2013 was 19 per 100,000 population, down from 39 per 100,000 in 2000.

Climate

Moscow, Jan. –9·4°C, July 18·3°C. Annual rainfall 630 mm. Arkhangelsk, Jan. –15°C, July 13·9°C. Annual rainfall 503 mm. St Petersburg, Jan. –8·3°C, July 17·8°C. Annual rainfall 488 mm. Vladivostok, Jan. –14·4°C, July 18·3°C. Annual rainfall 599 mm.

Constitution and Government

The Russian Soviet Federative Socialist Republic (RSFSR) adopted a declaration of republican sovereignty by 544 votes to 271 in June 1990. It became a founding member of the Commonwealth of Independent States (CIS) in Dec. 1991, and adopted the name 'Russian Federation'. A law of Nov. 1991 extended citizenship to all who lived in Russia at the time of its adoption and to those in other Soviet republics who requested it.

According to the 1993 constitution the Russian Federation is a 'democratic federal legally-based state with a republican form of government'. The Federation consists of 85 federal subjects (administrative units), of which 22 are republics, one autonomous region, four autonomous districts, nine territories, 46 regions and three federal cities. This includes Crimea (a republic) and Sevastopol (a federal city), which acceded to Russia in March 2014. However, most of the international community still considers them to be officially part of Ukraine (*see* CRIMEA *on page* 1230). The state is secular. Individuals have freedom of movement within or across the boundaries of the Federation; there is freedom of assembly and association, and freedom to engage in any entrepreneurial activity not forbidden by law. The state itself is based upon a separation of powers and upon federal principles, including a Constitutional Court. The most important matters of state are reserved for the federal government, including socio-economic policy, the budget, taxation, energy, foreign affairs and defence. Other matters, including the use of land and water, education and culture, health and social security, are for the joint management of the federal and local governments, which also have the right to legislate within their spheres of competence. A central role is accorded to the *President*, who defines the 'basic directions of domestic and foreign policy' and represents the state internationally. The President is directly elected for a six-year term (since Dec. 2008—previously a four-year term), and for not more than two consecutive terms; he must be at least 35 years old, a Russian citizen, and a resident in Russia for the previous ten years. The President has the right to appoint the prime minister, and (on his nomination) to appoint and dismiss deputy prime ministers and ministers, and may dismiss the government as a whole. In the event of the death or incapacity of the President, the Prime Minister becomes head of state.

Parliament is known as the *Federal Assembly* (Federalnoe Sobranie). The 'representative and legislative organ of the Russian Federation', it consists of two chambers: the *Federation Council* (Sovet Federatsii) and the *State Duma* (Gosudarstvennaya Duma). The Federation Council, or upper house, consists of 170 deputies. The State Duma, or lower house, consists of 450 deputies elected for a five-year term. Starting with the elections in Dec. 2007 all deputies to the State Duma are elected from party lists by proportional representation. There is a 7% threshold for the party-list seats. To qualify for candidacy an individual must be nominated by a registered political party. Incumbent parties are automatically included in the ballot; others must obtain a minimum of 200,000 supporting signatures of which no more than 5% may come from any one region. Alternatively, non-incumbent parties may put forward a deposit of 60m. roubles, which is returned if the party manages to win at least 4% of the popular vote. Parties which gain at least 35 seats may register as a faction, which gives them the right to join the Duma Council and chair committees. Any citizen aged over 21 may be elected to the State Duma, but may not at the same time be a member of the upper house or of other representative bodies. The Federation Council considers all matters that apply to the Federation as a whole, including state boundaries, martial law, and the deployment of Russian forces elsewhere. The Duma approves nominations for Prime Minister, and adopts federal laws (they are also considered by the Federation Council but any objection may be overridden by a two-thirds majority; objections on the part of the President may be overridden by both houses on the same basis). The Duma can reject nominations for Prime Minister but after the third rejection it is automatically dissolved. It is also dissolved if it twice votes a lack of confidence in the government, or if it refuses to express confidence in the government when the matter is raised by the Prime Minister.

A law was approved in June 2001 to reduce the proliferation of political parties (numbering some 200 in 2001). It took effect in July 2003. The new law introduced stricter registration criteria and obliging existing parties to reregister within two years. In order to register, political parties are required to have at least 50,000 members and (since Jan. 2006) more than 45 regional branches with a minimum membership of 500 each. Multiple party membership is banned.

There is a 19-member *Constitutional Court*, whose functions under the 1993 constitution include making decisions on the constitutionality of federal laws, presidential and government decrees, and the constitutions and laws of the subjects of the Federation. It is governed by a Law on the Constitutional Court, adopted in July 1994. Judges are elected for non-renewable 12-year terms.

National Anthem

In Dec. 2000 the Russian parliament, on President Putin's initiative, decided that the tune of the anthem of the former Soviet Union should be reintroduced as the Russian national anthem. The music was composed by Alexander Alexandrov

in 1943 for Stalin. Then new words were written by Sergei Mikhalkov, who had written the original words for the Soviet anthem in 1943. The new anthem is 'Rossiya—svyashennaya nasha derzhava, Rossiya—lyubimaya nasha strana' ('Russia—our holy country, Russia—our beloved country'). Boris Yeltsin had introduced a new anthem during his presidency—'Patriotic Song', from an opera by Mikhail Glinka and arranged by Andrei Petrov.

Government Chronology

General/First Secretaries of the Central Committee of the USSR (1922–91) and Presidents of Russia (1991–)

1922–53	Joseph Stalin
1953–64	Nikita Sergeyevich Khrushchev
1964–82	Leonid Ilyich Brezhnev
1982–84	Yuri Vladimirovich Andropov
1984–85	Konstantin Ustinovich Chernenko
1985–91	Mikhail Sergeyevich Gorbachev
1991–99	Boris Nikolayevich Yeltsin
1999–2008	Vladimir Vladimirovich Putin
2008–12	Dmitry Anatolyevich Medvedev
2012–	Vladimir Vladimirovich Putin

Recent Elections

In the presidential elections held on 18 March 2018 President Vladimir Putin (ind.) was re-elected with 76·7% of the votes cast. Pavel Grudinin (Communist Party of the Russian Federation; KPRF) took 11·8% of the vote; Vladimir Zhirinovsky (Liberal Democratic Party; LDPR) 5·6%; Ksenia Sobchak (Civic Initiative) 1·7%; Grigory Yavlinsky (Russian United Democratic Party; Yabloko) 1·0%; Boris Titov (Party of Growth) 0·8%; and Maxim Suraykin (Communists of Russia; KR) and Sergey Baburin (Russian All-People's Union; ROS) 0·7% each. Turnout was 67·5%. Although most countries acknowledged Putin's victory, some observers suggested that 'irregularities' tarnished the election and some opposition parties refused to recognize the result.

Elections for the State Duma were held on 18 Sept. 2016. United Russia won 343 seats with 54·2% of the vote (up from 238 seats and 49·5% at the 2011 elections); the KPRF 42 seats with 13·3% (down from 92 and 19·2% in 2011); the LDPR 39 with 13·1% of the vote (down from 56 and 11·7% in 2011); A Just Russia 23 with 6·2% (down from 64 and 13·2% in 2011). Two smaller parties and an independent candidate won the remaining three seats. Turnout was a record low 47·9%.

Current Government

President: Vladimir Putin; b. 1952 (sworn in 7 May 2012 for a second time, having previously been in office from Dec. 1999–May 2008).

Prime Minister: Dmitry Medvedev; b. 1965 (sworn in 8 May 2012).

In Feb. 2019 the government comprised:

First Deputy Prime Minister: Anton Siluanov (also *Minister of Finance*).

Deputy Prime Ministers: Maxim Akimov; Yury Borisov; Tatyana Golikova; Olga Golodets; Alexei Gordeyev; Dmitry Kozak; Vitaly Mutko; Yury Trutnev; Konstantin Chuychenko (also *Chief of Staff of the Government*).

Minister of Agriculture: Dmitry Patrushev. *Civil Defence, Emergencies and Disaster Relief:* Yevgeny Zinichev. *Construction, Housing and Public Utilities:* Vladimir Yakushev. *Culture:* Vladimir Medinsky. *Defence:* Sergei Shoigu. *Digital Development, Communications and Mass Media:* Konstantin Noskov. *Economic Development:* Maxim Oreshkin. *Education:* Olga Vasilyeva. *Energy:* Alexander Novak. *Far East Development:* Alexander Kozlov. *Foreign Affairs:* Sergei Lavrov. *Healthcare:* Veronika Skvortsova. *Industry and Trade:* Denis Manturov. *Interior:* Vladimir Kolokoltsev. *Justice:* Alexander Konovalov. *Labour and Social Protection:* Maksim Topilin. *Natural Resources and Environment:* Dmitry Kobylkin. *North Caucasus Affairs:* Sergei Chebotarev. *Science and Higher Education:* Mikhail Kotyukov. *Sport:* Pavel Kolobkov. *Transport:* Yevgeny Ditrikh.

Chairman of the State Duma: Vyacheslav Volodin.

Office of the President: http://kremlin.ru

Current Leaders

Vladimir Vladimirovich Putin

Position
President

Introduction
Vladimir Putin became president again in March 2012, having previously served two presidential terms from 1999–2008 and one term as prime minister from 2008. His initial appointment as president at the end of 1999 had been the culmination of a rapid political rise in the post-Communist era. He has made a determined effort to re-establish a more influential world role for his country, but his opposition to the US-led war in Iraq from 2003 and US plans to expand its missile defence systems into Eastern Europe—together with Russia's annexation of the Crimean peninsula from Ukraine in early 2014 and his support for President Assad's regime in the Syrian civil war—have severely strained relations with Washington and the European Union. He has nevertheless maintained a high approval rating among most Russian voters, although his style of government has been perceived as authoritarian and imperial. Precluded from serving a third presidential term under the constitution, he oversaw the election of his chosen successor, Dmitry Medvedev, in March 2008 and he assumed the post of prime minister in May. In Sept. 2011 Putin was confirmed as United Russia's candidate for the presidential election scheduled for March 2012. Despite a significant fall in support for his United Russia party in parliamentary polls at the end of 2011, he regained the presidency and in May 2012 replaced Medvedev who in turn took over the premiership. In addition to political and security tensions with the West, his third presidential term was marked by economic and financial tremors resulting from a depressed oil export market and a currency crisis. He was nevertheless re-elected again for a further term in March 2018.

Early Life
Vladimir Putin was born in St Petersburg (then called Leningrad) on 7 Oct. 1952, the son of a war veteran who, with his wife, had survived the siege of Leningrad. Baptized into Russian Orthodoxy, he was an accomplished athlete. After graduating from law school in 1975, he began a 15-year career with the KGB's foreign intelligence arm, stationed in Leningrad and East Germany. When collapse threatened the Soviet Union, he retired as a colonel and embarked on a political career.

In the early 1990s Putin worked in local government in St Petersburg, becoming deputy mayor in 1994. In 1996 President Yeltsin brought him to Moscow and appointed him deputy chief Kremlin administrator. He took charge of relations with Russia's diverse regions and in 1998 became head of the Federal Security Service (successor of the KGB) and secretary of the presidential Security Council. In Aug. 1999 he was named acting prime minister.

Career in Office
Putin became the acting president of Russia after Yeltsin's resignation on 31 Dec. 1999 and was officially elected president on 26 March 2000, taking 53% of the vote. His election programme prioritized a 'dictatorship of law' to combat high crime rates, as well as pledging to tackle poverty and promote family values, patriotism and fair business conditions.

He quickly set about exercising firm control over local government and the economy, with a stated aim of reducing corruption. In a bid to centralize power in Moscow, he restructured 89 legislative regions into seven districts, each with a government-approved leader (the majority of whom had military or security backgrounds). He reversed tax concessions that Yeltsin had brought in to assist the regions and reserved the right to dismiss any democratically-elected politician found to have broken the law.

Putin also removed several high-profile business and media figures from official positions. Yeltsin's daughter was dismissed as a Kremlin adviser but immunity was granted to Yeltsin himself, one of the more controversial moves of the then acting president. Putin appointed former finance minister and Yeltsin ally Mikhail Kasyanov as prime minister while placing other supporters in key Kremlin positions. Putin's economic policy was influenced by his allegiance to Anatoly Chubais, who led the wave of privatization in Russia in the early 1990s.

In April 2001 Putin's Unity party merged with the opposition Fatherland bloc, led by the mayor of Moscow, Yury Luzhkov. To pass legislation the president needed a simple majority of 226, with the merger giving him at least 132. In the summer of 2001 new laws on land, labour and pensions were proposed. These were opposed by the Communists whose leader Gennady Zyuganov called for a national demonstration against the reforms.

After Oct. 2001 Russians were free to buy residential and commercial land for the first time since the Bolsheviks took power in 1917. Farm land, making up 98% of the total, was not covered by the law. Critics feared that a privileged few would buy up the land much as they bought privatized businesses in the 1990s. Supporters maintained that it would attract foreign investment, speed up economic reform and stop the illegal sale of land.

Putin's image was dented by the sinking of the Kursk nuclear submarine in Aug. 2000 when all 118 Russian sailors on board died. He was widely condemned for inaction, refusing to return from his holiday and turning down offers of help from Norway and the UK. He was subsequently dogged by allegations of an official cover-up.

Putin meanwhile used the war with Chechnya to establish his 'strong man' credentials, although heavy Russian losses cost him some support and alleged human rights abuses led to a suspension of Russia's voting rights in the Council of Europe. In Oct. 2002 Chechen rebels took 800 people hostage inside a Moscow theatre, demanding the immediate withdrawal of Russian troops from Chechnya. The siege lasted three days before the Russian military stormed the building using an anaesthetic gas which killed the rebels but also over 100 hostages. In March 2003 Putin promised greater autonomy for Chechnya. This followed a referendum in the republic supporting a new constitution that would keep Chechnya within Russia but provide for a president and parliament. Moscow claimed 96% support for the proposals although no international observers were present and the referendum was opposed by separatist groups. In May 2003, following two suicide bomb attacks, Putin reaffirmed his determination to defeat Chechnya's rebel forces. He offered an amnesty for rebels who handed over their weapons by 1 Aug. 2003 and for Russian troops accused of human rights violations.

Following the 11 Sept. 2001 attacks on New York and Washington, D.-C. there was a rapprochement between Russia and the USA, and Putin gave unprecedented support for UN military action in Afghanistan. His offers of military assistance to the Afghan Northern Alliance, the use of Russian airspace for humanitarian aid and his role in persuading Tajikistan and Uzbekistan to support the campaign were well received in the West where leaders were quick to downplay Russia's role in Chechnya. In May 2002 Putin and US President George W. Bush signed an anti-nuclear deal agreeing to reduce their respective strategic nuclear warheads by two-thirds over the next ten years.

However, tension between the two countries increased over the question of Iraq in late 2002. While President Bush attempted to garner support for military action in Iraq—with Russia holding a power of veto within the UN Security Council—he warned Putin at the same time that he would not support Russian military incursions into Georgia, which Russia claimed was tolerating hostile Chechen activity. Putin's political dealings with 'rogue' nations, including North Korea and Cuba, were also criticized, as was Russia's trading of nuclear fuel and weapons with India, Iran, Iraq and Syria.

When US-led forces began attacking Iraq in March 2003 Russia condemned the action and delayed ratifying the US-Russian strategic arms control treaty (*see above*) until the war was over. Putin refuted US accusations that Russia had breached UN sanctions by selling armaments, including anti-tank missiles and jamming equipment, to Iraq. In May 2003 Russia nevertheless voted to accept a UN resolution on Iraq's future jointly proposed by the USA, UK and Spain. In return for the immediate ending of sanctions, the UN was to co-operate with the occupying forces to form a new government. In addition Russia would be able to complete long-standing contracts with Iraq. Despite tension in Russia's relationship with the UK as a result of differences over Iraq, Putin made an official state visit to Britain, the first by a Russian leader for over a century.

Having previously avoided party politics, Putin publicly endorsed a pro-government party—United Russia—in the Dec. 2003 parliamentary elections. In the March 2004 presidential elections, he was criticized by the international press and by OSCE monitors for manipulating the Russian media to influence voting in his favour. He was re-elected in the poll, claiming 71% of the vote and leaving his closest rival, the Communist Nikolai Kharitonov, with less than 14%. In May 2004 Putin set out his goals for his second term—modernizing Russia and raising living standards while aiming for a more stable democracy able to pursue strategic interests abroad.

Chechen violence had continued in 2003. Following a referendum in which Chechens agreed to a Moscow-approved constitution, Putin announced that a presidential vote would go ahead. In Oct. 2003, with a turnout of 85%, the pro-Moscow leader Akhmad Kadyrov was elected. However, he was then killed in a bomb attack in Chechnya's capital in May 2004 and Putin pledged to send extra troops in response. Alu Alkhanov was elected president of Chechnya on 29 Aug. 2004, and in Chechen parliamentary elections in Nov. 2005 the pro-Moscow United Russia party claimed about 60% of the popular vote.

In the aftermath of the bloodbath that ended the Beslan school siege by Chechen militants in Sept. 2004 in which more than 350 people were killed, Putin controversially took control of the appointment of regional governors who had been directly elected for the previous decade. Critics saw the move as undermining democracy.

In May 2005 Mikhail Khodorkovsky, a billionaire former head of oil-exporting company Yukos, was sentenced to nine years' imprisonment for tax evasion and fraud. His conviction, following the effective renationalization of Yukos in 2004, was widely viewed as politically motivated, owing to his criticism of Putin's regime (although he was eventually pardoned on humanitarian grounds in 2013).

High oil and gas prices continued to underpin Russia's strong economic growth during Putin's presidency. There was increasing state influence over the energy industry, exercised through the giant gas monopoly Gazprom and through Rosneft (another state-run company that acquired the prime assets of Yukos in 2004). However, Russia's reputation as a reliable international energy trader was tarnished. Several cuts in Russian oil and gas supplies to neighbouring countries—particularly Ukraine and Belarus—from 2006, purportedly over pricing disputes but with suspected political overtones, in turn disrupted pipeline flows to EU countries and prompted high-level protests.

There was meanwhile growing concern for civil and political freedoms in Putin's Russia, with foreign commentators citing increasing authoritarianism, the lack of a genuine opposition or independent judiciary and more general lawlessness, including violent xenophobia. The deaths in late 2006 of two prominent government critics—campaigning journalist Anna Politkovskaya and former intelligence officer Alexander Litvinenko—fuelled widespread suspicions of official involvement. Litvinenko's poisoning in London in particular led to a sharp deterioration in Russian–UK relations.

Plans by the USA to expand its missile defences into the Eastern European member countries of NATO (which were subsequently scaled back) further soured Russian-US relations in Putin's second term of office. In Nov. 2007 he approved a law suspending Russia's participation in the 1990 Conventional Armed Forces in Europe (CFE) Treaty limiting military deployments.

In Dec. 2007 the United Russia party won a landslide victory in parliamentary elections. With his second term set to expire in 2008, Putin announced that he would nevertheless continue in politics as the next prime minister and that Dmitry Medvedev (the chair of Gazprom) would be his preferred successor as president after elections scheduled for March. Russian voters duly endorsed this political continuity at the polls and Putin and Medvedev were sworn into their respective posts in May 2008. Putin therefore remained a pivotal figure in the Russian leadership, having an increasingly centralized grip on power and policy with President Medvedev.

United Russia was again dominant in the parliamentary elections in Dec. 2011, although with a reduced majority of seats and slightly less than 50% of the vote. Reports of electoral fraud prompted unprecedented opposition protests on the streets of Moscow. Despite the apparent decline in his personal support, Putin stood successfully as United Russia's candidate for the presidential election in March 2012 and once more took over the office that he had vacated in 2008. He stepped down as leader of United Russia ahead of being sworn in as president in May 2012.

Putin initially opposed outside intervention in the civil war that had broken out in 2011 in Syria, Russia's long-standing ally in the Middle East, although he supported a UN programme for the elimination of Syria's chemical weapons in the face of threatened military action by the West against the Assad regime. Already tense relations with the USA were also aggravated in Aug. 2013 as then President Obama cancelled a proposed bilateral summit following Russia's decision to grant asylum to Edward Snowden, a former US contractor who had leaked information about US and UK global intelligence surveillance activities.

In Nov. 2013 the government of neighbouring Ukraine's decision to shelve an integration pact with the European Union was widely attributed to Putin's political and financial pressure. The consequent anti-government protests in Ukraine, removal from power of pro-Russian president Viktor Yanukovych and installation of a new administration intent of eventual integration into Western political and security structures prompted Moscow's alleged fomentation of pro-Russian separatism in eastern Ukraine and its annexation in March 2014 of the Crimea peninsula. The annexation incurred international condemnation and the imposition of Western sanctions which, coupled with a major decline in international oil prices—Russia's principal export revenue source—fuelled a currency crisis towards the end of that year and a subsequent economic contraction.

From Sept. 2015, in a dramatic escalation of the civil war in Syria, Russia intervened militarily with air strikes ostensibly against anti-government Islamic State (IS) jihadists in the country. However, Western nations claimed the attacks were directed more widely against moderate opponents of President Assad's regime. In Oct. that year the downing of a civil airliner over Egypt carrying mainly Russian tourists was seen as jihadist retaliation for the air strikes. Then in Nov. a Russian warplane operating over Syria was shot down by the Turkish military for allegedly violating Turkey's airspace, provoking a furious denunciation by Putin and punitive Russian sanctions.

Russia's air support for government forces in the Syrian war led by Dec. 2016 to the expulsion of rebel fighters from Aleppo, further enhancing Moscow's regional influence, while the Baltic states and Poland—all members of NATO—perceived an increasing military threat from their powerful eastern neighbour. At the same time, there was a surprising rapprochement in Russia's relations with President Erdoğan of Turkey, to the extent that in Jan. 2017 the two countries launched co-ordinated air strikes against IS targets in Syria in an unusual military partnership between Moscow and a NATO member. By Nov. 2017 Assad's military forces, backed by Russian air power, had retaken the last major town in Syria still under IS control and in April 2018 allegedly used chemical weapons against a rebel-held enclave of the capital Damascus, prompting a retaliatory missile strike by the USA, UK and France on Syrian military facilities.

Putin's relationship with the US administration had remained frosty through 2016, and deteriorated further as President Obama's term in office approached its conclusion. In response to Moscow's alleged cyber hacking interference in campaigning for the Nov. US presidential elections—ostensibly in support of the successful Republican candidate, Donald Trump—Obama expelled 35 Russian diplomats in Dec. as a reprisal measure. An ongoing investigation through 2017 into Russia's perceived political meddling led in July–Aug. to the US Congress' approval of new sanctions against Moscow and the subsequent tit-for-tat expulsion of diplomatic staff.

In Sept. 2016 Putin had further reinforced his domestic political authority as United Russia increased its parliamentary majority in elections. However, in Dec. 2017 he declared that he would seek another term as president as an independent candidate, signalling the end of his direct association with the party. Putin duly won the elections in March 2018 after the main opposition figure, Alexei Navalny, had been barred from standing in Dec. by the Electoral Commission following accusations of embezzlement. Also in March, an international diplomatic storm erupted following the attempted assassination of a former Russian double agent, Sergei Skripal, together with his daughter, in the city of Salisbury in the UK using a toxic nerve agent. The British authorities accused the Putin government of complicity in the attack, prompting an unprecedented wave of expulsions of Russian diplomats not only by the UK but also many other Western countries. Moscow continued to deny any responsibility for the episode, instead making counterclaims of UK fabrications, and took similar retaliatory diplomatic action.

In July 2018 Putin and US President Trump conducted their first-ever summit meeting in Helsinki, Finland, after which Trump initially praised the Russian leader and rejected US intelligence agency claims of Russian interference in the US elections in 2016 before changing his stance the following day.

Relations between Russia and Ukraine again deteriorated in Oct. 2018 as Russian forces seized three Ukrainian naval vessels and their crews in the Kerch Strait connecting the Sea of Azov and the Black Sea.

Dmitry Anatolyevich Medvedev

Position
Prime Minister

Introduction
Dmitry Medvedev's political career has been closely associated with Vladimir Putin's since the mid-1990s. In March 2008 Medvedev was elected by a landslide vote to the presidency as Putin's preferred successor after the latter had completed the two consecutive presidential terms allowed under the constitution. In 2012, after four years in office, Medvedev stood down as Putin ran successfully again for the presidency, and he was subsequently appointed by Putin as prime minister in May that year. He was reappointed as premier following Putin's re-election as president in March 2018.

Early Life
Medvedev was born in St Petersburg (then called Leningrad) on 14 Sept. 1965. Both his parents were university teachers. He studied law at Leningrad State University, graduating in 1987. After obtaining a PhD in private law in 1990, he worked as an assistant professor at the university until 1999. In 1990 he also worked at the Leningrad Soviet of People's Deputies. From 1991–95 he served as legal adviser to the chairman of Leningrad city council and to the

committee for external relations of the St Petersburg mayor's office, headed by Vladimir Putin. In Nov. 1993 he became legal affairs director of Ilim Pulp Enterprise and in 1998 he was elected to the board of governors of Bratskiy LPK paper mill.

Medvedev was appointed deputy head of the presidential administration by Putin in Dec. 1999. In 2000 he was promoted to the rank of first deputy chief of staff and during the 2000 election was in charge of the presidential campaign headquarters. In the same year Medvedev became chairman of the board of directors of Gazprom, Russia's largest company. From 2001 he served as deputy chairman until, in June 2002, he became chairman again. Under Medvedev, Gazprom acquired other energy companies and expanded overseas, increasing its significance both within the Russian economy and as an international supplier.

In 2003 Medvedev was appointed chief of staff of the presidential executive office and in Nov. 2005 Putin made him first deputy prime minister, giving him control of four national infrastructure projects: health care, education, housing and agriculture. Medvedev's initiatives included supporting foster families and developing pre-school education; he also attempted to reshape relationships between the Kremlin and Russia's billionaire oligarchs. In Dec. 2007, having served the constitutional maximum of two terms, Putin named Medvedev as his chosen successor. This was interpreted by many as an arrangement by which the two could continue to govern in partnership. Medvedev was elected president with 70% of the vote on 2 March 2008 and was sworn in on 7 May 2008.

Career in Office

As expected, Medvedev appointed Putin prime minister. Medvedev pledged to continue Putin's policies, indicating that he would encourage a diversification of the economy to reduce reliance on gas revenues. He also signalled his support for a free press and free judiciary and spoke of limiting the influence of the security services.

Early challenges internationally included a deterioration in relations with NATO and Russia's western neighbours. In Aug. 2008 he sent troops to South Ossetia and Abkhazia in Georgia, in response to Tbilisi's military attacks on separatist forces within the breakaway regions. A week of fierce fighting ended with a French-brokered peace deal. Russia's intervention received widespread international criticism, as did Medvedev's announcement of Russia's unilateral recognition of the independence of the two territories.

In his first state-of-the-nation address in Nov. 2008, Medvedev proposed a constitutional change to extend the presidential term of office from four to six years and that of parliament from four to five years, arguing that it was necessary to guarantee effective government. However, critics considered the move undemocratic and designed to perpetuate authoritarian rule from the Kremlin. In the same speech Medvedev threatened to deploy short-range missiles in Kaliningrad to counter the USA's proposed missile shield in central Europe (although a more conciliatory approach followed Barack Obama's assumption of the US presidency in Jan. 2009). He meanwhile claimed that the USA bore responsibility for the global financial crisis that had undermined the Russian banking system and destabilized markets. Also in Nov. 2008 Medvedev undertook an overseas tour of Latin America and Cuba.

Russia's relations with the USA improved from 2009 following the installation of a new US administration under President Obama. Medvedev met Obama in July as the latter made his first official visit to Moscow and they agreed to negotiate cuts in their countries' nuclear weapons arsenals in a new initiative to supersede the 1991 Strategic Arms Reduction Treaty. (A 30% cut was subsequently concluded under an agreement signed in April 2010.) In Sept. 2009 Medvedev welcomed the US decision not to site missile defence bases in Poland and the Czech Republic, the Russian military having earlier confirmed that plans to deploy short-range missiles in the Kaliningrad enclave were being shelved. Nevertheless, in Nov. 2010 he warned of the dangers of a new arms race unless NATO and Russia reached a co-operative accord within a decade on a joint missile-defence mechanism.

Medvedev had meanwhile called in Nov. 2009 for reform of the economy and re-emphasized the need for Russia to end its dependency on gas and oil exports. He also said that Russia's survival depended on rapid modernization, based on democratic institutions and an end to corruption.

In Nov. 2010 Medvedev became the first Russian leader to visit the Russian-occupied Kurile Islands, which have been the subject of a territorial dispute with Japan since the end of World War II.

In Sept. 2011 Vladimir Putin was confirmed as United Russia's candidate for the presidential election scheduled for March 2012. Following his expected victory, he succeeded Medvedev in May that year as the latter assumed the premiership at the head of the United Russia-dominated government.

By 2013 there were reports in the Western media of Medvedev's apparent isolation from Putin's increasingly centralized 'inner circle'. He was, nevertheless, the first senior Russian leader to visit Crimea following the peninsula's secession from Ukraine and annexation by Russia in March 2014. Then in Aug. that year he announced an immediate Russian ban on the import of certain Western agricultural products and raw materials in response to punitive sanctions imposed on Russia in the wake of the Ukraine crisis.

In Dec. 2015, following the Turkish military's shooting down of a Russian warplane near the Turkey–Syria border the previous month, Medvedev said that, in addition to trading sanctions already approved, Russia's visa-free regime for Turkish citizens would be suspended and that Russian employers could no longer hire Turkish nationals.

In Jan. 2016 Medvedev acknowledged the challenges encountered by the Russian economy over the previous year owing to 'plunging oil prices, the pressure from [Western] sanctions and the nascent change in the global economic paradigm'. He added, however, that 'the economic situation is not simple but manageable. There are several positive trends which we will be working to strengthen this year.'

Following the US elections in Nov. 2016, Medvedev said that Russia was ready to forge a new relationship with President Donald Trump and that further bilateral developments would depend on the stance of the new US administration. However, following the US Congress' approval of new sanctions on Moscow in mid-2017 for alleged Russian meddling in the elections, Medvedev accused the US government of declaring a 'full-scale trade war' on Russia.

In May 2018 Medvedev's government resigned but his renomination for a further term as prime minister by newly-re-elected President Putin was overwhelmingly confirmed by parliament by 374 votes to 56.

Defence

The President of the Republic is C.-in-C. of the armed forces. Conscription was reduced to 18 months for those drafted in 2007 and was further reduced to one year for those drafted from 1 Jan. 2008.

A presidential decree of 1997 ordered a cut in the armed forces of 200,000 men, reducing them to an authorized strength of 1,004,000 in 1999. In 2011 active armed forces totalled 956,000, plus 474,000 personnel in paramilitary forces. There were estimated to be around 20m. reserves (all armed forces) in 2011 of whom 2m. had seen service within the previous five years.

Defence expenditure totalled US$68,163m. in 2013 (just over a tenth of that of the USA), equivalent to US$478 per capita and representing 3·1% of GDP. Russia was the world's third biggest military spender in 2013. In the meantime spending has grown to such an extent that as a share of GDP Russia's defence expenditure in 2015 was higher than at any other time since the break-up of the Soviet Union in 1991.

Nuclear Weapons

Russia's deployed nuclear warhead count stood at 1,600 in Jan. 2018 according to the Stockholm International Peace Research Institute. There are about a further 5,250 stored and other warheads, giving a total stockpile of around 6,850 warheads.

At the height of the Cold War each side possessed over 10,000 nuclear warheads. The START I arms-control treaty, signed in 1991, limited to approximately 6,000 the number of nuclear warheads that Russia and the USA may each deploy on long-range, or 'strategic', land-based missiles, submarine-launched missiles and bombers. The 1993 START II treaty would have obliged both sides to reduce their stocks of strategic weapons to 3,500 nuclear warheads. However, instruments of ratification were never exchanged and the treaty lapsed. Russia retracted acceptance in June 2002 after the USA withdrew from the Anti-Ballistic Missile treaty. START I expired on 5 Dec. 2009. On 24 May 2002 the USA and Russia signed the Strategic Offensive Reductions Treaty (or Moscow Treaty) to reduce the number of US and Russian warheads to between 1,700 and 2,200 each. The treaty was in force from June 2003 until Feb. 2011. It was then superseded by the Measures for the Further Reduction and Limitation of Strategic Offensive Arms (known as New START), signed by the Russian and US presidents in April 2010 and ratified by the US Senate in Dec. 2010 and the Russian Federal Assembly in Jan. 2011. Under its terms, both Russia and the USA were limited to 1,550 warheads, a 30% drop on previous levels, to be implemented within seven years. Both nations met their obligations by the deadline of Feb. 2018. However, with the agreement due to end in 2021, no extension had been agreed as of March 2019. Moreover, that month Russia's President Putin aggravated international tensions when he briefed the Russian parliament on the country's military arsenal, including the development of long-range missiles capable of carrying conventional or nuclear warheads that he claimed were practically impossible to intercept. Then, in Oct. 2018 President Trump announced his intention to withdraw the USA from an intermediate-range nuclear forces treaty with Russia signed in 1987, banning ground-launched medium-range missiles with a range between 500 and 5,500km. Trump claimed Russia had been in violation of its terms 'for many years'.

Chemical and Biological Weapons

Russia has converted or destroyed its former chemical weapon production facilities and is currently working to complete destruction of its chemical weapon stockpile in accordance with the provisions of the 1993 Chemical Weapons Convention. Russia has the largest declared stockpile of chemical weapons, originally totalling 40,000 tonnes although over 30,000 tonnes have since been destroyed.

The Soviet Union had perhaps the world's largest biological weapon programme until at least the 1980s. Russia has reiterated its commitment to the 1972 Biological and Toxin Weapons Convention.

Arms Trade

Russia is the world's second largest exporter of arms after the USA, with 23% of the global major weapons total over the period 2012–16.

Army

In 2013 Army personnel numbered around 285,000 (including about 80,000 conscripts). There were over 30,000 Russian troops stationed outside Russia in 2013, the majority in various states of the former USSR.

The Army is deployed in five military districts: West, Centre, South and East, plus an Arctic Joint Strategic Command (established in Dec. 2014). Equipment in 2013 included 2,550 main battle tanks (T-72s, T-80s and T-90s) plus some 18,000 in store. There were also more than 7,300 armoured infantry fighting vehicles and 9,700 armoured personnel carriers.

Strategic Nuclear Ground Forces

In 2012 there were three rocket armies. Each rocket army is divided into launcher groups with ten silos and one control centre. Inter-continental ballistic missiles numbered 506. Personnel, 40,000.

Navy

The Russian Navy continues to reduce steadily and levels of sea-going activity remain very low with activity concentrated on a few operational units in each fleet. The safe deployment and protection of the reduced force of ballistic missile submarines remains its first priority; and the defence of the Russian homeland its second. The strategic missile submarine force operates under command of the Strategic Nuclear Force commander whilst the remainder come under the Main Naval Staff in Moscow, through the Commanders of the fleets.

The Northern and Pacific fleets count the entirety of the ballistic missile submarine force, all nuclear-powered submarines, the sole operational aircraft carrier (the *Admiral Kuznetsov*) and most major surface warships. The Baltic Fleet organization is based in the St Petersburg area and in the Kaliningrad exclave. The Black Sea Fleet is based at facilities in Crimea, which came under Russia's direct control following its annexation of the peninsula in March 2014. Amid heightened tensions in the aftermath of the annexation (during which Russia temporarily took possession of a number of Ukrainian vessels moored in Crimea), Moscow announced plans in Sept. 2014 to add a further 80 warships to the Black Sea Fleet by 2020, making a total of some 206 ships and vessels. The additional ships are expected to be based at new naval facilities in Novorossiisk, scheduled for completion by 2020. There is a small Caspian Sea flotilla.

The material state of all the fleets is suffering from continued inactivity and lack of spares and fuel. The nuclear submarine refitting and refuelling operations in the Northern and Pacific Fleets remain in disarray, given the large numbers of nuclear submarines awaiting defuelling and disposal. The strength of the submarine force has now essentially stabilized, but there are still large numbers of decommissioned vessels awaiting their turn for scrapping in a steadily deteriorating state. In Jan. 2003 it was announced that up to a fifth of the fleet was to be scrapped.

In Jan. 2015 there were 11 operational nuclear-fuelled ballistic-missile submarines (two of Delta-III class; five Delta-IV, plus one in overhaul; one Typhoon; three Borei). There was one Typhoon-class submarine in reserve, which was used as a test platform. After a series of test launches, a new submarine-launched ballistic missile 'Bulava' (SS-NX-30) was officially approved for service in Dec. 2011. It was deployed on the new 'Borei'-class nuclear submarines in Jan. 2013, with 150 expected to be operational by 2020. Ten 'Borei'-class submarines are planned in total.

The attack submarine fleet comprises a wide range of classes, from the enormous 16,250 tonne 'Oscar' nuclear-powered missile submarine to diesel boats of around 2,000 tonnes. The inventory of tactical nuclear-fuelled submarines comprises five 'Oscar'-class, nine 'Akula'-class, four 'Sierra'-class and four 'Victor III'-class submarines.

The diesel-powered 'Kilo' class, of which the Navy operates 19, is still building at a reduced rate mostly for export.

Cruisers are divided into two categories; those optimized for anti-submarine warfare (ASW) are classified as 'Large Anti-Submarine Ships' and those primarily configured for anti-surface ship operations are classified 'Rocket Cruisers'. In 2011 the principal surface ships of the Russian Navy included the following classes:

Aircraft Carrier. The *Admiral Kuznetsov* of 67,500 tonnes was completed in 1989. It is capable of embarking 20 aircraft and 15–17 helicopters. All other aircraft carriers have been decommissioned or scrapped.

Cruisers. The ships of this classification are headed by two ships of the Kirov-class, the largest combatant warships, apart from aircraft carriers, to be built since the Second World War. There are, in addition, three Slava-class and one of the Nikolaev ('Kara') class in operation.

Destroyers. There are eight Udaloy I-class, the first of which entered service in 1981, one Udaloy II-class and five Sovremenny-class guided missile destroyers in operation. In addition there is a single remaining 'modified Kashin'-class ship in operation.

Frigates. There are eight frigates in operation: four Steregushchiy-class ships—all of which have been commissioned since 2007—two Neustrashimy-class vessels, one Krivak I-class and one Krivak II-class.

The Russian Naval Aviation operated some 116 combat-capable aircraft in 2011 including Su-23s, Su-24s, Su-25s and Tu-142s. In 2011 there were also 90 anti-submarine warfare helicopters in operation.

Total Naval personnel in 2011 numbered around 154,000. Some 35,000 served in naval aviation in 2011 and there were 9,500 naval infantry/coastal defence troops.

Air Force

Air Force personnel is estimated at 160,600 and equipment includes some 1,850 combat aircraft and about 2,000 helicopters.

The Air Force was reorganized in 2009 and now consists of: Operational Strategic Command for Air-Space Defence; First Air Force and Air Defence Command; Second Air Force and Air Defence Command; Third Air Force and Air Defence Command; Fourth Air Force and Air Defence Command; Military Transport Aviation Command; and Long Range Aviation Command. An air force base opened in Kyrgyzstan in Oct. 2003.

Prior to the restructuring equipment of the 37th Air Army included 124 Tu-22Ms plus Tu-95s and Tu-160s.

Tactical Aviation comprised in 2006 (numbers in brackets) Su-24 (400) and Su-25 (275) fighter-bombers and MiG-29 (314), MiG-31 (279) and Su-27 (390) fighters. In addition MiG-25 and Su-24s are used for reconnaissance missions.

Military Transport Aviation Command comprised nine regiments in 2006 and has some 293 aircraft. Funding shortages have reduced serviceability drastically.

Economy

Agriculture accounted for 3·6% of GDP in 2013, industry 32·3% and services 64·1%.

Overview

Russia emerged from a decade of post-Soviet economic and political turmoil to reassert itself as a world power in the early 2000s, underpinned by its vast resources of oil and natural gas. The state-run gas monopoly, Gazprom, is the world's largest producer and exporter of hydrocarbons. Nonetheless, the economy experienced contractions of 2·8% in 2015 and 0·2% in 2016—the result of falling domestic demand, capital flight, low business confidence and a lack of economic diversification—before growth resumed in 2017 at 1·5%.

Impediments to Russia's medium- and long-term growth prospects include an uncertain external environment (exacerbated by strained relations with the West and several regional neighbours), poor educational standards, mismanagement of public finances and a lack of infrastructure investment. The economy has also been severely affected by international sanctions in response to the Russian government's role in unrest in Ukraine since 2013. This has contributed to a significant depreciation of the currency, alongside reduced access to international financial markets. Although a weaker rouble has supported Russia's export potential, the decline in global commodity prices (most notably oil, which fell by around 35% in 2015) has slashed revenues. As a result, there has been a fall in average real incomes, keeping domestic demand and household consumption depressed. Moscow is meanwhile grappling with the added cost of prolonged military intervention in the Syrian civil war.

Russia became a member of the World Trade Organization in 2012 after 18 years of negotiations. Future prosperity is dependent on an upsurge in oil revenues, the relaxation of sanctions and greater political stability, both domestically and internationally.

Currency

The unit of currency is the *rouble* (RUB), of 100 *kopeks*. In Jan. 1998 the rouble was redenominated by a factor of a thousand. Foreign exchange reserves were US$383,664m. in Sept. 2009 and gold reserves 19·00m. troy oz. In Feb. 2005 Russia abandoned its *de facto* dollar peg and switched to a euro-dollar basket. Inflation rates (based on IMF statistics):

2008	2009	2010	2011	2012	2013	2014	2015	2016	2017
14·1%	11·7%	6·9%	8·4%	5·1%	6·8%	7·8%	15·5%	7·1%	3·7%

Inflation had been 2,510% in 1992. Total money supply in Dec. 2008 was 7,419·7bn. roubles. In Nov. 2000 President Putin and President Lukashenka of Belarus agreed the introduction of a single currency, but plans to introduce the Russian rouble to Belarus have since been postponed indefinitely.

Budget

Budgetary central government revenue totalled 13,638bn. roubles in 2013 (13,997bn. roubles in 2012) and expenditure 12,349bn. roubles (12,062bn. roubles in 2012). Principal sources of revenue in 2013: taxes on international trade and transactions, 4,974bn. roubles; taxes on goods and services, 4,129bn. roubles. Main items of expenditure by economic type in 2013: grants, 5,650bn. roubles; compensation of employees, 2,445bn. roubles.

VAT is 18% (reduced rate, 10%).

Performance

Real GDP growth rates (based on IMF statistics):

2008	2009	2010	2011	2012	2013	2014	2015	2016	2017
5·2%	−7·8%	4·5%	5·1%	3·7%	1·8%	0·7%	−2·5%	−0·2%	1·5%

Real GDP rose by 2·3% in 2018 according to the Federal State Statistics Service. Total GDP was US$1,577·5bn. in 2017. In June 2002 Russia was acknowledged as a market economy under United States trade law, symbolically underscoring the country's transformation from a state-planned economy.

Banking and Finance

The central bank and bank of issue is the State Bank of Russia (*Chairman*, Elvira Nabiullina). The Russian Bank for Reconstruction and Development and the State Investment Company were created in 1993 to channel foreign and domestic investment. Foreign bank branches have been operating since Nov. 1992.

By 1995 the number of registered commercial banks had increased to around 5,000 but following the Aug. 1997 liquidity crisis, owing to the ensuing bankruptcies, mergers and the Central Bank's revoking of licences, the number fell to 2,500. This has since fallen to 908 at the end of 2016, of which only 575 were actually operating. Approximately 80% of the commercial banks were state-owned through ministries or state enterprises.

Sberbank is the leading bank with assets of US$553·2bn. in March 2014, followed by VTB Bank (formerly Vneshtorgbank) with assets of US$266·6bn. Both are state-owned, as is Gazprombank (the third largest bank). In Sept. 2011 there were 991 credit institutions with 2,825 branches.

In the wake of one of the worst financial crises that Russia's market economy had experienced, the central bank tripled interest rates to 150% in May 1998 in an effort to restore stability to the financial system.

External debt was US$384,740m. in 2010, representing 26·9% of GNI.

In 2017 Russia received US$25·3bn. worth of foreign direct investment, down from US$37·2bn. in 2016.

There are stock exchanges in Moscow, Novosibirsk, St Petersburg and Vladivostok.

Energy and Natural Resources

Environment

Russia's carbon dioxide emissions from the consumption of energy in 2011 accounted for 5·3% of the world total (the fourth highest after China, the USA and India), and were equivalent to 12·0 tonnes per capita. An *Environmental Performance Index* compiled in 2016 ranked Russia 32nd of 180 countries, with 83·5%. The index examined various factors in nine areas—agriculture, air quality, biodiversity and habitat, climate and energy, fisheries, forests, health impacts, water and sanitation, and water resources.

Electricity

In 2011 installed capacity was 223·0m. kW and electricity production 1,054·77bn. kWh (713·69bn. kWh thermal, 167·61bn. kWh hydro-electric and 172·94bn. kWh nuclear). Consumption per capita was 7,196 kWh in 2011. There were 35 nuclear reactors in use in March 2017.

Oil and Gas

Russia was the third largest oil producer in 2017 (after the USA and Saudi Arabia) and the largest exporter. In 2017 there were proven oil reserves of 106·2bn. bbls. 2017 production of oil was a record 554·4m. tonnes (12·6% of the world total). Oil production rose every year between 1998 and 2007 but fell slightly in 2008 before increasing again every year between 2009 and 2017. There is an extensive domestic oil pipeline system. The main export pipeline to Europe is the Druzhba pipeline (crossing Belarus before splitting into northern and southern routes). The main export terminal is at Novorossiisk on the Black Sea. A 964-km pipeline from Skovorodino in Russia to Daqing in China was inaugurated in Jan. 2011, allowing Russia—as the world's largest oil producer—to increase significantly its exports to China. Other export pipeline developments include the Baltic Pipeline System I and II and the Caspian Pipeline Consortium's pipeline from Tengiz (Kazakhstan) to Novorossiisk.

Output of natural gas was a record 635·6bn. cu. metres in 2017. Russia is now the world's second largest producer, having been surpassed as the largest producer by the USA in 2009. It has the largest reserves of natural gas—in 2017 it had proven reserves of 35·0trn. cu. metres (18·1% of the world total). There is a comprehensive domestic distribution system (run by state-owned Gazprom, in which the government has a 50·23% stake), as well as gas pipelines linking Russia with former Soviet republics. In Russia's biggest-ever takeover Gazprom agreed in Sept. 2005 to buy a 72·7% stake in Sibneft, a leading oil company. The main export pipelines run from western Siberia through Ukraine and Belarus to European markets. Russia is seeking to diversify its gas export routes and a number of pipeline projects are under development. However, work stopped in 2014 on the US$22bn. South Stream pipeline, designed to bring gas from Russia to southeast Europe without passing through Ukraine, against a backdrop of rising tensions with the West in the aftermath of the annexation of Crimea from Ukraine earlier in the year. Russia is also looking to export its natural gas to Asian markets.

Minerals

Russia contains great mineral resources, including: coal (18% of global coal reserves), iron ore, gold, platinum, copper, zinc, lead, tin and rare metals. Output in 2011 (in tonnes): coal, 258·0m.; iron ore, 104·0m.; lignite, 76·8m.; potash, 6·5m.; bauxite, 4·5m.; aluminium, 3·9m.; alumina, 2·9m.; salt, 1·8m.; copper, 839,130; chrome ore, 400,000; zinc, 275,000; nickel, 264,000; molybdenum, 3,900; gold, 199,650 kg. Diamond production, 2013: 37·8m. carats (the most of any country). Annual uranium production is around 3,000 tonnes.

Agriculture

A presidential decree of Dec. 1991 authorized the private ownership of land on a general basis, but excluded farmland. Nevertheless, large state and collective farms, inherited from the Soviet era, were forced officially to reorganize, with most becoming joint-stock companies. Farm workers could branch off as private farmers by obtaining a grant of land from their parent farm, although they lacked full ownership rights. In Jan. 2003 a new law came into force regulating the possession, use and disposal of land plots designated as agricultural land. The law provides that: the authorities may confiscate farmland if its owners are using it for non-agricultural purposes; regional authorities will have the first option to purchase farmland from its owners; and farmland can only be sold to third parties if authorities refuse their option to buy. The law also deprives foreigners of the right to own agricultural land, although they may lease it for up to 49 years. In 2012 there were an estimated 119·75m. ha. of arable land and 1·60m. ha. of permanent crops. There were 4·2m. ha. of irrigated land in 2008.

Output in 2009 (in 1,000 tonnes) included: wheat, 61,740; potatoes, 31,134; sugar beets, 24,892; barley, 17,881; sunflower seeds, 6,454; oats, 5,401; rye, 4,333; maize, 3,963; cabbages, Brussels sprouts, etc., 3,312; tomatoes, 2,170; onions, 1,602; apples, 1,596; carrots and turnips, 1,519. Russia was the world's largest producer of barley, oats, rye and sunflower seeds in 2009.

Livestock, 2009: cattle, 21·04m.; sheep, 19·60m.; pigs, 16·16m.; chickens, 366m.

Livestock products in 2009 (in tonnes): poultry meat, 2·3m.; pork and pork products, 2·2m.; beef and veal, 1·7m.; cow's milk, 32·3m.; goat's milk, 0·2m.; eggs, 2·2m.; cheese, 0·6m.

Forestry

Russia has the largest area covered by forests of any country in the world, with 814·9m. ha. in 2015 (50% of Russia's land area and 20% of the global forest area). In 2011 timber production was 149·87m. cu. metres. Russia was the world's largest exporter of roundwood in 2011, with 16·4% of the world total.

Fisheries

Total catch in 2015 was 4,463,825 tonnes (down from 8,069,956 tonnes in 1989). Approximately 94% of the fish caught are from marine waters.

Industry

As a result of Soviet central planning, Russian industry remains dominated by heavy industries, such as energy and metals. As of 1 Jan. 2010 there were 418,600 manufacturing enterprises and organizations (of which 383,300 were private) and 433,700 construction enterprises and organizations (413,400 private). Manufacturing accounted for 13·1% of GDP in 2009 and construction 4·8%.

The leading companies by market capitalization in Russia in May 2018 were: Sberbank (US$86·3bn.); Rosneft, an oil and gas company (US$69·0bn.); and LukOil, an oil company (US$60·4bn.).

Output in 2007 (unless otherwise indicated) includes: (in tonnes) crude steel, 72·4m.; residual fuel oil (2009), 69·6m.; distillate fuel oil (2009), 67·2m.; cement, 59·9m.; rolled steel, 59·7m.; pig iron, 51·5m.; petrol, 35·1m.; coke, 32·3m.; jet fuel, 10·7m.; sulphuric acid (2006), 9·5m.; steel pipe, 8·7m.; bread, 7·9m.; paper and paperboard (2011), 7·6m.; sugar (2010), 3·0m.; clays, 2·2m.; caustic soda, 1·3m.; (in cu. metres) sawnwood (2008), 21·6m.; plywood, 2·8m.; (in sq. metres) cotton fabrics, 2,108m.; woollen fabrics, 28·7m.; (in units) cigarettes (2009), 413bn.; bricks, 13,090m.; televisions (2009), 4·8m.; refrigerators and freezers, 3·5m.; washing and drying machines (2009), 2·3m.; microwaves, 2·5m.; bicycles, 1·5m.; passenger cars, 1·3m.; trucks (2009), 91,676; combine harvesters, 8,060; tractors, 7,500; (in litres) beer (2009), 10,911m.; soft drinks, 5,982m.; mineral water, 3,632m.; spirits and liqueurs, 1,315m.

Labour

In 2010 the economically active population numbered 75·45m. (38·58m. males and 36·87m. females). Of those in employment in 2010, 18·1% worked in wholesale and retail trade/repair of motor vehicles, motorcycles and personal and household goods, 15·4% in manufacturing, 9·6% in agriculture and forestry, 8·8% in education, 7·9% in transport, 7·8% in construction and 7·0% in health and social work. The unemployment rate was 9·9% in May 2009—with 7·5m. people unemployed using International Labour Organization methodology—down from 10·2% in April 2009 although up from 6·1% in Oct. 2008. Average monthly wages were 20,952·2 roubles in 2010 (compared to 8,554·9 roubles in 2005); the monthly minimum wage in 2010 was 4,330 roubles (up from 132 roubles in 2000). In 2010, 18·5m. people, or 13·1% of the population, had an average per capita money income lower than the subsistence minimum (down from 29·0% of the population in 2000). The state Federal Employment Service was set up in 1992. Unemployment benefits are paid by the Service for 12 months, payable at: 75% of the average monthly wage during the last two months preceding unemployment for the first three months; 60% for the next four months; and 45% for the last five months. Annual paid leave is 24 working days. In 2013, just 200 working days were lost through strikes compared with 85,900 in 2005. Retirement age is 55 years for women, 60 for men.

Russia had 0·52m. people living in slavery according to the Walk Free Foundation's 2013 *Global Slavery Index*, the sixth highest total of any country.

International Trade

In Jan. 2010 Russia joined a customs union with Belarus and Kazakhstan, which was superseded by the Eurasian Economic Union in Jan. 2015.

Imports and Exports

The following table shows the value of Russia's foreign trade (in US$1bn.):

	2006	2007	2008	2009	2010
Imports c.i.f.	137·8	199·8	267·1	167·3	229·1
Exports f.o.b.	301·2	351·9	467·6	301·7	396·6

Of imports in 2010, 44·4% by value was machinery and transport equipment, 16·1% chemicals products and rubber, 15·9% foodstuffs and agricultural raw materials, and 7·4% metals and precious stones. Of exports, 68·4% by value was mineral products, 12·8% metals and precious stones, 6·2% chemical products and rubber, and 5·4% machinery and transport equipment. China provided 13·4% of imports in 2009, Germany 12·4%, USA 5·4%, Ukraine 5·3% and France 4·9%. In 2009 the Netherlands accounted for 12·0% of exports, Italy 8·3%, Germany 6·2%, Belarus 5·5% and China 5·5%. China is Russia's leading trading partner overall.

Communications

Roads

There were 933,000 km of roads in 2006, of which 80·9% were hard surfaced. In 2007, 78bn. passenger-km were travelled by road. There were 29,249,000 passenger cars in use in 2007 plus 4,730,000 lorries and vans and 861,000 buses and coaches. In 2013 there were 27,000 road deaths.

Rail

Length of railways in 2010 was 86,000 km, of which about half is electrified. In 2011, 933·1m. passengers and 1,381·3m. tonnes of freight were carried by rail; passenger-km travelled came to 140bn. and freight tonne-km to 2,128bn. There are metro services in Moscow (309 km), St Petersburg (105 km), Nizhny Novgorod (15 km), Novosibirsk (14 km), Samara (10 km), Ekaterinburg (9 km) and Kazan (7 km). Kazan's metro opened in 2005, making it the first metro to be opened in Russia since the break-up of the Soviet Union.

Civil Aviation

The main international airports are at Moscow (Domodedovo, Sheremetyevo and Vnukovo) and St Petersburg (Pulkovo). The national carrier is Aeroflot International Russian Airlines (51% state-owned), which carried 26·1m. scheduled passengers in 2015. Rossiya, S7 Airlines and UTair also operate internationally.

In 2009 scheduled airline traffic of Russian-based carriers flew 836m. km, carrying 34,403,000 passengers (11,992,000 on international flights). The three busiest airports all serve Moscow. Domodedovo is Russia's busiest airport in terms of passenger traffic (22,255,000 in 2010, a 19% increase on 2009). Sheremetyevo handled 19,329,000 passengers in 2010 (up 31% on 2009), and Vnukovo handled 9,460,000 in 2010 (up 22% on 2009). The fourth busiest airport is Pulkovo, which serves St Petersburg and handled 8,444,000 passengers in 2010 (up 25% on 2009).

Shipping

In Jan. 2014 there were 1,324 ships of 300 GT or over registered, totalling 4·76m. GT. Of the 1,324 vessels registered, 814 were general cargo ships, 410 oil tankers, 66 bulk carriers, 25 passenger ships and nine container ships. The Russian-controlled fleet comprised 1,547 vessels of 1,000 GT or over in July 2014, of which 1,051 were under the Russian flag and 496 under foreign flags. In 2010, 16m. passengers and 102m. tonnes of freight were carried on 101,000 km of inland waterways. The busiest ports are Novorossiisk (which handled 73,657,000 tonnes in 2013), Primorsk (63,822,000 tonnes in 2013) and St Petersburg (57,972,000 tonnes in 2013).

Telecommunications

In 2013 there were 40,473,000 main (fixed) telephone lines. Active mobile phone subscriptions numbered 208,065,000 in 2012 (1,453·3 per 1,000 persons). There were 61·5m. internet users in 2011. In March 2012 there were 5·2m. Facebook users.

Social Institutions

Out of 178 countries analysed in the 2017 *Fragile States Index*—a list published jointly by the Fund for Peace and *Foreign Policy* magazine—Russia was ranked the 67th most vulnerable to conflict or collapse. The index is based on 12 indicators of state vulnerability across social, political and economic categories.

Justice

The Supreme Court is the highest judicial body on civil, criminal and administrative law. The Supreme Arbitration Court deals with economic cases. The KGB, and the Federal Security Bureau which succeeded it, were replaced in Dec. 1992 by the Federal Counter-Intelligence Service. The legal system is, however, crippled by corruption.

A new civil code was introduced in 1993 to replace the former Soviet code. It guarantees the inviolability of private property and includes provisions for the freedom of movement of capital and goods.

12-member juries were introduced in a number of courts after Nov. 1993, but in the years that followed jury trials were not widely used. However, on 1 Jan. 2003 jury trials began to be phased in nationwide. A new criminal code came into force on 1 Jan. 1997, based on respect for the rights and freedoms of the individual and the sanctity of private property. A further new code that entered force on 1 July 2002 introduced new levels of protection for defendants and restrictions on law enforcement officials. The death penalty is retained for five crimes against the person. It is not applied to minors, women or men over 65.

In 2010, 2,629,000 crimes were recorded, including 15,600 murders and attempted murders (down from 31,800 in 2000), 1,108,000 thefts and 4,900 rapes and attempted rapes. In 1996 there were 140 executions (86 in 1995; 1 in 1992). Then President Yeltsin placed a moratorium on capital punishment in 1996 when Russia joined the Council of Europe, but parliament has refused to abolish the death penalty. The last execution was in Aug. 1996. The prison population in May 2011 was 806,100 (568 per 100,000 population—the second highest rate in the world after the USA). In 2010 there were 1,052 prison establishments and institutions. In 2015 the World Justice Project *Rule of Law Index*, which provides data on how the rule of law is experienced by the general public across eight categories, ranked Russia 74th of 102 countries for criminal justice and 60th for civil justice.

Education

Adult literacy rate in 2010 was 99·7%. In 2009 there were 5·02m. pupils in primary schools, 9·61m. in secondary schools and 9·33m. students in tertiary education (56·6% of whom were females). There were 5·23m. children in 45,300 pre-school establishments in 2009.

In 2012 public expenditure on education came to 4·2% of GDP.

Russia's largest university is the M. V. Lomonosov Moscow State University. Founded in 1755, it now has 30 faculties and 15 research centres. It has an annual enrolment of 31,000 students. The Russian Academy of Sciences, founded in 1724 and reorganized in 1925 as the Academy of Sciences of the Union of Soviet Socialist Republics, was restored under its present name in 1991. It is the highest scientific self-governing institution in Russia and has 18 divisions on particular areas of science. The Academy also has three regional branches: the Urals Branch, the Siberian Branch and the Far East Branch.

Health

Doctors numbered 703,000 in 2012, equivalent to 49 doctors per 10,000 population. There were 45,628 dentists, 1,214,292 nurses and midwives and 11,521 pharmacists in 2006. In 2012 there were 93 hospital beds per 10,000 inhabitants. Expenditure on health in 2009 was 5·4% of GDP. Russia had 62,581 newly diagnosed HIV infections in 2010 (44·1 cases per 100,000 of population). As at Sept. 2012 there were over 682,000 registered HIV-infected patients. In 2012 there were 74 cases of tuberculosis per 100,000 people. In 2009, 39·1% of Russian adults smoked (males, 60·2%; females, 21·7%). Cigarette consumption is among the highest of any country.

In *Water: At What Cost? The State of the World's Water 2016*, WaterAid reported that 3·1% of the population does not have access to safe water.

Welfare

State welfare provision includes: old age, disability and survivor pensions; sickness and maternity benefits; work injury payments; unemployment benefits; and family allowances. The basic pension is a flat amount provided to all those reaching retirement age (60 for males and 55 for females) with a minimum contribution record of five years. The old-age pension is calculated as the sum of three components. In 2010 the basic monthly flat-rate amount for pensioners under the age of 80 varied from 2,622 roubles to 5,124 roubles according to the number of dependents; the basic monthly flat-rate amount for a pensioner age 80 or older varied from 5,124 roubles to 7,686 roubles according to the number of dependents.

Religion

The Russian Orthodox Church is the largest religious association in the country. In early 2010 it had 160 dioceses with over 30,000 parishes, more than 200 bishops and 28,000 priests and about 790 monasteries. A survey conducted in 2012 by the Levada-Center (an independent, non-governmental polling and sociological research organization) estimated that some 74% of the population are Orthodox believers and 7% Muslims; 76% of Russians who described themselves as Orthodox believers were church-goers. There are still many Old Believers, whose schism from the Orthodox Church dates from the 17th century. The Russian Church is headed by the Patriarch of Moscow and All Rus' (Patriarch Kirill I—Metropolitan Kirill of Smolensk and Kaliningrad, b. 1946; elected Jan. 2009). Muslims represent the second largest religious community in Russia. In Feb. 2010 the Supreme Co-ordinating Council of Russian Muslims was established to be co-chaired by the heads of the three major organizations—the Central Spiritual Board of Muslims, the Council of Muftis of Russia and the Co-ordinating Muslim Council of the North Caucasus.

Culture

World Heritage Sites

Russia's World Heritage sites as classified by UNESCO (with year entered on list) are: the Historic Centre of St Petersburg (1990); the Kremlin and Red Square in Moscow (1990); Khizi Pogost (1990); the Historic Monuments of Novgorod and surroundings (1992); Cultural and Historic Ensemble of the Solovetsky Islands (1992); the White Monuments of Vladimir and Suzdal (1992); Architectural Ensemble of the Trinity Sergius Lavra in Sergiev Posad (1993); the Church of the Ascension, Kolomenskoye (1994); Virgin Komi Forests (1995); Lake Baikal (1996); Volcanoes of Kamchatka (1996, 2001); Golden Mountains of Altai (1998); Western Caucasus (1999); the Ensemble of Ferapontov Monastery (2000); Historic and Architectural Complex of the Kazan Kremlin (2000); Central Sikhote-Alin (2001, 2018); the Citadel, Ancient City and Fortress Buildings of Derbent (2003); Ensemble of the Novodevichy Convent in southwest Moscow (2004); Natural System of Wrangel Island Reserve (2004); the Historical Centre of the City of Yaroslavl (2005); the Putorana Plateau (2010); the Lena Pillars Nature Park (2012); Bolgar Historical and Archaeological Complex (2014); and Assumption Cathedral and Monastery of the town-island of Sviyazhsk (2017).

The Russian Federation also shares four UNESCO sites: the Curonian Spit with Lithuania (2000); Uvs Nuur Basin with Mongolia (2003); the Struve Geodetic Arc (2005), a chain of survey triangulations spanning from Norway to the Black Sea that helped establish the exact shape and size of the earth, with nine other countries; and Landscapes of Dauria (2017), an outstanding example of the Daurian Steppe eco-region, shared with Mongolia.

Press

In 2012 there were 546 daily newspapers. There were 27,801 non-daily newspapers in 2012. The most popular daily newspaper in 2013 was *Komsomolyskaya Pravda*, with an average daily readership of 2·5m., followed by *Moskovsky Komsomolets*, with a readership of 1·4m. In 2012, 116,888 new or revised books were published.

Tourism

In 2011 arrivals of non-resident visitors—including Russians living abroad—totalled 24,932,000 (22,281,000 in 2010), of which 2,336,000 were tourists (2,134,000 in 2010). There were 7,866 hotels and similar establishments in 2011, with 537,000 beds.

Festivals

One of the most popular festivals is the White Nights Festival, which is held from May to July in St Petersburg and combines ballet, opera and music performances. The Annual Summer Ballet Festival runs from June to Sept. in Moscow while the Moscow International Film Festival takes place in June. The biggest rock and pop festival is Nashestvie, which is held annually near Moscow in Aug.

Diplomatic Representatives

Of Russia in the United Kingdom (13 Kensington Palace Gdns, London, W8 4QX)

Ambassador: Alexander Vladimirovich Yakovenko.

Of the United Kingdom in Russia (Smolenskaya Naberezhnaya 10, 121099 Moscow)

Ambassador: Dr Laurie Bristow, CMG.

Of Russia in the USA (2650 Wisconsin Ave., NW, Washington, D.C., 20007)

Ambassador: Anatoly Ivanovich Antonov.

Of the USA in Russia (Bolshoy Deviatinsky Pereulok No. 8, 121099 Moscow)

Ambassador: Jon M. Huntsman, Jr.

Of Russia to the United Nations

Ambassador: Vassily A. Nebenzia.

Of Russia to the European Union

Ambassador: Vladimir A. Chizhov.

The Republics

Status

The 22 republics that with Russia itself constitute the Russian Federation were (except for Crimea; *see* CRIMEA *on page* 1230) part of the RSFSR in the Soviet period. On 31 March 1992 the federal government concluded treaties with the then 20 republics, except Checheno-Ingushetia and Tatarstan, defining their mutual responsibilities. Crimea became the 22nd republic in March 2014 although most of the international community does not accept the validity of its accession. The *Council of the Heads of the Republics* is chaired by the Russian President and includes the Russian Prime Minister. Its function is to provide an interaction between the federal government and the republican authorities.

Adygeya

Part of Krasnodar Territory.Area, 7,600 sq. km (2,950 sq. miles); population (2010 census), 439,996. Ethnic Russians constituted 63·6% of the population in 2010. Capital, Maikop (2010 census, 144,249). Established 27 July 1922; granted republican status in 1991.

Head of the Republic: Murat Kumpilov.

Prime Minister: AleksandrNarolin.

Chief industries are timber, woodworking and food processing; there is some engineering and gas production. Agriculture consists primarily of crops (beets, wheat, maize), on partly irrigated land. In 2015 gross regional product amounted to 82,583·7m. roubles. Public administration, defence, education, human health and social work activities accounted for 21·6% of gross value added in 2015, ahead of wholesale and retail trade, transport, accommodation and food services with 21·1% and industry with 20·4%.

Altai

Part of Altai Territory.Area, 92,600 sq. km (35,750 sq. miles); population (2010 census), 206,168. Ethnic Russians constituted 56·6% of the population in 2010. Capital, Gorno-Altaisk (2010 census, 56,933). Established 1 June 1922 as Oirot Autonomous Region; renamed 7 Jan. 1948; granted republican status in 1991 and renamed in 1992.

Head of the Republic and Chairman of the Government: AleksandrBerdnikov.

Cattle breeding predominates. Chief industries are clothing and footwear, foodstuffs, gold mining, timber, chemicals and dairying.

In 2015 gross regional product amounted to 41,776·8m. roubles. Public administration, defence, education, human health and social work activities accounted for 31·9% of gross value added in 2015, ahead of wholesale and retail trade, transport, accommodation and food services with 19·5% and agriculture, forestry and fishing with 16·9%.

Bashkortostan

Area 143,600 sq. km (55,450 sq. miles), population (2010 census), 4,072,292. Capital, Ufa (2010 census population, 1,062,319). Bashkiria was annexed to Russia in 1557. It was constituted as an Autonomous Soviet Republic on 23 March 1919. A declaration of republican sovereignty was adopted in 1990, and a declaration of independence on 28 March 1992. A treaty of Aug. 1994 with Russia preserves the common legislative framework of the Russian Federation while defining mutual areas of competence. The main ethnic groups are Russians, Tatars and Bashkirs. Ethnic Russians constituted only 36·1% of the population in 2010. There are also Chuvash and Mari minorities.

A constitution was adopted on 24 Dec. 1993. It states that Bashkiria conducts its own domestic and foreign policy, that its laws take precedence in Bashkiria, and that it forms part of the Russian Federation on a voluntary and equal basis.

Head of the Republic (acting): Rady Khabirov.

Prime Minister: Rustem Mardanov.

The most important industries are oil and oil products; there are also engineering, glass and building materials enterprises. Agriculture specializes in wheat, barley, oats and livestock. In 2015 gross regional product amounted to 1,317,431·4m. roubles. Industry accounted for 36·3% of gross value added in 2015, ahead of wholesale and retail trade, transport, accommodation and food services with 24·4% and public administration, defence, education, human health and social work activities with 12·4%.

Buryatia

Area is 351,300 sq. km (135,650 sq. miles). The Buryat Republic, situated to the south of Sakha, adopted the Soviet system on 1 March 1920. This area was penetrated by the Russians in the 17th century and finally annexed from China by the treaties of Nerchinsk (1689) and Kyakhta (1727). Population (2010 census), 972,021. Capital, Ulan-Ude (2010 census population, 404,426). The main ethnic groups are Russians, followed by Buryats. Ethnic Russians constituted 66·1% of the population in 2010. There are also Ukrainian, Tatar and Belarusian minorities.

There is a 65-member parliament, the *People's Hural*.

Head of the Republic: Alexei Tsydenov.

The main industries are engineering, brown coal and graphite, timber, building materials, sheep and cattle farming. In 2015 gross regional product amounted to 204,156·2m. roubles. Wholesale and retail trade, transport, accommodation and food services accounted for 29·9% of gross value added in 2015, ahead of industry with 26·9% and public administration, defence, education, human health and social work activities with 23·2%.

Chechnya

The area of the Republic of Chechnya is 15,000 sq. km (5,800 sq. miles). The population at the 2010 census was 1,268,989. Ethnic Russians constituted only 1·9% of the population in 2010. Capital, Dzhohar (since March 1998; previously known as Grozny; 2010 census population, 271,573). The Chechens and Ingushes were conquered by Russia in the late 1850s. In 1920 each nationality were constituted areas within the Soviet Mountain Republic and the Chechens became an Autonomous Region on 30 Nov. 1922. In Jan. 1934 the two regions were united, and on 5 Dec. 1936 constituted as the Checheno-Ingush Autonomous Republic. This was dissolved in 1944 and the population was deported en masse, allegedly for collaboration with the German occupation forces. It was reconstituted on 9 Jan. 1957: 232,000 Chechens and Ingushes returned to their homes in the next two years.

In 1991 rebel leader Jokhar Dudayev seized control of Chechnya and won elections. In Nov. he declared an independent Chechen Republic. Ingush desire to separate from Chechnya led to fighting along the Chechen-Ingush border and a deployment of Russian troops. An agreement to withdraw was reached between Russia and Chechnya on 15 Nov. 1992. The separation of Chechnya and Ingushetia was formalized in Dec. 1992. In April 1993 President Dudayev dissolved parliament. Hostilities continued throughout 1994 between the government and forces loosely grouped under the 'Provisional Chechen Council'. The Russian government, which had never recognized the Chechen declaration of independence of Nov. 1991, moved troops and armour into Chechnya on 11 Dec. 1994. Grozny was bombed and attacked by Russian ground forces at the end of Dec. 1994 and the presidential palace was captured on 19 Jan. 1995, but fighting continued. On 30 July 1995 the Russian and Chechen authorities signed a ceasefire. However, hostilities, raids and hostage-taking continued; Dudayev was killed in April 1996 and a ceasefire was agreed on 30 Aug. 1996.

Fighting broke out again, however, in Sept. 1999 as Russian forces launched attacks on 'rebel bases'. Fighting intensified and more than 200,000 civilians were forced to flee, mostly to neighbouring Ingushetia. By Feb. 2000 much of Grozny had been destroyed and was closed by the Russians. In June 2000 Vladimir Putin declared direct rule. The conflict continues, with estimates of the number of deaths varying from 6,500 to 15,000. Over 4,000 Russian soldiers have been killed. However, on 18 Nov. 2001 the first official meeting between negotiators for the Russian government and Chechen separatists took place. In Oct. 2002 a group of Chechen rebels took control of a Moscow theatre and held hostage 800 people for three days, before Russian troops stormed the building. An anaesthetic gas, used to combat the rebels, also killed many of the hostages.

On 23 March 2003 a referendum was held on a new constitution that would keep Chechnya within Russia but give it greater autonomy, and provide a new president and parliament for the republic. Although 96% of votes cast were in favour of the new constitution there was criticism of the conduct of the referendum. Presidential elections held on 5 Oct. 2003 were won by the Kremlin-backed candidate Akhmad Kadyrov, with 80·8% of the vote, but there was widespread condemnation of the electoral process. President Kadyrov was assassinated on 9 May 2004. Presidential elections held on 29 Aug. 2004, widely seen as rigged, were won by the Kremlin-backed Alu Alkhanov with 73·5% of the vote, against 5·9% for Movsur Khamidov, head of the Chechen department of the Federal Security Service. There were five other candidates. Turnout was 85·2%. On 27 Nov. 2005 the first parliamentary elections took place since Russian troops restored Moscow's control over Chechnya in 1999. In the elections to the People's Assembly (lower chamber) the United Russia party won 19 of 38 seats with 60·7% of the vote, the Communist Party 3 with 12·2%, the Union of Rightist Forces 1 with 12·4%, the Eurasian Union 1 with 3·9%; independents won 14 seats. In the Council of the Republic (upper chamber), United Russia won 14 of 20 seats, the Communist Party 3 and the Union of Rightist Forces 3.

Separatist President Aslan Maskhadov was killed by Russian troops on 8 March 2005, as was his successor Abdul-Khalim Sadulayev on 17 June 2006.

Moscow-backed Head of the Republic: Ramzan Kadyrov.

Prime Minister: Muslim Khuchiyev.

Chechnya's economy has been destroyed as a result of years of conflict with Russia. Following the conclusion of the second Chechen war in May 2000, it was estimated that over 90% of the working population lacked regular employment. The region is rich in oil—Chechnya's oil reserves are estimated at some 220m. bbls. In 2014 oil production was 448,000 tonnes. In 2015 gross regional product amounted to 160,503·2m. roubles. Public administration, defence, education, human health and social work activities accounted for 37·2% of gross value added in 2015, ahead of wholesale and retail trade, transport, accommodation and food services with 26·6% and construction with 14·8%. In 2011 there were a total of 368 medical facilities.

Chuvashia

Area, 18,300 sq. km (7,050 sq. miles); population (2010 census), 1,251,619. Capital, Cheboksary (2010 census population, 453,721). The territory was annexed by Russia in the middle of the 16th century. On 24 June 1920 it was constituted as an Autonomous Region, and on 21 April 1925 as an Autonomous Republic. The main ethnic groups are Chuvash, followed by Russians. Ethnic Russians constituted only 26·9% of the population in 2010. There are also Tatar and Mordovian minorities. Republican sovereignty was declared in Sept. 1990.

Head of the Republic: Mikhail Ignatyev.

Prime Minister: Ivan Motorin.

The timber industry antedates the Soviet period. Other industries include railway repair works, electrical and other engineering industries, building materials, chemicals, textiles and food industries. Grain crops account for nearly two-thirds of all sowings and fodder crops for nearly a quarter. Chuvashia is Russia's main producer of hops and the republic has a significant brewing industry. In 2015 gross regional product amounted to 250,408·9m. roubles. Industry accounted for 29·2% of gross value added in 2015, ahead of wholesale and retail trade, transport, accommodation and food services with 21·9% and public administration, defence, education, human health and social work activities with 16·2%.

Dagestan

Area, 50,300 sq. km (19,400 sq. miles); population (2010 census), 2,910,249. Capital, Makhachkala (2010 census population, 572,076). Over 30 nationalities inhabit this republic apart from Russians; the most numerous are Dagestanis and there are also Azerbaijani, Chechen and Jewish minorities. Ethnic Russians constituted only 3·6% of the population in 2010. Annexed from Persia in 1723, Dagestan was constituted an Autonomous Republic on 20 Jan. 1921. In 1991 the Supreme Soviet declared the area of republican, rather than autonomous republican, status. Many of the nationalities who live in Dagestan have organized armed militias, and in May 1998 rebels stormed the government building in Makhachkala. In Aug. 1999 Dagestan faced attacks from Islamic militants who invaded from Chechnya. Although Russian troops tried to restore order and discipline, the guerrilla campaign has continued with a series of bombings targeting Russian military personnel.

Acting Head of the Republic: Vladimir Vasilyev.

Prime Minister: Artyom Zdunov.

There are engineering, oil, chemical, woodworking, textile, food and other light industries. Agriculture is varied, ranging from wheat to grapes, with sheep farming and cattle breeding. In 2015 gross regional product amounted to 559,673·1m. roubles. Wholesale and retail trade, transport, accommodation and food services accounted for 40·6% of gross value added in 2015, ahead of construction with 17·6% and public administration, defence, education, human health and social work activities with 15·9%.

Ingushetia

The history of Ingushetia is interwoven with that of Chechnya (*see* CHECHNYA: General Details). Ingush desire to separate from Chechnya led to fighting along the Chechen-Ingush border and a deployment of Russian troops. The separation of Ingushetia from Chechnya was formalized by an amendment of Dec. 1992 to the Russian Constitution. On 15 May 1993 an extraordinary congress of the peoples of Ingushetia adopted a declaration of state sovereignty within the Russian Federation. Skirmishes between Ingush refugees and local police broke out in Aug. 1999 and tensions remained high with the danger of further outbreaks of fighting. The Russian attacks on neighbouring Chechnya in Sept. 1999 led to thousands of Chechen refugees fleeing to Ingushetia. In April 2004 President Murat Zyazikov survived an assassination attempt, as did Prime Minister Ibragim Malsagov in Aug. 2005.

The capital is Magas (2010 census population, 2,502).

Area, 4,300 sq. km (1,700 sq. miles); population (2010 census), 412,529. Ethnic Russians constituted only 0·8% of the population in 2010.

There is a 27-member parliament. On 27 Feb. 1994 presidential elections and a constitutional referendum were held. Turnout was 70%. At the referendum 97% of votes cast approved a new constitution stating that Ingushetia is a democratic law-based secular republic forming part of the Russian Federation on a treaty basis.

Head of the Republic: Yunus-bek Yevkurov.

Prime Minister: Ruslan Gagiev.

In 2015 gross regional product amounted to 54,330·4m. roubles. Public administration, defence, education, human health and social work activities accounted for 42·6% of gross value added in 2015, ahead of wholesale and retail trade, transport, accommodation and food services with 17·4% and construction with 13·9%. A special economic zone for Russian residents was set up in 1994, and an 'offshore' banking tax haven in 1996.

Kabardino-Balkaria

Area, 12,500 sq. km (4,850 sq. miles); population (2010 census), 859,939. Capital, Nalchik (2010 census population, 240,203). Kabarda was annexed to Russia in 1557. The republic was constituted on 5 Dec. 1936. The main ethnic groups are Kabardinians, followed by Russians and Balkars. Ethnic Russians constituted only 22·5% of the population in 2010. There are also Ukrainian, Ossetian and German minorities.

A treaty with Russia of 1 July 1994 defines their mutual areas of competence within the legislative framework of the Russian Federation. The recent history of Kabardino-Balkaria has been marked by the instability that has plagued the whole of the north Caucasus. In Oct. 2005 militants staged a large-scale assault on government buildings in Nalchik, an act for which Chechen rebel leader Shamil Besayev claimed responsibility.

Head of the Republic (acting): Kazbek Kokov.

Prime Minister: Aly Musukov.

Main industries are ore-mining, timber, engineering, coal, food processing, timber and light industries, building materials. Grain, livestock breeding, dairy farming and wine-growing are the principal branches of agriculture. In 2015 gross regional product amounted to 125,393·1m. roubles. Wholesale and retail trade, transport, accommodation and food services accounted for 26·4% of gross value added in 2015, ahead of public administration, defence, education, human health and social work activities with 25·9% and agriculture, forestry and fishing with 17·1%.

Kalmykia

Area, 76,100 sq. km (29,400 sq. miles); population (2010 census), 289,481. Capital, Elista (2010 census population, 103,749). The population is mainly Kalmyk and Russian, with small Chechen, Kazakh and German minorities. Ethnic Russians constituted 30·2% of the population in 2010.

The Kalmyks migrated from western China to Russia (Nogai Steppe) in the early 17th century. The territory was constituted an Autonomous Region on 4 Nov. 1920, and an Autonomous Republic on 22 Oct. 1935; this was dissolved in 1943. On 9 Jan. 1957 it was reconstituted as an Autonomous Region and on 29 July 1958 as an Autonomous Republic once more. In Oct. 1990 the republic was renamed the Kalmyk Soviet Socialist Republic; it was given its present name in Feb. 1992.

Head of the Republic: Aleksey Orlov.

Prime Minister: Igor Zotov.

In April 1993 the Supreme Soviet was dissolved and replaced by a professional parliament consisting of 25 of the former deputies. On 5 April 1994 a specially-constituted 300-member constituent assembly adopted a 'Steppe Code' as Kalmykia's basic law. This is not a constitution and renounces the declaration of republican sovereignty of 18 Oct. 1990. It provides for a *President* elected for five-year terms with the power to dissolve parliament, and a 27-member parliament, the *People's Hural,* elected every four years. It stipulates that Kalmykia is an equal member and integral part of the Russian Federation, functioning in accordance with the Russian constitution.

Main industries are oil and gas production, canning and building materials. Cattle breeding and irrigated farming (mainly fodder crops) are the principal branches of agriculture. Overgrazing during the Soviet period led to the desertification of Kalmykia's pastures and agricultural output declined substantially. In 2015 gross regional product amounted to 47,291·7m. roubles. Agriculture, forestry and fishing accounted for 28·8% of gross value added in 2015, ahead of wholesale and retail trade, transport, accommodation and food services with 28·1% and public administration, defence, education, human health and social work activities with 24·2%.

The main religion is Buddhism.

Karachai-Cherkessia

Area, 14,300 sq. km (5,500 sq. miles); population (2010 census), 477,859. Ethnic Russians constituted only 31·6% of the population in 2010. Capital, Cherkessk (2010 census population, 129,069). A Karachai Autonomous Region was established on 26 April 1926 (out of a previously united Karachaevo-Cherkess Autonomous Region created in 1922), and dissolved in 1943. A Cherkess Autonomous Region was established on 30 April 1928. The present Autonomous Region was re-established on 9 Jan. 1957. The Region declared itself a Soviet Socialist Republic in Dec. 1990. Tension between the two ethnic groups increased after the first free presidential election in April 1999 was won by Vladimir Semyonov, an ethnic Karachay. Despite numerous allegations of fraud the result was upheld by the Supreme Court. There were subsequently fears that the ethnic Cherkess opposition would attempt to set up breakaway government bodies.

Head of the Republic: Rashid Temrezov.

Prime Minister: Aslan Ozov.

There are ore-mining, engineering, chemical and woodworking industries. The Kuban-Kalaussi irrigation scheme irrigates 200,000 ha. Livestock breeding and grain growing predominate in agriculture. Conflict in the north Caucasus has had a serious impact on the economy and the agricultural sector is supported by central government. In 2015 gross regional product amounted to 67,355·2m. roubles. Public administration, defence, education, human health and social work activities accounted for 28·0% of gross value added in 2015, ahead of agriculture, forestry and fishing with 25·1% and industry with 18·6%.

Karelia

The Karelian Republic, capital Petrozavodsk (2010 census population, 261,897), covers an area of 172,400 sq. km, with a 2010 census population of 643,548. Ethnic Russians constituted 82·2% of the population in 2010. There are also populations of Karelians, Belarusians and Ukrainians.

Karelia (formerly Olonets Province) became part of the RSFSR after 1917. In June 1920 a Karelian Labour Commune was formed and in July 1923 this was transformed into the Karelian Autonomous Soviet Socialist Republic (one of the autonomous republics of the RSFSR). On 31 March 1940, after the Soviet-Finnish war, practically all the territory (with the exception of a small section in the neighbourhood of the Leningrad area) which had been ceded by Finland to the USSR was added to Karelia, and the Karelian Autonomous Republic was transformed into the Karelo-Finnish Soviet Socialist Republic as the 12th republic of the USSR. In 1946, however, the southern part of the republic, including its whole seaboard and the towns of Viipuri (Vyborg) and Keksholm, was attached to the RSFSR, reverting in 1956 to autonomous republican status within the RSFSR. In Nov. 1991 it declared itself the 'Republic of Karelia'.

Head of the Republic: Artur Parfenchikov.

Prime Minister: Aleksandr Chepik.

Karelia has a wealth of timber, some 70% of its territory being forest land. It is also rich in other natural resources, having large deposits of mica, diabase, spar, quartz, marble, granite, zinc, lead, silver, copper, molybdenum, tin, baryta and iron ore. Its lakes and rivers are rich in fish.

There are timber mills, paper-cellulose works, mica, chemical plants, power stations and furniture factories. In 2015 gross regional product amounted to 211,133·6m. roubles. Wholesale and retail trade, transport, accommodation and food services accounted for 30·4% of gross value added in 2015, ahead of industry with 28·9% and public administration, defence, education, human health and social work activities with 21·7%.

Khakassia

Area, 61,900 sq. km (23,900 sq. miles); population (2010 census), 532,403. Ethnic Russians constituted 81·7% of the population in 2010. Capital, Abakan (2010 census population, 165,214). Established 20 Oct. 1930; granted republican status in 1991.

Head of the Republic and Chairman of the Government: Valentin Konovalov.

There are coal- and ore-mining, timber and woodworking industries. The region is linked by rail with the Trans-Siberian line. In 2015 gross regional product amounted to 171,663·9m. roubles. Industry accounted for 40·5% of gross value added in 2015, ahead of wholesale and retail trade, transport, accommodation and food services with 23·5% and public administration, defence, education, human health and social work activities with 17·1%.

Komi

Area, 415,900 sq. km (160,550 sq. miles); population (2010 census), 901,189. Capital, Syktyvkar (2010 census population, 235,006). Annexed by the princes of Moscow in the 14th century, the territory was constituted as an Autonomous Region on 22 Aug. 1921 and as an Autonomous Republic on 5 Dec. 1936. The largest ethnic group are Russians (65·1% of the population in 2010), followed by Komis, with Ukrainian and Belarusian minorities.

A declaration of sovereignty was adopted by the republican parliament in Sept. 1990, and the designation 'Autonomous' dropped from the republic's official name.

Head of the Republic: Sergey Gaplikov.

Acting Chair of the Government: Larisa Maksimova.

There are coal, oil, timber, gas, asphalt and building materials industries, and light industry is expanding. Livestock breeding (including dairy farming) is the main branch of agriculture. In 2015 gross regional product amounted to 523,211·2m. roubles. Industry accounted for 50·5% of gross value added in 2015, ahead of wholesale and retail trade, transport, accommodation and food services with 15·2% and public administration, defence, education, human health and social work activities with 13·8%.

Mari-El

Area, 23,200 sq. km (8,950 sq. miles); population (2010 census), 696,459. Capital, Yoshkar-Ola (2010 census population, 248,782). The Mari people were annexed to Russia, with other peoples of the Kazan Tatar Khanate, when the latter was overthrown in 1552. On 4 Nov. 1920 the territory was constituted as an Autonomous Region, and on 5 Dec. 1936 as an Autonomous Republic. The republic renamed itself the Mari Soviet Socialist Republic in Oct. 1990, and adopted a new constitution in June 1995. In Dec. 1991 Vladislav Zotin was elected the first president. The main ethnic groups are Russians (47·4% of the population in 2010), followed by Maris, with some Tatars.

Head of the Republic: Aleksandr Yevstifeyev.

Coal is mined. The main industries are metalworking, timber, paper, woodworking and food processing. Crops include grain, flax, potatoes, fruit and vegetables. In 2015 gross regional product amounted to

165,531·0m. roubles. Industry accounted for 31·4% of gross value added in 2015, ahead of agriculture, forestry and fishing with 18·8% and wholesale and retail trade, transport, accommodation and food services with 15·2%.

Mordovia

Area, 26,200 sq. km (10,100 sq. miles); population (2010 census), 834,755. Capital, Saransk (2010 census population, 297,415). By the 13th century the Mordovian tribes had been subjugated by Russian princes. In 1928 the territory was constituted as a Mordovian Area within the Middle-Volga Territory, on 10 Jan. 1930 as an Autonomous Region and on 20 Dec. 1934 as an Autonomous Republic. The main ethnic groups are Russians (53·4% of the population in 2010), followed by Mordovians, with some Tatars.

Head of the Republic: Vladimir Volkov.

Prime Minister: Vladimir Sushkov.

Industries include wood-processing and the production of building materials, furniture, textiles and leather goods. Agriculture is devoted chiefly to grain, sugar beet, sheep and dairy farming. In 2015 gross regional product amounted to 187,397·3m. roubles. Industry accounted for 28·3% of gross value added in 2015, ahead of wholesale and retail trade, transport, accommodation and food services with 18·3% and public administration, defence, education, human health and social work activities with 18·2%.

North Ossetia-Alania

Area, 8,000 sq. km (3,100 sq. miles); population (2010 census), 712,980. Capital, Vladikavkaz (2010 census population, 311,693). North Ossetia was annexed by Russia from Turkey and named the Terek region in 1861. On 4 March 1918 it was proclaimed an Autonomous Soviet Republic, and on 20 Jan. 1921 set up with others as the Mountain Autonomous Republic, with North Ossetia as the Ossetian (Vladikavkaz) Area within it. On 7 July 1924 the latter was constituted as an Autonomous Region and on 5 Dec. 1936 as an Autonomous Republic. In the early 1990s there was a conflict with neighbouring Ingushetia to the east, and to the south the decision of the Georgian government to disband the republic of South Ossetia led to ethnic war, with North Ossetia supporting the South Ossetians. Pressure for Ossetian reunification continues. In Sept. 2004 hostage takers seized a school in the town of Beslan. A three-day standoff ended with more than 350 people killed, nearly half of them children. Chechen rebels claimed responsibility for the siege.

A new constitution was adopted on 12 Nov. 1994 under which the republic reverted to its former name, Alania. Ossetians are the largest ethnic group, followed by Russians (20·8% of the population in 2010), with some Chechens, Armenians and Ukrainians.

Head of the Republic: Vyacheslav Bitarov.

Prime Minister: Taimuraz Tuskayev.

The main industries are non-ferrous metals (mining and metallurgy), maize processing, timber and woodworking, textiles, building materials, distilleries and food processing. There is also a varied agriculture. In 2015 gross regional product amounted to 127,543·9m. roubles. Public administration, defence, education, human health and social work activities accounted for 30·3% of gross value added in 2015, ahead of wholesale and retail trade, transport, accommodation and food services with 26·7% and agriculture, forestry and fishing with 16·4%.

Sakha

The area is 3,103,200 sq. km (1,197,750 sq. miles), making Sakha—also known as Yakutia—the largest republic in the Russian Federation; population (2010 census), 958,528. Capital, Yakutsk (2010 census population, 269,601). The Yakuts were subjugated by the Russians in the 17th century. The territory was constituted an Autonomous Republic on 27 April 1922. The largest ethnic group are Russians (37·8% of the population in 2010), followed by Yakuts, with Ukrainian and Tatar minorities.

Acting Head of the Republic: Aysen Nikolayev.

Prime Minister: Yevgeny Chekin.

The principal industries are mining (gold, tin, mica, coal) and livestock-breeding. Silver- and lead-bearing ores and coal are worked. Large diamond fields have been opened up; Sakha produces most of the Russian Federation's output. Timber and food industries are developing. Trapping and breeding of fur-bearing animals (sable, squirrel, silver fox) are an important source of income. In 2015 gross regional product amounted to 749,987·5m. roubles. Industry accounted for 54·9% of gross value added in 2015, ahead of wholesale and retail trade, transport, accommodation and food services

with 15·8% and public administration, defence, education, human health and social work activities with 15·0%.

Tatarstan

Area, 68,000 sq. km (26,250 sq. miles); population (2010 census), 3,786,488. Capital, Kazan (2010 census population, 1,143,535). From the 10th to the 13th centuries this was the territory of the Volga-Kama Bulgar State; conquered by the Mongols, it became the seat of the Kazan (Tatar) Khans when the Mongol Empire broke up in the 15th century, and in 1552 was conquered again by Russia. On 27 May 1920 it was constituted as an Autonomous Republic. The main ethnic groups are Tatars and Russians (ethnic Russians constituted only 39·7% of the population in 2010), with Chuvash, Ukrainian and Mordovian minorities.

In Oct. 1991 the Supreme Soviet declared independence. At a referendum in March 1992, 61·4% of votes cast were in favour of increased autonomy. A constitution was adopted in April 1992, which proclaims Tatarstan a sovereign state which conducts its relations with the Russian Federation on an equal basis. On 15 Feb. 1994 the Russian and Tatar presidents signed a treaty defining Tatarstan as a state united with Russia on the basis of the constitutions of both. On 26 June 2007 Tatarstan's relationship with Russia was further defined, and its autonomy consolidated with the signing of a treaty between the two governments.

President: Rustam Minnikhanov.

Acting Prime Minister: Aleksey Pesoshin.

The republic has engineering, oil and chemical, timber, building materials, textiles, clothing and food industries. Tatarstan is one of the fastest-growing Russian republics. In 2015 gross regional product amounted to 1,833,214·5m. roubles. Industry accounted for 43·3% of gross value added in 2015, ahead of wholesale and retail trade, transport, accommodation and food services with 21·2% and real estate activities with 9·7%.

Tuva

Area, 170,500 sq. km (65,800 sq. miles); population (2010 census), 307,930. Capital, Kyzyl (2010 census population, 109,918). Tuva was incorporated in the USSR as an autonomous region on 11 Oct. 1944 and elevated to an Autonomous Republic on 10 Oct. 1961. The largest ethnic group are Tuvans, followed by Russians. Ethnic Russians constituted only 16·3% of the population in 2010. Tuva renamed itself the 'Republic of Tuva' in Oct. 1991.

A new constitution was promulgated on 22 Oct. 1993 which adopts the name 'Tyva' for the republic. This constitution provides for a 32-member parliament (*Supreme Hural*), and a *Grand Hural* alone empowered to change the constitution, asserts the precedence of Tuvan law and adopts powers to conduct foreign policy. It was approved by 62·2% of votes cast at a referendum on 12 Dec. 1993.

Head of the Republic and Chairman of the Government: Sholban Kara-ool.

Tuva is well-watered and hydro-electric resources are important. The Tuvans are mainly herdsmen and cattle farmers and there is much good pastoral land. There are deposits of gold, cobalt and asbestos. The main exports are hair, hides and wool. There are mining, woodworking, garment, leather, food and other industries. In 2015 gross regional product amounted to 47,287·3m. roubles. Public administration, defence, education, human health and social work activities accounted for 47·6% of gross value added in 2015, ahead of industry with 16·5% and wholesale and retail trade, transport, accommodation and food services with 13·2%.

Udmurtia

Area, 42,100 sq. km (16,250 sq. miles); population (2010 census), 1,521,420. Capital, Izhevsk (2010 census population, 627,734). The Udmurts (formerly known as 'Votyaks') were annexed by the Russians in the 15th and 16th centuries. On 4 Nov. 1920 the Votyak Autonomous Region was constituted (the name was changed to Udmurt in 1932), and on 28 Dec. 1934 was raised to the status of an Autonomous Republic. The main ethnic group are Russians (62·2% of the population in 2010), followed by Udmurts, with Tatar, Ukrainian and Mari minorities. A declaration of sovereignty and the present state title were adopted in Sept. 1990.

A new parliament was established in Dec. 1993 consisting of a 50-member upper house, the *Council of Representatives*, and a full-time 35-member lower house.

Head of the Republic: Aleksandr Brechalov.

Prime Minister: Yaroslav Semyonov.

Heavy industry includes the manufacture of locomotives, machine tools and other engineering products, most of them for the defence industries, as well as timber and building materials. There are also light industries: clothing, leather, furniture and food. In 2015 gross regional product amounted to 497,685·0m. roubles. Industry accounted for 45·6% of gross value added in 2015, ahead of wholesale and retail trade, transport, accommodation and food services with 17·1% and public administration, defence, education, human health and social work activities with 12·6%.

Autonomous Districts and Provinces

Chukot
Situated in Magadan region (Far East); area, 737,700 sq. km, population (2010 census), 50,526. Capital, Anadyr. Formed 1930. Population chiefly Russian, also Chukchi, Koryak, Yakut, Even. Minerals are extracted in the north, including gold, tin, mercury and tungsten.

Khanty-Mansi
Situated in Tyumen region (western Siberia); area, 523,100 sq. km, population (2010 census), 1,532,243, chiefly Russians but also Khants and Mansi. Capital, Khanty-Mansiisk. Formed 1930.

Nenets
Situated in Archangel region (Northern Russia); area, 176,700 sq. km, population (2010 census), 42,090. Capital, Naryan-Mar. Formed 1929.

Yamalo-Nenets
Situated in Tyumen region (western Siberia); area, 750,300 sq. km, population (2010 census), 522,904. Capital, Salekhard. Formed 1930.

Yevreyskaya (Jewish) Autonomous Oblast (Province)
Part of Khabarovsk Territory. Area, 36,000 sq. km (13,895 sq. miles); population (2010 census), 176,558, chiefly Russians, but also Ukrainians and Jews. Capital, Birobijan. Established as Jewish National District in 1928. There is a Yiddish national theatre, newspaper and broadcasting service.

Further Reading

Russia
Rossiiskii Statisticheskii Ezhegodnik. Annual (title varies)

Acton, E., *et al.*, *Critical Companion to the Russian Revolution.* 1997

Aslund, Anders, (ed.) *Economic Transformation in Russia.* 1994.—*Building Capitalism: the Transformation of the Former Soviet Bloc.* 2002

Bacon, Edwin, *Securitising Russia: The Domestic Politics of Putin.* 2006.—*Contemporary Russia.* 3rd ed. 2014

Brady, Rose, *Kapitalizm: Russia's Struggle to Free its Economy.* 2000

Cadier, David and Light, Margot, (eds) *Russia's Foreign Policy.* 2015

Cambridge Encyclopedia of Russia and the Former Soviet Union. 1995

Clover, Charles, *Black Wind, White Snow: The Rise of Russia's New Nationalism.* 2016

Dawisha, Karen, *Putin's Kleptocracy: Who Owns Russia?* 2014

Evans, Alfred B., *Russian Civil Society: A Critical Assessment.* 2005

Forsberg, Tuomas and Haukkala, Hiski, *The European Union and Russia.* 2016

Fowkes, B. (ed.) *Russia and Chechnia: The Permanent Crisis, Essays on Russo-Chechen Relations.* 1998

Freeze, G. (ed.) *Russia: A History.* 1997

Gall, C. and de Waal, T., *Chechnya: Calamity in the Caucasus.* 1998

Gessen, Masha, *The Man Without a Face: The Unlikely Rise of Vladimir Putin.* 2012

Granville, Brigitte and Oppenheimer, Peter, (eds) *Russia's Post-Community Economy.* 2001

Gustafson, Thane, *Capitalism Russian-Style.* 2000

Hill, Fiona and Gaddy, Clifford G., *Mr. Putin: Operative in the Kremlin.* 2013

Hollander, Paul, *Political Will and Personal Belief: The Decline and Fall of Soviet Communism.* 2000

Holmes, Stephen, *The State After Communism: Governance in the New Russia.* 2006

Hosking, Geoffrey, *Russia and the Russians, A History from Rus to the Russian Federation.* 2001

Judah, Ben, *Fragile Empire: How Russia Fell In and Out of Love with Vladimir Putin.* 2013

Kanet, Roger E. (ed.) *Russia: Re-Emerging Great Power.* 2007

Kochan, L. and Keep, J., *The Making of Modern Russia.* 3rd ed. 1997

Kotkin, Stephen, *Armageddon Averted: the Soviet Collapse 1970–2000.* 2001

Ledeneva, Alena V., *Can Russia Modernise?: Sistema, Power Networks and Informal Governance.* 2013

Lieven, A., *Chechnya: Tombstone of Russian Power.* 1998

Lipman, Maria and Petrov, Nikolay, (eds) *Russia 2025: Scenarios for the Russian Future.* 2013

Lloyd, J., *Rebirth of a Nation.* 1998

Lo, Bobo, *Russia and the New World Disorder.* 2015

Lucas, Edward, *The New Cold War: Putin's Russia and the Threat to the West.* 3rd ed. 2014

Marks, Steven, *How Russia Shaped the Modern World: From Art to Anti-Semitism, Ballet to Bolshevism.* 2002

Mendras, Marie, *Russian Politics: The Paradox of a Weak State.* 2012

Ostrovsky, Arkady, *The Invention of Russia: The Journey from Gorbachev's Freedom to Putin's War.* 2015

Paxton, J., *Encyclopedia of Russian History.* 1993.—*Leaders of Russia and the Soviet Union.* 2004

Ponsard, Lionel, *Russia, NATO and Cooperative Security.* 2006

Pursiainen, Christer, (ed.) *At the Crossroads of Post-Communist Modernisation: Russia and China in Comparative Perspective.* 2012

Putin, Vladimir, *First Person*; interviews, translated from Russian. 2000

Remington, Thomas F., *Politics in Russia.* 2005

Remnick, D., *Resurrection: The Struggle for a New Russia.* 1998

Riasanovsky, N. V., *A History of Russia.* 8th ed. 2010

Sakwa, R., *Russian Politics and Society.* 4th ed. 2008.—*Communism in Russia.* 2010

Service, Robert, *A History of Twentieth-Century Russia.* 1997.—*Lenin: A Biography.* 2000.—*Russia: Experiment with a People.* 2002

Shevtsova, Lilia, *Putin's Russia.* 2003

Shiraev, Eric, *Russian Government and Politics.* 2nd ed. 2013

Shiraev, Eric and Khudoley, Konstantin, *Russian Foreign Policy.* 2018

Shriver, G. (ed. and transl.) *Post-Soviet Russia, A Journey Through the Yeltsin Era.* 2000

Stent, Angela, *The Limits of Partnership: US–Russian Relations in the Twenty-First Century.* 2014

Studin, Irvin (ed.), *Russia: Strategy, Policy and Administration.* 2018

Taubman, William, *Gorbachev: His Life and Times.* 2017

Tsygankov, Andrei P., *Russia's Foreign Policy: Change and Continuity in National Identity.* 2006

Webber, Stephen L., *Military and Society in Post-Soviet Russia.* 2006

Westwood, J. N., *Endurance and Endeavour: Russian History, 1812–2001.* 5th ed. 2002

White, Stephen, Sakwa, Richard and Hale, Henry E. (eds) *Developments in Russian Politics 9.* 2018

National Statistical Office: Federal State Statistics Service, 39 Miasnitskaya St., 103450 Moscow. *Head:* Pavel Malkov.

Website: http://www.gks.ru

Chechnya
Jagielski, Wojciech, *Towers of Stone: The Battle of Wills in Chechnya.* 2009

Lieven, A. and Bradner, H., *Chechnya: Tombstone of Russian Power.* 1999

Rwanda

Republika y'u Rwanda (Republic of Rwanda)

Capital: Kigali
Population projection, 2020: 13·09m.
GNI per capita, 2017: (PPP$) 1,811
HDI/world rank, 2017: 0·524/158
Internet domain extension: .rw

Key Historical Events

The Twa—hunter-gatherer pygmies—were the first people to inhabit Rwanda. They now comprise 1% of the population. The Hutu were the next group to settle in Rwanda. They arrived at some point between AD 500 and 1100. They were small-scale agriculturalists, led by a king who ruled over clan groups. The final group to migrate was the Tutsi around 1400. Their ownership of cattle and their combat skills allowed them to gain control of the country. A feudalistic system developed where the Tutsi lent cows to the Hutu in return for labour and military service. At the apex was the Tutsi king, the mwami (pl., abami), believed to be of divine origin. The abami consolidated their power by centralizing the monarchy and reducing the power of neighbouring chiefs. Mwami Kigeri IV (reigned 1853–95) established the borders of Rwanda in the 19th century.

The Conference of Berlin in 1885 placed Rwanda under German control. However, no German actually reached the area until 1894 when Count von Götzen became the governor of German East Africa. The Belgians and British had ambitions in the area owing to its strategic position at the juncture of their separate empires. However, by 1910 German rule was accepted.

A consequence of German influence was the arrival of the Catholic Church through the mission of the White Fathers, who established schools and missions from 1899. Germany maintained the mwami political structure, and Yuhi V (reigned 1896–1931) accepted German overlordship. However, in 1916—during the First World War—Rwanda was occupied by Belgian forces and was declared a Belgian mandate in Aug. 1923 by the League of Nations. The Belgians ruled more directly than the Germans, curtailing the mwami's power and favouring the Tutsi minority on racial grounds. From 1952 the UN ordered Belgium to integrate Rwandans into the political system. The Belgians continued their policy of favouring the Tutsi and placed them in a position of domination over the Hutu majority. Civil unrest erupted into a civil war by 1959. A state of Ruanda-Urundi was established in 1960, under Belgian trusteeship, following an election. In 1961, while abroad, Mwami Kigeli V was exiled by the Belgians despite pressure from the UN. On 27 June 1962 the parliament voted to terminate the trusteeship and on 1 July 1962 Rwanda became independent.

Independence

The independent state of Rwanda was first governed by the Parmehutu party (a Hutu party representing the 85% Hutu population), led by Grégoire Kayibanda, but was not accepted by some Tutsis. An attempted invasion in 1963 by Tutsis who had fled to Uganda and Burundi was repelled. In retaliation over 12,000 Tutsis in Rwanda were massacred by the Hutu. The next massacre in 1972-73 was partly in response to the persecution of Hutus in neighbouring Tutsi-dominated Burundi. An attempt by Kayibanda to revive his waning popularity, the violence instead spurred Maj.-Gen. Juvénal Habyarimana, a senior army commander, to launch a bloodless coup. In 1975 Habyarimana formed *le Mouvement Révolutionaire National pour le Développement* (MRND), and turned Rwanda into a one-party police state, discriminating against the Tutsi in favour of the Hutu.

In 1990 the Rwandan Patriotic Front (RPF), of between 5,000 and 10,000 Tutsis, invaded Rwanda from Uganda, starting a civil war. A ceasefire was agreed on 29 March 1991 and on 14 July 1992 the Arusha Accords were signed. These allowed other political parties to stand for election and share power.

Many Hutus opposed Arusha. Multi-partyism led to the rise of far-right Hutu power groups who believed that the only solution to Hutu-Tutsi problems was the extermination of the Tutsi. The assassination of the first legitimately elected Hutu president of Burundi (21 Oct. 1993) by Tutsi army officers and the massacre of over 150,000 Hutus in Burundi served to further destabilize Rwanda. The assassination of Habyarimana in a plane crash on 6 April 1994, probably shot down by Hutu extremists, was the first step in a carefully premeditated genocide which killed around 1m. Rwandans in three months and forced over 2m. to flee to neighbouring countries.

Among the victims was the moderate Hutu prime minister, Agathe Uwilingiyimana. Gangs of *interahamwe* (civilian death squads) roamed the capital, Kigali, killing, looting and raping Tutsis and politically-moderate Hutus. When the RPF, led by Paul Kagame, reached Kigali the killings spread to other parts of the country. The UN sent a peacekeeping force (UNAMIR) but a lack of resources, an unclear mandate and international apathy made it impotent as the genocide took hold. France dispatched 2,000 troops on a humanitarian mission on 22 June 1994 to maintain a 'safe zone', which owing to France's affinity with the French-speaking Hutu former government, served as an escape route to Zaïre (now the Democratic Republic of the Congo) for Hutu extremists.

The RPF declared the war over on 17 July 1994 and was quickly recognized as the new government. Genocide trials began in Arusha, Tanzania in Dec. 1996. In Sept. 1998 Jean Kambanda, the former prime minister (April–July 1994), was sentenced to life imprisonment.

Rwanda was destabilized by the presence of Hutu refugee camps on the Zaïre borders. Amongst the 1·1m. refugees were *interahamwe* who used the camps as bases for attacks on Rwanda. These were broken up by Laurent Kabila in May 1997, before he assumed power in Zaïre.

In April 2000 Paul Kagame (the Tutsi vice president and defence minister) was elected president by parliament, replacing Pasteur Bizimungu, a Hutu who had been appointed by the RPF, in July 1994. Kagame was re-elected president in Aug. 2003 in Rwanda's first democratic elections since the atrocities.

Territory and Population

Rwanda is bounded south by Burundi, west by the Democratic Republic of the Congo, north by Uganda and east by Tanzania. A mountainous state of 25,314 sq. km (9,774 sq. miles), its western third drains to Lake Kivu on the border with the Democratic Republic of the Congo and thence to the Congo river, while the rest is drained by the Kagera river into the Nile system.

The population was 7,164,994 at the 1991 census, of whom over 90% were Hutu, 9% Tutsi and 1% Twa (pygmy). Following the genocide of 1994 ethnicity was not enumerated at the 2002 census, when the population was 8,128,553. Population at the 2012 census, 10,515,973; density, 415·4 per sq. km.

The UN gives a projected population for 2020 of 13·09m.

In 2011 the population was 19·2% urban.

Since Jan. 2006 Rwanda has been reorganized into five provinces (*intara*). It had previously been composed of 12 provinces that were less multiethnic. Among the reasons given for the change were the reduction of ethnic divisions and the suppression of reminders of the 1994 genocide. Areas and populations at the 2012 census were:

Province	Area (in sq. km)	Population (2012 census)
Eastern	9,458	2,595,703
Kigali	730	1,132,686
Northern	3,276	1,726,370
Southern	5,963	2,589,975
Western	5,883	2,471,239

Kigali, the capital, had a population of 1,132,686 in 2012; other towns are Butare, Gisenyi, Gitarama and Ruhengeri.

Kinyarwanda, which is the language of the entire population, along with English and French are the official languages. In 2008 English replaced

© Springer Nature Limited 2020
Palgrave Macmillan (ed.), *The Statesman's Yearbook 2020*,
https://doi.org/10.1057/978-1-349-95940-2_159

French as the language of instruction in schools. Swahili is spoken in the commercial centres.

Social Statistics

2008 estimates: births, 400,000; deaths, 141,000. Estimated birth rate in 2008 was 41·1 per 1,000 population; estimated death rate, 14·5. Annual population growth rate, 2005–10, 2·8%. Life expectancy at birth during the period 2005–10 was 61·1 years for females and 58·5 for males, up from 24·8 years for females and 21·4 years for males in 1990–95 (at the height of the civil war). Infant mortality has fallen considerably, from 70 per 1,000 live births in 2005 to 33 per 1,000 live births in 2014. Rwanda has also made some of the best progress in recent years in reducing child mortality. The number of deaths per 1,000 live births among children under five was reduced from 152 in 1990 to 52 in 2013. The number of deaths per 100,000 live births among mothers has also dropped considerably, from 567 in 2005 to 304 in 2014. Fertility rate, 2014, 3·9 births per woman.

Climate

Despite the equatorial situation, there is a highland tropical climate. The wet seasons are from Oct. to Dec. and March to May. Highest rainfall occurs in the west, at around 70" (1,770 mm), decreasing to 40–55" (1,020–1,400 mm) in the central uplands and to 30" (760 mm) in the north and east. Kigali, Jan. 67°F (19·4°C), July 70°F (21·1°C). Annual rainfall 40" (1,000 mm).

Constitution and Government

Under the 1978 constitution the MRND was the sole political organization.

A new constitution was promulgated in June 1991 permitting multi-party democracy.

The Arusha Agreement of Aug. 1994 provided for a transitional 70-member National Assembly, which began functioning in Nov. 1994. The seats won by the MRNDD (formerly MRND) were taken over by other parties on the grounds that the MRNDD was culpable of genocide.

A referendum was held on 26 May 2003 which approved a draft constitution by 93·4% (turnout was 87%). The new constitution, subsequently approved by the Supreme Court, provides for an 80-member *Chamber of Deputies* and a 26-member *Senate*, with the provision that no party may hold more than half of cabinet positions. 53 members of the Chamber of Deputies are directly elected, 24 women are elected by provincial councils, two members are elected by the National Youth Council and one is elected by a disabilities organization.

In 2015 a constitutional amendment reduced the length of presidential terms from seven years to five years and maintained a two-term limit. However, the relevant legislation allowed incumbent president Paul Kagame to be exempted, enabling him to seek a third seven-year term in 2017, potentially followed by two further five-year terms. The proposals won 98% support in a referendum.

National Anthem

'Rwanda Nziza' ('Beautiful Rwanda'); words by F. Murigo, tune by Capt. J.-B. Hashakaimana.

Recent Elections

Presidential elections were held on 4 Aug. 2017. Paul Kagame was re-elected president for a third seven-year term with 98·8% of the vote. Philippe Mpayimana, an independent candidate, and Frank Habineza of the Democratic Green Party won 0·7% and 0·5% respectively. Turnout was 98·2%.

In parliamentary elections held on 2–3 Sept. 2018 President Kagame's Rwandan Patriotic Front (RPF) and its coalition partners took 74·0% of the vote and won 40 of the 53 directly elected seats (but lost its absolute majority in the Chamber of Deputies), the Social Democratic Party (PSD) 5, the Liberal Party 4, the Democratic Green Party 2 and the Social Party Imberakuri also 2. Following the Sept. 2018 election, of the 80 Members of Parliament there were 49 women (61·3%) and 31 men (38·7%).

Current Government

President: Paul Kagame; b. 1957 (RPF; sworn in 22 April 2000 having been acting president since 24 March 2000, and re-elected in Aug. 2003, Aug. 2010 and Aug. 2017).

The government consisted of the following in Feb. 2019:

Prime Minister: Édouard Ngirente; b. 1973 (PSD; sworn in 30 Aug. 2017).

Minister of Agriculture and Animal Resources: Géraldine Mukeshimana. *Defence:* Maj.-Gen. Albert Murasira. *Education:* Eugène Mutimura. *Emergency Management:* Germaine Kamayirese. *Environment:* Vincent Biruta. *Finance and Economic Planning:* Uzziel Ndagijimana. *Foreign Affairs and International Relations:* Richard Sezibera. *Gender and Family Promotion:* Solina Nyirahabimana. *Health:* Diane Gashumba. *Information Communication Technology and Innovation:* Paula Ingabire. *Infrastructure:* Claver Gatete. *Justice and Attorney General:* Johnston Businge. *Local Government:* Anastase Shyaka. *Public Service and Labour:* Fanfan Kayirangwa Rwanyindo. *Sports and Culture:* Espérance Nyirasafari. *Trade and Industry:* Soraya Hakuziyaremye. *Youth:* Rosemary Mbabazi. *Minister in the President's Office:* Judith Uwizeye. *Minister of Cabinet Affairs in the Office of the Prime Minister:* Marie Solange Kaysire.

Ministers of State: Alvera Mukabaramba (*in Charge of Social Affairs*); Isaac Munyakazi (*in Charge of Primary and Secondary Education*); Patrick Ndimubanzi (*in Charge of Public Health and Primary Healthcare*); Olivier Nduhungirehe (*in Charge of the East African Community*); Claudine Uwera (*in Charge of Economic Planning*); Jean de Dieu Uwihanganye (*in Charge of Transport*); Evode Uwizeyimana (*in Charge of Constitutional and Legal Affairs*).

Government Website: http://www.go.rw

Current Leaders

Paul Kagame

Position
President

Introduction

Paul Kagame was elected president by the transitional National Assembly in April 2000 and democratic elections in 2003 cemented his mandate. He is leader of the ruling Rwandan Patriotic Front (RPF) and the first member of the Tutsi minority to be president since Rwanda gained independence in 1962. Although a leading force in the country, he is a low-key public figure. He has openly criticized the United Nations, arguing it could have done more to avoid the genocide of 1994 when around 1m. Rwandans were killed, and also accused France of complicity. He was re-elected president for further seven-year terms by overwhelming margins in Aug. 2010 and Aug. 2017.

Early Life

Kagame was born in Oct. 1957 in the Gitarama prefecture. Following ethnic violence in Rwanda, his family fled to Uganda in 1960 where he grew up in a refugee camp and then studied at Makerere University in Kampala. In 1979 Kagame joined the National Salvation Front (FRONASA), led by Yoweri Museveni, which took part in the Tanzanian removal of Idi Amin's regime in 1979. In 1980 he became a founding member of Museveni's National Resistance Army (NRA) and fought against the dictatorship of Milton Obote in Uganda. He became head of intelligence of the NRA in 1986 and the following year established the Rwandan Patriotic Front (RPF), with support from Museveni, which launched a guerrilla war against President Juvénal Habyarimana and his Hutu government. In 1993 a peace agreement was signed, but the death of Habyarimana in 1994 triggered the Hutu massacres of the Tutsi. The RPF resumed the civil war and soon gained control over the country. The new government of national unity, formed in July 1994, was led by Pasteur Bizimungu, a Hutu, with Kagame as vice president and defence minister.

Career in Office

Rwanda's involvement in the Democratic Republic of the Congo (DRC; known as Zaïre until 1997) began covertly in 1996 with an agreement with Uganda to oust the Zaïrean president Mobutu Sese Seko. Kagame and Museveni then sent troops back into the east of the DRC in 1998 to assist rebel groups against President Laurent Kabila and to eliminate the *interahamwe* (death squads from the 1994 genocide in Rwanda). In Nov. 1998 Kagame publicly admitted that Rwandan forces were active in the DRC for reasons of national security. However, divisions began to appear between Kagame and Museveni, who saw the enlargement and reorganization of the Rwandan forces as a direct threat.

In March 2000 President Bizimungu resigned, claiming that he was hounded from office for being a Hutu. Elected president by the transitional National Assembly in April 2000, Kagame attempted to portray himself as a civilian and neutral candidate, calling for ethnic peace and reconciliation.

Following the assassination of Laurent Kabila (president of the DRC) in Jan. 2001, his son and successor, Joseph Kabila, met Kagame who accused the DRC of harbouring Hutu militias. Kabila blamed Rwanda for killing more than 3·5m. inhabitants of the DRC and refused to co-operate until Rwandan troops were withdrawn. However, on 30 July 2002 the two nations signed a peace deal in South Africa under which the DRC agreed to disarm and arrest Hutu rebels and Rwanda withdrew its troops from the DRC in Oct. 2002.

Kagame was elected president by a popular democratic vote on 25 Aug. 2003. His win—with 95% of the vote—initially prompted allegations of irregularities from his main rival, Faustin Twagiramungu, although he accepted the victory the following month. Museveni's attendance at Kagame's inauguration ceremony demonstrated the easing of tensions between the two men. In 2007 Kagame authorized the release of several thousand prisoners accused of genocide. He also awarded a presidential pardon to Pasteur Bizimungu, who had served three years of a 15-year prison sentence for attempting to form a militia and for embezzlement. Parliamentary elections in Sept. 2008 returned the ruling coalition led by Kagame's RPF to power with almost 79% of the vote.

In Nov. 2006 a French investigative judge had accused Kagame of ordering the assassination of President Habyarimana in 1994. Kagame responded by cutting diplomatic links with France. Then, in Aug. 2008, a Rwandan report commissioned by Kagame made a counter-accusation of complicity by French politicians (including former president François Mitterrand) and army officers in the genocide. However, diplomatic ties were eventually restored in Nov. 2009 and French President Nicolas Sarkozy paid an official visit to Rwanda in Feb. 2010.

From Aug. 2008 fighting in the DRC intensified between the army and the mainly Tutsi insurgents loyal to Laurent Nkunda. Kabila's government had for some time claimed that Kagame was giving Rwandan support to Nkunda. However, in an apparent reversal of Rwandan policy, troops from both countries launched a joint offensive in Jan. 2009 against Nkunda's headquarters in the DRC and the rebel leader was arrested when he fled into Rwanda. Following the operation, relations between Rwanda and the DRC stabilized, but in 2012 there were further allegations of Rwandan support for rebel forces opposed to the Kabila regime, prompting the USA, UK and the Netherlands to suspend aid contributions.

In Nov. 2009 Rwanda was admitted to the Commonwealth despite (like Mozambique) not having had colonial or constitutional ties to the United Kingdom.

In Aug. 2010 Kagame was re-elected as president with another landslide share of the vote, although the opposition claimed that the election was not free and fair. In polling in Sept. 2013 the RPF retained its absolute parliamentary majority. In Oct. 2015 parliament agreed to a constitutional amendment that would allow Kagame to remain in power beyond the end of the constitutionally-specified two-term limit (in 2017, with elections that were scheduled for and duly took place in Aug.). The controversial proposal received overwhelming backing in a referendum in Dec. 2015.

Earlier, in July 2014, Kagame nominated Anastase Murekezi of the PSD as the new prime minister after dismissing Pierre Damien Habumuremyi. Kagame's tight political grip was reinforced by another landslide victory in the Aug. 2017 presidential election, after which he appointed Édouard Ngirente, also of the PSD, in place of Murekezi as premier. In parliamentary elections in Sept. 2018 the RPF again maintained its control of the Chamber of Deputies, securing about 74% of the vote.

In Jan. 2018 Kagame took over the year-long chairmanship of the African Union.

Édouard Ngirente

Position
Prime Minister

Introduction
Édouard Ngirente became prime minister on 30 Aug. 2017, despite being relatively unknown in public life.

Early Life
Ngirente was born in 1973 and studied at the National University of Rwanda, before gaining a doctorate in agricultural economics from the Catholic University of Louvain in Belgium. He took a post at the National University before joining the ministry of finance and economic planning, and then moved to Washington, D.C. to serve as an adviser to the executive director of the World Bank.

When Paul Kagame won a third presidential term in Aug. 2017, he named Ngirente as prime minister in succession to Anastase Murekezi, who had held the post since July 2014.

Career in Office
Ngirente spoke of his desire to lead a government representing all Rwandans. In Sept. 2017 he presented a seven-year economic programme aiming to create new jobs, develop key sectors to stimulate growth and trade, and undertake large-scale sanitation and electrification infrastructure projects. He also stated his ambition that 35% of Rwandans should be living in cities by 2024.

Among his chief challenges are endemic corruption, the mismanagement of government funds and concerns about human rights abuses.

Defence

In 2013 defence expenditure totalled US$82m. (US$7 per capita), representing 1·1% of GDP.

As at 31 May 2016 Rwanda had 6,144 personnel serving in UN peace-keeping operations (the fifth largest contingent of any country, after Ethiopia, India, Pakistan and Bangladesh).

Army
Strength (2011), 32,000. There were local defence forces of some 2,000 in 2011.

Economy

Agriculture accounted for 30·8% of GDP in 2013, industry 18·3% and services 50·9%.

Overview
Since the 1994 genocide and civil war, Rwanda has registered strong economic growth and macroeconomic stability. Subsistence agriculture dominates, and accounted for 33% of GDP, over 70% of employment and more than 45% of export earnings between 2006 and 2015. The effects of the global financial crisis reduced GDP growth from a peak of 11·2% in 2008 to 6·2% in 2009. However, the economy has prospered since then, largely driven by the services sector. Annual GDP growth averaged 7·5% between 2010 and 2015.

According to the World Bank, upwards of 30% of Rwanda's budget is financed by international aid. The poverty rate declined from 57% in 2005–06 to 39% in 2014. An economic development and poverty reduction strategy is aiming to elevate Rwanda to a lower-middle income economy by 2020 through improved infrastructure, rural development, increased productivity and youth employment, and responsible governance. In the World Bank's 2016 *Doing Business* survey Rwanda ranked as the most improved economy in sub-Saharan Africa, its ranking rising from 139th in 2009 to 62nd in 2015.

Currency
The unit of currency is the *Rwanda franc* (RWF) notionally of 100 *centimes*. The currency is not convertible. Foreign exchange reserves were US$312m. in July 2005. Broad money supply totalled 1,391bn. Rwanda francs in Dec. 2016. Inflation was 15·4% in 2008, and more recently 5·7% in 2016 and 4·8% in 2017.

Budget
Budgetary central government revenues in 2011 totalled 982,062m. Rwanda francs (provisional); expenditures totalled 578,363m. Rwanda francs (provisional). Grants accounted for 41·6% of revenue with taxes on goods and services contributing 27·1%; main items of expenditure by economic type were grants (38·1%) and use of goods and services (29·5%).

VAT is 18%.

Performance
Real GDP growth was 24·5% in 1995, following two years of negative growth including a rate of −41·9% in 1994 at the height of the civil war.

From 2000–08 growth averaged 8·6%. Real GDP growth was 8·9% in 2015, 6·0% in 2016 and 6·1% in 2017. Total GDP in 2017 was US$9·1bn.

Banking and Finance

The central bank is the National Bank of Rwanda (founded 1960; *Governor*, John Rwangombwa). There are seven commercial banks (Banque de Kigali, Banque de Commerce et de Développement Industriel, Banque Continentale Africaine au Rwanda, Banque à la Confiance d'Or, Banque Commerciale du Rwanda, Caisse Hypothécaire du Rwanda and Compagnie Générale de Banque), one development bank and one credit union system.

Foreign debt totalled US$795m. in 2010, representing 14·2% of GNI.

A stock exchange opened in Kigali in Jan. 2011.

Energy and Natural Resources

Environment

Carbon dioxide emissions from the consumption of energy in 2011 were the equivalent of 0·1 tonnes per capita.

Electricity

Installed capacity was 89,000 kW in 2011. Production was 346m. kWh in 2011 and consumption per capita was 38 kWh.

Oil and Gas

In 2013 proven natural gas reserves were 57bn. cu. metres.

Minerals

Production (2013 estimates): limestone for use in cement production, 96,000 tonnes; pozzolanic materials, 30,000 tonnes; sandstone, 12,000 tonnes. Niobium, tantalum, tin and tungsten are also mined. Rwanda is one of the world's largest producers of tantalum, which is used in the electronics industry.

Agriculture

There were an estimated 1·2m. ha. of arable land in 2012 and 250,000 ha. of permanent crops. Production (2012, in 1,000 tonnes): plantains, 3,219; cassava, 2,716; potatoes, 2,338; sweet potatoes, 1,005; maize, 573; dry beans, 433; pumpkins and squash, 236 (estimate); avocados, 145 (estimate); sorghum, 139; taro, 131.

In 2013 there were an estimated 2,680,000 goats, 1,140,000 cattle, 990,000 pigs, 810,000 sheep and 4·7m. chickens.

Forestry

Forests covered 0·48m. ha. (20% of the land area) in 2015. Timber production in 2011 was 6·21m. cu. metres.

Fisheries

The catch in 2012 totalled 19,475 tonnes, entirely from inland waters.

Industry

There are about 100 small-sized modern manufacturing enterprises in the country. Food manufacturing is the dominant industrial activity (64%) followed by construction (15%) and mining (9%). There is a large modern brewery.

Labour

The labour force in 2013 was 5,537,000 (4,173,000 in 2003). 87·2% of the population aged 15–64 was economically active in 2013. In the same year 0·6% of the population was unemployed.

Rwanda had 80,000 people living in slavery according to the Walk Free Foundation's 2013 *Global Slavery Index*.

International Trade

Imports and Exports

In 2010 imports (f.o.b.) amounted to US$1,274m.; exports (f.o.b.) US$238m. Imports doubled between 2006 and 2009. Leading imports in 2010 (US$1m.): machinery and transport equipment, 449·2; manufactured goods, 265·4; chemicals and related products, 170·3. Major exports in 2010 (US$1m.): tin, 66·9; coffee, 58·4; tea, 34·4. Main import suppliers, 2010 (US$1m.): Sweden, 120·0; UAE, 89·4; Kenya, 79·6. Main export markets, 2010 (US$1m.): Switzerland, 54·4; Kenya, 39·3; Belgium, 26·7.

Communications

Roads

Rwanda has some 14,000 km of roads. There are road links with Burundi, Uganda, Tanzania and the Democratic Republic of the Congo. In 2006 there were 4,130 motorcycles, 1,813 cars and jeeps, and 1,270 trucks and pick-ups. There were 308 road deaths in 2007.

Civil Aviation

There is an international airport at Kigali (Grégoire Kayibanda), which handled 458,807 passengers (382,766 on international flights) in 2012. A national carrier, Rwandair Express (since renamed RwandAir), began operations in 2003. In 2013 RwandAir served 16 destinations and carried 408,000 passengers (385,000 on international flights).

Telecommunications

Rwanda had 45,338 fixed telephone lines in 2013 and 6,689,000 mobile phone subscriptions. An estimated 8·7% of the population were internet users in 2013. In June 2012 there were 144,000 Facebook users.

Social Institutions

Out of 178 countries analysed in the 2017 *Fragile States Index*—a list published jointly by the Fund for Peace and *Foreign Policy* magazine— Rwanda was ranked the 34th most vulnerable to conflict or collapse. The index is based on 12 indicators of state vulnerability across social, political and economic categories.

Justice

A system of Courts of First Instance and provincial courts refer appeals to Courts of Appeal and a Court of Cassation situated in Kigali. The death penalty was last used in 1998 and was abolished in 2007. A number of people were executed for genocide in the civil war in 1994, including 22 at five different locations throughout the country on 24 April 1998.

The population in penal institutions in Dec. 2012 was 55,618, many thousands of whom were sentenced or awaiting trial in connection with the 1994 genocide.

Education

In 2008–09 there were 33,000 primary school teachers for 2·3m. pupils; 347,000 secondary pupils with 15,000 teachers; and 55,000 students at university level with 3,000 academic staff. Adult literacy rate in 2008 was 70%.

In 2007 public expenditure on education came to 4·9% of GDP and accounted for 19·0% of total government spending.

Health

In 2015 there were 742 physicians, 127 dentistry personnel and 9,661 nursing and midwifery personnel. There were 42 hospitals and 389 health centres in 2007.

In *Water: At What Cost? The State of the World's Water 2016*, WaterAid reported that 23·9% of the population does not have access to safe water.

Religion

In 2010 an estimated 93·4% of the population was Christian according to the Pew Research Center's Forum on Religion & Public Life, with 3·6% having no religious affiliation. Of the Christians in 2010, an estimated 53% were Catholics and 46% Protestants.

Culture

Press

The English-language *New Times* is published six days a week, with its sister publication the *Sunday Times* appearing on Sundays.

Tourism

In 2012 there were 815,000 international tourist arrivals (excluding same-day visitors), up from 688,000 in 2011.

Diplomatic Representatives

Of Rwanda in the United Kingdom (120–122 Seymour Pl., London, W1H 1NR)
High Commissioner: Yamina Claris Karitanyi.

Of the United Kingdom in Rwanda (Parcelle No. 1131, Blvd de l'Umuganda, Kacyiru-Sud, BP 576, Kigali)
High Commissioner: Jo Lomas.

Of Rwanda in the USA (1875 Connecticut Ave., NW, Suite 540, Washington, D.C., 20009)
Ambassador: Mathilde Mukantabana.

Of the USA in Rwanda (2657 Ave. de la Gendarmerie, Kigali)
Ambassador: Peter H. Vrooman.

Of Rwanda to the United Nations
Ambassador: Valentine Rugwabiza.

Of Rwanda to the European Union
Ambassador: Amandin Rugira.

Further Reading

Barnett, Michael, *Eyewitness to a Genocide: The United Nations and Rwanda.* 2003

Dallaire, Romeo, *Shake Hands with the Devil: The Failure of Humanity in Rwanda.* 2005

Dorsey, L., *Historical Dictionary of Rwanda.* 1995

Melson, Robert, *Genocide and Crisis in Central Africa: Conflict Roots, Mass Violence and Regional War.* 2001

Melvern, Linda, *A People Betrayed: The Role of the West in Rwanda's Genocide.* 2000

Prunier, G., *The Rwanda Crisis: History of a Genocide.* 1995

Waugh, Colin M., *Paul Kagame and Rwanda: Power, Genocide and the Rwandan Patriotic Front.* 2004

National Statistical Office: National Institute of Statistics of Rwanda, KN 2 Ave., Kigali.

Website: http://www.statistics.gov.rw

St Kitts and Nevis

Federation of St Kitts and Nevis

Capital: Basseterre
Population projection, 2020: 57,000
GNI per capita, 2017: (PPP$) 23,978
HDI/world rank, 2017: 0·778/72
Internet domain extension: .kn

Key Historical Events

The islands of St Kitts (formerly St Christopher) and Nevis were discovered and named by Columbus in 1493. They were settled by Britain in 1623 and 1628, but ownership was disputed with France until 1783. In Feb. 1967 colonial status was replaced by an 'association' with Britain, giving the islands full internal self-government. St Kitts and Nevis became fully independent on 19 Sept. 1983. In Oct. 1997 the five-person Nevis legislature voted to end the federation with St Kitts. However, in a referendum held on 10 Aug. 1998 voters rejected independence, only 62% voting for secession when a two-thirds vote in favour was needed. In Sept. 1998 Hurricane Georges caused devastation, leaving 25,000 people homeless, with some 80% of the houses in the islands damaged.

Territory and Population

The two islands of St Kitts and Nevis are situated at the northern end of the Leeward Islands in the eastern Caribbean. Nevis lies 3 km to the southeast of St Kitts. Population, 2011 census, 46,398. In 2011, 32·6% of the population were urban.

	Sq. km	Census 2001	Census 2011	Chief town	Population (2011 estimate)
St Kitts	168·0	35,217	34,983	Basseterre	13,000
Nevis	93·3	11,108	11,415	Charlestown	1,700
	261·3	46,325	46,398		

The UN gives a projected population for 2020 of 57,000.

Around 92% of the population is African-Caribbean. English is the official and spoken language.

Social Statistics

Births, 2008, 709; deaths, 357. Rates, 2008 (per 1,000 population): births, 13·8; deaths, 7·0. Infant mortality, 2010 (per 1,000 live births), 7. Life expectancy in 2012 was 73·3 years. Annual population growth rate, 2000–08, 1·3%; fertility rate, 2008, 1·8 births per woman.

Climate

Temperature varies between 21·4–30·7°C, with a sea breeze throughout the year and low humidity. Average annual rainfall is between 1,270 mm and 1,905 mm.

Constitution Government

The British sovereign is the head of state, represented by a Governor-General. The 1983 constitution described the country as 'a sovereign democratic federal state'. It allowed for a unicameral Parliament consisting of 11 elected Members (eight from St Kitts and three from Nevis), three appointed Senators and one *ex officio* member. Nevis was given its own Island Assembly and the right to secession from St Kitts.

The *Nevis Island* legislature comprises an Assembly of three nominated members and five elected members (one from each electoral district on the Island), and an Administration consisting of the Premier and two other persons appointed by the Deputy Governor-General.

National Anthem

'O Land of beauty! Our country where peace abounds'; words and tune by K. A. Georges.

Recent Elections

At the National Assembly elections on 16 Feb. 2015 the People's Action Movement won 4 seats, the Labour Party 3, the Concerned Citizens' Movement 2, the Nevis Reformation Party 1 and the People's Labour Party 1. Turnout was 72·2%.

Current Government

Governor-General: Samuel Weymouth Tapley Seaton, GCMG, CVO, QC, JP (since 20 May 2015—acting until 2 Sept. 2015).

In Feb. 2019 the government comprised:

Prime Minister, and Minister of Finance, Sustainable Development, National Security, People Empowerment and Constituency Empowerment: Timothy Harris; b. 1964 (People's Labour Party; sworn in 18 Feb. 2015).

Deputy Prime Minister, and Minister of Education, Youth, Sport and Culture: Shawn Richards.

Senior Minister, and Minister of Nevis Affairs, Labour, Social Security and Ecclesiastical Affairs: Vance Amory. *Agriculture, Human Settlement, Co-operatives and Environment:* Eugene Hamilton. *Foreign Affairs and Aviation:* Mark Brantley. *Public Infrastructure, Posts, Urban Development and Transport:* Ian 'Patches' Liburd. *Tourism, International Trade, Industry and Commerce:* Lindsay Grant. *Attorney General and Minister of Justice, Legal Affairs and Communications:* Vincent Byron. *Minister of State Responsible for Community Development, Gender Affairs, Social Services and Health:* Wendy Phipps.

The Premier of *Nevis* is Mark Brantley.

Government Website: http://www.gov.kn

Current Leaders

Timothy Harris

Position
Prime Minister

Introduction
Timothy Harris of the People's Labour Party (PLP) became prime minister in Feb. 2015 at the head of a three-party coalition government, ending the 20-year tenure of Denzil Douglas.

Early Life
Timothy Harris was born on 18 Jan. 1964 in Tabernacle, St Kitts. He graduated in accountancy from the University of the West Indies (UWI) in Barbados in 1988. He then worked for a manufacturing, retail and shipping company before studying for a master's degree in accountancy from UWI, Trinidad from 2000–02.

He was elected as a Labour MP in the 1995 general election, becoming minister of agriculture, lands and housing in Douglas's government. From 2001 he served as minister of education, labour and social services, and from 2004 as minister of foreign affairs and education. In 2007 he became minister of foreign affairs, international trade, industry and commerce. The following year he ceded the role of foreign minister to Douglas, taking on the finance portfolio in its place.

In Feb. 2010 he was appointed senior minister and minister of international trade, industry, commerce, agriculture, marine resources, consumer affairs and constituency empowerment. In Jan. 2013, following a series of policy disagreements with Douglas, Harris was fired from the cabinet. Later that year he founded the PLP and in Sept. 2013 became leader of Team Unity,

Palgrave Macmillan (ed.), *The Statesman's Yearbook 2020*,
https://doi.org/10.1057/978-1-349-95940-2_160

an alliance of the PLP, the People's Action Movement and the Concerned Citizens' Movement. In Feb. 2015 Team Unity fought a successful general election campaign, promising to boost local economies, provide permanent jobs and increase transparency in government.

Career in Office

Harris took office on 18 Feb. 2015. His challenges included maintaining an effective coalition government while delivering on pledges to increase prosperity. In April 2016 he signed the landmark Paris Agreement on Climate Change. In May 2018 he faced calls from demonstrators to step down as premier after his name was mentioned in an alleged bribery scandal and in Dec. he survived a parliamentary no-confidence motion.

Economy

Agriculture accounted for 1·5% of GDP in 2013, industry 25·7% and services 72·8%.

Overview

The economy has been in transition since the government's closure of the sugar industry in 2005, a move encouraged by the European Union and World Trade Organization after years of heavy losses. The most important sources of revenue are service industries, offshore finance and tourism but the country is vulnerable to shocks, notably natural disasters and shifts in the tourism market.

The economy contracted annually between 2009 and 2012 following falls in tourism receipts and foreign investment in construction activity. An increasing fiscal deficit led to the implementation of revenue reforms, including the introduction of VAT and excise tax changes in 2010, as well as expenditure cuts, including a freeze on public wages. GDP growth then averaged 5% per year from 2013–16, on the back of strong recovery in the tourism and construction sectors, plus an inflow of investment via the government's Citizenship-by-Investment (CBI) programme. Debt restructuring lowered public debt levels from 164% of GDP in 2010 to 66% in 2016. Nonetheless, over-reliance on CBI revenues renders long-term prospects uncertain.

Currency

The *East Caribbean dollar* (XCD) (of 100 *cents*) is in use. There was deflation of 0·3% in 2016 and then zero inflation in 2017. In July 2005 foreign exchange reserves were US$75m. Total money supply was EC$200m. in June 2005.

Budget

Budgetary central government revenues in 2014 were EC$551m. and expenditures EC$514m. Taxes accounted for 84·8% of revenues in 2014; compensation of employees accounted for 48·2% of expenditures.

Performance

The economy expanded by 2·7% in 2015, 2·9% in 2016 and 2·1% in 2017. Total GDP was US$0·9bn. in 2017.

Banking and Finance

The Eastern Caribbean Central Bank (*Governor*, Timothy Antoine) is located in St Kitts. It is a regional bank that serves the OECS countries. The Eastern Caribbean Central Bank has five clearing banks in St Kitts and Nevis (Bank of Nevis, Bank of Nova Scotia, CIBC FirstCaribbean International Bank, Royal Bank of Canada and St Kitts-Nevis-Anguilla National Bank).

Foreign debt in 2007 amounted to US$274m.

St Kitts and Nevis is a member of the Eastern Caribbean Securities Exchange, based in Basseterre.

Energy and Natural Resources

Environment

Carbon dioxide emissions from the consumption of energy in 2011 were the equivalent of 5·4 tonnes per capita.

Electricity

Installed capacity was 40,000 kW in 2011. Production in 2011 was an estimated 196m. kWh.

Minerals

In 2007 an estimated 223,000 tonnes of sand and gravel and 131,000 tonnes of crushed stone were produced.

Agriculture

Sugarcane was a mainstay of the agricultural sector until the sugar industry was closed down following the 2005 harvest after years of losses at the state-run sugar company. In 2012 there were an estimated 5,000 ha. of arable land. Most of the farms are small-holdings and there are a number of coconut estates amounting to some 400 ha. under public and private ownership. Production, 2012 estimates (in tonnes): coconuts, 3,012; sweet potatoes, 250; tomatoes, 200; potatoes, 170; watermelons, 170; pineapples, 165. Production of other fresh tropical fruit amounted to an estimated 1,906 tonnes in 2012.

Livestock (2013 estimates): goats, 9,100; sheep, 7,100; pigs, 7,000; cattle, 6,500; chickens, 80,000.

Forestry

The area under forests in 2015 was 11,000 ha., or 42% of the total land area.

Fisheries

The estimated catch in 2012 was 21,802 tonnes.

Industry

There are three industrial estates on St Kitts and one on Nevis. Export products include electronics and data processing equipment, and garments for the US market. Other small enterprises include food and drink processing, and construction.

Labour

The unemployment rate was 6·0% in 2009.

International Trade

Imports and Exports

Imports (c.i.f.), 2008, US$324·8m.; exports (f.o.b.), US$51·2m. The USA is by far the biggest trading partner. In 2008, 60·1% of imports were from the USA and 84·6% of exports went to the USA. Trinidad and Tobago is the second largest import supplier and the United Kingdom the second largest export destination. Main imports include machinery, manufactures, food and precious jewellery. Major exports are machinery, transport equipment, printed matter and beer.

Communications

Roads

There are about 380 km of roads.

Rail

In 2005 there were 50 km of railway, formerly operated by the sugar industry but now used for tourist purposes.

Civil Aviation

The main airport is the Robert Llewellyn Bradshaw International Airport (just over 3 km from Basseterre). In 2010 there were flights to Antigua, Atlanta, British Virgin Islands, Charlotte, London, Miami, Nevis (Newcastle), New York, Puerto Rico, Sint Maarten and the US Virgin Islands.

Shipping

There are two deep water ports located on the Basseterre harbour: the Birdrock Deepwater Port and Port Zante. In Jan. 2014 there were 178 ships of 300 GT or over registered, totalling 931,000 GT. The government maintains a commercial motor boat service between the islands.

Telecommunications

In March 2013 there were an estimated 77,000 mobile phone subscriptions and an estimated 19,200 main (fixed) telephone lines. In 2013 there were 24·5 fixed broadband subscriptions per 100 inhabitants and 5·5 mobile broadband subscriptions per 100 inhabitants.

Social Institutions

Justice

Justice is administered by the Supreme Court and by Magistrates' Courts. They have both civil and criminal jurisdiction. St Kitts and Nevis was one of ten countries to sign an agreement in Feb. 2001 establishing a Caribbean Court of Justice to replace the British Privy Council as the highest civil and criminal court. In the meantime the number of signatories has risen to 12. The court was inaugurated at Port of Spain, Trinidad on 16 April 2005 but has not yet been accepted as St Kitts and Nevis' final court of appeal.

The death penalty is in force and was used in 2008 for the first time since 1998.

The population in penal institutions in Aug. 2013 was 330 (equivalent to 611 per 100,000 of national population, the third highest rate in the world).

Education

Adult literacy was 97·8% in 2006. Education is compulsory between the ages of 5 and 16. In 2007 there were 2,360 pupils in pre-primary schools with 357 teaching staff, 6,172 pupils with 372 teaching staff in primary schools and 4,522 pupils with 447 teaching staff in secondary schools.

The main post-secondary institution is the Clarence Fitzroy Bryant College (formerly the St Kitts and Nevis College of Further Education). There are six divisions: Adult and Continuing Education; Arts, Sciences and General Studies; Health Science; Hospitality Studies; Teacher Education; and Technical and Vocational Education and Management Studies.

In 2005 public expenditure on education came to 10·9% of GNI.

Health

In the period 2000–10 there were 11 physicians per 10,000 inhabitants, 47 nursing and midwifery personnel per 10,000 persons and four dentistry personnel per 10,000. In 2008 there were four hospitals and 17 health centres. There were 48 hospital beds per 10,000 population in 2010.

In *Water: At What Cost? The State of the World's Water 2016*, WaterAid reported that 1·7% of the population does not have access to safe water.

Religion

According to the Pew Research Center's Forum on Religion & Public Life, an estimated 94·6% of the population were Christians in 2010 with 1·6% religiously unaffiliated. Anglicans are the largest denomination.

Culture

World Heritage Sites

There is one site on the UNESCO World Heritage List: Brimstone Hill Fortress National Park (inscribed on the list in 1999), a well-preserved example of 17th and 18th century British military architecture.

Press

In 2008 there was one daily newspaper with a circulation of 2,000. There were also four non-dailies.

Tourism

In 2010 there were 610,084 visitors in total including 514,825 cruise ship passengers and 91,561 staying visitors.

Diplomatic Representatives

Of St Kitts and Nevis in the United Kingdom (10 Kensington Court, London, W8 5DL)
    High Commissioner: Kevin Isaac.

Of the United Kingdom in St Kitts and Nevis
    High Commissioner: Janet Douglas, CMG (resides in Bridgetown, Barbados).

Of St Kitts and Nevis in the USA (1627 K St., NW, Suite 1200, Washington, D.C., 20006)
    Ambassador: Thelma Phillip-Browne.

Of the USA in St Kitts and Nevis
    Ambassador: Linda S. Taglialatela (resides in Bridgetown, Barbados).

Of St Kitts and Nevis to the United Nations
    Ambassador: Sam Condor.

Of St Kitts and Nevis to the European Union
    Ambassador: Len Monica Ishmael.

Further Reading

Statistics Division. *National Accounts.* Annual.—*St Kitts and Nevis Quarterly.*
Dyde, Brian, *St Kitts: Cradle of the Caribbean.* 1999
Hubbard, Vince, *A History of St Kitts.* 2002
National library: Public Library, Burdon St., Basseterre.
National Statistical Office: Statistics Division, Ministry of Sustainable Development, Church St., Basseterre.

St Lucia

Capital: Castries
Population projection, 2020: 181,000
GNI per capita, 2017: (PPP$) 11,695
HDI/world rank, 2017: 0·747/90=
Internet domain extension: .lc

Key Historical Events

The island was probably discovered by Columbus in 1502. An unsuccessful attempt to colonize by the British took place in 1605 and again in 1638 when settlers were soon murdered by the Caribs who inhabited the island. France claimed the right of sovereignty and ceded it to the French West India Company in 1642. St Lucia regularly and constantly changed hands between Britain and France, until it was finally ceded to Britain in 1814 by the Treaty of Paris. Since 1924 the island has had representative government. In March 1967 St Lucia gained full control of its internal affairs while Britain remained responsible for foreign affairs and defence. On 22 Feb. 1979 St Lucia achieved independence, opting to remain in the British Commonwealth.

Territory and Population

St Lucia is an island of the Lesser Antilles in the eastern Caribbean between Martinique and St Vincent, with an area of 617 sq. km (238 sq. miles). Population (2010 census, provisional) 166,526; density, 269·9 per sq. km. In 2011 the population was 28·1% urban.

Areas and populations of the districts at the 2010 census (provisional) were:

Districts	Sq. km	Population
Anse-la-Raye	31	6,247
Canaries	16	2,044
Castries	79	65,656
Choiseul	31	6,098
Dennery	70	12,599
Gros Inlet	101	25,210
Laborie	38	6,701
Micoud	78	16,284
Soufrière	51	8,472
Vieux Fort	44	16,284
Central Forest Reserve	78	—

The UN gives a projected population for 2020 of 181,000.

The official language is English, but 80% of the population speak a French Creole.

In 2010, 85% of the population was African/Black, 11% were of mixed race and 2% of East Indian ethnic origin.

The capital is Castries (population, 2010, 22,000).

Social Statistics

2011: births, 2,009; deaths, 983. Rates, 2011 (per 1,000 population): births, 12·0; deaths, 5·9. Infant mortality, 2010 (per 1,000 live births), 14. Expectation of life in 2013 was 72·2 years for males and 77·5 for females. Annual population growth rate, 2005–10, 1·4%; fertility rate, 2013, 1·9 births per woman.

Climate

The climate is tropical, with a dry season from Jan. to April. Most rain falls in Nov.–Dec.; annual amount varies from 60" (1,500 mm) to 138" (3,450 mm). The average annual temperature is about 80°F (26·7°C).

Constitution and Government

The head of state is the British sovereign, represented by an appointed Governor-General. There is an 18-seat *House of Assembly* (17 members elected for five years plus the Speaker) and an 11-seat *Senate* appointed by the Governor-General.

National Anthem

'Sons and daughters of St Lucia'; words by C. Jesse, tune by L. F. Thomas.

Recent Elections

At the elections of 6 June 2016 the opposition United Workers' Party won 11 seats with 54·8% of votes cast against six for the Saint Lucia Labour Party (44·1%).

Current Government

Governor-General: Sir Neville Cenac; b. 1939 (since 12 Jan. 2018).

In Feb. 2019 the government comprised:

Prime Minister, and Minister of Finance, Economic Growth, Job Creation and External Affairs: Allen Chastanet (United Workers' Party; sworn in 7 June 2016).

Minister of Agriculture, Fisheries, Physical Planning, Natural Resources and Co-operatives: Ezechiel Joseph. *Commerce, Industry, Investment, Enterprise Development and Consumer Affairs:* Bradley Felix. *Economic Development, Housing, Urban Renewal, Transport and Civil Aviation:* Guy Joseph. *Education, Innovation, Gender Relations and Sustainable Development:* Gale Rigobert. *Equity, Social Justice, Local Government and Empowerment:* Lenard Montoute. *Health and Wellness:* Mary Isaac. *Home Affairs, Justice and National Security:* Hermangild Francis. *Infrastructure, Ports, Energy and Labour:* Stephenson King. *Public Service:* Ubaldus Raymond. *Tourism, Information, Broadcasting, Culture and Creative Industries:* Dominic Fedee. *Youth Development and Sports:* Edmund Estephane. *Minister in the Office of the Prime Minister Responsible for External Affairs:* Sarah Flood Beaubrun.

Government Website: http://www.stlucia.gov.lc

Current Leaders

Allen Chastanet

Position
Prime Minister

Introduction
Allen Chastanet became prime minister in June 2016. A businessman, hotelier and politician, he is leader of the United Workers' Party (UWP).

Early Life
Born the son of a prominent businessman, Allen Chastanet graduated in economics and political science from Bishop's University, Quebec, in 1984 before taking a master's degree in development banking at the American University, Washington, D.C., in 1990.

After a number of senior marketing and sales roles from 1990 in the tourism and hotel business, including as director of the Saint Lucia tourist board from 1991–93, he was appointed managing director of Coco Resorts in St Lucia from 2003 until 2006 when he became chairman of the Caribbean Tourism Organization.

Between 2006 and 2011 he served as minister of tourism and civil aviation under the UWP administration. However, he failed in his attempt to be elected to parliament at the Dec. 2011 general election, in which the UWP was defeated by Kenny Anthony's Saint Lucia Labour Party.

In 2013 Chastanet was chosen as leader of the UWP and was elected to parliament at the general election of June 2016. His party claimed 11 of 17 seats and Chastanet duly assumed the premiership.

© Springer Nature Limited 2020
Palgrave Macmillan (ed.), *The Statesman's Yearbook 2020*,
https://doi.org/10.1057/978-1-349-95940-2_161

Career in Office

Chastanet pledged to scrap the Labour Party's value-added tax measures as part of a programme to accelerate economic recovery. He also vowed to improve law and order by employing more judges and increasing the number of courthouses. However, he has been criticized by opponents for reducing the cost of 'Citizenship by Investment'—a programme designed to attract foreign capital and business people in return for right of residence and citizenship—from US$200,000 to US$100,000, as well as revoking the requirement that such applicants declare their net worth. He was re-elected unopposed as leader of the UWP in Nov. 2018.

Economy

In 2015 agriculture contributed 2·4% of GDP, industry 13·0% and services 84·6%.

Overview

St Lucia's economy, the largest in the East Caribbean Currency Union, depends primarily on revenue from tourism and banana production, although small-scale manufacturing is also significant. The other main industry is oil refining, based on a plant with an operational capacity of 10m. bbls per year.

An outbreak of banana leaf disease between 2009 and 2011, together with the damage from Hurricane Tomas that struck in 2010, caused cuts in agricultural production and jobs. Against the backdrop of the global downturn, the economy contracted by 1·6% in 2010. Growth then averaged 1·2% per year from 2011–16 in spite of negative growth in 2015. Public debt increased from 52·1% of GDP to 69·2% between 2008 and 2016.

The introduction of a value added tax in Oct. 2012 led to a jump in inflation, which averaged 2·7% in the period 2011–14.

Currency

The *East Caribbean dollar* (XCD) (of 100 *cents*) is in use. US dollars are also normally accepted. There was deflation of 3·1% in 2016 but then inflation of 0·1% in 2017.

Budget

The fiscal year ends on 31 March. Revenues were EC$936·9m. in the fiscal year 2013–14 and expenditures EC$1,206·3m.

VAT was reduced from 15% to 12·5% from Feb. 2017. The reduced rate is 10%.

Performance

The economy shrank by 0·9% in 2015 before a recovery saw growth rates of 3·4% in 2016 and 3·0% in 2017. Total GDP in 2017 was US$1·7bn.

Banking and Finance

The Eastern Caribbean Central Bank based in St Kitts and Nevis functions as a central bank. The *Governor* is Timothy Antoine. There are three domestic banks (Caribbean Banking Corporation, St Lucia Co-operative Bank, East Caribbean Financial Holding Company) and three foreign banks.

External debt totalled US$464m. in 2010 and represented 54·0% of GNI.

St Lucia is a member of the Eastern Caribbean Securities Exchange, based in Basseterre.

Energy and Natural Resources

Environment

Carbon dioxide emissions from the consumption of energy in 2011 were the equivalent of 2·6 tonnes per capita.

Electricity

Installed capacity in 2011 was 76,000 kW. Production in 2011 was 385m. kWh; consumption per capita in 2011 was 2,149 kWh.

Agriculture

In 2013 St Lucia had approximately 3,000 ha. of arable land and 7,000 ha. of permanent crops. Bananas, cocoa, breadfruit and mango are the principal crops, but changes in the world's trading rules and changes in taste are combining to depress the banana trade. Farmers are experimenting with okra, tomatoes and avocados to help make up for the loss. Production, 2013 estimates (in 1,000 tonnes): coconuts (estimate), 15; bananas, 4.

Livestock (2013 estimates): pigs, 38,000; goats, 13,000; cattle, 11,000; sheep, 9,000; chickens, 450,000.

Forestry

In 2015 the area under forests was 20,000 ha. (33% of the total land area).

Fisheries

In 2015 the total catch was 2,083 tonnes.

Industry

The main areas of activity are clothing, assembly of electronic components, beverages, corrugated cardboard boxes, tourism, lime processing and coconut processing.

Labour

The labour force in 2013 was 96,000 (80,000 in 2003). 74·8% of the population aged 15–64 was economically active in 2013.

International Trade

Imports and Exports

Imports and exports for calendar years in US$1m.:

	2003	2004	2005	2006
Imports c.i.f.	407·7	421·6	485·8	592·4
Exports f.o.b.	62·5	79·8	64·2	93·7

Main imports in 2006: machinery and transport equipment, 25·8%; food and live animals, 15·9%; petroleum and petroleum products, 12·1%; chemicals and related products, 6·9%. Main exports, 2006: petroleum and petroleum products, 21·7%; bananas, 19·0%; machinery and transport equipment, 18·2%; beer, 14·0%. Main import suppliers, 2006: USA, 39·2%; Trinidad and Tobago, 16·9%; UK, 6·9%; Japan, 6·3%. Main export markets, 2006: Trinidad and Tobago, 30·1%; UK, 20·7%; USA, 20·6%; Barbados, 6·6%.

Communications

Roads

The island has about 1,200 km of roads, mainly unpaved.

Civil Aviation

There are two international airports: Hewanorra International (near Vieux-Fort) and George F. L. Charles (near Castries). In 2009 Hewanorra handled 513,959 passengers (483,632 in 2008) and George F. L. Charles—which handles inter-Caribbean flights—309,132 passengers (358,313 in 2008).

Shipping

There are two ports, Castries and Vieux Fort.

Telecommunications

Fixed telephone lines numbered 36,800 in 2012 (203·7 per 1,000 persons) and there were 216,500 mobile phone subscriptions in 2011 (or 1,207·8 per 1,000 inhabitants). Fixed internet subscriptions totalled 21,700 in 2011. As of 2013 there were 59,600 wireless broadband subscriptions (326·8 per 1,000 inhabitants).

Social Institutions

Justice

The island is divided into two judicial districts, and there are nine magistrates' courts. Appeals lie to the Eastern Caribbean Supreme Court of Appeal. St Lucia was one of ten countries to sign an agreement in Feb. 2001 establishing a Caribbean Court of Justice to replace the British Privy Council as the highest civil and criminal court. In the meantime the number of signatories has risen to 12. The court was inaugurated at Port of Spain, Trinidad on 16 April 2005. It has not yet replaced the Privy Council as St Lucia's final court of appeal.

The population in penal institutions in Dec. 2010 was 551 (315 per 100,000 of national population). The International Centre for Prison Studies estimated in 2014 that 59·0% of prisoners had yet to receive a trial.

Education

Primary education is free and compulsory. In 2008–09 there were 1,000 teachers for 20,000 pupils at primary school level; and 16,000 pupils and an estimated 1,000 teachers at secondary level. There is a community college.

In 2006 public expenditure on education came to 6·9% of GNI and 19·1% of total government spending.

Health

In the period 2006–12 there were 16 hospital beds per 10,000 population. There were 4·7 physicians per 10,000 inhabitants over the period 2000–10 and 21·6 nursing and midwifery personnel per 10,000.

In *Water: At What Cost? The State of the World's Water 2016*, WaterAid reported that 3·7% of the population does not have access to safe water.

Religion

According to estimates by the Pew Research Center's Forum on Religion & Public Life, 91·1% of the population in 2010 was Christian and 6·0% had no religious affiliation. In Feb. 2019 there was one cardinal.

Culture

World Heritage Sites

There is one UNESCO World Heritage site in St Lucia: Pitons Management Area (inscribed on the list in 2004). The site near the town of Soufrière includes the Pitons, two volcanic spires rising side by side from the sea, linked by the Piton Mitan ridge.

Press

There are no daily newspapers. In 2008 there were six paid-for non-daily newspapers: the thrice-weekly *The Voice* and *The Star*; and the weekly *The Mirror*, *The Crusader*, *The Vanguard* and *One Caribbean*.

Tourism

In 2010 there were 305,937 tourist arrivals by air, up from 278,491 in 2009. St Lucia received 670,043 cruise ship visitors in 2010 (when there were 380 cruise ship calls), down from 699,306 in 2009. There were 7,613 other same-day visitors in 2010.

Diplomatic Representatives

Of St Lucia in the United Kingdom (1 Collingham Gdns, London, SW5 0HW)
High Commissioner: Guy Mayers.

Of the United Kingdom in St Lucia
High Commissioner: Janet Douglas, CMG (resides in Bridgetown, Barbados).

Of St Lucia in the USA (1629 K St., NW, Suite 1250, Washington, D.C., 20006)
Ambassador: Anton Edsel Edmunds.

Of the USA in St Lucia
Ambassador: Linda S. Taglialatela (resides in Bridgetown, Barbados).

Of St Lucia to the United Nations
Ambassador: Cosmos Richardson.

Of St Lucia to the European Union
Ambassador: Len Monica Ishmael.

Further Reading

National Statistical Office: Central Statistical Office, Chreiki Building, Micoud Street, Castries.
Website: http://www.stats.gov.lc

St Vincent and the Grenadines

Capital: Kingstown
Population projection, 2020: 111,000
GNI per capita, 2017: (PPP$) 10,499
HDI/world rank, 2015: 0·723/99
Internet domain extension: .vc

Key Historical Events

St Vincent was discovered by Columbus on 22 Jan. (St Vincent's Day) 1498. British and French settlers occupied parts of the islands after 1627. In 1773 the Caribs recognized British sovereignty and agreed to a division of territory between themselves and the British. Resentful of British rule, the Caribs rebelled in 1795, aided by the French, but the revolt was subdued within a year. On 27 Oct. 1969 St Vincent became an Associated State with the UK responsible for foreign policy and defence. On 27 Oct. 1979 the colony gained full independence as St Vincent and the Grenadines.

Territory and Population

St Vincent is an island of the Lesser Antilles, situated in the eastern Caribbean between St Lucia and Grenada, from which latter it is separated by a chain of small islands known as the Grenadines. The total area of 389 sq. km (150 sq. miles) comprises the island of St Vincent itself (345 sq. km) and those of the Grenadines attached to it, of which the largest are Bequia, Mustique, Canouan, Mayreau and Union Island.

The population at the 2012 census was 109,991 (provisional), of whom 99,757 lived on St Vincent; density, 283 per sq. km. In 2011, 49·8% of the population lived in urban areas.

The UN gives a projected population for 2020 of 111,000.

The capital, Kingstown, had 26,721 inhabitants in June 2012 (provisional, including suburbs). The population is mainly of African descent (71·2% in 2012) and mixed heritage (23·0%), with smaller numbers of indigenous people, East Indians/Indians and Whites/Caucasians.

English is the official language, although French patois is widely spoken.

Social Statistics

Births, 2008 estimate, 1,900; deaths, 800. 2008 estimated rates (per 1,000 population): births, 17·6; deaths, 7·5. Infant mortality, 2010, 19 per 1,000 live births. Life expectancy, 2013, was 70·4 years for males and 74·7 years for females. Annual population growth rate, 2000–08, 0·1%; fertility rate, 2008, 2·1 births per woman.

Climate

The climate is tropical marine, with northeast trades predominating and rainfall ranging from 150" (3,750 mm) a year in the mountains to 60" (1,500 mm) on the southeast coast. The rainy season is from June to Dec., and temperatures are equable throughout the year.

Constitution and Government

The head of state is Queen Elizabeth II, represented by a Governor-General. Parliament is unicameral with a 23-member *House of Assembly* consisting of 15 members directly elected for a five-year term from single-member constituencies, six senators appointed by the Governor-General (four on the advice of the Prime Minister and two on the advice of the Leader of the Opposition) and two *ex officio* members.

National Anthem

'St Vincent, land so beautiful'; words by Phyllis Punnett, tune by J. B. Miguel.

Recent Elections

At the elections to the House of Assembly on 9 Dec. 2015 the ruling Unity Labour Party (ULP, social democratic) won 8 of the 15 elected seats with 52·3% of the vote, against 7 (47·4%) for the opposition New Democratic Party (NDP, conservative).

Current Government

Governor-General: Sir Frederick Ballantyne (since 2 Sept. 2002).

In Feb. 2019 the government comprised:

Prime Minister, and Minister of National Security, Air and Sea Port Development, Grenadines Affairs, Immigration and Legal Affairs: Dr Ralph E. Gonsalves; b. 1946 (ULP; sworn in 29 March 2001 and re-elected in Dec. 2005, Dec. 2010 and Dec. 2015).

Deputy Prime Minister, and Minister of Foreign Affairs, Trade and Commerce: Sir Louis Straker.

Minister of Agriculture, Forestry, Fisheries, Rural Transformation, Industry and Labour: Saboto Caesar. *Education, National Reconciliation, Ecclesiastical Affairs and Information:* St Clair 'Jimmy' Prince. *Finance, Economic Planning, Sustainable Development and Information Technology:* Camillo Gonsalves. *Health, Wellness and the Environment:* Robert L. Browne. *Housing, Informal Human Settlements, Lands and Surveys, and Physical Planning:* Montgomery Daniel. *National Mobilization, Social Development, Family, Gender Affairs, Persons with Disabilities and Youth:* Frederick Stephenson. *Tourism, Sports and Culture:* Cecil Mckie. *Transport, Works, Urban Development, Local Government and Postal Services:* Julian Francis.

Government Website: http://www.gov.vc

Current Leaders

Dr Ralph E. Gonsalves

Position
Prime Minister

Introduction
Dr Ralph E. Gonsalves became prime minister in 2001 after his Unity Labour Party (ULP) won an election brought forward from 2003 following anti-government protests in 2000. He won further terms in 2005, 2010 and 2015.

Early Life
'Comrade Ralph' was born in 1946. He studied at the University of the West Indies in Jamaica, gaining a PhD in political science. He later graduated in law from the University of the West Indies in Barbados, before returning home. In 1982 he founded the left-wing Movement for National Unity, which in 1994 amalgamated with the St Vincent Labour Party to form the ULP. Gonsalves succeeded the ULP's first leader, Vincent Beache, in 1998 and led the party to electoral victory in 2001, ending 15 years of New Democratic Party rule.

Career in Office
Gonsalves has sought to tackle the problems of money laundering, gun violence and drug-related crime. In June 2003 St Vincent and the Grenadines was removed from a list of uncooperative countries in the fight against money laundering throughout the Caribbean islands.

The country's economy is reliant on the banana trade and the government continues to pay large subsidies to farmers. However, a decline in banana prices and demand has led to some diversification. In June 2004 Gonsalves announced the launch of National Investments Promotions Incorporated to attract investment and boost exports, and the tourism sector has seen significant growth.

Gonsalves has maintained close ties with Taiwan and Cuba. In May 2005 Taiwan made a gift of computer equipment to his government to enhance efficiency. It also helped to build facilities for the 2007 Cricket World Cup.

Palgrave Macmillan (ed.), *The Statesman's Yearbook 2020*,
https://doi.org/10.1057/978-1-349-95940-2_162

In Jan. 2005 Gonsalves met with Fidel Castro to announce that new diplomatic missions would be established in their respective countries. Castro promised Cuban assistance to Gonsalves's campaign to increase national literacy rates. In 2008 diplomatic relations were established with Iran.

Feb. 2005 saw the launch of the World Bank-assisted HIV/AIDS prevention and control project, with the St Vincent government expected to invest at least US$1·7m. over five years. In April 2005 Gonsalves signed agreements with St Lucia and Dominica to introduce measures to combat climate change in the coastal areas of the three Windward Islands (with substantial funding from the USA and Japan). In May 2005 his government ratified the Kyoto protocol.

In parliamentary elections in Dec. 2005 the ULP retained the 12 seats (of 15) won in 2001. Gonsalves was sworn in for a second term and took over the national security portfolio. In May 2007 his government introduced VAT to increase public revenue (with a reduced rate for hotel accommodation to help protect the tourist industry). Plans for a new constitution and the establishment of a republic, for which Gonsalves campaigned for acceptance, were rejected by 55% of voters in a referendum in Nov. 2009. The ULP only narrowly retained its parliamentary majority in elections in Dec. 2010 and Dec. 2015, taking eight seats on both occasions, but the party's victories gave Gonsalves a third and fourth consecutive term as premier. In a cabinet reshuffle in Nov. 2017, Gonsalves's son Camillo took over the finance portfolio from his father while retaining his earlier responsibility for economic planning and sustainable development.

Economy

Agriculture accounted for 7·8% of GDP in 2014, industry 17·4% and services 74·8%.

Overview

St Vincent and the Grenadines is a lower-middle income country with a relatively underdeveloped economy. It is heavily dependent on agriculture, especially banana production. This enjoyed preferential access to EU markets until 2007 and still accounts for around a third of export earnings.

Economic growth has traditionally fluctuated with agricultural output and world market prices. Annual growth averaged 5·8% from 2004–08, supported by construction and public sector activity. However, the global slowdown led to reduced levels of tourism and foreign direct investment, with growth contracting in 2009 by 2·1% and 2010 by 3·4%. Nonetheless, the economy returned to growth in the period 2011–16, averaging 1·1% per year. Growth in 2017 remained relatively flat at 0·7%, although the projected boost in tourism arrivals in the second half of the year following the inauguration of the country's first international airport in Feb. offset a decline in the first half of the year.

The government has encouraged diversification into tourism, financial services and call centres. With its improved transport infrastructure and new hotel openings, it is hoped tourism in particular will contribute to healthy medium-term prosperity.

Currency

The currency in use is the *East Caribbean dollar* (XCD). There was deflation of 0·2% in 2016 but then inflation of 2·2% in 2017. Foreign exchange reserves were US$66m. in July 2005. Total money supply was EC$319m. in June 2005.

Budget

In 2013 revenues totalled EC$502·5m. and expenditures EC$624·9m.

VAT is 16% (reduced rate, 10%).

Performance

The economy grew by 0·8% in both 2015 and 2016, and 0·7% in 2017. In 2017 total GDP was US$0·8bn.

Banking and Finance

The Eastern Caribbean Central Bank is the bank of issue. The *Governor* is Timothy Antoine. There are branches of Barclays Bank PLC, the Caribbean Banking Corporation, FirstCaribbean International, the Canadian Imperial Bank of Commerce and the Bank of Nova Scotia. Locally-owned banks: First St Vincent Bank, Owens Bank, New Bank, the National Commercial Bank and St Vincent Co-operative Bank. There is a substantive offshore sector, which has moved to adopt international regulatory standards and is carefully vetted and properly regulated.

Foreign debt was US$287m. in 2013.

St Vincent and the Grenadines is a member of the Eastern Caribbean Securities Exchange, based in Basseterre.

Energy and Natural Resources

Environment

Carbon dioxide emissions from the consumption of energy in 2011 were the equivalent of 1·9 tonnes per capita.

Electricity

Installed capacity was an estimated 41,000 kW in 2011. Production in 2011 was about 142m. kWh; consumption per capita in 2011 was an estimated 1,298 kWh.

Agriculture

In 2007 the agricultural population was an estimated 23,000, of which 11,000 were economically active. There were an estimated 7,000 ha. of arable land and 5,000 ha. of permanent crops in 2007. The sugar industry was closed down in 1985 although some sugarcane is grown for rum production. Production (2013, in 1,000 tonnes): bananas (estimate), 58; sugarcane (estimate), 18; sweet potatoes, 3; yams, 3; plantains, 2; coconuts, 2; mangoes and guavas, 2.

Livestock (2013, in 1,000): goats, 9; sheep, 7; pigs, 6; cattle, 4.

Forestry

Forests covered 27,000 ha. in 2015, or 69% of the land area.

Fisheries

Total catch, 2014, 81,413 tonnes (all from sea fishing).

Industry

Industries include assembly of electronic equipment, manufacture of garments, electrical products, animal feeds and flour, corrugated galvanized sheets, exhaust systems, industrial gases, concrete blocks, plastics, soft drinks, beer and rum, wood products and furniture, and processing of milk, fruit juices and food items.

Labour

The labour force in 2013 was 55,000 (50,000 in 2003). 72·2% of the population aged 15–64 was economically active in 2013.

International Trade

Imports and Exports

Imports (c.i.f.) in 2010 totalled US$379·5m. and exports (f.o.b.) US$41·5m. Principal imports are basic manufactures, machinery and transport equipment, and food products. Principal exports are bananas, packaged flour and packaged rice. Main import suppliers, 2005: USA, 33·3%; Trinidad and Tobago, 23·6%; UK, 9·4%. Main export markets, 2005: UK, 26·8%; Barbados, 12·8%; Trinidad and Tobago, 12·3%.

Communications

Roads

There are more than 800 km of roads, around half of which are paved. Vehicles in use (2008): 9,250 passenger cars, 12,900 vans and lorries, and 1,220 motorcycles and mopeds.

Civil Aviation

Argyle International Airport on mainland St Vincent—the country's first international airport—was inaugurated in Feb. 2017. There are regional airports on Bequia, Canouan, Mustique and Union Island in the Grenadines.

Shipping

In Jan. 2014 there were 359 ships of 300 GT or over registered, totalling 2·09m. GT. Among the 359 vessels registered were 250 general cargo ships, 44 bulk carriers and 29 passenger ships.

Telecommunications

In 2013 there were 125,400 mobile phone subscriptions (1,146·3 for every 1,000 inhabitants) and 19,100 fixed telephone lines. In the same year an estimated 52·0% of the population were internet users.

Social Institutions

Justice

Law is based on UK common law as exercised by the Eastern Caribbean Supreme Court on St Lucia. Final appeal lies to the UK Privy Council. St Vincent and the Grenadines was one of 12 countries to sign an agreement establishing a Caribbean Court of Justice to replace the British Privy Council as the highest civil and criminal court. The court was inaugurated at Port of Spain, Trinidad on 16 April 2005 but has yet to be accepted as the final court of appeal for St Vincent and the Grenadines. Strength of police force (2009), 750.

The population in penal institutions in 2012 was 410 (376 per 100,000 of national population).

Education

In 2007 there were 3,894 children in pre-primary schools with 340 teaching staff, 15,928 pupils in primary schools with 933 teaching staff and (2005) 9,780 pupils in secondary schools. There is a community college.

In 2005 public expenditure on education came to 8·6% of GNI and 16·1% of total government spending.

Health

In 2007 there were 35 hospital beds per 10,000 persons. In 2009 there were 59 physicians, nine dentists, 299 nurses and 27 pharmacists.

In *Water: At What Cost? The State of the World's Water 2016*, WaterAid reported that 4·9% of the population does not have access to safe water.

Religion

In 2010 an estimated 88·7% of the population were Christians according to the Pew Research Center's Forum on Religion & Public Life and 3·4% Hindus, with a further 2·5% religiously unaffiliated.

Culture

Press

In 2008 there was one daily newspaper, *The Herald*. There were also nine weekly papers.

Tourism

There were 72,478 tourist arrivals by air in 2010, down from 97,432 in 2006. Cruise passenger arrivals numbered 110,954 in 2010 and there were also 42,603 yacht passengers.

Diplomatic Representatives

Of St Vincent and the Grenadines in the United Kingdom (10 Kensington Court, London, W8 5DL)
High Commissioner: Cenio Elwin Lewis.

Of the United Kingdom in St Vincent and the Grenadines (Francis Compton Building, 2nd Floor, Waterfront, Castries)
High Commissioner: Janet Douglas, CMG (resides in Bridgetown, Barbados).

Of St Vincent and the Grenadines in the USA (1627 K St., NW, Suite 1202, Washington, D.C., 20006)
Ambassador: Lou-Anne Gaylene Gilchrist.

Of the USA in St Vincent and the Grenadines
Ambassador: Linda S. Taglialatela (resides in Bridgetown, Barbados).

Of St Vincent and the Grenadines to the United Nations
Ambassador: Inga Rhonda King.

Of St Vincent and the Grenadines to the European Union
Ambassador: Len Monica Ishmael.

Further Reading

Sutty, L., *St Vincent and the Grenadines.* 1993
National Statistical Office: Statistical Office, Central Planning Division, Ministry of Finance & Economic Planning, Kingstown.
Website: http://www.stats.gov.vc

Samoa

O le Malo Tutoatasi o Samoa (Independent State of Samoa)

Capital: Apia
Population projection, 2020: 200,000
GNI per capita, 2017: (PPP$) 5,909
HDI/world rank, 2017: 0·713/104
Internet domain extension: .ws

Key Historical Events

Polynesians settled in the Samoan group of islands in the southern Pacific from about 1000 BC. Although probably sighted by the Dutch in 1722, the first European visitor was French in 1768. Treaties were signed between the Chiefs and European nations in 1838–39. Continuing strife among the chiefs was compounded by British, German and US rivalry for influence. In the Treaty of Berlin 1889 the three powers agreed to Western Samoa's independence and neutrality. When unrest continued, the treaty was annulled and Western Samoa became a German protectorate until in 1914 it was occupied by a New Zealand expeditionary force. The island was administered by New Zealand from 1920 to 1961. On 1 Jan. 1962 Western Samoa gained independence. In July 1997 the country renamed itself the Independent State of Samoa.

Territory and Population

Samoa lies between 13° and 15° S. lat. and 171° and 173° W. long. It comprises the two large islands of Savai'i and Upolu, the small islands of Manono and Apolima, and several uninhabited islets lying off the coast. The total land area is 2,935 sq. km (1,130 sq. miles), of which 1,825 sq. km (705 sq. miles) are in Savai'i and 1,100 sq. km (425 sq. miles) in Upolu (including Manono and Apolima). The islands are of volcanic origin, and the coasts are surrounded by coral reefs. Rugged mountain ranges form the core of both main islands. The large area laid waste by lava-flows in Savai'i is a primary cause of that island supporting less than one-third of the population of the islands despite its greater size than Upolu.

The population was 195,979 at the 2016 census; density, 67 per sq. km. The population at the 2016 census was 152,419 in Upolu (including Manono and Apolima) and 43,560 in Savai'i. The capital and chief port is Apia in Upolu (population 37,391 in 2016). In 2015, 19·1% of the population lived in urban areas.

The UN gives a projected population for 2020 of 200,000.

The official languages are Samoan and English.

Social Statistics

2006: births, 4,935; deaths, 728. Rates, 2006 (per 1,000 population): births, 27·3; deaths, 4·0. Expectation of life in 2007 was 68·4 years for males and 74·7 for females. Annual population growth rate, 2005–10, was 0·7%. Infant mortality, 2010, 17 per 1,000 live births; fertility rate, 2006, 4·2 births per woman.

Climate

A tropical marine climate, with cooler conditions from May to Nov. and a rainy season from Dec. to April. The rainfall is unevenly distributed, with south and east coasts having the greater quantities. Average annual rainfall is about 100" (2,500 mm) in the drier areas. Apia, Jan. 80°F (26·7°C), July 78°F (25·6°C). Annual rainfall 112" (2,800 mm).

Constitution and Government

HH Malietoa Tanumafili II, who was Head of State for life, died on 11 May 2007. The Head of State is henceforth elected by the Legislative Assembly and holds office for five-year terms.

The executive power is vested in the *Head of State*, who swears in the *Prime Minister* (who is elected by the Legislative Assembly) and, on the Prime Minister's advice, the Ministers to form the Cabinet. The Constitution also provides for a *Council of Deputies* of three members, of whom the chairman is the Deputy Head of State.

The *Legislative Assembly* contains 50 members serving five-year terms. 49 are directly elected (with 47 seats reserved for ethnic Samoans and two open to members of other communities) and a requirement that 10% of MPs are women meant that in March 2016 one extra woman was awarded a seat.

National Anthem

'Samoa, tula'i ma sisi ia laufu'a ('Samoa, Arise and Raise your Banner'); words and tune by S. I. Kuresa.

Recent Elections

In elections on 4 March 2016 the Human Rights Protection Party (HRPP) won 44 seats against two for the Tautua Samoa Party. Independents won three seats.

Tuimaleali'ifano Va'aletoa Sualauvi II was elected head of state unanimously by the Legislative Assembly on 5 July 2017.

Current Government

Head of State: Tuimaleali'ifano Va'aletoa Sualauvi II; b. 1947 (in office since 21 July 2017).

In Feb. 2019 the cabinet was composed as follows:

Prime Minister, and Minister of Foreign Affairs and Trade: Tuila'epa Sailele Malielegaoi; b. 1945 (Human Rights Protection Party; sworn in 23 Nov. 1998, and re-elected in March 2001, March 2006, March 2011 and March 2016).

Deputy Prime Minister, and Minister of Natural Resources and Environment: Fiame Naomi Mata'afa.

Minister of Agriculture and Fisheries: Lopao'o Natanielu Mua. *Commerce, Industry and Labour, and Public Enterprises:* Lautafi Fio Selafi Purcell. *Communications and Information Technology:* Afamasaga Lepuiai Rico Tupai. *Education, Sports and Culture:* Loau Sola Keneti Sio. *Finance:* Sili Epa Tuioti. *Health:* Dr Tuitama Leao Talalelei Tuitama. *Justice and Courts Administration:* Faaolesa Katopau T. Ainuu. *Police:* Sala Fata Pinati. *Revenue, and Prison and Correction Services:* Tialavea Feo Leniu Tionisio Hunt. *Women, Community and Social Development:* Faimalotoa Kika Lemaima Stowers. *Works, Transport and Infrastructure:* Papaliitele Niko Lee Hang.

Government Website: http://www.samoagovt.ws

Current Leaders

Tuila'epa Sailele Malielegaoi
Position
Prime Minister

Introduction
Tuila'epa Sailele Malielegaoi became prime minister in Nov. 1998 and won further terms in March 2001, March 2006, March 2011 and March 2016. He is leader of the Human Rights Protection Party (HRPP), the traditional ruling party of Samoa since 1982.

© Springer Nature Limited 2020
Palgrave Macmillan (ed.), *The Statesman's Yearbook 2020*,
https://doi.org/10.1057/978-1-349-95940-2_163

Early Life

Tuila'epa Sailele Malielegaoi was born on 14 April 1945 in Lepa, Samoa. He was educated in Samoa and at New Zealand's Auckland University, graduating with a master's degree (the first Samoan to do so) in commerce in 1969.

In 1978 he moved to Brussels to work for the European Economic Community. He entered Samoa's parliament two years later while working as a partner in the accounting firm Coopers and Lybrand. He was elected to the premiership after former prime minister Tofilau Eti Alesana retired in 1998.

Career in Office

Malielegaoi has aimed to diversify an economy dependent on fishing and agriculture and susceptible to natural disasters, focusing particularly on the tourism industry. In Aug. 2004 his government introduced internet access to assist economic development.

Malielegaoi has also been keen to promote education in Samoa. There is a scholarship scheme offering study opportunities in New Zealand, Australia and Fiji, and in Jan. 2003 a new inter-denominational Christian secondary school was opened. The police and health sectors have also received increased funding. In Jan. 2004 parliament voted to abolish the death penalty and in the same year Australia provided \$A7m. to fund training of Samoan security forces.

In foreign relations, Malielegaoi has pursued close relations with China. China agreed to help build an aquatic centre in Samoa for the 2007 South Pacific Games and has been aiding the construction of new buildings for the Samoan parliament and Justice Department. Japan has also invested in Samoa, providing funding for education and vocational training and for land redevelopment. In 2004 Samoa hosted the 35th Pacific Forum, which concentrated on regional economic and political co-operation and the Pacific-wide campaign to tackle HIV and AIDS.

Malielegaoi was re-elected for a third term when his Human Rights Protection Party won the March 2006 election. In May 2007 King Malietoa Tanumafili II died after 45 years on the throne, having been appointed king for life at independence in 1962. Under the constitution, his successor, Tuiatua Tupua Tamasese Efi, was elected for a five-year term by the Legislative Assembly in June 2007 (and re-elected unopposed in July 2012).

Opposition to controversial road traffic legislation by Malielegaoi (changing the driving side from right to left), which took effect in Sept. 2009, had earlier led to defections from the HRPP and to the formation in 2008 of two new political parties—the Tautua Samoa Party and the People's Party. In elections in March 2011 the HRRP won a landslide victory, heralding a fourth term for the premier.

At the end of 2011 Samoa crossed westward over the international date line for trading reasons (to align with Australia and New Zealand) and effectively erased a day from its calendar. In May 2012 Samoa acceded to the World Trade Organization as its 155th member, and in June that year the country celebrated 50 years of independence from New Zealand.

In March 2016 Malielegaoi was sworn in to a fifth term following the victory of the HRRP at elections.

In Dec. 2018 Samoa was included on a list of countries identified by the EU as tax havens that have failed to match up to international financial standards.

Economy

Trade, hotels and restaurants accounted for 34·0% of GDP in 2014, followed by services 10·3%, construction 10·2% and manufacturing 10·1%.

Overview

The economy is historically heavily dependent on agriculture (principally coconuts and its by-products, plus coffee) and fishing, which annually account for 90% of exports and employ more than two-thirds of the labour force. As a result, Samoa is vulnerable to climate shocks.

Efforts to diversify the economy have started to take effect. Following an economic contraction of 1·9% in 2013, average annual growth between 2014 and 2017 was recorded at 3·1%. Tourism is an increasingly important sector (contributing around 25% of GDP annually) and greater visitor numbers helped reverse economic downturns that followed an earthquake in 2009 and Cyclone Evan in 2012. Samoa attracted a record 139,000 visitors in 2015 when it hosted the Commonwealth Youth Games, and there was a further rise to 145,000 in 2016. Meanwhile, deregulation has spurred growth in the financial sector, while light manufacturing has also attracted foreign direct investment.

Currency

The unit of currency is the *tala* (WST) of 100 *sene*. There was inflation of 0·1% in 2016 and 1·3% in 2017. Foreign exchange reserves were US\$94m. in July 2005. Total money supply was 133m. tala in June 2005.

Budget

The fiscal year begins on 1 July. For 2015–16 budgetary central government revenue was SAT\$595·6m. (taxes, 83·5%); expenditure, SAT\$503·9m. (grants, 32·5%; compensation of employees, 32·4%).

There is a Value Added Goods and Services Tax (VAGST) of 15%.

Performance

The economy grew by 1·6% in 2015, 7·1% in 2016 and 2·5% in 2017. Total GDP in 2017 was US\$0·9bn.

Banking and Finance

The Central Bank of Samoa (founded 1984) is the bank of issue. The *Governor* is Atalina Enari. There is one development bank. Commercial banks include: ANZ, Industrial Bank, International Business Bank Corporation, National Bank of Samoa, Samoa Commercial Bank and Westpac Bank Samoa.

External debt totalled US\$308m. in 2010 and represented 56·6% of GNI.

Energy and Natural Resources

Environment

Samoa's carbon dioxide emissions from the consumption of energy in 2011 were the equivalent of 0·8 tonnes per capita.

Electricity

Installed capacity in 2011 was estimated at 42,000 kW. Production was 114m. kWh. in 2011 and consumption per capita 608 kWh.

Agriculture

In 2013 there were an estimated 8,000 ha. of arable land and 22,000 ha. of permanent cropland. The main products (2012 estimates, in 1,000 tonnes) are coconuts (178), bananas (20), taro (20), copra (5), mangoes and guavas (4), and pineapples (4).

Livestock (2013 estimates): pigs, 201,000; cattle, 30,000; asses, 7,000; chickens, 620,000.

Forestry

Forests covered 0·17m. ha. (60% of the land area) in 2015. Timber production was 76,000 cu. metres in 2011.

Fisheries

Fish landings in 2015 came to an estimated 8,700 tonnes.

Industry

Some industrial activity is being developed associated with agricultural products and forestry.

Labour

In 2012 there were 34,530 employed persons (21,787 males and 12,743 females). The unemployment rate in 2012 was 8·7%.

International Trade

Imports and Exports

In 2015 imports (c.i.f.) were valued at US\$370·6m. and exports (f.o.b.) at US\$58·9m. Main imports are machinery and transport equipment, foodstuffs and basic manufactures. Principal exports are coconuts, palm oil, taro and taamu, coffee and beer. New Zealand is the principal import source, accounting for 26·9% of imports in 2015. Australia is the largest export market, accounting for 48·0% of exports in 2015. Singapore was the second biggest supplier of imports in 2015 and New Zealand the second biggest export market.

Communications

Roads

The road network covers around 1,150 km. In 2005 there were 5,920 passenger cars plus 4,600 lorries and vans in use.

Civil Aviation

There is an international airport at Apia (Faleolo), which handled 321,973 passengers and 1,175 tonnes of freight in 2009. The national carrier is Virgin Samoa, known until 2011 as Polynesian Blue. In 2007 it operated domestic services and international flights to Auckland, Brisbane and Sydney.

Telecommunications

There are three radio communication stations at Apia. Radio telephone service connects Samoa with American Samoa, Fiji, New Zealand, Australia, Canada, USA and UK. In 2008 there were 28,800 main (fixed) telephone lines; mobile phone subscribers numbered 124,000 in 2008 (69·3 per 100 persons). There were 9,000 internet users in 2008.

Social Institutions

Out of 178 countries analysed in the 2017 *Fragile States Index*—a list published jointly by the Fund for Peace and *Foreign Policy* magazine—Samoa was ranked the 68th least vulnerable to conflict or collapse. The index is based on 12 indicators of state vulnerability across social, political and economic categories.

Justice

The population in penal institutions in 2012 was approximately 430 (228 per 100,000 of national population). The death penalty, not used in more than 50 years, was abolished in 2004.

Education

There were 30,000 pupils at primary schools in 2008–09 with 1,000 teaching staff and 25,000 pupils at secondary schools with 1,000 teaching staff. The University of the South Pacific has a School of Agriculture in Samoa, at Apia. A National University was established in 1984. In 2006 it had 2,298 students and 151 academic staff. There is also a Polytechnic Institute that provides mainly vocational and training courses.

The adult literacy in 2009 was estimated at 98·8%.

In 2008 public expenditure on education came to 5·7% of GDP and 13·4% of total government spending.

Health

In the period 2005–12 there were five physicians per 10,000 inhabitants, 19 nursing and midwifery personnel per 10,000 persons and one dentist per 10,000. Over the same period there were ten hospital beds per 10,000 inhabitants.

In *Water: At What Cost? The State of the World's Water 2016*, WaterAid reported that 1·0% of the population does not have access to safe water.

Religion

According to the Pew Research Center's Forum on Religion & Public Life, an estimated 96·8% of the population were Christians in 2010 with 2·5% having no religious affiliation.

Culture

Press

There are two dailies, plus a weekly, a fortnightly and a monthly. The most widely read newspaper is the independent *Samoa Observer*.

Tourism

In 2014 there were 131,795 visitor arrivals (124,673 in 2013).

Diplomatic Representatives

Of Samoa in the United Kingdom and to the European Union
   High Commissioner: Fatumanava Dr Pa'olelei Luteru (resides in Brussels).
   Honorary Consul: Prunella Scarlett, LVO (Church Cottage, Pedlinge, Nr Hythe, Kent, CT12 5JL).

Of the United Kingdom in Samoa
   High Commissioner: Laura Clarke (resides in Wellington).

Of Samoa in the USA and to the United Nations (800 Second Ave., Suite 400D, New York, NY 10017)
   Ambassador: Ali'ioaiga Feturi Elisaia.

Of the USA in Samoa
   Ambassador: Scott Brown (resides in Wellington).

Of Samoa to the European Union
   Ambassador: Fatumanava Dr Pa'olelei Luteru.

Further Reading

National Statistical Office: Samoa Bureau of Statistics (SBS), Ministry of Finance, Level 1, Government Building (MFMII), P. O. Box 1151, Apia.
Website: http://www.sbs.gov.ws

San Marino

Repubblica di San Marino (Republic of San Marino)

Capital: San Marino
Population projection, 2020: 34,000
GNI per capita, 2015: (PPP$) 50,063
Internet domain extension: .sm

Key Historical Events

San Marino is a small republic situated on the Adriatic side of central Italy. According to tradition, St Marinus and a group of Christians settled there to escape persecution. By the 12th century San Marino had developed into a commune ruled by its own statutes and consul. Unsuccessful attempts were made to annex the republic to the papal states in the 18th century and when Napoleon invaded Italy in 1797 he respected the rights of the republic and even offered to extend its territories. In 1815 the Congress of Vienna recognized the independence of the republic. On 22 March 1862 San Marino concluded a treaty of friendship and co-operation, including a *de facto* customs union, with Italy, thus preserving its independence although it is completely surrounded by Italian territory.

Territory and Population

San Marino is a land-locked state in central Italy, 20 km from the Adriatic. Area is 61·19 sq. km (23·6 sq. miles) and the population (Dec. 2017), 33,328; population density, 544·7 per sq. km. At July 2010, 12,722 citizens lived abroad.

The UN gives a projected population for 2020 of 34,000.

In 2010, 94·1% of the population were urban. The capital, San Marino, has 4,043 inhabitants (Dec. 2017); the largest town is Serravalle (10,877 in Dec. 2017), an industrial centre in the north. The official language is Italian.

Social Statistics

Births registered in 2009, 306; deaths, 233; marriages, 238; divorces, 63. Birth rate, 2009 (per 1,000 population), 9·3; death rate, 6·9. Annual population growth rate, 2003–13, 0·9%; fertility rate, 2013, 1·5 births per woman; infant mortality rate, 2010, two per 1,000 live births (one of the lowest rates in the world).

Climate

Temperate climate with cold, dry winters and warm summers.

Constitution and Government

The legislative power is vested in the *Great and General Council* of 60 members elected every five years by popular vote, two of whom are appointed every six months to act as *Captains Regent*, who are the heads of state.

Executive power is exercised by the ten-member *Congress of State*, presided over by the Captains Regent. The *Council of Twelve*, also presided over by the Captains Regent, is appointed by the Great and General Council to perform administrative functions.

National Anthem

No words, tune monastic, transcribed by F. Consolo.

Recent Elections

In parliamentary elections on 20 Nov. 2016 the San Marino First coalition won 25 of 60 seats with 41·7% of the vote (with Sammarinese Christian Democratic Party taking 16 seats, Socialist Party taking 5 seats and Party of Socialists and Democrats taking 4 seats); the Adesso.sm coalition won 20 seats with 31·4% (with Democratic Socialist Left taking 8, Repubblica Futura taking 6 and Civic 10 taking 6); the Democracy in Motion won 15 seats with 23·2% (with RETE Movement taking 12 and Democratic Movement San Marino Together taking 3). Turnout was 59·7%. As a majority was not reached in the Great and General Council, a run-off was held on 4 Dec. 2016 between the top two coalitions. The second round saw Adesso. sm take 57·9% of the vote, resulting in them having 35 of the 60 seats, while San Marino First took 42·0%, which resulted in them having 16 seats. The remaining nine seats were allocated to the Democracy in Motion. Turnout in the run-off was 50·1%.

Current Government

Captains Regent: Luca Santolini (since 1 Oct. 2018); Mirco Tomassoni (since 1 Oct. 2018).

In Feb. 2019 the Congress of State comprised:

Minister of Foreign Affairs, Political Affairs and Justice: Nicola Renzi. *Internal Affairs and Public Service:* Guerrino Zanotti. *Finance, Budget, Post, Transport and Economic Planning:* Simone Celli. *Industry, Crafts and Trade, Work, Co-operation and Telecommunications:* Andrea Zafferani. *Land and Environment, Agriculture, Tourism, Civil Protection and Youth Policy:* Augusto Michelotti. *Health and Social Security, Equal Opportunities, and Social Affairs:* Franco Santi. *Education, Culture and Universities, Research, Information, Sport and Technological Innovation:* Marco Podeschi.

Parliament Website (Italian only): http://www.consigliograndeegenerale.sm

Current Leaders

Luca Santolini
Position
Captain Regent

Introduction
Luca Santolini, a communications specialist, was sworn in for his first term as a Captain Regent on 1 Oct. 2018.

Early Life
Luca Santolini was born in Borgo Maggiore, San Marino, on 22 Feb. 1985. He graduated in international relations from the University of Bologna, Italy, and later studied journalism and publishing at the University of Urbino. His work in communications included advising Civic 10, a political party advocating democratic socialism, environmentalism and e-democracy. Santolini was first elected to the Great and General Council in 2012, representing Civic 10, which formed part of the opposition Active Citizenship alliance.

Career in Office
Santolini is one of 35 representatives of the ruling left-leaning Adesso.sm coalition, which emerged victorious in the general election of Nov. 2016. He is head of the San Marino delegation to the Organization for Security and Co-operation in Europe and a member of the justice commission.

Mirco Tomassoni
Position
Captain Regent

Introduction
Mirco Tomassoni, a police officer, was sworn in for his second term as a Captain Regent on 1 Oct. 2018.

Early Life
Mirco Tomassoni was born in Borgo Maggiore, San Marino, on 24 April 1969. Educated in San Marino, he joined the country's Civil Police Force in 1992. Following a car crash in 1999 he was left disabled. Having served on his local council—Castello di Montegiardino—during the 1990s and early 2000s, Tomassoni was first elected to the Great and General Council in 2006.

© Springer Nature Limited 2020
Palgrave Macmillan (ed.), *The Statesman's Yearbook 2020*,
https://doi.org/10.1057/978-1-349-95940-2_164

He represented the centre-left Party of Socialist and Democrats, which governed in coalition with the Popular Alliance and United Left.

Career in Office

Tomassoni was elected Captain Regent for the first time in Oct. 2007, alongside Alberto Selva. He campaigned to improve access for disabled people, initially while in office and subsequently through the Attiva-Mente association. He remains an employee of the Civil Police Force and serves on the commissions for health, sport, social security and the environment.

Defence

Military service is not obligatory, but all citizens between the ages of 16 and 55 can be called upon to defend the State. They may also serve as volunteers in the Military Corps. There is a military Gendarmerie.

Economy

Overview

The economy is integrated with that of Italy via a monetary and customs union, close trade links and labour mobility. It relies principally on manufacturing, financial services and tourism. The country attracts around 2m. visitors a year.

The global financial crisis, coupled with pressure to improve banking transparency, resulted in an economic contraction of over 43% between 2008 and 2016. An Italian amnesty on tax evasion in 2009–10 prompted an outflow of bank deposits. Whilst manufacturing and commercial activity improved moderately from early 2011, unemployment increased from 5% to 8% between 2009 and 2016, peaking at nearly 9% in 2014.

The financial sector has undergone deep restructuring and attempts to normalize international links since 2010 have proved fruitful. The government has signed Tax Information Exchange Agreements with many leading countries to promote international co-operation, and a monetary agreement with the European Union was activated in 2012. Prospects for recovery were boosted when San Marino was removed from Italy's tax blacklist in Feb. 2014 but near-zero inflation rates since 2015 pose a medium-term challenge to reviving economic fortunes.

Currency

Since 1 Jan. 2002 San Marino has been using the *euro* (EUR). Italy has agreed that San Marino may mint a small part of the total Italian euro coin contingent with their own motifs. Inflation was 0·6% in 2016 and 1·0% in 2017. Total money supply in June 2005 was €906m.

Budget

Revenues totalled €553·3m. in 2012 and expenditures €557·7m. Social contributions accounted for 29·6% of revenue in 2012 with taxes on goods and services accounting for 21·4%; social benefits accounted for 35·3% of expenditure in 2012 with wages and salaries accounting for 31·6%.

Performance

Following six years of negative growth from 2009–14 the economy grew by 0·6% in 2015, 2·2% in 2016 and 1·9% in 2017. Total GDP was US$1·7bn. in 2017.

Banking and Finance

The Banca Centrale della Repubblica di San Marino (*President*, Renato Clarizia) was established in 2005 as an amalgamation of the Istituto di Credito Sammarinese and the Ispettorato per il Credito e le Valute (the Inspectorate for Credit and Currencies). Many of its functions have since been taken over by the European Central Bank and it has taken on a more supervisory role. Commercial banks include: Banca di San Marino, Credito Industriale Sammarinese, Cassa di Risparmio della Repubblica di San Marino and the Banca Agricola Commerciale della Repubblica di San Marino.

Energy and Natural Resources

Electricity

Electricity is supplied by Italy.

Agriculture

There were 1,000 ha. of arable land in 2011. Wheat, barley, maize and vines are grown.

Industry

Labour

Out of 20,530 people in employment in 2006, 6,247 worked in manufacturing and 2,901 in wholesale and retail trade. In 2006 there were 473 registered unemployed persons.

International Trade

Imports and Exports

Import commodities are a wide range of consumer manufactures and foodstuffs. Export commodities are building stone, lime, wine, baked goods, textiles, varnishes and ceramics. San Marino maintains a customs union with the European Union.

Communications

Roads

A bus service connects San Marino with Rimini. There are 252 km of public roads and 40 km of private roads, and (2006) 32,263 passenger cars and 5,907 commercial vehicles.

Civil Aviation

The nearest airport is Rimini, 10 km to the east in Italy, which had scheduled flights in 2010 to Cologne-Bonn, Frankfurt, Hamburg, Karlsruhe, Liverpool, London Stansted, Luxembourg, Münster, Munich, Nuremberg, Stuttgart, Tirana and Vienna.

Telecommunications

San Marino had 18,800 fixed telephone subscriptions in 2013 and 36,800 mobile phone subscriptions. In the same year an estimated 50·8% of the population were internet users.

Social Institutions

Justice

Judges are appointed permanently by the Great and General Council; they may not be San Marino citizens. Petty civil cases are dealt with by a justice of the peace; legal commissioners deal with more serious civil cases, and all criminal cases and appeals lie to them from the justice of the peace. Appeals against the legal commissioners lie to two appeals judges as a court of third instance.

Education

Education is compulsory up to 16 years of age. In 2005 there were 15 nursery schools with 1,054 pupils and 141 teachers, 14 elementary schools with 1,497 pupils and 245 teachers, three junior high schools with 805 pupils and 144 teachers, and one high school with 1,289 pupils and 77 teachers. The University of San Marino began operating in 1988.

Health

In 2014 there were 201 physicians. In the same year there were 35·8 hospital beds per 10,000 population.

Religion

A 2010 study by the Pew Research Center's Forum on Religion & Public Life estimated that 91·6% of the population were Roman Catholics, with 7·2% religiously unaffiliated.

Culture

World Heritage Sites

There is one UNESCO World Heritage site in San Marino: San Marino Historic Centre and Mount Titano (inscribed on the list in 2008).

Press

San Marino had four paid-for daily newspapers in 2008 (including one sports paper). There are also three dailies published in Italy that include pages on San Marino.

Tourism

In 2011, 2,038,400 tourists visited San Marino (1,385,700 Italians and 652,700 other foreigners).

Diplomatic Representatives

Of San Marino in the United Kingdom
  Ambassador: Silvia Marchetti (resides in San Marino).
  Honorary Consul: Eduardo Teodorani-Fabri (Flat 51, 162 Sloane St., London, SW1X 9BS).

Of the United Kingdom in San Marino
  Ambassador: Jill Morris, CMG (resides in Rome).

Of San Marino in the USA and to the United Nations (1711 N St., NW, 2nd Floor, Washington, D.C., 20036).
  Ambassador: Damiano Beleffi.

Of the USA in San Marino
  Ambassador: Lewis M. Eisenberg (resides in Rome).

Of San Marino to the European Union
  Ambassador: Antonella Benedettini.

Further Reading

National Statistical Office: Ufficio Programmazione Economica e Centro Elaborazione Dati e Statistica, Via 28 Luglio, 192–47893 Borgo Maggiore.
Website: http://www.statistica.sm

São Tomé and Príncipe

República Democrática de São Tomé e Príncipe
(Democratic Republic of São Tomé and Príncipe)

Capital: São Tomé
Population projection, 2020: 218,000
GNI per capita, 2017: (PPP$) 2,941
HDI/world rank, 2017: 0·589/143
Internet domain extension: .st

Key Historical Events

The islands of São Tomé and Príncipe off the west coast of Africa were colonized by Portugal in the fifteenth century. There may have been a few African inhabitants earlier but most of the population arrived during the centuries when the islands served as a slave-trading depot for South America. In the 19th century the islands became the first parts of Africa to grow cocoa. In 1876 Portugal officially abolished slavery but in practice it continued with many Angolans, Mozambicans and Cabo Verdians brought in to work on the cocoa plantations. Because the slave-descended population was cut off from African culture, São Tomé had a higher proportion than other Portuguese colonies of *assimilados* (Africans acquiring full Portuguese culture and some rights). São Tomé saw serious riots against Portuguese rule in 1953. From 1960 a Movement for the Liberation of São Tomé e Príncipe operated from neighbouring African territories. In 1970 Portugal formed a 16-member legislative council and a provincial consultative council. Following the Portuguese revolution of 1974 a transitional government was formed. Independence came on 12 July 1975. Independent São Tomé and Príncipe officially proclaimed Marxist-Leninist policies but maintained a non-aligned foreign policy and has received aid from Portugal.

The government was overthrown by a coup on 16 July 2003 while President Fradique de Menezes and his foreign minister were abroad. The coup leader, Major Fernando Pereira, installed a junta but accepted a general amnesty from parliament on 24 July after agreeing to allow the ousted president to form a government of national unity.

Territory and Population

The republic, which lies about 200 km off the west coast of Gabon, in the Gulf of Guinea, comprises the main islands of São Tomé (845 sq. km) and Príncipe and several smaller islets including Pedras Tinhosas and Rolas. It has a total area of 1,001 sq. km (387 sq. miles). Population (census, 2012) 179,200; density, 179 per sq. km. In 2011, 63·0% of the population were urban.

The UN gives a projected population for 2020 of 218,000.

Areas and populations of the two provinces:

Province	Sq. km	Census 2012	Chief town
São Tomé	859	171,856	São Tomé
Príncipe	142	7,344	Santo António

The capital, São Tomé, had an estimated population of 64,000 in 2011. The official language is Portuguese. Lungwa São Tomé, a Portuguese Creole, and Fang, a Bantu language, are the spoken languages.

Social Statistics

2006: births, 5,072; deaths, 1,111. Rates, 2006 (per 1,000 population): birth, 33·4; death, 7·3; infant mortality (2010), 53 per 1,000 live births. Expectation of life, 2006, 63·5 years for males and 68·5 years for females. Annual population growth rate, 2010–15, 2·3%; fertility rate, 2008, 3·8 births per woman.

Climate

The tropical climate is modified by altitude and the effect of the cool Benguela current. The wet season is generally from Oct. to May, but rainfall varies considerably, from 40" (1,000 mm) in the hot and humid northeast to 150–200" (3,800–5,000 mm) on the plateau. São Tomé, Jan. 79°F (26·1°C), July 75°F (23·9°C). Annual rainfall 38" (951 mm).

Constitution and Government

The 1990 constitution was approved by 72% of votes at a referendum of March 1990 and became effective in Sept. 1990. It abolished the monopoly of the Movement for the Liberation of São Tomé and Príncipe (MLSTP). The *President* must be over 34 years old, and is elected by universal suffrage for one or two (maximum) five-year terms. He or she is also head of government and appoints a Council of Ministers. The 55-member *National Assembly* is elected for four years.

Since April 1995 **Príncipe** has enjoyed internal self-government, with a five-member regional government and an elected assembly.

National Anthem

'Independência total, glorioso canto do povo' ('Total independence, glorious song of the people'); words by A. N. do Espírito Santo, tune by M. de Sousa e Almeida.

Recent Elections

At the first round of presidential elections on 17 July 2016 former prime minister Evaristo Carvalho (Independent Democratic Action/ADI) won 49·9% of votes cast against incumbent president Manuel Pinto da Costa (ind.) with 24·8%, Maria das Neves (Movement for the Liberation of São Tomé and Príncipe-Social Democratic Party/MLSTP-PSD) with 24·3%, Manuel do Rosário (ind.) with 0·7% and Hélder Barros (ind.) with 0·3%. Turnout was 64·3%. A second round run-off had been scheduled for 7 Aug. However, Pinto da Costa withdrew after claiming that the first round had been fraudulent. Carvalho was therefore elected unopposed.

At the National Assembly elections on 7 Oct. 2018 the ADI won 25 of 55 seats with 41·8% of the vote, the MLSTP-PSD 23 with 40·3%, Democratic Convergence Party-Union for Democracy and Development-Democratic Movement Force of Change (PCD-MDFM-UDD) 5 with 9·5% and Movement of Independent Citizens of São Tomé and Príncipe (MCISTP) 2 with 2·1%. Turnout was 80·7%.

Current Government

President: Evaristo Carvalho; b. 1941 (ADI; sworn in 3 Sept. 2016).

In Feb. 2019 the government comprised:

Prime Minister: Jorge Bom Jesus (MLSTP-PSD; sworn in 3 Dec. 2018).

Minister of the Presidency, the Council of Ministers and Parliamentary Affairs: Wuando Borge Castro. *Agriculture, Fisheries and Rural Development:* Francisco Martins dos Ramos. *Defence and Internal Order:* Óscar Sousa. *Education and Higher Education:* Julieta Izidro Rodrigues. *Foreign Affairs, Co-operation and Communities:* Elsa Pinto. *Health:* Edgar Neves. *Justice, Public Administration and Human Rights:* Ivete da Graça Correia. *Labour, Solidarity, Family and Vocational Training:* Adlander Costa Mato. *Planning, Finance and the Blue Economy:* Osvaldo Vaz. *Public Works, Infrastructure, Natural Resources and Environment:* Osvaldo D'Abreu. *Tourism, Culture, Trade and Industry:* Maria da Graça Lavres. *Youth, Sport and Entrepreneurship:* Vinicius Xavier de Pina.

Parliament Website: http://www.parlamento.st

© Springer Nature Limited 2020
Palgrave Macmillan (ed.), *The Statesman's Yearbook 2020*,
https://doi.org/10.1057/978-1-349-95940-2_165

Current Leaders

Evaristo Carvalho

Position
President

Introduction
Evaristo Carvalho became president on 3 Sept. 2016 after the incumbent, Manuel Pinto da Costa, boycotted a run-off poll amid accusations of electoral fraud. Carvalho had previously served as prime minister twice before and ran unsuccessfully against Pinto da Costa for the presidency in 2011.

Early Life
Carvalho was born on 22 Oct. 1941, when São Tomé and Príncipe was still a Portuguese colony. After the nation won independence, Pinto da Costa served as its first president, holding office from 1975 until 1991. Carvalho was drafted into the Cabinet and went on to hold a number of prominent positions, including minister of defence and internal order and minister of construction, transport and communications.

Pinto da Costa's authoritarian tenure—which left the country's economy in a debilitated state—ended in 1991 when he opted not to contest elections after introducing a multi-party democratic system. Carvalho, however, continued to rise through the political ranks, serving as prime minister for six months in 1994 and again from Sept. 2002 until March 2003. He was also appointed vice-president of the Independent Democratic Action (ADI) party.

Carvalho stood in the 2011 election but was defeated by Pinto da Costa, who had previously run repeatedly, but unsuccessfully, for the presidency since surrendering office in 1991. The two contested the presidency again in 2016, with Carvalho winning on a platform of economic rejuvenation.

Career in Office
Although the presidency is a largely ceremonial role, Carvalho soon made his presence felt on the international stage by realigning São Tomé and Príncipe away from Taiwan and towards the People's Republic of China after Taiwan vetoed a US$100m. aid package to the country.

In the Oct. 2018 National Assembly elections, the ruling ADI party lost its parliamentary majority and the following month Carvalho named Jorge Bom Jesus of the opposition MLSTP-PSD as prime minister of a new coalition government.

Economy

In 2013 trade and hotels contributed 26·8% to GDP; followed by finance, real estate, public administration, defence and services, 21·7%; agriculture, forestry and fishing, 21·1%; and transport and communications, 14·4%.

Overview

São Tomé and Príncipe is among the world's poorest countries, with high levels of public debt and 66% of the population living in poverty. Heavily reliant on foreign aid and cocoa exports (and, more recently, coffee and palm oil), it receives debt relief under the IMF Heavily Indebted Poor Countries Initiative and signed a three-year US$6·2m. Extended Credit Facility (ECF) in 2015.

Annual growth averaged 5% between 2001 and 2007, but slowed in 2009 after the global financial crisis prompted sharp declines in foreign direct investment, remittances, tourist arrivals and donor assistance. Increases in international food and fuel prices also hit the economy hard. However, growth subsequently recovered, averaging 4% per year between 2012 and 2015.

Following the first review of the ECF in July 2016, the government received a US$0·9m. disbursement, helping to promote more inclusive growth. However, the country's oil industry prospects remain uncertain following oil giant Total's withdrawal from further exploration.

Currency

The unit of currency is the *dobra* (STN) of 100 *centimos*. It was redenominated on 1 Jan. 2018 at a rate of 1,000 old *dobras* to 1 new *dobra*. Inflation was 5·4% in 2016 and 5·7% in 2017. In Dec. 2017 foreign exchange reserves were US$59m. Broad money totalled 2·59bn. dobras in Jan. 2018.

Budget

Revenues in 2014 were 1,808·5bn. dobras (tax revenue, 48·6%) and expenditures 1,797·7bn. dobras (current expenditure, 58·9%).

Performance

Real GDP growth was 3·8% in 2015, 4·2% in 2016 and 3·9% in 2017. In 2017 total GDP was US$0·4bn.

Banking and Finance

In 1991 the Banco Central de São Tomé e Príncipe (*Governor*, Hélio Silva Almeida) replaced the Banco Nacional as the central bank and bank of issue. A private commercial bank, the Banco Internacional de São Tomé e Príncipe, began operations in 1993. Foreign debt amounted to US$170m. in 2010, representing 85·3% of GNI.

Energy and Natural Resources

Environment

In 2011 carbon dioxide emissions from the consumption of energy were the equivalent of 0·8 tonnes per capita.

Electricity

Installed capacity, 2011, 18,000 kW. Production was estimated at 60m. kWh in 2011, with consumption per capita an estimated 328 kWh.

Oil and Gas

There are large oil reserves around São Tomé and Príncipe that could greatly add to the country's wealth; the Joint Development Zone was set up with Nigeria to administer the exploitation because the reserves are located in shared waters. The first licence to begin exploration was granted in 2004. However, oil production has yet to commence.

Agriculture

After independence all landholdings over 200 ha. were nationalized into 15 state farms. These were partially privatized in 1985 by granting management contracts to foreign companies, and distributing some state land as small private plots. There were an estimated 9,000 ha. of arable land in 2013 and 39,000 ha. of permanent crops. Production (2013 in 1,000 tonnes): coconuts (estimate), 54; bananas, 41; palm fruit oil (estimate), 16; taro, 8; palm oil (estimate), 4; cocoa beans, 3; yams (estimate), 2. Livestock, 2013: 33,000 pigs; 5,700 goats (estimate); 3,200 sheep (estimate); 1,100 cattle; 265,000 chickens (estimate).

Forestry

In 2015 forests covered 54,000 ha., or 56% of the land area. In 2011, 122,000 cu. metres of timber were cut.

Fisheries

There are rich tuna shoals. The total catch in 2015 amounted to 11,448 tonnes.

Industry

Manufacturing contributed 4% of GDP in 2013. There are a few small factories in agricultural processing (including beer and palm oil production), timber processing, bricks, ceramics, printing, textiles and soap-making.

Labour

The unemployment rate was 13·9% in 2012.

International Trade

Imports and Exports

Trade figures for 2006: imports, US$70·9m.; exports, US$3·8m. Cocoa accounts for two-thirds of all exports.

In 2006 the main import suppliers were Portugal (63·6%), Angola (18·3%) and Belgium (4·6%); main export markets were Portugal (33·3%), the Netherlands (27·1%) and Belgium (14·3%).

Communications

Roads

There were 500 km of roads in 2009, 375 km of which were paved. Approximately 4,500 passenger cars, 2,183 motorcycles and over 1,800 trucks and vans were in use in 2008.

Civil Aviation

São Tomé airport had flights in 2010 to Libreville, Lisbon, Luanda, Port-Gentil and Praia. In 2007 São Tomé handled 50,625 passengers. There is a light aircraft service to Príncipe.

Shipping

São Tomé is the main port, but it lacks a deep water harbour. Neves handles oil imports and is the main fishing port. In Jan. 2014 there were nine ships of 300 GT or over registered, totalling 7,000 GT.

Telecommunications

In 2013 there were 7,000 fixed telephone subscriptions; mobile phone subscriptions numbered 125,300 that year (64·9 per 100 persons). In 2013 an estimated 23·0% of the population were internet users.

Social Institutions

Out of 178 countries analysed in the 2017 *Fragile States Index*—a list published jointly by the Fund for Peace and *Foreign Policy* magazine—São Tomé and Príncipe was ranked the 82nd least vulnerable to conflict or collapse. The index is based on 12 indicators of state vulnerability across social, political and economic categories.

Justice

Members of the Supreme Court are appointed by the National Assembly. There is no death penalty. The population in penal institutions in 2012 was 217 (128 per 100,000 of national population).

Education

Adult literacy was 88% in 2008. Education is free and compulsory. In 2007–08 there were 90 primary schools and 32,616 pupils, and ten secondary schools and 8,380 pupils; 96% of primary age children were attending school in 2006. There are two institutions of higher education.

Health

Over the period 2006–12 São Tomé and Príncipe had 29 hospital beds per 10,000 population.

In *Water: At What Cost? The State of the World's Water 2016*, WaterAid reported that 2·9% of the population does not have access to safe water.

Religion

In 2010 an estimated 82·2% of the population were Christians according to the Pew Research Center's Forum on Religion & Public Life, with 12·6% religiously unaffiliated. Of the Christians in 2010, an estimated 86% were Catholics and 14% Protestants.

Culture

Press

In 2008 there was one daily newspaper. Two government-owned and six independent papers were published irregularly.

Tourism

In 2011 there were 12,000 non-resident tourists.

Diplomatic Representatives

Of São Tomé and Príncipe in the United Kingdom
 Ambassador: Vacant (resides in Brussels).
 Chargé d'Affaires a.i.: Armindo de Brito.

Of the United Kingdom in São Tomé and Príncipe
 Ambassador: Jessica Hand (resides in Luanda, Angola).

Of São Tomé and Príncipe in the USA and to the United Nations
 Ambassador: Vacant.
 Chargé d'Affaires a.i.: Alcínio Cravid e Silva.

Of the USA in São Tomé and Príncipe
 Ambassador: Joel Danies (resides in Libreville, Gabon).

Of São Tomé and Príncipe to the European Union
 Ambassador: Maria d'Assunção de Barros Amaral Aguiar.

Further Reading

National Statistical Office: Instituto Nacional de Estatística, Largo das Alfândegas, Cx. Postal 256, São Tomé
Website (Portuguese only): http://www.ine.st

Saudi Arabia

Al-Mamlaka al-Arabiya as-Saudiya (Kingdom of Saudi Arabia)

Capital: Riyadh
Population projection, 2020: 34·71m.
GNI per capita, 2017: (PPP$) 49,680
HDI/world rank, 2017: 0·853/39=
Internet domain extension: .sa

Key Historical Events

Nomadic tribes have existed across the Arabian peninsula for thousands of years. The pre-Islamic period saw the development of civilizations based on trade in frankincense and spices, notably, from about the 12th century BC, the Minaeans in the southwest of what is now Saudi Arabia and Yemen. The Sabaean and Himyarite kingdoms flourished from around 650 BC and 115 BC respectively, their loose federations of city states lasting until the 6th century AD. Although increased trade brought these civilizations into contact with the Roman and Persian empires—the two great regional powers before the advent of Islam—they remained, for the most part, politically independent. The Nabataeans, an Aramaic people whose capital was at Petra, modern-day Jordan, spread into northern Arabia over a period covering the 1st century BC and the 1st AD before annexation of their territory by Rome. Persian influence was prevalent along Arabia's eastern coast, centred on Dilmun which covered parts of the mainland and the island of Bahrain.

By the 6th century AD the Hejaz region in northwestern Arabia was becoming increasingly powerful and an important link in the overland trade route from Egypt and the Byzantine Empire to the wider East. One of the principal cities of Hejaz was Makkah (Mecca), a staging post on the camel train routes and site of pilgrimage to numerous pre-Islamic religious shrines. The leading tribe in the city was the Quraysh, into which the Prophet Muhammad was born in 570. Muhammad and his followers (known as Muslims) took control of Makkah in 630. He had earlier declared himself a prophetic reformer, destroying the city's pagan idols and declaring it a centre of Muslim pilgrimage dedicated to the worship of Allah (God) alone. Muhammad died in AD 632, by then commanding the loyalty of almost all of Arabia.

The leaders who succeeded Muhammad, known as caliphs, spread the Islamic faith throughout and beyond the Arab world. However, Arabia itself began to fragment and by the latter part of the 7th century it had become a province of the Islamic realm, although the holy cities of Makkah and Madinah retained their spiritual focus. Meanwhile, increasingly remote from the main centres of Islamic authority under the Umayyad and Abbasid caliphate dynasties, Arabia became an arena for sectarian divisions—Shia, Sunni and Kharijite—which developed within the Islamic faith.

After 1269 most of the Hejaz region came under the suzerainty of the Egyptian Mameluks. The Ottoman Turks conquered Egypt in 1517 and, to counter the influence of the Christian Portuguese presence in the Gulf region, extended their nominal control over the whole Arabian Peninsula. Portuguese traders were followed by British, Dutch and French merchants during the 17th and 18th centuries, the British gradually securing political and commercial supremacy in the Gulf and southern Arabia through a system of protectorates and local treaties.

Saudi Arabia's origins as a political entity lay in the rise of the puritanical Wahhabi movement of the 18th century, which called for a return to the original principles of Islam and gained the allegiance of the powerful Al-Saud dynasty (founded in the 15th century) in the Nejd region of central Arabia. By 1811 the Al-Saud/Wahhabi armies controlled most of the peninsula and were seen as a threat to the Ottoman Turkish overlord. The Sultan called on his viceroy in Egypt, Mehmet Ali, to suppress the Wahhabis, who were defeated between 1811 and 1818. Nevertheless, the house of Al-Saud continued to hold sway over the interior of Arabia until 1891 when, after a long period of tribal warfare, the rival Al-Rashid family, with Ottoman support, seized control of the city of Riyadh.

The Al-Saud family was exiled to Kuwait but Abdulaziz bin Abdul Rahman (known to Europeans as Ibn Saud) restored Wahhabi fortunes, recapturing Riyadh in 1902 and reasserting Al-Saud control over Nejd by 1906. On the eve of the First World War Abdulaziz gained the al Hasa region east of Nejd on the Gulf from the Ottoman Turks. In 1920 he captured the Asir region and in 1921 added the Jebel Shammar territory (northwest of Nejd) of the Al-Rashid family. In 1925 Abdulaziz completed his conquest of Hejaz, overthrowing Hussein, Sharif of Makkah and a member of the Hashimi family. Abdulaziz became both Sultan of Nejd and King of the Hejaz. Britain recognized Abdulaziz as an independent ruler by the Treaty of Jeddah on 20 May 1927, and in 1932 Nejd and Hejaz were unified as the Kingdom of Saudi Arabia, ruled as an absolute monarchy under Islamic law.

Abdulaziz (died 9 Nov. 1953) concentrated on the political consolidation and modernization of the country. Oil was discovered in 1938 and its exploitation was developed with the support of the USA after the Second World War. Crown Prince Saud succeeded his father and ruled until Nov. 1964, when he was effectively deposed by his brother Faisal. During his reign Saudi relations with the pan-Arabist Nasser regime in Egypt deteriorated, most notably over the 1962 revolution in Yemen.

As king and prime minister, Faisal used oil production revenues to build up the country's economic base. In 1970 came the first of the five-year economic development programmes. Meanwhile, financial support was given to other Arab states in their conflict with Israel. Leading on from the Oct. 1973 Arab-Israeli war Arab producers, including Saudi Arabia, cut supplies to the USA and other Western countries, causing a fourfold increase in oil prices. However, Faisal subsequently adopted a more conciliatory stance than the more radical members of the Organization of Petroleum Exporting Countries (OPEC, founded in 1960) and the close Saudi economic relationship with the USA was reinforced with a co-operation agreement in 1974. In March 1975, when Faisal was assassinated by a nephew, believed to be mentally unstable, his half-brother Khalid became king.

Khalid continued Faisal's policies promoting Islamic solidarity and Arab unity in the wake of hostilities with Israel. In practice his moderate stance was in marked contrast to the militancy of many other Arab states, particularly over oil pricing by OPEC and opposition to Egypt's 1978 peace treaty with Israel. Khalid was also involved in early efforts to stop the civil war in Lebanon and, in 1981, he inaugurated the Gulf Co-operation Council (GCC). Domestically, he maintained his family's absolute political control and the conservative Islamic character of the country. However, opposition to his regime was demonstrated in Nov. 1979 when Sunni Muslim fundamentalists occupied the Grand Mosque at Makkah. A two-week siege ended with over 200 deaths. The second and third five-year development plans (1975–79 and 1980–84), both launched by Khalid, created much of the country's current economic infrastructure. Owing to Khalid's poor health throughout his reign much of his executive responsibility was assumed by his younger half-brother, Crown Prince Fahd.

Fahd succeeded to the throne on 13 June 1982. Like his predecessors, he maintained absolute power but broadened the process of political consultation and decision-making by setting up the Consultative Council (*Majlis Al-Shura*) of royal appointees from 1993. In 1986 he assumed the title of 'Custodian of the Two Holy Mosques' but the Saudi role in protecting religious pilgrims incurred international criticism in 1987 when 400 Iranian worshippers were killed in clashes in Makkah with security forces and again in 1994 when 270 pilgrims died in a stampede. Internationally, Fahd adopted a moderate policy on regional problems and closely allied the kingdom with the USA. Fahd was a key participant in diplomatic efforts to end the Iran-Iraq war in 1988 and, in 1989, he participated in the Taif reconciliation accord ending the 14-year Lebanese civil war. His pro-Western stance and co-operation in the 1990–91 Gulf crisis were crucial to the deployment and successful military operations of the US-led multinational force raised against Iraq following its invasion of Kuwait.

However, anti-Western disaffection among Saudi nationals has become more overt in recent years. In 1996 a bomb exploded at a US military complex at Dhahran, killing 19 and wounding over 300. In 2000 a series of bomb blasts, blamed by Saudi officials on British nationals engaged in

© Springer Nature Limited 2020
Palgrave Macmillan (ed.), *The Statesman's Yearbook 2020*,
https://doi.org/10.1057/978-1-349-95940-2_166

criminal activity, was widely believed abroad to be the work of Saudi dissidents. Up to 15 Saudi nationals were involved in the attacks on New York and Washington, D.C. on 11 Sept. 2001, co-ordinated by Saudi dissident Osama bin Laden and his al-Qaeda network. In Nov. 2002 the Saudi government refused permission for the US to use its military facilities to attack Iraq, even if sanctioned by the United Nations. In May 2003 suicide bombers killed ten US citizens and many others at housing compounds for Western expatriate workers in Riyadh. In April 2003 the US agreed to pull out most of its troops from the kingdom, while stressing that the two countries would remain allies.

As King Fahd's health declined, his half-brother, Crown Prince Abdullah bin Abdulaziz Al-Saud, assumed responsibility for government in 1996. When Fahd died on 1 Aug. 2005, Abdullah was appointed his successor. In Feb. 2013, 30 women were sworn on to the Shura consultative council—the first time females have held public office in Saudi Arabia. Saudi Arabia joined four fellow Arab states and the USA in launching air strikes on Islamic State strongholds in Syria from Sept. 2014. In Jan. 2015 King Abdullah died and was succeeded by another half-brother, Salman bin Abdulaziz Al-Saud.

Territory and Population

Saudi Arabia, which occupies nearly 80% of the Arabian peninsula, is bounded in the west by the Red Sea, east by the Persian Gulf, Qatar and the United Arab Emirates, north by Jordan, Iraq and Kuwait and south by Yemen and Oman. For the border dispute with Yemen *see* YEMEN: Territory and Population. The total area is 2,149,690 sq. km (829,995 sq. miles). Riyadh is the political, and Makkah (Mecca) the religious, capital.

Population at the census of April 2016, 27,236,156; density, 12·7 per sq. km. Approximately 31% of the population are foreigners. In 2011, 82·3% of the population lived in urban areas.

The UN gives a projected population for 2020 of 34·71m.

Principal cities (with 2010 provisional census populations in 1m.): Riyadh, 5·19; Jeddah, 3·43; Makkah, 1·53; Madinah, 1·10; Dammam, 0·90; Hofuf, 0·66.

The Neutral Zone (5,700 sq. km, 3,560 sq. miles), jointly owned and administered by Kuwait and Saudi Arabia from 1922 to 1966, was partitioned between the two countries in 1966, but the exploitation of the oil and other natural resources continues to be shared.

The official language is Arabic.

Social Statistics

2008 estimates: births, 590,000; deaths, 92,000. Birth rate (2008 estimate) was 23·4 per 1,000 population; death rate, 3·6. 75% of the population is under the age of 30. Expectation of life at birth, 2013, was 73·9 years for males and 77·6 years for females. Annual population growth rate, 2000–08, 2·4%. Infant mortality, 2010, was 15 per 1,000 live births, down from 58 in the years 1980–85. Fertility rate, 2008, 3·1 births per woman. Saudi Arabia was ranked 134th in a gender gap index of 145 countries compiled by the World Economic Forum for its *Global Gender Gap Report 2015*. The annual index considers economic, political, education and health criteria.

Climate

A desert climate, with very little rain and none at all from June to Dec. The months May to Sept. are very hot and humid, but winter temperatures are quite pleasant. Riyadh, Jan. 58°F (14·4°C), July 108°F (42°C). Annual rainfall 4" (100 mm). Jeddah, Jan. 73°F (22·8°C), July 87°F (30·6°C). Annual rainfall 3" (81 mm).

Constitution and Government

The reigning King, **Salman bin Abdulaziz Al-Saud** (b. 1935), Custodian of the two Holy Mosques, succeeded in Jan. 2015, after King Abdullah's death. *Crown Prince:* Prince Mohammed bin Salman bin Abdulaziz Al-Saud (b. 1985). The Saudi royal family is around 8,000-strong.

Constitutional practice derives from Sharia law. There is no formal constitution, but three royal decrees of 1 March 1992 established a Basic Law which defines the systems of central and municipal government, and

set up a 60-man Consultative Council (*Majlis Al-Shura*) of royal nominees in Aug. 1993. The *Chairman* is Abdullah Al-Asheikh. In July 1997 the King decreed an increase of the Consultative Council to a chairman plus 90 members, selected from men of science and experience; in 2001 it was increased again to a chairman plus 120 members and in 2005 further to a chairman plus 150 members. A Royal Order of Jan. 2013 specified that at least 20% of the members should be women. The King swore in the first 30 female members of the Consultative Council in Feb. 2013.

The Council does not have legislative powers.

Saudi Arabia is an absolute monarchy; executive power is discharged through a *Council of Ministers,* consisting of the King, Deputy Prime Minister, Second Deputy Prime Minister and Cabinet Ministers.

The King has the post of *Prime Minister* and can veto any decision of the Council of Ministers within 30 days.

In Oct. 2003 the government announced that municipal elections would be held in 2004 for the first time (although they were subsequently postponed until 2005), followed by city elections and partial elections to the *Majlis Al-Shura* in the following years. In March 2011 the government announced that the second municipal elections, previously scheduled for 2009, would be held in Sept. 2011. Women were eligible to vote and stand for office for the first time at the elections of Dec. 2015.

National Anthem

'Sarei lil majd walaya' ('Onward towards the glory and the heights'); words by Ibrahim Khafaji, tune by Abdul Rahman al Katib.

Government Chronology

Kings since 1932.

1932–53	Abdulaziz bin Abdul Rahman Al-Saud
1953–64	Saud bin Abdulaziz Al-Saud
1964–75	Faisal bin Abdulaziz Al-Saud
1975–82	Khalid bin Abdulaziz Al-Saud
1982–2005	Fahd bin Abdulaziz Al-Saud
2005–15	Abdullah bin Abdulaziz Al-Saud
2015–	Salman bin Abdulaziz Al-Saud

Recent Elections

Municipal elections were held on 12 Dec. 2015 for two-thirds of the seats on the councils of 284 municipalities. For the first time ever, women were permitted to stand for election and vote. 20 women were elected to councils. There are no political parties.

Current Government

In Feb. 2019 the Council of Ministers comprised:

Prime Minister: King Salman bin Abdulaziz Al-Saud; b. 1935.

Deputy Prime Minister and Minister of Defence: Prince Mohammed bin Salman bin Abdulaziz Al-Saud.

Minister of Civil Service: Sulaiman Al-Hamdan. *Commerce and Investment, and Municipal and Rural Affairs (acting):* Majid bin Abdullah Al-Qasabi. *Communications and Information Technology:* Abdullah bin Ammar Al-Sawahlah. *Culture:* Prince Badr bin Abdullah bin Farhan Al-Saud. *Economy and Planning:* Mohammed Al-Tuwaijri. *Education:* Hamad Al-Sheikh. *Energy, Industry and Natural Resources:* Khalid bin Abdulaziz Al-Falih. *Environment, Water and Agriculture:* Abdurrahman Abdul Mohsen Al-Fadli. *Finance:* Mohammed Al-Jadaan. *Foreign Affairs:* Ibrahim Al-Assaf. *Hajj and Umra:* Muhammad Saleh Benten. *Health:* Tawfiq bin Fawzan Al-Rabiah. *Housing:* Majed bin Abdullah bin Hamad Al-Haqail. *Interior:* Prince Abdulaziz bin Saud bin Naif. *Islamic Affairs, Endowments, Call and Guidance:* Abdullatif bin Abdulaziz bin Abdulrahman Al-Sheikh. *Justice:* Walid bin Mohammad bin Saleh Al-Samaani. *Labour and Social Development:* Ahmed bin Suleiman Al-Rajhi. *Media:* Turki Al-Shabana. *National Guard:* Abdullah bin Bandar bin Abdul Aziz. *Transport:* Nabil bin Mohammed Al-Amudi.

Majlis Website (Arabic only): http://www.shura.gov.sa

Current Leaders

King Salman bin Abdulaziz Al-Saud

Position
King

Introduction
A member of the ruling Saud family, King Salman acceded to the throne in Jan. 2015 following the death of his half-brother, King Abdullah.

Early Life
Salman was born on 31 Dec. 1935 in Riyadh and was educated at the city's Princes' School. In 1963 he became governor of Riyadh and remained in the position for the next 48 years. During this time, Riyadh's population increased from 200,000 to over 5m. and it became a centre for foreign investment. Salman earned a reputation as a mediator within the Saud family, and won recognition for his support of various humanitarian causes.

He was named defence minister in 2011 and became crown prince in 2012. In this latter role, he undertook many official trips abroad on behalf of the monarchy.

Career in Office
Salman acceded to the throne on 23 Jan. 2015 and in April he appointed Prince Mohammad bin Naif, who had been interior minister since 2012, as crown prince and first deputy prime minister. This was the first time a grandchild of the Saudi Kingdom's founding monarch, Abdulaziz, had entered the order of succession.

Salman vowed to improve educational standards, health care and housing, while urging businesses to do their 'national duty' in creating jobs for the growing younger population. Numerous advisory bodies were streamlined into two councils—one headed by Prince Mohammad bin Naif focusing on politics and security, and the other overseen by defence minister Prince Mohammed bin Salman concerned with economic and development policy. In Dec. 2015 women were allowed to vote and stand for public office for the first time in municipal elections.

Internationally, Salman has been confronted by political instability in neighbouring Yemen and increasing rivalry with Iran. Since March 2015 a Saudi-led regional coalition of Gulf Arab states has conducted a military campaign of air strikes against an Iranian-backed insurgency by rebel Shia Houthi forces in Yemen. The consequent friction with Iran was aggravated further in Jan. 2016 when the Saudi execution of a prominent Shia cleric led to the ransacking by protesters of the Saudi embassy in the Iranian capital and the retaliatory severing of diplomatic relations with Iran by the Saudi government. The Saudi military has since been accused of atrocities in its bombing campaign in Yemen, fuelling international pressure for a ceasefire and peace talks, which were tentatively initiated in Dec. 2018.

In Sept. 2015 hundreds of people died in two fatal incidents in the country—the first when a crane collapsed at the Grand Mosque in the holy city of Makkah during bad weather and the second in a stampede by Muslim worshippers attending the annual Hajj pilgrimage.

In June 2017 Saudi Arabia, the United Arab Emirates, Bahrain and Egypt broke off diplomatic relations and cut transport links with Qatar, accusing the country of promoting international terrorism and aligning with Iran. In the same month Salman named his seemingly reform-minded son, Prince Mohammed bin Salman bin Abdulaziz Al-Saud, as the crown prince in place of Mohammad bin Naif. Subsequently, in Sept., a royal decree announced that the ban on women driving motor vehicles would end in 2018 (from June), and in Nov. the crown prince instigated a crackdown on high-level corruption in the country with the arrest of scores of people including prominent royal family and business figures.

In Oct. 2018 Jamal Khashoggi, a journalist and prominent critic of the Saudi regime, was allegedly murdered and dismembered after entering the Saudi consulate in İstanbul, Turkey, prompting not only an unprecedented diplomatic backlash from the Turkish government and the Arab kingdom's Western allies but also accusations of the crown prince's personal involvement and demands for an investigation.

Defence

In 2013 defence expenditure totalled US\$59,560m. (up from US\$48,531m. in 2011), with spending per capita US\$2,211. Saudi Arabia's annual defence expenditure is the third largest after that of the USA and China. The 2013 expenditure represented 8·0% of GDP.

5,000 US troops were stationed in Saudi Arabia after the 1991 Gulf War and were joined by a further 20,000 during the 2003 conflict. However, virtually all US troops have now been withdrawn. In March 2011 the Gulf Co-operation Council's Peninsula Shield Force, which is based in Saudi Arabia and whose mission is to protect the security of member states from any external aggression, consisted of approximately 40,000 troops.

Army

Strength (2011) was 75,000. There is a paramilitary Border Guard (10,500) and a National Guard (*see below*).

Navy

The Royal Saudi Naval Forces fleet includes three destroyers, four frigates and four corvettes. Naval Aviation forces operate 46 helicopters.

The main naval bases are at Riyadh (HQ Naval Forces), Jeddah (Western Fleet) and Jubail (Eastern Fleet). Naval personnel in 2011 totalled 13,500, including 3,000 marines.

Air Force

Current combat aircraft include F-15s, F-5Bs, F-5Fs, Panavia Tornados and Eurofighter Typhoons. The Air Force operated 296 combat-capable aircraft in total and numbered 20,000 personnel in 2011.

Air Defence Force

This separate Command was formerly part of the Army. In 2011 it operated surface-to-air missile batteries and had a strength of 16,000.

National Guard

The total strength of the National Guard amounted to 100,000 (75,000 active, 25,000 tribal levies) in 2011. The National Guard's primary role is the protection of the Royal Family and vital points in the Kingdom. It is directly under royal command. The UK provides small advisory teams to the National Guard in the fields of general training and communications.

Industrial Security Force

This force was established in 2007 to protect state oil facilities in response to attacks in 2006 on the Abqaiq oil processing plant. Strength in 2011 was more than 9,000.

Economy

Agriculture accounted for 1·9% of GDP in 2013, industry 60·0% and services 38·1%. Manufacturing's share of total GDP was 10·0%.

Overview

The economy is dominated by the oil sector, which accounts for over 85% of total export revenue annually. Saudi Arabia is the world's largest oil producer and exporter, with almost a fifth of the world's proven oil reserves and over 60% of spare capacity in global oil supply. The industrial sector is based on hydrocarbon resources, although the country also has deposits of iron ore, phosphates, bauxite and copper.

In 1998 US and European oil companies were allowed to invest in the energy sector for the first time. The stock market was then opened to foreign investors and tax and customs regulations were reformed. The improvements facilitated full membership of the World Trade Organization in 2005. A tourism authority was also established.

In the 1980s the economy had posted negative annual growth rates over five years. In the 1990s annual growth then averaged 3·1% (still low compared to developing countries, particularly in the Asia–Pacific region), while in 2001 and 2002 the economy barely grew at all. However, rising oil prices boosted performance in 2003 and annual growth accelerated to 7·9%. Over half of the 2004 fiscal surplus was used to reduce central government debt by 16% to 66% of GDP, while the rest was put into a fund to finance investment in priority areas over a five-year period.

Oil production fell in 2008 and the global financial crisis caused the stock market to decline by 46% in the last quarter of that year. Nonetheless, high oil prices contributed to real GDP growth averaging 4·9% per annum between 2008 and 2012. Recovery in global demand meant that the non-oil sector also grew 7·5% per annum from 2010–12, with the manufacturing, retail and transport industries seeing double-digit growth. Government debt was 7·5% of GDP in 2011. When Libyan oil output was disrupted that year, Saudi Arabia increased its production to offset shortfalls. Per capita GDP also grew robustly in 2011, with the World Bank recording a level of over US$24,000. Inflation meanwhile stayed in single figures as a result of a flexible labour market and an open trade system.

The steep drop in oil prices in 2014–15 prompted a year-on-year decline in GDP. A record fiscal deficit of 15% was registered in 2015, down from a surplus of 5·8% in 2013. The rise in the budget deficit was also paralleled by an increase in government debt, from 1·6% of GDP at the end of 2014 to 12·4% in 2016. The fall in fiscal revenues emphasized the need to counteract the increasing vulnerability of the economy to oil price movements and to capitalize on growth opportunities in the private sector.

In response, the government launched an ambitious reform programme in 2016. Saudi Vision 2030 aims to reduce the reliance on oil through cutting public spending and subsidies for the oil sector and directing funds to non-oil dependent economic sectors, including manufacturing and finance. The programme, envisaging 80 planned projects in three five-year phases, received a positive response from the IMF, which nevertheless cautioned against rushed implementation.

The labour market is divided, with Saudis largely employed in the public sector and non-Saudis dominating the private sector. The government has invested in tertiary education and implemented reforms to boost Saudi nationals' competitiveness and access to high-paying jobs in the private sector. However, joblessness remains a serious problem, with youth unemployment over 40% and female unemployment around 33% at the end of 2014. The World Bank ranked Saudi Arabia 92nd out of 190 economies for ease of doing business in its 2018 index.

Currency

The unit of currency is the *rial* (SAR) of 100 *halalah*. Foreign exchange reserves totalled US$27,637m. in Sept. 2009 and gold reserves were 4·60m. troy oz. Total money supply in June 2009 was SAR474,307m. Inflation rates (based on IMF statistics):

2008	2009	2010	2011	2012	2013	2014	2015	2016	2017
6·1%	4·2%	3·8%	3·8%	2·9%	3·5%	2·2%	1·3%	2·0%	−0·9%

Budget

In 2012 revenues totalled SAR1,239·5bn. and expenditures SAR853·0bn. Oil revenues accounted for 92·0% of revenue in 2012; current expenditures accounted for 66·6% of expenditure.

VAT of 5% was introduced on 1 Jan. 2018.

Performance

Real GDP growth rates (based on IMF statistics):

2008	2009	2010	2011	2012	2013	2014	2015	2016	2017
6·3%	−2·1%	5·0%	10·0%	5·4%	2·7%	3·7%	4·1%	1·7%	−0·9%

Total GDP in 2017 was US$683·8bn.

Banking and Finance

The Saudi Arabian Monetary Agency (*Governor*, Ahmed Al-Khulaifi), established in 1953, functions as the central bank and the government's fiscal agent. In 2016, 12 Saudi banks and 13 foreign banks were licensed with the Saudi Arabian Monetary Authority. The leading banks are National Commercial Bank (assets in 2008 of US$59·1bn.), Samba Financial Group (US$47·7bn. in 2008) and Al-Rajhi Bank (US$44·0bn. in 2008). Sharia (the religious law of Islam) forbids the charging of interest; Islamic banking is based on sharing clients' profits and losses and imposing service charges. In 2005 total assets of commercial banks were US$202·4bn.

A number of industry sectors are closed to foreign investors, including petroleum exploration, defence-related activities and financial services.

There is a stock exchange in Riyadh.

Energy and Natural Resources

Environment

Saudi Arabia's carbon dioxide emissions from the consumption of energy in 2011 were the equivalent of 21·1 tonnes per capita. An *Environmental Performance Index* compiled in 2016 ranked Saudi Arabia 95th of 180 countries, with 68·6%. The index examined various factors in nine areas—agriculture, air quality, biodiversity and habitat, climate and energy, fisheries, forests, health impacts, water and sanitation, and water resources.

Electricity

Installed capacity was 51·1m. kW in 2011. Currently all electricity is thermally generated, but Saudi Arabia plans to build 16 nuclear power reactors under Russia's supervision. Production was 250·08bn. kWh in 2011; consumption per capita in 2011 was 9,008 kWh.

Oil and Gas

Proven oil reserves in 2017 were 266·2bn. bbls, the second highest after those of Venezuela and around 16% of world resources. However, Saudi Arabia has far more readily available reserves than Venezuela. Oil production began in 1938 by Aramco, which is now 100% state-owned and accounts for about 99% of total crude oil production. It is the world's largest oil company in terms of output. Production in 2017 totalled 561·7m. tonnes and accounted for 13% of the global oil output. Saudi Arabia lost its status as the world's largest oil producer to Russia in 2009 but regained it in 2011. However, in 2017 the USA became the largest producer. In 2015 petroleum oil export revenues were US$158bn., the highest of any country.

Production comes from 14 major oilfields, mostly in the Eastern Province and offshore, and including production from the Neutral Zone. The Ghawar oilfield, located between Riyadh and the Persian Gulf, is the largest in the world, with estimated reserves of 70bn. bbls. Oil reserves are expected to run out in approximately 2075. In April 2016 plans were unveiled in 'Vision 2030' to end the country's dependence on oil. 'Vision 2030' also calls for the partial privatization of Aramco.

In 2017 natural gas reserves were 8·0trn. cu. metres; output in 2017 was 111·4bn. cu. metres. The gas sector has been opened up to foreign investment.

Water

Efforts are under way to provide adequate supplies of water for urban, industrial, rural and agricultural use. Most investment has gone into sea-water desalination. In 2006 desalination plants produced 2·8m. cu. metres of water a day. Irrigation for agriculture consumes the largest amount, from fossil reserves (the country's principal water source) and from surface water collected during seasonal floods. In 2006 there were 230 dams with a holding capacity of 850·3m. cu. metres. Treated urban waste water is an increasing resource for both agricultural and industrial purposes.

Minerals

Production began in 1988 at Mahd Al-Dahab gold mine, the largest in the country. In 2010 total gold production was 4,476 kg. Deposits of iron, phosphate, bauxite, uranium, silver, tin, tungsten, nickel, chrome, zinc, lead, potassium ore and copper have also been found.

Agriculture

Land ownership is under the jurisdiction of the ministry of municipal and rural affairs.

Since 1970 the government has spent substantially on desert reclamation, irrigation schemes, drainage and control of surface water and of moving sands. Undeveloped land has been distributed to farmers and there are research and extension programmes. Large-scale private investment has concentrated on wheat, poultry and dairy production.

In 2013 there were an estimated 3·07m. ha. of arable land and 227,000 ha. of permanent cropland. Approximately 1·62m. ha. were equipped for irrigation in 2013. In 2015, 6% of employed persons were engaged in agriculture.

Production of leading crops, 2013 (in 1,000 tonnes): dates, 1,095; wheat, 660; melons and watermelons, 631; tomatoes, 544; potatoes, 390; cucumbers and gherkins, 247; grapes, 134; pumpkins and squash, 120; onions, 112; sorghum, 110.

Livestock (2013): sheep, 11·5m.; goats, 3·4m.; cattle, 456,000; camels, 233,000; chickens (estimate), 182m. Livestock products (2013 estimates, in 1,000 tonnes): milk, 2,338; meat, 795; eggs, 222.

Forestry

The area under forests was 0·98m. ha. (0·5% of the land area) in 2015.

Fisheries

In 2011 the total catch was 64,481 tonnes, entirely from sea fishing. Imports of fishery commodities were valued at US$487m. in 2011.

Industry

The largest companies in Saudi Arabia by market capitalization in May 2018 were SABIC (Saudi Basic Industries), at US$91·8bn.; Saudi Telecom (US$42·8bn.); and National Commercial Bank (US$35·3bn.).

In 2005 manufacturing accounted for 9·5% of GDP and construction 4·7%. The government encourages the establishment of manufacturing industries. Its policy focuses on establishing industries that use petroleum products, petrochemicals and minerals. Petrochemical and oil-based industries have been concentrated at eight new industrial cities, with the two principal cities at Jubail and Yanbu. Products include chemicals, plastics, industrial gases, steel and other metals. In 2016 there were 7,741 factories employing 1,037,845 workers.

Labour

The labour force in the first half of 2015 totalled 11,912,200. In 2015 females constituted 15·8% of the labour force—one of the lowest percentages of females in the workforce of any country. In the first half of 2015, 15·7% of the employed population were engaged in public administration and defence/compulsory social security, 13·0% in construction, 12·5% in wholesale and retail trade/repair of motor vehicles, and 12·3% in education. There are 9m. foreign workers, including over 1m. Egyptians and over 1m. Indians. In the period Jan.–June 2015 unemployment was 5·7% overall but 11·6% for Saudis.

Saudi Arabia had 58,000 people living in slavery according to the Walk Free Foundation's 2013 *Global Slavery Index*.

International Trade

Saudi Arabia, along with Bahrain, Kuwait, Oman, Qatar and the United Arab Emirates entered into a customs union in Jan. 2003.

Imports and Exports

Trade in US$1m.:

	2006	2007	2008	2009	2010
Imports c.i.f.	69,800	90,214	115,134	95,552	106,863
Exports f.o.b.	211,306	234,951	313,462	192,314	251,143

The principal export is crude oil; refined oil, petrochemicals, fertilizers, plastic products and wheat are other major exports. Saudi Arabia is the world's largest exporter of oil, accounting for 85·4% of all the country's exports in 2006. Crude oil exports in 2010 were 6·6m. bbls a day. Major import suppliers, 2006: USA, 14·5%; China, 8·6%; Germany, 8·1%; Japan, 8·1%. Main export destinations, 2006: Japan, 16·5%; USA, 15·1%; South Korea, 9·2%; China, 6·3%.

Communications

Roads

In 2005 there was a total road network of 221,372 km (21·5% paved), including 3,891 km of motorway. A causeway links Saudi Arabia with Bahrain. Passenger cars in use in 2005 numbered 3,206,000 and there were 1,127,900 lorries and vans. Although there was no specific law prohibiting women from driving, the Saudi interior ministry did not in the past issue licences to female drivers. In Sept. 2017 King Salman lifted the ban, which took effect in June 2018. In 2016–17 there were 460,488 road accidents resulting in 7,489 deaths.

Rail

In 2010, 1,412 km of 1,435 mm gauge lines linked Riyadh and Dammam with stops at Hofuf and Abqaiq. The network has since been extended, consisting of links from Riyadh to Jauf (and in due course to the Jordanian border), and from Makkah to Madinah. The line from Makkah to Madinah via Jeddah, which opened in Oct. 2018, is Saudi Arabia's first high-speed rail link. In 2012 railways carried 1·3m. passengers and 4·5m. tonnes of freight. The first line of a metro system in Makkah opened in 2010, covering 18·1 km. A metro is under construction in Riyadh, with the first phase expected to open during 2019.

Civil Aviation

The national carrier is the part-privatized Saudi Arabian Airlines, which in 2006 owned 139 aircraft and served 76 destinations. In 2005 scheduled airline traffic of Saudi-based carriers flew 117·1m. km and carried 11,126,300 passengers. There are four major international airports, at Jeddah (King Abdulaziz), Dhahran, Riyadh (King Khaled) and Dammam (King Fahd). There are also 23 domestic airports. Jeddah handled 25,785,463 passengers in 2012 (17,547,530 on international flights) and 265,629 tonnes of freight in 2011. Riyadh was the second busiest airport in 2012, handling 17,690,764 passengers (8,720,576 on domestic flights) and 305,943 tonnes of freight.

Shipping

The ports of Dammam and Jubail are on the Persian Gulf and Jeddah, Yanbu and Jizan on the Red Sea. There is a deepwater oil terminal at Ras Tanura. In 2014 Jeddah handled 60·4m. tonnes of cargo, Jubail 56·1m. tonnes and Yanbu 43·0m. tonnes. In Jan. 2014 there were 72 ships of 300 GT or over registered (including 38 oil tankers, 15 passenger ships and ten general cargo ships), totalling 1·45m. GT.

Telecommunications

In 2013 there were 4·9m. main (fixed) telephone lines. In the same year mobile phone subscriptions numbered 53·1m. (1,842·0 per 1,000 persons). The government sold a 30% stake in Saudi Telecom Company (STC) in Dec. 2002. STC lost its monopoly in the mobile phone market in 2005 and in landline services in 2007. In 2013 an estimated 60·5% of the population were internet users. In March 2012 there were 5·1m. Facebook users.

Social Institutions

Out of 178 countries analysed in the 2017 *Fragile States Index*—a list published jointly by the Fund for Peace and *Foreign Policy* magazine—Saudi Arabia was ranked the 78th least vulnerable to conflict or collapse. The index is based on 12 indicators of state vulnerability across social, political and economic categories.

Justice

The religious law of Islam (Sharia) is the common law of the land, and is administered by religious courts, at the head of which is a chief judge, who is responsible for the Department of Sharia Affairs. Sharia courts are concerned primarily with family inheritance and property matters. However, following judicial reforms of Oct. 2007 a newly established Supreme Court replaced the Supreme Judiciary Council as the highest judicial authority. Specialized courts are also to be established to operate alongside the Sharia courts and there are plans to codify Sharia and introduce the principle of precedent into court practice. The Committee for the Settlement of Commercial Disputes is the commercial court. Other specialized courts or committees include one dealing exclusively with labour and employment matters; the Negotiable Instruments Committee, which deals with cases relating to cheques, bills of exchange and promissory notes; and the Board of Grievances, whose preserve is disputes with the government or its agencies and which also has jurisdiction in trademark-infringement cases and is the authority for enforcing foreign court judgments.

The death penalty is in force for murder, rape, sodomy, armed robbery, sabotage, drug trafficking, adultery and apostasy; executions may be held in public. There were at least 139 executions in 2018, including at least three females. The population in penal institutions in Feb. 2013 was 47,000 (162 per 100,000 of national population). 58·7% of prisoners had yet to receive a trial according to 2014 estimates by the International Centre for Prison Studies.

Education

The educational system provides students with free education, books and health services. General education consists of kindergarten, six years of primary school and three years each of intermediate and high school. In 2005–06 there were: 1,449 pre-primary schools with 10,150 teachers and 97,137 pupils; 13,163 primary schools with 213,355 teachers and 2,417,811 pupils; 7,086 intermediate schools with 104,675 teachers and 1,071,747 pupils; 4,215 secondary schools with 79,754 teachers and 954,141 pupils. Students can attend either high schools offering programmes in arts and sciences, or vocational schools. Girls' education has traditionally been administered separately, but in Sept. 2009 the country's first mixed-gender university was opened and in Oct. 2009 a trial of mixed-gender education in 15 private elementary schools was launched. In 2005 there were 903 institutions for special needs pupils with 18,958 students. The adult literacy rate in

2009 was an estimated 86·1% (90·0% among males and 81·1% among females). Although Saudi girls were not even allowed to attend school until 1964 women now make up nearly 60% of Saudi Arabia's higher education students.

In 2005 there were 3,775 adult education centres. In 2005–06 there were 11 universities (including two Islamic universities and one university of petroleum and minerals); there were 603,767 students in total in higher education and 26,827 teachers.

Health

In 2013 Saudi Arabia had 22 hospital beds per 10,000 population. There were 79,313 physicians in 2014 (25·7 per 10,000 population), plus 160,811 nursing and midwifery personnel, 12,301 dentistry personnel and 21,639 pharmaceutical personnel. Expenditure on health in 2014 was 5·1% of GDP.

In *Water: At What Cost? The State of the World's Water 2016*, WaterAid reported that 3·0% of the population does not have access to safe water.

Welfare

The retirement age is 60 (men) or 55 (women), with eligibility based on 120 months of contributions. The minimum monthly old-age pension is SAR1,500, calculated as 2·5% of the average monthly wage during the previous two years multiplied by the number of years of contributions. A 1969 law requires employers with more than 20 employees to pay 100% of wages for the first 30 days of sick leave and 75% of wages for the next 60 days. Unemployment benefits of SAR2,000 (US$535) a month were introduced in 2011 for applicants who proved they were looking for work or undergoing training.

Workers' medical benefits include medical, dental and diagnostic treatment, hospitalization, medicines, appliances, transportation and rehabilitation.

Religion

According to the Pew Research Center's Forum on Religion & Public Life, in 2010 an estimated 78–83% of the total population were Sunni Muslims, 10–15% Shias, 4% Christians and 1% Hindus. The *Grand Mufti*, Sheikh Abdul Aziz bin Abdullah bin Mohammed Al-Sheikh, has cabinet rank. A special police force, the Mutaween, exists to enforce religious norms.

The annual *Hajj*, the pilgrimage to Makkah, takes place from the 8th to the 13th day of Dhu al Hijjah, the last month of the Islamic year. It attracts more than 1·8m. pilgrims annually. In the current Islamic year, 1441, the *Hajj* is scheduled to begin on 29 July 2020 in the Gregorian calendar.

Culture

World Heritage Sites

Saudi Arabia has five sites on the UNESCO World Heritage List: the archaeological site of Madain Salih (Al-Hijr) was inscribed in 2008; the At-Turaif District in Ad-Dir'iyah, founded in the 15th century and the first capital of the Saudi dynasty, was inscribed in 2010; Historic Jeddah, the Gate to Makkah, which is situated on the eastern shore of the Red Sea, was inscribed in 2014; Rock Art in the Hail Region of Saudi Arabia, a property made up of two components and situated in a desert landscape, was inscribed in 2015; and Al-Ahsa Oasis, an Evolving Cultural Landscape, was inscribed in 2018.

Press

In 2008 there were 16 daily newspapers with a combined circulation of 1,420,000. The most widely read newspapers are the Saudi-owned London-based *Asharq Al-Awsat* ('The Middle East'), *Al-Riyadh* and *Al-Watan*.

Tourism

There were 14,276,000 international tourists in 2012; spending by tourists in 2012 totalled US$8·4bn.

Calendar

In Oct. 2016 Saudi Arabia switched from using the lunar-based *Hjri* calendar to the Gregorian calendar.

Diplomatic Representatives

Of Saudi Arabia in the United Kingdom (30 Charles St., London, W1J 5DZ)
    Ambassador: Prince Mohammed bin Nawaf bin Abdulaziz Al-Saud.

Of the United Kingdom in Saudi Arabia (PO Box 94351, Riyadh 11693)
    Ambassador: Simon Collis, CMG.

Of Saudi Arabia in the USA (601 New Hampshire Ave., NW, Washington, D.C., 20037)
    Ambassador: Prince Khalid bin Salman bin Abdulaziz.

Of the USA in Saudi Arabia (PO Box 94309, Riyadh 11693)
    Ambassador: Vacant.
    Chargé d'Affaires a.i.: Christopher Henzel.

Of Saudi Arabia to the United Nations
    Ambassador: Abdallah Yahya Al-Mouallimi.

Of Saudi Arabia to the European Union
    Ambassador: Saad Bin Mohammed Alarify.

Further Reading

Aarts, Paul, *Saudi Arabia in the Balance: Political Economy, Society, Foreign Affairs.* 2006

Al-Rasheed, Madawi, *A History of Saudi Arabia.* 2002

Al-Rasheed, Madawi and Vitalis, Robert, (eds) *Counter-Narratives: History, Contemporary Society, and Politics in Saudi Arabia and Yemen.* 2004

Bradley, John R., *Saudi Arabia Exposed.* Revised ed. 2006

Hegghammer, Thomas, *Jihad in Saudi Arabia: Violence and Pan-Islamism since 1979.* 2010

Kostiner, J., *The Making of Saudi Arabia: from Chieftaincy to Monarchical State.* 1994

Lacey, Robert, *Inside the Kingdom: Kings, Clerics, Modernists, Terrorists and the Struggle for Saudi Arabia.* 2009

Mackey, Sandra, *The Saudis: Inside the Desert Kingdom.* Revised ed. 2003

Manea, Elham, *Regional Politics in the Gulf: Saudi Arabia, Oman and Yemen.* 2005

Murphy, Caryle, *A Kingdom's Future: Saudi Arabia through the Eyes of its Twentysomethings.* 2013

Peterson, J. E., *Historical Dictionary of Saudi Arabia.* 1994

Vassiliev, Alexei, *King Faisal of Saudi Arabia: Personality, Faith and Times.* 2012

Wright, J. W. (ed.) *Business and Economic Development in Saudi Arabia: Essays with Saudi Scholars.* 1996

National Statistical Office: Ministry of Economy and Planning, Central Department of Statistics and Information, Riyadh.

Website: http://www.stats.gov.sa

Senegal

République du Sénégal (Republic of Senegal)

Capital: Dakar
Population projection, 2020: 17·20m.
GNI per capita, 2017: (PPP$) 2,384
HDI/world rank, 2017: 0·505/164
Internet domain extension: .sn

Key Historical Events

For much of the 1st millennium AD Senegal was under the influence of the gold-rich Ghana Empire of the Soninke people. In western Senegal the Takrur state was established in the 9th century. Islam was introduced in the 11th century by the Zenega Berbers of southern Mauritania, who gave their name to the region. The power of the Malinke (Madingo) in present-day Mali expanded in the 13th and 14th centuries, especially under Mansa Musa, who subjugated Takrur and the Tukulor in Senegal. The west was dominated by the Jolof empire, which fragmented into four kingdoms in the 16th century.

Portuguese trading colonies were established on Gorée Island and at Rufisque in around 1444, encouraging the growth of the slave trade. The Dutch took control of Senegalese trade in the 17th century, only to be evicted in 1677 by the French, based at Saint-Louis at the mouth of the Sénégal River. Inland, the Tukulor created a Muslim theocracy in Fouta Toro, usurping the Denianké Dynasty in 1776. Tukulor power grew in the 1850s under al-Hajj Umar Tal, whose *jihad* was contained by treaty with the French in 1857. Britain accepted French hegemony in the region in 1814 after half a century of colonial rivalry, while retaining the Gambia River. Railway construction in 1879 cemented French control over western Senegal and Dakar became the capital of French West Africa in 1904. Casamance and eastern Senegal were conquered in the 1890s.

Senegalese service in the French army in the First World War secured representation in Paris and French citizenship for Africans in certain communes. The colonial administration followed a moderate liberalization programme, including the right to form political parties and trade unions. However, the decline in the groundnut trade in the 1930s increased poverty in Senegal. The expansion of the vote after the Second World War gave support to the Democratic Bloc (BDS), which joined the Socialist Party to become the Progressive Union (UPS), dominating the 1959 elections in the newly autonomous Senegal. Membership of the French Community lasted until independence on 20 June 1960 as part of the Federation of Mali with French Soudan (Mali); the Federation was dissolved on 20 Aug. 1960.

Leopold Sédar Senghor, the BDS founder and leader of the UPS, was elected president on 5 Sept. 1960. Relations with his prime minister, Mamadou Dia, deteriorated and Senghor had him arrested in Dec. 1962 after an attempted coup. Presidential power was augmented by referendum in 1963, allowing Senghor to ban all other parties in 1966. Senghor appointed Abdou Diouf prime minister in 1973 and began relaxing political restrictions. Abdoulaye Wade founded the Democratic Party (PDS) and a Marxist-Leninist party was formed. Recession and political agitation forced Senghor's resignation in Dec. 1980; Diouf succeeded and was confirmed by elections in 1983, 1988 and 1993.

Diouf pursued a vigorous foreign policy via the Organization of African Unity and the Economic Community of West African States. He reinstated the Gambian president, Sir Dawda Jawara, in 1981, creating the Senegambian confederation, which lasted until 1989. Unrest in the southern Casamance region escalated into secessionist civil war in the early 1990s. A skirmish on the Mauritanian border in 1989 resulted in the death of Senegalese and Mauritanians expatriates and the closing of the border, a dispute not resolved until 1994. The deterioration of the economy and the Casamance crisis led to electoral defeat in 2000. He conceded peacefully, handing power to his long-term rival, PDS leader Abdoulaye Wade. Wade was re-elected in 2007 and received legal dispensation to contest a third term in 2012, despite the constitution of 2001 limiting presidents to two terms of office. The decision prompted popular protests, leading to Macky Sall defeating Wade to become the new president in April 2012.

Territory and Population

Senegal is bounded by Mauritania to the north and northeast, Mali to the east, Guinea and Guinea-Bissau to the south and the Atlantic to the west with The Gambia forming an enclave along that shore. A short section of the boundary with The Gambia is undefined. Area, 196,712 sq. km, including 4,190 sq. km of inland water. Population (2013 census), 13,508,715 (50·1% female). Density, 70·2 per sq. km. In 2011 the population was 42·7% urban.

The UN gives a projected population for 2020 of 17·20m.

About 2m. Senegalese live abroad, particularly in France, Italy, Spain and the USA.

The areas, populations and capitals of the regions are:

Region	Area (in sq. km)	Population 2013 census	Capital
Dakar	547	3,137,196	Dakar
Diourbel	4,824	1,497,455	Diourbel
Fatick	6,849	714,392	Fatick
Kaffrine	11,262	566,992	Kaffrine
Kaolack	5,357	960,875	Kaolack
Kédougou	16,800	151,357	Kédougou
Kolda	13,771	662,456	Kolda
Louga	24,889	874,193	Louga
Matam	29,445	562,538	Matam
Saint-Louis	19,241	908,942	Saint-Louis
Sédhiou	7,341	452,994	Sédhiou
Tambacounda	42,364	681,310	Tambacounda
Thiès	6,670	1,788,864	Thiès
Ziguinchor	7,352	549,151	Ziguinchor

Dakar, the capital, had a census population in 2013 of 2,646,503. Other large cities (with 2013 census population figures) are: Touba (753,315), Thiès (317,763), Kaolack (233,708), Mbour (232,777), Rufisque (221,066) and Saint-Louis (209,752).

Ethnic groups are the Wolof (36% of the population), Fulani (16%), Serer (16%), Diola (9%), Tukulor (9%), Bambara (6%), Malinké (6%) and Sarakole (2%).

The official language is French; Wolof is widely spoken.

Social Statistics

2005 estimates: births, 430,000; deaths, 132,000. Rates, 2005 estimates (per 1,000 population): births, 39·4; deaths, 12·1. Annual population growth rate, 2000–05, 2·8%; infant mortality, 2010, 50 per 1,000 live births. Life expectancy in 2007 was 53·9 years for men and 56·9 for women. Fertility rate, 2008, 5·0 births per woman. 51% of the population were living in poverty in 2005.

Climate

A tropical climate with wet and dry seasons. The rains fall almost exclusively in the hot season, from June to Oct., with high humidity. Dakar, Jan. 72°F (22·2°C), July 82°F (27·8°C). Annual rainfall 22" (541 mm).

Constitution and Government

A new constitution was approved by a referendum held on 7 Jan. 2001. The head of state is the *President*, elected by universal suffrage for not more than two five-year terms (previously two seven-year terms). However, in 2008 the National Assembly approved a change back to seven-year terms,

© Springer Nature Limited 2020
Palgrave Macmillan (ed.), *The Statesman's Yearbook 2020*,
https://doi.org/10.1057/978-1-349-95940-2_167

before an amendment approved by referendum in 2016 restored the five-year provision. The *President* has the power to dissolve the National Assembly, without the agreement, as had been the case, of a two-thirds majority. The new constitution also abolished the upper house (the Senate), confirmed the status of the prime minister and for the first time gave women the right to own land. Senegal has a unicameral legislature—the 165-member *National Assembly*, with all members directly elected. The Senate was re-established in Jan. 2007 six years after being dissolved. In Sept. 2012 parliament voted to abolish it after severe floods hit Senegal, with the money that would be saved going towards improving the country's flood defences and aid for flood victims.

National Anthem

'Pincez tous vos koras, frappez les balafos' ('All pluck the koras, strike the balafons'); words by Léopold Sédar Senghor, tune by Herbert Pepper.

Recent Elections

Presidential elections took place on 24 Feb. 2019. Incumbent Macky Sall won 58·3% of the vote, ahead of former prime minister Idrissa Seck with 20·5%, Ousmane Sonko with 15·7%, Issa Sall with 4·1% and Madické Niang with 1·6%. Two leading opposition figures were both barred from contesting the election. Turnout was 66·2%.

Parliamentary elections were held on 30 July 2017. Turnout was 53·7%. The United in Hope coalition backing President Macky Sall took 125 of the 165 seats in the National Assembly. The Manko Wattu Sénégal coalition backing former President Abdoulaye Wade took 19 seats and Manko Taxawu Sénégal led by Dakar's mayor Khalifa Sall won seven, with 11 smaller parties taking three seats or fewer.

Current Government

President: Macky Sall; b. 1961 (Alliance for the Republic; sworn in 2 April 2012).

In Feb. 2019 the government was composed as follows:

Prime Minister: Mohamed Dionne; b. 1959 (Alliance for the Republic; took office 6 July 2014).

Minister of African Integration, NEPAD and La Francophonie: Mbagnick Ndiaye. *Agriculture and Rural Infrastructure:* Papa Abdoulaye Seck. *Air Transport and Development of Airport Infrastructure:* Maimouna Ndoye Seck. *Armed Forces:* Augustin Tine. *Civil Service, Rationalization of the Workforce and Public Service Renewal:* Mariama Sarr. *Commerce, Consumption, Informal Sector, and Small and Medium-Sized Enterprises:* Alioune Sarr. *Communication, Telecommunications, Posts and Digital Economy:* Abdoulaye Bibi Baldé. *Culture:* Abdou Latif Coulibaly. *Economy, Finance and Planning:* Amadou Ba. *Employment, Professional Insertion and Workforce:* Aboulaye Diop. *Environment and Sustainable Development:* Mame Thierno Dieng. *Fisheries and Maritime Affairs:* Oumar Guèye. *Foreign Affairs and Senegalese Abroad:* Sidiki Kaba. *Good Governance and Child Protection:* Ndeye Ramatoulaye Gueye Diop. *Health and Social Action:* Abdoulaye Diouf Sarr. *Higher Education and Research:* Mary Teuw Niane. *Industry:* Moustapha Diop. *Infrastructure, Land Transport and Rural Access Development:* Abdoulaye Daouda Diallo. *Interior and Public Security:* Aly Ngouille Ndiaye. *Investment Promotion, Partnerships and Development of Government Services:* Khoudia Mbaye. *Justice and Keeper of the Seals:* Ismaïla Madior Fall. *Labour, Social Dialogue, Professional Organizations and Institutional Relations:* Samba Sy. *Livestock and Livestock Products:* Aminata Mbengue Ndiaye. *Local Governance, Development and Planning:* Yaya Abdoul Kane. *Mines and Geology:* Aïssatou Sophie Gladima Siby. *National Education:* Serigne Mbaye Thiam. *Petroleum and Energy:* Mansour Elimane Kane. *Professional Training, Learning and Crafts:* Mamadou Talla. *Solidarity Economy and Microfinance:* Aminata Angélique Manga. *Sports:* Matar Ba. *Tourism:* Mame Mbaye Niang. *Urban Development, Housing and Living Environment:* Diène Farba Sarr. *Water and Sanitation:* Mansour Faye. *Women, Family and Gender:* Ndèye Saly Diop Dieng. *Youth, Citizenship Building and Volunteering Promotion:* Pape Gorgui Ndong. *Minister in Charge of the Plan Sénégal Emergent:* Cheikh Kante.

Government Website (French only): http://www.gouv.sn

Current Leaders

Macky Sall

Position

President

Introduction

Macky Sall, a former prime minister under President Wade and founder of the liberal Alliance for the Republic (APR), was elected president in March 2012. Having broken with Wade's administration over issues of transparency and public spending, Sall pledged to cut the size of government and tackle Senegal's long-standing problems of unemployment, poor infrastructure and food insecurity. He was re-elected in Feb. 2019.

Early Life

Macky Sall was born on 11 Dec. 1961 in Fatick, western Senegal. After graduating in geological engineering from Cheikh Anta Diop University, Dakar, he completed further studies in geophysics at the French Petroleum Institute in Paris from 1992–93. He worked for the state-owned oil company PETROSEN from 1994–2000.

A member of Wade's Senegalese Democratic Party (PDS), Sall became general secretary of its Fatick regional convention in 1998. Following the PDS victory at elections in 2000, he served as director general of PETROSEN from Dec. 2000 until July 2001. He was special presidential adviser on energy and mines from April 2000 to May 2001, and from 2001–03 served as minister for mines, energy and hydraulics.

Sall became mayor of Fatick in 2002 and from 2003–04 was minister of the interior and government spokesperson. In April 2004 he was appointed prime minister by President Wade. He served until June 2007, when he was elected president of the National Assembly. In Nov. 2007, after Sall initiated an enquiry into spending by an agency headed by the president's son, the term of the National Assembly president was reduced to one year, prompting his resignation.

In Dec. 2008 Sall founded the APR and in 2009 was again elected mayor of Fatick. Against a background of rising public discontent with the government and anger at Wade's decision to circumvent constitutional limits and stand for a third term as president, Sall ran a vigorous 2012 presidential campaign. Arguing for cuts in public spending and increased transparency, he proposed halving the size of government and reducing Senegal's diplomatic representation abroad, using the savings to reduce food prices. He also promised to attract foreign investment to boost the economy and develop infrastructure.

After claiming second place in the first round of voting, Sall won the support of 12 eliminated opposition candidates and on 25 March 2012 took almost 66% of the vote in a run-off. Wade conceded defeat and Sall was sworn in on 2 April 2012.

Career in Office

Sall took office promising to tackle corruption and deliver economic growth, while dealing with severe food crises in the drought-stricken Sahel region. He was also expected to enter negotiations with neighbouring The Gambia to end three decades of conflict in the southern Casamance region (where a ceasefire was subsequently declared in May 2014). In Sept. 2013 he dismissed the prime minister, Abdoul Mbaye, and replaced him with Aminata Touré, previously the justice minister, who became the country's second woman premier. However, she was dismissed in July 2014 and was replaced by Mohamed Dionne, a technocrat.

A constitutional amendment to reduce the presidential term of office from seven to five years was approved in a referendum in March 2016 and, despite anti-government protests in the capital in April 2017 demanding the release of political prisoners, the United in Hope coalition supporting Sall won a substantial majority in National Assembly elections in July that year. Although there were signs of increasing political disaffection through 2018 amid fears of Sall's subversion of democracy, he was re-elected as president with about 58% of the vote in Feb. 2019.

Defence

There is selective conscription for two years. Defence expenditure totalled US$231m. in 2013 (US$17 per capita), representing 1·6% of GDP.

Army

There are four military zones. The Army had a strength of 11,900 (including conscripts) in 2011. There is also a paramilitary force of gendarmerie and customs of 5,000.

Navy

Personnel (2011) totalled 950, and bases are at Dakar and Casamance.

Air Force

The Air Force, formed with French assistance, has one combat-capable aircraft. Personnel (2011) 770.

Economy

Agriculture accounted for 17% of GDP in 2012, industry 24% and services 59%.

Overview

In contrast to many of its West African neighbours, Senegal enjoys social and political stability and is open to the outside world. However, the economy has historically been plagued by a weak business environment, poor infrastructure and an inefficient energy sector. Annual GDP growth averaged 3·3% from 2006 to 2013, markedly below the sub-Saharan average of 6·0% and down from 4·5% between 1995 and 2006. A development strategy launched in Nov. 2014, known as Plan Sénégal Emergent (PSE), aims to transform the lower-middle income nation into an emerging economy by 2035. A central plank of the plan is to attract private and foreign direct investment. Between 2015 and 2017 Senegal averaged GDP growth of 6·6% per year, driven by PSE reforms, low oil prices and favourable weather conditions.

The service sector accounted for 58·8% of GDP in 2014, having grown rapidly since the 1990s (especially transportation and telecommunications). Construction and agriculture are also important, although the agricultural sector is in long-term decline. The mining and energy sectors have also experienced a surge in production in recent years.

In 2000 Senegal became eligible for the Heavily Indebted Poor Countries initiative, reaching the completion point of the initiative in 2004 and so earning debt relief totalling US$850m. However, the International Monetary Fund and the World Bank have identified the public debt, which reached 62% of GDP in 2017, as a potential challenge to future prosperity.

The port of Dakar serves as an important centre of trade in West Africa. A 20-ha. dry port project was completed in 2009 while Jafza International of Dubai is developing a Special Economic Zone adjacent to Dakar International Airport. Oil exploration in the Casamance region offers potential for future revenue streams, although work has been hampered by weak transportation links and civil unrest.

Currency

The unit of currency is the *franc CFA* (XOF) with a parity of 655·957 francs CFA to one euro. In June 2005 total money supply was 930,246m. francs CFA and foreign exchange reserves totalled US$1,380m. There was inflation of 0·8% in 2016 and 1·3% in 2017.

Budget

Revenues in 2012 totalled 1,723bn. francs CFA (tax revenue, 82·5%) and expenditures 2,157bn. francs CFA (current expenditure, 59·4%).

VAT is 18%.

Performance

Real GDP growth was 6·4% in 2015, 6·2% in 2016 and 7·2% in 2017. Total GDP in 2017 was US$16·4bn.

Banking and Finance

The Banque Centrale des Etats de l'Afrique de l'Ouest is the bank of issue of the franc CFA for all the countries of the West African Economic and Monetary Union (Benin, Burkina Faso, Côte d'Ivoire, Guinea-Bissau, Mali, Niger, Senegal and Togo) but has had its headquarters in Dakar, the Senegalese capital, since 1973. Its *Governor* is Tiémoko Meyliet Koné. There are eight commercial banks, the largest including Banque Internationale pour le Commerce et l'Industrie and Banque de l'Habitat. There are also four development banks and an Islamic bank. Only about 5% of the population have bank accounts.

External debt amounted to US$3,677m. in 2010. As a share of GNI, external debt fell from 78·7% in 2000 to 28·5% in 2010.

Senegal is affiliated to the regional BRVM stock exchange (serving the member states of the West African Economic and Monetary Union), based in Abidjan, Côte d'Ivoire.

Energy and Natural Resources

Environment

Senegal's carbon dioxide emissions from the consumption of energy in 2011 were the equivalent of 0·5 tonnes per capita.

Electricity

In 2011 installed capacity was an estimated 0·6m. kW. Production in 2011 was 2·71bn. kWh and consumption per capita 222 kWh.

Minerals

Output, 2008, included (in tonnes): sand, 6·4m.; calcium phosphate, 645,000; salt, 241,000. Annual gold production was approximately 600 kg for many years but increased to over 5,000 tonnes in 2009 following the opening of a new mine in 2008.

Agriculture

Because of erratic rainfall 25% of agricultural land needs irrigation. Most land is owned under customary rights and holdings tend to be small. In 2007 the economically active population engaged in agriculture was an estimated 3,750,000. In 2006 approximately 2·99m. ha. were used as arable land and 52,000 ha. for permanent crops. An estimated 63,000 ha. were irrigated in 2006. There were about 700 tractors in use in 2006 and 155 harvester-threshers. Production, 2005–06 (in 1,000 tonnes): sugarcane, 829; groundnuts, 703; millet, 609; maize, 400; rice, 289; cassava, 281; watermelons, 241; tomatoes, 161; sorghum, 144; onions, 76; mangoes, 62.

Livestock (2006): 5·00m. sheep; 4·26m. goats; 3·14m. cattle; 518,000 horses; 415,000 asses; 318,000 pigs.

Meat production (2006, in 1,000 tonnes): beef and veal, 50; chicken meat, 32; lamb and mutton, 19; goat meat, 11; pork and pork products, 10. Milk production (2006, in 1,000 litres): cow's milk, 135; goat's milk, 46; sheep's milk, 31.

Forestry

Forests covered 8·27m. ha. in 2015 (43% of the land area). Roundwood production in 2011 amounted to 6·26m. cu. metres.

Fisheries

In 2012 the total catch was an estimated 461,000 tonnes, around 93% of which came from sea fishing.

Oil and Gas

In May 2017 it was announced that an offshore gas field had been discovered off the coast of Senegal. The Greater Tortue Complex's reserves are estimated at 700bn. cu. metres, with production expected to begin in 2021. In Feb. 2018 the governments of Mauritania and Senegal signed an agreement pledging co-operation over the field, which straddles their maritime boundary.

Significant deposits of oil were discovered offshore in 2014. Senegal is aiming to be an oil producer by 2023.

Industry

Predominantly agricultural and fish processing, phosphate mining, petroleum refining and construction materials.

Labour

The labour force in 2013 was 6,118,000 (4,484,000 in 2003). 78·0% of the population aged 15–64 was economically active in 2013. In the same year 10·3% of the population was unemployed.

Senegal had 0·10m. people living in slavery according to the Walk Free Foundation's 2013 *Global Slavery Index*.

International Trade

Imports and Exports

In 2010 imports (f.o.b.) totalled US$4,782·2m. and exports (f.o.b.) US$2,088·1m. Chief imports: petroleum and petroleum products, food and live animals, and machinery and transport equipment. Chief exports: fish, petroleum and petroleum products, and chemicals and related products. Main import suppliers, 2010: France, 19·7%; Nigeria, 10·2%; China, 8·3%; Netherlands, 5·3%; UK, 4·9%; Main export markets, 2010: Mali, 26·1%; India, 10·0%; Switzerland, 7·9%; Bunkers and ship stores, 7·6%; France, 4·6%.

Communications

Roads

The length of roads in 2006 was 14,805 km, of which 29·3% were paved. In 2008 there were 205,704 passenger cars, 56,795 trucks and vans and 15,982 coaches. There were 320 deaths as a result of road accidents in 2007.

Rail

There were previously four railway lines but the total length of the track fell from 1,034 km (metre gauge) in 1986 to 645 km in 2005. Only the Dakar–Kidira line (continuing in Mali) is still theoretically in service although traffic was suspended in 2003 and again since 2009 owing to the poor state of the track. There is also a suburban rail service linking Dakar and Rufisque, which carried 4·9m. passengers in 2009. In 2009, 364,000 tonnes of freight were carried.

Civil Aviation

The international airport is at Dakar (Blaise Diagne International Airport). It opened in 2017 to replace Léopold Sédar Senghor International Airport, which has now become a military airport. The main airline is Transair, which serves 11 destinations from Blaise Diagne International Airport, including four within Senegal.

Shipping

In Jan. 2014 there were three ships of 300 GT or over registered, totalling 5,000 GT. 12·2m. tonnes of freight were handled in the port of Dakar in 2013.

Telecommunications

In 2013 there were 343,700 main (fixed) telephone lines; mobile phone subscriptions numbered 13,134,000 that year (92·9 per 100 persons). In 2013 an estimated 20·9% of the population were internet users. In June 2012 there were 666,000 Facebook users.

Social Institutions

Out of 178 countries analysed in the 2017 *Fragile States Index*—a list published jointly by the Fund for Peace and *Foreign Policy* magazine—Senegal was ranked the 60th most vulnerable to conflict or collapse. The index is based on 12 indicators of state vulnerability across social, political and economic categories.

Justice

There are *juges de paix* in each *département* and a court of first instance in each region. Assize courts are situated in Dakar, Kaolack, Saint-Louis and Ziguinchor, while the Court of Appeal resides in Dakar. The death penalty, last used in 1967, was abolished in Dec. 2004.

The population in penal institutions in Dec. 2012 was 8,428 (64 per 100,000 of national population). In 2015 the World Justice Project *Rule of Law Index*, which provides data on how the rule of law is experienced by the general public across eight categories, ranked Senegal 52nd of 102 countries for criminal justice and 46th for civil justice.

Education

The adult literacy rate in 2006 was 42%. In 2007 there were 1,572,178 pupils (45,957 teaching staff) in primary schools; 505,097 pupils (20,007 teaching staff) in secondary schools; and 76,949 students in tertiary education. There are two public universities (Cheikh Anta Diop and Gaston Berger) and three private universities (Dakar Bourguiba, Sahel and Suffolk).

In 2006 public expenditure on education came to 4·9% of GNI and 26·3% of total government spending.

Health

In 2006 there were 22 hospitals, 68 health centres and 949 health posts. There were six physicians per 100,000 population and 42 nurses and midwives per 100,000 in the period 2006–13. Senegal has been one of the most successful countries in Africa in the prevention of AIDS. Levels of infection have remained low, with the anti-AIDS programme having started as far back as 1986. The infection rate has been kept below 2%.

In *Water: At What Cost? The State of the World's Water 2016*, WaterAid reported that 21·5% of the population does not have access to safe water.

Religion

According to a study by the Pew Research Center's Forum on Religion & Public Life, in 2010 there were an estimated 11·98m. Muslims (equivalent to 96·4% of the population). Most Muslims in Senegal are members of Sufi brotherhoods—Sufis are often described as being 'mystic' Sunnis. There were also an estimated 450,000 Christians in 2010, around 93% of whom were Catholics. There was one Roman Catholic cardinal in Feb. 2019.

Culture

World Heritage Sites

Gorée Island, off the coast of Senegal, was added to the UNESCO World Heritage List in 1978. It was formerly the largest slave trading centre on the African coast. The Djoudj Sanctuary in the Senegal River delta (added in 1981), protects 1·5m. birds, including the white pelican, the purple heron, the African spoonbill, the great egret and the cormorant. Niokolo-Koba National Park, along the banks of the Gambia River (added in 1981), is home to the Derby eland (largest of the antelopes), chimpanzees, lions, leopards and a large population of elephants as well as many birds, reptiles and amphibians. The Island of Saint-Louis joined the UNESCO list in 2000 (reinscribed in 2007), as a reminder of its status as the capital between 1872 and 1957. The Saloum Delta (2011) comprises brackish channels encompassing over 200 islands and islets and is marked by numerous shellfish mounds produced by its human inhabitants over 2,000 years. The Bassari Country, comprising the Bassari–Salémata area, the Bedik–Bandafassi area and the Fula–Dindéfello area, was added to the UNESCO list in 2012. The site houses original and still vibrant cultures of the Bassari, Fula and Bedik peoples, featuring their original traits of agro-pastoral, social, ritual and spiritual practices.

Senegal shares a UNESCO site with The Gambia: the Stone Circles of Senegambia (added in 2006) are a collection of 93 stone circles, tumuli and burial mounds from between the 3rd century BC and the 16th century AD.

Press

In 2008 there were 26 daily newspapers with a total average circulation of 123,000 copies and 30 non-dailies.

Tourism

In 2011 there were 968,000 international tourist arrivals (excluding same-day visitors), up from 900,000 in 2010.

Diplomatic Representatives

Of Senegal in the United Kingdom (39 Marloes Rd, London, W8 6LA)
    Ambassador: Cheikh Ahmadou Dieng.

Of the United Kingdom in Senegal (BP 6025, Dakar)
    Ambassador: George Hodgson.

Of Senegal in the USA (2215 M St., NW, Washington, D.C., 20037)
    Ambassador: Momar Diop.

Of the USA in Senegal (Route des Almadies, PO Box 49, Dakar)
    Ambassador: Tulinabo S. Mushingi.

Of Senegal to the United Nations
    Ambassador: Cheikh Niang.

Of Senegal to the European Union
    Ambassador: Amadou Diop.

Further Reading

Adams, A. and So, J., *A Claim in Senegal, 1720–1994.* 1996
Gellar, Sheldon, *Democracy in Senegal: Tocquevillian Analytics in Africa.* 2005
Phillips, L. C., *Historical Dictionary of Senegal.* 2nd ed, revised by A. F. Clark. 1995
National Statistical Office: Direction de la Prévision et de la Statistique, BP 116, Dakar.
Website (French only): http://www.ansd.sn

Serbia

Republika Srbija (Republic of Serbia)

Capital: Belgrade
Population projection, 2020: 8·70m.
GNI per capita, 2017: (PPP$) 13,019
HDI/world rank, 2017: 0·787/67
Internet domain extension: .rs

Key Historical Events

The Serbs were converted to Orthodox Christianity by the Byzantines in 891, before becoming a prosperous independent state under Stevan Nemanja (1167–96). A Serbian Patriarchate was established at Peć during the reign of Stevan Dušan (1331–55). Dušan's attempted conquest of Constantinople failed and after he died many Serbian nobles accepted Turkish vassalage. The reduced Serbian state under Prince Lazar received the coup de grace at Kosovo on St Vitus's Day, 1389. However, Turkish preoccupations with a Mongol invasion and wars with Hungary delayed the incorporation of Serbia into the Ottoman Empire until 1459.

The Turks tolerated the Orthodox church though the Patriarchate was abolished in 1776. The native aristocracy was eliminated and replaced by a system of fiefdoms held in return for military or civil service. Local self-government based on rural extended family units (*zadruga*) continued. In its heyday the Ottoman system was no harder on the peasantry than the Christian feudalism it had replaced, but with the gradual decline of Ottoman power, corruption, oppression and reprisals led to economic deterioration and social unrest.

In 1804, murders carried out by mutinous Turkish infantry provoked a Serbian rising under Đorđe Petrović (Karađorđe). By the Treaty of Bucharest (1812) Russia agreed that Serbia, known as Servia until 1918, should remain Turkish. The Turks reoccupied Serbia with ferocious reprisals. A rebellion in 1815 was led by Miloš Obrenović who, with Russian support, won autonomy for Serbia within the Ottoman empire. Obrenović had Karađorđe murdered in 1817. After he was forced to grant a constitution establishing a state council he abdicated in 1839. In 1842 a coup overthrew the Obrenovićs and Alexander Karađorđević was elected ruler. He was deposed in 1858.

During the reign of the western-educated Michael Obrenović (1860 until his assassination in 1868) the foundations of a modern centralized and militarized state were laid, and the idea of a 'Great Serbia', first enunciated in Prime Minister Garašanin's *Draft Programme* of 1844, took root. Milan Obrenović, adopting the title of king, proclaimed formal independence in 1882. He suffered defeats against Turkey (1876) and Bulgaria (1885) and abdicated in 1889. After Alexander Obrenović was assassinated in 1903 Peter Karađorđević brought in a period of stable constitutional rule.

Serbia's aim to secure an outlet to the sea was thwarted by Austria. Annexing Bosnia in 1908, Austria forced the Serbs to withdraw from the Adriatic after the first Balkan war (1912).

The assassination of Archduke Franz Ferdinand of Austria in Sarajevo on 28 June 1914 precipitated the First World War. In the winter of 1915–16 the Serbian army was forced to retreat to Corfu, where the government aimed at a centralized, Serb-run state. But exiles from Croatia and Slovenia wanted a South Slav federation. This was accepted by the victorious Allies as the basis for the new state. The Croats were forced by the pressure of events to join Serbia and Montenegro on 1 Dec. 1918. From 1918–29 the country was known as the Kingdom of the Serbs, Croats and Slovenes.

A constitution of 1921 established an assembly but the trappings of parliamentary rule could not bridge the gulf between Serbs and Croats. The Croat peasant leader, Radić, was assassinated in 1928; his successor, Vlatko Maček, set up a separatist assembly in Zagreb. Faced with the threat of his kingdom's dissolution, on 6 Jan. 1929 the king suspended the constitution and established a royal dictatorship, redrawing provincial boundaries without regard for ethnicity and renaming the country Yugoslavia. In Oct. 1934 he was murdered by a Croat extremist while on an official visit to France.

During the regency of Prince Paul, the government pursued a pro-fascist line. On 25 March 1941 Paul was persuaded to adhere to the Axis Tripartite Pact. On 27 March he was overthrown by military officers in favour of the boy king Peter. Germany invaded on 6 April. Within ten days Yugoslavia surrendered; king and government fled to London. Resistance was led by a royalist group and the communist-dominated partisans of Josip Broz, nicknamed Tito. Having succeeded in liberating Yugoslavia, Tito set up a Soviet-type constitution but he was too independent for Stalin who sought to topple him. However, Tito made a *rapprochement* with the west and it was the Soviet Union under Khrushchev that had to extend the olive branch in 1956. Yugoslavia was permitted to evolve its 'own road to socialism'. Collectivization of agriculture was abandoned and Yugoslavia became a champion of international 'non-alignment'. A collective presidency came into being with the death of Tito in 1980.

Dissensions in Kosovo between Albanians and Serbs, and in parts of Croatia between Serbs and Croats, reached crisis point after 1988. In 1988 the Serbian presidency fell to the nationalist Slobodan Milošević, who aimed at the creation of an enlarged Serbian state. On 25 June 1991 Croatia and Slovenia declared independence. Fighting began in Croatia between Croatian forces and Serb irregulars from Serb-majority areas of Croatia. On 25 Sept. the UN Security Council imposed a mandatory arms embargo on Yugoslavia. A three-month moratorium agreed at EU peace talks on 30 June having expired, both Slovenia and Croatia declared their independence from the Yugoslav federation on 8 Oct. After 13 ceasefires had failed, a fourteenth was signed on 23 Nov. under UN auspices. A Security Council resolution of 27 Nov. proposed the deployment of a UN peacekeeping force if the ceasefire was kept. Fighting, however, continued. On 15 Jan. 1992 the EU recognized Croatia and Slovenia as independent states. Bosnia and Herzegovina was recognized on 7 April 1992 and Macedonia (now called North Macedonia) on 8 April 1993. A UN delegation began monitoring the ceasefire on 17 Jan. and the UN Security Council on 21 Feb. voted to send a 14,000-strong peacekeeping force to Croatia and Yugoslavia. On 27 April 1992 Serbia and Montenegro created a new federal republic of Yugoslavia.

On 30 May, responding to further Serbian military activities in Bosnia and Croatia, the UN Security Council voted to impose sanctions. In mid-1992 NATO committed air, sea and eventually land forces to enforce sanctions and protect humanitarian relief operations in Bosnia. At a joint UN-EC peace conference on Yugoslavia held in London on 26–27 Aug. some 30 countries and all the former republics of Yugoslavia endorsed a plan to end the fighting in Croatia and Bosnia, install UN supervision of heavy weapons, recognize the borders of Bosnia and Herzegovina and return refugees. At a further conference at Geneva on 30 Sept. the Croatian and Yugoslav presidents agreed to make efforts to bring about a peaceful solution in Bosnia, but fighting continued. Following the Bosnian-Croatian-Yugoslav (Dayton) agreement all UN sanctions were lifted in Nov. 1995.

In July 1997 Slobodan Milošević switched his power base to become president of federal Yugoslavia. The former Yugoslav foreign minister, Milan Milutinović, succeeded Milošević as Serbian President. Meanwhile, in Montenegro, the pro-western Milo Đukanović succeeded a pro-Milošević president.

Following the break-up of Yugoslavia, in March 1998 a coalition government was formed between the Socialist Party of Slobodan Milošević and the ultra-nationalist Serb Radical Party.

Kosovo

In 1998 unrest in Kosovo, with its largely Albanian population, led to a bid for outright independence. Violence flared resulting in what a US official described as 'horrendous human rights violations', including massive shelling of civilians and destruction of villages. A US-mediated agreement for negotiations to proceed during an interim period of autonomy allowed for food and medicine to be delivered to refugees. American support for a degree of autonomy (short of independence), accepted in principle by President Milošević, lifted the immediate threat of NATO air strikes. Further outbreaks of violence in early 1999 were followed by the departure of the 800-strong team of international 'verifiers' of the fragile peace. Peace talks in Paris broke down without a settlement though subsequently Albanian freedom fighters accepted terms allowing them broad autonomy. The sticking point on the Serbian side was the international insistence on having 28,000 NATO-led

© Springer Nature Limited 2020
Palgrave Macmillan (ed.), *The Statesman's Yearbook 2020*,
https://doi.org/10.1057/978-1-349-95940-2_168

peacemakers in Kosovo to keep apart the warring factions. Meanwhile, the scale of Serbian repression in Kosovo persuaded the NATO allies to take direct action. On the night of 24 March 1999 NATO aircraft began a bombing campaign against Yugoslavian military targets. Further Serbian provocation in Kosovo caused hundreds of thousands of ethnic Albanians to seek refuge in neighbouring countries. On 9 June after 78 days of air attacks NATO and Yugoslavia signed an accord on the Serb withdrawal from Kosovo, and on 11 June NATO's peacekeeping force, KFOR, entered Kosovo.

When the general election held on 24 Sept. 2000 resulted in a victory for the opposition democratic leader Vojislav Koštunica, President Milošević demanded a second round of voting. A strike by miners at the Kolubara coal mine on 29 Sept. was followed by a mass demonstration in Belgrade on 5 Oct. when the parliament building was set on fire. On 6 Oct. Slobodan Milošević accepted defeat. He was arrested on 1 April 2001 after a 30-hour confrontation with the authorities. On 28 June he was handed over to the United Nations War Crimes Tribunal in The Hague to face charges of crimes against humanity. Prime Minister Zoran Žižić resigned the next day. On 12 Feb. 2002 the trial of Slobodan Milošević, on charges of genocide and war crimes in the Balkans over a period of nearly ten years, began at the International Criminal Tribunal in The Hague. However, Milošević's death in March 2006 from heart failure while in the custody of the Tribunal brought proceedings to a close.

On 14 March 2002 Serbia and Montenegro agreed to remain part of a single entity called Serbia and Montenegro, thus relegating the name Yugoslavia to history. The agreement was ratified in principle by the federal parliament and the republican parliaments of Serbia and Montenegro on 9 April 2002. The new union came into force on 4 Feb. 2003. The country's fragile political structures came under the spotlight on 12 March 2003 when the Serbian prime minister Zoran Đinđić, a key figure in the toppling of the Milošević regime, was shot dead on the stairway of Serbia's chief government building.

After 4 Feb. 2006 Serbia and Montenegro had the right to vote for independence. Following a referendum on 21 May 2006, Montenegro declared independence and was recognized as such by Serbia on 15 June. As a result of Montenegro's vote, Serbia's parliament formally proclaimed Serbia to be independent for the first time since 1918 on 5 June 2006.

Territory and Population

Serbia is bounded in the northwest by Croatia, in the north by Hungary, in the northeast by Romania, in the east by Bulgaria, in the south by North Macedonia and in the west by Albania, Montenegro and Bosnia and Herzegovina. According to the constitution it includes the two provinces of Kosovo and Metohija in the south and Vojvodina in the north. With these Serbia's area is 88,361 sq. km; without, 55,968 sq. km. Population at the 2011 census was (with Vojvodina but without Kosovo and Metohija) 7,186,862; population density per sq. km, 92·8. Population at the 2011 census without both Vojvodina and Kosovo and Metohija was 5,255,053. The population was 56·4% urban in 2011. June 2017 population estimate: 7,020,858.

The UN gives a projected population for 2020 of 8·70m.

The capital is Belgrade (2011 census population, 1,166,763). Populations (2011 census) of principal towns:

Belgrade	1,166,763
Novi Sad	231,798
Priština	200,000[1]
Niš	183,164
Kragujevac	150,835
Subotica	97,910
Zrenjanin	76,511
Pančevo	76,203
Čačak	73,331
Novi Pazar	66,527

[1]2011 estimate.

The official language is Serbian.

Social Statistics

In 2008 there were a total of 69,083 live births in Serbia (without Kosovo and Metohija), a rate of 9·4 per 1,000 inhabitants. There were 102,711 deaths (14·0 per 1,000) and 38,285 marriages (5·2 per 1,000). Population growth rate, 2005–10, –0·6%. Life expectancy in 2013 was 71·3 years for men and 76·9 for women. Infant mortality was 6 per 1,000 live births in 2010.

Climate

Most parts have a central European type of climate, with cold winters and hot summers. Belgrade, Jan. 1·4°C, July 23·0°C. Annual rainfall 687 mm.

Constitution and Government

A new constitution was approved in a referendum held on 28–29 Oct. 2006, with 53·0% of the electorate (and 96·6% of those voting) supporting the proposed constitution. It declares the province of Kosovo and Metohija an integral part of Serbia and grants Vojvodina financial autonomy. Kosovo Albanians were not able to vote. Turnout was 54·9%. The *President* is elected by universal suffrage for not more than two five-year terms. There is a 250-member single-chamber *National Assembly*.

National Anthem

'Bože pravde' ('God of Justice'); words by Jovan Đorđević, tune by Davorin Jenko.

Recent Elections

Presidential elections were held on 2 April 2017. Prime Minister Aleksandar Vučić (Serbian Progressive Party/SNS) was elected with 56·0% of the vote against 16·6% for Saša Janković (ind.), 9·6% for Luka Maksimović (ind.), 5·7% for Vuk Jeremić (ind.), 4·6% for Vojislav Šešelj (Serbian Radical Party/SRS) and 2·3% for Boško Obradović (Dveri). There were five other candidates who all received less than 2% of the vote. Turnout was 54·4%.

Parliamentary elections were held on 24 April 2016. The coalition led by the SNS won 131 seats (48·2% of the vote); the Socialist Party of Serbia–United Serbia–Greens–Communist Party (SPS–JS–ZS–KP) coalition, 29 (11·0%); the SRS, 22 (8·1%); Enough is Enough, 16 (6·0%); the coalition led by the Democratic Party (DS), 16 (6·0%). The remaining seats went to smaller parties. Turnout was 56·1%.

Current Government

President: Aleksandar Vučić; b. 1970 (SNS; sworn in 31 May 2017).

In Feb. 2019 the centre-right coalition government comprised:

Prime Minister: Ana Brnabić; b. 1975 (ind.; since 29 June 2017).

First Deputy Prime Minister and Minister of Foreign Affairs: Ivica Dačić. *Deputy Prime Minister and Minister of Interior:* Nebojša Stefanović. *Deputy Prime Minister and Minister of Construction, Transport and Infrastructure:* Zorana Mihajlović. *Deputy Prime Minister and Minister of Trade, Tourism and Telecommunications:* Rasim Ljajić.

Minister of Finance: Siniša Mali. *Economy:* Goran Knežević. *Agriculture, Forestry and Water Management:* Branislav Nedimović. *Environmental Protection:* Goran Trivan. *Mining and Energy:* Aleksandar Antić. *European Integration:* Jadranka Joksimović. *Justice:* Nela Kuburović. *Public Administration and Local Self-Government:* Branko Ružić. *Labour, Employment, Veteran and Social Affairs:* Zoran Đorđević. *Education, Science and Technological Development:* Mladen Šarčević. *Health:* Zlatibor Lončar. *Defence:* Aleksandar Vulin. *Youth and Sport:* Vanja Udovičić. *Culture and Media:* Vladan Vukosavljević. *Minister without Portfolio Responsible for Population Policy:* Slavica Đukić-Dejanović. *Minister without Portfolio Responsible for Regional Development and Co-ordination of the Work of Public Companies:* Milan Krkobabić. *Minister without Portfolio Responsible for Innovation and Technology:* Nenad Popović.

Government Website: http://www.srbija.gov.rs

Current Leaders

Aleksandar Vučić

Position
President

Introduction
Aleksandar Vučić became president in May 2017, having previously been prime minister since April 2014. Formerly a nationalist who served as minister of information in the Milošević government of the 1990s, Vučić

leads the centrist Serbian Progressive Party (SNS) and has promoted Serbian accession to the European Union.

Early Life

Born on 5 March 1970, Vučić graduated in law from the University of Belgrade and spent a further year studying in the UK. In 1993 he joined the nationalist Serbian Radical Party (SRS) and was elected to parliament, becoming a vocal supporter of ethnic Serb leaders during the war in Bosnia that ran from 1992 until 1995. In 1994 he became secretary general of the SRS, and in 1996 was appointed director of the publically-funded Pinki centre for sports and business in Belgrade.

From 1998–2000 he served as minister of information under President Milošević, introducing controversial curbs on press freedom, including fines for journalists who criticized the government and a ban on broadcasts by foreign radio and television networks. Following the SRS's defeat at the 2000 general election and the departure of its leader Vojislav Šešelj in 2003 to face war crimes charges, Vučić worked with deputy leader Tomislav Nikolić to steer the party away from its extreme nationalist position. In 2008 Vučić joined Nikolić's newly-founded SNS, becoming its deputy leader. Following victory for the SNS-led coalition in the 2012 general election, Nikolić won the presidency in May 2012. Vučić took over the party leadership in Sept. 2012, having been elected to the post unopposed.

From July 2012–Aug. 2013 Vučić was defence minister and first deputy prime minister under Prime Minister Ivica Dačić of the Socialist Party. Vučić also had responsibility for tackling corruption and crime. During this period, he led negotiations to normalize Serbian–Kosovan relations, agreement on which was a prerequisite for Serbia's accession to the EU. Shortly after formal accession talks began, Nikolić called a snap election with a view to winning the SNS a greater mandate. Vučić campaigned on pledges to combat corruption and boost the economy and won a landslide victory in March 2014.

Vučić renewed the SNS–Socialist coalition and was sworn in as prime minister on 27 April 2014. Domestically, he has faced the challenges of implementing austerity measures at a time of hardship, while also tackling corruption and meeting EU requirements on civil rights issues. Internationally, relations with neighbouring states remain delicate, with additional tensions in the traditionally close ties with Russia caused by Serbia's desire for EU membership. In Nov. 2014 the International Monetary Fund agreed a standby arrangement to bolster economic reform in Serbia. In the same month, against the backdrop of continuing bilateral tensions over the status of Kosovo, Edi Rama made the first visit by an Albanian prime minister to Serbia in nearly 70 years.

Like several other regional neighbours, Serbia was confronted in 2015 with an influx of foreign migrants—many from war-torn Syria—heading for the more prosperous northern EU countries. In Aug. Vučić maintained that he would not close Serbia's borders to refugees but called on EU leaders to frame a plan for dealing with the tide.

Seeking an early mandate to continue reforms required for EU membership, Vučić and the SNS claimed victory in parliamentary elections in April 2016 and resumed the government alliance with the Socialists.

Career in Office

Having won elections for the state presidency in April 2017 with 56% of the vote, Vučić stood down as premier on 30 May 2017 and was sworn in as president the next day. In June that year Vučić nominated Ana Brnabić as the new independent and pro-European Union prime minister at the head of a centre-right coalition government that was approved by parliament and sworn into office at the end of the month.

Ana Brnabić

Position

Prime Minister

Introduction

Ana Brnabić is the first female and openly gay prime minister to serve in Serbia. She has no party affiliation.

Early Life

Born on 28 Sept. 1975 in Belgrade, she studied business administration at Northwood University, Michigan, in the USA before gaining an MBA from the University of Hull in the UK in 2001. During her studies, she worked for the Serbian Information Centre in a public relations and administrative capacity.

Brnabić returned to Serbia in 2002 and worked briefly as an adviser to presidential candidate Miroljub Labus. She then worked as a public relations officer for the national agrarian development programme, co-ordinating local and international stakeholders, including international organizations, foreign investors, local self-government and the public sector in Serbia. From 2007 to 2010 she advised on developing Serbian regional co-operation with the United States Agency for International Development, along with other international organizations (including the European Union) and foreign governments.

In 2010 she became an executive director of the PEXIM Foundation, a private, non-profit organization supporting talented students from Serbia and Macedonia (now called North Macedonia) to study at the University of Cambridge in the UK. In 2011 she joined the US company Continental Wind Serbia, serving as director from 2013–15 and overseeing a €300m. investment in a wind farm in the municipality of Kovin. In 2016 she was named minister of public administration and local self-government, introducing an e-governance system designed to cut down on bureaucracy.

Career in Office

On 29 June 2017, Brnabić was sworn in as prime minister, having been nominated for the post by President Aleksandar Vučić. As a modernizer, she pledged to continue reforms needed for Serbia to gain accession to the EU, such as improving relations with Kosovo, as well as reforming the judiciary and promoting minority and gay rights.

Defence

Conscription was abolished with effect from 1 Jan. 2011. In 2013 defence expenditure totalled US$681m. (US$94 per capita), representing 1·6% of GDP.

Army

Strength (2011) 12,260 including 1,800 conscripts. Equipment in 2011 included 212 main battle tanks and 323 armoured infantry fighting vehicles.

Air Force

The Air Force and Air Defence had a strength in 2011 of 4,262 including 477 conscripts. There were 84 combat-capable aircraft in 2011.

Economy

Agriculture accounted for 9% of GDP in 2012, industry 30% and services 61%.

Overview

The economy contracted by over 3% in 2009 as a result of the global financial crisis, having enjoyed over 5% annual growth between 2005 and 2008, and averaged only a 0·4% per annum increase between 2010 and 2015. Unemployment rose from 11% in 2008 to 24% in 2011 but had fallen back to 20% by the first quarter of 2016. 8·9% of the population was living under the poverty line in 2014. With 90% of exports sold in Europe and 55% in the eurozone, ongoing eurozone instability has been an impediment to mid- to long-term economic health.

Government debt rose from 28% of GDP in 2008 to 73% in 2015, while foreign debt stood at 79% of GDP in 2014. The government aims to secure membership of the EU, with candidate status agreed in 2013.

Currency

The unit of currency of Serbia is the *dinar* (RSD) of 100 *paras*. On 1 Jan. 2001 Yugoslavia adopted a managed float regime. The National Bank of Yugoslavia began setting the exchange rate of the dinar daily in the foreign exchange market on the previous day. In Kosovo both the dinar and the euro are legal tender. Inflation was 1·1% in 2016 and 3·1% in 2017.

Budget

Revenues in 2014 totalled 1,551·6bn. dinars (of which tax revenue, 88·3%) and expenditures 1,739·1bn. dinars (of which current expenditure, 93·6%).

VAT is 20% (reduced rate 10%).

Performance

The economy grew by 0·8% in 2015, 2·8% in 2016 and 1·9% in 2017. Total GDP was US$41·4bn. in 2017.

Banking and Finance

The National Bank is the bank of issue responsible for the monetary policy, stability of the currency of Serbia, the dinar, control of the money supply and prescribing the method of maintaining internal and external liquidity. The dinar became fully convertible in May 2002. The present *Governor* of the National Bank of Serbia is Jorgovanka Tabaković.

Foreign debt amounted to US$32,222m. in 2010, representing 84·3% of GNI.

There is a stock exchange in Belgrade.

Energy and Natural Resources

Electricity

In 2011 installed capacity was an estimated 8·5m. kW. Production in 2011 was 38·60bn. kWh and consumption per capita 3,993 kWh.

Minerals

(Excluding Kosovo and Metohija, in 1,000 tonnes). 2012: brown coal and lignite, 38,587; copper ore, 14,346.

Agriculture

(Excluding Kosovo and Metohija). In 2007 the sown area was 3,095,006 ha. Yields in 2008 (in 1,000 tonnes): maize, 6,158; sugar beets, 2,300; wheat (2007), 1,864; potatoes, 844; plums, 607; sunflower seeds, 454; grapes, 373; soybeans, 351; barley (2007), 259; apples, 236. Livestock in 2009 (in 1,000): cattle, 1,002; pigs, 3,631; sheep, 1,504; poultry, 22,821.

Forestry

Forests covered 2·72m. ha. in 2015 (31% of the land area). Of the total area under forests 92% was naturally regenerated forest in 2015 and 8% planted forest. Timber cut in 2011: 7,706,000 cu. metres.

Fisheries

Total catch, 2012, 4,798 tonnes (all from inland fishing).

Environment

Carbon dioxide emissions from the consumption of energy in 2011 were the equivalent of 6·0 tonnes per capita.

Industry

Production, 2008 (excluding Kosovo and Metohija, in 1,000 tonnes): cement, 2,843; crude steel, 1,662; pig iron, 1,582. 2007: cotton fabrics, 19,557,000 sq. metres; woollen fabrics, 11,000 sq. metres; passenger cars, 9,400 units; trucks, 473 units.

Labour

In April 2010 there were 2,412,106 workers employed (without Kosovo and Metohija), including 549,816 in agriculture, forestry and water management; 405,485 in manufacturing; 346,038 in wholesale and retail trade and repair; 170,146 in health and social work; 148,943 in education; and 142,514 in transport, storage and communications. In April 2010 there were 1,582,455 employees and 641,712 self-employed persons. Average annual salary in 2009 (without Kosovo and Metohija) was 31,733 dinars. Unemployment in April 2010 (without Kosovo and Metohija) was running at 19·2%.

Serbia had 26,000 people living in slavery according to the Walk Free Foundation's 2013 *Global Slavery Index*.

International Trade

Imports and Exports

In 2007 imports (c.i.f.) totalled US$18,553·6m. (US$13,172·3m. in 2006); exports (f.o.b.), US$8,824·7m. (US$6,427·9m. in 2006). The leading import sources in 2007 were Russia (14·2%), Germany (11·8%), Italy (9·7%) and China (7·4%). Principal export markets in 2007 were Italy (12·4%), Bosnia and Herzegovina (11·8%), Montenegro (10·8%) and Germany (10·6%). The main imports are machinery and transport equipment, chemicals, petroleum, and iron and steel. Main exports are food and livestock, machinery and transport equipment, iron and steel, and chemicals.

Communications

Roads

The length of roads in 2007 was 39,184 km, including 374 km of motorway and 5,133 km of main roads. In 2007 there were 1,476,600 passenger cars in use, 162,900 lorries and vans, 24,900 motorcycles and mopeds, and 8,900 buses and coaches. There were 962 deaths as a result of road accidents in 2007.

Rail

Railways are operated by Železnice Srbije; total length of network in 2011 (excluding Kosovo and Metohija) was 3,809 km. In 2009, 8·4m. passengers and 10·4m. tonnes of freight were carried (without Kosovo and Metohija). In Sept. 2010 the state-owned railway companies of Serbia, Croatia and Slovenia announced the creation of a joint venture called Cargo 10 to improve the management of freight trains along the route known as Corridor 10 that passes through all three countries.

Civil Aviation

The national airline (and the former national carrier of Yugoslavia) is Air Serbia, known as Jat Airways until Oct. 2013. In Jan. 2010 it flew to 30 destinations in 23 countries. The main airport is Belgrade Nikola Tesla Airport, which handled 4,776,164 passengers and 13,067 tonnes of cargo in 2015.

Telecommunications

There were 3,110,300 landline telephone subscriptions in 2010 (383·0 per 1,000 inhabitants) and 9,915,300 mobile phone subscriptions (1,220·8 per 1,000 inhabitants). An estimated 40·2% of households had a computer in 2010 and 51·5% of the population were internet users in 2013. In March 2012 there were 3·2m. Facebook users.

Social Institutions

Out of 178 countries analysed in the 2017 *Fragile States Index*—a list published jointly by the Fund for Peace and *Foreign Policy* magazine— Serbia was ranked the 72nd least vulnerable to conflict or collapse. The index is based on 12 indicators of state vulnerability across social, political and economic categories.

Justice

In 2013 Serbia had a Constitutional Court, a Supreme Court of Cassation, four Appellate Courts, 25 higher courts and 66 basic courts. There were also one Administrative Court, one Commercial Appellate Court, 16 Commercial Courts, one Misdemeanour Appellate Court and 44 Misdemeanour Courts. Serbia was ranked 63rd of 102 countries for criminal justice and 72nd for civil justice in the 2015 World Justice Project *Rule of Law Index*, which provides data on how the rule of law is experienced by the general public across eight categories.

Education

In 2008–09 there were: 158,000 pupils and 11,000 teaching staff in pre-primary education; 282,000 pupils and 17,000 teaching staff in primary education; 604,000 pupils and 60,000 teaching staff in secondary education; and 236,000 students and 15,000 teaching staff in tertiary education.

Health

In the period 2007–13 there were 21·1 physicians for every 10,000 population and 2·3 dentistry personnel per 10,000.

In *Water: At What Cost? The State of the World's Water 2016*, WaterAid reported that 0·8% of the population does not have access to safe water.

Religion

Serbia has been traditionally Orthodox. Muslims are found in the south as a result of the centuries-long Turkish occupation. The Serbian Orthodox Church with its seat in Belgrade has five metropolitanates (including one covering Australia and New Zealand), 34 eparchies (dioceses) and one autonomous archeparchy. Its *Patriarch* is Irinej (enthroned 23 Jan. 2010).

Culture

World Heritage Sites

There are five sites on the UNESCO World Heritage List: Stari Ras and Sopoćani (inscribed on the list in 1979); Studenica Monastery (1986); Medieval monuments in Kosovo (2004 and 2006); and Gamzigrad-Romuliana, the palace of Galerius (2007).

Serbia shares the Stećci Medieval Tombstones Graveyards (2016) with Bosnia and Herzegovina, Croatia and Montenegro.

Press

In 2010 there were 12 daily newspapers (11 paid-for and one free). The most widely read newspapers are *Blic* and *Kurir*.

Tourism

In 2011, 764,000 non-resident tourists stayed in holiday accommodation (up from 682,000 in 2010 and 645,000 in 2009). There were 280 hotels in 2011, with 16,034 rooms and 25,841 beds.

Festivals

The National Day is 15 Feb. The two biggest music festivals are the Exit Festival (July) in Novi Sad and Guča Trumpet Festival (Aug.). Jazz festivals are held annually in Belgrade (Oct.) and Novi Sad (Nov.) Belgrade Summer Festival (BELEF) is held throughout July and Aug. and features theatre, music and art. FEST (the international film festival in Belgrade) is in Feb.–March and the International Theatre Festival of Belgrade (BITEF) takes place in Sept.

Diplomatic Representatives

Of Serbia in the United Kingdom (28 Belgrave Sq., London, SW1X 8QB)
Ambassador: Aleksandra Joksimović.

Of the United Kingdom in Serbia (Resavska 46, 11000 Belgrade)
Ambassador: Denis Keefe, CMG.

Of Serbia in the USA (2233 Wisconsin Ave., NW, Washington, D.C., 20007)
Ambassador: Đerđ Matković.

Of the USA in Serbia (Bulevar kneza Aleksandra Karadjordjevica 92, 11040 Belgrade)
Ambassador: Kyle Randolph Scott.

Of Serbia to the United Nations
Ambassador: Milan Milanović.

Of Serbia to the European Union
Ambassador: Ana Hrustanović.

Kosovo and Metohija

Key Historical Events

Kosovo has a large ethnic Albanian majority. Following Albanian-Serb conflicts, the Kosovo and Serbian parliaments adopted constitutional amendments in March 1989 surrendering much of Kosovo's autonomy to Serbia. Renewed Albanian rioting broke out in 1990. The Prime Minister and six other ministers resigned in April 1990 over ethnic conflicts. In July 1990, 114 of the 130 Albanian members of the National Assembly voted for full republican status for Kosovo but the Serbian National Assembly declared this vote invalid and unanimously voted to dissolve the Kosovo Assembly. Direct Serbian rule was imposed causing widespread violence. Western demands for negotiations in granting Kosovo some kind of special status were rejected. Ibrahim Rugova, the leader of the main Albanian party, the Democratic League of Kosovo (LDK), declared himself 'president' demanding talks on independence. In 1998 armed conflict between Yugoslavia and the Kosovo Liberation Army led 200,000 people, or a tenth of the population of the province, to flee the fighting. Further repression by Serbian forces led to the threat of NATO direct action. Air strikes against Yugoslavian military targets began on 24 March 1999. Retaliation against Albanian Kosovars led to a massive exodus of refugees. On 9 June after 78 days of air attacks NATO and Yugoslavia signed an accord on the Serb withdrawal from Kosovo, and

on 11 June NATO's peacekeeping force, KFOR, entered Kosovo. In Nov. 2001 the Organization for Security and Co-operation in Europe mounted elections for a provincial assembly that were deemed fair and democratic.

The worst fighting between Serbs and Albanians since the end of the war claimed 19 lives in March 2004. The following March President Ramush Haradinaj resigned when he was indicted to face charges of war crimes at the UN tribunal in The Hague. In 2006 the UN sponsored talks on the future status of Kosovo and ethnic Serbian and Kosovan leaders met for the first time since 1999. In Oct. 2006 Serbia held a referendum that approved a new constitution keeping Kosovo as an integral part of the country. However, the Kosovan Albanian majority rejected the poll. In Feb. 2007 the UN announced plans for Kosovo's eventual independence that were immediately rejected by Serbia and heavily revised in July 2007 after Russian protests.

In Nov. 2007 Hashim Thaçi's Democratic Party of Kosovo won elections that were boycotted by the Serb minority. On 17 Feb. 2008 Kosovo made a unilateral declaration of independence though international recognition was patchy. Independence was recognized by the USA and EU member countries including Germany, France and the UK. However, Serbia rejected the declaration as did Russia, while Spain refused to support it and China expressed 'grave concern'. As such, Kosovo lacks recognition as a sovereign country by the UN and the EU although on 22 July 2010 the UN International Court of Justice gave an advisory ruling that the independence declaration was legal.

In April 2013 Serbia and Kosovo reached an EU-brokered agreement. While not recognizing Kosovo as an independent state, Serbia conceded its legal authority over the territory. In return, four Serb-majority areas in the north of Kosovo were to be granted limited autonomy. Both Serbia and Kosovo agreed that 'neither side will block, or encourage others to block, the other side's progress in their respective EU paths'.

Territory and Population

Area: 10,887 sq. km. The capital is Priština. Censuses carried out in Serbia in 1991 and 2002 were not taken in Kosovo. The 1991 and 2002 censuses were not taken. According to the census of March 2011 the population was 1,780,021; density, 163 per sq. km. About 4% of the population are Serbs, mostly in the north of the country. Population of Priština, 2011, 145,149. Other major towns are Prizren, Gjilan, Peć and Kosovska Mitrovica. Dec. 2017 population estimate: 1,798,506.

Social Statistics

Statistics for 2011: live births, 34,262; deaths, 7,556; marriages, 17,343; divorces, 1,469.

Constitution and Government

The constitution of Serbia defines the autonomous province of Kosovo and Metohija as an 'integral part' of the territory of Serbia with 'substantial autonomy'.

In April 2008 Kosovo's 120-member multi-ethnic parliamentary assembly (first convened on 10 Dec. 2001) approved a new constitution, which came into force on 15 June 2008. Its promulgation followed Kosovo's unilateral declaration of independence from Serbia in Feb. 2008 as the Republic of Kosovo. The constitution envisages a handover of executive power from the UN, which has been responsible for administration in the region since 1999, to the majority ethnic Albanian parliament, under the supervision of an EU team. It also specifies that Kosovo will 'have no territorial claim against, and shall seek no union with' any other state. However, the constitution was rejected by Serbia as it considers Kosovo to be part of its sovereign territory, while Russia claimed any EU involvement would be illegal as it had yet to be approved by the UN Security Council. In June 2008 an ethnic Serb assembly set up a rival administration in Mitrovica. The UN referred the declaration of independence to the International Court of Justice in Oct. 2008.

Kosovo came under interim international administration on 10 June 1999, in accordance with the terms of UN Security Council resolution 1244. The United Nations Interim Administration Mission in Kosovo (UNMIK) administered Kosovo following the arrival of KFOR (NATO-led peacekeeping force) and remained in place even after the Feb. 2008 declaration of independence. The unilateral declaration received a mixed response from the international community, with Serbia, Russia and Spain prominent among those nations who refused to recognize it. In Dec. 2008 EULEX, the European Union Rule of Law Mission in Kosovo, took over responsibility from the UN for policing, justice and customs services, with the agreement of Serbia.

There is a 120-member multi-ethnic parliamentary assembly, which first convened on 10 Dec. 2001. The new assembly brought together representatives of Kosovo's ethnic Albanian majority and its Serbian minority for the first time in more than a decade. Of the 120 members, 100 are directly elected with ten seats reserved for ethnic Serbs and ten for other ethnic minorities.

Recent Elections

Parliamentary elections were held on 11 June 2017; turnout was 41·2%. An alliance of parties led by the Democratic Party of Kosovo won 39 seats with 33·7% of the vote, Self-Determination 32 seats with 27·5%, a coalition of parties led by the Democratic League of Kosovo 29 with 25·5% and the Serb List 9 with 6·1%. Nine other parties won two seats or fewer.

Hashim Thaçi was elected president by parliament on 26 March 2016, receiving 71 out of a possible 120 votes in the third round of voting.

Current Government

President: Hashim Thaçi; b. 1975 (ind.; since 7 April 2016).

Prime Minister: Ramush Haradinaj; b. 1968 (Alliance for the Future of Kosovo; since 9 Sept. 2017, having previously been prime minister from Dec. 2004–March 2005).

Head of EULEX Kosovo: Alexandra Papadopoulou (Greece; since 1 Sept. 2016).

Office of the President: http://www.president-ksgov.net

International Relations

As at Feb. 2019 Kosovo was recognized as an independent state by 102 of the 193 UN members.

Economy

Budget

General government revenue in 2016 was €1,622m. (€1,479m. in 2015) and expenditure €1,285m. (€1,201m. in 2015).

VAT is 18% (reduced rate, 8%).

Performance

Total GDP was US$6·7bn. in 2016. Real GDP growth was 3·2% in 2010, 5·2% in 2011 and 2·3% in 2012.

Banking and Finance

In Aug. 1999 the Deutsche Mark became legal tender alongside the Yugoslav dinar, and on 1 Jan. 2002 the euro became the official currency of Kosovo. The Serb dinar is also legal tender in Kosovo but is used only by ethnic Serbs.

Energy and Natural Resources

Electricity

Electricity production in 2015 was 5·50bn. kWh.

Minerals

Production (2010): lignite, 7,958,000 tonnes; limestone, 2,606,000 cu. metres.

Agriculture

Production in 2008 (in 1,000 tonnes): cereals (including rice), 438; vegetables, 176. Livestock, 2008 (in 1,000): cattle, 342; sheep and goats, 180; pigs, 27.

Forestry

Timber cut in Kosovo in 2007 was 192,000 cu. metres according to official data; however, significant illegal logging also takes place.

Industry

Production (2012): cement, 535,000 tonnes (estimate).

Labour

In 2009 the employment rate was 26·1% (39·7% among males but only 12·5% among females). Youth and long-term unemployment are very high, at 73% and 82% of all those unemployed in 2010 respectively. A standard monthly minimum wage of €170 was introduced in 2011.

Communications

Roads

In 2015 there were 2,013 km of main and regional roads in Kosovo. Total vehicle registrations in 2015 were 342,142.

Rail

Total length of railways in 2007 was 430 km, of which 97 km were freight only. In 2005 the state-owned Kosovo Railways was established to take over the running of railways from the UN Mission in Kosovo.

Civil Aviation

There is an international airport at Priština (Adem Jashari), which handled 1,527,134 passengers in 2012.

Telecommunications

At the end of March 2017 there were 1·77m. mobile phone subscriptions and 334,452 fixed telephone lines.

Social Institutions

Justice

In 2016 there were a Supreme Court, a Court of Appeals and seven basic courts with 20 branch courts.

Education

In 2011–12 there were 24,945 children in pre-schools, 294,419 pupils in primary and lower secondary schools, 109,513 in upper secondary schools, 782 in primary and lower secondary special schools and 133 in upper secondary special schools. There were six public universities in 2012, the oldest and largest of which is the University of Priština. There are also several private universities and colleges.

Religion

The population of Kosovo is predominantly Muslim.

Culture

World Heritage Sites

Kosovo and Metohija has one site on the UNESCO World Heritage List: medieval monuments in Kosovo (inscribed on the list in 2004 and 2006) that contain frescoes dating from the 13th through to the 17th century.

Vojvodina

After the Battle of Kosovo in 1389 Turkish attacks on the Balkans led to a mass migration of Serbians to Vojvodina. Turkish rule ended after the 1716–18 war with Austria and, in exchange for acting as frontier protectors, the Austrians granted Vojvodina religious autonomy. However, in 1848 a revolution led to a Serbian alliance with the Croats. Vojvodina was briefly declared an independent dukedom. After the First World War the territory became part of the first Yugoslav state and was later granted autonomy in 1974. In 1989 the Serbian government, led by Slobodan Milošević, stripped Vojvodina of most of its autonomous rights and secured Serbian control, but its autonomy was restored by statute in Dec. 2009 and Novi Sad was defined as the province's chief administrative centre. Vojvodina can establish representative offices in Europe with the consent of the Serbian government.

Area: 21,506 sq. km; population, 1,931,809 (2011 census: 1,289,635 Serbs; 251,136 Hungarians); density, 89·8 per sq. km. The capital is Novi Sad. Official languages: Serbian, Hungarian, Slovak, Romanian, Croatian and Rusyn.

President of the Assembly: István Pásztor.

Chairman of the Government: Igor Mirović.

Further Reading

Serbia

Anzulovic, Branimir, *Heavenly Serbia: From Myth to Genocide.* 1999
Cox, John, *The History of Serbia.* 2002

Judah, Tim, *The Serbs: History, Myth and the Destruction of Yugoslavia.* 1997

Pavolwitch, Stevan K., *Serbia: The History of an Idea.* 2002

Stojanovic, Svetozar, *Serbia: The Democratic Revolution.* 2003

Thomas, Robert, *Serbia Under Milošević: Politics in the 1990s.* 1999

Vladisavljević, Nebojša, *Serbia's Antibureaucratic Revolution: Milošević, the Fall of Communism and Nationalist Mobilization.* 2008

National Statistical Office: Statistical Office of the Republic of Serbia, 5 Milana Rakića St., 11000 Belgrade.

Website: http://www.stat.gov.rs

Kosovo and Metohija

Judah, Tim, *Kosovo: War and Revenge.* 2000

King, Iain and Mason, Whit, *Peace at any Price: How the World Failed Kosovo.* 2006

Malcolm, N., *Kosovo: a Short History.* 2nd ed. 2002

Vickers, M., *Between Serb and Albanian: A History of Kosovo.* 1998

National Statistical Office: Kosovo Agency of Statistics, Rr Zenel Salihu Nr 4, 10000 Priština.

Website: http://ask.rks-gov.net/en/kosovo-agency-of-statistics

Seychelles

Republic of Seychelles

Capital: Victoria
Population projection, 2020: 96,000
GNI per capita, 2017: (PPP$) 26,077
HDI/world rank, 2017: 0·797/62
Internet domain extension: .sc

Key Historical Events

The Seychelles were colonized by the French in 1756 to establish spice plantations to compete with the Dutch monopoly. The islands were captured by the English in 1794. Subsequently, Britain offered to return Mauritius and its dependencies (which included the Seychelles) to France if that country would renounce all claims in India. France refused and the Seychelles were formally ceded to Britain as a dependency of Mauritius. In Nov. 1903 the Seychelles archipelago became a separate British Crown Colony. Internal self-government was achieved on 1 Oct. 1975 and independence as a republic within the British Commonwealth on 29 June 1976.

The first president, James Mancham, was deposed in a coup on 5 June 1977. Under the new constitution, the Seychelles People's Progressive Front became the sole legal party. There were several attempts to overthrow the regime but in 1979 and 1984 Albert René was the only candidate in the presidential elections. Under the new constitution approved in June 1993, President René was re-elected against two opponents. He stood down in 2004 and was succeeded by James Michel.

Territory and Population

The Seychelles consist of 115 islands in the Indian Ocean, north of Madagascar, with a combined area of 455 sq. km (175 sq. miles) in two distinct groups and a 2010 census population of 90,945. July 2018 estimate: 96,800. The Granitic group of 40 islands cover 244 sq. km (94 sq. miles); the principal island is Mahé, with 160 sq. km (62 sq. miles) and 78,539 inhabitants (2010 census), the other inhabited islands of the group being Praslin, La Digue, Silhouette, Fregate, North and Denis, which together had 12,406 inhabitants in 2010.

The UN gives a projected population for 2020 of 96,000.

The Outer or Coralline group comprises 75 islands spread over a wide area of ocean between the Mahé group and Madagascar, with a total land area of 211 sq. km (81 sq. miles). The main islands are the Amirante Isles (including Desroches, Poivre, Daros and Alphonse), Coetivy Island and Platte Island, all lying south of the Mahé group; the Farquhar, St Pierre and Providence Islands, north of Madagascar; and Aldabra, Astove, Assumption and the Cosmoledo Islands, about 1,000 km southwest of the Mahé group. Aldabra (whose lagoon covers 142 sq. km), Farquhar and Desroches were transferred to the new British Indian Ocean Territory in 1965, but were returned by Britain to the Seychelles on the latter's independence in 1976.

Victoria, the chief town, had a census population of 26,450 in 2010. In 2011, 55·9% of the population were urban.

The official languages are Creole, English and French but 91% of the population speak Creole.

Social Statistics

2012 births, 1,645; deaths, 651. 2012 rates per 1,000 population, birth, 18·6; death, 7·4; infant mortality (2010), 12 per 1,000 births. Annual population growth rate, 2005–10, 0·9%. Life expectancy at birth in the period 2005–10 was 68·1 years for males and 77·3 years for females. Fertility rate, 2013, 2·2 births per woman.

Climate

Though close to the equator, the climate is tropical. The hot, wet season is from Dec. to May, when conditions are humid, but southeast trades bring cooler conditions from June to Nov. Temperatures are high throughout the year, but the islands lie outside the cyclone belt. Victoria, Jan. 80°F (26·7°C), July 78°F (25·6°C). Annual rainfall 95" (2,287 mm).

Constitution and Government

Under the 1979 constitution the Seychelles People's Progressive Front/SPPF (renamed the People's Party in 2009) was the sole legal Party. There is a unicameral People's Assembly consisting of 33 seats, of which 25 are directly elected by simple majority vote and eight are allocated on a proportional basis, and an executive *President* directly elected for a five-year term (with a maximum of three successive terms). A constitutional amendment of Dec. 1991 legalized other parties. A commission was elected in July 1992 to draft a new constitution. The electorate was some 50,000; turnout was 90%. The SPPF gained 14 seats on the commission, the Democratic Party, eight; the latter, however, eventually withdrew. At a referendum in Nov. 1992 the new draft constitution failed to obtain the necessary 60% approval votes. The commission was reconvened in Jan. 1993. At a further referendum on 18 June 1993 the constitution was approved by 73·6% of votes cast. The elections of 1993 were the first multi-party ones since 1974.

National Anthem

'Koste Seselwa' ('Come Together Seychellois'); words and tune by D. F. M. André and G. C. R. Payet.

Recent Elections

In parliamentary elections held on 8–10 Sept. 2016 the Linyon Demokratik Seselwa alliance won 19 seats with 49·6% of the vote and the People's Party 14 with 49·2%. Turnout was 87·5%.

In presidential elections held on 3–5 Dec. 2015 incumbent James Michel (People's Party) won 47·8% of the vote against Wavel Ramkalawan (Seychelles National Party) with 33·9%, Patrick Pillay (Lalyans Seselwa) with 14·2%, David Pierre (Popular Democratic Movement) 2·1%, Alexcia Amesbury (Seychelles Party for Social Justice and Democracy) 1·3% and Philippe Boullé (ind.) with 0·7%. Turnout was 87·4%. Michel won the second round run-off on 16–18 Dec. 2015 with 50·2% of the vote against Ramkalawan with 49·8%. Turnout in the second round was 90·1%.

Current Government

President: Danny Faure; b. 1962 (People's Party; took office on 16 Oct. 2016). The President is *Minister of Public Administration, Legal Affairs and Defence.*

Vice-President and Minister Responsible for Foreign Affairs, Information Communication Technology, Information, Blue Economy, and Industry and Entrepreneurship Development: Vincent Meriton.

In Feb. 2019 the government comprised:

Minister of Education and Human Resource Development: Jeanne Simeon. *Employment, Immigration and Civil Status:* Myriam Telemaque. *Environment, Energy and Climate Change:* Wallace Cosgrow. *Family:* Mitcy Larue. *Finance, Trade, Investment and Economic Planning:* Maurice Loustau-Lalanne. *Fisheries and Agriculture:* Charles Bastienne. *Habitat, Lands, Infrastructure and Land Transport:* Pamela Charlotte. *Health:* Jean-Paul Adam. *Home Affairs, Local Government, Youth, Sports, Culture, and Risk and Disaster Management:* Macsuzy Mondon. *Tourism, Civil Aviation, Ports and Marine:* Didier Dogley.

Office of the President: http://www.statehouse.gov.sc

© Springer Nature Limited 2020
Palgrave Macmillan (ed.), *The Statesman's Yearbook 2020*,
https://doi.org/10.1057/978-1-349-95940-2_169

Current Leaders

Danny Faure

Position
President

Introduction
Danny Antoine Rollen Faure of the People's Party (PP) became president in Oct. 2016 following the resignation of James Michel.

Early Life
Faure was born on 8 May 1962 to Seychellois parents in the western Ugandan town of Kilembe. Having earned a degree in political science in Cuba, he worked for the Seychelles People's Progressive Front (SPPF, later renamed the People's Party), becoming chairman of its youth wing and a member of the party's central committee. In 1985 he took a job at the Seychelles ministry of education and he also worked as a lecturer at the National Youth Service (NYS) and the Seychelles Polytechnic. In 1989 he became director of the NYS.

After the reintroduction of multi-party democracy in 1993, Faure became leader of government business in the National Assembly, serving in that capacity until 1998. In April that year he was appointed minister of education, adding the youth portfolio three years later. In 2006 he became finance minister and oversaw a raft of economic reforms recommended by the International Monetary Fund. Having become secretary general of the PP in 2009, in July 2010 he was named vice-president to James Michel (while remaining minister for finance and trade, public administration and information communication technology).

In parliamentary elections in Sept. 2016 the opposition Linyon Demokratik Seselwa alliance took control of the legislature from the ruling PP for the first time in the country's history. Michel announced his resignation later that month, with power transferring to Faure with effect from 16 Oct. despite opposition calls for fresh presidential elections.

Career in Office
Faure called for national unity and promised to work with the National Assembly, which for the first time no longer had a majority from the president's own party.

However, in Aug. 2017 and again in Nov. 2018 Linyon Demokratik Seselwa supporters took to the streets of the capital, Victoria, expressing their dissatisfaction with Faure and demanding his resignation.

Defence

The Seychelles People's Defence Force comprises all services. Personnel (2011) Army, 200; paramilitary national guard, 250; paramilitary coastguard, 200 including 80 marines.

Defence expenditure totalled US$12m. in 2013 (US$127 per capita), representing 1·0% of GDP.

Coastguard

The Seychelles Coast Guard superseded the former navy and air force in 1992. Based at Port Victoria it operates nine patrol and coastal combatants.

Economy

Trade and hotels contributed 22·4% to GDP in 2014; followed by services, 17·5%; transport and communications, 14·6%; finance and real estate, 9·9%; and manufacturing, 8·3%.

Overview

Tourism and fisheries are the main pillars of the economy. The Seychelles has access to one of the world's largest tuna fishing grounds, and tuna fishing and processing accounts for 5% of GDP, 7% of employment and 35% of exports annually. A further 25% of GDP comes from tourism, although this sector is dependent on an economic resurgence in Europe (the primary source of visitors to the Seychelles) for its mid- to long-term prospects.

Despite one of the lowest poverty rates in the world, the economy lacks diversification and relies on imported raw materials, consumer products and professional services. In 2015 imports were valued at 84·7% of total GDP. The lack of land, capital and human resources restricts the potential of the economy.

After the fiscal deficit and public debt levels reached 8% and 131% of GDP respectively in 2007, the government embarked on a process of reform and fiscal consolidation. Generous debt relief and tighter fiscal policy prompted accelerated growth. The government also sought to boost the private sector by limiting the role of the state in economic activities. However, infrastructure needs further investment, as does the education system where standards are low. In addition, climate change will likely have a dramatic future impact, with rising sea levels increasing the prospect of major flooding and threatening the fishery and tourism industries. Given its geographic constraints, greater integration with a wide range of larger countries is crucial to future economic development.

Currency

The unit of currency is the *Seychelles rupee* (SCR) divided into 100 *cents.* In July 2005 foreign exchange reserves were US$44m. and total money supply was 1,220m. rupees. There was deflation of 1·0% in 2016 but then inflation of 2·9% in 2017.

Budget

In 2015 (provisional) budgetary central government revenues totalled 6,349m. rupees (of which taxes 5,428m. rupees) and expenditures 5,346m. rupees. Main items of expenditure by economic type in 2015 (provisional): subsidies, 1,438m. rupees; compensation of employees, 1,209m. rupees; use of goods and services, 1,089m. rupees.

VAT at 15% was introduced on 1 Jan. 2013.

Performance

There was a recession in both 2003 and 2004, with the economy contracting by 5·9% and 2·9% respectively. A significant economic recovery occurred between 2005 and 2007, but real GDP growth was negative again in both 2008 and 2009. The economy has expanded every year since, with growth of 4·9% in 2015, 4·5% in 2016 and 5·3% in 2017. Total GDP was US$1·5bn. in 2017.

Banking and Finance

The Central Bank of Seychelles (established in 1983; *Governor*, Caroline Abel), which is the bank of issue, and the Development Bank of Seychelles provide long-term lending for development purposes. There are also six commercial banks, including two local banks (the Seychelles Savings Bank and the Seychelles International Mercantile Banking Co-operation or NOUVOBANQ), and four branches of foreign banks (Barclays Bank, Banque Française Commerciale, Habib Bank and Bank of Baroda).

External debt totalled US$1,510m. in 2010 and represented 176·7% of GNI.

Energy and Natural Resources

Environment

Carbon dioxide emissions from the consumption of energy were the equivalent of 13·9 tonnes per capita in 2011.

Electricity

Installed capacity on Mahé and Praslin combined was 89,000 kW in 2011. Production in 2011 was 324m. kWh and consumption per capita 3,528 kWh.

Water

There are two raw water reservoirs, the Rochon Dam and La Gogue Dam, which have a combined holding capacity of 1·05bn. litres.

Agriculture

Since the rise of the tourism industry in the 1970s there has been a general decline in the production of traditional cash crops. The main crops (2012 estimates, in tonnes) are coconuts (2,800), bananas (2,000) and tomatoes (400). The staple food crop, rice, is imported from Asia. Livestock, 2012 estimates: 5,500 pigs, 5,400 goats and 142,000 chickens. In 2013 there were approximately 80 ha. of arable land and 1,400 ha. of permanent crop land.

Forestry

In 2015 forests covered 41,000 ha., or 88% of the total land area. Of the total area under forests 5% was primary forest in 2015, 83% other naturally regenerated forest and 12% planted forest. The ministry of environment has a number of ongoing forestry projects that aim at preserving and upgrading the local system. There are also a number of terrestrial nature reserves including three national parks, four special reserves and an 'area of outstanding natural beauty'.

Fisheries

The fisheries sector is the Seychelles' largest foreign exchange earner. In 2006 it accounted for 52% of export revenue. Total catch in 2015 was 102,695 tonnes, exclusively from sea fishing. 2006 fish production (in tonnes) included: canned tuna, 40,222; fish landed, 4,050; crustaceans, 606. Fisheries exports in 2006 amounted to 1,096·8m. rupees, of which: canned tuna, 1,030·4m.; fish meal 25·1m.; frozen prawns, 23·7m.

Industry

The Seychelles has the largest tuna canning factory in the world; in 2015 canned tuna output totalled 32,068 tonnes. Mineral water production totalled 11·4m. litres in 2015. Other important activities include production of cigarettes (58m. in 2015), soft drink production, beer and stout production, paints and animal feed.

Labour

Some 76% of employed persons work in the services sector. In 2015, 9,093 people worked in accommodation and food service activities. In 2015, 33,344 were formally employed in the private sector, 9,317 in the public sector and 5,762 in the parastatal sector.

International Trade

Imports and Exports

In 2005 imports (c.i.f.) totalled 3,712·2m. rupees (2,731·8m. rupees in 2004); exports (f.o.b.), 1,868·6m. rupees (1,599·9m. rupees in 2004). Domestic exports constitute around two-thirds of exports and re-exports a third. Principal imports: mineral fuel; food and live animals; machinery and transport equipment; manufactured goods; chemicals. Principal origins of imports, 2005: Saudi Arabia (23·0%), Spain (7·8%), Singapore (7·6%), France (6·5%). Principal exports: canned tuna; petroleum products; medicaments and medical appliances; fish meal (animal feed); frozen prawns. Main export markets (for domestic exports), 2005: UK (45·4%), France (23·1%), Italy (12·4%), Germany (10·2%).

Communications

Roads

In 2006 there were 502 km of roads, of which 96·0% were surfaced. There were 6,800 private cars in 2006 (80 per 1,000 inhabitants), 2,600 commercial vehicles, 300 taxis and 215 buses.

Rail

There are no railways in the Seychelles.

Civil Aviation

Seychelles International airport is on Mahé. In 2010 Air Seychelles flew on domestic routes and to Cape Town, Doha, Dubai, Frankfurt, Johannesburg, London, Mauritius, Milan, Nairobi, Paris, Réunion, Rome, Singapore and Zürich. In 2013 it carried 356,000 passengers (188,000 on international flights). Seychelles International handled 650,928 passengers (517,542 on international flights) in 2012 and 4,500 tonnes of freight.

Shipping

The main port is Victoria, which is also a tuna-fishing and fuel and services supply centre. In Jan. 2014 there were 13 ships of 300 GT or over registered, totalling 297,000 GT.

Telecommunications

In 2013 there were 136,800 mobile phone subscriptions (equivalent to 147·3 per 100 inhabitants) and 21,800 fixed telephone subscriptions (23·4 per 100 inhabitants). In the same year an estimated 50·4% of the population were internet users.

Social Institutions

Out of 178 countries analysed in the 2017 *Fragile States Index*—a list published jointly by the Fund for Peace and *Foreign Policy* magazine—the Seychelles was ranked the 54th least vulnerable to conflict or collapse. The

index is based on 12 indicators of state vulnerability across social, political and economic categories.

Justice

The death penalty was abolished for all crimes in 1993. The population in penal institutions in June 2014 was 786, including 59 foreigners (giving a rate of 826 per 100,000 of national population, the highest of any country).

Education

Adult literacy was an estimated 91·8% in 2009 (91·4% among males and 92·3% among females). Education is free from five to 12 years in primary schools, and 13 to 17 in secondary schools. There are three private schools providing primary and secondary education and one dealing only with secondary learning. Education beyond 18 years of age is funded jointly by the government and parents. The University of Seychelles opened in Sept. 2009. In 2014 there were 662 teaching staff for 8,812 pupils in primary schools, 7,277 pupils at secondary level with 550 teaching staff and 478 students at tertiary level with 56 academic staff.

Public expenditure on education came to 6·6% of GNI in 2006 or 12·6% of total government spending.

Health

In 2012 there were 93 physicians, 14 dentistry personnel, and 419 nursing and midwifery personnel. The Seychelles had six hospitals in 2009 with 338 beds. The health service is free.

In *Water: At What Cost? The State of the World's Water 2016*, WaterAid reported that 4·3% of the population does not have access to safe water.

Welfare

Social security is provided for people of 63 years and over, for the disabled and for families needing financial assistance. There is also assistance via means testing for those medically unfit to work and for mothers who remain out of work for longer than their designated maternity leave. Orphanages are also subsidized by the government.

Religion

82% of the inhabitants are Roman Catholic, the remainder of the population being followers of other religions (mainly Anglicans, with some Seventh-day Adventists, Bahá'ís, Muslims, Hindus, Pentecostalists and Jehovah's Witnesses) or religiously unaffiliated.

Culture

World Heritage Sites

Entered on the UNESCO World Heritage List in 1982, the four coral islands of Aldabra Atoll protect a shallow lagoon. A heritage site since 1983, the Vallée de Mai Nature Reserve is a natural palm forest on the small island of Praslin.

Press

In 2008 there was one daily newspaper (circulation of 3,000), as well as three weekly papers.

Tourism

Tourism is the main foreign exchange earner. Visitor numbers were a record 208,034 in 2012, up from 194,753 in 2011.

Festivals

There are numerous religious festivals including Thaipoosam Kavadi, an annual procession organized by the Seychelles Hindu Kovil Sangam. Secular festivals include the annual Youth Festival, Jazz Festival, Creole Festival, Kite Festival and the Subios Festival, a celebration of the underwater world.

Diplomatic Representatives

Of the Seychelles in the United Kingdom (130–132 Buckingham Palace Rd, London, SW1W 9SA)

High Commissioner: Derick Ally.

Of the United Kingdom in the Seychelles (3rd Floor, Oliaji Trade Centre, Francis Rachel St., Victoria, Mahé)
  High Commissioner: Caron Röhsler.

Of the Seychelles in the USA and to the United Nations (800 Second Ave., Suite 400C, New York, NY 10017)
  Ambassador: Ronald Jean Jumeau.

Of the USA in the Seychelles
  Ambassador: David Reimer (resides in Port Louis, Mauritius).

Of the Seychelles to the European Union
  Ambassador: Beryl Samson.

Further Reading

Scarr, D., *Seychelles Since 1970: History of a Slave and Post-Slavery Society.* 2000
National Statistical Office: Statistics and Database Administration Section (MISD), P. O. Box 206, Victoria, Mahé. *Seychelles in Figures*
Website: http://www.nbs.gov.sc

Sierra Leone

Republic of Sierra Leone

Capital: Freetown
Population projection, 2020: 8·05m.
GNI per capita, 2017: (PPP$) 1,240
HDI/world rank, 2017: 0·419/184
Internet domain extension: .sl

Key Historical Events

The ancestors of the Bulom, Nalou, Baga and Krim people are thought to have been the earliest settlers in coastal Sierra Leone. The Kissi and Gola lived inland to the east and the Limba inhabited the foothills of the Wara Wara mountains from at least the 10th century AD. Following the break-up of the Malian empire in the late 14th century much of Sierra Leone was settled by the Mande whose domination and interaction with the original inhabitants gave rise to new ethnic groups, including the Vai and Loko.

The Portuguese mariner Alvaro Fernandez sailed into the Rokel estuary near present-day Freetown in 1447 and located a source of fresh water. The inlet became a trading post for Portuguese, Dutch, French and British explorers on their way to and from India. Having established plantations in America and the Caribbean, European colonists sought labour from the Atlantic slave trade, much of it centred on Sierra Leone. In 1672 British traders from the Royal African Company established trading forts along the coast, although they repeatedly came under attack from European rivals.

When Britain outlawed slavery in 1772 the government established Granville Town (later Freetown) as a home for freed slaves. In 1791 the Sierra Leone Company was founded as a trading concession, with Sierra Leone becoming a British crown colony in 1808. By 1850 more than 40,000 freed slaves, many of them from Nova Scotia and Jamaica, had settled in Freetown and surrounding areas, intermarrying with natives and Europeans to forge the 'Krio' culture. British administrators and Krio traders led expeditions inland in the late 19th century and on 21 Aug. 1896 the hinterland was declared a British protectorate, governed by Frederic Cardew. The early years of the 20th century saw the development of the country's interior while Lebanese merchants increasingly dominated business and trade.

Milton Margai became the prime minister in 1960 and led the country to independence on 27 April 1961. In 1967 Dr Siaka Stevens' All People's Congress (APC) came to power via the ballot box, despite an attempted military coup. Sierra Leone became a republic on 19 April 1971 with Stevens as executive president. Following a referendum in June 1978 a new constitution was instituted under which the ruling APC became the sole legal party.

On 28 Nov. 1985 Joseph Saidu Momoh succeeded Stevens as president. He presided over an economic collapse and the rise of the Revolutionary United Front (RUF). Under the leadership of Foday Sankoh (and with alleged links to the Liberian president, Charles Taylor), the RUF began taking control of diamond mines in the east of the country. President Momoh was overthrown in a military coup led by Valentine Strasser on 29 April 1992 and a National Provisional Ruling Council (NPRC) was set up, although it was unable to prevent the country's slide into civil war. By 1995 the RUF controlled much of the countryside and the NPRC sought assistance from foreign mercenaries.

The NPRC agreed to presidential and parliamentary elections in April 1996 to establish a civilian government. Ahmad Tejan Kabbah became president but was ousted in May 1997 by the Armed Forces Revolutionary Council, led by Maj. Johnny Paul Koroma. In Feb. 1998 a Nigerian-led intervention force (ECOMOG) launched an offensive against the military junta. On 10 March President Kabbah returned from exile in Guinea promising a 'new beginning' but in Jan. 1999 the country again erupted into civil war.

In July 1999 the government reached an agreement with the rebel movement to bring the civil war to an end. Under the terms of the accord, the RUF was to gain four key government posts along with control of the country's mineral resources in return for surrendering its weapons. However,

civil war resumed in early 2000 and, responding to a government appeal, British forces were sent to back up the UN peacekeeping force (UNAMSIL). Foday Sankoh was captured and handed over to UN forces in May 2000. In July 2001 the RUF formally recognized the civil government of President Kabbah. In Jan. 2002 Kabbah declared the war over. Re-elected in May 2002, he has been at the forefront of reconstruction efforts although corruption remains an obstacle to progress. The last UN peacekeeping troops left Sierra Leone in Dec. 2005.

Territory and Population

Sierra Leone is bounded on the northwest, north and northeast by Guinea, on the southeast by Liberia and on the southwest by the Atlantic Ocean. The area is 71,740 sq. km (27,699 sq. miles). 2015 census population, 7,092,113; density, 98·9 per sq. km. In 2011, 38·8% of the population were urban.

The UN gives a projected population for 2020 of 8·05m.

The capital is Freetown, with a 2015 census population of 1,055,964.

Area, population and capitals of the three provinces and one area at the time of the 2015 census:

	Sq. km	Census 2015	Capital	Census 2015
Eastern Province	15,553	1,642,370	Kenema	200,443
Northern Province	35,936	2,508,201	Makeni	124,634
Southern Province	19,694	1,441,308	Bo	174,369
Western Area	557	1,500,234	Freetown	1,055,964

A fourth province, North West Province, was created in 2017 from Northern Province. The provinces are divided into districts as follows: Kailahun, Kenema, Kono (Eastern Province); Kambia, Karene, Port Loko, Western Area Rural, Western Area Urban (North West Province); Bombali, Falaba, Koinadugu, Tonkolili (Northern Province); Bo, Bonthe, Moyamba, Pujehun (Southern Province).

The principal peoples are the Mendes (26% of the total) in the south, the Temnes (25%) in the north and centre, the Konos, Fulanis, Bulloms, Korankos, Limbas and Kissis. English is the official language; a Creole (Krio) is spoken.

Social Statistics

2008 estimates: births, 224,000; deaths, 88,000. Estimated birth rate in 2008 was 40·3 per 1,000 population; estimated death rate, 15·8. Annual population growth rate, 2000–08, 3·4%. Expectation of life at birth in 2013 was 45·8 years for females and 45·3 years for males (giving Sierra Leone the lowest life expectancy for females, for males and overall). The World Health Organization's *World Health Statistics 2014* put Sierra Leone in last place in a 'healthy life expectancy' list, with an expected 39 years of healthy life for babies born in 2012. Infant mortality was 114 per 1,000 live births in 2010 (the highest in the world). Fertility rate, 2008, 5·2 births per woman.

Climate

A tropical climate, with marked wet and dry seasons and high temperatures throughout the year. The rainy season lasts from about April to Nov., when humidity can be very high. Thunderstorms are common from April to June and in Sept. and Oct. Rainfall is particularly heavy in Freetown because of the effect of neighbouring relief. Freetown, Jan. 80°F (26·7°C), July 78°F (25·6°C). Annual rainfall 135" (3,434 mm).

Constitution and Government

In a referendum in Sept. 1991 some 60% of the 2·5m. electorate voted for the introduction of a new constitution instituting multi-party democracy. The constitution has been amended several times since. The president, who is both head of state and head of government, is elected by popular vote for not more than two terms of five years. There is a 146-seat *National Assembly* (132 members elected by popular vote and 14 filled by paramount chiefs).

There is a *Supreme Council of State (SCS)* and a *Council of State Secretaries.*

National Anthem

'High We Exalt Thee, Realm of the Free'; words by C. Nelson Fyle, tune by J. J. Akar.

Recent Elections

Presidential and parliamentary elections were held on 7 March 2018.

In the first round of the presidential elections, Julius Maada Bio of the Sierra Leone People's Party (SLPP) received 43·3% of the vote, Samura Kamara of the All People's Congress (APC) 42·7%, Kandeh Yumkella of the National Grand Coalition (NGC) 6·9%, Samuel Sam-Sumana of the Coalition for Change (C4C) 3·5% and Mohamed Kamaraimba Mansaray of the Alliance Democratic Party (ADP) 1·1%. There were 11 other candidates who received less than 1% of the vote each. Bio won the second round run-off on 31 March 2018 with 51·8% against Kamara with 48·2%. Turnout was 84·2% in the first round and 81·1% in the second.

In the parliamentary elections, the All People's Congress won 68 of the available 132 seats; the Sierra Leone People's Party, 48; Coalition for Change, 8; National Grand Coalition, 4; ind., 3. One seat remained vacant. In addition 12 seats were allocated for elected chiefs.

Current Government

President: Julius Maada Bio; b. 1964 (SLPP; sworn in 4 April 2018).

Vice-President: Mohamed Juldeh Jalloh.

In Feb. 2019 the government comprised:

Chief Minister: David Francis. *Minister of Agriculture and Forestry:* Joseph J. Ndanema. *Energy:* Kanja Sesay. *Finance:* Jacob Saffa. *Foreign Affairs and International Co-operation:* Alie Kabba. *Health and Sanitation:* Alpha Wurie. *Information and Communications:* Mohamed Swarray. *Internal Affairs:* Edward Soluku. *Justice and Attorney General:* Priscilla Schwarz. *Labour:* Adekunle King. *Lands, Housing and Environment:* Dennis Sandy. *Local Government and Rural Development:* Anthony Y. Brewah. *Marine Resources:* Emma Kowa-Jalloh. *Mines and Mineral Resources:* Morie Manyeh. *Planning and Economic Development:* Nabeela F. Tunis. *Political and Public Affairs:* Foday Yumkella. *Primary and Secondary Education:* Alpha Timbo. *Social Welfare, Gender and Children's Affairs:* Baindu Dassama. *Sports:* Ibrahim Nyelenkeh. *Technical and Higher Education:* Aiah Gbakima. *Tourism and Cultural Affairs:* Memunatu B. Pratt. *Trade and Industry:* Peter Bayuku Konteh. *Transport and Aviation:* Kabineh M. Kallon. *Water Resources:* Jonathan Tengbe. *Works and Public Assets:* Raymond Ernest Denison de'Souza George. *Youth Affairs:* Mohamed Orman Bangura. *Deputy Minister for Defence:* Brig. (retd) Simeon Sheriff.

Office of the President: http://www.statehouse.gov.sl

Current Leaders

Julius Maada Bio

Position

President

Introduction

Julius Maada Bio, a member of the Sierra Leone People's Party (SLPP), was sworn in as president on 4 April 2018, succeeding Ernest Bai Koroma.

Early Life

Bio was born on 12 May 1964 in Tihun in Southern Province. In 1987 he graduated from the Armed Forces military academy at Benguema, near Freetown, as a second lieutenant in the Army. His various deployments included tackling incursions on the border with Guinea, training with United Nations forces in aviation security, participating in the West African

peacekeeping force in Liberia and countering Revolutionary United Front rebels on the border with Liberia.

On 29 April 1992 Bio took part in a military coup that deposed the All People's Congress (APC) government of Joseph Saidu Momoh. Bio was appointed secretary of state for the South in the new administration under Capt. Valentine Strasser. He was later appointed secretary of state for information and broadcasting. On 16 Jan. 1996 he led a further coup that ousted Strasser. He then moved to the USA, where he took a master's degree in international affairs at American University, Washington, D.C.

Bio joined the SLPP in 2005, and in July 2011 was selected as the SLPP candidate for the presidential election in 2012. He lost the vote but returned for the 2018 contest, winning a run-off poll on 31 March with 51·8% of the vote against 48·2% for Samura Kamara of the APC.

Career in Office

Upon his election, Bio reached out to his opponents with a view to promoting national unity. Among his chief challenges were dealing with the aftermath of the Ebola virus outbreak, bolstering a fragile economy undermined by widespread corruption and a slump in world commodity prices, and increasing access to education. In Dec. 2018 the International Monetary Fund approved a new US$172m. loan programme for Sierra Leone to help the country combat rising inflation and the lacklustre economic outlook.

Defence

In 2013 military expenditure totalled US$14m. (US$3 per capita), representing 0·3% of GDP.

Army

Following the civil war, the Army has disbanded and a new National Army has been formed with a strength of 10,500.

Navy

Based in Freetown there is a small naval force of around 200 operating one patrol boat.

Economy

Agriculture, forestry and fishing contributed 49·0% to GDP in 2013; followed by mining and quarrying, 15·8%; services, 9·1%; and trade and hotels, 8·3%.

Overview

The economy has made substantial progress since the end of civil war in 2002. Real GDP grew annually by just over 7% on average between 2004 and 2007, aided by remittances and investments from citizens working abroad. Agriculture, mining, construction and the services sectors make up the bulk of the economy. Foreign aid has helped finance the current account deficit, while programmes such as the Poverty Reduction and Growth Facility (2001–04) have improved public finance management.

However, growth decelerated in 2008 and 2009 as a result of the global economic downturn. In June 2010, the IMF approved a three-year Extended Credit Facility to spur growth in the medium-term. Structural reform priorities include improving tax administration, broadening the tax base, developing deeper financial services and further strengthening public financial management. Social indicators remain poor, with the country ranked 184th of 189 countries in the 2017 *Human Development Index*. GDP growth has also been highly erratic, recording record growth of 20·7% in 2013 and a record contraction of 21·1% in 2015. Poverty is widespread, particularly in rural areas where 79% are estimated to live below the poverty line.

Currency

The unit of currency is the *leone* (SLL) of 100 *cents*. Inflation was 10·9% in 2016, rising to 18·2% in 2017. Total money supply in July 2005 was 346,027m. leones and foreign exchange reserves were US$94m.

Budget

In 2014 total revenue was 3,353bn. leones (22·1% grants and 21·5% income tax) and total expenditures 4,273bn. leones (59·7% current expenditures).

Performance

GDP per capita was US$154 in 2000 compared to US$389 in 1982, although it has since risen back up to US$590 in 2012. Owing to the persistent Ebola epidemic and the collapse of iron ore prices, the economy contracted by 20·5% in 2015 (the worst performance of any country that year). However, there has been a recovery since then with real GDP growth of 6·3% in 2016 and 3·7% in in 2017. Total GDP in 2017 was US$3·8bn.

Banking and Finance

The bank of issue is the Bank of Sierra Leone which was established in 1964 (*Governor*, Kelfala Kallon). There are four commercial banks (two foreign).

Foreign debt totalled US$778m. in 2010, representing 40·8% of GNI.

Energy and Natural Resources

Environment

Carbon dioxide emissions from the consumption of energy in 2011 were the equivalent of 0·3 tonnes per capita.

The *Climate Change and Environmental Risk Atlas 2014* produced by Maplecroft, a risk analytics company, ranked Sierra Leone as the country facing the third highest economic and social risk from climate change by 2025.

Electricity

Installed capacity was 77,000 kW in 2011. Production in 2011 was 176m. kWh; consumption per capita in 2011 was 30 kWh.

Minerals

The chief minerals mined are diamonds (estimated at 438,000 carats in 2010) and rutile (68,200 tonnes in 2010). There are also deposits of gold, iron ore and bauxite. The presence of rich diamond deposits partly explains the close interest of neighbouring countries in the politics of Sierra Leone.

Agriculture

In 2007 the agricultural population was an estimated 3·34m., of which approximately 1·26m. were economically active. Cattle production is important in the north. Production (2013, in 1,000 tonnes): cassava, 3,810; rice, 1,256; sweet potatoes, 225; palm fruit oil (estimate), 210; groundnuts, 86; sugarcane (estimate), 77. In 2007 there were an estimated 900,000 ha. of arable land and 80,000 ha. of permanent crops.

Livestock (2013): goats (estimate), 896,000; sheep, 851,000; cattle, 688,000; horses (estimate), 428,000; chickens, 13m.

Forestry

In 2015 forests covered 3·04m. ha., or 43% of the total land area. Timber production in 2011 was 5·74m. cu. metres.

Fisheries

In 2014, 206,477 tonnes of fish were caught (mainly saltwater fish).

Industry

There are palm oil and rice mills; sawn timber, joinery products and furniture are produced.

Labour

The labour force in 2013 was 2,373,000 (1,672,000 in 2003). 68·8% of the population aged 15–64 was economically active in 2013. In the same year 3·4% of the population was unemployed.

Sierra Leone had 45,000 people living in slavery according to the Walk Free Foundation's 2013 *Global Slavery Index*.

International Trade

Imports and Exports

Total trade for 2012: imports, 5,113,562m. leones; exports (f.o.b.), 4,871,105m. leones. Main imports are crude materials and manufactured articles; main exports are iron ore, rutile, diamonds, cocoa and bauxite. A UN-mandated diamond export certification scheme is in force. The Security Council has commended Sierra Leone's government for its efforts in monitoring trade to prevent diamonds from becoming a future source of conflict. The main import suppliers in 2012 were Benin (13·3%), UAE (12·2%), Senegal (9·2%) and Côte d'Ivoire (8·1%). Principal export markets in 2012 were China (33·3%), UK (15·0%), Eswatini (2·7%) and Belgium (2·1%).

Communications

Roads

There were 11,300 km of roads in 2007 (8% paved). In May 2016 Sierra Leone's first functioning traffic light since the end of the civil war in 2002 was installed. All of the country's traffic lights had been looted for scrap during the conflict. In 2007 there were 16,400 passenger cars in use and 14,100 vans and lorries. There were 71 deaths as a result of road accidents in 2007.

Civil Aviation

Freetown Airport (Lungi) is the international airport. The national carrier is Leone Airways, operated by Arik Air (a Nigerian airline) under a joint venture agreement. In 2012 scheduled airline traffic of Sierra Leone-based carriers flew 2·6m. km; passenger-km totalled 153·7m. in the same year.

Shipping

The port of Freetown has one of the largest natural harbours in the world. Iron ore is exported through Pepel, and there is a small port at Bonthe. In Jan. 2014 there were 291 ships of 300 GT or over registered, totalling 1·01m. GT.

Telecommunications

In 2009 Sierra Leone had an estimated 1,160,000 mobile phone subscriptions and 32,800 main (fixed) telephone lines. The country's telecommunications network was virtually destroyed during the civil war, but since then the sector has been one of Sierra Leone's main successes. In 2009 there were an estimated 2·6 internet users per 1,000 inhabitants.

Social Institutions

Out of 178 countries analysed in the 2017 *Fragile States Index*—a list published jointly by the Fund for Peace and *Foreign Policy* magazine— Sierra Leone was ranked the 38th most vulnerable to conflict or collapse. The index is based on 12 indicators of state vulnerability across social, political and economic categories.

Justice

The High Court has jurisdiction in civil and criminal matters. Subordinate courts are held by magistrates in the various districts. Native Courts, headed by court Chairmen, apply native law and custom under a criminal and civil jurisdiction. Appeals from the decisions of magistrates' courts are heard by the High Court. Appeals from the decisions of the High Court are heard by the Sierra Leone Court of Appeal. Appeal lies from the Sierra Leone Court of Appeal to the Supreme Court, which is the highest court.

The death penalty is in force, but has not been used since Oct. 1998. 59·0% of prisoners had yet to receive a trial according to 2014 estimates by the International Centre for Prison Studies. Sierra Leone was ranked 85th of 102 countries for both criminal justice and civil justice in the 2015 World Justice Project *Rule of Law Index*, which provides data on how the rule of law is experienced by the general public across eight categories.

The population in penal institutions in Sept. 2013 was 3,281 (52 per 100,000 of national population).

Education

The adult literacy rate in 2008 was 40%. Primary education is partially free but not compulsory. In 2010–11 there were 5,931 primary schools with 1,194,503 pupils and 38,125 teachers, and 1,096 secondary schools with 352,732 pupils and 17,194 teachers. As a result of the 2005 Universities Act there are now two universities. The University of Sierra Leone comprises Fourah Bay College, the College of Medicine and Allied Health Sciences, and the Institute of Public Administration and Management. Njala University, until 2005 a constituent college of the University of Sierra Leone, is now an autonomous institution.

In 2005 public expenditure on education came to 3·9% of GNI.

Health

Sierra Leone had 136 doctors, 1,017 nurses and midwives, and 114 pharmacists in 2014; and six dentists in 2010. There were four hospital beds per 10,000 population in 2006. The Ebola outbreak of 2014–15 resulted in 3,956 deaths.

In *Water: At What Cost? The State of the World's Water 2016*, WaterAid reported that 37·4% of the population does not have access to safe water.

Religion

According to estimates by the Pew Research Center's Forum on Religion & Public Life, 78·0% of the population in 2010 were Muslims (mostly Sunnis) and 20·9% were Christians (mainly Protestants).

Culture

Press

In 2008 there were ten paid-for dailies with an average circulation of 22,000, plus 40 non-dailies.

Tourism

Tourism is in the initial stages of development. In 2012 there were 60,000 non-resident tourist arrivals by air (32,000 in 2007).

Diplomatic Representatives

Of Sierra Leone in the United Kingdom (41 Eagle St., London, WC1R 4TL)
  High Commissioner: Tamba John Sylvernus Lamina.

Of the United Kingdom in Sierra Leone (6 Spur Rd, Freetown)
  High Commissioner: Guy Warrington.

Of Sierra Leone in the USA (1701 19th St., NW, Washington, D.C., 20009)
  Ambassador: Vacant.
  Chargé d'Affaires a.i.: Isatu Isha Sillah.

Of the USA in Sierra Leone (Leicester, Freetown IVG 798-5000)
  Ambassador: Maria E. Brewer.

Of Sierra Leone to the United Nations
  Ambassador: Francis Mustapha Kai-Kai.

Of Sierra Leone to the European Union
  Ambassador: Ibrahim Sorie.

Further Reading

Abdullah, Ibrahim, (ed.) *Between Democracy and Terror: The Sierra Leone Civil War.* 2004
Conteh-Morgan, E. and Dixon-Fyle, M., *Sierra Leone at the End of the Twentieth Century: History, Politics, and Society.* 1999
Ferme, M., *The Underneath of Things: Violence, History, and the Everyday in Sierra Leone.* 2001
National Statistical Office: Statistics Sierra Leone, A. J. Momoh Street, Tower Hill, P.M.B. 595, Freetown.
Website: http://www.statistics.sl

Singapore

Republik Singapura (Republic of Singapore)

Population projection, 2020: 5·94m.
GNI per capita, 2017: (PPP$) 82,503
HDI/world rank, 2017: 0·932/9
Internet domain extension: .sg

Key Historical Events

The first known written account of the island of Singapore was by a Chinese explorer in the 3rd century AD. In a strategic location at the tip of the Malay peninsula, the island is likely to have been a port of call for sailors navigating the Melaka straits, although there is no evidence of settlement until the town of Temasek was described in the 13th century. Temasek was controlled by the Srivijaya Empire, centred on Palembang in Sumatra, during the 14th century, before falling to the Javanese Majapahit Empire. When Sultan Iskandar Shah founded the Melaka Sultanate in the 1390s, he established a trading post on Singapore Island. After Portuguese forces sacked Melaka in 1511 the island came under the influence of the newly created Johor Sultanate. In 1613 Singapore's main settlement was burnt down by Portuguese raiders and the island slipped into obscurity, with the ports of Melaka and Johor dominating the lucrative shipping routes that linked Europe and India with China and the East Indies.

In 1819 Sir Thomas Stamford Raffles, an administrator of the British East India Company based at the garrison of Bencoolen (Benkulu) in southwest Sumatra, established a trading settlement on Singapore Island to challenge Dutch supremacy of the region's ports. Raffles negotiated a deal with the ruling Sultan of Johor and left Col. William Farquhar in charge of the new settlement which was designated a free port. It grew rapidly, attracting Chinese, Malay, Bugis and Arab merchants who wanted to avoid the trade restrictions imposed at Dutch-controlled ports. In Aug. 1824 claims to Singapore by Britain and the East India Company were confirmed in treaties with the Dutch government and the Sultanate of Johor. Two years later Penang, Melaka and Singapore were combined as the Straits Settlements. With the opening of the Suez Canal in 1869 and the advent of ocean-going steamships, an era of prosperity began for Singapore. Growth was fuelled by the export of tin and rubber from the Malay peninsula, facilitated by the construction of a railway linking Singapore with Bangkok.

On 15 Feb. 1942, after capturing Malaya from the British in less than two months, Singapore was occupied by Japanese troops. Britain's return after Japan's surrender in 1945 was accompanied by growing nationalist sentiment. Britain formed the Federation of Malaya, administered by a high commissioner in Kuala Lumpur, and a separate Crown Colony of Singapore with a civil administration. Elections in both states in March 1948 were followed by outbreaks of anti-British violence, with the ethnic Chinese-dominated Malayan Communist Party demanding immediate independence and equality for all races. The British responded to 'the Emergency' by imposing hard-line restrictions on left-wing groups. Nevertheless, there was a gradual move towards self-government in Singapore in the 1950s and in June 1959, following the victory of the People's Action Party in the first legislative elections, Lee Kuan Yew became Singapore's first prime minister.

Singapore joined the Federation of Malaysia when it was formed in Sept. 1963 but tensions soon rose and in Aug. 1965 the Malaysian prime minister, Tunku Abdul Rahman, expelled Singapore from the Federation. It became an independent republic, which, under the authoritarian leadership of Lee Kuan Yew, saw rapid and sustained export-driven growth. Lee's resignation in Nov. 1990 saw Goh Chok Tong become prime minister. He served until Aug. 2004, when Lee Hsien Loong succeeded him.

Territory and Population

The Republic of Singapore consists of Singapore Island and some 63 smaller islands. Singapore Island is situated off the southern extremity of the Malay peninsula, to which it is joined by a 1·1-km causeway carrying a road,

railway and water pipeline across the Strait of Johor and by a 1·9-km bridge at Tuas, opened in Jan. 1998. The Straits of Johor between the island and the mainland are 914 metres wide. The island is 721·5 sq. km in area, including the offshore islands. At the time of Singapore's independence in 1965 the area was 581·5 sq. km, but ongoing land reclamation has seen the area grow by over 20% since then.

Census of population (2010): Chinese residents 2,793,980 (74·1%), Malays 503,868 (13·4%), Indians 348,119 (9·2%) and others 125,754 (3·3%); resident population, 3,771,721. Estimated total population in June 2018 was 5,638,676. The population is 100% urban. Population density, 7,815 per sq. km.

The UN gives a projected population for 2020 of 5·94m.

Malay, Chinese (Mandarin), Tamil and English are the official languages; Malay is the national language and English is the language of administration.

Social Statistics

2013 births, 39,720; deaths, 18,938. Birth rate per 1,000 resident population, 2013, 9·3; death rate per 1,000 resident population, 4·6. Population growth rate in the year ended 30 June 2014, 1·3%; infant mortality, 2010, two per 1,000 live births (one of the lowest in the world); life expectancy, 2013, 79·8 years for males and 84·7 years for females. The World Health Organization's *World Health Statistics 2014* put Singapore in first place in a 'healthy life expectancy' list, with an expected 76 years of healthy life for babies born in 2012. Fertility rate, 2013, 1·3 births per woman (the joint lowest in the world). In 2010 the most popular age range for marrying was 25–29 years for both males and females.

Source: Singapore Department of Statistics

Climate

The climate is equatorial, with relatively uniform temperature, abundant rainfall and high humidity. Rain falls throughout the year but tends to be heaviest from Nov. to Jan. Average daily temperature is 26·8°C with a maximum daily average of 30·9°C and a minimum daily average of 23·9°C. Mean annual rainfall is 2,345 mm.

Constitution and Government

Singapore is a republic with a parliamentary system of government. The organs of state—the executive, the legislature and the judiciary—are provided for by a written constitution. The Constitution is the supreme law of Singapore and any law enacted after the date of its commencement, which is inconsistent with its provisions, is void. The present constitution came into force on 3 June 1959 and was amended in 1965.

The Head of State is the *President*. The administration of the government is vested in the Cabinet headed by the *Prime Minister*. The Prime Minister and the other Cabinet Members are appointed by the President from among the Members of Parliament (MPs). The Cabinet is collectively responsible to Parliament. A constitutional amendment of Nov. 2016 reserved presidential elections for particular ethnic groups if no one from a particular group has been president for five consecutive terms.

Parliament is unicameral consisting of 89 elected members and three Non-Constituency MPs (NCMPs), elected by secret ballot from single-member and group representation constituencies, as well as nine Nominated Members of Parliament (NMPs) who are appointed for a term of two and a half years on the recommendation of a Special Select Committee of Parliament. With the customary exception of those serving criminal sentences, all citizens over 21 are eligible to vote. Voting in an election is compulsory. Group representation constituencies may return up to six Members of Parliament (four before 1996), one of whom must be from the Malay community, the Indian or other minority communities. To ensure representation of parties not in the government, provision is made for the appointment of three (or up to a maximum of six) NCMPs. The number of NCMPs is reduced by

© Springer Nature Limited 2020
Palgrave Macmillan (ed.), *The Statesman's Yearbook 2020*,
https://doi.org/10.1057/978-1-349-95940-2_171

one for each opposition candidate returned. There is a common roll without communal electorates.

A Presidential Council to consider and report on minorities' rights was established in 1970. The particular function of this council is to draw attention to any bill or to any subsidiary legislation which, in its opinion, discriminates against any racial or religious community.

Salaries for leading Singaporean politicians are the highest in the world. In 2017 the prime minister's salary was S$2·2m. (US$1·6m.)—four times that of President Donald Trump.

National Anthem

'Majulah Singapura' ('Onward Singapore'); words and tune by Zubir Said.

Government Chronology

Prime Ministers since 1959. (PAP = People's Action Party)

1959–90	PAP	Lee Kuan Yew
1990–2004	PAP	Goh Chok Tong
2004–	PAP	Lee Hsien Loong

Recent Elections

In parliamentary elections held on 11 Sept. 2015 the ruling People's Action Party (PAP) won 83 of 89 seats (with 69·9% of votes cast). The Workers' Party took six seats (12·5%). Seven other parties failed to gain any seats.

The 2017 presidential elections were Singapore's first reserved elections. After a constitutional amendment of Nov. 2016 only candidates from the Malay community were to run for the election. On 13 Sept. 2017 Halimah Yacob was declared president; she was the only candidate to be declared eligible by the Presidential Elections Committee.

Current Government

President: Halimah Yacob; b. 1954 (sworn in 14 Sept. 2017).

In Feb. 2019 the cabinet comprised:

Prime Minister: Lee Hsien Loong; b. 1952 (PAP; sworn in 12 Aug. 2004).

Deputy Prime Ministers: Teo Chee Hean (*Co-ordinating Minister for National Security*); Tharman Shanmugaratnam (*Co-ordinating Minister for Economic and Social Policies*).

Minister for Communications and Information: S. Iswaran. *Culture, Community and Youth:* Grace Fu Hai Yien. *Defence:* Ng Eng Hen. *Education:* Ong Ye Kung. *Environment and Water Resources:* Masagos Zulkifli. *Finance:* Heng Swee Keat. *Foreign Affairs:* Vivian Balakrishnan. *Health:* Gan Kim Yong. *Home Affairs and Law:* K. Shanmugam. *Manpower:* Josephine Teo. *National Development:* Lawrence Wong. *Social and Family Development:* Desmond Lee. *Trade and Industry:* Chan Chun Sing. *Transport and Co-ordinating Minister for Infrastructure:* Khaw Boon Wan. *Ministers in the Prime Minister's Office:* Ng Chee Meng; Indranee Thurai Rajah

Government Website: http://www.gov.sg

Current Leaders

Lee Hsien Loong
Position
Prime Minister

Introduction
When Lee Hsien Loong was sworn in as prime minister of Singapore on 12 Aug. 2004, it was only the second time the southeast Asian city-state had changed its leader since independence in the 1960s. His father, Lee Kuan Yew, was the country's charismatic leader for 31 years and oversaw a transformation from a third-world colony to a prosperous export-driven economy. Lee Hsien Loong, a former military strategist-turned-politician, pledged to sustain the vibrant economy while maintaining a cohesive society. In Sept. 2015 his People's Action Party won parliamentary elections for the 12th successive time since independence.

Early Life
Lee Hsien Loong was born in Singapore on 10 Feb. 1952, the eldest son of a wealthy and well-connected Hakka-Chinese family. His father, Lee Kuan Yew, was Singapore's first prime minister, and led the former British colony as head of the People's Action Party (PAP) from its first period of self-governance in 1959, through independence in 1965, until 1990. Lee Hsien Loong attended state primary and secondary schools in Singapore, and was awarded a president's scholarship to study mathematics and computer science at Cambridge University in England. He graduated in 1974 with first class honours and returned to serve in the Singapore Armed Forces, rising through the ranks to become a Brig.-Gen. He gained a reputation for his analytical and problem-solving skills. He entered politics as an MP representing the PAP in the general election of Sept. 1984. The election was the first occasion since 1963 that two opposition parties—the Workers' Party and the Singapore Democratic Party—were able to win seats from the ruling PAP. Lee was elected to the Central Executive Committee of the PAP in 1986.

Lee Kuan Yew resigned in Nov. 1990 after 31 years in power and Goh Chok Tong became prime minister, appointing Lee Hsien Loong his deputy with responsibility for economic and civil service affairs. After three decades of authoritarian rule, Singapore underwent a cautious liberalization. Lee held his parliamentary seat in the 1991 and 1997 general elections, which were landslide victories for the PAP. In Jan. 1998 he was appointed chairman of the Monetary Authority of Singapore. When, in line with other southeast Asian economies, Singapore faced an economic downturn in 1998, the government responded by cutting wages, allowing its currency to adjust downward and positioning the country as a leading international financial centre. Despite continued economic pressures, the PAP won the 2001 general election by a large majority. Lee was re-elected, and was appointed minister of finance in Nov. 2001. He pursued a tax-cutting agenda and brought in pension reforms and policies to liberalize the financial sector.

Career in Office
On 12 Aug. 2004 Lee was sworn in as prime minister, handing the chairmanship of the Monetary Authority to Goh Chok Tong who became senior minister in the cabinet. Lee said his goal was to build a vibrant and competitive economy and he pledged to maintain the open, consultative style of the Goh Chok Tong era. He also signalled that social liberalization would continue, reflecting the demands of a highly-educated and increasingly less tractable population, as well as the government's realization that Singapore must move beyond manufacturing into 'knowledge-based' industries that depend more on individual creativity and entrepreneurship.

In April 2005 Lee announced his government's controversial decision to legalize gambling, paving the way for the building of two large casino resorts and perhaps hinting at a more permissive atmosphere within the country. Nevertheless, in 2007 parliament voted against a proposal to decriminalize sex between men, and international appeals for clemency failed to prevent the execution of two Nigerians for drug smuggling.

Singapore's usually fraught relations with neighbouring Malaysia improved in Jan. 2005 when the two countries settled a dispute over land reclamation work in their border waters.

In the first electoral test since his appointment in 2004, Lee's party won the May 2006 parliamentary elections overwhelmingly. In 2008 his government's budget included tax incentives to enhance business competition, but Singapore's export-led economy was one of the first in Asia to feel the impact of the global financial downturn. In Jan. 2009 the government announced a S$20·5bn. stimulus package to bolster the economy and by July that year the country was emerging from its deepest recession on record.

In May 2011 the PAP was re-elected with a large majority but with a lower share of the popular vote, which opposition parties portrayed as a significant shift in the political landscape. The first ethnic rioting in the country in decades broke out in Dec. 2013, sparked by the death of an immigrant Indian worker in a traffic incident. Lee was re-elected as prime minister in Sept. 2015 following the success of the PAP with another unassailable majority in parliamentary elections held the same month. In Dec. 2016 the government announced that only ethnic Malays would be permitted to contest the 2017 elections for Singapore's largely ceremonial post of president, which were subsequently won in Sept. by Halimah Yacob who became the first female to hold the office.

A major cabinet reshuffle in April 2018 saw younger PAP political figures take the helm of nearly two-thirds of government ministries, fuelling speculation about the likely identity of Lee's eventual successor as prime minister after the next general election.

Defence

Compulsory military service in peacetime for all male citizens and permanent residents was introduced in 1967. The period of service is 22 to 24 months. Reserve liability continues to age 50 for officers, 40 for other ranks. In 2011 the SAF (Singapore Armed Forces) comprised 312,500 Operationally Ready National Servicemen and an estimated 72,500 regulars and Full-Time National Servicemen.

An agreement with the USA in Nov. 1990 provided for an increase in US use of naval and air force facilities.

Singapore is a member of the Five Powers Defence Arrangement, with Australia, New Zealand, Malaysia and the UK.

In 2013 defence expenditure totalled US$9,864m. (US$1,807 per capita—the highest of any Asian country), representing 3·4% of GDP.

Army

Strength (2011) 50,000 (including 35,000 conscripts) plus 300,000 reserves. Paramilitary forces consist of a Civil Defence Force (61,300 active personnel in 2011 including approximately 54,000 volunteers, plus 23,000 reservists), a Singapore Police Force (12,000 active personnel in 2011, plus 21,000 reservists) and a Singapore Gurkha Contingent (1,800 personnel in 2011).

Navy

The Republic of Singapore Navy comprises five commands: Fleet, Maritime Security Task Force, Maritime Training and Doctrine Command, Naval Logistics Command and Naval Diving Unit. The fleet includes five diesel submarines. The Navy numbers an estimated 9,000 personnel (1,800 conscripts, 2,200 regulars and 5,000 active reservists). There are two naval bases: Tuas Naval Base and Changi Naval Base.

Air Force

The Republic of Singapore Air Force (RSAF) has fighter squadrons comprising the F-16 Fighting Falcon, the F-15 Strike Eagle and the F5S/T Tiger.

Personnel strength (2011) about 13,500 (3,000 conscripts). Equipment includes 148 combat-capable aircraft and 19 attack helicopters.

Economy

Services accounted for 73% of GDP in 2012 and industry 27%.

According to the anti-corruption organization Transparency International, Singapore ranked equal third in the world in a 2018 survey of the countries with the least corruption in business and government. It received 85 out of 100 in the annual index.

Overview

Singapore had the second most competitive economy in the world in 2015 according to the World Economic Forum. A booming free-market and strong macro-economic management resulted in growth averaging 8·6% annually between 2004 and 2007. The global financial crisis then prompted a contraction of 0·6% in 2009, representing the biggest output decline in 20 years. Having rebounded strongly in 2010 as a result of high foreign demand for electronic exports, growth slowed again from 2011 to average 4% per year up to 2015.

Singapore is also the busiest port in the world. The workforce is highly skilled and educated, although foreign labour has been encouraged because of the low indigenous birth rate. Electronic manufacturing and financial services are the main drivers of growth; 28% of the population was employed in manufacturing and 72% in services in 2015. The government has encouraged business creation via a favourable tax regime and a regulatory system that sees the average start-up taking only three days to establish. The trade-to-GDP ratio is one of the highest in the world, at 326·1% in 2015, and the economy has one of the highest *per capita* gross national incomes, measuring US$80,270 in 2015. In March 2018 Singapore and ten other countries bordering the Pacific (although not the USA) signed the Comprehensive and Progressive Agreement for Trans-Pacific Partnership.

Currency

The unit of currency is the *Singapore dollar* (SGD) of 100 *cents*. It is managed against a basket of currencies of Singapore's main trading partners.

In Aug. 2009 foreign exchange reserves totalled US$174,606m. and total money supply was S$89,258m. Inflation rates (based on IMF statistics):

2008	2009	2010	2011	2012	2013	2014	2015	2016	2017
6·6%	0·6%	2·8%	5·2%	4·6%	2·4%	1·0%	−0·5%	−0·5%	0·6%

Budget

The fiscal year begins on 1 April. In 2016–17 budgetary central government revenue totalled S$78,511m. (S$74,244m. in 2015–16) and expenditure S$69,106m. (S$72,244m. in 2015–16).

Principal sources of revenue in 2016–17 were: taxes on income, profits and capital gains, S$26,378m.; taxes on goods and services, S$18,639m.; taxes on property, S$4,360m. Main items of expenditure by economic type in 2016–17: grants, S$15,297m.; social benefits, S$14,902m.; use of goods and services, S$14,412m.

There is a Goods and Services Tax (GST) of 7%.

Performance

Real GDP growth rates (based on IMF statistics):

2008	2009	2010	2011	2012	2013	2014	2015	2016	2017
1·8%	−0·6%	15·2%	6·4%	4·1%	5·1%	3·9%	2·2%	2·4%	3·6%

Total GDP was US$323·9bn. in 2017. Singapore was ranked third in the World Economic Forum's *Global Competitiveness Report 2017–2018* index. The index analyses 12 areas of competitiveness for over 100 countries including macroeconomy, higher education and training, institutions, innovation and infrastructure. In the 2018 *World Competitiveness Yearbook*, compiled by the International Institute for Management Development, Singapore came third in the world ranking. This annual publication ranks and analyses how a nation's business environment creates and sustains the competitiveness of enterprises.

Banking and Finance

The Monetary Authority of Singapore (*Chairman*, Tharman Shanmugaratnam) performs the functions of a central bank, except the issuing of currency which is the responsibility of the Board of the Commissioners of Currency.

The Development Bank of Singapore and POSB (formerly the Post Office Savings Bank) were merged in 1998 to become the largest bank in southeast Asia and one of the leading banks in Asia. In 2003 the company was rebranded as DBS Bank although POSB still operates as a recognizable brand within the enterprise with a customer base of over 3·2m. in Singapore in 2009. Customer deposits at DBS Bank totalled S$183·9bn. in the second quarter of 2010 and total assets S$276·3bn.

In Oct. 2010 there were 120 commercial banks in Singapore, of which seven were local. There were 31 representative offices, 26 foreign banks with full licences, 49 with 'wholesale' licences and 38 with 'offshore' licences. The total assets/liabilities amounted to S$749,703·1m. in July 2010. Total deposits of non-bank customers in July 2010 amounted to S$408,837·5m. and loans and advances including bills financing totalled S$298,693·2m. There were 46 merchant banks in Oct. 2010.

Gross external debt amounted to US$1,113,298m. in June 2012.

In 2017 Singapore received US$62·0bn. worth of foreign direct investment, down from a record US$77·5bn. in 2016.

The Singapore Exchange (SGX), a merger of the Stock Exchange of Singapore and the Singapore International Monetary Exchange, was officially launched on 1 Dec. 1999.

Energy and Natural Resources

Environment

Singapore's carbon dioxide emissions from the consumption of energy in 2011 were the equivalent of 39·2 tonnes per capita.

Electricity

Installed capacity was an estimated 10·2m. kW in 2011. Production (2011) 45,994m. kWh. Consumption per capita (2011) 8,858 kWh.

Oil and Gas

Replacing the Kallang Gasworks, the Senoko Gasworks started operations in Oct. 1996. It had a total gas production capacity of 1·6m. cu. metres per day.

In Jan. 2001 a 640-km gas pipeline linking Indonesia's West Natuna field with Singapore came on stream. It is expected to provide Singapore with US$8bn. worth of natural gas over a 20-year period.

Water

Singapore uses an average of 1·25m. cu. metres of water per day. Singapore's water supply comes from local sources and sources in Johor, Malaysia. The total water supply system comprises 19 raw water reservoirs, nine treatment works, 15 storage or service reservoirs and 5,150 km of pipelines.

Agriculture

Only about 0·9% of the total area is used for farming. Most of the food consumed has to be imported. 21,785 tonnes of vegetables, 6,775 tonnes of seafood and 438m. hen's eggs were produced in 2013. In the same year Singapore imported 182,123 tonnes of chicken, 104,554 tonnes of pork, 140,348 tonnes of fish and other seafood, 514,574 tonnes of vegetables, 414,774 tonnes of fruit and 1·25bn. hen's eggs.

Agro-technology parks house large-scale intensive farms to improve production of fresh food. A total of 1,465 ha. of land in Murai, Sungei Tengah, Nee Soon, Loyang, Mandai and Lim Chu Kang had been developed into Agro-technology Parks. As at Sept. 2010, 704 ha. had been allocated to 227 farms for the production of livestock, eggs, milk, aquarium and food fish, vegetables, fruits, orchids, ornamental and aquatic plants, as well as for the breeding of birds and dogs.

Forestry

In 2015 forests covered 16,000 ha., or 23% of the total land area.

Fisheries

The total catch in 2015 amounted to 1,265 tonnes. Imports of fishery commodities were valued at US$807·0m. in 2009.

Industry

The leading companies by market capitalization in Singapore in May 2018 were: DBS Group, a banking and financial services corporation (US$56·6bn.); Singtel, a telecommunications company (US$43·3bn.); and OCBC Bank (US$41·2bn.).

The largest industrial area is at Jurong. In 2007 there were an estimated 160,000 enterprises of which 99% were small and medium enterprises (SMEs). Only about 5% of SMEs are in the manufacturing sector but they generated 17% of SMEs' value-added in 2007.

Output, 2009 (in S$1m.), totalled 213,699·8: including electronic products and components, 67,226·1; refined petroleum products, 31,860·3; chemicals and chemical products, 25,873·3; machinery and equipment, 18,922·7; pharmaceutical products, 18,093·9; transport equipment, 16,431·7; fabricated metal products, 8,185·8; food, beverages and tobacco, 6,637·2.

According to the World Bank's *Doing Business 2018* Singapore is the second easiest country in which to do business and the sixth easiest in which to start a business.

Labour

The labour force in 2013 was 3,067,000 (2,105,000 in 2003). 73·7% of the population aged 15–64 was economically active in 2013. In the same year 2·8% of the population was unemployed. Of those in employment in 2013, 80·1% worked in services and 18·6% in industry. In that year 44·2% of the labour force was female. 30·3% of the labour force had a secondary education as the highest level and 49·9% had a tertiary education.

Legislation regulates the principal terms and conditions of employment such as hours of work, sick leave and other fringe benefits. Young people of 14–16 years may work in industrial establishments, and children of 12–14 years may be employed in approved apprenticeship schemes. A trade dispute may be referred to the Industrial Arbitration Court. Singapore does not have a minimum wage.

International Trade

Foreign investment of up to 40% of the equity of domestic banks is permitted.

Imports and Exports

Total imports were S$333,191m. in 2005; and total exports S$382,532m. in 2005. Exports in 2005 were worth 244% of GDP.

Imports and exports (in S$1m.), by country, 2005:

	Imports (c.i.f.)	*Exports (f.o.b.)*
Australia	4,850	14,045
China	34,170	32,909
Germany	9,915	10,504
Hong Kong	7,009	35,849
India	6,788	9,817
Indonesia	17,400	36,817
Japan	32,034	20,874
Korea, South	14,323	13,412
Malaysia	45,527	50,612
Saudi Arabia	14,894	708
Taiwan	19,720	14,938
Thailand	12,516	15,662
UK	6,554	10,525
USA	38,793	39,024

Main imports (2005, in S$1m.): machinery and equipment, 185,980; mineral fuels, 59,145; manufactured goods, 25,040; chemicals and chemical products, 20,744; food, 6,680; beverages and tobacco, 2,190; crude materials, 2,190; animal and vegetable oils, 479; miscellaneous manufactures, 26,526.

Main exports (2005, in S$1m.): machinery and transport equipment, 224,980; mineral fuels, 57,414; chemicals and chemical products, 43,611; manufactured goods, 17,498; food, 3,865; crude materials, 2,257; beverages and tobacco, 2,053; animal and vegetable oils, 422; miscellaneous manufactures, 26,049.

In May 2003 the USA and Singapore signed a free trade agreement removing tariffs on trade worth an estimated US$33bn. per annum.

Communications

Roads

In 2007 there were 3,297 km of public roads (100% asphalt-paved). Singapore has one of the densest road networks in the world. In 2007 there were 517,000 passenger cars, 14,500 buses and coaches, 151,000 vans and lorries, and 144,300 motorcycles and scooters.

Only the UAE ranked ahead of Singapore for quality of road infrastructure in the World Economic Forum's *Global Competitiveness Report 2017–2018*.

Rail

Woodlands Train Checkpoint is the southern terminus of the Malaysian Keretapi Tanah Melayu (KTM) rail network. A main line used to run on through Singapore but ceased operating in 2011. Branch lines serve the port of Singapore and the industrial estates at Jurong. The total rail length of the Mass Rapid Transit (SMRT) metro is 93·2 km. The 20 km North-East Line (operated by SBS Transit), the world's first fully automated heavy metro, became operational in 2003. In late 1999 the Light Rapid Transit System (LRT) began operations, linking the Bukit Panjang Estate with Choa Chu Kang in the North West region.

Singapore was ranked fourth for rail infrastructure in the World Economic Forum's *Global Competitiveness Report 2017–2018*.

Civil Aviation

As of Sept. 2010, Singapore Changi Airport was served by 96 airlines with more than 5,100 weekly flights to and from some 200 cities in 60 countries and territories worldwide. A total of 37,203,978 passengers and 1,633,791 tonnes of freight were handled in 2009. The national airline is Singapore Airlines, which carried 16,480,000 passengers in 2009–10. Its subsidiary, Silk Air, serves Asian destinations. Other Singapore-based carriers are Jetstar Asia and Scoot.

In the World Economic Forum's *Global Competitiveness Report 2017–2018*, Singapore ranked first for quality of air transport infrastructure.

Shipping

Singapore has a large container port, the world's second busiest in terms of containers handled and shipping tonnage in 2012, second only to Shanghai. The economy is dependent on shipping and entrepôt trade. A total of 134,883 vessels of 2·4bn. gross tonnes (GT) entered Singapore during 2014. In 2014, 4,595 vessels with a total of 82·2m. GT were registered in Singapore. The Singapore merchant fleet ranked fifth among the principal merchant fleets of the world in 2014. Total cargo handled in 2014 was 581·3m. freight tons, and total container throughput was 33,869,300 TEUs (twenty-foot equivalent units).

Only the Netherlands ranked ahead of Singapore for quality of port facilities in the World Economic Forum's *Global Competitiveness Report 2017–2018*.

Telecommunications

In 2013 there were 1,967,000 main (fixed) telephone lines. In the same year mobile phone subscriptions numbered 8,438,000 (1,559·2 per 1,000 persons). In 1997 Singapore Telecom, one of the largest companies in Asia, lost its monopoly with the entry of a new mobile phone operator. Singapore had three mobile phone operators in 2012—SingTel Mobile (owned by Singapore Telecom), M1 and StarHub Mobile. In 2013 there were 1,493·3 mobile broadband subscriptions per 1,000 inhabitants and 260·3 fixed broadband subscriptions for every 1,000 inhabitants. In March 2012 there were 2·6m. Facebook users.

According to the World Economic Forum's *Global Information Technology Report 2013* Singapore is ranked second in the world in exploiting global information technology developments.

Social Institutions

Out of 178 countries analysed in the 2017 *Fragile States Index*—a list published jointly by the Fund for Peace and *Foreign Policy* magazine—Singapore was ranked the 18th least vulnerable to conflict or collapse. The index is based on 12 indicators of state vulnerability across social, political and economic categories.

Justice

There is a Supreme Court in Singapore which consists of the High Court and the Court of Appeal. The Supreme Court is composed of a Chief Justice and 11 Judges. The High Court has unlimited original jurisdiction in both civil and criminal cases. The Court of Appeal is the final appellate court. It hears appeals from any judgement or order of the High Court in any civil matter. The Subordinate Courts consist of a total of 47 District and Magistrates' Courts, the Civil, the Family and Crime Registries, the Primary Dispute Resolution Centre, and the Small Claims Tribunal. The right of appeal to the UK Privy Council was abolished in 1994.

Penalties for drug trafficking and abuse are severe, including a mandatory death penalty. In 1994 there were 76 executions, although since then the average annual number has generally been declining. There were eight executions in 2017 and six in 2018. Crime rates are very low, with the homicide rate just 0·2 per 100,000 inhabitants in 2012—the lowest of any country apart from those with extremely small populations.

The Technology Court was introduced in 1995 where documents were filed electronically. This process was implemented in Aug. 1998 in the Magistrates appeal and the Court of Appeal.

The population in penal institutions as at 31 Dec. 2012 was 12,504 (230 per 100,000 of national population). In 2015 the World Justice Project *Rule of Law Index*, which provides data on how the rule of law is experienced by the general public across eight categories, ranked Singapore third of 102 countries for both criminal justice and civil justice.

Education

The general literacy rate rose from 84% in 1980 to an estimated 94·7% in 2009 (male 97·5%; female 92·0%). Kindergartens are private and fee-paying. Compulsory primary state education starts at six years and culminates at 11 or 12 years with an examination which influences choice of secondary schooling. There are 17 autonomous and eight private fee-paying secondary schools. Tertiary education at 16 years is divided into three branches: junior colleges leading to university; four polytechnics; and ten technical institutes.

In 2007 there were 301,101 pupils with 14,743 teaching staff in primary schools, 232,100 pupils with 13,686 teaching staff in secondary schools and 183,627 students with 14,209 academic staff in tertiary education.

There are six publicly-funded universities, of which the largest are the National University of Singapore (founded in 1905 and established as the National University of Singapore in 1980) with 34,715 students in 2015–16 and the Nanyang Technological University (founded in 1981 and established as the Nanyang Technological University in 1991) with 33,166 in 2015–16. Singapore Management University was established in 2000, the private but publicly-funded SIM University in 2005 and both the Singapore University of Technology and Design and the Singapore Institute of Technology in 2009.

In 2009 public expenditure on education came to 3·1% of GDP and accounted for 11·6% of total government expenditure.

According to the OECD's 2015 PISA (Programme for International Student Assessment) study, 15-year-olds in Singapore rank first among OECD and other major countries and cities in all three of the areas covered—mathematics, reading and science. The three-yearly study compares educational achievement of pupils in over 70 countries.

Health

There were 26 hospitals and speciality centres in 2014 with 11,230 beds. In 2014 there were 11,733 doctors, 1,905 dentists, and 37,618 registered nurses and midwives. Private practitioners provide 80% of primary health care services.

Of the 18,938 deaths in 2013 the leading causes were cancer (30·5%), pneumonia (18·5%) and coronary heart disease (15·5%).

Welfare

The Central Provident Fund (CPF) was set up in 1955 to provide financial security for workers upon retirement or when they are no longer able to work. In 2013 there were 3,507,645 members with total balances of S$252,969m.

Religion

According to the 2010 census, 33·3% of the population were Buddhists, 18·3% Christians, 14·7% Muslims, 10·9% Taoists and 5·1% Hindus; 0·7% belonged to other religions and 17·0% had no religion. A report published in April 2014 by the Pew Research Center ranked Singapore as the world's most religiously diverse country.

Culture

The National Arts Council (NAC) was established in 1991 to spearhead the development of the arts.

Press

In 2014 there were ten daily newspapers, with a total daily circulation of 1,355,000 copies. The most popular paid-for daily is *The Straits Times*, with an average daily circulation of 309,000 in 2014. Its online edition had 667,000 unique monthly visitors in 2014.

Tourism

International visitor arrivals totalled 15·6m. in 2013, up from 14·5m. in 2012. Tourism receipts rose from S$23·1bn. in 2012 to S$23·5bn. in 2013. In Dec. 2013 there were 196 gazetted hotels, providing 47,113 rooms.

Festivals

Every Jan. or Feb. the Lunar New Year is celebrated. Other Chinese festivals include Qing Ming (a time for the remembrance of ancestors), Yu Lan Jie (Feast of the Hungry Ghosts) and the Mid-Autumn Festival (Mooncake or Lantern festival).

Muslims in Singapore celebrate Hari Raya Puasa (to celebrate the end of a month-long fast) and Hari Raya Haji (a day of prayer and commemoration of the annual Mecca pilgrimage). There are also Muharram (a New Year celebration) and Maulud (Prophet Muhammad's birthday).

Hindus celebrate the Tamil New Year in mid-April. Thaipusam is a penitential Hindu festival popular with Tamils; and Diwali, the Festival of Lights, is celebrated by Hindus and Sikhs. Other festivals include Thimithi (a fire-walking ceremony) and Navarathiri (nine nights' prayer).

Buddhists observe Vesak Day, which commemorates the birth, enlightenment and Nirvana of the Buddha, and falls on the full moon day in May. Christmas, Good Friday and Easter Sunday are also recognized.

World Heritage Sites

Singapore has one site on the UNESCO World Heritage List: Singapore Botanical Gardens (2015), a site created in 1859 that includes a variety of historic features, plantings and buildings.

Diplomatic Representatives

Of Singapore in the United Kingdom (9 Wilton Cres., London, SW1X 8SP)
High Commissioner: Foo Chi Hsia.

Of the United Kingdom in Singapore (100 Tanglin Rd, Singapore 247919)
High Commissioner: Scott Wightman, CMG.

Of Singapore in the USA (3501 International Pl., NW, Washington, D.C., 20008)
Ambassador: Ashok Kumar.

Of the USA in Singapore (27 Napier Rd, Singapore 258508)
Ambassador: Vacant.
Chargé d'Affaires a.i.: Stephanie Syptak-Ramnath.

Of Singapore to the United Nations
Ambassador: Burhan Gafoor.

Of Singapore to the European Union
Ambassador: Jaya Ratnam.

Further Reading

Department of Statistics. *Monthly Digest of Statistics.—Yearbook of Statistics.*

The Constitution of Singapore. 1992

Ministry of Trade and Industry, *Economic Survey of Singapore.* (Quarterly and Annual)

Chee-Kiong, T., *The Making of Singapore Sociology: State and Society.* 2002

Chew, E. C. T., *A History of Singapore.* 1992

Huff, W. G., *Economic Growth of Singapore: Trade and Development in the Twentieth Century.* 1994

Myint, S., *The Principles of Singapore Law.* 4th ed. 2001

Tan, C. H., *Financial Markets and Institutions in Singapore.* 11th ed. 2005

National library: National Library of Singapore, 100 Victoria Street, Singapore 188064.

National Statistical Office: Department of Statistics, 100 High St. #05-01, The Treasury, Singapore 179434.

Website: http://www.singstat.gov.sg

Slovakia

Slovenská Republika (Slovak Republic)

Capital: Bratislava
Population projection, 2020: 5·45m.
GNI per capita, 2017: (PPP$) 29,467
HDI/world rank, 2017: 0·855/38
Internet domain extension: .sk

Key Historical Events

There is evidence of human habitation from 270,000 BC. In the Bronze Age the region was a centre for copper manufacture and was ruled by Carpathian, Celtic and Germanic tribes. The date of the Slavic arrival is contested but there is evidence of their presence from the sixth century under the Roman Empire. Waves of invasion and migration followed Roman withdrawal and control fell variously to the Avars, Franks and Magyars.

The first brief period of Slavic rule was the Samo Empire (623–658) followed by the Moravian Empire from 833–907. The region subsequently became part of the Kingdom of Hungary. In 1241 the region was invaded by Mongols and was stricken with famine but grew in prosperity through the medieval period. From the 16th–19th centuries Slovakia was at the centre of Hungary under the Habsburg dynasty. After 1867 it became part of the Austro-Hungarian Empire and underwent 'Magyarization', a repressive attempt to impose Magyar culture. In response, a nationalist movement at home and among immigrants in America gained momentum in the First World War.

On 28 Oct. 1918, after the dissolution of Austria-Hungary, the Czechoslovak State was founded. Two days later the Slovak National Council voted to unite with the Czechs. The Treaty of St Germain-en-Laye (1919) recognized the Czechoslovak Republic, consisting of the Czech lands (Bohemia, Moravia, part of Silesia) and Slovakia. The new state was numerically dominated by Czechs, giving rise to some tensions and calls for Slovakian independence. In 1939 negotiations between European powers resulted in Germany incorporating the Czech lands into the Reich as the 'Protectorate of Bohemia and Moravia'. Meanwhile the German-sponsored Slovak government declared independence. A government-in-exile, headed by Dr Edvard Beneš, was set up in London during the war. In 1944 Slovak resistance fighters began an uprising; liberation was completed by Soviet and US forces in May 1945. Territories taken by Germans, Poles and Hungarians were restored to Czech sovereignty.

Elections in May 1946 returned a coalition government, under communist prime minister Klement Gottwald. On 20 Feb. 1948, 12 non-communist ministers resigned in protest at the infiltration of communists into the police. Gottwald formed a predominantly communist government and in May 1948, after the government won an 89% majority in rigged parliamentary elections, President Beneš resigned. During the next two decades the government banned other parties and followed Stalinist policies. On 14 May 1955 Czechoslovakia signed the Warsaw Pact, allying itself with the Soviet Union and other Eastern Bloc countries.

In 1968 pressure for liberalization culminated in the overthrow of the Stalinist leadership and under Alexander Dubček, new first secretary of the communist party, the 'Prague Spring' saw sweeping reforms including the abolition of censorship. Between May and Aug. 1968 the USSR put pressure on the government to abandon reforms. Finally, Warsaw Pact troops occupied Czechoslovakia on 21 Aug. The government was forced to reverse reforms and accept the stationing of Soviet troops. In April 1969, with Soviet support, Dubček was replaced by Gustáv Husák.

Demands for reform persisted and mass demonstrations began in Nov. 1989. When authorities used violence to break up a demonstration on 17 Nov., the communist leadership resigned. On 30 Nov. the federal assembly abolished the communists' sole right to govern. A new government was formed on 3 Dec. and another followed a week later as the protest movement grew. Gustáv Husák resigned as president and was replaced by Václav Havel by the unanimous vote of 323 members of the federal assembly on 29 Dec. This bloodless overthrow of communist rule became known as the 'Velvet Revolution'.

At the June 1992 elections the Movement for Democratic Slovakia, led by Vladimír Mečiar, campaigned for Slovak independence. On 17 July the Slovak National Council adopted a declaration of sovereignty by 113 to 24 votes, the 'Velvet Divorce'. Havel resigned as federal president on 20 July. A constitution ratified on 1 Sept. 1992 paved the way for independent Slovakia to come into being on 1 Jan. 1993. Economic property was divided between Slovakia and the Czech Republic, with government real estate remaining with the republic in which it was located. Other property was divided by special commissions in the proportion of two (Czech Republic) to one (Slovakia), on the basis of population size. Military equipment was also divided on the two-to-one principle and military personnel were invited to choose in which army to serve.

In the 1990s Slovakia resisted calls for economic reforms and closer ties with Western Europe. However, following the election of a coalition government under Mikuláš Dzurinda in Oct. 1998, the country implemented reforms and attracted foreign investment. It responded to criticism about its human rights record by improving conditions for its Romany and Hungarian minorities. Slovakia joined NATO in March 2004 and the European Union, in May 2004. It elected a new coalition government under Prime Minister Robert Fico in June 2006. Fico was succeeded by Iveta Radičová in 2010 before reclaiming the premiership in March 2012.

Territory and Population

Slovakia is bounded in the northwest by the Czech Republic, north by Poland, east by Ukraine, south by Hungary and southwest by Austria. Its area is 49,034 sq. km (18,932 sq. miles). Census population in 2011 was 5,397,036 (2,769,264 females and 2,627,772 males); density, 110·1 per sq. km. In Dec. 2017 the population was estimated at 5,443,120.

The UN gives a projected population for 2020 of 5·45m.

In 2011, 54·9% of the population lived in urban areas. There are eight administrative regions *(Kraj)*, one of which is the capital, Bratislava. They have the same name as the main city of the region.

Region	Area in sq. km	2016 estimated population
Banská Bystrica	9,455	651,509
Bratislava	2,053	641,892
Košice	6,753	798,103
Nitra	6,343	680,779
Prešov	8,993	822,310
Trenčín	4,501	588,816
Trnava	4,148	561,156
Žilina	6,788	690,778

The capital, Bratislava, had an estimated population in 2016 of 425,923. The population of other principal towns (2016, in 1,000): Košice, 239; Prešov, 90; Žilina, 81; Banská Bystrica, 79; Nitra, 77; Trnava, 66; Trenčín, 56; Martin, 55.

The population is 80·7% Slovak, 8·5% Hungarian, 2·0% Roma, 0·6% Czech and 0·6% Ruthenian, with some Germans, Moravians, Poles and Ukrainians.

A law of Nov. 1995 makes Slovak the sole official language.

Social Statistics

Live births, 2015, 55,602; deaths, 53,826; marriages, 28,755; divorces, 9,786. Rates (per 1,000 population), 2015: live birth, 10·3; death, 9·9; marriage, 5·3; divorce, 1·8. Expectation of life, 2015, was 73·0 years for males and 79·7 for females. In 2015 the most popular age range for marrying

© Springer Nature Limited 2020
Palgrave Macmillan (ed.), *The Statesman's Yearbook 2020*,
https://doi.org/10.1057/978-1-349-95940-2_172

was 25–29 for both males and females. Annual population growth rate, 2010–14, 0·1%. Infant mortality, 2015 (per 1,000 live births), 5·1. Fertility rate, 2015, 1·4 births per woman.

Climate

A humid continental climate, with warm summers and cold winters. Precipitation is generally greater in summer, with thunderstorms. Autumn, with dry, clear weather and spring, which is damp, are each of short duration. Bratislava, Jan. –0·7°C. June 19·1°C. Annual rainfall 649 mm.

Constitution and Government

The constitution became effective on 1 Jan. 1993, creating a parliamentary democracy with universal suffrage from the age of 18. Parliament is the unicameral *National Council*. It has 150 members elected by proportional representation to serve four-year terms. The constitution was amended in Sept. 1998 to allow for the direct election of the *President*, who serves for a five-year term. The President may serve a maximum of two consecutive terms.

The Judicial Branch consists of a *Supreme Court*, whose judges are elected by the National Council, and a *Constitutional Court*, whose judges are appointed by the President from a group of nominees approved by the National Council.

Citizenship belongs to all citizens of the former federal Slovak Republic; other residents of five years standing may apply for citizenship. Slovakia grants dual citizenship.

National Anthem

'Nad Tatrou sa blýska' ('Storm over the Tatras'); words by J. Matúška, tune anonymous.

Government Chronology

(DU = Democratic Union; HZD = Movement for Democracy; HZDS = Movement for a Democratic Slovakia; KDH = Christian Democratic Movement; SDK = Slovak Democratic Coalition; SDKÚ = Slovak Democratic and Christian Union; SDKÚ–DS = Slovak Democratic and Christian Union–Democratic Party; Smer–SD = Direction–Social Democracy; SOP = Party of Civic Understanding; n/p = non-partisan)

Presidents since 1993.		
1993–98	n/p	Michal Kováč
1999–2004	SOP, n/p	Rudolf Schuster
2004–14	HZD, n/p	Ivan Gašparovič
2014–	n/p	Andrej Kiska

Prime Ministers since 1993.		
1993–94	HZDS	Vladimír Mečiar
1994	DU	Jozef Moravčík
1994–98	HZDS	Vladimír Mečiar
1998–2006	KDH/SDK, SDKÚ	Mikuláš Dzurinda
2006–10	Smer–SD	Robert Fico
2010–12	SDKÚ–DS	Iveta Radičová
2012–18	Smer–SD	Robert Fico
2018–	Smer–SD	Peter Pellegrini

Recent Elections

Elections to the National Council were held on 5 March 2016. Direction–Social Democracy (Smer–SD) won 49 seats with 28·3% of votes cast, ahead of Freedom and Solidarity 12·1% (21 seats), Ordinary People and Independent Personalities 11·0% (19), the Slovak National Party (SNS) 8·6% (15), Kotleba–People's Party Our Slovakia 8·0% (14), We Are Family 6·6% (11), Most–Híd 6·5% (11) and Network (Sieť) 5·6% (10). Turnout was 59·8%.

In the first round of presidential elections on 15 March 2014, incumbent prime minister Robert Fico of the Direction–Social Democracy party (Smer–SD) won 28·0% of the vote against 24·0% for independent candidate Andrej Kiska and 21·2% for Radoslav Procházka, also an independent candidate. There were 11 other candidates. Turnout was 43·4%. In the run-off held on 29 March Kiska won 59·4% against 40·6% for Fico. Turnout in the second round was 50·5%.

European Parliament

Slovakia has 13 representatives. At the May 2014 elections turnout was 13·1%—the lowest in the EU—down from 19·6% in 2009. Smer–SD won 4 seats with 24·1% of votes cast (political affiliation in European Parliament: Progressive Alliance of Socialists and Democrats); KDH, 2 with 13·2% (European People's Party); SDKÚ–DS, 2 with 7·8% (European People's Party); Ordinary People, 1 with 7·5% (European Conservatives and Reformists); New Majority, 1 seat with 6·8% (European Conservatives and Reformists); Freedom and Solidarity, 1 seat with 6·7% (Alliance of Liberals and Democrats for Europe); Party of the Hungarian Community, 1 seat with 6·5% (European People's Party); Most–Híd, 1 seat with 5·8% (European People's Party).

Current Government

President: Andrej Kiska; b. 1963 (ind.; sworn in 15 June 2014).

The government was composed as follows in Feb. 2019:

Prime Minister: Peter Pellegrini; b. 1975 (Smer–SD; sworn in 22 March 2018).

Deputy Prime Minister and Minister of Finance: Peter Kažimir (Smer–SD). *Deputy Prime Minister and Minister of Agriculture and Rural Development:* Gabriela Matečná (ind.). *Deputy Prime Minister and Minister of Environment:* László Sólymos (Most–Híd). *Deputy Prime Minister for Investments and the Information Society:* Richard Raši (Smer–SD).

Minister of Culture: Ľubica Laššáková (Smer–SD). *Defence:* Peter Gajdoš (ind.). *Economy:* Peter Žiga (Smer–SD). *Education, Science, Research and Sport:* Martina Lubyová (ind.). *Foreign Affairs:* Miroslav Lajčák (ind.). *Health:* Andrea Kalavská (ind.). *Interior:* Denisa Saková (Smer–SD). *Justice:* Gábor Gál (Most–Híd). *Labour, Social Affairs and the Family:* Ján Richter (Smer–SD). *Transport, Construction and Regional Development:* Árpád Érsek (Most–Híd).

Government Website: http://www.government.gov.sk

Current Leaders

Andrej Kiska
Position
President

Introduction
Andrej Kiska became president in June 2014 following a successful career as a businessman and philanthropist. Despite opinion polls indicating voter satisfaction with his tenure, he announced in May 2018 that he would not be a candidate in the presidential elections the following March and that he would stand down on the expiry of his term of office in June 2019.

Early Life
Kiska was born in Poprad, northern Slovakia on 2 Feb. 1963. He graduated in electrical engineering in 1986 from the Slovak Technical University in Bratislava. He moved to the USA following the Velvet Revolution in 1990, returning to Slovakia 18 months later. Having set up two successful hire-purchase companies in 1996, he sold his stake in both in 2005 and co-founded the charitable organization *Dobrý anděl* (Good Angel) the following year. It became the most successful non-corporate charity in Slovakia, providing financial aid to families in which a member had a life-threatening illness.

Career in Office
In 2014 Kiska ran for president as an independent candidate on an anti-corruption platform. He beat the leftist prime minister, Robert Fico, after a second round of voting in March 2014 and was inaugurated on 15 June, becoming the first president since independence to be unaffiliated with the Communist Party. Kiska's stance as a non-partisan candidate won popularity following several scandals involving the political elite in recent years.

He nominated just one out of the six candidates proposed by parliament as constitutional court judges, arguing that the other candidates were not suitably qualified. He also announced plans for a referendum on gay rights following a constitutional amendment in 2014 that excluded homosexual couples from marriage.

Kiska has indicated support for granting Kosovo official recognition as a sovereign state independent from Serbia and, unlike Fico, backed US sanctions against Russia following the crisis in Ukraine.

Following parliamentary elections in March 2016, Kiska asked incumbent prime minister Robert Fico to form a new government. However, in March 2018 Fico resigned amid popular anger over corruption and the murder of an investigative journalist and Kiska tasked Peter Pellegrini with the formation of a new government.

Peter Pellegrini

Position
Prime Minister

Introduction
Peter Pellegrini was sworn in as prime minister on 22 March 2018. A member of the pro-European, Direction–Social Democracy party (Smer–SD) party, he took office amid a national scandal over political corruption that forced the resignation of his predecessor, Robert Fico.

Early Life
Peter Pellegrini was born on 6 Oct. 1975 in Banská Bystrica, in what was then Czechoslovakia. He studied finance at Matej Bel University and the Technical University of Košice before working as an adviser to Ľubomír Vážny, a member of the National Council, between 2002 and 2006.

In 2006, the year in which Robert Fico began his first term as prime minister, Pellegrini was elected to the National Council as a representative of Smer–SD. Rising rapidly through the party ranks, he was made state secretary for finance in 2012 and then minister for education, science, research and sport in July 2014. His status as a close ally of Fico was confirmed by his appointment as the National Council's Speaker later in the same year. After the March 2016 parliamentary elections, in which Smer–SD won 49 out of 150 seats, the party formed a coalition with the Slovak National Party, Most–Híd and Network. Under Fico, Pellegrini served as deputy prime minister for investments and the information society.

In Feb. 2018 the home of Ján Kuciak, a journalist investigating links between high-level Slovakian politicians and organized crime, was broken into and he and his fiancée were murdered. The posthumous publication of Kuciak's findings, and the release of several suspects, prompted nationwide protests. After President Andrej Kiska said that fresh elections or a radical overhaul of the government were required to restore public trust, Fico offered his resignation on condition that the coalition was allowed to complete its term in parliament. Pellegrini subsequently replaced him on 22 March.

Career in Office
Pellegrini's cabinet was approved by the National Council on 26 March despite widespread public distrust as to whether its members would impartially investigate the murder of Kuciak, and there was also speculation over the continued influence of Fico amid calls in the media for early elections.

Defence

Since 1 Jan. 2006 Slovakia has had an all-volunteer professional army. In 2013 defence spending totalled US$995m. (US$181 per capita), representing 1·0% of GDP.

Army

Strength (2011), 6,230. In addition there were 2,545 central staff personnel in 2011 and 3,080 support and training personnel. Equipment in 2011 included 69 main battle tanks and 253 armoured infantry fighting vehicles.

Air Force

Personnel (2011), 3,944. Equipment in 2011 included 22 combat-capable aircraft (MiG-29 fighters).

International Relations

A referendum held on 16–17 May 2003 approved accession to the EU, with 92·5% of votes cast for membership and 7·5% against. Turnout was 52·2%. Slovakia became a member of NATO on 29 March 2004 and the EU on 1 May 2004.

Slovakia has had a long-standing dispute with Hungary over the Gabčíkovo-Nagymaros Project, involving the building of dam structures in both countries for the production of electric power, flood control and improvement of navigation on the Danube as agreed in a treaty signed in 1977 between Czechoslovakia and Hungary. In late 1998 Slovakia and Hungary signed a protocol easing tensions between the two nations and settling differences over the dam.

Economy

Agriculture accounted for 4·4% of GDP in 2014, industry 33·6% and services 62·0%.

Overview

Slovakia has undergone almost constant restructuring since 1998 when policy shifted from state intervention towards pro-market reforms. Following economic transition, the heavy industry and agriculture sectors shrank while the service sector increased its share of GDP (reaching 61% in 2010).

From 1998–2008 the economy enjoyed rapid growth, driven by strong exports and foreign direct investment, particularly in the automotive industry. GDP grew at approximately 4% per annum and peaked in 2007 at 10·5% on the back of strong domestic demand and buoyant exports. Slovakia entered the European exchange rate mechanism in 2005 and adopted the euro in Jan. 2009. However, the global financial crisis resulted in a 5·3% contraction in GDP that year. The government introduced a range of measures to counteract the effects of the downturn, which, combined with the recovery in global demand for manufactured goods, saw a resurgence from the second half of 2009.

The government managed to reduce the budget deficit by nearly five percentage points to 2·6% between 2010 and 2013, facilitating the country's exit from the European Union's Excessive Deficit Procedure. Nonetheless, growth declined from 2·7% in 2011 to 1·4% in 2013 owing to a weak external environment. Unemployment remained high at around 13% in 2014, with youth unemployment registering 33%.

However, there was a rebound with the economy expanding by 2·8% and 3·9% in 2014 and 2015 as household consumption grew on the back of labour market buoyancy. By 2016 the unemployment rate had dipped below 10%. Although public investment has been hit by slow disbursement of EU funds, business investment has been boosted by expanding exports, especially in the automotive industry (which produces over 1m. cars per year). Surging foreign direct investment into the automotive and electronics sectors further helped boost productivity, prompting faster economic convergence with the OECD average.

Nevertheless, the benefits of growth have not been equally shared across society. Long-term unemployment remains high by international standards. Notably, the Roma population is not well integrated, with many either in or at risk of poverty. Moreover, labour shortages are spreading despite relatively high unemployment. In order to make growth more inclusive, the government needs to pursue much needed reforms in education and skills development, as well as to facilitate Roma integration.

Currency

On 1 Jan. 2009 the *euro* (EUR) replaced the Slovak koruna (SKK) as the legal currency of Slovakia at the irrevocable conversion rate of 30·126 koruny to one euro. Foreign exchange reserves in Sept. 2009 were US$54m. (US$17,493m. in Sept. 2008) and gold reserves 1·02m. troy oz. There was deflation of 0·5% in 2016 but then inflation of 1·3% in 2017. Total money supply in Dec. 2008 was €545,969m.

Budget

General government revenue in 2016 (provisional) totalled €31,910m. and expenditure €34,015m.

Principal sources of revenue in 2016 (provisional) were: social security contributions, €11,201m.; taxes on goods and services, €8,539m.; taxes on income, profits and capital gains, €5,690m. Main items of expenditure by economic type in 2016 (provisional): social benefits, €15,520m.; compensation of employees, €7,400m.; use of goods and services, €4,459m.

Slovakia's budget deficit in 2017 was 0·8% of GDP (2016, 2·2%; 2015, 2·6%). The required target set by the EU is a budget deficit of no more than 3%.

VAT, personal and company income tax, real estate taxes and inheritance taxes came into force in Jan. 1993. VAT is 20% (reduced rate, 10%).

Performance

Real GDP growth was 3·9% in 2015, 3·3% in 2016 and 3·4% in 2017. Slovakia's total GDP in 2017 was US$95·8bn.

Banking and Finance

The central bank and bank of issue is the Slovak National Bank, founded in 1993 (*Governor*, Jozef Makúch). It has an autonomous statute modelled on the German Bundesbank, with the duties of maintaining control over monetary policy and inflation, ensuring the stability of the currency, and supervising commercial banks. However, it is now proposed to amend the central bank law to allow the government to appoint half the members of the board and force the bank to increase its financing of the budget deficit.

In Oct. 1998 the Slovak National Bank abandoned its fixed exchange rate system, whereby the crown's value was fixed within a fluctuation band against a number of currencies, and chose to float the currency.

Decentralization of the banking system began in 1991, and private banks began to operate. The two largest Slovak banks were both privatized in 2001. The Austrian bank Erste Bank bought an 87·18% stake in Slovenská Sporiteľňa (Slovak Savings Bank) and the Italian bank IntesaBci bought a 94·47% stake in Všeobecná úverová banka (General Credit Bank). In 2011 Slovenská Sporiteľňa had assets of €11·3bn. and Všeobecná úverová banka €10·8bn. In 2013 there were 29 commercial banks including three building savings banks.

Gross external debt amounted to US$65,592m. in June 2012.

There is a stock exchange in Bratislava.

Energy and Natural Resources

In 2011, 9·7% of energy consumption came from renewables (wind power, solar power, hydro-electric power, tidal power, geothermal energy and biomass), compared to the European Union average of 13·0%. A target of 14% has been set by the EU for 2020.

Environment

Slovakia's carbon dioxide emissions from the consumption of energy in 2011 were the equivalent of 6·4 tonnes per capita.

Electricity

Installed capacity in 2011 was 8·1m. kW, of which 2·5m. kW was hydro-electric and 1·9m. kW nuclear. Production in 2011 was 28·66bn. kWh, with consumption per capita 5,401 kWh. There were four nuclear reactors in use in 2011. In 2011 about 54% of electricity was nuclear-generated, making Slovakia one of the most nuclear-dependent nations in the world.

Oil and Gas

In 2013 natural gas reserves were 14bn. cu. metres; oil reserves were 9m. bbls in 2011. Natural gas production in 2011 amounted to 123m. cu. metres. Slovakia relies on Russia for almost all of its oil and gas.

Minerals

Output in 2014 (in 1,000 tonnes): limestone, 4,333; gravel, 3,863; lignite, 2,188; dolomite, 857. There are also reserves of copper, lead, zinc, iron, rock salt and others.

Agriculture

In 2015 there were 1·35m. ha. of arable land and 18,457 ha. of permanent crops. In 2015, 3·2% of employed persons were engaged in agriculture.

Production, 2015 (in 1,000 tonnes): wheat, 2,082·1; sugar beets, 1,205·5; maize, 929·2; barley, 688·6; rapeseed, 320·6; sunflower seeds, 174·3; potatoes, 144·6; soybeans (2014), 83·9; rye (2014), 53·5; grapes, 50·2.

Livestock, 2015: pigs, 633,000; cattle, 458,000; sheep, 382,000; chickens, 12·8m. Livestock products, 2013 estimates (in 1,000 tonnes): meat, 150; milk, 977; cheese, 41; eggs, 81.

Forestry

The area under forests in 2015 was 1·94m. ha., or 40% of the total land area. In 2011 timber production was 9·21m. cu. metres.

Fisheries

In 2015 the total catch was 1,971 tonnes, exclusively freshwater fish.

Industry

The main industries in Slovakia are machine engineering, chemical products, electrical apparatus, textiles, clothing and footwear, metallurgy, food and beverages, paper, wood and woodworking. Output (2014 unless otherwise indicated, in 1,000 tonnes) included: cement, 5,070; crude steel, 4,705; pig iron (2013), 3,617; distillate fuel oil (2012), 2,732; coke (2012), 1,560; petrol (2012), 1,348; residual fuel oil (2012), 616; flour, 343; ferroalloys, 103; toilet paper, 85; malt beer, 265m. litres. Motor vehicle production reached (2014) 908,074 units. Slovakia has the highest per capita car production of any country.

Labour

Out of 2,351,400 people in employment in 2011, 568,000 were in manufacturing, 304,000 in wholesale and retail trade/repair of motor vehicles, motorcycles and personal and household goods, 243,700 in construction and 164,200 in education. The average monthly salary in 2011 was €855. In Jan. 2011 the monthly minimum wage was €317. Unemployment stood at 19·2% in 2001, but then fell to 16·2% in 2005 and still further to 9·6% in 2008. It rose again to 14·5% in 2010 but had dropped to 6·1% by Dec. 2018. Youth unemployment was 33·2% in 2011. Long-term unemployment is also very high, with 63·9% of jobless Slovakians in 2011 having been out of work for more than a year (although the rate has fallen from 73·1% in 2006). In 2011 part-time work accounted for around 4% of all employment in Slovakia.

Slovakia had 19,000 people living in slavery according to the Walk Free Foundation's 2013 *Global Slavery Index*.

International Trade

Imports and Exports

In 2015 imports (f.o.b.) totalled €64,361m. (€60,019m. in 2014); exports (f.o.b.) €67,680m. (€64,721m. in 2014). Principal import sources in 2015 were: Germany, 15·7%; Czech Republic, 11·2%; China, 8·7%; Republic of Korea, 6·6%; Russia, 5·4%. The leading export markets in 2015 were: Germany, 22·4%; Czech Republic, 12·4%; Poland, 8·3%; Austria, 6·0%; Hungary, 5·6%. In 2015 machinery and transport equipment accounted for 47·3% of Slovakia's imports and 59·6% of exports; manufactured goods classified chiefly by material 15·0% of imports and 16·7% of exports; miscellaneous manufactured articles 12·6% of imports and 9·6% of exports; chemicals 8·8% of imports and 4·6% of exports.

Communications

Roads

In 2014 there were 54,801 km of roads, including 420 km of motorways. There were 1,949,055 passenger cars in use in 2014, plus 265,424 vans and lorries, 8,876 buses and coaches and 80,791 motorcycles and mopeds. In 2014 there were 13,307 road accidents resulting in 229 fatalities.

Rail

In 2011 the length of railway routes was 3,624 km. Most of the network is 1,435 mm gauge with short sections on three other gauges. In 2011, 47·5m. passengers were carried and 43·7m. tonnes of freight. There are tram/light rail networks in Bratislava, Košice and Trenčianske Teplice.

Civil Aviation

The main international airport is at Bratislava (M. R. Stefánik), which handled 1,413,193 passengers in 2012 and 22,565 tonnes of freight. There are also some international flights from Košice. Slovak Airlines (formerly the Slovak flag carrier) ceased operations in Feb. 2007, as did Air Slovakia in March 2010. SkyEurope (central Europe's first low-cost airline), which operated domestic services and also flew to a number of destinations in Europe, ceased operations in Sept. 2009. Danube Wings, launched in 2008, ceased operations in Dec. 2013.

Shipping

In 2012 vessels registered by Slovak enterprises numbered 218. Transport of goods on inland waterways in 2012 totalled 8·2m. tonnes, of which 5·3m. tonnes were transit goods and 2·9m. tonnes international.

Telecommunications

In 2013 there were 6,208,000 mobile phone subscriptions (1,139·1 per 1,000 inhabitants) and 967,000 fixed telephone lines. In 2000 Deutsche Telekom bought a 51% stake in the state-owned Slovak Telekom, with the Slovakian government retaining 49% of shares in the company. In 2015 Deutsche Telekom acquired these shares, resulting in Slovak Telekom now being fully owned by Deutsche Telekom. In 2013 an estimated 77·9% of the population aged 16–74 were internet users. In March 2012 there were 1·9m. Facebook users.

Social Institutions

Out of 178 countries analysed in the 2017 *Fragile States Index*—a list published jointly by the Fund for Peace and *Foreign Policy* magazine—Slovakia was ranked the 35th least vulnerable to conflict or collapse. The index is based on 12 indicators of state vulnerability across social, political and economic categories.

Justice

The post-Communist judicial system was established by a federal law of July 1991. This provided for a unified system of four types of court: civil, criminal, commercial and administrative. Commercial courts arbitrate in disputes arising from business activities. Administrative courts examine the legality of the decisions of state institutions when appealed by citizens. In addition, there are military courts which operate under the jurisdiction of the ministry of defence. There is a Supreme Court, and a hierarchy of courts under the ministry of justice at republic, region and district level. District courts are courts of first instance. Cases are usually decided by Senates comprising a judge and two associate judges, although occasionally by a single judge. (Associate judges are citizens in good standing over the age of 25 who are elected for four-year terms). Regional courts are courts of first instance in more serious cases and also courts of appeal for district courts. Cases are usually decided by a Senate of two judges and three associate judges, although again occasionally by a single judge. The Supreme Court interprets law as a guide to other courts and functions also as a court of appeal. Decisions are made by Senates of three judges. The judges of the Supreme Court are nominated by the President; other judges are appointed by the National Council.

The population in penal institutions in Aug. 2013 was 10,152 (187 per 100,000 of national population).

Education

In 2014–15 there were 2,896 pre-school institutions with 156,402 children and 15,175 teachers, 2,133 primary schools with 425,731 pupils and 29,646 teachers, 242 grammar schools with 75,512 students and 5,598 teachers, 448 vocational schools with 151,757 pupils and 11,183 teachers, and 425 special schools with 35,796 children and 4,917 teachers. There were 36 universities or university-type institutions with 173,320 students.

In 2012 spending on education was 9·8% of total government expenditure.

The adult literacy rate in 2015 was 99·6% (99·6% among both males and females).

Health

In 2013 there were 18,355 physicians, 2,586 dentists, 32,903 nurses and midwives, and 3,333 pharmacists. There were 42,245 beds in health establishments in total in 2013, of which 24,413 were in general hospitals. In 2013 Slovakia spent 7·5% of its GDP on health.

Welfare

The age of retirement is 62 for men and is rising for women, to be 62 by 2024. The average individual monthly old-age pension in 2015 was €411 with approximately 743,000 beneficiaries. Maternity benefit is paid for a total of 34 weeks or 37 weeks for a single mother and 43 weeks for multiple births. State unemployment benefit is 50% of previous earnings during the first four or six months, depending on the duration of unemployment insurance.

Religion

A federal Czechoslovakian law of July 1991 provides the basis for church-state relations and guarantees the religious and civic rights of citizens and churches. Churches must register to become legal entities but operate independently of the state. In 2011, 62·0% of the population were Roman Catholic, 5·9% members of the Evangelical Church of the Augsburg Confession, 5·8% Greek Catholic and 1·8% Calvinist. In Feb. 2019 there was one cardinal.

Culture

World Heritage Sites

There are seven UNESCO sites in Slovakia: Vlkolínec (inscribed on the list in 1993), a group of 45 traditional log houses; Banská Štiavnica (1993), a medieval mining town; Levoča, Spišský and the Associated Cultural Monuments (1993 and 2009)—13th century Spiš Castle is one of the largest castle complexes in central Europe; Bardejov Town Conservation Reserve (2000), a medieval fortified town; and Wooden Churches of the Slovak part of the Carpathian Mountain Area (2008).

Slovakia shares two UNESCO sites with other countries: the Caves of Aggtelek and Slovak Karst (1995, 2000 and 2008) with Hungary and Ancient and Primeval Beech Forests of the Carpathians and Other Regions of Europe (2007 and 2017) with Albania, Austria, Belgium, Bulgaria, Croatia, Germany, Italy, Romania, Slovenia, Spain and Ukraine.

Press

Slovakia had nine paid-for daily newspapers in 2013 with a combined average daily circulation of 300,000.

Tourism

In 2010, 1,327,000 non-resident tourists stayed in holiday accommodation (1,298,000 in 2009); there were 3,126 accommodation establishments in 2010 with 57,406 rooms and 147,492 beds.

Festivals

The Bratislava Rock Festival takes place in June and the Bratislava Music Festival and Interpodium is in Oct. The Myjava Folklore Festival is held each June, the Zvolen Castle Games in June–July, Theatrical Nitra is in Sept., and there is an annual Spring Music Festival in Košice.

Diplomatic Representatives

Of Slovakia in the United Kingdom (25 Kensington Palace Gdns, London, W8 4QY)
Ambassador: Ľubomír Rehák.

Of the United Kingdom in Slovakia (Panská 16, 81101 Bratislava)
Ambassador: Andrew Garth.

Of Slovakia in the USA (3523 International Court, NW, Washington, D.C., 20008)
Ambassador: Ivan Korčok.

Of the USA in Slovakia (Hviezdoslavovo Sq. 5, PO Box 309, 81499 Bratislava)
Ambassador: Adam Sterling.

Of Slovakia to the United Nations
Ambassador: Michal Mlynár.

Of Slovakia to the European Union
Permanent Representative: Peter Javorčik.

Further Reading

Fisher, Sharon, *Political Change in Post-Communist Slovakia and Croatia: From Nationalist to Europeanist.* 2006
Kirschbaum, S. J., *A History of Slovakia: the Struggle for Survival.* 1995
National Statistical Office: Statistical Office of the Slovak Republic, Miletičova 3, 82467 Bratislava.
Website: https://slovak.statistics.sk

Slovenia

Republika Slovenija (Republic of Slovenia)

Capital: Ljubljana
Population projection, 2020: 2·08m.
GNI per capita, 2017: (PPP$) 30,594
HDI/world rank, 2017: 0·896/25
Internet domain extension: .si

Key Historical Events

The region was settled by Celts and Illyrians in pre-Roman times and fell to Rome in the 1st century AD. In the 6th century Slavic tribes arrived and part of the territory came under the Slavic Duchy of Karantania in the 7th century. In 745 Karantania became part of the Frankish Empire as an independent country with its own laws and language. After passing under the rule of Bavarian dukes and the Republic of Venice, it joined its neighbouring Slovene-inhabited areas to become part of the Habsburg dynasty in the 14th century.

The Slovenes retained a strong national identity, aided by the printing of the first Slovenian books in 1550 and the translation of the Protestant Bible into Slovenian in 1584. A 12-day peasant revolt in 1573 was bloodily suppressed. In the 19th century a nationalist movement developed, demanding Slovenian autonomy within the Habsburg monarchy. Administrative autonomy was granted in the province of Carinthia while Slovenes in other areas gained some cultural rights. With the demise of the Habsburg monarchy, Slovenia became part of Austria-Hungary. Following Germany's defeat in the First World War, the Slovenes joined their Slav neighbours in the Kingdom of the Serbs, Croats and Slovenes on 1 Dec. 1918. The country was renamed Yugoslavia in 1929. During the Second World War Slovenian territory was divided and annexed by the Axis powers. In 1945 Slovenia became a constituent republic of the Socialist Federal Republic of Yugoslavia under Josep Tito.

In the 1980s nationalism grew stronger throughout Yugoslavia, spearheaded by the Serbs' call for Serbian unity. In Oct. 1989 the Slovene Assembly passed a constitutional amendment giving it the right to secede from Yugoslavia and in a referendum on 23 Dec. 1990, 88·5% voted for independence. Slovenia unilaterally declared independence on 25 June 1991 but, at EU-sponsored peace talks, suspended the claim for three months. Fighting between Slovenia and federal troops ended with a federal withdrawal and on 8 Oct. 1991 Slovenia again declared its independence.

In 1992 Slovenia removed more than 18,000 non-Slovene residents from its records and cancelled their rights. Under pressure from the EU, which Slovenia joined in May 2004, partial restoration of citizenship was granted to about 12,000 people, though a 2004 referendum rejected proposals to restore full retrospective rights. Slovenia joined NATO in March 2004 and became the first former communist bloc country to adopt the euro in Jan. 2007.

Territory and Population

Slovenia is bounded in the north by Austria, in the northeast by Hungary, in the southeast and south by Croatia and in the west by Italy. The length of coastline is 47 km. Its area is 20,273 sq. km. In Jan. 2011 the population at the register-based census was 2,050,189 (1,035,626 females); density per sq. km, 101·1. The capital is Ljubljana: 2011 census population, 272,220. Maribor (population of 95,171 in 2011) is the other major city. In 2011, 49·5% of the population lived in urban areas. In Jan. 2018 the population was estimated at 2,066,880.

The UN gives a projected population for 2020 of 2·08m.

The official language is Slovene.

In April 2004 voters rejected plans to restore the civil rights of Slovenia's ethnic minorities, mainly nationals of other former Yugoslav republics, which were 'erased' in 1992.

Social Statistics

Statistics for calendar years:

	Live births	Deaths	Natural increase per 1,000	Marriages	Divorces
2011	21,947	18,699	1·6	6,671	2,298
2012	21,938	19,257	1·3	7,057	2,509
2013	21,111	19,334	0·9	6,254	2,351
2014	21,165	18,886	1·1	6,571	2,469
2015	20,641	19,834	0·4	6,449	2,432

Rates, 2015 (per 1,000 population): birth, 10·0; death, 9·6. Infant mortality, 2015: 1·6 per 1,000 live births (one of the lowest rates in the world). There were 425 suicides in 2015 (21·4 per 100,000 population).

In 2015 the most popular age range for marrying was 25–29 females and 30–34 years for males. Expectation of life, 2015, was 77·6 years for males and 83·5 for females. Annual population growth rate, 2010–14, 0·1%. Total fertility rate, 2015, 1·6 births per woman.

Climate

Summers are warm, winters are cold with frequent snow. Ljubljana, Jan. –4°C, July 22°C. Annual rainfall 1,383 mm.

Constitution and Government

The constitution became effective on 23 Dec. 1991. Slovenia is a parliamentary democratic republic with an executive that consists of a directly-elected president and a prime minister, aided by a council of ministers. It has a bicameral parliament (*Skupščina Slovenije*), consisting of a 90-member *National Assembly* (*Državni Zbor*), 88 members elected for four-year terms by proportional representation with a 4% threshold and two members elected by ethnic minorities; and a 40-member, advisory *State Council* (*Državni Svet*), elected for five-year terms by interest groups and regions. It has veto powers over the National Assembly. Administratively the country is divided into 212 municipalities of which 11 are urban municipalities.

The Judicial branch consists of a *Supreme Court*, whose judges are elected by the National Assembly, and a *Constitutional Court*, whose judges are elected for nine-year terms by the National Assembly and nominated by the president.

National Anthem

'Zdravljica' ('A Toast'); words by Dr France Prešeren, tune by Stanko Premrl.

Government Chronology

(LDS = Liberal Democracy of Slovenia; LMŠ = Marjan Šarec List; NSi = New Slovenia Christian People's Party; PS = Positive Slovenia; SD = Social Democrats; SDS = Slovenian Democratic Party; SKD = Slovenian Christian Democrats; SLS+SKD = Slovenian People's Party; SMC = Party of Miro Cerar; n/p = non-partisan)

Presidents since 1990.

1990–2002	n/p	Milan Kučan
2002–07	LDS	Janez Drnovšek
2007–12	n/p	Danilo Türk
2012–	SD	Borut Pahor

© Springer Nature Limited 2020
Palgrave Macmillan (ed.), *The Statesman's Yearbook 2020*,
https://doi.org/10.1057/978-1-349-95940-2_173

Prime Ministers since 1990.

1990–92	SKD	Lojze Peterle
1992–2000	LDS	Janez Drnovšek
2000	SLS+SKD, NSi	Andrej Bajuk
2000–02	LDS	Janez Drnovšek
2002–04	LDS	Anton (Tone) Rop
2004–08	SDS	Janez Janša
2008–12	SD	Borut Pahor
2012–13	SDS	Janez Janša
2013–14	PS	Alenka Bratušek
2014–18	SMC	Miro Cerar
2018–	LMŠ	Marjan Šarec

Recent Elections

Presidential elections were held on 22 Oct. and 12 Nov. 2017. The turnout in the first round was 44·2% and in the second round 42·1%. Borut Pahor (ind.) won 47·2% of the vote in the first round, Marjan Šarec (Marjan Šarec List) 24·8% and Romana Tomc (Slovenian Democratic Party) 13·7%. There were six other candidates. In the run-off held on 12 Nov. 2017 Borut Pahor received 53·1% of votes cast against 46·9% for Marjan Šarec.

Elections were held for the National Assembly on 3 June 2018; turnout was 52·6%. The Slovenian Democratic Party (SDS) won 25 seats with 24·9% of votes cast; the Marjan Šarec List (LMŠ), 13 with 12·6%; the Social Democrats (SD), 10 with 9·9%; the Modern Centre Party (SMC), 10 with 9·7%; The Left, 9 with 9·3%; New Slovenia-Christian Democrats (NSi), 7 with 7·2%; the Party of Alenka Bratušek (SAB), 5 with 5·1%, the Democratic Party of Pensioners of Slovenia (DeSUS), 5 with 4·9%; the Slovenian National Party (SNS), 4 with 4·2%. In addition, two seats were allocated to the Italian and Hungarian national minorities.

Current Government

President: Borut Pahor; b. 1963 (Social Democrats; sworn in 22 Dec. 2012 and re-elected 12 Nov. 2017).

In Feb. 2019 the five-party coalition government comprised:

Prime Minister: Marjan Šarec; b. 1977 (LMŠ; sworn in 13 Sept. 2018).

Deputy Prime Ministers: Andrej Bertoncelj (also *Minister of Finance*); Alenka Bratušek (also *Minister of Infrastructure*); Miro Cerar (also *Minister of Foreign Affairs*); Karl Erjavec (also *Minister of Defence*); Jernej Pikalo (also *Minister of Education, Science and Sport*).

Minister of Agriculture, Forestry and Food: Aleksandra Pivec. *Culture:* Dejan Prešiček. *Economic Development and Technology:* Zdravko Počivalšek. *Environment and Spatial Planning:* Jure Leben. *Health:* Samo Fakin. *Interior:* Boštjan Poklukar. *Justice:* Andreja Katič. *Labour, Family, Social Affairs and Equal Opportunities:* Ksenija Klampfer. *Public Administration:* Rudi Medved. *Minister without Portfolio Responsible for Development, Strategic Projects and Cohesion:* Marko Bandelli. *Minister without Portfolio Responsible for Slovenians Abroad:* Peter Jožef Česnik.

Office of the President: http://www.up-rs.si

Current Leaders

Borut Pahor

Position
President

Introduction
Borut Pahor of the Social Democrats was elected president (the youngest to hold the office) in Dec. 2012, defeating the incumbent Danilo Türk, and was re-elected for a further term in Nov. 2017. He had previously served as prime minister at the head of a centre-left coalition from Nov. 2008 until Jan. 2012.

Early Life
Pahor was born in 1963 in Postojna, southeast of Ljubljana. He studied political science at the University of Ljubljana and, at the age of 26, became the youngest-ever member of the central committee of the Slovenian branch of the Communist Party, gaining a reputation as a reformist. In 1992, after the

collapse of communism in Eastern Europe and the fragmentation of Yugoslavia, he was elected a deputy in the National Assembly of the newly independent Slovenia.

A year later Pahor became deputy leader of the newly formed United List of Social Democrats (ZLSD). At the third ZLSD conference in March 1997 he was elected party leader on a centrist, 'third way' platform. At the 2000 elections, having led his party into a coalition with Janez Drnovšek's Liberal Democracy of Slovenia, Pahor won a third term in the National Assembly and became its president. In 2004 he was elected to the European Parliament, where he joined the Socialist Group. In the same year the centre-left coalition of which he was a member lost to the centre-right alliance led by the Slovenian Democratic Party. In 2005, on his initiative, the ZLSD was renamed the Social Democrats.

Parliamentary elections held on 21 Sept. 2008 saw the Social Democrats gain 29 of the 90 available seats to become the country's largest party. It formed a coalition government with Zares, Liberal Democracy of Slovenia and the Democratic Party of Pensioners of Slovenia. Pahor was sworn in as premier on 21 Nov. 2008.

Career in Office
Pahor promised to cut taxes, reform the national health and pension systems and increase investment incentives, but was forced to redraft the 2009 national budget in the wake of the global financial crisis, allowing for a significant increase in the budget deficit.

In Dec. 2008, owing to an unresolved border dispute, Slovenia obstructed Croatia's accession to the European Union and, in March 2009, was the last member of NATO to ratify Croatia's accession to the alliance. However, in Sept. 2009 Pahor said that the dispute would no longer prejudice Croatia's EU accession negotiations and in Nov. Slovenia lifted its embargo. In March 2010 he agreed to opposition demands for a referendum on allowing the border issue to go to international arbitration, and in June that year voters narrowly backed the plan.

Following a gas dispute between Russia and Ukraine in 2009, Pahor moved to diversify Slovenia's energy supply, so reducing dependence on Russia, and established the Strategic Energy Council to advise the government. He has also stated his commitment to the fight against climate change.

On 20 Sept. 2011, amid internal coalition disputes and an inability to implement economic reforms, parliament voted 51–36 against a motion of confidence. Pahor's government fell and assumed a caretaker role. Following inconclusive elections in Dec. 2011 he was succeeded as premier by former prime minister, Janez Janša.

Pahor nevertheless continued in politics and announced his candidacy for the presidential elections held in Nov. and Dec. 2012, in which he won a second round victory with 67% of the vote.

Following parliamentary elections in July 2014, in which the newly-formed Party of Miro Cerar emerged as the largest party, Pahor appointed its leader, Miro Cerar, as prime minister in Aug. at the head of a centre-left coalition. In Nov. 2017 Pahor won 53% of the vote in a run-off poll to secure re-election as president for a further five-year term.

Marjan Šarec

Position
Prime Minister

Introduction
Marjan Šarec became prime minister in Sept. 2018, with his Marjan Šarec List the second largest group in parliament. He took office when the anti-immigration Slovenian Democratic Party (SDS) failed to form a government. He leads a broad centre-left coalition.

Early Life
Šarec was born on 2 Dec. 1977 and graduated from the Academy of Theatre, Radio, Film and Television in 2001. He became a familiar figure on national television and radio, developing a reputation as a comedian, political satirist and mimic while also working as a journalist and editor.

In 2010 he was elected mayor of Kamnik in north-central Slovenia. He then joined Positive Slovenia under Zoran Janković before creating his own political party, the Marjan Šarec List, in 2014.

At parliamentary elections in 2018 his party won 12·6% of the vote, giving them 13 seats, the second largest contingent after the SDS. After prolonged negotiations, Šarec formed a coalition encompassing his List, the Social Democrats, the Modern Centre Party, the Democratic Party of

Pensioners of Slovenia and the Party of Alenka Bratušek, with parliamentary support of the nine MPs of The Left. Šarec took office on 13 Sept.

Career in Office

Apart from moving forward the sale of Slovenia's largest bank in return for European Commission approval of state aid, Šarec faces the challenge of confronting a surge in anti-immigration feeling. Also, amid a fevered political atmosphere, he must strive to hold together his fragile coalition with a view to bringing through a raft of economic and social reforms, not least to the health care system.

Defence

Compulsory military service for seven months ended in Sept. 2003. The army became fully professional in 2010 when the compulsory reserve was replaced by a new system of voluntary reserve service.

In 2013 defence spending totalled US$474m. (US$238 per capita), representing 1·0% of GDP.

Army

Personnel (2011), 7,600 and an army reserve of 1,600. There is a paramilitary police force of 4,500 with 5,000 reserves.

Navy

There is an Army Maritime element numbering 47 personnel in 2011.

Air Force

The Army Air element numbers 530 with nine combat-capable aircraft.

International Relations

Slovenia held a referendum on EU membership on 23 March 2003, in which 89·6% of votes cast were in favour of accession. It became a member of NATO on 29 March 2004 and the EU on 1 May 2004.

Economy

Agriculture accounted for 2% of GDP in 2012, industry 32% and services 66%.

Overview

Slovenia was among the most developed of the ten countries that joined the EU in 2004. However, the global financial crisis resulted in a prolonged economic recession owing to poor bank balance sheets and weak domestic demand.

Sound monetary and fiscal policies in the years prior to the crisis contributed to a small fiscal deficit and single-digit inflation but there was heavy dependence on exports, 69% of which went to EU markets in 2008. This left the country exposed as the eurozone struggled for stability. Despite its pre-2008 success, Slovenia has also been criticized for an inefficient business environment and the excessive number of state-owned enterprises.

The economy contracted by 8·0% in 2009 prompting a government stimulus package, but after a modest rebound in 2011 it contracted again by an average of 1·6% per year in 2012 and 2013. A raft of austerity measures prompted mass protests which, along with a corruption scandal, led to the fall of Janez Janša's government in Feb. 2013. Annual average growth of 2·8% was then recorded between 2014 and 2016.

In Dec. 2013 Slovenia narrowly avoided an EU bailout after it was announced that the ailing banking sector required funding of €4·8bn. to meet capital targets. A fire sale of national assets followed, culminating in privatization of the majority state-owned brewing giant, Lasko, in April 2015.

Slovenia offers generous welfare protection and the European Commission has warned of the heavy future cost of the pension system, which is expected to reach 13% of GDP by 2050. Reforms are urgently required to recapitalize the banking sector, tackle rising unemployment and spur export growth.

Currency

On 1 Jan. 2007 the *euro* (EUR) replaced the *tolar* (SLT) as the legal currency of Slovenia at the irrevocable conversion rate of 239·64 tolars to one euro. There was deflation of 0·1% in 2016 but then inflation of 1·4% in 2017.

Foreign exchange reserves were US$552m. and gold reserves 103,000 troy oz in Aug. 2010. Total money supply in July 2005 was 1,032·3bn. tolars.

Budget

General government revenue in 2016 (provisional) totalled €17,484m. and expenditure €18,146m.

Principal sources of revenue in 2016 (provisional) were: taxes on goods and services, €5,909m.; social security contributions, €5,785m.; taxes on income, profits and capital gains, €2,740m. Main items of expenditure by economic type in 2016 (provisional): social benefits, €7,075m.; compensation of employees, €4,581m.; use of goods and services, €2,600m.

Slovenia had a budget deficit in 2017 of 0·1% of GDP. There had been a budget deficit in 2016 of 1·9% of GDP and in 2015 of 2·8% of GDP. The required target set by the EU is a budget deficit of no more than 3%.

VAT is 22·0% (reduced rate, 9·5%).

Performance

Real GDP growth was 2·3% in 2015, 3·1% in 2016 and 5·0% in 2017. Of all the central and Eastern European countries that joined the European Union in May 2004, Slovenia has the highest per capita GDP at 85% of the EU average in 2010 (higher than in Portugal and only marginally lower than in Greece). Total GDP in 2017 was US$48·8bn.

Banking and Finance

The central bank and bank of issue, the Bank of Slovenia, was founded on 25 June 1991 upon independence. The *Governor* is Boštjan Vasle, appointed in Dec. 2018 for a term of six years. In Dec. 2014 there were 17 banks in Slovenia, including seven direct subsidiaries of Eurosystem banks and three savings banks. The largest banks are Nova Ljubljanska banka (NLB), Nova Kreditna Banka Maribor (NKBM) and Abanka.

In Dec. 2013 Slovenia avoided the need for a potential EU–IMF bailout after the government announced that it could meet the costs of a €4·8bn. rescue of the country's three largest banks, which had accumulated billions of euros of bad loans.

In June 2012 gross external debt amounted to US$52,416m.

Foreign debt amounted to €41,616m. at Aug. 2010. In 1997 Slovenia accepted 18% of the US$4,400m. commercial bank debt of the former Yugoslavia, thus gaining access to international capital markets.

There is a stock exchange in Ljubljana (LjSE).

Energy and Natural Resources

In 2011, 18·8% of energy consumption came from renewables (wind power, solar power, hydro-electric power, tidal power, geothermal energy and biomass), compared to the European Union average of 13·0%. A target of 25% has been set by the EU for 2020.

Environment

Slovenia's carbon dioxide emissions from the consumption of energy were the equivalent of 8·0 tonnes per capita in 2011. An *Environmental Performance Index* compiled in 2016 ranked Slovenia 5th of 180 countries, with 89·0%. The index examined various factors in nine areas—agriculture, air quality, biodiversity and habitat, climate and energy, fisheries, forests, health impacts, water and sanitation, and water resources.

Electricity

Installed capacity was 3·3m. kW in 2011. There was one nuclear power station in operation. The total amount of electricity produced in 2011 was 16,057m. kWh (6,215m. kWh nuclear, 6,074m. kWh thermal and 3,703m. kWh hydro-electric). Consumption per capita in 2011 was 7,175 kWh.

Minerals

Brown coal production was 4,430,000 tonnes in 2010.

Agriculture

Only around 1·9% of the population worked in agriculture, forestry and fisheries in 2011. Output (in 1,000 tonnes) in 2011: maize, 349; wheat, 153; grapes, 121; apples, 105; potatoes, 96.

Livestock in 2011: cattle, 462,300; pigs, 347,310; sheep, 119,976; poultry, 4,006,718.

In 2011 there were 168,744 ha. of arable land and 26,867 ha. of permanent crops.

Forestry

In 2015 the area under forests was 1·25m. ha., or 62% of the total land area. Timber production in 2011 was 3·39m. cu. metres.

Fisheries

Sea catch, 2015: 196 tonnes. Freshwater catch, 2015: 141 tonnes. Aquaculture production totalled 1,590 tonnes in 2015.

Industry

Industry contributed 21·9% of GDP in 2012. Traditional industries are metallurgy, furniture-making and textiles. The manufacture of electric goods and transport equipment is being developed.

Output of main products in 2012 (in 1,000 tonnes): basic iron and steel and ferro alloys, 1,528; ready mixed concrete, 984; cement (confidential); paper and paperboard, 672; aluminium and aluminium products, 452; plastics in primary form, 163; passenger cars, 126,836 units.

Labour

The registered labour force was 920,184 in 2012, with 110,183 registered unemployed. The unemployment rate in Dec. 2018 was 5·2% (compared to 6·6% in 2017 as a whole). In 2012 the average monthly gross wage per employee was €1,525·47.

International Trade

Imports and Exports

Imports of goods (c.i.f.) in 2011 were worth US$31,253·8m. and exports of goods (f.o.b.) US$28,984·5m. Exports of goods accounted for 58·8% of GDP in 2011.

Major imports of goods in 2011 were petroleum and petroleum products (10·9%), road vehicles (9·6%), electrical machinery, apparatus and appliances (6·4%), and iron and steel (4·7%). Major exports of goods in 2011 were road vehicles (12·4%), electrical machinery, apparatus and appliances (10·4%), and medical and pharmaceutical products (9·2%).

Share of imports from principal markets in 2011: Germany, 18·7%; Italy, 17·8%; Austria, 11·6%; France, 4·7%; Hungary, 4·2%. Exports: Germany, 21·1%; Italy, 11·9%; Austria, 7·8%; France, 6·8%; Croatia, 6·7%. About 74% of trade is with fellow EU countries.

Communications

Roads

In 2012 there were 38,985 km of road including 676 km of motorways. There were in Dec. 2013: 1,063,795 passenger cars; 2,465 buses; 90,560 goods motor vehicles; and 92,986 motorcycles and mopeds. 533m. passenger-km were travelled by road in 2012. There were 18,904 road traffic accidents with material damage in 2013 in which 125 persons were killed. In 2013 there were 6·1 road deaths per 100,000 population.

Rail

There were 1,209 km of 1,435 mm gauge in 2014, of which 500 km were electrified. In 2014, 14·8m. passengers and 18·0m. tonnes of freight were carried. In Sept. 2010 the state-owned railway companies of Slovenia, Croatia and Serbia announced the creation of a joint venture called Cargo 10 to improve the management of freight trains along the route known as Corridor 10 that passes through all three countries.

Civil Aviation

There is an international airport at Ljubljana (Ljubljana Jože Pučnik Airport), which handled 1,436,003 passengers (all on international flights) and 10,099 tonnes of freight in 2015. The national air carrier, Adria Airways, has flights to most major European cities. It carried 1,112,857 passengers in 2014 (1,026,839 in 2013).

Shipping

A total of 4,177 vessels arrived at or departed from Slovenia's ports in 2014 (3,739 cargo-carrying vessels and 438 passenger vessels), including 3,831 at Koper. Goods traffic at Koper, the country's only cargo port, totalled 18·0m. tonnes in 2014.

Telecommunications

In 2009 there were 2,100,000 mobile phone subscriptions (1,039·8 per 1,000 inhabitants) and 1,034,000 fixed telephone lines. The leading telecommunications operator is the state-owned Telekom Slovenije. In 2009 there were 577,000 mobile broadband subscriptions and 479,000 fixed broadband internet subscriptions. In March 2012 there were 671,000 Facebook users.

Social Institutions

Out of 178 countries analysed in the 2017 *Fragile States Index*—a list published jointly by the Fund for Peace and *Foreign Policy* magazine—Slovenia was ranked the 17th least vulnerable to conflict or collapse. The index is based on 12 indicators of state vulnerability across social, political and economic categories.

Justice

There are 44 district courts, 11 regional courts, four higher courts, an administrative court and a supreme court. There are also four labour and social courts, and a higher labour and social court. The population in penal institutions in Sept. 2013 was 1,357 (66 per 100,000 of national population). In 2015 the World Justice Project *Rule of Law Index*, which provides data on how the rule of law is experienced by the general public across eight categories, ranked Slovenia 24th of 102 countries for criminal justice and 25th for civil justice.

Education

In the school year 2012–13 there were 109,218 pupils (full- and part-time) and 6,468 classroom teachers (full- and part-time) in primary education; and 54,565 pupils and 7,498 classroom teachers in lower secondary education. In upper secondary education there were 92,998 students (full- and part-time) and 7,159 classroom teachers (full- and part-time). There were 97,706 students and 7,189 academic staff in tertiary education in the academic year 2012–13. There are three public universities—at Koper (University of Primorska), Ljubljana and Maribor—and one private university, the University of Nova Gorica.

In 2012 public expenditure on education came to 6·3% of GNI and 13·1% of total government spending.

Health

In 2014 there were 29 hospitals with 9,356 beds. In the same year there were 5,760 doctors, 1,370 dentists, 17,809 nurses and 1,352 pharmacists. Slovenia spent 9·1% of its GDP on health in 2013.

In *Water: At What Cost? The State of the World's Water 2016*, WaterAid reported that 0·5% of the population does not have access to safe water.

Welfare

There were 551,258 people receiving pensions in 2008, of which 342,992 were old-age pensioners. The average retirement ages in 2008 were 61 years and 11 months for men and 57 years and 7 months for women. Plans to speed up the process of increasing the retirement age to 65 for both men and women, a move highlighted as key to long-term fiscal sustainability by the EU and the IMF, were put to the vote in a referendum in June 2011 but received only 28·0% backing. In 2013 spending on social protection accounted for 24·9% of GDP.

Religion

A study by the Pew Research Center's Forum on Religion & Public Life estimated that 78·4% of the population in 2010 were Christians and 3·6% Muslims, with 18·0% having no religious affiliation. Of the Christians in 2010, 94% were Catholics. In Feb. 2019 there was one cardinal.

Culture

World Heritage Sites

Slovenia has four sites on the UNESCO World Heritage List: Škocjan Caves (inscribed on the list in 1986), consisting of limestone caves, passages and waterfalls more than 200 metres deep; Ancient and Primeval Beech Forests of the Carpathians and Other Regions of Europe (2007 and 2017), shared with Albania, Austria, Belgium, Bulgaria, Croatia, Germany, Italy, Romania, Slovakia, Spain and Ukraine; the Prehistoric Pile dwellings around the Alps (2011), shared with Austria, France, Germany, Italy and Switzerland; and Heritage of Mercury: Almadén and Idrija (2012), shared with Spain.

Press

In 2013 there were nine daily newspapers with a combined circulation of 251,000 and 135 non-dailies. The most popular paid-for daily is *Slovenske novice*, with an average daily readership in 2013 of 278,000.

Tourism

In 2010, 1,869,000 non-resident tourists stayed in holiday accommodation (1,824,000 in 2009) including: 412,000 from Italy; 202,000 from Austria; 194,000 from Germany; 103,000 from Croatia.

Festivals

Kurentovanje is a ten-day carnival to chase away the winter, which ends on Mardi Gras—the biggest celebrations occur in the town of Ptuj. Lent Festival in Maribor is a major performing arts festival held in late June to early July and similar summer festivals take place in Ljubljana and in the region of Primorska throughout July and Aug. Two of the biggest music festivals are the Druga Godba world music festival in Ljubljana in May–June and Rock Otočec at Novo Mesto in July.

Diplomatic Representatives

Of Slovenia in the United Kingdom (17 Dartmouth St., London, SW1H 9BL)
   Ambassador: Tadej Rupel.

Of the United Kingdom in Slovenia (3 Trg Republike, 1000 Ljubljana)
   Ambassador: Sophie Honey.

Of Slovenia in the USA (2410 California St., NW, Washington, D.C., 20008)
   Ambassador: Stanislav Vidovič.

Of the USA in Slovenia (Prešernova 31, 1000 Ljubljana)
   Ambassador: Vacant.
   Chargé d'Affaires a.i.: Gautam Rana.

Of Slovenia to the United Nations
   Ambassador: Darja Bavdaž Kuret.

Of Slovenia to the European Union
   Permanent Representative: Janez Lenarčič.

Further Reading

Cox, John K., *Slovenia.* 2005
Fink-Hafner, Danica and Robbins, John R. (eds) *Making a New Nation: Formation of Slovenia.* 1997
National Statistical Office: National Statistical Office, Vožarski Pot 12, 1000 Ljubljana.
Website: http://www.stat.si

Solomon Islands

Capital: Honiara
Population projection, 2020: 647,000
GNI per capita, 2017: (PPP$) 1,872
HDI/world rank, 2017: 0·546/152
Internet domain extension: .sb

Key Historical Events

The Solomon Islands were discovered by Europeans in 1568 but 200 years passed before contact was made again. The southern Solomon Islands were placed under British protection in 1893; the eastern and southern outliers were added in 1898 and 1899. Santa Isabel and the other islands to the north were ceded by Germany in 1900. Full internal self-government was achieved on 2 Jan. 1976 and independence on 7 July 1978.

In 1997 Bartholomew Ulufa'alu, a Malaitan, was elected prime minister. The following year, fighting broke out between the Isatabu Freedom Movement, which claimed to be representative of the native peoples of the island of Guadalcanal, and the Malaitan Eagle Force. In 2000 the Malaita Eagles led a coup which deposed Ulufa'alu, who was held at gunpoint for two days. After the failure of a 2001 peace accord, conflict between the Malaita Eagles and the Isatabu Freedom Movement escalated in 2003 and an Australian-led peacekeeping force landed to restore order. After some initial success the force was scaled back towards the end of the year.

In 2006 Manasseh Sogavare became prime minister, having previously held the office following the 2000 coup. His appointment was marked by rioting in Honiara and the destruction of the city's Chinatown as tensions rose over the political and business influence of the local Chinese population. After losing a vote of confidence in Dec. 2007, Sogavare was replaced by Derek Sikua, who held office until Danny Philip was elected premier in Aug. 2010. He in turn was replaced by Gordon Darcy Lilo in Nov. the following year. However, when Lilo lost his parliamentary seat at the Nov. 2014 general election, Sogavare returned to head a new coalition.

Territory and Population

The Solomon Islands lie within the area 5° to 12° 30' S. lat. and 155° 30' to 169° 45' E. long. The group includes the main islands of Guadalcanal, Malaita, New Georgia, San Cristobal (now Makira), Santa Isabel and Choiseul; the smaller Florida and Russell groups; the Shortland, Mono (or Treasury), Vella La Vella, Kolombangara, Ranongga, Gizo and Rendova Islands; to the east, Santa Cruz, Tikopia, the Reef and Duff groups; Rennell and Bellona in the south; Ontong Java or Lord Howe to the north; and many smaller islands. The land area is estimated at 28,370 sq. km (10,954 sq. miles). The larger islands are mountainous and forest clad, with flood-prone rivers of considerable energy potential. Guadalcanal has the largest land area and the greatest amount of flat coastal plain. Population at the census of Nov. 2009, 515,870 (251,415 females); density, 18·2 per sq. km. In 2011, 18·9% of the population lived in urban areas.

The UN gives a projected population for 2020 of 647,000.

The islands are administratively divided into nine provinces plus a Capital Territory. Area, population and capital:

Province	Sq. km	2009 census	Capital
Capital Territory	22	64,602	—
Central Islands	615	26,051	Tulagi
Choiseul	3,837	26,379	Taro
Guadalcanal	5,336	93,613	Honiara
Isabel	4,136	26,158	Buala
Makira and Ulawa	3,188	40,419	Kirakira
Malaita	4,225	137,596	Auki

(continued)

Province	Sq. km	2009 census	Capital
Rennell and Bellona	671	3,041	Tigoa
Temotu	895	21,362	Lata (Santa Cruz)
Western	5,475	76,649	Gizo

The capital, Honiara, on Guadalcanal, is the largest urban area, with a population in 2009 of 64,602. 93% of the population are Melanesian; other ethnic groups include Polynesian, Micronesian, European and Chinese.

English is the official language, and is spoken by 1–2% of the population. In all 120 indigenous languages are spoken; Melanesian languages are spoken by 85% of the population.

Social Statistics

2008 estimates: births, 16,000; deaths, 3,000. Estimated birth rate in 2008 was 30·4 per 1,000 population; estimated death rate, 6·2. Life expectancy, 2013, 69·2 years for women and 66·3 for men. Annual population growth rate, 2000–08, 2·6%. Infant mortality, 2010, 23 per 1,000 live births; fertility rate, 2008, 3·9 births per woman.

Climate

An equatorial climate with only small seasonal variations. Southeast winds cause cooler conditions from April to Nov., but northwest winds for the rest of the year bring higher temperatures and greater rainfall, with annual totals ranging between 80" (2,000 mm) and 120" (3,000 mm).

Constitution and Government

The Solomon Islands are a constitutional monarchy with the British Sovereign (represented locally by a Governor-General, who must be a Solomon Island citizen) as Head of State. Legislative power is vested in the single-chamber *National Parliament* composed of 50 members, elected by universal adult suffrage for four years. Parliamentary democracy is based on a multi-party system. Executive authority is effectively held by the Cabinet, led by the Prime Minister.

The *Governor-General* is appointed for up to five years, on the advice of Parliament, and acts in almost all matters on the advice of the Cabinet. The Prime Minister is elected by and from members of Parliament. Other Ministers are appointed by the Governor-General on the Prime Minister's recommendation, from members of Parliament. The Cabinet is responsible to Parliament. Emphasis is laid on the devolution of power to provincial governments, and traditional chiefs and leaders have a special role within the arrangement.

National Anthem

'God save our Solomon Islands from shore to shore'; words and tune by P. Balekana.

Recent Elections

National elections were held on 19 Nov. 2014. The Democratic Alliance Party won 7 seats, United Democratic Party 5, People's Alliance Party 3, Kadare Party of Solomon Islands 1, Solomon Islands Party for Rural Advancement 1 and Solomon Islands People First Party 1. Independent candidates took 32 seats. Manasseh Sogavare was elected prime minister on 9 Dec. 2014, defeating Jeremiah Manele by 31 votes to 19 in the parliamentary vote.

Sir Frank Kabui was re-elected to a second term as governor-general by parliament on 6 May 2014. He defeated David Vunagi and Andrew Mua.

© Springer Nature Limited 2020
Palgrave Macmillan (ed.), *The Statesman's Yearbook 2020*,
https://doi.org/10.1057/978-1-349-95940-2_174

Current Government

Governor-General: Sir Frank Kabui (since 7 July 2009).

In Feb. 2019 the government comprised:

Prime Minister: Rick Hou; b. 1958 (sworn in 15 Nov. 2017).

Deputy Prime Minister: Manasseh Sogavare (also *Minister of Finance and Treasury*).

Minister of Agriculture and Livestock: Augustine Auga. *Commerce, Industries, Labour and Immigration:* William Bradford Marau. *Communication and Aviation:* Peter Shanel Agovaka. *Culture and Tourism:* Bartholomew Parapolo. *Development Planning and Aid Co-ordination:* Jeremiah Manele. *Education and Human Resource Development:* John Dean Kuku. *Environment and Conservation:* Culwick Togamana. *Fisheries and Marine Resources:* John Maneniaru. *Foreign Affairs and External Trade:* Milner Tozaka. *Forestry and Research:* Samuel Manetoali. *Health and Medical Services:* Dr Tautai Angikimua Kaitu'u. *Home Affairs:* Commins Aston Mewa. *Infrastructure Development:* Stanley Festus Sofu. *Justice and Legal Affairs:* Derrick Manuari. *Lands and Housing:* Andrew Manepora'a. *Mines and Energy:* Bradley Tovosia. *National Unity, Reconciliation and Peace:* Ishmael Mali Avui. *Police and National Security:* Moses Garu. *Provincial Government and Institutional Strengthening:* Nestor Ghiro. *Public Service:* Connelly Sandakabatu. *Rural Development and Indigenous Affairs:* Dudley Kopu. *Women, Youth and Children's Affairs:* Lanelle Tanangada.

Solomon Islands Parliament: http://www.parliament.gov.sb

Current Leaders

Rick Hou

Position

Prime Minister

Introduction

Rick Houenipwela (generally known as Rick Hou), a former governor of the Central Bank, was elected prime minister on 15 Nov. 2017 following the ousting of long-time leader Manasseh Sogavare.

Early Life

Rick Hou was born on 8 Aug. 1958 on Malaita, when the Solomon Islands was a British Protectorate. He studied accountancy at Papua New Guinea University of Technology and earned a graduate diploma in development administration from the Australian National University. He joined the newly established Central Bank of Solomon Islands in 1983 and was promoted to deputy governor five years later. Appointed governor in 1993, he went on to serve three terms. Having stepped down in 2008, he worked as a senior advisor to the executive director of the World Bank in Washington, D.C.

Hou was first elected to the Solomon Islands' parliament in Aug. 2010 as a member of the Democratic Party. He briefly worked as minister for public service, before becoming minister for finance and treasury in Nov. 2011. From 2014 he served as chairman of the public accounts committee. When Manasseh Sogavare, the long-standing prime minister, was ousted in a vote of no confidence in Nov. 2017, Hou entered the contest to succeed him. On 15 Nov. 2017 he was elected prime minister by 33 parliamentary votes to 16, defeating John Moffat Fugui.

Career in Office

Hou outlined his priorities as securing political stability, rectifying the weak fiscal situation and stamping out corruption. He was expected to back infrastructure programmes as a means of resuscitating the economy, including the reopening of health clinics and the completion of a deal to lay a submarine cable linking the capital, Honiara, with Sydney in Australia (the first phase of a funding contract for which was signed in June 2018).

Defence

The marine wing of the Royal Solomon Islands Police operates three patrol boats and a number of fast crafts for surveillance of fisheries and maritime boundaries. There is also an RSI Police Field Force stationed at the border with Papua New Guinea.

In July 2003 an Australian-led peacekeeping force, the Regional Assistance Mission to Solomon Islands (RAMSI), landed to restore stability after years of ethnic fighting and high-level corruption. The force included troops from Fiji,

New Zealand, Papua New Guinea and Tonga. With the security situation having become more stable, the military component ended in July 2013.

Economy

Agriculture accounted for 39% of GDP in 2009, industry 6% and services 55%.

Overview

The Solomon Islands has a small, open economy vulnerable to external shocks. Food production accounts for over 50% of GDP. Timber is the main export, and gold-mining operations relaunched in March 2010 with production beginning a year later. Tourism accounts for less than 2% of GDP. Almost 23% of the population lived in poverty in 2014 and only 47·9% of the population had access to electricity in 2016.

The global financial crisis led to a decline in commodity exports that brought about a contraction in growth of nearly 5% in 2009, as well as the depletion of international currency reserves. An 18-month credit arrangement with the International Monetary Fund was approved in June 2010 and extended for three years in Dec. 2012, helping to restore economic stability. A surge in logging production from 2010 saw GDP growth rebound to nearly 6·9% that year and 13·0% in 2011.

In mid-2011 the trade balance shifted from deficit to surplus for the first time since 2004. China accounted for almost 40% of the country's exports in 2012. Severe flooding in April 2014 caused damage worth an estimated US$108m. (equivalent to 9% of GDP) and also forced the closure of a gold mine responsible for 20% of net exports, with expectations that it would remain closed for the foreseeable future. Annual growth nevertheless averaged 3·2% from 2012 to 2017, driven principally by the logging sector. The fiscal deficit reached 4·0% of GDP in 2017, while inflation was recorded at an annual rate of 1·6% in Oct. that year.

Growth in the mid-term will require spending on infrastructure (especially in energy supply, transportation and telecommunications), along with investment in the fisheries and agriculture sectors, since logging production is slowing down.

Currency

The *Solomon Island dollar* (SBD) of 100 *cents* was introduced in 1977. It was devalued by 20% in Dec. 1997 and 25% in March 2002. There was inflation of 0·5% in both 2016 and 2017. In July 2005 foreign exchange reserves were US$83m. and total money supply was SI$447m.

Budget

In 2015 budgetary central government revenues totalled SI$4,375m. and expenditures were SI$3,175m. Taxes accounted for 60·9% of revenues in 2015; use of goods and services accounted for 47·7% of expenditures and compensation of employees 33·4%.

Performance

The economy grew by 2·5% in 2015 and then 3·5% in both 2016 and 2017. Total GDP in 2017 was US$1·3bn.

Banking and Finance

The Central Bank of Solomon Islands is the bank of issue; its *Governor* is Denton Rarawa. There are three commercial banks and a development bank.

External debt totalled US$215m. in 2010 and represented 38·8% of GNI.

Energy and Natural Resources

Environment

Carbon dioxide emissions from the consumption of energy in 2011 were the equivalent of 0·4 tonnes per capita.

Electricity

Installed capacity in 2011 was an estimated 36,000 kW. Production in 2011 was 83m. kWh and consumption per capita 154 kWh.

Oil and Gas

The potential for oil, petroleum and gas production has yet to be tapped.

Minerals

In 1999 gold output from mining totalled 3,456 kg and silver output 2,138 kg. The only mine in the Solomon Islands closed in 2000 owing to civil unrest.

However, in March 2010 the mine was revived and production began again in March 2011. It was closed again in April 2014 following severe flooding in the area. Gold output in 2012 totalled 2,180 kg and silver output 932 kg.

Agriculture

Land is held either as customary land (88% of holdings) or registered land. Customary land rights depend on clan membership or kinship. Only Solomon Islanders own customary land; only Islanders or government members may hold perpetual estates of registered land. Coconuts, cocoa, rice and other minor crops are grown. Production, 2013 estimates (in 1,000 tonnes): coconuts, 384; palm fruit oil, 240; sweet potatoes, 100; yams, 45; taro, 43; palm oil, 37; palm kernels, 13. In 2013 there were an estimated 20,000 ha. of arable land and 860,000 ha. of permanent crops.

Livestock (2013 estimates): pigs, 55,000; cattle, 15,000.

Forestry

Forests covered 2·19m. ha. in 2015 (78% of the land area). Of the total area under forests 51% was primary forest in 2015, 48% other naturally regenerated forest and 1% planted forest. Timber production was 2·10m. cu. metres in 2011.

Fisheries

The Solomon Islands' waters are among the richest in tuna. The total catch in 2015 was 72,851 tonnes (more than double the 2009 total).

Industry

Industries include palm oil manufacture, processed fish production, rice milling, fish canning, fish freezing, saw milling, food, tobacco and soft drinks. Other products include wood and rattan furniture, fibreglass articles, boats, clothing and spices.

Labour

The estimated economically active population in 2010 was 123,000 (69% males), up from 105,000 in 2005.

International Trade

Imports and Exports

Imports 2007, US$285·0m.; exports, US$158·5m. Main imports, 2007: machinery and transport equipment, 28·4%; mineral fuels and lubricants, 24·9%; food and live animals, 17·6%. Main exports, 2007: timber, 66·6%; fish products, 13·0%; palm oil, 8·8%. Principal import suppliers (2007): Australia, 31·5%; Singapore, 27·0%; Japan, 8·2%. Principal export markets (2007): China, 46·5%; Thailand, 7·2%; South Korea, 6·1%.

Communications

Roads

In 2010 there was estimated to be a total of 1,875 km of roads, of which 104 km were paved. The rest of the network is surfaced with gravel, coral or earth.

Civil Aviation

A new terminal has been opened at Henderson International Airport in Honiara. The national carrier is Solomon Airlines. In 2006 scheduled airline traffic of Solomon Islands-based carriers flew 3m. km, carrying 101,000 passengers (32,000 on international flights).

Shipping

There are international ports at Honiara, Yandina in the Russell Islands and Noro in New Georgia, Western Province. In Jan. 2014 there were two ships of 300 GT or over registered, totalling 1,000 GT.

Telecommunications

Telecommunications are operated by Solomon Telekom, a joint venture between the government of Solomon Islands and Cable & Wireless (UK). Telecommunications between Honiara and provincial centres are facilitated by modern satellite communication systems. In 2014 there were 7,500 main (fixed) telephone lines; mobile phone subscriptions numbered 376,700 (658 per 1,000 persons). In 2011 an estimated 6% of the population were internet users.

Social Institutions

Out of 178 countries analysed in the 2017 *Fragile States Index*—a list published jointly by the Fund for Peace and *Foreign Policy* magazine—the Solomon Islands was ranked the joint 52nd most vulnerable (along with the Comoros) to conflict or collapse. The index is based on 12 indicators of state vulnerability across social, political and economic categories.

Justice

Civil and criminal jurisdiction is exercised by the High Court of the Solomon Islands, constituted 1975. A Solomon Islands Court of Appeal was established in 1982. Jurisdiction is based on the principles of English law (as applying on 1 Jan. 1981). Magistrates' courts can try civil cases on claims not exceeding SI$6,000, and criminal cases with penalties not exceeding 14 years' imprisonment. Certain crimes, such as burglary and arson, where the maximum sentence is for life, may also be tried by magistrates. There are also local courts, which decide matters concerning customary titles to land; decisions may be put to the Customary Land Appeal Court. There is no capital punishment.

The population in penal institutions in Sept. 2013 was 321 (55 per 100,000 of national population).

Education

In 2011 there were 121,720 pupils at primary and 42,783 pupils at secondary level (27,258 at junior secondary and 15,525 at senior secondary). The adult literacy rate in 2009 was 89% among males and 79% among females.

Training of teachers and trade and vocational training is carried out at the College of Higher Education. The University of the South Pacific Centre is at Honiara. Other rural training centres run by churches are also involved in vocational training.

In 2009 total expenditure on education came to 9·0% of GDP and accounted for 16·8% of total government spending.

Health

A free medical service is supplemented by the private sector. An international standard immunization programme is conducted in conjunction with the WHO for infants. Tuberculosis has been eradicated but malaria remains a problem. In 2009 there were 118 physicians, and 1,080 nursing and midwifery personnel. There were 15 hospitals beds per 10,000 inhabitants in 2005.

In *Water: At What Cost? The State of the World's Water 2016*, WaterAid reported that 19·2% of the population does not have access to safe water.

Religion

According to estimates by the Pew Research Center's Forum on Religion & Public Life, 97·4% of the population in 2010 were Christians (mainly Protestants).

Culture

World Heritage Sites

The Solomon Islands has one site on the UNESCO World Heritage List: East Rennell (inscribed on the list in 1998), the largest raised coral atoll in the world.

Press

There are three main newspapers in circulation. *The Solomon Star* (circulation: 5,000) is daily and the *Solomon Express* and *The Island Sun* are weekly. The Government Information Service publishes a monthly issue of the *Solomon Nius* that exclusively disseminates news of government activities. Non-government organizations such as the Solomon Islands Development Trust (SIDT) also publish monthly papers on environmental issues.

Tourism

Tourism in the Solomon Islands is still in a development stage. The emphasis is on establishing major hotels in the capital and provincial centres, to be supplemented by satellite eco-tourism projects in the rural areas. In 2011 there were 22,941 foreign tourists.

Festivals

Festivities and parades in the capital and provincial centres normally mark the National Day of Independence. The highlight is the annual National Trade and Cultural Show.

Diplomatic Representatives

Of the Solomon Islands in the United Kingdom (Room 229–230, 10 Greycoat Pl., London SW1P 1SB)
  High Commissioner: Eliam Tangirongo.

Of the United Kingdom in the Solomon Islands (Gallery 3 & 4, First Floor, Heritage Park Hotel Ltd, Mendana Ave., PO Box 676, Honiara)
  High Commissioner: David Ward.

Of the Solomon Islands in the USA and to the United Nations (800 Second Ave., Suite 400L, New York, NY 10017)
  Ambassador: Robert Sisilo.

Of the USA in the Solomon Islands
  Ambassador: Catherine Ebert-Gray (resides in Port Moresby, Papua New Guinea).

Of the Solomon Islands to the European Union
  Ambassador: Moses Kouni Mose.

Further Reading

Bennett, J. A., *Wealth of the Solomons: A History of a Pacific Archipelago, 1800–1978.* 1987

Fraenkel, Jonathan, *Manipulation of Custom: From Uprising to Intervention in the Solomon Islands.* 2005

White, Geoffrey M., *Identity Through History: Living Stories in a Solomon Islands Society.* 2003

National Statistical Office: Solomon Islands National Statistical Office, PO Box G6, Department of Finance, Honiara.

Website: http://www.statistics.gov.sb

Somalia

Jamhuuriyadda Federaalka Soomaaliya (Federal Republic of Somalia)

Capital: Mogadishu
Population projection, 2020: 16·11m.
GNI per capita, 2015: (PPP$) 294
Internet domain extension: .so

Key Historical Events

The origins of the Somali people can be traced back 2,000 years when they displaced an Arabic people. They converted to Islam in the 10th century and were organized in loose Islamic states by the 19th century. The northern part of Somaliland became a British protectorate in 1884. The southern part belonged to two local rulers who, in 1889, accepted Italian protection for their lands. Italy invaded Ethiopia in 1935 from Somaliland and in 1936 Somaliland was incorporated with Eritrea and Ethiopia into Italian East Africa. In 1940 Italian forces invaded British Somaliland but in 1941 the British, with South African and Indian troops, recaptured this territory and occupied Italian Somaliland. After the Second World War British Somaliland reverted to its colonial status and ex-Italian Somaliland became the UN Trust Territory of Somaliland, administered by Italy.

The independent Somali Republic was established on 1 July 1960 with the merger of the British Somaliland Protectorate, which first became independent on 26 June 1960, and the Italian Trusteeship Territory of Somaliland. On 21 Oct. 1969 Maj.-Gen. Mohammed Siyad Barre seized power, prompting a bloody civil war. Barre fled in Jan. 1991 but fighting continued. In Aug. 1992 a new coalition government agreed a UN military presence to back up relief efforts to help the estimated 1·5–2m. victims of famine. In Dec. 1992 the leaders of the two most prominent warring factions, Ali Mahdi Muhammad and Muhammad Farah Aidid, agreed to a peace plan. At the end of March 1993 the warring factions agreed to disarm and form a National Transitional Council. In Nov. 1994 the UN began to withdraw its forces.

The principal insurgent group in the north of the country, the Somali National Movement, unilaterally declared an independent **'Somaliland Republic'** on 17 May 1991. Muhammad Aidid's forces launched a campaign to reoccupy the 'Republic' in Jan. 1996. Aidid was assassinated in July 1996 and succeeded by his son Hussein Aidid. In July 1998 leaders in the northeast of Somalia proclaimed an 'autonomous state' named **Puntland**.

Peace efforts in neighbouring Djibouti culminated in July 2000 in a power-sharing agreement and a constitution valid for a three-year transition. The election of a civilian government followed in Aug. 2000, and in Oct. the government returned to Somalia from Djibouti. In April 2002 **'Southwestern Somalia'** broke away from Mogadishu, creating a third autonomous state. It was dissolved in 2005 but a reconfigured **Southwestern State** was constituted in Nov. 2014. **Galmudug** became an autonomous state in Aug. 2006, with **Jubaland** declaring its autonomy in April 2011 (gaining formal recognition in Aug. 2013). A sixth autonomous state, **Hirshabelle**, claimed autonomy in Oct. 2016.

In June 2006 an Islamic militia, the Islamic Courts Union, took control of Mogadishu and a large part of southern Somalia. Faced with government and Ethiopian forces, the Islamist militias withdrew from Mogadishu in Dec. 2006.

In June 2012 separatist leaders from Somaliland agreed to talks with the Somali government in London. In Aug. 2012 a Somali-elected parliament convened in Mogadishu for the first time in 20 years. It elected Hassan Sheikh Mohamud as president. In Oct. 2012 a mix of government and African Union troops ejected the Al-Shabaab militant Islamist group from Kismayo, its last major urban stronghold.

Territory and Population

Somalia is bounded north by the Gulf of Aden, east and south by the Indian Ocean, and west by Kenya, Ethiopia and Djibouti. Total area 637,657 sq. km (246,201 sq. miles). A census has not been held since 1987, when the population was 7,114,431. The United Nations gave an estimated population for 2013 of 13·13m.; density, 20·6 per sq. km. Population counting is complicated owing to large numbers of nomads and refugee movements as a result of famine and clan warfare. Over 1·1m. Somalis are displaced within the country and in 2016 there were 1·1m. Somali refugees living abroad, mainly in Kenya.

The UN gives a projected population for 2020 of 16·11m.

In 2011, 37·9% of the population were urban.

The country is administratively divided into 18 regions (with chief cities): Awdal (Baki), Bakol (Xuddur), Bay (Baydhabo), Benadir (Mogadishu), Bari (Bosaso), Galguduud (Duusa Marreeb), Gedo (Garbaharrey), Hiran (Beledweyne), Jubbada Dhexe (Jilib), Jubbada Hoose (Kismayo), Mudug (Gaalkacyo), Nogal (Garowe), Woqooyi Galbeed (Hargeisa), Sanaag (Ceerigabo), Shabeellaha Dhexe (Jowhar), Shabeellaha Hoose (Marka), Sol (Las Anod), Togder (Burao). Somaliland comprises the regions of Awdal, Woqooyi Galbeed, Togder, Sanaag and Sol. Puntland consists of Bari, Nogal and northern Mudug. Southwestern State consists of Bay, Bakol and Shabeellaha Hoose. Galmudug comprises Galguduud and southern Mudug, Jubaland includes Gedo, Jubbada Dhexe and Jubbada Hoose, while Hirshabelle consists of Hiran and Shabeellaha Dhexe.

The capital is Mogadishu (2014 population estimate, 2,014,000). Other large towns are Baidoa, Bosaso, Gaalkacyo and Hargeisa.

The official language is Somali. Arabic, English and Italian are widely spoken.

Social Statistics

Births, 2008 estimate, 394,000; deaths, 140,000. Rates, 2008 estimate (per 1,000 population): birth, 44·1; death, 15·7. Infant mortality, 2010, 108 per 1,000 live births. Annual population growth rate, 2000–08, 2·4%. Life expectancy at birth, 2013, was 53·4 years for men and 56·7 years for women. Fertility rate, 2008, 6·4 births per woman.

Climate

Much of the country is arid, although rainfall is more adequate towards the south. Temperatures are very high on the northern coasts. Mogadishu, Jan. 79°F (26·1°C), July 78°F (25·6°C). Annual rainfall 17" (429 mm). Berbera, Jan. 76°F (24·4°C), July 97°F (36·1°C). Annual rainfall 2" (51 mm).

Constitution and Government

A new constitution was promulgated on 1 Aug. 2012 after over 20 years of non-functioning government. It replaced the constitution of 1979 that itself had lost authority after the ousting of President Siyad Barre in 1991. The 2012 constitution was adopted by the National Constitutional Assembly with 96% backing from the 645 community leaders present at the vote (from a total of 825).

A bicameral federal parliament was created in 2016. The new parliamentary structure is comprised of a 54-member *Upper House* and a 275-member *House of the People*, with all members indirectly elected for four-year terms. Both houses reserve 30% of the seats for women. Seats in the Upper House are allocated based on region while the House of the People employs a power-sharing formula, based on the four major clans and an alliance of minority clans. Parliament elects the *President*, who in turn appoints a *Prime Minister*.

The Somali government—with the support of the United Nations Assistance Mission in Somalia (UNSOM)—is preparing for direct universal elections in 2020.

Galmudug

Galmudug, in the centre of the country, was established in Aug. 2006. It covers 142,400 sq. km and the capital city is Dhusamareb. Ahmed Duale Gelle was elected president in May 2017.

© Springer Nature Limited 2020
Palgrave Macmillan (ed.), *The Statesman's Yearbook 2020*,
https://doi.org/10.1057/978-1-349-95940-2_175

Hirshabelle

Hirshabelle, in the south-central part of the country, was established in Oct. 2016. The capital is Jowhar. Mohamed Abdi Waare has been president since Oct. 2017.

Jubaland

Jubaland, in the south of the country, declared autonomy in April 2011. It covers an area of 110,300 sq. km and had an estimated population of 4·5m. in 2017. The capital is Bu'ale. Ahmed Mohamed Islam was elected president in May 2013.

Puntland

Puntland, in the northeast of Somalia, declared itself an 'autonomous state' in July 1998. It covers 300,000 sq. km and had an estimated population in 2009 of 3·9m. The capital is Garowe. Said Abdullahi Deni became president in Jan. 2019.

Somaliland

An independent Somaliland Republic, in the north of Somalia, was established on 17 May 1991 based on the territory of the former British protectorate that ran from 1884 until Somali independence in 1960. It covers an area of 176,100 sq. km. The capital is Hargeisa and the population in 2014 was estimated at 3·5m. Musa Bihi Abdi was elected president in Nov. 2017.

Southwestern State

Southwestern State, in the southwest of the country, initially declared autonomy in April 2002 but was dissolved in 2005 before being reconstituted in Nov. 2014. In 2015 it had an estimated population of 5·3m. Baidoa is the capital. Abdiaziz Hassan Mohamed was elected president in Dec. 2018.

National Anthem

'Qolobaa Calankeed' ('Every nation has its own flag'); words and tune by Abdullahi Qarshe.

Recent Elections

Somalia's parliament elected Mohamed Abdullahi Mohamed president on 8 Feb. 2017. In the first round Hassan Sheikh Mohamud—the incumbent president—received 88 votes, ahead of Mohamed Abdullahi Mohamed (the prime minister from Nov. 2010 to June 2011) with 72 votes, Sharif Sheikh Ahmed (the president between Jan. 2009 and Aug. 2012) with 49 votes and Omar Abdirashid Ali Sharmarke—the incumbent prime minister—with 37 votes. Sharmarke then pulled out of the second round, in which Mohamed Abdullahi Mohamed won with 184 votes against 97 for Hassan Sheikh Mohamud and 46 for Sharif Sheikh Ahmed.

The first elections for the new parliamentary system—composed of a 54-member *Upper House* and 275-member *House of the People*—were held in Oct.–Nov. 2016, with members of the Upper House elected by regional assemblies and members of the House of the People elected by 275 electoral colleges. Each of the newly-formed electoral colleges—appointed by 135 Elders—is comprised of 51 regional delegates and includes a minimum of 16 women and 10 youth, as well as representatives from all of the sub-clans local to the respective seat.

The 2016 elections are considered by the United Nations Assistance Mission in Somalia (UNSOM) to be a milestone in the path to universal elections—whereas in 2012 the parliament was selected by 135 male Elders with voting restricted to the capital city, in 2016 parliament was elected by more than 14,000 citizens (30% of whom were female) at six locations across the country.

Current Government

President: Mohamed Abdullahi Mohamed; b. 1962 (Tayo Political Party; sworn in 8 Feb. 2017).

In Feb. 2019 the government comprised:

Prime Minister: Hassan Ali Kheyre; b. 1968 (ind.; sworn in 1 March 2017).

Deputy Prime Minister: Mahdi Ahmed Guled.

Minister of Agriculture: Said Hussein Iid. *Commerce and Industry:* Mohamed Abdi Hayir. *Constitutional Affairs:* Adirahman Hoosh Jibril. *Defence:* Hassan Ali Mohamed. *Education:* Abdirahman Dahir Osman. *Energy and Water:* Abdulaziz Abdullahi Mohamed. *Finance:* Abdirahman Dualle Beyleh. *Fisheries and Marine Resources:* Abdirahman Mohamed

Abdi Hashi. *Foreign Affairs:* Ahmed Isse Awad. *Health and Social Care:* Fowsiya Abiikar Nur. *Humanitarian Affairs and Disaster Management:* Hamza Said Hamza. *Information:* Dahir Mohamud Gelleh. *Interior, Federal Affairs and Reconciliation:* Mohamed Abdi Sabriye. *Internal Security:* Muhamed Abukar Islow Duale. *Justice:* Hassan Hussein Hajji. *Labour:* Salah Ahmed Jama. *Livestock:* Sheikh Nur Mohamed Hassan. *Petroleum and Mineral Resources:* Abdirashid Mohamed Ahmed. *Planning, Investment and Economic Promotion:* Jamal Mohamed Hassan. *Ports and Marine Transport:* Maryan Aweys. *Posts and Telecommunications:* Abdi Anshur Hassan. *Public Works and Housing:* Abdifitah Mohamed Ibrahim. *Religious Affairs:* Hassan Moalim Hussein. *Transport and Civil Aviation:* Mohamed Abdullahi Salad. *Women and Human Rights:* Deeqa Yasin Hajji Yusuf. *Youth and Sports:* Khadija Mohamed Diriye.

Office of the President (Arabic and Somali only): https://www.villasomalia.gov.so

Current Leaders

Mohamed Abdullahi Mohamed

Position

President

Introduction

A dual Somali-US citizen, Mohamed Abdullahi Mohamed—widely known as Farmaajo—took office as president on 16 Feb. 2017 after defeating incumbent President Hassan Sheikh Mohamud in a second round parliamentary vote.

Early Life

Mohamed Abdullahi Mohamed was born in Mogadishu on 11 March 1962. After completing his schooling, he entered the civil service, including a stint at the ministry of foreign affairs. In 1985 he moved to the USA as first secretary at the Somali embassy in Washington, D.C. Later, in 1993, he graduated in history from the State University of New York (SUNY)–Buffalo.

Mohamed then worked for various state agencies in the USA. He was finance chairman for Buffalo's municipal housing authority from 1994–97 and equal employment manager at the New York State department of transportation from 2002–10. He also taught conflict resolution at Erie Community College.

Returning to Somalia in 2010, he was appointed prime minister in Oct. that year following the resignation of Omar Ali Sharmarke. He embarked upon a series of reforms, including reducing the number of cabinet positions, requiring ministers to disclose their personal assets and establishing an anti-corruption commission. Following political infighting between the then President Sharif Ahmed and the speaker of parliament, Mohamed resigned in June 2011 and briefly returned to work in the United States.

Having been beaten in the first round of Somalia's 2012 presidential election, Mohamed then successfully fought the 2017 election promising to confront corruption, defeat the militant Islamist al-Shabaab group and promote food security.

Career in Office

In his inaugural address, Mohamed acknowledged the 'daunting' task ahead of him, claiming: 'This is the beginning of the era of unity, the democracy of Somalia and the. . . fight against corruption.'

Despite the government's increasing control across Somali territory, the overall security situation remained volatile as attacks by al-Shabaab jihadists persisted in 2017 and 2018. In a bid to counter the terror threat, in Aug. 2018 Mohamed reshuffled key security officials, including new appointments as commander of the Somali National Army, deputy director of the National Intelligence Security Agency and director of presidential security.

In July 2018 Somalia and Eritrea announced that they would establish diplomatic relations and exchange ambassadors after years of animosity. Then in Sept. the World Bank approved US$80m. in grants to Somalia, marking the first such disbursement to the Somali government in 30 years.

Defence

Army

Following the 1991 revolution there were no national armed forces for many years. However, in 2013 a first national army division was reinstated in a major step towards reviving the Somali Armed Forces. The Somali National Army reportedly comprised an estimated 20,000 personnel in mid-2014.

Economy

Agriculture accounts for approximately 59% of GDP, industry 10% and services 31%.

Somalia was rated the most corrupt country in the world in a 2018 survey of 180 countries carried out by the anti-corruption organization Transparency International.

Overview

Somalia has experienced decades of civil conflict, which saw the collapse of central government in 1991 and parliament only reconvening in the capital 21 years later. A large private sector, trading locally and with Asian partners, has compensated for a weak public sector. Remittances, amounting to around US$1·3bn. in 2016, have helped stimulate private investment in a number of commercial ventures, as well as partially offsetting a decline in per capita income. The formal economy is extremely fragile. Although GDP reached US$6·5bn. in 2017 (a 2·4% increase on 2016), growth was retarded by drought that year and remains too weak to significantly reduce widespread poverty. Somalia was ranked the most corrupt country in the world in 2016, 2017 and 2018 according to Transparency International.

The public external debt is high (estimated at more than 75% of GDP) and the servicing of that debt is not assured. Unemployment, especially among the young, is chronic. The country remains dependent on international aid. Somalia is one of three member states to remain in protracted arrears to the International Monetary Fund (IMF), accounting for 17% of total arrears to the Fund. Reviews of its overdue financial obligations have been postponed since Oct. 1990, owing to the absence of a functioning government and ongoing political and security problems, although the IMF resumed relations with the country in April 2013 after a 22-year gap.

Currency

The unit of currency is the *Somali shilling* (SOS) of 100 *cents*.

Budget

A budget for 2012 of US$126m. was reportedly approved in Dec. 2011.

Performance

Real GDP growth was 3·9% in 2015, 4·4% in 2016 and 2·3% in 2017. Total GDP in 2017 was US$7·4bn.

Banking and Finance

The bank of issue is the Central Bank of Somalia (*Governor*, Bashir Isse Ali). The separatist Somaliland Republic has its own functioning central bank in Hargeisa, the Bank of Somaliland (*Governor*, Ali Ibrahim Jama). Remittance companies (*hawala*) took the place of banks in the 1990s, channelling approximately US$800m. a year. Al-Barakaat, the largest *hawala*, was shut down in Nov. 2001. All national banks were bankrupted by 1990. The Universal Bank of Somalia, the first commercial bank in Mogadishu since 1990, opened with European backing in Jan. 2002.

In 2010 external debt totalled US$2,942m.

Energy and Natural Resources

Environment

Carbon dioxide emissions from the consumption of energy in 2011 were the equivalent of 0·1 tonnes per capita. An *Environmental Performance Index* compiled in 2016 ranked Somalia last of 180 countries, with 27·7%. The index examined various factors in nine areas—agriculture, air quality, biodiversity and habitat, climate and energy, fisheries, forests, health impacts, water and sanitation, and water resources.

Electricity

In 2011 installed capacity was 80,000 kW. Production (2011): 330m. kWh.

Oil and Gas

Proven natural gas reserves were 5·7bn. cu. metres in 2013.

Minerals

There are deposits of chromium, coal, copper, gold, gypsum, lead, limestone, manganese, nickel, sepiolite, silver, titanium, tungsten, uranium and zinc.

Agriculture

Somalia is essentially a pastoral country, and about 80% of the inhabitants depend on livestock-rearing. Half the population is nomadic. Agricultural land totalled around 44·0m. ha. in 2012. In the same year there were about 1·0m. ha. of arable land and 25,000 ha. of permanent crops. An estimated 200,000 ha. were equipped for irrigation in 2012. Output, 2013 estimates (in 1,000 tonnes): sorghum, 231; sugarcane, 220; maize, 149; cassava, 90; sesame seeds, 27. Livestock (2013 estimates): 12·3m. sheep; 11·6m. goats; 7·1m. camels; 4·9m. cattle. Somalia has the greatest number of camels of any country in the world.

Forestry

In 2015 the area under forests was 6·36m. ha., or 10% of the total land area. In 2011, 14·07m. cu. metres of roundwood were cut. Frankincense and myrrh are produced.

Fisheries

An estimated 30,000 tonnes of fish were caught in 2015, almost entirely from marine waters.

Industry

A few small industries exist including sugar refining, food processing and textiles. Raw sugar production was an estimated 15,000 tonnes in 2005.

Labour

The estimated economically active population in 2010 was 3,627,000 (59% males), up from 3,267,000 in 2005.

Somalia had 73,000 people living in slavery according to the Walk Free Foundation's 2013 *Global Slavery Index*.

International Trade

Imports and Exports

Imports in 2015 were estimated at US$2·1bn. and exports at US$0·5bn. Main imports: vegetables, raw sugar and rice. Main exports: sheep and goats, bovine animals and other animals. India is the principal import supplier, ahead of China. Saudi Arabia is the biggest export market, with Oman the second largest.

Communications

Roads

Before the start of the Somali Civil War in the mid-1980s the network had a total length of more than 21,000 km. In 2006, 90% of the road network was considered to be in a poor or a very poor state of repair. As the country begins to recover after years of conflict main roads are being repaired in order to facilitate the movement of goods and people.

Civil Aviation

There are international airports at Mogadishu and Hargeisa. In 2010 there were flights to Aden, Djibouti, Dubai, Jeddah, Nairobi, Sharjah and Wajir in addition to internal services.

Shipping

There are ports at Berbera, Bosaso, Kismayo, Marka and Mogadishu.

Piracy off the coast of Somalia was intensifying for several years with 215 attacks in the waters off Somalia recorded in 2009, 219 in 2010 and 236 in 2011. There were 14 actual hijacks in 2012, down from 28 in 2011 and 49 in 2010. The problem has become much less serious in the meantime, largely thanks to more patrolling of the waters off East Africa by international navies. However, NATO's anti-piracy initiative ended in Dec. 2016 and in March 2017 a commercial ship was attacked by Somali pirates for the first time since 2012.

Telecommunications

Somalia had 70,000 fixed telephone lines in 2012 (6·9 per 1,000 persons); mobile phone subscriptions numbered 1·8m. in 2011 (181·7 per 1,000 persons). In 2013 an estimated 1·5% of the population were internet users.

Social Institutions

According to the 2017 *Fragile States Index*—a list published jointly by the Fund for Peace and *Foreign Policy* magazine—Somalia was ranked as the country second most vulnerable to conflict or collapse. The index is based on 12 indicators of state vulnerability across social, political and economic categories.

Justice

There are 84 district courts, each with a civil and a criminal section. There are eight regional courts and two Courts of Appeal (at Mogadishu and Hargeisa), each with a general section and an assize section. The Supreme Court is in Mogadishu. The death penalty is in force; there were five judicial executions in 2018.

Education

The nomadic life of a large percentage of the population inhibits educational progress. Adult literacy was estimated at 38% in the period 2000–06 (50% among males and 26% among females). In 2007 there were 457,132 pupils in primary schools and 86,929 in secondary schools. In 2006, 23·5% of primary age children and 26·2% of secondary age children were attending school. The longest-established university was for many years the Somali National University in Mogadishu (founded 1954), but it was extensively damaged in the civil war and classes have been suspended indefinitely. A private university, Mogadishu University, was opened in 1997.

Health

In 2006 there were 300 physicians (3·5 per 100,000 population) and 965 nursing and midwifery personnel.

Somalia has among the highest percentages of undernourished people of any country, at 62% in the period 2005–07.

Religion

The population is almost entirely Sunni Muslims.

Culture

Press

There were seven daily newspapers in 2008. Average daily circulation of newspapers in 2008 totalled 21,000. In the 2013 *World Press Freedom Index* compiled by Reporters Without Borders, Somalia was ranked 175th out of 179 countries.

Tourism

Tourism was unknown for many years during the worst of the civil war, but visitor numbers have been increasing slowly as some sense of normality returns to the country. Somaliland's relative safety compared to the rest of Somalia has allowed a slightly more advanced tourism industry to develop there.

Diplomatic Representatives

Of the United Kingdom in Somalia (Near Mogadishu International Airport, Mogadishu)
Ambassador: David Concar.

Of Somalia in the USA (1705 DeSales St., NW, Suite 300, Washington, D.C., 20036–4421)
Ambassador: Vacant.
Chargé d'Affaires a.i.: Run Said Korshel.

Of the USA in Somalia
Ambassador: Donald Y. Yamamoto.

Of Somalia to the United Nations
Ambassador: Abukar Dahir Osman.

Of Somalia to the European Union
Ambassador: Ali Saeed Fiqi.

Further Reading

Fergusson, James, *The World's Most Dangerous Place: Inside the Outlaw State of Somalia.* 2013
Hansen, Stig Jarle, *Al-Shabaab in Somalia: The History and Ideology of a Militant Islamist Group, 2005–2012.* 2013
Lewis, Alexandra, *Security, Clans and Tribes: Unstable Governance in Somaliland, Yemen and the Gulf of Aden.* 2014
Lewis, I. M., *A Modern History of the Somali: Nation and State in the Horn of Africa.* 2002
Woodward, Peter, *The Horn of Africa: Politics and International Relations.* 2002
National Statistical Office: Central Statistical Department, State Planning Commission, Mogadishu.

South Africa

Republic of South Africa

Capitals: Pretoria/Tshwane (Administrative), Cape Town (Legislative), Bloemfontein (Judicial)
Seat of parliament: Cape Town
Seats of government: Cape Town, Pretoria
Population projection, 2020: 58·72m.
GNI per capita, 2017: (PPP$) 11,923
HDI/world rank, 2017: 0·699/113=
Internet domain extension: .za

Key Historical Events

The San and the Khoikhoi were the indigenous peoples of southern Africa. The San were nomadic hunter-gatherers who had lived from the land at the edge of the Kalahari desert for thousands of years. The Khoikhoi shared customs with the San and spoke related languages but also herded cattle and lived in more settled communities. The Khoikhoi settlements were most numerous in the Orange River valley and around the Cape. From the 4th century AD the eastern part of southern Africa was settled by Bantu-speaking groups, moving south from the continent's drier interior. They were mixed farmers: herding sheep and cattle, hunting game, cultivating sorghum and making tools and weapons from iron.

The hunting and herding communities of southern Africa came into contact with the wider world at the end of the fifteenth century. Portuguese mariners first rounded the Cape peninsula in 1487 and opened a trade route into the Indian Ocean. A century later the route was used by Spanish, English, Dutch and French seafarers. They landed occasionally on the Cape peninsula and bartered sheep and cattle with Khoikhoi pastoralists in return for iron and copper goods. In 1649 the Dutch East India Company, the world's most powerful trading corporation, established a trading post at the Cape. Three years later Jan van Riebeeck arrived with orders to establish a fort at Table Bay and supply passing ships with meat, fruit and vegetables. Within a decade slaves were brought in to work on building and maintaining the infrastructure, and settlers began to arrive from the Netherlands. Relations between the Dutch and the Khoikhoi soon deteriorated: quarrels over rights to graze cattle escalated into warfare as early as 1659.

Over the next century the population of the Cape Colony reached 10,000. It was a diverse community, where traders from Europe and Asia converged and exchanged goods and news. Large farms, cultivating vines and grain, were established in the fertile valleys to the east of Cape Town. Devastated by smallpox in 1713, the Khoikhoi population was unable to prevent *trekboers* (Dutch pastoral farmers) from moving to the north and east of the Cape colony. By 1770 trekboers were grazing their cattle as far east as the Fish river, where they came into contact with Xhosa farmers. More numerous and powerful than the Khoikhoi, and with greater resistance to European diseases, the Xhosa fought the Dutch settlers in a series of 'Frontier Wars'.

By the late 18th century Dutch sea power was on the wane. Vying with France for control of the main trade routes to Asia and the Americas, the British first seized Cape Town in 1795. Following the peace treaties of 1814, which ended the Napoleonic Wars, British sovereignty over the colony was confirmed. For the British, the main purpose of their acquisition was to provide a stepping-stone to their increasingly important colonies in Asia.

In the first two decades of the 19th century the Zulu people of the northeastern region (Natal) strengthened their power-base under their leader, Shaka. In response to a prolonged drought the Zulus conquered lands from rival Nguni groups, which culminated in widespread havoc and destruction, known as the *Mfecane*. From the chaos new kingdoms emerged, notably Gaza and Swaziland, while the Sotho, under King Moshoeshoe, formed the mountain territory now known as Lesotho.

The *Mfecane* led to the migration of thousands of Basotho and Batswana from the High Veld and Xhosa from the coastal plains into the Cape Colony. In the 1830s Boer settlers, increasingly dissatisfied with British rule and, realising that the *Mfecane* had caused the depopulation of land to the north and east, began to move there. In the 'Great Trek' that began in 1836, the Afrikaners were seeking a free and independent state which they achieved in the establishment of the Orange Free State and Transvaal in 1854.

Meanwhile, the British strengthened their hold over the Cape Colony and Natal by bringing in new settlers. Between 1860 and 1866, 6,000 Indians arrived in Natal from Madras and Calcutta to work as indentured labourers on the new sugar plantations. The population of the Cape Colony included many Afrikaners as well as the 'coloured' community (descendants of Khoikhoi, white settlers and Malay slaves). Most 'Coloureds' spoke Afrikaans, an offshoot of Dutch.

Britain annexed the Transvaal in 1877, and in 1879 fought the Zulus. Under King Ketshwayo the Zulus were victorious at Isandhlwana but were then defeated at Ulundi. Britain restored independence to the Transvaal (the South African Republic) in 1884 and annexed Zululand in 1887. Both the British and the Boers (a cultural subgroup of the Afrikaners) fought African resistance for many years, the last major rising being in Natal in 1906. However, the British and Boers continued to be rivals, especially after the discovery of diamonds at Kimberley in 1867 and of gold in the Transvaal in 1884. This led to an economic boom. Cecil Rhodes, owner of the De Beers company and for a time prime minister of the Cape, was the dominant entrepreneurial figure.

Boer War

In the 1890s the British, under Rhodes, sought control over the Transvaal goldfields. Despite being thwarted in their attempts to spark off rebellion amongst the Afrikaners of the South African Republic, the British continued to press for control. The Afrikaners, led by Paul Kruger, decided they would have to fight to keep their independence and declared war on Britain in late 1899. The contest appeared unequal, with the might of the British army against only 35,000 Boer soldiers. The Boers suffered a heavy defeat at Paardeberg in 1900, but then switched to guerrilla warfare. The British army, led by Gen. Kitchener, responded by setting up concentration camps and destroying crops and farmsteads. The 'scorched earth' policy was strongly criticized in Europe, but had the desired effect—in 1902 the Boer republics signed the Treaty of Vereeniging and came under British rule. They were given self-government in 1907 and on 31 May 1910 the Cape Colony, Natal, the Transvaal and the Orange Free State combined to form the Union of South Africa, a self-governing dominion under the British Crown.

The first general election in 1910 demonstrated the power of the Afrikaners within the new union—the South African party won 67 seats compared with 39 seats for the mainly English-speaking Unionist Party. Louis Botha became prime minister and Jan Smuts was made Minister of the Interior, Mines and Defence. The Union's economy was based on gold and diamond mining, for which there was organized recruitment of migrant African labourers from Union territory and other parts of Africa. Pass Laws were in operation, controlling Africans' movements in the towns and industrial areas, where they were regarded officially as temporary residents and segregated in 'townships'. Following the Land Act of 1913, 87% of the land was reserved for white ownership while Africans farmed as tenants or squatters. White miners' annual earnings were 12 times those of their black counterparts in 1911. African protests at segregation and absence of political rights were led by the South African Native National Congress (SANNC), founded in 1912 and renamed the African National Congress (ANC) in 1923.

African rights were further suppressed after the coming to power in 1924 of the Afrikaner Nationalist Party, led by J. B. Hertzog. The government secured recognition of full independence for South Africa by the Statute of Westminster on 11 Dec. 1931. It also promoted the status of the Afrikaans language and introduced new segregation measures such as the Native Laws Amendment Act of 1937, which set limits on the numbers of blacks who could live in urban areas. Jan Smuts came to power in 1939 heading a coalition government broadly in favour of the war against Nazi Germany.

Apartheid

In 1948 Smuts's Unionist Party was sensationally defeated by the right-wing National Party which had campaigned for *apartheid*, a new policy for dealing with the 'racial problem'. After 1948 the term apartheid soon developed from a political slogan into a systematic programme of social engineering championed by Hendrik Verwoerd, who became prime minister in 1958. A plethora of new laws from the Group Areas Act to the Prohibition of Mixed Marriages Act strengthened existing segregation and increased racial inequality. Blacks were divided into one of ten tribal groups, and forced to move to so-called Homelands (Bantustans), which were intended to become self-sufficient, self-governing states. Chief Buthelezi was pivotal in the Inkatha movement which attempted, but ultimately failed, to unite Homeland leaders. The massacre by police of 69 protesters against the Pass Laws at Sharpeville on 21 March 1960 led to a major crisis from which, however, the government emerged even stronger. The ANC and the Pan African Congress were banned and the leaders, including Nelson Mandela, were jailed in 1964. After withdrawing from the British Commonwealth in 1961, South Africa became increasingly isolated. To the north, former European colonies were becoming independent, often socialist, republics.

On 16 June 1976 thousands of students demonstrated in Soweto, an African township outside Johannesburg, against mandatory schooling in Afrikaans. Many died when police broke up the demonstration and rioting spread throughout the country. When P. W. Botha became prime minister in 1978, elements of the apartheid system were modified. Africans were allowed to form legal trade unions and the acts banning marriage and sexual relations between people of different races were repealed.

A new constitution, approved in a referendum of white voters on 2 Nov. 1983 and in force from 3 Sept. 1984, created a three-part parliament, with a House of Assembly for the Whites, a House of Representatives for the Coloureds and a House of Delegates for the Indians; Africans remained without representation. From late 1984 blacks in the cities and industrial areas staged large-scale protests. In June 1986 a state of emergency was imposed. Foreign condemnation led to the first economic sanctions against South Africa, imposed by a number of countries including the USA and Britain.

By 1989 a start had been made on dismantling apartheid and the government, led by F. W. de Klerk, announced its willingness to consider the extension of black South Africans' political rights. In Feb. 1990 a 30-year ban on the ANC was lifted and Nelson Mandela was released from prison on 11 Feb. 1990. In the Whites-only referendum on 17 March 1992, on the granting of constitutional equality to all races, 1,924,186 (68·7%) votes were in favour; 875,619 against.

On 22 Dec. 1993 parliament approved (by 237 votes to 45) a transitional constitution paving the way for a new multi-racial parliament which was elected on 29 April 1994. There was a decisive victory for the ANC and on 9 May 1994 Nelson Mandela was elected president. The new government included six ministers from the National Party and three from the Inkatha Freedom Party.

In 1997 the Truth and Reconciliation Commission, chaired by Archbishop Desmond Tutu, began hearings on human rights violations between 1960 and 1993. The commission promised amnesty to those who confessed their crimes under the apartheid system. Nelson Mandela, whose term as president cemented his reputation as a world statesman, retired in 1999. His deputy, Thabo Mbeki, elected president in a landslide vote, had already assumed many of Mandela's governing responsibilities. Wrestling with a developing economy, continuing inequality and a high crime rate, Mbeki received widespread criticism for his slowness in addressing the nation's AIDS epidemic. He stood down from the presidency in Sept. 2008 amid claims he had interfered in a corruption case against ANC leader Jacob Zuma.

The ANC dominated the general election of April 2009 and the following month parliament appointed Zuma president. Nelson Mandela's death in Dec. 2013 focused national and international attention on South Africa's post-apartheid progress. Zuma began a new term as president after the ANC won elections in May 2014, but he resigned in Feb. 2018 in the wake of persistent corruption allegations and was replaced by deputy president Cyril Ramaphosa.

Territory and Population

South Africa is bounded in the north by Namibia, Botswana and Zimbabwe, northeast by Eswatini and Mozambique, east by the Indian Ocean, and south and west by the South Atlantic, with Lesotho forming an enclave. Land area: 1,220,813 sq. km. This includes the uninhabited Prince Edward Island (41 sq. km) and Marion Island (388 sq. km), lying 1,900 km southeast of Cape Town. The islands were handed over to South Africa in Dec. 1947 to prevent

their falling into hostile hands. In 1994 Walvis Bay was ceded to Namibia, and Transkei, Bophuthatswana, Venda and Ciskei were reintegrated into South Africa.

At the census of 2011 the population was 51,770,560 (26,581,769 females), consisting of: Black African, 41,000,938 (79·2% of total population); Coloured, 4,615,401 (8·9%); White, 4,586,838 (8·9%); Indian/Asian, 1,286,930 (2·5%). The population has increased more than would have been expected since 2001 as huge numbers of migrants have entered South Africa from Zimbabwe, many of them undocumented. According to the 2011 census there were 2·2m. foreign-born people living in South Africa. In July 2018 the population was estimated at 57,725,600.

The UN gives a projected population for 2020 of 58·72m.

62·2% of the population were urban in 2011. In 2011 cities with the largest populations were: Johannesburg (Gauteng), 7,860,781; Cape Town (Western Cape), 3,430,992; Durban (KwaZulu-Natal), 2,786,046; Pretoria/Tshwane (Gauteng), 1,763,336; Port Elizabeth (Eastern Cape), 876,436. The metropolitan municipalities of eThekwini and Ekurhuleni had populations in 2011 of 3,442,361 and 3,178,470 respectively.

There were 1,283 permanent residence permits issued in 2012 and 141,550 temporary residence permits. Zimbabwe was the source country of the highest number of both permanent and temporary residence permits in 2012.

Population by province, according to the 2011 census:

Province	Total (including unspecified)	Black African	White	Coloured	Indian/ Asian
Eastern Cape	6,562,053	5,660,230	310,450	541,850	27,929
Free State	2,745,590	2,405,533	239,026	83,844	10,398
Gauteng	12,272,263	9,493,684	1,913,884	423,594	356,574
KwaZulu-Natal	10,267,300	8,912,921	428,842	141,376	756,991
Limpopo	5,404,868	5,224,754	139,359	14,415	17,881
Mpumalanga	4,039,939	3,662,219	303,595	36,611	27,917
Northern Cape	1,145,861	576,986	81,246	461,899	7,827
North-West	3,509,953	3,152,063	255,385	71,409	20,652
Western Cape	5,822,734	1,912,547	915,053	2,840,404	60,761

There are 11 official languages. Numbers of mother-tongue speakers at the 2011 census: isiZulu, 11,587,374 (22·7% of population); isiXhosa, 8,154,258 (16·0%); Afrikaans, 6,855,082 (13·5%); English, 4,892,623 (9·6%); Sepedi, 4,618,576 (9·1%); Setswana, 4,067,248 (8·0%); Sesotho, 3,849,563 (7·6%); Xitsonga, 2,277,148 (4·5%); SiSwati, 1,297,046 (2·5%); Tshivenda, 1,209,388 (2·4%); isiNdebele, 1,090,223 (2·1%). The use of any of these languages is a constitutional right 'wherever practicable'. Each province may adopt any of these as its official language. English is the sole language of command and instruction in the armed forces.

Social Statistics

Total number of registered live births in 2016 was 969,415 (down from a high of 1,677,415 in 2003).

The number of registered deaths increased from 317,236 in 1997 to 613,198 in 2006, with AIDS as the factor underlying much of the increase. Since then the increasing use of antiretroviral drugs has caused the number of registered deaths to fall to 480,476 in 2012. In 2012, 17·9% of all adults between 15 and 64 were infected with HIV. Estimated population growth rate, 2011–12, 1·3%. Fertility rate, 2009, 2·5 births per woman. Life expectancy at birth in 2013 was 58·2 years for males and 62·1 for females. It had been 59 years for males and 66 for females in the early 1990s but fell in the late 1990s and in the early part of the 21st century as a consequence of the AIDS epidemic. It was just 50·2 years for males and 53·9 for females in 2005 but has now risen again thanks to the development and improved availability of medical treatments for HIV.

Infant mortality, 2010, 41 per 1,000 live births.

From 1998, under a new bill, customary and traditional marriages are recognized in law as registered by the civil registration system. Same-sex marriage was legalized in Nov. 2006. Marriages in 2016 totalled 139,512 (184,8601 in 2006). Of the total marriages officially recorded in 2016, 43,359

(31·1%) were solemnized in religious ceremonies. In 2010 the most popular age range for marrying was 30–34 for males and 25–29 for females. Divorces granted in 2016 totalled 25,326 (31,270 in 2006).

Climate

There is abundant sunshine and relatively low rainfall. The southwest has a Mediterranean climate, with rain mainly in winter, but most of the country has a summer maximum, although quantities show a decrease from east to west. Pretoria, Jan. 73·4°F (23·0°C), July 53·6°F (12·0°C). Annual rainfall 26·5" (674 mm). Bloemfontein, Jan. 73·4°F (23·0°C), July 45·9°F (7·7°C). Annual rainfall 22" (559 mm). Cape Town, Jan. 69·6°F (20·9°C), July 54·0°F (12·2°C). Annual rainfall 20·3" (515 mm). Johannesburg, Jan. 68·2°F (20·1°C), July 50·7°F (10·4°C). Annual rainfall 28·1" (713 mm).

Constitution and Government

An Interim *Constitution* came into effect on 27 April 1994 and was in force until 3 Feb. 1997. Under it, the National Assembly and Senate formed a Constitutional Assembly, which had the task of drafting a definitive constitution. This was signed into law in Dec. 1996 and took effect on 4 Feb. 1997. The 1996 constitution defines the powers of the President, Parliament (consisting of the National Assembly and the National Council of Provinces—NCOP), the national executive, the judiciary, public administration, the security services and the relationship between the three spheres of government. It incorporates a Bill of Rights pertaining to, *inter alia*, education, housing, food and water supply, and security, in addition to political rights. All legislation must conform to the Constitution and the Bill of Rights. The Constitution was amended in 2001 to provide that Constitutional Court judges are appointed for a non-renewable 12-year term of office, or until they reach the age of 70 years, except where an Act of Parliament extends the term of office of a Constitutional Court judge. This Constitution Amendment Act also made the head of the Constitutional Court the Chief Justice. The head of the Supreme Court of Appeal is now the President of that Court.

A *Constitutional Court*, consisting of a president, a deputy president and nine other judges, was inaugurated in Feb. 1995. The Court's judges are appointed by the President of the Republic from a list provided by the Judicial Service Commission, after consulting the President of the Constitutional Court (now the Chief Justice) and the leaders of parties represented in the National Assembly.

Parliament is the legislative authority and has the power to make laws for the country in accordance with the Constitution. It consists of the National Assembly and the NCOP. Parliamentary sittings are open to the public.

The *National Assembly* consists of 400 members directly elected for five years, 200 from national party lists and 200 from regional party lists. In terms of the 1993 Constitution, which still regulated the 1999 elections, the nine provincial legislatures are elected at the same time and candidates may stand for both. If elected to both, they have to choose between sitting in the national or provincial assembly. In the former case, the runner-up is elected to the Provincial Assembly.

The *National Council of Provinces* (NCOP) consists of 54 permanent members and 36 special delegates and aims to represent provincial interests in the national sphere of government. Delegations from each province consist of ten representatives. Bills (except finance bills) may be introduced in either house but must be passed by both. A finance bill may only be introduced in the National Assembly. If a bill is rejected by one house it is referred back to both after consideration by a joint National Assembly-NCOP committee called the Mediation Committee. Bills relating to the provinces must be passed by the NCOP.

The Constitution mandates the establishment of *Traditional Leaders* by means of either provincial or national legislation. The National House of Traditional Leaders was established in April 1997. Each provincial House of Traditional Leaders nominated three members to be represented in the National House. The National House advises national government on the role of traditional leaders and on customary law. Following a six-year study by the Commission on Traditional Leadership Disputes and Claims, in July 2010 then President Jacob Zuma announced that only seven of the 13 kingships would be officially recognized and six would be abolished. Five of the seven kingships and their kings were confirmed by the commission. The remaining two were awaiting the commission's recommendation on the rightful incumbent. In terms of the commission's findings, existing kings who were found not to qualify for the status of kingship were to be allocated a principal traditional leadership.

National Anthem

A combination of shortened forms of 'Die Stem van Suid-Afrika'/'The Call of South Africa' (words by C. J. Langenhoven; tune by M. L. de Villiers) and the ANC anthem 'Nkosi sikelel' iAfrika'/'God bless Africa' (words and tune by Enoch Sontonga).

Government Chronology

Presidents from 1961. (ANC = African National Congress; NP = National Party; UP = United Party)

1961–67	NP	Charles Robberts Swart
1968–75	NP	Jacobus Johannes Fouché
1975–78	NP	Nicolaas Johannes Diederichs
1978–79	NP	Balthazar Johannes Vorster
1979–84	NP	Marais Viljoen
1984–89	NP	Pieter Willem Botha
1989–94	NP	Frederik Willem de Klerk
1994–99	ANC	Nelson Rolihlahla Mandela
1999–2008	ANC	Thabo Mvuyelwa Mbeki
2008–09	ANC	Kgalema Petrus Motlanthe
2009–18	ANC	Jacob Gedleyihlekisa Zuma
2018–	ANC	Matamela Cyril Ramaphosa

Prime Ministers since 1939.

1939–48	military/UP	Jan Christiaan Smuts
1948–54	NP	Daniël François Malan
1954–58	NP	Johannes Gerhardus Strijdom
1958–66	NP	Hendrik Frensch Verwoerd
1966–78	NP	Balthazar Johannes Vorster
1978–84	NP	Pieter Willem Botha

Recent Elections

Parliamentary elections were held on 7 May 2014. Turnout was 73·4%. The African National Congress (ANC) won 249 seats in Parliament's National Assembly with 62·1% of votes cast (264 seats and 65·9% in 2009), Democratic Alliance (DA) 89 with 22·2% (67 seats and 16·7% in 2009), Economic Freedom Fighters (EFF) 25 with 6·4%, Inkatha Freedom Party (IFP) 10 with 2·4%, National Freedom Party (NFP) 6 with 1·6%, United Democratic Movement (UDM) 4 with 1·0%, Freedom Front Plus (VF+) 4 with 0·9%, Congress of the People (COPE) 3 with 0·7%, African Christian Democratic Party (ACDP) 3 with 0·6%, African Independent Congress (AIC) 3 with 0·5% and Agang SA 2 with 0·3%. Two smaller parties took one seat each.

Current Government

President: Cyril Ramaphosa; b. 1952 (ANC; since 14 Feb. 2018—acting until 15 Feb. 2018).

Deputy President: David Mabuza.

In Feb. 2019 the government comprised:

Minister of Agriculture, Forestry and Fisheries: Senzeni Zokwana. *Arts and Culture:* Nkosinathi Emmanuel Mthethwa. *Basic Education:* Matsie Angelina Motshekga. *Communications:* Stella Ndabeni-Abrahams. *Co-operative Governance and Traditional Affairs:* Zweli Mkhize. *Defence and Military Veterans:* Nosiviwe Noluthando Mapisa-Nqakula. *Economic Development:* Ebrahim Patel. *Energy:* Jeffrey Thamsanqa Radebe. *Environment:* Nomvula Mokonyane. *Finance:* Tito Mboweni. *Health:* Dr Pakishe Aaron Motsoaledi. *Higher Education and Training:* Grace Naledi Mandisa Pandor. *Home Affairs:* Siyabonga Cyprian. *Human Settlements:* Nomaindiya Mfeketo. *International Relations and Co-operation:* Lindiwe Nonceba Sisulu. *Justice and Correctional Services:* Tshililo Michael Masutha. *Labour:* Mildred Oliphant. *Mineral Resources:* Gwede Mantashe. *Police:* Bheki Cele. *Public Enterprises:* Pravin Jamnadas Gordhan. *Public Service and Administration:* Ayanda Dlodlo. *Public Works:* Thembelani Thulas Nxesi. *Rural Development and Land Reform:* Maite Nkoana-Mashabane. *Science and Technology:* Mmamoloko Kubayi-Ngubane. *Small Business*

Development: Lindiwe Zulu. *Social Development:* Susan Shabangu. *Sport and Recreation:* Tokozile Xasa. *State Security:* Dipuo Letsatsi-Duba. *Tourism:* Derek Hanekom. *Trade and Industry:* Rob Davies. *Transport:* Bonginkosi Emmanuel 'Blade' Nzimande. *Water and Sanitation:* Gugile Nkwinti. *Minister in the Presidency Responsible for National Planning, Monitoring and Evaluation:* Nkosazana Dlamini-Zuma. *Minister in the Presidency Responsible for Women:* Bathabile Dlamini.
Government Website: http://www.gov.za

Current Leaders

Cyril Ramaphosa
Position
President

Introduction
Cyril Ramaphosa, widely seen as the natural successor to Nelson Mandela, became president in succession to Jacob Zuma on 15 Feb. 2018.

Early Life
Cyril Ramaphosa was born on 17 Nov. 1952 in Soweto, Johannesburg. He graduated in law from the University of the North in Limpopo Province, where he joined the South African Students' Organisation and the Black People's Convention. He was twice detained by the authorities for his part in organizing pro-FRELIMO (Liberation Front of Mozambique) rallies in 1974 and for participation in the Soweto riots in 1976.

After continuing his law studies at the University of South Africa, he joined the Council of Unions of South Africa and helped to form the South African National Union of Mineworkers. He later became chairman of the National Reception Committee which co-ordinated arrangements for the release of Nelson Mandela. Having become a member of Parliament in 1994, he withdrew from politics in Jan. 1997 after losing the presidential race to Thabo Mbeki. He then pursued his many business interests, which included food and beverages (McDonald's and Coca-Cola), telecommunications and cattle farming.

On 18 Dec. 2012 he returned to frontline politics as deputy president. On 3 June 2014 he became Chairman of the National Planning Commission and helped to craft the National Development Plan designed to transform South Africa by 2030.

He was elected to succeed Zuma as ANC president in Dec. 2017 and when Zuma resigned as president ahead of a parliamentary no-confidence motion, Ramaphosa succeeded him on 15 Feb. 2018.

Career in Office
Ramaphosa faced a formidable array of challenges, including reviving the rule of law, battling corruption, reassuring investors and improving public services. His election pledges included establishing a judicial commission to investigate corruption among state officials, and he promptly reshuffled the cabinet to remove many of the members who had been controversial through the Zuma era. He also named the deputy ANC president, David Mabuza, as the country's deputy president. However, the burst of optimism when he became president had given way to economic gloom by Sept. as South Africa entered its first recession since 2009 amid weak growth, continued high unemployment and downgrading of the country's sovereign debt to junk status. In Nov. 2018 Ramaphosa reiterated that the constitution would be changed to explicitly allow for the expropriation of white-owned land without compensation.

Defence

The South African National Defence Force (SANDF) comprises four services, namely the SA Army, the SA Air Force, the SA Navy and the SA Military Health Service (SAMHS). In 2012 the SANDF consisted of 62,082 active members (excluding 12,382 civilian employees). SAMHS personnel totalled 9,159 (including around 1,115 reservists) in 2011. South Africa ended conscription in 1994.

Defence expenditure totalled US$4,848m. in 2013 (equivalent to US$100 per capita), and represented 1·3% of GDP. Defence expenditure in 1985 had represented 3·8% of GDP. In 2013 South Africa was responsible for 21% of Africa's total defence expenditure.

Army
Army personnel totalled 37,141 in 2011. Reserves numbered 12,264 in 2011. The army territorial reserve was disbanded in 2009.

Navy
Navy personnel in 2011 totalled 6,244, with 861 reserves. The fleet is based at the naval bases at Simon's Town on the west coast, Port Elizabeth on the south and Durban on the east and includes three submarines and four frigates.

Air Force
Strength (2011) 10,653, with 831 reserves. In 2011 the Air Force had 42 combat-capable aircraft (Saab *Gripens* and British Aerospace *Hawks*) and 11 combat-capable helicopters.

Economy

Agriculture accounted for 2·3% of GDP in 2013, industry 29·9% and services 67·8%.

Overview
South Africa is an upper-middle income country. Although it no longer has Sub-Saharan Africa's largest economy—having been overtaken by Nigeria in 2014—South Africa continues to be an important regional economic power. It has a well-capitalized banking system, abundant natural resources and established regulatory systems, as well as good research and development capabilities and a solid manufacturing base.

Average annual GDP growth was 5·2% between 2004 and 2007, although the ten-year mean to 2014 was only 3%. By 2017 growth had slipped to 1·3%, the result of a combination of lower domestic and export demand, increased political risk, decreasing commodity prices and a slowdown in the Chinese economy—the country's largest trade partner.

In 2015, against the backdrop of a weak mid-term fiscal outlook, the government announced expenditure savings and tax increases (each equivalent to 0·6% of GDP) to reduce the budget deficit from 4·0% of GDP in 2014–15 to 2·5% in 2017–18. Despite this, however, the budget deficit was recorded at 4·6% in 2017. The government has also aimed to stabilize the gross debt burden at about 50% of GDP, seeking to minimize pressure on the sovereign rating, but gross national debt was estimated to be above the target, at 53%, in 2017.

The pro-poor orientation of public spending has seen significant social development since 1994. Around 3·5% of GDP has been spent annually on social welfare—twice the median spent by other developing economies. Life expectancy, after falling dramatically from 62 years in 1992 to 53 years in 2010, recovered to 62 years by 2017. This has largely reflected the rapid expansion of antiretroviral treatment programmes to fight HIV/AIDS, supported by broader declines in both adult and infant mortality. Nonetheless, South Africa continues to have one of the highest rates of income inequality in the world.

Currency
The unit of currency is the *rand* (ZAR) of 100 *cents*. A single free-floating exchange rate replaced the former two-tier system on 13 March 1995. Inflation rates (based on IMF statistics):

2008	2009	2010	2011	2012	2013	2014	2015	2016	2017
11·0%	7·1%	4·3%	5·0%	5·6%	5·8%	6·1%	4·6%	6·3%	5·3%

Foreign exchange reserves were US$32,251m. in Sept. 2009 (US$4,171m. in 1998) and gold reserves 4·01m. troy oz. Total money supply was R419,506m. in Aug. 2009.

Budget
Budgetary central government revenue in 2014–15 totalled R1,018bn. and expenditure R1,165bn. Principal sources of revenue in 2014–15 were: taxes on income, profits and capital gains, R562bn.; taxes on goods and services, R367bn.; taxes on international trade and transactions, R40bn. Main items of expenditure by economic type in 2014–15: grants, R694bn.; social benefits, R129bn.; compensation of employees, R121bn.

VAT was raised from 14% to 15% in April 2018.

South Africa's fiscal year runs from 1 April to 31 March.

Performance

Real GDP growth rates (based on IMF statistics):

2008	2009	2010	2011	2012	2013	2014	2015	2016	2017
3·2%	−1·5%	3·0%	3·3%	2·2%	2·5%	1·8%	1·3%	0·6%	1·3%

In 2009 South Africa experienced its first recession in 17 years. Total GDP in 2017 was US$349·4bn.

Banking and Finance

The central bank and bank of issue is the South African Reserve Bank (SARB; established 1920), which functions independently. Its *Governor* is Lesetja Kganyago. The Banks Act 1990 governs the operations and prudential requirements of banks.

At the end of Dec. 2014, 33 banks (including three mutual banks) were registered with the Office of the Registrar of Banks. Furthermore, 40 foreign banks had authorized representative offices in South Africa. The combined assets of the banking institutions amounted to R4,179bn. (31 Dec. 2014), total liabilities to R3,234bn. and total equity to R318bn. Total assets of the four largest commercial banks (Standard Bank, FirstRand, Absa and Nedbank) came to R3,478bn.

Foreign debt totalled US$45,165m. in 2010, representing 12·7% of GNI.

The stock exchange, the JSE Securities Exchange, is based in Johannesburg. Foreign nationals have been eligible for membership since Nov. 1995.

Energy and Natural Resources

Environment

South Africa's carbon dioxide emissions from the consumption of energy in 2011 were the equivalent of 9·6 tonnes per capita.

Electricity

South African households use over 25% of the country's energy. Coal supplies 75% of primary energy requirements, followed by oil (21%), nuclear (3%) and natural gas (1%). There is one nuclear power station (Koeberg) with two reactors, two gas turbine generators, two conventional hydro-electric plants and two pumped storage stations. The two nuclear reactors are projected to close in 2024 and 2025. Eskom, a public utility, generates 95% of the country's electricity (as well as two-thirds of the electricity for the African continent) and owns and operates the national transmission system. In 2011, 222,710 GWh of electricity were delivered throughout South Africa by Eskom.

Eskom electrified 149,914 homes in 2011, bringing the total number of homes connected since the start of the electrification programme in 1991 to 3,901,054. The Government aims to achieve universal access to electricity by 2025. Capacity shortages from late 2007 forced Eskom into emergency reductions to protect the power system from potential failure and a national electricity crisis was declared in Jan. 2008. South Africa continues to suffer from frequent power cuts. In 2011, 84·7% of households used electricity for lighting.

The energy sector contributes about 15% to GDP and employs about 250,000 people. Because of South Africa's large coal deposits, the country is one of the cheapest electricity suppliers in the world.

The first wind-energy farm in Africa was opened at Klipheuwel in the Western Cape in Feb. 2003.

Oil and Gas

South Africa has limited oil reserves and relies on coal for much of its oil production. It has a highly developed synthetic fuels industry. Sasol and PetroSA are the two major players in the synthetic fuel market. Synfuels meet approximately 40% of local demand. Natural gas production in 2011 amounted to 1·3bn. cu. metres.

PetroSA is responsible for exploration of both offshore natural gas and onshore coal-bed methane. The EM gas field complex off Mossel Bay in the Western Cape started production in 2000. PetroSA's gas-to-liquid plant supplies about 7% of South Africa's liquid fuel needs.

South Africa is one of the major oil refining nations in Africa with a crude refining capacity of 511,000 bbls per day.

Minerals

Total sales of primary minerals increased to R370·6bn. in 2011; the value of exports of primary minerals increased to a record R282·0bn. Mining contributed 8·6% of GDP in 2010, up from 7·6% in 2001.

In 2011 employment in the mining sector rose by 2·9% from 498,906 in 2010 to 513,211. Some 53 different minerals were produced in 2011 from 1,592 mines and quarries.

Mineral production (in tonnes), 2010: coal, 254·5m.; iron ore, 58·7m.; limestone and dolomite, 17·9m.; chromium ore, 10·8m.; manganese ore, 7·2m.; aluminium (2011), 809,000; copper, 83,600; nickel, 40,000; zinc, 36,100; and (in kg) platinum-group metals, 287,300 (of which platinum, 147,800); gold, 188,700; silver, 79,300. Diamond production, 2010: 8,868,400 carats. Gold production in 2010 was at its lowest level in over a century although sales revenue rose to a record high of R53·1bn. Production in 2010 was less than half than that of 2002. South Africa is the world's leading producer of platinum and also has the largest reserves.

Agriculture

South Africa has a dual agricultural economy, comprising a well-developed commercial sector and a predominantly subsistence-orientated sector. Much of the land suitable for mechanized farming has unreliable rainfall. Of the total farming area, natural pasture occupies 81% (69·6m. ha.) and planted pasture 2% (2m. ha.). About 12% of South Africa's surface area can be used for crop production. High potential arable land comprises only 22% of the total arable land. Annual crops and orchards are cultivated on 9·9m. ha. of dry land and 1·3m. ha. under irrigation. In 2015–16 gross farming income totalled R237·3bn.

Production:

(*Field crops, 2016 unless otherwise indicated, in 1,000 tonnes*): sugar-cane (2015–16), 14,900; maize (2015–16), 7,537; wheat, 1,734; sunflower seeds, 755; soybeans, 742; malting barley, 292; canola, 102; grain sorghum, 74; dry beans (2015–16), 35; groundnuts (2015–16), 19.

(*Horticulture, 2015–16 unless otherwise indicated, in 1,000 tonnes*): potatoes (2015), 2,487; oranges, 1,753; apples, 949; onions, 687; tomatoes, 561; pears, 418; bananas, 401; grapefruit, 391. Wine production totalled 1,080m. litres in 2017, ranking South Africa eighth in the world.

(*Animal products, 2015–16*): 5,236,472 sheep and lambs slaughtered; 2,998,733 cattle slaughtered; 2,797,127 pigs slaughtered; 1,005m. broilers slaughtered (2015 estimate); fresh milk (2015), 3,051m. litres; wool, 34·8m. kg.

Gross income from animal products, in 2015–16 (R1,000), 116,658,000; horticulture, 70,340,000; field crops, 50,318,000.

Agricultural exports contribute about 7% of total imports and 11% of total exports. In 2015–16 the estimated value of agricultural imports was R76·5bn. and exports R83·0bn.

Forestry

South Africa has developed one of the largest man-made forestry resources in the world with plantations covering an area of 1·3m. ha. Production from these plantations in 2011 amounted to 18·5m. cu. metres, valued at R7·0bn., the most important products by value being pulpwood (R4·9bn.) and sawlogs (R1·7bn.). In terms of volume, 12·6m. cu. metres and 4·2m. cu. metres of the aforementioned products were produced respectively. About 92,700 staff were employed in the primary sector in 2011 (growing and harvesting) and a further 73,200 in the processing industries (sawmilling, pulp and paper, mining timber and poles, and board products). In 2011 the forestry and forest products industry contributed 1·2% to South Africa's GDP.

In 2015 the area under all types of forests was 9·2m. ha. Of this, planted forest covered 1·8m. ha., primary forest 0·9m. ha. and other naturally regenerated forest the remaining 6·5m. ha. In 2010 the private sector owned or controlled 1,057,279 ha. (83%) of the plantation area of 1,273,357 ha. as well as (in 2010–11) 188 of the 192 primary processing plants in the country. The remaining 17% (216,078 ha.) were owned by the state.

The industry was a net exporter to the value of R4·5bn. in 2011, more than 99% of which was in the form of converted value-added products. The forest products industry contributed 2·1% of total exports and 1·5% of total imports in 2011. In that year pulp product exports were the most important (R7·06bn. or 47% of the total), followed by paper (R4·62bn. or 31% of the total), solid wood products (R2·74bn. or 18% of the total) and other products (R0·55bn. or 4% of the total). Woodchip exports, mainly to Japan, accounted for 62% (R1·70bn.) of the total solid wood products exports.

Fisheries

The commercial marine fishing industry is valued at approximately R6bn. annually and employs 27,000 people directly.

In 2012 there were over 2,900 fishing rights allocated to 1,788 vessels in 21 different fisheries, a decrease in the size of the fleet since 2002 in line with the international trend to reduce pressure on resources. The total catch in 2014 was 596,040 tonnes, over 99% of which came from marine fishing.

Industry

The leading companies by market capitalization in South Africa in May 2018 were: Naspers, a multinational media company (US$112·8bn.); FirstRand, a financial services provider (US$30·3bn.); and Standard Bank Group (US$28·5bn.).

Actual value of sales of the principal groups of industries (in R1m.) in 2010: petroleum, chemical products, rubber and plastic products, 281·2; basic iron and steel, non-ferrous metal products, metal products and machinery, 267·4; food and beverages, 247·9; motor vehicles, parts and accessories and other transport equipment, 162·4; wood, paper, publishing and printing, 108·3; textiles, clothing, leather and footwear, 37·4. Total actual value including other groups, R1,253·0m. In 2013 industry accounted for 29·9% of GDP, with manufacturing contributing 13·2%.

Labour

The Employment Equity Act, 1998 signalled the beginning of the final phase of transformation in the job market, which began with the implementation of the Labour Relations Act. It aims to avoid all discrimination in employment. The Basic Conditions of Employment Act, 1997 applies to all workers except for the South African National Defence Force (SANDF), the South African Secret Service (SASS) and the National Intelligence Agency (NIA). The new provisions include a reduction in the maximum hours of work from 46 to 45 hours per week (however, the Act allows for the progressive reduction of working hours to 40 per week).

The labour force in South Africa numbered 20·2m. in the fourth quarter of 2014, of which 4·9m. were unemployed. In the fourth quarter of 2014 the official unemployment rate was 24·3%, compared to 24·1% in the fourth quarter of 2009.

The Unemployment Insurance Fund (UIF) provides benefits to workers who become unemployed. All employees who work for more than 24 hours a month and their employers contribute to the Fund. In the year ending March 2014 there were 10·0m. contributors (9·8m. in 2013). In the same period the UIF paid benefits to 762,385 beneficiaries, a total amount of R7·1bn.

South Africa had 45,000 people living in slavery according to the Walk Free Foundation's 2013 *Global Slavery Index*.

International Trade

South Africa's four main trading partners in 2012 were China, USA, Germany and Japan. China was South Africa's number one trading partner in terms of total trade (the sum of exports and imports) recorded in 2012. Exports to China rose from R58·6bn. in 2010 to R85·3bn. in 2011 (although they fell to R81·1bn. in 2012). Imports from China increased from R84·1bn. in 2010 to R103·1bn. in 2011 and further to R120·1bn. in 2012.

In 2011 the European Union accounted for 24·9% (R152·3bn.) of South Africa's total exports and 30·8% (R222·8bn.) of total imports. A trade, development and co-operation agreement (TDCA) came into force on May 2004, under the terms of which South Africa grants duty-free access to 86% of EU imports over a period of 12 years, while the EU liberalizes 95% of South Africa's imports over a ten-year period. The Agreement provides for ongoing EU financial assistance in grants and loans for development co-operation, which amounts to some R900m. per annum.

In 2010 the total value of South Africa's exports destined for Africa was R85·0bn. and imports R45·9bn. Within the Southern African Development Community (SADC), a smaller group of countries including South Africa, Botswana, Eswatini, Lesotho and Namibia have organized themselves into the Southern African Customs Union (SACU), sharing a common tariff regime without any internal barriers. Exports to SADC countries increased to R60·8bn. in 2010. Imports from within the region in 2010 totalled R23·7bn.

Imports and Exports
Trade in US$1m.:

	2007	2008	2009	2010
Imports (f.o.b.)	79,872·6	87,593·1	63,766·1	80,139·3
Exports (f.o.b.)	64,026·6	73,965·5	53,863·9	71,484·3

Main imports (in US$1m.):

	2008	2009	2010
Machinery and transport equipment	30,670	22,201	28,400
(Office and telecom equipment)	7,371	5,971	8,077
(Automotive products)	6,138	4,340	6,843
Fuels	19,555	13,663	15,723
(Petroleum and petroleum products)	18,513	12,949	14,769
Chemicals	8,550	6,674	8,663

Main exports (in US$1m.):

	2008	2009	2010
Machinery and transport equipment	16,229	10,787	13,451
(Automotive products)	7,737	5,087	6,702
Non-ferrous metals, including platinum	12,578	8,614	11,973
(Platinum group metals)	9,801	6,767	9,377
Iron and steel	8,860	5,116	7,735
Fuels	7,120	6,023	7,198

Communications

The public company Transnet SOC Ltd (formerly Transnet Limited) was established on 1 April 1990. In the financial year ended 31 March 2012 it handled 201m. tonnes of rail freight and 4,352,000 TEUs through the harbours, while 16·7m. litres were pumped through its petrol pipelines. In the same year, Transnet reported a profit of R4,113m. (R4,119m. for 2010–11). In March 2012 it had assets totalling R178·0bn.

Roads

In 2011 the South African road network comprised some 747,000 km of roads and streets. Toll roads cover around 3,120 km of the national network. South Africa has the longest road network in Africa. As at 31 Oct. 2010 there were 9,797,413 registered motor vehicles. In 2013 an estimated 13,300 people were killed in traffic accidents.

Rail

The Passenger Rail Agency of South Africa (PRASA) was formed in March 2009 as an umbrella organization to oversee the day-to-day running of rail services in South Africa. PRASA operates Metrorail, offering commuter rail services in urban areas and transporting 1·7m. passengers on weekdays to 478 stations over 2,400 km of track; and Shosholoza Meyl, providing regional and long-distance rail transport. South Africa's first high-speed rail service, Gautrain, was inaugurated in June 2010. It links Johannesburg's O. R. Tambo International Airport and the centre of the city with Pretoria.

Freight train services are provided by Transnet Freight Rail (formerly Spoornet), a public company owned solely by the South African government. Transnet transports 17% of the nation's freight annually and employs over 25,000 people.

Civil Aviation

Responsibility for civil aviation safety and security lies with the South African Civil Aviation Authority (SACAA). The Airports Company South Africa (ACSA) owns and operates South Africa's principal airports. The main international airports are: Johannesburg, Cape Town, Durban, Bloemfontein, Port Elizabeth, Pilanesberg, Lanseria and Upington. In April 2003 the Cabinet approved the status of the Kruger Mpumalanga Airport, near Nelspruit, as an international airport. ACSA also has a 35-year concession to operate Pilanesberg International Airport near Sun City in North-West Province.

The flag carrier South African Airways (SAA), along with Airlink, Comair, Interair and SA Express, operate scheduled international air services. Several other operators provide internal flights and cargo services.

In 2014 O. R. Tambo International Airport (formerly Johannesburg International) handled 18,820,988 passengers (9,257,225 on domestic flights), Cape Town handled 8,392,989 passengers (6,879,919 on domestic flights) and Durban (King Shaka) handled 4,465,088 passengers (4,179,121 on domestic flights). O. R. Tambo Airport is also the busiest airport for freight, handling around 390,000 tonnes of cargo in 2014.

Shipping

The South African Maritime Safety Authority (SAMSA) was established on 1 April 1998 as the authority responsible for ensuring the safety of life at sea and the prevention of sea pollution from ships. Approximately 98% of South Africa's exports are conveyed by sea.

The National Ports Authority supervises South Africa's major ports. The largest ports include the deep water ports of Richards Bay, with its multi-product dry bulk handling facilities, multi-purpose terminal and the world's largest bulk coal terminal, and Saldanha featuring a bulk ore terminal adjacent to a bulk oil jetty with extensive storage facilities. Durban, Cape Town and Port Elizabeth provide large container terminals for deep-sea and coastal container traffic. The Port of Durban handles 2·5m. containers per annum. East London, the only river port, has a multi-purpose terminal and dry dock facilities. Mossel Bay is a specialized port serving the south coast fishing industry and offshore gas fields. During 2014 the seven major ports handled a total of 220·0m. tonnes of cargo (Richards Bay, 94·2m. tonnes; Saldanha, 64·7m. tonnes; Durban, 45·2m. tonnes).

In Jan. 2014 there were five ships of 300 GT or over registered, totalling 12,000 GT.

Telecommunications

In 2013 there were 3·9m. main (fixed) telephone lines. In the same year mobile phone subscriptions numbered 76·9m. (1,456·4 per 1,000 persons). The largest mobile phone networks are Vodacom and MTN. In 2011, 88·9% of households had a mobile phone; landline telephone, 14·5%.

Between 1997 and 2002 Telkom SA, for many years the national operator, concentrated on replacing analogue lines with digital technology, under the terms of its final exclusive licence; the transmission network is now almost wholly digital. Under the Telecommunications Acts of 1996 and 2001, South Africa has liberalized its telecommunications industry. Telkom lost its monopoly on the fixed-line market in 2006 with the launch of Neotel, the country's second national operator. Telkom was offered on the Johannesburg Securities Exchange and the New York Stock Exchange in March 2003, realizing R3·9bn. on the first day.

A new 14,000-km submarine cable, the West Africa Cable System, became operational in May 2012, allowing South Africa to greatly increase the capacity of its mobile phone and internet networks.

In 2013 an estimated 48·9% of the population were internet users. In June 2012 there were 5·0m. Facebook users.

Social Institutions

Out of 178 countries analysed in the 2017 *Fragile States Index*—a list published jointly by the Fund for Peace and *Foreign Policy* magazine—South Africa was ranked the 83rd least vulnerable to conflict or collapse. The index is based on 12 indicators of state vulnerability across social, political and economic categories.

Justice

All law must be consistent with the Constitution and its Bill of Rights. Judgments of courts declaring legislation, executive action, or conduct to be invalid are binding on all organs of state and all persons. The common law of the Republic is based on Roman-Dutch law—that is the uncodified law of Holland as it was at the date of the cession of the Cape to the United Kingdom in 1806. South African law has, however, developed its own unique characteristics.

Judges hold office until they attain the age of 70 or, if they have not served for 15 years, until they have completed 15 years of service or have reached the age of 75, when they are discharged from active service. A judge discharged from active service must be ready to perform service for an aggregate of three months a year until the age of 75. The Chief Justice of South Africa, the Deputy Chief Justice, the President of the Supreme Court of Appeal and the Deputy President of the Supreme Court of Appeal are appointed by the President after consulting the Judicial Service Commission. In the case of the Chief Justice and Deputy Chief Justice, the President must also consult the leaders of parties represented in the National Assembly. The President on the advice of the Judicial Service Commission (JSC) appoints all other judges.

The higher courts include: 1) *The Constitutional Court* (CC), which consists of the Chief Justice of South Africa, the Deputy Chief Justice of South Africa and nine other judges. It is the highest court in all matters in which the interpretation of the Constitution or its application to any law, including the common law, is relevant; 2) *The Supreme Court of Appeal*, consisting of a President, a Deputy President and the number of judges of appeal determined by an Act of Parliament. It is the highest court of appeal in all other matters; 3) *The High Courts*, which may decide constitutional matters other than those which are within the exclusive jurisdiction of the Constitutional Court, and any other matter other than one assigned by Parliament to a court of a status similar to that of a High Court. Each High Court is presided over by a Judge President who may divide the area under his jurisdiction into circuit districts. In each such district there shall be held at least twice in every year and at such times and places determined by the Judge President, a court which shall be presided over by a judge of the High Court. Such a court is known as the circuit court for the district in question; 4) *The Land Claims Court*, established under the Restitution of Land Rights Act of 1994 deals with claims for restitution of rights in land to persons or communities dispossessed of such rights after 1913 as a result of past racially discriminatory laws or practices. It has jurisdiction throughout the Republic and the power to determine such claims and related matters such as compensation and rights of occupation; 5) *The Labour Court*, established under the Labour Relations Act 1995 deals with labour disputes. It is a superior court that has authority, inherent powers and standing in relation to matters under its jurisdiction, equal to that the High Court has in relation to matters under its jurisdiction. Appeals from decisions of the Labour Court lie to the Labour Appeal Court which has authority in labour matters equivalent to that of the Supreme Court of Appeal in other matters.

The lower courts are called Magistrates' Courts. Magisterial districts have been grouped into 13 clusters headed by chief magistrates. From the magistrates court there is an appeal to the High Court having jurisdiction in that area, and then to the Supreme Court of Appeal.

In a departure from the Roman-Dutch legal system, jury trials were introduced in 1831 and continued until 1969. However, in practice trial by jury was rarely used after 1954 following amendments to the criminal code. They were officially abolished in 1969, partly owing to fears of potential racial prejudice among jurors—a concern that was compounded by the country's apartheid system.

The death penalty was abolished in June 1995, with the last execution carried out by the South African government having taken place in 1989. In 2013–14 there were 17,068 murders (down from a peak of 26,877 murders in 1995–96 although up from 15,609 in 2011–12). South Africa's murder rate has steadily declined accordingly and is now less than half the rate of 1995–96, at 32 per 100,000 in 2013–14. Budgeted spending on police, prisons and justice services for 2012–13 was R95·7bn. The population in penal institutions in Aug. 2013 was 156,370 (294 per 100,000 of national population). In 2015 the World Justice Project *Rule of Law Index*, which provides data on how the rule of law is experienced by the general public across eight categories, ranked South Africa 38th of 102 countries for criminal justice and 39th for civil justice.

Education

The South African Schools Act 1996 became effective on 1 Jan. 1997 and provides for: compulsory education for students between the ages of seven and 15 years of age, or students reaching the ninth grade, whichever occurs first. Pupils normally enrol for Grade 1 education at the beginning of the year in which they turn seven years of age although earlier entry at the age of six is allowed if the child meets specified criteria indicating that they have reached a stage of school readiness.

In 2014 the South African public education system accommodated 12·1m. school pupils, 969,165 university students (of which 161,493 at universities of technology) and 702,383 further education and training college students. There were 25,741 primary, secondary, combined and intermediate schools with 425,090 educators.

In the 2010–11 financial year R165bn. was allocated to education. In 2011 public expenditure on education came to 6·1% of GDP and 18·9% of total government spending.

As a result of a major restructure of South African higher education during 2002–04, 36 universities and technikons (non-university higher education institutions) were reduced by means of mergers and incorporations to 17 universities and six universities of technology. The University of South Africa (UNISA) is the oldest and largest university in South Africa and one of the largest distance education institutions in the world. In 2014 UNISA had a total of 328,493 students and 4,953 permanent staff. In 2014 North-West University had 63,135 students, Tshwane University of Technology 56,785, University of Pretoria 56,376, University of Johannesburg 49,789, University of KwaZulu-Natal 45,466 and Cape Peninsula University of Technology 33,187.

The adult literacy rate in 2012 was 93·7% (95·0% for males and 92·6% for females).

Health

Some 40% of South Africans live in poverty and 75% of these live in rural areas with limited access to health services. There is an extensive network of public health clinics providing free public health services, plus mobile clinics run by the government to provide primary and preventive health care.

36,912 doctors were registered with the Health Profession Council of South Africa (HPCSA) in 2010. These include doctors working for the state, doctors in private practice and specialists. Doctors train at the medical schools of eight universities and the majority go on to practise privately. In 2010, 110,518 enrolled nurses and enrolled nursing auxiliaries were registered with the South African Nursing Council (SANC); there were 5,320 dental practitioners registered with the HPCSA. In 2010, 12,218 pharmacists were registered with the South African Pharmacy Council. Chris Hani Baragwanath Hospital, situated to the southwest of Johannesburg, with its 3,200 beds, is the largest hospital in the world.

In Oct. 1998 the first traditional hospital was opened in Mpumalanga—the Samuel Traditional Hospital. There are about 200,000 traditional healers in South Africa providing services to between 60% and 80% of their communities.

Approximately 5·5m. South Africans are HIV-infected, the highest number in the world (equivalent to nearly 12% of the population of South Africa and some 17% of global HIV/AIDS cases). Government expenditure on HIV and AIDS increased substantially from R3bn. in 2005–06 to R11bn. in 2013–14. In Aug. 2003 the government announced plans to roll out the provision of anti-retrovirals (ARVs) in the public health sector that would see 1·4m. people on treatment. By 2008 a further target of having at least one service point in every local municipality across the country had been achieved. South Africa now runs the world's largest treatment programme and in 2014 over 2·7m. people were receiving ARVs.

In *Water: At What Cost? The State of the World's Water 2016*, WaterAid reported that 6·8% of the population does not have access to safe water.

Welfare

As at 31 Dec. 2014 the department of social development was disbursing grants through its provincial offices to 16·4m. beneficiaries. Recipients are means-tested to determine their eligibility. At that time 11·6m. people received the child support grant (CSG) of R320 per month. The age of children eligible for the CSG has been progressively increased to cover children up to and including the age of 17 years since 1 Jan. 2012. At 31 Dec. 2014, 3·1m. received old-age grants of R1,350 per month. There were plans to phase out the old-age grant means test by 2016, but this was subsequently delayed. The age for male eligibility was lowered in phases over a two-year period from 65 to 60 in April 2010, the same as for women.

Other benefits paid are the disability, foster child, care dependency and war veterans' grants as well as institutional grants and grants in aid.

The total budget allocation for the payment of social assistance was R118bn. in 2013–14.

Religion

South Africa is a secular state and freedom of worship is guaranteed by the Constitution. According to estimates by the Pew Research Center's Forum on Religion & Public Life, 81·2% of the population in 2010 were Christians but 14·9% did not have any religious affiliation. There are small numbers of Hindus and Muslims. Among the Christians, 90% in 2010 were Protestants and 9% Catholics. In 1992 the Anglican Church of Southern Africa voted by 79% of votes cast for the ordination of women. In Feb. 2019 there was one cardinal.

Culture

World Heritage Sites

UNESCO World Heritage sites under South African jurisdiction (with year entered on list) are: Greater St Lucia Wetland Park (1999), encompassing marine, wetland and savannah environments; Robben Island (1999), used since the 17th century as a prison, hospital and military base—it was the location for Nelson Mandela's incarceration; fossil hominid sites of Sterkfontein, Swartkrans, Kromdraai and environs (1999 and 2005), offering evidence of human evolution over 3·5m. years; Mapungubwe Cultural Landscape (2003), a savannah landscape at the confluence of the Limpopo and Shashe rivers and the site of the largest kingdom in Africa in the 14th century; Cape Floral Region Protected Areas (2004 and 2015); Vredefort Dome (2005), part of a meteorite impact structure; Richtersveld cultural and botanical landscape (2007), covering 160,000 ha. of mountainous desert; the

‡Khomani Cultural Landscape (2017), a large expanse of sand containing evidence of human occupation from the Stone Age to the present; and Barberton Makhonjwa Mountains (2018), an area containing volcanic and sedimentary rock more than 3bn. years old. Shared with Lesotho, Maloti-Drakensberg Park (2013) is a transboundary site composed of the uKhahlamba Drakensberg National Park and the Sehlathebe National Park in Lesotho.

Press

In 2013 there were 21 paid-for dailies, 12 paid-for Sunday newspapers, 67 paid-for non-daily newspapers and 226 free non-dailies. The newspapers with the highest circulation figures are *Sunday Times*, *Soccer Laduma* and *Daily Sun*. There were 92 newspaper online editions in 2013.

Tourism

In 2013 there were a record 9·62m. international tourist arrivals (excluding same-day visitors), up from 9·19m. in 2012. Most visitors in 2012 came from Zimbabwe, Lesotho, Mozambique, Eswatini and Botswana. International tourist receipts in 2012 totalled US$10·0bn., up from US$9·5bn. in 2011. The number of people employed directly in tourism rose to 598,000 in 2011 from 567,000 in 2010.

Festivals

Best-known arts festivals: the Klein Karoo Festival (Oudtshoorn, Western Cape), which has a strong Afrikaans component, is held in April; the Grahamstown Arts Festival in the Eastern Cape is held in June/July; the Mangaung African Cultural Festival (Macufe) is held in Sept. in Bloemfontein; and the Aardklop Arts Festival, in Potchefstroom in the North-West province, is held in Sept. The Encounters South African International Documentary Festival has been held since 1999.

Diplomatic Representatives

Of South Africa in the United Kingdom (South Africa House, Trafalgar Square, London, WC2N 5DP)
    High Commissioner: Nomatemba Gugulethu Pudnixia Olivia Tambo.

Of the United Kingdom in South Africa (255 Hill St., Arcadia, Pretoria 0002)
    High Commissioner: Nigel Casey, MVO.

Of South Africa in the USA (3051 Massachusetts Ave., NW, Washington, D.C., 20008)
    Ambassador: Mninwa Johannes Mahlangu.

Of the USA in South Africa (877 Pretorius St., Arcadia, Pretoria)
    Ambassador: Vacant.
    Chargé d'Affaires a.i.: Jessye Lapenn.

Of South Africa to the United Nations
    Ambassador: Jerry Matthews Matjila.

Of South Africa to the European Union
    Ambassador: Baso Sangqu.

South African Provinces

In 1994 the former provinces of the Cape of Good Hope, Natal, the Orange Free State and the Transvaal, together with the former 'homelands' or 'TBVC countries' of Transkei, Bophuthatswana, Venda and Ciskei, were replaced by nine new provinces. Transkei and Ciskei were integrated into Eastern Cape, Venda into Northern Province (now Limpopo), and Bophuthatswana into Free State, Mpumalanga and North-West.

Eastern Cape

The area is 169,580 sq. km. The population in 2011 was 6,562,053 (3,472,353 female), the third largest population in South Africa. Of that number: Black African, 5,660,230 (86% of the population); Coloured, 541,850 (8%); White, 310,450 (5%). Density (2011), 39 per sq. km. In 2011, 78·8% spoke isiXhosa as their first language, 10·6% Afrikaans and 5·6% English. The provincial capital is Bhisho.

At the provincial elections held on 7 May 2014, 45 of 63 seats were won by the African National Congress, ten by the Democratic Alliance, four by the United Democratic Movement, two by the Economic Freedom Fighters, and one each by the Congress of the People and the African Independent Congress.

Premier: Phumulo Masualle (took office on 21 May 2014).

In 2011, 75·0% of households used electricity for lighting (the lowest percentage of any South African province). There were 596,573 agricultural households in total in 2011; 35·4% of households in the province were engaged in agriculture. Manufacturing is based mainly in Port Elizabeth and East London with motor manufacturing as the prime industry. In the fourth quarter of 2014 the labour force numbered 1,884,000, of whom 549,000 were unemployed (29·1%).

Total road network in 2008 was around 78,000 km. The province has four airports: Port Elizabeth, East London, Umtata and Bulembu (Bhisho). There are three deep-water ports: Port Elizabeth, East London and Coega. In 2011, 81·9% of households had a mobile phone; landline telephone, 9·8%; and computer, 11·9%.

In 2014 there were 1,946,885 children enrolled in schools and 64,258 teaching staff. The Province has four universities: Walter Sisulu University, Rhodes University, the University of Fort Hare and Nelson Mandela University. In 2009 there were 90 hospitals in the public sector with 14,456 beds.

Free State

The area is 129,480 sq. km. The province is the third largest in South Africa but has the second smallest population and the second lowest population density. The population in 2011 was 2,745,590 (1,416,623 female). Of that number: Black African, 2,405,533 (87·6% of the population); White, 239,026 (8·7%); Coloured, 83,844 (3·1%). Density (2011), 21 per sq. km. In 2011, 64·2% (1,717,881) of the population spoke Sesotho as their first language, 12·7% (340,490) Afrikaans, 7·5% (201,145) isiXhosa and 5·2% (140,228) Setswana. The provincial capital is Bloemfontein.

At the provincial elections held on 7 May 2014 the African National Congress retained its majority winning 22 of the 30 seats; the Democratic Alliance five; the Economic Freedom Fighters two; and Freedom Front Plus one.

Premier: Sisi Ntombela (took office on 27 March 2018).

In 2011, 89·9% of households used electricity for lighting. The province contributes about 16·5% of South Africa's total mineral output. There were 201,286 agricultural households in total in 2011; 24·4% of households in the province were engaged in agriculture. Free State produces about 40% of total maize and 50% of total wheat output in South Africa. In the fourth quarter of 2014 the labour force numbered 1,138,000, of whom 367,000 were unemployed (32·2%—the highest unemployment rate of any province).

Total road network in 2008 was around 111,000 km. In 2011, 87·9% of households had a mobile phone; landline telephone, 10·0%; and computer, 17·9%.

In 2014 there were 672,290 pupils enrolled in schools and 24,552 teaching staff. The Province has two universities: the University of the Free State and the Central University of Technology, Free State. In 2009 there were 32 public hospitals with 4,958 beds.

Gauteng

Gauteng is the smallest province in South Africa, covering an area of 17,010 sq. km (approximately 1·4% of the total land surface of South Africa). In 2011 the population was 12,272,263 (6,082,388 female). Of that number: Black African, 9,493,684 (77%); White, 1,913,884 (16%); Coloured, 423,594 (3%); Indian/Asian, 356,574 (3%). Density (2011), 721 per sq. km. In 2011, 19·8% spoke isiZulu as their first language, 13·3% English, 12·4% Afrikaans, 11·6% Sesotho and 10·6% Sepedi. The provincial capital is Johannesburg.

At the provincial elections held on 7 May 2014, 40 of 73 seats were won by the African National Congress, 23 by the Democratic Alliance, eight by the Economic Freedom Fighters and one each by Freedom Front Plus and the Inkatha Freedom Party.

Premier: David Makhura (took office on 21 May 2014).

In 2011, 87·4% of households used electricity for lighting. There were 279,110 agricultural households in total in 2011; 7·1% of households in the province were engaged in agriculture. In the fourth quarter of 2014 the labour force numbered 6,473,000, of whom 1,593,000 were unemployed (24·6%).

Total road network in 2008 was around 55,000 km. In 2009 Gauteng had 3,680,158 registered vehicles, more than any other province. O. R. Tambo International Airport is the main airport in the province. In 2011, 93·8% of households had a mobile (the highest percentage of any province); landline telephone, 18·0%; and computer, 31·1%.

In 2014 there were 2,191,475 children enrolled in schools with a total of 77,265 teaching staff. The Province has seven universities: Sefako Makgatho Health Sciences University, University of South Africa, University of Johannesburg, University of Pretoria, University of the Witwatersrand, Tshwane University of Technology and Vaal University of Technology. In 2009 there were 31 public hospitals and 16,816 hospital beds. In 2008 there were 81 private hospitals with 13,454 beds.

Kwazulu-Natal

The area is 92,100 sq. km. The population in 2011 was 10,267,300 (5,388,625 female). Of that number: Black African, 8,912,921 (87% of the population); Indian/Asian, 756,991 (7%); White, 428,842 (4%); Coloured, 141,376 (1%). Density (2011), 111 per sq. km. In 2011, 77·8% spoke isiZulu as their first language, 13·2% English, 3·4% isiXhosa and 1·6% Afrikaans. The provincial capital is Pietermaritzburg.

At the provincial elections held on 7 May 2014, 52 of 80 seats were won by the African National Congress, ten by the Democratic Alliance, nine by the Inkatha Freedom Party, six by the National Freedom Party, two by the Economic Freedom Fighters and one by the Minority Front.

Premier: Willies Mchunu (ANC; took office on 24 May 2016—acting until 25 May 2016).

In 2011, 77·9% of households used electricity for lighting. There were 717,006 agricultural households in total in 2011; 28·2% of households in the province were engaged in agriculture. Sugarcane and maize are the principal crops. In the fourth quarter of 2014 the labour force numbered 3,183,000, of whom 663,000 were unemployed (20·8%).

Total road network in 2008 was around 98,000 km. Durban International Airport is the main airport. Durban harbour is the busiest in South Africa and one of the ten largest harbours in the world. In 2011, 87·6% of households had a mobile phone; landline telephone, 16·0%; and computer, 16·4%.

In 2014 there were 2,901,697 children enrolled in schools with 95,560 teaching staff. The Province has four universities: University of KwaZulu-Natal, University of Zululand, Durban University of Technology and Mangosuthu University of Technology. In 2009 there were 75 public hospitals with 23,142 beds.

Limpopo

The area is 123,910 sq. km. In 2011 the population was 5,404,868 (2,880,732 female). Of that number: Black African, 5,224,754 (96·7% of the population); White, 139,359 (2·6%); Indian/Asian, 17,881 (0·3%); Coloured, 14,415 (0·3%). Density (2011), 44 per sq. km. In 2011 52·9% spoke Sepedi as their first language, 17·0% Xitsonga, 16·7% Tshivenda, 2·6% Afrikaans and 2·0% isiNdebele. The provincial capital is Polokwane (Pietersburg).

At the provincial elections held on 7 May 2014, 39 of 49 seats were won by the African National Congress, six by the Economic Freedom Fighters, three by the Democratic Alliance and one by Congress of the People.

Premier: Stanley Mathabatha (sworn in 18 July 2013).

In 2011, 87·3% of households used electricity for lighting. There were 468,494 agricultural households in total in 2011; 33·0% of households in the province were engaged in agriculture. In the fourth quarter of 2014 the labour force numbered 1,469,000, of whom 234,000 were unemployed (15·9%—the lowest unemployment rate of any province).

Total road network in 2008 was around 66,000 km. In 2011, 88·5% of households had a mobile phone; landline telephone, 3·8%; and computer, 12·4%.

In 2014 there were 1,720,585 children enrolled in schools with 57,256 teaching staff. The Province has two universities: the University of Limpopo and the University of Venda. In 2009 there were 41 public hospitals with 7,866 hospital beds.

Mpumalanga

The area is 78,490 sq. km. In 2011 the population was 4,039,939 (2,065,883 female). Of that number: Black African, 3,662,219 (90·7% of the population); White, 303,595 (7·5%); Coloured, 36,611 (0·9%); Indian/Asian, 27,917 (0·7%). Density (2011), 51 per sq. km. In 2011, 27·7% spoke SiSwati as their first language, 24·1% isiZulu, 10·4% Xitsonga, 10·1% isiNdebele, 9·3% Sepedi, 7·2% Afrikaans, 3·5% Sesotho, 3·1% English, 1·8% Setswana and 1·2% isiXhosa. The provincial capital is Nelspruit.

At the provincial elections held on 7 May 2014, 24 of 30 seats were won by the African National Congress, three by the Democratic Alliance, two by the Economic Freedom Fighters and one by the Bushbuckridge Residents Association.

Premier: Refilwe Mtsweni (since 27 Feb. 2018—acting until 20 March 2018).

In 2011, 86·4% of households used electricity for lighting. The province is rich in coal reserves and produces about 80% of the country's supplies. There were 263,391 agricultural households in total in 2011; 24·5% of households in the province were engaged in agriculture. In the fourth quarter of 2014 the labour force numbered 1,550,000, of whom 412,000 were unemployed (26·6%).

Total road network in 2008 was around 56,000 km. In 2011, 91·1% of households had a mobile phone; landline telephone, 6·3%; and computer, 16·3%.

In 2014 there were 1,057,788 children enrolled in schools with 35,000 teaching staff. A new university, the University of Mpumalanga, opened in Feb. 2014. In 2005 there were 24 public hospitals, plus 198 clinics and 34 community health centres, with 4,173 beds.

Northern Cape

The area is 361,830 sq. km and the population in 2011 was 1,145,861 (580,889 female). Of that number: Black African, 576,986 (50% of the population); Coloured, 461,899 (40%); White, 81,246 (7%). Density (2011), 3 per sq. km. In 2011, 53·8% spoke Afrikaans as their first language, 33·1% Setswana, 5·3% isiXhosa and 3·4% English. Kimberley is the provincial and economic capital.

At the provincial elections held on 7 May 2014, 20 of 30 seats were won by the African National Congress, seven by the Democratic Alliance, two by the Economic Freedom Fighters and one by the Congress of the People.

Premier: Sylvia Lucas (since 30 April 2013—acting until 23 May 2013).

In 2011, 85·4% of households used electricity for lighting. Diamonds are found in shallow water at Port Nolloth, Hondeklipbaai and Lamberts Bay, and also mined inland along the entire coastal strip from the Orange river mouth in the north to Lamberts Bay in the south. There were 55,150 agricultural households in total in 2011; 18·3% of households in the province were engaged in agriculture. In the fourth quarter of 2014 the labour force numbered 450,000, of whom 129,000 were unemployed (28·7%).

Total road network in 2008 was around 111,000 km. Five airports are used for scheduled flights—Kimberley, Upington, Aggeneys, Springbok and Alexander Bay. In 2011, 81·1% of households had a mobile phone; landline telephone, 12·7%; and computer, 16·5%.

In 2014 there were 289,004 children enrolled in schools with a total of 9,182 teaching staff. Northern Cape's first university, Sol Plaatje University, opened in Kimberley in Feb. 2014. In 2009 there were 21 public hospitals with 1,958 beds.

North-West

The area is 116,320 sq. km with a population in 2011 of 3,509,953 (1,730,049 female). Of that number: Black African, 3,152,063 (89·8%); White, 255,385 (7·3%); Coloured, 71,409 (2·0%). Density (2011), 30 per sq. km. In 2011, 63·4% spoke Setswana as their first language, 9·0% Afrikaans, 5·8% Sesotho, 5·5% isiXhosa, 3·7% Xitsonga, 3·5% English, 2·5% isiZulu and 2·4% Sepedi. The provincial capital is Mmabatho.

At the provincial elections held on 7 May 2014 the African National Congress won 23 of 33 seats, the Economic Freedom Fighters five, the Democratic Alliance four and Freedom Front Plus one.

Premier: Job Mokgoro (sworn in 22 June 2018).

In 2011, 84·0% of households used electricity for lighting. Gold is mined at Klerksdorp, and diamonds at Lichtenburg, Koster, Christiana and Bloemhof. There were 214,049 agricultural households in total in 2011; 20·2% of households in the province were engaged in agriculture. In the fourth quarter of 2014 the labour force numbered 1,268,000, of whom 320,000 were unemployed (25·2%).

Total road network in 2008 was around 73,000 km. In 2011, 86·8% of households had a mobile phone; landline telephone, 6·2%; and computer, 14·4%.

In 2014 there were 800,316 children enrolled in schools with 26,086 teaching staff. There is one university, the North-West University. In 2009 there were 20 public hospitals with 4,507 beds.

Western Cape

The area is 129,370 sq. km. Population in 2011, 5,822,734 (2,964,228 female). Of that number: Coloured, 2,840,404 (48·8%); Black African, 1,912,547 (32·8%); White, 915,053 (15·7%). Density (2011), 45 per sq. km. In 2011, 49·7% spoke Afrikaans as their first language, 24·7% isiXhosa and 20·2% English. The capital is Cape Town.

At the provincial elections held on 7 May 2014, 26 of 42 seats were won by the Democratic Alliance (DA), 14 by the African National Congress, and one each by the Economic Freedom Fighters and the African Christian Democratic Party.

Premier: Helen Zille (DA; took office on 6 May 2009).

In 2011, 93·4% of households used electricity for lighting (the highest percentage of any province). There were 84,574 agricultural households in total in 2011; 5·2% of households in the province were engaged in agriculture. The Western Cape is one of the world's finest grape-growing regions. The Klein Karoo region is the centre of the South African ostrich-farming industry. In the fourth quarter of 2014 the labour force numbered 2,813,000, of whom 643,000 were unemployed (22·9%).

Total road network in 2008 was around 92,000 km. Cape Town International Airport is the main airport in the province. In 2011, 88·9% of households had a mobile phone; landline telephone, 30·8% (the highest percentage of any province); and computer, 34·4% (also the highest percentage of any province).

In 2014 there were 1,075,396 children enrolled in schools with 35,931 teaching staff. The Province has four universities: the University of the Western Cape, the University of Cape Town, Stellenbosch University and the Cape Peninsula University of Technology. In 2009 there were 58 public hospitals with 9,858 beds.

Further Reading

South Africa

Government Communication and Information System (GCIS), including extracts from the *South Africa Yearbook 2016/17*, compiled and published by GCIS.

Beinart, W., *Twentieth Century South Africa.* 1994

Butler, Anthony, *Contemporary South Africa.* 3rd ed. 2017

Davenport, T. R. H., *South Africa: a Modern History.* 5th ed. 2000

De Klerk, F. W., *The Last Trek—A New Beginning.* 1999

Ellis, Stephen, *External Mission: The ANC in Exile, 1960-1990.* 2012

Fine, B and Rustomjee, Z., *The Political Economy of South Africa.* 1996

Giliomee, Hermann, *The Afrikaners: Biography of a People.* 2003

Guelke, Adrian, *Rethinking the Rise of Apartheid.* 2004

Hough, M. and Du Plessis, A. (eds) *Selected Documents and Commentaries on Negotiations and Constitutional Development in the RSA, 1989–1994.* 1994

Johnson, R. W. and Schlemmer, L. (eds) *Launching Democracy in South Africa: the First Open Election, 1994.* 1996

Mandela, N., *Long Walk to Freedom: the Autobiography of Nelson Mandela.* 1994

Meredith, M., *South Africa's New Era: the 1994 Election.* 1994

Picard, Louis A., *The State of the State: Institutional Transformation, Capacity and Political Change in South Africa.* 2005

Sparks, Allister, *Beyond the Miracle: Inside the New South Africa.* 2006

Thompson, Leonard, *A History of South Africa.* 4th ed. 2014

The Truth and Reconciliation Commission of South Africa Report. 5 vols.

Waldmeir, P., *Anatomy of a Miracle: the End of Apartheid and the Birth of the New South Africa.* 1997

Who's Who in South African Politics. Online only

National Statistical Office: Statistics South Africa, 170 Thabo Sehume St., Pretoria 0002.

Website: http://www.statssa.gov.za

South Sudan

(Republic of South Sudan)

Capital: Juba
Population projection, 2020: 13·61m.
GNI per capita, 2017: (PPP$) 963
HDI/world rank, 2017: 0·388/187
Internet domain extension: .ss

Key Historical Events

South Sudan was administered separately from the north under Egyptian and British rule until 1946 when the British unified the regions. When independence as a single state was granted in 1956 and southern autonomy was compromised, tensions between the predominantly Muslim, Arabic north and the Christian and animist south escalated into civil war. An agreement between the government and the Southern Sudan Liberation Front signed in Addis Ababa in 1972 brought a brief respite from the fighting but in 1983 hostilities recommenced. They lasted 19 years and resulted in 1·9m. civilian deaths in the south of Sudan before a ceasefire was declared in Jan. 2002. A comprehensive peace agreement was signed between the Khartoum government and the southern rebels led by the Sudan People's Liberation Movement in Jan. 2005. They entered a unity government, despite ongoing arguments over disputed areas, and a southern autonomous government was formed. In a referendum on independence for the south on 9–15 Jan. 2011, 98·8% of votes cast were in favour. South Sudan became an independent country on 9 July 2011. On 14 July 2011 it became the 193rd member of the United Nations.

Tensions with Sudan over oil fees and sovereignty in the oil-rich Abyei territory led to the creation of a demilitarized buffer zone in March 2013. In July 2013 President Kiir dismissed his cabinet including Vice President Machar, which provoked a coup attempt in Dec. that exacerbated existing inter-ethnic friction and resulted in the subsequent deaths of thousands of people, mass displacements and famine. In Aug. 2015 Kiir accepted an internationally-mediated peace deal in which Machar would return to office in a unity government. However, in July 2016 Kiir again dismissed Machar prompting renewed fighting that killed hundreds. In response the African Union agreed to deploy troops in the country with a broader mandate than that of the existing 12,000-strong UN peacekeeping force.

Territory and Population

South Sudan is bounded in the north by Sudan, east by Ethiopia, southeast by Kenya, south by Uganda, southwest by the Democratic Republic of the Congo and west by the Central African Republic. Its area is 644,329 sq. km. In 2008 the census population was 8,260,490 (disputed). More than half (51%) of the population is below the age of 18. 83% of the population is rural.

The UN gives a projected population for 2020 of 13·61m.

The country is composed of 32 states (with capitals): Akobo (Akobo), Amadi (Mundri), Aweil (Aweil), Aweil East (Wanyjok), Bieh (Waat), Boma (Pibor), Central Upper Nile (Malakal), Eastern Lakes (Yirol), Fangak (Ayod), Fashoda (Kodok), Gbudwe (Yambio), Gogrial (Kuajok), Gok (Cueibet), Imatong (Torit), Jonglei (Bor), Jubek (Juba), Kapoeta (Kapoeta), Latjoor (Nasir), Lol (Raja), Maiwut (Maiwut), Maridi (Maridi), Northern Liech (Bentiu), Northern Upper Nile (Renk), Ruweng (Pariang), Southern Liech (Leer), Tambura (Tambura), Terekeka (Terekeka), Tonj (Tonj), Twic (Mayen Abun), Wau (Wau), Western Lakes (Rumbek), Yei River (Yei).

The capital, Juba, had a population of 230,000 in 2008. Other major cities are Wau (118,000), Malakal (115,000), Yei (111,000) and Yambio (106,000).

The official language is English.

Climate

South Sudan's climate is tropical with wet and dry seasons. The winter is relatively cool and dry while the rainy season usually takes place from April to Dec. with most rain falling in the summer months. Juba, Jan. 81°F (27·3°C), July 76°F (24·5°C). Annual rainfall 38" (965 mm). Wau, Jan. 79°F (25·9°C), July 78°F (25·3°C). Annual rainfall 44" (1,118 mm).

Constitution and Government

An interim constitution was ratified shortly before independence and came into force on 7 July 2011. Under the constitution the *President* is the Head of State, Head of Government and Commander-in-Chief of the armed forces and serves a four-year term. The National Legislature consists of two Houses: the *National Legislative Assembly,* comprising members of the former Southern Sudan Legislative Assembly and all South Sudanese who were members of the National Assembly of Sudan; and the *Council of States,* which consists of South Sudanese who had seats in the Council of States of Sudan plus 20 members appointed by the President. Members of both houses serve four-year terms.

National Anthem

'South Sudan Oyee'; words and tune by students and teachers of Juba University.

Current Government

In Feb. 2019 the government comprised:

President: Salva Kiir Mayardit; b. 1951 (Sudan People's Liberation Movement; sworn in 9 July 2011).

First Vice President: Taban Deng Gai. *Second Vice President:* James Wani Igga.

Minister of Agriculture and Food Security: Onyoti Adigo Nyikwec. *Cabinet Affairs:* Martin Elia Lomuro. *Culture, Youth and Sport:* Nadia Arop Dudi. *Defence and Veteran Affairs:* Kuol Manyang Juuk. *Energy and Dams:* Dhieu Mathok Diing. *Environment and Forestry:* Josephine Napwon. *Federal Affairs:* Richard K. Mulla. *Finance and Economic Planning:* Salvatore Garang Mabiordit. *Foreign Affairs and International Co-operation:* Nhial Deng Nhial. *Gender, Child and Social Welfare:* Awut Deng Acuil. *General Education and Instruction:* Deng Deng Hoch. *Health:* Riek Gai Kok. *Higher Education, Science and Technology:* Yien Tut. *Humanitarian Affairs and Disaster Management:* Hussein Mar Nyuot. *Information, Communication, Technology and Postal Services:* Michael Makuei Lueth. *Interior:* Michael Tiangjiek Mut. *Justice:* Paulino Wanawilla Onango. *Labour, Public Services and Human Resource Development:* James Hoth Mai. *Lands, Housing and Urban Development:* Alfred Lado Gore. *Livestock and Fisheries:* James Duku. *Mining:* Gabriel Thok Deng. *Parliamentary Affairs:* Peter Bashir Gbandi. *Petroleum:* Ezekiel Lul. *Roads and Bridges:* Rebecca Joshua Okwaci. *Trade and Industry:* Paul Mayom Akec. *Transport:* John Luk Jok. *Water Resources and Irrigation:* Sofia Gai. *Wildlife Conservation and Tourism:* Jemma Nunu Kumba. *Minister in the Office of the President for National Security Service:* Obuto Mamur Mete. *Minister in the Office of the President:* Mayik Ayii Deng.

Government Website: http://www.goss-online.org

Current Leaders

Salva Kiir Mayardit

Position
President

Introduction
Salva Kiir Mayardit became president of the newly independent Republic of South Sudan in July 2011. A veteran of Sudan's long civil war, he helped establish the dominant Marxist rebel movement in southern Sudan in the 1980s, leading its military wing. A political power struggle between Kiir and former vice president Riek Machar continued to fuel intermittent bitter fighting from late 2013, although a power-sharing agreement was reached

in Aug. 2018 in a bid to end the conflict that has killed tens of thousands of people and displaced millions.

Early Life

Salva Kiir Mayardit was born into the Dinka ethnic group in Bahr Al Ghazal state in southern Sudan in 1951. He became active in the Anya-Nya southern rebel movement in the civil war in the late 1960s. Following a settlement on regional autonomy in 1972, Kiir joined the Sudanese Army, graduating from its Military College at Omdurman.

The southern rebellion reignited in 1983 after President Nimeiry imposed Sharia law. Kiir joined John Garang in defecting from the Army and co-founded the Sudanese People's Liberation Movement (SPLM) that year. The Marxist-Leninist organization became the dominant southern rebel force.

Peace talks between the SPLM and Sudan's president, Omar al-Bashir, began in 2002. They culminated in a peace agreement of 2005, ending the war that had claimed 2m. lives and recognizing southern autonomy. Kiir became vice president of the Government of Southern Sudan (GOSS) in Juba. He became president following Garang's death in a helicopter accident in July 2005. His ability to unite rival factions was underlined when he was re-elected president of the GOSS in April 2010 with 93% support. Nearly 99% of voters in the Jan. 2011 referendum then elected to separate from Sudan and, following approval from Khartoum, the Republic of South Sudan was formally established on 9 July that year, with Kiir as head of state.

Career in Office

In his inaugural address Kiir said the South Sudanese would forgive but not forget past injustices. He made conciliatory gestures to southern rebel groups previously opposed to the SPLM, and asked the United Nations for help to lift South Sudan from the 'abyss of poverty and deprivation'.

However, following deepening tensions with the Bashir regime in Sudan over oil transit fees (for South Sudan's only export route north to the Red Sea) and revenue-sharing, South Sudan shut down oil exports in early 2012, seriously undermining the economies of both countries until an agreement to resume oil pumping was reached in March 2013. Meanwhile, in April 2012 Sudan's air force had raided its neighbour after South Sudanese troops occupied the disputed border region of Abyei and the Heglig oilfields. The UN threatened sanctions against both countries if they did not stop the escalating violence and return to negotiations. Kiir met President Bashir in Ethiopia in Sept. in an attempt to resolve the crisis. In March 2013 they agreed to a troop withdrawal and demilitarization of the border area.

In July 2013 Kiir dismissed his cabinet, including Vice President Machar, and made a series of new appointments. This controversial move provoked an apparent coup attempt in Dec. by military forces loyal to Machar, prompting a wave of ethnic violence, atrocities against civilians, mass displacements and increasing famine. Conflict continued throughout 2014 and into 2015 as general elections were called off owing to the security situation, and a constitutional amendment was passed by parliament extending Kiir's presidential mandate by three years. Despite reservations, in Aug. 2015 Kiir accepted under threat of UN sanctions an internationally-mediated peace deal with the rebels in which Machar would return as vice president in a unity government. There were nevertheless further tensions and sporadic ceasefire violations following Kiir's unilateral decision in Oct. that year to increase the number of states in the country from ten to 28, potentially undermining the power-sharing basis of the peace agreement. In July 2016 Kiir again dismissed Machar from the vice presidency, appointing Taban Deng Gai in his place, and the year ended with further conflict between rival supporters.

In Feb. 2017 the UN declared a famine in parts of the country as aid agencies warned that war and economic collapse had left many thousands of people facing starvation. Then, in May that year, Kiir announced a unilateral ceasefire by his forces and launched a national dialogue in a bid to end the prolonged crisis. A steering committee, overseen by Kiir, was sworn in to conduct consultations but Machar was excluded from the dialogue, which was consequently rejected by his rebel supporters.

In July 2018 the Parliament approved an extension of Kiir's term for another three years with the main objective of stabilizing the country's political situation amid ongoing peace negotiations with the armed opposition. Then in Aug. Kiir signed a power-sharing accord with Machar and other opposition groups.

Defence

On independence in 2011 the former rebel Sudan People's Liberation Army changed its name to the South Sudan Armed Forces. The United Nations Mission in the Republic of South Sudan (UNMISS) has been in South Sudan since independence to consolidate peace and security and to help establish conditions for development. It had 7,900 uniformed personnel in Feb. 2018.

In 2013 defence expenditure totalled US$714m. (US$64 per capita), representing 5·3% of GDP.

Economy

South Sudan featured among the ten most corrupt countries in the world in a 2018 survey of 180 countries carried out by the anti-corruption organization Transparency International.

Overview

Oil exports began in 1999 and have been essential to the fortunes of what is now South Sudan, accounting for almost all exports and over 90% of government revenues. About 70% of what was formerly Sudan's oil production is located in the territory of the South.

Despite a 2005 agreement to share oil revenues equally, there have been clashes between North and South over oil-rich border regions, such as Abyei. Oil production was consequently shut down in Jan. 2012, creating a large fiscal deficit. Against a backdrop of austerity measures, and despite reforms designed to increase non-oil revenues, the economy contracted by 52·4% in 2012. Other contentious issues have included border definition and debt servicing.

Oil production had been expected to resume in 2013 and lead to significant growth, but civil war, which began in Dec. 2013, undermined prospects for economic recovery. Growth of 2·9% in 2014 was followed by a return to recession in 2015, which continued in 2016 and 2017.

Despite its oil wealth, South Sudan is among Africa's least developed economies, with conflict and instability having impoverished the country. The infrastructure is poor, with few paved roads. Corruption is also a problem, and social indicators are weak. However, there is growth potential, with sizeable livestock, fishery and forestry resources, and fertile conditions that make agriculture a promising non-oil sector.

Currency

The official unit of currency is the *South Sudan pound* (SSP) of 100 *piastres*, introduced on 18 July 2011. Inflation was 379·8% in 2016 (the highest rate of any country in the world that year) and 187·9% in 2017 (the second highest rate, behind that of Venezuela).

Performance

Following a halt in oil production in the wake of a dispute with neighbouring Sudan over transit fees, the economy shrank by 52·4% in 2012 (South Sudan's first full year as an independent country). However, it made a significant recovery in 2013, growing by 29·3%. More recently South Sudan has been in recession as a consequence of the internal conflict with the economy shrinking by 13·9% in 2016 and 5·1% in 2017. Total GDP in 2016 was US$2·9bn.

Banking and Finance

The Bank of South Sudan (BOSS) serves as the country's central bank. Its *Governor* is Dier Tong Ngor.

Energy And Natural Resources

Environment

The *Climate Change and Environmental Risk Atlas 2014* produced by Maplecroft, a risk analytics company, ranked South Sudan as the country facing the fifth highest economic and social risk from climate change by 2025.

Electricity

In 2016 only 9% of the population had access to electricity.

Oil and Gas

Oil production was 1·5m. tonnes in 2012. South Sudan currently exports all of its crude oil via a pipeline through Sudan, although flows have been disrupted because of continuing disputes between the two countries. However, plans to construct a pipeline through Uganda, Kenya and Rwanda announced in 2014 would provide South Sudan with an alternative means of export.

Agriculture

South Sudan has some 31m. head of livestock, more than three times the number of humans.

Forestry

In 2015 the area under forests was 7·16m. ha., or 11% of the total land area. Timber cut in 2012: 4·38m. cu. metres.

Minerals

Mineral deposits include copper, dolomite, gold, iron ore, lead, manganese, marble, uranium and zinc. However, levels of commercial extraction are insignificant.

Communications

Roads

Only a small proportion of South Sudan's road network is paved, but in Sept. 2012 a 192 km highway linking Juba, the capital, with Nimule, on the Ugandan border, was inaugurated.

Rail

Total length of railway is 248 km, running from the Sudanese border to Wau.

Civil Aviation

There is an international airport at Juba with connections to Addis Ababa, Cairo, Entebbe, Khartoum and Nairobi. Other major airports include those at Malakal, Rumbek and Wau. South Supreme Airlines operates both domestic and international flights.

Social Institutions

According to the 2017 Fragile States Index—a list published jointly by the Fund for Peace and *Foreign Policy* magazine—South Sudan was ranked as the state most vulnerable to conflict or collapse. The Index is based on 12 indicators of state vulnerability across social, political and economic categories.

Justice

The Judiciary of Southern Sudan (JOSS) oversees the court systems of South Sudan. The highest court is the Supreme Court. The second tier of justice consists of three Courts of Appeal. Each state has a High Court, as well as county, town and city courts.

The death penalty is in force and was used in 2018, when at least seven executions were carried out.

The population in penal institutions in April 2013 was approximately 7,000 (65 per 100,000 of national population).

Education

Primary school enrolment in 2009 was 1,380,580. Secondary school enrolment (ages 14–17) was 44,027 in 2009. Higher education institutions include the University of Juba (founded in 1977), the University of Bahr el Ghazal (1991) in Wau and Upper Nile University (1991) in Malakal. The literacy rate for people aged 15 and above was 27% in 2009.

Health

There are three teaching hospitals, seven state hospitals and 16 county hospitals.

In *Water: At What Cost? The State of the World's Water 2016*, WaterAid reported that 41·3% of the population does not have access to safe water.

Religion

A large percentage of South Sudan's population are Christian—primarily Roman Catholic, Anglican and Presbyterian. There are also followers of African traditional animist religions as well as Muslims.

Diplomatic Representatives

Of South Sudan in the United Kingdom (Winchester House, 259–269 Old Marylebone Rd, London, NW1 5RA)
   Ambassador: Vacant.
   Chargé d'Affaires a.i.: Maker Ayuel Deng.

Of the United Kingdom in South Sudan (EU Compound, Kololo Rd, Thom Ping, Juba)
   Ambassador: Alison Blackburne.

Of South Sudan in the USA (1015 31st St., NW, Suite 300, Washington, D.C., 20007)
   Ambassador: Philip Jada Natana.

Of the USA in South Sudan (Kololo Rd, Juba)
   Ambassador: Thomas J. Hushek.

Of South Sudan to the United Nations
   Ambassador: Akuei Bona Malwal.

Of South Sudan to the European Union
   Ambassador: Emmanuel Lomoro LoWilla.

Further Reading

Copnall, James, *A Poisonous Thorn in Our Hearts: Sudan and South Sudan's Bitter and Incomplete Divorce.* 2014

Johnson, Hilde F., *South Sudan: The Untold Story from Independence to Civil War.* 2016

Martell, Peter, *First Raise a Flag: How South Sudan Won the Longest War but Lost the Peace.* 2018

Vertin, Zach, *A Rope from the Sky: The Making and Unmaking of the World's Newest State.* 2018

National Statistical Office: National Bureau of Statistics, Near South Sudan High Court, May St., Juba.

Website: http://ssnbs.org

Spain

Reino de España (Kingdom of Spain)

Capital: Madrid
Population projection, 2020: 46·46m.
GNI per capita, 2017: (PPP$) 34,258
HDI/world rank, 2017: 0·891/26
Internet domain extension: .es

Key Historical Events

A bridge between Europe and Africa, the Iberian peninsula has absorbed influences from both regions. The original inhabitants were Iberians, who spoke a non Indo-European language, and Celtic peoples, who were mainly to the north and west of the peninsula. From the 8th century BC the Phoenicians established trading colonies such as Gades (Cádiz), importing metalworking skills, music and literacy in the form of a semi-syllabic script. The Greeks established a trading settlement in Catalonia named Empirion (now Ampurias) around 575 BC, and there is evidence of other Greek and Phoenician settlements along the Mediterranean coast.

From 241 BC the Iberian peninsula came under the influence of Carthage in North Africa. The Carthaginians, led by Hamilcar Barca, landed at Cádiz and moved north and east. They eventually founded a new capital at Cartagena: the city grew rapidly and had a population of around 30,000 by 215 BC. A Roman presence began at this time, further north in Catalonia. The first legionnaires established their base at Tarragona, from where they waged war on the Carthaginians. Fighting between the two powers ebbed and flowed for years, until the Carthaginians were forced off the peninsula in 206 BC. Roman laws and customs were gradually adopted over the following six centuries, but there were frequent rebellions among the native peoples.

Roman rule was on the wane throughout Europe by AD 400, and Roman Hispania was no exception. In 409 Visigoths, Suevi and Vandals crossed the Pyrenees and began to establish themselves as the new rulers. By 470 most of the leading families were of Germanic origin. Toledo became the capital and seat of successive Visigothic monarchs until the early 700s. At this time, the Romans were defeated in North Africa by Muslim armies, who began to turn their attention to the Iberian peninsula. Toledo fell to Arab and Berber forces and the death of King Roderic in 711 marked the end of Visigothic hegemony.

Islam came to dominate large parts of the peninsula for the next 500 years, though there were sizeable Jewish communities in the southern and eastern towns and some Christian principalities in the north. The Umayyad dynasty used Córdoba as the administrative centre of al-Andalus ('Land of the Vandals') until 1031. New trade links were established with most of the Islamic world and Córdoba and Seville became beacons of modernity and creativity.

While al-Andalus prospered, the Christian principalities in places such as Asturias, the Basque territories and northern Catalonia remained relatively poor and agrarian. However, from about 900 there was a gradual expansion southwards towards al-Andalus, described as the start of the *Reconquista*, or reconquest of Spain by the Christians. By 1000 there was considerable contact between the Christian principalities and France: Norman knights fought in Catalonia and French settlers arrived in towns along the pilgrimage route to Santiago de Compostela.

From the 1120s the Muslim governors of al-Andalus found themselves under threat from both northern Christian rulers and native Andalusi. Alfonso VII of Leon-Castile eventually conquered Córdoba in 1146 and the strategically important Almería, on the Mediterranean coast, in 1147. Following these victories, the three most powerful Christian kingdoms of Aragon, Castile and Portugal pushed south and east and by 1300 the last remaining Islamic dominion was the emirate of Granada. Muslim inhabitants were expelled from many towns and cities, though in rural areas the Islamic faith and Arabic language survived for centuries. While Córdoba declined, Barcelona emerged as an economic powerhouse on a par with Genoa and Venice.

Castile and Aragon were the dominant kingdoms by the early 1300s, but they were characterized by infighting and rebellion. King Pedro the Cruel of Castile, backed by the English, was challenged by a coalition of nobles led by his half brother Enrique de Trastámara and others with French support. Enrique eventually prevailed, and was crowned Enrique II in 1369.

The Modern State

The Spanish monarchy was founded in 1469 following the marriage of Isabel (Isabella), princess of Castile and Fernando (Ferdinand), heir to the throne of Aragon. Under their joint reign, they laid the foundations for a unified Spain. In 1478 they established the notorious Spanish Inquisition, expelling and executing thousands of Jews and other non-Christians. Four years later the last Islamic territory of Granada was besieged. It surrendered in 1492, the year in which Christopher Columbus reached the New World.

When Fernando and Isabel's son Juan died in 1497, the succession to the Spanish crowns passed to his sister, Juana *la loca* (the Mad). Juana married Philip (Felipe) the Handsome, heir through his father, Emperor Maximilian I, to the Habsburg domains in Germany and Flanders. When Fernando died in 1516, Juana and Felipe's son, Charles of Ghent, inherited Spain, its colonies in the New World, Naples and, following the death of Maximilian I in 1519, the Habsburg territories. Shortly afterwards he was elected Holy Roman Emperor, a title he held as Charles V (Carlos I of Spain). In the space of only a few years, Charles commanded one of the most extensive empires since Rome.

Columbus paved the way for the Spanish colonies in the New World but for 30 years after his discoveries attention focused solely on the Caribbean. It was only in 1521 that Hernando Cortés overthrew the Aztecs, with help from native Indian allies. After 1540 gold and silver began pouring into Spanish coffers from mines in Peru and Mexico. Sugar plantations were established in the Caribbean and the indigenous populations were gradually wiped out. To maintain control of the new empire Charles V relied heavily on co-operation from Italians, Flemings and Germans. The rise of Spain as a military power began in the 1560s in the reign of Felipe II. He built a powerful navy and annexed Portugal in 1580. The new fleet patrolled the American supply routes, fending off attacks from the English, and set up new colonies in the Philippines and at Buenos Aires.

Spain's Golden Age began to lose its lustre in the late 16th century, following a popular uprising in the Netherlands under William of Orange. The Dutch were beginning to establish their own colonies in Asia and started making inroads in Brazil. Spain was weakened by the cost of defending its empire against France and England and in 1640 the unity of the Iberian peninsula itself came under threat by rebellions in Catalonia and Portugal. The crowning of Carlos II, a disabled child, in 1665 symbolized Spain's growing vulnerability.

Carlos II died without issue in 1700 and left the throne to Philippe, duke of Anjou and grandson of King Louis XIV of France. Felipe (Philippe) V was the first in a line of five Bourbon monarchs, who reigned in Spain until 1833. Under Felipe V, and his successor Fernando VI, Spain restored some of its influence in Europe, particularly in Italy, where Naples and Sicily were recovered from Austria in 1734. In the 1760s educational reforms led many universities to replace conservative Jesuit doctrines with modern physics, astronomy and political theory. The 1780s, when Spain was ruled by Carlos III, was a period of stability and prosperity. Catalonia became a centre of early industrialization with its booming textile trade and Madrid saw a flowering of artistic expression encapsulated by the work of Goya. In 1793 the new revolutionary French Republic turned its attention to neighbouring Spain and Britain. In 1794–95 French forces invaded Catalonia and the Basque provinces, following which King Carlos IV of Spain formed an alliance with France under its new emperor, Napoleon. Hostilities with Britain, however, saw defeat for the Franco–Spanish naval forces at the Battle of Trafalgar, which further undermined Spain's links with its colonies and damaged its economy.

In 1808 the weak and unpopular Carlos IV abdicated and the Spanish crown passed to Fernando VII, though his right to the throne was ceded to Napoleon later that year. However, Napoleon misjudged the mood of the Spanish public who began a five-year war of independence. In 1813 the French forces were finally expelled but ideas from revolutionary France had begun to take root. The medieval *Cortes* (parliament) was revived and a Liberal reformist group secured Spain's first constitution. The following year

© Springer Nature Limited 2020
Palgrave Macmillan (ed.), *The Statesman's Yearbook 2020*,
https://doi.org/10.1057/978-1-349-95940-2_178

Fernando VII was restored to the Spanish throne, but his reactionary 20-year reign oversaw the re-establishment of the Inquisition, persecution of the Liberals and repression of free speech. Spain meanwhile endured a severe economic recession.

End of Empire

Queen Isabel II inherited the Spanish throne as a child in 1833. During her reign there were various attempts by the Liberals and progressives to reinstate a constitution and in 1868 she was deposed. Amadeo I of Savoy was chosen as monarch but he was unable to adapt to Spanish politics and abdicated in 1873. The Cortes immediately proclaimed a republic, but in less than a year a coup restored the Bourbon monarchy, with Alfonso XII, the son of exiled Isabel II, as king.

The disastrous Spanish-American War of 1898 marked the end of the Spanish Empire. Spain was defeated by the USA, resulting in the loss of Cuba, Puerto Rico, Guam and the Philippines. Neutral in the First World War, Spain enjoyed a trade and industry boom, but prosperity did not benefit all levels of society and workers demonstrated against high food prices. In 1923 Gen. Miguel Primo de Rivera, Marquis of Estella, led a military coup and closed down the Cortes in his determination to clear out what he saw as corrupt, self-serving politicians. Although there were improvements under de Rivera in the nation's infrastructure, his public works programmes were hit by financial difficulties in 1929 and he resigned the following year.

1931 marked the beginning of a new genuinely democratic era for Spain. Municipal elections were held and won by a republican-socialist coalition. King Alfonso XIII went into exile and the Second Republic was declared. The 1936 elections saw the country split in two, with the Republican government and its supporters on one side (an uneasy alliance of communists, socialists and anarchists) and the Nationalists (the army, the Catholic Church, monarchists and the fascist-style Falange Party) on the other.

Civil War

The assassination of the opposition leader José Calvo Sotelo by Republican police officers in July 1936 gave the army, led by Gen. Francisco Franco, an excuse to stage a coup. The failure of the military to overthrow the government led to a protracted civil war. The Nationalists received extensive military and financial support from fascist Germany and Italy, while the Republican government received backing from the Soviet Union and, to a lesser degree, from the International Brigades, made up of foreign volunteers.

By 1939 the Nationalists, led by Franco, had prevailed. More than 350,000 Spaniards died in the fighting and an estimated 100,000 Republicans were subsequently executed or died in prison. Franco's cure for Spain's 'sick' economy was withdrawal from world markets and the establishment of a self-sufficient autarky which remained neutral in the Second World War. However, by the late 1940s inflation was rising steeply and Spain was losing ground to other European countries. Franco allowed a gradual liberalization of the economy, but despite this and the readmission of Spain to the UN in 1955 the economy remained in deep trouble. The desperate conditions endured by hundreds of thousands of workers led to nationwide strikes, growing opposition to the Franco regime among university students and intellectuals and demands for independence in Catalonia and the Basque Country.

Franco died in 1975, having earlier named Juan Carlos, the grandson of Alfonso XIII, his successor as king. Under Juan Carlos, Spain made the transition back to democracy. The first elections were held in 1977 and a new constitution was approved by referendum in 1978. In Feb. 1981 there was a futile fascist coup attempt and the following year saw a spectacular victory for the Socialist Party which presided over a rapid expansion in the economy during its 14 years in power. In 1986 Spain joined the European Economic Community, cementing the nation's status as a popular location for foreign investors and tourists, though its international reputation suffered from the ongoing violent campaign waged by ETA, the separatist terrorist group attempting to secure an independent Basque homeland.

In 1996 Spaniards voted in a conservative People's Party administration under the leadership of José María Aznar, whose re-election in March 2000 with an absolute majority was attributed to the buoyant state of the Spanish economy, which had averaged in excess of 4% annual growth during his first term of office.

Madrid suffered Spain's worst terrorist attack on 11 March 2004 when four commuter trains were bombed, killing 191 and injuring over 1,800 people. The government initially blamed ETA but suspicion quickly moved to Islamist extremists. On 14 March the Socialists, led by José Luis Rodríguez Zapatero, defeated the People's Party in general elections.

In March 2006 ETA announced a permanent ceasefire but the truce ended in Dec. that year when the group carried out a car bomb attack at Madrid's Barajas airport. (ETA subsequently agreed to a further ceasefire in Sept. 2010 and in Nov. 2012 offered to hold talks with the Spanish government on a definitive end to its operations, but the offer was rejected.)

In Nov. 2007 parliament passed legislation formally denouncing the rule of Franco. Zapatero won a further term in office in parliamentary elections in March 2008. The following year Spain suffered a deep economic downturn, ushering in a period of austerity that met with large-scale popular protests. Mariano Rajoy, head of the Popular Party, became premier in Dec. 2011. Although his government had to seek emergency financial assistance in 2012 from Spain's eurozone partners, the country emerged from recession in 2013. Despite winning the Dec. 2015 election, Rajoy's party fell short of a parliamentary majority and unsuccessful coalition negotiations forced a further election in June 2016. Again, no party secured a majority but Rajoy was eventually confirmed as prime minister in Oct. at the head of a minority administration.

In April 2017 ETA effectively ceased its armed campaign. In Oct. the authorities in Catalonia held an independence referendum in defiance of the central government in Madrid and hundreds of people were injured in clashes with police. The vote was overwhelmingly in favour of independence—subsequently declared by the Catalan government. The Madrid government responded by imposing direct rule. However, in regional parliamentary elections in Dec., pro-independence parties won a majority of seats, further aggravating the secession crisis.

Territory and Population

Spain is bounded in the north by the Bay of Biscay, France and Andorra, east and south by the Mediterranean and the Straits of Gibraltar, southwest by the Atlantic and west by Portugal and the Atlantic. Continental Spain has an area of 493,491 sq. km, and including the Balearic and Canary Islands and the towns of Ceuta and Melilla on the northern coast of Africa, 505,693 sq. km (195,249 sq. miles). Population (census, 2011), 46,815,916 (23,711,613 females). By the beginning of 2014 the resident population had fallen to 46,771,341, mainly owing to immigrants who had come to Spain in earlier years leaving as a result of the economic crisis and spiralling unemployment. The number of migrants coming from Latin America to Spain in 2012 was less than a third of the 2007 total, whereas the number of migrants going from Spain to Latin America in 2012 was nearly three times the 2007 figure. In 2011, 77·6% of the population lived in urban areas; population density in 2011 was 93 per sq. km. In 2011 foreigners resident in Spain numbered 5,252,473 (up from 3,730,610 in 2005), including 798,104 from Romania, 773,966 from Morocco, 316,756 from Ecuador, 312,098 from the UK and 250,087 from Colombia. Foreigners constituted 11·2% of the population in 2011 (8·5% in 2005 and 2·3% in 2000). The estimated population on 1 Jan. 2017 was 46,572,132.

The UN gives a projected population for 2020 of 46·46m.

The growth of the population has been as follows:

Census year	Population	Rate of annual increase
1860	15,655,467	0·34
1910	19,927,150	0·72
1920	21,303,162	0·69
1930	23,563,867	1·06
1940	25,877,971	0·98
1950	27,976,755	0·81
1960	30,903,137	1·05
1970	33,823,918	0·95
1981	37,746,260	1·05
1991	38,872,268	0·30
2001	40,847,371	0·51
2011	46,815,916	1·46

Area and population of the autonomous communities (in italics) and provinces at the 2011 census:

Autonomous community/ Province	Area (sq. km)	Population	Per sq. km
Andalucía	*87,597*	*8,371,270*	*96*
Almería	8,774	688,736	78
Cádiz	7,436	1,244,732	167
Córdoba	13,771	802,575	58
Granada	12,647	922,100	73
Huelva	10,128	519,895	51
Jaén	13,496	667,484	49
Málaga	7,308	1,594,808	218
Sevilla (Seville)	14,036	1,930,941	138
Aragón	*47,720*	*1,344,509*	*28*
Huesca	15,636	225,962	14
Teruel	14,810	143,162	10
Zaragoza (Saragossa)	17,275	975,385	56
Asturias	*10,604*	*1,075,183*	*101*
Baleares	*4,992*	*1,100,503*	*220*
Basque Country	*7,230*	*2,185,393*	*302*
Álava (Araba-Álava)	3,032	320,778	106
Guipúzcoa (Gipuzkoa)	1,980	708,425	358
Vizcaya (Bizkaia)	2,217	1,156,190	522
Canary Islands	*7,494*	*2,082,655*	*278*
Palmas de Gran Canaria, Las	4,066	1,087,225	267
Santa Cruz de Tenerife	3,381	995,429	294
Cantabria	*5,321*	*592,542*	*111*
Castilla-La Mancha	*79,462*	*2,106,331*	*27*
Albacete	14,926	401,580	27
Ciudad Real	19,813	526,628	27
Cuenca	17,141	215,165	13
Guadalajara	12,212	257,442	21
Toledo	15,370	705,516	46
Castilla y León	*94,227*	*2,540,188*	*27*
Ávila	8,050	171,647	21
Burgos	14,291	372,538	26
León	15,582	493,312	32
Palencia	8,053	170,513	21
Salamanca	12,350	350,018	28
Segovia	6,923	163,171	24
Soria	10,307	94,610	9
Valladolid	8,110	532,765	66
Zamora	10,561	191,613	18
Catalonia	*32,091*	*7,519,843*	*234*
Barcelona	7,728	5,522,565	715
Girona (Gerona)	5,910	751,806	127
Lleida (Lérida)	12,150	438,428	36
Tarragona	6,303	807,044	128
Extremadura	*41,635*	*1,104,499*	*27*
Badajoz (Baajós)	21,766	691,799	32
Cáceres	19,868	412,701	21
Galicia	*29,575*	*2,772,928*	*94*
Coruña, La (Coruña, A)	7,950	1,141,286	144
Lugo	9,857	348,067	35
Ourense (Orense)	7,273	328,697	45
Pontevedra	4,495	954,877	212
Madrid	*8,028*	*6,421,874*	*800*
Murcia	*11,314*	*1,462,128*	*129*
Navarra	*10,390*	*640,129*	*62*
Rioja, La	*5,045*	*321,173*	*64*
Valencian Community	*23,254*	*5,009,931*	*215*

(*continued*)

Autonomous community/ Province	Area (sq. km)	Population	Per sq. km
Alicante (Alacant)	5,817	1,852,166	318
Castellón (Castelló)	6,632	594,423	90
Valencia (València)	10,806	2,563,342	237
Ceuta[1]	*19*	*83,517*	*4,176*
Melilla[1]	*13*	*81,323*	*6,777*
Total	*505,963*	*46,815,916*	*93*

[1]Ceuta and Melilla gained limited autonomous status in 1994.

The capitals of the autonomous communities are: *Andalucía:* Seville (Sevilla); *Aragón:* Zaragoza (Saragossa); *Asturias:* Oviedo; *Baleares:* Palma de Mallorca; *Basque Country:* Vitoria-Gasteiz; *Canary Islands:* dual capitals, Las Palmas de Gran Canaria and Santa Cruz de Tenerife; *Cantabria:* Santander; *Castilla-La Mancha:* Toledo; *Castilla y León: de facto* capital, Valladolid; *Catalonia:* Barcelona; *Extremadura:* Mérida; *Galicia:* Santiago de Compostela; *Madrid:* Madrid; *Murcia:* Murcia (but regional parliament in Cartagena); *Navarra:* Pamplona (Iruña); *La Rioja:* Logroño; *Valencian Community:* Valencia (València).

The capitals of the provinces are the towns from which they take the name, except in the cases of Álava/Araba-Álava (capital, Vitoria-Gasteiz), Guipúzcoa/Gipuzkoa (San Sebastián) and Vizcaya/Bizkaia (Bilbao/Bilbo).

The islands that form the Balearics include Majorca (Mallorca), Minorca (Menorca), Ibiza and Formentera. Those which form the Canary Archipelago are divided into two provinces, under the name of their respective capitals: Santa Cruz de Tenerife and Las Palmas de Gran Canaria. The province of Santa Cruz de Tenerife is constituted by the islands of Tenerife, La Palma, Gomera and Hierro; that of Las Palmas by Gran Canaria, Lanzarote and Fuerteventura, with the small barren islands of Alegranza, Roque del Este, Roque del Oeste, Graciosa, Montaña Clara and Lobos.

Places under Spanish sovereignty in Africa (Alhucemas, Ceuta, Chafarinas, Melilla and Peñón de Vélez) constitute the two provinces of Ceuta and Melilla.

Populations of principal towns in 2011:

Town	Population
Albacete	171,999
Alcalá de Henares	200,505
Alcobendas	110,351
Alcorcón	167,217
Algeciras	117,695
Alicante (Alacant)	329,325
Almería	189,680
Badajoz (Baajós)	151,214
Badalona	219,241
Barakaldo	100,064
Barcelona	1,611,013
Bilbao (Bilbo)	351,356
Burgos	178,864
Cádiz	124,014
Cartagena	215,757
Castellón de la Plana (Castelló de la Plana)	176,298
Córdoba	328,326
Coruña, La (Coruña, A)	245,053
Dos Hermanas	128,433
Elche (Elx)	227,417
Fuenlabrada	196,986
Getafe	168,642
Gijón (Xixón)	276,969
Granada	241,003
Huelva	147,808
Jaén	116,469

(*continued*)

Town	Population
Jerez de la Frontera	211,784
Leganés	185,758
León	131,411
L'Hospitalet de Llobregat	256,509
Lleida (Lérida)	137,283
Logroño	152,698
Madrid	3,198,645
Málaga	561,435
Marbella	135,124
Mataró	123,367
Móstoles	203,493
Murcia	437,667
Ourense (Orense)	107,314
Oviedo	225,005
Palma de Mallorca	402,044
Palmas de Gran Canaria, Las	381,271
Pamplona (Iruña)	195,943
Parla	122,045
Reus	106,849
Sabadell	206,949
Salamanca	151,658
San Cristóbal de La Laguna	152,025
San Sebastián (Donostia)	185,512
Santa Coloma de Gramenet	119,391
Santa Cruz de Tenerife	204,476
Santander	178,095
Seville (Sevilla)	698,042
Tarragona	133,223
Telde	101,080
Terrassa	214,406
Torrejón de Ardoz	123,213
Valencia (València)	792,054
Valladolid	311,682
Vigo	295,623
Vitoria-Gasteiz	240,753
Zaragoza (Saragossa)	678,115

Languages

The Constitution states that 'Castilian is the Spanish official language of the State', but also that 'All other Spanish languages will also be official in the corresponding Autonomous Communities'. At the last linguistic census (2011) Catalan (an official EU language since 1990) was spoken in Catalonia by 73·2% of people and understood by 95·1%. It is also spoken in Baleares, Valencian Community (where it is frequently called Valencian) and in parts of Aragón, a narrow strip close to the Catalonian and Valencian Community boundaries, and Murcia, to the south of the Valencian Community. Galician, a language very close to Portuguese, was understood in 2007 by 98·0% of people in Galicia aged 15 and over and spoken to a high or moderate standard by 89·4%; Basque by a significant and increasing minority in the Basque Country, and by a small minority in northwest Navarra. It is estimated that one-third of all Spaniards speaks one of the other three official languages as well as standard Castilian. In bilingual communities, both Castilian and the regional language are taught in schools and universities.

Social Statistics

Statistics for calendar years:

	Births	Deaths	Marriages[1]	Divorces
2012	454,648	402,950	165,101	104,262
2013	425,715	390,419	153,375	95,427

(*continued*)

	Births	Deaths	Marriages[1]	Divorces
2014	427,595	395,830	159,279	100,746
2015	420,290	422,568	165,172	96,562
2016	410,583	410,611	171,023	96,824

[1]Excluding same-sex marriage, which was permitted from 2005.

Rate per 1,000 population, 2016: births, 8·8; deaths, 8·8; marriages, 3·7; divorces, 2·1. In 2010 the most popular age range for marrying was 30–34 for both males and females. Annual population growth rate, 2010–15, −0·2%. Suicide rate (per 100,000 population), 2015: 7·5. Expectation of life, 2007, was 77·5 years for males and 84·0 for females. Infant mortality, 2010, four per 1,000 live births; fertility rate, 2008, 1·4 births per woman. In 2009 Spain received 3,007 asylum applications, down from 7,662 in 2007.

In 2007–08, 19·6% of 15 to 34-year-olds used cannabis and 5·1% cocaine. A 2009 report found that use of cocaine in Spain was the highest in the European Union.

Climate

Most of Spain has a form of Mediterranean climate with mild, moist winters and hot, dry summers, but the northern coastal region has a moist, equable climate, with rainfall well distributed throughout the year, mild winters and warm summers, and less sunshine than the rest of Spain. The south, in particular Andalucía, is dry and prone to drought.

Madrid, Jan. 41°F (5°C), July 77°F (25°C). Annual rainfall 16·8" (419 mm). Barcelona, Jan. 46°F (8°C), July 74°F (23·5°C). Annual rainfall 21" (525 mm). Cartagena, Jan. 51°F (10·5°C), July 75°F (24°C). Annual rainfall 14·9" (373 mm). La Coruña, Jan. 51°F (10·5°C), July 66°F (19°C). Annual rainfall 32" (800 mm). Seville, Jan. 51°F (10·5°C), July 85°F (29·5°C). Annual rainfall 19·5" (486 mm). Palma de Mallorca, Jan. 51°F (11°C), July 77°F (25°C). Annual rainfall 13·6" (347 mm). Santa Cruz de Tenerife, Jan. 64°F (17·9°C), July 76°F (24·4°C). Annual rainfall 7·72" (196 mm).

Constitution and Government

Following the death of General Franco in 1975 and the transition to a democracy, the first democratic elections were held on 15 June 1977. A new constitution was approved by referendum on 6 Dec. 1978, and came into force 29 Dec. 1978. It has been amended twice since, in 1992 and 2011. It established a parliamentary monarchy.

The reigning King is **Felipe VI** (Don Felipe de Borbón y Grecia), born 30 Jan. 1968, who succeeded his father, Juan Carlos I (Juan Carlos de Borbón), on 19 June 2014. Felipe was married on 22 May 2004 to Letizia Ortiz Rocasolano. *Offspring*: Leonor, b. 8 Nov. 2005 (heiress presumptive); Sofia, b. 29 April 2007. Juan Carlos married Princess Sophia of Greece on 14 May 1962. The two retained their respective titles of King and Queen even after Juan Carlos's abdication on 18 June 2014. Besides Felipe, the couple have two other *offspring*: Elena, born 20 Dec. 1963, married 18 March 1995 Jaime de Marichalar, divorced 25 Nov. 2009 (*offspring*: Felipe, b. 17 July 1998; Victoria, b. 9 Sept. 2000); Cristina, born 13 June 1965, married 4 Oct. 1997 Iñaki Urdangarín (*offspring*: Juan, b. 29 Sept. 1999; Pablo, b. 6 Dec. 2000; Miguel, b. 30 April 2002; Irene, b. 5 June 2005).

The King receives an allowance, part of which is taxable, approved by parliament each year. For 2018 this was €7·9m. There is no formal court; the (private) *Diputación de la Grandeza* represents the interests of the aristocracy.

Legislative power is vested in the *Cortes Generales*, a bicameral parliament composed of the Congress of Deputies (lower house) and the Senate (upper house). The *Congress of Deputies* has not less than 300 nor more than 400 members (350 in the 2016 election) elected in a proportional system under which electors choose between party lists of candidates in multi-member constituencies.

The *Senate* has 266 members of whom 208 are elected by a majority system: the 47 mainland provinces elect four senators each, regardless of population; the larger islands (Gran Canaria, Majorca and Tenerife) elect three senators and each of the smaller islands or groups of islands (Ibiza-Formentera, Minorca, Fuerteventura, Gomera, Hierro, Lanzarote and La Palma) elect one senator. To these each self-governing community appoints one senator, and an additional senator for every million inhabitants in their respective territories. Currently 58 senators are appointed by the self-governing communities. Deputies and senators are elected by universal secret suffrage for four-year terms. The Prime Minister is elected by the Congress of Deputies.

The *Constitutional Court* is empowered to solve conflicts between the State and the Autonomous Communities; to determine if legislation passed by the Cortes is contrary to the Constitution; and to protect the constitutional rights of individuals violated by any authority. Its 12 members are appointed by the monarch. It has a nine-year term, with a third of the membership being renewed every three years.

In 2006 a revised Statute of Autonomy of Catalonia (one of the nation's 17 autonomous communities) received 73·9% support in a referendum of the Catalan electorate, giving the regional parliament increased powers over taxation and judicial matters. In late 2013 the Catalan government announced a referendum on independence from Spain. However, after such a referendum was declared illegal by the Spanish Constitutional Court, Catalonia held a non-binding informal vote in Nov. 2014 on separation from Spain. Turnout was around 39%, with 81% of votes cast in favour of independence.

National Anthem

'Marcha Real' ('Royal March'); no words, tune anonymous.

Government Chronology

Heads of government since 1939. (PP = Popular Party; PSOE = Spanish Socialist Workers' Party; UCD = Central Democratic Union)

1939–73	military	Francisco Franco
1973	military	Luis Carrero
1973–76	civilian	Carlos Arias Navarro
1976	military	Fernando de Santiago
1976–81	UCD	Adolfo Suárez
1981–82	UCD	Leopoldo Calvo-Sotelo
1982–96	PSOE	Felipe González
1996–2004	PP	José María Aznar
2004–11	PSOE	José Luis Rodríguez Zapatero
2011–18	PP	Mariano Rajoy Brey
2018–	PSOE	Pedro Sánchez

Recent Elections

Since no party was able to secure a majority at the Dec. 2015 elections, and with talks between parties failing to produce a coalition government, a general election took place on 26 June 2016. Turnout was 69·8%. In the *Congress of Deputies* the Popular Party (PP) won 137 seats with 33·0% of votes cast; the Spanish Socialist Workers' Party (PSOE), 85 with 22·7%; Podemos (including En Comú Podem, Compromís and En Marea), 71 with 21·1%; Citizens (Ciudadanos), 32 with 13·1%; Republican Left of Catalonia (ERC–CAT SÍ), 9 with 2·6%; Democratic Convergence of Catalonia (CDC), 8 with 2·0%; the Basque Nationalist Party (EAJ–PNV), 5 with 1·2%; Euskal Herria Bildu (Basque Country Unite), 2 with 0·8%; Canarian Coalition–Canarian Nationalist Party (CCa–PNC), 1 with 0·3%. In the *Senate*, the PP won 130 seats; PSOE, 43; Podemos (including En Comú Podem, Compromís and En Marea), 16; ERC–CAT SÍ, 10; EAJ–PNV, 5; CDC, 2; CCa–PNC, 1; Gomera Socialist Group (ASG), 1.

European Parliament

Spain has 54 representatives. At the May 2014 elections turnout was 45·8% (44·9% in 2009). The PP won 16 seats with 26·1% of votes cast (political affiliation in European Parliament: European People's Party); the PSOE, 14 with 23·0% (Progressive Alliance of Socialists and Democrats); Plural Left (a coalition of national and regional left-wing parties), 6 with 10·0% (five with European United Left/Nordic Green Left and one with Greens/European Free Alliance); Podemos (We Can), 5 with 8·0% (European United Left/Nordic Green Left); UPyD, 4 with 6·5% (Alliance of Liberals and Democrats for Europe); the Coalition for Europe (a coalition of regionalist parties), 3 with 5·4% (two with Alliance of Liberals and Democrats for Europe and one with European People's Party); Left for the Right to Decide (Catalan separatist coalition), 2 with 4·0% (Greens/European Free Alliance); Citizens–Party of the Citizenry, 2 with 3·2% (Alliance of Liberals and Democrats for Europe); the People Decide (left-wing regionalist coalition), 1 with 2·1% (European United Left/Nordic Green Left);

Primavera Europea (coalition of green left-wing parties), 1 with 1·9% (Greens/European Free Alliance).

Current Government

In Feb. 2019 the coalition government comprised:

President of the Council and Prime Minister: Pedro Sánchez; b. 1972 (PSOE; sworn in 2 June 2018).

Vice-President of the Council, and Minister of the Presidency, Relations with Parliament and Equality: Carmen Calvo.

Minister for Agriculture, Fisheries, and Food: Luis Planas. *Culture and Sport:* José Guirao Cabrera. *Defence:* Margarita Robles. *Development:* José Luis Ábalos Meco. *Ecological Transition:* Teresa Ribera. *Economy and Business:* Nadia Calviño. *Education and Vocational Training, and Spokesperson of the Government:* Isabel Celaá. *Finance:* María Jesús Montero. *Foreign Affairs, European Union Affairs and Co-operation:* Josep Borrell. *Health, Consumption and Social Welfare:* María Luisa Carcedo. *Industry, Trade and Tourism:* Reyes Maroto. *Interior:* Fernando Grande-Marlaska. *Justice:* Dolores Delgado. *Labour, Migration and Social Security:* Magdalena Valerio. *Science, Innovation and Universities:* Pedro Duque. *Territorial Policy and Public Administration:* Meritxell Batet.

President of the Congress of Deputies: Ana Pastor Julián.

Of the 18 cabinet ministers, 11 are currently women.

Government Website: http://www.lamoncloa.gob.es

Current Leaders

Pedro Sánchez

Position

Prime Minister

Introduction

Pedro Sánchez of the Spanish Socialist Workers' Party (PSOE) became prime minister on 2 June 2018. He is the first Spanish politician to unseat a premier through a vote of no confidence without holding a seat in parliament.

Early Life

Born on 29 Feb. 1972 in Madrid, Pedro Sánchez Pérez-Castejón graduated in economics and business from the city's Complutense University. He joined the PSOE in 1993, rising to become secretary-general in 2014. In 1998 he earned a master's degree from the Free University of Brussels in Belgium and in 2012 was awarded his doctorate in economics and business from Madrid's Camilo José Cela University, where he later taught.

Before embarking on a career in regional and national politics, Sánchez worked as a parliamentary assistant in the European Parliament and as chief-of-staff to the United Nations' high representative in Bosnia during the Kosovo War. In 2000 he returned to Spain, working variously as an economic adviser to the PSOE's federal executive committee and as a self-employed consultant advising foreign businesses. Between 2004 and 2009 he was also a Madrid city councillor.

In 2009 he was elected to the Congress of Deputies representing Madrid, before losing his seat in 2011 and resuming his academic career. In 2013 he returned to parliament and was elected party leader in 2014, the first PSOE secretary-general to be elected directly by members. In the 2015 elections his party came second behind Mariano Rajoy's Popular Party, which fell short of winning a majority. This pushed Sánchez to make a failed bid for the premiership. In the 2016 elections the PSOE suffered the worst defeat in its history, winning just 85 out of 350 seats, while the Popular Party again emerged the largest party with Rajoy returning to office. Sánchez resigned as leader of the PSOE and relinquished his seat in parliament in Oct. 2016 after refusing to support the formation of Rajoy's conservative coalition.

Sánchez subsequently won the party primaries to be reinstated as secretary-general in May 2017. On 31 May 2018 the PSOE filed a no-confidence motion against Rajoy following a corruption scandal centred on a secret campaign fund that the Popular Party ran from 1999 until 2005. The motion passed with the support of the PSOE, Podemos, and Basque, Valencian and Catalan regionalist and nationalist parties. Rajoy thus became the first prime minister in modern Spanish history to be defeated in a no-confidence motion.

Career in Office

With Rajoy forced from office, Sánchez was sworn in as his successor on 2 June 2018. He pledged to increase unemployment benefits and to reinstate dialogue with the Catalan independence movement.

Defence

Conscription was abolished in 2001. The government had begun the phased abolition of conscription in 1996. In 2002 the armed forces became fully professional. However, a shortfall in recruitment in Spain meant that descendants of Spanish migrants, many of whom had never been to Europe, began to join. Since 1989 women have been accepted in all sections of the armed forces.

In 2013 defence expenditure totalled US$11,593m. (US$245 per capita), representing 0·8% of GDP (compared to the NATO target of 2%).

Army

Strength (2013) 70,800 active personnel and 3,000 reservists. In the same year the army operated 327 main battle tanks, 875 armoured personnel carriers and six attack helicopters.

Guardia Civil

The paramilitary *Guardia Civil* numbered 79,950 in 2013.

Navy

The principal amphibious ship of the Navy is the light vertical/short take-off and landing multi-purpose *Juan Carlos I*, commissioned in 2010. It carries AV-8B Harrier combat aircraft. There are also two landing platform dock ships, three French-designed submarines, five destroyers and six frigates. The country's only aircraft carrier was withdrawn from service in 2013.

In 2013 Naval Aviation operated 17 combat-capable aircraft and 38 helicopters. Personnel numbered 800 in 2013. There are 5,300 marines.

Main naval bases are at Cartagena, Ferrol, Rota and San Fernando.

In 2013 personnel totalled 22,200 including the marines and Naval Aviation. There were 9,000 naval reservists in 2013.

Air Force

The Air Force is organized as an independent service, dating from 1939. It is administered through three operational commands. These comprise Central Air Command, Combat Air Command and Canary Islands Air Command.

There were 157 combat-capable aircraft in 2013 including Eurofighter *Typhoons* and EF/A-18s.

Strength (2013) 20,600. There were 2,200 air force reservists in 2013.

Economy

Agriculture accounted for 2% of GDP in 2012, industry 24% and services 74%.

Spain's 'shadow' (black market) economy is estimated to constitute approximately 17·2% of the country's official GDP.

In 2017 Spain gave US$2·6bn. in international aid. This represented 0·19% of GDP.

Overview

Spain joined the European Community (forerunner of the European Union) in 1986 and subsequently made significant economic progress. The economy grew consistently for 16 years until 2009 when the global financial crisis prompted a contraction. Before the crash Spain was considered to have one of the most dynamic economies in the eurozone, with the service sector's share of total GDP expanding at the expense of the traditionally strong agriculture, forestry and fishing industries.

Strong demand for tourist-related facilities, foreign demand for property and high levels of investment in infrastructure combined to make the pre-crisis construction sector twice as large as in other major European economies in terms of share of GDP. Consequently, the bursting of the housing bubble was a major contributory factor in the downturn in 2009. The economy contracted by 3·6% that year, with public finances recording a deficit of over 11% of GDP. GDP shrank further until 2013, by which time unemployment measured 26·1%. However, a rebound saw annualized growth of 2·8% between 2014 and 2017, driven by buoyant domestic demand.

After several years of substantial fiscal consolidation—including expenditure cuts and corporate tax reforms—the budget deficit decreased to 3·1% of GDP in 2017 from 4·5% the previous year. However, with public debt at around 98% of GDP, the scope for fiscal expansion remains limited and inflation is expected to increase as the impact of low oil prices diminishes. Although the jobless rate is declining, it is still high, standing at 15·3% in 2018. Addressing long-term and youth unemployment remains an acute challenge.

The business climate has improved in the post-crisis period, reflecting favourable financial conditions, reduced indebtedness and increasing demand. Exporters have benefited from gains in competitiveness (in part owing to restrained wage growth) and from a significant expansion of export potential. Nonetheless, sustaining the recovery remains a challenge, particularly in light of upheaval in the EU as a result of the UK's 'Brexit' vote—factors that may dampen private sector confidence.

Currency

On 1 Jan. 1999 the *euro* (EUR) became the legal currency in Spain at the irrevocable conversion rate of 166·386 pesetas to one euro. The euro, which consists of 100 cents, has been in circulation since 1 Jan. 2002. On the introduction of the euro there was a 'dual circulation' period before the peseta ceased to be legal tender on 28 Feb. 2002.

Foreign exchange reserves were US$12,657m. in Sept. 2009 (US$52,490m. in 1998) and gold reserves 9·05m. troy oz. Inflation rates (based on OECD statistics):

2008	2009	2010	2011	2012	2013	2014	2015	2016	2017
4·1%	−0·2%	2·0%	3·0%	2·4%	1·5%	−0·2%	−0·6%	−0·3%	2·0%

Total money supply was €506,714m. in Aug. 2009.

Budget

In 2014 general government revenues totalled €395bn. and expenditures €462bn. Principal sources of revenue in 2014: social security contributions, €119bn.; taxes on goods and services, €109bn.; taxes on income, profits and capital gains, €101bn. Main items of expenditure by economic type in 2014: social benefits, €199bn.; compensation of employees, €111bn.; use of goods and services, €53bn.

Spain's budget deficit in 2017 was 3·1% of GDP (2016, 4·5%; 2015, 5·3%). The required target set by the EU is a budget deficit of no more than 3%.

VAT is 21%, with a rate of 10% on certain services (catering and hospitality) and 4% on basic foodstuffs.

Performance

Real GDP growth rates (based on OECD statistics):

2008	2009	2010	2011	2012	2013	2014	2015	2016	2017
1·1%	−3·6%	0·0%	−1·0%	−2·9%	−1·7%	1·4%	3·6%	3·2%	3·0%

Total GDP (2017): US$1,311·3bn.

Banking and Finance

The central bank is the Bank of Spain (*Governor*, Luis María Linde) which gained autonomy under an ordinance of 1994. Its Governor is appointed for a six-year term. The Banking Corporation of Spain, *Argentaria*, groups together the shares of all state-owned banks, and competes in the financial market with private banks. In 1993 the government sold 49·9% of the capital of Argentaria; the remainder in two flotations ending on 13 Feb. 1998.

Spanish banking is dominated by two main banks—Santander and BBVA (Banco Bilbao Vizcaya Argentaria). Santander had assets of US$1,533·2bn. in 2013 and BBVA assets of US$823·9bn.

Gross external debt amounted to US$2,264,614m. in June 2012.

Total foreign direct investment in 2017 was US$19·1bn., down from a record US$77·0bn. in 2008.

There are stock exchanges in Madrid, Barcelona, Bilbao and Valencia.

Energy and Natural Resources

In 2011, 15·1% of energy consumption came from renewables (wind power, solar power, hydro-electric power, tidal power, geothermal energy and biomass), compared to the European Union average of 13·0%. A target of 20% has been set by the EU for 2020.

Environment

In 2011 Spain's carbon dioxide emissions from the consumption of energy were the equivalent of 6·8 tonnes per capita.

Electricity

Installed capacity was 110·1m. kW in 2011. The total electricity output in 2011 amounted to 291·2bn. kWh, of which 51·3% was thermal, 19·8% nuclear, 11·3% hydro-electric and 17·6% other (notably wind). In 2010 there were eight nuclear reactors in operation. Consumption per capita in 2011 was 6,133 kWh.

Oil and Gas

Spain is heavily dependent on imported oil; Mexico is its largest supplier. Crude oil production (2011), 0·7m. bbls.

The government sold its remaining stake in the oil, gas and chemicals group Repsol in 1997. Natural gas production (2011) totalled 52m. cu. metres. Ever increasing consumption means that Spain has to import large quantities of natural gas, primarily from Algeria.

Wind

Spain is one of the world's largest wind-power producers, with an installed capacity of 23,025 MW in 2015 (the fourth highest after China, the USA and Germany). Production of wind-generated electricity was 55·7bn. kWh in 2013.

Minerals

Coal production (2011), 6·62m. tonnes; other principal minerals (in 1,000 tonnes): limestone (2008 estimate), 270,000; dolomite (2008 estimate), 15,000; gypsum and anhydrite (2008 estimate), 15,000; marl (2008 estimate), 10,000; salt (2008), 4,141; feldspar (2008), 690; potash (2008), 435; aluminium (2008), 408; fluorspar (2008), 149; nickel (2008), 8. Gold production, 2008, 3,400 kg; silver production, 2008, 3,400 kg.

Agriculture

There were 965,000 farms in Spain in 2013. Agriculture employed 4·5% of the workforce in 2013. Food and live animals accounted for 12·2% of exports and 8·1% of imports in 2010.

There were an estimated 12·57m. ha. of arable land in 2012 and 4·97m. ha. of permanent crops.

Principal crops	Area (in 1,000 ha.)			Yield (in 1,000 tonnes)		
	2010	2011	2012	2010	2011	2012
Barley	2,886	2,701	2,691	8,154	8,287	5,956
Wheat	1,948	1,995	2,188	5,941	6,877	5,190
Maize	315	369	390	3,325	4,200	4,262
Tomatoes	59	51	49	4,313	3,864	4,046
Sugar beets	43	45	39	3,535	4,189	3,482
Potatoes	78	80	72	2,298	2,455	2,192
Onions	23	25	23	1,105	1,308	1,170

Production of wine in 2012 totalled 31,122,560 hectolitres (12·1% of the world total), ranking Spain third behind France and Italy.

Fruit production (2012, in tonnes): grapes, 5,332,000; oranges, 2,942,000; tangerines, mandarins, clementines and satsumas, 1,871,000; peaches and nectarines, 1,172,000; lemons and limes, 684,000; apples, 481,000; pears, 407,000.

Production of olives, 2012, 3,849,000 tonnes; olive oil, 653,000 tonnes. Spain is the world's leading producer both of olives and olive oil.

Livestock (2013): pigs, 25·49m.; sheep, 16·12m.; cattle, 5·80m.; goats, 2·61m.; chickens (estimate), 138m.; asses and mules (estimate), 0·25m.; horses (estimate), 0·25m. Livestock products (2013, in 1,000 tonnes): pork and pork products, 3,431; beef and veal, 581; lamb and mutton, 118; poultry meat, 1,329; milk, 7,404; cheese (estimate), 225; eggs, 743.

Forestry

In 2015 the area under forests was 18·42m. ha., or 37% of the total land area. In 2011 timber production was 15·43m. cu. metres.

Fisheries

Spain is one of the leading fishing nations in the EU; it is also the EU's leading importer of fishery commodities. Fishing vessels had a total tonnage of 387,503 GT in 2012, the highest in the EU and representing nearly a quarter of the total tonnage; fleets have been gradually reduced from 18,385 boats in 1995 to 10,143 in 2012. Total catch in 2015 amounted to 973,240 tonnes, almost exclusively sea fish. Imports of fishery commodities were valued at US$7,309m. in 2011 (the fourth highest in the world) and exports at US$4,186m. (the ninth highest).

Industry

The leading companies by market capitalization in Spain in May 2018 were: Banco Santander (US$106·3bn.); Inditex, a fashion distributor (US$99·5bn.); and BBVA-Banco Bilbao Vizcaya (US$54·4bn.).

In 2007 industry accounted for 30% of GDP, with manufacturing contributing 15%.

Industrial products, 2007 unless otherwise indicated (in tonnes): cement (2008), 43·1m.; distillate fuel oil, 23·9m.; crude steel (2008), 18·6m.; residual fuel oil, 9·3m.; petrol, 9·2m.; paper and paperboard, 6·7m.; pig iron (estimate), 4·2m.; jet fuel, 2·6m.; lime (estimate), 2·0m.; nitrogenous fertilizers, 836,270; cigarettes, 41·91bn. units.

Output of other products, 2007: passenger cars, 2,385,210 units; TV receivers, 3·01m. units; washing and drying machines; 2·48m. units; fridge-freezers, 1·15m. units. In 2007, 6,765·6m. litres of mineral water, 5,888·0m. litres of soft drinks and 3,350·2m. litres of beer were produced.

Labour

The labour force in 2013 was 23,420,000 (19,689,000 in 2003). 74·2% of the population aged 15–64 was economically active in 2013. Of those in employment in 2013, 75·9% worked in services, 19·8% in industry and 4·2% in agriculture. In that year 45·5% of the labour force was female. 23·4% of the labour force had a secondary education as the highest level and 36·3% had a tertiary education. The retirement age was traditionally 65 years but in July 2011 the government agreed to raise the age to 67. The change, which is being phased in gradually, started on 1 Jan. 2013 in a process that is set to continue through to 2027. In 2016 the minimum wage was €655·08 a month.

Spain's unemployment rate exceeded 22% in 1994 but then fell steadily, declining to 8·2% in 2007. However, as a result of the global economic crisis the unemployment rate rose by eight percentage points in the space of 12 months from March 2008. In the period Jan.–March 2009 an average of 8,600 jobs were lost every day. Unemployment peaked at 26·3% in July 2013. In Dec. 2018 the rate stood at 14·3%, down from 17·2% in 2017 as a whole and 19·2% in 2016 (and the lowest since 2008). Spain had the second highest unemployment rate in the EU in Dec. 2017 (only below that of Greece). Youth unemployment—those under 25—is particularly high, at 47·5% in Nov. 2015 (although it was 55·8% in July 2013).

Spain had 6,000 people living in slavery according to the Walk Free Foundation's 2013 *Global Slavery Index*.

International Trade

Imports and Exports

Trade in US$1m.:

	2012	2013	2014	2015	2016
Imports c.i.f.	325,835	332,267	350,978	305,266	302,539
Exports f.o.b.	285,936	310,964	318,649	278,122	281,777

Principal imports in 2016 were machinery and transport equipment (33·1%), followed by miscellaneous manufactured articles (14·9%) and chemicals (14·3%); main exports in 2016 were machinery and transport equipment (35·0%), food, animals and beverages (15·2%) and manufactured goods classified chiefly by material (14·9%).

Leading import sources in 2016 were Germany (12·8%), France (11·0%) and China (8·3%); leading export markets in 2016 were: France (15·4%), Germany (10·8%) and Italy (7·5%). In 2016 the EU accounted for 61·7% of Spain's imports and 66·6% of exports.

Trade Fairs

Barcelona ranked as the third most popular convention city in 2016 according to the International Congress and Convention Association. Barcelona hosted 181 international association meetings that year.

Communications

Roads

In 2007 the total length of roads was 667,064; the network included 13,014 km of motorways, 12,832 km of highways/national roads and 140,165 km of secondary roads. In 2015 road transport totalled 363,942m. passenger-km; freight transport totalled 209,387m. tonne-km in 2015. Number of passenger cars in use (2007), 21,760,200; lorries and vans, 5,140,600; buses and coaches, 61,000; motorcycles and mopeds, 2,311,300. In 2007, 3,823 persons were killed in road accidents (5,604 in 1997).

Rail

The total length of the state railways in 2011 was 15,680 km, mostly broad (1,668 mm) gauge (9,488 km electrified). The state railway system was divided in two in 2005; Administrador de Infraestructuras Ferroviarias (ADIF) now manages the infrastructure and Renfe Operadora runs train operations. There is an ever-expanding high-speed standard gauge (1,435 mm) network, totalling 3,100 km in 2013. Only China has a longer high-speed rail network. The first high-speed line, from Madrid to Seville, opened in 1992. It was extended northwards from Madrid initially to Lleida, with passenger services beginning in 2003, and further to Tarragona (2006), Barcelona (2008) and the border with France (2013). A number of other high-speed lines connecting different parts of the country have been built since then. Passenger-km travelled in 2011 came to 22·7bn. and freight tonne-km to 8·0bn. There are metros in Madrid (287 km), Valencia (152 km), Barcelona (105 km), Bilbao (38 km), Seville (18 km) and Palma de Mallorca (7 km).

In 2003 the construction of two 38 km-long rail tunnels under the Straits of Gibraltar was agreed in principle with Morocco. As of late 2016 a joint research committee was analysing the technological feasibility and economic viability of the project.

Civil Aviation

Spain's 15 busiest airports by passenger traffic in 2013 were: Madrid (Barajas), Barcelona (El Prat), Palma de Mallorca, Málaga, Gran Canaria, Alicante, Tenerife (South), Ibiza, Lanzarote, Valencia, Fuerteventura, Bilbao, Seville, Tenerife (North) and Girona. A small airport in Seo de Urgel serves Andorra and is 12 km from the border. Madrid (Barajas) handled 39,735,618 passengers in 2013, Barcelona (El Prat) 35,216,828 and Palma de Mallorca 22,768,032. Madrid (Barajas) is the busiest airport by cargo traffic, handling 366,969 tonnes of freight and mail in 2013, ahead of Barcelona (El Prat) with 98,087 tonnes and Zaragoza with 71,565 tonnes. The former national carrier Iberia Airlines completed its privatization process in April 2001, when shares were listed for the first time on the stock exchange. In April 2010 it signed a deal with British Airways to merge and create a new company called International Airlines Group, which was founded in Jan. 2011. However, both carriers still operate under their own brands. Of other airlines, the largest are the low-cost carrier Vueling Airlines (which is also part of International Airlines Group) and Air Europa. Services are also provided by about 70 foreign airlines.

Shipping

In Jan. 2014 there were 149 ships of 300 GT or over registered, totalling 2·43m. GT. Of the 149 vessels registered, 52 were passenger ships, 41 general cargo ships, 39 oil tankers, 13 liquid gas tankers, two bulk carriers and two container ships. The Spanish-controlled fleet comprised 188 vessels of 1,000 GT or over in July 2014, of which 97 were under the Spanish flag and 91 under foreign flags. The leading ports are Algeciras (91,150,000 tonnes of cargo in 2013), Barcelona, Bilbao, Cartagena, Las Palmas de Gran Canaria, Santa Cruz de Tenerife, Tarragona and Valencia.

Telecommunications

In 2013 there were 19,384,000 main (fixed) telephone lines. In the same year mobile phone subscriptions numbered 50,159,000 (1,068·9 per 1,000 persons). The government disposed of its remaining 21% stake in Telefónica in 1997, bringing 1·4m. shareholders into the company's equity base. A second operator, Retevisión, accounts for 3% of the domestic market, which was wholly deregulated in 1998. The mobile phone business was deregulated in 1995; the leading mobile network operators are Movistar, Vodafone, Orange and Yoigo.

In 2013 an estimated 76·2% of the population were internet users. There were 53·0 mobile broadband subscriptions per 100 inhabitants in 2012 and 24·4 fixed broadband subscriptions per 100 inhabitants. In March 2012 there were 15·7m. Facebook users.

Social Institutions

Out of 178 countries analysed in the 2017 *Fragile States Index*—a list published jointly by the Fund for Peace and *Foreign Policy* magazine—Spain was ranked the 24th least vulnerable to conflict or collapse. The index is based on 12 indicators of state vulnerability across social, political and economic categories.

Justice

Justice is administered by Tribunals and Courts, which jointly form the Judicial Power. Judges and magistrates cannot be removed, suspended or transferred except as set forth by law. The constitution of 1978 established the *General Council of the Judicial Power*, consisting of a President and 20 magistrates, judges, attorneys and lawyers, governing the Judicial Power in full independence from the state's legislative and executive organs. Its members are appointed by the *Cortes Generales*. Its President is that of the Supreme Court (*Tribunal Supremo*), who is appointed by the monarch on the proposal of the General Council of the Judicial.

The Judicature is composed of the Supreme Court; 17 Higher Courts of Justice, one for each autonomous community; 52 Provincial High Courts; Courts of First Instance; Courts of Judicial Proceedings, not passing sentences; and Penal Courts, passing sentences.

The Supreme Court consists of a President, and various judges distributed among seven chambers: one for civil matters, three for administrative purposes, one for criminal trials, one for social matters and one for military cases. The Supreme Court has disciplinary faculties; is court of appeal in all criminal trials; for administrative purposes decides in first and second instance disputes arising between private individuals and the State; and in social matters makes final decisions.

A new penal code came into force in May 1996, replacing the code of 1848. It provides for a maximum of 30 years imprisonment in specified exceptional cases, with a normal maximum of 20 years. Sanctions with a rehabilitative intent include fines adjusted to means, community service and weekend imprisonment. The death penalty was abolished by the 1978 constitution. The prison population in Aug. 2013 was 68,220 (147 per 100,000 of national population). In 2012, 2,268,900 crimes were recorded by the police (2,285,500 in 2011). A jury system commenced operating in Nov. 1995 in criminal cases (first trials in May 1996). Juries consist of nine members. In 2015 the World Justice Project *Rule of Law Index*, which provides data on how the rule of law is experienced by the general public across eight categories, ranked Spain 26th of 102 countries for criminal justice and 24th for civil justice.

A juvenile criminal law of 1995 lays emphasis on rehabilitation. It raised the age of responsibility from 12 to 14 years. Criminal conduct on the part of children under 14 is a matter for legal protection and custody. 14- and 15-year-olds are classified as 'minors'; 16- and 17-year-olds as 'young persons'; and the legal majority for criminal offences is set at 18 years. Persons up to the age of 21 may, at the courts' discretion, be dealt with as juveniles.

The *Audiencia Nacional* deals with terrorism, monetary offences and drug-trafficking where more than one province is involved. Its president is appointed by the General Council of the Judicial Power.

There is an Ombudsman (*Defensor del Pueblo*), who is elected for a five-year term (currently Francisco Fernández Marugán in an acting capacity; b. 1946).

Education

In 1991 the General Regulation of the Educational System Act came into force. This Act gradually extends the school-leaving age to 16 years and determines the following levels of education: infants (3–5 years of age), primary (6–11), secondary (12–15) and baccalaureate or vocational and technical (16–17). Primary and secondary levels of education are now compulsory and free. Religious instruction is optional.

In Sept. 1997 a joint declaration with trade unions, parents' and schools' associations was signed in support of a new finance law guaranteeing that spending on education will reach 6% of GDP within five years, thus protecting it from changes in the political sphere. In 2006 public expenditure on education came to 4·4% of GNI and 11·1% of total government spending.

A new compulsory secondary education programme has replaced the Basic General Education programme which was in force since 1970. In addition, university entrance exams underwent reform in 1997, resulting in greater emphasis now being placed on the teaching of Humanities at secondary level.

In 2015 pre-primary education was undertaken by 1,398,107 pupils; primary or basic education: 3,010,404 pupils. In 2015 there were 99,581 teaching staff in pre-primary and 228,299 teachers in primary schools. Secondary education, including high schools and technical schools, was undertaken by 3,313,127 pupils and 276,487 teachers in 2015.

In 2011 there were 76 universities: 50 public state universities and 26 private universities (including Catholic establishments). In 2006–07 there were 1,265,480 students at state universities; 140,414 at private universities.

The adult literacy rate is at least 99%.

Health

In 2009 there were 219,031 doctors, 63,337 pharmacists, 26,725 dentists and stomatologists, and 255,445 graduate nurses. Number of hospitals (2009), 770, with 146,310 beds. In 2012 Spain spent 8·9% of its GDP on health, with public spending accounting for 71·7% of total expenditure on health and private spending 28·3%.

Welfare

Social expenditure totalled €271,018m. in 2013 including old age €98,314m., health €65,719m. and unemployment €32,031m. The minimum retirement pension in 2015 was €7,851·20 per year, made in 14 payments.

In 2016 the system of contributions to the social security and employment scheme was: for old age, disability and survivors, and sickness and maternity, a contribution of 28·3% of the basic wage (23·6% paid by the employer, 4·7% by the employee); for unemployment benefit, a contribution of 7·05% (5·5% paid by the employer, 1·55% by the employee). There are also minor contributions for work injuries.

Religion

There is no official religion. In 2010 Roman Catholicism was the religion of 75·2% of the population according to estimates by the Pew Research Center's Forum on Religion & Public Life. In Feb. 2019 there were 14 cardinals. There are 70 dioceses and archdioceses including the archdiocese of Toledo, where the Primate resides. The Pew Research Center estimated that 2·1% of the population were Muslims, 2·0% were Orthodox Christians and 19·0% did not have any religious affiliation. While Spain is not traditionally an Orthodox country, numbers began to grow in the early 1990s when there was an influx of migrant workers from Eastern Europe (particularly from Romania).

Culture

World Heritage Sites

There are 47 UNESCO sites in Spain: the works of Antoni Gaudí in and around Barcelona (inscribed in 1984 and 2005), Burgos Cathedral (1984), Historic Centre of Córdoba (1984 and 1994), Alhambra, Generalife and Albayzín, Granada (1984 and 1994), Monastery and site of the Escurial, Madrid (1984), Altamira Cave (1985 and 2008), Old Town of Segovia and its Aqueduct (1985), Monuments of Oviedo and the Kingdom of the Asturias (1985 and 1998), Santiago de Compostela (Old Town) (1985), Old Town of Ávila, with its Extra-Muros churches (1985 and 2007), Mudéjar Architecture of Aragón (1986 and 2001), Historic City of Toledo (1986), Garajonay National Park (1986), Old Town of Cáceres (1986), Cathedral, Alcazar and Archivo de Indias in Seville (1987), Old City of Salamanca (1988), Poblet Monastery (1991), Archaeological Ensemble of Mérida (1993), Royal Monastery of Santa María de Guadalupe (1993), Route of Santiago de Compostela (1993 and 2015), Doñana National Park (1994 and 2005), Historic Walled Town of Cuenca (1996), La Lonja de la Seda de Valencia (1996), Las Médulas (1997), the Palau de la Música Catalana and the Hospital de Sant Pau, Barcelona (1997 and 2008), San Millán Yuso and Suso Monasteries (1997), University and Historic Precinct of Alcalá de Henares (1998), Rock-Art of the Mediterranean Basin on the Iberian Peninsula (1998), Ibiza, Biodiversity and Culture (1999), San Cristóbal de La Laguna (1999), the Archaeological Ensemble of Tárraco (2000), the Palmeral of Elche (2000), the Roman Walls of Lugo (2000), Catalan Romanesque Churches of the Vall de Boí (2000), Archaeological Site of Atapuerca (2000), Aranjuez Cultural Landscape (2001), Renaissance monumental ensembles of Úbeda and Baeza (2003), Vizcaya Bridge (2006), Teide National Park, Tenerife (2007), the Tower of Hercules, La Coruña (2009), the Cultural Landscape of the Serra de Tramuntana (2011), Antequera Dolmens Site (2016) and the Caliphate City of Medina Azahara (2018).

Spain shares the Pyrénées—Mount Perdu (1997 and 1999) with France, the Prehistoric Rock Art Sites in the Côa Valley and Siega Verde (1998) with Portugal, Ancient and Primeval Beech Forests of the Carpathians and Other Regions of Europe (2007 and 2017) with Albania, Austria, Belgium, Bulgaria, Croatia, Germany, Italy, Romania, Slovakia, Slovenia and Ukraine, and Heritage of Mercury: Almadén and Idrija (2012) with Slovenia.

Press

In 2014 there were 110 paid-for daily newspapers with a total daily circulation of 2·35m. copies. The main paid-for titles are *El País* (average daily circulation 260,000 in 2014) and *El Mundo* (150,000), along with the dedicated sports papers *Marca* (172,000) and *As* (149,000). The leading free paper, *20 Minutos*, has a much larger circulation than the leading paid-for dailies. All of the paid-for dailies had online editions in 2014.

In 2009, 96,955 printed books were published.

Tourism

In 2016 Spain was behind only France and the USA in the number of international tourist arrivals, and behind only the USA for tourism receipts. In 2016, 75·3m. tourists visited Spain; receipts for 2016 amounted to US$60·5bn. In 2013 most tourists were from the UK (14·3m.), followed by Germany (9·9m.), France (9·5m.) and Italy (3·2m.). The main destinations within Spain were Catalonia (15·6m.), the Balearics (11·1m.), the Canary Islands (10·6m.) and Andalucía (7·9m.).

Festivals

Religious Festivals: Epiphany (6 Jan.), the Feast of the Assumption (15 Aug.), All Saints Day (1 Nov.) and Immaculate Conception (8 Dec.) are all public holidays. Cultural Festivals: Day of Andalucía (28 Feb.), the Feast of San José in Valencia (19 March) is the culmination of a 13-day festival; the Festival of the Sardine in Murcia is an end of Easter parade in which a huge papier mâché sardine is burned; Feria de Abril is a major festival in Seville at the end of April featuring flamenco dancing and bullfighting; the San Fermines Festival, which takes place in mid-July, is most famous for the running of the bulls in the streets of Pamplona; La Tomatina, a battle of revellers armed with 50 tonnes of tomatoes, takes place on the last Wednesday in Aug. and is the highlight of the annual fiesta in Buñol, Valencia; National Day of Catalonia (11 Sept.); Spanish National Day (12 Oct.). The largest rock and pop music festivals are Festival Arte-Nativo Viña Rock in Villarrobledo (April), Primavera Sound in Barcelona (May), Sónar in Barcelona (June), Bilbao BBK Live (July) and Benicàssim International Festival (July).

Diplomatic Representatives

Of Spain in the United Kingdom (39 Chesham Pl., London, SW1X 8SB)
Ambassador: Carlos Bastarreche.

Of the United Kingdom in Spain (Torre Espacio, Paseo de la Castellana 259D, 28046 Madrid)
Ambassador: Simon Manley, CMG.

Of Spain in the USA (2375 Pennsylvania Ave., NW, Washington, D.C., 20037)
Ambassador: Santiago Cabanas Ansorena.

Of the USA in Spain (Calle de Serrano 75, 28006 Madrid)
Ambassador: Richard Duke Buchan III.

Of Spain to the United Nations
Ambassador: Agustín Santos Maraver.

Of Spain to the European Union
Permanent Representative: Pablo García-Berdoy.

Further Reading

Balfour, Sebastian, *The Politics of Contemporary Spain.* 2004
Barton, Simon, *A History of Spain.* 2nd ed. 2009
Carr, Raymond, (ed.) *Spain: A History.* 2000
Chaqués Bonafont, Laura, Palau, Anna M. and Baumgartner, Frank R., *Agenda Dynamics in Spain.* 2015
Closa, Carlos and Heywood, Paul, *Spain and the European Union.* 2004

Conversi, D., *The Basques, The Catalans and Spain.* 1997

Elliott, John H., *Scots and Catalans: Union and Disunion.* 2018

Gunther, Richard, *Democracy in Modern Spain.* 2004

Gunther, Richard and Montero, José Ramón, *The Politics of Spain.* 2009

Harrison, Joseph and Corkhill, David, *Spain: A Modern European Economy.* 2004

Heywood, P., *The Government and Politics of Spain.* 1995

Hooper, John, *The New Spaniards.* 2nd ed. revised. 2006

Minder, Raphael, *The Struggle for Catalonia.* 2017

Payne, Stanley G., *Spain: A Unique History.* 2011

Péréz-Díaz, V. M., *The Return of Civil Society: the Emergence of Democratic Spain.* 1993

Phillips, William D., Jr and Phillips, Carla Rahn, *A Concise History of Spain.* 2010

Pierson, Peter, *The History of Spain.* 2008

Royo, Sebastian, *Lessons from the Economic Crisis in Spain.* 2013

Salvadó, Francisco J. Romero, *Twentieth-Century Spain: Politics and Society in Spain, 1898–1998.* 1999

Smith, Angel, *The Origins of Catalan Nationalism, 1770–1898.* 2014

National library: Biblioteca Nacional, Paseo de Recoletos, 20–22, 28071 Madrid.

National Statistical Office: Instituto Nacional de Estadística (INE), Paseo de la Castellana, 183, Madrid. *President:* Gregorio Izquierdo Llanes.

Website: http://www.ine.es

Sri Lanka

Sri Lanka Prajathanthrika Samajavadi Janarajaya (Democratic Socialist Republic of Sri Lanka)

Capitals: Sri Jayawardenapura Kotte (Administrative and Legislative), Colombo (Commercial)
Population projection, 2020: 21·08m.
GNI per capita, 2017: (PPP$) 11,326
HDI/world rank, 2017: 0·770/76
Internet domain extension: .lk

Key Historical Events

Archaeological evidence suggests Sri Lanka has been inhabited since at least the Mesolithic era 34,000 years ago. Its recorded history begins in 483 BC, when, according to the Sinhalese chronicle *Mahavamsa*, several hundred men led by Vijaya, a prince from Bengal, reached the island. Anuradhapura was founded in 377 BC, becoming the principal settlement. Introduced in 250 BC by the Indian Emperor, Ashoka, Buddhism was gradually adopted, becoming central to the developing Sinhalese culture even while its influence in India declined. South Indian Chola kings controlled Anuradhapura in the second century BC until King Dutugemunu wrested control in 161 BC.

A spate of attacks from south India in the 8th century AD prompted King Aggabodhi IV to move Sri Lanka's seat of government to Polonnaruwa. A Chola army under Rajarja I then destroyed Anuradhapura in 993, although Sinhalese control was re-established in 1070. Trade with southeast Asia flourished in the 12th century under Parakramabahu I and Sinhalese civilization reached its height under Nissanka Mala (1187–96), the last Polonnaruwa king to rule the whole island. During the 13th century a Tamil kingdom was established in the northeast, centred on Jaffna. The seat of Sinhalese power gradually shifted to the southwest, where coastal provinces thrived on the spice trade with Arab merchants.

The arrival of Portuguese mariners in 1505 heralded a new era of European influence, initially centred in the southwest before other coastal provinces, including Jaffna, came under Portuguese rule from 1600. Dutch seafarers had meanwhile established a presence from the 1590s, and gradually took control of Portuguese forts and Sri Lanka's maritime regions from 1658. In 1670 the Dutch East Indian Company (VOC) declared a monopoly over exports including elephants and pearls and imports such as cotton. Dutch power in Asia subsequently waned as its possessions came under attack from British and French forces. In 1796 Colombo, Trincomalee, Jaffna and Kalpitya surrendered to British rule, with control initially routed through Madras in India. In 1802 a separate colony (Ceylon) under the British Crown was constituted. Although an attempt to capture Kandy in 1803 failed, the province was later annexed to British Ceylon under the Kandyan Convention of 1815.

Ceylon was then unified under a single administration for the first time in 400 years. As in other British colonies, the education system created an English-speaking elite as ethnic and caste rivalries continued. Nationalist sentiment gained ground after the First World War and internal self-government under a directly elected State Council was granted in 1931. Ceylon's economy was hit hard in the 1930s, prompting demands for full independence. This followed on 4 Feb. 1948 with dominion status in the British Commonwealth.

In 1956 Solomon Bandaranaike became prime minister at the head of the People's United Front, advocating neutrality and the promotion of Sinhalese national culture. Tamil demands for official recognition of their language and a separate state under a federal system caused riots in 1958. Bandaranaike was assassinated in Sept. 1959. His widow, Sirimavo Bandaranaike, succeeded him at the head of an increasingly left-wing government. In May 1972 Ceylon became a republic and adopted the name Sri Lanka.

In July 1977 the United National Party (dominant from 1948 until 1956) returned to power and in 1978 a new constitution set up a presidential system. The problem of communal unrest remained unsolved and

Tamil separatists were active. In 1983 Tamil United Liberation Front members of parliament were asked to renounce their objective for a separate Tamil state in the north and the east of the country. They refused and withdrew from parliament. Militant Tamils then began armed action that developed into civil war. President Ranasinghe Premadasa was assassinated on 1 May 1993.

A ceasefire was signed on 3 Jan. 1995 but fighting broke out again in April. The Tamil stronghold of Jaffna in the far north of the country was captured by government forces in Dec. 1995. In April 2000 the Tamil Tigers captured a military garrison at Elephant Pass, the isthmus that links Jaffna to the rest of Sri Lanka, threatening a recapture of the Jaffna peninsula. On 22 Feb. 2002 the government and Tamil Tiger leaders agreed to an internationally-monitored ceasefire, paving the way to the first full-scale peace talks for seven years. An estimated 61,000 people had died during the previous 19 years of conflict. In late 2002 the Tamil Tigers abandoned their ambitions for a separate state, settling instead for regional autonomy.

On 26 Dec. 2004 Sri Lanka, along with a number of other south Asian countries, was hit by a devastating tsunami. The death toll in Sri Lanka was put at 35,000.

A series of incidents in early 2006 brought the country back to the brink of civil war. Fighting intensified throughout the year, with the government claiming success in the east of the country. The government withdrew from the 2002 ceasefire agreement in Jan. 2008. In early 2009 Sri Lankan military forces launched a major offensive on the Tamil Tigers and on 19 May 2009 then President Mahinda Rajapaksa formally declared an end to hostilities. The UN estimated that around 7,000 Tamil civilians were killed in the 2009 military action, with some 135,000 displaced.

After a period of relative stability, in Aug. 2011 the government lifted a state of emergency in place since Aug. 2005. There was a further 12-day state of emergency declared in March 2018 in response to a wave of sectarian violence directed against the Muslim community.

Territory and Population

Sri Lanka is an island in the Indian Ocean, south of the Indian peninsula from which it is separated by the Palk Strait. On 28 June 1974 the frontier between India and Sri Lanka in the Palk Strait was redefined, giving to Sri Lanka the island of Kachchativu.

Area (in sq. km) and population (2012 census):

District	Area	Population
Ampara	4,415	649,402
Anuradhapura	7,179	860,575
Badulla	2,861	815,405
Batticaloa	2,854	526,567
Colombo	669	2,324,349
Galle	1,652	1,063,334
Gampaha	1,387	2,304,833
Hambantota	2,609	599,903
Jaffna	1,025	583,882
Kalutara	1,598	1,221,948
Kandy	1,940	1,375,382
Kegalle	1,693	840,648
Kilinochchi	1,279	113,510
Kurunegala	4,816	1,618,465
Mannar	1,996	99,570
Matale	1,993	484,531
Matara	1,283	814,048

(*continued*)

© Springer Nature Limited 2020
Palgrave Macmillan (ed.), *The Statesman's Yearbook 2020*,
https://doi.org/10.1057/978-1-349-95940-2_179

District	Area	Population
Moneragala	5,639	451,058
Mullaitivu	2,617	92,238
Nuwara Eliya	1,741	711,644
Polonnaruwa	3,293	406,088
Puttalam	3,072	762,396
Ratnapura	3,275	1,088,007
Trincomalee	2,727	379,541
Vavuniya	1,967	172,115
Total	65,610	20,359,439

Major ethnic groups in 2012: Sinhalese (75%), Sri Lankan Tamils (11%), Sri Lankan Moors (9%), Indian Tamils (4%).

Of the population of 20,359,439 in 2012, 10,502,805 were females. Density, 310 per sq. km. In 2011, 14·3% of the population lived in urban areas.

The UN gives a projected population for 2020 of 21·08m.

During the 25-year-long civil war from 1983 to 2009 approximately 800,000 Tamils left the country, either as refugees to India or to seek political asylum in the West.

Colombo (the largest city) had 561,314 inhabitants in 2012. Other major towns and their populations (2012) are: Kaduwela, 252,041; Maharagama, 196,423; Kesbewa, 185,122; Dehiwela-Mt Lavinia, 184,468; Moratuwa, 168,280; Negombo, 142,449; Sri Jayawardenapura Kotte (now the administrative and legislative capital), 107,925.

Sinhala and Tamil are the official languages; English is in use.

Social Statistics

Statistics for 2008: births, 373,575; deaths, 123,814. 2008 rates per 1,000 population: birth, 18·5; death, 6·1; infant mortality rate, 2010 (per 1,000 live births), 14. Life expectancy, 2013, 77·4 years for females and 71·2 for males. Annual population growth rate, 2005–10, 0·8%. Fertility rate, 2008, 2·3 births per woman. Sri Lanka has the third oldest population in Asia, after Japan and Singapore, thanks largely to relatively good health and a low fertility rate.

Climate

Sri Lanka, which has an equatorial climate, is affected by the Northeast Monsoon (Dec. to Feb.), the Southwest Monsoon (May to July) and two inter-monsoons (March to April and Aug. to Nov.). Rainfall is heaviest in the southwest highlands while the northwest and southeast are relatively dry. Colombo, Jan. 79·9°F (26·6°C), July 81·7°F (27·6°C). Annual rainfall 95·4" (2,424 mm). Trincomalee, Jan. 78·8°F (26°C), July 86·2°F (30·1°C). Annual rainfall 62·2" (1,580 mm). Kandy, Jan. 73·9°F (23·3°C), July 76·1°F (24·5°C). Annual rainfall 72·4" (1,840 mm). Nuwara Eliya, Jan. 58·5°F (14·7°C), July 60·3°F (15·7°C). Annual rainfall 75" (1,905 mm).

On 26 Dec. 2004 an undersea earthquake centred off the Indonesian island of Sumatra caused a huge tsunami that flooded large areas along the southern and eastern coasts of Sri Lanka resulting in 35,000 deaths. In total there were more than 225,000 deaths in 14 countries.

Constitution and Government

A new constitution for the Democratic Socialist Republic of Sri Lanka was promulgated on 7 Sept. 1978.

The executive *President* is directly elected for a six-year term renewable once.

Parliament consists of one chamber, composed of 225 members (196 elected and 29 from the National List). Election is by proportional representation by universal suffrage at 18 years. The term of Parliament is six years. The Prime Minister and other Ministers, who must be members of Parliament, are appointed by the President.

National Anthem

'Sri Lanka Matha, Apa Sri Lanka' ('Mother Sri Lanka, thee Sri Lanka'); words and tune by A. Samarakoon. There is a Tamil version, 'Sri Lanka thaaya, nam Sri Lanka'; words anonymous.

Government Chronology

(NDF = New Democratic Front; SLFP = Sri Lanka Freedom Party; SLMP = Sri Lanka People's Party; SLPP = Sri Lanka Podujana Peramuna; UNP = United National Party; n/p = non-partisan)

Presidents since 1972.

1972–78	n/p	William Gopallawa
1978–89	UNP	Junius Richard Jayewardene
1989–93	UNP	Ranasinghe Premadasa
1993–94	UNP	Dingiri Banda Wijetunge
1994–2005	SLMP/SLFP	Chandrika Bandaranaike Kumaratunga
2005–15	SLFP	Mahinda Rajapaksa
2015–	NDF	Maithripala Sirisena

Prime Ministers since 1948.

1948–52	UNP	Don Stephen Senanayake
1952–53	UNP	Dudley Shelton Senanayake
1953–56	UNP	John Lionel Kotalawela
1956–59	SLFP	Solomon Ridgeway Dias Bandaranaike
1959–60	SLFP	Vijayananda Dahanayake
1960	UNP	Dudley Shelton Senanayake
1960–65	SLFP	Sirimavo Ratwatte Dias Bandaranaike
1965–70	UNP	Dudley Shelton Senanayake
1970–77	SLFP	Sirimavo Ratwatte Dias Bandaranaike
1977–78	UNP	Junius Richard Jayewardene
1978–89	UNP	Ranasinghe Premadasa
1989–93	UNP	Dingiri Banda Wijetunge
1993–94	UNP	Ranil Wickremesinghe
1994	SLMP/SLFP	Chandrika Bandaranaike Kumaratunga
1994–2000	SLFP	Sirimavo Ratwatte Dias Bandaranaike
2000–01	SLFP	Ratnasiri Wickremanayake
2001–04	UNP	Ranil Wickremesinghe
2004–05	SLFP	Mahinda Rajapaksa
2005–10	SLFP	Ratnasiri Wickremanayake
2010–15	SLFP	Dissanayake Mudiyansalage Jayaratne
2015–18	UNP	Ranil Wickremesinghe
2018	SLPP	Mahinda Rajapaksa (disputed)
2018–	UNP	Ranil Wickremesinghe

Recent Elections

Presidential elections were held on 8 Jan. 2015. Maithripala Sirisena of the New Democratic Front was elected with 51·3% of the vote, ahead of incumbent president Mahinda Rajapaksa of the United People's Freedom Alliance (made up of several parties including the Sri Lanka Freedom Party) with 47·6%. There were 17 other candidates. Turnout was 81·5%.

Parliamentary elections were held ten months ahead of schedule on 17 Aug. 2015. The United National Front for Good Governance alliance (led by the United National Party) gained 106 seats with 45·7% of the vote; the United People's Freedom Alliance (led by the Sri Lanka Freedom Party) 95 with 42·4%; the Tamil National Alliance 16 with 4·6%; and Janata Vimukthi Peramuna 6 with 4·9%. The Sri Lanka Muslim Congress and the Eelam People's Democratic Party won one seat each. Turnout was 77·7%.

Current Government

In Feb. 2019 the cabinet comprised:

President and Minister of Defence, and Mahaweli Development and Environment: Maithripala Sirisena; b. 1951 (New Democratic Front; sworn in 9 Jan. 2015).

Prime Minister, and Minister of National Policies and Economic Affairs, Rehabilitation and Prison Reforms, Northern Development, Vocational Training, Skill Development and Youth Affairs: Ranil Wickremesinghe; b. 1949 (United National Party; sworn in 16 Dec. 2018, having previously been prime minister from May 1993–Aug. 1994, Dec. 2001–April 2004 and Jan. 2015–Oct. 2018).

Minister of Tourism Development, Wildlife and Christian Religious Affairs: John Amarathunga. *Buddhist Affairs, and North Western Province Development:* Gamini Jayawickrema Perera. *Finance and Mass Media:* Mangala Samaraweera. *Public Enterprise, Upcountry Heritage and Kandy Development:* Lakshman Kiriella. *City Planning, Water Supply and Higher Education:* Rauff Hakeem. *Foreign Affairs:* Tilak Marapana. *Health, Nutrition and Indigenous Medicine:* Dr Rajitha Senaratne. *Power, Energy and Business Development:* Ravi Karunanayake. *Internal and Home Affairs, and Provincial Councils and Local Government:* Vajira Abeywardhane. *Industry and Commerce, and Resettlement and Co-operative Development:* Rishad Bathiudeen. *Large City Development and Western Development:* Patali Champika Ranawaka. *Plantation Industries:* Navin Dissanayake. *Agriculture, Rural Economic Affairs, Livestock Development, Irrigation, and Fisheries and Aquatic Resources Development:* Pelisge Harrison. *Highways and Road Development, and Petroleum Resources Development:* Kabeer Hashim. *Public Administration and Disaster Management:* Ranjith Madduma Bandara. *Lands and Parliamentary Reforms:* Gayantha Karunathilaka. *Housing, Construction and Cultural Affairs:* Sajith Premadasa. *Transport and Civil Aviation:* Arjuna Ranatunga. *Upcountry New Villages, Infrastructure and Community Development:* Palani Digambaram. *Women and Children's Affairs, and Development of Dry Zones:* Chandrani Bandara. *Justice and Prison Reforms:* Thalatha Atukorala. *Education:* Akila Viraj Kariyawasam. *Postal Services and Muslim Affairs:* M. H. A. Haleem. *Ports and Shipping, and Southern Development:* Sagala Ratnayake. *Telecommunications, Digital Infrastructure, Foreign Employment and Sport:* Harin Fernando. *National Integration, Official Languages, Social Progress and Hindu Affairs:* Mano Ganesan. *Labour, Trade Union Relations and Social Empowerment:* Daya Gamage. *Development Strategies, International Trade, Science, Technology and Research:* Malik Samarawickrema.

Government Website: https://www.gov.lk

Current Leaders

Maithripala Sirisena
Position
President

Introduction
Maithripala Sirisena became president on 9 Jan. 2015 after defeating incumbent Mahinda Rajapaksa. He vowed to serve only a single term in office.

Early Life
Sirisena was born on 3 Sept. 1951 and grew up in Polonnaruwa. In 1967 he joined the youth wing of the Sri Lanka Freedom Party (SLFP). Four years later he received a 15-month prison sentence for alleged involvement in a Marxist insurrection.

In 1979 he became SLFP secretary in Polonnaruwa and also received another prison term for his political activities. In 1980 he graduated in political science from Russia's Maxim Gorky Academy.

Having entered parliament in 1989 he became a minister in 1997, in charge of Mahaweli development and parliamentary affairs, and in 2001 was named SLFP general secretary. Three years later he joined with Janatha Vimukthi Peramuna to form the United People's Freedom Alliance (UPFA), which subsequently formed the government. Sirisena was minister of Mahaweli River Basin and Rajarata development, and also leader of the house. He later served variously as minister of agriculture, irrigation, environment and health. He also had five spells as acting minister of defence, including during the final days of the civil war in 2009.

Sirisena announced that he would contest the presidential election of Jan. 2015 in opposition to the authoritarian incumbent SLFP president, Mahinda Rajapaksa. Sirisena claimed he 'could not stay any more with a leader who had plundered the country, government, and national wealth', and fought the election for the New Democratic Front. In a run-off on 8 Jan. 2015 he received 51·3% of the vote to 47·6% for Rajapaksa.

Career in Office
Sirisena was sworn in a day later and appointed Ranil Wickremesinghe as premier. Pledging to serve only a single term, Sirisena promised to investigate alleged crimes during the civil war, rein in presidential powers, fight corruption and guarantee press freedom. He also had to maintain his

disparate coalition and distance himself from the failings of the previous regime, of which he had been a part.

In May 2015 he secured the introduction of constitutional changes curtailing presidential powers and reimposing a two-term limit. Also, despite opposition from legislators loyal to Rajapaksa, he dissolved parliament in June that year in preparation for fresh elections in Aug., which were won by the United National Front for Good Governance. In May 2017 Sirisena announced his first cabinet reshuffle since he assumed the presidency, making nine ministerial changes. Then in Aug. foreign minister Ravi Karunanayake was replaced in the wake of corruption allegations. In Oct. 2018 Sirisena sparked a constitutional crisis as he dismissed Wickremesinghe as premier, replacing him by former president Rajapaksa, and subsequently called for fresh elections. However, in Dec. the Supreme Court overruled Sirisena's actions as unconstitutional and parliament passed a vote of confidence in Wickremesinghe who was reinstated as prime minister.

Ranil Wickremesinghe
Position
Prime Minister

Introduction
Ranil Wickremesinghe, the leader of the United National Party (UNP), was returned to office as prime minister for a third term in Jan. 2015, having served two previous terms from May 1993–Aug. 1994 and from Dec. 2001–April 2004.

Early Life
Ranil Wickremesinghe was born on 24 March 1949 in Colombo. His uncle, J. R. Jayewardene, had become Sri Lanka's first executive president in 1978.

After secondary education, Wickremesinghe studied law and qualified as an attorney of the Supreme Court of Sri Lanka in 1972. In 1977 he entered parliament and, despite his youth and political inexperience, was appointed deputy minister for foreign affairs in Jayawardene's government. In 1978 he joined the cabinet as minister of youth affairs and employment and took on additional responsibility as minister of education in 1980.

In 1989, following the election of Ranasinghe Premadasa to the presidency, Wickremesinghe became the leader of the house in parliament and minister of industries. After the assassination of Premadasa in May 1993, a new UNP government was formed with Dingiri Wijetunge as president and Wickremesinghe, aged 44, as the country's youngest ever prime minister.

Career in Office
Although his first period in office was only to last for 16 months, he advanced export-oriented trade liberalization and kick-started economic growth for the ensuing decade. Ousted from power in Aug. 1994 with the UNP's electoral defeat, he became party leader in Nov. after the assassination of former leaders Premadasa and Gamini Dissanayake by the Liberation Tigers of Tamil Eelam (LTTE).

His early co-operation with the newly-formed People's Alliance government won him credit as a statesman, although he opposed the government's plans for devolution to the northeastern Tamil-occupied areas. Talks launched in 2000 with President Chandrika Kumaratunga to agree a new constitution also fell through when Wickremesinghe withdrew support at a late stage. One year earlier, he had lost out in presidential elections to Kumaratunga, and from that time the balance of presidential and parliamentary powers became a contentious political issue.

Wickremesinghe returned to office as premier when the UNF won the general elections in Dec. 2001 as the largest parliamentary group. The elections were undermined by violence and the alleged prevention by the army of 80,000 people in the LTTE-held northeast from accessing balloting posts in government-held areas. International observers nevertheless approved the polls and Wickremesinghe was sworn in as prime minister, maintaining his role as leader of the UNP. Although the constitution previously allowed the president jurisdiction over the formation of the government, Wickremesinghe successfully pressured Kumaratunga to allow him to name his own cabinet. Kumaratunga abrogated control over the ministries of defence and finance but remained commander-in-chief of defence forces.

Wickremesinghe's second term focused on establishing a workable peace deal with the LTTE and revitalizing Sri Lanka's economy. In Feb. 2002 an internationally-monitored ceasefire was agreed with the LTTE, whose leader announced in April an end to suicide bombings in return for the lifting of the ban on the Tamil Tigers. Defying Kumaratunga, Wickremesinghe agreed to this, culminating in Dec. 2002 in a deal granting Tamil autonomy in return for peace.

Relations between Kumaratunga and Wickremesinghe remained frosty through 2003 and in Feb. 2004 the president dissolved parliament. In the April elections the UPFA won 105 seats to the UNP's 82. Although the polls produced a hung parliament, Kumaratunga appointed Mahinda Rajapaksa, her own party's parliamentary leader, as prime minister. Wickremesinghe remained leader of the opposition UNP and contested the 2005 presidential election, losing to the then incumbent prime minister Rajapaksa.

In 2015 Wickremesinghe regained the premiership following presidential elections that were won by Maithripala Sirisena of the UNP-led coalition. He also assumed the policy planning, economic affairs, child, youth and cultural affairs portfolios, while pledging to promote employment, health and education and to investigate past fraud and corruption. In Jan. 2016 he presented a resolution in parliament to establish a new Constitutional Assembly and steering committee to seek public input and make recommendations for a revised constitution. In July that year the government announced that it would seek to end the military's involvement in Sri Lanka's civil life and in Aug. approved legislation to establish an agency to investigate the disappearance of Tamils during the civil war. In Nov. 2017 Wickremesinghe appeared before a commission of inquiry investigating alleged irregularities in the issuance of government bonds by the central bank, dubbed the 'biggest financial scam in Sri Lanka's history' by the opposition.

In Oct. 2018 President Sirisena prompted political turmoil as he dismissed Wickremesinghe as premier, replacing him by former president Rajapaksa, and dissolved parliament. However, Wickremesinghe rejected his sacking as unconstitutional and illegitimate and in Dec. the Supreme Court overruled Sirisena after parliament had passed a vote of confidence in Wickremesinghe's continued premiership.

Defence

Defence expenditure in 2013 totalled US$1,793m. (US$83 per capita), representing 2·8% of GDP.

Army
Strength (2011), 117,900 (including 39,900 recalled reservists). In addition there were 1,100 reserves. Paramilitary forces consist of the Ministry of Defence Police (31,200, plus 30,400 reservists), the Home Guard (13,000), the National Guard (some 15,000) and an anti-guerrilla Special Task Force (3,000).

Navy
The main naval bases are at Colombo and Trincomalee. Personnel in 2011 numbered 15,000, including a reserve of about 2,400.

Air Force
The Air Force has four zonal commands: Eastern, Northern, Southern and Western. Total strength (2011) 18,000 with 31 combat-capable aircraft and 11 attack helicopters. Main attack aircraft types included *Kfirs*, F-7s and MiG-27s.

Economy

Agriculture accounted for 8·2% of GDP in 2016, industry 29·6% and services 62·2%.

The conflict with the minority separatists, the Tamil Tigers, which lasted some 25 years, is estimated to have cost the country between 1–1·5% in growth per year.

Overview
Three decades of civil war disrupted inter-regional commerce, damaged infrastructure and weakened public finances. Nonetheless, the economy maintained growth, generating higher per capita income than neighbouring India. GDP growth averaged 5·8% from 2010–17, although it reached a 16-year low of 3·3% in 2017 largely as the result of drought.

With the start of the peace process in Feb. 2002, the government embarked on reforms to revive the economy, including exchange rate and trade liberalization, privatization and the introduction of VAT. In May 2009 the civil war ended, boosting economic prospects and providing renewed opportunity for reform, and in July the IMF approved a US$2·6bn. loan to help the economy weather the effects of the global financial crisis and to rebuild war-torn regions.

The main sources of growth have been domestic consumption, tourism, and textile and garment exports. Tourism arrivals increased by 46·1% year-on-year in 2010, reflecting the end of fighting. Although the poverty rate has been in consistent decline, the cost of post-conflict relief and reconstruction has held back the rate of decrease.

Annual inflation rose from 2·8% in 2014 to 6·5% in 2017. Public debt also increased, albeit slightly, from 75·5% of GDP in 2014 to 77·6% in 2017. Some 44% of Sri Lankan exports go to Europe and the USA, making the economy vulnerable to declines in demand from these regions.

Currency
The unit of currency is the *Sri Lankan rupee* (LKR) of 100 *cents*. Foreign exchange reserves were US$2,236m. and gold reserves 167,000 troy oz in June 2005. Inflation was 4·0% in 2016 and 6·5% in 2017. Total money supply in March 2005 was Rs 208,095m.

Budget
Budgetary central government revenue in 2016 (provisional) totalled Rs 1,693bn. (taxes, Rs 1,464bn.) and expenditure Rs 2,007bn. (interest, Rs 611bn.; compensation of employees, Rs 576bn.; social benefits, Rs 317bn.).

VAT is 15%.

Performance
Real GDP growth was 5·0% in 2015, 4·5% in 2016 and 3·3% in 2017. Total GDP in 2017 was US$87·2bn.

Banking and Finance
The Central Bank of Sri Lanka is the bank of issue (*Governor*, Indrajit Coomaraswamy). There are 23 commercial banks. This includes two state-owned banks, the Bank of Ceylon and People's Bank, which account for about 40% of assets, and 12 foreign banks. There are 14 specialized banks including the National Savings Bank.

Sri Lanka's foreign debt amounted to US$20,452m. in 2010, up from US$11,372m. in 2005 and US$9,087m. in 2000. However, as a proportion of GNI it declined from 56·7% in 2000 to 47·2% in 2005 and further to 41·8% in 2010.

There is a stock exchange in Colombo.

Energy and Natural Resources

Environment
Carbon dioxide emissions from the consumption of energy in 2011 were the equivalent of 0·7 tonnes per capita.

Electricity
Installed capacity (2011), 3·1m. kW. Production, 2011, 11·6bn. kWh (40% hydro-electric). Consumption per capita in 2011 was 554 kWh.

Oil and Gas
There are plans for a huge oil refinery as part of the Hambantota port development. It is expected to be completed by 2023.

Minerals
Gems are among the chief minerals mined and exported (particularly sapphires). Output of principal products (2013 estimates): sapphires, 1,500,000 carats; limestone, 1,400,000 tonnes; phosphate rock, 53,000 tonnes; ilmenite, 43,000 tonnes; quartzite, 38,000 tonnes. Salt extraction is the oldest industry; the method is the solar evaporation of sea-water. Production, 2013, 13,000 tonnes.

Agriculture
There were approximately 970,000 ha. of arable land and 950,000 ha. of permanent crops in 2007. In 2006, 32·2% of the economically active population were engaged in agriculture. Main crops in 2013 (in 1,000 tonnes): rice, 4,621; coconuts, 2,513; sugarcane, 960; bananas and plantains, 605; tea, 340; cassava, 303; maize, 209. Sri Lanka ranks fourth in the world for tea production, behind China, India and Kenya.

Livestock in 2013: 1,169,000 cattle; 381,000 buffaloes; 331,000 goats; 17m. chickens.

Forestry
The area under forests in 2015 was 2·07m. ha., or 33% of the land area. Of the total area under forests 8% was primary forest in 2015, 82% other

naturally regenerated forest and 10% planted forest. In 2011, 5·75m. cu. metres of roundwood were cut.

Fisheries
Total catch in 2015 was 506,636 tonnes (of which 87% was from marine waters).

Industry

The main industries are the processing of rubber, tea, coconuts and other agricultural commodities, tobacco, textiles, clothing and leather goods, chemicals, plastics, cement and petroleum refining. Industrial production rose by 10·3% in 2011.

Labour
The labour force in 2013 was 8,451,000 (7,914,000 in 2003). 59·4% of the population aged 15–64 was economically active in 2013. In the same year 4·4% of the population was unemployed.

Sri Lanka had 19,000 people living in slavery according to the Walk Free Foundation's 2013 *Global Slavery Index*.

International Trade

Imports and Exports
Trade in US$1m.:

	2005	2006	2007	2008	2009
Imports c.i.f.	8,307	9,773	11,386	13,629	9,432
Exports f.o.b.	6,160	6,760	7,661	8,177	7,122

Principal imports in 2009: petroleum and petroleum products, 18·5%; machinery and transport equipment, 16·6%; textile yarn, fabrics and finished articles, 15·2%; food and livestock, 14·2%. Principal exports in 2009: clothing and apparel, 45·9%; tea, 16·5%; diamonds and other precious and semiprecious stones, 5·1%; machinery and transport equipment, 4·3%.

In 2009 the leading import suppliers were India (18·0%), Singapore (11·7%), China (9·3%), Iran (9·0%) and Hong Kong (5·5%). The leading export markets in 2009 were the USA (22·3%), UK (14·4%), Italy (6·1%), Belgium (5·2%) and Germany (4·9%).

Communications

Roads
In 2006 the road network totalled 91,907 km in length, including 11,716 km of national roads and 15,532 km of secondary roads. Number of motor vehicles, 2006, 2,269,575, comprising 338,608 passenger cars, 77,233 buses and coaches, 431,594 trucks and vans and 1,422,140 motorcycles and mopeds. There were 2,239 fatalities in road accidents in 2006.

Rail
In 2007 there were 1,463 km of railway (1,676 mm gauge). Passenger-km travelled in 2007 came to 4·77bn. and freight tonne-km to 135m.

Civil Aviation
There is an international airport at Colombo (Bandaranaike). The national carrier is SriLankan Airlines, which has been part-owned and managed by Emirates since 1998. Mihin Lanka, a low-cost airline fully owned and funded by the government, was launched in 2007 but ceased operations in 2016. In 2006 SriLankan Airlines carried 2,900,068 passengers (all on international flights). Colombo handled 4,740,187 passengers and 169,038 tonnes of freight in 2006.

Shipping
In Jan. 2014 there were 30 ships of 300 GT or over registered, totalling 140,000 GT. Colombo is a modern container port; Galle and Trincomalee are natural harbours. The first of three phases of a new port at Hambantota was inaugurated in Nov. 2010. On completion it is set to be Sri Lanka's largest port.

Telecommunications
In Dec. 2012 there were 3,449,000 main (fixed) telephone lines; mobile phone subscriptions numbered 20,315,000 in 2013 (95·5 per 100 persons). In 2013 an estimated 21·9% of the population were internet users. In March 2012 there were 1·2m. Facebook users.

Social Institutions

Out of 178 countries analysed in the 2017 *Fragile States Index*—a list published jointly by the Fund for Peace and *Foreign Policy* magazine—Sri Lanka was ranked the 47th most vulnerable to conflict or collapse. The index is based on 12 indicators of state vulnerability across social, political and economic categories.

Justice
The systems of law which are valid are Roman-Dutch, English, Tesawalamai, Islamic and Kandyan.

Kandyan law applies in matters relating to inheritance, matrimonial rights and donations; Tesawalamai law applies in Jaffna as above and in sales of land. Islamic law is applied to all Muslims in respect of succession, donations, marriage, divorce and maintenance. These customary and religious laws have been modified by local enactments.

The courts of original jurisdiction are the High Court, Provincial Courts, District Courts, Magistrates' Courts and Primary Courts. District Courts have unlimited civil jurisdiction. The Magistrates' Courts exercise criminal jurisdiction. The Primary Courts exercise civil jurisdiction in petty disputes and criminal jurisdiction in respect of certain offences.

The Constitution of 1978 provided for the establishment of two superior courts, the Supreme Court and the Court of Appeal.

The Supreme Court is the highest and final superior court of record and exercises jurisdiction in respect of constitutional matters, jurisdiction for the protection of fundamental rights, final appellate jurisdiction in election petitions and jurisdiction in respect of any breach of the privileges of Parliament. The Court of Appeal has appellate jurisdiction to correct all errors in fact or law committed by any court, tribunal or institution.

The population in penal institutions in Sept. 2013 was 27,000 (132 per 100,000 of national population). The death penalty, last used in 1976, was reactivated in Nov. 2004 after a 28-year moratorium. In 2015 the World Justice Project *Rule of Law Index*, which provides data on how the rule of law is experienced by the general public across eight categories, ranked Sri Lanka 46th of 102 countries for criminal justice and 69th for civil justice.

Education
Education is free and is compulsory from age five to 14 years. The literacy rate in 2008 was 91%. Sri Lanka's rate compares very favourably with the rates of 65% in India and 54% in Pakistan.

In 2008 there were 9,335 schools with primary classes and 69,499 primary teachers for 1,626,285 pupils. The number of pupils in secondary classes in 2008 was 1,897,350, with 98,582 teachers. There were 401,666 students and 21,715 teachers in advanced level classes in 2008. There are 16 universities, including the Open University (distance) and the Buddhist and Pali University. In 2008, excluding at the two aforementioned universities, there were 66,675 undergraduates enrolled.

Health
Over the period 2006–12 Sri Lanka had 36 hospital beds per 10,000 population. In the period 2006–13 there were seven doctors for every 10,000 population, 16 nursing and midwifery personnel per 10,000 population and one dentist per 10,000. Expenditure on health in 2014 was 2·8% of GDP.

In *Water: At What Cost? The State of the World's Water 2016*, WaterAid reported that 4·4% of the population does not have access to safe water.

Welfare
To qualify for an old-age pension an individual must be above the age of 55 for men or 50 for women. However, a grant is payable at any age if the person is emigrating permanently. Old-age benefits are made up of a lump sum equal to total employee and employer contributions, plus interest.

The family allowances programme is being implemented in stages. Families earning below Rs 1,000 a month are entitled to Rs 100–Rs 1,000 a month benefit, depending on family size and income.

Religion

In 2012 the population was 70% Buddhist, 13% Hindu, 10% Muslim and 6% Roman Catholic. In Feb. 2019 there was one Roman Catholic cardinal.

Culture

World Heritage Sites

Sri Lanka has eight sites on the UNESCO World Heritage List: Sacred City of Anuradhapura (inscribed on the list in 1982); Ancient City of Polonnaruwa (1982); Ancient City of Sigiriya (1982); Sinharaja Forest Reserve (1988); Sacred City of Kandy (1988); Old Town of Galle and its Fortifications (1988); the Golden Temple of Dambulla (1991); and the Central Highlands (2010).

Press

In 2011 there were 17 paid-for daily newspapers with a combined circulation of 590,000. There were five newspaper online editions in 2011.

Tourism

In 2014 there were a record 1,527,000 foreign tourists (up from 448,000 in 2009), bringing revenue of US$3,278m.

Diplomatic Representatives

Of Sri Lanka in the United Kingdom (13 Hyde Park Gdns, London, W2 2LU)
High Commissioner: Manisha Gunasekera.

Of the United Kingdom in Sri Lanka (389 Bauddhaloka Mawatha, Colombo 7)
High Commissioner: James Dauris.

Of Sri Lanka in the USA (3025 Whitehaven St., NW, Washington, D.C., 20008)
Ambassador: Vacant.
Chargé d'Affaires a.i.: Sarath Dissanayake.

Of the USA in Sri Lanka (210 Galle Rd, Colombo 3)
Ambassador: Alaina Teplitz.

Of Sri Lanka to the United Nations
Ambassador: Amrith Rohan Perera.

Of Sri Lanka to the European Union
Ambassador: Rodney Perera.

Further Reading

De Silva, C. R., *Sri Lanka: a History.* 1991
Nira, Wickramasinghe, *Sri Lanka in the Modern Age: A History of Contested Identity.* 2005
Winslow, Deborah and Woost, Michael D., *Economy, Culture and Civil War in Sri Lanka.* 2004
National Statistical Office: Department of Census and Statistics, POB 563, Colombo 7.
Website: http://www.statistics.gov.lk

Sudan

Jamhuryat es-Sudan (The Republic of The Sudan)

Capital: Khartoum
Population projection, 2020: 43·54m.
GNI per capita, 2017: (PPP$) 4,119
HDI/world rank, 2017: 0·502/167
Internet domain extension: .sd

Key Historical Events

The earliest inhabitants of Sudan were Mesolithic hunter-gatherers, who lived and travelled in the region around Khartoum from as early as 30,000 BC. They had domesticated animals by 4000 BC. Cultural influences from Egypt rippled through to Nubia in north-eastern Sudan from around 3000 BC as Egypt's first dynasty moved south along the river Nile in search of construction materials and slaves. By 2000 BC it had reached as far south as the river Nile's fourth cataract, more than 700 km beyond Aswan. Egyptian-controlled Nubia was divided into Wawat in the north (centred on Aswan) and Kush in the south (based at Nepata, or the modern Marawi). When Egypt's power waned in the 11th century BC (the end of the New Kingdom) Kush, with its Egyptian and African influences, mineral resources and its position on trade routes linking the Nile to the Red Sea, became a powerful kingdom. At its height, under King Piantkhi in 750 BC, the whole of Egypt was brought under Kushite control. However, the invasion of Egypt by Assyrian forces in 671 BC forced a retreat to Nepata. From there, the kingdom of Kush continued to exert control over the middle Nile for much of the next millennium, developing a distinctive culture and language. By AD 200 Kush was in decline and was finally overthrown in 350 by the king of Aksum from the Ethiopian highlands.

Sudan was brought back into contact with the Mediterranean world in the 6th century by the arrival of Coptic Christian missionaries. They travelled south along the Nile and established churches in the three middle-Nile kingdoms that had superseded Kush: Nobatia in the north and Maqurrah and 'Alwah in the south, near modern Khartoum. Egypt was invaded by Arabs in 639 and came under Muslim rule. Raiding parties moved up the Nile and absorbed Nobatia. The king of Maqurrah engineered a truce at Dunqulah with an Arab military expedition, commanded by 'Abd Allah ibn Sa'd, preserving the kingdom for a further six centuries.

In 1250 Egypt came under the control of Mamluk sultans, supported by a caste of warrior slaves. They pushed south into Nubia, bringing chaos and devastation to Maqurrah and opening it up to waves of Arab immigrants, particularly the Juhaynah people. They intermarried with the Nubians and introduced Arab Muslim culture. Alwah, to the south, retained its Christian traditions until 1500 when, weakened by Bedouin raids, it collapsed under an Arab confederation led by Abd Allah Jamma. The Arabs themselves came under attack in the region around modern Khartoum from warriors of the Funj dynasty, a kingdom that had its origins in the Blue Nile's upper reaches. The Funj established their supremacy in the Al Jazirah region by 1607 and expanded northwards under Badi II Abu Daqn later in the 17th century. It was a relatively peaceful and stable period and the teaching of Islam flourished in schools and mosques along the Nile. The Funj themselves adopted Islam but retained a number of traditional African customs and beliefs.

Egyptian Ascendancy

In 1820 Muhammad Ali, viceroy of Egypt under the Ottoman Turks, sent an army southward to conquer Sudan. The Funj kingdom collapsed and within a year Ali's forces had taken control of the Nile valley from Nubia to the Ethiopian foothills. There was initial resistance but the appointment of Ali Kurshid Agha as governor general in 1826 led to the establishment of Khartoum as the administrative capital, improvements to agriculture and the development of the trade in slaves and ivory. Ismail Pasha became viceroy of Egypt in 1863 and announced a grand scheme to modernize and control the entire Nile river system from the Mediterranean to the Great Lakes of East Africa. Ismail needed the financial help of the European powers who, in return, demanded an end to the slave trade. The British had a particular interest in Egyptian affairs following the opening of the Suez Canal in 1869. Ismail commissioned the Englishmen Samuel Baker and, later, Charles Gordon to establish Egyptian control in southern Sudan and Central Africa and to crush slavery. The controllers of the slave trade were powerful and proved hard to defeat, especially away from the Nile. In addition, there was unease among Muslims over the crusading style of the English anti-slavers. In 1879, amid rising discontent, Ismail's financial backing collapsed and his grand project was abandoned. Ismail was exiled and Gordon resigned.

Rise of the Mahdi

The power vacuum was filled by Muhammad Ahmad in 1881; he declared himself the Mahdi ('divinely guided one') and led a movement that sought an end to Egyptian (Ottoman) influence and a return to the simplicity of early Islam. By 1882 the Mahdi had garnered the support of a least 30,000 armed followers (the Ansar). They captured the town of Al Abayyid, which led to a British order for the evacuation of Egyptians and foreigners from Khartoum, where the military commander was Charles Gordon. The campaign failed disastrously: Gordon was killed by Mahdists in early 1885. The Mahdi died in the same year, but his successor, the Khalifa Abdallahi, continued to build up the Mahdist state.

In the 1890s the European powers were vying for control of Africa and the British made plans for the control of the Nile valley and the reconquest of Sudan. In a series of attacks between 1896 and 1898, an Anglo-Egyptian force of 25,800 men under Herbert (later Lord) Kitchener destroyed the Mahdist state. Anglo-Egyptian agreements in 1899 established a joint (condominium) government of Sudan: in theory it was administered by a governor-general, appointed by Egypt with the consent of Great Britain. In practice the governor-general, Sir Reginald Wingate, controlled the condominium government from Khartoum. Sudanese resentment over colonial rule erupted in various Mahdist uprisings but with insufficient support to pose a threat to the government. In 1911 the Sudan Plantations syndicate launched a scheme to irrigate the Al Jazirah region and establish a large cotton plantation for Britain's textile industry. The cotton crop became the mainstay of the economy.

Sudanese nationalist sentiment grew in the early 1920s when 'Ali 'Abd al Latif, inspired by Egyptian nationalists, founded the White Flag League. When Governor-General Sir Lee Stack was assassinated in 1924 in Cairo (capital of newly independent Egypt), the British ordered all Egyptian troops out of Sudan. British rule continued unchallenged until after the Second World War. The broad policy was to treat Sudan as two countries with the aim of integrating the southern provinces with their largely Christian and animist peoples with British East Africa. However, in 1948 a predominantly elective Legislative Assembly was convened for the whole territory. In the 1948 elections the Independence Front, which favoured the creation of an independent republic, gained a majority over the National Front, which aimed for union with Egypt.

Independence

Following the 1952 revolution in Egypt, Sudan became a parliamentary republic in 1956.

Sudan's democracy proved to be short-lived as the political parties became mired in internecine fighting. At the same time, a revolt raged in the south over Islamic domination. In 1958 Gen. Ibrahim Abboud led a military coup that ended the parliamentary system. In 1964, unable to improve Sudan's poor economic performance or to end the southern revolt, Abboud agreed to the re-establishment of civilian government. A coalition, headed by Muhammad Ahmad Mahjub, was weakened by factional disputes and little progress was made in solving the country's economic and social problems.

In 1969 Col. Gaafur Muhammad al-Nimeiry staged a successful coup. He banned all political parties and nationalized banks and numerous industries. The civil war was ended by an agreement between the government and the Southern Sudan Liberation Front signed in Addis Ababa in 1972. In the same year the Sudanese Socialist Union, the country's only political organization,

© Springer Nature Limited 2020
Palgrave Macmillan (ed.), *The Statesman's Yearbook 2020*,
https://doi.org/10.1057/978-1-349-95940-2_180

elected a People's Assembly to draw up a new constitution, adopted in 1973. Nimeiry's regime was blamed for worsening economic conditions and came under Islamist attack for its support for Egypt's role in the Camp David Accords with Israel; in the late 1970s Nimeiry dismissed his cabinet and closed universities in an attempt to quell opposition.

Accelerating Violence

From the early 1980s political instability in southern Sudan worsened. Nimeiry responded by imposing Sharia law in 1983, inflaming a renewed civil war with the largely Christian and animist Sudan People's Liberation Movement (SPLM) led by John Garang. Having survived numerous earlier coup attempts, Nimeiry was overthrown in 1985. Following elections in 1986 a civilian government led by Sadiq al-Mahdi ruled until he was ousted three years later in a bloodless military coup. The new regime of Lieut.-Gen. Omar Ahmed al-Bashir strengthened ties with Libya, Iran, and Iraq, reinforced Islamic law, banned opposition parties and continued to pursue the war with the south against the backdrop of a stagnant economy and a catastrophic famine. Bashir officially became president in 1993 but significant political power was held by the National Islamic Front, a fundamentalist political organization led by Hassan al-Turabi, who became speaker of parliament. In 1999 Bashir declared a state of emergency during a power struggle with Turabi, who was eventually toppled and parliament dissolved. Turabi subsequently formed his own opposition party, the Popular National Congress, although he and other party members were arrested in early 2001. He was released in Oct. 2003, only to be rearrested in March 2004 over an alleged coup plot. He was freed again in June 2005.

In Jan. 2002 a ceasefire was declared to allow relief aid to be distributed in the drought-stricken south-central region. In July 2002 the government and the SPLM agreed to a framework for peace providing for autonomy for the south and a referendum on independence after six years. Nevertheless, hostilities continued, particularly in the Darfur region of western Sudan where conflict between local African rebels and the army and government-backed Arab militias intensified from early 2003.

Having agreed on the division of oil wealth in post-war Sudan and on further power-sharing protocols, the government and the SPLM finally signed a comprehensive peace agreement on 9 Jan. 2005. It provided for a government of national unity (headed by Bashir but including northern and southern political groups) during a six-year transition period; self-determination for the South, with a referendum on secession at the end of the transition period; a permanent ceasefire; and the disengagement of forces. In more than 20 years of civil war, over 2m. people were thought to have died and more than 4m. made refugees. The agreement was briefly undermined in July 2005 when John Garang, SPLM leader and first vice-president in the power-sharing government, was killed in an air crash, provoking clashes between southern Sudanese and northern Arabs in Khartoum. His SPLM deputy, Salva Kiir Mayardit, took over as first vice-president in Aug. The power-sharing government was formed officially in Sept. 2005 and a devolved government of southern Sudan was established in Oct.

Although the comprehensive peace agreement focused mainly on the north-south civil war, some of its provisions for power-sharing and decentralization are applicable to Darfur. However, despite ongoing peace talks and UN and other international intervention to stop the violence, the conflict has continued. The government and Arab militias have been accused of systematic abuses of human rights, crimes that the UN Security Council referred to the International Criminal Court in March 2005. The targeting of civilians in the conflict has resulted in up to 300,000 deaths and the displacement of some 2·7m. people since 2003.

A referendum on full independence for the South took place on 9–15 Jan. 2011; 98·8% of votes were cast in favour of secession. South Sudan became an independent country on 9 July 2011.

Within Sudan, simmering opposition to Bashir's long-standing dictatorship sparked widespread street protests from Dec. 2018 that led the president to dissolve the federal government and declare a repressive one-year state of emergency in Feb. 2019.

Territory and Population

Sudan is bounded in the north by Egypt, northeast by the Red Sea, east by Eritrea and Ethiopia, south by South Sudan, southwest by the Central African Republic, west by Chad and northwest by Libya. Its area is 1,881,000 sq. km. In 2008—when present-day South Sudan was still part of Sudan—the census population was 39,154,490. In 2011, 40·8% of the population were urban.

The UN gives a projected population for 2020 of 43·54m.

The country is administratively divided into 18 states (with capitals): Al Qadarif (Al Qadarif), Blue Nile (Al Damazin), Central Darfur (Zalingei), East Darfur (Ed Daein), Gezira (Wadi Medani), Kassala (Kassala), Khartoum (Khartoum), North Darfur (Al Fashir), North Kordufan (Al Obeid), Northern (Dongula), Red Sea (Port Sudan), River Nile (Al Damar), Sennar (Singa), South Darfur (Nyala), South Kordufan (Kadugli), West Darfur (Geneina), West Kordufan (Al Fula), White Nile (Rabak).

The capital, Khartoum, had a provisional census population of 1,410,858 in 2008. Other major cities, with 2008 provisional population, are Omdurman (1,849,659), Khartoum North (1,012,211), Nyala (492,984), Port Sudan (394,561), Al Obeid (345,126), Kassala (298,529), Wadi Medani (289,482) and Al Qadarif (269,395).

The country is mainly populated by Arab and Nubian peoples. Arabic and English are both official languages.

Social Statistics

2009 estimates: births, 1,402,000; deaths, 382,000. Rates, 2009 estimates (per 1,000 population): birth, 9; death, 33. Infant mortality, 2010 (per 1,000 live births), 66. Expectation of life in 2013 was 63·9 years for females and 60·3 for males. Annual population growth rate, 2005–10, 2·4%. Fertility rate, 2013, 4·4 births per woman.

Climate

Lying wholly within the tropics, the country has a continental climate and only the Red Sea coast experiences maritime influences. Temperatures are generally high for most of the year, with May and June the hottest months. Winters are virtually cloudless and night temperatures are consequently cool. Summer is the rainy season inland, with amounts increasing from north to south, but the northern areas are virtually a desert region. On the Red Sea coast, most rain falls in winter. Khartoum, Jan. 64°F (18·0°C), July 89°F (31·7°C). Annual rainfall 6" (157 mm). Annual rainfall 39" (968 mm). Port Sudan, Jan. 74°F (23·3°C), July 94°F (34·4°C). Annual rainfall 4" (94 mm). Wadi Halfa, Jan. 50°F (10·0°C), July 90°F (32·2°C). Annual rainfall 0·1" (2·5 mm).

Constitution and Government

The constitution was suspended after the 1989 coup and a 12-member Revolutionary Council then ruled. A 300-member Provisional National Assembly was appointed in Feb. 1992 as a transitional legislature pending elections. These were held in March 1996. On 26 May 1998 President Omar Hassan Ahmed al-Bashir approved a new constitution. Notably this lifted the ban on opposition political parties, although the government continued to monitor and control criticism until the constitution came legally into effect. The constitution was partially suspended in Dec. 1999.

Sudan has a bicameral legislature. There is a lower house, the 426-seat *National Assembly* with members directly elected, and an upper house, the *Council of States*, consisting of a maximum of 56 members of whom 54 are indirectly elected.

National Anthem

'Nahnu Jundullah, Jundu Al-Watlan' ('We are the Army of God and of Our Land'); words by A. M. Salih, tune by A. Murjan.

Government Chronology

(DUP = Democratic Unionist Party; NCP = National Congress party; NUP = National Unionist Party; SSU = Sudan Socialist Union; Umma = 'Community of the Believers' Party; n/p = non-partisan)

Heads of State since 1956.	
Commission of Sovereignty	
1956–58	Abd al-Fattah Mohammad al-Mughrabi; Mohammad Uthman ad-Dardiri; Ahmad Mohammad Yasin; Ahmad Mohammad Salih; Siricio Iro Wani
Chairman of the Supreme Council of the Armed Forces	
1958–64	military Ibrahim Abboud
Commission of Sovereignty (I)	
1964–65	Abd al-Halim Mohammad; Tijani al-Mahi; Mubarak Shaddad; Ibrahim Yusuf Sulayman; Luigi Adwok Bong Gicomeho

(*continued*)

Commission of Sovereignty (II)	
1965	Ismail al-Azhari; Abd Allah al-Fadil al-Mahdi, Luigi Adwok Bong Gicomeho; Abd al-Halim Mohammad; Khidr Hamad

Chairman of the Council of Sovereignty

1965–69	NUP	Ismail al-Azhari

Chairmen of the Revolutionary Command Council

1969–71	military, SSU	Gaafur Muhammad al-Nimeiry
1971	military, SSU	Abu Bakr an-Nur Uthman
1971	military, SSU	Gaafur Muhammad al-Nimeiry

President

1971–85	military, SSU	Gaafur Muhammad al-Nimeiry

Chairman of the Transitional Military Council
1985–86 military Abd ar-Rahman Siwar ad-Dhahab

Chairman of the Council of Sovereignty

1986–89	DUP	Ahmad Ali al-Mirghani

Chairman of the Revolutionary Command Council of National Salvation

1989–93 military Omar Hassan Ahmed al-Bashir
President

1993–	military, NCP	Omar Hassan Ahmed al-Bashir

Heads of Government since 1952.

Chief Ministers

1952–53	Umma	Abd ar-Rahman al-Mahdi
1954–56	NUP	Ismail al-Azhari

Prime Ministers

1954–56	NUP	Ismail al-Azhari
1956–58	Umma	Abd Allah Khalil
1958–64	military (*de facto*)	Ibrahim Abboud
1964–65	n/p	Sirr al-Khatim al-Khalifah
1965–66	Umma	Muhammad Ahmad Mahgoub
1966–67	Umma	Sadiq al-Mahdi
1967–69	Umma	Muhammad Ahmad Mahgoub
1969	n/p	Babiker Awadalla
1969–76	military, SSU	Gaafur Muhammad al-Nimeiry
1976–77	SSU	Rashid Bakr
1977–85	military, SSU	Gaafur Muhammad al-Nimeiry
1985–86	n/p	al-Jazuli Dafallah
1986–89	Umma	Sadiq al-Mahdi
2017–18	NCP	Bakri Hassan Saleh
2018–19	NCP	Motazz Moussa
2019–	NCP	Mohamed Tahir Ayala

Recent Elections

The first elections since the secession of South Sudan were held from 13–16 April 2015. However, they were boycotted by several of the main opposition parties who cited the government's repressive measures against civil society and the media. In presidential elections, incumbent Omar Hassan Ahmed al-Bashir was re-elected with 94·0% of votes cast against 15 other candidates.

In concurrent National Assembly elections the National Congress Party (NCP) of President Bashir won 323 of 426 seats, the original Democratic Unionist Party (DUP) 25, the DUP (led by Jalal al-Digair) 15 and other smaller parties 44. 19 seats went to independents.

Current Government

President: Field Marshal Omar Hassan Ahmed al-Bashir; b. 1944 (NCP; appointed 1989, re-elected in March 1996, Dec. 2000, April 2010 and April 2015).

Prime Minister: Mohamed Tahir Ayala. *First Vice-President and Minister of Defence:* Gen. Awad Mohamed Ahmed bin Auf. *Second Vice-President:* Osman Mohamed Yousif Kibir.

In Feb. 2019 the government comprised:
Minister of Agriculture and Forests: Hassab al-Nabi Mussa. *Culture, Tourism and Archaeology:* Omar Suleiman Adam Ibrahim. *Education:* Mashair Al-Dawalab. *Federal Government:* Hamid Mumtaz. *Finance:* Mustafa Youssef. *Foreign Affairs:* Al-Dirdiri Mohamed Ahmed. *Health:* Mohamed Abu Zaid. *Higher Education:* Sadiq al-Hadi al-Mahdi. *Industry and Trade:* Musa Mohamed Karama. *Information, Telecommunications and Information Technology:* Bushara Aro Jummaa. *Interior:* Ahmed Bilal Othman. *Justice:* Mohamed Ahmed Salim. *Labour, Administrative Reform and Human Resources Development:* Bahar Idris Abu Garda. *Petroleum, Gas and Minerals:* Azhari Abdel Qader. *Presidency:* Fadul Abdallah. *Social Security and Development:* Widad Yagoub Ibrahim Osman. *Transportation and Urban Development:* Hatim al-Sir. *Water Resources, Irrigation and Electricity:* Khadhir Gassimal-Seed. *Minister of the Council of Ministers:* Ahmed Saad Omar.

Government Website (limited English): http://www.sudan.gov.sd

Current Leaders

Field Marshal Omar Hassan Ahmed al-Bashir
Position
President

Introduction
Omar al-Bashir is one of Africa's longest-serving presidents, having seized power in 1989. He has since been re-elected four times—in 1996, 2000, 2010 and 2015—although the polls were boycotted by the main opposition groups. His rule has been characterized by civil war and genocide, particularly in the western province of Darfur. He nevertheless signed a significant peace agreement in Jan. 2005 to end the long-running insurrection in South Sudan, which heralded the territory's drive to national independence in 2011. Since Dec. 2018 he has been confronted by escalating domestic public discontent over the rising cost of living and demands for an end to his regime.

Early Life
Bashir was born to a family of Sudanese peasants in 1944. He went to primary school in his home village before his family moved to Khartoum, where he completed secondary education. Having joined the Sudanese air force as a teenager, he soon made the grade as an officer and was sent to a military college in Egypt. He later served with a Sudanese unit that fought against Israel alongside Egyptian forces in the 1973 war. Promotions followed quickly and by the early 1980s he was a general. His political life began with the military coup of 1989 when, together with a group of middle-ranking officers, he overthrew the elected government of Sadiq al-Mahdi and installed a Revolutionary Command Council.

Career in Office
The National Islamic Front (later renamed the National Congress Party; NCP), led by Hassan al-Turabi, supported Bashir's new regime. Influenced by Turabi, and by the campaigns in South Sudan against animist and Christian secessionist rebels, Bashir began the Islamization of Sudan and introduced Sharia law. He moved Sudan into the radical Arab camp, inviting political and economic isolation and aggravating the distress caused by instability and civil war.

In 1993 Bashir declared himself president. Long-promised elections were held in March 1996, when Bashir was elected head of state in a poll that was regarded internationally as deeply flawed. For a time Sudan provided a haven for radical Islamic refugees who included al-Qaeda's Osama bin Laden. By 1998 Sudan was regarded as a pariah state by the USA. In that year, US missiles destroyed a pharmaceutical factory in Khartoum that was suspected, wrongly as it turned out, of producing chemical weapons.

In 1999 Bashir declared a state of emergency during a power struggle with Turabi, then the speaker of parliament, who had moved to reduce the president's powers. Turabi was toppled and parliament dissolved. In Dec. 2000 Bashir was re-elected as president, although the main opposition parties again boycotted the poll.

In the wake of the 11 Sept. 2001 attacks in the USA, Bashir made an effort to gain international acceptability. However, Sudan continued to be regarded by many in the West as a rogue state, crippled by poverty and conflict, and was also cited by the United Nations for gross human rights violations.

Meanwhile, the civil war in the South continued, by this time having claimed over 2m. lives and displaced more than 4m. refugees. In Jan. 2005, after three years of talks, Bashir's government and the Sudan People's Liberation Movement (SPLM) finally signed a comprehensive peace agreement. It provided for a government of national unity (headed by Bashir but also comprising members of the NCP, the SPLM and other northern and southern political forces), self-determination for the South, a permanent ceasefire and the disengagement of forces. In July 2005 the agreement was briefly threatened when John Garang, the leader of the SPLM and first vice-president in the power-sharing government, was killed in a helicopter accident, provoking clashes between Sudanese in the south and Arab northerners. Garang was replaced as first vice-president by his deputy, Salva Kiir Mayardit, in Aug.

The formation of the national unity government was announced in Sept. 2005 and a devolved government in south Sudan was established in Oct. In Oct. 2007 the SPLM suspended its participation in the national unity administration, accusing the northern Sudanese of failing to honour the 2005 accord, but rejoined in Dec. In Jan. 2011 the results of a referendum in South Sudan on secession from the North showed an overwhelming vote in favour of self-determination. Bashir had earlier confirmed that he would accept the result, but the countdown to actual independence in July that year was marred by mutual recriminations between the North and South and violent clashes between their respective forces, particularly around the disputed oil-rich border area of Abyei. Post-independence, both sides agreed in Oct. to establish joint committees in an attempt to resolve outstanding flashpoints. However, in April 2012 Sudan's air force raided its neighbour after South Sudanese troops occupied the Abyei region and the Heglig oilfields. The United Nations threatened sanctions against both countries if they did not stop the escalating violence and return to negotiations. Bashir met the South Sudan president in Ethiopia in Sept. in an attempt to resolve the crisis, and although they concluded agreements on trade, security and a resumption of oil exports, they failed to resolve contested border issues. In Oct. 2013 the residents of Abyei voted overwhelmingly in an unofficial referendum to join South Sudan.

In addition to the civil war in the South, Bashir's regime has overseen fierce fighting in the western province of Darfur between government-backed Arab militias and local black rebel forces. The conflict escalated from 2003 despite international attempts to stop the violence, provoking a refugee and humanitarian crisis. A UN report in March 2007 accused the government of orchestrating 'gross and systematic' human rights abuses in Darfur and complained that the response of the international community had been 'inadequate and ineffective'. After months of negotiations Bashir finally agreed on 31 Dec. 2007 to the deployment of a hybrid African Union–UN peacekeeping force (UNAMID, under UN control) in Darfur to replace an existing smaller African Union mission. The Darfur conflict also undermined Sudan's already fractious relations with neighbouring Chad until Jan. 2010, when both sides stated their readiness to normalize relations. The International Criminal Court has indicted Bashir for genocide and war crimes in Darfur—accusations that the Sudanese government has rejected. Violence across the region has nevertheless continued to generate further casualties and internal displacement, prompting Amnesty International to accuse the government of launching chemical weapon attacks on the civilian population in 2016.

In April 2010 Bashir won another presidential term and the National Congress Party won a comfortable parliamentary majority in the country's first multi-party elections in 24 years, but the poll was criticized by international monitors. Popular discontent over economic austerity measures imposed from 2011 in response to falling oil revenues, together with

allegations of government corruption, undermined Bashir's authority during 2013, and in Oct. that year dissident NCP members broke away to form a new party. His term as president was nevertheless extended again in April 2015 following his victory at the first elections to take place since the secession of South Sudan in 2011. In Oct. 2015 he launched a national dialogue, largely boycotted by opposition and rebel groups, on government, the economy and the conflicts in Sudan's border regions, which officially closed a year later. Then in March 2017 he appointed First Vice-President Bakri Hassan Saleh to the additional reinstated post of prime minister. In May Saleh announced a 'government of national consensus' tasked with drafting a new constitution. The government was nevertheless still dominated by the NCP.

On the international stage, in Jan. 2014 Bashir had given cautious support to the South Sudan government in the wake of an alleged attempted coup in Dec. 2013 that prompted a wave of violence in that country, while in 2015 he instigated a surprising reversal of three decades of close Sudanese–Iranian relations. In March that year he opted to back military intervention by a Saudi Arabian-led regional coalition of Gulf Arab states against an Iranian-backed insurgency by rebel Shia Houthi forces in Yemen. In Jan. 2016, following the ransacking of the Saudi embassy in the Iranian capital of Tehran, Sudan broke off diplomatic relations with Iran in support of the Saudi government. Commentators speculated that Bashir's change of policy reflected his need of Saudi aid to rescue Sudan's struggling economy. In Oct. 2017 the US government lifted economic sanctions on Sudan (in force since 1997) in recognition of 'positive actions' by the Bashir regime against terrorism, potentially transforming Sudan's trade and inward investment prospects.

In Sept. 2018 Bashir replaced Bakri Hassan Saleh with Motazz Moussa as prime minister and a new cabinet was announced. However, from Dec. festering discontent with the government over the high cost of living and food and fuel shortages prompted widespread street protests by demonstrators demanding an end to Bashir's 30-year rule, which were met by a security crackdown and mass arrests. In Feb. 2019, as popular opposition escalated, the president declared a state of emergency, dismissing Motazz Moussa's government and naming a caretaker administration with Mohamed Tahir Ayala as premier.

Defence

There is conscription for one to two years. Defence expenditure totalled US$1,516m. in 2013 (US$43 per capita), representing 3·0% of GDP.

In Aug. 2007 the Sudanese government agreed to a joint African Union/ United Nations peacekeeping force being deployed in Darfur. The mission, known as UNAMID or UN-AU Mission in Darfur, began operations on 31 Dec. 2007 and had 10,673 deployed personnel in Jan. 2019.

Army

Strength (2011) 105,000 (around 20,000 conscripts). There is a paramilitary People's Defence Force of 17,500 and an additional 85,000 reservists.

Navy

The navy operates in the Red Sea and also on the River Nile. Personnel in 2011 numbered 1,300. The major base is at Port Sudan.

Air Force

Personnel totalled (2011) 3,000, with 61 combat-capable aircraft, including A-5s (Chinese-built versions of MiG-19s), Su-25s and MiG-29s, and 29 attack helicopters.

Economy

Agriculture accounted for 39·0% of GDP, industry 2·9% and services 58·1% in 2016.

Sudan featured among the ten most corrupt countries in the world in a 2018 survey of 180 countries carried out by the anti-corruption organization Transparency International.

Overview

Sudan is rich in natural resources but its economy lags behind many of its neighbours, largely owing to its long history of conflict. The economy was almost entirely agrarian until 1999, when an oil pipeline from the Muglad Basin to a Red Sea export terminal was opened. Sudan was able to begin exporting crude oil and recorded its first trade surplus. It has since become dependent on oil production, with agriculture and mining playing secondary roles, and prospered on the back of high oil prices and significant foreign direct investment.

However, with the secession of South Sudan in 2011 Sudan lost almost three-quarters of its oil revenues, half of its fiscal revenues, two-thirds of its foreign exchange earnings and 95% of its exports. The situation was compounded by a weak policy response and ongoing disputes with the South over territorial rights and the division of oil revenues and debt responsibilities. In 2012 the economy contracted by 3·4%, inflation rose to high double-digit levels and fuel prices increased, triggering country-wide protests.

In June 2012 a three-year economic adjustment programme was introduced in an effort to diversify the economy. The authorities focused investment in the agricultural and gold mining sectors, committing 20% of public expenditure to agricultural infrastructure and technology alone. A programme of fiscal consolidation was also initiated to control the large national deficit. In the four years to 2016, GDP growth averaged 3·7% annually.

The country nonetheless suffers from high levels of poverty and income inequality. It is particularly vulnerable to fluctuations in the oil price and in remittances from expatriates working in Gulf countries. Meanwhile, the conflict in Darfur and tense relations with South Sudan remain long-term obstacles to sustained development.

Currency

The unit of currency is the *Sudanese pound* (SDG) of 100 *piastres*, introduced in Jan. 2007 to replace the *Sudanese dinar* (SDD) at a rate of 1 Sudanese pound = 100 Sudanese dinars. The dinar ceased to be legal tender on 30 June 2007. Inflation was 17·8% in 2016 and 32·4% in 2017. There has been double-digit inflation every year since 2008. Foreign exchange reserves were US$2,107m. in July 2005 and total money supply was 705,505m. dinars.

Budget

In 2012 revenues totalled 24,588m. Sudanese pounds and expenditures 31,561m. Sudanese pounds.

VAT is 17%.

Performance

The economy expanded by 1·3% in 2015, 3·0% in 2016 and 1·4% in 2017. Sudan's total GDP in 2017 was US$117·5bn.

Banking and Finance

The Bank of Sudan (*Governor*, Mohamed Khair al-Zubair) opened in Feb. 1960 with an authorized capital of £S1·5m. as the central bank and bank of issue. Banks were nationalized in 1970 but in 1974 foreign banks were allowed to open branches. The application of Islamic law from 1 Jan. 1991 put an end to the charging of interest in official banking transactions, and seven banks are run on Islamic principles. Mergers of seven local banks in 1993 resulted in the formation of the Khartoum Bank, the Industrial Development Bank and the Savings Bank.

Sudan's external debt totalled US$21,846m. in 2010, up from US$17,474m. in 2005 and US$15,983m. in 2000. However, as a share of GNI it fell from 141·4% in 2000 to 67·1% in 2005 and further to 39·1% in 2010.

A stock exchange opened in Khartoum in 1995.

Energy and Natural Resources

Environment

Sudan's carbon dioxide emissions from the consumption of energy in 2010 were the equivalent of 0·4 tonnes per capita.

Electricity

Installed capacity was 3·0m. kW in 2011. Production in 2011 was 8·60bn. kWh, with consumption per capita 184 kWh.

Oil and Gas

In 2012 oil reserves totalled 1·5bn. bbls. In June 1998 Sudan began exploiting its reserves and on 31 Aug. 1999 it officially became an oil producing country; production in 2012 totalled 4·1m. tonnes. An oil refinery at Al-Jayli, with a capacity of 2·5m. tonnes, opened in 2000. Natural gas reserves in 2010 were 85bn. cu. metres.

Minerals

Mineral deposits include chromite, feldspar, fluorite, gold, gypsum, kaolin, laterite, manganese ore, marble, mica, quartz, salt and silver. Production (in tonnes, 2013): laterite, 339,000; gypsum, 132,000; feldspar, 32,000; chromite, 31,000. Gold (25,000 kg in 2013) is also produced.

Agriculture

80% of the population depends on agriculture. Land tenure is based on customary rights; land is ultimately owned by the government. There were about 19·32m. ha. of arable land in 2007 and 225,000 ha. of permanent crops. 1·15m. ha. were irrigated in 2007. There were ten tractors and one harvester-thresher per 10,000 ha. in 2006.

Production (2013) in 1,000 tonnes: sugarcane, 6,798; sorghum, 4,524; groundnuts, 1,767; millet, 1,090; onions (estimate), 1,037; bananas, 758; mangoes and guavas, 636; sesame seeds, 562; tomatoes, 530.

Livestock (2013): sheep, 39·6m.; goats, 31·0m.; cattle, 30·0m.; camels, 4·8m.; chickens, 46m.

Livestock products (2013) in 1,000 tonnes: beef and veal (estimate), 358; lamb and mutton, 249; camel meat (estimate), 150; goat meat, 115; chicken meat, 55; cow's milk, 2,795; goat's milk, 1,105; sheep's milk, 398; cheese, 108; eggs, 45.

Forestry

Forests covered 19·21m. ha. in 2015, or 10% of the total land area. Of the total area under forests 7% was primary forest in 2015, 61% other naturally regenerated forest and 32% planted forest. In 2012, 15·55m. cu. metres of roundwood were cut.

Fisheries

In 2015 the total catch was an estimated 33,000 tonnes, of which approximately 95% were freshwater fish.

Industry

Production figures (2007 unless otherwise indicated, in 1,000 tonnes): distillate fuel oil, 1,873; petrol, 1,639; wheat and blended flour (2006), 1,200; raw sugar, 743; residual fuel oil, 677; cement, 326; jet fuel, 303; soap, 80. In 2000 an industrial complex assembling 12,000 vehicles a year opened.

Labour

The estimated total workforce in 2010 was 13,885,000 (70% males), up from 11,997,000 in 2005.

Sudan had 0·26m. people living in slavery according to the Walk Free Foundation's 2013 *Global Slavery Index*.

International Trade

Imports and Exports

In 2009 imports (c.i.f.) amounted to US$8,589·9m. and exports (f.o.b.) to US$9,079·5m. The main imports are petroleum products, machinery and equipment, foodstuffs, manufactured goods, medicines and chemicals. Main exports are oil (which accounts for about 87% of export revenues), cotton, gum arabic, oil seeds, sorghum, livestock, sesame, gold and sugar. The main import sources in 2006 were China (18·8%), Saudi Arabia (8·9%), Japan (8·1%), India (6·7%) and United Arab Emirates (5·6%). Principal export markets in 2006 were China (78·9%), Japan (5·5%), United Arab Emirates (5·1%), Saudi Arabia (2·8%) and Egypt (1·3%).

Communications

Roads

The road network covers around 32,400 km. There were an estimated 768,000 passenger cars and 300,000 trucks and vans in 2007.

Rail

Total length in 2005 was 4,578 km. In 2008 the railways carried 100,000 passengers and 1·1m. tonnes of freight.

Civil Aviation

There is an international airport at Khartoum, which handled 2,178,097 passengers and 59,299 tonnes of freight in 2009. The national carrier is the government-owned Sudan Airways, which operates domestic and international services. In 2006 scheduled airline traffic of Sudan-based carriers flew 9m. km, carrying 563,000 passengers (365,000 on international flights).

Shipping

Supplementing the railways are regular steamer services of the Sudan Railways. Port Sudan is the major seaport; Suakin port opened in 1991. In Jan. 2014 there were two ships of 300 GT or over registered, totalling 20,000 GT.

Telecommunications

In 2013 there were 416,000 fixed telephone subscriptions; mobile phone subscriptions numbered 27,658,000 that year (728·5 per 1,000 persons). There were 34,200 fixed broadband subscriptions in 2012 and 10·2m. wireless broadband subscriptions in 2013. 21·0% of the population aged 15 and over were internet users in 2012.

Social Institutions

Out of 178 countries analysed in the 2017 *Fragile States Index*—a list published jointly by the Fund for Peace and *Foreign Policy* magazine— Sudan was ranked the joint fifth most vulnerable (along with Syria) to conflict or collapse. The index is based on 12 indicators of state vulnerability across social, political and economic categories.

Justice

The judiciary is a separate independent department of state, directly and solely responsible to the President of the Republic. The general administrative supervision and control of the judiciary is vested in the High Judicial Council.

Civil Justice is administered by the courts constituted under the Civil Justice Ordinance, namely the High Court of Justice—consisting of the Court of Appeal and Judges of the High Court, sitting as courts of original jurisdiction—and Province Courts—consisting of the Courts of Province and District Judges. The law administered is 'justice, equity and good conscience' in all cases where there is no special enactment. Procedure is governed by the Civil Justice Ordinance.

Justice for the Muslim population is administered by the Islamic law courts, which form the Sharia Divisions of the Court of Appeal, High Courts and Kadis Courts; President of the Sharia Division is the Grand Kadi. In Dec. 1990 the government announced that Sharia would be applied in the non-Muslim southern parts of the country as well.

Criminal Justice is administered by the courts constituted under the Code of Criminal Procedure, namely major courts, minor courts and magistrates' courts. Serious crimes are tried by major courts, which are composed of a President and two members and have the power to pass the death sentence. There were three executions in 2018. Major Courts are, as a rule, presided over by a Judge of the High Court appointed to a Provincial Circuit or a Province Judge. There is a right of appeal to the Chief Justice against any decision or order of a Major Court, and all its findings and sentences are subject to confirmation by him.

Lesser crimes are tried by Minor Courts consisting of three Magistrates and presided over by a Second Class Magistrate, and by Magistrates' Courts.

The population in penal institutions in 2011 was 20,000 (56 per 100,000 of national population).

Education

In 2007 there were 28,185 teaching staff for 490,808 pupils at pre-primary schools; 107,933 teaching staff for 3·96m. pupils at primary schools; and 79,122 secondary school teaching staff for 1·46m. pupils. In 2006 there were 29 public higher education institutions (including two Islamic universities, one university of science and technology, and an institute of advanced banking) and eight private higher education institutions. Adult literacy rate was 69% in 2008.

Health

In 2006 there were 11,083 physicians, 944 dentists, 33,354 nurses and midwives and 1,531 pharmacists. Hospital bed provision in 2006 was seven per 10,000 population.

Religion

Islam is the state religion. A study by the Pew Research Center's Forum on Religion & Public Life estimated that there were 30·49m. Muslims in 2010 (mostly Sunnis), 1·81m. Christians and 950,000 followers of folk religions. A further 350,000 people had no religious affiliation. Catholics account for around 55% of Christians and Protestants 40%. In Feb. 2019 the Roman Catholic Church had one cardinal.

Culture

World Heritage Sites

Sudan has three sites on the UNESCO World Heritage List: Gebel Barkal and the Sites of the Napatan Region (inscribed on the list in 2003), a collection of tombs, pyramids and palaces of the Second Kingdom of Kush (900 BC to AD 350); the Archaeological Sites of the Island of Meroe (2011), once the heartland of the Kingdom of Kush that includes the royal city of the Kushite kings at Meroe; and Sanganeb Marine National Park and Dungonab Bay— Mukkawar Island Marine National Park (2016), a property consisting of two separate areas: Sanganeb and a combination of Dungonab Bay and Mukkawar Island. It includes a diverse system of coral reefs, mangroves, seagrass beds, beaches and islets.

Press

In 2008 there were 29 paid-for daily newspapers with a combined circulation of 90,000. Opposition newspapers are permitted although they are vetted by an official censor.

Tourism

In 2011 there were 536,000 international tourist arrivals (excluding same-day visitors), spending a total of US$185m.

Diplomatic Representatives

Of Sudan in the United Kingdom (3 Cleveland Row, London, SW1A 1DD)
  Ambassador: Mohammed Abdalla Ali Eltom.

Of the United Kingdom in Sudan (off Sharia Al Baladiya, Khartoum, PO Box 801)
  Ambassador: Irfan Siddiq, OBE.

Of Sudan in the USA (2210 Massachusetts Ave., NW, Washington, D.C., 20008)
  Ambassador: Vacant.
  Chargé d'Affaires a.i.: Mohamed Atta al-Moula Abbas.

Of the USA in Sudan (Kilo Asharah, Soba, Khartoum)
  Ambassador: Vacant.
  Chargé d'Affaires a.i.: Steven Koutsis.

Of Sudan to the United Nations
  Ambassador: Omer Dahab Fadl Mohamed.

Of Sudan to the European Union
  Ambassador: Mutrif Siddig Ali.

Further Reading

Copnall, James, *A Poisonous Thorn in Our Hearts: Sudan and South Sudan's Bitter and Incomplete Divorce.* 2014

Idris, Amir, *Conflict and Politics of Identity in Sudan.* 2006

Iyob, Ruth, *Sudan: The Elusive Quest for Peace.* 2006

Sidahmed, Alsir, *Sudan.* 2004

Woodward, Peter, *The Horn of Africa: Politics and International Relations.* 2002

National Statistical Office: Central Bureau of Statistics. PO Box 700, Khartoum.

Website: http://cbs.gov.sd/index.php/en

Suriname

Republiek Suriname (Republic of Suriname)

Capital: Paramaribo
Population projection, 2020: 578,000
GNI per capita, 2017: (PPP$) 13,306
HDI/world rank, 2017: 0·720/100
Internet domain extension: .sr

Key Historical Events

Arawak and Carib groups lived in coastal areas of present-day Suriname and along the Marowijne River from at least 3,000 BC. The forested interior was home to other Amerindians including the Acurio, Trio and Warau. Christopher Columbus explored the coast in 1498, followed by Amerigo Vespucci and Alonso de Ojeda the following year. Spanish and Dutch seafarers attempted to establish settlements, but the first documented community was at Marshall's Creek, founded by British puritans in 1630.

In 1650 the British governor of Barbados, Lord Willoughby, sent three ships to Suriname to build a new colony, which was briefly known as Willoughbyland. By the early 1660s tobacco, sugar and cotton plantations extended across some 120 sq. km, supporting several thousand settlers, including Jews from Brazil. In Feb. 1667 the colony was captured by Dutch forces, led by Abraham Crijnessen, and renamed Fort Zeelandia. The Treaty of Breda, signed in July 1667, gave the Dutch control of the colony in exchange for British rule in New Amsterdam (subsequently New York in the United States).

Suriname was administered by the States of Zeeland until 1683, when it was supervised by the Society of Suriname—itself divided between three participants: the city of Amsterdam, the van Sommelsdijk family and the Dutch West India Company. The town of Paramaribo was laid out on a grid pattern from 1683, close to Fort Zeelandia. During the late 17th and early 18th centuries thousands of slaves were shipped from West Africa to work on the plantations. In 1795 Suriname was united with the three Dutch colonies of Berbice, Essequibo and Demerara to the east.

Having vied for control of the region for several years, British forces were able to take Suriname during the Napoleonic Wars of 1799–1802 and 1804–16. Following the defeat of Napoleon, the Anglo–Dutch Treaty of 1816 returned Suriname to the Netherlands, while the other three Dutch colonies were merged to form British Guiana in 1830. Slavery was finally abolished by the Dutch authorities in 1863, after which thousands of people were brought from the Dutch East Indies (notably Java), southern China (via Macau) and British India to work on the plantations.

Mineral extraction gathered pace in Suriname during the first part of the 20th century. A brief gold rush in 1905 was followed by exploration for bauxite by the US firm Alcoa. Mining began in 1916, with Suriname becoming one of the world's leading bauxite producers. During the Second World War the colony was briefly occupied by the USA to protect bauxite reserves. In 1954 Suriname was granted regional autonomy, along with Aruba and the Netherlands Antilles. In 1973 the local government began negotiations on full independence, which was gained on 25 Nov. 1975. The former governor, Johan Ferrier, served as the first president and Henck Arron was prime minister.

In Feb. 1980 Arron's government was ousted in a coup and a National Military Council (NMC) established. A further coup in Aug. that year deposed several members of the NMC and the president. More attempted coups took place in 1981 and 1982, with the NMC retaining control under Dési Bouterse. In Oct. 1987 a new constitution was approved by referendum.

Suriname returned to democracy in Jan. 1988 but on 24 Dec. 1990 another military coup deposed the government. Civilian rule was re-established in 1991, which led to a peace agreement with rebel groups in Aug. 1992. Jules Wijdenbosch, an ally of Bouterse, was elected president in May 1996. He was ousted in 2000 by Ronald Venetiaan, who served for ten years before Bouterse was elected president in July 2010.

Territory and Population

Suriname is located on the northern coast of South America between 2–6° North latitude and 54–59° West longitude. It is bounded in the north by the Atlantic Ocean, east by French Guiana, west by Guyana, and south by Brazil. Area, 163,820 sq. km. Census population, 2012, 541,638; density, 3·3 per sq. km.

The UN gives a projected population for 2020 of 578,000.

The capital, Paramaribo, had (2012 census) 240,924 inhabitants.

Suriname is divided into ten districts. They are (with 2012 census population and chief town): Brokopondo, population 15,909 (Brokopondo); Commewijne, 31,420 (Nieuw Amsterdam); Coronie, 3,391 (Totness); Marowijne, 18,294 (Albina); Nickerie, 34,233 (Nieuw Nickerie); Para, 24,700 (Onverwacht); Paramaribo, 240,924—representing 44% of Suriname's total population (Paramaribo); Saramacca, 17,480 (Groningen); Sipaliwini, 37,065 (local authority in Paramaribo); Wanica, 118,222 (Lelydorp).

There is an ongoing unresolved dispute between Suriname and Guyana for the return of a triangle of uninhabited rainforest in Guyana between the New River and the Courantyne River, near the Brazilian border. In Sept. 2007 the UN settled a long-standing maritime boundary dispute between the two countries. The coastal area off both countries is believed to hold significant oil and gas deposits.

Major ethnic groups in percentages of the population in 2012: East Indian, 27·4%; Maroon (descendants of African runaway slaves from Dutch plantations in the late 17th and early 18th centuries), 21·7%; Creole, 15·7%; Javanese, 13·7%; Mixed, 13·4%. 93·3% of the population in 2010 were Surinamese, 1·9% Dutch, 1·5% Guyanese and 0·9% Brazilian. 69·8% of the population lived in urban areas in 2011.

The official language is Dutch. English is widely spoken next to Hindi, Javanese and Chinese as inter-group communication. A vernacular, called 'Sranan' or 'Surinamese', is used as a *lingua franca*. In 1976 it was decided that Spanish was to become the nation's principal working language.

Social Statistics

2007: births, 9,769; deaths, 3,374. Rates per 1,000 population: birth rate, 19·2; death rate, 6·6. Expectation of life, 2007, was 65·3 years for males and 72·5 for females. Annual population growth rate, 2000–05, 1·5%. Infant mortality, 2010, 27 per 1,000 live births; fertility rate, 2008, 2·4 births per woman. Abortion is illegal.

Climate

The climate is equatorial, with uniformly high temperatures and rainfall. The temperature is an average of 27°C throughout the year; there are two rainy seasons (May–July and Nov.–Jan.) and two dry seasons (Aug.–Oct. and Feb.–April). Paramaribo, Jan. 21°C, July 32·4°C. Average rainfall 182·3 mm.

Constitution and Government

The current constitution was ratified on 30 Sept. 1987. Parliament is a 51-member *National Assembly*. The head of state is the *President*, elected for a five-year term by a two-thirds majority by the National Assembly, or, failing that, by an electoral college, the United People's Assembly, enlarged by the inclusion of regional and local councillors, by a simple majority.

National Anthem

'God zij met ons Suriname' ('God be with our Suriname'); words by C. A. Hoekstra, tune by J. C. de Puy. There is a Sranan version, 'Opo kondreman oen opo'; words by H. de Ziel.

© Springer Nature Limited 2020
Palgrave Macmillan (ed.), *The Statesman's Yearbook 2020*,
https://doi.org/10.1057/978-1-349-95940-2_181

Recent Elections

Parliamentary elections were held on 25 May 2015. The National Democratic Party won 26 of the available 51 seats (45·6% of the vote), the V7 alliance won 18 with 37·2%, A-Combination took 5 (10·5%), the Party for Democracy and Development through Unity took 1 (4·3%) and the Progressive Workers' and Farmers' Union took 1 (0·7%). The National Democratic Party's victory marked the first time that a party had achieved an absolute majority since Suriname became independent in 1975.

On 14 July 2015 former dictator and incumbent president Dési Bouterse was re-elected president by the National Assembly. Since he stood unopposed, there was no need for a formal vote.

Current Government

President: Dési Bouterse; b. 1945 (National Democratic Party; sworn in 12 Aug. 2010 and re-elected in July 2015).

Vice-President: Ashwin Adhin.

In Feb. 2019 the government comprised:

Minister of Agriculture, Animal Husbandry and Fisheries: Lekhram Soerdjan. *Defence:* Ronni Benschop. *Education, Science and Culture:* Lilian Ferrier. *Finance:* Gillmore Hoefdraad. *Foreign Affairs:* Yldiz Pollack-Beighle. *Home Affairs:* Faizel Mohamed 'Mike' Noersalim. *Justice and Police:* Stuart Getrouw. *Labour:* Soewarto Moestadja. *Natural Resources:* Regilio Dodson. *Physical Planning, Land and Forestry Management:* Roline Samsoedien. *Public Health:* Antoine Elias. *Public Works:* Jerry Miranda. *Regional Development:* Edgar Dikan. *Social Affairs and Housing:* Cristien Polak. *Sport and Youth Affairs:* Lalinie Gopal. *Trade, Industry and Tourism:* Stephen Tsang. *Transport and Communication:* Patrick Pengel.

National Assembly Website (Dutch only): http://www.dna.sr

Current Leaders

Desiré Delano 'Dési' Bouterse

Position
President

Introduction
Former military dictator Dési Bouterse was sworn in as president in Aug. 2010 following his election by the National Assembly in July. He had earlier led the National Democratic Party to victory within the Mega Combination coalition at parliamentary elections in May that year. He was re-elected in July 2015.

Early Life
Bouterse was born on 13 Oct. 1945 in Domburg, Suriname. After attending the Middelbare Handelsschool, he moved to the Netherlands for military training.

On 25 Feb. 1980 a group of Surinamese army sergeants, including Bouterse, led a coup. By Aug. they had forced out President Johan Ferrier, who had overseen the nation's transition to independence from Dutch rule five years earlier. The military took over the government and declared a socialist republic, with Bouterse named chairman of the National Military Council. Over the next seven years he appointed puppet presidents while ruling as *de facto* leader.

Democratic elections in 1988 stripped Bouterse of much of his power, though a new constitution in 1987 confirmed his control of the military. In Dec. 1990 he dismissed the government, holding power until elections the following year. His position weakened as civil war took hold and a strong ethnic Maroon rebel movement developed under Ronnie Brunswijk, a former bodyguard of Bouterse.

Bouterse gradually entered into mainstream politics as leader of the National Democratic Party, which he had established in 1987. However, he was dogged by allegations of extra judicial murders following the 1980 coup. He was also later convicted *in absentia* in the Netherlands for drug trafficking offences and sentenced in 1999 to 11 years' imprisonment.

Campaigning on a populist platform, he secured the support of several small parties and formed the Mega Combination coalition to contest the general election of May 2010, winning 23 of a possible 51 seats. In the presidential election of July 2010, Bouterse secured 36 parliamentary votes, exceeding the two-thirds majority needed to defeat the minister of justice, Chandrikapersad Santokhi.

Career in Office
Bouterse's election was widely criticized, with claims that his run for the presidency was motivated by a desire to secure immunity from criminal prosecution. In April 2012 the National Assembly passed an amnesty law covering alleged violations under his earlier military rule. However, in June 2016 a military court ruled the law unconstitutional, potentially paving the way for further criminal proceedings against him. Earlier, in March 2015, Bouterse's son was sentenced in the USA to at least 16 years' imprisonment having been convicted of drug and arms smuggling offences.

Bouterse was reappointed president by parliament in July 2015, following parliamentary elections in May in which the National Democratic Party won a narrow overall majority.

In May 2016, with the support of the World Bank, the government announced a programme of fiscal and monetary policy adjustments to stabilize the economy and reforms to promote private sector activity. However, the economy has since struggled with a decline in foreign exchange reserves in the aftermath of a commodity export boom and the cancellation in May 2017 of a loan arrangement with the International Monetary Fund.

In April 2018 Bouterse made a number of cabinet changes, consolidating his political control ahead of elections scheduled for 2020 despite continuing legal proceedings over his alleged involvement in murders following the military coup in 1980.

Defence

In 2011 defence expenditure totalled an estimated US$55m. (approximately US$100 per capita), representing 1% of GDP.

Army
Total strength was 1,400 in 2011.

Navy
In 2011 personnel, based at Paramaribo, totalled around 240.

Air Force
Estimated personnel (2011): 200. There were four combat-capable aircraft.

Economy

In 2011 agriculture contributed 10% of GDP, industry 38% and services 52%.

Overview
Suriname is rich in natural resources. Oil, gold and alumina jointly account for around 80% of exports and over 30% of GDP. The public sector accounts for more than half of total employment.

After years of turmoil, the economy strengthened from the early 2000s thanks to sustained political stability and, at that time, buoyant international commodity prices. Annual growth averaged 4·3% from 2004–14, driven by the extractive industries, services and the construction sector. However, the economy then contracted by 2·6% in 2015 and 5·1% in 2016 as a result of high inflation, currency depreciation and the slow recovery from a commodity price decline. Also, the fiscal position has been weakened since 2013 by wage hikes and increased capital spending, with a deficit of 7·9% of GDP in 2016. Public debt increased from around 18% of GDP in 2008 to 43·3% in 2016. Heavy reliance on commodity exports leaves Suriname vulnerable to price shocks, and the high poverty rate (estimated at around 47%) is an ongoing concern.

Currency
The unit of currency is the *Suriname dollar* (SRD) of 100 *cents*, introduced on 1 Jan. 2004 to replace the *Suriname guilder* (SRG) at a rate of one Suriname dollar = 1,000 Suriname guilders. Foreign exchange reserves totalled US$140m. and gold reserves were 29,000 troy oz in July 2005. Total money supply in June 2005 was 777m. Suriname dollars. The rate of inflation was 55·5% in 2016 (the third highest in the world that year) and 22·0% in 2017.

Budget

In 2011 budgetary central government revenue totalled 3,707m. Suriname dollars and expenditure 3,014m. Suriname dollars. Principal sources of revenue in 2011: taxes on goods and services, 1,134m. Suriname dollars; taxes on income, profits and capital gains, 1,040m. Suriname dollars. Main items of expenditure by economic type in 2011: compensation of employees, 1,209m. Suriname dollars; use of goods and services, 900m. Suriname dollars.

VAT is 10% for goods and 8% for services.

Performance

Real GDP growth was 3·0% in 2009 at the height of the global recession, but more recently falling commodity prices led to a recession when real GDP contracted by 2·6% in 2015 and 5·1% in 2016. A slight recovery then saw the economy grow by 1·9% in 2017. Total GDP in 2017 was US$3·3bn.

Banking and Finance

The Central Bank of Suriname (*Governor*, Robert-Gray van Trikt) is a bankers' bank and also the bank of issue. There are three commercial banks; the Suriname People's Credit Bank operates under the auspices of the government. There are a post office savings bank, a mortgage bank, an investment bank, a long-term investments agency, a National Development Bank and an Agrarian Bank.

Energy and Natural Resources

Environment

Suriname's carbon dioxide emissions from the consumption of energy in 2011 were the equivalent of 4·0 tonnes per capita.

Electricity

Installed capacity in 2011 was 0·4m. kW. Production was an estimated 1·95bn. kWh in 2011 and consumption per capita an estimated 3,683 kWh.

Oil and Gas

Crude oil production (2011), 5·1m. bbls. Reserves in 2014 were 93m. bbls.

Minerals

Bauxite is the most important mineral. Suriname ranks among the ten largest bauxite producers in the world. Production (2011), 3,236,000 tonnes.

Agriculture

Agriculture is restricted to the alluvial coastal zone; in 2013 there were an estimated 60,000 ha. of arable land and 6,000 ha. of permanent crops. The staple food crop is rice: production, 224,000 tonnes in 2012. Other crops (2012 in 1,000 tonnes): sugarcane (estimate), 120; bananas, 92; plantains, 19; oranges, 16; cassava, 4; coconuts, 4. Livestock in 2012 (estimates): cattle, 57,000; pigs, 32,000; sheep, 6,000; goats, 4,000; chickens, 6m.

Forestry

Forests covered 15·33m. ha. in 2015, or 95% of the land area. In terms of percentage coverage, Suriname was the world's most heavily forested country in 2015. Of the total area under forests 91% in 2015 was primary forest and 9% other naturally regenerated forest. Production of roundwood in 2011 was 413,000 cu. metres.

Fisheries

The catch in 2014 amounted to 38,358 tonnes, almost entirely from marine waters.

Industry

There is no longer any aluminium smelting, but there are food-processing and wood-using industries. Production: alumina (2007), 2,181,000 tonnes; residual fuel oil (2007), 360,000 tonnes; cement (2008 estimate), 65,000 tonnes; distillate fuel oil (2007), 41,000 tonnes; sawnwood (2007), 57,000 cu. metres.

Labour

The labour force in 2013 was 211,000 (175,000 in 2003). 59·3% of the population aged 15–64 was economically active in 2013. In the same year 6·6% of the population was unemployed.

International Trade

Imports and Exports

Trade in US$1m.:

	2012	2013	2014
Imports c.i.f.	1,732·8	2,308·5	1,826·7
Exports f.o.b.	2,380·5	2,204·4	1,917·7

Principal imports are machinery and transport equipment, and mineral fuels and lubricants. Principal exports are crude oil, alumina and gold.

In 2014 imports (in US$1m.) were mainly from the USA (501·7), the Netherlands (263·7), Trinidad and Tobago (194·3) and China (122·6); exports were mainly to the USA (466·6), the UAE (421·9), Switzerland (261·2) and Belgium (162·3).

Communications

Roads

The road network covers some 4,000 km. In 2006 there were 81,778 passenger cars, 25,745 trucks and vans, 3,029 buses and coaches and 40,889 motorcycles and mopeds. There were 82 fatalities in road accidents in 2012.

Rail

There are two single-track railways.

Civil Aviation

There are two international airports. The larger airport (Johan Adolf Pengel) is 45 km south of Paramaribo while the smaller Zog en Hoop is 5 km west of Paramaribo. The national carrier is Surinam Airways, which in 2010 had flights to Amsterdam, Aruba, Curaçao, Miami and Port of Spain. In 2012 scheduled airline traffic of Suriname-based carriers flew 1·9m. km; passenger-km totalled 1·3bn. in the same year.

Shipping

In Jan. 2014 there were three ships of 300 GT or over registered, totalling 3,000 GT. The main port is Nieuwe Haven.

Telecommunications

In 2013 there were 868,600 mobile phone subscriptions (1,610·7 per 1,000 inhabitants) and 84,900 fixed telephone lines. In the same year an estimated 37·4% of the population were internet users.

Social Institutions

Out of 178 countries analysed in the 2017 *Fragile States Index*—a list published jointly by the Fund for Peace and *Foreign Policy* magazine—Suriname was ranked the joint 65th least vulnerable (along with Kazakhstan) to conflict or collapse. The index is based on 12 indicators of state vulnerability across social, political and economic categories.

Justice

Members of the court of justice are nominated by the President. There are three cantonal courts. Suriname was one of ten countries to sign an agreement in Feb. 2001 establishing a Caribbean Court of Justice to replace the British Privy Council as the highest civil and criminal court. In the meantime the number of signatories has risen to 12. The court was inaugurated at Port of Spain, Trinidad on 16 April 2005 but it has not yet been accepted as Suriname's final court of appeal.

The population in penal institutions in 2012 was 994 (186 per 100,000 of national population). 50·0% of prisoners had yet to receive a trial according to 2014 estimates by the International Centre for Prison Studies. The death penalty, which was last used in 1982, was abolished in March 2015.

Education

Adult literacy was 94·6% in 2008 (95·5% among males and 93·8% among females). In 2013, 336 primary schools had 5,114 teachers and 70,254 pupils; 142 secondary schools had 4,086 teachers and 52,109 pupils. Anton de Kom University, founded in 1968 and the country's only university, comprises faculties of humanities, mathematical and physical sciences, medical sciences, social sciences and technological sciences. There are also a number of higher professional education institutes.

Health

In 2010 there were 31 hospital beds per 10,000 population. In the period 2000–10 there were 4·5 physicians per 10,000 inhabitants.

In *Water: At What Cost? The State of the World's Water 2016*, WaterAid reported that 5·2% of the population does not have access to safe water.

Religion

A study by the Pew Research Center's Forum on Religion & Public Life estimated that in 2010 there were 270,000 Christians (including 150,000 Roman Catholics and 110,000 Protestants), 100,000 Hindus, 80,000 Muslims and 30,000 folk religionists. People with no religious affiliation also numbered 30,000 in 2010.

Culture

World Heritage Sites

Suriname has two sites on the UNESCO World Heritage List: Central Suriname Nature Reserve (inscribed on the list in 2000); and the Historic Inner City of Paramaribo (2002).

Press

There were four daily newspapers in 2008 with a combined circulation of 55,000.

Tourism

In 2010 there were 204,000 international tourist arrivals (excluding same-day visitors), spending a total of US$61m.

Festivals

The people of Suriname celebrate Chinese New Year (Jan.); Phagwa, a Hindu celebration (March–April); Id-Ul-Fitre, the sugar feast at the end of Ramadan (May); Avondvierdaagse, a carnival (during the Easter holidays); Suriflora, a celebration of plants and flowers (April–May); Keti koti, an Afro-Surinamese holiday to commemorate the abolition of slavery (1 July); Suri-pop, a popular music festival (July); Nationale Kunstbeurs, arts and crafts (Oct.–Nov.); Diwali, the Hindu ceremony of light (Nov.); Djaran Kepang, a Javanese dance held on feast days; Winti-prey, a ceremony for the Winti gods.

Diplomatic Representatives

Of Suriname in the United Kingdom
Ambassador: Reggy Martiales Nelson (resides in Paris).
Honorary Consul: Dr Amwedhkar Jethu (127 Pier House, 31 Cheyne Walk, London, SW3 5HN).

Of the United Kingdom in Suriname
Ambassador: Greg Quinn (resides in Georgetown, Guyana).

Of Suriname in the USA (4201 Connecticut Ave., NW, Suite 400, Washington, D.C., 20008)
Ambassador: Niermala Sakoentala Badrising.

Of the USA in Suriname (165 Kristalstraat, Paramaribo)
Ambassador: Karen Lynn Williams.

Of Suriname to the United Nations
Ambassador: Vacant.
Chargé d'Affaires a.i.: Kitty Sweeb.

Of Suriname to the European Union
Ambassador: Wilfred Eduard Christopher.

Further Reading

Dew, E. M., *Trouble in Suriname, 1975–1993.* 1995
National Statistical Office: Algemeen Bureau voor de Statistiek, Klipstenenstraat 5, POB 244, Paramaribo.
Website (Dutch only): http://www.statistics-suriname.org

Sweden

Konungariket Sverige (Kingdom of Sweden)

Capital: Stockholm
Population projection, 2020: 10·12m.
GNI per capita, 2017: (PPP$) 47,766
HDI/world rank, 2017: 0·933/7=
Internet domain extension: .se

Key Historical Events

Sweden was covered by a thick ice cap until 14,000 years ago, when the ice began to retreat. The first human traces, in southern Sweden, date from 10,000 BC. Between 8000 and 6000 BC the country was populated by hunters and fishermen, using simple stone tools. Artefacts found in graves show that the Bronze Age was marked by a relatively advanced culture. From 500 BC to AD 800 agriculture became the basis for society and the economy. The Viking Age (800–1050) took expansion eastwards. Swedish Vikings reached into today's Russia, where they set up trading stations and principalities, such as Novgorod and Rurik. The Vikings also travelled to the Black and Caspian Seas and developed trading links with the Byzantine Empire and the Arabs.

In 830 the Frankish monk Ansgar introduced Christianity to Sweden but made few converts. In the 11th century, English missionaries had greater success and by the end of the century the country was fully Christianized. Olof Skötkonung, who proclaimed himself ruler of Sweden, supported the new religion.

By 1200 Sweden had become a united kingdom with largely the same borders as it has today, except that Skåne, Halland and Blekinge in the south of Sweden formed part of Denmark, and Jämtland, Härjedalen and Bohuslän in the west belonged to Norway. There was a struggle for power between the Sverker and Erik families, who ruled alternately in 1160–1250. However, by the middle of the 13th century with the building of royal castles and introduction of provincial administration, the crown was able to assert the authority of the central government and impose laws valid for the whole kingdom. Among the most important figures of the 13th century was Birger Jarl, who promoted the newly founded city of Stockholm. At a time when Hanseatic merchants traded in Sweden, Stockholm contained a large German population while, on the southeast coast, Kalmar and Gotland were controlled by German immigrants. The Hanseatic trading posts to the east included Finland, which was brought into the Swedish kingdom. A new code of law, for the entire country, was introduced in 1350 by King Magnus Eriksson. In 1340 Valdemar Atterdag, King of Denmark, went to war with Sweden over the southern provinces of Skåne, Halland and Blekinge. He attacked Gotland in 1361 in one of the bloodiest battles in Nordic history, to secure a base for further assaults on Sweden and to overthrow the Hanseatic League.

In the 14th century trade increased and until the mid-16th century the Hanseatic League dominated Sweden's trade. In 1350 the Black Death decimated the population. Inheritance and marriage ties united the crowns of Denmark, Norway and Sweden in 1389, under the rule of Queen Margaret of Denmark. In 1397 the loose association known as the Union of Kalmar confirmed her five-year old nephew, Erik of Pomerania, as ruler of the three countries. The Swedish nationalist Sten Sture, who was made king of Sweden in 1470, defeated the Danes at the Battle of Brunkeberg in Stockholm. Following this success, Sten Sture promoted nationalistic sentiment by the public display of a great wood carving of St George slaying the dragon (now placed in Stockholm cathedral) and the setting up of the first Swedish university at Uppsala. The union period (1397–1521) was characterized by a struggle for power between the king, the nobility and the burghers and peasants. These conflicts culminated in the Stockholm Bloodbath in 1520, when eighty leading men in Sweden were executed on orders of the Danish king, Christian II. In 1521 Christian II was overthrown by Gustav Vasa, a Swedish nobleman, who was elected king in 1523.

Empire Building

Gustav Vasa (ruled 1523–60) laid the foundations of the Swedish national state. With the Reformation, Sweden was converted to Lutheranism and the church became a national institution. At the same time power was concentrated in the hands of the king and in 1544 a hereditary monarchy was established. By the 16th century Scandinavia was divided into two states, Sweden-Finland and Denmark-Norway. Since the dissolution of the union with Denmark and Norway, Swedish foreign policy focused on dominating the Baltic Sea, and this led to wars with Denmark from the 1560s.

In 1611 Gustavus Adolphus (Gustaf II Adolf) consolidated Sweden's position on the Russian side of the Baltic Sea. Sweden defeated Denmark in two wars (1643 and 1657) to take control of the previously Danish provinces of Skåne, Halland, Blekinge and Gotland and the Norwegian provinces of Bohuslän, Jämtland and Härjedalen. Gustavus Adolphus gave his support to the Protestant alliance in the Thirty Years War. This cost him his life but earned Sweden territory in the north of Germany. Finland and the present-day Baltic republics also belonged to Sweden making it a great power in northern Europe.

Following the death of King Karl XII in 1718 the Swedish Parliament (Riksdag) introduced a constitution that abolished royal absolutism. But royal authority was soon reasserted. After defeat in the Great Northern War (1700–21) against Denmark, Poland and Russia, Sweden lost most of its Baltic territories, including a part of Finland and all its north-German possessions except west Pomerania. During the Napoleonic Wars, Sweden lost Finland to Russia and withdrew from its remaining German provinces. In 1810 Napoleon's marshal Jean-Baptiste Bernadotte assumed power as Karl XIV Johan. He tried to win back Finland from Russia, but had to make do with a union of Sweden and Norway, confirmed by the treaty of Kiel in 1814.

The short war against Norway in 1814 was Sweden's last military adventure. Since then Sweden has favoured neutrality. For this reason, there was no early application to join the EEC (European Economic Community). But in line with a commitment to liberalize trade, Sweden was a founder member of EFTA (European Free Trade Agreement) in 1959. After the Cold War and the collapse of the Soviet Union, the policy of neutrality was seen by many as obsolete. Sweden became a member of the EU (European Union) in 1995.

Following constitutional reforms in 1974 the remaining powers of the king were reduced to purely ceremonial functions. Carl XVI Gustaf, who succeeded the throne in 1973, is the first Swedish king to be bound by the new constitution. In 1980 the order of succession was amended to allow for a female member of the royal family to inherit the crown. Consequently, Princess Victoria is the heir apparent rather than her younger brother Prince Carl Philip.

Modern Economy

After the Napoleonic Wars, Sweden suffered economic stagnation. The country was poor with 90% of the population living off the land. Out of a population of five million, over one million emigrated between 1866 and 1914, mostly to North America. Industry did not start to grow until the 1890s. However, it then developed rapidly and after the Second World War Sweden was transformed into one of the leading industrial nations in Europe. In the six years to 1951 the country's GNP rose by 20%. Economic success was partly thanks to the early utilization of hydro-electric power which supported the pulp and paper industries of the northern forests. Swedish inventors created the ball-bearing, the adjustable spanner, the primus stove and the cream separator, as well as the safety match and dynamite. By 1956 the economy was booming, poverty had almost disappeared and unemployment was at a minimum. Sweden was one of the richest countries in Europe.

Social democracy began as the political offshoot of the trade unions. The working class was supported by intellectuals, such as the scientist Hjalmar Branting, who was the first Scandinavian socialist prime minister. The first representative of social democracy entered the government in 1917. Universal suffrage was introduced for men in 1909 and for women in 1921. In the 1930s, when the Social Democrats had become the governing party, plans for the welfare society were laid. Reforms included restrictions on child and

© Springer Nature Limited 2020
Palgrave Macmillan (ed.), *The Statesman's Yearbook 2020*,
https://doi.org/10.1057/978-1-349-95940-2_182

female labour, free elementary education and old-age pensions. A four-party coalition for the duration of the Second World War was succeeded by a Social Democrat government with Per Albin Hansson as prime minister. Following his death in 1946, Tage Erlander became prime minister and stayed in office until 1969. He was succeeded by Olof Palme who was prime minister between 1969 and 1976. Owing to the rise in oil prices in 1973, unemployment increased. From the mid-1970s, improvements in living standards slowed. Economic crisis drove the Social Democrats out of government and in 1976 a non-socialist coalition was formed under Centre Party chairman, Thorbjörn Fälldin. Conflicts over the expansion of nuclear power led to several government reshuffles. In 1982 the Social Democrats resumed office with Olof Palme as prime minister. The assassination of Palme in 1986 shook the country which had been spared political violence for nearly 200 years. Ingvar Carlsson took over as head of government. In the 1990s industrial production fell and unemployment rose, which led to a high budget deficit and increased national debt. Popular dissatisfaction showed in the 1991 election, when a non-socialist coalition government was formed with Carl Bildt as prime minister. Launching a programme of deregulation and privatization, Bildt did much to prepare the economy for closer involvement with Europe. Capital gains taxes were reduced, as too were social benefits. But the government failed to reduce unemployment, the budget deficit or the national debt. Hence, the 1994 election put the Social Democrats back in power, with Ingvar Carlsson again as prime minister. In 1996 he stepped down to be replaced by Göran Persson. Persson led a series of minority governments. His third term, which began in 2002, was marked by the murder of his foreign minister, Anna Lindh, in 2003 and the rejection by referendum of Sweden's entry into the single European currency.

In Sept. 2006 the Social Democrats emerged from elections as the single biggest party but Fredrik Reinfeldt of the Moderate Party was able to form a centre-right 'Alliance for Sweden' coalition to end 12 years of Social Democratic government. No party secured a majority at the parliamentary elections of 2010, polls in which the Sweden Democrats became the first Swedish far-right party to win parliamentary representation. Later that year, the government applied to the UK for the extradition of WikiLeaks founder Julian Assange, who had been accused of sexual offences. In response Assange took refuge in London's Ecuadorian embassy, where he remained as of late 2018. Meanwhile, Reinfeldt formed a minority administration but when no party achieved a majority at the general election of Sept. 2014, he was replaced as premier by Stefan Löfven at the head of a centre-left coalition.

Territory and Population

Sweden is bounded in the west and northwest by Norway, east by Finland and the Gulf of Bothnia, southeast by the Baltic Sea and southwest by the Kattegat. The area is 447,420 sq. km, including inland water (96,000 lakes) totalling 40,080 sq. km. The area including territorial waters is 528,447 sq. km. At the last census, in 1990, the population was 8,587,353. Parliament decided in 1995 to change to a register-based method of calculating the population. The recorded population at 31 Dec. 2017 was 10,120,242; density 24·8 per sq. km. In 2011, 84·8% of the population lived in urban areas.

The UN gives a projected population for 2020 of 10·12m.

Area, population and population density of the counties (*län*):

	Land area (in sq. km)	Population (1990 census)	Population (31 Dec. 2017)	Density per sq. km (31 Dec. 2017)
Blekinge	2,931	150,615	159,371	54
Dalarna	28,030	288,919	286,165	10
Gävleborg	18,119	289,346	285,637	16
Gotland	3,134	57,132	58,595	19
Halland	5,427	254,568	324,825	60
Jämtland	48,945	135,724	129,806	3
Jönköping	10,438	308,294	357,237	34
Kalmar	11,166	241,149	243,536	22
Kronoberg	8,425	177,880	197,519	23
Norrbotten	97,257	263,546	251,295	3
Örebro	8,504	272,474	298,907	35

(*continued*)

	Land area (in sq. km)	Population (1990 census)	Population (31 Dec. 2017)	Density per sq. km (31 Dec. 2017)
Östergötland	10,545	402,849	457,496	43
Skåne	10,969	1,068,587	1,344,689	123
Södermanland	6,076	255,546	291,341	48
Stockholm	6,526	1,640,389	2,308,143	354
Uppsala	8,192	268,503	368,971	45
Värmland	17,517	283,148	280,399	16
Västerbotten	54,672	251,846	268,465	5
Västernorrland	21,552	261,099	245,968	11
Västmanland	5,118	258,544	271,095	53
Västra Götaland	23,797	1,458,166	1,690,782	71

There are some 17,000 Sami (Lapps).

On 31 Dec. 2008 foreign-born persons in Sweden numbered 1,281,581. Of these, 269,681 were from Nordic countries; 459,139 from the rest of Europe; 90,733 from Africa; 28,750 from North America; 60,878 from South America; 361,333 from Asian countries; 6,437 from the former USSR; 3,957 from Oceania; and 673 country unknown. Of the total 175,113 were born in Finland. 13·8% of the population of Sweden in Dec. 2008 was foreign-born, the highest proportion in any of the Nordic countries. At 23 refugees per 1,000 inhabitants in Dec. 2016, Sweden has the sixth highest number of refugees compared to the national population of the host country and the highest of any industrialized country.

Immigration: 2007, 99,485; 2008, 101,171; 2009, 102,280. Emigration: 2007, 45,418; 2008, 45,294; 2009, 39,240.

Population of the 50 largest communities, 31 Dec. 2017:

Stockholm	949,761
Gothenburg (Göteborg)	564,039
Malmö	333,633
Uppsala	219,914
Linköping	158,520
Örebro	150,291
Västerås	150,134
Helsingborg	143,304
Norrköping	140,927
Jönköping	137,481
Umeå	125,080
Lund	121,274
Borås	111,026
Huddinge	110,003
Eskilstuna	104,709
Nacka	101,231
Gävle	100,603
Halmstad	99,752
Sundsvall	98,810
Södertälje	96,032
Botkyrka	91,925
Karlstad	91,120
Växjö	91,060
Haninge	88,037
Kristianstad	84,151
Kungsbacka	81,986
Solna	79,707
Luleå	77,470
Järfälla	76,453
Skellefteå	72,723
Sollentuna	71,848
Täby	70,405

(*continued*)

Kalmar	67,451
Karlskrona	66,666
Mölndal	66,121
Varberg	62,755
Östersund	62,601
Norrtälje	60,808
Gotland	58,595
Falun	58,340
Trollhättan	58,238
Örnsköldsvik	56,139
Uddevalla	55,763
Nyköping	55,467
Skövde	54,975
Hässleholm	52,003
Borlänge	51,964
Sundbyberg	49,424
Tyresö	47,304
Lidingö	47,185

The *de facto* official language is Swedish.

Social Statistics

Statistics for calendar years:

	Total living births	To mothers single, divorced or widowed	Stillborn	Marriages	Divorces	Deaths exclusive of stillborn
2004	100,928	55,991	318	43,088	20,106	90,532
2005	101,346	56,238	301	44,381	20,000	91,710
2006	105,913	58,820	319	45,551	20,295	91,177
2007	107,421	58,819	326	47,898	20,669	91,729
2008	109,301	59,832	396	50,332	21,377	91,449

Rates, 2008, per 1,000 population: births, 11·9; deaths, 9·9; marriages, 5·4; divorces, 2·3. Sweden has one of the highest rate of births outside marriage in Europe, at 55% in 2008. In 2008 the average age at first marriage was 35·1 years for males and 32·5 years for females. Expectation of life in 2013: males, 79·7 years; females, 83·9. Annual population growth rate, 2005–10, 0·8%. Infant mortality, 2010, two per 1,000 live births (one of the lowest rates in the world). Fertility rate, 2008, 1·9 births per woman. Sweden legalized same-sex marriage in May 2009. Sweden was ranked fourth in a gender gap index of 145 countries compiled by the World Economic Forum for its *Global Gender Gap Report 2015*. The annual index considers economic, political, education and health criteria. In 2015 Sweden received 162,877 asylum seekers at the height of the European migrant crisis, up from 81,301 in 2014 and 17,530 in 2005.

Climate

The north has severe winters, with snow lying for 4–7 months. Summers are fine but cool, with long daylight hours. Further south, winters are less cold, summers are warm and rainfall well distributed throughout the year, although slightly higher in the summer. Stockholm, Jan. −2·8°C, July 17·2°C. Annual rainfall 385 mm.

Constitution and Government

The reigning King is **Carl XVI Gustaf**, b. 30 April 1946, succeeded on the death of his grandfather Gustaf VI Adolf, 15 Sept. 1973, married 19 June 1976 to Silvia Renate Sommerlath, b. 23 Dec. 1943 (Queen of Sweden). *Daughter* and *Heir Apparent:* Crown Princess Victoria Ingrid Alice Désirée, Duchess of Västergötland, b. 14 July 1977, married 19 June 2010 to Daniel Westling, b. 15 Sept. 1973 (*offspring:* Princess Estelle Silvia Ewa Mary, b. 23

Feb. 2012; Prince Oscar Carl Olaf, b. 2 March 2016); *son:* Prince Carl Philip Edmund Bertil, Duke of Värmland, b. 13 May 1979, married 13 June 2015 to Sofia Kristina Hellqvist, b. 6 Dec. 1984 (*offspring:* Prince Alexander Erik Hubertus Bertil, b. 19 April 2016; Prince Gabriel Carl Walther, b. 31 Aug. 2017); *daughter:* Princess Madeleine Thérèse Amelie Josephine, Duchess of Hälsingland and Gästrikland, b. 10 June 1982, married 8 June 2013 to Christopher O'Neill, b. 27 June 1974 (*offspring:* Princess Leonore Lilian Maria, b. 20 Feb. 2014; Prince Nicolas Paul Gustaf, b. 15 June 2015; Princess Adrienne Josephine Alice, b. 9 March 2018). *Sisters of the King.* Princess Margaretha, b. 31 Oct. 1934, married 30 June 1964 to John Ambler, died 31 May 2008; Princess Birgitta (Princess of Sweden), b. 19 Jan. 1937, married 25 May 1961 (civil marriage) and 30 May 1961 (religious ceremony) to Johann Georg, Prince of Hohenzollern, died 2 March 2016; Princess Désirée, b. 2 June 1938, married 5 June 1964 to Baron Niclas Silfverschiöld; Princess Christina, b. 3 Aug. 1943, married 15 June 1974 to Tord Magnuson. *Uncles of the King.* Count Sigvard Bernadotte of Wisborg, b. 7 June 1907, died 4 Feb. 2002; Count Carl Johan Bernadotte of Wisborg, b. 31 Oct. 1916, died 5 May 2012.

Under the 1975 constitution Sweden is a representative and parliamentary democracy. The King is Head of State, but does not participate in government. Parliament is the single-chamber *Riksdag* of 349 members elected for a period of four years in direct, general elections.

The manner of election to the *Riksdag* is proportional. The country is divided into 29 constituencies. In these constituencies 310 members are elected. The remaining 39 seats constitute a nationwide pool intended to give absolute proportionality to parties that receive at least 4% of the votes. A party receiving less than 4% of the votes in the country is, however, entitled to participate in the distribution of seats in a constituency if it has obtained at least 12% of the votes cast there.

A parliament, the *Sameting*, was instituted for the Sami (Lapps) in 1993.

National Anthem

'Du gamla, du fria' ('Thou ancient, thou free'); words by R. Dybeck; folk-tune.

Government Chronology

Prime Ministers since 1936. (C = Centre Party; FP = Liberal Party; M = Moderate Party; SAP = Swedish Social Democratic Party)

1936–46	SAP	Per Albin Hansson
1946–69	SAP	Tage Fritiof Erlander
1969–76	SAP	Sven Olof Joachim Palme
1976–78	C	Thorbjörn Fälldin
1978–79	FP	Ola Ullsten
1979–82	C	Thorbjörn Fälldin
1982–86	SAP	Sven Olof Joachim Palme
1986–91	SAP	Ingvar Gösta Carlsson
1991–94	M	Carl Bildt
1994–96	SAP	Ingvar Gösta Carlsson
1996–2006	SAP	Göran Persson
2006–14	M	John Fredrik Reinfeldt
2014–	SAP	Stefan Löfven

Recent Elections

In parliamentary elections held on 9 Sept. 2018 the ruling Swedish Social Democratic Party (SAP) won 100 seats with 28·3% of votes cast (down from 113 with 31·0% in 2014), the Moderate Party 70 with 19·8% (down from 84 with 23·3%), the far-right Sweden Democrats 62 with 17·5% (up from 49 with 12·9%), the Centre Party 31 with 8·6% (22 with 6·1%), the Left Party 28 with 8·0% (21 with 5·7%), the Christian Democratic Party 22 with 6·3% (16 with 4·6%), the Liberal Party 20 with 5·5% (19 with 5·4%) and the Green Party 16 with 4·4% (25 with 7·3%). Turnout was 87·2%.

European Parliament

Sweden has 20 representatives. At the May 2014 elections turnout was 51·1% (45·5% in 2009). The SAP won 5 seats with 24·4% of votes cast (political affiliation in European Parliament: Progressive Alliance of Socialists and Democrats); the Green Party, 4 with 15·3% (Greens/European Free Alliance); the Moderate Party, 3 with 13·6% (European People's Party); the Liberal Party, 2 with 10·0% (Alliance of Liberals and Democrats for Europe); the Sweden Democrats, 2 with 9·7% (Europe of Freedom and Direct Democracy); the Centre Party, 1 with 6·5% (Alliance of Liberals and Democrats for Europe); the Left Party, 1 with 6·3% (European United Left/Nordic Green Left); the Christian Democratic Party, 1 with 6·0% (European People's Party); the Feminist Initiative, 1 with 5·3% (Progressive Alliance of Socialists and Democrats).

Current Government

Following parliamentary elections in Sept. 2014 a new minority centre-left coalition government consisting of the Social Democrats and the Greens was formed. It was renewed following the Sept 2018 election. In Feb. 2019 the cabinet comprised:

Prime Minister: Stefan Löfven; b. 1957 (Social Democrats; sworn in 3 Oct. 2014).

Deputy Prime Minister, and Minister of Environment and Climate: Isabella Lövin.

Minister of Culture and Democracy: Amanda Lind. *Defence:* Peter Hultqvist. *Education:* Anna Ekström. *Employment:* Ylva Johansson. *Energy and Digital Development:* Anders Ygeman. *Enterprise:* Ibrahim Baylan. *EU Affairs:* Hans Dahlgren. *Finance:* Magdalena Andersson. *Financial Markets and Housing:* Per Bolund. *Foreign Affairs:* Margot Wallström. *Foreign Trade:* Ann Linde. *Gender Equality:* Åsa Lindhagen. *Health and Social Affairs:* Lena Hallengren. *Higher Education and Research:* Matilda Ernkrans. *Home Affairs:* Mikael Damberg. *Infrastructure:* Tomas Eneroth. *International Development Co-operation:* Peter Eriksson. *Justice and Migration:* Morgan Johansson. *Public Administration:* Ardalan Shekarabi. *Rural Affairs:* Jennie Nilsson. *Social Security:* Annika Strandhäll.

Of the 23 ministers, 12 are currently women.

Government Website: http://www.government.se

Current Leaders

Stefan Löfven

Position
Prime Minister

Introduction
Veteran trade unionist and leader of the Swedish Social Democratic Party (SAP) Stefan Löfven became prime minister in Oct. 2014 at the head of a centre-left coalition. Löfven refused to invite the far-right Sweden Democrats (SD) into government, opting instead to form a minority administration. Following inconclusive elections in Sept. 2018, which delivered a hung parliament, he lost a confidence vote in the *Riksdag* but continued in office in a caretaker capacity pending the formation of a new government. Following inconclusive elections in Sept. 2018, which delivered a hung parliament, he lost a confidence vote in the *Riksdag* but continued in office in a caretaker capacity until he was again nominated and endorsed as premier by the legislature in Jan. 2019.

Early Life
Stefan Löfven was born on 21 July 1957 in Stockholm. After finishing school, he trained for a year as a welder before studying social work at Umeå University. In 1976 he began working in the post office, then at a sawmill, and in 1979 joined a vehicle manufacturer as a welder. He became active in the Swedish Metalworkers' Union from the early 1980s, serving as a local branch president in 1988 and a member of the union's national council the following year.

From 2002–05 he was vice-president of the union, taking over as president in 2006 when it became IF Metall. From 2003 he also served on the executive board of the Swedish Trade Union Confederation. He gained a reputation as a skilled negotiator, particularly in the aftermath of the economic crisis of 2008. In 2005 he was appointed to the executive committee of the SAP, serving until 2012, and from 2007–09 chaired its welfare policy review group. In Jan. 2012 he was elected party leader and entered the 2014 general election campaign pledging to increase spending on health and education and to raise taxes, in contrast to the incumbent government's austerity programme. The SAP emerged as the largest party and formed a

coalition with other centre-left parties, having declined to invite the far-right SD to join them.

Career in Office
Löfven took office on 3 Oct. 2014, vowing to reduce unemployment, especially among young people, and to invest in infrastructure. However, the minority government experienced early difficulties when, in Dec. 2014, parliament failed to pass the cabinet's budget. In response, Löfven initially called a further election for March 2015, but later in the month struck a deal in which he agreed to follow a modified version of the centre-right opposition's budget for the following year and to cancel the March polls. The agreement was intended to sideline the SD.

On the international stage, Löfven announced in Oct. 2014 that Sweden would officially recognize the State of Palestine, prompting Israel to recall its ambassador from Stockholm in protest.

In 2015, in response to the escalating foreign migrant influx into Europe towards the more prosperous northern EU member states, the government introduced tighter border controls and other restrictions in the last quarter of the year to stem the unprecedented flow into the country. In April 2017, in a suspected Islamist terror attack in Stockholm, an immigrant from Uzbekistan drove a delivery truck into a department store killing four people.

The stability of Löfven's minority coalition was undermined in July 2017 as his interior and infrastructure ministers resigned over a serious data security breach scandal surrounding the Swedish Transport Agency. The Sept. 2018 elections then delivered a hung parliament, allowing neither the centre-left nor centre-right to form an immediate coalition, but which subsequently approved a motion of no confidence against Löfven in a 204–142 vote. He nevertheless continued in office on a caretaker basis until the parliament approved his renomination as premier on 18 Jan. 2019.

Defence

The Supreme Commander is, under the government, in command of the three services. The Supreme Commander is assisted by the Swedish Armed Forces HQ. There is also a Swedish Armed Forces Logistics Organization.

Conscripted military service was phased out and ended officially on 1 July 2010. However, in March 2017 it was announced that conscription would be reintroduced for men and women from Jan. 2018. Women had not previously been subject to conscription.

In 2013 defence expenditure totalled US$6,633m., with spending per capita of US$727. The 2013 expenditure represented 1·2% of GDP. Sweden's national security policy is currently undergoing a shift in emphasis. Beginning with the decommissioning of obsolete units and structures, the main thrust of policy is the creation of contingency forces adaptable to a variety of situations.

When Sweden joined the European Union in 1995 the government stressed that membership did not imply any change in the country's traditional policy of non-participation in military alliances, with the option of staying neutral in the event of war in its vicinity.

Sweden has modern air raid shelters with capacity for some 7m. people. Since this falls short of providing protection for the whole population, evacuation and relocation operations would be necessary in the event of war.

The Swedish Civil Contingencies Agency is responsible for civil protection and emergency preparedness and has a mandate spanning the entire spectrum of threats and risks, including wartime defence.

Army

Army strength, 2013, 5,500. Voluntary auxiliary organizations numbered 22,000. Equipment in 2013 included 132 main battle tanks and 354 armoured infantry fighting vehicles.

Navy

In 2013 the Navy operated six submarines, 156 amphibious landing craft and 22 patrol and coastal combatant vessels.

The personnel of the Navy in 2013 totalled 3,000 (including 850 amphibious). In addition there was a paramilitary coast guard numbering 800.

Air Force

Strength (2013) 3,300. There were 134 combat-capable aircraft in 2013 (JAS 39 *Gripens*).

In 1998 the helicopter units of the Swedish Army and Navy were merged with those of the Air Force to form a single helicopter wing, which since 2003 has fallen under the direct authority of the Air Force.

International Relations

In a referendum held on 14 Sept. 2003 Swedish voters rejected their country's entry into the common European currency, 56·1% opposing membership of the euro against 41·8% voting in favour. Turnout was 81·2%.

Economy

Services accounted for 72% of GDP in 2012, industry 27% and agriculture 1%.

According to the anti-corruption organization Transparency International, Sweden ranked equal third in the world in a 2018 survey of the countries with the least corruption in business and government. It received 85 out of 100 in the annual index.

Sweden gave US$5·6bn. in international aid in 2017, which at 1·02% of GNI made it the most generous developed country as a percentage of its gross national income. Sweden was one of only five industrialized countries to meet the UN target of 0·7% in 2017.

Overview

Sweden is a highly developed post-industrial economy with one of the highest GDP per capita ratios in the world. Tax revenue as a percentage of GDP is also one of the world's highest, which affords Swedes an advanced welfare system and a high standard of living. In Sept. 2003 a referendum rejected adoption of the European single currency (euro).

After the 2001 global 'dotcom' technology crash that damaged Ericsson, one of Sweden's largest companies, the economy experienced an upswing with strong recovery in the telecommunications and automobile sectors fuelling export-led growth from 2003–07. Increased exports combined with rising production and low interest rates prompted a revival in business investment. Growth was further buoyed by increased consumer spending.

The economy weathered the global financial crisis that began in 2008, thanks to strong macroeconomic and fiscal fundamentals and a well-diversified private sector. Sweden is one of the few advanced economies where output had exceeded 2008 levels by 2015. Despite sluggish economic conditions in the eurozone, the economy averaged annual growth of 2·5% between 2010 and 2014, underpinned by strong domestic demand in the context of a weak export market. In 2015 GDP growth reached 4·3%, followed by 3·1% in 2016. However, household debt is high and rising, while over-inflated house prices and ease of access to low-amortization mortgages pose risks to consumption should the housing market implode.

In 2017 public debt was relatively low, at under 40%, and robust job creation saw unemployment fall to 6·7%, although labour shortages have intensified in various industries, most notably construction. Youth joblessness also remains persistently high, and the IMF has predicted higher unemployment in the short term in the wake of refugee inflows related to the European migrant crisis, which saw the Swedish population surge by 1·5%.

A number of sectors, including electricity, telecommunications and areas of transport, have been deregulated. However, Sweden is facing pressure from the EU to privatize its state monopolies in the pharmaceutical, construction and alcoholic beverage sectors.

Currency

The unit of currency is the *krona* (SEK), of 100 *öre*. Inflation rates (based on OECD statistics):

2008	2009	2010	2011	2012	2013	2014	2015	2016	2017
3·4%	−0·5%	1·2%	3·0%	0·9%	0·0%	−0·2%	0·0%	1·0%	1·8%

Foreign exchange reserves were US$38,704m. and gold reserves 4·04m. troy oz in Sept. 2009. Total money supply was 1,486·7bn. kr. in Aug. 2009.

Budget

General government revenue in 2015 (provisional) totalled 2,070bn. kr. and expenditure 2,017bn. kr.

Principal sources of revenue in 2015 (provisional) were: taxes on income, profits and capital gains, 759bn. kr.; taxes on goods and services, 520bn. kr. Main items of expenditure by economic type in 2015 (provisional): social benefits, 715bn. kr.; compensation of employees, 523bn. kr.

Sweden had a budget surplus of 1·6% of GDP in 2017. There was also a surplus in 2016 (1·1%) and in 2015 (0·2%). The required target set by the EU is a budget deficit of no more than 3%.

VAT is 25% (reduced rates, 12% and 6%).

Performance

Real GDP growth rates (based on OECD statistics):

2008	2009	2010	2011	2012	2013	2014	2015	2016	2017
−0·7%	−5·1%	5·7%	2·7%	0·0%	1·2%	2·7%	4·2%	2·5%	2·4%

Sweden's total GDP in 2017 was US$538·0bn.

Banking and Finance

The central bank and bank of issue is the Sveriges Riksbank. The bank has 11 trustees, elected by parliament, and is managed by a directorate, including the governor, appointed by the trustees. The *Governor* is Stefan Ingves, appointed for a six-year term. In 2008 there were 118 banks (30 Swedish commercial banks, 33 foreign banks, 53 savings banks and two co-operative banks). Bank deposits from the public in 2008 amounted to 2,201bn. kr.; lending to the public in 2008 amounted to 3,033bn. kr. The largest banks are Nordea Bank AB (generally known as Nordea; previously MeritaNorbanken, formed in 1997 when Nordbanken of Sweden merged with Merita of Finland), Handelsbanken, Skandinavska Enskilda Banken (generally known as SEB) and Swedbank (formerly FöreningsSparbanken). In April 2000 MeritaNordbanken acquired Denmark's Unidanmark, thereby becoming the Nordic region's biggest bank in terms of assets. It became Nordea Bank AB in Dec. 2001. By 2009 approximately 71% of the Swedish population were using online banking.

In June 2012 Sweden's gross external debt totalled US$1,006,665m.

There is a stock exchange in Stockholm.

Energy and Natural Resources

In 2007 Sweden obtained 31% of its energy from oil, down from 77% in 1970. It aims to end fossil fuel dependency completely by 2020. In 2011, 46·8% of energy consumption came from renewables (wind power, solar power, hydro-electric power, tidal power, geothermal energy and biomass), compared to the European Union average of 13·0%. Sweden has by some margin the highest proportion of its energy consumption coming from renewables of any EU member country. A target of 49% has been set by the EU for 2020.

Environment

Carbon dioxide emissions from the consumption of energy in 2011 were the equivalent of 5·9 tonnes per capita (compared to the European average of 7·1 tonnes per capita). Sweden's greenhouse gas emissions fell by 34·8% between 1990 and 2012.

An *Environmental Performance Index* compiled in 2016 ranked Sweden third in the world behind Finland and Iceland, with 90·4%. The index examined various factors in nine areas—agriculture, air quality, biodiversity and habitat, climate and energy, fisheries, forests, health impacts, water and sanitation, and water resources. In 2012, 47% of municipal waste was recycled or composted (compared to the European Union average of 42%) with only 1% going to landfill.

Electricity

Sweden is rich in hydro-power resources. Installed capacity was 35,227 MW in 2011, including 16,577 MW in hydro-electric plants, 9,323 MW in nuclear plants and 6,546 MW in thermal plants. Electricity production in 2011 was 150,376m. kWh; consumption was 143,143 kWh. In 2011 consumption per capita was 15,149 kWh. Renewable sources accounted for 61·8% of electricity consumption in 2013 (up from 53·6% in 2008). A referendum of 1980 called for the phasing out of nuclear power by 2010. In Feb. 1997 the government began denuclearization by designating one of the 12 reactors for decommissioning. However, in Feb. 2009 the government announced an end to the 30-year ban on nuclear plant construction. In 2014 there were ten nuclear reactors in operation.

Minerals

Sweden is a leading producer of iron ore with around 2% of the world's total output. It is the largest iron ore exporter in Europe. There are also deposits of copper, gold, lead, zinc and alum shale containing oil and uranium. Iron ore produced, 2005, 23·3m. tonnes; zinc (mine output, zinc content), 214,600 tonnes; copper (mine output, copper content), 97,800 tonnes.

Agriculture

In 2005 agricultural land totalled 3,216,839 ha. There were 2,703,333 ha. of arable land in 2005 and 513,505 ha. of natural pasture on agricultural holdings of more than 2 ha. Of the land used for arable farming in 2007, 2–5 ha. holdings covered a total area of 49,162 ha.; 5·1–10 ha. holdings covered 99,272 ha.; 10·1–20 ha., 194,006; 20·1–30 ha., 175,331; 30·1–50 ha., 322,764; 50·1–100 ha., 629,899 and holdings larger than 100 ha. covered 1,177,258 ha. There were 72,609 agricultural enterprises in 2007 compared to 150,014 in 1971 and 282,187 in 1951. Around 37% of the enterprises were between 5 and 20 ha. In 2005 Sweden set aside 222,268 ha. (7·3% of its agricultural land—one of the highest proportions in the world) for the growth of organic crops.

Agriculture accounts for 5·8% of exports and 7·9% of imports. The agricultural sector employs 3% of the workforce.

Chief crops	Area (1,000 ha.)			Production (1,000 tonnes)		
	2006	2007	2008	2006	2007	2008
Ley	1,055·1	1,081·1	1,114·3	2,425·0	2,720·8	2,326·1
Wheat	360·9	361·6	361·5	1,967·4	2,255·7	2,202·2
Sugar beet	44·2	40·7	36·8	2,189·0	2,137·7	1,974·9
Barley	315·1	326·7	405·8	1,110·6	1,439·0	1,671·6
Potatoes	28·2	28·4	26·9	777·8	789·0	853·2
Oats	206·1	207·9	227·6	624·4	889·8	820·0
Rye	23·5	24·7	27·6	115·4	137·6	168·8

Production (in 1,000 tonnes) in 2008: milk, 3,019; meat, 406; cheese, 114; butter, 39.

Livestock, 2008: pigs, 1,609,289; cattle, 1,558,381; sheep and lambs, 524,780; poultry, 7,194,759. There were 249,191 reindeer in Sami villages in 2007. Harvest of moose during open season 2008: 83,554.

Forestry

Forests form one of the country's greatest natural assets. The growing stock includes 42% spruce, 39% pine and 16% broad-leaved. In 2015 forests covered 28·07m. ha. (68% of the land area). Sweden's largest forest owner is Sveaskog, with holdings of 4·3m. ha. Since 2001 the company has been completely state-owned after taking over the part-privatized AssiDomän corporation. Public ownership (including the state) accounts for 19% of the forests, limited companies own 25% and the remaining 56% is in private hands. In 2011, 71·90m. cu. metres of roundwood were cut.

Fisheries

Total catch in 2012 was 151,609 tonnes (150,117 tonnes from marine waters and 1,492 tonnes from inland waters). In 2012 the fishing fleet consisted of 1,401 vessels totalling 30,705 GT. Imports of fishery commodities were valued at US$3,633m. in 2011 and exports at US$2,852m.

Industry

The leading companies by market capitalization in Sweden in May 2018 were: Atlas Copco, a global industrial group of companies (US$49·5bn.); Nordea Bank AB (US$43·0bn.); and Volvo Group, a multinational manufacturing company (US$37·1bn.).

Manufacturing is mainly based on metals and forest resources. Chemicals (especially petrochemicals), building materials and decorative glass and china are also important.

Industry groups	Sales value of production (gross) in 1m. kr. (2007)
Manufacturing industry	1,601,718
Food products, beverages and tobacco	123,671
Textiles and textile products, leather and leather products	11,965

(continued)

Industry groups	Sales value of production (gross) in 1m. kr. (2007)
Wood and wood products	90,112
Pulp, paper and paper products, publishers and printers	181,237
Coke, refined petroleum products and nuclear fuel	13,854
Chemicals, chemical products and man-made fibres	118,795
Rubber and plastic products	39,601
Other non-metallic mineral products	31,672
Basic metals	156,552
Fabricated metal products, machinery and equipment	787,711
Other manufacturing industries	46,549
Mines and quarries	28,166

Labour

The labour force in 2013 was 5,118,000 (4,631,000 in 2003). 80·9% of the population aged 15–64 was economically active in 2013. The female labour force participation rate is among the highest of any industrialized country, at 78·8% in 2013. Of those in employment in 2013, 78·3% worked in services, 19·3% in industry and 1·8% in agriculture. In that year 47·4% of the labour force was female. 52·4% of the labour force had a secondary education as the highest level and 35·3% had a tertiary education. The unemployment rate in Dec. 2018 was 6·4% (down slightly from 6·7% in 2017 as a whole); youth unemployment was 24·0% in the third quarter of 2012.

International Trade

Imports and Exports

Imports and exports (in 1m. kr.):

	2004	2005	2006	2007	2008
Imports	739,203	833,757	939,730	1,030,100	1,088,990
Exports	904,532	977,280	1,089,095	1,140,032	1,194,559

Breakdown by Standard International Trade Classification (SITC, revision 3) categories (value in 1bn. kr.):

	Imports		Exports	
	2006	2007	2006	2007
0. Food and live animals	59·7	64·6	31·4	33·4
1. Beverages and tobacco	7·6	8·1	5·8	6·5
2. Crude materials	31·4	37·3	63·9	69·7
3. Fuels and lubricants	117·5	113·6	64·4	63·0
4. Animal and vegetable oils	3·5	3·0	1·5	1·2
5. Chemicals	98·2	110·5	125·2	126·1
6. Manufactured goods	143·6	165·5	218·3	238·5
7. Machinery and transport equipment	366·4	398·8	481·2	502·2
8. Miscellaneous manufactured items	111·4	118·7	94·3	97·8
9. Other	0·5	1·1	3·2	3·1

Principal imports in 2007 (in 1bn. kr.): road vehicles, 111·7; petroleum and petroleum products, 98·9; electrical machines, apparatus and appliances, 65·5; telecommunications, sound recording and similar appliances, 54·6; iron and steel, 50·1. Principal exports in 2007 (in 1bn. kr.): road vehicles, 154·8; iron and steel, 77·4; telecommunications, sound recording and similar appliances, 77·0; paper, paperboard and manufactures thereof, 73·2; medical and pharmaceutical preparations, 59·2. Machinery and transport equipment accounts for some 44% of Swedish exports. This includes the mobile phone sector, which is the largest product group in the Swedish export market.

Imports and exports by countries (value in 1bn. kr.):

	Imports from		Exports to	
	2007	2008	2007	2008
Denmark	94·1	102·7	84·1	88·3
Finland	64·0	62·4	71·3	75·8
France	50·8	54·6	57·0	58·4
Germany	188·6	190·9	119·1	123·9
Netherlands	62·5	64·7	57·6	60·9
Norway	88·0	97·2	107·3	113·5
UK	74·8	68·8	81·6	87·5
USA	32·0	33·7	86·5	78·7

In 2008 fellow EU member countries accounted for 69·7% of imports and 60·0% of exports.

Communications

A 16-km long fixed link with Denmark was opened in July 2000 when the Öresund motorway and railway bridge between Malmö and Copenhagen was completed.

Roads

In 2009 there were 215,597 km of roads open to the public of which 98,467 km were state-administered roads (main roads, 15,329 km; secondary roads, 83,138 km). There were also 1,855 km of motorway. 79% of all roads in 2005 were surfaced. Motor vehicles in 2008 included 4,279,000 passenger cars, 510,000 lorries, 13,000 buses and 489,000 motorcycles and mopeds. There were 1,015,997 Volvos, 434,757 Saabs, 343,060 Fords and 327,379 Volkswagens registered in 2006. Sweden has the lowest death rate in road accidents of any industrialized country, at 2·7 deaths per 100,000 people in 2013. 260 people were killed in traffic accidents in 2013.

Rail

Total length of railways at 31 Dec. 2012 was 11,136 km (8,194 km electrified). In 2012, 193m. passengers and 66m. tonnes of freight were carried. There is a metro in Stockholm (110 km), and tram/light rail networks in Stockholm (8 km), Gothenburg (118 km) and Norrköping (13 km).

Civil Aviation

The main international airports are at Stockholm (Arlanda), Gothenburg (Landvetter), Stockholm (Skavsta) and Malmö (Sturup). The Scandinavian Airlines System (SAS) resulted from the 1950 merger of the three former Scandinavian airlines. It is now known as Scandinavian Airlines. SAS Sverige AB is the Swedish partner (SAS Denmark A/S and SAS Norge ASA being the other two). The Swedish government is the principal shareholder of SAS with a 14·8% share. The government of Denmark owns 14·2%. The remaining shares are listed on the stock exchanges of Stockholm, Copenhagen and Oslo. SAS had a market capitalization in Oct. 2009 of 11,918m. kr. and an operating revenue in 2008 of 53,195m. kr.

Braathens Regional Airlines (BRA), a Sweden-based carrier, operates domestic flights and also flies to Helsinki in Finland.

In 2008 Stockholm (Arlanda) handled 18,136,165 passengers (13,281,466 on international flights) and 187,000 tonnes of freight. Gothenburg (Landvetter) was the second busiest airport, handling 4,303,722 passengers (3,158,822 on international flights) and 100,000 tonnes of freight. Malmö handled 1,882,428 passengers in 2006 (1,181,970 on domestic flights).

Shipping

The mercantile marine consisted on 31 Dec. 2008 of 1,036 vessels of 4·53m. GT. Cargo vessels entering Swedish ports in 2008 numbered 19,396 (125·74m. GT) while there were 75,343 passenger ferries (1,011·83m. GT). The number of cargo vessels leaving Swedish ports in 2008 totalled 19,389 (125·47m. GT) and the number of passenger ferries leaving was 75,636 (1,015·82m. GT).

The busiest port is Gothenburg. In 2007 a total of 42·33m. tonnes of goods were loaded and unloaded there (39·46m. tonnes unloaded from and loaded to foreign ports). Other major ports are Brofjorden, Trelleborg, Malmö and Luleå.

Telecommunications

In 2012 there were 4,169,000 main (fixed) telephone lines. In the same year mobile phone subscriptions numbered 11,848,000 (1,254·7 per 1,000 persons). In June 2000 the state sold off a 30% stake in the Swedish telecommunications operator Telia. In Dec. 2002 Telia and the Finnish telecommunications operator Sonera merged to become TeliaSonera. The Swedish state owns 37·3%. In 2013, 94·8% of the population aged 16–74 were internet users. In the same year there were 110·3 wireless broadband subscriptions per 100 inhabitants and 32·6 fixed broadband subscriptions per 100. In March 2012 there were 4·5m. Facebook users.

According to the World Economic Forum's *Global Information Technology Report 2010–11* Sweden is ranked first in the world in benefitting from global information technology developments.

Social Institutions

According to the 2017 *Fragile States Index*—a list published jointly by the Fund for Peace and *Foreign Policy* magazine—Sweden was ranked as the country fifth least vulnerable to conflict or collapse. The index is based on 12 indicators of state vulnerability across social, political and economic categories.

Justice

Sweden has two parallel types of courts—general courts that deal with criminal and civil cases and general administrative courts that deal with cases related to public administration. The general courts have three instances: district courts, courts of appeal and the Supreme Court. There are 60 district courts, of which 23 also serve as real estate courts and four courts of appeal. The administrative courts also have three instances: 23 county administrative courts, four administrative courts of appeal and the Supreme Administrative Court. In addition, a number of special courts and tribunals have been established to hear specific kinds of cases and matters.

Every district court, court of appeal, county administrative court and administrative court of appeal has a number of lay judges. These take part in the adjudication of both specific concrete issues and matters of law; each has the right to vote.

Criminal cases are normally tried by one judge and three lay judges. Civil disputes are normally heard by a single judge or three judges. In the courts of appeal, criminal cases are determined by three judges and two lay judges. Civil cases are tried by three or four judges. In the settlement of family cases, lay judges take part in the proceedings in both the district court and in the court of appeal. Proceedings in the general administrative courts are in writing; i.e. the court determines the case on the basis of correspondences between the parties. Nevertheless, it is also possible to hold a hearing. The cases are determined by a single judge or one judge and three lay judges. In the administrative court of appeal, cases are normally heard by three judges or three judges and two lay judges.

Those who lack the means to take advantage of their rights are entitled to legal aid. Everyone suspected of a serious crime or taken into custody has the right to a public counsel (advocate). The title advocate can only be used by accredited members of the Swedish Bar Association. Qualifying as an advocate requires extensive theoretical and practical training. All advocates in Sweden are employed in the private sector.

The control over the way in which public authorities fulfil their commitments is exercised by the Parliamentary Ombudsmen and the Chancellor of Justice. In 2008–09 the Ombudsmen received 6,918 cases altogether, of which 68 were instituted on their own initiative. Sweden has no constitutional court. However, in each particular case the courts do have a certain right to ascertain whether a statute meets the standards set out by superordinate provisions.

The population in penal institutions in Oct. 2012 was 6,364 (67 per 100,000 of national population). There are 56 prisons spread throughout the country. Sweden was ranked seventh of 102 countries for criminal justice and sixth for civil justice in the 2015 World Justice Project *Rule of Law Index*, which provides data on how the rule of law is experienced by the general public across eight categories.

There were 209 incidents of murder, manslaughter and assault resulting in death in 2008 (121 in 1990 and 258 in 2007).

Education

In 2008–09 there were 906,189 pupils in 4,755 compulsory schools. In secondary education at the higher stage (the integrated upper secondary school) there were 396,336 pupils in Oct. 2008 (excluding pupils in the fourth year of the technical course regarded as third-level education). The folk high schools, 'people's colleges', had 27,508 pupils on courses of more than 15 weeks in the autumn of 2008. Around a fifth of pupils attend independent schools ('free schools'), which are non-fee paying public schools owned and run by a variety of educational providers.

In municipal adult education there were 170,318 students in 2007–08.

There are also special schools for pupils with visual and hearing impairments (516 pupils in 2008) and for those who are intellectually disabled (22,595 pupils).

In 2007–08 there were 384,733 students enrolled for undergraduate studies in integrated institutions for higher education. The number of students enrolled for postgraduate studies in 2008 was 16,922.

In 2010 public expenditure on education came to 7·0% of GDP (and accounted for 13·4% of total government expenditure). The adult literacy rate is at least 99%.

Health

In 2008 there were 29,100 doctors, 4,100 dentists, 71,400 nurses and midwives and 25,899 hospital beds. In 2008 Sweden spent 9·4% of its GDP on health.

In 2010, 14% of Swedes aged 15 and over smoked on a daily basis (males, 13%; females, 15%), among the lowest percentages of any industrialized country.

Welfare

Social insurance benefits are granted mainly according to uniform statutory principles. All persons resident in Sweden are covered, regardless of citizenship. All schemes are compulsory, except for unemployment insurance. Benefits are usually income-related. Most social security schemes are at present undergoing extensive discussion and changes.

Type of social insurance scheme	Payments 2008 (in 1m. kr.)
Old-age pension	219,376
Sickness insurance	96,748
Parental insurance	28,705
Child allowance	23,389
Attendance allowance	19,858
Survivor's pension	16,700
Unemployment insurance	13,592
Housing supplement	11,472
Work injury insurance	5,425

Under a Pension Reform Plan Sweden is one of the world's leaders in the shift to private pension systems. In the new system each worker's future pension will be based on the amount of money accumulated in two separate individual accounts. The bulk of retirement income will come from a notional account maintained by the government on behalf of the individual, but a significant portion of retirement income will come from a private individual account. There are two types of pension—the income pension and the premium pension. The income pension comes under a pay-as-you-go system, with the premium pension based on contributions invested in a fund chosen by the insured person.

There is also a guarantee pension for those aged 65 and resident in Sweden for the last three years but without an earnings-related pension. Its value in 2010 was 90,312 kr. for a single pensioner and 80,560 kr. for a married pensioner.

Religion

The Swedish Lutheran Church was disestablished in 2000. It is headed by Archbishop Antje Jackelén (b. 1955) and has its metropolitan see at Uppsala. In 2008 there were 13 bishoprics and 1,802 parishes. The clergy are chiefly supported from the parishes and the proceeds of the church lands. Around 70% of the population, equivalent to 6·6m. people, belong to the Church of Sweden. Other denominations, in 2010: Pentecostal Movement, 82,769 members; The Mission Covenant Church of Sweden, 60,445; InterAct, 32,138; Salvation Army, 5,159 soldiers; The Baptist Union of Sweden, 17,441; Swedish Alliance Mission, 13,687. There were also 96,950 Roman Catholics (under a Bishop resident at Stockholm). The Orthodox and Oriental churches number around 120,000 members. In Feb. 2019 there was one Roman Catholic cardinal.

Although there are no official statistics on the number of Muslims, their numbers were estimated at 450,000–500,000 in 2010. An estimated 20,000 Jews lived in Sweden in 2010.

Culture

World Heritage Sites

There are 15 sites under Swedish jurisdiction that appear on the UNESCO World Heritage List: the royal palace of Drottningholm (1991); the Viking settlements of Birka and Hovgården (1993); the Engelsberg ironworks (1993); the Bronze Age rock carvings in Tanum (1994); Skogskyrkogården cemetery (1994); the Hanseatic town of Visby (1995); the Lapponian area (home of the Sami people in the Arctic circle) (1996); the church town of Gammelstad in Luleå (1996); the naval port of Karlskrona (1998); the Kvarken Archipelago and High Coast (2000 and 2006), shared with Finland; the agricultural landscape of Southern Öland (2000); the Mining Area of the Great Copper Mountain in Falun (2001); the Varberg Radio Station (2004) at Grimeton in southern Sweden; the Struve Geodetic Arc (2005), a chain of survey triangulations spanning from Norway to the Black Sea that helped establish the exact shape and size of the earth and is shared with nine other countries; and the Decorated Farmhouses of Hälsingland (2012), an ensemble of timber buildings in northeastern Sweden, a fusion of local building and folk art traditions.

Press

In 2014 there were 84 daily newspapers (of which 79 were paid-for and five were free) with an average daily circulation of 3,082,000. There were also 186 non-dailies in 2014. The leading paper in terms of circulation in 2014 was the free *Lokaltidningen Mitt i*, with an average daily circulation of 859,000 copies. The paid-for daily papers with the highest circulation are *Dagens Nyheter*, with an average daily circulation of 283,000 in 2013, and *Göteborgs-Posten*, with an average daily circulation of 177,000 in 2014. In 2011 there were 70 newspaper online editions with 10,080,000 unique monthly visitors. In 2010 a total of 21,631 book titles were published.

Tourism

In 2013 Swedes stayed 22,557,815 nights in hotels in Sweden and 11,223,586 at campsites; and foreign visitors stayed 6,874,759 nights in hotels and 3,273,264 at campsites. The leading countries of residence of the foreign visitors in 2013 were Norway (2,961,772 nights in hotels and at campsites), Germany, Denmark and the United Kingdom.

Festivals

Important traditional festivals include Lucia, held in Dec., and Walpurgis Night, a spring celebration held in April. The eight-day Malmö Festival includes live music and other cultural events and is held annually in Aug.

Diplomatic Representatives

Of Sweden in the United Kingdom (11 Montagu Pl., London, W1H 2AL)
Ambassador: Torbjörn Sohlström.

Of the United Kingdom in Sweden (Skarpögatan 6–8, Box 27819, S-115 93 Stockholm)
Ambassador: David Cairns.

Of Sweden in the USA (2900 K St., NW, Washington, D.C., 20007)
Ambassador: Karin Ulrika Olofsdotter.

Of the USA in Sweden (Dag Hammarskjölds Väg 31, S-115 89 Stockholm)
Ambassador: Vacant.
Chargé d'Affaires a.i.: Clifford Bond.

Of Sweden to the United Nations
Ambassador: Olof Skoog.

Of Sweden to the European Union
Permanent Representative: Lars Danielsson.

Further Reading

Statistics Sweden. *Statistik Årsbok/Statistical Yearbook of Sweden.—Historisk statistik för Sverige* (Historical Statistics of Sweden). 1914–2014.—*Allmän månadsstatistik* (Monthly Digest of Swedish Statistics). 1969–2002.—*Statistiska meddelanden* (Statistical Reports). From 1963

Henrekson, M., *An Economic Analysis of Swedish Government Expenditure.* 1992

Nordstrom, Byron J., *The History of Sweden.* 2002

Petersson, O., *Swedish Government and Politics.* 1994

Schön, Lennart, *An Economic History of Sweden.* 2012

Sejersted, Francis, *The Age of Social Democracy: Norway and Sweden in the Twentieth Century.* 2011

Sveriges statskalender. Annual, from 1813

National library: Kungliga Biblioteket, PO Box 5039, SE–102 41 Stockholm.

National Statistical Office: Statistics Sweden, PO Box 24300, SE–104 51 Stockholm.

Website: http://www.scb.se

Swedish Institute Website: http://www.si.se

Switzerland

Schweizerische Eidtgenossenschaft—Confédération Suisse—Confederazione Svizzera (Swiss Confederation)

Capital: Berne
Population projection, 2020: 8·67m.
GNI per capita, 2017: (PPP$) 57,625
HDI/world rank, 2017: 0·944/2
Internet domain extension: .ch

Key Historical Events

Neolithic settlements from around 3,000 BC have been found. Celtic clans settled in fertile valleys in parts of present-day Switzerland from around 1,500 BC, with the Raetians in the east and the Helvetti to the west. A Bronze Age Celtic civilization reached its height around 100 BC. An attempt by the Helvetti to spread west into Gaul was quashed by Julius Caesar in 58 BC. As the Roman Empire expanded northward and westward, Switzerland came under its domain, centred on Aventicum (Avenches). The Romans constructed a road network from the strategically important Alpine passes but attempts to conquer Germanic tribes to the north and east of the Rhine were thwarted in 9 AD. Garrisons along the Rhine from Lake Constance to Basle were maintained until Roman forces withdrew in 401.

The Germanic Alemanni tribe became dominant in northern and central Switzerland as Rome's influence declined, while Latin-speaking Burgundians held sway in the Jura mountains. Celtic tribes were gradually subsumed over the following centuries. Frankish rulers established monasteries, enabling the spread of Christianity and feudalism throughout west-central Europe in the seventh and eighth centuries. Following the signing of the Treaty of Verdun in 840 western and southwest Switzerland came under the jurisdiction of the Burgundian king, Lothair I, and the north and east formed part of the domain of Louis the German. The Burgundian lands became part of the Holy Roman Empire in 1033, while various independent dukedoms emerged in the north and east, notably Swabia, Zahringen, Savoy and Kyberg. The Kyberg domains of central Switzerland passed to the Habsburgs in 1264. The expansion of this dynasty led to three mountain-based clans—the Uri, the Schwyz and the Unterwalden—forming a defensive league. Their agreement, renewed in 1291, is considered the founding document of the Swiss nation. The league defeated the Habsburgs at Mortgarten in 1315 and by 1353 the confederation had added the cantons of Glarus and Zug and the city states of Lucerne, Zürich and Berne, forming the 'Old Federation' of eight states within the Holy Roman Empire.

Defeat at the hands of French forces at Marignano in 1515 led the Swiss confederation to form a 'perpetual alliance' with France and marked the start of a neutral stance. Relations between the cantons deteriorated in the 16th century and during the Reformation, when the city-states of Zürich, Berne, Basle and St Gallen adopted Protestantism while Catholicism was retained in the four forest cantons. The 1531 Treaty of Kappel ended the civil war and preserved Catholicism in the rural south, though religious tensions continued in the late 16th century with the rural cantons and city states linked only by neutrality in the Thirty Years War. The War's end in 1648 and the subsequent Peace of Westphalia saw Switzerland declared independent of the Holy Roman Empire.

Geneva, Basle, Berne and Zürich grew prosperous in the 18th century, becoming Enlightenment centres of intellectual and cultural achievement. Power remained with the oligarchs until the arrival of French Revolutionary troops in their offensive against Austrian and Russian forces in 1798. Napoleon's Act of Mediation in 1803 partially restored political power to the cantons but it was not until 1815 that the Congress of Vienna re-established Switzerland's independence, its perpetual neutrality guaranteed by Austria, France, Great Britain, Portugal, Prussia, Spain and Sweden.

In 1848 a new constitution was approved following disputes between Protestant and Catholic cantons. The 22 cantons were linked by a federal government (consisting of a bicameral parliament that elected a seven-member governing council) and a federal tribunal to rule on intra-cantonal disputes. This constitution was revised in 1874 to allow for national and local referenda on a range of issues.

Switzerland maintained its status of armed neutrality in the First World War but was unable to avoid mass unemployment, leading to a national strike in 1918 and demands for social security. The 1919 Treaty of Versailles reaffirmed Switzerland's neutrality and a year later it joined the League of Nations (based in Geneva). The Federal Council issued a declaration of neutrality at the start of the Second World War and much effort went in to shoring up defences and remaining self-sufficient while surrounded by the Axis powers. The Swiss government subsequently expressed regrets about the country's behaviour in the Second World War following a report by an independent panel of historians on relations with the Nazis.

In 1959 Switzerland became a founding member of the European Free Trade Association but has remained outside the European Union. It joined the UN by a narrow majority in a referendum in 2002. In 2005 Switzerland signed up to the Schengen accord.

Territory and Population

Switzerland is bounded in the west and northwest by France, north by Germany, east by Austria and Liechtenstein and south by Italy. Area and population by canton (with date of establishment):

Canton	Area (sq. km)	Population (31 Dec. 2016)
Uri (1291)	1,077	36,145
Schwyz (1291)	908	155,863
Obwalden (1291)	491	37,378
Nidwalden (1291)	276	42,556
Lucerne (1332)	1,493	403,397
Zürich (1351)	1,729	1,487,969
Glarus (Glaris) (1352)	685	40,147
Zug (1352)	239	123,948
Fribourg (Freiburg) (1481)	1,671	311,914
Solothurn (Soleure) (1481)	791	269,441
Basel-Town (Bâle-V.) (1501)	37	193,070
Basel-Country (Bâle-C.) (1501)	518	285,624
Schaffhausen (Schaffhouse) (1501)	298	80,769
Appenzell-Outer Rhoden (1513)	243	54,954
Appenzell-Inner Rhoden (1513)	173	16,003
Berne (Bern) (1553)	5,959	1,026,513
St Gallen (St Gall) (1803)	2,026	502,552
Graubünden (Grisons) (1803)	7,105	197,550
Aargau (Argovie) (1803)	1,404	663,462
Thurgau (Thurgovie) (1803)	991	270,709
Ticino (Tessin) (1803)	2,812	354,375
Vaud (Waadt) (1803)	3,212	784,822
Valais (Wallis) (1815)	5,224	339,176
Neuchâtel (Neuenburg) (1815)	803	178,567
Geneva (Genève) (1815)	282	489,524
Jura (1979)	838	73,122
Total	*41,285*	*8,419,550*

Switzerland last had a traditional decennial census in 2000; it now has an annual census using a register-based method of calculating the population.

In Dec. 2016 there were 4,246,113 females and 2,101,146 resident foreign nationals out of a total population of 8,419,550. In the same year foreign nationals made up 25% of the population, one of the highest proportions in Western Europe. In 2011, 73·7% of the population lived in urban areas. Population density in 2016 was 204 per sq. km.

The UN gives a projected population for 2020 of 8·67m.

German, French, Italian and Romansch (which is spoken mostly in Graubünden) are the official languages. German is spoken by the majority of inhabitants in 19 of the 26 cantons, French in Fribourg, Vaud, Valais, Neuchâtel, Jura and Geneva, and Italian in Ticino. In 2013, 64·5% of the population aged over 15 gave German as their main language, 22·6% French, 8·3% Italian and 0·5% Romansch.

At the end of 2016 the five largest cities were Zürich (402,800); Geneva (199,000); Basle (171,000); Lausanne (137,800); Berne (133,100). In 2016 the population figures of conurbations were: Zürich, 1,354,100; Geneva, 585,400; Basle, 545,300; Lausanne, 415,600; Berne, 415,500; other towns, 2016 (and their conurbations), Winterthur, 109,800 (140,200); Lucerne, 81,600 (228,300); St Gallen, 75,500 (166,400); Lugano, 63,900 (151,700); Biel, 54,500 (105,400).

Social Statistics

Statistics for calendar years:

	Live births	Marriages	Divorces	Deaths
2011	80,808	42,083	17,566	62,091
2012	82,164	42,654	17,550	64,173
2013	82,731	39,794	17,119	64,961
2014	85,287	41,891	16,737	63,938
2015	86,559	41,437	16,960	67,606

Rates (2014, per 1,000 population): birth, 10·4; death, 7·8; marriage, 5·1; divorce, 2·0. In 2015 the most popular age range for marrying was 30–34 for males and 25–29 for females. Expectation of life, 2014: males, 81·0 years; females, 85·2. In 2014 the suicide rate per 100,000 population was 10·5 (males, 15·8; females, 5·6). Annual population growth rate, 2010–15, 1·1%. Infant mortality, 2014, 3·9 per 1,000 live births; fertility rate, 2014, 1·5 births per woman. In 2015 Switzerland received 39,523 asylum applications, up from 23,765 in 2014.

Climate

The climate is largely dictated by relief and altitude, and includes continental and mountain types. Summers are generally warm, with quite considerable rainfall; winters are fine, with clear, cold air. Berne, Jan. 32°F (0°C), July, 65°F (18·5°C). Annual rainfall 39·4" (986 mm).

Constitution and Government

A new constitution was accepted on 18 April 1999 in a popular vote and came into effect on 1 Jan. 2000, replacing the constitution dating from 1874. Switzerland is a republic. The highest authority is vested in the electorate, i.e. all Swiss citizens over 18. This electorate, besides electing its representatives to the Parliament, has the voting power on amendments to, or on the revision of, the Constitution as well as on Switzerland joining international organizations for collective security or supranational communities (mandatory referendum). It also takes decisions on laws and certain international treaties if requested by 50,000 voters or eight cantons (facultative referendum), and it has the right of initiating constitutional amendments, the support required for such demands being 100,000 voters (popular initiative). The Swiss vote in more referendums—three or four a year—than any other nation. A mandatory referendum and a constitutional amendment demanded by popular initiative require a double majority (a majority of the voters and a majority of the cantons voting in favour of the proposal) to be accepted while a facultative referendum is accepted if a majority of the voters vote in favour of the proposal. Between 1848 and Feb. 2019, 216 initiatives were put to the vote but only 22 were adopted. The highest turnout for a popular initiative has been 86·3% and the lowest 26·7%.

The Federal government is responsible for legislating matters of foreign relations, defence (within the framework of its powers), professional education and technical universities, protection of the environment, water, public works, road traffic, nuclear energy, foreign trade, social security, residence and domicile of foreigners, civil law, banking and insurance, monetary policy and economic development. It is also responsible for formulating policy concerning statistics gathering, sport, forests, fishery and hunting, post and telecommunications, radio and television, private economic activity, competition policy, alcohol and gambling.

The legislative authority is vested in a parliament of two chambers: the Council of States (*Ständerat/Conseil des États*) and the National Council (*Nationalrat/Conseil National*). The Council of States is composed of 46 members, chosen and paid by the 23 cantons of the Confederation, two for each canton. The mode of their election and the term of membership depend on the canton. Three of the cantons are politically divided—Basle into Town and Country, Appenzell into Outer-Rhoden and Inner-Rhoden, and Unterwalden into Obwalden and Nidwalden. Each of these 'half-cantons' sends one member to the State Council. The Swiss parliament is a militia/semi-professional parliament.

The National Council has 200 members directly elected for four years, in proportion to the population of the cantons, with the proviso that each canton or half-canton is represented by at least one member. The members are paid from federal funds. The parliament sits for at least four ordinary three-week sessions annually. Extraordinary sessions can be held if necessary and if demanded by the Federal Council, 25% of the National Council or five cantons.

The 200 seats are distributed among the cantons according to population size:

Zürich	34
Berne	26
Vaud (Waadt)	18
Aargau (Argovie)	15
St Gallen (St Gall)	12
Geneva	11
Lucerne	10
Ticino (Tessin)	8
Basel-Country (Bâle-C.)	7
Fribourg (Freiburg)	7
Solothurn (Soleure)	7
Valais (Wallis)	7
Thurgau (Thurgovie)	6
Basel-Town (Bâle-V.)	5
Graubünden (Grisons)	5
Neuchâtel (Neuenburg)	5
Schwyz	4
Zug	3
Jura	2
Schaffhausen (Schaffhouse)	2
Appenzell Inner-Rhoden	1
Appenzell Outer-Rhoden	1
Glarus	1
Nidwalden	1
Obwalden	1
Uri	1

A general election takes place by ballot every four years. Every citizen of the republic aged 18 or over is entitled to a vote, and any voter may be elected a deputy. Laws passed by both chambers may be submitted to direct popular vote, when 50,000 citizens or eight cantons demand it; the vote can be only 'Yes' or 'No'. This principle, called the *referendum*, is frequently acted on.

The chief executive authority is deputed to the *Bundesrat* (*Conseil Fédéral* or Federal Council), consisting of seven members, elected for four years by the *United Federal Assembly*, i.e. joint sessions of both chambers, such as to represent both the different geographical regions and language communities. The members of this council must not hold any other office in the Confederation or cantons, nor engage in any calling or business. In the

Federal Parliament legislation may be introduced either by a member, or by either chamber, or by the Federal Council (but not by the people). Every citizen who has a vote for the National Council is eligible to become a member of the executive.

The *President* of the Federal Council (called President of the Confederation) and the *Vice-President* are the first magistrates of the Confederation. Both are elected by the United Federal Assembly for one calendar year from among the Federal Councillors, and are not immediately re-eligible to the same offices. The Vice-President, however, may be, and usually is, elected to succeed the outgoing President.

The seven members of the Federal Council act as ministers, or chiefs of the seven administrative departments of the republic. The city of Berne is the seat of the Federal Council and the central administrative authorities.

National Anthem

'Trittst im Morgenrot daher'/'Sur nos monts quand le soleil'/'Quando il ciel' di porpora' ('When the morning skies grow red'); German words by Leonhard Widmer, French by Charles Chatelanat, Italian by Camillo Valsangiacomo, tune by Alberich Zwyssig.

Government Chronology

Presidents since 1945. (BDP/PBD = Conservative Democratic Party of Switzerland; CVP/PDC = Christian Democratic People's Party; FDP/PLR = FDP.The Liberals; FDP/PRD = Free Democratic Party/Radical Democratic Party; SPS/PSS = Social Democratic Party of Switzerland; SVP/UDC = Swiss People's Party/Centre Democratic Union)

1945	SVP/UDC	Adolf Eduard von Steiger
1946	FDP/PRD	Karl Kobelt
1947	CVP/PDC	Philipp Etter
1948	CVP/PDC	Enrico Celio
1949	SPS/PSS	Ernst Nobs
1950	FDP/PRD	Max-Édouard Petitpierre
1951	SVP/UDC	Adolf Eduard von Steiger
1952	FDP/PRD	Karl Kobelt
1953	CVP/PDC	Philipp Etter
1954	FDP/PRD	Rodolphe Rubattel
1955	FDP/PRD	Max-Édouard Petitpierre
1956	SVP/UDC	Markus Feldmann
1957	FDP/PRD	Hans Streuli
1958	CVP/PDC	Thomas Emil Leo Holenstein
1959	FDP/PRD	Paul Chaudet
1960	FDP/PRD	Max-Édouard Petitpierre
1961	SVP/UDC	Friedrich Traugott Wahlen
1962	FDP/PRD	Paul Chaudet
1963	SPS/PSS	Willy Spühler
1964	CVP/PDC	Ludwig von Moos
1965	SPS/PSS	Hans-Peter Tschudi
1966	FDP/PRD	Hans Schaffner
1967	CVP/PDC	Roger Bonvin
1968	SPS/PSS	Willy Spühler
1969	CVP/PDC	Ludwig von Moos
1970	SPS/PSS	Hans-Peter Tschudi
1971	SVP/UDC	Rudolf Gnägi
1972	FDP/PRD	Nello Celio
1973	CVP/PDC	Roger Bonvin
1974	FDP/PRD	Ernst Brugger
1975	SPS/PSS	Pierre Graber
1976	SVP/UDC	Rudolf Gnägi
1977	CVP/PDC	Kurt Furgler
1978	SPS/PSS	Willi Ritschard
1979	CVP/PDC	Hans Hürlimann
1980	FDP/PRD	Georges-André Chevallaz

(*continued*)

1981	CVP/PDC	Kurt Furgler
1982	FDP/PRD	Fritz Honegger
1983	SPS/PSS	Pierre Aubert
1984	SVP/UDC	Leon Schlumpf
1985	CVP/PDC	Kurt Furgler
1986	CVP/PDC	Alphons Egli
1987	SPS/PSS	Pierre Aubert
1988	SPS/PSS	Otto Stich
1989	FDP/PRD	Jean-Pascal Delamuraz
1990	CVP/PDC	Arnold Koller
1991	CVP/PDC	Flavio Cotti
1992	SPS/PSS	René Felber
1993	SVP/UDC	Adolf Ogi
1994	SPS/PSS	Otto Stich
1995	FDP/PRD	Kaspar Villiger
1996	FDP/PRD	Jean-Pascal Delamuraz
1997	CVP/PDC	Arnold Koller
1998	CVP/PDC	Flavio Cotti
1999	SPS/PSS	Ruth Dreifuss
2000	SVP/UDC	Adolf Ogi
2001	SPS/PSS	Moritz Leuenberger
2002	FDP/PRD	Kaspar Villiger
2003	FDP/PRD	Pascal Couchepin
2004	CVP/PDC	Joseph Deiss
2005	SVP/UDC	Samuel Schmid
2006	SPS/PSS	Moritz Leuenberger
2007	SPS/PSS	Micheline Calmy-Rey
2008	FDP/PRD	Pascal Couchepin
2009	FDP/PLR	Hans-Rudolf Merz
2010	CVP/PDC	Doris Leuthard
2011	SPS/PSS	Micheline Calmy-Rey
2012	BDP/PBD	Eveline Widmer-Schlumpf
2013	SVP/UDC	Ueli Maurer
2014	FDP/PLR	Didier Burkhalter
2015	SPS/PSS	Simonetta Sommaruga
2016	FDP/PLR	Johann Schneider-Ammann
2017	CVP/PDC	Doris Leuthard
2018	SPS/PSS	Alain Berset
2019	SVP/UDC	Ueli Maurer

Recent Elections

In elections to the National Council on 18 Oct. 2015 the Swiss People's Party/Centre Democratic Union (SVP) took 29·4% of the vote (65 seats), the Social Democratic Party of Switzerland (SPS) 18·8% (43), FDP.The Liberals (FDP) 16·4% (33), the Christian Democratic People's Party (CVP) 11·6% (27), the Green Party (GPS) 7·1% (11), the Green Liberal Party (GLP) 4·6% (7), the Conservative Democratic Party of Switzerland (BDP) 4·1% (7), the Evangelical People's Party (EVP) 1·9% (2) and the Ticino League (LdT) 1·0% (2). The Christian Social Party, the Geneva Citizens' Movement and the Swiss Party of Labour won one seat each. Turnout was 48·4%.

In elections to the Council of States on the same day the CVP and the FDP both won 13 seats, the SPS 12, the SVP 5, the GPS 1 and the BDP 1. An independent also won a seat.

At an election held in the United Federal Assembly on 5 Dec. 2018 Ueli Maurer was elected president for 2019 with 201 votes out of 209; Simonetta Sommaruga was elected vice-president.

Current Government

In Feb. 2019 the Federal Council comprised:

President of the Confederation and Head of the Department of Finance: Ueli Maurer; b. 1950 (Swiss People's Party/SVP; sworn in 1 Jan. 2019).

Vice-President and Minister of Environment, Transport, Energy and Communications: Simonetta Sommaruga (Social Democratic Party of Switzerland/SPS; sworn in 1 Jan. 2019).

Minister of Defence, Civil Protection and Sport: Viola Amherd (CVP). *Economic Affairs, Education and Research:* Guy Parmelin (SVP). *Foreign Affairs:* Ignazio Cassis (FDP.The Liberals). *Home Affairs:* Alain Berset (SPS). *Justice and Police:* Karin Keller-Sutter (FDP.The Liberals). *Federal Authorities Website:* http://www.admin.ch

---

Current Leaders

Ueli Maurer

Position

President

Introduction

Ueli Maurer has twice served as president of the Swiss Federal Council, as well as heading up the Council's defence and finance departments.

Early Life

Maurer was born on 1 Dec. 1950 in Wetzikon, in the canton of Zürich. He served a commercial apprenticeship and managed a farmers' co-operative from 1974 to 1994. He was elected to the town council of Hinwil in 1978 and five years later entered the cantonal parliament of Zürich. In 1991 he became president of the cantonal parliament and was elected to the National Council. He was manager of the Zürich Farmers' Association from 1994–2008, leaving to become president of the Swiss Vegetable Producers' Association (a role he relinquished on nomination to the Federal Council).

In 1996 Maurer was chosen as president of the Swiss People's Party (SVP). Initially regarded as an acolyte of Christoph Blocher, the figurehead of the party's nationalist wing, Maurer proved himself an effective political operator. Under his leadership—which included controversially bullish stances on Switzerland's relations with the European Union, immigration and women's rights—the party became the country's most popular, doubling its share of the vote.

In Oct. 2007 Maurer resigned the SVP leadership after taking the party to its largest ever electoral victory. After narrowly failing to win a seat in the Council of States (the Federal Assembly's upper house), he took on the presidency of the SVP's Zürich division. Elected to the Federal Council in Dec. 2008 he assumed responsibility for the defence, civil protection and sports portfolios.

Career in Office

In the parliamentary vote to decide the new president held on 5 Dec. 2012, Maurer received 148 of a possible 202 votes and received backing from all parliamentary groups except the Green Party. During his presidency, Switzerland limited the number of residence permits granted to citizens from 17 EU countries.

Maurer joined the Federal Council once more on 8 Dec. 2015, and was voted to the Council presidency for a second time on 5 Dec. 2018, to serve in 2019. In Jan. 2019 he spoke of his desire to renegotiate the Swiss–EU framework agreement and to secure a free trade accord with the USA.

Defence

There are fortifications in all entrances to the Alps and on the important passes crossing the Alps and the Jura. Large-scale destruction of bridges, tunnels and defiles are prepared for an emergency.

Conscripts complete 18–21 weeks of basic training and then regular annual refresher training up to a set number of service days. In 2013 defence spending totalled US$5,038m. (US$630 per capita), representing 0·8% of GDP.

Army

There are about 4,000 regular soldiers, but some 220,000 conscripts undergo training annually (18 or 21 weeks recruit training at 20, six or seven refresher courses of 19 days every year between 21 and 30). Proposals ('Army XXI') implemented in 2004 envisaged an Armed Forces based on the three areas of promoting peace, defence and general civil affairs support. Troop levels were cut to 220,000 (120,000 conscripts, 20,000 recruits, 80,000 reservists).

Since 2004 Switzerland has a Chief of the Armed Forces in the rank of a lieutenant-general. In peacetime the Army has no general; in time of war the Federal Assembly in joint session of both Houses appoints a general.

In 1999 for the first time a small Swiss contingent was deployed outside the country, in Kosovo.

Navy

There is no Navy in the Swiss Armed Forces but the Land Forces include a small Marine component with patrol boats.

Air Force

The Air Force has five air base commands. The fighter squadrons are equipped with Swiss-built F-5E Tiger IIs and F/A-18s. Personnel (2011), 22,500 including air defence units and military airfield guard units, with 87 combat-capable aircraft.

International Relations

In a referendum in 1986 the electorate voted against UN membership, but in a further referendum on 4 March 2002, 54·6% of votes cast were in favour of joining. Switzerland officially became a member at the UN's General Assembly in Sept. 2002. An official application for membership of the EU was made in May 1992, but in Dec. 1992 the electorate voted against joining the European Economic Area. At a referendum in March 2001, 76·7% of voters rejected membership talks with the EU, with just 23·3% in favour; turnout was 55·1%.

Economy

Agriculture accounted for 0·7% of GDP in 2013, industry 26·1% and services 73·2%.

According to the anti-corruption organization Transparency International, Switzerland ranked equal third in the world in a 2018 survey of the countries with the least corruption in business and government. It received 85 out of 100 in the annual index.

Overview

Switzerland has a small economy but one of the highest living standards in the world. Owing to a lack of raw materials, prosperity is built on labour skills, a business-friendly environment and technological expertise. As well as banking and insurance, the economy is focused on micro-technology, hi-tech industry, biotechnology and pharmaceuticals. Small- and medium-sized businesses dominate. The favourable business climate attracted foreign direct investment (FDI) averaging 2·6% of GDP between 2010 and 2014. FDI in 2015 was put at US$68·8bn.

The central government oversees foreign policy, defence, pensions, postal services, telecommunications, railway services and currency management. All other responsibilities are dealt with at the canton level, notably economic regulation, education, health care and the judiciary. This system has led to large income disparities across cantons, with tax revenue per capita differing by as much as a factor of two. In 2004 a referendum approved the New Financial Equalization System, which provided a clearer division between federal and local responsibilities.

In 2000 the National Bank introduced a monetary policy framework aimed at keeping inflation below 2%. Inflation has remained low for many years, contained primarily by strong retail competition and a flexible labour market. It averaged 0·1% per year in the decade to 2017. In 2004 the authorities launched a reform agenda to open up sheltered sectors (i.e. sectors protected from foreign competition), reduce the role of the state, encourage external economic relations and improve the education system in a bid to boost competition and growth. Following these reforms growth accelerated and became broad-based, benefiting from buoyant global markets and supported by strong investment and private consumption.

Switzerland hosts the world's third largest financial market (with the financial sector accounting for approximately 12% of GDP in 2015 and employing 5·7% of the working population at the end of 2014). Consequently, it suffered in the global financial crisis when banks made large losses and the country's largest bank, UBS, had to be rescued by the government in late 2008. The economy went into recession in 2009, but strong growth in emerging markets (notably China, with which Switzerland has a free trade agreement) offset reduced demand from EU countries, which had normally absorbed half of all exports. Economic growth averaged 2·0% between 2010 and 2014, before falling back to closer to 1·5% in 2015 and 2016.

Financial regulations adopted in Jan. 2012 demanded that UBS and Credit Suisse bank hold additional capital and liquidity, and a countercyclical capital buffer requiring banks to build capital gradually as imbalances in the credit market develop was implemented in July 2012.

The Swiss National Bank (SNB) implemented a minimum exchange rate floor in Sept. 2011 to contain spillovers from the eurozone sovereign debt crisis. Deflation was initially avoided but in late 2014 inflows of capital forced the SNB to intervene more heavily to defend the floor. In Jan. 2015 the SNB exited the floor and the exchange rate appreciated substantially before dropping back during 2017. The SNB's balance sheet equated to around 127% of GDP in 2017.

In the pension and health care sectors pressures are building in the face of a projected 16% increase in the old-age dependency ratio by 2035. Solving long-term fiscal problems is proving highly challenging, despite a VAT increase to finance social security.

Currency

The unit of currency is the *Swiss franc* (CHF) of 100 *centimes* or *Rappen*. Foreign exchange reserves were US$78,864m. in Sept. 2009 and gold reserves were 33·44m. troy oz (77·79m. troy oz in 2000). Inflation rates (based on OECD statistics):

2008	2009	2010	2011	2012	2013	2014	2015	2016	2017
2·4%	−0·5%	0·7%	0·2%	−0·7%	−0·2%	0·0%	−1·1%	−0·4%	0·5%

Total money supply in July 2009 was 339,809m. Swiss francs. The Swiss franc was pegged to the euro in Sept. 2011 but the Central Bank ended the currency ceiling in Jan. 2015.

Budget

Revenue and expenditure of the Confederation, in 1m. Swiss francs, for calendar years:

	2010	2011	2012	2013[1]	2014[1]
Revenue	63,465	65,201	64,416	67,011	64,920
Expenditure	60,335	64,497	62,731	64,540	64,726

[1]Provisional.

VAT is 7·7%, with reduced rates of 3·7% and 2·5%.

Performance

Real GDP growth rates (based on OECD statistics):

2008	2009	2010	2011	2012	2013	2014	2015	2016	2017
2·1%	−2·2%	2·9%	1·8%	1·0%	1·9%	2·5%	1·3%	1·6%	1·7%

Total GDP was US$678·9bn. in 2017.

Switzerland was ranked first in the World Economic Forum's *Global Competitiveness Report 2017–2018* index. The index analyses 12 areas of competitiveness for over 100 countries including macroeconomy, higher education and training, institutions, innovation and infrastructure. In the 2018 *World Competitiveness Yearbook*, compiled by the International Institute for Management Development, Switzerland came fifth in the world ranking. This annual publication ranks and analyses how a nation's business environment creates and sustains the competitiveness of enterprises.

Banking and Finance

The National Bank, with headquarters divided between Berne and Zürich, opened on 20 June 1907. It has the exclusive right to issue banknotes. The *Chairman* is Thomas Jordan.

In 2017 there were 253 banks with total assets of 3,249,438m. Swiss francs. Of these 24 were cantonal banks, four big banks, 62 regional and saving banks, one Raiffeisen bank and 162 other banks. The number of banks has come down from 625 in 1990.

In 2018 the largest banks in order of market capitalization were UBS (US$61·8bn.) and Crédit Suisse Group (US$43·7bn.). UBS ranks sixth in Europe by market capitalization and is Europe's tenth largest bank by assets, which totalled US$960·1bn. in 2018. Finance and insurance is one of Switzerland's most important industries, and contributed 9·4% of value added in 2017.

Total foreign direct investment in 2017 was US$41·0bn.

In Dec. 2017 Switzerland's gross external debt totalled US$1,842,288m.

The stock exchange system has been reformed under federal legislation of 1990 on securities trading and capital market services. The four smaller exchanges have been closed and activity concentrated on the major exchanges of Zürich, Basle and Geneva, which harmonized their operations with the introduction of the Swiss Electronic Exchange (EBS) in 1995. Zürich is a major international insurance centre.

In Aug. 1998 Crédit Suisse and UBS AG agreed a deal to pay US$1·25bn. (£750m.) to Holocaust survivors over a three-year-period in an out-of-court settlement. The deal brought to an end the issue of money left in Holocaust victims' Swiss Bank accounts that were allowed to remain dormant after the war.

Energy and Natural Resources

Environment

In 2012 carbon dioxide emissions from the consumption of energy were the equivalent of 6·4 tonnes per capita. An *Environmental Performance Index* compiled in 2016 ranked Switzerland 16th of 180 countries, with 86·9%. The index examined various factors in nine areas—agriculture, air quality, biodiversity and habitat, climate and energy, fisheries, forests, health impacts, water and sanitation, and water resources.

Switzerland is one of the world leaders in recycling. In 2012, 50% of all household waste was recycled, including 96% of glass and 92% of aluminium cans.

Electricity

Installed capacity was 20·0m. kW in 2011. Production was 64·6bn. kWh in 2011. 52·8% of electricity produced in 2011 was hydro-electric, 41·3% nuclear and 5·5% conventional thermal. In 1990, 54% of citizens voted for a ten-year moratorium on the construction of new nuclear plants. A referendum was held in 2003 on proposals to write a commitment to phase out nuclear power altogether into the constitution. However, the proposal was rejected. In May 2011 the government decided to abandon plans to build any further nuclear reactors in the wake of the Fukushima disaster in Japan. There are currently five nuclear reactors in use. Consumption per capita in 2011 was 8,455 kWh.

Minerals

In 2016, 4,800 people were employed in mining and quarrying. Production, 2013 (in 1,000 tonnes): salt, 652; gypsum (estimate), 340; lime (estimate), 118.

Agriculture

The country is self-sufficient in milk. Agriculture is partly protected by subsidies and imports are regulated according to WTO standards. In 2012 agriculture occupied 3·6% of the total workforce. There were 269,500 ha. of open arable land in 2012, 133,600 ha. of cultivated grassland and 611,200 ha. of natural grassland and pastures. In 2012 there were 13,100 ha. of vineyards. There were 56,600 farms in 2012 (56% in mountain or hill regions), of which 2,400 were under 1 ha., 20,800 over 20 ha. and 16,300 in part-time use. In 2012 there were 403,000 ha. of arable land and 23,700 ha. of permanent crops. Approximately 11·6% of all agricultural land is used for organic farming—one of the highest proportions in the world.

Area harvested, 2012 (in 1,000 ha.): cereals, 147; sugar beets, 19; potatoes, 11. Production, 2012 (in 1,000 tonnes): sugar beets, 1,673; wheat, 502; potatoes, 451; barley, 185; maize, 147; rapeseed, 66; carrots, 46. Fruit production (in 1,000 tonnes) in 2012 was: apples, 232; grapes, 127; pears, 48. Wine is produced in 25 of the cantons. In 2012 vineyards produced 100m. litres of wine.

Livestock on farms, 2012 (in 1,000): cattle, 1,565; pigs, 1,544; sheep, 417; goats, 88; horses, 58; chickens, 9,878. Livestock products, 2012 (in 1,000 tonnes): milk, 4,111; meat, 487; cheese, 181.

Forestry

In 2015 the area under forests was 1·25m. ha., or 31% of the total land area. In 2011, 4·86m. cu. metres of roundwood were cut.

Fisheries

Total catch, 2015, 2,023 tonnes, exclusively freshwater fish.

Industry

The leading companies by market capitalization in Switzerland in May 2018 were: Nestlé SA, a food and beverages company (US$237·3bn.); Novartis AG, a pharmaceutical company (US$203·0bn.); and Roche AG, another pharmaceutical company (US$189·7bn.).

The chief food producing industries, based on Swiss agriculture, are the manufacture of cheese, butter, sugar and meat. Among the other industries, construction, the manufacture of chemicals and pharmaceutical products, the production of machinery (including electrical machinery and scientific and optical instruments) and watch and clock making are the most important. The leading industries in 2012 in terms of value added (in 1m. Swiss francs) were: construction, 31,245 (5·0% of GDP); pharmaceutical products, 23,704 (3·8%); computer, electronic and optical products, 23,651 (3·8%); food and tobacco products, 12,228 (2·0%); machinery and equipment, 11,119 (1·8%); electricity, gas, steam and air conditioning supply, 9,304 (1·5%).

Labour

In 2017 the total working population was 4,637,000, of whom 663,000 people were in health, 633,000 in manufacturing and 573,000 in trade. The unemployment rate in the third quarter of 2018 was 4·3%. In 2017, 84·3% of men and 75·2% of women between the ages of 15 and 64 were in employment. The percentage of men in employment is one of the highest among the major industrialized nations.

The foreign labour force was 1,707,000 in 2017 (799,000 women). Of these 281,000 were Italian, 261,000 German, 219,000 Portuguese and 106,000 French. In 2017 approximately 1,187,000 EU citizens worked in Switzerland.

International Trade

Legislation of 1991 increased the possibilities of foreign ownership of domestic companies.

Imports and Exports

Imports and exports, excluding gold (bullion and coins) and silver (coins), were (in 1m. Swiss francs):

	2008	2009	2010	2011	2012
Imports	197,521	168,998	183,436	184,540	185,409
Exports	215,984	187,448	203,484	208,203	211,808

In 2012 the EU accounted for 74·6% of imports (138·3bn. Swiss francs) and 55·7% of exports (118·0bn. Swiss francs). Main import suppliers in 2012 (share of total trade): Germany, 29·6%; Italy, 10·2%; France, 8·4%; USA, 5·7%; China, 5·5%. Main export markets: Germany, 19·8%; USA, 11·1%; Italy, 7·1%; France, 7·0%; UK, 5·4%.

Main imports in 2012 (in 1m. Swiss francs): consumer goods, 78,225; raw materials and semi-manufactures, 40,946; capital goods, 40,165.

Main exports in 2012 (in 1m. Swiss francs): chemicals, 79,012; precision instruments, clocks and watches and jewellery, 44,040; machinery and electronics, 33,307.

Communications

Roads

In 2016 there were 71,540 km of roads, comprising 1,447 km of motorways, 18,247 km of highways and national roads and 51,846 km of secondary and local roads. Motor vehicles in 2016 (in 1,000): passenger cars, 4,524; motorcycles and mopeds, 896; vans and lorries, 406; buses and coaches, 15. Freight transported by road in 2016 totalled 17·0bn. tonne-km. Switzerland has one of the lowest death rates in road accidents of any industrialized country, at 2·6 deaths per 100,000 people in 2016. Road accidents injured 21,392 people in 2016 and killed 216 (down from 954 in 1990).

Switzerland was ranked third for its road infrastructure in the World Economic Forum's *Global Competitiveness Report 2017–2018*.

Rail

In 2015 the length of the general traffic railways was 5,177 km. Swiss Federal Railways, the largest rail company in the country, had a route length of 3,002 km in 2015. In 2016 Swiss and foreign railway companies carried 607m. passengers and 68m. tonnes of freight. In Oct. 2010 the final breakthrough of the world's longest rail tunnel took place—the 57 km long tunnel under the Gotthard mountain range in the Alps linking Erstfeld and Bodio. The tunnel was officially opened in June 2016. There are a number of tram/light rail networks, notably in Basle, Berne, Geneva, Lausanne and Zürich.

Switzerland was ranked first for rail infrastructure in the World Economic Forum's *Global Competitiveness Report 2017–2018*.

Civil Aviation

There are seven airports with international scheduled and charter traffic: Basle (the binational Euroairport, which also serves Mulhouse in France), Berne (Belp), Geneva (Cointrin), Lugano (Agno), Sion, St Gallen (Altenrhein) and Zürich (Kloten). In 2013 these airports handled 45,501,533 passengers and 403,250 tonnes of freight and mail. Swissair, the former national carrier, faced collapse and grounded flights in Oct. 2001. In April 2002 a successor airline, Swiss International Air Lines (Swiss), took over as the national carrier. Services were also provided in 2013 by over 80 foreign airlines. Zürich is the busiest airport, handling 24,853,679 passengers in 2013 and 327,055 tonnes of freight. Geneva handled 14,328,107 passengers and 36,276 tonnes of freight in 2013. Together these two airports accounted for 86% of Swiss passenger traffic in 2013.

Shipping

In 2016, 5·9m. tonnes of freight were transported on the Rhine. A merchant marine was created in 1941, the place of registry of its vessels being Basle. At the end of 2016 it comprised 50 ships totalling 1,756,020 DWT.

Telecommunications

In 2012 there were 4·7m. main (fixed) telephone lines. In the same year mobile phone subscriptions numbered 10·6m. (1,320·6 per 1,000 persons). There were 63·4 mobile broadband subscriptions per 100 inhabitants in 2013 and 42·5 fixed broadband subscriptions per 100 inhabitants. In March 2012 there were 2·7m. Facebook users.

Social Institutions

According to the 2017 *Fragile States Index*—a list published jointly by the Fund for Peace and *Foreign Policy* magazine—Switzerland was ranked as the country third least vulnerable to conflict or collapse. The index is based on 12 indicators of state vulnerability across social, political and economic categories.

Justice

The Federal Court, which sits at Lausanne, consists of 30 judges and 30 supplementary judges, elected by the Federal Assembly for six years and eligible for re-election; the President and Vice-President serve for two years and re-election is not practised. The Tribunal has original and final jurisdiction in suits between the Confederation and cantons; between different cantons; between the Confederation or cantons and corporations or individuals; between parties who refer their case to it; or in suits which the constitution or legislation of cantons places within its authority. It is a court of appeal against decisions of other federal authorities, and of cantonal authorities applying federal laws. The Tribunal comprises two courts of public law, two civil courts, a chamber of bankruptcy, a chamber of prosecution, a court of criminal appeal, a court of extraordinary appeal and a Federal Criminal Court.

A Federal Insurance Court sits in Lucerne, and comprises 11 judges and 11 supplementary judges elected for six years by the Federal Assembly.

A federal penal code replaced cantonal codes in 1942. It abolished capital punishment except for offences in wartime; this latter proviso was abolished in 1992.

The population in penal institutions in Sept. 2012 was 6,599 (82 per 100,000 population).

Education

Education is administered by the confederation, cantons and communes. The cantons and their local municipalities finance 90% of public expenditure on education. The total compulsory school period amounts to 11 years. The primary level comprises eight years and the lower secondary level takes three years. In the canton of Ticino, the lower secondary level (*scuola media*) lasts for four years. Generally, compulsory education sets in for children at the age of four.

After the end of their compulsory school years roughly two-thirds of young people in Switzerland switch to a form of education that combines classroom instruction at a vocational school with an apprenticeship in a training company (dual-track system), This provides them with a VET (vocational education and training) certificate and can also be concluded with a federal vocational baccalaureate. Around one-third opt for continuing school education at a specialized upper secondary or a baccalaureate school, which prepare students for tertiary education at a university.

The tertiary level comprises universities (including universities of applied sciences and universities of teacher education) and, as a second important pillar, institutions providing professional education and training.

In 2013–14 there were 910,285 pupils in compulsory education (162,154 in pre-primary schools, 450,350 at primary, 263,709 at lower secondary and 34,072 at special schools), 361,737 in Stage II secondary education and 289,699 students in higher education, including 142,164 students at universities and 87,291 at universities of applied sciences.

There are ten universities (date of foundation and students in 2014–15): Basle (1460, 13,238), Berne (1528, 16,477), Fribourg (1889, 10,422), Geneva (1559, 15,781), Lausanne (1537, 14,089), Lucerne (16th century, 2,821), Neuchâtel (1866, 4,348), St Gallen (1899, 8,449), Svizzera italiana (1996, 3,016), Zürich (1523, 26,338); two institutions of technology: Federal Institute of Technology Lausanne (1853, 9,710), Federal Institute of Technology Zürich (1854, 18,185); and two institutions of equivalent status recently created: Kurt Bösch Institut in Sion and Fern Studien Schweiz in Brig (combined total of 1,087 students). There are nine universities of applied sciences (date of foundation and enrolment figures for 2014–15): Berne (1997, 6,923); Central Switzerland (1997, 6,739); Eastern Switzerland (1997, 5,449); Kalaidos (2005, 1,798); Les Roches-Gruyère (2008, 226); Northwestern Switzerland (1997, 11,833); Southern Switzerland (1997, 4,581); Western Switzerland (1997, 19,390); Zürich (2007, 20,014). There were 12,703 students enrolled at universities of teacher education in 2014–15.

19% of university students in 2014–15 were foreign (with foreign school education).

In 2011 public expenditure on education came to 5·3% of GDP and accounted for 15·7% of total government expenditure.

The adult literacy rate is at least 99%.

Health

There were 34,348 doctors in 2014, and 4,181 dentists and 4,350 pharmacists in 2012. There were 293 hospitals with 37,836 beds in 2013. In 2012, 28·2% of the population were smokers. In 2011 Switzerland spent 8·1% of its GDP on health. Although active euthanasia is illegal in Switzerland, doctors may help patients die if they have given specific consent.

Welfare

The Federal Insurance Law against accident and illness, of 13 June 1911, entitled all citizens to insurance against illness; foreigners could also be admitted to the benefits. Major reform of the law was ratified in 1994 and came into effect in 1996, making it compulsory for all citizens. Subsidies are paid by the Confederation and the Cantons only for insured persons with low incomes. Also compulsory are the Old-Age and Survivors' Insurance (OASI, since 1948), Invalidity Insurance (II, since 1960) and Accident Insurance (1984/1996). Unemployment Insurance (1984) and Occupational benefit plans (Second Pillar, 1985) are compulsory for employees only.

The following amounts (in 1m. Swiss francs) were paid in social protection benefits:

	2014	2015
Occupational pension plans	34,399	35,247
Old-age and survivors' insurance	40,486	41,387
Mandatory health insurance	24,758	26,085
Disability insurance	8,123	8,157
Accident insurance for employees	5,648	5,744
Family allowances (cantonal law)	5,476	5,623
Unemployment insurance	5,505	5,827
Supplementary benefits (OASI/II)	4,689	4,782
Total (including other benefits)	157,061	161,929

Religion

There is liberty of conscience and of creed. The leading religion confessions in 2016 were the Roman Catholic Church (36·5% of the population) and the Swiss Reformed Church (24·5%). Other Christians accounted for 5·9% of the population in 2016 and Muslims 5·2%, while 24·9% did not have any religious affiliation. In Feb. 2019 the Roman Catholic Church had two cardinals.

Culture

World Heritage Sites

There are 12 sites in Switzerland that appear on the UNESCO World Heritage List. They are (with the year entered on list): the Abbey-Cathedral of St Gallen (1983), the 9th-century Benedictine convent of St John at Müstair (1983), the Old City of Berne (1983), the three castles and city walls of Bellinzona (2000), the Jungfrau-Aletsch-Bietschhorn mountain region (2001 and 2007), Monte San Giorgio (2003), the Lavaux vineyard terraces (2007), the Swiss Tectonic Arena Sardona (2008) and La Chaux-de-Fonds/Le Locle watchmaking town-planning (2009). The Rhaetian Railway in the Albula/Bernina Landscapes (2008) is shared with Italy, the Prehistoric Pile dwellings around the Alps (2011) is shared with Austria, France, Germany, Italy and Slovenia, and the Architectural Work of Le Corbusier, an Outstanding Contribution to the Modern Movement (2016), is shared with Argentina, Belgium, France, Germany, India and Japan.

Press

There were 79 daily newspapers in 2013 and 93 paid-for non-daily papers. The average circulation of paid-for daily papers in 2013 was 1,810,000 and of free dailies 1,039,000. There were 52 newspaper online editions in 2013. The number of newspaper online unique monthly visitors rose from 89,099,000 in 2010 to 195,105,000 in 2013.

Tourism

Tourism is an important industry. In 2013 there were 8·97m. non-resident tourists staying at hotels and similar establishments, bringing revenue of US$20,440m. Overnight stays by tourists in hotels and health establishments totalled 35,624,000 in 2013 (19,735,000 by foreigners). The main countries of origin of foreign tourists were Germany (4,573,000 overnight stays in 2013), the UK (1,640,000) and the USA (1,585,000). 13·60m. Swiss citizens travelled abroad in 2013.

Festivals

The Lucerne Festival is one of Europe's leading cultural events and since 2001 has been split into three festivals: Ostern during Lent, Sommer in Aug.–Sept. and Piano in Nov. The 2013 summer festival was attended by 85,000 people. The Montreux Jazz Festival is held annually in July. It attracts over 250,000 people per year. The biggest rock and pop festivals are OpenAir St Gallen (June), Paléo Festival in Nyon (July), Gurtenfestival in Berne (July) and Rock Oz'Arènes in Avenches (Aug.).

Diplomatic Representatives

Of Switzerland in the United Kingdom (16–18 Montagu Pl., London, W1H 2BQ)
Ambassador: Alexandre Fasel.

Of the United Kingdom in Switzerland (Thunstrasse 50, 3005 Berne)
Ambassador: Jane Owen.

Of Switzerland in the USA (2900 Cathedral Ave., NW, Washington, D.C., 20008)
Ambassador: Martin Werner Dahinden.

Of the USA in Switzerland (Sulgeneckstrasse 19, 3007 Berne)
Ambassador: Edward McMullen, Jr.

Of Switzerland to the United Nations
Ambassador: Jürg Lauber.

Of Switzerland to the European Union
Ambassador: Urs Bucher.

Further Reading

Office Fédéral de la Statistique. *Annuaire Statistique de la Suisse.*

Bewes, Diccon, *Swiss Watching: Inside Europe's Landlocked Island.* 2010

Breiding, R. James, *Swiss Made: The Untold Story Behind Switzerland's Success.* 2012

Butler, Michael, Pender, Malcolm and Charnley, Joy, *Making of Modern Switzerland, 1848–1998.* 2000

Church, Clive H., *Politics and Government of Switzerland*. 2004
Church, Clive H. and Head, Randolph C., *A Concise History of Switzerland*. 2013
Jenni, Sabine, *Switzerland's Differentiated European Integration: The Last Gallic Village?*. 2016
Kriesi, Hanspeter, Farago, Peter, Kohli, Martin and Zarin-Nejadan, Milad, *Contemporary Switzerland*. 2005
Kriesi, Hanspeter and Trechsel, Alexander H., *The Politics of Switzerland*. 2008

Linder, Wolf, *Swiss Democracy: Possible Solutions to Conflict in Multicultural Societies*. 3rd ed. 2010
Skenderovic, Damir, *The Radical Right in Switzerland: Continuity and Change, 1945–2000*. 2009
National library: Bibliothèque Nationale Suisse, Hallwylstr. 15, 3003 Berne.
National Statistical Office: Office Fédéral de la Statistique, Espace de l'Europe 10, 2010 Neuchâtel.
SFSO Information Service email: information@bfs.admin.ch
Website: http://www.bfs.admin.ch

Syria

Jumhuriya al-Arabya as-Suriya (Syrian Arab Republic)

Capital: Damascus
Population projection, 2020: 18·92m.
GNI per capita, 2017: (PPP$) 2,337
HDI/world rank, 2017: 0·536/155
Internet domain extension: .sy

Key Historical Events

Ancient Syria, a region encompassing modern Israel, Palestine, Lebanon and Jordan, was home to some of the world's earliest civilizations. From the city of Ebla, founded around 3000 BC, the Semitic empire developed. This was succeeded around 2260 BC by the Akkadian empire, then by the Amorites whose cities fell to the Hittites in the mid-2nd millennium BC. During the next 500 years Canaanites, Phoenicians, Aryans, Aramaeans and Hebrews settled different parts of the region. From the 9th–7th centuries BC the Assyrian empire dominated until, weakened by Cimmerian and Scythian immigration, it gave way to Babylonian rule.

The Babylonian empire, which saw the enslavement of the Jews, was defeated in 539 BC by the Persian King Cyrus. In the 4th century BC Alexander the Great overthrew the Persians and Syria came under Greek rule until the expansion of Rome in the early 2nd century BC. Syria became a Roman province in 64 BC. The Greek cities of the interior (the Decapolis) were rebuilt, including Damascus. Palmyra, a key city on the trade routes to the Euphrates, rose against Rome under Queen Zenobia but was defeated in AD 272.

Syria became an important frontier zone under Diocletian, who established lines of defence (*limes*) against eastern invaders. Syrian cities such as Edessa had contained the earliest Christian communities, and Antioch, where St Peter preached, grew in significance when Emperor Constantine moved the seat of the Empire east to Byzantium in 303. In 451 it was made a patriarchate.

Syria prospered under Byzantium until the Persian invasions of the 6th century. In the 620s Emperor Heraclius briefly regained the region for Byzantium, before ceding it to Muslim Arab forces at the Battle of the Yarmuk River in 636. Syria was at the heart, geographically and politically, of the Ummayad empires for the next 100 years. From 661 Damascus was capital of the Ummayad Caliphate, though its influence declined after 750 when the Abbasid Caliphate moved the capital to Baghdad.

From 969 the resurgent Byzantine Empire challenged for control of the region, twice conquering its principal cities. In 1085 Syria was conquered by the Seljid Turks. With the beginning of the Crusades Muslim-held strongholds were repeatedly attacked by Christian invaders. Antioch and Edessa fell to the crusaders in 1098 and Jerusalem in 1099. In the 12th century Muslim tribes won back much land under the successive leaderships of Zengi of Mosul, Nur-ad Din and Salah ad-Din (Saladin). Salah ad-Din founded the Ayyubid dynasty and in 1187 his forces recaptured Jerusalem from the Christians.

In 1260 a series of Mongol invasions began from the east, destroying cities and agriculture before being repelled by the Egyptian Mamluks. The Mamluks also drove the last crusaders from the Holy Land in 1302. The area remained under Mamluk rule until it fell to the Ottoman Turks in 1516. In the 1830s Egyptian forces invaded Syria as part of a wider war against the Ottomans. European powers became involved, brokering several agreements and finally forcing Egypt to withdraw in 1840.

During the First World War, in which Turkey joined the Central Powers, the French and British drew up the Sykes–Picot agreement, which planned the division of the Middle East into areas of French and British control. After the end of the war, the Ottoman Empire was dissolved and Lebanon, Palestine and Transjordan were made separate territories, reducing Syria to its modern borders.

In March 1920 Faisal ibn Husayn of Mecca became king of Syria but was deposed by the French, who were awarded the Syrian mandate by the League of Nations later that year. A widespread revolt against French rule was suppressed in 1925, with French troops bombarding Damascus. An abortive attempt to negotiate independence in 1936 was followed by more fruitful discussions in 1941, when British and Free French forces occupied the country. Syria held elections in 1943, electing the nationalist Shukri al-Kuwatli as president. Syrian independence was recognized on 1 Jan. 1944 and European forces withdrew in 1946.

A series of military coups from 1949–54 interrupted civilian government. The 1948 Arab–Israeli War, in which Syria fought for the Palestinians, ushered in decades of mutual hostility with neighbouring Israel. In 1956 the Suez Crisis prompted a period of martial law. In the same year Syria signed a pact with the Soviet Union which ensured supplies of military equipment in return for Communist influence. Popular enthusiasm for the Pan-Arabist movement led Syria to unite with Egypt in 1958, creating the United Arab Republic. However, Syria seceded in Sept. 1961 and a series of military coups ensued, culminating in the Ba'ath Party taking power in 1963. After the Syrian Ba'athists split from the Iraqi Ba'athists in 1966, long-term tensions arose between the two countries and led to Syrian support for Iran.

The 1967 war with Israel resulted in the loss of the Golan Heights. In 1970 Hafez al-Assad (of the minority Alawite sect) seized power. He was elected president in 1971 and embarked on a 'corrective' movement to end corruption. Domestic opposition was suppressed and the Sunni fundamentalist Muslim Brotherhood was destroyed along with the city of Hamah in 1982. Syrian forces invaded Lebanon in 1976 to prevent a Palestinian victory over the Maronite Christians, with whom Syria had political ties.

Assad joined the international coalition against the Iraqi occupation of Kuwait in 1991 and engaged in unsuccessful talks with Israel in the 1990s. His son, Bashar, took over on Assad's death in 2000. In 2003 Syria refused to back the US-led invasion of Iraq and relations with Washington were further strained over US accusations of Syrian support for terrorism. Though Syrian influence in Lebanon remained strong, it withdrew its last troops from the country in 2005, after involvement in the assassination of the former Lebanese prime minister, Rafiq al-Hariri. Following French-brokered talks, in Oct. 2008 Syria established diplomatic relations with Lebanon for the first time.

Beginning in March 2011 there were popular anti-government protests throughout the country, echoing similar demonstrations across the Middle East and North Africa. Assad's dismissal of the government and lifting in April of the state of emergency in place since 1963 failed to stem dissent, and his regime adopted an increasingly repressive response to the opposition. This prompted the USA and the EU to impose sanctions from May 2011 and in Nov. that year Syria was suspended from the Arab League. At the end of 2012 the USA joined other nations including France, Turkey, the UK and several Gulf states in recognizing the rebel National Coalition as the legitimate Syrian government, and in March 2013 the UK and USA agreed to provide rebel forces with non-military aid. However, the Assad regime has proved resilient and by May 2014 government forces had successfully retaken the strategically and symbolically important city of Homs after a three-year occupation by insurgents.

The escalating conflict has resulted in some 200,000 deaths since 2011 while around 4m. people have left the country as refugees. The crisis has also prompted an upsurge in activity by international militant organizations, including al-Qaeda and the jihadist Islamic State of Iraq and Syria (since renamed Islamic State). In June 2014 Islamic State declared that it was incorporating territory in Syria and Iraq over which it had taken control into a new caliphate. In Aug. 2014 the UN accused the organization of 'mass atrocities' and in Sept. US led-forces began air strikes against jihadist targets in the cities of Aleppo and Raqqah. Conflict between Assad's forces, with Russian and Iranian military backing, against disparate opposition groups including Islamic State dragged on through 2015 and 2016. However, government forces began to make decisive inroads into rebel strongholds and by early 2018 Assad's control over the country had been largely restored.

Territory and Population

Syria is bounded by the Mediterranean and Lebanon in the west, by Israel and Jordan in the south, by Iraq in the east and by Turkey in the north. The frontier between Syria and Turkey was settled by the Franco-Turkish agreement of 22 June 1929. The area is 185,180 sq. km (71,498 sq. miles). The population at the last census, in 2004, was 17,920,844. The estimated population in 2011 was 21,377,000; density, 115 per sq. km. In 2011, 56·2% of the population lived in urban areas. An estimated 6·6m. Syrians are displaced within the country as a consequence of the civil conflict that began in 2011.

The UN gives a projected population for 2020 of 18·92m.

Area and population (2011 estimate, in 1,000) of the 14 districts (mohafaza):

	Sq. km	Population
Aleppo (Halab)	18,500	4,868
Damascus City	105	1,754
Dará	3,730	1,027
Deir Ez-Zor	33,060	1,239
Hamah	8,883	1,628
Hasakah	23,334	1,512
Homs (Hims)	42,223	1,803
Idlib	6,097	1,501
Lattakia (Ladhiqiyah)	2,297	1,008
Qunaytirah	1,861	90
Raqqah	19,616	944
Rif Dimashq	18,032	2,836
Suwaydá	5,550	370
Tartous	1,892	797

The capital is Damascus (Dimashq), with an estimated population in 2010 of 2,401,000. Other major towns are Aleppo, Homs, Hamah, Lattakia, Raqqah and Tartous.

Over 1m. Iraqi refugees entered Syria between 2003 and 2007, although many started to return in late 2007. There were an estimated 18,000 refugees in Syria in 2018, down from 755,000 in 2011, with most having left in the wake of the civil war.

Arabic is the official language, spoken by 90% of the population, while 9% speak Kurdish (chiefly in Hasakah in the northeast of the country) and 1% other languages.

Social Statistics

2008 births, estimate, 594,000; deaths, 72,000. Rates, 2008 estimate (per 1,000 population): birth, 28·0; death, 3·4. Infant mortality, 2010 (per 1,000 live births), 14. Expectation of life, 2013, was 71·8 years for males and 77·8 for females. Annual population growth rate, 2000–08, 3·1%. Fertility rate, 2008, 3·2 births per woman.

Climate

The climate is Mediterranean in type, with mild wet winters and dry, hot summers, though there are variations in temperatures and rainfall between the coastal regions and the interior, which even includes desert conditions. The more mountainous parts are subject to snowfall. Damascus, Jan. 38·1°F (3·4°C), July 77·4°F (25·2°C). Annual rainfall 8·8" (217 mm). Aleppo, Jan. 36·7°F (2·6°C), July 80·4°F (26·9°C). Annual rainfall 10·2" (258 mm). Homs, Jan. 38·7°F (3·7°C), July 82·4°F (28°C). Annual rainfall 3·4" (86·7 mm).

Constitution and Government

A new constitution was adopted on 27 Feb. 2012, after receiving 89·4% support in a referendum with a turnout of 57·4%. It replaced the previous constitution promulgated in 1973. Among the new constitution's provisions is the removal of a previous clause confirming the Arab Socialist Renaissance (Ba'ath) Party, in power since 1963, as the 'leading party in the State and society'. The constitution proceeds to outlaw parties established on a 'religious, sectarian, tribal [or] regional' basis. The President is limited to two seven-year terms, although this clause may not be retroactively applied, allowing the incumbent, President Bashar al-Assad, to remain in office for potentially four terms. At a referendum on 27 May 2007 Bashar al-Assad (b. 1965) was confirmed as President for a second term, receiving 97·6% of the vote. Presidential elections may be contested, though any candidate must be a Muslim. The description of Syria as a 'planned socialist economy' in the 1973 constitution has been replaced by an assertion that the economy 'shall be based on the principle of developing public and private economic activity through economic and social plans'.

The amended constitution was widely perceived as an attempt by President Assad to appease the opposition movement that emerged during the 2011 Arab Spring and placate international opinion against him. Nonetheless, the referendum was boycotted by leading opposition groups and received little support from the international community. Legislative power is held by a 250-member People's Assembly (Majlis al-Sha'ab), renewed every four years in 15 multi-seat constituencies.

National Anthem

'Humata al Diyari al aykum salaam' ('Defenders of the Realm, on you be peace'); words by Khalil Mardam Bey, tune by M. S. and A. S. Flayfel.

Government Chronology

Heads of State since 1943. (HS = People's Party; HSQ = Syrian National Party; KW = National Bloc)

President		
1943–49	KW	Shukri al-Kuwatli
Chairmen of Supreme Military Council		
1949	military	Husni al-Zaim
1949	military	Muhammad Sami Hilmi al-Hinnawi
President		
1949–51	KW	Hashim Bay Khalid al-Atassi
Chairman of Supreme Military Council		
1951	military	Adib ash-Shishakli
Presidents		
1951–53	military	Fawzi Silu
1953–54	military	Adib ash-Shishakli
1954–55	KW	Hashim Bay Khalid al-Atassi
1955–58	HSQ	Shukri al-Kuwatli
United Arab Republic		
1958–61		
President		
1961–63	HS	Nazim al-Qudsi
Chairmen of National Revolutionary Command Council		
1963	military/Ba'ath	Lu'ayy al-Atassi
1963–64	military/Ba'ath	Muhammad Amin al-Hafez
Chairman of Presidential Council		
1964–66	military/Ba'ath	Muhammad Amin al-Hafez
Heads of State		
1966–70	Ba'ath	Nur ad-Din Mustafa al-Atassi
1970–71	Ba'ath	Ahmad al-Hasan al-Khatib
1971	military/Ba'ath	Abu Sulayman Hafez al-Assad
Presidents		
1971–2000	Ba'ath	Abu Sulayman Hafez al-Assad
2000–	Ba'ath	Bashar al-Assad

Recent Elections

Elections were held on 13 April 2016. The ruling National Progressive Front (led by the Ba'ath Party) won 200 of 250 seats. Turnout was 57·6%. Opposition parties boycotted the election. It was reported that over 140,000 refugees crossed the border from Lebanon to vote.

In presidential elections held on 3 June 2014, incumbent president Bashar al-Assad (Ba'ath Party) won 88·7% of the vote, against Hassan al-Nouri (National Initiative for Administration and Change in Syria) with 4·3% and

Maher Hajjar (ind.) with 3·2%. Turnout was 73·4%. Despite being Syria's first multi-candidate presidential election in more than four decades it was widely criticized by the international community, with the European Union describing Assad's victory as illegitimate.

Current Government

Following the death of Lieut.-Gen. Hafez al-Assad on 10 June 2000, a presidential referendum was held on 10 July 2000. The former president's son Bashar al-Assad won 97·3% of the vote.

President: Bashar al-Assad; b. 1965 (Ba'ath; sworn in 17 July 2000).

Vice-Presidents: Farouk al-Shara; Najah al-Attar.

In Feb. 2019 the government comprised:

Prime Minister: Imad Khamis; b. 1961 (Ba'ath; sworn in 3 July 2016).

Deputy Prime Minister and Minister of Foreign Affairs and Expatriates: Walid Muallem. *Deputy Prime Minister:* Gen. Fahd Jassem al-Freij.

Minister of Administrative Development: Salam Mohammad al-Saffaf. *Agriculture and Agrarian Reform:* Ahmad al-Qadri. *Awqaf:* Mohammad Abdel-Sattar Sayyed. *Communications and Technology:* Iyad Mohammad al-Khatib. *Culture:* Mohammad al-Ahmad. *Defence:* Gen. Ali Abdullah Ayyoub. *Economy and Foreign Trade:* Mohammad Samer Abdelrahman al-Khalil. *Education:* Emad Mowaffaq al-Azab. *Electricity:* Zuheir Kharboutli. *Finance:* Maamoun Hamdan. *Health:* Dr Nizar Wehbe Yazigi. *Higher Education:* Bassam Bashir Ibrahim. *Industry:* Mohammad Maan Zain al-Abidine. *Information:* Imad Abullah Sarah. *Interior:* Mohammad Khalid Rahmoun. *Internal Trade and Consumer Protection:* Atef Nadaf. *Justice:* Hisham Mohammad Mamdouh al-Shaar. *Local Administration:* Hussein Makhlouf. *Oil and Mineral Resources:* Ali Ghanem. *Presidential Affairs:* Mansour Fadlallah Azzam. *Public Works and Housing:* Suhail Mohammad Abdel Latif. *Social Affairs and Labour:* Rima al-Qadiri. *Tourism:* Mohammad Rami Radwan Martini. *Transport:* Ali Hammoud. *Water Resources:* Hussein Arnous.

Syrian Parliament (Arabic only): http://www.parliament.gov.sy

Current Leaders

Bashar al-Assad

Position

President

Introduction

Bashar al-Assad was confirmed as president in a national referendum in July 2000 following the death of his father the previous month. He had not been groomed for a political career, pursuing instead a medical education in England. However, on the death of his elder brother Basil—their father's chosen successor—in an accident in 1994, Assad was recalled to Damascus. Thereafter he rose through the senior ranks of the armed forces, consolidating his influence and authority within his father's regime to achieve the first-ever father-to-son succession to the highest office in an Arab republic. From March 2011 his repressive rule was dogged by street protests, echoing those in several other Arab states. By early 2012 the discontent had descended into open civil war between the security forces and disparate opposition groups across the country. Conflict dragged on relentlessly, but from late 2016 government forces, with Russian and Iranian military backing, made decisive inroads into rebel strongholds and by the end of 2018 Assad's control over the country had been virtually restored—at the estimated cost of around 600,000 lives.

Early Life

Assad was born in Damascus on 11 Sept. 1965. After attending high school in the capital, he went to London, England, to study ophthalmology. Having returned to Syria upon the death of his brother, he became commander of the Syrian army's armoured division. Assad reportedly used this position to install his own supporters and remove ageing senior figures and potential rivals from the army and security services. He was appointed to the rank of colonel in 1999.

When President Hafez al-Assad died suddenly on 10 June 2000, Syria's political establishment was quick to demonstrate support for his son. The People's Assembly voted to change the constitution to lower the minimum age for a president from 40 to 34—Assad's age at that time. The Assembly and the dominant Ba'ath Party approved his nomination for the presidency (as the only candidate) and the party elected him as its secretary-general. He was also declared commander-in-chief of the armed forces, his military rank having been elevated to lieutenant-general. In a national referendum held on 10 July 2000, Assad was endorsed as president with 97·3% of the votes cast.

Career in Office

In his inaugural address to the People's Assembly, Assad spoke of the need for economic reform. He called for the restructuring of the state-dominated economy and improved competitiveness, the dismantling of bureaucracy and the ending of corruption. Private investment has since been encouraged. However, initial signs of political liberalization—a partial lifting of censorship, the release of some political prisoners, tolerance of criticism of the government and party, and the limited introduction of the internet—faded in 2001 as dissidents were again arrested and detained. On the international stage, peace with Israel remained elusive, given Syria's stipulation that the Israelis give up the whole of the Golan Heights seized in the Six-Day War of 1967. Also, the renewed Palestinian *intifada* against Israeli occupation polarized the already volatile politics of the Middle East and made a Syrian-Israeli accord increasingly unlikely.

In 2002–03 Syria opposed US military threats against Iraq, fearing the consequences of another war in the Middle East, and claimed that the UN Security Council did not endorse an invasion. US-led forces nevertheless invaded Iraq in March 2003 and Saddam Hussein was toppled the following month. The USA subsequently threatened Assad with economic, diplomatic or other undefined sanctions, suggesting that Syria was harbouring members of Saddam Hussein's regime and had been involved in the development of chemical weapons.

In Jan. 2004 Assad visited Turkey, the first Syrian leader to do so, improving several decades of cool relations between the two countries. The following May the USA imposed economic sanctions on Syria for alleged support for terrorism and failure to stop militants entering Iraq. A UN Security Council resolution adopted in Sept. 2004 and the subsequent assassination of former Lebanese prime minister Rafiq al-Hariri in Beirut in Feb. 2005 (allegedly with Syrian involvement) increased the international pressure on Assad to remove Syria's forces from Lebanon completely. Although the withdrawal was completed in April that year, the UN continued to probe al-Hariri's murder, implicating senior Syrian officials and chiding Assad's government for its perceived lack of co-operation with UN investigators. Syria's frosty diplomatic relationship with the USA was aggravated by Assad's support for Hizbollah during the radical Lebanese militia's war against the Israeli military in July–Aug. 2006.

Following the restoration of Iraqi-Syrian diplomatic ties in Nov. 2006, President Jalal Talabani became the first Iraqi head of state to visit Damascus for 30 years in Jan. 2007. In March the European Union reopened a dialogue with the Syrian government, and in May the US Secretary of State met the Syrian foreign minister in Egypt for the first high-level bilateral contact in two years. Relations with Israel, however, deteriorated further after an Israeli air strike against an undefined site in northern Syria in Sept. (which US intelligence sources claimed in April 2008 to have been a covert nuclear reactor plant).

Despite the ruling National Progressive Front's overwhelming victory in parliamentary elections in April 2007 and Assad's endorsement as president for a further term in a national referendum in May, a crackdown on dissent remained in force. During that year several government critics and human rights campaigners were sentenced to terms of imprisonment, and in Jan. 2008 Syria's leading dissident, Riyad Seif, was detained by security services.

In Oct. 2008 Syria and Lebanon signed an accord establishing diplomatic relations for the first time in their turbulent post-independence history. After several postponements, the Damascus stock exchange was launched in March 2009, marking a further step in the liberalization of Syria's state-controlled economy.

From March 2011 Assad faced popular protests against his rule, echoing similar demonstrations in countries throughout North Africa and the Middle East. The initial release of several dozen political prisoners failed to quell discontent, which spread rapidly from Damascus to other major cities. In April 2011 he lifted the state of emergency in place for 48 years, but violent repression of the uprising by government forces continued in defiance of international opinion. The USA and EU imposed sanctions, including asset freezing and travel bans, and the Arab League suspended Syria's membership. However, China and particularly Russia vetoed UN Security Council resolutions critical of Syria, lending apparent support to Assad's assertion that his opponents were terrorists under foreign direction and did not reflect Syrian public opinion. In late 2012 anti-Assad groups united to form the Syrian National Coalition for Revolutionary and Opposition Forces, which promptly gained diplomatic recognition from the major Western nations, the

Gulf states and also from Turkey (the Assad regime's relations with which had by then been further soured by a number of violent border incidents and the tide of Syrian refugees).

From 2013, as the civil war intensified, Syrian government forces were accused of deploying chemical weapons against rebel-held areas in contravention of international law and there was an upsurge in activity by international militant organizations, including al-Qaeda and the jihadist Islamic State (IS). In June 2014 IS declared that it was incorporating territory in Syria and Iraq over which it had taken control into a new caliphate. In Aug. the UN accused the organization of 'mass atrocities' and from Sept. that year US led-international forces, including several Arab states, began air strikes against IS positions. The civil war persisted through 2015 and from Sept. the Russian military joined the hostilities with air strikes ostensibly against IS targets, although Western countries suspected they were directed more widely against moderate Syrian opponents of the Assad regime. In addition, the UK parliament voted in Dec. to extend British air strikes against IS to Syrian territory (reversing an earlier vote in 2013). In late 2016 the tide of the war began to turn in Assad's favour as his forces, supported by Russian air power and Iranian-sponsored militias, forged a western corridor of territory under their control that culminated in the expulsion of rebel fighters from the city of Aleppo. In April 2017 the USA launched a missile strike on a Syrian military base in response to a chemical weapon attack on a rebel-held town in Idlib district, and in Oct. US-backed rebel and Kurdish forces took control of the IS stronghold of Raqqah. Assad's forces nevertheless reasserted territorial control over much of the country by April 2018, when another alleged government chemical weapon attack prompted a further retaliatory air strike by the USA, UK and France on Syrian military facilities.

As it became increasingly likely through 2018 that Assad would remain in power, Syria's neighbours—initially the United Arab Emirates and Bahrain in Dec.—began moves to restore diplomatic ties after years of estrangement. Also in Dec., US President Donald Trump ordered the withdrawal of 2,000 US troops in Syria, claiming that Islamic State extremists had been defeated, although the decision was criticized by US allies and prompted the resignation of his defence secretary.

Meanwhile, in June 2014 Assad had been returned for another seven-year presidential term by voters in government-controlled areas of the country in the first multi-candidate elections for over 40 years. However, the poll was dismissed by the rebel opposition and Western powers as illegitimate.

Defence

Before the start of the Syrian Civil War, military service was compulsory for a period of 18 months. Defence expenditure in 2010 totalled US$2,296m. (US$103 per capita), representing 3·9% of GDP. Syria had 14,000 troops based in Lebanon in early 2005, but in March 2005 the two countries agreed that Syria would begin to redeploy the troops to the Bekaa Valley in the east of the country. They were subsequently all withdrawn from Lebanon.

In Sept. 2007 an Israeli air strike destroyed a suspected nuclear reactor in the Deir Ez-Zor region.

Army

At the time of the start of Syria's civil war in 2011, personnel numbered about 220,000 (including conscripts) with a further 280,000 available reservists. In addition there was a gendarmerie of 8,000 and a Workers Militia of approximately 100,000.

Navy

The Navy included 32 patrol and coastal combatants in 2011. A small naval aviation branch of the Air Force operated 13 anti-submarine warfare helicopters. Personnel in 2011 numbered 5,000.

Air Force

The Air Force, including Air Defence Command, had (2011) 70,000 personnel plus 30,000 reservists. Air Defence Command numbered 60,000 in 2011 (including 20,000 reservists). There were 365 combat-capable aircraft (including MiG-21, MiG-23, MiG-25 and MiG-29 supersonic interceptors and Su-22 and Su-24 fighter-bombers), and 33 attack helicopters.

International Relations

Syria was the world's largest recipient of overseas development assistance in both 2015 and 2016. It received US$4·9bn. worth in 2015 and US$8·9bn. in 2016.

Economy

In 2009 manufacturing, mining and public utilities contributed 31·4% to GDP; followed by agriculture, 21·1%; trade, restaurants and hotels, 17·0%; and transport and communications, 10·1%.

Syria featured among the ten most corrupt countries in the world in a 2018 survey of 180 countries carried out by the anti-corruption organization Transparency International.

Overview

The civil war in Syria that began in 2011 has significantly damaged the economy, with ongoing instability and violence hampering prospects for reconstruction. Before the conflict, reforms had spurred growth in the state-dominated economy by just under 5% per year between 2005 and 2010. However, the growth was not socially inclusive, with little job creation or poverty reduction. Rural society became increasingly marginalized and susceptible to external shocks such as drought, despite contributing some 20% to overall GDP. Expansion was largely dependent on oil revenues, but exports have collapsed since violence erupted in 2011.

With over 250,000 people killed, 7·7m. people internally displaced and another 4·8m. leaving the country by Sept. 2017 because of the conflict, an economic recovery faces major obstacles. The rate of extreme poverty has increased sharply, with the UN reporting a rise from 14% in 2010 to more than 50% in 2015. In 2017 the pro-Assad Damascus Center for Research and Studies estimated the rate at 67%. Welfare services have also been drastically cut. Should peace be restored, short- and medium-term economic challenges include improving output (with an estimated US$180bn. needed to restore pre-conflict GDP levels), stabilizing the currency, reducing unemployment and rebuilding infrastructure and homes. The government would also have to focus on reforming public services and developing the non-oil sector to diversify the economy.

Currency

The monetary unit is the *Syrian pound* (SYP) of 100 *piastres*. Inflation was 15·2% in 2008, falling to 2·8% in 2009 and rising to 4·4% in 2010. Since the onset of the civil war in 2011 data has been unavailable. Gold reserves were 830,000 troy oz in June 2011. Broad money supply in Dec. 2011 was £Syr.1,881·6bn.

Budget

The fiscal year is the calendar year. In 2009 revenues were £Syr.533·0bn. and expenditures £Syr.666·4bn.

Performance

The economy had experienced a growth of 5·9% in 2009 and 3·4% in 2010 before the onset of the Syrian civil war, but subsequent data for real GDP is unavailable. Total GDP in 2012 was US$73·7bn.

Banking and Finance

The Central Bank is the bank of issue. Commercial banks were nationalized in 1963. The *Governor* of the Central Bank is Hazem Karfoul. In 2007 there were nine private banks.

Foreign debt totalled US$4,729m. in 2010, equivalent to 8·2% of GNI.

A stock exchange opened in Damascus in March 2009 with six listed companies.

Energy and Natural Resources

Environment

Syria's carbon dioxide emissions from the consumption of energy in 2011 were the equivalent of 2·8 tonnes per capita.

Electricity

Installed capacity was 8·2m. kW in 2011. Production in 2011 was 41·08bn. kWh and consumption per capita 1,871 kWh.

Oil and Gas

Oil reserves in 2012 were 2·5bn. bbls; production in 2012 (8·2m. tonnes) fell by 49·9% from the 2011 total of 16·3m. tonnes as a result of Syria's civil war. Natural gas reserves (2012), 300bn. cu. metres; production, 7·6bn. cu. metres.

Minerals

Phosphate production, 2012, 460,000 tonnes; other minerals are gypsum (328,000 tonnes in 2012) and salt (34,000 tonnes in 2012). There are indications of lead, copper, antimony, nickel, chrome and other minerals widely distributed.

Agriculture

The arable area in 2013 was 4·66m. ha. and there were 1·07m. ha. of permanent cropland. 1·31m. ha. were irrigated in 2013. Production of principal crops, 2013 (in 1,000 tonnes): wheat, 3,182; olives, 842; oranges, 792; tomatoes, 500; potatoes, 442; sugar beets, 317; seed cotton, 169; cottonseed, 110. Livestock (2013, in 1,000): sheep, 18,019; goats, 2,294; cattle, 1,113; asses, 835; chickens, 26,984. Livestock products, 2013 (in 1,000 tonnes): milk, 2,364; meat, 359; eggs, 123.

Forestry

In 2015 there were 0·49m. ha. of forest (3% of the land area). Timber production in 2011 was 68,000 cu. metres.

Fisheries

The total catch in 2015 was an estimated 4,100 tonnes (59% freshwater fish).

Industry

Production (in tonnes): cement (2009), 5,497,000; residual fuel oil (2007), 4,862,000; distillate fuel oil (2007), 3,824,000; petrol (2007), 1,278,000; virgin olive oil (2011), 208,000; cotton yarn (2008), 137,000; nitrogenous fertilizers (2008), 116,000; refrigerators (2008), 248,000 units; washing machines (2008), 94,000 units; carpets (2008), 11·7m. sq. metres.

Labour

The labour force in 2013 was 6,025,000 (5,147,000 in 2003). 45·7% of the population aged 15–64 was economically active in 2013. In the same year 11·3% of the population was unemployed.

Syria had 19,000 people living in slavery according to the Walk Free Foundation's 2013 *Global Slavery Index*.

International Trade

Imports and Exports

Imports (c.i.f.) in 2010 totalled US$17,562m. (US$15,443m. in 2009) and exports (f.o.b.) US$11,353m. (US$9,694m. in 2009). Main imports: seed oils, wheat flours and wheat. Main exports: spice seeds, apples and pears, and calcium phosphates. Turkey is the principal import supplier, ahead of China. Egypt is the biggest export market, with Jordan the second largest.

Communications

Roads

In 2006 there were 40,032 km of roads, including 1,103 km of motorways, 5,971 km of main roads and 31,849 km of secondary roads; 95·8% of roads were paved. There were in 2007 a total of 446,100 passenger cars in use (22 per 1,000 inhabitants), 50,800 buses and coaches and 528,300 vans and lorries. In 2007 there were 13,465 road accidents involving injury resulting in 2,818 deaths.

Rail

In 2008 the Syrian Railways operated 1,801 km of 1,435 mm gauge; in 2010 the smaller Hedjaz-Syrian Railway operated 338 km of 1,050 mm gauge. Passenger-km travelled on the Syrian Railways in 2008 came to 1·1bn. and freight tonne-km to 2·4bn.; passenger-km travelled on the Hedjaz-Syrian Railway in 2009 came to 665,000 and freight tonne-km to 0·2m. Some passenger services resumed in 2015 after the rail network had been closed down following damage during the civil war starting in 2011.

Civil Aviation

Damascus airport has ceased operations on several occasions amid fierce fighting since the outbreak of the civil war in 2011. No major international air carriers currently fly to Damascus.

Shipping

In Jan. 2014 there were 18 ships of 300 GT or over registered, totalling 59,000 GT. The main port is Lattakia.

Telecommunications

In 2014 there were 14,039,000 mobile phone subscriptions (638·6 per 1,000 inhabitants). Syria had 3,629,000 fixed telephone lines in 2014. In the same year 28·1% of the population were internet users.

Social Institutions

Out of 178 countries analysed in the 2017 *Fragile States Index*—a list published jointly by the Fund for Peace and *Foreign Policy* magazine—Syria was ranked the joint fifth most vulnerable (along with Sudan) to conflict or collapse. The index is based on 12 indicators of state vulnerability across social, political and economic categories.

Justice

Syrian law is based on both Islamic and French jurisprudence. There are two courts of first instance in each district, one for civil and one for criminal cases. There is also a Summary Court in each sub-district, under Justices of the Peace. There is a Court of Appeal in the capital of each governorate, with a Court of Cassation in Damascus. The death penalty is still in force, but owing to the ongoing conflict it is not known if judicial executions are still taking place.

50·5% of prisoners had yet to receive a trial according to 2014 estimates by the International Centre for Prison Studies.

Education

In 2007 there were 145,781 pre-primary school children, 2,310,168 primary school pupils and 2,549,444 secondary school pupils. Adult literacy in 2009 was an estimated 84·2% (male, 90·4%; female, 78·0%).

In 2005–06 there were five universities: Al-Baath University, the Syrian Virtual University, Tishreen University, the University of Aleppo and the University of Damascus. The establishment of private universities has been permitted since 2001.

In 2007 total expenditure on education came to 4·9% of GDP and accounted for 16·7% of total government expenditure.

Health

In the period 2005–11 Syria had 15 hospital beds per 10,000 population. There were 30,702 physicians, 16,169 dentists, 38,070 nurses and midwives and 16,579 pharmacists in 2008.

In *Water: At What Cost? The State of the World's Water 2016*, WaterAid reported that 9·9% of the population does not have access to safe water.

Religion

According to the Pew Research Center's Forum on Religion & Public Life, in 2010 the population was an estimated 92·8% Muslim and 5·2% Christian. Most Muslims in 2010 were Sunnis but there were also significant numbers of Alawites (an offshoot of Shia Islam), including President Assad. Sunnis make up nearly three-quarters of the total population.

Culture

World Heritage Sites

There are six UNESCO sites in Syria: the old city of Damascus, dating from the 3rd millennium BC and including the Umayyid Mosque (inscribed in 1979); the old city of Bosra, once the capital of the Roman province of Arabia and an important stopover on the ancient caravan routes (1980); Palmyra (Tadmur), a desert oasis northeast of Damascus, containing the ruins of a city that was one of the most prosperous centres of the ancient world (1980—partly demolished by Islamic State forces in 2015); the old city of Aleppo, located at the crossroads of various trade routes since the 2nd millennium BC (1986); the two castles of Crac des Chevaliers and Qal'at Salah El-Din (2006); and the Ancient Villages of Northern Syria (2011), which date from the 1st to the 7th centuries AD.

Press

In 2008 there were four national daily newspapers with a combined circulation of 130,000 plus five regional and local dailies. In the 2013 *World Press Freedom Index* compiled by Reporters Without Borders, Syria ranked 176th out of 179 countries.

Tourism

In 2010 there were a record 8,546,000 international tourist arrivals (excluding same-day visitors), spending a total of US$6·19bn. Tourist numbers have, however, declined considerably since 2010 as a result of the civil war.

Diplomatic Representatives

Of Syria in the United Kingdom (8 Belgrave Sq., London, SW1X 8PH)
Temporarily closed.

Of the United Kingdom in Syria
All staff have been withdrawn.

Of Syria in the USA (embassy in Washington, D.C. closed in March 2014).

Of the USA in Syria (embassy in Damascus closed in Feb. 2012).

Of Syria to the United Nations
Ambassador: Bashar Jaafari.

Of Syria to the European Union
Ambassador: Vacant.

Further Reading

Cockburn, Patrick, *The Rise of Islamic State: ISIS and the New Sunni Revolution.* 2015
Goodarzi, Jubin, *Syria and Iran: Diplomatic Alliance and Power Politics in the Middle East.* 2006
Guo, Luc, *Understanding Syria: History, Geography, Economy.* 2011
Hinnebusch, Raymond, *Syria: Revolution From Above.* 2002
Hitti, Philip K., *History of Syria Including Lebanon and Palestine.* 2002
Kienle, Eberhard, *Contemporary Syria: Liberalization Between Cold War and Peace.* 1997
Lesch, David W., *The New Lion of Damascus: Bashar Al Asad and Modern Syria.* 2005
Moubayed, Sami, *Steel and Silk: Men and Women Who Shaped Syria 1900–2000.* 2005
Perthes, Volker, *Syria Under Bashar Al-Asad: Modernisation and the Limits of Change.* 2005
Starr, Stephen, *Revolt in Syria: Eye-Witness to the Uprising.* 2012
Van Dam, Nikolaos, *The Struggle for Power in Syria: Politics and Society Under Asad and the Ba'th Party.* 2011
Weiss, Michael and Hassan, Hassan, *ISIS: Inside the Army of Terror.* 2015
National Statistical Office: Central Bureau of Statistics, Nizar Kabbani St., Abu Romanneh, Damascus.
Website: http://www.cbssyr.sy

Tajikistan

Jumkhurii Tojikiston (Republic of Tajikistan)

Capital: Dushanbe
Population projection, 2020: 9·48m.
GNI per capita, 2017: (PPP$) 3,317
HDI/world rank, 2017: 0·650/127=
Internet domain extension: .tj

Key Historical Events

The Tajik Soviet Socialist Republic was formed from those regions of Bokhara and Turkestan where the population consisted mainly of Tajiks. It was admitted as a constituent republic of the Soviet Union on 5 Dec. 1929. In Aug. 1990 the Tajik Supreme Soviet adopted a declaration of republican sovereignty and in Sept. 1991 Tajikistan declared independence. In Dec. 1991 the republic became a member of the CIS. After demonstrations and fighting, the Communist government was replaced by a Revolutionary Coalition Council on 7 May 1992. Following further demonstrations, President Nabiyev was ousted on 7 Sept. Civil war broke out, and the government resigned on 10 Nov. On 30 Nov. it was announced that a CIS peacekeeping force would be sent to Tajikistan. A state of emergency was imposed in Jan. 1993. On 23 Dec. 1996 a ceasefire was signed. A further agreement on 8 March 1997 provided for the disarmament of the Islamic-led insurgents, the United Tajik Opposition, and their eventual integration into the regular armed forces. A peace agreement brokered by Iran and Russia was signed in Moscow on 27 June 1997 stipulating that the opposition should have 30% of ministerial posts in a Commission of National Reconciliation. President Rakhmon (formerly Rakhmonov), first elected in 1994, won a second term in 1999. The country's first multi-party parliamentary election was held in Feb. 2000, although it was criticized by observers for failing to meet democratic standards. Rakhmon won further terms in 2006 and 2013.

Ethnic conflict and Islamist militancy have plagued Tajikistan in the post-Soviet era, with the Rasht Valley and the Fergana Valleys—a region disputed by ethnic Tajiks, Uzbeks and Kyrgyz groups—being areas of particular concern.

Territory and Population

Tajikistan is bordered in the north and west by Uzbekistan and Kyrgyzstan, in the east by China and in the south by Afghanistan. Area, 143,100 sq. km (55,200 sq. miles). It includes two regions (Sughd and Khatlon), one autonomous region (Gorno-Badakhshan Autonomous Region), the city of Dushanbe and regions of republican subordination. 2010 census population, 7,564,502; density, 53 per sq. km. 84·3% of the population in 2010 were Tajiks, 12·2% Uzbeks, 0·8% Kyrgyz and 0·5% Russians. In Jan. 2014 the population was estimated at 8,161,100.

The UN gives a projected population for 2020 of 9·48m.

In 2011 only 26·4% of the population lived in urban areas, making it the most rural of the former Soviet republics.

The capital is Dushanbe (2010 population, 724,844). Other large towns are Khujand (formerly Leninabad), Kulyab (Kulob) and Kurgan-Tyube.

The official language is Tajik, written in Arabic script until 1930 and after 1992 (the Roman alphabet was used 1930–40; the Cyrillic, 1940–92).

Social Statistics

Estimates, 2008: births, 192,000; deaths, 44,000. Rates, 2008 estimate (per 1,000 population): births, 28·1; deaths, 6·4. Life expectancy, 2013, 64·1 years for men and 70·8 for women. Annual growth, 2000–08, 1·3%. Infant mortality, 2010, 52 per 1,000 live births; fertility rate, 2008, 3·4 births per woman.

Climate

Considering its altitude, Tajikistan is a comparatively dry country. July to Sept. are particularly dry months. Winters are cold but spring comes earlier than farther north. Dushanbe, Jan. –10°C, July 25°C. Annual rainfall 375 mm.

Constitution and Government

In Nov. 1994 a new Constitution was approved by 90% of the electorate. The head of state is the *President*, elected by universal suffrage. When the 1994 constitution took effect, the presidential term of office was five years. However, an amendment to the Constitution prior to the 1999 election extended the term to seven years, although a president could only serve one term. Following another referendum in June 2003, President Rakhmonov (now Rakhmon) was allowed to serve two additional terms after the expiry (in Nov. 2006) of the one that he was serving, theoretically enabling him to remain in office until 2020. The Organization for Security and Co-operation in Europe and the USA expressed concerns at the result. In 2015 Rakhmon was granted 'Leader of the Nation' status by parliament, providing him and his family with permanent immunity from prosecution. In May 2016 a reported 96·6% of voters in a further referendum endorsed a raft of 41 constitutional amendments. These included removing term limits on the presidency for Rakhmon, reducing the minimum age to hold the office to 30 and barring religion-based political parties. Tajikistan has a bicameral legislature. The lower chamber is the 63-seat *Majlisi Namoyandagon* (*Assembly of Representatives*), with 41 members elected in single-seat constituencies and 22 by proportional representation for five-year terms. The upper chamber is the 34-seat *Majlisi Milliy* (*National Assembly*), with 25 members chosen for five-year terms by local deputies, eight appointed by the president and one reserved for the former president.

National Anthem

'Zinda bosh, ey Vatan, Tochikistoni ozodi man' ('Live long, O Nation, my free Tajikistan'); words by Gulnazar Keldi, tune by Suleiman Yudakov.

Recent Elections

At presidential elections on 6 Nov. 2013 President Rakhmon was re-elected with 83·9% of votes cast. The main opposition party boycotted the vote after potentially the most significant rival candidate, female rights lawyer Oinikhol Bobonazarova, was barred from standing.

In elections to the Assembly of Representatives held on 1 March 2015 the People's Democratic Party of Tajikistan (PDPT) won 51 of 63 seats (65·4% of the vote), Agrarian Party 5 (11·7%), the Party of Economic Reforms 3 (7·5%), the Communist Party (CP) 2 (2·2%), the Socialist Party 1 (5·5%) and the Democratic Party 1 (1·7%). Turnout was 87·7%. Elections to the National Assembly were held on 27 March 2015. 25 of the 33 seats were voted for by local majlisi deputies and eight were appointed by the president.

Current Government

President: Emomalii Rakhmon; b. 1952 (PDPT; as Speaker elected by the former Supreme Soviet 19 Nov. 1992, re-elected 6 Nov. 1994, 6 Nov. 1999, 6 Nov. 2006 and 6 Nov. 2013).

In Feb. 2019 the government comprised:

Prime Minister: Qohir Rasulzoda; b. 1961 (PDPT; sworn in 23 Nov. 2013).

First Deputy Prime Minister: Davlatali Said. *Deputy Prime Ministers:* Mahmadtoir Zokirzoda; Azim Ibrohim.

Minister of Agriculture: Izatullo Sattori. *Culture:* Shamsiddin Orumbekzoda. *Defence:* Sherali Mirzo. *Economic Development and Trade:* Nematullo Hikmatullozoda. *Education and Science:* Nuriddin Said. *Energy and Water Resources:* Usmonal Usmonzoda. *Finance:* Faiziddin Qahhorzoda.

Foreign Affairs: Sirojidin Aslov. *Health and Social Protection:* Nasim Khoja Olimzoda. *Industry and New Technologies:* Zarobiddin Fayzullozoda. *Internal Affairs:* Ramazon Rahimzoda. *Justice:* Rustam Shohmurod. *Labour, Migration and Employment:* Sumangul Taghoizoda. *Transport:* Khudoyor Khudoyorzoda. *Office of the President:* http://www.prezident.tj

Current Leaders

Emomalii Rakhmon

Position
President

Introduction
Emomalii Rakhmon (formerly Rakhmonov), a former cotton-farm administrator, became Tajikistan's head of state in Nov. 1992, after the country's first post-Soviet leader, Rakhmon Nabiyev, was forced to resign. Rakhmon has survived civil war and an assassination attempt, but reforming institutions and raising living standards in one of the region's poorest countries has proved a hard challenge. In March 2007 he announced that he was dropping the Russian suffix (-ov) from his surname. He was re-elected for a further seven-year term in Nov. 2013.

Early Life
Emomalii Sharipovich Rakhmon was born on 5 Oct. 1952 in the Danghara district of the Kulob province of the Tajik Soviet Socialist Republic (SSR). He studied electronics and from 1969 worked at a vegetable-oil extraction factory in Qurghonteppa. After three years in the Soviet navy, Rakhmon became an administrator at Lenin *Kholkov* (collective farm) in Danghara, constructing a power base as chairman of the farm's trade union committee.

He studied economics by correspondence and in 1982 graduated from the Tajik State University. He was elected people's deputy of the supreme council of the Tajik SSR in 1990. Tajikistan declared independence in Sept. 1991 but hopes of an economically viable state were undermined by civil war. On 19 Nov. 1992, following Nabiev's forced resignation and the annulment of the office of president, Rakhmon was elected chairman of the supreme council and head of state. On 6 Nov. 1994, following inter-Tajik peace talks, he won presidential elections, claiming 58·3% of the vote.

Career in Office
Civil war continued through the early years of Rakhmon's presidency and by the time hostilities between the Islamist-led opposition and his Moscow-backed administration ended in June 1997, at least 50,000 people had died. In March 1998 he joined the centrist People's Democratic Party of Tajikistan (PDPT). He was re-elected president on 6 Nov. 1999 with 97% of the vote, and on 22 June 2003 won a referendum to allow him to run for two further seven-year terms. Rakhmon's grip on power was underlined in the general elections of Feb. 2005 and Feb. 2010 when his PDPT won landslide parliamentary victories. The opposition Islamic and communist parties alleged fraud in both polls and observers said the vote failed to meet international standards. Meanwhile, Rakhmon was again re-elected overwhelmingly to the presidency in Nov. 2006 as the opposition boycotted the vote.

Tajikistan suffered a particularly severe winter in 2007–08 and also faced an energy crisis. Many industries were forced to shut down, some rural areas had no electricity and even the capital faced food shortages. In April 2008 the International Monetary Fund ordered the Tajik authorities to repay IMF disbursements that had been obtained on the basis of false data and misreporting. Rakhmon subsequently removed some senior National Bank officials from their positions.

Tensions increased between Tajikistan and Uzbekistan through 2012 as the Tajik government accused its neighbour of disrupting gas and electricity deliveries, while the Uzbek government objected to Tajik plans for a large dam project (work on which began in Oct. 2016) fearing that it would restrict access to regional water resources.

In Oct. 2012 Tajikistan agreed to extend Russia's lease on a Soviet-era army base, scheduled to expire in 2014, for 30 more years.

Rakhmon's re-election in Nov. 2013 was criticized by observers from the Organization for Security and Co-operation in Europe, who highlighted a lack of pluralism and genuine electoral choice. Following the poll he dismissed Akil Akilov, the prime minister since 1999, and replaced him with Qohir Rasulzoda. In parliamentary elections in March 2015 the PDPT again won an overwhelming majority of seats.

In May 2016 a nationwide referendum approved constitutional amendments including the scrapping of the limit on presidential terms and also the outlawing of faith-based political parties, particularly targeting Islamic

militancy. Although Rakhmon's political dominance has been confirmed, economic discontent fuelled by poverty and unemployment has nevertheless encouraged radicalization among the younger population.

Defence

Conscription is compulsory for two years. In 2011 the active armed forces had a strength of 8,800. Paramilitary forces totalled 7,500 including 3,800 interior troops and 2,500 emergencies ministry troops. 5,000 Russian Army personnel were stationed in the country in 2011.

Defence expenditure in 2013 totalled US$189m. (US$24 per capita), representing 2·2% of GDP.

Army
Personnel strength (2011) 7,300.

Air Force
Air Force/Air Defence strength (2011) 1,500.

Economy

Agriculture accounted for 26·6% of GDP in 2012, industry 22·5% and services 50·9%.

Overview
Although arable land accounts for only 10% of its total area, Tajikistan is primarily an agrarian economy, with the sector employing almost half of the labour force and contributing 25% of GDP in 2016. As a result of war and unstable government in the 1990s, the economy deteriorated faster than in other former Soviet satellite states. In 1996 a reform programme was launched, supported by the IMF and the World Bank. Despite a slow start and the Russian financial crisis of 1998, the focus on reconstruction stimulated a market-driven economy.

Economic growth, which averaged 8·6% annually from 2000–08, has depended on cotton and aluminium exports, as well as rising remittances (principally from Russia). Sound macroeconomic management has enabled inflation to be brought under control, having reached levels between 30% and 40% in the period 1998–2001. Other achievements include the halving of foreign debt, stabilization of the exchange rate and a reduction in the poverty level from 83% in 1999 to 42% in 2011.

The global financial crisis saw growth slow to 3·9% in 2009, caused by a sharp reduction in remittances (down 31% from the previous year) and lower prices and demand for aluminium and cotton. Larger remittance inflows led to GDP growth of 7·5% in 2012 and reached a record high of US$4·1bn. in 2013, fuelling investment and private consumption.

Although Tajikistan maintained high levels of growth between 2010 and 2015—6% or above annually—the services sector has faced decline in recent years as a result of low external trade. Additionally, private consumption has since contracted owing to currency depreciation, although its effect has been offset in part by increases in fixed investment. A lack of developed infrastructure, the weak rule of law and sprawling bureaucracy (especially in the tax system) pose long-term challenges to the economy.

In March 2013 the country joined the World Trade Organization.

Currency
The unit of currency is the *somoni* (TJS) of 100 *dirams*, which replaced the Tajik rouble on 30 Oct. 2000 at 1 somoni = 1,000 Tajik roubles. The introduction of the new currency was intended to strengthen the national banking system. The IMF voiced its support for the new currency, which it believed would contribute to macroeconomic stability and expedite the transition to a market economy. Inflation in 1993 was 2,601%, declining to 418% in 1996 and still further to 7·2% in 2004, the reduction being helped by a US$22m. IMF loan in 1996 and maintenance of a tighter monetary regime. Although the rate had risen back up to 20·4% in 2008, more recently it was 5·9% in 2016 and 7·3% in 2017. Broad money supply totalled 12·5bn. somoni in June 2016. Gold reserves stood at 47,000 troy oz in July 2005.

Budget
General government revenues in 2014 totalled 11,550m. somoni and expenditures 13,234m. somoni.

VAT is 20%.

Performance

Annual real GDP growth was negative for four consecutive years in the mid-1990s. Since then the economy has recovered—more recently there has been growth of 6·0% in 2015, 6·9% in 2016 and 7·1% in 2017. Total GDP in 2017 was US$7·1bn. According to World Bank data for 2017, Tajikistan is the country third most reliant on remittances from abroad, accounting for 31·6% of total GDP.

Banking and Finance

The central bank and bank of issue is the National Bank (*Chairman*, Jamshed Nurmahmadzoda). In Sept. 2014 there were 17 commercial banks, including one fully state-owned institution and seven majority foreign-owned institutions.

Foreign debt totalled US$2,955m. in 2010, representing 53·1% of GNI.

Energy and Natural Resources

Environment

In 2011 Tajikistan's carbon dioxide emissions from the consumption of energy accounted for 0·4 tonnes per capita.

Electricity

Installed capacity in 2011 was 5·1m. kW. Production was 16·4bn. kWh in 2011 and consumption per capita 2,081 kWh.

Oil and Gas

Natural gas output in 2011 was 40 cu. metres; reserves were 5·7bn. cu. metres in 2013.

Minerals

There are deposits of coal, lead, zinc, iron ore, antimony, mercury, gold, silver, tungsten and uranium. Production, 2010, in 1,000 tonnes: aluminium, 349; hard coal, 177.

Agriculture

In 2013 there were approximately 735,000 ha. of arable land and 140,000 ha. of permanent crops. Cotton is the major cash crop, with various fruits, sugarcane, jute, silk, rice and millet also being grown.

Output of main agricultural products (in 1,000 tonnes) in 2013: potatoes, 1,116; wheat, 947; watermelons, 495; onions, 435; seed cotton, 393; tomatoes, 368. Livestock, 2013: 3·10m. sheep; 2·10m. cattle; 1·83m. goats; 5m. chickens. Livestock products, 2013 estimates (in 1,000 tonnes): meat, 88; milk, 902.

Forestry

Forests covered 0·41m. ha. in 2015, or 3% of the land area. Timber production in 2011 was 90,000 cu. metres.

Fisheries

The total catch in 2012 was 923 tonnes, exclusively from inland waters.

Industry

Major industries: aluminium, electro-chemical plants, textile machinery, carpet weaving, silk mills, refrigerators, hydro-electric power. Output in 2007 (unless otherwise specified): cement (2011), 299,400 tonnes; multi-nutrient fertilizer, 24,500 tonnes; cotton woven fabrics, 30·5m. sq. metres; woven carpets and other floor coverings, 941,700 sq. metres; woven silk fabrics, 40,900 sq. metres; footwear, 172,400 pairs.

Labour

The labour force in 2013 was 3,578,000 (2,585,000 in 2003). 70·7% of the population aged 15–64 was economically active in 2013. In the same year 11·2% of the population was unemployed.

Tajikistan had 24,000 people living in slavery according to the Walk Free Foundation's 2013 *Global Slavery Index*.

International Trade

Imports and Exports

In 2014 imports were valued at US$4,297·4m. (US$4,150·7m. in 2013) and exports at US$977·3m. (US$1,161·8m. in 2013). Main imports are petroleum products, wheat and cars; main exports are aluminium, cotton fibre and electricity. Principal import suppliers are China, Kazakhstan, Russia and Uzbekistan. Principal export markets are Kazakhstan, Switzerland, Turkey and Uzbekistan.

Communications

Roads

The road network covers an estimated 30,000 km, nearly all of which was built in the Soviet era. There were 357,869 registered vehicles in use in 2010 (297,341 cars, 37,395 heavy trucks, 14,653 buses, and 8,480 motorcycles and mopeds). In 2010 there were 411 fatalities as a result of road accidents.

Rail

Length of railways, 2011, 621 km. Passenger-km travelled in 2011 came to 32m. and freight tonne-km in 2009 to 1·3bn.

Civil Aviation

There are international airports at Dushanbe and Khujand. The national carrier is Tajik Air, which has flights to 11 international destinations as well as operating domestic services. In 2012 scheduled airline traffic of Tajik-based carriers flew 10·4m. km; passenger-km totalled 2·9bn. in the same year.

Telecommunications

In 2013 there were an estimated 425,000 fixed telephone subscriptions in Tajikistan and mobile phone subscriptions numbered an estimated 7,537,000 (918 per 1,000 persons). In the same year an estimated 16·0% of the population were internet users.

Social Institutions

Out of 178 countries analysed in the 2017 *Fragile States Index*—a list published jointly by the Fund for Peace and *Foreign Policy* magazine—Tajikistan was ranked the 61st most vulnerable to conflict or collapse. The index is based on 12 indicators of state vulnerability across social, political and economic categories.

Justice

In 2012, 16,593 crimes were reported (12,754 in 2002). The population in penal institutions in Dec. 2010 was 9,317 (130 per 100,000 of national population). The death penalty is retained but has been subject to a moratorium since July 2004.

Education

The adult literacy rate in 2008 was over 99%. In 2007 there were 680,308 pupils and 31,482 teaching staff at primary schools; 1,012,275 pupils and 61,186 teaching staff at secondary schools; and 147,294 students and 7,761 academic staff at higher education institutions. There were 32 higher education institutions in total in 2007.

In 2007 public expenditure on education came to 3·5% of GNI and 18·2% of total government spending.

Health

In 2006 there were 61 hospital beds per 10,000 inhabitants. There were 13,267 physicians in 2006, 1,003 dentistry personnel and 33,165 nursing and midwifery personnel.

In *Water: At What Cost? The State of the World's Water 2016*, WaterAid reported that 26·2% of the population does not have access to safe water.

Welfare

At the beginning of 2009 there were 537,700 pensioners; average monthly pension was 87·36 somoni.

Religion

The Tajiks are predominantly Sunni Muslims (80%); Shia Muslims, 5%.

Culture

World Heritage Sites

Tajikistan has two sites on the UNESCO World Heritage List: the Proto-urban site of Sarazm (inscribed on the list in 2010), an archaeological site displaying some of the early human settlements in Central Asia; and Tajik

National Park (2013), which covers over 2·5m. ha. and offers the opportunity for the study of plate tectonics and subduction phenomena.

Press

Media freedom suffered during the civil war between 1992 and 1997 when around 60 journalists were killed and many others fled the country. *Imruz News*, the first daily newspaper since 1992, was launched in Aug. 2010.

Tourism

There were 244,000 non-resident visitors in 2012 (183,000 in 2011).

Diplomatic Representatives

Of Tajikistan in the United Kingdom (3 Shortlands, London, W6 8DA)
  Ambassador: Masud Khalifazoda.

Of the United Kingdom in Tajikistan (65 Mirzo Tursunzoda St., 734002 Dushanbe)
  Ambassador: Hugh Philpott, OBE.

Of Tajikistan in the USA (1005 New Hampshire Ave., NW, Washington, D.C., 20037)
  Ambassador: Farhod Salim.

Of the USA in Tajikistan (109-A Ismoili Somoni Ave., Dushanbe)
  Ambassador: Vacant.
  Chargé d'Affaires a.i.: Kevin Covert.

Of Tajikistan to the United Nations
  Ambassador: Mahamadamin Mahmadaminov.

Of Tajikistan to the European Union
  Ambassador: Erikinkhon Rahmatullozoda.

Gorno-Badakhshan Autonomous Region

The region was established initially in 1925 as the Special Pamir Province, along the borders of Afghanistan and China. Area, 63,700 sq. km (24,590 sq. miles). Population (mainly Tajiks with a Kirghiz minority), 218,000 (2007). Capital, Khorog. The inhabitants are predominantly Ismaili Muslims.

There is mining for gold, rock crystal, mica, coal and salt. Wheat, fruit and fodder crops are grown, and cattle and sheep are bred in the western parts.

The area is the most impoverished in Tajikistan; the majority of the population exists below the poverty line and many are employed abroad, mainly in the Russian Federation.

The Khorog State University was founded in 1992. The private University of Central Asia has a campus located in Khorog (the other two being in Tekeli, Kazakhstan and Naryn, Kyrgyzstan).

Further Reading

Tajikistan

Abdullaev, K. and Akbarzadeh, S., *Historical Dictionary of Tajikistan.* 2002
Akiner, S., *Tajikistan: Disintegration or Reconciliation?* 2001
Djalili, M. R. (ed.) *Tajikistan: The Trials of Independence.* 1998
Jonson, Lena, *Tajikistan in the New Central Asia: Geopolitics, Great Power Rivalry and Radical Islam.* 2006
National Statistical Office: Statistical Agency under President of the Republic of Tajikistan, 17 Bokhtar St., Dushanbe.
Website: http://www.stat.tj

Tanzania

Jamhuri ya Muungano wa Tanzania (United Republic of Tanzania)

Capital: Dodoma
Population projection, 2020: 62·77m.
GNI per capita, 2017: (PPP$) 2,655
HDI/world rank, 2017: 0·538/154
Internet domain extension: .tz

Key Historical Events

Archaeological evidence suggests that present-day Tanzania was inhabited by Khoisan-speaking hunter-gatherers from at least 10,000 BC. The Sandawe and Hadze of north-central Tanzania are descendants of these groups. Cushitic-speaking cattle herders migrated south from Ethiopia and Sudan from around 1000 BC. Beginning in the first millennium AD, Tanzania was settled by Bantu-speaking iron-working farmers, whose origins are considered to be in the borderlands of present-day Nigeria and Cameroon.

Seafarers from Arabia established a trading settlement on the coast at Kilwa around AD 800, and Persian merchants settled on the islands of Zanzibar and Pemba. Nilotic-speaking pastoralists (including the Maasai and Luo) moved south into Tanzania between AD 900 and AD 1700. Sultan Hassan bin Sulaiman I established control of Kilwa around 1270. Islam spread and a thriving Afro-Arab 'Swahili' culture took hold in coastal areas.

Portuguese explorers arrived off Kilwa in 1500, heralding two centuries of Portuguese control over various East African trading ports. Zanzibar came under Omani control in the 1650s and prospered as a centre of the slave trade, extending its influence over the coastal hinterland and into the mainland interior. Britain attempted to end the slave trade by signing the Treaty of Moresby with the Sultan of Zanzibar in 1822. During the 1880s the German imperialist, Dr Carl Peters, founded German East Africa by signing agreements with local rulers. A series of agreements between Britain and Germany and the Sultan of Zanzibar saw Germany become the dominant influence over most of mainland Tanzania, while the Sultan of Zanzibar retained control of a strip of coastal territories and Britain ruled Zanzibar as a protectorate.

German East Africa was conquered by the Allies in the First World War and subsequently divided between the Belgians, the Portuguese and the British. The country was administered as a League of Nations mandate until 1946, and then as a UN trusteeship territory until 9 Dec. 1961. Tanganyika achieved responsible government in Sept. 1960 and full self-government on 1 May 1961. On 9 Dec. 1961 Tanganyika became a sovereign independent member state of the Commonwealth of Nations. On 9 Dec. 1962 the country adopted a republican form of government (still within the British Commonwealth) and Dr Nyerere was elected as the first president.

Zanzibar gained internal self-government on 24 June 1963, followed by full independence on 9 Dec. 1963. On 12 Jan. 1964 the sultanate was overthrown by a revolt of the Afro-Shirazi Party leaders who established the People's Republic of Zanzibar. Also in Jan. 1964 there was an attempted coup against Nyerere who had to seek British military help. On 26 April 1964 Tanganyika, Zanzibar and Pemba combined to form the United Republic of Tanzania. The first multi-party elections were held in 1995.

Territory and Population

Tanzania is bounded in the northeast by Kenya, north by Lake Victoria and Uganda, northwest by Rwanda and Burundi, west by Lake Tanganyika, southwest by Zambia and Malaŵi, and south by Mozambique. Total area 942,799 sq. km (364,017 sq. miles), including the offshore islands of Zanzibar (1,554 sq. km) and Pemba (906 sq. km) and inland waters. 2012 census population, 44,928,923, giving a density of 50·8 per sq. km.

The UN gives a projected population for 2020 of 62·77m.

In 2011, 26·9% of the population lived in urban areas. In 2000 Tanzania hosted the highest number of refugees in Africa (mainly from Burundi), with a population of over 680,000. By 2012 repatriation programmes had allowed the number of refugees to drop to only just over 100,000.

The chief towns (2012 census populations) are Dar es Salaam, the chief port and former capital (4,364,541), Mwanza (706,453), Zanzibar (501,459), Arusha (416,442), Mbeya (385,279). Dodoma, the capital, had a population of 213,636 in 2012.

The United Republic is divided into 31 administrative regions of which 26 are in mainland Tanzania, three in Zanzibar and two in Pemba. Land areas and populations of the regions:

Region	Land area (sq. km)	Population (2012 census)
Arusha	37,576	1,694,310
Dar es Salaam	1,393	4,364,541
Dodoma	41,311	2,083,588
Geita	20,054	1,739,530
Iringa	35,503	941,238
Kagera	25,265	2,458,023
Katavi	45,843	564,604
Kigoma	37,040	2,127,930
Kilimanjaro	13,250	1,640,087
Lindi	66,040	864,652
Manyara	44,522	1,425,131
Mara	21,760	1,743,830
Mbeya[1]	60,350	2,707,410
Morogoro	70,624	2,218,492
Mtwara	16,710	1,270,854
Mwanza	9,467	2,772,509
Njombe	21,347	702,097
Pwani (Coast)	32,547	1,098,668
Rukwa	22,792	1,004,539
Ruvuma	63,669	1,376,891
Shinyanga	18,901	1,534,808
Simiyu	25,212	1,584,157
Singida	49,340	1,370,637
Tabora	76,150	2,291,623
Tanga	26,677	2,045,205
Zanzibar and Pemba	*2,460*	*1,303,569*
Pemba North	574	211,732
Pemba South	332	195,116
Zanzibar North	470	187,455
Zanzibar South	854	115,588
Zanzibar West	230	593,678

[1]In 2016 Songwe Region was created from the western part of Mbeya Region.

The official languages are Swahili (spoken as a mother tongue by only 8·8% of the population, but used as a *lingua franca* by 91%) and English.

Social Statistics

2008 estimates: births, 1,765,000; deaths, 482,000. Rates, 2008 estimates (per 1,000 population): births, 41·5; deaths, 11·4. Annual population growth rate, 2000–08, 2·7%. Life expectancy in 2013 was 60·2 years for men and 62·9 for women. 45% of the population was below 15 years old in 2008. Infant mortality, 2010, 50 per 1,000 live births; fertility rate, 2008, 5·6 births per woman.

Climate

The climate is very varied and is controlled largely by altitude and distance from the sea. There are three climatic zones: the hot and humid coast, the drier central plateau with seasonal variations of temperature, and the semi-temperate mountains. Dodoma, Jan. 75°F (23·9°C), July 67°F (19·4°C). Annual rainfall 23" (572 mm). Dar es Salaam, Jan. 82°F (27·8°C), July 74°F (23·3°C). Annual rainfall 43" (1,064 mm).

Constitution and Government

The current constitution dates from 25 April 1977 but underwent major revisions in Oct. 1984. The *President* is head of state, chairman of the party and commander-in-chief of the armed forces. The *Prime Minister* is also the leader of government business in the National Assembly.

The 393-member *Bunge (National Assembly)* is composed of 264 constituency representatives, 113 appointed women, ten Union presidential nominees (five of whom must be women), five representatives of the Zanzibar House of Representatives (two women), and one *ex officio* member (the Attorney General). In Dec. 1979 a separate constitution for Zanzibar was approved. Although at present under the same Constitution as Tanzania, Zanzibar has, in fact, been ruled by decree since 1964. The formation of a government of national unity was approved by 66·4% of voters in a referendum in July 2010.

National Anthem

'God Bless Africa/Mungu ibariki Afrika'; words collective, tune by M. E. Sontonga and V. E. Webster.

Government Chronology

Presidents since 1964. (CCM = Chama Cha Mapinduzi (Revolutionary State Party); TANU = Tanganyika African National Union)

1964–85	TANU/CCM	Julius Kambarage Nyerere
1985–95	CCM	Ali Hassan Mwinyi
1995–2005	CCM	Benjamin William Mkapa
2005–15	CCM	Jakaya Mrisho Kikwete
2015–	CCM	John Pombe Magufuli

Recent Elections

Presidential and parliamentary elections were held on 25 Oct. 2015. John Magufuli of Chama Cha Mapinduzi (Revolutionary State Party) won the presidential election with 58·5% of votes cast against Edward Lowassa of Chama Cha Demokrasia na Maendeleo (Party for Democracy and Progress) with 40·0% and six other candidates. Following the parliamentary elections, seats in the National Assembly were distributed as follows: Chama Cha Mapinduzi, 253; Chama Cha Demokrasia na Maendeleo, 70; Chama Cha Wananchi (Civic United Front), 42; Chama Cha Wazalendo (Alliance for Change and Transparency), 1; Chama Cha Mageuzi na Ujenzi wa Taifa (NCCR-Mageuzi), 1. Chama Cha Mapinduzi is Africa's longest-ruling party, having been in power since Tanzania gained independence in 1964.

Current Government

President: John Magufuli; b. 1959 (Chama Cha Mapinduzi/CCM; sworn in 5 Nov. 2015).

Vice-President: Samia Suluhu.

In March 2019 the government consisted of:

Prime Minister: Kassim Majaliwa; b. 1960 (CCM; sworn in 20 Nov. 2015).

President of Zanzibar: Dr Ali Mohamed Shein.

Minister of Agriculture: Charles Tizeba. *Constitutional Affairs and Justice:* Augustine Mahiga. *Defence and National Service:* Hussein Mwinyi. *Education, Science, Technology and Vocational Training:* Joyce Ndalichako. *Energy:* Medard Kalemani. *Finance and Planning:* Philip Mpango. *Foreign Affairs, East African Community Affairs, and Regional and International Co-operation:* Palamagamba Kabudi. *Health, Community Development, Seniors and Children:* Ummy Mwalimu. *Home Affairs:* Kangi Lugola. *Industry, Trade and Investment:* Charles Mwijage. *Information, Culture,*

Artists and Sports: Harrison Mwakyembe. *Lands, Housing and Human Settlements:* William Lukuvi. *Livestock and Fisheries:* Luhaga Mpina. *Minerals:* Anghellah Kairuki. *Natural Resources and Tourism:* Hamisi Kigwangalla. *Water and Irrigation:* Makame Mbarawa. *Works, Transport and Communication:* Isack Kamwelwe.

Government Website: http://www.tanzania.go.tz

Current Leaders

John Magufuli

Position

President

Introduction

A teacher and chemist, John Magufuli is a member of Tanzania's dominant party, Chama Cha Mapinduzi (CCM, or Revolutionary State Party). Having won the Oct. 2015 presidential election, he was sworn in the following month.

Early Life

John Pombe Joseph Magufuli was born on 29 Oct. 1959 in the northwestern district of Chato. Between 1982 and 1983 he worked as a teacher of chemistry and mathematics at a secondary school. He then studied science and education at the the University of Dar es Salaam, graduating in 1988. A year later he joined the Nyanza Co-operative Union Ltd as an industrial chemist, remaining there until 1995. He earned a master's degree and then a doctorate in chemistry from the University of Dar es Salaam in 1994 and 2009 respectively.

Magufuli was first elected to parliament as the representative for Chato in 1995. In 2000 he retained his seat and was promoted from deputy minister of works to minister. In 2006, under President Jakaya Kikwete, he was named minister of lands and human settlement. From 2008–10 he was minister of livestock and fisheries, and then served a second term at the ministry of works until 2015. He earned the nickname 'The Bulldozer' for leading a road-building programme across the country.

On 12 July 2015 Magufuli was nominated CCM candidate for that year's presidential election, ahead of justice minister and former UN deputy secretary-general Asha-Rose Migiro and African Union ambassador to the USA Amina Salum Ali. Despite the strong challenge from opposition candidate Edward Lowassa in the election held on 25 Oct. 2015, Magufuli received 58% of the vote to Lowassa's 40% and was declared the winner four days later. He was sworn in to office on 5 Nov. 2015.

Career in Office

Magufuli pledged to implement a range of cost-cutting measures to combat wasteful public spending. He banned unnecessary foreign travel by government officials and cancelled Independence Day celebrations, freeing up funds for sanitation projects designed to prevent the spread of cholera. On 10 Dec. 2015 he announced his cabinet which, with 19 ministries, had 11 fewer posts than the previous government. Magufuli also promised to impose anti-corruption measures and to exploit Tanzania's gas resources to tackle power shortages across the country. He has since outlined ambitious plans to improve public sector efficiency and living standards despite fiscal limitations, but has nevertheless drawn criticism from Western nations for his alleged political authoritarianism and intolerance in social matters. In Nov. 2018 he declared that he preferred Chinese investment, aid and loans to Western assistance as it was offered with fewer conditions or demands.

Defence

Defence expenditure totalled US$327m. in 2013 (US$7 per capita), representing 1·0% of GDP.

As at 31 May 2016 Tanzania had 2,330 personnel (including 2,230 troops) serving in UN peacekeeping operations.

Army

Strength in 2011 was an estimated 23,000. Equipment in 2011 included 45 main battle tanks, although their serviceability was in doubt. In the meantime Tanzania has taken delivery of a range of new hardware from China, including amphibious light tanks. There is a paramilitary Police Field Force of 1,400.

Navy

Personnel in 2011 totalled about 1,000, with eight patrol and coastal combatants.

Air Force

Tanzania Air Force Command personnel totalled around 3,000 in 2011. Although there were a reported 22 combat-capable aircraft in 2011 virtually no air defence assets were serviceable.

International Relations

In Nov. 1999 a treaty was signed between Tanzania, Kenya and Uganda to create a new East African Community as a means of developing East African trade, tourism and industry and laying the foundations for a future common market and political federation.

Economy

Agriculture accounted for 33·3% of GDP in 2013, industry 24·2% and services 42·5%.

Overview

From the late 1960s to the mid-1980s the economy stagnated under corrupt state control. However, from 1985 popular discontent encouraged the government of Ali Hassan Mwinyi to loosen control over prices and trade. Subsequent banking reforms and a developing private sector spurred growth.

Robust GDP growth averaged 7.0% annually between 2013 and 2016 and measured 6·0% in 2017, driven by the construction, mining, transport and communications sectors. Public investment, particularly the implementation of larger infrastructure projects, is expected to further boost the economy in the mid-term. However, private-sector investment has been hindered by uncertainty in the business environment and stalling credit growth, which fell from 24·8% in 2015 to 7·2% in 2016 and to 0·3% as of Aug. 2017, in response to which the central bank loosened monetary policy to address liquidity constraints. Meanwhile, fiscal deficits of 3·7% and 2·1% of GDP were recorded in 2016 and 2017, respectively.

The government has made considerable efforts to contain recurrent and inefficient spending, including reducing the public-sector payroll and non-priority expenditure while increasing development investment. Nonetheless, the country faces significant challenges, including high poverty and youth unemployment levels and large infrastructure deficiencies. Sustained reforms are needed to maintain continued growth and job creation, led by the private sector as targeted in the government's development plan.

Currency

The monetary unit is the *Tanzanian shilling* (TZS) of 100 *cents*. Foreign exchange reserves were US$3,533m. in Sept. 2009. Inflation, which had been 26·8% in 1995, was down to 4·1% in 2004, the lowest rate for more than 20 years. More recently it was 5·2% in 2016 and 5·3% in 2017. Total money supply in Aug. 2009 was Sh. 3,429·5bn.

Budget

The fiscal year ends 30 June. Budgetary central government revenues in 2012–13 were Sh. 11,582bn. and expenditures Sh. 13,282bn. Taxes contributed 81·0% of revenues in 2012–13 and grants 12·7%; grants represented 50·6% of expenditures in 2012–13 with compensation of employees accounting for 19·7%.

VAT is 18%.

Performance

Real GDP growth was 7·0% in both 2015 and 2016, and then 6·0% in 2017. Total GDP was US$52·1bn. in 2017 (mainland Tanzania only).

Banking and Finance

The central bank is the Bank of Tanzania (*Governor*, Florens Luoga).

On 6 Feb. 1967 all commercial banks with the exception of National Co-operative Banks were nationalized, and their interests vested in the National Bank of Commerce on the mainland and the Peoples' Bank in Zanzibar. However, in 1993 private-sector commercial banks were allowed to open. In 1997 the National Bank of Commerce (NBC) was split into a trade bank, a regional rural bank and a micro-finance bank. It was privatized in 2000, with the South African concern Absa Group Limited purchasing a 55% stake. The government retained 30% with the International Finance Corporation holding 15%. In 2010 it had 53 branches; total assets at 31 Dec. 2009, Sh. 1,294,606m. The NBC's market dominance has severely declined since 1997. In Dec. 2008 the Co-operatives Rural and Development Bank (CRDB) held 17% of the banking sector's total assets, making it the market leader (the National Microfinance Bank held 16% and the NBC 13%). In Oct. 2010 there were 28 commercial banks registered in Tanzania.

Foreign debt totalled US$8,664m. in 2010, representing 37·7% of GNI.

A stock exchange opened in Dar es Salaam in 1996.

Energy and Natural Resources

Environment

Tanzania's carbon dioxide emissions from the consumption of energy in 2011 were the equivalent of 0·2 tonnes per capita.

Electricity

Installed capacity was 1·0m. kW in 2011. Production in 2011 was 5·30bn. kWh, with consumption per capita 116 kWh. In 2016, 33% of the population had access to electricity (up from 15% in 2010).

Oil and Gas

A number of international companies are exploring for both gas and oil. In 2013 proven natural gas reserves were 6·5bn. cu. metres.

Minerals

Tanzania's mineral resources include gold, nickel, cobalt, silver and diamonds. International funds injected to improve Tanzania's economy have resulted in notable increases, particularly in gold production. The first commercial gold mine began operating in Mwanza in 1998. By 2005 the value of gold exports had reached US$642m., up from US$121m. in 2000. Gold production in 2005 totalled 52,236 kg. Large deposits of coal and tin exist but mining is on a small scale. Diamond production in 2013 was 171,391 carats.

Agriculture

About 80% of the workforce are engaged in agriculture, chiefly in subsistence farming. Agricultural produce contributes around 85% of exports. There were an estimated 13·5m. ha. of arable land in 2013 and 2·2m. ha. of permanent crops. Approximately 364,000 ha. were equipped for irrigation in 2013.

Production of main agricultural crops in 2013 (in 1,000 tonnes) was: maize, 5,356; cassava, 4,755; sweet potatoes, 3,470; sugarcane, 2,992; bananas, 2,679; rice, 2,195; potatoes, 1,768; sunflower seeds, 1,630; groundnuts, 1,425; dry beans, 1,114; sesame seeds, 1,050; sorghum, 832; plantains (estimate), 578; coconuts (estimate), 530. Zanzibar is a major producer of cloves.

Livestock (2013): 24·5m. cattle; 16·0m. goats; 7·7m. sheep; 35·5m. chickens (estimate).

Livestock products (2013, in 1,000 tonnes): beef and veal, 300; goat meat (estimate), 38; lamb and mutton (estimate), 25; pork and pork products (estimate), 14; chicken meat, 87; cow's milk, 1,922; goat's milk (estimate), 111; eggs, 35; honey (estimate), 30.

Forestry

Forests covered 46·06m. ha. in 2015 (52% of the total land area). In 2011, 25·38m. cu. metres of roundwood were cut.

Fisheries

Catch (2012) 327,257 tonnes, of which 314,945 tonnes were from inland waters.

Industry

Industry is limited, and is mainly textiles, petroleum and chemical products, food processing, tobacco, brewing and paper manufacturing.

Labour

Tanzania had 0·33m. people living in slavery according to the Walk Free Foundation's 2013 *Global Slavery Index*.

International Trade

Imports and Exports

Goods imports were US$12,691·1m. in 2014 (US$12,525·4m. in 2013) and goods exports US$5,704·7m. (US$4,412·5m. in 2013).

The main imports are mineral fuels and lubricants, and machinery and transport equipment. Gold accounted for about a quarter of export revenues in 2014. Cashew nuts, cloves, coffee, cotton, tea and tobacco are also important exports.

The leading import source in 2010 was India (11·2%), followed by China and South Africa; the leading export market in 2010 was Switzerland (17·5%), followed by China and South Africa.

Communications

Roads

In 2008 there were 87,524 km of roads, including 10,042 km of highways or national roads. Passenger cars in use in 2007 numbered 80,900; there were also 369,900 lorries and vans, 23,100 buses and coaches, and 52,000 motor-cycles and mopeds.

Rail

In 1977 the independent Tanzanian Railway Corporation was formed. The network totalled 2,707 km (metre gauge) in 2005, excluding the joint Tanzania-Zambia (Tazara) railway's 961 km in Tanzania (1,067 mm gauge) operated by a separate administration. In 2008 the state railway carried 0·5m. passengers and 0·5m. tonnes of freight, and in 2005 the Tazara carried 0·9m. passengers and 0·6m. tonnes of freight. There are plans for a new railway linking Dar es Salaam with Kigali in Rwanda and Musongati in Burundi.

In 1998 a transhipment facility for containers opened at Kidatu, south-west of Dar es Salaam, providing a link between the 1,067 mm gauge railways of the southern part of Africa and the 1,000 mm gauge lines of the north.

Civil Aviation

There are three international airports: Dar es Salaam, Zanzibar and Kilimanjaro (Moshi/Arusha). Although Air Tanzania is the national carrier, Precision Air carries far more passengers (743,000 in 2013) and serves more destinations (ten in 2013). Dar es Salaam is the busiest airport, handling 2,088,282 passengers in 2012 (1,100,666 on international flights), followed by Zanzibar with 787,813 (388,231 on domestic flights).

Shipping

In Jan. 2014 there were 181 ships of 300 GT or over registered, totalling 6,257,000 GT. Of the 181 vessels registered, 95 were general cargo ships, 60 oil tankers, 11 passenger ships, eight bulk carriers, six container ships and there was one liquid gas tanker. The main seaports are Dar es Salaam, Mtwara, Tanga and Zanzibar. There are also ports on the lakes. There are plans for a new port to be built at Bagamoyo, which would potentially become not only the largest port in Tanzania but also in East Africa as a whole.

Telecommunications

In 2013 there were 165,000 main (fixed) telephone lines; mobile phone subscriptions numbered 27,443,000 that year (557·2 per 1,000 persons). In 2013 an estimated 4·4% of the population were internet users. In June 2012 there were 518,000 Facebook users.

Social Institutions

Out of 178 countries analysed in the 2017 *Fragile States Index*—a list published jointly by the Fund for Peace and *Foreign Policy* magazine—Tanzania was ranked the joint 65th most vulnerable (along with Kyrgyzstan) to conflict or collapse. The index is based on 12 indicators of state vulnerability across social, political and economic categories.

Justice

The Judiciary is independent in both judicial and administrative matters and is composed of a four-tier system of Courts: Primary Courts; District and Resident Magistrates' Courts; the High Court; and the Court of Appeal. The Chief Justice is head of the Court of Appeal and the Judiciary Department. The Court's main registry is at Dar es Salaam; its jurisdiction includes Zanzibar. The Principal Judge is head of the High Court, also headquartered at Dar es Salaam, which has resident judges at seven regional centres.

The population in penal institutions in Jan. 2013 was 36,552 (178 per 100,000 of national population). The International Centre for Prison Studies estimated in 2014 that 50·1% of prisoners had yet to receive a trial. Tanzania was ranked 67th of 102 countries for criminal justice and 57th for civil justice in the 2015 World Justice Project *Rule of Law Index*, which provides data on how the rule of law is experienced by the general public across eight categories.

Education

Primary education is compulsory and lasts seven years, and has been free since 2002. The official entry age is seven. In 2012 there were 1,034,729 children in pre-primary education with (2010) 16,349 teachers, 8,247,172 pupils in primary education with 180,987 teaching staff and 2,118,067 pupils in secondary education with 80,250 teaching staff. Secondary education has been free since 2016. There were 166,014 students in tertiary education in 2012.

There were 16 public and ten private universities in 2012. The University of Dar es Salaam, which gained university status in 1970, is the oldest and largest university.

Adult literacy rate in 2010 was an estimated 67·8% (male, 75·5%; female, 60·8%). In 2010 total expenditure on education came to 6·2% of GDP and 21·2% of total government spending.

Health

Over the period 2006–12 Tanzania had seven hospital beds per 10,000 population. There were 1,157 physicians in 2014 (two per 100,000 population), plus 21,552 nursing and midwifery personnel, 1,037 dentistry personnel and 1,839 pharmaceutical personnel. Expenditure on health in 2014 was 6·4% of GDP.

In *Water: At What Cost? The State of the World's Water 2016*, WaterAid reported that 44·4% of the population does not have access to safe water (the ninth highest percentage of any nation). Tanzania ranked as the country with the seventh largest number of people living without access to safe water (23·2m. in 2015).

Religion

In 2010 an estimated 61·4% of the population was Christian and 35·2% Muslim according to the Pew Research Center's Forum on Religion & Public Life. Of the Christians in 2010, an estimated 53% were Catholics and 46% Protestants. Most Muslims are Sunnis but there are significant Shia and Ahmadi minorities. In Feb. 2019 the Roman Catholic Church had one cardinal.

Culture

World Heritage Sites

Tanzania has seven sites on the UNESCO World Heritage List: Ngorongoro Conservation Area (inscribed on the list in 1979); the Ruins of Kilwa Kisiwani and of Songo Mnara (1981); Serengeti National Park (1981); Selous Game Reserve (1982); Kilimanjaro National Park (1987); the Stone Town of Zanzibar (2000); and the Kondoa Rock-Art sites (2006).

Press

In 2008 there were 14 dailies with a combined circulation of 125,000.

Tourism

There were 16 national parks in Tanzania in 2014. In 2010 there were 754,000 international tourist arrivals (excluding same-day visitors), bringing revenue of US$1,255m. Tourism is the country's second largest foreign exchange earner after agriculture.

Diplomatic Representatives

Of Tanzania in the United Kingdom (3 Stratford Pl., London, W1C 1AS)
  High Commissioner: Asha-Rose Migiro.

Of the United Kingdom in Tanzania (Umoja House, Hamburg Ave., PO Box 9200 Dar es Salaam)
  High Commissioner: Sarah Cooke.

Of Tanzania in the USA (1232 22nd St., NW, Washington, D.C., 20037)
  Ambassador: Wilson Mutagaywa Masilingi.

Of the USA in Tanzania (686 Old Bagamoyo Rd, Msasani, Dar es Salaam)
  Ambassador: Vacant.
  Chargé d'Affaires a.i.: Inmi Patterson.

Of Tanzania to the United Nations
  Ambassador: Modest Jonathan Mero.

Of Tanzania to the European Union
  Ambassador: Joseph E. Sokoine.

Further Reading

National Statistical Office: National Bureau of Statistics, Box 796, Dar es Salaam.
Website: http://www.nbs.go.tz

Thailand

Prathet Thai (Kingdom of Thailand)

Capital: Bangkok
Population projection, 2020: 69·41m.
GNI per capita, 2017: (PPP$) 15,516
HDI/world rank, 2017: 0·755/83=
Internet domain extension: .th

Key Historical Events

Excavations at Ban Chiang on the Khorat plateau in northeast Thailand suggest rice farming was under way by as early as 2500 BC. From around 300 BC the Indianized Funan kingdom held sway across much of southeast Asia, including eastern and central Thailand. Artifacts discovered at the Funan capital of Ba Phnom, in modern Cambodia, point to trading links with China and India and as far as the Middle East and Rome. At its height in the 6th century AD, Funan control included part of the Malay peninsula.

Mon, Tai and Khmer peoples first entered northern and eastern Thailand from southern China in the 5th century AD. Taking advantage of Funan's decline after the 6th century, the Mon began to establish independent kingdoms. Among them was Dvaravarti, which in the 10th century was absorbed by the Indian-influenced Khmer empire, centred on Angkor. Mongol incursions into Yunnan in southern China in the mid-13th century forced a new wave of Tai migration that culminated in the Sukhothai kingdom of north-central Thailand. Under Ramkhamhaeng (1279–98), its influence stretched southward to the Malay peninsula. Trade with India and China flourished and the Siamese language developed in written form.

The Tai kingdom of Lan Na emerged as the dominant power in northern Thailand in the 14th century while further south the declining Sukhothai came under the influence of Rama Tibodi, prince of U Tong, who, around 1350, established a Buddhist dynasty centred on Ayutthaya. Rice cultivation and trade brought prosperity and power to Siam over the next four centuries, though tempered by frequent warfare with the Khmer empire and the Lao state of Chiang Mai. Trade with Europe, the Middle East, China and Japan expanded considerably in the 16th and 17th centuries, notably under King Narai (1656–88). Relations with France developed in the 1680s but soured amid attempts to convert Narai to Christianity: French troops were expelled in 1688 and most foreigners were barred from Siam over the next century.

Ayutthaya suffered a series of attacks from Burma in the mid-1700s and fell in 1767 although Thai forces, led by Gen. Phya Tak (King Taksin), re-established control with the help of Chinese merchants within a decade. His successor, Chao Phraya Chakkri (Rama I), established Bangkok as his capital and restored the Buddhist religion during his reign (1782–1809). Subsequent Chakkri kings resumed relations with the West but, through skilful diplomacy, managed to preserve Siam's independence. The nation remained an absolute monarchy until 24 June 1932 when a group of rebels calling themselves the People's Party precipitated a bloodless coup. After King Prajadhipok tried to dissolve the newly appointed general assembly the army moved against him to become the dominant political force, a position it has held ever since. In 1939 Field Marshal Pibulsonggram became premier and embarked on a pro-Japanese policy that brought Thailand into the Second World War on Japan's side.

After 1945 periods of military rule were interspersed with attempts at democratic, civilian government. Democratic government was reintroduced for a short time after 1963 and again from 1969–71, until a military coup was staged aimed at checking crime and the communist insurgence. A moderately democratic constitution was introduced in 1978. On 23 Feb. 1991 a military junta seized power in Thailand's 17th coup since 1932. Following the appointment of Gen. Suchinda Kraprayoon as prime minister on 17 April 1992 there were violent anti-government demonstrations. Gen. Suchinda resigned and in May the Legislative Assembly voted that future prime ministers should be elected by its members rather than appointed by the military. The 1995 election was fought against a background of political and financial corruption. After the 1996 election a new constitution was drafted

allowing for the separation of the executive, legislative and judicial branches of government.

On 26 Dec. 2004 Thailand, along with a number of other south Asian countries, was hit by a devastating tsunami. The death toll in Thailand was put at 8,000. The government of Thaksin Shinawatra was overthrown in a bloodless military coup on 19 Sept. 2006. Elections held in Dec. 2007 were won by the People's Power Party (PPP), the successor to Thaksin's banned Thai Rak Thai party. Samak Sundaravej became prime minister in Feb. 2008, marking a return to civilian rule. When a Constitutional Court ruling removed him from office in Sept. 2008 he was replaced by Somchai Wongsawat. Wongsawat in turn had to step down in Dec. 2008 when the Constitutional Court disbanded the ruling PPP following accusations of electoral fraud. Opposition leader Abhisit Vejjajiva formed a parliamentary coalition and was elected to the premiership.

The pro-Thaksin United Front for Democracy against Dictatorship ('redshirts') held anti-government protests in April 2009 and again in March–May 2010, prompting the government to impose a state of emergency. In July 2011 the Pheu Thai Party triumphed in elections and its leader—and Thaksin's sister—Yingluck Shinawatra was sworn in as premier. In 2012 anti-government 'yellow-shirt' protesters called for the overthrow of Yingluck. In Nov. 2013 an amnesty bill that opponents claimed would allow Thaksin to return from exile without facing further punishment prompted a new wave of protests. The following month, Yingluck announced that elections would be brought forward to Feb. 2014. A two-month state of emergency was declared in Jan. 2014 and the leading opposition group, the Democrat Party, boycotted the election, which was severely disrupted by anti-government protesters and subsequently invalidated by the Constitutional Court in March. On 7 May 2014 Yingluck was dismissed from office by the Constitutional Court following investigations into the mishandling of a national rice pledging scheme and unconstitutional political appointments made during her time as premier.

Thailand returned to military rule on 22 May 2014 when army chief Gen. Prayuth Chan-ocha launched a coup d'état against the acting government in place since Yingluck's impeachment. An interim constitution was presented to then King Bhumibol Adulyadej by the military junta, and signed into law two months later.

Territory and Population

Thailand is bounded in the west by Myanmar, north and east by Laos and southeast by Cambodia. In the south it becomes a peninsula bounded in the west by the Indian Ocean, south by Malaysia and east by the Gulf of Thailand. The area is 513,120 sq. km (198,117 sq. miles).

At the 2010 census the population was 65,981,659; density, 128·6 per sq. km. In 2011, 34·4% of the population lived in urban areas.

The UN gives a projected population for 2020 of 69·41m.

Thailand is divided into six regions, 76 provinces and Bangkok, the capital. Population of Bangkok (2010 estimate), 8,213,000. Other towns (2010 estimates): Samut Prakan (1,093,000), Udon Thani (399,000), Chonburi (371,000), Nonthaburi (368,000), Nakhon Ratchasima (305,000), Lampang (282,000), Hat Yai (269,000), Rayong (230,000).

Thai is the official language, spoken by 53% of the population as their mother tongue. 27% speak Lao (mainly in the northeast), 12% Chinese (mainly in urban areas), 3·7% Malay (mainly in the south) and 2·7% Khmer (along the Cambodian border). There are more Lao speakers in Thailand than in Laos.

Social Statistics

2005–06 births, 705,639; deaths, 440,024; marriages (2005), 345,234; divorces (2005), 90,688. Rates (per 1,000 population, 2005–06): birth, 10·9; death, 6·8; marriage (2005), 5·2; divorce (2005), 1·4. Annual population growth rate, 2000–05, 1·0%. Expectation of life (2007): 65·4 years for men; 72·1 years for women. Infant mortality, 2010, 11 per 1,000 live births; fertility rate, 2008, 1·8 births per woman.

© Springer Nature Limited 2020
Palgrave Macmillan (ed.), *The Statesman's Yearbook 2020*,
https://doi.org/10.1057/978-1-349-95940-2_187

Climate

The climate is tropical, with high temperatures and humidity. Over most of the country, three seasons may be recognized. The rainy season is June to Oct., the cool season from Nov. to Feb. and the hot season is March to May. Rainfall is generally heaviest in the south and lightest in the northeast. Bangkok, Jan. 78°F (25·6°C), July 83°F (28·3°C). Annual rainfall 56" (1,400 mm).

On 26 Dec. 2004 an undersea earthquake centred off the Indonesian island of Sumatra caused a huge tsunami that flooded coastal areas in western Thailand resulting in 8,000 deaths. In total there were more than 225,000 deaths in 14 countries.

Constitution and Government

Bhumibol Adulyadej, who was born 5 Dec. 1927, died on 13 Oct. 2016, having reigned as king for 70 years and 126 days. His son and heir apparent, Crown Prince **Vajiralongkorn**, ascended to the throne on 1 Dec. as King Rama X.

Following the coup of May 2014, the existing constitution was superseded on 22 July by an interim replacement drafted by the military junta and signed into law by the King without public consultation. The interim constitution (the 19th since the overthrow of absolute monarchy in 1932) recognized the status of the junta—the National Council for Peace and Order (NCPO)—as Thailand's legitimate executive authority, whilst granting it powers to recommend appointments to a new committee drafting a permanent constitution. A new parliament, a *National Legislative Assembly* of up to 220 members appointed by the NCPO (increased in 2016 to 250 members), was established to replace the previous 150-seat Senate and 500-seat House of Representatives.

In Sept. 2015 the military-appointed National Reform Council rejected the draft of a new constitution. A Constitution Drafting Commission presented a new draft to the public in March 2016 and a referendum on its adoption was held on 7 Aug. that year, when it received 61·4% support, with turnout at 59·4%. The promulgation process saw the prime minister, Prayuth Chan-ocha, approve the constitution on 8 Nov. and submit it for royal endorsement, which was granted in April 2017 after amendments consolidating royal powers were made. The constitution allows for the NCPO to appoint a panel to select all members of the 250-seat Senate, with six seats reserved for the heads of the army, navy, air force and police, plus the supreme commander of the military and the permanent secretary of defence. The Senate may call a vote of no confidence in the lower house and under certain circumstances could also impose a prime minister who is not a member of parliament.

National Anthem

'Prathet Thai ruam nua chat chua Thai' ('Thailand, cradle of Thais wherever they may be'); words by Luang Saranuprapan, tune by Phrachen Duriyang.

Government Chronology

Heads of Government since 1944. (PCT = Thai Nation Party; PKS = Social Action Party; PKWM = New Aspiration Party; PP = Democrat Party; PPP = People's Power Party; PTP = Pheu Thai Party; SP = United Thai People's Party; ST = Free Thai Movement; TRT = Thai Rak Thai; n/p = non-partisan)

Prime Ministers		
1944–45	military	Khuang Aphaiwong
1945	n/p	Tawee Boonyaket
1945–46	ST	Seni Pramoj
1946	military	Khuang Aphaiwong
1946	n/p	Pridi Phanomyong
1946–47	military	Thamrong Nawasawat
1948–57	military	Plaek Pibulsongkram
1957	n/p	Pote Sarasin
1958	military	Thanom Kittikachorn
1959–63	military	Sarit Thanarat
1963–73	military, SP	Thanom Kittikachorn
1973–75	n/p	Sanya Thammasak

(continued)

1975	PP	Seni Pramoj
1975–76	PKS	Kukrit Pramoj
1976	PP	Seni Pramoj
Chairman of the National Administrative Reform Council		
1976–80	military (*de facto* ruler)	Sangad Chaloryu
Prime Ministers		
1976–77	n/p	Thanin Kraivichien
1977–80	military	Kriangsak Chomanan
1980–88	military	Prem Tinsulanonda
1988–91	PCT	Chatichai Choonhavan
Chairman of the National Peacekeeping Council		
1991	military	Sunthorn Kongsompong
Prime Ministers		
1991–92	n/p	Anand Panyarachun
1992	military	Suchinda Kraprayoon
1992	n/p	Anand Panyarachun
1992–95	PP	Chuan Leekpai
1995–96	PCT	Banharn Silpa-Archa
1996–97	PKWM	Chavalit Yongchaiyudh
1997–2001	PP	Chuan Leekpai
2001–06	TRT	Thaksin Shinawatra
2006	TRT	Chidchai Vanasatidya (acting for Thaksin Shinawatra)
Chairman of the Council for Democratic Reform under Constitutional Monarchy		
2006	military	Sonthi Boonyaratkalin
Prime Ministers		
2006–08	n/p	Surayud Chulanont
2008	PPP	Samak Sundaravej
2008	PPP	Somchai Wongsawat
2008	PPP	Chaovarat Chanweerakul (acting)
2008–11	PP	Abhisit Vejjajiva
2011–14	PTP	Yingluck Shinawatra
Chairman of the National Council for Peace and Order		
2014	military	Prayuth Chan-ocha
Prime Minister		
2014–	military	Prayuth Chan-ocha

Recent Elections

At the elections to the House of Representatives on 3 July 2011 the Pheu Thai Party (PTP) won a majority with 265 seats out of 500 and 53·0% of the vote, ahead of the ruling Democrat Party with 159 seats (31·8%), Bhumjaithai with 34 seats (6·8%), Chartthaipattana with 19 (3·8%), the Chart Pattana Puea Pandin Party with 7 (1·4%) and the Phalang Chon Party also with 7 and 1·4%. Five other parties won four seats or fewer. Turnout was 66%. In a special session of the House of Representatives held on 5 Aug. 2011 the Thai parliament elected Yingluck Shinawatra prime minister by 296 to 3 with 197 abstentions.

Early elections to the House of Representatives were called after Yingluck Shinawatra dissolved parliament in Dec. 2013. They were held on 2 Feb. 2014, but were declared invalid on 21 March by Thailand's Constitutional Court after it emerged that voting did not take place on the same day across the country, in violation of the constitution. In March 2018 Prime Minister Prayuth Chan-ocha indicated that delayed elections would be held in Feb. 2019 (although they were later postponed until March 2019).

There were elections to the 150-seat Senate on 30 March 2014. 77 members were directly elected with the remaining 73 appointed by a selection committee.

Current Government

Army chief Gen. Prayuth Chan-ocha seized power from the caretaker government on 22 May 2014. Prayuth leads the military government known as the National Council for Peace and Order (NCPO) and was expected to rule until the appointment of a new interim government. However, in Aug. 2014 he was named as interim prime minister pending the holding of fresh elections.

In Feb. 2019 the government comprised:

Prime Minister: Prayuth Chan-ocha; b. 1954 (since 25 Aug. 2014—also Leader of National Council for Peace and Order since 22 May 2014).

Deputy Prime Ministers: Gen. Prawit Wongsuwan (also *Minister of Defence*); Wissanu Krea-ngam; Prajin Juntong (also *Minister of Justice*); Somkid Jatusripitak; Chatchai Sarikulya.

Minister of Agriculture and Co-operatives: Krissada Boonraj. *Commerce:* Sonthirat Sonthijirawong. *Culture:* Veera Rojpojanarat. *Digital Economy and Society:* Pichet Durongkaveroj. *Education:* Teerakiat Jaroensettasin. *Energy:* Siri Jirapongphan. *Finance:* Apisak Tantivorawong. *Foreign Affairs:* Don Pramudwinai. *Industry:* Uttama Savanayana. *Interior:* Anupong Paochinda. *Labour:* Adul Saengsikaew. *Natural Resources and Environment:* Surasak Kanchanarat. *Public Health:* Piyasakol Sakolsatayadorn. *Science and Technology:* Suvit Maesincee. *Social Development and Human Security:* Anantaphon Kanchanarat. *Tourism and Sports:* Weerasak Kowsurat. *Transport:* Arkhom Termpittyapaisith. *Ministers in the Prime Minister's Office:* Suwaphan Tanyuvardhana; Kobsak Pootrakool. *Government Website:* http://www.thaigov.go.th

Current Leaders

Prayuth Chan-ocha

Position

Prime Minister

Introduction

Prayuth Chan-ocha, leader of the May 2014 coup in Thailand, was designated prime minister by the National Legislative Assembly (NLA) the following Aug. He has remained in office pending the outcome of delayed elections in March 2019.

Early Life

Prayuth was born on 21 March 1954 in Nakhon Ratchasima province. In 1976 he graduated from the Chulachomklao Royal Military Academy and joined the 21st Infantry Regiment, also known as the Queen's Guard, where he spent most of his military career. In 2006 he was appointed Commanding General of 1st Army Area and was chosen to participate in the military-backed NLA following the removal of Thaksin Shinawatra from office that year. In 2008 Prayuth became Army Chief of Staff and in 2009 was named its Deputy Commander in Chief. Considered a hard-liner, he supported the military's tough stance against the Thaksin-supporting 'Red Shirt' protesters in April 2009 and April–May 2010.

In Oct. 2010 Prayuth was appointed Commander in Chief of the Army. Despite his opposition to Thaksin Shinawatra, Prayuth was seen as co-operative towards his sister, Yingluck Shinawatra, after she won the July 2011 parliamentary polls. When political tensions began to rise in Nov. 2013, Prayuth was initially reluctant to order army involvement. However, after Yingluck was removed from office by the Constitutional Court, Prayuth launched a coup on 22 May 2014. Heading the newly-established National Council for Peace and Order, he ordered a clampdown on dissent, declared a nationwide curfew and issued an interim constitution granting the military sweeping powers. On 31 July 2014 a new NLA was established, with many of its legislators handpicked by Prayuth from military and police backgrounds. On 24 Aug. 2014 he was designated prime minister by the NLA.

Career in Office

Prayuth retired from the army on 30 Sept. 2014. Having promised reforms to prevent a return to the political instability that has undermined the nation for years, he drew up a new draft constitution that was approved in a national referendum in Aug. 2016 and that reinforced the military's authority over politics. However, in a surprising move in Jan. 2017 King Vajiralongkorn, who had succeeded his late father Bhumibol Adulyadej in Dec. 2016, requested changes to the draft before eventually giving royal assent to the constitution in April. In June 2017 the National Legislative Assembly approved legislation designed to extend the political influence of the military beyond 2018, although a delayed general election in March 2019 was expected to return nominal powers to a civilian government.

In Aug. 2015 a terrorist bomb, seemingly targeting tourists, had killed 20 people at a Hindu shrine in Bangkok.

Defence

Conscription is for two years; if there are not enough volunteers a conscription lottery is held to fill the quota. In 2013 defence expenditure totalled US$6,213m. (US$92 per capita), representing 1·5% of GDP.

Army

Strength (2011) 190,000 (including around 70,000 conscripts). In addition there were 45,000 National Security Volunteer Corps, around 20,000 *Thahan Phran* ('Hunter Soldiers', a volunteer irregular force), 41,000 Border Police and a 50,000 strong paramilitary provincial police force (including an estimated 500-strong special action force).

Navy

The Royal Thai Navy is, next to the Chinese, the most significant naval force in the South China Sea. The fleet includes a small Spanish-built vertical/short-take-off-and-land carrier *Chakri Naruebet,* which entered service in 1997 and operates nine ex-Spanish AV-8A Harrier aircraft (although their serviceability is in doubt) and helicopters, and ten frigates. Manpower was 69,900 (2011) including 25,800 conscripts and 1,200 naval aviation personnel.

The main bases are at Ban Pak Nam, Bangkok, Sattahip, Songkla and Phang Nga, with the riverine forces based at Nakhon Phanom.

Air Force

The Royal Thai Air Force had a strength (2011) of an estimated 46,000 personnel and 163 combat-capable aircraft, including F-16s and F-5Es. The RTAF is made up of four air divisions.

Economy

Agriculture accounted for 11·3% of GDP in 2013, industry 37·0% and services 51·7%.

Thailand's 'shadow' (black market) economy is estimated to constitute approximately 48% of the country's official GDP.

Overview

Thailand began its transformation into a diverse, industrialized economy in the 1980s. An export-oriented, labour-intensive manufacturing sector developed largely owing to foreign investment, which in 2015 amounted to US$7·1bn. Exports accounted for 69% of national income in 2015—the major trading partners being China, Japan and the USA—while the services sector (dominated by travel and tourism) accounted for around 19%.

The Asian financial crisis of the late 1990s saw GDP contract by 10·5% in 1998 against a backdrop of high inflation and rising unemployment and poverty. A prudent macroeconomic policy, low public debt and falling inflation then helped Thailand to recover, with GDP growth averaging 5% annually from 2002 to 2007. However, the global financial crisis saw the economy contract again, and at one of the steepest rates in southeast Asia in 2009. Growth has since been erratic, supported by a boost in tourism and demand for electronics and automobiles, but hampered by floods in 2011 and the impact of political tensions that culminated in a military coup in May 2014.

The World Bank raised Thailand's economic status to an upper-middle income nation in 2011 with the country set to reach most of its UN Millennium Development targets. However, despite the government raising the minimum wage (to over US$8·40 per day since 2013) and cutting corporation tax from 23% to 20%, poverty remains high in rural areas and inequality is rife compared to many of Thailand's regional neighbours.

Risks to long-term prosperity include a slowdown in emerging market growth, political unrest and militancy.

Currency

The unit of currency is the *baht* (THB) of 100 *satang.* After being pegged to the US dollar, the baht was devalued and allowed to float on 2 July 1997. It was the devaluation of the baht that sparked the financial turmoil that spread throughout the world over the next year. Foreign exchange reserves were US$127,165m. in Sept. 2009 (US$28,434m. in 1998) and gold reserves 2·70m. troy oz. Total money supply in Aug. 2009 was 1,022·2bn. baht. Inflation rates (based on IMF statistics):

2008	2009	2010	2011	2012	2013	2014	2015	2016	2017
5·5%	−0·8%	3·3%	3·8%	3·0%	2·2%	1·9%	−0·9%	0·2%	0·7%

Budget

The fiscal year runs from 1 Oct.–30 Sept. In 2014–15 budgetary central government revenue was 2,483bn. baht and expenditure 2,470bn. baht. Main sources of revenue in 2014–15: taxes on goods and services, 1,102bn. baht; taxes on income, profits and capital gains, 895bn. baht. Main items of expenditure by economic type in 2014–15: compensation of employees, 742bn. baht; grants, 571bn. baht.

VAT is 7%.

Performance

Real GDP growth rates (based on IMF statistics):

2008	2009	2010	2011	2012	2013	2014	2015	2016	2017
1·7%	−0·7%	7·5%	0·8%	7·2%	2·7%	1·0%	3·0%	3·3%	3·9%

Thailand's total GDP in 2017 was US$455·2bn.

Banking and Finance

The Bank of Thailand (founded in 1942) is the central bank and bank of issue, an independent body although its capital is government-owned. Its assets in 2014 were 3,527,289m. baht and its liabilities 4,227,783m. baht. Its *Governor* is Veerathai Santiprabhob. In 2013 there were 15 commercial banks. There are four major banks: Bangkok Bank (with assets in Dec. 2013 of US$79,340m.), KASIKORNBANK, Krung Thai Bank (which is state-owned) and Siam Commercial Bank.

External debt amounted to US$71,263m. in 2010, up from US$46,342m. in 2005 although down from US$79,720m. in 2000. As a share of GNI foreign debt declined from 66·0% in 2000 to 27·6% in 2005 and further to 23·4% in 2010.

There is a stock exchange (SET) in Bangkok.

Energy and Natural Resources

Environment

Thailand's carbon dioxide emissions from the consumption of energy in 2011 were the equivalent of 4·4 tonnes per capita.

Electricity

Installed capacity, 2011, was an estimated 47·5m. kW. Output, 2011, 151·60bn. kWh, with consumption per capita 2,420 kWh.

Oil and Gas

Proven oil reserves in 2012 were 0·4bn. bbls. Production of oil in 2012 was a record 16·2m. tonnes. Thailand and Vietnam settled an offshore dispute in 1997 that stretched back to 1973. Demarcation allowed for petroleum exploration in the Gulf of Thailand, with each side required to give the other some revenue if an underground reservoir is discovered that straddles the border.

Production of natural gas in 2012 reached a record 41·4bn. cu. metres. Reserves, 2012, 300bn. cu. metres. In April 1998 Thailand and Malaysia agreed to share equally the natural gas jointly produced in an offshore area (the Malaysian-Thailand Joint Development Area) that both countries claim as their own territory.

Minerals

The mineral resources include antimony, cassiterite (tin ore), copper, diatomite, dolomite, gold, gypsum, kaolin, lignite, limestone, manganese, marl, potash, rubies, sapphires, silica sand, silver and zinc. Production, 2005 unless otherwise indicated (in tonnes): limestone (2008), 142·12m.; lignite, 21·43m.; gypsum, 7·11m.; salt, 1·17m.; feldspar, 1·15m.; kaolin, 746,000; iron ore (metal content), 116,000 (estimate); zinc ore (metal content), 31,000 (estimate).

Agriculture

In 2013 there were an estimated 16·8m. ha. of arable land and 4·5m. ha. of permanent cropland. About 6·4m. ha. were equipped for irrigation in 2013. The chief produce is rice, a staple of the national diet. Output of the major crops in 2013 was (in 1,000 tonnes): sugarcane, 100,096; rice, 36,762; cassava, 30,228; palm fruit oil, 12,374; maize, 4,876; natural rubber, 4,305; mangoes and guavas, 3,421; pineapples, 2,068; bananas, 1,031; coconuts, 1,010. Thailand is the world's leading producer of natural rubber. Livestock, 2013: pigs, 7,606,000; cattle, 5,148,000; buffaloes, 1,289,000; chickens, 259m.; ducks, 15m.

Forestry

Forests covered 16·40m. ha. in 2015, or 32% of the land area. Of the total area under forests 41% was primary forest in 2015, 35% other naturally regenerated forest and 24% planted forest. Teak and other hardwoods grow in the deciduous forests of the north; elsewhere tropical evergreen forests are found, with the timber yang the main crop (a source of yang oil). In 2011, 33·79m. cu. metres of roundwood were cut.

Fisheries

In 2012 the total catch came to 1,834,573 tonnes with marine fishing accounting for 88% of all fish caught. Thailand is the third largest exporter of fishery commodities in the world (after China and Norway), with exports in 2011 totalling US$9·46bn. Imports of fishery commodities in 2011 totalled US$2·72bn. Aquaculture production in 2010 was the sixth highest in the world, at 1,286,122 tonnes.

Industry

The leading companies by market capitalization in Thailand in May 2018 were: PTT PCL, an oil and gas company (US$50·9bn.); Airports of Thailand, a company that manages Thailand's international and some smaller airports (US$32·0bn.); and CP All, an operator of convenience stores (US$24·1bn.).

Production (2008 unless otherwise indicated): 31·65m. tonnes of cement, 18·38m. tonnes of distillate fuel oil (2007), 9·79m. tonnes of sugar (2013), 7·33m. tonnes of residual fuel oil (2007), 6·85m. tonnes of hot-rolled steel products (2013), 6·31m. tonnes of petrol (2007), 3·58m. tonnes of crude steel (2013), 174,000 tonnes of tin plate (2012), 2·32m. sq. metres of knitted or crocheted fabrics, 2,192·7m. litres of soft drinks, 2,160·0m. litres of beer, 30·5bn. cigarettes, 945,100 passenger cars and 1,484,000 commercial vehicles (2012), and 5,881,000 televisions.

Labour

The labour force in 2013 was 39,873,000 (36,471,000 in 2003). 78·3% of the population aged 15–64 was economically active in 2013. In the same year 0·7% of the population was unemployed. There is no nationwide minimum wage but a minimum wage is set at different levels at the provincial level. It varied between 159 baht and 221 baht per day in July 2011.

Thailand had 0·47m. people living in slavery according to the Walk Free Foundation's 2013 *Global Slavery Index*, the seventh highest total of any country.

International Trade

Imports and Exports

In 2015 imports (c.i.f.) totalled US$202,019·4m.; exports (f.o.b.), US$210,883·4m. Main imports in 2015: machinery and transport equipment, 37·8%; manufactured goods classified chiefly by material, 17·1%; mineral fuels and lubricants, 14·9%. Exports, 2015: machinery and transport equipment, 44·9%; food, animals and beverages, 13·4%; manufactured goods classified chiefly by material, 12·6%. The principal import source in 2007 was Japan (20·3%), followed by China and the USA. The principal export market in 2007 was the USA (12·6%), followed by Japan and China. In the meantime China has become Thailand's largest trading partner.

Communications

Roads

In 2006 there were 180,053 km of roads, of which 450 km were motorways. Vehicles in use in 2006 included: 3·80m. passenger cars, 4·99m. lorries and vans and 15·67m. motorcycles and mopeds. Thailand has among the world's highest road death rates, at an estimated 36·2 per 100,000 population in 2012.

Rail

The State Railway totalled 4,041 km in 2012. Passenger-km travelled in 2011 came to 7·5bn.; freight tonne-km transported in 2011 totalled 2·5bn. A metro ('Skytrain'), or elevated transit system, was opened in Bangkok in 1999. A second (underground) mass transit system in Bangkok, the Bangkok Subway, was opened in 2004.

Civil Aviation

The main international airports are at Bangkok (Suvarnabhumi and Don Muang), Chiang Mai, Phuket and Hat Yai. The national carrier, Thai Airways International, is 51·03% state-owned. In 2005 scheduled airline traffic of Thai-based carriers flew 213·8m. km, carrying 21,507,900 passengers. Suvarnabhumi, which only opened in 2006, handled 53,002,328 passengers in 2012 (39,358,339 on international flights) and 1,345,490 tonnes of freight. Phuket is the second busiest airport, with 9,541,552 passengers in 2012 (5,052,218 on international flights) and 34,055 tonnes of freight.

Shipping

In Jan. 2014 there were 539 ships of 300 GT or over registered, totalling 3,090,000 GT. Of the 539 vessels registered, 231 were oil tankers, 140 general cargo ships, 90 liquid gas tankers, 39 bulk carriers, 21 passenger ships and 18 container ships. The busiest ports are Laem Chabang and Bangkok.

Telecommunications

In 2013 there were 6·1m. main (fixed) telephone lines. In the same year mobile phone subscriptions numbered 93·8m. (1,400·5 per 1,000 persons). In 2013 an estimated 28·9% of the population aged six years and over were internet users. In March 2012 there were 14·2m. Facebook users.

Social Institutions

Out of 178 countries analysed in the 2017 *Fragile States Index*—a list published jointly by the Fund for Peace and *Foreign Policy* magazine—Thailand was ranked the 82nd most vulnerable to conflict or collapse. The index is based on 12 indicators of state vulnerability across social, political and economic categories.

Justice

The judicial power is exercised in the name of the King, by *(a)* courts of first instance, *(b)* the court of appeal *(Uthorn)* and *(c)* the Supreme Court *(Dika)*. The King appoints, transfers and dismisses judges, who are independent in conducting trials and giving judgment in accordance with the law.

Courts of first instance are subdivided into 20 magistrates' courts *(Kwaeng)* with limited civil and minor criminal jurisdiction; 85 provincial courts *(Changwad)* with unlimited civil and criminal jurisdiction; the criminal and civil courts with exclusive jurisdiction in Bangkok; the central juvenile courts for persons under 18 years of age in Bangkok.

The court of appeal exercises appellate jurisdiction in civil and criminal cases from all courts of first instance. From it appeals lie to Dika Court on any point of law and, in certain cases, on questions of fact.

The Supreme Court is the supreme tribunal of the land. Besides its normal appellate jurisdiction in civil and criminal matters, it has semi-original jurisdiction over general election petitions. The decisions of Dika Court are final. Every person has the right to present a petition to the government who will deal with all matters of grievance.

The death penalty is still in force; an execution in June 2018 was the first since 2009. The population in penal institutions in March 2011 was 224,292 (328 per 100,000 of national population). Thailand was ranked 53rd of 102 countries for criminal justice and 74th for civil justice in the 2015 World Justice Project *Rule of Law Index*, which provides data on how the rule of law is experienced by the general public across eight categories.

Education

Education is compulsory for children for nine years and is free in local municipal schools. In 2007 there were 5,703,756 primary school pupils with 321,930 teaching staff. There were 4,789,339 secondary school pupils in 2007 with 227,929 teaching staff. There were 1,005,481 students in vocational education in 2005. In higher education there were 2,503,572 students in 2007 with 66,431 academic staff. In 2005 there were 78 public and 61 private institutions of higher education, 146 industry and community colleges, 110 technical colleges, 54 polytechnic colleges and 44 agricultural and technology colleges.

The adult literacy rate in 2005 was 94%.

In 2007 public expenditure on education came to 4·0% of GNI and 20·9% of total government spending.

Health

Thailand had 21 hospital beds per 10,000 population in 2010; there were 26,244 doctors in the same year plus 11,847 dentists, 8,700 pharmacists and 138,710 registered nurses (most of whom were nurse-midwives). Thailand is considered to be the most successful country in the world in preventing the spread of HIV/AIDS. The number of annual new HIV cases has fallen to under 10,000 from a high of 140,000 in the mid-1990s.

In *Water: At What Cost? The State of the World's Water 2016*, WaterAid reported that 2·2% of the population does not have access to safe water.

Religion

According to the Pew Research Center's Forum on Religion & Public Life, 93·2% of the population in 2010 was Buddhist, 5·5% Muslim and 0·9% Christian. Only Cambodia has a higher percentage of Buddhists in its population, and only China has more Buddhists. Most Muslims are Sunnis and among Christians there are more Protestants than Catholics. In Feb. 2019 the Roman Catholic Church had two cardinals.

Culture

World Heritage Sites

There are five UNESCO sites in Thailand. They are: the Thung Yai-Huai Kha Khaeng wildlife sanctuaries (inscribed in 1991); the palace, temples, Buddhas, etc. of the historic town of Sukhothai (1991); the 15th–18th century historic town of Ayutthaya (1991); the Bronze Age Ba Chiang archaeological site (1992); and the mountainous Dong Phayayen-Khao Yai forest complex (2005).

Press

In 2008 there were 46 daily newspapers (45 paid-for and one free), with a combined circulation of 7·4m. The newspapers with the highest circulation figures are *Thai Rath*, *Daily News* and *Kom Chad Luek*.

Tourism

In 2010 there were 15,936,000 tourist arrivals, up from 14,150,000 in 2009. Tourist numbers have doubled since 1998. The leading nationalities of tourists in 2010 were Malaysia (2,059,000), China (1,122,000), Japan (994,000) and the United Kingdom (811,000).

Festivals

Songkran, celebrated on 13 April each year, is the traditional Thai New Year festival, although 1 Jan. was made the official New Year in 1940. Other notable festivals include: the colourful Bosang Umbrella Fair in Jan. and a Flower Carnival in Feb., both in Chiang Mai; a Candle Festival held in Ubon Ratchathani on Khao Phansa Day in July (the day after the full moon of the eighth lunar month, marking the start of Buddhist Lent); Buffalo Races, held during Oct. at Chonburi; and an annual Elephant Round-up in the third week of Nov. at Surin.

Diplomatic Representatives

Of Thailand in the United Kingdom (29–30 Queen's Gate, London, SW7 5JB)
  Ambassador: Pisanu Suvanajata.

Of the United Kingdom in Thailand (14 Wireless Rd, Lumpini, Pathumwan, Bangkok 10330)
  Ambassador: Brian Davidson.

Of Thailand in the USA (1024 Wisconsin Ave., NW, Washington, D.C., 20007)
  Ambassador: Virachai Plasai.

Of the USA in Thailand (95 Wireless Rd, Bangkok 10330)
  Ambassador: Vacant.
  Chargé d'Affaires a.i.: Peter Haymond.

Of Thailand to the United Nations
  Ambassador: Vitavas Srivihok.

Of Thailand to the European Union
  Ambassador: Manasvi Srisodapol.

Further Reading

National Statistical Office. *Thailand Statistical Yearbook.*
Krongkaew, M. (ed.) *Thailand's Industrialization and its Consequences.*
  1995

National Statistical Office: National Statistical Office, The Government
  Complex, Building B, Chang Watthana Rd, Laksi, Bangkok 10210.
  Website: http://www.nso.go.th

Timor-Leste

República Democrática de Timor-Leste (Democratic Republic of Timor-Leste)

Capital: Dili
Population projection, 2020: 1·38m.
GNI per capita, 2017: (PPP$) 6,846
HDI/world rank, 2017: 0·625/132
Internet domain extension: .tl

Key Historical Events

The island of Timor probably served as a stepping stone in the migration of modern humans from Africa to Australasia. The Jerimalai cave in Timor-Leste was inhabited at least 42,000 years ago, and stone tools and fishing equipment discovered there point to seafaring traditions. Settlement by Melanesians took place on Timor from around 3,000 BC and further waves of migration from south China (Hakka people) and the Malay Peninsula date from around 2,500 BC. Trade links with China and elsewhere in southeast Asia developed over centuries—with sandalwood, honey, beeswax and slaves exchanged for rice, textiles and metal goods. In the mid-14th century the island came under the influence of the Javanese Majapahit empire, which reached its zenith under Hayam Wuruk (1350–89).

Portuguese mariners reached present-day Timor-Leste near the modern town of Pante Makasar in 1515. Early settlers established the port of Lifau and the Dominican friar Antonio Taveiro began missionary work among the local Ambeno, Mena and Amanuban kingdoms in the 1560s. The powerful Da Costa and Hornay families, who helped to establish the colonies of Goa, Malacca and Batavia, developed a lucrative trade in sandalwood during the 17th century. The period was marked by frequent clashes with rival Dutch forces—the Dutch East India Company established a base on the island of Solor in 1613. The arrival of a governor, António Coelho Guerreiro, in 1702 raised tensions between the two leading families and the Portuguese authorities. Following clashes, the colonial base was moved east to Dili in 1769 and the Dutch were able to expand their influence in western Timor. From around 1815 coffee, sugarcane and cotton plantations were established among the remnants of the sandalwood forests. The Treaty of Lisbon in 1869 formally divided the island of Timor into Portuguese Timor and the Dutch East Indies, although the definitive border was not agreed until 1916.

Resistance to Portuguese rule grew in the early years of the 20th century. A Timorese rebellion from 1911–12 was only quelled when the authorities brought in reinforcements from Mozambique and Macao. More than 3,000 Timorese and close to 300 Portuguese were killed. In late 1941 Portuguese Timor was occupied by small numbers of Australian, British and Dutch troops. They were overwhelmed by a Japanese invasion at Dili in Feb. 1942. A guerrilla campaign, waged by Australian forces along with Timorese and Portuguese fighters, was eventually crushed and by the time of the Japanese surrender in Sept. 1945 an estimated 50,000 had died.

Investment in infrastructure, agriculture, education and health care remained limited in the aftermath of the Second World War. Following the fall of António Salazar in 1968, the new government of Portugal sought a gradual decolonization. An independence movement, the Revolutionary Front for an Independent East Timor (FRETILIN), declared independence on 28 Nov. 1975. Nine days later the territory was occupied by Indonesia, which claimed it as the province of Timor Timur.

The United Nations did not recognize Indonesian sovereignty over the territory. FRETILIN maintained a guerrilla resistance to the Indonesian government, which resulted in large-scale casualties and alleged atrocities. On 24 July 1998 Indonesia announced a withdrawal of troops from Timor-Leste and an amnesty for some political prisoners, although no indication was given of how many of the estimated 12,000 troops and police would pull out. On 5 Aug. 1998 Indonesia and Portugal reached agreement on the outlines of an autonomy plan which would give the Timorese the right to self-government except in foreign affairs and defence.

In a referendum on the future of Timor-Leste held on 30 Aug. 1999 the electorate was some 450,000 and turnout was nearly 99%. 78·5% of voters opted for independence, but pro-Indonesian militia gangs wreaked havoc both before and after the referendum. The militias accused the UN of rigging the poll. There was widespread violence in and around Dili, the provincial capital, with heavy loss of life, and thousands of people were forced to flee intimidation. Timor-Leste's first democratic election took place on 30 Aug. 2001 in a ballot run by the UN, with FRETILIN winning 57% of the vote and 55 of the 88 seats in the new constituent assembly. Timor-Leste became an independent country on 20 May 2002.

In 2006 the UN established a non-military peacekeeping mission (UNMIT) in the country. A report presented to the UN in the same year found that the Indonesian occupation had directly resulted in the deaths of 100,000 East Timorese. In Feb. 2008 the then president, José Ramos-Horta, survived an assassination attempt at his official residence by disaffected soldiers. In Dec. 2012, with Timor-Leste by then relatively peaceful, UNMIT was withdrawn from the country.

Territory and Population

Timor-Leste (East Timor) has a total land area of 14,954 sq. km (5,774 sq. miles), consisting of the mainland (13,987 sq. km), the enclave of Oecussi in West Timor (817 sq. km), and the islands of Atauro to the north (140 sq. km) and Jaco to the east (10 sq. km). The mainland area incorporates the eastern half of the island of Timor. Oecussi lies westwards, separated from the main portion of Timor-Leste by a distance of some 100 km. The island is bound to the south by the Timor Sea and lies approximately 500 km from the Australian coast.

Provisional population at the census of July 2015, 1,183,643 (601,112 males); density, 79 per sq. km. The largest city is Dili, Timor-Leste's capital. In 2015 its population was 244,584. In 2011, 28·6% of the population were urban.

The UN gives a projected population for 2020 of 1·38m.

The ethnic East Timorese form the majority of the population. Non-East Timorese, comprising Portuguese and West Timorese as well as persons from Sumatra, Java, Sulawesi and other parts of Indonesia, are estimated to constitute approximately 20% of the total population.

During Indonesian occupation the official language was Indonesian (Bahasa Indonesia). Timor-Leste's constitution designates Portuguese and Tetum (an Austronesian language influenced by Portuguese) as the official languages, and English and Indonesian as working languages.

Social Statistics

2008 estimates: births, 44,000; deaths, 9,500. Rates, 2008 estimates (per 1,000 population): births, 40·0; deaths, 8·7. Annual population growth rate in 2000–08, 3·7%. Fertility rate, 2008, 6·5 children per woman. In 2013 life expectancy at birth was 66·0 years for males and 69·1 years for females.

From having the world's highest rate of infant mortality in the early 1980s, Timor-Leste's infant mortality rate dropped to 46 per 1,000 live births in 2010, although the figure varies widely between urban and rural areas.

Climate

In the north there is an average annual temperature of over 24°C (75°F), weak precipitation—below 1,500 mm (59") annually—and a dry period lasting five months. The mountainous zone, between the northern and southern parts of the island, has high precipitation—above 1,500 mm (59")—and a dry period of four months. The southern zone has precipitation reaching 2,000 mm (79") and is permanently humid. The monsoon season extends from Nov. to May.

© Springer Nature Limited 2020
Palgrave Macmillan (ed.), *The Statesman's Yearbook 2020*,
https://doi.org/10.1057/978-1-349-95940-2_188

Constitution and Government

The constitution promulgated in 2002 created a unicameral system with a *National Parliament* with a minimum requirement of 52 directly-elected seats and a maximum of 65. For the first term after independence the parliament had 88 members but this was reduced after the June 2007 legislative elections.

The *President* is directly elected for a period of five years and may not serve more than two terms.

National Anthem

'Pátria, Pátria, Timor-Leste, nossa Nação' ('Fatherland, fatherland, East Timor our Nation'); words by F. Borja da Costa, tune by A. Araujo.

Recent Elections

Presidential elections were held on 20 March 2017. Francisco Guterres of the ruling FRETILIN (Revolutionary Front for an Independent East Timor) party was elected with 57·1% of votes cast, ahead of António da Conceição of the Democratic Party with 32·5% of the vote, José Luís Guterres of Frenti-Mudança with 2·6%, José Neves and Luís Alves Tilman (both independent) with 2·3% and 2·2% respectively, Antonio Maher Lopes of the Socialist Party of Timor with 1·8%, and Ángela Freitas of the Timorese Workers' Party and Amorim Vieira (another independent candidate) with 0·8% each. Turnout was 71·2%.

Elections to the 65-member National Parliament took place on 12 May 2018. The Alliance for Change and Progress (AMP) won 49·6% of votes cast and 34 seats, ahead of FRETILIN with 34·2% of the votes and 23 seats, the Democratic Party 8·1% and 5 seats and the Democratic Development Forum 5·5% and 3 seats. Turnout was 81·0%.

Current Government

President: Francisco Guterres; b. 1954 (FRETILIN; since 20 May 2017).

In Feb. 2019 the government comprised the following:

Prime Minister: Taur Matan Ruak; b. 1956 (People's Liberation Party; took office 22 June 2018).

Minister of State: Agio Pereira (also *Minister at the Presidency of the Council of Ministers*).

Minister of Agriculture and Fisheries: Joaquim José Gusmão dos Reis Martins. *Defence:* Filomeno Paixão. *Education, Youth and Sports:* Dulce de Jesus Soares. *Finance (acting):* Sara Lopes Brites. *Foreign Affairs and Co-operation:* Dionísio Babo Soares. *Higher Education, Science and Culture:* Longhinhos dos Santos. *Justice:* Manuel Cárceres da Costa. *Legislative Reform and Parliamentary Affairs:* Fidelis Magalhães. *Public Works:* Salvador Soares dos Reis Pires. *Social Solidarity and Inclusion:* Armanda Berta dos Santos. *Transport and Communications:* José Agostinho da Silva.

Government Website: http://timor-leste.gov.tl

Current Leaders

Francisco Guterres

Position
President

Introduction
Francisco Guterres was sworn in as president in May 2017, the first member of FRETILIN (Revolutionary Front for an Independent East Timor) to hold the post.

Early Life
Francisco Guterres was born on 7 Sept. 1954 in Ossú and completed his secondary education in Dili in 1973. Popularly known as Lú-Olo ('pigeon'), Guterres served with the FRETILIN resistance movement following its establishment in 1974. He became a guerrilla fighter following Indonesia's invasion in 1975, rising through FRETILIN's ranks to hold various senior political roles in the organization.

In 1998 he was voted general co-ordinator of the FRETILIN presidential council and two years later acceded to the group's presidency. In Sept. 2001 he was named president of the national Constituent Assembly ahead of Timor-Leste's independence in 2002. He then became president of the National Parliament, serving in the role until 2007. He stood unsuccessfully as the FRETILIN candidate for the national presidency in both 2007 and

2012. At his third attempt, in March 2017, his bid was supported by Xanana Gusmão, the former president and prime minister. At the polls he won 57% of the vote to claim the presidency.

Career in Office
Guterres was sworn in on 20 May. He highlighted the need for the country to diversify its economy as oil and gas reserves dwindle. He was also expected to address the issue of disputed mineral reserves in the Timor Sea with Australia.

At parliamentary elections in July 2017 FRETILIN emerged as the largest party and formed a minority government in Sept. in alliance with the Democratic Party under Prime Minister Mari Alkatiri. However, Alkatiri's administration was unable to muster support for its policy programme and in Jan. 2018 Guterres dissolved parliament and ordered fresh elections. The subsequent polling in May ended the prevailing political stalemate as a three-party coalition—the Alliance for Change and Progress, led by Taur Matan Ruak who became prime minister in June—won an outright parliamentary majority.

Taur Matan Ruak

Position
Prime Minister

Introduction
Taur Matan Ruak became prime minister in June 2018, after more than a year of political deadlock. He had previously served as president from 2012–17, when he left to become leader of the People's Liberation Party (PLP).

Early Life
Born José Maria de Vasconcelhos on 10 Oct. 1956 in Baucau District, the prime minister is popularly known by his *nom de guerre*, Taur Matan Ruak, meaning 'two sharp eyes' in the local Tetun language.

During the Indonesian invasion in Dec. 1975, Ruak joined FALINTIL, the military wing of FRETILIN (Revolutionary Front for an Independent East Timor). In March 1979 he was captured by Indonesian troops but escaped after 23 days. He became chief-of-staff of FALINTIL in 1992, commander in 1998 and commander-in-chief in 2000. With the dissolution of FALINTIL, Ruak became a brigadier general in the newly established national army on 1 Feb. 2001 and was promoted to major general in 2009.

Having resigned from the army in Sept. 2011, he successfully ran for the presidency and was sworn in on 20 May 2012, the tenth anniversary of Timor-Leste's independence. Despite having no executive powers, he co-operated with the government on issues including diversification of the economy, national defence strategy and forging closer ties with regional partners. He relinquished the presidency in May 2017 at the end of his term.

He then became the leader of the PLP ahead of elections in July 2017, which resulted in FRETILIN heading an ineffective minority government. In the face of legislative stalemate, parliament was dissolved in Jan. 2018 and a fresh poll held in May. An outright majority was won by the Alliance for Change and Progress—a three-party coalition that included the PLP—ending months of political gridlock. Ruak emerged as the coalition's prime ministerial nominee and was sworn in on 22 June 2018.

Career in Office
Ruak's key challenges include reducing poverty, stamping out corruption and developing the country's rich oil and gas resources, all without upsetting the coalition's delicate harmony. However, his administration got off to a shaky start after the president, Francisco Guterres, refused to swear in various cabinet ministers amid allegations that they were implicated in corruption cases.

Defence

The Timor-Leste Defence Force comprises an army and a small naval element. In 2013 the army had 1,250 personnel and the naval element around 80. Defence spending totalled US$67m. in 2013 (US$57 per capita), representing 1·6% of GDP.

In 2006 the UN initiated the 'Integrated Mission in East Timor' (UNMIT) in a bid to bring stability to the country. Totalling 2,745 personnel in mid-2012, it was withdrawn at the end of Dec. 2012. The Australian-led International Stabilisation Force, also deployed in 2006, left in March 2013.

Economy

Overview

Since 2006, when the UN established a non-military peacekeeping force in the country, the economy has benefited from greater political stability and the implementation of far-reaching reforms. There has been a move from public to private sector-led growth, and some petroleum revenues have been channelled into infrastructure schemes and other development programmes of national importance. There has meanwhile been a near-halving of infant and child mortality rates, significant advances in health and education standards, and increasing citizen participation. However, even though high oil prices saw the country advance to lower-middle income status in 2011, poverty remains high, especially in rural areas where the majority of the population lives.

To ensure long-term prosperity, the government must seek to diversify the economy, encourage further private investment, improve health and education services, and create more job opportunities for the young—particularly given that revenues from declining natural resources are finite. To this end, a national strategic development plan for 2011–30 aims to address questions of social capital, infrastructure improvement and institutional reform.

Currency

The official currency is the *US dollar*. The Australian dollar and the Indonesian rupiah, both previously used, no longer serve as legal tender. There was deflation of 1·3% in 2016 but then inflation of 0·6% in 2017.

Budget

Budgetary central government revenues in 2016 were US$1,455m. (US$1,452m. in 2015) and expenditures US$1,018m. (US$1,028m. in 2015). Grants accounted for 85·6% of revenue in 2016 with taxes contributing 10·8%; main items of expenditure by economic type in 2016 were use of goods and services (34·6%) and grants (22·6%).

Performance

Total GDP in 2017 was US$3·0bn. Timor-Leste's economy grew by 4·0% in 2015 and 5·3% in 2016, but the economy then shrank by 4·6% in 2017 as a result of political uncertainty holding back public spending and private investment.

Energy and Natural Resources

Environment

Timor-Leste's carbon dioxide emissions from the consumption of energy were the equivalent of 0·3 tonnes per capita in 2011.

Electricity

Electricity produced in 2011 totalled of 140m. kWh; consumption per capita was 128 kWh.

Oil and Gas

Crude oil production in 2011 totalled 35m. bbls. The oil and gas sector provides about 90% of state revenues. The Timor Gap, an area of offshore territory between Timor-Leste and Australia, is one of the richest oilfields in the world outside the Middle East. The area is split into three zones with a central 'zone of occupation' (occupying 61,000 sq. km). Royalties on oil discovered within the central zone were split equally between Indonesia and Australia following the Timor Gap Treaty which came into force on 9 Feb. 1991. Questions over Timor-Leste's rights to oil revenue from the area have arisen following the 1999 independence referendum. There are also extensive offshore gas fields, but the region generally remains underexplored.

Minerals

Gold, iron sands, copper and chromium are present.

Agriculture

Although the presence of sandalwood was one of the principal reasons behind Portuguese colonization, its production has declined in recent years. In 2012 there were an estimated 160,000 ha. of arable land and 74,000 ha. of permanent crops. Principal crops are rice, maize, cassava, sweet potatoes, dry beans, coconuts and coffee.

Forestry

Forests covered 0·69m. ha. in 2015, representing 46% of the total land area. Timber production in 2011 was 115,000 cu. metres.

Fisheries

The total fish catch in 2011 was an estimated 3,200 tonnes.

Industry

Labour

In 2010 unemployment was officially 9·8% of the labour force between 15 and 64.

International Trade

Imports and Exports

Imports totalled US$268·5m. in 2008 and exports US$49·2m. Major imports are mineral fuels, motor vehicles and cereals. Oil, coffee and textiles are important exports. Leading import suppliers are Indonesia, Singapore, Australia and Vietnam. Leading export destinations are Germany, the USA, Indonesia and Singapore.

Communications

Civil Aviation

There is an international airport at Dili (Presidente Nicolau Lobato International Airport).

Telecommunications

In 2011 there were 614,151 mobile phone subscriptions (560·2 per 1,000 inhabitants) and 3,054 landline telephone subscriptions (2·8 per 1,000 inhabitants).

Social Institutions

Out of 178 countries analysed in the 2017 *Fragile States Index*—a list published jointly by the Fund for Peace and *Foreign Policy* magazine—Timor-Leste was ranked the 35th most vulnerable to conflict or collapse. The index is based on 12 indicators of state vulnerability across social, political and economic categories.

Justice

In the wake of Timor-Leste's pro-independence referendum vote in 1999, the Indonesian judicial system was replaced by a temporary UN-administered system using international judicial officers and advisers, alongside a cohort of 60 Timorese legal trainees. Four district courts of first instance—in Dili, Suai, Oecussi and Baucau—were re-established to rule on ordinary crimes. An appeals court was also set up, along with a mechanism to judge, for example, war crimes and crimes against humanity.

Following independence in 2002, the government made steps to adopt the Portuguese judicial system. New penal and civil law codes were promulgated in 2009 and 2011. However, in Oct. 2014 this transition was thrown into turmoil following the decision to dismiss all international personnel (including judges and prosecutors) within 48 hours.

Health

In 2009 there were six hospitals, 65 community health centres, 183 health posts and 162 mobile health clinics, staffed by 2,500 Timorese health workers with the support of 300 Cuban doctors.

In *Water: At What Cost? The State of the World's Water 2016*, WaterAid reported that 28·1% of the population does not have access to safe water.

Religion

Over 90% of Timor-Leste's population are Roman Catholic, with Protestants, Muslims, Hindus and Buddhists accounting for the remainder.

Culture

Press

In 2007 there were three daily newspapers: *Suara Timor Lorosae*, *Timor Post* and *Jornal Nacional Diario*. There were also three non-dailies in 2007.

Tourism

In 2014, 60,000 non-resident tourists—excluding same-day visitors—arrived by air (down from a record 79,000 in 2013).

Diplomatic Representatives

Of Timor-Leste in the United Kingdom (6th Floor, 83 Victoria St., London, SW1H 0HW)
Ambassador: Joaquim António María Lopes da Fonseca.

Of the United Kingdom in Timor-Leste (embassy in Dili closed in Oct. 2006)
Ambassador: Moazzam Malik (resides in Jakarta, Indonesia).

Of Timor-Leste in the USA (4201 Connecticut Ave., NW, Suite 504, Washington, D.C., 20008)
Ambassador: Domingos Sarmento Alves.

Of the USA in Timor-Leste (Avenida de Portugal, Pantai Kelapa, Dili)
Ambassador: Kathleen M. Fitzpatrick.

Of Timor-Leste to the United Nations
Ambassador: Maria Helena Lopes de Jesus Pires.

Of Timor-Leste to the European Union
Ambassador: Francisco Tilman Cepeda.

Further Reading

Berlie, Jean A. (ed.), *East Timor's Independence, Indonesia and ASEAN.* 2017
Dunn, James, *East Timor: A Rough Passage to Independence.* 2003
Hainsworth, Paul and McCloskey, Stephen, (eds) *The East Timor Question: The Struggle for Independence from Indonesia.* 2000
Kingsbury, Damien and Leach, Michael, (eds) *East Timor: Beyond Independence.* 2007
Kohen, Arnold S., *From the Place of the Dead: Bishop Belo and the Struggle for East Timor.* 2000
Nevins, Joseph, *A Not-So-Distant Horror: Mass Violence in East Timor.* 2005
Robinson, Geoffrey, *"If You Leave Us Here, We Will Die": How Genocide Was Stopped in East Timor.* 2009
Tanter, Richard, Ball, Desmond and Van Klinken, Gerry, (eds) *Masters of Terror: Indonesia's Military and Violence in East Timor.* 2006
National Statistical Office: Direcção Nacional de Estatística, Rua de Caicoli, P. O. Box 10, Dili.
Website: http://www.statistics.gov.tl

Togo

République Togolaise (Togolese Republic)

Capital: Lomé
Population projection, 2020: 8·38m.
GNI per capita, 2017: (PPP$) 1,453
HDI/world rank, 2017: 0·503/165=
Internet domain extension: .tg

Key Historical Events

Eleventh century records relate Togo's settlement by a succession of tribes. The Kwa people from the Volta region were joined by the Ewe people from the Niger Valley, while later migrations included the Ana, Mina and Guin people from Ghana and the Ivory Coast, and the Nawdba from the east, who settled in northern Togo.

During 1471–72 Portuguese explorers and traders began trading along the coast in gold, silver and pepper. In the 16th century Britain, Denmark, Holland, France, Germany, Sweden and Portugal all shipped slaves from the region in co-operation with tribal leaders. The 18th century saw conflicts with the Akwamu Confederacy and the Ashanti Kingdom in the west, and the Kingdom of Dahomey in the east, as tribal rulers tried to consolidate their territory. Meanwhile, Britain, France and Germany became the dominant European powers in the region.

Following the abolition of slavery in the 19th century, British, French and German traders built up a flourishing palm oil export trade from Anecho, Agoue and Porto Seguro. As a result several Togolese families of partly Brazilian or Portuguese origin came to prominence, some retaining considerable influence to the present day.

Despite competition from Britain and France, Germany signed a treaty with chief Mlapa III on 5 July 1884 to establish colonial rule on the coast. Control was then extended inland and, following agreement with Britain and France, the borders of German Togoland were defined. Using slave labour, Germany developed the agricultural sector, focusing on cacao, coffee and cotton.

In 1914 the Allies overran German Togoland and in 1922 it was partitioned into a western British Mandated Territory and an eastern French Mandated Territory under the League of Nations. In 1946, following the Second World War, British Togoland and French Togoland became Trust territories under the United Nations. On 9 May 1956 a UN-sponsored referendum in British Togoland resulted in a majority vote for union with the neighbouring colony of Gold Coast. The territory soon merged with Gold Coast to become Ghana, despite objections from the southern Togolese, most of whom had voted for union with French Togo. In 1956 French Togo was granted partial self-government to become the Republic of Togo. It gained full independence on 27 April 1960.

Sylvanus Olympio was elected president in 1958. In 1961 a new constitution established broad executive powers for the presidency, alongside an elected National Assembly. Olympio won the 1961 election and his party, Unité Togolaise (UT), took all 51 National Assembly seats. In 1962 Olympio disbanded the main opposition parties. On 13 Jan. 1963 Olympio was assassinated and the army voted in Nicolas Grunitsky as head of state. A military coup ousted Grunitsky in Jan. 1967 and on 14 April 1967 Gen. (then Col.) Etienne Gnassingbé Eyadéma took the presidency.

Eyadéma developed the country's investment banking sector and its phosphates exports, before recession in the 1980s caused a price collapse. Eyadéma ruled as head of Togo's only officially recognized political party, the Rassemblement du Peuple Togolais (RPT), and survived several attempted coups. In Aug. 1991 a national conference of Togo's leading political movements led to a reduction in Eyadéma's executive powers. A transitional administration, the High Council of the Republic, was installed, led by Kokou Koffigoh.

In Nov. 1991 the new government banned the RPT and the army, which backed Eyadéma, attempted a coup. Eyadéma negotiated the return of some of his powers and won an election in Aug. 1992, though its validity was disputed. In 1994 a coalition of the Comité d'Action pour le Renouveau and

the Union Togolaise pour la Démocratie won a majority in the National Assembly elections. The RPT returned to power in the election of June 1998 and Eyadéma retained the presidency until his death in Feb. 2005.

On Eyadéma's death the military installed his son, Faure Gnassingbé, as president and the following day the constitution was amended to legalize his succession. Under domestic and international pressure he stepped down on 25 Feb. 2005 and parliament speaker Abbas Bonfoh became interim president. Faure Gnassingbé won the presidential election held in April 2005 but the opposition alleged vote rigging and 400–500 people died in riots. Gnassingbé was subsequently confirmed as president. He won further terms in 2010 and 2015 but on each occasion the opposition alleged electoral fraud and refused to recognize his victories.

Territory and Population

Togo is bounded in the west by Ghana, north by Burkina Faso, east by Benin and south by the Gulf of Guinea. The area is 56,600 sq. km. 2010 census population, 6,191,155 (3,182,060 females); density, 109 per sq. km.

The UN gives a projected population for 2020 of 8·38m.

In 2011, 44·1% of the population lived in urban areas. In 2010, 42% were below the age of 15. The capital is Lomé (2010 census population, 837,437), other towns being Sokodé (95,070), Kara (94,878), Kpalimé (75,084), Atakpamé (69,261), Dapaong (58,071) and Tsévié (54,474).

Area, 2010 census population and chief town of the five regions:

Region	Area in sq. km	Population	Chief town
Centrale	13,317	617,871	Sokodé
De La Kara	11,738	769,940	Kara
Des Plateaux	16,975	1,375,165	Atakpamé
Des Savanes	8,470	828,224	Dapaong
Maritime	6,100	2,599,955	Lomé

There are 37 ethnic groups. The south is largely populated by Ewe-speaking peoples (forming 23% of the population), Watyi (10%) and other related groups, while the north is mainly inhabited by Hamitic groups speaking Kabre (14%), Tem (6%) and Gurma (3%). The official language is French but Ewe and Kabre are also taught in schools.

Social Statistics

2008 estimates: births, 212,000; deaths, 53,000. Estimated rates, 2008 (per 1,000 population): births, 32·9; deaths, 8·2. Expectation of life (2013) was 55·6 years for males and 57·4 for females. Annual population growth rate, 2005–10, 2·6%. Infant mortality, 2010, 66 per 1,000 live births; fertility rate, 2008, 4·3 births per woman.

Climate

The tropical climate produces wet seasons from March to July and from Oct. to Nov. in the south. The north has one wet season, from April to July. The heaviest rainfall occurs in the mountains of the west, southwest and centre. Lomé, Jan. 81°F (27·2°C), July 76°F (24·4°C). Annual rainfall 35" (875 mm).

Constitution and Government

A referendum on 27 Sept. 1992 approved a new constitution by 98·1% of votes cast. Under this the *President* and the *National Assembly* were directly elected for five-year terms. On 30 Dec. 2002 parliament approved an amendment to the constitution lifting the restriction on the number of times that the president may be re-elected. The National Assembly has 91 seats and is elected for a five-year term.

National Anthem

'Terre de nos aïeux' ('Land of our forefathers'); words and music by A. Casimir-Dosseh.

Recent Elections

In presidential elections held on 25 April 2015 Faure Gnassingbé was re-elected with 58·8% of the vote, ahead of Jean-Pierre Fabre of the National Alliance for Change (Alliance Nationale pour le Changement) with 35·2% and Tchaboure Gogue of the Alliance of Democrats for Integral Development (Alliance des Démocrates pour le Développement Intégral) with 4·0%. There were two other candidates. Turnout was 60·9%.

At the parliamentary elections on 20 Dec. 2018 the ruling Union for the Republic (UNIR) won 59 of 91 seats, the Union of Forces for Change 7, the New Togolese Commitment 3, the Patriotic Movement for Democracy and Development 2, the Movement of Centrist Republicans 1 and the Pan-African Democratic Party 1. Independents took 18 seats. Turnout was 59·3%.

Current Government

President, and Minister of Defence and War Veterans: Faure Gnassingbé; b. 1966 (UNIR—formerly RPT; sworn in 4 May 2005 and re-elected 4 March 2010 and 25 April 2015).

In Feb. 2019 the government comprised:

Prime Minister: Komi Sélom Klassou; b. 1960 (UNIR; sworn in 5 June 2015).

Minister of Agriculture, Animal Production and Fisheries: Noël Koutéra Bataka. *Basic Development, Handicrafts and Youth:* Victoire Tomégah Dogbé. *Cities, Urban Planning, Housing and Sanitation:* Koko Ayéva. *Communication, Sports and Civic Education:* Folly Bazi Katari. *Culture, Tourism and Recreation:* Kossivi Egbetognon. *Development Planning and Co-operation:* Demba Tignokpa. *Economy and Finance:* Sani Yaya. *Environment, Sustainable Development and Natural Protection:* Olatokoun Wonou David. *Foreign Affairs, African Integration and Togolese Abroad:* Robert Dussey. *Health and Public Hygiene:* Moustapha Midjiyawa. *Higher Education and Research:* Koffi Akpagana. *Human Rights:* Christian Trimua. *Infrastructure and Transport:* Zouréatou Tchakondo-Kassa-Traoré. *Justice and Keeper of the Seals:* Puis Agbetomey. *Mines and Energy:* Dèdèriwè Ably-Bidamon. *Posts, Digital Economy and Technological Innovation:* Cina Lawson. *Public Service, Labour, Administrative Reform and Social Protection:* Gilbert Bawara. *Security and Civil Protection:* Gen. Damehane Yark. *Social Action, Promotion of Women and Literacy:* Tchabinandi Kolani Yentcharé. *Technical Education, Training and Professional Integration:* Tairou Babiègue. *Territorial Administration, Decentralization and Local Government:* Payadowa Boukpéssi. *Trade, Industry, Private Sector Development and Promotion of Local Consumption:* Kodjo Adedze. *Water, Rural Infrastructure and Rural Hydraulics:* Antoine Lekpa Gbegbeni. *Minister in the Presidency:* Arouna Batiem Silly Kpabre.

Government Website (French only): http://www.republicoftogo.com

Current Leaders

Faure Gnassingbé

Position
President

Introduction
Faure Gnassingbé was installed as president in 2005 after the death of his father who had held power since 1967. His initial appointment in Feb. led to violent protests and international condemnation. Forced to step down, he contested a presidential election and emerged victorious in April 2005. Having then sought political reconciliation, he was re-elected to the presidency in March 2010 and again in April 2015.

Early Life
Faure Essozimna Gnassingbé was born in Afagnan on 6 June 1966. He attended school in the capital, Lomé, followed by the Sorbonne University in Paris and the George Washington University in the USA. On returning to Togo in the mid-1990s, he began work as a civil servant.

He entered politics in 2002, when he was elected the representative of the ruling Togolese People's Assembly (RPT; since reconfigured as the UNIR),

and in June 2003 he took office as minister of public works, mines and telecommunications.

On 6 Feb. 2005, the day after his father's death, Faure was proclaimed as his successor by the Togolese army, sparking widespread protest. Amid mounting international criticism, Faure announced that a presidential election would be held on 24 April 2005 and stepped down from office. Official results gave Faure over 60% of the vote at the subsequent elections and, despite violence erupting in Lomé amid claims of electoral fraud, he was sworn in as president on 4 May 2005.

Career in Office
Faure promised to push for economic growth, to reform institutions and to improve Togo's image abroad. Although most of the key government posts went to members of the ruling party, Edem Kodjo, the leader of a moderate opposition party, was named prime minister in June 2005. In Sept. 2006 Faure appointed another veteran opposition leader, Yawovi Madji Agboyibo of the Action Committee for Renewal, as prime minister with the task of forming a unity government. In Oct. 2007 the ruling RPT won parliamentary elections in which opposition parties took part for the first time in almost two decades and which were declared by international observers to be free and fair. Faure then appointed Komlan Mally prime minister and a new government was formed in Dec. When Mally resigned in Sept. 2008, Faure appointed Gilbert Houngbo, an independent, as the new premier. Faure was returned to office in presidential elections on 4 March 2010. In May that year veteran opposition leader Gilchrist Olympio agreed to join a government of national unity, ending years of hostility towards the then RPT but causing a deep split within his Union of Forces for Change which had alleged widespread fraud in the election.

Parliamentary elections scheduled for Oct. 2012 were postponed after violent protests in June that year against electoral law amendments that demonstrators claimed favoured the ruling UNIR. The following month Faure appointed Kwesi Ahoomey-Zunu as prime minister following the resignation of Gilbert Houngbo. The delayed elections were finally held in July 2013, returning the UNIR with a majority of parliamentary seats. There were opposition claims of polling irregularities, but international observers deemed the elections fair.

Faure was re-elected for a further presidential term in elections in April 2015, following which in June he named Komi Sélom Klassou as the new premier at the head of a largely unchanged cabinet. However, there has since been growing popular pressure for political reform and demands for the restoration of the 1992 constitution limiting the number of presidential terms of office to two. In the Dec. 2018 parliamentary elections the UNIR again secured a majority but lost some seats despite the poll being largely shunned by the opposition parties.

Defence

There is selective conscription that lasts for two years. Defence expenditure totalled US$72m. in 2013 (US$10 per capita), representing 1·8% of GDP.

Army

Strength (2011) around 8,100, with a further 750 in a paramilitary gendarmerie.

Navy

In 2011 the Naval wing of the armed forces numbered about 200 and was based at Lomé.

Air Force

The Air Force—established with French assistance—numbered (2011) 250, with ten combat aircraft although their serviceability is in doubt.

Economy

Agriculture contributed 31% of GDP in 2011, industry 16% and services 53%.

Overview

Togo's economic performance is among the weakest in sub-Saharan Africa, with poverty increasing significantly since the early 1980s. Social indicators are low, with the country ranked 165th out of 189 on the 2017 UN Human Development Index. In the World Bank's *Doing Business 2017* report, Togo also ranked only 154th of 190 countries. The main economic activities are mining, agriculture and re-exporting. Natural resources, port activities and public investment have been the drivers of growth in recent years.

After civil and economic turmoil in the early 1990s, a structural redevelopment programme was launched in 1994. Following a downturn in 2005, the government acted to restore fiscal discipline and strengthen governance. However, flooding and the surge in global food and fuel prices in 2008 hurt the economy. Further flooding in large parts of the country in Sept. and Oct. 2010 caused more damage to infrastructure and crops.

In Dec. 2010 Togo completed the Heavily Indebted Poor Countries (HIPC) process, leading to a cancellation of around 82% of its external debt. As a result, total government debt fell from 67% of GDP to about 30%.

Currency

The unit of currency is the *franc CFA* (XOF) with a parity of 655·957 francs CFA to one euro. Foreign exchange reserves were US$270m. in June 2005 and total money supply was 177,138m. francs CFA. There was inflation of 0·9% in 2016 but then deflation of 0·7% in 2017.

Budget

In 2016 budgetary central government revenues were 695bn. francs CFA and expenditures 580bn. francs CFA. Taxes accounted for 82·2% of revenues in 2016; use of goods and services accounted for 37·8% of expenditures and compensation of employees 31·6%.

VAT is 18%.

Performance

Real GDP growth was 5·7% in 2015, 5·1% in 2016 and 4·4% in 2017. Total GDP in 2017 was US$4·8bn.

Banking and Finance

The bank of issue is the Central Bank of West African States (BCEAO). The *Governor* is Tiémoko Meyliet Koné. In 2016 there were 13 commercial banks. Foreign debt totalled US$1,728m. in 2010, representing 61·1% of GNI.

Energy and Natural Resources

Environment

Togo's carbon dioxide emissions from the consumption of energy in 2011 were the equivalent of 0·2 tonnes per capita.

Electricity

Installed capacity in 2011 was an estimated 85,000 kW. In 2011 production totalled 139m. kWh. Over 80% of the electricity consumed is imported, mainly from Ghana. Consumption per capita in 2011 was 138 kWh.

Minerals

Output of phosphate rock in 2011 was 866,000 tonnes. Other minerals are limestone, iron ore and marble.

Agriculture

Agriculture supports about 80% of the population. There were an estimated 2·65m. ha. of arable land in 2013 and 0·17m. ha. of permanent crops. There are considerable plantations of oil and cocoa palms, coffee, cacao, kola, cassava and cotton. Production, 2013 (in 1,000 tonnes): cassava, 903; maize, 693; yams, 661; sorghum, 285; rice, 260; palm fruit oil (estimate), 147; dry beans, 105; seed cotton, 78; millet, 64; cottonseed (estimate), 45; palm kernels, 41.

Livestock (2013, in 1,000): goats, 2,728; sheep (estimate), 2,200; cattle, 443; pigs (estimate), 400; chickens (estimate), 25,000.

Forestry

Forests covered 0·19m. ha. in 2015, or 4% of the land area. Teak plantations covered 8,600 ha. In 2011, 4·59m. cu. metres of roundwood were cut.

Fisheries

The catch in 2010 totalled 21,497 tonnes (77% from marine waters).

Industry

Industry is small-scale. Cement and textiles are produced and food processed. In 2011 industry accounted for 16% of GDP, with manufacturing contributing 8%.

Labour

In 2010 the estimated labour force was 3,059,000 (56% males), up from 2,182,000 in 2000. In Aug. 2008 the statutory monthly minimum wage was raised to 28,000 francs CFA.

Togo had 49,000 people living in slavery according to the Walk Free Foundation's 2013 *Global Slavery Index*.

International Trade

Imports and Exports

In 2008 imports (c.i.f.) amounted to US$1,540m.; exports (f.o.b.) US$790m. The main import suppliers in 2005 were France (17·6%), China (13·2%) and Côte d'Ivoire (6·5%). Principal export destinations in 2005 were Ghana (20·3%), Burkina Faso (18·4%) and Benin (11·6%). Leading imports are food, refined petroleum, and chemicals and chemical products; main exports are cement, phosphates and cotton.

Communications

Roads

There were 11,652 km of roads in 2007, including 3,067 km of highways or national roads. In 2007 there were 10,600 passenger cars in use, 2,200 lorries and vans and 34,200 motorcycles and mopeds.

Rail

There are four railways (metre gauge) connecting Lomé, with Aného (continuing to Cotonou in Benin), Kpalimé, Tabligbo and (via Atakpamé) Blitta; total length in 2005, 532 km. In 2005 the railways carried 1·1m. tonnes of freight. There has been no passenger rail service since 1996.

Civil Aviation

In 2010 ASKY Airlines (a pan-African airline with its hub in Lomé) flew from Lomé-Tokoin airport to Abidjan, Accra, Bamako, Banjul, Brazzaville, Cotonou, Dakar, Douala, Kinshasa, Lagos, Libreville and Ouagadougou. There were international flights in 2010 with other airlines to Abidjan, Accra, Addis Ababa, Bamako, Casablanca, Cotonou, Dakar, Libreville, Ouagadougou, Paris and Tripoli (Libya). In 2012 Tokoin handled 472,313 passengers (417,672 on international flights) and 7,256 tonnes of freight.

Shipping

In Jan. 2014 there were 133 ships of 300 GT or over registered, totalling 626,000 GT.

Telecommunications

In 2013 there were 62,500 main (fixed) telephone lines in Togo; mobile phone subscriptions numbered 4,263,000 that year (625·3 per 1,000 persons). In 2013 an estimated 4·5% of the population were internet users.

Social Institutions

Out of 178 countries analysed in the 2017 *Fragile States Index*—a list published jointly by the Fund for Peace and *Foreign Policy* magazine—Togo was ranked the 56th most vulnerable to conflict or collapse. The index is based on 12 indicators of state vulnerability across social, political and economic categories.

Justice

The Supreme Court and two Appeal Courts are in Lomé, one for criminal cases and one for civil and commercial cases. Each receives appeal from a series of local tribunals.

The death penalty was abolished in June 2009. The population in penal institutions in Oct. 2010 was 4,116 (59 per 100,000 of national population). 65·2% of prisoners had yet to receive a trial according to 2014 estimates by the International Centre for Prison Studies.

Education

The adult literacy rate in 2008 was 65%. In 2007 there were 1,021,617 pupils and 26,103 teaching staff in primary schools, and 408,964 pupils in secondary schools with 11,518 teaching staff. In 2006 there were 32,502 students in higher education and 455 academic staff. In 2007 about 77% of children of primary school age were attending school. The University of

Benin at Lomé (founded in 1970) is the leading institution of tertiary education.

In 2007 public expenditure on education came to 3·8% of GNI and accounted for 17·2% of total government expenditure.

Health

In 2005 hospital bed provision was nine per 10,000 population. In 2008 there were 349 physicians, 1,816 nursing and midwifery personnel, 19 dentistry personnel and 11 pharmaceutical personnel.

In *Water: At What Cost? The State of the World's Water 2016*, WaterAid reported that 36·9% of the population does not have access to safe water.

Religion

A study by the Pew Research Center's Forum on Religion & Public Life estimated that there were 2·64m. Christians in 2010, 2·15m. folk religionists and 840,000 Muslims. A further 370,000 people had no religious affiliation. Of the Christians in 2010, an estimated 60% were Catholics and 39% Protestants.

Culture

World Heritage Sites

There is one UNESCO site in Togo: Koutammakou, the land of the Batammariba (inscribed on the list in 2004).

Press

There is one government-controlled daily newspaper, *Togo-Presse* (circulation of 5,000 in 2008).

Tourism

In 2010 there were 202,000 international tourists staying at hotels and similar establishments; spending by tourists totalled US$66m. in the same year.

Diplomatic Representatives

Of Togo in the United Kingdom (Units 3, 7 & 8 Lysander Mews, Lysander Grove, London, N19 3QP)
Ambassador: Vacant.
Chargé d'Affaires a.i.: Abra Dackey.

Of the United Kingdom in Togo
Ambassador: Iain Walker (resides in Accra, Ghana).

Of Togo in the USA (2208 Massachusetts Ave., NW, Washington, D.C., 20008)
Ambassador: Frédéric Edem Hegbe.

Of the USA in Togo (4332 Blvd Eyadéma, BP 852, Lomé)
Ambassador: David R. Gilmour.

Of Togo to the United Nations
Ambassador: Kokou Kpayedo.

Of Togo to the European Union
Ambassador: Félix Kodjo Sagbo.

Further Reading

National Statistical Office: Direction Générale de la Statistique et de la Comptabilité Nationale, B. P. 118, Lomé.
Website (French only): http://www.stat-togo.org

Tonga

Pule'anga Fakatu'i 'o Tonga (Kingdom of Tonga)

Capital: Nuku'alofa
Population projection, 2020: 111,000
GNI per capita, 2017: (PPP$) 5,547
HDI/world rank, 2017: 0·726/98
Internet domain extension: .to

Key Historical Events

The Tongatapu group of islands in the south western Pacific Ocean were discovered by Tasman in 1643. The Kingdom of Tonga attained unity under Taufa'ahau Tupou (George I) who became ruler of his native Ha'apai in 1820, of Vava'u in 1833 and of Tongatapu in 1845. By 1860 the kingdom had converted to Christianity. In 1862 the king granted freedom from arbitrary rule of minor chiefs and extended land rights. These institutional changes, together with the establishment of a parliament of chiefs, paved the way towards a democratic constitution. By the Anglo–German Agreement of 14 Nov. 1899, the Tonga Islands became a British protectorate. The protectorate was dissolved on 4 June 1970 when Tonga, the only ancient kingdom surviving from the pre-European period in Polynesia, achieved independence within the Commonwealth.

Territory and Population

The Kingdom consists of some 169 islands and islets with a total area, including 30 sq. km of inland waters plus uninhabited islands, of 748 sq. km (289 sq. miles), and lies between 15° and 23° 30' S. lat and 173° and 177° W. long, its western boundary being the eastern boundary of Fiji. The islands are split up into the following groups (reading from north to south): the Niuas, Vava'u, Ha'apai, Tongatapu and 'Eua. The three main groups, both from historical and administrative significance, are Tongatapu in the south, Ha'apai in the centre and Vava'u in the north. Census population (2016), 100,651; density, 140 per sq. km. In 2011, 23·5% of the population lived in urban areas.

The UN gives a projected population for 2020 of 111,000.

The capital is Nuku'alofa on Tongatapu; population (2016), 23,221.

There are five divisions comprising 23 districts:

Division	Sq. km	Census 2016	Capital
Niuas	72	1,232	Hihifo
Vava'u	121	13,738	Neiafu
Ha'apai	109	6,125	Pangai
Tongatapu	260	74,611	Nuku'alofa
'Eua	87	4,945	Ohonua

Both Tongan and English are recognized as official languages.

Social Statistics

Births, 2008 estimates, 2,900; deaths, 600; marriages (Tongatapu only), 892; divorces, 95. Expectation of life, 2013: males, 69·8 years; females, 75·7. Annual population growth rate, 2000–08, 0·6%. Infant mortality, 2010, 13 per 1,000 live births. Fertility rate, 2008, 4·0 births per woman.

Climate

Generally a healthy climate, although Jan. to March hot and humid, with temperatures of 90°F (32·2°C). Rainfall amounts are comparatively high, being greatest from Dec. to March. Nuku'alofa, Jan. 25·8°C, July 21·3°C. Annual rainfall 1,643 mm. Vava'u, Jan. 27·3°C, July 23·4°C. Annual rainfall 2,034 mm.

Constitution and Government

The reigning King is **Tupou VI ('Aho'eitu 'Unuaki'otonga Tuku'aho Tupou VI)**, born 12 July 1959, succeeded on 18 March 2012 on the death of his brother, George Tupou V.

The current Constitution is based on the one granted in 1875. It was last amended in 2010 in order to enact electoral reforms, to provide parliament with greater constitutional powers and to reduce monarchical influence on executive matters. There is a Privy Council, Cabinet, Legislative Assembly and Judiciary. The *Legislative Assembly*, of a maximum of 30 members, is composed of 17 elected representatives of the people, nine nobles elected by their peers and up to four *ex officio* members.

National Anthem

'E 'Otua, Mafimafi, ko ho mau 'eiki Koe' ('Oh Almighty God above, thou art our Lord and sure defence'); words by Prince Uelingtoni Ngu Tupoumalohi, tune by C. G. Schmitt.

Recent Elections

Elections were held on 16 Nov. 2017 for the 17 elected seats. The Democratic Party of the Friendly Islands won 14 seats and independent candidates three. Turnout was 67·0%.

Current Government

In Feb. 2019 the government comprised:

Prime Minister, and Minister of Foreign Affairs: 'Akilisi Pohiva; b. 1941 (in office since 30 Dec. 2014).

Deputy Prime Minister, and Minister of Infrastructure and Tourism: Semisi Lafu Kioa Sika.

Minister of Agriculture, Food, Forests and Fisheries: Semisi Tauelangai Fakahau. *Commerce, Consumer Affairs, Trade, Innovation and Labour:* Tevita Tu'i Uata. *Education and Training:* Penisimani 'Epenisa Fifita. *Finance and National Planning:* Pohiva Tu'i'onetoa. *Health, and Public Enterprises:* Dr Saia Ma'u Piukala. *Internal Affairs and Sports:* Losaline Ma'asi. *Justice and Prisons:* Sione Vuna Fa'otusia. *Lands and Natural Resources, and His Majesty's Armed Forces:* Lord Ma'afu Tuku'i'aulahi. *Meteorology, Energy, Information, Disaster Management, Environment, Climate Change and Communications:* Poasi Mataele Tei. *Revenue and Customs, and Police, Fire and Emergency Services:* Mateni Tapueluelu.

Government Website: http://www.tongaportal.gov.to

Current Leaders

Samiuela 'Akilisi Pohiva

Position
Prime Minister

Introduction
'Akilisi Pohiva became Tonga's first democratically-elected prime minister on 30 Dec. 2014. Following early parliamentary elections he was reinstalled for a second term on 18 Dec. 2017. The former teacher has campaigned for democracy and restraints on monarchical power for decades.

Early Life
'Akilisi Pohiva was born on 7 April 1941 in Fakakakai, a village in Tonga's Ha'apai archipelago. Having earned a certificate from Tupou College in 1961, he began a teaching career. He graduated in education from the University of the South Pacific in 1978 and taught in various institutions until 1982, when he took a job at the National Office for Disaster Relief and Reconstruction. At this time Pohiva became active in Tonga's pro-democracy movement. He became known as a whistleblower against official corruption, leaving him a target for the ruling elite, particularly King Taufa'ahau Tupou IV.

© Springer Nature Limited 2020
Palgrave Macmillan (ed.), *The Statesman's Yearbook 2020*,
https://doi.org/10.1057/978-1-349-95940-2_190

Elected to Tonga's legislature in 1987, Pohiva co-founded the Friendly Islands Human Rights & Democracy Movement. In 1996 he and the editor of the *Tonga Times* were arrested and imprisoned after publishing an article alleging that the king had a secret fortune. Charged with sedition, Pohiva was subsequently acquitted but was arrested again in 2007 for an alleged role in riots in the capital, Nuku'alofa, the previous year that claimed eight lives.

Pohiva's demands for democratic reform became more potent after the global financial crisis in 2008–09, which hit Tonga hard. Rates of unemployment and poverty spiralled and there were frequent breakdowns in law and order amid corruption scandals. Having narrowly lost the 2010 parliamentary election to Lord Tu'ivakano, Pohiva took on the incumbent deputy prime minister, Samiu Vaipulu, in legislative polls on 27 Nov. 2014. After almost five weeks of political wrangling, he emerged victorious, collecting 15 of 26 parliamentarians' votes to become the country's first democratically-elected prime minister.

Career in Office
Pohiva said that his priority was to 'create a political framework in which every Tongan is held in equal value, and justice is served for everyone'. He vowed to boost the ailing economy, which is largely dependent on foreign aid and remittances from overseas. He was also expected to focus on increasing productivity in agriculture, fisheries and tourism, and promised to reduce spending on official travel and diplomatic missions. In Aug. 2017 the king dissolved parliament and dismissed Pohiva, accusing his government of trying to usurp the powers of the monarchy. Fresh parliamentary elections in Nov. were then won by the Democratic Party of the Friendly Islands, which took 14 of the 17 popularly elected seats, and Pohiva was subsequently reappointed as premier the following month. In Jan. 2018 he was admitted to hospital with an undisclosed illness, but was later said to be in a stable condition in an intensive care unit.

Defence

Army
The Tonga Defence Services number around 450 troops.

Navy
A coastal naval force operating several small patrol boats is based at Touliki, in Nuku'alofa.

Air Force
An Air Force was created in 1996. There is also a small naval aviation unit.

Economy

In 2016 agriculture accounted for 19·8% of GDP, industry 19·9% and services 60·3%.

Overview
Tonga has a small, open island economy heavily reliant on foreign aid and remittances. Although the country has enjoyed several years of robust growth and macroeconomic stability, the short-term outlook has been undermined by the devastating effects of tropical Cyclone Gita, which struck in Feb. 2018.

The dominance of the public sector has led to a low level of economic dynamism despite a workforce that is considered among the best educated in the Pacific Island nations. Agricultural produce and fish make up two-thirds of total exports. Tourism is the second-largest source of hard currency earnings following remittances. High labour costs, limited export diversification and lack of long-term investment must be addressed in order to secure sustainable growth.

The economy weathered the effects of the global financial crisis of 2008 and 2009, although GDP contracted by 1·1% in 2012 and 0·6% in 2013 as remittances declined steeply and the cost of food and fuel imports rose. Growth rebounded to an average of 2·9% per year between 2014 and 2017, driven by donor-funded construction and infrastructure projects as well as increased tourism. Inflation spiked in 2017 at 7·4% owing to a new import tax and an increase in domestic food prices. However, the rate is expected to decline as the effect of the import tax subsides.

Currency
The unit of currency is the *pa'anga* (TOP) of 100 *seniti*. There was inflation of 2·6% in 2016, rising to 7·4% in 2017. In July 2005 foreign exchange reserves were US$49m. and total money supply was T$65m.

Budget
Budgetary central government revenues were T$364m. in 2015–16, with expenditures T$284m.

There is a consumption tax of 15%.

Performance
The economy grew by 3·5% in 2015, 4·2% in 2016 and 2·5% in 2017. Total GDP in 2017 was US$0·4bn. According to World Bank data for 2017, Tonga is the country most reliant on remittances from abroad, accounting for 34·2% of total GDP.

Banking and Finance
The National Reserve Bank of Tonga (*Governor*, Sione Ngongo Kioa) was established in 1989 as a bank of issue and to manage foreign reserves. The Bank of Tonga and the Tonga Development Bank are both situated in Nuku'alofa with branches in the main islands. Other commercial banks in Nuku'alofa are ANZ Banking Group Ltd, the MBF Bank Ltd, the National Reserve Bank of Tonga and the Westpac Banking Corp.

External debt totalled US$144m. in 2010 and represented 39·7% of GNI.

Energy and Natural Resources

Environment
Tonga's carbon dioxide emissions from the consumption of energy in 2011 were the equivalent of 1·7 tonnes per capita.

Electricity
Production (2011) 53m. kWh. Installed capacity (2011 estimate) 14,000 kW.

Agriculture
In 2014 there were approximately 18,000 ha. of arable land and 11,000 ha. of permanent crops. Production (2013 estimates, in 1,000 tonnes): coconuts, 130; pumpkins and squash, 20; cassava, 8; sweet potatoes, 7; yams, 5; taro, 3; plantains, 2; lemons and limes, 2.

Livestock (2013 estimates): pigs, 83,000; goats, 13,000; cattle, 12,000; horses, 11,000.

Forestry
Forests covered 9,000 ha. in 2015, or 13% of the land area.

Fisheries
In 2015 the total catch was 1,781 tonnes.

Industry

The main industries produce food and beverages, paper, chemicals, metals and textiles.

International Trade

Imports and Exports
In 2010 imports (c.i.f.) were valued at US$158·8m. and exports (f.o.b.) at US$8·3m. Main imports are food and live animals, basic manufactures, machinery and transport equipment, and mineral fuels and lubricants; main exports are coconut oil, vanilla beans, root crops, desiccated coconut and watermelons. The leading import suppliers in 2006 were New Zealand (33·1%), Fiji (28·2%), Australia (12·5%) and the USA (9·8%); principal export markets were Japan (40·6%), USA (25·0%), Australia (14·6%) and South Korea (8·3%).

Communications

Roads
There are about 680 km of roads. Registered vehicles in 2010 numbered 5,806, including 4,411 cars and four-wheeled light vehicles, 1,285 heavy trucks and 62 motorized two- and three-wheelers.

Civil Aviation
There is an international airport at Nuku'alofa on Tongatapu. The national carrier was the state-owned Royal Tongan Airlines, but it ceased operations in May 2004 owing to financial difficulties. In 2009 Nuku'alofa (Fua'Amotu International) handled 222,612 passengers and 1,417 tonnes of freight.

Shipping

In Jan. 2014 there were 16 ships of 300 GT or over registered, totalling 37,000 GT. The main port is Nuku'alofa.

Telecommunications

The operation of the National Telecommunication Network and Services is the responsibility of the Tonga Telecommunication Commission (TCC). In 2011 there were 30,000 main (fixed) telephone lines; mobile phone subscriptions numbered 55,000 that year (52·6 per 100 persons). In 2013 an estimated 35·0% of the population were internet users. Ucall mobile GSM digital has been in operation in Tonga since Dec. 2001.

Social Institutions

Justice

The judiciary is presided over by the Chief Justice. The enforcement of justice is the responsibility of the Attorney-General and the Minister of Police. In 1994 the UK ceased appointing Tongan judges and subsidizing their salaries.

The population in penal institutions in Dec. 2012 was 158 (150 per 100,000 of national population).

Education

In 2014 there were a total of 17,093 pupils with 782 teachers in primary schools and 14,961 pupils with 1,316 teachers in secondary schools. There is an extension centre of the University of the South Pacific at Nuku'alofa. 'Atenisi Institute comprises 'Atenisi University (Tonga's only private university) and the 'Atenisi Foundation for the Performing Arts.

The literacy rate in 2011 was 98%.

Health

In 2012 there were four hospitals and 286 hospital beds. There were 62 physicians, 378 nursing and midwifery personnel, 37 dentistry personnel and 15 pharmaceutical personnel in 2009.

In *Water: At What Cost? The State of the World's Water 2016*, WaterAid reported that 0·4% of the population does not have access to safe water.

Religion

Christianity is the main religion, with the Free Wesleyan Church being the largest denomination. There are also significant numbers of Later-day Saints and Catholics as well as followers of other religions. In Feb. 2019 there was one Roman Catholic cardinal.

Culture

Press

There are no daily newspapers. There were three paid-for non-daily newspapers in 2008: the *Tonga Chronicle* (a government-owned weekly), the *Times of Tonga* and *Matangi Tonga*.

Tourism

There were 46,040 tourist arrivals by air in 2011. Tourism receipts in 2011 totalled US$32m.

Diplomatic Representatives

Of Tonga in the United Kingdom (36 Molyneux St., London, W1H 5BQ)
    High Commissioner: Titilupe Fanetupouvava'u Tu'ivakano.

Of the United Kingdom in Tonga (High Commission in Nuku'alofa closed in March 2006)
    High Commissioner: Melanie Hopkins (resides in Suva, Fiji).

Of Tonga in the USA and to the United Nations (250 E. 51st St., New York, NY 10022)
    Ambassador: Viliami Va'inga Tone.

Of the USA in Tonga
    Ambassador: Vacant.
    Chargé d'Affaires a.i.: Michael Goldman (resides in Suva, Fiji).

Of Tonga to the European Union
    Ambassador: Sione Ngongo Kioa.

Further Reading

Campbell, I. C., *Island Kingdom: Tonga, Ancient and Modern.* 1994
Wood-Ellem, E., *Queen Salote of Tonga, The Story of an Era 1900–1965.* 2000
National Statistical Office: Tonga Statistics Department, P.O. Box 149, Nuku'alofa.
Website: http://tonga.prism.spc.int

Trinidad and Tobago

Republic of Trinidad and Tobago

Capital: Port of Spain
Population projection, 2020: 1·38m.
GNI per capita, 2017: (PPP$) 28,622
HDI/world rank, 2017: 0·784/69
Internet domain extension: .tt

Key Historical Events

When Columbus visited Trinidad in 1498 the island was inhabited by Arawak Indians. Tobago was occupied by the Caribs. Trinidad remained a neglected Spanish possession for almost 300 years until it was surrendered to a British naval expedition in 1797. The British first attempted to settle Tobago in 1721 but the French captured the island in 1781 and transformed it into a sugar-producing colony. In 1802 the British acquired Tobago and in 1899 it was administratively combined with Trinidad. When slavery was abolished in the late 1830s, the British subsidized immigration from India to replace plantation labourers. Sugar and cocoa declined towards the end of the 19th century. Oil and asphalt became the main sources of income. On 31 Aug. 1962 Trinidad and Tobago became an independent member of the Commonwealth. A Republican Constitution was adopted on 1 Aug. 1976.

The government shut down the sugar industry after the 2007 harvest. The industry underpinned the economy for centuries but had become unsustainable after the withdrawal of EU subsidies. In Aug. 2011 Prime Minister Kamla Persad-Bissessar declared a state of emergency in a bid to confront the increasingly violent threat posed by the illegal drugs and weapons trade. Lasting until Dec. 2011, it was the first state of emergency since 1990, when the Jamaat al Muslimeen group unsuccessfully attempted a coup.

Territory and Population

The island of Trinidad is situated in the Caribbean Sea, about 12 km off the northeast coast of Venezuela; several islets, the largest being Chacachacare, Huevos, Monos and Gaspar Grande, lie in the Gulf of Paria which separates Trinidad from Venezuela. The smaller island of Tobago lies 30·7 km further to the northeast. Altogether, the islands cover 5,128 sq. km (1,980 sq. miles), of which Trinidad (including the islets) has 4,828 sq. km (1,864 sq. miles) and Tobago 300 sq. km (116 sq. miles). In 2011 the census population was 1,328,019 (Trinidad, 1,267,145; Tobago, 60,874); density, 259 per sq. km.

The UN gives a projected population for 2020 of 1·38m.

In 2011, 14·2% of the population lived in urban areas. Capital, Port of Spain (2011 census, 37,074); other important towns, Chaguanas (83,516), San Fernando (48,838), Arima (33,606) and Point Fortin (20,235). The main towns on Tobago are Scarborough and Plymouth. Distribution of population by ethnic group (2011): East Indian, 35·4%; African, 34·2%; mixed races, 22·8%; others, 7·6%.

The official language is English.

Social Statistics

2008 births, 19,888; deaths, 10,463. 2008 birth rate (per 1,000 population), 15·2; death rate, 8·0. Expectation of life, 2013, was 66·4 years for males and 73·6 for females. Annual population growth rate, 1998–2008, 0·4%. Infant mortality, 2010, 24 per 1,000 live births; fertility rate, 2008, 1·6 births per woman.

Climate

A tropical climate cooled by the northeast trade winds. The dry season runs from Jan. to June, with a wet season for the rest of the year. Temperatures are uniformly high the year round. Port of Spain, Jan. 76·3°F (24·6°C), July 79·2°F (26·2°C). Annual rainfall 1,870 mm.

Constitution and Government

The 1976 constitution provides for a bicameral legislature of a *Senate* and a *House of Representatives*, who elect the *President*, who is head of state. The *Senate* consists of 31 members, 16 being appointed by the President on the advice of the *Prime Minister*, six on the advice of the Leader of the Opposition and nine at the discretion of the President.

The *House of Representatives* consists of 41 (39 for Trinidad and two for Tobago) elected members and a Speaker elected from within or outside the House.

Executive power is vested in the Prime Minister, who is appointed by the President, and the Cabinet.

National Anthem

'Forged from the love of liberty'; words and music by P. Castagne.

Government Chronology

Presidents since 1976.

1976–87	Ellis Emmanuel Innocent Clarke
1987–97	Noor Mohammed Hassanali
1997–2003	Arthur Napoleon Raymond Robinson
2003–13	George Maxwell Richards
2013–18	Anthony Thomas Aquinas Carmona
2018–	Paula-Mae Weekes

Prime Ministers since independence. (NAR = National Alliance for Reconstruction; PNM = People's National Movement; UNC = United National Congress)

1962–81	PNM	Eric Eustace Williams
1981–86	PNM	George Michael Chambers
1986–91	NAR	Arthur Napoleon Raymond Robinson
1991–95	PNM	Patrick Augustus Mervyn Manning
1995–2001	UNC	Basdeo Panday
2001–10	PNM	Patrick Augustus Mervyn Manning
2010–15	UNC	Kamla Persad-Bissessar
2015–	PNM	Keith Rowley

Recent Elections

Indirect presidential elections were held on 19 Jan. 2018. Paula-Mae Weekes stood unopposed and was duly elected.

In parliamentary elections held on 7 Sept. 2015 the opposition People's National Movement (PNM) won 23 of 41 seats with 51·7% of votes cast against the People's Partnership coalition (comprising the United National Congress, the Congress of the People, the Tobago Organization of the People and the National Joint Action Committee) with 18 seats and 46·6%. Turnout was 66·8%.

Current Government

President: Paula-Mae Weekes; b. 1958 (ind.; sworn in 19 March 2018).

In Feb. 2019 the cabinet comprised:

Prime Minister: Keith Rowley; b. 1949 (PNM; sworn in 9 Sept. 2015).

Minister of Agriculture, Land and Fisheries: Clarence Rambharat. *Communications, National Security, and Minister in the Office of the Prime Minister:* Stuart Young. *Community Development, Culture and the Arts:* Nyan Gadsby-Dolly. *Education:* Anthony Garcia. *Energy and Energy Affairs:* Franklin Khan. *Finance:* Colm Imbert. *Foreign and CARICOM*

Palgrave Macmillan (ed.), *The Statesman's Yearbook 2020*,
https://doi.org/10.1057/978-1-349-95940-2_191

Affairs: Dennis Moses. *Health:* Terrence Deyalsingh. *Housing and Urban Development:* Edmund Dillon. *Labour and Small and Micro Enterprise Development:* Jennifer Baptiste-Primus. *Planning and Development:* Camille Robinson-Regis. *Public Administration:* Marlene McDonald. *Public Utilities:* Robert Le Hunte. *Rural Development and Local Government:* Kazim Hosein. *Social Development and Family Services:* Cherrie-Ann Crichlow-Cockburn. *Sport and Youth Affairs:* Shamfa Cudjoe. *Tourism:* Randall Mitchell. *Trade and Industry:* Paula Gopee-Scoon. *Works and Transport:* Rohan Sinanan. *Minister in the Office of the Attorney General and Minister of Legal Affairs:* Fitzgerald Hinds. *Attorney General:* Faris Al-Rawi.

Government Website: http://www.gov.tt

Current Leaders

Paula-Mae Weekes

Position

President

Introduction

Paula-Mae Weekes was sworn in as president in March 2018. A barrister who has served at the highest levels of the judiciary and worked in the private sector, she is the country's first female president.

Early Life

Weekes was born on 23 Dec. 1958 in Port of Spain, when Trinidad and Tobago was a British colony. She graduated in law in 1980 from the Cave Hill campus of the University of the West Indies in Barbados. Two years later, following further study at Hugh Wooding Law School, she joined the office of the director of public prosecutions as state counsel. She remained there until 1993 when she entered private practice, eventually establishing her own chambers.

Appointed to the Judiciary in 1996, Weekes presided over the trial courts for the next nine years. She was promoted to the Court of Appeal in 2005 and briefly served as acting Chief Justice in 2012, before retiring in 2016. Later that year she was invited to join the Judiciary of the Turks and Caicos Islands.

In Jan. 2018 she was nominated as a candidate for the presidency by the People's National Movement government, led by Prime Minister Keith Rowley. Later endorsed by opposition leader Kamla Persad-Bissessar, she was the only nominated candidate on election day and so was deemed elected without the need of a vote. She replaced Anthony Carmona as president on 19 March 2018.

Career in Office

In her inaugural address, Weekes promised to tackle the country's high levels of crime, corruption and unemployment, saying that she would 'mobilize forces and resources to step out boldly and make Trinidad and Tobago a better place for us and our children'.

Keith Rowley

Position

Prime Minister

Introduction

A veteran member of the People's National Movement (PNM), Keith Rowley became prime minister in Sept. 2015 after defeating the incumbent People's Partnership coalition.

Early Life

Keith Rowley was born on 24 Oct. 1949 in Mason Hall. After studying geology and geography at the University of the West Indies (UWI) in Jamaica, he returned to the university's campus in Trinidad and Tobago, where he attained a PhD in geochemistry. He worked in volcanology research at UWI, rising to be head of the seismic research unit, and also served as manager of the state-owned National Quarries Company Ltd.

After unsuccessfully contesting the seat of Tobago West in 1981, Rowley served in parliament as an opposition senator from 1987–90 before being elected as MP for Diego Martin West in 1991. He served as minister of agriculture, land and marine sources from 1992–95. After a period in opposition, he was then minister of planning and development from 2001–03, minister of housing from 2003–07, and minister of trade and industry from 2007–08. He was fired from this last post by the then prime minister, Patrick Manning, amid disagreements about the oversight of a state-owned development corporation.

Following the PNM's defeat at elections in 2010 and Manning's subsequent resignation, Rowley was elected party leader. He led the party to victory in the Sept. 2015 general election, pledging to reform public administration.

Career in Office

Rowley took office on 9 Sept. 2015, with the PNM having won 23 out of 41 seats. His early months saw him steer his budget through parliament against a backdrop of worsening economic conditions that prompted the Central Bank to declare a recession. His main challenges have included addressing the impact of falling oil prices on the national economy, as well as delivering on his promises to make government more accountable.

Defence

The Trinidad and Tobago Defence Force consists of the Trinidad and Tobago Regiment, the Coast Guard, the Air Guard and the Defence Force Reserves. Personnel in 2011 totalled around 4,100.

In 2013 defence expenditure totalled US$400m. (US$326 per capita), representing 1·5% of GDP.

Army

The Trinidad and Tobago Regiment (the Army) is part of the Trinidad and Tobago Defence Force. It has approximately 2,000 personnel organized into a Regiment Headquarters and four battalions.

Navy

In 2011 there was a Coast Guard of 1,063.

Air Force

The Air Guard, formerly part of the Coast Guard, had 50 personnel, three aircraft and one helicopter in 2011.

Economy

Industry accounted for 57% of GDP in 2012, services 42% and agriculture 1%.

Overview

Trinidad and Tobago has the fifth highest level of per capita income in the Latin American and Caribbean region, according to the World Bank. It is a major regional financial centre and leader in economic integration, playing a key role in the CARICOM Single Market and Economy since its establishment in 2006. Tourism is also an important source of national revenue.

The islands are rich in natural resources, with oil and gas exploitation accounting for 32% of GDP, 84% of merchandise exports and 52% of government revenue in 2016. However, the country is vulnerable to international market fluctuations. Additionally, only a minority have benefited from the wealth created by the oil and gas sector, which employs about one-fifth of the of the labour force, while an estimated 20% of the population still lives in poverty.

The global financial crisis from 2008 caused a sharp decline in the prices of major exports, including oil, resulting in a lengthy recession. The largest privately-held conglomerate in the country, the CL Financial Group, received a government bailout in 2009. The debt-to-GDP ratio also increased sharply from 2008, with public sector debt standing at 57·6% of GDP in the last quarter of 2017.

Currency

The unit of currency is the *Trinidad and Tobago dollar* (TTD) of 100 *cents*. Inflation was 3·1% in 2016 and 1·9% in 2017. In April 1994 the TT dollar was floated and managed by the Central Bank at TT$6·06 to US$1·00. Foreign exchange reserves in July 2005 were US$3,918m. and gold reserves 61,000 troy oz. Total money supply in May 2005 was TT$9,438m.

Budget

The fiscal year for the budget is 1 Oct. to 30 Sept. In 2011–12 central government revenue was TT$52,204m. and expenditure was TT$49,787m. Taxes accounted for 83·5% of revenues; compensation of employees accounted for 24·2% of expenditures, use of goods and services 22·0% and grants 21·9%.

VAT is 12·5%.

Performance

The economy grew by 1·7% in 2015 but shrank by 6·1% in 2016 and 2·6% in 2017 as a consequence of prolonged supply disruptions in the energy sector. Total GDP in 2017 was US$22·1bn.

Banking and Finance

The Central Bank of Trinidad and Tobago began operations in 1964 (*Governor*, Alvin Hilaire). In Sept. 2012 its assets totalled TT$76,152m., liabilities TT$74,649m. and equity TT$1,503m. There are eight commercial banks. Central government external debt totalled US$2,170·8m. in Sept. 2015. The stock exchange in Port of Spain participates in the regional Caribbean exchange.

Energy and Natural Resources

Environment

Carbon dioxide emissions from the consumption of energy were the equivalent of 42·5 tonnes per capita in 2011.

Electricity

In 2011 the installed capacity was 2·30m. kW, electricity production was 8·87bn. kWh and consumption per capita 6,652 kWh.

Oil and Gas

Oil production is one of Trinidad's leading industries. Commercial production began in 1908; production of oil in 2012 was 6·0m. tonnes. Reserves in 2012 totalled 0·8bn. bbls. Crude oil is also imported for refining.

In 2012 production of natural gas was 42·2bn. cu. metres; proven reserves of natural gas were 400bn. cu. metres. A major discovery of approximately 50bn. cu. metres was made by BP in 2000, followed by a further discovery of approximately 30bn. cu. metres in 2002.

Agriculture

In 2007 the agricultural population was an estimated 94,000, of which some 49,000 were economically active. Production of main crops (2013, in 1,000 tonnes): coconuts (estimate), 21; plantains (estimate), 5; bananas (estimate), 4; taro, 3; maize (estimate), 3; cassava, 3; rice, 3; pumpkins and squash, 3. There were around 25,000 ha. of arable land and 22,000 ha. of permanent cropland in 2007. Livestock (2013): pigs (estimate), 35,000; cattle (estimate), 35,000; sheep, 21,000; goats, 18,000; chickens (estimate), 35m. Livestock products, 2013: chicken meat, 67,000 tonnes; pork and pork products, 3,000 tonnes; milk, 4,000 tonnes.

Forestry

Forests covered 0·23m. ha. in 2015, or 46% of the land area. Timber production for 2011 was 80,000 cu. metres.

Fisheries

The catch in 2013 totalled 13,212 tonnes.

Industry

Major industries include petroleum and petroleum products, liquefied natural gas, methanol, ammonia, urea, steel products, beverages, food processing and cement. Trinidad and Tobago ranks among the world's largest producers of ammonia and methanol. The petroleum industry contributed 38·9% of GDP in 2012; in the same year industry as a whole accounted for 57% of GDP, with manufacturing contributing 6%.

Labour

The labour force in 2013 was 685,000 (617,000 in 2003). 71·0% of the population aged 15–64 was economically active in 2013. In the same year 3·6% of the population was unemployed.

International Trade

Imports and Exports

In 2010 imports (c.i.f.) totalled US$6,479·6m. and exports (f.o.b.) US$10,981·7m. In 2005 crude petroleum accounted for 19% of imports, and refined petroleum 29% of exports. Trinidad and Tobago is the world's leading exporter of ammonia and methanol. The principal import sources in 2005 were the USA (29·2%), Brazil (13·5%), Venezuela (6·0%) and Colombia (5·6%). The main export markets in 2005 were the USA (58·6%), Jamaica (7·5%), France (4·4%) and Barbados (4·3%).

Communications

Roads

In 2010 there were 8,320 km of roads, of which 51·1% were paved. There were 468,255 vehicles in use in 2007.

Civil Aviation

There is an international airport at Port of Spain (Piarco) and in Tobago (A. N. R. Robinson International Airport). In 2012 Piarco handled 2,724,888 passengers (1,723,835 on international flights) and 53,935 tonnes of freight. The national carrier is Caribbean Airlines, which has flights to 18 international destinations as well as operating domestic services. In 2012 scheduled airline traffic of Trinidad and Tobago-based carriers flew 52·8m. km; passenger-km totalled 9·2bn. in the same year.

Shipping

In Jan. 2014 there were 11 ships of 300 GT or over registered, totalling 20,000 GT. The largest port is Port of Spain. The other main harbour is Point Lisas. There is a deep-water harbour at Scarborough (Tobago). A ferry service links Port of Spain with Scarborough.

Telecommunications

International and domestic communications are provided by Telecommunications Services of Trinidad and Tobago (TSTT). In 2013 there were 291,300 main (fixed) telephone lines; mobile phone subscriptions numbered 1,944,000 that year (1,449·4 per 1,000 persons). In 2013 an estimated 63·8% of the population were internet users. In Dec. 2011 there were 441,000 Facebook users.

Social Institutions

Out of 178 countries analysed in the 2017 *Fragile States Index*—a list published jointly by the Fund for Peace and *Foreign Policy* magazine—Trinidad and Tobago was ranked the joint 50th least vulnerable (along with Mongolia) to conflict or collapse. The index is based on 12 indicators of state vulnerability across social, political and economic categories.

Justice

The High Court consists of the Chief Justice and 11 puisne judges. In criminal cases a judge of the High Court sits with a jury of 12 in cases of treason and murder, and with nine jurors in other cases. The Court of Appeal consists of the Chief Justice and seven Justices of Appeal. In hearing appeals, the Court is comprised of three judges sitting together except when the appeal is from a Summary Court or from a decision of a High Court judge in chambers. In such cases two judges would comprise the Court. There is a limited right of appeal from it to the British Privy Council. There are three High Courts and 12 magistrates' courts. There is an *Ombudsman*. Trinidad and Tobago was one of ten countries to sign an agreement in Feb. 2001 establishing a Caribbean Court of Justice (CCJ) to replace the British Privy Council as the highest civil and criminal court. In the meantime the number of signatories has risen to 12. The court was inaugurated at Port of Spain on 16 April 2005. However, despite its location Trinidad and Tobago has yet to accept the CCJ as its final court of appeal.

The death penalty is authorized. There were ten executions in 1999, although none since. There were 407 murders in 2013, down from 550 in 2008 although up from just 98 in 1998.

The average daily population in penal institutions in 2012 was 3,800 (281 per 100,000 of national population). 59·0% of prisoners had yet to receive a trial according to 2014 estimates by the International Centre for Prison Studies.

Education

In 2007 there were 130,242 pupils enrolled in primary schools with 8,171 teaching staff and 98,490 pupils in secondary schools with 7,041 teaching staff. In 2005 there were 16,920 students in higher education and 1,800 academic staff. The University of the West Indies campus in St Augustine (2006–07) had 13,629 students and 572 academic staff. 1,358 of the students were from other countries.

Adult literacy was estimated at 98·7% in 2009.

In 2010–11 spending on education accounted for 12·2% of total central government expenditure.

Health

In 2009 there were 1,543 physicians (11·7 per 10,000 population) and 4,677 nursing and midwifery personnel (35·5 per 10,000); there were 641 licensed pharmacists in 2007. In 2011 there were 21 hospitals (11 public and ten private).

In *Water: At What Cost? The State of the World's Water 2016*, WaterAid reported that 4·9% of the population does not have access to safe water.

Religion

An estimated 65·9% of the population in 2010 were Christians (mainly Protestants), 22·7% Hindus and 5·5% Muslims according to the Pew Research Center's Forum on Religion & Public Life.

Culture

Press

There were three daily newspapers in 2008—*Trinidad and Tobago Express*, *Trinidad and Tobago Guardian* and *Trinidad and Tobago Newsday*—with a total circulation of 140,000. There were also nine paid-for non-dailies in 2008.

Tourism

In 2008 there were 432,551 tourist arrivals by air (of which 187,515 were from the USA), down from 449,453 in 2007. There were a record 119,600 cruise passenger arrivals in 2009.

Festivals

Religious festivals: the Feast of La Divina Pastora, or Sipari Mai, a Catholic and Hindu celebration of the Holy Mother Mary; Saint Peter's Day Celebration, the Patron Saint of Fishermen; Hosein, or Hosay, a Shia Muslim festival; Phagwah, a Hindu spring festival; Santa Rosa, a Caribbean Amerindian festival; Eid-al-Fitr, the Muslim festival at the end of Ramadan; Diwali, the Hindu festival of light; Christmas. Cultural festivals: Carnival (on 24 and 25 Feb. in 2020); Spiritual Baptist Shouter Liberation Day, a recognition of the Baptist religion; Indian Arrival Day, commemorating the arrival of the first East Indian labourers; Sugar and Energy Festival; Pan Ramajay, a music festival of all types; Emancipation, a recognition of the period of slavery; Tobago Heritage Festival, celebrating Tobago's traditions and customs; Parang Festival, traditional folk music of Christmas; Pan Jazz Festival; Music Festival, predominantly classical music but Indian and Calypso are included.

Diplomatic Representatives

Of Trinidad and Tobago in the United Kingdom (42 Belgrave Sq., London, SW1X 8NT)
High Commissioner: Orville London.

Of the United Kingdom in Trinidad and Tobago (19 St Clair Ave., St Clair, Port of Spain)
High Commissioner: Tim Stew, MBE.

Of Trinidad and Tobago in the USA (1708 Massachusetts Ave., NW, Washington, D.C., 20036)
Ambassador: Anthony Wayne Jerome Phillips-Spencer.

Of the USA in Trinidad and Tobago (15 Queen's Park West, Port of Spain)
Ambassador: Joseph N. Mondello.

Of Trinidad and Tobago to the United Nations
Ambassador: Pennelope Althea Beckles.

Of Trinidad and Tobago to the European Union
Ambassador: Colin Michael Connelly.

Further Reading

Meighoo, Kirk, *Politics in a Half-Made Society: Trinidad and Tobago, 1925–2001.* 2003

Williams, E., *History of the People of Trinidad and Tobago.* 1993

Central library: The Central Library of Trinidad and Tobago, Queen's Park East, Port of Spain.

National Statistical Office: Central Statistical Office, 47 Frederick St., Port of Spain.

Website: http://cso.gov.tt

Tunisia

Jumhuriya at-Tunisiya (Republic of Tunisia)

Capital: Tunis
Population projection, 2020: 11·90m.
GNI per capita, 2017: (PPP$) 10,275
HDI/world rank, 2017: 0·735/95=
Internet domain extension: .tn

Key Historical Events

Tunisia's earliest inhabitants included the semi-nomadic Berbers, whose descendants still live in North Africa's Atlas Mountains. Phoenician merchants established trading settlements throughout the central and western Mediterranean from the 10th century BC and founded the port of Carthage in 814 BC. By the 5th century Carthage had become the most powerful city in the western Mediterranean with an empire extending from present-day Morocco to Egypt and controlling Sardinia, the Balearic Islands, Malta and much of Sicily. A rival to the Roman Empire, the city was eventually destroyed in the Third Punic War. From 146 BC Tunisia was absorbed into the Roman Empire and its people sold into slavery.

Emperor Augustus supervised the reconstruction of Carthage in the 2nd century AD, although frequent revolts broke out as the Roman Empire waned. In 429 Tunisia was captured by the Vandals until ousted by the Byzantines in 534. Uqba ibn Nafa led an Arab Muslim army into Tunisia in 670 and founded the city of Kairouan. Most of the indigenous Berber population converted to Islam and the region, known as Ifriqiya, became part of the powerful caliphate centred on Baghdad where it reached its apotheosis under Harun al Rashid (786–809). Tunisia subsequently came under the control of the local Aghlabid dynasty and then under the Fatimids from 909. Bedouin Arabs from the Nile Valley (the Banu Hilal) entered the region around 1000 and from the 12th century Tunisia came under the orbit of the al-Muwahhid empire. The Berber general Abd al-Wahid ibn Abi Hafs wrested control in 1207, heralding three centuries of rule by the Hafsid dynasties. The port of Tunis was made capital and the term 'Tunisia' gradually replaced 'Ifriqiya'.

Ottoman troops advanced from the east in the early 16th century, forcing the Hafsids into an alliance with the Spanish Habsburgs in 1534. However, the Ottomans seized Tunis in 1574. Direct control from İstanbul was superseded by rule through local governors known as beys, such as the Muradid beys who made powerful alliances in the Tunisian hinterland and held sway from the 1640s to 1705. Al-Husayn ibn Ali (ruled 1705–40) founded the Husaynid dynasty and oversaw a period of prosperity through trade and piracy.

As the Ottoman Empire declined Tunisia became increasingly autonomous but attempts to establish a republic in the mid-19th century failed owing to a weak economy and political unrest. In 1869 Tunisia declared itself bankrupt and an international commission from France, Great Britain and Italy took over the country's finances. In 1881 Tunisia was invaded by France which alleged that Tunisian troops had been threatening the French colony of Algeria. Tunisia became a French protectorate despite Italian opposition.

Nationalist sentiment increased after the First World War and the Destour (Constitutional) Party was set up in 1920. Its more radical successor, the Neo-Destour Party, was established by Habib Bourguiba in 1934. Seen as a threat to colonial rule, Bourguiba was imprisoned in 1938. After the Second World War France offered increased autonomy. Nationalists, dismayed at the slow pace of reform, staged mass strikes and demonstrations in 1950. Violent protest increased until France granted internal self-government in 1955, with full independence on 20 March 1956. A constitutional assembly was established and Bourguiba became prime minister. The monarchy was abolished and a republic established the following year, with Bourguiba as president.

Taking a socialist secular line, Bourguiba promoted social and economic development. In 1975 the constitution was amended so that Bourguiba could be president-for-life. The late 1970s saw hardship and growing discontent. A general strike in Jan. 1978 erupted into riots and violence flared again in 1980 and 1984. Islamist groups became increasingly influential and Bourguiba was overthrown in a bloodless coup in 1987. His successor, Zine El Abidine Ben Ali, introduced democratic reforms, eased restrictive press laws and opened negotiations with Islamic groups, although he refused to recognize the prominent al-Nahda party. He was re-elected president in 1994, 1999, 2004 and 2009. However, widespread anti-government protests in Dec. 2010 and Jan. 2011—often referred to as the Jasmine Revolution—led to Ben Ali going into exile. A national unity government took power in his place. A state of emergency declared in Jan. 2011 was lifted in March 2014. However, a new state of emergency was declared in Nov. 2015 following a series of Islamist extremist attacks during that year. It was extended for a further seven months in March 2018 and has been extended several times since then.

Territory and Population

Tunisia is bounded in the north and east by the Mediterranean Sea, west by Algeria and south by Libya. The area is 163,610 sq. km, including 8,350 sq. km of inland waters. Census population, 2014: 10,982,754, giving a density of 70·7 per sq. km. July 2017 population estimate: 11,435,000. In 2011, 67·7% of the population were urban.

The UN gives a projected population for 2020 of 11·90m.

The areas and populations (2014 census) of the 24 governorates:

	Area in sq. km	Population
Aryanah (Ariana)	498	576,088
Bajah (Béja)	3,558	303,032
Banzart (Bizerte)	3,685	568,219
Bin Arus (Bin Arous)	761	631,842
Jundubah (Jendouba)	3,102	401,477
Kaf (Le Kef)	4,965	243,156
Madaniyin (Médénine)	8,588	479,520
Mahdiyah (Mahdia)	2,966	410,812
Manubah (Manouba)	1,060	379,518
Munastir (Monastir)	1,019	548,828
Nabul (Nabeul)	2,788	787,920
Qabis (Gabès)	7,175	374,300
Qafsah (Gafsa)	8,990	337,331
Qasrayn (Kassérine)	8,066	439,243
Qayrawan (Kairouan)	6,712	570,559
Qibili (Kebili)	22,084	156,961
Safaqis (Sfax)	7,545	955,421
Sidi Bu Zayd (Sidi Bouzid)	6,994	429,912
Silyanah (Siliana)	4,631	223,087
Susah (Sousse)	2,621	674,971
Tatawin (Tataouine)	38,889	149,453
Tawzar (Tozeur)	4,719	107,912
Tunis	346	1,056,247
Zaghwan (Zaghouan)	2,768	176,945

Tunis, the capital, had 638,845 inhabitants at the 2014 census. Other main cities (2014 census in 1,000): Sfax, 272·8; Sousse, 221·5; Ettadhamen, 143·0; Kairouan, a holy city of the Muslims, 139·1; Bizerte, 136·9; Gabès, 131·0; La Soukra, 129·7.

The official language is Arabic but French is the main language in the media, commercial enterprise and government departments. Berber-speaking people form less than 1% of the population.

© Springer Nature Limited 2020
Palgrave Macmillan (ed.), *The Statesman's Yearbook 2020*,
https://doi.org/10.1057/978-1-349-95940-2_192

Social Statistics

2008 estimates: births, 183,000; deaths, 61,000; marriages (2005), 74,000. Rates (2008 estimates): birth, 18 per 1,000 population; death, 6. Annual population growth rate, 2000–05, 1·0%. In 2005 the most popular age range for marrying was 30–34 for males and 25–29 for females. Expectation of life, 2007, was 71·8 years for males and 76·0 for females. Infant mortality, 2010, 14 per 1,000 live births; fertility rate, 2008, 1·8 births per woman.

Climate

The climate ranges from warm temperate in the north, where winters are mild and wet and the summers hot and dry, to desert in the south. Tunis, Jan. 48°F (8·9°C), July 78°F (25·6°C). Annual rainfall 16" (400 mm). Bizerte, Jan. 52°F (11·1°C), July 77°F (25°C). Annual rainfall 25" (622 mm). Sfax, Jan. 52°F (11·1°C), July 78°F (25·6°C). Annual rainfall 8" (196 mm).

Constitution and Government

Following the revolution of Jan. 2011 and the ousting of President Zine El Abidine Ben Ali, elections were held in Oct. that year for a Constituent Assembly with a mandate to draft and approve a new constitution. On 26 Jan. 2014 parliament approved the new constitution, achieving the required majority of two-thirds support from the Assembly with 200 of 216 votes cast. The constitution states that elections are to be held every five years. While Islam is acknowledged as the state religion, there is no reference to Islamic law as a source of legislation. Freedom of worship is guaranteed, as are the equal rights of men and women before the law. Executive power is divided between the *Prime Minister* and the *President*. There is a unicameral parliament—the *Assembly of the Representatives of the People*—consisting of 217 members.

National Anthem

'Humata al Hima' ('Defenders of the Homeland'); words by Mustapha al Rafi and Aboul Kacem Chabbi, tune by M. A. Wahab.

Government Chronology

Presidents since 1957. (CPR = Congress for the Republic; ND = Neo-Destour Party; NT = Call of Tunisia/Nidaa Tounes; PSD = Socialist Destourian Party; RCD = Constitutional Democratic Rally; n/p = non-partisan)

1957–87	ND, PSD	Habib Ali Bourguiba
1987–2011	PSD, RCD	Zine El Abidine Ben Ali
2011	n/p	Foued Mebazaa (acting)
2011–14	CPR	Moncef Marzouki (interim)
2014–	NT	Beji Caid Essebsi

Recent Elections

Parliamentary elections were held on 26 Oct. 2014. They were the first to take place since the adoption of a new constitution in Jan. 2014 creating an Assembly of the Representatives of the People. Call of Tunisia (Nidaa Tounes) won 85 seats with 37·6%; Ennahda, 69 with 27·8%; Free Patriotic Union (UPL), 16 with 4·1%; Popular Front, 15 with 3·6%; Tunisian Aspiration (Afek Tounes), 8 with 3·0%. 11 other parties gained four seats or fewer and three independents were elected. Turnout was 64·6%.

In the first round of presidential elections held on 23 Nov. 2014, Beji Caid Essebsi of Call of Tunisia/Nidaa Tounes won 39·5% of the vote against incumbent interim president Moncef Marzouki (Congress for the Republic) with 33·4%, Hamma Hammami (Popular Front) 7·8%, Hechmi Hamdi (Current of Love) 5·8% and Slim Riahi (UPL) 5·6%. 22 other candidates took less than 2% of the vote each. Essebsi won the run-off held on 21 Dec. with 55·7% of the vote against 44·3% for Marzouki. Turnout in the first round was 62·9% and in the second 60·1%.

Current Government

President: Beji Caid Essebsi; b. 1926 (Nidaa Tounes; since 31 Dec. 2014).
In March 2019 the government comprised:

Prime Minister: Youssef Chahed; b. 1975 (Nidaa Tounes; since 27 Aug. 2016).

Minister of Agriculture, Water Resources and Fisheries: Samir Taieb. *Civil Service, Modernization of Administration and Public Policy:* Kamel Morjane. *Commerce:* Omar Behi. *Communications Technology and the Digital Economy:* Anouar Maarouf. *Cultural Affairs:* Mohamed Zine El Abidine. *Development, Investment and International Co-operation:* Zied Ladhari. *Education:* Hatem Ben Salem. *Finance:* Mohamed Ridha Chalghoum. *Foreign Affairs:* Khémaies Jhinaoui. *Higher Education and Scientific Research:* Slim Khalbous. *Industry and Small and Medium-Sized Enterprises:* Slim Feriani. *Infrastructure, Housing and Spatial Planning:* Noureddine Selmi. *Interior:* Hichem Fourati. *Justice:* Karim Jamoussi. *Local Affairs and Environment:* Mokhtar Hammami. *National Defence:* Abdelkarim Zbidi. *Religious Affairs:* Ahmed Adhoum. *Social Affairs:* Mohamed Trabelsi. *State Property and Land Affairs:* Hédi Mekni. *Tourism and Handicrafts:* Roni Trabelsi. *Transport:* Hichem Ben Ahmed. *Vocational Training and Employment:* Saida Ounissi. *Women's Affairs, Family and Children:* Naziha Laabidi. *Youth and Sport, and Health (acting):* Sonia Ben Cheikh.

Government Website (French and Arabic only): http://www.ministeres.tn

Current Leaders

Beji Caid Essebsi

Position
President

Introduction
Beji Caid Essebsi became Tunisia's first democratically-elected president on 21 Dec. 2014. A lawyer, he has been an influential figure throughout Tunisia's history as an independent nation.

Early Life
Beji Caid Essebsi was born on 29 Nov. 1926 in the port of Sidi Bouzid in the French Protectorate of Tunisia. Graduating in law from the University of Paris in 1950, he went on to start a legal practice in Tunis. Following Tunisian independence in 1956, he became an adviser to the new president, Habib Bourguiba.

Appointed legal director of the ministry of the interior, he went on to head the department for national security and, in 1965, became interior minister. During this period, the Bourguiba administration became notorious for the harsh repression of dissenting voices. In the early 1970s Essebsi pushed, largely unsuccessfully, for economic and democratic reforms. He served as secretary to the prime minister, Mohamed Mzali, from 1980 until Mzali's dismissal in 1986 amid rioting sparked by government-mandated price rises.

Elected to parliament in 1989, Essebsi served as Speaker from 1990–91. He continued to argue the case for democratic and economic reforms but made little progress under President Zine El Abidine Ben Ali. When frustration boiled over into riots that toppled Ben Ali and swept across much of the Arab world in Jan. 2011, Essebsi was appointed premier and charged with forming an interim government.

Following elections for the Constituent Assembly in Oct. 2011, which were won by the moderate Islamist Ennahda party, Essebsi founded Nidaa Tounes (Call of Tunisia), a secular grouping representing a wide political spectrum as well as trade unionists and businessmen. Critics complained that it was dominated by former members of Ben Ali's Constitutional Democratic Rally (RCD), but Nidaa Tounes gained ground amid mounting disappointment with stalled reforms and against a backdrop of simmering insecurity. Essebsi announced that he would contest the 2014 presidential elections and in the second round of voting on 21 Dec. he defeated the incumbent, Moncef Marzouki, taking 55·7% of the vote on a 60% turnout.

Career in Office
Essebsi promised to restore stability and strengthen Tunisia's institutions after several years of political and economic turmoil under a moderate Islamist government. The peaceful handover of power won international approval, but tackling the high unemployment rate has posed a considerable challenge for the administration. Also, when Essebsi raised concerns about a change to the law requiring that past human rights abuses be investigated, critics accused him of attempting to avoid scrutiny of his role as interior minister in the 1960s. There were subsequent demonstrations in May 2017

against a proposed government amnesty for business figures and public servants accused of corruption under the former regime.

In March 2015 Essebsi admitted to shortcomings in the country's security system while urging national unity following an attack by Islamist militants on a museum in Tunis that saw 21 foreign tourists and one policeman killed. In another attack in June extremists killed a further 38 people, again mainly tourists (mostly British), at a beach resort in Sousse, while in Nov. 2015 a bus carrying presidential guards in the capital was blown up by a suicide bomber.

In Aug. 2016 parliament voted to remove Habib Essid as prime minister and Essebsi charged Youssef Chahed, also of Nidaa Tounes, with forming a national unity coalition government. However, the government has since been weakened by divisions between coalition partners, while the additional fragmentation of Nidaa Tounes—the largest party—has reflected the growing estrangement of Essebsi and Chahed and their respective factions.

Youssef Chahed

Position
Prime Minister

Introduction
Youssef Chahed became prime minister in Aug. 2016, the country's youngest head of government since Tunisia gained independence.

Early Life
Youssef Chahed was born on 18 Sept. 1975 in Tunis. He graduated in 1998 from the Institut national agronomique de Tunisie before continuing his studies in environmental economy and natural resources in France, receiving his doctorate in 2003. He then worked as a visiting professor in Brazil, France and Japan.

Between 2003 and 2015 Chahed served as a consultant for, among others, the United Nations Food and Agriculture Organization and several EU-related organs. He has also worked with various governmental and non-governmental organizations to ensure greater food security and the development of co-operatives in Tunisia.

After the 2011 revolution in his homeland, Chahed became a founding member of the centrist Republican Party (Al Joumhouri), before co-founding the secularist Call of Tunisia (Nidaa Tounes) a year later. In Feb. 2015 he became state secretary to the minister of agriculture, hydraulic resources and fishing, and in Jan. 2016 was awarded his own ministerial portfolio—that of local affairs. On 3 Aug. 2016 President Beji Caid Essebsi named Chahed as successor to Habib Essid, who had been dismissed as prime minister following a parliamentary no-confidence vote in July. Parliament approved Chahed's new coalition government on 27 Aug.

Career in Office
Chahed has been confronted with multiple challenges in office. His fragile administration has been undermined by growing factional dissension within Nidaa Tounes stemming from his fractious relationship with President Essebsi. In an effort to reassert his political authority, he carried out a major government reshuffle in Nov. 2018.

He has also had to contend with a struggling economy, high youth unemployment and a tourism industry still recovering from a devastating terror attack in 2015 when 38 people were murdered by a gunman in the city of Sousse. He warned of an unavoidable austerity programme if the economic situation did not rapidly improve, and he also stressed the need to tackle corruption—one of the primary sources of discontent leading up to the 2011 uprising. In Jan. 2018 simmering public impatience with poverty levels, joblessness and government-imposed tax and price rises had prompted street protests in several Tunisian cities and violent clashes with security forces.

Defence

Selective conscription is for one year. Defence expenditure in 2013 totalled US$769m. (US$71 per capita), representing 1·6% of GDP.

Army

Strength (2011) 27,000 (22,000 conscripts). There is also a National Guard numbering 12,000.

Navy

In 2011 naval personnel totalled around 4,800. Forces are based at Bizerte, Sfax and Kelibia.

Air Force

The Air Force operated 24 combat-capable aircraft in 2011, including ten F-5E/F Tiger II fighters and nine Aero L-59s. Personnel (2011) 4,000.

Economy

In 2011 services accounted for 59·8% of GDP, industry 31·3% and agriculture 8·9%.

Overview

Tunisia's economic record compares favourably with other developing nations, particularly those on the African continent. After a balance of payments crisis in the mid-1980s, steps were taken to improve macroeconomic policy, foster the private sector and liberalize prices and controls. In the 1990s the economy grew steadily at an average annual rate of 5%. However, the Jasmine Revolution of 2011 prompted a contraction in GDP of 1·9% that year and a prolonged period of instability, exacerbated by a sharp fall in foreign investment.

Persistent macroeconomic imbalances in the public finances, along with delays in the implementation of structural reforms, have continued to hold back sustained growth. In 2016 GDP grew by only 1·0%, while unemployment rose to 15·6% from 15·1% the previous year.

Major challenges include launching the development projects and structural reforms outlined in the government's 2016–20 economic programme, as well as an overhaul of public administration.

Currency

The unit of currency is the *Tunisian dinar* (TND) of 1,000 *millimes*. The currency was made convertible on 6 Jan. 1993. Foreign exchange reserves were US$4,069m. and gold reserves 218,000 troy oz in July 2005. Inflation was 3·7% in 2016 and 5·3% in 2017. Total money supply was 8,339m. dinars in June 2005.

Budget

The fiscal year is the calendar year. Budgetary central government revenue totalled 16,940m. dinars in 2012 and expenditure 19,345m. dinars. Taxes accounted for 87·7% of total revenues in 2012. Principal sources of revenue in 2012: taxes on goods and services, 6,928m. dinars; taxes on income, profits and capital gains, 6,062m. dinars; taxes on international trade and transactions, 1,334m. dinars. Main items of expenditure by economic type in 2012: compensation of employees, 8,617m. dinars; subsidies, 4,917m. dinars; interest, 1,272m. dinars.

VAT is 19% (reduced rates, 13% and 7%).

Performance

Real GDP expanded by 1·2% in 2015, 1·1% in 2016 and 2·0% in 2017. Tunisia's total GDP in 2017 was US$40·3bn.

Banking and Finance

The Central Bank of Tunisia (*Governor*, Marouane El Abassi) is the bank of issue. In 2014 there were 22 commercial banks, two merchant banks and seven 'offshore' banks.

In 2010 external debt totalled US$21,584m., equivalent to 51·1% of GNI.

There is a small stock exchange (51 companies trading in 2007).

Energy and Natural Resources

Environment

Tunisia's carbon dioxide emissions from the consumption of energy in 2011 were the equivalent of 1·9 tonnes per capita.

Electricity

Installed capacity was an estimated 4·0m. kW in 2011. Production in 2011 was 16·50bn. kWh; consumption per capita was 1,531 kWh.

Oil and Gas

Oil production (2012) was 3·1m. tonnes with 0·4bn. bbls in proven reserves. Natural gas production (2011), 2·6bn. cu. metres; proven reserves were 65bn. cu. metres in 2013.

Minerals

Mineral production (in 1,000 tonnes) in 2012: phosphate rock, 2,762; salt, 1,132; iron ore, 117.

Agriculture

There are five agricultural regions: the *north*, mountainous with large fertile valleys; the *northeast*, with the peninsula of Cap Bon, suited for the cultivation of oranges, lemons and tangerines; the *Sahel*, where olive trees abound; the *centre*, a region of high tablelands and pastures; and the *desert* of the south, where dates are grown.

In 2007 the economically active agricultural population was an estimated 787,000. Large estates predominate; smallholdings are tending to fragment, partly owing to inheritance laws. In 2006 356,000 ha. were irrigated. There were 2·76m. ha. of arable land in 2007 and 2·17m. ha. of permanent crops. There were 140 tractors and ten harvester-threshers per 10,000 ha. of arable land in 2006. The main crops are cereals, citrus fruits, tomatoes, melons, olives, dates and grapes. Production, 2013 (in 1,000 tonnes): olives, 1,100; tomatoes, 1,079; wheat, 975; melons and watermelons (estimate), 599; potatoes, 385; chillies and green peppers, 384; barley, 289; shallots (estimate), 261; carrots and turnips, 222; dates, 195; onions (estimate), 174; grapes, 132; oranges, 130; peaches and nectarines, 127; apples, 120; grapefruit, 96.

Livestock, 2013 (in 1,000): sheep, 6,856; goats, 1,248; cattle, 646; asses (estimate), 240; camels (estimate), 237; mules (estimate), 82; horses (estimate), 57. Livestock products, 2013 estimates (in 1,000 tonnes): meat, 327; milk, 1,191; eggs, 99.

Forestry

In 2015 there were 1·04m. ha. of forests (7% of the land area). Timber production in 2011 was 2·41m. cu. metres.

Fisheries

In 2015 the catch amounted to 118,762 tonnes, almost exclusively from marine waters.

Industry

Production (2011, in 1,000 tonnes): cement, 7,055; phosphoric acid, 568; lime, 282; distillate fuel oil, 254; residual fuel oil, 236; crude steel, 119. There were 5,837 industrial enterprises of ten employees or more in 2010 employing a total of 498,929 people. In 2011 manufacturing accounted for 18·1% of GDP.

Labour

The labour force in 2013 was 3,978,000 (3,355,000 in 2003). 51·2% of the population aged 15–64 was economically active in 2013. In the same year 13·3% of the population was unemployed. In 2013, 26·9% of the labour force was female.

International Trade

In Feb. 1989 Tunisia signed a treaty of economic co-operation with the other countries of Maghreb: Algeria, Libya, Mauritania and Morocco. Tunisia was the first country to sign a partnership agreement with the European Union, becoming fully integrated in its free trade zone in Jan. 2008.

Imports and Exports

Trade in US$1m.:

	2011	2012	2013	2014	2015
Imports c.i.f.	23,952	24,471	24,266	24,793	20,223
Exports f.o.b.	17,847	17,007	17,061	16,760	14,074

Principal imports in 2015 were machinery and transport equipment (32·2%) followed by manufactured goods classified chiefly by material (19·8%) and mineral fuels and lubricants (14·2%); main exports in 2015 were machinery and transport equipment (35·0%), miscellaneous manufactured articles (25·4%) and manufactured goods classified chiefly by material (9·5%).

The main import suppliers in 2015 were France (17·4%), Italy (14·7%) and China (7·2%). Main export markets in 2015 were France (27·9%), Italy (18·7%) and Germany (9·9%).

Communications

Roads

The road network covered 19,371 km in 2008, including 359 km of motorways and 4,738 km of national roads. In 2007 there were 746,700 passenger cars, 300,500 lorries and vans, 10,100 buses and coaches, and 5,300 motorcycles and mopeds. There were 10,681 road accidents in 2007 resulting in 1,497 fatalities.

Rail

In 2007 there were 2,165 km of railways on metre and 1,435 mm gauge track. Passenger-km travelled in 2007 came to 1,487m. and freight tonne-km to 2,197m. There is a tramway in Tunis (32 km).

Civil Aviation

The national carrier, Tunisair, is 64·9% state-owned and in 2013 carried 3,710,000 passengers. There are eight international airports. In 2012 Tunis-Carthage handled 5,249,411 passengers (4,903,506 on international flights) and 16,666 tonnes of freight. Enfidha-Hammamet, which opened in 2009, handled 2,087,122 passengers in 2012 and Djerba 1,969,043.

Shipping

There are ports at Tunis, its outer port Tunis-Goulette, Sfax, Sousse and Bizerte, all of which are directly accessible to ocean-going vessels. The ports of La Skhirra and Gabès are used for the shipping of Algerian and Tunisian oil. In Jan. 2014 there were 18 ships of 300 GT or over registered, totalling 191,000 GT.

Telecommunications

In 2009 there were 9,797,000 mobile phone subscriptions (953·8 per 1,000 inhabitants) and 1,279,000 fixed telephone lines. There were 340·7 internet users for every 1,000 inhabitants in 2009. In June 2012 there were 3·1m. Facebook users.

Social Institutions

Out of 178 countries analysed in the 2017 *Fragile States Index*—a list published jointly by the Fund for Peace and *Foreign Policy* magazine—Tunisia was ranked the 89th most vulnerable to conflict or collapse. The index is based on 12 indicators of state vulnerability across social, political and economic categories.

Justice

There are 51 magistrates' courts, 13 courts of first instance, three courts of appeal (in Tunis, Sfax and Sousse) and the High Court in Tunis.

A Personal Status Code was promulgated on 13 Aug. 1956 and applied to Tunisians from 1 Jan. 1957. This raised the status of women, made divorce subject to a court decision, abolished polygamy and decreed a minimum marriage age.

The population in penal institutions in 2012 was 21,300 (199 per 100,000 of national population). 54·0% of prisoners had yet to receive a trial according to 2014 estimates by the International Centre for Prison Studies. Tunisia was ranked 41st of 102 countries for criminal justice and 49th for civil justice in the 2015 World Justice Project *Rule of Law Index*, which provides data on how the rule of law is experienced by the general public across eight categories.

Education

The adult literacy rate in 2008 was 78%. All education is free from primary schools to university. Attendance at school is compulsory between the ages of six and 16. In 2007 there were 1,068,822 pupils in primary schools with 58,879 teaching staff and 1,268,219 pupils in secondary schools with 79,735 teaching staff.

In 2007 there were 13 public universities including the Virtual University of Tunis. There are a number of other public and private higher education institutions. There were 326,185 students in higher education in 2007 with 18,117 academic staff.

In 2005 public expenditure on education came to 7·2% of GDP and accounted for 20·8% of total government expenditure.

Health

There were 172 hospitals and 2,079 basic health centres in 2007 with a capacity of 17,998 beds. In 2006 there were 9,653 doctors, 1,858 dentists, 30,812 paramedical staff and 2,255 pharmacists.

In *Water: At What Cost? The State of the World's Water 2016*, WaterAid reported that 2·3% of the population does not have access to safe water.

Religion

The constitution recognizes Islam as the state religion. According to estimates by the Pew Research Center's Forum on Religion & Public Life, more than 99% of the population are Muslims (mostly Sunnis).

Culture

World Heritage Sites

Tunisia has eight sites on the UNESCO World Heritage List: the Amphitheatre of El Jem (inscribed on the list in 1979); the Site of Carthage (1979); the Medina of Tunis (1979); Ichkeul National Park (1980); the Punic Town of Kerkuane and its Necropolis (1985 and 1986); the Medina of Sousse (1988); Kairouan (1988); and Dougga/Thugga (1997).

Press

In 2009 there were nine paid-for daily newspapers (four in Arabic and five in French).

Tourism

Tourism accounts for 15% of GDP. In 2011 there were 4,785,000 international tourist arrivals, excluding same-day visitors (down from 6,903,000 in 2010 in the wake of the revolution of early 2011). Numbers have fallen since 2008, when a record 7,050,000 tourists visited the country. Spending by tourists in 2011 totalled US$1,914m. Visitor numbers fell again in 2015 in the wake of two attacks on foreign tourists during the year.

Diplomatic Representatives

Of Tunisia in the United Kingdom (29 Prince's Gate, London, SW7 1QG)
Ambassador: Nabil Ben Khedher.

Of the United Kingdom in Tunisia (Rue du Lac Windermere, Les Berges du Lac, 1053, Tunis)
Ambassador: Louise De Sousa.

Of Tunisia in the USA (1515 Massachusetts Ave., NW, Washington, D.C., 20005)
Ambassador: Fayçal Gouia.

Of the USA in Tunisia (Les Berges du Lac, 1053 Tunis)
Ambassador: Daniel H. Rubinstein.

Of Tunisia to the United Nations
Ambassador: Mohamed Khaled Khiari.

Of Tunisia to the European Union
Ambassador: Ridha Ben Mosbah.

Further Reading

Hanau Santini, Ruth, *Limited Statehood in Post-Revolutionary Tunisia: Citizenship, Economy and Security.* 2018
Hassan, Fareed M. A., *Tunisia: Understanding Successful Socioeconomic Development.* 2005
Murphy, Emma C., *Economic and Political Change in Tunisia: From Bourguiba to Ben Ali.* 2003
National Statistical Office: Institut National de la Statistique, 70 Rue Ech-cham, BP 265 CEDEX, Tunis.
Website: http://www.ins.nat.tn

Turkey

Türkiye Cumhuriyeti (Republic of Turkey)

Capital: Ankara
Population projection, 2020: 83·84m.
GNI per capita, 2017: (PPP$) 24,804
HDI/world rank, 2017: 0·791/64
Internet domain extension: .tr

Key Historical Events

There is evidence of human habitation in Anatolia (Asia Minor) from around 7500 BC. Catal Huyuk (on the Konya Plain) flourished between 6500 and 5800 BC to become one of the world's largest and most important Neolithic sites. Between 1800 and 1200 BC much of Anatolia came under Hittite rule, initially centred on Cappadocia. The artistic work of the Hittites shows a high level of culture with Babylonian and Assyrian influence. Greek colonies were established around the Anatolian coast from around 700 BC including Byzantium, which was founded by Greeks from Megara in 667 BC. Anatolia was conquered by Persians in the 6th century BC.

Alexander the Great defeated the Persians around 330 BC. After his death there was a long civil war between the Seleucids and the Ptolemies, while the kingdoms of Galatia, Armenia, Pergamum, Cappadocia, Bithynia and Pontus all established footholds in the region. Rome gained dominance around the 2nd century BC and brought stability and prosperity. Turkey was home to some of the earliest centres of Christianity, such as Antioch (modern Antalya) and Ephesus. In AD 324 the Emperor Constantine began the construction of a new capital at Byzantium. Constantinople became the centre of the Byzantine (Eastern Roman) Empire, which peaked under Justinian in the mid-6th century.

Muslim Arab forces attacked Constantinople in the 670s and besieged the city again in 716 but were repelled, thwarting the expansion of the Umayyad Caliphate ruled by Umar II. Constantine V (741–75) led Christian Byzantine forces eastward to recover lands in Anatolia. The Seljuk Turks, whose origins were in central Asia, established dominance over much of Anatolia during the 11th century, led by Alp Arslan. They came under threat during the Crusades and were overrun by the Mongol hordes from 1243. The Ottoman principality was one of a number of small Turkish states that emerged in Anatolia amid the retreat of the Mongols and the waning of the Seljuk and Byzantine empires. Osman I led the early phase of Ottoman expansion, conquering Byzantine towns in northwest Anatolia in the early 14th century. Sultan Mehmed II seized Constantinople in 1453 and went on to establish Ottoman dominance in the Balkans and the Aegean. The empire expanded to its fullest extent under Suleiman the Magnificent (1494–1566), taking in North Africa, the Levant, Persia, Anatolia, the Balkans and the Caucasus.

From the early 17th century the Ottoman empire fell into a long decline, its power weakening rapidly in the 19th century. The Kingdom of Greece broke away from Ottoman rule in 1832, with Serbs, Romanians, Armenians, Albanians, Bulgarians and Arabs demanding independence soon afterwards. Attempts by Turkey to redefine itself were further hindered in the 20th century by the First World War, during which it sided with Germany. In fighting with Greece over disputed territory from 1920–22, the Turkish National Movement was led by Mustafa Kemal (Atatürk: 'Father of the Turks'), who wanted a republic based on a modern secular society. Turkey became a republic on 29 Oct. 1923, with Ankara its capital. Islam ceased to be the official state religion in 1928 and women were given the same rights to employment and education as men, although they were not able to vote in national elections until 1934. İsmet İnönü became president following Kemal's death in 1938 and steered a neutral course through the Second World War. The 1950s were marked by a policy of firm alignment with the West, and Turkey joined NATO in 1952.

On 27 May 1960 the Turkish army overthrew the government and party activities were suspended. A new constitution was approved in a referendum held on 9 July 1961. On 20 July 1974 Turkish forces invaded Cyprus, leading to the unilateral establishment of the 'Turkish Republic of Northern Cyprus' in 1983. The question of Cypriot governance has been a source of tension with Greece ever since. (*See* CYPRUS: Key Historical Events *for further information.*)

On 12 Sept. 1980 the Turkish armed forces again drove the government in Ankara from office. A new constitution was enforced after a national referendum on 7 Nov. 1982. In the face of mounting Islamization of government policy, the Supreme National Security Council reaffirmed its commitment to the secular state. On 6 March 1997 Prime Minister Necmettin Erbakan, leader of the pro-Islamist Welfare Party, promised to combat Muslim fundamentalism but in June he was forced to resign by a campaign led by the army.

His successor, Ahmet Mesut Yılmaz, was in office until 1999 when he was replaced by Mustafa Bülent Ecevit of the Democratic Left Party. Ecevit had previously served three spells as premier in the 1970s. The Justice and Development Party (AKP) came to power in 2002, with Abdullah Gül heading the government until Recep Tayyip Erdoğan took over the premiership in 2003.

In Feb. 2000 the Kurdish Workers' Party (PKK) formally abandoned its 15-year rebellion and adopted the democratic programme urged by its imprisoned leader, Abdullah Öçalan. Despite being a long-term ally of the USA, the Turkish parliament voted against allowing US troops to attack Iraq from its southeastern border in 2003, with the incumbent AKP government harbouring concerns about the possibility of an independent Kurdish state arising from a divided Iraq.

An associate member of the European Union since 1964, Turkey has aspired to accession pending the completion of negotiations. However, significant hurdles remain, including the status of Northern Cyprus, the issue of human rights in Turkey and lukewarm support for its full membership in some EU states.

In Aug. 2007 Abdullah Gül became president, following several months of political wrangling over concerns, particularly in the military, that his Islamist background might compromise Turkey's constitutional secularism. In 2011 the AKP was returned to power, with Erdoğan claiming a third term as premier. Relations with Syria were subsequently strained as Erdoğan became an outspoken critic of Syrian President Assad's regime. Turkey has taken in over 2·9m. refugees from its civil war-ravaged neighbour against a backdrop of sporadic border skirmishes.

In Aug. 2014 Erdoğan won the first direct popular election for the presidency. Islamic State (IS) claimed responsibility for a number of fatal attacks on Turkish soil in 2015 and 2016. In July 2016 a failed coup against Erdoğan prompted mass arrests along with a media clampdown.

Territory and Population

Turkey is bounded in the west by the Aegean Sea and Greece, north by Bulgaria and the Black Sea, east by Georgia, Armenia and Iran, and south by Iraq, Syria and the Mediterranean. The area is 783,562 sq. km (302,535 sq. miles), including 13,930 sq. km (5,378 sq. miles) of inland waters. The last traditional census was in 2000. In 2007 an address-based population registration system was established to replace ten-yearly censuses. The population at 31 Dec. 2017 using this method was 80,810,525, giving a density of 105·0 per sq. km. In 2011, 70·1% of the population lived in urban areas.

The UN gives a projected population for 2020 of 83·84m.

Turkish is the official language. Kurdish and Arabic are also spoken.

Some 14m. Kurds live in Turkey. In Feb. 1991 limited use of the Kurdish language was sanctioned, and in Aug. 2002 parliament legalized Kurdish radio and television broadcasts. There were 2·87m. refugees (primarily from Syria) at the end of 2016—the highest number in any country and 17% of the global total—many of whom had fled from Islamic State fighters over the border.

Land area and population of the 81 provinces at the 2012 census:

	Area in sq. km	Population
Adana	13,915	2,125,635
Adıyaman	7,033	595,261
Afyonkarahisar	14,314	703,948

(continued)

Palgrave Macmillan (ed.), *The Statesman's Yearbook 2020*, https://doi.org/10.1057/978-1-349-95940-2_193

	Area in sq. km	Population
Ağrı	11,470	552,404
Aksaray	7,570	379,915
Amasya	5,690	322,283
Ankara	24,521	4,965,542
Antalya	20,723	2,092,537
Ardahan	4,842	106,643
Artvin	7,367	167,082
Aydın	7,851	1,006,541
Balıkesir	14,299	1,160,731
Bartın	2,080	188,436
Batman	4,659	534,205
Bayburt	3,739	75,797
Bilecik	4,302	204,116
Bingöl	8,253	262,507
Bitlis	7,021	337,253
Bolu	8,320	281,080
Burdur	6,840	254,341
Bursa	10,422	2,688,171
Çanakkale	9,933	493,691
Çankırı	7,490	184,406
Çorum	12,792	529,975
Denizli	11,692	950,557
Diyarbakır	15,058	1,592,167
Düzce	2,567	346,493
Edirne	6,074	399,708
Elazığ	8,455	562,703
Erzincan	11,619	217,886
Erzurum	25,323	778,195
Eskişehir	13,842	789,750
Gaziantep	6,819	1,799,558
Giresun	6,832	419,555
Gümüşhane	6,437	135,216
Hakkâri	7,179	279,982
Hatay	5,828	1,483,674
Iğdır	3,588	190,409
Isparta	8,276	416,663
İstanbul	5,196	13,854,740
İzmir	12,012	4,005,459
Kahramanmaraş	14,346	1,063,174
Karabük	4,109	225,145
Karaman	8,845	235,424
Kars	10,127	304,821
Kastamonu	13,153	359,808
Kayseri	17,043	1,274,968
Kilis	1,428	124,320
Kırıkkale	4,534	274,727
Kırklareli	6,278	341,218
Kırşehir	6,352	221,209
Kocaeli	3,612	1,634,691
Konya	38,873	2,052,281
Kütahya	11,977	573,421
Malatya	11,776	762,366
Manisa	13,096	1,346,162
Mardin	8,806	773,026
Mersin	15,485	1,682,848
Muğla	12,851	851,145
Muş	8,059	413,260
Nevşehir	5,379	285,190

(*continued*)

	Area in sq. km	Population
Niğde	7,352	340,270
Ordu	5,952	741,371
Osmaniye	3,124	492,135
Rize	3,922	324,152
Sakarya	4,838	902,267
Samsun	9,083	1,251,722
Şanlıurfa	18,765	1,762,075
Siirt	5,473	310,879
Sinop	5,792	201,311
Şırnak	7,152	466,982
Sivas	28,549	623,535
Tekirdağ	6,313	852,321
Tokat	9,958	613,990
Trabzon	4,664	757,898
Tunceli	7,432	86,276
Uşak	5,341	342,269
Van	19,299	1,051,975
Yalova	847	211,799
Yozgat	14,072	453,211
Zonguldak	3,304	606,527

Population of cities of over 250,000 inhabitants in 2012:

İstanbul	13,522,528
Ankara	4,417,522
İzmir	2,803,418
Bursa	1,734,705
Adana	1,628,725
Gaziantep	1,421,359
Konya	1,107,886
Antalya	994,306
Diyarbakır	892,713
Mersin	876,958
Kayseri	865,393
Eskişehir	659,924
Gebze	559,954
Urfa	526,247
Denizli	525,497
Samsun	510,678
Kahramanmaraş	443,575
Sakarya	439,602
Malatya	426,381
Erzurum	384,399
Van	370,190
Batman	348,963
Elazığ	347,857
Sivas	312,587
Manisa	309,050
İzmit	302,960
Balıkesir	267,903

Social Statistics

Births, 2009, 1,241,617; deaths, 367,971. 2009 birth rate per 1,000 population, 17·3; death rate, 5·1. 2009 marriages, 591,472 (rate of 8·2 per 1,000 population); divorces, 114,162 (rate of 1·6 per 1,000 population). Population growth rate, 2009, 1·3%. Expectation of life, 2013, was 71·8 years for males and 78·7 for females. Infant mortality, 2010, 12 per 1,000 live births, declining significantly from 66 per 1,000 live births in 1990. Fertility rate,

2013, 2·0 births per woman. In 2009 the most popular age for marrying was 25–29 for males and 20–24 for females.

Climate

Coastal regions have a Mediterranean climate, with mild, moist winters and hot, dry summers. The interior plateau has more extreme conditions, with low and irregular rainfall, cold and snowy winters, and hot, almost rainless summers. Ankara, Jan. 32·5°F (0·3°C), July 73°F (23°C). Annual rainfall 14·7" (367 mm). İstanbul, Jan. 41°F (5°C), July 73°F (23°C). Annual rainfall 28·9" (723 mm). İzmir, Jan. 46°F (8°C), July 81°F (27°C). Annual rainfall 28" (700 mm).

Constitution and Government

On 7 Nov. 1982 a new constitution was adopted, which has subsequently undergone several revisions. Following a referendum on 21 Oct. 2007, it was amended so that the *President* would be directly elected by the people, instead of by *Parliament*, as had been the case. Furthermore, the president is now able to serve for up to two five-year terms, rather than being limited to a single seven-year term. This reform came into force at the presidential election of Aug. 2014. Further amendments were introduced after acceptance in a referendum on 12 Sept. 2010. Under their terms, military officers accused of crimes against the state may be tried in civilian courts. Legal protection previously granted to participants in the 1980 coup was removed. Government workers are granted the right to collective bargaining and restrictions on striking were loosened. The *Constitutional Court* was expanded, with the president and parliament having a greater say in judicial appointments.

According to the current constitution the presidency is not an executive position and the president may not be linked to a political party but can veto laws and official appointments. There is a 600-member Turkish Grand National Assembly (550 members prior to the 2018 elections), elected by universal suffrage (at 18 years and over) for four-year terms by proportional representation. In April 2017 President Recep Tayyip Erdoğan secured approval in a further national referendum for a sweeping extension of his constitutional powers that would transform Turkey's governance from a parliamentary system to an executive presidency. The changes were due to come into effect at elections scheduled for 2019 but actually came into force in June 2018 when elections were brought forward.

National Anthem

'Korkma! Sönmez bu şafaklarda yüzen al sancak' ('Be not afraid! Our flag will never fade'); words by Mehmet Akif Ersoy, tune by Zeki Üngör.

Government Chronology

(AKP = Justice and Development Party; ANAP = Motherland Party; AP = Justice Party; CGP = Republican Reliance Party; CHP = Republican People's Party; DP = Democrat Party; DSP = Democratic Left Party; DYP = True Path Party; RP = Welfare Party; n/p = non-partisan)

Heads of State since 1938.

Presidents of the Republic		
1938–50	CHP	İsmet İnönü
1950–60	DP	Mahmut Celal Bayar
Chairman of the Committee of National Unity (MBK) and Head of State		
1950–61	military	Cemal Gürsel
Presidents of the Republic		
1961–66	n/p (ex-military)	Cemal Gürsel
1966–73	n/p (ex-military)	Cevdet Sunay
1973–80	n/p (ex-military)	Fahri Korutürk
Chairman of the National Security Council (MGK) and Head of State		
1980–82	military	Kenan Evren
Presidents of the Republic		
1982–89	n/p (ex-military)	Kenan Evren
1989–93	ANAP	Turgut Özal
1993–2000	DYP	Süleyman Demirel

(*continued*)

2000–07	n/p	Ahmet Necdet Sezer
2007–14	AKP	Abdullah Gül
2014–	AKP	Recep Tayyip Erdoğan

Prime Ministers since 1921.

1921–22	military	Mustafa Fevzi Çakmak
1922–23	n/p	Hüseyin Rauf Bey
1923–23	CHP	Ali Fethi Okyar
1923–24	CHP	Mustafa İsmet İnönü
1924–25	CHP	Ali Fethi Okyar
1925–37	CHP	Mustafa İsmet İnönü
1937–39	CHP	Mahmut Celal Bayar
1939–42	CHP	Refik İbrahim Saydam
1942–46	CHP	Mehmet Şükrü Saraçoğlu
1946–47	CHP	Mehmet Recep Peker
1947–49	CHP	Hasan Saka
1949–50	CHP	Mehmet Şemsettin Günaltay
1950–60	DP	Adnan Menderes
1960–61	military	Cemal Gürsel
1961–65	CHP	Mustafa İsmet İnönü
1965	n/p	Suat Hayri Ürgüplü
1965–71	AP	Süleyman Demirel
1971–72	n/p	İsmail Nihat Erim
1972–73	CGP	Ferit Melen
1973–74	n/p	Mehmet Naim Talu
1974–74	CHP	Mustafa Bülent Ecevit
1975–77	AP	Süleyman Demirel
1977–77	CHP	Mustafa Bülent Ecevit
1977–78	AP	Süleyman Demirel
1978–79	CHP	Mustafa Bülent Ecevit
1979–80	AP	Süleyman Demirel
1980–83	n/p	Saim Bülent Ulusu
1983–89	ANAP	Turgut Özal
1989–91	ANAP	Yıldırım Akbulut
1991	ANAP	Ahmet Mesut Yılmaz
1991–93	DYP	Süleyman Demirel
1993–96	DYP	Tansu Çiller
1996	ANAP	Ahmet Mesut Yılmaz
1996–97	RP	Necmettin Erbakan
1997–99	ANAP	Ahmet Mesut Yılmaz
1999–2002	DSP	Mustafa Bülent Ecevit
2002–03	AKP	AbdullahGül
2003–14	AKP	Recep Tayyip Erdoğan
2014–16	AKP	Ahmet Davutoğlu
2016–18	AKP	Binali Yıldırım

Recent Elections

On 24 June 2018 Turkey held its second direct presidential election since legislation passed in 2012 meant that Turkey's head of state would be elected by the public, rather than members of parliament. Incumbent president Recep Tayyip Erdoğan (Justice and Development Party/AKP) won in a single round of voting with 52·6% of votes, against Muharrem İnce of the Republican People's Party (CHP) with 30·6%, Selahattin Demirtaş of the People's Democratic Party (HDP) with 8·4%, Meral Akşener of the İyi Party (İYI) with 7·3%, Temel Karamollaoğlu of the Felicity Party (SP) with 0·9% and Doğu Perinçek of the Patriotic Party (VP) with 0·2%. Turnout was 86·2%.

Snap parliamentary elections were held on the same day. The People's Alliance won a parliamentary majority by taking 344 of the 600 seats with 53·7% of votes cast (295 seats for the ruling AKP and 49 for the Nationalist Movement Party), against 189 seats and 33·9% for the Nation Alliance (with the CHP taking 146 seats and the İYI 43) and 67 seats and 11·7% for the

HDP. Three other parties failed to secure the 10% of votes needed to gain parliamentary representation. Turnout was 86·2%.

Current Government

President: Recep Tayyip Erdoğan; b. 1954 (AKP; sworn in 28 Aug. 2014 and re-elected 24 June 2018).

In Feb. 2019 the government comprised:

Vice President: Fuat Oktay.

Minister of Agriculture and Forestry: Bekir Pakdemirli. *Commerce:* Ruhsar Pekcan. *Culture and Tourism:* Mehmet Ersoy. *Defence:* Hulusi Akar. *Energy and Natural Resources:* Fatih Dönmez. *Environment and Urban Affairs:* Murat Kurum. *Foreign Affairs:* Mevlüt Çavuşoğlu. *Health:* Fahrettin Koca. *Industry and Development:* Mustafa Varank. *Interior:* Süleyman Soylu. *Justice:* Abdülhamit Gül. *Labour, Social Services and Family:* Zehra Zümrüt Selçuk. *National Education:* Ziya Selçuk. *Transport and Infrastructure:* Mehmet Cahit Turhan. *Treasury and Finance:* Berat Albayrak. *Youth and Sports:* Mehmet Muharrem Kasapoğlu.

Office of the President: http://www.tccb.gov.tr

Current Leaders

Recep Tayyip Erdoğan

Position
President

Introduction
Recep Tayyip Erdoğan won the country's first direct presidential elections in Aug. 2014, having previously served as AKP prime minister since 2003. For many years a prominent Islamist, he sought to remould himself as a pro-European moderate but continued to cause unease among secularists. He has also been viewed as increasingly authoritarian. In foreign relations he identified Turkey's admission to the European Union as his government's top priority, but negotiations have been hampered by Turkey's refusal to recognize the government of Greek Cyprus. He has meanwhile overseen a deterioration in relations with neighbouring Syria, while continuing to confront Kurdish separatism along Turkey's southeastern border, and there has also been diplomatic friction with Israel, Russia and the USA. In 2016 he initiated a purge of suspected opposition figures and critics following a failed coup in July, and in April 2017 he secured approval in a national referendum for a sweeping extension of his presidential powers. His direct re-election for a second term in June 2018 completed Turkey's transition to an executive presidency.

Early Life
Erdoğan was born in 1954 in Rize. He attended a Koranic college before graduating in economics in 1981 from Marmara University in İstanbul. From the mid-1980s he became active in the pro-Islamist Welfare Party and in 1994 he was made mayor of İstanbul.

The Welfare Party was outlawed in 1998 for contravening Turkey's secularist constitution. In the same year Erdoğan was imprisoned for four months for reading a pro-Islamist poem at a political rally. Following the banning of the Virtue Party (the successor to Welfare) in June 2001, he established the AKP, espousing pro-Western and democratic policies, and the party won an outright victory at the Nov. 2002 elections. Erdoğan remained AKP leader with Abdullah Gül, his deputy, as prime minister until he won a by-election in Feb. 2003 (following constitutional changes that rescinded his ineligibility for office owing to a criminal conviction) and replaced Gül as premier.

Career in Office
Turkey's wish for EU accession was undermined by the failure of the Greek and Turkish sectors of Cyprus to agree on the divided island's reunification. To fulfil the criteria for EU membership, Erdoğan pushed legislative and constitutional reforms through parliament and also made a deal accepting Cyprus as an EU member. The European Council consequently agreed to open accession negotiations that began in 2005. However, in 2006 the EU partially suspended them because of the Turkish government's failure to open its ports and airports to Cypriot traffic.

In early 2007 Erdoğan decided not to stand for election to the state presidency and instead put forward foreign minister Abdullah Gül as the AKP candidate. However, Gül was equally unpalatable to secular and particularly military opinion, leading to a political stand-off in the National Assembly. Erdoğan consequently called an early general election for July that year, which returned the AKP to power, and in Aug. the new parliament endorsed Gül as president. Tensions between the AKP and the secular opposition have since continued. In Sept. 2010 Erdoğan's government won a referendum on constitutional reforms increasing parliamentary control over the army and judiciary, and in Aug. 2013 several generals were sentenced to life imprisonment for allegedly plotting to overthrow the AKP administration, although the convictions were overturned in March 2015.

Erdoğan has adopted a hard line towards Kurdish separatist insurgents based in northern Iraq. In July 2010 the PKK indicated its willingness to consider a truce in return for greater political and cultural rights, but the offer met with no official response. There was instead an escalation of Turkish military and penal measures against the PKK and pro-Kurdish activists in 2011 and 2012. In March 2013 the imprisoned PKK leader, Abdullah Öcalan, called for a ceasefire and ordered a withdrawal of PKK fighters from Turkey to advance peace negotiations with the government. Turkish military operations against the PKK nevertheless intensified.

In foreign affairs, Erdoğan clashed publicly in 2009 with the president of Israel over Israeli military action in the Palestinian Gaza Strip. Relations were damaged further in 2010 as nine Turkish activists were killed in an Israeli commando raid on a flotilla of ships carrying aid and supplies to Gaza (although the prospect of lucrative Mediterranean gas exploitation deals was to prompt a normalization of ties in 2016). Turkey's diplomatic ties with the USA and France also came under strain at this time over US congressional and French parliamentary recognition of the mass killing of Armenians in 1915 during Ottoman rule as genocide. In 2011, while critical of NATO's military action against the Gaddafi regime in Libya, Erdoğan was supportive of the 'Arab Spring' protest movements that erupted against established regimes across much of the Middle East and North Africa.

The civil war in Syria since 2011 has led to a serious deterioration in Turkey's relations with the neighbouring regime of President Assad and, for a period, with Russia. Turkey has had to contend with a surge of Syrian refugees, while Ankara's reluctance to aid Syria's Kurds against the military advance of Islamic State (IS) Sunni jihadists has fuelled resentment among the restive Kurdish population in Turkey towards the Erdoğan government. Numerous terror attacks in Turkey since 2015 by suspected IS and Kurdish extremists have continued to incur Turkish military retaliation, while Russia's aerial involvement over Syria in support of the Assad regime from Sept. 2015 led to the shooting down of a Russian warplane in Oct. that year for allegedly violating Turkish airspace. Russia, as Turkey's second largest trading partner, retaliated with economic sanctions. However, despite the assassination in Ankara of Russia's ambassador to Turkey in Dec. 2016 there was a rapprochement between the two countries in 2017, including co-ordinated air strikes against IS targets in Syria in an unusual military partnership between Moscow and a NATO member as well as Turkey's intended purchase of a missile defence system from Russia. In 2018 the Turkish government stepped up military intervention in northern Syria in its campaign against Kurdish separatism, which in turn led to increasing friction in Erdoğan's relations with US President Donald Trump who has sought to protect Kurdish and other rebel forces opposed to the Syrian regime.

In May and June 2013 there had been violent clashes in İstanbul and several other cities between environmental demonstrators and riot police, prompting accusations of heavy-handedness by Erdoğan's government and criticism from the EU. In Dec. that year a political crisis was triggered by a corruption scandal allegedly involving senior political and business figures and an apparent government attempt to suppress police investigations.

On 1 July 2014 Erdoğan was named the AKP's candidate in Turkey's first ever direct presidential elections. He was elected on 10 Aug. with 51·8% of the vote and sworn in on 28 Aug. with Ahmet Davutoğlu, also of the AKP, replacing him as prime minister. However, in Dec. 2014 a wave of arrests of journalists on charges of establishing a terrorist group was described by the opposition CHP as a coup against democracy, which further undermined EU confidence in the Turkish government's respect for the rule of law and fuelled concerns over a concentration of political power in Erdoğan's hands. Parliamentary elections in June 2015 deprived the AKP of a majority but, after governing as an interim administration until Nov. that year, the party won an unexpected and decisive victory in further polling marred by violence and media restrictions.

In March 2016 EU leaders struck a deal with Turkey to restrict the passage of non-EU migrants into Europe in return for funding and political concessions, while in May that year Davutoğlu resigned as prime minister to be replaced by Binali Yıldırım.

In July 2016 disgruntled army factions attempted a coup against Erdoğan but it was defeated within a day, during which around 300 people were killed. Erdoğan subsequently authorized the mass arrests of thousands of suspected opponents under emergency rule and sought to silence criticism in the media, while in Jan. 2017 he secured the passage through parliament of a constitutional reform bill giving him unfettered executive powers, which was narrowly approved in a referendum the following April.

Despite a struggling economy, a currency crisis and accusations of increasing political intolerance, Erdoğan called snap elections in June 2018 in which he was returned in a single round of voting for another term under a new presidential system eliminating the post of prime minister.

Defence

The President of the Republic is C.-in-C. of the armed forces. The *National Security Council*, chaired by the president and comprising military leaders and the ministers of defence and the economy, also functions as a *de facto* constitutional watchdog. Reforms passed in July 2003 in preparation for EU membership aimed to reduce the influence of the military in the political system. In Oct. 2003 the Turkish parliament voted to send 10,000 troops to Iraq, which would have made it the third largest force in the country after the USA and the UK, but the Iraqi Governing Council rejected the plan.

Conscription is 12 months for privates, and for those with four-year university degrees or higher either 12 months as reserve officers or six months as short-term privates.

In 2013 defence expenditure totalled US$10,742m., with spending per capita US$133. The 2013 expenditure represented 1·3% of GDP.

Army

Strength (2011) 660,700 (including around 325,000 conscripts and 258,700 reservists). There is also a paramilitary gendarmerie-cum-national guard of 150,000. In addition around 36,000 Turkish troops are stationed in Northern Cyprus.

Navy

The fleet in 2011 included 14 diesel submarines, 18 frigates and six corvettes. The main naval base is at Gölcük in the Gulf of İzmit.

There is a naval air component with ten anti-submarine warfare helicopters and seven light aircraft in 2011. There is a 3,100-strong Marine Regiment. The Coast Guard numbers 3,250 (including 1,400 conscripts).

Personnel in 2011 totalled 48,600 (34,500 conscripts) including marines and coast guard.

Air Force

The Air Force is being restructured, with the former 1st and 2nd Tactical Air Force Commands being merged into a new Combat Air Force and Air Missile Defence Command controlled from Eskişehir in central Turkey. There were around 338 combat-capable aircraft in operation in 2011 including F-5A/Bs, F-4E Phantoms and F-16C/Ds.

Personnel strength (2011), 60,000.

International Relations

Relations between Turkey and Iraq have long been strained over activity in the borderlands of northern Iraq by Kurdish separatist movements including the PKK. In Dec. 2007 Turkey launched air strikes on Iraqi territory against the PKK and in Feb. 2008 Turkish troops made a week-long incursion into northern Iraq to fight rebels.

There is an ongoing dispute with Greece over the division of Cyprus, oil rights under the Aegean Sea and ownership of uninhabited islands close to the Turkish coast.

Turkey has applied to join the EU and was awarded candidate status in 1999. Talks on membership began in Oct. 2005 but Turkey is unlikely to achieve full membership in the foreseeable future.

After civil war broke out in Syria in 2011, Turkey's relations with its neighbour came under renewed strain, with tensions spilling over into sporadic border skirmishes.

Economy

In 2014 finance and real estate contributed 16·2% to GDP; followed by manufacturing, 15·8%; trade and hotels, 14·5%; and transport and communications, 13·9%.

Overview

The largest industrial sector is textiles, although the automotive and electronics industries have grown strongly, and agriculture still accounts for roughly 20% of total employment. The financial sector withstood the global downturn from 2008 well, and Turkey was the only country in the OECD not to provide state support to the banking sector. The country also has a successful tourism industry.

In 2000 Turkey committed to a three-year exchange rate-based stabilization programme, including wide-ranging structural reforms and strong fiscal adjustment. However, a currency crisis the following year caused its collapse and brought the country to the brink of debt default. A revised programme was introduced in May 2001 with IMF support, promoting market liberalization and a stronger banking sector. Reflecting tighter fiscal policies and central bank independence, annual growth from 2003–07 averaged nearly 7% and public debt fell from 74% to 39% of GDP. However, the global financial crisis, combined with domestic political tensions, saw growth in 2008 drop to 0·9%, and in 2009 the economy contracted by nearly 5%. It then recovered in 2010 and unemployment fell back to its pre-crisis level of around 10%.

GDP growth averaged 8·2 from 2010–13. In 2014 it was 5·2%, while inflation measured 8·9% and public debt stood at 33·6% of GDP (down from 42·3% in 2010). Growth accelerated from 3·2% in 2016 to 5·1% in the first half of 2017. However, the inflation rate reached 10·2% in Aug. that year—the first time it had reached double digits in a decade. Unemployment had also risen to 10·2% by May, although the jobless rate among those aged 15–24 reached 19·8%, almost 2·5 percentage points higher than in May 2016. Meanwhile, Turkey's ranking in the World Economic Forum's *Global Competitiveness Report* for 2016–17 fell to 55th from 43rd in 2012–13.

Although Turkey's growth prospects are reasonably robust, it faces challenges to achieve high-income status. A deteriorating geopolitical environment since 2015 has negatively impacted exports, investment and growth, while elections, cabinet changes and an attempted coup have all affected the government's reform momentum. At the same time, a series of terrorist attacks have weakened tourist arrivals and foreign investment.

Currency

The unit of currency is the Turkish *lira* (TRY) of 100 *kuruş*. It was introduced on 1 Jan. 2005 as the new Turkish lira—officially abbreviated as YTL—replacing the Turkish lira (TRL) at 1 new Turkish lira = 1m. Turkish lira. On 1 Jan. 2009 the 'new' was removed and its official name is again just 'Turkish lira' (since 2012 indicated by the symbol ₺). Gold reserves were 3·73m. troy oz in Sept. 2009 and foreign exchange reserves US$69,387m. Inflation rates (based on IMF statistics):

2008	2009	2010	2011	2012	2013	2014	2015	2016	2017
10·4%	6·3%	8·6%	6·5%	8·9%	7·5%	8·9%	7·7%	7·8%	11·1%

Total money supply in July 2009 was ₺88,267m.

Budget

The fiscal year is the calendar year. Budgetary central government revenue totalled ₺564bn. in 2016 (₺492bn. in 2015) and expenditure ₺569bn. (₺479bn. in 2015). Tax revenues were ₺477bn. in 2016. The leading items of expenditure in 2016 were wages and salaries (₺143bn.), followed by grants (₺96bn.) and social benefits (₺93bn.).

VAT is 18%, with reduced rates of 8% and 1%.

Performance

Real GDP growth rates (based on IMF statistics):

2008	2009	2010	2011	2012	2013	2014	2015	2016	2017
0·8%	−4·7%	8·5%	11·1%	4·8%	8·5%	5·2%	6·1%	3·2%	7·4%

Total GDP was US$851·1bn. in 2017.

Banking and Finance

The Central Bank (Merkez Bankası; *Governor*, Murat Çetinkaya) is the bank of issue. In 2015 there were 52 banks, including 34 deposit banks and 13 development and investment banks. The deposit banks included three state-owned banks and nine privately-owned banks. The largest banks are Ziraat Bankası (with assets of US$103·8bn. in Dec. 2015), İşbank (assets of US$94·5bn. in Dec. 2015), Garanti Bank, Akbank and Yapı Kredi.

In 2010 external debt totalled US$293,872m., equivalent to 40·4% of GNI.

There is a stock exchange in İstanbul (ISE).

Energy and Natural Resources

Environment

In 2011 Turkey's carbon dioxide emissions from the consumption of energy were the equivalent of 3·7 tonnes per capita. Turkey's greenhouse gas emissions rose by 163·3% between 1990 and 2012.

Electricity

In 2011 installed capacity was 52·91m. kW (17·14m. kW hydro-electric); production in 2011 was 229·4bn. kWh and consumption per capita 3,152 kWh. There are plans to build three nuclear plants to meet the country's growing energy needs, with the first projected to become operational in 2023. Work on the first plant began in April 2018.

Oil and Gas

Crude oil production (2011) was 25m. bbls. Reserves in 2014 were 295m. bbls. In 2012, net imports of crude petroleum totalled 230·6m. bbls. Natural gas output was 781m. cu. metres in 2011.

Accords for the construction of an oil pipeline from Azerbaijan through Georgia to the Mediterranean port of Ceyhan in southern Turkey (the BTC pipeline) were signed in Nov. 1999. Work on the pipeline began in Sept. 2002 and it was officially opened in May 2005.

A gas pipeline from Baku in Azerbaijan (the South Caucasus pipeline) through Georgia to Erzurum was commissioned in June 2006.

Minerals

Turkey is rich in minerals, and is a major producer of chrome.

Production of principal minerals (in 1,000 tonnes, in 2007 unless otherwise indicated) was: lignite, 72,902; iron, 4,849; copper (gross weight), 4,806; boron, 4,407; coal, 2,462; salt, 2,366; magnesite (2006), 2,088; chrome, 1,679.

Agriculture

In 2015, 20·4% of employed persons were engaged in agriculture. In 2013 Turkey had 20·57m. ha. of arable land and 3·23m. ha. of permanent crops. 5·2m. ha. were equipped for irrigation in 2013.

Production (2013, in 1,000 tonnes) of principal crops: wheat, 22,050; sugar beets, 16,489; tomatoes, 11,820; barley, 7,900; maize, 5,900; melons and watermelons, 5,587; grapes, 4,011; potatoes, 3,948; apples, 3,128; seed cotton, 2,250; chillies and green peppers, 2,159; onions, 1,905; oranges, 1,781; cucumbers and gherkins, 1,755; olives, 1,676; sunflower seeds, 1,523; cottonseed, 1,287; tangerines, mandarins, clementines and satsumas, 942; rice, 900; cotton lint, 878; aubergines, 827; apricots, 812; lemons and limes, 726. Turkey is the largest producer of apricots.

Livestock, 2013 (in 1,000): sheep, 29,284; cattle, 14,415; goats, 9,226; asses, 181; horses, 136; buffaloes, 118; chickens, 266,000. Livestock products, 2013 estimates (in 1,000 tonnes): milk, 18,224; meat, 2,995; eggs, 1,031; cheese, 204; honey, 95.

Forestry

There were 11·72m. ha. of forests in 2015, or 15% of the total land area. Timber production was 21·04m. cu. metres in 2011.

Fisheries

The catch in 2015 totalled 431,909 tonnes (397,733 tonnes from marine waters). Aquaculture production in 2010 came to 167,721 tonnes.

Industry

The leading companies by market capitalization in May 2018 were: Garanti Bank (US$9·0bn.); Erdemir, a steel producer (US$8·4bn.); and Koç Holding, an industrial conglomerate with varied interests, notably oil and gas (US$8·0bn.).

Production in 2005 (in 1,000 tonnes unless otherwise stated): cement, 41,100; crude steel, 20,965; iron and steel bars, 11,854; distillate fuel oil (2007), 7,016; residual fuel oil (2007), 6,399; petrol (2007), 4,098; coke (2007), 3,335; sugar, 1,928; nitrogenous fertilizers, 1,525; paper and paperboard, 1,005; cotton yarn, 459; olive oil, 301; polyethylene, 274; pig iron, 178; cotton woven fabrics, 609m. metres; woollen woven fabrics, 32m.

metres; carpets, 58,034,681 sq. metres; TV sets, 20,790,123 units; refrigerators, 5,098,866 units; cars, 635,137 units; lorries, 39,324 assembled units; tractors, 38,800 units; cigarettes, 104,170 tonnes.

Labour

The labour force in 2013 was 27,355,000 (21,910,000 in 2003). 53·5% of the population aged 15–64 was economically active in 2013. In that year 30·7% of the labour force was female. Of those in employment in 2012, 51·2% worked in services, 26·6% in industry and 22·2% in agriculture. The unemployment rate in Oct. 2018 was 11·5%, up from 10·9% in 2017 as a whole. The gross monthly minimum wage was ₺1,071 in Jan. 2014.

Turkey had 0·12m. people living in slavery according to the Walk Free Foundation's 2013 *Global Slavery Index*.

International Trade

A customs union with the EU came into force on 1 Jan. 1996.

Imports and Exports

Imports (c.i.f.) in 2010 totalled US$185,541m. (US$140,869m. in 2009) and exports (f.o.b.) US$113,980m. (US$102,139m. in 2009). Chief imports (2005) in US$1m.: machinery and transport equipment, 37,809; manufactured goods, 19,990; chemicals and related products, 16,167; petroleum and petroleum products, 12,413; crude materials excluding fuels, 7,661. Chief exports: machinery and transport equipment, 21,509; apparel and clothing accessories, 11,833; textile yarn, fabrics and finished articles, 7,076; food and live animals, 6,512; iron and steel, 5,827.

The main import suppliers in 2006 (in US$1m.) were: Russia, 17,645; Germany, 14,653; China, 9,601; Italy, 8,597; France, 7,212; USA, 6,221. Main export markets, 2006: Germany, 9,684; UK, 6,813; Italy, 6,753; USA, 5,061; France, 4,604; Spain, 3,721. In the meantime trade with Iraq has increased to such an extent that it is now Turkey's second largest export market. The EU accounted for 40·7% of imports and 54·3% of exports in 2006.

Communications

Roads

In 2006 there were 427,099 km of roads, including 1,987 km of motorway. In 2007 road vehicles in use included 6,472,200 passenger cars, 2,619,700 lorries and vans, 561,700 buses and coaches and 2,003,500 motorcycles and mopeds. There were 5,002 fatalities from road accidents in 2007.

Rail

Total length of railway lines in 2011 was 9,642 km (1,435 mm gauge), of which 2,789 km were electrified. Turkey's first high-speed line was opened in 2009 between Ankara and Eskişehir. The first phase of construction of an undersea rail tunnel linking European and Asian Turkey, named Marmaray, was completed in Oct. 2013; the second phase is expected to become operational during 2019 following a number of delays. Passenger-km travelled in 2011 came to 5·82bn. and freight tonne-km to 11·30bn. There are metro systems operating in Adana, Ankara, Bursa, İstanbul and İzmir.

Civil Aviation

There are international airports at İstanbul (İstanbul and Sabiha Gökçen), Dalaman (Muğla), Ankara (Esenboga), İzmir (Adnan Menderes), Adana and Antalya. The national carrier is Turkish Airlines, which is 49·1% state-owned. In 2014 it carried 54,675,000 passengers (31,967,000 on international flights) and flew 106,787m. revenue passenger-km. In 2015 it served 110 countries, more than any other airline. In 2009 İstanbul's Atatürk Airport handled 29,854,119 passengers and 381,174 tonnes of freight. Antalya was the second busiest airport for passenger traffic, with 18,403,617 passengers and İstanbul's Sabiha Gökçen Airport third with 6,640,230 passengers. A third airport serving İstanbul (İstanbul Airport) was opened in Oct. 2018, capable of handling 90m. passengers per year and expected to eventually handle 150m. Atatürk Airport was set to close to commercial flights when the new hub became fully operational. Following a number of delays this was expected to happen in the second quarter of 2019. Atatürk Airport would then only be used for aviation fairs and training activities.

Shipping

In Jan. 2014 there were 915 ships of 300 GT or over registered, totalling 6·13m. GT. Among the 915 vessels registered were 414 general cargo ships,

182 oil tankers and 170 passenger ships. The Turkish-controlled fleet comprised 1,381 vessels of 1,000 GT or over in July 2014, of which 583 were under the Turkish flag and 798 under foreign flags. In 2014 Turkish ports handled 378·4m. tonnes of cargo.

In 2013 work began on Kanal İstanbul, a major waterway connecting the Black Sea to the Sea of Marmara aimed at reducing marine traffic through the Bosphorus. It is scheduled to open in 2023.

Telecommunications

In 2013 there were 13,552,000 main (fixed) telephone lines. In the same year mobile phone subscriptions numbered 69,661,000 (929·6 per 1,000 persons). In Nov. 2005 the government sold a 55% stake in Türk Telecom to a consortium led by Saudi Arabia's Oger Telecom and Telecom Italia. The government's stake fell to 30% in May 2008 through a public offering. In 2013 an estimated 46·3% of the population aged 16–74 were internet users. In March 2012 there were 31·0m. Facebook users.

Social Institutions

Out of 178 countries analysed in the 2017 *Fragile States Index*—a list published jointly by the Fund for Peace and *Foreign Policy* magazine—Turkey was ranked the 64th most vulnerable to conflict or collapse. The index is based on 12 indicators of state vulnerability across social, political and economic categories.

Justice

The unified legal system consists of: (1) justices of the peace (single judges with limited but summary penal and civil jurisdiction); (2) courts of first instance (single judges, dealing with cases outside the jurisdiction of (3) and (4)); (3) central criminal courts (a president and two judges, dealing with cases where the crime is punishable by imprisonment over five years); (4) commercial courts (three judges); (5) state security courts, to prosecute offences against the integrity of the state (a president and two judges).

The civil and military High Courts of Appeal sit at Ankara. The Council of State is the highest administrative tribunal; it consists of five chambers. Its 31 judges are nominated from among high-ranking personalities in politics, economy, law, the army, etc. The Military Administrative Court deals with the judicial control of administrative acts and deeds concerning military personnel. The Court of Jurisdictional Disputes is empowered to resolve disputes between civil, administrative and military courts. The Supreme Council of Judges and Public Prosecutors appoints judges and prosecutors to the profession and has disciplinary powers.

The Civil Code and the Code of Obligations have been adapted from the corresponding Swiss codes. The Penal Code is largely based upon the Italian Penal Code, and the Code of Civil Procedure closely resembles that of the Canton of Neuchâtel. The Commercial Code is based on the German.

The population in penal institutions in Sept. 2013 was 137,133 (179 per 100,000 of national population). In 2015 the World Justice Project *Rule of Law Index*, which provides data on how the rule of law is experienced by the general public across eight categories, ranked Turkey 76th of 102 countries for criminal justice and 63rd for civil justice.

The death penalty, not used since 1984, was abolished in peacetime in Aug. 2002. The government signed a European Convention protocol abolishing the death penalty entirely in Jan. 2004.

Education

Adult literacy in 2009 was 90·8% (male, 96·4%; female, 85·3%). Compulsory primary and secondary education is free of charge in state schools between the ages of six and 18. In Aug. 2002 parliament legalized education in Kurdish. In 2014–15 there were 2,614 *İmam-hatip* (religious) schools with 932,273 pupils (96,851 in 2004–05).

Statistics for 2005–06	Number	Teachers	Students
Pre-school institutions	18,539	20,910	550,146
Primary schools	34,990	389,859	10,673,935
High schools	3,406	102,581	2,075,617
Vocational and technical high schools	4,029	82,736	1,182,637

In 2007–08 there were 53 state universities, including two higher institutes of technology, and 24 private universities. In 2008 there were 2,532,622 students in tertiary education and 98,766 academic staff. In 2010, 49,116 students were studying abroad.

In 2006 public expenditure on education came to 2·9% of GDP.

Health

In 2006 there were 116,014 physicians, 23,798 dentists, 217,685 nurses and midwives and 24,740 pharmacists. There were 1,347 hospitals with 179,649 beds in 2009.

Welfare

Distribution of main non-means tested social protection benefits in 2012 was as follows: old age, ₺90,622m.; sickness/health care, ₺55,562m.; survivors, ₺21,841m.; unemployment, ₺2,263m. Total (including others): ₺173,627m. Total social protection expenditure amounted to ₺195,419m. in 2012.

Religion

Islam ceased to be the official religion in 1928. The Constitution guarantees freedom of religion but forbids its political exploitation or any impairment of the secular character of the republic.

In 2010 the population was an estimated 98·0% Muslim (around 85–90% Sunni and 10–15% Shia) according to the Pew Research Center's Forum on Religion & Public Life. There are small numbers of Orthodox Christians and other Christians.

Culture

World Heritage Sites

UNESCO World Heritage sites under Turkish jurisdiction (with year entered on list) are: Historic Areas of İstanbul (1985), including the ancient Hippodrome of Constantine, the 6th-century Hagia Sophia and the 16th-century Süleymaniye Mosque; Göreme National Park and the Rock Sites of Cappadocia (1985); Great Mosque and Hospital of Divriği (1985), founded in the early 13th century; Hattusha (1986), the former capital of the Hittite Empire; Nemrut Dağ (1987), including the 1st century BC mausoleum of Antiochus I; Xanthos-Letoon (1988), the capital of Lycia; Hierapolis-Pamukkale (1988), including mineral forests, petrified waterfalls and the ruins of ancient baths, temples and other Greek monuments; City of Safranbolu (1994), a caravan station from the 13th century; Archaeological Site of Troy (1998); the Selimiye Mosque and its Social Complex (2011) in Edirne, the former capital of the Ottoman Empire; the Neolithic Site of Çatalhöyük (2012), vast archaeological remains of Neolithic occupation dating from 7400–6200 BC, a unique illustration of the evolution of social organization and cultural practices as humans adapted to a sedentary life; Bursa and Cumalıkızık: the birth of the Ottoman Empire (2014), a site that illustrates the creation of an urban and rural system establishing the Ottoman Empire in the early 14th century; Pergamon and its Multi-Layered Cultural Landscape (2014), a site that rises high above the Bakırçay Plain in the Aegean Region; Diyarbakır Fortress and Hevsel Gardens Cultural Landscape (2015), a site that encompasses the inner castle, the Amida Mound and the city walls of Diyarbakır; Ephesus (2015), which is composed of Hellenistic and Roman settlements founded on new locations; the Archaeological Site of Ani (2016), a medieval site combining residential, religious and military structures; Aphrodisias (2017), an area consisting of the archaeological site of Aphrodisias and marble quarries; and Göbekli Tepe (2018), a site containing monumental circular and rectangular megalithic structures.

Press

In 2014 there were 80 daily newspapers with a combined average daily circulation of 4·9m. In the 2016 *World Press Freedom Index* compiled by Reporters Without Borders, Turkey ranked 151st out of 180 countries. In Dec. 2016, 81 journalists were in prison—more than in any other country.

Tourism

In 2015, 39·5m. international tourists visited Turkey (down slightly from a record 39·8m. in 2014), making it the sixth most popular tourist destination. However, terrorist incidents and political instability since then have led to a steep decline in tourist numbers. Receipts from tourism in 2014 totalled US$29·5bn.

Festivals

Republic Day is on 29 Oct. The most important Islamic festivals are Şeker Bayramı ('sugar festival', Eid al-Fitr) at the end of Ramadan and Kurban Bayramı (Eid al-Adha). Their dates vary depending on the Islamic calendar.

İstanbul hosts a variety of festivals including International İstanbul Film Festival (April), the One Love music festival (June), the International İstanbul Music Festival (June), International İstanbul Jazz Festival (July) and the Rock'n Coke music festival (July). Aspendos International Opera and Ballet Festival takes place in Antalya in June–July.

Diplomatic Representatives

Of Turkey in the United Kingdom (43 Belgrave Sq., London, SW1X 8PA)
Ambassador: Ümit Yalçın.

Of the United Kingdom in Turkey (Şehit Ersan Caddesi 46/A, Çankaya, Ankara)
Ambassador: Sir Dominick Chilcott, KCMG.

Of Turkey in the USA (2525 Massachusetts Ave., NW, Washington, D.C., 20008)
Ambassador: Serdar Kılıç.

Of the USA in Turkey (110 Atatürk Blvd, Kavaklıdere, 06100 Ankara)
Ambassador: Vacant.
Chargé d'Affaires a.i.: Jeffrey M. Hovenier.

Of Turkey to the United Nations
Ambassador: Feridun Hadi Sinirlioğlu.

Of Turkey to the European Union
Ambassador: Mehmet Kemal Bozay.

Further Reading

State Institute of Statistics. *Türkiye İstatistik Yilliği/Statistical Yearbook of Turkey* (now discontinued).—*Diş Ticaret İstatistikleri/Foreign Trade Statistics* (Annual).—*Aylik İstatistik Bülten* (Monthly).

Abramowitz, Morton, (ed.) *Turkey's Transformation and American Policy.* 2000

Aydın-Düzgit, Senem and Tocci, Nathalie, *Turkey and the European Union.* 2015

De Waal, Thomas, *Great Catastrophe: Armenians and Turks in the Shadow of Genocide.* 2015

Genç, Kaya, *Under the Shadow: Rage and Revolution in Modern Turkey.* 2016

Gözen Ercan, Pınar, *Turkish Foreign Policy: International Relations, Legality and Global Reach.* 2017

İnalcık, H., Faroqhi, S., McGowan, B., Quataert, D. and Pamuk, Ş., *An Economic and Social History of the Ottoman Empire.* 1994

Jenkins, Gareth, *Political Islam in Turkey: Running West, Heading East.* 2008

Kalaycioğlu, Ersin, *Turkish Dynamics: Bridge Across Troubled Lands.* 2006.—*Turkish Democracy Today.* 2006

Keyman, E. Fuat and Gumüşçu, Sebnem, *Democracy, Identity and Foreign Policy in Turkey.* 2014

LaGro, Esra and Jørgensen, Knud Erik, *Turkey and the European Union: Prospects for a Difficult Encounter.* 2007

Stone, Norman, *Turkey: a Short History.* 2011

National Statistical Office: Turkstat, Necatibey Caddesi no. 114, 06100 Ankara.

Website: http://www.tuik.gov.tr

Turkmenistan

Türkmenistan

Capital: Ashgabat
Population projection, 2020: 6·03m.
GNI per capita, 2017: (PPP$) 15,594
HDI/world rank, 2017: 0·706/108=
Internet domain extension: .tm

Key Historical Events

Until 1917 Russian Central Asia was divided politically into the Khanate of Khiva, the Emirate of Bokhara and the Governor-Generalship of Turkestan. The Khan of Khiva was deposed in Feb. 1920 and a People's Soviet Republic was set up. In Aug. 1920 the Amir of Bokhara suffered the same fate. The former Governor-Generalship of Turkestan was constituted an Autonomous Soviet Socialist Republic within the RSFSR on 11 April 1921. In the autumn of 1924 the Soviets of the Turkestan, Bokhara and Khiva Republics decided to redistribute their territories on a nationality basis. The redistribution was completed in May 1925 when the new states of Uzbekistan, Turkmenistan and Tadzhikistan were accepted into the USSR as Union Republics. Following the break-up of the Soviet Union, Turkmenistan declared independence in Oct. 1991. Saparmurad Niyazov was elected president and founded the Democratic Party of Turkmenistan, the country's only legal party. Also prime minister and supreme commander of the armed forces, parliament proclaimed Niyazov head of state for life in Dec. 1999. He held the official title of 'Turkmenbashi', leader of all Turkmen. In July 2000 Niyazov introduced a law requiring all officials to speak Turkmen. He died of a heart attack in Dec. 2006. Gurbanguly Berdymukhammedov succeeded him.

Territory and Population

Turkmenistan is bounded in the north by Kazakhstan, in the north and northeast by Uzbekistan, in the southeast by Afghanistan, in the southwest by Iran and in the west by the Caspian Sea. Area, 448,100 sq. km (186,400 sq. miles). The 1995 census population was 4,483,251; density 10·0 per sq. km. Estimate, 2010, 5·04m. A census was carried out in 2012 but as at March 2018 the results had yet to be officially released, although some data was unofficially published online in Feb. 2015. The vast majority of citizens are Turkmen, but there are some Russians and Uzbeks. A dual-citizenship treaty between Turkmenistan and Russia has been rescinded. In 2011, 50·0% of the population lived in rural areas.

The UN gives a projected population for 2020 of 6·03m.

There are five administrative regions (*velayaty*): Ahal, Balkan, Dashoguz, Lebap and Mary. Ashgabat, the capital, is an administrative and territorial unit with province-wide powers. The estimated population of Ashgabat (formerly Ashkhabad) in 2012 was 701,000. Other large towns are Turkmenabat (formerly Chardzhou), Mary (Merv), Balkanabad (Nebit-Dag) and Dashoguz.

The official language is Turkmen, spoken by 77% of the population; Uzbek is spoken by 9% and Russian by 7%.

Social Statistics

2008 estimates: births, 111,000; deaths, 39,000. Estimated rates, 2008 (per 1,000 population): births, 21·9; deaths, 7·7. Annual population growth rate, 2000–08, 1·4%. Life expectancy, 2013: 61·4 years for males and 69·8 for females. Infant mortality, 2010, 47 per 1,000 live births; fertility rate, 2008, 2·5 births per woman.

Climate

The summers are warm to hot but the humidity is relatively low. The winters are cold but generally dry and sunny over most of the country. Ashgabat, Jan. –1°C, July 25°C. Annual rainfall 375 mm.

Constitution and Government

A new constitution was adopted on 14 Sept. 2016. Among its provisions is an extension of the presidential term from five to seven years, and the removal of an upper age limit of 70 for presidential candidates. A new position of human rights commissioner was created. The *Majlis* (Assembly), the sole legislative body, comprises 125 members and the constitution allows for a multi-party system. Turkmenistan's international neutrality is also enshrined.

National Anthem

'Janym gurban sana, erkana yurdum' ('I am ready to give life for our native hearth'); composed by Veli Muhatov.

Recent Elections

In the presidential election of 12 Feb. 2017 incumbent Gurbanguly Berdymukhammedov was re-elected with 97·7% of the vote (97·1% in 2012). Turnout was 97·3%.

Majlis elections were held on 25 March 2018. The Democratic Party won 55 of 125 seats, the Agrarian Party 11 and the Party of Industrialists and Entrepreneurs 11; groups of citizens took 48 seats. The Party of Industrialists and Entrepreneurs is the only nominal opposition party. All three parties align themselves with the President Berdymukhammedov's policies. Turnout was 91·7%.

Current Government

President and Prime Minister: Gurbanguly Berdymukhammedov; b. 1957 (DP; in office since 21 Dec. 2006—acting until 14 Feb. 2007).

In Feb. 2019 the government comprised:

Deputy Prime Ministers: Bakhargul Abdyeva; Purli Agamyradov; Dadebay Amangeldiyev; Mammetkhan Chakyev; Chary Gylyjov; Myratgeldi Meredov; Rashid Meredov (also *Minister of Foreign Affairs*); Gochmyrat Myradov.

Minister of Agriculture and Water Resources: Magtymguly Bayramdurdyyev. *Communications:* Bairamgeldy Ovezov. *Construction and Architecture:* Soenchnazar Selimov. *Culture:* Atagely Shamuradov. *Defence:* Begench Gundogdyev. *Education:* Mammetmyrat Geldiniyazov. *Energy:* Charymyrat Purchekov. *Finance and Economy:* Batyr Bazarov. *Health and Medical Industry:* Nurmuhammet Amannepesov. *Industry:* Khosgeldi Mergenov. *Internal Affairs:* Isgender Mulikov. *Justice:* Begmyrat Muhammedov. *Labour and Social Welfare:* Muhammetseyit Sylapov. *National Security:* Yalym Berdyev. *Nature Protection:* Babageldi Annabayramov. *Oil and Gas:* Myratgeldi Meredov. *Public Utilities:* Kakageldy Gurbanov. *Railways:* Azat Atamyradov. *Road Transport:* Orazdurdy Suhanov. *Sports and Youth Policy:* Dayanch Gulgeldiev. *Textile Industry:* Resul Rejepov. *Trade and Foreign Economic Relations:* Amandurdy Ishanov.

Government Website: http://www.turkmenistan.gov.tm

Current Leaders

Gurbanguly Berdymukhammedov

Position
President

Introduction
Gurbanguly Berdymukhammedov came to power in 2006 following the death of President Saparmurad Niyazov, known as Turkmenbashi. Berdymukhammedov had served as minister of health in Niyazov's government since 1997, implementing the closure of rural hospitals. Though not initially regarded as a frontrunner for the presidency, he became acting president when Niyazov's constitutional successor, Ovezgeldi Atayev, was charged with criminal offences. Having won the Feb. 2007 presidential election, Berdymukhammedov began to strengthen ties with the outside world and introduced some constitutional reforms, although critics

© Springer Nature Limited 2020
Palgrave Macmillan (ed.), *The Statesman's Yearbook 2020*,
https://doi.org/10.1057/978-1-349-95940-2_194

questioned their democratic validity. He was re-elected in Feb. 2012 and again in Feb. 2017.

Early Life
Berdymukhammedov was born in Babaarap village in the region of Ashgabat in 1957. He graduated in dentistry from the Turkmen state medical institute in 1979 and later completed a PhD in medical sciences in Moscow. In 1995 he was appointed head of the dentistry centre of the ministry of health and became associate professor and dean of the dentistry faculty of the state medical institute. He was Niyazov's personal dentist and in 1997 entered political life as the minister for health and the medical industry.

In April 2001 Berdymukhammedov was appointed deputy chairman of the council of ministers. Under Niyazov's autocratic regime the health service suffered acute financial problems. In April 2004 Niyazov announced that since state health care workers were not being paid, Berdymukhammedov would also forfeit his pay for three months. In the same year Berdymukhammedov implemented drastic cuts, closing all rural hospitals and sacking 15,000 health care workers, replacing them with untrained army conscripts.

When Niyazov died of a heart attack on 21 Dec. 2006, the Turkmen constitution provided for Ovezgeldi Atayev, chairman of the *Khalk Maslakhaty* (People's Council), to become acting president. However, Berdymukhammedov assumed the role and announced that Atayev was the subject of criminal investigation. On 26 Dec. an extraordinary session of the *Khalk Maslakhaty* amended the constitution to allow the acting president to stand in presidential elections. It also blocked the candidacy of leading opposition figures based abroad.

Berdymukhammedov was said to have the backing of Akmurad Rejepo, head of the presidential security service, and although five other candidates stood in the elections, his victory was widely predicted. During his campaign Berdymukhammedov promised to reform the agricultural sector and to improve living conditions. He pledged that the government would continue to provide free natural gas, electricity, salt and water, and that salaries and pensions would be increased regularly.

Career in Office
On 11 Feb. 2007 Berdymukhammedov was elected president with nearly 90% of the vote. While making no decisive break with Niyazov's isolationist policies, there were early indications of a more outward-looking stance. Representatives of many foreign governments attended his inauguration and he subsequently received delegations from China, Russia and the USA. He confirmed that Turkmenistan would honour its gas contracts with Russia and moved towards stronger relations with neighbouring Afghanistan. The government also announced that it was reinforcing commercial ties with Iran.

Berdymukhammedov extended the period of formal schooling, reintroduced foreign languages to the curriculum and lifted restrictions on travel within Turkmenistan. He raised the prospect of reopening rural hospitals and promised to widen Internet access (available to only 1% of the population when he came to power). However, these reforms would be dependent on an economic upturn. A new constitution was adopted in Sept. 2008 that increased the number of parliamentary seats to 125 and increased the influence of the *Majlis*. Nevertheless, Berdymukhammedov's hold on power was reinforced as parliamentary elections in Dec. that year returned an overwhelming number of candidates from his dominant Democratic Party.

The cult of personality around the presidency has lessened under Berdymukhammedov, but the government retains tight control over political organizations. It also continues to attract criticism for human rights and a lack of transparency in the electoral system, under which the president was returned for a second term in Feb. 2012.

The government has sought to diversify its gas markets and break free of Russian dominance of the export routes. An export pipeline to China was inaugurated in Dec. 2009 and in Jan. 2010 a second pipeline to Iran opened.

In Aug. 2013 Berdymukhammedov announced that he was stepping down as leader of the ruling DP while in office, stating that he wanted to be above partisan politics while promoting a multi-party political system. Parliamentary elections in Dec. 2013 were won by the DP and parties sympathetic to the president, although human rights campaigners were critical of the results. In Jan. 2015, amid a slump in oil and gas prices, the central bank devalued the currency by 19% against the US dollar (the first such change since May 2008) which prompted an increase in inflation and constrained consumer demand. Unemployment and lay-offs also rose during the year and there were shortages of basic goods in some provinces.

In Sept. 2016 constitutional changes extended the presidential term from five to seven years and ended the 70-year age limit for the office-holder. Berdymukhammedov was subsequently returned for a third presidential term in elections staged in Feb. 2017 in which he claimed almost 98% of the vote, and in the parliamentary elections in March 2018 the DP remained the dominant party of power.

It was reported at the end of 2017 that the president had banned women from driving cars.

Defence

Conscription is compulsory for two years. Defence expenditure in 2012 totalled US$539m. (US$107 per capita), representing 1·6% of GDP.

Army
In 2011 the Army was 18,500-strong.

Navy
In 2011 the Navy numbered 500 and operated from a minor base at Turkmenbashi on the Caspian Sea with six patrol and coastal combatants. The Caspian Sea Flotilla is operating as a joint Russian, Kazakh and Turkmen flotilla under Russian command. It is based at Astrakhan.

Air Force
The Air Force, with 3,000 personnel (including Air Defence), had 94 combat-capable aircraft in 2011 including Su-17s and MiG-29s.

Economy

In 2010 agriculture accounted for 11·5% of GDP, industry 60·0% and services 28·5%.

Overview
Turkmenistan has the world's fourth largest gas reserves. Hydrocarbons comprise 80% of exports and are the chief factor in the country's recent economic upturn. Other major exports include textiles and raw cotton.

GDP growth averaged 11·6% per year from 2011 to 2014, leading to a steady increase in average income levels that saw the country move to upper-middle income status. However, growth slowed to 6·5% in 2015 as a result of the decrease in global energy prices, while the current account deficit reached 11·8% of GDP. Diversifying the highly concentrated export sector is necessary to offset output volatility and create jobs to absorb a young and growing working-age population.

Despite a privatization programme launched in 1994, most businesses remain state-run and foreign investment levels are low.

Turkmenistan agreed to supply natural gas to Russia in 2003 and to China and Iran in 2005. However, deliveries were constrained by a lack of export routes and a reliance on Russian pipelines. To moderate Russia's influence, a pipeline to China opened in 2009 and another to Iran the following year.

Despite historically high poverty rates, social indicators in Turkmenistan have improved. The government's national development programme for 2011–30 aims for inclusive growth, modernization of the country's infrastructure and the promotion of foreign direct investment.

Currency
The unit of currency is the *new manat* (TMT) of 100 *tenge*, introduced on 1 Jan. 2009 to replace the *manat* (TMM) at a rate of 1 TMT = 5,000 TMM. The manat was devalued by 18% in Jan. 2015. There was inflation of 3·6% in 2016, rising to 8·0% in 2017.

Budget
Revenues were 10·1bn. manat in 2008 and expenditures 5·4bn. manat.
VAT is 15%.

Performance
Total GDP in 2017 was US$42·4bn. Real GDP contracted by an average of 10·5% every year between 1993 and 1997. However, a spectacular revival led to double-digit growth every year between 1999 and 2008, with the economy growing by an average of 15·3% annually. More recently real GDP growth was 6·5% in 2015, 6·2% in 2016 and 6·5% in 2017. The rapid growth of recent years is largely down to large-scale gas exports to Russia.

Banking and Finance

There are two types of bank in Turkmenistan—state commercial banks and joint stock open-end commercial banks. The central bank is the State Central Bank of Turkmenistan (*Chairman*, Merdan Annadurdyev). There were 11 banks in 2015. In 2010 foreign debt totalled US$422m., equivalent to just 2·1% of GNI.

Energy and Natural Resources

Environment

Carbon dioxide emissions from the consumption of energy in 2011 accounted for 11·0 tonnes per capita.

Electricity

Installed capacity in 2011 was an estimated 3·2m. kW. Production was 17·22bn. kWh in 2011, with consumption per capita 2,873 kWh.

Oil and Gas

Turkmenistan possesses the world's fourth largest reserves of natural gas and substantial oil resources. The Galkynysh gas field, in the southeast of the country, was discovered in 2006 and is the second largest in the world. The 1,833-km Turkmenistan–China gas pipeline, taking natural gas to Xinjiang in China via Kazakhstan and Uzbekistan, was inaugurated in Dec. 2009. Oil production in 2012 was 11·0m. tonnes.

Natural gas reserves were 19·5trn. cu. metres in 2017 and oil reserves 0·6bn. bbls in 2012. In 2012 natural gas production was 64·4bn. cu. metres.

Minerals

There are reserves of coal, sulphur, magnesium, potassium, lead, barite, viterite, bromine, iodine and salt.

Agriculture

Cotton and wheat account for two-thirds of agricultural production. Barley, maize, corn, rice, wool, silk and fruit are also produced. Production of main crops (2013 estimates, in 1,000 tonnes): wheat, 1,600; seed cotton, 600; tomatoes, 397; cottonseed, 396; potatoes, 323; grapes, 272; watermelons, 251; sugar beets, 238; cotton lint, 198. There were approximately 1·94m. ha. of arable land in 2013 and 60,000 ha. of permanent crops.

Livestock, 2013 estimates: sheep, 14·0m.; goats, 2·29m.; cattle, 2·27m.; camels, 120,000; chickens, 16m.

Forestry

There were 4·13m. ha. of forests (9% of the land area) in 2015.

Fisheries

There are fisheries in the Caspian Sea. The estimated total catch in 2011 was 15,000 tonnes, exclusively freshwater fish.

Industry

Main industries: oil refining, gas extraction, chemicals, manufacture of machinery, fertilizers, textiles and clothing. Output, 2007 (in tonnes): distillate fuel oil, 2,908,000; residual fuel oil, 2,020,000; petrol, 1,464,000; cement, 941,000.

Labour

The estimated labour force in 2010 totalled 2,509,000 (53% males), up from 1,826,000 in 2000.

Turkmenistan had 15,000 people living in slavery according to the Walk Free Foundation's 2013 *Global Slavery Index*.

International Trade

Imports and Exports

Imports, 2013, US$16,090m.; exports, US$18,854m. Main imports: machinery and mechanical appliances, base metals and articles of base metal, transport equipment and products of the chemical or allied industries. Main exports: natural gas, petroleum products, crude oil and cotton fibre. The main import suppliers in 2010 were: Turkey (30·1%); China, including Hong Kong and Taiwan (11·5%); Russia (9·3%); United Arab Emirates (9·0%); Iran (8·5%). In 2010 the leading export markets were: Iran (32·9%); Russia

(25·4%); China, including Hong Kong and Taiwan (10·1%); Georgia (6·7%); Italy (5·3%).

Communications

Roads

The total road network covers around 14,000 km. In 2006 there were 650 fatalities as a result of road accidents.

Rail

Length of railways in 2011, 3,115 km of 1,520 mm gauge. A rail link to Iran was opened in 1996. In 2008, 6·2m. passengers and 25·4m. tonnes of freight were carried.

Civil Aviation

Turkmenistan Airlines, founded in 1992, is the flag carrier. In 2005 scheduled airline traffic of Turkmenistan-based carriers flew 9·5m. km, carrying 1,899,800 passengers. A new international airport was inaugurated at Ashgabat in Sept. 2016.

Shipping

In Jan. 2014 there were 16 ships of 300 GT or over registered, totalling 52,000 GT. The main port is Turkmenbashi, on the Caspian Sea.

Telecommunications

In 2013 there were an estimated 6,125,000 mobile phone subscriptions (1,168·9 per 1,000 inhabitants) and an estimated 602,000 fixed telephone lines. There were an estimated 9·6 internet users for every 100 inhabitants in 2013. Internet usage was banned under the former president, Saparmurad Niyazov, and has only been available since 2007.

Social Institutions

Out of 178 countries analysed in the 2017 *Fragile States Index*—a list published jointly by the Fund for Peace and *Foreign Policy* magazine—Turkmenistan was ranked the joint 86th most vulnerable (along with the Maldives) to conflict or collapse. The index is based on 12 indicators of state vulnerability across social, political and economic categories.

Justice

The population in penal institutions in 2013 was 30,568 (583 per 100,000 of national population). The death penalty was abolished in 1999 (there were over 100 executions in 1996).

Education

Compulsory education lasts 12 years from age 6 to 17. The duration of higher education programmes is generally five years (longer in the case of medicine and some other disciplines). In 2014 there were 188,518 children in pre-primary schools, 359,064 pupils at primary schools and 650,998 pupils at secondary schools. There were 44,411 students at institutions of higher education in 2014.

In 2009 adult literacy was estimated at 99·6%.

Health

In 2006 there were 43 hospital beds per 10,000 inhabitants. There were 12,210 physicians, 703 dentistry personnel and 23,026 nursing and midwifery personnel in 2006.

Welfare

A Social Security Code was adopted in 2007. In 2010 there were 274,171 pensioners; in Jan. 2010 the minimum pension was 121 new manat a month and the maximum pension 532 new manat.

Religion

In 2010 an estimated 93·0% of the population were Muslims (mainly Sunnis) according to the Pew Research Center's Forum on Religion & Public Life, with 6·4% Christians (mainly Orthodox).

Culture

World Heritage Sites

Turkmenistan has three sites on the UNESCO World Heritage List: the State Historical and Cultural Park 'Ancient Merv' (inscribed on the list in 1999), the oldest and best-preserved Central Asian Silk Route city, dominated by Seljuk architecture; Kunya-Urgench (2005), the ancient capital of the Khorezem region; and the Parthian Fortresses of Nisa (2007), the site of one of the earliest and most important cities of the Parthian Empire.

Press

In 2008 there were two daily newspapers with a combined average circulation of 56,000. Approval is required from the president's office before publication. In the 2013 *World Press Freedom Index* compiled by Reporters Without Borders, Turkmenistan ranked 177th out of 179 countries.

Tourism

In 2005 there were 12,000 non-resident tourists.

Calendar

In Aug. 2002 then President Saparmurad Niyazov renamed the days of the week and the months, for example with Jan. becoming 'Turkmenbashi' after the president's official name, meaning 'head of all the Turkmen'. April was renamed in honour of the president's mother. Tuesday was renamed 'Young Day' and Saturday 'Spiritual Day'. However, in April 2008 President Gurbanguly Berdymukhammedov reversed his predecessor's decisions.

Diplomatic Representatives

Of Turkmenistan in the United Kingdom (131 Holland Park Ave., London, W11 4UT)
    Ambassador: Yazmurad N. Seryaev.

Of the United Kingdom in Turkmenistan (3rd Floor Office Building, Four Points Ak Altyn Hotel, Ashgabat 744001)
    Ambassador: Thorda Abbott-Watt.

Of Turkmenistan in the USA (2207 Massachusetts Ave., NW, Washington, D.C., 20008)
    Ambassador: Meret Orazov.

Of the USA in Turkmenistan (9 1984 St., Ashgabat 744000)
    Ambassador: Allan Mustard.

Of Turkmenistan to the United Nations
    Ambassador: Aksoltan T. Ataeva.

Of Turkmenistan to the European Union
    Ambassador: Ata Oveznepesovich Serdarov.

Further Reading

Abazov, Rafis, *Historical Dictionary of Turkmenistan.* 2005
National Statistical Office: State Statistical Committee of Turkmenistan, 72 Magtymgyly Ave., Ashgabat 744000.
Website (Turkmen and Russian only): http://www.stat.gov.tm

Tuvalu

Capital: Fongafale
Population projection, 2020: 11,000
GNI per capita, 2017: (PPP$) 5,888
Internet domain extension: .tv

Key Historical Events

Formerly known as the Ellice Islands, Tuvalu is a group of nine islands in the western central Pacific. Joining the British controlled Gilbert Islands Protectorate in 1916, they became the Gilbert and Ellice Islands colony.

After the Japanese occupied the Gilbert Islands in 1942, US forces occupied the Ellice Islands. A referendum held in 1974 produced a large majority in favour of separation from the Gilbert Islands. In 1975 the Ellice Islands were renamed Tuvalu. Independence was achieved on 1 Oct. 1978. Early in 1979 the USA signed a treaty of friendship with Tuvalu and relinquished its claim to the four southern islands in return for the right to veto any other nation's request to use any of Tuvalu's islands for military purposes. In 2011 a state of emergency was declared on two occasions; the first in Jan. as a result of protests and the second in Oct. owing to a shortage of clean drinking water.

Territory and Population

Tuvalu lies between 5° 30' and 11° S. lat. and 176° and 180° E. long. and comprises Nanumea, Nanumaga, Niutao, Nui, Vaitupu, Nukufetau, Funafuti (administrative centre; 2012 census population, 5,879), Nukulaelae and Niulakita. Population (census 2012) 10,640, excluding an estimated 1,500 who were working abroad, mainly in Nauru and Kiribati. Area approximately 26 sq. km (10 sq. miles). Density, 2012, 409 per sq. km.

The UN gives a projected population for 2020 of 11,000.

In 2011, 50·9% of the population lived in urban areas. The population is of a Polynesian race.

The official languages are Tuvaluan and English.

Social Statistics

2005 births (est.), 230; deaths (est.), 60. Infant mortality, 2010, 27 per 1,000 live births. Expectation of life, 2008: males, 64 years; females, 63. Annual population growth rate, 1998–2008, 0·5%; fertility rate, 2008, 3·2 births per woman.

Climate

A pleasant but monotonous climate with temperatures averaging 86°F (30°C), though trade winds from the east moderate conditions for much of the year. Rainfall ranges from 120" (3,000 mm) to over 160" (4,000 mm). Funafuti, Jan. 84°F (28·9°C), July 81°F (27·2°C). Annual rainfall 160" (4,003 mm). Although the islands are north of the recognized hurricane belt they were badly hit by hurricanes in the 1990s, raising fears for the long-term future of Tuvalu as the sea level continues to rise.

Constitution and Government

The Head of State is the British sovereign, represented by an appointed Governor-General. The Constitution provides for a Prime Minister and the cabinet ministers to be elected from among the 15 members of the *Fale I Fono* (*Parliament*).

National Anthem

'Tuvalu mote Atua' ('Tuvalu for the Almighty'); words and tune by A. Manoa.

Recent Elections

Parliamentary elections were held on 31 March 2015. Only non-partisans were elected as there are no political parties. On 10 April 2015 incumbent Enele Sopoaga was sworn in again as prime minister.

Current Government

Governor-General: Sir Iakoba Taeia Italeli (sworn in 16 April 2010 and re-elected 31 March 2015).

In Feb. 2019 the cabinet comprised:

Prime Minister, and Minister of Public Utilities and Infrastructure: Enele Sopoaga; b. 1956 (took office on 5 Aug. 2013).

Deputy Prime Minister, and Minister of Finance and Economic Development: Maatia Toafa.

Minister of Communications and Transport: Monise Laafai. *Education, Youth and Sports:* Fauoa Maani. *Foreign Affairs, Trade, Tourism, Environment and Labour:* Taukelina Finikaso. *Health:* Satini Tulaga Manuella. *Home Affairs and Rural Development:* Namoliki Sualiki Neemia. *Natural Resources:* Puakena Boreham.

Government Website: http://www.tuvaluislands.com/gov_info.htm

Current Leaders

Enele Sopoaga

Position
Prime Minister

Introduction
Enele Sopoaga was sworn in as prime minister on 5 Aug. 2013, ending a constitutional crisis in which his predecessor, Willy Telavi, was dismissed from office by the governor-general. Sopoaga's elder brother, Saufatu, had served as prime minister between 2002 and 2004. Enele was returned for a second term of office following parliamentary elections in March 2015.

Early Life
Born on 10 Feb. 1956, Sopoaga began his civil service career in 1980 in the ministry of social services. Awarded a post-graduate certificate in diplomatic studies by Oxford University in the UK in 1990, he moved to the ministry of foreign affairs in 1992 and became its head. In addition, he served as Tuvalu's ambassador to the UN and as vice chairman of the Alliance of Small Island States (which he represented at the 2009 UN Climate Change Conference in Copenhagen). His reputation as a climate change spokesman was reinforced when he headed the Tuvaluan delegation to the Cancún climate change conference in 2010.

He first stood for election to the non-partisan national parliament at the 2010 general election and was appointed minister of foreign affairs, environment and labour in the government of Maatia Toafa. On 21 Dec. 2010, after Toafa was brought down by a motion of no confidence, Sopoaga challenged for the premiership but was narrowly defeated by Willy Telavi. Installed as leader of the opposition, Sopoaga protested that a culture of censorship existed in the Tuvaluan media, prompting him to set up the *Tala o Matagi* newspaper in 2011.

A political crisis was sparked by the death of the finance minister, Lotoala Metia, in Dec. 2012. Prime Minister Telavi, who no longer commanded a majority, declined to recall parliament on the grounds that he was only legally obliged to convene the house once a year. Responding to calls from the opposition, Governor-General Sir Iakoba Italeli (who represents Queen Elizabeth II, the country's head of state) exercised his reserve powers in forcing parliament to meet and debate a no-confidence motion. Telavi reacted by writing to Queen Elizabeth to inform her that he was dismissing Italeli.

The vote of no confidence nonetheless went ahead on 2 Aug. 2013, with Telavi's government defeated by eight votes to four. On 4 Aug. parliament elected Sopoaga as prime minister and he was sworn in the following day.

Palgrave Macmillan (ed.), *The Statesman's Yearbook 2020*,
https://doi.org/10.1057/978-1-349-95940-2_195

Career in Office

At the Sept. 2013 Pacific Islands Forum summit in Majuro in the Marshall Islands, Sopoaga urged the international community to co-ordinate an effective response to climate change and the threat it poses to low-lying countries including Tuvalu. He was sworn in as prime minister again in April 2015 following elections in March at the head of a cabinet unchanged in key positions. In late 2018 he again stressed the dangers of climate change to his country's future and called upon Australia to block a contentious coal-mining project in the state of Queensland and to make deeper cuts to its carbon emissions.

Economy

Agriculture, forestry and fishing contributed 23·8% to GDP in 2012; followed by finance and real estate, 19·4%; services, 17·2%; public administration and defence, 15·1%; trade, hotels and restaurants, 11·3%.

Overview

With few natural resources, the economy is dependent on revenue derived from the licensing of the '.tv' internet suffix via a US-based company, foreign aid, the sale of tuna fishing licences and interest from the Tuvalu Trust Fund (which was established in 1987 by Australia, New Zealand and the UK). GDP grew in 2011 for the first time since the global financial crisis, while public debt stood at 41% of GDP at end of 2013.

The private sector accounted for about 25% of GDP in 2010. Maritime industries provide most private employment but were badly affected by the global financial crisis and have yet to recover. The IMF has recommended overseas seasonal employment as an alternative for those previously employed at sea. Remittances are the largest source of foreign exchange but they declined from about 30% of GDP in 2001–03 to 10% in 2014. Cyclone Pam devastated much of the country in March 2015, causing an estimated US$10m. worth of damage, equivalent to 30% of GDP. In spite of this the economy grew by 9·1% in 2015.

Climate change, rising sea-levels and the lack of economies of scale pose long-term challenges to prosperity.

Currency

The unit of currency is the Australian *dollar* although Tuvaluan coins up to $A1 are in local circulation. Inflation was 3·5% in 2016 and 4·1% in 2017.

Budget

In 2012 revenues totalled $A32·4m. and expenditures $A30·7m.

Performance

The economy grew by 9·1% in 2015, 3·0% in 2016 and 3·2% in 2017. In 2017 total GDP was US$40m.

Banking and Finance

The Tuvalu National Bank was established at Funafuti in 1980, and is a joint venture between the Tuvalu government and Westpac International. There is also a development bank.

Energy and Natural Resources

Electricity

Installed capacity was an estimated 2,000 kW in 2011; production was around 5m. kWh.

Agriculture

Coconut palms are the main crop. Production of coconuts (2013 estimate), 1,800 tonnes. Fruit and vegetables are grown for local consumption. Livestock, 2014 estimate: pigs, 14,100; chickens, 54,000.

Fisheries

Total catch, 2011, 11,093 tonnes. A seamount was discovered in Tuvaluan waters in 1991 and is a good location for deep-sea fish. The sale of fishing licences to American, Japanese, New Zealand, South Korean and Taiwanese fleets provides a significant source of income, in some years contributing up to 50% of total government revenue.

Industry

Small amounts of copra, handicrafts and garments are produced.

International Trade

Imports and Exports

Main sources of income are copra, stamps, handicrafts and remittances from Tuvaluans abroad. 2007 imports, $A18·5m.; 2007 exports, $A0·1m. Leading import suppliers are Australia, China and Japan. Significant export destinations are Australia, India and Indonesia.

Communications

Roads

In 2013 there were just 8 km of roads.

Civil Aviation

In 2010 Air Pacific operated two flights a week from Funafuti International to Suva in Fiji.

Shipping

Funafuti is the only port and a deep-water wharf was opened in 1980. In Jan. 2014 there were 86 ships of 300 GT or over registered, totalling 1·10m. GT. Of the 86 vessels registered, 39 were oil tankers, 28 general cargo ships, 15 bulk carriers, two passenger ships and there was one container ship and one liquid gas tanker. Tuvalu is a 'flag of convenience' country.

Telecommunications

In 2013 there were approximately 1,450 main telephone lines in operation. There were an estimated 3,400 mobile phone subscriptions, and some 37·0% of the population used the internet that year.

Social Institutions

Justice

There is a High Court presided over by the Chief Justice of Fiji. A Court of Appeal is constituted if required. There are also eight Island Courts with limited jurisdiction.

Education

There were 1,872 pupils at ten primary schools in 2014 and 750 pupils at two secondary schools. Education is free and compulsory from the ages of six to 15. There is a Maritime Training School at Funafuti, and the University of the South Pacific, based in Fiji, has an extension centre at Funafuti.

In 2012 the education budget represented 1·2% of GDP.

Health

In 2015 there was one central hospital situated at Funafuti and clinics on each of the other inhabited islands. Over the period 2006–13 there were 1·1 physicians for every 1,000 population, 5·8 nursing and midwifery personnel per 1,000 population and 0·4 dentistry personnel per 1,000.

In *Water: At What Cost? The State of the World's Water 2016*, WaterAid reported that 2·3% of the population does not have access to safe water.

Religion

The majority of the population are Protestants who are members of the Congregational Christian Church of Tuvalu (also known as the Church of Tuvalu). There are also small numbers of Roman Catholics, Seventh-day Adventists, Jehovah's Witnesses, Bahá'ís, Muslims and Latter-day Saints (Mormons).

Culture

Press

The Government Broadcasting and Information Division produces *Tuvalu Echoes*, a fortnightly publication, and *Te Lama*, a monthly religious publication.

Tourism

There were 1,232 visitor arrivals in 2011, down from a record 1,665 in 2008.

Diplomatic Representatives

Of Tuvalu in the United Kingdom (Tuvalu House, 230 Worple Rd, London, SW20 8RH)

Honorary Consul: Sir Iftikhar A. Ayaz.

Of the United Kingdom in Tuvalu
High Commissioner: Melanie Hopkins (resides in Suva, Fiji).

Of Tuvalu in the USA and to the United Nations (800 Second Ave., Suite 400D, New York, NY 10017)
Ambassador: Samuelu Laloniu.

Of the USA in Tuvalu
Ambassador: Vacant.
Chargé d'Affaires a.i.: Michael Goldman (resides in Suva, Fiji).

Of Tuvalu to the European Union
Ambassador: Aunese Makoi Simati.

Further Reading

Bennetts, P. and Wheeler, T., *Time and Tide: The Islands of Tuvalu.* 2001
National Statistical Office: Ministry of Finance and Economic Planning, Private Bag, Vaiaku, Funafuti.
Website: http://tuvalu.prism.spc.int

Uganda

Jamhuri ya Uganda (Republic of Uganda)

Capital: Kampala
Population projection, 2020: 47·19m.
GNI per capita, 2017: (PPP$) 1,658
HDI/world rank, 2017: 0·516/162
Internet domain extension: .ug

Key Historical Events

Bantu-speaking mixed farmers first migrated into southwest Uganda from the west around 500 BC. There is evidence that they smelted iron for tools and weapons. In the following centuries Nilotic-speaking pastoralists entered northern Uganda from the upper Nile valley (now southern Sudan). By AD 1300 several kingdoms (the Chwezi states) had been established in southern Uganda. In 1500 Nilotic-speaking Luo people invaded the Chwezi states and established the kingdoms of Buganda, Bunyoro and Ankole. At this time, northern Uganda became home to the Alur and Acholi ethnic groups. During the 17th century Bunyoro was southern Uganda's most powerful state, controlling an area that stretched into present-day Rwanda and Tanzania. From about 1700 the kingdom of Buganda expanded (largely at the expense of Bunyoro), and a century later it dominated a large territory bordering Lake Victoria from the Victoria Nile to the Kagera River. The *kabaka* (king) maintained a large court and a powerful army and traded in cattle, ivory and slaves.

Arab traders from Zanzibar on Africa's east coast reached Lake Victoria by 1844. A prominent trader, Ahmad bin Ibrahim, introduced the kabaka to foreign trade; imported cloth and firearms were exchanged for ivory and slaves. Ibrahim also introduced Islam to the region. In 1862 John Speke, a British explorer who was attempting to find the source of the Nile, became the first European to visit Buganda, by then a highly developed state supported by an army of more than 150,000 and a navy.

He met with Kabaka Mutesa I; as did Henry Stanley, who reached Buganda in 1875. Mutesa, fearful of attacks from Egypt, agreed to Stanley's proposal to allow Christian missionaries to enter his realm. Members of the British Protestant Church Missionary Society arrived in 1877 and were followed two years later by representatives of the French Roman Catholic White Fathers. Both were successful in attracting converts but by the 1880s they were in fierce competition. Trade with the Indian Ocean ports continued, bringing with it greater Islamic influence.

Mutesa was succeeded by Mwanga in 1884. He was wary of the new foreign ideologies and attempted to halt their spread but was deposed by Christian and Muslim converts in 1888. He was later reinstated but with considerably reduced power and influence. In 1889 Mwanga was visited by Carl Peters, a German doctor, and the kabaka subsequently signed a treaty of friendship with Germany. Britain was concerned by the growth of German influence and the potential threat to its position on the Nile. In 1890 the two European powers signed a treaty giving Britain rights to what was to become Uganda and giving Germany control over land to the southeast (now Tanzania). Frederick Lugard, acting as an agent of the Imperial British East Africa Company (IBEA), arrived in Buganda with a detachment of troops and in 1892 he backed Protestant converts in an attack on the French Catholic mission.

British Rule

In 1894 Britain made Uganda a protectorate. Allying with the Protestant Baganda chiefs, the British set about conquering the rest of the country, assisted by Nubian mercenary troops, formerly in the service of the khedive of Egypt. The British deposed Mwanga and replaced him with his infant son Daudi Chwa. Bunyoro had been spared the religious civil wars of Buganda and was firmly united by its king, Kabarega. Following five years of conflict, the British occupied Bunyoro and conquered Acholi and the northern region. Other African chiefdoms, such as Ankole in the southwest, signed treaties with the British, as did the chiefdoms of Busoga. In 1900 an agreement was signed between the British administration under Sir Harry Johnston and Buganda, giving the kingdom considerable autonomy and transforming it into a constitutional monarchy controlled largely by Protestant chiefs. Half of Bunyoro's conquered territory was also awarded to Buganda, including the historic heartland of the kingdom containing several royal tombs. Buganda doubled in size from ten to 20 counties (*sazas*), but the 'lost counties' of Bunyoro remained a grievance.

Economic Development

In 1901 a railway from Mombasa on the Indian Ocean reached Kisumu, on Lake Victoria, connected by boat with Uganda. The railway was later extended to Kampala. The railway had cost far more than was anticipated and the British, anxious for a return on their investment, turned to cotton to provide raw materials for British mills. Buganda, with its strategic location on the north shore of Lake Victoria, reaped the benefits of cotton growing; it soon became the major export crop and made the Buganda kingdom relatively prosperous. Coffee and sugar production accelerated in the 1920s. The country attracted few permanent European settlers and the cash crops were mostly produced by African smallholders, rather than the plantation system used in other colonies. Many South Asians were encouraged to settle in Uganda, where they played a leading role in the country's commerce. In 1921 a legislative council for the protectorate was established (although its first African member was admitted only in 1945).

The colonial government regulated the buying and processing of cash crops, setting prices and reserving the role of intermediary for Asians, who were thought to be more efficient. The British and Asians repelled African attempts to break into cotton ginning, leading to resentment among the Baganda. In addition, on the Asian-owned sugar plantations established in the 1920s, labour for sugarcane and other cash crops was increasingly provided by migrants from the fringes of Uganda and beyond. In 1949 discontented Baganda rioted and burned down the houses of pro-government chiefs in Kampala. The rioters had three demands: the right to bypass government price controls on the sales of cotton, the removal of the Asian monopoly over cotton ginning, and the right to have their own representatives in local government. They were also critical of the young kabaka, Frederick Walugembe Mutesa II. The British governor, Sir John Hall, regarded the riots as the work of communist-inspired agitators such as the Uganda African Farmers Union (UAFU), founded by I. K. Musazi in 1947. The UAFU was banned and none of the requested reforms were implemented. Musazi's Uganda National Congress replaced the UAFU in 1952 but remained a discussion group rather than an organized political party.

Meanwhile, the British began to prepare for an independent Uganda. Britain's post-war withdrawal from India, nationalism in West Africa and a more liberal philosophy all had an effect. Sir Andrew Cohen was installed as governor in 1952 and pursued economic and political reforms: removing obstacles to African cotton ginning, encouraging co-operatives, establishing the Uganda Development Corporation and reorganizing the Legislative Council to include Africans elected from districts across the country for the first time. There was also talk of a future federation of east African territories (Kenya, Uganda and Tanganyika). However, there was resistance among the Baganda, who feared the erosion of their power-base. Mutesa II refused to co-operate with Cohen's plan for an integrated Buganda. Cohen deported him to exile in London, setting off a storm of protest. Two year later Mutesa II was reinstated, officially as a constitutional monarch, but in reality having considerable political clout. In 1960 a political organizer from Lango, Milton Obote, formed a new party, the Uganda People's Congress (UPC), as a coalition of all those who opposed Buganda dominance (apart from the Catholic-dominated Democratic Party (DP)).

Independence

On 9 Oct. 1962 Uganda became independent, with Obote as prime minister and the kabaka as head of state. Buganda was given considerable autonomy. In 1963 Uganda became a republic and Mutesa II was elected president. The first years of independence were dominated by a struggle between the central government and Buganda. In 1966 Obote introduced a new constitution that

Palgrave Macmillan (ed.), *The Statesman's Yearbook 2020*,
https://doi.org/10.1057/978-1-349-95940-2_196

ended Buganda's autonomy and restored the 'lost counties' to the Bunyoro. Obote then captured the kabaka's palace at Mengo and forced the kabaka to flee the country. In 1967 a new constitution was introduced giving the central government—especially the president—greater power and dividing Buganda into four districts. The traditional kingships were also abolished (in the case of Buganda retroactive to 1966). The 1960s saw a steady build-up of military power in Uganda, under Major Gen. Idi Amin Dada.

In Jan. 1971 Obote was deposed in a coup by Idi Amin. Amin was faced with opposition within the army by officers and troops loyal to Obote but by the end of 1971 he was in firm control. In 1972 he ordered Asians who were not citizens of Uganda to leave the country and within three months all 60,000 had left, most of them for Britain. Their expulsion hit the Ugandan economy hard. Amin's rule became increasingly dictatorial and brutal; it is estimated that over 300,000 Ugandans were killed during the 1970s. His corrupt administration led to divisions in the military and a number of coup attempts. Israel conducted a successful raid on the Entebbe airport in 1976 to rescue passengers on a plane hijacked by Palestinian terrorists. Amin's expulsion of Israeli technicians won him the support of Arab nations such as Libya.

In 1976 Amin declared himself president for life and two years later he invaded Tanzania in an attempt to annex the Kagera region. The following year Tanzania launched a successful counter-invasion, unifying anti-Amin forces under the Uganda National Liberation Front (UNLF). Amin's forces were driven out and he fled to exile in Saudi Arabia. Tanzania left an occupation force in Uganda. Yusufu Lule was installed as president but was quickly replaced by Godfrey Binaisa, who was then overthrown in a military coup on 10 May 1980, headed by Paulo Muwanga. Shortly after the Muwanga 1980 coup, Obote made a triumphant return from Tanzania and rallied his former UPC supporters. His main opponents were the DP, led by Paul Kawanga Ssemogerere. The DP were announced as winners on 10 Dec. 1980 but Muwanga seized control of the Electoral Commission and announced a UPC victory 18 hours later, verified by the Commonwealth Observer Group.

In Feb. 1981, shortly after the new Obote government took office, with Paulo Muwanga as vice-president and minister of defence, a former Military Commission member, Yoweri Museveni, and his armed supporters declared themselves the National Resistance Army (NRA). Museveni vowed to overthrow Obote by means of a popular rebellion, and what became known as 'the war in the bush' began. Approximately 200,000 Ugandans sought refuge in neighbouring Rwanda, Zaïre and Sudan. In 1985 a military coup deposed Obote and Lieut.-Gen. Tito Okello became head of state. When it was not given a role in the new regime, the NRA continued its guerrilla campaign. It took Kampala in 1986 and Museveni became the new president. He concentrated on rebuilding the ruined economy by cutting back the army and civil service and reforming agriculture and industry. In 1993 Museveni permitted the restoration of traditional kings, including Ronald Muwenda Mutebi II as kabaka. In May 1996 Museveni was returned to office in the country's first direct presidential elections. A new parliament, chosen in elections in June, was dominated by Museveni supporters.

Museveni was re-elected in March 2001, following a period of relative stability and economic growth. However, his popularity was diminished by discontent with Uganda's intervention in civil war in the Democratic Republic of the Congo (formerly Zaïre) and signs of corruption in the government. Uganda's forces were largely withdrawn from the Democratic Republic of the Congo by the end of 2002. In 2005 the International Court in The Hague ordered Uganda to pay compensation to the DRC for its activities there between 1998 and 2003.

In Feb. 2006 Museveni won a new presidential term. In July 2006 peace talks commenced between the government and the Lord's Resistance Army (LRA), a fanatically religious group led by Joseph Kony that has terrorized northern Uganda for many years. A ceasefire was declared in Aug. 2006 but subsequent talks have been marred by disputes and walkouts.

Territory and Population

Uganda is bounded in the north by South Sudan, in the east by Kenya, in the south by Tanzania and Rwanda, and the west by the Democratic Republic of the Congo. Total area 241,551 sq. km, including 41,740 sq. km of inland waters.

The 2014 census population was 34,634,650 (17,060,832 males, 17,573,818 females); density, 143·4 per sq. km. The largest city is Kampala, the capital (census population of 1,507,080 in 2014). Other major towns are Nansana, Kira, Makindye Ssabagabo, Mbarara, Mukono and Gulu. In 2011, 13·5% of the population lived in urban areas.

The UN gives a projected population for 2020 of 47·19m.

The country is administratively divided into one city and 111 districts, which are grouped in four geographical regions (which do not have administrative status). Area and population of the regions at the census of 2014:

Region	Area in sq. km	2014 population (in 1,000)
Central Region	61,403	9,529·2
Eastern Region	39,479	9,042·4
Northern Region	85,392	7,188·1
Western Region	55,277	8,874·9

The official languages are English and (since 2005) Kiswahili. About 70% of the population speak Bantu languages; Nilotic languages are spoken in the north and east.

Social Statistics

2008 estimates: births, 1,461,000; deaths, 401,000. Rates, 2008 estimates (per 1,000 population): births, 46·2; deaths, 12·7. Uganda has one of the youngest populations of any country, with 76% of the population under the age of 30 and 48% under 15. Uganda's life expectancy at birth in 2013 was 58·0 years for males and 60·4 years for females. Life expectancy declined dramatically until the late 1990s, largely owing to the huge number of people in the country with HIV. However, for both males and females expectation of life is now starting to rise again. Annual population growth rate, 2000–08, 3·2%. Infant mortality, 2010, 63 per 1,000 live births; fertility rate, 2008, 6·3 births per woman.

Climate

Although in equatorial latitudes, the climate is more tropical because of its elevation, and is characterized by two distinct rainy seasons, March–May and Sept.–Nov. In comparison, June–Aug. and Dec.–Feb. are relatively dry. Temperatures vary little over the year. Kampala, Jan. 74°F (23·3°C), July 70°F (21·1°C). Annual rainfall 46·5" (1,180 mm). Entebbe, Jan. 72°F (22·2°C), July 69°F (20·6°C). Annual rainfall 63·9" (1,624 mm).

Constitution and Government

The *President* is head of state and head of government, and is elected for a five-year term by adult suffrage. In Aug. 2005 Parliament amended the constitution to allow an incumbent to hold office for more than two terms, thus enabling President Museveni to serve another term in office. Having lapsed in 1966, the kabakaship was revived as a ceremonial office in 1993. Ronald Muwenda Mutebi (b. 13 April 1955) was crowned Mutebi II, 36th Kabaka, on 31 July 1993.

Until 1994 the national legislature was the 278-member National Resistance Council, but this was replaced by a 284-member *Constituent Assembly* in March 1994. A new constitution was adopted on 8 Oct. 1995 and the Constituent Assembly dissolved. Uganda's unicameral *Parliament* now consists of 465 members (422 members directly elected, 25 indirectly elected from special interest groups—including women and the army—and 18 non-voting *ex officio* members appointed by the President). A referendum on the return of multi-party democracy was held on 29 June 2000, but 88% of voters supported President Museveni's 'no-party' Movement system of government. Turnout was 51%. In Feb. 2003 President Museveni pledged to lift the ban on political parties. In a referendum held on 28 July 2005, 92·4% of voters backed the restoration of a multi-party political system, although the opposition called for a boycott. Formerly the constitution limited the president to two terms but in July 2005 parliament voted to lift the restriction on the number of times that the president may be re-elected.

National Anthem

'Oh, Uganda, may God uphold thee'; words and tune by G. W. Kakoma.

Recent Elections

Presidential elections were held on 18 Feb. 2016. President Museveni was re-elected winning 60·6% of votes cast, with his main rival, Kizza Besigye, receiving 35·6% of the vote. There were six other candidates. Turnout was 67·6%.

Parliamentary elections were held on the same day. The National Resistance Movement won 279 seats, the Forum for Democratic Change 34, the Democratic Party 11, Uganda People's Congress 9 and the Conservative Party and the Justice Forum both gained one seat each. 37 seats went to independents. Turnout was 59·3%.

Current Government

President: Yoweri K. Museveni; b. 1944 (sworn in 27 Jan. 1986 and re-elected in 1996, 2001, 2006, 2011 and 2016).

In Feb. 2019 the government comprised:

Vice-President: Edward Kiwanuka Ssekandi; b. 1943 (sworn in 24 May 2011).

Prime Minister: Ruhakana Rugunda; b. 1949 (sworn in 18 Sept. 2014).

First Deputy Prime Minister and Deputy Leader of Government Business in Parliament: Moses Ali. *Second Deputy Prime Minister and Minister of East African Affairs:* Kirunda Kivejinja.

Minister of Agriculture, Animal Industry and Fisheries: Vincent Ssempijja. *Defence and Veterans' Affairs:* Adolf Mwesige. *Disaster Preparedness and Refugees:* Hilary Onek. *Education and Sports:* Janet Kataaha Museveni. *Energy and Minerals:* Irene Muloni. *Finance and Economic Affairs:* Matia Kasaija. *Foreign Affairs:* Sam Kutesa. *Gender, Labour and Social Affairs:* Janat Mukwaya. *Health:* Jane Aceng. *Information, ICT and Communications:* Frank Tumwebaze. *Internal Affairs:* Jeje Odongo. *Justice and Constitutional Affairs:* Kahinda Otafiire. *Kampala City Authority:* Betty Kamya. *Karamoja Affairs:* John Byabagambi. *Lands, Housing and Urban Development:* Betty Amongi. *Local Development:* Tom Butime. *Presidency:* Esther Mbulakubuza Mbayo. *Public Service:* Muruli Mukasa. *Science, Technology and Innovation:* Elioda Tumwesigye. *Security:* Gen. Elly Tumwine. *Tourism, Wildlife and Antiquities:* Ephraim Kamuntu. *Trade, Industry and Co-operatives:* Amelia Kyambadde. *Water and Environment:* Sam Cheptoris. *Works and Transport:* Monica Azuba Ntege. *Minister in Charge of General Duties in the Office of the Prime Minister:* Mary Karooro Okurut. *Minister without Portfolio:* Hajji Nadduli. *Attorney General:* William Byaruhanga. *Government Chief Whip:* Ruth Nankabirwa.

Government Website: http://www.gou.go.ug

Current Leaders

Yoweri Museveni

Position
President

Introduction
Yoweri Museveni became president of Uganda in 1986 and has been largely credited with transforming the country's economy after the years of misrule by Idi Amin Dada and Milton Obote. He won the first direct presidential elections in 1996 and was re-elected in 2001. In July 2005 a national referendum approved the lifting of restrictions on multi-party politics (in force since Museveni came to power) and the National Assembly abolished a constitutional limit on presidential terms. He won further terms in Feb. 2006, Feb. 2011 and Feb. 2016.

Early Life
Yoweri Kaguta Museveni was born in 1944 in Ankole, western Uganda, where he attended Mbarara High School and Ntare School. He studied economics and political science at the University of Dar es Salaam, Tanzania, graduating in 1970. While at university Museveni was politically active and became the chairman of a leftist student group linked to African liberation movements. In 1971 Idi Amin Dada came to power in Uganda and Museveni went back to Tanzania. He was a founder of the Front for National Salvation, one of the rebel groups that overthrew Amin in 1979. Museveni held various ministerial posts before running for president in 1980. Defeated by Milton Obote, he formed the National Resistance Army, which took power on 26 Jan. 1986 when Museveni declared himself president and minister of defence.

Career in Office
For much of his presidency, Museveni has been favoured by Western nations and foreign aid donors for opening up the Ugandan economy and reducing poverty. Primary school education increased markedly and, thanks to anti-AIDS campaigns, he has succeeded in reducing HIV levels. However, Museveni's image has been tarnished internationally by Ugandan military

interference in neighbouring Democratic Republic of the Congo and by human rights concerns.

After coming to power, Museveni claimed that political parties divided poor countries like Uganda into ethnic, religious and tribal groups. His preferred system therefore had individuals competing for political office on individual merit. However, after 2001 calls for a return to multi-party democracy in Uganda became more persistent, and this was approved in a national referendum in July 2005, although the turnout was low. Museveni's government nevertheless supported the restoration. Parliament meanwhile voted to lift the constitutional limit on the office of president. Museveni stood for re-election in Feb. 2006 and won a further term with almost 60% of the vote.

In Oct. 2005 Kizza Besigye—Museveni's main opposition rival in the 2001 presidential poll which had been tainted by violence—returned to Uganda from exile in South Africa to contest the 2006 elections. His subsequent arrest for treason provoked violent street protests before his release on bail in Jan. 2006. Meanwhile, concern over alleged human rights abuses by Museveni's government led the UK and other European countries to suspend direct development aid in Dec. 2005. Britain later agreed to resume aid in Nov. 2007 at the biennial Commonwealth Heads of Government conference hosted by Museveni in Kampala.

In July 2006 the government opened peace talks with the rebel Lord's Resistance Army (LRA), which has conducted an insurgency in northern Uganda since the 1980s involving atrocities against the local population. A truce was signed in Aug. that year, but subsequent political progress was limited amid reported divisions within the LRA itself. In early 2008 the LRA announced that its leader, Joseph Kony, was ready to sign a peace agreement. Optimism proved unfounded, however, leading to a new offensive in Dec. against the rebels by troops from Uganda, Sudan and the Democratic Republic of the Congo. In Jan. 2009 the LRA called for a new ceasefire and in March Ugandan troops ended their offensive. Museveni's government claimed that the campaign had seriously hampered LRA capabilities and also rescued many kidnap victims. However, the LRA, and more recently the rebel Allied Democratic Forces (which also violently oppose Museveni), have remained destabilizing forces in Uganda and neighbouring countries.

Following the announcement in Jan. 2009 of a significant oil discovery in Uganda by a British exploration company, Museveni said that the income from the oil could transform the country's economy and development. Subsequent allegations of bribery in the award of oil contracts led parliament to suspend new oil deals in Oct. 2011 and Museveni to publicly reject claims that government ministers were engaged in corrupt practices. At the same time, however, Sam Kutesa resigned as foreign minister ahead of an investigation (although he was reinstated in Aug. 2012).

In Sept. 2009 there were riots in Kampala by supporters of Ronald Mutebi, the king of Buganda (one of five ancient kingdoms that had been restored by Museveni) and leader of Uganda's largest ethnic group. Tensions between Museveni's government and Buganda grew when parliament passed new land legislation that the king had opposed because it eroded his ownership rights.

In Dec. 2009 the National Resistance Movement endorsed Museveni as its candidate for the presidential election in Feb. 2011. He secured a further term, taking 68% of the vote, but Kizza Besigye, his main challenger again, rejected the result amid claims of vote-rigging. In April and May Besigye organized opposition protests in Kampala, partly in reaction to rising food and fuel prices, but they were met with a heavy-handed response by security forces and Besigye himself was attacked and injured.

In late 2012 there were further allegations from the United Nations of Ugandan support for rebel forces opposed to the Kabila regime in the Democratic Republic of the Congo. In Nov. the Ugandan government responded by declaring that its troops would be withdrawn from UN-sponsored peacekeeping missions. Museveni did, however, sign a UN-brokered international accord in Feb. 2013 pledging non-interference in its neighbour's affairs.

In Dec. 2013 the Ugandan parliament passed legislation toughening penalties, to include life imprisonment, for homosexual behaviour. Museveni ratified the bill in Feb. 2014 despite international criticism and cuts in aid funding, but in Aug. that year the constitutional court ruled the law null and void.

In Sept. 2014 Museveni sacked Prime Minister Amama Mbabazi amid reported divisions within the National Resistance Movement and replaced him with Ruhakana Rugunda, previously the health minister. Mbabazi, along with veteran presidential candidate Besigye, subsequently stood unsuccessfully against Museveni in the elections held in Feb. 2016, when the president secured another landslide victory amid opposition and international concerns over polling transparency. In Jan. 2018 the 73-year-old Museveni signed into law a controversial and unpopular bill removing from the constitution the age limit of 75 for candidates in presidential elections, therefore allowing him to stand again in 2021 and possibly to retain the office for life.

Defence

Defence expenditure in 2013 totalled US$342m. (US$10 per capita), representing 1·6% of GDP.

Army

The Uganda People's Defence Forces (UPDF) had a strength estimated at 40,000–45,000 in 2011. There is a Border Defence Unit about 600-strong and local defence units estimated at 10,000.

Navy

There is a Marine unit of the police (about 400-strong in 2011).

Air Force

In 2011 the UPDF Air Wing operated 14 combat-capable aircraft (although the serviceability of some was in doubt) and one attack helicopter. There was also a police air wing around 800-strong.

International Relations

In Nov. 1999 Uganda, Tanzania and Kenya created a new East African Community to develop East African trade, tourism and industry and to lay the foundations for a future common market and political federation.

Economy

In 2016 agriculture accounted for 25·8% of GDP, industry 22·5% and services 51·7%.

Overview

Uganda experienced a period of consistent growth from 1987–2010 as a result of pro-market structural reforms implemented against a backdrop of relative political stability after years of civil strife. Real GDP grew at an annual average of 7% throughout the 1990s and into the 2000s. Even given increasing domestic economic volatility in the decade to 2015, growth remained at an annual average of 6%. However, the struggling global economy in this period reduced demand for Ugandan exports, with the oil sector suffering particularly badly despite the benefits of improved industry infrastructure.

To attain long-term prosperity and to address the country's wealth disparity (with poverty prevalent in the Northern region), the government must address comparatively low levels of economic productivity, while also improving infrastructure (in particular, confronting chaotic urban development) and increasing access to credit.

Currency

The monetary unit is the *Uganda shilling* (UGX) notionally divided into 100 *cents*. In 1987 the currency was devalued by 77% and a new 'heavy' shilling was introduced worth 100 old shillings. Inflation was 5·5% in 2016 and 5·6% in 2017. Foreign exchange reserves in June 2005 were US$1,326m. Total money supply in July 2005 was Shs 1,513·0bn.

Budget

The financial year runs from 1 July–30 June. Budgetary central government revenues in 2015–16 were Shs 12,647bn. and expenditures Shs 11,567bn. Main sources of revenue in 2015–16 were: taxes on goods and services, Shs 5,989bn.; taxes on income, profits and capital gains, Shs 3,810bn.; taxes on international trade and transactions, Shs 1,320bn. Main items of expenditure by economic type in 2015–16: grants, Shs 4,085bn.; use of goods and services, Shs 3,397bn.; compensation of employees, Shs 1,970bn.

VAT is 18%.

Performance

Real GDP growth was 5·7% in 2015, 2·3% in 2016 and 4·8% in 2017. Between 2001 and 2011 Uganda's economy grew at more than 5% every year. Uganda's total GDP in 2017 was US$25·9bn.

Banking and Finance

The Bank of Uganda (*Governor*, Emmanuel Tumusiime Mutebile) was established in 1966 and is the central bank and bank of issue. In addition there are five foreign, six commercial and two development banks. There is also the state-owned Uganda Development Bank, which is scheduled for eventual privatization.

External debt totalled US$2,994m. in 2010, representing 17·9% of GNI.

Energy and Natural Resources

Environment

Uganda's carbon dioxide emissions from the consumption of energy were the equivalent of 0·1 tonnes per capita in 2011.

Electricity

Installed capacity in 2011 was 0·6m. kW, about 76% of which was provided by the Owen Falls Extension Project (a hydro-electric scheme). Production (2011 estimate) 2·59bn. kWh. Per capita consumption (2011 estimate) 72 kWh.

Oil and Gas

Oil was first discovered in Uganda in 2006. There was a further major find in 2009, when the Jobi-Rii oil field was considered to be the largest onshore discovery in sub-Saharan Africa in over 20 years. Reserves have been estimated at 2·5bn. bbls. Production was expected to begin in 2012 but it is now not forecast to start until 2021.

Minerals

In Nov. 1997 extraction started on the first of an estimated US$400m. worth of cobalt from pyrites. Tungsten and tin concentrates are also mined. There are also significant quantities of clay and gypsum.

Agriculture

80% of the workforce is involved with agriculture. In 2007 the agricultural area included an estimated 5·5m. ha. of arable land and about 2·2m. ha. of permanent crops. Agriculture is one of the priority areas for increased production, with many projects funded both locally and externally. It contributes 90% of exports. Production (2013) in 1,000 tonnes: plantains, 4,375; sugarcane (estimate), 3,350; cassava, 2,979; maize, 2,748; sweet potatoes, 1,811; dry beans, 941; bananas (estimate), 562; sorghum, 299; onions (estimate), 298; groundnuts, 295; sunflower seeds, 238. Coffee is the mainstay of the economy, accounting for more than 50% of the annual commodity export revenue. Coffee production has more than doubled since 1990. Uganda is the world's leading producer of plantains.

Livestock (2013): goats, 14·6m.; cattle, 13·0m.; pigs (estimate), 2·5m.; sheep (estimate), 2·0m.; chickens, 32m. Livestock products, 2013 estimates (in 1,000 tonnes): milk, 1,504; meat, 455.

Forestry

In 2015 the area under forests was 2·08m. ha., or 10% of the total land area. Exploitable forests consist almost entirely of hardwoods. Timber production in 2011 totalled 44·39m. cu. metres. Uganda has great potential for timber-processing for export, manufacture of high-quality furniture and wood products, and various packaging materials.

Fisheries

In 2015 fish landings totalled 396,205 tonnes, entirely from inland waters. Fish farming (especially catfish and tilapia) is a fast-growing industry, with production having increased from 5,539 tonnes in 2004 to 76,654 tonnes in 2009. Exports of fishery commodities, valued at US$109m. in 2009, are now one of Uganda's leading foreign currency earners.

Industry

Production (in 1,000 tonnes): cement (2013), 2,023; sugar (2012), 315; beer (2012), 254·5m. litres. In 2013–14 industry accounted for 26·3% of GDP, with manufacturing contributing 7·7%. Industrial production grew by 5·6% in 2013–14.

Labour

The labour force in 2013 was 14,589,000 (10,709,000 in 2003). 78·1% of the population aged 15–64 was economically active in 2013. In the same year 4·2% of the population was unemployed.

Uganda had 0·25m. people living in slavery according to the Walk Free Foundation's 2013 *Global Slavery Index*.

International Trade

Imports and Exports

In 2010 imports (c.i.f.) amounted to US$4,664·3m. (US$4,247·4m. in 2009); exports (f.o.b.) US$1,618·6m. (US$1,567·6m. in 2009). Coffee, fish and fish products are the principal exports. Major imports are machinery and transport equipment, and food, beverages and tobacco products. The main import suppliers in 2006 were Kenya (15·7%), UAE (12·7%) and India (8·2%). In 2006 the main export markets were UAE (19·4%), Sudan (9·5%) and Kenya (9·1%).

Communications

Roads

The road network totals around 140,000 km (4% paved). In 2014 Uganda had 20,544 km of national roads. There were 81,300 passenger cars in use in 2007, 79,300 lorries and vans, 40,500 buses and coaches, and 176,500 motorcycles and mopeds. In 2007 there were 17,428 road accidents resulting in 2,779 deaths.

In 2007 the government established the Uganda Road Fund, a body responsible for financing road maintenance. The estimated budget in 2007–08 totalled US$111·35m.

Rail

In 2005 the railway network totalled 1,241 km (metre gauge). In 1996 passenger services were suspended and have not been reinstated in the meantime. Freight tonne-km in 2015 came to 189m.

Civil Aviation

There is an international airport at Entebbe, 40 km from Kampala. Air Uganda, formed in 2007, was the national airline until July 2014. It ceased operations when the issuer of its air operator's certificate, the Ugandan Civil Aviation Authority, failed an audit carried out by the International Civil Aviation Organization. In 2012 scheduled airline traffic of Uganda-based carriers flew 3·8m. km; passenger-km totalled 444·9m. in the same year.

Telecommunications

In June 2013 there were 207,500 main (fixed) telephone lines; mobile phone subscriptions numbered 16,569,000 in June 2013 (44·1 per 100 persons). In 2013 an estimated 16·2% of the population were internet users. In June 2012 there were 415,000 Facebook users.

Social Institutions

Out of 178 countries analysed in the 2017 *Fragile States Index*—a list published jointly by the Fund for Peace and *Foreign Policy* magazine—Uganda was ranked the 24th most vulnerable to conflict or collapse. The index is based on 12 indicators of state vulnerability across social, political and economic categories.

Justice

The Supreme Court of Uganda, presided over by the Chief Justice, is the highest court. There are a Court of Appeal and a High Court below that. Subordinate courts, presided over by Chief Magistrates and Magistrates of the first, second and third grade, are established in all areas: jurisdiction varies with the grade of Magistrate. Chief and first-grade Magistrates are professionally qualified; second- and third-grade Magistrates are trained to diploma level at the Law Development Centre, Kampala. Chief Magistrates exercise supervision over and hear appeals from second- and third-grade courts, and village courts.

The population in penal institutions in Aug. 2010 was 30,312 (89 per 100,000 of national population). The death penalty is still in force. There were two executions in 2006 but none since. The International Centre for Prison Studies estimated in 2014 that 55·0% of prisoners had yet to receive a trial. In 2015 the World Justice Project *Rule of Law Index*, which provides data on how the rule of law is experienced by the general public across eight categories, ranked Uganda 80th of 102 countries for criminal justice and 68th for civil justice.

Education

In 2011 there were 8,098,177 pupils and 169,503 teaching staff at primary schools. 67·5% of primary schools were government-aided in 2013 and 32·5% private. There were 1,175,648 students and an estimated 63,400 teaching staff at secondary schools in 2008. In 2013 tertiary institutions included five public universities, 29 private universities, and 61 business and commerce institutions (of which 56 were private). Uganda had 289,545 students in tertiary education in 2011 and 5,724 academic staff. In 2013 there were 34,694 students at colleges of commerce and business studies and related study centres with 1,918 lecturers and tutors, and 8,056 students at teachers' colleges with 326 lecturers and tutors. The adult literacy rate was 71·4% in 2006 (81·4% among males and 62·1% among females).

School attendance has trebled since Yoweri Museveni became president in 1986. In 1997 free primary education was introduced, initially for four children in every family; in 2003 this was extended to cover all children. In 2008–09 public expenditure on education came to 3·2% of GDP and 15·0% of total government spending.

Health

In 2012–13 there were 148 public hospitals, 5,077 public health centres and 112 public district health offices. There were 1,488 private health care facilities in 2012–13. In 2015 there were 4,811 physicians, and 55,206 nurses and midwives. Uganda has had significant success in the fight against AIDS. A climate of free debate, with President Museveni recognizing the threat as early as 1986 and making every government department take the problem seriously, resulted in HIV prevalence among adults declining from approximately 13% in the early 1990s to 7% in 2012.

In *Water: At What Cost? The State of the World's Water 2016*, WaterAid reported that 21·0% of the population does not have access to safe water.

Religion

According to the Pew Research Center's Forum on Religion & Public Life the population was 86·7% Christian in 2010, with Muslims accounting for 9·1%. Of the Christians, 51% in 2010 were Protestants and 49% Catholics. In Feb. 2019 there was one Roman Catholic cardinal.

Culture

World Heritage Sites

Uganda has three sites on the UNESCO World Heritage List: Bwindi Impenetrable National Park (inscribed on the list in 1994); Rwenzori Mountains National Park (1994); and the Tombs of the Buganda Kings at Kasubi (2001).

Press

There were five daily newspapers in 2008 with a combined average daily circulation of 110,000.

Tourism

In 2011 there were 1,151,000 international tourist arrivals (excluding day-visitors); spending by tourists totalled US$950m.

Festivals

Cultural festivals include Martyrs' Day (3 June), Heroes' Day (9 June) and Independence Day (9 Oct.).

Diplomatic Representatives

Of Uganda in the United Kingdom (Uganda House, 58–59 Trafalgar Sq., London, WC2N 5DX)
High Commissioner: Julius Peter Moto.

Of the United Kingdom in Uganda (4 Windsor Loop, PO Box 7070, Kampala)
High Commissioner: Peter West.

Of Uganda in the USA (5911 16th St., NW, Washington, D.C., 20011)
Ambassador: Sebujja Mull Katende.

Of the USA in Uganda (1577 Ggaba Rd, Kampala)
  Ambassador: Deborah R. Malac.

Of Uganda to the United Nations
  Ambassador: Adonia Ayebare.

Of Uganda to the European Union
  Ambassador: Mirjam Blaak.

Further Reading

Museveni, Y., *What is Africa's Problem?* 1993.
Mutibwa, P., *Uganda since Independence: a Story of Unfulfilled Hopes.* 1992
Ofcansky, Thomas P., *Uganda: Tarnished Pearl of Africa.* 1999
National Statistical Office: Uganda Bureau of Statistics, P. O. Box 7186, Kampala.
Website: http://www.ubos.org

Ukraine

Ukraina

Capital: Kyiv (formerly Kiev)
Population projection, 2020: 43·58m.
GNI per capita, 2017: (PPP$) 8,130
HDI/world rank, 2017: 0·751/88
Internet domain extension: .ua

Key Historical Events

Kyiv (formerly Kiev) was the centre of the Rus principality in the 11th and 12th centuries and is still known as the Mother of Russian cities. The western Ukraine principality of Galicia was annexed by Poland in the 14th century. At about the same time, Kyiv and the Ukrainian principality of Volhynia were conquered by Lithuania before being absorbed by Poland. Poland, however, could not subjugate the Ukrainian cossacks, who allied themselves with Russia. Ukraine, except for Galicia (part of the Austrian Empire, 1772–1919), was incorporated into the Russian Empire after the second partition of Poland in 1793.

In 1917, following the Bolshevik revolution, the Ukrainians in Russia established an independent republic. Austrian Ukraine proclaimed itself a republic in 1918 and was federated with its Russian counterpart. The Allies ignored Ukrainian claims to Galicia, however, and in 1918 awarded that area to Poland. From 1922 to 1932, drastic efforts were made by the USSR to suppress Ukrainian nationalism. Ukraine suffered from the forced collectivization of agriculture and the expropriation of foodstuffs; the result was the famine of 1932–33 when more than 7m. people died. Following the Soviet seizure of eastern Poland in Sept. 1939, Polish Galicia was incorporated into the Ukrainian SSR. When the Germans invaded Ukraine in 1941 hopes that an autonomous or independent Ukrainian republic would be set up under German protection were disappointed. Ukraine was retaken by the USSR in 1944. The Crimean region was joined to Ukraine in 1954. A power-generating facility at Chernobyl was the site of a major nuclear accident in 1986.

On 5 Dec. 1991 the Supreme Soviet declared Ukraine's independence. Ukraine was one of the founder members of the Commonwealth of Independent States in Dec. 1991. After independence, Crimea—which was part of Russia until 1954—became a source of contention between Moscow and Kyiv. The Russian Supreme Soviet laid claim to the Crimean port city of Sevastopol, the home port of the 350-ship Black Sea Fleet, despite an agreement to divide the fleet. There was also conflict between Ukraine and Russia over possession and transfer of nuclear weapons, delivery of Russian fuel to Ukraine and military and political integration within the CIS. Leonid Kuchma was elected president in 1994 and re-elected in 1999. Support for him fell after public demonstrations against maladministration including the accusation that he was responsible for the murder of a radical journalist. Conflicts between the presidential administration and government led to the sacking of reform-minded prime minister Viktor Yushchenko in April 2001, who was replaced by Kuchma loyalist Anatolii Kinakh at the end of May.

The Pope's historic visit to Ukraine in June 2001 was accompanied by disturbances, particularly in the capital, reflecting long-standing distrust between Catholics and Orthodox Christians. Presidential elections in Oct. and Nov. 2004 were won by Kuchma's chosen successor, Viktor Yanukovych, who defeated Viktor Yushchenko in the second round run-off. But observers claimed the election failed to meet democratic standards and in Kyiv widespread protests came to be known as the 'Orange Revolution'. After the poll was declared invalid Yushchenko was elected president in a repeat of the run-off. However, infighting between the leaders of the revolution led to growing popular discontent. In Feb. 2010 Yanukovych was elected president, defeating Yuliya Tymoshenko, a figurehead of the 2004 protests. Tymoshenko was imprisoned in Oct. 2011 for alleged abuse of power in relation to a 2009 gas deal with Russia. In April 2013 the European Court of Human Rights declared her arrest and detention unlawful.

In Nov. 2013 the government abandoned plans to sign an association agreement with the European Union. In Feb. 2014 President Victor Yanukovych was impeached by the Ukrainian parliament following widespread popular opposition to his efforts to develop closer political and economic relations with Russia. In response, Russian ground forces occupied strategic points around Ukraine's Crimean peninsula, citing a need to protect both its Black Sea naval fleet—which is stationed in the region—and ethnic Russians living in Crimea. Russia's actions were widely condemned by Western leaders. A referendum in Crimea in March 2014 saw 97% of votes cast in favour of the region joining Russia and seceding from Ukraine. Later the same month, the government in Moscow enacted legislation absorbing Crimea into the Russian Federation despite international condemnation.

In May 2014 unauthorized referenda held in Donetsk and Luhansk provinces indicated popular support for both to declare themselves independent republics. However, the polls lacked recognition from the government in Kyiv and from most of the international community (although Russia expressed 'respect' for the results). Fighting ensued in both provinces (collectively known as the Donbass Region) between Ukrainian troops and pro-Russian separatist forces. A ceasefire agreed in Sept. 2014 failed to hold, but a second, internationally-brokered peace deal was negotiated in Feb. 2015. Nonetheless, sporadic fighting continued, with an upsurge in hostilities between Ukrainian troops and Moscow-backed rebels in the region reported in early 2017.

Territory and Population

Ukraine is bounded in the east by the Russian Federation, north by Belarus, west by Poland, Slovakia, Hungary, Romania and Moldova, and south by the Black Sea and Sea of Azov. Area, 603,549 sq. km (233,032 sq. miles). At the last census, in 2001, the population was 48,457,102 of whom 26,015,758 were female. A census was to be held in 2011, but it has been postponed on five occasions and has now been rescheduled for 2020. Population estimate, Jan. 2018: 44,736,804, giving a density of 74 per sq. km. Most of the population are Ukrainians, with some Russians and small numbers of Moldovans, Belarusians, Bulgarians, Hungarians, Poles and Crimean Tatars—most of the Tatars were forcibly transported to Central Asia in 1944 for anti-Soviet activities during the Second World War. Ukraine's population is projected to drop to 42·45m. by 2025 (the same population as in the late 1950s). In 2011, 69·1% of the population lived in urban areas.

The UN gives a projected population for 2020 of 43·58m.

As of 1 Jan. 2014 Ukraine was divided into 24 provinces, two municipalities (Kyiv and Sevastopol) and the Autonomous Republic of Crimea. In March 2014 Crimea was annexed by Russia in a move lacking international recognition. In May 2014 separatists in Donetsk and Luhansk provinces unilaterally declared independence but the Ukrainian government and the wider international community have rejected the legitimacy of these declarations. Area and estimated population in Jan. 2018:

	Area (sq. km)	Population
Cherkasy	20,916	1,220,363
Chernihiv	31,903	1,020,078
Chernivtsi	8,096	906,701
Crimea	26,081	1,913,731
Dnipropetrovsk	31,923	3,231,140
Donetsk	26,517	4,200,461
Ivano-Frankivsk	13,927	1,377,496
Kharkiv	31,418	2,694,007
Kherson	28,461	1,046,981
Khmelnitsky	20,629	1,274,409
Kirovohrad	24,588	956,250
Kyiv Municipality	836	2,934,522
Kyiv	28,121	1,754,284
Luhansk	26,683	2,167,802

(continued)

© Springer Nature Limited 2020
Palgrave Macmillan (ed.), *The Statesman's Yearbook 2020*,
https://doi.org/10.1057/978-1-349-95940-2_197

	Area (sq. km)	Population
Lviv	21,831	2,529,608
Mykolaïv	24,585	1,141,324
Odesa	33,314	2,383,075
Poltava	28,750	1,413,829
Rivne	20,051	1,160,647
Sevastopol Municipality	864	436,670
Sumy	23,832	1,094,284
Ternopil	13,824	1,052,312
Vinnytsya	26,492	1,575,808
Volyn	20,144	1,038,457
Zakarpattia	12,753	1,258,155
Zaporizhzhya	27,183	1,723,171
Zhytomyr	29,827	1,231,239

The capital is Kyiv (estimated population 2,934,522 in Jan. 2018). Other towns with Jan. 2018 estimated populations over 0·2m. are:

	Population
Kharkiv	1,450,082
Odesa	1,011,494
Dnipropetrovsk	1,000,506
Donetsk	918,917
Zaporizhzhya	745,432
Lviv	726,772
Kryvy Rih	629,695
Mykolaïv	486,255
Mariupol	444,493
Luhansk	406,729
Sevastopol	382,878
Vinnytsya	371,855
Makiïvka	344,793
Simferopol	341,799
Kherson	291,428
Poltava	289,544
Chernihiv	289,399
Cherkasy	277,944
Khmelnitsky	268,417
Zhytomyr	266,936
Chernivtsi	265,682
Sumy	264,483
Rivne	246,574
Horlivka	245,724
Ivano-Frankivsk	235,355
Dniprodzerzhynsk	235,066
Kirovohrad	228,630
Kremenchuk	221,251
Ternopil	218,653
Lutsk	216,505
Bila Tserkva	209,176

The 1996 constitution made Ukrainian the sole official language. Russian (the language of 33% of the population, mainly in the south and east), Romanian, Polish and Hungarian are also spoken. Additionally, the 1996 constitution abolished dual citizenship, previously available if there was a treaty with the other country (there was no such treaty with Russia). Anyone resident in Ukraine since 1991 may be naturalized.

Social Statistics

2009 births, 512,525; deaths, 706,739; marriages, 318,198; divorces, 145,439. Rates (per 1,000 population), 2009: births, 11·1; deaths, 15·3. Annual population growth rate, 2000–05, −0·9%. Life expectancy, 2007:

males, 62·7 years, females, 73·8. In 2006 the most popular age range for marrying was 20–24 for both males and females. Infant mortality, 2010, 11 per 1,000 live births; fertility rate, 2008, 1·3 births per woman (one of the lowest rates of any country).

Climate

Temperate continental with a subtropical Mediterranean climate prevalent on the southern portions of the Crimean Peninsula. The average monthly temperature in winter ranges from 17·6°F to 35·6°F (−8°C to 2°C), while summer temperatures average 62·6°F to 77°F (17°C to 25°C). The Black Sea coast is subject to freezing, and no Ukrainian port is permanently ice-free. Precipitation generally decreases from north to south; it is greatest in the Carpathians where it exceeds more than 58·5" (1,500 mm) per year, and least in the coastal lowlands of the Black Sea where it averages less than 11·7" (300 mm) per year.

Constitution and Government

In a referendum on 1 Dec. 1991, 90·3% of votes cast were in favour of independence. Turnout was 83·7%.

A new constitution was adopted on 28 June 1996. It defines Ukraine as a sovereign, democratic, unitary state governed by the rule of law and guaranteeing civil rights. The head of state is the *President*, elected directly by the people for a five-year term. An amendment to the constitution that came into effect on 1 Jan. 2006 gives increased powers to parliament, including the right to appoint and dismiss the prime minister. However, after parliament dismissed the prime minister and the cabinet on 10 Jan. 2006 the then President Yushchenko stated that only the new parliament that was to be elected in March 2006 would have such powers.

Parliament is the 450-member unicameral *Verkhovna Rada* (*Supreme Council*). Prior to the March 2006 election half of the members were chosen from party lists by proportional vote and half from individual constituencies, but in accordance with a constitutional amendment for the 2006 election all 450 members were chosen from party lists. The same method applied for the elections in 2007 but for the 2012 election it was decided to revert to the pre-2006 mixed voting system.

There is an 18-member *Constitutional Court*, six members being appointed by the President, six by parliament and six by a panel of judges. Constitutional amendments may be initiated at the President's request to parliament, or by at least one-third of parliamentary deputies. The Communist Party was officially banned in the country in 1991, but was renamed the Socialist Party of Ukraine. Hard-line Communists protested against the ban, which was rescinded by the Supreme Council in May 1993.

For information on Crimea's constitutional status, see CRIMEA *on page* 1230. In May 2014 the provinces of Donetsk and Luhansk held referenda that lacked recognition from the national government or from the international community but that nonetheless showed support for unilateral declarations of independence.

National Anthem

'Shche ne vmerla, Ukraïny i slava, i volya' ('Ukraine's freedom and glory has not yet perished'); words by P. Chubynsky, tune by M. Verbytsky.

Government Chronology

Presidents since 1991.

1991–94	Leonid Makarovich Kravchuk
1994–2005	Leonid Danylovich Kuchma
2005–10	Viktor Andriyovich Yushchenko
2010–14	Viktor Fedorovych Yanukovych
2014	Oleksandr Valentynovych Turchynov (acting)
2014–	Petro Oleksiyovych Poroshenko

Prime Ministers since 1990.

1990–92	Vitold Pavlovich Fokin
1992	Valentyn Kostyantynovich Symonenko
1992–93	Leonid Danylovich Kuchma
1994–95	Vitaliy Anriyovich Masol

(continued)

1995–96	Yevhen Kyrylovich Marchuk
1996–97	Pavlo Ivanovich Lazarenko
1997–99	Valeriy Pavlovich Pustovoytenko
1999–2001	Viktor Andriyovich Yushchenko
2001–02	Anatolii Kyrylovich Kinakh
2002–05	Viktor Fedorovych Yanukovych
2005	Yuliya Volodymyrivna Tymoshenko
2005–06	Yuriy Ivanovich Yekhanurov
2006–07	Viktor Fedorovych Yanukovych
2007–10	Yuliya Volodymyrivna Tymoshenko
2010–14	Mykola Yanovych Azarov
2014	Serhiy Hennadiyovych Arbuzov (acting)
2014–16	Arseniy Petrovych Yatsenyuk
2016–	Volodymyr Borysovych Groysman

Recent Elections

Presidential elections were held on 25 May 2014. Originally scheduled to take place in March 2015, the date was moved forward following the 2014 Ukrainian revolution and subsequent ousting of Viktor Yanukovych from the presidency. Petro Poroshenko won 54·7% of the vote against 12·8% for former prime minister Yuliya Tymoshenko, 8·3% for Oleh Lyashko, 5·5% for Anatoliy Hrytsenko and 5·2% for Serhiy Tihipko. There were 16 other candidates. Turnout was 60·2%.

In parliamentary elections held on 26 Oct. 2014 the Petro Poroshenko Bloc won 132 of the 423 contested seats, the People's Front of Prime Minister Arseniy Yatsenyuk 82, Self Reliance Party 33, Opposition Bloc 29, Radical Party of Oleh Lyashko 22, All-Ukrainian Union 'Fatherland' 19 and the far-right Svoboda (Freedom) party 6. Four other parties won one seat each and 96 seats went to independents. Turnout was 52·4%.

Current Government

President: Petro Poroshenko; b. 1965 (ind.; since 7 June 2014).

In Feb. 2019 the government comprised:

Prime Minister: Volodymyr Groysman; b. 1978 (Petro Poroshenko Bloc; since 14 April 2016).

First Vice Prime Minister: Stepan Kubiv (also *Minister of Economic Development and Trade*). *Vice Prime Ministers:* Vyacheslav Kyrylenko; Hennadiy Zubko (also *Minister of Regional Development, Construction, Housing and Utilities*); Volodymyr Kistion; Ivanna Klympush-Tsintsadze (also *Minister for European Integration*); Pavlo Rozenko.

Minister of Agrarian Policy and Food (acting): Olga Trofimtseva. *Culture:* Yevhen Nishchuk. *Defence:* Col.-Gen. Stepan Poltorak. *Ecology and Natural Resources:* Ostap Semerak. *Education and Science:* Lilia Hrynevych. *Energy and Coal Industry:* Ihor Nasalyk. *Finance:* Oksana Markarova. *Foreign Affairs:* Pavlo Klimkin. *Health (acting):* Ulana Suprun. *Information Policy:* Yuriy Stets. *Infrastructure:* Volodymyr Omelyan. *Interior:* Arsen Avakov. *Justice:* Pavlo Petrenko. *Social Policy:* Andrii Reva. *Temporarily Occupied Territories and Internally Displaced Persons:* Vadym Chernysh. *Veterans' Affairs:* Irina Friz. *Youth and Sports:* Ihor Zhdanov. *Minister of the Cabinet of Ministers:* Olexandr Saienko.

Government Website: http://www.kmu.gov.ua

Current Leaders

Petro Poroshenko

Position

President

Introduction

Petro Poroshenko, one of Ukraine's richest businessmen, was voted president in the May 2014 election. A pro-European, his chief priorities have been to try and re-establish stability in the country following the collapse of the Victor Yanukovych regime and to address the need for urgent economic reforms, but relations with neighbouring Russia have remained hostile in the wake of Moscow's alleged backing for violent separatist unrest in eastern Ukraine and a more recent military provocation in Nov. 2018.

Early Life

Petro Oleksiyovych Poroshenko was born on 26 Sept. 1965 in Bolhrad. He graduated in economics from Taras Shevchenko National University of Kyiv in 1989. He then undertook three years' postgraduate studies at the same institution, after which he co-founded and chaired Ukrprominvest, an investment company dealing mainly in confectionary. Over the next decade Ukrprominvest acquired several state-owned enterprises, creating the largest confectionery manufacturing operation in Ukraine and earning Poroshenko the nickname of 'the Chocolate King'.

In 1998 Poroshenko was voted into parliament as a member of the pro-Russian Social Democratic Party. In 2000 he established the Solidarity party but left in 2001 when he became campaign chief for Viktor Yushchenko's Our Ukraine Bloc. Poroshenko retained his parliamentary seat at the March 2002 polls. During the Orange Revolution of 2004 he was a key financial supporter for the pro-democracy movement and, following Yushchenko's 2004 presidential election victory, was named secretary of the National Security and Defence Council.

In March 2006 he was re-elected to parliament with the support of Our Ukraine and was given the chair of the parliamentary committee on finance and banking. From 2007–12 he was head of the board of the national bank, and from 2009–10 he served as minister of foreign affairs. In early 2012 Poroshenko served briefly as minister of trade and economic development under Viktor Yanukovych. In Oct. 2012 he returned to parliament as an independent candidate and was an active supporter of the pro-European protests that swept the country the following year. After winning the May 2014 presidential election with an outright majority (attracting almost 55% of the vote, making a run-off poll unnecessary), he was sworn into office on 7 June.

Career in Office

Poroshenko has aligned Ukraine's future with Europe (including the possibility of EU membership by 2025), advocated devolution of power to regional governments and tabled economic reforms to improve investment opportunities. His intentions to mend relations with Russia, however, have been hindered by Moscow's aggressive absorption of Crimea into the Russian Federation in March 2014 and the simmering conflict in the eastern provinces of Donetsk and Luhansk between Ukrainian troops and pro-Russian separatist forces (despite a fragile ceasefire agreement in force since Feb. 2015).

In Oct. 2014 Poroshenko called snap parliamentary elections that paved the way for a new government and effectively removed the remnants of Yanukovych's support. Following the elections Arseniy Yatsenyuk of the pro-Western People's Front, who had become acting prime minister in Feb. 2014, was reappointed as premier in Nov. at the head of a coalition government with the Petro Poroshenko Bloc supporting the president. However, in the wake of endemic corruption, political paralysis and a worsening economy, Poroshenko sought Yatsenyuk's resignation in Feb. 2016. The prime minister resisted until April when he announced his departure, and Poroshenko nominated parliamentary speaker Volodymyr Groysman as his successor. Groysman was sworn in on 14 April.

In Sept. 2017 Ukraine's delayed Association Agreement with the European Union, which had been signed in 2014, entered into force having earlier been ratified by all the signatories. Also in 2017, it was reported that around 2,400 Soviet-era statues and monuments across Ukraine had been dismantled in compliance with a ban on such symbols that Poroshenko had signed into law in 2015.

Tensions with Russia continued through 2018 ahead of Ukrainian presidential elections scheduled for the end of March 2019. In a major escalation in Nov., Poroshenko's government imposed martial law for 30 days after Russian forces seized three Ukrainian naval vessels and their crews in the strategic Kerch Strait connecting the Sea of Azov and the Black Sea. Also, speaking at a special council of orthodox priests in Kyiv in Dec. 2018, Poroshenko announced the creation of an independent Orthodox Church of Ukraine, marking a historic split from the Russian Orthodox Church and a symbolic rejection of Moscow's political influence.

Volodymyr Groysman

Position

Prime Minister

Introduction

Volodymyr Groysman became prime minister on 14 April 2016 at the age of just 38, having been a former mayor of Vinnytsya and speaker of the national parliament. He rose to national prominence in the anti-Yanukovych revolution of 2014 and is regarded as an ally of President Petro Poroshenko.

Early Life

Volodymyr Borysovych Groysman was born on 20 Jan. 1978 in Vinnytsya. Before finishing secondary school, he had begun working in his father's company. In 2002, while studying jurisprudence at the Interregional Academy of Personnel Management, he was elected to the Vinnytsya City Council. He graduated in law in 2003 and a year later joined the pro-Western Our Ukraine Party.

In 2005 Groysman was elected head of the council in Vinnytsya and in 2006, backed by Our Ukraine and the Yuliya Tymoshenko Party, he became the youngest-ever mayor of a Ukrainian administrative centre. In 2010, representing the small Conscience of Ukraine Party, he was re-elected mayor with a strong majority. During his tenure he was credited with improving infrastructure and attracting European investment to the city. He also forged a relationship with Poroshenko, who owned a confectionary factory in the city.

Groysman garnered national attention during the 2014 uprising when in Feb. that year he was brought to Kyiv to join the coalition government headed by Prime Minister Arseniy Yatsenyuk. As minister of regional development, construction and housing and communal services he worked on emergency measures formulated in response to Russia's annexation of Crimea and ongoing fighting in the east of Ukraine. In July 2014 Groysman also chaired the Ukrainian Special Government Commission investigating the downing of a Malaysian commercial airliner while it was flying over Ukraine.

In Nov. 2014, with Poroshenko as president, Groysman was elected speaker of parliament (*Verkhovna Rada*). As the government under Yatsenyuk unravelled in early 2016 Groysman was chosen as prime minister by parliament in April.

Career in Office

Groysman has faced a number of challenges including how to maintain the fragile ceasefire in the east between government forces and Russian-backed separatists. He has also had to address an economy in recession while juggling the demands for reform required to secure support from the International Monetary Fund (in the form of loans worth US$18bn.) and the European Union. Groysman has additionally identified rampant corruption and ineffective governance as threats to internal security. However, his critics have argued that his proximity to Poroshenko damages his ability to tackle cronyism, with several reformist ministers having left government on Groysman's accession to the premiership.

Defence

In 2011 the armed forces numbered 129,925 personnel, with 1m. reserves. Conscription was abolished in Oct. 2013, with Ukraine hoping to develop an all-professional military. However, it was reintroduced on 1 May 2014 in response to the escalating conflict with the pro-Russian insurgency in eastern Ukraine. Conscription for males aged 20–27 is now 18 months for the Army and the Air Force, and 24 months for the Navy. When it became independent in 1991 Ukraine had around 1,700–1,900 Soviet strategic nuclear warheads deployed on its territory. By mid-1996 all Soviet-era strategic warheads had been transferred to Russia for elimination.

Military expenditure in 2013 totalled US$2,418m. (US$54 per capita), representing 1·3% of GDP.

Army

In 2011 ground forces numbered 70,753. Equipment included 2,988 main battle tanks (T-55s, T-64s, T-72s, T-80s and T-84s) and 139 attack helicopters.

In addition there were around 39,900 Ministry of Internal Affairs troops, 45,000 Border Guards and some 9,500 civil defence troops.

Navy

The Navy numbered 13,932 in 2011, including some 2,500 Naval Aviation and 3,000 naval infantry. Equipment in 2011 included one frigate and three corvettes.

In 2011 the aviation forces of the former Soviet Black Sea Fleet under Ukrainian command operated ten combat-capable aircraft and 77 helicopters. In March 2014 several Ukrainian vessels based in Crimea were seized by Russia following Russia's annexation of the region. Although agreement was

reached between the two countries regarding the return of the ships, the Russian State Duma voted in the same month to terminate earlier treaties between Moscow and Kyiv governing the use of naval facilities in the region.

Air Force

Equipment in 2011 included 211 combat-capable aircraft (MiG-29s, Su-24s, Su-25s and Su-27s). Personnel numbered 45,240 in 2011.

Economy

In 2016 agriculture accounted for 13·7% of GDP, industry 27·1% and services 59·2%.

Overview

Following independence in 1991, Ukraine's transition to a market economy was tumultuous. The economy was in recession for much of the 1990s, losing 60% of GDP between 1991 and 1999. Prices stabilized after the introduction of a new currency, the *hryvnia*, in 1996 and structural reforms helped bring the economy under control by 2000. Despite a sharp slowdown in 2005 following the political upheaval of the 2004 presidential elections, economic growth averaged 7·0% between 2001 and 2008, the second highest rate in Europe after Latvia over that period.

The global financial crisis sparked a withdrawal of investment and a collapse in the price of steel (a major industry) in 2008. Despite an IMF-approved US$16·4bn. loan in Oct. that year, GDP shrank by more than 15% in 2009, reflecting the collapse of steel output and declines in the construction and retail sectors. The *hryvnia* lost 40% of its value against the US dollar.

Economic growth resumed in 2010 following moderate improvements in external demand. Trade with European Union countries has since exceeded that with Russia, although Russia remains Ukraine's main single-nation trading partner. However, following the collapse of the Yanukovych government in Feb. 2014 after widespread public protests against its decision to end EU association talks, the country's finances were plunged into new turmoil. Russia's annexation of Crimea and the ensuing civil war in the eastern provinces of Donetsk and Luhansk have further destabilized the economy. GDP contracted by 6·6% in 2014 and 9·8% in 2015, and inflation surpassed 40% as the value of the *hryvnia* plummeted and corruption remained rife. In March 2015 the IMF issued a US$17·5bn. bailout package over four years to help support the economy through the ongoing crisis.

Real GDP growth of 2·4% year-on-year in the first half of 2017 followed expansion of 2·4% in 2016. However, growth remains modest in the face of unfinished structural reforms and the fallout from hostilities in eastern Ukraine. Nonetheless, fiscal expenditures and revenues grew strongly, by 13·5% and 22·8% respectively, in the first half of 2017. As a result, the fiscal balance in that period recorded a surplus of 0·9% of full-year GDP, although public debt continued to grow, reaching 85% of GDP in July 2017 owing to the high cost of bank recapitalization.

Deeper anti-corruption reforms, further improvements to the business environment and progress on privatization are key to strengthening investor confidence and attracting foreign investment. Long-term prospects remain vulnerable to delays in the reform agenda and any renewed escalation of conflict within the country.

Currency

The unit of currency is the *hryvnia* (UAH) of 100 *kopiykas*, which replaced karbovanets on 2 Sept. 1996 at 100,000 karbovanets = 1 hryvnia. 2000 saw the introduction of a floating exchange rate for the hryvnia. There was inflation of 13·9% in 2016 and 14·4% in 2017 (the highest rate in Europe that year). Inflation had been 4,735% in 1993. Foreign exchange reserves in Sept. 2009 were US$25,189m., gold reserves were 864,000 troy oz and total money supply was 221,530m. hryvnias.

Budget

Budgetary central government revenue and expenditure (in 1m. hryvnias), year ending 31 Dec.:

	2014	*2015*	*2016*
Revenue	356,196	525,753	616,092
Expenditure	425,638	550,500	665,843

Principal sources of revenue in 2016 were: taxes on goods and services, 335,254m. hryvnias; taxes on income, profits and capital gains, 114,155m. hryvnias. Main items of expenditure by economic type in 2016 were: grants, 339,947m. hryvnias; compensation of employees, 105,352m. hryvnias.

VAT is 20% (reduced rate, 7%).

Performance

Ukraine's economy experienced a major downturn in the wake of the global financial crisis, with negative growth in 2009 of 15·1%. More recently it shrank by 9·8% in 2015 as a consequence of Ukraine's conflict with Russia before a slight recovery saw growth of 2·4% in 2016 and 2·5% in 2017. Ukraine's total GDP in 2017 was US$112·2bn.

Banking and Finance

A National Bank was founded in March 1991. It operates under government control, its Governor being appointed by the President with the approval of parliament. The *Governor* is Yakiv Smoliy. There were 198 banks in all as at 1 Jan. 2012, with assets totalling 1,054,280m. hryvnias. The largest banks are PrivatBank, Ukreximbank and Oschadbank.

In 2010 external debt totalled US$116,808m., equivalent to 85·9% of GNI.

There is a stock exchange in Kyiv.

Energy and Natural Resources

Environment

Carbon dioxide emissions from the consumption of energy in 2011 accounted for 6·6 tonnes per capita. Ukraine's greenhouse gas emissions fell by 57·1% between 1990 and 2012, mainly owing to the decline of polluting industries from the Soviet era.

Electricity

Installed capacity was 54·6m. kW in 2011. In 2011 production was 194·95bn. kWh; consumption per capita in 2011 was 4,119 kWh. A Soviet programme to greatly expand nuclear power-generating capacity in the country was abandoned in the wake of the 1986 accident at Chernobyl. Chernobyl was closed down on 15 Dec. 2000. In 2011 there were 15 nuclear reactors in use supplying 46·3% of output.

Oil and Gas

In 2011 output of crude petroleum was 18m. bbls; in 2012 production of natural gas was 18·6bn. cu. metres, with 600bn. cu. metres of proven natural gas reserves.

Minerals

Ukraine's industrial economy, accounting for more than a quarter of total employment, is based largely on the republic's vast mineral resources. The Donetsk Basin contains huge reserves of coal, and the nearby iron ore reserves of Kryvy Rih are equally rich. Among Ukraine's other mineral resources are manganese, bauxite, nickel, titanium and salt. Production in 2013 (in 1m. tonnes): hard coal, 68·8; iron ore (estimate), 45·9; salt, 5·8; manganese (estimate), 0·5.

Agriculture

Ukraine has extremely fertile black-earth soils in the central and southern portions, totalling nearly two-thirds of the territory. In 2013 there were 32·53m. ha. of arable land and 0·89m. ha. of permanent crops. Output (in 1,000 tonnes) in 2013: maize, 30,950; wheat, 22,279; potatoes, 22,259; sunflower seeds, 11,050; sugar beets, 10,789; barley, 7,562; soybeans, 2,774; rapeseeds, 2,352; cabbages, Brussels sprouts, etc., 2,083; tomatoes, 2,051. Livestock, 2013: 7,577,000 pigs; 4,646,000 cattle; 1,073,000 sheep; 665,000 goats; 195m. chickens; 11m. ducks. Livestock products, 2013 (in 1,000 tonnes): pork and pork products, 748; beef and veal, 428; poultry meat, 1,168; milk, 11,488; eggs, 1,139.

Forestry

The area under forests in Ukraine in 2015 was 9·66m. ha. (17% of the total land area). In 2011, 17·51m. cu. metres of timber were produced.

Fisheries

In 2015 the catch totalled 120,372 tonnes, of which 100,256 tonnes were from sea fishing. The total catch in 1988 had been 968,972 tonnes.

Industry

Industrial production grew by 10·2% in 2007. Output, 2007 (in tonnes unless otherwise stated): pig iron, 35·6m.; crude steel, 29·0m.; rolled ferrous metals, 24·5m.; cement, 15·0m.; petrol, 4·2m.; distillate fuel oil, 4·1m.; residual fuel oil, 3·4m.; mineral fertilizer, 2·8m.; bread and bakery products, 2·0m.; sugar, 1·9m.; sulphuric acid, 1·6m.; fabrics, 114m. sq. metres; footwear, 22·5m. pairs; refrigerators, 824,000 units; television sets, 507,000 units; passenger cars, 380,000 units; washing machines, 173,000 units; cigarettes, 129bn. units.

In 2007 industry accounted for 28·2% of GDP, with manufacturing contributing 20·5%.

Labour

In 2011 a total of 20,324,000 persons aged 15 to 70 were in employment. The principal areas of activity were (in 1,000): wholesale and retail trade, and restaurants and hotels, 4,865; agriculture, hunting, forestry and fishing, 3,394; manufacturing, 3,353. In 2011 there were 1,733,000 unemployed and the level of unemployment was 7·9%.

Ukraine had 0·11m. people living in slavery according to the Walk Free Foundation's 2013 *Global Slavery Index*.

International Trade

Imports and Exports

The following table shows the value of Ukraine's foreign trade (in US$1m.):

	Imports (c.i.f.)	Exports (f.o.b.)
2011	82,607·5	68,393·0
2012	84,657·0	68,684·2
2013	76,986·0	63,320·5
2014	54,381·4	53,913·3
2015	37,516·2	38,127·0

Main import suppliers in 2015: Russia, 25·7%; China, 10·1%; Germany, 9·5%. Main exports markets in 2015: Russia, 19·1%; Turkey, 6·5%; China, 5·0%.

Principal imports in 2015 were mineral fuels and lubricants (29·0%), machinery and transport equipment, and chemicals; main exports in 2015 were manufactured goods classified chiefly by material (28·4%), food, animals and beverages, and crude materials and animal and vegetable oils.

Communications

Roads

In 2007 there were 169,422 km of roads, including 20,497 km of national roads. There were 5,939,600 passenger cars in use in 2007 and 714,300 motorcycles and mopeds. There were 63,554 road accidents involving injury in 2007 (9,574 fatalities).

Rail

Total length was 22,302 km in 2009. Passenger-km travelled in 2009 came to 48·3bn. and freight tonne-km to 196·2bn. There are metros in Kyiv, Kharkiv, Kryvy Rih and Dnipropetrovsk.

Civil Aviation

The main international airport is Kyiv (Boryspil), and there are international flights from seven other airports. The flag carrier is Ukraine International Airlines. It operated international flights in 2005 to Amsterdam, Barcelona, Berlin, Brussels, Dubai, Düsseldorf, Helsinki, Kuwait, Lisbon, London, Madrid, Paris, Rome, Vienna and Zürich.

In 2012 Kyiv handled 8,478,091 passengers (7,432,008 on international flights) and 38,642 tonnes of freight. In the same year Simferopol (under Russian control since the annexation of Crimea in 2014) handled 1,113,900 passengers and Odesa 907,600 passengers.

Shipping

In Jan. 2014 there were 142 ships of 300 GT or over registered, totalling 359,000 GT. The main seaports are Illichivsk, Izmail, Mariupol, Mykolaïv, Odesa and Yuzhny. Odesa is the leading port, in 2013 handling 23,100,000 tonnes of freight.

Telecommunications

In 2009 there were 55,333,000 mobile phone subscriptions (1,210·6 per 1,000 inhabitants) and 13,026,000 fixed telephone lines. There were 2,649,000 fixed internet subscriptions in 2009 and 1,733,000 mobile broadband subscriptions. In March 2012 there were 1·7m. Facebook users.

Social Institutions

Out of 178 countries analysed in the 2017 *Fragile States Index*—a list published jointly by the Fund for Peace and *Foreign Policy* magazine—Ukraine was ranked the 89th least vulnerable to conflict or collapse. The index is based on 12 indicators of state vulnerability across social, political and economic categories.

Justice

A new civil code came into force in Jan. 2004. Justice is administered by the Constitutional Court of Ukraine and by courts of general jurisdiction. The Supreme Court of Ukraine is the highest judicial organ of general jurisdiction. The death penalty was abolished in 1999. There were 169 executions in 1996 and the last executions took place in 1997. The population in penal institutions in Sept. 2013 was 137,965 (305 per 100,000 of national population). Ukraine was ranked 71st of 102 countries for criminal justice and 65th for civil justice in the 2015 World Justice Project *Rule of Law Index*, which provides data on how the rule of law is experienced by the general public across eight categories.

Education

In 2016–17 the number of pupils in 16,900 primary and secondary schools was 3·8m.; 287 further education establishments had 1,369,400 students, and 370 technical colleges had 217,300 students; 1,300,000 children were attending pre-school institutions.

In 2005–06 there were 16 universities including an international university of information systems, management and business.

Adult literacy rate in 2008 was over 99%.

In 2006 public expenditure on education came to 6·2% of GDP and 19·3% of total government spending.

Health

In 2007 there were 223,294 physicians, 25,450 dentists, 340,986 nurses, 23,645 midwives and 21,745 pharmacists. There were 439,549 beds in 2,843 hospitals in 2007.

In *Water: At What Cost? The State of the World's Water 2016*, WaterAid reported that 3·8% of the population does not have access to safe water.

Welfare

There were 10·6m. old-age pensioners as at 1 Jan. 2012 and 3·2m. other pensioners. The total included 881,636 Chernobyl victims. In 2012 general government spending on social protection amounted to 46·0% of total general government expenditure.

Religion

According to the Pew Research Center's Forum on Religion & Public Life an estimated 83·8% of the population in 2010 were Christians (over 90% of which were Orthodox), with 14·7% religiously unaffiliated. The Pew Research Center's study estimated that there were 34·9m. Orthodox Christians in 2010. In 2018 there were an estimated 300,000 Jews.

A new independent Orthodox Church of Ukraine (OCU) was officially established in Jan. 2019 following a special unification council in Dec. 2018 between the existing Ukrainian Autocephalous Orthodox Church, the Ukrainian Orthodox Church—Kyivan Patriarchate and a minority of the hierarchy of the Ukrainian Orthodox Church—Moscow Patriarchate. Metropolitan Epifaniy (Dumenko), a former bishop of the Kyivan Patriarchate, was elected Metropolitan of Kyiv and All Ukraine (Primate) of the new Church. The Ukrainian Autocephalous Orthodox Church and the Ukrainian Orthodox Church—Kyivan Patriarchate were dissolved but the Ukrainian Orthodox Church—Moscow Patriarchate, headed by Metropolitan Onufriy (Berezovsky) and an autonomous branch of the Russian Orthodox Church, still exists. The establishment of the OCU marked a further rejection of Russian influence in Ukraine.

The hierarchy of the Roman Catholic Church (*Primate*, Cardinal Mieczysław Mokrzycki, Archbishop Metropolitan of Lviv) was restored by the Pope John Paul II's confirmation of ten bishops in 1991. In Feb. 2019 there was one cardinal. The Ukrainian Greek Catholic Church (*Head*, Bishop Sviatoslav Shevchuk, Major Archbishop, Metropolitan of Kyiv-Halych) is a Church of the Byzantine rite, which is in full communion with the Roman Church. Catholicism is strong in the western half of the country.

Culture

World Heritage Sites

Ukraine has eight sites on the UNESCO World Heritage List: Kyiv—Saint Sophia Cathedral and Related Monastic Buildings, Kyiv—Pechersk Lavra (inscribed on the list in 1990 and 2005); Lviv—the Ensemble of the Historic Centre (1998 and 2008); the Struve Geodetic Arc (2005), a chain of survey triangulations spanning from Norway to the Black Sea that helped establish the exact shape and size of the earth, which is shared with nine other countries; Ancient and Primeval Beech Forests of the Carpathians and Other Regions of Europe (2007 and 2017), shared with Albania, Austria, Belgium, Bulgaria, Croatia, Germany, Italy, Romania, Slovakia, Slovenia and Spain; the Residence of Bukovinian and Dalmatian Metropolitans (2011), a property built from 1864–82; the ancient City of Tauric Chersonese and its chora (2013), located on the Heraclean Peninsula in southwest Crimea; and the wooden *tserkvas* (churches) of the Carpathian region (2013), comprising 16 *tservkas* in the eastern fringe of Central Europe, shared with Poland.

Press

In 2013 there were 55 daily newspapers with an estimated average combined circulation of 2·4m. There were nine newspaper online editions in 2013. The number of newspaper online unique monthly visitors rose from 1,003,000 in 2010 to 1,402,000 in 2013.

Tourism

There were 23,013,000 non-resident tourists in 2012; total receipts were US$5,988m.

Festivals

The arts festival Day of Kyiv occurs on the last weekend of May. The main music festivals are the Koktebel Jazz Festival (Sept.) and Jazz Carnival in Odesa (Sept.). The Molodist International Film Festival takes place in Kyiv in Oct.

Diplomatic Representatives

Of Ukraine in the United Kingdom (60 Holland Park, London, W11 3SJ)
    Ambassador: Natalia Galibarenko.

Of the United Kingdom in Ukraine (9 Desyatynna St., 01901 Kyiv)
    Ambassador: Judith Gough, CMG.

Of Ukraine in the USA (3350 M St., NW, Washington, D.C., 20007)
    Ambassador: Valerii Chalyi.

Of the USA in Ukraine (4 A. I. Sikorsky St., 04112 Kyiv)
    Ambassador: Marie L. Yovanovitch.

Of Ukraine to the United Nations
    Ambassador: Volodymyr Yelchenko.

Of Ukraine to the European Union
    Ambassador: Mykola Tochytskyi.

Crimea

The Crimean peninsula extends southwards into the Black Sea. Area, 26,100 sq. km; population, 2,284,400 (2014); ethnic groups: Russians, 65·4%; Ukrainians, 15·1%; Tatars, 12·2%. The capital is Simferopol.

Crimea was occupied by Tatars in 1239, conquered by Ottoman Turks in 1475 and retaken by Russia in 1783. In 1921 after the Communist revolution it became an autonomous republic, but was transformed into a province (oblast) of the Russian Federation in 1945 after the deportation of the Tatar population in 1944 for alleged collaboration with the German invaders in the Second World War. Crimea was transferred to Ukraine in 1954 and became an autonomous republic in 1991. After the ousting of Ukraine's President Yanukovych in Feb. 2014, pro-Russian forces occupied Simferopol and strategic sites throughout the region. In March that year Crimea's parliament voted in favour of seceding from Ukraine and joining Russia, a proposal that was endorsed in a regional referendum the same month. However, Crimea's absorption into the Russian Federation has lacked international recognition and Russia has incurred sanctions from the European Union and the USA. Parliamentary elections were held on 14 Sept. 2014 following Crimea's annexation and were won by President Putin's United Russia party.

Head of the Republic: Sergey Aksyonov.

Further Reading

Ukraine

Encyclopedia of Ukraine. 5 vols. 1984–93

Applebaum, Anne, *Red Famine: Stalin's War on Ukraine.* 2017

Aslund, Anders, *Revolution in Orange: The Origins of Ukraine's Democratic Breakthrough.* 2006

D'Anieri, Paul, *Economic Interdependence in Ukrainian–Russian Relations.* 2000.—*Understanding Ukrainian Politics: Power, Politics and Institutional Design.* 2006

Dragneva, Rilka and Wolczuk, Kataryna, *Ukraine Between the EU and Russia: the Integration Challenge.* 2015

Haaland Matláry, Janne and Heier, Tormod, (eds) *Ukraine and Beyond: Russia's Strategic Security Challenge to Europe.* 2016

Kuzio, Taras, Kravchuk, Robert and D'Anieri, Paul, *State and Institution Building in Ukraine.* 2000

Magocsi, P. R., *A History of Ukraine.* 1997

Motyl, A. J., *Dilemmas of Independence: Ukraine after Totalitarianism.* 1993

Nahaylo, B., *Ukrainian Resurgence.* 2nd ed. 2000

Plokhy, Serhii, *The Gates of Europe: A History of Ukraine.* 2015

Reid, A., *Borderland: A Journey Through the History of Ukraine.* 1997

Wilson, Andrew, *The Ukrainians: Unexpected Nation.* 2000.—*Ukraine's Orange Revolution.* 2006

National Statistical Office: State Committee of Statistics of Ukraine, 3 Shota Rustavely St., Kyiv 01023.

Website: http://www.ukrstat.gov.ua

United Arab Emirates

Imarat al-Arabiya al-Muttahida

Capital: Abu Dhabi
Population projection, 2020: 9·81m.
GNI per capita, 2017: (PPP$) 67,805
HDI/world rank, 2017: 0·863/34
Internet domain extension: .ae

Key Historical Events

Archaeological evidence indicates that in the 3rd millennium BC a culture known as Umm al-Nar developed in modern-day Abu Dhabi. There was trade with both the Mesopotamian civilization and the Indus culture, particularly the export of copper. Later settlements, with Hellenistic features and dating from between the 3rd century BC and the 3rd century AD, have been discovered at Meleiha, near the Sharjah coast, and at Al-Dur in the emirate of Umm al Qaiwain. There are indications that the coastal areas of the United Arab Emirates (UAE) and Oman came under Sassanian (Persian) influence from the 4th century AD until the early 7th century when the Islamic era began. Tribes in the Dibba region along the eastern coast rebelled before Islamic forces won a decisive battle in AD 632.

In the Middle Ages much of the region was part of the Persian Kingdom of Hormuz (from 1300), which controlled the approach to the Gulf and most of the trade. European intervention in the Gulf began in the early 16th century when the Portuguese established a commercial monopoly, building a number of forts including Julfar (in modern-day Ras al-Khaimah). Portuguese ascendancy was later challenged by the Dutch and then by the British, who exercised their naval power in the Gulf in the 18th century to protect trade with India.

By that time two major tribal confederations had grown powerful along the coast of the lower Gulf. The largest, the Bani Yas, was established on the coast by the late 16th century. A large Bani Yas settlement was founded in Abu Dhabi in the 1760s, and in 1793 it became the seat of government of the al-Nahyan branch of the tribal confederation. There is further evidence of elements of the Bani Yas population extending from Qatar in the west to Dubai in the east and inland to the Liwa oasis belt. The Qawasim, a branch of the Huwalah tribe, were a maritime people (largely operating from Ras al-Khaimah) who emerged as an important group once the Omani empire of the late 17th and early 18th centuries was destroyed at the end of the Omani-Persian war in 1720. They established control over other strands of the Huwalah between Sharjah and Musandam and with a large fleet, posed a serious challenge to British shipping.

Piracy was rife until the early 19th century when the British suppressed the raiders. In 1820 Britain signed the General Treaty of Peace with the principal Arab sheikhdoms. From this and later agreements the area became known as the Trucial Coast from the 1850s (the term Trucial referring to the fact that the component sheikhdoms were bound by the truces concluded with Britain). Britain assumed responsibility for the defence of the territory under the maritime treaty of 1853 and, under the exclusive treaties of 1892, for external relations of each of the Trucial sheikhdoms. The sheikhdoms were otherwise autonomous and followed the traditional form of Arab monarchy, with each ruler having virtually absolute power.

The collapse of the pearl market and the world economic depression of the early 20th century undermined the economies of the Trucial States. Their subsequent transformation began with the discovery of oil off the coast of Abu Dhabi. Sheikh Shakhbut bin Sultan al-Nahyan, the ruler of Abu Dhabi from 1928–66, granted the first of several oil exploration concessions to foreign companies in 1939. However, the Second World War delayed exploration. The first commercial discovery was made in the late 1950s and the first exports began in 1962.

Sheikh Shakhbut, who was seen as an obstacle to the development of the oil industry, was deposed in 1966 in favour of his younger brother Sheikh Zayed bin Sultan al-Nahyan. The president of the UAE for more than 30 years until his death in 2004, he was re-elected by the rulers of the other emirates at five-year intervals. In the late 1960s oil was discovered in Dubai and in Sharjah, and then in Ras al-Khaimah in the 1980s.

In Jan. 1968 Britain announced the withdrawal of its military forces from the area by 1971. In March the Trucial States joined Bahrain and Qatar (which were also under British protection) in what was named the Federation of Arab Emirates. It was intended that the Federation should become fully independent but the interests of Bahrain and Qatar proved to be incompatible with those of the other sheikhdoms and both seceded from the Federation in 1971 to become separate independent entities. Six of the Trucial States (Abu Dhabi, Dubai, Sharjah, Umm al Qaiwain, Ajman and Fujairah) had agreed a federal constitution for achieving independence as the United Arab Emirates. The British accordingly terminated its special treaty relationship, and the UAE became independent on 2 Dec. 1971. The remaining sheikhdom, Ras al-Khaimah, joined the UAE in Feb. 1972. At independence Sheikh Zayed of Abu Dhabi took office as the first President of the loose federation. Sheikh Rashid bin Said al-Maktoum, the ruler of Dubai for over 30 years from 1958, became Vice-President. The al-Maktoum family, like the al-Nahyan rulers of Abu Dhabi, are a dynastic line of the Bani Yas tribe. The UAE instituted the Federal National Council, a 40-member consultative body appointed by the seven rulers. After the oil price increases of 1973–74—the UAE having given support to the Arab cause in the 1973 war with Israel—the economy and wealth of the new federation developed rapidly.

An attempted coup took place in Sharjah in 1987. Sheikh Sultan Bin Mohammad al-Qassimi abdicated in favour of his brother after admitting mismanagement of the emirate's economy but was restored to power by the Supreme Council of Rulers. In 1991 the UAE became involved in a major international financial scandal when the Bank of Credit and Commerce International (BCCI), in which the Abu Dhabi ruling family held a controlling 77% interest, collapsed. Abu Dhabi sued BCCI for damages in 1993 and several executives were convicted of fraud, given prison sentences and ordered to pay compensation.

Sheikh Rashid bin Said al-Maktoum died in 1990 and was succeeded by his son Sheikh Maktoum bin Rashid al-Maktoum as ruler of Dubai and UAE vice-president. In June 1996 the Federal National Council approved a permanent constitution replacing the provisional document that had been renewed every five years since 1971. At the same time, Abu Dhabi City was designated as the UAE's permanent capital.

In foreign relations the UAE has adopted a largely pro-Western and anti-Iranian stance. Following the fall of the Shah of Iran in 1979 and the outbreak of the Iran–Iraq war in 1980, the stability of the entire region was threatened. Partly in response to Iranian threats to close the Strait of Hormuz to shipping carrying oil exports from Gulf countries, the UAE joined with five other states to form the Gulf Co-operation Council (GCC) in 1981 to work towards political and economic integration. There has been further tension with Iran relating to territorial claims over the island of Abu Musa and the Greater and Lesser Tunb islands, strategically located in the Strait of Hormuz. Iran claimed sovereignty over the islands in the early 1990s and rejected a proposal by the GCC for the claim to be resolved by the International Court of Justice. In 1996 Iran opened an airport on Abu Musa and a power station on Greater Tunb, further damaging relations. Following UAE criticism of a rapprochement between Saudi Arabia and Iran, the GCC reiterated its support for the Emirates in the dispute in 2001. Iran rejected what it claimed was a biased decision. An agreement on the demarcation of the border between the UAE and Oman was ratified in 2003.

UAE forces joined the US-led international coalition against Iraq after the invasion of Kuwait in 1990. Following the Sept. 2001 attacks in the USA, the UAE's banking sector was subject to international scrutiny, and the government consequently ordered financial institutions to freeze the assets of 62 organizations and individuals suspected of funding terrorist movements. The USA stationed forces in the UAE during the invasion of Iraq in March 2003.

After the death of Sheikh Zayed bin Sultan al-Nahyan in 2004, his son Sheikh Khalifa bin Zayed al-Nahyan succeeded him as president. In Dec. 2006 the country held its first national elections, although with a restricted voter pool. From Sept. 2014 the UAE took part in US-led air strikes against

© Springer Nature Limited 2020
Palgrave Macmillan (ed.), *The Statesman's Yearbook 2020*,
https://doi.org/10.1057/978-1-349-95940-2_198

Islamic State militants in Syria and from March 2015 joined Saudi Arabian-led military action against Shia Houthi insurgents in Yemen.

Territory and Population

The Emirates are bounded in the north by the Persian Gulf, northeast by Oman, east by the Gulf of Oman and Oman, and south and west by Saudi Arabia. Their area is approximately 83,600 sq. km (32,300 sq. miles), excluding over 100 offshore islands. The total population at the last census in 2005 census was 4,106,427 (68·3% male); density, 49 per sq. km. Estimate, 1 July 2016, 9,121,000. About one-tenth are nomads. In 2011, 84·4% of the population lived in urban areas. Approximately 88% of the population are international migrants.

The UN gives a projected population for 2020 of 9·81m. The population of the United Arab Emirates has trebled since 2000.

Populations of the seven Emirates, 2015 estimates unless otherwise indicated (in 1,000): Abu Dhabi, 2,784; Ajman, 263 (2010 estimate); Dubai, 2,447; Fujairah, 214; Ras al-Khaimah, 470; Sharjah, 1,406; Umm al Qaiwain, 65 (2010 estimate). The chief cities are Dubai (2015 estimated population of 2,401,067), Abu Dhabi, the federal capital (estimated population of 1,202,756 in 2015), Sharjah and Al Ain.

The official language is Arabic; English is widely spoken.

Social Statistics

2008 births, 68,779; deaths, 9,775. 2008 birth rate (per 1,000 population), 14·4; death rate, 1·6; infant mortality rate (per 1,000 live births), 6 (2010). Life expectancy, 2013, 76·1 years for men and 78·2 years for women. Annual population growth rate, 1998–2008, 4·4%; fertility rate, 2013, 1·9 births per woman. The UAE has had one of the largest reductions in its fertility rate of any country in the world over the past quarter of a century, having had a rate of 4·4 births per woman in 1990.

Climate

The country experiences desert conditions, with rainfall both limited and erratic. The period May to Sept. is generally rainless. Abu Dhabi, Jan. 65°F (18·3°C), July 95°F (35·0°C). Annual rainfall 3·5" (89 mm). Dubai, Jan. 66°F (18·9°C), July 94°F (34·4°C). Annual rainfall 3·7" (94 mm).

Constitution and Government

The Emirates is a federation, headed by a *Supreme Council of Rulers* which is composed of the seven rulers which elects from among its members a *President* and *Vice-President* for five-year terms, and appoints a *Council of Ministers*. The Council of Ministers drafts legislation and a federal budget; its proposals are submitted to a *Federal National Council* of 40 members (20 appointed and 20 elected through councils for each of the seven Emirates) which may propose amendments but has no executive power. There is a *National Consultative Council* made up of citizens.

The current constitution came into force on 2 Dec. 1971 and was made permanent in 1996.

National Anthem

'Ishy Biladi' (Long live my Homeland); words by Abdullah Al Hassan, tune by Mohamed Abdel Wahab.

Government Chronology

Presidents since 1971.

| 1971–2004 | Sheikh Zayed bin Sultan al-Nahyan |
| 2004– | Sheikh Khalifa bin Zayed al-Nahyan |

Recent Elections

A parliamentary election was held on 3 Oct. 2015, with 20 seats in the Federal National Council elected by the population and the other 20 chosen by the rulers of the Emirates. There are no political parties. Turnout was 35·3%.

Current Government

President: HH Sheikh Khalifa bin Zayed al-Nahyan, Ruler of Abu Dhabi (b. 1948; appointed 3 Nov. 2004).

Members of the Supreme Council of Rulers:

President: HH Sheikh Khalifa bin Zayed al-Nahyan.

Vice-President and Prime Minister: HH Sheikh Muhammad bin Rashid al-Maktoum, Ruler of Dubai (b. 1949).

HH Dr Sheikh Sultan bin Mohammed al-Qassimi, Ruler of Sharjah.

HH Sheikh Saud ibn Saqr al-Qasimi, Ruler of Ras al-Khaimah.

HH Sheikh Hamad bin Mohammed al-Sharqi, Ruler of Fujairah.

HH Sheikh Humaid bin Rashid al-Nuaimi, Ruler of Ajman.

HH Sheikh Saud bin Rashid al-Mualla, Ruler of Umm al Qaiwain.

In Feb. 2019 the cabinet comprised:

Prime Minister and Minister of Defence: HH Sheikh Muhammad bin Rashid al-Maktoum; b. 1949 (sworn in 5 Jan. 2006).

Deputy Prime Ministers: HH Maj.-Gen. Sheikh Saif bin Zayed al-Nahyan (also *Minister of the Interior*); HH Sheikh Mansour bin Zayed al-Nahyan (also *Minister of Presidential Affairs*).

Minister of Finance: HH Sheikh Hamdan bin Rashid al-Maktoum. *Foreign Affairs and International Co-operation:* Sheikh Abdullah bin Zayed al-Nahyan. *Tolerance:* Sheikh Nahyan bin Mubarak al-Nahyan. *Cabinet Affairs and the Future:* Mohammed bin Abdullah Al Gergawi. *Economy:* Sultan bin Said al-Mansouri. *Health and Prevention:* Abdul Rahman Mohammad al-Owais. *Energy and Industry:* Suhail Mohammad al-Mazroui. *Education:* Hussain bin Ibrahim al-Hamadi. *Infrastructure Development:* Abdullah Bel Haif al-Nuaimi. *Justice:* Sultan bin Saeed al-Badi. *Culture and Knowledge Development:* Noura bint Mohammed al-Kaabi. *Climate Change and Environment:* Thani al-Zeyoudi. *Human Resources and Emiratization:* Nasser bin Thani Juma al-Hamli. *Community Development:* Hessa bint Essa Buhumaid. *Secretary General of the Cabinet:* Abdullah Mohammad Saeed bin Touq.

Government Website: http://www.government.ae

Current Leaders

Sheikh Khalifa bin Zayed al-Nahyan

Position
President

Introduction
Sheikh Khalifa bin Zayed al-Nahyan was appointed president on 3 Nov. 2004, following the death of his father, Sheikh Zayed. Sheikh Khalifa has continued his father's policies of co-operation with neighbouring Arab countries and with the USA, and reducing the UAE's economic dependence on oil and gas extraction.

Early Life
Sheikh Khalifa bin Zayed al-Nahyan was born in 1948 in Al Ain, Abu Dhabi. In 1966, following his father's promotion to the post of Ruler of Abu Dhabi, he was appointed as Ruler's Representative in the Emirate's eastern province and in 1969 was nominated as Crown Prince and head of Abu Dhabi's new department of defence.

Following Sheikh Zayed's initiative in 1971 to bring together the rulers of the Trucial States to form the UAE (and his assumption of the federation presidency), Sheikh Khalifa became deputy prime minister in the federal cabinet and chairman of the Abu Dhabi Executive Council. He oversaw massive infrastructure development in Abu Dhabi, funded by oil revenues, and in 1976 was nominated as deputy supreme commander of the unified UAE Armed Forces.

In 1981 Sheikh Khalifa established the Abu Dhabi Department of Social Services and Commercial Buildings to offer loans for house building. From the late 1980s, he was Chairman of the Supreme Petroleum Council, and helped develop the UAE's petrochemicals and industrial complex at Ruwais. He also served as chairman of the Abu Dhabi Fund for Development (responsible for overseas aid), chairman of the Abu Dhabi Investment Authority and head of the Environmental Research and Wildlife Development Agency. In late 1991 and early 1992 he and his father were mired in the fraud scandal surrounding the collapse of the BCCI bank, 77% of which was owned by the Abu Dhabi government. Sheikh Khalifa's scheme to compensate creditors resulted in a payout of US$1·8bn.

When Sheikh Zayed's health declined in the late 1990s, Sheikh Khalifa became the public face of the UAE, along with Sheikh Maktoum, Ruler of Dubai. On 3 Nov. 2004, the day after Zayed's death, Sheikh Khalifa was appointed president of the UAE.

Career in Office

In Dec. 2005 Sheikh Khalifa announced plans for the UAE's first elections, in which half of the members of the consultative Federal National Council would be elected by a limited number of citizens. The non-party elections were held in Dec. 2006 ostensibly heralding extended political participation.

Despite Sheikh Khalifa's strong support of the Gulf Co-operation Council (GCC), in May 2009 the UAE withdrew from plans for Gulf monetary union. This move followed the decision to locate the headquarters of the GCC Monetary Council in Saudi Arabia. Meanwhile, the UAE and particularly Dubai were adversely affected by the global financial crisis. In Feb. 2009, and again in Dec., the Abu Dhabi government intervened to support the banking sector, to prevent a debt default by Dubai and to reassure the financial markets.

The government expanded the voter franchise for elections to the Federal National Council in Sept. 2011. There was, however, increasing nervousness from 2012 over regional pressures for political liberalization and the rise of Islamist movements, prompting arrests of activists. Further non-partisan parliamentary elections took place in Oct. 2015.

In 2011 the UAE joined the NATO-led military operation that helped dislodge the Gaddafi regime in Libya. In Aug. 2014 the government intervened again in Libya, taking part in air strikes against Islamist militants, and then from Sept. that year participated in the US-led air campaign against Islamic State jihadists in Syria. Since March 2015 the UAE has joined other Gulf Arab states in a Saudi Arabian-led military campaign of air strikes against an Iranian-backed insurgency by rebel Shia Houthi forces in Yemen and, following the ransacking by protesters of the Saudi embassy in the Iranian capital of Tehran in Jan. 2016, the UAE downgraded its diplomatic relations with Iran. In June 2017 the UAE, Saudi Arabia, Bahrain and Egypt broke off diplomatic relations and cut transport links with Qatar, accusing the country of promoting international terrorism and aligning with Iran. Efforts to resolve the diplomatic crisis have since failed, casting some doubt on the future viability of the GCC.

In April 2016 Sheikh Khalifa was among numerous prominent world figures whose extensive secret wealth in offshore tax havens was revealed in a leak of documents belonging to a specialist Panamanian law firm—dubbed the *Panama Papers*—to investigative journalists.

Defence

Conscription was introduced in June 2014, and required all male high-school graduates aged 18 to 30 to serve in the armed forces for nine months. Those who have not completed secondary school serve for two years. In 2011 defence expenditure totalled US$9,320m. (US$1,810 per capita), representing 2·7% of GDP.

Army

The strength was (2011) 44,000 (including Dubai independent forces).

Navy

In 2011 the combined naval flotilla of the Emirates included 17 patrol and coastal combatants. Personnel in 2011 numbered around 2,500. The main base is at Abu Dhabi, with minor bases in the other Emirates.

Air Force

Equipment in 2011 included 178 combat-capable aircraft (including F-16s, Mirage 2000s and British Aerospace *Hawks*) and some 31 multi-role helicopters. Personnel numbered 4,500 in 2011.

Economy

Crude petroleum and natural gas contributed 38·9% to GDP in 2013; followed by finance and real estate, 16·7%; trade and hotels, 12·2%; construction, 9·0%.

Overview

The UAE is the third largest exporter of oil in the world and has one of the highest per capita incomes. Oil and natural gas contribute approximately 30% of GDP annually. Recognizing the longer-term importance of economic

diversification, the authorities have sought to encourage investment in tourism, finance, transport and manufacturing. In 2015 the government laid out plans to increase the contribution to GDP of non-oil sectors to 80% by 2030.

The government sought to reduce its spending after a sharp increase in the aftermath of the 2008 global financial crisis (when the economy contracted sharply) and subsequent Arab Spring uprisings in 2011. That year government expenditure accounted for 26·9% of GDP, before falling to 26·3% in 2012 and 23·3% in 2014. Although the economy recovered from 2010, mid-term prospects have been threatened by a steep decline in oil prices in 2015. GDP growth consequently tapered from 5·1% that year to 3·0% in 2016 and only 0·8% in 2017.

Currency

The unit of currency is the *dirham* (AED) of 100 *fils*. Gold reserves are negligible. In March 2009 foreign exchange reserves were US$34,040m. and total money supply was DH 211,314m. Inflation rates (based on IMF statistics):

2008	2009	2010	2011	2012	2013	2014	2015	2016	2017
12·3%	1·6%	0·9%	0·9%	0·7%	1·1%	2·3%	4·1%	1·6%	2·0%

Budget

The fiscal year is the calendar year. General government revenue in 2012 totalled DH 391,323m. and expenditure DH 294,339m. Revenue is principally derived from oil-concession payments. Defence, education, and public order and safety are the main items of expenditure.

VAT of 5% was introduced on 1 Jan. 2018.

The United Arab Emirates has the highest corporate tax rate of any country, at 55% in 2014.

Performance

Real GDP growth rates (based on IMF statistics):

2008	2009	2010	2011	2012	2013	2014	2015	2016	2017
3·2%	−5·2%	1·6%	6·9%	4·5%	5·1%	4·4%	5·1%	3·0%	0·8%

In 2017 total GDP was US$382·6bn.

Banking and Finance

The UAE Central Bank was established in 1980 (*Governor*, Mubarak al-Mansouri). The largest banks are the National Bank of Abu Dhabi, with assets of US$102·4bn. in March 2015, Emirates NBD (assets of US$98·8bn.) and First Gulf Bank (US$57·8bn.). In April 2017 the National Bank of Abu Dhabi and First Gulf Bank merged as the National Bank of Abu Dhabi.

There are stock exchanges in Abu Dhabi and Dubai.

Energy and Natural Resources

Environment

In 2011 carbon dioxide emissions from the consumption of energy were the equivalent of 44·4 tonnes per capita, the highest of any sovereign country in the world.

Electricity

Installed capacity was 26·1m. kW in 2011. Production in 2011 was 99·14bn. kWh, with consumption per capita (2011) 10,200 kWh. Construction of the first of four nuclear plants began in July 2012. The United Arab Emirates is the first country to begin construction of its first nuclear power plant since construction was started on China's first plant in 1985. The first plant is expected to become operational in late 2019 or early 2020. All four plants are projected to be completed by 2021.

Oil and Gas

Oil and gas provided about 34·3% of GDP in 2014. Oil production, 2017, 176·3m. tonnes. The UAE had reserves in 2017 amounting to 97·8bn. bbls. Abu Dhabi has 95% of the UAE's total oil reserves.

Abu Dhabi also has reserves of natural gas, nationalized in 1976. There is a gas liquefaction plant on Das Island. Proven natural gas reserves (2017) were 5·9trn. cu. metres. Natural gas production, 2012, 51·7bn. cu. metres.

Minerals

Sulphur, gypsum, chromite and lime are mined.

Agriculture

The fertile Buraimi Oasis, known as Al Ain, is largely in Abu Dhabi territory. There is a programme of fostering agriculture by desalination, dam-building and tree-planting. In 2012 there were 37,000 ha. of arable land and 40,000 ha. of permanent cropland. Output, 2013 (in 1,000 tonnes): dates, 238; sorghum, 54; cucumbers and gherkins, 34; tomatoes, 33; onions and shallots (estimate), 24.

Livestock products, 2013 estimates (in 1,000 tonnes): meat, 141; milk, 151; eggs, 30. Livestock (2013): sheep, 2·08m.; goats, 1·85m.; camels, 393,000; cattle, 85,000; chickens (estimate), 21·5m.

Forestry

In 2015, 0·32m. ha. were under forests (4% of the total land area).

Fisheries

Total catch, 2014, 73,203 tonnes (exclusively marine fish).

Industry

The largest companies in the United Arab Emirates by market capitalization in May 2018 were Etisalat, a telecommunications services provider (US$38·2bn.); First Abu Dhabi Bank (US$33·8bn.); and DP World, a global port operator (US$18·3bn.).

In 2013 manufacturing accounted for 8·5% of GDP. Industrial products include aluminium, cable, cement, chemicals, fertilizers (Abu Dhabi), rolled steel and plastics (Dubai, Sharjah), and tools and clothing (Dubai). The diamond business is becoming increasingly important in Dubai.

Labour

The labour force in 2013 was 6,232,000 (2,196,000 in 2003). 80·2% of the population aged 15–64 was economically active in 2013. In the same year 3·8% of the population was unemployed. In 2012, 12·9% of the labour force was female.

The United Arab Emirates had 19,000 people living in slavery according to the Walk Free Foundation's 2013 *Global Slavery Index*.

International Trade

There are free trade zones at Jebel Ali (administered by Dubai), Sharjah and Fujairah. Foreign companies may set up wholly owned subsidiaries. In 2010 there were over 6,400 companies in the Jebel Ali zone.

The United Arab Emirates, along with Bahrain, Kuwait, Oman, Qatar and Saudi Arabia entered into a customs union in Jan. 2003.

Imports and Exports

Imports (c.i.f.) in 2014 totalled US$282·2bn.; exports (f.o.b.) were US$367·6bn. Petroleum exports in 2014 totalled US$97·2bn. Principal imports: machinery and transport equipment, food, chemicals and jewellery. Crude petroleum and natural gas are the main exports. Main import suppliers are China, the USA, India and Germany. Main export markets are Japan, India, South Korea and Thailand.

Communications

Roads

In 2008 there were 4,080 km of roads. There were 1,279,100 passenger cars (293 per 1,000 inhabitants), 48,200 buses and coaches and 39,400 lorries and vans in 2007.

The UAE was the top ranked nation for road infrastructure in the World Economic Forum's *Global Competitiveness Report 2017–2018.*

Rail

Etihad Rail, a rail network linking the seven Emirates, is currently under construction. Commercial operations on the first of three phases began in Dec. 2015.

A metro system opened in Dubai in Sept. 2009.

Civil Aviation

There are international airports at Abu Dhabi, Al Ain, Dubai, Fujairah, Ras al-Khaimah and Sharjah. Dubai is the busiest airport, handling 66,431,533 passengers and 2,435,567 tonnes of freight in 2013 (up from 37,441,440 passengers and 1,824,992 tonnes of freight in 2008). Dubai was the seventh busiest airport in the world overall and the second busiest for international passenger traffic in 2013. However, in 2014 it overtook London Heathrow as the world's busiest airport for international traffic. As recently as 2006 it did not even rank among the 30 busiest airports in the world. A second airport in Dubai (Dubai World Central—al-Maktoum International Airport) opened in June 2010. Initially only handling cargo flights, it began to be used for passenger traffic in Oct. 2013. Dubai set up its own airline, Emirates, in 1985. In 2013–14 it flew 215,353m. international scheduled passenger-km, the most of any airline; it carried 44·5m. passengers in 2013–14. Etihad Airways, the national airline of the United Arab Emirates, began operations in Nov. 2003. Air Arabia is a low-cost airline based in Sharjah, flying to 35 destinations (mainly in Asia).

In the World Economic Forum's *Global Competitiveness Report 2017–2018* the UAE ranked third for quality of air transport infrastructure.

Shipping

There are 15 commercial seaports, of which five major ports are on the Persian Gulf (Zayed in Abu Dhabi, Rashid and Jebel Ali in Dubai, Khalid in Sharjah, and Saqr in Ras al-Khaimah) and two on the Gulf of Oman: Fujairah and Khor Fakkan. Rashid and Fujairah are important container terminals. In Jan. 2014 there were 113 ships of 300 GT or over registered, totalling 501,000 GT.

The UAE was ranked fourth in the World Economic Forum's *Global Competitiveness Report 2017–2018* for the quality of its port facilities.

Telecommunications

In 2013 there were 2·1m. main (fixed) telephone lines. In the same year active mobile phone subscriptions numbered 16·1m. (1,718·7 per 1,000 persons). In 2013 an estimated 88·0% of the population were internet users. In March 2012 there were 2·9m. Facebook users.

Social Institutions

Out of 178 countries analysed in the 2017 *Fragile States Index*—a list published jointly by the Fund for Peace and *Foreign Policy* magazine—the United Arab Emirates was ranked the 32nd least vulnerable to conflict or collapse. The index is based on 12 indicators of state vulnerability across social, political and economic categories.

Justice

The basic principles of the law are Islamic. Each Emirate has its own penal code. A federal code takes precedence and ensures compatibility. There are federal courts with appellate powers, which function under federal laws. Emirates have the option to merge their courts with the federal judiciary.

The death penalty is in force; there was one execution in 2017 but none in 2018. The United Arab Emirates was ranked ninth of 102 countries for criminal justice and 29th for civil justice in the 2015 World Justice Project *Rule of Law Index*, which provides data on how the rule of law is experienced by the general public across eight categories.

Education

In 2007 there were 100,269 pre-primary pupils with 4,823 teaching staff, 284,034 primary pupils with 16,523 teaching staff and 310,999 secondary pupils with 24,152 teaching staff. In 2005–06 there were 14,984 students at the United Arab Emirates University and 2,925 students at the five colleges of Zayed University. The largest higher education institution is the system of the Higher Colleges of Technology, with 16,894 students in 2005–06. The adult literacy rate in 2005 was 90·0%. In 2009 public expenditure on education came to 1·2% of GDP and 23·4% of total government spending.

Health

In 2012 there were 65 private hospitals and 31 public hospitals. In the period 2000–10 there were 19·3 physicians for every 10,000 population, 40·9 nursing and midwifery personnel per 10,000 population, 4·3 dentistry personnel per 10,000 and 5·9 pharmaceutical personnel per 10,000. There were 11 hospital beds per 10,000 population in the period 2006–12.

In *Water: At What Cost? The State of the World's Water 2016*, WaterAid reported that 0·4% of the population does not have access to safe water.

Religion

Most inhabitants are Sunni Muslims, with a small Shia minority.

Culture

Dubai is scheduled to host Expo 2020 under the theme 'Connecting Minds, Creating the Future' from Oct. 2020 to April 2021.

World Heritage Sites
The Cultural Sites of Al Ain (Hafit, Hili, Bidaa Bint Saud and Oases Areas), dating back to 2500 BC, was inscribed on the UNESCO World Heritage List in 2011.

Press
In 2008 there were 13 daily newspapers (12 paid-for and one free) with a combined circulation of 943,000.

Tourism
In 2014 Dubai received 13·2m. tourists. In 2013, 2·8m. people stayed at hotels and hotel apartments in Abu Dhabi.

Diplomatic Representatives

Of the UAE in the United Kingdom (1–2 Grosvenor Cres., London, SW1X 7EF)
  Ambassador: Sulaiman Hamid Salem Almazroui.

Of the United Kingdom in the UAE (Khalid bin Al Waleed St., Street 22, POB 248, Abu Dhabi)
  Ambassador: Patrick Moody.

Of the UAE in the USA (3522 International Court, NW, Washington, D.C., 20008)
  Ambassador: Yousef Mana Saeed Ahmed Al Otaiba.

Of the USA in the UAE (POB 4009, Abu Dhabi)
  Ambassador: Vacant.
  Chargé d'Affaires a.i.: Steven C. Bondy

Of the UAE to the United Nations
  Ambassador: Lana Nusseibeh.

Of the UAE to the European Union
  Ambassador: Mohamed Issa Hamad Abushahab.

Further Reading

Davidson, Christopher M., *The United Arab Emirates: A Study in Survival.* 2005
Vine, P. and Al Abed, I., *United Arab Emirates: A New Perspective.* 2001
Federal Competitiveness and Statistics Authority: P.O. Box 127000, Dubai.
Website: http://fcsa.gov.ae

United Kingdom of Great Britain and Northern Ireland

Capital: London
Population projection, 2020: 67·33m.
GNI per capita, 2017: (PPP$) 39,116
HDI/world rank, 2017: 0·922/14
Internet domain extension: .uk

Key Historical Events

Remains of Stone Age settlements of hunters and fishermen suggest that the first inhabitants crossed from the low countries of Continental Europe on one or more wide causeways. By the time their successors had turned to subsistence farming, the land links to the continent had disappeared under the sea. These offshore islands created at the ending of the Ice Age shared, with nearside Europe, a slowly evolving agricultural economy using bronze and iron tools. The Ancient Britons were Celts, whose ancestors had migrated from the valleys of the Rhine, the Rhône and the Danube. Having asserted their command of northern Italy and France (Gaul), the Celts established a bridgehead to Ireland and thence to Britain. By 600 BC they were the undisputed dominant force of Western Europe and were to remain so until challenged by the Romans.

The Romans were dominant from AD 78. From the 3rd century they were increasingly harried by tribes of Celts from Scotland and Ireland and by Angles and Saxons from northern Germany. Celtic tradition, presided over by druids (religious leaders) and bards (storytellers), survived most successfully in Ireland and Wales where Roman influence was barely visible. Scotland resisted the Roman legions; Hadrian's Wall was built as a northern frontier between the Tyne and Solway Firth in the early 2nd century AD. Roman authority was challenged, notably by Boudicca, queen of the Iceni tribe of East Anglia. The rebellion and the brutal repression that followed led to a long period of peaceful settlement, during which the Romans established a road network linking new towns such as Londinium (London) and Eboracum (York). But by the 5th century Roman Britain had disintegrated into a collection of warring kingdoms. The English and Welsh economies thrived on the export of silver, lead, gold, iron and other minerals. With the spread of Christianity, chiefly by Irish missionaries, came the beginnings of an education and legal system.

After the withdrawal of the Roman legions in the early 5th century, the Romano-British were pushed back to higher land in the west by waves of invading Saxons, Angles and Jutes. Danish invasions in 865 established the Danelaw in northern England. Alfred the Great of Wessex resisted Danish expansion, strengthening Anglo-Saxon unity.

Norman Conquest

William, duke of Normandy, led the Norman Conquest and was crowned king in 1066. When William died in 1087 he left Normandy to his eldest son Robert, thus separating it from England. The French dialect known as Anglo-Norman was spoken by the ruling class in England for two centuries after the Conquest. The Norman heritage was preserved also in the overlap between French and English feudal lords. Henry II, the founder of the Plantagenet dynasty, was feudatory lord of half of France. But most of the French possessions were lost by Henry's son John. Thereafter, the Norman baronage came to regard themselves as English. The ambitions of Edward III began and those of Henry V renewed the Hundred Years War (1338–1453) with France, which ended with the loss of all the remaining French possessions except Calais.

The dynastic struggle between the rival houses of York and Lancaster was concluded by the invasion of Henry (VII) Tudor in 1485. His son, Henry VIII, asserted royal authority over the church and rejected papal authority. Tudor power reached its zenith with Elizabeth I, under whom Protestantism became firmly established in England. The Spanish Armada—an attempt by Catholic Spain to return England to the papal fold—was repelled in 1588.

The accession of James VI of Scotland to the English throne in 1603 brought the two countries into dynastic union. A struggle for supremacy between Crown and Parliament culminated in the Civil War, which started in 1642. Charles I was executed by Parliament in 1649, beginning the rule of Protector Oliver Cromwell. The Stuart monarchy was restored in 1660, on terms which conceded financial authority and thus decision-making power to Parliament. The attempt of James II, a Catholic, to restore the royal prerogative led to the intervention of William of Orange. James fled the country and the crown was taken by William (III) and his wife Mary as queen regnant. The accession of William involved England in a protracted war against France.

The parliaments of England and Scotland were united in 1707 under Queen Anne, the first British monarch. With the accession of the Hanoverian George I in 1714, the system of Parliamentary party government took hold. By the mid-18th century London had taken over from Amsterdam as the leading financial centre. With easy access to capital, entrepreneurs were able to invest in new, improved methods of production. With the harnessing of steam power made possible by the engineering genius of Thomas Newcomen and James Watt, economic enterprise shifted away from the southeast to the north of England, Scotland and South Wales where there were large reserves of coal. The demand for raw materials and the pursuit of markets for finished goods opened up trade throughout the civilized world and extended British influence.

American Colonies

Britain's first successful colonies in North America were established in the reign of James I of England (1603–25) and, soon afterwards, Bermuda, St Kitts, Barbados and Nevis were colonized. By the mid-17th century, Britain controlled the American east coast and had strong bases in India and in the West Indies, where the sugar economy was dependent on slave labour imported from West Africa. Critical to imperial expansion was Britain's rivalry with France. Britain emerged much strengthened from the War of the League of Augsburg (1689–97) and the War of Spanish Succession (1702–13) while French ambitions in Europe and beyond were severely curtailed. But it was the Seven Years' War (1756–63), in which France and Prussia were the chief contenders, that deprived France of her remaining territorial claims in North America and India and confirmed Britain as the world's leading maritime power.

Relations between Parliament and Crown went through an unsettled period in the reign of George III, who was blamed for the loss of the American colonies. The War of Independence ended with Britain's recognition of American right to self-government in 1783. In 1793 revolutionary France declared war and was not finally defeated until 1815. The demands of war further stimulated the new, steam-powered industries. Despite Britain finding itself the pre-eminent world power, after 1815 there was frequent unrest as an increasingly urban and industrial society found its interests poorly represented by a parliament composed chiefly of landowners. The Reform Act of 1832 extended representation in Parliament and further acts (1867, 1884, 1918 and 1928) led gradually to universal adult suffrage.

Ireland was brought under direct rule from Westminster in 1801, creating the United Kingdom of Great Britain and Ireland. The accession of Victoria in 1837 was the beginning of an era of unprecedented material progress. Early industrial development produced great national wealth but its distribution was uneven and the condition of the poor improved slowly. Whereas early Victorian reforms were responses to obvious distress, governments after 1868 were more inclined towards preventive state action.

The Victorian empire included India, Canada, Australasia and vast territories in Africa and Eastern Asia. There was war with Russia in Crimea (1854–56); most wars, however, were fought to conquer or pacify colonies. After 1870 the Suez Canal enabled Britain to control the empire more efficiently; Britain became a 40% shareholder in 1875 and the controlling power in Egypt in 1882. The most serious imperial wars were the Boer Wars of 1881 and 1899–1902 against the Dutch settlers in South Africa. After a less than glorious victory, Britain negotiated a Union of South Africa, by which South Africa enjoyed the same autonomy agreed for Canada (1867), Australia (1901) and later New Zealand (1907). The 'dominion status' of these countries was clarified by the Statute of Westminster (1931).

Palgrave Macmillan (ed.), *The Statesman's Yearbook 2020*,
https://doi.org/10.1057/978-1-349-95940-2_199

With the spread of trade unionism and the emergence of the Labour Party, the gap between right- and left-wing politics widened after 1900. Labour had to wait until 1924 to form its first government but the Liberal landslide of 1906 carried forward the programme of social reform. David Lloyd George's People's Budget led to the abolition of the House of Lords' right to override the House of Commons while a contributory insurance scheme to cover basic health care, a modest benefit for the unemployed, free school meals and non-contributory old age pensions were all introduced.

On 3 Aug. 1914 Germany invaded Belgium. Britain was obliged by treaty to retaliate by declaring war. Four years of bloody trench warfare ensued in northern France and Belgium, with American intervention in 1917 helping to break the stalemate. The United Kingdom alone lost 715,000 soldiers and another 200,000 from the empire. Rebellions broke out in Ireland, born of the failure of successive attempts to agree a formula for Irish Home Rule. The issue was complicated by factional disagreement in southern Ireland and the wish of northern Ireland (Ulster) to remain in the United Kingdom. In 1920, after four years' conflict, the Government of Ireland Act partitioned the country. The northern six counties remained British, a parliament was created and a Unionist government took office. The southern 26 counties moved by stages to complete independence as the Irish Free State in 1922.

Second World War

A post-war boom was followed by a lengthy recession and heavy unemployment, exacerbated by the reluctance of politicians to adopt Keynesian economics. Germany revived as a military power in the 1930s, unchecked by reluctant neighbours after the punitive Treaty of Versailles. British Prime Minister Neville Chamberlain agreed to the German acquisition of parts of Czechoslovakia at the Munich Agreement in 1938. His policy of appeasement was much criticized, though it is arguable that Britain was in no position to go to war in 1938. Germany invaded Poland on 1 Sept. 1939. Britain, bound once more by treaty, declared war. In May 1940 Chamberlain was replaced as prime minister by Winston Churchill, who formed a national unity government. Although British military casualties were less than in the 1914–18 war, the civilian population was hit much worse during the Second World War; over 90,000 died, many as a result of German bombing in the Battle of Britain in 1940.

The war ended with German and Japanese defeat in 1945, by which stage the United Kingdom was virtually bankrupt. In 1939 the country had had assets of around £3,000m. By the end of the war, it owed about the same amount. A pre-war balance of payments deficit averaging £43m. a year had jumped to £750m. It was a time of great social upheaval. In the 1945 election a Labour government under Clement Attlee was returned with a large majority and a socialist programme, which emphasized wealth distribution above wealth creation, was implemented. It undertook to establish a free National Health Service, an ambitious housing programme and the state control of major industries. Subsequent governments modified but generally accepted the changes.

With Britain bankrupted, the United States stepped into the breach as the now undisputed free world leader. Fearing a European breakdown and a Communist takeover, the Marshall Plan was implemented by the USA, providing massive investment to rebuild Europe. An essential condition of the Marshall Plan was a joint effort of the participating nations to put their economies in order. But when continental leaders made the first tentative moves towards European unity, the UK was unwilling to be closely involved. With the independence of India (and Pakistan), the centrepiece of the British Empire, in 1947, decolonization took root, reaching its climax in the 1960s. Rather than to Europe, Britain now looked instead to a Commonwealth of freely associated states, recognizing the British monarch as symbolic Commonwealth head (some states chose to retain the monarch as head of state), and to the 'special relationship' with the United States.

In March 1957 France, Germany, Italy, Belgium, the Netherlands and Luxembourg signed the Treaty of Rome, which laid down terms for the European Economic Community (EEC). Two years later seven of the European countries outside the Common Market—Austria, Denmark, Norway, Portugal, Sweden, Switzerland and the UK—formed the European Free Trade Association. When the United Kingdom moved to join the EEC in 1962, five of the six members of the Community were willing to support the application but France vetoed it. A second application, in 1967, also failed but admission was achieved in 1973 under the Conservative government of Edward Heath. Membership of the Community was endorsed by referendum in 1975.

On the wider international scene, the limits of independent military action were made clear by the Suez crisis of 1956 when the UK, in collusion with France and Israel, used force to stop President Nasser of Egypt nationalizing the Suez Canal. Assumed American support was not forthcoming and the enterprise collapsed when the UK was left alone to cope with a potentially disastrous run on sterling. In the 1960s and 1970s the UK began to come to terms with advanced technology. Old-established industries such as textiles, shipbuilding, iron and steel and coal mining, the leaders of the first industrial revolution, gave way to manufacturing that relied on the microchip. Service industries, particularly in the financial sector, occupied an increasing share of the economy and trade restrictions were dismantled throughout the world.

In 1979 a Conservative government led by Margaret Thatcher came to power, committed to a free market economy. State industry was returned to private enterprise, the trade unions (blamed for the crippling 1978–79 Winter of Discontent) lost much of their power to direct government policy, and high earners were to benefit from lower taxation. A period of readjustment climaxed with a coal miners' strike during 1984–85 that turned into a trial of strength between the government and organized labour. The Labour Party and allied unions, themselves in the process of modernization, distanced themselves from the socialist rhetoric of the miners' leaders and the strike collapsed.

Despite rising living standards, there was concern about the quality of essential services such as education and health and disillusionment with a Conservative administration unable to construct a coherent European policy. In 1997 a Labour government, led by Tony Blair, was returned with a large Commons majority. Like Thatcher, he believed in the free market. In addition he introduced reforms in the system of government including the abolition of voting rights of hereditary peers in the House of Lords and the setting up of directly elected assemblies for Scotland, Wales and Northern Ireland. Blair showed greater enthusiasm for involvement in Europe while the war in Iraq went some way to rejuvenating the 'special relationship' with the USA. Fears of terrorist reprisals for British involvement in the Iraq war were realized on 7 July 2005 when bombs planted on three London underground trains and a bus killed 52 people. Gordon Brown, the chancellor during Blair's premiership, succeeded him as prime minister in June 2007. He was replaced by Conservative leader David Cameron, who took office in May 2010 in a coalition with the Liberal Democrats to end 13 years of Labour rule.

Cameron's tenure was dominated by the UK's faltering economy in the wake of the global financial crisis, which prompted severe cuts to public expenditure. In 2013 the prime minister pledged to hold a referendum following the 2015 general election—were the Conservatives to be returned to power—on whether to maintain British membership of the European Union. In Sept. 2014 Scottish voters rejected independence from the UK in a fiercely contested referendum. Cameron was re-elected to a second term as prime minister following the May 2015 general election in which, contrary to expectations, the Conservatives won a majority of seats.

In the promised referendum on EU membership in June 2016, the UK electorate defied predictions and voted to leave, prompting Cameron's resignation. He was replaced by former home secretary Theresa May, whose government was charged with negotiating the terms of the British withdrawal and forging the UK's new position in the world order. Following parliamentary endorsement in March 2017, the prime minister activated Article 50 of the EU Lisbon treaty to formally commence the exit process. However, her political authority was compromised in June 2017 when, having called a snap general election, the Conservative Party lost its overall majority in the House of Commons and subsequently had to conclude an informal pact with Democratic Unionist Party Members of Parliament from Northern Ireland.

Territory and Population

Area (in sq. km) and population at the census taken on 27 March 2011:

Divisions	Area	Population
England	130,432	53,012,456
Wales	20,780	3,063,456
Scotland	78,808	5,295,403
Northern Ireland	14,130	1,810,863
	244,150	*63,182,178*

Population of the United Kingdom (present on census night) at the four previous decennial censuses:

Divisions	1971	1981	1991	2001
England[1]	46,018,371	46,226,100[2]	46,382,050	49,138,831
Wales	2,731,204	2,790,500[2]	2,811,865	2,903,085
Scotland	5,228,963	5,130,700	4,998,567	5,062,011
Northern Ireland	1,536,065	1,532,196[3]	1,577,836	1,685,267
United Kingdom	55,514,603	55,679,496	55,770,318	58,789,194

[1]Areas now included in Wales formed the English county of Monmouthshire until 1974.
[2]The final counts for England and Wales are believed to be over-stated as a result of an error in processing. The preliminary counts presented here rounded to the nearest hundred are thought to be more accurate.
[3]There was a high level of non-enumeration in Northern Ireland during the 1981 census mainly as a result of protests in Catholic areas about the Republican hunger strikes.

The land area of the United Kingdom in 2011 was 242,509 sq. km; density, 261 per sq. km. 79·8% of the population lived in urban areas in 2011. London had a 2011 population of 8,174,000.

UK mid-2017 population estimate: 66,040,229 (32,581,801 males; 33,458,428 females).

The UN gives a projected population for 2020 of 67·33m.

Population of the United Kingdom by sex at census day 2011:

Divisions	Males	Females
England	26,069,148	26,943,308
Wales	1,504,228	1,559,228
Scotland	2,567,444	2,727,959
Northern Ireland	887,323	923,540
United Kingdom	31,028,143	32,154,035

Households in the United Kingdom at the 2011 census: England, 22,063,000; Wales, 1,303,000; Scotland, 2,373,000; Northern Ireland, 703,000.

The age distribution in the United Kingdom at census day in 2011 was as follows (in 1,000):

Age-group	England and Wales	Scotland	Northern Ireland	United Kingdom
Under 5	3,497	293	124	3,914
5 and under 10	3,136	270	111	3,517
10 and under 15	3,259	292	119	3,669
15 and under 20	3,539	331	126	3,996
20 and under 25	3,807	364	126	4,297
25 and under 35	7,521	667	244	8,432
35 and under 45	7,831	735	254	8,820
45 and under 55	7,702	787	249	8,738
55 and under 65	6,561	667	194	7,422
65 and under 70	2,674	261	82	3,017
70 and under 75	2,179	221	63	2,463
75 and under 85	3,116	303	87	3,505
85 and upwards	1,255	106	31	1,392

In 2011, 17·6% of the population of the UK were under the age of 15, 66·0% between 15 and 64 and 16·4% aged 65 and over. In 1911 only 5·3% of the population had been 65 and over.

England and Wales

The census population (present on census night) of England and Wales 1801 to 2011:

Date of enumeration	Population	Pop. per sq. mile[1]
1801	8,892,536	152
1811	10,164,256	174
1821	12,000,236	206
1831	13,896,797	238
1841	15,914,148	273
1851	17,927,609	307
1861	20,066,224	344
1871	22,712,266	389
1881	25,974,439	445
1891	29,002,525	497
1901	32,527,843	558
1911	36,070,492	618
1921	37,886,699	649
1931	39,952,377	685
1951	43,757,888	750
1961	46,104,548	791
1971	48,749,575	323
1981	49,016,600	325
1991	49,193,915	330
2001	52,041,916	345
2011	56,075,909	371

[1]Per sq. km from 1971.

The birthplaces of the population of England and Wales at census day 2011 were: England, 44,882,858; Wales, 2,732,624; Scotland, 733,218; Northern Ireland, 214,988; Ireland, 407,357; other European Union countries, 2,035,619 (including: Poland, 579,121; Germany, 273,564; Italy, 134,619; France, 129,804); elsewhere, 5,062,034 (including: India, 694,148; Pakistan, 482,137; Bangladesh, 211,500; Nigeria, 191,183).

Ethnic Groups

The 1991 census was the first to include a question on ethnic status.

Percentage figures from the 2011 census relating to ethnicity in England and Wales:

	England and Wales (%)	England (%)	Wales (%)
White			
British	80·6	79·8	93·2
Irish	1·0	1·0	0·5
Other	0·6	0·6	0·3
Mixed			
White and Black Caribbean	0·8	0·8	0·4
White and Black African	0·3	0·3	0·1
White and Asian	0·6	0·6	0·3
Other Mixed	0·1	0·1	0·1
Asian or Asian British			
Indian or British Indian	2·5	2·6	0·6
Pakistani or British Pakistani	2·0	2·1	0·4
Bangladeshi or British Bangladeshi	0·8	0·8	0·3

(continued)

	England and Wales (%)	England (%)	Wales (%)
Chinese	0·7	0·7	0·5
Other Asian	0·1	0·2	0·0
Arab	0·4	0·4	0·3
Black or Black British			
African	1·9	2·0	0·4
Caribbean	1·1	1·1	0·1
Other Black	0·1	0·1	0·0
Other ethnic groups	0·1	0·1	0·0

In Scotland 4·0% of the population in 2011 were from a minority (non-White) ethnic group, compared with 2·0% in 2001 and 1·3% in 1991. Pakistanis, Pakistani Scottish or Pakistani British formed the largest such group in 2011, constituting 0·9%.

The following table shows the distribution of the urban and rural population in the United Kingdom since 1960:

	Population in thousands		Percentage	
	Urban areas	Rural areas	Urban	Rural
1960	41,218	11,327	78·4	21·6
1970	42,912	12,734	77·1	22·9
1980	44,187	12,116	78·5	21·5
1990	44,708	12,507	78·1	21·9
2000	46,305	12,569	78·7	21·3
2010	49,323	12,712	79·5	20·5

British Citizenship

Under the British Nationality Act 1981 there are three main forms of citizenship: citizenship for persons closely connected with the UK; British Dependent Territories citizenship; British Overseas citizenship. British citizenship is acquired automatically at birth by a child born in the UK if his or her mother or father is a British citizen or is settled in the UK. A child born abroad to a British citizen is a British citizen by descent. British citizenship may be acquired by registration for stateless persons, and for children not automatically acquiring such citizenship or born abroad to parents who are citizens by descent; and, for other adults, by naturalization. Requirements for the latter include five years' residence (three years for applicants married to a British citizen). The Hong Kong (British Nationality) Order 1986 created the status of British National (Overseas) for citizens connected with Hong Kong before 1997, and the British Nationality (Hong Kong) Act 1990 made provision for up to 50,000 selected persons to register as British citizens.

Emigration and Immigration

Immigration is mainly governed by the Immigration Act 1970 and Immigration Rules made under it. British and Commonwealth citizens with the right of abode before 1983 are not subject to immigration control, nor are citizens of European Economic Area countries. Other persons seeking to work or settle in the UK must obtain a visa or entry clearance.

Total international migration estimates for recent years are as follows. Inflows (in 1,000):

	Total	British	Non-British
2014	632	81	551
2015	631	84	548
2016	589	74	515
2017	644	81	563

Outflows (in 1,000):

	Total	British	Non-British
2014	319	137	182
2015	299	124	175
2016	340	134	206
2017	360	129	231

The number of immigrants into the UK in 2017, at 644,000, was the highest on record for a calendar year. The number of emigrants from the UK in 2008, at 427,000, was the highest on record for a calendar year. The number of emigrants in 2015 was the lowest since 1999. Net migration—the difference between immigration and emigration—was 332,000 in 2015 (the highest on record for a calendar year). Emigration from the UK last exceeded immigration into the UK in 1993.

In the year ending Sept. 2014 there were 107,565 grants of settlement in the UK (down from 241,586 in year ending Sept. 2010). In 2013, of the 154,689 permissions granted 36% were to nationals of South Asia and 24% to nationals of Sub-Saharan Africa. Main individual countries were: India, 26,198; Pakistan, 18,905; Nigeria, 7,699; China, 7,244; South Africa, 5,778; USA, 5,420. In 2013, 7·7% of the UK's population were foreign citizens, compared to the EU-wide average of 4·1%.

Asylum

In 2014 there were 24,914 applications for asylum, down from the high of 84,132 in 2002. The main countries of origin in 2014 were Eritrea, Pakistan, Syria, Iran and Albania. While respecting its obligations to political refugees under the UN Convention and Protocol relating to the status of Refugees, the government has powers under the Asylum and Immigration Act 1996 to weed out applicants seeking entry for non-political reasons and to designate certain countries as not giving risk of persecution.

Coleman, D. and Salt, J., *The British Population: Patterns, Trends and Processes.* 1992

See also ENGLAND, SCOTLAND, WALES *and* NORTHERN IRELAND: Territory and Population.

Language

Although there is no legally defined official language in the United Kingdom, English is the *de facto* official language.

Social Statistics

UK statistics, 2016: births, 774,835; deaths, 597,206; marriages (2014), 289,841; divorces (2014), 122,651. UK rates (per 1,000 population), 2016: birth, 11·8; death, 9·1; marriage (2014), 4·4; divorce (2014), 1·9. The number of births in the UK in 2012 was the highest since 1972; the number of deaths in 2011 (552,232) was the lowest since 1930, while the number of deaths in 2015 was the highest since 2003. The divorce rate in 2014 was at its lowest since the early 1970s. In 1976, for the only time in the 20th century, deaths in the UK (680,800) exceeded births (675,500). In 2012 cancer caused 166,000 deaths (29% of all deaths in the UK), making it the biggest killer, ahead of respiratory diseases at 80,000 (14%), and coronary heart disease at 74,000 (13%). UK life expectancy, 2014–16: males, 79·2 years; females, 82·9. The World Health Organization's *World Health Statistics 2017* put the UK in joint 21st place in a 'healthy life expectancy' list, with an expected 71·4 years of healthy life for babies born in 2015. Annual population growth rate, 2010–15, 0·7%. In 2011, 16·8% of the total population was over 65, up from 14·2% in 1971. In 2016 there were 5,965 suicides (4,508 of whom were men), giving a suicide rate of 10·4 per 100,000 population. Infant mortality, 2016, 3·9 per 1,000 live births. Fertility rate, 2016, 1·8 births per woman. Of the 776,352 live births in the UK in 2014, 47·6% were to unmarried women, up from 6% in 1961 and 20% in 1986. In 1999 for the first time there were more births to women in the 30–34 age group in the UK than in the 25–29 bracket. 64% of dependent children lived in married (both opposite and same sex) couple families in the UK in 2017 and 21% in single-parent families. In 2017 the average household in the UK consisted of 2·4 people, the same percentage as in 2010. UNICEF reported that 19·7% of children in the UK in 2014 lived in relative poverty (living in a household in which disposable income—when adjusted for family size and composition—is less than 60% of the national median income), compared to 9·2% in Denmark (the world's lowest rate).

Great Britain statistics, 2016: births, 750,759; deaths, 581,776; marriages (2014), 281,291; divorces (2014), 120,196.

England and Wales statistics (in 1,000), 2016: births, 696; deaths, 525; marriages (2015), 246; divorces, 107. In 2012 the annual number of births in England and Wales was at its highest level since the early 1970s although it has fallen slightly since then. The rate of births to females aged 15–19 was

13·7 per 1,000 women in 2016 (the lowest on record); it has fallen every year since 2008 and has halved since 2001. By 2016 the number of centenarians had reached an estimated 13,710 in England and Wales. The median age of marriage in England and Wales in 2015 was 33·9 years for men and 31·7 years for women, up from 25·0 years for men and 22·6 years for women in 1975. 74% of marriages in England and Wales in 2015 were civil and 26% religious, compared to 51% religious and 49% civil in 1991. Same-sex civil partnerships were legalized in Dec. 2005 in the UK as a whole; same-sex marriage was legalized in England and Wales in July 2013 with the first such weddings taking place in March 2014.

Compared to the rest of the European Union, Britain has relatively high rates of drug use, although overall drug usage is falling. Figures released in 2014 showed that 15·8% of schoolchildren aged 15 years old in England had used cannabis at least once in the previous year. In 2015–16, 15·8% of 16 to 24-year-olds had used cannabis and 4·4% cocaine. A 2014 report found that in the previous year cocaine use in England and Wales among adults was the second highest in the European Union after Spain. There were 3,744 drug-related deaths (involving both legal and illegal drugs) registered in England and Wales in 2016 (the highest annual total since comparable records began in 1993). Male drug misuse deaths (involving illegal drugs) increased from 1,843 in 2015 to 1,896 in 2016. Female drug misuse deaths increased from 636 in 2015 to 697 in 2016.

See also NORTHERN IRELAND: Social Statistics.

Climate

The climate is cool temperate oceanic, with mild conditions and rainfall evenly distributed over the year, though the weather is very changeable because of cyclonic influences. In general, temperatures are higher in the west and lower in the east in winter and rather the reverse in summer. Rainfall amounts are greatest in the west, where most of the high ground occurs.

London, Jan. 39°F (3·9°C), July 64°F (17·8°C). Annual rainfall 25" (635 mm). Aberdeen, Jan. 38°F (3·3°C), July 57°F (13·9°C). Annual rainfall 32" (813 mm). Belfast, Jan. 40°F (4·5°C), July 59°F (15·0°C). Annual rainfall 37·4" (950 mm). Birmingham, Jan. 38°F (3·3°C), July 61°F (16·1°C). Annual rainfall 30" (749 mm). Cardiff, Jan. 40°F (4·4°C), July 61°F (16·1°C). Annual rainfall 42·6" (1,065 mm). Edinburgh, Jan. 38°F (3·3°C), July 58°F (14·5°C). Annual rainfall 27" (686 mm). Glasgow, Jan. 39°F (3·9°C), July 59°F (15·0°C). Annual rainfall 38" (965 mm). Manchester, Jan. 39°F (3·9°C), July 61°F (16·1°C). Annual rainfall 34·5" (876 mm).

Constitution and Government

The reigning Queen and Head of the Commonwealth is **Elizabeth II** Alexandra Mary, b. 21 April 1926, daughter of King George VI and Queen Elizabeth; married on 20 Nov. 1947 Lieut. Philip Mountbatten (formerly Prince Philip of Greece), created Duke of Edinburgh, Earl of Merioneth and Baron Greenwich on the same day and created Prince Philip, Duke of Edinburgh, 22 Feb. 1957; succeeded to the crown on the death of her father, on 6 Feb. 1952 (making her currently the world's longest-reigning monarch).

Offspring

Prince Charles Philip Arthur George, Prince of Wales (Heir Apparent), b. 14 Nov. 1948; married Lady Diana Frances Spencer on 29 July 1981; after divorce, 28 Aug. 1996, Diana, Princess of Wales (died in Paris in a road accident on 31 Aug. 1997); married Camilla Parker Bowles on 9 April 2005. *Offspring of first marriage:* William Arthur Philip Louis, b. 21 June 1982; married Catherine 'Kate' Middleton on 29 April 2011 (*offspring:* George Alexander Louis, b. 22 July 2013; Charlotte Elizabeth Diana, b. 2 May 2015; Louis Arthur Charles, b. 23 April 2018); Henry Charles Albert David 'Harry', b. 15 Sept. 1984; married Rachel Meghan 'Meghan' Markle on 19 May 2018. Princess Anne Elizabeth Alice Louise, the Princess Royal, b. 15 Aug. 1950; married Mark Anthony Peter Phillips on 14 Nov. 1973; divorced, 1992; married Cdr Timothy Laurence on 12 Dec. 1992. *Offspring of first marriage:* Peter Mark Andrew, b. 15 Nov. 1977; married Autumn Patricia Kelly on 17 May 2008 (*offspring:* Savannah Phillips, b. 29 Dec. 2010; Isla Elizabeth Phillips, b. 29 March 2012); Zara Anne Elizabeth, b. 15 May 1981; married Michael James 'Mike' Tindall on 30 July 2011 (*offspring:* Mia Grace Tindall, b. 17 Jan. 2014; Lena Elizabeth Tindall, b. 18 June 2018). Prince Andrew Albert Christian Edward, created Duke of York, 23 July 1986, b. 19 Feb. 1960; married Sarah Margaret Ferguson on 23 July 1986; after divorce, 30 May

1996, Sarah, Duchess of York. *Offspring:* Princess Beatrice Mary, b. 8 Aug. 1988; Princess Eugenie Victoria Helena, b. 23 March 1990; married Jack Christopher Stamp Brooksbank on 12 Oct. 2018. Prince Edward Antony Richard Louis, created Earl of Wessex and Viscount Severn, 19 June 1999, b. 10 March 1964; married Sophie Rhys-Jones, Countess of Wessex, on 19 June 1999. *Offspring:* Louise Alice Elizabeth Mary, Lady Louise Windsor, b. 8 Nov. 2003; James Alexander Philip Theo, Viscount Severn, b. 17 Dec. 2007.

The Queen's legal title rests on the statute of 12 and 13 Will. III, ch. 3, by which the succession to the Crown of Great Britain and Ireland was settled on the Princess Sophia of Hanover and the 'heirs of her body being Protestants'. By proclamation of 17 July 1917 the royal family became known as the House and Family of Windsor. On 8 Feb. 1960 the Queen issued a declaration varying her confirmatory declaration of 9 April 1952 to the effect that while the Queen and her children should continue to be known as the House of Windsor, her descendants, other than descendants entitled to the style of Royal Highness and the title of Prince or Princess, and female descendants who marry and their descendants should bear the name of Mountbatten-Windsor.

Lineage to the throne

1) Prince of Wales. 2) Prince William of Wales. 3) Prince George of Cambridge. 4) Princess Charlotte of Cambridge. 5) Prince Louis of Cambridge.

By letters patent of 30 Nov. 1917 the titles of Royal Highness and Prince or Princess are restricted to the Sovereign's children, the children of the Sovereign's sons and the eldest living son of the eldest son of the Prince of Wales.

Traditionally provision has been made for the support of the royal household, after the surrender of hereditary revenues, by the settlement of the Civil List soon after the beginning of each reign. The Civil List Act of 1 Jan. 1972 provided for a decennial, and the Civil List (Increase of Financial Provision) Order 1975 for an annual review of the List, but in July 1990 it was again fixed for one decade. The Civil List of 2012 provided for an annuity of £7,900,000 to the Queen annually; and £359,000 to Prince Philip. These amounts were the same as for the periods 2001–10 and 1991–2000. The income of the Prince of Wales derives from the Duchy of Cornwall. The Civil List was exempted from taxation in 1910. The Queen has paid income tax on her private income since 1993. In Oct. 2010 then Chancellor George Osborne announced that from 2013 the Civil List would be abolished. It has been replaced by a Sovereign Support Grant combining the Civil List and three Grants-in-Aid into one payment, with the Queen receiving 15% of the profits from the Crown Estate but two years in arrears. The Sovereign Grant is set at £82·4m. for 2019–20.

The supreme legislative power is vested in Parliament, which consists of the Crown, the House of Lords and the House of Commons, and evolved into something resembling its present form in the mid-14th century. A bill which is passed by both Houses and receives Royal Assent becomes an Act of Parliament and part of statute law.

Parliament is summoned, and a General Election is called, by the sovereign on the advice of the Prime Minister. Under the Fixed Term Parliaments Act 2011 a Parliament normally lasts five years, divided into annual sessions. A session is ended by prorogation, and most public bills which have not been passed by both Houses then lapse, unless they are subject to a carry over motion. A Parliament normally ends by dissolution at the end of five years, unless a motion of no confidence is passed and no alternative government is found or if a motion for an early general election is agreed by at least two-thirds of the House of Commons.

Under the Parliament Act 1911 all money bills (so certified by the Speaker of the House of Commons), if not passed by the Lords without amendment, may become law without their concurrence within one month of introduction in the Lords. Under the Parliament Acts 1911 and 1949 public bills introduced in the House of Commons, other than money bills or a bill extending the maximum duration of Parliament, if passed by the Commons in two successive sessions and rejected each time by the Lords, may become law without being passed by the Lords provided that one year has elapsed between Commons second reading in the first session and passing of the bill by the Commons in the second session, and that the bill reaches the Lords at least one month before the end of the second session. The Parliament Acts have been used four times since 1949: in 1991 for the War Crimes Act, in 1999 for the European Parliamentary Elections Act, in 2000 for the Sexual Offences (Amendment) Act and for the Hunting Act in 2004.

Peerages are created by the sovereign, on the advice of the Prime Minister, with no limits on their number. The following are the main categories of membership of the House of Lords (composition at 5 Sept. 2017, excluding 16 members who were on leave of absence and eight disqualified as senior members of the judiciary):

Party	Life Peers	Excepted Hereditary Peers	Bishops	Total
Conservative	205	49	...	254
Labour	195	4	...	199
Liberal Democrat	97	4	...	101
Crossbench	145	32	...	177
Archbishops and Bishops	...	...	24	24
Other	43	2	...	45
Total	*685*	*91*	*24*	*800*

Composition by party or group:

Conservative	254 (63 women)
Labour	199 (64 women)
Liberal Democrat	101 (34 women)
Crossbench	177 (41 women)
Archbishops and Bishops	24 (2 women)
Other	45 (6 women)
Total	*800*

The House of Commons consists of Members of Parliament (MPs) representing constituencies determined by the Boundary Commissions. MPs must be over 18 years of age (since July 2006—formerly 21 years), and be either a British citizen, a citizen of the Republic of Ireland or a citizen of a commonwealth country who does not require leave to enter or remain in the UK, or has indefinite leave to remain in the UK. Certain groups of people are not eligible to stand as an MP, these include: civil servants, members of the regular armed forces, policemen, judges and other office-holders named in the House of Commons (Disqualification) Act 1975. In general hereditary peers are no longer disqualified from membership of the Commons, following the passage of the House of Lords Act 1999. However, the hereditary peers who still sit in the Lords remain disqualified, as do the few hereditary peers who were given life peerages after the passing of the 1999 Act. Life peers are disqualified from membership of the House of Commons.

In order to vote at elections in the United Kingdom a person must be on the electoral register. No person may vote in more than one constituency at a general election. All persons may apply to vote by post if they are unable to vote in person, or if they fulfil certain legal requirements they may also be entitled to vote by proxy. UK Parliamentary elections are held under the first-past-the-post system, in which the candidate who receives the most votes is elected.

All persons over 16 years old and not subject to any legal incapacity to vote and who are either British citizens or citizens of the Republic of Ireland resident in the UK, or Commonwealth citizens resident in the UK are entitled to be included in the register of electors for the constituency containing the address at which they were residing on the qualifying date for the register, and at the age of 18 are entitled to vote at elections held during the period for which the register remains in force.

Members of the armed forces and their spouses are entitled, if otherwise qualified, to be registered as 'service voters' provided they make a 'service declaration'. There are also special arrangements for Crown Servants employed overseas. British citizens living overseas may be registered to vote in the constituency where they were previously registered for up to 15 years after they left the UK.

Parliamentary constituency boundaries are reviewed periodically. This is to account for population changes and realign constituency boundaries with other administrative boundaries that may have changed in intervening years. The reviews are carried out by four Boundary Commissions, one for each part of the UK. They are independent and impartial but must follow the rules for redistribution of seats set out in legislation passed by Parliament in 1986 and amended in 2011 by the *Parliamentary Voting System* and *Constituencies Act*. The *Parliamentary Voting System* and *Constituencies Act 2011* also abolished the power of the Boundary Commissions to carry out interim reviews, and provided for boundary reviews to take place every five years. The Sixth Review, known as the 2013 Review, was to be the first to use the new rules for redistribution and would have reduced the number of seats in the House of Commons from 650 to 600. However, the Electoral Registration and Administration Act 2013 effectively provided that the 2013 review should be postponed until 2018. The Seventh review, known as the 2018 Review, was launched in Feb. 2016 and in Sept. 2018 all four Boundary Commissions submitted their final reports and recommendations for new Parliamentary constituency boundaries to the Government.

The parliamentary electorate of the United Kingdom and Northern Ireland in the register in Dec. 2017 numbered 46,148,035 (38,693,859 in England, 2,261,233 in Wales, 3,950,643 in Scotland and 1,242,300 in Northern Ireland).

At the UK general election held on 8 June 2017, 650 members were returned: 533 from England, 59 from Scotland, 40 from Wales and 18 from Northern Ireland. Every constituency returns a single member.

On 5 May 2011 a referendum was held on proposals to replace the 'first past the post' electoral system (in which each constituency returns the candidate polling the largest number of votes) with an 'alternative vote' system (AV). The promise of a referendum on the issue was a key condition for the Liberal Democrats joining the coalition government following the 2010 general election. Under the AV system, voters rank candidates in order of preference, with the votes of the candidate receiving least support redistributed until one candidate has over 50% of votes. The Liberal Democrats and the Labour Party campaigned in support of moving to AV while the Conservatives opposed it. Turnout was 42·0%, with 67·9% of votes against the change and 32·1% in favour.

A further referendum, with considerably greater constitutional and international repercussions, took place on 23 June 2016 in the wake of growing public scepticism about the benefits of continued British membership of the European Union after 43 years. Following a controversial campaign, with divisive consequences for both the Conservative and Labour parties, voters backed an exit from the Union by a majority of 51·9% to 48·1%, triggering a complex process of withdrawal.

One of the main aspects of the former Labour government's programme of constitutional reform was Scottish and Welsh devolution. In the referendum on Scottish devolution on 11 Sept. 1997, 1,775,045 votes (74·3%) were cast in favour of a Scottish parliament and 614,400 against (25·7%). The turnout was 60·4%, so around 44·8% of the total electorate voted in favour. For the second question, on the Parliament's tax-raising powers, 1,512,889 votes were cast in favour (63·5%) and 870,263 against (36·5%). This represented 38·4% of the total electorate. On 18 Sept. 2014 a referendum on independence from the United Kingdom was held. 55·3% voted against independence and 44·7% in favour. Turnout was 84·6%, with 4,283,392 people registered to vote.

On 18 Sept. 1997 in Wales there were 559,419 votes cast in favour of a Welsh assembly (50·3%) and 552,698 against (49·7%). The turnout was 51·3%.

For MPs' salaries *see below*. Members of the House of Lords are unsalaried but may recover expenses incurred in attending sittings of the House by claiming a flat rate attendance allowance of £150 or £300. Additionally, Members of the House who are disabled may recover the extra cost of attending the House incurred by reason of their disablement. In connection with attendance at the House and parliamentary duties within the UK, Lords may also recover the cost of travelling to and from home.

The executive government is vested nominally in the Crown, but practically in a committee of Ministers, called the Cabinet, which is dependent on the support of a majority in the House of Commons. The head of the Cabinet is the *Prime Minister*, a position first constitutionally recognized in 1905. The Prime Minister's colleagues in the Cabinet are appointed on his or her recommendation.

Salaries

In 2018–19 Members of Parliament received an annual salary of £77,379. This then went up by 2·7% to £79,468 for 2019–20. Ministers who are MPs also receive a ministerial salary. In 2018–19 the Prime Minister was entitled to an annual salary (additional to the MPs' salary) of £78,223 and Cabinet Ministers £70,137. However, in line with the ministerial pay freeze announced by David Cameron at the beginning of the 2015 Parliament, ministers waived their salary increases and received £75,440 and £67,505 respectively. Following a scandal over MPs' abuse of expenses, the Parliamentary Standards Act 2009 was passed in July 2009 creating the Independent Parliamentary Standards Authority (IPSA). Reforms to the expenses system were introduced by the IPSA in May.

The Privy Council

Before the development of the Cabinet System, the Privy Council was the chief source of executive power, but now its functions are largely formal. It advises the monarch to approve Orders in Council and on the issue of royal proclamations, and has some independent powers such as the supervision of the registration of the medical profession. It consists of all Cabinet members, the Archbishops of Canterbury and York, the Speaker of the House of Commons and senior British and Commonwealth statesmen. There are a number of advisory Privy Council committees. The Judicial Committee is the final court of appeal from courts of the UK dependencies, the Channel Islands and the Isle of Man, and some Commonwealth countries.

Freedom of Information Act

The Freedom of Information Act 2000 was implemented gradually between Nov. 2002 and Jan. 2005 when the General Right of Access to all information became law. Not to be confused with the Data Protection Act of 1998, the FOIA allows individuals to gain access to information held by public authorities in England, Wales and Northern Ireland. A separate Act applies in Scotland. Some information is exempted from release, for example security-related documents. An independent Commissioner for Information oversees the process.

See also NORTHERN IRELAND: Constitution and Government.

Local Government

Administration is carried out by four types of bodies: (i) local branches of some central ministries, such as the Departments of Health and Social Security; (ii) local sub-managements of nationalized industries; (iii) specialist authorities such as the National Rivers Authority; and (iv) the system of local government described below. The phrase 'local government' has come to mean that part of the local administration conducted by elected councils. There are separate systems for England, Wales, Scotland and Northern Ireland.

The Local Government Act 1992 provided for the establishment of new unitary councils (authorities) in England, responsible for all services in their areas, though the two-tier structure of district and county councils remained for much of the country. In 1996 all of Wales and Scotland was given unitary local government systems. In April 2009 a further nine single-tier unitary authorities were created in a bid to simplify the system.

Local authorities have statutory powers and claims on public funds. Relations with central government are maintained through the ministry of housing, communities and local government in England, and through the Welsh and Scottish Executives. In England the Home Office is concerned with some local government functions. (These are performed by departments within the Welsh and Scottish Offices.) Ministers have powers of intervention to protect individuals' rights and safeguard public health, and the government has the power to cap (i.e. limit) local authority budgets.

The chair of the council (known as the Mayor in boroughs and cities) is traditionally one of the councillors elected by the rest. However, the Mayor of London has been directly elected since 1999 and following the Local Government Act 2000, 16 councils in England now have direct mayoral elections as do seven combined authorities. Mayors of cities may have the title of Lord Mayor conferred on them. 51 towns in England, seven in Scotland, six in Wales and five in Northern Ireland have the status of city. Brighton and Hove, Wolverhampton and Inverness were awarded city status in 2000. In 2002 Preston, Newport, Stirling, Lisburn and Newry were given city status to mark Queen Elizabeth II's golden jubilee; and in 2012 Chelmsford, Perth and St Asaph were granted city status to mark her diamond jubilee. This status is granted by the personal command of the monarch and confers no special privileges or powers. In Scotland, the chair of city councils is deemed Lord Provost, and is elsewhere known as Convenor or Provost. In Wales, the chair is called Chairman in counties and Mayor in county boroughs. Any parish or community council can by simple resolution adopt the style 'town council' and the status of town for the parish or community.

Functions

Legislation in the 1980s initiated a trend for local authorities to provide services by, or in collaboration with, commercial or voluntary bodies rather than provide them directly. In England, county councils are responsible for strategic planning, transport planning, non-trunk roads and regulation of traffic, personal social services, consumer protection, disposal of waste, the fire and library services and, partially, for education. District councils are responsible for environmental health, housing, local planning applications (in the first instance) and refuse collection. Unitary authorities combine functions of both levels.

Finance

Revenue is derived from the Council Tax, which supports about one-fifth of current expenditure, the remainder being funded by central government grants and by the redistribution of revenue from the national non-domestic rate (property tax). Capital expenditure is financed by borrowing within government-set limits and sales of real estate.

Elections

England: The 36 metropolitan districts are divided into wards, each one of which is represented by three councillors. One-third of councillors are elected each year for three years out of four, except for Doncaster which moved to whole council elections in 2015. 34 metropolitan districts had an election on 3 May 2018, with only Doncaster and Rotherham not doing so. The 201 district councils and the 56 English unitary authorities are divided into wards. Each chooses either to follow the metropolitan district system, or to have all seats contested once every four years, or to elect by halves every two years. On 4 May 2017 there were elections in seven unitary authorities and for six directly-elected mayors. Elections were held in 67 district councils and 17 unitary authorities on 3 May 2018, along with mayoral elections for five local authorities and the combined Sheffield City Region. The 27 county councils have one councillor for each electoral division, elected every four years. County council elections were last held on 4 May 2017.

In London there are 33 councils (including the City of London), the whole of which are elected every four years. The Greater London Authority has a 25-member Assembly, elected using AMS (Additional Member System), and a directly elected mayor, elected by the SV (Supplementary Vote) system. For the election of London Assembly members London is divided into 14 constituencies. Each constituency elects one member, in addition to which there are 11 'London Member' seats. Sadiq Khan (Lab.) was elected mayor on 5 May 2016. Elections for all 32 London boroughs were held on 3 May 2018.

Wales: The 22 unitary authorities are split between single and multi-member wards, elected every four years. Elections for all 22 authorities were held on 4 May 2017.

Scotland: The 32 unitary authorities generally hold elections every four years. The last elections were held on 4 May 2017.

Northern Ireland: On 22 May 2014 elections were held for councils in 11 districts that were to replace the previous 26 districts delineated in 1973. The old and new councils ran in tandem until the end of March 2015, when the old councils ceased to operate.

Resident citizens of the UK, Ireland, a Commonwealth country or an EU country may vote and stand for election at age 18.

Election Results

English elections for 34 metropolitan boroughs, 32 London Boroughs, 17 unitary authorities and 67 districts on 3 May 2018 resulted in Labour control of 74 councils, Conservative 46, Liberal Democrat 9 and no overall control in 21. Labour gained 77 seats (2,350 overall), the Conservatives lost 33 (total 1,332), the Liberal Democrats gained 75 (total 536) and UKIP lost 123 (total 3). Others gained 4 (total 183).

English elections for 35 councils (of which 27 non-metropolitan county councils, one metropolitan borough and seven unitary authorities including the Isles of Scilly) were held on 4 May 2017. Excluding the Isles of Scilly—where all the councillors are independents—the Conservatives secured control over 27 councils (a net gain of 10), Labour 2 (a net loss of 1) and no overall control in the remaining 5. The Conservatives gained 319 seats (for a total of 1,439), Labour lost 142 (418), the Liberal Democrats lost 28 (312), UKIP lost 143 (1) and others lost 6 (199).

English elections for 35 metropolitan boroughs, 19 unitary authorities and 70 districts on 5 May 2016 resulted in Labour control of 58 councils, Conservative 38, Liberal Democrat 4 and no overall control in 24. Labour lost 18 seats (1,326 overall), the Conservatives lost 48 seats (total 842), the Liberal Democrats gained 45 (total 378), UKIP gained 25 (total 58) and others lost 4 (total 165).

English elections for 36 metropolitan boroughs, 49 unitary authorities and 194 districts on 7 May 2015 resulted in Conservative control of 163 councils, Labour 74, Liberal Democrat 4, UK Independence Party (UKIP) 1, others 1 and no overall control in 36. The Conservatives gained 541 seats (5,521 overall), Labour lost 203 (total 2,278), the Liberal Democrats lost 411 (total 658), UKIP gained 176 (total 202) and others lost 122 (total 667).

Elections for 22 Welsh unitary authorities held on 4 May 2017 resulted in Labour control of seven councils, independent control of three, Plaid Cymru control of one, Conservative control of one and no overall control in ten councils.

Elections for all 32 unitary authorities in Scotland held on 4 May 2017 resulted in independent control of 3 councils, with no overall control in the remaining 29. The Scottish National Party won 431 seats; the Conservatives, 276; Labour, 262; the Liberal Democrats, 67; the Greens, 19; and others, 172.

Elections for 11 new local district councils were held in Northern Ireland on 22 May 2014. None of the parties took control of a council. The Democratic Unionist Party took 130 seats, Sinn Féin 105, Ulster Unionist Party 88, Social Democratic and Labour Party 66, Alliance Party 32 and Traditional Unionist Voice 13. Independents and others took 26 seats.

Elections for London's Mayor and a 25-member London Assembly took place on 5 May 2016. Sadiq Khan (Lab.) won with 56·9% of the vote (including second preferences). He gained 1,310,143 votes (1,148,716 as first votes) against 994,614 votes (909,755 as first votes) for Conservative candidate Zac Goldsmith.

National Anthem

'God Save the Queen' (King) (words and tune anonymous; earliest known printed source, 1744).

Government Chronology

Prime Ministers since the Second World War (Con = Conservative Party; Lab = Labour Party):

1945–51	Lab	Clement Attlee
1951–55	Con	Winston Churchill
1955–57	Con	Sir Anthony Eden
1957–63	Con	Harold Macmillan
1963–64	Con	Sir Alec Douglas-Home
1964–70	Lab	Harold Wilson
1970–74	Con	Edward Heath
1974–76	Lab	Harold Wilson
1976–79	Lab	James Callaghan
1979–90	Con	Margaret Thatcher
1990–97	Con	John Major
1997–2007	Lab	Tony Blair
2007–10	Lab	Gordon Brown
2010–16	Con	David Cameron
2016–	Con	Theresa May

Recent Elections

At the general election of 8 June 2017 the Conservative Party won 318 seats with 42·4% of votes cast (331 with 36·9% in 2015); the Labour Party 262 with 40·0% (232 with 30·4% in 2015); the Liberal Democrats 12 with 7·4% (8 with 7·9%); Green Party 1 with 1·6% (1 with 3·8%); ind. 1. Regional parties (Scotland): the Scottish National Party 35 (56 in 2015); (Wales): Plaid Cymru 4 (3); (Northern Ireland): the Democratic Unionist Party 10 (8); Sinn Féin 7 (4). Turnout was 68·7% (66·1% in 2015).

European Parliament

The United Kingdom has 73 representatives. At the May 2014 elections turnout was 34·2% (34·7% in 2009). The UK Independence Party won 24 seats with 27·5% of votes cast (political affiliation in European Parliament: Europe of Freedom and Direct Democracy); the Labour Party, 20 with 25·4% (Progressive Alliance of Socialists and Democrats); the Conservative Party, 19 with 23·9% (European Conservatives and Reformists); the Green Party, 3 with 7·9% (Greens/European Free Alliance); the Scottish National Party, 2 with 2·5% (Greens/European Free Alliance); the Liberal Democrats, 1 with 6·9% (Alliance of Liberals and Democrats for Europe); Plaid Cymru, 1 with 0·7% (Greens/European Free Alliance). Voting for these parties was on a proportional system. Voting in Northern Ireland was by the transferable vote system: Sinn Féin (European United Left/Nordic Green Left), the Democratic Unionist Party (non-attached) and the Ulster Unionist Party (European Conservatives and Reformists) gained 1 seat each.

Current Government

In March 2019 the Conservative Party cabinet consisted of the following:

(a) 23 MEMBERS OF THE CABINET

Prime Minister, First Lord of the Treasury and Minister for the Civil Service: Theresa May, b. 1956.

Chancellor of the Duchy of Lancaster and Minister for the Cabinet Office: David Lidington, b. 1956.

Chancellor of the Exchequer: Philip Hammond, b. 1955.

Secretary of State for the Home Department: Sajid Javid, b. 1969.

Secretary of State for Foreign and Commonwealth Affairs: Jeremy Hunt, b. 1966.

Secretary of State for Exiting the European Union: Stephen Barclay, b. 1972.

Secretary of State for Defence: Gavin Williamson, b. 1976.

Lord Chancellor and Secretary of State for Justice: David Gauke, b. 1971.

Secretary of State for Health and Social Care: Matthew Hancock, b. 1978.

Secretary of State for Business, Energy and Industrial Strategy: Greg Clark, b. 1967.

Secretary of State for International Trade and President of the Board of Trade: Liam Fox, b. 1961.

Secretary of State for Work and Pensions: Amber Rudd, b. 1963.

Secretary of State for Education: Damian Hinds, b. 1969.

Secretary of State for Environment, Food and Rural Affairs: Michael Gove, b. 1967.

Secretary of State for Housing, Communities and Local Government: James Brokenshire, b. 1968.

Secretary of State for Transport: Chris Grayling, b. 1962.

Leader of the House of Lords and Lord Privy Seal: Baroness Evans of Bowes Park, b. 1975.

Secretary of State for Scotland: David Mundell, b. 1962.

Secretary of State for Wales: Alun Cairns, b. 1970.

Secretary of State for Northern Ireland: Karen Bradley, b. 1970.

Secretary of State for International Development: Penny Mordaunt, b. 1973 (also *Minister for Women and Equalities*).

Secretary of State for Digital, Culture, Media and Sport: Jeremy Wright, b. 1972.

Minister without Portfolio: Brandon Lewis, b. 1971.

(Non-cabinet members but attend cabinet meetings): Elizabeth Truss, b. 1975, *Chief Secretary to the Treasury;* Andrea Leadsom, b. 1963, *Lord President of the Council and Leader of the House of Commons;* Julian Smith, b. 1971, *Chief Whip (Parliamentary Secretary to the Treasury);* Geoffrey Cox, b. 1960, *Attorney General;* Claire Perry, b. 1964, *Minister of State for Energy and Clean Growth;* Caroline Nokes, b. 1972, *Minister of State for Immigration.*

(b) LAW OFFICERS

Attorney General: Geoffrey Cox b. 1960 (also attends Cabinet meetings).

Solicitor General: Robert Buckland, b. 1968.

Advocate General for Scotland: Richard Keen, Baron Keen of Elie, QC, b. 1954.

(c) MINISTERS OF STATE (BY DEPARTMENT)

Department for Business, Energy and Industrial Strategy: Claire Perry, b. 1964, *Minister of State for Energy and Clean Growth;* Chris Skidmore, b. 1981 (also *Department for Education*), *Minister of State for Universities, Science, Research and Innovation.*

Ministry of Defence: Earl Howe, b. 1951 (also *Deputy Leader of the House of Lords*), *Minister of State for Defence;* Mark Lancaster, b. 1970, *Minister of State for the Armed Forces.*

Department for Digital, Culture, Media and Sport: Margot James, b. 1957, *Minister for Digital and the Creative Industries.*

Department for Education: Nick Gibb, b. 1960, *Minister of State for School Standards;* Anne Milton, b. 1955, *Minister of State for Apprenticeships and Skills;* Chris Skidmore, b. 1981 (also *Department for Business, Energy and Industrial Strategy*), *Minister of State for Universities, Science, Research and Innovation.*

Department for Environment, Food and Rural Affairs: Robert Goodwill, b. 1956, *Minister of State for Agriculture, Fisheries and Food.*

Department for Exiting the European Union: Lord Callanan, b. 1961.

Foreign and Commonwealth Office: Sir Alan Duncan, b. 1957, *Minister of State for Europe and the Americas;* Alistair Burt, b. 1955 (also *Department for International Development*), *Minister of State for the Middle East;*

Lord Ahmad of Wimbledon, b. 1968, *Minister of State for the Common-wealth and the UN;* Mark Field, b. 1964, *Minister of State for Asia and the Pacific;* Harriett Baldwin, b. 1960 (also *Department for International Development*), *Minister of State for Africa.*

Department of Health and Social Care: Stephen Hammond, b. 1962, *Minister of State for Health;* Caroline Dinenage, b. 1971, *Minister of State for Care.*

Home Office: Caroline Nokes, b. 1972, *Minister of State for Immigration;* Ben Wallace, b. 1970, *Minister of State for Security and Economic Crime;* Nick Hurd, b. 1962, *Minister of State for Policing and the Fire Service* (also *Minister for London*); Baroness Williams of Trafford, b. 1967 (also *Department for International Development*), *Minister of State for Countering Extremism.*

Ministry of Housing, Communities and Local Government: Kit Malthouse, b. 1966, *Minister of State for Housing.*

Department for International Development: Alistair Burt, b. 1955 (also *Foreign and Commonwealth Office*); Harriett Baldwin, b. 1960 (also *Foreign and Commonwealth Office*); Lord Bates, b. 1961.

Department for International Trade: George Hollingbery, b. 1963, *Minister of State for Trade Policy;* Baroness Fairhead, b. 1961, *Minister of State for Trade and Export Promotion.*

Ministry of Justice: Rory Stewart, b. 1973.

Northern Ireland Office: John Penrose, b. 1964.

Department for Transport: Jesse Norman, b. 1962, *Minister of State for Transport.*

Department for Work and Pensions: Alok Sharma, b. 1967, *Minister of State for Employment;* Sarah Newton, b. 1961, *Minister of State for Disabled People, Health and Work.*

(d) PARLIAMENTARY SECRETARIES AND UNDERSECRETARIES (BY DEPARTMENT)

Department for Business, Energy and Industrial Strategy: Kelly Tolhurst, b. 1978, *Minister for Small Business, Consumers and Corporate Responsibility;* Richard Harrington, b. 1957, *Minister for Business and Industry;* Lord Henley, b. 1953.

Cabinet Office: Oliver Dowden, b. 1978, *Minister for Implementation;* Chloe Smith, b. 1982, *Minister for the Constitution.*

Ministry of Defence: Tobias Ellwood, b. 1966, *Minister for Defence People and Veterans;* Stuart Andrew, b. 1971, *Minister for Defence Procurement.*

Department for Digital, Culture, Media and Sport: Lord Ashton of Hyde, b. 1958; Michael Ellis, b. 1967; Mims Davies, b. 1975.

Department for Education: Lord Agnew, b. 1961; Nadhim Zahawi, b. 1967.

Department for Environment, Food and Rural Affairs: Thérèse Coffey, b. 1971; Lord Gardiner of Kimble, b. 1956; David Rutley, b. 1961.

Department for Exiting the European Union: Robin Walker, b. 1978; Chris Heaton-Harris, b. 1967; Kwasi Kwarteng, b. 1975.

Department of Health and Social Care: Steve Brine, b. 1974; Jackie Doyle-Price, b. 1969; Baroness Blackwood, b. 1970.

Home Office: Victoria Atkins, b. 1976 (also *Department for International Development*).

Ministry of Housing, Communities and Local Government: Jake Berry, b. 1978, *Minister for the Northern Powerhouse and Local Growth;* Heather Wheeler, b. 1959, *Minister for Housing and Homelessness;* Rishi Sunak, b. 1980, *Minister for Local Government;* Lord Bourne of Aberystwyth, b. 1952 (also *Wales Office*), *Minister for Faith.*

Department for International Development: Victoria Atkins, b. 1976 (also *Home Office*), *Minister for Women;* Baroness Williams of Trafford, b. 1967 (also *Home Office*), *Minister for Equalities.*

Department for International Trade: Graham Stuart, b. 1962.

Ministry of Justice: Lucy Frazer, b. 1972; Edward Argar, b. 1977.

Northern Ireland Office: Lord Duncan of Springbank, b. 1973 (also *Scotland Office*).

Scotland Office: Lord Duncan of Springbank, b. 1973 (also *Northern Ireland Office*).

Department for Transport: Baroness Sugg, b. 1977; Nusrat Ghani, b. 1972; Andrew Jones, b. 1963.

HM Treasury: Mel Stride, b. 1961, *Financial Secretary;* Robert Jenrick, b. 1982, *Exchequer Secretary;* John Glen, b. 1974, *Economic Secretary.*

Wales Office: Lord Bourne of Aberystwyth, b. 1952 (also *Ministry of Housing, Communities and Local Government*); Nigel Adams, b. 1966.

Department for Work and Pensions: Guy Opperman, b. 1965; Baroness Buscombe, b. 1954; Justin Tomlinson, b. 1976.

(e) OPPOSITION FRONT BENCH

Leader of the Opposition: Jeremy Corbyn, b. 1949.

Leader of the Opposition in the House of Lords: Baroness Smith of Basildon, b. 1959.

The *Speaker* of the House of Commons is John Bercow (Con.), elected on 22 June 2009.

Government Website: http://www.direct.gov.uk

Current Leaders

Theresa May

Position
Prime Minister

Introduction
On 13 July 2016 Theresa May became prime minister after David Cameron resigned following referendum backing for the United Kingdom to leave the European Union. Her main challenges included overseeing the anticipated exit from the EU (commonly referred to as 'Brexit') and attempting to unite the country in the light of political and social tensions that emerged in the run-up to, and after, the referendum. However, her decision to hold an early general election in June 2017, with expectations of victory, backfired as her Conservative Party lost its overall majority in the House of Commons. Her subsequent parliamentary vulnerability, together with internal Conservative divisions over her perceived leadership shortcomings and the UK's ultimate aims in the ensuing Brexit negotiations, fuelled speculation about the longer-term viability of her tenure as premier.

Early Life
May was born Theresa Brasier on 1 Oct. 1956 in Eastbourne, Sussex, and was brought up, the daughter of a vicar, in Oxfordshire. She graduated in geography from the University of Oxford, in 1977. She subsequently joined the Bank of England and from 1985–97 worked for the Association for Payment Clearing Services (APACS). She also served as a Conservative councillor for the London Borough of Merton from 1986–97. At the 1992 general election May unsuccessfully contested the seat of North West Durham and in 1994 failed to win a by-election in Barking. However, in 1997 she was elected member of Parliament for Maidenhead, and has held the seat ever since.

In 1999 she joined William Hague's shadow cabinet as shadow secretary of state for education and employment. She went on to serve in the shadow cabinets of Iain Duncan Smith, Michael Howard and David Cameron, variously holding the portfolios for transport and work and pensions. From 2002–03 she served as the first female chair of the Conservative Party, and in 2010 was appointed home secretary in the Conservative–Liberal coalition government under Cameron. She was reappointed to the post following the Conservative victory at the 2015 polls, going on to become the longest serving home secretary in 60 years. During her tenure she oversaw the controversial deportation of the radical Muslim cleric Abu Qatada to Jordan, the creation of the National Crime Agency, and the introduction of elected police and crime commissioners. She also received criticism for failure to meet the government's net immigration target of below 100,000 per year. Ahead of the June 2016 referendum on the UK's future relationship with the EU, May supported retaining membership but kept a relatively low profile during the campaign. Cameron resigned after his call for remaining a member was rejected in the referendum, triggering a party leadership election race. May emerged as a strong contender as other prominent candidates—most notably Boris Johnson and Michael Gove—quickly fell by the wayside. She won the first polling round with 165 votes, and the second with 199 votes. On 11 July Andrea Leadsom, May's remaining rival in the race, withdrew and May automatically became party leader. On 13 July she accepted the Queen's invitation to form a government.

Career in Office
The overriding focus of May's first year in power was the initiation of the UK's withdrawal from the EU. Reiterating her position that 'Brexit means Brexit', she stated that she would aim to invoke Article 50 of the Lisbon Treaty (heralding a two-year withdrawal period) by the end of March 2017 and also made clear that the government would promptly seek to realign the UK in the wider world trading order. However, she met legal and political obstacles along the way. In Jan. the UK Supreme Court upheld an earlier court ruling that the government must obtain parliamentary approval for

triggering the withdrawal process, and she also had to concede opposition calls for a White Paper (a government statement on policy) on negotiating strategy. Nevertheless, in Feb. the House of Commons voted overwhelmingly in favour of a bill allowing the government to initiate exit negotiations and—following endorsement of the legislation by the House of Lords—May invoked the EU treaty procedure on 29 March.

In late Jan. 2017 the prime minister became the first foreign leader to visit the new US president, Donald Trump, in the White House. She stressed her commitment to the so-called 'special relationship' between the UK and USA, but provoked some dissension within the British parliament and the wider country for her invitation to the president to make a visit to the UK, which was subsequently scheduled despite concerns over potential opposition for July 2018. Meanwhile, UK commercial relations with China seemingly strengthened in early 2018 as the prime minister signed lucrative trade deals during a three-day visit to Beijing.

Seeking to reinforce her political mandate ahead of formal Brexit negotiations due to start on 19 June 2017, and emboldened by apparent internal divisions within the opposition Labour Party, May called a snap election for 8 June 2017, prompting media predictions of a Conservative landslide victory. However, Jeremy Corbyn, the Labour leader, unexpectedly bridged the divides within his party and garnered sufficient voter support to deny the Conservatives their previous overall parliamentary majority. May's political authority was consequently undermined and she was further criticized during the month for a perceived inadequate response to the trauma generated by a major social housing fire in London.

Forced to seek broader parliamentary support, May turned to the ten Democratic Unionist Party (DUP) MPs from Northern Ireland (where devolved power-sharing had collapsed in Jan. 2017) and signed an informal 'confidence and supply' arrangement with them on 26 June following the Queen's Speech the previous week in which her government's Brexit-dominated legislative programme—shorn of several major manifesto commitments—was outlined.

Many months of contentious Brexit negotiations followed, aggravated by continuing uncertainty in the EU about the UK's ambitions and by domestic political upheaval. May's efforts to establish a government consensus on acceptable terms for withdrawal were consistently undermined by the hostility of hard-line Conservative MPs to any lasting UK subjection to EU jurisdiction and structures, which prompted a series of damaging cabinet and other ministerial resignations, and by DUP demands over the island of Ireland's future border arrangements. A withdrawal agreement reached in Nov. 2018 between May and the other EU government heads was consequently rejected (by a record margin) in the House of Commons in Jan. 2019 and again in two further votes during March (albeit by reduced majorities). The EU meanwhile granted a limited, and conditional, extension to the UK's planned departure date of 29 March, and May promised to resign as premier if parliament would endorse her agreement (having previously survived a motion of no confidence in her party leadership triggered in Dec. by disgruntled Conservatives). Considerable public hostility was directed towards MPs from all parties—who had failed in a series of indicative votes to chart any alternative way forward and also rejected a no-deal divorce from the EU—as the promised leaving date was derailed amid the political and constitutional impasse. Such confusion also raised the possibility of a much longer extension of the withdrawal process, a revocation of Article 50 or perhaps a general election.

Defence

The Defence Council was established on 1 April 1964 under the chairmanship of the Secretary of State for Defence, who is responsible to the Sovereign and Parliament for the defence of the realm. Vested in the Defence Council are the functions of commanding and administering the Armed Forces. The Secretary of State heads the Department of Defence.

Defence policy decision-making is a collective governmental responsibility. Important matters of policy are considered by the full Cabinet or, more frequently, by the Defence and Overseas Policy Committee under the chairmanship of the Prime Minister.

Total number of the UK forces services personnel at 1 Jan. 2015 was 194,600 (down from 199,600 on 1 Jan. 2014), of which 154,200 were UK regular forces. There were an estimated 30,000 volunteer reservists. Women numbered 15,500 (10·1%) of the regular forces. In 2011 UK armed forces abroad included 18,150 personnel based in Germany and 2,430 in Cyprus. Deaths in the UK regular armed forces totalled 72 in 2016, down from 205 in 2009. The last British troops left Iraq in July 2009. In Sept. 2014 there were

approximately 3,900 British troops serving with the International Security Assistance Force (ISAF) in Afghanistan, although the mission's mandate expired at the end of the year. As at May 2017 the UK contributed some 500 troops to the more than 13,500 personnel charged with training, advising and assisting the Afghan National Security Forces under the aegis of Operation *Resolute Support*. British troop deaths in Iraq between 2003 and July 2009 totalled 179; deaths in Afghanistan between 2001 and Dec. 2014 when the ISAF mission ended totalled 453 (with the last ones in April 2014). Three deaths in 2015 brought the total up to 456 as at March 2019.

In Nov. 2010 the UK and France signed a Defence and Security Cooperation Treaty providing for the creation of a rapid reaction force, with troops from both nations called up as required after a joint political decision. Aircraft carriers may be jointly used under certain circumstances and there will be joint training exercises, pooling of resources for the maintenance and logistics of the A400M transport aircraft, and joint work on several other projects. The treaty provides for collaboration and co-operation through shared facilities to maintain the safety of the two countries' independent nuclear deterrents. As part of the requirements under the treaty, a new Technology Development Centre is being built at Aldermaston in the UK. This will support a joint Anglo/French Hydrodynamics Research Facility being developed at Valduc in France. Known as the EPURE facility, it is replacing existing facilities in both countries.

The ban on gays and lesbians serving in the armed forces, which had been upheld by a House of Commons vote in May 1996, was suspended in Sept. 1999 after the European Court of Human Rights ruled that the current ban was unlawful.

Defence Budget

In accordance with the 2018 Autumn Budget the planned defence budget for 2019–20 is £38·8bn. (£29·0bn. resource budget). Defence spending in 2013 represented 2·4% of GDP (above the NATO target of 2%), down from 5·2% in 1985. Per capita defence expenditure in 2013 totalled £551 (US$900).

Nuclear Weapons

Having carried out its first test in 1952, there have been 45 tests in all (the last in 1991). The nuclear arsenal consisted of about 120 Trident submarine-launched ballistic missile warheads in Jan. 2018 according to the Stockholm International Peace Research Institute. In addition there were some 95 non-deployed weapons in the nuclear stockpile.

Arms Trade

The UK is a net exporter of arms and over the period 2012–16 was the world's sixth largest exporter, with 4·6% of the global major weapons total.

Army

The Chief of the General Staff (CGS) is the 4-star commander and professional head of the Army and is responsible for implementing departmental decisions within it. He provides advice to ministers on managerial and operational issues and sets the strategic direction for the Army. CGS is also accountable for the efficiency and fighting effectiveness of the Army and the delivery of military capability.

CGS commands the Army through a single Army Staff that works out of the Army Headquarters in Andover, Hants. Subordinate to CGS are three 3-star commanders: Commander Land Forces (CLF); the Adjutant General (AG); and Commander Force Development and Capability (FD&Cap). CLF trains and commands the formations and units of the Army—the Land Forces. AG is the Principal Personnel Officer and leads the personnel and infrastructure areas. Comd FD&Cap leads on the development and delivery of optimum Army capability, including equipment and its support. Once soldiers are deployed abroad on operations, they are commanded from the tri-service Permanent Joint Headquarters (PJHQ) at Northwood, north London.

In line with the 2010 Strategic Defence and Security Review, the Army is reorganizing into a new structure called 'Army 2020'. The number of regular personnel is in the process of reducing to around 82,000 while the reserves are increasing to a trained strength of 30,000 to make a fully integrated Army of 112,000 by 2020. Women serve throughout the Army. In 2016 the UK government permitted women to apply for all close ground combat jobs from the end of 2018 (women having previously been excluded from infantry and armoured roles). All roles were opened to women from Oct. 2018.

The British Army's four core purposes are to: protect the United Kingdom; fight the UK's enemies; prevent conflict; and deal with disaster.

The British Army is currently equipped with a wide range of equipment to meet present-day threats. This includes the tracked range of Challenger 2 main battle tanks, Warrior Armoured Infantry Fighting vehicles, AS90 self-propelled artillery and the new Scout range of vehicles. The wheeled fleet includes Mastiff, Ridgeback, Husky, Jackal and Foxhound vehicles, proven on operations in Iraq and Afghanistan. Additionally the British Army has a fleet of AH-64D Apache and Wildcat helicopters.

Chandler, David G. and Beckett, Ian, (eds.) *The Oxford History of the British Army.* 2003

Haswell, Maj. Jock and Lewis-Stempel, John, *A Brief History of the British Army.* 2016

Mallinson, Allan, *The Making of the British Army.* 2009

Navy

Control of the Royal Navy is vested in the Defence Council and is exercised through the Admiralty Board, chaired by the Secretary of State for Defence.

The First Sea Lord and Chief of Naval Staff is the professional head of the Royal Navy and is responsible to the Secretary of State for Defence for the fighting effectiveness, efficiency and morale of the Naval Service. Subordinate to the First Sea Lord, the Fleet Commander, based at Navy Command Headquarters (NCHQ) in Portsmouth, Hants, is responsible for operations, while the Second Sea Lord is responsible for naval personnel. Main naval bases are at Devonport, Portsmouth and Faslane.

The roles of the Royal Navy are war-fighting, maritime security and international engagement. The Navy are also the custodians of the UK's Continuous-At-Sea-Deterrent (CASD).

The strength of the fleet's major units in the respective years:

	2007	2008	2009	2010	2011	2012
Strategic Submarines	4	4	4	4	4	4
Nuclear Submarines	9	9	8	7	6	5
Aircraft Carriers	2	2	2	2	1	1
Destroyers	8	7	6	6	6	6
Frigates	17	17	17	17	13	13
Landing Platform Docks	2	2	2	2	2	2
Landing Platform Helicopters	1	1	1	1	1	1

The four Trafalgar class nuclear submarines in active service are scheduled to be replaced by seven *Astute* class nuclear submarines by 2024. In 2014, two of the new *Astute* class submarines (HMS *Astute* and HMS *Ambush*) were launched following successful sea trials. A third, HMS *Artful*, was commissioned in March 2016 following successful sea trials in 2015. A further four *Astute* class submarines are planned or under construction and set to be commissioned by 2024.

The Continuous-At-Sea-Deterrent is borne by four Vanguard class Trident submarines—*Vanguard*, *Victorious*, *Vigilant* and *Vengeance*. They are each capable of deploying 16 US-built Trident II D5 missiles. The last remaining *Invincible* class ship, HMS *Illustrious*, was decommissioned in Aug. 2014. *Ark Royal*, its sister ship, was decommissioned in Jan. 2011 following the government's Strategic Defence and Security Review in 2010, and a third ship in the class, *Invincible*, was decommissioned in 2005. The Invincible class is set to be replaced by two large *Queen Elizabeth* class aircraft carriers. The first, HMS *Queen Elizabeth*, launched for sea trials in June 2017 and was commissioned in Dec. 2017. Her sister ship, HMS *Prince of Wales*, is scheduled to be handed over to the Navy during 2019 and is expected to enter full service from 2023. A Helicopter Carrier, HMS *Ocean*, specifically designed for amphibious operations, entered service in 1998 and was joined by two amphibious Landing Platform Docks (LPD), HMS *Albion* and HMS *Bulwark*, in 2003 and 2004 respectively. HMS *Ocean* was decommissioned in March 2018. In 2016 it was announced that the Vanguard class would be replaced by a fleet of Dreadnought class submarines armed with Trident II D5 missiles. Construction on these new vessels—the Royal Navy's largest ever submarines, measuring over 150 metres and weighing 17,500 tonnes—began in Oct. 2016. They are expected to be operational by the 2030s.

The current class of Type 23 Frigates are set to be replaced by the Type 26 Global Combat Ship in the early 2020s. Along with six Type 45 Destroyers, these ships will form the backbone of the future surface fleet.

The Fleet Air Arm is currently going through a period of transition. The search and rescue role previously provided by Sea King helicopters was taken over by contractor-provided services in late 2015. The last active Sea Kings were retired in Sept. 2018. Their airborne surveillance and control capability is being transferred to the new 'Crowsnest' system fitted in Merlin Mk 2s. The Navy has taken delivery of its first Wildcat helicopters (which replace the now decommissioned Lynx Mk3 and 8 helicopters) and the Merlin Mk2 (replacing the Merlin Mk1). Alongside the Royal Air Force, the Royal Navy will operate a Carrier Strike capability with a fleet of F-35 Lightning IIs (otherwise known as the Joint Strike Fighter), which are scheduled to deploy from the *Queen Elizabeth* class aircraft carriers in 2020.

The Maritime Reserve (MR) comprises the Royal Naval Reserve (RNR) and the Royal Marines Reserve (RMR), which are volunteer forces that currently number around 2,700 but are expected to grow to 4,150 by 2020. The MR provides trained personnel to supplement regular forces.

The Royal Marines Command, 6,750-strong in Feb. 2017, provides a commando brigade comprising three commando groups. The Special Boat Squadron and specialist defence units complete their operational strength.

The total number of trained naval service personnel was 29,500 in Feb. 2017.

Redford, Duncan and Grove, Philip D., *The Royal Navy: A History Since 1900.* 2014

Air Force

The Royal Air Force was formed on 1 April 1918 through the merger of the Royal Flying Corps and the Royal Naval Air Service. It consists of one Command (AIR), which is divided into three Groups.

Number 1 Group, with bases such as Coningsby (Lincs), Lossiemouth (Moray) and Marham (Norfolk), is home to combat aircraft, support helicopters, and Intelligence, Surveillance, Target Acquisition and Reconnaissance platforms.

The Typhoon has replaced the Tornado F3 in the air defence role and continues to develop a potent air-to-ground capability, with the new Paveway IV bomb as well as Stormshadow missiles for long-range attack. The Harrier was retired in Dec. 2010 following the government's Strategic Defence and Security Review; its successor, the F-35 Lightning II (otherwise known as the Joint Strike Fighter or Joint Combat Aircraft), began flight trials on the *Queen Elizabeth* aircraft carrier din Oct. 2018. Attack versions of the Tornado have been upgraded and fitted with RAPTOR (Reconnaissance Airborne Pod for Tornado). Remotely Piloted Air Systems (RPAS) continue to be widely employed in support of operations in Afghanistan.

There are two main pillars within Number 2 Group: Air Transport (AT)/Air-to-Air Refuelling (AAR) and Force Protection. AT/AAR provides rapid strategic and tactical reach, including the delivery of the airbridge to the Middle East and South Atlantic. Force protection comprises the RAF Regiment and RAF Police. The Operational Support Squadrons of the Royal Auxiliary Air Force are also included in No. 2 Group, as are Regiment Auxiliaries and the Mountain Rescue Service.

Mainstays of the AT and AAR force are the Hercules, TriStar and C-17s based at Brize Norton (Oxon). The A330 Voyager entered service in April 2012 and will gradually supplant the TriStar tankers and the Vickers VC-10 jetliners (the latter of which were retired in Sept. 2013) as part of the Future Strategic Tanker Aircraft programme. The A400M Atlas entered operational service in Sept. 2015 to replace the Hercules fleet, which is due to be withdrawn from service by 2022.

The UK Air Surveillance and Control Systems (ASACS) Force retains a fixed, static structure and continues to hold responsibility for the security of UK airspace; in platform terms this mission is delivered through Quick Reaction Alert Typhoons operating in the air-to-air role. In addition the Force has a deployable radar capability provided through No. 1 Air Control Centre, which has provided valuable support to ongoing operations in Afghanistan. Another key element is the space surveillance and missile warning radar at Fylingdales (N. Yorks).

Number 22 (Training) Group recruits and provides trained specialist personnel, and is also responsible for the Air Cadet Organisation and the University Air Squadrons. No. 22 Group also has responsibility both for the Royal Air Force Aerobatic Team (the Red Arrows) and the Royal Air Force Battle of Britain Memorial Flight.

In terms of personnel, on 1 Jan. 2015 Royal Air Force strength stood at 35,030 (8,010 officers).

Nesbit, Roy Conyers, *Royal Air Force: An Illustrated History from 1918.* 1998

Economy

In 2015 services accounted for 79·9% of GDP, industry 19·4% and agriculture 0·7% (69·4%, 29·2% and 1·4% respectively in 1990). Manufacturing's share of GDP fell from 17·5% in 1990 to 9·8% in 2015.

According to the anti-corruption organization Transparency International, in 2018 the United Kingdom ranked equal 11th in the world in a survey of the countries with the least corruption in business and government. It received 80 out of 100 in the annual index.

In 2017 the UK gave US$18·1bn. in international aid, representing 0·70% of its GNI. In actual terms this made the UK the third most generous country in the world, and as a percentage of GNI the fifth most generous and one of only five industrialized countries to meet or exceed the UN target of 0·7%.

Overview

The UK's economy ranks among the world's largest. From 1993–2004 the country enjoyed sustained non-inflationary growth, the longest period of expansion in 30 years. Light market regulation and labour market flexibility had meanwhile prompted higher levels of foreign direct investment than in most other European countries. However, the economy was severely dented by the global financial crisis that began in 2008. After two years of recession, GDP growth averaged 1·9% per year in the period 2010–14 against a backdrop of radical public spending cuts. As of 2018 the UK was still emerging from the economic turmoil prompted by the crisis, and also faced new uncertainty in light of its pending withdrawal from the European Union (commonly referred to as 'Brexit') after over 40 years of membership following a national referendum in June 2016. GDP grew by 1·7% in 2017 and 1·4% in 2018 as the clock ran down on securing a Brexit deal with the EU by 29 March 2019. According to the IMF, reverting to World Trade Organization trading rules, even in an orderly manner, would lead to long-run output losses for the UK of around 5% to 8% of GDP compared to a non-Brexit scenario.

Despite almost closing the GDP per capita gap with other major European countries, the disparity with the most successful OECD members (Canada, the USA and Australia) has remained, partly because of weaker productivity levels in the UK. Annualized growth in output per hour worked between 2010 and 2014 averaged 0·4%, compared to 2·2% in the decade preceding the financial crisis. In the year to the second quarter of 2018, the total number of hours worked shrank by 0·2% year-on-year, the first decline since the end of 2011.

The service sector was responsible for 80·2% of GDP in 2016, with insurance and finance comprising 32% of total services exports that year (higher than in any other G7 country). These services remain a major pillar of the economy thanks to the strength of the City of London and despite the impact of the financial crisis. In 2017 manufacturing accounted for 10% of the economy in terms of gross value added. The UK is the world's eighth largest producer of manufactured goods, with pharmaceuticals, electronics and the automotive industry making important contributions. The country also has a 17% global market share in aerospace, second only to the USA. Despite the fall in manufacturing's share of overall output in absolute terms (the sector having accounted for over 30% of GDP in 1970), it had increased decade by decade until its peak in 2007. In 2014 nearly 70% of all R&D expenditure accrued to the sector and, according to global advisory firm KPMG, the UK was ranked second (alongside China and behind only the USA) as a top destination for global companies to derive manufacturing sales growth over the preceding two years.

The sustained weakness of the pound since the Brexit vote has prompted increased sales of British goods and services abroad while also improving tourist inflows. The depreciation has also raised the prices of imports, which pushed up inflation to 3·0% in Dec. 2017. However, inflation had slowed to 2·4% by Sept. 2018, driven by lower food and drink prices.

In the three months to Aug. 2018, the UK's trading deficit narrowed by £4·7bn. to £2·8bn. Nonetheless, the outlook for UK exporters was unclear amid Brexit uncertainty, slowing growth in key markets and global trade tensions.

The Brexit vote had followed almost a decade of economic stagnation that began with the British bank Northern Rock being taken into 'temporary' public ownership in Feb. 2008 as a result of credit problems. In Oct. that year continued instability in the financial markets had prompted a government injection of £37bn. into three of the UK's biggest banks—Royal Bank of Scotland, Lloyds TSB and Halifax Bank of Scotland. In an attempt to stave off a deep recession, the Bank of England reduced interest rates six times from Oct. 2008 to 0·5% in March 2009, and by July 2012 the Bank had injected a total of £375bn. into the economy through its 'quantitative easing' asset-purchase programme. To further boost the economy and encourage spending in the wake of the Brexit decision, the Bank of England injected a further £70bn. in Aug. 2016 and cut its benchmark interest rate to a new record low of 0·25%. However, in Nov. 2017 the Bank voted to increase the rate for the first time since 2008, by 0·25%, in a bid to stave off inflationary pressures.

Having fallen into recession following contractions in the second and third quarters of 2008, the economy continued to shrink up to Sept. 2009 (recording a drop of 4·2% over the year as a whole). Recovery in 2011 was impeded by high commodity prices and the effects of the eurozone debt crisis—the value of shipments to eurozone countries, the destination of 40% of British exports, fell significantly. Although the UK relapsed into recession in the first half of 2012, the London Olympic Games provided a boost in the third quarter of that year and the economy then grew by 2·0% in 2013, its fastest pace since 2007 (propelled by improved consumer confidence and the easing of credit conditions). The IMF confirmed that growth in 2014 was faster than in any other advanced economy, although the current account deficit reached a 50-year high of 5·1% before declining to 4·1% in 2015. GDP growth was 2·3% in 2015 and 1·8% in 2016.

Although unemployment had risen to 8·4% by Dec. 2011—its highest level in over 15 years—a subsequent rapid rise in new jobs (albeit largely on a less permanent or part-time basis) meant that the jobless rate fell substantially to stand at 4·3% in the three months to Nov. 2017—the lowest rate since 1975. It fell further, to 4·0%, in the second quarter 2018—below the equilibrium level of 4·25% that the Bank of England considers sustainable—although that decline was mostly driven by an increase in the number of people dropping out of the labour force rather than any major rise in employment.

The Code for Fiscal Stability, introduced in 1998, had stipulated that the government could borrow only to invest and not to support current spending. The 'sustainable investment' or 'golden' rule looked to maintain the public sector net debt below 40% of GDP over the economic cycle. However, in April 2009 the then Chancellor, Alistair Darling, had confirmed in his Budget Report that borrowing would be taken to record levels to help the government manage the escalating economic crisis. By Sept. 2009 overall government debt stood at 57·5% of GDP, its highest level since 1974. In June 2010 the new Chancellor, George Osborne, introduced an emergency Budget to tackle the deficit, which reached £155bn. in 2009–10. In Oct. 2010 he revealed details of a spending review which would see public sector job losses, an increase in the retirement age from 65 to 66 by 2020 and £7bn. in additional welfare budget cuts. He subsequently announced progressive increases in tax-free allowances for individuals, a reduction in the top rate of income tax from 50% to 45% and several freezes to fuel duty, while it was hoped that measures against tax avoidance and evasion would raise £12bn. in extra revenue over the lifetime of the parliament. The implementation of welfare reforms—including plans to introduce a 'universal credit' system merging several benefits into a single monthly payment—began to roll out, although proposed changes to entitlements for the sick and disabled have since proved particularly controversial.

Current spending on health care and education has been around the OECD average but public services are overstretched. Nonetheless, the UK's benefit system is more strongly targeted to supporting low-income groups than in most other OECD countries. As an increasing number of companies close final salary pension schemes, the government has also encouraged individuals to take more responsibility for their retirement. The then Chancellor, George Osborne, announced a new lifetime ISA in his 2016 Budget with the aim of making saving more flexible for the younger generations. Under the scheme, anyone under the age of 40 can save up to £4,000 annually up to the age of 50, with the government contributing an additional £1 for each £4 saved.

The budget deficit fell to 2·5% of GDP at the end of 2016, with the goal of reducing the structural deficit to 2% of GDP by 2021 likely to be achieved earlier than planned. Moreover, reduced debt service costs owing to very low interest rates, the transfer of interest payments collected by the Bank of England under its quantitative easing programme and the longest maturity of public debt in the OECD (above 15 years) has helped eased fiscal pressure. The UK's longer-term economic outlook will be heavily influenced by the success or otherwise of its withdrawal from the EU. The result of the Brexit referendum caused immediate upheaval in the financial markets. Inflation climbed to 1% in Sept. 2016 (from 0·3% in May), with the Institute of Fiscal

Studies stating that the increase in the price of goods would adversely affect lower income families as a consequence of tax credits and benefits being frozen in cash terms until 2020. The value of the currency tumbled and by Oct. 2016 sterling had dropped to a six-year low against the euro. While the potential impact of Brexit on the City of London remains unclear, investment banks such as Goldman Sachs and Morgan Stanley have pledged to relocate thousands of jobs in the event that Britain loses its 'passport' rights to the EU single market. In his Budget speech in March 2017 new Chancellor Philip Hammond pledged to cut corporation tax from 28% to 19% in a bid to improve the country's competitiveness on the international business stage—especially in light of the uncertainty wrought by the Brexit vote. His plans to raise national insurance contributions for self-employed people, however, met stiff political opposition and were withdrawn. Although the Nov. 2017 and March 2018 financial statements saw the Chancellor stick to his fiscal targets, ruling out an immediate end to austerity, his 2018 Autumn Budget marked the beginning of a less restrictive fiscal policy.

Following the resignation of Prime Minister David Cameron after the Brexit referendum, Theresa May took over as premier. Despite a series of legal and parliamentary challenges, she triggered the formal leaving process from the EU (via Article 50 of the Treaty of Lisbon) at the end of March 2017, with a view to completion of Brexit in March 2019. However, in Jan. 2019 parliament voted against her draft plan for withdrawal—agreed with the EU in Nov. 2017—increasing the chances of a 'no deal' Brexit. UK MPs backed a call to replace the controversial Northern Ireland 'backstop' clause in the agreement (relating to the Irish border) with alternative legal arrangements, and a further round of negotiations with the EU began. May's slightly amended deal was rejected again in March, with MPs also voting against a 'no deal' Brexit, although that vote was non-binding.

The failure to reach an acceptable withdrawal agreement with the EU is the greatest risk to the UK's economic outlook. OECD analysis suggests that a no-deal scenario could cut over 2% from real GDP over two years. The lack of details on the future relationship between the UK and the EU or the extension of the transition period, and the resulting uncertainties, has led to significant investor nervousness.

Currency

The unit of currency is the *pound sterling* (£; GBP) of 100 *pence* (p.). Before decimalization on 15 Feb. 1971 £1 = 20 shillings (*s*) of 12 pence (*d*). A gold standard was adopted in 1816, the sovereign, a £1, or twenty-shilling gold coin, weighing 7·98805 grams. It is eleven-twelfths pure gold and one-twelfth alloy. Currency notes for £1 and 10*s*. were first issued by the Treasury in 1914, replacing the circulation of sovereigns. The issue of £1 and 10*s*. notes was taken over by the Bank of England in 1928. 10*s*. notes ceased to be legal tender in 1970 and £1 notes (in England and Wales) in 1988. Sterling was a member of the exchange rate mechanism of the European Monetary System from 8 Oct. 1990 until 16 Sept. 1992 ('Black Wednesday'), when the UK government could not maintain the value of the currency above the European Exchange Rate Mechanism's agreed lower limit.

Inflation

Consumer Price Index (CPI) inflation rates (based on OECD statistics):

2008	2009	2010	2011	2012	2013	2014	2015	2016	2017
3·6%	2·2%	3·3%	4·5%	2·8%	2·6%	1·5%	0·1%	0·6%	2·7%

Coinage

Estimated number of coins in circulation at 31 March 2016 was 30,139m., of which: £2, 479m.; £1, 1,671m.; 50p, 1,053m.; 20p, 3,004m.; 10p, 1,713m.; 5p, 4,075m.; 2p, 6,714m.; 1p, 11,430m. Total value: £4,644m.

Banknotes

The Bank of England issues notes in denominations of £5, £10, £20 and £50 up to the amount of the fiduciary issue. Under the provisions of the Currency Act 1983 the amount of the fiduciary issue is limited, but can be altered by direction of HM Treasury on the advice of the Bank of England.

All current series Bank of England notes are legal tender in England and Wales. Some banks in Scotland (Bank of Scotland, Clydesdale Bank and the Royal Bank of Scotland) and Northern Ireland (Bank of Ireland, First Trust Bank, Danske Bank—formerly Northern Bank—and Ulster Bank) have note-issuing powers.

The total amount of Bank of England notes in circulation at 28 Feb. 2017 was £73,198m.

Foreign currency reserves were US$115,213m. and gold reserves 9·98m. fine oz in Sept. 2017 (22·98m. fine oz in April 1999, before the Treasury's announcement of its intention to sell nearly 60% of UK gold reserves over the medium term).

Budget

The fiscal year runs from 6 April to 5 April. The Oct. 2018 Budget estimated public sector net borrowing for 2017–18 at £39·8bn., with a forecast of £25·5bn. in 2018–19, then £31·8bn. in 2019–20, £26·7bn. in 2020–21 and £23·8bn. in 2021–22. Public sector net debt as a proportion of GDP was put at 85·0% for 2017–18, 83·7% in 2018–19 and then falling further to 75·7% in 2021–22 and 75·0% in 2022–23. As a share of GDP, this will see borrowing fall from 1·9% in 2017–18 to 0·9% in 2022–23.

Public sector current spending for 2018–19 is set at £731·5bn., increasing to £824·4bn. by 2022–23. Net investment is to be unchanged in 2018–19 from 2017–18 at £41·2bn., before rising to £51·2bn. by 2022–23. The United Kingdom's budget deficit in 2017 was 1·8% of GDP (down from 2·9% in 2016 and 4·2% in 2015).

The independent Office for Budget Responsibility forecasts economic growth of 1·6% in 2019, followed by 1·4% in both 2020 and 2021.

The Oct. 2018 Budget's provisions included an additional £2bn. per year for mental health funding by 2023–24, as part of an additional £20·5bn. over five years for the National Health Service as a whole. There was an extra £700m. for local councils to fund care of the elderly and those with disabilities, and an additional £1bn. for the ministry of defence for the rest of 2018 and 2019 to fund its cyber capability and nuclear submarine programme. Counter-terrorism police were also to be allocated £160m. more, while schools were promised a one-off 'bonus' of £400m. to aid the purchase of 'the little extras they need'.

The National Living Wage was to be raised from £7·83 to £8·21 per hour from April 2019. Fuel duty was frozen for the ninth year in a row. An extra £1bn. was set aside to assist welfare claimants transferring to universal credit, and an additional £500m. was made available to assist preparations for exiting the European Union. A commemorative 50-pence piece was scheduled to be minted to mark Brexit. The Chancellor also suggested that the Spring 2019 budget statement could be upgraded to a full budget if required.

From April 2020 digital technology companies with global sales in excess of £500m. per year will face a 2% tax on money made in the UK market. A provision of £900m. was made for business rates relief for small enterprises and a Future High Streets Fund, worth £675m. and intended to bolster the physical retail sector, was announced. The Chancellor also outlined a new tax on plastic packaging containing less than 30% recyclable material.

The government will no longer sign any new private finance initiative contracts. An additional £500m. for the Housing Infrastructure Fund was announced, with a view to assisting the building of some 650,000 new homes. In addition, stamp duty was abolished for first-time buyers purchasing shared-equity homes worth up to £500,000, and the 'Help to Buy' home ownership scheme was extended to 2023 for first-time buyers. Plans were also set out for £30bn. of spending on England's road infrastructure.

The *Financial Times* commented on the budget: 'In normal circumstances, Philip Hammond, chancellor of the exchequer, would have been in a far more comfortable position in delivering his Budget on Monday than he or his predecessors since the financial crisis 10 years ago. As he repeatedly reminded his listeners, the fiscal squeeze was coming to an end. Above all, he had more money to play with than he expected. Alas, these are not normal circumstances. The uncertainty of Brexit hangs over prospects. . . Mr Hammond is indicating to his colleagues that, provided they. . . give prime minister Theresa May the latitude she needs to reach a Brexit deal, sunlit uplands of growth and fiscal largesse lie ahead... But, if Brexit turns into a disaster, that may well not remain true.' (*Financial Times*, 29 October 2018).

Current Budget (in £1bn.)	2017–18 Outturn	2018–19 Forecast	2019–20 Forecast
Current Receipts	754·0	787·3	809·8
Public Sector Current Expenditure	711·5	731·5	751·9

Surplus on Current Budget (in £1bn.)	2017–18 Outturn	2018–19 Forecast	2019–20 Forecast
	1·4	15·7	16·6

Current Receipts (in £1bn.)	2017–18 Outturn	2018–19 Forecast	2019–20 Forecast
National Accounts Taxes	700·7	736·1	755·8
Current Receipts	754·0	787·3	809·8

Departmental Expenditure Limits (Resource Budget, in £1bn.)	2018–19 Planned	2019–20 Planned
Defence	28·4	29·0
Single Intelligence Account	2·2	2·0
Home Office	10·8	10·7
Foreign and Commonwealth Office	2·2	1·2
International Development	7·7	8·2
Health (including NHS)	123·3	129·6
Work and Pensions	6·0	5·4
Education	62·5	63·5
Business, Energy and Industrial Strategy	1·7	1·8
Transport	2·1	2·9
Exiting the European Union	0·1	0·1
Digital, Culture, Media and Sport	1·5	1·5
HCLG Communities	2·6	2·3
HCLG Local Government	4·7	5·9
Scotland	14·7	15·7
Wales	13·3	11·6
Northern Ireland	10·3	10·3
Justice	6·3	6·0
Law Officers' Departments	0·6	0·6
Environment, Food and Rural Affairs	1·6	1·5
HM Revenue and Customs	3·4	3·2
HM Treasury	0·2	0·2
Cabinet Office	0·4	0·3
International Trade	0·4	0·3
Small and Independent Bodies	1·5	1·3

VAT, introduced on 1 April 1973, was raised from 17·5% to 20·0% in Jan. 2011. The reduced rate is 5·0%.

Rates of Income Tax for 2018–19:

Income between	%[1]
£11,851–£46,350 (basic rate)[2]	20
Between £46,351–£150,000 (higher rate)	40
Over £150,000	45

[1]The standard rate of tax applicable to savings income (subject to the level of an individual's other income sources) is 0% for income up to £5,000, then 20% up to the basic rate limit, 40% to the higher rate limit and thereafter 45%. The rates applicable to dividends are 7·5% for income up to the basic rate limit, 32·5% to the higher rate limit and 38·1% above that. [2]There is a standard personal allowance threshold (£11,850 in 2018–19), below which income tax is not payable.

Performance
In 2017 total GDP was US$2,622·4bn. (£2,033·8bn.), the fifth highest in the world.

Real GDP growth rates (based on OECD statistics):

2008	2009	2010	2011	2012	2013	2014	2015	2016	2017
–0·3%	–4·2%	1·7%	1·6%	1·4%	2·0%	2·9%	2·3%	1·8%	1·7%

The provisional real GDP growth rate in 2018 according to the Office of National Statistics was 1·4%. With the economy contracting in both the second and third quarters of 2008 the UK went into recession for the first time since 1991. There were five consecutive quarters of negative growth before the economy expanded by 0·4% in the third quarter of 2009. It shrank again in the fourth quarter of 2010, by 0·4%. After a slight recovery there was a further recession in late 2011 and early 2012.

The UK was ranked eighth in the World Economic Forum's *Global Competitiveness Report 2017–2018* index. The index analyses 12 areas of competitiveness for over 100 countries including macro-economy, higher education and training, institutions, innovation and infrastructure.

Banking and Finance
The Bank of England is the government's banker and the 'banker's bank'. It has the sole right of note issue in England and Wales. It was founded by Royal Charter in 1694 and nationalized in 1946. The capital stock has, since 1 March 1946, been held by HM Treasury. The *Governor* (appointed for eight-year terms) is Mark Carney (b. 1965; took office July 2013).

In addition to the statutory Weekly Report a consolidated balance sheet is published quarterly. End June figures are as follows (in £1m.):

	Notes in circulation	Reserve balances	Other liabilities
2014	61,761	302,868	39,424
2015	65,561	313,598	37,714
2016	71,287	318,549	40,323

Major British Banking Groups' statistics at end Aug. 2017: total sterling deposits, £2,377bn.; total foreign currency deposits, £1,198bn.; total sterling liabilities, £2,712bn.; total foreign currency liabilities, £1,374bn.; total liabilities, £4,085bn.; total sterling assets, £2,738bn.; total foreign currency assets, £1,347bn.; total assets, £4,085bn.

In April 2016 Britain's largest bank both by market capitalization and assets was HSBC with US$133·0bn. and US$2,409·7bn. respectively.

50% of the adult population were using online banking in 2013, up from 35% in 2008.

In May 1997 the power to set base interest rates was transferred from the Treasury to the Bank of England. The government continues to set the inflation target but the Bank has responsibility for setting interest rates to meet the target. Base rates are now set by a nine-member Monetary Policy Committee (MPC) at the Bank; members include the Governor. Membership of the Court (the governing body) was widened. The 1998 Act provides for the Court to consist of the Governor, two Deputy Governors and 16 Directors. The Act also established the MPC as a Committee of the Bank and sets a framework for its operations. The Bank of England's Prudential Regulation Authority (PRA) works alongside the Financial Conduct Authority (FCA) creating a 'twin peaks' regulatory structure in the UK. The PRA is responsible for the prudential regulation of major financial institutions, regulating their 'financial safety' and 'soundness'. The FCA is a separate institution and not part of the Bank of England. The FCA is responsible for promoting effective competition, ensuring that relevant markets function well and for the conduct regulation of all financial services firms. The bank rate was lowered from 0·5% to 0·25% on 4 Aug. 2016 (the lowest since the Bank of England was founded in 1694), but then raised back up to 0·5% on 2 Nov. 2017.

The London Stock Exchange (called International Stock Exchange until May 1991) originated over 300 years ago, although a regulated stock exchange did not come into existence until 1801. In July 1991 the 91 shareholders voted unanimously for a new memorandum and articles of association which devolves power to a wider range of participants in the securities industry, and replaces the Stock Exchange Council with a 14-member board. The Financial Times Stock Exchange 100 (FTSE 100) ended 2018 at 6,728·1, down from 7,687·8 at the end of 2017 (falling 12·5% during the year).

Gross external debt totalled US$8,647,109m. in Dec. 2017 (compared to US$7,499,252m. in Dec. 2016).

The UK received US$15·1bn. worth of foreign direct investment in 2017, down from a record US$196·1bn. in 2016.

National Savings and Investments
Statistics for 2015–16 and 2016–17:

Conaghan, Dan, *The Bank: Inside the Bank of England.* 2012

Kynaston, David, *Till Time's Last Sand: A History of the Bank of England 1694–2013.* 2017

Roberts, R. and Kynaston, D. (eds.) *The Bank of England: Money, Power and Influence, 1694–1994.* 1995

Amounts	Premium bonds		Savings certificates		Total (including other accounts and bonds)	
	2015–16 in £1,000	2016–17 in £1,000	2015–16 in £1,000	2016–17 in £1,000	2015–16 in £1,000	2016–17 in £1,000
—Received	15,219,121	14,149,735	195,595	790,022	31,465,355	35,025,913
—Interest and prizes earned by investors	807,320	773,960	398,709	716,655	2,067,732	2,333,765
—Paid	(8,330,052)	(7,666,403)	(2,027,657)	(5,033,551)	(22,273,169)	(25,567,871)
Invested at 31 March	69,556,624	61,860,235	27,501,756	23,966,034	135,148,451	146,940,258

Energy and Natural Resources

In 2011 just 3·8% of energy consumption came from renewables (wind power, solar power, hydro-electric power, tidal power, geothermal energy and biomass), compared to the European Union average of 13·0%. A target of 15% has been set by the EU for 2020.

Environment

The UK's carbon dioxide emissions from the consumption of energy in 2014 were the equivalent of 6·5 tonnes per capita. The UK's total emission of greenhouse gases is estimated to have fallen from 809m. tonnes in 1990 to 568m. tonnes by 2013. An *Environmental Performance Index* compiled in 2016 ranked the UK 12th in the world, with 87·4%. The index examined various factors in six areas—air pollution, biodiversity and habitat, climate change, environmental health, productive natural resources and water resources. In 2012 an estimated 46% of municipal waste was recycled or composted, compared to the European Union average of 42%.

Electricity

The Electricity Act of 1989 implemented the restructuring and privatization of the electricity industry. In 1999 the domestic electricity market (peak load below 100 kW) was opened to competition.

Generators

Under the 1989 Act, National Power and Powergen took over the fossil fuel and hydro-electric power stations previously owned by the Central Electricity Generating Board, and were privatized in 1991. A succession of takeovers and mergers saw the rapid diversification of the UK generation market. There were a total of 15 nuclear reactors in use in the UK at eight nuclear power stations in March 2019, all of which are operated by EDF Energy. It plans to build several new nuclear power stations in the UK. Construction of the first of these, at Hinkley Point in Somerset, was approved in Oct. 2013 with work commencing in Dec. 2018.

Transmission

Since 2005 the electricity systems of England, Wales and Scotland have been integrated and operate under the British Electricity Trading and Transmission Arrangements (BETTA). National Grid became the operator of the UK transmission networks under the new arrangements.

Distribution and Supply

The 12 Area Boards were replaced under the 1989 Act by regional electricity companies (RECs), which were privatized in 1990; 14 public electricity suppliers then came into operation which, under the terms of the Utilities Act of 2000, needed separate licences for their supply businesses and distribution networks. Subsequent market liberalization has seen a sharp increase in the number of electricity suppliers in operation, the largest of which are British Gas, EDF Energy, E.ON UK, npower, ScottishPower and SSE.

See also SCOTLAND.

Electricity Associations

The Electricity Association, formerly the trade association of the UK electricity companies, was replaced in Oct. 2003 by three industry bodies. The Energy Networks Association (ENA) represents the transmission and distribution companies for both gas and electricity. The Association of Electricity Producers (AEP) represented companies that generate electricity using coal, gas and nuclear power as well as renewable sources such as wind, biomass and water. The Energy Retail Association (ERA) represented Britain's domestic electricity and gas suppliers in the internal market. AEP and ERA were merged with the UK Business Council for Sustainable Energy (UKBCSE) in April 2012 to create Energy UK. A trade association for both the electricity and the gas sector, it represents a wide range of interests. It includes small, medium and large companies working in electricity generation, energy networks and gas and electricity supply, as well as a number of businesses that provide equipment and services to the industry.

Regulation

The Office of Electricity Regulation ('OFFER') was set up under the 1989 Act to protect consumer interests following privatization. In 1999 it was merged with the Office of Gas Supply ('Ofgas') to form the Office of Gas and Electricity Markets ('Ofgem'), reflecting the opening up of all markets for electricity and gas supply to full competition from May that year, with many suppliers now offering both gas and electricity to customers.

Statistics

The electricity industry contributed about 0·95% of the UK's Gross Domestic Product in 2012. The installed capacity of all UK power stations in 2013 was 82,928 MW. In 2012 the fuel generation mix was: coal 38%, gas 28%, nuclear 18%, wind and solar 6%, other renewables 4%, hydro 1%, oil and other fuels 1%, and net imports 3%. At its peak in the 1990s nuclear power accounted for over a quarter of electricity generation. In the second quarter of 2015, 25·3% of UK power was generated from renewable—i.e. wind, solar, biomass and hydro-electric—sources (up from 16·7% in April–June 2014) compared with 20·5% from coal (down from 28·2% year-on-year). It was the first time the share from renewables was greater than that of coal; gas was the largest power source, at 30·2%. Final consumption in 2012 totalled 325·4 TWh, of which domestic users took 35·3%, industrial users 30·2%, and service and energy industry users 34·6%. Consumption per capita in 2013 was 5,407 kWh.

Electrica Services. *Electricity Industry Review.* Annual

Surrey, J. (ed.) *The British Electricity Experience: Privatization—the Record, the Issues, the Lessons.* 1996

Oil and Gas

Production in 1,000 tonnes, in 2017: throughput of crude and process oils, 60,245; total refinery fuel use, 3,407. Refinery output: gas/diesel oil, 20,303; motor spirit, 17,416; aviation turbine fuel, 5,031; butane, propane and other petroleum gases, 4,622; fuel oil, 3,893; naphtha, 2,280; burning oil, 2,047; bitumen, 817. Total output of refined products, 59,824. Total indigenous oil production (2017), 46·9m. tonnes. The UK had proven oil reserves of 2·8bn. bbls in 2015. The UK became a net importer of oil in 2005, having been a net exporter since 1980.

The first significant offshore gas discovery was made in 1965 in the North Sea, followed in 1969 by the first commercial oil offshore. Offshore production of gas began in 1967 and oil in 1975.

Oil and gas have played an important part in providing the UK's energy needs. In 2017, either through direct use or as a source of energy to produce electricity, oil and gas accounted for some 76% (29% gas and 48% oil) of total UK energy consumption, with UK-based production supplying some 70% of all the oil and gas consumed. However, oil production peaked in 1999 as did natural gas production in 2000, and annual production of both has gradually been declining in the years since then. As of 2015 the UK ranked 22nd among the world's largest gas producers and 21st among the largest oil producers.

Oil products also provide important contributions to other industries, such as feedstocks for the petrochemical industry and lubricants for various uses. While the importance of oil as a source of energy for electrical generation and use by industry and commercial operations has declined with the increasing use of gas, oil still makes up around 18% of total industrial uses of energy. Its prime importance is in the transport sector, where it provides 97% of the total energy used.

The reform of the old nationalized gas industry began with the Gas Act of 1986, which paved the way for the privatization later that year of the British Gas Corporation, and established the Director General of Gas Supply

(DGGS) as the independent regulator. This had a limited effect on competition, as British Gas retained a monopoly on tariff (domestic) supply. Competition progressively developed in the industrial and commercial (non-tariff) market.

The Gas Act 1995 amended the 1986 Act to prepare the way for full competition, including the domestic market. It created three separate licences—for Public Gas Transporters who operate pipelines, for Shippers (wholesalers) who contract for gas to be transported through the pipelines, and for Suppliers (retailers) who then market gas to consumers. It also placed the DGGS under a statutory duty to secure effective competition.

The domestic market was progressively opened to full competition from 1996 until May 1998.

In 1997 British Gas took a commercial decision to de-merge its trading business. Centrica plc (a new company) was formed to handle the gas sales, gas trading, services and retail businesses of BG, together with the gas production businesses of the North and South Morecambe Field. The remaining parts of the business, including transportation and storage and the international downstream activities, were contained in BG plc. As a result of subsequent changes, National Grid Gas plc now owns and operates the UK's national gas transmission system.

The Department of Energy and Climate Change (DECC) was created in Oct. 2008 to oversee the UK oil and gas industry, and in July 2016 was merged to become the Department for Business, Energy and Industrial Strategy (BEIS). The regulator for Britain's gas and electricity industries is Ofgem (Office of the Gas and Electricity Markets), created in 1999 through the merger of Ofgas (Office of Gas Supply) and OFFER (Office of Electricity Regulation). Its role is to protect and advance the interests of consumers by promoting competition where possible.

A second European Directive was published in June 2003 with rules for the internal market in natural gas. Member states were allowed one year to execute its provisions; the UK implemented the directive in July 2004.

The UK became a net importer of gas in 2004. To help ensure a secure gas supply as the UK becomes more dependent on imported gas, several gas infrastructure projects have been developed. These supply the UK with gas from a number of sources, including Norway and the Netherlands. There is already a pipeline (the Interconnector) linking the UK and European gas grids via Belgium. This link to Continental Europe opened in Oct. 1998 and has an export capacity of 20·0bn. cu. metres a year and an import capacity of 25·5bn. cu. metres a year.

Proven natural gas reserves in 2015 were 200bn. cu. metres. Production was 42·3bn. cu. metres in 2017. The UK's natural gas output declined every year from 2000 (when it totalled 108·4bn. cu. metres) to 2013 before rising slightly each year since 2014. In 2017, 34% of the UK's total gas supply was used by domestic users and 33% by electricity generators—a figure that has risen since the move away from the use of coal for electricity generation accelerated in 2016.

Wind

The UK is the sixth largest wind power producer, behind the USA, China, Germany, Spain and India. Production of wind-generated electricity in 2014 totalled 32·0bn. kWh. Installed capacity at the end of 2014 totalled 13,037 MW, of which 8,536 MW onshore and 4,501 MW offshore. The UK has the largest offshore wind capacity of any country.

Minerals

Legislation to privatize the coal industry was introduced in 1994 and established the Coal Authority to take over certain activities from British Coal Corporation. The Coal Authority is the owner of almost all the UK's coal reserves; it licenses private coal mining and disposes of property not required for operational purposes. The Coal Authority also deals with the historic legacy of coal mining including handling subsidence claims in former mining areas, treating mine water discharges and dealing with surface hazards. In 2014 there were three underground coal mines and 31 opencast coal mines in operation. The last underground mine closed in Dec. 2015.

Total production from deep mines was 6·2m. tonnes in 2012 (204·7m. tonnes in 1958 and 83·8m. tonnes in 1988). Output from opencast sites in 2012 was 10·1m. tonnes (15·0m. tonnes in 1958 and 20·3m. tonnes in 1988). In 2013 inland coal consumption was 60·4m. tonnes.

Output of non-fuel minerals in Great Britain, 2014 (in 1,000 tonnes): limestone (estimate), 66,300; sand and gravel (estimate), 61,000; igneous rock (estimate), 43,700; sandstone (estimate), 12,500; clay and shale, 6,806; salt, 4,690; silica sand, 3,948; dolomite, 3,730; chalk, 3,312; gypsum (estimate), 1,200.

Steel and Metals
Steel production in recent years (in 1m. tonnes):

2009	10·1
2010	9·7
2011	9·5
2012	9·5
2013	11·9
2014	12·0
2015	10·9

Deliveries of finished steel products from UK mills in 2012 were 9·3m. tonnes, the same as in 2011, and comprised 4·2m. tonnes to the UK domestic market and 5·1m. tonnes for export. About 53% of UK steel exports went to other EU countries. UK steel imports in 2012 were about 5·5m. tonnes, with 72% coming from other EU countries. UK steel demand totalled 9·7m. tonnes in 2012, down from 10·2m. tonnes in 2011. The main markets for steel in the UK are construction, engineering, automotive and metal goods.

The steel contained in imported goods was 9·4m. tonnes in 2012, down from 9·9m. tonnes in 2011.

Since late 2015 the UK steel industry has been in crisis as a result of global overproduction and several major British manufacturing plants have been faced with closure. Annual production today is less than half the 1970 total.

Agriculture
Land use in 2014: agriculture, 71%; other, 29%. In 2014 agricultural land in the UK totalled (in 1,000 ha.) 18,456, comprising agricultural holdings, 17,257; and common rough grazing, 1,199. Land use of agricultural holdings in 2014 (in 1,000 ha.): permanent grassland (including rough grazing), 9,755; crops, 4,722; temporary grass under five years old, 1,396; uncropped arable land, 160; other, 1,224. Area sown to crops in 2014 (in 1,000 ha.): arable crops, 4,559 (of which wheat, 1,936; barley, 1,080; oilseed rape, 675); horticultural crops (including fruit), 164.

In 2014 there were 6·28m. ha. of arable land and 32,000 ha. of orchard fruit, soft fruit and wine grapes.

The area of fully organic farmland in the UK in 2014 was 548,000 ha. Including land in conversion, 3·2% of the agricultural land was managed organically in 2014. Organic food sales for the UK in 2013 totalled £1·66bn., unchanged from 2012.

The number of people working on agricultural holdings in June 2014 was 476,000, of whom 294,000 were farmers, partners, directors or spouses; 11,000 salaried managers; and 170,000 other workers including 66,000 seasonal, casual or gang workers. Of the 170,000 regular workers, 40,000 were part-time. There were some 212,000 commercial farm holdings in 2014. Average size of holdings, 81 ha.

Total income from farming was £5·4bn. in 2014 (£5·5bn. in 2013). Trade in food, feed and drink accounted for 6·1% of exports and 9·5% of imports in 2014, up from 5·8% of exports and 8·8% of imports in 2010.

Area given over to principal crops in the UK:

	Area (1,000 ha.)					
	Wheat	Barley	Sugar beets	Potatoes	Oilseed rape	Oats
2012	1,992	1,002	120	149	756	122
2013	1,615	1,213	117	139	715	177
2014	1,936	1,080	116	141	675	137
2015	1,832	1,101	90	129	652	131

(continued)

	Area (1,000 ha.)					
	Wheat	Barley	Sugar beets	Potatoes	Oilseed rape	Oats
2016	1,823	1,122	86	139	579	141

Production of principal crops in the UK:

	Total production (1,000 tonnes)					
	Wheat	Barley	Sugar beets	Potatoes	Oilseed rape	Oats
2012	13,261	5,522	7,291	4,658	2,557	627
2013	11,921	7,092	8,432	5,754	2,128	964
2014	16,606	6,911	9,310	5,923	2,460	820
2015	16,444	7,370	6,218	5,644	2,542	799
2016	14,383	6,655	5,687	5,395	1,775	816

Horticultural crops
2016 output (in 1,000 tonnes): carrots, 724; onions, 372; apples, 260; cabbage, 232; peas, 154; strawberries, 120; lettuce, 102; turnips and swedes, 88; cauliflowers, 83.

Livestock in the UK as at June in each year (in 1,000):

	2007	2008	2009	2010	2011
Sheep	33,946	33,131	31,445	31,084	31,634
Cattle	10,370	10,163	10,082	10,170	9,988
—dairy	(1,937)	(1,892)	(1,838)	(1,830)	(1,796)
—beef	(1,709)	(1,678)	(1,633)	(1,668)	(1,687)
Pigs	4,834	4,714	4,540	4,460	4,441
Poultry	167,667	166,200	152,753	163,867	162,551

Livestock products in 2014, provisional (1,000 tonnes): beef and veal, 871; pork and pork products, 820; lamb and mutton, 307; poultry meat, 1,648; cheese, 414. Hens' eggs, 864m. dozen in 2014 (provisional). Milk production in 2014 (provisional) totalled 14,656m. litres.

In Feb. 2001 the UK was hit by a major foot-and-mouth disease epidemic for the first time since 1967–68, with 2,030 confirmed cases and 4,050,000 animals being slaughtered during the months which followed. In the 1967–68 epidemic there had been 2,364 cases with approximately 434,000 animals slaughtered.

Forestry
In March 2017 the area of woodland in the United Kingdom was 3,166,000 ha., of which the Forestry Commission/Natural Resources Wales/Forest Service owned or managed 863,000 ha. In the year to March 2017, 6,500 ha. of new woodland was created (1,100 ha., Forestry Commission/Natural Resources Wales/Forest Service; 5,500 ha., private woodlands) and 17,100 ha. restocked after harvesting. UK production of roundwood in 2015 was 10·6m. cu. metres.

In 2016 imports of wood and panels were 11·3m. cu. metres; imports of pulp and paper were 7·2m. tonnes and wood pellets 6·8m. tonnes. In 2016 exports of wood and panels were 1·4m. cu. metres; exports of pulp and paper were 5·7m. tonnes.

Forestry Commission. *Forestry Facts and Figures.* Annual

Fisheries
Quantity (in 1,000 tonnes) and value (in £1m.) of all fish landings into the UK and UK vessels' landings abroad:

Quantity	2007	2008	2009	2010	2011
Wet fish	466·2	437·8	447·0	454·7	441·9
Shell fish	147·7	150·4	137·3	153·5	157·7
Total	613·9	588·2	584·3	608·2	599·6
Value					

(*continued*)

Quantity	2007	2008	2009	2010	2011
Wet fish	365·2	370·4	437·2	453·4	537·4
Shell fish	281·1	265·2	242·3	266·5	290·8
Total	646·3	635·6	679·5	719·9	828·2

In Dec. 2016 the fishing fleet comprised 6,191 registered vessels. Major fishing ports: (England) Plymouth, Brixham, Newlyn; (Scotland) Peterhead, Lerwick, Fraserburgh, Scrabster; (Northern Ireland) Ardglass. Peterhead is the UK's leading port, with 106,600 tonnes of fish landed by UK vessels in 2011 (with a value of £132·5m.).

In 2015 the average person in the UK consumed 24·3 kg of fish and fishery products a year, compared to the European Union average of 25·1 kg.

Industry
The UK's largest company by market capitalization on 26 March 2019 was Royal Dutch Shell (British/Dutch) at £199·0bn. (US$262·7bn.), with HSBC the second largest at £123·3bn. (US$162·7bn.) and BP the third largest at £112·1bn. (US$148·0bn.).

In 2013 there were 137,045 manufacturing firms, of which 435 employed 500 persons or more, and 80,230 employed four or fewer. Manufacturing contributed 9·8% of GDP in 2015.

Chemicals and chemical products. Manufacturers' sales (in £1m.) in 2012: primary plastics and other plastic products, 18,577; pharmaceutical preparations and basic pharmaceutical products, 12,289; paints, etc., 2,950; organic basic chemicals, 2,940; perfumes and toilet products, 2,392; soap, detergents, and cleaning and polishing preparations, 1,784; fertilizers, etc., 1,603; rubber products (excluding tyres and tubes), 1,602.

Construction. Total value (in £1m.) of constructional work in Great Britain in 2011 was 121,737, including new work, 77,590 (of which housing, 21,322). Cement production, 2011, 8,529,000 tonnes; building brick production, 2011, 1,554m. units.

Electrical Goods. Manufacturers' sales (in £1m.) in 2012: electric motors, generators and transformers, 3,060; electricity distribution and control apparatus, 2,173; electronic and electric wires and cables, 1,425; electric lighting equipment, 1,334; electric domestic appliances, 1,156.

Engineering, machinery and instruments. Manufacturers' sales (in £1m.) in 2012: motor vehicles, 28,004; aircraft and spacecraft and related machinery, 17,265; electrical and electronic equipment for motor vehicles, and parts and accessories, 9,140; instruments and appliances for measuring, testing and navigation, 5,658; machinery for mining, quarrying and construction, 4,471; engines and turbines (excluding aircraft, vehicle and cycle engines), 4,232; repair and maintenance of aircraft and spacecraft, 3,333; installation of industrial machinery and equipment, 3,273; repair of machinery, 3,034; medical and dental instruments and supplies, 2,629; lifting and handling equipment, 2,326; non-domestic cooling and ventilation equipment, 2,260. Car production, 2012, 1,464,906 units (up 7·7% from 2011).

Foodstuffs, etc. Manufacturers' sales (in £1m.) in 2012: operation of dairies and cheese making, 6,792; meat processing and preservation, 5,835; bread, fresh pastry goods and cakes, 5,752; production of meat and poultry meat products, 5,593; mineral water and soft drinks, 4,103; cakes, biscuits, preserved pastry goods and rusks, 3,958; prepared feeds for farm animals, 3,787; grain mill products, 3,736; distilled, rectified and blended spirits, 3,723; beer, 3,269; poultry processing and preservation, 2,947; fruit and vegetable processing and preservation, 2,900; cocoa, chocolate and sugar confectionery, 2,613; fish and fish products processing and preservation, 2,220; condiments and seasonings, 1,812; tobacco products, 1,793. Alcoholic beverage production, 2014: beer, 4,120·4m. litres (5,746·1m. litres in 2004); wine, 1,256·2m. litres (1,272·5m. litres in 2004); spirits, 866·8m. litres (408·1m. litres in 2004).

Metals. Manufacturers' sales (in £1m.) in 2012: metal structures and parts of structures, 5,463; machining, 4,559; forging, pressing, stamping and roll forming of metal, 1,968; weapons and ammunition, 1,881; tubes, pipes and other products of steel, 1,557; light metal packaging, 1,395; doors and windows of metal, 1,286.

Textiles and clothing. Manufacturers' sales (in £1m.) in 2012: finished textile articles (excluding apparel), 1,169; weaving and finishing of textiles, 1,100; outerwear (excluding workwear) and underwear, 1,010.

Wood products, furniture, paper and printing. Manufacturers' sales (in £1m.) in 2012: printing (excluding newspapers), 7,722; corrugated paper and paperboard, and containers of paper and paperboard, 3,921; furniture (excluding office, shop and kitchen furniture), 3,208; builders' carpentry and joinery, 2,983; paper and paperboard, 2,481.

Labour

In the fourth quarter of 2016 the UK's total economically active population (i.e. all persons in employment plus the claimant unemployed in the age ranges of 16 to 64 for men and 16 to 59 for women) was (in 1,000) 31,394 (14,347 females), of whom 29,839 (13,661 females) were in employment. UK employees by form of employment in Dec. 2016 (in 1,000) included: wholesale and retail trade/repair of motor vehicles and motorcycles, 5,082; human health and social work activities, 4,312; professional scientific and technical activities, 3,024; education, 3,011; administrative and support service activities, 2,972; manufacturing, 2,623; accommodation and food service activities, 2,317; construction, 2,242; transport and storage, 1,684; public administration and defence/compulsory social security, 1,466; information and communication, 1,411; financial and insurance activities, 1,074; arts, entertainment and recreation, 1,016; real estate activities, 566; agriculture, forestry and fishing, 408; water supply, sewerage, waste and remediation activities, 210; electricity, gas, steam and air conditioning supply, 151.

Registered unemployed in UK (in 1,000; figures seasonally adjusted): 2011, 2,593 (8·1%); 2012, 2,572 (8·0%); 2013, 2,474 (7·6%); 2014, 2,026 (6·2%); 2015, 1,781 (5·4%); 2016, 1,634 (4·9%). Of the 1,634,000 unemployed people in 2016, 890,000 were men and 743,000 women. In the period Nov. 2018–Jan. 2019 the unemployment rate was 3·9% (down from 4·3% in Nov. 2017–Jan. 2018 and 4·7% in Nov. 2016–Jan. 2017). In the period Nov. 2016–Jan. 2017, 554,000 young people in the UK aged 16–24 were unemployed (a rate of 12·3%), down from 632,000 in Nov. 2015–Jan. 2016 and the lowest rate since the period Aug.–Oct. 2004. In 2012 the UK was one of only three OECD countries (the others being Hungary and Ireland) in which the share of 15–24 year-olds who were unemployed or inactive and neither in education nor training was higher for the native rather than foreign-born population. Long-term unemployment rose from 22·6% of the labour force between 16 and 64 having been out of work for more than a year in the period Oct.–Dec. 2008 to 35·9% in the period Nov. 2013–Jan. 2014.

There were 4,794,000 private sector businesses in the UK at the start of 2012 (up from 3,559,000 in 2002), of which 4,788,000 were small and medium-sized enterprises (fewer than 250 employees) and 4,580,000 had fewer than ten employees. 2·6m. businesses were registered at Companies House in March 2012.

Workers (in 1,000) involved in industrial stoppages (and working days lost): 2009, 209 (0·46m.); 2010, 133 (0·37m.); 2011, 1,530 (1·39m.); 2012, 237 (0·25m.); 2013, 395 (0·44m.). In 1975, 6m. working days had been lost through stoppages. Between 2007 and 2013 strikes cost Britain an average of 25 working days per 1,000 employees a year.

The Wages Councils set up in 1909 to establish minimum rates of pay (in 1992 of 2·5m. workers) were abolished in 1993. The former Labour government that came to power in May 1997 was committed to the introduction of a National Minimum Wage and established a Low Pay Commission to advise on its implementation. It is currently £7·70 for 21–24 year olds, £6·15 for 18–20 year olds and £4·35 for 16–17 year olds. A National Living Wage was introduced in April 2016 for workers aged 25 and above who were not in the first year of an apprenticeship. It was increased to £8·21 an hour from 1 April 2019. In April 2016 the median gross salary for full-time employees was £28,195 (£30,550 for men and £24,831 for women). Median hourly pay for full-time employees excluding overtime in April 2016 in the UK was £13·59 (£14·16 for males and £12·82 for females). Estimated median weekly earnings in April 2016 were highest in London, at £671, and lowest in the East Midlands, at £483.

Britons in full-time employment worked an average of 41·3 hours a week in 2012, compared to the EU average of 40·7 hours. In the period Oct.–Dec. 2013, 3·35m. Britons (2·47m. men and 876,000 women) worked more than an average of 48 hours a week, with 104,000 working more than 78 hours a week.

The UK had 4,000 people living in slavery according to the Walk Free Foundation's 2013 *Global Slavery Index.*

International Trade

Imports and Exports

Imports of goods in 2016 totalled £437,458m. and exports £302,067m. In 2016 the UK's goods imports from other EU member countries totalled £241,921m. and from non-EU member countries £195,537m., compared to £225,888m. and £181,508m. respectively in 2015. Goods exports to other EU member countries in 2016 totalled £145,471m. and to non-EU member countries £156,596m., compared to £138,865m. and £149,905m. respectively in 2015.

In 2016 other EU members accounted for 52·4% of the UK's foreign trade in goods (55·3% of imports and 48·2% of exports), with the USA accounting for 11·4% of foreign trade and the rest of the world 36·2%. Germany was the UK's biggest trading partner overall in 2016, followed by the USA, the Netherlands, China and France.

Figures for trade in goods by country and groups of countries (in £1m.):

	Imports		Exports	
Country	2015	2016	2015	2016
—EU-28 countries	225,888	241,921	138,865	145,471
Austria	3,060	3,287	1,625	1,834
Belgium	21,361	23,491	12,015	11,831
Bulgaria	377	303	362	457
Croatia	97	103	148	184
Cyprus	162	183	387	325
Czech Republic	4,953	5,466	2,048	2,220
Denmark	3,501	4,040	2,418	2,543
Estonia	189	249	227	236
Finland	2,079	2,262	1,337	1,314
France	24,871	25,503	18,606	20,003
Germany	61,465	65,790	31,770	33,068
Greece	727	809	968	937
Hungary	2,556	2,773	1,326	1,370
Ireland	12,741	13,556	17,416	17,235
Italy	15,948	17,467	8,820	10,078
Latvia	496	712	223	238
Lithuania	788	773	290	364
Luxembourg	473	444	205	212
Malta	187	205	391	399
Netherlands	31,601	36,194	17,601	18,651
Poland	8,222	9,358	3,786	4,281
Portugal	2,389	2,719	1,315	1,467
Romania	1,567	1,805	1,027	1,053
Slovakia	2,028	2,727	464	549
Slovenia	331	422	212	249
Spain	16,799	14,799	9,260	9,691
Sweden	6,920	6,481	4,618	4,682
Other foreign countries				
—Europe				
Iceland	469	476	220	584
Norway	12,325	13,736	3,144	3,180
Russia	4,220	4,009	2,758	2,906
Serbia	146	219	131	133
Switzerland	8,721	10,126	9,832	8,602
Turkey	7,038	7,457	3,483	4,451
Ukraine	247	305	283	393

(*continued*)

	Imports		Exports	
Country	2015	2016	2015	2016
Other in Europe	283	431	1,218	1,254
Africa—				
Egypt	671	674	1,039	1,323
Morocco	589	995	507	880
South Africa	2,867	3,052	2,252	2,414
Other in Africa	5,951	4,338	4,650	4,864
Asia—				
China	36,344	40,547	12,773	13,478
Hong Kong	6,579	6,691	5,835	6,336
India	6,097	6,369	4,018	3,703
Indonesia	1,096	1,283	470	559
Israel	1,055	1,046	1,116	1,186
Japan	6,822	8,241	4,528	5,041
Korea, South	4,413	4,762	4,880	4,594
Malaysia	1,866	1,852	1,369	1,365
Pakistan	1,076	1,194	525	651
Philippines	412	493	401	422
Saudi Arabia	1,878	1,555	4,638	4,571
Singapore	1,912	2,575	3,818	4,707
Taiwan	3,188	3,188	1,185	1,203
Thailand	2,597	2,873	1,252	1,141
Other in Asia	14,000	15,119	12,755	13,331
Oceania—				
Australia	1,911	2,078	3,864	4,108
New Zealand	911	883	580	743
Other in Oceania	151	155	65	95
Americas—				
Argentina	600	673	297	321
Brazil	2,008	1,990	2,175	1,975
Canada	6,056	5,375	3,901	4,876
Chile	584	673	460	477
Colombia	610	495	371	273
Mexico	1,016	1,075	1,307	1,320
USA	33,124	36,625	45,898	47,420
Venezuela	200	129	211	109
Other in America	1,475	1,780	1,696	1,607
Total, foreign countries	407,396	437,458	288,770	302,067

In 2016 finished manufactured goods accounted for 55·0% of the UK's imports and 54·4% of exports; semi-manufactured goods 23·0% of imports and 25·9% of exports; food, beverages and tobacco 9·5% of imports and 6·7% of exports; and oil 5·9% of imports and 6·8% of exports.

The UK's trade deficit in goods in 2016 totalled £135,391m., up from £78,807m. in 2006 and £14,895m. in 1996. The largest deficit in goods in 2016 was with Germany (£32·7bn.) and the largest surplus with the USA (£10·8bn.). The last trade surplus in goods was in 1982. The trade surplus in services in 2016 was £92,378m., giving a trade deficit in goods and services combined of £43,013m. The last trade surplus in goods and services combined was in 1997. The UK is the tenth biggest exporter of goods but the fourth biggest importer, and the second biggest exporter of services (after the USA) but the fifth biggest importer.

Communications

Roads

Responsibility for the construction and maintenance of trunk roads belongs to central government. Roads not classified as trunk roads are the responsibility of county or unitary councils.

In 2015 there were 395,703 km of public roads in Great Britain, classified as: motorways, 3,654 km; A-roads, 8,478 km; other major roads, 38,298 km; minor roads, 345,274 km.

In 2013 journeys by car, vans and taxis totalled 641bn. passenger km (less than 60bn. in the early 1950s). Even in the mid-1950s passenger km in cars, vans and taxis exceeded the annual total in 2013 by rail. Licensed motor vehicles in 2014 included 28,183,000 private cars, 1,067,000 mopeds, scooters and motorcycles, 109,000 buses and 3,890,000 other private and light goods vehicles. In 2014, 76% of households had access to a car with 32% of households having use of two or more cars. New vehicle registrations in 2014: 2,973,700. Driving tests, 2014–15 (in 1,000): applications, 1,659; tests held, 1,533; tests passed, 719; pass rate, 47% (51% among males and 44% among females). The driving test was extended in 1996 to include a written examination.

Road casualties in Great Britain in 2014, 194,477 (the first increase in casualties since 1997) including 1,775 killed. Britain has one of the lowest death rates in road accidents of any industrialized country, at 2·9 deaths per 100,000 people in 2014.

Journeys by bus and coach in 2013 totalled 40bn. passenger-km. Passenger journeys by local bus services, 2013–14, 5,206m. For London buses see Transport for London under Rail, below.

Rail

In 1994 the nationalized railway network was restructured to allow for privatization. Ownership of the track, stations and infrastructure was vested in a government-owned company, Railtrack, which was privatized in May 1996.

Passenger operations were reorganized into 25 train-operating companies, which were transferred to the private sector by Feb. 1997. By March 1997 all freight operations were also privatized. On 3 Oct. 2002 a new private sector not-for-dividend company limited by guarantee, Network Rail, took over from Railtrack plc as network owner and operator. The train-operating companies pay Network Rail for access to the rail network, and lease the rolling stock from three private-sector companies.

The rail network comprises 15,754 route km (around a third electrified). Annual passenger-km were a record 59·2bn. in 2013. There were 1·59bn. passenger journeys in 2013–14 on franchised operated services (the highest total since the 1920s and more than double the 735·1m. of 1994–95). The amount of freight moved declined gradually over many years to 13·0bn. tonne-km in 1994–95 but has generally since risen and totalled 22·7bn. tonne-km in 2013–14, the highest total since the early 1970s. In 2013–14 a total of seven people (excluding trespassers) were fatally injured on the railways and nine people on level crossings (compared to 1,713 deaths in road accidents in 2013).

Eurotunnel PLC holds a concession from the government to operate the Channel Tunnel (49·4 km), through which vehicle-carrying and Eurostar passenger trains are run in conjunction with French and Belgian railways. Since Nov. 2007 a new dedicated high-speed line connects the Channel Tunnel to London St Pancras. Domestic trains began using the line on regular services in Dec. 2009.

Transport for London (TfL) is accountable to the Mayor of London and is responsible for implementing his Transport Strategy as well as planning and delivering a range of transport facilities. TfL's remit covers London Underground, London Overground, London Buses, the Docklands Light Railway and Croydon Tramlink. It is also responsible for London River Services, Victoria Coach Station and London's Transport Museum, and provides transport for users with reduced mobility via Dial-a-Ride. As well as running the central London congestion charging scheme, TfL manages a 580 km network of London's main roads, all 4,600 traffic lights and the private hire trade. It also provides grants to London Boroughs to fund local transport improvements.

Every weekday in Greater London, 5·4m. journeys are made on London's buses, 3m. on the underground, 7m. on foot, 0·3m. by bicycle, 0·2m. by taxi, 160,000 on the Docklands Light Railway and 60,000 on Croydon Tramlink.

The privately franchised Docklands Light Railway is operated in east inner London.

There are metros in Glasgow and Newcastle, and light rail/tram systems in Birmingham/Wolverhampton, Blackpool, Edinburgh, Manchester, Nottingham and Sheffield.

Civil Aviation

All UK airports handled a total of 251·7m. passengers in 2015 (238·6m. in 2014). London area airports (Heathrow, Gatwick, London City, Luton, Southend and Stansted) handled 155·3m. passengers in 2015.

Busiest airports in 2015:

	Passengers			
	Total	On international flights		Freight (tonnes)
Heathrow	74,985,748	69,812,535	Heathrow	1,496,551
Gatwick	40,269,087	36,663,907	East Midlands International	291,689
Manchester	23,136,047	20,713,032	Stansted	207,996
Stansted	22,519,178	20,768,053	Manchester	100,021
Luton	12,263,505	11,317,069	Gatwick	73,371

Heathrow was the world's third busiest airport for passenger traffic in 2013 and Europe's busiest. For many years more international passengers used Heathrow than any other airport in the world, but in 2014 it lost this status to Dubai.

Following the Civil Aviation Act 1971, the Civil Aviation Authority (CAA) was established as an independent public body responsible for the economic and safety regulation of British civil aviation. A CAA wholly owned subsidiary, National Air Traffic Services, operates air traffic control. Highlands and Islands Airports Ltd is owned by the Scottish Ministers and operates 11 airports.

There were 20,161 civil aircraft registered in the UK at 3 Oct. 2011. British Airways is the largest UK airline in terms of numbers of aircraft and distance flown, with a total of 259 aircraft in service at 31 Dec. 2013. It operates long- and short-haul international services, as well as an extensive domestic network. British Airways also has franchise agreements with two other operators: Comair and Sun-Air of Scandinavia. In April 2010 it signed a deal with the Spanish airline Iberia to merge and create a new company called International Airlines Group, which was formed in Jan. 2011. However, both carriers still operate under their own brands. Other major airlines in 2013 (with numbers of aircraft): easyJet (198); Flybe (64); Jet2.com (49); Monarch Airlines (39); Thomas Cook Airlines (31); Thomson Airways (63); Virgin Atlantic (39). Monarch Airlines ceased operations in Oct. 2017. According to CAA airline statistics, in 2008 easyJet overtook British Airways in terms of passengers carried to become the largest airline as measured by passenger numbers—in 2013 easyJet carried 50,963,923 passengers (44,722,874 on international flights) and flew 407·2m. km while British Airways carried 38,318,147 passengers in 2013 (33,154,062 on international flights), although it flew 673·9m. km. In April 2003 British Airways announced that Concorde, the world's first supersonic jet which began commercial service in 1976, would be permanently grounded from Oct. 2003. In recent years low-cost airlines such as Ryanair and easyJet have become increasingly popular. Serving mostly domestic and European destinations, they recovered quickly from the slump of the airline business following the attacks on New York and Washington on 11 Sept. 2001.

The most frequently flown route into and out of the UK in 2015 was Heathrow–New York John F. Kennedy and vice-versa (3,050,499 passengers), followed by Heathrow–Dubai and vice-versa (2,451,738) and Heathrow–Dublin and vice-versa (1,682,855).

Shipping

The UK-owned merchant fleet (trading vessels over 100 GT) in Dec. 2012 totalled 675 ships of 21·6m. DWT and 20·4m. GT. These included 109 fully cellular container vessels, 107 general cargo vessels, 92 bulk carriers and 56 oil tankers. The UK-owned and registered fleet totalled 331 ships of 6·8m. DWT.

The shipping industry is estimated to have made a £5·6bn. value-added contribution to the UK GDP in 2011. 73% of shipping revenue in 2011 came from freight (including freight transported by passenger vessels) and 27% from carrying passengers.

The principal ports in terms of freight are (with 1m. tonnes of cargo handled in 2012): Grimsby and Immingham (60·1), London (43·7), Milford Haven (39·8), Southampton (38·1), Tees and Hartlepool (34·0). Total traffic in 2012 was 500·9m. tonnes. Felixstowe is by far the busiest container port, handling 3,249 TEUs (twenty-foot equivalent units) in 2011. Southampton handled 1,590 TEUs in 2011. Dover is by far the busiest port for passenger traffic

(11,918,000 international passenger movements in 2012, although down from 16,329,000 in 2002), with Holyhead the second busiest (1,898,000 in 2012).

Inland Waterways

There are approximately 3,500 miles (5,630 km) of navigable canals and river navigations in Great Britain. In July 2012 a new waterways charity, the Canal & River Trust (CRT), took over the management of the network of waterways in England and Wales from British Waterways. In Scotland the 137 miles (220 km) of inland waterways remain under the control of British Waterways (operating as Scottish Canals), which is a stand-alone public body of the Scottish government.

River navigations and canals managed by other authorities include the Thames, Great Ouse and Nene, Norfolk Broads and Manchester Ship Canal.

The Association of Inland Navigation Authorities (AINA) represents some 30 navigation authorities providing an almost complete UK coverage.

Telecommunications

In 2015 there were four main mobile networks—EE, O2, Vodafone and Three. BT (then British Telecom) was established in 1981 to take over the management of telecommunications from the Post Office. In 1984 it was privatized as British Telecommunications plc, changing its trading name from British Telecom to BT in 1991. For many years it was the only fixed line provider, but there are now a large number of other providers with increased choice for consumers and a wide range of packages and deals.

By 1998 all of the BT system was served by digital exchanges. In 2013 there were 33,384,000 fixed telephone subscriptions (equivalent to 528·8 per 1,000 population). 84% of UK households had a fixed telephone in 2012, a fall from a peak of 95% in the late 1990s as increasingly UK consumers use email, speaking on a mobile phone and in particular text messaging. At the end of 2013, 75% of fixed lines were residential and 25% business. There were 67,000 public payphones in 2012 (146,000 in 2002). BT had the largest share of the landline phone market at the end of 2015 with 37%, followed by Virgin Media with 13%. The other main providers are Sky and TalkTalk.

In 2013 there were 82·7m. mobile phone subscriptions in the UK, up from 43·5m. in 2000 and 1·1m. in 1990. 15% of people lived in a mobile-only household in 2013. In 2012 each mobile subscriber sent on average 153 text messages per month. However, the volume of mobile originated calls fell by 1% year-on-year to 122bn. minutes.

Telecommunications services are regulated by the Office of Communications ('*Ofcom*') in the interests of consumers. According to its *Communications Market Report 2012*, 58% of adults in a survey stated that they use text messaging to communicate with friends and family at least once a day, 49% face-to-face, 47% voice call on a mobile phone, 32% social networking, 30% email, 29% voice call on a landline and 26% instant messaging. Among those aged 16–24, 90% stated that they used text messaging, 63% face-to-face, 67% voice call on a mobile phone, 73% social networking, 43% email, 15% voice call on a landline and 62% instant messaging.

In March 2012 there were 30·5m. Facebook users (48% of the total population of the UK).

Internet

At 30 June 2012 there were 52·7m. internet users in the UK (the third highest total in Europe after Russia and Germany), just over 83% of the total population. In 2013, 88% of households had a computer. 80% of households in Great Britain had internet access in 2012, up from 57% in 2006; 93% of households with internet access were using fixed broadband, up from 69% in 2006. According to a report published in 2011, 67% of children aged 5–7, 82% of 8–11 year olds and 90% of 12–15 year olds used the internet at home. In 2011, 45% of internet users used a mobile phone to connect to the internet, up from 23% in 2009. E-commerce amounted to £50bn. in 2011, the second highest in the world after the USA. In 2013 there were 87·2 wireless broadband subscriptions per 100 inhabitants and 35·8 fixed broadband subscriptions per 100.

Social Institutions

Out of 178 countries analysed in the 2017 *Fragile States Index*—a list published jointly by the Fund for Peace and *Foreign Policy* magazine—the UK was ranked the 19th least vulnerable to conflict or collapse. The index is based on 12 indicators of state vulnerability across social, political and economic categories.

Justice

England and Wales

The legal system of England and Wales, divided into civil and criminal courts, has at the head of the superior courts, as the ultimate court of appeal, the Supreme Court of the United Kingdom, which hears appeals for all civil law cases in the UK and for all criminal cases in England, Wales and Northern Ireland (Scotland's highest court for criminal cases is the High Court of Justiciary). The Supreme Court was created as a result of the Constitutional Reform Act 2005 and came into being on 1 Oct. 2009, replacing the Appellate Committee of the House of Lords. In order that civil cases may go from the Court of Appeal (or Court of Session in Scotland) to the Supreme Court, it is necessary to obtain the leave of either the respective lower court, although in certain limited cases an appeal may lie direct to the Supreme Court from the decisions of the High Courts. Appeals may be brought to the Supreme Court provided that the lower Court is satisfied that a point of law 'of general public importance' is involved, and that it is in the public interest that a further appeal should be brought. As a judicial body, the Supreme Court consists of 12 Justices drawn from the different jurisdictions of the United Kingdom, and is led by the President of the Supreme Court, the Rt Hon. the Lord Neuberger of Abbotsbury. The final court of appeal for certain of the Commonwealth countries, the UK overseas territories and the British Crown dependencies is the Judicial Committee of the Privy Council which includes Justices of the Supreme Court, other Lords of Appeal and Privy Councillors who hold or have held high judicial office in the UK or Privy Councillors who are or have been Chief Justices or Judges of certain Superior Courts of Commonwealth countries.

Civil Law
The main courts of original civil jurisdiction are the High Court and county courts.

The High Court has exclusive jurisdiction to deal with specialist classes of case, e.g. judicial review. It has concurrent jurisdiction with county courts in cases involving contract and tort although it will only hear those cases where the issues are complex or important. The High Court also has appellate jurisdiction to hear appeals from lower tribunals.

The judges of the High Court are attached to one of its three divisions: Chancery, Queen's Bench and Family; each with its separate field of jurisdiction. The Heads of the three divisions are the Lord Chief Justice (Queen's Bench), the Vice-Chancellor (Chancery) and the President of the Family Division. In addition there are 107 High Court judges (100 men and seven women). For the hearing of cases at first instance, High Court judges sit singly. Appellate jurisdiction is usually exercised by Divisional Courts consisting of two (sometimes three) judges, though in certain circumstances a judge sitting alone may hear the appeal. High Court business is dealt with in the Royal Courts of Justice and by over 130 District Registries outside London.

County courts can deal with all contract and tort cases, and recovery of land actions, regardless of value. They have upper financial limits to deal with specialist classes of business such as equity and Admiralty cases. Certain county courts have been designated to deal with family, bankruptcy, patents and discrimination cases.

There are about 220 county courts located throughout the country, each with its own district. A case may be heard by a circuit judge or by a district judge. Defended claims are allocated to one of three tracks—the small claims track, the fast track and the multi-track. The small claims track provides a simple and informal procedure for resolving disputes, mainly in claims for debt, where the value of the claim is no more than £5,000. Parties should be able to do this without the need for a solicitor. Other claims valued between £5,000 and £15,000 will generally be allocated to the fast track, and higher valued claims which could not be dealt with justly in the fast track may be allocated to the multi-track.

Specialist courts include the Patents Court, which deals only with matters concerning patents, registered designs and appeals against the decision of the Comptroller General of Patents. Cases suitable to be heard by a county court are dealt with at Central London County Court.

The Court of Appeal (Civil Division) hears appeals in civil actions from the High Court and county courts, and tribunals. Its President is the Master of the Rolls, aided by up to 38 Lord or Lady Justices of Appeal (as at June 2018). Cases are generally heard by three judges.

Civil proceedings are instituted by the aggrieved person, but as they are a private matter, they are frequently settled by the parties through their lawyers before the matter comes to trial. In very limited classes of dispute (e.g. libel and slander), a party may request a jury to sit to decide questions of fact and the award of damages.

Criminal Law
At the base of the system of criminal courts in England and Wales are the magistrates' courts which deal with over 95% of criminal cases. In general,

in exercising their summary jurisdiction, they have power to pass a sentence of up to six months' imprisonment (or 12 months for consecutive sentences) and to impose a fine of up to £5,000 on any one offence. They also deal with the preliminary hearing of cases triable at the Crown Court. In addition to dealing summarily with over 2·0m. cases, which include thefts, assaults, drug abuse, etc., they also have a limited civil and family jurisdiction.

Magistrates' courts normally sit with a bench of three lay justices. Although unpaid they are entitled to loss of earnings and travel and subsistence allowance. They undergo training after appointment and they are advised by a professional legal adviser. Full-time District Judges (magistrates' courts), formerly known as stipendiary magistrates, also deal with cases in magistrates' courts. Generally they possess the same powers as the lay bench, but they sit alone. On 1 April 2016 the total strength of the lay magistracy was 17,552 including 9,299 women. Justices of the Peace are appointed on behalf of the Queen by the Lord Chancellor.

Justices are selected and trained specially to sit in Youth and Family Proceedings Courts. Youth Courts deal with cases involving children and young persons up to the age of 18 charged with criminal offences (other than homicide and other grave offences). These courts normally sit with three justices, including at least one man and one woman, and are accommodated separately from other courts.

Family Proceedings Courts deal with matrimonial applications and Children Act matters, including care, residence and contact and adoption. These courts normally sit with three justices including at least one man and one woman.

Above the magistrates' courts is the Crown Court. This was set up by the Courts Act 1971 to replace quarter sessions and assizes. Unlike quarter sessions and assizes, which were individual courts, the Crown Court is a single court which is capable of sitting anywhere in England and Wales. It has power to deal with all trials on indictment and has inherited the jurisdiction of quarter sessions to hear appeals, proceedings on committal of persons from the magistrates' courts for sentence, and certain original proceedings on civil matters under individual statutes.

The jurisdiction of the Crown Court is exercisable by a High Court judge, a Circuit judge or a Recorder (a part-time judge) sitting alone, or, in specified circumstances, with Justices of the Peace. The Lord Chief Justice has given directions as to the types of case to be allocated to High Court judges (the more serious cases) and to Circuit judges or Recorders respectively.

Appeals from magistrates' courts go either to a Divisional Court of the Queen's Bench Division of the High Court (when a point of law alone is involved) or to the Crown Court where there is a complete rehearing on appeals against conviction and/or sentence. Appeals from the Crown Court in cases tried on indictment lie to the Court of Appeal (Criminal Division). Appeals on questions of law go by right, and appeals on other matters by leave. The Lord Chief Justice or a Lord Justice of Appeal sits with judges of the High Court to constitute this court. Thereafter, appeals in England and Wales can be made to the Supreme Court.

There remains as a last resort the invocation of the royal prerogative of mercy exercised on the advice of the Home Secretary. In 1965 the death penalty was abolished for murder and in 1998 abolished for all crimes.

All contested criminal trials, except those which come before the magistrates' courts, are tried by a judge and a jury consisting of 12 members. The jury decides whether the accused is guilty or not. The judge is responsible for summing up on the facts and directing the jury on the relevant law. He or she sentences offenders who have been convicted by the jury (or who have pleaded guilty). If, after at least two hours and ten minutes of deliberation, a jury is unable to reach a unanimous verdict it may, on the judge's direction—and provided that in a full jury of 12 at least ten of its members are agreed—bring in a majority verdict. The failure of a jury to agree on a unanimous verdict or to bring in a majority verdict may involve the retrial of the case before a new jury.

The Employment Appeal Tribunal
The Employment Appeal Tribunal, which is a superior Court of Record with the like powers, rights, privileges and authority of the High Court, was set up in 1976 to hear appeals on questions of law against decisions of employment tribunals and of the Certification Officer. The appeals are heard by a judge sitting alone or with two members (in exceptional cases four) appointed for their special knowledge or experience of industrial relations either on the employer or the trade union side, with always an equal number on each side. The great bulk of their work is concerned with the problems which can arise between employees and their employers.

Military Courts

Under the Armed Forces Act 2006, criminal offences and disciplinary offences alleged against service personnel subject to service law (or civilians overseas who are subject to service discipline) may be tried in the Court Martial. Lower-level offences by service personnel may be dealt with at a summary hearing by their commanding officer, subject to appeal to the Summary Appeal Court.

The Personnel of the Law

All judicial officers are independent of Parliament and the Executive. They are appointed by the Crown on the advice of the Prime Minister or the Lord Chancellor, or directly by the Lord Chancellor himself, and hold office until retiring age. Under the Judicial Pensions and Retirement Act 1993 judges normally retire by age 70 years.

The legal profession is divided; barristers, who advise on legal problems and can conduct cases before all courts, usually act for the public only through solicitors, who deal directly with the legal business brought to them by the public and have rights to present cases before certain courts. The distinction between the two branches of the profession has been weakened since the passing of the Courts and Legal Services Act 1990, which has enabled solicitors to obtain the right to appear as advocates before all courts. Long-standing members of both professions are eligible for appointment to most judicial offices.

For all judicial appointments up to and including the level of Circuit Judge, it is necessary to apply in writing to be considered for appointment. Vacancies are advertised. A panel consisting of a judge, an official and a lay member decide whom to invite for interview and also interview the shortlisted applicants. They make recommendations to the Lord Chancellor, who retains the right of final recommendation to the Sovereign or appointment, as appropriate.

Legal Services

The system of legal aid in England and Wales was established after the Second World War under the Legal Aid and Advice Act 1949. The Legal Aid Board was then set up under the Legal Aid Act 1988 and took over the administration of legal aid from the Law Society in 1989. The Legal Services Commission (LSC) was set up (as a non-departmental public body) under the Access to Justice Act 1999 and replaced the Legal Aid Board on 1 April 2000. The LSC was then abolished as a result of the Legal Aid, Sentencing and Punishment of Offenders Act (LASPO) 2012 and replaced from 1 April 2013 with the Legal Aid Agency (LAA), which is an executive agency of the Ministry of Justice. A new office of the Director of Legal Casework was created to ensure independence of decision-making.

The Legal Aid Agency includes contracted solicitors and advice agencies that provide civil and family legal advice and representation. It manages Civil Legal Advice, which includes telephone and internet-based services, and contracts with quality assured providers to deliver face-to-face civil legal aid services across a range of categories such as debt and housing. It aimed to reduce spending on legal aid in 2013–14 by 7·7% from £2·0bn. in 2012–13 to £1·8bn. It was also aiming to have administration costs totalling £86·1m. for the financial year, down 12·3% on the Legal Services Commission's 2012–13 budget.

The Agency also provides legal advice and representation to people being investigated or charged with a criminal offence. It manages the duty solicitor schemes for police stations and magistrates' courts so that those who need advice and representation can see a solicitor, and funds services in the higher courts. The Public Defender Service provides criminal defence services directly to the public.

See also SCOTLAND.

CIVIL JUDICIAL STATISTICS
ENGLAND AND WALES

	Number of cases 2016
Appellate Courts	
Judicial Committee of the Privy Council	51
Supreme Court	73
Court of Appeal	1,029

(*continued*)

CIVIL JUDICIAL STATISTICS
ENGLAND AND WALES

High Court of Justice (appeals and special cases from inferior courts)	60

Courts of First Instance (excluding Magistrates' Courts and Tribunals)

High Court of Justice:	
—Chancery Division	25,168
—Queen's Bench Division	9,274
County courts: Matrimonial suits	114,825[1]
County courts: Non-family work	1,802,286

[1]Includes dissolutions of civil partnerships.

CRIMINAL STATISTICS
ENGLAND AND WALES

	Total number of offenders (in 1,000)	
	2015	2016
Proceeded against in Magistrates' Courts	1,492	1,456
—Indictable offences	324	293
—Summary offences	1,169	1,163
Found guilty at all courts	1,249	1,240
—Indictable offences	267	246
—Summary offences	982	994
Offenders sentenced	1,247	1,238
—Fines	892	911
—Community sentence	114	103
—Immediate custody	90	90
—Other	150	135
Out of court disposals	331	285
—Cautions	126	103
—Community resolutions	119	111
—Other	86	70

Crime Survey for England and Wales British (CSEW) interviews in 2013–14 estimate that there were 7·1m. crimes against adults aged 16 or over living in private households in England and Wales, down from 8·4m. in 2012–13 and a peak of over 19·1m. in the mid-1990s. Property crime accounted for 82% of CSEW crime in 2013–14 and violence 18%. The 2013–14 total was the lowest since the forerunner of the CSEW, the British Crime Survey, was introduced in 1981. There were about 3·7m. crimes recorded by the police in both 2012–13 and 2013–14, the lowest total since the late 1980s. The number of recorded homicides in England and Wales in 2012–13 was 551, up from 530 in 2011–12 although in both cases the lowest since 1989.

In Sept. 2015 the prison population was 85,886 (95·5% of which were male), down from a high of 88,167 in Nov. 2011 although up from around 45,000 in 1990 and just over 20,000 in 1950. The annual average prison population rose 30% between 2001 and 2011, from 66,301 to 85,951. Although crimes have fallen considerably since the mid-1990s the prison population has risen considerably over the same period. Between 2001 and 2011 the annual average female prison population rose by 12%, from 3,740 to 4,188; the annual average male population rose by 31%, from 62,560 to 81,763. These figures do not include prisoners held in police cells. The UK was ranked 11th of 102 countries for criminal justice and 13th for civil justice in the 2015 World Justice Project *Rule of Law Index*, which provides data on how the rule of law is experienced by the general public across eight categories.

See also SCOTLAND *and* NORTHERN IRELAND.

Police

In England and Wales there are 43 police forces, each maintained by a police authority typically comprising nine local councillors, three magistrates and five independent members. London is policed by the Metropolitan Police Service (responsible to the Mayor's Office for Policing and Crime, headed by the Mayor) and the City of London Police (whose police authority is the City of London Corporation). In Scotland the Scottish Police Authority holds the national police service, Police Scotland, to account.

Figures show that the total strength of the police service in England and Wales at 30 Sept. 2016 was 198,228. 122,859 police officers were supported by 64,805 police staff and designated officers (investigation officers, detention officers and escort officers). In addition there were 10,551 PCSOs (police community support officers) on 30 Sept. 2016. There were 14,864 special constables in Sept. 2016. As of March 2015, 28·2% of officers were female and 5·5% of officers came from an ethnic minority.

Education

Adult Literacy and Numeracy
In 2001 the Labour government at the time published the *Skills for Life Strategy* in response to the recommendations in the 1999 Moser report (*A Fresh Start. Improving Literacy and Numeracy*). The strategy covered adults aged 16 and above at skills levels of pre-entry up to and including Level 2. The results of the 2011 *Skills for Life Survey* showed that in England 5·1m. adults aged 16–65 (14·9% of the population in this age bracket) had literacy levels below Level 1—equivalent to the level expected of an average 11-year-old—and 16·8m. had numeracy skills (49·1% of those in the same age range) below Level 1. From April 2001 to June 2008, 2,276,000 learners achieved at least one qualification in literacy, numeracy or language against a target set in 2001 of 2·25m. by July 2010.

The Publicly Maintained System of Education
Compulsory schooling begins at the age of five (four in Northern Ireland). The minimum leaving age for all pupils was 16 but as a result of the Education and Skills Act of Nov. 2008 this was raised in stages to 18. Since the summer of 2015 all young people in England born on or after 1 Sept. 1997 have to remain in education or training to 18. No tuition fees are payable in any publicly maintained school (but parents can choose to pay for their children to attend independent schools run by individuals, companies or charitable institutions). The post-school or tertiary stage, which is voluntary, includes universities, further education establishments and other higher education establishments, as well as adult education and youth services. Financial assistance (grants and loans) is generally available to students in higher education and to some students on other courses in further education.

National Curriculum
The National Curriculum was introduced in 1988 and has undergone a number of revisions—the latest taking place in 2014. It determines the content of what will be taught, sets attainment targets for learning and determines how performance will be assessed and reported.

The National Curriculum comprises the core subjects of English, mathematics and science; and foundation subjects of information communication technology, design and technology, history, geography, modern foreign languages, art and design, music, physical education and citizenship.

At Key Stage 4 (ages 14–16) schools must provide access for each pupil to a minimum of one course in the arts (art and design, music, dance, drama and media arts); one course in the humanities (history and geography); at least one modern foreign language; and design and technology. However, since Sept. 2004 these subject areas are no longer compulsory for key stage 4 pupils.

In addition, pupils must be taught religious education during all four key stages, although parents have the right to withdraw their children from this provision. Careers and sex education are compulsory at Key Stages 3 and 4, and work-related learning is compulsory at Key Stage 4. The subject of personal, social and health education is not statutory but should be taught across all four key stages. Every school must also provide a form of daily collective worship, but with the right to withdraw.

In Sept. 2008 the Early Years Foundation Stage (EYFS) replaced the Foundation Stage curriculum which was a distinct phase of education for children aged three to the end of the reception year of primary school. The EYFS is a national play-based framework for supporting the learning, development and safety of children from birth to the age of five. The EYFS does not form part of the National Curriculum. All state and independent schools and 'registered' early years providers are required to meet the learning and development requirements of the EYFS.

Early Learning
All three- and four-year-olds are entitled to 15 hours per week of free early learning for 38 weeks per year until they reach compulsory school age. Free early-learning places can be delivered by state nursery schools; nursery classes in primary schools and reception classes; and private, voluntary and independent providers and registered childminders who are part of a quality assured network. There are around 38,900 sites currently involved in delivering free early-learning. Local authorities have a duty to ensure that there are sufficient free early learning places for all three- and four-year-olds.

Primary Schools
These provide compulsory education for pupils from the age of five (four in Northern Ireland) up to the age of 11 (12 in Scotland). Most public sector primary schools take boys and girls in mixed classes. Some pre-compulsory age pupils attend nursery classes within primary schools, however, and in England some middle schools cater for pupils at either side of the secondary education transition age. In 2013–14 there were 21,040 public sector mainstream primary schools in the United Kingdom, with an average of 20·5 pupils per teacher.

Middle Schools
A number of local authorities operate a middle school system. These provide for pupils from the age of eight, nine or ten up to the age of 12, 13 or 14, and are deemed either primary or secondary according to the age range of the pupils.

Secondary Schools
In 2013–14 there were 4,116 state-funded secondary schools in the United Kingdom providing for pupils from the age of 11 upwards. Some local authorities have retained a selective admissions policy at age 11 (mainly for entry to grammar schools), and some 232 state-funded secondary schools in the United Kingdom operate a selective admissions policy. There are 51 secondary modern schools in England providing a general education up to the minimum school leaving age of 16, although some pupils stay on beyond that age. In state-funded secondary schools in the United Kingdom there are an average 15·4 pupils per teacher.

Almost all local authorities operate a system of comprehensive schools to which pupils are admitted without reference to ability or aptitude. With the development of comprehensive education, various patterns of secondary schools have come into operation. Principally these are: 1) All-through schools with pupils aged 11 to 18 or 11 to 16; pupils over 16 being able to transfer to an 11 to 18 school or a sixth form college providing for pupils aged 16 to 19. (Since 1 April 1993, sixth form colleges have been part of the further education sector—there were 94 sixth form colleges in 2012–13). 2) Local authorities operating a three-tier system involving middle schools where transfer to secondary school is at ages 12, 13 or 14. These correspond to 12 to 18, 13 to 18 and 14 to 18 comprehensive schools respectively. 3) In areas where there are no middle schools a two-tier system of junior and senior comprehensive schools for pupils aged 11 to 18, with optional transfer to these schools at age 13 or 14.

Academies
Following passage of the Academies Act in 2010, all publicly-funded schools were invited to become academies. Academies are independent state schools funded directly from the government, rather than the local council. Each academy is run by a trust that employs staff directly. Academies can set their own term times and do not need to follow the national curriculum. Some are sponsored by businesses, universities, faith groups, voluntary groups or other schools. In May 2012 there were more than 1,800 academies in England.

Free Schools
The 2010 Academies Act also allowed for the creation of free schools. These are schools set up by groups of parents or teachers, charities, trusts, voluntary groups or faith groups if they believe the local state school provision is inadequate. They are funded and operate exactly as academies do. In early 2014 there were more than 170 free schools in England.

Faith Schools
A faith school is one associated with a particular religion. Most are run like other state schools and must follow the national curriculum except for religious studies, in which subject they are free to teach only about their own religion. Although anyone is free to apply for a place at a faith school, each school may have its own specific admissions criteria and staffing policies.

City Technology Colleges

CTCs are independent all-ability secondary schools established in partnership between government and business sponsors under the Education Reform Act 1988. They teach the full National Curriculum but give special emphasis to technology, science and mathematics. The government meets all recurrent costs. Although there were originally 15 CTCs, there are now only three remaining as 12 have been converted to Academies.

Music and Dance Scheme (formerly the Music and Ballet Scheme)

The 'Aided Pupil Scheme' for boys and girls with outstanding talent in music or dance (principally ballet) helps parents with the fees and boarding costs at eight specialist private schools in England. Since 2004 the scheme has been developed to include 21 centres for advanced training and a national grants scheme for out-of-school-hours training.

Independent Schools

Independent schools which belong to an association affiliated to the Independent Schools Council (accounting for 80% of pupils) are subject to an inspection regime agreed between the government and the ISC. The Schools Inspection Service inspects schools affiliated to the Focus Learning Trust, and the Bridge Schools Inspectorate inspects schools affiliated to the Christian Schools Trust and the Association of Muslim Schools, also under arrangements agreed with the government. Non-association schools are inspected by Ofsted on a regular cycle.

The earliest of the independent schools were founded by medieval churches. Many were founded as 'grammar' (classical) schools in the 16th century, receiving charters from the reigning sovereign. Reformed mainly in the middle of the 19th century, among the best-known are Eton College, founded in 1440 by Henry VI; Winchester College (1394), founded by William of Wykeham, Bishop of Winchester; Harrow School, founded in 1560 as a grammar school by John Lyon, a yeoman; and Charterhouse (1611). Among the earliest foundations are King's School, Canterbury, founded 600; King's School, Rochester (604) and St Peter's, York (627).

Special Education

It is estimated that, nationally, 20% of the school population will have special educational needs at some time during their school career. For some 2·7% of pupils the local authority will need to make a statutory assessment of special educational needs under the Education Act 1996 and draw up a legal document, the statement, which sets out the extra provision a child needs. (In Scotland pupils are assessed for a Coordinated Support Plan.)

Maintained schools must use their best endeavours to make provision for such pupils. The new *Special educational needs and disability code of practice: 0 to 25 years*, which came into force on 1 Sept. 2014 and replaced an earlier Code, gives practical guidance.

Youth Work

The priority age group for agencies and services providing youth work is 13- to 19-year-olds, but the target age group may extend to 11- to 25-year-olds. Provision is usually in the form of positive activities delivered in youth clubs and centres, or through 'detached' or outreach work aimed at young people at risk from alcohol or drug misuse, or of drifting into crime. There is an increasing emphasis on youth workers working with disaffected, and socially excluded, young people and providing services at times and in places where young people want them. Youth work can be delivered by local authority youth services, the voluntary and community sector, and other specialist youth agencies.

Teachers

Qualified teacher status (QTS) is obtained through either an undergraduate or postgraduate course of initial teacher training. Training courses are either college-based or employment-based, the latter allowing trainees to teach as unqualified teachers and also study for QTS at the same time. As well as meeting common professional standards, trainees must also pass computerized skills tests in information and communication technology, numeracy and literacy in order to be awarded QTS. Newly qualified teachers are then required to complete an induction programme during their first year of teaching.

Those who are recognized as qualified teachers in Scotland or Northern Ireland are also entitled to apply to the General Teaching Council for England or the General Teaching Council for Wales for QTS without undertaking further training. Nationals of European Economic Area (EEA) countries who are recognized as schoolteachers in an EEA member state can apply to the GTCE for QTS without undertaking further training.

Teachers who qualified as teachers in countries outside of the EEA are allowed to teach for four years in state maintained and non-maintained special schools in England. This is subject to satisfying Home Office rules on employing overseas workers. They are only allowed to teach beyond four years if they have been awarded QTS which can be obtained through undertaking an employment-based training programme.

In 2013–14, 506,100 full-time teachers (353,700 females) were employed in maintained nursery, primary and secondary schools in the United Kingdom; there were also 85,700 full-time equivalent of part-time teachers.

Further Education (Non-University)

The English Further Education (FE) system provides a wide range of education and training opportunities for individuals and employers. Learning opportunities are provided, from age 14 upwards, at all levels from basic skills to higher education. The FE system's primary purpose is to help people gain the skills they need to improve their employability.

Following the abolition of the former Learning and Skills Council, from April 2010 responsibility for funding full- and part-time education and training provision for people aged 16 to 19 fell to local education authorities and the Young People's Learning Agency (YPLA). Under the Education Act 2011 the YPLA, which was sponsored by the Department for Education and supported the delivery of training and education to 16- to 19-year-olds in England, was to close on 31 March 2012. On 1 April 2012 responsibilities of the YPLA were transferred to the Education Funding Agency (EFA). The Education and Skills Funding Agency (ESFA) was formed on 1 April 2017 following the merger of the EFA and the Skills Funding Agency and is an executive agency sponsored by the Department for Education. It is now the single agency accountable for funding education and training for children, young people and adults.

Further education is the largest sector providing educational opportunities for the over 16s. In 2012–13 there were 396 FE colleges in the UK.

Higher Education

In 2012–13 there were 2·5m. students in the UK at 160 higher education institutions, of which 132 were universities. The higher education student population was 56·1% female in 2012–13. 37% of the UK population between the ages of 25 and 34 have attained a tertiary qualification (OECD average, 34%), compared to only 25% of those aged between 55 and 64.

Total income for higher education institutions in the UK was £30·7bn. in 2013–14. Of this £6·1bn. came from funding body grants; £13·7bn. from tuition fees and education grants and contracts; £5·1bn. from research grants and contracts; £0·3bn. from endowment and investment income; and £5·6bn. from other sources. Higher education institutions are funded by four UK bodies, one each for England, Scotland, Wales and Northern Ireland. Their roles include: allocating funds for teaching and research; promoting high-quality education and research; advising government on the needs of higher education; informing students about the quality of higher education available; and ensuring the proper use of public funds.

The *Open University* (OU) received its Royal Charter on 23 April 1969 and is an independent, self-governing institution, awarding its own degrees at undergraduate and postgraduate level. It is financed by students' fees and by the government through the Higher Education Funding Council for England for its students in England, Northern Ireland and other EU countries, the Scottish Funding Council and the Higher Education Funding Council for Wales.

Study materials provided may include specially written textbooks, online teaching materials, audio CDs, DVDs and computer software. The OUAnywhere initiative allows students to access learning materials through their smartphones and tablets. Support is usually provided by tutors or study advisers who are available to students through group tutorials and seminars, online or by telephone.

No formal qualifications are required for entry to the majority of undergraduate courses. 69% of undergraduates have no previous higher education qualifications on entry. The University launched with 25,000 students and in 2011–12 there were 246,626 students (including 37,121 on OU validated programmes). 342 undergraduate modules are offered by the OU along with 141 postgraduate modules. There are 13 national and regional centres in addition to 350 study centres across the UK and more than 6,340 associate lecturers. 80 of the FTSE 100 companies have sponsored staff to study with the OU. In 2010–11 the OU attracted more than £17·5m. in external research income.

The only university independent of the state system is the *University of Buckingham*, which opened in 1976 and received its Royal Charter in 1983. It offers two-year honours degrees, the academic year commencing in Jan. or Sept., and consisting of four 10-week terms. There are a wide variety of subjects available, the most popular being in business, humanities, law and science. The University also offers a 4·5 year Medical School MB ChB programme and a range of postgraduate programmes, including professional, PGCE and master's level courses for teachers. In Jan. 2019 there were over 3,000 students at the University.

All universities charge fees, but financial help is available to students from several sources, and the majority of students receive some form of financial assistance.

Higher Education (HE) Student Support

All students are expected to make a contribution towards their tuition fees. In Dec. 2010 the then coalition government agreed to increase the maximum tuition fee rate to £9,000 for 2012–13 for students beginning their studies in Sept. 2012 or later. No eligible student (new or existing) has to pay their fees either before or during their course, as a Tuition Fee Loan is available. Students in the fifth or later years of medical or dental courses and on NHS-funded courses in professions allied to medicine may be eligible for a means-tested grant from the NHS Bursary system. Postgraduate trainee teachers may be eligible for tax-free bursaries; these range from £3,000 to £30,000 depending on the teaching subject. Non-repayable Maintenance Grants of up to £3,387 for students from lower income backgrounds were replaced from Aug. 2016 by additional loans, repayable once graduates earn more than £21,000. Previously, universities and colleges wishing to charge maximum fees were required to make bursaries available to students in receipt of the full Maintenance Grant.

A Maintenance Loan is available to help with students' living costs. All students are entitled to 72% of the maximum loan, with the balance subject to income assessment. The maximum loans available for students who started their courses in 2015–16 are: £8,009 (living away from home and studying in London); £5,740 (living away from home and studying outside London); and £4,565 (living at home). For those who started their courses in 2016–17 the maximum loans available are: £10,702 (living away from home and studying in London); £8,200 (living away from home and studying outside London); and £6,904 (living at home). For students who started their courses in 2017–18 the maximum loans available are: £11,002 (living away from home and studying in London); £8,430 (living away from home and studying outside London); and £7,097 (living at home). For students who started their courses in 2018–19 the maximum loans are: £11,354 (living away from home and studying in London); £8,700 (living away from home and studying outside London); £7,324 (living at home). Neither the Tuition Fee Loan nor the Maintenance Loan has to be repaid until the student has left university or college and is earning over £21,000.

Applications for student finance are made through Local Authorities or, under a pilot scheme operating in some areas, direct to the Student Loans Company. The Student Loans Company manages loan accounts and the payment of the student finance package.

Postgraduate studentships and research grants are available from the Arts and Humanities Research Council (AHRC) or similar councils. There are six other grant-awarding Research Councils which each report to the Department of Business, Innovation and Skills. They offer awards to students studying within the broad spectrum of economics, engineering, astronomy and medical, biological and physical sciences.

The AHRC receives approximately £102m. annually from the government to support research and postgraduate study in the arts and humanities, from languages and law, archaeology and English literature to design and creative and performing arts. In any one year the AHRC makes approximately 700 research awards and around 1,350 postgraduate awards. Awards are made after a rigorous peer review process, to ensure that only applications of the highest quality are funded.

Professional and Career Development Loans (CDLs)

These loans are specifically designed to help individuals acquire and improve vocational skills, and are aimed at those who would otherwise not have reasonable or adequate access to the funds. Loans of between £300 and £10,000 can be applied for to support up to two years of education or learning (plus up to one year's practical work experience where it forms part of the course).

Finance

Total public education expenditure in the United Kingdom for 2013–14 was £88·3bn. representing 5·1% of GDP, compared with £44·4bn. and 4·3% of GDP in 2000–01.

See also ENGLAND, SCOTLAND *and* NORTHERN IRELAND.

British Council

The British Council is the UK's international organization for cultural relations and educational opportunities. The British Council works with over 100 countries in the fields of arts and culture, English language, education and civil society. In 2017–18 it reached more than 75m. people directly and 758m. people overall including online, through broadcasts and publications. It has around 10,000 employees worldwide. Its total turnover in 2017–18 was £1,172m., of which £168m. (14·3%) was a grant-in-aid from the Foreign and Commonwealth Office. The remainder was generated through trading activities such as English-language teaching.

Chair: Christopher Rodrigues, CBE.

Chief Executive: Sir Ciarán Devane.

Headquarters: 10 Spring Gdns, London, SW1A 2BN.

Health

The National Health Service (NHS) in England and Wales started on 5 July 1948. There is a separate Act for Scotland.

The NHS is a charge on the national income in the same way, for example, as the armed forces. Every person normally resident in the UK is entitled to use any part of the service, and no insurance qualification is necessary.

Since its inception, the NHS has been funded from general taxation and National Insurance (NI) contributions, and the present government has maintained the original principle that the NHS should be a service provided to all those who need it, regardless of their ability to pay or where they live. In 2011 the NHS in England was funded 17·9% by NI contributions, 80·9% by general taxation with the remainder coming from charges and receipts, including land sales and proceeds from income generation schemes. Health authorities may raise funds from voluntary sources; hospitals may take private, paying patients.

Health is the second largest government spending sector after social protection. In 2015–16 NHS expenditure on health was £143·7bn. In 2016 the UK spent 9·8% of its GDP on health, with public spending amounting to 79·4% of the total.

Organization

The Health and Social Care Act 2012 provided for a major restructuring of the NHS. On 1 April 2013 the ten Strategic Health Authorities (SHAs), responsible for implementing Department of Health policy at regional level and overseeing the operations of NHS trusts at the local level since 2002, were abolished. Primary Care Trusts—introduced in 2000 to control local health care and hold to account provider organizations for delivery of services that they commissioned—also ceased to exist.

Under the terms of the 2012 Act, responsibility for commissioning NHS care was given over to more than 200 clinical commissioning groups (CCGs), each made up of GPs and other clinicians. CCGs are directly responsible for a combined budget of some £60bn. Every GP practice is required to be a member of a CCG. Each CCG has a governing body comprising at least one registered nurse and a secondary care specialist alongside GPs.

CCGs are supported by the NHS Commissioning Board, which authorizes clinical commissioning groups, allocates resources and commissions certain services itself, such as primary care. The Commissioning Board operates 27 area teams.

The NHS Trust Development Authority oversees the performance and governance of NHS Trusts, including clinical quality and managing their progress towards NHS Foundation Trusts (which have greater managerial and financial independence than NHS Trusts). The Quality Care Commission, meanwhile, guarantees the safety and quality of services, and Monitor regulates economic efficiency. Separate bodies have overall responsibility for professional education, training and public health programmes.

Services

The NHS broadly consists of hospital and specialist services, general medical, dental and ophthalmic services, pharmaceutical services, community health services and school health services. In general these services are free of charge; the main exceptions are prescriptions, spectacles, dental and optical examination, dentures and dental treatment, amenity beds in hospitals, and some community services, for which contributory charges are made with certain exemptions.

Private

In recent years increasing numbers of people have turned to private medical insurance. This covers the costs of private medical treatment (PMI) for curable short-term medical conditions. PMI includes the costs of surgery, specialists, nursing and accommodation at a private hospital or in a private ward of an NHS hospital. Approximately 13% of the UK population have private medical insurance. The leading companies are BUPA Healthcare, AXA PPP Healthcare and PruHealth.

In 2013, 18·7% of the population of the UK aged 18 and over smoked. In 1974 the percentage had been 45%, with 51% of males and 41% of females smoking. Over the years the difference between the percentage of men and of women who smoke has been declining—in 2013 the rates were 21·1% for men and 16·5% for women. The overall percentage of the UK population who are smokers is similar to the average for the EU as a whole, but among men the percentage of smokers in the UK is lower than in the EU as a whole whereas among women it is higher. Alcohol consumption has fallen slightly in recent years. The average British adult consumed 11·4 litres of pure alcohol a year in the period 2015–17, down from 12·3 litres in 2009–11.

There were 88,769 people living with HIV in the UK who accessed HIV care in 2015 (compared to 51,449 in 2006).

See also NORTHERN IRELAND.

Personal Social Services

Under the Local Authority Social Services Act 1970, and in Scotland the Social Work (Scotland) Act 1968, the welfare and social work services provided by local authorities were made the responsibility of a new local authority department—the Social Services Department in England and Wales, and Social Work Departments in Scotland headed by a Director of Social Work, responsibility in Scotland passing in 1975 to the local authorities. The social services thus administered include: the fostering, care and adoption of children, welfare services and social workers for people with learning difficulties and the mentally ill, the disabled and the aged, and accommodation for those needing residential care services. Legislation of 1996 permits local authorities to make cash payments as an alternative to community care. In Scotland the Social Work Departments' functions also include the supervision of persons on probation, of adult offenders and of persons released from penal institutions or subject to fine supervision orders.

Expenditure is reviewed by the Social Services Inspectorate and the Audit Commission (in Scotland by the Social Work Services Inspectorate and the Accounts Commission).

Welfare

The National Insurance Act 1965 now operates under the Social Security Contributions and Benefits Act 1992 and the Social Security Administration Act 1992.

Since 1975 Class 1 contributions have been related to the employee's earnings and are collected with PAYE (Pay As You Earn) income tax. Class 2 and Class 3 contributions remain flat-rate, but, in addition to Class 2 contributions, those who are self-employed may be liable to pay Class 4 contributions, which for the year 2017–18 were at the rate of 9% on profits or gains between £8,164 and £45,000 (with a further 2% contribution on any profit exceeding the upper limit), which are assessable for income tax under Schedule D. The non-employed and others whose contribution record is not sufficient to give entitlement to benefits were able to pay a Class 3 contribution of £14·25 per week in 2017–18 voluntarily, to qualify for a limited range of benefits. Class 2 weekly contributions for 2017–18 for men and women were £2·85. Class 1A contributions are paid by employers who provide employees with a car and fuel for their private use.

The Social Security Pensions Act 1975 introduced earnings-related retirement, invalidity and widows' pensions. Members of occupational pension schemes may be contracted out of the earnings-related part of the state scheme relating to retirement and widows' benefits. Employee's national insurance contribution liability depends on whether he/she is in contracted-out or not contracted-out employment.

Full-rate contributions for non-contracted-out employment in 2017–18:

Weekly Earnings (in £1)	Employee (primary) pays	Employer (secondary) pays
Below 113 (Lower Earnings Limit)[1]	Nil	Nil
113–157 (Primary Threshold)[2]	Nil	13·8%

(continued)

Weekly Earnings (in £1)	Employee (primary) pays	Employer (secondary) pays
157–866 (Primary Threshold to Upper Earnings Limit)	12%	13·8%
Over 866 (Upper Earnings Limit)	2%	13·8%

[1]Below £157 (Secondary Threshold) for employer.
[2]Above £157 (Secondary Threshold) for employer.

For contracted-out employment, the contracted-out rebate for primary contributions (employee's contribution) is 1·4% of earnings between the lower earnings limit and the upper earnings limit for all forms of contracting-out; the contracted-out rebate for secondary contributions (employer's contributions) is 3·4% of earnings between the lower earnings limit and the upper earnings limit.

Contributions together with interest on investments form the income of the *National Insurance Fund* from which benefits are paid. 29,390,000 persons (13,420,000 women) paid contributions in 2008–09, including 25,210,000 employees at standard rate.

Receipts, 2009–10 (in £1m.), 129,320, including: contributions, 73,817; investment income, 1,684; transfers from Great Britain, 395; compensation for Statutory Sick Pay/Statutory Maternity Pay, 237. Disbursements (in £1m.), 79,793, including: retirement pensions, 66,442; Incapacity, 6,177; Personal Pensions, 2,623; administration, 1,401; Jobseeker's Allowance (Contributory), 1,106; Bereavement Benefits, 647; redundancy payments, 531; transfers to Northern Ireland, 395; maternity, 343.

Statutory Sick Pay (SSP)

Employers are responsible for paying SSP to their employees who are absent from work through illness or injury for up to 28 weeks in any three-year period. All employees aged between 16 and 65 (60 for women) with earnings above the Lower Earnings Limit are covered by the scheme whenever they are sick for four or more days consecutively. The weekly rate (2017–18) was £89·35. For most employees SSP completely replaces their entitlement to state incapacity benefit which is not payable as long as any employer's responsibility for SSP remains.

Contributory Benefits

Qualification for these depends upon fulfilment of the appropriate contribution conditions, except that persons who are incapable of work as the result of an industrial accident may receive incapacity benefit followed by invalidity benefit without having to satisfy the contributions conditions.

Jobseeker's Allowance

Unemployed persons claiming the allowance must sign a 'Jobseeker's Agreement' setting out a plan of action to find work. The allowance is not payable to persons who left their job voluntarily or through misconduct. Claimants with sufficient National Insurance contributions are entitled to the allowance for six months regardless of their means; otherwise, recipients qualify through a means test and the allowance is fixed according to family circumstances, at a rate corresponding to Income Support for an indefinite period. In May 2018 there were 446,000 people receiving the Jobseeker's Allowance (268,200 males). Payments start (2017–18) at £57·90 per week.

Statutory Maternity Pay

Pregnant working women may be eligible to receive Statutory Maternity Pay directly from their employer for a maximum of 39 weeks if average gross earnings are £113 a week or more (2017–18). There are two rates: a higher rate (90% of average earnings for the first six weeks), and a lower rate of £140·98 in 2017–18 or 90% of earnings (whichever is less) for up to 33 weeks. For women who do not qualify for Statutory Maternity Pay, including self-employed women, there is a Maternity Allowance.

A payment of £500 (Sure Start Maternity Grant) may be available if the mother or her partner are receiving Income Support, income-based Jobseeker's Allowance, Pension Credit, Child Tax Credit (at a rate higher than the family element) or Working Tax Credit (in cases of disability). It is also available if a parent adopts a baby, is granted a parental order on a surrogate birth or is granted a residence order on a child (subject to certain conditions). It is restricted to the first child in a family.

Statutory Paternity Pay

Since 6 April 2003 working fathers have had the right to two weeks paid paternity leave providing average earnings are £113 a week or more (2017–18). This will be paid at the same rate as the lower rate of Statutory Maternity Pay (£140·98 a week in 2017–18 or 90% of average weekly earnings if this is less than £140·98).

Statutory Adoption Pay

Paid adoption leave is for up to 39 weeks at the same rate as Statutory Paternity Pay. It is available to employed people adopting a child on their own, or for one member of a couple adopting together. Parents adopting from overseas are also eligible, although conditions may differ.

Bereavement Benefits

Available to both men and women, Bereavement Benefits were introduced from 9 April 2001 to replace the former Widows' Benefit scheme. There are three main types of Bereavement Benefits available to men and women widowed on or after 9 April 2001: bereavement payment, widowed parent's allowance and bereavement allowance. *Bereavement Payment* is a single tax-free lump sum of £2,000 payable immediately on bereavement. A widower/widow may be able to get this benefit if their late spouse has paid enough National Insurance Contributions (NIC) and was under 60 at death; or was not getting a Category A State Retirement Pension at death. *Widowed Parent's Allowance* is a weekly benefit payable when the widower/widow is receiving Child Benefit. The amount of Widowed Parent's Allowance is based on the late spouse's NIC record. He/she may also get benefit for the eldest dependent child and further higher benefit for each subsequent child; also an additional pension based on their late spouse's earnings. If the late spouse was a member of a contracted-out occupational scheme or a personal pension scheme, that scheme is responsible for paying the whole or part of the additional pensions. Widowed Parent's Allowance is taxable. *Bereavement Allowance* is a weekly benefit payable to widows and widowers without dependent children and is payable between age 45 and State Pension age. The amount of Bereavement Allowance payable to a widower/widow between 45 and 54 is related to their age at the date of entitlement. Their weekly rate is reduced by 7% for each year they are aged under 55 so that they get 93% rate at age 54, falling to 30% at age 45. Those aged 55 or over at the date of entitlement will get the full rate of Bereavement Allowance. The amount of Bereavement Allowance is based on the late spouse's NIC record and is payable for a maximum of 52 weeks from the date of bereavement. A widower/widow cannot get a Bereavement Allowance at the same time as a Widowed Parent's Allowance. Women widowed before 9 April 2001 continue to receive their Widows' Benefit entitlement on the arrangements that existed before that date so long as they continue to satisfy the qualifying conditions. There were 66,357 recipients of Bereavement Benefits in May 2017.

Retirement Pension

The state retirement ('old-age') pension scheme has two components: a basic pension and an additional state pension (state second pension or S2P). The amount of the first is subject to National Insurance contributions made; the amount of the second is earnings-related although it is scheduled to become a flat-rate top-up payment by 2030. Payments are made automatically when the basic pension is claimed. Qualifying National Insurance contributions are made for employed persons earning over a lower threshold (£5,876 in 2017–18), anyone looking after children under the age of 12 and in receipt of Child Benefit, carers working more than 20 hours a week claiming Carer's Credit and foster carers claiming Carer's Credit, and persons receiving certain other benefits as a result of illness or disability.

Pensions are payable to men at 65 years of age. Until April 2010 they were payable to women at 60 years of age but since then the state pension age for women has been gradually rising, with the age differential in the process of being phased out. Under the 2011 Pensions Act the equalization of the state pension age will take place by Nov. 2018 (instead of April 2020) and the state pension age for both men and women will be increased to 66 by Oct. 2020. Under the Pensions Act 2014 the State Pension age for men and women will now increase to 67 between 2026 and 2028. The State Pension age is then expected to increase to 68 between 2037 and 2039. There are standard rates for single persons and for married couples. Proportionately reduced pensions are payable where contribution records are deficient.

Employees may contract out of the additional state pension if they join an employers contracted-out occupational pension scheme or have an appropriate stakeholder or personal pension scheme. The self-employed,

unemployed, those in full-time training and anyone earning below a lower threshold (£5,876 in 2017–18) do not qualify.

Self- and non-employed persons may contribute voluntarily for retirement pension.

In Jan. 2013 the government announced plans to introduce a revised state pension scheme. The new state pension—which came into effect in April 2016—applies to men born on or after 6 April 1951 and woman born on or after 6 April 1953. The full flat-rate pension for 2017–18 was £159·55 per week. People who receive the new state pension are not eligible for the additional state pension. Claimants must have made 35 years of National Insurance contributions to receive the full new pension, up from the previously required 30 years.

Persons who defer claiming their pension during the five years following retirement age are paid an increased amount, as do men and women who had paid graduated contributions. 12,277,360 persons were receiving National Insurance retirement pensions in May 2009 (7,650,400 women and 4,626,960 men). The full basic state pension for 2017–18—which applies to people who reached state pension age before 6 April 2016—was £122·30 per week for a single person and £195·60 per week for a couple. Since 1 Oct. 1989 the pension for which a person has qualified may be paid in full whether a person continues in work or not irrespective of the amount of earnings. The official retirement age for males in 2017 was 65, with the average actual retirement age among males that year being 65·1 years (up from 64·6 years in 2010). For women the average actual retirement age rose from 62·3 years to 63·6 years between 2010 and 2017. At the age of 80 a small age addition is payable. In addition non-contributory pensions are now payable, subject to residence conditions, to persons aged 80 and over who do not qualify for a retirement pension or qualify for one at a low rate.

Pensioners whose pension is insufficient to live on may qualify for Income Support.

Non-Contributory Benefits

Universal Credit

Universal Credit has been trialled since April 2013 on a limited basis and has been gradually introduced nationally since then, although the process has not yet been completed. It replaces Child Tax Credit, Housing Benefit, Income Support, Income-related Employment Support and Allowance, Income-related Jobseeker's Allowance and Working Tax Credit.

Child Benefit

Child Benefit is a tax-free cash allowance normally paid to the mother. The weekly rates are highest for the eldest qualifying child (£20·70 weekly in 2017–18) and less for each other child (£13·70 weekly in 2017–18). Child Benefit is payable for children under 16, for 16- and 17-year-olds registered for work or training, and for those under 20 receiving full-time non-advanced education. Some 7,376,965 families received benefit in Aug. 2017. From Jan. 2013 families with at least one partner earning £50,000 or more were not able to claim the total amount of child benefit.

Child Support Agency

The Child Support Agency (CSA) is responsible for calculating, collecting and enforcing child maintenance payments. The non-resident parent pays 15% of their net income if they have one child, 20% for two and 30% for three or more children. The agency currently deals with around 1·5m. child support cases. In Dec. 2006 the Child Maintenance White Paper announced the establishment of a new and radically different organization called the Child Maintenance and Enforcement Commission. It assumed responsibility for the Child Support Agency in Nov. 2008, and was to introduce a tougher enforcement regime that encouraged parents to take greater responsibility for the financial support of their children. However, it was abolished in July 2012, with the CSA becoming the delivery arm of the Child Maintenance Group within the Department for Work and Pensions.

Working Tax Credit

This tackles poor work incentives and persistent poverty among working people. For families with children, credit is available for those with low incomes. It also extends support to low-income working people without children aged 25 or over working 30 hours or more a week. The Working Tax Credit is not just restricted to those with children; the amount of the award varies considerably depending on the prevailing circumstances. Both single persons and couples may be eligible.

Child Tax Credit

The Child Tax Credit aims at creating a single system of support for families with children, payable irrespective of the work status of the adults in the household. This means that the Child Tax Credit forms a stable and secure income bridge as families move off welfare and into work. It also provides a common framework of assessment, so that all families are part of the same inclusive system. The Child Tax Credit provides a family element of up to £545 per year and a child element of up to £2,780 per child per year in addition to Child Benefit. The amount paid varies depending on the number of children and the gross annual joint income.

Guardian's Allowance

A person responsible for an orphan child may be entitled to a Guardian's Allowance in addition to Child Benefit. Normally, both the child's parents must be dead but when they never married or were divorced, or one is missing or serving a long sentence of imprisonment, the allowance may be paid on the death of one parent only. The weekly rate of Guardian's Allowance was £16·70 in 2017–18.

Attendance Allowance

This is a tax-free Social Security benefit for disabled people over 65 who need help with personal care. The rates are increased for the terminally ill. There were 1,614,270 recipients in May 2010.

Carers' Allowance

This is a taxable benefit paid to those who care for a disabled person for at least 35 hours per week. The carer must be at least 16, not in full-time education of 21 hours or more per week, and not earn more than £100 per week after certain deductions have been made—such as income tax. This is a weekly rate (£62·70 in 2017–18), with increases for dependants. In May 2010 there were 536,900 recipients.

Disability Living Allowance

This is a non-taxable benefit available to people disabled before the age of 65, who need help with getting around or with personal care for at least three months. The mobility component has two weekly rates, the care component has three. There were 3,157,310 recipients in May 2010. From 8 April 2013 Disability Living Allowance is being gradually phased out and replaced by Personal Independence Payment.

Industrial Injuries Disablement Benefit

The scheme provides a system of insurance against 'personal injury by accident arising out of and in the course of employment' and against certain prescribed diseases and injuries owing to the nature of the employment. It is payable where, as the result of an industrial accident or prescribed disease, there is a loss of physical or mental faculty. The loss of faculty will be assessed as a percentage by comparison with a person of the same age and sex whose condition is normal. If the assessment is between 14–100% benefit will be paid as weekly pension. The rates vary from 20% disabled to 100% disablement. Assessments of less than 14% do not normally attract basic benefit except for certain progressive chest diseases. Pensions for persons under 18 are at a reduced rate. When injury benefit was abolished for industrial accidents occurring and prescribed diseases commencing on or after 6 April 1983, a common start date was introduced for the payment of Disablement Benefit 90 days (excluding Sundays) after the date of the relevant accident or onset of the disease. There are no contribution conditions for the payment of benefit. There were 203,650 recipients in March 2016.

War Pensions

Pensions are payable for disablement or death as a result of service in the armed forces. Similar schemes exist for other groups such as merchant seamen injured as a result of war or for civilians injured by enemy action in the Second World War. The amount depends on the degree of disablement. There were 123,593 recipients in March 2017.

Housing Benefit

The Housing Benefit scheme assists persons who need help to pay their rent, using general assessment rules and benefit levels similar to those for the income support scheme. The scheme sets a limit of £16,000 on the amount of capital a person may have and still remain entitled. Restrictions on the granting of benefit to persons under 25 were introduced in 1995. In May 2018 there were 4,177,820 beneficiaries. Since April 2013 claimants in social housing have their Housing Benefit reduced by 14% if they have one spare bedroom and by 25% if they have two or more spare bedrooms.

Income Support

Income Support is a non-contributory benefit for people aged 16 or over, not working 16 hours or more a week or with a partner not working more than 24 hours or more per week, and not required to be available for employment. These include single parents, long-term sick or disabled persons, and those caring for them who qualify for Invalid Care Allowance. Income Support is not payable if the claimant (or claimant and partner together) has capital assets that total more than £16,000. These include savings, investments or property other than their home. Savings/capital assets worth under £6,000 are ignored. Savings between £6,000 and £16,000 are treated as if each £250 or part of £250 brings in an income of £1 per week. From 6 Oct. 2003 a new Pension Credit replaced the Minimum Income Guarantee (Income Support for people aged 60 and over). In Oct. 2008 Income Support paid on the grounds of incapacity was replaced by Employment and Support Allowance for all new claims. In May 2017 there were 1,822,123 Pension Credit claimants. There were 560,000 Income Support claimants in Feb. 2018. Weekly payments start at £57·90.

Council Tax Support

Council tax support replaced council tax benefit in April 2013 to provide financial assistance to low income households in paying council tax. Each local authority operates its own scheme.

Sure Start Maternity Grants

This is a payment of up to £500 for the first baby expected, born or adopted, payable to persons receiving Income Support, Income-based Jobseeker's Allowance, Child Tax Credit, Working Tax Credit or Pension Credit.

Funeral Payments

This is a payment of fees levied by the burial authorities and crematoria, plus up to £700 for other funeral expenses, to persons receiving Income Support, Income-based Jobseeker's Allowance, Housing Benefit, Child Tax Credit, Working Tax Credit or Pension Credit.

Cold Weather Payments

This is a payment of £25 for any consecutive seven days when the temperature is below freezing to persons receiving income support who are pensioners, disabled or have a child under five.

Winter Fuel Payments

This is a payment of between £100 and £300 to every household with a person aged 65 or over providing they are not living long-term in a hospital or care home, with those aged 80 and over qualifying for the higher rate.

Community Care Grants

These are payments to help persons receiving income support to move into the community or avoid institutional care.

Budgeting Loans

These are interest-free loans to persons receiving income support for expenses difficult to budget for.

Fraser, Derek, *The Evolution of the British Welfare State: A History of Social Policy since the Industrial Revolution.* 2009

Harris, Bernard, *The Origins of the British Welfare State: Social Welfare in England and Wales, 1800–1945.* 2004

Hill, M., *The Welfare State in Britain: a Political History since 1945.* 1993

Lowe, Rodney, *The Welfare State in Britain since 1945.* 2004

Timmins, N., *The Five Giants: a Biography of the Welfare State.* 1995

Religion

The Anglican Communion originated from the Church of England and parallels in its fellowship of autonomous churches the evolution of British influence beyond the seas from colonies to dominions and independent nations. The Archbishop of Canterbury presides as *primus inter pares* at the meetings of the bishops of the Anglican Communion at the Lambeth Conference and at the biennial meetings of the Primates and the Anglican Consultative Council. The Lambeth Conference is normally decennial. A Conference was held in 2008 in Canterbury and was attended by 670 bishops, but the one that would normally have taken place in 2018 was delayed and is now expected to take place in 2020. Average attendance at Sunday worship in 2013 numbered 1·0m., compared to 3·5m. in 1950. There were 1,085,600 Anglicans on the electoral roll in 2013.

The Anglican Communion (Anglican Episcopal family) consists of an estimated 80m. Christians who are members of 45 different Churches (including five Extra-Provincial Dioceses). These are: The Anglican Church in Aotearoa, New Zealand and Polynesia; The Anglican Church of Australia; The Church of Bangladesh; The Anglican Church of Bermuda (Extra-Provincial to the Archbishop of Canterbury); The Anglican Episcopal Church of Brazil; The Anglican Church of Burundi; The Anglican Church of Canada; The Church of the Province of Central Africa; The Anglican Church of the Central America Region; The Church of Ceylon (Sri Lanka) (Extra-Provincial to the Archbishop of Canterbury); The Anglican Church of Chile; The Province of the Anglican Church of the Congo; The Church of England; The Parish of the Falkland Islands (Extra-Provincial to the Archbishop of Canterbury); Hong Kong Sheng Kung Hui; The Church of the Province of the Indian Ocean; The Church of Ireland; The Nippon Sei Ko Kai; The Episcopal Church in Jerusalem and the Middle East; The Anglican Church of Kenya; The Anglican Church of Korea; The Lusitanian Church (Portugal) (Extra-Provincial to the Archbishop of Canterbury); The Church of the Province of Melanesia; The Anglican Church of Mexico; The Church of the Province of Myanmar (Burma); The Church of Nigeria (Anglican Communion); The Church of North India; The Church of Pakistan; The Anglican Church of Papua New Guinea; The Episcopal Church in the Philippines; The Episcopal Church of Rwanda; The Scottish Episcopal Church; The Anglican Church of South America; The Church of the Province of South East Asia; The Church of South India; The Province of the Episcopal Church of South Sudan; The Anglican Church of Southern Africa; The Reformed Episcopal Church of Spain (Extra-Provincial to the Archbishop of Canterbury); The Province of the Episcopal Church of Sudan; The Anglican Church of Tanzania; The Church of the Province of Uganda; The Episcopal Church in the United States of America; The Church in Wales; The Church of the Province of West Africa; and The Church in the Province of the West Indies. New provinces are also currently in formation. Churches in Communion include the Mar Thoma Syrian Church, the Philippine Independent Church, and some Lutheran and Old Catholic Churches in Europe. The Church in China is known as a 'post-denominational' Church whose formation included Anglicans in the Holy Catholic Church in China.

England and Wales
The established Church of England, which baptizes about 13% of infants born in England (i.e. excluding Wales but including the Isle of Man and the Channel Islands), is Anglican. Civil disabilities on account of religion do not attach to any class of British subject. Under the Welsh Church Acts, 1914 and 1919, the Church in Wales and Monmouthshire was disestablished as from 1 April 1920, and Wales was formed into a separate Province.

The Queen is, under God, the supreme governor of the Church of England, with the right, regulated by statute, to nominate to the vacant archbishoprics and bishoprics. The Queen, on the advice of the First Lord of the Treasury, also appoints to such deaneries, prebendaries and canonries as are in the gift of the Crown, while a large number of livings and also some canonries are in the gift of the Lord Chancellor.

There are two archbishops (at the head of the two Provinces of Canterbury and York), and 44 diocesan sees including the diocese in Europe, which is part of the Province of Canterbury. Justin Welby was enthroned as *Archbishop of Canterbury* on 21 March 2013. Each archbishop also has his own particular diocese, wherein he exercises episcopal, as in his Province he exercises metropolitan, jurisdiction. In 2016 there were 38 serving bishops, 71 suffragan bishops, 42 deans of cathedrals and 117 archdeacons. The *General Synod*, which replaced the Church Assembly in 1970 in England, consists of a House of Bishops, a House of Clergy and a House of Laity, and has power to frame legislation regarding Church matters. The first two Houses consist of the members of the Convocations of Canterbury and York, each of which consists of the diocesan bishops and elected representatives of the suffragan bishops, five for Canterbury province and three for York (forming an Upper House); deans and archdeacons, and a certain number of proctors elected as the representatives of the priests and deacons in each diocese, together with, in the case of Canterbury Convocation, four representatives of the Universities of Oxford, Cambridge, London and the Southern Universities, and in the case of York two representatives of the Universities of Durham and Newcastle and the other Northern Universities, and three archdeacons to the Armed Forces, the Chaplain General of Prisons

and two representatives of the Religious Communities (forming the Lower House). The House of Laity is elected by the lay members of the Deanery Synods but also includes two representatives of the Religious Communities. The Houses of Clergy and Laity also include a small number of *ex officio* members. Every Measure passed by the General Synod must be submitted to the Ecclesiastical Committee, consisting of 15 members of the House of Lords nominated by the Lord Chancellor and 15 members of the House of Commons nominated by the Speaker. This committee reports on each Measure to Parliament, and the Measure receives the Royal Assent and becomes law if each House of Parliament resolves that the Measure be presented to the Queen.

Parochial affairs are managed by annual parochial church meetings and parochial church councils. In 2008 there were 12,702 ecclesiastical parishes, inclusive of the Isle of Man and the Channel Islands. These parishes do not, in many cases, coincide with civil parishes. Although most parishes have their own churches, not every parish nowadays can have its own incumbent or priest. About 3,290 non-stipendiary clergy hold a bishop's licence to officiate at services.

In 2016 there were 4,036 incumbents excluding dignitaries, 1,748 other clergy of incumbent status and 1,504 assistant ministers or curates working in the parishes.

Women have been admitted to Holy Orders as deacons since 1987 and as priests since 1994. In July 2014 the General Synod voted to allow women to become bishops for the first time. On 26 Jan. 2015 Libby Lane became the Church of England's first female bishop when she was consecrated Bishop of Stockport. In 2016 there were 1,888 full-time stipendiary women clergy, 1,784 of whom were in the parochial ministry. In the years following the vote in 1992 in favour of the ordination of women, 441 clergymen resigned because they disagreed with the decision. 11 clergymen subsequently re-entered the Church of England ministry and of the 441 who resigned, 260 are estimated to have joined the Roman Catholic Church and 30 the Orthodox Church. In Nov. 2010 five bishops (two retired) resigned in opposition to plans to admit women to the Episcopate.

Private persons possess the right of presentation to over 2,000 benefices; the patronage of the others belongs mainly to the Queen, the bishops and cathedrals, the Lord Chancellor, the colleges of the Universities of Oxford and Cambridge and other patronage trusts. More than 750 benefices include patronage trusts among their patrons. In addition to the dignitaries and parochial clergy already identified there were, in 2016, 110 other full-time cathedral staff and 103 full-time non-parochial clergy working within the diocesan framework, giving a total of 7,253 full-time stipendiary clergy working within the diocesan framework in 2016. In addition there were 535 part-time stipendiary clergy. Although these figures account for the majority of active clergy in England, there are many others serving in institutions and elsewhere who cannot be quantified with any certainty. They include 1,113 chaplains in hospitals, the forces, prisons, schools and colleges, as well as those in mission agencies and religious communities.

Of the 40,405 buildings registered for the solemnization of marriages at 30 June 2007 (statistics from the Office of National Statistics), 16,418 belonged to the Church of England and the Church in Wales, and 23,987 to other religious denominations (Methodist, 6,362; Roman Catholic, 3,310; Baptist, 3,075; United Reformed, 1,587; Congregationalist, 1,245; Calvinistic Methodist, 1,057, Jehovah's Witnesses, 830; Brethren, 741; Salvation Army, 722; Unitarians, 161; other Christian, 4,291; Sikhs, 161; Muslims, 164; other non-Christian, 281). Of the 235,794 marriages celebrated in 2008 (331,150 in 1990), 57,057 were in the Established Church and the Church in Wales (115,328 in 1990), 21,444 in other denominations (43,837 in 1990) and 157,296 were civil marriages in Register Offices (156,875 in 1990).

The Roman Catholic population in England and Wales (the number of adherents) was 4,084,351 in 2009; 898,852 regularly attended Mass in England and Wales in 2009. There are 22 dioceses in five provinces and one Bishopric of the Forces (also covers Scotland), and the Personal Ordinariate of Our Lady of Walsingham. Vincent Nichols was installed as *Archbishop of Westminster* on 21 May 2009. In March 2019 there was one Roman Catholic cardinal. In England and Wales there are five archbishops and 17 other diocesan bishops. In 2009 there were 4,645 priests in active ministry, 2,524 parish churches and 1,036 convents.

Religious affiliation figures for England and Wales according to the 2001 and 2011 censuses:

Religion	2001 census	2011 census	% of population in 2011
Christian	37,338,000	33,243,000	59·3
No religion	7,709,000	14,097,000	25·1
Muslim	1,547,000	2,706,000	4·8
Hindu	552,000	817,000	1·5
Sikh	329,000	423,000	0·8
Jewish	260,000	263,000	0·5
Buddhist	144,000	248,000	0·4
Other religion	151,000	241,000	0·4
Not stated	4,011,000	4,038,000	7·2

In Scotland according to the 2011 census 53·8% of the population stated their religion as Christian and 36·7% stated that they had no religion; the largest grouping was the Church of Scotland with 32·4% while 15·9% identified as being Roman Catholic.

In 2010 there were 5,515,000 members of Christian churches in the UK (5,845,000 in 2005), equivalent to 11·2% of the population (12·3% in 2005).

The Salvation Army is an international Christian church and charity, working in 128 countries, and offers unconditional friendship, support and practical help to people of all ages, backgrounds and needs. In the UK and the Republic of Ireland (as at 2017) this work includes more than 800 community churches and social centres with more than 4,000 employees, some 1,500 ministers of religion and 50,000 members.

There is a 300-member Board of Deputies of British Jews.

In 2015 there were approximately 1·66m. visits to Westminster Abbey, London, 1·61m. to St Paul's Cathedral, London, and 957,000 to Canterbury Cathedral.

See also SCOTLAND and NORTHERN IRELAND.

Bradley, I., *Marching to the Promised Land: Has the Church a Future?* 1992

Chapman, Mark, *Anglicanism: A Very Short Introduction.* 2006

Davie, Martin, *A Guide to the Church of England.* 2008

De La Noy, M., *The Church of England: a Portrait.* 1993

Culture

World Heritage Sites

Sites under UK jurisdiction which appear on UNESCO's World Heritage List are (with year entered on list): Giant's Causeway and Causeway Coast (1986), rock formations on the Antrim Plateau in Northern Ireland; Durham Castle and Cathedral (1986 and 2008), the largest example of a Norman cathedral; Ironbridge Gorge (1986), built in the 18th century and considered the emblem of the industrial revolution; Studley Royal Park, including the Ruins of Fountains Abbey (1986), developed from the 18th century on the site of a former Cistercian abbey in Yorkshire; Stonehenge, Avebury and Associated Sites (1986 and 2008), among the world's most famous pre-historic monoliths; Castles and Town Walls of King Edward in Gwynedd (1986), a testament to the early period of English colonization in the late 13th century; St Kilda (1986, 2004 and 2005), a volcanic archipelago on the coast of the Hebrides; Blenheim Palace (1987), seat of the Dukes of Marlborough near Oxford and birthplace of Sir Winston Churchill; City of Bath (1987), with remains from its time as a Roman spa town, and home to many examples of neo-classical Georgian architecture; Westminster Palace, Westminster Abbey and Saint Margaret's Church (1987 and 2008)—the palace is the medieval seat of parliament rebuilt in the 19th century, the abbey the site of all coronations since the 11th century and Saint Margaret's is a small medieval gothic church; Henderson Island (1988), a South Pacific atoll; Tower of London (1988), a Norman fortress built to guard London; Canterbury Cathedral, St Augustine's Abbey and St Martin's Church (1988), the spiritual seat of the Church of England; Old and New Towns of Edinburgh (1995), the Scottish capital; Gough and Inaccessible Islands (1995 and 2004), two of the least disturbed islands and marine eco-systems in the South Atlantic; Maritime Greenwich (1997), including Britain's first Palladian building, designed by Inigo Jones, Christopher Wren's Royal Naval College and the Royal Observatory; Heart of Neolithic Orkney (1999), comprising several important neolithic monuments; Historic Town of St George's and Related Fortifications, Bermuda (2000), an example of early English New World colonialism; Blaenavon Industrial Landscape (2000), a symbol of South Wales's role as a coal and iron provider in the 19th century; Dorset and East Devon Coast (2001), which demonstrate rock formations and fossil remains from the Mesozoic Era; Derwent Valley Mills (2001), 18th-century cotton mills at the forefront of the Industrial Revolution; New Lanark (2001), Robert Owen's model industrial community and cotton mills of the early 19th century; Saltaire (2001), a mid-19th century planned industrial community for the textile industry; Royal Botanical Gardens, Kew (2003), containing important botanical collections in a historic landscape; Liverpool—Maritime Mercantile City (2004); the Cornwall and West Devon mining landscape (2006); the Pontcysyllte Aqueduct and Canal near Wrexham (2009), a feat of civil engineering by Thomas Telford during the Industrial Revolution; the Forth Bridge (2015), a railway bridge that had the world's longest span when opened in 1890 and that continues to carry freight and passengers today; Gorham's Cave Complex (2016), consisting of four caves in Gibraltar that provide evidence of Neanderthal occupation over a span of more than 100,000 years; and the English Lake District (2017), a mountainous area in northwest England.

The UK also shares the Frontiers of the Roman Empire sites (1987, 2005 and 2008) with Germany, containing the border line of the Roman Empire at its greatest extent in the 2nd century AD (specifically Hadrian's Wall).

Press

In Jan. 2017 there were ten national dailies with a combined average daily circulation of 6,274,905 and nine national Sunday newspapers (5,433,695). In Jan. 2014 there were also 114 morning, evening and Sunday regional newspapers and 929 weeklies (345 of these for free distribution). In 2010 there were 3,212 consumer magazines and 4,765 business magazines. The most widely read daily is the tabloid *The Sun*, with an average daily circulation of 1,666,715 in Jan. 2017. The most widely read Sunday paper is *The Sun on Sunday*, with an average circulation of 1,375,539 in Jan. 2017.

In 2014 the Independent Press Standards Organisation (IPSO) replaced the former Press Complaints Commission. IPSO is the independent regulator of the newspaper and magazine industry. It is financed by the Regulatory Funding Committee, which is funded by member publications. Its chair is Sir Alan Moses.

In 2013 a total of 184,000 book titles were published in the UK (an 8% increase from 2012).

Tourism

In 2015 British residents made 124·4m. trips within Great Britain, passing 377·1m. nights in accommodation and spending £24,825m. Of these, 56·0m. trips were holiday tourism and 46·6m. for visiting friends and relatives. Visits from foreign tourists to the UK totalled a record 36·1m. in 2015. Spending was £22·1bn. in the same year. In 2014 the UK ranked eighth for international tourism arrivals behind France, the USA, Spain, China, Italy, Turkey and Germany. The main countries of origin for foreign visitors in 2015 were: France (4·2m.), USA (3·3m.), Germany (3·2m.), Ireland (2·6m.) and Spain (2·2m.).

In 2014 there were 3·0m. people working in tourism-related industries.

UK residents made 65·7m. trips abroad in 2015 (31·2m. in 1990 and 69·5m. in 2006). Spain was the most popular destination in 2015 for Britons travelling abroad (13·0m. visits), followed by France (8·8m.), and Ireland, Italy and the USA (all 3·5m.).

Festivals

Among the most famous music festivals are the Promenade Concerts or 'Proms', which take place at the Royal Albert Hall in London every year from July to Sept.; the Glyndebourne season in Sussex (May to Aug.); the Aldeburgh Festival in Suffolk (June); the Glastonbury Festival in Somerset (June); the Download Festival at Donington Park in Leicestershire (June); the Buxton Festival in Derbyshire (July); and the Reading and Leeds Festivals (Aug.). The annual London Film Festival takes place in Oct. Literary festivals include the Oxford Literary Festival in March, the Hay Festival at Hay-on-Wye in Powys (late May/early June) and the Cheltenham Festival of Literature in Gloucestershire (Oct.). The Edinburgh Festival and the Fringe Festival both take place in Aug./early Sept. and are major international festivals of culture. The Brighton Festival in May is England's largest arts festival. The multicultural Notting Hill Carnival in London takes place at the end of Aug. Other major events in the annual calendar are the New Year's Day Parade in London, the Crufts Dog Show at the Birmingham National Exhibition Centre (March), the Ideal Home Exhibition in London (March-April), the London Marathon (April), the Chelsea Flower Show (May), Royal Ascot (horse racing, in June), Wimbledon (tennis, in July), Henley Royal Regatta (July), Cowes (yachting, in Aug.) and the Lord Mayor's Show in London (Nov.).

Diplomatic Representatives

Of the USA in the United Kingdom (33 Nine Elms Lane, London, SW11 7US)
Ambassador: Robert Wood 'Woody' Johnson IV.

Of the United Kingdom in the USA (3100 Massachusetts Ave., NW, Washington, D.C., 20008)
Ambassador: Sir Kim Darroch, KCMG.

Of the United Kingdom to the United Nations
Ambassador: Karen Pierce, DCMG.

Of the United Kingdom to the European Union
Permanent Representative: Sir Tim Barrow, KCMG, LVO, MBE.

England

Key Historical Events

Emperor Claudius's invasion in AD 43 established Roman rule in southern England. After the failed rebellions in AD 60 of Queen Boudicca of the Iceni and the suppression of Wales by AD 78, there was a long period of peaceful settlement, during which the Romans established new towns such as Londinium (London) and Eboracum (York). After the withdrawal of the Roman legions in the early 5th century, Pictish and Saxon raiders harassed the British towns. Defensive Saxon settlements were at first encouraged by the authorities but their rebellion soon threatened the Roman way of life. The Romano-British were pushed back to higher land in the west by waves of invading Saxons, Angles and Jutes. After a period of Mercian supremacy under Offa in the 8th century, the West Saxons (Wessex) dominated southern England. Danish invasions in 865 established the Danelaw in northern England. Alfred the Great of Wessex and his son Edward resisted Danish expansion, strengthening Anglo-Saxon unity under Alfred's successors—Athelstan became the first king of all England in 927.

Danish rule over England was reasserted by Sweyn in 994 and his son, Canute. The Anglo-Saxon restoration was short-lived; William, duke of Normandy led the Norman Conquest in 1066, defeating Harold II at the Battle of Hastings. When William died in 1087, he left Normandy to his eldest son Robert, thus separating it from England. Henry II, the founder of the Plantagenet dynasty, was feudatory lord of half of France but Henry's son John lost most of the French possessions. The barons forced John to seal the Magna Carta in 1215, later interpreted as the source of English civil liberties. Thereafter, the Norman baronage came to regard themselves as English.

The Hundred Years War (1338–1453) with France ended with the loss of all remaining French possessions except Calais. In 1387 and in later outbreaks, the Black Death reduced the population by over a third. A dynastic struggle between the rival houses of York and Lancaster was concluded by the invasion of Henry Tudor in 1485. His son, Henry VIII, asserted royal authority over the church, breaking with Rome. Tudor power reached its zenith with Elizabeth I. Philip II's Spanish Armada, destroyed in 1588, was sent to turn back the Protestant tide in England and to counter English ambitions in the New World.

The accession of James VI of Scotland to the English throne in 1603 brought the two countries into personal union. Charles I's defeat in the Civil War resulted in a republican Commonwealth but the Stuart monarchy was restored in 1660. England and Scotland were united in 1707 under Anne, queen of Great Britain.

Territory and Population

At the census taken on 27 March 2011 the area of England was 130,432 sq. km (of which land 130,278 sq. km) and the population 53,012,456, giving a density of 407 per sq. km. England covers 53·4% of the total area of the United Kingdom. Households at the 2011 census: 22,063,368. Mid-2017 population estimate: 55,619,430 (27,481,053 males; 28,138,377 females).

Population (present on census night) at the four previous decennial censuses:

1971	1981	1991	2001
46,018,371[1]	46,226,100[2]	46,382,050	49,138,831

[1] Area now included in Wales formed the English county of Monmouthshire until 1974. [2] The final count is believed to be over-stated as a result of an error in processing. The preliminary counts presented here rounded to the nearest hundred are thought to be more accurate.

Population at census day 2011:

Males	Females	Total
26,069,148	26,943,308	53,012,456

For further statistical information, see under Territory and Population, UNITED KINGDOM.

The population on census day in 2011 in the nine English Government Office regions (created in 1994) was as follows: East, 5,846,965; East Midlands, 4,533,222; London, 8,173,941; North East, 2,596,886; North West, 7,052,177; South East, 8,634,750; South West, 5,288,935; West Midlands, 5,601,847; Yorkshire and the Humber, 5,283,733.

Following the local government reorganization in the mid-1990s, there is a mixed pattern to local government in England. Apart from Greater London, England is divided into 27 counties with two tiers of administration; a county council and district councils. There are six metropolitan county areas containing 36 single-tier metropolitan districts.

In addition, there are 56 single-tier unitary authorities which, with the exception of the Isle of Wight, were formerly district councils in the shire counties of England. The Isle of Wight is a unitary county council. The Isles of Scilly have a unitary council but are considered a district of 'Cornwall and the Isles of Scilly'.

As a consequence of the establishment of the 56 unitary authorities, a number of county areas were abolished. These were Avon, Cleveland and Humberside. Berkshire County Council was also abolished but the county itself is retained for ceremonial purposes. Greater London comprises 32 boroughs and the City of London.

Area in sq. km of English counties and unitary authorities, and population at census day 2011:

	Land area (sq. km)	Population
Metropolitan counties		
Greater Manchester	1,276	2,682,528
Merseyside	645	1,381,189
South Yorkshire	1,552	1,343,601
Tyne and Wear	540	1,104,825
West Midlands	902	2,736,460
West Yorkshire	2,029	2,226,058
Non-metropolitan counties		
Buckinghamshire (Bucks)	1,565	505,283
Cambridgeshire (Camb)	3,046	621,210
Cumbria	6,767	499,858
Derbyshire	2,547	769,686
Devon	6,564	746,399
Dorset	2,542	412,905
East Sussex	1,709	526,671
Essex	3,464	1,393,587
Gloucestershire (Gloucs)	2,653	596,984
Hampshire (Hants)	3,679	1,317,788
Hertfordshire (Herts)	1,643	1,116,062
Kent	3,544	1,463,740
Lancashire (Lancs)	2,903	1,171,339
Leicestershire (Leics)	2,083	650,489
Lincolnshire (Lincs)	5,921	713,653
Norfolk	5,371	857,888
Northamptonshire (Northants)	2,364	691,952
North Yorkshire (N. Yorks)	8,038	598,376
Nottinghamshire (Notts)	2,085	785,802
Oxfordshire (Oxon)	2,605	653,798
Somerset (Som)	3,451	529,972

(continued)

	Land area (sq. km)	Population
Staffordshire (Staffs)	2,620	848,489
Suffolk	3,800	728,163
Surrey	1,663	1,132,390
Warwickshire	1,975	545,474
West Sussex	1,990	806,892
Worcestershire	1,741	566,169
Unitary Authorities		
Bath and North East Somerset	346	176,016
Bedford	476	157,479
Blackburn with Darwen	137	147,489
Blackpool	35	142,065
Bournemouth	46	183,491
Bracknell Forest	109	113,205
Brighton and Hove	83	273,369
Bristol, City of	110	428,234
Central Bedfordshire	716	254,381
Cheshire East	1,166	370,127
Cheshire West & Chester	917	329,608
Cornwall	3,546	532,273
Darlington	197	105,564
Derby	78	248,752
Durham	2,226	513,242
East Riding of Yorkshire	2,408	334,179
Halton	79	125,746
Hartlepool	94	92,028
Herefordshire, County of	2,180	183,477
Isle of Wight	380	138,265
Isles of Scilly	16	2,203
Kingston upon Hull, City of	71	256,406
Leicester	73	329,839
Luton	43	203,201
Medway	192	263,925
Middlesbrough	54	138,412
Milton Keynes	309	248,821
North East Lincolnshire	192	159,616
North Lincolnshire	846	167,446
North Somerset	374	202,566
Northumberland	5,013	316,028
Nottingham	75	305,680
Peterborough	343	183,631
Plymouth	80	256,384
Poole	65	147,645
Portsmouth	40	205,056
Reading	40	155,698
Redcar and Cleveland	245	135,177
Rutland	382	37,369
Shropshire	3,197	306,129
Slough	33	140,205
South Gloucestershire	497	262,767
Southampton	50	236,882
Southend-on-Sea	42	173,658
Stockton-on-Tees	204	191,610
Stoke-on-Trent	93	249,008
Swindon	230	209,156
Telford and Wrekin	290	166,641
Thurrock	163	157,705
Torbay	63	130,959

(continued)

	Land area (sq. km)	Population
Warrington	181	202,228
West Berkshire	704	153,822
Wiltshire (Wilts)	3,255	470,981
Windsor and Maidenhead	197	144,560
Wokingham	179	154,380
York	272	198,051

Source: Office of National Statistics

In 2011 London had a population of 8,173,941. Populations of next largest cities in 2011 were: Birmingham, 1,073,045; Leeds, 751,485; Sheffield, 552,698; Bradford, 522,452; Manchester, 503,127; Liverpool, 466,415; Bristol, 428,234.

Greater London Boroughs
Total area 1,572 sq. km. Population at census day 2011: 8,173,941 (inner London, 3,231,901). Population by borough (census day 2011):

Barking and Dagenham	185,911
Barnet	356,386
Bexley	231,997
Brent	311,215
Bromley	309,392
Camden[1]	220,338
Croydon	363,378
Ealing	338,449
Enfield	312,466
Greenwich	254,557
Hackney[1]	246,270
Hammersmith and Fulham[1]	182,493
Haringey[1]	254,926
Harrow	239,056
Havering	237,232
Hillingdon	273,936
Hounslow	253,957
Islington[1]	206,125
Kensington and Chelsea[1]	158,649
Kingston upon Thames	160,060
Lambeth[1]	303,086
Lewisham[1]	275,885
Merton	199,693
Newham[1]	307,984
Redbridge	278,970
Richmond upon Thames	186,990
Southwark[1]	288,283
Sutton	190,146
Tower Hamlets[1]	254,096
Waltham Forest	258,249
Wandsworth[1]	306,995
Westminster, City of[1]	219,396

[1]Inner London borough.
Source: Office of National Statistics

The City of London (677 acres) is administered by its Corporation which retains some independent powers. Population at census day 2011: 7,375.

Climate

For more detailed information, see under Climate, UNITED KINGDOM.

London, Jan. 39°F (3·9°C), July 64°F (17·8°C). Annual rainfall 25" (635 mm). Birmingham, Jan. 38°F (3·3°C), July 61°F (16·1°C). Annual rainfall 30" (749 mm). Manchester, Jan. 39°F (3·9°C), July 61°F (16·1°C). Annual rainfall 34·5" (876 mm).

Constitution and Government

The Parliamentary electorate of England in the register in Dec. 2017 numbered 38,693,859.

Recent Elections

At the UK general election held on 8 June 2017, 533 members were returned from England.

See also Constitution and Government, Recent Elections *and* Current Government *in* UNITED KINGDOM.

Defence

For information on defence, see UNITED KINGDOM.

Economy

For information on the economy, see UNITED KINGDOM.

Energy and Natural Resources

For information on energy and natural resources, see UNITED KINGDOM.

Water

The Water Act of Sept. 1989 privatized the nine water and sewerage authorities in England. In March 2017 there were nine water and sewerage companies in total in England as well as 14 water supply-only companies. The Act also inaugurated the National Rivers Authority, with environmental and resource management responsibilities, and the 'regulator' *Office of Water Services (Ofwat)*, charged with protecting consumer interests.

Industry

Labour

The International Labour Organization unemployment rate in the period Oct.–Dec. 2013 was 7·2%, the same as the UK as a whole. Unemployment was lowest in the southeast (5·1%) and highest in the northeast (10·0%).

International Trade

For information on international trade, see UNITED KINGDOM.

Communications

For information on communications, see UNITED KINGDOM.

Shipping

In 2013 English ports handled 347·1m. tonnes of traffic, down from 386·5m. tonnes in 2008.

Social Institutions

Education

For details on the nature and types of school, see under Education, UNITED KINGDOM.

In 2012–13 education expenditure by central and local government in England was £109bn.

In Jan. 2014 there were 414 public sector nursery schools and one direct grant nursery school in England with provision for children under five; 39,915 pupils under five were attending public sector nursery schools. Some of these children were attending part-time.

In Jan. 2014 there were 4,416,710 pupils at 16,788 primary schools in England. Nearly all primary schools take both boys and girls. 13% of primary schools had 100 full-time pupils or fewer.

In Jan. 2014 there were 3,329 state-funded secondary schools in England with 3·2m. pupils of which 57% were academies (including free schools, university technical colleges and studio schools). Almost all local education authorities operate a system of comprehensive schools to which pupils are admitted without reference to ability or aptitude. In Jan. 2014 there were 1,249 such schools in England with 1·2m. pupils (2,704 schools and 2·8m. pupils in Jan. 2008). Some local authorities continue to operate a selective admissions policy at age 11, as do 163 state-funded secondary schools in England (135 of these being converter academies). All-through schools have pupils aged three to 18; pupils over 16 being able to transfer to an 11 to 18 school or a sixth form college providing for pupils aged 16 to 19—there are currently 93 official or designated sixth form colleges in England. In Jan. 2014 there were 176 middle schools deemed secondary.

Under the Education Act 1996 children have special educational needs if they have a learning difficulty that calls for special educational provision to be made for them. In some cases the local authority will need to make a statutory assessment of special educational needs under the Education Act 1996, which may ultimately lead to a 'statement'. In England the total number of pupils with statements in Jan. 2014 was 232,190. In Jan. 2014 there were 964 maintained special schools and 69 non-maintained special schools.

Outside the state system of education there were 2,411 independent schools (excluding direct grant nursery schools) in England in Jan. 2014, ranging from large prestigious schools to small local ones. Some provide boarding facilities but the majority include non-resident day pupils. There were 578,975 pupils in these schools in Jan. 2014, which represent about 7% of the total pupil population in England.

In 2013–14, 26,103 trainees began college-based initial teacher training courses and a further 6,676 trainees entered School Direct training.

Further Education (Non-University)

Participation in FE and Skills learning totalled 4·5m. in 2012–13, with 2·9m. students enrolled at FE colleges, 851,500 in apprenticeships and 759,600 in workplace and community learning. Total funding for the FE and Skills sector in England for 2012–13 was £4·0bn.

Higher Education

In 2011–12 there were 131 higher education institutions in England, including the individual colleges of the University of London. There were a total of 89 universities in England in 2011–12. Since then a further 11 institutions have been granted university status (*see* footnotes to sections c) and d) *below*). The main funding body is the Higher Education Funding Council for England (HEFCE), which distributes public money for teaching and research to universities and colleges. It works in partnership with the higher education sector and advises government on higher education policy. In 2011–12 HEFCE distributed a total of £6·51bn., including £4·34bn. for teaching and £1·56bn. for research.

a) *Universities*

Name (Location)	No. of students (2011–12)	No. of academic staff (2011–12)
Anglia Ruskin University (Chelmsford)	21,605	1,235
Aston University (Birmingham)	10,200	765
University of Bath	15,135	1,140
Bath Spa University	8,550	580
University of Bedfordshire	22,275	665
University of Birmingham	31,070	2,690
Birmingham City University	23,165	1,325
University of Bolton	8,485	300
Bournemouth University (Poole)	19,750	725
University of Bradford	14,210	610
University of Brighton	22,075	1,560
University of Bristol	19,145	2,390
Brunel University (Uxbridge)[1]	15,885	1,210
University of Buckingham[2]	1,885	130
Buckinghamshire New University	9,775	395
University of Cambridge[3]	19,945	4,765
Canterbury Christ Church University	19,105	655
University of Central Lancashire (Preston)	31,530	1,205
University of Chester	15,215	505
University of Chichester	5,640	420
City University (London)[4]	19,340	1,620
Coventry University	31,045	1,655
Cranfield University[5]	5,240	650
University for the Creative Arts (Canterbury, Epsom, Farnham, Maidstone and Rochester)	5,750	295

(*continued*)

University of Cumbria (Carlisle)	10,710	425
De Montfort University (Leicester)	21,795	1,140
University of Derby	18,495	965
University of Durham	16,570	1,505
University of East Anglia (Norwich)	17,610	2,225
University of East London	23,225	850
Edge Hill University (Ormskirk)	22,350	925
University of Essex (Colchester)	15,215	1,075
University of Exeter	18,720	1,425
University of Gloucestershire (Cheltenham)	9,080	535
University of Greenwich (London)	26,445	1,240
University of Hertfordshire (Hatfield)	27,320	1,640
University of Huddersfield	22,340	1,145
University of Hull	23,315	970
Imperial College London	16,000	3,690
Keele University (Newcastle-under-Lyme)	10,665	775
University of Kent (Canterbury)	20,310	1,660
Kingston University (Kingston upon Thames)	26,055	1,895
University of Lancaster	13,075	1,430
University of Leeds	32,510	2,940
Leeds Metropolitan University[6]	27,985	1,625
University of Leicester	17,055	2,030
University of Lincoln	13,120	815
University of Liverpool	21,875	2,200
Liverpool Hope University	7,745	245
Liverpool John Moores University	24,455	1,265
University of the Arts London	17,300	2,120
University of London[3]	142,190	19,515
London Metropolitan University	23,280	835
London South Bank University	23,350	970
Loughborough University	16,025	1,520
University of Manchester	40,680	4,415
Manchester Metropolitan University	34,430	2,150
Middlesex University (London)	23,540	790
University of Newcastle upon Tyne	21,055	2,360
University of Northampton	14,605	795
University of Northumbria at Newcastle	29,300	1,345
University of Nottingham	35,630	3,280
Nottingham Trent University	27,930	1,520
Open University[7]	201,270	7,385
University of Oxford[3]	25,595	5,660
Oxford Brookes University	18,425	1,240
University of Plymouth	31,105	1,160
University of Portsmouth	23,705	1,490
University of Reading	13,505	1,525
Roehampton University	9,255	450
University of Salford	21,755	1,470
University of Sheffield	25,965	2,615
Sheffield Hallam University	37,160	2,065
University of Southampton	24,135	2,625
Southampton Solent University[8]	12,530	705
Staffordshire University (Stoke-on-Trent)	21,760	860
University of Sunderland	17,380	740
University of Surrey (Guildford)	15,055	1,510
University of Sussex (Brighton)	13,130	1,590
Teesside University (Middlesbrough)	27,980	710

(*continued*)

University of Warwick (Coventry)	27,440	1,795
University of the West of England, Bristol	30,390	1,525
University of West London	12,400	595
University of Westminster (London)	21,500	1,335
University of Winchester	6,330	540
University of Wolverhampton	21,510	800
University of Worcester	10,695	535
University of York	17,405	1,410
York St John University	5,975	260

[1]Renamed Brunel University London in 2014.
[2]Private.
[3]See listing of colleges below.
[4]Renamed City, University of London in 2016 when it became part of the University of London.
[5]Postgraduate only.
[6]Renamed Leeds Beckett University in 2014.
[7]Entirely distance learning—*see* page 1262.
[8]Renamed Solent University in 2018.

b) *University of Cambridge; University of London; University of Oxford*
University of Cambridge Colleges:

Christ's College; Churchill College; Clare College; Clare Hall[1]; Corpus Christi College; Darwin College[1]; Downing College; Emmanuel College; Fitzwilliam College; Girton College; Gonville and Caius College; Homerton College; Hughes Hall; Jesus College; King's College; Lucy Cavendish; Magdalene College; Murray Edwards College[2]; Newnham College; Pembroke College; Peterhouse; Queen's College; Robinson College; St Catharine's College; St Edmund's College; St John's College; Selwyn College; Sidney Sussex College; Trinity College; Trinity Hall; Wolfson College.

[1]Postgraduate only.
[2]Formerly New Hall.

University of London Colleges (total no. of students 2013–14/no. of full-time academic staff 2013–14):

Birkbeck (15,545/450); Courtauld Institute of Art (460/35); Goldsmiths College (8,110/335); Heythrop College (800/40); Institute of Cancer Research (290/515[1]); Institute of Education[2] (5,690/250); King's College London (27,645/3,085); London Business School (1,905/105); London School of Economics and Political Science (10,145/810); London School of Hygiene and Tropical Medicine (1,250/535); Queen Mary, University of London (15,420/1,575); Royal Academy of Music (745/20); Royal Central School of Speech and Drama (985/35); Royal Holloway, University of London (9,670/605); Royal Veterinary College (2,155/220); St George's (5,505/385); School of Oriental and African Studies[3] (5,415/335); University College London (28,430/4,745). In 2013–14 the University of London had 54,323 external programme students.

[1]Includes researchers who meet the official description of academic staff.
[2]Merged with University College London in 2014.
[3]Renamed SOAS University of London in 2016.

University of Oxford Colleges:

All Souls College; Balliol College; Brasenose College; Christ Church; Corpus Christi College; Exeter College; Green Templeton College[1]; Harris Manchester College; Hertford College; Jesus College; Keble College; Kellogg College[1]; Lady Margaret Hall; Linacre College[1]; Lincoln College; Magdalen College; Mansfield College; Merton College; New College; Nuffield College[1]; Oriel College; Pembroke College; The Queen's College; St Anne's College; St Antony's College[1]; St Catherine's College; St Cross College[1]; St Edmund Hall; St Hilda's College; St Hugh's College; St John's College; St Peter's College; Somerville College; Trinity College; University College; Wadham College; Wolfson College[1]; Worcester College. *Permanent Private Halls:* Blackfriars; Campion Hall; Greyfriars; Regent's Park College; St Benet's Hall; St Stephen's House; Wycliffe Hall.

[1]Postgraduate only.

c) *Colleges of Art, Dance, Drama and Music*

2011–12: Arts University College at Bournemouth[1]; Conservatoire for Dance and Drama (London)[2]; Guildhall School of Music and Drama (London); Leeds College of Art[3]; Liverpool Institute for Performing Arts; Norwich University College of the Arts[4]; Ravensbourne (Bromley)[5]; Rose Bruford College of Theatre & Performance (Sidcup); Royal College of Art (London); Royal College of Music (London); Royal Northern College of Music (Manchester); Trinity Laban Conservatoire of Music and Dance (London).

[1]Awarded university status as Arts University Bournemouth in 2012.
[2]Affiliate schools: Bristol Old Vic Theatre School; Central School of Ballet; London Academy of Music and Dramatic Art; London Contemporary Dance School; National Centre for Circus Arts; Northern School of Contemporary Dance; Rambert School of Ballet and Contemporary Dance; Royal Academy of Dramatic Art.
[3]Awarded university status as Leeds Arts University in 2017.
[4]Awarded university status as Norwich University of the Arts in 2013.
[5]Awarded university status as Ravensbourne University London in 2018.

d) *Other Institutions*

2011–12: University College Birmingham[1]; Bishop Grosseteste University College (Lincoln)[2]; University College Falmouth Incorporating Dartington College of Arts[3]; Harper Adams University College (Newport)[4]; Leeds Trinity University College[5]; University of London (Institutes and Activities); Newman University College (Birmingham)[6]; University College Plymouth St Mark and St John[7]; Royal Agricultural College (Cirencester)[8]; St Mary's University College, Twickenham[9]; University Campus Suffolk[10]; Writtle College (Chelmsford)[11].

[1]Awarded university status in 2012.
[2]Awarded university status as Bishop Grosseteste University in 2012.
[3]Awarded university status as Falmouth University in 2012.
[4]Awarded university status as Harper Adams University in 2012.
[5]Awarded university status as Leeds Trinity University in 2012.
[6]Awarded university status as Newman University, Birmingham in 2013.
[7]Awarded university status as University of St Mark & St John in 2013.
[8]Awarded university status as Royal Agricultural University in 2013.
[9]Awarded university status as St Mary's University, Twickenham in 2014.
[10]Awarded university status as University of Suffolk in 2016.
[11]Renamed Writtle University College in 2016.

Health

As at 30 Sept. 2013 there were 35,561 general medical practitioners in England excluding registrars and retainers (35,120 in Sept. 2010), with an average of 1,787 patients per doctor. There were 22,920 NHS dentists in England in 2011–12. In England in 2013 there were 347,944 qualified nursing, midwifery and health visiting staff and 23,833 GP practice nurses. As at 30 Sept. 2013 there were 41,220 consultants in England (37,752 in Sept. 2010) and 4,404 GP registrars. There was an average of 135,949 available hospital beds in England in 2013–14 (142,470 in 2010–11).

In 2013, 26·0% of men and 23·8% of women were obese (having a body mass index over 30), compared with 13·2% and 16·4% in 1993 respectively. In 2010, 20% of men and 19% of women aged 16 and over in England were smokers. Among 11- to 15-year-olds it was estimated that 6% of girls but only 4% of boys were regular smokers in 2010.

Personal Social Services staff numbered 140,700 in England at 30 Sept. 2013. The total expenditure (2012–13) for PSS was £14·6bn.

Culture

Tourism
The leading free admission attraction in 2015 was the British Museum, with 6·8m. visits. The leading tourist attractions charging admission in 2015 were: the Tower of London, with 2·8m. visits; Westminster Abbey, with 1·7m.; the Royal Botanic Gardens, Kew, with 1·6m.; St Paul's Cathedral, with 1·6m.; and Chester Zoo, with 1·5m.

Scotland

Key Historical Events

Earliest evidence of human settlement in Scotland dates from the Middle Stone Age. Hunters and fishermen on the west coast were succeeded by farming communities as far north as Shetland. The Romans, who were active in the 1st century AD, built Hadrian's Wall between the Tyne and Solway Firth as their northern frontier. At this time, the Picts formed two kingdoms north of the Firth of Clyde. From the 6th century, the Celtic Scots from Dalriada, in the north of Ireland, fought with Angles and Britons for control of southern Scotland.

In 843 Kenneth MacAlpin united the Scots and the Picts to found the kingdom of Scotland. A legal and administrative uniformity was established by David I (reigned 1124–53). William the Lion abandoned claims to Northumbria in 1209 but began the alliance with France. In 1286 Edward I of England asserted his claim as overlord of Scotland and appointed his son to succeed to the crown. Resistance to English rule was led by William Wallace and later by Robert Bruce, who defeated the English at Bannockburn in 1314. His grandson, Robert II, became the first Stewart (Stuart) king in 1371.

Royal minorities undermined the authority of the crown in the 15th century until the accession of James IV in 1488. Relations with England improved after his marriage to Margaret Tudor in 1503 but when Henry VIII invaded France, James attacked England and was killed at the Battle of Flodden in 1513. The young James V was assailed by conflicting pressures from pro-French and pro-English factions but having secured his personal rule, he entered into two successive French marriages. His daughter, Mary Queen of Scots, married the French Dauphin in 1558. Protestant opposition to French influence was bolstered by Elizabeth I of England, who sent troops. Mary was in France when the Scottish parliament renounced papal authority, bolstering the reformist movement, led by John Knox. Returning to Scotland after her husband's death in 1561, Mary was forced to take refuge in England. Her son, James VI, survived the animosity between his own and his mother's followers to make an alliance with England. Deemed a threat because of her claim to the English throne, Mary was executed on Elizabeth's orders in 1587.

Elizabeth died without issue in 1603 and was succeeded by James. Although he styled himself 'king of Great Britain', England and Scotland remained independent. Charles I alienated much of the Scottish nobility and was defeated in the Bishops' Wars by the Covenanters, who rejected English interference in the Scottish church. Scottish armies fought for both sides in the English Civil War, which led to the execution of Charles I in 1649. However, the Scots soon united to accept Charles II as their king. Having established dominance in England, Cromwell moved against Scotland forcing Charles II into exile. His restoration in 1660 was welcomed in both kingdoms. His successor, James VII (James II of England), was less astute in managing religious and political differences. The collapse of his regime in 1688 and the arrival of William of Orange confirmed the Protestant ascendancy in Scotland and England.

The union of parliament in 1707 brought Scotland more directly under English authority. However, Scotland retained its own legal and ecclesiastical systems. The remaining supporters of James VII, the Jacobites, led two abortive risings on behalf of James's son and grandson (the old and young Pretenders) but were defeated decisively at Culloden in 1746.

For more recent Scottish history, see UNITED KINGDOM: Key Historical Events.

Territory and Population

The total area of Scotland is 78,808 sq. km (2011), including its islands—186 in number—and inland water. Scotland covers 32·3% of the total area of the United Kingdom.

Population (including military in the barracks and seamen on board vessels in the harbours) at the dates of each census:

Date of enumeration	Population	Pop. per sq. mile[1]
1801	1,608,420	53
1811	1,805,864	60
1821	2,091,521	70
1831	2,364,386	79
1841	2,620,184	88
1851	2,888,742	97
1861	3,062,294	100
1871	3,360,018	113
1881	3,735,573	125
1891	4,025,647	135
1901	4,472,103	150
1911	4,760,904	160

(continued)

Date of enumeration	Population	Pop. per sq. mile[1]
1921	4,882,497	164
1931	4,842,980	163
1951	5,096,415	171
1961	5,179,344	174
1971	5,228,963	67
1981	5,130,735	66
1991	4,998,567	60
2001	5,062,011	65
2011	5,295,403	68

[1]Per sq. km from 1971.

Population at census day 2011:

Males	Females	Total
2,567,444	2,727,959	5,295,403

Mid-2017 population estimate: 5,424,800 (2,640,300 males; 2,784,500 females).

In 2011, 24,974 people spoke Gaelic and 55,817 spoke Scots (comprising dialects from the Lowlands and Northern Isles). Households in 2011: 2,373,000.

The age distribution in Scotland at census day in 2011 was as follows (in 1,000):

Age-group	
Under 5	293
5 and under 10	270
10 and under 15	292
15 and under 20	331
20 and under 25	364
25 and under 35	667
35 and under 45	735
45 and under 55	787
55 and under 65	667
65 and under 70	261
70 and under 75	221
75 and under 85	303
85 and upwards	106

Land area and population (27 March 2011) by administrative area:

Council Area	Area (sq. km)	Population
Aberdeen City	186	222,793
Aberdeenshire	6,313	252,973
Angus	2,182	115,978
Argyll and Bute	6,909	88,166
Clackmannanshire	159	51,442
Dumfries and Galloway	6,426	151,324
Dundee City	60	147,268
East Ayrshire	1,262	122,767
East Dunbartonshire	174	105,026
East Lothian	679	99,717
East Renfrewshire	174	90,574
Edinburgh, City of	263	476,626
Eilean Siar[1]	3,060	27,684
Falkirk	297	155,990
Fife	1,325	365,198
Glasgow City	175	593,245
Highland	25,684	232,132
Inverclyde	160	81,485

(continued)

Council Area	Area (sq. km)	Population
Midlothian	354	83,187
Moray	2,238	93,295
North Ayrshire	885	138,146
North Lanarkshire	470	337,727
Orkney Islands	990	21,349
Perth and Kinross	5,286	146,652
Renfrewshire	262	174,908
Scottish Borders	4,732	113,870
Shetland Islands	1,467	23,167
South Ayrshire	1,222	112,799
South Lanarkshire	1,772	313,830
Stirling	2,187	90,247
West Dunbartonshire	159	90,720
West Lothian	427	175,118
Total	77,937	5,295,403

[1]Formerly Western Isles.

Glasgow is Scotland's largest city, with a population of 593,000 in 2011, followed by Edinburgh, the capital (477,000), and Aberdeen, with 223,000.

The birthplaces of the 2011 census day population in Scotland were: Scotland, 4,411,884; England, 459,486; Poland, 55,231; Northern Ireland, 36,655; India, 23,489; Ireland 22,952; Germany, 22,274; Pakistan, 20,039; Wales, 17,381; elsewhere, 226,012.

Social Statistics

	Estimated resident population at 30 June	Total births	Live births outside marriage	Deaths	Marriages	Divorces, annulments and dissolutions[1]
2009	5,231,900	59,046	29,710	53,856	27,524	11,538
2010	5,262,200	58,791	29,528	53,967	28,480	10,750
2011	5,299,900	58,590	29,888	53,661	29,135	10,115
2012	5,313,600	58,027	29,795	54,937	30,534	9,879
2013	5,327,700	56,014	28,816	54,700	27,547	9,571
2014	5,347,600	56,725[2]	28,821[2]	54,239[2]	29,070[2]	9,809

[1]Figures are for financial year ending 31 March in the year in question.
[2]Provisional.

2014 rates per 1,000 population (provisional): birth, 10·6; death, 10·2; marriage, 5·5; infant mortality per 1,000 live births, 3·6; sex ratio, 1,050 male births to 1,000 female. Average age of marriage in 2014: males, 33·2, females, 31·4. Expectation of life, 2013–15: males, 77·1 years; females, 81·1.

Climate
For more detailed information, see under Climate, UNITED KINGDOM.

Aberdeen, Jan. 38°F (3·3°C), July 57°F (13·9°C). Annual rainfall 32" (813 mm). Edinburgh, Jan. 38°F (3·3°C), July 58°F (14·5°C). Annual rainfall 27" (686 mm). Glasgow, Jan. 39°F (3·9°C), July 59°F (15°C). Annual rainfall 38" (965 mm).

Constitution and Government
In a referendum on devolution on 11 Sept. 1997, Scotland's voters opted for devolved government, calling for the reinstatement of a separate parliament in Scotland, the first since union with England in 1707. 1,775,045 votes (74·3%) were cast in favour of a Scottish parliament and 614,400 against (25·7%). On a turnout of 60·4%, around 44·8% of the total electorate voted in favour. For the second question, on the Parliament's tax-raising powers, 1,512,889 votes were cast in favour (63·5%) and 870,263 against (36·5%). This represented 38·4% of the total electorate.

A referendum on independence from the United Kingdom was held on 18 Sept. 2014. In response to the question 'Should Scotland be an independent country?', 55·3% answered 'no' with 44·7% answering 'yes'. 4,283,392 people were registered to vote; turnout was 84·6%. For the first time in the United Kingdom 16- and 17-year-olds could vote in a major ballot.

The Scottish Parliament is made up of 129 members and managed a budget of £34·7bn. in 2013–14. The parliament may pass laws and has limited tax raising powers; it is also responsible for devolved issues, including health, education, police and fire services; however, 'reserved issues' (foreign policy, constitutional matters, and many domestic areas including social security, trade and industry, and employment legislation) remain the responsibility of the British Parliament in Westminster.

The Parliamentary electorate of Scotland in the register in Dec. 2017 numbered 3,950,643.

Recent Elections

At the UK general election held on 8 June 2017, 59 members were returned from Scotland. The Scottish National Party won 35 seats; Conservative, 13; Labour, 7; Liberal Democrats, 4.

In elections to the Scottish Parliament on 5 May 2016, the Scottish National Party (SNP) won 63 seats (4 by regional list), against 31 (24 by regional list) for the Conservatives, 24 (21 by regional list) for Labour, 6 (all by regional list) for the Greens and 5 (one by regional list) for the Liberal Democrats. Of the 129 seats, 73 were won on a first-past-the-post basis and 56 through proportional representation (regional list). The election delivered a third consecutive parliament in which the SNP was the largest party (although two seats short of a majority) and also saw the Conservatives surpass Labour in Scotland for the first time since the opening of the Scottish Parliament in 1999.

See also Constitution and Government, Recent Elections *and* Current Government *in* UNITED KINGDOM.

Current Government

First Minister: Nicola Sturgeon; b. 1970 (Scottish National Party).
Presiding Officer: Ken Macintosh.
Scottish Government: http://www.gov.scot

Defence

For information on defence, see UNITED KINGDOM.

Economy

For information on the economy, see UNITED KINGDOM.

Overview

After legislative powers were devolved to a reconstituted Scottish Parliament in 1999, the economy achieved a degree of financial autonomy, including the power to determine the cost of university education and to vary the level of income tax.

Traditionally, heavy industry—including mining, shipbuilding and engineering—had dominated the economy. Subsequent industrial decline during the second half of the 20th century was countered by the discovery of oil reserves in the North Sea in the mid-1960s and a shift towards a services-orientated economy. The services sector accounts for some three-quarters of the economy, with tourism and financial services key contributors. Primary exports include textiles, whisky and shortbread.

In 2008 the near collapse of the Royal Bank of Scotland and HBOS (the holding company of the Bank of Scotland) threatened a UK financial sector meltdown until both institutions were bailed out by the government. Alongside the rest of the UK economy, Scotland returned to positive growth in 2010. However, given its dependence on oil production, the economy slowed significantly after oil prices fell in 2015. Growth in Scotland lagged behind the UK-wide rate by 1·5% in the first half of 2017. To counter this trend, government policy has focused on reviving the manufacturing sector.

A referendum in Sept. 2014 resulted in a majority vote against Scottish independence from the UK. Analysts had predicted that independence would have bleak economic consequences for the nation, owing to declining oil revenues, an ageing population and uncertainty over the sterling currency union and membership of the European Union. Following the referendum, the UK government set out plans to devolve more responsibility to the Scottish Parliament, including greater local tax-raising and spending powers. In light of Scotland's predominant 'remain' vote in the 2016 EU membership referendum—in contrast to the UK-wide decision to leave—Scotland's long-term political and economic prospects were again thrown into doubt.

Currency

The Bank of Scotland, Clydesdale Bank and the Royal Bank of Scotland have note-issuing powers.

Budget

Government expenditure in Scotland came to £66·4bn. in 2013–14 (including social protection £22·3bn., health £11·5bn. and education and training £7·6bn.). Revenues (excluding North Sea revenue) totalled £50·0bn. (including income tax £11·4bn., VAT £10·1bn. and national insurance contributions £8·7bn.).

Performance

The real GDP growth rate in 2010 was 0·9%.

Energy and Natural Resources

Environment

44·3% of household waste was recycled in 2015.

Electricity

The Electricity Act 1989 led to the privatization of the industry in Scotland and the creation of three new companies: ScottishPower, Scottish Hydro-Electric and Scottish Nuclear. After a series of acquisitions and mergers, in Dec. 1998 Scottish Hydro-Electric became part of the newly formed Scottish and Southern Energy (rebranded to SSE in 2010), a vertically integrated company that covers generation, transmission, distribution and supply in northern Scotland. ScottishPower runs distribution in central and southern Scotland and in 2007 became a subsidiary of the Spanish company Iberdrola. Scottish Nuclear, responsible for operating the two Scottish nuclear power stations, merged with British Energy in 1996, which in turn became a subsidiary of EDF in Jan. 2009.

Water

Water supply is the responsibility of the Regional and Island local authorities. The Scottish Environment Protection Agency (SEPA) is responsible for environmental management.

Agriculture

In 2010 total agricultural area was 5,643,054 ha., of which 3,191,593 ha. were used for rough grazing and 1,932,274 ha. for crops and grass.

Selected crop production, 2010 (in 1,000 tonnes): barley, 1,665; potatoes, 1,472; wheat, 918; oats, 135.

Livestock, 2010 (in 1,000): sheep, 6,753; cattle, 1,826; pigs, 409; poultry, 14,593.

Forestry

Total forest area in March 2017 was 1,440,000 ha., of which 470,000 ha. was owned or managed by the Forestry Commission.

Fisheries

The major fishing ports in terms of value of fish landed are Peterhead, Lerwick, Fraserburgh and Aberdeen. In 2014 there were 2,030 fishing vessels that landed 481,000 tonnes of fish worth £514m.

Industry

Labour

In the period Nov. 2014–Jan. 2015 the economically active population numbered 2,773,000 (1,357,000 females), of whom 162,000 (63,000 females) were unemployed. The International Labour Organization unemployment rate in the period Oct.–Dec. 2013 was 7·1% (compared to 7·2% in the UK as a whole). In the fourth quarter of 2014, 21·0% of employee jobs were in the public sector. In 2014, of the employed workforce 25·1% were in retail, wholesale, and accommodation and food service activities, 9·3% in manufacturing, and 9·1% in administrative and support service activities.

Communications

Roads

Responsibility for the construction and maintenance of trunk roads belongs to the Scottish Office. Roads not classified as trunk roads are the responsibility of county or unitary councils. In 2014 there were 55,987 km of public roads, of which 600 km were motorways. As of 31 Dec. 2014 there were 2·50m. licensed private and light goods vehicles.

Rail
Total railway length in 2013–14 was 2,763 km. In 2013–14 a total of 86·3m. passengers travelled by rail and, in 2012–13, 8·4m. tonnes of freight were carried. There are a metro in Glasgow and a tram network in Edinburgh.

Civil Aviation
There are major airports at Aberdeen, Edinburgh, Glasgow and Prestwick. In 2014 Edinburgh was the sixth busiest for passenger traffic in the UK, with 10,158,906 passengers (4,810,866 on domestic flights) and Glasgow was the eighth busiest with 7,708,867 (3,760,616). In 2014, 24,076,045 passengers and 55,126 tonnes of freight were carried by Scottish airports.

Shipping
The principal Scottish port is Forth (including Grangemouth, Leith and Rosyth), which handled 25·3m. tonnes of cargo in 2012.

Social Institutions

Justice
The High Court of Justiciary is the supreme criminal court in Scotland and has jurisdiction in all cases of crime committed in any part of Scotland, unless expressly excluded by statute. It consists of the Lord Justice General, the Lord Justice Clerk and 30 other judges, who are the same judges who preside in the Court of Session, the Scottish Supreme Civil Court. One judge is seconded to the Scottish Law Commission. The Court is presided over by the Lord Justice General, whom failing, by the Lord Justice Clerk, and exercises an appellate jurisdiction as well as being a court of first instance. The home of the High Court is Edinburgh, but the court visits other towns and cities in Scotland on circuit and indeed the busiest High Court sitting is in Glasgow. The court sits in Edinburgh both as a Court of Appeal (the *quorum* being two judges if the appeal is against sentence or other disposals, and three in all other cases) and on circuit as a court of first instance. Although the decisions of the High Court are not subject to review by the Supreme Court of the United Kingdom, with the Scotland Act 1998 coming into force on 20 May 1999, there is a limited right of appeal against the termination of a devolution issue to the Supreme Court of the United Kingdom. One judge sitting with a jury of 15 persons can, and usually does, try cases, but two or more judges (with a jury) may do so in important or complex cases. The court has a privative jurisdiction over cases of treason, murder, rape, breach of duty by magistrates and certain statutory offences under the Official Secrets Act 1911 and the Geneva Conventions Act 1957. It also tries the most serious crimes against person or property and those cases in which a sentence greater than imprisonment for three years is likely to be imposed.

The Sheriff Court has an inherent universal criminal jurisdiction (as well as an extensive civil one), limited in general to crimes and offences committed within a sheriffdom (a specifically defined region), which has, however, been curtailed by statute or practice under which the High Court of Justiciary has exclusive jurisdiction in relation to the crimes mentioned above. The Sheriff Court is presided over by a sheriff principal or a sheriff, who when trying cases on indictment sits with a jury of 15 people. His powers of awarding punishment involving imprisonment are restricted to a maximum of three years, but he may under certain statutory powers remit the prisoner to the High Court for sentence if this is felt to be insufficient. The sheriff also exercises a wide summary criminal jurisdiction and when doing so sits without a jury; and he has concurrent jurisdiction with every other court within his Sheriff Court district in regard to all offences competent for trial in summary courts. The great majority of offences which come before courts are of a more minor nature and as such are disposed of in the Sheriff Summary Courts or in the District Courts (*see below*). Where a case is to be tried on indictment either in the High Court of Justiciary or in the Sheriff Court, the judge may, before the trial, hold a preliminary or first diet to decide questions of a preliminary nature, whether relating to the competency or relevancy of proceedings or otherwise. Any decision at a preliminary diet (other than a decision to adjourn the first or preliminary diet or discharge trial diet) can be the subject of an appeal to the High Court of Justiciary prior to the trial. The High Court also has the exclusive power to provide a remedy for all extraordinary occurrences in the course of criminal business where there is no other mode of appeal available. This is known as the Nobile Officium powers of the High Court and all petitions to the High Court as the Nobile Officium must be heard before at least three judges.

In cases to be tried on indictment in the Sheriff Court a first diet is mandatory before the trial diet to decide questions of a preliminary nature and to identify cases which are unlikely to go to trial on the date programmed. Likewise in summary proceedings, an intermediate diet is again mandatory before trial. In High Court cases such matters may be dealt with at a preliminary diet.

District Courts have jurisdiction in more minor offences occurring within a district which before recent local government reorganization corresponded to district council boundaries. These courts are presided over by lay magistrates, known as justices, who have limited powers for fine and imprisonment. In Glasgow District there are also stipendiary magistrates, who are legally qualified, and who have the same sentencing powers as sheriffs.

The Court of Session, presided over by the Lord President (the Lord Justice General in criminal cases), is divided into an inner-house comprising two divisions of five judges each with a mainly appellate function, and an outer-house comprising 22 single judges sitting individually at first instance; it exercises the highest civil jurisdiction in Scotland, with the Supreme Court of the United Kingdom as the final Court of Appeal.

CIVIL JUDICIAL STATISTICS

	2013–14
Supreme Court (Appeals from Court of Session)	16
Court of Session:	
General Department—initiated	3,517
Petition Department—initiated	1,197
Sheriff Courts:	
Ordinary Cause—initiated	24,026
Summary Cause—initiated	18,852
Small Claim—initiated	29,633

CRIMINAL STATISTICS

	2011–12	2012–13	2013–14
Crimes and offences[1] recorded by the police:			
All crimes	314,188	273,053	270,397
Non-sexual crimes of violence	9,533	7,530	6,785
All offences	542,315	543,768	501,281[2]
Persons with a charge proved in court:			
All crimes and offences[1]	108,424	101,018	105,656
All crimes	40,671	36,978	36,202
Persons aged 8–15[3]	47	36	16
Average prison population	8,179	8,057	7,894

[1]Contraventions of Scottish criminal law are divided for statistical purposes into crimes and offences. The term 'crime' is generally used for more serious criminal acts; and 'offence' for less serious ones, although the term 'offence' may also be used in relation to serious breaches of criminal law. The distinction is made only for working purposes and the 'seriousness' is generally related to the maximum sentence that can be imposed.
[2]Owing to a change in recording practices, data for 2013–14 offences is not comparable with the two previous years' totals.
[3]Except for serious offences which qualify for solemn proceedings, children aged 8–15 are not proceeded against in Scottish courts. Children within this age group that commit crime are generally referred to the reporter of the children's panel or are given a police warning.

Police
In Scotland, the unitary councils have the role of police authorities. The actual strength at 30 Sept. 2010 was 17,371 officers. There were 1,567 special constables. Total police funding in Scotland for 2010–11 was £1,412m.

Education
In Sept. 2013 there were 2,569 publicly funded (local authority, grant-aided and self-governing) primary, secondary and special schools. All teachers employed in these schools are required to be qualified.

Pre-school Education
In Sept. 2013 there were 2,504 pre-school centres that were in partnership with their local authority and 102,871 pupils enrolled in these centres.

Primary Education
In Sept. 2013 there were 2,056 publicly funded primary schools with 377,382 pupils and 22,905 full-time equivalent teachers.

Secondary Education
In Sept. 2013 there were 364 publicly funded secondary schools with 289,164 pupils and 23,695 full-time equivalent teachers. Pupils who start their secondary education in schools that do not cater for a full range of courses may be transferred at the end of their second or fourth year to schools where a full range of courses is provided.

Independent schools
There were 102 independent schools in Dec. 2013. In Sept. 2014 there were 30,687 pupils in 72 independent schools that belonged to the Scottish Council of Independent Schools. A small number of the Scottish independent schools are of the 'public school' type, but they are not known as 'public schools' since in Scotland this term is used to denote education authority (i.e. state) schools.

Special Education
In Sept. 2013 there were 149 publicly funded special schools with 6,984 pupils.

Further Education
Under the Further and Higher Education (Scotland) Act 1992 funding of the Further Education colleges was transferred to central government in 1993. Scotland's FE colleges are funded by the Scottish Funding Council (SFC), which replaced the Scottish Further Education Funding Council and the Scottish Higher Education Funding Council in Oct. 2005.

There are 43 incorporated FE colleges as well as the FE colleges in Orkney and Shetland, which are run by the local education authorities, and two privately managed colleges, Sabhal Mor Ostaig and Newbattle Abbey College. The colleges offer training in a wide range of vocational areas and co-operate with the Scottish Qualifications Authority, the Enterprise, Energy and Lifelong Learning Directorate and the Education Directorate of the Scottish Executive in the development of new courses. The qualifications offered by colleges aim to improve the skills of the nation's workforce and increase the country's competitiveness.

In 2010–11 there were 314,585 students and a total of 383,005 enrolments on courses at Scotland's 43 further education institutions; the full-time equivalent staff number in the colleges was 12,291.

Full-time students resident in Scotland (and EU students) undertaking non-advanced (further education) courses are mainly supported through discretionary further education bursaries that are administered locally by further education colleges within National Policy Guidelines issued by the SFC. The Colleges have delegated discretionary powers for some aspects of the bursary support award.

In May 2000 the Scottish Executive announced the abolition of tuition fees for all eligible Scottish (and EU) full-time further education students from autumn 2000. The Executive also made a commitment to take steps to align, from autumn 2001, the levels of support available on a weekly basis for FE students with those that will apply for HE students and to begin to align the systems of assessment of parental/family contributions.

Higher Education
In Scotland in 2011–12 there were 19 institutions of higher education funded by the Scottish Funding Council. Included in this total is the Open University. University education in Scotland has a long history. Four universities—St Andrews, Glasgow, Aberdeen and Edinburgh, known collectively as the 'ancient Scottish universities'—were founded in the 15th and 16th centuries. Four further universities—Strathclyde, Heriot-Watt, Stirling and Dundee—were formally established as independent universities between 1964 and 1967, and three others—Napier (now Edinburgh Napier University), Paisley (now the University of the West of Scotland) and Robert Gordon—were granted the title of university in 1992, with Glasgow Caledonian and Abertay Dundee being added in 1993 and 1994 respectively. Two more of the present-day universities followed in 2007 when the University of Paisley and Bell College merged to become the University of the West of Scotland and Queen Margaret University College became Queen Margaret University. Most recently the University of the Highlands and Islands, which evolved from the higher education institution UHI Millennium Institute and is a federation of 13 colleges and research institutions, was granted university status in 2011.

The remaining higher education institutions, which all offer courses at degree level (although not themselves universities), were formerly Central Institutions: Glasgow School of Art; Royal Conservatoire of Scotland (Glasgow); and SRUC (Scotland's Rural College), with campuses in a number of locations.

Further education colleges may also provide higher education courses.

University and HE student and staff figures:

Name (and Location)	Students (2011–12)	Staff (2011–12)
Aberdeen Univ.	15,515	1,620
Abertay Dundee Univ.	4,930	200
Dundee Univ.	16,500	1,450
Edinburgh Napier Univ.	14,060	765
Edinburgh Univ.	27,675	3,350
Glasgow Caledonian Univ.	16,120	720
Glasgow School of Art	1,720	155
Glasgow Univ.	26,295	2,655
Heriot-Watt Univ. (Edinburgh)	10,870	685
Queen Margaret University (Edinburgh)	5,245	205
Robert Gordon Univ. (Aberdeen)	12,700	660
Royal Conservatoire of Scotland (Glasgow)	895	270
St Andrews Univ.	9,850	1,040
SRUC (Aberdeen, Ayr, Broxburn, Cupar, Dumfries and Edinburgh)[1]	990	210
Stirling Univ.	11,120	855
Strathclyde Univ. (Glasgow)	19,755	1,320
Univ. of the Highlands and Islands (Inverness)	7,225	30
Univ. of the West Scotland (Ayr, Dumfries, Hamilton and Paisley)	14,845	540

[1]Created in Oct. 2012 through the merger of the Scottish Agricultural College and three further education colleges.

All the higher education institutions are independent and self-governing. In addition to funding through the higher education funding councils, they receive tuition fees from the Students Awards Agency for Scotland for students domiciled in Scotland, and through local education authorities for students domiciled in England and Wales. Institutions which carry out research may also receive funding through the five Research Councils administered by the Office of Science and Technology.

Health
As at 30 Sept. 2014 there were 4,918 general medical practitioners in Scotland. In Sept. 2014 there were 3,883 general dental practitioners in Scotland.

In 2014, 25% of men and 28% of women aged 16–64 were obese (having a body mass index of 30 or over), up from 22% and 26% in 2003 respectively.

Scottish social service workforce numbered 199,670 in Dec. 2014. Scotland's expenditure on social work (2013–14) was £3,856m.

Welfare
In Feb. 2010 there were 1,003,760 retirement pensioners, 213,460 beneficiaries of incapacity benefit, 340,540 recipients of disability living allowance, 185,990 claimants of income support, 278,480 of pension credit, 147,030 recipients of attendance allowance and 141,840 claimants of Jobseeker's Allowance. A total of 468,960 households were receiving housing benefit in July 2010 and 562,680 council tax benefit. There were 345,500 families with child tax credit or working tax credit awards, or with children and receiving out-of-work benefits, in Dec. 2014.

Religion
The Church of Scotland, which was reformed in 1560, subsequently developed a presbyterian system of church government which was established in 1690 and has continued to the present day.

The supreme court is the General Assembly, which now consists of some 750 voting members, ministers and elders in equal numbers, together with some members of the diaconate, all commissioned by presbyteries. It meets annually in May, under the presidency of a Moderator appointed by the Assembly. The Queen is normally represented by a Lord High Commissioner, but has occasionally attended in person. The royal presence in a special throne gallery in the hall (but outside the Assembly) symbolizes the independence from state control of what is nevertheless recognized as the national Church in Scotland.

There are also 43 presbyteries in Scotland, providing governance and supervision at regional level, together with the presbyteries of England, Europe and Jerusalem. At the base of this conciliar structure of Church courts are the Kirk Sessions overseeing the local congregations, of which there were 1,379 on 31 Dec. 2014. The total communicant membership of the Church on 31 Dec. 2014 was 380,163.

The Scottish Episcopal Church is a province of the Anglican Communion and is one of the historic Scottish churches. It consists of seven dioceses. As at 31 Dec. 2014 it had 313 churches, 520 clergy and 32,634 members, of whom 23,145 were communicants.

There are in Scotland some small outstanding Presbyterian bodies and also Baptists, Congregationalists, Methodists and Unitarians.

The Roman Catholic Church had in Scotland (in 2014) two archbishops, five bishops, eight bishops emeriti, 66 permanent deacons, 664 priests and 445 parishes. The estimated Catholic population in 2014 was 658,450.

Of the 29,069 marriages in Scotland in 2014, 15·5% were conducted by the Church of Scotland, 12·2% by the Humanist Society of Scotland and 5·4% by the Roman Catholic Church. 51·6% were civil marriages and the rest were in other Churches and organizations.

Culture

World Heritage Sites

Scotland has five sites on UNESCO's World Heritage List (with year entered on list): St Kilda (1986, 2004 and 2005), a volcanic archipelago on the coast of the Hebrides; Old and New Towns of Edinburgh (1995), the Scottish capital; the Heart of Neolithic Orkney (1999), comprising several important neolithic monuments; New Lanark (2001), Robert Owen's model industrial community and cotton mills of the early 19th century; and the Forth Bridge (2015), a railway bridge that had the world's longest span when opened in 1890 and that continues to carry freight and passengers today.

Press

Average daily circulation in Jan. 2011 for the daily *Scotsman* was 43,362 and the *Daily Record* 306,872; and for *Scotland on Sunday* 56,256 and the *Sunday Mail* 366,325.

Tourism

There were 2·7m. overseas visitors to Scotland in 2014, spending £1·8bn. Overall tourism receipts totalled £4·8bn. The leading free admission attraction was the National Museum of Scotland in Edinburgh, with 1·6m. visitors in 2014. The leading tourist attraction charging admission in 2014 was Edinburgh Castle, with 1·5m. visits. In 2015, 8·5% of the workforce was employed in the tourism and hospitality industry.

Festivals

St Andrew's Day on 30 Nov. is Scotland's official national day. However, Burns Night on 25 Jan. to commemorate the life and works of Scots poet Robert Burns has become the day on which Scottish culture is celebrated throughout the UK. The Edinburgh Festival and the Fringe Festival both take place in Aug./early Sept. and are major international festivals of culture. The leading rock and pop festival is the TRNSMT festival, which is held in Glasgow. New Year's Eve is known as Hogmanay and the largest celebrations occur in Edinburgh.

Wales

Key Historical Events

After the Roman evacuation, Wales divided into tribal kingdoms. Cunedda Wledig, a prince from southern Scotland, founded a dynasty in the northwest region of Gwynedd—to become the focus for Welsh unity—while the Irish exerted an influence in the kingdom of Dyfed. Offa's Dyke, a defensive earthwork, was the dividing line between England and Wales. In the late 9th century the kings of southern Wales swore fealty to Alfred of Wessex, a relationship assumed by the English crown. Gruffydd ap Llywelyn of Gwynedd briefly united Wales from 1055–63. His death was followed by Norman expansion into southern Wales, where the Marcher lordships were created.

With the accession of Llywelyn the Great (1194–1240), the house of Gwynedd overcame rival claims from Powys and Deheubarth to forge a stable political state under English suzerainty. His grandson, Llywelyn ap Gruffydd (1246–82), was recognized as Prince of Wales by Henry III but Llywelyn intrigued against Edward I, who reduced Gwynedd's hegemony. Wales was annexed and subdued by a network of castles. Edward's infant son, born at Caernarfon, was made Prince of Wales.

Loyalty to Henry VIII, who was of Welsh descent, was rewarded with political influence. The 'Act of Union' in 1536 made English law general, admitted Welsh representatives to Parliament and established the Council of Wales and the Marches.

For more recent Welsh history, see UNITED KINGDOM: Key Historical Events.

Territory and Population

At the census taken on 27 March 2011 the population was 3,063,456. The area of Wales is 20,780 sq. km. (of which land 20,735 sq. km). Population density, 2011 census: 148 per sq. km. Wales covers 8·5% of the total area of the United Kingdom.

Population at census day 2011:

Males	Females	Total
1,504,228	1,559,228	3,063,456

Population (present on census night) at the four previous decennial censuses:

1971	1981	1991	2001
2,731,204[1]	2,790,500[2]	2,811,865	2,903,805

[1]Areas now recognized as Monmouthshire and small sections of various other counties formed the county of Monmouthshire in England until 1974.
[2]The final count is believed to be over-stated as a result of an error in processing. The preliminary counts presented here rounded to the nearest hundred are thought to be more accurate.

Mid-2017 population estimate: 3,125,165 (1,540,200 males; 1,584,965 females).

Cardiff, the capital and largest city, had a population in 2011 of 346,090; Swansea, the second largest city, had a population of 239,023.

In 2011, 630,062 people aged three and over were able to speak, read or write Welsh. Households at the 2011 census: 1,302,676.

For further statistical information, see under Territory and Population, UNITED KINGDOM.

Wales is divided into 22 unitary authorities (cities and counties, counties and county boroughs).

Designations, areas and populations of the unitary authority areas at census day 2011:

Unitary Authority	Designation	Land area (sq. km)	Population
Blaenau Gwent	County Borough	109	69,814
Bridgend	County Borough	251	139,178
Caerphilly	County Borough	277	178,806
Cardiff	City and County	140	346,090
Carmarthenshire	County	2,370	183,777
Ceredigion	County	1,785	75,922
Conwy	County Borough	1,126	115,228
Denbighshire	County	837	93,734
Flintshire	County	438	152,506

(continued)

Unitary Authority	Designation	Land area (sq. km)	Population
Gwynedd	County	2,535	121,874
Isle of Anglesey	County	711	69,751
Merthyr Tydfil	County Borough	111	58,802
Monmouthshire	County	849	91,323
Neath Port Talbot	County Borough	441	139,812
Newport	County Borough	191	145,736
Pembrokeshire	County	1,619	122,439
Powys	County	5,180	132,976
Rhondda Cynon Taff	County Borough	424	234,410
Swansea	City and County	380	239,023
Torfaen	County Borough	126	91,075
Vale of Glamorgan	County Borough	331	126,336
Wrexham	County Borough	504	134,844

Social Statistics

2014: births, 33,544 (10·8 per 1,000 population); deaths, 31,439 (10·2 per 1,000 population); infant deaths, 123 (3·7 per 1,000 live births); marriages (2013), 12,794

Climate

For more detailed information, see under Climate, UNITED KINGDOM.

Cardiff, Jan. 40°F (4·4°C), July 61°F (16·1°C). Annual rainfall 42·6" (1,065 mm).

Constitution and Government

One of the main aspects of the former British Labour government's programme of constitutional reform was devolution. On 18 Sept. 1997 in the referendum there were 559,419 votes cast in favour of a Welsh assembly (50·3%) and 552,698 against (49·7%). The turnout was 51·3%.

The Parliamentary electorate of Wales in the register in Dec. 2017 numbered 2,261,233.

Recent Elections

At the UK general election on 8 June 2017, 40 members were returned from Wales. Labour won 28 seats (25 in 2015), Conservatives 8 seats (11), Plaid Cymru 4 seats (3).

At the 2014 European Parliamentary elections the Conservatives, Labour, Plaid Cymru and UKIP won one seat each.

In the elections to the Welsh Assembly on 5 May 2016, Labour won 29 seats (2 by regional list), followed by Plaid Cymru with 12 (6 by regional list), the Conservatives with 11 (5 by regional list), UKIP with 7 (all by regional list) and the Liberal Democrats with 1. Of the 60 seats, 40 seats were won on a first-past-the-post basis and 20 through proportional representation (regional list).

See also Constitution and Government, Recent Elections *and* Current Government *in* UNITED KINGDOM.

Current Government

First Secretary: Mark Drakeford; b. 1954 (Labour).
Presiding Officer: Elin Jones.
Welsh Government: https://gov.wales

Defence

For information on defence, see UNITED KINGDOM.

Economy

For information on the economy, see UNITED KINGDOM.

Overview

Wales has enjoyed increased economic autonomy since the Welsh Assembly was created by legislation in 1998. In 2006 extended powers were delegated from the Westminster Parliament to the Assembly and a referendum held in March 2011 approved law-making powers similar to those of the Scottish Parliament.

With rich mineral deposits, development in the 19th and early 20th centuries centred on coal, slate and steel exports. Steel also supported a substantial manufacturing industry. The post-Second World War era marked a shift away from traditional heavy industry. However, manufacturing has enjoyed a renaissance so that it accounted for 16% of the economy in 2015, double the rate for the UK as a whole. In contrast, the financial and insurance sectors have grown by only 1% since 2008 to comprise just 4% of the economy in 2015. The tourism sector—which is largely made up of accommodation and food service activities—grew by 24·4% in the same period and contributed £3·1bn. to GDP in 2013. The public sector—notably health, education and public administration—contributed £14·5bn. in 2015.

In 2015 gross value added (GVA—a measure of goods and services produced less all production costs) for the economy was £55·7bn., accounting for 3·4% of the UK's GVA total. This equated to £18,002 per head, the lowest GVA per head in UK and only 68·8% of the UK average that year. However, its growth per head between 2014 and 2015 was the highest of the UK nations at 2·8%. Wales had one of the lowest rates of unemployment in the UK in 2015 at 4·3%, down from 8·2% in 2013, although a large proportion of work carried out is not considered high value or highly skilled. The small population and lack of large metropolitan centres have been cited as factors in uneven development across the principality.

Energy and Natural Resources

For information on energy and natural resources, see UNITED KINGDOM.

Environment

54·3% of municipal waste was recycled in 2013–14.

Water

The Water Act of Sept. 1989 privatized Welsh Water (Dŵr Cymru), along with the nine water authorities in England.

Agriculture

In 2014 there were 35,252 agricultural holdings. Of these, 11,250 were under 5 ha., 8,075 were between 5 and 20 ha., 6,193 were between 20 and 50 ha. and 9,734 were over 50 ha. The average size of a holding in Wales in 2014 was 46 ha.

The area of tillage in 2014 was 86,728 ha. (85,789 ha. for crops and 939 ha. bare fallow). Major crops, 2014 (1,000 tonnes, provisional): wheat, 164; barley, 116; potatoes, 86; oats, 29.

Livestock, 2014: sheep and lambs, 9,738,871; cattle and calves, 1,102,768; pigs, 28,370; poultry, 8,997,200.

Forestry

In March 2017 there were 117,000 ha. of Natural Resources Wales woodland and 190,000 ha. of other woodland.

Fisheries

The major fishing port is Milford Haven. In 2014, in all ports in Wales, 9,900 tonnes of fish and shellfish worth £13·4m. were landed. There were 466 fishing vessels registered in Wales in 2014.

Industry

Main industrial production (gross value added), 2012 in £1m. (provisional): basic metals and metal products, 1,136; food products, beverages and tobacco, 1,064; transport equipment, 871; rubber and plastic products, 716; computer, electronic and optical products, 662.

Labour

In the year ending 31 March 2012 there were 1,305,500 people in employment, of whom 178,900 were self-employed. The number of claimant count unemployed in March 2012 was 79,800. The largest sectors in terms of jobs in 2011 were: wholesale and retail trade, 212,000; human health and social work activities, 209,000; manufacturing, 144,000; education, 134,000. As a proportion of total employment, just over half (51%) of the workforce in 2011 were in these four industry sectors. The International Labour Organization unemployment rate in the period Oct.–Dec. 2013 was 7·1% (compared to 7·2% in the UK as a whole). In 2011, 128,000 working days were lost as a result of industrial disputes.

International Trade

For information on international trade, see UNITED KINGDOM.

Communications

Roads

Responsibility for the construction and maintenance of trunk roads belongs to the Welsh Assembly Government. Roads not classified as trunk roads are the responsibility of county or unitary councils. In 2014 there were 133 km of motorway, 1,576 km of trunk roads and 2,752 km of principal roads. 1,774,500 vehicles were licensed in 2013, including 1,525,200 private and light goods vehicles. In 2013 there were 5,895 reported accidents that led to 8,335 casualties, including 111 deaths.

Civil Aviation

Cardiff Airport handled 1,023,932 passengers in 2014 (857,755 on international flights) and 36 tonnes of freight.

Shipping

The principal ports are (with 1m. tonnes of cargo handled in 2013): Milford Haven (41·1) and Port Talbot (8·5).

Social Institutions

Justice

As at 31 March 2013 police strength amounted to 6,761. During the year ending March 2014 there were 172,689 recorded offences including 17 homicides, 18,946 other crimes involving violence with injury and 3,366 sexual offences. The clear-up rate was 35%. 17,815 people were found guilty of indictable offences in Magistrates' Courts in 2011 and 3,903 in Crown Courts.

Education

In April 2006 ACCAC (the qualification, curriculum and assessment authority), Dysg (the Welsh operation of the Learning and Skills Development Agency), ELWa (the National Council for Education and Training Wales) and the Wales Youth Agency merged with the Welsh Assembly Government's Department for Training and Education to form a new department, the Department for Children, Education, Lifelong Learning and Skills (DCELLS) in the Welsh Assembly Government.

There were 25 maintained nursery schools in Jan. 2010, and 67,093 pupils under five years provided for in nursery schools and in nursery or infants classes in primary schools.

In Jan. 2010 there were 257,445 pupils at 1,462 primary schools. Of these, 476 primary schools use Welsh as the sole or main medium of instruction. Such schools are to be found in all parts of Wales but are mainly concentrated in the predominantly Welsh-speaking areas of west and northwest Wales. Generally, children transfer from primary to secondary schools at 11 years of age.

In Jan. 2010 there were 223 secondary schools. All maintained secondary schools are classified as comprehensive; there are no middle schools in Wales. In 2009–10, 58 of the secondary schools were classed as Welsh-speaking as defined in section 354(b) of the Education Act 1996.

Under the Education Act 1996, children have special educational needs if they have a learning difficulty that calls for special educational provision to be made for them. In a minority of cases the local education authority will need to make a statutory assessment of special educational needs under the Education Act 1996, which may ultimately lead to a 'statement of Special Educational Needs'. The total number of pupils with statements in Jan. 2010 was 14,327. Since April 2002 Special Educational Needs (SEN) guidance for Wales has been set out in the SEN Code of Practice for Wales.

In Jan. 2010, 8,943 full-time pupils and 279 part-time pupils attended 64 independent schools.

Post-16 Learning

The responsibilities of DCELLS (*see above*) include the funding, planning and promotion of children's services, education, learning and skills in Wales. In 2010–11 DCELLS funding for post-16 education and training Wales (excluding higher education provision) providers totalled £577m. This is split between FE institutions, school sixth forms, work-based learning providers, HE institutions and Local Authority (LA) community learning providers. In 2013–14, 48,055 full-time students and 101,135 students studying part-time in the further education sector (excluding work-based learning) were supported at 16 further

education institutions. There were 22,685 further education enrolments at higher education institutions. The proportion of working age adults with no qualifications fell from 15% in 2009 to 10% in 2014; and 57% of working age adults had the equivalent of a National Qualification Framework Level 3 or above in 2014, compared to 49% in 2009.

Higher Education

In 2013–14 there were eight higher education institutions in Wales with a total income of £1·38bn., of which 18·1% came from funding council grants. There were 137,145 students in the higher education sector in 2013–14, including those registered with the Open University in Wales, of which 94,250 were full-time and 42,895 part-time students, excluding those enrolled on higher education provision at further education colleges.

Higher Education Institutes (HEIs)	HE students at HEIs (2013–14)	No. of full-time academic staff (2013–14)
Aberystwyth University	11,170	545
Bangor University	10,645	665
Cardiff Metropolitan University	13,395	380
Cardiff University	30,180	2,145
Glyndwr University (Wrexham)	8,405	205
Swansea University	14,820	985
University of South Wales (Cardiff, Newport and Pontypridd)	29,195	705
University of Wales Trinity Saint David (Carmarthen, Lampeter and Swansea)	11,320	300

Health

As at 30 Sept. 2014 there were 2,006 general medical practitioners in Wales, with an average of 1,582 patients per doctor. As at 30 Sept. 2012 there were 28,080 whole-time equivalent nursing, midwifery and health visiting staff. At 31 March 2014 there were 1,438 general dental practitioners in Wales. The average daily number of hospital beds available in 2013–14 was 11,242, of which 9,653 were occupied. In 2012–13, 502,439 in-patient cases were reported, with stays lasting an average 7·5 days. At 31 March 2011, 354,766 people were waiting to start treatment of whom 20,744 had waited for more than 26 weeks.

The 2014 Welsh Health Survey found that 22% of adults were obese (having a body mass index over 30).

Personal Social Services (PSS) staff numbered 23,780 in Wales at 31 March 2014. The total expenditure (2013–14) for PSS was £1,640m. in Wales.

Welfare

In Aug. 2014, 651,970 people received state retirement pensions. There were 47,710 people receiving income support in Aug. 2014 and 135,800 receiving pension credit; in Aug. 2013, 363,525 families received child benefit.

Religion

Under the Welsh Church Acts, 1914 and 1919, the Church in Wales and Monmouthshire was disestablished as from 1 April 1920, and Wales was formed into a separate Province.

Culture

World Heritage Sites

Wales has three sites on UNESCO's World Heritage List (with year entered on list): Castles and Town Walls of King Edward in Gwynedd (1986), a testament to the early period of English colonization in the late 13th century; Blaenavon Industrial Landscape (2000), a symbol of South Wales's role as a coal and iron provider in the 19th century; and the Pontcysyllte Aqueduct and Canal near Wrexham (2009), a feat of civil engineering by Thomas Telford during the Industrial Revolution.

Tourism

In 2014 there were some 7·5m. domestic trips (from elsewhere in the UK) into Wales. Visitors stayed 29·1m. nights and spent £1·4bn. The leading free admission attraction in 2014 was the Wales Millennium Centre in Cardiff with 1·2m. visits. The leading paid admission attraction was the LC, a leisure complex and waterpark in Swansea, with 774,617 visitors in 2014.

Festivals

Every year there are local and national *eisteddfods* (festivals for musical competitions, etc.). The National Eisteddfod of Wales takes place every Aug., traditionally alternating between north and south Wales. In 2020 it will be held in Tregaron, in Ceredigion.

Northern Ireland

Key Historical Events

The Government of Ireland Act 1920 granted Northern Ireland its own bicameral parliament (Stormont). The rejection of home rule by the rest of Ireland (which pursued independence) forced a separation along primarily religious lines, with a large Catholic minority in the six northern counties. Between 1921–72 Stormont had full responsibility for local affairs except for taxation and customs; Northern Ireland was on the whole neglected by Westminster, allowing the virtual exclusion of Catholics from political office. The (predominantly Protestant) Unionist government ignored demands from London and the Catholic community to end communal discrimination.

In the late 1960s a Civil Rights campaign and reactions to it escalated into serious rioting and sectarian violence involving the Irish Republican Army (IRA, a terrorist organization aiming to unify Northern Ireland with the Republic of Ireland) and loyalist paramilitary organizations, such as the Ulster Defence Association. The British Army was deployed to protect civilians and was at first welcomed by the Catholic community. However, British soldiers shot dead 13 Catholic civil rights protesters in (London)Derry on 30 Jan. 1972—'Bloody Sunday'—prompting the Republic of Ireland's foreign minister to demand United Nations intervention. 467 people died in 1972, on account of 'the Troubles', and nearly 1,800 between 1971–77. The Northern Ireland government resigned and direct rule from Westminster was imposed.

Attempts have been made by successive governments to find a means of restoring greater power to Northern Ireland's political representatives on a widely acceptable basis, including a Constitutional Convention (1975–76), a Constitutional Conference (1979–80) and 78-member Northern Ireland Assembly elected by proportional representation in 1982. This was dissolved in 1986, partly in response to Unionist reaction to the Anglo-Irish Agreement signed on 15 Nov. 1985, which established an Intergovernmental Conference of British and Irish ministers to monitor issues of concern to the nationalist community. The Provisional IRA bombing of a Remembrance Day service in Enniskillen in 1987 killed 11. Universally condemned, it galvanized the anti-violence campaign.

On 15 Dec. 1993 the British and Irish prime ministers, John Major and Albert Reynolds, issued a joint declaration as a basis for all-party talks to achieve a political settlement. They invited Sinn Féin, the political wing of the IRA, to join the talks in an All-Ireland Forum after the cessation of terrorist violence. The IRA announced 'a complete cessation of military operations' on 31 Aug. 1994. On 13 Oct. 1994 the anti-IRA Combined Loyalist Military Command also announced a ceasefire 'dependent upon the continued cessation of all nationalist republican violence'.

Elections were held on 30 May 1996 to constitute a 110-member forum to take part in talks with the British and Irish governments. The Ulster Unionist Party won 30 seats, the Democratic Unionist Party 24 seats, the Social Democratic and Labour Party 21 seats and Sinn Féin 17 seats. Opening plenary talks, excluding Sinn Féin, began under the chairmanship of US Senator George Mitchell on 12 June 1996. A marathon negotiating struggle on 9–10 April 1998 led to agreement on a framework for sharing power designed to satisfy Protestant demands for a reaffirmation of their national identity as British, Catholic desires for a closer relationship with the Republic of Ireland and Britain's wish to return to Northern Ireland the powers London assumed in 1972.

Under the Good Friday Agreement, there was to be a democratically elected legislature in Belfast, a ministerial council giving the governments of Northern Ireland and Ireland joint responsibilities in areas like tourism, transportation and the environment, and a consultative council meeting twice a year to bring together ministers from the British and Irish parliaments, and the three assemblies being created in Northern Ireland and in Scotland and Wales. The Irish government eliminated from its constitution its territorial claim on Northern Ireland.

In the referendum on 22 May 1998, 71·1% of votes in Northern Ireland were cast in favour of the Good Friday peace agreement and 94·4% in the Republic of Ireland. As a consequence, in June, Northern Ireland's 1·2m. voters elected the first power-sharing administration since the collapse of the Sunningdale Agreement in 1974.

On 15 Aug. 1998 a 200 kg bomb exploded in the centre of Omagh. The dissident republican group the 'Real IRA' claimed responsibility. 29 people died and over 200 were injured, making it the single bloodiest incident of the Troubles—about 3,500 deaths had been recorded since the Troubles began by the end of 2001.

In Nov. 1999 the Mitchell talks finally produced an agreement between the Ulster Unionists and Sinn Féin, paving the way for devolved government. The new Northern Ireland Assembly met on 29 Nov. 1999 and on 2 Dec. legislative powers were fully devolved from London to Belfast. However, on 11 Feb. 2000 the Assembly was suspended following a breakdown in negotiations on the decommissioning of IRA weapons. Direct rule from London was restored. Devolved government resumed on 30 May after the IRA agreed to open their arms dumps to independent inspection. First Minister David Trimble resigned on 30 June 2001 to pressure republicans over decommissioning but on 22 Oct. Sinn Féin president Gerry Adams announced that he had recommended a 'ground-breaking' step on the arms issue. The IRA made a start on decommissioning arms, ammunition and explosives. David Trimble was re-elected first minister on 6 Nov. 2001.

On 15 Oct. 2002 the Assembly executive was again suspended over allegations of IRA spying at the Northern Ireland Office, although all charges were dropped in Jan. 2006. Direct rule from London was reimposed and on 30 Oct. the IRA cut off its links with the weapons decommissioning body. The Ulster Volunteer Force followed suit on 17 Jan. 2003. Elections for the Northern Ireland Assembly took place on 26 Nov. 2003. The theft of £26·5m. from the Northern Bank in Belfast in Dec. 2004 suggested closer than acknowledged associations between Sinn Féin and the IRA. Controversy surrounding the raid put the peace process on hold. In July 2005 the IRA formally announced an end to its armed campaign. In Sept. 2005 it claimed to have destroyed its arsenal of weapons.

The Stormont assembly met in May 2006 for the first time in more than three years, charged with restoring devolution by 24 Nov. that year. On that date a transitional assembly was established and in Jan. 2007 Sinn Féin voted to support policing policies in Northern Ireland, a key requirement for a workable power-sharing agreement. The transitional assembly was dissolved at the end of that month ahead of assembly elections in March 2007, in which the loyalist DUP and republican Sinn Féin polled most votes. Both parties came under pressure to compromise and on 26 March reached an historic agreement to share power from 8 May with a devolved Northern Ireland government replacing direct rule from London. In a symbolic moment for the peace process, Queen Elizabeth II met and shook hands with then deputy first minister and former IRA commander Martin McGuinness in June 2012. Despite the political progress, sporadic sectarian violence and attacks by dissident groups have continued.

In Jan. 2017 the devolved Northern Ireland government collapsed following the resignation of McGuinness in protest at a scandal over a renewable energy scheme. His departure sparked an Assembly election, held in March 2017, in which Unionist parties failed to secure a majority of seats for the first time since partition in 1921. Subsequent inter-party negotiations failed to restore a power-sharing administration by March 2019.

Territory and Population

Population of Northern Ireland at census day in 2011 and areas of districts in 2011 were as follows:

District[1]	Population	Area in ha. (including inland water)
Antrim	53,428	57,686
Ards	78,078	37,799
Armagh	59,340	67,060
Ballymena	64,044	63,202
Ballymoney	31,224	41,820
Banbridge	48,339	45,263
Belfast	280,962	10,998
Carrickfergus	39,114	8,181
Castlereagh	67,242	8,514
Coleraine	59,067	48,352
Cookstown	37,013	62,244

(*continued*)

District[1]	Population	Area in ha. (including inland water)
Craigavon	93,023	37,842
Derry (Londonderry)	107,877	37,986
Down	69,731	64,825
Dungannon	57,852	78,360
Fermanagh	61,805	187,126
Larne	32,180	33,579
Limavady	33,536	58,562
Lisburn	120,165	44,684
Magherafelt	45,038	57,280
Moyle	17,050	49,419
Newry and Mourne	99,480	90,070
Newtownabbey	85,139	15,056
North Down	78,937	8,150
Omagh	51,356	113,045
Strabane	39,843	85,868
Northern Ireland	1,810,863	1,412,972

[1]On 1 April 2015 the 26 districts were reorganized into 11 local government districts: Fermanagh and Omagh; Derry and Strabane; Mid Ulster; Causeway Coast and Glens; Mid and East Antrim; Antrim and Newtownabbey; Ards and North Down; Armagh City, Banbridge and Craigavon; Lisburn and Castlereagh; Newry, Mourne and Down; Belfast.

Northern Ireland's area of 14,130 sq. km represents 5·8% of the total area of the United Kingdom. Chief town (census, 2011): Belfast, 280,962.

Population at census day 2011:

Males	Females	Total
887,323	923,540	1,810,863

Mid-2017 population estimate: 1,870,834 (920,248 males; 950,586 females).

Social Statistics

In 2010 there were 25,315 births, 14,457 deaths, 8,156 marriages and 2,600 divorces.

Climate

For more detailed information, see under Climate, UNITED KINGDOM.

Belfast, Jan. 40°F (4·5°C), July 59°F (15·0°C). Annual rainfall 37·4" (950 mm).

Constitution and Government

Under the Northern Ireland Act 1998 power that was previously exercised by the NI Departments was devolved to the Northern Ireland Assembly and its Executive Committee of Ministers. In April 2010 a new justice department came into existence to take responsibility for policing and judicial matters, which had previously been under the jurisdiction of the Secretary of State. Constitutional and national security issues along with firearms and explosives licensing and legislation remain the domain of the Secretary of State, who is also involved in public inquiries and some policy-making decisions.

The Parliamentary electorate of Northern Ireland in the register in Dec. 2017 numbered 1,242,300.

Secretary of State for Northern Ireland: Karen Bradley.

Recent Elections

At the general election of 8 June 2017, 18 members were returned from Northern Ireland. The Democratic Unionist Party won 10 seats (8 in 2015); Sinn Féin 7 (4); others 1 (1).

In the Northern Ireland Assembly elections on 2 March 2017 the Democratic Unionist Party won 28 seats (28·1% of first preference votes); Sinn Féin 27 (27·9%); the Social and Democratic Labour Party 12 (11·9%); the Ulster Unionist Party 10 (12·9%); the Alliance Party 8 (9·1%); the Green Party in Northern Ireland 2 (2·3%); the Traditional Unionist Voice 1 (2·6%); People Before Profit Alliance 1 (1·8%); ind. 1 (1·8%). Turnout was 64·8%.

At the May 2014 European Parliament elections, voting was by the single transferable vote system: Sinn Féin (25·5%), the Democratic Unionist Party (20·9%) and the Ulster Unionist Party (13·3%) gained 1 seat each. Turnout was 51·8%.

Current Government

First Minister: Vacant.

Deputy First Minister: Vacant.

Northern Ireland Executive: http://www.northernireland.gov.uk

Economy

For information on the economy, see UNITED KINGDOM.

Overview

Northern Ireland has the smallest of the economies within the United Kingdom. Traditionally it has been led by manufacturing, heavy industry and agriculture, but there has been a shift towards a more service-based economy since the 1980s. There is a strong dependence on the public sector, which accounted for 27·9% of all jobs at the end of 2013. Low wages and low labour productivity levels are a legacy of 30 years of domestic civil conflict, an unfavourable demographic structure and a relatively peripheral geographical location. Nonetheless, the economy has benefited from the peace process that culminated in the 1998 Good Friday Agreement, despite subsequent difficulties in implementation of the treaty.

Northern Ireland's share of UK gross value added (GVA; a measure of goods and services produced less all production costs) grew by 2·0% in 2015 (to £34·4bn.), the second smallest level among the 12 statistical regions of the UK. In the same year, GVA per capita was £18,584, lower than in all other regions except for Wales, owing to low productivity levels and high rates of economic inactivity. While local employment has returned to pre-financial crisis levels (70% of 16 to 64-year-olds were employed in 2016), output has remained below its pre-crisis peak. However, tourism is an increasingly important sector and offers potential for further expansion.

The economy is closely linked with that of the neighbouring Republic of Ireland, which in 2016 took 56% of Northern Ireland's exports to the EU and 31% of all its goods exports by value. Exports contributed 20% of Northern Ireland's GVA in 2015, as against 17% for the UK as a whole. Machinery and transport equipment was the principal export commodity group in 2016, accounting for 33% of total goods exports by value.

Brexit negotiations on the UK's withdrawal from the EU have serious implications for Northern Ireland. Establishing the status of its border with the Republic of Ireland is essential to safeguarding industries, such as the agri-food sector. It is felt to be vital that the Northern Ireland Assembly is functioning and politically stable in order to articulate the needs of the province and prepare the economy for whatever changes Brexit ushers in.

Currency

Banknotes are issued by Bank of Ireland, First Trust Bank, Danske Bank (formerly Northern Bank) and Ulster Bank.

Banking and Finance

Among the Department of Finance and Personnel's primary functions are the control of expenditure of Northern Ireland departments; liaising with HM Treasury, the European Commission and the Northern Ireland Office on financial matters; reviewing and developing rating policy and legislation; formulating policy and co-ordinating arrangements for central personnel management including monitoring equal opportunities policy for the Civil Service; promoting energy efficiency in the public sector through provision of funding for energy efficiency projects and monitoring energy consumption and emissions; formulating building regulations policy and legislation; formulating policy and providing a procurement service for the Northern Ireland public sector.

Public income of Northern Ireland (in £1,000 sterling):

	2009–10	2010–11	2011–12
Receipts from UK government	11,836,000	13,373,000	13,332,000
Regional and district rates	961,324	1,016,391	1,064,896
Interest on loans made from the Consolidated Fund	70,647	62,211	54,587
Interest on government loans	27,584	27,972	27,733

(*continued*)

	2009–10	2010–11	2011–12
Other central receipts	13,523	6,418	22,799
Other departmental receipts	203,501	620,621	93,915
Total public income	*13,112,579*	*15,106,613*	*14,595,930*

Energy and Natural Resources

Electricity
There are three power stations with an installed capacity of some 2,100 MW.

In addition, electricity is also supplied through a 500 MW interconnector linking the Northern Ireland Electricity (NIE) and Scottish Power networks and a number of interconnectors linking the NIE network with the Electricity Supply Board (ESB) network in the Republic of Ireland.

Oil and Gas
In Sept. 2001 the Northern Ireland executive approved grant support for the development of the gas network outside the Greater Belfast area, to the North/North West region and for the construction of a South/North pipeline. A North West gas pipeline, completed in late 2004, supplies gas for the Combined Cycle Turbine power station at Coolkeeragh outside Londonderry, which opened in June 2005. A South/North pipeline was commissioned in Oct. 2006, connecting the grids of Northern Ireland and the Republic of Ireland for the first time. The Northern Ireland Authority for Energy Regulation has granted a licence to supply gas to the major towns along the route of both these.

Minerals
Output of minerals (in 1,000 tonnes), 2010: sandstone, 2,768; basalt and igneous rock (other than granite), 5,438; limestone, 3,689; sand and gravel, 2,178; other minerals (rock salt, fireclay, dolomite, granite and chalk), 2,087. There are extensive lignite deposits but they have not yet been developed. The United Kingdom's only operational gold mine, located near Omagh, opened in 2007; production in 2011 was 202 kg. Silver production in 2011 was 531 kg.

Agriculture
Provisional gross output in 2011:

	Quantity	Value (£1m.)
Cattle and calves	463,288	375·2
Sheep and lambs	693,457	55·0
Pigs	1,020,600	104·0
Poultry (1,000 tonnes)	258·1	239·0
Eggs (m. dozen)	82·3	55·4
Milk (1m. litres)	1,966·0	542·9
Other livestock products	—	13·0
Cereals (1,000 tonnes)	239·8	44·1
Potatoes (1,000 tonnes)	196·3	23·4
Fruit (1,000 tonnes)	48·1	7·4
Vegetables (1,000 tonnes)	37·4	17·4
Mushrooms (1,000 tonnes)	15·3	18·5
Other crops	—	12·1
Flowers, ornamentals and nursery stock	—	10·9
Capital formation	—	97·2
Contract work	—	72·0
Other items	—	17·6
Gross output	—	*1,705·1*

Area (in 1,000 ha.) on farms:

	2009	2010	2011
Cereals	39	38	38
Potatoes	5	5	5

	2009	2010	2011
Horticulture	3	3	3
Other crops	10	9	8
Grass	791	780	777
Rough grazing	142	141	141
Other land	18	18	19
Total area	*1,008*	*994*	*991*

Livestock (in 1,000 heads) on farms at June census:

	2009	2010	2011
Dairy cows	285	281	283
Beef cows	257	258	270
Other cattle	1,057	1,065	1,038
Ewes	892	876	895
Sows	38	39	38
Laying hens	2,316	2,099	2,430
Broilers	11,418	11,915	14,069

Industry

Labour
The main sources of employment statistics are the Census of Employment, conducted every two years, and the Quarterly Employment Survey. In Sept. 2012 there were 692,516 employees, of whom 336,137 were males. Employment in services amounted to 566,726 (82% of all employees in employment) and in manufacturing and construction to 103,537 (15%). There were 71,876 people working in manufacturing and 31,661 in construction. The International Labour Organization unemployment rate in the period Oct.–Dec. 2013 was 7·4% (compared to 7·2% in the UK as a whole).

Communications

Roads
In April 2014 the total length of public roads was 25,837 km, graded for administrative purposes as follows: motorway, 230 km (excluding 19 km slip roads); 'A' roads dual carriageway, 420 km; 'A' roads single carriageway, 2,079 km; 'B' roads, 2,906 km; 'C' roads, 4,726 km; unclassified, 15,476 km.

The number of motor vehicles licensed at 31 Dec. 2011 was 1,053,338, including private light goods vehicles, 879,787; heavy goods vehicles, 23,084; motorcycles, scooters and mopeds, 25,196.

The Northern Ireland Transport Holding Company (NITHC) oversees the provision of public transport services in Northern Ireland. Its subsidiary companies, Ulsterbus, Citybus and Northern Ireland Railways, are responsible for the delivery of most bus and rail services under the brand name of Translink.

Rail
Northern Ireland Railways, a subsidiary of the Northern Ireland Transport Holding Company, provides rail services within Northern Ireland and cross-border services to Dublin, jointly with Irish Rail (Iarnród Éireann). The number of track km operated is 340. In 2013–14 railways carried 12·5m. passengers, generating passenger receipts of £41·3m.

Civil Aviation
There are scheduled air services to three airports in Northern Ireland: Belfast International, George Best Belfast City and City of Derry. Scheduled services are provided by Aer Lingus, ASL Airlines Ireland, BH Air, British Airways, CityJet, easyJet, Flybe, Icelandair, Jet2.com, KLM, Norwegian, Ryanair, Thomas Cook, Thomson, Virgin Atlantic and Wizz Air. In 2014 the airports collectively handled approximately 6·9m. passengers. Belfast International, the busiest airport, is Northern Ireland's main charter airport. Belfast International handled 4·0m. passengers in 2014.

Belfast City Airport offers services to 18 regional airports in Great Britain including services to London Heathrow. The City of Derry Airport provides services from the northwest of Ireland to four United Kingdom destinations including London Stansted. There are two other licensed airfields at St Angelo and Newtownards.

(continued)

Shipping

There are five commercial ports in Northern Ireland. Belfast is the largest port, competing with Larne for the majority of the passenger and Roll-on Roll-off services that operate to and from Northern Ireland. Passenger services are currently available to Liverpool, Cairnryan and Troon. In addition, Belfast, Londonderry and Warrenpoint ports offer bulk cargo services mostly for British and European markets. They also occasionally service other international destinations direct.

Total tonnage of goods through the principal ports in Northern Ireland in 2013 was 25·3m. tonnes. Belfast handled 16·8m. tonnes of cargo in 2013.

Social Institutions

Justice

The Lord Chief Justice of Northern Ireland is President of the Courts of Northern Ireland and Head of the Judiciary and as such is responsible for assigning the judiciary to the courts. The Lord Chief Justice is also Chairman of the Judicial Appointments Commission which is responsible for selecting and recommending to the Lord Chancellor candidates for judicial appointment in Northern Ireland. The court structure in Northern Ireland has three tiers: the Court of Judicature of Northern Ireland (comprising the Court of Appeal, the High Court and the Crown Court), the County Courts and the Magistrates' Courts. There are 21 Petty Sessions districts which when grouped together for administration purposes form seven County Court Divisions and four Crown Court Circuits.

The County Court has general civil jurisdiction subject to an upper monetary limit. Appeals from the Magistrates' Courts lie to the County Court, or to the Court of Appeal on a point of law, while appeals from the County Court lie to the High Court or, on a point of law, to the Court of Appeal.

Police

Following legislation introduced in the House of Commons in May 2000, the name of the Royal Ulster Constabulary was changed to the Police Service of Northern Ireland (PSNI). The Police Authority for Northern Ireland has been replaced by the Northern Ireland Policing Board. The Police Service continues to undergo significant changes arising from the recommendations of the Commission into the future of policing in Northern Ireland published in 1999. In 2010 the PSNI comprised 7,212 regular officers including those student officers undergoing training, 305 full-time reserve officers and 677 part-time reserves. The proportion of Catholic regular officers, which was around 19·1% by Jan. 2006, had increased to 29·6% by Dec. 2010.

The population in penal institutions in Sept. 2013 was 1,851 (101 per 100,000 population).

Education

Public education, other than university education, is presently administered by the Department of Education, the Department of Employment and Learning, and locally by five Education and Library Boards. The Department of Education is concerned with the range of education from nursery education through to secondary, youth services and for the development of community relations within and between schools. The Department of Employment and Learning is responsible for higher education, further education, student support, postgraduate awards, and the funding of teacher training.

Integrated Schools

The Department of Education has a statutory duty to encourage and facilitate the development of integrated education. It does not seek to impose integration but responds to parental demand for new integrated schools where this does not involve unreasonable public expenditure. The emphasis for future development of the integrated sector has increasingly been on the transformation of existing schools to integrated status. In 2011–12 there were 62 integrated schools, with a total enrolment of 21,747 pupils (6% of all pupils).

Irish Medium Education

Following a commitment in the Belfast Agreement, the 1998 Education Order placed a statutory duty on the Department to encourage and facilitate the development of Irish-medium education. It also provided for the funding of an Irish-medium promotional body, and funding of Irish-medium schools on the same basis as integrated schools. In 2011–12 there were 25 Irish-medium primary schools, one post-primary and 13 units (four of which are post-primary) catering for 3,635 pupils.

Pre-school Education

This is provided in nursery schools or nursery classes in primary schools, reception classes and in funded places in voluntary and private settings.

There were 97 nursery schools in 2011–12 with 5,911 pupils, and 8,608 nursery pupils in primary schools. A further 444 reception pupils were enrolled in primary schools. In addition there were 8,149 children in funded places in voluntary and private pre-school education centres in 2011–12.

Primary Education

This is from four to 11 years. In 2011–12 there were 839 primary schools with 153,740 pupils. There were also 15 preparatory departments of grammar schools with 1,954 pupils. In 2009–10 there were 7,808 FTE primary school teachers and 141 FTE preparatory department teachers.

Secondary Education

This is compulsory from 11 to 16 years. In 2011–12 there were 68 grammar schools with 62,554 pupils and 148 other secondary schools with 84,193 pupils. In 2009–10 there were 4,137 FTE grammar school teachers and 5,970 FTE other secondary school teachers.

Further Education

In Aug. 2007 six regional colleges of further education were formed from the former 16 FE institutions: Belfast Metropolitan College, Northern Regional College, North West Regional College, Southern Regional College, South Eastern Regional College, South West College. In 2011–12 there were over 4,100 lecturers and support staff, 27,905 full-time enrolments and 125,175 part-time enrolments.

Special Education

The Education and Library Boards provide for children with special educational needs up to the age of 19. This provision may be made in ordinary classes in primary or secondary schools or in special units attached to those schools, or in special schools. In 2010–11 there were 43 special schools with 4,658 pupils. This includes two hospital schools.

Universities

There are two universities: Queen's University Belfast (founded in 1849 as a college of the Queen's University of Ireland and reconstituted as a separate university in 1908), which had 22,985 students, 1,375 full-time and 140 part-time academic staff in 2011–12; and Ulster University, formed on 1 Oct. 1984, which has campuses in Belfast, Coleraine, Jordanstown and Londonderry. In 2011–12 it had 26,560 students, 1,060 full-time and 405 part-time academic staff.

Full-Time Initial Teacher Education

This is takes place at both universities and at two university colleges of education—Stranmillis and St Mary's—the latter mainly for the primary school sector, in respect of which four-year (Hons) BEd courses are available. The training of teachers for secondary schools is provided, in the main, in the education departments of the two universities, but four-year (Hons) BEd courses are also available in the colleges for intending secondary teachers of religious education, business studies and craft, design and technology. There were a total of 2,360 students (1,814 women) in training at the two university colleges and the two universities during 2011–12.

Health

The Department of Health, Social Services and Public Safety has three main business responsibilities: Health and Personal Social Services (HPSS), which includes policy and legislation for hospitals, family practitioner services, and community health and personal social services; Public Health, which covers policy, legislation and administrative action to promote and protect the health and well-being of the population; and Public Safety, which covers policy and legislation for fire, rescue and ambulance services.

The four Health and Social Services Boards commission health and personal social services for their resident populations from providers including HSS Trusts, and voluntary and private sector bodies. The 19 Health and Social Services Trusts, established under the Health and Personal Social Services (NI) Order 1991, are managerially independent but accountable to the Minister. They are the main providers of health and personal social services as commissioned by the HSS Boards and are responsible for the management of staff and services of hospitals and other health and personal social services establishments. Seven provide hospital services only, five provide community and personal social services only and six provide both. In 2013 there were 1,171 doctors (principals) with an average of 1,639 patients each.

The 2011/12 Health Survey Northern Ireland found that around 23% of adults were obese (having a body mass index over 30).

Welfare

The Social Security Agency's remit is now part of the Department for Communities, and social security schemes are similar to those in Great Britain.

National Insurance

During the year ended 31 March 2014 payments from the National Insurance Fund at £2,020m. exceeded receipts by £353m. Total benefit expenditure was £2,335m. Jobseeker's Allowance contributions amounted to £19·1m. State Pensions amounted to £1,971·9m. and Bereavement Benefits to £21·1m. Incapacity Benefits totalled £75·5m. Maternity Allowance of £11·8m. was paid and employers were reimbursed £65·2m. in respect of Statutory Sick, Maternity, Adoption and Paternity Pay. £0·9m. was given to personal pension plan providers.

Child Benefit

In 2012–13 a total of £391m. was paid in Child Benefit and Guardian's Allowance. As at April 2014, 167,100 families benefited from Child and Working Tax Credits.

Religion

According to the 2011 census there were: Roman Catholics, 738,033; Presbyterians, 345,101; Church of Ireland, 248,821; Methodists, 54,253; other Christian, 104,380; other religions, 14,859. There were also 305,416 persons with no religion or religion was not stated.

Culture

World Heritage Sites

Northern Ireland has one site on UNESCO's World Heritage List: the Giant's Causeway and Causeway Coast (inscribed on the list in 1986), a series of rock formations on the Antrim Plateau.

Tourism

There were 2·1m. non-resident visitors to Northern Ireland in 2013 (excluding day trips), contributing £531m. to the economy. Holiday-makers from Northern Ireland contributed a further £192m. Eight Areas of Outstanding Natural Beauty and 47 National Nature Reserves have been declared, and there are many country and regional parks. The leading paid admission attraction in 2013 was the Giant's Causeway World Heritage Site with 754,000 visits. The leading free admission attraction (excluding country parks, parks and gardens) was the Ulster Museum with 416,000 visits in 2013.

Isle of Man

Key Historical Events

The Isle of Man was first inhabited 10,000 years ago. Part of Norway in the 9th century, in 1266 it was ceded to Scotland but came under English control in 1333.

The Isle of Man has been a British Crown dependency since 1765, with the British government responsible for its defence and foreign policy. Otherwise it has extensive right of self-government.

A special relationship exists between the Isle of Man and the European Union providing for free trade, and adoption by the Isle of Man of the EU's external trade policies with third countries. The island remains free to levy its own taxes.

Territory and Population

Area, 572 sq. km (221 sq. miles); resident population census in April 2016, 83,314, giving a density of 145·7 per sq. km. In 2011 an estimated 78% of the population lived in urban areas. The principal towns are (April 2016 population) Douglas (26,997), Onchan (adjoining Douglas; 9,128), Ramsey (7,845) and Peel (5,374). Just over half the population at the 2011 census was born outside of the island.

Social Statistics

2011: births, 890; deaths, 799. Annual growth rate, 2006–11, 1·0%.

Climate

Lying in the Irish Sea, the island's climate is temperate and lacking in extremes. Thunderstorms, snow and frost are infrequent, although the island tends to be windy. July and Aug. are the warmest months with an average daily maximum temperature of around 17·6°C (63°F).

Constitution and Government

As a result of Revestment in 1765, the Isle of Man became a dependency of the British Crown. The UK government is responsible for the external relations of the island, including its defence and international affairs, and the island makes a financial contribution to the cost of these services. The Isle of Man has a special relationship with the European Union. It neither contributes funds to, nor receives money from, the EU. The Isle of Man is not represented in either the UK or European Parliaments.

The island is administered in accordance with its own laws by the High Court of *Tynwald*, consisting of the President of Tynwald, the *Legislative Council* and the *House of Keys*. The Legislative Council is composed of the Lord Bishop of Sodor and Man, eight members selected by the House of Keys and the Attorney General, who has no vote. The House of Keys is an assembly of 24 members chosen by adult suffrage. The minimum age for voting was lowered to 16 in 2006. The President of Tynwald is chosen by the Legislative Council and the House of Keys, sitting together as Tynwald. An open-air Tynwald ceremony is held in early July each year at St Johns. Until 1990 the Lieut.-Governor, appointed by the UK government, presided over Tynwald.

A Council of Ministers was instituted in 1990, replacing the Executive Council which had acted as an advisory body to the Lieut.-Governor. The Council of Ministers consists of the Chief Minister (elected for a five-year term) and the ministers of the nine major departments, being the Treasury; Agriculture, Fisheries and Forestry; Education; Health and Social Security; Home Affairs; Local Government and the Environment; Tourism and Leisure; Trade and Industry; and Transport.

Recent Elections

Elections to the House of Keys were held on 22 Sept. 2016. Independents took 21 of the 24 seats and the Liberal Vannin Party 3.

Current Government

Lieut.-Governor: Sir Richard Gozney.

President: Stephen Rodan (elected July 2016).

In Feb. 2019 the *Chief Minister* was Howard Quayle. *Treasury Minister:* Alfred Cannan.

Government Website: http://www.gov.im

Economy

Currency

The Isle of Man government issues its own notes and coins on a par with £1 sterling. Various commemorative coins have been minted. Inflation was 2·8% in 2012.

Budget

The Isle of Man is statutorily required to budget for a surplus of revenue over expenditure. Revenue is raised from income tax, taxes on expenditure, health and social security contributions, and fees and charges for services.

The standard rate of tax is 10% for personal income, and there is a higher rate of 18%. Banking and land property businesses are liable at 10% on their first £100m. of taxable income and 18% on the balance.

There is a Customs and Excise Agreement with the UK, and rates of tax on expenditure are the same as those in the UK with very few exceptions. In addition, there is a reciprocal agreement on social security with the UK, and the rates of most health and social security (National Insurance) contributions are the same as in the UK.

In 2007–08 the Isle of Man government budgeted for expenditure of £809m. and revenue of £845m.

Performance

In 2014–15 GDP was £4,514m. Real GDP growth in 2011–12 was 2·0%. 88% of national income is generated from services with the finance sector being the single largest contributor (36%).

Banking and Finance

The banking sector is regulated by the Financial Supervision Commission. It is responsible for the licensing and supervision of banks, deposit-takers and financial intermediaries giving financial advice, and for receiving client monies for investment and management. A compensation fund to protect investors was set up in 1991 under the Commission.

In June 2013 the deposit base was £45bn., and there were 30 licensed deposit takers, 54 investment businesses and 303 corporate and trust service providers.

The insurance industry is regulated by the Insurance and Pensions Authority. In June 2012 there were 142 insurance companies.

Energy and Natural Resources

Electricity
The Manx Electricity Authority generates most of the island's electricity by oil-fired power stations although there is a small hydro-electric plant. A cable link with the UK power grid came into operation in Nov. 2000. In 2006, 379m. kWh were sold.

Minerals
Although lead and tin mining industries were major employers in the past, they have long since shut down and the only mining activity in the island is now for aggregates. The Lady Isabella, built in 1854 to drain the mines above Laxey, is one of the largest waterwheels in Europe.

Agriculture
The area farmed is about 104,000 acres, being 74% of a total land area of around 141,500 acres. 65,000 acres are grassland with a further 27,000 acres for rough grazing. There are approximately 137,000 sheep, 30,000 cattle, 20,000 poultry and 600 pigs on the island's 658 farms. Agriculture now contributes less than 2% of the island's GDP.

Forestry
The Department of Agriculture, Fisheries and Forestry has a forestry estate of some 6,800 acres. Commercial forestry is directed towards softwood production. The Manx National Glens and other amenity areas are maintained for public use by the Department, which owns some 18,000 acres of the island's hills and uplands open for public use.

Fisheries
The Isle of Man is noted for the Manx kipper, a gutted smoked herring. Scallops and the related queen scallops (queenies) are the economic mainstay of the Manx fishing fleet. In 2012 the total catch was 6,172 tonnes.

Industry

Labour
The economically active population in 2006 was 41,793, of whom 6,381 were self-employed and 1,010 were unemployed. Employment by sector: finance, 23%; professional services, 20%; distributive services, 11%; construction, 8%; manufacturing, 5%.

At the end of 2006 there were 577 persons on the unemployment register, giving an unemployment rate of 1·4%.

International Trade
The Isle of Man forms part of the customs union of the European Union, although the island is not part of the EU itself. The relationship with the EU provides for free trade and the adoption of the EU's external trade policies and tariffs with non-EU countries.

Imports and Exports
The Isle of Man is in customs and excise union with the United Kingdom, which is also its main trading partner.

Communications

Roads
There are 800 km of good roads. At the end of March 2010 there were 81,985 licensed vehicles, with 72,621 of these being private cars. Bus services operate to all parts of the island. The TT (Tourist Trophy) motorcycle races take place annually on the 60·75 km Mountain Circuit.

Rail
Several novel transport systems operate on the island during the summer season from May to Sept. Horse-drawn trams run along Douglas promenade, and the Manx Electric Railway links Douglas, Laxey, Ramsey and Snaefell Mountain (621 metres) in the north. The Isle of Man Steam Railway also operates between Douglas and Port Erin in the south.

Civil Aviation
Ronaldsway Airport in the south handles scheduled services linking the island with Belfast, Birmingham, Bristol, Dublin, Edinburgh, Geneva, Glasgow, Liverpool, London and Manchester. Air taxi services also operate.

Shipping
Car ferries run between Douglas and the UK and the Irish Republic. In 2014 there were 391 merchant vessels on the island's shipping register.

Telecommunications
Manx Telecom Limited, a wholly owned subsidiary of O2, holds the telecommunications licence issued by the Communications Commission for the Isle of Man.

Social Institutions

Justice
The First Deemster is the head of the Isle of Man's judiciary. The Isle of Man Constabulary numbered 329 all ranks in 2014.

The population in penal institutions in Oct. 2014 was 80 (94 per 100,000 of national population).

Education
Education is compulsory between the ages of five and 16. In 2013 the Isle of Man had 6,275 pupils in primary education and 5,523 in secondary education, across five secondary schools and 32 primary schools. The Department also runs a college of further education and a special school. Government expenditure on education was budgeted to be £90m. in 2014–15. The island has a private primary school, a private secondary school and an international business school.

Health
The island has had its own National Health Service since 1948, providing medical, dental and ophthalmic services. In 2012–13 government expenditure on the NHS was budgeted to be £125m. There are two hospitals. At the end of 2013 there were 164 full-time equivalent physicians, 34 full-time and 18 part-time general practitioners, 32 full-time and four part-time dentists, and 23 pharmacies.

Welfare
Numbers receiving certain benefits at Dec. 2013: Retirement Pension 18,646; Child Benefit, 9,592; Sick and Disablement Benefits, 4,643; Income Support, 4,003; Jobseekers' Allowance, 856. Total government expenditure on social security benefits in 2013–14 was budgeted to be £260m.

Religion
The island has a rich heritage of Christian associations, and the Diocese of Sodor and Man, one of the oldest in the British Isles, has existed since 476.

Culture

Press
In 2008 there were two paid-for weekly newspapers and one free weekly.

Tourism
During the late 19th century through to the middle of the 20th century, tourism was one of the island's main sources of income and employment. In 2013 there were 290,754 visitors (294,460 in 2012); tourism expenditure in 2013 totalled £106·8m.

Channel Islands

Key Historical Events
The Channel Islands consist of Jersey, Guernsey and the following dependencies of Guernsey: Alderney, Brechou, Great Sark, Little Sark, Herm, Jethou and Lihou. They were an integral part of the Duchy of Normandy at the time of the Norman Conquest of England in 1066. Since then they have belonged to the British Crown and are not part of the UK. The islands have created their own self-government, with the British government at Westminster being responsible for defence and foreign policy. The Lieut.-Governors of Jersey and Guernsey,

appointed by the Crown, are the personal representatives of the Sovereign as well as being the commanders of the armed forces. The legislature of Jersey is 'The States of Jersey', and that of Guernsey is 'The States of Deliberation'.

Left undefended from 1940 to 1945 the islands were the only part of Britain to fall to Germany.

Territory and Population

The Channel Islands cover a total of 194 sq. km (75 sq. miles), and in 2011 had a population of approximately 163,000.

The official languages are French and English, but English is now the main language.

Climate

The climate is mild, with an average temperature for the year of 11·5°C. Average yearly rainfall totals: Jersey, 862·9 mm; Guernsey, 858·9 mm. The wettest months are in the winter. Highest temperatures recorded: Jersey (St Helier), 36·0°C; Guernsey (airport), 33·7°C. Maximum temperatures usually occur in July and Aug. (daily maximum 20·8°C in Jersey, slightly lower in Guernsey). Lowest temperatures recorded: Jersey, –10·3°C; Guernsey, –7·4°C. Jan. and Feb. are the coldest months (mean temperature approximately 6°C).

Constitution and Government

The Lieut.-Governors and Cs.-in-C. of Jersey and Guernsey are the personal representatives of the Sovereign, the Commanders of the Armed Forces of the Crown, and the channel of communication between the Crown and the insular governments. They are appointed by the Crown and have a voice but no vote in the islands' legislatures.

Economy

Performance
Total GDP in 2007 was US$11·5bn.

Energy and Natural Resources

Fisheries
Total catch in 2015 was 2,574 tonnes, exclusively from sea fishing.

International Trade

External Economic Relations
The Channel Islands are not members of the European Union but under a special relationship accept a number of European laws, including certain EU customs regulations. Trade with the UK is classed as domestic.

Communications

Civil Aviation
Scheduled air services are maintained by Aer Lingus, Aurigny Air Services, Blue Islands, British Airways, easyJet, Emirates, Flybe, Jet2.com and SkyWork Airlines.

Shipping
Passenger and cargo services between Jersey, Guernsey, England (Poole and Portsmouth) and France (St Malo) are maintained by Condor Ferries. Local companies run between Guernsey, Alderney and England, and between Guernsey and Sark.

Social Institutions

Justice
Justice is administered by the Royal Courts of Jersey and Guernsey, each of which consists of the Bailiff and 12 Jurats (magistrates), the latter being elected by an electoral college. There is an appeal from the Royal Courts to the Courts of Appeal of Jersey and of Guernsey. A final appeal lies to the Privy Council in certain cases. A stipendiary magistrate in each, Jersey and Guernsey, deals with minor civil and criminal cases.

Religion

Jersey and Guernsey each constitutes a deanery under the jurisdiction of the Bishop of Winchester. The rectories (12 in Jersey; 10 in Guernsey) are in the gift of the Crown. The Roman Catholic and various Nonconformist Churches are represented.

Jersey

Territory and Population

The area is 118·2 sq. km (45·6 sq. miles). Resident population (2011 census), 97,857 (49,561 females); density, 828 per sq. km. The chief town is St Helier on the south coast. It had a population of 33,522 in 2011.

The official language is English (French until 1960). The island has its own language, known as Jersey French, or Jérriaise. French is used in the courts of law and by the legal profession while there are significant numbers of Portuguese- and Polish-speakers thanks to immigration, largely since the 1990s.

Social Statistics

There were 997 live births and 784 deaths in 2015 and 484 marriages in 2013. Life expectancy, 2015: males, 81 years; females, 86 years.

Constitution and Government

The island parliament is the *States of Jersey*. The States comprises the Bailiff, the Lieut.-Governor, the Dean of Jersey, the Attorney-General and the Solicitor-General, and 51 members elected by universal suffrage: ten Senators (four elected for a three-year term only), the Constables of the 12 parishes (every third year) and 29 Deputies (every third year). They all have the right to speak in the Assembly, but only the 51 elected members have the right to vote; the Bailiff has a casting vote. Except in specific instances, enactments passed by the States require the sanction of the Queen-in-Council. The Lieut.-Governor has the power of veto on certain forms of legislation.

A new post of Chief Minister was inaugurated in 2005. The Chief Minister, who is elected by the States, presides over a nine-member Council of Ministers responsible for government policy.

Recent Elections

On 14 Nov. 2011 parliament elected Ian Gorst Chief Minister by 27 votes to 24. He was re-elected on 3 Nov. 2014.

Current Government

Lieut.-Governor and C.-in-C. of Jersey: Air Chief Marshal Sir Stephen Dalton, GCB, ADC.
    Chief of Staff to the Lieut.-Governor: Justin Oldridge.
    Bailiff of Jersey and President of the States: William Bailhache.
    Chief Minister: John Le Fondré, Jr.
Government Website: http://www.gov.je

Economy

Currency
The States issue banknotes in denominations of £50, £20, £10, £5 and £1. Coinage from 1p to £1 is struck in the same denominations as the UK. There were £70m. worth of States of Jersey banknotes in circulation in 2013. Inflation in Dec. 2013 was 1·9%.

Budget
2015 general revenue income, £692m.; departmental expenditure, £697m.
    Parochial rates are payable by owners and occupiers.

Performance
In 2009 total GDP was £3·7bn.

Banking and Finance
In 2013 there were 42 banks; combined deposits were £145·2bn. Jersey is a leading offshore financial centre.
    A 0% rate of company tax was introduced on 1 Jan. 2009.

Energy and Natural Resources

Agriculture
2015 total agricultural exports, £39,106,958 (of which Jersey Royal potatoes, £27,554,627). Agricultural land made up 51·9% of the island's land area in 2015. In 2015 there were 2,807 cows and heifers in milk, 1,015 sheep and 432 pigs.

Fisheries
There were 160 fishing vessels in 2010. The total catch of shellfish in 2009 was 1,181 tonnes and of wet fish 72 tonnes. Aquaculture production (oysters,

mussels and scallops) totalled 1,007 tonnes in 2009. The value of the fishing industry at first sale in 2010 was £7m.

Industry

Principal activities: light industry, mainly electrical goods, textiles and clothing.

Labour

In Dec. 2011, 53,790 persons were economically active; 1,540 persons were registered unemployed. Financial and legal services was the largest employment sector, followed by wholesale and retail trades and the public sector.

External Economic Relations

Imports and Exports

Principal imports: machinery and transport equipment, manufactured goods, food, mineral fuels, and chemicals. Principal exports: machinery and transport equipment, food, and manufactured goods.

Communications

Roads

In Dec. 2014 there were 121,551 registered motor vehicles. There were 1·50 cars/vans per private household in 2011.

Civil Aviation

Jersey airport is situated at St Peter. It covers approximately 375 acres. In 2011 the airport handled 1,474,373 passengers.

Shipping

All vessels arriving in Jersey from outside Jersey waters report at St Helier or Gorey on first arrival. There is a harbour of minor importance at St Aubin. There were 730,000 passenger arrivals and departures in 2009; 395,000 tonnes of freight (exports and imports) were shipped through St Helier harbour.

Telecommunications

The Jersey Competition Regulatory Authority (JCRA) is the general competition, postal and telecommunications regulatory authority. JT (formerly Jersey Telecom) is the leading company providing fixed, mobile and broadband services. In 2010 main telephone lines numbered 73,800. Mobile phone services are provided by JT, Sure and Airtel-Vodafone.

Social Institutions

Justice

Justice is administered by the Royal Court, consisting of the Bailiff and 12 Jurats (magistrates). There is a final appeal in certain cases to the Sovereign in Council. There is also a Court of Appeal, consisting of the Bailiff and two judges. Minor civil and criminal cases are dealt with by a stipendiary magistrate.

In 2009 there were 4,529 crimes recorded. Customs and Excise was responsible for 108 drug seizures with a street value of £2·6m. in 2009 (up from 92 seizures and a street value of £1·3m. in 2008). In 2009 the daily average prison population was 184.

Education

In 2013 there were six States secondary schools (two fee-paying), one high school and two special needs secondary schools. There were 22 States primary schools, nine of which have provisions for special needs pupils. There were seven private primary schools in 2013. The total number of pupils in Jersey's schools in the same year was 13,241 (7,109 in primary schools and 6,132 in secondary schools).

Health

Gross revenue expenditure on health and social services in 2011 was £188,687,500. In 2010 there was one general hospital with about 245 beds. In 2011 there were 95 doctors (general practitioners).

Welfare

A contributory Health Insurance Scheme is administered by the Social Security Department. In 2009 expenditure on benefits paid out from the Social Security Fund was £172m., and income from contributions, supplementation, interest and rent was £217m. Over 25,000 people received Old Age Pension and 1,012 claimed Maternity Allowance.

Culture

Tourism

In 2011 there were 689,700 visitors to the island, spending £242m.

Guernsey

Territory and Population

The area is 63·5 sq. km. Population (March 2017) 64,540. The main town is St Peter Port (March 2017 population of 18,694).

English is the most widely spoken language. A Norman-French dialect (called Guernsey French or Guernesiais) is spoken by a small number of (mainly older) people. It is now being reintroduced into some school curriculums. Some schools raise awareness of Guernsey French within the curriculum and it is also taught as an extra-curricular activity in others.

Social Statistics

Births during 2011 were 605; deaths, 503.

Constitution and Government

The States of Deliberation, the Parliament of Guernsey, is composed of the following members: the Bailiff, who is President *ex officio*; H.M. Procureur and H.M. Comptroller (Law Officers of the Crown), who have a voice but no vote; 38 People's Deputies elected by popular franchise; ten Douzaine Representatives elected by their Parochial Douzaines; two representatives of the States of Alderney. In May 2004 a slimmed-down States of Deliberation, and an executive form of government was introduced with a Chief Minister for the first time.

The States of Election, an electoral college, elects the Jurats (magistrates). It is composed of the following members: the Bailiff (President *ex officio*); the 12 Jurats or 'Jurés-Justiciers'; H.M. Procureur and H.M. Comptroller; the 38 People's Deputies and 34 representatives from the 10 Parochial Douzaines.

Since Jan. 1949 all legislative powers and functions (with minor exceptions) formerly exercised by the Royal Court have been vested in the States of Deliberation. Projets de Loi (Bills) require the sanction of The Queen-in-Council.

Recent Elections

Elections for People's Deputies were held on 27 April 2016.

Current Government

Bailiff of Guernsey and President of the States: Richard Collas.

Lieut.-Governor and C.-in-C. of Guernsey and its Dependencies: Vice Adm. Ian Corder, CB.

President of the Policy and Resources Committee: Gavin St Pier.
Government Website: http://www.gov.gg

Economy

Budget

Year ended 31 Dec. 2013: revenue £361·3m.; expenditure, £345·7m. The standard rate of income tax is 20p in the pound. States and parochial rates are very moderate. No super-tax or death duties are levied.

Banking and Finance

In March 2016 there were 372 employers in the finance and legal sector, employing a total of 6,825 people. Financial services accounts for approximately 33% of Guernsey's GDP. Guernsey is a leading offshore financial centre.

The general rate of income tax payable by Guernsey companies, formerly 20%, has been 0% since 1 Jan. 2008.

External Economic Relations

Imports and Exports

In 2012 a total of 366,360 tonnes of freight was imported into Guernsey and 38,805 tonnes were exported. The majority of freight is transported by sea. Just 1% (including mail and newspapers) is transported by air.

Communications

Civil Aviation

In 2012 a total of 920,889 passengers used Guernsey's airport, which is situated at La Villiaze. There were direct flights in 2012 to Alderney, Birmingham, Bristol, Dinard, Dublin, Düsseldorf, East Midlands, Exeter, Geneva, Hannover, Isle of Man, Jersey, London (Gatwick and Stansted), Manchester, Rotterdam, Southampton and Zürich.

Shipping

The principal port is St Peter Port. There is also a harbour at St Sampson's (mainly for commercial shipping). In 2015 sea passenger movements totalled 357,625. There were 169 fishing vessels registered in 2015 and more than 5,000 other craft.

Telecommunications

There were around 45,100 main telephone lines in 2010. Sure (formerly C & W Guernsey) offers landline, mobile and broadband services. JT and Airtel-Vodafone offer mobile and broadband services.

Social Institutions

Justice

The total number of criminal offences reported to the police in 2015 was 1,527, down from 1,728 in 2014 and 3,465 in 2005. In 2015 the average prison population was 98 (unchanged from 2014).

Education

There are two public schools, one grammar school, a number of modern secondary and primary schools, and a College of Further Education. The total number of schoolchildren in Jan. 2015 was 8,747. Facilities are available for the study of art, domestic science and many other subjects of a technical nature.

Health

Guernsey is not covered by the UK National Health Service. In 2012 acute services were based at the Princess Elizabeth Hospital, elderly care services at King Edward VII Hospital and mental health services at Castel Hospital. A new mental health facility opened in 2015.

Culture

Press

The *Guernsey Evening Press* is published daily except Sundays.

Tourism

There were 331,600 visitors to Guernsey in 2012. Of those, 168,700 were holidaymakers, 84,800 were business visitors and 49,900 were visiting friends or relatives. The remaining 28,200 were visiting the Island for other purposes.

Alderney

Population (2013 census), 1,903. The main town is St Anne's. The island has an airport.

The Constitution of the island (reformed 1987) provides for its own popularly elected President and States (10 members), and its own Court. Elections were held for the five members of the States in Nov. 2016. Alderney levies its taxes at Guernsey rates and passes the revenue to Guernsey, which charges for the services it provides.

President of the States: Stuart Trought.
Chief Executive: Andrew Muter.
*Greffier:*Jonathan Anderson.

Sark

The population was 542 in Jan. 2014. In order to comply with European human rights legislation, the constitution was amended in Jan. 2008 to make the Chief Pleas (parliament) democratically electable. Previously 40 out of 52 seats were reserved for land-owners. Elections took place in Dec. 2008 for a fully-elected 28-seat chamber. In addition, the powers of the Seigneur (who is head of the island) were restricted. These changes were a decisive move away from the previously feudal system. In 2017 the number of members was reduced from 28 to 18, with nine to be elected every two years.The most recent election took place in Dec. 2018. Sark has no income tax. Motor vehicles, except tractors, are not allowed.

Seigneur: Maj. Christopher Beaumont.
Seneschal: Jeremy La Trobe-Bateman.
President of Chief Pleas: Arthur Rolfe.

United Kingdom Overseas Territories

There are 14 British Overseas Territories: Anguilla; Bermuda; British Antarctic Territory; British Indian Ocean Territory; British Virgin Islands; Cayman Islands; Falkland Islands; Gibraltar; Montserrat; Pitcairn Islands; St Helena, Ascension and Tristan da Cunha; South Georgia and the South Sandwich Islands; the Sovereign Base Areas of Akrotiri and Dhekelia in Cyprus; and the Turks and Caicos Islands. Three (British Antarctic Territory, British Indian Ocean Territory and South Georgia and the South Sandwich Islands) are administered by a Commissioner instead of a Governor.

Gibraltar borders the south coast of Spain, the Sovereign Base Areas are in Cyprus and the remaining territories are islands in the Caribbean, Pacific, Indian Ocean and South Atlantic. Gibraltar and the Falkland Islands are claimed by Spain and Argentina respectively.

The Territories are not part of the UK constitutionally. Most have elected governments with varying authority over domestic matters. The Governor, appointed by, and representing, HM the Queen, oversees external affairs, internal security, defence, and in most cases the public service.

In 1999 the UK government outlined four principles to underlie the Territories' relationship with Britain: self-determination; mutual obligations and responsibilities; freedom to run their own affairs wherever possible; and the UK's commitment to help them develop economically and to assist in emergencies. In addition, in 2002 the British Overseas Territories Act came into force, granting UK citizenship to the citizens of all the Territories (except those who derived their British nationality by virtue only of a connection with the Sovereign Base Areas of Akrotiri and Dhekelia in Cyprus).

UK government ministers and heads of Territory governments meet annually in the Overseas Territories Consultative Council (established in 1999) to discuss key policy issues.

Anguilla

Anguilla was inhabited by Arawaks for several centuries before the arrival of Europeans. Having been colonized in 1650 by English settlers, it was subsequently administered as part of the Leeward Islands, and from 1825 was closely associated with neighbouring St Kitts. In 1875 a petition requesting separate status for Anguilla and direct rule from Britain was rejected, and a further request in 1958 for the dissolution of political and administrative ties with St Kitts also failed. From 1958 to 1962 Anguilla was part of the Federation of the West Indies. Opposition to rule from St Kitts erupted in 1967 as Anguilla refused to recognize the authority of the State government any longer. During 1968–69 the UK government maintained a 'Senior British Official' to advise the local Anguilla Council and devise a solution to the problem. In 1969, following the ejection from the island of a high-ranking British civil servant, British security forces occupied Anguilla and a Commissioner was installed as Anguilla became *de facto* a separate UK dependency. Its status was then formalized under the Anguilla Act 1980 when it separated from the territory of St Kitts-Nevis-Anguilla. A new constitution came into effect in 1982 providing for a large measure of autonomy under the Crown.

Anguilla is the most northerly of the Leeward Islands, some 112 km (70 miles) to the northwest of St Kitts and 8 km (5 miles) to the north of St Martin/Sint Maarten. The territory also comprises the island of Sombrero and several other off-shore islets or cays. The total area is about 155 sq. km (60 sq. miles). There is a tropical oceanic climate and storms and hurricanes may occur between July and Nov.

Census population (2011): 13,572; density: 87·6 per sq. km. People of African descent make up 90% of the population, mixed origins 5% and white 4%. The official language is English.

The *House of Assembly* consists of a Speaker, Deputy Speaker, seven directly elected members for five-year terms, two nominated members and two *ex officio* members: the Deputy Governor and the Attorney-General. The Governor discharges his executive powers on the advice of an Executive Council comprising a Chief Minister, three Ministers, the Deputy Governor, Attorney-General and the Secretary to the Executive Council.

Governor: Tim Foy (took office on 21 Aug. 2017).

Chief Minister: Victor Banks (Anguilla United Front; sworn in 23 April 2015).

The currency is the *East Caribbean dollar* (*see* ANTIGUA AND BARBUDA: Currency). The main sources of revenue are custom duties, tourism and bank licence fees. There is little taxation. The Eastern Caribbean Central Bank based in St Kitts and Nevis functions as a central bank. There is a small offshore banking sector. The main industries are tourism, financial services and fishing. Agriculture is limited and the island relies on imports for food.

Wallblake is the airport for the capital, The Valley. Anguilla is linked to neighbouring islands by services operated by American Airlines, Coastal Air Transport, LIAT and WINAIR. The main seaports are Sandy Ground and Blowing Point, the latter serving passenger and cargo traffic to and from St Martin.

Justice is based on UK common law as exercised by the Eastern Caribbean Supreme Court on St Lucia and final appeal lies to the UK Privy Council. Primary and secondary education is free and compulsory and higher education is provided at regional universities and similar institutions. Religious observance is largely Anglican and Methodist.

Bermuda

The islands were discovered by Spanish sea captain Juan Bermúdez, probably in 1503, but were uninhabited until British colonists were wrecked there in 1609. In 1684 the Crown took over the government. A referendum in 1995 rejected independence from the UK.

Bermuda consists of a group of 138 islands and islets (about 20 inhabited), situated in the western Atlantic (32° 18' N. lat., 64° 46' W. long.); the nearest point of the mainland, 940 km distant, is Cape Hatteras (North Carolina). The area is 53·3 sq. km (20·6 sq. miles). The climate is warm and humid. In June 1995 the USA surrendered its lease on land used since 1941 for naval and air force bases. Census population (2016): 64,628 (Black, 52%; White and others, 48%); density: 1,213 per sq. km. The official language is English.

Under the 1968 constitution the *Governor*, appointed by the Crown, has special responsibility for external affairs, defence, internal security and the police. The legislature, which is responsible for domestic matters, consists of a *Senate* of 11 members—five appointed by the Governor on the recommendation of the Premier, three by the Governor on the recommendation of the Opposition Leader and three by the Governor at his own discretion—and the *House of Assembly*, with 36 members elected by universal suffrage.

Governor: John Rankin (took office on 5 Dec. 2016).

Premier: David Burt (sworn in 19 July 2017).

Bermuda has one of the highest per capita incomes of any country. The territory is a leading offshore financial centre with tax exemption facilities, and is the world's third largest reinsurance market after London and New York. There is also a stock exchange, the BSX. The unit of currency is the *Bermuda dollar* (BMD), at parity with the US dollar. The main sources of state revenue are payroll taxes, customs duty and taxes on international companies. Tourism is also important to the economy.

L. F. Wade International Airport (formerly known as Bermuda International Airport) is 19 km from the capital, Hamilton. Air Canada, American Airlines, British Airways, Delta Air Lines, jetBlue, United Airlines, US Airways and WestJet serve Bermuda with regular scheduled services. There are three ports—Hamilton, St George's and Dockyard—and there is an open shipping registry.

Education is compulsory between the ages of five and 16, and the adult literacy rate is at least 98%. Religious observance reflects the Anglican, Methodist, Roman Catholic, Seventh-day Adventist, African Methodist Episcopal and Baptist faiths.

The Historic Town of St George's and Related Fortifications, an example of early English New World colonialism, were inscribed on UNESCO's World Heritage List in 2000.

British Antarctic Territory

The British Antarctic Territory was established on 3 March 1962, as a consequence of the entry into force of the Antarctic Treaty, to separate those areas of the then Falkland Islands Dependencies which lay within the Treaty area from those which did not (i.e. South Georgia and the South Sandwich Islands).

The territory encompasses the lands and islands within the area south of 60°S latitude lying between 20°W and 80°W longitude (approximately due south of the Falkland Islands and the Dependencies). It covers an area of some 1,700,000 sq. km, and its principal components are the South Orkney and South Shetland Islands, the Antarctic Peninsula (Palmer Land and Graham Land), the Filchner and Ronne Ice Shelves and Coats Land.

There are no indigenous or permanent residents, although an itinerant population of some 300 scientists and logistics staff man a number of research stations.

Commissioner: Ben Merrick (non-resident).

Administrator: Henry Burgess.

British Indian Ocean Territory

This territory was established to meet UK and US defence requirements by an Order in Council in 1965, consisting then of the Chagos Archipelago (formerly administered from Mauritius) and the islands of Aldabra, Desroches and Farquhar (all formerly administered from the Seychelles). The latter islands became part of the Seychelles when that country achieved independence in 1976. In 2000 the High Court ruled that the 2,000 Ilois people (native to the archipelago) deported between 1967 and 1973 to accommodate a US military base on Diego Garcia had been removed unlawfully. Chagos islanders subsequently lost a UK High Court case for compensation and the right to return in 2003, although further High Court rulings in 2006 and 2007 went against the UK government. Also, in Feb. 2019, the International Court of Justice ruled that the islands had not been lawfully separated from Mauritius and that British control should end. However, the UK government viewed that decision as an 'advisory opinion' and not a judgment. Return by the Ilois to the archipelago (excepting Diego Garcia) is unlikely until all appeal processes have been exhausted. In 2010 the UK government had unilaterally imposed a marine protected area around the archipelago, a decision challenged by the Mauritian government at the Permanent Court of Arbitration in 2014.

The group, with a total land area of 60 sq. km (23 sq. miles), comprises five coral atolls (Diego Garcia, Peros Banhos, Salomon, Eagle and Egmont), of which the largest and southernmost, Diego Garcia, covers 44 sq. km (17 sq. miles) and lies 725 km (450 miles) south of the Maldives. A US Navy support facility has been established on Diego Garcia. There is no permanent population.

Commissioner: Ben Merrick (non-resident).

Administrator: Linsey Billing.

British Virgin Islands

Discovered by Columbus on his second voyage in 1493, the British Virgin Islands were first settled by the Dutch in 1648 and taken over in 1666 by a group of English planters. The islands were annexed to the British Crown in 1672. Constitutional government was granted in 1773, but was later surrendered in 1867. A Legislative Council formed in that year was abolished in 1902. In 1950 a partly nominated and partly elected Legislative Council was restored. A ministerial system of government was introduced in 1967.

The Islands form the eastern extremity of the Greater Antilles and number 60, of which 16 are inhabited. The largest are Tortola, Virgin Gorda, Jost Van Dyke and Anegada. Total area: 151 sq. km (58 sq. miles). There is a moderate, tropical climate, although the Islands were devastated by two hurricanes in Sept. 2017. Census population (2010): 28,054. The capital, Road Town, is on Tortola. The official language is English, although Spanish and Creole are also spoken.

The constitution became effective on 15 June 2007. It granted the Islands greater autonomy and self-determination. There is a *Premier* (formerly *Chief Minister*) and a *House of Assembly* (formerly *Legislative Council*). The Premier is appointed by the *Governor*. The House of Assembly consists of 13 members elected for a four-year term (five directly-elected members from constituencies and four members from 'at large' seats covering the territory as a whole), a Speaker and the Attorney General *ex officio*. The Cabinet consists of the Premier, four other Ministers and the Attorney General *ex officio*.

Governor: Gus Jaspert (took office on 22 Aug. 2017).

Premier: Andrew Fahie (Virgin Islands Party; sworn in 26 Feb. 2019).

The economy is based on international financial services and tourism. In 2015 there were six commercial banks and more than 2,000 registered mutual funds. The financial services industry accounts for over 60% of government revenue. The Islands' financial probity has, however, been questioned by allegations that portray the territory as a popular tax haven for the world's rich and powerful elite. The official unit of currency is the US dollar. The construction industry is a significant employer, but local manufacturing and agricultural production are limited.

Beef Island Airport, about 16 km from Road Town, is capable of receiving short-take-off-and-landing jet aircraft. Several airlines serve the Islands, notably LIAT. There are scheduled flights to the US territory of Puerto Rico and a number of other islands in the Eastern Caribbean. There are two deep-water harbours, Port Purcell and Road Town, and four other ports.

Justice is based on UK common law. There are courts of first instance and the appeal court is in the UK. Education is free and compulsory from five to 16 years. There are government schools, private schools and also the H. Lavity Stoutt Community College located on Tortola. In 1986 a branch of the Hull University (England) School of Education was established. There are Anglican, Methodist, Seventh-day Adventist, Roman Catholic, Baptist, Pentecostal and other Christian churches in the Territory, together with Jehovah's Witness and Hindu congregations.

Cayman Islands

The Islands were discovered by Columbus on 10 May 1503 and (with Jamaica) were recognized as British possessions by the Treaty of Madrid in 1670. They were administered by Jamaica from 1863, but remained under British sovereignty when Jamaica became independent in 1962. They consist of Grand Cayman (settled in 1734), Cayman Brac and Little Cayman (settled in 1833). They are located in the Caribbean Sea, about 305 km (190 miles) northwest of Jamaica; area, 259 sq. km (100 sq. miles). The climate is tropical maritime, and hurricanes may be experienced between July and Nov. Census population (2010): 55,456; density: 214 per sq. km. Population estimate (Dec. 2014): 58,238. The official language is English. The chief town is George Town.

The Cayman Islands are a self-governing UK overseas territory. A new constitution granting the Islands more political autonomy took effect on 6 Nov. 2009, creating the office of *Premier* who is limited to two consecutive four-year terms of office. There is a *Legislative Assembly* of 19 members.

Governor: Martyn Roper.

Premier: Alden McLaughlin (sworn in 29 May 2013).

Financial services, the principal industry, are monitored by the Cayman Islands Monetary Authority, although the Islands have been criticized as an alleged haven for tax avoiders. Most of the world's leading banks have branches or subsidiaries in the Islands. Tourism is the next most important industry. The unit of currency is the *Cayman Island dollar* (KYD), usually written as CI$.

There are international airports at George Town (Owen Roberts) and on Grand Cayman and Cayman Brac (Gerrard Smith). Cayman Airways provides a regular inter-island service and also flies to the USA, Cuba and Jamaica. Some additional international airlines provide services to the UK, Canada, The Bahamas, Honduras, Jamaica and the USA. Motor vessels ply regularly between the Cayman Islands, Cuba, Jamaica and Florida.

There is a Grand Court, sitting six times a year for criminal sessions at George Town under a Chief Justice and two puisne judges. There are three Magistrates presiding over the Summary Court. There are government and private schools, and four institutions provide tertiary education. The healthcare system includes public and private service providers.

Residents are primarily of Christian faiths. Other religions, including Baha'i, Buddhism, Hinduism, Islam and Judaism, are also represented.

Falkland Islands

France and then Britain established settlements in the Islands in 1764 and 1765. Subsequently, the British, French and Spanish periodically had forces stationed there until 1811 when all the garrisons were withdrawn. Following the overthrow of Spanish rule in Argentina, the Argentines in 1820 claimed to succeed Spain in the French and British settlements. The British objected and reclaimed their settlement in 1833 as a Crown Colony. On 2 April 1982 Argentine armed forces occupied the Falkland Islands and the United Nations (UN) Security Council called for Argentina's withdrawal the following day. After a military campaign, without a formal declaration of war, the UK regained possession on 14–15 June when Argentina surrendered. In April 1990 Argentina's Congress declared the Falkland and other British-held South Atlantic islands part of the new Argentine province of Tierra del Fuego. However, there has been no threat of further hostilities. Since 1982 there has been a standing garrison of British armed service personnel in addition to a local volunteer defence force. A new constitution came into force in Jan. 2009, reaffirming the Territory's right of self-determination contained in international covenants, and 99·8% of the electorate voted in a referendum in March 2013 to maintain British Overseas Territory status.

The Territory comprises numerous islands situated in the South Atlantic Ocean about 480 miles northeast of Cape Horn covering about 12,200 sq. km (East Falkland Island, 6,760 sq. km; West Falkland, 5,410 sq. km, including the adjacent small islands). There is a cool temperate and windy climate. Census population (2016): 3,032 (nearly all of British descent). The official language is English. The only town is Stanley, in East Falkland.

Domestic policy is the responsibility of the *Executive Council* although the Governor can override it and decide policy 'in the interests of good governance' or in matters relating to external affairs, defence, internal security (including police), the administration of justice, audit and public service management. There is a *Legislative Council* consisting of eight elected members together with the *ex officio* Chief Executive and Financial Secretary. Only elected members have a vote.

Governor: Nigel Phillips, CBE (took office on 12 Sept. 2017).

Chief Executive: Barry Rowland.

The economy has traditionally been based on agriculture (principally sheep farming) and fishing. However, with substantial oil reserves believed to exist around the Islands, licensed exploration began in 1996. Drilling was then abandoned in 1998 in response to falling crude prices before interest revived from 2008 as prices recovered. Given the potential oil riches, Argentina has appealed to the UN to bring the UK into renewed talks over the status of the Islands. Trade is predominantly with the UK, the rest with Latin America and particularly Chile. Main imports are refined petroleum oils and surveying, hydrographic, oceanographic, hydrological, meteorological or geophysical instruments and appliances. Significant exports are molluscs, frozen fish and wool. The unit of currency is the *Falkland Islands pound* (FKP), at parity with £1 sterling. The only bank presence is Standard Chartered Bank.

An airport is sited at Mount Pleasant on East Falkland. The Ministry of Defence operates non-commercial flights from the UK via Ascension Island. LATAM Airlines runs commercial services to and from the Islands.

There is a Supreme Court, and a Court of Appeal sits in the UK; appeals may go from that court to the judicial committee of the Privy Council. The senior resident judicial officer is the Senior Magistrate. There are an Attorney General and a Senior Crown Counsel. Education is compulsory between the ages of five and 16 years. The Government Medical Department is responsible for all medical services to civilians. Health care facilities are based at the King Edward VII Memorial Hospital, the only hospital on the Islands.

Gibraltar

The Rock of Gibraltar was settled by Moors in 711. In 1462 it was taken by Spaniards from Grenada, but then captured by British forces in 1704 and ceded to Great Britain in 1713 by the Treaty of Utrecht. The cession was confirmed by the treaties of Paris (1763) and Versailles (1783). In 1830 Gibraltar became a British crown colony. In 1973 Gibraltar joined the European Community as a UK dependent territory. Spain has maintained its historic claim to outright control over the territory. However, in 1967 the majority of the inhabitants voted in a referendum to retain their link with the UK and, in a further (unofficial) vote in 2002, rejected joint British and Spanish sovereignty. Gibraltarians have full UK citizenship. The UK Ministry of Defence maintains a tri-service garrison on the Rock.

Gibraltar is situated in latitude 36°07' N and longitude 05°21' W. Area, 6·5 sq. km (2·5 sq. miles) including port and harbour. The climate is warm temperate. The population is mostly of mixed Genoese, Portuguese, Maltese and Spanish descent. Census population (2012): 32,577; density: 5,012 per sq. km. The official language is English; Spanish is also spoken.

A new constitution came into effect in Jan. 2007, giving Gibraltar full internal self-government. The legislature consists of the Queen as head of state and the *Gibraltar Parliament*. The *Governor* is Commander-in-Chief and has direct constitutional responsibility for matters relating to defence, external affairs and some aspects of internal security. The *Council of Ministers* is headed by the Chief Minister, appointed by the Governor. The Gibraltar Parliament consists of a Speaker and at least 17 elected members. A Mayor of Gibraltar is elected by the members of parliament (excluding the Speaker).

Governor and C.-in-C: Lieut.-Gen. Edward Davis, CB, CBE (took office on 19 Jan. 2016).

Chief Minister: Fabian Picardo (Gibraltar Socialist Labour Party; elected in Dec. 2011).

The economy is mainly based on service industries (financial services, offshore banking, tourism), port facilities and transhipment. Gibraltar is also a world-leading centre for online gambling. The *Gibraltar pound* (GIP) is at parity with the UK £1 sterling (both legal tender). The main revenue sources are income tax, import duties, company taxes and general rates. The majority of authorized credit institutions are subsidiaries or branches of major UK or other European Economic Area (EEA) credit institutions. The territory is dependent on imported foodstuffs and fuels. The UK is the largest source of imports. Other major trade partners include Spain, the Netherlands and Germany. Exports are mainly re-exports of petroleum and petroleum products supplied to shipping, manufactured goods, wines, spirits, malt and tobacco. Gibraltar North Front is the international airport, with scheduled flights to UK and Moroccan destinations. The Strait of Gibraltar is a principal gateway between the Mediterranean and Black Sea areas and the rest of the world.

The judicial system is based on the English model. There are a Court of Appeal, a Supreme Court (presided over by the Chief Justice), a Court of First Instance and a Magistrates' Court. Free compulsory education is provided between the ages of four and 15 years. There are 14 schools and one college of further education. The Gibraltar Health Authority is responsible for providing health care and there is a comprehensive social security system. Roman Catholicism is the predominant religious faith.

Gorham's Cave Complex, consisting of four caves that provide evidence of Neanderthal occupation over a span of more than 100,000 years, was inscribed on UNESCO's World Heritage List in 2016.

Montserrat

Montserrat was discovered by Columbus in 1493 and colonized in 1632 by Britain, which brought Irish settlers to the island. It formed part of the federal colony of the Leeward Islands from 1871 until 1958, when it became a separate colony following the dissolution of the federation.

Montserrat is situated in the Caribbean Sea, 43 km southwest of Antigua. Area: 102·3 sq. km (39·5 sq. miles). The climate is tropical, with a hurricane season between July and Nov. What was previously the capital, Plymouth, is now deserted as a result of the continuing activity of the Soufriere Hills volcano (which erupted in 1995 and again in 1997 with devastating human and economic consequences). The safe area is in the north of the island, where Brades, the *de facto* capital, is located. Census population (2011): 4,922. The official language is English.

The head of state is Queen Elizabeth II, represented by a *Governor*. The constitution promulgated in 2011 provides for greater control of international relations by the government of Montserrat, the strengthening of fundamental rights and freedoms, and a national advisory council along with commissions to deal with complaints, integrity, elections and clemency. The *Legislative Assembly* consists of nine elected members and two *ex officio* members (the Attorney-General and Financial Secretary). The cabinet includes a minimum membership of the *Premier*, three other ministers and the two *ex officio* members.

Governor: Andrew Pearce (took office on 1 Feb. 2018).

Premier: Donaldson Romeo (took office on 12 Sept. 2014).

The currency is the *East Caribbean dollar* (*see* ANTIGUA AND BARBUDA: Currency). The Eastern Caribbean Central Bank based in St Kitts and Nevis functions as a central bank. Having previously been an economic mainstay, tourism was devastated by the 1997 volcanic eruption and Montserrat has since relied heavily on aid from the UK and European Union, although the USA is the island's main trading partner. A new airport opened in Feb. 2005. Plymouth is the port of entry, but alternative anchorage was provided at Old Bay Road during the volcanic crisis.

The justice system is based on UK common law as exercised by the Eastern Caribbean Supreme Court. Final appeal lies to the UK Privy Council. Law is administered by the West Indies Associated States Court, a Court of Summary Jurisdiction and Magistrate's Courts. In 2013–14 there were four primary schools and one secondary school. The main religion is Christianity,

with Anglicans, Methodists, Pentecostalists, Roman Catholics and Seventh-day Adventists being the leading denominations.

Pitcairn Island

Pitcairn was discovered by British naval Capt. Philip Carteret in 1767, but remained uninhabited until 1790, when it was occupied by nine mutineers of HMS *Bounty*, with 12 women and six men from Tahiti. Nothing was known of their existence until the island was visited in 1808.

In 2004 six men, comprising some 12% of the island's resident population and including several prominent public figures, were convicted of child sex offences. The scandal divided the island, with defendants arguing that English law did not have jurisdiction on Pitcairn and that underage sex was a long-standing tradition. Sentences ranged up to six-and-a-half years in prison.

Pitcairn Island (4·6 sq. km; 1·75 sq. miles), with an equable climate, is situated in the Pacific Ocean, nearly equidistant from New Zealand and Panama (25° 04' S. lat., 130° 06' W. long.). Adamstown is the only settlement. The estimated population in 2015 was 57. The uninhabited islands of Henderson (31 sq. km), Ducie (3·9 sq. km) and Oeno (5·2 sq. km) were annexed in 1902. English is the official language but Pitkern is also spoken.

The *Island Council* has ten members, seven of whom (five Councillors, the Mayor and Deputy Mayor) are elected by popular vote. The other three are the *ex officio* Administrator (who serves as both the head of government and the representative of the Governor), the Governor (who is also the British High Commissioner to New Zealand) and the Deputy Governor. The Councillors and the Deputy Mayor all serve two-year terms. The Mayor is elected for three years and is eligible to serve a second term, while the Administrator is appointed by the Governor for an indefinite term. No political parties exist.

Governor: Laura Clarke (took office in Jan. 2018).

Mayor: Shawn Christian (took office in Jan. 2014).

Economic activity includes fishing, agriculture and postage stamp sales. New Zealand currency is used. In a bid to preserve the environment and boost tourism, a marine reserve around the territory measuring 830,000 sq. km was established in Sept. 2016. Henderson Island was inscribed on the UNESCO World Heritage List in 1988.

St Helena, Ascension and Tristan da Cunha

The island of St Helena was uninhabited when discovered by the Portuguese in 1502. It was administered by the East India Company from 1659 and became a British colony in 1834. French Emperor Napoleon died there in exile in 1821. Area: 416 sq. km (161 sq. miles). Census population (2016): 5,714.

St Helena, of volcanic origin, 3,100 km from the west coast of Africa. Area: 122 sq. km (47 sq. miles), with a cultivable area of 243 ha. Census population (2016): 4,615. The capital and port is Jamestown. The official language is English.

Ascension, small island of volcanic origin, 1,100 km (700 miles) northwest of St Helena. Area: 88 sq. km (34 sq. miles). The island hosts sea turtles, rabbits, the sooty tern or 'wideawake' and feral donkeys. A cable station connects the island with St Helena, Sierra Leone, St Vincent, Rio de Janeiro and Buenos Aires. There is an airstrip (Miracle Mile) near the settlement of Georgetown; the Royal Air Force maintains an air link with the Falkland Islands.

Tristan da Cunha, the largest of a small group of islands in the South Atlantic, lying 2,124 km (1,320 miles) southwest of St Helena, of which they became dependencies in 1938. Area: 98 sq. km; Population (2016): 293, all living in the settlement of Edinburgh of the Seven Seas. Inaccessible Island (10 sq. km) lies 20 miles to the west, and the three Nightingale Islands (2 sq. km) lie 20 miles to the south; they are uninhabited. Gough Island (90 sq. km) is 220 miles to the south and has a meteorological station. Tristan consists of a volcano rising to a height of 2,060 metres, with a circumference at its base of 34 km. The volcano, believed to be extinct, erupted unexpectedly in Oct. 1961. The original inhabitants were shipwrecked sailors and soldiers who remained behind when the garrison from St Helena was withdrawn in 1817.

In 1944 Tristan da Cunha was commissioned as a warship, HMS *Atlantic Isle*, and became an important meteorological and radio station. An Administrator was appointed in 1948. The Island Council, set up in 1932, consists of a Chief Islander, three nominated and eight elected members, under the chairmanship of the Administrator.

Under the terms of a new constitution that came into force in Sept. 2009, the territory changed its official name from St Helena and Dependencies to St

Helena, Ascension and Tristan da Cunha. The constitution included a bill of rights, allowing citizens to appeal to local courts on human rights issues rather than address the European Court of Human Rights as they had done previously. Constraints were placed on the powers of the Governor (who no longer holds the title of 'Commander-in-Chief'), while the independence of the judiciary and public service were constitutionally enshrined.

The territory's *Legislative Council* consists of 12 elected members, three non-voting *ex officio* members (the Chief Secretary, the Financial Secretary and the Attorney General) and the Speaker and Deputy Speaker. The Governor is advised by an *Executive Council* comprising the three non-voting *ex officio* members and five elected members from the Legislative Council. The Governor must, except in certain prescribed circumstances, act in accordance with the advice of the Executive Council.

Governor: Lisa Phillips (took office on 25 April 2016).
Administrator of Ascension: Justine Allan.
Administrator of Tristan da Cunha: Sean Burns.
An international airport was opened in 2016.
The population is mainly Anglican.
St Helena, Ascension and Tristan da Cunha has one site on UNESCO's World Heritage List: Gough and Inaccessible Islands (inscribed on the list in 1995 and 2004), two of the least disturbed islands and marine eco-systems in the South Atlantic.

South Georgia and the South Sandwich Islands

The first landing and exploration was undertaken by Capt. James Cook, who formally took possession in the name of the British Crown in 1775. Seal hunting reached its peak in 1800 and whalers were active from 1904 to 1966. A German team was the first to carry out scientific studies there in 1882–83. Argentine forces occupied South Georgia on 3 April 1982 until a British naval task force recovered the Island three weeks later.

South Georgia lies 1,300 km southeast of the Falkland Islands (area: 3,760 sq. km) and the South Sandwich Islands are 760 km southeast of South Georgia (area: 340 sq. km). The climate is wet and cold, with strong winds. In 1993 crown sovereignty and jurisdiction were extended from 19 km (12 miles) to 322 km (200 miles) around the islands. There is no permanent population. The British Antarctic Survey operates a fisheries science facility at King Edward Point and a biological station on Bird Island. The South Sandwich Islands are uninhabited.

Under the constitution that came into force in 1985 the Territories ceased to be dependencies of the Falkland Islands. The Government of South Georgia and the South Sandwich Islands (GSGSSI) administers the islands. The local administration is the responsibility of the Government Officer based at King Edward Point. Executive power is vested in a Commissioner, who is also the Governor of the Falkland Islands (Nigel Phillips, CBE, since Sept. 2017). The Commissioner consults the officer commanding British Forces in the South Atlantic on defence matters and the Executive Council of the Falkland Islands on the exercise of his functions that might affect that territory. There is no Legislative Council. Laws are made by the Commissioner.

The bases at King Edward Point and Bird Island have modern satellite communication systems. King Edward Point is regularly visited by the GSGSSI Fishery Patrol Vessel. Other visiting vessels include cruise ships, BAS research ships, warships and auxiliaries, fishing vessels and yachts.

There is a Supreme Court for the Territories and a Court of Appeal in the UK. Appeals may go from that court to the Judicial Committee of the Privy Council. The British Antarctic Survey base commander at King Edward Point is usually appointed a magistrate.

Sovereign Base Areas of Akrotiri and Dhekelia in Cyprus

The Sovereign Base Areas (SBAs) are those parts of the island of Cyprus that stayed under UK jurisdiction and remained British sovereign territory when the 1960 Treaty of Establishment created the independent Republic of Cyprus. The Akrotiri facility formed a strategic part of the West's nuclear capacity during the Cold War. The SBAs were used for the deployment of troops in the Gulf War in 1991. Military intelligence is now the key role of the SBAs. The construction of massive antennae at the RAF communications base at Akrotiri sparked violent riots in 2001 and 2002, led by a Greek Cypriot MP. In Feb. 2003 the UK Government offered to surrender approximately half the area of the SBAs as an incentive for a settlement between the Greek and Turkish administrations in Cyprus.

The SBAs, with a total land area of 254 sq. km (98 sq. miles), comprise the Western SBA (123 sq. km), including Episkopi Garrison and RAF Akrotiri (opened 1956), and the Eastern SBA (131 sq. km), including Dhekelia Garrison. The SBAs cover 3% of the land area of the island of Cyprus. The UK Government has declared that it will not develop the SBAs other than for military purposes. Citizens and residents of the Republic of Cyprus are guaranteed freedom of access and communications to and through the SBAs.

The SBAs are administered as military bases reporting to the ministry of defence in London. The Administrator is the Commander British Forces Cyprus. The joint force headquarters are at Episkopi.

Commander British Forces Cyprus: Maj.-Gen. James Illingworth (since 15 Feb. 2017).

The Turks and Caicos Islands

After a long period of rival French and Spanish claims, the islands were secured to the British Crown in 1766. They became a separate colony in 1973 after association with the colonies of The Bahamas and Jamaica. In 2009 the UK government imposed direct rule after allegations of widespread corruption among the islands' rulers.

The Islands are situated between 21° and 22°N. lat. and 71° and 72°W. long, about 80 km east of The Bahamas, of which they are geographically an extension. There are over 40 islands, covering an estimated area of 500 sq. km (193 sq. miles). Only seven are inhabited: Grand Caicos, the largest, is 48 km long by 3 to 5 km broad; Grand Turk, the capital and main political and administrative centre, is 11 km long by 2 km broad. Population (2012): 31,618; Grand Turk, 4,831; Middle Caicos, 168; North Caicos, 1,312; Parrot Cay, 131; Providenciales, 23,769; Salt Cay, 108; South Caicos, 1,139. Despite a generally equable climate, the Islands were pummelled by a category 5 hurricane (the highest level) in Sept. 2017. The official language is English.

A new constitution entered force in Aug. 2006. It granted the Islands further self-government, made provision for the establishment of an Advisory National Security Council, and changed the title of Chief Minister and Deputy Chief Minister to Premier and Deputy Premier. Following a corruption scandal in 2009, the UK government dissolved the cabinet and the House of Assembly and placed the Islands under direct rule that continued until 2012. The *Cabinet* (formerly *Executive Council*) comprises the Governor, the Premier, no more than six other Ministers, the Deputy Governor and the Attorney General. The *House of Assembly* (formerly *Legislative Council*) consists of a Speaker, the Attorney General, 15 elected members and four appointed members.

Governor: John Freeman (took office 17 Oct. 2016).
Premier: Sharlene Cartwright Robinson (sworn in 20 Dec. 2016).

The economy is based on free-market private sector-led development. The focus is on the service sector, with tourism and offshore finance still the dominant industries, together with fishing. The US dollar is the official currency. The international airports are on Grand Turk and Providenciales. An internal air service provides regular daily flights between the inhabited islands. The main ports are at Grand Turk, Cockburn Harbour and Providenciales.

Laws are a mixture of Statute and Common Law. There is a Magistrates Court and a Supreme Court. Appeals lie from the Supreme Court to the Court of Appeal which sits in Nassau, The Bahamas. There is a further appeal in certain cases to the Privy Council in London. Education is free between the ages of five and 14. There are Anglican, Catholic, Methodist, Baptist and Evangelist faith groups.

Further Reading

United Kingdom of Great Britain and Northern Ireland

The Office for National Statistics publishes data online at http://www.ons. gov.uk. The Stationery Office (TSO), formerly HMSO, offers publications covering legislation, official reports, and government and parliamentary papers.

Bache, Ian and Jordan, Andrew, *The Europeanization of British Politics.* 2006

Baker, David and Schnapper, Pauline, *Britain and the Crisis of the European Union.* 2015

Beech, Matt and Lee, Simon, (eds) *Ten Years of New Labour.* 2008

Black, Jeremy, *A History of the British Isles.* 3rd ed. 2012

Bogdanor, Vernon, *Devolution in the United Kingdom.* 1999.—*The New British Constitution. 2009*

Cairncross, A., *The British Economy Since 1945: Economic Policy and Performance, 1945–1995.* 2nd ed. 1995

Casey, Terence, (ed.) *The Blair Legacy: Politics, Policy, Governance, and Foreign Affairs.* 2009

Clark, Alistair, *Political Parties in the UK.* 2nd ed. 2018

Cowley, Philip and Kavanagh, Dennis, *The British General Election of 2017.* 2018

Davies, Norman, *The Isles: A History.* 1999

Denver, David, Carman, Christopher and Johns, Robert, (eds) *Elections and Voters in Britain.* 3rd ed. 2012

Dorey, Peter and Garnett, Mark, *The British Coalition Government, 2010–2015: A Marriage of Inconvenience.* 2016

Evans, Geoffrey and Menon, Anand, *Brexit and British Politics.* 2017

Floud, Roderick and Johnson, Paul, (eds) *The Cambridge Economic History of Modern Britain.* 3 vols. 2004

Gascoigne, B. (ed.) *Encyclopedia of Britain.* 1994

Geddes, Andrew, *Britain and the European Union.* 2013

Glencross, Andrew, *Why the UK Voted for Brexit: David Cameron's Great Miscalculation.* 2016

Griffiths, Simon and Leach, Robert, *British Politics.* 3rd ed. 2018

Hannay, David, *Britain's Quest for a Role: A Diplomatic Memoir from Europe to the UN.* 2012

Harrison, B., *The Transformation of British Politics, 1860–1995.* 1996

Heffernan, Richard, Hay, Colin, Russell, Meg and Cowley, Philip, (eds) *Developments in British Politics 10.* 2016

Heywood, Andrew, *Essentials of UK Politics.* 4th ed. 2017

Kellner, Peter, *Democracy: 1,000 Years in Pursuit of British Liberty.* 2009

Leese, Peter, *Britain Since 1945.* 2006

Leventhal, F. M. (ed.) *20th-Century Britain: an Encyclopedia.* 1995

Marquand, David, *Britain Since 1918: The Strange Career of British Democracy.* 2008

McCormick, John, *Contemporary Britain.* 4th ed. 2018

Moran, Michael, *Politics and Governance in the UK.* 3rd ed. 2015—*The End of British Politics?* 2017

Mortimore, Roger and Blick, Andrew, (eds) *Butler's British Political Facts.* 2018

Oakland, John, *British Civilization: an Introduction.* 8th ed. 2015

Oxford History of the British Empire. 2 vols. 1999

Palmer, A. and Palmer, V., *The Chronology of British History.* 1995

Penguin History of Britain. 9 vols. 1996

Preston, P. W., *Britain After Empire.* 2014

Robbins, Keith, *A Bibliography of British History 1914–1989.* 1996

Roberts, Andrew, *Churchill: Walking with Destiny.* 2018

Sanders, David and Houghton, David Patrick, *Losing an Empire, Finding a Role: British Foreign Policy Since 1945.* 2nd ed. 2016

Shipman, Tim, *All Out War: The Full Story of How Brexit Sank Britain's Political Class.* 2016

Simms, Brendan, *Britain's Europe: A Thousand Years of Conflict and Cooperation.* 2016

Wall, Stephen, *A Stranger in Europe: Britain and the EU from Thatcher to Blair.* 2008.—*The Official History of Britain and the European Community, Volume II: From Rejection to Referendum, 1963–75.* 2012

Waller, R. and Criddle, B., *The Almanac of British Politics.* 8th ed. 2007

Wilson, David and Game, Chris, *Local Government in the United Kingdom.* 5th ed. 2011

Other more specialized titles are listed under TERRITORY AND POPULATION; ARMY; NAVY; AIR FORCE; BANKING AND FINANCE; ELECTRICITY; WELFARE; *and* RELIGION, *above. See also* Further Reading *in* SCOTLAND, WALES *and* NORTHERN IRELAND.

National Statistical Office: UK Statistics Authority, Statistics House, Tredegar Park, Newport, Gwent, NP10 8XG. *National Statistician:* John Pullinger, CB.

Website: http://www.statistics.gov.uk

England

See Further Reading *in* UNITED KINGDOM.

Scotland

Scottish *Government. State of the Economy.* Twice yearly—*Scottish Abstract of Statistics* (now discontinued). Annual

Brown, A., *et al.*, *Politics and Society in Scotland.* 1996

Cairney, Paul and McGarvey, Neil, *Scottish Politics.* 2nd ed. 2013

Devine, T. M. and Finlay, R. J. (eds) *Scotland in the 20th Century.* 1996

Elliott, John H., *Scots and Catalans: Union and Disunion.* 2018

Harvie, C., *Scotland and Nationalism: Scottish Society and Politics, 1707 to the Present.* 4th ed. 2004

Hassan, Gerry, *Independence of the Scottish Mind.* 2014

Keay, J. and J., *Collins Encyclopedia of Scotland: The Story of a Nation.* 2000

Macleod, J., *Highlanders: A History of the Gaels.* 1997

Magnusson, M., *Scotland: The Story of a Nation.* 2000

McCaffrey, J. F., *Scotland in the Nineteenth Century.* 1998

Mitchell, James, *Governing Scotland.* 2003

Statistical office: Room 1N.04, St Andrew's House, Regent Road, Edinburgh, EH1 3DG.

Website: https://www2.gov.scot/Topics/Statistics

Wales

National Assembly. Digest of Welsh Statistics (now discontinued).

Davies, J., *History of Wales.* 1993

Jenkins, G. H., *The Foundations of Modern Wales 1642–1780.* 1993.—*The Welsh Language and its Social Domains 1801–1911: A Social History of the Welsh Language.* 2000

Jones, G. E., *Modern Wales: a Concise History.* 2nd ed. 1994

Morgan, K. and Mungham, G., *Redesigning Democracy. The Making of the Welsh Assembly.* 2000

Williams, G., *Renewal and Reformation Wales c. 1415–1642.* 1993

Statistical office: Statistical Directorate, Welsh Assembly Government, Cathays Park, Cardiff CF10 3NQ.

Website: https://statswales.gov.wales

Northern Ireland

Adshead, Maura and Tonge, Jonathan, *Politics in Ireland: Convergence and Divergence in a Two-Polity Island.* 2009

Armstrong, Charles I., Herbert, David and Mustad, Jan Erik (eds), *The Legacy of the Good Friday Agreement: Northern Irish Politics, Culture and Art after 1998.* 2018

Aughey, A. and Morrow, D. (eds) *Northern Ireland Politics.* 1996

Bardon, Jonathan, *A History of Ulster.* 1992

Bloomfield, D., *Peacemaking Strategies in Northern Ireland.* 1998

Bourke, Richard, *Peace in Ireland: The War of Ideas.* 2003

Bow, P. and Gillespie, G., *Northern Ireland: a Chronology of the Troubles, 1968–1993.* 1993

Dixon, Paul, *Northern Ireland: The Politics of War and Peace.* 2nd ed. 2008

Fay, Marie-Thérèse, Morrisey, Mike and Smyth, Marie, *Northern Ireland's Troubles.* 1999

Hennessey, T., *A History of Northern Ireland 1920–96.* 1998

Loughlin, James, *The Ulster Question Since 1945.* 1998

McGarry, J. and O'Leary, B. (eds) *Explaining Northern Ireland: Broken Images.* 1995

Neumann, Peter R., *Britain's Long War: British Strategy in the Northern Ireland Conflict, 1969–98.* 2003

Patterson, Henry, *Ireland Since 1939: The Persistence of Conflict.* 2006.—*Ireland's Violent Frontier: The Border and Anglo–Irish Relations During the Troubles.* 2013

Rose, Peter, *How the Troubles Came to Northern Ireland.* 1999

Ruane, J. and Todd, J., *The Dynamics of Conflict in Northern Ireland: Power, Conflict and Emancipation.* 1997

Tonge, Jonathan, *The New Northern Irish Politics?* 2004

Statistical office: Northern Ireland Statistics and Research Agency (NISRA), McAuley House, 2–14 Castle St., Belfast BT1 1SA.

Website: http://www.nisra.gov.uk

Isle of Man

Additional information is available from: Economic Affairs Division, Illiam Dhone House, 2 Circular Rd, Douglas, Isle of Man, IM1 1PQ. *Email:* economics@gov.im

Isle of Man in Numbers. Annual

Belchem, J. (ed.) *A New History of the Isle of Man, Volume V—The Modern Period 1830–1999.* 2000

Kermode, D. G., *Offshore Island Politics: The Constitutional and Political Development of the Isle of Man in the Twentieth Century.* 2001

Moore, A. W., *A History of the Isle of Man.* 1900; reprinted 1992

Manx National Heritage publishes a series of booklets including *Early Maps of the Isle of Man*, *The Art of the Manx Crosses*, *The Ancient & Historic Monuments of the Isle of Man*, *Pre-historic Sites of the Isle of Man*.

Channel Islands

Lemprière, R., *History of the Channel Islands.* Rev. ed. 1980

Turner, Barry, *Outpost of Occupation: How the Channel Islands Survived Nazi Rule, 1940–45*. 2010

Jersey

Balleine, G. R., *A History of the Island of Jersey.* Rev. ed. 1981

States of Jersey Library: Halkett Place, St Helier.

Statistical Office: Statistics Unit, P. O. Box 140, Cyril Le Marquand House, The Parade, St Helier, Jersey, JE4 8QT.

Website: https://www.gov.je/Government/JerseyInFigures/Pages/index.aspx

Guernsey

Marr, L. J., *A History of Guernsey.* 1982

Statistical office: Policy and Research Unit, Sir Charles Frossard House, La Charroterie, St. Peter Port, GY1 1FH.

Website: http://www.gov.gg/pru

Alderney

Coysh, V., *Alderney.* 1974

Sark

Hathaway, S., *Dame of Sark: An Autobiography.* 1961

United States of America

Capital: Washington, D.C.
Population projection, 2020: 331·43m.
GNI per capita, 2017: (PPP$) 54,941
HDI/world rank, 2017: 0·924/13
Internet domain extension: .us

Key Historical Events

It is believed that the name America was first used on a map of the New World created by German cartographer Martin Waldseemüller in 1507, reputedly in recognition of the Italian explorer, Amerigo Vespucci, who had made a series of voyages to the region in the late 15th and early 16th centuries. The earliest inhabitants of the north American continent can be traced back to Palaeolithic times. The Pueblo culture in modern-day Colorado and New Mexico flourished from the 11th to the 14th century AD. In the 12th century permanent settlements appeared in the east where cultivation and fishing supported major fortified towns. The first Europeans to make their presence felt were the Spanish, who based themselves in Florida before venturing north and west. Santa Fe in New Mexico was founded in 1610. But by the mid-17th century there was competition centred on Quebec from the French who colonized the banks of the St Lawrence River.

Elizabethan adventurers were eager to exploit the New World but it was not until 1607 that an English colony was established. This was at Jamestown in what is now southern Virginia. After a perilous start when disease and malnutrition carried off most of the settlers, Virginia's population grew rapidly to meet the European demand for tobacco. Maryland, originally a refuge for persecuted Catholics, also thrived on the tobacco trade. To make up for the shortage of labour, slaves were imported from Africa.

In 1620 a hundred pilgrims landed at Plymouth Rock to found a Puritan enclave, which became the colony of Massachusetts. Other settlements soon followed, accommodating a broad range of Christian radicals fleeing persecution. Not all were tolerant of beliefs that differed from their own. Pennsylvania, the colony named after the Quaker William Penn, was exceptional in offering freedom of worship to 'all persons who confess and acknowledge the one almighty and eternal God'. In 1664 the British took control of neighbouring Dutch colonies. New Amsterdam became New York. Almost all of the eastern seaboard was now claimed by British settlers who were also venturing inland.

Their main European rivals were the French who claimed a vast area around and to the southwest of the Great Lakes. With American Indian tribes allied to both sides, there was heavy fighting in 1744 and 1748. But within a decade British forces had captured most of the French strongholds. After the Treaty of Paris in 1763, Britain commanded the whole of North America east of the Mississippi while Spain, having surrendered Florida, gained Louisiana from France. For a brief period colonization was restricted to the area east of the Appalachians, the rest of the territory being reserved for American Indian tribes. This soon became a point of issue between the settlers who were intent on expansion and the government in London, which wanted a settled, self-supporting community benefiting British trade. Having disposed of the French threat, the colonists felt confident enough to defy orders that ignored their interests. In particular, they objected to the Navigation Acts which required goods to be carried in British vessels and to various taxes imposed without consultation. 'No taxation without representation' became a rallying cry for disaffected colonists. The centre of opposition was Boston, scene of the infamous 'tea party' when, in 1773, militants destroyed a cargo of East India tea. In 1775 the arrest of rebel ringleaders served only to provoke the 13 colonies to co-operate in further acts of rebellion, including the setting up of a *de facto* government which appointed George Washington commander of American forces.

Independence

The War of Independence (Revolutionary War) was by no means a clear-cut affair. British forces, never more than 50,000 strong, were supported by a powerful body of colonists who remained loyal to the Crown. The war lasted for seven years from 1776 with both sides often getting close to a conclusive victory. The decisive moment came at last with the surrender of Gen. Burgoyne and his 8,000 troops in upper New York state in Oct. 1777, a defeat that persuaded a cautious France to enter the war. Under the peace terms secured in 1783 Britain kept Canada, leaving the new United States with territory stretching from the Atlantic to the Mississippi. A constitution based on democratic principles buttressed by inalienable rights including the ownership of property came into force in 1789. It allowed for a federal government headed by a president and executive, a legislature with a House of Representatives and a Senate, and a judiciary with ultimate authority on constitutional matters exercised by a Supreme Court. The first president was George Washington, who was elected in 1789. In 1800 Washington, D.C. was declared the national capital.

Hostilities with Britain resumed in 1812 amidst accusations that Britain was using the excuse of the Napoleonic wars to harass American shipping and to encourage American Indian resistance to expansion into the Midwest. Most of the fighting took place on the Canadian border where an attempted invasion was decisively repulsed. But Louisiana, having reverted to French rule and subsequently sold to the USA, was secured for the Union. With the exception of Louisiana, other American territories that had once been part of the Spanish empire fell to Mexico. But not for long. In 1836 Texas broke away from Mexico, surviving as an independent republic until 1845 when it was annexed by the USA. This provoked war with Mexico which ended in 1848 with the USA taking over what are now the states of California, Arizona, Colorado, Utah, Nevada and New Mexico. Any temptation there might have been for European involvement in the struggle was removed by the Monroe Doctrine, a declaration by President Monroe that interference from the Old World in matters concerning the western hemisphere would not be tolerated. It was a measure of the growing military and economic self-confidence of the USA that such a warning, delivered in 1823, was taken seriously.

The westward expansion began soon after independence but accelerated with the destruction of American Indian power and the removal of the native population to designated reservations. In 1846 a long-running dispute with Britain confirming US title to Oregon acted as a spur to migration as did the Californian gold rush of 1848. By the 1850s the railway network was bringing people and economic prosperity to the mid-west. The population quadrupled between 1815 to 1860, from 8m. to almost 31m. In 1862 the Homestead Act allocated 160 acres to anyone who was ready to farm it. By 1890 the expansion into the west was largely complete.

Civil War

The transition from a rural society to an industrial power of world importance created tensions, not least between the slave-owning southern states and the rest of the Union which favoured the abolition of slavery. Economic as well as humanitarian factors were in play since the North resented the advantage cheap labour gave to the South. The opposing view held that the South, by now the world's largest cotton producer, depended on slavery for its commercial survival. Mutual antagonism came to a head with the secession of the southern states from the Union in 1860–61 and their formation as a Confederacy. Despite sporadic outbreaks of violence, civil war was not in prospect until Confederate troops fired on the US flag at Fort Sumter. President Abraham Lincoln ordered a blockade of the South. The recruitment of rival armies followed within weeks. The war turned out to be much bloodier than anyone had expected. More American lives were lost in the Civil War than in the two world wars combined. The military balance was maintained until 1863 when the North secured a crushing victory at the Battle of Gettysburg. However, the war continued until April 1865 when Robert E. Lee surrendered to Ulysses S. Grant at Appomattox Courthouse in Virginia. A few days later Lincoln was assassinated, a loss that the southern states had subsequent cause to regret. Contrary to Lincoln's hopes, a generous settlement was now out of the question. Instead of a gradual transition to a new society, the South was rushed into a social revolution. This in turn led to terrorist violence and acts of vengeance against freed slaves. From this carnage emerged the notorious Ku Klux Klan as the standard bearer of lynch law. While the 13th amendment (1865) prohibited slavery, political freedom was denied to the Black community by state-imposed literacy tests and discriminatory property taxes.

That America had interests beyond its own borders was made evident by the Spanish war of 1898 which resulted in the USA becoming the dominant power in the Caribbean. However, the effort to take over in the Philippines came up against Filipino resistance and led to a heavy death toll.

By 1900 the USA rivalled Britain and Germany as the world's dominant power. With vast natural resources and a manufacturing capacity that secured 11% of world trade, it was clear that Europe was soon to lose its grip on world affairs. Ironically, though, it was Europe as the chief supplier of labour that gave the USA the impetus it needed to fulfil its promise. Between 1881 and 1920, 23m. immigrants entered the USA, the largest population movement ever recorded.

Given the heterogeneous background of the American population in the early 20th century it is scarcely surprising that popular opinion was against involvement in the First World War. But events, including German U-boat harassment of American shipping, soon proved that isolationism was not an option. It was not until 1917 that America joined the hostilities but the resurgence of energy created by the arrival of the American Expeditionary Force was critical to the Allied breakthrough.

Post-war America, relatively unscathed by the European conflict, was unquestionably the most powerful nation and as such was able to dictate terms at the Versailles peace conference. But President Wilson's 'fourteen points' which set out a plan for collective security policed by a League of Nations failed to win support in the one country that was critical to its success. The Treaty was rejected by the Senate in 1920 and America retreated once again into isolationism.

A resumption of economic growth was accompanied by a struggle to impose a common set of values, chiefly white and Protestant, on a diverse population. To outsiders the most extraordinary experiment in social engineering was Prohibition, a federally-imposed attempt to outlaw all alcoholic drinks. Whatever gain there was to the health of the nation, the chief beneficiaries were the bosses of organized crime.

New Deal

Dreams of everlasting prosperity were shattered by the 1929 Stock Market Crash. A succession of bank failures was followed by widespread bankruptcies and mass unemployment which sent the economy into a further downward spin. The beginning of the end to the agony came with the election to the presidency of Franklin D. Roosevelt, who pushed through Congress a series of radical measures known collectively as the New Deal, aimed at revitalizing the nation. The abandonment of the gold standard, cheap loans to restart factories and farms and huge investment in public works proved to be the key to recovery. Nonetheless, unemployment remained high until production was boosted by the demands of another world war. In 1935 Roosevelt's social security act provided the bare bones of an American welfare state.

Roosevelt was well aware of the dangers to the USA if the fascist dictators were allowed to triumph, but as in 1914, there was formidable popular opposition to direct involvement. Roosevelt compromised by supplying Britain with much needed armaments on favourable terms. But it was events in Asia rather than in Europe that eventually persuaded America of the need for direct action. Opposition to Japanese expansion into China and southeast Asia, including an oil embargo and a freezing of Japanese assets in the USA, brought a savage retaliation at Pearl Harbor in 1941, when much of the US fleet was destroyed. America declared war on Japan while Germany declared war on America. The US military effort focused initially on the Pacific but after 1942 American forces were also committed to the campaign in north Africa and Europe. With the D-Day landings in June 1944, US troops led the attack on Germany and in May 1945, within a month of Roosevelt's death, Germany surrendered. By then Vice-President Harry Truman had been confirmed as Roosevelt's successor and forced a Japanese surrender by sacrificing Hiroshima and Nagasaki to the atomic bomb.

This time, in the aftermath of war, the USA needed no encouragement to assume the leadership of the free world. The threat of a Soviet takeover in Europe was countered by the formation of NATO in 1949 and the provision of dollar aid under the 1947 Marshall Plan to kick-start European economic recovery. In addition, the Truman doctrine provided a $400m. aid package for the Turkish and Greek governments. The risk of a return to isolationism receded still further when China fell to communism in 1949. In 1950 American troops went to the aid of South Korea when it was invaded by the communist North. Though technically under the aegis of the UN, the campaign was an almost entirely American affair led by Gen. Douglas

MacArthur. When Chinese forces became involved, MacArthur spoke openly of extending the war to the Chinese mainland, a threat countered strongly by President Truman who forced MacArthur's resignation to establish undisputed political control over the military.

A ceasefire was negotiated after Dwight Eisenhower was elected president in 1953. The USA took the lead in setting up the South East Asia Treaty Organization on the same lines as NATO. Eisenhower had a decisive influence on the Suez crisis in 1956 when he refused to support the invasion of Egypt by British, French and Israeli forces. Domestically, he made little headway against a powerful Democratic opposition in both Houses of Congress. His attempts to thaw the Cold War also met with frustration. He handed over the Republican presidential candidacy to his vice-president Richard Nixon, who lost the 1960 election by a slim margin to John F. Kennedy.

Civil Rights

In the early 1960s civil rights were high on the political agenda. The thuggish tactics of Senator Joe McCarthy and the House Committee on Un-American Activities during the previous decade brought into focus basic democratic freedoms guaranteed by the Constitution while growing protests against racial discrimination led to legislation to enforce equality of opportunity in education and employment. The civil rights movement peaked in the early 1960s when the imposition of federal law in the South led to acts of violence against liberal protesters. Foremost among the campaigners for racial equality was Martin Luther King, Jr, who was awarded the Nobel Peace Prize in 1964 and who was assassinated four years later.

Social tensions were exacerbated by the Cold War confrontation. In his first year of office Kennedy was embarrassed by the failed Bay of Pigs invasion when anti-Castro Cubans, trained and supported by the CIA, attempted to overthrow the country's communist regime. The building of the Berlin Wall in Aug. 1961 symbolized a hardening of the Cold War. In 1962 Kennedy had to confront the prospect of the Soviets placing missiles in Cuba. The prospect of world war was only too real until an agreement between the two nations allowed for a withdrawal of the missiles on the condition of a US promise not to invade Cuba. The incident prompted a thawing in East–West relations and in 1963 the USA, UK and USSR signed the Limited Test Ban Treaty which, for the first time, put a brake on the spread of nuclear weapons. Less hopeful was the acceleration of the conflict in Vietnam. Kennedy increased the American military presence in South Vietnam from 700 at the beginning of his term in office to 15,000 to counter the threat of communist domination by the North. Domestically, Kennedy's government pledged $1·2bn. for social and housing programmes.

Kennedy was assassinated in Dallas in Nov. 1963 and his vice-president, Lyndon Johnson, was inaugurated as his successor. Johnson oversaw the implementation of civil rights legislation initiated by the Kennedy administration, epitomized by the Voting Rights Act, and also introduced Medicare (health insurance for the elderly). By 1966 over 350,000 American troops were in Vietnam and by the following year almost 80,000 Americans had been killed or wounded. The public turned against involvement in southeast Asia, not least because increased military expenditure led to a delay in domestic reforms.

Watergate

Johnson decided not to contest the 1968 presidential election. His likely successor for the Democrat nomination was John Kennedy's brother, Bobby, but he was assassinated in June of that year. The Republican nominee, Richard Nixon, won the presidency. With falling support for US involvement in Vietnam, he reduced the number of troops stationed there from 550,000 in 1969 to 30,000 three years later but authorized military operations in North Vietnam, Laos and Cambodia in the hope of forcing North Vietnam to the negotiating table. Elsewhere, he signed the Strategic Arms Limitation Treaty (SALT) with Moscow in 1972 and relaxed trade restrictions against China.

Nixon was re-elected as president in 1973 and shortly afterwards agreed a ceasefire with North Vietnam. However, his second term of office was cut short by the Watergate scandal. The charges against him centred on White House-released taped transcripts of discussions in which Nixon authorized a cover-up of a break-in at the Democratic party headquarters in the Watergate complex, Washington, D.C. in 1972. Threatened with Congressional impeachment, Nixon announced his resignation in Aug. 1974.

Gerald Ford, who replaced Nixon, granted his predecessor a controversial 'full, free and absolute pardon'. Ford lost the 1976 presidential election to Democrat Jimmy Carter. Perceived as a Washington outsider, Carter's often strained relations with Congress and the Senate obstructed his domestic agenda. The economy suffered and by 1980 inflation and unemployment were both running high. Internationally, he secured the neutrality of the Panama Canal and brokered the influential Camp David talks between Egypt and Israel. He also re-established diplomatic ties with China. Henry Kissinger, who was secretary of state for part of Nixon's and all of Carter's years in office, oversaw America's withdrawal from southeast Asia, winning the Nobel Peace Prize jointly with his North Vietnamese counterpart Le Duc Tho in 1974. Attempts at further improving US–Soviet relations were scuppered when the signing of the Strategic Arms Limitation Treaty (SALT II) was postponed because of the Soviet invasion of Afghanistan in 1979. The incursion also led to a US boycott of the 1980 Moscow Olympics. Radical Iranian students stormed the US embassy in Tehran in late 1979 and seized over 50 US hostages. After a year of negotiations, a secret US military rescue mission failed and contributed to Republican Ronald Reagan's landslide victory at the 1980 presidential polls.

Reagan's economic policies, known as 'Reaganomics', redefined American society in the 1980s. In his first year of office he introduced a 25% tax cut for individuals and corporations. He slashed welfare but increased military expenditure. In terms of governmental structure, he was intent on delegating many federal programmes to state and local levels. A recession in 1982 prompted tax increases and set the pattern of boom and bust that characterized his tenure. In 1986 he reduced the number of tax rates, abolishing tax altogether for many low-income earners. In Oct. 1987 the stock market collapsed, losing a third of its value over two months, and by the end of his presidency, Reagan had seen the national debt more than triple to $2·5trn.

End to the Cold War

Relations between the USA and USSR deteriorated in the early 1980s. The shooting down of a South Korean airliner carrying American citizens in 1983 led to a further deployment of US missiles in Western Europe while US proposals for the Strategic Defense Initiative (known as 'Star Wars') added to tensions. In 1983 the USA invaded Grenada, scene of a coup, in a bid to curb Soviet–Cuban influence in the Caribbean. However, relations between the two superpowers improved in the mid-eighties after successful negotiations on nuclear arms limitations. Reagan met Soviet leader Mikhail Gorbachev in 1985 and in 1987 the two leaders signed a treaty in Washington, D.C. agreeing to destroy a range of intermediate-range nuclear weapons.

Reagan's foreign policy elsewhere was unstinting in its protection of US interests. In 1986 he bombed Tripoli after Libya was accused of involvement in the bombing of a nightclub in West Berlin which killed two American servicemen. The following year he became embroiled in the Iran-Contra affair. The CIA was found to have sold arms to Iran to fund anti-communist guerrillas in Nicaragua. Reagan and his deputy, George Bush, were cleared of direct involvement but Reagan was censured for allowing the affair to develop.

Bush took over the presidency in 1989 and continued an active foreign policy. At the end of 1989 he authorized the invasion of Panama to remove Gen. Manuel Antonio Noriega from power. The collapse of the Soviet empire in 1990 extended US economic aid to Eastern Europe and Bush signed a non-aggression pact with Soviet leader Mikhail Gorbachev which effectively ended the Cold War. In 1990–91 Bush led a coalition of European and Arab states to counter the Iraqi invasion of Kuwait. Around 500,000 US troops were stationed in the Persian Gulf and when trade embargoes and diplomacy failed to persuade Iraq to withdraw, Bush authorized a military offensive in Jan. 1991. By the end of Feb. Kuwaiti independence had been restored. Domestically, Bush was badly damaged when he was forced to raise taxes despite his election promise of 'no new taxes'.

The Democrats regained control of the White House with the election of Bill Clinton in 1992. Clinton combined economic recovery at home with an active foreign policy which underlined America's role as the only superpower. He secured the passage of the North American Free Trade Agreement, which created a free-trade zone between the United States, Canada and Mexico, cut the United States budget deficit by 50% in his first term and in his second term authorized America's first tax cut since 1981. Unemployment reached its lowest levels since the late-1960s and in 1998 there was a federal budget surplus for the first time in almost 30 years. His social legislation included anti-crime provisions, the Family and Medical Leave Act, a welfare reform bill and an increase in the minimum wage. He also appointed Madeleine Albright as the first-ever female secretary of state.

On the international scene Clinton brokered talks between the Palestinian leader Yasser Arafat and Israeli Prime Minister Yitzhak Rabin which resulted in limited Palestinian self-rule. He sent peacekeeping troops both to Bosnia and Herzegovina and to Haiti. In 1995 he was instrumental in securing the Dayton accords that offered peace between Yugoslavia, Croatia and Bosnia and Herzegovina. Relations with Vietnam were normalized and diplomatic and trade links with China much improved. He was also an important figure in the formulation of the 1998 Good Friday agreement which sought to reach a peace settlement in Northern Ireland.

Clinton retained a hard-line stance against Iraq, sending forces against Saddam Hussein in 1994, 1996 and 1998. Sudan and Afghanistan were attacked in 1998 having been linked with the al-Qaeda terrorist network held responsible for the bombing of US embassies in Tanzania and Kenya. In 1999 there was a Clinton-led NATO campaign of air strikes against Yugoslavia when the country's leaders refused to end a campaign of violence against ethnic Albanians in Kosovo. Yugoslav president Slobodan Milošević was forced to withdraw his troops and allow an international peacekeeping force in Kosovo.

However, Clinton's second term of office was dominated by scandal. He reached an out-of-court agreement with Paula Jones, a state government employee who had accused him of sexual harassment. Clinton and his wife, Hillary, were also accused of criminal wrongdoing over a land deal in Arkansas, known as Whitewater, though they were both eventually cleared of the charges. Most damagingly, Clinton had an affair with Monica Lewinsky, a White House intern. Having denied the sexual nature of the affair under oath, Clinton was impeached for perjury and obstruction of justice although the Senate trial ended when neither motion gained a simple majority.

In 2000 Clinton's vice-president, Al Gore, lost the presidential election to George W. Bush, son of the earlier President George Bush. Gore was defeated despite winning the popular vote. In 2001 Bush's first budget included a $1·25trn. tax cut. He attracted international criticism in his early months in office for refusing to ratify the Kyoto Agreement on global warming and climate change and for his bid to replace the 1972 Anti-Ballistic Missile Treaty with a new accord allowing for a missile defence system in the United States. Following talks with Russian President Vladimir Putin in June 2001 the two leaders signed an anti-nuclear deal to reduce their respective strategic nuclear warheads by two-thirds over the next ten years.

'War on Terror'

On 11 Sept. 2001 the heart of New York City was devastated after hijackers flew two jet airliners into the World Trade Center. A plane also crashed into the Pentagon, in Washington, D.C., and a fourth hijacked plane crashed near the town of Shanksville, Pennsylvania. The death toll, initially put at 6,700, was eventually lowered to 2,753, with 67 countries reporting dead or missing citizens. Osama bin Laden, the Saudi dissident leader of the al-Qaeda terrorist network and believed to be living in Afghanistan at the invitation of the ruling Taliban, immediately became the chief suspect and military action against Afghanistan followed, with air strikes beginning on 7 Oct. 2001. Despite the UN establishing a fragile multi-party government in Afghanistan, the USA continues to carry out special missions against Taliban and al-Qaeda targets.

In early 2002 Bush declared North Korea, Iran and Iraq 'an axis of evil' and by Sept. 2002 was pressing the UN to act against Iraq. Bush's foreign policy was played out against a background of domestic recession. On 20 March 2003 US forces, supported by the UK, launched attacks on Iraq, and initiated a war aimed at 'liberating Iraq'. On 9 April 2003 American forces took control of central Baghdad, effectively bringing an end to Saddam Hussein's rule. In Nov. 2004 Bush won a second term as president, which was dominated by continuing military engagement in Iraq and Afghanistan and by the collapse in 2007 of the US sub-prime mortgage sector. He was succeeded by the Democrat Barack Obama, who won the election of 2008 to become the country's first African American president.

Obama took office with the global financial system in turmoil. In March 2010 he oversaw the passage of landmark legislation reforming health care insurance. In May 2011 he ordered the military strike that led to the death of Osama bin Laden in Pakistan. He won a second term with victory in the 2012 presidential election. From June 2013 his administration was undermined by revelations of controversial widespread surveillance of US citizens and foreign allies by the National Security Agency. In Oct. 2013 the government shut down for 16 days following Congress's refusal to sign off the budget.

From 2014 US air strikes targeted Islamic State jihadists in Iraq and Syria. Also that year social unrest in Ferguson, Missouri, sparked a national debate on relations between the police and the Black community. Tensions continued in 2015 and 2016 amid a number of high-profile incidents in which unarmed Black men were shot and killed by police. A protest in Dallas in July 2016 culminated in the deaths of five police officers.

In July 2015 the USA sanctioned a multinational deal with Iran, curbing nuclear weapons development by Tehran. In the same month, the USA and Cuba normalized their diplomatic relations. 2016 was dominated by the presidential election in Nov., when Republican candidate Donald Trump defeated Democrat Hillary Clinton. Trump campaigned on a divisive populist agenda of protectionist economic policies and tighter border controls. After taking office in Jan. 2017, his early tenure was dominated by legal challenges to executive orders he had signed imposing a travel ban on several Muslim-majority nations. He also introduced new regulations governing visa applications and trade between US citizens and Cuban firms, confirming a renewed cooling in relations with its island neighbour.

Territory and Population

The United States is bounded in the north by Canada, east by the North Atlantic, south by the Gulf of Mexico and Mexico, and west by the North Pacific Ocean. The area of the 50 states of the USA plus the District of Columbia is 3,796,742 sq. miles (9,833,517 sq. km), of which 3,531,905 sq. miles (9,147,593 sq. km) are land and 264,837 sq. miles (685,924 sq. km) are water (comprising Great Lakes, inland and coastal water).

Population at each census from 1790 to 2010 (including Alaska and Hawaii from 1960). Figures do not include Puerto Rico, Guam, American Samoa or other Pacific islands, or the US population abroad. Residents of Indian reservations not included before 1890.

	White	Black	Other races	Total
1790	3,172,464	757,208	—	3,929,672
1800	4,306,446	1,002,037	—	5,308,483
1810	5,862,073	1,377,808	—	7,239,881
1820	7,866,797	1,771,562	—	9,638,359
1830	10,537,378	2,328,642	—	12,866,020
1840	14,195,805	2,873,648	—	17,069,453
1850	19,553,068	3,638,808	—	23,191,876
1860	26,922,537	4,441,830	78,954	31,443,321
1870	34,337,292	5,392,172	88,985	39,818,449
1880	43,402,970	6,580,793	172,020	50,155,783
1890	55,101,258	7,488,676	357,780	62,947,714
1900	66,868,508	8,834,395	509,265	76,212,168
1910	81,812,405	9,828,667	587,459	92,228,531
1920	94,903,540	10,463,607	654,421	106,021,568
1930	110,395,753	11,891,842	915,065	123,202,660
1940	118,357,831	12,865,914	941,384	132,165,129
1950	135,149,629	15,044,937	1,131,232	151,325,798
1960	158,831,732	18,871,831	1,619,612	179,323,175
1970	177,748,975	22,580,289	2,882,662	203,211,926
1980	188,371,622	26,495,025	11,679,158	226,545,805
1990	199,686,070	29,986,060	19,037,743	248,709,873
2000[1]	211,460,626	34,658,190	35,303,090	281,421,906
2010[1]	223,553,265	38,929,319	46,262,954	308,745,538

[1]'White' refers to the White-alone population, 'Black' to the Black-alone population and 'Other races' to the population in all the remaining race groups, including those reporting two or more races.

The mid-year population estimate for 2018 was 327,167,434.

The 2010 census population of 308,745,538 represented an increase of 9·7% since 2000 (the smallest percentage increase between ten-yearly US censuses since the Second World War). Minorities accounted for 92% of the growth. There were 156,964,212 females at the 2010 census, or 50·8% of the total population.

The UN gives a projected population for 2020 of 331·43m.

2010 density, 33·8 per sq. km (87·4 per sq. mile). Urban population (persons living in places with at least 2,500 inhabitants) at the 2010 census was 249,253,271 (80·7%); rural, 59,492,267. In 2000 it was 79·0%; in 1990, 75·2%; in 1980, 73·7%; in 1970, 73·6%.

Sex distribution by race of the population in 2013:

	Males	Females
White	121,636,000	123,957,000
Black or African American	19,946,000	21,768,000
American Indian and Alaska Native	1,974,000	1,935,000
Asian	8,000,000	8,804,000
Native Hawaiian and Other Pacific Islander	369,000	356,000
Two or More Races	3,817,000	3,936,000
Total	*155,741,000*	*160,756,000*

Alongside these racial groups, and applicable to all of them, a category of 'Hispanic origin' comprised 50,477,594 persons in 2010 (including 31,798,258 of Mexican ancestry), up 15,171,776 from 35,305,818 in 2000. Hispanics are now the largest ethnic minority in the USA. The rapid growth in the Hispanic and Asian populations led the US Census Bureau to suggest in 2014 that by around 2044 Whites will constitute less than half the total population.

Among ten-year age groups the 45–54 age group contained the most people according to the 2010 census, with a total of 45,006,716 (14·6% of the population). At the 2000 census the 35–44 age group had the most people.

At the 2010 census there were 116,716,292 households, up from 105,480,101 in 2000. There were 31·7m. single-person households in 2010 representing 27% of all households, up from 9% in 1950.

There were 53,364 people aged 100 or over according to the 2010 census, compared to 50,454 in 2000. Females accounted for 82·8% of the centenarians in 2010, up from 80·1% in 2000.

The USA does not have an official language, although English has been provided with official status in 30 states. A survey covering the period 2009–13 showed that 60·4m. persons five years and over spoke a language other than English in the home, including Spanish or Spanish Creole by 37·5m.; Chinese by 2·9m.; French or French Creole by 2·0m.; Tagalog (a Filipino language) by 1·6m.; Vietnamese by 1·4m.; Korean by 1·1m.; and German by 1·1m. 79·3% of the population has English as its mother tongue.

The following table includes population statistics, the year in which each of the original 13 states (Connecticut, Delaware, Georgia, Maryland, Massachusetts, New Hampshire, New Jersey, New York, North Carolina, Pennsylvania, Rhode Island, South Carolina, Virginia) ratified the constitution, and the year when each of the other states was admitted into the Union. Two-letter abbreviated postal codes for use in addresses are shown in brackets.

The USA is divided into four geographic regions comprised of nine divisions. These are, with their 2010 census populations: Northeast (comprised of the New England and Middle Atlantic divisions), 53,317,240; Midwest (East North Central, West North Central), 66,927,001; South (South Atlantic, East South Central, West South Central), 114,555,744; West (Mountain, Pacific), 71,945,553.

Geographic divisions and states		*Land area: sq. miles, 2010*	*Census population, 1 April 2010*	*Pop. per sq. mile, 2010*
United States		3,531,905[1]	308,745,538	87·4
New England		*62,689*	*14,444,865*	*230·4*
Connecticut (1788)	(CT)	4,842	3,574,097	738·1
Maine (1820)	(ME)	30,843	1,328,361	43·1
Massachusetts (1788)	(MA)	7,800	6,547,629	839·4
New Hampshire (1788)	(NH)	8,953	1,316,470	147·0
Rhode Island (1790)	(RI)	1,034	1,052,567	1,018·1
Vermont (1791)	(VT)	9,217	625,741	67·9
Middle Atlantic		*99,223*	*40,872,375*	*411·9*
New Jersey (1787)	(NJ)	7,354	8,791,894	1,195·5

(continued)

Geographic divisions and states		Land area: sq. miles, 2010	Census population, 1 April 2010	Pop. per sq. mile, 2010
New York (1788)	(NY)	47,126	19,378,102	411·2
Pennsylvania (1787)	(PA)	44,743	12,702,379	283·9
East North Central		242,903	46,421,564	191·1
Illinois (1818)	(IL)	55,519	12,830,632	231·1
Indiana (1816)	(IN)	35,826	6,483,802	181·0
Michigan (1837)	(MI)	56,539	9,883,640	174·8
Ohio (1803)	(OH)	40,861	11,536,504	282·3
Wisconsin (1848)	(WI)	54,158	5,686,986	105·0
West North Central		507,621	20,505,437	40·4
Iowa (1846)	(IA)	55,857	3,046,355	54·5
Kansas (1861)	(KS)	81,759	2,853,118	34·9
Minnesota (1858)	(MN)	79,627	5,303,925	66·6
Missouri (1821)	(MO)	68,742	5,988,927	87·1
Nebraska (1867)	(NE)	76,824	1,826,341	23·8
North Dakota (1889)	(ND)	69,001	672,591	9·7
South Dakota (1889)	(SD)	75,811	814,180	10·7
South Atlantic		265,062	59,777,037	225·5
Delaware (1787)	(DE)	1,949	897,934	460·8
Dist. of Columbia (1791)[2]	(DC)	61	601,723	9,856·2
Florida (1845)	(FL)	53,625	18,801,310	350·6
Georgia (1788)	(GA)	57,513	9,687,653	168·4
Maryland (1788)	(MD)	9,707	5,773,552	594·8
North Carolina (1789)	(NC)	48,618	9,535,483	196·1
South Carolina (1788)	(SC)	30,061	4,625,364	153·9
Virginia (1788)	(VA)	39,490	8,001,024	202·6
West Virginia (1863)	(WV)	24,038	1,852,994	77·1
East South Central		178,289	18,432,505	103·4
Alabama (1819)	(AL)	50,645	4,779,736	94·4
Kentucky (1792)	(KY)	39,486	4,339,367	109·9
Mississippi (1817)	(MS)	46,923	2,967,297	63·2
Tennessee (1796)	(TN)	41,235	6,346,105	153·9
West South Central		425,066	36,346,202	85·5
Arkansas (1836)	(AR)	52,035	2,915,918	56·0
Louisiana (1812)	(LA)	43,204	4,533,372	104·9
Oklahoma (1907)	(OK)	68,595	3,751,351	54·7
Texas (1845)	(TX)	261,232	25,145,561	96·3
Mountain		855,767	22,065,451	25·8
Arizona (1912)	(AZ)	113,594	6,392,017	56·3

(continued)

Geographic divisions and states		Land area: sq. miles, 2010	Census population, 1 April 2010	Pop. per sq. mile, 2010
Colorado (1876)	(CO)	103,642	5,029,196	48·5
Idaho (1890)	(ID)	82,643	1,567,582	19·0
Montana (1889)	(MT)	145,546	989,415	6·8
Nevada (1864)	(NV)	109,781	2,700,551	24·6
New Mexico (1912)	(NM)	121,298	2,059,179	17·0
Utah (1896)	(UT)	82,170	2,763,885	33·6
Wyoming (1890)	(WY)	97,093	563,626	5·8
Pacific		895,287	49,880,102	55·7
Alaska (1959)	(AK)	570,641	710,231	1·2
California (1850)	(CA)	155,779	37,253,956	239·1
Hawaii (1960)	(HI)	6,423	1,360,301	211·8
Oregon (1859)	(OR)	95,988	3,831,074	39·9
Washington (1889)	(WA)	66,456	6,724,540	101·2
Outlying Territories, total		4,032	4,100,954	1,017·1
American Samoa		76	55,519	730·5
Guam		210	159,358	758·8
Johnston Atoll[3]		1	0[3]	0
Midway Islands[3]		2	0[3]	0
Northern Marianas		182	53,883	296·1
Puerto Rico		3,424	3,725,789	1,088·1
Virgin Islands		134	106,405	794·1
Wake Island[3]		3	0[3]	0

[1]Overall figure for area does not equal sum of totals for individual states and divisions because of rounding.

[2]District of Columbia selected as site of national government in 1791.

[3]No permanent residents. There may be occasional visits from military and scientific personnel.

In 2016 there were 43,070,000 foreign-born persons, representing 13·5% of the population; of these 22·45m. were from Latin America (including 11·70m. from Mexico), 12·83m. from Asia and 4·52m. from Europe. The percentage of the population that is foreign-born has more than doubled since 1980. In fiscal year 2015 a total of 1,051,031 persons obtained legal permanent resident status (1,266,129 in fiscal year 2006 and a record 1,826,595 in 1991).

Population of cities with over 100,000 inhabitants at the censuses of 2000 and 2010:

Cities	Census 2000	Census 2010
New York, NY	8,008,278	8,175,133
Los Angeles, CA	3,694,820	3,792,621
Chicago, IL	2,896,016	2,695,598
Houston, TX	1,953,631	2,099,451

(continued)

Cities	Census 2000	Census 2010
Philadelphia, PA	1,517,550	1,526,006
Phoenix, AZ	1,321,045	1,445,632
San Antonio, TX	1,144,646	1,327,407
San Diego, CA	1,223,400	1,307,402
Dallas, TX	1,188,580	1,197,816
San Jose, CA	894,943	945,942
Indianapolis, IN	791,926	829,718
Jacksonville, FL	735,617	821,784
San Francisco, CA	776,733	805,235
Austin, TX	656,562	790,390
Columbus, OH	711,470	787,033
Fort Worth, TX	534,694	741,206
Louisville/Jefferson County, KY	256,231	741,096
Charlotte, NC	540,828	731,424
Detroit, MI	951,270	713,777
El Paso, TX	563,662	649,121
Memphis, TN	650,100	646,889
Nashville-Davidson, TN	569,891	626,681
Baltimore, MD	651,154	620,961
Boston, MA	589,141	617,594
Seattle, WA	563,374	608,660
Washington, DC	572,059	601,723
Denver, CO	554,636	600,158
Milwaukee, WI	596,974	594,833
Portland, OR	529,121	583,776
Las Vegas, NV	478,434	583,756
Oklahoma City, OK	506,132	579,999
Albuquerque, NM	448,607	545,852
Tucson, AZ	486,699	520,116
Fresno, CA	427,652	494,665
Sacramento, CA	407,018	466,488
Long Beach, CA	461,522	462,257
Kansas City, MO	441,545	459,787
Mesa, AZ	396,375	439,041
Virginia Beach, VA	425,257	437,994
Atlanta, GA	416,474	420,003
Colorado Springs, CO	360,890	416,427
Omaha, NE	390,007	408,958
Raleigh, NC	276,093	403,892
Miami, FL	362,470	399,457
Cleveland, OH	478,403	396,815
Tulsa, OK	393,049	391,906
Oakland, CA	399,484	390,724
Minneapolis, MN	382,618	382,578
Wichita, KS	344,284	382,368
Arlington, TX	332,969	365,438
Bakersfield, CA	247,057	347,483
New Orleans, LA	484,674	343,829
Urban Honolulu, HI[1, 2]	—	337,256
Anaheim, CA	328,014	336,265
Tampa, FL	303,447	335,709
Aurora, CO	276,393	325,078
Santa Ana, CA	337,977	324,528
St Louis, MO	348,189	319,294
Pittsburgh, PA	334,563	305,704
Corpus Christi, TX	277,454	305,215
Riverside, CA	255,166	303,871
Cincinnati, OH	331,285	296,943

(continued)

Cities	Census 2000	Census 2010
Lexington-Fayette, KY	260,512	295,803
Anchorage, AK[3]	260,283	291,826
Stockton, CA	243,771	291,707
Toledo, OH	313,619	287,208
St Paul, MN	287,151	285,068
Newark, NJ	273,546	277,140
Greensboro, NC	223,891	269,666
Buffalo, NY	292,648	261,310
Plano, TX	222,030	259,841
Lincoln, NE	225,581	258,379
Henderson, NV	175,381	257,729
Fort Wayne, IN	205,727	253,691
Jersey City, NJ	240,055	247,597
St Petersburg, FL	248,232	244,769
Chula Vista, CA	173,556	243,916
Norfolk, VA	234,403	242,803
Orlando, FL	185,951	238,300
Chandler, AZ	176,581	236,123
Laredo, TX	176,576	236,091
Madison, WI	208,054	233,209
Winston-Salem, NC	185,776	229,617
Lubbock, TX	199,564	229,573
Baton Rouge, LA	227,818	229,493
Durham, NC	187,035	228,330
Garland, TX	215,768	226,876
Glendale, AZ	218,812	226,721
Reno, NV	180,480	225,221
Hialeah, FL	226,419	224,669
Paradise, NV[1]	186,070	223,167
Chesapeake, VA	199,184	222,209
Scottsdale, AZ	202,705	217,385
North Las Vegas, NV	115,488	216,961
Irving, TX	191,615	216,290
Fremont, CA	203,413	214,089
Irvine, CA	143,072	212,375
Birmingham, AL	242,820	212,237
Rochester, NY	219,773	210,565
San Bernardino, CA	185,401	209,924
Spokane, WA	195,629	208,916
Gilbert, AZ[4]	109,697	208,453
Arlington, VA[1]	189,453	207,627
Montgomery, AL	201,568	205,764
Boise City, ID	185,787	205,671
Richmond, VA	197,790	204,214
Des Moines, IA	198,682	203,433
Modesto, CA	188,856	201,165
Fayetteville, NC	121,015	200,564
Augusta-Richmond County, GA	199,775	200,549
Shreveport, LA	200,145	199,311
Akron, OH	217,074	199,110
Tacoma, WA	193,556	198,397
Aurora, IL	142,990	197,899
Oxnard, CA	170,358	197,899
Fontana, CA	128,929	196,069
Yonkers, NY	196,086	195,976
Mobile, AL	198,915	195,111
Little Rock, AR	183,133	193,524
Moreno Valley, CA	142,381	193,365

(continued)

Cities	Census 2000	Census 2010	Cities	Census 2000	Census 2010
Glendale, CA	194,973	191,719	Sunnyvale, CA	131,760	140,081
Amarillo, TX	173,627	190,695	Alexandria, VA	128,283	139,966
Huntington Beach, CA	189,594	189,992	Mesquite, TX	124,523	139,824
Columbus, GA	186,291	189,885	Metairie, LA[1]	146,136	138,481
Sunrise Manor, NV[1]	156,120	189,372	Hampton, VA	146,437	137,436
Grand Rapids, MI	197,800	188,040	Pasadena, CA	133,936	137,122
Salt Lake City, UT	181,743	186,440	Orange, CA	128,821	136,416
Tallahassee, FL	150,624	181,376	Savannah, GA	131,510	136,286
Worcester, MA	172,648	181,045	Cary, NC[4]	94,536	135,234
Newport News, VA	180,150	180,719	Fullerton, CA	126,003	135,161
Huntsville, AL	158,216	180,105	Warren, MI	138,247	134,056
Knoxville, TN	173,890	178,874	Clarksville, TN	103,445	132,929
Spring Valley, NV[1]	117,390	178,395	McKinney, TX	54,369	131,117
Providence, RI	173,618	178,042	McAllen, TX	106,414	129,877
Santa Clarita, CA	151,088	176,320	New Haven, CT	123,626	129,779
Grand Prairie, TX	127,427	175,396	Sterling Heights, MI	124,471	129,699
Brownsville, TX	139,722	175,023	West Valley City, UT	108,896	129,480
Jackson, MS	184,256	173,514	Columbia, SC	116,278	129,272
Overland Park, KS	149,080	173,372	Killeen, TX	86,911	127,921
Garden Grove, CA	165,196	170,883	Topeka, KS	122,377	127,473
Santa Rosa, CA	147,595	167,815	Thousand Oaks, CA	117,005	126,683
Chattanooga, TN	155,554	167,674	East Los Angeles, CA[1]	124,283	126,496
Oceanside, CA	161,029	167,086	Cedar Rapids, IA	120,758	126,326
Fort Lauderdale, FL	152,397	165,521	Olathe, KS	92,962	125,872
Rancho Cucamonga, CA	127,743	165,269	Elizabeth, NJ	120,568	124,969
Port St Lucie, FL	88,769	164,603	Waco, TX	113,726	124,805
Ontario, CA	158,007	163,924	Hartford, CT	121,578	124,775
Vancouver, WA	143,560	161,791	Visalia, CA	91,565	124,442
Tempe, AZ	158,625	161,719	Gainesville, FL	95,447	124,354
Springfield, MO	151,580	159,498	Simi Valley, CA	111,351	124,237
Lancaster, CA	118,718	156,633	Stamford, CT	117,083	122,643
Eugene, OR	137,893	156,185	Bellevue, WA	109,569	122,363
Pembroke Pines, FL	137,427	154,750	Concord, CA	121,780	122,067
Salem, OR	136,924	154,637	Miramar, FL	72,739	122,041
Cape Coral, FL	102,286	154,305	Coral Springs, FL	117,549	121,096
Peoria, AZ	108,364	154,065	Lafayette, LA	110,257	120,263
Sioux Falls, SD	123,975	153,888	Charleston, SC	96,650	120,083
Springfield, MA	152,082	153,060	Carrollton, TX	109,576	119,097
Elk Grove, CA[2]	—	153,015	Roseville, CA	79,921	118,788
Rockford, IL	150,115	152,871	Thornton, CO	82,384	118,772
Palmdale, CA	116,670	152,750	Beaumont, TX	113,866	118,296
Corona, CA	124,966	152,374	Allentown, PA	106,632	118,032
Salinas, CA	151,060	150,441	Surprise, AZ	30,848	117,517
Pomona, CA	149,473	149,058	Evansville, IN	121,582	117,429
Pasadena, TX	141,674	149,043	Abilene, TX	115,930	117,063
Joliet, IL	106,221	147,433	Frisco, TX	33,714	116,989
Paterson, NJ	149,222	146,199	Independence, MO	113,288	116,830
Kansas City, KS	146,866	145,786	Athens-Clarke County, GA	101,489	116,714
Torrance, CA	137,946	145,438	Santa Clara, CA	102,361	116,468
Syracuse, NY	147,306	145,170	Springfield, IL	111,454	116,250
Bridgeport, CT	139,529	144,229	Vallejo, CA	116,760	115,942
Hayward, CA	140,030	144,186	Victorville, CA	64,029	115,903
Fort Collins, CO	118,652	143,986	Peoria, IL	112,936	115,007
Escondido, CA	133,559	143,911	Lansing, MI	119,128	114,297
Lakewood, CO	144,126	142,980	Ann Arbor, MI	114,024	113,934
Naperville, IL	128,358	141,853	El Monte, CA	115,965	113,475
Dayton, OH	166,179	141,527	Denton, TX	80,537	113,383
Hollywood, FL	139,357	140,768	Berkeley, CA	102,743	112,580

(*continued*)   (*continued*)

Cities	Census 2000	Census 2010
Provo, UT	105,166	112,488
Downey, CA	107,323	111,772
Midland, TX	94,996	111,147
Norman, OK	95,694	110,925
Waterbury, CT	107,271	110,366
Costa Mesa, CA	108,724	109,960
Inglewood, CA	112,580	109,673
Manchester, NH	107,006	109,565
Murfreesboro, TN	68,816	108,755
Columbia, MO	84,531	108,500
Enterprise, NV[1]	14,676	108,481
Elgin, IL	94,487	108,188
Clearwater, FL	108,787	107,685
Miami Gardens, FL[2]	—	107,167
Rochester, MN	85,806	106,769
Pueblo, CO	102,121	106,595
Lowell, MA	105,167	106,519
Wilmington, NC	75,838	106,476
Arvada, CO	102,153	106,433
San Buenaventura (Ventura), CA	100,916	106,433
Westminster, CO	100,940	106,114
West Covina, CA	105,080	106,098
Gresham, OR	90,205	105,594
Fargo, ND	90,599	105,549
Norwalk, CA	103,298	105,549
Carlsbad, CA	78,247	105,328
Fairfield, CA	96,178	105,321
Cambridge, MA	101,355	105,162
Wichita Falls, TX	104,197	104,553
High Point, NC	85,839	104,371
Billings, MT	89,847	104,170
Green Bay, WI	102,313	104,057
West Jordan, UT	68,336	103,712
Richmond, CA	99,216	103,701
Brandon, FL[1]	77,895	103,483
Murrieta, CA	44,282	103,466
Burbank, CA	100,316	103,340
Palm Bay, FL	79,413	103,190
Everett, WA	91,488	103,019
Flint, MI	124,943	102,434
Antioch, CA	90,532	102,372
Erie, PA	103,717	101,786
South Bend, IN	107,789	101,168
Daly City, CA	103,621	101,123
Centennial, CO[2]	—	100,377

[1]Designated by the United States Census Bureau as a CDP (census designated place) and not incorporated as a city.
[2]Incorporated since the 2000 census.
[3]Officially designated as a Municipality.
[4]Officially designated as a Town.

Immigration and naturalization

The Immigration and Nationality Act, as amended, provides for the numerical limitation of most immigration. The Immigration Act of 1990 established major revisions in the numerical limits and preference system regulating legal immigration. The numerical limits are imposed on visas issued and not admissions. The maximum number of visas allowed to be issued under the preference categories in fiscal year 2012 was 370,951: 226,000 for family-sponsored immigrants and 144,951 for employment-based immigrants. Within the overall limitations the per-country limit for independent countries is set to 7% of the total family and employment limits, while dependent areas are limited to 2% of the total. Immigrants not subject to any numerical limitation are spouses, children, and parents of US citizens who are 21 years of age or older; certain former US citizens; ministers of religion; certain long-term US government employees; refugees and asylum-seekers adjusting to immigrant status; and certain other groups of immigrants.

Immigrants obtaining lawful permanent residence, by country or region of birth, for fiscal years:

Country or region of birth	Immigrants admitted			
	2012	2013	2014	2015
All countries	1,031,631	990,553	1,016,518	1,051,031
Europe	*81,671*	*86,556*	*83,266*	*85,803*
Germany	5,812	6,032	5,584	5,436
Poland	6,300	6,430	5,689	5,275
Russia	9,969	9,753	9,079	8,799
Ukraine	7,642	8,193	7,752	7,987
UK	12,014	12,984	12,225	12,592
Other	39,934	43,164	42,937	45,714
Asia	*429,599*	*400,548*	*430,508*	*419,297*
Afghanistan	1,617	2,196	10,527	8,328
Bangladesh	14,705	12,099	14,645	13,570
Bhutan	10,198	8,954	7,298	6,325
China (mainland)	81,784	71,798	76,089	74,558
India	66,434	68,458	77,908	64,116
Iran	12,916	12,863	11,615	13,114
Iraq	20,369	9,552	19,153	21,107
Japan	6,061	5,925	5,545	5,395
Korea (South)	20,846	23,166	20,423	17,138
Myanmar	17,383	12,565	11,144	12,808
Nepal	11,312	13,046	12,357	12,926
Pakistan	14,740	13,251	18,612	18,057
Philippines	57,327	54,446	49,996	56,478
Taiwan	5,331	5,385	4,697	4,888
Thailand	9,459	7,583	6,197	7,502
Uzbekistan	4,726	4,382	5,194	3,977
Vietnam	28,304	27,101	30,283	30,832
Other	46,087	47,778	48,825	48,178
North and Central America	*327,771*	*315,660*	*324,354*	*366,126*
Canada	12,932	13,181	11,586	12,673
Cuba	32,820	32,219	46,679	54,396
Dominican Republic	41,566	41,311	44,577	50,610
El Salvador	16,256	18,260	19,273	19,487
Guatemala	10,341	10,224	10,238	11,773
Haiti	22,818	20,351	15,274	16,967
Honduras	6,884	8,898	8,156	9,274
Jamaica	20,705	19,400	19,026	17,642
Mexico	146,406	135,028	134,052	158,619
Other	17,043	16,788	15,493	14,685
South America	*79,401*	*80,945*	*73,715*	*72,309*
Brazil	11,441	11,033	10,429	11,424
Colombia	20,931	21,131	18,175	17,316
Ecuador	9,342	10,591	10,960	10,187
Guyana	5,683	5,897	6,267	5,543
Peru	12,609	12,564	10,606	10,148
Venezuela	9,387	9,572	8,427	9,144
Other	10,008	10,157	8,851	8,547
Africa	*107,241*	*98,304*	*98,413*	*101,415*

(continued)

Country or region of birth	Immigrants admitted			
	2012	2013	2014	2015
Egypt	8,988	10,294	11,477	12,085
Ethiopia	14,544	13,097	12,300	11,394
Ghana	10,592	10,265	7,115	6,186
Kenya	7,043	6,123	5,884	5,602
Liberia	4,109	3,334	3,874	3,795
Nigeria	13,575	13,840	12,828	11,542
Somalia	5,204	3,764	5,190	6,796
Other	43,186	37,587	39,745	44,015
Unknown	1,206	3,263	1,150	677

The total number of immigrants admitted from 1820 to 2017 was 83,861,792, with most coming from Mexico, Germany and Italy. One of the consequences of the economic downturn of the late 2000s is that immigration from Mexico declined considerably and the net migration flow also slowed. In 2013 for the first time Mexico was overtaken as the leading sending country for immigrants to the USA, with more coming from both China and India. Illegal immigration remains a concern. In the 2013 fiscal year the USA deported some 370,000 undocumented immigrants. In the 2014 fiscal year 67,339 unaccompanied children were detained crossing the US–Mexico border (of which more came from Honduras, Guatemala and El Salvador than Mexico itself), up from 38,045 in the previous fiscal year and 24,120 in the 2012 fiscal year. The number of immigrants admitted for legal permanent residence in the United States in fiscal year 2017 was 1,127,627. Included in this total were 578,081 new arrivals who entered the country with legal permanent resident status. The remaining 549,546 were status adjusters, who had arrived earlier as non-immigrants (including students and temporary workers). The USA has by far the largest annual net gain in migrants of any country. It also receives the most asylum seekers on an annual basis.

A total of 707,265 persons were naturalized in fiscal year 2017 (including 118,559 persons born in Mexico).

The refugee admissions ceiling for fiscal year 2017 was fixed by then President Obama at 110,000 (the highest total since 1995). For the fiscal year 2018, President Trump—who campaigned for the presidency on a platform of immigration control—requested a cap of 45,000.

Social Statistics

Figures from Alaska and Hawaii are only shown from 1960 onwards.

	Live births	Deaths	Marriages	Divorces	Deaths under 1 year
1900	—	343,217	709,000	56,000	—
1910	2,777,000	696,856	948,000	83,000	—
1920	2,950,000	1,118,070	1,274,476	170,505	170,911
1930	2,618,000	1,327,240	1,126,856	195,961	143,201
1940	2,559,000	1,417,269	1,595,879	264,000	110,984
1950	3,632,000	1,452,454	1,667,231	385,144	103,825
1960	4,257,850	1,711,982	1,523,000	393,000	110,873
1970	3,731,386	1,921,031	2,158,802	708,000	74,667
1980	3,612,258	1,989,841	2,390,252	1,189,000	45,526
1990	4,158,212	2,148,463	2,443,489	1,182,000	38,351
2000	4,058,814	2,403,351	2,315,000	—	28,035
2001	4,025,933	2,416,425	2,326,000	—	27,568
2002	4,021,726	2,443,387	2,290,000	—	28,034
2003	4,089,950	2,448,288	2,245,000	—	28,025
2004	4,112,052	2,397,615	2,279,000	—	27,936
2005	4,138,349	2,448,017	2,249,000	—	28,440
2006	4,265,555	2,426,264	2,193,000[1]	—	28,527
2007	4,316,233	2,432,712	2,197,000	—	29,138
2008	4,247,694	2,471,984	2,157,000	—	28,059

(continued)

	Live births	Deaths	Marriages	Divorces	Deaths under 1 year
2009	4,130,665	2,437,163	2,080,000	—	26,412
2010	3,999,386	2,468,435	2,096,000	—	24,586
2011	3,953,590	2,515,458	2,118,000	—	23,985
2012	3,952,841	2,543,279	2,131,000	—	23,629
2013	3,932,181	2,596,993	2,081,301[2]	—	23,440
2014	3,988,076	2,626,418	2,140,272[2]	—	23,515
2015	3,978,497	2,712,630	2,221,579	—	23,455
2015	3,978,497	2,712,630	2,221,579	—	23,455
2016	3,945,875	2,744,248	2,251,411	—	23,161
2017	3,855,500	2,813,503	2,236,496[3]	—	22,335

[1]Excluding Louisiana.
[2]Excluding Georgia.
[3]Provisional.

The number of births in 2017 was the lowest since 1987, while the number of deaths in 2017 was the highest in a single year ever recorded.

Rates (per 1,000 population):

	Birth	Death	Marriage
2000	14·4	8·5	8·2
2001	14·1	8·5	8·2
2002	13·9	8·5	8·0
2003	14·1	8·4	7·7
2004	14·0	8·2	7·8
2005	14·0	8·3	7·6
2006	14·2	8·1	7·5[1]
2007	14·3	8·0	7·3
2008	14·0	8·1	7·1
2009	13·5	7·9	6·8
2010	13·0	8·0	6·8
2011	12·7	8·1	6·8
2012	12·6	8·1	6·8
2013	12·4	8·2	6·8[2]
2014	12·5	8·2	6·9[2]
2015	12·4	8·5	6·9
2016	12·2	8·5	7·0
2017	11·8	8·6	6·9[3]

[1]Excluding Louisiana. [2]Excluding Georgia. [3]Provisional.

The birth rate in 2017 was the lowest ever recorded. Although divorce figures are not available since 1997 as not all states maintain complete statistics, it is estimated that the rate fell from 4·3 per 1,000 population in 1997 to 3·1 per 1,000 in 2015 (the lowest rate since 1968). Rate of natural increase per 1,000 population: 5·9 in 2000; 5·0 in 2010; 3·2 in 2017. Population growth rate, 2003–13, 0·9%.

Even though the marriage rate shows a gradual decline, it remains much higher than in most other industrial countries. In 2017 the median age at first marriage was 29·5 for males and 27·4 for females. In 2014, 7% of Black men were married to a White woman and 4% of Black women were married to a White man. Following a Supreme Court ruling, same-sex marriage became legal nationwide in June 2015.

The number of births to unmarried women in 2014 was 1,604,870 (40·2% of all births), compared to 665,747 in 1980 and a peak of 1,726,566 in 2008. The rate of births to teenagers was 22·3 per 1,000 women in 2015 (the lowest on record); it has halved since 2001. The number of babies born to women aged 15–19 was 249,078 in 2014, down from 409,802 in 2009 and the fewest reported since the end of the Second World War. Between 1970 and 2009 the proportion of all births outside of marriage rose from 11% to 41% with increases in all age groups (although it has fallen slightly in the meantime—the percentage of all births to unmarried women was 40·3% in 2015). The birth rate for unmarried women fell for the seventh consecutive year to 43·4 per 1,000 women aged 15–44 in 2015. In 2016, 31·3% of children under 18 years lived in households with only one parent or neither parent.

Infant mortality rates, per 1,000 live births: 29·2 in 1950; 12·9 in 1980; 5·9 in 2016. Fertility rate, 2016, 1·8 births per woman (the lowest since the mid-1980s).

There were a reported 926,190 abortions in 2014, down from a peak in 1990 of an estimated 1,608,600. The number of abortions per 1,000 women aged 15–44 in 2014 was 14·6, the lowest since 1972.

Expectation of life, 1970: males, 67·1 years; females, 74·7 years. 2016: males, 76·1 years; females, 81·1 years. The overall figure for 2016 of 78·6 years represented the second consecutive fall (from 78·7 years in 2015 and 78·9 years in 2014).

Numbers of deaths by principal causes, 2014 (and as a percentage of all deaths): heart disease, 614,348 (23·4%); cancer, 591,699 (22·5%); chronic lower respiratory disease, 147,101 (5·6%); accidents, 136,053 (5·2%); stroke, 133,103 (5·1%); Alzheimer's disease, 93,541 (3·6%); diabetes, 76,488 (2·9%); pneumonia and influenza, 55,227 (2·1%); kidney diseases, 48,146 (1·8%); suicide, 42,773 (1·6%). The age-adjusted suicide rate in 2014, at 13·0 per 100,000 population (20·7 per 100,000 among males and 5·5 per 100,000 among females), was the highest since the mid-1980s.

The number of Americans living in poverty in 2015 was 43·1m. or 13·5% of the total population, down from 46·7m. and 14·8% in 2014 but up from 11·3% in 2000.

Climate

For temperature and rainfall figures, *see* entries on individual states as indicated by regions, below, of mainland USA.

Pacific Coast

The climate varies with latitude, distance from the sea and the effect of relief, ranging from polar conditions in North Alaska through cool to warm temperate climates further south. The extreme south is temperate desert. Rainfall everywhere is moderate. *See* Alaska, California, Oregon, Washington.

Mountain States

Very varied, with relief exerting the main control; very cold in the north in winter, with considerable snowfall. In the south, much higher temperatures and aridity produce desert conditions. Rainfall everywhere is very variable as a result of rain-shadow influences. *See* Arizona, Colorado, Idaho, Montana, Nevada, New Mexico, Utah, Wyoming.

High Plains

A continental climate with a large annual range of temperature and moderate rainfall, mainly in summer, although unreliable. Dust storms are common in summer and blizzards in winter. *See* Nebraska, North Dakota, South Dakota.

Central Plains

A temperate continental climate, with hot summers and cold winters, except in the extreme south. Rainfall is plentiful and comes at all seasons, but there is a summer maximum in western parts. *See* Mississippi, Missouri, Oklahoma, Texas.

Mid-West

Continental, with hot summers and cold winters. Rainfall is moderate, with a summer maximum in most parts. *See* Indiana, Iowa, Kansas.

Great Lakes

Continental, resembling that of the Central Plains, with hot summers but very cold winters because of the freezing of the lakes. Rainfall is moderate with a slight summer maximum. *See* Illinois, Michigan, Minnesota, Ohio, Wisconsin.

Appalachian Mountains

The north is cool temperate with cold winters, the south warm temperate with milder winters. Precipitation is heavy, increasing to the south but evenly distributed over the year. *See* Kentucky, Pennsylvania, Tennessee, West Virginia.

Gulf Coast

Conditions vary from warm temperate to sub-tropical, with plentiful rainfall, decreasing towards the west but evenly distributed over the year. *See* Alabama, Arkansas, Florida, Louisiana.

Atlantic Coast

Temperate maritime climate but with great differences in temperature according to latitude. Rainfall is ample at all seasons; snowfall in the north can be heavy. *See* Delaware, District of Columbia, Georgia, Maryland, New Jersey, New York State, North Carolina, South Carolina, Virginia.

New England

Cool temperate, with severe winters and warm summers. Precipitation is well distributed with a slight winter maximum. Snowfall is heavy in winter. *See* Connecticut, Maine, Massachusetts, New Hampshire, Rhode Island, Vermont. *See* also Hawaii and Outlying Territories.

Constitution and Government

The form of government of the USA is based on the constitution adopted on 17 Sept. 1787 and effective from 4 March 1789.

By the constitution the government of the nation is composed of three co-ordinate branches, the executive, the legislative and the judicial.

The Federal government has authority in matters of general taxation, treaties and other dealings with foreign countries, foreign and inter-state commerce, bankruptcy, postal service, coinage, weights and measures, patents and copyright, the armed forces (including, to a certain extent, the militia), and crimes against the USA; it has sole legislative authority over the District of Columbia and the possessions of the USA.

The 5th article of the constitution provides that Congress may, on a two-thirds vote of both houses, propose amendments to the constitution, or, on the application of the legislatures of two-thirds of all the states, call a convention for proposing amendments, which in either case shall be valid as part of the constitution when ratified by the legislatures of three-fourths of the several states, or by conventions in three-fourths thereof, whichever mode of ratification may be proposed by Congress. Ten amendments (called collectively 'the Bill of Rights') to the constitution were added 15 Dec. 1791; two in 1795 and 1804; a 13th amendment, 6 Dec. 1865, abolishing slavery; a 14th in 1868, including the important 'due process' clause; a 15th, 3 Feb. 1870, establishing equal voting rights for White and Black; a 16th, 3 Feb. 1913, authorizing the income tax; a 17th, 8 April 1913, providing for popular election of Senators; an 18th, 16 Jan. 1919, prohibiting alcoholic liquors; a 19th, 18 Aug. 1920, establishing women's suffrage; a 20th, 23 Jan. 1933, advancing the date of the President's and Vice-President's inauguration and abolishing the 'lameduck' sessions of Congress; a 21st, 5 Dec. 1933, repealing the 18th amendment; a 22nd, 27 Feb. 1951, limiting a President's tenure of office to two terms, or two full terms in the case of a Vice-President who has succeeded to the office of President and has served two years or less of another President's term, or one full term in the case of a Vice-President who has succeeded to the office of President and has served more than two years of another President's term; a 23rd, 30 March 1961, granting citizens of the District of Columbia the right to vote in national elections; a 24th, 4 Feb. 1964, banning the use of the poll-tax in federal elections; a 25th, 10 Feb. 1967, dealing with Presidential disability and succession; a 26th, 22 June 1970, establishing the right of citizens who are 18 years of age and older to vote; a 27th, 7 May 1992, providing that no law varying the compensation of Senators or Representatives shall take effect until an election has taken place.

National Motto

'In God we trust'; formally adopted by Congress 30 July 1956.

Presidency

The executive power is vested in a president, who holds office for four years, and is elected, together with a vice-president chosen for the same term, by electors from each state, equal to the whole number of Senators and Representatives to which the state may be entitled in the Congress. The President must be a natural-born citizen, resident in the country for 14 years, and at least 35 years old.

The presidential election is held every fourth (leap) year on the Tuesday after the first Monday in Nov. Technically, this is an election of presidential electors, not of a president directly; the electors thus chosen meet and give their votes (for the candidate to whom they are pledged, in some states by law, but in most states by custom and prudent politics) at their respective state capitals on the first Monday after the second Wednesday in Dec. next following their election; and the votes of the electors of all the states are opened and counted in the presence of both Houses of Congress on the sixth day of Jan. The total electorate vote is one for each Senator and Representative. Electors may not be a member of Congress or hold federal office. If no candidate secures the minimum 270 college votes needed for outright victory, the 12th Amendment to the Constitution applies, and the House of Representatives chooses a president from among the first three finishers in the electoral college. (This last happened in 1824).

If the successful candidate for President dies before taking office the Vice-President-elect becomes President; if no candidate has a majority or if the successful candidate fails to qualify, then, by the 20th amendment, the Vice-President acts as President until a president qualifies. The duties of the Presidency, in absence of the President and Vice-President by reason of death, resignation, removal, inability or failure to qualify, devolve upon the Speaker of the House under legislation enacted on 18 July 1947. In case of absence of a Speaker for like reason, the presidential duties devolve upon the President *pro tempore* of the Senate and successively upon those members of the cabinet in order of precedence, who have the constitutional qualifications for President.

The presidential term, by the 20th amendment to the constitution, begins at noon on 20 Jan. of the inaugural year. This amendment also installs the newly elected Congress in office on 3 Jan. instead of—as formerly—in the following Dec. The President's salary is $400,000 per year (taxable), with an additional $50,000 to assist in defraying expenses resulting from official duties. Also he may spend up to $100,000 non-taxable for travel and $19,000 for official entertainment. In 1999 the presidential salary was increased for the president taking office in Jan. 2001, having remained at $200,000 a year since 1969. The office of Vice-President carries a salary of $230,700 and $20,000 allowance for expenses, all taxable. The Vice-President is *ex officio* President of the Senate, and in the case of 'the removal of the President, or of his death, resignation, or inability to discharge the powers and duties of his office', he becomes the President for the remainder of the term.

Cabinet

The administrative business of the nation has been traditionally vested in several executive departments, the heads of which, unofficially and *ex officio*, formed the President's cabinet. Beginning with the Interstate Commerce Commission in 1887, however, an increasing amount of executive business has been entrusted to some 30 so-called independent agencies, such as the Central Intelligence Agency, the Federal Reserve System, etc.

All heads of departments and of the administrative agencies are appointed by the President, but must be confirmed by the Senate.

Congress

The legislative power is vested by the Constitution in a Congress, consisting of a Senate and House of Representatives.

Electorate

By amendments of the constitution, disqualification of voters on the ground of race, colour or sex is forbidden. The electorate consists of all citizens over 18 years of age. Literacy tests have been banned since 1970. In 1972 durational residency requirements were held to violate the constitution. In 1973 US citizens abroad were enfranchised.

With limitations imposed by the constitution, it is the states which determine voter eligibility. In general states exclude from voting: persons who have not established residency in the jurisdiction in which they wish to vote; persons who have been convicted of felonies whose civil rights have not been restored; persons declared mentally incompetent by a court.

Illiterate voters are entitled to receive assistance in marking their ballots. Minority-language voters in jurisdictions with statutorily prescribed minority concentrations are entitled to have elections conducted in the minority language as well as English. Disabled voters are entitled to accessible polling places. Voters absent on election days or unable to go to the polls are generally entitled under state law to vote by absentee ballot.

The Constitution guarantees citizens that their votes will be of equal value under the 'one person, one vote' rule.

Senate

The Senate consists of two members from each state (but not from the District of Columbia), chosen by popular vote for six years, approximately one-third retiring or seeking re-election every two years. Senators must be no less than 30 years of age; must have been citizens of the USA for nine years, and be residents in the states for which they are chosen. The Senate has complete freedom to initiate legislation, except revenue bills (which must originate in the House of Representatives); it may, however, amend or reject any legislation originating in the lower house. The Senate is also entrusted with the power of giving or withholding its 'advice and consent' to the ratification of all treaties initiated by the President with foreign powers, a two-thirds majority of Senators present being required for approval. (However, it has no control over 'international executive agreements' made by the President with foreign governments; such 'agreements' cover a wide range and are more numerous than formal treaties.)

The Senate has 16 Standing Committees to which all bills are referred for study, revision or rejection. The House of Representatives has 20 such committees. In both Houses each Standing Committee has a chairman and a majority representing the majority party of the whole House; each has numerous sub-committees. The jurisdictions of these Committees correspond largely to those of the appropriate executive departments and agencies. Both Houses also have a few select or special Committees with limited duration.

House of Representatives

The House of Representatives consists of 435 members elected every second year. The number of each state's Representatives is determined by the decennial census, in the absence of specific Congressional legislation affecting the basis. The number of Representatives for each state in the 116th congress, which began in Jan. 2019 (based on the 2010 census), is given below:

Alabama	7
Alaska	1
Arizona	9
Arkansas	4
California	53
Colorado	7
Connecticut	5
Delaware	1
Florida	27
Georgia	14
Hawaii	2
Idaho	2
Illinois	18
Indiana	9
Iowa	4
Kansas	4
Kentucky	6
Louisiana	6
Maine	2
Maryland	8
Massachusetts	9
Michigan	14
Minnesota	8
Mississippi	4
Missouri	8
Montana	1
Nebraska	3
Nevada	4
New Hampshire	2
New Jersey	12
New Mexico	3
New York	27
North Carolina	13
North Dakota	1
Ohio	16
Oklahoma	5
Oregon	5
Pennsylvania	18
Rhode Island	2
South Carolina	7
South Dakota	1

(*continued*)

Tennessee	9
Texas	36
Utah	4
Vermont	1
Virginia	11
Washington	10
West Virginia	3
Wisconsin	8
Wyoming	1

The constitution requires congressional districts within each state to be substantially equal in population. Final decisions on congressional district boundaries are taken by the state legislatures and governors. By custom the Representative lives in the district from which he is elected. Representatives must be not less than 25 years of age, citizens of the USA for seven years and residents in the state from which they are chosen.

In addition, five delegates (one each from the District of Columbia, American Samoa, Guam, the US Virgin Islands and Puerto Rico) are also members of Congress. They have a voice but no vote, except in committees. The delegate from Puerto Rico is the resident commissioner. Puerto Ricans vote at primaries, but not at national elections. Each of the two Houses of Congress is sole 'judge of the elections, returns and qualifications of its own members'; and each of the Houses may, with the concurrence of two-thirds, expel a member. The period usually termed 'a Congress' in legislative language continues for two years, terminating at noon on 3 Jan.

The salary of a Senator is $174,000 per annum, with tax-free expense allowance and allowances for travelling expenses and for clerical hire. The salary of the Speaker of the House of Representatives is $223,500 per annum, with a taxable allowance. The salary of a Member of the House is $174,000. The salary for the Majority and Minority Leaders of the Senate and the House of Representatives is $193,400.

No Senator or Representative can, during the time for which he is elected, be appointed to any *civil* office under authority of the USA which shall have been created or the emoluments of which shall have been increased during such time; and no person holding *any* office under the USA can be a member of either House during his continuance in office. No religious text may be required as a qualification to any office or public trust under the USA or in any state.

American Indians
By an Act passed on 2 June 1924 full citizenship was granted to all American Indians born in the USA, though those remaining in tribal units were still under special federal jurisdiction. The Indian Reorganization Act of 1934 gave the tribal Indians, at their own option, substantial opportunities of self-government and the establishment of self-controlled corporate enterprises empowered to borrow money and buy land, machinery and equipment; these corporations are controlled by democratically elected tribal councils. Recently a trend towards releasing American Indians from federal supervision has resulted in legislation terminating supervision over specific tribes. In 1988 the federal government recognized that it had a special relationship with, and a trust responsibility for, federally recognized American Indian entities in continental USA and tribal entities in Alaska. In 2015 the Bureau of Indian Affairs listed 566 'Indian Entities Recognized and Eligible to Receive Services'. Total American Indian and Alaska Native population at the 2010 census was 2,932,248, of which California (362,801), Oklahoma (321,687), Arizona (296,529) and New Mexico (193,222) accounted for more than 40%.

The **District of Columbia,** ceded by the State of Maryland for the purposes of government in 1791, is the seat of the US government. It includes the city of Washington, and embraces a land area of 61 sq. miles. The Reorganization Plan No. 3 of 1967 instituted a Mayor Council form of government with appointed officers. In 1973 an elected Mayor and elected councillors were introduced; in 1974 they received power to legislate in local matters. Congress retains power to enact legislation and to veto or supersede the Council's acts. Since 1961 citizens have had the right to vote in national elections. In 1978 the Senate approved a constitutional amendment giving the District full voting representation in Congress but it was not ratified by the requisite three-quarters of the states within seven years and so expired in 1985.

The **Commonwealth of the Northern Mariana Islands,** the **Commonwealth of Puerto Rico, American Samoa, Guam** and the **Virgin Islands of the United States** each have a local legislature, whose acts may be modified or annulled by Congress, though in practice this has seldom been done. Puerto Rico, since its attainment of commonwealth status on 25 July 1952, enjoys practically complete self-government, including the election of its governor and other officials. The conduct of foreign relations, however, is still a federal function and federal bureaux and agencies still operate in the island.

General supervision of territorial administration is exercised by the Office of Territories in the Department of Interior.

Local Government
The Union comprises 13 original states, seven states which were admitted without having been previously organized as territories, and 30 states which had been territories—50 states in all. Each state has its own constitution (which the USA guarantees shall be republican in form), deriving its authority, not from Congress, but from the people of the state. Admission of states into the Union has been granted by special Acts of Congress, either (1) in the form of 'enabling Acts' providing for the drafting and ratification of a state constitution by the people, in which case the territory becomes a state as soon as the conditions are fulfilled, or (2) accepting a constitution already framed, and at once granting admission.

Each state is provided with a legislature of two Houses (except Nebraska, which since 1937 has had a single-chamber legislature), a governor and other executive officials, and a judicial system. Both Houses of the legislature are elective, but the senators (having larger electoral districts usually covering two or three counties compared with the single county or, in some states, the town, which sends one representative to the Lower House) are less numerous than the representatives, while in 38 states their terms are four years; in 12 states the term is two years. Of the four-year Senates, Illinois, Montana and New Jersey provide for two four-year terms and one two-year term in each decade. Terms of the lower houses are usually shorter; in 45 states, two years. The trend is towards annual sessions of state legislatures; most meet annually now whereas in 1939 only four did.

The Governor is elected by direct vote of the people over the whole state for a term of office ranging in the various states from two to four years and with a salary ranging from $70,000 (Maine) to $201,680 (California). The Governor's duty is to see to the faithful administration of the law, and he has command of the military forces of the state. He may recommend measures but does not present bills to the legislature. In some states he presents estimates. In all but one of the states (North Carolina) the Governor has a veto upon legislation, which may, however, be overridden by the two Houses, in some states by a simple majority, in others by a three-fifths or two-thirds majority. In some states the Governor, on his death or resignation, is succeeded by a Lieut.-Governor who was elected at the same time and has been presiding over the state Senate. In several states the Speaker of the Lower House succeeds the Governor.

National Anthem
The Star-spangled Banner, 'Oh say, can you see by the dawn's early light'; words by F. S. Key, 1814, tune by J. S. Smith; formally adopted by Congress 3 March 1931.

Government Chronology

Presidents of the USA

Name	Party[1]	From state	Term of service	Born	Died
George Washington	(F.)	Virginia	1789–97	1732	1799
John Adams	(F.)	Massachusetts	1797–1801	1735	1826
Thomas Jefferson	(D.)	Virginia	1801–09	1743	1826
James Madison	(D.)	Virginia	1809–17	1751	1836
James Monroe	(D.)	Virginia	1817–25	1759	1831
John Quincy Adams	(n.p.)	Massachusetts	1825–29	1767	1848
Andrew Jackson	(D.)	Tennessee	1829–37	1767	1845

(continued)

Name	Party[1]	From state	Term of service	Born	Died
Martin Van Buren	(D.)	New York	1837–41	1782	1862
William H. Harrison	(W.)	Ohio	Mar.–April 1841	1773	1841
John Tyler	(W.)	Virginia	1841–45	1790	1862
James K. Polk	(D.)	Tennessee	1845–49	1795	1849
Zachary Taylor	(W.)	Louisiana	1849–July 1850	1784	1850
Millard Fillmore	(W.)	New York	1850–53	1800	1874
Franklin Pierce	(D.)	New Hampshire	1853–57	1804	1869
James Buchanan	(D.)	Pennsylvania	1857–61	1791	1868
Abraham Lincoln	(R.)	Illinois	1861–April 1865	1809	1865
Andrew Johnson	(D.)	Tennessee	1865–69	1808	1875
Ulysses S. Grant	(R.)	Illinois	1869–77	1822	1885
Rutherford B. Hayes	(R.)	Ohio	1877–81	1822	1893
James A. Garfield	(R.)	Ohio	Mar.–Sept. 1881	1831	1881
Chester A. Arthur	(R.)	New York	1881–85	1830	1886
Grover Cleveland	(D.)	New York	1885–89	1837	1908
Benjamin Harrison	(R.)	Indiana	1889–93	1833	1901
Grover Cleveland	(D.)	New York	1893–97	1837	1908
William McKinley	(R.)	Ohio	1897–Sept. 1901	1843	1901
Theodore Roosevelt	(R.)	New York	1901–09	1858	1919
William H. Taft	(R.)	Ohio	1909–13	1857	1930
Woodrow Wilson	(D.)	New Jersey	1913–21	1856	1924
Warren Gamaliel Harding	(R.)	Ohio	1921–Aug. 1923	1865	1923
Calvin Coolidge	(R.)	Massachusetts	1923–29	1872	1933
Herbert C. Hoover	(R.)	California	1929–33	1874	1964
Franklin D. Roosevelt	(D.)	New York	1933–April 1945	1882	1945
Harry S. Truman	(D.)	Missouri	1945–53	1884	1972
Dwight D. Eisenhower	(R.)	New York	1953–61	1890	1969
John F. Kennedy	(D.)	Massachusetts	1961–Nov. 1963	1917	1963
Lyndon B. Johnson	(D.)	Texas	1963–69	1908	1973
Richard M. Nixon	(R.)	California	1969–74	1913	1994
Gerald R. Ford	(R.)	Michigan	1974–77	1913	2006
James Earl Carter	(D.)	Georgia	1977–81	1924	—
Ronald W. Reagan	(R.)	California	1981–89	1911	2004

Name	Party[1]	From state	Term of service	Born	Died
George H. W. Bush	(R.)	Texas	1989–93	1924	2018
Bill (William J.) Clinton	(D.)	Arkansas	1993–2001	1946	—
George W. Bush	(R.)	Texas	2001–09	1946	—
Barack H. Obama	(D.)	Illinois	2009–17	1961	—
Donald J. Trump	(R.)	New York	2017–	1946	—

[1]F. = Federalist; D. = Democrat; n.p. = no party; W. = Whig; R. = Republican.

Vice-Presidents of the USA

Name	Party[1]	From state	Term of service	Born	Died
John Adams	(F.)	Massachusetts	1789–97	1735	1826
Thomas Jefferson	(R.)	Virginia	1797–1801	1743	1826
Aaron Burr	(R.)	New York	1801–05[2]	1756	1836
George Clinton	(R.)	New York	1805–12	1739	1812
Elbridge Gerry	(R.)	Massachusetts	1813–14[2]	1744	1814
Daniel D. Tompkins	(R.)	New York	1817–25	1774	1825
John C. Calhoun	(NR./D.)	South Carolina	1825–32[2]	1782	1850
Martin Van Buren	(D.)	New York	1833–37	1782	1862
Richard M. Johnson	(D.)	Kentucky	1837–41	1780	1850
John Tyler	(W.)	Virginia	Mar.–April 1841[2]	1790	1862
George M. Dallas	(D.)	Pennsylvania	1845–49	1792	1864
Millard Fillmore	(W.)	New York	1849–50[2]	1800	1874
William R. King	(D.)	Alabama	Mar.–April 1853[2]	1786	1853
John C. Breckinridge	(D.)	Kentucky	1857–61	1821	1875
Hannibal Hamlin	(R.)	Maine	1861–65	1809	1891
Andrew Johnson	(D.)	Tennessee	Mar.–April 1865[2]	1808	1875
Schuyler Colfax	(R.)	Indiana	1869–73	1823	1885
Henry Wilson	(R.)	Massachusetts	1873–75[2]	1812	1875
William A. Wheeler	(R.)	New York	1877–81	1819	1887
Chester A. Arthur[2]	(R.)	New York	Mar.–Sept. 1881	1830	1886
Thomas A. Hendricks	(D.)	Indiana	Mar.–Nov. 1885[2]	1819	1885
Levi P. Morton	(R.)	New York	1889–93	1824	1920
Adlai Stevenson	(D.)	Illinois	1893–97	1835	1914
Garret A. Hobart	(R.)	New Jersey	1897–99[2]	1844	1899
Theodore Roosevelt	(R.)	New York	Mar.–Sept. 1901[2]	1858	1919
Charles W. Fairbanks	(R.)	Indiana	1905–09	1855	1920

(continued)

(continued)

Name	Party[1]	From state	Term of service	Born	Died
James S. Sherman	(R.)	New York	1909–12[2]	1855	1912
Thomas R. Marshall	(D.)	Indiana	1913–21	1854	1925
Calvin Coolidge	(R.)	Massachusetts	1921–Aug. 1923[2]	1872	1933
Charles G. Dawes	(R.)	Illinois	1925–29	1865	1951
Charles Curtis	(R.)	Kansas	1929–33	1860	1935
John N. Garner	(D.)	Texas	1933–41	1868	1967
Henry A. Wallace	(D.)	Iowa	1941–45	1888	1965
Harry S. Truman	(D.)	Missouri	1945–April 1945[2]	1884	1972
Alben W. Barkley	(D.)	Kentucky	1949–53	1877	1956
Richard M. Nixon	(R.)	California	1953–61	1913	1994
Lyndon B. Johnson	(D.)	Texas	1961–Nov. 1963[2]	1908	1973
Hubert H. Humphrey	(D.)	Minnesota	1965–69	1911	1978
Spiro T. Agnew	(R.)	Maryland	1969–73	1918	1996
Gerald R. Ford	(R.)	Michigan	1973–74	1913	2006
Nelson Rockefeller	(R.)	New York	1974–77	1908	1979
Walter Mondale	(D.)	Minnesota	1977–81	1928	—
George H. W. Bush	(R.)	Texas	1981–89	1924	2018
Danforth Quayle	(R.)	Indiana	1989–93	1947	—
Albert Gore	(D.)	Tennessee	1993–2001	1948	—
Richard B. Cheney	(R.)	Wyoming	2001–09	1941	—
Joseph R. Biden	(D.)	Delaware	2009–17	1942	—
Michael Pence	(R.)	Indiana	2017–	1959	—

[1]F. = Federalist; R. = Republican; NR. = National Republican; D. = Democrat; W. = Whig.
[2]Position vacant thereafter until commencement of the next presidential term.

Recent Elections

At the presidential election on 8 Nov. 2016 Donald Trump (Republican) was elected president. Trump won 306 electoral college votes in states where he won the popular vote and Hillary Clinton (Democrat) won 232. However, the final tally was 304 for Trump and 227 for Clinton as seven college electors chose to vote for candidates other than the two front-runners.

Electoral college votes by state in 2016:

a) Won by Trump

State	Electoral college votes
Alabama	9
Alaska	3
Arizona	11
Arkansas	6
Florida[1]	29
Georgia	16
Idaho	4
Indiana	11
Iowa[1]	6
Kansas	6

(continued)

State	Electoral college votes
Kentucky	8
Louisiana	8
Michigan[1]	16
Mississippi	6
Missouri	10
Montana	3
Nebraska	5
North Carolina	15
North Dakota	3
Ohio[1]	18
Oklahoma	7
Pennsylvania[1]	20
South Carolina	9
South Dakota	3
Tennessee	11
Texas	38
Utah	6
West Virginia	5
Wisconsin[1]	10
Wyoming	3

[1]Won by Obama in 2012.

b) Won by Clinton

State	Electoral college votes
California	55
Colorado	9
Connecticut	7
Delaware	3
D.C.	3
Hawaii	4
Illinois	20
Maine	4
Maryland	10
Massachusetts	11
Minnesota	10
Nevada	6
New Hampshire	4
New Jersey	14
New Mexico	5
New York	29
Oregon	7
Rhode Island	4
Vermont	3
Virginia	13
Washington	12

Following the mid-term elections of 6 Nov. 2018 the 116th Congress (2019–21) is constituted as follows: Senate—53 Republicans, 45 Democrats and 2 ind. who caucus with the Democrats (51 Republicans, 47 Democrats and 2 ind. for the 115th Congress before the 2018 elections); House of Representatives—235 Democrats and 199 Republicans with one vacant (235 Republicans and 193 Democrats with seven vacant for the 115th Congress before the 2018 elections).

The Speaker of the House of Representatives is Nancy Pelosi (D.). The Majority Leader of the Senate is Mitch McConnell (R.).

Denton, Robert E., Jr, (ed.) *The 2016 US Presidential Campaign: Political Communication and Practice.* 2017

Current Government

President of the United States: Donald Trump, of New York; b. 1946. Graduated in economics from the Wharton School of the University of Pennsylvania (1968); real estate developer and television presenter.

Vice-President: Mike Pence, b. Indiana, 1959. First elected to Congress in 2000; chairman of the House Republican Conference (2009–11); governor of Indiana (2013–17).

In Feb. 2019 the cabinet consisted of the following:

1. *Secretary of State* (created 1789). Mike Pompeo; b. 1963.
2. *Secretary of the Treasury* (1789). Steven Mnuchin; b. 1962.
3. *Acting Secretary of Defense* (1947). Patrick Shanahan; b. 1962.
4. *Attorney General* (Department of Justice, 1870). William P. Barr; b. 1950.
5. *Acting Secretary of the Interior* (1849). David Bernhardt; b. 1969.
6. *Secretary of Agriculture* (1889). Sonny Perdue; b. 1946.
7. *Secretary of Commerce* (1903). Wilbur Ross; b. 1937.
8. *Secretary of Labor* (1913). Alexander Acosta; b. 1969.
9. *Secretary of Health and Human Services* (1953). Alex Azar; b. 1967.
10. *Secretary of Housing and Urban Development* (1966). Ben Carson; b. 1951.
11. *Secretary of Transportation* (1967). Elaine Chao; b. 1953.
12. *Secretary of Energy* (1977). Rick Perry; b. 1950.
13. *Secretary of Education* (1979). Betsy DeVos; b. 1958.
14. *Secretary of Veterans' Affairs* (1989). Robert Wilkie; b. 1962.
15. *Secretary of Homeland Security* (2002). Kirstjen M. Nielsen; b. 1972.

Each of the above cabinet officers receives an annual salary of $210,700 and holds office during the pleasure of the President.

The following also have cabinet status:

White House Chief of Staff (acting): Mick Mulvaney; US Trade Representative: Robert Lighthizer; Director of National Intelligence: Daniel Coats; US Ambassador to the United Nations (acting): Jonathan Cohen; Director of the Office of Management and Budget: Mick Mulvaney; Director of the Central Intelligence Agency: Gina Haspel; Environmental Protection Agency Administrator: Andrew R. Wheeler; Administrator of the Small Business Administration: Linda McMahon.

Office of the President: http://www.whitehouse.gov

Current Leaders

Donald Trump

Position

President

Introduction

Donald Trump, a wealthy entrepreneur and television personality, surprisingly won the 2016 presidential race as the Republican Party candidate and was sworn into office on 20 Jan. 2017. His first two years in office saw the pursuit of his 'America First' election campaign agenda as well as the adoption of other more contentious policies, some of which have generated considerable opposition across the country and beyond.

Early Life

Trump was born on 14 June 1946 in the Queens borough of New York. His father established a successful business in real estate development and construction. At the age of 13 he enrolled at the New York Military Academy, where he completed his high school education. In 1964 he started at Fordham University and then moved to the Wharton School of Finance and Commerce at the University of Pennsylvania, from where he graduated in economics in 1968. During this time, he also began working for his father's company.

Trump took over his father's business in 1971, renaming it the Trump Organization. He regularly attracted media attention with high-profile projects such as Trump Tower (the Manhattan skyscraper completed in 1983 that is now his business headquarters), Trump University (which ran for five years from 2005), and his involvement in the Miss Universe and Miss USA beauty pageants.

From the 1980s Trump sporadically expressed an interest in entering politics, variously mentioning ambitions to stand for the US presidency or the mayoralty of New York.

He was a vocal critic of Barack Obama's two-term Democratic tenure from 2009, even suggesting that Obama had not been eligible to stand for the presidency on the spurious grounds that he was born abroad (an allegation the White House refuted by releasing Obama's birth certificate).

On 16 June 2015 Trump formally announced his decision to stand in the presidential primaries, promising to 'Make America Great Again'. He became the presumptive nominee following a landslide victory in the Indiana primary on 3 May 2016, after which all his remaining Republican

rivals withdrew. On 15 July he announced Indiana governor Mike Pence as his running mate and both were nominated at the Republican National Convention four days later.

Trump attracted much media focus on his business history, celebrity reputation, social attitudes and abrasive campaigning style, while his contentious policy standpoints included strict controls on immigration and the exclusion of foreign Muslims, and the building of a wall along the border with neighbouring Mexico—payment for which he claimed would be Mexico's responsibility. Trump also stated his intention to repeal Obama's affordable medical care legislation, to negotiate new bilateral trade deals abroad and to withhold defensive support to NATO partners that he considered made an insufficient contribution to defence costs. In addition, he praised the autocratic presidential tenure of Vladimir Putin in Russia.

Trump variously described the Democratic presidential candidate, Hillary Clinton, as 'crooked' and physically unfit for office. His victory at the polls on 8 Nov. was regarded as one of the greatest upsets in US presidential election history.

Career in Office

Trump was inaugurated as the 45th president in Jan. 2017. Apparent discord in the White House, and some allegations of impropriety, have since prompted a frequent turnover of senior government figures and presidential aides, while Trump has also favoured the use of a social media platform over traditional channels of information dissemination and state diplomacy, which on several occasions has generated criticism and resentment overseas. Meanwhile, he has sought to implement the reversal of much of his predecessor's legacy on trade, the environment and health care, and to strengthen US defences, immigration controls and deportation guidelines. In June 2017 he announced that he would withdraw the USA from the 2015 landmark United Nations agreement reached in Paris on climate change. However, his efforts to suspend the entry of citizens from several Muslim-majority countries in the Middle East and Africa were blocked by the courts until June 2018 when the Supreme Court ruled that the ban could be enforced. His demands for federal funding for the construction of a border wall with Mexico to block illegal immigration were resisted by the resurgent Democrats in the House of Representatives following their majority victory in the mid-term congressional elections in Nov. 2018. The consequent political stand-off led to the longest shutdown of the federal government in history, from late Dec. 2018 until its temporary suspension for three weeks from late Jan. 2019 and the negotiation of a limited compromise agreement in mid-Feb. Trump subsequently declared a national emergency as a means of securing extra funding to build the wall, although the legality of his action was promptly and widely challenged.

On the diplomatic front, Trump's sometimes critical attitude towards NATO and the European Union has caused consternation among the USA's European allies. He has also made plain his confrontational stance towards Iran (withdrawing the USA in May 2018 from the multilateral agreement of 2015 containing Iran's nuclear development in return for the lifting of sanctions) and distanced himself from the long-standing US commitment to a separate Palestinian state alongside Israel. Moreover, in Dec. 2017 he announced that the USA would officially recognize Jerusalem as the capital of Israel and transfer its embassy to the city. He did, however, endorse the 'one China' principle defining US relations with Beijing. Meanwhile, there remains ongoing speculation over his ambivalence towards Russia's President Putin, as claims about alleged Russian cyber backing for Trump's election campaign have continued to undermine his fractious relationship with the US federal security agencies and the media. He nevertheless announced in Oct. 2017 that he intended to withdraw the USA from the 1987 arms limitation agreement with Russia on intermediate-range nuclear weapons in Europe, accusing the Russians of breaking its terms. In regard to Cuba, Trump has adopted a harder line than his predecessor, banning US citizens from conducting business with any entity with links to the Cuban military, intelligence or security agencies and tightening visa restrictions. He has also sought to undermine the regime of the leftist president of Venezuela, Nicolás Maduro, and in Jan. 2019, amid increasing civil unrest, recognized Juan Guaidó, the head of the Venezuelan National Assembly, as the country's interim leader. In response to alleged chemical weapon attacks in March 2017 and April 2018 in Syria's civil war attributed to President Assad's regime, Trump ordered missile strikes on Syrian military targets, but later announced in Dec. that he would withdraw US troops operating in Syria against Islamic State extremists, prompting the resignation of his defence secretary. He initially pursued an aggressive policy to communist North Korea's military threat to neighbouring states, warning of overwhelming retaliatory action. However, he then staged an historic meeting with his counterpart, Kim Jong-un, in June 2018, at which they agreed to work towards denuclearization of the Korean peninsula. Despite little apparent diplomatic progress by the year's end, a second summit took place in late Feb. 2019 but ended without any significant advances being made.

Regarding economic policy, Trump instigated major changes in taxation and budgetary spending, further stimulating an already growing economy. In Dec. 2017 he signed into law a radical US$1·5trn. tax reform plan, cutting corporate tax rates in particular, while in Feb. 2018, in a significant departure from traditional Republican fiscal orthodoxy, he proposed a $4·4trn. budget outlining steep changes to domestic programmes, large increases in military expenditure and a significant rise in the federal deficit. Meanwhile, his disdain for the international trade order prompted his withdrawal of the USA from the Trans-Pacific Partnership (the trade agreement concluded by the Obama administration with 11 other Pacific region countries) and the renegotiation of the 24-year-old trilateral North American Free Trade Agreement between the USA, Canada and Mexico. He also threatened to ignite a damaging trade war between the USA and China after progressively imposing trade tariffs on Chinese products to stop what he claimed had been the systematic theft of US intellectual property. China similarly retaliated before both sides agreed a temporary suspension of further punitive action in Dec. 2018 to allow for further negotiations.

Defence

The President is C.-in-C. of the Army, Navy and Air Force.

The National Security Act of 1947 provides for the unification of the Army, Navy and Air Forces under a single Secretary of Defense with cabinet rank. The President is also advised by a National Security Council and the Office of Civil and Defense Mobilization.

Defence expenditure in 2013 totalled $600,400m. ($1,896 per capita). Defence spending in 2013 represented 3·7% of GDP (down from 37·8% in 1944, 14·2% in 1953, 9·4% in 1968 and 6·2% of GDP in 1986 although up from the post-war low of 3·0% in 1999). The USA spent more on defence in 2013 than the next 12 biggest spenders combined. US expenditure was 33·5% of the world total, although its population is less than 5% of the world total. In 1997 the Quadrennial Defense Review (QDR) was implemented—a plan to transform US defence strategy and military forces.

Conscription was first introduced during the American Civil War in 1862 and operated during all subsequent major periods of conflict including World Wars I and II, the Korean War and the Vietnam War. A limited draft was also employed in peacetime in the Cold War and early 1960s. The final draft ended in 1973 when the USA converted to an all-volunteer military. Although conscription is not currently in force the Military Selective Service Act requires all males between the ages of 18 and 26 to register for compulsory military service should the need arise.

Active duty military personnel in Feb. 2017 numbered 1,291,817, of which 204,376 were women. In Dec. 2016 US armed forces abroad numbered 239,830, including 11,281 in and around Afghanistan and 25,168 in and around Iraq. In Dec. 2011 the last US troops left Iraq although 4,000 remained in neighbouring Kuwait. However, US troops have been redeployed in Iraq since June 2014 to oppose Islamic State forces active in the country. In Dec. 2016 some 6,800 US troops were on active duty in Iraq. There were 31 active duty military deaths in the US armed forces participating in Operation Enduring Freedom (Afghanistan) and Operation New Dawn (Iraq) in 2018 (37 in 2017). In June 2011 then President Obama announced that 10,000 troops would be withdrawn from Afghanistan by the end of 2011 and a further 23,000 by the end of Sept. 2012. There were 29,000 US troops serving with the International Security Assistance Force (ISAF) in Afghanistan in Sept. 2014, although the mission's mandate expired at the end of the year. As of Feb. 2019 the USA contributed some 8,500 troops to more than 17,000 personnel charged with training, advising and assisting the Afghan National Security Forces under the aegis of Operation *Resolute Support*. After President Trump agreed in Aug. 2017 to send some 3,500 additional troops, there were more than 14,000 US forces in Afghanistan overall in Nov. 2017 including troops for use in counter-terrorism operations. US troop deaths in Iraq between 2003 and March 2019 totalled 4,568 (peaking at 904 in 2007);

deaths in Afghanistan between 2001 and March 2019 totalled 2,421 (peaking at 498 in 2010).

The USA is the world's largest exporter of arms, with 33% of the global major weapons total over the period 2012–16.

The USA's last nuclear test was in 1993. The deployed nuclear warhead count stood at 1,750 in Jan. 2018 according to the Stockholm International Peace Research Institute. There are about a further 4,700 stored and other warheads, giving a total stockpile of around 6,450 warheads. At the height of the Cold War each side possessed over 10,000 nuclear warheads. The START I arms-control treaty, signed in 1991, limited to approximately 6,000 the number of nuclear warheads that the USA and Russia may each deploy on long-range, or 'strategic', land-based missiles, submarine-launched missiles and bombers. The 1993 START II treaty would have obliged both sides to reduce their stocks of strategic weapons to 3,500 nuclear warheads. However, instruments of ratification were never exchanged and the treaty lapsed. Russia retracted acceptance in June 2002 after the USA withdrew from the Anti-Ballistic Missile treaty. START I expired on 5 Dec. 2009. In July 2007 the Bush administration decided not to extend the treaty beyond the original expiry date. In May 2001 then President Bush called for the development of an anti-missile shield to move beyond the constraints of the Anti-Ballistic Missile Treaty. In Dec. 2001 he announced that the USA was unilaterally abandoning the Treaty. On 24 May 2002 the USA and Russia signed the Strategic Offensive Reductions Treaty (or Moscow Treaty) to reduce the number of US and Russian warheads to between 1,700 and 2,200 each. The treaty was in force from June 2003 until Feb. 2011. It was then superseded by the Measures for the Further Reduction and Limitation of Strategic Offensive Arms (known as New START), signed by the US and Russian presidents in April 2010 and ratified by the US Senate in Dec. 2010 and the Russian Federal Assembly in Jan. 2011. It laid out terms for the number of warheads on each side to be limited to 1,550 by Feb. 2018, a 30% drop on previous levels. Both nations met their obligations by the deadline but, with the agreement due to end in 2021, no extension had been agreed as of March 2019. Meanwhile, in Oct. 2018 President Trump announced his intention to withdraw the USA from an intermediate-range nuclear forces treaty with Russia signed in 1987, banning ground-launched medium-range missiles with a range between 500 and 5,500 km. Trump claimed Russia had been in violation of its terms 'for many years'.

In May 2010 the Obama administration announced that the USA had a total of 5,113 active nuclear warheads, down from a peak of 31,225 in 1967. In Jan. 2018 strategic nuclear delivery vehicles were made up as follows:

Intercontinental ballistic missiles: 400 Minuteman III.

Submarine-launched ballistic missiles: 240 Trident II.

Bombers: 44 B-52H; 16 B-2A.

Estimates of the number of firearms in the country are around 310m., equivalent to 99 firearms for every 100 people, making the USA the world's most heavily armed country.

With a total of 3·2m. employees in 2015, the Department of Defense is the world's largest employer.

Army

Secretary of the Army
Mark T. Esper.

The Secretary of the Army is the head of the Department of the Army. Subject to the authority of the President as C.-in-C. and of the Secretary of Defense, he is responsible for all affairs of the Department.

The Army consists of the Active Army, the Army National Guard of the US, the Army Reserve and civilian workforce; and all persons appointed to or enlisted into the Army without component; and all persons serving under call or conscription, including members of the National Guard of the States, etc., when in the service of the US. The active duty strength of the Army was 565,463 (79,694 women) in Sept. 2011.

The Army budget for fiscal year 2019 was $178,886m., with a request for fiscal year 2020 of $191,397m.

Starting in 2006 the Army undertook its widest-ranging reorganization since the end of the Second World War in order to allow it to deploy continuously in different parts of the world. Subsequent cuts to the defence budget saw the Pentagon announce in Feb. 2014 plans to reduce active troop numbers from 520,000 to between 440,000 and 450,000, its lowest level since 1940 (before the USA entered the Second World War).

The US Army Forces Command (FORSCOM), with headquarters at Fort Bragg, North Carolina, is the largest United States Army Command and consists of more than 750,000 Active Army, US Army Reserve and Army National Guard soldiers. The other Army Commands are US Army Training and Doctrine Command (TRADOC) and US Army Materiel Command (AMC). The Army Service Component Commands are: United States Army Cyber Command/Second Army; United States Army Central (USARCENT)/Third Army; United States Army North (USARNORTH)/Fifth Army; United States Army South (USARSO)/Sixth Army; United States Army Europe (USAREUR)/Seventh Army; United States Army Africa (USARAF)/Ninth Army; United States Army Pacific (USARPAC); United States Army Special Operations Command (USASOC); Military Surface Deployment and Distribution Command (SDDC).

The United States Army Space and Missile Defense Command (SMDC), created in 1997 and with its headquarters at Redstone Arsenal, Alabama, is a specialized major command within the United States Army. The First United States Army now serves as a mobilization, readiness and training command.

Approximately 32% of the Active Army is deployed outside the continental USA. Several divisions, which are located in the USA, keep equipment in Germany and can be flown there in 48–72 hours. Headquarters of US Seventh and Eighth Armies are in Europe and Korea respectively.

Combat vehicles of the US Army are the tank, armoured personnel carrier, infantry fighting vehicle, and the armoured command vehicle. The Army's main battle tank is the M1A2 Abrams; its standard infantry fighting vehicle is the M2A3 Bradley.

The Army has nearly 4,900 aircraft, all but about 300 of them helicopters, including AH-1 Cobra and AH-64 Apache attack helicopters.

Over 95% of recruits enlisting in the Army have a high school education and over 50% of the Army is married. Women serve in both combat support and combat service support units.

The National Guard is a reserve military component with both a state and a federal role. Enlistment is voluntary. The members are recruited by each state, but are equipped and paid by the federal government (except when performing state missions). As the organized militia of the several states, the District of Columbia, Puerto Rico and the Territories of the Virgin Islands and Guam, the Guard may be called into service for local emergencies by the chief executives in those jurisdictions; and may be called into federal service by the President to thwart invasion or rebellion or to enforce federal law. In its role as a reserve component of the Army, the Guard is subject to the order of the President in the event of national emergency. In 2011 it numbered 465,071 (Army, 358,391; Air Force, 106,680).

The Army Reserve is designed to supply qualified and experienced units and individuals in an emergency. Members of units are assigned to the Ready Reserve, which is subject to call by the President in case of national emergency without declaration of war by Congress. The Standby Reserve and the Retired Reserve may be called only after declaration of war or national emergency by Congress. In 2011 the Army Reserve numbered 198,000.

Navy

Secretary of the Navy
Richard V. Spencer.

The Navy's Operating Forces include the Atlantic Fleet, divided between the 2nd fleet (home waters) and 6th fleet (Mediterranean) and the Pacific Fleet, similarly divided between the 3rd fleet (home waters), the 7th fleet (West Pacific) and the 5th fleet (Indian Ocean), which was formally activated in 1995 and maintained by units from both Pacific and Atlantic.

The Navy budget for fiscal year 2019 was $195,627m., with a request for fiscal year 2020 of $205,572m.

The active duty strength of the Navy was 325,123 (53,385 women) in Sept. 2011.

The active ship force levels of the Navy in the year indicated:

Category	2000	2005	2010	2011
Aircraft Carriers	12	12	11	11
Cruisers	27	23	22	22
Destroyers	54	46	59	61

(continued)

Category	2000	2005	2010	2011
Frigates	35	30	29	26
Littoral Combat Ships	—	—	2	2
Surface Warships	*128*	*111*	*123*	*122*
Attack Submarines	56	54	53	53
Ballistic Missile-Carrying Submarines (SSBNs)	*18*	*14*	*14*	*14*
Guided-Missile Submarines (SSGNs)	—	4	4	4
Mine Warfare	18	17	14	14
Amphibious	41	37	33	31
Auxiliary	57	45	47	47
Total Active	*318*	*282*	*288*	*285*

Ships in the Naval Reserve Force, Military Sealift Command and Naval Fleet Auxiliary Force are included in this table.

Submarine Forces
A principal part of the US naval task is to deploy the seaborne strategic deterrent from nuclear-powered ballistic missile-carrying submarines (SSBN), of which there were 14 in 2012, all of the Ohio class. The listed total of 57 tactical submarines in 2012 comprised four Ohio class guided-missile submarines, plus 41 attack submarines of the Los Angeles class, three of the Seawolf class and nine of the Virginia class.

Surface Combatant Forces
The surface combatant forces are comprised of modern cruisers, destroyers and frigates. These ships provide multi-mission capabilities to achieve maritime dominance in the crowded and complex littoral warfare environment.

As of 2012 the cruiser force consisted of 22 Ticonderoga class ships. There were 62 active guided-missile Arleigh Burke Aegis class destroyers and 22 active Oliver Hazard Perry class guided-missile frigates.

Aircraft Carriers
There were ten nuclear-powered Nimitz class carriers in 2012, the first of which, USS *Nimitz*, was commissioned on 3 May 1975 and the tenth and last of which, USS *George H. W. Bush*, was commissioned on 10 Jan. 2009. USS *Enterprise,* completed in 1961, was the prototype nuclear-powered carrier and was in service until Dec. 2012 when it was retired, temporarily reducing the number of aircraft carriers to ten. The Navy's newest nuclear-powered aircraft carrier, USS *Gerald R. Ford*, was commissioned in July 2017. The USS *Ronald Reagan* is the only aircraft carrier whose home port is not in the USA—since Oct. 2015 its home port has been Yokosuka, in Japan. Each of the Nimitz class carriers can carry between 85 and 90 fixed-wing aircraft and helicopters. Strike fighter planes are primarily F/A-18 Hornets and Super Hornets.

Naval Aviation
The principal function of the naval aviation organization (strength in 2013 of 98,600) is to train and provide combat ready aviation forces. The main carrier-borne combat aircraft in the 2013 inventory were 820 F/A-18 Hornet dual-purpose fighter/attack aircraft out of a total of 1,089 combat-capable aircraft.

The Marine Corps
While administratively part of the Department of the Navy, the Corps ranks as a separate armed service, with the Commandant serving in his own right as a member of the Joint Chiefs of Staff, and responsible directly to the Secretary of the Navy. Its strength (including active reservists) was 199,350 in 2013.

The role of the Marine Corps is to provide specially trained and equipped amphibious expeditionary forces. The Corps includes an autonomous aviation element numbering 34,700 in 2013.

The US Coast Guard
The Coast Guard operates under the Department of Homeland Security in time of peace and as part of the Navy in time of war or when directed by the President. The act of establishment stated the Coast Guard 'shall be a military service and branch of the armed forces of the United States at all times'.

The Coast Guard is the country's oldest continuous sea-going service and its missions include maintenance of aids to navigation, icebreaking, environmental response (oil spills), maritime law enforcement, marine licensing, port security, search and rescue and waterways management.

The workforce in 2013 was made up of 41,200 military personnel augmented by 7,600 civilians. On an average Coast Guard day the service conducts 45 search and rescue cases, saves ten lives and over $1·2m. in property, seizes 874 lb of cocaine and 214 lb of marijuana, interdicts 17 illegal migrants, conducts 24 security boardings in and around US ports, investigates 35 pollution incidents, and facilitates movement of $8·7bn. worth of goods and commodities through the maritime transportation system.

Air Force

Secretary of the Air Force
Heather Wilson.

The Department of the Air Force was activated within the Department of Defense on 18 Sept. 1947, under the terms of the National Security Act of 1947.

The USAF has the mission to defend the USA through control and exploitation of air, space and cyberspace. For operational purposes the service is divided into nine major commands, 35 field operating agencies and four direct-reporting units. In addition there are two reserve components: the Air Force Reserve and the Air National Guard.

Major commands accomplish designated phases of USAF worldwide activities. They also organize, administer, equip and train their subordinate elements. In descending order, elements of major commands include numbered air forces, wings, groups, squadrons and flights. The basic unit for generating and employing combat capability is the wing, considered to be the Air Force's prime war-fighting instrument. The bulk of the combat forces are grouped under the Air Combat Command, which controls strategic bombing, tactical strike, air defence and reconnaissance assets in the USA.

Air Force bombers include the B-1B Lancer, the B-2A Spirit and the B-52H Stratofortress, which has been the primary manned strategic bomber for 50 years. In the fighter category are the F-22A Raptor, F-15 Eagle and Strike Eagle and the F-16 Fighting Falcon.

The Air Force budget for fiscal year 2019 was $192,920m., with a request for fiscal year 2020 of $204,757m.

The active duty strength of the Air Force was 333,370 (63,552 women) in Sept. 2011—19·1% of personnel were women, compared to 16·4% in the Navy and 13·6% in the Army. Since 1991 women have been authorized to fly combat aircraft, but not until 1993 were they allowed to fly fighters.

Economy

Services accounted for 78·0% of GDP in 2014, industry 20·7% and agriculture 1·3%.

Per capita personal income in 2015 was $47,669, more than double the 1994 total of $22,538.

In 2017 the USA gave $34·7bn. in international aid, the highest figure of any country. In terms of a percentage of GNI, however, the USA was one of the least generous major industrialized countries, giving just 0·18% (compared to more than 0·6% in the early 1960s).

Overview

The USA remains an economic powerhouse, producing around 20% of total global output. However, based on GDP measured by Purchasing Power Parity, China's economy became the world's largest in 2014—a position previously held by the USA for over a century. The USA's volume of trade is the largest in the world, although the value of the external sector as a percentage of GDP is relatively low. It is self-sufficient in most raw materials, with the notable exception of oil (although it is predicted that domestic shale oil production will lead to self-sufficiency by the 2030s). Core industries include motor vehicles, steel, aerospace, chemicals, telecommunications, electronics, computers and military equipment. Since 1992 the economy has grown at higher average rates than in the other OECD and G7 countries in most years, and per capita GDP is higher than in other G7 states. The economy, however, is constrained by imbalances, including a low savings rate, a heavy reliance on consumer spending and a sizeable current account deficit. The global economy remains fragile following the 2008 financial crisis triggered by the collapse of the US sub-prime housing market. The ripple effects of the crisis continue to impact the USA as it struggles to maintain its leading status within the changing world economy.

By 1995 labour productivity in advanced Western European countries had reached US levels, but since then US labour and total factor productivity growth has outpaced that of other advanced economies. The principal sectors in which the USA outperforms its rivals are retail, wholesale and finance. It has also been able to extract greater efficiency gains from information technology-related investments. US firms enjoy greater flexibility than their counterparts in Western Europe and Asia in laying off workers and in introducing labour-saving technology. However, income inequality is higher than in other advanced economies and the gap between skilled and unskilled labour incomes has been growing over the last three decades. The USA also has a significant gender pay gap and it showed the widest disparity of all the 38 developed countries surveyed in the International Labour Organization's *Global Wage Report 2014/15*. In 2013 over 45m. Americans lived below the poverty line (with a disproportionate percentage of these being African-Americans), although by 2017 the figure had declined to 39·7m. people.

The attacks of 11 Sept. 2001 posed serious challenges to the dollar payment system and stock market. Business investment relative to GDP plummeted in 2001–02, having reached record highs in the previous fiscal year. The collapse of the giant energy company Enron in Dec. 2002 was followed by other accounting scandals. However, in the third quarter of 2003 the economy recorded an annualized growth rate of 6·9%, fuelled by tax cuts, low interest rates and increased consumer and business spending. Interest rates began rising from then historic lows of 1·0% in 2003 with the federal funds rate reaching 5·25% by the end of 2006. Growth remained strong through 2006 despite the impact of Hurricane Katrina and high oil prices.

The sub-prime mortgage crisis of 2007 seriously damaged the wider economy. A sharp rise in defaults and foreclosures as a result of the rapid decline in house prices, which had begun in 2006, spread panic through the banking sector. A government stimulus package enacted in early 2008 (consisting of targeted tax rebates and investment incentives), together with interest rate cuts amounting to 5% by Dec. 2008, were aimed at raising confidence in the financial markets. However, market nervousness increased, prompting tougher lending criteria and declining asset prices. In Sept. 2008 Lehman Brothers became the first major bank to collapse since the start of the crisis. The government announced financial rescue packages for mortgage-lending giants Fannie Mae and Freddie Mac—between them responsible for half of the outstanding mortgages in the economy—along with American International Group, the country's biggest insurance company.

In Oct. 2008 the House of Representatives approved a $700bn. plan aimed at purchasing bad debts of failing institutions. Continued market turmoil then resulted in a further $250bn. investment that gave the government stakes in a range of banks. Interest rates reached their lowest recorded level at between 0–0·25% in Dec. 2008. In Feb. 2009 Congress approved the then President Obama's $787bn. economic stimulus plan, comprising tax breaks and money for social programmes, a move that substantially increased the fiscal deficit. The cost of military action in Iraq and Afghanistan, meanwhile, put further strain on the economy. Growth of 1·5% in the third quarter of 2009 brought an end to the recession. The fragile recovery was underpinned by the government stimulus measures, a rebound in world trade (with increasing demand from large emerging-market economies) and housing market stabilization. The economy nonetheless contracted by 2·5% in 2009 as a whole, while real annual GDP growth in the first ten years of the century, at an average of 1·7%, was the lowest in a full decade since the 1930s. Further recovery was hampered by a combination of external events, such as rising oil prices, a debt crisis in the eurozone, and weak domestic drivers including low consumer spending and the sluggish housing market. However, GDP grew by 2·6% in 2010, and by early 2012 positive employment and retail sales figures saw the stock market jump to its highest level since May 2008.

Fiscal pressures have emerged with the retirement of the post-Second World War baby-boom generation and the rise in life expectancy, increasing the strain on welfare entitlement programmes. In March 2010 the then

President Obama signed into law a health care reform measure—the Affordable Care Act (ACA)—to extend health insurance to an additional 32m. Americans, impose new taxes on the wealthy and outlaw restrictive insurance practices. According to the Congressional Budget Office, efficiencies contained in the reform were expected to cut the federal deficit by $138bn. over ten years. The US Department of Health and Human Services reported in March 2016 that approximately 20m. Americans had gained health coverage under the Act since 2010. However, after several unsuccessful attempts in 2017 to repeal and replace the ACA (with a programme based around refundable tax credits to support insurance purchases), the new populist president, Donald Trump, signed an executive order in Oct. scaling back some of the Act's provisions.

In Feb. 2011 Obama had unveiled his 2012 Budget, which aimed to cut $1·1trn. from the US deficit over the following decade. However, political wrangling over raising the debt ceiling caused disruption on the financial markets as fears mounted that the economy would default. In Aug. 2011 Congress approved a bipartisan compromise deal that raised the debt ceiling by $2·4trn. from $14·3trn. and paved the way for savings of at least $2·1trn. over ten years. The international credit-rating agency Standard & Poor's downgraded the USA's AAA credit-rating to AA+ days after the deal had been reached, causing further volatility in the markets. This rating was reaffirmed in Oct. 2016.

Against a background of congressional disagreements, a combination of scheduled tax increases and automatic spending cuts—known as the 'fiscal cliff'—threatened to push the economy into recession again at the start of 2013. Failure to reach an accord on the budget by 31 Dec. 2012 would have triggered automatic tax increases of over $500bn. and spending cuts of over $100bn. from domestic and military programmes, amounting to a 4–5% cut in output. However, a deal was reached on the eve of the deadline, based on a package of measures including limited tax rises for wealthier families and individuals and a short-term extension of unemployment benefits.

On 1 Oct. 2013 following a repeated failure by Congress to agree a budget for the next fiscal year, the government entered a partial shutdown of operations for the first time in 17 years. A short-term fiscal deal was struck on 17 Oct., funding the government until 15 Jan. 2014 and raising the debt ceiling until 7 Feb. Congress then agreed to raise the borrowing limit for another year in Feb. 2014. According to Standard & Poor's, the Oct. shutdown shaved $24bn. off the economy and cut growth significantly in the fourth quarter of 2013. To prevent a repeat shutdown, an omnibus spending bill was passed in Jan. 2014 to provide the government with funding of $1·1trn. for the 2014 fiscal year. In Oct. 2015 Congress passed a budget agreement that allowed for the debt ceiling to be raised until March 2017.

In April 2014 Janet Yellen, the then chair of the Federal Reserve Board, cut back the Board's quantitative easing programme. She then closed monthly bond purchases with a final $15bn. buying round in Oct. that year. The programme, which began in 2009, was the largest emergency economic stimulus in history and added over $3·5trn. to the Federal Reserve's balance sheet deficit—an amount roughly equal to the size of the German economy.

Economic recovery gained momentum from the second quarter of 2013 and throughout 2014 and 2015. Annual GDP growth averaged 2·4% in the period 2013–15, rendering the economy 10% larger than its 2007 pre-crisis level. In the third quarter of 2017, GDP increased at an annual rate of 2·8% despite the impact of hurricanes Harvey and Irma in Aug. and Sept., respectively. Stock and asset prices had also improved following the recession, while unemployment fell by around 0·8% each year between 2010 and 2016. The more optimistic economic outlook resulted from a combination of the hydraulic fracturing energy boom, a rebound in the housing market, robust real consumer spending (which reached an all-time high in the fourth quarter of 2016) and an improved fiscal situation. By March 2019 the jobless rate had dropped to 3·8%, although the Labor Department indicated that it might not be as favourable as it appeared, pointing to an increase in the number of Americans receiving unemployment benefits over the previous ten months. Meanwhile, the Federal Reserve's benchmark interest rate, which had been raised by a quarter percentage point in Dec. 2015 (for the first time since 2006 and from a record low level), was increased by the same amount again in Dec. 2016, three times in 2017 and four times in 2018. In its March 2019 meeting the Federal Reserve agreed to keep interest rates steady, pointing toward low inflation, among other factors. Uncertainty remained as to whether interest rates would be increased later in the year, ultimately

depending on inflation. In mid-2018 the government passed a bill aimed at loosening the banking rules implemented after the financial crisis and assisting small- to medium-sized banks.

Nonetheless, the economic rebound has been more fragile than any following previous recessions, since damage to the financial sector has not been fully repaired. Furthermore, government spending has created a fiscal drag and the long-expected retirement of baby-boomers has depressed the labour supply. The economy continues to face a number of risks, including slow growth in emerging world markets and international political volatility. The election of President Trump in Nov. 2016 and the potential changes to monetary and fiscal policy added further uncertainty, although he promised to increase annual GDP growth to 4·0% by cutting taxes, increasing infrastructure spending and removing regulation. The US government ended fiscal year 2017 in Sept. with a deficit more than $82bn. higher than that in the previous year. After the fiscal year 2018 budget narrowly passed Congress the following month, a proposal for significant tax reform was then approved by the Senate in Dec. 2017. It was the largest tax overhaul in over 30 years, effectively reducing the corporate tax rate from 35% to 21%. Although Trump's tax reform gave the economy an expected short-term boost, the ultimate economic impacts of its changes continue to be debated.

In March 2018 President Trump ordered tariffs of 10% on foreign aluminium imports and 25% on foreign steel imports. The US also imposed three rounds of tariffs that year on Chinese imports (totalling more than $250bn.), prompting Chinese retaliatory measures before both sides agreed a temporary suspension of further punitive action in Dec. to allow for negotiations to defuse a damaging trade war. A study published by the National Bureau of Economic Research suggested that the trade dispute with China cost the US economy $7·8bn. over the course of 2018. Meanwhile, the US trade deficit reached an all-time high in early 2019.

GDP growth in 2018 was 2·9%, falling just short of the Trump administration's 3% goal. This exceeded most economists' expectations given the negative impacts of the trade conflict with China and the unexpected drop in consumer spending that occurred in the final quarter of 2018. Furthermore, in the autumn of 2018 the US stock market experienced the largest drops since the 2008 financial crisis. The S&P stock market index dropped 6·2% while the Dow Jones Industrial Average index dropped 5·6%, although there was a recovery from the end of the year. Despite what then became the longest federal government shutdown in the country's history, lasting a total of 35 days between Dec. 2018 and Jan. 2019, the Federal Reserve reported in Feb. 2019 that consumer and business confidence remained favourable, but acknowledged that some economic indicators had 'softened' since the autumn.

Currency

The unit of currency is the *dollar* (USD) of 100 *cents*. Notes are issued by the 12 Federal Reserve Banks, which are denoted by a branch letter (A = Boston, MA; B = New York, NY; C = Philadelphia, PA; D = Cleveland, OH; E = Richmond, VA; F = Atlanta, GA; G = Chicago, IL; H = St Louis, MO; I = Minneapolis, MN; J = Kansas City, MO; K = Dallas, TX; L = San Francisco, CA).

Inflation rates (based on OECD statistics):

2008	2009	2010	2011	2012	2013	2014	2015	2016	2017
3·8%	−0·3%	1·6%	3·1%	2·1%	1·5%	1·6%	0·1%	1·3%	2·1%

Foreign exchange reserves in Dec. 2014 were $41,944m. and gold reserves were 261·50m. troy oz. The USA has the most gold reserves of any country, and more than the combined reserves of the next two (Germany and Italy). Broad money supply totalled $15,624·8bn. in Dec. 2014.

Budget

The budget covers virtually all the programmes of federal government, including those financed through trust funds, such as for social security, Medicare and highway construction. Receipts of the government include all income from its sovereign or compulsory powers; income from business-type or market-orientated activities of the government is offset against outlays. The fiscal year ends on 30 Sept. (before 1977 on 30 June). Budget receipts and outlays, including off-budget receipts and outlays (in $1m.):

Fiscal year ending in	Receipts	Outlays	Surplus (+) or deficit (−)
1950	39,443	42,562	−3,119
1960	92,492	92,191	+301
1970	192,807	195,649	−2,842
1980	517,112	590,941	−73,830
1990	1,031,958	1,252,993	−221,036
2000	2,025,191	1,788,950	+236,241
2010	2,162,706	3,457,079	−1,294,373
2011	2,303,466	3,603,065	−1,299,599
2012	2,449,990	3,536,945	−1,086,955
2013	2,775,105	3,454,647	−679,542
2014	3,021,491	3,506,091	−484,600
2015	3,249,887	3,688,383	−438,496
2016	3,267,961	3,852,612	−584,651

The last budget surplus was in fiscal year 2001, when there was a surplus of $128,236m.

Budget and off-budget receipts, by source, for fiscal years (in $1m.):

Source	2015	2016
Individual income taxes	1,540,802	1,546,075
Corporate income taxes	343,797	299,571
Social insurance and retirement receipts	1,065,257	1,115,065
Excise taxes	98,279	95,026
Other	201,752	212,224
Total	3,249,887	3,267,961

Budget and off-budget outlays, by function, for fiscal years (in $1m.):

Function	2015	2016
National defence	589,659	593,372
Education, training, employment and social service	122,061	109,737
Health	482,230	511,317
Medicare	546,202	594,536
Income security	508,843	514,139
Social security	887,753	916,067
Veterans' benefits and services	159,738	174,516
Energy	6,838	3,719
Natural resources and environment	36,034	39,534
Commerce and housing credit	−37,905	−34,077
Transportation	89,533	92,566
Community and regional development	20,669	20,140
Net interest	223,181	240,033
International affairs	48,576	45,306
General science, space and technology	29,412	30,174
Agriculture	18,500	18,342
Administration of justice	51,906	55,768
General government	20,956	22,674
Undistributed offsetting receipts	−115,803	−95,251
Total	3,688,383	3,852,612

Budget and off-budget outlays, by agency, for fiscal years (in $1m.):

Agency	2015	2016
Legislative Branch	4,321	4,347
Judicial Branch	7,137	7,499
Agriculture	139,115	138,161

(continued)

Agency	2015	2016
Commerce	8,956	9,165
Defence—Military	562,499	565,370
Education	90,029	76,978
Energy	25,424	25,860
Health and Human Services	1,027,514	1,102,965
Homeland Security	42,572	45,196
Housing and Urban Development	35,527	26,388
Interior	12,340	12,583
Justice	26,906	29,523
Labor	45,217	41,364
State	26,498	29,449
Transportation	75,425	78,423
Treasury	485,623	526,116
Veterans' Affairs	159,216	174,019
Corps of Engineers	6,685	6,388
Defence—Civil	62,966	64,508
Environmental Protection Agency	7,008	8,725
Executive Office of the President	397	397
General Services Administration	−890	−735
International Assistance Programmes	20,950	16,240
National Aeronautics and Space Administration	18,268	18,828
National Science Foundation	6,837	6,902
Office of Personnel Management	91,734	91,318
Small Business Administration	−746	−445
Social Security Administration	944,122	976,785
Other independent agencies	14,327	11,657
Undistributed offsetting receipts	−257,594	−241,362
Total	3,688,383	3,852,612

National Debt

Federal debt held by the public (in $1m.), and per capita debt (in $1) on 30 June to 1976 and on 30 Sept. since then:

	Public debt	Per capita
1920	24,299	229
1930	16,185	132
1940	42,772	324
1950	219,023	1,447
1960	236,840	1,321
1970	283,198	1,394
1980	711,923	3,143
1990	2,411,558	9,696
2000	3,409,804	12,084
2010	9,018,882	29,155
2011	10,128,187	32,499
2012	11,281,131	35,928
2013	11,982,713	37,892
2014	12,779,899	40,110
2015	13,116,692	40,857
2016	14,167,725	43,808

National Income

The Bureau of Economic Analysis of the Department of Commerce prepares detailed estimates on the national income and product. In Dec. 2003 the Bureau revised these accounts back to 1929. The principal tables are published monthly in *Survey of Current Business;* the complete set of national income and product tables are published in the *Survey* normally each Aug., showing data for recent years.

Gross Domestic Product	(in $1,000m.)				
	2012	2013	2014	2015	2016
Gross domestic product	16,155·3	16,691·5	17,427·6	18,120·7	18,624·5
Personal consumption expenditures	11,050·6	11,361·2	11,863·7	12,332·3	12,820·7
Goods	3,739·1	3,834·5	3,970·5	4,033·2	4,121·4
Durable goods	1,191·9	1,241·7	1,296·4	1,367·1	1,411·0
Nondurable goods	2,547·2	2,592·8	2,674·1	2,666·0	2,710·4
Services	7,311·5	7,526·7	7,893·2	8,299·1	8,699·3
Gross private domestic investment	2,511·7	2,706·3	2,916·4	3,093·6	3,057·2
Fixed investment	2,449·9	2,613·9	2,838·4	2,981·6	3,022·1
Nonresidential	2,007·7	2,094·4	2,268·3	2,336·2	2,316·3
Structures	448·0	463·6	537·5	537·5	516·2
Equipment	937·9	982·8	1,046·5	1,081·9	1,043·9
Intellectual property products	621·7	647·9	684·3	716·8	756·2
Residential	442·2	519·5	570·2	645·4	705·9
Change in private inventories	61·8	92·4	78·0	111·9	35·1
Net exports of goods and services	−565·7	−492·0	−509·5	−524·0	−521·2
Exports	2,198·2	2,276·6	2,373·6	2,264·9	2,214·6
Goods	1,526·0	1,562·7	1,617·9	1,497·2	1,446·0
Services	672·2	713·9	755·7	767·7	768·5
Imports	2,763·8	2,768·6	2,883·2	2,789·0	2,735·8
Goods	2,305·8	2,301·5	2,396·1	2,290·5	2,224·2
Services	458·0	467·1	487·1	498·5	511·6
Government consumption expenditures and gross investment	3,158·6	3,116·1	3,157·0	3,218·9	3,267·8
Federal	1,292·5	1,229·5	1,218·1	1,224·0	1,231·5
National defence	817·8	767·0	745·6	731·6	728·9
Nondefence	474·7	462·5	472·5	492·4	502·6
State and local	1,866·1	1,886·6	1,938·9	1,994·9	2,036·3

Relation of Gross Domestic Product, Gross National Product, Net National Product, National Income and Personal Income	(in $1,000m.)				
	2012	2013	2014	2015	2016
Gross domestic product	16,155·3	16,691·5	17,427·6	18,120·7	18,624·5
Plus: Income receipts from the rest of the world	801·5	825·5	847·2	812·9	844·3
Less: Income payments to the rest of the world	563·9	581·3	612·6	608·4	647·2
Equals: Gross national product	16,392·8	16,935·8	17,662·1	18,325·2	18,821·6
Less: Consumption of fixed capital	2,534·2	2,628·9	2,748·0	2,841·5	2,916·7
Private	2,038·0	2,122·4	2,231·2	2,319·6	2,390·5
Domestic business	1,633·4	1,694·7	1,775·0	1,846·9	1,895·3
Capital consumption allowances	1,652·2	1,731·7	1,837·1	1,946·9	2,005·6
Less: Capital consumption adjustment	18·8	37·0	62·1	100·0	110·3
Households and institutions	404·6	427·7	456·1	472·7	495·3
Government	496·2	506·5	516·9	521·9	526·2
General government	436·1	444·5	453·0	456·7	459·8
Government enterprises	60·1	62·0	63·9	65·2	66·4
Equals: Net national product	13,858·6	14,306·9	14,914·1	15,483·7	15,904·8
Less: Statistical discrepancy	−203·3	−137·9	−229·9	−255·9	−147·2
Equals: National income	14,061·9	14,444·8	15,144·0	15,739·6	16,052·0
Less: Corporate profits with inventory valuation and capital consumption adjustments	11,998·2	2,032·9	2,140·6	2,117·5	2,073·5
Taxes on production and imports less subsidies	1,074·0	1,115·6	1,163·6	1,198·5	1,226·2
Contributions for government social insurance (domestic)	951·6	1,104·6	1,155·3	1,208·0	1,245·3
Net interest and miscellaneous payments on assets	527·7	504·6	535·0	583·4	570·6
Business current transfer payments (net)	104·7	118·4	138·9	165·0	164·0
Current surplus of government enterprises	−19·3	−20·9	−17·9	−14·3	−10·1

(*continued*)

Relation of Gross Domestic Product, Gross National Product, Net National Product, National Income and Personal Income	(in $1,000m.)				
	2012	2013	2014	2015	2016
Plus: Personal income receipts on assets	2,123·8	2,056·1	2,245·1	2,387·1	2,377·8
Personal current transfer receipts	2,366·3	2,428·0	2,544·4	2,684·4	2,768·4
Equals: Personal income	13,915·1	14,073·7	14,818·2	15,553·0	15,928·7
Addenda:					
Gross domestic income	16,358·5	16,829·5	17,657·5	18,376·6	18,771·6
Gross national income	16,596·1	17,073·7	17,892·1	18,581·1	18,968·7
Gross national factor income	15,436·7	15,860·6	16,607·6	17,232·0	17,588·6
Net domestic product	13,621·0	14,062·6	14,679·6	15,279·2	15,707·8
Net domestic income	13,824·3	14,200·6	14,909·5	15,535·1	15,854·9
Net national factor income	12,902·5	13,231·7	13,859·5	14,390·4	14,671·9
Net domestic purchases	14,186·7	14,554·6	15,189·1	15,803·2	16,229·0

	(in $1,000m.)				
National Income by Type of Income	2012	2013	2014	2015	2016
National income	14,061·9	14,444·8	15,144·0	15,739·6	16,052·0
Compensation of employees	8,609·9	8,842·4	9,256·5	9,708·3	9,978·6
Wages and salaries	6,930·3	7,116·7	7,476·8	7,858·9	8,085·2
Government	1,198·2	1,208·0	1,236·9	1,275·6	1,307·5
Other	5,732·0	5,908·7	6,239·9	6,583·3	6,777·8
Supplements to wages and salaries	1,679·6	1,725·8	1,779·7	1,849·4	1,893·4
Employer contributions for employee pension and insurance funds	1,165·3	1,199·0	1,231·7	1,278·0	1,309·8
Employer contributions for government social insurance	514·3	526·8	548·0	571·4	583·6
Proprietors' income with inventory valuation and capital consumption adjustments	1,241·4	1,284·7	1,315·8	1,318·8	1,341·9
Farm	61·6	87·8	68·1	53·7	43·2
Nonfarm	1,179·8	1,197·0	1,247·7	1,265·1	1,298·7
Rental income of persons with capital consumption adjustment	525·3	567·1	611·7	662·5	707·3
Corporate profits with inventory valuation and capital consumption adjustments	1,998·2	2,032·9	2,140·6	2,117·5	2,073·5
Taxes on corporate income	447·6	467·7	505·3	507·4	471·0
Profits after tax with inventory valuation and capital consumption adjustments	1,550·5	1,565·2	1,635·3	1,610·0	1,602·4
Net dividends	859·4	929·4	986·4	1,039·9	981·9
Undistributed profits with inventory valuation and capital consumption adjustments	691·2	635·8	648·9	570·1	620·6
Net interest and miscellaneous payments	527·7	504·6	535·0	583·4	570·6
Taxes on production and imports	1,132·1	1,174·9	1,221·6	1,255·8	1,288·0
Less: Subsidies	58·0	59·3	58·1	57·3	61·8
Business current transfer payments (net)	104·7	118·4	138·9	165·0	164·0
To persons (net)	42·7	41·1	45·6	53·1	57·4
To government (net)	72·6	90·8	102·2	112·4	105·9
To the rest of the world (net)	−10·6	−13·5	−9·0	−0·6	0·7
Current surplus of government enterprises	−19·3	−20·9	−17·9	−14·3	−10·1
Addenda for corporate cash flow:					
Net cash flow with inventory valuation adjustment	2,049·6	2,042·0	2,111·3	2,098·4	2,179·3
Undistributed profits with inventory valuation and capital consumption adjustments	691·2	635·8	648·9	570·1	620·6
Consumption of fixed capital	1,351·0	1,400·5	1,465·7	1,525·1	1,563·2
Less: Capital transfers paid (net)	−7·4	−5·7	3·3	−3·2	4·4
Addenda:					
Proprietors' income with inventory valuation and capital consumption adjustments	1,241·4	1,284·7	1,315·8	1,318·8	1,341·9
Farm	61·6	87·8	68·1	53·7	43·2
Proprietors' income with inventory valuation adjustment	67·4	93·6	74·2	59·7	49·2
Capital consumption adjustment	−5·9	−5·8	−6·0	−6·0	−6·1

(*continued*)

National Income by Type of Income	(in $1,000m.)				
	2012	2013	2014	2015	2016
Nonfarm	1,179·8	1,197·0	1,247·7	1,265·1	1,298·7
Proprietors' income (without inventory valuation and capital consumption adjustments)	1,024·3	1,011·7	1,048·7	1,038·6	1,075·7
Inventory valuation adjustment	−1·8	0·4	0·9	9·2	−0·3
Capital consumption adjustment	157·3	184·9	198·0	217·3	223·4
Rental income of persons with capital consumption adjustment	525·3	567·1	611·7	662·5	707·3
Rental income of persons (without capital consumption adjustment)	539·5	582·6	629·0	680·4	726·1
Capital consumption adjustment	−14·2	−15·5	−17·3	−17·9	−18·8
Corporate profits with inventory valuation and capital consumption adjustments	1,998·2	2,032·9	2,140·6	2,117·5	2,073·5
Corporate profits with inventory valuation adjustment	2,116·6	2,159·4	2,253·2	2,210·9	2,161·6
Profits before tax (without inventory valuation and capital consumption adjustments)	2,130·8	2,156·1	2,249·1	2,158·5	2,158·9
Taxes on corporate income	447·6	467·7	505·3	507·4	471·0
Profits after tax (without inventory valuation and capital consumption adjustments)	1,683·2	1,688·4	1,743·8	1,651·1	1,687·9
Net dividends	859·4	929·4	986·4	1,039·9	981·9
Undistributed profits (without inventory valuation and capital consumption adjustments)	823·8	759·0	757·4	611·2	706·0
Inventory valuation adjustment	−14·2	3·3	4·1	52·4	2·7
Capital consumption adjustment	−118·5	−126·6	−112·6	−93·5	−88·2

Real Gross Domestic Product	(in 1,000m. chained [2009] dollars)[1]				
	2012	2013	2014	2015	2016
Gross domestic product	15,354·6	15,612·2	16,013·3	16,471·5	16,716·2
Personal consumption expenditures	10,413·2	10,565·4	10,868·4	11,264·3	11,572·1
Goods	3,504·3	3,613·5	3,753·5	3,927·3	4,072·2
Durable goods	1,236·2	1,312·7	1,403·1	1,511·8	1,595·1
Nondurable goods	2,277·5	2,316·1	2,373·0	2,446·8	2,514·3
Services	6,908·1	6,951·3	7,115·5	7,340·1	7,507·3
Gross private domestic investment	2,465·7	2,616·5	2,761·7	2,905·4	2,858·3
Fixed investment	2,400·4	2,521·4	2,677·3	2,782·7	2,803·4
Nonresidential	1,964·1	2,032·9	2,172·7	2,223·5	2,210·4
Structures	423·1	428·8	474·0	465·4	446·4
Equipment	939·2	982·3	1,047·4	1,084·5	1,047·8
Intellectual property products	603·8	624·5	653·1	677·8	720·4
Residential	436·5	488·3	505·2	556·9	587·4
Change in private inventories	54·7	78·7	67·8	100·5	33·4
Net exports of goods and services	−447·1	−404·9	−427·7	−545·3	−586·3
Exports	1,963·2	2,031·5	2,118·4	2,127·1	2,120·1
Goods	1,344·2	1,385·7	1,448·9	1,443·1	1,447·5
Services	618·7	645·7	669·3	683·2	672·8
Imports	2,410·2	2,436·4	2,546·1	2,672·4	2,706·3
Goods	1,972·2	1,995·4	2,093·1	2,201·1	2,220·0
Services	437·1	439·9	451·2	469·3	484·0
Government consumption expenditures and gross investment	2,941·6	2,857·6	2,839·1	2,878·5	2,900·2
Federal	1,213·5	1,142·8	1,115·0	1,114·1	1,114·6
National defence	768·2	715·7	686·8	672·0	667·0
Nondefence	445·3	427·0	427·9	441·6	447·0
State and local	1,728·1	1,714·1	1,723·0	1,762·8	1,783·6
Residual	−19·7	−23·7	−37·5	−44·8	−49·8

[1]In 1996 the chain-weighted method of estimating GDP replaced that of constant base-year prices. In chain-weighting the weights used to value different sectors of the economy are continually updated to reflect changes in relative prices.

Performance

Total GDP in 2017 was $19,390·6bn. (making the USA by some way the world's largest economy), representing 24% of the world's total GDP (although in 2000 the USA's share of global GDP was 31%).

Real GDP growth rates (based on OECD statistics):

2008	2009	2010	2011	2012	2013	2014	2015	2016	2017
−0·1%	−2·5%	2·6%	1·6%	2·2%	1·8%	2·5%	2·9%	1·6%	2·2%

The real GDP growth rate in 2018 according to the Bureau of Economic Analysis was 2·9%. The USA's economy shrank by 1·9% in the third quarter of 2008, by 8·2% in the fourth quarter (the steepest quarterly fall since 1958) and by 5·4% in the first quarter of 2009. There was also negative growth in the second quarter of 2009, of 0·5%. The recession ended with growth of 1·3% in the third quarter of 2009.

The USA was ranked second in the World Economic Forum's *Global Competitiveness Report 2017–2018* index, up from third in the 2016–2017 report. The index analyses 12 areas of competitiveness for over 100 countries including macroeconomy, higher education and training, institutions, innovation and infrastructure. In the 2018 *World Competitiveness Yearbook*, compiled by the International Institute for Management Development, the USA came first in the world ranking (up from fourth in 2017). This annual publication ranks and analyses how a nation's business environment creates and sustains the competitiveness of enterprises.

Banking and Finance

The Federal Reserve System, established under The Federal Reserve Act of 1913, comprises the Board of seven Governors, the 12 regional Federal Reserve Banks with their 24 branches, and the Federal Open Market Committee. The seven members of the Board of Governors are appointed by the President with the consent of the Senate. Each Governor is appointed to a full term of 14 years or an unexpired portion of a term, one term expiring every two years. The Board exercises broad supervisory authority over the operations of the 12 Federal Reserve Banks, including approval of their budgets and of the appointments of their presidents and first vice presidents; it designates three of the nine directors of each Reserve Bank including the Chair and Deputy Chair. The Chair of the Federal Reserve Board is appointed by the President for four-year terms. The *Chair* is Jerome H. Powell. The Board has supervisory and regulatory responsibilities over banks that are members of the Federal Reserve System, bank holding companies, bank mergers, Edge Act and agreement corporations, foreign activities of member banks, international banking facilities in the USA, and activities of the US branches and agencies of foreign banks. Legislation of 1991 requires foreign banks to prove that they are subject to comprehensive consolidated supervision by a regulator at home, and have the Board's approval to establish branches, agencies and representative offices. The Board also assures the smooth functioning and continued development of the nation's vast payments system. Another area of the Board's responsibilities involves the implementation by regulation of major federal laws governing consumer credit.

From 1968 the Congress passed a number of consumer financial protection acts, the first of which was the Truth in Lending Act, for which it has directed the Board to write implementing regulations and assume partial enforcement responsibility. Others include the Equal Credit Opportunity Act, Home Mortgage Disclosure Act, Consumer Leasing Act, Fair Credit Billing Act, Truth in Savings Act and Electronic Fund Transfer Act. To manage these responsibilities the Board has established a Division of Consumer and Community Affairs. To assist it, the Board consults with a Consumer Advisory Council, established by the Congress in 1976 as a statutory part of the Federal Reserve System.

Another statutory body, the Federal Advisory Council, consists of 12 members (one from each district); it meets in Washington, D.C. four times a year to advise the Board of Governors on economic and banking developments. Following the passage of the Monetary Control Act of 1980, the Board of Governors established the Thrift Institutions Advisory Council to provide information and views on the special needs and problems of thrift institutions. The group is comprised of representatives of mutual savings banks, savings and loan associations, and credit unions.

All depository institutions (commercial and savings banks, savings and loan associations, credit unions, US agencies and branches of foreign banks, and Edge Act and agreement corporations) must meet reserve requirements set by the Federal Reserve and hold the reserves in the form of vault cash or deposits at Federal Reserve Banks.

Banks which participate in the federal deposit insurance fund have their deposits insured against loss up to $100,000 for each account. The fund is administered by the Federal Deposit Insurance Corporation established in 1933; it obtains resources through annual assessments on participating banks. All members of the Federal Reserve System are required to insure their deposits through the Corporation, and non-member banks may apply and qualify for insurance.

The Federal Deposit Insurance Corporation Improvement Act of 1992 originated with bank reform initiatives. It imposed new capital rules on banks, new reporting requirements and a code of 'safety and soundness' standards. The main aim of the Act is to reduce risk through rigorous enforcement of capital requirements. Regulators are required to take action where banks fail to observe these standards.

In April 2017 the largest banks in the USA in terms of market value were: J. P. Morgan Chase ($305·9bn.); Wells Fargo ($273·9bn.); and Bank of America ($231·2bn.).

The key stock exchanges are the New York Stock Exchange (NYSE Euronext) and the Nasdaq Stock Exchange (NASDAQ). They are the two largest stock exchanges in the world by market capitalization, with the New York Stock Exchange having a market capitalization larger than the next three biggest combined. There are several other stock exchanges, in Philadelphia, Boston, San Francisco (Pacific Stock Exchange) and Chicago, although trading is very limited in them.

Gross external debt totalled $19,019,303m. in Dec. 2017 (compared to $18,025,120m. in Dec. 2016).

The USA received $275·4bn. worth of foreign direct investment in 2017, down from $457·1bn. in 2016 and a record $465·8bn. in 2015. By the end of 2017 the total stock of foreign direct investment was $7,807·0bn.

By Aug. 2013, 61% of internet users in the USA were using online banking.

Energy and Natural Resources

In 2015 fossil fuels accounted for 81% of primary energy consumption (of which petroleum 37%, natural gas 29% and coal 16%), renewables (including biomass, hydro-power, wind, geothermal and solar) 10% and nuclear power 9%. Consumption of renewables surpassed nuclear power in 2011, since when its share in consumption has gradually increased.

Environment

The USA's carbon dioxide emissions from the consumption of energy in 2014 accounted for 14·5% of the world total (the second highest after China) and were equivalent to 16·5 tonnes per capita (down from 19·6 tonnes per capita in 2001). The population of the USA is only 4·6% of the world total. An *Environmental Performance Index* compiled in 2016 ranked the USA 26th of 180 countries, with 84·7%. The index examined various factors in nine areas—agriculture, air quality, biodiversity and habitat, climate and energy, fisheries, forests, health impacts, water and sanitation, and water resources.

In March 2001 then President Bush rejected the 1997 Kyoto Protocol, which aimed to combat the rise in the earth's temperature through the reduction of industrialized nations' carbon dioxide emissions from the consumption and flaring of fossil fuels by an average 5·2% below 1990 levels by 2012. In Feb. 2002 he unveiled an alternative climate change plan to the Kyoto Protocol, calling for voluntary measures to reduce the rate of increase of US carbon dioxide emissions from the consumption and flaring of fossil fuels.

In 2009 then President Obama endorsed an American Clean Energy and Security bill that laid out plans for an emissions trading scheme echoing the EU model. It was passed by the House of Representatives in 2009 but did not become law owing to inaction in the Senate. Obama had previously called for a reduction in US greenhouse gas emissions of 80% on 1990 levels by 2050.

In 2017 President Trump's budget proposals included a 31% funding cut to the Environmental Protection Agency, although Congress eventually approved a cut of only 1%. In June 2017 Trump announced the USA's withdrawal NB curly apostrophe in USA's (as in Trump's two lines higher up) from the 2015 Paris Agreement on climate change. He has pledged his support for the USA's domestic fossil fuel industries.

The USA recycled 34·5% of its municipal solid waste in 2012.

Electricity

Net installed capacity in 2014 was 1,073·4m. kW. In 2016 natural gas surpassed coal for the first time as the leading source of electricity production, with 34% of the total compared to 30% for coal. Nuclear contributed 20% of the total in 2016 and renewables (notably hydro and wind) 15%. The USA has more nuclear reactors in use than any other country in the world. In 2016 the USA had a nuclear generating capacity of 99,535 MW, with 99 nuclear reactors. Two reactors are under construction in Georgia that are expected to become operational in 2021 and 2022. Electricity generation in 2014 was 4,339,210m. kWh, the second highest in the world behind China. Consumption per capita in 2013 was 12,988 kWh.

Oil and Gas

Crude oil production (2018), 4,001m. bbls, the highest ever annual total. Up until 2008 production had been gradually declining since the mid-1980s, when annual production was 3,275m. bbls. In 2008 production was at its lowest level since 1946, at 1,830m. bbls. However, it has since risen sharply, largely thanks to the development of hydraulic fracturing (or 'fracking') and horizontal drilling. By 2017 the USA had become the world's largest oil producer. Proven crude oil reserves were 39·2bn. bbls in 2017. Offshore oil accounts for about 16% of total production. Crude oil imports began to exceed production in 1993 and in 2015 totalled 2,683m. bbls, with Canada supplying over 40% of US oil imports. In Oct. 2002 the USA took its first delivery of Russian oil for its Strategic Petroleum Reserve as a consequence of an energy dialogue declared by then President George W. Bush and Vladimir Putin at their summit in May 2002. The USA is by far the largest single consumer of oil (19·4m. bbls per day in 2015). In 2011 the USA exported more petroleum products than it imported on an annual basis for the first time since 1949.

The USA is by some distance the greatest single consumer of natural gas and also the largest producer (having overtaken Russia in 2010). Dry natural gas production, 2018, was a record 30·44trn. cu. ft. Shale gas production was 15·2trn. cu. ft in 2015 (46% of total US natural gas production), up from 0·4trn. cu. ft in 2000. Proven natural gas reserves in 2017 totalled 464·3trn. cu. ft. In 2017 natural gas exports exceeded imports for the first time in 60 years.

Wind

The USA is the largest producer of wind power, with 190·9bn. kWh in 2015 (up from 94·7bn. kWh in 2010 and 26·6bn. kWh in 2006). In 2014 total installed capacity amounted to 65,877 MW, second only behind China.

Ethanol

The USA is the largest producer of ethanol (from maize). Production totalled 13,300m. gallons in 2012 (13,929m. gallons in 2011 and 13,298m. gallons in 2010).

Water

The total area within the 50 states of the USA plus the District of Columbia covered by water is 264,837 sq. miles. Total average annual water usage is nearly 67,000 cu. ft per person—more than twice the average for an industrialized nation.

Non-Fuel Minerals

The USA is wholly dependent upon imports for columbium, bauxite, mica sheet, manganese, strontium and graphite, and imports over 80% of its requirements of industrial diamonds, fluorspar, platinum, tantalum, tungsten, chromium and tin.

Total value of non-fuel minerals produced in 2017 was an estimated $75·2bn. ($39·5bn. in 1997). Details of some of the main minerals produced are given in the following tables.

Production of metals (2012):

	Unit	Quantity
Aluminium	1,000 tonnes	2,070
Copper	1,000 tonnes	1,170
Gold	tonnes	235

(continued)

	Unit	Quantity
Iron ore	1m. tonnes	54
Lead	1,000 tonnes	345
Silver	tonnes	1,060
Uranium	tonnes	1,596
Zinc	1,000 tonnes	738

In 2015 the value of metal mine production was $26·6bn.

Precious metals are mined mainly in California and Utah (gold); and Nevada, Arizona and Idaho (silver).

Production of non-metals (2012):

	Unit	Quantity
Barite	1,000 tonnes	666
Boron	1,000 tonnes	confidential
Bromine	1,000 tonnes	confidential
Cement	1,000 tonnes	74,900
Clays	1,000 tonnes	25,800
Diatomite	1,000 tonnes	735
Feldspar	1,000 tonnes	525
Garnet (industrial)	1,000 tonnes	47
Gypsum	1m. tonnes	16
Lime	1m. tonnes	19
Phosphate rock	1m. tonnes	30
Pumice	1,000 tonnes	397
Salt	1m. tonnes	37
Sand and gravel	1m. tonnes	824[1]
Stone (crushed/broken)	1m. tonnes	1,170

[1]2013.

Coal

Proven recoverable coal reserves were 277,382m. short tons at the end of 2016, 22·1% of the world total. Output in 2015 (in 1m. short tons): 896·9 including bituminous coal, 403·7; sub-bituminous coal, 419·5; lignite, 71·6; anthracite, 2·1. Production dropped 10·3% in 2015 compared to 2014 and the number of producing mines declined to 853 from 985 in 2014. The USA is the world's second largest coal producer, after China.

Agriculture

Agriculture in the USA is characterized by its ability to adapt to widely varying conditions, and still produce an abundance and variety of agricultural products. From colonial times to about 1920 the major increases in farm production were brought about by adding to the number of farms and the amount of land under cultivation. During this period nearly 320m. acres of virgin forest were converted to crop land or pasture, and extensive areas of grasslands were ploughed. Improvident use of soil and water resources was evident in many areas.

During the next 20 years the number of farms reached a plateau of about 6·5m., and the acreage planted to crops held relatively stable around 330m. acres. The major source of increase in farm output arose from the substitution of power-driven machines for horses and mules. Greater emphasis was placed on development and improvement of land, and the need for conservation of basic agricultural resources was recognized. A successful conservation programme, highly co-ordinated and on a national scale—to prevent further erosion, to restore the native fertility of damaged land and to adjust land uses to production capabilities and needs—has been in operation since early in the 1930s.

Since the Second World War the uptrend in farm output has been greatly accelerated by increased production per acre and per farm animal. These increases are associated with a higher degree of mechanization; greater use of lime and fertilizer; improved varieties, including hybrid maize and grain sorghums; more effective control of insects and disease; improved strains of livestock and poultry; and wider use of good husbandry practices, such as nutritionally balanced feeds, use of superior sites and better housing. During this period land included in farms decreased slowly, crop land harvested declined somewhat more rapidly, but the number of farms declined sharply.

All land in farms totalled less than 500m. acres in 1870, rose to a peak of over 1,200m. acres in the 1950s and had declined to 912m. acres by 2015, even with the addition of the new States of Alaska and Hawaii in 1960. The number of farms declined from 6·35m. in 1940 to 2·11m. in 2012, as the average size of farms doubled. The average size of farms in 2012 was 434 acres, but ranged from a few acres to many thousand acres. In 2012 the total value of land and buildings was $2,268,537m. The average value of land and buildings per acre in 2012 was $2,481.

In 2012 there were 1,828,946 farms managed by families or individuals (86·7% of all farms); 1,428,351 farms (67·7% of all farms) were managed by full owners (farmers who own all the land they operate). Hired farmworkers numbered 2,736,417 in 2012. There were 4·2m. tractors in 2012, 731,771 hay balers and 346,632 self-propelled grain and bean combines. In 2012 there were an estimated 155·11m. ha. of arable land and 2·60m. ha. of permanent crops. 22·6m. ha. of farmland was irrigated in 2012.

Cash receipts from farm marketings and government payments (in $1bn.):

	Crops	Livestock and livestock products	Total
2013	220·8	182·7	403·6
2014	211·4	212·8	424·2
2015	185·7	189·8	375·4

Net farm income was $80·9bn. in 2015 ($92·6bn. in 2014).

The harvest area and production of the principal crops for 2014 and 2015 were:

	2014			2015		
	Harvested 1m. acres	Production 1m.	Yield per acre	Harvested 1m. acres	Production 1m.	Yield per acre
Corn for grain (bu.)	83·1	14,215·5	171·0	80·8	13,602·0	168·4
Soybeans (bu.)	82·6	3,927·1	47·5	81·7	3,926·3	48·0
Wheat (bu.)	46·4	2,026·3	43·7	47·3	2,061·9	43·6
Cotton (bales)[1]	9·3	16·3	838	8·1	12·9	766
Potatoes (cwt.)	1·1	442·2	421	1·1	441·2	418
Hay (sh. tons)	57·1	139·9	2·5	54·4	134·5	2·5

[1]Yield in lb.

The USA is the world's leading producer of maize and sorghum.

Fruit
Production, in 1,000 tons:

	2013	2014	2015
Apples	5,216	5,907	5,002
Grapes	8,632	7,884	7,677
Lemons	824	904	890
Oranges	6,768	6,353	5,911
Strawberries	1,524	1,511	1,161
Tangerines and mandarins	732	863	935

The farm value of the above crops in 2015 was: apples, $3,394m.; grapes, $5,562m.; lemons, $734m.; oranges, $1,711m.; strawberries, $2,239m.; tangerines and mandarins, $637m. The USA is the world's second largest producer of apples.

In 2016 there were 2,714,498 acres of organic crops. Certified organic farms numbered 14,217 in 2016.

Organic food sales for the USA in 2015 totalled $39·7bn.

Dairy produce
In 2015 production of milk was 208,633m. lb; cheese, 11,838m. lb; butter, 1,858m. lb; ice cream, 898m. gallons; non-fat dry milk, 1,822m. lb; yoghurt, 4,742m. lb. The USA is the world's largest producer of both cheese and milk.

Livestock
In 2013 there were 8,525m. broilers and 240m. turkeys. Eggs produced, 2013, 96·4bn.

Value of production (in $1m.) was:

	2013	2014	2015
Cattle and calves	48,479	59,922	59,858
Hogs and pigs	21,666	24,153	19,283
Broilers	30,762	32,728	28,710
Turkeys	4,840	5,305	5,708
Eggs	8,679	10,258	13,500

Livestock numbered, in 2015 (1m.): cattle and calves (including dairy cows), 89·1; hogs and pigs, 68·9; sheep and lambs, 5·3. Approximate value of livestock (in $1bn.), 2015: cattle, 141·2; hogs and pigs, 6·6; sheep and lambs, 1·1.

Forestry
Forests covered a total area of 766·26m. acres (310·10m. ha.) in 2015, or 34% of the land area. Of the total area under forests 68% was timber land. The 154 national forests had an area of 188,323,491 acres in 2017. Timber production was 14,091m. cu. ft in 2015. The USA is the world's largest producer of roundwood (10·8% of the world total in 2015).

In 2014 there were 758 designated wilderness areas throughout the USA, covering a total of 109·5m. acres (44·3m. ha.). More than half of the total area covered is in Alaska (52%), followed by California (14%), Idaho, Arizona and Washington.

Fisheries
In 2013 the domestic catch was 9,880m. lb, valued at $5,490m. (including 1,257m. lb of shellfish valued at $2,858m.). Main species landed in terms of value ($1m.): salmon, 757; crabs, 714; shrimp, 565; lobsters, 518. Disposition of the domestic catch in 2013 (1m. lb): fresh or frozen, 8,019; canned, 365; cured, 45; reduced to meal or oil, 1,451. The USA's imports of fishery commodities in 2011 ($17·47bn.) were the largest of any country; exports of fishery commodities totalled $5·79bn. (the fifth highest in the world).

Tennessee Valley Authority
Established by Act of Congress, 1933, the TVA is a multiple-purpose federal agency which carries out its duties in an area embracing some 41,000 sq. miles in the seven Tennessee River Valley states: Tennessee, Kentucky, Mississippi, Alabama, North Carolina, Georgia and Virginia. In addition, 76 counties outside the Valley are served by TVA power distributors. It is the largest public power company in the USA. Its three directors are appointed by the President, with the consent of the Senate; headquarters are in Knoxville (TN).

Industry
The largest companies in the USA by market capitalization on 26 March 2019 were: Microsoft ($904·6bn.), a technology company; Apple Inc. ($880·8bn.), a computer company; and Amazon ($876·2bn.), a technology company. They were also the three largest companies by market value in the world in March 2019. According to a survey published by the New York-based Interbrand in Oct. 2018, Apple is the world's most valuable brand, worth $214·48bn.

The following table presents industry statistics of manufactures as reported at various censuses from 1909 to 1980 and from the Annual Survey of Manufactures for years in which no census was taken.

The Annual Surveys of Manufactures carry forward the key measures of manufacturing activity which are covered in detail by the Census of Manufactures.

	Production workers (average for year)	Production workers' wages total ($1,000)	Value added by manufacture ($1,000)
1909	3,261,736	3,205,213	8,160,075
1919	9,464,916	9,664,009	23,841,624

(continued)

	Production workers (average for year)	Production workers' wages total ($1,000)	Value added by manufacture ($1,000)
1929	8,369,705	10,884,919	30,591,435
1933	5,787,611	4,940,146	14,007,540
1939	7,808,205	8,997,515	24,487,304
1950	11,778,803	34,600,025	89,749,765
1960	12,209,514	55,555,452	163,998,531
1970	13,528,000	91,609,000	300,227,600
1980	13,900,100	198,164,000	773,831,300
1990	12,232,700	275,208,400	1,346,970,100
2000	11,943,646	363,380,819	1,973,622,421
2010	7,513,272	305,085,547	2,149,584,183
2013	7,756,977	341,602,352	2,356,025,285
2014	7,729,203	350,741,168	2,387,163,183
2015	7,807,966	360,741,434	2,430,098,147

The total number of employees in the manufacturing industry in 2015 was 11,166,953; there were 297,191 manufacturing establishments in 2012 (350,828 in 2002). In 2015 manufacturing contributed 12·1% of GDP, down from 15·1% of GDP in 2000. The leading industries in 2015 in terms of value added by manufacture (in $1bn.) were: chemicals, 377·3; computer and electronic products, 278·2; food and beverage and tobacco products, 257·5; motor vehicles and parts, 163·1; petroleum and coal products, 161·8; machinery, 153·1. In 2015 a total of 12,105,000 motor vehicles were made in the USA (the highest total since 2002), continuing an upward trend since the height of the recession in 2009 when only 5,710,000 were produced.

In 2015 principal commodities produced (by value of shipments, in $1m.) were: transportation equipment, 948,208; food, 775,591; chemicals, 751,623; petroleum and coal products, 507,907; machinery, 384,579.

Net profits (2015) for manufacturing corporations were $505bn. after tax. Hourly earnings of production workers in Aug. 2017 were $20·93 in manufacturing and $26·80 in construction.

The USA is the second largest beer producer after China, with 5,940m. gallons in 2013.

Iron and Steel

Output of the iron and steel industries (in 1m. net tons of 2,000 lb) in recent years was:

	Pig iron	Raw steel	Steel by method of production[1]	
			Electric[1]	Basic oxygen
2011	30·2	86·4	52·1	34·3
2012	30·1	88·7	52·4	36·3
2013	30·3	86·9	52·7	34·2
2014	29·4	88·2	55·2	33·0
2015	25·4	78·8	49·6	29·2

[1]The sum of these two items should equal the total in the preceding column; any difference is due to rounding.

In May 2016 iron and steel mills and ferroalloy manufacturing employed 83,890 persons. The median hourly wage was $22·88.

Labour

According to the Bureau of Labor Statistics there were 157·1m. people in the civilian labour force in 2015 (83·6m. men and 73·5m. women). There were 26·3m. foreign-born persons in the labour force in 2015, representing 16·7% of the total. Undocumented immigrants constitute 5% of the labour force. The unemployment rate was 3·8% in Feb. 2019, down from 4·1% in Feb. 2018, 9·0% in Feb. 2011 and 10·0% in Oct. 2009 (which was the highest rate since 1983). Payroll employment increased by 216,000 in Jan. 2017 reflecting job gains in retail trade, construction and financial activities (having fallen by 793,000 in Jan. 2009 in the largest monthly fall since 1945). In 2009 as a whole 5·1m. jobs were lost—the highest number since records began in 1939. Long-term unemployment rose from 6·1% of the labour force between 16 and 64 having been out of work for more than a year in 2001 to

10·0% in 2006 and 31·3% in 2011. In Jan. 2010 for the first time there were more women (64·2m.) than men (63·4m.) on US payrolls. In 2016 employed persons (16 years and over) numbered 151·4m. (46·8% women; 34·7% Black or African American/Asian/Hispanic or Latino).

Employed persons by industry, 2016:

Industry Group	Employed (1,000 persons)	Female (%)	Black or African American/Asian/ Hispanic or Latino (%)
Agriculture, forestry, fisheries, and hunting	2,460	25·3	28·3
Mining/quarrying/oil and gas extraction	792	13·4	26·5
Construction	10,328	9·1	36·6
Manufacturing	15,408	28·9	32·9
Wholesale and retail trade	20,218	44·5	34·3
Transportation and utilities	8,012	23·5	40·6
Information	2,855	40·6	30·0
Financial activities	10,404	52·3	29·6
Professional and business services	18,325	41·4	34·6
Education and health services	34,263	74·6	33·0
Leisure and hospitality	14,193	50·6	42·0
Other services	7,320	52·2	36·4
Public administration	6,857	45·1	33·4

A total of 12 strikes and lockouts of 1,000 workers or more occurred in 2015, involving 47,000 workers and 740,000 idle days.

On 24 July 2007 the federal hourly minimum wage was raised from $5·15 to $5·85 an hour. It had been $5·15 for nearly ten years, having previously been increased from $4·75 an hour on 1 Sept. 1997. It was raised again on 24 July 2008, to $6·55 an hour, and on 24 July 2009, to $7·25 (still valid as of March 2019). Americans worked an average 1,789 hours per person in 2014. Median weekly earnings in 2016 were $915 among men and $749 among women).

Labour relations are legally regulated by the National Labor Relations Act, amended by the Labor–Management Relations (Taft–Hartley) Act 1947 as amended by the Labor–Management Reporting and Disclosure Act 1959, again amended in 1974, and the Railway Labor Act of 1926, as amended in 1934 and 1936.

The USA had 60,000 people living in slavery according to the Walk Free Foundation's 2013 *Global Slavery Index*.

International Trade

The North American Free Trade Agreement (NAFTA) between the USA, Canada and Mexico was signed on 7 Oct. 1992 and came into effect on 1 Jan. 1994. The Central America-Dominican Republic-United States Free Trade Agreement (CAFTA-DR) between the USA, Costa Rica, the Dominican Republic, El Salvador, Guatemala, Honduras and Nicaragua entered into force for the USA on 1 March 2006.

Imports and Exports

Total value of imports and exports of goods (in $1bn.):

	Imports	Exports	Trade balance
2008	2,141·3	1,308·8	−832·5
2009	1,580·0	1,070·3	−509·7
2010	1,939·0	1,290·3	−648·7
2011	2,239·9	1,498·9	−741·0
2012	2,303·7	1,562·6	−741·1
2013	2,294·2	1,593·7	−700·5
2014	2,385·5	1,635·6	−749·9
2015	2,273·2	1,511·4	−761·9

(*continued*)

	Imports	Exports	Trade balance
2016	2,208·0	1,457·0	−751·1
2017	2,360·9	1,553·4	−807·5

The USA's international trade deficit increased from $502·0bn. in 2016 to $552·3bn. in 2017. The goods deficit increased from $751·1bn. in 2016 to $807·5bn. in 2017, while the services surplus increased from $249·1bn. in 2016 to $255·2bn. in 2017. The last recorded trade surplus in goods was in 1975. The USA is the world's leading importer and up until 2013 the leading trading nation, although China overtook the USA that year as the largest trading nation overall. The USA is also the second largest exporter after China. In 2014 its trade in goods accounted for 12·6% of the world's imports and 8·5% of exports. Its deficit with China, which stood at just $83·9bn. in 2000, was $347·0bn. in 2016.

Imports and exports (in $1m.) by category including main components by value, 2016:

	Imports	Exports
Food and live animals	*100,040*	*96,173*
Meat and preparations	8,561	16,244
Fish and preparations	19,331	5,076
Cereals and preparations	9,040	22,966
Vegetables and fruit	32,635	21,692
Beverages and tobacco	*24,048*	*6,488*
Crude materials (except fuels)	*29,612*	*71,597*
Oil seeds and oleaginous fruits	1,034	24,725
Metalliferous ores and metal scrap	5,844	16,119
Mineral fuels and lubricants	*154,040*	*93,473*
Petroleum products and preparations	142,854	75,458
Natural and manufactured gas	7,981	13,189
Animal and vegetable oils	*6,063*	*2,623*
Chemicals and related products	*217,323*	*186,259*
Organic chemicals	47,179	31,176
Inorganic chemicals	10,927	10,126
Medicinal/pharmaceutical products	95,465	47,206
Essential oils and resinoids	14,328	15,273
Plastics (primary and non-primary)	23,732	43,288
Chemical materials and products	16,585	29,086
Manufactured goods by material	*232,436*	*101,854*
Rubber manufactures	20,099	8,373
Paper and paperboard	16,063	14,605
Textile yarn/fabrics	27,522	11,806
Nonmetallic mineral manufactures	45,834	13,428
Iron and steel	27,379	12,602
Nonferrous metals	33,455	13,477
Manufactures of metals	49,831	24,382
Machinery and transport equipment	*954,276*	*492,932*
Power generating machinery	64,473	33,741
Specialized industrial machinery	42,514	38,056
General industrial machinery	89,981	58,606
Office machines	110,535	19,341
Telecommunications equipment	157,905	20,702
Electrical machinery	168,434	78,309
Road vehicles	277,250	111,568
Transport equipment	33,881	127,881
Miscellaneous manufactured articles	*366,735*	*117,747*
Furniture	47,142	6,233
Clothing and accessories	88,232	3,063
Footwear	25,634	788
Scientific and controlling equipment	53,659	46,783
Photographic equipment	14,226	6,120

(*continued*)

	Imports	Exports
Miscellaneous articles	113,917	51,643
Miscellaneous commodities	*104,611*	*60,240*
Re-exports	—	*224,336*

Imports and exports by selected countries for the calendar years 2015 and 2016 (in $1m.):

	General imports		Exports incl. re-exports	
Country	2015	2016	2015	2016
Australia	10,894	9,534	25,036	22,225
Belgium	19,482	17,020	34,160	32,271
Brazil	27,468	26,176	31,651	30,297
Canada	296,156	278,067	280,609	266,827
China	483,245	462,813	116,072	115,775
Colombia	14,075	13,796	16,287	13,099
France	47,815	46,765	30,104	30,941
Germany	124,820	114,227	49,971	49,362
Hong Kong	6,796	7,386	37,167	34,908
India	44,792	45,998	21,452	21,689
Indonesia	19,602	19,203	7,121	6,037
Ireland	39,336	45,504	8,931	9,556
Israel	24,478	22,203	13,539	13,197
Italy	44,159	45,210	16,204	16,754
Japan	131,364	132,202	62,443	63,264
South Korea	71,759	69,932	43,446	42,266
Malaysia	33,971	36,687	12,277	11,867
Mexico	296,408	294,151	235,745	230,959
Netherlands	16,836	16,152	40,196	40,377
Saudi Arabia	22,081	16,926	19,739	18,023
Singapore	18,267	17,801	28,472	26,868
Spain	14,130	13,468	10,310	10,373
Switzerland	31,397	36,374	22,185	22,701
Taiwan	40,908	39,313	25,860	26,045
Thailand	28,632	29,493	11,231	10,573
United Arab Emirates	2,469	3,371	23,006	22,401
United Kingdom	57,962	54,326	56,115	55,396
Vietnam	38,016	42,099	7,101	10,100

Communications

Roads

On 31 Dec. 2012 the total public road mileage was 4,092,730 miles (urban, 1,113,018; rural, 2,979,711). Urban roads in 2012 included 16,910 miles of interstate highways, 11,469 miles of other freeways and expressways, and 791,832 miles of local roads. Rural roads in 2012 included 30,522 miles of interstate highways, 4,395 miles of other freeways and expressways, and 2,036,976 miles of local roads. State highway funds were $168,242m. in 2015.

Motor vehicles registered in 2012: 245,184,447, of which 111,289,906 automobiles, 764,509 buses and 133,130,032 trucks. There were 211,814,830 licensed drivers in 2012 and 8,429,988 motorcycle registrations. The average distance travelled by a motor vehicle in 2012 was 11,705 miles. In 2015 there were 35,092 fatalities in road accidents (the highest total since 2008), up from 32,675 in 2014.

Rail

Freight service is provided by nine major independent railroad companies and several hundred smaller operators. The largest companies are the Union Pacific Railroad and the BNSF Railway (formerly the Burlington Northern and Santa Fe Railway). Long-distance passenger trains are run by the National Railroad Passenger Corporation (Amtrak), which is federally assisted. Amtrak was set up in 1971 to maintain a basic network of long-distance passenger trains, and is responsible for almost all non-commuter services. In 2013 the operational Amtrak rail system measured 21,356 miles.

Outside the major conurbations, there are almost no regular passenger services other than those of Amtrak, which carried 30·8m. passengers in fiscal year 2015.

Civil Aviation

The busiest US airport in 2016 was Atlanta (Hartsfield–Jackson), which handled 104,171,935 passengers. The second busiest was Los Angeles International with 80,921, 527 passengers, followed by Chicago (O'Hare) with 77,960,588. As well as being the three busiest airports in the USA for passenger traffic, they also rank among the busiest in the world. The six busiest in the world in 2016 were Atlanta, Beijing Capital International, Dubai, Los Angeles, Tokyo Haneda and Chicago O'Hare. New York (John F. Kennedy) was the busiest airport in the USA for international passengers in 2015, with 30,020,301, ahead of Miami International with 21,206,577.

There were 23 airports with more than 10m. enplanements in 2013. These were, in descending order: Atlanta (Hartsfield–Jackson); Los Angeles; Chicago (O'Hare); Dallas/Fort Worth; Denver; New York (John F. Kennedy); San Francisco; Charlotte/Douglas; Las Vegas (McCarran); Phoenix (Sky Harbor); Miami; Houston (George Bush Intercontinental); Newark (Liberty); Orlando; Seattle (Seattle–Tacoma); Minneapolis–St Paul; Detroit (Metropolitan Wayne County); Boston (Logan); Philadelphia; New York (La Guardia); Fort Lauderdale/Hollywood International; Baltimore/Washington, D.-C. (Thurgood Marshall); Washington, D.C. (Dulles).

The leading airports in 2016 on the basis of aircraft movements were Atlanta Hartsfield-Jackson (898,356); Chicago O'Hare (867,635); Los Angeles (697,138); Dallas/Fort Worth (672,748).

In 2017 the largest airlines ranked by enplaned passengers both in the USA and in the world were Southwest Airlines (157·7m.), Delta Air Lines (145·6m.) and American Airlines (144·9m.). Delta Air Lines filed for bankruptcy in Sept. 2005, but emerged from bankruptcy protection in April 2007. AMR, the parent company for American Airlines, filed for bankruptcy in Nov. 2011. It then merged with US Airways Group in Dec. 2013 to form American Airlines Group, Inc. In 2015 US flag carriers in scheduled service enplaned 798·4m. revenue passengers.

Shipping

In Jan. 2014 there were 347 ships of 300 GT or over registered, totalling 7·61m. DWT. These included 156 passenger ships, 68 container ships, 63 general cargo ships and 52 oil tankers. The US-controlled fleet comprised 1,022 vessels of 1,000 GT or over in July 2014. Only 201 of the 1,022 vessels in July 2014 were flying the US flag.

The busiest port is South Louisiana, which handled 261·9m. tons of cargo in 2016. Other major ports are Houston (248·0m. tons in 2016), New York-New Jersey (133·4m. tons in 2016), New Orleans, Beaumont, Corpus Christi, Long Beach and Baton Rouge. South Louisiana handles the most domestic cargo ahead of Houston, but Houston the most foreign trade cargo ahead of South Louisiana.

Telecommunications

Regional private companies formed from the American Telephone and Telegraph Co. after its dissolution in 1995 ('Baby Bells') operate the telephone and electronic transmission services system at the national and local levels. Telegram services are still available through iTelegram. In 2012 there were 138·6m. main telephone lines in operation (436·5 per 1,000 inhabitants), down from 182·9m. in 2003. There were 304·8m. cellphone subscriptions in 2012 (960·1 per 1,000 persons), up from 160·6m. in 2003. In addition the proportion of households that only have cellphones has rapidly increased, to such an extent that by Dec. 2008 the number of cellphone-only households had surpassed landline-only households, with 20% of households being cellphone-only. The leading cellphone operators are Verizon Wireless (with more than 115m. subscribers), AT&T Mobility, Sprint Nextel and T-Mobile. In 2013 an estimated 84·2% of the population were internet users. 75·6% of households had a computer in 2011, with 71·7% of households having internet access at home. In 2014 e-commerce amounted to $304·9bn. In 2012 there were 89·8 wireless broadband subscriptions per 100 inhabitants and only 28·4 fixed broadband subscriptions per 100. In Dec. 2011 there were 157·4m. Facebook users (about three times as many as any other country and 50% the total population of the USA).

Social Institutions

Out of 178 countries analysed in the 2017 *Fragile States Index*—a list published jointly by the Fund for Peace and *Foreign Policy* magazine—the USA was ranked the 21st least vulnerable to conflict or collapse. The index is based on 12 indicators of state vulnerability across social, political and economic categories.

Justice

Legal controversies may be decided in two systems of courts: the federal courts, with jurisdiction confined to certain matters enumerated in Article III of the Constitution, and the state courts, with jurisdiction in all other proceedings. The federal courts have jurisdiction exclusive of the state courts in criminal prosecutions for the violation of federal statutes, in civil cases involving the government, in bankruptcy cases and in admiralty proceedings, and have jurisdiction concurrent with the state courts over suits between parties from different states, and certain suits involving questions of federal law.

The highest court is the Supreme Court of the US, which reviews cases from the lower federal courts and certain cases originating in state courts involving questions of federal law. It is the final arbiter of all questions involving federal statutes and the Constitution; and it has the power to invalidate any federal or state law or executive action which it finds repugnant to the Constitution. This court, consisting of nine justices appointed by the President who receive salaries of $255,300 a year (the Chief Justice, $267,000), meets from Oct. until June every year. For the term beginning Oct. 2012 it disposed of 7,602 cases, deciding 76 on their merits. In the remainder of cases it either summarily affirms lower court decisions or declines to review. A few suits, usually brought by state governments, originate in the Supreme Court, but issues of fact are mostly referred to a master.

The US courts of appeals number 13 (in 11 circuits composed of three or more states and one circuit for the District of Columbia and one Court of Appeals for the Federal Circuit); the 179 circuit judges receive salaries of $220,600 a year. Any party to a suit in a lower federal court usually has a right of appeal to one of these courts. In addition, there are direct appeals to these courts from many federal administrative agencies. In the year ending 30 Sept. 2013, 56,475 appeals were filed in the courts of appeals, in addition to 1,259 in the US Court of Appeals for the Federal Circuit.

The trial courts in the federal system are the US district courts, of which there are 94 in the 50 states, one in the District of Columbia and one each in the Commonwealth of Puerto Rico and the Territories of the Virgin Islands, Guam and the Northern Marianas. Each state has at least one US district court, and three states have four apiece. Each district court has from one to 28 judgeships. There are 677 US district judges ($208,000 a year), who received 284,604 civil cases in 2012–13.

In addition to these courts of general jurisdiction, there are special federal courts of limited jurisdiction. The US Court of Federal Claims (16 judges at $205,100 a year) decides claims for money damages against the federal government in a wide variety of matters; the Court of International Trade (13 judges at $208,000) determines controversies concerning the classification and valuation of imported merchandise.

The judges of all these courts are appointed by the President with the approval of the Senate; to assure their independence, they hold office 'during good behaviour' (meaning that they cannot be discharged but may be impeached for misconduct) and cannot have their salaries reduced. This does not apply to judges in the Territories, who hold their offices for a term of ten years or to judges of the US Court of Federal Claims. The judges may retire with full pay at the age of 70 years if they have served a period of ten years, or at 65 if they have 15 years of service, but they are subject to call for such judicial duties as they are willing to undertake.

Among the 284,604 civil cases filed in the district courts in 2012–13, 63,316 were personal injury cases, 56,955 were prisoner petitions, 35,307 were civil rights cases and 28,571 were contract actions. In the year ending Sept. 2015, 860,182 cases were filed in the US Bankruptcy Courts (down 10·7% from 963,739 in 2014 and the lowest since fiscal year 2007), 835,197 of which involved individuals or non-businesses.

In 2000 the number of lawyers in the USA passed the 1m. mark, the equivalent of 363 per 100,000 people, reaching 1·3m. by 2015.

There were 75,861 criminal cases filed for the year ending March 2017 of which 24,104 involved drugs, 20,602 immigration and 10,171 property offences.

Persons convicted of federal crimes may be fined, released on probation under the supervision of the probation officers of the federal courts, confined in prison, or confined in prison with a period of supervised release to follow, also under the supervision of probation officers of the federal courts. Federal prisoners are confined in 87 institutions incorporating various security levels that are operated by the Bureau of Prisons. On 31 Dec. 2012 the total number of prisoners under the jurisdiction of federal or state adult correctional authorities was 1,570,397, down slightly from 1,598,248 in Dec. 2007. A total of 2,228,000 inmates were held in state or federal prisons or local jails in 2012 (down from a peak of 2,308,000 in 2008), giving a rate of 710 per 100,000 population (the second highest in the world). Although the USA has less than 5% of the world's population it has around 24% of the world's prisoners. Blacks make up 37% of the prison population, although they only account for 14% of the general population. The USA was ranked 23rd of 102 countries for criminal justice and 21st for civil justice in the 2015 World Justice Project *Rule of Law Index*, which provides data on how the rule of law is experienced by the general public across eight categories.

The state courts have jurisdiction over all civil and criminal cases arising under state laws, but decisions of the state courts of last resort as to the validity of treaties or of laws of the USA, or on other questions arising under the Constitution, are subject to review by the Supreme Court of the US. The state court systems are generally similar to the federal system, to the extent that they generally have a number of trial courts and intermediate appellate courts, and a single court of last resort. The highest court in each state is usually called the Supreme Court or Court of Appeals with a Chief Justice and Associate Justices, usually elected but sometimes appointed by the Governor with the advice and consent of the State Senate or other advisory body; they usually hold office for a term of years, but in some instances for life or during good behaviour. The lowest tribunals are usually those of Justices of the Peace; many towns and cities have municipal and police courts, with power to commit for trial in criminal matters and to determine misdemeanours for violation of the municipal ordinances.

There were no executions from 1968 to 1976. The US Supreme Court had held the death penalty, as applied in general criminal statutes, to contravene the eighth and fourteenth amendments of the US constitution, as a cruel and unusual punishment when used so irregularly and rarely as to destroy its deterrent value. The death penalty was reinstated by the Supreme Court in 1976, but has not been authorized in Alaska, the District of Columbia, Hawaii, Iowa, Kansas, Maine, Massachusetts, Michigan, Minnesota, New Jersey, New York, North Dakota, Rhode Island, Vermont, West Virginia and Wisconsin. At 1 July 2017 there were 2,817 (including 53 women) prisoners under sentence of death. 39 people were sentenced to death in 2017. In 2018 there were 25 executions (up from 23 in 2017 but down from a peak of 98 in 1999). From 1976–2018 there were 1,490 executions of which 558 were in Texas and 113 in Virginia. The death penalty for offenders under the age of 18 was abolished in March 2005. For the first time since 1963, there were two executions under federal jurisdiction in 2001. In Sept. 2003 the federal Court of Appeals in San Francisco overturned over 100 death sentences in Arizona, Idaho and Montana on the grounds that judges, not juries, had passed sentence, contravening a Supreme Court ruling of 2002.

There were 17,413 murders in 2016, the highest total since 1997 and up from 14,164 in 2014 (which had been the lowest annual total since 1968). The murder rate in 2016 was 5·3 per 100,000 persons, up from 4·4 per 100,000 in 2014 although down from 10·2 per 100,000 in 1980. 73% of all murders in 2016 were carried out with firearms.

Education
The adult literacy rate is at least 99%.

Based on the results from the Program for the International Assessment of Adult Competencies (PIAAC), in 2012 some 18% of US adults ages 16 to 65 scored at or below level 1 proficiency on the literacy scale compared to the average of 15% for the countries participating in PIAAC. (The scale ranged from below level 1 to level 5, with level 1 literacy proficiency requiring 'knowledge and skill in recognizing basic vocabulary, evaluating the meaning of sentences, and reading of paragraph text.')

Elementary and secondary education is mainly a state responsibility. Each state and the District of Columbia has a system of free public schools, established by law, with courses covering 12 years plus kindergarten. There are three structural patterns in common use; the K8-4 plan, meaning kindergarten plus eight elementary grades followed by four high school grades; the K6-3-3 plan, or kindergarten plus six elementary grades followed by a three-year junior high school and a three-year senior high school; and the K5-3-4 plan, kindergarten plus five elementary grades followed by a three-year middle school and a four-year high school. All plans lead to high-school graduation, usually at age 17 or 18. Vocational education is an optional part of secondary education. Each state has delegated some degree of control of the educational programme to local school districts (numbering 13,567 in school year 2011–12), each with a board of education (usually three to nine members) selected locally and serving mostly without pay. The policies of the local school districts must be in accord with the laws and the regulations of their state departments of education. While regulations differ from one jurisdiction to another, in general it may be said that school attendance is compulsory from age seven to 16. All states operate both two-year and four-year public colleges, with the two-year colleges typically offering programmes at lower cost. Private schools and college operate independently throughout the USA and are funded primarily by tuition.

'Charter schools' are public schools that operate outside the school boards' administration. They retain the basics of public school education, but may offer unconventional curricula and hours of attendance. Founders may be parents, teachers, public bodies or commercial firms. Organization and conditions depend upon individual states' legislation. The first charter schools were set up in Minnesota in 1991. By 2012, 6,079 charter schools were operating in 40 states and Washington, D.C.

In 2012 some 18% of US adults age 16 to 65 scored at or below level 1 proficiency on the PIAAC literacy scale (*see* above). By race/ethnicity, 10% of Whites, 35% of Blacks and 43% of Hispanics scored at or below level 1 proficiency. In March 2013, 88·2% of all persons 25 years old and over had completed four years of high school or more, and 31·7% had completed a bachelor's or higher degree. In the age group 25 to 29, 89·9% had completed four years of high school or more, and 33·6% had completed a bachelor's or higher degree. However, according to a study conducted in 2013 about a third of American fourth graders (aged 9–10) are unable to read at a basic level.

In the fall of 2012, 20·6m. students (12·7m. full-time and 11·7m. women) were enrolled in 4,726 colleges and universities; 3·0m. were first-time students. It is projected that in 2023 the student population will number 23·8m.

In 2015–16 total expenditure on education came to $1,254bn. (7·0% of GDP); spending on elementary and secondary education totalled $707bn. (3·9% of GDP) and that on tertiary education was $548bn. (3·0% of GDP). Current expenditure per pupil in public elementary and secondary schools in 2013–14 was $11,226. At the post-secondary level, the USA spent $29,700 per full-time equivalent student in 2014, compared to the OECD average of $16,400.

Estimated expenditures in 2015–16 for private elementary and secondary schools and private post-secondary institutions were $52bn. and $204bn., respectively. In 2011–12 the federal government contributed about 18% of total revenue for public institutions; state governments, 24%; student tuition and fees, 21%; and local sources, 6%. Federal support for vocational education in fiscal year 2012 amounted to about $1·7bn.

Summary of statistics of regular schools (public and private), teachers and pupils for 2011–12 (compiled by the US National Center for Education Statistics):

Schools by level	Number of schools	Teachers (in 1,000)	Enrolment (in 1,000)
Elementary and secondary schools:			
Public	98,328	3,103	49,522
Private	30,861	421	5,268
Higher education:			
Public	2,011	953	15,110
Private	5,223	570	5,884
Total	*136,423*	*5,048*	*75,784*

In the fall of 2012 there were 16·0 pupils per teacher in public schools in the USA and 12·5 pupils per teacher in private schools.

The majority of the private elementary and secondary schools are affiliated with religious denominations. In 2011–12 there were 6,870 Catholic schools with 2,088,000 pupils and 138,000 teachers, and 14,210 schools of other religious affiliations with 1,992,000 pupils and 163,000 teachers.

During the school year 2011–12 high-school graduates numbered 3,452,000 (of whom 3·1m. were from public schools). Institutions of higher education conferred 1,840,000 bachelor's degrees during the year 2012–13; 1,007,000 associate's degrees; 752,000 master's degrees; and 175,000 doctorates degrees. In the fiscal year 2013 US Department of Education outlays in support of student grant, loan and work study programmes totalled $43bn. An additional $107bn. in loans was made available through these outlays to support students in postsecondary education.

During the academic year 2011–12, 764,500 foreign students were enrolled in American colleges and universities. The countries with the largest numbers of students in American colleges were: China, 194,000; India, 100,300; South Korea, 72,300; Saudi Arabia, 34,100; Canada, 26,800; Taiwan, 23,300; Japan, 20,000.

In 2012, 66,000 US students were enrolled in degree programmes in colleges and universities outside of the USA. The country attracting the most students from the USA was the United Kingdom, with 17,000. In addition to these students, some 274,000 US college students attend short programmes in other countries every year.

School enrolment, Oct. 2012, encompassed 93·2% of the children who were 5 and 6 years old; 98·0% of the children aged 7–13 years; 97·0% of those aged 14–17; 69·0% of those aged 18–19; and 40·2% of those aged 20–24.

The US National Center for Education Statistics estimates the total enrolment in the fall of 2014 at all of the country's elementary, secondary and higher educational institutions (public and private) at 75·7m. (68·7m. in the fall of 2000).

The number of teachers in public and private elementary and secondary schools in 2012 was about 3,525,000. The estimated average annual salary of public school teachers was $56,400 in 2012–13.

Health

Admission to the practice of medicine (for both doctors of medicine and doctors of osteopathic medicine) is controlled in each state by examining boards directly representing the profession and acting with authority conferred by state law. Although there are a number of variations, the usual time now required to complete training is eight years beyond the secondary school with up to three or more years of additional graduate training. Certification as a specialist may require between three and five more years of graduate training plus experience in practice. In 2013 the total number of physicians in the USA, Puerto Rico and outlying US areas was 1,045,910 (813,770 in 2000 and 393,742 in 1975); active doctors numbered 854,698.

Dentists in 2015 numbered 195,722 (163,345 in 2001).

Number of hospitals listed by the American Hospital Association in 2014 was 5,627, with 902,202 beds. Of the total, 213 hospitals with 38,893 beds were operated by the federal government; 1,003 with 116,411 beds by state and local government; 2,870 with 534,554 beds by non-profit organizations (including church groups); 1,053 with 135,909 beds were investor-owned. Non-federal hospitals (comprising psychiatric and respiratory disease facilities, and long-term and short-term general and other special hospitals) numbered 5,414, with 863,309 beds in 2014.

Patient admissions to community hospitals in 2014 totalled 33,067,000; average length of stay was 5·5 days. There were 693·1m. outpatient visits.

Personal health expenditure in 2015 totalled $2,717·2bn., including: hospital care, $1,036·1bn.; professional services, $840·2bn.; prescription drugs, $324·6bn.; nursing-home care, $156·8bn.; home health care, $88·8bn.; medical durables, $48·5bn. Total national health spending in 2015 amounted to $3,205·6bn. In 2014 the USA spent 16·5% of its GDP on health—nearly 5% more than any other leading industrialized nation. Public spending on health amounted to 48·2% of total health spending in 2013 (the lowest percentage of any major industrialized nation). In March 2010 then President Obama secured the passage of a controversial health care reform package that was expected to increase insurance coverage to a further 32m. citizens. Implementation of the Patient Protection and Affordable Care Act (popularly known as 'Obamacare') began in Oct. 2013. By May 2014 it was estimated that 20m. Americans had gained health insurance coverage under the Act. The proportion of uninsured people dropped from 18·0% to 11·4% between the third quarter of 2013 and the second quarter of 2015. The US Census Bureau had estimated in 2008 that 46·3m. people in America were uninsured. However, Obama's presidential successor, Donald Trump, has vowed to repeal large parts of the Obamacare legislation.

In 2016, 15·5% of American adults (17·5% of males and 13·5% of females) were smokers, down from a peak of over 42% in 1965. In 2013–14, 37·9% of the adult population were considered obese (having a body mass index over 30), compared to 14·6% in the early 1970s.

In *Water: At What Cost? The State of the World's Water 2016*, WaterAid reported that 0·8% of the population does not have access to safe water.

Welfare

Social welfare legislation was chiefly the province of the various states until the adoption of the Social Security Act of 14 Aug. 1935. This as amended provides for a federal system of old-age, survivors and disability insurance; health insurance for the aged and disabled; supplemental security income for the aged, blind and disabled; federal state unemployment insurance; and federal grants to states for public assistance (medical assistance for the aged and aid to families with dependent children generally and for maternal and child health and child welfare services).

Legislation of Aug. 1996 began the transfer of aid administratic back to the states, restricted the provision of aid to a maximum period of five years, and abolished benefits to immigrants (both legal and illegal) for the first five years of their residence in the USA. The Social Security Administration (formerly part of the Department of Health and Human Services but an independent agency since March 1995) has responsibility for a number of programmes covering retirement, disability, Medicare, Supplemental Security Income and survivors. The Administration for Children and Families (ACF), an agency of the Department of Health and Human Services, is responsible for federal programmes which promote the economic and social wellbeing of families, children, individuals and communities. ACF has federal responsibility for the following programmes: Temporary Assistance for Needy Families; low income energy assistance; Head Start; child care; child protective services; and a community services block grant. The ACF also has federal responsibility for social service programmes for children, youth, native Americans and persons with developmental disabilities.

The Administration on Aging (AoA), an agency in the US Department of Health and Human Services, is one of the nation's largest providers of home- and community-based care for older persons and their caregivers. Created in 1965 with the passage of the Older Americans Act (OAA), AoA is part of a federal, state, tribal and local partnership called the Aging Network. It serves about 10m. older persons and their caregivers, and includes 56 state and territorial units on aging, 622 Area Agencies on Aging, 260 Title VI Native American aging programmes and tens of thousands of service providers. These organizations provide assistance and services to older individuals and their families in urban, suburban, and rural areas throughout the USA.

The Centers for Medicare and Medicaid Services (formerly the Health Care Financing Administration), an agency of the Health and Human Services Department, has federal responsibility for health insurance for the aged and disabled. Unemployment insurance is the responsibility of the Department of Labor.

In 2015–16 an average of 1,206,820 families were receiving payments under Temporary Assistance for Needy Families; total payments amounted to $30,868m. (including 23·9% for basic assistance, 16·6% for child care, and 9·2% for work, education and training activities). The role of the Office of Child Support Enforcement (OCSE) is to ensure that children are supported by their parents. Money collected is for children who live with only one parent because of divorce, separation or birth outside marriage. In 2015–16, $32,700m. was collected for child support; total OCSE expenditures were $5·7bn. ($3·4bn. in federal funds and $2·3bn. in state funds).

The Social Security Act provides for protection against the cost of medical care through Medicare, a two-part programme of health insurance for people age 65 and over, people of any age with permanent kidney failure and for certain disabled people under age 65 who receive Social Security disability benefits. In 2014 payments totalling $269,300m. were made under the hospital portion of Medicare. Medicare enrolment in 2014 totalled 54·1m.

Full retirement benefits are payable from age 66 for Americans born between 1943 and 1954. For those born in 1955 the full retirement age (normal retirement age) will be 66 years and 2 months. The full retirement age will continue to rise in two-month increments each year until it reaches 67 for everyone born in 1960 or later. Pensions may also be deferred up to age 70. In June 2018 there were 43·1m. retired workers receiving an average monthly benefit of $1,413 ($1,198 for disabled workers); retired workers and their dependants accounted for 72% of total benefits paid, with disabled workers and dependants accounting for 13%. The minimum social security benefit was eliminated in Jan. 1982 for all workers becoming eligible for retirement or disability insurance benefits after Dec. 1981. A means-tested supplemental income benefit is available to over-65s and disabled and blind individuals with limited income and limited resources.

Medicaid is a jointly-funded, federal-state health insurance programme for certain low-income and vulnerable people. It covered 73·7m. individuals in 2013 including children under 21 (40·4%), adults aged 65 and over (5·6%) and blind and/or disabled (13·0%).

In Dec. 2016, 8·25m. persons were receiving Supplementary Security Income payments. 1,164,589 aged persons received $501·5m. in benefits; 68,344 blind people received $39·4m.; and 7,018,228 disabled people received $4,199·4m. Payments, including supplemental amounts from various states, totalled $4,740·3m. in 2016.

In 2015–16 the Supplemental Nutrition Assistance Program (formerly the Food Stamp Program) helped 44,219,000 persons at a cost of $70,915m.; and an average of 30·4m. persons received help from the national school lunch programme (73·3% for free or at a reduced price).

The USA is one of the few countries in the world not to have guaranteed paid maternity leave. Only 12% of Americans have access to the paid parental leave.

Religion

The leading religious bodies according to the *2010 U.S. Religion Census: Religious Congregations & Membership Study* and based on the number of adherents are as follows:

Religious bodies	Tradition	Adherents	Congregations
Catholic Church[1]	Catholic	58,927,887	20,589
Southern Baptist Convention	Evangelical Protestant	19,896,279	50,816
Non-denominational (Christian)	Evangelical Protestant	12,241,329	35,496
United Methodist Church	Mainline Protestant	9,860,653	33,323
Church of Jesus Christ of Latter-day Saints	Latter-day Saint	6,144,582	13,601
Evangelical Lutheran Church in America	Mainline Protestant	4,181,219	9,846
Assemblies of God	Evangelical Protestant (Pentecostal)	2,944,887	12,258
Muslim	Islamic	2,600,082[2]	2,106
Presbyterian Church (USA)	Mainline Protestant	2,451,980	10,487
Lutheran Church—Missouri Synod	Evangelical Protestant	2,270,921	6,040

[1]In Feb. 2019 there were 15 cardinals. [2]Estimate.

In 2010 there were 2,257,000 Jews (estimate), 1,184,249 Jehovah's Witnesses, 992,000 Buddhists (estimate) and 641,186 Hindus. Other major religious bodies with at least 1m. adherents are: Episcopal Church; National Baptist Convention, USA, Inc.; Churches of Christ; American Baptist Churches in the USA; Christian Churches and Churches of Christ; United Church of Christ; Seventh-day Adventist Church; Church of God (Cleveland, Tennessee); African Methodist Episcopal Church.

FitzGerald, Frances, *The Evangelicals: The Struggle to Shape America*. 2017

Culture

World Heritage Sites

There are 23 sites under American jurisdiction that appear on the UNESCO World Heritage List. They are (with year entered on list): Mesa Verde National Park, Colorado (1978); Yellowstone National Park, Wyoming/Idaho/Montana (1978); Everglades National Park, Florida (1979); Grand Canyon National Park, Arizona (1979); Independence Hall, Pennsylvania (1979); Redwood National and State Parks, California (1980); Mammoth Cave National Park, Kentucky (1981); Olympic National Park, Washington State (1981); Cahokia Mounds State Historic Site, Illinois (1982); Great Smoky Mountains National Park, North Carolina/Tennessee (1983); San Juan National Historic Site and La Fortaleza, Puerto Rico (1983); the Statue of Liberty, New York (1984); Yosemite National Park, California (1984);

Monticello and the University of Virginia, Charlottesville, Virginia (1987); Chaco Culture National Historic Park, New Mexico (1987); Hawaii Volcanoes National Park, including Mauna Loa, Hawaii (1987); Pueblo de Taos, New Mexico (1992); Carlsbad Caverns National Park, New Mexico (1995); Papahanaumokuakea, Hawaii (2010); Monumental Earthworks of Poverty Point, Louisiana (2014); San Antonio Missions, Texas (2015).

Two UNESCO World Heritage sites fall under joint US and Canadian jurisdiction: Kluane/Wrangell-St Elias/Glacier Bay/Tatshenshini-Alsek (1979, 1992 and 1994), parks in Alaska, Yukon and British Columbia; Waterton Glacier International Peace Park (1995), in Montana and Alberta.

Press

In 2014 there were 1,355 daily newspapers with a combined daily circulation of 42·7m., the fourth highest in the world behind India, China and Japan. There were 953 morning papers and 402 evening papers, plus 923 Sunday papers (circulation, 42·8m.). Unlike China and India, where circulation is rising, in the USA it has fallen since 1985, when daily circulation was 62·8m. The most widely read newspapers are *USA Today* (average daily circulation in 2014 of 4·1m.), followed by the *Wall Street Journal* (2·3m.) and the *New York Times* (2·1m.). According to a Pew Research Centre 2018 report an estimated 93% of Americans obtained national and international news from the internet. As of Sept. 2014 the USA's three most used online news sites were *The Huffington Post* (68·5m. unique desktop users per month), CNN (67·7m.) and *The New York Times* (41·6m.). In the *2018 World Press Freedom Index* compiled by Reporters Without Borders, the USA was ranked 45th out of 180 countries.

In 2015 a total of 338,986 book titles were produced (excluding self-published titles). However, there were at least 625,327 self-published books released in 2015. In 2017 the book publishing industry generated an estimated $26·2bn. in net revenue.

Tourism

In 2013 the USA received a record 69,995,000 foreign visitors (66,657,000 in 2012 and 62,821,000 in 2011), of whom 23,407,000 were from Canada and 14,547,000 from Mexico. 18% of all tourists were from Europe. Only France received more tourists than the USA in 2013.

In 2013 visitors to the USA spent $172·9bn., giving the USA by far the highest annual revenue from tourists of any country (Spain, which received the second most, had $62·6bn.). Expenditure by US travellers in foreign countries for 2013 was $104·1bn., second only to spending by Chinese travellers in foreign countries.

Festivals

Independence Day is celebrated on 4 July and Thanksgiving on the fourth Thursday of Nov. There are major opera festivals at Cooperstown (Glimmerglass), New York State (July–Aug.); Santa Fe, New Mexico (June–Aug.); and Seattle, Washington State (Aug.). Among the many famous film festivals are the Sundance Film Festival in Jan. and the New York Film Festival in late Sept./early Oct. Leading rock and pop festivals include SXSW in Austin, Texas (March), Coachella in Palm Springs, California (April), Bonnaroo in Manchester, Tennessee (June), Summerfest in Milwaukee, Wisconsin (June–July) and Lollapalooza in Chicago, Illinois (Aug.). The Burning Man art, music and performance festival takes place every year (Aug.–Sept.) in the Black Rock Desert, Nevada.

Diplomatic Representatives

Of the USA in the United Kingdom (33 Nine Elms Lane, London, SW11 7US)
    Ambassador: Robert Wood Johnson IV.

Of the United Kingdom in the USA (3100 Massachusetts Ave., NW, Washington, D.C., 20008)
    Ambassador: Sir Kim Darroch, KCMG.

Of the United States to the United Nations
    Ambassador: Vacant.
    Chargé d'Affaires a.i.: Jonathan Cohen.

Of the United States to the European Union
    Ambassador: Gordon D. Sondland.

States and Territories

Against the names of the Governors, Lieut.-Governors and the Secretaries of State, (D.) stands for Democrat and (R.) for Republican.

See also Local Government on page 1308.

Alabama

Key Historical Events

The early European explorers were Spanish, but the first permanent European settlement was French, as part of French Louisiana after 1699. During the 17th and 18th centuries the British, Spanish and French all fought for control of the territory; it passed to Britain in 1763 and thence to the USA in 1783, except for a Spanish enclave on Mobile Bay, which lasted until 1813. Alabama was organized as a Territory in 1817 and was admitted to the Union as a state on 14 Dec. 1819.

The economy was then based on cotton, grown in white-owned plantations by black slave labour imported since 1719. Alabama seceded from the Union at the beginning of the Civil War (1861) and joined the Confederate States of America; its capital Montgomery became the Confederate capital. After the defeat of the Confederacy the state was readmitted to the Union in 1878. Attempts made during the reconstruction period to find a role for the newly freed black slaves—who made up about 50% of the population—largely failed, and when whites regained political control in the 1870s a strict policy of segregation came into force. At the same time Birmingham began to develop as an important centre of iron- and steel-making. Most of the state was still rural. In 1915 a boll-weevil epidemic attacked the cotton and forced diversification into other farm produce. More industries developed from the power schemes of the Tennessee Valley Authority in the 1930s. The black population remained mainly rural, poor and without political power, until the 1960s when confrontations on the issue of civil rights produced reforms.

Territory and Population

Alabama is bounded in the north by Tennessee, east by Georgia, south by Florida and the Gulf of Mexico and west by Mississippi. Land area, 50,645 sq. miles (131,171 sq. km); water area, 1,775 sq. miles (4,597 sq. km). Census population, 1 April 2010, was 4,779,736, an increase of 7·5% since 2000. July 2018 estimate, 4,887,871.

Population in five census years was:

	White	Black	American Indian	Asian	Total	Per sq. mile
1930	1,700,844	944,834	465	105	2,646,248	51·3
			All others			
1980	2,872,621	996,335	24,932		3,893,888	74·9
1990	2,975,797	1,020,705	44,085		4,040,587	79·6
2000	3,162,808	1,155,930	128,362		4,447,100	87·6
2010	3,275,394	1,251,311	253,031		4,779,736	94·4

Of the total population in 2010, 2,459,548 were female and 3,647,277 were 18 years old or older. In 2010 the Hispanic population was 185,602, up from 75,830 in 2000 (an increase of 144·8%).

The large cities (2010 census) were (with metropolitan areas in brackets): Birmingham, 212,237 (Birmingham–Hoover metropolitan area, 1,128,047); Montgomery (the capital), 205,764 (374,536); Mobile, 195,111 (412,992); Huntsville, 180,105 (417,593); Tuscaloosa, 90,468 (219,461).

Social Statistics

Births, 2014, 59,422 (12·3 per 1,000 population); deaths, 2014, 50,215 (10·4). Infant deaths, 2013, 8·6 per 1,000 live births. 2014: marriages, 7·8 per 1,000 population; divorces and annulments, 3·8.

Climate

Birmingham, Jan. 46°F (7·8°C), July 80°F (26·7°C). Annual rainfall 54" (1,372 mm). Mobile, Jan. 52°F (11·1°C), July 82°F (27·8°C). Annual rainfall 62" (1,575 mm). Montgomery, Jan. 49°F (9·4°C), July 81°F (27·2°C). Annual rainfall 52" (1,321 mm). The growing season ranges from 190 days

(north) to 270 days (south). Alabama belongs to the Gulf Coast climate zone (*see* UNITED STATES: Climate).

Constitution and Government

The current constitution dates from 1901; it has had 892 amendments (as at 2014). The legislature consists of a Senate of 35 members and a House of Representatives of 105 members, all elected for four years. The Governor and Lieut.-Governor are elected for four years.

For the 116th Congress, which convened in Jan. 2019, Alabama sends seven members to the House of Representatives. It is represented in the Senate by Richard Shelby (D. 1987–94; R. 1994–2023) and Doug Jones (D. 2018–21).

Applicants for registration must take an oath of allegiance to the United States and fill out an application showing evidence that they meet State voter registration requirements.

Montgomery is the capital.

Recent Elections

In the 2016 presidential election Donald Trump took Alabama with 62·9% of the vote (Mitt Romney won it in 2012).

Current Government

Governor: Kay Ivey (R.), 2019–23 (salary: $120,395).
  Lieut.-Governor: Will Ainsworth (R.), 2019–23.
  Secretary of State: John Merrill (R.), since Jan. 2015.
Government Website: https://www.alabama.gov

Economy

Per capita personal income (2015) was $38,965.

Budget

In 2011 total state revenue was $26,305m. Total expenditure was $28,061m. (education, $10,938m.; public welfare, $5,962m.; hospitals, $1,948m.; highways, $1,616m.; health, $609m.). Outstanding debt in 2011, $9,067m.

Performance

Gross Domestic Product by state was $199,656m. in 2015, ranking Alabama 27th in the United States. In 2015 state real GDP growth was 0·9%.

Energy and Natural Resources

Electricity

In 2015 production was 152·5bn. kWh, of which 55·8bn. kWh was from natural gas.

Oil and Gas

In 2014 Alabama produced 9·8m. bbls of crude petroleum; marketed production of natural gas totalled 181bn. cu. ft.

Water

The total area covered by water is 1,775 sq. miles.

Minerals

Principal minerals, 2013 (in 1,000 short tons): crushed stone, 40,100; coal, 18,620; sand and gravel, 10,520; lime, 2,500. Value of non-fuel mineral production in 2009 was $1,020m.

Agriculture

The number of farms in 2009 was 48,500, covering 9·0m. acres; the average farm had 186 acres and was valued at $2,100 per acre (Jan. 2010).

Cash receipts from farm marketings, 2009: crops, $883m.; livestock and poultry products, $3,335m.; total, $4,218m. The net farm income in 2009 was $1,019m. Principal sources: broilers, cattle and calves, eggs, hogs, dairy products, greenhouse and nursery products, peanuts, soybeans, cotton and vegetables. In 2009 broilers accounted for the largest percentage of cash receipts from farm marketings; cattle and calves were second; and eggs third.

Forestry

Alabama had 22·91m. acres of forested land in 2013 of which 746,153 acres were national forest. Harvest volumes in 2013, 234·41m. cu. ft pine saw timber, 47·67m. cu. ft hardwood saw timber, 891·57m. cu. ft pulp wood and

14·34m. cu. ft poles. Total harvest, 2013, was 1,187·99m. cu. ft. Georgia is the only state with a larger annual harvest. The estimated delivered timber value of forest products in 2013 was $1·5bn.

Fisheries

Alabama had aquaculture sales worth $111·2m. in 2013, ranking it third behind Washington and Mississippi.

Industry

In 2012 the state's 9,836 manufacturing establishments had 553,000 employees, earning $25,916m. Total value added by manufacturing in 2013 was $47,357m. Alabama is both an industrial and service-oriented state. The chief industries are lumber and wood products, food and kindred products, textiles and apparel, non-electrical machinery, transportation equipment and primary metals.

Labour

In 2010, 1,869,000 were employed in non-agricultural sectors, of whom 386,800 were in government; 360,100 in trade, transportation and utilities; 236,100 in manufacturing; 214,400 in education and health services; 208,300 in professional and business services. In Dec. 2010 the unemployment rate was 9·1%.

International Trade

Imports and Exports

In 2015 imports into Alabama totalled $21·9bn. (down from $22·2bn. in 2014). In the same year exports from Alabama totalled $19·3bn., down from $19·5bn. in 2014. The leading source for imports in 2015 was South Korea ($4·7bn.), ahead of Germany ($4·1bn.). The leading destination for exports in 2015 was Canada ($4·1bn.), followed by China ($3·1bn.).

Communications

Roads

Total road length in 2012 was 101,811 miles, comprising 76,620 miles of rural road and 25,191 miles of urban road. Registered motor vehicles numbered 4,712,167.

Rail

In 2012 there were 3,194 miles of freight railroad (excluding trackage rights). There were 26 freight railroads operating in 2012. Rail traffic originating in Alabama in 2012 totalled 38·2m. tons and rail traffic terminating in the state came to 51·1m. tons.

Civil Aviation

In 2011 there were five primary airports (commercial service airports with more than 10,000 passenger boardings annually) with a combined total of 2,566,909 enplanements, up from 2,562,567 in 2010.

Shipping

There are 1,600 miles of navigable inland water and 50 miles of Gulf Coast. The only deep-water port is Mobile, with a large ocean-going trade; total tonnage (2014), 64·3m. tons. The Alabama State Docks also operates a system of ten inland docks; there are several privately run inland docks.

Social Institutions

Justice

In Dec. 2014 the prison population totalled 31,771. Following the reinstatement of the death penalty by the US Supreme Court in 1976 death sentences have been awarded since 1983. There were three executions in 2017 and two in 2018.

Education

In 2012–13 there were 1,637 public elementary and secondary schools with 51,877 teachers and 744,637 students enrolled in grades K–12. Average public school teacher salary in 2012–13 was $47,949. Spending per student in 2010–11 was $8,726.

In 2012–13 there were 77 degree-granting institutions (39 public and 38 private). Total enrolment (fall 2012) was 310,311 students. Enrolment for four-year courses (fall 2014) at University of Alabama at Tuscaloosa totalled

36,047, Auburn University 25,912, Troy University 19,041, University of Alabama at Birmingham 18,698 and University of South Alabama at Mobile 15,805. Columbia Southern University at Orange Beach, a private online university, had 21,359 students in fall 2014.

Health

Alabama had 3·1 community hospital beds for every 1,000 population in 2013. In the same year there were 22·4 active physicians per 10,000 civilian population and 4·4 dentists per 10,000.

Welfare

Medicare enrolment in July 2012 totalled 898,707. In fiscal year 2012 a total of 957,500 people in Alabama received Medicaid. In Dec. 2014 there were 1,095,925 Old-Age, Survivors, and Disability Insurance (OASDI) beneficiaries. A total of 50,757 people were receiving payments under Temporary Assistance for Needy Families (TANF) in Dec. 2012.

Religion

The main religious traditions in 2010 were: Evangelical Protestants, with 2,009,448 members; Mainline Protestants, 388,252; Black Protestants, 346,519; Catholics, 200,657; Latter-day Saints (Mormons), 36,820.

Alaska

Key Historical Events

Discovered in 1741 by Vitus Bering, Alaska's first settlement, on Kodiak Island, was in 1784. The area known as Russian America with its capital (1806) at Sitka was ruled by a Russo-American fur company and vaguely claimed as a Russian colony. Alaska was purchased by the United States from Russia under the treaty of 30 March 1867 for $7·2m. Settlement was boosted by gold workers in the 1880s. In 1884 Alaska became a 'district' governed by the code of the state of Oregon. By Act of Congress approved 24 Aug. 1912 Alaska became an incorporated Territory; its first legislature in 1913 granted votes to women, seven years in advance of the Constitutional Amendment.

During the Second World War the Federal government acquired large areas for defence purposes and for the construction of the strategic Alaska Highway. In the 1950s oil was found. Alaska became the 49th state of the Union on 3 Jan. 1959. In the 1970s new oilfields were discovered and the Trans-Alaska pipeline was opened in 1977. The state obtained most of its income from petroleum by 1985.

Questions of land-use predominate; there are large areas with valuable mineral resources, other large areas held for the native peoples and some still held by the Federal government. The population increased by over 400% between 1940 and 1980.

Territory and Population

Alaska is bounded north by the Beaufort Sea, west and south by the Pacific and east by Canada. The total area is 665,384 sq. miles (1,723,337 sq. km), making it the largest state of the USA; 570,641 sq. miles (1,477,953 sq. km) are land and 94,743 sq. miles (245,383 sq. km) are water. It is also the least densely populated state. The federal government owned 225,848,164 acres in 2010 (the largest area in any state), equivalent to 61·8% of the state area (the third highest percentage after Nevada and Utah). Census population, 1 April 2010, was 710,231, an increase of 13·3% since 2000. July 2018 estimate, 737,438.

Population in five census years was:

	White	Black	All others	Total	Per sq. mile
1950	92,808	—	35,835	128,643	0·23
1980	309,728	13,643	78,480	401,851	1·00
1990	415,492	22,451	112,100	550,043	1·00
2000	434,534	21,787	170,611	626,932	1·10
2010	473,576	23,263	213,392	710,231	1·24

Of the total population in 2010, 369,628 were male and 522,853 were 18 years old or older. Alaska's Hispanic population was 39,249 in 2010, up from 25,852 in 2000. As of 2010, 14·8% of Alaska's population was identified as Alaska Native or American Indian (the highest percentage of any US state).

The largest county equivalent and city is in the borough of Anchorage, which had a 2010 census population of 291,826. Census populations of the other 14 county equivalents, 2010: Fairbanks North Star, 97,581; Matanuska-Susitna, 88,995; Kenai Peninsula, 55,400; Juneau (the capital), 31,275; Bethel, 17,013; Kodiak Island, 13,592; Ketchikan Gateway, 13,477; Valdez-Cordova, 9,636; Nome, 9,492; North Slope, 9,430; Sitka, 8,881; Northwest Arctic, 7,523; Wade Hampton, 7,459; Southeast Fairbanks, 7,029. Largest incorporated places in 2010 were: Anchorage, 291,826; Fairbanks, 31,535; Juneau, 31,275; Sitka, 8,881; Ketchikan, 8,050; Wasilla, 7,831; Kenai, 7,100; Kodiak, 6,130; Bethel, 6,080; Palmer, 5,937.

Social Statistics

Births, 2014, 11,392 (15·5 per 1,000 population); deaths, 2014, 4,128 (5·6—the lowest rate in any US state). Infant mortality, 2013, 5·8 per 1,000 live births. 2014: marriages, 7·5 per 1,000 population; divorces and annulments, 4·0. Same-sex marriage became legal in Oct. 2014.

Climate

Anchorage, Jan. 12°F (–11·1°C), July 57°F (13·9°C). Annual rainfall 15" (371 mm). Fairbanks, Jan. –11°F (–23·9°C), July 60°F (15·6°C). Annual rainfall 12" (300 mm). Sitka, Jan. 33°F (0·6°C), July 55°F (12·8°C). Annual rainfall 87" (2,175 mm). Alaska belongs to the Pacific Coast climate zone (*see* UNITED STATES: Climate).

Constitution and Government

The state has the right to select 103·55m. acres of vacant and unappropriated public lands in order to establish 'a tax basis'; it can open these lands to prospectors for minerals, and the state is to derive the principal advantage in all gains resulting from the discovery of minerals. In addition, certain federally administered lands reserved for conservation of fisheries and wild life have been transferred to the state. Special provision is made for federal control of land for defence in areas of high strategic importance.

The constitution of Alaska was adopted by public vote, 24 April 1956. The state legislature consists of a Senate of 20 members (elected for four years) and a House of Representatives of 40 members (elected for two years).

For the 116th Congress, which convened in Jan. 2019, Alaska sends one member to the House of Representatives. It is represented in the Senate by Lisa Murkowski (R. 2002–23) and Daniel Sullivan (R. 2015–21). The franchise may be exercised by all citizens over 18.

The capital is Juneau.

Recent Elections

In the 2016 presidential election Donald Trump took Alaska with 52·9% of the vote (Mitt Romney won it in 2012).

Current Government

Governor: Mike Dunleavy (R.), Dec. 2018–Dec. 2022 (salary: $145,000).
Lieut.-Governor: Kevin Meyer (R.), Dec. 2018–Dec. 2022.
Government Website: http://www.alaska.gov

Economy

Per capita personal income (2015) was $55,940.

Budget

In 2011 total state revenue was $14,921m. Total expenditure was $11,320m. (education, $2,475m.; public welfare, $1,918m.; highways, $1,412m.; government administration, $586m.; natural resources, $391m.). Outstanding debt in 2011, $6,418m.

Performance

2015 Gross Domestic Product by state was $52,747m., ranking Alaska 46th in the United States. In 2015 state real GDP growth was –0·6%.

Energy and Natural Resources

Oil and Gas

Alaska ranks fourth among the leading oil producers in the USA (behind Texas, North Dakota and California), although production is steadily declining and is now less than a quarter of what it was in 1988. Commercial production of crude petroleum began in 1959 and by 1961 had become the most important mineral by value. Production in 2014 totalled 181m. bbls. Oil comes mainly from Prudhoe Bay, the Kuparuk River field and several Cook Inlet fields. Oil from the Prudhoe Bay Arctic field is now carried by the Trans-Alaska pipeline to Prince William Sound on the south coast, where there is a tanker terminal at Valdez.

Natural gas marketed production, 2014, 345bn. cu. ft.

Water

The total area covered by water is 94,743 sq. miles (the most of any state), of which 19,304 sq. miles are inland.

Minerals

Estimated value of production, 2012, in $1m.: gold, 1,537·5; zinc, 1,139·6; silver, 383·6; lead, 234·8; coal and peat, 72·5; industrial minerals (sand, gravel and rock), 68·1. Total estimated 2012 value, $3,436·1m. Value of non-fuel mineral production in 2009 was $2,620m.

Agriculture

In some parts of the state the climate during the brief spring and summer (about 100 days in major areas and 152 days in the southeastern coastal area) is suitable for agricultural operations, thanks to the long hours of sunlight, but Alaska is a food-importing area. In 2007 there were 686 farms covering a total of 882,000 acres. The average farm had 1,285 acres in 2007 and was valued at $391 per acre.

Farm income, 2009: crops, $26m.; livestock and products, $6m. The net farm income in 2009 was $8m. Principal sources: greenhouse and nursery products, hay and potatoes.

In 2007 there were 14,823 cattle and calves, 522 sheep and lambs, 757 hogs and pigs, and 3,600 laying hens.

Forestry

Of the 126·87m. forested acres of Alaska (the highest acreage of any state), 10·87m. acres are national forest land. The interior forest covers 115m. acres; more than 13m. acres are considered commercial forest, of which 3·4m. acres are in designated parks or wilderness and unavailable for harvest. The coastal rain forests provide the bulk of commercial timber volume; of their 13·6m. acres, 7·6m. acres support commercial stands, of which 1·9m. acres are in parks or wilderness and unavailable for harvest.

In 2014 there were 758 designated wilderness areas throughout the USA, covering a total of 109·5m. acres (44·3m. ha.). More than 52% of the system is in Alaska (57·4m. acres or 23·2m. ha.).

Fisheries

In 2017 commercial fishing landed 6,005m. lb of fish and shellfish at a value of $1·8bn. Alaska is by the far the most important state for fishery landings, accounting for 60·5% of the total by weight in 2017.

Industry

In 2012 the state's 1,446 manufacturing establishments had 42,000 employees, earning $1,699m. Total value added by manufacturing in 2013 was $1,726m. The largest manufacturing sectors are wood processing, seafood products and printing and publishing.

Labour

Total non-agricultural employment, 2010: 324,400. Employees by branch, 2010: government, 85,200; trade, transportation and utilities, 62,800; education and health services, 41,700; leisure and hospitality, 31,500; professional and business services, 26,200. The unemployment rate in Dec. 2010 was 7·9%.

International Trade

Imports and Exports

In 2015 imports into Alaska totalled $2,494m. (up from $2,016m. in 2014). In the same year exports from Alaska totalled $4,620m., down from $5,111m. in 2014. The leading source for imports in 2015 was China ($663m.), ahead of Canada ($612m.). The leading destination for exports in 2015 was also China ($1,203m.), followed by Japan ($964m.).

Communications

Roads

Alaska's highway and road system, 2012, totalled 16,301 miles comprising 2,423 miles of urban road and 13,878 miles of rural road. Registered motor vehicles numbered 743,305.

The Alaska Highway extends 1,523 miles from Dawson Creek, British Columbia, to Fairbanks, Alaska. It was built by the US Army in 1942, at a cost of $138m. The greater portion of it, because it lies in Canada, is maintained by Canada.

Rail

There is a railroad from Skagway to the town of Whitehorse, the White Pass and Yukon route, in the Canadian Yukon region (this service operates seasonally, although only the section between Skagway and Carcross is in service). The government-owned Alaska Railroad runs from Seward to Fairbanks. This is a freight service with only occasional passenger use. In 2012 there was one freight railroad operating with 506 miles of freight railroad (excluding trackage rights). Rail traffic originating in Alaska in 2012 totalled 5·6m. tons and rail traffic terminating in the state also came to 5·6m. tons.

Civil Aviation

Alaska's largest international airports are Anchorage and Fairbanks. There were 29 primary airports in 2012 (commercial service airports with more than 10,000 passenger boardings annually), more than in any other state. General aviation aircraft in the state per 1,000 population is about ten times the US average. Anchorage handled 2,543,105 tonnes of freight in 2011 (including transit freight), ranking it second in the USA behind Memphis for cargo handled (and fourth in the world). Alaska Airlines carried 27·4m. passengers in 2013 (25·9m. in 2012). There were 4,537,477 passenger enplanements statewide in 2012.

Shipping

Regular shipping services to and from the USA are furnished by two steamship and several barge lines operating out of Seattle and other Pacific coast ports. A Canadian company also furnishes a regular service from Vancouver, BC. Anchorage is the main port.

A 1,435 nautical-mile ferry system for motor cars and passengers (the 'Alaska Marine Highway') operates from Bellingham, Washington and Prince Rupert (British Columbia) to Juneau, Haines (for access to the Alaska Highway) and Skagway. A second system extends throughout the south-central region of Alaska linking the Cook Inlet area with Kodiak Island and Prince William Sound.

Social Institutions

Justice

The death penalty was abolished in Alaska in 1957. In Dec. 2014 the jail and prison population totalled 5,216.

Education

In 2013–14 there were 507 public schools in Alaska serving over 130,000 students. There were also 8,195 full- and part-time teachers who earned an average salary of $65,891. Total audited K-12 operating and selected special revenue funds for public schools in the 2012–13 school year were $2·32bn., a figure that includes State of Alaska retirement payments.

There are seven degree-granting institutions (five public and two private). The University of Alaska (founded in 1922) had 28,760 students at fall 2014 at its three campuses (Anchorage, Fairbanks and Southeast); there are six teaching units at the main campus in Anchorage.

Health

Alaska had 2·1 community hospital beds for every 1,000 population in 2013. In the same year there were 25·0 active physicians per 10,000 civilian population and 7·8 dentists per 10,000.

Welfare

Medicare enrolment in July 2012 totalled 73,833. In fiscal year 2012 a total of 137,055 people in Alaska received Medicaid. In Dec. 2014 there were 89,047 Old-Age, Survivors, and Disability Insurance (OASDI) beneficiaries. A total of 9,872 people were receiving payments under Temporary Assistance for Needy Families (TANF) in Dec. 2012.

Religion

The main religious traditions in 2010 were: Evangelical Protestants, with 100,960 members; Catholics, 50,866; Mainline Protestants, 32,550; Latter-day Saints (Mormons), 32,671; Orthodox Christians, 13,480.

Arizona

Key Historical Events

Spaniards looking for sources of gold or silver entered Arizona in the 16th century finding there American natives, including Tohono O'odham, Navajo, Hopi and Apache. The first Spanish Catholic mission was founded in the early 1690s by Father Eusebio Kino. Settlements were made in 1752 and a Spanish army headquarters was set up at Tucson in 1776. The area was governed by Mexico after the collapse of Spanish colonial power. Mexico ceded it to the USA in the Treaty of Guadalupe Hidalgo after the Mexican-American war (1848). Arizona was then part of New Mexico; the Gadsen Purchase (of land south of the Gila River) was added to it in 1853. The whole was organized as the Arizona Territory on 24 Feb. 1863.

Miners and ranchers began settling in the 1850s. Conflicts between American Indian and immigrant populations intensified when troops were withdrawn to serve in the Civil War. The Navajo surrendered in 1865, but the Apache continued to fight, under Geronimo and other leaders, until 1886. Arizona was admitted to the Union as the 48th state in 1912.

Large areas of the state have been retained as Indian reservations and as parks to protect the exceptional desert and mountain landscape. In recent years this landscape and the American Indian traditions have been used to attract tourists.

Territory and Population

Arizona is bounded north by Utah, east by New Mexico, south by Mexico, west by California and Nevada. Total area is 113,990 sq. miles (295,234 sq. km) of which 113,594 sq. miles (294,207 sq. km) are land. Of the total area in 2009, 28% was Indian Reservation, 18% was in individual or corporate ownership, 17% was held by the US Bureau of Land Management, 15% by the US Forest Service, 13% by the State and 10% by others. In 2010 American Indian lands covered 31,646 sq. miles (reservations plus off-reservation trust land), the largest area of any state. Census population, 1 April 2010, was 6,392,017, an increase of 24·6% since 2000. The rate of Arizona's population increase during the 2000s was the second fastest in the USA (behind Nevada). July 2018 estimate, 7,171,646.

Population in five census years:

	White	Black	American Indian/ Alaska Native	Chinese	Japanese	Total	Per sq. mile
1910	171,468	2,009	29,201	1,305	371	204,354	1·8
				All others			
1980	2,260,288	74,159	162,854	383,768		2,718,215	23·9
1990	2,963,186	110,524	203,527	387,991		3,665,228	32·3
2000	3,873,611	158,873	255,879	842,269		5,130,632	45·2
2010	4,667,121	259,008	296,529	1,169,359		6,392,017	56·3

Of the total population in 2010, 3,216,194 were female and 4,763,003 were 18 years old or older. Arizona's Hispanic population was 1,895,149 in 2010 (29·6%) up from 1,295,617 in 2000 (an increase of 46·3%).

The large cities (2010 census) were: Phoenix (the capital) 1,445,632; Tucson, 520,116; Mesa, 439,041; Chandler, 236,123; Glendale, 226,721; Scottsdale, 217,385; Gilbert, 208,453; Tempe, 161,719; Peoria, 154,065; Surprise, 117,517. The Phoenix–Mesa–Glendale metropolitan area had a 2010 census population of 4,192,887.

Social Statistics

Births, 2014, 86,887 (12·9 per 1,000 population); deaths, 2014, 51,538 (7·7). Infant mortality, 2013, 5·3 per 1,000 live births. 2014 marriages, 5·8 per 1,000 population; divorces and annulments, 3·9. Same-sex marriage became legal in Oct. 2014.

Climate

Phoenix, Jan. 53·6°F (12°C), July 93·5°F (34°C). Annual rainfall 7·66" (194 mm). Yuma, Jan. 56·5°F (13·6°C), July 93·7°F (34·3°C). Annual rainfall 3·17" (80 mm). Flagstaff, Jan. 28·7°F (−1·8°C), July 66·3°F (19·1°C). Annual rainfall 22·8" (579 mm). Arizona belongs to the Mountain States climate zone (see UNITED STATES: Climate).

Constitution and Government

The state constitution (1911, with 146 amendments) placed the government under direct control of the people through the initiative, referendum and the recall provisions. The state Senate consists of 30 members, and the House of Representatives consists of 60, all elected for two years.

For the 116th Congress, which convened in Jan. 2019, Arizona sends nine members to the House of Representatives. It is represented in the Senate by Kyrsten Sinema (D. 2019–25) and Martha McSally (R. 2019–2023).

The state capital is Phoenix. The state is divided into 15 counties.

Recent Elections

In the 2016 presidential election Donald Trump took Arizona with 49·5% of the vote (Mitt Romney won it in 2012).

Current Government

Governor: Douglas A. 'Doug' Ducey (R.), 2019–23 (salary: $95,000).
Secretary of State: Katie Hobbs (D.), since Jan. 2019.
Government Website: https://az.gov

Economy

Per capita personal income (2015) was $39,060.

Budget

In 2011 total state revenue was $36,611m. Total expenditure was $32,875m. (public welfare, $9,511m.; education, $9,122m.; highways, $2,038m.; health, $1,822m.; correction, $906m.). Outstanding debt in 2011, $14,163m.

Performance

Gross Domestic Product by state was $290,903m. in 2015, ranking Arizona 22nd in the United States. In 2015 state real GDP growth was 1·4%.

Energy and Natural Resources

Primary energy sources are coal (35·2%), nuclear (24·5%), gas (19·5%) and hydro-electric (18·9%).

Electricity

In 2015 production was 113·1bn. kWh, of which 36·2bn. kWh was from coal, 33·7bn. kWh from natural gas and 32·5bn. kWh from nuclear energy.

Water

The total area covered by water is 396 sq. miles.

Minerals

The mining industry historically has been and continues to be a significant part of the economy. By value the most important mineral produced is copper. Production in 2007 was 731,000 tonnes. Most of the state's silver and gold are recovered from copper ore. Other minerals include sand and gravel, molybdenum, coal and gemstones. Value of non-fuel mineral production in 2009 was $5,180m.

Agriculture

Arizona, despite its dry climate, is well suited for agriculture along the watercourses and where irrigation is practised on a large scale from great reservoirs constructed by the USA as well as by the state government and private interests. Irrigated area in 2007 was 876,158 acres. The wide pasture lands are favourable for the rearing of cattle and sheep, but numbers are either stationary or declining compared with 1920.

In 2007 Arizona contained 15,637 farms and ranches and the total farm and pastoral area was 26·1m. acres; in 2007 there were 1,205,425 acres of crop land. In 2007 the average farm was 1,670 acres (the fifth largest average size in the USA) and was valued at $748 per acre. Farming is highly commercialized and mechanized and concentrated largely on cotton picked by machines.

Area under cotton in 2009: upland cotton, 145,000 acres (440,000 bales harvested); American Pima cotton, 1,700 acres (4,000 bales harvested).

In 2009 the cash receipts from crops were $1,766m., and from livestock and products $1,178m. The net farm income in 2009 was $203m. Most important cereals are wheat, corn and barley; most important crops include lettuce, cotton, citrus fruit, broccoli, spinach, cauliflower, melons, onions, potatoes and carrots. In Dec. 2009 there were 930,000 cattle, 167,000 hogs, 160,000 sheep and 43,000 goats.

Forestry

The state had a forested area of 18,587,000 acres in 2013, of which 7,732,000 acres were national forest.

Industry

In 2012 the state's 8,582 manufacturing establishments had 264,000 employees, earning $16,406m. Total value added by manufacturing in 2013 was $27,451m.

Labour

In 2010 total non-agricultural employment was 2,377,000. Employees by branch, 2010 (in 1,000): trade, transportation and utilities, 468; government, 417; education and health services, 344; professional and business services, 339; leisure and hospitality, 253. The unemployment rate in Dec. 2010 was 9·6%.

International Trade

Imports and Exports

In 2015 imports into Arizona totalled $19,749m. (up from $19,744m. in 2014). In the same year exports from Arizona totalled $22,655m., up from $21,247m. in 2014. The leading source for imports in 2015 was Mexico ($7,640m.), ahead of China ($2,651m.). The leading destination for exports in 2015 was also Mexico ($9,162m.), followed by Canada ($2,303m.).

Communications

Roads

In 2012 there were 65,262 miles of roads comprising 23,876 miles of urban road and 41,386 miles of rural road. There were 5,014,259 registered vehicles.

Rail

In 2012 there were 1,643 miles of freight railroad (excluding trackage rights). There were nine freight railroads operating in 2012. Rail traffic originating in Arizona in 2012 totalled 3·3m. tons and rail traffic terminating in the state came to 26·1m. tons. A light rail system opened in Phoenix in 2008.

Civil Aviation

In 2011 Arizona had nine primary airports (commercial service airports with more than 10,000 passenger boardings annually) with a combined total of 22,735,131 enplanements, up from 21,834,569 in 2010. The busiest airport, Phoenix Sky Harbor International, had 19,750,306 enplanements in 2011 (ranking it ninth in the USA).

Social Institutions

Justice

A 'right-to-work' amendment to the constitution, adopted 5 Nov. 1946, makes illegal any concessions to trade-union demands for a 'closed shop'.

In Dec. 2014 the prison population totalled 42,259. Chain gangs were reintroduced into prisons in 1995. The death penalty is authorized. There was one execution in 2014 but none since.

Education

School attendance is compulsory between the ages of six and 16. There were 2,399 public elementary and secondary schools in 2012–13 with 48,866 teachers and 1,089,384 students. There were 53,120 students enrolled at 340 private schools with 3,810 teachers in fall 2011. In 2010–11 the total expenditure on public elementary and secondary education was $9,889m. Arizona has three public universities: the University of Arizona (Tucson) with (fall 2014) 42,236 students; Northern Arizona University (Flagstaff) with 27,705; Arizona State University (five campuses) with 83,260. In 2012–13 there were 87 degree-granting institutions in total, including 63 private institutions.

Health

Arizona had 2·0 community hospital beds for every 1,000 population in 2013. In the same year there were 25·5 active physicians per 10,000 civilian population and 5·5 dentists per 10,000.

Welfare

Medicare enrolment in July 2012 totalled 999,494. In fiscal year 2011 a total of 1,990,332 people in Arizona received Medicaid. In Dec. 2014 there were

1,207,102 Old-Age, Survivors, and Disability Insurance (OASDI) beneficiaries. A total of 39,184 people were receiving payments under Temporary Assistance for Needy Families (TANF) in Dec. 2012.

Religion

The principal religious traditions in 2010 were: Catholics, with 930,702 members; Evangelical Protestants, 762,376; Latter-day Saints (Mormons), 394,844; Mainline Protestants, 171,792; Hindus, 32,887.

Culture

Tourism

In 2011 overseas visitors to Arizona—excluding those from Canada and Mexico—numbered 864,000, up from 765,000 in 2010 and 563,000 in 2006.

Arkansas

Key Historical Events

In the 16th and 17th centuries French and Spanish explorers encountered tribes of Chaddo, Osage and Quapaw. The first European settlement was French, at Arkansas Post in 1686, and the area became part of French Louisiana. The USA bought Arkansas from France as part of the Louisiana Purchase in 1803; it was organized as a Territory in 1819 and entered the Union on 15 June 1836 as the 25th state.

The eastern plains by the Mississippi were settled by white plantation-owners who grew cotton with black slave labour. The rest of the state attracted a scattered population of small farmers. The plantations were the centre of political power. Arkansas seceded from the Union in 1861 and joined the Confederate States of America. At that time the slave population was about 25% of the total.

In 1868 the state was readmitted to the Union. Attempts to integrate the black population into state life achieved little, and a policy of segregation was rigidly adhered to until the 1950s. In 1957 federal authorities ordered that high school segregation must end. The state governor called on the state militia to prevent desegregation; there was rioting, and federal troops entered Little Rock, the capital, to restore order. It was another ten years before school segregation finally ended.

The main industrial development followed the discovery of large reserves of bauxite.

Territory and Population

Arkansas is bounded north by Missouri, east by Tennessee and Mississippi, south by Louisiana, southwest by Texas and west by Oklahoma. Land area, 52,035 sq. miles (134,771 sq. km); water area, 1,143 sq. miles (2,961 sq. km). Census population, 1 April 2010, was 2,915,918, an increase of 9·1% since 2000. July 2018 estimate, 3,013,825.

Population in five census years was:

	White	Black	American Indian	Asian	Total	Per sq. mile
1910	1,131,026	442,891	460	472	1,574,449	30·0
			All others			
1980	1,890,332	373,768	22,335		2,286,435	43·9
1990	1,944,744	373,912	32,069		2,350,725	45·1
2000	2,138,598	418,950	115,852		2,673,400	51·3
2010	2,245,229	449,895	220,794		2,915,918	56·0

Of the total population in 2010, 1,484,281 were female and 2,204,443 were 18 years old or older. In 2010 the Hispanic population of Arkansas was 186,050, up from 86,866 in 2000, an increase of 114·2%.

Little Rock (capital) had a population of 193,524 in 2010; Fort Smith, 86,209; Fayetteville, 73,580; Springdale, 69,797; Jonesboro, 67,263; North Little Rock, 62,304; Conway, 58,908; Rogers, 55,964. The population of the largest metropolitan statistical areas in 2010 was: Little Rock–North Little Rock–Conway, 699,757; Fayetteville–Springdale–Rogers, 463,204; Fort Smith, 298,592; Texarkana, 136,027; Jonesboro, 121,026; Pine Bluff, 100,258.

Social Statistics

Births, 2014, were 38,551 (13·0 per 1,000 population); deaths, 2014, 30,467 (10·3). Infant mortality, 2013, 7·9 per 1,000 live births. 2014: marriages, 10·1 per 1,000.

Climate

Little Rock, Jan. 39·9°F, July 84°F. Annual rainfall 52·4". Arkansas belongs to the Gulf Coast climate zone (*see* UNITED STATES: Climate).

Constitution and Government

The General Assembly consists of a Senate of 35 members elected for four years, partially renewed every two years, and a House of Representatives of 100 members elected for two years. The sessions are biennial and usually limited to 60 days. The Governor and Lieut.-Governor are elected for four years.

For the 116th Congress, which convened in Jan. 2019, Arkansas sends four members to the House of Representatives. It is represented in the Senate by John Boozman (R. 2011–23) and Tom Cotton (R. 2015–21).

The state is divided into 75 counties; the capital is Little Rock.

Recent Elections

In the 2016 presidential election Donald Trump took Arkansas with 60·4% of the vote (Mitt Romney won it in 2012).

Current Government

Governor: Asa Hutchinson (R.), 2019–23 (salary: $143,820).
　　Lieut.-Governor: Tim Griffin (R.), 2019–23.
　　Secretary of State: John Thurston (R.), since Jan. 2019.
Government Website: https://portal.arkansas.gov

Economy

Per capita personal income (2015) was $39,107.

Budget

In 2011 total revenue was $22,808m. Total expenditure was $18,862m. (education, $7,508m.; public welfare, $4,494m.; highways, $1,081m.; hospitals, $857m.; government administration, $576m.). Outstanding debt in 2011, $3,749m.

Performance

2015 Gross Domestic Product by state was $118,907m., ranking Arkansas 34th in the United States. In 2015 state real GDP growth was 0·5%.

Energy and Natural Resources

Oil and Gas

In 2014 Arkansas produced 6·8m. bbls of crude petroleum; marketed production of natural gas totalled 1,124bn. cu. ft.

Water

The total area covered by water is 1,143 sq. miles.

Minerals

Employment in mining, quarrying, and oil and gas extraction totalled 6,364 in March 2007. Crushed stone was the leading mineral commodity produced, in terms of value, followed by bromine. Value of domestic non-fuel mineral production in 2009 was $636m.

Agriculture

In 2007, 49,346 farms had a total area of 13·9m. acres; average farm was 281 acres and was valued at $2,343 per acre. 7·37m. acres were harvested cropland. Arkansas ranked first in the acreage and production of rice in 2007 (48·4% of US total production), second in the production of broilers (1,172m. birds) and third in turkeys (29·2m. birds).

Farm income, 2009: crops, $3,226m.; livestock and products, $3,964m. The net farm income in 2009 was $1,524m.

Forestry

In 2013 the state had a forested area of 18,966,000 acres, of which 2,499,000 acres were national forest.

Industry

In 2012 the state's 6,544 manufacturing establishments had 379,000 employees, earning $15,030m. Total value added by manufacturing in 2013 was $25,152m.

Labour

Total non-agricultural employment, 2010: 1,613,200. Employees by branch, 2010 (in 1,000): trade, transportation and utilities, 234;

government, 218; education and health services, 166; manufacturing, 160; professional and business services, 118. The unemployment rate in Dec. 2010 was 7·9%.

International Trade

Imports and Exports
In 2015 imports into Arkansas totalled $7,911m. (up from $7,610m. in 2014). In the same year exports from Arkansas totalled $5,869m., down from $6,866m. in 2014. The leading source for imports in 2015 was China ($2,576m.), ahead of France ($1,682m.). The leading destination for exports in 2015 was Canada ($1,206m.), followed by Mexico ($844m.).

Communications

Roads
Total road mileage (2012), 100,123 miles—urban, 13,428; rural, 86,695. There were 2,403,830 registered motor vehicles.

Rail
In 2012 there were 2,698 miles of freight railroad (excluding trackage rights). There were 24 freight railroads operating in 2012. Rail traffic originating in Arkansas in 2012 totalled 14·5m. tons and rail traffic terminating in the state came to 27·4m. tons.

Civil Aviation
There were four primary airports—commercial service airports with more than 10,000 passenger boardings annually—in 2011 with a combined total of 1,715,357 enplanements, down from 1,757,190 in 2010.

Shipping
There are about 1,000 miles of navigable rivers, including the Mississippi, Arkansas, Red, White and Ouachita Rivers. The Arkansas River/Kerr-McClellan Channel flows diagonally eastward across the state and gives access to the sea via the Mississippi River.

Social Institutions

Justice
In Dec. 2014 there were 17,874 federal and state prisoners. There were four executions in April 2017—the first since 2005. In a state-wide vote held on the same day as the presidential election in Nov. 2016, medical use of marijuana was legalized.

Education
In 2012–13 there were 1,128 public elementary and secondary schools with 486,157 enrolled pupils and 34,131 teachers. Total expenditure on public elementary and secondary education in 2010–11 was $5,392m.; average teacher salary was $46,632 in 2012–13. Spending per student in 2010–11 was $9,496.

In 2012–13 there were 33 public and 19 private degree-granting institutions; total student enrolment in fall 2012 was 176,458 (157,224 public and 19,234 private). The Arkansas State University System (founded in 1909) includes the Jonesboro, Beebe, Mountain Home and Newport campuses; total student enrolment was 21,154 in fall 2014.

Health
Arkansas had 3·2 community hospital beds for every 1,000 population in 2013. In the same year there were 21·5 active physicians per 10,000 civilian population and 4·1 dentists per 10,000.

Welfare
Medicare enrolment in July 2012 totalled 561,480. In fiscal year 2012 a total of 797,161 people in Arkansas received Medicaid. In Dec. 2014 there were 673,193 Old-Age, Survivors, and Disability Insurance (OASDI) beneficiaries. A total of 16,908 people were receiving payments under Temporary Assistance for Needy Families (TANF) in Dec. 2012.

Religion
The principal religious traditions in 2010 were: Evangelical Protestants, with 1,136,611 members; Mainline Protestants, 205,332; Catholics, 122,662; Black Protestants, 107,202; Latter-day Saints (Mormons), 29,645.

California

Key Historical Events
There were many small American Indian tribes, but no central power, when the area was discovered in 1542 by the Spanish navigator Juan Cabrillo. The Spaniards did not begin to establish missions until the 18th century, when the Franciscan friar Junipero Serra settled at San Diego in 1769. The missions became farming and ranching villages with large American Indian populations. When the Spanish empire collapsed in 1821, the area was governed from newly independent Mexico.

The first wagon-train of American settlers arrived from Missouri in 1841. In 1846, during the war between Mexico and the USA, Americans in California proclaimed it to be part of the USA. The territory was ceded by Mexico on 2 Feb. 1848 and became the 31st state of the Union on 9 Sept. 1850.

Gold was discovered in 1848–49 and there was an immediate influx of population. The state remained isolated, however, until the development of railways in the 1860s. From then on the population doubled on average every 20 years. The sunny climate attracted fruit-growers, market-gardeners and wine producers. In the early 20th century the bright lights and cheap labour attracted film-makers to Hollywood, Los Angeles.

Southern California remained mainly agricultural with an American Indian or Spanish-speaking labour force until after the Second World War. Now more than 90% of the population is urban, with the manufacturing emphasis on hi-technology equipment, much of it for the aerospace, computer and office equipment industries.

Territory and Population
Land area, 155,779 sq. miles (403,466 sq. km); water area, 7,916 sq. miles (20,501 sq. km). California is the third largest US state behind Alaska and Texas. The federal government owned 47,797,533 acres in 2010, equivalent to 47·7% of the state area. Census population, 1 April 2010, was 37,253,956, an increase of 10·0% since 2000. The growth rate reflects continued high though somewhat reduced natural increase (excess of births over deaths) as well as substantial net immigration. California's population is 12·1% of the total US population. July 2018 estimate, 39,557,045.

Population in five census years was:

	White	Black	Japanese	Chinese	Total (incl. all others)	Per sq. mile
1910	2,259,672	21,645	41,356	36,248	2,377,549	15·2
1960	14,455,230	883,861	157,317	95,600	15,717,204	100·8

	White	Black	Asian/ other	Hispanic	Total	Per sq. mile
1990	20,524,327	2,208,801	7,026,893	7,687,938	29,760,021	190·8
2000	20,170,059	2,263,882	11,437,707	10,966,556	33,871,648	217·2
2010	21,453,934	2,299,072	13,500,950	14,013,719	37,253,956	239·1

Of the total population in 2010, 18,736,126 were female and 27,958,916 were 18 years old or older.

In addition to having the highest population of any state in the USA, California has the largest Hispanic population of any state in terms of numbers and the third largest in terms of percentage of population. In 2010 there were 14,013,719 Hispanics living in California (37·6% of the overall population), up from 10,966,556 in 2000, the largest numeric rise of any state over the same period. By 2020 Hispanics are projected to form a majority.

The 50 largest cities (2012 population estimates) are:

Los Angeles	3,825,297
San Diego	1,321,315
San Jose	971,372
San Francisco	812,538
Fresno	505,009
Sacramento (capital)	470,956
Long Beach	464,662
Oakland	395,341
Bakersfield	354,480
Anaheim	343,793
Santa Ana	327,731

(continued)

Riverside	308,511
Stockton	295,707
Chula Vista	249,382
Irvine	223,729
Fremont	217,700
San Bernardino	211,674
Modesto	203,085
Oxnard	200,390
Fontana	199,898
Moreno Valley	196,495
Glendale	192,654
Huntington Beach	192,524
Santa Clarita	177,445
Garden Grove	172,648
Rancho Cucamonga	169,498
Oceanside	169,319
Santa Rosa	168,841
Ontario	166,134
Lancaster	157,826
Elk Grove	155,937
Corona	154,520
Palmdale	153,708
Salinas	152,401
Pomona	149,950
Hayward	147,113
Torrance	146,115
Escondido	146,064
Sunnyvale	142,896
Pasadena	139,222
Orange	138,010
Fullerton	137,481
Thousand Oaks	128,031
Visalia	126,864
Simi Valley	125,317
Concord	123,206
Roseville	122,060
Victorville	119,059
Santa Clara	118,813
Vallejo	115,928

Largest metropolitan areas (2010 census): Los Angeles–Long Beach–Santa Ana, 12,828,837; San Francisco–Oakland–Fremont, 4,335,391; Riverside–San Bernardino–Ontario, 4,224,851; San Diego–Carlsbad–San Marcos, 3,095,313; Sacramento–Arden-Arcade–Roseville, 2,149,127; San Jose–Sunnyvale–Santa Clara, 1,836,911; Fresno, 930,450.

Social Statistics

Births, 2014, 502,879 (13·0 per 1,000 population); deaths, 2014, 245,929 (6·3). Marriages, 2014, 6·4 per 1,000 population. Infant deaths, 2013, 4·8 per 1,000 live births. California was the second state after Massachusetts to allow same-sex marriage when it became legal in June 2008, but the ruling was nullified when 52·5% of votes cast in a referendum held on 4 Nov. 2008 were in favour of a ban. On 4 Aug. 2010 a federal court declared the ban unconstitutional, a decision which was upheld by the United States Court of Appeals for the Ninth Circuit on 7 Feb. 2012. Same-sex marriages resumed in June 2013.

Climate

Los Angeles, Jan. 58°F (14·4°C), July 74°F (23·3°C). Annual rainfall 15" (381 mm). Sacramento, Jan. 45°F (7·2°C), July 76°F (24·4°C). Annual rainfall 18" (457 mm). San Diego, Jan. 57°F (13·9°C), July 71°F (21·7°C). Annual rainfall 10" (259 mm). San Francisco, Jan. 51°F (10·6°C), July 59°F (15°C). Annual rainfall 20" (508 mm). Death Valley, Jan. 52°F (11°C), July 100°F (38°C). Annual rainfall 1·6" (40 mm). California belongs to the Pacific Coast climate zone (see UNITED STATES: Climate).

Constitution and Government

The present constitution became effective from 4 July 1879; it has had numerous amendments since 1962. The Senate is composed of 40 members elected for four years—half being elected every two years—and the Assembly, of 80 members, elected for two years. Two-year regular sessions convene in Dec. of each even numbered year. The Governor and Lieut.-Governor are elected for four years.

For the 116th Congress, which convened in Jan. 2019, California sends 53 members to the House of Representatives. It is represented in the Senate by Dianne Feinstein (D. 1993–2025) and Kamala Harris (D. 2017–23).

The capital is Sacramento. The state is divided into 58 counties.

Recent Elections

In the 2016 presidential election Hillary Clinton took California with 61·5% of the vote (Barack Obama won it in 2012).

Current Government

Governor: Gavin Newsom (D.), 2019–23 (salary: $201,680).
  Lieut.-Governor: Eleni Kounalakis (D.), 2019–23.
  Secretary of State: Alex Padilla (D.), since Jan. 2015.
Government Website: https://www.ca.gov

Economy

Per capita personal income (2015) was $52,651.

California's economy, one of the largest and most diverse in the world, has major components in high-technology, trade, entertainment, finance, agriculture, manufacturing, government, tourism, construction and services. California's economy is very dependent on international trade.

Farm production in California has risen despite declines in acreage. Farm-related sales have more than quadrupled over the past three decades. Largest production categories are fruits and nuts, livestock and poultry, vegetables and melons.

Budget

For the year ending 30 June 2011, total state revenues were $122·5bn. Total expenditures were $131·0bn. (education, $50·1bn.; health and human services, $41·9bn.; corrections and rehabilitation, $9·7bn.). Debt outstanding (2012) $84·4bn.

Performance

California's economy, the largest among the 50 states and one of the largest in the world, has major components in high technology, trade, entertainment, agriculture, manufacturing, tourism, construction and services. California is home to leading innovators and entrepreneurs and to firms like Apple, Cisco and Intel in technology; eBay, Facebook, Google and Yahoo in pioneering the use of the internet; Amgen and Genentech in biotech; and DreamWorks and Pixar in combining technology and entertainment. California experienced a severe economic recession that began at the end of 2007, although the state has now fully recovered from this. The principal cause of the recession was a financial crisis instigated by risky financial activity that led to the bursting of the housing bubble.

If California were a country in its own right it would be the world's fifth largest economy. 2017 Gross Domestic Product by state was $2,746,873m., the highest in the United States and representing 14·3% of the USA's total GDP. In 2017 state real GDP growth was 3·0%. Taxable sales in 2017 totalled $675,699m.

Banking and Finance

As of 30 June 2014 there were 7,135 offices of commercial banks, 1,644 offices of credit unions, 131 offices of savings institutions and one US branch of a foreign bank. As of that date California-headquartered savings institutions had deposits of $10·8bn., and mortgage loans also of $10·8bn. Insured commercial banks headquartered in the state had demand deposits of $50·6bn. and time and savings deposits of $372·0bn. Total loans reached $373·3bn. of which real estate loans were $256·7m. Credit unions had assets totalling $145·3bn., and total loans outstanding were $80·2bn.

Energy and Natural Resources

Electricity

In 2011 production was 200,414m. kWh of which 90,751m. kWh was from natural gas, 36,666m. kWh from nuclear energy and 42,727m. kWh from conventional hydroelectric energy. California leads the nation in electricity generation from non-hydroelectric renewable energy sources. California generates electricity using wind, geothermal, solar, fuel wood and municipal solid waste/landfill gas resources. The world's largest solar power facility operates in California's Mojave Desert. Consumption is growing at a rate of 2% annually.

Oil and Gas

California is the nation's third largest oil producing state. Total onshore and offshore production fell to an average of 539,200 bbls per day in 2011. Net natural gas production in 2011 was 243bn. cu. ft.

Water

The total area covered by water is approximately 7,916 sq. miles. Water quality is judged to be good along 83% of the 960 miles of assessed coastal shoreline.

Minerals

Gold production was 160,767 troy oz in 2015 (compared to less than 20,000 troy oz in 2007). The value of gold production increased to $187·5m. from $183·3m. in 2014. Bentonite clay (including hectorite), common clay, crushed stone, dimension stone, feldspar, fuller's earth, gemstones, gypsum, industrial sand and gravel, iron ore, kaolin clay, lime, magnesium compounds, masonry cement, pumice, pumicite, salt, silver, soda ash, sodium sulphate and zeolites are also produced.

In 2015 California ranked sixth among the states in non-fuel mineral production, accounting for approximately 4·2% of the US total. California was the leading state in the production of construction sand, gravel and diatomite, and was the only producer of boron compounds and rare earth elements. The only metals produced in California were gold and silver. The market value of non-fuel minerals produced was $3·6bn.; the mining industry employed around 26,800 persons in 2011 (compared to 48,000 in the early 1980s).

Agriculture

California is the most diversified agricultural economy in the world, producing more than 400 agricultural commodities. It is by far the largest agricultural producer and exporter in the United States. The state grows nearly half of the nation's total of fruits, nuts and vegetables. Many of these commodities are specialty crops and almost solely produced in California. In 2017 there were 77,100 farms totalling 25·3m. acres of farmland. The net farm income in 2017 was $17,709m. (the largest of any state). In 2017 cash income from marketings reached $50·1bn. (13·3% of the US total). Fruit and nut cash receipts, at $21·98bn. in 2017, were 6·4% above the previous year and comprised 44% of the total. Vegetable receipts were also up 6·4% from the previous year at $8·37bn., comprising 17% of total sales. Livestock and poultry receipts rose 7% from 2016 at $10·63bn. and comprised 21% of total sales. California's leading commodity in cash receipts in 2017 was milk and cream with $6·56bn., followed by grapes at $5·79bn.; almonds at $5·60bn.; and strawberries at $3·10bn.

Production of cotton lint in 2011 was 321,800 short tons; other field and seed crops included (in 1m. short tons): hay and alfalfa, 8; rice, 2; sugar beets, 1; wheat, 1. Principal fruit, nut and vegetable crops in 2011 (in 1,000 short tons): tomatoes, 12,562; grapes, 6,612; lettuce, 3,247; oranges, 2,500; strawberries, 1,023; almonds, 1,015; broccoli, 1,012; onions, 973; carrots, 945; lemons, 820; celery, 773; peaches, 773.

In 2011 there were 1·7m. dairy cows; 5·2m. all cattle and calves; 570,000 sheep and lambs; and 105,000 hogs and pigs.

Forestry

In 2011 California had 32·94m. acres of forested land—of which 20,802,641 acres were national forest. There are about 16·6m. acres of productive forest land, from which about 2,900m. bd ft are harvested annually. Total value of timber harvest, 2011, $272m. Lumber production, 2011, 1,288m. bd ft.

Fisheries

The catch in 2011 was 408m. lb; leading species in landings were sardine, squid, anchovy, mackerel, crab, urchin, sole, whiting, sablefish and tuna.

Industry

The professional and business services, manufacturing and information services industries—which include many high-paying jobs involving computer and software design, data processing and hosting, motion picture production and engineering—accounted for 33% of California's total output in 2017, followed by 22% from the finance, insurance and real estate sector and 13% from trade and transportation services. Total output from manufacturing was $300·35bn. in 2017. There were 36,117 manufacturing firms in California in 2015.

Labour

In 2011 the civilian labour force was 18·4m., of whom 16·2m. were employed. A total of 126,200 jobs were added in 2011, mainly in professional and business services, educational and health services, trade, transportation and utilities, and leisure and hospitality. The unemployment rate was 10·1% in Oct. 2012.

International Trade

Imports and Exports

In 2015 imports into California totalled $408·2bn. (up from $403·8bn. in 2014). In the same year exports from California totalled $165·4bn., down from $173·9bn. in 2014. California's imports in 2015 were the most of any state and its exports the second largest after those of Texas. Imports in 2015 were 18·2% of all US imports and exports 11·0% of all US exports. The leading source for imports in 2015 was China ($143·6bn.), ahead of Mexico ($45·1bn.). The leading destination for exports in 2015 was Mexico ($26·8bn.), followed by Canada ($17·3bn.).

Communications

Roads

In 2011 California had 172,202 miles of public roads (including 15,133 of state highways). There were a total of 32,903,847 registered motor vehicles in 2013. Motor vehicle collision fatalities in 2012 were 2,758.

Rail

In addition to Amtrak's long-distance trains, local and medium-distance passenger trains run in the San Francisco Bay area sponsored by the California Department of Transportation, and a network of commuter trains around Los Angeles opened in 1992. There are metro and light rail systems in San Francisco and Los Angeles, and light rail lines in Sacramento, San Diego and San Jose. In 2012 there were 5,295 miles of freight railroad (excluding trackage rights). There were 24 freight railroads operating in 2012. Rail traffic originating in California in 2012 totalled 59·1m. tons and rail traffic terminating in the state came to 98·9m. tons.

Civil Aviation

In 2011 there were a total of 968 public and private airports, heliports, stolports and seaplane bases.

A total of 61,862,052 passengers (16,731,324 international; 45,130,728 domestic) embarked/disembarked at Los Angeles airport in 2011. It handled approximately 1,853,658 tonnes of freight. At San Francisco airport, in 2011, 40,800,352 passengers (9,013,021 international; 31,787,331 domestic) embarked/disembarked, and 421,096 tonnes of freight were handled. There were a total of 51,311,722 passenger enplanements at Los Angeles and San Francisco in 2011.

Shipping

The chief ports are Long Beach and Los Angeles. In 2014 Long Beach was the fifth busiest port in the USA, handling 85·0m. tons of cargo, and Los Angeles the tenth busiest, with 61·0m. tons.

Social Institutions

Justice

A 'three strikes law', making 25-years-to-life sentences mandatory for third felony offences, was adopted in 1994 after an initiative (i.e. referendum) was 72% in favour. However, the state's Supreme Court ruled in June 1996 that judges may disregard previous convictions in awarding sentences. In Nov. 2012 voters approved Proposition 36, which modifies the three strikes law, to impose a life sentence only when the third felony conviction is 'serious or violent' and authorizes resentencing for offenders currently serving life sentences if their third strike conviction was not serious or violent. In Nov. 2017 there were 35 adult prisons. As of Dec. 2016 there were 6,919 adult inmates serving 'three strikes' sentences. There were 131,109 state prisoners in Nov. 2017, down from 173,479 in Oct. 2006. The death penalty is authorized following its reinstatement by the US Supreme Court in 1976.

Since 1978 the state has executed 13 condemned inmates. The most recent execution was in 2006. A moratorium on death sentences was ordered in Dec. 2006 but in a statewide referendum on the same ballot as the presidential election in Nov. 2016, a proposed repeal of the death penalty was rejected. As of Nov. 2017 the California Department of Corrections and Rehabilitation housed 744 condemned inmates (more than any other state). In another statewide referendum also held in Nov. 2016, the recreational use of marijuana was legalized.

Education

Full-time attendance at school is compulsory for children from six to 18 years of age for a minimum of 175 days per annum. In fall 2015 there were 6·7m. pupils enrolled in both public and private elementary and secondary schools. Total state expenditure on public education, 2015–16, was $63·8bn. Average teacher salary in 2015 was $77,179 (the second highest in the USA).

Community colleges had 2,127,444 students in fall 2015.

California has two publicly-supported higher education systems: the University of California (1868) and the California State University and Colleges. In fall 2015 the University of California, with ten campuses for resident instruction and research including Berkeley, Los Angeles (UCLA) and San Francisco, had 257,438 students. California State University, with 23 campuses including Sacramento, Long Beach, Los Angeles and San Francisco, had 474,571 students. There were 147 public degree-granting institutions for higher education in 2015–16; there were 307 private degree-granting institutions that had a total estimated enrolment of 498,215 in the fall of 2015.

Health

California had 1·8 community hospital beds for every 1,000 population in 2013. In the same year there were 27·8 active physicians per 10,000 civilian population and 7·7 dentists per 10,000.

Welfare

Medicare enrolment in July 2012 totalled 5,126,609. In fiscal year 2013 a total of 12,329,162 people in California received Medicaid. On 1 Jan. 1974 the federal government (Social Security Administration) assumed responsibility for the Supplemental Security Income/State Supplemental Program, which replaced the State Old-Age Security. The SSI/SSP provides financial assistance for needy aged (65 years or older), blind or disabled persons. An individual recipient may own assets up to $2,000; a couple up to $3,000, subject to specific exclusions. In Sept. 2017 there were 1·26m. SSI recipients. In fiscal year 2015–16 the caseload of the welfare programme CalWORKS averaged 495,554, a decrease of 18·5% from fiscal year 1997–98 (the year CalWORKS was implemented).

Religion

The principal religious traditions in 2010 were: Catholics, with 10,234,036 members; Evangelical Protestants, 3,502,250; Mainline Protestants, 880,981; Latter-day Saints (Mormons), 770,437; Buddhists, 326,940.

Culture

Tourism

The travel and tourism industry provides 2·5% of the state's $2·7trn. economy. Visitors in 2017 spent $120·1bn. generating $7·9bn. in state and local tax revenues. Tourist spending has increased at an average annual rate of 4·1% since 2010. California was the state most visited by overseas travellers in 2017, when international tourists spent $27·1bn. (approximately 20% of all tourist spending).

Colorado

Key Historical Events

Spanish explorers claimed the area for Spain in 1706; it was then the territory of the Arapaho, Cheyenne, Ute and other Plains and Great Basin Indians. Eastern Colorado, the hot, dry plains, passed to France in 1802 and then to the USA as part of the Louisiana Purchase in 1803. The rest remained Spanish, becoming Mexican when Spanish power in the Americas ended. In 1848, after war between Mexico and the USA, Mexican Colorado was ceded to the USA. A gold rush in 1859 brought a great influx of population, and in 1861 Colorado was organized as a Territory. The Territory officially supported the Union in the Civil War of 1861–65, but its settlers were divided and served on both sides.

Colorado became a state in 1876. Mining and ranching were the mainstays of the economy. In the 1920s the first large projects were undertaken to exploit the Colorado River. The Colorado River Compact was agreed in 1922, and the Boulder Dam (now Hoover Dam) was authorized in 1928. Since then irrigated agriculture has overtaken mining as an industry and is as important as ranching. In 1945 the Colorado-Big Thompson project diverted water by tunnel beneath the Rocky Mountains to irrigate 700,000 acres (284,000 ha.) of northern Colorado. Now more than 80% of the population is urban, with the majority engaged in telecommunications, aerospace and computer technology. Colorado and Washington became the first US states to legalize the recreational possession and sale of marijuana following voter referendums in Nov. 2012. The first so-called 'pot shops' opened on 1 Jan. 2014.

Territory and Population

Colorado is bounded north by Wyoming, northeast by Nebraska, east by Kansas, southeast by Oklahoma, south by New Mexico and west by Utah. Total area is 104,094 sq. miles (269,601 sq. km) of which 103,642 sq. miles (268,431 sq. km) are land.

Census population, 1 April 2010, was 5,029,196, an increase of 16·9% since 2000. July 2018 estimate, 5,695,564.

Population in five census years was:

	White	Black	American Indian	Asian	Total	Per sq. mile
1910	783,415	11,453	1,482	2,674	799,024	7·7
			All others			
1980	2,571,498	101,703	216,763		2,889,964	27·9
1990	2,905,474	133,146	255,774		3,294,394	31·8
2000	3,560,005	165,063	576,193		4,301,261	41·5
2010	4,089,202	201,737	738,257		5,029,196	48·5

Of the total population in 2010, 2,520,662 were male and 3,803,587 were 18 years old or older. The Hispanic population in 2010 was 1,038,687, up from 735,601 in 2000 (an increase of 41·2%). Large cities, with 2008 populations: Denver City (the capital), 566,974; Colorado Springs, 372,437; Aurora, 305,582; Lakewood, 140,024; Fort Collins, 129,467; Westminster, 105,753; Arvada, 104,830; Pueblo, 103,730.

Main metropolitan areas (2008): Denver–Aurora, 2,506,626; Colorado Springs, 617,714; Boulder, 293,161; Fort Collins–Loveland, 292,825; Greeley, 249,715; Pueblo, 156,737; Grand Junction, 143,171.

Social Statistics

Births, 2014, were 65,830 (12·3 per 1,000 population); deaths, 2014, 35,237 (6·6). Infant mortality, 2013, 5·1 per 1,000 live births. 2014: marriages, 7·1 per 1,000 population; divorces and annulments, 3·9. Same-sex marriage became legal in Oct. 2014.

Climate

Denver, Jan. 31°F (–0·6°C), July 73°F (22·8°C). Annual rainfall 14" (358 mm). Pueblo, Jan. 30°F (–1·1°C), July 83°F (28·3°C). Annual rainfall 12" (312 mm). Colorado belongs to the Mountain States climate zone (*see* UNITED STATES: Climate).

Constitution and Government

The constitution adopted in 1876 is still in effect with (2017) 152 amendments. The General Assembly consists of a Senate of 35 members elected for four years, one-half retiring every two years, and of a House of Representatives of 65 members elected for two years. Sessions are annual, beginning 1951. Qualified as electors are all citizens, male and female (except convicted, incarcerated criminals), 18 years of age, who have resided in the state and the precinct for 32 days immediately preceding the election. There is a seven-member State Supreme Court.

For the 116th Congress, which convened in Jan. 2019, Colorado sends seven members to the House of Representatives. It is represented in the Senate by Michael Bennet (D. 2009–23) and Cory Gardner (R. 2015–21).

The capital is Denver. There are 64 counties.

Recent Elections

In the 2016 presidential election Hillary Clinton took Colorado with 47·2% of the vote (Barack Obama won it in 2012).

Current Government

Governor: Jared Polis (D.), 2019–23 (salary: $90,000).
  Lieut.-Governor: Dianne Primavera (D.), 2019–23.
  Secretary of State: Jena Griswold (D.), since Jan. 2019.
Government Website: https://www.colorado.gov

Economy

Per capita personal income (2015) was $50,410.

Budget

In 2011 total revenue was $30,248m. and total expenditure $29,169m. Major areas of expenditure were: education, $9,250m.; public welfare, $5,663m.; highways, $1,436m.; health, $1,232m.; correction, $1,024m. Debt outstanding, in 2011, was $16,335m.

Performance

2015 Gross Domestic Product by state was $313,748m., ranking Colorado 19th in the United States. In 2015 state real GDP growth was 3·2%.

Energy and Natural Resources

Oil and Gas

In 2014 Colorado produced 95·2m. bbls of crude petroleum; marketed production of natural gas totalled 1,631bn. cu. ft.

Water

The Rocky Mountains of Colorado form the headwaters for four major American rivers: the Colorado, Rio Grande, Arkansas and Platte. The total area covered by water is 452 sq. miles.

Minerals

Coal (2009): 28·3m. short tons were produced. In 2008 there were 29,900 people employed in mining, including 7,882 in extracting oil and natural gas. Value of domestic non-fuel mineral production in 2009 was $1,420m.

Agriculture

In 2009 farms and ranches numbered 36,200, with a total of 31·3m. acres of agricultural land. 5,781,000 acres were harvested crop land; average farm, 865 acres. Average value of farmland and buildings per acre in Jan. 2010 was $1,080. Cash receipts from farm marketings, 2009: from crops, $2,230m.; from livestock and products, $3,323m. The net farm income in 2009 was $745m.

Production of principal crops in 2009: corn for grain, 151·5m. bu.; wheat, 100·6m. bu.; barley, 10·4m. bu.; sorghum for grain, 6·8m. bu.; millet, 5·3m. bu.; hay, 4,778,000 tons; corn for silage, 1,998,000 tons; sugar beets, 945,000 tons; potatoes, 23·6m. cwt.

In Dec. 2009 the number of farm animals was: 2,600,000 cattle and calves, 710,000 swine and 375,000 sheep. Wool production in 2007 totalled 2,916,000 lb.

Forestry

The state had a forested area of 22,891,000 acres in 2013, of which 11,156,000 acres were national forest.

Industry

In 2012 the state's 10,430 manufacturing establishments had 235,000 employees, earning $12,683m. Total value added by manufacturing in 2013 was $23,683m.

Labour

Total non-agricultural employment, 2010: 2,220,000. Employees by branch, 2010 (in 1,000): trade, transportation and utilities, 397; government, 393; professional and business services, 329; education and health services, 265; leisure and hospitality, 263. The unemployment rate in Dec. 2010 was 8·9%.

International Trade

Imports and Exports

In 2015 imports into Colorado totalled $13,509m. (down from $14,260m. in 2014). In the same year exports from Colorado totalled $7,950m., down from $8,364m. in 2014. The leading source for imports in 2015 was Canada ($3,211m.), ahead of China ($2,428m.). The leading destination for exports in 2015 was also Canada ($1,408m.), followed by Mexico ($1,077m.).

Trade Fairs

The National Western Stock Show and Rodeo is the largest event of its kind in the USA, drawing over 600,000 visitors.

Communications

Roads

In 2012 there were 88,524 miles of road, of which 19,610 miles were urban roads and 68,914 miles rural roads. There were 4,378,015 motor vehicle registrations.

Rail

In 2012 there were 2,662 miles of freight railroad (excluding trackage rights). There were 14 freight railroads operating in 2012. Rail traffic originating in Colorado in 2012 totalled 30·6m. tons and rail traffic terminating in the state came to 29·7m. tons. A light rail system opened in Denver in 1994.

Civil Aviation

In 2012 Colorado had ten primary airports (commercial service airports with more than 10,000 passenger boardings annually) with a combined total of 27,664,844 enplanements, up from 27,575,461 in 2011. Denver International Airport, the largest airport in the state and 11th busiest in the world, handled 52,699,298 passengers in 2011.

Social Institutions

Justice

In Dec. 2014 there were 20,646 federal and state prisoners. The death penalty is authorized but has not been used since 1997.

Education

In 2012–13 there were 1,844 public elementary and secondary schools with 863,561 pupils and 48,922 teachers. In 2012–13 teachers' salaries averaged $49,844.

Enrolments in four-year state universities and colleges in fall 2014 were: University of Colorado at Boulder, 32,432 students; University of Colorado at Denver, 22,791; University of Colorado at Colorado Springs, 11,761; Colorado State University (Fort Collins), 31,354; Colorado State University Global Campus (Greenwood Village—online only), 9,259; Colorado State University (Pueblo), 7,256; Metropolitan State University of Denver, 21,674; University of Northern Colorado (Greeley), 12,050; Colorado Mesa University (Grand Junction), 9,116; Colorado School of Mines (Golden), 5,962; Colorado Mountain College (Glenwood Springs), 5,705; United States Air Force Academy (Colorado Springs), 3,952; Fort Lewis College (Durango), 3,791; Adams State University (Alamosa), 3,154; Western State Colorado University (Gunnison), 2,584.

Total enrolment in private degree-granting universities and colleges in fall 2012 was 90,491.

Health

Colorado had 2·0 community hospital beds for every 1,000 population in 2013. In the same year there were 29·1 active physicians per 10,000 civilian population and 6·9 dentists per 10,000.

Welfare

Medicare enrolment in July 2012 totalled 686,012. In fiscal year 2011 a total of 737,469 people in Colorado received Medicaid. In Dec. 2014 there were 794,937 Old-Age, Survivors, and Disability Insurance (OASDI) beneficiaries. A total of 38,277 people were receiving payments under Temporary Assistance for Needy Families (TANF) in Dec. 2012.

Religion

The principal religious traditions in 2010 were: Catholics, with 811,630 members; Evangelical Protestants, 601,009; Mainline Protestants, 246,706; Latter-day Saints (Mormons), 145,033; Buddhists, 23,920.

Culture

Tourism

In 2011 overseas visitors to Colorado—excluding those from Canada and Mexico—numbered 446,000, up from 343,000 in 2010.

Connecticut

Key Historical Events

Formerly territory of Algonquian-speaking Indians, Connecticut was first colonized by Europeans during the 1630s, when English Puritans moved there from Massachusetts Bay. Settlements were founded in the Connecticut River Valley at Hartford, Saybrook, Wethersfield and Windsor in 1635. They formed an organized commonwealth in 1637. A further settlement was made at New Haven in 1638 and was united to the commonwealth under a royal charter in 1662. The charter confirmed the commonwealth constitution, drawn up by mutual agreement in 1639 and called the Fundamental Orders of Connecticut.

The area was agricultural and its population of largely English descent until the early 19th century. After the War of Independence, Connecticut was one of the original 13 states of the Union. Its state constitution came into force in 1818 and lasted with amendments until 1965 when a new one was adopted.

In the early 1800s a textile industry thrived on water power. By 1850 the state had more employment in industry than in agriculture, and immigration from Europe (and especially from southern and Eastern Europe) grew rapidly throughout the 19th century. Some immigrants worked in whaling and iron-mining, but most sought industrial employment. Settlement was spread over a large number of small towns, with no single dominant culture.

Yale University was founded at New Haven in 1701. The US Coastguard Academy was founded in 1876 at New London, a former whaling port.

Territory and Population

Connecticut is bounded in the north by Massachusetts, east by Rhode Island, south by the Atlantic and west by New York. Land area, 4,842 sq. miles (12,542 sq. km); water area, 701 sq. miles (1,816 sq. km).

Census population, 1 April 2010, was 3,574,097, an increase of 4·9% since 2000. July 2018 estimate, 3,572,665.

Population in five census years was:

	White	Black	American Indian	Asian		Total	Per sq. mile
1910	1,098,897	15,174	152	533		1,114,756	231·3
1980	2,799,420	217,433	4,533	18,970		3,107,576	634·3

	White	Black	American Indian/ Alaska Native	Asian	Others	Total	Per sq. mile
1990	2,859,353	274,269	6,654	50,078	96,762	3,287,116	678·6
2000	2,780,355	309,843	9,639	82,313	148,567	3,405,565	702·9
2010	2,772,410	362,296	11,256	135,565	292,570	3,574,097	738·1

Of the total population in 2010, 1,834,483 were female and 2,757,082 were 18 years old or older. The Hispanic population in 2010 was 479,087, up from 320,323 in 2000 (an increase of 49·6%).

The chief cities and towns are (2010 census populations):

Bridgeport	144,229
New Haven	129,779
Hartford (capital)	124,775
Stamford	122,643
Waterbury	110,366
Norwalk	85,603
Danbury	80,893
New Britain	73,206
West Hartford	63,268
Meriden	60,868
Bristol	60,477
West Haven	55,564

Social Statistics

Births, 2014, 36,285 (12·3 per 1,000 population); deaths, 2014, 29,860 (8·3). Infant mortality rate, 2013, 4·8 per 1,000 live births. 2014: marriages, 5·4 per 1,000 population; divorces and annulments, 2·6. Connecticut became the third state after Massachusetts and California to allow same-sex marriage when it became legal in Nov. 2008.

Climate

New Haven: Jan. 25°F (−3·8°C), July 74°F (23·4°C). Annual rainfall 45" (1,143 mm). Connecticut belongs to the New England climate zone (*see* UNITED STATES: Climate).

Constitution and Government

The 1818 constitution was revised in 1955. On 30 Dec. 1965 a new constitution went into effect, having been framed by a constitutional convention in the summer of 1965 and approved by the voters in Dec. 1965.

The General Assembly consists of a Senate of 36 members and a House of Representatives of 151 members. Members of each House are elected for the term of two years. Legislative sessions are annual.

For the 116th Congress, which convened in Jan. 2019, Connecticut sends five members to the House of Representatives. It is represented in the Senate by Richard Blumenthal (D. 2011–23) and Christopher Murphy (D. 2013–25).

There are eight counties. The state capital is Hartford.

Recent Elections

In the 2016 presidential election Hillary Clinton took Connecticut with 54·5% of the vote (Barack Obama won it in 2012).

Current Government

Governor: Ned Lamont (D.), 2019–23 (salary: $150,000).
   Lieut.-Governor: Susan Bysiewicz (D.), 2019–23.
   Secretary of the State: Denise Merrill (D.), since Jan. 2011.
Government Website: https://portal.ct.gov

Economy

Per capita personal income (2015) was $66,972, the second highest in the country (after the District of Columbia).

Budget

In 2011 total state revenue was $28,928m. Total expenditure was $28,094m. (education, $6,748m.; public welfare, $6,362m.; hospitals, $1,476m.; government administration, $1,178m.; highways, $1,013m.). Outstanding debt in 2011, $30,524m.

Performance

Gross Domestic Product by state in 2015 was $252,930m., ranking Connecticut 23rd in the United States. In 2015 state real GDP growth was 0·7%.

Energy and Natural Resources

Water

The total area covered by water is 701 sq. miles.

Minerals

The state has some mineral resources: crushed stone, sand, gravel, clay, dimension stone, feldspar and quartz. Total non-fuel mineral production in 2009 was valued at more than $160m.

Agriculture

In 2007 the state had 4,916 farms with a total area of 405,616 acres; the average farm size was 83 acres, valued at $12,667 per acre in 2007. Farm income, 2009: crops $384m., and livestock and products $152m. The net farm income in 2009 was $116m. Principal crops are greenhouse and nursery products, dairy products and chicken eggs.

In 2007 there were 50,213 all cattle (value $81·7m.), 5,767 sheep and 3,645 swine.

Forestry

Total forested area was 1,799,000 acres in 2013.

Industry

In 2012 the state's 8,700 manufacturing establishments had 328,000 employees, earning $21,092m. Total value added by manufacturing in 2013 was $34,068m.

Labour

Total non-agricultural employment, 2010, 1,608,000. Employees by branch, 2010 (in 1,000): education and health services, 307; trade, transportation and utilities, 289; government, 245; professional and business services, 190; manufacturing, 166. The average annual wage per employee in 2009 was $57,771—the highest of any state. The unemployment rate in Dec. 2010 was 9·0%.

International Trade

Imports and Exports
In 2015 imports into Connecticut totalled $25,968m. (up from $23,919m. in 2014). In the same year exports from Connecticut totalled $15,242m., down from $15,963m. in 2014. The leading source for imports in 2015 was the United Kingdom ($5,551m.), ahead of Canada ($3,452m.). The leading destination for exports in 2015 was France ($1,943m.), followed by Germany ($1,654m.).

Communications

Roads
The total length of highways in 2012 was 21,431 miles comprising 15,202 miles of urban road and 6,229 miles of rural road. Motor vehicles registered in 2012 numbered 2,623,127.

Rail
In 2012 there were 364 miles of freight railroad (excluding trackage rights). There were eight freight railroads operating in 2012. Rail traffic originating in Connecticut in 2012 totalled 1·3m. tons and rail traffic terminating in the state also came to 1·3m. tons.

Civil Aviation
In 2011 there were two primary airports (commercial service airports with more than 10,000 passenger boardings annually). The main airport is Bradley International at Windsor Locks, which had 2,772,315 enplanements in 2011.

Social Institutions

Justice
In Dec. 2014 the jail and prison population totalled 16,636. In April 2012 Connecticut became the 17th US state to abolish the death penalty.

Education
Instruction is free for all children and young people between the ages of four and 21 years, and compulsory for all children between the ages of five and 18 years. In 2012–13 there were 1,169 public schools with 550,954 pupils and 43,931 teachers. In 2010–11 total expenditure on public elementary and secondary education was $9,944m. Private schools numbered 410 in fall 2011. Average teacher salary was $69,766 in 2012–13. In 2010–11 spending per pupil was $16,224.

In fall 2009 there were 124,185 students enrolled in the state's public colleges and universities (five state universities, one external degree college, 12 community colleges and a US Coast Guard Academy). The University of Connecticut (founded in 1881), with a main campus at Storrs and six smaller campuses, had 29,517 students in fall 2009. The Connecticut State University System (founded in 1983 but with its oldest institution established in 1849) comprises four universities and had 36,503 students in fall 2009. Enrolment in independent institutions of higher education in 2009 totalled 69,028 students. In fall 2014 Yale University, New Haven (founded in 1701) had 12,336 students; University of Hartford (1877), 6,817; Wesleyan University, Middletown (1831), 3,224; Trinity College, Hartford (1823), 2,408; and Connecticut College, New London (1915), 1,900. There were 24 private degree-granting four-year institutions in 2012–13 and one private degree-granting two-year institution as well as four seminaries and Lincoln College of New England.

Health
Connecticut had 2·2 community hospital beds for every 1,000 population in 2013. In the same year there were 38·4 active physicians per 10,000 civilian population and 7·6 dentists per 10,000.

Welfare
Medicare enrolment in July 2012 totalled 599,165. In fiscal year 2012 a total of 750,087 people in Connecticut received Medicaid. In Dec. 2014 there were 654,533 Old-Age, Survivors, and Disability Insurance (OASDI) beneficiaries. A total of 30,048 people were receiving payments under Temporary Assistance for Needy Families (TANF) in Dec. 2012.

Religion

The principal religious traditions in the state in 2010 were: Catholics, with 1,254,340 members; Mainline Protestants, 281,174; Evangelical Protestants, 157,336; Jews, 47,639; Black Protestants, 22,969.

Culture

Tourism
Overseas visitors to Connecticut—excluding those from Canada and Mexico—numbered 307,000 in 2011, up from 290,000 in 2010.

Delaware

Key Historical Events

Delaware was the territory of Algonquian-speaking Indians who were displaced by European settlement in the 17th century. The first settlers were Swedes who came in 1638 to build Fort Christina (now Wilmington), and colonize what they called New Sweden. In 1655 their colony was taken by the Dutch, who were based in New Amsterdam. In 1664 the British took the whole New Amsterdam colony, including Delaware, and called it New York.

In 1682 Delaware was granted to William Penn, who wanted access to the coast for his Pennsylvania colony. Union of the two colonies was unpopular, and Delaware gained its own government in 1704, although it continued to share a royal governor with Pennsylvania until the War of Independence. Delaware then became one of the 13 original states of the Union and the first to ratify the federal constitution (on 7 Dec. 1787).

The population was of Swedish, Finnish, British and Irish extraction. The land was low-lying and fertile, and the use of slave labour was legal. There was a significant number of black slaves, but Delaware was a border state during the Civil War (1861–65) and did not leave the Union.

19th-century immigrants were mostly European Jews, Poles, Germans and Italians. The north became industrial and densely populated, more so after the Second World War with the rise of the petrochemical industry. Industry in general profited from the opening of the Chesapeake and Delaware Canal in 1829; it was converted to a toll-free deep channel for ocean-going ships in 1919.

Territory and Population

Delaware is bounded in the north by Pennsylvania, northeast by New Jersey, east by Delaware Bay, south and west by Maryland. Land area 1,949 sq. miles (5,047 sq. km); water area, 540 sq. miles (1,399 sq. km). Census population, 1 April 2010, was 897,934, an increase of 14·6% since 2000. July 2018 estimate, 967,171. Population in five census years was:

	White	Black	American Indian	Asian	Total	Per sq. mile
1910	171,102	31,181	5	34	202,322	103·0
			All others			
1980	488,002	96,157	10,179		594,338	290·8
1990	535,094	112,460	18,614		666,168	325·9
2000	584,773	150,666	48,161		783,600	401·0
2010	618,617	191,814	87,503		897,934	460·8

Of the total population in 2010, 462,995 were female and 692,169 were 18 years old or older. The Hispanic population in 2010 was 73,221, up from 37,277 in 2000 (an increase of 96·4%).

The 2010 census figures show Wilmington with a population of 70,851; Dover (the capital), 36,047; Newark, 31,454; Bear, 19,371; Middletown, 18,871.

Social Statistics

Births, 2014, 10,972 (11·7 per 1,000 population); deaths, 2014, 8,260 (8·8). 2013 infant mortality, 6·4 per 1,000 live births. 2014: marriages, 6·0 per 1,000 population; divorces and annulments, 3·3. Same-sex marriage was legalized in May 2013, with effect from July 2013.

Climate

Wilmington, Jan. 31°F (–0·6°C), July 76°F (24·4°C). Annual rainfall 43" (1,076 mm). Delaware belongs to the Atlantic Coast climate zone (*see* UNITED STATES: Climate).

Constitution and Government

The present constitution (the fourth) dates from 1897, and has had 51 amendments; it was not ratified by the electorate but promulgated by the Constitutional Convention. The General Assembly consists of a Senate of 21 members elected for four years and a House of Representatives of 41 members elected for two years.

For the 116th Congress, which convened in Jan. 2019, Delaware sends one member to the House of Representatives. It is represented in the Senate by Thomas Carper (D. 2001–25) and Christopher Coons (D. 2011–21).

The state capital is Dover. Delaware is divided into three counties.

Recent Elections

In the 2016 presidential election Hillary Clinton took Delaware with 53·4% of the vote (Barack Obama won it in 2012).

Current Government

Governor: John C. Carney, Jr (D.), 2017–21 (salary: $171,000).
Lieut.-Governor: Bethany Hall-Long (D.), 2017–21.
Secretary of State: Jeffrey W. Bullock (D.), since Jan. 2009.
Government Website: https://delaware.gov

Economy

Per capita personal income (2015) was $47,662.

Budget

In 2011 total revenue was $9,106m. Total expenditure was $7,936m. (education, $2,544m.; public welfare, $1,762m.; highways, $461m.; government administration, $440m.; health, $395m.). Debt outstanding in 2011, $5,808m.

Performance

2015 Gross Domestic Product by state was $68,724m., ranking Delaware 41st in the United States. In 2015 state real GDP growth was 2·7%.

Banking and Finance

Delaware National Bank has branches statewide. Also based in Delaware, MBNA is the world's largest independent credit card issuer.

Energy and Natural Resources

Water

The total area covered by water is 540 sq. miles.

Minerals

The mineral resources of Delaware are not extensive, consisting chiefly of clay products, stone, sand and gravel and magnesium compounds. Total non-fuel mineral production in 2009 was valued at more than $25m.

Agriculture

There were 510,000 acres in 2,546 farms in 2007. The average farm was 200 acres and was valued (land and buildings) at $10,347 per acre in 2007. Farm income, 2007: crops $209m., and livestock and products $795m. The net farm income in 2009 was $193m. The major product is broilers, with a value of $734·9m. in 2007.

The chief crops are corn for feed, greenhouse products and soybeans.

Forestry

Total forested area was 362,000 acres in 2013.

Industry

In 2012 the state's 1,146 manufacturing establishments had 53,000 employees, earning $2,786m. Total value added by manufacturing in 2013 was $5,923m. Main manufactures are chemicals, transport equipment and food.

Labour

Total non-agricultural employment, 2010, 413,000. Employees by branch, 2010 (in 1,000): trade, transportation and utilities, 74; education and health services, 65; government, 64; professional and business services, 55; financial activities, 43. The unemployment rate in Dec. 2010 was 8·5%.

International Trade

Imports and Exports

In 2015 imports into Delaware totalled $9,234m. (down from $10,739m. in 2014). In the same year exports from Delaware totalled $5,408m., up from $5,267m. in 2014. The leading source for imports in 2015 was Belgium ($1,339m.), ahead of France ($1,106m.). The leading destination for exports in 2015 was the United Kingdom ($882m.), followed by Saudi Arabia ($705m.).

Communications

Roads

In 2012 there were 6,377 miles of roads comprising 3,021 miles of urban road and 3,356 miles of rural road. In 2012 total vehicles registered numbered 912,912.

Rail

In 2012 there were 250 miles of freight railroad (excluding trackage rights). There were seven freight railroads operating in 2012. Rail traffic originating in Delaware in 2012 totalled 0·8m. tons and rail traffic terminating in the state came to 4·4m. tons. An important component of Delaware's freight infrastructure is the rail access to the Port of Wilmington.

Civil Aviation

Delaware is the only state not to have a primary airport (a commercial service airport with more than 10,000 passenger boardings annually). It had four general aviation airports in 2011.

Social Institutions

Justice

In Dec. 2014 the jail and prison population totalled 6,955. The last execution was in 2012. Delaware's Supreme Court ruled the state's death penalty unconstitutional in Aug. 2016.

Education

The state has free public schools and compulsory school attendance to age 16. In 2012–13 the 225 elementary and secondary public schools had 129,026 enrolled pupils and 9,257 teachers. Another 25,090 children were enrolled in 120 private schools in fall 2011. Total expenditure for public elementary and secondary education in 2010–11 was $1,855m. and average teacher salary in 2012–13 was $59,679. Expenditure per pupil was $12,467 in 2010–11.

The state supports the University of Delaware at Newark (founded in 1834) which (in fall 2014) had 1,112 full-time faculty members and 22,680 students; Delaware State University, Dover (1891), with 287 full-time faculty members and 4,397 students; and the campuses of Delaware Technical Community College at Stanton and Wilmington with 6,700 students, Georgetown with 4,296 and Dover with 2,939.

Health

Delaware had 2·2 community hospital beds for every 1,000 population in 2013. In the same year there were 27·4 active physicians per 10,000 civilian population and 4·5 dentists per 10,000.

Welfare

Medicare enrolment in July 2012 totalled 160,921. In fiscal year 2012 a total of 238,997 people in Delaware received Medicaid. In Dec. 2014 there were 192,187 Old-Age, Survivors, and Disability Insurance (OASDI) beneficiaries. A total of 14,383 people were receiving payments under Temporary Assistance for Needy Families (TANF) in Dec. 2012.

Religion

The main religious traditions in the state in 2010 were: Catholics, with 182,532 members; Mainline Protestants, 86,858; Evangelical Protestants, 64,625; Black Protestants, 13,371; Hindus, 7,805.

District of Columbia

Key Historical Events

The District of Columbia, organized in 1790, is the seat of the government of the USA, for which the land was ceded by the states of Maryland and Virginia to the USA as a site for the national capital. It was established under Acts of Congress in 1790 and 1791. Congress first met in it in 1800 and federal authority over it became vested in 1801. In 1846 the land ceded by Virginia (about 33 sq. miles) was given back.

Territory and Population

The District forms an enclave on the Potomac River, where the river forms the southwest boundary of Maryland. The land area of the District of Columbia is 61 sq. miles (158 sq. km); water area, 7 sq. miles (19 sq. km).

Census population, 1 April 2010, was 601,723, an increase of 5·2% since 2000. July 2018 estimate, 702,455. The population was 100% urban in 2010. Metropolitan area of Washington, D.C.–Arlington–Alexandria (2010), 5,582,170. The Hispanic population in 2010 was 54,749, up from 44,953 in 2000 (an increase of 21·8%). Of the total population in 2010, 317,501 were female and 500,908 were 18 years old or older.

Population in five census years was:

	White	Black	American Indian	Chinese and Japanese	Total	Per sq. mile
1910	236,128	94,446	68	427	331,069	5,517·8
			All others			
1980	171,768	448,906	17,659		638,333	10,464·4
1990	179,667	339,604	87,629		606,900	9,949·2
2000	176,101	343,312	52,646		572,059	9,378·0
2010	231,471	305,125	65,127		601,723	9,856·5

Blacks constituted 50·7% of the population at the 2010 census—the highest proportion in the USA.

Social Statistics

Births, 2014, 9,509 (14·4 per 1,000 population); deaths, 2014, 4,723 (7·2). Infant mortality rate, 2013, 6·7 per 1,000 live births. 2014: marriages, 11·8 per 1,000 population; divorces and annulments, 2·6. The abortion rate, at 33 for every 1,000 women aged 15 to 44 in 2014, is the highest in the USA. Same-sex marriage became legal in March 2010.

Climate

Washington, Jan. 34°F (1·1°C), July 77°F (25°C). Annual rainfall 43" (1,064 mm). The District of Columbia belongs to the Atlantic Coast climate zone (*see* UNITED STATES: Climate).

Constitution and Government

Local government, from 1 July 1878 until Aug. 1967, was that of a municipal corporation administered by a board of three commissioners, of whom two were appointed from civil life by the President, and confirmed by the Senate, for a term of three years each. The other commissioner was detailed by the President from the Engineer Corps of the Army. The Commission form of government was abolished in 1967 and a new Mayor Council instituted with officers appointed by the President with the advice and consent of the Senate. On 24 Dec. 1973 the appointed officers were replaced by an elected Mayor and councillors, with full legislative powers in local matters as from 1974. Congress retains the right to legislate, to veto or supersede the Council's acts. The 23rd amendment to the federal constitution (1961) conferred the right to vote in national elections. The District has one delegate and one shadow delegate to the House of Representatives and two shadow senators. The Congressman may participate but not vote on the House floor.

Recent Elections

In the 2016 presidential election Hillary Clinton took the District of Columbia with 92·8% of the vote (Barack Obama won it in 2012).

Current Government

Mayor: Muriel Bowser (D.), 2019–23 (salary: $200,000).
　Secretary of the District: Lauren C. Vaughan (D.), since Jan. 2015.
Government Website: https://dc.gov

Economy

Per capita personal income (2015) was $71,496, the highest in the country.

Budget

The District's revenues are derived from a tax on real and personal property, sales taxes, taxes on corporations and companies, licences for conducting various businesses and from federal payments. The District of Columbia has no bonded debt not covered by its accumulated sinking fund.

Performance

Gross Domestic Product by state in 2015 was $122,146m. In 2015 state real GDP growth was 2·2%.

Energy and Natural Resources

Water

The total area covered by water is 7 sq. miles.

Industry

In 2012 there were 226 manufacturing establishments with 2,700 employees, earning $123m. Total value added by manufacturing in 2013 was $151m. The main industries are communications, finance, government service, insurance, real estate, services, transport, utilities, and wholesale and retail trade.

Labour

Total non-agricultural employment, 2010, 711,000. Employees by branch, 2010 (in 1,000): government, 246; professional and business services, 149; education and health services, 108; leisure and hospitality, 59; trade, transportation and utilities, 27. In Dec. 2010 the unemployment rate was 9·6%.

International Trade

Imports and Exports

In 2015 imports into the District of Columbia totalled $913m. (down from $1,105m. in 2014). In the same year exports from the District of Columbia totalled $1,088m., up from $940m. in 2014. The leading source for imports in 2015 was Japan ($164m.), ahead of India ($140m.). The leading destination for exports in 2015 was the United Arab Emirates ($686m.), followed by Oman ($72m.).

Communications

Roads

In 2012 there were 1,502 miles of roads. There were 318,206 registered vehicles in 2012.

Rail

In 2012 there were 20 miles of freight railroad (excluding trackage rights). There were three freight railroads operating in 2012. Rail traffic originating in District of Columbia in 2012 totalled 37,000 tons and rail traffic terminating in the state came to 17,000 tons. There is a metro in Washington extending to 130 km, and two commuter rail networks.

Civil Aviation

The District is served by three general airports; across the Potomac River in Arlington County, Va., is Ronald Reagan Washington National Airport; in Dulles, Va., is Washington Dulles International Airport; and in Maryland is Baltimore/Washington International Thurgood Marshall Airport.

Social Institutions

Justice

The death penalty was declared unconstitutional in the District of Columbia on 14 Nov. 1973.

The District's Court system is the Judicial Branch of the District of Columbia. It is the only completely unified court system in the United States, because of the District's unique city-state jurisdiction. Until the District of Columbia Court Reform and Criminal Procedure Act of 1970, the judicial system was almost entirely in the hands of Federal government. Since that time, the system has been similar in most respects to the autonomous systems of the states.

Education

In 2012–13 there were 76,140 pupils enrolled at 244 elementary and secondary public schools with 5,925 teachers. Expenditure per pupil in 2010–11 was $20,793.

Higher education is given through the Consortium of Universities of the Metropolitan Washington Area, which consists of 14 universities: American University; Catholic University of America; Gallaudet University; George Mason University; George Washington University; Georgetown University; Howard University; Marymount University; National Defense University;

National Intelligence University; Trinity Washington University; Uniformed Services University of the Health Sciences; University of the District of Columbia (the only public university in Washington, D.C.); University of Maryland College Park. There were 20 degree-granting institutions altogether in 2012–13.

Health

The District of Columbia had 5·6 community hospital beds for every 1,000 population in 2013. In the same year there were 74·7 active physicians per 10,000 civilian population and 8·9 dentists per 10,000.

Welfare

Medicare enrolment in July 2012 totalled 83,322. In fiscal year 2011 a total of 235,665 people in the District of Columbia received Medicaid. In Dec. 2014 there were 79,716 Old-Age, Survivors, and Disability Insurance (OASDI) beneficiaries. A total of 17,436 people were receiving payments under Temporary Assistance for Needy Families (TANF) in Dec. 2012.

Religion

The main religious traditions in 2010 were: Mainline Protestants, with 82,388 members; Catholics, 75,948; Evangelical Protestants, 75,306; Black Protestants, 50,602; Jews, 17,664.

Florida

Key Historical Events

Of the French and Spanish settlements in Florida in the 16th century, the Spanish, at St Augustine from 1565, survived. Florida was claimed by Spain until 1763 when it passed to Britain. Although regained by Spain in 1783, the British used it as a base for attacks on American forces during the war of 1812. Gen. Andrew Jackson captured Pensacola for the USA in 1818. In 1819 a treaty was signed which ceded Florida to the USA with effect from 1821 and it became a Territory of the USA in 1822.

Florida had been the home of the Apalachee and Timucua Indians. After 1770, groups of Creek Indians began to arrive as refugees from the European-American Indian wars. These 'Seminoles' or runaways attracted other refugees including slaves, the recapture of whom was the motive for the first Seminole War of 1817–18. A second war followed in 1835–42, when the Seminoles retreated to the Everglades swamps. After a third war in 1855–58 most Seminoles were forced or persuaded to move to reserves in Oklahoma.

Florida became a state in 1845. About half of the population were black slaves. At the outbreak of Civil War in 1861 the state seceded from the Union.

During the 20th century Florida continued to grow fruit and vegetables, but real estate development (often for retirement) and the growth of tourism and the aerospace industry set it apart from other ex-plantation states.

Territory and Population

Florida is a peninsula bounded in the west by the Gulf of Mexico, south by the Straits of Florida, east by the Atlantic, north by Georgia and northwest by Alabama. Land area, 53,625 sq. miles (138,887 sq. km); water area, 12,133 sq. miles (31,424 sq. km). Census population, 1 April 2010, was 18,801,310, an increase of 17·6% since 2000. July 2018 estimate, 21,299,325.

Population in five federal census years was:

	White	Black	All others	Total	Per sq. mile
1950	2,166,051	603,101	2,153	2,771,305	51·1
1980	8,319,448	1,342,478	84,398	9,746,324	180·1
1990	10,749,285	1,759,534	429,107	12,937,926	238·9
2000	12,465,029	2,335,505	1,181,844	15,982,378	296·4
2010	14,109,162	2,999,862	1,692,286	18,801,310	350·6

Of the total population in 2010, 9,611,955 were female and 14,799,219 were 18 years old or older. The Hispanic population in 2010 was 4,223,806, up from 2,682,715 in 2000 (a rise of 57·4% and the third largest numeric increase of any state in the USA).

The largest cities in the state, 2010 census, are: Jacksonville, 821,784; Miami, 399,457; Tampa, 335,709; St Petersburg, 244,769; Orlando, 238,300; Hialeah, 224,669; Tallahassee (the capital), 181,376; Fort Lauderdale, 165,521; Port St Lucie, 164,603; Pembroke Pines, 154,750; Cape Coral, 154,305; Hollywood, 140,768; Gainesville, 124,354; Miramar, 122,041; Coral Springs, 121,096; Clearwater, 107,685; Miami Gardens, 107,167; Brandon, 103,483; Palm Bay, 103,190; West Palm Beach, 99,919; Pompano Beach, 99,845; Spring Hill, 98,621; Lakeland, 97,422; Davie, 91,992; Miami Beach, 87,779; Lehigh Acres, 86,784; Deltona, 85,182; Plantation, 84,955; Sunrise, 84,439; Boca Raton, 84,392.

Population of the largest metropolitan areas (2010): Miami–Fort Lauderdale–Pompano Beach, 5,564,635; Tampa–St Petersburg–Clearwater, 2,783,243; Orlando–Kissimmee–Sanford, 2,134,411; Jacksonville, 1,345,596.

Social Statistics

Births, 2014, 219,991 (11·1 per 1,000 population); deaths, 2014, 185,956 (9·3). Infant mortality, 2013, 6·1 per 1,000 live births. 2014: marriages, 7·3 per 1,000 population; divorces and annulments, 4·0. Same-sex marriage became legal in Jan. 2015.

Climate

Jacksonville, Jan. 55°F (12·8°C), July 81°F (27·2°C). Annual rainfall 54" (1,353 mm). Key West, Jan. 70°F (21·1°C), July 83°F (28·3°C). Annual rainfall 39" (968 mm). Miami, Jan. 67°F (19·4°C), July 82°F (27·8°C). Annual rainfall 60" (1,516 mm). Tampa, Jan. 61°F (16·1°C), July 81°F (27·2°C). Annual rainfall 51" (1,285 mm). Florida belongs to the Gulf Coast climate zone (*see* UNITED STATES: Climate).

Constitution and Government

The 1968 Legislature revised the constitution of 1885. The state legislature comprises the Senate and House of Representatives. The Senate has 40 members elected for four years. Half of the membership is elected every two years. The House has 120 members, all of whom are elected every two years during elections held in even-numbered years. Sessions of the legislature are held annually, and are limited to 60 days. Senate and House districts are based on population, with each senator and member representing approximately the same number of residents. The Senate and House are reapportioned every ten years when the federal census is released. In addition to the Governor and Lieut.-Governor (who are elected for four years), the constitution provides for a cabinet composed of an attorney general, a chief financial officer and a commissioner of agriculture.

For the 116th Congress, which convened in Jan. 2016, Florida sends 27 members to the House of Representatives. It is represented in the Senate by Marco Rubio (R. 2011–23) and Rick Scott (R. 2019–25).

The state capital is Tallahassee. The state is divided into 67 counties.

Recent Elections

In the 2016 presidential election Donald Trump took Florida with 49·1% of the vote (Barack Obama won it in 2012).

Current Government

Governor: Ron DeSantis (R.), 2019–23 (salary: $130,273).
　Lieut.-Governor: Jeanette Núñez (R.), 2019–23.
　Secretary of State: Laurel Lee (R.), since Jan. 2019.
Government Website: http://www.myflorida.com

Economy

Per capita personal income (2015) was $44,101.

Budget

In 2011 total state revenue was $106,166m. Total expenditure was $84,633m. (including: education, $24,883m.; public welfare, $22,303m.; highways, $5,449m.; health, $3,750m.; government administration, $2,758m.). Outstanding debt in 2011, $43,472m.

Performance

2015 Gross Domestic Product by state was $888,087m., ranking Florida 4th in the United States. In 2015 state real GDP growth was 4·0%.

Banking and Finance

In 2014 there were 179 financial institutions in Florida insured by the US Federal Deposit Insurance Corporation, with assets worth $160,397m.

Energy and Natural Resources

Electricity

In 2015 production was 237·4bn. kWh, of which 155·8bn. kWh was from natural gas.

Oil and Gas

In 2014 Florida produced 2·2m. bbls of crude petroleum.

Water

The total area covered by water is 12,133 sq. miles (the third largest of any state after Alaska and Michigan), of which 5,027 sq. miles are inland.

Minerals

Total non-fuel mineral production for 2009 was valued at $4,250m. Phosphate rock was the leading mineral commodity produced in 2009. Florida produces more than four times as much phosphate rock as the next highest producing state. Production of crushed stone, portland cement, construction sand and gravel, and zirconium concentrates is also important.

Agriculture

In 2007 there were 9·23m. acres of farmland; 47,463 farms with an average of 195 acres per farm. The total value of land and buildings was $52,054m. in 2007; average value (2007) of land and buildings per acre, $5,639.

Farm income from crops and livestock (2009) was $7,100m., of which crops provided $5,998m. and livestock and products $1,102m. Major crop contributors are greenhouse products, oranges, sugarcane, tomatoes, grapefruit, peppers, other winter vegetables and indoor and landscaping plants. The net farm income in 2009 was $1,281m. In 2007 the state had 1·71m. cattle, including 119,900 dairy cows, and 19,900 hogs and pigs, plus 11·79m. laying hens.

Forestry

In 2013 Florida had 17·27m. acres of forested land (11·14m. acres privately-owned), including 1·18m. acres of national forests.

Industry

In 2012 the state's 26,088 manufacturing establishments had 568,000 employees, earning $29,156m. Total value added by manufacturing in 2013 was $51,285m. Main industries include: printing and publishing, machinery and computer equipment, apparel and finished products, fabricated metal products, and lumber and wood products.

Labour

Total non-agricultural employment, 2010, 7,175,000. Employees by branch, 2010 (in 1,000): trade, transportation and utilities, 1,455; government, 1,115; education and health services, 1,079; professional and business services, 1,036; leisure and hospitality, 918. In Dec. 2010 the unemployment rate was 12·0%.

International Trade

Imports and Exports

In 2015 imports into Florida totalled $73·4bn. (up from $71·9bn. in 2014). In the same year exports from Florida totalled $53·9bn., down from $58·4bn. in 2014. The leading source for imports in 2015 was China ($11·8bn.), ahead of Mexico ($5·6bn.). The leading destination for exports in 2015 was Canada ($3·9bn.), followed by Brazil ($3·7bn.).

Communications

Roads

The state (2012) had 121,829 miles of highways, roads and streets (81,496 miles being urban roads and 40,333 rural). In 2012 there were 15,046,834 vehicle registrations and 2,424 traffic accident fatalities.

Rail

In 2012 there were 2,900 miles of freight railroad (excluding trackage rights). There were 14 freight railroads operating in 2012. Rail traffic originating in Florida in 2012 totalled 43·7m. tons and rail traffic terminating in the state came to 66·7m. tons. There is a metro of 22 miles, a peoplemover and a commuter rail route in Miami.

Civil Aviation

In 2011 Florida had 19 primary airports (commercial service airports with more than 10,000 passenger boardings annually), seven of which had more than 1m. passenger enplanements. There were 69,319,400 passenger enplanements at the primary airports in 2011 (up from 66,716,652 in 2010). The busiest airports in 2011 were Miami International (18,342,158 enplanements), Orlando International (17,250,415) and Fort Lauderdale/Hollywood International (11,332,466).

Shipping

There are 14 deepwater ports: those on the Gulf coast handle mainly domestic trade and those on the Atlantic coast primarily international trade and cruise ship traffic. The major ports are Tampa (which handled 35·2m. short tons of cargo in 2014), Port Everglades (22·4m. short tons in 2014), Jacksonville and Miami.

Social Institutions

Justice

The state resumed the use of the death penalty in 1979. There were 97 executions between 1977 and 2018, including three in 2017 and two in 2018. In Dec. 2014 there were 102,870 federal and state prisoners, up from 85,530 in Dec. 2004. Chain gangs were introduced in 1995. In a state-wide vote held on the same day as the presidential election in Nov. 2016, medical use of marijuana was legalized.

Education

Attendance at school is compulsory between six and 16. In 2012–13 there were 4,388 public elementary and secondary schools with 2,692,162 enrolled pupils and 176,537 teachers. Total expenditure on public elementary and secondary education in 2010–11 was $27,434m. and spending per pupil was $9,030. The average teacher salary was $46,944 in 2012–13.

In 2012–13 there were 239 degree-granting institutions (41 public and 198 private); there were 804,693 students at public degree-granting institutions in fall 2012. There are 12 institutions in the State University System of Florida: University of Central Florida (founded 1963) at Orlando with 60,767 students in fall 2014; Florida International University at Miami (founded 1965) with 49,610; University of Florida at Gainesville (founded 1853) with 49,459; University of South Florida at Tampa (founded 1960) with 41,938; Florida State University at Tallahassee (founded in 1857) with 41,226; Florida Atlantic University (founded 1964) at Boca Raton with 30,297; University of North Florida at Jacksonville (founded 1972) with 15,984; Florida Gulf Coast University (founded 1997) at Fort Myers with 14,473; University of West Florida at Pensacola (founded 1963) with 12,602; Florida A. & M. (Agricultural and Mechanical) University at Tallahassee (founded 1887) with 10,241; New College of Florida (founded 2001) at Sarasota with 834: and Florida Polytechnic University (founded 2012) at Lakeland with 540. There are 30 private colleges and universities belonging to the Independent Colleges and Universities of Florida (ICUF), an association serving more than 150,000 degree-seeking students.

Health

Florida had 2·7 community hospital beds for every 1,000 population in 2013. In the same year there were 27·2 active physicians per 10,000 civilian population and 5·1 dentists per 10,000.

Welfare

Medicare enrolment in July 2012 totalled 3,598,595. In fiscal year 2011 a total of 3,829,173 people in Florida received Medicaid. In Dec. 2014 there were 4,223,274 Old-Age, Survivors, and Disability Insurance (OASDI) beneficiaries. A total of 99,825 people were receiving payments under Temporary Assistance for Needy Families (TANF) in Dec. 2012.

Religion

The principal religious traditions in the state in 2010 were: Evangelical Protestants, with 3,049,524 members; Catholics, 2,515,243; Mainline Protestants, 870,959; Black Protestants, 333,390; Muslims, 165,000 (estimate).

Culture

Tourism

Overseas visitors to Florida—excluding those from Canada and Mexico—numbered 9,540,000 in 2016 (down from 9,667,000 in 2015). There were 3,672,000 visits by Canadians in 2015. Florida ranks among the most visited states and Miami and Orlando among the most visited cities.

Georgia

Key Historical Events

Originally the territory of Creek and Cherokee tribes, Georgia was first settled by Europeans in the 18th century. James Oglethorpe founded Savannah in 1733, intending it as a colony offering a new start to debtors, convicts and the poor. Settlement was slow until 1783, when growth began in the cotton-growing areas west of Augusta. The American Indian population was cleared off the rich cotton land and moved beyond the Mississippi. Georgia became one of the original 13 states of the Union.

A plantation economy developed rapidly, using slave labour. In 1861 Georgia seceded from the Union and became an important source of supplies for the Confederate cause, although some northern areas never accepted secession and continued in sympathy with the Union during the Civil War. At the beginning of the war 56% of the population were white, descendants of British, Austrian and New England immigrants; the remaining 44% were black slaves.

The city of Atlanta, which grew as a railway junction, was destroyed during the war but revived to become the centre of southern reconstruction in the post-war period. It was confirmed as the state capital in 1877. Successive movements for black freedom in social, economic and political life have developed in the city, notably the Southern Christian Leadership Conference, led by Martin Luther King, who was assassinated in 1968.

Territory and Population
Georgia is bounded north by Tennessee and North Carolina, northeast by South Carolina, east by the Atlantic, south by Florida and west by Alabama. Land area, 57,513 sq. miles (148,959 sq. km); water area, 1,912 sq. miles (4,951 sq. km). Census population, 1 April 2010, was 9,687,653, an increase of 18·3% since 2000. July 2018 estimate, 10,519,475.

Population in five census years was:

	White	Black	American Indian	Asian	Total	Per sq. mile
1910	1,431,802	1,176,987	95	237	2,609,121	44·4
			All others			
1980	3,948,007	1,465,457	50,801		5,464,265	92·7
1990	4,600,148	1,746,565	131,503		6,478,216	110·0
2000	5,327,281	2,349,542	509,630		8,186,453	141·4
2010	5,787,440	2,950,435	949,778		9,687,653	168·4

Of the total population in 2010, 4,958,482 were female and 7,196,101 were 18 years old or older. The estimated Hispanic population was 853,689 in 2010, up from 435,277 in 2000 (an increase of 96·1%).

The largest cities are: Atlanta (capital), with a population (2010 census) of 420,003; Augusta-Richmond County, 200,549; Columbus, 189,885; Savannah, 136,286; Athens-Clarke County, 116,714. The Atlanta–Sandy Springs–Marietta metropolitan area had a 2010 census population of 5,268,860; Augusta-Richmond County, 556,877; Savannah, 347,611.

Social Statistics
Births, 2014, 130,946 (13·0 per 1,000 population); deaths, 2014, 76,887 (7·6). Infant mortality, 2013, 8·1 per 1,000 live births. Marriages, 2012, 6·5 per 1,000 population.

Climate
Atlanta, Jan. 43°F (6·1°C), July 78°F (25·6°C). Annual rainfall 49" (1,234 mm). Georgia belongs to the Atlantic Coast climate zone (see UNITED STATES: Climate).

Constitution and Government
A new constitution was approved on 25 Sept. 1981, ratified on 2 Nov. 1982 and became effective on 1 July 1983. The General Assembly consists of a Senate of 56 members and a House of Representatives of 180 members, both elected for two years. Legislative sessions are annual, beginning the 2nd Monday in Jan. and lasting for 40 days.

Georgia was the first state to extend the franchise to all citizens 18 years old and above.

For the 116th Congress, which convened in Jan. 2019 Georgia sends 14 members to the House of Representatives. It is represented in the Senate by Johnny Isakson (R. 2005–23) and David Perdue (R. 2015–21).

The state capital is Atlanta. Georgia is divided into 159 counties.

Recent Elections
In the 2016 presidential election Donald Trump took Georgia with 51·3% of the vote (Mitt Romney won it in 2012).

Current Government
Governor: Brian Kemp (R.), 2019–23 (salary: $139,339).
Lieut.-Governor: Geoff Duncan (R.), 2019–23.
Secretary of State: Brad Raffensperger (R.), since Jan. 2019.
Government Website: https://georgia.gov

Economy
Per capita personal income (2015) was $40,551.

Budget
In 2011 total state revenue was $52,295m. Total expenditure was $44,750m. (education, $17,429m.; public welfare, $10,367m.; highways, $1,641m.; correction, $1,462m.; health, $1,159m.). Outstanding debt in 2011, $13,403m.

Performance
Gross Domestic Product by state was $497,944m. in 2015, ranking Georgia 9th in the United States. In 2015 state real GDP growth was 2·6%.

Energy and Natural Resources
Electricity
In 2015 production was 128·8bn. kWh, of which 50·5bn. kWh was from natural gas.

Water
The total area covered by water is 1,912 sq. miles.

Minerals
Georgia is the leading producer of kaolin. The state ranks first in production of crushed and dimensional granite, and second in production of fuller's earth and marble (crushed and dimensional). Total value of non-fuel mineral production for 2009 was $1,410m.

Agriculture
In 2007, 47,846 farms covered 10·15m. acres; the average farm was of 212 acres. In 2007 the average value of farmland and buildings was $3,117 per acre. The major product is broilers; in 2007, 1·40bn. were produced (the most in any state) with a value of $3·19bn. For 2007 cotton output was 1·6m. bales (of 480 lb). Other major crops include tobacco, corn, wheat, soybeans, peanuts and pecans. Cash receipts from farm marketings, 2009: crops, $2,556m.; livestock and products, $4,291m.; total, $6,847m. The net farm income in 2009 was $2,359m.

In 2007 farm animals included 1·12m. cattle and 236,500 swine; there were also 19·27m. laying hens.

Forestry
The forested area in 2013 was 24·74m. acres with 822,000 acres of national forest. Georgia has the largest acreage of forest available for commercial use in the country, and the forest industry is the second largest industry in the state. Softwood lumber output in 2011 was 1,914m. bd ft.

Industry
In 2012 the state's 16,460 manufacturing establishments had 731,000 employees, earning $33,013m. Total value added by manufacturing in 2013 was $66,159m.

Labour
Total non-agricultural employment, 2010, 3,826,000. Employees by branch, 2010 (in 1,000): trade, transportation and utilities, 808; government, 678; professional and business services, 519; education and health services, 486; leisure and hospitality, 374. Georgia's unemployment rate in Dec. 2010 was 10·4%.

International Trade
Imports and Exports
In 2015 imports into Georgia totalled $88·7bn. (up from $83·9bn. in 2014). In the same year exports from Georgia totalled $38·6bn., down from $39·4bn. in 2014. The leading source for imports in 2015 was China ($19·8bn.), ahead of Germany ($16·4bn.). The leading destination for exports in 2015 was Canada ($6·5bn.), followed by Mexico ($3·5bn.).

Communications

Roads

In 2012 there were 125,523 miles of roads comprising 40,476 miles of urban road and 85,047 miles of rural road. There were 7,445,788 motor vehicles registered.

Rail

In 2012 there were 4,653 miles of freight railroad, including 3,251 miles of Class I railroads. There were 24 freight railroads operating in 2012. Rail traffic originating in Georgia in 2012 totalled 31·8m. and rail traffic terminating in the state came to 67·7m. tons. There is a 48-mile heavy-rail subway system serving Metropolitan Atlanta, and a 2·7 mile tramway that opened in Atlanta in Dec. 2014.

Civil Aviation

In 2011 there were seven primary airports (commercial service airports with more than 10,000 passenger boardings annually) with a combined total of 45,649,069 enplanements, up from 44,347,182 in 2010. Hartsfield–Jackson Atlanta International Airport handled a record 44,414,121 passenger enplanements in 2011—the highest number of any airport in the world.

Shipping

There are deepwater ports at Savannah, the principal port, and Brunswick.

Social Institutions

Justice

In Dec. 2014 there were 52,949 federal and state prisoners. The death penalty is authorized for capital offences. There were two executions in 2018.

Education

Since 1945 education has been compulsory; tuition is free until the age of 18 and school attendance is compulsory for pupils between the ages of six and 16 years. In 2012–13 there were 2,425 public elementary and secondary schools with 1·7m. pupils and 109,365 teachers; total expenditure on public elementary and secondary education (2010–11) was $17,178m. Teachers' salaries averaged $52,880 in 2012–13.

The University of Georgia (Athens) was founded in 1785 and was the first chartered State University in the USA (35,197 students in fall 2014). Other higher education institutions (with fall 2014 student enrolment) include Georgia State University, Atlanta (32,556); Kennesaw State University, Kennesaw (25,714 students); Georgia Institute of Technology, Atlanta (23,109); Georgia Southern University, Statesboro (20,517). The Atlanta University Center, devoted primarily to Black education, includes co-educational Clark Atlanta University (3,485); Spelman College (2,135), the first liberal arts college for Black women in the USA; Morehouse College (2,109), a liberal arts college for men; and Morehouse School of Medicine (398). Wesleyan College (711), near Macon, is the oldest chartered women's college in the world.

Health

Georgia had 2·5 community hospital beds for every 1,000 population in 2013. In the same year there were 23·4 active physicians per 10,000 civilian population and 4·7 dentists per 10,000.

Welfare

Medicare enrolment in July 2012 totalled 1,354,637. In fiscal year 2012 a total of 2,168,283 people in Georgia received Medicaid. In Dec. 2014 there were 1,676,778 Old-Age, Survivors, and Disability Insurance (OASDI) beneficiaries. A total of 37,318 people were receiving payments under Temporary Assistance for Needy Families (TANF) in Dec. 2012.

Religion

The principal religious traditions in the state in 2010 were: Evangelical Protestants, with 2,853,360 members; Mainline Protestants, 855,259; Catholics, 596,384; Black Protestants, 381,421; Latter-day Saints (Mormons), 78,177.

Culture

Tourism

Overseas visitors to Georgia in 2011—excluding those from Canada and Mexico—numbered 669,000, down from 817,000 in 2010 although up from 520,000 in 2006.

Hawaii

Key Historical Events

The islands of Hawaii were settled by Polynesian immigrants, probably from the Marquesas Islands, about AD 400. A second major immigration, from Tahiti, occurred around 800–900. In the late 18th century all the islands were united into one kingdom by Kamehameha I. Western exploration began in 1778, and Christian missions were established after 1820. Europeans called Hawaii the Sandwich Islands. The USA, Britain and France all claimed an interest. Kamehameha III placed Hawaii under US protection in 1851. US sugar-growing companies became dominant and in 1887 the USA obtained a naval base at Pearl Harbor. A struggle developed between forces for and against annexation by the USA. In 1893 the monarchy was overthrown. The republican government agreed to be annexed to the USA in 1898, and Hawaii became a US Territory in 1900.

The islands and the naval base were of great strategic importance during the Second World War, when the Japanese attack on Pearl Harbor brought the USA into the war.

Hawaii became the 50th state of the Union in 1959. The 19th-century plantation economy encouraged the immigration of workers, especially from China and Japan. Hawaiian laws, religions and culture were gradually adapted to the needs of the immigrant community.

Territory and Population

The Hawaiian Islands lie in the North Pacific Ocean, between 18° 54' and 28° 15' N. lat. and 154° 40' and 178° 25' W. long., about 2,090 nautical miles southwest of San Francisco. There are 137 named islands and islets in the group, of which seven major and five minor islands are inhabited. Land area, 6,423 sq. miles (16,635 sq. km); water area, 4,509 sq. miles (11,678 sq. km). Census population, 1 April 2010, was 1,360,301, an increase of 12·3% since 2000. July 2018 estimate, 1,420,491. Of the total population in 2010, 681,243 were male and 1,056,483 were 18 years old or older.

The principal islands are Hawaii, 4,028 sq. miles, population 2010, 185,079; Maui, 727 sq. miles, population 144,444; Oahu, 600 sq. miles, population 953,207; Kauai, 552 sq. miles, population 66,921; Molokai, 260 sq. miles, population 7,345; Lanai, 141 sq. miles, population 3,135; Niihau, 70 sq. miles, population 170; Kahoolawe, 45 sq. miles (uninhabited). The capital Honolulu—on the island of Oahu—had a population in 2010 of 387,170.

Figures for main racial groups, 2010, were: 336,599 White; 197,497 Filipino; 185,502 Japanese; 80,337 Native Hawaiian; 54,955 Chinese; 24,203 Korean; 21,424 Black or African American; 18,287 Samoan; 9,779 Vietnamese.

Social Statistics

Births, 2014, 18,550 (13·1 per 1,000 population); deaths, 2014, 10,767 (7·6). Infant deaths, 2013, were at a rate of 6·4 per 1,000 live births. Marriages, 2014, 17·7 per 1,000 population. Inter-marriage between the races is common. In 2007, of the 9,401 resident couples married, 55·1% were inter-racial. 65·6% were non-resident marriages. Same-sex marriage was legalized by the State Legislature in Dec. 2013.

Climate

All the islands have a tropical climate, with an abrupt change in conditions between windward and leeward sides, most marked in rainfall. Temperatures vary little. Average temperatures in Honolulu: Jan. 73·0°F, July 80·8°F. Average annual rainfall in Honolulu: 18·29".

Constitution and Government

Hawaii was officially admitted into the United States on 21 Aug. 1959. However, the constitution of the State of Hawaii was created by the 1950 Constitutional Convention, ratified by the voters of the Territory on 7 Nov. 1950, and amended on 27 June 1959. The Legislature consists of a Senate of 25 members elected for four years and a House of Representatives of 51 members elected for two years. There have been two constitutional conventions since 1950, in 1968 and 1978. In addition to amendments proposed by these conventions the Legislature is able to propose amendments to voters during the general election. This has resulted in numerous amendments.

For the 116th Congress, which convened in Jan. 2019, Hawaii sends two members to the House of Representatives. It is represented in the Senate by Brian Schatz (D. 2012–23) and Mazie Hirono (D. 2013–25).

The state capital is Honolulu. There are five counties.

Recent Elections

In the 2016 presidential election Hillary Clinton took Hawaii with 62·3% of the vote (Barack Obama won it in 2012).

Current Government

Governor: David Ige (D.), Dec. 2018–Dec. 2022 (salary: $152,544).
    Lieut.-Governor: Josh Green (D.), Dec. 2018–Dec. 2022.
Government Website: http://www.ehawaii.gov

Economy

Per capita personal income (2015) was $47,753.

Budget

Revenue is derived mainly from taxation of sales and gross receipts, real property, corporate and personal income, and inheritance taxes, licences, public land sales and leases.

In 2011 total state revenue was $12,932m. Total expenditure was $11,476m. (education, $3,345m.; public welfare, $2,087m.; hospitals, $667m.; health, $620m.; government administration, $417m.). Outstanding debt in 2011, $7,913m.

Performance

2015 Gross Domestic Product by state was $80,376m., ranking Hawaii 38th in the United States. In 2015 state real GDP growth was 2·3%.

Energy and Natural Resources

Oil and Gas

In 2011, $139·5m. was generated by gas sales.

Water

The total area covered by water is 4,509 sq. miles.

Minerals

Production in 2008: crushed stone, 7·5m. tonnes; construction sand and gravel, 1·4m. tonnes. Total value of non-fuel mineral production in 2009 was $116m.

Agriculture

Farming is highly commercialized and highly mechanized. In 2007 there were 7,521 farms covering an area of 1·12m. acres; average number of acres per farm, 149, valued at $7,688 per acre.

Greenhouse products, pineapples, sugarcane and macadamia nuts are the staple crops. Farm income, 2009, from crop sales was $510m., and from livestock $72m. The net farm income in 2009 was $133m.

Forestry

Hawaii had 1·92m. acres of forested land in 2010 (of which 1·78m. acres were non-federal and 0·14m. acres federal).

Fisheries

In 2009 the commercial fish catch was 26·91m. lb with a value of $71·2m.

Industry

In 2012 the state's 1,592 manufacturing establishments had 23,000 employees, earning $930m. Total value added by manufacturing in 2013 was $1,140m.

Labour

Total non-agricultural employment amounted to 587,000 in 2010. Employees by branch, 2010 (in 1,000): government, 125; trade, transportation and utilities, 109; leisure and hospitality, 100; education and health services, 76; professional and business services, 71. The unemployment rate in Dec. 2010 was 6·3%.

International Trade

Imports and Exports

In 2015 imports into Hawaii totalled $3,756m. (down from $5,329m. in 2014). In the same year exports from Hawaii totalled $1,896m., up from $1,447m. in 2014. The leading source for imports in 2015 was Indonesia ($816m.), ahead of Russia ($477m.). The leading destination for exports in 2015 was Australia ($1,278m.), followed by Vietnam ($102m.).

Communications

Roads

In 2012 there were 4,416 miles of roads comprising 2,364 miles of urban road and 2,052 miles of rural road. There were 1,196,215 registered motor vehicles.

Civil Aviation

Hawaii had seven primary airports in 2011 (commercial service airports with more than 10,000 passenger boardings annually), with a combined total of 14,603,529 enplanements. The busiest airport, Honolulu International, had 8,689,699 enplanements in 2011 (down from 8,740,077 in 2010). Hawaiian Airlines carried a record 8,666,319 passengers in 2011, up from 8,424,288 in 2010.

Shipping

Several lines of steamers connect the islands with the mainland USA, Canada, Australia, the Philippines, China and Japan. In 2012, 976 overseas and 2,705 inter-island vessels entered the port of Honolulu.

Social Institutions

Justice

The death penalty was abolished in Hawaii in 1948. In Dec. 2014 the jail and prison population totalled 5,866.

Education

Education is free and compulsory between the ages of six and 18. The language in the schools is English. In 2012–13 there were 288 public schools with 184,760 pupils and 11,608 teachers. In fall 2011 there were 130 private schools with 37,530 pupils and 3,010 teachers. In 2010–11, $2,343m. was spent on public elementary and secondary education; average teacher salary was $54,300 in 2012–13. In fall 2012 the number of students enrolled in degree-granting institutions was 78,456.

Health

Hawaii had 2·0 community hospital beds for every 1,000 population in 2013. In the same year there were 30·8 active physicians per 10,000 civilian population and 7·5 dentists per 10,000.

Welfare

Medicare enrolment in July 2012 totalled 222,572. In fiscal year 2011 a total of 313,630 people in Hawaii received Medicaid. In Dec. 2014 there were 251,591 Old-Age, Survivors, and Disability Insurance (OASDI) beneficiaries. A total of 28,783 people were receiving payments under Temporary Assistance for Needy Families (TANF) in Dec. 2012.

Religion

The principal religious traditions in the state in 2010 were: Catholics, with 249,619 members; Evangelical Protestants, 130,265; Latter-day Saints (Mormons), 69,872; Buddhists, 65,759; Mainline Protestants, 40,833.

Culture

Tourism

Tourism is outstanding in Hawaii's economy. There were 6·4m. tourist arrivals by air in 2009. Tourist expenditure (air visitors only) contributed $9,794·3m. to the state's economy in 2009. There were 240,245 cruise ship passenger arrivals in 2012.

Idaho

Key Historical Events

Kutenai, Kalispel, Nez Percé and other tribes lived on the Pacific watershed of the northern Rocky Mountains. European exploration began in 1805, and after 1809 there were trading posts and small settlements, with fur-trapping as the primary activity. The area was disputed between Britain and the USA until 1846 when British claims were dropped. In 1860 the discovery of gold and silver brought a rush of immigrant prospectors. An area including present-day Montana was created a Territory in March 1863. Montana was separated from it in 1864. Population growth was stimulated by refugees from the Confederate states after the Civil War and by settlements of Mormons from Utah.

Fur-trapping and mining gave way to arable farming. Idaho became a state in 1890, with its capital at Boise. The population of the Territory capital,

Idaho City, a gold-mining boom town in the 1860s (about 40,000 at its height), was the largest in the Pacific Northwest. By 1869 the population was down to 1,000.

In the 20th century the American Indian population shrank to 1%. The Mormon community has grown to include much of southeastern Idaho and more than half the church-going population of the state.

The Snake River of southern Idaho has supported hydro-electricity and irrigation. Food processing, minerals and timber are important. So too are the high technology companies in Idaho's metropolitan areas. Much of the state, however, remains sparsely populated and rural.

Territory and Population

Idaho is within the Rocky Mountains and bounded north by Canada, east by Montana and Wyoming, south by Nevada and Utah, west by Oregon and Washington. Total area is 83,569 sq. miles (216,443 sq. km) of which 82,643 sq. miles (214,045 sq. km) are land. In 2010 the federal government owned 61·7% of the state area. Census population, 1 April 2010, was 1,567,582, an increase of 21·1% since 2000. July 2018 estimate, 1,754,208.

Population in five census years was:

	White	Black	American Indian/ Alaska Native	Asian	Total (including others)	Per sq. mile
1910	319,221	651	3,488	2,234	325,594	3·9
1980	901,641	2,716	10,521	5,948	943,935	11·3
1990	950,451	3,370	13,780	9,365	1,006,749	12·2
2000	1,177,304	5,456	17,645	13,197	1,293,953	15·6
2010	1,396,487	9,810	21,441	19,069	1,567,582	19·0

Of the total population in 2010, 785,324 were male and 1,138,510 were 18 years old or older. In 2010 Idaho's Hispanic population was 175,901, up from 101,690 in 2000 (an increase of 73·0%).

The largest cities are: Boise City (the capital), with a 2010 population of 205,671; Nampa, 81,557; Meridian, 75,092; Idaho Falls, 56,813; Pocatello, 54,255; Caldwell, 46,237; Coeur d'Alene, 44,137; Twin Falls, 44,125; Lewiston, 31,894.

Social Statistics

Births, 2014, 22,876 (14·0 per 1,000 population); deaths, 2014, 12,613 (7·7). Infant mortality rate, 2013, 5·6 per 1,000 live births. 2014: marriages, 8·4 per 1,000 population; divorces and annulments, 4·2. Same-sex marriage became legal in Oct. 2014.

Climate

Boise City, Jan. 29°F (−1·7°C), July 74°F (23·3°C). Annual rainfall 12" (303 mm). Idaho belongs to the Mountain States climate zone (see UNITED STATES: Climate).

Constitution and Government

The constitution adopted in 1890 is still in force; it has had 132 amendments as of Sept. 2016. The Legislature consists of a Senate of 35 members and a House of Representatives of 70 members, all the legislators being elected for two years. It meets annually.

For the 116th Congress, which convened in Jan. 2019, Idaho sends two members to the House of Representatives. It is represented in the Senate by Michael Crapo (R. 1999–2023) and James Risch (R. 2009–21).

The state is divided into 44 counties. The capital is Boise City.

Recent Elections

In the 2016 presidential election Donald Trump took Idaho with 59·2% of the vote (Mitt Romney won it in 2012).

Current Government

Governor: Brad Little (R.), 2019–23 (salary: $124,436).
  Lieut.-Governor: Janice McGeachin (R.), 2019–23.
  Secretary of State: Lawerence Denney (R.), since Jan. 2015.
Government Website: http://www.idaho.gov

Economy

Per capita personal income (2015) was $37,509.

Budget

In 2011 total state revenue was $10,776m. Total expenditure was $8,733m. (education, $2,701m.; public welfare, $2,175m.; highways, $836m.; government administration, $273m.; correction, $219m.). Outstanding debt in 2011, $3,928m.

Performance

Gross Domestic Product by state in 2015 was $65,549m., ranking Idaho 42nd in the United States. In 2015 state real GDP growth was 2·7%.

Energy and Natural Resources

Water

The total area covered by water is 926 sq. miles.

Minerals

Principal non-fuel minerals are processed phosphate rock, silver, gold, molybdenum and sand and gravel. Value of non-fuel mineral output for 2009 was $935m.

Agriculture

Agriculture is the second largest industry, despite a great part of the state being naturally arid. Extensive irrigation works have been carried out, bringing an estimated 3·5m. acres under irrigation, and there are over 50 soil conservation districts.

In 2009 there were 25,500 farms with a total area of 11·4m. acres; average value per acre (Jan. 2010), $2,100. In 2009 the average farm was 447 acres.

Value of crop production in 2009, $2,664m.; and livestock and products, $2,549m. The most important crops are potatoes and wheat. Other crops are sugar beets, hay, barley, field peas and beans, onions and apples. The net farm income in 2009 was $927m. In Dec. 2009 there were 2·1m. cattle and calves, 220,000 sheep and 36,000 hogs and pigs. There were 30m. food-sized trout produced on fish farms in 2009. The dairy industry is the fastest-growing sector in Idaho agriculture.

Forestry

In 2012 there were a total of 21·48m. acres of forest, of which 16·23m. acres were national forest.

Fisheries

73% of the commercial trout processed in the USA was produced in Idaho in 2009. Idaho ranked first in state trout production by producing fish to a value of $35·6m.

Industry

In 2012 Idaho's 3,944 manufacturing establishments had 113,000 employees, with a payroll of $5,291m. Total value added by manufacturing in 2013 was $8,815m.

Labour

Total non-agricultural employment, 2010, 603,000. Employees by branch, 2010 (in 1,000): trade, transportation and utilities, 121; government, 119; education and health services, 84; professional and business services, 73; leisure and hospitality, 58. The unemployment rate in Dec. 2010 was 9·7%.

International Trade

Imports and Exports

In 2015 imports into Idaho totalled $5,166m. (down from $5,696m. in 2014). In the same year exports from Idaho totalled $4,295m., down from $5,138m. in 2014. The leading source for imports in 2015 was China ($1,583m.), ahead of Canada ($912m.). The leading destination for exports in 2015 was Canada ($979m.), followed by China ($561m.).

Communications

Roads

In 2012 there were 48,492 miles of public roads (42,940 miles rural, 5,552 urban). There were 1,580,264 registered motor vehicles in 2012.

Rail

The state had (2012) 1,623 miles of freight railroad. There were 12 freight railroads operating in 2012. Rail traffic originating in Idaho in 2012 totalled 7·1m. tons and rail traffic terminating in the state came to 7·4m. tons.

Civil Aviation

There were 68 municipally-owned airports in 2009. There were 1,904,446 passenger enplanements statewide in 2008.

Shipping

Water transport is provided from the Pacific to the port of Lewiston, by way of the Columbia and Snake rivers, a distance of 464 miles.

Social Institutions

Justice

The death penalty may be imposed for first degree murder or aggravated kidnapping, but the judge must consider mitigating circumstances before imposing a sentence of death. Since 1976 there have only been three executions, in 1994, 2011 and 2012. In Dec. 2014 there were 8,117 prisoners in federal and state prisons.

Education

In 2012–13 there were 756 public schools with 284,834 pupils and 14,563 teachers; average salary of teachers was $49,734. Total expenditure on public elementary and secondary education in 2010–11 was $2,107m.

The University of Idaho, founded at Moscow in 1889, had 928 faculty in fall 2009, and a total enrolment of 11,957. Boise State University had 611 faculty in fall 2009 and a total enrolment of 18,936. Idaho State University had 602 full-time faculty in fall 2009 and a total enrolment of 13,493. Total enrolment in degree-granting institutions in fall 2012 was 108,008 (78,781 in public institutions).

Health

Idaho had 2·1 community hospital beds for every 1,000 population in 2013. In the same year there were 19·2 active physicians per 10,000 civilian population and 5·8 dentists per 10,000.

Welfare

Medicare enrolment in July 2012 totalled 248,633. In fiscal year 2011 a total of 261,014 people in Idaho received Medicaid. Old-age, Survivors, and Disability Insurance (OASDI) is granted to persons if they paid sufficiently into the system or meet other qualifications; in Dec. 2014 there were 306,264 beneficiaries. A total of 2,927 people were receiving payments under Temporary Assistance for Needy Families (TANF) in Dec. 2012.

Religion

In 2010 the chief religious traditions were: Latter-day Saints (Mormons), with 410,289 members; Evangelical Protestants, 201,546; Catholics, 123,400; Mainline Protestants, 57,056.

Illinois

Key Historical Events

Home to Algonquian-speaking tribes, Illinois was explored first by the French in 1673. France claimed the area until 1763 when, after the French and Indian War, it was ceded to Britain along with all the French land east of the Mississippi. In 1783 Britain recognized US claims to Illinois, which became part of the North West Territory of the USA in 1787, and of Indiana Territory in 1800. Illinois became a Territory in its own right in 1809, and a state in 1818.

Immigration increased greatly with the opening in 1825 of the Erie Canal from New York, along which farmer settlers could move west and their produce back east for sale. Chicago was incorporated as a city in 1837 and quickly became the transport, trading and distribution centre of the mid-west. Industrial growth brought a further wave of immigration in the 1840s, mainly of European refugees. This movement continued with varying force until the 1920s, when it was largely replaced by immigration of black work-seekers from the southern states.

In the 20th century the population was urbanized and heavy industry was established along a network of rail and waterway routes. Chicago recovered from a destructive fire in 1871 to become the hub of this network and at one time the second largest American city.

Territory and Population

Illinois is bounded north by Wisconsin, northeast by Lake Michigan, east by Indiana, southeast by the Ohio River (forming the boundary with Kentucky), and west by the Mississippi River (forming the boundary with Missouri and Iowa). Land area, 55,519 sq. miles (143,793 sq. km); water area, 2,395 sq. miles (6,202 sq. km). Census population, 1 April 2010, was 12,830,632, an increase of 3·3% since 2000. July 2018 estimate, 12,741,080.

Population in five census years was:

	White	Black	American Indian	All others		Total	Per sq. mile
1910	5,526,962	109,049	188	2,392		5,638,591	100·6
				All others			
1980	9,233,327	1,675,398	—	517,793		11,426,518	203·0
	White	Black	American Indian/ Alaska Native	Asian/ Native Hawaiian/ Pacific Islander	Other	Total	Per sq. mile
1990	8,957,923	1,690,855	24,077	284,944	472,803	11,430,602	205·6
2000	9,125,471	1,876,875	31,006	428,213	957,728	12,419,293	223·4
2010	9,177,877	1,866,414	43,963	590,984	1,151,394	12,830,632	231·1

Of the total population in 2010, 6,538,356 were female and 9,701,453 were 18 years old or older. In 2010 the Hispanic population was 2,027,578 (1,530,262 in 2000).

The most populous cities (2010) are: Chicago, 2,695,598; Aurora, 197,899; Rockford, 152,871; Joliet, 147,433; Naperville, 141,853; Springfield (the capital), 116,250; Peoria, 115,007; Elgin, 108,188; Waukegan, 89,078.

Largest metropolitan area populations, 2010 census: Chicago–Joliet–Naperville, 9,461,105; Peoria, 379,186; Rockford, 349,431; Champaign–Urbana, 231,891; Springfield, 210,170.

Social Statistics

Births, 2014, 158,556 (12·3 per 1,000 population); deaths, 2014, 105,293 (8·2). Infant mortality rate, 2013, 6·0 per 1,000 live births. 2014: marriages, 6·2 per 1,000 population; divorces and annulments, 2·2. Same-sex marriage was legalized by the State Legislature in June 2014.

Climate

Chicago, Jan. 25·3°F (–3·7°C), July 75·4°F (24·1°C). Annual rainfall 38·0". Illinois belongs to the Great Lakes climate zone (see UNITED STATES: Climate).

Constitution and Government

The present constitution became effective on 1 July 1971. The General Assembly consists of a House of Representatives of 118 members elected for two years, and a Senate of 59 members who are divided into three groups; in one, they are elected for terms of four years, four years, and two years; in the next, for terms of four years, two years, and four years; and in the last, for terms of two years, four years, and four years. Sessions are annual. The state is divided into legislative districts, in each of which one senator is chosen; each district is divided into two representative districts, in each of which one representative is chosen.

For the 116th Congress, which convened in Jan. 2019, Illinois sends 18 members to the House of Representatives. It is represented in the Senate by Richard Durbin (D. 1997–2021) and Tammy Duckworth (D. 2017–23).

The capital is Springfield.

Recent Elections

In the 2016 presidential election Hillary Clinton took Illinois with 55·4% of the vote (Barack Obama won it in 2012).

Current Government

Governor: J. B. Pritzker (D.), 2019–23 (salary: $177,412).
Lieut.-Governor: Juliana Stratton (D.), 2019–23.
Secretary of State: Jesse White (D.), since Jan. 1999.
Government Website: https://www2.illinois.gov

Economy
Per capita personal income (2015) was $49,471.

Budget
In 2011 total state revenues amounted to $79,512m. Total expenditure was $74,655m. (public welfare, $19,508m.; education, $17,131m.; highways, $5,110m.; health, $2,234m.; correction, $1,514m.). Debt outstanding, in 2011, $64,801m.

Performance
Gross Domestic Product by state in 2015 was $776,882m., ranking Illinois 5th in the United States. In 2015 state real GDP growth was 1·8%.

Energy and Natural Resources

Electricity
In 2015 production was 194·0bn. kWh, of which 97·0bn. kWh was from nuclear energy.

Oil and Gas
In 2014 Illinois produced 9·5m. bbls of crude petroleum; marketed production of natural gas totalled 2·6bn. cu. ft.

Water
The total area covered by water is 2,395 sq. miles.

Minerals
The chief mineral product is coal. In 2009 there were 22 operative mines; output was 33·7m. short tons. Mineral production also includes sand, gravel and limestone. Value of non-fuel mineral production in 2009 was $929m.

Agriculture
In 2007 there were 76,860 farms in Illinois that contained 26·78m. acres of land. The average farm had 348 acres in 2007 and was valued at $3,792 per acre. In 2007 cash receipts from farm marketings in Illinois totalled $11·68bn. The net farm income in 2007 was $3,244m. In 2008 Illinois was the second largest producer among US states of corn and soybeans, producing 2·13bn. bu. and 428m. bu. respectively. Cash receipts for corn totalled $9·3bn. in 2007; for soybeans, $3·7bn. In 2007 there were 4·30m. hogs and pigs, 1·23m. cattle including 429,100 beef cows and 99,700 dairy cows, and 52,400 sheep and lambs.

Forestry
In 2013 there were a total of 4·90m. acres of forest (4·05m. acres private), of which 297,000 acres were national forest. Timberland area totalled 4·58m. acres in 2013.

Industry
Important industries include financial services, manufacturing, retail and transportation. In 2012 the state's 29,090 manufacturing establishments had 1,143,000 employees, earning $59,293m. Total value added by manufacturing in 2013 was $112,179m.

Labour
Total non-agricultural employment, 2010, 5,611,000. Employees by branch, 2010 (in 1,000): trade, transportation and utilities, 1,125; government, 857; education and health services, 833; professional and business services, 799; manufacturing, 559. In Dec. 2010 the unemployment rate was 9·2%.

International Trade

Imports and Exports
In 2015 imports into Illinois totalled $121·3bn. (down from $140·4bn. in 2014). In the same year exports from Illinois totalled $63·4bn., down from $68·4bn. in 2014. The leading source for imports in 2015 was China ($31·2bn.), ahead of Canada ($29·6bn.). The leading destination for exports in 2015 was Canada ($17·5bn.), followed by Mexico ($9·1bn.).

Communications

Roads
In 2012 there were 144,337 miles of roads, comprising 45,895 miles of urban road and 98,442 miles of rural road. There were 9,767,228 registered motor vehicles in 2012.

Rail
Union Station, Chicago is the home of Amtrak's national hub. Amtrak trains provide service to cities in Illinois to many destinations in the USA. Illinois is also served by a metro (CTA) system, and by seven groups of commuter railroads controlled by METRA, which has many stations and serves several Illinois counties. In 2012 there were 6,986 miles of freight railroad (excluding trackage rights), including 5,851 miles of Class I railroads. Only Texas among US states has a larger rail network. There were 40 freight railroads operating in 2012. Rail traffic originating in Illinois in 2012 totalled 115·9m. tons (the second highest after Wyoming) and rail traffic terminating in the state came to 157·8m. tons (the second highest after Texas). There is also a metro system in Chicago (108 miles).

Civil Aviation
In 2011 Illinois had nine primary airports (commercial service airports with more than 10,000 passenger boardings annually) with a combined total of 42,242,807 enplanements, up from 41,944,295 in 2010. The busiest airport, Chicago O'Hare International, had 31,892,301 enplanements in 2011 (ranking it second in the USA behind Hartsfield–Jackson Atlanta International). Chicago Midway International had 9,134,576 enplanements in 2011.

Shipping
The port of Chicago handled 17,482,673 tons of cargo in 2014.

Social Institutions

Justice
There were 48,278 federal and state prisoners in Dec. 2014.

Executions began in 1990 following the US Supreme Court's reinstatement of capital punishment in 1976, with the most recent execution being in March 1999. However, on 31 Jan. 2000 the death penalty was suspended and it was formally abolished on 9 March 2011.

A Civil Rights Act (1941), as amended, bans all forms of discrimination by places of public accommodation, including inns, restaurants, retail stores, railroads, aeroplanes, buses, etc., against persons on account of 'race, religion, color, national ancestry or physical or mental handicap'; another section similarly mentions 'race or color'.

The Fair Employment Practices Act of 1961, as amended, prohibits discrimination in employment based on race, colour, sex, religion, national origin or ancestry, by employers, employment agencies, labour organizations and others. These principles are embodied in the 1971 constitution.

The Illinois Human Rights Act (1979) prevents unlawful discrimination in employment, real property transactions, access to financial credit and public accommodations, by authorizing the creation of a Department of Human Rights to enforce, and a Human Rights Commission to adjudicate, allegations of unlawful discrimination.

Education
Education is free and compulsory for children between seven and 17 years of age. In 2012–13 there were 4,372 public schools (elementary, junior high, secondary, special education and others) with 2,072,880 students and 135,700 teachers. In fall 2011, 271,030 students were enrolled in 1,570 private schools with 19,150 teachers. In 2012–13 the average teacher salary was $59,113. Total expenditure on public elementary and secondary education in 2010–11 was $27,621m.; spending per pupil amounted to $11,742. In fall 2012 degree-granting institutions had a total enrolment of 867,110. There were 186 degree-granting institutions (60 public, 83 not-for-profit independent and 43 for-profit independent) in 2012–13.

Major colleges and universities (fall 2014):

Founded	Name	Place	Control	Enrolment
1851	Northwestern University	Evanston	Independent	21,554
1857	Illinois State University	Normal	Public	20,615
1867	University of Illinois	Urbana/ Champaign	Public	45,140

(*continued*)

Founded	Name	Place	Control	Enrolment
		Springfield (1969)		5,431
		Chicago (1982)		27,969
1867	Chicago State University	Chicago	Public	5,211
1867	Northeastern Illinois University	Chicago	Public	10,275
1869	Southern Illinois University	Carbondale	Public	17,989
		Edwardsville (1957)		13,972
1870	Loyola University of Chicago	Chicago	Roman Catholic	15,902
1890	University of Chicago	Chicago	Independent	15,097
1895	Eastern Illinois University	Charleston	Public	8,913
1895	Northern Illinois University	DeKalb	Public	20,611
1897	Bradley University	Peoria	Independent	5,300
1899	Western Illinois University	Macomb	Public	11,458
1940	Illinois Institute of Technology	Chicago	Independent	7,898
1945	Roosevelt University	Chicago	Independent	6,069
1969	Governors State University	University Park	Public	5,776

Health

Illinois had 2·5 community hospital beds for every 1,000 population in 2013. In the same year there were 30·1 active physicians per 10,000 civilian population and 6·7 dentists per 10,000.

Welfare

Medicare enrolment in July 2012 totalled 1,947,504. In fiscal year 2012 a total of 3,061,914 people in Illinois received Medicaid. In Dec. 2014 there were 2,155,290 Old-Age, Survivors, and Disability Insurance (OASDI) beneficiaries. A total of 44,385 people were receiving payments under Temporary Assistance for Needy Families (TANF) in Dec. 2012.

Religion

In 2010 the chief religious traditions were: Catholics, with 3,648,907 members; Evangelical Protestants, 1,649,402; Mainline Protestants, 933,690; Muslims, 359,000 (estimate); Black Protestants, 220,435.

Culture

Tourism

In 2011 overseas visitors to Illinois—excluding those from Canada and Mexico—numbered 1,255,000, up from 1,186,000 in 2010 and 1,083,000 in 2006.

Indiana

Key Historical Events

The area was inhabited by Algonquian-speaking tribes when the first European explorers (French) laid claim to it in the 17th century. They established fortified trading posts but there was little settlement. In 1763 the area passed to Britain, with other French-claimed territory east of the Mississippi. In 1783 Indiana became part of the North West Territory of the USA; it became a separate territory in 1800 and a state in 1816. Until 1811 there was continuing conflict with the American Indian inhabitants, who were then defeated at Tippecanoe.

Early farming settlement was by families of British and German descent, including Amish and Mennonite communities. Later industrial development offered an incentive for more immigration from Europe, and, subsequently, from the southern states. In 1906 the town of Gary was laid out by the United States Steel Corporation and named after its chairman, Elbert H. Gary. The industry benefited from navigable water to supplies of iron ore and of coal. Indiana Port on Lake Michigan was a thriving trade centre, especially after the opening of the St Lawrence Seaway in 1959. The Ohio River also carried freight.

Indianapolis was built after 1821 and became the state capital in 1825. Natural gas was discovered in the neighbourhood in the late 19th century. This stimulated the growth of a motor industry, celebrated by the Indianapolis 500 race, held annually since 1911.

Territory and Population

Indiana is bounded west by Illinois, north by Michigan and Lake Michigan, east by Ohio and south by Kentucky across the Ohio River. Total area is 36,420 sq. miles (94,326 sq. km) of which 35,826 sq. miles (92,789 sq. km) are land. Census population, 1 April 2010, was 6,483,802, an increase of 6·6% since 2000. July 2018 estimate, 6,691,878.

Population in five census years was:

	White	Black	American Indian/ Alaska Native	Asian	Other	Total	Per sq. mile
1930	3,125,778	111,982	285	458	—	3,238,503	89·4
1980	5,004,394	414,785	7,836	20,557	42,652	5,490,224	152·8
1990	5,020,700	432,092	12,720	37,617	41,030	5,544,159	154·6
2000	5,320,022	510,034	15,815	61,131	173,483	6,080,485	169·5
2010	5,467,906	591,397	18,462	102,474	303,563	6,483,802	181·0

Of the total population in 2010, 3,294,065 were female and 4,875,504 were 18 years old or older. Indiana's Hispanic population was 389,707 in 2010, an 81·7% increase on the 2000 total of 214,536.

The largest cities with census population, 2010, are: Indianapolis (capital), 820,445; Fort Wayne, 253,691; Evansville, 117,429; South Bend, 101,168; Hammond, 80,830; Bloomington, 80,405; Gary, 80,294; Carmel, 79,191; Fishers, 76,794; Muncie, 70,085.

Social Statistics

Births, 2014, 84,080 (12·7 per 1,000 population); deaths, 2014, 60,940 (9·2). Infant mortality rate, 2013, 7·2 per 1,000 live births. Marriages, 2014, 7·1 per 1,000 population. Same-sex marriage became legal in Oct. 2014.

Climate

Indianapolis, Jan. 29°F (−1·7°C), July 76°F (24·4°C). Annual rainfall 41" (1,034 mm). Indiana belongs to the Mid-West climate zone (see UNITED STATES: Climate).

Constitution and Government

The present constitution (the second) dates from 1851. The General Assembly consists of a Senate of 50 members elected for four years, and a House of Representatives of 100 members elected for two years. It meets annually.

For the 116th Congress, which convened in Jan. 2019, Indiana sends nine members to the House of Representatives. It is represented in the Senate by Todd Young (R. 2017–23) and Mike Braun (R. 2019–25).

The state capital is Indianapolis. The state is divided into 92 counties and 1,008 townships.

Recent Elections

In the 2016 presidential election Donald Trump took Indiana with 57·2% of the vote (Mitt Romney won it in 2012).

Current Government

Governor: Eric Holcomb (R.), 2017–21 (salary: $121,233).
    Lieut.-Governor: Suzanne Crouch (R.), 2017–21.
    Secretary of State: Connie Lawson (R.), since March 2012.
Government Website: https://www.in.gov

Economy

Per capita personal income (2015) was $40,998.

Budget

In 2011 total state revenue was $38,895m. Total expenditure was $35,262m. (including: education, $14,055m.; public welfare, $8,397m.; highways,

$2,680m.; correction, $661m.; health, $566m.). Outstanding debt in 2011, $22,144m.

Performance
In 2015 Gross Domestic Product by state was $336,053m., ranking Indiana 16th in the United States. In 2015 state real GDP growth was 1·4%.

Energy and Natural Resources

Electricity
In 2015 production was 104·0bn. kWh, of which 78·2bn. kWh was from coal.

Oil and Gas
In 2014 Indiana produced 2·5m. bbls of crude petroleum; marketed production of natural gas totalled 6·6bn. cu. ft.

Water
The total area covered by water is 593 sq. miles.

Minerals
The state produced 44,100,000 tonnes of crushed stone and 206,000 tonnes of dimension stone in 2009. Production of coal (2010) was 35·3m. short tons. Value of domestic non-fuel mineral production in 2009 was $806m.

Agriculture
Indiana is largely agricultural, about 64% of its total land area being in farms. In 2013, 58,700 farms had 14·70m. acres (average, 250 acres). The average value of land and buildings per acre was $6,400 in 2013.

Farm income 2012: crops, $8·6bn.; livestock and products, $3·5bn.; total, $12·1bn. The net farm income in 2012 was $3,291m. The four most important products were corn, soybeans, hogs and dairy products. Cash receipts for corn totalled $4·8bn. in 2012; for soybeans, $3·2bn. The livestock in 2013 included 810,000 cattle and calves, 55,000 sheep and lambs, 3·65m. hogs and pigs, and 26·64m. laying hens.

Forestry
In 2013 there were 4·88m. acres of forest including 206,000 acres of national forest.

Industry

In 2012 Indiana's 17,636 manufacturing establishments had 979,000 employees, earning $49,485m. Total value added by manufacturing in 2013 was $100,326m. The steel industry is the largest in the country.

Labour
Total non-agricultural employment, 2010, 2,793,000. Employees by branch, 2010 (in 1,000): trade, transportation and utilities, 541; manufacturing, 446; government, 438; education and health services, 425; professional and business services, 275. The unemployment rate in Dec. 2010 was 9·5%.

International Trade

Imports and Exports
In 2015 imports into Indiana totalled $49·1bn. (up from $48·9bn. in 2014). In the same year exports from Indiana totalled $33·8bn., down from $35·6bn. in 2014. The leading source for imports in 2015 was China ($8·3bn.), ahead of Canada ($7·9bn.). The leading destination for exports in 2015 was Canada ($11·0bn.), followed by Mexico ($4·9bn.).

Communications

Roads
In 2012 there were 97,288 miles of public roads (69,439 miles rural). There were 5,781,263 registered motor vehicles.

Rail
In 2012 there were 4,075 miles of freight railroad of which 2,510 miles were Class I. There were 41 freight railroads operating in 2012. Rail traffic originating in Indiana in 2012 totalled 54·2m. tons and rail traffic terminating in the state came to 56·5m. tons.

Civil Aviation
Of airports in 2011, 113 were for public use and 631 were for private use. There were 7,006,250 passenger enplanements statewide in 2010. The busiest airport, Indianapolis International, had 3,728,698 enplanements in 2010.

Social Institutions

Justice
Following the US Supreme Court's reinstatement of the death penalty in 1976, death sentences have been given since 1980. No executions have taken place since 2009 when one was carried out. In Dec. 2014, 29,271 prisoners were under the jurisdiction of state and federal correctional authorities.

The Civil Rights Act of 1885 forbids places of public accommodation to bar any persons on grounds not applicable to all citizens alike; no citizen may be disqualified for jury service 'on account of race or color'. An Act of 1947 makes it an offence to spread religious or racial hatred.

A 1961 Act provided 'all of its citizens equal opportunity for education, employment and access to public conveniences and accommodations' and created a Civil Rights Commission.

Education
School attendance is compulsory from seven to 18 years. In 2012–13 there were 1,944 public schools with 1,041,369 pupils and 59,863 teachers. The average expenditure per pupil was $9,251 in 2010–11. Teachers' salaries averaged $51,456 (2012–13). Total expenditure for public elementary and secondary education in 2010–11 was $11,038m.

Some leading institutions for higher education were (2009):

Founded	Institution	Control	Students
1801	Vincennes University	State	13,947
1824	Indiana University, Bloomington	State	42,347
1832	Wabash College, Crawfordsville	Independent	883
1837	De Pauw University, Greencastle	Methodist	2,396
1842	University of Notre Dame	R.C.	11,816
1847	Earlham College, Richmond	Quaker	1,266
1850	Butler University, Indianapolis	Independent	4,505
1859	Valparaiso University, Valparaiso	Evangelical Lutheran Church	4,065
1870	Indiana State University, Terre Haute	State	10,534
1874	Purdue University, Lafayette	State	41,052
1898	Ball State University, Muncie	State	21,401
1902	University of Indianapolis, Indianapolis	Methodist	5,055
1963	Ivy Tech Community College, Indianapolis	State	110,359
1969	Indiana University-Purdue University, Indianapolis	State	30,383
1985	University of Southern Indiana, Evansville	State	10,516

Health
Illinois had 2·6 community hospital beds for every 1,000 population in 2013. In the same year there were 23·3 active physicians per 10,000 civilian population and 4·7 dentists per 10,000.

Welfare
Medicare enrolment in July 2012 totalled 1,068,485. In fiscal year 2012 a total of 1,278,012 people in Indiana received Medicaid. In Dec. 2014 there were 1,286,099 Old-Age, Survivors, and Disability Insurance (OASDI) beneficiaries. A total of 27,253 people were receiving payments under Temporary Assistance for Needy Families (TANF) in Dec. 2012.

Religion

In 2010 the chief religious traditions were: Evangelical Protestants, with 1,238,154 members; Catholics, 747,706; Mainline Protestants, 689,902; Black Protestants, 94,705; Latter-day Saints (Mormons), 42,608.

Iowa

Key Historical Events

Originally the territory of the Iowa Indians, the area was explored by the Frenchmen Marquette and Joliet in 1673. French trading posts were set up, but there were few other settlements. In 1803 the French sold their claim to Iowa to the USA as part of the Louisiana Purchase. The land was still occupied by Indians but, in the 1830s, the tribes sold their land to the US government and migrated to reservations. Iowa became a US Territory in 1838 and a state in 1846.

The state was settled by immigrants drawn mainly from neighbouring states to the east. Later there was more immigration from Protestant states of northern Europe. The land was extremely fertile and most immigrants came to farm. Not all the American Indian population had accepted the cession and there were some violent confrontations, notably the murder of settlers at Spirit Lake in 1857. The capital, Des Moines, was founded in 1843 as a fort to protect American Indian rights. It expanded rapidly along with coal mining after 1910.

Territory and Population

Iowa is bounded east by the Mississippi River (forming the boundary with Wisconsin and Illinois), south by Missouri, west by the Missouri River (forming the boundary with Nebraska), northwest by the Big Sioux River (forming the boundary with South Dakota) and north by Minnesota. Total area is 56,273 sq. miles (145,746 sq. km) of which 55,857 sq. miles (144,669 sq. km) are land. Census population, 1 April 2010, was 3,046,355, an increase of 4·1% since 2000. July 2018 estimate, 3,156,145.

Population in five census years was:

	White	Black	American Indian	Asian	Total	Per sq. mile
1870	1,188,207	5,762	48	3	1,194,020	21·5
			All others			
1980	2,839,225	41,700	32,882		2,913,808	51·7
1990	2,683,090	48,090	45,575		2,776,755	49·7
2000	2,748,640	61,853	115,831		2,926,324	52·4
2010	2,781,561	89,148	175,646		3,046,355	54·5

Of the total population in 2010, 1,538,036 were female and 2,318,362 were 18 years old or older. In 2010 the Hispanic population was 151,544, up from 82,473 in 2000 (an increase of 83·7%).

The largest cities in the state, with their population in 2010, are: Des Moines (capital), 203,433; Cedar Rapids, 126,326; Davenport, 99,685; Sioux City, 82,684; Waterloo, 68,406; Iowa City, 67,862; Council Bluffs, 62,230; Ames, 58,965; Dubuque, 57,637; West Des Moines, 56,609; Ankeny, 45,582; Urbandale, 39,463; Cedar Falls, 39,260; Marion, 34,768; Bettendorf, 33,217.

Social Statistics

Births, 2014, 39,687 (12·8 per 1,000 population); deaths, 2014, 29,190 (9·4). Infant mortality, 2013, 4·3 per 1,000 live births. 2014: marriages, 6·9 per 1,000 population; divorces and annulments, 1·5. Same-sex marriage became legal in April 2009.

Climate

Cedar Rapids, Jan. 17·6°F, July 74·2°F. Annual rainfall 34". Des Moines, Jan. 19·4°F, July 76·6°F. Annual rainfall 33". Iowa belongs to the Mid-West climate zone (see UNITED STATES: Climate).

Constitution and Government

The constitution of 1857 still exists; it has had 48 amendments as of Sept. 2016. The General Assembly comprises a Senate of 50 and a House of Representatives of 100 members, meeting annually for an unlimited session. Senators are elected for four years, half retiring every second year:

Representatives for two years. The Governor and Lieut.-Governor are elected for four years.

For the 116th Congress, which convened in Jan. 2019, Iowa sends four members to the House of Representatives. It is represented in the Senate by Chuck Grassley (R. 1981–2023) and Joni Ernst (R. 2015–21).

Iowa is divided into 99 counties; the capital is Des Moines.

Recent Elections

In the 2016 presidential election Donald Trump took Iowa with 51·8% of the vote (Barack Obama won it in 2012).

Current Government

Governor: Kim Reynolds (R.), 2019–23 (salary: $130,000).

Lieut.-Governor: Adam Gregg (R.), 2019–23.

Secretary of State: Paul Pate (R.), since Jan. 2015.

Government Website: https://www.iowa.gov

Economy

Per capita personal income (2015) was $44,971.

Budget

In 2011 total state revenue amounted to $24,089m. Total state expenditure was $19,937m. (education, $6,270m.; public welfare, $4,901m.; highways, $1,591m.; hospitals, $1,090m.; government administration, $551m.). Outstanding debt in 2011, $7,574m.

Performance

Gross Domestic Product by state was $174,030m. in 2015, ranking Iowa 30th in the United States. In 2015 state real GDP growth was 1·3%.

Energy and Natural Resources

Water

The total area covered by water is 416 sq. miles.

Minerals

Production in 2008: crushed stone, 37·8m. tonnes; sand and gravel, 15·6m. tonnes. The value of domestic non-fuel mineral products in 2009 was $590m.

Agriculture

Iowa is the wealthiest of the agricultural states, partly because nearly the whole area (92%) is arable and included in farms. The total farm area, 2007, is 30·7m. acres. The average farm in 2007 was 331 acres. The average value of buildings and land per acre was, in 2007, $3,388. The number of farms has declined since 1960, from 174,000 to 92,856 in 2007.

Farm income, 2007: crops, $10,180m.; livestock and products, $8,857m.; total, $19,037m. (the third highest total, behind California and Texas). The net farm income in 2007 was $5,334m. In 2007 production of corn was 2,377m. bu.[1], value $10,197m.; and soybeans, 449m. bu.[1], value $4,712m. In 2007 livestock included: swine, 19·3m.[1]; dairy cows, 215,000; all cattle, 3·98m.; sheep and lambs, 209,000; laying hens, 53·79m.[1] Wool production in 2007 totalled 1·25m. lb.

[1]More than any other state.

Forestry

Total forested area was 2·97m. acres in 2013.

Industry

In 2012 Iowa's 9,846 manufacturing establishments had 532,000 employees, earning $25,524m. Total value added by manufacturing in 2013 was $45,848m.

Labour

Total non-agricultural employment, 2010, 1,469,000. Employees by branch, 2010 (in 1,000): trade, transport and utilities, 300; government, 254; education and health services, 214; manufacturing, 200; leisure and hospitality, 130. Iowa had an unemployment rate of 6·1% in Dec. 2010.

International Trade

Imports and Exports

In 2015 imports into Iowa totalled $9,363m. (down from $10,087m. in 2014). In the same year exports from Iowa totalled $13,234m., down from

$15,112m. in 2014. The leading source for imports in 2015 was Canada ($2,749m.), ahead of Mexico ($1,612m.). The leading destination for exports in 2015 was also Canada ($3,873m.), again followed by Mexico ($2,100m.).

Communications

Roads
In 2012 there were 114,438 miles of streets and highways, of which 103,013 miles were rural and 11,425 urban. There were 3,330,987 motor vehicle registrations.

Rail
In 2012 there were 3,869 miles of freight railroad (excluding trackage rights). There were 14 freight railroads operating in 2012. Rail traffic originating in Iowa in 2012 totalled 46·3m. tons and rail traffic terminating in the state came to 35·4m. tons.

Civil Aviation
In 2011 Iowa had seven primary airports (commercial service airports with more than 10,000 passenger boardings annually) with a combined total of 1,473,744 enplanements, up from 1,465,337 in 2010. The busiest airport, Des Moines International, had 932,828 enplanements in 2011.

Social Institutions

Justice
The death penalty was abolished in Iowa in 1965. There were 8,838 federal and state prisoners in Dec. 2014.

Education
School attendance is compulsory for 24 consecutive weeks annually during school age (6–16). In 2010–11 there were 1,396 public primary and secondary schools with 473,493 pupils in attendance and 33,916 teachers. There were 198 private schools with 33,804 pupils and 2,410 teachers in 2010–11. Average teacher's salary in 2010–11 was $49,794. In the 2009–10 school year the state spent an average of $8,603 on each elementary and secondary school student.

Leading institutions for higher education enrolment figures (fall 2010) were:

Founded	Institution	Control	Professors	Full-time students
1843	Clarke College, Dubuque	Independent	128	1,255
1846	Grinnell College, Grinnell	Independent	156	1,655
1847	University of Iowa, Iowa City	State	2,156	30,825
1851	Coe College, Cedar Rapids	Independent	80	1,343
1852	Wartburg College, Waverly	Evangelical Lutheran	109	1,775
1853	Cornell College, Mount Vernon	Independent	119	1,191
1854	Upper Iowa University, Fayette	Independent	83	6,765
1858	Iowa State University, Ames	State	1,766	28,682
1859	Luther College, Decorah	Evangelical Lutheran	249	2,481
1876	Univ. of Northern Iowa, Cedar Falls	State	824	13,201
1881	Drake University, Des Moines	Independent	362	5,616
1882	St Ambrose University, Davenport	Roman Catholic	356	3,663

(continued)

Founded	Institution	Control	Professors	Full-time students
1891	Buena Vista University, Storm Lake	Presbyterian	97	2,706
1894	Morningside College, Sioux City	Methodist	77	1,991

Health
Iowa had 3·2 community hospital beds for every 1,000 population in 2013. In the same year there were 23·2 active physicians per 10,000 civilian population and 5·2 dentists per 10,000.

Welfare
Medicare enrolment in July 2012 totalled 539,336. In fiscal year 2012 a total of 559,027 people in Iowa received Medicaid. In Dec. 2014 there were 616,301 Old-Age, Survivors, and Disability Insurance (OASDI) beneficiaries. A total of 39,715 people were receiving payments under Temporary Assistance for Needy Families (TANF) in Dec. 2012.

Religion
The chief religious traditions in Iowa in 2010 were: Mainline Protestants, with 666,637 members; Catholics, 503,080; Evangelical Protestants, 402,376; Latter-day Saints (Mormons), 32,283; Black Protestants, 17,902.

Kansas

Key Historical Events
The area was explored from Mexico in the 16th century, when Spanish travellers encountered Kansas, Wichita, Osage and Pawnee tribes. The French claimed Kansas in 1682, establishing a valuable fur trade with local tribes in the 18th century. In 1803 the area passed to the USA as part of the Louisiana Purchase and became a base for pioneering trails further west. After 1830 it was 'Indian Territory' and a number of tribes displaced from eastern states were settled there. In 1854 the Kansas Territory was created and opened for white settlement. The early settlers were farmers from Europe or New England, but the Territory's position also brought it into contact with southern culture. Slavery was prohibited by the Missouri Compromise of 1820 but the 1854 Kansas-Nebraska Act affirmed the principle of 'popular sovereignty' to settle the issue, which was then fought out by opposing factions throughout 'Bleeding Kansas'.

Kansas entered the Union (as a non-slave state) in 1861, minus the territory that is now in Colorado.

The economy was based on cattle-ranching and railways. Herds were driven to the railheads and shipped from vast stockyards, or slaughtered and processed in railhead meat-packing plants. Wheat and sorghum also became important once the plains could be ploughed on a large scale.

Territory and Population
Kansas is bounded north by Nebraska, east by Missouri, with the Missouri River as boundary in the northeast, south by Oklahoma and west by Colorado. Total area is 82,278 sq. miles (213,100 sq. km) of which 81,759 sq. miles (211,754 sq. km) are land. Census population, 1 April 2010, was 2,853,118, an increase of 6·1% since 2000. July 2018 estimate, 2,911,505.

Population in five federal census years was:

	White	Black	American Indian	Asian	Total	Per sq. mile
1870	346,377	17,108	914	—	364,399	4·5
			All others			
1980	2,168,221	126,127	69,888		2,364,236	28·8
1990	2,231,986	143,076	102,512		2,477,574	30·3
2000	2,313,944	154,198	220,276		2,688,418	32·9
2010	2,391,044	167,864	294,210		2,853,118	34·9

Of the total population in 2010, 1,437,710 were female and 2,126,179 were 18 years old or older. In 2010 the Hispanic population was 300,042, up from 188,252 in 2000 (an increase of 59·4%).

Cities, with 2010 census population: Wichita, 382,368; Overland Park, 173,372; Kansas City, 145,786; Topeka (capital), 127,473; Olathe, 125,872; Lawrence, 87,643.

Social Statistics

Births, 2014, 39,223 (13·5 per 1,000 population); deaths, 2014, 25,793 (8·9). Infant mortality, 2013, 6·5 per 1,000 live births. 2014: marriages, 6·1 per 1,000 population; divorces and annulments, 3·0. Same-sex marriage became legal in Nov. 2014.

Climate

Dodge City, Jan. 29°F (−1·7°C), July 78°F (25·6°C). Annual rainfall 21" (518 mm). Kansas City, Jan. 30°F (−1·1°C), July 79°F (26·1°C). Annual rainfall 38" (947 mm). Topeka, Jan. 28°F (−2·2°C), July 78°F (25·6°C). Annual rainfall 35" (875 mm). Wichita, Jan. 31°F (−0·6°C), July 81°F (27·2°C). Annual rainfall 31" (777 mm). Kansas belongs to the Mid-West climate zone (*see* UNITED STATES: Climate).

Constitution and Government

The year 1861 saw the adoption of the present constitution; it has had 183 amendments. The Legislature includes a Senate of 40 members, elected for four years, and a House of Representatives of 125 members, elected for two years. Sessions are annual.

For the 116th Congress, which convened in Jan. 2019, Kansas sends four members to the House of Representatives. It is represented in the Senate by Pat Roberts (R. 1997–2021) and Jerry Moran (R. 2011–23).

The capital is Topeka. The state is divided into 105 counties.

Recent Elections

In the 2016 presidential election Donald Trump took Kansas with 57·2% of the vote (Mitt Romney won it in 2012).

Current Government

Governor: Laura Kelly (D.), 2019–23 (salary: $99,636).
　Lieut.-Governor: Lynn Rogers (D.), 2019–23.
　　Secretary of State: Scott Schwab (R.), since Jan. 2019.
Government Website: https://portal.kansas.gov

Economy

Per capita personal income (2015) was $45,876.

Budget

In 2011 total state revenue was $18,613m. Total expenditure was $16,687m. (including: education, $5,966m.; public welfare, $3,531m.; highways, $1,239m.; hospitals, $1,228m.; government administration, $456m.). Outstanding debt in 2011, $6,893m.

Performance

Gross Domestic Product by state in 2015 was $149,641m., ranking Kansas 31st in the United States. In 2015 state real GDP growth was 0·8%.

Energy and Natural Resources

Oil and Gas

In 2014 Kansas produced 49·5m. bbls of crude petroleum; marketed production of natural gas totalled 286bn. cu. ft.

Water

The total area covered by water is 520 sq. miles.

Minerals

Important fuel minerals are coal, petroleum and natural gas. Principal non-fuel minerals are cement, salt and crushed stone. Total value of non-fuel mineral output in 2009 was $953m.

Agriculture

Kansas is pre-eminently agricultural, but sometimes suffers from lack of rainfall in the west. In 2012 there were 65,500 farms with a total acreage of 46·0m. Average number of acres per farm was 702. Average value of farmland and buildings per acre, in 2012, was $1,632. Farm income 2011:

from crops, $6,318m.; and from livestock and products, $8,729m. Chief crops: wheat, corn and soybeans. The net farm income in 2011 was $2,156m. Wheat production was 378·0m. bu. in 2012. Kansas was the USA's largest wheat producer in 2012. There is an extensive livestock industry, including, in 2013, 6·6m. cattle (third in the USA), 75,000 sheep, and 1·77m. hogs and pigs.

Forestry

The state had a forested area of 5·2m. acres in 2012.

Industry

In 2012 the state's 6,860 manufacturing establishments had 338,000 employees, earning $16,537m. Total value added by manufacturing in 2013 was $28,874m.

Labour

Total non-agricultural employment, 2010, 1,323,000. Employees by branch, 2010 (in 1,000): government, 262; trade, transportation and utilities, 251; education and health services, 180; manufacturing, 160; professional and business services, 142. In Dec. 2010 the state unemployment rate was 6·8%.

International Trade

Imports and Exports

In 2015 imports into Kansas totalled $11,773m. (down from $11,809m. in 2014). In the same year exports from Kansas totalled $10,690m., down from $12,022m. in 2014. The leading source for imports in 2015 was China ($2,625m.), ahead of Canada ($1,595m.). The leading destination for exports in 2015 was Canada ($2,368m.), followed by Mexico ($1,798m.).

Communications

Roads

In 2012 there were 140,614 miles of roads (127,573 miles rural). There were 2,367,652 registered motor vehicles.

Rail

There were 4,855 miles of freight railroad in 2012. There were 13 freight railroads operating in 2012. Rail traffic originating in Kansas totalled 17·9m. tons and rail traffic terminating in the state came to 23·4m. tons.

Civil Aviation

There were four primary airports in 2011 (commercial service airports with more than 10,000 passenger boardings annually) with a combined total of 822,434 enplanements, up from 815,385 in 2010.

Social Institutions

Justice

In Dec. 2014 there were 9,663 federal and state prisoners. The death penalty was declared unconstitutional in Kansas in 2004. The last execution was in 1965.

Education

In 2012–13 there were 1,367 public elementary and secondary schools with 489,043 pupils enrolled and 41,243 teachers. Total expenditure on public elementary and secondary education in 2010–11 was $5,825m.; average teacher salary was $47,464 in 2012–13. Spending per pupil in 2010–11 was $9,802.

The Kansas Board of Regents governs six state universities: Kansas State University, Manhattan (founded in 1863); University of Kansas, Lawrence (1864); Emporia State University, Emporia; Pittsburg State University, Pittsburg; Fort Hays State University, Hays; and Wichita State University, Wichita. It also supervises and co-ordinates 19 community colleges, five technical colleges, six technical schools and a municipal university.

Health

Kansas had 3·5 community hospital beds for every 1,000 population in 2013. In the same year there were 25·4 active physicians per 10,000 civilian population and 5·0 dentists per 10,000.

Welfare

Medicare enrolment in July 2012 totalled 456,220. In fiscal year 2011 a total of 403,694 people in Kansas received Medicaid. In Dec. 2014 there were

521,955 Old-Age, Survivors, and Disability Insurance (OASDI) beneficiaries. A total of 22,336 people were receiving payments under Temporary Assistance for Needy Families (TANF) in Dec. 2012.

Religion
In 2010 the chief religious traditions were: Evangelical Protestants, with 516,818 members; Catholics, 426,611; Mainline Protestants, 386,980; Black Protestants, 41,666; Latter-day Saints (Mormons), 40,251.

Kentucky

Key Historical Events
Lying west of the Appalachians and south of the Ohio River, the area was the meeting place and battleground for the eastern Iroquois and the southern Cherokees. Northern Shawnees were also present. The first successful white settlement took place in 1769 when Daniel Boone reached the Bluegrass plains from the eastern, trans-Appalachian, colonies. After 1783 immigration from the east was rapid, settlers travelling by river or crossing the mountains by the Cumberland Gap. The area was originally attached to Virginia but became a separate state in 1792.

Large plantations dependent on slave labour were established, as were small farms worked by white owners. The state became divided on the issue of slavery, although plantation interests (mainly producing tobacco) dominated state government. In fact the state did not secede in 1861, and the majority of citizens supported the Union. Public opinion was more favourable to the south in the hard times of the reconstruction period.

The eastern mountains became an important coal mining area, tobacco-growing continued and the Bluegrass plains produced livestock, including especially fine thoroughbred horses.

Territory and Population
Kentucky is bounded in the north by the Ohio River (forming the boundary with Illinois, Indiana and Ohio), northeast by the Big Sandy River (forming the boundary with West Virginia), east by Virginia, south by Tennessee and west by the Mississippi River (forming the boundary with Missouri). Total area is 40,408 sq. miles (104,656 sq. km) of which 39,486 sq. miles (102,269 sq. km) are land. Census population, 1 April 2010, was 4,339,367, an increase of 7·4% since 2000. July 2018 estimate, 4,468,402.

Population in five census years was:

	White	Black	All others	Total	Per sq. mile
1930	2,388,364	226,040	185	2,614,589	65·1
1980	3,379,006	259,477	22,294	3,660,777	92·3
1990	3,391,832	262,907	30,557	3,685,296	92·8
2000	3,640,889	295,994	104,886	4,041,769	101·7
2010	3,809,537	337,520	192,310	4,339,367	109·9

Of the total population in 2010, 2,204,415 were female and 3,315,996 were 18 years old or older. Kentucky's Hispanic population was 132,836, up 121·6% on the 2000 census figure of 59,939.

The principal cities with census population in 2010 are: Louisville, 597,337; Lexington-Fayette, 295,803; Bowling Green, 58,067; Owensboro, 57,265; Covington, 40,640; Hopkinsville, 31,577; Richmond, 31,364; Florence, 29,951; Georgetown, 29,098; Henderson, 28,757; Elizabethtown, 28,531; Nicholasville, 28,015; Jeffersontown, 26,595; Frankfort (capital), 25,527.

Social Statistics
Births, 2014, 56,170 (12·7 per 1,000 population); deaths, 2014, 44,838 (10·2). Infant mortality, 2013, 6·4 per 1,000 live births. 2014: marriages, 6·9 per 1,000 population; divorces and annulments, 3·8.

Climate
Kentucky is in the Appalachian Mountains climatic zone (see UNITED STATES: Climate). It has a temperate climate. Temperatures are moderate during both winter and summer, precipitation is ample without a pronounced dry season, and winter snowfall amounts are variable. Mean annual temperatures range from 52°F in the northeast to 58°F in the southwest. Annual rainfall averages at about 45". Snowfall ranges from 5 to 10" in the southwest of the state, to 25" in the northeast, and 40" at higher altitudes in the southeast.

Constitution and Government
The constitution dates from 1891; there had been three preceding it. The 1891 constitution was promulgated by convention and provides that amendments be submitted to the electorate for ratification. The General Assembly consists of a Senate of 38 members elected for four years, one half retiring every two years, and a House of Representatives of 100 members elected for two years. It has annual sessions. All citizens of 18 or over are qualified as electors.

For the 116th Congress, which convened in Jan. 2019, Kentucky sends six members to the House of Representatives. It is represented in the Senate by Mitch McConnell (R. 1985–2021) and Rand Paul (R. 2011–23).

The capital is Frankfort. The state is divided into 120 counties.

Recent Elections
In the 2016 presidential election Donald Trump took Kentucky with 62·5% of the vote (Mitt Romney won it in 2012).

Current Government
Governor: Matt Bevin (R.), Dec. 2015–Dec. 2019 (salary: $145,992).
  Lieut.-Governor: Jenean Hampton (R.), Dec. 2015–Dec. 2019.
    Secretary of State: Alison Lundergan Grimes (D.), since Jan. 2012.
Government Website: https://kentucky.gov

Economy
Per capita personal income (2015) was $38,989.

Budget
In 2011 total state revenue was $31,056m. Total expenditure was $29,370m. (including: education, $9,415m.; public welfare, $7,334m.; highways, $1,936m.; hospitals, $1,135m.; government administration, $880m.). Debt outstanding in 2011, $14,522m.

Performance
Gross Domestic Product by state in 2015 was $193,274m., ranking Kentucky 28th in the United States. In 2015 state real GDP growth was 1·4%.

Energy and Natural Resources

Electricity
In 2015 production was 83,544m. kWh, of which 72,620m. kWh was from coal.

Oil and Gas
In 2014 Kentucky produced 3·4m. bbls of crude petroleum; marketed production of natural gas totalled 79bn. cu. ft.

Water
The total area covered by water is 921 sq. miles.

Minerals
The principal mineral is coal: 107·3m. short tons were mined in 2009, value $6·3bn. In 2008, 51·0m. tonnes of crushed stone were mined, value $411m.; 7·6m. tonnes of sand and gravel, value $41·6m.; 0·4m. tonnes of clay, value $8·2m. Other minerals include fluorspar, ball clay, gemstones, dolomite, cement and lime. Total value of non-fuel mineral production for 2009 was $668m.

Agriculture
In 2007, 85,260 farms covered an area of 13·99m. acres. The average farm was 164 acres. In 2007 the average value of farmland and buildings per acre was $2,682.

Farm income, 2009: from crops, $1,829m.; and from livestock, $2,429m. The net farm income in 2009 was $1,332m. The chief crop is tobacco: production, in 2007, 196·3m. lb. Kentucky is the USA's second largest tobacco producer, after North Carolina. Other principal crops include corn (172m. bu. in 2007), soybeans, hay and wheat.

Stock-raising is important in Kentucky, which has long been famous for its horses. There were 175,500 horses in the state in 2007, a number exceeded only by Texas. The livestock in 2007 included 2·40m. all cattle and calves, 90,000 dairy cows, 37,000 sheep, 348,000 swine and 4·58m. laying hens.

Forestry

In 2012 Kentucky had 12·51m. acres forested land, of which 816,000 acres were national forest.

Industry

In 2012 Kentucky's 9,096 manufacturing establishments had 508,000 employees, earning $23,647m. The value added by manufacture in 2013 was $44,475m.

Labour

Total non-agricultural employment, 2010, 1,770,000. Employees by branch, 2010 (in 1,000): trade, transportation and utilities, 359; government, 331; education and health services, 250; manufacturing, 209; professional and business services, 180. The unemployment rate in Dec. 2010 was 10·3%.

International Trade

Imports and Exports

In 2015 imports into Kentucky totalled $38,658m. (down from $39,353m. in 2014). In the same year exports from Kentucky totalled $27,644m., down from $27,757m. in 2014. The leading source for imports in 2015 was Mexico ($6,089m.), ahead of China ($6,059m.). The leading destination for exports in 2015 was Canada ($7,260m.), followed by the United Kingdom ($2,558m.).

Communications

Roads

In 2012 there were 79,321 miles of roads comprising 12,620 miles of urban road and 66,701 miles of rural road. There were 3,570,060 registered motor vehicles.

Rail

In 2012 there were 2,608 miles of freight railroad (excluding trackage rights). There were 13 freight railroads operating in 2012. Rail traffic originating in Kentucky in 2012 totalled 59·2m. tons and rail traffic terminating in the state came to 36·8m. tons.

Civil Aviation

In 2011 Kentucky had five primary airports—commercial service airports with more than 10,000 passenger boardings annually—with a combined total of 5,642,399 enplanements, down from 6,133,451 in 2010. The busiest airports are Cincinnati/Northern Kentucky International (which had 3,422,466 enplanements in 2011) and Louisville International (1,650,707 enplanements in 2011). Louisville handled 2,188,422 tonnes of freight in 2011, ranking it third in the USA for cargo handled behind Memphis and Anchorage.

Shipping

There is barge traffic on the 1,100 miles of navigable rivers. There are six public river ports, over 30 contract terminal facilities and 150 private terminal operations. Kentucky's waterways have access to the junction of the upper and lower Mississippi, Ohio and Tennessee-Tombigbee navigation corridors.

Social Institutions

Justice

There are 12 adult prisons within the Department of Corrections Adult Institutions and three privately run adult institutions. In Dec. 2014 there were 21,657 prison inmates. The death penalty is authorized for murder and kidnapping. As of Dec. 2011 there were 35 persons (including one female) under sentence of death. There was one execution in 2008 but none since.

Education

Attendance at school between the ages of six and 16 years (inclusive) is compulsory, the normal term being 175 days. In 2012–13 there were 685,167 pupils and 42,769 teachers in 1,583 public elementary and secondary schools; teachers' salaries (2012–13) averaged $50,326. The average total expenditure per pupil in 2010–11 was $9,228. There were also 5,240 teachers working in 330 private elementary and secondary schools with 69,410 students in fall 2011.

In 2012–13 the state had 24 public, 27 not-for-profit independent and 29 for-profit independent degree-granting institutions. There were 224,092 students at public degree-granting institutions in fall 2012 and 58,033 students at private degree-granting institutions. The largest of the institutions of higher learning are (fall 2014): University of Kentucky, with 29,203 students; University of Louisville, 21,561; Western Kentucky University, 20,171; Eastern Kentucky University, 16,305; Northern Kentucky University, 15,090; Murray State University, 11,207; Morehead State University, 11,052. Five of the several privately-endowed colleges of standing are Berea College, Berea; Centre College, Danville; Transylvania University, Lexington; Georgetown College, Georgetown; and Bellarmine College, Louisville.

Health

Kentucky had 3·2 community hospital beds for every 1,000 population in 2013. In the same year there were 24·6 active physicians per 10,000 civilian population and 5·7 dentists per 10,000.

Welfare

Medicare enrolment in July 2012 totalled 807,868. In fiscal year 2012 a total of 1,087,727 people in Kentucky received Medicaid. In Dec. 2014 there were 954,284 Old-Age, Survivors, and Disability Insurance (OASDI) beneficiaries. A total of 62,497 people were receiving payments under Temporary Assistance for Needy Families (TANF) in Dec. 2012.

Religion

The principal religious traditions in the state in 2010 were: Evangelical Protestants, with 1,448,947 members; Catholics, 359,783; Mainline Protestants, 305,955; Black Protestants, 64,958; Latter-day Saints (Mormons), 32,559.

Louisiana

Key Historical Events

Originally the territory of Choctaw and Caddo tribes, the area was claimed for France in 1682. In 1718 the French founded New Orleans which became the centre of a crown colony in 1731. France ceded the area west of the Mississippi (most of the present state) to Spain in 1762 and the eastern area, north of New Orleans, to Britain in 1763. The British section passed to the USA in 1783 but France bought back the rest from Spain in 1800, including New Orleans and the mouth of the Mississippi. The USA, fearing exclusion from a strategically important and commercially promising shipping area, persuaded France to sell Louisiana in 1803. The present states of Missouri, Arkansas, Iowa, North Dakota, South Dakota, Nebraska and Oklahoma were included in the purchase.

The area became the Territory of New Orleans in 1804 and was admitted to the Union as a state in 1812. The economy initially depended on cotton and sugarcane plantations. The population was of French, Spanish and black descent, with a growing number of American settlers. Plantation interests succeeded in achieving secession in 1861 but New Orleans was occupied by the Union in 1862. Planter influence was reasserted in the late 19th century, imposing rigid segregation and denying black rights.

The state has become mainly urban industrial, with the Mississippi ports growing rapidly. There is petroleum and natural gas, and a strong tourist industry based on the French culture and Caribbean atmosphere of New Orleans.

Louisiana, and New Orleans in particular, suffered widespread damage and loss of life after Hurricane Katrina struck the Gulf Coast on 31 Aug. 2005.

Territory and Population

Louisiana is bounded north by Arkansas, east by Mississippi, south by the Gulf of Mexico and west by Texas. Land area, 43,204 sq. miles (111,898 sq. km); water area, 9,174 sq. miles (23,761 sq. km). Census population, 1 April 2010, was 4,533,372, an increase of 1·4% since 2000. July 2018 estimate, 4,659,978.

Population in five census years was:

	White	Black	American Indian	Asian	Total	Per sq. mile
1930	1,322,712	776,326	1,536	1,019	2,101,593	46·5

(*continued*)

	White	Black	American Indian	Asian	Total	Per sq. mile
			All others			
1980	2,911,243	1,237,263	55,466		4,205,900	93·5
1990	2,839,138	1,299,281	81,554		4,219,973	96·9
2000	2,856,161	1,451,944	160,871		4,468,976	102·6
2010	2,836,192	1,452,396	244,784		4,533,372	104·9

Of the total population in 2010, 2,314,080 were female and 3,415,357 were 18 years old or older. The Hispanic population was 192,560 in 2010, an increase of 78·7% on the 2000 census figure of 107,738.

The largest cities with their 2010 census population are: New Orleans, 343,829 (484,764 in 2000); Baton Rouge (the capital), 229,493; Shreveport, 199,311; Metairie, 138,481; Lafayette, 120,623; Lake Charles, 71,993; Kenner, 66,702; Bossier City, 61,315; Monroe, 48,815. In Jan. 2006 the population of New Orleans was estimated at 144,000 in the wake of Hurricane Katrina, making Baton Rouge temporarily the most populous city in Louisiana. Although the population of New Orleans has risen steadily back up since then, it has still not reached pre-Katrina levels.

Social Statistics
Births, 2014, 64,497 (13·9 per 1,000 population); deaths, 2014, 43,869 (9·4). Infant deaths, 2013, 8·7 per 1,000 live births. Marriages, 2014, 6·9 per 1,000 population; divorces and annulments, 2·3.

Climate
New Orleans, Jan. 54°F (12·2°C), July 83°F (28·3°C). Annual rainfall 58" (1,458 mm). Louisiana belongs to the Gulf Coast climate zone (*see* UNITED STATES: Climate).

Constitution and Government
The present constitution dates from 1974. The Legislature consists of a Senate of 39 members and a House of Representatives of 105 members, both chosen for four years. Sessions are annual; a fiscal session is held in even years.

For the 116th Congress, which convened in Jan. 2019, Louisiana sends six members to the House of Representatives. It is represented in the Senate by Bill Cassidy (R. 2015–21) and John Kennedy (R. 2017–23).

Louisiana is divided into 64 parishes (corresponding to the counties of other states). The capital is Baton Rouge.

Recent Elections
In the 2016 presidential election Donald Trump took Louisiana with 58·1% of the vote (Mitt Romney won it in 2012).

Current Government
Governor: John Bel Edwards (D.), 2016–20 (salary: $130,000).
   Lieut.-Governor: Billy Nungesser (R.), 2016–20.
   Secretary of State: Kyle Ardoin (R.), since May 2018—acting until Dec. 2018.
Government Website: http://www.louisiana.gov

Economy
Per capita personal income (2015) was $43,252.

Budget
In 2011 total revenue was $33,975m. Total expenditure was $33,396m. (including: education, $8,904m.; public welfare, $6,426m.; hospitals, $2,205m.; highways, $2,185m.; government administration, $982m.). Debt outstanding, in 2011, $18,447m.

Performance
Gross Domestic Product by state in 2015 was $239,305m., ranking Louisiana 24th in the United States. In 2015 state real GDP growth was 1·0%.

Energy and Natural Resources
Electricity
In 2015 production was 107·8bn. kWh, of which 66·2bn. kWh was from natural gas.

Oil and Gas
In 2014 Louisiana produced 68·4m. bbls of crude petroleum; marketed production of natural gas totalled 1,980bn. cu. ft (fourth in the USA behind Texas, Pennsylvania and Oklahoma).

Water
The total area covered by water is 9,174 sq. miles, of which 4,562 sq. miles are inland.

Minerals
Principal non-fuel minerals are salt, sand, gravel and lime. Total non-fuel mineral production in 2009 was more than $460m.

Agriculture
The state is divided into two parts, the uplands and the alluvial and swamp regions of the coast. A delta occupies about one-third of the total area. Manufacturing is the leading industry, but agriculture is important. The number of farms in 2007 was 30,106 covering 8·11m. acres; the average farm had 269 acres. Average value of farmland per acre, in 2007, was $2,058.

Farm income, 2009: from crops, $1,762m.; and from livestock, $778m. The net farm income in 2009 was $689m. Principal crops, 2007 production, were: soybeans, 24·72m. bu.; sugarcane, 14·09m. tons; rice, 23·12m. cwt; corn, 114·67m. bu.; cotton, 699,000 bales; sorghum, 22·40m. bu.

Forestry
In 2013 the state had 14·97m. acres of forested land, of which 692,000 acres were national forest. Private, non-industrial landowners own 62% of the state's forestland, forest products industries own 29% and the general public owns 9%. Production 2011: sawtimber, 828,637,892 bd ft; cordwood, 5,844,089 standard cords. The economic impact of forestry and forest products industries in Louisiana was $3·1bn. in 2010.

Fisheries
In 2017 Louisiana's commercial fisheries catch for all species totalled 898·5m. lb, valued at $370·2m. Louisiana's commercial fishery landings in terms of weight are second only behind those of Alaska. Louisiana had aquaculture sales worth $90·6m. in 2013, ranking it fourth behind Washington, Mississippi and Alabama.

Industry
Louisiana's leading manufacturing activity is the production of chemicals, followed, in order of importance, by the processing of petroleum and coal products, the production of transportation equipment and production of paper products. In 2012 the state's 6,994 manufacturing establishments had 287,000 employees, earning $17,602m. Total value added by manufacturing in 2013 was $57,752m.

Labour
Total non-agricultural employment, 2010, 1,884,000. Employees by branch, 2010 (in 1,000): government, 366; trade, transportation and utilities, 364; education and health services, 271; leisure and hospitality, 194; professional and business services, 193. The unemployment rate was 7·7% in Dec. 2010.

International Trade
Imports and Exports
In 2015 imports into Louisiana totalled $35·2bn. (down from $57·6bn. in 2014). In the same year exports from Louisiana totalled $48·7bn., down from $64·8bn. in 2014. The leading source for imports in 2015 was Saudi Arabia ($5·9bn.), ahead of Venezuela ($4·6bn.). The leading destination for exports in 2015 was China ($6·6bn.), followed by Mexico ($5·9bn.).

Communications
Roads
In 2012 there were 61,326 miles of road (44,356 miles rural). Registered motor vehicles numbered 3,821,119.

Rail
In 2012 there were 2,927 miles of freight railroad (excluding trackage rights). There were 18 freight railroads operating in 2012. Rail traffic originating in Louisiana in 2012 totalled 29·3m. tons and rail traffic terminating in the state came to 44·6m. tons. There is a tramway in New Orleans.

Civil Aviation

In 2011 there were seven primary airports—commercial service airports with more than 10,000 passenger boardings annually—with a combined total of 5,496,614 enplanements, up from 5,274,620 in 2010. By far the busiest airport, Louis Armstrong New Orleans International, had 4,255,411 enplanements in 2011.

Shipping

The port of South Louisiana is the busiest in the country and the second busiest after Houston for foreign trade cargo. In 2014 South Louisiana handled 267·4m. tons of cargo (141·6m. tons of domestic cargo and 125·8m. tons of foreign trade cargo). Other major ports are New Orleans, Baton Rouge, Lake Charles and Plaquemines, which ranked as the USA's 7th, 9th, 12th and 13th busiest ports respectively in 2014. Louisiana has some 5,000 miles of navigable rivers, bayous, creeks and canals.

Social Institutions

Justice

In Dec. 2014 there were 38,030 federal and state prisoners. There have been no executions since one was carried out in 2010.

Education

School attendance is compulsory between the ages of seven and 18. In 2012–13 there were 1,456 public schools with 710,903 pupils and 46,493 teachers. There were 390 private schools in fall 2011 with 125,720 pupils and 8,830 teachers. Teachers' average salary in 2012–13 was $51,381. In 2012–13 the state had 35 public and 37 private degree-granting institutions. There were 220,971 students at public degree-granting institutions in fall 2012 and 37,854 at private degree-granting institutions.

Enrolment (fall 2014) in the University of Louisiana System was 88,693 (Lafayette, 17,195; Southeastern, 14,487; Louisiana Tech., 11,225; New Orleans, 9,234; Northwestern, 9,002; Monroe, 8,517; McNeese, 8,237; Nicholls, 6,292; Grambling, 4,504); Louisiana State University, 44,368 (with campuses at Alexandria, Baton Rouge, Eunice, New Orleans and Shreveport); Southern University System, 12,029 (with campuses at Baton Rouge, New Orleans and Shreveport). Major private institutions (fall 2014): Tulane University, 12,603; Loyola University, 4,330; Xavier University, 2,976.

Health

Louisiana had 3·4 community hospital beds for every 1,000 population in 2013. In the same year there were 27·2 active physicians per 10,000 civilian population and 4·8 dentists per 10,000.

Welfare

Medicare enrolment in July 2012 totalled 730,917. In fiscal year 2011 a total of 1,298,343 people in Louisiana received Medicaid. In Dec. 2014 there were 854,211 Old-Age, Survivors, and Disability Insurance (OASDI) beneficiaries. A total of 19,735 people were receiving payments under Temporary Assistance for Needy Families (TANF) in Dec. 2012.

Religion

The principal religious traditions in the state in 2010 were: Catholics, with 1,200,900 members; Evangelical Protestants, 1,064,486; Black Protestants, 217,176; Mainline Protestants, 202,751; Latter-day Saints (Mormons), 29,107.

Maine

Key Historical Events

Originally occupied by Algonquian-speaking tribes, the Territory was disputed between groups of British settlers, and between the British and French, throughout the 17th and most of the 18th centuries. After 1652 Maine was governed as part of Massachusetts, and French claims finally failed in 1763. Most of the early settlers were English and Protestant Irish, with many Quebec French.

The Massachusetts settlers gained control when the first colonist, Sir Ferdinando Gorges, supported the losing royalist side in the English civil war. During the English-American war of 1812, Maine residents claimed that the Massachusetts government did not protect them against British raids. Maine was separated from Massachusetts and entered the Union as a state in 1820.

Maine is a mountainous state and even the coastline is rugged, but the coastal belt is where most settlement has developed. In the 19th century there were manufacturing towns making use of cheap water-power and the rocky shore supported a shell-fish industry. The latter still flourishes, together with intensive horticulture, producing potatoes and fruit. The other main economic activity is forestry for timber, pulp and paper.

The capital is Augusta, a river trading post which was fortified against American Indian attacks in 1754, incorporated as a town in 1797 and chosen as capital in 1832.

Territory and Population

Maine is bounded west, north and east by Canada, southeast by the Atlantic, south and southwest by New Hampshire. Land area, 30,843 sq. miles (79,883 sq. km); water area, 4,537 sq. miles (11,750 sq. km). Census population, 1 April 2010, was 1,328,361, an increase of 4·2% since 2000. July 2018 estimate, 1,338,404.

Population for five census years was:

	White	Black	American Indian	Asian	Total	Per sq. mile
1910	739,995	1,363	992	121	742,371	24·8
			All others			
1980	1,109,850	3,128	12,049		1,125,027	36·3
1990	1,208,360	5,138	14,430		1,227,928	39·8
2000	1,236,014	6,760	2,149		1,274,923	41·3
2010	1,264,971	15,707	7,683		1,328,361	43·1

Of the total population in 2010, 678,305 were female and 1,053,828 were 18 years old or older. In 2010 the Hispanic population was 16,935, an increase of 80·9% on the 2000 census figure of 9,360. Only North Dakota and Vermont have fewer persons of Hispanic origin in the USA.

The largest city in the state is Portland, with a census population of 66,194 in 2010. Other cities (with population in 2010) are: Lewiston, 36,592; Bangor, 33,039; South Portland, 25,002; Auburn, 23,055; Biddeford, 21,277; Augusta (capital), 19,136; Saco, 18,482; Westbrook, 17,494.

Social Statistics

Births, 2014, 12,698 (9·5 per 1,000 population); deaths, 2014, 13,510 (10·2). Maine was one of only two states in the USA where deaths exceeded births in 2014, the other being West Virginia. Infant mortality rate, 2013, 7·1 per 1,000 live births. 2014: marriages, 7·7 per 1,000 population; divorces and annulments, 3·6. Same-sex marriage became legal in Dec. 2012 after it had been approved in a referendum the previous month on the same day as the presidential election.

Climate

Average maximum temperatures range from 56·3°F in Waterville to 48·3°F in Caribou, but record high (since c. 1950) is 103°F. Average minimum ranges from 36·9°F in Rockland to 28·3°F in Greenville, but record low (also in Greenville) is –42°F. Average annual rainfall ranges from 48·85" in Machias to 36·09" in Houlton. Average annual snowfall ranges from 118·7" in Greenville to 59·7" in Rockland. Maine belongs to the New England climate zone (see UNITED STATES: Climate).

Constitution and Government

The constitution of 1820 is still in force, but it has been amended 172 times (most recently in 2011).

The Legislature consists of the Senate with 35 members and the House of Representatives with 151 members, both Houses being elected simultaneously for two years. Sessions are annual.

For the 116th Congress, which convened in Jan. 2019, Maine sends two members to the House of Representatives. It is represented in the Senate by Susan Collins (R. 1997–2021) and Angus King (Independent, 2013–25).

The capital is Augusta. The state is divided into 16 counties.

Recent Elections

In the 2016 presidential election Hillary Clinton took Maine with 47·9% of the vote (Barack Obama won it in 2012)

Current Government

Governor: Janet Mills (D.), 2019–23 (salary: $70,000).
    Senate President: Troy Jackson (D.), 2018–20.
    Secretary of State: Matthew Dunlap (D.), since Jan. 2013.
Government Website: https://www.maine.gov

Economy

Per capita personal income (2015) was $42,077.

Budget

In 2011 total state revenue was $10,611m. Total expenditure was $9,099m. (public welfare, $2,905m.; education, $2,121m.; highways, $647m.; health, $446m.; government administration, $286m.). Outstanding debt in 2011, $5,904m.

Performance

Gross Domestic Product by state was $57,297m. in 2015, ranking Maine 43rd in the United States. In 2015 state real GDP growth was 1·1%.

Energy and Natural Resources

Water

The total area covered by water is 4,537 sq. miles.

Minerals

Minerals include sand and gravel, stone, lead, clay, copper, peat, silver and zinc. Total value of non-fuel mineral production for 2009 was $125m.

Agriculture

In 2007, 8,136 farms occupied 1·35m. acres; the average farm was 166 acres. Average value of farmland and buildings per acre in 2007 was $2,203. Farm income, 2009: from crops, $320m.; and from livestock and products, $258m. The net farm income in 2009 was $139m. Principal commodities are potatoes, dairy products and chicken eggs.

Forestry

There were 17·64m. acres of forested land in 2013, of which 58,000 acres were national forests. Commercial forest includes pine, spruce and fir. Wood products industries are of great economic importance.

Fisheries

In 2009 the commercial catch was 184·6m. lb, valued at $285·9m.

Industry

In 2012 the state's 4,518 manufacturing establishments had 132,000 employees, earning $6,437m. Total value added by manufacturing in 2013 was $7,942m.

Labour

Total non-agricultural employment, 2010, 593,000. Employees by branch, 2010 (in 1,000): education and health services, 119; trade, transportation and utilities, 117; government, 103; leisure and hospitality, 60; professional and business services, 56. The unemployment rate in Dec. 2010 was 7·5%.

International Trade

Imports and Exports

In 2015 imports into Maine totalled $3,687m. (down from $3,867m. in 2014). In the same year exports from Maine totalled $2,763m., down from $2,811m. in 2014. The leading source for imports in 2015 was Canada ($1,950m.), ahead of China ($467m.). The leading destination for exports in 2015 was also Canada ($1,305m.), again followed by China ($212m.).

Communications

Roads

In 2012 there were 22,871 miles of road (19,863 miles rural). There were 1,126,824 registered motor vehicles.

Rail

In 2012 there were 1,116 miles of freight railroad (excluding trackage rights). There were eight freight railroads operating in 2012. Rail traffic originating in Maine in 2012 totalled 2·1m. tons and rail traffic terminating in the state came to 2·6m. tons.

Civil Aviation

There are international airports at Portland and Bangor. In 2012 Maine had five primary airports (commercial service airports with more than 10,000 passenger boardings annually) with a combined total of 1,139,884 enplanements, down from 1,268,056 in 2011.

Social Institutions

Justice

In Dec. 2014 there were 2,242 federal and state prisoners. Capital punishment was abolished in 1887. In a state-wide vote held on the same day as the presidential election in Nov. 2016, the recreational use of marijuana was legalized.

Education

Education is free for pupils from five to 21 years of age, and compulsory from seven to 17. In 2012–13 there were 185,739 pupils and 15,222 teachers in 626 public elementary and secondary schools. Expenditure on public education in 2010–11 was $2,631m.

In 2012–13 there were 32 degree-granting institutions (15 public); there were 72,810 students enrolled in fall 2012 (50,270 in public institutions). The University of Maine System, created by Maine's state legislature in 1968, consists of seven universities: the University of Maine (founded in 1865); the University of Maine at Augusta (1965), at Farmington (1864), at Fort Kent (1878), at Machias (1909), at Presque Isle (1903); and the University of Southern Maine (1878, campuses at Portland, Gorham and Lewiston-Auburn).

There are several independent universities, including: Bowdoin College, founded in 1794 at Brunswick; Bates College at Lewiston; Colby College at Waterville; Husson College at Bangor; Westbrook College at Westbrook; Unity College at Unity; and the University of New England (formerly St Francis College) at Biddeford.

Health

Maine had 2·6 community hospital beds for every 1,000 population in 2013. In the same year there were 33·7 active physicians per 10,000 civilian population and 5·2 dentists per 10,000.

Welfare

Medicare enrolment in July 2012 totalled 283,066. In fiscal year 2011 a total of 329,837 people in Maine received Medicaid. In Dec. 2014 there were 325,496 Old-Age, Survivors, and Disability Insurance (OASDI) beneficiaries. A total of 15,742 people were receiving payments under Temporary Assistance for Needy Families (TANF) in Dec. 2012.

Religion

The principal religious traditions in 2010 were: Catholics, with 190,106 members; Mainline Protestants, 93,580; Evangelical Protestants, 59,052; Latter-day Saints (Mormons), 11,704.

Maryland

Key Historical Events

The first European visitors found Algonquian-speaking tribes, often under attack by Iroquois from further north. The first white settlement was made by the Calvert family, British Roman Catholics, in 1634. The settlers received some legislative rights in 1638. In 1649 their assembly passed the Act of Toleration, granting freedom of worship to all Christians. A peace treaty was signed with the Iroquois in 1652, after which it was possible for farming settlements to expand north and west. The capital (formerly at St Mary's City) was moved to Annapolis in 1694. Baltimore, which became the state's main city, was founded in 1729.

The first industry was tobacco-growing, which was based on slave-worked plantations. There were also many immigrant British small farmers, tradesmen and indentured servants.

At the close of the War of Independence, the treaty of Paris was ratified in Annapolis. Maryland became a state of the Union in 1788. In 1791 the state ceded land for the new federal capital, Washington, and its economy has depended on the capital's proximity ever since. Baltimore also grew as a port and industrial city, attracting European immigration in the 19th century. Although in sympathy with the south, Maryland remained in the Union in the Civil War albeit under the imposition of martial law.

Territory and Population

Maryland is bounded north by Pennsylvania, east by Delaware and the Atlantic, south by Virginia and West Virginia, with the Potomac River forming most of the boundary, and west by West Virginia. Chesapeake Bay almost cuts off the eastern end of the state from the rest. Land area, 9,707 sq. miles (25,142 sq. km); water area, 2,699 sq. miles (6,990 sq. km). Census population, 1 April 2010, was 5,773,552, an increase of 9·0% since 2000. July 2018 estimate, 6,042,718.

Population for five federal censuses was:

	White	Black	American Indian	Asian	Total	Per sq. mile
1920	1,204,737	244,479	32	400	1,449,661	145·8
1960	2,573,919	518,410	1,538	5,700	3,100,689	314·0
			All others			
1990	3,393,964	1,189,899	197,605		4,781,468	489·2
2000	3,391,308	1,477,411	427,767		5,296,486	541·9
2010	3,359,284	1,700,298	713,970		5,773,552	594·8

Of the total population in 2010, 2,981,790 were female and 4,420,588 were 18 years old or older. In 2010 Maryland's Hispanic population was 470,632, up from 227,916 in 2000 (an increase of 106·5%).

The largest city in the state (containing 10·8% of the population) is Baltimore, with 620,961 (2010 census). Baltimore–Towson, metropolitan area, 2,710,4894 (2010). Other main population centres (2010 census) are Columbia (99,615); Germantown (86,395); Silver Spring (71,452); Waldorf (67,752); Glen Burnie (67,639); Ellicott City (65,834); Frederick (65,239); Dundalk (63,597); Rockville (61,209); Bethesda (60,858). Annapolis (the capital) had a population of 38,394 in 2010.

Social Statistics

Births, 2014, 73,921 (12·4 per 1,000 population); deaths, 2014, 45,867 (7·7). Infant mortality, 2013, 6·6 per 1,000 live births. 2014: marriages, 6·5 per 1,000 population; divorces and annulments, 2·5. Same-sex marriage became legal in Jan. 2013 after it had been approved in a referendum in Nov. 2012 on the same day as the presidential election.

Climate

Baltimore, Jan. 36°F (2·2°C), July 79°F (26·1°C). Annual rainfall 42" (1,066 mm). Maryland belongs to the Atlantic Coast climate zone (*see* UNITED STATES: Climate).

Constitution and Government

The present constitution dates from 1867; it has had 233 amendments as of Sept. 2016. Amendments are proposed and considered annually by the General Assembly and must be ratified by the electorate. The General Assembly consists of a Senate of 47, and a House of Delegates of 141 members, both elected for four years, as are the Governor and Lieut.-Governor. Voters are citizens who have the usual residential qualifications.

For the 116th Congress, which convened in Jan. 2019, Maryland sends eight members to the House of Representatives. It is represented in the Senate by Benjamin Cardin (D. 2007–25) and Chris Van Hollen (D. 2017–23).

The state capital is Annapolis. The state is divided into 23 counties and Baltimore City.

Recent Elections

In the 2016 presidential election Hillary Clinton took Maryland with 60·5% of the vote (Barack Obama won it in 2012).

Current Government

Governor: Larry Hogan (R.), 2019–23 (salary: $170,000).
  Lieut.-Governor: Boyd Rutherford (R.), 2019–23.
  Secretary of State: John C. Wobensmith (R.), since Jan. 2015.
Government Website: http://www.maryland.gov

Economy

Per capita personal income (2015) was $56,127. Maryland had the highest average household income in 2014, at $73,971.

Budget

In 2011 total state revenue was $41,717m. Total expenditure was $37,673m. (education, $11,213m.; public welfare, $9,274m.; highways, $2,196m.; health, $1,849m.; correction, $1,384m.). Outstanding debt in 2011, $25,250m.

Performance

Gross Domestic Product by state in 2015 was $365,356m., ranking Maryland 15th in the United States. In 2015 state real GDP growth was 2·0%.

Energy and Natural Resources

Water

The total area covered by water is approximately 2,699 sq. miles.

Minerals

Value of non-fuel mineral production in 2009 was more than $300m. The leading mineral commodities by weight are crushed stone (24·8m. tonnes in 2008) and sand and gravel (12·0m. tonnes in 2008). Stone is the leading mineral commodity by value followed by Portland cement, coal, and sand and gravel. In 2007 output of crushed stone was valued at $282m. and Portland cement at an estimated $265m. Coal output was 2·31m. short tons in 2009.

Agriculture

In 2007 there were 12,834 farms with an area of 2·05m. acres. The average number of acres per farm was 160. The average value per acre in 2007 was $7,034.

Livestock, 2012: cattle and calves, 194,524; hogs and pigs, 19,869; sheep and lambs, 19,265; laying hens, 2·36m. Farm income cash receipts, 2009: crops, $751m.; livestock and products, $905m.; total, $1,656m. The net farm income in 2009 was $299m. Broilers (2007 value, $732·3m.), greenhouse and nursery products ($396·1m. in 2007) and dairy products ($207·6m. in 2007) are the leading agricultural commodities.

Forestry

Total forested area was 2·46m. acres in 2013.

Fisheries

In 2009, 55·8m. lb of seafood was landed at a dockside value of $67·3m. In 2011 there were 70 processing plants employing 1,217 people.

Industry

In 2012 the state's 6,406 manufacturing establishments had 207,000 employees, earning $12,084m. Total value added by manufacturing in 2013 was $22,098m.

Labour

Total non-agricultural employment, 2010, 2,513,000. Employees by branch, 2010 (in 1,000): government, 501; trade, transportation and utilities, 438; education and health services, 400; professional and business services, 386; leisure and hospitality, 229. The unemployment rate in Dec. 2010 was 7·4%.

International Trade

Imports and Exports

In 2015 imports into Maryland totalled $31·5bn. (up from $30·1bn. in 2014). In the same year exports from Maryland totalled $10·1bn., down from $12·2bn. in 2014. The leading source for imports in 2015 was Germany ($5·4bn.), ahead of China ($3·4bn.). The leading destination for exports in 2015 was Canada ($1·5bn.), followed by Saudi Arabia ($0·8bn.).

Communications

Roads

In 2012 there were 32,372 miles of road comprising 17,973 miles of urban road and 14,399 miles of rural road. There were 3,861,428 registered vehicles in 2012.

Rail

Maryland is served by CSX Transportation, Norfolk Southern Railroad as well as by six short-line railroads. Metro lines also serve Maryland in suburban Washington, D.C. Amtrak provides passenger service linking Baltimore and BWI Airport to major cities on the Atlantic Coast. MARC commuter rail serves the Baltimore–Washington metropolitan area. In 2012 there were 758 miles of freight railroad (excluding trackage rights). There were nine freight railroads operating in 2012. Rail traffic originating in Maryland in 2012 totalled 5·8m. tons and rail traffic terminating in the state came to 35·5m. tons.

Civil Aviation

In 2011 there were two primary airports (commercial service airports with more than 10,000 passenger boardings annually). The main airport, Baltimore/Washington International Thurgood Marshall, had 11,067,319 enplanements in 2011.

Shipping

In 2014 Baltimore handled 37·2m. tons of cargo. It is located about 200 miles further inland than any other Atlantic seaport.

Social Institutions

Justice

Prisons in Dec. 2014 held 21,011 inmates. Maryland's prison system has conducted a work-release programme for selected prisoners since 1963. All institutions have academic and vocational training programmes. There was one execution in 2004, the first since 1998, and one in 2005, but the death penalty was suspended in 2006 and formally abolished for future offenders in May 2013.

Education

Education is compulsory from five to 16 years of age. In 2012–13 there were 1,456 public schools with 859,638 pupils and 57,718 teachers. Average teacher salary in 2012–13 was $65,265. Total expenditure on public elementary and secondary education in 2010–11 was $13,252m. Spending per pupil in 2010–11 was $14,123.

In 2012–13 there were 64 degree-granting institutions (29 public and 35 private). The largest is the University System of Maryland (created in 1988), with about 160,000 students (fall 2014), consisting of 12 institutions, two regional higher education centres and a system office. The USM institutions are: Bowie State University; Coppin State University; Frostburg State University; Salisbury University; Towson University; University of Baltimore; and the six constituents of the University of Maryland (Baltimore, Baltimore County, College Park, Eastern Shore, University College and the Center for Environmental Science).

Health

Maryland had 2·1 community hospital beds for every 1,000 population in 2013. In the same year there were 40·9 active physicians per 10,000 civilian population and 7·2 dentists per 10,000.

Welfare

Medicare enrolment in July 2012 totalled 850,299. In fiscal year 2012 a total of 1,046,597 people in Maryland received Medicaid. In Dec. 2014 there were 936,372 Old-Age, Survivors, and Disability Insurance (OASDI) beneficiaries. A total of 56,079 people were receiving payments under Temporary Assistance for Needy Families (TANF) in Dec. 2012.

Religion

Maryland was the first US state to give religious freedom to all who came within its borders. The principal religious traditions in 2010 were Catholics (837,338 members), Evangelical Protestants (693,990 members), Mainline Protestants (500,112 members), Black Protestants (157,854 members) and Jews (83,284 members).

Culture

Cultural venues include: Frostburg Performing Arts Center, Strathmore Hall Arts Center and Center Stage. Performing arts institutions include the Baltimore Opera Company, Peabody Music Conservatory and Arena Players.

Tourism

In 2011 there were 335,000 overseas visitors to Maryland, excluding those from Canada and Mexico.

Massachusetts

Key Historical Events

The first European settlement was at Plymouth, where the *Mayflower* landed its English religious separatists in 1620. In 1626–30 more colonists arrived, the main body being English Puritans who founded a Puritan commonwealth. This commonwealth, of about 1,000 colonists led by John Winthrop, became the Massachusetts Bay Colony and was founded under a company charter. Following disagreement between the English government and the colony, the charter was withdrawn in 1684, but in 1691 a new charter united a number of settlements under the name of Massachusetts Bay. The colony's government was rigidly theocratic.

Shipbuilding, iron-working and manufacturing were more important than farming, the land being poor. The colony was Protestant and of English descent until the War of Independence. The former colony adopted its present constitution in 1780. In the struggle which ended in the separation of the American colonies from the mother country, Massachusetts took the foremost part, and on 6 Feb. 1788 became the 6th state to ratify the US constitution. The state acquired its present boundaries (having previously included Maine) in 1820.

During the 19th century, industrialization and immigration from Europe increased while Catholic Irish and Italian immigrants began to change the population's character. The main inland industry was textile manufacture, the main coastal occupation, whaling; both have now gone. Boston has remained the most important city of New England, attracting a large black population since 1950.

Territory and Population

Massachusetts is bounded north by Vermont and New Hampshire, east by the Atlantic, south by Connecticut and Rhode Island and west by New York. Land area, 7,800 sq. miles (20,202 sq. km); water area, 2,754 sq. miles (7,134 sq. km). Census population, 1 April 2010, was 6,547,629, an increase of 3·1% since 2000. July 2018 estimate, 6,902,149.

Population at five federal census years was:

	White	Black	Other	Total	Per sq. mile
1950	4,611,503	73,171	5,840	4,690,514	598·4
1980	5,362,836	221,279	152,922	5,737,037	732·0
1990	5,405,374	300,130	310,921	6,016,425	767·6
2000	5,367,286	343,454	638,357	6,349,097	809·8
2010	5,265,236	434,398	847,995	6,547,629	839·4

Of the total population in 2010, 3,381,001 were female and 5,128,706 were 18 years old or older. In 2010 the Hispanic population was 627,654, up from 428,729 in 2000 (an increase of 46·4%).

Population of the largest cities at the 2010 census: Boston (the capital), 617,594; Worcester, 181,045; Springfield, 153,060; Lowell, 106,519; Cambridge, 105,162; New Bedford, 95,072; Brockton, 93,810; Quincy, 92,271; Lynn, 90,329; Fall River, 88,857; Newton, 85,146. The Boston–Cambridge–Quincy metropolitan area had a 2010 census population of 4,552,402; Worcester, 798,552; Springfield, 692,942.

Social Statistics

Births, 2014, 71,908 (10·7 per 1,000 population); deaths, 2014, 55,200 (8·2). Infant mortality, 2013, 4·2 per 1,000 live births. 2014: marriages, 5·6 per 1,000 population; divorces and annulments, 2·7. Massachusetts was the first state to allow same-sex marriage, beginning in May 2004.

Climate

Boston, Jan. 28°F (–2·2°C), July 71°F (21·7°C). Annual rainfall 41" (1,036 mm). Massachusetts belongs to the New England climate zone (*see* UNITED STATES: Climate).

Constitution and Government

The constitution dates from 1780 and has had 120 amendments as of Jan. 2016. The legislative body, styled the General Court of the Commonwealth of Massachusetts, meets annually, and consists of the Senate with 40 members and the House of Representatives of 160 members, both elected for two years.

For the 116th Congress, which convened in Jan. 2019, Massachusetts sends nine members to the House of Representatives. It is represented in the Senate by Elizabeth Warren (D. 2013–25) and Edward J. Markey (D. 2013–21), who succeeded John Kerry (D. 1985–2013) following the latter's appointment as Secretary of State. Markey won a special election in June 2013 to take on the remainder of Kerry's term, which was set to end in Jan. 2015.

The capital is Boston. The state has 14 counties.

Recent Elections

In the 2016 presidential election Hillary Clinton took Massachusetts with 60·8% of the vote (Barack Obama won it in 2012).

Current Government

Governor: Charlie Baker (R.), 2019–23 (salary: $151,800).

    Lieut.-Governor: Karyn Polito (R.), 2019–23.

      Secretary of the Commonwealth: William F. Galvin (D.), since Jan. 1995.

Government Website: https://www.mass.gov

Economy

Per capita personal income (2015) was $61,032, the third highest in the country.

Budget

In 2011 total state revenue was $56,637m. Total expenditure was $52,551m. (public welfare, $14,716m.; education, $12,334m.; highways, $1,908m.; government administration, $1,648m.; health, $1,112m.). Outstanding debt in 2011, $74,316m.

Performance

Gross State Product by state in 2015 was $484,943m., ranking Massachusetts 11th in the United States. In 2015 state real GDP growth was 3·8%.

Energy and Natural Resources

Water

The total area covered by water is 2,754 sq. miles.

Minerals

Total domestic non-fuel mineral output in 2009 was valued at more than $210m., most of which came from sand, gravel, crushed stone and lime.

Agriculture

In 2007 there were 7,691 farms with an average area of 67 acres and a total area of 517,879 acres. Average value per acre in 2007 was $12,313. Farm income, 2009: from crops, $380m.; and from livestock and products, $101m. Principal commodities are greenhouse products, cranberries and dairy products. The net farm income in 2009 was $108m.

Forestry

In 2013 forests covered 3,036,000 acres, of which timberland was 2,902,000 acres. Commercially important hardwoods are sugar maple, northern red oak and white ash; softwoods are white pine and hemlock.

Fisheries

In 2009 commercial fishing produced 356·0m. lb of fish with a value of $400·2m.

Industry

In 2012 the state's 13,648 manufacturing establishments had 468,000 employees, earning $28,795m. Total value added by manufacturing in 2013 was $46,539m.

Labour

Total non-agricultural employment, 2010, 3,186,000. Employees by branch, 2010 (in 1,000): education and health services, 664; trade, transportation and utilities, 544; professional and business services, 461; government, 438; leisure and hospitality, 306. The state unemployment rate was 8·3% in Dec. 2010.

International Trade

Imports and Exports

In 2015 imports into Massachusetts totalled $33·7bn. (down from $34·5bn. in 2014). In the same year exports from Massachusetts totalled $25·3bn., down from $27·4bn. in 2014. The leading source for imports in 2015 was Canada ($7·7bn.), ahead of China ($4·4bn.). The leading destination for exports in 2015 was also Canada ($3·2bn.), followed by Mexico ($2·6bn.).

Communications

Roads

In 2012 there were 36,330 miles of public road (30,141 miles urban, 6,164 rural). There were approximately 4,826,000 registered motor vehicles.

Rail

In 2012 there were 973 miles of freight railroad (excluding trackage rights). There were 12 freight railroads operating in 2012. Rail traffic originating in Massachusetts in 2012 totalled 2·8m. tons and rail traffic terminating in the state came to 6·7m. tons. There are metro, light rail, tramway and commuter networks in and around Boston.

Civil Aviation

In 2011 there were seven primary airports (commercial service airports with more than 10,000 passenger boardings annually) with a combined total of 14,532,785 enplanements, up from 13,963,433 in 2010. By far the busiest airport is General Edward Lawrence Logan International, Boston's airport, with 14,180,730 enplanements in 2011.

Shipping

The state has three deep-water harbours, the busiest of which is Boston (with 17·0m. tons of cargo in 2014—11·9m. tons of foreign trade cargo and 5·1m. tons of domestic trade cargo). Other ports are Fall River and New Bedford.

Social Institutions

Justice

There were 10,713 federal and state prisoners in Dec. 2014. The death penalty was abolished in 1984. In a state-wide vote held on the same day as the presidential election in Nov. 2016, the recreational use of marijuana was legalized.

Education

School attendance is compulsory for ages six to 16. In 2012–13 there were 1,866 public elementary and secondary schools with 954,773 pupils and 70,636 teachers; total expenditure on public schools in 2010–11 was $14,716m. Teachers' salaries in 2012–13 averaged $73,129, the highest in any US state.

    Some leading higher education institutions are:

Year opened	Name and location of universities and colleges	Students (fall 2009)
1636	Harvard University, Cambridge	27,651
1839	Framingham State College	5,989
1839	Westfield State College	5,675
1840	Bridgewater State College	10,774
1852	Tufts University, Medford[1]	10,252
1854	Salem State College	10,125
1861	Mass. Institute of Technology, Cambridge	10,384
1863	University of Massachusetts, Amherst	27,016
1863	Boston College (RC), Chestnut Hill	15,036
1865	Worcester Polytechnic Institute, Worcester	4,961
1869	Boston University, Boston	31,960
1874	Worcester State College	5,473
1894	Fitchburg State College	7,043
1894	University of Massachusetts, Lowell	13,602
1895	University of Massachusetts, Dartmouth	9,302
1898	Northeastern University, Boston[2]	27,537
1899	Simmons College, Boston[3]	5,003
1905	Wentworth Institute of Technology	3,808
1906	Suffolk University	9,148
1917	Bentley University[4]	5,628
1919	Western New England College	3,710

(continued)

Year opened	Name and location of universities and colleges	Students (fall 2009)
1919	Babson College	3,445
1947	Merrimack College	2,090
1948	Brandeis University, Waltham	5,598
1964	University of Massachusetts, Boston	14,912

[1]Includes Jackson College for women. [2]Includes Forsyth Dental Center School. [3]For women only. [4]Name change from Bentley College, effective Oct. 2008.

Health
Massachusetts had 2·5 community hospital beds for every 1,000 population in 2013. In the same year there were 47·0 active physicians per 10,000 civilian population and 7·8 dentists per 10,000.

Welfare
Medicare enrolment in July 2012 totalled 1,130,305. In fiscal year 2011 a total of 1,720,444 people in Massachusetts received Medicaid. In Dec. 2014 there were 1,224,469 Old-Age, Survivors, and Disability Insurance (OASDI) beneficiaries. A total of 95,277 people were receiving payments under Temporary Assistance for Needy Families (TANF) in Dec. 2012.

Religion
The principal religious traditions in 2010 were Catholics (2,940,199 members), Mainline Protestants (308,286 members), Evangelical Protestants (224,726 members), Jews (80,502 members) and Orthodox Christians (61,544 members).

Culture

Tourism
Overseas visitors to Massachusetts (excluding those from Canada and Mexico) numbered 1,422,000 in 2011, up from 1,292,000 in 2010 and 1,105,000 in 2006.

Michigan

Key Historical Events
The French were the first European settlers, establishing a fur trade with the local Algonquian Indians in the late 17th century. They founded Sault Ste Marie in 1668 and Detroit in 1701. In 1763 Michigan passed to Britain, along with other French territory east of the Mississippi, and from Britain it passed to the USA in 1783. Britain, however, kept a force at Detroit until 1796, and recaptured Detroit in 1812. Regular American settlement did not begin until later. The Territory of Michigan (1805) had its boundaries extended after 1818 and 1834. It was admitted to the Union as a state (with its present boundaries) in 1837.

During the 19th century there was rapid industrial growth, especially in mining and metalworking. The largest groups of immigrants were British, German, Irish and Dutch. Other groups came from Scandinavia, Poland and Italy. Many settled as miners, farmers and industrial workers. The motor industry became dominant, especially in Detroit. Lake Michigan ports shipped bulk cargo of iron ore and grain.

Detroit was the capital until 1847, when that function passed to Lansing. Detroit remained, however, an important centre of flour-milling and shipping and, after the First World War, of the motor industry.

Territory and Population
Michigan is divided into two by Lake Michigan. The northern part is bounded south by the lake and by Wisconsin, west and north by Lake Superior, east by the North Channel of Lake Huron; between the two latter lakes the Canadian border runs through straits at Sault Ste Marie. The southern part is bounded in the west and north by Lake Michigan, east by Lake Huron, Ontario and Lake Erie, south by Ohio and Indiana. Total area is 96,714 sq. miles (250,487 sq. km) of which 56,539 sq. miles (146,435 sq. km) are land and 40,175 sq. miles (104,052 sq. km) water. Census population, 1 April 2010, was 9,883,640, a fall of 0·6% since 2000. Michigan was the only state whose population fell between 2000 and 2010. July 2018 estimate, 9,995,195.

Population of five federal census years was:

	White	Black	American Indian	Asian	Total	Per sq. mile
1910	2,785,247	17,115	7,519	292	2,810,173	48·9
			All others			
1980	7,872,241	1,199,023	190,814		9,262,078	162·6
1990	7,756,086	1,291,706	247,505		9,295,297	160·0
2000	7,966,053	1,412,742	559,649		9,938,444	175·0
2010	7,803,120	1,400,362	680,158		9,883,640	174·8

Of the total population in 2010, 5,035,526 were female and 7,539,572 were 18 years old or more. In 2010 the Hispanic population was 436,358, up from 323,877 in 2000 (an increase of 34·7%).

Populations of the chief cities in 2010 were: Detroit, 713,777; Grand Rapids, 188,040; Warren, 134,056; Sterling Heights, 129,699; Lansing (the capital), 114,297; Ann Arbor, 113,934; Flint, 102,434; Dearborn, 98,153. The Detroit–Warren–Livonia metropolitan area had a 2010 census population of 4,296,250.

Social Statistics
Births, 2014, 114,375 (11·5 per 1,000 population); deaths, 2014, 93,914 (9·5). Infant mortality, 2013, 7·1 per 1,000 live births. 2014: marriages, 5·8 per 1,000 population; divorces and annulments, 3·0.

Climate
Detroit, Jan. 23·5°F (–5·0°C), July 72°F (22·5°C). Annual rainfall 32" (810 mm). Grand Rapids, Jan. 22°F (–5·5°C), July 71·5°F (22·0°C). Annual rainfall 34" (860 mm). Lansing, Jan. 22°F (–5·5°C), July 70·5°F (21·5°C). Annual rainfall 29" (740 mm). Michigan belongs to the Great Lakes climate zone (see UNITED STATES: Climate).

Constitution and Government
The present constitution became effective on 1 Jan. 1964. The Senate consists of 38 members, elected for four years, and the House of Representatives of 110 members, elected for two years. Sessions are biennial.

For the 116th Congress, which convened in Jan. 2019, Michigan sends 14 members to the House of Representatives. It is represented in the Senate by Debbie Stabenow (D. 2001–25) and Gary Peters (D. 2015–21).

The capital is Lansing. The state is organized in 83 counties.

Recent Elections
In the 2016 presidential election Donald Trump took Michigan with 47·6% of the vote (Barack Obama won it in 2012).

Current Government
Governor: Gretchen Whitmer (D.), 2019–23 (salary: $159,300).
Lieut.-Governor: Garlin Gilchrist (D.), 2019–23.
Secretary of State: Jocelyn Benson (D.), since Jan. 2019.
Government Website: https://www.michigan.gov

Economy
Per capita personal income (2015) was $42,427.

Budget
In 2011 total state revenue was $64,440m. Total expenditure was $63,109m. (education, $23,146m.; public welfare, $14,927m.; hospitals, $2,522m.; highways, $2,464m.; correction, $1,663m.). Outstanding debt in 2011, $30,975m.

Performance
Gross Domestic Product by state in 2015 was $468,334m., ranking Michigan 13th in the United States. In 2015 state real GDP growth was 1·6%.

Energy and Natural Resources

Electricity
In 2015 production was 113·0bn. kWh, of which 52·9bn. kWh was from coal.

Oil and Gas

In 2014 Michigan produced 7·3m. bbls of crude petroleum; marketed production of natural gas totalled 115bn. cu. ft.

Water

The total area covered by water is 40,175 sq. miles (the second largest area covered by water after Alaska).

Minerals

Domestic non-fuel mineral output in 2009 was valued at $1,760m. according to the US Geological Survey. Output was mainly iron ore, cement, crushed stone, sand and gravel.

Agriculture

The state, formerly agricultural, is now chiefly industrial. It contained 55,000 farms in 2008 with a total area of 10·0m. acres; the average farm was 182 acres. The farm real estate average value per acre in 2009 was $3,750. Principal crops are corn, soybeans, wheat, sugar beets, dry beans, potatoes and hay. Principal fruit crops include apples, blueberries, cherries (tart and sweet), grapes, peaches and strawberries. In 2008 there were 353,000 dairy cows, 92,000 beef cows and 1·02m. pigs. Output in 2008 included 110m. lb of blueberries, 22·2m. pots of geraniums and 1·7m. cwt of black beans. Farm income in 2008: total, $6,607m.; crops, $4,078m.; livestock and products, $2,529m. The net farm income in 2008 was $2·03bn.

Forestry

Forests covered 20·4m. acres in 2013, with 2·7m. acres of national forest. In 2013, 19·4m. acres was timberland acreage. Three-quarters of the timber volume was hardwoods, principally hard and soft maples, aspen, oak and birch. Christmas trees are another important forest crop.

Fisheries

In 2012 recreational fishing licences were purchased by 930,092 residents and 204,167 non-residents. Recreational fishing revenue (2011) was estimated at $4·4bn. ($2·4bn. from retail sales, $1·4bn. in wages and salaries, and $0·6bn. in tax revenues).

Industry

Manufacturing is important; among principal products are motor vehicles and trucks, machinery, fabricated metals, primary metals, cement, chemicals, furniture, paper, foodstuffs, rubber, plastics and pharmaceuticals. In 2012 Michigan's 26,688 manufacturing establishments had 1,080,000 employees, earning $57,443m. Total value added by manufacturing in 2013 was $98,438m.

Labour

Total non-agricultural labour force in 2010 was 3,861,400. Employees by branch, 2010 (in 1,000): trade, transportation and utilities, 709; government, 636; education and health services, 617; professional and business services, 514; manufacturing, 474. The unemployment rate in Dec. 2010 was 11·1%.

International Trade

Imports and Exports

In 2015 imports into Michigan totalled $124·2bn. (up from $123·0bn. in 2014). In the same year exports from Michigan totalled $54·0bn., down from $57·6bn. in 2014. The leading source for imports in 2015 was Canada ($45·7bn.), ahead of Mexico ($44·0bn.). The leading destination for exports in 2015 was also Canada ($23·5bn.), again followed by Mexico ($11·8bn.).

Communications

Roads

In 2012 there were 122,051 miles of road (86,009 miles of rural road and 36,042 miles of urban road). Vehicle registrations in 2012 numbered 7,531,943.

Rail

In 2012 there were 3,542 miles of freight railroad in Michigan (excluding trackage rights) and a 3-mile light rail peoplemover in Detroit. There were 27 freight railroads operating in 2012. Rail traffic originating in Michigan in 2012 totalled 21·9m. tons and rail traffic terminating in the state came to 32·7m. tons.

Civil Aviation

There are major international airports at Detroit, Flint and Grand Rapids. In 2012 Michigan had 15 primary airports (commercial service airports with more than 10,000 passenger boardings annually) with a combined total of 17,892,542 enplanements, down from 18,132,602 in 2011.

Shipping

The major ports are Detroit (which handled 14·1m. short tons of cargo in 2014), Presque Isle (9·1m. short tons in 2014), St Clair and Calcite.

Social Institutions

Justice

A Civil Rights Commission was established, and its powers and duties were implemented by legislation in the extra session of 1963. Statutory enactments guaranteeing civil rights in specific areas date from 1885. The legislature has a unique one-person grand jury system. The Michigan Supreme Court consists of seven non-partisan elected justices. In Dec. 2014 there were 43,390 prisoners in state or federal correctional institutions. Capital punishment was officially abolished in 1964 but there has never been an execution in Michigan.

Education

Education is compulsory for children from six to 16 years of age. In 2012–13 there were 1,555,370 pupils and 86,154 teachers in 3,657 public schools. Total expenditure on public elementary and secondary education in 2010–11 was $19,445m.; average teacher salary was $61,560 in 2012–13. Spending per pupil in 2010–11 was $10,577.

In 2012–13 there were 116 degree-granting institutions (46 public and 70 private); there were 663,825 students in total in fall 2012 (540,242 at public institutions).

Universities and students (fall 2009):

Founded	Name	Students
1817	University of Michigan, Ann Arbor	41,674
(1956	University of Michigan, Flint	7,773)
(1959	University of Michigan, Dearborn	8,379)
1849	Eastern Michigan University	22,893
1855	Michigan State University	47,071
1868	Wayne State University	31,786
1884	Ferris State University	13,865
1885	Michigan Technological University	7,136
1892	Central Michigan University	27,247
1899	Northern Michigan University	9,428
1903	Western Michigan University	24,576
1946	Lake Superior State University	2,588
1957	Oakland University	18,918
1960	Grand Valley State University	24,408
1963	Saginaw Valley State University	10,498

Health

Michigan had 2·5 community hospital beds for every 1,000 population in 2013. In the same year there were 31·5 active physicians per 10,000 civilian population and 6·1 dentists per 10,000.

Welfare

Medicare enrolment in July 2012 totalled 1,763,430. In fiscal year 2012 a total of 2,253,486 people in Michigan received Medicaid. In Dec. 2014 there were 2,121,776 Old-Age, Survivors, and Disability Insurance (OASDI) beneficiaries. A total of 96,860 people were receiving payments under Temporary Assistance for Needy Families (TANF) in Dec. 2012.

Religion

The principal religious traditions in the state in 2010 were: Catholics, with 1,717,296 members; Evangelical Protestants, 1,277,144; Mainline Protestants, 653,898; Black Protestants, 214,114; Muslims, 120,000 (estimate).

Minnesota

Key Historical Events

Minnesota remained an American Indian territory until the middle of the 19th century, the main groups being Chippewa and Sioux. In the 17th century there had been some French exploration, but no permanent settlement. After passing under the nominal control of France, Britain and Spain, the area became part of the Louisiana Purchase and was sold to the USA in 1803.

Fort Snelling was founded in 1819. Early settlers came from other states, especially New England, to exploit the great forests. Lumbering gave way to homesteading, and the American settlers were joined by Germans, Scandinavians and Poles. Agriculture, mining and forest industries became the mainstays of the economy. Minneapolis, founded as a village in 1856, grew first as a lumber centre, processing the logs floated down the Minnesota River, and then as a centre of flour-milling and grain marketing. St Paul, its twin city across the river, became Territorial capital in 1849 and state capital in 1858. St Paul also stands at the head of navigation on the Mississippi which rises in Minnesota.

The Territory (1849) included parts of North and South Dakota, but at its admission to the Union in 1858, the state of Minnesota had its present boundaries.

Territory and Population

Minnesota is bounded north by Canada, east by Lake Superior and Wisconsin, with the Mississippi River forming the boundary in the southeast, south by Iowa, west by South and North Dakota, with the Red River forming the boundary in the northwest. Land area, 79,627 sq. miles (206,232 sq. km); water area, 7,309 sq. miles (18,930 sq. km). Census population, 1 April 2010, was 5,303,925, an increase of 7·8% since 2000. July 2018 estimate, 5,611,179.

Population in five census years was:

	White	Black	American Indian	Asian	Total	Per sq. mile
1910	2,059,227	7,084	9,053	344	2,075,708	25·7
			All others			
1980	3,935,770	53,344	86,856		4,075,970	51·4
1990	4,130,395	94,944	149,760		4,375,099	55·0
2000	4,400,282	171,731	347,466		4,919,479	61·8
2010	4,524,062	274,412	505,451		5,303,925	66·6

Of the total population in 2010, 2,671,793 were female and 4,019,862 were 18 years old or older. In 2010 the Hispanic population was 250,258, up from 143,382 in 2000 (an increase of 74·5%).

The largest cities (with 2010 census population) are Minneapolis (382,578), St Paul (the capital; 285,068), Rochester (106,769), Duluth (86,265) and Bloomington (82,893). The Minneapolis–St Paul–Bloomington metropolitan area had a 2010 census population of 3,279,833.

Social Statistics

Births, 2014, 69,904 (12·8 per 1,000 population); deaths, 2014, 41,445 (7·6). Infant mortality, 2013, 5·1 per 1,000 live births. Marriages, 2014, 5·9 per 1,000 population. Same-sex marriage was legalized in May 2013, with effect from Aug. 2013.

Climate

Duluth, Jan. 8°F (−13·3°C), July 63°F (17·2°C). Annual rainfall 29" (719 mm). Minneapolis–St. Paul, Jan. 12°F (−11·1°C), July 71°F (21·7°C). Annual rainfall 26" (656 mm). Minnesota belongs to the Great Lakes climate zone (see UNITED STATES: Climate).

Constitution and Government

The original constitution dated from 1857; it was extensively amended and given a new structure in 1974. The Legislature consists of a Senate of 67 members, elected for four years, and a House of Representatives of 134 members, elected for two years. It meets for 120 days within each two years.

For the 116th Congress, which convened in Jan. 2019, Minnesota sends eight members to the House of Representatives. It is represented in the Senate by Amy Klobuchar (D. 2007–25) and Tina Smith (D. 2018–21). Smith filled the seat formerly held by Al Franken following his resignation in Jan. 2018.

The capital is St Paul. There are 87 counties.

Recent Elections

In the 2016 presidential election Hillary Clinton took Minnesota with 46·9% of the vote (Barack Obama won it in 2012).

Current Government

Governor: Tim Walz (Democratic–Farmer–Labor), 2019–23 (salary: $127,629).

Lieut.-Governor: Peggy Flanagan (Democratic–Farmer–Labor), 2019–23.

Secretary of State: Steve Simon (Democratic–Farmer–Labor), since Jan. 2015.

Government Website: https://www.mn.gov/portal

Economy

Per capita personal income (2015) was $50,541.

Budget

In 2011 total state revenue was $45,684m. Total expenditure was $38,488m. (education, $12,406m.; public welfare, $10,872m.; highways, $2,565m.; government administration, $905m.; natural resources, $691m.). Outstanding debt in 2011, $12,897m.

Performance

In 2015 Gross Domestic Product by state was $328,340m., ranking Minnesota 17th in the United States. In 2015 state real GDP growth was 1·9%.

Energy and Natural Resources

Water

The total area covered by water is 7,309 sq. miles, of which 4,763 sq. miles are inland.

Minerals

The iron ore and taconite industry is important in the USA. Production of usable iron ore in 2007 was 38·8m. tons, value $2,320m. Other important minerals are sand and gravel, crushed and dimension stone, clays and peat. Total value of non-fuel mineral production in 2009 was $2,050m.

Agriculture

In 2007 there were 80,992 farms with a total area of 26·92m. acres; the average farm was of 332 acres. Average value of land and buildings per acre, 2007, $2,569. Farm income, 2009: from crops, $8,423m.; and from livestock and products, $4,902m. The net farm income in 2009 was $3,020m. Important products: corn, soybeans, sugar beets, spring wheat, processing sweetcorn, oats, dry milk, cheese, mink, turkeys, wild rice, butter, eggs, flaxseed, dairy cows, barley, swine, cattle for market, honey, potatoes, rye, chickens, sunflower seed and dry edible beans. In 2007 there were 2·40m. cattle (460,000 dairy cows), 7·65m. hogs and pigs and 144,600 sheep and lambs.

Forestry

In 2013 Minnesota had 17,378,000 acres of forested land, including 2,601,000 acres of national forest.

Industry

In 2012 the state's 16,368 manufacturing establishments had 664,000 employees, earning $34,528m. Total value added by manufacturing in 2013 was $55,721m.

Labour

Total non-agricultural employment, 2010, 2,637,000. Employees by branch, 2010 (in 1,000): trade, transportation and utilities, 490; education and health services, 458; government, 417; professional and business services, 313; manufacturing, 292. In Dec. 2010 the unemployment rate was 6·9%.

International Trade

Imports and Exports

In 2015 imports into Minnesota totalled $28·6bn. (down from $34·7bn. in 2014). In the same year exports from Minnesota totalled $20·0bn., down from $21·4bn. in 2014. The leading source for imports in 2015 was China ($10·0bn.), ahead of Canada ($8·6bn.). The leading destination for exports in 2015 was Canada ($4·5bn.), followed by Mexico ($2·4bn.).

Communications

Roads

In 2012 there were 138,832 miles of public roads (117,931 miles rural). There were 4,857,239 registered motor vehicles in 2012.

Rail

In 2012 there were 4,450 miles of freight railroad (excluding trackage rights). There were 18 freight railroads operating in 2012. Rail traffic originating in Minnesota in 2012 totalled 90·3m. tons and rail traffic terminating in the state came to 70·3m. tons.

Civil Aviation

In 2011 Minnesota had seven primary airports (commercial service airports with more than 10,000 passenger boardings annually) with a combined total of 16,221,481 enplanements, up from 15,846,286 in 2010. By far the busiest airport is Minneapolis–St Paul International (MSP), with 15,895,653 enplanements in 2011.

Social Institutions

Justice

In Dec. 2014 there were 10,637 federal and state prisoners. Capital punishment was abolished in 1911.

Education

In 2012–13 there were 845,404 students and 53,585 teachers in public elementary and secondary schools; there were 2,444 public schools in total including charter schools. There were 87,620 students enrolled in 500 private schools with 6,420 teachers in fall 2011.

The Minnesota State Colleges and Universities System (created in 1995) is the largest single provider of higher education in the state. The system includes 31 institutions (seven state universities and 24 technical and community colleges) spanning 54 campuses and serving over 435,000 students annually. In fall 2012 enrolled students at public degree-granting institutions numbered 272,290. The seven state universities are: St Cloud State University, with 18,123 students in fall 2009; Minnesota, Mankato, 14,955; Winona, 8,657; Minnesota, Moorhead, 7,510; Metropolitan State University (in Minneapolis and St Paul), 7,354; Bemidji State University, 5,175; Southwest Minnesota State University (in Marshall), 6,740. Minnesota State University's Akita campus in Japan closed in 2003.

The University of Minnesota (founded in 1851) has five campuses at Crookston, Duluth, Morris, Rochester and Twin Cities.

Health

Minnesota had 2·7 community hospital beds for every 1,000 population in 2013. In the same year there were 31·1 active physicians per 10,000 civilian population and 6·1 dentists per 10,000.

Welfare

Medicare enrolment in July 2012 totalled 837,750. In fiscal year 2012 a total of 1,070,994 people in Minnesota received Medicaid. In Dec. 2014 there were 965,018 Old-Age, Survivors, and Disability Insurance (OASDI) beneficiaries. A total of 46,900 people were receiving payments under Temporary Assistance for Needy Families (TANF) in Dec. 2012.

Religion

The principal religious traditions in the state in 2010 were: Catholics, with 1,150,367 members; Mainline Protestants, 974,156; Evangelical Protestants, 744,910; Latter-day Saints (Mormons), 31,569; Jews, 23,940.

Mississippi

Key Historical Events

Mississippi was one of the territories claimed by France and ceded to Britain in 1763. The indigenous people were Choctaw and Natchez. French settlers at first traded amicably, but in the course of three wars (1716, 1723 and 1729) the French allied with the Choctaw to drive the Natchez out. The Natchez massacred the settlers of Fort Rosalie, which the French had founded in 1716 and which was later renamed Natchez.

In 1783 the area became part of the USA except for Natchez which was under Spanish control until 1798. The United States then made it the capital of the Territory of Mississippi. The boundaries of the Territory were extended in 1804 and again in 1812. In 1817 it was divided into two territories, with the western part becoming the state of Mississippi. (The eastern part became the state of Alabama in 1819.) The city of Jackson was laid out in 1822 as the new state capital.

A cotton plantation economy developed, based on black slave labour and by 1860 the majority of the population was black. Mississippi joined the Confederacy during the Civil War. After defeat and reconstruction there was a return to rigid segregation and denial of black rights. This situation lasted until the 1960s. There was a black majority until the Second World War, when out-migration began to change the pattern. By 1990 about 35% of the population was black, and manufacture (especially clothing and textiles) had become the largest single employer of labour.

Mississippi suffered widespread damage and loss of life after Hurricane Katrina struck the Gulf Coast on 31 Aug. 2005.

Territory and Population

Mississippi is bounded in the north by Tennessee, east by Alabama, south by the Gulf of Mexico and Louisiana, and west by the Mississippi River forming the boundary with Louisiana and Arkansas. Land area, 46,923 sq. miles (121,531 sq. km); water area, 1,509 sq. miles (3,907 sq. km). Census population, 1 April 2010, was 2,967,297, an increase of 4·3% since 2000. July 2018 estimate, 2,986,530.

Population of five federal census years was:

	White	Black	American Indian	Asian	Total	Per sq. mile
1910	786,111	1,009,487	1,253	263	1,797,114	38·8
			All others			
1980	1,615,190	887,206	18,242		2,520,638	53·0
1990	1,633,461	915,057	24,698		2,573,216	54·8
2000	1,746,099	1,033,809	64,750		2,844,658	60·6
2010	1,754,684	1,098,385	114,228		2,967,297	63·2

Of the total population in 2010, 1,526,057 were female and 2,211,742 were 18 years old or older. In 2010 Mississippi's Hispanic population was 81,481, up from 39,569 in 2000 (an increase of 105·9%).

The largest city (2010 census) is Jackson (the capital), 173,514. Others (2010 census) are: Gulfport, 67,793; Southaven, 48,982; Hattiesburg, 45,989; Biloxi, 44,054; Meridian, 41,148; Tupelo, 34,546; Greenville, 34,400; Olive Branch, 33,484; Horn Lake, 26,066; Clinton, 25,216.

Social Statistics

2014: births, 38,736 (12·9 per 1,000 population); deaths, 2014, 30,557 (10·2 per 1,000 population). Infant mortality, 2013, 9·6 per 1,000 live births. 2014: marriages, 6·9 per 1,000 population; divorces and annulments, 3·4.

Mississippi has the highest proportion of people living in poverty of any state, at 21·8% in 2010.

Climate

Jackson, Jan. 45°F (7·2°C), July 81°F (27·2°C). Annual rainfall 56" (1,422 mm). Vicksburg, Jan. 47°F (8·3°C), July 82°F (28·0°C). Annual rainfall 58" (1,473 mm). Mississippi belongs to the Central Plains climate zone (*see* UNITED STATES: Climate).

Constitution and Government

The present constitution was adopted in 1890 without ratification by the electorate; there were 123 amendments by 2009.

The Legislature consists of a Senate (52 members) and a House of Representatives (122 members), both elected for four years. Electors are all citizens who have resided in the state, in the county and in the election district for 30 days prior to the election and have been registered according to law.

For the 116th Congress, which convened in Jan. 2019, Mississippi sends four members to the House of Representatives. It is represented in the Senate by Roger Wicker (R. 2007–25) and Cindy Hyde-Smith (R. 2018–21). Hyde-Smith was appointed by Governor Phil Bryant to fill the seat formerly held by Thad Cochran, who had resigned for health reasons.

The capital is Jackson; there are 82 counties.

Recent Elections

In the 2016 presidential election Donald Trump took Mississippi with 58·3% of the vote (Mitt Romney won it in 2012).

Current Government

Governor: Phil Bryant (R.), 2016–20 (salary: $122,160).
  Lieut.-Governor: Tate Reeves (R.), 2016–20.
    Secretary of State: Delbert Hosemann (R.), since Jan. 2008.
Government Website: https://www.ms.gov

Economy

Per capita personal income (2015) was $35,444, the lowest in the country. Mississippi also had the lowest average household income in 2015, at $40,593.

Budget

In 2011 total state revenue was $23,606m. Total expenditure was $20,157m. (education, $5,519m.; public welfare, $5,437m.; highways, $1,378m.; hospitals, $1,073m.; health, $434m.). Outstanding debt in 2011, $6,768m.

Performance

Gross Domestic Product by state in 2015 was $105,819m., ranking Mississippi 36th in the United States. In 2015 state real GDP growth was 0·5%.

Energy and Natural Resources

Oil and Gas

Petroleum and natural gas account for about 90% (by value) of mineral production. Output of petroleum, 2010, was 21m. bbls and of natural gas 86bn. cu. ft. There are three oil refineries.

Water

The total area covered by water is 1,509 sq. miles.

Minerals

The value of domestic non-fuel mineral production in 2010 was $183m.

Agriculture

Agriculture is the leading industry of the state because of the semi-tropical climate and a rich productive soil. In 2010 farms numbered 42,400 with an area of 11·2m. acres. Average size of farm was 263 acres. This compares with an average farm size of 176 acres in 1967. Average value of farm land and farm buildings per acre in 2011 was $2,120.

Cash income from all crops and livestock in 2010 was $4,890m. Cash income from crops was $1,914m., and from livestock and products $2,975m. The net farm income in 2010 was $1,407m. The chief product is soybeans, cash income (2010) $856m. from 1,980,000 acres producing 76,230,000 bu. Cotton, rice, corn, hay, wheat, oats, sorghum, peanuts, pecans, sweet potatoes, peaches, blueberries, other vegetables, nursery and forest products continue to contribute.

On 1 Jan. 2010 there were 900,000 head of cattle and calves on Mississippi farms. In Dec. 2010 dairy cows totalled 17,000; beef cows, 495,000; hogs and pigs, 385,000. Of cash income from livestock and products, 2010, $169m. was credited to cattle and calves. Cash income from poultry and eggs, 2010, totalled $2·5bn.; swine, $96m.; dairy products, $74m.

Forestry

In 2010 income from forestry amounted to $1·04bn. Output (2010): pine logs 897m. bd ft; hardwood lumber, 319m. bd ft; pulpwood, 5·08m. cords. There were 19·5m. acres of forest in 2013, with 1·3m. acres of national forest area.

Fisheries

Commercial catch, in 2010, totalled 111m. lb of fish with a value of $21·9m. Mississippi had aquaculture sales worth $203·6m. in 2013, ranking it second behind Washington.

Industry

In 2012 the state's 5,640 manufacturing establishments had 338,000 employees, earning $14,485m. The average annual wage was $42,863. Total value added by manufacturing in 2013 was $22,522m.

Labour

In 2010 total non-agricultural employment was 1,084,900. Employees by branch, 2010 (in 1,000): government, 249; services, 168; wholesale and retail trade, 167; manufacturing, 137. The unemployment rate in Dec. 2010 was 10·2%.

International Trade

Imports and Exports

In 2015 imports into Mississippi totalled $14·1bn. (down from $17·3bn. in 2014). In the same year exports from Mississippi totalled $10·8bn., down from $11·5bn. in 2014. The leading source for imports in 2015 was China ($3·9bn.), ahead of Mexico ($1·4bn.). The leading destination for exports in 2015 was Canada ($2·0bn.), followed by Mexico ($1·1bn.).

Communications

Roads

The state as of 1 July 2011 maintained 14,609 miles of highways, of which 14,606 miles were paved. In fiscal year 2011, 1·8m. passenger vehicles and pick-ups were registered.

Rail

In 2012 there were 2,452 miles of freight railroad (excluding trackage rights). There were 27 freight railroads operating in 2012. Rail traffic originating in Mississippi in 2012 totalled 7·7m. tons and rail traffic terminating in the state came to 13·6m. tons.

Civil Aviation

There were 80 public airports in 2010, 73 of them general aviation airports. There were 1,231,879 passenger enplanements statewide in 2010.

Social Institutions

Justice

The death penalty is authorized; there were six executions in 2012 but none since. In Dec. 2014 there were 18,793 federal and state prisoners.

Education

Attendance at school is compulsory as laid down in the Education Reform Act of 1982. The public elementary and secondary schools in 2009–10 had 447,806 pupils and 33,210 classroom teachers. In 2009–10 teachers' average salary was $42,308. The expenditure per pupil in average daily attendance, 2009–10, was $8,930.

There are 18 universities and senior colleges, of which eight are state-supported. In fall 2010 the University of Mississippi, Oxford had 1,846 faculty and 19,954 students; Mississippi State University, Starkville, 1,289 faculty and 19,725 students; Mississippi University for Women, Columbus, 174 faculty and 2,730 students; University of Southern Mississippi, Hattiesburg, 885 faculty and 17,254 students; Jackson State University, Jackson, 504 faculty and 9,615 students; Delta State University, Cleveland, 254 faculty and 4,416 students; Alcorn State University, Lorman, 226 faculty and 3,682 students; Mississippi Valley State University, Itta Bena, 154 faculty and 2,840 students. State support for the universities (2010–11) was $400,842,200.

Community and junior colleges had (2009–10) 80,550 full-time equivalent students and 2,534 full-time instructors. The state appropriation for junior colleges, 2009–10, was $168,422,707.

Health

Mississippi had 4·3 community hospital beds for every 1,000 population in 2013. In the same year there were 19·5 active physicians per 10,000 civilian population and 4·3 dentists per 10,000.

Welfare

Medicare enrolment in July 2012 totalled 525,530. The Division of Medicaid paid (fiscal year 2011) $3·62bn. for medical services, including $617·5m. for hospital services, $727m. for skilled nursing home care and $302m. for drugs. There were 66,990 persons eligible for Aged Medicaid benefits as of 30 June 2011 and 165,523 persons eligible for Disabled Medicaid benefits. In the fiscal year 2010–11, 11,609 families with 17,896 dependent children received $1,617,869 in the Temporary Assistance to Needy Families programme. The average monthly payment was $139·85 per family or $66·26 per recipient.

Religion

The principal religious traditions in 2010 were: Evangelical Protestants, with 1,168,450 members; Mainline Protestants, 244,121; Black Protestants, 182,556; Catholics, 112,488; Latter-day Saints (Mormons), 22,308.

Culture

Tourism

Total receipts in 2010 amounted to $5·97bn.; an estimated 12m. overnight tourists visited the state.

Missouri

Key Historical Events

Territory of several American Indian groups, including the Missouri, the area was not settled by European immigrants until the 18th century. The French founded Ste Genevieve in 1735, partly as a lead-mining community. St Louis was founded as a fur-trading base in 1764. The area was nominally under Spanish rule from 1770 until 1800 when it passed back to France. In 1803 the USA bought it as part of the Louisiana Purchase.

St Louis was made the capital of the whole Louisiana Territory in 1805, and of a new Missouri Territory in 1812. In that year American immigration increased markedly. The Territory became a state in 1821. Bitter disputes between slave-owning and anti-slavery factions led to the former obtaining statehood without the prohibition of slavery required of all other new states north of latitude 36° 30'. This was achieved by the Missouri Compromise of 1820. The Compromise was repealed in 1854 and declared unconstitutional in 1857. During the Civil War the state held to the Union side, although St Louis was placed under martial law.

With the development of steamboat traffic on the Missouri and Mississippi rivers, and the expansion of railways, the state became the transport hub of all western movement. Lead and other mining remained important, as did livestock farming. European settlers came from Germany, Britain and Ireland.

Territory and Population

Missouri is bounded north by Iowa, east by the Mississippi River forming the boundary with Illinois and Kentucky, south by Arkansas, southeast by Tennessee, southwest by Oklahoma, west by Kansas and Nebraska, with the Missouri River forming the boundary in the northwest. Total area is 69,707 sq. miles (180,540 sq. km) of which 68,742 sq. miles (178,040 sq. km) are land.

Census population, 1 April 2010, was 5,988,927, an increase of 7·0% since 2000. July 2018 estimate, 6,126,452.

Population of five federal census years was:

	White	Black	American Indian	Asian	Total	Per sq. mile
1930	3,403,876	223,840	578	1,073	3,629,367	52·4
			All others			
1980	4,345,521	514,276	56,889		4,916,686	71·3
1990	4,486,228	548,208	82,637		5,117,073	74·3
2000	4,748,083	629,391	217,737		5,595,211	81·2
2010	4,958,770	693,391	336,766		5,988,927	87·1

Of the total population in 2010, 3,055,450 were female and 4,563,491 were 18 years old or older. In 2010 Missouri's Hispanic population was 212,470, up from 118,592 in 2000 (an increase of 79·2%).

The principal cities at the 2010 census were:

Kansas City	459,787
St Louis	319,294
Springfield	159,498
Independence	116,830
Columbia	108,500
Lee's Summit	91,364
O'Fallon	79,329
St Joseph	76,780

(*continued*)

St Charles	65,794
Blue Springs	52,575
St Peters	52,575
Florissant	52,158

The capital, Jefferson City, had a population in 2010 of 43,079.

Largest metropolitan areas, 2010: St Louis, 2,812,896; Kansas City, 2,035,334; Springfield, 436,712.

Social Statistics

Births, 2014, 75,360 (12·4 per 1,000 population); deaths, 2014, 58,320 (9·6). Infant mortality, 2013, 6·5 per 1,000 live births. 2014: marriages, 6·7 per 1,000 population; divorces and annulments, 3·3.

Climate

Kansas City, Jan. 30°F (−1·1°C), July 79°F (26·1°C). Annual rainfall 38" (947 mm). St Louis, Jan. 32°F (0°C), July 79°F (26·1°C). Annual rainfall 40" (1,004 mm). Missouri belongs to the Central Plains climate zone (*see* UNITED STATES: Climate).

Constitution and Government

A new constitution, the fourth, was adopted on 27 Feb. 1945; it has had 108 amendments in the meantime. The General Assembly consists of a Senate of 34 members elected for four years (half for re-election every two years), and a House of Representatives of 163 members elected for two years. The Governor and Lieut.-Governor are elected for four years.

For the 116th Congress, which convened in Jan. 2019, Missouri sends eight members to the House of Representatives. It is represented in the Senate by Roy Blunt (R. 2011–23) and Josh Hawley (R. 2019–25).

Jefferson City is the state capital. The state is divided into 114 counties and the city of St Louis.

Recent Elections

In the 2016 presidential election Donald Trump took Missouri with 57·1% of the vote (Mitt Romney won it in 2012).

Current Government

Governor: Mike Parson (R.), 2018–21 (salary: $133,821).

  Lieut.-Governor: Mike Kehoe (R.), 2018–21.

  Secretary of State: Jay Ashcroft (R.), since Jan. 2017.

Government Website: https://www.mo.gov

Economy

Per capita personal income (2015) was $42,752.

Budget

In 2011 total state revenue was $38,607m. Total expenditure was $30,647m. (education, $8,855m.; public welfare, $7,587m.; highways, $2,033m.; hospitals, $1,493m.; health, $1,402m.). Outstanding debt in 2011, $20,682m.

Performance

In 2015 Gross Domestic Product by state was $294,491m., ranking Missouri 21st in the United States. In 2015 state real GDP growth was 1·7%.

Energy and Natural Resources

Water

The total area covered by water is 965 sq. miles.

Minerals

The three leading mineral commodities are lead, Portland cement and crushed stone. Value of domestic non-fuel mineral production was $1,810m. in 2009.

Agriculture

In 2012 there were 106,500 farms in Missouri producing crops and livestock on more than 29m. acres; the average farm had 269 acres. In the same year Missouri farmers produced 5·4m. acres of soybeans, 3·6m. acres of corn, 790,000 acres of winter wheat, 350,000 acres of cotton and 180,000 acres of rice; they raised 3·9m. cattle and 2·8m. hogs and pigs. Missouri's cash receipts exceeded $9·5bn. in 2012, with $5·43bn. from crops and $4·07bn. from livestock.

Forestry
The state had a forested area of 15,452,450 acres in 2013, of which 1,508,156 acres were national forest.

Industry
In 2012 the state's 14,242 manufacturing establishments had 559,000 employees, earning $26,599m. Total value added by manufacturing in 2013 was $46,364m.

Labour
Total non-agricultural employment, 2010, 2,647,000. Employees by branch, 2010 (in 1,000): trade, transportation and utilities, 510; government, 451; education and health services, 406; professional and business services, 319; leisure and hospitality, 271. The unemployment rate was 9·6% in Dec. 2010.

International Trade

Imports and Exports
In 2015 imports into Missouri totalled $18·5bn. (up from $18·3bn. in 2014). In the same year exports from Missouri totalled $13·6bn., down from $14·2bn. in 2014. The leading source for imports in 2015 was China ($4·8bn.), ahead of Canada ($3·4bn.). The leading destination for exports in 2015 was Canada ($4·5bn.), followed by Mexico ($2·5bn.).

Communications

Roads
In 2012 there were 131,978 miles of road (107,926 miles rural) and 5,508,795 registered motor vehicles.

Rail
In 2012 there were 3,957 miles of freight railroad (excluding trackage rights). There were 17 freight railroads operating in 2012. Rail traffic originating in Missouri in 2012 totalled 16·7m. tons and rail traffic terminating in the state came to 68·9m. tons. There is a light rail line in St Louis.

Civil Aviation
There were five primary airports—commercial service airports with more than 10,000 passenger boardings annually—in 2011 with a combined total of 11,587,550 enplanements, up from 11,414,476 in 2010. The busiest airports are Kansas City International and Lambert-St Louis International.

Social Institutions

Justice
In Dec. 2014 there were 31,942 federal and state prisoners. The death penalty was reinstated in 1978. Executions were suspended between June 2006 and June 2007. There was one execution in both 2016 and 2017 but none in 2018. The Missouri Law Enforcement Assistance Council was created in 1969 for law reform. With reorganization of state government in 1974 the duties of the Council were delegated to the Department of Public Safety. The Department of Corrections was organized as a separate department of State by an Act of the Legislature in 1981.

Education
School attendance is compulsory for children from seven to 16 years. In 2012–13 there were 2,419 public schools (kindergarten through grade 12) with 917,900 pupils and 66,248 teachers. Total expenditure on public elementary and secondary education in 2010–11 was $10,072m.; teacher salaries averaged $47,517 in 2012–13. Spending per pupil in 2010–11 was $9,461.

The higher education system in Missouri is an informal, loose federation of institutions, comprised of distinct sectors and numerous campuses, centres and off-campus locations. In 2013 there were ten public four-year universities with a total fall enrolment of 149,354 (including the University of Missouri with 75,272 students at four campuses), 13 public two-year colleges with a total fall enrolment of 104,084 and a state technical college with a fall enrolment of 1,293 for a total of 254,731 enrolled students. In addition, there are 25 comprehensive independent, not-for profit universities and colleges with a total fall 2013 enrolment of 134,467 and 155 private career or proprietary schools certified to operate by the Coordinating Board for Higher Education with an enrolment of over 70,000 students.

Health
Missouri had 3·1 community hospital beds for every 1,000 population in 2013. In the same year there were 28·9 active physicians per 10,000 civilian population and 4·8 dentists per 10,000.

Welfare
Medicare enrolment in July 2012 totalled 1,060,077. In fiscal year 2012 a total of 1,151,473 people in Missouri received Medicaid. In Dec. 2014 there were 1,246,269 Old-Age, Survivors, and Disability Insurance (OASDI) beneficiaries. A total of 80,293 people were receiving payments under Temporary Assistance for Needy Families (TANF) in Dec. 2012.

Religion
The principal religious traditions in 2010 were: Evangelical Protestants, with 1,518,847 members; Catholics, 724,315; Mainline Protestants, 462,246; Black Protestants, 93,900; Latter-day Saints (Mormons), 92,248.

Montana

Key Historical Events
Originally the territory of many American Indian hunters including the Sioux, Cheyenne and Chippewa, Montana was not settled by American colonists until the 19th century. The area passed to the USA with the Louisiana Purchase of 1803, but the area west of the Rockies was disputed with Britain until 1846. Trappers and fur-traders were the first immigrants, and the fortified trading post at Fort Benton (1846) became the first permanent settlement. Colonization increased when gold was found in 1862. Montana was created a separate Territory (out of Idaho and Dakota Territories) in 1864. In 1866 large-scale grazing of sheep and cattle provoked violent confrontation with the indigenous people whose hunting lands were invaded. American Indian wars led to the defeat of federal forces at Little Bighorn in 1876 and at Big Hole Basin in 1877, but by 1880 the American Indians had been moved to reservations. Montana became a state in 1889.

Helena, the capital, was founded as a mining town in the 1860s. In the early 20th century there were many European immigrants who settled as farmers or as copper-miners, especially at Butte.

Territory and Population
Montana is bounded north by Canada, east by North and South Dakota, south by Wyoming and west by Idaho and the Bitterroot Range of the Rocky Mountains. Land area, 145,546 sq. miles (376,962 sq. km); water area, 1,494 sq. miles (3,869 sq. km). In 2010 American Indian lands covered 13,171 sq. miles (reservations plus off-reservation trust land). Census population, 1 April 2010, was 989,415, an increase of 9·7% since 2000. July 2018 estimate, 1,062,305.

Population in five census years was:

	White	Black	American Indian/ Alaska Native	Asian	Total (including others)	Per sq. mile
1910	360,580	1,834	10,745	2,870	376,053	2·6
1980	740,148	1,786	37,270	2,503	786,690	5·3
1990	741,111	2,381	47,679	4,259	799,065	5·4
2000	817,229	2,692	56,068	5,161	902,195	6·2
2010	884,961	4,027	62,555	6,253	989,415	6·8

Of the total population in 2010, 496,667 were male and 765,852 were 18 years old or older. Median age, 39·8 years. Households, 409,607. In 2010 Montana's Hispanic population was 28,565, up from 18,081 in 2000 (an increase of 58·0%).

The largest cities, 2010, are Billings, 104,170; Missoula, 66,788; Great Falls, 58,505; Bozeman, 37,280; Butte-Silver Bow, 33,525; Helena (capital), 28,190; Kalispell, 19,927.

Social Statistics
Births, 2014, 12,432 (12·1 per 1,000 population); deaths, 2014, 9,381 (9·2). Infant mortality rate, 2013, 5·6 per 1,000 live births. 2014: marriages, 7·9 per 1,000 population; divorces and annulments, 3·4. Same-sex marriage became legal in Nov. 2014.

Climate

Helena, Jan. 18°F (−7·8°C), July 69°F (20·6°C). Annual rainfall 13" (325 mm). Montana belongs to the Mountain States climate zone (*see* UNITED STATES: Climate).

Constitution and Government

A new constitution came into force on 1 July 1973. The Senate consists of 50 senators, elected for four years, one-half at each biennial election. The 100 members of the House of Representatives are elected for two years.

For the 116th Congress, which convened in Jan. 2019, Montana sends one member to the House of Representatives. It is represented in the Senate by Jon Tester (D. 2007–25) and Steve Daines (R. 2015–21).

The capital is Helena. The state is divided into 56 counties.

Recent Elections

In the 2016 presidential election Donald Trump took Montana with 56·5% of the vote (Mitt Romney won it in 2012).

Current Government

Governor: Steve Bullock (D.), 2017–21 (salary: $115,505).
  Lieut.-Governor: Mike Cooney (D.), 2017–21.
    Secretary of State: Corey Stapleton (R.), since Jan. 2017.
Government Website: https://www.mt.gov

Economy

Per capita personal income (2015) was $41,280.

Budget

In 2011 total state revenue was $7,951m. Total expenditure was $7,105m. (education, $1,841m.; public welfare, $1,390m.; highways, $709m.; government administration, $420m.; natural resources, $260m.). Outstanding debt in 2011, $4,267m.

Performance

Gross Domestic Product by state in 2015 was $45,237m., ranking Montana 48th in the United States. In 2015 state real GDP growth was 2·0%.

Energy and Natural Resources

Oil and Gas

Montana has vast technically recoverable oil reserves in the northeast of the state in an area known as the Bakken Formation. In 2014 Montana produced 29·9m. bbls of crude petroleum; marketed production of natural gas totalled 60bn. cu. ft.

Water

The total area covered by water is 1,494 sq. miles.

Minerals

The total value of non-fuel mineral production for 2009 was $982m. Principal minerals include copper, gold, platinum-group metals, molybdenum and silver. Production of coal (2009) was 39·5m. short tons.

Agriculture

In 2007 there were 29,524 farms and ranches with an area of 61·39m. acres. Large-scale farming predominates; in 2007 the average size per farm was 2,079 acres. The average value per acre in 2007 was $775. Area harvested, 2007, 9,163,867 acres, including 5·1m. acres of wheat.

The chief crops are wheat, hay, barley, oats, sugar beets, potatoes, corn, dry beans and cherries. Wheat production in 2007 totalled 147·5m. bu., a figure exceeded only by North Dakota and Kansas. Farm income, 2009: from crops, $1,516m.; and from livestock and products, $1,049m. In 2007 there were 2·59m. cattle and calves, 182,000 hogs and pigs and 272,000 sheep and lambs. The net farm income in 2009 was $248m.

Forestry

In 2012 there were 25·60m. acres of forested land with 15·31m. acres in ten national forests.

Industry

In 2012 the state's 3,282 manufacturing establishments had 40,000 employees, earning $1,750m. Total value added by manufacturing in 2013 was $3,592m.

Labour

Total non-agricultural employment, 2010, 428,000. Employees by branch, 2010 (in 1,000): government, 91; trade, transportation and utilities, 87; education and health services, 64; leisure and hospitality, 56; professional and business services, 39. In Dec. 2010 the unemployment rate was 7·4%.

International Trade

Imports and Exports

In 2015 imports from Montana totalled $4,063m. (down from $6,238m. in 2014). In the same year exports totalled $1,404m., down from $1,545m. in 2014. The leading source for imports in 2015 was Canada ($3,505m.), ahead of Germany ($152m.).The leading destination for exports in 2015 was also Canada ($523m.), followed by South Korea ($172m.).

Communications

Roads

In 2012 there were a total of 74,905 miles of road comprising 3,183 miles of urban road and 71,722 miles of rural road. There were 1,329,735 registered motor vehicles.

Rail

In 2012 there were 3,200 miles of freight railroad (excluding trackage rights). There were eight freight railroads operating in 2012. Rail traffic originating in Montana in 2012 totalled 38·3m. tons and rail traffic terminating in the state came to 4·8m. tons.

Civil Aviation

There were seven primary airports—commercial service airports with more than 10,000 passenger boardings annually—in 2011 with a combined total of 1,570,469 enplanements, up from 1,496,777 in 2010.

Social Institutions

Justice

In Dec. 2014 there were 3,699 prison inmates. The death penalty is authorized; there was one execution in 2006, the first since 1998, but none since.

Education

In 2012–13 the 827 public elementary and secondary schools had 142,908 pupils and 10,200 teachers. Total expenditure on public school education in 2010–11 was $1,653m.; average teacher salary was $49,999 in 2012–13. Spending per pupil in 2010–11 was $10,719.

In fall 2012 there were 53,254 students enrolled at 22 degree-granting institutions (17 public). The Montana State University System (created in 1994) is comprised of 16 public universities and colleges, including (fall 2014 enrolment): Montana State University at Bozeman (14,982 students), founded in 1893; the University of Montana at Missoula, founded in 1893 (13,952); Montana State University-Billings (4,768); Montana Tech at Butte (2,085); Great Falls College Montana State University (1,772); Helena College University of Montana at Helena (1,564); the University of Montana-Western at Dillon (1,375); and Montana State University-Northern at Havre (1,230). The private University of Great Falls (founded in 1932) had 1,117 students in fall 2014.

Health

Montana had 3·7 community hospital beds for every 1,000 population in 2013. In the same year there were 23·1 active physicians per 10,000 civilian population and 5·9 dentists per 10,000.

Welfare

Medicare enrolment in July 2012 totalled 181,881. In fiscal year 2012 a total of 140,283 people in Montana received Medicaid. In Dec. 2014 there were 212,535 Old-Age, Survivors, and Disability Insurance (OASDI) beneficiaries. A total of 8,061 people were receiving payments under Temporary Assistance for Needy Families (TANF) in Dec. 2012.

Religion

The principal religious traditions in 2010 were: Catholics, with 127,612 members; Evangelical Protestants, 121,064; Mainline Protestants, 76,869; Latter-day Saints (Mormons), 47,380.

Nebraska

Key Historical Events

The Nebraska region was first reached by Europeans from Mexico under the Spanish general Coronado in 1541. It was ceded by France to Spain in 1763, returned to France in 1801, and sold by Napoleon to the USA as part of the Louisiana Purchase in 1803. During the 1840s the Platte River valley was the trail for thousands of pioneers' wagons heading for Oregon and California. The need to serve and protect the trail led to the creation of Nebraska as a Territory in 1854. In 1862 the Homestead Act opened the area for settlement, but colonization was slow until the Union Pacific Railroad was completed in 1869. Omaha, developed as the starting point of the Union Pacific, became one of the largest railway towns in the country.

Nebraska became a state in 1867, with approximately its present boundaries except that it later received small areas from the Dakotas. Many early settlers were from Europe, brought in by railway-company schemes, but from the late 1880s eastern Nebraska suffered catastrophic drought. Crop and stock farming recovered but crop growing was only established in the west by means of irrigation.

Territory and Population

Nebraska is bounded in the north by South Dakota, with the Missouri River forming the boundary in the northeast and the boundary with Iowa and Missouri to the east, south by Kansas, southwest by Colorado and west by Wyoming. Total area is 77,348 sq. miles (200,330 sq. km) of which 76,824 sq. miles (198,974 sq. km) are land. Census population, 1 April 2010, was 1,826,341, an increase of 6·7% since 2000. July 2018 estimate, 1,929,268.

Population in five census years was:

	White	Black	American Indian	Asian	Total	Per sq. mile
1910	1,180,293	7,689	3,502	730	1,192,214	15·5
			All others			
1980	1,490,381	48,390	31,054		1,569,825	20·5
1990	1,480,558	57,404	40,423		1,578,385	20·5
2000	1,533,261	68,541	109,461		1,711,263	22·3
2010	1,572,838	82,885	170,618		1,826,341	23·8

Of the total population in 2010, 920,045 were female and 1,367,120 were 18 years old or older. In 2010 the estimated Hispanic population of Nebraska was 167,405, up from 94,425 in 2000 (a rise of 77·3%). The largest cities in the state are: Omaha, with a census population, 2010, of 408,958; Lincoln (the capital), 258,379; Bellevue, 50,137; Grand Island, 48,520; Kearney, 30,787; Fremont, 26,397; Hastings, 24,907; North Platte, 24,733; Norfolk, 24,210.

Social Statistics

Births, 2014, 26,794 (14·2 per 1,000 population); deaths, 2014, 15,978 (8·5). Infant mortality rate, 2013, 5·2 per 1,000 live births. 2014: marriages, 6·4 per 1,000 population; divorces and annulments, 3·1.

Climate

Omaha, Jan. 22°F (−5·6°C), July 77°F (25°C). Annual rainfall 29" (721 mm). Nebraska belongs to the High Plains climate zone (see UNITED STATES: Climate).

Constitution and Government

The present constitution was adopted in 1875; it had been amended 194 times by 2011. By an amendment of 1934 Nebraska has a single-chambered legislature (elected for four years) of 49 members elected on a non-party ballot and classed as senators—the only state in the USA to have one. It meets annually.

For the 116th Congress, which convened in Jan. 2019, Nebraska sends three members to the House of Representatives. It is represented in the Senate by Deb Fischer (R. 2013–25) and Ben Sasse (R. 2015–21).

The capital is Lincoln. The state has 93 counties.

Recent Elections

In the 2016 presidential election Donald Trump took Nebraska with 60·3% of the vote (Mitt Romney won it in 2012).

Current Government

Governor: Pete Ricketts (R.), 2019–23 (salary: $105,000).
    Lieut.-Governor: Mike Foley (R.), 2019–23.
    Secretary of State: Bob Evnen (R.), since Jan. 2019.
Government Website: http://www.nebraska.gov

Economy

Per capita personal income (2015) was $48,006.

Budget

In 2011 total state revenue was $11,523m. Total expenditure was $9,356m. (education, $3,330m.; public welfare, $2,091m.; highways, $602m.; health, $456m.; hospitals, $261m.). Outstanding debt in 2011, $2,346m.

Performance

Gross Domestic Product by state was $113,282m. in 2015, ranking Nebraska 35th in the United States. In 2015 state real GDP growth was 0·9%.

Energy and Natural Resources

Oil and Gas

In 2014 Nebraska produced 3·1m. bbls of crude petroleum.

Water

The total area covered by water is 524 sq. miles.

Minerals

Output of non-fuel minerals, 2008 (in 1,000 tonnes): sand and gravel for construction, 13,700; stone, 7,960; clays, 109 (estimate). Other minerals include limestone, potash, pumice, slate and shale. Total value of non-fuel mineral output in 2009 was $248m.

Agriculture

Nebraska is one of the most important agricultural states. In 2007 it contained 47,712 farms, with a total area of 45·48m. acres. The average farm was 953 acres and was valued in 2007 at $1,159 per acre. In 2007 the total acreage harvested was 18·17m. acres.

In 2009 net farm income was $3,276m. Farm income, 2009: from crops, $8,026m.; and from livestock and products, $7,283m. Principal commodities are cattle, corn, soybeans and hogs. Livestock, 2007: cattle, 6·58m.; hogs and pigs, 3·27m.; sheep and lambs, 76,400; laying hens, 10·49m.

Forestry

The state had a forested area of 1,539,000 acres in 2013, of which 50,000 acres were national forest.

Industry

In 2012 the state's 4,512 manufacturing establishments had 215,000 employees, earning $9,252m. Total value added by manufacturing in 2013 was $20,041m.

Labour

Total non-agricultural employment, 2010, 939,000. Employees by branch in 2010 (in 1,000): trade, transportation and utilities, 196; government, 169; education and health services, 136; professional and business services, 101; manufacturing, 92. In Dec. 2010 the unemployment rate was 4·3%.

International Trade

Imports and Exports

In 2015 imports into Nebraska totalled $4,136m. (up from $4,055m. in 2014). In the same year exports from Nebraska totalled $6,663m., down from $7,890m. in 2014. The leading source for imports in 2015 was China ($1,021m.), ahead of Canada ($950m.). The leading destination for exports in 2015 was Canada ($1,467m.), followed by Mexico ($1,261m.).

Communications

Roads

In 2012 there were 93,797 miles of road (87,279 miles rural). Registered motor vehicles in 2012 numbered 1,835,625.

Rail

In 2012 there were 3,375 miles of freight railroad (excluding trackage rights). There were 12 freight railroads operating in 2012. Rail traffic originating in Nebraska in 2012 totalled 27·0m. tons and rail traffic terminating in the state came to 23·3m. tons.

Civil Aviation

There were five primary airports—commercial service airports with more than 10,000 passenger boardings annually—in 2011 with a combined total of 2,251,850 enplanements, down from 2,296,210 in 2010. The busiest airport, Eppley Airfield (Omaha's airport), had 2,047,055 enplanements in 2011.

Social Institutions

Justice

A 'Civil Rights Act' revised in 1969 provides that all people are entitled to a full and equal enjoyment of public facilities. In Dec. 2014 there were 5,441 prison inmates. The death penalty was abolished in May 2015, at which time there had not been an execution since 1997. However, following a petition campaign by supporters of capital punishment a referendum on the abolition was held in Nov. 2016 and the death penalty reinstated. In Aug. 2018 Nebraska carried out its first execution since 1997.

Education

School attendance is compulsory for children from six to 18 years of age. There were 1,101 public elementary and secondary schools in 2012–13 with 303,505 pupils and 22,103 teachers. In fall 2011 there were 40,750 pupils in 220 private schools with 2,840 teachers. Total expenditure on public elementary and secondary education in 2010–11 was $3,739m.; spending per pupil was $11,540. Total enrolment in public degree-granting institutions in fall 2012 was 104,166; there were also 35,412 students in private degree-granting institutions. The largest institutions are:

Founded	Institution	Students (fall 2014)
1867	Peru State College	2,499
	University of Nebraska (State)	50,831
1869	—Lincoln	25,006
1902	—Medical Center	3,696
1905	—Kearney	6,902
1908	—Omaha	15,227
1878	Creighton University, Omaha (Roman Catholic)	8,236
1887	Nebraska Wesleyan University (Private)	2,083
1894	Concordia University Nebraska, Seward (Lutheran)	2,332
1910	Wayne State College	3,470
1911	Chadron State College	3,033
1966	Bellevue University (Private)	9,879
1971	Nebraska Community Colleges (Local government)	39,484
	—Central Area	6,377
	—Metropolitan Area	14,675
	—Mid Plains Area	2,143
	—Northeast Area	5,061
	—Southeast Area	9,392

Health

Nebraska had 3·6 community hospital beds for every 1,000 population in 2013. In the same year there were 26·0 active physicians per 10,000 civilian population and 6·4 dentists per 10,000.

Welfare

Medicare enrolment in July 2012 totalled 292,577. In fiscal year 2012 a total of 292,966 people in Nebraska received Medicaid. In Dec. 2014 there were 326,078 Old-Age, Survivors, and Disability Insurance (OASDI) beneficiaries. A total of 12,896 people were receiving payments under Temporary Assistance for Needy Families (TANF) in Dec. 2012.

Religion

The principal religious traditions in 2010 were: Catholics, with 372,838 members; Mainline Protestants, 297,522; Evangelical Protestants, 288,965; Latter-day Saints (Mormons), 25,611; Black Protestants, 13,106.

Nevada

Key Historical Events

The area was part of Spanish America until 1821 when it became part of the newly independent state of Mexico. Following a war between Mexico and the USA, Nevada was ceded to the USA as part of California in 1848. Settlement began in 1849 and the area was separated from California and joined with Utah Territory in 1850. In 1859 a rich deposit of silver was found in the Comstock Lode. Virginia City was founded as a mining town and immigration increased rapidly. Nevada Territory was formed in 1861. During the Civil War the Federal government, allegedly in order to obtain the wealth of silver for the Union cause, agreed to admit Nevada to the Union as the 36th state. This was in 1864. Areas of Arizona and Utah Territories were added in 1866–67.

The mining boom lasted until 1882, by which time cattle ranching in the valleys, where the climate is less arid, had become equally important. Carson City, the capital, developed in association with the nearby mining industry. The largest cities, Las Vegas and Reno, grew in the 20th century with the building of the Hoover dam, the introduction of legal gambling and of easy divorce.

After 1950 much of the desert area was adopted by the Federal government for weapons testing and other military purposes.

Territory and Population

Nevada is bounded north by Oregon and Idaho, east by Utah, southeast by Arizona, with the Colorado River forming most of the boundary, south and west by California. Total area is 110,572 sq. miles (286,380 sq. km) of which 109,781 sq. miles (284,332 sq. km) are land. In 2010 the federal government owned 56,961,778 acres, equivalent to 81·1% of the state area (the highest percentage in any state).

Census population, 1 April 2010, was 2,700,551, an increase of 35·1% since 2000. Nevada had the fastest-growing population of any state between the censuses of 2000 and 2010, continuing a trend stretching back to 1950. July 2018 estimate, 3,034,392.

Population in five census years was:

	White	Black	American Indian/ Alaska Native	Asian	Total (including others)	Per sq. mile
1910	74,276	513	5,240	1,846	81,875	0·7
1980	700,360	50,999	13,308	35,841	800,508	7·2
1990	1,012,695	78,771	19,637	90,730	1,201,833	10·9
2000	1,501,886	135,477	26,420	334,474	1,998,257	18·2
2010	1,786,688	218,626	32,062	195,436	2,700,551	24·6

Of the total population in 2010, 1,363,616 were male and 2,035,543 were 18 years old or older. In 2010 the Hispanic population was 716,501, up from 393,970 in 2000 (an increase of 81·9%).

The largest cities in 2010 were: Las Vegas, 583,756; Henderson, 257,729; Reno, 225,221; North Las Vegas, 216,961; Sparks, 90,264; Carson City (the capital), 55,274.

Social Statistics

Births, 2014, were 35,861 (12·6 per 1,000 population); deaths, 2014, 21,793 (7·7). Infant mortality rate, 2013, 5·3 per 1,000 live births. 2014: marriages, 31·9 per 1,000 population; divorces and annulments, 5·3. Nevada's marriage rate in 2014 was nearly double that of any other state. Same-sex marriage became legal in Oct. 2014.

Climate

Las Vegas, Jan. 57°F (14°C), July 104°F (40°C). Annual rainfall 4·13" (105 mm). Reno, Jan. 45°F (7°C), July 91°F (33°C). Annual rainfall 7·53"

(191 mm). Nevada belongs to the Mountain States climate zone (*see* UNITED STATES: Climate).

Constitution and Government

The constitution adopted in 1864 is still in force, with 130 amendments as of Sept. 2016. The Legislature meets biennially (and in special sessions) and consists of a Senate of 21 members elected for four years, with half their number elected every two years, and an Assembly of 42 members elected for two years. The Governor may be elected for two consecutive four-year terms.

For the 116th Congress, which convened in Jan. 2019, Nevada sends four members to the House of Representatives. It is represented in the Senate by Catherine Cortez Masto (D. 2017–23) and Jacky Rosen (D. 2019–25).

The state capital is Carson City. There are 16 counties and one independent city (Carson City).

Recent Elections

In the 2016 presidential election Hillary Clinton took Nevada with 47·9% of the vote (Barack Obama won it in 2012).

Current Government

Governor: Steve Sisolak (D.), 2019–23 (salary: $149,573).

Lieut.-Governor: Kate Marshall (D.), 2019–23.

Secretary of State: Barbara Cegavske (R.), since Jan. 2015.

Government Website: http://www.nv.gov

Economy

Per capita personal income (2015) was $42,185.

Budget

In 2011 total state revenue was $17,597m. Total expenditure was $13,203m. (including: education, $4,148m.; public welfare, $2,128m.; highways, $773m.; government administration, $283m.; correction, $276m.). Outstanding debt in 2011, $4,201m.

Performance

Gross Domestic Product by state in 2015 was $139,724m., ranking Nevada 33rd in the United States. In 2015 state real GDP growth was 1·6%.

Energy and Natural Resources

Water

The total area covered by water is 791 sq. miles.

Minerals

Nevada has led the nation in gold production since 1981, producing 76% of gold in 2008. It is ranked second in silver production, accounting for 19% of the nation's silver in 2008. In 2008 Nevada produced 178,000 kg of gold and 235,000 kg of silver. Nevada also produces other minerals such as aggregates, clays, copper, diatomite, dolomite, geothermal energy, gypsum, lapidary, lime and limestone. The total value of Nevada's non-fuel mineral production in 2009 was $6,020m.

Agriculture

In 2011 there were 2,950 farms with a total area of 5·85m. acres. Farms averaged 1,983 acres. Average value per acre in 2011 was $613.

Farm income from crops in 2011 totalled $281m., and cash receipts for livestock and products totalled $399m. The four most important commodities were cattle ($251m.); feed crops ($149m.); dairy products ($136m.); and onions ($71m.). The net farm income in 2011 was $223m.

In 2011 there were 441,629 cattle and 65,581 sheep and lambs.

Forestry

Nevada had, in 2012, 11·17m. acres of forested land with 5·77m. acres of national forest.

Industry

The main industry is the service industry, especially tourism and legalized gambling. Gaming industry total revenue for 2013 was $11,143m. In June 2012 there were 2,859 active licences in force, including 443 for non-restricted casinos (those with more than 15 slot machines and/or gaming tables).

In 2012 Nevada's 3,446 manufacturing establishments had 77,000 employees, earning $3,982m. Total value added by manufacturing in 2013 was $8,720m.

Labour

Total non-agricultural employment in 2010 was 1,116,000. Employees by branch in 2010 (in 1,000): leisure and hospitality, 309; trade, transportation and utilities, 209; government, 155; professional and business services, 136; education and health services, 100. The unemployment rate in Dec. 2010 was 14·9%, the highest of any US state.

International Trade

Imports and Exports

In 2015 imports into Nevada totalled $9,595m. (up from $7,857m. in 2014). In the same year exports from Nevada totalled $8,666m., up from $7,692m. in 2014. The leading source for imports in 2015 was China ($4,568m.), ahead of Canada ($779m.). The leading destination for exports in 2015 was Switzerland ($2,426m.), followed by India ($1,721m.).

Communications

Roads

In 2012 there were 38,567 miles of road, of which 30,314 miles were rural roads and 8,253 urban. Vehicle registrations in 2012 numbered 2,060,690.

Rail

In 2012 there were 1,192 miles of freight railroad (excluding trackage rights). There were two freight railroads operating in 2012. Rail traffic originating in Nevada in 2012 totalled 2·1m. tons and rail traffic terminating in the state came to 5·1m. tons. Las Vegas has a 4-mile monorail metro system.

Civil Aviation

In 2011 Nevada had four primary airports (commercial service airports with more than 10,000 passenger boardings annually) with a combined total of 21,907,927 enplanements, up from 21,046,012 in 2010. By far the busiest airport is McCarran International (the airport for Las Vegas), with 19,872,617 enplanements in 2011.

Social Institutions

Justice

Capital punishment was reintroduced in 1978, and executions began in 1979. There was one execution in 2006 but none since. In Dec. 2014 there were 12,537 prison inmates in state or federal correctional institutions. In a statewide vote held on the same day as the presidential election in Nov. 2016, the recreational use of marijuana was legalized.

Education

School attendance is compulsory for children from seven to 18 years of age. In fall 2011 there were 664 public elementary and secondary schools with 439,634 pupils and 21,132 teachers; 39 charter elementary and secondary schools had 18,391 pupils. Expenditure per pupil in fiscal year 2010–11 was $8,411. Teachers' salaries in public schools in 2011–12 averaged $55,957. In fall 2011 there were 160 private elementary and secondary schools with 26,130 pupils and 1,590 teachers.

The Nevada System of Higher Education (NSHE) consists of two research universities, one State college, four community colleges and one research institute. Institutions are the University of Nevada, Reno, the University of Nevada, Las Vegas, the Nevada State College (at Henderson), the College of Southern Nevada (at Las Vegas, North Las Vegas and Henderson), Great Basin College (at Elko), Truckee Meadows Community College (at Reno), Western Nevada College (at Carson City, Minden and Fallon) and the Desert Research Institute (at Reno and Las Vegas). In fall 2012 there were 118,300 students in degree-granting institutions.

Health

Nevada had 2·0 community hospital beds for every 1,000 population in 2013. In the same year there were 20·3 active physicians per 10,000 civilian population and 5·2 dentists per 10,000.

Welfare

Medicare enrolment in July 2012 totalled 390,686. In fiscal year 2012 a total of 377,288 people in Nevada received Medicaid. In Dec. 2014 there were 475,811 Old-Age, Survivors, and Disability Insurance (OASDI) beneficiaries. A total of 27,185 people were receiving payments under Temporary Assistance for Needy Families (TANF) in Dec. 2012.

Religion

The principal religious traditions in the state in 2010 were: Catholics, with 451,070 members; Evangelical Protestants, 213,188; Latter-day Saints (Mormons), 175,466; Mainline Protestants, 41,558; Buddhists, 14,727.

Culture

Tourism

In 2011 overseas visitors to Nevada—excluding those from Canada and Mexico—numbered 2,872,000, up from 2,504,000 in 2010 and 1,690,000 in 2006. Nevada ranks among the most visited states and Las Vegas among the most visited cities.

New Hampshire

Key Historical Events

The area was part of a grant by the English crown to John Mason and fellow-colonists and was first settled in 1623. In 1629 an area between the Merrimack and Piscatagua rivers was called New Hampshire. More settlements followed, and in 1641 they were taken under the jurisdiction of the governor of Massachusetts. New Hampshire became a separate colony in 1679.

After the War of Independence New Hampshire was one of the 13 original states of the Union, ratifying the US constitution in 1788. The state constitution, which dates from 1776, was almost totally rewritten in 1784 and amended again in 1792.

The settlers were Protestants from Britain and Northern Ireland. They developed manufacturing industries, especially shoe-making, textiles and clothing, to which large numbers of French Canadians were attracted after the Civil War.

Portsmouth, originally a fishing settlement, was the colonial capital and is the only seaport. In 1808 the state capital was moved to Concord (having had no permanent home since 1775); Concord produced the Concord Coach which was widely used on the stagecoach routes of the West until 1900.

Territory and Population

New Hampshire is bounded in the north by Canada, east by Maine and the Atlantic, south by Massachusetts and west by Vermont. Total area is 9,349 sq. miles (24,214 sq. km) of which 8,953 sq. miles (23,187 sq. km) are land. Census population, 1 April 2010, was 1,316,470, an increase of 6·5% since 2000. July 2018 estimate, 1,356,458.

Population at five federal censuses was:

	White	Black	American Indian	Asian	Total	Per sq. mile
1910	429,906	564	34	68	430,572	47·7
			All others			
1980	910,099	3,990	6,521		920,610	101·9
1990	1,087,433	7,198	14,621		1,109,252	123·7
2000	1,186,851	9,035	39,900		1,235,786	137·8
2010	1,236,050	15,035	65,385		1,316,470	147·0

Of the total population in 2010, 667,076 were female and 1,029,236 were 18 years old or older. In 2010 the Hispanic population was 36,704, up from 20,489 in 2000 (an increase of 79·1%). The largest city in the state is Manchester, with a 2010 census population of 109,565. The capital is Concord, 42,695. Other main cities and towns (with 2010 populations) are: Nashua, 86,494; Dover, 29,987; Rochester, 29,752; Keene, 23,409; Derry, 22,015; Portsmouth, 20,779; Laconia, 15,951.

Social Statistics

Births, 2014, 12,302 (9·3 per 1,000 population—the lowest rate in any US state); deaths, 2014, 11,516 (8·7). Infant mortality rate, 2013, 5·6 per 1,000 live births. 2014: marriages, 7·2 per 1,000 population; divorces and annulments, 3·5. Same-sex marriage became legal in Jan. 2010.

Climate

New Hampshire is in the New England climate zone (*see* UNITED STATES: Climate). Manchester, Jan. 22°F (–5·6°C), July 70°F (21·1°C). Annual rainfall 40" (1,003 mm).

Constitution and Government

While the present constitution dates from 1784, it was extensively revised in 1792 when the state joined the Union. Since 1775 there have been 16 state conventions with 49 amendments adopted to change the constitution.

The Legislature (called the General Court) consists of a Senate of 24 members, elected for two years, and a House of Representatives, of 400 members, elected for two years. It meets annually. The Governor and five administrative officers called 'Councillors' are also elected for two years.

For the 116th Congress, which convened in Jan. 2019, New Hampshire sends two members to the House of Representatives. It is represented in the Senate by Jeanne Shaheen (D. 2009–21) and Margaret Wood Hassan (D. 2017–23).

The capital is Concord. The state is divided into ten counties.

Recent Elections

In the 2016 presidential election Hillary Clinton took New Hampshire with 47·6% of the vote (Barack Obama won it in 2012).

Current Government

Governor: Chris Sununu (R.), 2019–23 ($127,443).
    Senate President: Donna Soucy (R.), since Dec. 2018.
    Secretary of State: William M. Gardner (D.), since Dec. 1976.
Government Website: https://www.nh.gov

Economy

Per capita personal income (2015) was $54,817.

Budget

New Hampshire has no general sales tax or state income tax but does have local property taxes. Other government revenues come from rooms and meals tax, business profits tax, motor vehicle licences, fuel taxes, fishing and hunting licences, state-controlled sales of alcoholic beverages, and cigarette and tobacco taxes.

In 2011 total state revenue was $8,521m. Total expenditure was $7,638m. (including: education, $2,016m.; public welfare, $1,945m.; highways, $553m.; government administration, $256m.; correction, $113m.). Outstanding debt in 2011, $8,450m.

Performance

Gross Domestic Product by state in 2015 was $73,867m., ranking New Hampshire 40th in the United States. In 2015 state real GDP growth was 1·4%.

Energy and Natural Resources

Water

The total area covered by water is 397 sq. miles.

Minerals

Minerals are little worked; they consist mainly of sand and gravel, stone, and clay for building and highway construction. Value of domestic non-fuel mineral production in 2009 was $108m.

Agriculture

In 2012 there were 4,391 farms covering 474,065 acres; average farm was 108 acres. Average value per acre in 2012, $4,167. Farm income, 2009: from crops, $104m.; from livestock and products, $75m. The net farm income in 2009 was $19m.

The chief field crops are hay and vegetables; the chief fruit crop is apples. Livestock, 2012: cattle and calves, 33,392; sheep and lambs, 8,079; hogs and pigs, 3,287; laying hens, 221,446.

Forestry

In 2013 the state had a forested area of 4,783,477 acres, of which 793,384 acres were national forest.

Fisheries

2009 commercial fishing landings amounted to 13·9m. lb worth $17·7m.

Industry

Principal manufactures: electrical and electronic goods, machinery and metal products. In 2012 the state's 3,850 manufacturing establishments had 135,000 employees, earning $7,930m. Total value added by manufacturing in 2013 was $10,628m.

Labour

Total non-agricultural employment, 2010, 623,000. Employees by branch, 2010 (in 1,000): trade, transportation and utilities, 132; education and health services, 110; government, 97; manufacturing, 66; professional and business services, 64. In Dec. 2010 the unemployment rate was 5·6%.

International Trade

Imports and Exports

In 2015 imports into New Hampshire totalled $9,313m. (down from $11,232m. in 2014). In the same year exports from New Hampshire totalled $4,001m., down from $4,233m. in 2014. The leading source for imports in 2015 was Canada ($4,900m.), ahead of China ($1,149m.). The leading destination for exports in 2015 was also Canada ($537m.), followed by Mexico ($503m.).

Communications

Roads

In 2012 there were 16,105 miles of road (11,375 miles rural). There were approximately 1,223,000 registered motor vehicles in 2011.

Rail

In 2012 there were 344 miles of freight railroad (excluding trackage rights). There were nine freight railroads operating in 2012. Rail traffic originating in New Hampshire in 2012 totalled 0·3m. tons and rail traffic terminating in the state came to 0·8m. tons.

Civil Aviation

New Hampshire's only primary airport—a commercial service airport with more than 10,000 passenger boardings annually—is Manchester. In 2011 it had 1,342,308 enplanements.

Social Institutions

Justice

There were 2,963 prison inmates in Dec. 2014. The death penalty was abolished in May 2000—the last execution had been in 1939.

Education

School attendance is compulsory for children from six to 18 years of age (since 1 July 2009—previously school attendance had only been compulsory to 16). Employed illiterate minors between 16 and 21 years of age must attend evening or special classes, if provided by the district.

In 2012–13, 486 public elementary and secondary schools had 188,974 pupils and 14,925 teachers. Teachers' salaries in 2012–13 averaged $55,599. An average of $13,548 was spent on public education per pupil in 2010–11.

The largest four-year institutions are Southern New Hampshire University (founded in 1932, was New Hampshire College), with 43,274 in fall 2014; the University of New Hampshire (1866), 15,117; Dartmouth College (1769), 6,298; Keene State College (1909), 4,957; Plymouth State University (1871), 4,855. There were 27 degree-granting institutions in 2012–13; total enrolment, fall 2012, was 82,678.

Health

New Hampshire had 2·1 community hospital beds for every 1,000 population in 2013. In the same year there were 32·0 active physicians per 10,000 civilian population and 6·4 dentists per 10,000.

Welfare

Medicare enrolment in July 2012 totalled 237,729. In fiscal year 2012 a total of 163,357 people in New Hampshire received Medicaid. In Dec. 2014 there were 283,983 Old-Age, Survivors, and Disability Insurance (OASDI) beneficiaries. A total of 7,745 people were receiving payments under Temporary Assistance for Needy Families (TANF) in Dec. 2012.

Religion

The principal religious traditions in the state in 2010 were: Catholics, with 311,028 members; Mainline Protestants, 81,111; Evangelical Protestants, 47,128; Latter-day Saints (Mormons), 8,231; Orthodox Christians, 4,926.

New Jersey

Key Historical Events

Originally the territory of Delaware Indians, the area was settled by immigrant colonists in the early 17th century, when Dutch and Swedish traders established fortified posts on the Hudson and Delaware Rivers. The Dutch gave way to the English in 1664. In 1676 the English divided the area; the eastern portion was assigned to Sir George Carteret and the western granted to Quaker settlers. This lasted until 1702 when New Jersey was united as a colony of the Crown and placed under the jurisdiction of the governor of New York. It became a separate colony in 1738.

During the War of Independence crucial battles were fought at Trenton, Princeton and Monmouth. New Jersey became the 3rd state of the Union in 1787. Trenton, the state capital since 1790, began as a Quaker settlement and became an iron-working town. Industrial development grew rapidly, there and elsewhere in the state, after the opening of canals and railways in the 1830s. Princeton, also a Quaker settlement, became an important post on the New York road; the college of New Jersey (Princeton University) was transferred there from Newark in 1756.

The need for supplies in the Civil War stimulated industry and New Jersey became a manufacturing state. The growth of New York and Philadelphia, however, encouraged commuting to employment in both centres. By 1980 about 60% of the state's population lived within 30 miles of New York.

Territory and Population

New Jersey is bounded north by New York, east by the Atlantic with Long Island and New York City to the northeast, south by Delaware Bay and west by Pennsylvania. Land area, 7,354 sq. miles (19,047 sq. km); water area, 1,368 sq. miles (3,544 sq. km). Census population, 1 April 2010, was 8,791,894, an increase of 4·5% since 2000. July 2018 estimate, 8,908,520.

Population at five federal censuses was:

	White	Black	Asian	Others	Total	Per sq. mile
1910	2,445,894	89,760	1,345	168	2,537,167	337·7
1980	6,127,467	925,066	103,848	208,442	7,364,823	986·2
1990	6,130,465	1,036,825	272,521	290,377	7,730,188	1,042·0
2000	6,104,705	1,141,821	483,605	684,219	8,414,350	1,134·4
2010	6,029,248	1,204,826	725,726	832,094	8,791,894	1,195·5

Of the total population in 2010, 4,512,294 were female and 6,726,680 were 18 years old or older. In 2010 the Hispanic population was 1,555,144, up from 1,117,191 in 2000 (an increase of 39·2%).

Census populations of the largest cities and towns in 2010 were:

Newark	277,140
Jersey City	247,597
Paterson	146,199
Elizabeth	124,969
Edison	99,967
Toms River	88,791
Trenton (capital)	84,913
Clifton	84,136
Camden	77,344
Brick Township	75,072
Passaic	69,781
Union City	66,455
East Orange	64,270
Bayonne	63,024
North Bergen Township	60,773
Vineland	60,724

(continued)

Union Township	56,642
New Brunswick	55,181
Wayne	54,717
Irvington	53,926
Lakewood	53,805
Parsippany-Troy Hills Township	53,238
Perth Amboy	50,814
Hoboken	50,005

Social Statistics

Births, 2014, 103,305 (11·6 per 1,000 population); deaths, 2014, 71,316 (8·0). Infant mortality, 2013, 4·5 per 1,000 live births. 2014: marriages, 5·4 per 1,000 population; divorces and annulments, 2·8. Same-sex marriage became legal in Oct. 2013.

Climate

Jersey City, Jan. 31°F (–0·6°C), July 75°F (23·9°C). Annual rainfall 41" (1,025 mm). Trenton, Jan. 32°F (0°C), July 76°F (24·4°C). Annual rainfall 40" (1,003 mm). New Jersey belongs to the Atlantic Coast climate zone (*see* UNITED STATES: Climate).

Constitution and Government

The present constitution, ratified by the registered voters on 4 Nov. 1947, has been amended 45 times. There is a 40-member Senate and an 80-member General Assembly. Assembly members serve two years, senators four years, except those elected at the election following each census, who serve for two years. Sessions are held throughout the year.

For the 116th Congress, which convened in Jan. 2019, New Jersey sends 12 members to the House of Representatives. It is represented in the Senate by Robert Menendez (D. 2007–25) and Cory Booker (D. 2013–21).

The capital is Trenton. The state is divided into 21 counties, which are subdivided into 565 municipalities—cities, towns, boroughs, villages and townships.

Recent Elections

In the 2016 presidential election Hillary Clinton took New Jersey with 55·0% of the vote (Barack Obama won it in 2012).

Current Government

Governor: Phil Murphy (D.), 2018–22 (salary: $175,000).
  Lieut.-Governor: Sheila Oliver (D.), 2018–22.
  Secretary of State: Tahesha Way (D.), since Jan. 2018.
Government Website: https://www.nj.gov

Economy

Per capita income (2015) was $59,782, the fourth highest in the country.

Budget

In 2011 total state revenue was $70,798m. Total expenditure was $67,114m. (including: education, $15,710m.; public welfare, $14,214m.; highways, $3,179m.; hospitals, $2,119m.; government administration, $1,690m.). Outstanding debt in 2011, $64,005m.

Performance

Gross Domestic Product by state in 2015 was $567,738m., ranking New Jersey 8th in the United States. In 2015 state real GDP growth was 2·0%.

Energy and Natural Resources

Water

The total area covered by water is 1,368 sq. miles.

Minerals

In 2008 the chief minerals were stone (17·9m. tons, value $155m.) and sand and gravel (15·1m. tons, value $191m.); others are clays, peat and gemstones. New Jersey is a leading producer of greensand marl, magnesium compounds and peat. Total value of domestic non-fuel mineral products for 2009 was more than $270m.

Agriculture

Horticulture, fruit and vegetable production and the raising of livestock are pursued. In 2007 there were 10,327 farms covering a total of 733,000 acres with an average farm size of 71 acres. Average value per acre in 2013 was $12,700—making it the most valuable land per acre in the USA.

Cash receipts from farm marketings, 2011: crops, $994·6m.; livestock and products, $126·8m. The net farm income in 2012 was $339·6m. Principal commodities are nursery/greenhouse products, blueberries, peaches, tomatoes, peppers and cranberries.

Livestock, 2012: 7,500 dairy cows, 31,000 all cattle and 8,000 swine. 2007: 14,835 sheep and lambs, and 1·6m. laying hens.

Forestry

Total forested area was 2,002,000 acres in 2013.

Fisheries

2009 commercial fishing landings amounted to 161·6m. lb worth $149·0m.

Electricity

In 2015 production was 74,609m. kWh, of which 36,974m. kWh was from natural gas and 33,262m. kWh from nuclear energy.

Industry

In 2012 the state's 15,516 manufacturing establishments had 461,000 employees, earning $28,190m. Total value added by manufacturing in 2013 was $43,341m.

Labour

Total non-agricultural employment, 2010, 3,855,000. Employees by branch, 2010 (in 1,000): trade, transportation and utilities, 808; government, 643; education and health services, 606; professional and business services, 582; leisure and hospitality, 335. The unemployment rate in Dec. 2010 was 9·1%.

International Trade

Imports and Exports

In 2015 imports into New Jersey totalled $119·6bn. (down from $126·5bn. in 2014). In the same year exports from New Jersey totalled $32·1bn., down from $36·6bn. in 2014. The leading source for imports in 2015 was China ($18·6bn.), ahead of Japan ($10·5bn.). The leading destination for exports in 2015 was Canada ($6·6bn.), followed by Mexico ($2·6bn).

Communications

Roads

In 2012 there were 39,272 miles of road, of which 33,388 miles were urban. There were approximately 7,579,000 registered vehicles in 2012.

Rail

In 2012 there were 981 miles of freight railroad (excluding trackage rights). There were 17 freight railroads operating in 2012. Rail traffic originating in New Jersey in 2012 totalled 11·8m. tons and rail traffic terminating in the state came to 23·6m. tons.

There is a metro link to New York (22 km), a light rail line (7 km) and extensive commuter railroads around Newark.

Civil Aviation

In 2011 there were two primary airports (commercial service airports with more than 10,000 passenger boardings annually). The main airport is Newark Liberty International, with 16,814,092 enplanements in 2011 (up from 16,571,754 in 2010). Atlantic City International had 668,930 enplanements in 2011 (down from 669,470 in 2010).

Social Institutions

Justice

In Dec. 2014 there were 21,590 prison inmates. The death penalty was abolished on 17 Dec. 2007, after its initial suspension in Jan. 2006. The death penalty was last used in 1963.

Education

Elementary instruction is compulsory for all from six to 16 years of age and free to all from five to 20 years of age. In 2012–13 there were 2,625 public elementary and secondary schools with 1,372,203 pupils and 110,929 teachers; total expenditure on public schools in 2010–11 was $25,309m. Spending per pupil in 2010–11 came to $16,855. Teachers' salaries averaged $68,797 in 2012–13.

There are 31 public universities and colleges (including 19 community colleges) in New Jersey. In fall 2009 public institutions had 348,934 students (177,173 in community colleges). Enrolment in fall 2009: Rutgers, the State University (founded as Queen's College in 1766), had 54,648 students at campuses in Camden, Newark and New Brunswick; College of New Jersey (1855; formerly Trenton State College), 6,980; Kean University, at Union City (1855), 15,051; Montclair State University (1908), 18,171; Rowan University, at Glassboro (1923), 11,006; William Paterson University, at Wayne (1855), 10,820.

There are 32 independent institutions, of which 14 are senior colleges and universities with a public mission, two independent two-year religious colleges, ten rabbinical schools and theological seminaries, and six proprietary institutions with degree-granting authority. Independent institutions had 83,233 students in fall 2009: Fairleigh Dickinson University, at Teaneck (1941), had 8,804 students; Princeton University (founded in 1746), 7,592; Seton Hall University, at South Orange (1856), 9,616.

Health
New Jersey had 2·4 community hospital beds for every 1,000 population in 2013. In the same year there were 33·5 active physicians per 10,000 civilian population and 8·1 dentists per 10,000.

Welfare
Medicare enrolment in July 2012 totalled 1,408,437. In fiscal year 2012 a total of 1,521,078 people in New Jersey received Medicaid. In Dec. 2014 there were 1,568,016 Old-Age, Survivors, and Disability Insurance (OASDI) beneficiaries. A total of 78,798 people were receiving payments under Temporary Assistance for Needy Families (TANF) in Dec. 2012.

Religion
The principal religious traditions in the state in 2010 were: Catholics, with 3,235,290 members; Mainline Protestants, 502,797; Evangelical Protestants, 380,347; Jews, 216,706; Muslims, 161,000 (estimate).

Culture

Tourism
Overseas visitors to New Jersey (excluding those from Canada and Mexico) numbered 976,000 in 2011, up from 975,000 in 2010 and 845,000 in 2006.

New Mexico

Key Historical Events
The first European settlement was established in 1598. Until 1771 New Mexico was the Spanish 'Kingdom of New Mexico'. In 1771 it was annexed to the northern province of New Spain. When New Spain won its independence in 1821, it took the name of Republic of Mexico and established New Mexico as its northernmost department. Ceded to the USA in 1848 after war between the USA and Mexico, the area was recognized as a Territory in 1850, by which time its population was Spanish and American Indian. There were frequent conflicts between new settlers and raiding parties of Navajo and Apaches. The American Indian war lasted from 1861–66, and from 1864–68 about 8,000 Navajo were imprisoned at Bosque Redondo.

The boundaries were altered several times when land was taken into Texas, Utah, Colorado and lastly (1863) Arizona. New Mexico became a state in 1912.

Settlement proceeded by means of irrigated crop-growing and Mexican-style ranching. During the Second World War the desert areas were used as testing zones for atomic weapons. Mineral related industries developed after the discovery of uranium and petroleum.

Territory and Population
New Mexico is bounded north by Colorado, northeast by Oklahoma, east by Texas, south by Texas and Mexico and west by Arizona. Total area is 121,590 sq. miles (314,917 sq. km) of which 121,298 sq. miles (314,161 sq. km) are land. In 2010 American Indian lands covered 12,085 sq. miles (reservations plus off-reservation trust land).

Census population, 1 April 2010, was 2,059,179, an increase of 13·2% since 2000. July 2018 estimate, 2,095,428. Of the total population in 2010, 1,041,758 were female and 1,540,507 were 18 years old or older.

The population in five census years was:

	White	Black	American Indian/ Alaska Native	Asian/ Native Hawaiian/ Pacific Islander	Other	Total	Per sq. mile
1910	304,594	1,628	20,573	506	—	327,301	2·7
1980	977,587	24,020	106,119	6,825	188,343	1,302,894	10·7
1990	1,146,028	30,210	134,355	14,124	190,352	1,515,069	12·5
2000	1,214,253	34,343	173,483	20,758	376,209	1,819,046	15·0
2010	1,407,876	42,550	193,222	30,018	385,513	2,059,179	17·0

Before 1930 New Mexico was largely a Spanish-speaking state, but after 1945 an influx of population from other states considerably reduced the percentage of persons of Spanish origin or descent. However, in recent years the percentage of the Hispanic population has begun to rise again. In 2010 the Hispanic population was 953,403, up from 765,386 in 2000 (an increase of 24·6%). At 46·3%, New Mexico has the largest percentage of persons of Hispanic origin of any state in the USA.

The largest cities are Albuquerque, with a 2010 census population of 545,852; Las Cruces, 97,618; Rio Rancho, 87,521; Santa Fe (the capital), 67,947; Roswell, 48,366.

Social Statistics
Births, 2014, 26,052 (12·5 per 1,000 population); deaths, 2014, 17,579 (8·4). Infant mortality, 2013, 5·3 per 1,000 live births. 2014: marriages, 8·1 per 1,000 population; divorces and annulments, 3·6. Same-sex marriage became legal in Dec. 2013.

Climate
Santa Fe, Jan. 26·4°F (−3·1°C), July 68·4°F (20°C). Annual rainfall 15·2" (386 mm). New Mexico belongs to the Mountain States climate zone (*see* UNITED STATES: Climate).

Constitution and Government
The constitution of 1912 is still in force with 171 amendments as of Sept. 2016. The state Legislature, which meets annually, consists of 42 members of the Senate, elected for four years, and 70 members of the House of Representatives, elected for two years.

For the 116th Congress, which convened in Jan. 2019, New Mexico sends three members to the House of Representatives. It is represented in the Senate by Tom Udall (D. 2009–21) and Martin Heinrich (D. 2013–25).

The state capital is Santa Fe. The state is divided into 33 counties.

Recent Elections
In the 2016 presidential election Hillary Clinton took New Mexico with 48·3% of the vote (Barack Obama won it in 2012).

Current Government
Governor: Michelle Lujan Grisham (D.), 2019–23 (salary: $110,000).
Lieut.-Governor: Howie Morales (D.), 2019–23.
Secretary of State: Maggie Toulouse Oliver (D.), since Dec. 2016.
Government Website: http://www.newmexico.gov

Economy
Per capita personal income (2015) was $38,457.

Budget
In 2011 total state revenue was $19,867m. Total expenditure was $17,865m. (including: education, $5,392m.; public welfare, $4,329m.; health, $921m.; highways, $806m.; government administration, $637m.). Outstanding debt in 2011, $8,119m.

Performance
Gross Domestic Product by state in 2015 was $93,339m., ranking New Mexico 37th in the United States. In 2015 state real GDP growth was 1·7%.

Energy and Natural Resources

Oil and Gas
In 2014 New Mexico produced 123·7m. bbls of crude petroleum; marketed production of natural gas totalled 1,181bn. cu. ft.

Water
The total area covered by water is 292 sq. miles.

Minerals
New Mexico is one of the largest energy producing states in the USA. In 2015 potash production was 1,433,245 short tons (with a production value of $659·5m.); copper, 397,441,145 lb ($996·8m.); coal, 19,676,277 short tons ($691·0m.). New Mexico is the country's leading potash producer and ranked second for copper production in 2015.

Agriculture
New Mexico produces grains, vegetables, hay, livestock, milk, cotton and pecans. In 2007 there were 20,930 farms covering 43·24m. acres; average farm size 2,066 acres. In 2007 average value of farmland and buildings per acre was $337.

2009 cash receipts from crops, $701m.; and from livestock products, $1,998m. The net farm income in 2009 was $432m. Principal commodities are dairy products, cattle, hay and pecans. Farm animals in 2007 included 326,000 dairy cows, 1·53m. all cattle, 127,000 sheep and lambs, and 2,000 swine.

Forestry
The state had a forested area of 24,839,000 acres in 2013, of which 7,808,000 acres were national forest.

Industry
In 2012 the state's 2,888 manufacturing establishments had 54,000 employees, earning $2,729m. Total value added by manufacturing in 2013 was $13,790m.

Labour
Total non-agricultural employment, 2010, 802,000. Employees by branch, 2010 (in 1,000): government, 199; trade, transportation and utilities, 133; education and health services, 120; professional and business services, 98; leisure and hospitality, 84. The unemployment rate in Dec. 2010 was 8·6%.

International Trade

Imports and Exports
In 2015 imports into New Mexico totalled $2,249m. (up from $2,233m. in 2014). In the same year exports from New Mexico totalled $3,781m., down from $3,802m. in 2014. The leading source for imports in 2015 was China ($789m.), ahead of Mexico ($635m.). The leading destination for exports in 2015 was Mexico ($1,683m.), followed by Israel ($1,083m.).

Communications

Roads
In 2012 there were 68,384 miles of road (60,494 miles rural). There were 1,739,124 registered motor vehicles.

Rail
In 2012 there were 1,837 miles of freight railroad (excluding trackage rights). There were six freight railroads operating in 2012. Rail traffic originating in New Mexico in 2012 totalled 12·1m. tons and rail traffic terminating in the state came to 3·8m. tons.

Civil Aviation
In 2011 there were four primary airports—commercial service airports with more than 10,000 passenger boardings annually—with a combined total of 2,865,348 enplanements, down from 2,924,466 in 2010. By far the busiest airport, Albuquerque International Sunport, had 2,768,435 enplanements in 2011.

Social Institutions

Justice
In Dec. 2014 there were 7,021 prison inmates in state or federal correctional institutions. The death penalty was abolished with effect from 1 July 2009 for crimes committed after that date, although two prisoners remained on death row. It was most recently used in 2001 (one execution) for the first time since 1960.

Since 1949 the denial of employment by reason of race, colour, religion, national origin or ancestry has been forbidden. A law of 1955 prohibits discrimination in public places because of race or colour. An 'equal rights' amendment was added to the constitution in 1972.

Education
Elementary education is free, and compulsory between five and 18 years. In 2012–13 there were 338,220 students in 880 public elementary and secondary schools with 22,201 teachers; average teacher salary in 2012–13 was $46,573. Total expenditure on public school education in 2010–11 was $3,642m. Spending per pupil in 2010–11 was $9,250.

In fall 2012 there were 146,792 students attending public degree-granting institutions and 9,632 at private institutions. The main state-supported four-year universities are (fall 2014 enrolment):

Name and place	Students
University of New Mexico, Albuquerque	27,844
New Mexico State University, Las Cruces	15,829
Eastern New Mexico University, Portales	5,879
Western New Mexico University, Silver City	3,557
New Mexico Highlands University, Las Vegas	3,546
New Mexico Institute of Mining and Technology, Socorro	2,127
Navajo Technical University, Crownpoint	2,075

Health
New Mexico had 1·8 community hospital beds for every 1,000 population in 2013. In the same year there were 25·2 active physicians per 10,000 civilian population and 5·1 dentists per 10,000.

Welfare
Medicare enrolment in July 2012 totalled 337,771. In fiscal year 2012 a total of 559,950 people in New Mexico received Medicaid. In Dec. 2014 there were 399,987 Old-Age, Survivors, and Disability Insurance (OASDI) beneficiaries. A total of 40,798 people were receiving payments under Temporary Assistance for Needy Families (TANF) in Dec. 2012.

Religion
The principal religious traditions in 2010 were: Catholics, with 584,941 members; Evangelical Protestants, 277,326; Mainline Protestants, 71,118; Latter-day Saints (Mormons), 68,192; Buddhists, 8,180.

New York State

Key Historical Events
The first European immigrants came in the 17th century, when there were two powerful American Indian groups in rivalry: the Iroquois confederacy (Mohawk, Oneida, Onondaga, Cayuga and Seneca) and the Algonquian-speaking Mohegan and Munsee. The Dutch made settlements at Fort Orange (now Albany) in 1624 and at New Amsterdam in 1625, trading with the American Indians for furs. In the 1660s there was conflict between the Dutch and the British in the Caribbean; as part of the concluding treaty the British, in 1664, received Dutch possessions in the Americas, including New Amsterdam, which they renamed New York.

In 1763 the Treaty of Paris ended war between the British and the French in North America (in which the Iroquois had allied themselves with the British). Settlers of British descent in New England then felt confident enough to expand westward. The climate of northern New York being severe, most settled in the Hudson river valley. After the War of Independence New York became the 11th state of the Union (1778), having first declared itself independent of Britain in 1777.

The economy depended on manufacturing, shipping and other means of distribution and trade. During the 19th century New York became the most important city in the USA. Its industries, especially clothing, attracted thousands of European immigrants. Industrial development spread along the Hudson-Mohawk valley, which was made the route of the Erie Canal (1825) linking New York with Buffalo on Lake Erie and thus with the developing farmlands of the middle west.

On 11 Sept. 2001 two hijacked commercial airliners were flown into the World Trade Center in central New York. The complex was destroyed in the attack and 2,753 people died.

Territory and Population

New York is bounded west and north by Canada with Lake Erie, Lake Ontario and the St Lawrence River forming the boundary; east by Vermont, Massachusetts and Connecticut, southeast by the Atlantic, south by New Jersey and Pennsylvania. Land area, 47,126 sq. miles (122,057 sq. km); water area, 7,429 sq. miles (19,240 sq. km). Census population, 1 April 2010, was 19,378,102, an increase of 2·1% since 2000. July 2018 estimate, 19,542,209.

Population in five census years was:

	White	Black	American Indian	Asian	Total	Per sq. mile
1910	8,966,845	134,191	6,046	6,532	9,113,614	191·2
			All others			
1980	13,961,106	2,401,842	1,194,340		17,557,288	367·0
1990	13,385,255	2,859,055	1,746,145		17,990,455	381·0
2000	12,893,689	3,014,385	3,068,383		18,976,457	401·9
2010	12,740,974	3,073,800	3,563,328		19,378,102	411·2

Of the total population in 2010, 10,000,955 were female and 15,053,173 were 18 years old or older. In 2010 the Hispanic population was 3,416,922, up from 2,867,583 in 2000 (an increase of 19·2%).

The population of New York City, by boroughs, census of 1 April 2010 was: Bronx, 1,385,108; Brooklyn, 2,504,700; Manhattan, 1,585,873; Queens, 2,230,722; Staten Island, 468,730; total, 8,175,133.

Population of other large cities and incorporated places at the 2010 census was:

Buffalo	261,310
Rochester	210,565
Yonkers	195,976
Syracuse	145,170
Albany (capital)	97,856
New Rochelle	77,062
Cheektowaga	75,178
Mount Vernon	67,292
Schenectady	66,135
Utica	62,235
Brentwood	60,664
Tonawanda	58,144
White Plains	56,853
Hempstead	53,891
Levittown	51,881
Irondequoit	51,692
Niagara Falls	50,193
Troy	50,129
Binghamton	47,376
West Seneca	44,711
West Babylon	43,213
Freeport	42,860
Hicksville	41,547
Coram	39,113
East Meadow	38,132
Valley Stream	37,511
Brighton	36,609
Commack	36,124

The New York–Northern New Jersey–Long Island metropolitan area had, in 2010, a population of 18,897,109. Other large urbanized areas, census 2010; Buffalo–Niagara Falls, 1,135,509; Rochester, 1,054,323; Albany–Schenectady–Troy, 870,716.

Social Statistics

Births, 2014, 238,773 (12·1 per 1,000 population); deaths, 2014, 149,944 (7·6). Infant mortality rate, 2013, 4·9 per 1,000 live births. 2014: marriages, 6·7 per 1,000 population; divorces and annulments, 2·8. Same-sex marriage became legal in July 2011.

Climate

Albany, Jan. 24°F (−4·4°C), July 73°F (22·8°C). Annual rainfall 34" (855 mm). Buffalo, Jan. 24°F (−4·4°C), July 70°F (21·1°C). Annual rainfall 36" (905 mm). New York, Jan. 30°F (−1·1°C), July 74°F (23·3°C). Annual rainfall 43" (1,087 mm). New York belongs to the Atlantic Coast climate zone (see UNITED STATES: Climate).

Constitution and Government

New York State has had five constitutions, adopted in 1777, 1821, 1846, 1894 and 1938. The constitution produced by the 1938 convention (which was substantially a modification of the 1894 one), forms the fundamental law of the state (as modified by subsequent amendments). A proposed new constitution in 1967 was rejected by the electorate. In 1997 voters rejected a proposal to hold a new constitutional convention.

The Legislature comprises the Senate, with 62 members, and the Assembly, with 150. All members are elected in even-numbered years for two-year terms. The Legislature meets every year, typically for several days a week from Jan.–June and, if recalled by leaders of the Legislature, at other times during the year. The Governor can also call the Legislature into extraordinary session. The state capital is Albany. For local government the state is divided into 62 counties, five of which constitute the city of New York.

Each of the state's 62 cities is incorporated by charter, under special legislation. The government of New York City is vested in the mayor (Bill de Blasio), elected for four years, and a city council, whose president and members are elected for four years. The council has a President and 51 members, each elected from a district wholly within the city. The mayor appoints all the heads of departments, except the comptroller (the chief financial officer), who is elected. Each of the five city boroughs (Manhattan, Bronx, Brooklyn, Queens and Staten Island) has a president, elected for four years. Each borough is also a county, although Manhattan borough, as a county, is called New York, Brooklyn is called Kings, and Staten Island is called Richmond.

For the 116th Congress, which convened in Jan. 2019, New York State sends 27 members to the House of Representatives. It is represented in the Senate by Charles Schumer (D. 1999–2023) and Kirsten Gillibrand (D. 2009–25), who succeeded Hillary Clinton (D. 2001–09) following the latter's appointment as Secretary of State. Gillibrand won a special election in Nov. 2010 to take on the remainder of Clinton's term, which was set to end in Jan. 2013.

Recent Elections

In the 2016 presidential election Hillary Clinton took New York State with 58·8% of the vote (Barack Obama won it in 2012).

Current Government

Governor: Andrew Cuomo (D.), 2019–23 (salary: $179,000).
   Lieut.-Governor: Kathy Hochul (D.), 2019–23.
   Secretary of State: Rossana Rosado (D.), since Feb. 2016.
Government Website: https://www.ny.gov

Economy

Per capita personal income (2015) was $57,705.

Budget

In 2011 total state revenue was $205,546m. Total expenditure was $184,009m. (including: public welfare, $51,132m.; education, $45,219m.; health, $8,828m.; hospitals, $6,114m.; government administration, $5,699m.). Outstanding debt in 2011 was $134,929m.

Performance

Gross Domestic Product by state was $1,433,531m. in 2015, ranking New York State third after California and Texas. In 2015 state real GDP growth was 0·9%.

Banking and Finance
In 2014 there were 159 financial institutions in New York State insured by the US Federal Deposit Insurance Corporation, with assets worth $903,358m.

Energy and Natural Resources

Electricity
In 2015 production was 138·6bn. kWh, of which 56·9bn. kWh was from natural gas.

Oil and Gas
In 2014 New York produced 341,000 bbls of crude petroleum; marketed production of natural gas totalled 20bn. cu. ft.

Water
The total area covered by water is 7,429 sq. miles.

Minerals
Principal minerals are: sand and gravel, salt, titanium concentrate, talc, abrasive garnet, wollastonite and emery. Quarry products include trap rock, slate, marble, limestone and sandstone. Value of domestic non-fuel mineral output in 2009 was $1,370m.

Agriculture
New York State has large agricultural interests. In 2007 it had 36,352 farms, with a total area of 7·17m. acres; average farm was 197 acres. Average value per acre in 2007 was $2,275.

Farm income, 2009: from crops, $1,680m.; and from livestock, $1,996m. The net farm income in 2009 was $553m. Dairying is an important type of farming. Field crops comprise maize, winter wheat, oats and hay. New York ranks second in the USA in the production of apples and maple syrup. Other products are grapes, tart cherries, peaches, pears, plums, strawberries, raspberries, cabbage, onions, potatoes and maple sugar. Farm animals, 2007, included 1,443,000 all cattle, 626,000 dairy cows, 85,700 hogs and pigs, 63,000 sheep and lambs, and 3·95m. laying hens.

Forestry
Total forested area was 18,950,000 acres in 2013, of which 14,000 acres were national forest. There were state parks and recreation areas covering 330,000 acres in 2011.

Industry

Leading industries are clothing, non-electrical machinery, printing and publishing, electrical equipment, instruments, food and allied products and fabricated metals. In 2012 the state's 33,692 manufacturing establishments had 885,000 employees, earning $45,679m. Total value added by manufacturing in 2013 was $72,861m.

Labour
Total non-agricultural employment, 2010, 8,553,300. Employees by branch, 2010 (in 1,000): education and health services, 1,704; government, 1,510; trade, transportation and utilities, 1,457; professional and business services, 1,100; leisure and hospitality, 733. In Dec. 2010 the unemployment rate was 8·2%.

International Trade

Imports and Exports
In 2015 imports into New York State totalled $133·1bn. (down from $134·7bn. in 2014). In the same year exports from New York State totalled $83·1bn., down from $88·8bn. in 2014. The leading source for imports in 2015 was China ($23·0bn.), ahead of Canada ($18·0bn.). The leading destination for exports in 2015 was Canada ($14·9bn.), followed by Hong Kong ($9·6bn.).

Communications

Roads
In 2012 there were 114,709 miles of road (66,201 miles rural). The New York State Thruway comprises six highways totalling 570 miles; it includes a 496-mile long mainline running from New York City to Ripley in the far west of the state where New York and Pennsylvania meet. The Adirondack Northway, a 176-mile toll-free highway, is a connecting road from the Thruway at Albany to the Canadian border at Champlain, Quebec.

There were approximately 10,103,000 motor vehicle registrations in 2011 and 1,168 traffic accident fatalities in 2012.

Rail
In 2012 there were 3,447 miles of freight railroad (excluding trackage rights). There were 39 freight railroads operating in 2012. Rail traffic originating in New York State in 2012 totalled 7·4m. tons and rail traffic terminating in the state came to 20·6m. tons. New York City has NYCTA and PATH metro systems, and commuter railroads run by Metro-North, New Jersey Transit and Long Island Rail Road. Buffalo has a 6-mile metro line.

Civil Aviation
There were 14 primary airports—commercial service airports with more than 10,000 passenger boardings annually—in New York State in 2011 with a combined total of 44,211,872 enplanements, up from 43,617,917 in 2010. Five of the primary airports had more than 1m. passenger enplanements in 2011: New York City's John F. Kennedy International (with 23,664,832 enplanements, ranking it sixth in the USA), New York City's La Guardia (11,989,227), Buffalo Niagara International (2,582,597), Albany International (1,216,626) and Greater Rochester International (1,190,967).

Shipping
The canals of the state, combined in 1918 in what is called the Improved Canal System, have a length of 524 miles, of which the Erie or Barge canal has 340 miles.

Social Institutions

Justice
The State Human Rights Law was approved on 12 March 1945, effective on 1 July 1945. The State Division of Human Rights is charged with the responsibility of enforcing this law. The division may request and utilize the services of all governmental departments and agencies; adopt and promulgate suitable rules and regulations; test, investigate and pass judgment upon complaints alleging discrimination in employment, in places of public accommodation, resort or amusement, education, and in housing, land and commercial space; hold hearings, subpoena witnesses and require the production for examination of papers relating to matters under investigation; grant compensatory damages and require repayment of profits in certain housing cases among other provisions; apply for court injunctions to prevent frustration of orders of the Commissioner.

In Dec. 2014 there were 52,518 state and federal prisoners, down from 63,751 in Dec. 2004.

The death penalty was declared unconstitutional in New York State in 2004; the last inmate was removed from death row in 2007. The last execution was in 1963.

Education
Education is compulsory between the ages of six and 16. In 2012–13 the 4,823 public elementary and secondary schools had 2,710,703 pupils and 207,060 teachers. There were 487,810 pupils at 1,930 private schools in fall 2011.

The state's educational system, including public and private schools and secondary institutions, universities, colleges, libraries, museums, etc., constitutes (by legislative act) the 'University of the State of New York', which is governed by a Board of Regents consisting of 15 members appointed by the Legislature. Within the framework of this 'University' was established in 1948 a 'State University' (SUNY), which controls 64 colleges and educational centres, 30 of which are locally operated community colleges. The 'State University' is governed by a board of 16 Trustees, appointed by the Governor with the consent and advice of the Senate.

In fall 2009 there were 269 degree-granting colleges and universities in New York State; enrolled students numbered 1,248,908.

Student enrolment (fall 2009) in degree-granting institutions in the state included:

Founded	Name and place	Students
1754	Columbia University, New York City	24,230
1795	Union College, Schenectady and Albany	2,194
1824	Rensselaer Polytechnic Institute, Troy	6,901
1829	Rochester Institute of Technology, Rochester	15,445

(*continued*)

Founded	Name and place	Students
1831	New York University, New York City	43,404
1836	Alfred University, Alfred	2,319
1841	Manhattanville College, New York City	2,993
1846	Colgate University, Hamilton	2,837
1846	Fordham University, New York City	14,544
1847	The City University of New York (CUNY), New York City	259,515
1848	University of Rochester, Rochester	9,506
1854	Polytechnic Institute of New York University, New York City	4,514
1856	St Lawrence University, Canton	2,401
1859	Cooper Union for the Advancement of Science and Art, NYC	995
1861	Vassar College, Poughkeepsie	2,453
1863	Manhattan College, New York City	3,461
1865	Cornell University, Ithaca	20,633
1870	Syracuse University, Syracuse	19,638
1870	St John's University, New York City	20,352
1892	Ithaca College, Ithaca	6,894
1906	Pace University, New York City and Westchester	12,706
1926	Long Island University	21,682
1929	Marist College, Poughkeepsie	6,179
1935	Hofstra University, Hempstead	12,068
1948	State University of New York (SUNY)	464,981

Health

New York State had 2·9 community hospital beds for every 1,000 population in 2013. In the same year there were 39·4 active physicians per 10,000 civilian population and 7·3 dentists per 10,000.

Welfare

Medicare enrolment in July 2012 totalled 3,160,615. In fiscal year 2012 a total of 5,801,537 people in New York State received Medicaid. In Dec. 2014 there were 3,482,978 Old-Age, Survivors, and Disability Insurance (OASDI) beneficiaries. A total of 281,726 people were receiving payments under Temporary Assistance for Needy Families (TANF) in Dec. 2012.

Religion

The principal religious traditions in 2010 were: Catholics, with 6,287,618 members; Mainline Protestants, 1,027,403; Evangelical Protestants, 871,326; Jews, 784,106; Muslims, 393,000 (estimate).

Culture

Tourism

Overseas visitors to New York State—excluding those from Canada and Mexico—numbered 10,014,000 in 2016 (the most of any state), down from 10,385,000 in 2015. There were 3,368,000 visits by Canadians in 2015.

North Carolina

Key Historical Events

The early inhabitants were Cherokees. European settlement was attempted in 1585–87, following an exploratory visit by Sir Walter Raleigh, but this failed. Settlers from Virginia came to the shores of Albemarle Sound after 1650 and in 1663 Charles II chartered a private colony of Carolina. In 1691 the north was put under a deputy governor who ruled from Charleston in the south. The colony was formally separated into North and South Carolina in 1712. In 1729 control was taken from the private proprietors and vested in the Crown, whereupon settlement grew, and the boundary between north and south was finally fixed (1735).

After the War of Independence, North Carolina became one of the original 13 states of the Union. The city of Raleigh was laid out as the new capital. Having been a plantation colony North Carolina continued to develop as a plantation state, growing tobacco with black slave labour. It was also an important source of gold before the western gold-rushes of 1848.

In 1861 at the outset of the Civil War, North Carolina seceded from the Union, but General Sherman occupied the capital unopposed. A military governor was admitted in 1862, and civilian government restored with readmission to the Union in 1868.

Territory and Population

North Carolina is bounded north by Virginia, east by the Atlantic, south by South Carolina, southwest by Georgia and west by Tennessee. Land area, 48,618 sq. miles (125,920 sq. km); water area, 5,201 sq. miles (13,471 sq. km). Census population, 1 April 2010, was 9,535,483, an increase of 18·5% since 2000. July 2018 estimate, 10,383,620.

Population in five census years was:

	White	Black	American Indian	Asian	Total	Per sq. mile
1910	1,500,511	697,843	7,851	82	2,206,287	45·3
			All others			
1980	4,453,010	1,316,050	105,369		5,874,429	111·5
1990	5,008,491	1,456,323	163,823		6,628,637	136·1
2000	5,804,656	1,737,545	507,112		8,049,313	165·2
2010	6,528,950	2,048,628	957,905		9,535,483	196·1

Of the total population in 2010, 4,889,991 were female and 7,253,848 were 18 years old or older. In 2010 North Carolina's Hispanic population was 800,120, up from 378,963 in 2000. This represented a rise of 111·1%.

The principal cities (with census population in 2010) are: Charlotte, 731,424; Raleigh (the capital), 403,892; Greensboro, 269,666; Winston-Salem, 229,617; Durham, 228,330; Fayetteville, 200,564; Cary, 135,234; Wilmington, 106,476; High Point, 104,371.

Social Statistics

Births, 2014, 120,975 (12·2 per 1,000 population); deaths, 2014, 85,367 (8·6). Infant mortality rate, 2013, 7·0 per 1,000 live births. 2014: marriages, 6·9 per 1,000 population; divorces and annulments, 3·4. Same-sex marriage became legal in Oct. 2014.

Climate

Climate varies sharply with altitude; the warmest area is in the southeast near Southport and Wilmington; the coldest is Mount Mitchell (6,684 ft). Raleigh, Jan. 42°F (5·6°C), July 79°F (26·1°C). Annual rainfall 46" (1,158 mm). North Carolina belongs to the Atlantic Coast climate zone (see UNITED STATES: Climate).

Constitution and Government

The present constitution dates from 1971 (previous constitutions, 1776 and 1868); it has had 38 amendments as of 2016. The General Assembly consists of a Senate of 50 members and a House of Representatives of 120 members; all are elected by districts for two years. It meets in odd-numbered years in Jan.

The Governor and Lieut.-Governor are elected for four years; they can be elected to only one additional consecutive term. There are also 19 executive departments—eight have elected heads (for four-year terms) and ten have heads appointed by the Governor; the other department is the North Carolina Community College System, under a president.

For the 116th Congress, which convened in Jan. 2019, North Carolina sends 13 members to the House of Representatives. It is represented in the Senate by Richard Burr (R. 2005–23) and Thom Tillis (R. 2015–21).

The capital is Raleigh. There are 100 counties.

Recent Elections

In the 2016 presidential election Donald Trump took North Carolina with 50·5% of the vote (Mitt Romney won it in 2012).

Current Government

Governor: Roy Cooper (D.), 2017–21 (salary: $144,349).
Lieut.-Governor: Dan Forest (R.), 2017–21.
Secretary of State: Elaine Marshall (D.), since Jan. 1997.
Government Website: https://www.nc.gov

Economy

Per capita personal income (2015) was $40,656.

Budget

In 2011 total state revenue was $63,199m. Total expenditure was $53,089m. (education, $19,311m.; public welfare, $11,619m.; highways, $3,433m.; hospitals, $1,622m.; health, $1,567m.). Outstanding debt in 2011, $18,556m.

Performance

Gross Domestic Product by state in 2015 was $495,402m., ranking North Carolina 10th in the United States. In 2015 state real GDP growth was 2·0%.

Energy and Natural Resources

Electricity

In 2015 production was 128·4bn. kWh, of which 42·1bn. kWh was from nuclear energy, 39·9bn. kWh from coal and 36·5bn. kWh from natural gas.

Water

The total area covered by water is 5,201 sq. miles, of which 4,052 sq. miles are inland.

Minerals

Principal minerals are stone, sand and gravel, phosphate rock, feldspar, lithium minerals, olivine, kaolin and talc. North Carolina is a leading producer of bricks, making more than 1bn. bricks a year. Value of domestic non-fuel mineral production in 2009 was $846m.

Agriculture

In 2007 there were 52,913 farms covering 8·47m. acres; average size of farms was 160 acres and average value per acre in 2007 was $4,096.

Farm income, 2009: from crops, $3,478m.; and from livestock and products, $5,710m. The net farm income in 2009 was $2,739m. Principal commodities are broilers, hogs, and greenhouse and dairy products. North Carolina is the USA's largest tobacco producer (366·0m. lb in 2007, representing 47% of overall production).

Livestock, 2007: cattle, 820,000; hogs and pigs, 10·13m.; laying hens, 12·75m.

Forestry

Forests covered 18·61m. acres in 2013, with 1·28m. acres of national forest. Main products are hardwood veneer and hardwood plywood, furniture woods, pulp, paper and lumber.

Fisheries

Commercial fish catch, 2009, had a value of approximately $77·2m. and produced 69·0m. lb. The catch is mainly of blue crab, menhaden, Atlantic croaker, flounder, shark, sea trout, mullet, blue fish and shrimp.

Industry

The leading industries by employment are textiles, clothing, furniture, electrical machinery and equipment, non-electrical machinery and food processing. In 2012 the state's 18,932 manufacturing establishments had 871,000 employees, earning $38,618m. Total value added by manufacturing in 2013 was $106,757m.

Labour

Total non-agricultural employment, 2010, 3,862,000. Employees by branch, 2010 (in 1,000): trade, transport and utilities, 711; government, 704; education and health services, 539; professional and business services, 481; manufacturing, 431. The unemployment rate in Dec. 2010 was 9·8%.

International Trade

Imports and Exports

In 2015 imports into North Carolina totalled $51·3bn. (down from $52·9bn. in 2014). In the same year exports from North Carolina totalled $30·2bn., down from $31·4bn. in 2014. The leading source for imports in 2015 was China ($11·1bn.), ahead of Mexico ($4·5bn.). The leading destination for exports in 2015 was Canada ($6·9bn.), followed by Mexico ($3·2bn.).

Communications

Roads

In 2012 there were 106,063 miles of road (68,518 miles rural). There were approximately 7,593,000 registered motor vehicles.

Rail

In 2012 there were 3,258 miles of freight railroad (excluding trackage rights). There were 23 freight railroads operating in 2012. Rail traffic originating in North Carolina in 2012 totalled 10·4m. tons and rail traffic terminating in the state came to 47·9m. tons.

Civil Aviation

In 2011 North Carolina had nine primary airports (commercial service airports with more than 10,000 passenger boardings annually) with a combined total of 25,751,825 enplanements, up from 25,331,266 in 2010. By far the busiest airport is Charlotte/Douglas International, with 19,022,535 enplanements in 2011.

Shipping

There are two ocean ports, Wilmington and Morehead City.

Social Institutions

Justice

There were five executions in 2005 and four in 2006, but the death penalty was suspended in Jan. 2007. In Dec. 2014 there were 37,096 federal and state prisoners.

Education

School attendance is compulsory between seven and 16. In 2012–13 there were 1,518,465 pupils and 98,590 teachers at 2,614 public schools; there were 119,070 pupils at 640 private schools. Total expenditure on public schools was $13,278m. in 2010–11; teachers' salaries in 2012–13 averaged $45,947.

The 16 senior universities are all part of the University of North Carolina system (with 222,322 enrolled students in fall 2009). The largest institution is the North Carolina State University (founded 1887), at Raleigh, with 33,819 students. The University of North Carolina at Chapel Hill (founded in 1789; the first state university to open in America in 1795) had 28,916 students in fall 2009; East Carolina University (founded in 1907), at Greenville, had 27,654. There were 74 private degree-granting institutions in 2012–13; enrolment totalled 112,347 in fall 2012.

Health

North Carolina had 2·3 community hospital beds for every 1,000 population in 2013. In the same year there were 26·4 active physicians per 10,000 civilian population and 4·8 dentists per 10,000.

Welfare

Medicare enrolment in July 2012 totalled 1,602,851. In fiscal year 2012 a total of 2,065,596 people in North Carolina received Medicaid. In Dec. 2014 there were 1,948,531 Old-Age, Survivors, and Disability Insurance (OASDI) beneficiaries. A total of 40,905 people were receiving payments under Temporary Assistance for Needy Families (TANF) in Dec. 2012.

Religion

The principal religious traditions in 2010 were: Evangelical Protestants, with 2,585,530 members; Mainline Protestants, 1,130,241; Catholics, 392,912; Black Protestants, 248,257; Latter-day Saints (Mormons), 77,627.

Culture

Tourism

In 2011 overseas visitors to North Carolina—excluding those from Canada and Mexico—numbered 335,000, down from 343,000 in 2010.

North Dakota

Key Historical Events

The original inhabitants were Plains Indians. French explorers and traders were active in the 18th century, often operating from French possessions in Canada. France claimed the area until 1803, when it passed to the USA as part of the Louisiana Purchase, except for the northeastern part which was held by the British until 1818.

Trading with the American Indians, mainly for furs, continued until the 1860s, with American traders succeeding the French. In 1861 the Dakota Territory (North and South) was established. In 1862 the Homestead Act was passed (allowing 160 acres of public land free to any family who had worked and lived on it for five years) and this greatly stimulated settlement. Farming settlers came to the wheat lands in great numbers, many of them from Canada, Norway and Germany.

Bismarck, the capital, began as a crossing-point on the Missouri and was fortified in 1872 to protect workers building the Northern Pacific Railway. There followed a gold-rush nearby and the town became a service centre for prospectors. In 1889 North and South Dakota were admitted to the Union as separate states with Bismarck as the Northern capital. The largest city, Fargo, was also a railway town, named after William George Fargo, the express-company founder.

The population grew rapidly until 1890 and steadily until 1930 by which time it was about one-third European in origin. Between 1930 and 1970 there was a steady population drain, increasing whenever farming was affected by the extremes of the continental climate. The discovery of oil in the state in 2006 has since prompted an economic boom that has generated a population rise more than three times the rate in the USA overall since 2010.

Territory and Population

North Dakota is bounded north by Canada, east by the Red River (forming a boundary with Minnesota), south by South Dakota and west by Montana. Land area, 69,001 sq. miles (178,711 sq. km); water area, 1,698 sq. miles (4,397 sq. km). Census population, 1 April 2010, was 672,591, an increase of 4·7% since 2000. Following the discovery of oil in 2006 the population rose by 7·6% between 2010 and 2013, the fastest rate of growth in the country. July 2018 population estimate, 760,077.

Population at five census years was:

	White	Black	American Indian	Asian	Total	Per sq. mile
1910	569,855	617	6,486	98	577,056	8·2
			All others			
1980	625,557	2,568	24,692		652,717	9·5
1990	604,142	3,524	31,134		638,800	9·3
2000	593,182	3,916	45,102		642,200	9·3
2010	605,449	7,960	59,182		672,591	9·7

Of the total population in 2010, 339,864 were male and 522,720 were 18 years old or older. Only Vermont has fewer persons of Hispanic origin than North Dakota. In 2010 the Hispanic population was 13,467, up from 7,786 in 2000 (an increase of 73·0%).

The largest cities are Fargo with a population, census 2010, of 105,549; Bismarck (capital), 61,272; Grand Forks, 52,838; and Minot, 40,888.

Social Statistics

Births, 2014, 11,359 (15·4 per 1,000 population); deaths, 2014, 6,184 (8·4). Infant mortality rate, 2013, 6·0 per 1,000 live births. 2014: marriages, 6·3 per 1,000 population; divorces and annulments, 2·8.

Climate

Bismarck, Jan. 8°F (−13·3°C), July 71°F (21·1°C). Annual rainfall 16" (402 mm). Fargo, Jan. 6°F (−14·4°C), July 71°F (21·1°C). Annual rainfall 20" (503 mm). North Dakota belongs to the High Plains climate zone (*see* UNITED STATES: Climate).

Constitution and Government

The present constitution dates from 1889; it has had 154 amendments as of 2011. The Legislative Assembly consists of a Senate of 47 members elected for four years, and a House of Representatives of 94 members elected for four years. The Governor and Lieut.-Governor are elected for four years.

For the 116th Congress, which convened in Jan. 2019, North Dakota sends one member to the House of Representatives. It is represented in the Senate by John Hoeven (R. 2011–23) and Kevin Cramer (R. 2019–25).

The capital is Bismarck. The state has 53 organized counties.

Recent Elections

In the 2016 presidential election Donald Trump took North Dakota with 64·1% of the vote (Mitt Romney won it in 2012).

Current Government

Governor: Doug Burgum (R.), 2016–20 (salary: $129,096).
  Lieut.-Governor: Brent Sanford (R.), 2016–20.
    Secretary of State: Alvin A. Jaeger (R.), since Jan. 1993.
Government Website: https://www.nd.gov

Economy

Per capita personal income (2015) was $54,376.

Budget

In 2011 total state revenue was $7,806m. Total expenditure was $5,516m. (education, $1,781m.; public welfare, $913m.; highways, $717m.; natural resources, $262m.; government administration, $160m.). Outstanding debt in 2011, $2,061m.

Performance

Gross Domestic Product by state in 2015 was $55,860m., ranking North Dakota 45th in the United States. In 2015 state real GDP growth was −2·6% (the biggest fall of any state, as a consequence of the global drop in oil prices). In 2014 growth had been 6·3%, the highest rate of any state, thanks to North Dakota's booming oil production at the time.

Energy and Natural Resources

Oil and Gas

Oil was discovered in 1951. North Dakota is now the USA's second largest oil-producing state, after Texas (accounting for 12% of output). Crude petroleum production has increased tenfold since 2005 and doubled since 2011, and in 2015 was 429m. bbls. However, provisional figures for 2016 suggest that it fell to below the 2014 total of 394m. bbls. Marketed production of natural gas in 2012 totalled 179bn. cu. ft.

Water

The total area covered by water is 1,698 sq. miles.

Minerals

Production of lignite (2009) was 29·9m. short tons. Total value of domestic non-fuel mineral production in 2009 was more than $50m.

Agriculture

In 2007 there were 31,970 farms (61,963 in 1954) in an area of 39·67m. acres and with an average farm acreage of 1,241. In 2007 the average value of farmland and buildings per acre was $771.

Farm income, 2009: from crops, $5,581m.; and from livestock, $771m. The net farm income in 2009 was $1,936m. Production, 2007, included: wheat, 293·5m. bu. (the most in any state); corn, 275·3m. bu.; soybeans, 106·6m. bu.; barley, 75·4m. bu. (the most in any state); honey, 31m. lb (the most in any state).

The state has also an active livestock industry, chiefly cattle raising. Livestock, 2007: cattle, 1·81m.; hogs and pigs, 181,700; sheep, 89,000; laying hens, 109,300.

Forestry

Forest area, 2014, was 797,000 acres, of which 96,000 acres were national forest.

Industry

Although the state is still mainly agricultural it is diversifying into high tech and information technology industries. In 2012 the state's 1,918 manufacturing establishments had 60,000 employees, earning $2,611m. Total value added by manufacturing in 2013 was $5,729m.

Labour

Total non-agricultural employment, 2010, 376,000. Employees by branch, 2010 (in 1,000): government, 80; trade, transportation and utilities, 80; education and health services, 55; leisure and hospitality, 34; professional and business services, 28. The unemployment rate in Dec. 2012 was just 3·2%, the lowest of any US state.

International Trade

Imports and Exports

In 2015 imports into North Dakota totalled $3,137m. (down from $3,828m. in 2014). In the same year exports from North Dakota totalled $4,027m., down from $5,513m. in 2014. The leading source for imports in 2015 was Canada ($1,923m.), ahead of South Korea ($210m.). The leading destination for exports in 2015 was also Canada ($2,923m.), followed by Mexico ($294m.).

Communications

Roads

In 2012 there were 86,851 miles of road (84,929 miles rural). There were 776,344 registered motor vehicles.

Rail

In 2012 there were 3,330 miles of freight railroad (excluding trackage rights). There were eight freight railroads operating in 2012. Rail traffic originating in North Dakota in 2012 totalled 49·5m. tons and rail traffic terminating in the state came to 22·0m. tons.

Civil Aviation

In 2011 there were six primary airports—commercial service airports with more than 10,000 passenger boardings annually—with a combined total of 861,139 enplanements, up from 798,204 in 2010.

Social Institutions

Justice

In Dec. 2014 there were 1,718 federal and state prisoners, up 9·0% from 1,576 in Dec. 2013—the largest rise in any state over the same period. The Missouri River Correctional Center is a minimum custody institution. The death penalty was abolished in 1973. In a state-wide vote held on the same day as the presidential election in Nov. 2016, medical use of marijuana was legalized.

Education

School attendance is compulsory between the ages of seven and 16. In 2012–13 there were 525 public schools with 101,111 pupils and 8,677 teachers. State expenditure per pupil in elementary and secondary schools in 2010–11 was $10,898. Average teacher salary was $47,344 in 2012–13.

The University of North Dakota in Grand Forks, founded in 1883, had 14,906 students in fall 2014; North Dakota State University in Fargo had 14,747. There were 21 degree-granting institutions in 2012–13 (14 public and seven private); total enrolment in fall 2012 was 55,169.

Health

North Dakota had 4·0 community hospital beds for every 1,000 population in 2013. In the same year there were 25·3 active physicians per 10,000 civilian population and 5·4 dentists per 10,000.

Welfare

Medicare enrolment in July 2012 totalled 112,385. In fiscal year 2012 a total of 90,837 people in North Dakota received Medicaid. In Dec. 2014 there were 124,372 Old-Age, Survivors, and Disability Insurance (OASDI) beneficiaries. A total of 3,776 people were receiving payments under Temporary Assistance for Needy Families (TANF) in Dec. 2012.

Religion

The main religious traditions in 2010 were: Mainline Protestants, with 196,839 members; Catholics, 167,349; Evangelical Protestants, 78,607; Latter-day Saints (Mormons), 7,206.

Ohio

Key Historical Events

The land was inhabited by Delaware, Miami, Shawnee and Wyandot Indians. It was explored by French and British traders in the 18th century and confirmed as part of British North America in 1763. After the War of Independence it became part of the Northwest Territory of the new United States. Former independence fighters came in from New England in 1788 to make the first permanent white settlement at Marietta, at the confluence of the Ohio and Muskingum rivers. In 1803 Ohio was separated from the rest of the Territory and admitted to the Union as the 17th state.

In the early 19th century there was steady immigration from Europe, mainly of Germans, Swiss, Irish and Welsh. Industrial growth began with the processing of farm, forest and mining products; it increased rapidly with the need to supply the Union armies in the Civil War of 1861–65.

As the industrial cities grew, so immigration began again, with many whites from Eastern Europe and the Balkans and blacks from the southern states looking for work in Ohio.

Cleveland, which developed rapidly as a Lake Erie port after the opening of commercial waterways to the interior and the Atlantic coast (1825, 1830 and 1855), became an iron-and-steel town during the Civil War.

Territory and Population

Ohio is bounded north by Michigan and Lake Erie, east by Pennsylvania, southeast and south by the Ohio River (forming a boundary with West Virginia and Kentucky) and west by Indiana. Land area, 40,861 sq. miles (105,829 sq. km); water area, 3,965 sq. miles (10,269 sq. km). Census population, 1 April 2010, was 11,536,504, an increase of 1·6% since 2000. July 2018 estimate, 11,689,442.

Population at five census years was:

	White	Black	American Indian	Asian	Total	Per sq. mile
1910	4,654,897	111,452	127	645	4,767,121	117·0
			All others			
1980	9,597,458	1,076,748	123,424		10,797,630	263·2
1990	9,521,756	1,154,826	170,533		10,847,115	264·5
2000	9,645,453	1,301,307	406,380		11,353,140	277·3
2010	9,539,437	1,407,681	589,386		11,536,504	282·3

Of the total population in 2010, 5,904,348 were female and 8,805,753 were 18 years old or older. In 2010 the Hispanic population was 354,674, up from 217,123 in 2000 (an increase of 63·4%).

Census population of chief cities on 1 April 2010 was:

Columbus (capital)	787,033
Cleveland	396,815
Cincinnati	296,943
Toledo	287,208
Akron	199,110
Dayton	141,527
Parma	81,601
Canton	73,007
Youngstown	66,982
Lorain	64,097
Hamilton	62,477
Springfield	60,608
Kettering	56,163
Elyria	54,533
Lakewood	52,131
Cuyahoga Falls	49,652
Euclid	48,920
Middletown	48,694
Mansfield	47,821
Newark	47,573
Mentor	47,159
Cleveland Heights	46,121
Beavercreek	45,193
Strongsville	44,750
Fairfield	42,510
Dublin	41,751
Warren	41,557
Findlay	41,202

Largest metropolitan areas, 2010 census: Cincinnati–Middleton, 2,130,151; Cleveland–Elyria–Mentor, 2,077,240; Columbus (the capital), 1,836,536; Dayton, 841,502; Akron, 703,200; Toledo, 651,429; Youngstown–Warren–Boardman, 565,773; Canton–Massillon, 404,422.

Social Statistics

Births, 2014, 139,467 (12·0 per 1,000 population); deaths, 2014, 114,509 (9·9). Infant mortality, 2013, 7·3 per 1,000 live births. 2014: marriages, 5·8 per 1,000 population; divorces and annulments, 3·2.

Climate

Cincinnati, Jan. 30·6°F, July 76·8°F, annual rainfall 39·6"; Cleveland, Jan. 25·7°F, July 71·9°F, annual rainfall 38·7"; Columbus, Jan. 28·3°F, July 74·7°F, annual rainfall 40·0". Ohio belongs to the Great Lakes climate zone (*see* UNITED STATES: Climate).

Constitution and Government

The question of a general revision of the constitution drafted by an elected convention is submitted to the people every 20 years. The constitution dates from 1851, since when there have been 161 amendments adopted to change the constitution.

The Senate consists of 33 members and the House of Representatives of 99 members. The Senate is elected for four years, half every two years; the House is elected for two years; the Governor, Lieut.-Governor and Secretary of State for four years. Qualified as electors are (with necessary exceptions) all citizens 18 years of age who have the usual residential qualifications.

For the 116th Congress, which convened in Jan. 2019, Ohio sends 16 members to the House of Representatives. It is represented in the Senate by Sherrod Brown (D. 2007–25) and Rob Portman (R. 2011–23).

The capital (since 1816) is Columbus. Ohio is divided into 88 counties.

Recent Elections

In the 2016 presidential election Donald Trump took Ohio with 52·1% of the vote (Barack Obama won it in 2012).

Current Government

Governor: Mike DeWine (R.), 2019–23 (salary: $148,886).
    Lieut.-Governor: Jon Husted (R.), 2019–23.
    Secretary of State: Frank LaRose (R.), since Jan. 2019.
Government Website: https://ohio.gov

Economy

Per capita personal income (2015) was $43,478.

Budget

In 2011 total state revenue was $98,560m. Total expenditure was $79,153m. (education, $22,408m.; public welfare, $18,422m.; highways, $3,494m.; hospitals, $2,660m.; health, $2,482m.). Outstanding debt in 2011, $30,926m.

Performance

In 2015 Gross Domestic Product by state was $610,928m., ranking Ohio 7th in the United States. In 2015 state real GDP growth was 1·8%.

Energy and Natural Resources

Electricity

In 2015 production was 121·9bn. kWh, of which 71·7bn. kWh was from coal.

Oil and Gas

In 2014 Ohio produced 14·9m. bbls of crude petroleum; marketed production of natural gas totalled 519bn. cu. ft.

Water

Lake Erie supplies northern Ohio with its water. The total area covered by water is 3,965 sq. miles.

Minerals

Ohio has extensive mineral resources, of which coal is the most important by value: production (2011), 27,929,089 short tons. Coal production in 2011 was valued at $1,194,931,060. Production of other minerals totalled 88,556,399 short tons, of which limestone, dolomite, sand and gravel accounted for 91%. The remainder was comprised of various amounts of salt, sandstone, clay, shale, gypsum and peat. The combined value of all non-fuel industrial minerals in 2011 was $886,417,044.

Agriculture

Ohio is extensively devoted to agriculture. In 2012, 75,500 farms covered 14·0m. acres. The average size of a farm in 2012 was 185 acres. Average value of farmland and buildings per acre in 2010 was $3,900.

Farm income, 2009: from crops, $4,601m.; from livestock, $2,234m.; total, $6,836m. The net farm income in 2009 was $2,122m. Production (2012): corn for grain (436·8m. bu.), soybeans (202·0m. bu.), wheat (31·0m. bu.), oats (2·6m. bu.). In 2012 there were 2·06m. pigs, 1·24m. cattle and 112,000 sheep.

Forestry

Forest area, 2011, 8,162,000 acres. National forest lands area, 2011, 266,000 acres.

Industry

In 2012, 30,496 manufacturing establishments employed 1,322,000 persons, earning $69,279m. Total value added by manufacturing in 2013 was $124,349m. The largest industries were manufacturing of transport equipment, fabricated metal products and machinery.

Labour

Total non-agricultural employment, 2010, 5,031,000. Employees by branch, 2010 (in 1,000): trade, transportation and utilities, 947; education and health services, 843; government, 782; professional and business services, 623; manufacturing, 620. In Dec. 2010 the unemployment rate was 9·5%.

International Trade

Imports and Exports

In 2015 imports into Ohio totalled $68·9bn. (down from $70·4bn. in 2014). In the same year exports from Ohio totalled $51·2bn., down from $52·6bn. in 2014. The leading source for imports in 2015 was Canada ($13·8bn.), ahead of China ($13·4bn.). The leading destination for exports in 2015 was also Canada ($20·3bn.), followed by Mexico ($6·7bn.).

Communications

Roads

In 2012 there were 123,281 miles of road; there were 9,776,560 registered motor vehicles in the same year.

Rail

In 2012 there were 5,288 miles of freight railroad (excluding trackage rights). There were 34 freight railroads operating in 2012. Rail traffic originating in Ohio in 2012 totalled 66·2m. tons and rail traffic terminating in the state came to 77·3m. tons. Cleveland has a 19-mile metro system.

Civil Aviation

In 2011 there were six primary airports—commercial service airports with more than 10,000 passenger boardings annually—with a combined total of 9,715,163 enplanements, down from 9,873,248 in 2010. The busiest airports, Cleveland-Hopkins International and Port Columbus International, had 4,401,033 and 3,134,379 enplanements respectively in 2011.

Shipping

Ohio has more than 700 miles of navigable waterways, with Lake Erie having a 265-mile shoreline. The ports of Cincinnati and Northern Kentucky handled 49·9m. tons of cargo in 2014.

Social Institutions

Justice

In Dec. 2014 there were 51,519 federal and state prisoners (47,311 males). Ohio had 144 death row inmates in July 2017. There was one execution in 2018.

Education

School attendance during full term is compulsory for children from six to 18 years of age. In 2012–13 there were 1,729,916 enrolled pupils in 3,751 schools. Teachers' salaries averaged $58,092. Estimated public expenditure on elementary and secondary schools for 2010–11 was $23,500m.

In 2012–13 there were 60 public colleges and universities. Total enrolment (fall 2012) was 524,338 students; independent colleges and universities enrolled 185,480 students.

Main public campuses, fall 2014:

Founded	Institutions	Enrolments
1804	Ohio University, Athens	29,217
1809	Miami University, Oxford	18,620
1819	University of Cincinnati	35,313
1870	University of Akron	23,962
1870	Ohio State University, Columbus	58,322
1872	University of Toledo	20,626
1908	Youngstown State University	12,503
1910	Bowling Green State University	16,554
1910	Kent State University	29,477
1964	Cleveland State University	16,936
1964	Wright State University, Dayton	16,842

The largest private universities are the University of Dayton (11,343 students in fall 2014) and Case Western Reserve University, at Cleveland (10,771 students in fall 2014).

Health
Ohio had 2·9 community hospital beds for every 1,000 population in 2013. In the same year there were 31·4 active physicians per 10,000 civilian population and 5·2 dentists per 10,000.

Welfare
Medicare enrolment in July 2012 totalled 2,010,774. In fiscal year 2012 a total of 2,500,418 people in Ohio received Medicaid. In Dec. 2014 there were 2,267,508 Old-Age, Survivors, and Disability Insurance (OASDI) beneficiaries. A total of 144,691 people were receiving payments under Temporary Assistance for Needy Families (TANF) in Dec. 2012.

Religion

The principal religious traditions in Ohio in 2010 were: Catholics, with 1,992,567 members; Evangelical Protestants, 1,491,845; Mainline Protestants, 1,154,461; Black Protestants, 170,388; Jews, 64,479.

Culture

Tourism
Overseas visitors to Ohio—excluding those from Canada and Mexico—numbered 279,000 in 2011, down from 316,000 in 2010 and 390,000 in 2006.

Oklahoma

Key Historical Events

Francisco Coronado led a Spanish expedition in 1541, claiming the land for Spain. There were several American Indian groups but no strong political unit. In 1714 Juchereau de Saint Denis made the first French contact. During the 18th century French fur-traders were active. A French and Spanish struggle for control was resolved by the French withdrawal in 1763. France returned briefly in 1800–03, and the territory then passed to the USA as part of the Louisiana Purchase.

In 1828 the Federal government set aside the area of the present state as Indian Territory (a reservation and sanctuary for American Indian tribes who had been driven off their lands elsewhere by white settlement). About 70 tribes came, among whom were Creeks, Choctaws and Cherokees from the southeastern states, and Plains Indians.

In 1889 the government took back about 2·5m. acres of the Territory and opened it to white settlement. About 10,000 homesteaders gathered at the site of Oklahoma City on the Santa Fe Railway in the rush to stake their land claims. The settlers' area, and others subsequently opened to settlement, were organized as the Oklahoma Territory in 1890. In 1907 the Oklahoma and Indian Territories were combined and admitted to the Union as a state. Indian reservations were established within the state.

The economy first depended on ranching and farming, with packing stations on the railways. A mining industry grew in the 1870s attracting foreign immigration, mainly from Europe. In 1901 oil was found near Tulsa.

Territory and Population

Oklahoma is bounded north by Kansas, northeast by Missouri, east by Arkansas, south by Texas (the Red River forming part of the boundary) and, at the western extremity of the 'panhandle', by New Mexico and Colorado. Land area, 68,595 sq. miles (177,660 sq. km); water area, 1,304 sq. miles (3,377 sq. km). Census population, 1 April 2010, was 3,751,351, an increase of 8·7% since 2000. July 2018 estimate, 3,943,079.

The population at five federal censuses was:

	White	Black	American Indian/ Alaska Native	Other	Total	Per sq. mile
1930	2,130,778	172,198	92,725	339	2,396,040	34·6
1980	2,597,783	204,658	169,292	53,557	3,025,486	43·2
1990	2,583,512	233,801	252,420	119,723	3,189,456	44·5
2000	2,628,434	260,968	273,230	288,022	3,450,654	50·3
2010	2,706,845	277,644	321,687	445,175	3,751,351	54·7

Of the total population in 2010, 1,894,374 were female and 2,821,685 were 18 years old or older. Oklahoma is home to 39 recognized American Indian tribes. In 2010 Oklahoma's Hispanic population was 332,007, up from 179,304 in 2000 (an increase of 85·2%).

The most important cities with population, 2010, are Oklahoma City (capital), 579,999; Tulsa, 391,906; Norman, 110,925; Broken Arrow, 98,850; Lawton, 96,867; Edmond, 81,405; Moore, 55,081; Midwest City, 54,371; Enid, 49,379; Stillwater, 45,688; Muskogee, 39,223; Bartlesville, 35,750.

Social Statistics

Births, 2014, 53,339 (13·8 per 1,000 population); deaths, 2014, 38,464 (10·0). Infant mortality rate, 2013, 6·7 per 1,000 live births. 2014: marriages, 7·1 per 1,000 population; divorces and annulments, 4·5. Same-sex marriage became legal in Oct. 2014.

Climate

Oklahoma City, Jan. 34°F (1°C), July 81°F (27°C). Annual rainfall 31·9" (8,113 mm). Tulsa, Jan. 34°F (1°C), July 82°F (28°C). Annual rainfall 33·2" (8,438 mm). Oklahoma belongs to the Central Plains climate zone (*see* UNITED STATES: Climate). Oklahoma's average temperature in July 2011 was 88·9°F (31·6°C), the highest for any state in US history.

Constitution and Government

The constitution, dating from 1907, provides for amendment by initiative petition and legislative referendum; it has had numerous amendments since then.

The Legislature consists of a Senate of 48 members, who are elected for four years, and a House of Representatives elected for two years and consisting of 101 members. The Governor and Lieut.-Governor are elected for four-year terms; the Governor can only be elected for two terms in succession. Electors are (with necessary exceptions) all citizens 18 years or older, with the usual qualifications.

For the 116th Congress, which convened in Jan. 2019, Oklahoma sends five members to the House of Representatives. It is represented in the Senate by James Inhofe (R. 1994–2021) and James Lankford (R. 2015–23). Lankford was elected to fill the seat formerly held by Tom Coburn, who had resigned for health reasons.

The capital is Oklahoma City. The state has 77 counties.

Recent Elections

In the 2016 presidential election Donald Trump took Oklahoma with 65·3% of the vote (Mitt Romney won it in 2012).

Current Government

Governor: Kevin Stitt (R.), 2019–23 (salary: $147,000).
  Lieut.-Governor: Matt Pinnell (R.), 2019–23.
  Secretary of State: Michael Rogers (R.), since Jan. 2019.
Government Website: https://www.ok.gov

Economy

Per capita personal income (2015) was $44,272.

Budget

In 2011 total state revenue was $26,225m. Total expenditure was $22,378m. (education, $7,491m.; public welfare, $5,457m.; highways, $2,049m.; health, $804m.; government administration, $590m.). Outstanding debt in 2011, $10,255m.

Performance

Gross Domestic Product by state in 2015 was $185,981m., ranking Oklahoma 29th in the United States. In 2015 state real GDP growth was 2·2%.

Energy and Natural Resources

Oil and Gas

In 2014 Oklahoma produced 127·0m. bbls of crude petroleum (ranking it fifth in the USA after Texas, North Dakota, California and Alaska); marketed production of natural gas totalled 2,310bn. cu. ft (third in the USA behind Texas and Pennsylvania).

Water

The total area covered by water is 1,304 sq. miles.

Minerals

Coal production (2009), 956,000 short tons. Principal minerals are: crushed stone, cement, sand and gravel, iodine, glass sand, gypsum. Other minerals are helium, clay and sand, zinc, lead, granite, tripoli, bentonite, lime and volcanic ash. Total value of domestic non-fuel minerals produced in 2009 was $675m.

Agriculture

In 2007 the state had 86,565 farms and ranches with a total area of 35·09m. acres; average size was 405 acres and average value per acre was $1,157. Area harvested, 2007, 7,650,080 acres. Livestock, 2007: cattle, 5·39m.; sheep and lambs, 76,200; hogs and pigs, 2·40m.; laying hens, 3·32m.

Farm income, 2009: from crops, $1,260m.; from livestock and products, $3,584m. The net farm income in 2009 was $130m. The major cash grain is wheat (167m. bu. in 2008 with a value of $1,082m.). Other crops include barley, oats, rye, grain, corn, soybeans, grain sorghum, cotton, peanuts and peaches. Value of cattle and calves produced, 2008, $1,954m.

The Oklahoma Conservation Commission works with 91 conservation districts, universities, and state and federal government agencies. The early work of the conservation districts, beginning in 1937, was limited to flood and erosion control: since 1970, they also include urban areas.

Irrigated production has increased in the Oklahoma 'panhandle'. The Ogallala aquifer is the primary source of irrigation water there and in western Oklahoma, a finite source because of its isolation from major sources of recharge. Declining groundwater levels necessitate the most effective irrigation practices.

Forestry

There were 12,363,000 acres of forested land in 2013, with 306,000 acres of national forest. The forest products industry is concentrated in the 118 eastern counties. There are three forest regions: Ozark (oak, hickory); Ouachita highlands (pine, oak); Cross-Timbers (post oak, black jack oak). Southern pine is the chief commercial species, at almost 80% of saw-timber harvested annually. Replanting is essential.

Electricity

In 2015 production was 76,136m. kWh, of which 34,286m. kWh was from natural gas and 24,867m. kWh from coal.

Industry

In 2012 Oklahoma's 8,100 manufacturing establishments had 297,000 employees, earning $14,162m. Total value added by manufacturing in 2013 was $24,257m.

Labour

Total non-agricultural employment in 2010 was 1,526,000. Employees by branch, 2010 (in 1,000): government, 340; trade, transportation and utilities, 277; education and health services, 204; professional and business services, 169; leisure and hospitality, 138. Oklahoma's unemployment rate was 6·8% in Dec. 2010.

International Trade

Imports and Exports

In 2015 imports into Oklahoma totalled $11·0bn. (down from $13·6bn. in 2014). In the same year exports from Oklahoma totalled $5·3bn., down from $6·3bn. in 2014. The leading source for imports in 2015 was Canada ($4·4bn.), ahead of China ($2·5bn.). The leading destination for exports in 2015 was also Canada ($1·6bn.), followed by Mexico ($0·6bn.).

Communications

Roads

In 2012 there were 112,821 miles of road comprising 16,146 miles of urban road and 96,675 miles of rural road. There were 3,312,256 registered motor vehicles.

Rail

In 2012 there were 3,273 miles of freight railroad (excluding trackage rights). There were 19 freight railroads operating in 2012. Rail traffic originating in Oklahoma in 2012 totalled 18·3m. tons and rail traffic terminating in the state came to 34·8m. tons.

Civil Aviation

There were three primary airports—commercial service airports with more than 10,000 passenger boardings annually—in 2011 with a combined total of 3,148,469 enplanements, down from 3,161,942 in 2010. The main airport is Will Rogers World, at Oklahoma City, which had 1,738,438 enplanements in 2011.

Shipping

The McClellan-Kerr Arkansas Navigation System provides access from east central Oklahoma to New Orleans through the Verdigris, Arkansas and Mississippi rivers. Commodities shipped are mainly chemical fertilizer, farm produce, petroleum products, iron and steel, coal, sand and gravel.

Social Institutions

Justice

There were 27,650 federal and state prisoners in Dec. 2014. The death penalty was suspended in 1966 and reimposed in 1976. In a referendum held in Nov. 2016, the state's commitment to the death penalty was reaffirmed after the state attorney general had suspended executions the previous year. There was one execution in 2015 but then none since. Oklahoma had 112 executions between 1977 and 2018—the third highest total in the USA behind Texas and Virginia.

Education

Public elementary and secondary schools numbered 1,796 in 2012–13; there were 673,483 pupils and 41,775 teachers. The average teacher salary per annum was $44,128 in 2012–13. In 2010–11 total expenditure on public elementary and secondary education was $5,619m. There were 66 degree-granting establishments (29 public) in 2012–13; enrolment totalled 228,464 in fall 2012.

Public institutions of higher education include:

Founded	Name	Place	2014 enrolment
1890	University of Oklahoma	Norman	27,261
1890	Oklahoma State University	Stillwater	25,962
		Oklahoma City (1961)	6,712
1890	University of Central Oklahoma	Edmond	16,840
1897	Northeastern State University	Tahlequah	8,310
1897	Southwestern Oklahoma State University	Weatherford	4,994
1901	Northern Oklahoma College	Tonkawa	4,766
1908	Cameron University	Lawton	5,537

(continued)

Founded	Name	Place	2014 enrolment
1909	East Central University	Ada	4,428
1909	Rogers State University	Claremore	4,030
1909	Southeastern Oklahoma State University	Durant	3,878
1946	Oklahoma State University Institute of Technology	Okmulgee	3,379
1969	Rose State College	Midwest City	6,891
1970	Tulsa Community College	Tulsa	17,861
1972	Oklahoma City Community College	Oklahoma City	13,444

The largest private institution of higher education is the University of Tulsa (founded in 1894), with 4,682 students in fall 2014.

Health
Oklahoma had 3·0 community hospital beds for every 1,000 population in 2013. In the same year there were 22·3 active physicians per 10,000 civilian population and 5·0 dentists per 10,000.

Welfare
Medicare enrolment in July 2012 totalled 637,480. In fiscal year 2012 a total of 981,568 people in Oklahoma received Medicaid. In Dec. 2014 there were 749,794 Old-Age, Survivors, and Disability Insurance (OASDI) beneficiaries. A total of 18,633 people were receiving payments under Temporary Assistance for Needy Families (TANF) in Dec. 2012.

Religion
The principal religious traditions in the state in 2010 were: Evangelical Protestants, with 1,531,381 members; Mainline Protestants, 383,786; Catholics, 178,430; Black Protestants, 51,621; Latter-day Saints (Mormons), 46,693.

Oregon

Key Historical Events
The area was divided between many American Indian tribes including the Chinook, Tillamook, Cayuse and Modoc. In the 18th century English and Spanish visitors tried to establish claims, based on explorations of the 16th century. The USA also laid claim by right of discovery when an expedition entered the mouth of the Columbia River in 1792.

Oregon was disputed between Britain and the USA. An American fur trading settlement established at Astoria in 1811 was taken by the British in 1812. The Hudson Bay Company was the most active force in Oregon until the 1830s when American pioneers began to migrate westwards along the Oregon Trail. The dispute between Britain and the USA was resolved in 1846 with the boundary fixed at 49°N. lat. Oregon was organized as a Territory in 1848 but with wider boundaries; it became a state with its present boundaries in 1859.

Early settlers were mainly American. They came to farm in the Willamette Valley and to exploit the western forests. Portland developed as a port for ocean-going traffic, although it was 100 miles inland at the confluence of the Willamette and Columbia rivers. Industries followed when the railways came and the rivers were exploited for hydro-electricity. The capital of the Territory from 1851 was Salem, a mission for American Indians on the Willamette river; it was confirmed as state capital in 1864. Salem became the processing centre for the farming and market-gardening of the Willamette Valley.

Territory and Population
Oregon is bounded in the north by Washington, with the Columbia River forming most of the boundary, east by Idaho, with the Snake River forming most of the boundary, south by Nevada and California and west by the Pacific. Land area, 95,988 sq. miles (248,608 sq. km); water area, 2,391 sq. miles (6,191 sq. km). In 2010 the federal government owned 53·0% of the state area. Census population, 1 April 2010, was 3,831,074, an increase of 12·0% since 2000. July 2018 estimate, 4,190,713.

Population at five federal censuses was:

	White	Black	American Indian	Asian	Total	Per sq. mile
1930	938,598	2,234	4,776	8,179	953,786	9·9
1980	2,490,610	37,060	27,314	34,775	2,633,105	27·3
	White	Black	American Indian/ Alaska Native	All Others	Total	Per sq. mile
1990	2,636,787	46,178	38,496	120,860	2,842,321	29·6
2000	2,961,623	55,662	45,211	358,903	3,421,399	35·6
2010	3,204,614	69,206	53,203	504,051	3,831,074	39·9

Of the total population in 2010, 1,935,072 were female and 2,964,621 were 18 years old or older. In 2010 the Hispanic population was 450,062, up from 275,314 in 2000 (an increase of 63·5%).

The largest cities (2010 census figures) are: Portland, 583,776; Eugene, 156,185; Salem (the capital), 154,637; Gresham, 105,594; Hillsboro, 91,611; Beaverton, 89,803; Bend, 76,639; Medford, 74,907; Springfield, 59,403; Corvallis, 54,462; Albany, 50,158. Primary statistical (metropolitan) areas: Portland–Vancouver–Hillsboro, 2,226,009; Salem, 390,738; Eugene–Springfield, 351,715.

Social Statistics
Births, 2014, 45,556 (11·5 per 1,000 population); deaths, 2014, 34,151 (8·6). Infant mortality rate, 2013, 4·9 per 1,000 live births. 2014: marriages, 6·8 per 1,000 population; divorces and annulments, 3·4. Same-sex marriage was legalized in May 2014.

Climate
Jan. 32°F (0°C), July 66°F (19°C). Annual rainfall 28" (710 mm). Oregon belongs to the Pacific coast climate zone (see UNITED STATES: Climate).

Constitution and Government
The present constitution dates from 1859; some 250 items in it have been amended. The Legislative Assembly consists of a Senate of 30 members, elected for four years (half their number retiring every two years), and a House of 60 representatives, elected for two years. The Governor is elected for four years. The constitution reserves to the voters the rights of initiative and referendum and recall.

For the 116th Congress, which convened in Jan. 2019, Oregon sends five members to the House of Representatives. It is represented in the Senate by Ron Wyden (D. 1996–2023) and Jeff Merkley (D. 2009–21).

The capital is Salem. There are 36 counties in the state.

Recent Elections
In the 2016 presidential election Hillary Clinton took Oregon with 51·7% of the vote (Barack Obama won it in 2012).

Current Government
Governor: Kate Brown (D.), 2019–23 (salary: $98,600).

Secretary of State (acting): Leslie Cummings (R.), since Feb. 2019.

Government Website: https://www.oregon.gov

Economy
Per capita personal income (2015) was $42,974.

Budget
In 2011 total state revenue was $34,991m. Total expenditure was $27,335m. (including: education, $7,102m.; public welfare, $6,027m.; highways, $1,672m.; hospitals, $1,629m.; government administration, $786m.). Outstanding debt in 2011, $14,069m.

Performance
Gross Domestic Product by state was $217,629m. in 2015, ranking Oregon 25th in the United States. In 2015 state real GDP growth was 4·9%, the highest increase of any state.

Energy and Natural Resources

Water
The total area covered by water is 2,391 sq. miles.

Minerals
Mineral resources include gold, silver, lead, mercury, chromite, sand and gravel, stone, clays, lime, silica, diatomite, expansible shale, scoria, pumice and uranium. There is geothermal potential. The total value of non-fuel mineral production in 2009 was $314m.

Agriculture
Oregon, which has an area of 61,557,184 acres, is divided by the Cascade Range into two distinct climate zones. West of the Cascade Range there is a good rainfall and almost every variety of crop common to the temperate zone is grown; east of the Range stock-raising and wheat-growing are the principal industries and irrigation is needed for row crops and fruits.

There were, in 2013, 35,000 farms with an acreage of 16·5m. and an average farm size of 471 acres; most are family-owned corporate farms. Average value per acre (2012), $1,882.

Farm income in 2009: from crops, $2,995m.; from livestock and products, $898m. The net farm income in 2009 was $563m. Oregon's top commodities in 2012 were greenhouse and nursery ($745·1m.), cattle and calves ($653·8m.), hay ($638·1m.), wheat ($472·1m.) and grass seed ($411·1m.).

Forestry
Forestland is land that is capable of having at least 10% cover of trees. Roughly 80% of forestland is classified as timberland, which can grow commercial-grade timber. Oregon land area: 63m. acres; forestland, 30·4m. acres; timberland, 24·7m. acres. Only California has more forestland. In 2011 forest/timberland ownership was as follows: federal and state government, 34·5m. acres; private ownership, 19·8m. acres; tribal ownership, 821,000 acres.

The Oregon Department of Forestry (ODF) estimates logging totalled 3·6bn. bd ft in 2011. According to the Oregon Employment Department's covered employment statistics, the forestry and logging subsector's 766 worksites employed 9,385 people statewide and added about $474m. in payroll to Oregon's economy in 2011. Trees vary from the coastal forest of hemlock and spruce to the state's primary species, Douglas fir, throughout much of western Oregon. In eastern Oregon, ponderosa pine, lodgepole pine and true firs are found. Here, along the Cascade summit and in the mountains of northeast Oregon, alpine species are found.

Fisheries
Commercial fish and shellfish landings in 2008 was 260·3m. lb and amounted to a value of $126·5m. The most important are: ground fish, crab, shrimp, tuna, whiting and salmon.

Oil and Gas
In 2014 marketed production of natural gas totalled 950m. cu. ft.

Electricity
In 2015 production was 57,867m. kWh, of which 31,254m. kWh was from conventional hydro-electric energy and 16,237m. kWh from natural gas.

Industry

Forest products manufacturing is Oregon's leading industry, followed by high technology. In 2012 the state's 10,802 manufacturing establishments had 298,000 employees, earning $15,012m. Total value added by manufacturing in 2013 was $37,145m.

Labour
Total non-agricultural employment, 2010, 1,600,000. Employees by branch, 2010 (in 1,000): trade, transportation and utilities, 308; government, 300; education and health services, 228; professional and business services, 181; manufacturing, 164. The unemployment rate was 10·6% in Dec. 2010.

International Trade

Imports and Exports
In 2015 imports into Oregon totalled $14·8bn. (up from $13·8bn. in 2014). In the same year exports from Oregon totalled $20·1bn., down from $20·9bn. in

2014. The leading source for imports in 2015 was Canada ($2·7bn.), ahead of China ($2·5bn.). The leading destination for exports in 2015 was China ($4·8bn.), followed by Canada ($2·6bn.).

Communications

Roads
In 2012 there were 59,262 miles of road (46,390 miles rural). There were 3,441,114 registered vehicles in 2012.

Rail
In 2012 there were 2,396 total miles of freight railroad (excluding trackage rights). There were 18 freight railroads operating in 2012. Rail traffic originating in Oregon in 2012 totalled 10·2m. tons and rail traffic terminating in the state came to 19·3m. tons. There is a light rail network in Portland.

Civil Aviation
There were six primary airports in 2011 (commercial service airports with more than 10,000 passenger boardings annually) with a combined total of 7,772,049 enplanements, up from 7,533,325 in 2010. The busiest airport is Portland International, with 6,808,486 enplanements in 2011.

Shipping
Portland is a major seaport for large ocean-going vessels and is 101 miles inland from the mouth of the Columbia River. In 2014 Portland handled 25,142,613 tons of cargo; Coos Bay, the second busiest port, handled 1,859,026 tons of cargo in 2014.

Social Institutions

Justice
There are 14 correctional institutions in Oregon. In Dec. 2014 there were 15,075 federal and state prisoners. The sterilization law, originally passed in 1917, was amended in 1967 and abolished in 1993. In 1994 Oregon became the first US state to legalize some categories of euthanasia, although implementation of legislation was delayed until 1997.

The death penalty is authorized but there have been no executions since 2001.

Education
School attendance is compulsory from seven to 18 years of age if the twelfth year of school has not been completed; those between the ages of 16 and 18 years, if legally employed, may attend part-time or evening schools. Others may be excused under certain circumstances. In fall 2011 the 1,355 public elementary and secondary schools had 561,698 students and 30,157 teachers; average salary for teachers (2010–11), $56,203. The State's share of the K-12 education budget was $5·75bn. for the two years ending 30 June 2011. For the same two years the Federal Government is estimated to have provided $1·5bn. for Oregon K-12 programmes.

Leading state-supported institutions of higher education (fall 2012) included:

	Students
Portland State University, Portland	28,731
Oregon State University, Corvallis	26,393
University of Oregon, Eugene	24,593
Southern Oregon University, Ashland	6,481
Western Oregon University, Monmouth	6,187
Eastern Oregon University, La Grande	4,208
Oregon Institute of Technology, Klamath Falls	4,001

In 2014 Oregon's higher education system consisted of seven public universities, 17 public community colleges, 67 private for-profit and independent colleges and universities, and hundreds of private career and trade schools. Total enrolment for the Oregon University System campuses in fall 2013 was 103,074.

2013 enrolment in Oregon's 19 private colleges and universities (members of the Oregon Alliance of Independent Colleges and Universities) totalled 35,000 students.

Health

Oregon had 1·7 community hospital beds for every 1,000 population in 2013. In the same year there were 30·7 active physicians per 10,000 civilian population and 6·9 dentists per 10,000.

Welfare

Medicare enrolment in July 2012 totalled 670,095. In fiscal year 2012 a total of 759,972 people in Oregon received Medicaid. In Dec. 2014 there were 798,156 Old-Age, Survivors, and Disability Insurance (OASDI) beneficiaries. A total of 62,051 people were receiving payments under Temporary Assistance for Needy Families (TANF) in Dec. 2012.

Religion

The principal religious traditions in the state in 2010 were: Evangelical Protestants, with 447,009 members; Catholics, 399,440; Latter-day Saints (Mormons), 150,097; Mainline Protestants, 140,248; Buddhists, 14,785.

Pennsylvania

Key Historical Events

Pennsylvania was occupied by four powerful tribes in the 17th century: Delaware, Susquehannock, Shawnee and Iroquois. The first white settlers were Swedish, arriving in 1643. The British became dominant in 1664 and in 1681 William Penn, an English Quaker, was given a charter to colonize the area as a sanctuary for his fellow Quakers. Penn's ideal was peaceful co-operation with the American Indians and religious toleration within the colony. Several religious groups were attracted to Pennsylvania, including Protestant sects from Germany and France. In the 18th century, co-operation with the American Indians failed as the settlers extended their territory.

The Declaration of Independence was signed in Philadelphia while Pennsylvania became one of the original 13 states of the Union. In 1812 the state capital was moved to its current location in Harrisburg, originally a trading post and ferry point on the Susquehanna River in the south-central part of the state. The Mason-Dixon line, the state's southern boundary, was the dividing line between free and slave states in the build-up to the Civil War. Gettysburg and other crucial battles were fought in the state. Industrial growth was rapid after the war. Pittsburgh, founded as a British fort in 1761 during war with the French, had become an iron-making town by 1800 and grew rapidly when canal and railway links opened in the 1830s. The American Federation of Labor was founded in Pittsburgh in 1881, by which time the city was of national importance producing coal, iron, steel and glass.

At the beginning of the 20th century, industry attracted immigration from Italy and Eastern Europe. In farming areas the early sect communities survive, notably Amish and Mennonites. (The Pennsylvania 'Dutch' are of German extraction.)

Territory and Population

Pennsylvania is bounded north by New York, east by New Jersey, south by Delaware and Maryland, southwest by West Virginia, west by Ohio and northwest by Lake Erie. Land area, 44,743 sq. miles (115,883 sq. km); water area, 1,312 sq. miles (3,397 sq. km). Census population, 1 April 2010, was 12,702,379, an increase of 3·4% since 2000. July 2018 estimate, 12,807,060.

Population at five census years was:

	White	Black	American Indian	All others	Total	Per sq. mile
1910	7,467,713	193,919	1,503	1,976	7,665,111	171·0
			All others			
1980	10,652,320	1,046,810	164,765		11,863,895	264·7
1990	10,520,201	1,089,795	271,647		11,881,643	265·1
2000	10,484,203	1,224,612	572,239		12,281,054	274·0
2010	10,406,288	1,377,689	918,402		12,702,379	283·9

Of the total population in 2010, 6,512,016 were female and 9,910,224 were 18 years old or older. In 2010 Pennsylvania's Hispanic population was 719,660, up from 394,088 in 2000 (a rise of 82·6%).

The population of the largest cities and townships, 2010 census, was:

Philadelphia	1,526,006
Pittsburgh	305,704
Allentown	118,032
Erie	101,786
Reading	88,082
Scranton	76,089
Bethlehem	74,982
Lancaster	59,322
Levittown	52,983

The Philadelphia–Camden–Wilmington metropolitan area had a 2010 census population of 5,965,343. The capital, Harrisburg, had a population in 2010 of 49,528.

Social Statistics

Births, 2014, 142,268 (11·1 per 1,000 population); deaths, 2014, 128,434 (10·0). Infant mortality, 2013, 6·7 per 1,000 live births. 2014: marriages, 5·8 per 1,000 population; divorces and annulments, 2·7. Same-sex marriage was legalized in May 2014.

Climate

Philadelphia, Jan. 32°F (0°C), July 77°F (25°C). Annual rainfall 40" (1,006 mm). Pittsburgh, Jan. 31°F (–0·6°C), July 74°F (23·3°C). Annual rainfall 37" (914 mm). Pennsylvania belongs to the Appalachian Mountains climate zone (see UNITED STATES: Climate).

Constitution and Government

The present constitution dates from 1968. The General Assembly consists of a Senate of 50 members chosen for four years, one-half being elected biennially, and a House of Representatives of 203 members chosen for two years. The Governor and Lieut.-Governor are elected for four years. Every citizen 18 years of age, with the usual residential qualifications, may vote. Registered voters in Nov. 2012, 8,508,015.

For the 116th Congress, which convened in Jan. 2019, Pennsylvania sends 18 members to the House of Representatives. It is represented in the Senate by Robert Casey, Jr (D. 2007–25) and Patrick Toomey (R. 2011–23).

The state capital is Harrisburg. The state is organized in counties (numbering 67), cities, boroughs, townships and school districts.

Recent Elections

In the 2016 presidential election Donald Trump took Pennsylvania with 48·8% of the vote (Barack Obama won it in 2012).

Current Government

Governor: Tom Wolf (D.), 2019–23 (salary: $194,850).

Lieut.-Governor: John Fetterman (D.), 2019–23.

Secretary of the Commonwealth (acting): Kathy Boockvar (D.), since Jan. 2019.

Government Website: https://www.pa.gov

Economy

Per capita personal income (2015) was $49,180.

Budget

In 2011 total state revenue was $91,705m. Total expenditure was $90,792m. (including: public welfare, $23,707m.; education, $22,849m.; highways, $7,790m.; hospitals, $3,531m.; government administration, $2,957m.). Outstanding debt in 2011, $45,267m.

Performance

Gross Domestic Product by state in 2015 was $709,762m., ranking Pennsylvania 6th in the United States. In 2015 state real GDP growth was 2·8%.

Energy and Natural Resources

Electricity

In 2015 production was 214·6bn. kWh, of which 80·5bn. kWh was from nuclear energy, 64·6bn. kWh from coal and 59·5bn. kWh from natural gas.

Oil and Gas
In 2014 Pennsylvania produced 6·7m. bbls of crude petroleum; marketed production of natural gas totalled 4,215bn. cu. ft (second in the USA behind Texas).

Water
The total area covered by water is 1,312 sq. miles.

Minerals
Pennsylvania is almost the sole producer of anthracite coal. Production, 2007: crushed stone, 122m. tons; construction sand and gravel, 20m. tons. Bituminous coal production in 2009 totalled 56,248,000 tons; anthracite coal production in 2009, 1,731,000 tons. Non-fuel mineral production was worth more than $1,620m. in 2009.

Agriculture
Agriculture, market-gardening, fruit-growing, horticulture and forestry are pursued within the state. In 2007 there were 63,163 farms with a total farm area of 7·81m. acres. Average number of acres per farm in 2007 was 124 and the average value per acre was $4,775. Cash receipts, 2007: from crops, $1,929m.; and from livestock and products, $3,831m. The net farm income in 2007 was $2,155m.

In 2007–08 Pennsylvania ranked first in the USA for the production of mushrooms (496·7m. lb, value in 2007 $486·7m.). Cash receipts for other leading commodities in 2007: dairy products, $2,219·2m.; cattle and calves, $462·3m.; chicken eggs, $389·1m.; broilers, $381·0m.; corn, $380·5m.

In 2007 there were on farms: 1·61m. cattle and calves, 96,900 sheep and lambs, 1·17m. hogs and pigs and 21·98m. laying hens.

Forestry
In 2013 the total forested area was 16,999,000 acres, of which 502,000 acres were national forest. In 2009 state forest land totalled 2,145,804 acres; state park land, 274,105 acres; state game land, 1,400,000 acres.

Industry
In 2012 the state's 29,262 manufacturing establishments had 1,135,000 employees, earning $58,155m. Total value added by manufacturing in 2013 was $103,791m.

Labour
Total non-agricultural employment, 2010, 5,616,000. Employees by branch, 2010 (in 1,000): education and health services, 1,136; trade, transportation and utilities, 1,080; government, 757; professional and business services, 685; manufacturing, 561. The unemployment rate in Dec. 2010 was 8·5%.

International Trade

Imports and Exports
In 2015 imports into Pennsylvania totalled $79·8bn. (down from $83·2bn. in 2014). In the same year exports from Pennsylvania totalled $39·4bn., down from $40·4bn. in 2014. The leading source for imports in 2015 was China ($20·2bn.), ahead of Canada ($10·7bn.). The leading destination for exports in 2015 was Canada ($11·7bn.), followed by Mexico ($4·2bn.).

Communications

Roads
In 2012 highways and roads in the state (federal, local and state combined) totalled 119,846 miles (73,592 miles rural). Registered motor vehicles numbered 10,052,131.

Rail
In 2012 there were 5,151 miles of freight railroad (excluding trackage rights), including 2,428 miles of Class I railroads. There were 57 freight railroads operating in 2012 (the most in any state). Rail traffic originating in Pennsylvania in 2012 totalled 51·6m. tons and rail traffic terminating in the state came to 54·5m. tons. There are metro, light rail and tramway networks in Philadelphia and Pittsburgh, and commuter networks around Philadelphia.

Civil Aviation
In 2011 there were nine primary airports (commercial service airports with more than 10,000 passenger boardings annually) with a combined total of 20,584,069 enplanements, up from 20,540,939 in 2010. By far the busiest airport is Philadelphia International, with 14,883,180 enplanements in 2011.

Shipping
The major ports are Pittsburgh (which handled 31·5m. tons of cargo in 2014), Philadelphia (18·5m. tons in 2014), Marcus Hook, Penn Manor and Chester.

Social Institutions

Justice
Governor Tom Wolf imposed a moratorium on the death penalty in Feb. 2015. The last execution was in 1999, but there were 169 death row inmates as at 1 July 2017. There were 50,694 prisoners in federal and state correctional institutions in Dec. 2014.

Education
School attendance is compulsory for children eight to 17 years of age. In 2012–13 there were 3,229 public elementary and secondary schools with 1,763,677 pupils and 123,147 teachers; total expenditure on public elementary and secondary education in 2010–11 was $27,394m. Teachers' salaries averaged $63,521 in 2012–13.

Leading higher education institutions include:

Founded	Institutions	Students (fall 2014)
1740	University of Pennsylvania (non-sect.)	24,806
1787	University of Pittsburgh (all campuses)	35,199
1832	Lafayette College, Easton (Presbyterian)	2,503
1833	Haverford College	1,194
1842	Villanova University (R.C.)	10,735
1846	Bucknell University (Baptist)	3,624
1851	St Joseph's University, Philadelphia (R.C.)	8,974
1852	California University of Pennsylvania	7,978
1855	Pennsylvania State University (all campuses)	90,350
1855	Millersville University of Pennsylvania	8,047
1863	La Salle University, Philadelphia (R.C.)	6,242
1864	Swarthmore College	1,542
1866	Lehigh University, Bethlehem (non-sect.)	7,119
1871	West Chester University of Pennsylvania	16,086
1875	Indiana University of Pennsylvania	14,534
1878	Duquesne University, Pittsburgh (R.C.)	9,648
1884	Temple University, Philadelphia	37,485
1885	Bryn Mawr College	1,709
1888	University of Scranton (R.C.)	5,589
1891	Drexel University, Philadelphia	26,359
1900	Carnegie-Mellon University, Pittsburgh	12,587

Health
Pennsylvania had 3·1 community hospital beds for every 1,000 population in 2013. In the same year there were 35·1 active physicians per 10,000 civilian population and 6·0 dentists per 10,000.

Welfare
Medicare enrolment in July 2012 totalled 2,395,790. In fiscal year 2012 a total of 2,499,089 people in Pennsylvania received Medicaid. In Dec. 2014 there were 2,722,892 Old-Age, Survivors, and Disability Insurance (OASDI) beneficiaries. A total of 182,834 people were receiving payments under Temporary Assistance for Needy Families (TANF) in Dec. 2012.

Religion
The principal religious traditions in 2010 were Catholics (3,503,028 members), Mainline Protestants (1,773,491 members), Evangelical Protestants (1,078,477 members), Black Protestants (114,337 members) and Jews (102,312 members).

Culture

Tourism

In 2011 overseas visitors to Pennsylvania—excluding those from Canada and Mexico—numbered 920,000, down from 923,000 in 2010 but up from 672,000 in 2006.

Rhode Island

Key Historical Events

The earliest white settlement was founded by Roger Williams, an English Puritan who was expelled from Massachusetts because of his dissident religious views and his insistence on the land-rights of the American Indians. At Providence he bought land from the Narragansetts and founded a colony there in 1636. A charter was granted in 1663. Religious toleration attracted Jewish and nonconformist settlers; later there was French Canadian settlement.

Shipping and fishing developed strongly, especially at Newport and Providence. These two cities were twin capitals until 1900, when the capital was fixed at Providence.

Significant actions took place in Rhode Island during the War of Independence. In 1790 the state accepted the federal constitution and was admitted to the Union.

Early farming development was most successful in dairying and poultry. Early industrialization from the 1790s was mainly in textiles. Thriving on abundant water power, the industry began to decline after the First World War. British, Irish, Polish, Italian and Portuguese workers settled in the state, working in the mills or in the shipbuilding, shipping, fishing and naval ports. The growth of the cities led to the abolition of the property qualification for the franchise in 1888.

Territory and Population

Rhode Island is bounded north and east by Massachusetts, south by the Atlantic and west by Connecticut. Land area, 1,034 sq. miles (2,678 sq. km); water area, 511 sq. miles (1,324 sq. km). Census population, 1 April 2010, was 1,052,567, an increase of 0·4% since 2000. July 2018 estimate, 1,057,315.

Population of five census years was:

	White	Black	American Indian/ Alaska Native	Asian	Total	Per sq. mile
1910	532,492	9,529	284	305	542,610	508·5
			All others			
1980	896,692	27,584	22,878		947,154	903·0
					Total (including others)	
1990	917,375	38,861	4,071	18,325	1,003,164	960·3
2000	891,191	46,908	5,121	24,232	1,048,319	1,003·2
2010	856,869	60,189	6,058	30,457	1,052,567	1,018·1

Of the total population in 2010, 544,167 were female and 828,611 were 18 years old or older. In 2010 the Hispanic population was 130,655, up from 90,820 in 2000 (an increase of 43·9%).

The chief cities and their population (census, 2010) are Providence (the capital), 178,042; Warwick, 82,672; Cranston, 80,387; Pawtucket, 71,148; East Providence, 47,037.

Social Statistics

Births, 2014, 10,823 (10·3 per 1,000 population); deaths, 2014, 9,770 (9·3). Infant mortality rate, 2013, 6·5 per 1,000 live births. 2014: marriages, 6·7 per 1,000 population; divorces and annulments, 2·8. Same-sex marriage was legalized in May 2013, with effect from Aug. 2013.

Climate

Providence, Jan. 28°F (−2·2°C), July 72°F (22·2°C). Annual rainfall 43" (1,079 mm). Rhode Island belongs to the New England climate zone (*see* UNITED STATES: Climate).

Constitution and Government

The present constitution dates from 1843; it has had 63 amendments. The General Assembly consists of a Senate of 38 members and a House of Representatives of 75 members, both elected for two years. The Governor and Lieut.-Governor are now elected for four years. Every citizen, 18 years of age, who has resided in the state for 30 days, and is duly registered, is qualified to vote.

For the 116th Congress, which convened in Jan. 2019, Rhode Island sends two members to the House of Representatives. It is represented in the Senate by Jack Reed (D. 1997–2021) and Sheldon Whitehouse (D. 2007–25).

The capital is Providence. The state has five counties but no county governments. There are 39 municipalities, each having its own form of local government.

Recent Elections

In the 2016 presidential election Hillary Clinton took Rhode Island with 55·4% of the vote (Barack Obama won it in 2012).

Current Government

Governor: Gina Raimondo (D.), 2019–23 (salary: $139,695).
     Lieut.-Governor: Daniel McKee (D.), 2019–23.
     Secretary of State: Nellie Gorbea (D.), since Jan. 2015.
Government Website: https://www.ri.gov

Economy

Per capita personal income (2015) was $50,080.

Budget

In 2011 total state revenue was $9,372m. Total expenditure was $8,271m. (including: public welfare, $2,403m.; education, $1,815m.; government administration, $321m.; highways, $255m.; correction, $182m.). Outstanding debt in 2011, $9,174m.

Performance

Gross Domestic Product in 2015 was $56,052m., ranking Rhode Island 44th in the United States. In 2015 state real GDP growth was 1·4%.

Energy and Natural Resources

Water

The total area covered by water is 511 sq. miles.

Minerals

The small non-fuel mineral output—mostly stone, sand and gravel—was valued at more than $40m. in 2009.

Agriculture

In 2007 there were 1,219 farms with an area of 68,000 acres. The average size of a farm was 56 acres. In 2013 the average value of land and buildings per acre was $11,800—making it the second most valuable after New Jersey. Farm income, 2009: from crops, $53m.; livestock and products, $9m. The net farm income in 2009 was $14m. Principal commodities are greenhouse and nursery products, dairy products and sweetcorn.

Forestry

Total forested area was 367,000 acres in 2013.

Fisheries

In 2009 the commercial catch was 84·5m. lb valued at $61·7m.

Industry

Manufacturing is the chief source of income and the largest employer. Principal industries are jewellery and silverware, electrical machinery, electronics, plastics, metal products, instruments, chemicals and boat building. In 2012 the state's 3,018 manufacturing establishments had 79,000 employees, earning $4,153m. Total value added by manufacturing in 2013 was $6,053m.

Labour

In 2010 total non-agricultural employment was 458,800. Employees by branch, 2010 (in 1,000): education and health services, 102; trade, transportation and utilities, 73; government, 62; professional and business services,

53; leisure and hospitality, 50; manufacturing, 40. The unemployment rate in Dec. 2010 was 11·5%.

International Trade

Imports and Exports
In 2015 imports into Rhode Island totalled $8,237m. (down from $8,357m. in 2014). In the same year exports from Rhode Island totalled $2,133m., down from $2,388m. in 2014. The leading source for imports in 2015 was Germany ($2,358m.), ahead of Mexico ($1,214m.). The leading destination for exports in 2015 was Canada ($531m.), followed by Mexico ($181m.).

Communications

Roads
In 2012 there were 6,480 miles of roads (5,256 miles urban). There were approximately 821,000 registered motor vehicles.

Rail
In 2012 there were 19 miles of freight railroad (excluding trackage rights). There was one freight railroad operating in 2012. Rail traffic originating in Rhode Island in 2012 totalled 49,000 tons and rail traffic terminating in the state came to 836,000 tons. Amtrak's New York–Boston route runs through the state, serving Providence.

Civil Aviation
In 2011 there were two primary airports (commercial service airports with more than 10,000 passenger boardings annually). The main airport is Theodore Francis Green Memorial State at Warwick, near Providence, which had 1,920,699 enplanements in 2011.

Shipping
The leading port is Providence, which handled 8·1m. tons of cargo in 2014.

Social Institutions

Justice
In Dec. 2014 the jail and prison population totalled 3,359. The last execution was in 1845. Capital punishment was abolished in 1852, but reinstated in 1872 for murder committed by a life prisoner. However, it was never carried out and the death penalty was completely abolished in 1984.

Education
In 2012–13 there were 311 public elementary and secondary schools with 142,481 pupils and 9,871 teachers. In fall 2011, 25,420 pupils were enrolled in 140 private schools that had 2,360 teachers. Total expenditure on public elementary and secondary education in 2010–11 was $2,316m.; spending per pupil was $14,948.

There were 13 degree-granting institutions (three public and ten private) in 2012–13. The public institutions are the University of Rhode Island, Kingston, with 16,571 students in fall 2014; the Community College of Rhode Island, Warwick, with 17,553; and Rhode Island College, Providence, with 8,641. Among the private institutions, Johnson & Wales University at Providence, founded in 1914, had 9,955 students in fall 2014; Brown University at Providence, founded in 1764, had 9,181; Roger Williams University at Bristol had 4,884; Providence College at Providence had 4,533; and Bryant University at Smithfield had 3,462.

Health
Rhode Island had 2·1 community hospital beds for every 1,000 population in 2013. In the same year there were 40·2 active physicians per 10,000 civilian population and 5·4 dentists per 10,000.

Welfare
Medicare enrolment in July 2012 totalled 192,259. In fiscal year 2012 a total of 226,119 people in Rhode Island received Medicaid. In Dec. 2014 there were 216,069 Old-Age, Survivors, and Disability Insurance (OASDI) beneficiaries. A total of 15,343 people were receiving payments under Temporary Assistance for Needy Families (TANF) in Dec. 2012.

Religion
The principal religious traditions in the state in 2010 were: Catholics, with 466,598 members; Mainline Protestants, 57,103; Evangelical Protestants, 26,242; Jews, 8,845; Orthodox Christians, 7,625.

South Carolina

Key Historical Events
Originally the territory of Yamasee Indians, the area attracted French and Spanish explorers in the 16th century. There were attempts at settlement on the coast, none of which lasted. Charles I of England made a land grant in 1629 but the first permanent white settlement began at Charles Town in 1670, moving to Charleston in 1680. This was a proprietorial colony including North Carolina until 1712; both passed to the Crown in 1729.

The coastlands developed as plantations worked by slave labour. In the hills there were small farming settlements and many trading posts, dealing with American Indian suppliers.

After active campaigns during the War of Independence, South Carolina became one of the original states of the Union in 1788.

In 1793 the cotton gin was invented, enabling the speedy mechanical separation of seed and fibre. This made it possible to grow huge areas of cotton and meet the rapidly-growing needs of new textile industries. Plantation farming spread widely and South Carolina became hostile to the anti-slavery campaign which was strong in northern states. The state first attempted to secede from the Union in 1847, but was not supported by other southern states until 1860, when secession led to civil war.

At that time the population was about 703,000, of whom 413,000 were black. During the reconstruction periods there was some political power for black citizens but control was back in white hands by 1876. The constitution was amended in 1895 to disenfranchise most black voters and they remained with hardly any voice in government until the Civil Rights movement of the 1960s. Columbia became the capital in 1786.

Territory and Population
South Carolina is bounded in the north by North Carolina, east and southeast by the Atlantic, southwest and west by Georgia. Land area, 30,061 sq. miles (77,857 sq. km); water area, 1,960 sq. miles (5,076 sq. km). Census population, 1 April 2010, was 4,625,364, an increase of 15·3% since 2000. July 2018 estimate, 5,084,127.

The population in five census years was:

	White	Black	American Indian	Asian	Total	Per sq. mile
1910	679,161	835,843	331	65	1,515,400	49·7
			All others			
1980	2,150,507	948,623	22,703		3,121,833	100·3
1990	2,406,974	1,039,884	39,845		3,486,703	115·8
2000	2,695,560	1,185,216	131,236		4,012,012	133·2
2010	3,060,000	1,290,684	274,680		4,625,364	153·9

Of the total population in 2010, 2,375,263 were female and 3,544,890 were 18 years old or older. In 2010 the Hispanic population of South Carolina was 235,682, up from 95,076 in 2000 (an increase of 147·9%, the largest percentage rise in any US state).

Populations of large towns in 2010: Columbia (capital), 129,272; Charleston, 120,083; North Charleston, 97,471; Mount Pleasant, 67,843; Rock Hill, 66,154; Greenville, 58,409.

Social Statistics
Births, 2014, 57,627 (11·9 per 1,000 population); deaths, 2014, 45,454 (9·4). Infant deaths, 2013, 6·9 per 1,000 live births. 2014: marriages, 7·6 per 1,000 population; divorces and annulments, 2·9. Same-sex marriage became legal in Nov. 2014.

Climate
Columbia, Jan. 44·7°F (7°C), Aug. 80·2°F (26·9°C). Annual rainfall 49·12" (1,247·6 mm). South Carolina belongs to the Atlantic Coast climate zone (*see* UNITED STATES: Climate).

Constitution and Government
The present constitution dates from 1895, when it went into force without ratification by the electorate. The General Assembly consists of a Senate of 46 members, elected for four years, and a House of Representatives of 124 members, elected for two years. It meets annually. The Governor and Lieut.-Governor are elected for four years.

For the 116th Congress, which convened in Jan. 2019, South Carolina sends seven members to the House of Representatives. It is represented in the Senate by Lindsey Graham (R. 2003–21) and Tim Scott (R. 2013–23). Scott was appointed to fill the seat formerly held by Jim DeMint until a special election scheduled for 4 Nov. 2014. DeMint's term was to end in 2017.

The capital is Columbia. There are 46 counties.

Recent Elections
In the 2016 presidential election Donald Trump took South Carolina with 54·9% of the vote (Mitt Romney won it in 2012).

Current Government
Governor: Henry McMaster (R.), 2019–23 (salary: $106,078).
   Lieut.-Governor: Pamela Evette (R.), 2019–23.
   Secretary of State: Mark Hammond (R.), since Jan. 2003.

Economy
Per capita personal income (2015) was $38,041.

Budget
In 2011 total state revenue was $31,733m. Total expenditure was $29,352m. (including: education, $8,081m.; public welfare, $6,831m.; hospitals, $1,478m.; highways, $1,171m.; health, $952m.). Outstanding debt in 2011, $15,341m.

Performance
Gross Domestic Product by state was $201,005m. in 2015, ranking South Carolina 26th in the United States. In 2015 state real GDP growth was 2·5%.

Energy and Natural Resources
Electricity
In 2015 production was 96·5bn. kWh, of which 53·2bn. kWh was from nuclear energy.

Water
The total area covered by water is 1,960 sq. miles.

Minerals
Gold is found, though non-metallic minerals are of chief importance: value of non-fuel mineral output in 2009 was more than $440m., chiefly from cement (Portland), stone and gold. Production of kaolin, vermiculite and scrap mica is also important.

Agriculture
In 2007 there were 25,867 farms covering a farm area of 4·89m. acres. The average farm was of 189 acres. The average value of farmland and buildings per acre was $2,858 in 2007.

Farm income, 2007: from crops, $785m.; from livestock and products, $1,242m. The net farm income in 2007 was $535m. Cash receipts for leading commodities in 2007: broilers, $666·0m.; greenhouse products, $272·9m.; turkeys, $198·5m.; cattle and calves, $133·4m.; corn, $105·8m.

Livestock on farms, 2007: 401,000 all cattle, 293,800 hogs and pigs, 8,000 sheep and lambs, and 4·71m. laying hens.

Forestry
The forest industry is important; total forest land (2013), 13·04m. acres. National forests amounted to 602,000 acres.

Industry
In 2012 the state's 8,190 manufacturing establishments had 445,000 employees, earning $21,368m. Total value added by manufacturing in 2013 was $39,443m.

Labour
Total non-agricultural employment, 2010, 1,805,000. Employees by branch, 2010 (in 1,000): government, 345; trade, transportation and utilities, 344; professional and business services, 214; education and health services, 213; manufacturing, 207. The unemployment rate in Dec. 2010 was 10·9%.

International Trade
Imports and Exports
In 2015 imports into South Carolina totalled $39·0bn. (up from $37·8bn. in 2014). In the same year exports from South Carolina totalled $31·0bn., up from $29·8bn. in 2014. The leading source for imports in 2015 was Germany ($7·5bn.), ahead of China ($5·9bn.). The leading destination for exports in 2015 was China ($4·4bn.), followed by Germany ($3·9bn.).

Communications
Roads
In 2012 there were 66,244 miles of road comprising 16,368 miles of urban road and 49,876 miles of rural road. There were 3,784,593 registered motor vehicles.

Rail
In 2012 there were 2,311 miles of freight railroad (excluding trackage rights). There were 15 freight railroads operating in 2012. Rail traffic originating in South Carolina totalled 12·1m. tons in 2012 and rail traffic terminating in the state came to 27·8m. tons.

Civil Aviation
There were six primary airports—commercial service airports with more than 10,000 passenger boardings annually—in 2011 with a combined total of 3,593,332 enplanements, up from 3,082,283 in 2010. The main airport is Charleston International, which had 1,247,459 enplanements in 2011.

Shipping
The state has three deep-water ports.

Social Institutions
Justice
In Dec. 2014 there were 21,401 federal and state prisoners. The death penalty is authorized. There have been no executions since 2011, when one was carried out.

Education
In 2012–13 there were 735,998 pupils and 48,072 teachers in 1,254 public schools. Total expenditure on public elementary and secondary education in 2010–11 was $7,920m.; spending per pupil was $8,903. Average teaching salary was $47,924 in 2012–13. In fall 2011 there were 380 private schools with total enrolment of 60,890 pupils and 5,000 teachers.

Among the public higher education institutions are: the University of South Carolina (USC), founded at Columbia in 1801, with (fall 2014 enrolment) 32,971 students; USC Spartanburg, with 5,585; USC Aiken, with 3,444; Clemson University, founded in 1889, with 21,857; Coastal Carolina University, at Conway, with 9,976; Winthrop University, at Rock Hill, with 6,024; Francis Marion University, at Florence, with 3,944; South Carolina State University, at Orangeburg, with 3,331; Medical University of South Carolina, at Charleston, with 2,898; Lander University, at Greenwood, with 2,787; the College of Charleston, with 11,456; and Citadel Military College of South Carolina, at Charleston, with 3,592.

Health
South Carolina had 2·7 community hospital beds for every 1,000 population in 2013. In the same year there were 24·1 active physicians per 10,000 civilian population and 4·8 dentists per 10,000.

Welfare
Medicare enrolment in July 2012 totalled 839,183. In fiscal year 2012 a total of 985,528 people in South Carolina received Medicaid. In Dec. 2014 there were 1,040,971 Old-Age, Survivors, and Disability Insurance (OASDI) beneficiaries. A total of 30,766 people were receiving payments under Temporary Assistance for Needy Families (TANF) in Dec. 2012.

Religion
The principal religious traditions in 2010 were: Evangelical Protestants, with 1,410,988 members; Mainline Protestants, 482,103; Black Protestants, 256,178; Catholics, 181,743; Latter-day Saints (Mormons), 37,863.

South Dakota

Key Historical Events
The area was part of the hunting grounds of nomadic Dakota (Sioux) Indians. French explorers visited the site of Fort Pierre in 1742–43 and claimed the area for France. In 1763 the claim, together with French claims to all land

west of the Mississippi, passed to Spain. Spain held the Dakotas until defeated by France in the Napoleonic Wars when France regained the area and sold it to the USA as part of the Louisiana Purchase in 1803.

Fur-traders were active but there was no settlement until Fort Randall was founded on the Missouri river in 1856. In 1861 North and South Dakota were united as the Dakota Territory. The Homestead Act of 1862 stimulated settlement, mainly in the southeast until there was a gold-rush in the Black Hills of the west in 1875–76. Colonization was by farming communities in the east with miners and ranchers in the west. Livestock farming predominated, attracting European settlers from Scandinavia, Germany and Russia.

In 1889 the North and South were separated and admitted to the Union as states. Pierre, founded as a railhead in 1880, was confirmed as the capital in 1904. It faces Fort Pierre, the former centre of the fur trade, across the Missouri river. During the 20th century there have been schemes to exploit the Missouri for power and irrigation.

Territory and Population

South Dakota is bounded in the north by North Dakota, east by Minnesota, southeast by the Big Sioux River (forming the boundary with Iowa), south by Nebraska (with the Missouri River forming part of the boundary) and west by Wyoming and Montana. Land area, 75,811 sq. miles (196,350 sq. km); water area, 1,305 sq. miles (3,379 sq. km). In 2010 American Indian lands covered 15,837 sq. miles (reservations plus off-reservation trust land).

Census population, 1 April 2010, was 814,180, an increase of 7·9% since 2000. July 2018 estimate, 882,235.

Population in five federal censuses was:

	White	Black	American Indian	Asian	Total	Per sq. mile
1910	563,771	817	19,137	163	583,888	7·6
			All others			
1980	638,955	2,144	49,079		690,178	9·0
			American Indian/ Alaska Native	Asian/ other		
1990	637,515	3,258	50,575	4,656	696,004	9·2
2000	669,404	4,685	62,283	18,472	754,844	9·9
2010	699,392	10,207	71,817	32,764	814,180	10·7

Of the total population in 2010, 407,381 were male and 611,383 were 18 years old or older. In 2010 the Hispanic population was 22,119, up from 10,903 in 2000 (an increase of 102·9%).

Population of the chief cities (census of 2010) was: Sioux Falls, 153,888; Rapid City, 67,956; Aberdeen, 26,091; Brookings, 22,056; Watertown, 21,482; Mitchell, 15,254; Pierre (the capital), 13,646.

Social Statistics

Births, 2014, 12,283 (14·4 per 1,000 population); deaths, 2014, 7,507 (8·8). Infant deaths, 2013, 6·5 per 1,000 live births. 2014: marriages, 7·1 per 1,000 population; divorces and annulments, 2·8.

Climate

Rapid City, Jan. 25°F (−3·9°C), July 73°F (22·8°C). Annual rainfall 19" (474 mm). Sioux Falls, Jan. 14°F (−10°C), July 73°F (22·8°C). Annual rainfall 25" (625 mm). South Dakota belongs to the High Plains climate zone (see UNITED STATES: Climate).

Constitution and Government

Voters are all citizens 18 years of age or older. The people reserve the right of the initiative and referendum. The Senate has 35 members, and the House of Representatives 70 members, all elected for two years; the Governor and Lieut.-Governor are elected for four years.

For the 116th Congress, which convened in Jan. 2019, South Dakota sends one member to the House of Representatives. It is represented in the Senate by John Thune (R. 2005–23) and Mike Rounds (R. 2015–21).

The capital is Pierre. The state is divided into 66 organized counties.

Recent Elections

In the 2016 presidential election Donald Trump took South Dakota with 61·5% of the vote (Mitt Romney won it in 2012).

Current Government

Governor: Kristi Noem (R.), 2019–23 (salary: $112,214).
Lieut.-Governor: Larry Rhoden (R.), 2019–23.
Secretary of State: Steve Barnett (R.), since Jan. 2019.
Government Website: http://www.sd.gov.

Economy

Per capita personal income (2015) was $45,002.

Budget

In 2011 total state revenue was $6,017m. Total expenditure was $4,498m. (education, $1,300m.; public welfare, $966m.; highways, $607m.; government administration, $171m.; natural resources, $165m.). Outstanding debt in 2011, $3,545m.

Performance

Gross Domestic Product by state in 2015 was $47,244m., ranking South Dakota 47th in the United States. In 2015 state real GDP growth was 2·6%.

Energy and Natural Resources

Oil and Gas

In 2014 South Dakota produced 1·8m. bbls of crude petroleum; marketed production of natural gas totalled 15bn. cu. ft.

Water

The total area covered by water is 1,305 sq. miles.

Minerals

Gold is one of the leading mineral commodities, with 1,900 kg produced in 2008. Gross value rose from $29m. in 2003 to $53m. in 2008. In 2008 sand and gravel was the major non-metallic industrial mineral commodity with 12·3m. tonnes produced. Other major minerals were: crushed stone (5·4m. tonnes); limestone (2·8m.); sandstone and quartzite (2·1m.); clays (155,000). Value of non-fuel mineral production in 2009 was $230m.

Agriculture

In 2007 there were 31,169 farms with an acreage of 43·67m. and an average farm size of 1,401 acres. Average value of farmland and buildings per acre in 2007 was $896. Cash receipts, 2011: from crops, $6,207m.; from livestock and products, $4,002m. The net farm income in 2009 was $2,376m.

Principal commodities, with 2012 production figures, are: corn, 535m. bu.; soybeans, 141m. bu.; wheat, 102m. bu.; cattle (2007), 1,472m. lb. The farm livestock in 2012 included 3·85m. cattle; 1·20m. hogs and pigs; and 275,000 sheep and lambs. In 2012, 17·0m. lb of honey were produced, a total exceeded only by North Dakota.

Forestry

South Dakota had 1,929,000 acres of forested land in 2011, of which 1,014,000 acres were national forest.

Industry

In 2012 the state's 2,554 manufacturing establishments had 98,000 employees, earning $4,086m. Total value added by manufacturing in 2013 was $6,483m.

Labour

Total non-agricultural employment, 2010, 403,000. Employees by branch, 2010 (in 1,000): trade, transportation and utilities, 81; government, 79; education and health services, 64; leisure and hospitality, 43; manufacturing, 37. The average annual wage per employee in 2009 was $33,352—the lowest of any state. The state unemployment rate in Dec. 2010 was 4·7%.

International Trade

Imports and Exports

In 2015 imports into South Dakota totalled $1,140m. (up from $1,043m. in 2014). In the same year exports from South Dakota totalled $1,420m., down from $1,578m. in 2014. The leading source for imports in 2015 was Canada ($543m.), ahead of Brazil ($158m.). The leading destination for exports in 2015 was also Canada ($526m.), followed by Mexico ($389m.).

Communications

Roads
In 2012 there were 82,536 miles of road comprising 3,074 miles of urban road and 79,462 miles of rural road. There were 930,219 registered vehicles.

Rail
In 2012 there were 1,753 miles of freight railroad (excluding trackage rights). There were nine freight railroads operating in 2012. Rail traffic originating in South Dakota totalled 14·3m. tons in 2012 and rail traffic terminating in the state came to 4·8m. tons.

Civil Aviation
There were four primary airports in 2011 (commercial service airports with more than 10,000 passenger boardings annually) with a combined total of 716,885 enplanements, up from 674,840 in 2010.

Social Institutions

Justice
In Dec. 2014 the jail and prison population totalled 3,608. The death penalty is authorized and was used in 2007 for the first time in 60 years. Since then there have been two executions in 2012 and one in 2018.

Education
School attendance is compulsory between the ages of six and 18 (since 1 July 2009—previously school attendance had only been compulsory to 16). In 2012–13 there were 130,471 pupils at 714 public schools with 9,334 teachers. The 70 private schools had 12,490 pupils and 970 teachers in fall 2011. Public school teacher salaries in 2012–13 averaged $39,580. In 2010–11 total expenditure on public elementary and secondary education was $1,347m.; spending per pupil was $8,931.

Higher (public) institutions include South Dakota State University, founded at Brookings in 1881, with (fall 2014 enrolment) 12,543 students; University of South Dakota, founded at Vermillion in 1882, 10,061; Black Hills State University, founded at Spearfish in 1883, 4,489; Northern State University at Aberdeen, 3,531; Dakota State University at Madison, 3,047; and South Dakota School of Mines and Technology at Rapid City, 2,798 students. There were 13 private degree-granting institutions in 2012–13; enrolment in fall 2012 totalled 11,873 students.

Health
South Dakota had 4·9 community hospital beds for every 1,000 population in 2013. In the same year there were 24·6 active physicians per 10,000 civilian population and 5·4 dentists per 10,000.

Welfare
Medicare enrolment in July 2012 totalled 143,582. In fiscal year 2012 a total of 136,023 people in South Dakota received Medicaid. In Dec. 2014 there were 165,499 Old-Age, Survivors, and Disability Insurance (OASDI) beneficiaries. A total of 6,725 people were receiving payments under Temporary Assistance for Needy Families (TANF) in Dec. 2012.

Religion
The principal religious traditions in 2010 were: Mainline Protestants, with 196,001 members; Catholics, 148,883; Evangelical Protestants, 118,142; Latter-day Saints (Mormons), 10,001.

Tennessee

Key Historical Events
Bordered on the west by the Mississippi, Tennessee was part of an area inhabited by Cherokee. French, Spanish and British explorers navigated the Mississippi to trade with the Cherokee in the late 16th and 17th centuries. French claims were abandoned in 1763. Colonists from the British colonies of Virginia and Carolina then began to cross the Appalachians westwards, but there was no organized Territory until after the War of Independence. In 1784 there was a short-lived, independent state called Franklin. In 1790 the South West Territory (including Tennessee) was formed and Tennessee entered the Union as a state in 1796.

The state was active in the war against Britain in 1812. After the American victory, colonization increased and pressure for land mounted. The Cherokee were forcibly removed during the 1830s and taken to Oklahoma, a journey on which many died.

Tennessee was a slave state and seceded from the Union in 1861, although eastern Tennessee was against secession. There were important battles at Shiloh, Chattanooga, Stone River and Nashville. In 1866 Tennessee was readmitted to the Union.

Nashville, the capital since 1843, Memphis, Knoxville, and Chattanooga all developed as river towns, Memphis becoming an important cotton and timber port. Growth was greatly accelerated by the creation of the Tennessee Valley Authority in the 1930s, producing power for industry. With an expanding economy, by 1970, the southern pattern of emigration and population loss had been reversed.

Territory and Population
Tennessee is bounded north by Kentucky and Virginia, east by North Carolina, south by Georgia, Alabama and Mississippi and west by the Mississippi River (forming the boundary with Arkansas and Missouri). Total area is 42,144 sq. miles (109,153 sq. km) of which 41,235 sq. miles (106,798 sq. km) are land. Census population, 1 April 2010, was 6,346,105, an increase of 11·5% since 2000. July 2018 estimate, 6,770,010.

Population in five census years was:

	White	Black	American Indian	Asian	Total	Per sq. mile
1910	1,711,432	473,088	216	53	2,184,789	52·4
			All others			
1980	3,835,452	725,942	29,726		4,591,120	111·6
1990	4,048,068	778,035	51,082		4,877,185	115·7
2000	4,563,310	932,809	193,164		5,689,283	138·0
2010	4,921,948	1,057,315	366,842		6,346,105	153·9

Of the total population in 2010, 3,252,601 were female and 4,850,104 were 18 years old or older. In 2010 the Hispanic population of Tennessee was 290,059, up from 123,838 in 2000 (an increase of 134·2%).

The cities, with population (2010) are Memphis, 646,889; Nashville (capital), 601,222; Knoxville, 178,874; Chattanooga, 167,674; Clarksville, 132,929; Murfreesboro, 108,755; Jackson, 65,211; Johnson City, 63,152; Franklin, 62,487; Bartlett, 54,613; Hendersonville, 51,372. Largest Metropolitan Statistical Areas, with 2010 populations: Nashville-Davidson–Murfreesboro–Franklin, 1,589,934; Memphis, 1,316,100; Knoxville, 698,030; Johnson City, 198,716; Chattanooga, 528,143; Clarksville, 273,949.

Social Statistics
Births, 2014, 81,602 (12·5 per 1,000 population); deaths, 2014, 64,661 (9·9). Infant mortality, 2013, 6·8 per 1,000 live births. 2014: marriages, 8·4 per 1,000 population; divorces and annulments, 3·8.

Climate
Memphis, Jan. 41°F (5°C), July 82°F (27·8°C). Annual rainfall 49" (1,221 mm). Nashville, Jan. 39°F (3·9°C), July 79°F (26·1°C). Annual rainfall 48" (1,196 mm). Tennessee belongs to the Appalachian Mountains climate zone (*see* UNITED STATES: Climate).

Constitution and Government
The state has operated under three constitutions, the last of which was adopted in 1870 and has been since amended 38 times (first in 1953). Voters at an election may authorize the calling of a convention limited to altering or abolishing one or more specified sections of the constitution. The General Assembly consists of a Senate of 33 members and a House of Representatives of 99 members, senators elected for four years and representatives for two years. Qualified as electors are all citizens (usual residential and age (18) qualifications).

For the 116th Congress, which convened in Jan. 2019, Tennessee sends nine members to the House of Representatives. It is represented in the Senate by Lamar Alexander (R. 2003–21) and Marsha Blackburn (R. 2019–25).

The capital is Nashville. The state is divided into 95 counties.

Recent Elections
In the 2016 presidential election Donald Trump took Tennessee with 61·1% of the vote (Mitt Romney won it in 2012).

Current Government

Governor: Bill Lee (R.), 2019–23 (salary: $119,116).
  Lieut.-Governor: Randy McNally (R.), 2019–23.
    Secretary of State: Tre Hargett (R.), since Jan. 2009.
Government Website: https://www.tn.gov

Economy

Per capita personal income (2015) was $42,069.

Budget

In 2011 total state revenue was $34,681m. Total expenditure was $30,841m. (including: public welfare, $10,747m.; education, $9,177m.; highways, $1,705m.; health, $1,119m.; correction, $796m.). Outstanding debt in 2011, $5,899m.

Performance

Gross Domestic Product by state in 2015 was $315,857m., ranking Tennessee 18th in the United States. In 2015 state real GDP growth was 2·7%.

Energy and Natural Resources

Water

The total area covered by water is 909 sq. miles.

Minerals

Domestic non-fuel mineral production was worth $675m. in 2009.

Agriculture

In 2007, 79,280 farms covered 10·97m. acres. The average farm was of 138 acres. In 2007 the average value of farmland and buildings per acre was $3,378.

    Farm income, 2009: from crops, $1,705m.; from livestock, $1,137m. The net farm income in 2009 was $613m. Main crops were soybeans, broilers and cattle.

    In 2007 there were on farms: 61,000 dairy cows, 2·12m. all cattle, 138,200 hogs and pigs, and 29,800 sheep and lambs.

Forestry

Forests occupied 13·92m. acres in 2012. The forest industry and industries dependent on it employ about 0·04m. workers. Wood products are valued at over $500m. per year. National forest system land (2012) 717,000 acres.

Oil and Gas

In 2014 Tennessee produced 330,000 bbls of crude petroleum; marketed production of natural gas totalled 5·3bn. cu. ft.

Electricity

In 2015 production was 72,215m. kWh, of which 30,586m. kWh was from coal and 24,960m. kWh from nuclear energy.

Industry

The manufacturing industries include iron and steel working, but the most important products are chemicals, including synthetic fibres and allied products, electrical equipment and food. In 2012 the state's 13,122 manufacturing establishments had 657,000 employees, earning $31,150m. Total value added by manufacturing in 2013 was $61,365m.

Labour

In 2010 total non-agricultural employment was 2,613,000. Employees by branch, 2010 (in 1,000): trade, transportation and utilities, 555; government, 432; education and health services, 373; professional and business services, 305; manufacturing, 298. The unemployment rate in Dec. 2010 was 9·4%.

International Trade

Imports and Exports

In 2015 imports into Tennessee totalled $77·0bn., (up from $69·8bn. in 2014). In the same year exports from Tennessee totalled $32·6bn., down from $33·3bn. in 2014. The leading source for imports in 2015 was Canada ($27·2bn.), ahead of Japan ($7·2bn.). The leading destination for exports in 2015 was also Canada ($8·7bn.), followed by Mexico ($4·9bn.).

Communications

Roads

In 2012 there were 95,523 miles of roads (70,009 miles rural). There were 5,225,095 registered motor vehicles.

Rail

In 2012 there were 2,649 miles of freight railroad (excluding trackage rights). There were 25 freight railroads operating in 2012. Rail traffic originating in Tennessee totalled 15·7m. tons in 2012 and rail traffic terminating in the state came to 26·6m. tons. There is a tramway in Memphis.

Civil Aviation

There were five primary airports—commercial service airports with more than 10,000 passenger boardings annually—in 2011 with a combined total of 10,383,482 enplanements, down from 10,663,323 in 2010. The main airports are Nashville International (which had 4,673,047 enplanements in 2011) and Memphis International (with 4,344,213 enplanements in 2011). Memphis International handled 3,916,410 tonnes of freight in 2011, ranking it second in the world behind Hong Kong (which surpassed Memphis as the world's busiest cargo airport in 2010).

Social Institutions

Justice

The death penalty is authorized. There were three executions in 2018 (the first since 2009). In Dec. 2014 there were 28,769 prison inmates.

Education

School attendance has been compulsory since 1925 and the employment of children under 16 years of age in workshops, factories or mines is illegal.

    In 2012–13 there were 1,835 public schools with 993,496 pupils and 66,406 teachers. Total expenditure on public elementary and secondary education was $9,294m. in 2010–11 and average teacher salary was $48,289 in 2012–13. Spending per pupil in 2010–11 was $8,484.

    Tennessee has 22 public colleges and universities (nine four-year and 13 two-year institutions). In fall 2014 the universities included the University of Tennessee, Knoxville (founded 1794) with 30,386 students; Middle Tennessee State University at Murfreesboro with 22,729; the University of Memphis with 21,059; East Tennessee State University at Johnson City with 14,434; the University of Tennessee at Chattanooga with 11,670; Tennessee Technological University at Cookeville with 11,339; Austin Peay State University at Clarksville with 10,111; Tennessee State University at Nashville with 9,027; University of Tennessee at Martin with 7,042. The largest private universities are Vanderbilt University, Nashville (founded 1873) with 12,686 students in fall 2014; and Belmont University, Nashville (1890) with 7,244.

Health

Tennessee had 3·1 community hospital beds for every 1,000 population in 2013. In the same year there were 27·7 active physicians per 10,000 civilian population and 5·0 dentists per 10,000.

Welfare

Medicare enrolment in July 2012 totalled 1,134,164. In fiscal year 2012 a total of 1,536,604 people in Tennessee received Medicaid. In Dec. 2014 there were 1,371,562 Old-Age, Survivors, and Disability Insurance (OASDI) beneficiaries. A total of 128,856 people were receiving payments under Temporary Assistance for Needy Families (TANF) in Dec. 2012.

Religion

The principal religious traditions in 2010 were: Evangelical Protestants, with 2,384,381 members; Mainline Protestants, 533,145; Black Protestants, 273,889; Catholics, 223,045; Latter-day Saints (Mormons), 47,391.

Texas

Key Historical Events

A number of American Indian tribes occupied the area before French and Spanish explorers arrived in the 16th century. In 1685 La Salle established a colony at Fort St Louis, but Texas was confirmed as Spanish in 1713. Spanish missions increased during the 18th century with San Antonio (1718) as their headquarters.

    In 1820 a Virginian colonist, Moses Austin, obtained permission to begin a settlement in Texas. In 1821 the Spanish empire in the Americas came to an end and Texas, together with Coahuila, formed a state of the newly independent Mexico. The Mexicans agreed to the Austin venture and settlers of British and American descent came in.

Discontented with Mexican government, the settlers declared independence in 1836. Warfare, including the siege of the Alamo fort, ended with the foundation of the independent Republic of Texas which lasted until 1845. During this period the Texas Rangers were organized as a police force and border patrol. Texas was annexed to the Union in Dec. 1845, as the Federal government feared its vulnerability to Mexican occupation. This led to war between Mexico and the USA from 1845 to 1848. In 1861 Texas left the Union and joined the southern states in the Civil War, being readmitted in 1869. Ranching and cotton-growing were the main activities before the discovery of oil in 1901.

Territory and Population

Texas is bounded north by Oklahoma, northeast by Arkansas, east by Louisiana, southeast by the Gulf of Mexico, south by Mexico and west by New Mexico. Land area, 261,232 sq. miles (676,587 sq. km); water area, 7,365 sq. miles (19,075 sq. km). Texas is the second largest US state behind Alaska. Census population, 1 April 2010, was 25,145,561, an increase of 20·6% since 2000. July 2018 estimate, 28,701,845.

Population for five census years was:

	White	Black	American Indian	Asian	Total	Per sq. mile
1910	3,204,848	690,049	702	943	3,896,542	14·8
			All others			
1980	11,197,663	1,710,250	1,320,470		14,228,383	54·2
			American Indian/ Alaska Native	All Others		
1990	12,774,762	2,021,632	65,877	2,124,239	16,986,510	64·9
2000	14,799,505	2,404,566	118,362	3,529,387	20,851,820	79·7
2010	17,701,552	2,979,598	170,972	4,293,439	25,145,561	96·3

Of the total population in 2010, 12,673,281 were female and 18,279,737 were 18 years old or older. In 2010 the Hispanic population was 9,460,921, up from 6,669,666 in 2000 (an increase of 41·8%). The numerical increase was the second largest in the Hispanic population of any state in the USA, after California. Only New Mexico has a greater percentage of Hispanics in the state population.

The largest cities, with census population in 2010, are:

Houston	2,099,451
San Antonio	1,327,407
Dallas	1,197,816
Austin (capital)	790,390
Fort Worth	741,206
El Paso	649,121
Arlington	365,438
Corpus Christi	305,215
Plano	259,841
Laredo	236,091
Lubbock	229,573
Garland	226,876
Irving	216,290
Amarillo	190,695
Grand Prairie	175,396
Brownsville	175,023
Pasadena	149,043
Mesquite	139,824
McKinney	131,117
McAllen	129,877
Killeen	127,921

(continued)

Waco	124,805
Carrollton	119,097
Beaumont	118,296
Abilene	117,063
Frisco	116,989
Denton	113,383
Midland	111,147
Wichita Falls	104,553

The population of the largest Metropolitan Statistical Areas in 2010 was: Dallas–Fort Worth–Arlington, 6,371,773; Houston–Sugarland–Baytown, 5,946,800; San Antonio–New Braunfels, 2,142,508; Austin–Round Rock–San Marcos, 1,716,289.

Social Statistics

Births, 2014, 399,766 (14·8 per 1,000 population); deaths, 2014, 183,912 (6·8). Infant mortality, 2013, 5·8 per 1,000 live births. 2014: marriages, 6·9 per 1,000 population; divorces and annulments, 2·7.

Climate

Dallas, Jan. 45°F (7·2°C), July 84°F (28·9°C). Annual rainfall 38" (945 mm). El Paso, Jan. 44°F (6·7°C), July 81°F (27·2°C). Annual rainfall 9" (221 mm). Galveston, Jan. 54°F (12·2°C), July 84°F (28·9°C). Annual rainfall 46" (1,159 mm). Houston, Jan. 52°F (11·1°C), July 83°F (28·3°C). Annual rainfall 48" (1,200 mm). Texas suffered its worst one-year drought on record in 2011, when the average rainfall for the state was 14·9" (378 mm). Texas belongs to the Central Plains climate zone (*see* UNITED STATES: Climate).

Constitution and Government

The present constitution dates from 1876; it has been amended 491 times as of 2015. The state legislature consists of the Senate and House of Representatives. The Senate has 31 members elected for four-year terms. Half of the membership is elected every two years. The House has 150 members, elected for two-year terms during polling held in even-numbered years. The legislature meets in regular session for about five months every other year. The session begins in Jan. of odd-numbered years and lasts no more than 140 days (although special sessions can be called by the Governor). The Governor and Lieut.-Governor are elected for four years.

For the 116th Congress, which convened in Jan. 2019, Texas sends 36 members to the House of Representatives. It is represented in the Senate by John Cornyn (R. 2002–21) and Ted Cruz (R. 2013–25).

The capital is Austin. The state has 254 counties.

Recent Elections

In the 2016 presidential election Donald Trump took Texas with 52·6% of the vote (Mitt Romney won it in 2012).

Current Government

Governor: Greg Abbott (R.), 2019–23 (salary: $153,750).
    Lieut.-Governor: Dan Patrick (R.), 2019–23.
    Secretary of State (acting): David Whitley (R.), since Dec. 2018.
Government Website: https://texas.gov

Economy

Per capita personal income (2015) was $46,745.

Budget

In 2011 total state revenue was $134,345m. Total expenditure was $125,940m. (education, $48,809m.; public welfare, $31,269m.; highways, $6,558m.; hospitals, $4,196m.; correction, $3,765m.). Outstanding debt in 2011, $38,530m.

Performance

In 2015 Gross Domestic Product by state was $1,630,082m., ranking Texas second after California. If Texas were a country in its own right it would be the world's 10th largest economy. In 2015 state real GDP growth was 4·8%, second only to Oregon.

Banking and Finance

In 2014 there were 507 financial institutions in Texas insured by the US Federal Deposit Insurance Corporation, with assets worth $445,806m.

As at Dec. 2014 there were 267 state-chartered banks operating in Texas, with total assets of $235,400m. The largest banks were Comerica Bank, Dallas (with assets of $69,310·2m.), Frost Bank, San Antonio (with assets of $28,327·5m.), Prosperity Bank, El Campo (with assets of $21,504·1m.), International Bank of Commerce, Laredo (with assets of $9,892·2m.) and PlainsCapital Bank, Dallas (with assets of $8,685·9m.).

Energy and Natural Resources

Electricity

In 2015 production was 449·8bn. kWh, of which 237·7bn. kWh was from natural gas.

Oil and Gas

Texas is the leading producer in the USA of both oil and natural gas. In 2014 it produced 36% of the country's oil and 29% of its natural gas. Output, 2014: crude petroleum, 1,156m. bbls; marketed production of natural gas, 7,953bn. cu. ft. Natural gasoline (a liquid form of natural gas), butane and propane gases are also produced.

Water

The total area covered by water is 7,365 sq. miles, of which 5,616 sq. miles are inland. Only Alaska has a larger area covered by inland water.

Minerals

Minerals include helium, crude gypsum, granite and sandstone, salt and cement. Production of coal (2009) was 35·1m. short tons. Total value of domestic non-fuel mineral products in 2009 was $2,650m.

Agriculture

Texas is one of the most important agricultural states. In 2007 it had 247,437 farms covering 130·40m. acres (up from 228,926 farms covering 129·88m. acres in 2002); average farm was of 527 acres. Both the number of farms and the total area covered are the highest in the USA. In 2007 land and buildings were valued at $1,270 per acre. Large-scale commercial farms, highly mechanized, dominate in Texas; farms of 1,000 acres or more in number far exceed that of any other state, but small-scale farming persists. Soil erosion is a serious problem in some parts.

Production: corn, barley, beans, cotton, hay, oats, peanuts, rye, sorghum, soybeans, sunflowers, wheat, oranges, grapefruit, peaches, sweet potatoes. Farm income, 2009: from crops, $5,932m.; from livestock and products, $10,641m. (the most of any state). The net farm income in 2009 was $2,124m.

The state has an important livestock industry, leading in the number of all cattle (13·71m.) and sheep (945,000); it also had 0·44m. dairy cows, 1·16m. hogs and pigs, and 19·12m. laying hens in 2007. Wool production in 2007 totalled 4·60m. lb, the most of any state.

Forestry

There were 61,797,000 acres of forested land in 2011, with 730,000 acres of national forest.

Industry

In 2012 the state's 41,802 manufacturing establishments had 1,609,000 employees, earning $88,427m. Total value added by manufacturing in 2013 was $239,012m.

Labour

Total non-agricultural employment, 2010, 10,342,000. Employees by branch, 2010 (in 1,000): trade, transportation and utilities, 2,050; government, 1,860; education and health services, 1,388; professional and business services, 1,273; leisure and hospitality, 1,006. The unemployment rate in Dec. 2010 was 8·3%.

International Trade

Imports and Exports

In 2015 imports into Texas totalled $252·1bn. (down from $302·9bn. in 2014). In the same year exports from Texas totalled $248·6bn., down from $285·6bn. in 2014. Imports in 2015 were the second largest of any US state after those of California and exports the largest. Imports in 2015 were 11·2% of all US imports and exports 16·5% of all exports. The leading source for imports in 2015 was Mexico ($84·0bn.), ahead of China ($41·0bn.). The leading destination for exports in 2015 was also Mexico ($92·9bn.), followed by Canada ($25·5bn.).

Communications

Roads

In 2012 there were 313,210 miles of road comprising 99,276 miles of urban road and 213,934 miles of rural road. There were 19,789,723 registered motor vehicles and 3,398 traffic accident fatalities.

Rail

In 2012 there were 10,469 miles of freight railroad (excluding trackage rights), including 8,369 miles of Class I railroads. Texas has more rail miles than any other state. There were 49 freight railroads operating in 2012. Rail traffic originating in Texas in 2012 totalled 92·9m. tons and rail traffic terminating in the state came to 206·6m. tons (the most of any state). There are light rail systems in Austin, Dallas and Houston.

Civil Aviation

There were 24 primary airports—commercial service airports with more than 10,000 passenger boardings annually—in Texas in 2011 with a combined total of 68,524,498 enplanements, up from 67,664,379 in 2010. Dallas/Fort Worth International had 27,518,358 enplanements in 2011 (ranking it fourth in the USA) and George Bush Intercontinental/Houston had 19,306,660. A further five primary airports had more than 1m. passenger enplanements in 2011: William P. Hobby (Houston's second airport), Austin-Bergstrom International, San Antonio International, Dallas Love Field and El Paso International.

Shipping

The port of Houston, connected by the Houston Ship Channel (50 miles long) with the Gulf of Mexico, is the second busiest in the country after South Louisiana and the busiest for foreign trade cargo. In 2014 it handled 234·3m. tons of cargo (160·5m. tons of foreign trade cargo and 73·8m. tons of domestic cargo). Other major ports are Beaumont, Corpus Christi, Texas City and Port Arthur, which ranked as the USA's 4th, 6th, 15th and 20th busiest ports respectively in 2014. There are more than 1,000 miles of inland waterways.

Social Institutions

Justice

In Dec. 2014 there were 166,043 state and federal prisoners, up from 157,617 in Dec. 2004. Between 1977 and 2018 Texas was responsible for 558 of the USA's 1,490 executions (more than four times as many as any other state), although it was not until 1982 that Texas reintroduced the death penalty. There were seven executions in 2017 and 13 in 2018. In 2000, 40 people had been executed, the highest number in a year in any state since the authorities began keeping records in 1930. Texas had 243 death row inmates as at 1 July 2017.

Education

School attendance is compulsory from six to 18 years of age.

In the 2012–13 school year there were 9,280 public elementary and secondary schools with 5,077,659 enrolled pupils; there were 327,356 teachers. Total expenditure on public schools in 2010–11 was $52,712m.

In 2012–13 there were 108 public degree-granting higher education institutions; enrolled students in fall 2012 totalled 1,347,860. The public University of Texas System, one of the largest in the USA, comprises eight academic and six health institutions and had over 225,000 students in fall 2014; the Texas A&M University System is made up of 11 universities, seven state agencies and a health science centre and had over 140,000 students in fall 2014; and the Texas State University System has eight component institutions and had over 80,000 students in fall 2014.

Other public universities and student enrolment, fall 2014:

Institutions	Students
University of Houston System	68,425
Texas Tech University System	46,583
University of North Texas System	41,304

(continued)

Institutions	Students
Texas Woman's University, Denton	15,071
Stephen F. Austin State University, Nacogdoches	12,801
Texas Southern University, Houston	9,233
Midwestern State University, Wichita Falls	5,874

There were 163 independent colleges and universities in 2012–13. Largest student enrolments, fall 2014:

Institutions	Students
Baylor University, Waco	16,263
Southern Methodist University, Dallas	11,272
Texas Christian University, Fort Worth	10,033
University of the Incarnate World, San Antonio	8,745
Rice University, Houston	6,621
Wayland Baptist University, Plainview	5,536
Dallas Baptist University, Dallas	5,445
University of Phoenix, Houston	5,254

Health

Texas had 2·3 community hospital beds for every 1,000 population in 2013. In the same year there were 23·2 active physicians per 10,000 civilian population and 5·1 dentists per 10,000.

Welfare

Medicare enrolment in July 2012 totalled 3,261,073. In fiscal year 2011 a total of 4,996,318 people in Texas received Medicaid. In Dec. 2014 there were 3,842,249 Old-Age, Survivors, and Disability Insurance (OASDI) beneficiaries. A total of 99,080 people were receiving payments under Temporary Assistance for Needy Families (TANF) in Dec. 2012.

Religion

In 2010 the leading religious traditions were: Evangelical Protestants, with 6,456,168 members; Catholics, 4,673,500; Mainline Protestants, 1,553,959; Muslims, 422,000 (estimate); Black Protestants, 345,998.

Culture

Tourism
In 2011 overseas visitors to Texas—excluding those from Canada and Mexico—numbered 1,283,000, up from 1,028,000 in 2010 and 975,000 in 2006.

Utah

Key Historical Events

Spanish Franciscan missionaries explored the area in 1776, finding Shoshoni Indians. Spain laid claim to Utah and designated it part of Spanish Mexico. As such it passed into the hands of the Mexican Republic when Mexico rebelled against Spain and gained independence in 1821.

In 1848, at the conclusion of war between the USA and Mexico, the USA received Utah along with other southwestern territory. Settlers had already arrived in 1847 when the Mormons (the Church of Jesus Christ of Latter-day Saints) arrived, having been driven on by hostility in Ohio, Missouri and Illinois. Led by Brigham Young, they entered the Great Salt Valley and colonized it. In 1849 they applied for statehood but were refused. In 1850 Utah and Nevada were joined as one Territory. The Mormon community continued to ask for statehood but this was only granted in 1896, after they had renounced polygamy and disbanded their People's Party.

Mining, especially of copper, and livestock farming were the basis of the economy. Settlement had to adapt to desert conditions and the main centres of population were in the narrow belt between the Wasatch Mountains and the Great Salt Lake. Salt Lake City, the capital, was founded in 1847 and laid out according to Joseph Smith's plan for the city of Zion. It was the centre of the Mormons' provisional 'State of Deseret' and Territorial capital from 1856 until 1896, except briefly in 1858 when federal forces occupied it during conflict between territorial and Union governments.

Territory and Population

Utah is bounded north by Idaho and Wyoming, east by Colorado, south by Arizona and west by Nevada. Land area, 82,170 sq. miles (212,818 sq. km); water area, 2,727 sq. miles (7,064 sq. km). In 2010 American Indian lands covered 8,954 sq. miles (reservations plus off-reservation trust land). The federal government owned 35,033,603 acres in 2010, equivalent to 66·5% of the state area (the second highest percentage after Nevada).

Census population, 1 April 2010, was 2,763,885, an increase of 23·8% since 2000. July 2018 estimate, 3,161,105.

Population at five federal censuses was:

	White	Black	American Indian/ Alaska Native	Asian	Total (including others)	Per sq. mile
1910	366,583	1,144	3,123	2,501	373,851	4·5
1980	1,382,550	9,225	19,256	15,076	1,461,037	17·7
1990	1,615,845	11,576	24,283	25,696	1,722,850	21·0
2000	1,992,975	17,657	29,684	37,108	2,233,169	27·2
2010	2,379,560	29,287	32,927	55,285	2,763,885	33·6

Of the total population in 2010, 1,388,317 were male and 1,892,858 were 18 years old or older. In 2010 the Hispanic population was 358,340, up from 201,559 in 2000 (an increase of 77·8%).

The largest cities are Salt Lake City (the capital), with a population (census, 2010) of 186,440; West Valley City, 129,480; Provo, 112,488; West Jordan, 103,712; Orem, 88,328; Sandy, 87,461.

Social Statistics

Births, 2014, 51,154 (17·4 per 1,000 population—the highest rate in any US state); deaths, 2014, 16,719 (5·7). Infant mortality rate, 2013, 5·2 per 1,000 live births. 2014: marriages, 7·3 per 1,000 population; divorces and annulments, 3·1. Utah has the highest fertility rate of any US state, at 2·3 births per woman in 2014. Same-sex marriage became legal in Oct. 2014.

Climate

Salt Lake City, Jan. 29°F (–1·7°C), July 77°F (25°C). Annual rainfall 16" (401 mm). Utah belongs to the Mountain States climate region (*see* UNITED STATES: Climate).

Constitution and Government

Utah adopted its present constitution in 1896; it has had numerous amendments since then. The Legislature consists of a Senate (in part renewed every two years) of 29 members, elected for four years, and of a House of Representatives of 75 members elected for two years. It sits annually in Jan. The Governor is elected for four years. The constitution provides for the initiative and referendum.

For the 116th Congress, which convened in Jan. 2019, Utah sends four members to the House of Representatives. It is represented in the Senate by Mike Lee (R. 2011–23) and Mitt Romney (R. 2019–25).

The capital is Salt Lake City. There are 29 counties in the state.

Recent Elections

In the 2016 presidential election Donald Trump took Utah with 45·9% of the vote (Mitt Romney won it in 2012).

Current Government

Governor: Gary R. Herbert (R.), 2017–21 (salary: $150,000).
Lieut.-Governor: Spencer J. Cox (R.), 2017–21.
Government Website: https://www.utah.gov

Economy

Per capita personal income (2015) was $39,045.

Budget
In 2011 total state revenue was $16,985m. Total expenditure was $16,683m. (including: education, $6,516m.; public welfare, $2,812m.; highways, $1,514m.; hospitals, $956m.; government administration, $800m.). Outstanding debt in 2011, $7,206m.

Performance
Gross Domestic Product by state in 2015 was $147,503m., ranking Utah 32nd in the United States. In 2015 state real GDP growth was 3·4%.

Energy and Natural Resources

Oil and Gas
In 2014 Utah produced 40·9m. bbls of crude petroleum; marketed production of natural gas totalled 453bn. cu. ft.

Water
The total area covered by water is 2,727 sq. miles.

Minerals
The principal minerals are: copper, gold, magnesium, petroleum, lead, silver and zinc. The state also has natural gas, clays, tungsten, molybdenum, uranium and phosphate rock. Production of coal (2009) was 21·7m. short tons. The value of domestic non-fuel mineral production in 2009 was $3,910m.

Agriculture
In 2007 Utah had 16,700 farms covering 11·09m. acres. Average number of acres per farm was 664 and the average value per acre was $1,249. Farm income, 2008: from crops, $527m.; and from livestock and products, $987m. The net farm income in 2008 was $252m. The principal crops are: barley, wheat (spring and winter), oats, potatoes, hay (alfalfa, sweet clover and lespedeza) and maize. Livestock, 2007: cattle, 843,000; hogs and pigs, 760,000; sheep and lambs, 278,000; laying hens, 3·59m.

Forestry
Forest area, 2012, was 18,299,000 acres and included 6,343,000 acres of national forest.

Industry
Leading manufactures by value added are primary metals, ordinances and transport, food, fabricated metals and machinery, and petroleum products. In 2012 Utah's 6,560 manufacturing establishments had 221,000 employees, earning $11,698m. Total value added by manufacturing in 2013 was $21,891m.

Labour
Total non-agricultural employment, 2010, 1,181,000. Employees by branch, 2010 (in 1,000): trade, transportation and utilities, 229; government, 216; education and health services, 155; professional and business services, 153; manufacturing, 111. The unemployment rate in Dec. 2010 was 7·5%.

International Trade

Imports and Exports
In 2015 imports into Utah totalled $12·1bn. (up from $11·1bn. in 2014). In the same year exports from Utah totalled $13·3bn., up from $12·2bn. in 2014. The leading source for imports in 2015 was Mexico ($3·3bn.), ahead of China ($2·2bn.). The leading destination for exports in 2015 was the United Kingdom ($3·0bn.), followed by Hong Kong ($1·9bn.).

Communications

Roads
In 2012 there were 45,891 miles of road (35,123 miles rural). There were 1,918,522 registered motor vehicles.

Rail
In 2012 there were 1,343 miles of freight railroad (excluding trackage rights). There were seven freight railroads operating in 2012. Rail traffic originating in Utah totalled 15·8m. tons in 2012 and rail traffic terminating in the state came to 10·8m. tons. A light rail system opened in Salt Lake City in 1999.

Civil Aviation
There is an international airport at Salt Lake City. In 2012 Utah had four primary airports (commercial service airports with more than 10,000 passenger boardings annually) with a combined total of 9,679,453 enplanements, down from 9,773,886 in 2011.

Social Institutions

Justice
In Dec. 2014 there were 7,026 prison inmates. The death penalty is authorized; there was one execution in 2010 (the first since 1999) but none since. In March 2015 the state reintroduced firing squads as a method of execution.

Education
School attendance is compulsory for children from six to 18 years of age. In 2012–13 there were 613,279 pupils and 26,610 teachers in 1,039 public elementary and secondary schools; teachers' salaries averaged $49,393. In 2010–11 total expenditure on public elementary and secondary education was $4,643m.; spending per pupil was $6,326.

In fall 2012 there were 267,309 students enrolled in public and private degree-granting institutions. Among the public institutions, the University of Utah (founded in 1850) in Salt Lake City had 31,515 students in fall 2014; Utah Valley University in Orem, 31,332; Utah State University in Logan, 27,662; Weber State University in Ogden, 25,954; Dixie State University in St George, 8,570; Southern Utah University in Cedar City, 7,656; Salt Lake Community College in Salt Lake City, 30,248; and Snow College in Ephraim, 4,779. The Mormon Church maintains the private Brigham Young University at Provo (1875) with 30,484 students in fall 2014.

Health
Utah had 1·8 community hospital beds for every 1,000 population in 2013. In the same year there were 22·6 active physicians per 10,000 civilian population and 6·5 dentists per 10,000.

Welfare
Medicare enrolment in July 2012 totalled 307,539. In fiscal year 2011 a total of 434,969 people in Utah received Medicaid. In Dec. 2014 there were 365,730 Old-Age, Survivors, and Disability Insurance (OASDI) beneficiaries. A total of 10,563 people were receiving payments under Temporary Assistance for Needy Families (TANF) in Dec. 2012.

Religion
In 2010 the leading religious traditions were: Latter-day Saints (Mormons), with 1,911,047 members; Catholics, 160,125; Evangelical Protestants, 63,040; Mainline Protestants, 23,546; Buddhists, 8,602.

Culture

Tourism
Overseas visitors to Utah (excluding those from Canada and Mexico) numbered 502,000 in 2011, up from 475,000 in 2010.

Vermont

Key Historical Events
The original American Indian hunting grounds of the Green Mountains and lakes was explored by the Frenchman, Samuel de Champlain, in 1609. He reached Lake Champlain on the northwest border. The first attempt at permanent settlement was also French, on Isle La Motte in 1666. In 1763 the British gained the area by the Treaty of Paris. The Treaty, which also brought peace with the American Indian allies of the French, opened the way for settlement, but in a mountain area transport was slow and difficult. Montpelier, the state capital from 1805, was chartered as a township site in 1781 to command the main pass through the Green Mountains.

In the War of Independence Vermont declared itself an independent state to avoid being taken over by New Hampshire and New York. In 1791 it became the 14th state of the Union.

Most early settlers were New Englanders of British and Protestant descent. After 1812 a granite-quarrying industry grew around the town of Barre, attracting immigrant workers from Italy and Scandinavia. French Canadians settled in Winooski. Textile and engineering industries developed in the 19th century attracted more European workers.

Vermont saw the only Civil War action north of Pennsylvania when a Confederate raiding party attacked from Canada in 1864.

During the 20th century the textile and engineering industries have declined but paper and lumber industries flourish. Settlement is still mainly rural or in small towns.

Territory and Population

Vermont is bounded in the north by Canada, east by New Hampshire, south by Massachusetts and west by New York. Total area is 9,616 sq. miles (24,906 sq. km) of which 9,217 sq. miles (23,871 sq. km) are land. Census population, 1 April 2010, was 625,741, an increase of 2·8% since 2000. July 2018 estimate, 626,299.

Population at five census years was:

	White	Black	American Indian/ Alaska Native	Asian	Total (including others)	Per sq. mile
1910	354,298	1,621	26	11	355,956	39·0
1980	506,736	1,135	984	1,355	511,456	55·1
1990	555,088	1,951	1,696	3,215[1]	562,758	60·8
2000	589,208	3,063	2,420	5,358[1]	608,827	65·8
2010	596,292	6,277	2,207	8,107[1]	625,741	67·9

[1]Includes Native Hawaiian and other Pacific Islander.

Of the total population in 2010, 317,535 were female and 496,508 were 18 years old or older. In 2000, 414,480 (66·2%) were rural, the highest rural population percentage of any state in the USA. In 2010 the Hispanic population was 9,208, the lowest total of any state. However, this figure represents a rise of 67·3% compared to the 2000 census figure of 5,504. The largest cities are Burlington, with a population (2010) of 42,417; South Burlington, 17,904; Rutland City, 16,495. The capital, Montpelier, had a population in 2010 of 7,855.

Social Statistics

Births, 2014, 6,130 (9·8 per 1,000 population); deaths, 2014, 5,623 (9·0). Infant deaths, 2013, 4·4 per 1,000 live births. 2014: marriages, 8·7 per 1,000 population; divorces and annulments, 3·5. Same-sex marriage became legal in Sept. 2009.

Climate

Burlington, Jan. 17°F (−8·3°C), July 70°F (21·1°C). Annual rainfall 33" (820 mm). Vermont belongs to the New England climate zone (see UNITED STATES: Climate).

Constitution and Government

The constitution was adopted in 1793 and has since been amended. Amendments are proposed by two-thirds vote of the Senate every four years, and must be accepted by two sessions of the legislature; they are then submitted to popular vote. The state Legislature, consisting of a Senate of 30 members and a House of Representatives of 150 members (both elected for two years), meets in Jan. every year. The Governor and Lieut.-Governor are elected for two years. Electors are all citizens who possess certain residential qualifications and have taken the freeman's oath set forth in the constitution.

For the 116th Congress, which convened in Jan. 2019, Vermont sends one member to the House of Representatives. It is represented in the Senate by Patrick Leahy (D. 1975–2023—making him currently the longest-serving senator) and Bernard (Bernie) Sanders (Independent, 2007–25). Sanders ran as a Democrat in the 2016 presidential primary elections but has otherwise served as an independent.

The capital is Montpelier. There are 14 counties and 255 political units or towns.

Recent Elections

In the 2016 presidential election Hillary Clinton took Vermont with 61·1% of the vote (Barack Obama won it in 2012).

Current Government

Governor: Phil Scott (R.), 2019–23 (salary: $172,619).
    Lieut.-Governor: David Zuckerman (Progressive/Democrat), 2019–23.
    Secretary of State: Jim Condos (R.), since Jan. 2011.
Government Website: https://vermont.gov/portal

Economy

Per capita personal income (2015) was $47,864.

Budget

In 2011 total state revenue was $6,506m. Total expenditure was $5,854m. (education, $2,323m.; public welfare, $1,463m.; highways, $419m.; health, $191m.; government administration, $138m.). Outstanding debt in 2011, $3,485m.

Performance

Gross Domestic Product by state was $30,038m. in 2015, ranking Vermont 50th in the United States. In 2015 state real GDP growth was 0·4%.

Energy and Natural Resources

Water

The total area covered by water is 400 sq. miles.

Minerals

Stone, chiefly granite, marble and slate, is the leading mineral produced in Vermont, contributing about 60% of the total value of mineral products. Other products include asbestos, talc, sand and gravel. Value of domestic non-fuel mineral products in 2009 was more than $120m.

Agriculture

Agriculture is the most important industry. In 2007 the state had 6,984 farms covering 1·23m. acres; the average farm was of 177 acres and the average value per acre of land and buildings was $2,903. In 2007 farm income from crops totalled $93m.; from livestock and products, $581m. The net farm income in 2007 was $263m. Principal commodities are dairy products (cash receipts of $517·9m. in 2007), cattle, greenhouse products and hay. In 2007 Vermont had 265,000 cattle and calves and 2,700 hogs and pigs.

Forestry

The state is 78% forest, with 17% in public ownership. In 2013 Vermont had 4,514,000 acres of forested land with 446,000 acres of national forest.

Industry

In 2012 the state's 2,618 manufacturing establishments had 76,000 employees, earning $3,761m. Total value added by manufacturing in 2013 was $3,885m.

Labour

Total non-agricultural employment, 2010, 298,000. Employees by branch, 2010 (in 1,000): education and health services, 59; trade, transportation and utilities, 56; government, 55; leisure and hospitality, 32; manufacturing, 31. The unemployment rate in Dec. 2010 was 5·8%.

International Trade

Imports and Exports

In 2015 imports into Vermont totalled $4,063m. (down from $4,765m. in 2014). In the same year exports from Vermont totalled $3,181m., down from $3,670m. in 2014. The leading source for imports in 2015 was Canada ($2,918m.), ahead of China ($265m.). The leading destination for exports in 2015 was also Canada ($1,172m.), followed by Hong Kong ($302m.).

Communications

Roads

In 2012 there were 14,291 miles of road comprising 1,470 miles of urban road and 12,821 miles of rural road. Motor vehicle registrations totalled 576,250.

Rail

In 2012 there were 590 miles of freight railroad (excluding trackage rights). There were eight freight railroads operating in 2012. Rail traffic originating in Vermont totalled 0·7m. tons in 2012 with rail traffic terminating in the state totalling 1·6m. tons.

Civil Aviation

Vermont's only primary airport—a commercial service airport with more than 10,000 passenger boardings annually—is Burlington International. In 2011 it had 636,019 enplanements.

Social Institutions

Justice
In Dec. 2014 the jail and prison population totalled 1,979. The death penalty was officially abolished in 1987 but effectively in 1964.

Education
School attendance during the full school term is compulsory for children from six to 16 years of age, unless they have completed the 10th grade or undergo approved home instruction. In 2012–13, 320 public elementary and secondary schools had 89,624 pupils and 8,403 teachers; average teacher's salary was $52,526. Total expenditure on public elementary and secondary education in 2010–11 totalled $1,516m.

In 2012–13 there were 24 degree-granting institutions (six public); enrolment totalled 44,703. In fall 2014 the University of Vermont (1791), in Burlington, had 12,856 students; Norwich University, in Northfield, had 3,672; the Community College of Vermont, in Winooski, had 6,019; and Champlain College, in Burlington, had 3,585.

Health
Vermont had 1·9 community hospital beds for every 1,000 population in 2013. In the same year there were 38·2 active physicians per 10,000 civilian population and 5·8 dentists per 10,000.

Welfare
Medicare enrolment in July 2012 totalled 120,295. In fiscal year 2012 a total of 188,283 people in Vermont received Medicaid. In Dec. 2014 there were 140,634 Old-Age, Survivors, and Disability Insurance (OASDI) beneficiaries. A total of 6,718 people were receiving payments under Temporary Assistance for Needy Families (TANF) in Dec. 2012.

Religion
The leading religious traditions in the state in 2010 were: Catholics, with 128,293 members; Mainline Protestants, 48,029; Evangelical Protestants, 22,630; Latter-day Saints (Mormons), 4,384.

Virginia

Key Historical Events
In 1607 a British colony was founded at Jamestown, on a peninsula in the James River, to grow tobacco. The area was marshy and unhealthy but the colony survived and in 1619 introduced a form of representative government. The tobacco plantations expanded and African slaves were imported. Jamestown was later abandoned but tobacco-growing continued and spread through the eastern part of the territory.

In 1624 control of the colony passed from the Virginia Company of London to the Crown. Growth was rapid during the 17th and 18th centuries. The movement for American independence was strong in Virginia; George Washington and Thomas Jefferson were both Virginians, and crucial battles of the War of Independence were fought there.

When the Union was formed, Virginia became one of the original states, but with reservations because of its attachment to slave-owning. In 1831 there was a slave rebellion. The tobacco plantations began to decline, and plantation owners turned to the breeding of slaves. While the eastern plantation lands seceded from the Union in 1861, the small farmers and miners of the western hills refused to secede and remained in the Union as West Virginia.

Richmond, the capital, became the capital of the Confederacy. Much of the Civil War took place in Virginia, with considerable damage to the economy. After the war the position of the black population was little improved. Blacks remained without political or civil rights until the 1960s.

Territory and Population
Virginia is bounded northwest by West Virginia, northeast by Maryland and the District of Columbia, east by the Atlantic, south by North Carolina and Tennessee and west by Kentucky. Land area, 39,490 sq. miles (102,279 sq. km); water area, 3,285 sq. miles (8,508 sq. km). Census population, 1 April 2010, was 8,001,024, an increase of 13·0% since 2000. July 2018 estimate, 8,517,685.

Population for five federal census years was:

	White	Black	American Indian/ Alaska Native	Asian/ Other	Total	Per sq. mile
1910	1,389,809	671,096	539	168	2,061,612	51·2
			All others			
1980	4,230,000	1,008,311	108, 517		5,346,818	134·7
1990	4,791,739	1,162,994	15,282	217,343	6,187,358	155·9
2000	5,120,110	1,390,293	21,172	546,940	7,078,515	178·8
2010	5,486,852	1,551,399	29,225	933,548	8,001,024	202·6

Of the total population in 2010, 4,075,041 were female and 6,147,347 were 18 years old or older. In 2010 the Hispanic population was 631,825, up from 329,540 in 2000 (an increase of 91·7%).

The population (2010 census population) of the principal cities was: Virginia Beach, 437,994; Norfolk, 242,803; Chesapeake, 222,209; Arlington CDP, 207,627; Richmond (the capital), 204,214; Newport News, 180,719; Alexandria, 139,966; Hampton, 137,436.

Social Statistics
Births, 2014, 103,300 (12·4 per 1,000 population); deaths, 2014, 63,598 (7·6). Infant mortality, 2013, 6·2 per 1,000 live births. 2014: marriages, 6·7 per 1,000 population; divorces and annulments, 3·5. Same-sex marriage became legal in Oct. 2014.

Climate
Average temperatures in Jan. are 41°F (5°C) in the Tidewater coastal area and 32°F (0°C) in the Blue Ridge mountains; July averages, 78°F (25·5°C) and 68°F (20°C) respectively. Precipitation averages 36" (914 mm) in the Shenandoah valley and 44" (1,118 mm) in the south. Snowfall is 5–10" (125–250 mm) in the Tidewater and 25–30" (625–750 mm) in the western mountains. Norfolk, Jan. 41°F (5°C), July 79°F (26°C). Annual rainfall 46" (1,145 mm). Virginia belongs to the Atlantic Coast climate zone (*see* UNITED STATES: Climate).

Constitution and Government
The present constitution became effective in 1971. The General Assembly consists of a Senate of 40 members, elected for four years, and a House of Delegates of 100 members, elected for two years. It sits annually in Jan. The Governor and Lieut.-Governor are elected for four years.

For the 116th Congress, which convened in Jan. 2019, Virginia sends 11 members to the House of Representatives. It is represented in the Senate by Mark Warner (D. 2009–21) and Tim Kaine (D. 2013–25).

The state capital is Richmond; the state contains 95 counties and 38 independent cities.

Recent Elections
In the 2016 presidential election Hillary Clinton took Virginia with 49·9% of the vote (Barack Obama won it in 2012).

Current Government
Governor: Ralph Northam (D.) 2018–22 (salary: $175,000).
Lieut.-Governor: Justin Fairfax (D.) 2018–22.
Secretary of the Commonwealth: Kelly Thomasson (D.), since April 2016.
Government Website: https://www.virginia.gov

Economy
Per capita personal income (2015) was $52,136.

Budget
In 2011 total state revenue was $50,782m. Total expenditure was $5,549m. (education, $14,372m.; public welfare, $9,348m.; highways, $3,328m.; health, $3,254m.; correction, $1,679m.). Outstanding debt in 2011, $26,479m.

Performance
Gross Domestic Product by state in 2015 was $481,084m., ranking Virginia 12th in the United States. In 2015 state real GDP growth was 2·0%.

Energy and Natural Resources

Water
The total area covered by water is 3,285 sq. miles.

Minerals
Coal is the most important mineral, with output (2009) of 21·2m. short tons. Lead and zinc ores, stone, sand and gravel, lime and titanium ore are also produced. Total domestic non-fuel mineral output was valued at $955m. in 2009.

Agriculture
In 2007 there were 47,383 farms with an area of 8·10m. acres; the average farm had 171 acres, and the average value per acre was $4,213. Farm income, 2009: from crops, $1,006m.; and from livestock and products, $1,635m. The net farm income in 2009 was $352m. The leading commodities are broilers (cash receipts of $559·4m. in 2007), cattle, dairy products and turkeys. Livestock, 2007: cattle and calves, 1·57m.; dairy cows, 99,000; sheep and lambs, 78,000; hogs and pigs, 371,200; laying hens, 3·21m.

Forestry
Forests covered 15,883,000 acres in 2012, including 1,750,000 acres of national forest.

Fisheries
Commercial catch (2009) totalled 426·3m. lb of fish, worth $152·7m.

Oil and Gas
In 2014 Virginia's marketed production of natural gas totalled 132bn. cu. ft.

Electricity
In 2015 production was 84,412m. kWh, of which 33,284m. kWh was from natural gas and 28,060m. kWh from nuclear energy.

Industry
The manufacture of cigars and cigarettes, of rayon and allied products, and the building of ships lead in value of products. In 2012 the state's 11,536 manufacturing establishments had 521,000 employees, earning $25,618m. Total value added by manufacturing in 2013 was $57,435m.

Labour
Total non-agricultural employment, 2010, 3,627,000. Employees by branch, 2010 (in 1,000): government, 703; professional and business services, 648; trade, transportation and utilities, 620; education and health services, 456; leisure and hospitality, 338. The unemployment rate in Dec. 2010 was 6·6%.

International Trade

Imports and Exports
In 2015 imports into Virginia totalled $25·1bn. (up from $24·3bn. in 2014). In the same year exports from Virginia totalled $17·8bn., down from $19·4bn. in 2014. The leading source for imports in 2015 was China ($6·9bn.), ahead of Canada ($1·8bn.). The leading destination for exports in 2015 was Canada ($3·4bn.), followed by China ($1·6bn.).

Communications

Roads
In 2012 there were 74,591 miles of roads (50,177 miles rural). There were 6,917,302 registered motor vehicles.

Rail
In 2012 there were 3,215 miles of freight railroad (excluding trackage rights). There were nine freight railroads operating in 2012. Rail traffic originating in Virginia totalled 32·2m. tons in 2012 and rail traffic terminating in the state came to 77·6m. tons. A light rail system opened in Norfolk in 2011.

Civil Aviation
There are international airports at Norfolk, Dulles, Richmond, Arlington and Newport News. In 2012 there were nine primary airports (commercial service airports with more than 10,000 passenger boardings annually) with a combined total of 24,467,633 enplanements, up from 24,415,798 in 2011.

Social Institutions

Justice
In Dec. 2014 there were 37,544 prison inmates. The death penalty is authorized. Between 1977 and 2018 there were 113 executions in Virginia—only Texas had more. There were two executions in 2017 but none in 2018.

Education
Elementary and secondary instruction is free, and for ages 5–18 attendance is compulsory.

There are 134 school districts. In 2012–13 there were 1,265,419 pupils in 2,203 elementary and secondary schools, with 89,389 teachers; average annual salary for public elementary and secondary teachers was $49,869. Total expenditure on public elementary and secondary education in 2010–11 was $14,292m.

In 2012–13 there were 132 degree-granting education institutions (40 public and 92 private). Leading institutions include:

Founded	Name and place of college	Students 2014
1693	College of William and Mary, Williamsburg (State)	8,437
1749	Washington and Lee University, Lexington	2,264
1776	Hampden-Sydney College, Hampden-Sydney (Presbyterian)	1,105
1819	University of Virginia, Charlottesville (State)	23,732
1832	Randolph-Macon College, Ashland (Methodist)	1,394
1832	University of Richmond, Richmond (Baptist)	4,182
1838	Virginia Commonwealth University, Richmond	30,848
1839	Virginia Military Institute Lexington (State)	1,700
1865	Virginia Union University, Richmond	1,715
1868	Hampton University	4,393
1872	Virginia Polytechnic Institute and State University, Blacksburg	31,224
1882	Virginia State University, Petersburg	5,025
1908	James Madison University, Harrisonburg	20,855
1910	Radford University (State)	9,798
1930	Old Dominion University, Norfolk	24,932
1935	Norfolk State University (State)	6,027
1957	George Mason University (State), Fairfax	33,729
1960	Christopher Newport University (State), Newport News	5,221
1971	Liberty University, Lynchburg	81,459

Health
Virginia had 2·2 community hospital beds for every 1,000 population in 2013. In the same year there were 28·1 active physicians per 10,000 civilian population and 6·3 dentists per 10,000.

Welfare
Medicare enrolment in July 2012 totalled 1,231,640. In fiscal year 2012 a total of 1,029,515 people in Virginia received Medicaid. In Dec. 2014 there were 1,415,661 Old-Age, Survivors, and Disability Insurance (OASDI) beneficiaries. A total of 66,532 people were receiving payments under Temporary Assistance for Needy Families (TANF) in Dec. 2012.

Religion
The principal religious traditions in the state in 2010 were: Evangelical Protestants, with 1,531,731 members; Mainline Protestants, 870,842; Catholics, 674,555; Muslims, 213,000 (estimate); Black Protestants, 111,028.

Culture

Tourism
In 2011 overseas visitors to Virginia—excluding those from Canada and Mexico—numbered 362,000, down from 369,000 in 2010.

Washington State

Key Historical Events

The strongest American Indian tribes in the 18th century were Chinook, Nez Percé, Salish and Yakima. The area was designated by European colonizers as part of the Oregon Country. Between 1775 and 1800 it was claimed by Spain, Britain and the USA; the dispute between the two latter nations was not settled until 1846.

The first small white settlements were American Indian missions and fur-trading posts. In the 1840s American settlers began to push westwards along the Oregon Trail, making a settlement with Britain a matter of urgency. When this was achieved the whole area was organized as the Oregon Territory in 1848. Washington was made a separate Territory in 1853.

Apart from trapping and fishing, the chief industry was supplying timber for the new settlements of California. After 1870 the westward extension of railways encouraged settlement. Statehood was granted in 1889. Settlers were mostly Americans from neighbouring states to the east and Canadians. Scandinavian immigrants followed. Seattle, laid out in 1853 as a saw-milling town, was named after the American Indian chief who had ceded the land and befriended the settlers. It grew as a port during the Alaskan and Yukon gold-rushes of the 1890s. The economy thrived on exploiting the Columbia River for hydro-electric power. Washington and Colorado became the first US states to legalize the recreational possession and sale of marijuana following voter referendums in Nov. 2012.

Territory and Population

Washington is bounded north by Canada, east by Idaho, south by Oregon with the Columbia River forming most of the boundary, and west by the Pacific. Land area, 66,456 sq. miles (172,119 sq. km); water area, 4,842 sq. miles (12,542 sq. km). Lands owned by the federal government, 2003, were 13,246,559 acres or 31·0% of the total area. Census population, 1 April 2010, was 6,724,540, an increase of 14·1% since 2000. July 2018 estimate, 7,535,591.

Population in five federal census years was:

	White	Black	American Indian/ Alaska Native	Asian/ Other	Total	Per sq. mile
1910	1,109,111	6,058	10,997	15,824	1,141,990	17·1
1980	3,779,170	105,574	60,804	186,608	4,132,156	62·1
1990	4,308,937	149,801	81,483	326,471	4,866,692	73·1
2000	4,821,823	190,267	93,301	788,730	5,894,121	88·6
2010	5,196,362	240,042	103,869	1,184,267	6,724,540	101·2

Of the total population in 2010, 3,374,833 were female and 5,143,186 were 18 years old or older. In 2010 the Hispanic population was 755,790, up from 441,509 in 2000 (a rise of 71·2%).

In 2010 American Indian lands covered 5,063 sq. miles (reservations plus off-reservation trust land).

Leading cities are Seattle, with a population in 2010 of 608,660; Spokane, 208,916; Tacoma, 198,397; Vancouver, 161,791; Bellevue, 122,363. Others: Everett, 103,019; Kent, 92,411; Yakima, 91,067; Renton, 90,927; Spokane Valley, 89,755; Federal Way, 89,306; Bellingham, 80,885; Kennewick, 73,917; Auburn, 70,180; Marysville, 60,020; Pasco, 59,781; Lakewood, 58,163; Redmond, 54,144; Shoreline, 53,007. The Seattle–Tacoma–Bremerton metropolitan area had a 2010 census population of 3,439,809. The capital, Olympia, had a population in 2010 of 46,478.

Social Statistics

Births, 2014, 88,585 (12·5 per 1,000 population); deaths, 2014, 52,099 (7·4). Infant mortality rate, 2013, 4·5 per 1,000 live births. 2014: marriages, 7·0 per 1,000 population; divorces and annulments, 3·6. Same-sex marriage became legal in Dec. 2012 after it had been approved in a referendum a month earlier on the same day as the presidential election.

Climate

Seattle, Jan. 40°F (4·4°C), July 63°F (17·2°C). Annual rainfall 34" (848 mm). Spokane, Jan. 27°F (−2·8°C), July 70°F (21·1°C). Annual rainfall 14" (350 mm). Washington belongs to the Pacific Coast climate zone (*see* UNITED STATES: Climate).

Constitution and Government

The constitution, adopted in 1889, has had 107 amendments as of Sept. 2016. The Legislature consists of a Senate of 49 members elected for four years, half their number retiring every two years, and a House of Representatives of 98 members, elected for two years. The Governor and Lieut.-Governor are elected for four years.

For the 116th Congress, which convened in Jan. 2019, Washington sends ten members to the House of Representatives. It is represented in the Senate by Patty Murray (D. 1993–2023) and Maria Cantwell (D. 2001–25).

The capital is Olympia. The state contains 39 counties.

Recent Elections

In the 2016 presidential election Hillary Clinton took Washington State with 54·4% of the vote (Barack Obama won it in 2012).

Current Government

Governor: Jay Inslee (D.), 2017–21 (salary: $171,898).
    Lieut.-Governor: Cyrus Habib (D.), 2017–21.
    Secretary of State: Kim Wyman (R.), since Jan. 2013.
Government Website: https://access.wa.gov

Economy

Per capita personal income (2015) was $51,146.

Budget

In 2011 total state revenue was $50,420m. Total expenditure was $46,000m. (education, $14,886m.; public welfare, $8,669m.; highways, $3,030m.; hospitals, $2,051m.; health, $1,797m.). Outstanding debt in 2011, $28,154m.

Performance

In 2015 Gross Domestic Product by state was $445,413m., ranking Washington 14th in the United States. In 2015 state real GDP growth was 3·0%.

Energy and Natural Resources

Electricity

In 2015 production was 109·3bn. kWh, of which 73·4bn. kWh was from conventional hydro-electric energy.

Water

The total area covered by water is 4,842 sq. miles.

Minerals

Mining and quarrying are not as important as forestry, agriculture or manufacturing. Total value of non-fuel mineral production in 2009 was $650m.

Agriculture

Agriculture is constantly growing in value as a result of more intensive and diversified farming, and because of the 1m.-acre Columbia Basin Irrigation Project.

In 2007 there were 39,284 farms with an acreage of 15·32m.; the average farm was 381 acres. Average value of farmland and buildings per acre in 2007 was $1,992. Apples, milk, wheat, cattle and calves and potatoes are the top five commodities. Washington is the USA's largest producer of apples, cherries and pears. In 2007 livestock included 1·09m. all cattle (274,000 beef cows and 243,100 dairy cows), 53,200 sheep and lambs, 28,500 hogs and pigs, and 5·79m. laying hens.

Farm income, 2009: from crops, $4,953m.; from livestock and products, $1,640m. The net farm income in 2009 was $962m.

Forestry

Forests covered 22·22m. acres in 2013, of which 8·4m. acres were national forest. In 2012 timber harvested totalled 2,740m. bd ft, 45% of which was Douglas fir.

Fisheries

Salmon and shellfish are important; total commercial catch, 2009, was 163·9m. lb and was worth $227·8m. Washington is the leading state for aquaculture production, which was valued at $233·0m. in 2013.

Industry

Principal manufactures are aircraft, pulp and paper, lumber and plywood, aluminium, processed fruit and vegetables. In 2012 the state's 14,440 manufacturing establishments had 502,000 employees, earning $29,135m. Total value added by manufacturing in 2013 was $62,637m.

Labour

In 2010 total non-agricultural employment was 2,777,000. Employees by branch, 2010 (in 1,000): government, 547; trade, transportation and utilities, 517; education and health services, 375; professional and business services, 326; leisure and hospitality, 266. The unemployment rate in Dec. 2010 was 9·3%.

International Trade

Imports and Exports

In 2015 imports into Washington totalled $51·1bn. (down from $52·5bn. in 2014). In the same year exports from Washington totalled $86·4bn., down from $90·6bn. in 2014. The leading source for imports in 2015 was Canada ($13·3bn.), ahead of China ($10·4bn.). The leading destination for exports in 2015 was China ($19·5bn.), followed by Canada ($8·0bn.).

Communications

Roads

In 2012 there were 83,878 miles of road comprising 23,742 miles of urban road and 60,136 miles of rural road. There were 5,632,644 registered motor vehicles.

Rail

In 2012 there were 3,192 miles of freight railroad (excluding trackage rights). There were 24 freight railroads operating in 2012. Rail traffic originating in Washington totalled 21·9m. tons in 2012 and rail traffic terminating in the state came 48·3m. tons. A light rail system opened in Seattle in 2009.

Civil Aviation

There are international airports at Seattle/Tacoma and Spokane. In 2012 Washington had ten primary airports (commercial service airports with more than 10,000 passenger boardings annually) with a combined total of 18,698,295 enplanements, up from 18,525,818 in 2011.

Social Institutions

Justice

In Dec. 2014 there were 18,120 prison inmates. There was one execution in 2010, the first since 2001, but none in the following three years. The death penalty was then suspended in Feb. 2014 and abolished in Oct. 2018.

Education

Education is given free to all children between the ages of five and 21 years, and is compulsory for children from eight to 18 years of age. In 2012–13 there were 1,051,694 pupils in public elementary and secondary schools with 53,699 teachers; teachers' salaries in 2012–13 averaged $53,571. In fall 2011 there were 93,630 pupils in 630 private schools.

In fall 2012 total enrolment in degree-granting post-secondary institutions was 365,514. The public University of Washington, founded 1861 and with campuses at Seattle, Tacoma and Bothell, had (in fall 2014) 54,223 students; Washington State University at Pullman, founded 1890, for science and agriculture, had 28,686 students. Western Washington University had 15,060; Eastern Washington University, 13,453; Central Washington University, 11,799; Gonzaga University, at Spokane, 7,352; Seattle University, 7,273.

Health

Washington had 1·7 community hospital beds for every 1,000 population in 2013. In the same year there were 28·4 active physicians per 10,000 civilian population and 7·1 dentists per 10,000.

Welfare

Medicare enrolment in July 2012 totalled 1,056,923. In fiscal year 2012 a total of 1,462,881 people in Washington received Medicaid. In Dec. 2014 there were 1,230,039 Old-Age, Survivors, and Disability Insurance (OASDI) beneficiaries. A total of 116,042 people were receiving payments under Temporary Assistance for Needy Families (TANF) in Dec. 2012.

Religion

The principal religious traditions in the state in 2010 were: Evangelical Protestants, with 820,643 members; Catholics, 784,332; Mainline Protestants, 308,292; Latter-day Saints (Mormons), 271,414; Buddhists, 49,065.

Culture

Tourism

In 2016 overseas visitors to Washington—excluding those from Canada and Mexico—numbered 729,000, down from 852,000 in 2015. There were 2,750,000 visits by Canadians in 2015.

West Virginia

Key Historical Events

In 1861 the slave-owning state of Virginia seceded from the Union. The 40 western counties, mostly hilly country and settled by miners and small farmers who were not slave-owners, were declared a new state. On 20 June 1863 West Virginia became the 35th state of the Union.

The capital, Charleston, was an 18th-century fortified post on the early westward migration routes across the Appalachians. In 1795 local brine wells were tapped and the city grew as a salt town. Coal, oil, natural gas and a variety of salt brines were all found in due course. Huntington, the next largest town, served the same industrial area as a railway terminus and port on the Ohio river. Wheeling, the original state capital, located on the major transportation routes of the Ohio River, Baltimore and Ohio Railroad and the National Road, was a well-established, cosmopolitan city when it hosted the statehood meetings in 1861.

Three-quarters of the state is forest. Settlement has been concentrated in the mineral-bearing Kanawha valley, along the Ohio river and in the industrial Monongahela valley of the north. More than half of the population is still classified as rural. However, the majority commute to industrial employment.

Territory and Population

West Virginia is bounded in the north by Pennsylvania and Maryland, east and south by Virginia, southwest by the Big Sandy River (forming the boundary with Kentucky) and west by the Ohio River (forming the boundary with Ohio). Total area is 24,230 sq. miles (62,756 sq. km) of which 24,038 sq. miles (62,259 sq. km) are land. Census population, 1 April 2010, was 1,852,994, an increase of 2·5% since 2000. July 2018 estimate, 1,805,832.

Population in five federal census years was:

	White	Black	American Indian/ Alaska Native	Asian/ Other	Total	Per sq. mile
1910	1,156,817	64,173	36	93	1,221,119	50·8
1980	1,874,751	65,051	1,610	5,194	1,949,644	80·3
1990	1,725,523	56,295	2,458	7,459	1,793,477	74·0
2000	1,718,777	57,232	3,606	9,834	1,808,344	75·1
2010	1,739,988	63,124	3,787	46,095	1,852,994	77·1

Of the total population in 2010, 939,408 were female and 1,465,576 were 18 years old or older. In 2010 the Hispanic population was 22,268, up from 12,279 in 2000 (an increase of 81·4%). Even with this increase West Virginia has the smallest Hispanic percentage in its population (at 1·2%) of any state.

The 2010 census population of the principal cities was: Charleston (the capital), 51,400; Huntington, 49,130. Others: Parkersburg, 31,492; Morgantown, 29,660; Wheeling, 28,486; Weirton, 19,746; Fairmont, 18,704; Beckley, 17,614; Martinsburg, 17,227; Clarksburg, 16,578.

Social Statistics

Births, 2014, 20,301 (11·0 per 1,000 population); deaths, 2014, 22,186 (12·0—the highest rate in any US state). West Virginia was one of only two states in the USA where deaths exceeded births in 2014, the other being Maine. Infant mortality, 2013, 7·6 per 1,000 live births. 2014: marriages, 6·7 per 1,000 population; divorces and annulments, 4·2. Same-sex marriage became legal in Oct. 2014.

Climate

Charleston, Jan. 34°F (1·1°C), July 76°F (24·4°C). Annual rainfall 40" (1,010 mm). West Virginia belongs to the Appalachian Mountains climate zone (*see* UNITED STATES: Climate).

Constitution and Government

The present constitution was adopted in 1872; it has had 17 amendments. The Legislature consists of the Senate of 34 members elected for a term of four years, one-half being elected biennially, and the House of Delegates of 100 members, elected biennially. The Governor is elected for four years and may serve one successive term.

For the 116th Congress, which convened in Jan. 2019, West Virginia sends three members to the House of Representatives. It is represented in the Senate by Joe Manchin III (D. 2011–25) and Shelley Moore Capito (R. 2015–21).

The state capital is Charleston. There are 55 counties.

Recent Elections

In the 2016 presidential election Donald Trump took West Virginia with 68·7% of the vote (Mitt Romney won it in 2012).

Current Government

Governor: Jim Justice (R.), 2017–21 (salary: $150,000).
  Senate President: Mitch Carmichael (R.), 2019–21.
  Secretary of State: Mac Warner (R.), since Jan. 2017.
Government Website: https://www.wv.gov

Economy

Per capita personal income (2015) was $37,047.

Budget

Total revenues in 2011 were $15,329m. Total expenditures were $13,000m. (education, $4,162m.; public welfare, $3,288m.; highways, $1,224m.; government administration, $418m.; health, $318m.). Outstanding debt in 2011, $7,406m.

Performance

Gross Domestic Product by state in 2015 was $74,321m., ranking West Virginia 39th in the United States. In 2015 state real GDP growth was 1·4%.

Energy and Natural Resources

Electricity

In 2015 total production was 72,295m. kWh, of which 94·1% was from coal (the highest percentage of any state).

Oil and Gas

In 2014 West Virginia produced 7·5m. bbls of crude petroleum; marketed production of natural gas totalled 1,040bn. cu. ft.

Water

The total area covered by water is 192 sq. miles.

Minerals

West Virginia is the nation's second largest coal-producing state after Wyoming; output was 137·0m. short tons in 2009. Coal-related employment (21,665 jobs in 2009) is higher than in any other state. Salt, sand and gravel, sandstone and limestone are also produced. The total value of non-fuel mineral production in 2009 was $215m.

Agriculture

In 2007 the state had 23,618 farms with an area of 3·70m. acres; average size of farm was 157 acres, valued at $2,385 per acre. Livestock farming predominates. Principal commodities are broilers, cattle, turkeys and dairy products.

Cash income, 2008: from crops was $96m.; from livestock and products, $429m. The net farm income in 2008 was $5m. The most important crops are hay, corn and apples.

Livestock on farms, 2007, included 411,000 cattle, of which 204,000 were beef cows and 12,000 dairy cows; sheep, 38,000; hogs and pigs, 9,000; laying hens, 1·22m.

Forestry

Forests covered 12,186,000 acres in 2013, with 1,048,000 acres of national forest. 78·5% of the state is woodland.

Industry

In 2012 the state's 3,064 manufacturing establishments had 120,000 employees, earning $6,258m. Total value added by manufacturing in 2013 was $10,912m.

Labour

Total non-agricultural employment, 2010, 746,000. Employees by branch, 2010 (in 1,000): government, 153; trade, transportation and utilities, 135; education and health services, 121; leisure and hospitality, 72; professional

and business services, 61. The state unemployment rate in Dec. 2010 was 9·7%.

International Trade

Imports and Exports

In 2015 imports into West Virginia totalled $3,782m. (down from $3,812m. in 2014). In the same year exports from West Virginia totalled $5,833m., down from $7,597m. in 2014. The leading source for imports in 2015 was Japan ($1,259m.), ahead of Canada ($1,161m.). The leading destination for exports in 2015 was Canada ($1,755m.), followed by China ($456m.).

Communications

Roads

In 2012 there were 38,684 miles of road (33,130 miles rural). There were 1,400,881 registered motor vehicles.

Rail

In 2012 there were 2,226 miles of freight railroad (excluding trackage rights). There were eight freight railroads operating in 2012. Rail traffic originating in West Virginia totalled 92·3m. tons in 2012 (the third highest after Wyoming and Illinois) with rail traffic terminating in the state totalling 14·3m. tons.

Civil Aviation

There were five primary airports—commercial service airports with more than 10,000 passenger boardings annually—in 2011 with a combined total of 435,193 enplanements, up from 414,317 in 2010.

Shipping

There are some 420·5 miles of navigable rivers.

Social Institutions

Justice

The state court system consists of a Supreme Court, 31 circuit courts, and magistrate courts in each county. The Supreme Court of Appeals, exercising original and appellate jurisdiction, has five members elected by the people for 12-year terms. Each circuit court has from one to seven judges (as determined by the Legislature on the basis of population and case-load) chosen by the voters within each circuit for eight-year terms.

In Dec. 2014, 6,896 prisoners were under the jurisdiction of state and federal correctional authorities. Capital punishment was abolished in 1965. The last execution was in 1959.

Education

School attendance is compulsory for all between the ages of six and 16. In 2012–13, 767 public elementary and secondary schools had 283,044 pupils and 20,101 teachers. Total expenditure on public elementary and secondary education in 2010–11 was $3,516m.; average teacher salary was $46,405 in 2012–13. Spending per pupil in 2010–11 was $11,978.

In 2012–13 there were 23 public and 20 private degree-granting institutions including:

Founded	Name and place	Students (fall 2014)
1837	Marshall University, Huntington	13,381[1]
1837	West Liberty University, West Liberty	2,694
1867	Fairmont State University, Fairmont	4,035
1868	West Virginia University, Morgantown	29,175
1872	Concord University, Athens	2,545
1872	Glenville State College, Glenville	1,802
1872	Shepherd University, Shepherdstown	4,041
1891	West Virginia State University, Institute	2,884
1895	West Virginia University Institute of Technology, Montgomery	1,261
1895	Bluefield State College, Bluefield	1,563
1901	Potomac State College of West Virginia University, Keyser	1,540

(*continued*)

Founded	Name and place	Students (fall 2014)
1961	West Virginia University at Parkersburg, Parkersburg	2,985
1991	American Public University System, Charles Town (online learning)	57,539

[1]Includes Marshall University–South Charleston Campus, founded in 1972.

Health
West Virginia had 3·8 community hospital beds for every 1,000 population in 2013. In the same year there were 27·1 active physicians per 10,000 civilian population and 4·8 dentists per 10,000.

Welfare
The Department of Health Human Resources, originating in the 1930s as the Department of Public Assistance, is both state and federally financed. Medicare enrolment in July 2012 totalled 398,602. In fiscal year 2012 a total of 404,533 people in West Virginia received Medicaid. In Dec. 2014 there were 464,823 Old-Age, Survivors, and Disability Insurance (OASDI) beneficiaries. A total of 20,112 people were receiving payments under Temporary Assistance for Needy Families (TANF) in Dec. 2012.

Religion
The principal religious traditions in the state in 2010 were: Mainline Protestants, with 274,766 members; Evangelical Protestants, 249,756; Catholics, 95,849; Latter-day Saints (Mormons), 17,555; Black Protestants, 11,505.

Wisconsin

Key Historical Events
The French were the first European explorers of the territory; Jean Nicolet landed at Green Bay in 1634, a mission was founded in 1671 and a permanent settlement at Green Bay followed. In 1763 French claims were surrendered to Britain. In 1783 Britain ceded the area to the USA which designated the Northwest Territory, of which Wisconsin was part. In 1836 a separate Territory of Wisconsin included the present Iowa, Minnesota and parts of the Dakotas.

In 1836 James Duane Doty founded Madison and, even before it was inhabited, successfully pressed its claim to be the capital of the Territory. In 1848 Wisconsin became a state, with its present boundaries.

The city of Milwaukee was founded on Lake Michigan when American Indian tribes gave up their claims to the land in 1831–33. It grew rapidly as a port and industrial town, attracting German settlers in the 1840s and Poles and Italians 50 years later. The Lake Michigan shore was developed as an industrial area; the rest of the south proved suitable for dairy farming; the north, mainly forests and lakes, has remained sparsely settled except for tourist bases.

Since the Second World War there has been black immigration from the southern states to the industrial lake-shore cities.

Territory and Population
Wisconsin is bounded north by Lake Superior and the Upper Peninsula of Michigan, east by Lake Michigan, south by Illinois, and west by Iowa and Minnesota, with the Mississippi River forming most of the boundary. Land area, 54,158 sq. miles (140,268 sq. km); water area, 11,339 sq. miles (29,367 sq. km). Census population, 1 April 2010, was 5,686,986, an increase of 6·0% since 2000. July 2018 estimate, 5,813,568.

Population in five census years was:

	White	Black	All others	Total	Per sq. mile
1910	2,320,555	2,900	10,405	2,333,860	42·2
1980	4,443,035	182,592	80,015	4,705,642	86·4
1990	4,512,523	244,539	134,707	4,891,769	90·1
2000	4,769,857	304,460	289,358	5,363,675	98·8
2010	4,902,067	359,148	425,771	5,686,986	105·0

Of the total population in 2010, 2,864,586 were female and 4,347,494 were 18 years old or older. In 2010 Wisconsin's Hispanic population was 336,056, up from 192,921 in 2000 (an increase of 74·2%).

Population of the large cities, 2010 census, was as follows:

Milwaukee	594,833
Madison (capital)	233,209
Green Bay	104,057
Kenosha	99,218
Racine	78,860
Appleton	72,623
Waukesha	70,718
Oshkosh	66,083
Eau Claire	65,883
Janesville	63,575
West Allis	60,411
La Crosse	51,320
Sheboygan	49,288
Wauwatosa	46,396
Fond du Lac	43,021
New Berlin	39,584
Wausau	39,106
Brookfield	37,920
Beloit	36,966
Greenfield	36,720

Population of largest metropolitan areas, 2010 census: Milwaukee–Waukesha–West Allis, 1,555,908; Madison, 568,593; Green Bay, 306,241.

Social Statistics
Births, 2014, 67,161 (11·7 per 1,000 population); deaths, 2014, 50,291 (8·7). Infant deaths, 2013, 6·3 per 1,000 live births. 2014: marriages, 5·7 per 1,000 population; divorces and annulments, 2·7. Same-sex marriage became legal in Oct. 2014.

Climate
Milwaukee, Jan. 19°F (−7·2°C), July 70°F (21·1°C). Annual rainfall 29" (727 mm). Wisconsin belongs to the Great Lakes climate zone (see UNITED STATES: Climate).

Constitution and Government
The constitution, which dates from 1848, has 141 amendments. The legislative power is vested in a Senate of 33 members elected for four years, one-half elected alternately, and an Assembly of 99 members all elected simultaneously for two years. The Governor and Lieut.-Governor are elected for four years.

For the 116th Congress, which convened in Jan. 2019, Wisconsin sends eight members to the House of Representatives. It is represented in the Senate by Ronald Johnson (R. 2011–23) and Tammy Baldwin (D. 2013–25).

The capital is Madison. The state has 72 counties.

Recent Elections
In the 2016 presidential election Donald Trump took Wisconsin with 47·9% of the vote (Barack Obama won it in 2012).

Current Government
Governor: Tony Evers (D.), 2019–23 (salary: $146,786).
Lieut.-Governor: Mandela Barnes (D.), 2019–23.
Secretary of State: Douglas La Follette (D.), since Jan. 1983.
Government Website: https://www.wisconsin.gov

Economy
Per capita personal income (2015) was $45,617.

Budget
Total state revenues in 2011 were $44,807m.; total expenditure, $39,350m. (including: education, $11,345m.; public welfare, $8,969m.; highways,

$2,432m.; hospitals, $1,188m.; correction, $1,161m.). Outstanding debt in 2011, $22,879m.

Performance
Gross Domestic Product by state in 2015 was $302,076m., ranking Wisconsin 20th in the United States. In 2015 state real GDP growth was 1·1%.

Energy and Natural Resources

Electricity
In 2015 production was 66,360m. kWh, of which 37,181m. kWh was from coal.

Water
The total area covered by water is 11,339 sq. miles.

Minerals
Construction sand and gravel, crushed stone, industrial or specialty sand and lime are the chief mineral products. Mineral production in 2009 was valued at $546m.

Agriculture
In 2012 there were 76,800 farms with a total of 15m. acres and an average size of 195 acres. In 2013 the average value of farm real estate, including land and buildings, was $4,400 per acre. Farm income, 2009: from crops, $2,831m.; from livestock and products, $4,779m. The net farm income in 2009 was $849m.

Dairy farming is important, with 1·27m. dairy cows in 2012. Production of cheese was 2·7bn. lb in 2012 and accounted for about a quarter of the USA's total. Other important commodities are corn, cattle, soybeans, potatoes and cranberries. Wisconsin is the leading cranberry producer, with 4·83m. bbls in 2012 accounting for 60% of the USA's total.

Forestry
Wisconsin had (2013) 17,101,000 acres of forested land, with 1,434,000 acres of national forest.

Industry

Wisconsin has much heavy industry, particularly in the Milwaukee area. Three-fifths of manufacturing employees work on durable goods. Industrial machinery is the major industrial group (17% of all manufacturing employment) followed by fabricated metals, food and kindred products, printing and publishing, paper and allied products, electrical equipment and transportation equipment. In 2012 the state's 20,532 manufacturing establishments had 984,000 employees, earning $48,309m. Total value added by manufacturing in 2013 was $83,725m.

Labour
Total non-agricultural employment, 2010, 2,735,000. Employees by branch, 2010 (in 1,000): trade, transportation and utilities, 508; manufacturing, 431; government, 421; education and health services, 418; professional and business services, 268. Average annual pay per worker (2009) was $39,131. The state unemployment rate in Dec. 2010 was 7·5%.

International Trade

Imports and Exports
In 2015 imports into Wisconsin totalled $23·0bn. (down from $23·6bn. in 2014). In the same year exports from Wisconsin totalled $22·4bn., down from $23·4bn. in 2014. The leading source for imports in 2015 was China ($6·2bn.), ahead of Canada ($4·2bn.). The leading destination for exports in 2015 was Canada ($7·3bn.), followed by Mexico ($3·0bn.).

Communications

Roads
In 2012 the state had 115,095 miles of road of which 92,123 miles were rural roads. There were 4,934,320 registered motor vehicles.

Rail
In 2012 there were 3,449 miles of freight railroad (excluding trackage rights). There were eight freight railroads operating in 2012. Rail traffic originating in Wisconsin totalled 20·6m. tons in 2012 with rail traffic terminating in the state totalling 57·5m. tons.

Civil Aviation
There were eight primary airports—commercial service airports with more than 10,000 passenger boardings annually—in 2011 with a combined total of 6,292,628 enplanements, down from 6,459,046 in 2010. By far the busiest airport is General Mitchell International (Milwaukee's airport), with 4,671,976 enplanements in 2011.

Shipping
By far the largest and busiest port on the Great Lakes, the port of Duluth-Superior handled 37·4m. tons of freight in 2014. It accommodates the maritime transportation needs of a wide range of industries ranging from agriculture, forestry, mining and manufacturing to construction, power generation and passenger cruising. Other major ports are Milwaukee (3·0m. tons in 2014) and Green Bay (2·5m. tons in 2014).

Social Institutions

Justice
In Dec. 2014 there were 22,597 prison inmates. The death penalty was abolished in 1853.

Education
All children between the ages of six and 18 are required to attend school full-time to the end of the school term in which they become 18 years of age. In 2012–13, 2,285 public elementary and secondary schools had 872,436 pupils; there were 57,551 teachers. In fall 2011 private schools enrolled 127,250 students. Average public school teacher salary in 2012–13 was $55,171. Total expenditure for public elementary and secondary education was $11,360m. in 2010–11. Spending per pupil in 2010–11 was $11,946.

There are three non-profit higher educational sectors in Wisconsin: the public colleges and universities, the technical colleges, and the private colleges and universities.

The University of Wisconsin, established in 1848, was joined by law in 1971 with the Wisconsin State Universities System to become the University of Wisconsin System with 13 degree granting campuses, 13 two-year campuses in the Center System and the state-wide University Extension. The system had, in 2009–10, 6,898 faculty members. In fall 2009, 178,909 students enrolled (11,216 at Eau Claire, 6,638 at Green Bay, 10,009 at La Crosse, 41,654 at Madison, 30,418 at Milwaukee, 13,192 at Oshkosh, 5,303 at Parkside, 7,803 at Platteville, 6,728 at River Falls, 9,209 at Stevens Point, 9,017 at Stout, 2,794 at Superior, 11,139 at Whitewater and 13,789 at the Center System freshman-sophomore centres).

The Wisconsin Technical College System has 16 technical college districts, which award two-year associate degrees, one- and two-year technical diplomas and short-term technical diplomas. Approximately 400,000 students enrol in the colleges each year.

UW-Extension enrolled 187,809 students in its continuing education programmes in year ending June 2009. Independent institutions of higher education include: Marquette University (Jesuit), in Milwaukee (with 11,689 students in fall 2009); Cardinal Strich University (Franciscan), with campuses in Milwaukee, Madison and Edina, Minnesota (6,276); Concordia University Wisconsin (Lutheran), in Mequon (7,178); and Lawrence University, Appleton (1,483). The state's educational and broadcasting service is licensed through the UW Board of Regents.

Health
Wisconsin had 2·2 community hospital beds for every 1,000 population in 2013. In the same year there were 27·9 active physicians per 10,000 civilian population and 5·6 dentists per 10,000.

Welfare
Medicare enrolment in July 2012 totalled 967,760. In fiscal year 2012 a total of 1,363,261 people in Wisconsin received Medicaid. In Dec. 2014 there were 1,153,149 Old-Age, Survivors, and Disability Insurance (OASDI) beneficiaries. A total of 58,009 people were receiving payments under Temporary Assistance for Needy Families (TANF) in Dec. 2012.

Religion

In 2010 the main religious traditions were: Catholics, with 1,425,523 members; Evangelical Protestants, 806,028; Mainline Protestants, 684,035; Black Protestants, 44,203; Latter-day Saints (Mormons), 25,738.

Wyoming

Key Historical Events

The territory was inhabited by Plains Indians (Arapahoes, Sioux and Cheyenne) in the early 19th century. There was some trading with white Americans, but very little white settlement. In the 1840s the great western migration routes, the Oregon and the Overland Trails, ran through the territory with Wyoming offering mountain passes accessible to wagons. Once migration became a steady flow forts were built to protect the route from American Indian attack.

In 1867 coal was discovered. In 1868 Wyoming was organized as a separate Territory and in 1869 the Sioux and Arapaho were confined to reservations. At the same time the route of the Union Pacific Railway brought railway towns to southern Wyoming. Settlement of the north was delayed until after the final defeat of hostile American Indians in 1876.

The economy was based on ranching. Cheyenne, made Territorial capital in 1869, also functioned as a railway town moving cattle. Casper, on the site of a fort on the Pony Express route, was also a railway town on the Chicago and North Western. Laramie started as a Union Pacific construction workers' shanty town in 1868. In 1890 oil was discovered at Casper, and Wyoming became a state the same year. Subsequently, mineral extraction became the leading industry, as natural gas, uranium, bentonite and trona were exploited as well as oil and coal.

Territory and Population

Wyoming is bounded north by Montana, east by South Dakota and Nebraska, south by Colorado, southwest by Utah and west by Idaho. Total area is 97,813 sq. miles (253,335 sq. km) of which 97,093 sq. miles (251,470 sq. km) are land. The Yellowstone National Park occupies about 2·22m. acres; the Grand Teton National Park has 307,000 acres. The federal government in 2003 owned 49,268 sq. miles (50·6% of the total area of the state). The Federal Bureau of Land Management administers 17·4m. acres.

Census population, 1 April 2010, was 563,626, an increase of 14·1% since 2000. Wyoming has the smallest population of any of the states of the USA, but in the year 1 July 2008–30 June 2009 the state's population showed the largest percentage growth of any in the USA. July 2018 estimate, 577,737.

Population in five census years was:

	White	Black	American Indian	Asian			Total	Per sq. mile
1910	140,318	2,235	1,486	1,926			145,965	1·5
			All others					
1980	446,488	3,364	19,705				469,557	4·8
	White	Black	American Indian/ Alaska Native	Asian/ Native Hawaiian/ Pacific Islander	Other	Total		Per sq. mile
1990	427,061	3,606	9,479	2,806	10,636	453,588		4·7
2000	454,670	3,722	11,133	3,073	21,184	493,782		5·1
2010	511,279	4,748	13,336	4,853	29,410	563,626		5·8

Of the total population in 2010, 287,437 were male and 428,224 were 18 years old or older. At the 2010 census the Hispanic population of Wyoming was 50,231, up from 31,669 in 2000 (an increase of 58·6%).

The largest towns (with 2010 census population) are Cheyenne (the capital), 59,466; Casper, 55,316; Laramie, 30,816; Gillette, 29,087; Rock Springs, 23,036; Sheridan, 17,444.

Social Statistics

Births, 2014, 7,696 (13·2 per 1,000 population); deaths, 2014, 4,666 (8·0). Infant mortality rate, 2013, 4·8 per 1,000 live births. 2014: marriages, 7·7 per 1,000 population; divorces and annulments, 4·6. The abortion rate, at 1 for every 1,000 women aged 15 to 44 in 2014, is the lowest of any US state. Same-sex marriage became legal in Oct. 2014.

Climate

Cheyenne, Jan. 25°F (−3·9°C), July 66°F (18·9°C). Annual rainfall 15" (376 mm). Yellowstone Park, Jan. 18°F (−7·8°C), July 61°F (16·1°C). Annual rainfall 18" (444 mm). Wyoming belongs to the Mountain States climate region (*see* UNITED STATES: Climate).

Constitution and Government

The constitution, drafted in 1890, has since had 76 amendments. The Legislature consists of a Senate of 30 members elected for staggered four-year terms, and a House of Representatives of 60 members elected for two years. It sits annually in Jan. or Feb. The Governor is elected for four years.

For the 116th Congress, which convened in Jan. 2019, Wyoming sends one member to the House of Representatives. It is represented in the Senate by Michael Enzi (R. 1997–2021) and John Barrasso (R. 2007–25).

The capital is Cheyenne. The state contains 23 counties.

Recent Elections

In the 2016 presidential election Donald Trump took Wyoming with 70·1% of the vote (Mitt Romney won it in 2012).

Current Government

Governor: Mark Gordon (R.), 2019–23 (salary: $105,000).
Secretary of State: Edward A. Buchanan (R.), since March 2018.
Government Website: http://www.wyo.gov

Economy

Per capita personal income (2015) was $55,303.

Budget

In 2011 total state revenue was $7,494m. Total expenditure was $5,674m. (education, $1,679m.; public welfare, $740m.; highways, $537m.; natural resources, $354m.; health, $282m.). Outstanding debt in 2011, $1,364m.

Performance

Gross Domestic Product by state was $39,864m. in 2015, ranking Wyoming 49th in the United States. In 2015 state real GDP growth was –0·1%.

Energy and Natural Resources

Oil and Gas

In 2014 Wyoming produced 76·1m. bbls of crude petroleum; marketed production of natural gas totalled 1,791bn. cu. ft (fifth in the USA behind Texas, Pennsylvania, Oklahoma and Louisiana).

Water

The total area covered by water is 720 sq. miles.

Minerals

In 2010 the output of coal was 442·1m. short tons; trona, 16·5m. short tons; uranium (2010 estimate), 1·8m. lb. Wyoming is the USA's leading coal and uranium producer, accounting for 40% of the country's coal output in 2010. It also has 40% of the country's recoverable coal reserves. Wyoming's recoverable coal reserves total more than 42bn. tons. Total value of non-fuel mineral production in 2010 was $1,860m.

Agriculture

Wyoming is semi-arid, and agriculture is carried on by irrigation and dry farming. In 2007 there were 11,069 farms and ranches; total farm area was 34·4m. acres; average size of farm in 2007 was 2,726 acres (the largest of any state). In 2007 the average value of farmland was $513 per acre.

Total value, 2008, of crops produced, $226m.; of livestock and products, $748m. The net farm income in 2008 was $92m. Principal commodities are cattle, hogs, hay, sheep, sugar beets, barley, wheat and corn. Animals on farms in 2007 included 1·31m. cattle, 413,000 sheep and lambs, and 107,000 hogs and pigs.

Forestry

The state had a forested area of 10,401,000 acres in 2012, of which 5,849,000 acres were national forest.

Industry

In 2012 the state's 1,468 manufacturing establishments had 25,000 employees, earning $1,542m. Total value added by manufacturing in 2013 was $2,797m. A large portion of the manufacturing in the state is based on natural resources, mainly oil and farm products.

Labour
Total non-agricultural employment, 2010, 283,000. Employees by branch, 2010 (in 1,000): government, 73; trade, transportation and utilities, 52; leisure and hospitality, 33; education and health services, 26; mining, 25.

International Trade

Imports and Exports
In 2015 imports into Wyoming totalled $1,145m. (down from $1,901m. in 2014). In the same year exports from Wyoming totalled $1,175m., down from $1,757m. in 2014. The leading source for imports in 2015 was Canada ($816m.), ahead of China ($139m.). The leading destination for exports in 2015 was Brazil ($195m.), followed by Canada ($192m.).

Communications

Roads
In 2012 there were 2,862 miles of urban roads and 25,554 miles of rural roads. There were 768,086 motor vehicle registrations in 2012.

Rail
In 2012 there were 1,860 miles of freight railroad (excluding trackage rights). There were four freight railroads operating in 2012. Rail traffic originating in Wyoming totalled 434·3m. tons in 2012 (the highest of any state) with traffic terminating in the state totalling 15·8m. tons.

Civil Aviation
In 2011 there were eight primary airports (commercial service airports with more than 10,000 passenger boardings annually) with a combined total of 496,642 enplanements, down from 498,358 in 2010.

Social Institutions

Justice
In Dec. 2014 there were 2,383 prison inmates. Capital punishment is authorized but has been used only once, in 1992, since the US Supreme Court reinstated the death penalty in 1976.

Education
In 2012–13, 365 public elementary and secondary schools had 91,533 pupils and 7,350 teachers. In fall 2011 pupils in private elementary and secondary schools numbered 2,740. In 2010–11 the average expenditure per pupil was $15,815; total expenditure on public elementary and secondary education was $1,643m.

In fall 2014 the University of Wyoming, founded at Laramie in 1887, had 12,820 students; there were also seven colleges (with 21,496 students) and three private higher education institutions.

Health
Wyoming had 3·3 community hospital beds for every 1,000 population in 2013. In the same year there were 19·5 active physicians per 10,000 civilian population and 5·3 dentists per 10,000.

Welfare
Medicare enrolment in July 2012 totalled 86,081. In fiscal year 2012 a total of 76,337 people in Wyoming received Medicaid. In Dec. 2014 there were 101,296 Old-Age, Survivors, and Disability Insurance (OASDI) beneficiaries. A total of 676 people were receiving payments under Temporary Assistance for Needy Families (TANF) in Dec. 2012.

Religion
In 2010 the main religious traditions were: Latter-day Saints (Mormons), with 63,316 members; Catholics, 61,222; Evangelical Protestants, 59,247; Mainline Protestants, 36,539.

Commonwealth of the Northern Mariana Islands

Key Historical Events
In 1889 Spain ceded Guam (largest and southernmost of the Marianas Islands) to the USA and sold the rest to Germany. Occupied by Japan in 1914, the islands were administered by Japan under a League of Nations mandate until occupied by US forces in Aug. 1944. In 1947 they became part of the US-administered Trust Territory of the Pacific Islands. On 17 June 1975 the electorate voted for a Commonwealth in association with the USA; this was approved by the US government in April 1976 and came into force on 1 Jan. 1978. In Nov. 1986 the islanders were granted US citizenship. The UN terminated the Trusteeship status on 22 Dec. 1990.

Territory and Population
The Northern Marianas form a single chain of 16 mountainous islands extending north of Guam for about 560 km, with a total area of 5,117 sq. km (1,976 sq. miles) of which 472 sq. km (182 sq. miles) are dry land, and with a population (2010 census) of 53,883.

The areas and populations of the islands are as follows:

Island(s)	Sq. km	2000 Census	2010 Census
Northern Group[1]	160	6	0
Saipan	119	62,392	48,220
Tinian (with Aguijan)	108[2]	3,540	3,136
Rota	85	3,283	2,527

[1]Pagan, Agrihan, Alamagan and nine uninhabited islands.
[2]Including uninhabited Aguijan.

In 2010, 33% of the population aged five or over spoke Philippine languages at home, 24% Chamorro and 17% English. English remains an official language along with Carolinian and Chamorro. The largest town is Chalan Kanoa on Saipan.

Social Statistics
Births, 2014, 517 (10·0 per 1,000 population); deaths, 2014, 202 (3·9).

Constitution and Government
The Constitution was approved by a referendum on 6 March 1977 and came into force on 9 Jan. 1978. The legislature comprises a nine-member *Senate*, with three Senators elected from each of the main three islands for a term of four years, and a 20-member *House of Representatives*, elected for a term of two years.

The Commonwealth is administered by a Governor and Lieut.-Governor. The term of the Governor is four years.

As from Jan. 2009 the Commonwealth sends one delegate to the US House of Representatives. The Congressman may participate but not vote on the House floor.

Recent Elections
At the elections of 13 Nov. 2018 the Republican Party won 13 seats in the House of Representatives and ind. 7.

In the gubernatorial elections also on 13 Nov. 2018 incumbent Ralph Torres received 62·2% of votes cast against Juan N. Babauta with 7·8%.

Current Government
Governor: Ralph Torres (R.), since Dec. 2015.
   Lieut.-Governor: Arnold Palacios (R.), since Jan. 2019.
Legislature Website: http://www.cnmileg.gov.mp

Energy and Natural Resources

Water
The total area covered by water is 1,793 sq. miles, of which 6 sq. miles are inland.

Fisheries
In 2015 total catch was 2,573,000 lb (1,167 tonnes), entirely from marine waters.

Industry

Labour
In 2014 there were 25,658 persons in employment including 3,848 in management, 3,189 in office and administrative support and 2,810 in sales and related activities.

International Trade

Imports and Exports

In 2012 imports totalled $496m. and exports $268m. Major imports are mineral fuels, fabric, and articles of leather and travel goods. Major exports are apparel and clothing accessories, iron and steel, and fish, crustaceans and molluscs.

Communications

Roads

There are about 381 km of roads.

Civil Aviation

In 2011 there were three primary airports (commercial service airports with more than 10,000 passenger boardings annually). The main airport, Francisco C. Ada/Saipan International, had 382,386 enplanements in 2011 (433,557 in 2010). The airports at Rota and Tinian have much smaller passenger numbers.

Social Institutions

Education

In fall 2007 there were 462 pupils enrolled in nursery school and pre-school, 689 in kindergarten, 6,989 in elementary school (grades 1–8), 3,159 in high school (grades 9–12) and 901 in higher education.

Health

There were 3·6 doctors per 10,000 inhabitants in 2008, 18·2 nursing personnel per 10,000 inhabitants and 0·7 midwifery personnel per 10,000. In 2007 there was one hospital with 86 beds and a public health wellness clinic. There are six private clinics.

Religion

The population is predominantly Roman Catholic.

Culture

Tourism

In 2011 there were 336,000 international tourist arrivals, excluding same-day visitors (375,000 in 2010).

Commonwealth of Puerto Rico

Key Historical Events

A Spanish dependency since the 16th century, Puerto Rico was ceded to the USA in 1898 after the Spanish defeat in the Spanish-American war. In 1917 US citizenship was conferred and in 1932 there was a name change from Porto Rico to Puerto Rico. In 1952 Puerto Rico was proclaimed a commonwealth with a representative government and a directly elected governor.

Territory and Population

Puerto Rico is the easternmost of the Greater Antilles and lies between the Dominican Republic and the US Virgin Islands. The total area is 13,791 sq. km (5,325 sq. miles), of which 8,868 sq. km (3,424 sq. miles) are dry land; the population, according to the census of 1 April 2010, was 3,725,789, a fall of 2·2% from 2000. The population has continued to decline since then, largely as a result of people emigrating because of the ongoing financial struggles. July 2018 estimate, 3,195,153. The urban population was 3,493,256 in 2010, representing 93·8% (94·3% in 2000) of the total population. Population density was 1,088 per sq. mile in 2010. Of the total population in 2010, 1,940,618 were female. The UN gives a projected population for 2020 of 3·65m.

Chief towns, 2010 census, are: San Juan (the capital), 395,326; Bayamón, 208,116; Carolina, 176,762; Ponce, 166,327; Caguas, 142,893.

The Puerto Rican island of Vieques, 10 miles to the east, has an area of 51·7 sq. miles and 9,301 (2010) inhabitants. The island of Culebra, between Puerto Rico and St Thomas, has an area of 10 sq. miles and 1,818 (2010) inhabitants. Both islands have good harbours.

Spanish and English are the joint official languages.

Social Statistics

Births, 2014, 34,434 (9·7 per 1,000 population); deaths, 2014, 30,152 (8·5). Marriages, 2006, 23,185; infant mortality rate, 2013, 7·1 per 1,000 live births. Population growth rate, 2007–08, 0·3%. In 2006 the most popular age range for marrying was 20–24 for both males and females. Fertility rate, 2014, 1·4 births per woman.

Climate

Warm, sunny winters with hot summers. The north coast experiences more rainfall than the south coast and generally does not have a dry season as rainfall is evenly spread throughout the year. San Juan, Jan. 25°C, July 28°C. Annual rainfall 1,246 mm.

Constitution and Government

Puerto Rico is a self-governing commonwealth (*Estado Libre Asociado*) in association with the United States. The chief of state is the President of the United States of America. The head of government is an elected Governor. There are two legislative chambers: the 51-member House of Representatives and the 27-member Senate. Both houses meet annually in Jan. The executive power is exercised by the Governor, elected every four years, who leads a cabinet of 15 ministers.

A new constitution was drafted by a Puerto Rican Constituent Assembly and approved by the electorate at a referendum on 3 March 1952. It was then submitted to Congress, which struck out Section 20 of Article 11 covering the 'right to work' and the 'right to an adequate standard of living'; the remainder was passed and proclaimed by the Governor on 25 July 1952.

Puerto Rico broadly has authority over its internal affairs, but the USA controls areas generally regulated by the federal government. Puerto Ricans are US citizens and possess most of the rights and obligations of citizens from the 50 states, such as paying Social Security and receiving federal welfare. Differences include Puerto Rico's local taxation system and partial exemption from Internal Revenue Code, its lack of voting representation in either house of the US Congress (they have one non-voting representative) and the ineligibility of Puerto Ricans to vote in presidential elections. Puerto Rican men are subject to subscription in the US Armed Forces, but the commonwealth sends independent teams to the Olympics.

The US Constitution remains the supreme legal document. Puerto Rico's authority over internal affairs is subject to the agreement of the US Congress and may, in theory, be rescinded at any time. Its status has long been the subject of debate in Washington and San Juan, centred on the options of remaining as a Commonwealth or adopting statehood, a compact of Free Association or independence.

At a plebiscite on 14 Nov. 1993 on Puerto Rico's future status, 48·6% of votes cast were for Commonwealth (status quo), 46·3% for Statehood (51st State of the USA) and 4·4% for full independence. In a further plebiscite in Dec. 1998, some 52·2% of voters backed the opposition's call for no change, while 46·5% supported statehood. Independence was supported by 2·5%, while free association received 0·3%. A Presidential Task Force on Puerto Rico's Status was established by then President Clinton in 2000 and continued to report during the tenures of George W. Bush and Barack Obama. During his tenure President Obama reiterated his commitment to its status being decided by the will of the people of Puerto Rico as expressed in a plebiscite or referendum.

A non-binding referendum of Puerto Rico's status was held on 6 Nov. 2012. Voters were asked two questions: firstly, whether they wished to continue with the current territorial status; and, secondly, which status they favoured of statehood, independence or sovereign nation in free association with the USA. Turnout approached 80%, with 54·0% voting no to the first question. Of those, 73·0% cast a vote on the second question, with 61·1% opting for statehood, 33·3% for sovereign free association and 5·5% for independence. Another non-binding referendum held in June 2017 was boycotted by independence supporters. With turnout recorded at just 23%, of those who did vote 97% were in favour of statehood. Nonetheless, before Puerto Rico can become the 51st state of the USA, legislation would be subject to approval by the Congress in Washington before being signed off by the President.

Recent Elections

At the gubernatorial election on 8 Nov. 2016 Ricardo Rosselló (New Progressive Party/PNP) won with 41·8% of the vote, ahead of David Bernier (Popular Democratic Party/PPD) with 38·9%, Alexandra Lúgaro (ind.) 11·1% and Manuel Cidre (ind.) 5·7%. There were two other candidates. Turnout was 55·1%.

In elections to the House of Representatives on the same day the New Progressive Party (PNP) won 34 of the 51 seats, the Popular Democratic

Party (PPD) 16 seats and the Puerto Rican Independence Party (PIP) one seat. In the Senate elections of the same day PNP took 21 seats, PPD 7, and PIP and an independent won a single seat each.

Current Government

Governor: Ricardo Rosselló (PNP), since Jan. 2017.

Secretary of State: Luis Rivera Marín (PNP), since Jan. 2017.

Government Website (Spanish only): http://www.gobierno.pr

Economy

Budget

Revenues in 2012 totalled $13,869·8m. Tax revenues accounted for 57·8% of revenue. Government budget expenditures totalled $28,894·1m. in fiscal year 2012. Main areas of expenditure were social development (51%), economic development (24%), debt service (11%) and protection and security (6%).

Per capita personal income (2012) was $16,934.

Total government debt in June 2012 was $67·7bn., equivalent to some two-thirds of GDP, leading to fears of a debt crisis. In Nov. 2013 Washington announced that it was sending a team of economic experts to advise the administration in San Juan. By June 2015 public debt had risen to $72bn.—equivalent to around $20,000 for every resident—and from late 2015 the government was unable to fully service its debt obligations. In June 2016 legislation passed in Washington allowed for the restructuring of the territory's debts, averting the immediate threat of a $2bn. default. Under the terms of the new legislation, in May 2017 Puerto Rico filed for bankruptcy—the largest in US history. Four months later Hurricane Maria caused widespread damage, destroying property estimated in the tens of billions of dollars. In Jan. 2018 the government projected that it would run a budget deficit until at least 2022, so ruling out debt repayments before that date. However, a revised fiscal plan delivered the following month was more optimistic, suggesting a $2·8bn. surplus over the period to 2023.

Performance

The economy contracted every year between 2005 and 2011, before recording growth of 0·5% in 2012. Total GDP in 2016 was $105·0bn. Over 46% of citizens live below the poverty line. Economic prospects were further hit in 2017 by Hurricane Maria, which saw the destruction of 80% of the island's crops and the mass closure of businesses (20% of which were still closed as of April 2018).

Energy and Natural Resources

Environment

Puerto Rico's carbon dioxide emissions from the consumption of energy in 2011 were the equivalent of 7·2 tonnes per capita.

Electricity

Installed capacity was an estimated 5·6m. kW in 2011. Production in 2011 was 22·3bn. kWh. Consumption per capita in 2011 was 6,013 kWh.

Water

The total area covered by water is 1,901 sq. miles, of which 76 sq. miles are inland.

Agriculture

Gross agricultural income in 2009 was $794m. In 2009, 1·6% of the economically active population was employed in agriculture. Production estimates in 2008 (in 1,000 tonnes): plantains, 80; bananas, 54; oranges, 20; tomatoes, 19; pineapples, 17; pumpkins and squash, 14; mangoes and guavas, 14. Livestock (2008 estimates): cattle, 380,000; pigs, 50,000; horses, 6,600; sheep, 6,300; chickens, 13m. Livestock products, 2008 estimates (in 1,000 tonnes): poultry, 50; pork, 11; beef, 10; milk, 350; eggs, 12.

Forestry

In 2015 the area under forests was 0·50m. ha., or 58% of the total land area.

Fisheries

The total catch in 2015 was 2,425,000 lb (1,100 tonnes), exclusively from sea fishing.

Industry

Manufacturing contributed $46,113·9m. to total GDP in 2012, including $28,047·4m. from pharmaceutical and medicine manufacturing.

Labour

There were 1,035,000 people in employment in 2012, including 231,000 in wholesale and retail trade, 225,000 in public administration and 95,000 in manufacturing. The unemployment rate was 10·1% in Aug. 2017—more than double the rate for the USA as a whole.

International Trade

Imports and Exports

In 2015 imports into Puerto Rico totalled $19·6bn. (down from $23·4bn. in 2014). In the same year exports from Puerto Rico totalled $20·2bn., down from $20·3bn. in 2014.

Puerto Rico is not permitted to levy taxes on imports.

Communications

Roads

In 2007 there were 16,397 miles of roads and 2,531,199 registered motor vehicles.

Rail

There are 96 km of railroad, although no passenger service. There is a 17·2 km urban train system in use.

Civil Aviation

There were six primary airports in 2011 (commercial service airports with more than 10,000 passenger boardings annually) with a combined total of 4,413,509 enplanements, down from 4,679,049 in 2010. By far the busiest airport is San Juan's Luis Muñoz Marín International, which had 3,983,130 enplanements in 2011.

Shipping

The leading ports are San Juan (which handled 10·8m. tons of cargo in 2014) and Ponce.

Telecommunications

In 2011 there were 826,100 landline telephone subscriptions (equivalent to 220·6 per 1,000 inhabitants) and 3,108,400 mobile phone subscriptions (or 829·9 per 1,000 inhabitants). In 2011, 48·0% of the population were internet users.

Social Institutions

Justice

The Judicial power of the commonwealth is vested in a unified judicial system with regard to jurisdiction, operation and administration. It consists of the Supreme Court, the Court of Appeals and the Court of First Instance, which jointly constitute the General Court of Justice. The Supreme Court is the court of last instance, and is composed of nine members (a chief justice and eight associate justices) named by the Governor with the consent of the Senate. Judgments on federal laws are subject to review by the US Supreme Court.

The Court of First Instance is a court of original general jurisdiction consisting of a Superior Court (253 judges) and municipal courts (85 judges). There are 13 judicial regions in the First Instance Court. Final judgments made by the Court of First Instance must be appealed at the Court of Appeals. The United States Court of Appeals for the First Circuit, based in Boston, Massachusetts, sits in San Juan for two weeks each year.

The population in penal institutions in Dec. 2011 was 11,452 (311 per 100,000 population).

Education

Education was made compulsory in 1899. The adult literacy rate was 92·0% in 2010. Total enrolment in public primary and secondary schools, 2015, was 402,691. Private primary and secondary schools had a total enrolment of 126,852 pupils in 2015. Enrolment has been steadily falling over a period of many years as a result of the island's economic downturn and associated population decline starting in the mid-2000s. This was then exacerbated by the departure of large numbers of families after Hurricane Maria struck Puerto Rico in Sept. 2017, resulting in the subsequent closure of more than 200 schools.

There were 240,878 students in tertiary education in 2015. The largest university, the University of Puerto Rico, was founded in 1903 and has 11 campuses with a total of 64,000 students. The largest private university is the Inter-American University of Puerto Rico, which was founded in 1912 as the Polytechnic Institute of Puerto Rico and has more than 40,000 students.

Health

There were 71 hospitals in 2009, with a hospital bed provision of 32 per 10,000 population. In the same year there were 12,698 non-federal physicians.

Religion

In 2010 there were approximately 3·63m. Roman Catholics (about 70% of the population) and around 2·62m. Protestants (25%) according to the Pew Research Center's Forum on Religion & Public Life.

Culture

Tourism

There were 4,379,200 non-resident visitors in 2010 (4,415,300 in 2009 and 5,213,100 in 2008) with spending from such visitors totalling $3,210·7m.

American Samoa

Key Historical Events

The first recorded visit by Europeans was in 1722. On 14 July 1889 a treaty between the USA, Germany and Great Britain proclaimed the Samoan Islands neutral territory, under a four-power government consisting of the three treaty powers and the local native government. By the Tripartite Treaty of 7 Nov. 1899, ratified 19 Feb. 1900, Great Britain and Germany renounced, in favour of the USA, all rights over the islands of the Samoan group east of 171° long. west of Greenwich. The islands to the west of that meridian, now the independent state of Samoa, were assigned to Germany. The islands of Tutuila and Aunu'u were ceded to the USA by their High Chiefs on 17 April 1900, and the islands of the Manu'a group on 16 July 1904. Congress accepted the islands under a Joint Resolution approved 20 Feb. 1929. Swain's Island, 210 miles north of the Samoan Islands, was annexed in 1925 and is administered as an integral part of American Samoa.

Territory and Population

The islands (Tutuila, Aunu'u, Ta'u, Olosega, Ofu and Rose) are approximately 650 miles east-northeast of Fiji. The total area is 1,505 sq. km (581 sq. miles), of which 198 sq. km (76 sq. miles) are dry land; population (2010 census), 55,519, nearly all Polynesians or part-Polynesians. Population density was 278 per sq. km in 2010.

In 2010, 88% of the population lived in urban areas. The capital is Pago Pago, which had a population of 3,656 in 2010. The island's three Districts are Eastern (population, 2010, 23,030), Western (31,329) and Manu'a (1,143). There is also Swain's Island, with an area of 1·9 sq. miles and 17 inhabitants (2010), which lies 210 miles to the northwest. Rose Island (uninhabited) is 0·4 sq. mile in area.

The official languages are Samoan and English.

Social Statistics

Births, 2014, 1,077 (19·8 per 1,000 population); deaths, 2014, 246 (3·9). Infant mortality, 2006, 11·8 per 1,000 live births.

Climate

A tropical maritime climate with a small annual range of temperature and plentiful rainfall. Pago Pago, Jan. 83°F (28·3°C), July 80°F (26·7°C). Annual rainfall 194" (4,850 mm).

Constitution and Government

American Samoa is constitutionally an unorganized, unincorporated territory of the USA administered under the Department of the Interior. Its indigenous inhabitants are US nationals and are classified locally as citizens of American Samoa with certain privileges under local laws not granted to non-indigenous persons. Polynesian customs (not inconsistent with US laws) are respected.

Fagatogo is the seat of the government.

On 25 Feb. 1948 a bicameral legislature was established, at the request of the Samoans, to have advisory legislative functions. With the adoption of the constitution of 22 April 1960, and the revised Constitution of 1967, the legislature was vested with limited law-making authority. The lower house, or House of Representatives, is composed of 20 members elected by universal adult suffrage and one non-voting member for Swain's Island. The upper house, or Senate, is comprised of 18 members elected, in the traditional

Samoan manner, in meetings of the chiefs. The Governor and Lieut.-Governor have been popularly elected since 1978. American Samoa also sends one delegate to the US House of Representatives. The Congressman may participate but not vote on the House floor.

Recent Elections

At elections to the House of Representatives on 8 Nov. 2016, only non-partisans were elected.

At gubernatorial elections held on 8 Nov. 2016 incumbent Lolo Matalasi Moliga took 60·2% of vote against 35·8% for Faoa Aitofele Sunia.

Current Government

Governor: Lolo Matalasi Moliga (ind.), since Jan. 2013.
   Lieut.-Governor: Lemanu Peleti Mauga (ind.), since Jan. 2013.
Government Website: https://www.americansamoa.gov

Economy

Overview

The Economic Development and Planning Office promotes economic expansion and outside investment.

Budget

The chief sources of revenue are annual federal grants from the USA, local revenues from taxes, duties, receipts from commercial operations (enterprise and special revenue funds), utilities, rents and leases, and liquor sales. In 2009–10 revenues were $267·4m. and expenditures $266·8m.

Energy and Natural Resources

Environment

American Samoa's carbon dioxide emissions from the consumption of energy in 2011 were the equivalent of 8·2 tonnes per capita.

Electricity

Installed capacity was 41,000 kW in 2011. Production in 2011 was about 155m. kWh. Per capita consumption in 2011 was 2,804 kWh. All the Manu'a islands have electricity.

Water

The total area covered by water is 505 sq. miles, of which 8 sq. miles are inland.

Agriculture

Of the 48,640 acres of land area, 12,000 acres are used for tropical crops; most commercial farms are in the Tafuna plains and west Tutuila. Principal crops are coconuts, taro, bread-fruit, yams and bananas.

   Livestock (2013 estimates): pigs, 10,500; chickens, 40,000.

Forestry

Forests covered a total area of 18,000 ha. in 2015, or 88% of the land area.

Fisheries

Total catch in 2015 was 6,660,000 lb (3,021 tonnes).

Industry

Fish canning is important, employing the second largest number of people (after government). Attempts are being made to provide a variety of light industries. Tuna fishing and local inshore fishing are both expanding.

Labour

In 2010 the civilian labour force numbered 18,300, of whom 16,616 were employed. The unemployment rate in 2010 was 9·2%.

International Trade

Imports and Exports

Imports in 2006 totalled $579m. and exports $439m.

   Chief imports are fish for canning, building materials, fuel oil, food, jewellery, machines and parts, alcoholic beverages and cigarettes. Chief exports are canned tuna, watches, pet foods and handicrafts.

Communications

Roads

There are about 150 km of paved roads and 200 km of unpaved roads in all. Motor vehicles registered, 2006, 9,215 (including 7,758 private vehicles).

Civil Aviation

American Samoa has one primary airport—a commercial service airport with more than 10,000 passenger boardings annually. Pago Pago International had 45,486 enplanements in 2011.

Shipping

The harbour at Pago Pago, which nearly bisects the island of Tutuila, is the only good harbour for large vessels in American Samoa.

Social Institutions

Justice

Judicial power is vested firstly in a High Court. The trial division has original jurisdiction of all criminal and civil cases. The probate division has jurisdiction of estates, guardianships, trusts and other matters. The land and title division decides cases relating to disputes involving communal land and Matai title court rules on questions and controversy over family titles. The appellate division hears appeals from trial, land and title, and probate divisions as well as having original jurisdiction in selected matters. The appellate court is the court of last resort. Two American judges sit with five Samoan judges permanently. In addition there are temporary judges or assessors who sit occasionally on cases involving Samoan customs. There is also a District Court with limited jurisdiction and there are 69 village courts.

The population in penal institutions in Dec. 2011 was 167 (equivalent to 240 per 100,000 population).

Education

Education is compulsory between the ages of six and 18. In 2006–07 there were 16,427 pupils in public elementary and secondary schools, of which 16,191 were in regular schools, 187 in vocational education and 49 in special education. There were 1,767 students in higher education in fall 2007.

Religion

According to the Pew Research Center's Forum on Religion & Public Life, in 2010 the population was an estimated 98·3% Christian. Around 61% of Christians are Protestants and 20% Catholics.

Culture

Tourism

In 2011 there were 28,403 visitor arrivals, including 5,682 tourists.

Guam

Key Historical Events

Magellan is said to have discovered the island in 1521; it was ceded by Spain to the USA by the Treaty of Paris (10 Dec. 1898). The island was captured by the Japanese on 10 Dec. 1941 and retaken by American forces following the Battle of Guam (21 July–8 Aug. 1944). Guam is of strategic importance; substantial numbers of naval and air force personnel occupy about one-third of the usable land.

Territory and Population

Guam is the largest and most southern island of the Marianas Archipelago, in 13° 26' N. lat., 144° 45' E. long. Total area, 210 sq. miles (543 sq. km). US bases occupy a third of the island. Hagåtña (previously Agaña), the seat of government, is about eight miles from the anchorage in Apra Harbor. The census in 2010 showed a population of 159,358; density, 290 per sq. km. In 2010 an estimated 93·2% of the population lived in urban areas. The UN gives a projected population for 2020 of 169,000. The Malay strain is predominant. Chamorro, the native language, and English are the official languages.

Social Statistics

Births, 2014, 3,395 (21·1 per 1,000 population); deaths, 2014, 939 (5·8). Infant mortality rate, 2013, 9·1 per 1,000 live births. Life expectancy at birth, 2005–10, was 73·3 years for males and 77·9 years for females. Fertility rate, 2010, 3·0 births per woman.

Climate

Tropical maritime, with little difference in temperatures over the year. Rainfall is copious at all seasons, but is greatest from July to Oct. Hagåtña, Jan. 81°F (27·2°C), July 81°F (27·2°C). Annual rainfall 93" (2,325 mm).

Constitution and Government

Guam's constitutional status is that of an 'unincorporated territory' of the USA. In Aug. 1950 the President transferred the administration of the island from the Navy Department to the Interior Department. The transfer conferred full citizenship on the Guamanians, who had previously been 'nationals' of the USA. There was a referendum on status on 30 Jan. 1982. 38% of eligible voters voted; 48·5% of those favoured Commonwealth status.

The Governor and Lieut.-Governor are elected for four-year terms. The legislature is a 15-member elected Senate; its powers are similar to those of an American state legislature. Guam sends one non-voting delegate (Madeleine Bordallo, D., 2017–19) to the US House of Representatives.

Recent Elections

At the election of 6 Nov. 2018 for the Guam Legislature the Democrats won ten seats and the Republicans won five. In gubernatorial elections, also held on 6 Nov. 2018, Lou Leon Guerrero (Democrat) won with 50·7% of the vote against Ray Tenorio (Republican) with 26·4% and Frank Aguon, Jr (Democrat) with 22·8%.

Current Government

Governor: Lou Leon Guerrero (D.), since Jan. 2019.
Lieut.-Governor: Josh Tenorio (D.), since Jan. 2019.

Economy

Budget

Total revenue (2010) $942·6m.; expenditure $1,081·6m. Around 60% of the economy is driven by tourism and 30% comes from the US military presence on the island.

Energy and Natural Resources

Environment

Guam's carbon dioxide emissions from the consumption of energy in 2011 were the equivalent of 12·7 tonnes per capita.

Electricity

Installed capacity was 0·6m. kW in 2011. Production was approximately 1,885m. kWh in 2011. Consumption per capita in 2011 was estimated at 11,718 kWh.

Water

The total area covered by water is 361 sq. miles, of which 8 sq. miles are inland.

Agriculture

The major products of the island are sweet potatoes, cucumbers, watermelons and beans. In 2013 there were approximately 1,000 acres of arable land and 9,000 acres of permanent cropland. Production (2013 estimates, in 1,000 tonnes): coconuts, 50; watermelons, 2. Livestock (2013 estimates) included 5,400 pigs and 800 goats. There is an agricultural experimental station at Inarajan.

Forestry

There were 25,000 ha. of forest in 2015, or 46% of the total land area.

Fisheries

In 2015 total catch was 2,892,000 lb (1,312 tonnes), exclusively from sea fishing.

Industry

Guam Economic Development Authority controls three industrial estates: Cabras Island (32 acres); Calvo estate at Tamuning (26 acres); Harmon estate (16 acres). Industries include textile manufacture, cement and petroleum distribution, warehousing, printing, plastics and ship-repair. Other main sources of income are construction and tourism.

Labour

There were 121,570 persons of employable age at the end of 2013, of whom 70,490 were in the workforce. 5,940 were unemployed.

International Trade

Guam is the only American territory which has complete 'free trade'; excise duties are levied only upon imports of tobacco, liquid fuel and liquor.

Imports and Exports

In 2012 imports were valued at $639m. and exports at $46m. Main export destinations in 2012 were Japan, 25%; Micronesia, 18%; Hong Kong, 13%. The USA is by far the biggest source of imports, ahead of Japan.

Communications

Roads

In 2008 there were 1,633 km of roads.

Civil Aviation

Guam has one primary airport (a commercial service airport with more than 10,000 passenger boardings annually). Guam International, which is at Tamuning, had 1,369,586 enplanements in 2011.

Shipping

There is a port at Apra Harbor.

Social Institutions

Justice

The Organic Act established a District Court with jurisdiction in matters arising under both federal and territorial law; the judge is appointed by the President subject to Senate approval. There are also a Supreme Court and a Superior Court; all judges are locally appointed except the Federal District judge. Misdemeanours are under the jurisdiction of the police court. The Spanish law was superseded in 1933 by five civil codes based upon California law.

The population in penal institutions in June 2013 was 696 (432 per 100,000 population).

Education

Education is compulsory from five to 16. Bilingual teaching programmes integrate the Chamorro language and culture into public school courses. Total primary and secondary school enrolment in fall 2008 was 39,875, including 30,329 in the public system and 7,053 in private schools; there were 34 public schools and 27 private schools. The University of Guam is in Mangilao and Guam Community College is in Barrigada.

Health

There are a hospital, eight nutrition centres, a school health programme and an extensive immunization programme. Emphasis is on disease prevention, health education and nutrition.

Religion

About 75% of the Guamanians are Roman Catholics; the other 25% are Baptists, Episcopalians, Bahá'ís, Lutherans, Latter-day Saints (Mormons), Presbyterians, Jehovah's Witnesses and members of the Church of Christ and Seventh-day Adventists.

Culture

Tourism

In 2011, 1,227,000 overseas visitors—excluding those from Canada and Mexico—visited Guam (down from 1,318,000 in 2010 although up from 1,170,000 in 2006). Most tourists come from Japan and South Korea.

Virgin Islands of the United States

Key Historical Events

The Virgin Islands of the United States, formerly known as the Danish West Indies, were named and claimed for Spain by Columbus in 1493. They were later settled by Dutch and English planters, invaded by France in the mid-17th century and abandoned by the French c. 1700, by which time Danish influence had been established. St Croix was held by the Knights of Malta between two periods of French rule.

The Virgin Islands were purchased from Denmark by the United States for $25m. on 31 March 1917. Their value was wholly strategic, inasmuch as they commanded the Anegada Passage from the Atlantic Ocean to the Caribbean Sea and the approach to the Panama Canal. Although the inhabitants were made US citizens in 1927, the islands are constitutionally an 'unincorporated territory'.

Territory and Population

The Virgin Islands group, lying about 40 miles due east of Puerto Rico, comprises the islands of St Thomas (31 sq. miles), St Croix (83 sq. miles), St John (20 sq. miles) and 65 small islets or cays, mostly uninhabited. The total area is 1,898 sq. km (733 sq. miles), of which 348 sq. km (134 sq. miles) are dry land.

The population according to the 2010 census was 106,405; density 794 per sq. mile. In 2010, 95% of the population was urban.

Population (2010 census) of St Thomas, 51,634; St Croix, 50,601; St John, 4,170. In 2010, 46·7% of the population was native born.

The UN gives a projected population for 2020 of 105,000.

The capital and only city, Charlotte Amalie, on St Thomas, had a population (2010 census) of 10,354. There are two towns on St Croix with 2010 census populations of: Christiansted, 2,433; Frederiksted, 859. The official language is English. Spanish is also spoken.

Social Statistics

Births, 2010, 1,600 (15·1 per 1,000 population); deaths, 2009, 675 (6·3). Infant mortality, 2005–07, 11·5 per 1,000 live births.

Climate

Average temperatures vary from 77°F to 82°F throughout the year; humidity is low. Average annual rainfall, about 45". The islands lie in the hurricane belt; tropical storms with heavy rainfall can occur in late summer.

Constitution and Government

The Organic Act of 22 July 1954 gives the US Department of the Interior full jurisdiction; some limited legislative powers are given to a single-chambered legislature, composed of 15 senators elected for two years representing the two legislative districts of St Croix and St Thomas-St John.

The Governor is elected by the residents. Since 1954 there have been four attempts to redraft the Constitution, to provide for greater autonomy. Each has been rejected by the electorate. The latest was defeated in a referendum in Nov. 1981, with 50% of the electorate participating.

For administration, there are 14 executive departments, 13 of which are under commissioners and the other, the Department of Justice, under an Attorney-General. The US Department of the Interior appoints a Federal Comptroller of government revenue and expenditure.

The franchise is vested in residents who are citizens of the United States, 18 years of age or over. They do not participate in the US presidential election but they have a non-voting representative in Congress.

The capital is Charlotte Amalie, on St Thomas Island.

Recent Elections

In elections for governor held on 20 Nov. 2018 Albert Bryan, Jr (Democrat) won 54·5% of the vote, against 45·1% for Kenneth Mapp (ind.) in a second round run-off. In Senate elections held on 6 Nov. 2018 the Democratic Party of the Virgin Islands won 13 out of 15 seats and independents 2.

Current Government

Governor: Albert Bryan, Jr (D.), since Jan. 2019.
   Lieut.-Governor: Tregenza Roach (D.), since Jan. 2019.
US Virgin Islands Government: https://vi.gov

Economy

Currency

United States currency became legal tender on 1 July 1934.

Budget

Under the 1954 Organic Act finances are provided partly from local revenues—customs, federal income tax, real and personal property tax, trade tax, excise tax, pilotage fees, etc.—and partly from Federal Matching Funds, being the excise taxes collected by the federal government on such Virgin Islands products transported to the mainland as are liable.

Per capita income, 2012, $35,844.
Revenues in 2014–15 totalled $1,203·9m.; expenditures were $1,547·0m.

Energy and Natural Resources

Environment
Carbon dioxide emissions from the consumption of energy in 2011 were the equivalent of 130·0 tonnes per capita, the second highest in the world.

Electricity
The Virgin Islands Water and Power Authority operates electrical generation and water desalination and reverse osmosis units on St Croix, St John and St Thomas. Production in 2011 was 951m. kWh. Per capita consumption in 2011 was 8,937 kWh. Installed capacity in 2011 was 345,000 kW.

Water
The total area covered by water is 599 sq. miles, of which 18 sq. miles are inland.

Agriculture
Land for fruit, vegetables and animal feed is available on St Croix, and there are tax incentives for development.
Livestock (2012 estimates): cattle, 8,000; goats, 4,000; pigs, 3,000; sheep, 3,000; chickens, 40,000.

Forestry
Forests covered 18,000 ha. in 2015, or 50% of the land area.

Fisheries
The total catch in 2015 was 833,000 lb (378 tonnes).

Industry
The main occupations on St Thomas are tourism and government service; on St Croix manufacturing is more important. Manufactures include rum (the most valuable product), watches, pharmaceuticals and fragrances. Industries in order of revenue: tourism, refining oil, watch assembly, rum distilling, construction.

Labour
At the end of 2014 the total labour force was 46,594, of whom 40,886 were employed. 5,708 were unemployed.

International Trade

Imports and Exports
In 2015 imports into the Virgin Islands totalled $131m. (down from $687m. in 2014). In the same year exports from the Virgin Islands totalled $149m., down from $1,405m. in 2014.

Communications

Roads
In 2008 the Virgin Islands had an estimated 1,260 km of roads. There were 74,500 vehicles registered in 2010.

Civil Aviation
In 2011 there were two primary airports (commercial service airports with more than 10,000 passenger boardings annually). The main airport is Cyril E. King at Charlotte Amalie on St Thomas, which had 596,832 enplanements in 2011. The smaller Henry E. Rohlsen airport at Christiansted on St Croix had 184,331 enplanements in 2011.

Shipping
The whole territory has free port status. There is an hourly boat service between St Thomas and St John and a 75-minute catamaran service between St Croix and St Thomas two to three times a day.

Social Institutions

Justice
The population in penal institutions in Jan. 2011 was 587 (539 per 100,000 population).

Education
In fall 2007 there were 10,770 in elementary school, 5,133 in high school and 2,384 students in higher education; there were 1,518 school teachers. In fall 2005 the University of the Virgin Islands (St Thomas and St Croix campuses, with an ecological research station on St John) had 2,392 students (1,263 full-time and 1,129 part-time) and 107 full-time instructional staff; 77% of the students were female.

Health
In 2018 there were 382 Virgin Island licensed medical professionals (excluding nurses). The Roy Lester Schneider Hospital on St Thomas had 169 beds in 2008. The Governor Juan F. Luis Hospital, Christiansted serves St Croix, with 188 beds in 2008.

Religion
According to the Pew Research Center's Forum on Religion & Public Life, in 2010 the population was an estimated 94·8% Christian. Around 69% of Christians are Protestants and 29% Catholics. There are places of worship of the Protestant, Roman Catholic and Jewish faiths in St Thomas and St Croix, and Protestant and Roman Catholic churches in St John.

Culture

Tourism
Tourism accounts for some 70% of GDP. In 2010 there were 691,559 visitor arrivals by air (excluding resident arrivals and inter-island traffic but including excursionists), up from 664,249 in 2009 although down slightly from 693,372 in 2007. There were 1,858,946 cruise passenger arrivals in 2010 (when there were 680 cruise ship calls), again down from 2007—when there had been 1,917,878 cruise passengers—before the global economic crisis had set in.

Other Unincorporated Territories

Baker Island
A small Pacific island 2,600 km southwest of Hawaii. Administered under the US Department of the Interior. Area 0·6 sq. mile; population (2010), nil. The islands are part of the Pacific Remote Islands Marine National Monument.

Howland Island
A small Pacific island 2,600 km southwest of Hawaii. Administered under the US Department of the Interior. Area 0·7 sq. mile; population (2010), nil. The islands are part of the Pacific Remote Islands Marine National Monument.

Jarvis Island
A small Pacific island 2,100 km south of Hawaii. Administered under the US Department of the Interior. Area 1·7 sq. miles; population (2010), nil. The islands are part of the Pacific Remote Islands Marine National Monument.

Johnston Atoll
Two small Pacific islands 1,100 km southwest of Hawaii, administered by the US Air Force. Area, 1·0 sq. mile; population (2010), nil. The islands are part of the Pacific Remote Islands Marine National Monument.

Kingman Reef
Small Pacific reef 1,500 km southwest of Hawaii, administered by the US Navy. Area one tenth of a sq. mile; population (2010), nil. The islands are part of the Pacific Remote Islands Marine National Monument.

Midway Islands
Two small Pacific islands at the western end of the Hawaiian chain, administered by the US Navy. Area, 2·4 sq. miles; in 2010 around 40 workers were present at any one time. The islands are part of the Papahanaumokuakea Marine National Monument.

Navassa Island
Small Caribbean island 48 km west of Haiti, administered by US Coast Guards. Area 1·4 sq. miles; population (2010), nil.

Wake Island
Three small Pacific islands 3,700 km west of Hawaii, administered by the US Air Force. Area, 2·5 sq. miles; in 2010 around 150 workers were present at any one time. The islands are part of the Pacific Remote Islands Marine National Monument.

Incorporated Territories

Palmyra Atoll

Small atoll 1,500 km southwest of Hawaii, administered by the US Department of the Interior. It is part federally-owned and part privately-owned. Area 4·6 sq. miles; population (2010), nil. The islands are part of the Pacific Remote Islands Marine National Monument.

Further Reading

United States of America

Official statistical information

The Office of Management and Budget, Washington, D.C., 20503 is part of the Executive Office of the President; it is responsible for co-ordinating all the statistical work of the different Federal government agencies. The Office does not collect or publish data itself. The main statistical agencies are as follows:

(1) Data User Services Division, Bureau of the Census, Department of Commerce, Washington, D.C., 20233. Responsible for decennial censuses of population and housing, quinquennial census of agriculture, manufactures and business; current statistics on population and the labour force, manufacturing activity and commodity production, trade and services, foreign trade, state and local government finances and operations. (Statistical Abstract of the United States [now discontinued], annual, and others).

(2) Bureau of Labor Statistics, Department of Labor, 441 G Street NW, Washington, D.C., 20212. (Monthly Labor Review and others).

(3) Information Division, Economic Research Service, Department of Agriculture, Washington, D.C., 20250. (*Agricultural Statistics*, annual, and others).

(4) National Center for Health Statistics, Department of Health and Human Services, 3700 East-West Highway, Hyattsville, MD 20782. (*Vital Statistics of the United States*, monthly and annual, and others).

(5) Bureau of Mines Office of Technical Information, Department of the Interior, Washington, D.C., 20241. (*Minerals Yearbook*, annual, and others).

(6) Office of Energy Information Services, Energy Information Administration, Department of Energy, Washington, D.C., 20461.

(7) Statistical Publications, Department of Commerce, Room 5062 Main Commerce, 14th St and Constitution Avenue NW, Washington, D.C., 20230; the Department's Bureau of Economic Analysis and its Office of Industry and Trade Information are the main collectors of data.

(8) Center for Education Statistics, Department of Education, 555 New Jersey Avenue NW, Washington, D.C., 20208.

(9) Public Correspondence Division, Office of the Assistant Secretary of Defense (Public Affairs P.C.), The Pentagon, Washington, D.C., 20301-1400.

(10) Bureau of Justice Statistics, Department of Justice, 633 Indiana Avenue NW, Washington, D.C., 20531.

(11) Public Inquiry, APA 200, Federal Aviation Administration, Department of Transportation, 800 Independence Avenue SW, Washington, D.C., 20591.

(12) Office of Public Affairs, Federal Highway Administration, Department of Transportation, 400 7th St., SW, Washington, D.C., 20590.

(13) Statistics Division, Internal Revenue Service, Department of the Treasury, 1201 E St. NW, Washington, D.C., 20224. Statistics on the economy are also published by the Division of Research and Statistics, Federal Reserve Board, Washington, D.C., 20551; the Congressional Joint Committee on the Economy, Capitol; the Office of the Secretary, Department of the Treasury, 1500 Pennsylvania Avenue NW, Washington, D.C., 20220.

Other official publications

Economic Report of the President. Annual. Bureau of the Census. *Statistical Abstract of the United States* (now discontinued). Annual. *Historical Statistics of the United States, Colonial Times to 1970.*

United States Government Manual. Annual.

The official publications of the USA are issued by the US Government Printing Office and are distributed by the Superintendent of Documents, who issued in 1940 a cumulative *Catalog of the Public Documents of the Congress and of All Departments of the Government of the United States.* This *Catalog* is kept up to date by *Monthly Catalog of United States Government Publications* with annual index and supplemented by *Price Lists.* Each *Price List* is devoted to a special subject or type of material.

Treaties and other International Acts of the United States of America (Edited by Hunter Miller). 8 vols. 1929–48. This edition stops in 1863. It may be supplemented by *Treaties, Conventions, International Acts, Protocols and Agreements Between the US and Other Powers, 1776–1937* (Edited by William M. Malloy and others). 4 vols. 1909–38. A new Treaty Series, *US Treaties and Other International Agreements,* was started in 1950.

Writings on American History. Washington, annual from 1902–90 (except 1904–05 and 1941–47).

Other publications

The Cambridge Economic History of the United States. vol. 1. 1996; vol. 2. 2000; vol. 3. 2000

Bacevich, Andrew J., *American Empire: The Realities and Consequences of US Diplomacy.* 2002

Bowles, Nigel and McMahon, Robert K., *Government and Politics of the United States.* 3rd ed. 2014

Brands, H. W., *Reagan: The Life.* 2015

Brogan, H., *The Longman History of the United States of America.* 2nd ed. 1999

Cannon, Lou, *The Reagan Paradox: The Conservative Icon and Today's GOP.* 2014.

Chollet, Derek, *The Long Game: How Obama Defied Washington and Redefined America's Role in the World.* 2016

Daalder, Ivo H. and Lindsay, James M., *America Unbound: the Bush Revolution in Foreign Policy.* 2003

Dallek, Robert, *Franklin D. Roosevelt: A Political Life.* 2017

Downing, Taylor, *1983: Reagan, Andropov and a World on the Brink.* 2018

Duncan, Russell and Goddard, Joseph, *Contemporary United States.* 5th ed. 2018

Fergusson, Niall, *Kissinger: 1923–1968: The Idealist.* 2015

Fitzgerald, David and Ryan, David, *Obama, US Foreign Policy and the Dilemmas of Intervention.* 2014

Foner, E. and Garraty, J. A. (eds) *The Reader's Companion to American History.* 1992

Grunwald, Michael, *The New New Deal: The Hidden Story of Change in the Obama Era.* 2012

Haass, Richard, *The Reluctant Sheriff: The United States After the Cold War.* 1998

Heilemann, John and Halperin, Mark, *Game Change: Obama and the Clintons, McCain and Palin, and the Race of a Lifetime.* 2010

Henriksen, Thomas H., *Cycles in US Foreign Policy since the Cold War.* 2017

Jenkins, Philip, *A History of the United States.* 4th ed. 2012

Jennings, F., *The Creation of America.* 2000

Jentleson, B. W. and Paterson, T. G. (eds) *Encyclopedia of US Foreign Relations.* 4 vols. 1997

Kuklick, Bruce, *A Political History of the USA.* 2009

Lepore, Jill, *These Truths: A History of the United States.* 2018

Little, Douglas, *American Orientalism: The United States and the Middle East since 1945.* 2002

Lord, C. L. and E. H., *Historical Atlas of the US.* Rev. ed. 1969

McGregor, Richard, *Asia's Reckoning: China, Japan and the Fate of US Power in the Pacific Century.* 2017

Merriam, L. A. and Oberly, J. (eds) *United States History: an Annotated Bibliography.* 1995

Morison, S. E. with Commager, H. S., *The Growth of the American Republic.* 2 vols. 5th ed. 1962–63

Norton, Mary Beth, Kamensky, Jane, Sheriff, Carol, Blight, David W., Chudacoff, Howard P., Logevall, Frederik and Bailey, Beth, *A People and a Nation: the History of the United States.* 10th ed. 2013

Peele, Gillian, Bailey, Christopher J., Herbert, Jon N., Cain, Bruce and Peters, B. Guy, (eds) *Developments in American Politics 8.* 2018

Pfucha, F. P., *Handbook for Research in American History: a Guide to Bibliographies and Other Reference Works.* 2nd ed. 1994

Prestowitz, Clyde, *Rogue Nation: American Unilateralism and the Failure of Good Intentions.* 2003

Remnick, David, *The Bridge: the Life and Rise of Barack Obama.* 2010

Srinivasan, Bhu, *Americana: A 400-Year History of American Capitalism.* 2017

Starr-Deelen, Donna G., *Counter-Terrorism from the Obama Administration to President Trump.* 2017

Stent, Angela, *The Limits of Partnership: US-Russian Relations in the Twenty-First Century.* 2014

Traynor, John, *Mastering Modern United States History.* 2nd ed. 2018

Wright, Lawrence, *The Looming Tower: Al Qaeda's Road to 9/11.* 2005

Who's Who in America. Annual

Other more specialized titles are listed under RECENT ELECTIONS *and* RELIGION, *above.*

National library: The Library of Congress, Independence Ave. SE, Washington, D.C., 20540. *Librarian:* Carla Hayden.

National statistical office: Bureau of the Census, Washington, D.C., 20233. *Director:* Steven Dillingham.

Website: http://www.census.gov

States and Territories

Official publications of the various states and insular possessions are listed in the *Monthly Check-List of State Publications,* issued by the Library of Congress since 1910.

The Book of the States. Biennial. 1953 ff.

State Government Finances. Annual. 1966 ff.

Bureau of the Census. *State and Metropolitan Area Data Book.* Irregular.— *County and City Data Book.* Irregular.

Hill, K. Q., *Democracy in the 50 States.* 1995

Alabama

Alabama Official and Statistical Register (now discontinued). Quadrennial

Alabama County Data Book. Annual

Directory of Health Care Facilities.

Alaska

Statistical Information: Department of Commerce and Economic Development, Economic Analysis Section, POB 110804, Juneau 99811. Publishes *The Alaska Economy Performance Report* (now discontinued).

Annual Financial Report.

Naske, C.-M. and Slotnick, H. E., *Alaska: a History of the 49th State.* 2nd ed. 1995

State library: POB 110571, Juneau, Alaska 99811-0571.

Arizona

Statistical information: College of Business and Public Administration, Univ. of Arizona, Tucson 85721. Publishes *Arizona Statistical Abstract* (now discontinued).

Arizona Department of Health Services, Center for Health Statistics. *Arizona Health Status and Vital Statistics 2016 Annual Report.* Online only

Arizona Historical Society. *1999/2000 Official Directory, Arizona Historical Museums and Related Support Organizations.* 1999

August, Jack L., *Vision in the Desert: Carl Hayden and the Hydropolitics in the American Southwest.* 1999

Leavengood, Betty, *Lives Shaped by Landscape: Grand Canyon Women.* 1999

Office of the Secretary of State. *Arizona Blue Book, 2011–12.* 2011

Shillingberg, William B., *Tombstone, A. T.: A History of Early Mining, Milling and Mayhem.* 1999

Arizona State Library, Archives and Public Records (ASLAPR): 1700 West Washington, Suite 200, Phoenix. *Website:* https://azlibrary.gov

Arkansas

Statistical information: Arkansas Institute for Economic Advancement, Univ. of Arkansas at Little Rock, Little Rock 72204. Publishes *Arkansas State and County Economic Data.*

Agricultural Statistics for Arkansas (now discontinued). Annual

Current Employment Developments (now discontinued). Monthly

Arkansas Department of Education. *Annual Statistical Report.* Annual

California

California Government and Politics (now discontinued). Hoeber, T. R., *et al.,* (eds) Annual

California Statistical Abstract (now discontinued). Annual; online only

Bean, W. and Rawls, J. J., *California: an Interpretive History.* 10th ed. 2011

Gerston, Larry N. and Christensen, Terry, *California Politics and Government: a Practical Approach.* 13th ed. 2015

State library: The California State Library, Library-Courts Bldg, Sacramento 95814.

Colorado

Statistical information: Business Research Division, Univ. of Colorado, Boulder 80309. Publishes *Statistical Abstract of Colorado* (now discontinued).

Griffiths, M. and Rubright, L., *Colorado: a Geography.* 1983

State library: Colorado State Library, 201 E. Colfax, Rm. 314, Denver 80203.

Connecticut

State Register and Manual. Annual

Halliburton, W. J., *The People of Connecticut.* 1985

State library: Connecticut State Library, 231 Capitol Avenue, Hartford (CT) 06105.

Business Incentives: Connecticut Economic Resource Center, 805 Brook St., Rocky Hill (CT) 06067.

Connecticut Tourism: Dept. of Economic and Community Development, 865 Brook St., Rocky Hill (CT) 06067.

Delaware

Statistical information: Delaware Economic Development Office, Dover, DE 19901. Publishes *Delaware Statistical Overview* (now discontinued).

State Manual, Containing Official List of Officers, Commissions and County Officers (now discontinued). Annual

Smeal, L., *Delaware Historical and Biographical Index.* 1984

District of Columbia

Greater Washington Board of Trade. *OPPTY.* Occasional

Reports of the Commissioners of the District of Columbia. 1874–1967

Bowling, K. R., *The Creation of Washington D.C.: the Idea and the Location of the American Capital.* 1991

Florida

Statistical information: Bureau of Economic and Business Research, Univ. of Florida, Gainesville 32611. Publishes *Florida Statistical Abstract* (now discontinued).

Benton, J. E. (ed.) *Government and Politics in Florida.* 3rd ed. 2008

Morris, A., *The Florida Handbook.* Biennial

State library: 500 S Bronough Street, Tallahassee 32399.

Georgia

Statistical information: Selig Center for Economic Growth, Univ. of Georgia, Athens 30602. Publishes *Georgia Statistical Abstract* (now discontinued).

State Law Library: Judicial Building, Capital Sq., Atlanta.

Hawaii

Statistical information: Hawaii State Department of Business, POB 2359, Honolulu 96804. Publishes *The State of Hawaii Data Book.*

Atlas of Hawaii. 3rd ed. 1998

Oliver, Anthony M., *Hawaii Facts and Reference Book: Recent Historical Facts and Events in the Fiftieth State.* 1995

Idaho

Statistical information: Idaho Commerce, 700 West State St., Boise 83720.

Schwantes, C. A., *In Mountain Shadows: a History of Idaho.* 1996

Illinois

Statistical information: Department of Commerce and Community Affairs, 620 Adams St., Springfield 62701. Publishes *Illinois State and Regional Economic Data Book* (now discontinued). Bureau of Economic and Business Research, Univ. of Illinois, 1206 South 6th St., Champaign 61820. Publishes *Illinois Statistical Abstract* (now discontinued).

Blue Book of the State of Illinois. Edited by Secretary of State. Biennial

Miller, D. L., *City of the Century: The Epic of Chicago and the Making of America.* 1996

The Illinois State Library: Springfield, IL 62756.

Indiana

Statistical information: Indiana Business Research Center, Indiana Univ., Indianapolis 46202. Publishes *Indiana Factbook* (now discontinued).

Gray, R. D. (ed.) *Indiana History: a Book of Readings.* 1994
Martin, J. B., *Indiana: an Interpretation.* 1992
State library: Indiana State Library, 140 North Senate, Indianapolis 46204.

Iowa

Annual Survey of Manufactures.
Government Finance.
Official Register. Secretary of State. Biennial
State Government Website: https://www.iowa.gov
State Library of Iowa: Des Moines 50319.

Kansas

Statistical information: Institute for Public Policy and Business Research, Univ. of Kansas, 607 Blake Hall, Lawrence 66045. Publishes *Kansas Statistical Abstract.*
Annual Economic Report of the Governor.
State library: Kansas State Library, Topeka.

Kentucky

Kentucky Deskbook of Economic Statistics (now discontinued). Kentucky Cabinet for Economic Development, Frankfort
Ulack, R. (ed.) *Atlas of Kentucky.* 1998

Louisiana

Louisiana State Census Data Center. Online only
Calhoun, Milburn and McGovern, Bernie, (eds) *Louisiana Almanac 2012 Edition.* 2012
Wall, Bennett H., *et al.*, (eds) *Louisiana: a History, Fifth Edition.* 2008
Wilds, J., *et al.*, (eds) *Louisiana Yesterday and Today: a Historical Guide to the State.* 1996
State library: The State Library of Louisiana, 701 North 4th St., Baton Rouge.

Maine

Statistical information: Maine Department of Economic and Community Development, State House Station 59, Augusta 04333. Publishes *Maine Economic Development Guide.*
Palmer, K. T., *et al.*, *Maine Politics and Government.* 1993

Maryland

Statistical Information: Maryland Department of Economic and Employment Development, 217 East Redwood St., Baltimore 21202.
DiLisio, J. E., *Maryland.* 1982
Rollo, V. F., *Maryland's Constitution and Government.* 1982
State library: Maryland State Library, Annapolis.

Massachusetts

Levitan, D. with Mariner, E. C., *Your Massachusetts Government.* 1984

Michigan

Michigan Manual. Biennial
Michigan Economic Development Corporation. *Economic Profiler* (now discontinued). Online only
Browne, W. P. and Verburg, K., *Michigan Politics and Government: Facing Change in a Complex State.* 1995
Dunbar, W. F. and May, G. S., *Michigan: A History of the Wolverine State.* 3rd ed. 1995
State Library Services: Library of Michigan, Lansing 48909.

Minnesota

Statistical Information: Department of Trade and Economic Development, 500 Metro Square, St Paul 55101. Publishes *Compare Minnesota: an Economic and Statistical Factbook* (now discontinued).—*Economic Report to the Governor* (now discontinued).
Legislative Manual. Biennial
Minnesota Agriculture Statistics (now discontinued). Annual

Mississippi

Secretary of State. *Mississippi Official and Statistical Register* (quadrennial).—*Blue Book:* http://www.sos.ms.gov/Education-Publications/Pages/Blue-Book.aspx
Mississippi Library Commission: 3881 Eastwood Drive, Jackson, MS 39211.

Missouri

Statistical information: Business and Public Administration Research Center, Univ. of Missouri, Columbia 65211. Publishes *Statistical Abstract for Missouri* (now discontinued).
Missouri Area Labor Trends (now discontinued). Monthly
Missouri Farm Facts (now discontinued). Annual
Report of the Public Schools of Missouri (now discontinued). Annual

Montana

Statistical information. Census and Economic Information Center, Montana Department of Commerce, 1425 9th Ave., Helena 59620.

Nebraska

Statistical information: Department of Economic Development, Box 94666, Lincoln 68509.
Nebraska Blue Book. Biennial
Olson, J. C., *History of Nebraska.* 3rd ed. 1997
State library: Nebraska State Library, PO Box 98931, State Capitol Bldg, Lincoln.

Nevada

Statistical information: Budget and Planning Division, Department of Administration, Capitol Complex, Carson City, Nevada 89710. Publishes *Nevada Statistical Abstract* (now discontinued). Biennial
Bowers, Michael W., *The Stagebrush State: Nevada's History, Government, and Politics.* 1996
Hulse, J. W., *The Nevada Adventure: a History.* 6th ed. 1990.—*The Silver State: Nevada's Heritage Reinterpreted.* 1998
State Government Website: http://www.nv.gov
Nevada State Library: Nevada State Library and Archives, Carson City.

New Hampshire

Delorme, D. (ed.) *New Hampshire Atlas and Gazetteer.* 2010

New Jersey

Statistical information: New Jersey State Data Center, Department of Labor, CN 388, Trenton 08625. Publishes *New Jersey Statistical Factbook* (now discontinued).
Legislative District Data Book. Annual
Manual of the Legislature of New Jersey. Annual
Cunningham, J. T., *New Jersey: America's Main Road.* Rev. ed. 1976
State library: 185 W. State Street, Trenton, CN 520, NJ 08625.

New Mexico

Bureau of Business and Economic Research, Univ. of New Mexico—*Census in New Mexico* (now discontinued).—*Economic Census: New Mexico* (now discontinued).—*New Mexico Business.* Monthly; annual review in Jan.–Feb. issue (now discontinued).
Etulain, R., *Contemporary New Mexico, 1940–1990.* 1994

New York State

Statistical information: Nelson Rockefeller Institute of Government, 411 State St., Albany 12203. Publishes *New York State Statistical Yearbook.*
New York Red Book. Biennial.
Legislative Manual (now discontinued). Biennial.
The Modern New York State Legislature: Redressing the Balance. 1991
State library: The New York State Library, Albany 12230.

North Carolina

Statistical information: Office of State Planning, 116 West Jones St., Raleigh 27603. Publishes *Statistical Abstract of North Carolina Counties* (now discontinued).
North Carolina Manual (now discontinued). Biennial
Fleer, J. D., *North Carolina: Government and Population.* 1995

North Dakota

Statistical information: Bureau of Business and Economic Research, Univ. of North Dakota, Grand Forks 58202. Publishes *Statistical Abstract of North Dakota* (now discontinued).
North Dakota Blue Book.

Ohio

Official Roster: Federal, State, County Officers and Department Information. Biennial

Shkurti, W. J. and Bartle, J. (eds) *Benchmark Ohio.* 1991

Oklahoma

Center for Economic and Management Research, Univ. of Oklahoma, 307 West Brooks St., Norman 73019. *Statistical Abstract of Oklahoma* (now discontinued).

Oklahoma Department of Libraries. *Oklahoma Almanac.* Biennial

Goins, Charles Robert and Goble, Danney, *Historical Atlas of Oklahoma.* 4th ed. 2006

State library: Oklahoma Department of Libraries, 200 Northeast 18th Street, Oklahoma City 73105.

Oregon

Oregon Blue Book. Biennial

Friedman, R., *The Other Side of Oregon.* 1993

McArthur, L. A., *Oregon Geographic Names.* 7th ed. 2003

Orr, E. L., *et al.*, *Geology of Oregon.* 1992

State library: The Oregon State Library, 250 Winter St. NE, Salem 97301–3950.

Pennsylvania

Statistical information: Pennsylvania State Data Center, 777 West Harrisburg Pike, Middletown 17057. Publishes *Pennsylvania Statistical Abstract.*

Downey, D. B. and Bremer, F. (eds) *Guide to the History of Pennsylvania.* 1994

Rhode Island

Statistical information: Rhode Island Economic Development Corporation, 1 West Exchange Street, Providence, RI 02903. Publishes *Rhode Island Basic Economic Statistics* (now discontinued).

Rhode Island Manual (now discontinued).

Wright, M. I. and Sullivan, R. J., *Rhode Island Atlas.* 1983

State library: Rhode Island State Library, State House, Providence 02908.

South Carolina

Statistical information: Budget and Control Board, R. C. Dennis Bldg, Columbia 29201. Publishes *South Carolina Statistical Abstract* (now discontinued).

South Carolina Legislative Manual. Annual

Edgar, W. B., *South Carolina in the Modern Age.* 1992

Graham, C. B. and Moore, W. V., *South Carolina Politics and Government.* 1995

State library: South Carolina State Library, Columbia.

South Dakota

Statistical information: State Data Center, Univ. of South Dakota, Vermillion 57069.

Governor's Budget Report. South Dakota Bureau of Finance and Management. Annual

South Dakota Historical Collections. 1902–82

South Dakota Legislative Manual. Biennial

Berg, F. M., *South Dakota: Land of Shining Gold.* 1982

State library: South Dakota State Library, 800 Governor's Drive, Pierre, S.D. 57501–2294.

Tennessee

Statistical information: Center for Business and Economic Research, Univ. of Tennessee, Knoxville 37996. Publishes *Tennessee Statistical Abstract*

Tennessee Blue Book.

Dykeman, W., *Tennessee.* Rev. ed. 1984

State library: State Library and Archives, 403 7th Avenue North, Nashville.

Texas

Texas Almanac. Biennial

Kingston, M., *Texas Almanac's Political History of Texas.* 1992

Newell, Charldean, Prindle, David F. and Riddlesperger, James, *Texas Politics.* 13th ed. 2015

Legislative Reference Library: Box 12488, Capitol Station, Austin, Texas 78711-2488.

Utah

Statistical information: Bureau of Economic and Business Research, Univ. of Utah, 401 Kendall D. Garff Bldg, Salt Lake City 84112. Publishes *Statistical Abstract of Utah* (now discontinued).

Utah Foundation. *Statistical Review of Government in Utah.* 1991

Vermont

Statistical information: Office of Policy Research and Coordination, Montpelier 05602

Legislative Directory. Biennial

Vermont Annual Financial Report. Annual

Vermont Atlas and Gazetteer. 12th ed. 2007

Vermont Year-Book, formerly Walton's Register (now discontinued). Annual

State library: Vermont Dept. of Libraries, 109 State St., Montpelier.

Virginia

Statistical information: Cooper Center for Public Service, Univ. of Virginia, 918 Emmet St. N., Suite 300, Charlottesville 22903-4832. Publishes *Virginia Statistical Abstract* (now discontinued).—*Population Estimates of Virginia Cities and Counties* (now discontinued).

Rubin, L. D., Jr, *Virginia: a Bicentennial History.* 1977

Salmon, E. J. and Campbell, E. D. C., Jr, *The Hornbook of Virginia History: A Ready-Reference Guide to the Old Dominion's People, Places, and Past.* 1994

State library: Library of Virginia, Richmond 23219.

Washington State

Statistical information: State Office of Financial Management, POB 43113, Olympia 98504-3113. Publishes *Washington State Data Book*

Dodds, G. B., *American North-West: a History of Oregon and Washington.* 1986

West Virginia

West Virginia Blue Book. Annual, since 1916

Rice, O. K., *West Virginia: A History.* 2nd ed. 1994

State library: Archives and History, Division of Culture and History, Charleston.

Wisconsin

Wisconsin Blue Book. Biennial

State Historical Society of Wisconsin: *The History of Wisconsin.* Vol. IV J. Buenker. 1999

State Information Agency: Legislative Reference Bureau, One East Main St., Suite 200, Madison, WI 53703-2037.

Website: http://legis.wisconsin.gov

Wyoming

Equality State Almanac 2010. Wyoming Department of Administration and Information. Division of Economic Analysis. Cheyenne, WY 82002

Wyoming Official Directory. Secretary of State. Annual

Treadway, T., *Wyoming.* 1982

Statistics Website: http://eadiv.state.wy.us

Commonwealth of Puerto Rico

Statistical Information: Government Development Bank for Puerto Rico, PO Box 42001, San Juan 00940-2001.

Website: http://www.gdb-pur.com/economy

Commonwealth Library: Univ. of Puerto Rico Library, Rio Piedras.

Guam

Report (Annual) of the Governor of Guam to the US Department of Interior (now discontinued).

Guam Annual Economic Review (now discontinued).

Rogers, R. F., *Destiny's Landfall: a History of Guam.* 1995

Wuerch, W. L. and Ballendorf, D. A., *Historical Dictionary of Guam and Micronesia.* 1995

Statistical Office: P.O. Box 2950, Hagåtña, Guam 96932.

Uruguay

República Oriental del Uruguay (Oriental Republic of Uruguay)

Capital: Montevideo
Population projection, 2020: 3·49m.
GNI per capita, 2017: (PPP$) 19,930
HDI/world rank, 2017: 0·804/55
Internet domain extension: .uy

Key Historical Events

From around 4000 BC Uruguay was populated principally by Charrúa and Guaraní Indians. The Charrúa migrated seasonally between coastal and inland areas, while the Guaraní settled in the eastern forests and in the north. Smaller groups also settled the region and lands were fought over vigorously. In 1516 the first Europeans to enter the territory, Spanish navigator Juan Díaz de Solis and his party, were killed. Other Spanish and Portuguese expeditions followed and in the late 16th century the Spanish laid claim to the Río de la Plata. In 1603 Spanish governor Hernando Arias de Saavedra is said to have shipped cattle and horses from the Paraguay region into Río de la Plata, and Spanish, Portuguese and English settlers began livestock farming. The native peoples resisted the European colonizers but were killed in large numbers in warfare and by European disease.

In 1680 the Portuguese established the settlement of Colonia do Sacramento on the Río de la Plata. In 1726 the Spanish founded San Felipe de Montevideo as a fortified port and settled its hinterland. For the next 50 years the two powers fought over the coastal region and in 1776 the Spanish established the viceroyalty of the Río de la Plata, with Buenos Aires as its capital. While the Napoleonic wars were weakening Spain, an autonomous junta was established in Montevideo and in 1810 *criollos* (ethnic Spanish born in South America) seized power from the Spanish in Buenos Aires. A federalist movement originating in the inland region of the Banda Oriental challenged both Montevideo and Buenos Aires. In the ensuing conflict Portuguese Brazil annexed the Banda Oriental from 1820–25, until Uruguayan federalists led a successful uprising and regained control. Banda Oriental declared its independence and its incorporation into the United Provinces of Río de la Plata on 25 Aug. 1825. Fighting continued until 1828 when negotiations began with Brazil and Argentina. On 18 July 1830 the constitution of the Oriental Republic of Uruguay was approved.

Conflict between the two main political parties, the *colorados* and *blancos*, dominated the next 90 years, factionalizing the nation and leading to the economically damaging War of the Triple Alliance (1864–70), fought between Paraguay and the unified forces of Uruguay, Argentina and Brazil. In 1905 the first democratic elections took place, returning the *colorados* to government under President José Batlle y Ordónez. In the early 20th century ranching brought prosperity and an influx of immigrants, and a welfare state was developed. In 1919 a new constitution aimed to protect against dictatorship by providing for a plural executive known as a *colegiado*. However, economic depression led to instability and in 1933 presidential government and quadrennial elections were introduced.

Collective leadership returned from 1951–56 but a series of strikes and riots in the 1960s led to the extension of army influence. The military took repressive measures and the presidency was restored in 1967. Marxist urban guerrillas, the Tupamaros, fought a violent campaign against the regime but were finally defeated in 1972. The military took over the government in 1973. A period of harsh repression followed during which thousands were arrested and human rights abuses were rife. Economic difficulties in the 1980s weakened the military government and the country returned to civilian rule in 1985. Economic growth in the 1990s was followed by a downturn from 1999–2002. In 2005 Uruguay elected its first left-wing leader, Tabaré Vázquez of the Progressive Encounter-Broad Front-New Majority coalition.

The military ruler from 1981–85, Gregorio Álvarez, was sentenced to 25 years in prison in Oct. 2009 for murder and human rights abuses during his rule. The following month José Mujica, a former guerrilla leader, was elected president. In Feb. 2010 Juan María Bordaberry, president from 1972–76, received a 30-year sentence for murder and constitutional violations while in office. In Dec. 2013 Uruguay became the first country in the world to legalize the sale, cultivation and distribution of marijuana.

Territory and Population

Uruguay is bounded on the northeast by Brazil, on the southeast by the Atlantic, on the south by the Río de la Plata and on the west by Argentina. The area is 176,215 sq. km (68,037 sq. miles), including 1,199 sq. km (463 sq. miles) of inland waters. The following table shows the area and the population of the 19 departments at census 2011:

Departments	Sq. km	Census 2011	Capital
Artigas	11,928	73,378	Artigas
Canelones	4,536	520,187	Canelones
Cerro-Largo	13,648	84,698	Melo
Colonia	6,106	123,203	Colonia
Durazno	11,643	57,088	Durazno
Flores	5,144	25,050	Trinidad
Florida	10,417	67,048	Florida
Lavalleja	10,016	58,815	Minas
Maldonado	4,793	164,300	Maldonado
Montevideo	530	1,319,108	Montevideo
Paysandú	13,922	113,124	Paysandú
Río Negro	9,282	54,765	Fray Bentos
Rivera	9,370	103,493	Rivera
Rocha	10,551	68,088	Rocha
Salto	14,163	124,878	Salto
San José	4,992	108,309	San José
Soriano	9,008	82,595	Mercedes
Tacuarembó	15,438	90,053	Tacuarembó
Treinta y Tres	9,529	48,134	Treinta y Tres

The total population at the 2011 census was 3,286,314; density, 18·8 per sq. km.

The UN gives a projected population for 2020 of 3·49m.

In 2011 Montevideo (the capital) accounted for 39·7% of the total population. It had a population in 2011 of 1,304,687. Other major cities are Salto (population of 104,011 in 2011) and Ciudad de la Costa (95,176 in 2011). 92·6% of the population lived in urban areas in 2011.

13% of the population are over 65; 24% are under 15; 63% are between 15 and 64.

The official language is Spanish.

Social Statistics

2009: births, 47,152; deaths, 32,179. Rates (per 1,000 population), 2009: birth, 14·1; death, 9·6. Annual population growth rate, 2005–10, 0·3%. Infant mortality, 2010 (per 1,000 live births), 9. Life expectancy in 2013 was 73·7 years among males and 80·6 years among females. Fertility rate, 2013, 2·0 births per woman. Uruguay legalized same-sex marriage in Aug. 2013. In Oct. 2012 it became the second Latin American country (after Cuba) to legalize abortion for all women.

Climate

A warm temperate climate, with mild winters and warm summers. The wettest months are March to June, but there is really no dry season. Montevideo, Jan. 72°F (22·2°C), July 50°F (10°C). Annual rainfall 38" (950 mm).

© Springer Nature Limited 2020
Palgrave Macmillan (ed.), *The Statesman's Yearbook 2020*,
https://doi.org/10.1057/978-1-349-95940-2_201

Constitution and Government

The Constitution was adopted on 27 Nov. 1966 and became effective in Feb. 1967; it has been amended in 1989, 1994, 1996 and 2004.

Congress consists of a *Senate* of 31 members and a *Chamber of Deputies* of 99 members, both elected by proportional representation for five-year terms although in the case of the Senate only 30 members are elected with one seat reserved for the Vice-President. The electoral system provides that the successful presidential candidate be a member of the party which gains a parliamentary majority. Electors vote for deputies on a first-past-the-post system, and simultaneously vote for a presidential candidate of the same party. The winners of the second vote are credited with the number of votes obtained by their party in the parliamentary elections. Referendums may be called at the instigation of 10,000 signatories. Voting is compulsory.

National Anthem

'Orientales, la patria o la tumba' ('Easterners, the fatherland or the tomb'); words by F. Acuña de Figueroa, tune by F. J. Debali.

Government Chronology

Heads of State since 1943. (FA = Broad Front; PC = Colorado Party; PN = National Party (Blancos); PS = Socialist Party of Uruguay)

Presidents of the Republic

1943–47	PC	Juan José Amézaga Landaraso
1947	PC	Tomás Berreta Gandolfo
1947–51	PC	Luis Conrado Batlle Berres
1951–52	PC	Andrés Martínez Trueba

Chairman of the 1st National Council of Government

1952–55	PC	Andrés Martínez Trueba

Chairmen of the 2nd National Council of Government

1955–56	PC	Luis Conrado Batlle Berres
1956–57	PC	Alberto Fermín Zubiría Urtiague
1957–58	PC	Arturo Lezama Bagez
1958–59	PC	Carlos Lorenzo Fischer Brusoni

Chairmen of the 3rd National Council of Government

1959–60	PN	Martín Recaredo Echegoyen Machicote
1960–61	PN	Benito Nardone Cetrulo
1961–62	PN	Eduardo Víctor Haedo
1962–63	PN	Faustino Harrison Usoz

Chairmen of the 4th National Council of Government

1963–64	PN	Daniel Fernández Crespo
1964–65	PN	Luis Giannattasio Finocchietti
1965–66	PN	Washington Beltrán Mullin
1966–67	PN	Alberto Heber Usher

Presidents of the Republic

1967	PC	Óscar Diego Gestido Pose
1967–72	PC	Jorge Pacheco Areco
1972–76	PC[1]	Juan María Bordaberry Arocena
1976–81	PN[2]	Aparicio Méndez Manfredini
1981–85	military	Gregorio Conrado Álvarez Armellino
1985–90	PC	Julio María Sanguinetti Coirolo
1990–95	PN	Luis Alberto Lacalle de Herrera
1995–2000	PC	Julio María Sanguinetti Coirolo

(continued)

2000–05	PC	Jorge Luis Batlle Ibáñez
2005–10	PS, FA	Tabaré Ramón Vázquez Rosas
2010–15	FA	José Alberto Mujica
2015–	FA	Tabaré Ramón Vázquez Rosas

[1]Civilian president under military rule 1973–76.
[2]Civilian president under military rule.

Recent Elections

Elections for the General Assembly were held on 26 Oct. 2014. In elections to the Chamber of Deputies, the Broad Front (FA) won 50 seats, the National Party (PN) 32, the Colorado Party (PC) 13, the Independent Party (PI) 3 and the Popular Assembly 1. In the Senate election FA won 15 seats, PN 10, PC 4 and PI 1.

In the presidential run-off held on 30 Nov. 2014, Tabaré Vázquez (FA) won with 56·6% of the vote against Luis Alberto Lacalle Pou (PN) with 43·4%. Seven other candidates had participated in the first round of voting on 26 Oct. 2014. Turnout was 90·5% in the first round and 88·6% in the second.

Current Government

President: Tabaré Ramón Vázquez Rosas; b. 1940 (FA; sworn in 1 March 2015, having previously been president from March 2005–March 2010).
Vice-President: Lucía Topolansky.
In Feb. 2019 the government comprised:
Minister of Defence: Jorge Menéndez. *Economy and Finance:* Danilo Astori. *Education and Culture:* María Julia Muñoz. *Foreign Relations:* Rodolfo Nin Novoa. *Housing, Land Management and Environment:* Eneida de León. *Industry, Energy and Mining:* Carolina Cosse. *Interior:* Eduardo Bonomi. *Livestock, Agriculture and Fisheries:* Enzo Benech. *Public Health:* Jorge Basso. *Social Development:* Marina Arismendi. *Tourism and Sports:* Liliam Kechichián. *Transport and Public Works:* Victor Rossi. *Work and Social Security:* Ernesto Murro.
Presidency Website (limited English): http://www.presidencia.gub.uy

Current Leaders

Tabaré Vázquez

Position
President

Introduction
Following his election success in Oct. 2004, Tabaré Vázquez was sworn in as the first left-wing president in Uruguay's history on 1 March 2005 and remained in office until 2010. A cancer specialist and former mayor of the capital, Montevideo, he promised to focus on helping the poor and creating jobs. He was elected for another presidential term in Nov. 2014, succeeding his fellow Broad Front member José Alberto Mujica.

Early Life
Tabaré Ramón Vázquez was born in a poor district of Montevideo on 17 Jan. 1940, the son of an oil refinery worker. Having graduated in medicine from the capital's University of the Republic in 1969, he then specialized in oncology and radiotherapy, beginning work in 1972. In 1976 Vázquez obtained a scholarship from the French government to study further at the Institut Gustave Roussy in Paris.

In 1985, the year in which civilian government was restored in Uruguay after 12 years of military dictatorship, Vázquez was nominated director of the department of oncology and radiotherapy at the University of the Republic. He subsequently published more than 100 scientific papers and attended numerous international conferences. Affiliated with the central committee of the Socialist Party from late 1987, he then joined the Broad Front (a left-wing coalition formed in 1971) and stood as their candidate in the election for the mayorship of Montevideo in Nov. 1989. He won and went on to become a popular and successful figure, re-elected throughout the 1990s and early 2000s with increasing majorities.

In 1994 Vázquez came within a handful of votes of winning the presidency as the candidate of the Progressive Encounter–Broad Front (EP–FA) alliance, just losing to the Colorado Party's Julio María Sanguinetti. Vázquez entered the 1999 presidential election with high hopes, promising to create jobs with increased spending. The election went to a run-off but was won by the Colorado candidate, Jorge Batlle. However, support for the ruling party fell sharply when Uruguay's economy plunged into recession in 2002. In the presidential election of Oct. 2004, Vázquez received 50·4% of votes cast, avoiding the need for a run-off. The EP–FA–NM coalition (by then including New Majority) also emerged victorious in the legislative elections—the first parliamentary election win for the political left in Uruguay's history. On 1 March 2005 Vázquez was inaugurated as president.

Career in Office

Having campaigned on a promise to fight poverty and tackle unemployment, Vázquez embarked on his five-year term by launching a US$100m. 'social emergency programme'. He pledged to distribute wealth more evenly by strengthening educational institutions and introducing a national minimum wage. He also signed an economic agreement with Venezuela, restored diplomatic relations with Cuba and set out to strengthen ties with other members of the MERCOSUR trade bloc to reduce the country's foreign debt. Demonstrating his popular touch, he announced that he would continue to see cancer patients throughout his term in office.

Vázquez promised to investigate the fate of the many thousands who disappeared during the military dictatorship of the 1970s and in Dec. 2005 forensic investigations unearthed the remains of victims believed to have been killed during that time. In Nov. 2006 the former president, Juan María Bordaberry Arocena, was detained in connection with the deaths of 14 political opponents in the 1970s and was later sentenced to 30 years' incarceration before his death in 2011. Also in late 2006, the Uruguayan government repaid all its outstanding debt to the International Monetary Fund.

Uruguay's relations with Argentina deteriorated sharply at the end of 2007 after Vázquez authorized the opening of a controversial paper pulp mill on the Uruguay River, which forms the border between the two countries. The Argentine government maintained that the plant would degrade the river and local environment.

In Nov. 2008 the Senate passed legislation that would decriminalize abortion, prompting Vázquez's resignation from the Socialist Party after he refused to endorse the bill. Barred from running for re-election in 2009 but leaving office with a 60% approval rating, he refused to rule out a return in 2014 and in Nov. that year he won the run-off poll as the Broad Front candidate, claiming almost 57% of the vote against Luis Lacalle Pou of the centre-right National Party. Sworn in for a second presidential term on 1 March 2015, Vázquez has since maintained the generous social welfare policies of his Broad Front predecessor, José Mujica, but has nevertheless faced growing public concern over rising crime, poor educational standards, the country's over-dependence on exports and a deteriorating fiscal deficit.

Defence

Defence expenditure totalled US$445m. in 2013 (US$134 per capita), representing 0·9% of GDP.

Army

The Army consists of volunteers who enlist for one to two years' service. There are four military regions with divisional headquarters. Strength (2011), 16,200. In addition there are government paramilitary forces, numbering 818 in 2011.

Navy

The Navy includes two frigates. A naval aviation service, with 211 personnel in 2011, operates one combat-capable aircraft. Personnel in 2011 totalled 5,400 including 450 naval infantry and 1,800 coast guards. The main base is at Montevideo.

Air Force

Organized with US aid, the Air Force had (2011) 3,000 personnel and 15 combat-capable aircraft.

Economy

Finance and real estate contributed 20·7% to GDP in 2014; followed by services, 14·1%; trade and hotels, 13·0%; and manufacturing, 12·3%.

Overview

Agriculture contributes 8% of GDP and 70% of total exports. The creation of the Southern Common Market in the 1990s sealed trade relations with South American partners—notably Brazil, which buys 18% of Uruguay's exports. China is the next largest export market and the largest import market; in 2011 total trade between the two countries was worth US$3·74bn., 20 times the level in 1988. Tourism is a key growth sector.

Annual GDP growth from 2004 to 2015 averaged 5·0%, despite negative growth in 2009 at the height of the global financial crisis; GDP per capita was US$13,944 in 2015. Unemployment stood at 6·6% in 2014. The economy is built on strong macro-principles of low debt, high domestic demand and diversified production. The government has also embarked on an economic liberalization programme, reducing tariffs, cutting government spending and encouraging private ownership. The government had aimed to provide at least 90% of its electricity supply from renewable sources by 2015, investing heavily in wind power; renewable sources actually provided 95% that year.

In the long term the government must strive to reduce public debt and diversify export markets away from South America in order to avoid a repeat of 2001 when the economy suffered badly as a result of Argentina's debt default.

Currency

The unit of currency is the *Uruguayan peso* (UYU), of 100 *centésimos*, which replaced the *nuevo peso* in March 1993 at 1 Uruguayan peso = 1,000 nuevos pesos. In June 2002 Uruguay allowed the peso to float freely. Inflation, which had been over 100% in 1990, was 9·6% in 2016 and 6·2% in 2017. In July 2005 total money supply was 22,794m. pesos, foreign exchange reserves were US$2,578m. and gold reserves were 8,000 troy oz (1·8m. troy oz in Nov. 1999).

Budget

In 2016 central government revenues totalled 574,052m. pesos (of which taxes 376,787m. pesos) and expenditures 610,652m. pesos. Main items of expenditure by economic type in 2016: social benefits, 250,647m. pesos; compensation of employees, 199,106m. pesos; use of goods and services, 61,849m. pesos.

Standard rate of VAT is 22% (reduced rate, 10%).

Performance

Uruguay depends heavily on its two large neighbours, Brazil and Argentina. Uruguay suffered four successive years of negative growth between 1999 and 2002, culminating in the economy shrinking by 7·1% in 2002, as the general downturn in the world economy was exacerbated by Argentina's crisis. More recently Brazil's economic problems have led to Uruguay having real GDP growth of only 0·4% in 2015, 1·7% in 2016 and 2·7% in 2017. Nevertheless, with the economy expanding every year since 2003 Uruguay is now experiencing the longest period of growth in the country's history. Total GDP in 2017 was US$56·2bn.

Banking and Finance

The Central Bank (*President*, Mario Bergara) was inaugurated on 16 May 1967. It is the bank of issue and supreme regulatory authority. In 2014 there were three state banks and ten private banks. In 2011 commercial banks had assets of US$28·9bn.

In 2010 foreign debt totalled US$11,347m., equivalent to 29·0% of GNI. There is a stock exchange in Montevideo.

Energy and Natural Resources

Environment

Uruguay's carbon dioxide emissions from the consumption of energy in 2011 were the equivalent of 2·5 tonnes per capita.

Electricity

Installed capacity was 2·8m. kW in 2011. Production in 2011 was 10·34bn. kWh; consumption per capita in 2011 was 3,192 kWh.

Agriculture

Rising investment has helped agriculture, which has given a major boost to the country's economy. Agricultural land makes up 87·2% of the country's land area. Some large *estancias* have been divided up into family farms; the average farm is about 250 acres. In 2012 there were approximately 1·76m. ha. of arable land and 39,000 ha. of permanent crops. An estimated 238,000 ha. were equipped for irrigation in 2013.

Main crops (in 1,000 tonnes), 2012 unless otherwise indicated: soybeans (2011), 1,830 (estimate); rice, 1,424; wheat, 982; maize, 528; sorghum, 372; sugarcane, 368; barley, 220; oranges, 140 (estimate); grapes, 130 (estimate); potatoes, 109; clementines, mandarins, satsumas and tangerines, 101 (estimate); apples, 80 (estimate); sweet potatoes, 76 (estimate); oats, 50 (estimate); lemons and limes, 40 (estimate).

Livestock, 2012 (estimates): cattle, 11·41m.; sheep, 8·23m.; horses, 407,000; pigs, 222,000; chickens, 18m.

Livestock products, 2011 estimates (in 1,000 tonnes): beef and veal, 479; lamb and mutton, 32; pork and pork products, 21; poultry meat, 86; milk 2,057; eggs, 54; greasy wool, 35. Slaughterings in 2013–14: cattle, 1·96m.; sheep, 1·66m.; pigs, 197,000; horses, 35,000.

Forestry

In 2015 the area under forests was 1·85m. ha. (mainly eucalyptus and pine), representing 11% of the total land area. In 2011, 10·43m. cu. metres of roundwood were cut.

Fisheries

The total catch in 2015 was 59,540 tonnes, almost entirely marine fish.

Industry

Manufacturing accounted for 13·8% of GDP in 2014. Industries include meat packing, oil refining, cement manufacture, foodstuffs, beverages, cigarettes, leather and textile manufacture, chemicals, light engineering and transport equipment.

Labour

In 1996 the retirement age was raised from 55 to 60 for women; it remains 60 for men. The labour force in 2013 was 1,750,000 (1,579,000 in 2003). 76·5% of the population aged 15–64 was economically active in 2013. In the same year 6·6% of the population was unemployed.

International Trade

Imports and Exports

Goods imports in 2013 totalled US$11,642·4m. (US$11,652·1m. in 2012) and goods exports US$9,065·8m. (US$8,709·2m. in 2012).

Principal imports in 2013 were machinery and transport (30·4%), mineral fuels and lubricants, and chemicals; main exports in 2013 were food, animals and beverages (44·8%), crude materials and animal and vegetable oils, and manufactured goods.

In 2013 Brazil was both the leading import supplier (17·7% of Uruguay's imports) and the leading export destination (19·6% of Uruguay's exports).

Communications

Roads

Uruguay has more than 75,000 km of roads, including 8,776 km of national roads in 2016. Passenger cars in 2007 numbered 553,200 (151 per 1,000 inhabitants in 2005). There were 150 fatalities as a result of road accidents in 2005.

Rail

The total railway system open for traffic in 2005 was 1,508 km of 1,435 mm gauge. Passenger services, which had been abandoned in 1988, were resumed on a limited basis in 1993. In 2007 the railways carried 600,000 passengers and 1·4m. tonnes of freight.

Civil Aviation

The largest international airport is at Montevideo (Carrasco). There were direct international services in 2010 to Asunción, Barcelona, Buenos Aires, Córdoba (Argentina), Curitiba, Florianópolis, Iguazu Falls, Lima, Madrid, Miami, Panama City, Porto Alegre, Rio de Janeiro, San Salvador, Santiago and São Paulo. The former national carrier, Pluna, ceased operations in July 2012. There were 11 international airports in 2014. Nine had paved runways, one was semi-paved and one unpaved. In 2010 airports in Uruguay handled 2,195,336 passengers, of which 2,011,601 were at Carrasco. 26,832 tonnes of freight passed through Carrasco in 2010. In 2012 scheduled airline traffic of Uruguayan-based carriers flew 34·5m. km; passenger-km totalled 1·5bn. in the same year.

Shipping

In Jan. 2014 there were 19 ships of 300 GT or over registered, totalling 85,000 GT. The chief port is Montevideo, which handled 10·6m. tonnes of foreign cargo in 2013.

Telecommunications

There were 5,268,000 mobile phone subscriptions in 2013 (1,546·2 per 1,000 inhabitants) and 1,048,000 fixed telephone lines in the same year. In 2013 Uruguay had 720,000 fixed broadband internet subscriptions and 1,552,000 mobile broadband subscriptions. In March 2012 there were 1·5m. Facebook users.

Social Institutions

Out of 178 countries analysed in the 2017 *Fragile States Index*—a list published jointly by the Fund for Peace and *Foreign Policy* magazine—Uruguay was ranked the 22nd least vulnerable to conflict or collapse. The index is based on 12 indicators of state vulnerability across social, political and economic categories.

Justice

The Supreme Court is elected by Congress; it appoints all other judges. There are six courts of appeal, each with three judges. There are civil and criminal courts. Montevideo has ten courts of first instance, Paysandú and Salto have two each and the other departments have one each. There are approximately 300 lower courts.

The population in penal institutions in July 2012 was 9,524 (281 per 100,000 of national population). 64·5% of prisoners had yet to receive a trial according to 2014 estimates by the International Centre for Prison Studies. In 2015 the World Justice Project *Rule of Law Index*, which provides data on how the rule of law is experienced by the general public across eight categories, ranked Uruguay 36th of 102 countries for criminal justice and 17th for civil justice.

Education

Adult literacy in 2006 was 98·3% (male, 97·6%; female, 98·6%). The female literacy rate is the second highest in South America, behind Chile. Primary education is obligatory; both primary and secondary education are free. In 2007 there were 122,089 pupils in pre-primary schools with 5,220 teaching staff, 359,439 primary school pupils with 23,175 teaching staff and at secondary level there were 294,852 pupils and 21,369 teaching staff.

There is one state university, one independent Roman Catholic university and one private institute of technology. In 2007 there were 158,841 students and 15,789 academic staff in tertiary education.

In 2006 public expenditure on education came to 3·0% of GNI and represented 11·6% of total government expenditure.

Health

In 2008 there were 13,197 physicians, 19,595 nursing and midwifery personnel, 2,476 dentistry personnel and 1,877 pharmaceutical personnel. In 2013 there were 3·9 public hospitals per 100,000 population. In the period 2006–12 Uruguay had a provision of 25 hospital beds per 10,000 population.

In *Water: At What Cost? The State of the World's Water 2016*, WaterAid reported that 0·3% of the population does not have access to safe water.

Welfare

The welfare state dates from the beginning of the 1900s. In 2013 there were 0·8m. recipients of pensions and benefits monthly. In Oct. 2013 the minimum monthly old-age pension was increased to 6,170 pesos. There is a mixed social insurance and individual account system (compulsory for employed and self-employed persons born after 1 April 1956 with monthly earnings greater than 31,618 pesos and optional for those with monthly earnings of 31,618 pesos or less) with a maximum monthly pension in 2013 of 26,085 pesos. A social insurance system only that covers all others had a maximum monthly pension in 2013 of 38,574 pesos.

Religion

State and Church are separate, and there is complete religious liberty. According to estimates by the Pew Research Center's Forum on Religion & Public Life, in 2010 the population was 57·9% Christian (mainly Catholics) with 40·7% not having any religious affiliation. In Feb. 2019 there was one cardinal.

Culture

World Heritage Sites
Uruguay has two sites on the UNESCO World Heritage List: the Historic Quarter of the City of Colonia del Sacramento (inscribed on the list in 1995), founded in 1680 by the Portuguese; and Fray Bentos Industrial Landscape (inscribed on the list in 2015), a site that illustrates the whole process of meat sourcing, processing, packing and dispatching.

Press
In 2008 there were 34 paid-for dailies with an average circulation of 145,000. The newspaper with the highest circulation is *El País*, which sold a daily average of 46,000 copies in 2008.

Tourism
There were 2,857,000 international tourist arrivals—excluding same-day visitors—in 2011 (2,349,000 in 2010). Receipts from tourism in 2011 totalled US$2,203m.

Diplomatic Representatives

Of Uruguay in the United Kingdom (150 Brompton Rd, London, SW3 1HX)
  Ambassador: Fernando López-Fabregat.

Of the United Kingdom in Uruguay (Calle Marco Bruto 1073, 11300 Montevideo)
  Ambassador: Ian Duddy.

Of Uruguay in the USA (1913 I St., NW, Washington, D.C., 20006)
  Ambassador: Carlos Alberto Gianelli Derois.

Of the USA in Uruguay (Lauro Müller 1776, Montevideo)
  Ambassador: Kelly A. Keiderling.

Of Uruguay to the United Nations
  Ambassador: Elbio Oscar Rosselli Frieri.

Of Uruguay to the European Union
  Ambassador: Carlos Pérez del Castillo.

Further Reading

González, L. E., *Political Structures and Democracy in Uruguay.* 1992

Sosnowski, S. (ed.) *Repression, Exile and Democracy: Uruguayan Culture.* 1993

National library: Biblioteca Nacional de Uruguay, 18 de julio de 1790, Montevideo.

National Statistical Office: Instituto Nacional de Estadística (INE), Rio Negro 1520, Montevideo.

Website (Spanish only): http://www.ine.gub.uy

Uzbekistan

Uzbekiston Respublikasy (Republic of Uzbekistan)

Capital: Tashkent
Population projection, 2020: 33·24m.
GNI per capita, 2017: (PPP$) 6,470
HDI/world rank, 2017: 0·710/105
Internet domain extension: .uz

Key Historical Events

Evidence of human settlement from at least 2200 BC is believed to be that of the Oxus civilization which extended across central Asia from Turkmenistan to Tajikistan. The region came under the influence of the first Persian Empire, centred on Persepolis, from around 550 BC when it was known as Sogdiana. Alexander the Great conquered Sogdiana and the ancient Greek kingdom of Bactria in 327 BC, marrying Roxane, daughter of a Sogdian chieftain.

Turkic nomads entered the area from the 5th century AD and control subsequently passed to Arabs, who introduced Islam to Transoxiana in the 8th century. The Persian Samanid dynasty, centred on the cities of Bukhara, Samarkand and Heart, held sway from around AD 875 for over a century, before falling to the Khara-Khanid Khanate.

Much of present-day Uzbekistan came under the control of Seljuk Turks from the 11th century. Led by Alp Arslan, they went on to conquer Georgia, Armenia, Syria and most of Anatolia. Khwarazm in northwest Uzbekistan gained independence from the Seljuks in the late 12th century, expanding westward as far as the Caspian Sea. Genghis Khan's Mongol Hordes overran Central Asia from 1221 and retained power until the rise of Timur, who made his native Samarkand the capital of an empire that by 1405 stretched from western India to the Black Sea. The subsequent Timurid dynasty was ruled by Shahrukh and, from 1447, by Ulugh-beg. Located on the trade routes between Europe, Persia, India and China, the oasis cities of Samarkand, Bukhara and Tashkent became prosperous centres of culture and learning.

The Uzbeks were Turkic-speaking tribes who moved into the region from the steppes to the north of the Aral Sea from the early 16th century. They established separate principalities, notably the Emirate of Bukhara and the Khanates of Khiva and Kokand. The fall of the Timurid Empire presaged the gradual decline of the Central Asian trade routes, partly as a result of the opening of shipping lines between Western Europe and India and East Asia.

During the 1850s the Russian empire began to expand into central Asia. In 1865 Russian forces seized the city of Tashkent and a year later the Khanate of Kokand was dissolved and incorporated into the Governor-Generalship of Turkestan. The Khanate of Khiva and the Emirate of Bukhara became protectorates. Russian colonists, settling throughout Central Asia, developed the region's infrastructure while exploiting the abundant minerals and promoting the growth of cash crops such as cotton. There were periodic revolts against Russian rule, notably the Andizhan Uprising of 1898. The chaos surrounding the Bolshevik Revolution of 1917 precipitated the growth of an Uzbek guerrilla army, 'the Basmachi', although their efforts to establish a democratic republic were unsuccessful. In 1924 the Khorezm and Bukhara People's Republics were incorporated into the Uzbekistan Soviet Socialist Republic (SSR), which also included Tajikistan until it became a separate SSR in 1929. The Soviet period brought collectivization and rapid industrialization, particularly around the capital, Tashkent, leading to an influx of Russian migrant workers. Uzbekistan SSR became the primary cotton-producing region of the Soviet Union, although the large-scale diversion of rivers for irrigation had disastrous consequences for the Aral Sea, which lost two-thirds of its volume.

On 20 June 1990 the Supreme Soviet adopted a declaration of sovereignty, although the Communist Party, led by Islam Karimov, remained the only official political party. Following the collapse of the Soviet Union, Uzbekistan was declared an independent republic on 31 Aug. 1991. In Dec. 1991 Uzbekistan became a member of the Commonwealth of Independent States and Karimov was elected president by popular vote. He subsequently cracked down on political opponents, notably the Birlik party and the Islamic Renaissance Party, citing the need for 'stability'.

Bomb blasts in Tashkent, one of which almost killed the president in Feb. 1999, were blamed on extremists from the Islamist Movement of Uzbekistan (IMU), which operates largely in the Ferghana valley and aims to create a pan-Central Asian Islamic state. The IMU leader, Juma Namangoniy, was reportedly killed in Aug. 2002. Nearly 50 people died in a series of bombings and shootings in March 2004, allegedly perpetrated by Islamic militants. Suicide bombers targeted the US and Israeli embassies in Tashkent in July 2004.

On 13 May 2005 several hundred demonstrators were killed in Andizhan after troops fired into a crowd protesting against the imprisonment of local businessmen. The USA joined calls for an international inquiry into the shootings. In Nov. 2005 the USA closed its military air base at Karshi-Khanabad which had been used for operations in Afghanistan.

Territory and Population

Uzbekistan is bordered in the north by Kazakhstan, in the east by Kyrgyzstan and Tajikistan, in the south by Afghanistan and in the west by Turkmenistan. Area, 444,103 sq. km (171,469 sq. miles), including 22,000 sq. km (8,500 sq. miles) of inland water. A census has not been held since 1989, when the population was 19,810,077. A 'mini-census' based on 10% of the population was conducted in April 2011 but there are no future plans for a full census. Estimate, Jan. 2017: 32,120,500, giving a density of 76·1 per sq. km. The vast majority of the population are Uzbeks, with small Tajik, Kazakh, Tatar and Russian minorities. In 2010, 63·8% of the population lived in rural areas.

The UN gives a projected population for 2020 of 33·24m.

The areas and populations of the 12 regions, the Karakalpak Autonomous Republic (Karakalpakstan) and the city of Tashkent are as follows (Uzbek spellings in brackets):

Region	Area (in sq. km)	Population (2017 estimate)	Capital	Population (2014 estimate)
Andizhan (Andijon)	4,303	2,962,500	Andizhan	403,900
Bukhara (Bukhoro)	41,937	1,843,500	Bukhara	272,500
Dzhizak (Jizzakh)	21,179	1,301,000	Dzhizak	163,200
Ferghana (Farghona)	7,005	3,564,800	Ferghana	264,900
Khorezm (Khorazm)	6,464	1,776,700	Urgench (Urganch)	137,300
Kashkadar (Qashqadaryo)	28,568	3,088,800	Karshi (Qarshi)	254,600
Karakalpak Autonomous Republic (Qoraqalpoghiston)	161,358	1,817,500	Nukus (Nuqus)	295,200
Namangan	7,181	2,652,400	Namangan	475,700
Navoi (Nawoiy)	109,375	942,800	Nawoiy	134,100
Samarkand (Samarqand)	16,773	3,651,700	Samarkand	509,000
Syr-Darya (Sirdaryo)	4,276	803,100	Gulistan (Guliston)	77,300[1]
Surkhan-Darya (Surkhondaryo)	20,099	2,462,300	Termez (Termiz)	136,200
Tashkent (Toshkent)	15,258	2,829,300	Tashkent	2,352,900
Tashkent City (Toshkent Shari)	327	2,424,100	—	—

[1]2010 estimate.

Regions are further subdivided into 227 districts and cities.

The capital is Tashkent (2014 population estimate, 2,352,900); other large towns are Namangan, Samarkand, Andizhan, Nukus, Bukhara, Karshi, Kokand, Ferghana, Margilan, Chirchik and Urgench.

© Springer Nature Limited 2020
Palgrave Macmillan (ed.), *The Statesman's Yearbook 2020*,
https://doi.org/10.1057/978-1-349-95940-2_202

The Roman alphabet (in use 1929–40) was reintroduced in 1994. The Arabic script was in use prior to 1929, and Cyrillic from 1940-94.

The official language is Uzbek. Russian and Tajik are also spoken.

Social Statistics

2009 births, 649,700; deaths, 130,700; marriages, 227,600; divorces, 17,200. Rates, 2009: birth (per 1,000 population), 23·3; death, 4·7; marriage, 10·0; divorce, 0·6. Life expectancy, 2013, 65·0 years for men and 71·7 for women. Annual population growth rate, 2003–13, 1·2%. Infant mortality, 2010, 44 per 1,000 live births; fertility rate, 2013, 2·3 births per woman.

Climate

The summers are warm to hot with low humidity. The winters are cold but generally dry and sunny. Tashkent, Jan. –1°C, July 25°C. Annual rainfall 14·8" (375 mm).

Constitution and Government

A new constitution was adopted on 8 Dec. 1992 stating that Uzbekistan is a pluralist democracy. The constitution restricts the president to standing for two five-year terms. In Jan. 2002 a referendum was held at which 91% of the electorate voted in favour of extending the presidential term from five to seven years. Voters were also in favour of changing from a single-chamber legislature to a bicameral parliament. Based on the constitution then President Karimov's term of office that started in Jan. 2000 ended in Jan. 2007, but according to election law a vote must be held in Dec. of the year in which the president's term expires. Pro-Karimov legislators maintained that he was eligible to stand again in the Dec. 2007 elections as he had only served one seven-year term despite having been president since 1990.

Uzbekistan switched to a bicameral legislature in Jan. 2005 with the establishment of the 100-member *Senate* (with 16 members appointed by the president and 84 elected from the ranks of regional, district and city legislative councils). The lower house is the 150-member *Oliy Majlis* (Supreme Assembly). 135 seats are elected by popular vote for five-year terms and 15 are reserved for the Ecological Movement.

National Anthem

'Serquyosh, hur o'lkam, elga baxt najot' ('Stand tall, my free country, good fortune and salvation to you'); words by Abdulla Aripov, tune by Mutal Burhanov.

Government Chronology

President since 1990. (LDP = Liberal Democratic Party; UNRDP = Uzbekistan National Revival Democratic Party; n/p = non-partisan)

1990–2016	n/p	Islam Abduganiyevich Karimov
2016	UNRDP	Nigmatilla Yuldashev (acting)
2016–	LDP	Shavkat Mirziyoyev

Recent Elections

In parliamentary elections held in two rounds on 21 Dec. 2014 and 4 Jan. 2015, the Liberal Democratic Party won 52 of the 150 seats, followed by the Uzbekistan National Revival Democratic Party with 36, the People's Democratic Party of Uzbekistan with 27 and the Justice Social Democratic Party with 20. A further 15 seats were reserved for the Ecological Movement of Uzbekistan. All parties taking part in the election were loyal to President Islam Karimov—opposition parties were barred from participating. Turnout was 88·9% in the first round and 76·9% in the second.

Presidential elections were held on 4 Dec. 2016 following the death of incumbent President Islam Karimov on 2 Sept. In accordance with the constitution, the election was to be held within three months of Karimov's death. Prime Minister Shavkat Mirziyoyev (Liberal Democratic Party) took 88·6% of the vote, against 3·7% for Khatamjon Ketmonov, 3·5% for Narimon Umarov and 2·4% for Sarvar Otamuradov. The OSCE noted cases of ballot box stuffing, widespread proxy voting and irregularities during counting. Turnout was 87·8%.

Current Government

President: Shavkat Mirziyoyev; b. 1957 (Liberal Democratic Party; since 8 Sept. 2016—acting until 14 Dec. 2016).

In Feb. 2019 the government comprised:

Prime Minister: Abdulla Aripov; b. 1961 (Liberal Democratic Party; since 14 Dec. 2016).

First Deputy Prime Minister: Achilbay Ramatov (also *Minister of Transport*).

Deputy Prime Ministers: Aziz Abduhakimov; Eliyor Ganiev; Jamshid Kuchkarov (also *Minister of Finance*); Tanzila Narbaeva.

Minister of Agriculture: Jamshid Khodjaev. *Culture:* Bakhtiyor Sayfullayev. *Defence:* Bakhodir Kurbanov. *Development of Information Technologies and Communications:* Shukhrat Sadikov. *Economy:* Batyr Khojayev. *Emergency Situations:* Rustam Juraev. *Employment Relations and Labour:* Sherzod Kudbiev. *Energy:* Alisher Sultanov. *Foreign Affairs:* Abdulaziz Kamilov. *Higher and Secondary Specialized Education:* Inom Majidov. *Internal Affairs:* Pulat Bobojonov. *Innovative Development:* Ibrohim Abdurahmonov. *Investment and Foreign Trade:* Sardor Umurzakov. *Justice:* Ruslanbek Davletov. *Physical Culture and Sports:* Dilmurod Nabiyev. *Preschool Education:* Agrippina Shin. *Public Education:* Sherzod Shermatov. *Public Health:* Alisher Shadmanov. *Water Management:* Shavkat Hamroyev.

Office of the President: http://www.gov.uz

Current Leaders

Shavkat Mirziyoyev

Position
President

Introduction
Shavkat Mirziyoyev was elected president on 4 Dec. 2016 after a three-month period as interim president following the death of Islam Karimov, who had dominated Uzbek politics since the country gained independence in 1991. As prime minister from 2003–16 and a loyal servant to Karimov, Mirziyoyev was expected to pursue similar policies.

Early Life
Mirziyoyev was born on 24 July 1957 in Soviet Uzbekistan. He received a doctorate in technological sciences from the Tashkent Institute of Irrigation and Melioration in 1981, where he subsequently won a fellowship before rising to become vice-rector for academic affairs. Mirziyoyev served as governor of the Dzhizak and Samarkand regions before being selected by Karimov to become premier in 2003.

Career in Office
Mirziyoyev maintained a low profile as prime minister, which an investigative media report suggested was the result of his desire not to provoke jealousy from the president. He was, however, a close confidante of Karimov and was therefore the clear favourite to succeed him in the presidency. When Karimov died in Sept. 2016, Mirziyoyev stepped into the role in a caretaker capacity ahead of elections held in Dec. Having claimed 88·6% support at the disputed polls, he was sworn into office pledging to build on his predecessor's legacy. He has nevertheless needed to win over an international community suspicious of Karimov's track record of oppression and intolerance. Having initially made several new cabinet appointments in Dec. 2017, including Abdulla Aripov as prime minister, Mirziyoyev subsequently dismissed Rustam Azimov as first deputy prime minister in June 2017 in a perceived move against an influential political rival.

Abroad, Mirziyoyev has taken steps to strengthen ties with Uzbekistan's neighbours. His visits to Turkmenistan and Kazakhstan shortly after his election and to Kyrgyzstan in Sept. 2017 raised hopes for broader regional economic co-operation, while in Feb. 2017 the first commercial flight for 20 years between Uzbekistan and Tajikistan took place. In April 2018 Mirziyoyev announced Uzbekistan's intention to join the Council of Co-operation of the Turkic-Speaking States, also known as the Turkic Council, founded by Azerbaijan, Kazakhstan, Kyrgyzstan and Turkey.

Defence

Conscription is for 12 months. Defence expenditure in 2010 totalled US$1,422m. (US$51 per capita), representing 3·7% of GDP.

Army

Personnel, 2011, 50,000. There are, in addition, paramilitary forces totalling up to 20,000.

Air Force

Personnel, 2011, 17,000. There were 135 combat-capable aircraft in operation (including Su-17s, Su-24s, Su-25s, Su-27s and MiG-29s) and 29 attack helicopters.

Economy

Agriculture accounted for 17·6% of GDP in 2016, industry 32·9% and services 49·5%.

Overview

After the collapse of the Soviet Union, Uzbekistan embarked on cautious economic reform. However, there remain state controls on planning, foreign exchange, trade and investment aimed at achieving import-substitution industrialization and self-sufficiency in food and energy. The land is rich in natural resources, and primary commodities account for the majority of exports. Uzbekistan is the world's second largest cotton exporter behind the USA.

Economic growth averaged 8·2% per year between 2008 and 2015. Despite a challenging external environment the outlook remains positive, based on a continuation of counter-cyclical policies, a bottoming-out of commodity prices and a gradual deepening of the reform agenda.

Although social indicators have improved, 13·7% of the population lived below the national poverty line in 2014. With the goal of becoming an industrialized, upper-middle income country by 2030, the government is continuing the transition towards a more market-oriented economy and plans further investment in infrastructure and social services.

Currency

A coupon for a new unit of currency, the *soum* (UZS), was introduced alongside the rouble on 15 Nov. 1993. This was replaced by the *soum* proper at 1 soum = 1,000 coupons on 1 July 1994. In 1994 inflation was 1,568%, but it reached more stable levels of 8·0% in 2016 and 12·5% in 2017.

Budget

In 2012 budgetary central government revenue amounted to 12,610bn. soums and expenditure to 10,837bn. soums.

VAT is 20%.

Performance

Real GDP growth was 7·9% in 2015, 7·8% in 2016 and 5·3% in 2017. Total GDP in 2017 was US$48·7bn.

Banking and Finance

The Central Bank is the bank of issue (*Chairman*, Mamarizo Nurmuratov). In 2015 there were 26 commercial banks, of which eight were privately owned. In 2010 foreign debt amounted to US$7,404m., equivalent to 19·0% of GNI.

Energy and Natural Resources

Environment

Irrigation of arid areas has caused the drying up of the Aral Sea. Uzbekistan's carbon dioxide emissions from the consumption of energy in 2011 were the equivalent of 4·2 tonnes per capita.

Electricity

Installed capacity was an estimated 12·4m. kW in 2011. Production was 52·4bn. kWh in 2011 and consumption per capita 1,858 kWh.

Oil and Gas

Oil production was 3·2m. tonnes in 2012; natural gas output was 56·9bn. cu. metres. In 2012 there were proven oil reserves of 0·6bn. bbls and natural gas reserves of 1·1trn. cu. metres.

Minerals

Lignite production in 2011 was 3·78m. tonnes. In 2010 an estimated 90 tonnes of gold and 59 tonnes of silver were produced. There are also large reserves of uranium, copper, lead, zinc and tungsten; all uranium mined (an estimated 2,500 tonnes in 2011) is exported.

Agriculture

Farming is intensive and based on irrigation. In 2013 there were an estimated 4·40m. ha. of arable land and 0·37m. ha. of permanent cropland. Approximately 4·22m. ha. were equipped for irrigation in 2013.

Areas harvested, 2013: wheat, 1·44m. ha.; seed cotton, 1·31m. ha.; grapes, 114,000 ha.; barley, 91,000 ha.; apples (estimate), 90,000 ha. Output of main agricultural products (2013, in 1,000 tonnes): wheat, 6,842; seed cotton, 3,361; tomatoes, 2,247; potatoes, 2,205; cottonseed (estimate), 1,849; carrots and turnips, 1,642; watermelons, 1,558; grapes, 1,322; cotton lint (estimate), 1,094; onions, 1,067; cabbages, kale, etc., 905; apples (estimate), 894. Livestock, 2013: 14·2m. sheep; 10·1m. cattle; 3·0m. goats; 46m. chickens (estimate). Livestock products, 2013 (in 1,000 tonnes): beef and veal, 750; lamb and mutton, 166; pork and pork products, 35; poultry meat, 45; cow's milk, 7,845; goat's milk (estimate), 39; eggs (estimate), 246.

Forestry

In 2015 the area under forests was 3·22m. ha., accounting for 7% of the total land area. Of the total area under forests 2% was primary forest in 2015, 73% other naturally regenerated forest and 25% planted forest. In 2011, 30,000 cu. metres of timber were produced.

Fisheries

The total catch in 2015 was 22,954 tonnes, exclusively freshwater fish.

Industry

Major industries include fertilizers, agricultural and textile machinery, aircraft, metallurgy, chemicals, food processing, building materials and the manufacture of textiles. Industrial production grew by 4·2% in 2012.

Labour

The labour force in 2013 was 13,303,000 (10,084,000 in 2003). 64·7% of the population aged 15–64 was economically active in 2013. In the same year 10·8% of the population was unemployed.

Uzbekistan had 0·17m. people living in slavery according to the Walk Free Foundation's 2013 *Global Slavery Index*.

International Trade

Imports and Exports

In 2010 imports were valued at US$8,386m. and exports at US$11,587m. The leading trading partners in 2010 were Russia, South Korea and China for imports, and Russia, Kazakhstan and China for exports. Principal imports are machinery and equipment, parts and components of motor vehicles, pharmaceutical products and petroleum oils. Main exports are gold, mineral fuels, mineral oils and distillation products, and cotton.

Communications

Roads

Length of roads, 2005, was 84,400 km (85% paved).

Rail

The total length of railway in 2011 was 4,258 km of 1,520 mm gauge (727 km electrified). In 2011, 16·0m. passengers and 80·9m. tonnes of freight were carried. There is a metro in Tashkent.

Civil Aviation

The main international airport is in Tashkent (Vostochny). Andizhan, Bukhara, Ferghana, Karshi, Namangan, Navoi, Nukus, Samarkand, Termez, Urgench and Zarafshan also have airports. The national carrier is the state-owned Uzbekistan Airways, which in 2010 operated domestic services and flew to Almaty, Amritsar, Ashgabat, Astana, Athens, Baku, Bangkok, Beijing, Bishkek, Delhi, Dubai, Ekaterinburg, Frankfurt, Geneva, İstanbul, Kazan, Krasnodar, Krasnoyarsk, Kuala Lumpur, Kyiv, Lahore, London, Milan, Mineralnye Vody, Moscow, New York, Novosibirsk, Osaka, Paris, Riga, Rome, Rostov, St Petersburg, Samara, Seoul, Sharjah, Simferopol, Sochi, Tel Aviv, Tokyo, Tyumen, Ufa and Urumqi. In 2012 scheduled airline traffic of Uzbekistan-based carriers flew 44·0m. km; passenger-km totalled 6·3bn. in the same year. In 2009 Tashkent handled 1,940,985 passengers and 35,791 tonnes of freight.

Telecommunications

In 2012 there were 1,980,000 main (fixed) telephone lines; mobile phone subscriptions numbered 20,274,000 in the same year (710·3 per 1,000 persons). In 2013 an estimated 38·2% of the population were internet users. In March 2012 there were 129,000 Facebook users.

Social Institutions

Out of 178 countries analysed in the 2017 *Fragile States Index*—a list published jointly by the Fund for Peace and *Foreign Policy* magazine—Uzbekistan was ranked the 63rd most vulnerable to conflict or collapse. The index is based on 12 indicators of state vulnerability across social, political and economic categories.

Justice

The upper level of the judicial system comprises the Constitutional Court, the Supreme Court and the High Economic Court. Lower court systems exist at the regional, district and town levels. The population in penal institutions in Dec. 2012 was approximately 42,000 (152 per 100,000 of national population). The death penalty, last used in 2005, was abolished in Jan. 2008. Uzbekistan was ranked 49th of 102 countries for criminal justice and 66th for civil justice in the 2015 World Justice Project *Rule of Law Index*, which provides data on how the rule of law is experienced by the general public across eight categories.

Education

In 2007 there were 562,000 pre-primary pupils with 60,642 teaching staff, 2·16m. primary pupils with 118,676 teaching staff and 4·60m. secondary pupils with 352,001 teaching staff. There were 288,550 students and 23,354 academic staff in tertiary education in 2007. There are universities and medical schools in Tashkent and Samarkand. Adult literacy rate in 2009 was estimated at 99·3% (99·6% among males and 99·1% among females).

Health

In 2013 there were 40 hospital beds per 10,000 population. There were 72,237 physicians in 2014 (24·5 per 10,000 population), plus 368,250 nursing and midwifery personnel, 4,520 dentistry personnel and 1,243 pharmaceutical personnel. Expenditure on health in 2014 was 5·9% of GDP.

Welfare

There is a statutory pension system consisting of two pillars: a public pay-as-you-go defined-benefit pension scheme and (since 2005) a mandatory public funded defined-contribution scheme. The larger pay-as-you-go pillar provides income to approximately 2·8m. people.

Religion

In 2010 an estimated 96·7% of the population were Muslims (mainly Sunnis) according to the Pew Research Center's Forum on Religion & Public Life, with 2·3% Christians.

Culture

World Heritage Sites

Uzbekistan has five sites on the UNESCO World Heritage List: Itchan Kala (inscribed on the list in 1990); the Historic Centre of Bukhara (1993); the Historic Centre of Shakhrisyabz (2000); Samarkand—Crossroads of Cultures (2001). Shared with Kazakhstan and Kyrgyzstan, Western Tien-Shan (2016) is a transnational property located in one of the largest mountain ranges in the world.

Press

In 2008 there were four paid-for daily newspapers with a combined circulation of 30,000.

Tourism

There were 975,000 non-resident tourist arrivals in 2010 (1,215,000 in 2009), excluding same-day visitors.

Diplomatic Representatives

Of Uzbekistan in the United Kingdom (41 Holland Park, London, W11 3RP)
    Ambassador: Alisher Shaykhov.

Of the United Kingdom in Uzbekistan (67 Gulyamov St., 100000 Tashkent)
    Ambassador: Christopher Allan.

Of Uzbekistan in the USA (1746 Massachusetts Ave., NW, Washington, D.C., 20036)
    Ambassador: Javlon Vakhabov.

Of the USA in Uzbekistan (3 Moyqorghon St., 5th Block, Yunusobod District, 100093 Tashkent)
    Ambassador: Vacant.
    Chargé d'Affaires a.i.: Alan D. Meltzer.

Of Uzbekistan to the United Nations
    Ambassador: Bakhtiyor Ibragimov.

Of Uzbekistan to the European Union
    Ambassador: Vladimir Norov.

Karakalpak Autonomous Republic (Karakalpakstan)

Under Russian rule from the second half of the 19th century, the territory was constituted within the then Kazakh Autonomous Republic (of the Russian Federation) as an Autonomous Region in 1925. In March 1932 it became an Autonomous Republic within the Russian Federation, and in Dec. 1936 it became part of the Uzbek SSR. Area, 166,600 sq. km (64,320 sq. miles); population, 1,692,800 (2012). Capital, Nukus. The main ethnic groups are Qoraqalpoghs, Uzbeks and Kazakhs. Manufacturing includes bricks, leather goods, furniture, canning and wine. Principal crops are rice and cotton, although the shrinking of the Aral Sea has had a detrimental effect on agriculture. In 2011 the poverty rate was 32%. Karakalpak State University was established in 1976.

Further Reading

Uzbekistan

Bohr, A. (ed.) *Uzbekistan: Politics and Foreign Policy.* 1998
Kalter, J. and Pavaloi, M., *Uzbekistan: Heir to the Silk Road.* 1997
Melvin, N. J., *Uzbekistan: Transition to Authoritarianism on the Silk Road.* 2000
Yalcin, Resul, *The Rebirth of Uzbekistan: Politics, Economy and Society in the Post-Soviet Era.* 2002
National Statistical Office: State Committee of the Republic of Uzbekistan on Statistics, Mustakillik Avenue 63, Tashkent 100077.
Website: https://stat.uz

Vanuatu

Ripablik blong Vanuatu (Republic of Vanuatu)

Capital: Port Vila
Population projection, 2020: 294,000
GNI per capita, 2017: (PPP$) 2,995
HDI/world rank, 2017: 0·603/138
Internet domain extension: .vu

Key Historical Events

Vanuatu occupies the group of islands formerly known as the New Hebrides, in the southwestern Pacific Ocean. Capt. Bligh and his companions, cast adrift by the *Bounty* mutineers, sailed through part of the island group in 1789. Sandalwood merchants and European missionaries came to the islands in the mid-19th century and were then followed by cotton planters—mostly French and British—in 1868. In response to Australian calls to annexe the islands, Britain and France agreed on joint supervision. Joint sovereignty was held over the indigenous Melanesian people but each nation retained responsibility for its own nationals according to a protocol of 1914. The island group escaped Japanese invasion during the Second World War and became an Allied base. On 30 July 1980 New Hebrides became an independent nation under the name of Vanuatu, meaning 'Our Land Forever'.

Territory and Population

Vanuatu comprises 83 islands (65 of which are inhabited), which lie roughly 800 km west of Fiji and 400 km northeast of New Caledonia. The estimated land area is 12,190 sq. km (4,706 sq. miles). The larger islands of the group are: Espiritu Santo, Malekula, Epi, Pentecost, Aoba, Maewo, Paama, Ambrym, Efate, Erromanga, Tanna and Aneityum. They also claim Matthew and Hunter islands. Population at the 2016 census, 272,459, giving a density of 22·4 per sq. km.

The UN gives a projected population for 2020 of 294,000.

In 2016, 75·1% of the population lived in rural areas. Port Vila (the capital) had a 2016 census population of 51,437 and Luganville 16,312.

39% of the population is under 15 years of age, 55% between the ages of 15 and 59 and 6% 60 or over.

The national language is Bislama (spoken by 57% of the population): English and French are also official languages; about 30,000 speak French.

Social Statistics

2008 estimates: births, 7,100; deaths, 1,200. Rates, 2008 estimates (per 1,000 population): births, 30·2; deaths, 5·0. Annual population growth rate, 2000–08, 2·6%. Life expectancy, 2013, was 69·7 years for males and 73·8 years for females. Infant mortality, 2010, 12 per 1,000 live births; fertility rate, 2008, 4·0 births per woman.

Climate

The climate is tropical, but moderated by oceanic influences and by trade winds from May to Oct. High humidity occasionally occurs and cyclones are possible. Rainfall ranges from 90" (2,250 mm) in the south to 155" (3,875 mm) in the north. Vila, Jan. 80°F (26·7°C), July 72°F (22·2°C). Annual rainfall 84" (2,103 mm).

Constitution and Government

Legislative power resides in a 52-member unicameral Parliament elected for a term of four years. The *President* is elected for a five-year term by an electoral college comprising Parliament and the presidents of the 11 regional councils. Executive power is vested in a Council of Ministers, responsible to Parliament, and appointed and led by a Prime Minister who is elected from and by Parliament.

There is also a *Council of Chiefs,* comprising traditional tribal leaders, to advise on matters of custom.

National Anthem

'Yumi, yumi, yumi i glat blong talem se, yumi, yumi, yumi i man blong Vanuatu' ('We, we, we are glad to tell, we, we, we are the people of Vanuatu'); words and tune by F. Vincent Ayssav.

Recent Elections

Tallis Obed Moses was elected president on 6 July 2017 by an electoral college after a series of votes in the fourth round of voting, receiving 40 of 57 votes. There were 15 other candidates in the election.

Parliamentary elections were held on 22 Jan. 2016. The Party of Our Land (Vanua'aka Pati/VP) won six of 52 seats, as did the Union of Moderate Parties (Union des Partis Moderés/UMP) and the Ground and Justice Party (Graon mo Jastis Pati/GJP); the National United Party/NUP and Iauko Group/IG both won four seats; Reunification of Movements for Change/RMC and Nagriamel/NAG both won three. A number of smaller parties each took one or two seats and eight went to independents.

Current Government

President: Tallis Obed Moses; b. 1954 (ind.; sworn in 6 July 2017).

In Feb. 2019 the government comprised:

Prime Minister: Charlot Salwai; b. 1963 (RMC; took office on 11 Feb. 2016).

Deputy Prime Minister, and Minister of Tourism, Commerce, Trades and ni-Vanuatu Business: Bob Loughman.

Minister of Agriculture, Forestry, Livestock, Fisheries and Biodiversity: Hosea Nevu. *Education:* Jean-Pierre Nirua. *Finance and Economic Management:* Gaetan Pikioune. *Foreign Affairs and External Trade:* Ralph Regenvanu. *Health:* Jack Norris. *Infrastructure and Public Utilities:* Christophe Emelee. *Internal Affairs:* Andrew Napuat. *Justice and Community Services:* Don Ken. *Lands and Natural Resources:* Alfred Maoh. *Planning and Climate Change Adaptation:* Ham Lini. *Youth and Sport:* Simeon Seule.

Government Website: http://www.gov.vu

Current Leaders

Charlot Salwai

Position
Prime Minister

Introduction
Charlot Salwai, a Francophone economist and politician, was elected prime minister by parliament at the head of a coalition government in Feb. 2016.

Early Life
A member of the French-speaking minority, Salwai was born on Pentecost Island. Having qualified as an accountant, he worked for a national development bank between 1988 and 1990. He subsequently became private secretary to the then prime minister, Maxime Carlot Korman, until 1995, before taking up a variety of governmental and advisory positions.

He was initially elected to parliament in 2002 for the Pentecost constituency, and was returned again in 2004, 2008, 2012 and 2016. Over this period he variously served as minister for trade and industry, lands and natural resources, education, finance and economic management, and internal affairs. In 2012 he founded a political party, the Reunification of Movements for Change.

Career in Office
On 11 Feb. 2016 Salwai was elected prime minister, leading the Unity for Change coalition of political parties. His appointment resulted from a snap

election held in Jan. 2016 following the dissolution of parliament in Nov. 2015 after numerous politicians were convicted of bribery.

Salwai is the third parliamentary representative from Pentecost to be premier since Vanuatu's independence in 1980. With two-thirds of parliament's members being newly elected, he claimed that the people of Vanuatu had 'voted for change'. He emphasized the need for national unity and pledged to champion several infrastructure development projects. He has also had to address the physical destruction wrought by a powerful cyclone in March 2015. In 2017 there was speculation about Salwai's state of health amid reports of a stroke, although the government denied that there was an issue. In Dec. that year, following a cabinet reshuffle, he survived a parliamentary no-confidence vote by a majority of 37 to 13.

In Jan. 2019 Scott Morrison became the first Australian prime minister to visit Vanuatu in nearly 30 years.

Defence

Vanuatu does not have an army but there is a Vanuatu Police Force and a paramilitary Vanuatu Mobile Force.

Economy

In 2011 agriculture accounted for 25·2% of GDP, industry 10·7% and services 64·1%.

Overview
The largest sectors are agriculture, fishing, offshore financial services and tourism. Efforts have been made to boost tourism by improving air travel connections and cruise ship facilities. The export base is narrow, consisting mainly of copra, beef, cocoa, timber and coffee. Remittances from seasonal workers in New Zealand are the country's second largest foreign exchange earner. Australia and New Zealand are the chief sources of foreign aid.

GDP grew at over 5% per year between 2005 and 2008 and even reached 3·5% in 2009 at the height of the global financial crisis (with growth particularly strong in telecommunications, agriculture and hospitality sectors). However, damaging tropical cyclones and growing political instability linked to corruption have since posed threats to Vanuatu's economic outlook. GDP fell by 0·8% in 2015, while public debt amounted to 21·5% of GDP.

Currency
The unit of currency is the *vatu* (VUV) with no minor unit. There was inflation of 0·8% in 2016 and 3·1% in 2017. Foreign exchange reserves in July 2005 were US$60m. and total money supply was 14,373m. vatu.

Budget
In 2016 budgetary central government revenues totalled 26,897m. vatu (including taxes, 14,231m. vatu) and expenditures 21,649m. vatu (including compensation of employees, 9,107m. vatu).

VAT is 15%.

Performance
Vanuatu experienced a two-year recession in 2001 and 2002, when the economy contracted by 3·4% and 5·2% respectively. More recently the economy expanded by 0·2% in 2015, 3·5% in 2016 and 4·2% in 2017. Total GDP in 2017 was US$0·9bn.

Banking and Finance
The Reserve Bank of Vanuatu (*Governor,* Simeon Athy) is the central bank and bank of issue. There is also the state-owned National Bank, plus three other banks—ANZ Bank Ltd, Westpac Banking Corp. and BRED. Total assets and liabilities of commercial banks at 31 Dec. 2009 were 80,527m. vatu.

External debt totalled US$148m. in 2010 and represented 20·9% of GNI.

Energy and Natural Resources

Environment
Vanuatu's carbon dioxide emissions from the consumption of energy in 2011 were the equivalent of 0·6 tonnes per capita.

Electricity
Electrical capacity in 2011 was 31,000 kW. Production in 2011 was about 68m. kWh and consumption per capita an estimated 280 kWh.

Agriculture

About 65% of the labour force are employed in agriculture. In 2014 there were approximately 20,000 ha. of arable land and 125,000 ha. of permanent crops. The main commercial crops are copra, coconuts, cocoa and coffee. Production (2013 estimates, in 1,000 tonnes): coconuts, 395; bananas, 16; groundnuts, 3; cocoa beans, 2. 80% of the population are engaged in subsistence agriculture; yams, taro, cassava, sweet potatoes and bananas are grown for local consumption.

Livestock (2013 estimates): cattle, 173,000; pigs, 94,000; goats, 25,000; chickens, 750,000.

Forestry
There were 0·44m. ha. of forest in 2015 (36% of the land area). In 2011, 119,000 cu. metres of roundwood were cut.

Fisheries
Fish landings in 2015 totalled 75,510 tonnes. The principal catch is tuna.

Industry

Principal industries include copra processing, meat canning and fish freezing, a saw-mill, soft drinks factories and a print works.

In 2011 industry accounted for 10·7% of GDP, with manufacturing contributing 4·8%.

International Trade

Imports and Exports
Merchandise imports in 2011 totalled US$280·6m. (US$276·0m. in 2010) and merchandise exports US$63·5m. (US$46·2m. in 2010).

Principal imports in 2011 were food, animals and beverages (24·5%), machinery and transport equipment, and mineral fuels and lubricants; main exports in 2011 were crude materials and animal and vegetable oils (49·4%), food, animals and beverages, and chemicals.

In 2007 the main import suppliers were Australia, New Zealand, Singapore, Fiji and China. The main export destinations were the Philippines, New Caledonia, Fiji, Japan and Singapore.

Communications

Roads
There are approximately 1,100 km of largely unpaved roads, mostly on Efate and Espiritu Santo. There were around 15,500 vehicles in use in 2008.

Civil Aviation
There is an international airport at Bauerfield Port Vila. In 2010 the state-owned Air Vanuatu flew to Auckland, Brisbane, Honiara, Nadi, Nouméa and Sydney as well as providing services between different parts of Vanuatu. In 2012 scheduled airline traffic of Vanuatu-based carriers flew 20·6m. km; passenger-km totalled 863·8m. in the same year.

Shipping
In Jan. 2014 there were 67 ships of 300 GT or over registered, totalling 1·34m. GT. Vanuatu is a 'flag of convenience' country. The chief ports are Port Vila and Santo.

Telecommunications
In 2012 there were 4,800 main (fixed) telephone lines; active mobile phone subscriptions numbered 146,000 in the same year (590·8 per 1,000 persons). In 2013 an estimated 11·3% of the population were internet users.

Social Institutions

Justice
The legal system is based on British common law and French civil law. There is a Supreme Court with a Chief Justice and a Magistrates Court.

The death penalty was abolished in 1980. The population in penal institutions in Dec. 2012 was 194 (76 per 100,000 of national population).

Education
In 2006 there were 1,316 pupils with 111 teaching staff in pre-primary schools. There were 38,000 pupils in primary schools in 2007 with 2,000 teaching staff, and 18,000 pupils in secondary schools in 2009.

There is a campus of the University of the South Pacific at Port Vila and a Vanuatu Institute of Technology. The adult literacy rate in 2009 was an estimated 82·0%. In 2009 public expenditure on education came to 5·0% of GDP.

Health

There were 46 physicians, 549 nursing and midwifery personnel, 17 dentistry personnel and 29 pharmaceutical personnel in 2012; and 41 hospital beds per 10,000 population in 2005.

In *Water: At What Cost? The State of the World's Water 2016*, WaterAid reported that 5·5% of the population does not have access to safe water.

Religion

In 2010 an estimated 93·3% of the population were Christians (mainly Protestants) and 4·1% folk religionists according to the Pew Research Center's Forum on Religion & Public Life.

Culture

World Heritage Sites

Vanuatu has one site on the UNESCO World Heritage List: Chief Roi Mata's Domain (inscribed on the list in 2008), three sites on the islands of Efate, Lelepa and Artok that contain the chief's residence and burial chamber.

Press

In 2008 there was one daily newspaper (the *Vanuatu Daily Post*) with a circulation of 3,000.

Tourism

In 2011 there were a record 248,898 non-resident visitor arrivals (154,938 by cruise ship and 93,960 by air), up from 237,648 in 2010 and 225,452 in 2009.

Diplomatic Representatives

Of Vanuatu in the United Kingdom
High Commissioner: Roy Mickey Joy (resides in Brussels).

Of the United Kingdom in Vanuatu
High Commissioner: David Ward (resides in Honiara, Solomon Islands).

Of Vanuatu in the USA and to the United Nations (685 Third Ave., Suite 1103, New York, NY 10017)
Ambassador: Odo Tevi.

Of the USA in Vanuatu
Ambassador: Catherine Ebert-Gray (resides in Port Moresby, Papua New Guinea).

Of Vanuatu to the European Union
Ambassador: John Licht.

Further Reading

Miles, W. F. S., *Bridging Mental Boundaries in a Postcolonial Microcosm: Identity and Development in Vanuatu*. 1998

National Statistical Office: Vanuatu Statistics Office, Private Mail Bag 019, Port Vila.

Website: https://vnso.gov.vu

Vatican City State

Stato della Città del Vaticano

Population projection, 2016: 836
Internet domain extension: .va

Key Historical Events

Ager Vaticanus was the name given to a marshy area to the west of the city of Rome, close to the river Tiber. Uninhabited for much of Rome's long history, the area was developed with villas and gardens during the first century, when the city expanded. At the peak of imperial power in the second century, Rome's population was estimated to have reached 1·6m.

Christian tradition holds that Saint Peter was crucified in Rome in AD 64 during a wave of Christian persecution ordered by Emperor Nero. Pilgrims flocked to his tomb, which, during the 4th century, became the centrepiece of a basilica commissioned by Emperor Constantine I. Constantine legalized Christianity in the Roman Empire in 313. A palace was constructed near the basilica early in the 5th century, during the pontificate of Pope Symmachus, although the Lateran Palace in southeast Rome served as the main papal residence for many centuries.

During the 7th century, as Byzantine power weakened across the Italian peninsula, the papacy—a major landowner—increasingly held sway over land beyond Rome. By 781 the pope had become temporal sovereign of territory (known as the Papal States) including Ravenna, the Duchy of the Pentapolis, parts of the Duchy of Benevento, Corsica, Lombardy, Tuscany and several Italian cities.

The papal court moved to Avignon in 1309, precipitated by a feud between Pope Boniface VIII and Philip IV of France. When Pope Gregory XI returned to Rome in 1377 his court took up residence at the Vatican, which remained the papal seat for the next two centuries. Plans to redevelop St Peter's basilica were drawn up in the mid-15th century but work did not begin until 1506, under Pope Julius II. The monumental new basilica—still the biggest church in Christendom—took 120 years to complete under the guidance of several designers and Renaissance masters, including Michelangelo.

When Rome was captured by Piedmont-led forces in 1871 and declared the capital of the Kingdom of Italy, papal temporal power was brought to an end. The Quirinale Palace, the papal residence since 1583, was confiscated and made the royal palace. Since then, popes have resided in the Vatican. On 11 Feb. 1929 a treaty with the Italian government recognized the sovereignty of the Holy See in the city of the Vatican. Both German and Allied forces respected the Vatican's neutrality during the Second World War.

In 1978 Karol Wojtyła, a Pole, was elected pope (taking the name John Paul II), becoming the first non-Italian to hold the position since 1523. When he died in 2005, he was succeeded by the German-born Cardinal Joseph Ratzinger (Pope Benedict XVI), who in 2013 became the first pope to resign the office since 1415. An Argentine cardinal, Jorge Bergoglio was elected next, adopting the papal name Francis. The first Latin American to be pope, he has faced the task of uniting a church beset by corruption and sexual abuse scandals and been confronted by a number of key doctrinal debates regarding the role of women in the church, the use of contraception and attitudes to same-sex marriage.

Territory and Population

The area of the Vatican City is 44 ha. or 0·44 sq. km (108·7 acres or 0·17 sq. miles), making it the smallest independent country in the world. It includes the Piazza di San Pietro (St Peter's Square), which is to remain normally open to the public and subject to the powers of the Italian police. It has its own railway station (for freight only), postal facilities, coins and radio. Twelve buildings in and outside Rome enjoy extra-territorial rights, including the Basilicas of St John Lateran, St Mary Major and St Paul without the Walls, the Pope's summer villa at Castel Gandolfo and a further Vatican radio station on Italian soil. *Radio Vaticana* broadcasts an extensive service in 40 languages from the transmitters in Vatican City and in Italy. The Holy See and the Vatican are not synonymous—the Holy See, referring to the primacy of the Pope, is located in Vatican City. The *de facto* official language is Latin. Vatican City had 836 inhabitants in 2016.

Constitution and Government

Vatican City State is governed by a Commission appointed by the Pope. The reason for its existence is to provide an extra-territorial, independent base for the Holy See, the government of the Roman Catholic Church. The Pope exercises sovereignty and has absolute legislative, executive and judicial powers. The judicial power is delegated to a tribunal in the first instance, to the Sacred Roman Rota in appeal and to the Supreme Tribunal of the Signature in final appeal.

A new Fundamental Law was promulgated by Pope John Paul II on 26 Nov. 2000 and became effective on 22 Feb. 2001; this replaced the first Fundamental Law of 1929. The Pope is elected by the College of Cardinals, meeting in secret conclave. The election is by scrutiny and requires a two-thirds majority.

National Anthem

'Inno e Marcia Pontificale' ('Hymn and Pontifical March'); words by Raffaello Lavagna, tune by Charles-François Gounod.

Government Chronology

Popes since 1939.

1939–58	Pius XII (Eugenio Maria Pacelli)	Italian
1958–63	John XXIII (Angelo Giuseppe Roncalli)	Italian
1963–78	Paul VI (Giovanni Battista Montini)	Italian
1978	John Paul I (Albino Luciani)	Italian
1978–2005	John Paul II (Karol Józef Wojtyła)	Polish
2005–13	Benedict XVI (Joseph Aloisius Ratzinger)	German
2013–	Francis (Jorge Mario Bergoglio)	Argentinian

Current Government

Supreme Pontiff: Francis (Jorge Mario Bergoglio), born in Buenos Aires, Argentina, 17 Dec. 1936. Archbishop of Buenos Aires 1998–2013, created Cardinal in 2001, elected Pope 13 March 2013, inaugurated 19 March 2013. Pope Francis is the first Latin American to be elected Pope, the first Jesuit and the first non-European Pope since 741.

> *Secretary of State:* Archbishop Pietro Parolin.
> *Secretary for Relations with Other States:* Archbishop Paul Gallagher.
> *Office of the Sovereign of the Vatican City:* http://w2.vatican.va

Current Leaders

Pope Francis

Introduction

Jorge Bergoglio became Pope Francis after being elected head of the Roman Catholic Church on 13 March 2013 following the resignation of Benedict XVI. He is the first pope from Latin America and the first Jesuit to hold the post. Seen as an outsider untarnished by the internal power struggles within the Curia and free from the taint of association with the Church's sex abuse scandals, he is known for his austerity. Bergoglio chose his papal name in honour of St Francis of Assisi, famous for his pledge of poverty and humility.

Early Life

Jorge Mario Bergoglio was born in the Flores district of Buenos Aires on 17 Dec. 1936 to Italian immigrant parents. Having completed a high school diploma in chemistry, in 1955 he enrolled at the Inmaculada Concepción

© Springer Nature Limited 2020
Palgrave Macmillan (ed.), *The Statesman's Yearbook 2020*,
https://doi.org/10.1057/978-1-349-95940-2_204

seminary in Buenos Aires. In March 1958 he joined the Society of Jesus (Jesuits) as a novice. In 1960 he graduated in philosophy from the Colegio Máximo San José.

On 13 Dec. 1969 Bergoglio was ordained as a priest. He completed his tertianship, a required period of strict discipline undertaken by Jesuits, at Alcalá de Henares in Spain and took his final vows on 22 April 1973. He served as the Jesuit Provincial Superior for Argentina from 1973–79 and as rector of the philosophical and theological faculty at the Jesuit University in San Miguel from 1980–86.

Bergoglio was appointed titular Bishop of Auca and Auxiliary of Buenos Aires in May 1992. In Feb. 1998 he became Archbishop of Buenos Aires. During his tenure, Bergoglio became known for his work with the poor and his tense relationship with the governments of Néstor Kirchner and Cristina Fernández de Kirchner, which championed liberal social measures including same-sex marriage. On 21 Feb. 2001 Bergoglio was proclaimed a Cardinal by John Paul II and at the 2005 conclave was regarded as a frontrunner for the papacy that eventually fell to Joseph Ratzinger. After Ratzinger resigned on 28 Feb. 2013, Bergoglio was elected his successor in the fifth ballot of the conclave.

Career in Office

The election of Francis was popularly received but his papacy has coincided with troubled times for the Church, including dwindling congregations and extensive sex abuse and corruption scandals involving Catholic clergy and Vatican officials. He has also been confronted with contentious social issues and the question of the role of women within the Church. Although a traditionalist, he has criticized obstructiveness within the Vatican bureaucracy and the Curia towards reform.

In June 2015 Francis wrote an encyclical calling for international action to address environmental degradation and climate change, for which he blamed apathy, the reckless pursuit of profit and political shortsightedness. Then in Aug. that year, commenting on the escalating influx into the European Union of refugees mainly from the Middle East and Africa, he branded the rejection of migrants fleeing violence 'an act of war'. While acknowledging that Europe was struggling to deal with the unprecedented flow, he insisted in Jan. 2016 that the continent had the capacity to absorb the refugees without sacrificing its security or culture. He also denounced all religiously-inspired violence.

Francis has travelled abroad extensively on pastoral visits since his election, attracting large attendances, and has been prepared to raise contentious issues in host countries.

Economy

Overview

The economy is supported by voluntary donations (known as 'Peter's Pence') from Roman Catholics across the world, the sale of tourist souvenirs, admission fees to museums and publication sales. Other sources of income include investments in bonds and currencies, plus income from real estate.

The Vatican Bank, officially called the Institute for the Works of Religion (IOR), was established in 1942 and is used by Vatican agencies, church organizations, bishops and religious orders around the world. It offers currency exchange services and interest-bearing accounts, and has an investment portfolio. The Bank's surplus is used for charitable purposes, including disaster relief and the support of churches in the developing world.

In Sept. 2010 Italian treasury police investigated the then president of the IOR for money-laundering. In Dec. that year measures to bring the Bank into line with international standards on transparency were established by Pope Benedict XVI, and have been continued by his successor, Pope Francis, who ordered a fresh banking enquiry in 2013. Between May 2013 and May 2014 the Bank closed 544 accounts that did not meet new standards for clients. In 2017 its net profits were reported as €31·9m., down from €36·0m. in 2016.

Currency

Since 1 Jan. 2002 the Vatican City has been using the *euro* (EUR). Italy has agreed that the Vatican City may mint a small part of the total Italian euro coin contingent with their own motifs.

Budget

Revenues in 2006 were €227·8m. and expenditures €225·4m.

Social Institutions

Justice

In 2006 the Vatican City's legal system hosted 341 civil cases and 486 criminal cases. Most of the offences are committed by outsiders, principally at St Peter's Basilica and the museums.

Religion

Roman Catholic Church

As the Vicar of Christ and the Successor of St Peter, the Pope is held to be by divine right the centre of all Catholic unity and exercises universal governance over the Church. He is also the sovereign ruler of Vatican City State. He has for advisers the College of Cardinals, consisting in Feb. 2019 of 223 cardinals from 88 countries (75 created by Pope John Paul II, 75 created by Pope Benedict XVI and 73 created by Pope Francis), of whom 123 are cardinal electors—those under the age of 80 who may enter into conclave to elect a new Pope. Cardinals, addressed by the title of 'Eminence', are appointed by the Pope from senior ecclesiastics who are either the bishops of important Sees or the heads of departments at the Roman Curia. In addition to the College of Cardinals, there is a Synod of Bishops, created by Pope Paul VI and formally instituted on 15 Sept. 1965. This consists of the Patriarchs and certain Metropolitans of the Catholic Church of Oriental Rite, of elected representatives of the national episcopal conferences and religious orders of the world, of the cardinals in charge of the Roman Congregations and of other persons nominated by the Pope. The Synod meets in both general (global) and special (regional) assemblies.

The central administration of the Roman Catholic Church is carried out by permanent organisms called Congregations, Council, Commissions and Offices. The Congregations are composed of cardinals and diocesan bishops (both appointed for five-year periods), with Consultors and Officials. There are nine Congregations, viz.: Doctrine, Oriental Churches, Bishops, the Sacraments and Divine Worship, Clergy, Religious, Catholic Education, Evangelization of the Peoples and Causes of the Saints. Pontifical Councils have replaced some of the previously designated Secretariats and Prefectures and now represent the Laity, Christian Unity, the Family, Justice and Peace, Cor Unum, Migrants, Health Care Workers, Interpretation of Legislative Texts, Inter-Religious Dialogue, Culture, Preserving the Patrimony of Art and History, and a Commission for Latin America.

Culture

World Heritage Sites

The Holy See has two sites on the UNESCO World Heritage List: Vatican City (inscribed on the list in 1984)—the centre of the Roman Catholic Church, it contains some of the greatest pieces of European art and architecture, including St Peter's Basilica.

The Historic Centre of Rome, the properties of the Holy See in that city enjoying extraterritorial rights (inscribed on the list in 1980 and 1990), is shared with Italy.

Press

In 2014 there was one daily, *L'Osservatore Romano. L'Osservatore della Domenica* is its Sunday supplement. Weekly editions of *L'Osservatore Romano* are published in several languages including English, Polish and Spanish.

Diplomatic Representatives

In its diplomatic relations with foreign countries the Holy See is represented by the Secretariat of State and the Second Section (Relations with States) of the Council for Public Affairs of the Church. It maintains permanent observers to the UN.

Of the Holy See in the United Kingdom (54 Parkside, London, SW19 5NE)
Apostolic Nuncio: Archbishop Edward Joseph Adams.

Of the United Kingdom at the Holy See (Via XX Settembre 80/a, 00187 Rome)
Ambassador: Sally Axworthy, MBE.

Of the Holy See in the USA (3339 Massachusetts Ave., NW, Washington, D.C., 20008)

   Apostolic Nuncio: Archbishop Christophe Pierre.

Of the USA at the Holy See (Via Sallustiana 49, 00187 Rome)

   Ambassador: Callista L. Gingrich.

Of the Holy See to the European Union

   Apostolic Nuncio: Archbishop Alain Paul Lebeaupin.

Further Reading

Collins, Roger, *Keepers of the Keys of Heaven: A History of the Papacy.* 2010

Hebblethwaite, Peter, *Paul VI: The First Modern Pope.* 1994.—*John XXIII: Pope of the Century.* 2005

Iverleigh, Austen, *The Great Reformer: Francis and the Making of a Radical Pope.* 2014

Norwich, John Julius, *The Popes: A History.* 2012

O'Connor, Garry, *Universal Father: A Life of Pope John Paul II.* 2006.—*Subdued Fires: An Intimate Portrait of Pope Benedict XVI.* 2013

Posner, Gerald, *God's Bankers: A History of Money and Power at the Vatican.* 2015

Reese, T., *Inside the Vatican.* 1997

Thavis, John, *The Vatican Diaries: A Behind-the-Scenes Look at the Power, Personalities and Politics at the Heart of the Catholic Church.* 2013

Vallely, Paul, *Pope Francis: Untying the Knots.* 2013

Permanent Observer Mission to the UN: https://holyseemission.org

Venezuela

República Bolivariana de Venezuela (Bolivarian Republic of Venezuela)

Capital: Caracas
Population projection, 2020: 33·17m.
GNI per capita, 2017: (PPP$) 10,672
HDI/world rank, 2017: 0·761/78
Internet domain extension: .ve

Key Historical Events

Present-day Venezuela was inhabited by hunter-gatherers from at least 3000 BC. The Arawaks and Carib lived mainly in the north and around the Orinoco river system. Christopher Columbus landed at Macuro on 5 Aug. 1498. A year later the area was explored by Alonso de Ojeda and Amerigo Vespucci. They named it Venezuela (Little Venice) after the indigenous villages built on stilts over water. Spanish settlements were established on the Caribbean coast from the early 16th century and ruled from Santo Domingo (Dominican Republic). Santiago de León de Caracas, founded in 1567, became the seat of the government of the province of Venezuela in 1578. Cocoa plantations developed slowly and much of the forested interior remained unexplored.

In 1717 Venezuela came under the Spanish Viceroyalty of New Granada, centred on Bogotá. In May 1795 discontent over Spanish rule erupted into a revolt, led by José Leonardo Chirino. Francisco de Miranda and Simón Bolívar led further rebellions from 1805 and, following Napoleon's defeat of Spain, independence was declared in 1811. Spanish control was restored but the colonial power's defeat in the battle of Carabobo in June 1821 ensured that Venezuela became part of the federal republic of Greater Colombia. Gen. José Páez led revolts, culminating in a congress in 1830 that created a constitution for a new Republic of Venezuela and elected Páez the first president.

Páez was succeeded by José Tadeo Monagas and then by his brother, José Gregorio Monagas, who governed until he was overthrown in 1858. Gen. Antonio Guzmán Blanco came to power in the April Revolution of 1870 and dominated for the next 18 years. He improved education, modernized the country's infrastructure and forced the separation of church and state. Blanco's autocratic rule was followed by the dictatorships of Joaquín Crespo (1892–98) and Cipriano Castro (1899–1908). Castro's unpopular administration prompted civil strife and, in 1902, a major international incident known as the Venezuela Claims when Great Britain, Germany and Italy dispatched a joint naval force to seek redress for unpaid loans.

The brutal dictatorship of Juan Vicente Gómez, which began in Dec. 1908 when he seized power from Castro, endured until his death in 1935 and saw the nation's oil industry develop. The election of Isaías Medina Angarita as president on 28 April 1941 led to the re-establishment of political parties, including *Acción Democrática* (AD), founded in Sept. 1941. In 1945 a revolt against the government of Gen. Isaías Medina led to constitutional and economic reforms. In 1947 the writer Rómulo Gallegos was elected president but it was a short-lived democratic spell as the government was overthrown in a military coup in Nov. 1948 and the subsequent dictatorship of Marcos Jiménez lasted until 1958.

In 1961 a new constitution provided for a presidential election every five years, a national congress, and state and municipal legislative assemblies. Twenty political parties participated in the 1983 elections, with the economy in crisis and corruption linked to drug trafficking widespread. In Feb. 1992 there were two abortive coups and a state of emergency was declared. In Dec. 1993 Dr Rafael Caldera Rodríguez's election as president reflected disenchantment with the established political parties. He took office in the early stages of a banking crisis that cost 15% of GDP. Fiscal tightening backed by the IMF brought rapid recovery. Hugo Chávez Frías, who became president in Feb. 1999, continued with economic reforms and amended the constitution to increase presidential powers. The country was renamed the Bolivarian Republic of Venezuela. In Dec. 1999 the north coast was hit by devastating floods and mudslides which resulted in 30,000 deaths.

President Chávez was deposed and arrested on 12 April 2002 in a coup following a general strike but was back in power within 48 hours. Opposition pressure intensified in 2002 and 2003 but when Chávez faced a referendum on 15 Aug. 2004 he emerged victorious. Having held power for 14 years, he died on 5 March 2013. His 'socialist revolution' and opposition to US policies won him support domestically and from regional partners but his long-term legacy is uncertain. His death triggered a presidential election in April 2013, narrowly won by the then acting president, Nicolás Maduro. In Dec. 2015 the Democratic Unity Roundtable secured a two-thirds majority in parliamentary elections, ending 16 years of socialist rule. Elections were held in July 2017 for a new constituent assembly convened controversially by presidential decree and charged with drafting a new constitution.

Maduro was re-elected for a second term in May 2018 despite an opposition boycott and claims of widespread vote-rigging, but his regime was increasingly challenged by anti-government protests in the early months of 2019.

Territory and Population

Venezuela is bounded to the north by the Caribbean with a 2,813 km coastline, east by the Atlantic and Guyana, south by Brazil, and southwest and west by Colombia. The area is 916,445 sq. km (353,839 sq. miles) including 72 islands in the Caribbean. Population at the 2011 census was 27,227,930 (13,678,178 females and 13,549,752 males); density, 29·7 per sq. km. Venezuela has the highest percentage of urban population in South America, with 93·4% living in urban areas in 2010.

The UN gives a projected population for 2020 of 33·17m.

The official language is Spanish. English is taught as a mandatory second language in high schools.

Area, population and capitals of the 23 states (*estados*), one federal dependency (*dependencias federales*) and one capital district (*distrito capital*):

State	Area (sq. km)	2011 census population	Capital	Density; inhabitants per sq. km
Distrito Capital	433	1,943,901	Caracas	4,489·4
Amazonas	177,617	146,480	Puerto Ayacucho	0·8
Anzoátegui	43,300	1,469,747	Barcelona	33·9
Apure	76,500	459,025	San Fernando	6·0
Aragua	7,014	1,630,308	Maracay	235·6
Barinas	35,200	816,264	Barinas	23·2
Bolívar	240,528	1,410,964	Ciudad Bolívar	5·9
Carabobo	4,650	2,245,744	Valencia	514·0
Cojedes	14,800	323,165	San Carlos	21·8
Delta Amacuro	40,200	167,676	Tucupita	4·2
Falcón	24,800	902,847	Coro	36·4
Guárico	64,986	747,739	San Juan de los Morros	11·5
Lara	19,800	1,774,867	Barquisimeto	89·6
Mérida	11,300	828,592	Mérida	73·3
Miranda	7,950	2,675,165	Los Teques	336·5
Monagas	28,900	905,443	Maturín	31·3

(continued)

© Springer Nature Limited 2020
Palgrave Macmillan (ed.), *The Statesman's Yearbook 2020*,
https://doi.org/10.1057/978-1-349-95940-2_205

State	Area (sq. km)	2011 census population	Capital	Density; inhabitants per sq. km
Nueva Esparta	1,150	491,610	La Asunción	427·5
Portuguesa	15,200	876,496	Guanare	57·7
Sucre	11,800	896,291	Cumaná	76·0
Táchira	11,100	1,168,908	San Cristóbal	105·3
Trujillo	7,400	686,367	Trujillo	92·8
Vargas	1,497	352,920	La Guaira	235·8
Yaracuy	7,100	600,852	San Felipe	84·6
Zulia	63,100	3,704,404	Maracaibo	73·7
Dependencias Federales	120	2,155	—	18·0

Around 2·3m. Venezuelans lived abroad in 2018 (notably in Colombia, Peru and Chile) as a consequence of the economic and political turmoil in the country, including 1·6m. who have left since 2015.

Caracas, Venezuela's largest city, is the political, financial, commercial, communications and cultural centre of the country. Caracas had a population of 1,942,652 in 2011. Maracaibo, the nation's second largest city (2011 population of 1,898,770), is located near Venezuela's most important petroleum fields and richest agricultural areas. Other major cities are Valencia, Barquisimeto and Ciudad Guayana.

Social Statistics

2008 births, 581,480; deaths, 124,062. 2008 birth rate per 1,000 population, 20·8; death rate, 4·4. Annual population growth rate, 2008–10, 1·6%. Life expectancy, 2013, was 71·7 years for males and 77·7 years for females. Infant mortality, 2010, 16 per 1,000 live births; fertility rate, 2008, 2·5 births per woman. In 2011 the most popular age for marrying was 25–29 for both men and women.

Climate

The climate ranges from warm temperate to tropical. Temperatures vary little throughout the year and rainfall is plentiful. The dry season is from Dec. to April. The hottest months are July and Aug. Caracas, Jan. 65°F (18·3°C), July 69°F (20·6°C). Annual rainfall 32" (833 mm). Ciudad Bolívar, Jan. 79°F (26·1°C), July 81°F (27·2°C). Annual rainfall 41" (1,016 mm). Maracaibo, Jan. 81°F (27·2°C), July 85°F (29·4°C). Annual rainfall 23" (577 mm).

Constitution and Government

The present constitution was approved in a referendum held on 15 Dec. 1999. Venezuela is a federal republic, comprising 23 states and one federal district, plus 235 islands and 75 islets and cays that constitute the federal dependencies. Executive power is vested in the *President*. The ministers, who together constitute the Council of Ministers, are appointed by the President and head various executive departments.

92% of votes cast in a referendum (the first in Venezuela's history) on 25 April 1999 were in favour of the plan to rewrite the constitution proposed by then President Hugo Chávez. In Dec. 1999 Chávez's plan to redraft the constitution was approved by over 70% of voters in a referendum. Consequently presidents were able to serve two consecutive six-year-terms instead of terms of five years which could not be consecutive, the Senate was abolished and greater powers were given to the state and the armed forces. Chávez effectively took over both the executive and the judiciary. After the Senate was dissolved, the 167-seat *National Assembly* (with members elected for five-year terms) became the unicameral legislature. There are 164 directly elected members with three seats reserved for the indigenous community.

The constitution provides for procedures by which the president may reject bills passed by Congress, as well as provisions by which Congress may override such presidential veto acts. In Aug. 2007 Chávez presented a set of constitutional reforms, including an end to presidential term limits. The proposals were rejected in a national referendum held on 2 Dec. 2007, with 49% of votes cast in favour of the amendments to the constitution and 51% against. However, another referendum on 15 Feb.

2009 to abolish presidential term limits (and those of various other elected officials including National Assembly deputies) was approved with 54% of votes cast in favour and 46% against.

In July 2017 elections were convened by President Maduro to return 545 members of a constituent assembly charged with drafting a new constitution. With opposition parties boycotting the elections amid claims that they were unconstitutional, the resulting assembly overwhelmingly comprised pro-government members. It subsequently declared itself the supreme authority in the country, although the National Assembly refused to subordinate itself. As a result, both bodies began passing legislation.

National Anthem

'Gloria al bravo pueblo' ('Glory to the brave people'); words by Vicente Salias, tune by Juan Landaeta.

Government Chronology

Heads of State since 1941. (AD = Democratic Action; CD = Democratic Convergence; COPEI = Social Christian Party; MVR = Movement for the Fifth Republic; PSUV = United Socialist Party of Venezuela; n/p = non-partisan)

President of the Republic		
1941–45	military	Isaías Medina Angarita

Revolutionary Junta of Government		
1945–48		Rómulo E. Betancourt Bello (AD) (chair); Luis Beltrán Prieto Figueroa (AD); Carlos Román Delgado Chalbaud (military); Raúl Leoni Otero (AD); Gonzalo Barrios Bustillos (AD); Mario Ricardo Vargas Cárdenas (military); Edmundo Fernández (n/p)

President of the Republic		
1948	AD	Rómulo Ángel Gallegos Freire

Junta of Government		
1948–52		Carlos Román Delgado Chalbaud (military); Germán Suárez Flamerich (n/p); Marcos Evangelista Pérez Jiménez (military); Luis Felipe Llovera Páez (military)

President of the Republic		
1952–58	military	Marcos Evangelista Pérez Jiménez

Junta of Government (I)		
1958		Wolfgang Enrique Larrazábal Ugueto (military) (chair); Pedro José Quevedo (military); Roberto Casanova (military); Carlos Luis Araque (military); Abel Romero Villate (military); Eugenio Mendoza Goiticoa (n/p); Blas Lamberti Cano (n/p); Arturo Sosa Fernández (n/p); Edgar Sanabria Arcia (n/p)

Junta of Government (II)		
1958–59		Edgard Sanabria Arcia (n/p) (chair); Arturo Sosa Fernández (n/p); Miguel J. Rodríguez Olivares (military); Carlos Luis Araque (military); Pedro José Quevedo (military)

Presidents of the Republic		
1959–64	AD	Rómulo Ernesto Betancourt Bello
1964–69	AD	Raúl Leoni Otero
1969–74	COPEI	Rafael Caldera Rodríguez
1974–79	AD	Carlos Andrés Pérez Rodríguez
1979–84	COPEI	Luis Antonio Herrera Campins
1984–89	AD	Jaime Lusinchi
1989–93	AD	Carlos Andrés Pérez Rodríguez
1994–99	CD	Rafael Caldera Rodríguez
1999–2013	MVR, PSUV	Hugo Rafael Chávez Frías
2013–	PSUV	Nicolás Maduro

Recent Elections

In presidential elections on 20 May 2018 incumbent Nicolás Maduro (Great Patriotic Pole/GPP, led by the United Socialist Party of Venezuela/PSUV) was re-elected president with 67·8% of the vote, ahead of Henri Falcón (Progressive Advance) with 20·9%, Javier Bertucci (ind.) with 10·8% and Reinaldo Quijada (Popular Political Unit 89) with 0·4%. Turnout was 46·1%. There were widespread allegations of fraud.

In elections to the Congress, held on 6 Dec. 2015, all 167 seats were contested. The opposition Unidad Democrática (Democratic Unity Roundtable, MUD) won 109 seats and the Partido Socialista Unido de Venezuela (United Socialist Party of Venezuela, PSUV) 55 with the remaining three seats reserved for indigenous peoples. Turnout was 74·2%.

Current Government

President (disputed): Nicolás Maduro; b. 1962 (PSUV; since 5 March 2013—acting until 19 April 2013).

  Vice-President: Delcy Rodríguez.

In Feb. 2019 the government comprised:

  Minister of Agricultural Production and Lands: Wilmar Castro Soteldo. *Basic, Strategic and Socialist Industries:* Juan Arias. *Communes and Social Movements:* Blanca Eekhout. *Communication and Information:* Jorge Rodríguez Gómez. *Culture:* Ernesto Villegas. *Defence:* Vladimir Padrino López. *Ecological Mining Development:* Víctor Cano. *Economy and Finance:* Simón Zerpa. *Ecosocialism:* Heryck Rangel. *Education:* Aristóbulo Istúriz. *Electricity:* Luis Motta Domínguez. *Fisheries and Aquaculture:* Dante Rivas. *Food:* Luis Medina Ramírez. *Foreign Affairs:* Jorge Arreaza. *Foreign Trade and Investment:* Yomana Koteich. *Health:* Carlos Alvarado. *Higher Education, Science and Technology:* Hugbel Roa. *Housing and Habitat:* Ildemaro Villarroel Arismendi. *Indigenous People:* Aloha Nuñez. *Internal Affairs, Justice and Peace:* Néstor Reverol. *Labour and Social Affairs:* Eduardo Piñate. *National Industries and Industrial Production:* Tareck El Aissami. *Penitentiary Services:* Iris Varela. *Petroleum:* Manuel Quevedo. *Planning:* Ricardo Menéndez. *Public Works:* Marleny Contreras. *Tourism:* Stella Lugo. *Transport:* Hipólito Abreu. *Urban Agriculture:* Mayerlin Arias. *Water Care:* Evelyn Vásquez. *Women and Gender Equality:* Caryl Bertho. *Youth and Sport:* Pedro Infante. *Secretariat of the Presidency:* Jorge Márquez.

Office of the President (Spanish only): http://www.presidencia.gob.ve

Current Leaders

Nicolás Maduro

Position
President

Introduction
Nicolás Maduro took office as interim president on 5 March 2013 following the death of Hugo Chávez. He was confirmed in the role when he won the presidential election held on 14 April 2013. A long-time ally of Chávez, he served as his minister of foreign affairs for seven years. Since Dec. 2015 he has been faced with a hostile majority in parliament following the opposition's overwhelming victory in National Assembly elections, in addition to public disaffection over declining living standards and shortages of basic essential commodities. He was re-elected for a second term in May 2018 in polling marred by an opposition boycott and claims of widespread vote-rigging, but his regime was increasingly challenged by anti-government protests in the early months of 2019.

Early Life
Nicolás Maduro was born on 23 Nov. 1962 in Caracas. The son of a prominent union leader, he was schooled in the capital city before becoming a bus driver. As a public transport workers' trade unionist, Maduro met Chávez in 1992 after the latter was imprisoned for his involvement in an attempted coup. Maduro campaigned for his release, meeting his future wife, Chávez's defence attorney Cilia Flores, in the process.

After Chávez was released in 1994, Maduro helped him establish the Movement for a Fifth Republic, the Bolivarian party that launched Chávez to the presidency in 1998. In the same year Maduro was elected to the Chamber of Deputies, the lower house of the old bicameral parliament. The following year a unicameral parliament was introduced, with Maduro appointed its Speaker in 2005. In Aug. 2006 he was named foreign minister, a position he held until March 2013. His tenure was characterized by the 'oil diplomacy' that saw Venezuela provide subsidized oil to neighbouring South American countries. He also attracted international attention by stating his support for Muammar Gaddafi's regime in Libya and promoted the creation of a union of emerging economies to counter US influence.

When Chávez won a third presidential term in Oct. 2012, he selected Maduro as his vice-president. In Dec. 2012 Chávez announced he was again suffering from cancer and named Maduro as his preferred successor. Chávez died in March 2013 and Maduro succeeded him on an interim basis. In the presidential election of 14 April 2013 Maduro took 50·7% of the vote, defeating Henrique Capriles, the candidate for a coalition of opposition groups.

Career in Office
In the aftermath of Chávez's death, Maduro publicly venerated his predecessor. He has maintained Chávez's political line but has been challenged by a soaring crime rate and an economy over-reliant on oil exports and subject to high inflation.

Any rapprochement with the USA was meanwhile undermined by Maduro's suggestion that Chávez's cancer (first diagnosed in June 2011) was the result of an attack by 'historic enemies' of the country and also by his expulsion of several US diplomats during 2013.

Despite attempts to curb popular anti-government protests, grievances over food shortages and rising crime rates continued through 2014 and 2015 as the oil-based economy was undermined by the rapidly falling international oil price, prompting a deepening recession and the risk of a debt default. Reflecting the rising discontent, National Assembly elections in Dec. 2015 returned the opposition Unidad Democrática (Democratic Unity Roundtable) with an overall majority. In May 2016 Maduro declared a 60-day state of economic emergency, while the imposition of unpopular price and currency measures against the backdrop of rampant corruption and burgeoning debt continued to fuel social unrest. In April 2017 the government announced the country's withdrawal from the Organization of American States, accusing the regional body of plotting against it. Then in July that year elections were held for a controversial new constituent assembly with the power to rewrite the constitution, although the opposition dismissed the poll as fraudulent and the new body as a hand-picked pro-Maduro vehicle designed to bypass the hostile National Assembly. International opinion was similarly critical. Meanwhile, the economy continued to slide under mounting debt, prompting international credit rating agencies to declare in Oct. 2017 that Venezuela was in 'selective default'.

Despite the deepening economic malaise, prompting the emigration of huge numbers of Venezuelans to neighbouring countries, Maduro claimed victory with about 68% of the vote in presidential elections in May 2018. Then in Aug. he survived an apparent assassination attempt using drones carrying explosives at a military parade in the capital.

Anti-government protests escalated in the first quarter of 2019 as Juan Guaidó, the head of the National Assembly, challenged Maduro's legitimacy and declared himself interim president with broad international recognition, including by the USA and most European Union and Latin American countries.

Defence

There is a 30-month conscript service obligation. Defence expenditure totalled US$5,240m. in 2013 (US$184 per capita), representing 1·5% of GDP.

Army

The Army has one general command, one aviation command and one logistics command, six divisions (four infantry, one armoured and one cavalry) and one combat engineer corps. Equipment in 2011 included 116 main battle tanks. Strength (2011) around 63,000. There were an additional 8,000 reserves.

A 23,000-strong volunteer National Guard is responsible for internal security.

Navy

Strength (2011) around 17,500 (3,200 conscripts). The combatant fleet comprises two submarines and six frigates. Naval Aviation, 500 strong, operated three combat-capable aircraft in 2011.

Air Force

The Air Force was 11,500 strong in 2011 and had 99 combat-capable aircraft. Main aircraft types are Su-30s, F-16A/Bs, F-5s, JL-8s and Embraer EMB 312s.

Economy

In 2014 services accounted for 52·6% of GDP, industry 41·8% and agriculture 5·6%.

Overview

Venezuela has the fifth largest economy and biggest mineral and oil reserves in Latin America, with oil providing over 95% of exports and nearly 50% of fiscal revenue in 2015. In the decade to 2014 the country benefited from historically high oil prices, which allowed for increased public spending on ambitious infrastructure programmes. However, an economy that had grown by 18·3% in 2004 then contracted by 3·2% in 2009 and 1·5% in 2010 as a result of the global financial crisis before growth recovered to average 3·7% annually between 2011 and 2013. Although the poverty rate declined from 50% in 1998 to approximately 30% in 2013, the decline in oil prices from 2014—along with inadequate macro- and microeconomic policies—have adversely affected economic wellbeing. Further contractions in GDP growth were recorded every year from 2014 to 2017, with the World Bank predicting little prospect of a short-term upturn.

The fiscal deficit was estimated at 20% of GDP at the end of 2015, with external financing needs estimated at between US$25bn. and US$35bn. in that year. Access to external financing is limited and the public deficit has been largely monetized, which along with price controls, restrictions on access to foreign currency and the collapse of the private sector in the provision of basic goods have cumulatively led to one of the world's highest inflation rates. The country implemented additional exchange rate controls in 2014 but with little success in stemming the outflow of foreign currency.

Among Venezuela's many challenges, one of the most pressing is to contain the major macroeconomic imbalances that are already reversing previous social advances. The country needs to rebuild private sector confidence by improving the investment climate, and must diversify its exports to reduce its extreme vulnerability to oil price fluctuations.

Currency

The unit of currency is the *bolívar soberano* (VES) of 100 *céntimos*. It was introduced on 20 Aug. 2018, replacing the *bolívar fuerte* (VEF) at a rate of one bolívar soberano = 100,000 bolívares fuerte. In Aug. 2009 foreign exchange reserves were US$18,559m., gold reserves were 11·46m. troy oz and total money supply was 186,679m. Bs.F. As of 2015 the government operated three official exchange rates—two preferential rates for the importation of essential goods including food, medicines and car parts, and a third for those who did not have permission to use the first two. There was also a black market rate that valued the bolívar more cheaply. In Feb. 2016, faced with triple-digit inflation and a deep recession, President Maduro announced plans to devalue the currency, eliminate the second of the preferential rates and increase the cost of gasoline for the first time in nearly 20 years. Inflation rates (based on IMF statistics):

2008	2009	2010	2011	2012	2013	2014	2015	2016	2017
31·4%	26·0%	28·2%	26·1%	21·1%	43·5%	57·3%	111·8%	254·4%	1,087·5%

Inflation has not been in single figures since 1983. The rates in both 2015 and 2017 were the highest of any country in both years. The rate in 2016 was the second highest in the world that year.

Budget

The fiscal year is the calendar year. In 2006 revenue totalled Bs 117,326bn. and expenditure Bs 117,255bn. Petroleum income accounted for 52·9% of revenues in 2006; current expenditure accounted for 75·0% of expenditures. The standard rate of VAT was increased from 12% to 16% with effect from 1 Sept. 2018.

Performance

Real GDP growth rates (based on IMF statistics):

2008	2009	2010	2011	2012	2013	2014	2015	2016	2017
5·3%	−3·2%	−1·5%	4·2%	5·6%	1·3%	−3·9%	−6·2%	−16·5%	−14·0%

Total GDP in 2013 was US$371·3bn.

Banking and Finance

A law of Dec. 1992 provided for greater autonomy for the Central Bank. Its *President*, currently Calixto Ortega Sánchez, is appointed by the President for five-year terms. In 2014 there were 23 universal banks and one commercial bank.

Venezuela's foreign debt totalled US$55,572m. in 2010, representing 14·3% of GNI.

The total stock of FDI at the end of 2012 was US$49·08bn.

There is a stock exchange in Caracas.

Energy and Natural Resources

Environment

Carbon dioxide emissions from the consumption of energy in 2011 were the equivalent of 6·2 tonnes per capita.

Electricity

Installed capacity in 2011 was 25·7m. kW; production was 122·06bn. kWh in 2011 and consumption per capita 4,129 kWh. Power shortages have become common.

Oil and Gas

Proven reserves of oil were 303·2bn. bbls in 2017, the most of any country and 17·9% of the world total. However, the reserves in Saudi Arabia—which ranks second behind Venezuela—are much more accessible. Venezuela has significant reserves of heavy crude oil, which is more expensive and difficult to extract than conventional crude oil. The oil sector was nationalized in 1976. Private and foreign investment were permitted after 1992, before then President Chávez instigated a 'renationalization' following strikes in Dec. 2002–Feb. 2003. In Feb. 2007 Chávez announced that the last foreign-controlled oil production sites would be brought under government control. Oil production in 2016 was 124·1m. tonnes. Oil provides about 50% of Venezuela's revenues. Natural gas production in 2016 was 34·3bn. cu. metres. Natural gas reserves in 2017 were 6·4trn. cu. metres, the largest in Latin America.

Minerals

Output (in 1,000 tonnes) in 2012: iron ore, 15,124 (estimate); iron ore and concentrate (metal content), 9,400 (estimate); limestone, 5,893; sand, 3,621; bauxite, 2,286; coal, 1,911; alumina, 808; gold, 1,981 kg.

Agriculture

Coffee, cocoa, sugarcane, maize, rice, wheat, tobacco, cotton, beans and sisal are grown. 50% of farmers are engaged in subsistence agriculture. There were an estimated 2·7m. ha. of arable land in 2013 and 0·7m. ha. of permanent crops. About 1·1m. ha. were equipped for irrigation in 2013.

Production in 2013 in 1,000 tonnes: sugarcane, 7,055; maize, 2,457; rice, 1,084; plantains, 535; pineapples, 462; bananas, 428; potatoes, 420; palm fruit oil, 397; oranges, 378; cassava, 368; melons and watermelons, 328; carrots and turnips, 227; papayas, 185.

Livestock (2013): cattle, 16·97m.; pigs, 3·81m.; goats, 1·43m.; sheep, 600,000; horses (estimate), 522,000; chickens (estimate), 122m.

Forestry

In 2015 the area under forests was 46·68m. ha., or 53% of the total land area. Timber production in 2011 was 5·35m. cu. metres.

Fisheries

In 2012 the total catch was 213,072 tonnes (mostly from marine waters).

Industry

Production (2007 unless otherwise indicated, in tonnes): petrol, 16·4m.; residual fuel oil, 14·6m.; distillate fuel oil, 14·3m.; cement (2007 estimate), 11m.; crude steel (2006), 4·9m.; raw sugar (2005), 690,000.

Labour

The labour force in 2013 was 14,050,000 (11,877,000 in 2003). 68·8% of the population aged 15–64 was economically active in 2013. In the same year 7·5% of the population was unemployed.

Venezuela had 80,000 people living in slavery according to the Walk Free Foundation's 2013 *Global Slavery Index*.

International Trade

Imports and Exports

Trade in US$1m.:

	2008	2009	2010
Imports c.i.f.	47,450	38,677	32,343
Exports f.o.b.	83,478	56,583	66,963

The main import sources are the USA, China, Brazil, Mexico and Colombia. The leading export destinations are the USA, China, Colombia, the Netherlands and Brazil.

Exports of petroleum in 2010 accounted for 95% of all export revenues. Machinery and transport accounted for 38% of imports in 2010, and chemicals and related products 20%.

Communications

Roads

The road network covers approximately 96,000 km. There were 2,952,100 passenger cars in use in 2007 (107 per 1,000 inhabitants) plus 84,000 lorries and vans. There were 6,218 fatalities as a result of road accidents in 2006.

Rail

The railway network comprises 742 km of 1,435 gauge track. Freight tonne-km in 2007 came to 81m. In 2006 Venezuela's first inter-city passenger service in nearly 70 years was opened with the inauguration of a line from Caracas to Cúa. Several other new lines are planned or currently under construction.

There are metros in Caracas, Los Teques, Maracaibo and Valencia.

Civil Aviation

The main international airport is at Caracas (Simon Bolívar), with some international flights from Maracaibo. The national carrier is Conviasa, founded in 2004 as the successor to Viasa, which had ceased operations in 1997. In 2005 scheduled airline traffic of Venezuela-based carriers flew 31·0m. km, carrying 3,240,200 passengers.

Shipping

In Jan. 2014 there were 74 ships of 300 GT or over registered, totalling 899,000 GT. La Guaira, Maracaibo, Puerto Cabello, Puerto Ordaz and Guanta are the chief ports. The principal navigable rivers are the Orinoco and its tributaries the Apure and Arauca.

Telecommunications

In 2012 there were 7,649,000 main (fixed) telephone lines; mobile phone subscriptions numbered 30,569,000 in the same year (1,020·5 per 1,000 persons). In 2012, 49·1% of the population were internet users. In June 2012 there were 9·7m. Facebook users.

Social Institutions

Out of 178 countries analysed in the 2017 *Fragile States Index*—a list published jointly by the Fund for Peace and *Foreign Policy* magazine—Venezuela was ranked the 58th most vulnerable to conflict or collapse. The index is based on 12 indicators of state vulnerability across social, political and economic categories.

Justice

A new penal code was implemented on 1 July 1999. The new, US-style system features public trials, verbal arguments, prosecutors, citizen juries and the presumption of innocence, instead of an inquisitorial system inherited from Spain that included secretive trials and long exchanges of written arguments.

In Aug. 1999 the new constitutional assembly declared a judicial emergency, granting itself sweeping new powers to dismiss judges and overhaul the court system. The assembly excluded the Supreme Court and the national Judicial Council from a commission charged with reorganizing the judiciary. Then President Chávez declared the assembly the supreme power in Venezuela.

The court system is plagued by chronic corruption and a huge case backlog. The population in penal institutions in 2014 was approximately 55,000 (178 per 100,000 population), a 186% increase from 2006. In Oct. 1999 over 100 judges accused of corruption were suspended. Hundreds more were removed from office over subsequent months and years, amid accusations that many appointments and suspensions were politically motivated. The country suffers from a shortfall in both numbers of judges and prosecutors. The International Centre for Prison Studies estimated in 2014 that 68·4% of prisoners had yet to receive a trial. In 2015 the World Justice Project *Rule of Law Index*, which provides data on how the rule of law is experienced by the general public across eight categories, ranked Venezuela last of 102 countries for criminal justice and 100th for civil justice.

Under the provisions of the Dec. 1999 constitution, the Supreme Court (which had been the highest court in the land) was replaced by the Supreme Tribunal of Justice. In 2012 a new penal code (the seventh of Hugo Chávez's tenure) allowed for trials to proceed in the event that a defendant fails to appear at court and that certain cases may be tried in private where a judge considers it necessary for the 'normal development' of the trial.

There were 21,752 homicides in 2016, equivalent to 70 per 100,000 people—the second highest rate of any country behind that of El Salvador.

Education

In 2007 there were 3,521,139 primary school pupils (184,409 teaching staff in 2005) and 2,174,619 secondary school pupils (187,737 teaching staff in 2005).

The leading institute of higher education is the Central University of Venezuela (Universidad Central de Venezuela), founded in 1721 in Caracas. The Bolivarian University of Venezuela (Universidad Bolivariana de Venezuela) was founded in 2003 by then President Chávez in order to give lower-income students the opportunity to study free of charge regardless of academic qualifications or prior education. More than 75% of students are from poor backgrounds. There were 1,381,126 students in tertiary education in 2006 with 108,594 academic staff.

Adult literacy was 95% in 2007.

Public expenditure on education came to 3·7% of GNI in 2007.

Health

In 2009 there were 11 hospital beds per 10,000 inhabitants. In the period 2000–10 there were 19 physicians per 10,000 persons, 11 nursing and midwifery personnel for every 10,000 and six dentists for every 10,000. Expenditure on health in 2011 came to 4·5% of GDP.

In *Water: At What Cost? The State of the World's Water 2016*, WaterAid reported that 6·9% of the population does not have access to safe water.

Welfare

The official retirement age is 60 years (men) or 55 years (women). However, the pensionable age is lower for those in arduous or unhealthy employment. The old-age pension is the minimum wage (9,648·18 Bs.F a month), plus 30% of the reference salary (20% of covered earnings in the last five years or 10% in the last ten years—whichever is higher) and an increment of 1% of earnings for every 50-week period of contributions beyond 750 weeks. The minimum pension is equal to the legal monthly minimum wage.

Unemployment benefit is 60% of the insured person's average monthly earnings during the previous 12 months. The benefit is paid for up to five months.

Religion

In 2010 there were an estimated 22·50m. Catholics and 2·92m. Protestants according to the Pew Research Center's Forum on Religion & Public Life, with 2·90m. people having no religious affiliation. The Roman Catholic Church has nine ecclesiastical provinces, each headed by an archbishop. There were two cardinals in Feb. 2019.

Culture

World Heritage Sites

Venezuela has three sites on the UNESCO World Heritage List: Coro and its Port (inscribed on the list in 1993); Canaima National Park (1994); and La Ciudad Universitaria de Caracas (2000).

Press

In 2008 there were 108 daily newspapers (106 paid-for and two free) with a circulation of 2·53m.

Tourism

In 2014 there were 857,000 non-resident tourists, down from 986,000 in 2013 although up from 562,000 in 2009.

Festivals

Among the country's most celebrated festivals is the Procession of the Holy Shepherdess (Jan.), which has run annually since 1856. Its centrepiece is a grand procession taking a statue of the divine shepherdess from Santa Rosa to the city of Barquisimeto, before the return trip is made at Easter. Celebrations to mark the initial declaration of independence from Spain in 1810 fall on 19 April, which is also designated as Day of the Indian. The Festival Internacional de Teatro in Caracas takes place in April and the Festival Internacional de Música El Hatillo is in Oct. Independence Day is observed on 5 July while the birthday of Simón Bolívar is celebrated on 24 July.

Diplomatic Representatives

Of Venezuela in the United Kingdom (1 Cromwell Rd, London, SW7 2HW)
Ambassador: Rocío Maneiro.

Of the United Kingdom in Venezuela (Torre La Castellana, Piso 11, Avenida Principal de La Castellana, Urbanización La Castellana, Caracas)
Ambassador: Andrew Soper.

Of Venezuela in the USA (1099 30th St., NW, Washington, D.C., 20007)
Ambassador: Vacant.

Chargé d'Affaires a.i.: Lissett Margarita Hernández Márquez.
Of the USA in Venezuela (Calle F con calle Suapure, Colinas de Valle Arriba, Caracas)
Ambassador: Vacant.
Chargé d'Affaires a.i.: James Story.

Of Venezuela to the United Nations
Ambassador: Samuel Moncada.

Of Venezuela to the European Union
Ambassador: Claudia Salerno Caldera.

Further Reading

Dirección General de Estadística, Ministerio de Fomento, Boletín Mensual de Estadística.—Anuario Estadístico de Venezuela (now discontinued). Annual
Canache, D., *Venezuela: Public Opinion and Protest in a Fragile Democracy.* 2002
Carroll, Rory, *Comandante: Hugo Chávez's Venezuela.* 2013
Frederick, Julia C. and Tarver, H. Micheal, *The History of Venezuela.* 2006
Rudolph, D. K. and Rudolph, G. A., *Historical Dictionary of Venezuela.* 2nd ed. 1995
Wilpert, Greg, *Changing Venezuela by Taking Power: the History and Policies of the Chavez Government.* 2006
National Statistical Office: Instituto Nacional de Estadística, Avenida Boyacá Edificio Fundación La Salle, Piso 4, Maripérez, Caracas.
Website (Spanish only): http://www.ine.gov.ve

Vietnam

Công Hòa Xã Hôi Chu Nghĩa Viêt Nam (Socialist Republic of Vietnam)

Capital: Hanoi
Population projection, 2020: 98·36m.
GNI per capita, 2017: (PPP$) 5,859
HDI/world rank, 2017: 0·694/116
Internet domain extension: .vn

Key Historical Events

Archaeological evidence suggests Neolithic settlements in northern Vietnam existed from around 5000 BC. There were small rice-dependent villages in the Red River Delta from around 2000 BC and by AD 1500 there was bronze working at Dong Dau, near present-day Hanoi.

Much of present-day northern Vietnam was closely linked with China from the third century BC, initially as part of Nam Viet, regionally-administered from Canton, and from 111 BC under Han dynasty control. Chinese rule of Vietnam's north continued under the Tsin (265–420), Sui (581–618) and T'ang (618–907) dynasties. There followed several short-lived kingdoms until relative stability was restored by the Ly dynasty (1010–1225), notably under Emperor Ly Thanh Tong (1127–38) who adopted the name Dai Viet. The region's political structure remained Chinese-influenced but independent, although it came under attack from Sino-Mongol forces in 1285 and succumbed to Ming Dynasty control for 20 years from 1407.

From the late 1420s the Le dynasty expanded southward. In 1471 Le Thanh Tong seized control of much of the Kingdom of Champa (now Vietnam's central area), although complete defeat of the Cham took several centuries. By the 1500s the Le dynasty was in decline and was overthrown in 1527. The powerful Mac, Trinh and Nguyen families then fought for control. By 1590 the Trinh had established dominance in the north, centred on Thang Long (Hanoi)—the kingdom of Tonkin. The Nguyen ruled the southern provinces from Hue, a kingdom that became known as Cochin-China.

Both kingdoms benefited from growing trade with China and Japan and, to a lesser extent, in the 17th century with Portuguese, Dutch and English merchants. Catholicism, introduced from Europe, took root across much of Vietnam while the Nguyen pushed south into the Mekong Delta, which was home to thousands of Chinese refugees fleeing after the collapse of the Ming dynasty.

In 1749 Cambodia ceded the remainder of the lower Mekong delta to Nguyen control. In the 1770s a rebellion led by three brothers from the village of Tay Son, in Quy Nhan province, toppled the Nguyen and the Trinh, although the Nguyen wrested back control in 1802. At the end of the 18th century, France helped establish Emperor Gia-Long as ruler of a unified Vietnam. French forces captured Saigon in 1859 and took control of Cochin-China. Tonkin and Annam became French protectorates in 1884 and, with Cambodia already annexed (1863), a union of Indochina was formed in 1887, with Laos added six years later.

A Marxist/Leninist-inspired nationalist movement grew during the 1920s. In 1930 Nguyen Ai Quoc (Ho Chi Minh) established the Indochinese Communist Party, which became the Viet Minh movement. In 1940 Vietnam was occupied by Japan but after Japanese defeat in 1945, the Viet Minh established a republic with its capital in Hanoi. On 6 March 1946 France recognized the Democratic Republic of Vietnam as a 'Free State within the Indo-Chinese Federation'. In Nov. 1946 French forces attacked the Viet Minh in Haiphong, sparking a war of resistance until a peace agreement was reached in July 1954.

By the Paris Agreement of Dec. 1954 France transferred sovereignty to Vietnam, which was divided along the 17th parallel into Communist North Vietnam and non-Communist South. From 1959 the North promoted insurgency in the south, and in 1963 the Viet Cong (Communist guerrillas operating in the south) defeated several units of the South Vietnamese Army, prompting the overthrow and execution of President Ngo Dinh Diem. The Gulf of Tonkin incident, in which two US destroyers were allegedly attacked by North Vietnam, prompted retaliation by Washington. Aerial bombing raids began in March 1965 and the first combat troops soon followed, peaking at 540,000 in 1968. Opposition to the war in America mounted from 1967.

On 27 Jan. 1973 an agreement was signed in Paris ending the war although hostilities continued between North and South until the latter's defeat in 1975. Between 150,000 and 200,000 South Vietnamese fled the country. North and South Vietnam unified as the Socialist Republic of Vietnam on 2 July 1976. Vietnam invaded Cambodia in Dec. 1978, prompting a bloody but indecisive war with Chinese forces in Feb.–March 1979.

In 1986 Vietnam began a shift towards a multi-sectoral market economy under state regulation. In 1995 Vietnam normalized relations with the USA and in July that year joined ASEAN and signed landmark trade agreements with the EU. The economy suffered during the Asian economic crisis of the late 1990s but trade with the USA was normalized in 2001. In 2007 the country joined the World Trade Organization after 12 years of talks.

Territory and Population

Vietnam is bounded in the west by Cambodia and Laos, north by China and east and south by the South China Sea. It has a total area of 330,951 sq. km and is divided into eight regions, 58 provinces and five municipalities (Can Tho, Da Nang, Hai Phong, Hanoi and Thanh Pho Ho Chi Minh). At the 2009 census the population was 85,846,997. July 2012 estimate: 88,772,900; density, 268 per sq. km. The areas and 2012 estimated populations were as follows:

Region/Province	Area (sq. km)	Estimated population 2012	Capital
Dac Nong	6,516	543,200	Gia Nghia
Dak Lak	13,125	1,796,700	Buon Me Thuot
Gia Lai	15,537	1,342,700	Play Cu
Kon Tum	9,690	462,400	Kon Tum
Lam Dong	9,774	1,234,600	Da Lat
Central Highlands	54,641	5,379,600	
An Giang	3,537	2,153,700	Long Xuyen
Bac Lieu	2,469	873,400	Bac Lieu
Ben Tre	2,358	1,258,500	Ben Tre
Ca Mau	5,295	1,217,100	Ca Mau
Can Tho	1,409	1,214,100	Can Tho
Dong Thap	3,377	1,676,300	Cao Lanh
Hau Giang	1,602	769,700	Vi Thanh
Kien Giang	6,348	1,726,200	Rach Gia
Long An	4,492	1,458,200	Tan An
Soc Trang	3,312	1,301,900	Soc Trang
Tien Giang	2,508	1,692,500	My Tho
Tra Vinh	2,341	1,015,300	Tra Vinh
Vinh Long	1,505	1,033,600	Vinh Long
Mekong River Delta	40,553	17,390,500	
Ha Tinh	5,998	1,230,500	Ha Tinh
Nghe An	16,491	2,952,000	Vinh
Quang Binh	8,065	857,900	Dong Hoi
Quang Tri	4,740	608,100	Dong Ha
Thanh Hoa	11,132	3,426,600	Thanh Hoa
Thua Thien–Hue	5,033	1,114,500	Hue

(continued)

© Springer Nature Limited 2020
Palgrave Macmillan (ed.), *The Statesman's Yearbook 2020*,
https://doi.org/10.1057/978-1-349-95940-2_206

Region/Province	Area (sq. km)	Estimated population 2012	Capital
North Central Coast	51,459	10,189,600	
Bac Can	4,859	301,000	Bac Can
Bac Giang	3,849	1,588,500	Bac Giang
Cao Bang	6,708	515,200	Cao Bang
Ha Giang	7,915	758,000	Ha Giang
Lang Son	8,321	744,100	Lang Son
Phu Tho	3,533	1,335,900	Viet Tri
Quang Ninh	6,102	1,177,200	Ha Long
Thai Nguyen	3,535	1,150,200	Thai Nguyen
Tuyen Quang	5,867	738,900	Tuyen Quang
North East	63,959	9,720,200	
Dien Bien	9,563	519,300	Dien Bien Phu
Hoa Binh	4,609	806,100	Hoa Binh
Lai Chau	9,069	397,500	Lai Chau
Lao Cai	6,384	646,800	Lao Cai
Son La	14,174	1,134,300	Son La
Yen Bai	6,886	764,400	Yen Bai
North West	37,415	2,857,200	
Bac Ninh	823	1,079,900	Bac Ninh
Ha Nam	860	790,000	Phu Ly
Hai Duong	1,656	1,735,100	Hai Duong
Hai Phong	1,524	1,904,100	Hai Phong
Hanoi	3,324	6,844,100	Hanoi
Hung Yen	926	1,145,600	Hung Yen
Nam Dinh	1,653	1,836,900	Nam Dinh
Ninh Binh	1,377	915,900	Ninh Binh
Thai Binh	1,570	1,787,300	Thai Binh
Vinh Phuc	1,236	1,020,600	Vinh Yen
Red River Delta	14,949	19,059,500	
Binh Dinh	6,051	1,501,800	Quy Nhon
Da Nang	1,285	973,800	Da Nang
Khanh Hoa	5,218	1,183,000	Nha Trang
Phu Yen	5,061	877,200	Tuy Hoa
Quang Nam	10,438	1,450,100	Tam Ky
Quang Ngai	5,153	1,227,900	Quang Ngai
South Central Coast	33,206	7,213,800	
Ba Ria (Vung Tau)	1,990	1,039,200	Ba Ria
Binh Duong	2,694	1,748,000	Thu Dau Mot
Binh Phuoc	6,872	912,700	Dong Xoai
Binh Thuan	7,813	1,193,500	Phan Thiet
Dong Nai	5,907	2,720,800	Bien Hoa
Ninh Thuan	3,358	576,700	Phan Rang–Thap Cham
Tay Ninh	4,040	1,089,900	Tay Ninh
Thanh Pho Ho Chi Minh	2,096	7,681,700	Ho Chi Minh City
South East	34,770	16,962,500	

31·0% of the population live in urban areas (2011).

The UN gives a projected population for 2020 of 98·36m.

Major cities (with 2009 populations): Ho Chi Minh City (5,880,615), Hanoi (2,316,772), Da Nang (770,911), Hai Phong (769,739), Can Tho (731,545).

86% of the population are Vietnamese (Kinh). There are also 53 minority groups thinly spread in the extensive mountainous regions. The largest minorities are: Tay, Thai, Muong, Khmer, Mong and Nung.

The official language is Vietnamese. Chinese, French and Khmer are also spoken.

Social Statistics

2008 estimates: births, 1,494,000; deaths, 469,000. Estimated birth rate in 2008 was 17·2 per 1,000 population; estimated death rate, 5·4. Life expectancy, 2013, was 71·3 years for males and 80·5 years for females. Annual population growth rate, 2010–15, 1·1%. Infant mortality, 2010, 19 per 1,000 live births; fertility rate, 2008, 2·1 births per woman. Vietnam has had one of the largest reductions in its fertility rate of any country in the world in recent years, having had a rate of 5·8 births per woman in 1975. Sanctions are imposed on couples with more than two children. The rate at which Vietnam has reduced poverty, from more than 58% of the population in 1993 to under 15% in 2008, is among the most dramatic of any country in the world.

Climate

The humid monsoon climate gives tropical conditions in the south, with a rainy season from May to Oct., and sub-tropical conditions in the north, though real winter conditions can affect the north when polar air blows south over Asia. In general, there is little variation in temperatures over the year. Hanoi, Jan. 62°F (16·7°C), July 84°F (28·9°C). Annual rainfall 72" (1,830 mm).

Constitution and Government

The National Assembly unanimously approved a new constitution on 15 April 1992. Under this the Communist Party retains a monopoly of power and the responsibility for guiding the state according to the tenets of Marxism-Leninism and Ho Chi Minh, but with certain curbs on its administrative functions. Vietnam is a one-party republic. The powers of the National Assembly are increased. The 500-member *National Assembly* is elected for five-year terms. Candidates may be proposed by the Communist Party or the Fatherland Front (which groups various social organizations), or they may propose themselves as individual Independents. The Assembly convenes three times a year and appoints a prime minister and cabinet. It elects the *President*, the head of state. The latter heads a *State Council* which issues decrees when the National Assembly is not in session.

The ultimate source of political power is the Communist Party of Vietnam, founded in 1930; it had 3·6m. members in 2011.

National Anthem

'Doàn quân Viêt Nam di chung lòng cúú quóc' ('Soldiers of Vietnam, we are advancing'); words and tune by Van Cao.

Government Chronology

General Secretaries of the Communist Party since 1976.

1976–86	Le Duan
1986	Truong Chinh
1986–91	Nguyen Van Linh
1991–97	Do Muoi
1997–2001	Le Kha Phieu
2001–11	Nong Duc Manh
2011–	Nguyen Phu Trong

Heads of State since 1976.

Presidents

1976–80	Ton Duc Thang
1980–81	Nguyen Huu Tho

Chairmen of the State Council

1981–87	Truong Chinh
1987–92	Vo Chi Cong

Presidents

1992–97	Le Duc Anh
1997–2006	Tran Duc Luong
2006–11	Nguyen Minh Triet
2011–16	Truong Tan Sang
2016–18	Tran Dai Quang
2018–	Nguyen Phu Trong

Prime Ministers since 1976.

1976–87	Pham Van Dong
1987–88	Pham Hung
1988	Vo Van Kiet
1988–91	Do Muoi
1991–97	Vo Van Kiet
1997–2006	Phan Van Khai
2006–16	Nguyen Tan Dung
2016–	Nguyen Xuan Phuc

Recent Elections

In parliamentary elections held on 22 May 2016 Communist Party members won 473 of 494 seats, with 21 seats going to non-party candidates. Turnout was more than 99%.

Nguyen Phu Trong was overwhelmingly elected president by the National Assembly on 23 Oct. 2018, receiving 476 of 477 votes.

Current Government

President (titular head of state): Nguyen Phu Trong; b. 1944 (in office since 23 Oct. 2018).

Vice-President: Dang Thi Ngoc Thinh.

Full members of the Politburo of the Communist Party of Vietnam: Nguyen Phu Trong (b. 1944; *General Secretary*); Nguyen Xuan Phuc; Nguyen Thi Kim Ngan; Ngo Xuan Lich; To Lam; Nguyen Thien Nhan; Pham Minh Chinh; Tong Thi Phong; Vuong Dinh Hue; Tran Quoc Vuong; Pham Binh Minh; Truong Thi Mai; Truong Hoa Binh; Nguyen Van Binh; Vo Van Thuong; Hoang Trung Hai.

In Feb. 2019 the government comprised:

Prime Minister: Nguyen Xuan Phuc; b. 1954 (in office since 7 April 2016).

Deputy Prime Ministers: Pham Binh Minh (also *Minister of Foreign Affairs*); Truong Hoa Binh; Vuong Dinh Hue; Vu Duc Dam; Trinh Dinh Dung.

Minister of National Defence: Ngo Xuan Lich. *Public Security:* To Lam. *Home Affairs:* Le Vinh Tan. *Finance:* Dinh Tien Dung. *Agriculture and Rural Development:* Nguyen Xuan Cuong. *Health:* Nguyen Thi Kim Tien. *Industry and Trade:* Tran Tuan Anh. *Education and Training:* Phung Xuan Nha. *Natural Resources and Environment:* Tran Hong Ha. *Culture, Sports and Tourism:* Nguyen Ngoc Thien. *Science and Technology:* Chu Ngoc Anh. *Planning and Investment:* Nguyen Chi Dung. *Labour, War Invalids and Social Affairs:* Dao Ngoc Dung. *Justice:* Le Thanh Long. *Construction:* Pham Hong Ha. *Transport:* Nguyen Van The. *Information and Communications:* Nguyen Manh Hung. *Chairman of the Committee for Ethnic Minority Affairs:* Do Van Chien. *Chairman of the Government Office:* Mai Tien Dung.

Government Website: http://www.gov.vn

Current Leaders

Nguyen Phu Trong

Position

State President and General Secretary of the Communist Party of Vietnam

Introduction

Nguyen Phu Trong was elected general secretary of the Communist Party of Vietnam in Jan. 2011 at the Party's 11th five-yearly national congress, replacing Nong Duc Manh. Chairman of the National Assembly since 2006, Trong was previously the party secretary for Hanoi. He was re-elected for a second term as general secretary in Jan. 2016 at the Party's 12th congress. In Oct. 2018 he was also elected as the country's new president, becoming the first holder of both posts since the 1960s.

Early Life

Trong was born in Hanoi on 14 April 1944. He attended the Nguyen Gia Thieu school in Hanoi district and from 1963–67 studied linguistics at the Hanoi General University. After graduating, Trong became a civil servant and in 1968 was inducted into the Communist Party of Vietnam. From 1968–73 he worked on the *Communist Review*, the party's official journal, and was a prominent representative of the party's youth contingent. He then undertook post-graduate studies at Ho Chi Minh National Academy of Politics and Public Administration before returning as editor of the *Communist Review* in 1976. In 1983 he graduated with a history PhD from the Soviet Academy of Social Sciences. He returned to the *Communist Review* and held senior posts, joining the editorial board in 1991 and serving as editor-in-chief until 1996.

In 1994 Trong became a member of the Communist Party central committee and from 1996–98 was deputy secretary of its Hanoi section. In 1997 he joined the politburo, focusing on political research and theory. He was appointed head of 'ideological-cultural and scientific-educational affairs' and from 2001–06 served as chairman of the 'theoretical council'.

From 2000–06 he was party secretary in Hanoi and from 2002–06 a deputy in the National Assembly. In 2006 he was elected secretary of the Assembly's party organization, as well as chairman of the Assembly itself, and became a member of the council for defence and security.

Career in Office

At 67 years of age, Trong was past the mandatory retirement age when he became general secretary and was considered a conservative hard-liner. He has adopted a tough stance towards the media and moved against critical journalism, including banning the use of unnamed sources. However, against a background of continuing scandals in state-owned enterprises, he has acknowledged the government's need to curb high-level corruption, particularly relating to PetroVietnam, the state oil giant. In Jan. 2016 he was re-elected general secretary of the Communist Party after the more reformist outgoing prime minister, Nguyen Tan Dung, withdrew his candidacy, and in Oct. 2018 he was additionally elected state president by the National Assembly in succession to Tran Dai Quang.

While Trong has sought closer ties with China—on which Vietnam is economically dependent—there have been continued bilateral tensions since 2014 over China's assertive sovereignty claims to contested islands in the South China Sea and over maritime oil drilling activities. Nevertheless, Trong and President Xi Jinping both stressed the close links between their two countries during reciprocal visits in April 2015 and Nov. 2017. In July 2015 Trong made an official visit to the USA at the invitation of then President Barack Obama's administration and, while on a return visit in May 2016, Obama announced that the long-standing embargo on US arms sales to Vietnam was to end. Trong also made the first visit by a Vietnamese communist leader to Indonesia in Aug. 2017.

Nguyen Xuan Phuc

Position

Prime Minister

Introduction

On 7 April 2016 Nguyen Xuan Phuc became prime minister after he received over 90% support in a parliamentary vote. He is scheduled to serve a five-year term as part of a governing triumvirate with Communist Party general secretary, Nguyen Phu Trong, and President Tran Dai Quang.

Early Life

Nguyen was born on 20 July 1954 in the commune of Que Phu in south central Vietnam. He graduated in economics from the National Economics University, Hanoi in 1978, after which he joined the economic management committee of Quang Nam province.

He became a Communist Party member in 1982, rising through the party ranks. He held various regional party roles including director of the department of planning and investment for Quang Nam-Da Nang from 1993–96, vice-president and vice-chairman of the People's Committee of Quang Nam province from 1997–2001 and chairman from 2001–06. He also became a deputy chief government inspector in 2006.

In June 2006 he was elected to the party central committee and in Aug. the following year he was named minister-chairman of the government office. He became deputy prime minister in June 2011. At the 12th National Party Congress held in Jan. 2016 Nguyen was selected to succeed Nguyen Tan Dung as premier, with his election endorsed by parliament in April.

Career in Office

Nguyen's government has sought to maintain Vietnam's vigorous economic growth, as well as the country's rapid integration into global commerce and its enviable inward foreign investment record. There has also been increasing pressure for reforms to overhaul the scandal-hit state-owned sector and banking system. In foreign policy, Nguyen has continued his predecessor's challenge to Chinese maritime and territorial claims in the South China Sea.

In July 2016 Nguyen was re-elected prime minister by the National Assembly, with key positions in his cabinet remaining the same. In May 2017 he visited the USA in an attempt to further develop trade relations with the new US administration under President Donald Trump and signed commercial transactions worth US$8bn.

Defence

Conscription is for two years (army) or three years (air force and navy). For specialists it is also three years.

In 2013 defence expenditure totalled US$3,800m. (US$41 per capita), representing 2·4% of GDP.

Army

There are nine military regions (including the capital). Strength (2011) was estimated to be 412,000. Paramilitary Local Defence forces number around 5m. and include the People's Self-Defence Force (urban) and the People's Militia (rural). There is also a paramilitary Border Defence Corps numbering some 40,000.

Navy

In 2011 the fleet included two diesel submarines (although their serviceability was in doubt), two frigates and seven corvettes. Vietnam ordered six *Kilo* class submarines from Russia in 2009. The first one was handed over in Nov. 2013 and the other five between March 2014 and Jan. 2017. In 2011 personnel was estimated at 13,000 plus an additional Naval Infantry force of about 27,000.

Air Force

In 2011 the People's Air Force had 30,000 personnel, with 235 combat-capable aircraft (Su-22s, Su-27s, Su-30s and MiG-21s) and 26 attack helicopters.

Economy

Agriculture accounted for 18·1% of GDP in 2016, industry 36·4% and services 45·5%.

Overview

GDP growth averaged 6·4% per year in the decade to 2012 but slowed to 5·4% in 2013 before rebounding to 6·7% in 2015, although it did then slow to 6·2% in 2016. Improvements in macroeconomic stability saw inflation fall from a peak of 23% in Aug. 2011 to 3·4% in Aug. 2017. Exports flourished between 2015 and 2017 (equating to 89·8% of GDP in 2015), compared with those of regional neighbours. The country received US$108bn. in foreign direct investment between 2007 (when it joined the World Trade Organization) and 2018. In March 2018 Vietnam and ten other countries bordering the Pacific (although not the USA) signed the Comprehensive and Progressive Agreement for Trans-Pacific Partnership.

The economy is moving away from traditional labour-intensive manufacturing sectors (garments, footwear and furniture) towards high-technology, higher-value products. The Social Economic Development Strategy for 2011–20 lays out plans for structural reforms, environmental sustainability and social equity. In particular, it aims to promote human resources, skills development and infrastructure expansion. The 12th Congress of the Communist Party that met in Jan. 2016 continued to affirm the country's integration into the global economy and its pursuance of a socialist-oriented market economy.

Currency

The unit of currency is the *dong* (VND). The dong was devalued by 5·4% in Nov. 2009, 3·4% in Feb. 2010, 2·1% in Aug. 2010 and 8·5% in Feb. 2011. Foreign exchange reserves were US$8,268m. in May 2005 and total money supply was 192,281bn. dong. Inflation was 23·1% in 2008, and more recently 2·7% in 2016 and 3·5% in 2017.

Budget

Budgetary central government revenues in 2013 totalled 781,954bn. dong (687,980bn. dong in 2012) and expenses were 772,863bn. dong (659,230bn. dong in 2012).

VAT is 10% (reduced rate, 5%).

Performance

Real GDP growth rates have been consistently strong since the late 1980s, only going below 5% during that time in 1999. The economy grew by 6·7% in 2015, 6·2% in 2016 and 6·8% in 2017. GDP per head, which was US$98 in 1990, had risen to US$1,755 by 2012. Vietnam's total GDP in 2017 was US$223·9bn.

Banking and Finance

The central bank and bank of issue is the State Bank of Vietnam (founded in 1951; *Governor*, Le Minh Hung). There were 42 banks in 2011. The leading commercial banks are Vietnam Bank for Agriculture and Rural Development (usually referred to as Agribank), Vietinbank, Bank for Investment and Development of Vietnam (BIDV) and Joint Stock Commercial Bank for Foreign Trade of Vietnam (Vietcombank).

External debt totalled US$35,139m. in 2010, representing 36·5% of GNI. Foreign direct investment in Vietnam increased every year between 2011 and 2017, when it reached a record US$14·1bn.

There are stock exchanges in Ho Chi Minh City, which opened in July 2000, and Hanoi, which opened in March 2005.

Energy and Natural Resources

Environment

Vietnam's carbon dioxide emissions from the consumption of energy were the equivalent of 1·5 tonnes per capita in 2011.

Electricity

Total installed capacity of power generation in 2011 was an estimated 25·7m. kW. In 2011, 105·22bn. kWh of electricity were produced (63·94bn. kWh thermal and 41·19bn. kWh hydro-electric); consumption per capita was 1,213 kWh. The proportion of households with electricity has doubled in the past 20 years, to 96·4% in 2012.

Oil and Gas

Oil reserves in 2012 totalled 4·4bn. bbls. In Aug. 2001 an offshore oil mine containing more than 400m. bbls of petroleum was discovered. Oil production in 2012, 17·0m. tonnes. Natural gas reserves in 2012 were 600bn. cu. metres; production was 9·4bn. cu. metres.

Minerals

Vietnam is endowed with an abundance of mineral resources such as coal (3·5bn. tonnes), bauxite (3bn. tonnes), apatite (1bn. tonnes), iron ore (700m. tonnes), chromate (10m. tonnes), copper (600,000 tonnes) and tin (70,000 tonnes); coal production was 34·1m. tonnes in 2005. There are also deposits of manganese, titanium, a little gold and marble. 2005 output (in 1,000 tonnes): sand and gravel, 146,400; lime, 1,718; salt, 925.

Agriculture

Agriculture employs 70% of the workforce. Ownership of land is vested in the state, but since 1992 farmers may inherit and sell plots allocated on 20-year leases. There were 6·41m. ha. of arable land in 2014 and 3·82m. ha. of permanent crops.

Production in 1,000 tonnes in 2013: rice, 44,040; sugarcane, 20,131; cassava, 9,758; maize, 5,191; bananas, 1,893; sweet potatoes, 1,358; coffee, 1,327; coconuts, 1,304; watermelons, 1,163; natural rubber, 965. Vietnam is the second largest coffee producer in the world after Brazil.

Livestock, 2013: pigs, 26·26m.; cattle, 5·16m.; buffaloes, 2·56m.; goats, 1·39m.; chickens, 235m.; ducks, 69m.

Livestock products (2013 estimates): meat, 4,321,000 tonnes; eggs, 378,000 tonnes; milk, 487,000 tonnes.

Forestry

In 2015 forests covered 14·77m. ha., or 48% of the land area. An export ban on logs has been in place since 1992. Timber production was 27·10m. cu. metres in 2011, nearly all of it for fuel.

Fisheries

Total catch, 2015, 2,757,314 tonnes (95% from sea fishing). Vietnam's aquaculture production is the third largest in the world behind those of China and India, at 2,845,600 tonnes in 2011. Exports of fishery commodities were valued at US$6,242m. in 2011 (the fourth highest in the world) and imports at US$706m.

Industry

Manufacturing accounted for 13·7% of GDP in 2015. The main industries are cement, chemical fertilizers, coal, food processing, garments, glass, machine building, mining, oil, paper, shoes, steel and tyres.

Labour

The labour force in 2013 was 53,444,000 (44,284,000 in 2003). 82·2% of the population aged 15–64 was economically active in 2013. In the same year 2·2% of the population was unemployed. The normal retirement age is 60 for men and 55 for women, but there are proposals to raise this to 62 for men and 60 for women.

Vietnam had 0·25m. people living in slavery according to the Walk Free Foundation's 2013 *Global Slavery Index*.

International Trade

In Feb. 1994 the USA lifted the trade embargo it had imposed in 1975, and in Nov. 2001 a trade agreement with the USA was ratified. The agreement allows Vietnam's exports access to the US market on the same terms as those enjoyed by most other countries. The 1992 constitution regulates joint ventures with western firms; full repatriation of profits and non-nationalization of investments are guaranteed.

Imports and Exports

Imports (c.i.f.) in 2010 totalled US$83,779m., up from US$36,761m. in 2005; exports (f.o.b.), US$72,237m., up from US$32,447m. in 2005. In 2009 the main imports were: machinery and transport equipment (31·3%), in particular electrical machinery, apparatus and appliances; manufactured goods (25·4%); chemicals and related products (14·6%); mineral fuels, lubricants and related materials (10·7%). Main exports in 2009: miscellaneous manufactured articles (34·8%), in particular articles of apparel and clothing accessories; food and live animals (20·1%); mineral fuels, lubricants and related materials (14·9%); machinery and transport equipment (13·0%).

The main import suppliers in 2009 were China (23·8%), Japan (10·7%), South Korea (10·0%) and Thailand (6·5%). Principal export markets in 2009 were the USA (20·0%), Japan (11·1%), China (9·5%) and Australia (4·2%).

Communications

Roads

There were 160,089 km of roads in 2007, of which 47·6% were paved. In 2007 there were 1,146,300 passenger cars in use and around 21·78m. motorcycles and mopeds. There were 13,200 fatalities in road accidents in 2007.

Rail

There were 2,347 km of railways in 2011, mostly metre gauge. Rail links with China were reopened in Feb. 1996. In 2011, 12·0m. passengers and 7·2m. tonnes of freight were carried. Metros are under construction in both Hanoi and Ho Chi Minh City, with Hanoi's expected to open during 2019 and Ho Chi Minh City's in 2020.

Civil Aviation

There are international airports at Hanoi (Noi Bai) and Ho Chi Minh City (Tan Son Nhat) and 13 domestic airports. The national carrier is Vietnam Airlines, which provides domestic services and in 2010 had international flights to more than 20 destinations. In 2012 scheduled airline traffic of Vietnam-based carriers flew 111·8m. km; passenger-km totalled 25·3bn. in the same year. The busiest airport is Ho Chi Minh City, which in 2012 handled 17,538,353 passengers and had 131,710 aircraft movements. Hanoi handled 11,341,039 passengers and had 84,304 aircraft movements in 2012.

Shipping

In Jan. 2014 there were 1,340 ships of 300 GT or over registered (including 1,039 general cargo ships and 148 bulk carriers), totalling 4,003,000 GT. The major ports are Hai Phong, Ho Chi Minh City and Da Nang. There are regular services to Hong Kong, Singapore, Thailand, Cambodia and Japan. There are some 19,500 km of navigable waterways.

Telecommunications

In 2011 there were 10,175,000 main (fixed) telephone lines; mobile phone subscriptions numbered 127,318,000 in the same year (1,416·0 per 1,000 persons). In 2011, 35·1% of the population were internet users. In June 2012 there were 9·7m. Facebook users. In March 2012 there were 3·2m. Facebook users.

Social Institutions

Out of 178 countries analysed in the 2017 *Fragile States Index*—a list published jointly by the Fund for Peace and *Foreign Policy* magazine—Vietnam was ranked the 74th least vulnerable to conflict or collapse. The index is based on 12 indicators of state vulnerability across social, political and economic categories.

Justice

A new penal code came into force on 1 Jan. 1986 'to complete the work of the 1980 constitution'. Penalties (including death) are prescribed for opposition to the people's power and for economic crimes. The judicial system comprises the Supreme People's Court, provincial courts and district courts. The president of the Supreme Court is responsible to the National Assembly, as is the Procurator-General, who heads the Supreme People's Office of Supervision and Control.

Vietnam does not normally divulge figures on its use of the death penalty, but the government reported to the National Assembly in Nov. 2018 that 85 people had been executed during the year.

The population in penal institutions in mid-2014 was 142,636 (154 per 100,000 of national population). Vietnam was ranked 39th of 102 countries for criminal justice and 76th for civil justice in the 2015 World Justice Project *Rule of Law Index*, which provides data on how the rule of law is experienced by the general public across eight categories.

Education

Adult literacy rate in 2009 was estimated at 92·8% (95·2% among males and 90·5% among females). Primary education consists of a ten-year course divided into three levels of four, three and three years respectively. In 2007 there were 7,041,312 pupils and 344,547 teaching staff in primary schools, and 9,845,407 pupils and 451,165 teaching staff at secondary schools. In 2008 less than 1% of the population aged 25–55 did not have any level of education attainment, down from 23% in 1992. There were 376 higher education institutions in 2009 (150 universities and 226 colleges), of which 81 (44 universities and 37 colleges) were private. In 2007 there were 1,587,609 students in higher education with 53,518 academic staff.

Health

In the period 2006–13 Vietnam had 11·6 physicians for every 10,000 population, 11·4 nursing and midwifery personnel per 10,000 population and 3·1 pharmaceutical personnel per 10,000. There were 20 hospital beds per 10,000 population in the period 2006–12.

In *Water: At What Cost? The State of the World's Water 2016*, WaterAid reported that 2·4% of the population does not have access to safe water.

Religion

Taoism is the traditional religion but Buddhism is widespread. At the census of 2009 the principal denominations were: Buddhists, 6,802,318; Catholics, 5,677,086; Hoa Hao (a tradition based on Buddhism), 1,433,252; Cao Dai (a synthesis of Christianity, Buddhism and Confucianism), 807,915; Protestants, 734,168; no religion, 70,193,377. In Feb. 2019 there were two cardinals. The Roman Catholic Church has 26 dioceses, including three archdioceses.

Culture

World Heritage Sites

Vietnam has eight sites on the UNESCO World Heritage List: the Complex of Hue Monuments (inscribed on the list in 1993); Ha Long Bay (1994 and 2000); Hoi An Ancient Town (1999); My Son Sanctuary (1999); Phong Nha-Ke Bang National Park (2003 and 2015); the Central Sector of the Imperial Citadel of Thang Long, Hanoi (2010); the Citadel of the Ho Dynasty (2011); and Trang An Landscape Complex (2014).

Press

In 2008 there were 55 paid-for daily newspapers with a combined circulation of 2·8m. The Communist Party controls all print media. In the 2015 *World Press Freedom Index* compiled by Reporters Without Borders, Vietnam was ranked 175th out of 180 countries.

Tourism

There were a record 6,014,000 international visitors in 2011 (up from 5,050,000 in 2010). Tourist numbers have doubled since 2003. The main nationalities of tourists in 2010 were China (905,000), South Korea (496,000) and Japan (442,000).

Diplomatic Representatives

Of Vietnam in the United Kingdom (12–14 Victoria Rd, London, W8 5RD)
  Ambassador: Tran Ngoc An.

Of the United Kingdom in Vietnam (Central Building, 4th Floor, 31 Hai Ba Trung, Hanoi)
  Ambassador: Gareth Ward.

Of Vietnam in the USA (1233 20th St., NW, Suite 400, Washington, D.C., 20036)
  Ambassador: Ha Kim Ngoc.

Of the USA in Vietnam (7 Lang Ha St., Hanoi)
  Ambassador: Daniel J. Kritenbrink.

Of Vietnam to the United Nations
  Ambassador: Dang Dinh Quy.

Of Vietnam to the European Union
  Ambassador: Vu Anh Quang.

Further Reading

Trade and Tourism Information Centre with the General Statistical Office. *Economy and Trade of Vietnam* [various 5-year periods]

Dumbrell, John, *Rethinking the Vietnam War.* 2012

Gilbert, Marc Jason, (ed.) *Why the North Won the Vietnam War.* 2002

Goscha, Christopher E., *Vietnam: A New History.* 2016

Harvie, C. and Tran Van Hoa V., *Reforms and Economic Growth.* 1997

Karnow, S., *Vietnam: a History.* 2nd ed. revised. 1997

London, Jonathan, *Politics in Contemporary Vietnam: Party, State, and Authority Relations.* 2014

Morgan, Ted, *Valley of Death: The Tragedy at Dien Bien Phu That Led America into the Vietnam War.* 2010

Morley, J. W. and Nishihara M., *Vietnam Joins the World.* 1997

National Statistical Office: General Statistical Office, 6B Hoang Dieu, Ba Dinh District, Hanoi.

Website: http://www.gso.gov.vn

Yemen

Jamhuriya al Yamaniya (Republic of Yemen)

Capitals: Sana'a (Legislative and Administrative), Aden (Commercial)
Population projection, 2020: 30·25m.
GNI per capita, 2017: (PPP$) 1,239
HDI/world rank, 2017: 0·452/178
Internet domain extension: .ye

Key Historical Events

One of the earliest recorded pre-Islamic Arab civilizations was the Sabaean culture, which flourished in what is now Yemen and southwestern Saudi Arabia during the 1st millennium BC. The wealth of the kingdom of Saba (or Sheba) was based on the incense and spice trade and on agriculture. Beginning in about 115 BC, the Himyarites gradually absorbed Saba and Hadhramaut (to the east) to claim control of all of the southwest Arabian peninsula by the 4th century AD. Himyarite dominance came to an end in the 6th century as Abyssinian (Ethiopian) forces invaded in AD 525. Abyssinian rule was overthrown in 575 by Persian military intervention, and Persian control then endured until the advent of Islam in 628.

Yemen became a province of the Muslim caliphate. Thereafter its fortunes reflected the fluctuating power of the imams (kings and spiritual leaders) of the Zaidi sect—who built the theocratic political structure of Yemen that endured from the 9th century until 1962—and of rival dynasties and conquerors. These included the Fatimid caliphs of Egypt, who occupied most of Yemen from about 1000 until 1175 and, subsequently, the Ayyubids, who ruled until about 1250. The Rasulids, who had served as governors of Yemen under the Ayyubid dynasty, then exercised a measure of sovereignty. However, central authority had fragmented by the time the Ottoman Turks, fearful of Christian Portuguese influence in southern Arabia, intervened in Yemen in the first half of the 16th century. They held nominal but tenuous sovereignty until the end of the First World War (when Yemen became independent), and conflict with the Zaidi imams was frequent.

The southern Yemeni port of Aden was a coveted commercial location on the trading routes to the wider East from ancient times. By the end of the 18th century its strategic importance had increased as Britain sought to contain the French threat to colonial communications with British India following Napoleon's conquest of Egypt. Britain's need for a military and refuelling base in the region led in 1839 to the British capture of Aden, attaching it administratively to India. The opening of the Suez Canal in 1869 further enhanced both Aden's strategic significance and British colonial consolidation.

In the early 1870s, tribal and religious warfare led the Ottoman Turks to reassert authority over northern Yemen, an occupation that lasted until 1918. After the Ottoman evacuation, Imam Yahya sought to expand Yemeni territory. However, in 1934, after brief hostilities with Saudi Arabia and skirmishes with British forces from Aden, a trilateral treaty to fix Yemen's boundaries was agreed. A generally peaceful coexistence lasted for the rest of Imam Yahya's reign. Aden, meanwhile, was formally made a British crown colony in 1937 and the surrounding region became known as the Aden protectorate. Imam Yahya was assassinated in Feb. 1948 and was succeeded by his son, Crown Prince Ahmad. Ahmad's reign was marked by repression, renewed friction over the British presence and growing pressure in the 1950s to support the Arab nationalist objectives of the new Nasser regime in Egypt. Following Ahmad's death his son, Muhammad al-Badr, was deposed a week after his accession in Sept. 1962 by rebels aided by Egypt who took control of the capital, Sana'a, and proclaimed the Yemen Arab Republic (YAR). Saudi Arabia and Jordan supported al-Badr's royalist forces against the new republic and conflict continued periodically until 1970. Despite its instability, the YAR regime retained power and secured international recognition.

In 1963 the Aden colony was merged into the Federation of South Arabia. A power struggle between rival nationalist groups after the British withdrawal in 1967 led to an independent Marxist state with Aden as the capital. This was renamed the People's Democratic Republic of Yemen (PDRY) in 1970. Frequent border clashes between the YAR and the PDRY characterized the next decade.

A coup in the YAR brought Lieut.-Col. Ibrahim al-Hamadi to power in 1974. However, he was assassinated in Oct. 1977, as was his successor, Lieut.-Col. Ahmad al-Ghashmi, in June 1978. The following month Lieut.-Col. Ali Abdullah Saleh was elected president by the Constitutional Assembly. In early 1979 a full-scale war erupted between North and South Yemen before Arab League mediation brought the hostilities to an end. Saleh was meanwhile re-elected as YAR President in May 1983 and again in July 1988 by a new Consultative Council.

In the PDRY the chairman of the Presidential Council, Salem Rubayyi Ali, was overthrown in June 1978. Prime Minister Ali Nasser Muhammad briefly assumed the chairmanship before Abdul Fattah Ismail, a hard-line orthodox Marxist, was elected as head of state by the new Presidium of the People's Supreme Assembly in Dec. 1978. Ismail resigned unexpectedly in April 1980 and was replaced by Ali Nasser Muhammad. While maintaining South Yemen's close relations with the Soviet Union, Muhammad favoured reconciliation with moderate Arab states to further a proposed merger with the YAR. In Feb. 1985 Muhammad resigned as prime minister but remained head of state and secretary-general of the dominant Yemeni Socialist Party. The rest of that year was marked by the re-emergence of political rivalries, which triggered a brief civil war in Jan. 1986. Muhammad fled into exile, after which a new government was formed.

In May 1988 the YAR and PDRY governments reached an agreement to pursue unification discussions and demilitarize their borders. Their respective leaders, Ali Abdullah Saleh and Ali Salem Albidh, agreed in late 1989 a draft unity constitution (originally drawn up in 1981) and on 22 May 1990 the Republic of Yemen was declared. A five-member Presidential Council assumed power and Saleh was appointed as president for a transitional period. By 1993 relations between the North and South had again deteriorated and sporadic military clashes escalated into full civil war in May 1994 between disaffected southern forces and Yemen's northern-based government. However, northern forces quickly prevailed and, following Aden's capture on 7 July 1994, southern leaders went into exile.

Having been confirmed in office by parliament in Oct. 1994 for a five-year term, President Saleh was re-elected by popular vote in Sept. 1999. An extension of his term from five to seven years was subsequently approved in a referendum in Feb. 2001 and he was again re-elected in 2006.

In foreign affairs Yemen suffered diplomatic isolation and economic sanctions in the early 1990s for its equivocal response to Iraq's invasion of Kuwait. In 1995 Yemen clashed with Eritrea over control of the Hanish Islands in the Red Sea. Following arbitration by an international panel, Yemen assumed control of the main islands in 1998.

Long-standing tensions with neighbouring Saudi Arabia were eased when a border dispute was settled in June 2000. Attacks on Western targets in Yemeni territory—most notably the suicide bombing of the US naval vessel *USS Cole* in Oct. 2000 and a bomb attack on a French supertanker, the *Limburg*, in Oct. 2002—fuelled concerns that Yemen might be a haven for Islamic extremists. Nevertheless, President Saleh pledged full support for the USA's global campaign against terrorism in the wake of the events of 11 Sept. 2001.

Attacks linked to al-Qaeda continued throughout the decade. In Jan. 2011 the US government expressed its 'urgent concern' at Yemen's extremist links. Popular anti-government protests starting the same month led to President Saleh relinquishing power in Nov. 2011. He was succeeded by Abd Rabbo Mansour Hadi, who won the presidential election held in Feb. 2012 unopposed. However, the country has remained in a volatile and unstable state. An insurgency by Shia Muslim Houthi rebels gathered momentum, provoking a military air campaign against them by a coalition of Sunni Muslim states led by Saudi Arabia from early 2015 that had claimed over 10,000 Yemeni lives by the end of 2016.

© Springer Nature Limited 2020
Palgrave Macmillan (ed.), *The Statesman's Yearbook 2020*,
https://doi.org/10.1057/978-1-349-95940-2_207

Territory and Population

Yemen is bounded in the north by Saudi Arabia, east by Oman, south by the Gulf of Aden and west by the Red Sea. The territory includes 112 islands including Kamaran (181 sq. km) and Perim (300 sq. km) in the Red Sea and Socotra (3,500 sq. km) in the Gulf of Aden. On 15 Dec. 1995 Eritrean troops occupied the islands of Greater and Lesser Hanish, and Yemen retaliated with aerial bombardments. A ceasefire was agreed at presidential level on 17 Dec. On 20 Dec. the UN resolved to send a good offices mission to the area. In an agreement of 21 May 1996 brokered by France, Yemen and Eritrea renounced the use of force to settle the dispute and agreed to submit it to arbitration. Following a ruling issued by the Permanent Court of Arbitration in The Hague, Yemen assumed control of the main islands in 1998. The area is 555,000 sq. km excluding the desert Empty Quarter (Rub Al-Khahi).

A dispute with Saudi Arabia broke out in Dec. 1994 over some 1,500–2,000 km of undemarcated desert boundary. A memorandum of understanding signed on 26 Feb. 1995 reaffirmed the border agreement reached at Taif in 1934, and on 12 June 2000 a 'final and permanent' border treaty between the two countries was signed. An agreement of June 1995 completed the demarcation of the border with Oman.

At the last census, in 2004, the population was 19,685,161. The United Nations gave an estimated population for 2014 of 26·25m.; density, 47 per sq. km. In 2011, 32·4% of the population lived in urban areas.

The UN gives a projected population for 2020 of 30·25m.

The country is administratively divided into 21 governorates and the municipality of Sana'a (city). The 21 governorates are (with capitals): Abyan (Zinjibar), Aden (Aden), Al-Baidha (Al-Baidha), Al-Dhale (Al-Dhale), Al-Hudaydah (Al-Hudaydah), Al-Jawf (Al-Hazm), Al-Mahrah (Al-Ghaydah), Al-Mahwit (Al-Mahwit), Amran (Amran), Dhamar (Dhamar), Hadhramaut (Mukalla), Hajjah (Hajjah), Ibb (Ibb), Lahj (Lahj), Mareb (Mareb), Raymah (Jabin), Sa'dah (Sa'dah), Sana'a (Sana'a), Shabwa (Ataq), Socotra (Hadibu), Ta'iz (Ta'iz).

The capital is Sana'a, with an estimated population in 2010 of 2,084,000. Other major towns are Aden (the commercial capital), Ta'iz, Al-Hudaydah, Ibb, Mukalla and Dhamar.

The official language is Arabic.

Social Statistics

2009 estimates: births, 886,000; deaths, 163,000. Rates, 2009 estimates (per 1,000 population): birth, 38; death, 7. Yemen has one of the youngest populations of any country, with 75% of the population under the age of 30 and 44% under 15. Life expectancy, 2013, was 61·8 years for males and 64·5 years for females. Infant mortality, 2010, 57 per 1,000 live births. Annual population growth rate, 2003–13, 2·5%; fertility rate, 2013, 4·1 births per woman.

Climate

A desert climate, modified by relief. Sana'a, Jan. 57°F (13·9°C), July 71°F (21·7°C). Aden, Jan. 75°F (24°C), July 90°F (32°C). Annual rainfall 20" (508 mm) in the north, but very low in coastal areas: 1·8" (46 mm).

Constitution and Government

Parliament consists of a 301-member *Assembly of Representatives* (*Majlis al-Nuwaab*), previously elected for a six-year term in single-seat constituencies—although parliamentary elections have not been held since April 2003—and a 111-member *Consultative Council (Majlis al-Shoora)*, appointed by the President for an indefinite term. A new people's transitional council was created in Feb. 2015 when the *Assembly of Representatives* was briefly suspended in the wake of the Houthi rebel uprising. The *Assembly* was reinstated following UN-brokered talks between rival factions.

The constitution was adopted in May 1991 but was drastically amended in 1994 following the civil war. On 28 Sept. 1994 the Assembly of Representatives unanimously adopted the amended constitution founded on Islamic law. It abolished the former five-member Presidential Council and installed a *President* elected by parliament for a five-year term, subsequently amended to a seven-year term through a referendum held on 20 Feb. 2001. As a result of the same referendum the term for MPs was extended from four to six years. After popular protests in 2011 unseated President Saleh, his successor, Abd Rabbo Mansour Hadi, was expected to oversee the drafting of

a new constitution. However, Hadi was himself the subject of a coup in early 2015 during which the Houthi rebels established a rival administration. Houthi representatives had earlier refused to enter negotiations on ratification of a draft constitution submitted in Jan. 2015.

National Anthem

'Raddidi Ayyatuha ad Dunya nashidi' ('Repeat, O World, my song'); words by A. Noman, tune by Ayub Tarish.

Government Chronology

(MSA = General People's Congress)
Heads of State since 1990.

Presidents

| 1990–12 | MSA | Ali Abdullah Saleh |
| 2012– | MSA | Abd Rabbo Mansour Hadi |

Head of the Revolutionary Committee

| 2015–16 | military | Muhammad Ali al-Houthi |

Head of the Supreme Political Council

| 2016–18 | military | Saleh Ali al-Sammad |
| 2018– | military | Mahdi al-Mashat |

Recent Elections

In presidential elections held on 21 Feb. 2012 the sole candidate, Vice President Abd Rabbo Mansour Hadi, won 99·8% of the vote. Turnout was 65·0%.

Parliamentary elections were last held on 27 April 2003, in which the General People's Congress (MSA) gained 238 seats, Yemeni Congregation for Reform (Islah) 46 seats, Yemeni Socialist Party 8 seats, Nasserite Unionist People's Organization (TWSN) 3 seats, the Arab Socialist Rebirth Party (Baath) 2 seats and ind. 4 seats. Turnout was 76·0%.

Current Government

In Jan. 2015 President Abd Rabbo Mansour Hadi and Prime Minister Khaled Mahfoodh Abdullah Bahah resigned following an uprising led by the Houthi rebel group. The cabinet was also forced to resign and an interim government was installed by the Houthis. However, in Feb. 2015 Hadi, who had fled to the southern region of Aden, retracted his resignation and claimed to be still in control of the country. Muhammad Ali al-Houthi and the Revolutionary Committee handed power to a rival Supreme Political Council in Aug. 2016. *De jure President:* Abd Rabbo Mansour Hadi (since 25 Feb. 2012).
Head of the Supreme Political Council: Mahdi al-Mashat (since 25 April 2018).

Current Leaders

Abd Rabbo Mansour Hadi

Position
De jure President

Introduction

Abd Rabbo Mansour Hadi, a career military officer from southern Yemen, became president in Feb. 2012, ending 33 years of rule by Ali Abdullah Saleh. Hadi resigned in Jan. 2015 following a takeover by Iranian-backed Houthi rebels of the capital, Sana'a, but a month later withdrew his resignation and has since sought to wrestle back control of the country from the Houthis. His government operates partly from Riyadh in Saudi Arabia and partly from Aden, but exercises limited authority.

Early Life

Hadi was born on 1 May 1945 in Thukian, Abyan. He attended Aden Protectorate Army School, graduating in 1964, and won a scholarship to the UK's Royal Military Academy at Sandhurst.

Following South Yemen's independence in Nov. 1967, Hadi served in an armoured division at the Al-Anad military base. He undertook further training in Cairo in 1970, before being posted to the Al-Dhale region and serving on the mediation committee that successfully resolved a conflict with North Yemen in 1972. For much of the 1970s he managed South Yemen's military training establishment and spent time in Moscow studying military leadership. Promoted to deputy chief of staff in 1983, he was responsible for military liaison with the then Soviet Union.

Following Yemen's unification in May 1990, Hadi was a leading figure in the republic's new army. During the 1994 civil war he supported Ali Abdullah Saleh (the president and former leader of North Yemen) and was subsequently appointed vice president and minister of defence—the most senior position in the government held by a southerner.

Saleh stood down in Nov. 2011 after more than ten months of popular unrest interspersed with violent government crackdowns. In accordance with a UN Security Council resolution, he agreed to transfer power to Hadi for an interim period ahead of presidential elections. On 21 Feb. 2012 Hadi, the sole candidate, was elected president, with a reported voter turnout of 65%.

Career in Office

Hadi was sworn in to office on 25 Feb. 2012. Initially a popular figure within Yemen, he also received support from many neighbouring states. However, he faced a trying tenure in view of continued threats from al-Qaeda, the Houthi rebellion, a secessionist movement in the south, a weak economy and crumbling infrastructure. A conference of 'national dialogue', convened in March 2013 in an effort to resolve Yemen's social, political and demographic divisions, came to an end in Jan. 2014 after inconclusive talks. Elections planned for Feb. 2014 were meanwhile postponed indefinitely.

Hadi resigned on 22 Jan. 2015 following the Houthi rebel takeover of the capital that saw Hadi placed under house arrest and a Houthi-run administration installed. Against a backdrop of calls from the UN for his reinstatement, a month later Hadi escaped to Aden, which he declared the *de facto* capital, and withdrew his resignation. However, the Houthi Revolutionary Committee has continued to contest his government's legitimacy and in Aug. 2016 installed a rival Supreme Political Council.

Since March 2015 a Saudi Arabian-led coalition of Gulf Arab states has supported Hadi's regime militarily with an air campaign against Houthi strongholds, which has caused thousands of Yemeni deaths amid a humanitarian crisis, including famine and a major cholera outbreak, and claims of crimes against humanity. Tentative peace talks were initiated between the Hadi government and the Houthis in Dec. 2018, at which both sides agreed to an exchange of prisoners and to a ceasefire in the Houthi-controlled Red Sea port city of Al-Hudaydah, potentially increasing the supply of crucial humanitarian aid.

Mahdi al-Mashat

Position
Head of the Supreme Political Council

Introduction
Mahdi al-Mashat was sworn in as president of Yemen's Supreme Political Council on 25 April 2018 following the death of Saleh Ali al-Sammad in an air strike by Saudi Arabia and its coalition allies. Al-Mashat assumed the leadership of the Iranian-backed Houthi movement that in Sept. 2014 had wrested control of the capital Sana'a from President Abd Rabbo Mansour Hadi's Saudi-backed government. The international community does not recognize the authority of the Supreme Political Council.

Early Life
Few details have emerged about Mahdi al-Mashat's early background beyond his reported birth around 1980 and his long-time adherence to Ansar Allah, a theological group founded in the 1990s to which the Shia Houthi movement is linked. In Sept. 2014 the Houthis had seized control of Sana'a and agreed to a UN-brokered deal to take part in a unity government. However, in Jan. 2015 they rejected proposals to divide the country into six regions and forced the resignation of President Hadi (which he later retracted). In Aug. 2016 al-Sammad announced the establishment of a ten-member presidential council to govern the capital and other parts of the country under Houthi control, which led to the breakdown of UN-sponsored peace talks.

Career in Office
With different Yemeni factions serving as proxies for other regional powers, al-Mashat took office amid the continuing military campaign to regain Sana'a by the Saudi-led coalition backing Aden-based President Hadi. Following his appointment, al-Mashat condemned the killing of Saleh Ali al-Sammad as a political assassination—blaming the USA as an accomplice through its support for the Saudis—and a violation of Yemen's national sovereignty under international law.

Defence

Defence expenditure in 2013 totalled US$1,812m. (US$71 per capita), representing 4·7% of GDP.

Estimates of the number of small arms in the country are around 12m., equivalent to 61 firearms for every 100 people, making Yemen second only behind the USA as the world's most heavily armed country.

Army
Strength (2011), 60,000 (including conscripts). In 2011 there were paramilitary tribal levies numbering at least 20,000 and a Ministry of Security force of 50,000.

Navy
Navy forces are based at Aden and Al-Hudaydah, with other facilities at Mukalla, Perim and Socotra. Personnel in 2011 numbered 1,700.

Air Force
Personnel (2011), 3,000. There were 79 combat-capable aircraft in 2011 (F-5s, Su-22s, MiG-21s and MiG-29s).

Economy

Agriculture accounted for 9·8% of GDP in 2015, industry 48·1% and services 42·1%.

Yemen featured among the ten most corrupt countries in the world in a 2018 survey of 180 countries carried out by the anti-corruption organization Transparency International.

Overview
Yemen is among the poorest countries in the Middle East, with little arable land and limited natural resources. More than half of the population live without food security, while water resources are below the average for the region. Long-standing political and social unrest continues to hinder economic stability, with the World Bank reporting in 2016 that 37·4% of the population was living on less than US$2 (PPP) per day.

The economy slipped into recession in 2011, before recovering with growth of 2·4% in 2012 and 4·8% in 2013. However, civil conflict since 2015 has led to a catastrophic economic and humanitarian crisis. The economy contracted by 16·7% in 2015, followed by 13·6% in 2016, and an estimated 2·5m. people had been displaced by the fighting as of 2017.

Oil production remains the main export and income source for the government, despite declining reserves.

Currency
The unit of currency is the *riyal* (YER) of 100 *fils*. During the transitional period to north-south unification the northern *riyal* of 100 *fils* and the southern *dinar* of 1,000 *fils* co-existed. There were three foreign exchange rates operating: an internal clearing rate, an official rate and a commercial rate. In 1996 the official rate was abolished. Total money supply in June 2005 was 372,105m. riyals, gold reserves totalled 50,000 troy oz and foreign exchange reserves were US$5,253m. There was deflation of 12·6% in 2016 but then inflation of 24·7% in 2017.

Budget
The fiscal year is the calendar year. General government revenues in 2012 were 2,063bn. riyals (1,383bn. riyals in 2011) and expenditures 2,108bn. riyals (1,876bn. riyals in 2011).

Performance
Real GDP grew by 7·7% in 2010, but contracted by 12·7% in 2011 in the wake of political turmoil in Yemen that year. The economy then began to recover, expanding by 2·4% in 2012 and 4·8% in 2013. However, Yemen has been in recession since then as the civil war intensified with the economy

shrinking by 13·6% in 2016 and 5·9% in 2017. Total GDP in 2016 was US$18·2bn.

Banking and Finance

The *Governor* of the Central Bank of Yemen is Mohammed Zammam. In Dec. 2012 there were 17 licensed banks (including five Islamic banks) and two micro finance institutions. Of the 12 conventional banks, three were state-controlled banks, four were domestic private banks and five were branches of foreign-owned banks. In 2009 foreign debt amounted to US$6,370m., which represented 25·6% of GNI.

Energy and Natural Resources

Environment

Yemen's carbon dioxide emissions from the consumption of energy were the equivalent of 0·8 tonnes per capita in 2011.

Electricity

Installed capacity was 1·5m. kW in 2011. Production in 2011 was 6·21bn. kWh; consumption per capita was 266 kWh.

Oil and Gas

In 2012 there were oil reserves of 3·0bn. bbls, mostly near the former north–south border. Oil production (2012): 8·3m. tonnes. Natural gas reserves in 2012 were 500bn. cu. metres; production was 7·6bn. cu. metres.

Minerals

In 2008, 65,000 tonnes of salt were produced. In 2008, 100,000 tonnes of gypsum were extracted and 4·95m. cu. metres of quarried stone (including marble).

Agriculture

In 2007 there were around 1·38m. ha. of arable land and 250,000 ha. of permanent cropland. 772,000 ha. were irrigated in 2006. In the south, agriculture is largely of a subsistence nature, sorghum, sesame and millet being the chief crops, and wheat and barley being widely grown at the higher elevations. Cash crops include cotton. Fruit is plentiful in the north. Production (2013, in 1,000 tonnes): sorghum, 439; mangoes and guavas, 382; potatoes, 282; wheat, 232; onions, 227; melons and watermelons, 215. Livestock in 2013: sheep, 9·6m.; goats, 9·3m.; cattle, 1·7m.; chickens (estimate), 63m. Livestock products, 2013 estimates (in 1,000 tonnes): meat, 384; milk, 368.

Forestry

There were 0·55m. ha. of forest in 2015 (1% of the total land area). Timber production in 2011 was 456,000 cu. metres.

Fisheries

Fishing is a major industry. Total catch in 2012 was 230,516 tonnes, exclusively marine fish.

Industry

Output (2007 unless otherwise indicated, in 1,000 tonnes): cement (2009), 2,118; petrol, 1,127; distillate fuel oil, 991; residual fuel oil, 676; jet fuel, 486; kerosene, 97. In 2006 industry accounted for 49·2% of GDP, with manufacturing contributing 7·8%.

Labour

The labour force in 2013 was 7,343,000 (4,824,000 in 2003). 50·4% of the population aged 15–64 was economically active in 2013. In the same year 17·7% of the population was unemployed.

Yemen had 41,000 people living in slavery according to the Walk Free Foundation's 2013 *Global Slavery Index*.

International Trade

Imports and Exports

Trade in US$1m.:

	2005	2006	2007	2008	2009
Imports c.i.f.	5,399·9	6,080·9	8,510·7	10,546·2	9,184·8
Exports f.o.b.	5,607·7	6,654·1	6,298·9	7,583·8	6,259·0

Main import suppliers, 2009: United Arab Emirates, 9·9%; China, 9·3%; USA, 6·4%; Japan, 5·6%. Main export markets, 2009: China, 25·2%; India, 20·1%; Thailand, 18·4%; Singapore, 6·9%.

Oil and fish are major exports, the largest imports being food and live animals, and transport and machinery equipment. Oil and oil products account for nearly 90% of exports. A large transhipment and entrepôt trade is centred on Aden, which was made a free trade zone in 1991.

Communications

Roads

There were 71,300 km of roads in 2005 (8·7% paved). In 2007 there were 777,700 vehicles in use.

Civil Aviation

There are international airports at Sana'a and Aden, but both have been periodically closed as a result of the civil war. In 2012 Sana'a handled 1,598,661 passengers (1,176,447 on international flights) and 18,119 tonnes of freight. The national carrier is Yemenia, which in 2010 operated internal services and had international flights to more than 20 destinations. In 2012 scheduled airline traffic of Yemen-based carriers flew 22·0m. km; passenger-km totalled 3·7bn. in the same year.

Shipping

In Jan. 2014 there were seven ships of 300 GT or over registered, totalling 22,000 GT. There are ports at Aden, Mokha, Al-Hudaydah, Mukalla and Nashtoon.

Telecommunications

In 2012 there were 1,104,000 main (fixed) telephone lines; mobile phone subscriptions numbered 13,900,000 in the same year (582·8 per 1,000 persons). In 2013 an estimated 20·0% of the population were internet users. In March 2012 there were 437,000 Facebook users.

Social Institutions

According to the 2017 *Fragile States Index*—a list published jointly by the Fund for Peace and *Foreign Policy* magazine—Yemen was ranked as the country fourth most vulnerable to conflict or collapse. The index is based on 12 indicators of state vulnerability across social, political and economic categories.

Justice

A civil code based on Islamic law was introduced in 1992. The death penalty is still in force. There were five confirmed judicial executions in 2018.

The International Centre for Prison Studies estimated in 2014 that 70·1% of prisoners had yet to receive a trial.

Education

In 2005 there were 17,993 children in pre-primary schools, 3·21m. pupils in primary schools and 1·46m. pupils in secondary schools. In 2006 there were 209,386 students in higher education. The adult literacy rate in 2009 was estimated at 62·4% (79·9% among males but only 44·7% among females, one of the biggest differences in literacy rates between the sexes of any country).

In 2008 total expenditure on education came to 5·2% of GDP and accounted for 16·0% of total government expenditure.

Health

In the period 2006–12 Yemen had seven hospital beds per 10,000 population. In the period 2007–13 there were 2·0 physicians for every 10,000 population, 6·8 nursing and midwifery personnel per 10,000 population, 0·4 dentistry personnel per 10,000 and 0·9 pharmaceutical personnel per 10,000.

Religion

More than 99% of the population in 2010 was Muslim (60–65% Sunnis and 35–40% Shias) according to the Pew Research Center's Forum on Religion & Public Life, with small Hindu and Christian minorities—an estimated 150,000 and 40,000 respectively.

Culture

World Heritage Sites

There are four sites under Yemeni jurisdiction that appear in the UNESCO World Heritage List. They are (with year entered on the list): the old walled city of Shibam (1982); the old city of Sana'a (1986); the historic town of Zabid (1993); and the Socotra Archipelago (2008).

Press

In 2008 there were five daily newspapers with a combined average daily circulation of 40,000.

Tourism

There were 829,000 international tourist arrivals—excluding same-day visitors—in 2011 (1,025,000 in 2010). Receipts from tourism in 2011 totalled US$783m.

Diplomatic Representatives

Of Yemen in the United Kingdom (57 Cromwell Rd, London, SW7 2ED)
  Ambassador: Yassin Saeed Noman Ahmed.

Of the United Kingdom in Yemen (938 Thahr Himyar St., East Ring Rd, Sana'a)
  Ambassador: Michael Aron (resides in Riyadh, Saudi Arabia).

Of Yemen in the USA (2319 Wyoming Ave., NW, Washington, D.C., 20008)
  Ambassador: Ahmed Awad Ahmed bin Mubarak.

Of the USA in Yemen (Sa'awan St., PO Box 22347, Sana'a)
  All staff have been withdrawn.

Of Yemen to the United Nations
  Ambassador: Abdullah Ali Fadhel Al-Saadi.

Of Yemen to the European Union
  Ambassador: Mohamed Taha Mustafa.

Further Reading

Central Statistical Organization. *Statistical Year Book* (now discontinued).

Al-Rasheed, Madawi and Vitalis, Robert, (eds) *Counter-Narratives: History, Contemporary Society, and Politics in Saudi Arabia and Yemen.* 2004

Bruck, Gabriele vom, *Islam, Memory and Morality in Yemen: Ruling Families in Transition.* 2005

Clark, Victoria, *Yemen: Dancing on the Heads of Snakes.* 2010

Dresch, Paul, *A History of Modern Yemen.* 2001

Leach, Hugh, *Seen in the Yemen: Travelling with Freya Stark and Others.* 2011

Lewis, Alexandra, *Security, Clans and Tribes: Unstable Governance in Somaliland, Yemen and the Gulf of Aden.* 2014

Mackintosh-Smith, T., *Yemen—Travels in Dictionary Land.* 1997

Manea, Elham, *Regional Politics in the Gulf: Saudi Arabia, Oman and Yemen.* 2005

National Statistical Office: Central Statistical Organization, Ministry of Planning and International Co-operation.

Zambia

Republic of Zambia

Capital: Lusaka
Population projection, 2020: 18·68m.
GNI per capita, 2017: (PPP$) 3,557
HDI/world rank, 2017: 0·588/144
Internet domain extension: .zm

Key Historical Events

The earliest known inhabitants were nomadic bushmen. From the 4th century AD, Bantu tribes farmed the region and established villages. Copper was mined from the 11th century, and trade developed with neighbouring regions in copper and textiles. From 1500–1900 the region was divided into four tribal kingdoms: the Kazembe-Lunda in the north, the Bemba in the northeast, the Chewa in the east and the Barotse, later known as the Lozi, in the west. An inland region, it was not penetrated by non-Africans until the late 18th century, when Portuguese traders arrived. The Scottish explorer David Livingstone followed in the mid-19th century, and in the 1880s the British colonialist and mining magnate, Cecil Rhodes, arrived.

Rhodes persuaded the British government to secure Bechuanaland in 1885, and in 1888 he obtained mining rights in the territory of the Ndebele, which reached to the Zambezi river. In 1890 the chief of the Lozi, Lewanika, granted Rhodes mining rights in return for British protection. In 1891 the British government granted Rhodes's British South Africa Company a charter to administer the area from the Zambezi river to Lake Tanganyika.

From 1900 the territory was administered as two separate protectorates, Northwestern and Northeastern Rhodesia. Lead, zinc and copper were discovered, attracting more European prospectors. In 1911 the two protectorates merged to become Northern Rhodesia and in 1924 the British Crown took over direct administration. The territory was governed through a legislative council elected by the European population. The detection of rich copper seams—known as the Copper Belt—led to a mining boom. The European population grow tenfold to 40,000 over the next three decades. Meanwhile, the African majority (98% of the country) increasingly voiced its opposition to European rule. In 1948 some African members were added to the legislative council and the country's first African political party, the Northern Rhodesian Congress, was established. Connected to the African National Congress (ANC), in 1951 it renamed itself the Northern Rhodesian African National Congress.

In 1953 the British government imposed a federation consisting of Northern Rhodesia, its southern self-governing neighbour Rhodesia and Nyasaland. The Federation was welcomed by most Europeans in the territories as a means of consolidating their economic and political control but was opposed by most Africans for the same reason. In 1958 Kenneth Kaunda led a breakaway group from the Northern Rhodesian ANC to found the more radical Zambian African National Congress. After he was jailed for civil disobedience, the United National Independence Party (UNIP) was formed and elected Kaunda its leader on his release in Jan. 1960. Membership grew rapidly, convincing the British to accept it as a negotiating partner. In London in Dec. 1960, Kaunda and other UNIP members secured a timetable for independence.

Elections in 1962 resulted in a UNIP–ANC coalition. The Federation was dissolved on 31 Dec. 1963 and in general elections held that year, with universal adult suffrage, UNIP won a clear victory. On 24 Oct. 1964 the country declared independence as the Republic of Zambia, named after the Zambezi river. The government oversaw a period of prosperity until copper prices collapsed in the 1970s. Further difficulties were caused by UN-imposed sanctions on Rhodesia—a key trading partner—and rising oil prices, so that by the late 1970s Zambia was greatly indebted to the IMF.

Amid domestic dissent, Kaunda brought in centralizing and authoritarian measures, including a new constitution making Zambia a one-party state. Living standards fell as copper production almost halved. Food riots and widespread unrest resulted in the 1991 electoral victory of the Movement for Multi-Party Democracy (MMD). However, allegations of corruption dogged the MMD government throughout successive terms, while the economy remained weak. Privatization of the copper mines and other market-orientated reforms in the early 2000s reduced inflation but food security has remained a serious issue.

In 2002 Levy Mwanawasa succeeded Frederick Chiluba, who had been president since 1991. Mwanawasa won a second term in 2006 but died two years later. Chiluba also died, in 2011, having spent years contesting corruption charges. Rupiah Banda held the presidency until 2011, when he was replaced by Michael Sata. In Oct. 2014 he too died in office and was replaced in Jan. 2015 by Edgar Lungu, who was charged with seeing out the rest of Sata's scheduled tenure. Following the general election of Aug. 2016, Lungu secured a further five-year term.

Territory and Population

Zambia is bounded by the Democratic Republic of the Congo in the north, Tanzania in the northeast, Malaŵi in the east, Mozambique in the southeast, Zimbabwe and Namibia in the south, and Angola in the west. The area is 752,612 sq. km (290,584 sq. miles). Population (2010 census), 13,092,666; population density, 17·4 per sq. km. In 2011, 35·9% of the population were urban.

The UN gives a projected population for 2020 of 18·68m.

The republic is divided into ten provinces. Area, population at the 2010 census and chief towns:

Province	Area (in sq. km)	Population	Chief Town
Central	94,394	1,307,111	Kabwe
Copperbelt	31,328	1,972,317	Ndola
Eastern	51,620	1,592,661	Chipata
Luapula	50,567	991,927	Mansa
Lusaka	21,896	2,191,225	Lusaka
Muchinga[1]	87,410	711,657	Chinsali
Northern	77,900	1,105,824	Kasama
North-Western	125,826	727,044	Solwezi
Southern	85,283	1,589,926	Choma
Western	126,386	902,974	Mongu

[1]Muchinga Province, consisting of districts from Northern and Eastern provinces, was established in 2011.

The capital is Lusaka, which had a census population in 2010 of 1,747,152. Other major towns (with 2010 census population in 1,000) are: Kitwe, 501; Ndola, 451; Kabwe, 202; Chingola, 185; Mufulira, 151; Livingstone, 134; Luanshya, 130.

The population consists of over 70 Bantu-speaking ethnic groups, with the main groups being the Bemba (18%), Tonga (10%), Nyanja (8%) and Lozi (6%). The official language is English.

Social Statistics

Estimates, 2008: births, 541,000; deaths, 218,000. Estimated birth rate in 2008 was 42·9 per 1,000 population; estimated death rate, 17·3. Zambia's life expectancy at birth in 2013 was 56·3 years for males and 60·0 for females. Life expectancy was declining for many years, largely owing to the huge number of people in the country with HIV, although it has now begun to rise again slowly. In 2009, 13·5% of all adults between 15 and 49 were infected with HIV. Annual population growth rate, 2000–08, 2·3%. Infant mortality, 2010, 69 per 1,000 live births; fertility rate, 2008, 5·8 births per woman.

Palgrave Macmillan (ed.), *The Statesman's Yearbook 2020*,
https://doi.org/10.1057/978-1-349-95940-2_208

Climate

The climate is tropical, but has three seasons. The cool, dry one is from May to Aug., a hot dry one follows until Nov., when the wet season commences. Frosts may occur in some areas in the cool season. Lusaka, Jan. 70°F (21·1°C), July 61°F (16·1°C). Annual rainfall 33" (836 mm). Livingstone, Jan. 75°F (23·9°C), July 61°F (16·1°C). Annual rainfall 27" (673 mm). Ndola, Jan. 70°F (21·1°C), July 59°F (15°C). Annual rainfall 52" (1,293 mm).

Constitution and Government

Zambia has a unicameral legislature. The *National Assembly* consists of 167 members (156 directly elected in single-member constituencies and eight appointed by the President, plus the Vice President, the Speaker and the First Deputy Speaker). The constitution was adopted on 24 Aug. 1991 and was amended in 1996 to restrict the President from serving more than two terms of office. Further amendments ratified in Jan. 2016 set a fixed date for elections, increased the size of parliament from 158 members and required the President to win an overall majority at the polls. Presidential candidates must also select a running-mate who automatically serves as Vice President and succeeds the President in the event of the President's death while in office. Provision was also made for individuals to hold dual citizenship and for the establishment of a constitutional court.

National Anthem

'Lumbanyeni Zambia' ('Stand and Sing of Zambia'); words collective, tune by M. E. Sontonga.

Recent Elections

Presidential elections took place on 11 Aug. 2016. Edgar Lungu (Patriotic Front/PF) was re-elected with 50·4% of the vote, beating Hakainde Hichilema (United Party for National Development/UPND) with 47·6%. Seven other candidates received less than 1% of the vote each. Turnout was 56·5%.

In the parliamentary elections held on the same day the Patriotic Front gained 80 of the 156 elected seats in the National Assembly; the United Party for National Development took 58, the Movement for Multi-Party Democracy 3 and the Forum for Democracy and Development 1. 14 seats went to independents. Turnout was 56·0%.

Current Government

President: Edgar Lungu; b. 1956 (PF; since 25 Jan. 2015).
   Vice President: Inonge Wina.
   In Feb. 2019 the government comprised:
   Minister of Agriculture: Micheal Zondani Katambo. *Chiefs and Traditional Affairs:* Lawrence John Sichalwe. *Commerce, Trade and Industry:* Christopher Yaluma. *Community Development and Social Welfare:* Olipa Mwansa Phiri. *Defence:* Davies Chama. *Energy:* Mathew Nkhuwa. *Finance:* Margaret Mwanakatwe. *Fisheries and Livestock:* Kampamba Mulenga Chilumba. *Foreign Affairs:* Joseph Malanji. *Gender:* Elizabeth Phiri. *General Education:* David Mabumba. *Health:* Chitalu Chilufya. *Higher Education:* Nkandu Luo. *Home Affairs:* Stephen Kampyongo. *Housing and Infrastructure Development:* Ronald Kaoma Chitotela. *Information and Broadcasting:* Dora Siliya. *Justice:* Given Lubinda. *Labour and Social Security:* Joyce Nonde-Simukoko. *Lands and Natural Resources:* Jean Kapata. *Local Government:* Vincent Mwale. *Lusaka Province:* Bowman Lusambo. *Mines and Minerals Development:* Richard Musukwa. *National Development and Planning:* Alexander Chiteme. *Presidential Affairs:* Chomba Freedom Sikazwe. *Religious Affairs and National Guidance:* Godfridah Sumaili. *Tourism and Arts:* Charles Romel Banda. *Transport and Communication:* Brian Mushimba. *Water Development, Sanitation and Environmental Protection:* Dennis Musuku Wanchinga. *Works and Supply:* Mutotwe Kafwaya. *Youth, Sport and Child Development:* Moses Mawere. *Minister in the Office of the Vice President:* Sylvia Bambala Chalikosa.
   Zambian Parliament: http://www.parliament.gov.zm

Current Leaders

Edgar Lungu

Position
President

Introduction
Edgar Chagwa Lungu became president in Jan. 2015. Lungu, who leads the Patriotic Front (PF), served out the rest of Michael Sata's term after Sata died in office in Oct. 2014. At elections held in Aug. 2016, he was returned for a five-year term.

Early Life
Lungu was born on 11 Nov. 1956 and grew up in Kitwe. Having graduated in law from the University of Zambia in 1982, he practised in the ministry of legal affairs before moving into the corporate sector.
   His political career began in 2001 when he joined Sata's newly-founded PF. When the PF won the 2011 elections, Lungu became a junior minister in the vice president's office. He was promoted to minister of home affairs in 2012, took over the defence portfolio a year later and was named minister of justice in 2014. He was acting president when Sata suffered ill health in 2013 and 2014. In Nov. 2014 Guy Scott, then serving as interim president, dismissed Lungu as secretary-general of the PF but the decision was reversed and Lungu was subsequently elected party leader. In Jan. 2015 he narrowly won the poll to determine who would serve out the remainder of Sata's term (and appointed Inonge Wina as Zambia's first ever female vice president) before being re-elected for a full presidential term in Aug. 2016.

Career in Office
Early accusations of Lungu's authoritarianism were fuelled in 2017 with the arrest in April of opposition leader Hakainde Hichilema on treason charges, the suspension in June of 48 UPND members of parliament, Lungu's declaration in July of a state of emergency on security grounds and his alleged interference in Nov. in the independence of the judiciary. Further political repression in 2018 was aggravated by increasing economic hardship, reflecting widespread corruption and a severe debt crisis.

Defence

In 2013 defence expenditure totalled US$390m. (US$27 per capita), representing 1·7% of GDP.

Army

Strength (2011) 13,500. There are also two paramilitary police units totalling 1,400.

Air Force

In 2011 the Air Force had 18 combat-capable aircraft (MiG-21s and K-8s). Serviceability of most types is reported to be low. Personnel (2011) 1,600.

Economy

In 2011 agriculture accounted for 19·5% of GDP, industry 37·4% and services 43·1%.

Overview

GDP growth averaged 7% per year in the decade to 2015 and the government has worked with the IMF to ensure macroeconomic stability, leading to a significant reduction in inflation. However, strong economic performance is yet to translate into significant poverty reduction—60% of the population lived below the poverty line in 2015 (77·9% of rural dwellers) and 42% in extreme poverty. A national development plan for 2017–21 aims to address this.
   Copper accounts for 75% of annual export earnings, making the country vulnerable to relatively small fluctuations in the world copper price. The decline of copper prices from a peak of US$10,100 per ton in Feb. 2011 to US$4,595 per ton in Feb. 2016 heightened the need to diversify the economy. Although the construction and communications sectors have been strong drivers of growth since the turn of the century, Zambia remains heavily dependent on foreign aid.

Currency

The unit of currency is the *new kwacha* (ZMW) of 100 *ngwee*. It replaced the *kwacha* (ZMK) on 1 Jan. 2013 at a rate of 1,000 *old kwacha* = 1 *new kwacha*. Foreign exchange reserves were US$477m. in July 2005. Inflation was 17·9% in 2016, falling to 6·6% in 2017. Total money supply in June 2005 was 2,140·3bn. kwacha.

Budget

The fiscal year is the calendar year. Budgetary central government revenues in 2016 totalled 39,514m. kwacha and expenditures 48,180m. kwacha. Taxes contributed 81·7% of revenue in 2016; wages and salaries accounted for 37·0% of expenditure, with use of goods and services accounting for 29·1%.

VAT is 16%.

Performance

Real GDP growth was 2·9% in 2015, 3·8% in 2016 and 3·4% in 2017. Total GDP in 2017 was US$25·8bn.

Banking and Finance

The central bank is the Bank of Zambia (*Governor*, Denny Kalyalya). In 2011 there were 19 commercial banks, including one foreign financial institution and 12 subsidiaries of a foreign bank. Non-banking financial institutions in 2012 included four building societies, one development finance institution and one development bank. The Bank of Zambia monitors and supervises the operations of financial institutions. Banks and building societies are governed by the Banking and Financial Services Act 1994. Foreign debt totalled US$3,689m. in 2010, representing 25·8% of GNI.

There is a stock exchange in Lusaka.

Energy and Natural Resources

Environment

Zambia's carbon dioxide emissions from the consumption of energy in 2011 were the equivalent of 0·2 tonnes per capita.

Electricity

Installed capacity in 2011 was 2·0m. kW. Production in 2011 was 11·46bn. kWh, almost exclusively hydro-electric; consumption per capita was 799 kWh.

Oil and Gas

Oil and gas were both discovered in the northwest of Zambia in 2006. Exploration licences have been issued both to local and to foreign companies.

Minerals

Minerals produced (in 1,000 tonnes): copper (2009), 697; cobalt (2009), 1·5; silver (2009 estimate), 6,000 kg; gold (2009 estimate), 3,100 kg. Zambia is well-endowed with gemstones, especially emeralds, amethysts, aquamarine, tourmaline and garnets. Zambia Consolidated Copper Mines, privatized in 2000, is the country's largest employer. In 2011, 220,000 tonnes of coal were produced.

Agriculture

70% of the population is dependent on agriculture. There were an estimated 3·80m. ha. of arable land in 2014 and 36,000 ha. of permanent crops. Principal agricultural products (2013, in 1,000 tonnes): sugarcane (estimate), 4,000; maize, 2,533; cassava, 1,115; wheat, 274; soybeans, 261; sweet potatoes, 188.

Livestock (2013): cattle, 4·0m.; goats (estimate), 2·5m.; pigs, 1·1m.; chickens (estimate), 38m.

Forestry

Forests covered 48·64m. ha. in 2015, or 65% of the total land area. Timber production in 2011 was 10·57m. cu. metres, most of it for fuel.

Fisheries

Total catch, 2015, 83,719 tonnes (exclusively from inland waters).

Industry

In 2011 industry accounted for 37·4% of GDP, with manufacturing contributing 8·4%. Industrial production grew by 4·4% in 2011. Zambia's economy is totally dependent upon its mining sector. Other industries include construction, foodstuffs, beverages, chemicals and textiles.

Labour

The labour force totalled 5,966,199 in 2012 (51·6% female); 52·2% of those in employment were engaged in agriculture. The unemployment rate was 7·8% in 2012.

Zambia had 96,000 people living in slavery according to the Walk Free Foundation's 2013 *Global Slavery Index*.

International Trade

Imports and Exports

Goods imports in 2014 totalled US$9,539·0m. (US$10,161·8m. in 2013) and goods exports US$9,687·9m. (US$10,594·1m. in 2013).

Principal imports in 2014 were machinery and transport (31·7%), crude materials and animal and vegetable oils, and manufactured goods; main exports in 2014 were manufactured goods (79·3%), food, animals and beverages, and chemicals. Copper accounts for around 75% of exports.

The leading import supplier in 2010 was South Africa (34·4%), followed by the Democratic Republic of the Congo and Kuwait; the leading export destination in 2010 was Switzerland (51·0%), followed by China and South Africa.

Communications

Roads

Zambia had a classified network of 67,671 km of public roads in 2014. In 2013, 534,532 vehicles were registered. There were 29,118 traffic accidents in 2013, with 1,851 fatalities.

Rail

In 2005 there were 1,271 km of the state-owned Zambia Railways (ZR) and 891 km of the Tanzania-Zambia (Tazara) Railway, both on 1,067 mm gauge. A 27 km stretch of railway linking Chipata in the east of the country with Mchinji in Malaŵi was opened in Aug. 2010. This links with the existing railway to Nacala, one of Mozambique's leading ports.

Civil Aviation

Zambia's leading airline is Proflight Zambia, which operates domestic services and international flights to Durban and Lilongwe. Lusaka is the principal international airport. In 2012 Lusaka International handled 925,077 passengers (684,548 on international flights) and 5,194 tonnes of freight. Scheduled airline traffic of Zambian-based carriers flew 1·8m. km in 2012; passenger-km totalled 28·7m. in the same year.

Telecommunications

In 2013 there were 116,000 main (fixed) telephone lines; mobile phone subscriptions numbered 10,396,000 in the same year (715·0 per 1,000 persons). In 2013 an estimated 15·4% of the population were internet users. In June 2012 there were 236,000 Facebook users.

Social Institutions

Out of 178 countries analysed in the 2017 *Fragile States Index*—a list published jointly by the Fund for Peace and *Foreign Policy* magazine—Zambia was ranked the 46th most vulnerable to conflict or collapse. The index is based on 12 indicators of state vulnerability across social, political and economic categories.

Justice

The Judiciary consists of the Supreme Court, the High Court and four classes of magistrates' courts; all have civil and criminal jurisdiction.

The Supreme Court hears and determines appeals from the High Court. Its seat is at Lusaka. The High Court exercises the powers vested in the High Court in England, subject to the High Court ordinance of Zambia. Its sessions are held where occasion requires, mostly at Lusaka and Ndola. All criminal cases tried by subordinate courts are subject to revision by the High Court.

The death penalty is authorized, although there have not been any executions since 1997. The population in penal institutions in Sept. 2013 was 17,021 (119 per 100,000 of national population). Zambia was ranked 65th of 102 countries for criminal justice and 71st for civil justice in the 2015 World Justice Project *Rule of Law Index*, which provides data on how the rule of law is experienced by the general public across eight categories.

Education

Schooling is for nine years. In April 2002 then President Mwanawasa announced the reintroduction of universal free primary education, abolished under former President Chiluba. In 2007 there were 2,790,312 pupils in primary schools with 56,557 teaching staff and 607,296 pupils in secondary schools with 14,246 teaching staff.

There are three universities and a National Institute of Public Administration. The University of Zambia, at Lusaka, was founded in 1965 and had 10,122 students in 2007. Copperbelt University, at Kitwe, founded in 1987, had 4,273 students in 2007. Mulungushi University, near Kabwe, was founded in 2008.

The adult literacy rate in 2009 was estimated at 70·9% (80·6% among males and 61·3% among females).

In 2008 public expenditure on education came to 1·3% of GDP.

Health

In 2016 there were 1,514 physicians, 6,627 nursing and midwifery personnel, 256 dentistry personnel and 1,159 pharmaceutical personnel. There were 109 hospitals in 2012, with a total of 25,806 beds.

In *Water: At What Cost? The State of the World's Water 2016*, WaterAid reported that 34·6% of the population does not have access to safe water.

Religion

In 1993 the then president declared Zambia to be a Christian nation, but freedom of worship is a constitutional right. In 2010 there were an estimated 8·87m. Protestants, 2·75m. Catholics and 1·11m. other Christians according to the Pew Research Center's Forum on Religion & Public Life.

Culture

World Heritage Sites

Zambia shares one site with Zimbabwe on the UNESCO World Heritage List: the Victoria Falls/Mosi-oa-Tunya (inscribed on the list in 1989), waterfalls on the Zambezi River.

Press

In 2008 there were three paid-for daily papers, *The Post*, the *Times of Zambia* and the *Zambia Daily Mail. The Post* is privately-owned and the *Times of Zambia* and the *Zambia Daily Mail* state-owned.

Tourism

There were a record 906,000 international tourist arrivals—excluding same-day visitors—in 2011. Receipts from tourism in 2011 totalled US$146m.

Diplomatic Representatives

Of Zambia in the United Kingdom (Zambia House, 2 Palace Gate, London, W8 5NG)

High Commissioner: Muyeba Shichapwa Chikonde.

Of the United Kingdom in Zambia (5210 Independence Ave., PO Box 50050, 15101 Ridgeway, Lusaka)

High Commissioner: Fergus Cochrane-Dyet, OBE.

Of Zambia in the USA (2200 R St., NW, Washington, D.C., 20008)

Ambassador: Ngosa Simbyakula.

Of the USA in Zambia (Eastern end of Kabulonga Rd, Ibex Hill, Lusaka)

Ambassador: Daniel L. Foote.

Of Zambia to the United Nations

Ambassador: Lazarous Kapambwe.

Of Zambia to the European Union

Ambassador: Grace Musonda Mutale Kabwe.

Further Reading

Central Statistical Office. *Monthly Digest of Statistics.*

Chiluba, F., *Democracy: the Challenge of Change.* 1995

Sardanis, Andrew, *Africa: Another Side of the Coin: Northern Rhodesia's Final Years and Zambia's Nationhood.* 2003

Simon, David J., Pletcher, James R. and Siegel, Brian V., *Historical Dictionary of Zambia.* 2008

National Statistical Office: Central Statistical Office, PO Box 31908, Lusaka.

Website: http://www.zamstats.gov.zm

Zimbabwe

Republic of Zimbabwe

Capital: Harare
Population projection, 2020: 17·68m.
GNI per capita, 2017: (PPP$) 1,683
HDI/world rank, 2017: 0·535/156
Internet domain extension: .zw

Key Historical Events

Archaeological evidence shows human settlement dating back several thousand years. The Khoisan people were early inhabitants of the region, followed from around AD 500 by the Bantu-speaking Gokomere. Trading civilizations flourished from the 9th century, culminating in the Mwene Mutapa Empire (Empire of Great Zimbabwe) from the 15th century. Its stronghold was a fortified stone town known as Great Zimbabwe ('houses of stone'), which was founded around 1000 and had a population of up to 18,000 at its peak. During the 16th and 17th centuries the area came under partial control by the Portuguese until the Shona people defeated them in 1693 and established the Rozwi Empire. This fell to the migrating Ndebele (Matabele) in 1834.

King Lobengula of Matabeleland signed the Rudd Concession on 13 Oct. 1888, giving the British mining rights. The British South Africa Company, under Cecil Rhodes, colonized the territory from 1890. European immigration increased after white settlers won the first Matabele war in 1893–94. Following unsuccessful Ndebele and Shona uprisings in 1896 and 1897, indigenous people were increasingly displaced from their land. In 1911 the region was divided into Southern and Northern Rhodesia (*see* ZAMBIA: Key Historical Events) and in 1923 became a self-governing colony. In 1953 Southern and Northern Rhodesia joined with Nyasaland to form the Federation of Rhodesia and Nyasaland, a move opposed by African nationalists who feared it would entrench white minority rule. The South Rhodesian African National Congress was founded in 1957 and campaigned for self-rule by the African majority until it was banned in 1960. After unrest mounted in Nyasaland and neighbouring states, the federation was dissolved on 31 Dec. 1963 and Southern Rhodesia reverted to self-governing colony status within the British Commonwealth under the name of Rhodesia.

On 11 Nov. 1965 Rhodesia's white-dominated government issued a unilateral declaration of independence (UDI) to forestall any British attempt to grant black majority rule. The British governor dismissed the prime minister, Ian Smith, and his cabinet, and the British government reasserted its formal responsibility for Rhodesia although the Smith cabinet was effectively left to run the country. Britain imposed economic sanctions, as did the UN in 1968. On 2 March 1970 the Smith government declared Rhodesia a republic and adopted a new constitution. From 1966–79 the Zimbabwe African People's Union (ZAPU) and its offshoot, the Zimbabwe African National Union (ZANU)—both of which were banned—led a sporadic guerrilla campaign. On 3 March 1978 Smith signed a constitutional agreement with the internationally-backed nationalist leaders. A draft constitution was published in Jan. 1979 and accepted by the white electorate in a referendum. Following the Commonwealth Conference in Lusaka in Aug. 1979, elections in March 1980 resulted in victory for ZANU. Southern Rhodesia became the Republic of Zimbabwe on 18 April 1980.

Political conflict between ZANU and ZAPU supporters in Matabeleland led to allegations of atrocities by government forces in 1983–84. Land reform—the redistribution of good farming land from the minority white population to the African population—became a pressing issue. President Mugabe's government bought 3·5m. ha. of land from white farmers, with the UK funding the £44m. bill. However, only 70,000 families benefited amid allegations of government profiteering. In early 2000 a policy of land occupation began, with black settlers taking over white-owned farms by force. President Mugabe ignored international pressure to restore the rule of law and violence escalated. During campaigning for the 2002 presidential election, which failed to meet international democratic standards, the opposition leader, Morgan Tsvangirai, was charged with treason. Zimbabwe was suspended from the Commonwealth in March 2002 over the conduct of the election and when the suspension was extended in 2003 it pulled out altogether.

In the early 2000s agricultural production fell drastically, the result of drought and of the continuing land seizures. In Sept. 2005 President Mugabe nationalized all land and ended the right of landowners to challenge government expropriations in the courts. In May 2005 the government began the mass demolition of urban slums, claiming it would improve law and order. Around 700,000 people were left homeless. The conduct of parliamentary and Senate elections in 2005, which resulted in victory for President Mugabe's party, was criticized by the international community and in March 2007 evidence that Morgan Tsvangirai had been tortured by police caused an international outcry. In 2006 and 2007 the population experienced mass hunger, with UNICEF estimating that 4m. needed aid. The country's AIDS pandemic continued to worsen in 2007, with 24% of children under 17 orphaned by the disease.

In 2008 elections held against a backdrop of hyperinflation, Mugabe's ZANU-PF lost their parliamentary majority—to the Movement for Democratic Change (MDC)—for the first time since independence. Mugabe retained the presidency when Morgan Tsvangirai, then leader of the MDC, pulled out of a run-off, claiming his supporters had suffered intimidation at the hands of Mugabe's supporters. An international outcry forced Mugabe into talks with Tsvangirai that resulted in a power-sharing agreement in Sept. 2008. The agreement faltered over the allocation of ministries until the composition of the new cabinet was finalized in Feb. 2009. By the end of 2008 millions of civilians relied on food relief, while a cholera outbreak had claimed over 2,000 lives by Jan. 2009, with 1,500 new cases a day being reported.

In July 2013 Mugabe won a seventh presidential term but he was forced to step down in Nov. 2017 after the army intervened following his dismissal of his vice-president, Emmerson Mnangagwa. Mnangagwa was subsequently sworn in as president.

Territory and Population

Zimbabwe is bounded in the north by Zambia, east by Mozambique, south by South Africa and west by Botswana and the Caprivi Strip of Namibia. The area is 390,757 sq. km (150,871 sq. miles). Population at the 2012 census, 13,061,239 (6,780,700 female); density, 33·4 per sq. km. In 2011, 38·8% of the population were urban. Although the population is still rising, it has done so at a lower rate than had been previously expected, partly owing to the large number of AIDS-related deaths and partly as a result of over 3m. Zimbabweans having left the country as President Mugabe's grip on power strengthened, with the vast majority choosing to live in South Africa. However, since 2010 the growth rate has accelerated again.

The UN gives a projected population for 2020 of 17·68m.

There are eight provinces and two cities, Harare and Bulawayo, with provincial status. Area and population (2012 census):

	Area (sq. km)	Population
Bulawayo	479	653,337
Harare	872	2,123,132
Manicaland	36,459	1,752,698
Mashonaland Central	28,347	1,152,520
Mashonaland East	32,230	1,344,955
Mashonaland West	57,441	1,501,656
Masvingo	56,566	1,485,090
Matabeleland North	75,025	749,017
Matebeleland South	54,172	683,893
Midlands	49,166	1,614,941

Palgrave Macmillan (ed.), *The Statesman's Yearbook 2020*,
https://doi.org/10.1057/978-1-349-95940-2_209

Harare, the capital, had a population in 2012 of 1,485,231. Other main cities (with 2012 census populations) were Bulawayo (653,337), Chitungwiza (356,840), Mutare (186,208) and Epworth (167,462). The population is approximately 98% African, 1% mixed and Asian and there are around 70,000 whites. The main ethno-linguistic groups are the Shona (71%), Ndebele (16%), Ndau (3%) and Nyanja (3%). Other smaller ones include Kalanga, Manyika, Tonga and Lozi.

The official language is English.

Social Statistics

2008 estimates: births, 373,000; deaths, 199,000. Rates (2008 estimates, per 1,000 population); birth, 29·9; death, 16·0. Annual population growth rate, 2000–08, 0·0%. Zimbabwe's expectation of life at birth in 2012 was 54·7 years for females and 52·6 for males, up from an average of 40·7 years in 2003 thanks to a sharp decline in the HIV prevalence attributed mainly to changes in sexual behaviour and to some extent to effective preventive programmes. Overall life expectancy had reached 61·9 years in 1985 before Zimbabwe was affected by the HIV/AIDS epidemic. In 2009, 14·3% of all adults between 15 and 49 were infected with HIV. Infant mortality, 2010, 51 per 1,000 live births; fertility rate, 2008, 3·4 births per woman.

Climate

Though situated in the tropics, conditions are remarkably temperate throughout the year because of altitude, and an inland position keeps humidity low. The warmest weather occurs in the three months before the main rainy season, which starts in Nov. and lasts until March. The cool season is from mid-May to mid-Aug. and, though days are mild and sunny, nights are chilly. Harare, Jan. 69°F (20·6°C), July 57°F (13·9°C). Annual rainfall 33" (828 mm). Bulawayo, Jan. 71°F (21·7°C), July 57°F (13·9°C). Annual rainfall 24" (594 mm). Victoria Falls, Jan. 78°F (25·6°C), July 61°F (16·1°C). Annual rainfall 28" (710 mm).

Constitution and Government

In May 2013 a new constitution was signed into law, replacing one that had been in force since 1980. In a referendum on 16 March 2013 it received 92·9% support and won the required two-thirds support in the House of Assembly and the Senate along with presidential approval two months later, having been supported by both ZANU-PF and the MDC.

Under its terms, the executive *President* is limited to two five-year terms (not to be implemented retrospectively, ensuring that the incumbent at the time, Robert Mugabe, qualified for up to a further two terms despite having held office since 1980). The *House of Assembly* is elected by universal suffrage for five-year terms and comprises 210 members elected by secret ballot in 210 constituencies plus, for the first two parliaments, 60 seats for women elected by proportional representation. The *Senate* is made up of 80 members (six each from ten provinces elected by proportional representation, 18 Chiefs and two representatives of disabled persons).

The 2013 constitution also abolished the post of prime minister, provided for a strengthened Bill of Rights, removed immunity for presidents once they have left office, strengthened the powers of the judiciary and established a National Peace and Reconciliation Commission.

National Anthem

'Kalibusiswe Ilizwe leZimbabwe' ('Blessed be the Land of Zimbabwe'); words by Dr Solomon M. Mutswairo; tune by Fred Changundega.

Government Chronology

Presidents since 1980. (ZANU = Zimbabwe African National Union; ZANU-PF = Zimbabwe African National Union-Patriotic Front)

1980–87	ZANU	Canaan Sodindo Banana
1987–17	ZANU-PF	Robert Gabriel Mugabe
2017–	ZANU-PF	Emmerson Dambudzo Mnangagwa

Prime Ministers since 1980. (MDC-T = Movement for Democratic Change-Tsvangirai; ZANU = Zimbabwe African National Union)

1980–87	ZANU	Robert Gabriel Mugabe
2009–13	MDC-T	Morgan Richard Tsvangirai

Recent Elections

Presidential and parliamentary elections took place on 30 July 2018. Incumbent Emmerson Mnangagwa won the presidential election with 50·8% of the vote. Nelson Chamisa finished second with 44·3%. There were 21 other candidates who received less than 1% of the vote each. International observers noted widespread fraud.

Of the 270 seats contested on the same day in the House of Assembly the Zimbabwe African National Union-Patriotic Front (ZANU-PF) won 179 seats, against 88 for the Movement for Democratic Change Alliance (MDC Alliance). Two other parties and an independent won one seat each. Of the 80 available seats in the Senate, the ZANU-PF won 34, the MDC Alliance 25 and the Movement for Democratic Change-Tsvangirai (MDC-T) 1. In addition 18 seats are allocated for chiefs and there are two seats for elected people with disabilities.

Current Government

President: Emmerson Mnangagwa; b. 1942 (ZANU-PF; sworn in 24 Nov. 2017).

In Feb. 2019 the government comprised:

First Vice-President: Constantino Chiwenga. *Second Vice-President:* Kembo Mohadi.

Minister of Defence and War Veterans: Oppah Muchinguri-Kashiri. *Energy and Power Development:* Joram Gumbo. *Environment, Tourism and Hospitality Industry:* Priscah Mupfumira. *Finance and Economic Planning:* Mthuli Ncube. *Foreign Affairs and International Trade:* Lieut.-Gen. (retd) Sibusiso Moyo. *Health and Child Care:* Obadiah Moyo. *Higher and Tertiary Education:* Amon Murwira. *Home Affairs and Cultural Heritage:* Cain Mathema. *Industry and Commerce:* Mangaliso Ndlovu. *Information Communication Technology and Courier Services:* Kazembe Kazembe. *Information, Publicity and Broadcasting Services:* Monica Mutsvangwa. *Justice, Legal and Parliamentary Affairs:* Ziyambi Ziyambi. *Lands, Agriculture, Water, Climate and Rural Resettlement:* Perence Shiri. *Local Government, Public Works and National Housing:* July Moyo. *Mines and Mining Development:* Winston Chitando. *Primary and Secondary Education:* Paul Mavima. *Public Service, Labour and Social Welfare:* Sekesai Nzenza. *Transport and Infrastructure Development:* Joel Matiza. *Women Affairs:* Sithembiso Nyoni. *Youth, Sport, Arts and Recreation:* Kirsty Coventry. *Government Website:* http://www.zim.gov.zw

Current Leaders

Emmerson Mnangagwa

Position
President

Introduction
Emmerson Mnangagwa became president on 24 Nov. 2017 following Robert Mugabe's resignation after 37 years in power. A long-time ally of Mugabe, Mnangagwa is a former justice minister with a reputation for toughness. He was re-elected president in July 2018, although international observers noted widespread fraud.

Early Life
Mnangagwa was born on 15 Sept. 1942 in Zvishavane (then in Southern Rhodesia). His family moved to Northern Rhodesia (now Zambia) in 1955, where he attended Hodgson Technical College in Lusaka. He joined the Zimbabwe African People's Union (ZAPU) in 1962, undertaking military training in China and Egypt. Reputedly part of the 'crocodile gang' charged with sabotaging colonial infrastructure, he was jailed in 1965 for ten years for plotting to blow up a train.

While imprisoned in Salisbury (now Harare), he became close to Mugabe and other leading independence figures. Released in 1975 and deported to Lusaka, he studied law at the University of Zambia and became a senior member of the Zimbabwe African National Union-Patriotic Front (ZANU-PF). He became head of national security under Zimbabwe's first Black majority government in 1980, but has denied suggestions of involvement in the Gukurahundi campaign—a civil war with ZAPU supporters that led to an estimated 20,000 deaths across Matabeleland.

Elected member of Parliament for Kwerkwe East in 1985, Mnangagwa was appointed minister of justice, legal and parliamentary affairs in 1988—a position he held for 12 years. He lost his seat to the opposition Movement for Democratic Change (MDC) in 2000 and was demoted to minister for rural housing and social amenities. However, after winning a seat again in 2008, Mnangagwa reportedly ran Mugabe's campaign in that year's disputed presidential election and brokered a power-sharing pact with opposition leader Morgan Tsvangirai. He was also named defence minister. When Mugabe was re-elected in 2013 he reappointed Mnangagwa justice minister. In 2014 he made Mnangagwa vice president.

Amid rumours of his ambitions to succeed Mugabe, he was replaced as justice minister in Oct. 2017 and dismissed as vice president the following month, seemingly to pave the way for Mugabe's wife, Grace, to succeed her husband. The move sparked military intervention and mounting calls for Mugabe to step down. Facing the threat of impeachment, Mugabe resigned on 21 Nov. 2017, with Mnangagwa sworn in to replace him three days later.

Career in Office

Mnangagwa pledged to rebuild Zimbabwe's shattered economy by creating jobs through partnerships with international investors, and he urged Western nations to consider lifting sanctions on Zimbabwe. However, the International Monetary Fund and the World Bank have withheld financial support unless Zimbabwe repays arrears to its multilateral creditors, while a deepening currency crisis has evoked earlier memories of hyperinflation under the Mugabe regime. Despite the economic malaise, Mnangagwa and ZANU-PF secured narrow re-election controversially in July 2018. However, violent anti-government street protests then erupted in Jan. 2019 over fuel price increases and the continuing decline in living standards.

Defence

In 2013 military expenditure totalled US$356m. (US$27 per capita), representing 3·2% of GDP.

Army

Strength in 2011 was estimated at 25,000. There were a further 21,800 paramilitary police including a police support unit of 2,300.

Air Force

The Air Force (ZAF) had a strength in 2011 of about 4,000 personnel. The headquarters of the ZAF and the main ZAF stations are in Harare; the second main base is at Gweru, with many secondary airfields throughout the country. There were 46 combat-capable aircraft (including F-7s and K-8s) in 2011 although the serviceability of some aircraft was in doubt, and six attack helicopters.

Economy

Agriculture accounted for 13% of GDP in 2012, industry 32% and services 55%.

Zimbabwe's 'shadow' (black market) economy is estimated to constitute approximately 63% of the country's official GDP, one of the highest percentages of any country in the world.

Overview

At independence Zimbabwe was the second largest economy in Africa but its prosperity has deteriorated sharply since the 1990s. Between 1999 and 2008 output fell by more than 45%. According to the IMF the economic decline was attributable to loose fiscal and monetary policies, an overvalued fixed exchange rate, excessive administrative controls and regulations, and chronic shortages of goods and foreign exchange. The combined effect was magnified by the collapse of the health and education systems, weak infrastructure, high rates of HIV infection, a fast-track land reform programme and recurring droughts. Political instability and spiralling external debt, which amounted to US$10·7bn. by 2011, prompted most Western donors to reduce or withdraw operations and confine financial support to humanitarian aid. While China remains a major donor of both finance and food, it too made some aid cuts in 2007 under pressure from Western governments.

The period 2009–12 was marked by a recovery following the introduction of the multiple currency system, with the economy growing at an average rate of 10·0% per annum. Inflation stabilized, while revenues and bank deposits rose sharply. However, GDP growth then slowed markedly from 10·6% in 2012 to just 1·1% in 2015, owing largely to trade imbalances and the effects of climate change.

Nonetheless, social services have recovered amid resurgent public and donor spending, while HIV prevalence fell to around 15% in 2014 from more than 40% in 1998. Life expectancy rose from a low of 40·7 years in 2003 to 53·6 years in 2012, while maternal and infant mortality rates had also improved dramatically by 2014.

With abundant natural resources and a well-educated workforce, Zimbabwe has good potential for sustained growth and poverty reduction. However, there is a pressing need for radical economic reform and improvements in basic services if long-term prosperity is to be achieved.

Currency

The use of the Zimbabwean dollar as an official currency was effectively abandoned on 12 April 2009, with currencies such as the South African rand, the Botswana pula, the pound sterling and the US dollar are used instead. The Zimbabwean dollar was officially withdrawn from circulation in Sept. 2015. Until 12 April 2009 the unit of currency was the *Zimbabwe fourth dollar* (ZWL), introduced on 2 Feb. 2009, with 12 zeros being removed to make 1trn. dollars (ZWR) equal to one new dollar. The *Zimbabwe third dollar* (ZWR) had replaced the *Zimbabwe second dollar* (ZWD) on 1 Aug. 2008, with a conversion rate of 1 revalued dollar = 10bn. old dollars (ZWD). The currency was devalued 17% in Jan. 1994 and made fully convertible. Its value dropped by 65% in 1998. It was devalued again in Aug. 2000 by 24%, in May 2005 by 45% and in July 2005 by 94%. It was further devalued by 60% in July 2006 and the following day the *Zimbabwean new (second) dollar* became the new currency. Inflation, which was 18·9% in 1997, rose to 133·2% in 2002 and 6,723·7% in 2007. The last official annual rate calculated in Zimbabwe dollars was 231,150,888·9% in July 2008. A multi-currency system was introduced in 2009. There was deflation of 1·6% in 2016 but then inflation of 0·9% in 2017. Total money supply was Z$425,445·0bn. in Dec. 2007, up from Z$0·4bn. in Dec. 2002 and Z$44·7bn. in Dec. 2005.

Budget

Revenues in 2015 totalled US$3,990m. and expenditures US$4,179m. Tax revenues accounted for 94·3% of total revenue in 2015; current expenditures accounted for 91·9% of total expenditure. VAT was reduced from 17·5% to 15% in Jan. 2006.

Performance

Real GDP growth was negative every year from 1999 through to 2008. However, from 2009–12 economic growth averaged 13·2%. It has since slowed, with growth rates of 1·4% in 2015, 0·7% in 2016 and 3·7% in 2017. Total GDP in 2017 was US$17·8bn.

Banking and Finance

The Reserve Bank of Zimbabwe is the central bank (established 1965; *Governor*, John Mangudya). It acts as banker to the government and to the commercial banks, is the note-issuing authority and co-ordinates the application of the government's monetary policy. The Infrastructure Development Bank of Zimbabwe focuses on the development and funding of both public and private sector infrastructure projects in all key sectors of the economy. In 2014 there were 13 commercial banks, three building societies, one merchant bank and one savings bank.

Zimbabwe's foreign debt totalled US$5,016m. in 2010, representing 71·8% of GNI.

In Aug. 2003 Zimbabwe's banks ran out of banknotes as inflation reached 360%.

There is a stock exchange in Harare.

Energy and Natural Resources

Environment

Carbon dioxide emissions from the consumption of energy were the equivalent of 0·8 tonnes per capita in 2011.

Electricity

Installed capacity was an estimated 2·1m. kW in 2011. Production in 2011 was 8·93bn. kWh. Consumption per capita in 2011 was 783 kWh.

Minerals

The mining sector accounts for about 4% of GDP. 2006 production: coal, 2·11m. tonnes; chromite (gross weight), 700,000 tonnes; asbestos, 97,000 tonnes; nickel, 8,825 tonnes; gold, 11·4 tonnes. Diamond production in 2005 totalled 251,152 carats. A huge diamond field was discovered near Mutare in 2006. In 2013 it provided about 13% of world rough diamond supply.

Agriculture

Agriculture is the largest employer, providing jobs for 25% of the workforce. In 2013 there were an estimated 4·0m. ha. of arable land and 0·1m. ha. of permanent crops. Approximately 0·2m. ha. were equipped for irrigation in 2013.

A constitutional amendment providing for the compulsory purchase of land for peasant resettlement came into force in March 1992. A provision to seize white-owned farmland for peasant resettlement was part of the government's new draft constitution that was rejected in the referendum of Feb. 2000. Various deadlines were given for white farmers to abandon their property during Aug. and Sept. 2002. The government claims that 300,000 landless black Zimbabweans have been resettled on seized land.

The staple food crop is maize, but 2012 production (at 999,000 tonnes) was less than a half of the 1997 figure. Tobacco is the largest export crop, although production fell from 215,000 tonnes in 1997 to 86,000 tonnes in 2012. Production of other leading crops, 2012, in 1,000 tonnes: sugarcane (estimate), 3,929; cassava (estimate), 228; cottonseed (estimate), 200; seed cotton, 170; cotton lint (estimate), 105; bananas (estimate), 100.

Livestock (2013 estimates): cattle, 6·15m.; goats, 5·00m.; asses, 620,000; pigs, 415,000; sheep, 320,000; chickens, 36m. Livestock products (2013 estimates, in 1,000 tonnes): milk, 410; meat, 268.

Forestry

In 2015 forests covered 14·06m. ha., or 36% of the total land area. Timber production in 2011 was 9·31m. cu. metres.

Fisheries

The catch in 2015 was approximately 10,500 tonnes (all from inland waters).

Industry

Metal products account for over 20% of industrial output. Important agro-industries include food processing, textiles, furniture and other wood products.

Labour

The labour force in 2013 was 7,533,000 (6,224,000 in 2003). 87·7% of the population aged 15–64 was economically active in 2013. In the same year 5·3% of the population was unemployed.

Zimbabwe had 94,000 people living in slavery according to the Walk Free Foundation's 2013 *Global Slavery Index*.

International Trade

Imports and Exports

Goods imports in 2014 totalled US$6,379·8m. (US$7,704·2m. in 2013) and goods exports US$3,063·7m. (US$3,507·3m. in 2013).

Principal imports in 2014 were mineral fuels and lubricants (24·5%), machinery and transport equipment, and chemicals; main exports in 2014 were food, animals and beverages (35·2%), manufactured goods, and crude materials and animal and vegetable oils.

The leading import supplier in 2014 was South Africa (50·2%), followed by the USA and China; the leading export destination in 2013 was South Africa (54·2%), followed by the UAE and China.

Communications

Roads

The road network covers some 97,000 km but much of it is in poor condition. Number of vehicles in use, 2007: passenger cars, 1,214,100; lorries and vans, 186,800; buses and coaches, 15,600; motorcycles and mopeds, 109,000. There were 1,037 road accident fatalities in 2006.

Rail

In 2005 the National Railways of Zimbabwe had 2,759 km (1,067 mm gauge) of route ways (483 km electrified). In 2005 the railways carried 3m. passengers and 6·1m. tonnes of freight (including the Beitbridge-Bulawayo Railway).

Civil Aviation

There are three international airports: Harare (the main airport), Bulawayo and Victoria Falls. Air Zimbabwe, the state-owned national carrier, ceased operations in Feb. 2012 but resumed flying on a limited basis in May. After the government took over Air Zimbabwe's debts it began flying on international routes again in Nov. 2012. In Oct. 2018 plans were announced to merge Air Zimbabwe with Zimbabwe Airways, the country's other airline. In 2012 scheduled airline traffic of Zimbabwe-based carriers flew 9·1m. km; passenger-km totalled 566·6m. in the same year. In 2009 Harare handled 612,208 passengers (674,281 in 2008).

Shipping

Zimbabwe's outlets to the sea are Maputo and Beira in Mozambique, Dar es Salaam, Tanzania and the South African ports.

Telecommunications

In 2013 there were 304,000 main (fixed) telephone lines; mobile phone subscriptions numbered 13,633,000 in the same year (963·5 per 1,000 persons). In 2013 an estimated 18·5% of the population were internet users. In June 2012 there were 236,000 Facebook users.

Social Institutions

Out of 178 countries analysed in the 2017 *Fragile States Index*—a list published jointly by the Fund for Peace and *Foreign Policy* magazine— Zimbabwe was ranked the joint 13th most vulnerable (along with Nigeria) to conflict or collapse. The index is based on 12 indicators of state vulnerability across social, political and economic categories.

Justice

The general common law of Zimbabwe is the Roman Dutch law as it applied in the Colony of the Cape of Good Hope on 10 June 1891, as subsequently modified by statute. Provision is made by statute for the application of African customary law by all courts in appropriate cases.

The death penalty is authorized, although it has not been used since 2005.

The Supreme Court consists of the Chief Justice and at least two Supreme Court judges. It is the final court of appeal. It exercises appellate jurisdiction in appeals from the High Court and other courts and tribunals; its only original jurisdiction is that conferred on it by the Constitution to enforce the protective provisions of the Declaration of Rights. The Court's permanent seat is in Harare but it also sits regularly in Bulawayo.

The High Court is also headed by the Chief Justice, supported by the Judge President and an appropriate number of High Court judges. It has full original jurisdiction, in both Civil and Criminal cases, over all persons and all matters in Zimbabwe. The Judge President is in charge of the Court, subject to the directions of the Chief Justice. The Court has permanent seats in both Harare and Bulawayo and sittings are held three times a year in three other principal towns.

Regional courts, established in Harare and Bulawayo but also holding sittings in other centres, exercise a solely criminal jurisdiction which is intermediate between that of the High Court and the Magistrates' courts. Magistrates' courts, established in 20 centres throughout the country, and staffed by full-time professional magistrates, exercise both civil and criminal jurisdiction.

Primary courts consist of village courts and community courts. Village courts are presided over by officers selected for the purpose from the local population, sitting with two assessors. They deal with specific classes of civil cases and have jurisdiction only where African customary law is applicable. Community courts are presided over by officers in full-time public service, who may also be assisted by assessors. They have jurisdiction in all civil cases determinable by African customary law and also deal with appeals from village courts. They also have limited criminal jurisdiction in respect of petty offences.

The population in penal institutions in Feb. 2013 was 16,902 (129 per 100,000 of national population). In 2015 the World Justice Project *Rule of Law Index*, which provides data on how the rule of law is experienced by the general public across eight categories, ranked Zimbabwe 72nd of 102 countries for criminal justice and 79th for civil justice.

Education

Education is compulsory. 'Manageable' school fees were introduced in 1991; primary education had hitherto been free to all. All instruction is given in

English. In 2012 there were 2,666,451 pupils at primary schools (74,355 teaching staff) and 936,734 pupils at secondary schools (41,759 teaching staff). In May 2004 the 45 private schools were closed down for increasing fees without state approval although they have for the most part since reopened. Private school fees are out of reach of the majority of families. Tens of thousands of teachers have left Zimbabwe and thousands more have left the profession. In 2009 the adult literacy rate was an estimated 91·9%. Both the overall rate and the rate for males are the highest in Africa.

There are 12 universities, the oldest and largest of which is the University of Zimbabwe, founded in 1952. Although historically well-regarded, the university experienced a series of problems ranging from staff shortages to electricity supply issues that resulted in its closure for much of 2008 and 2009.

In 2012 there were 94,012 students in tertiary education.

Health

There were 30 hospital beds per 10,000 inhabitants in 2006. All mission health institutions get 100% government grants-in-aid for recurrent expenditure. In 2011 there were 1,054 physicians, 17,022 nursing and midwifery personnel, 255 dentistry personnel and 467 pharmaceutical personnel. It is estimated that one in three adults is HIV infected.

In *Water: At What Cost? The State of the World's Water 2016*, WaterAid reported that 23·1% of the population does not have access to safe water.

Welfare

It is a statutory responsibility of the government in many areas to provide: processing and administration of war pensions and old age pensions; protection of children; administration of remand, probation and correctional institutions; registration and supervision of welfare organizations.

Religion

A study by the Pew Research Center's Forum on Religion & Public Life estimated that in 2010 there were 10·93m. Christians, 990,000 people with no religious affiliation, 480,000 folk religionists and 110,000 Muslims. Of the Christians in 2010, 85% were Protestants and 13% Catholics.

Culture

World Heritage Sites

Zimbabwe has five sites on the UNESCO World Heritage List: Mana Pools National Park, Sapi and Chewore Safari Areas (inscribed on the list in 1984); the Great Zimbabwe National Monument (1986); the Khambi Ruins National Monument (1986); and Matobo Hills (2003).

Zimbabwe shares with Zambia the Victoria Falls/Mosi-oa-Tunya (1989), waterfalls on the Zambezi River.

Press

In 2008 there were two daily newspapers, both controlled by the government, with a combined circulation of 28,000. In Jan. 2002 parliament passed an Access to Information Bill restricting press freedom, making it an offence to report from Zimbabwe unless registered by a state-appointed commission. In Sept. 2003 the independent *Daily News* was shut down for contraventions of the new press law. Zimbabwe's High Court ordered the government to allow its reopening but the order was ignored.

Tourism

International visitors numbered 2,423,000 in 2011 (2,239,000 in 2010 and 2,017,000 in 2009). Receipts in 2011 totalled US$664m.

Festivals

Of particular importance are the Harare International Festival of the Arts (April) and the Bulawayo Music Festival (May). The Zimbabwe International Film Festival is held in Harare in Aug./Sept.

Diplomatic Representatives

Of Zimbabwe in the United Kingdom (Zimbabwe House, 429 Strand, London, WC2R 0JR)
Ambassador: Christian Katsande.

Of the United Kingdom in Zimbabwe (3 Norfolk Rd, Mount Pleasant, Harare)
Ambassador: Melanie Robinson.

Of Zimbabwe in the USA (1608 New Hampshire Ave., NW, Washington, D.C., 20009)
Ambassador: Ammon Mutembwa.

Of the USA in Zimbabwe (172 Herbert Chitepo Ave., Harare)
Ambassador: Brian A. Nichols.

Of Zimbabwe to the United Nations
Ambassador: Frederick Musiiwa Makamure Shava.

Of Zimbabwe to the European Union
Ambassador: Tadeous Tafirenyika Chifamba.

Further Reading

Central Statistical Office. *Quarterly Digest of Statistics.*
Hatchard, J., *Individual Freedoms and State Security in the African Context: the Case of Zimbabwe.* 1993
Hill, Geoff, *What Happens After Mugabe? Can Zimbabwe Rise From the Ashes?* 2005
Meredith, Martin, *Mugabe: Power and Plunder in Zimbabwe.* 2002
Skålnes, T., *The Politics of Economic Reform in Zimbabwe: Continuity and Change in Development.* 1995
Weiss, R., *Zimbabwe and the New Elite.* 1994
National Statistical Office: Central Statistical Office, 20th Floor, Kaguvi Building, Cnr Fourth St./Central Ave., P. O. Box, CY 342, Causeway, Harare.

Statesman's Yearbook Select Sources

The Statesman's Yearbook references the following sources to maintain accuracy and currency of information contained in our content management system:

- 2017 Global Go To Think Tanks Report (https://repository.upenn.edu/cgi/viewcontent.cgi?article=1012&context=think_tanks)
- United Nations Statistical Yearbook (https://unstats.un.org/unsd/publications/statistical-yearbook)
- Euromonitor International (http://www.euromonitor.com/economic-research)
- United Nations Development Programme Human Development Report (http://hdr.undp.org/sites/default/files/2018_human_development_statistical_update.pdf)
- United Nations World Population Prospects (http://esa.un.org/unpd/wpp)
- United Nations World Urbanization Prospects (http://esa.un.org/unpd/wup)
- United Nations Demographic Yearbook (http://unstats.un.org/unsd/demographic/products/dyb/dyb2.htm)
- City population (http://www.citypopulation.de)
- Stockholm International Peace Research Institute Yearbook (http://www.sipri.org/yearbook)
- International Institute of Strategic Studies Military Balance (https://www.iiss.org/publications/the-military-balance)
- International Monetary Fund World Economic Outlook (https://www.imf.org/en/Publications/WEO/Issues/2018/09/24/world-economic-outlook-october-2018; https://www.imf.org/external/pubs/ft/weo/2018/02/weodata/index.aspx)
- Selected International Monetary Fund Reports
- Selected European Union Reports
- Eurostat (http://ec.europa.eu/eurostat)
- Selected World Bank Reports and Datasets
- Selected Organisation for Economic Co-operation and Development Reports and Datasets
- Selected World Trade Organization Reports
- International Monetary Fund Government Finance Statistics Yearbook (https://www.bookstore.imf.org/books/title/government-finance-statistics-yearbook-2017)
- World Investment Report (http://unctad.org/en/pages/DIAE/World%20Investment%20Report/WIR-Series.aspx)
- United Nations Energy Statistics Yearbook (http://unstats.un.org/unsd/energy/yearbook/default.htm)
- BP Statistical Review of World Energy (https://www.bp.com/content/dam/bp/business-sites/en/global/corporate/pdfs/energy-economics/statistical-review/bp-stats-review-2018-full-report.pdf)
- US Geological Society (http://minerals.usgs.gov/minerals)
- Food and Agricultural Organization Datasets (http://www.fao.org/faostat/en/#home)
- Food and Agricultural Organization Forest Products Yearbook (http://www.fao.org/forestry/statistics/80570/en)
- Food and Agricultural Organization Fishery Statistics – Capture Production (http://www.fao.org/fishery/statistics/global-capture-production/en)
- United Nations Industrial Commodity Statistics Yearbook (https://unstats.un.org/unsd/industry/Commodity/Yearbook.cshtml)
- International Labour Organization Statistics (http://www.ilo.org/ilostat)
- United Nations International Trade Statistics Yearbook (https://comtrade.un.org/pb/downloads/2017/VolI2017.pdf)
- International Road Federation World Road Statistics (http://worldroadstatistics.org)
- International Railway Statistics (http://www.uic.org/statistics)
- Railway Directory (http://www.railwaydirectory.net)
- Selected Airports Council International Reports (http://www.aci.aero/Data-Centre)
- Shipping Statistics Yearbook (http://www.infoline.isl.org)
- International Telecommunication Union Yearbook of Statistics (https://www.itu.int/en/ITU-D/Statistics/Pages/yb2018.aspx)
- World Prison Population List (http://www.prisonstudies.org/sites/default/files/resources/downloads/wppl_12.pdf)
- UNESCO Institute for Statistics (http://data.uis.unesco.org)
- World Health Statistics (http://www.who.int/gho/publications/world_health_statistics/en)
- Pew Research Center's Religion & Public Life Project (http://www.pewforum.org/2012/12/18/global-religious-landscape-exec)
- Religious Trends No 7
- World Association of Newspapers World Press Trends (http://www.wan-ifra.org/microsites/world-press-trends)
- National and regional statistical offices and yearbooks, government departments and international organizations throughout the world
- Selected print and online national and international news media

© Springer Nature Limited 2020
Palgrave Macmillan (ed.), *The Statesman's Yearbook 2020*,
https://doi.org/10.1057/978-1-349-95940-2

Abbreviations

ACP	African Caribbean Pacific		**GWh**	gigawatt hours
Adm.	Admiral		**ha.**	hectare(s)
Adv.	Advocate		**HDI**	Human Development Index
a.i.	ad interim		**IMF**	International Monetary Fund
Ave.	Avenue		**ind.**	independent(s)
b.	born		**ICT**	information and communication technology
bbls	barrels		**ISO**	International Organization for Standardization (domain names)
bd	board		**K**	kindergarten
Blvd	Boulevard		**kg**	kilogramme(s)
bn.	billion (one thousand million)		**kl**	kilolitre(s)
Brig.	Brigadier		**km**	kilometre(s)
bu.	bushel		**kW**	kilowatt
Capt.	Captain		**kWh**	kilowatt hours
Col.	Colonel		**lat.**	latitude
Cdr	Commander		**lb**	pound(s) (weight)
CFA	Communauté Financière Africaine		**Lieut.**	Lieutenant
CFP	Comptoirs Français du Pacifique		**long.**	longitude
CGT	compensated gross tonnes		**m.**	million
c.i.f.	cost, insurance, freight		**Maj.**	Major
C.-in-C.	Commander-in-Chief		**MW**	megawatt
CIS	Commonwealth of Independent States		**MWh**	megawatt hours
cm	centimetre(s)		**NA**	not available
Co.	County		**NATO**	North Atlantic Treaty Organization
Cres.	Crescent		**n.e.c.**	not elsewhere classified
cu.	cubic		**NRT**	net registered tones
CUP	Cambridge University Press		**NT**	net tonnes
cwt	hundredweight		**OUP**	Oxford University Press
D.	Democratic Party		**oz**	ounce(s)
DWT	dead weight tonnes		**PAYE**	Pay-As-You-Earn
EEA	European Economic Area		**Pl.**	Place
EEZ	Exclusive Economic Zone		**PPP**	Purchasing Power Parity
EMS	European Monetary System		**R.**	Republican Party
EMU	European Monetary Union		**Rd**	Road
ERM	Exchange Rate Mechanism		**retd**	retired
est.	estimate		**Rt Hon.**	Right Honourable
EU	European Union		**SADC**	Southern African Development Community
f.o.b.	free on board		**SDR**	Special Drawing Rights
FDI	foreign direct investment		**Sq.**	Square
ft	foot/feet		**sq.**	square
FTE	full-time equivalent		**St.**	Street
G7 Group	Canada, France, Germany, Italy, Japan, UK, USA		**SSI**	Supplemental Security Income
GDP	gross domestic product		**TAFE**	technical and further education
Gdns	Gardens		**TEU**	twenty-foot equivalent units
Gen.	General		**trn.**	trillion (one million million)
GNI	gross national income		**UN**	United Nations
GNP	gross national product		**Univ.**	University
GRT	gross registered tonnes		**VAT**	value-added tax
GT	gross tonnes		**v.f.d.**	value for duty
GW	gigawatt			

© Springer Nature Limited 2020
Palgrave Macmillan (ed.), *The Statesman's Yearbook 2020*,
https://doi.org/10.1057/978-1-349-95940-2

Current Leaders Index

© Springer Nature Limited 2020
Palgrave Macmillan (ed.), *The Statesman's Yearbook 2020*,
https://doi.org/10.1057/978-1-349-95940-2

Place and International Organizations Index

© Springer Nature Limited 2020
Palgrave Macmillan (ed.), *The Statesman's Yearbook 2020*,
https://doi.org/10.1057/978-1-349-95940-2

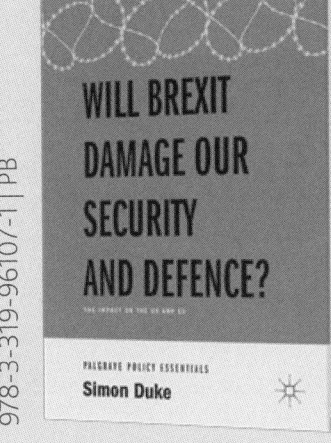